The **HUTCHINSON**
ENCYCLOPEDIA

The HUTCHINSON
ENCYCLOPEDIA

First published (as *Hutchinson's Twentieth Century Encyclopedia*) 1948
Second Edition 1951
Third Edition 1956
Fourth edition (as *Hutchinson's New 20th Century Encyclopedia*) 1964
Fifth edition 1970
Sixth edition (as *The New Hutchinson 20th Century Encyclopedia*) 1977
Seventh edition 1981
Eighth edition (as *The Hutchinson Encyclopedia*) 1988
Ninth edition 1990
Tenth edition 1992
1994 edition (revised and updated) 1993
Reprinted 1994
1995 edition (revised and updated) 1994
1996 edition (revised and updated) 1995
1997 edition (revised and updated) 1996
Reprinted 1997
Eleventh edition (1998 edition) 1997
Reprinted 1998
1999 edition (revised and updated) 1998
Reprinted 1999
2000 edition (revised and updated) 1999
2001 edition (revised and updated) 2000

Twelfth edition (2002 edition) 2001
2005 edition (revised and updated) 2004

Hodder Arnold
338 Euston Road
London
NW1 3BH
www.madaboutbooks.co.uk

ISBN: 0–340–88690–0

British Library Cataloguing in Publication Data
A catalogue record for this book is available from the British Library

Printed and bound in Dubai

Contents

FOCUS FEATURES

The Hutchinson Encyclopedia includes 15 Focus Features, the full set of
which has been created with relevance to Key Stages 3 or 4 of the UK
National Curriculum.

Introduction

The Hutchinson Encyclopedia, now in its twelfth edition, has been newly compiled from the vast resources of the Helicon databases and is fully revised and updated. As with its predecessors, this edition includes hundreds of new entries – and an entirely new selection of photographs, artworks, and diagrams. A new set of maps has been created for the encyclopedia, including maps of all the countries of the world.

The aim of *The Hutchinson Encyclopedia* remains that of providing the reader with the widest possible range of material within the limitations of space, and to provide it in clear and accessible language. With each edition, the inclusion policy has to adapt to the needs of the times; the many changes seen in the past decade are reflected in the considerable number of entries in areas such as computing and the Internet; advances in biotechnology; and popular culture.

This edition includes a new set of the popular 'Focus Features' on a selection of major topics, written by specialist contributors with relevance to Key Stages 3 and 4 of the National Curriculum; a thematically arranged 'Factfile' at the end of the book with dozens of lists and tables; a selection of quotations, fact boxes, and useful Web sites, and additional cross-referencing to help link entries and features more clearly.

How to use this book

ARRANGEMENT OF ENTRIES

Entries are ordered in strict alphabetical sequence, as if there were no spaces or punctuation between words, thus: *cold-blooded; cold, common; cold fusion*. There is one exception to this rule – biographical entries.

For biographical entries, where first and other forenames are given as part of the headword, alphabetization is organized strictly according to the family name / last name. First and other forenames are ignored, except in cases where a number of biographical entries have the same family/last name. So, we have *Brown, James; Brown, John; Brown, Robert, brown dwarf; Browne, Thomas.*

Parts of a person's name that are not generally used are enclosed in parentheses. These elements are ignored in deciding alphabetical sequence.

A purely mechanical alphabetization is also avoided in a few cases for ease of reference: for example, sovereigns with the same name are grouped according to country first and then by number, so that King George II of England comes before King George III of England rather than next to King George II of Greece. Words beginning 'Mc' are treated the same as 'Mac', and in placenames 'St' as if it were spelled 'Saint'. Saints themselves are alphabetized according to their name alone: *Clare (county of Ireland); Clare, St; Clare, John.* Where two or more entries have the same headword, they are ordered alphabetically according to subject, so, for example, memory in computing precedes memory in psychology.

FOREIGN NAMES AND TITLES

Names of foreign sovereigns and places are usually shown in their English form, except where the foreign name is more familiar; thus, there are entries for Charles III of Spain, but for Juan Carlos (not John Charles). Entries for titled people are under the name by which they are best known to the general reader; thus, Anthony Eden, not Lord Avon.

CROSS-REFERENCES AND BOLD TYPE

Within entries, cross-references (▷) immediately precede the word cross-referenced and indicate a reference to a feature on the same or a related topic. Cross-referencing is selective, with the aim of pointing the reader to an entry that is helpful. Common alternative spellings or names are also given as cross-references: thus, there is a cross-reference from *Mohammed* to *Muhammad*, and from *Yangtze* to *Chang Jiang*. Cross-references are not normally given to neighbouring entries. Page references are given for cross-references to 'Focus Features' and 'Factfile' tables.

Bold type is used for distinct types of the main term (for example, in the entry for *chemistry*, '**organic chemistry**' and '**inorganic chemistry**' are in bold type).

CHINESE NAMES

Pinyin, the preferred system for transcribing Chinese names for people and places, is generally used; thus there is an entry for *Mao Zedong*, not Mao *Tse-Tung*; an exception is made for a few names which are more familiar in their former (Wade-Giles) form, such as *Sun-Yat-sen* and *Chiang Kai-shek*. (Where confusion is likely, Wade-Giles forms are given as cross-references.)

MAPS

Place names are generally shown on the maps in their local form. Where a place name has a popular English language version, that version is shown in brackets on the map. The colour of individual country maps is linked to the colour of their continent as shown on the world political maps at the start of the book.

COUNTRY MAP LEGEND

(The continental map legend can be found on each continental map)

Cities, towns & capitals

▣ **CHICAGO**	over 3 million
◻ **HAMBURG**	1–3 million
○ **Bulawayo**	250 000–1 million
● Antofogasta	100 000–250 000
◉ Ajaccio	25 000–100 000
• Indian Springs	under 25 000
LONDON	country capital
Edinburgh	state or province capital

Political type & boundaries

ONTARIO	state or province
▬▬▬▬	international boundary
▬ ▬ ▬	international boundary in water
▬ · ▬ · ▬	undefined/disputed boundary or ceasefire/demarcation line
▬▬▬▬	state or province boundary

Cultural features

▪▪▪▪▪▪	ancient wall

Hydrographic features

～	river, canal
～	seasonal river
Niagara Falls	waterfall
Kariba Dam	dam
⬭	lake
⬭	seasonal lake
⬭	salt lake
⬭	seasonal salt lake

Communications

▬▬▬	motorway
▬▬▬	main road
▬▬▬	other road
▬ ▬ ▬	track
✈	international airport

Topographic features

▴ **Mount Ziel** 1510	elevation above sea level
⤬ **Khyber Pass** 1080	mountain pass

ABBREVIATIONS AND SYMBOLS

km = kilometres	GDP = gross domestic product
mi = miles	GNP = gross national product
m = metres	PPP = purchasing power parity
C = century	N, S, E, W = north, south, east, west
Cs = centuries	<15 = up to and including 15
c. = circa	>65 = over 65

SI (metric) units are used for scientific entries; commonly used measurements include an imperial equivalent.

WEB LINKS

All of the Web sites in this encyclopedia have been carefully selected and checked to ensure that they represent reliable sources of information. However the World Wide Web is a constantly evolving place, so the publisher cannot take responsibility for the fact that the content of sites may change beyond the scope of the description given.

The publisher also cannot take responsibility for the content displayed on these sites. The inclusion of a given site in this book should not be taken to mean that the publisher approves of, or endorses, any opinion given on the site, or any of the links accessible from it.

COMMENTS AND SUGGESTIONS

The continuing success and accuracy of *The Hutchinson Encyclopedia* have been helped by the many readers who have taken the trouble to write in, whether with suggestions for new entries or additional information, or with amendments to existing entries. Your feedback is invaluable for the continuing improvement of the encyclopedia.

Updates are included to March 2004.

Acknowledgements

CONTRIBUTORS

Owen Adikibi PhD, CIM, IBIM
Lesley Askins MPhil, FSA, MIFA
Roy Adkins MPhil, FSA, MIFA
Alain Anderton MA
Christine Avery MA, PhD
John Ayto MA
Paul Bahn PhD, FSA
Anne Barker BA
Tallis Barker DPhil, ARCM
Malcolm Bradbury MA, PhD, FRSL
Elizabeth Breuilly
Clare Collinson BA
Nigel Davis BSc
Ian Derbyshire MA, PhD, FRSL
J D Derbyshire PhD, FInstM
Michael Dewar MA
Dougal Dixon MSc

Mark Dreyer
Nigel Dudley BSc
Ingrid von Essen
Eric Farge
Anna Farkas MA
Peter W Fleming PhD
Karen Froud
Diana Gallannaugh BSc
Lawrence Garner BA
William Gould BA
Wendy Grossman
Jackie Herald
Michael Hitchcock DPhil
Chris Holdsworth MA, PhD
Stuart Holroyd
Lisa Isenman
Mawil Izzi Dien PhD

Sara Jenkins Jones
Charles W Kidd
Peter Lafferty MSc
Graham K H Ley MPhil
Carol Lister PhD, FSS
Graham Littler MSc, FSS
Tom McArthur PhD
John Mapps
Richard Martin PhD
David M Munro PhD, FSA (Scot)
Chris Murray
Joanne O'Brien MA
Maureen O'Connor BA
Robert Paisley PhD
Martin Palmer MA
Paulette Pratt
Tim Pulleine

Ben Ramos
Glyn Redworth MPhil
Ian Ridpath FRAS
Adrian Room MA, DipEd, FRGS
Simon Ross BA
Julian Rowe PhD
Jack Schofield MA
Emma Shackleton MA
Andrew Skilton DPhil
Joe Staines BA
Callum Storie BSc(Arch)
Catherine Thompson MA
Jason Tomes DPhil
Stephen Webster MPhil, PGCE
Elizabeth Whitelegg BSc
John Wright

FOCUS FEATURE AUTHORS

Paul Bray BA, freelance technology journalist who writes for the *Daily Telegraph*, *The Sunday Times*, and a number of computer magazines and Web sites.

Sarah Chester PhD, scientific writer and editor.

Ian Derbyshire MA, PhD, FCA, writer on history, government, and politics; coauthor of *Politics in Britain: from Callaghan to Thatcher* and *Political Systems of the World*.

Clive Gillman, lead artist and technical consultant of FACT (Foundation for Art and Creative Technology) in Liverpool.

Simon Hall MA, historical author and publishing project manager.

Martin Henig MA, DPhil, DLitt, FSA, visiting lecturer in Roman Art at the University of Oxford, Hon. Editor of the British Archaeological Association, author of *The Art of Roman Britain*.

Peter Higgins BA, BSc (Hons), PhD, professor of mathematics at the University of Essex, author of *Mathematics for the Curious*.

Richard James PhD, retired lecturer in astronomy at the University of Manchester, now a teaching fellow in the Department of Physics and Astronomy.

Charles Messenger, freelance military historian and defence analyst.

Eugene Ogan PhD, professor of anthropology (emeritus) at the University of Minnesota, author of *The Nasioi of Papua New Guinea* and *Endangered Peoples of Oceania*.

Jon Turney PhD, senior lecturer in science communication at the Department of Science and Technology Studies, University College, London.

Simon Torok BSc (Hons), Grad Dip Sci Com, PhD, external communications manager at the Tyndall Centre for Climate Change Research.

Matthew Walker MA, PhD, MRCP, Advanced Wellcome Fellow and lecturer in neurology at the Institute of Neurology, London.

Paul Wymer PhD, educationalist and science writer, established the National Centre for Biotechnology Education.

EDITORIAL AND PRODUCTION

EDITORIAL DIRECTOR
Hilary McGlynn

DEPUTY EDITORIAL DIRECTOR
Roger Tritton

PROJECT EDITOR
Fran Alexander

PROJECT MANAGERS
Sarah Hudson, Barbara Fraser

EDITORS

Ruth Austin
Andrew Bacon
Oliver Baird
Colin Baldwin
Julian Beecroft
Alison Brett
Gerry Brisch
Stuart Brown
Nicky Bull
Penuel Burchall
Gill Colver
Susan Dickson
Denise Dresner
Alan Foster
Georgina Giraldi
Pippa Kelly

Michael Lacewing
Joan Lait
Elizabeth Littler
Rachel Margolis
Nicky Matthews
Kathryn Pilgrem
Elisabeth Rees
Bryan Rogers
Catherine Shephard
Sandra Szivos
Catherine Thompson
Lisa Trueman
Ceri Warner
Liz Whiting

FOCUS FEATURE EDITOR
Alyson Lacewing

CONTENT DEVELOPMENT MANAGERS
Claire Lishman
Oliver Baird

CONTENT FULFILMENT MANAGERS
Tracey Auden
Rachel Margolis

SYSTEMS MANAGER
Lorraine Cotterell

DESIGN AND PRODUCTION
John Normansell
Stacey Penny

PICTURE RESEARCH
Sophie Evans
Gill Metcalfe

CARTOGRAPHIC PRODUCTION MANAGER
Caroline Dodds

CARTOGRAPHERS
Ben Brown
Rachel Hopper
Adam Meara
Olive Pearson
Nikki Sargeant

TYPOGRAPHY AND LAYOUT DESIGN
Ken Wilson

COMPUTER TYPESETTING
Florence Production Ltd, Tiverton, Devon, England

PAGE LAYOUT
Florence Production Ltd, Tiverton, Devon, England

REPRO
Hilite Design and Repro, Southampton, England

A

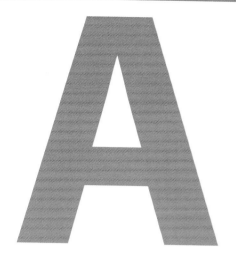

A in physics, symbol for ▷ampere, a unit of electrical current.

Aachen (French **Aix-la-Chapelle**) cathedral city and spa in the *Land* (state) of North Rhine-Westphalia, Germany, 64 km/40 mi southwest of Cologne, near the Dutch and Belgian borders; population (2003 est) 241,300. It has thriving electronic, glass, food, woollen textile, and rubber industries, and is one of Germany's principal railway junctions. It also lies at the centre of a coalmining district, although coal and lignite production is in decline. Aachen was the Roman **Aquisgranum** and was the site of baths in the 1st century. It has been visited for its thermal springs since Roman times, and the spa facilities continue today. Charlemagne, Holy Roman Emperor from 800, founded the cathedral in 796.

Related Web site: Aachen http://www-i5.informatik.rwth-aachen.de/mjf/stadt-aachen.html

Aalborg alternative form of ▷Ålborg, a port in Denmark.

Aalto, Alvar (Hugo Alvar Henrik) (1898–1976) Finnish architect and designer. He was a pioneer of the ▷Modern Movement in his native Finland. Initially working within the confines of the ▷International Style, he later developed a unique architectural style, characterized by asymmetry, curved walls, and contrast of natural materials. He invented a new form of laminated bent-plywood furniture in 1932 and won many design awards for household and industrial items.

Aalto's buildings include Baker House, a Hall of Residence at the Massachusetts Institute of Technology 1947–49; Technical High School, Otaniemi, 1962–65; and Finlandia Hall, Helsinki, 1972.

aardvark (Afrikaans 'earth pig') nocturnal mammal *Orycteropus afer*, the only species in the order Tubulidentata, found in central and southern Africa. A timid, defenceless animal about the size of a pig, it has a long head, a piglike snout, large ears, sparse body hair, a thick tail, and short legs.

It can burrow rapidly with its clawed front feet. It spends the day in its burrow, and at night digs open termite and ant nests, licking up the insects with its long sticky tongue. Its teeth are unique, without enamel, and are the main reason for the aardvark being placed in its own order. When fully grown, it is about 1.5 m/5 ft long and its tongue is 30 cm/12 in long.

aardwolf nocturnal mammal *Proteles cristatus* of the ▷hyena family, Hyaenidae. It is yellowish grey with dark stripes and, excluding its bushy tail, is around 70 cm/30 in long. It is found in eastern and southern Africa, usually in the burrows of the ▷aardvark. It feeds almost exclusively on termites, eating up to 300,000 per day, but may also eat other insects and small mammals.

Aarhus alternative form of ▷Århus, a port in Denmark.

abacus ancient calculating device made up of a frame of parallel wires on which beads are strung. The method of calculating with a handful of stones on a 'flat surface' (Latin *abacus*) was familiar to the Greeks and Romans, and used by earlier peoples, possibly even in ancient Babylon; it survives in the more sophisticated bead-frame form of the Russian *schoty* and the Japanese *soroban*. The abacus has been superseded by the electronic calculator.

The wires of a bead-frame abacus define place value (for example, in the decimal number system each successive wire, counting from right to left, would stand for ones, tens, hundreds, thousands, and so on) and beads are slid to the top of each wire in order to represent the digits of a particular number. On a simple decimal abacus, for example, the number 8,493 would be entered by sliding three beads on the first wire (three ones), nine beads on the second wire (nine tens), four beads on the third wire (four hundreds), and eight beads on the fourth wire (eight thousands).

Abadan Iranian oil port in Khuzestan province, situated on an island on the east side of the Shatt-al-Arab waterway at the head of the Gulf, 675 km/420 mi southwest of Tehran; population (1997 est) 308,000. Abadan is the chief refinery and shipping centre for Iran's oil industry, nationalized in 1951. This measure was the beginning of the worldwide movement by oil-producing countries to assume control of profits from their own resources. Oil installations were badly damaged during the Iran–Iraq war from 1980–88.

abalone edible marine snail of the worldwide genus *Haliotis*, family Haliotidae. Abalones have flattened, oval, spiralled shells, which have holes around the outer edge and a bluish mother-of-pearl lining. This lining is used in ornamental work.

Abba Swedish pop group 1973–81, one of the most successful groups in Europe during the 1970s. Their well-produced songs were characterized by the harmonies of the two female lead singers, and were aimed at a wide audience. Abba had a string of international hits beginning with 'Waterloo' (winner of the Eurovision Song Contest 1974) and including 'SOS' (1974), 'Fernando' (1976), 'Dancing Queen' (1976), and 'The Winner Takes It All' (1980).

Abbado, Claudio (1933–) Italian conductor. He was principal director of the Vienna State Opera from 1986 and of the Berlin Philharmonic Orchestra from 1989. Associated early in his career with the La Scala Opera, Milan, his wide-ranging repertoire includes a significant number of 20th-century composers, among them Schoenberg, Prokofiev, Janáček, Bartók, and Stockhausen. He has also conducted the European Youth Orchestra from its inception in 1977.

Abbās I, the Great (*c.* 1571–1629) Shah of Persia from 1587. He expanded Persian territory by conquest, defeating the Uzbeks near Herat in 1597 and also the Turks. At his death his empire reached from the River Tigris to the Indus River. He was a patron of the arts.

Abbasid dynasty Family of rulers of the Islamic empire, whose ▷caliphs reigned in Baghdad 750–1258. They were descended from Abbas, the prophet Muhammad's uncle, and some of them, such as Harun al-Rashid and Mamun (reigned 813–33), were outstanding patrons of cultural development. Later their power dwindled, and in 1258 Baghdad was burned by the Tatars.

abbey in the Christian church, a building or group of buildings housing a community of monks or of nuns, all dedicated to a life of celibacy and religious seclusion, governed by an abbot or abbess respectively. The word is also applied to a building that was once the church of an abbey; for example, Westminster Abbey, London.

Abbey Theatre playhouse in Dublin, Republic of Ireland, associated with the literary revival of the early 1900s, that was part of a general cultural Irish revival. The theatre opened in 1904 and staged the works of a number of Irish dramatists, including Lady Gregory, W B Yeats, J M Synge, and Seán O'Casey. Burned down in 1951, the Abbey Theatre was rebuilt in 1966.

> **Peter Abelard**
> *All acts are in themselves indifferent and only become good or evil according to the intention of their author.*
> J P Migne (ed.) *Patrologiae Latina* 178, 644a

Abbott and Costello Stage names of William Abbott (1895–1974) and Louis Cristillo (1906–1959). US comedy duo. Having formed a successful vaudevillian stage act during the 1930s, Abbott and Costello went on to make a number of films together that showcased their routines between 1940 and 1956.

Abd al-Hamid II (1842–1918) Last sultan of Turkey 1876–1909. In 1908 the ▷Young Turks under Enver Pasha forced Abd al-Hamid to restore the constitution of 1876 and in 1909 insisted on his deposition. He died in confinement. For his part in the ▷Armenian massacres suppressing the revolt of 1894–96 he was known as the 'Great Assassin'; his actions still motivate Armenian violence against the Turks.

Abd al-Malik Ibn Marwan (647–705) Fifth caliph of the Umayyad dynasty, who reigned 685–705, based in Damascus. He waged military campaigns to unite Muslim groups and battled against the Greeks. He instituted a purely Arab coinage and replaced Syriac, Coptic, and Greek with Arabic as the language for his lands. His reign was turbulent but succeeded in extending and strengthening the power of the dynasty. He was also a patron of the arts.

abdication crisis in British history, the constitutional upheaval of the period 16 November 1936 to 10 December 1936, brought about by the British king ▷Edward VIII's decision to marry Wallis ▷Simpson, a US divorcee. The marriage of the 'Supreme Governor' of the Church of England to a divorced person was considered unsuitable and the king abdicated on 10 December and left for voluntary exile in France. He was created Duke of Windsor and married Mrs Simpson on 3 June 1937.

abdomen in vertebrates, the part of the body below the ▷thorax, containing the digestive organs; in insects and other arthropods, it is the hind part of the body. In mammals, the abdomen is separated from the thorax by the ▷diaphragm, a sheet of muscular tissue; in arthropods, commonly by a narrow constriction. In mammals, the female reproductive organs are in the abdomen. In insects and spiders, it is characterized by the absence of limbs.

Abdullah ibn Hussein (1882–1951) King of Jordan 1946–51. In 1921, after the collapse of the Ottoman empire, he became emir of the British mandate of Transjordan, covering present-day Jordan, and became king when the mandate ended in May 1946. In May 1948 King Abdullah attacked the newly established state of Israel, capturing large areas. He retained the area called the West Bank (Arab Palestine) after a ceasefire in 1949 and renamed the country the Hashemite Kingdom of Jordan. He was assassinated in July 1951 by a Palestinian Arab fanatic.

Abdullah ibn Hussein (1962–) King of Jordan from 1999. Abdullah was crowned king of Jordan after his father, ▷Hussein ibn Talal, who had ruled the Hashemite Kingdom since 1952, died. Abdullah, who was an army major general, and untested in the affairs of state, became the fourth leader of this small but strategically vital state. He promised to maintain Hussein's legacy, continuing the course of moderation and commitment to Middle East peace.

Abdullah, Sheikh Muhammad (1905–1982) Indian politician, known as the 'Lion of Kashmir'. He headed the struggle for constitutional government against the Maharajah of Kashmir, and in 1948, following a coup, became prime minister. He agreed to the accession of the state to India, but was dismissed and imprisoned from 1953 (with brief intervals of freedom) until 1966, when he called for Kashmiri self-determination. He became chief minister of Jammu and Kashmir in 1975, accepting the sovereignty of India.

Abel In the Old Testament (Genesis 4), the second son of Adam and Eve; as a shepherd, he made burnt offerings of meat to God which were more acceptable than the fruits offered by his brother Cain; he was killed by the jealous Cain. This was the first death recounted in the Bible.

Abel, John Jacob (1857–1938) US biochemist, discoverer of ▷adrenaline. He studied the chemical composition of body tissues, and this led, in 1898, to the discovery of adrenaline, the first hormone to be identified, which Abel called epinephrine. He later became the first to isolate ▷amino acids from blood.

Abelard, Peter (1079–1142) (French **Pierre Abélard**) French scholastic philosopher who worked on logic and theology. His romantic liaison with his pupil ▷Héloïse caused a medieval scandal. Details of his life are contained in the autobiographical *Historia Calamitatum Mearum/The History of My Misfortunes*. Abelard, born in Pallet, near Nantes, became canon of Notre Dame in Paris and master of the cathedral school in 1115. When his seduction of Héloïse and secret marriage to her (shortly after the birth of a son) became known, she entered a convent. He was castrated at the instigation of her uncle Canon Fulbert, and became a monk. Resuming teaching a year later, he was cited for heresy and became a hermit at Nogent, where he built the oratory of the Paraclete, and later abbot of a monastery in Brittany. Also a musician and composer, he composed songs for Héloïse, planctus, and Latin lamentations.

Related Web site: Abelard http://www.nd.edu/Departments/Maritain/etext/abelard.htm

Abercrombie, (Leslie) Patrick (1879–1957) English architect. A pioneer of British town planning, he was involved in replanning British cities, including London, after damage in World War II. He initiated the ▷new town policy, which drew on the idea of the ▷garden city. He was knighted in 1945.

Aberdeen, George Hamilton Gordon, 4th Earl of Aberdeen (1784–1860) British Tory politician, prime minister from 1852 until 1855, when he resigned because of criticism provoked by the miseries and mismanagement of the ▷Crimean War.

Aberdeen City city and unitary authority in northeast Scotland. The unitary authority was created in 1996 from the district of the same name that was part of Grampian region from 1975; before that it was part of Aberdeenshire. The city of Aberdeen, as well as being the administrative headquarters of the Aberdeen City unitary authority, is the administrative headquarters of ▷Aberdeenshire unitary authority. It is now Scotland's third largest city.

area 185 sq km/71 sq mi **physical** low-lying coastal area on the banks of the rivers Dee and Don; it has 3 km/2 mi of sandy beaches **features** St Andrew's Episcopal Cathedral (consecrated in 1816);

King's College (from 1500) and Marischal College (founded in 1593, and housed in one of the world's largest granite buildings constructed in 1836), which together form Aberdeen University; Brig O'Balgownie (1314–18); Municipal Buildings (1867); St Machar Cathedral (from 1370). Aberdeen's granite buildings have given it the name of 'Silver City', although the last granite quarry, in Rubislaw, closed in 1971 **agriculture** white and salmon fishing **industries** North Sea oil (it is the main centre in Scotland and Europe for offshore oil exploration and there are shore-based maintenance and service depots for the North Sea oil rigs; an airport and heliport at Dyce, 9.6 km/6 mi northwest of the city, link the mainland to the rigs), oil and gas service industries, paper manufacturing, textiles, engineering, food processing, chemicals, fish processing **population** (2000 est) 213,100 **famous people** poet John Barbour, archdeacon of Aberdeen; Scottish historian Hector Boece (c. 1465–1536), principal of King's College; theologian George Campbell; the poet Lord ▷Byron received his early education at the grammar school here

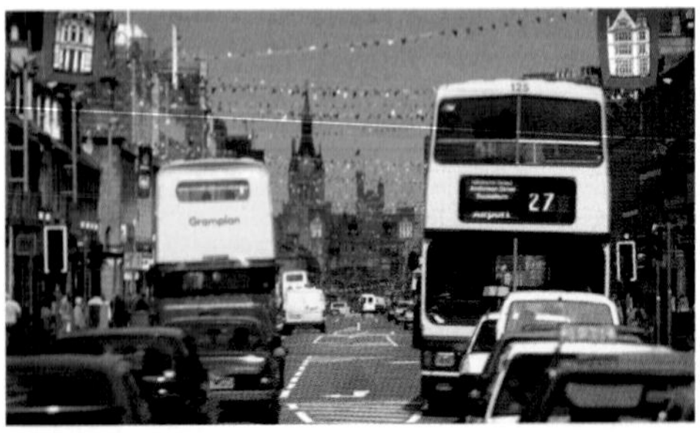

ABERDEEN CITY The city and historic royal burgh of Aberdeen, Scotland, is a busy seaport. This picture shows the bustle of the city centre in Union Street. *Image Bank*

Aberdeenshire unitary authority in northeast Scotland, created in 1996 from three districts within the former Grampian region; its administrative headquarters, Aberdeen, lies outside the authority. **area** 6,308 sq km/2,436 sq mi **towns** Banff, Fraserburgh, Huntly, Peterhead, Stonehaven, Inverurie **physical** area of contrast with mountainous western interior, intensively farmed core, and coastal plain; Cairngorm Mountains; rivers Deveron, Ythan, Don, and Dee **features** Balmoral Castle; Braemar Games **industries** oil and gas, papermaking, whisky distilling, seafood, tourism **agriculture** fishing, beef cattle, cereal crops **population** (1998 est) 226,300; the population has risen by 20% since 1981, largely as a result of employment-driven immigration, mainly because of the oil and gas industry

aberration of starlight apparent displacement of a star from its true position, due to the combined effects of the speed of light and the speed of the Earth in orbit around the Sun (about 30 km per second/18.5 mi per second). Aberration, discovered in 1728 by English astronomer James Bradley, was the first observational proof that the Earth orbits the Sun.

aberration, optical any of a number of defects that impair the image in an optical instrument. Aberration occurs because of minute variations in lenses and mirrors, and because different parts of the light ▷spectrum are reflected or refracted by varying amounts.

Aberystwyth commercial, tourist, and educational centre in Ceredigion, mid-Wales, situated at the mouths of the rivers Ystwyth and Rheidol in Cardigan Bay; population (2000 est) 13,000, of which 45% is Welsh-speaking. It is the site of the University College of Wales (1872), which dominates the town, and during term time the population swells to around 20,000 (2000 est). Aberystwyth is the largest town in mid-Wales and houses many of Wales's national organizations and institutions.

Abidjan port and former capital (until 1983) of the Republic of Côte d'Ivoire; population (1995 est) 2,722,000. There is an airport, communication by rail, as well as by sea, and the city has become increasingly important for its industries which include metallurgy, farm machinery, car and electrical assembly. Products include coffee, palm oil, cocoa, and timber (mahogany). There are tourist markets trading in handicrafts and traditional medicines.

ab init. abbreviation for **ab initio** (Latin 'from the beginning').

abiotic factor non-living variable within the ecosystem, affecting the life of organisms. Examples include temperature, light, and water. Abiotic factors can be harmful to the environment, as when sulphur dioxide emissions from power stations produce acid rain.

Abkhazia (or **Abkhaziya**) autonomous republic in northwestern ▷Georgia; area 8,600 sq km/3,320 sq mi; population (1991) 525,000. The region is located between the main range of the ▷Caucasus Mountains and the ▷Black Sea, with a subtropical climate on the latter's shores, and with densely wooded foothills. The capital is Sokhumi; other cities include Ochamchire and Gagra. Industries include the mining of tin and coal, and lumbering and sawmilling. Fruit, tobacco, and tea are cultivated, and tourism and health resorts are also important.

Abkhazia was inhabited traditionally by Abkhazis, an ethnic group converted from Christianity to Islam in the 17th century. By the 1980s some 17% of the population were Muslims and two-thirds were of Georgian origin.

Related Web site: Abkhazia Home Page http://hypatia.ss.uci.edu/gpacs/abkhazia/

Åbo Swedish name for ▷Turku, a port in southwest Finland.

abolitionism a movement culminating in the late 18th and early 19th centuries that aimed first to end the slave trade, and then to abolish the institution of ▷slavery and emancipate slaves.

In the USA, slavery was officially abolished by the ▷Emancipation Proclamation (1863) of President Abraham ▷Lincoln, but it could not be enforced until 1865 after the Union victory in the Civil War. The question of whether newly admitted states would allow slavery had been a major issue in the break-up of the Union.

In the UK, the leading abolitionist was William ▷Wilberforce, who secured passage of a bill abolishing the slave trade in 1807.

abominable snowman (or **yeti**) legendary creature, said to resemble a human, with long arms and a thickset body covered with reddish-grey hair. Reports of its existence in the Himalayas have been made since 1832, and they gained substance from a published photograph of a huge footprint in the snow in 1951. No further 'evidence' has been found. According to local legend, the creature brings bad luck to anyone who sees it.

Aboriginal art art of the Australian Aborigines. Traditionally almost entirely religious and ceremonial, it was directed towards portraying stories of the ▷Dreamtime, a creation mythology reflecting the Aboriginal hunter-gatherer lifestyle. Perishable materials were used, as in bark painting and carved trees and logs, and few early works of this type survive. A great deal of rock art remains intact, however, and forms one of the richest continuing traditions in the world. Abstract patterns and stylized figures predominate. Ground and body painting were also practised, chiefly as part of secret initiation rites.

aborigine (Latin *ab origine* 'from the beginning') any indigenous inhabitant of a region or country. The word often refers to the original peoples of areas colonized by Europeans, and especially to ▷Australian Aborigines.

abortion (Latin *aborire* 'to miscarry') ending of a pregnancy before the fetus is developed sufficiently to survive outside the uterus. Loss of a fetus at a later gestational age is termed premature stillbirth. Abortion may be accidental (▷miscarriage) or deliberate (termination of pregnancy).

Deliberate termination In the first nine weeks of pregnancy, medical termination may be carried out using the 'abortion pill' (▷mifepristone) in conjunction with a ▷prostaglandin. There are also various procedures for surgical termination, such as ▷dilatation and curettage, depending on the length of the pregnancy.

Worldwide, an estimated 150,000 unwanted pregnancies are terminated each day by induced abortion. One-third of these abortions are performed illegally and unsafely, and cause one in eight of all maternal deaths.

Abortion as birth control Abortion as a means of birth control has long been controversial. The argument centres largely upon whether a woman should legally be permitted to have an abortion and, if so, under what circumstances. Another aspect is whether, and to what extent, the law should protect the fetus.

Those who oppose abortion generally believe that human life begins at the moment of conception, when a sperm fertilizes an egg. This is the view held, for example, by the Roman Catholic Church. Those who support unrestricted legal abortion may believe in a woman's right to choose whether she wants a child, and may take into account the large numbers of deaths and injuries from unprofessional back-street abortions.

Others approve abortion for specific reasons. For example, if a woman's life or health is jeopardized, abortion may be recommended; and if there is a strong likelihood that the child will be born with severe mental or physical disability. Other grounds for abortion include pregnancy resulting from sexual assault such as rape or incest.

1967 Abortion Act In the UK an abortion must be carried out under the terms of the 1967 Abortion Act, which states that two doctors must agree that termination of the pregnancy is necessary, and the operation must be performed on approved premises.

In April 1990, after 15 unsuccessful attempts to alter the 1967 act, Parliament approved a measure to lower the time limit on abortions from 28 to 24 weeks. Pregnancy can still be terminated at a later date if the mother's life is in danger. In 1998, just under 178,000 abortions were performed in England and Wales and just over 12,000 in Scotland.

Aboukir Bay, Battle of also known as the **Battle of the Nile**; naval battle during the Napoleonic Wars between Great Britain and France, in which Admiral Horatio Nelson defeated Napoleon Bonaparte's fleet at the Egyptian seaport of Aboukir on 1 August 1798. The defeat put an end to French designs in the Middle East.

Abraham (lived *c.* 2300 BC) In the Old Testament, the founder of the Jewish nation. In his early life he was called Abram. God promised him heirs and land for his people in Canaan (Israel), renamed him Abraham ('father of many nations'), and tested his faith by a command (later retracted) to sacrifice his son Isaac.

Still childless at the age of 76, Abraham subsequently had a son (Ishmael) with his wife's maidservant Hagar, and then, at the age of 100, a son (Isaac) with his wife Sarah. God's promise to Abraham that his descendants would be a nation and Canaan their land was fulfilled when the descendants of Abraham's grandson Jacob were led out of Egypt by Moses.

Related Web site: Abraham http://www.newadvent.org/cathen/01051a.htm

Abraham, Plains of plateau near Québec, Canada, where the British commander ▷Wolfe defeated the French under ▷Montcalm, on 13 September 1759, during the French and Indian (or Seven Years) War (1754–63). The outcome of the battle established British supremacy in Canada.

abrasive (Latin 'to scratch away') substance used for cutting and polishing or for removing small amounts of the surface of hard materials. There are two types: natural and artificial abrasives, and their hardness is measured using the ▷Mohs scale. Natural abrasives include quartz, sandstone, pumice, diamond, emery, and corundum; artificial abrasives include rouge, whiting, and carborundum.

Abruzzi (or **Abruzzo**) mountainous region of southern central Italy, comprising the provinces of L'Aquila, Chieti, Pescara, and Teramo; area 10,800 sq km/4,169 sq mi; population (1999 est) 1,277,300. L'Aquila, the capital, and Pescara are the principal towns. Gran Sasso d'Italia, 2,914 m/9,564 ft, is the highest point of the ▷Apennines.

abscess collection of ▷pus in solid tissue forming in response to infection. Its presence is signalled by pain and inflammation.

abscissa in ▷coordinate geometry, the x-coordinate of a point – that is, the horizontal distance of that point from the vertical or y-axis. For example, a point with the coordinates (4, 3) has an abscissa of 4. The y-coordinate of a point is known as the ▷ordinate.

abscissin (or **abscissic acid**) plant hormone found in all higher plants. It is involved in the process of ▷abscission and also inhibits stem elongation, germination of seeds, and the sprouting of buds.

abscission in botany, the controlled separation of part of a plant from the main plant body – most commonly, the falling of leaves or the dropping of fruit controlled by ▷abscissin. In ▷deciduous plants the leaves are shed before the winter or dry season, whereas ▷evergreen plants drop their leaves continually throughout the year. Fruitdrop, the abscission of fruit while still immature, is a naturally occurring process.

absolute value (or **modulus**) in mathematics, the value, or magnitude, of a number irrespective of its sign. The absolute value of a number n is written $|n|$ (or sometimes as mod n), and is defined as the positive square root of n^2. For example, the numbers −5 and 5 have the same absolute value:

$$|5| = |-5| = 5$$

For a ▷complex number, the absolute value is its distance to the origin when it is plotted on an Argand diagram, and can be calculated (without plotting) by applying ▷Pythagoras' theorem. By definition, the absolute value of any complex number $a + ib$ (where a and b are real numbers and i is the square root of −1) is given by the expression:

$$|a + ib| = \sqrt{(a^2 + b^2)}$$

absolute zero lowest temperature theoretically possible according to kinetic theory, zero kelvin (0 K), equivalent to −273.15°C/−459.67°F, at which molecules are in their lowest energy state. Although the third law of ▷thermodynamics indicates the impossibility of reaching absolute zero in practice, temperatures of less than a billionth of a degree above absolute zero have been produced. Near absolute zero, the physical properties of some materials change substantially; for example, some metals lose their electrical resistance and become superconducting.

absolutism (or **absolute monarchy**) system of government in which the ruler or rulers have unlimited power and are subject to no constitutional safeguards or checks. The principle of an absolute monarch, given a right to rule by God (the ▷divine right of kings), was extensively used in Europe during the 17th and 18th centuries; it was based on an earlier theory of papal absolutism.

absorption in physics, taking up of matter of energy by a substance by another, such as a liquid by a solid (ink by blotting paper) or a gas by a liquid (ammonia by water). In physics, absorption is the phenomenon by which a substance retains the energy of radiation of particular wavelengths; for example, a piece of blue glass absorbs all visible light except the wavelengths in the blue part of the spectrum; it also refers to the partial loss of energy resulting from light and other electromagnetic waves passing through a medium. In nuclear physics, absorption is the capture by elements, such as boron, of neutrons produced by fission in a reactor.

abstract art nonrepresentational art. Ornamental art without figurative representation occurs in most cultures. The modern abstract movement in sculpture and painting emerged in Europe and North America between 1910 and 1920. Two approaches produce different abstract styles: images that have been 'abstracted' from nature to the point where they no longer reflect a conventional reality, and nonobjective, or 'pure', art forms, without any reference to reality.

History Abstract art began in the avant-garde movements of the late 19th century – ▷Impressionism, ▷Neo-Impressionism, and ▷post-Impressionism. These styles of painting reduced the importance of the original subject matter and began to emphasize the creative process of painting itself. In the first decade of the 20th century, some painters in Europe began to abandon the established Western conventions of imitating nature and of storytelling and developed a new artistic form and expression.

Abstract artists Wassily ▷Kandinsky is generally regarded as the first abstract artist. From 1910 to 1914 he worked on two series, *Improvisations* and *Compositions*, in which he moved gradually towards total abstraction. His highly coloured canvases influenced many younger European artists. In France around 1907, the cubists Pablo ▷Picasso and Georges ▷Braque also developed a semi-abstract style; their pictures, some partly collage, were composed mainly of fragmented natural images. By 1912 Robert ▷Delaunay had pushed cubism to complete abstraction.

Many variations of abstract art developed in Europe and Russia, as shown in the work of Piet ▷Mondrian, Kasimir Malevich, the ▷Futurists, the Vorticists, and the ▷Dadaists. Sculptors were inspired by the new freedom in form and content, and Constantin ▷Brancusi's versions of *The Kiss* (1907–12) are among the earliest semi-abstract sculptures. Cubist-inspired sculptors such as Raymond Duchamp-Villon and Jacques Lipchitz moved further towards abstraction, as did the Dadaist Hans Arp.

US art Two exhibitions of European art, one in New York in 1913 (the Armory Show), the other in San Francisco in 1917, opened the way for abstraction in US art. Many painters, including the young Georgia ▷O'Keeffe, experimented with new styles. Morgan Russell and Stanton Macdonald-Wright invented their own abstract style, Synchromism, a rival to Orphism, a similar style developed in France by Delaunay. Both movements emphasized colour over form.

Later developments Abstract art has dominated Western art from 1920 and has continued to produce many variations. In the 1940s it gained renewed vigour in the works of the abstract expressionists, and in the 1950s Minimal art developed as a more impersonal, simplified style of abstraction.

Related Web site: Pure Abstraction http://sunsite.unc.edu/wm/paint/tl/20th/pure-abs.html

abstract expressionism movement in US painting that was the dominant force in the country's art in the late 1940s and 1950s. It was characterized by the sensuous use of paint, often on very large canvases, to convey powerful emotions. Some of the artists involved painted pure abstract pictures, but others often retained figurative traces in their work. Most of the leading abstract expressionists were based in New York during the heyday of the movement (they are sometimes referred to as the New York School), and their critical and financial success (after initial opposition) helped New York to replace Paris as the world's leading centre of contemporary art, a position it has held ever since.

Related Web site: Abstract Expressionism http://sunsite.unc.edu/wm/ paint/tl/20th/abs-expr.html

Absurd, Theatre of the avant-garde drama originating with a group of dramatists in the 1950s, including Samuel Beckett, Eugène Ionesco, Jean Genet, and Harold Pinter. Their work expressed the belief that in a godless universe human existence has no meaning or purpose and therefore all communication breaks down. Logical construction and argument gives way to irrational and illogical speech and to its ultimate conclusion, silence, as in Beckett's play *Breath* (1970).

Abu Bakr (or Abu-Bekr) (573–634) Muslim ▷caliph (civic and religious leader of Islam) from 632 to 34. Born Abd-al-Ka'aba, he adopted the name Abu Bakr ('Father of the virgin') about 618 when the prophet ▷Muhammad married his daughter Ayesha.
He was a close adviser to Muhammad in 622–32 and succeeded the prophet as political leader at his death. As the first Muslim caliph he imposed Muslim authority over all the Arab tribes, added Mesopotamia to the Muslim world, and instigated expansion of Islam into Iraq and Syria.

Abu Dhabi sheikhdom in southwest Asia, on the Gulf, capital of the ▷United Arab Emirates; area 67,350 sq km/26,000 sq mi; population (1995) 928,400. Formerly under British protection, it has been ruled since 1971 by Sheikh Sultan Zayed bin al-Nahayan, who is also president of the Supreme Council of Rulers of the United Arab Emirates.

Related Web site: Abu Dhabi http://www.uaeforever.com/AbuDhabi/

Abuja capital of Nigeria (formally designated as such 1982, although not officially recognized until 1992); population of Federal Capital District (1991) 378,700; population of city alone (1992 est) 305,900. Shaped like a crescent, the city was designed by Japanese architect Kenzo Tange: building of the city began in 1976 as a replacement for Lagos, and it is still under construction. The main functions of the city are administrative, with only light industry.

Abu Simbel site of two ancient temples cut into the rock on the banks of the Nile in southern Egypt during the reign of Rameses II, commemorating him and his wife Nefertari. The temples were moved in sections in 1966–67 and rebuilt 60 m/200 ft above their original location before the site was flooded by the waters of the Aswan High Dam.

abutilon one of a group of 90 related species of tropical or semitropical ornamental plants. The Indian mallow or velvet leaf (*Abutilon theophrastus*) is one of the more common; it has bell-shaped yellow flowers and is the source of a jutelike fibre. Many of the species are pollinated by hummingbirds. (Genus *Abutilon*, family Malvaceae.)

abyssal zone dark ocean region 2,000–6,000 m/6,500–19,500 ft deep; temperature 4°C/39°F. Three-quarters of the area of the deep-ocean floor lies in the abyssal zone, which is too far from the surface for photosynthesis to take place. Some fish and crustaceans living there are blind or have their own light sources. The region above is the bathyal zone; the region below, the hadal zone.

Abyssinia former name of ▷Ethiopia.

abzyme in biotechnology, an artificially created antibody that can be used like an enzyme to accelerate reactions.

AC in physics, abbreviation for ▷alternating current.

a/c abbreviation for **account**.

acacia any of a large group of shrubs and trees that includes the thorn trees of the African savannah and the gum arabic tree (*Acacia senegal*) of North Africa, and several North American species of the southwestern USA and Mexico. The hardy tree commonly known as acacia is the false acacia (*Robinia pseudacacia*, of the subfamily Papilionoideae). True acacias are found in warm regions of the world, particularly Australia. (Genus *Acacia*, family Leguminosae.)

Related Web site: Acacia (False) http://www.botanical.com/botanical/mgmh/a/acaci005.html

Academy Award annual honour awarded since 1927 by the American Academy of Motion Picture Arts and Sciences in a number of categories that reflect the diversity and collaborative nature of film-making. The Academy Award is one of the highest accolades in the film industry, and a virtual guarantor of increased financial returns.

The trophy itself is a gold-plated statuette which since 1931 has been popularly nicknamed an 'Oscar'. The most prestigious awards are for Best Picture, Best Director, Best Actor, and Best Actress.

Related Web site: Academy of Motion Picture Arts and Sciences http://www.oscars.org/

Academy, French (or Académie Française) literary society concerned with maintaining the purity of the French language, founded by ▷Richelieu in 1635. Membership is limited to 40 'Immortals' at a time.

acanthus herbaceous plant with handsome lobed leaves. Twenty species are found in the Mediterranean region and Old World tropics, including bear's-breech (*Acanthus mollis*) whose leaves were used as a motif in classical architecture, especially on Corinthian columns. (Genus *Acanthus*, family Acanthaceae.)

a cappella (Italian 'in the style of the chapel') choral music sung without instrumental accompaniment. In modern music it is characteristic of ▷gospel music, ▷doo-wop, and the evangelical Christian church movement.

Acapulco (or Acapulco de Juarez) port and holiday resort in southern Mexico; population (1995 est) 657,000. The city lies in Guerrero state 310 km/193 mi southwest of Mexico City. It is one of the leading Mexican tourist resorts on what is known as the 'Mexican Riviera'. There is deep-sea fishing, and tropical products are exported.

Related Web site: Acapulco Today http://accessmexico.com/acapulco/

ACAS acronym for ▷Advisory, Conciliation, and Arbitration Service, a government-funded body in the UK.

acceleration rate of change of the velocity of a moving body. It is usually measured in metres per second per second ($m\ s^{-2}$) or feet per second per second ($ft\ s^{-2}$). Because velocity is a ▷vector quantity (possessing both magnitude and direction) a body travelling at constant speed may be said to be accelerating if its direction of motion changes. According to Newton's second law of motion, a body will accelerate only if it is acted upon by an unbalanced, or resultant, ▷force. Acceleration due to gravity is the acceleration of a body falling freely under the influence of the Earth's gravitational field; it varies slightly at different latitudes and altitudes. The value adopted internationally for gravitational acceleration is $9.806\ m\ s^{-2}/32.174\ ft\ s^{-2}$.

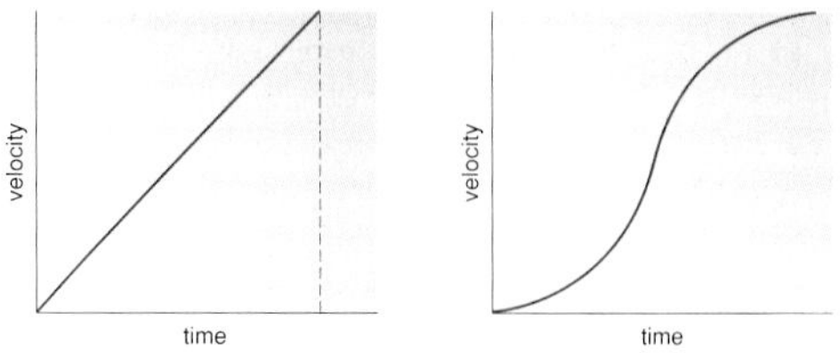

ACCELERATION Acceleration can be depicted graphically by mapping velocity against time. Where acceleration is constant the graph is a straight line.

accelerator in physics, a device to bring charged particles (such as protons and electrons) up to high speeds and energies, at which they can be of use in industry, medicine, and pure physics. At low energies, accelerated particles can be used to produce the image on a television screen and generate X-rays (by means of a ▷cathode-ray tube), destroy tumour cells, or kill bacteria. When high-energy particles collide with other particles, the fragments formed reveal the nature of the fundamental forces.

The first accelerators used high voltages (produced by ▷Van de Graaff generators) to generate a strong, unvarying electric field. Charged particles were accelerated as they passed through the electric field. However, because the voltage produced by a generator is limited, these accelerators were replaced by machines where the particles passed through regions of alternating electric fields, receiving a succession of small pushes to accelerate them. The first of these accelerators was the **linear accelerator** or **linac**. The linac consists of a line of metal tubes, called drift tubes, through which the particles travel. The particles are accelerated by electric fields in the gaps between the drift tubes. Another way of making repeated use of an electric field is to bend the path of a particle into a circle so that it passes repeatedly through the same electric field. The first accelerator to use this idea was the **cyclotron** pioneered in the early 1930s by US physicist Ernest Lawrence. One of the world's most powerful accelerators is the 2 km/1.25 mi diameter machine at ▷Fermilab near Batavia, Illinois, USA. The largest accelerator is the ▷Large Electron Positron Collider at ▷CERN near Geneva, operational 1989–2000. The world's longest linac is also a colliding beam machine: the Stanford Linear Collider, in California. Accelerators have been instrumental in revealing that protons and neutrons are made up of smaller elementary particles called ▷quarks.

accent way of speaking that identifies a person with a particular country, region, language, social class, or some mixture of these.

accent mark (´, ˇ, ˆ) used to indicate stress on a particular syllable or a difference in the pronunciation of a letter. English does not use accents, except in some words of foreign origin such as 'cliché', 'café', and 'fête'.

accessory in law, a criminal accomplice who aids in the commission of a crime committed by someone else. An accomplice may be either 'before the fact' (assisting, ordering, or procuring another to commit a crime) or 'after the fact' (giving assistance after the crime). An accomplice present when the crime is committed is an abettor.

access time (or **reaction time**) in computing, the time taken by a computer, after an instruction has been given, to read from or write to ▷memory.

acclimation (or **acclimatization**) the physiological changes induced in an organism by exposure to new environmental conditions. When humans move to higher altitudes, for example, the number of red blood cells rises to increase the oxygen-carrying capacity of the blood in order to compensate for the lower levels of oxygen in the air.

accommodation in biology, the ability of the ▷eye to focus on near or far objects by changing the shape of the lens.

accomplice in law, a person who acts with another in the commission or attempted commission of a crime, either as a principal or as an ▷accessory.

accordion musical instrument of the free-reed organ type, comprising left and right wind chests connected by flexible, pleated bellows. The accordionist's right hand plays the melody on a piano-style keyboard of 26–34 keys, while the left hand has a system of push buttons for selecting single notes or chord harmonies.

accountant person responsible for drawing up accounts, usually for a business organization. Accountants have traditionally concentrated on recording what has happened financially in the past. However, in management accounting, accountants are increasingly involved in helping to formulate policy for business organizations, providing information for decision-makers and frameworks for making those decisions.

accounting the principles and practice of systematically recording, presenting, and interpreting financial accounts; financial record keeping and management of businesses and other organizations, from balance sheets to policy decisions, for tax or operating purposes. Forms of inflation accounting, such as CCA (current cost accounting) and CPP (current purchasing power), are aimed at providing valid financial comparisons over a period in which money values change.

Accra capital and port of Ghana; population (1998) 1,446,000. It is an important political, commercial, and administrative centre. The port trades in cacao, gold, diamonds, and timber. Scrap metal is a major import and is the basis of local engineering businesses. Other industries include light engineering, brewing, and tobacco and food processing. Osu (Christiansborg) Castle is the presidential residence. The National Museum of Ghana is here, and the University of Ghana is at nearby Legon.

accumulator in computing, a special register, or memory location, in the ▷arithmetic and logic unit of the computer processor. It is used to hold the result of a calculation temporarily or to store data that is being transferred.

accumulator in electricity, a storage ▷battery – that is, a group of rechargeable secondary cells. A familiar example is the lead–acid car battery.

acer group of over 115 related species of trees and shrubs of the temperate regions of the northern hemisphere, many of them popular garden specimens. They include ▷sycamore and ▷maple. Some species have pinnate leaves (leaflets either side of a stem), including the box elder (*Acer negundo*) of North America. (Genus *Acer.*)

acetaldehyde common name for ▷ethanal.

acetate common name for ▷ethanoate.

acetic acid common name for ▷ethanoic acid.

acetone common name for ▷propanone.

acetylene common name for ▷ethyne.

Achaea (or Achaia) in ancient Greece, an area of the northern Peloponnese. The Achaeans were the predominant society during the Mycenaean period and are said by Homer to have taken part in the siege of Troy. The larger Roman province of Achaea was created after the defeat of the Achaean League in 146 BC; it included all mainland Greece south of a line drawn from the Ambracian to the Maliac Gulf.

Achaean League union in 280 BC of most of the cities of the northern Peloponnese, which managed to defeat ▷Sparta, but was itself defeated by the Romans in 146 BC.

Achebe, Chinua (Albert Chinualumogo) (1930–) Nigerian novelist. His themes include the social and political impact of European colonialism on African people, and the problems of newly independent African nations. Among his works are the seminal *Things Fall Apart* (1958), one of the first African novels to achieve a global reputation, and *Anthills of the Savannah* (1987).

achene dry, one-seeded ▷fruit that develops from a single ▷ovary and does not split open to disperse the seed. Achenes commonly occur in groups – for example, the fruiting heads of buttercup *Ranunculus* and clematis. The outer surface may be smooth, spiny, ribbed, or tuberculate, depending on the species.

Achernar (or Alpha Eridani) brightest star in the constellation Eridanus, and the ninth-brightest star in the sky. It is a hot, luminous, blue star with a true luminosity 250 times that of the Sun. It is 144 light years away from the Sun.

Acheson, Dean (Gooderham) (1893–1971) US politician. As undersecretary of state 1945–47 in Harry Truman's Democratic administration, he was associated with George C Marshall in preparing the ▷Marshall Plan, and succeeded him as secretary of state 1949–53.

> **Dean Acheson**
> *The first requirement of a statesman is that he be dull. This is not always easy to achieve.*
> The Observer 21 June 1970

Achilles Greek hero of Homer's *Iliad*. He was the son of Peleus, King of the Myrmidons in Thessaly, and of the sea nymph Thetis who, by dipping him in the River Styx, rendered him invulnerable, except for the heel by which she held him. Achilles killed ▷Hector at the climax of the *Iliad*, and according to subsequent Greek legends was himself killed by ▷Paris, who shot a poisoned arrow into Achilles' heel.

ACID RAIN The diagram shows how acid rain is formed in industrial areas and distributed over long distances, where it can kill trees and damage buildings and statues.

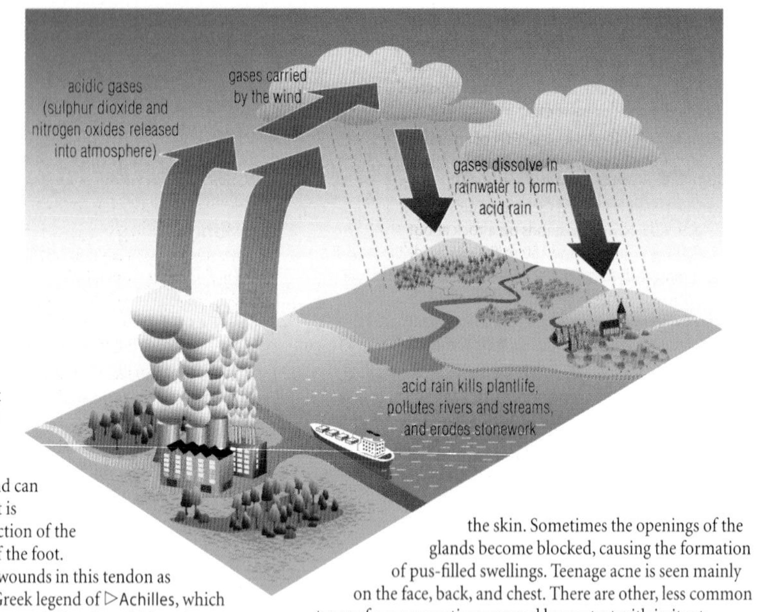
acidic gases
(sulphur dioxide and
nitrogen oxides released
into atmosphere)
gases carried
by the wind
gases dissolve in
rainwater to form
acid rain
acid rain kills plantlife,
pollutes rivers and streams,
and erodes stonework

Achilles tendon tendon at the back of the ankle attaching the calf muscles to the heel bone. It is one of the largest tendons in the human body, and can resist great tensional strain, but is sometimes ruptured by contraction of the muscles in sudden extension of the foot.

Ancient surgeons regarded wounds in this tendon as fatal, probably because of the Greek legend of ▷Achilles, which relates how the mother of the hero Achilles dipped him when an infant into the River Styx, so that he became invulnerable except for the heel by which she held him.

achromatic lens combination of lenses made from materials of different refractive indexes, constructed in such a way as to minimize chromatic aberration (which in a single lens causes coloured fringes around images because the lens diffracts the different wavelengths in white light to slightly different extents).

acid in chemistry, compound that releases hydrogen ions (H^+ or protons) in the presence of an ionizing solvent (usually water). Acids react with ▷bases to form salts, and they act as solvents. Strong acids are corrosive; dilute acids have a sour or sharp taste, although in some organic acids this may be partially masked by other flavour characteristics. The strength of an acid is measured by its hydrogen-ion concentration, indicated by the ▷pH value. All acids have a pH below 7.0.

Acids can be classified as monobasic, dibasic, tribasic, and so forth, according to their basicity (the number of hydrogen atoms available to react with a base) and degree of ionization (how many of the available hydrogen atoms dissociate in water). Dilute sulphuric acid is classified as a strong (highly ionized), dibasic acid.

Inorganic acids include boric, carbonic, hydrochloric, hydrofluoric, nitric, phosphoric, and sulphuric. Organic acids include ethanoic (acetic), benzoic, citric, methanoic (formic) lactic, oxalic, and salicylic, as well as complex substances such as ▷nucleic acids and ▷amino acids.

Sulphuric, nitric and hydrochloric acid are sometimes referred to as the mineral acids. Most naturally occurring acids are found as organic compounds, such as the fatty acids R-COOH and sulphonic acids $R\text{-}SO_3H$, where R is an organic group.

Related Web site: Acids http://www.purchon.co.uk/science/acids.htm
Definition Of Acids And Bases And The Role Of Water http://chemed.chem.purdue.edu/genchem/topicreview/bp/ch11/acidbaseframe.html

acid rain acidic precipitation thought to be caused principally by the release into the atmosphere of sulphur dioxide (SO_2) and oxides of nitrogen (NO_x), which dissolve in pure rainwater making it acidic. Sulphur dioxide is formed by the burning of fossil fuels, such as coal, that contain high quantities of sulphur; nitrogen oxides are contributed from various industrial activities and from car exhaust fumes.

acid salt chemical compound formed by the partial neutralization of a dibasic or tribasic ▷acid (one that contains two or three hydrogen atoms). Although a salt, it contains replaceable hydrogen, so it may undergo the typical reactions of an acid. Examples are sodium hydrogen sulphate ($NaHSO_4$) and acid phosphates.

aclinic line the magnetic equator, an imaginary line near the Equator, where a compass needle balances horizontally, the attraction of the north and south magnetic poles being equal.

acne skin eruption, mainly occurring among adolescents and young adults, caused by inflammation of the sebaceous glands which secrete an oily substance (sebum), the natural lubricant of the skin. Sometimes the openings of the glands become blocked, causing the formation of pus-filled swellings. Teenage acne is seen mainly on the face, back, and chest. There are other, less common types of acne, sometimes caused by contact with irritant chemicals (chloracne).

aconite (or monkshood or wolfsbane) herbaceous plant belonging to the buttercup family, with hooded blue–mauve flowers, native to Europe and Asia. It produces aconitine, a poison with pain-killing and sleep-inducing properties. (*Aconitum napellus*, family Ranunculaceae.)

acorn fruit of the ▷oak tree, a ▷nut growing in a shallow cup.

A Coruña (or Corunna) seaport and capital of A Coruña province in Galicia, northwest Spain, lying on a narrow peninsula between two bays; population (1998 est) 243,100. It is one of the most important European fishing ports, and is well known for its high quality fish and seafood. Other industries include tobacco, sugar refining, textiles, and glass. A Coruña has a large and busy harbour, and a 2 km/1.5 mi stretch of sandy beach in the heart of the city. The Spanish ▷Armada sailed from A Coruña in 1588, and the town was sacked by Francis Drake in 1589.

acouchi any of several small South American rodents, genus *Myoprocta*. They have white-tipped tails, and are smaller relatives of the ▷agouti.

acoustic term describing a musical instrument played without electrical amplification or assistance, for example an acoustic guitar or acoustic piano. It is also a term used by musicians to characterize room response, an important factor in performance. A so-called 'bright' acoustic provides a lively reverberation while a 'dry' or 'muddy' acoustic is lacking in response; see ▷acoustics.

acoustic coupler device that enables computer data to be transmitted and received through a normal telephone handset; the handset rests on the coupler to make the connection. A small speaker within the device is used to convert the computer's digital output data into sound signals, which are then picked up by the handset and transmitted through the telephone system. At the receiving telephone, a second acoustic coupler or modem converts the sound signals back into digital data for input into a computer.

acoustics in general, the experimental and theoretical science of sound and its transmission; in particular, that branch of the science that has to do with the phenomena of sound in a particular space such as a room or theatre. In architecture, the sound-reflecting character of an internal space.

Acoustical engineering is concerned with the technical control of sound, and involves architecture and construction, studying control of vibration, soundproofing, and the elimination of noise. It also includes all forms of sound recording and reinforcement, the hearing and perception of sounds, and hearing aids.

acquired immune deficiency syndrome full name for the disease ▷AIDS.

acquittal in law, the setting free of someone charged with a crime after a trial.

Acre former name of the Israeli seaport of ▷Akko.

acre traditional English land measure equal to 4,840 square yards (4,047 sq m/0.405 ha). Originally meaning a field, it was the size that a yoke of oxen could plough in a day. As early as Edward I's reign, the acre was standardized by statute for official use, although local variations in Ireland, Scotland, and some English counties continued. It may be subdivided into 160 square rods (one square rod equalling 25.29 sq m/30.25 sq yd).

acronym word formed from the initial letters and/or syllables of other words, intended as a pronounceable abbreviation; for example, NATO (North Atlantic Treaty Organization), radar (radio detecting and ranging), RAM (random-access memory) and FORTRAN (formula translation).

acropolis (Greek 'high city') citadel of an ancient Greek town. The Acropolis of Athens contains the ruins of the ▷Parthenon and surrounding complexes, built there during the days of the Athenian empire. The term is also used for analogous structures.

The Acropolis of Athens stands on a rock about 45 m/150 ft high, 350 m/1,150 ft long, and 150 m/500 ft broad. The first kings of Athens built their palace here, and a temple of Athene, the Hecatompedon, existed before the Persian invasion. The later edifices were the Parthenon, the Propylaea, designed by Mnesicles in 437 BC, a temple of Nike Apteros, the Erechtheum, the sanctuary of Artemis Brauronia, and the Pinacotheca.

THE ACROPOLIS The ruins of the Parthenon (built 447–438 BC), a temple dedicated to the goddess Athena, rise from the Acropolis in Athens, Greece. *Image Bank*

acrostic (Greek 'at the extremity of a line or row') a number of lines of writing, usually verse, whose initial letters (read downwards) form a word, phrase, or sentence. A **single acrostic** is formed by the initial letters of lines only; a **double acrostic** is formed by the first and last letters.

Acrux (or **Alpha Crucis**) brightest star in the constellation of Crux, marking one of the four points of the Southern Cross, and the 13th-brightest star in the night sky. It is a double star comprising two blue-white stars, and is 360 light years away from the Sun. Together with nearby Gacrux, it points towards the south celestial pole.

acrylic fibre synthetic fibre often used as a substitute for wool. It was first developed in the mid-1940s but was not produced in large quantities until the 1950s. Strong and warm, acrylic fibre is often used for sweaters and tracksuits and as linings for boots and gloves, as well as in furnishing fabrics and carpets. It is manufactured as a filament, then cut into short staple lengths similar to wool hairs, and spun into yarn. **Modacrylic** is a modified acrylic yarn.

acrylic paint any of a range of synthetic substitutes for ▷oil paint, mostly soluble in water. Acrylic paints are used in a variety of painting techniques, from wash to impasto. They dry quicker than oil paint and are waterproof and remain slightly flexible, but lack the translucency of natural substances.

ACT abbreviation for ▷Australian Capital Territory.

actinide any of a series of 15 radioactive metallic chemical elements with atomic numbers 89 (actinium) to 103 (lawrencium). Elements 89 to 95 occur in nature; the rest of the series are synthesized elements only. Actinides are grouped together because of their chemical similarities (for example, they are all bivalent), the properties differing only slightly with atomic number. The series is set out in a band in the ▷periodic table of the elements, as are the ▷lanthanides.

actinium (Greek *aktis* 'ray') white, radioactive, metallic element, the first of the actinide series, symbol Ac, atomic number 89, relative atomic mass 227; it is a weak emitter of high-energy alpha particles.

Actinium occurs with uranium and radium in ▷pitchblende and other ores, and can be synthesized by bombarding radium with neutrons. The longest-lived isotope, Ac-227, has a half-life of 21.8 years (all the other isotopes have very short half-lives). Chemically, it is exclusively trivalent, resembling in its reactions the lanthanides and the other actinides. Actinium was discovered in 1899 by the French chemist André Debierne.

action in law, one of the proceedings whereby a person or agency seeks to enforce rights or redress a wrong in a civil court.

action painting (or **gesture painting**) in abstract art, a form of abstract expressionism that emphasized the importance of the physical act of painting. Jackson ▷Pollock, the leading exponent, threw, dripped, and dribbled paint on to canvases fastened to the floor. He was known to attack his canvas with knives and trowels and bicycle over it. Another principal exponent was Willem de Kooning.

action potential in biology, a change in the ▷potential difference (voltage) across the membrane of a nerve cell when an impulse passes along it. A change in potential (from about −60 to +45 millivolts) accompanies the passage of sodium and potassium ions across the membrane.

Actium, Battle of naval battle in which Octavian defeated the combined fleets of ▷Mark Antony and ▷Cleopatra on 2 September 31 BC to become the undisputed ruler of the Roman world (as the emperor ▷Augustus). The site of the battle is at Akri, a promontory in western Greece.

Antony had encamped in Greece with a powerful force of infantry and cavalry, and was waiting for Octavian's smaller force to attack. However, engagements on land proved indecisive and in the meantime Octavian's naval commander Marcus Agrippa had managed to cut off Antony's supply route by sea, despite commanding a fleet of only 400 ships against Antony's 500. Antony and Cleopatra could have escaped overland to continue the fight but Cleopatra demanded to return to Egypt by sea and they were defeated in the ensuing sea battle. Having unsuccessfully requested peace terms, they fled to Egypt but Octavian pursued them the following year. Alexandria surrendered without a fight and they committed suicide.

Related Web site: Battle of Actium http://myron.sjsu.edu/romeweb/ROMARMY/art21.htm

activation energy in chemistry, the minimum energy required in order to start a chemical reaction. Some elements and compounds will react together merely by bringing them into contact (spontaneous reaction). For others it is necessary to supply energy (heat radiation, or electrical charge) in order to start the reaction. This initial energy is the activation energy.

act of Congress in the USA, a bill or resolution passed by both houses of Congress, the Senate and the House of Representatives, which becomes law with the signature of the president. If vetoed by the president, it may still become law if it returns to Congress again and is passed by a majority of two-thirds in each house.

act of God legal term meaning some sudden and irresistible act of nature that could not reasonably have been foreseen or prevented, such as floods or exceptionally high tides, storms, lightning, earthquakes, sharp frosts, or sudden death.

act of Parliament in Britain, a change in the law originating in Parliament and called a statute. Before an act receives the royal assent and becomes law it is a **bill**. The US equivalent is an ▷act of Congress.

actuary mathematician who makes statistical calculations concerning human life expectancy and other risks, on which insurance, life assurance, and pension premiums are based.

acupuncture in alternative medicine, a system of inserting long, thin metal needles into the body at predetermined points to relieve pain, as an anaesthetic in surgery, and to assist healing. The needles are rotated manually or electrically. The method, developed in ancient China and increasingly popular in the West, is thought to work by stimulating the brain's own painkillers, the ▷endorphins.

Related Web site: Acupuncture.com http://acupuncture.com/

acute in medicine, term used to describe a disease of sudden and severe onset which resolves quickly; for example, pneumonia and meningitis. In contrast, a **chronic** condition develops and remains over a long period.

acute angle an angle between 0° and 90°; that is, an amount of turn that is less than a quarter of a circle.

AD in the Christian chronological system, abbreviation for ▷anno Domini.

Ada high-level computer-programming language, developed and owned by the US Department of Defense, designed for use in situations in which a computer directly controls a process or machine, such as a military aircraft. The language took more than five years to specify, and became commercially available only in the late 1980s. It is named after English mathematician Ada Augusta Byron.

ACT OF PARLIAMENT The title page of an Elizabethan act of Parliament 1585. *Philip Sauvain Picture Collection*

Adam (Hebrew *adham* 'man') In the Old Testament (Genesis 2, 3), the first human. Formed by God from dust and given the breath of life, Adam was placed in the Garden of Eden, where ▷Eve was created from his rib and given to him as a companion. Because she tempted him, he tasted the forbidden fruit of the Tree of Knowledge of Good and Evil, for which trespass they were expelled from the Garden.

Adam Family of Scottish architects and designers. **William Adam** (1689–1748) was the leading Scottish architect of his day, and his son **Robert Adam** (1728–1792) is considered one of the greatest British architects of the late 18th century, responsible for transforming the prevailing Palladian fashion in architecture to a neoclassical style.

Adams, Gerry (1948–) Born Gerard Adams. Northern Irish politician, president of ▷Sinn Fein (the political wing of the Irish Republican Army, IRA) from 1978. Adams was born in Belfast, the son of an IRA activist. He was elected member of Parliament for Belfast West in 1983 but declined to take up his Westminster seat, as he refused to take an oath of allegiance to the British queen. He lost his seat in 1992 but regained it in 1997, still refusing to sit in the Westminster Parliament. He has been a key figure in Irish peace negotiations. In 1994 he was the main architect of the IRA ceasefire and in 1997 Adams entered into multiparty talks with the British government which, on Good Friday, 10 April 1998, resulted in an agreement accepted by all parties and subsequently endorsed in referenda held simultaneously in Northern Ireland and in the Irish Republic.

Adams was interned 1972–77 on suspicion of involvement in terrorist activity. In 1993 it was revealed that he had held talks about a possible political solution with the leader of the Social Democratic and Labour Party, John ▷Hume, and with representatives of the British government. In August 1994, when Adams announced an IRA ceasefire, the British government removed all restrictions on his public appearances and freedom to travel to mainland Britain (in force since 1988). The unwillingness of the IRA to decommission its arms prior to full British troop withdrawal from Northern Ireland led to a delay in the start of all-party peace talks in 1995, and the resumption of IRA violence in February 1996 damaged his credibility and cast doubt over the peace process.

Adams was criticized for failing to denounce the violence. Nevertheless, in September 1998, he met the Ulster Unionist leader, David Trimble, at Stormont, Belfast, in an historic meeting, the first of its kind for several generations.

Adams, John (1735–1826) 2nd president of the USA 1797–1801, and vice-president 1789–97. He was a member of the Continental Congress 1774–78 and signed the Declaration of Independence. In 1779 he went to France and negotiated the treaty of 1783 that ended the American Revolution. In 1785 he became the first US ambassador in London.

Related Web site: John Adams – Second President 1797–1801 http://www.whitehouse.gov/WH/glimpse/presidents/html/ja2.html

Adams, John Couch (1819–1892) English astronomer. He mathematically deduced the existence of the planet Neptune in 1845 from the effects of its gravitational pull on the motion of Uranus, although it was not found until 1846 by J G Galle. Adams also studied the Moon's motion, the Leonid meteors, and terrestrial magnetism.

Adams, John Quincy (1767–1848) 6th president of the USA 1825–29, eldest son of President John Adams. He negotiated the Treaty of Ghent to end the ▷War of 1812 (fought with Britain) on generous terms for the USA. In 1817 he became President James Monroe's secretary of state, formulating the ▷Monroe Doctrine in 1823. As president, Adams was an advocate of strong federal government.

Related Web site: John Quincy Adams – Sixth President 1825–1829 http://www.whitehouse.gov/WH/glimpse/presidents/html/ja6.html

Adams, Richard George (1920–) English novelist. He wrote *Watership Down* (1972), a story of rabbits who escape from a doomed warren and work together to establish a new one. *Tales from Watership Down* (1996) continues the mythology. His other novels using animals as main characters are *Shardik* (1974), *The Plague Dogs* (1977), and *Traveller* (1988), while *The Girl on the Swing* (1980) and *Maia* (1984) have human protagonists. He has also written *The Days Gone By: An Autobiography* (1990).

Adams, Samuel (1722–1803) US politician, the chief instigator of the Boston Tea Party (see ▷American Revolution). He was a signatory to the ▷Declaration of Independence, served in the ▷Continental Congress, and anticipated the French emperor Napoleon in calling the British a 'nation of shopkeepers'.

Adamson, Robert Scottish photographer. He collaborated with fellow Scottish photographer David Octavius Hill. See ▷Hill and Adamson.

Adana capital of Adana (Seyhan) province, southern Turkey; population (1990) 916,150. It is a major cotton-growing centre and Turkey's fourth-largest city. It is located in the middle of the Curukova plain, in the most fertile area of the country.

adaptation (Latin *adaptare* 'to fit to') in biology, any change in the structure or function of an organism that allows it to survive and reproduce more effectively in its environment. In ▷evolution, adaptation is thought to occur as a result of random variation in the genetic make-up of organisms coupled with ▷natural selection. Species become extinct when they are no longer adapted to their environment.

Related Web site: Desert Plant Survival http://www.desertusa.com/du_plantsurv.html

adaptive radiation in evolution, the formation of several species, with ▷adaptations to different ways of life, from a single ancestral type. Adaptive radiation is likely to occur whenever members of a species migrate to a new habitat with unoccupied ecological niches. It is thought that the lack of competition in such niches allows sections of the migrant population to develop new adaptations, and eventually to become new species.

The colonization of newly formed volcanic islands has led to the development of many unique species. The 13 species of Darwin's finch on the Galapagos Islands, for example, are probably descended from a single species from the South American mainland. The parent stock evolved into different species that now occupy a range of diverse niches.

Ad Dakhla port and southern region in Western Sahara; population (1994) 29,800. The town was first established as a Spanish trading port in 1476, when it was known as **Villa Cisneros**.

Addams, Charles Samuel (1912–1988) US cartoonist, creator of the ghoulish Addams family featured in the *New Yorker* magazine. A successful 1960s television comedy series and two feature-length films were based on these cartoons.

addax light-coloured ▷antelope *Addax nasomaculatus* of the family Bovidae. It lives in North Africa around the Sahara Desert where it exists without drinking on scanty vegetation. It is about 1.1 m/3.5 ft tall at the shoulder, and both sexes have spirally twisted horns. Its hooves are broad, enabling it to move easily on soft sand.

adder (Anglo-Saxon *naedre* 'serpent') European venomous snake, the common ▷viper *Vipera berus*. Growing on average to about 60 cm/24 in in length, it has a thick body, a triangular head, with a characteristic V-shaped mark and, often, zigzag markings along the back. It feeds on small mammals and lizards. The puff adder *Bitis arietans* is a large, yellowish, thick-bodied viper up to 1.6 m/5 ft long, living in Africa and Arabia.

The adder, a shy animal, is the only poisonous snake found in Britain. Two-thirds of adder bites produce symptoms no more severe than vomiting and localized swelling. Throughout Europe there have been only 95 deaths in the past 125 years; 14 of these have occurred in Britain.

The name 'adder' is often used for any snake that happens to look like an adder. Two such species live in Australia: the common death adder and the desert death adder. They belong to the genus *Acanthopihis*, and are not members of the viper family.

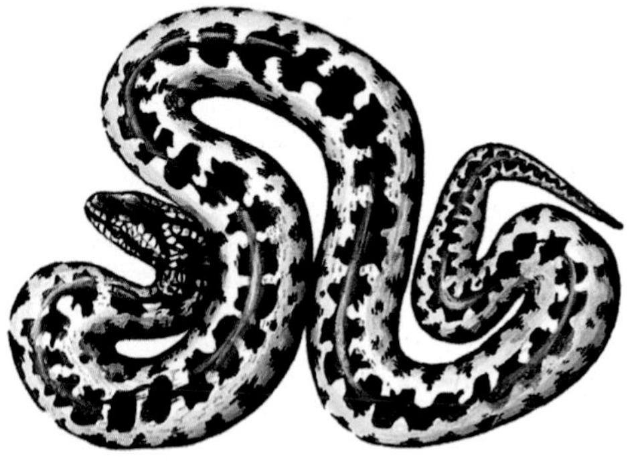

ADDER The common adder, or viper, is widely distributed in Europe as far east as Siberia.

addiction state of dependence caused by habitual use of drugs, alcohol, or other substances. It is characterized by uncontrolled craving, tolerance, and symptoms of withdrawal when access is denied. Habitual use produces changes in body chemistry and treatment must be geared to a gradual reduction in dosage.

adding machine device for adding (and usually subtracting, multiplying, and dividing) numbers, operated mechanically or electromechanically; now largely superseded by electronic calculators.

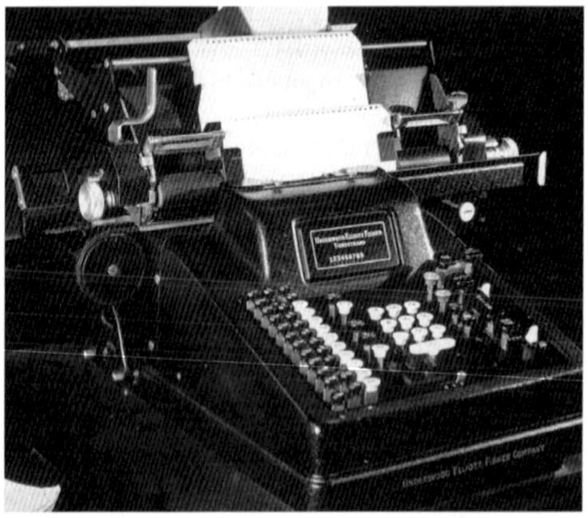

ADDING MACHINE An adding machine from the 1940s. *Archive Photos*

Addis Ababa (or Adis Abeba; Amharic 'new flower') capital of Ethiopia; population (1992) 2,213,000. The city is at an altitude of 2,500 m/8,200 ft. It was founded in 1887 by Menelik II, chief of Shoa, who ascended the throne of Ethiopia in 1889. His former residence, Menelik Palace, is now occupied by the government. Industries include light engineering, food processing, brewing, livestock processing, chemicals, cement, textiles, footwear, clothing, and handicrafts.

The city is the headquarters of the ▷Organization of African Unity (OAU) and the United Nations Economic Commission for Africa.

Joseph Addison

Thus I live in the world rather as a spectator of mankind than as one of the species.

Spectator no. 1

Addison, Joseph (1672–1719) English poet and dramatist, and one of the most celebrated of English essayists. In 1704 he commemorated ▷Marlborough's victory at Blenheim in a poem commissioned by the government, 'The Campaign'. He subsequently held political appointments and was a Member of Parliament for Malmesbury from 1708 until his death. From 1709 to 1711 he contributed to the *Tatler* magazine, begun by Richard ▷Steele, with whom he was cofounder in 1711–12 of the *Spectator*.

His neoclassical blank verse tragedy *Cato* (1713) was highly respected in the 18th century, but as a poet and dramatist Addison formerly held a much higher place than he now does. His essays, however, set a new standard of easy elegance in English prose and his work foreshadows modern journalism.

Related Web site: Selected Poetry of Joseph Addison http://www.library.utoronto.ca/utel/rp/authors/addison.html

addition in arithmetic, the operation of combining two numbers to form a sum; thus, 7 + 4 = 11. It is one of the four basic operations of arithmetic (the others are subtraction, multiplication, and division).

addition reaction chemical reaction in which the atoms of an element or compound react with a double bond or triple bond in an organic compound by opening up one of the bonds and becoming attached to it, for example:

$$CH_2{=}CH_2 + HCl \rightarrow CH_3CH_2Cl$$

Another example is the addition of hydrogen atoms to ▷unsaturated compounds in vegetable oils to produce margarine. Addition reactions are used to make polymers from ▷alkenes.

Adelaide capital and chief port of South Australia; population (2001 est) 1,072,600. Adelaide is situated on the River Torrens, 11 km/7 mi from the Gulf of St Vincent. The city is the economic and cultural centre of South Australia, and a major focus for rail, road, sea and air routes. This position, combined with the availability of many raw materials, has favoured considerable industrial development. Power sources include natural gas, piped into Adelaide from the Gidgealpa gas fields of the Cooper Basin. Industries include oil refining, shipbuilding, textiles, machinery, chemicals and electronics, and the manufacture of electrical goods, cars and motor components. Grain, wool, fruit, and wine, including much produce from the basin of the Murray River which has no port at its outlet to the sea, are exported from Port Adelaide, 11 km/7 mi northwest of the city, with facilities for both container and passenger traffic. Adelaide was founded in 1836 and named after the queen of William IV.

Aden (Arabic **'Adan**) main port and commercial centre of Yemen, on a rocky peninsula at the southwest corner of Arabia, commanding the entrance to the Red Sea; population (1995) 562,000. The city's economy is based on oil refining, fishing, and shipping. A British territory from 1839, Aden became part of independent South Yemen in 1967; it was the capital of South Yemen until 1990.

Adenauer, Konrad (1876–1967) German Christian Democrat politician, chancellor of West Germany 1949–63. With the French president Charles de Gaulle he achieved the post-war reconciliation of France and Germany and strongly supported all measures designed to strengthen the Western bloc in Europe.

Adenauer was mayor of his native city of Cologne from 1917 until his imprisonment by Hitler in 1933 for opposition to the Nazi regime.

adenoids masses of lymphoid tissue, similar to ▷tonsils, located in the upper part of the throat, behind the nose. They are part of a child's natural defences against the entry of germs but usually shrink and disappear by the age of ten.

adhesive substance that sticks two surfaces together. Natural adhesives (glues) include gelatin in its crude industrial form (made from bones, hide fragments, and fish offal) and vegetable gums. Synthetic adhesives include thermoplastic and thermosetting resins, which are often stronger than the substances they join; mixtures of ▷epoxy resin and hardener that set by chemical reaction; and elastomeric (stretching) adhesives for flexible joints. Superglues are fast-setting adhesives used in very small quantities.

adiabatic in biology and physics, describing a process that occurs without loss or gain of heat, especially the expansion or contraction of a gas in which a change takes place in the pressure or volume, although no heat is allowed to enter or leave.

Adige (German **Etsch**; ancient **Athesis**) second longest river (after the Po) in Italy, 410 km/255 mi in length. It rises in the Rhaetian Alps, crosses the Lombardy Plain and enters the Adriatic just north of the Po delta.

adipose tissue type of ▷connective tissue of vertebrates that serves as an energy reserve, and also pads some organs. It is commonly called fat tissue, and consists of large spherical cells filled with fat. In mammals, major layers are in the inner layer of skin and around the kidneys and heart.

Alfred Adler

Whenever a child lies you will always find a severe parent. A lie would have no sense unless the truth were felt to be dangerous.

The New York Times 1949

Adirondacks mountainous area in northeast New York State, USA, rising to 1,629 m/5,344ft at Mount Marcy; the source of the Hudson and Ausable rivers. The Adirondacks region is named after an American Indian people; it is now a summer resort area with good sports facilities, and is noted for its beautiful scenery.

adjournment in law, the postponement of the hearing of a case for later consideration. If a hearing is adjourned *sine die* ('without day') it is postponed for an indefinite period.

Adler, Alfred (1870–1937) Austrian psychologist. He saw the 'will to power' as more influential in accounting for human behaviour than the sexual drive. A dispute over this theory led to the dissolution of his ten-year collaboration with psychiatry's founder Sigmund ▷Freud. The concepts of inferiority complex and overcompensation originated with Adler.

administrative law law concerning the powers and control of government agencies or those agencies granted statutory powers of administration.

admiral butterfly any of several species of butterfly in the same family (Nymphalidae) as the tortoiseshells. The best-known is the **red admiral** (*Vanessa atalanta*), found worldwide in the northern hemisphere. It has black wings crossed by scarlet bands and marked with white and blue spots, and spanning 6 cm/2.5 in. It either hibernates, or migrates south each year from northern areas to subtropical zones.

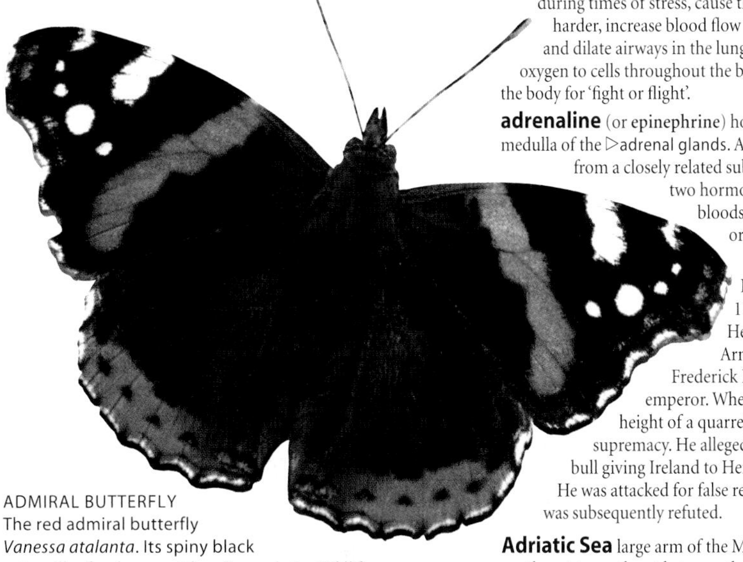

ADMIRAL BUTTERFLY The red admiral butterfly *Vanessa atalanta*. Its spiny black caterpillar feeds on nettles. *Premaphotos Wildlife*

Admiralty, Board of the in the UK, the controlling department of state for the Royal Navy from the reign of Henry VIII until 1964, when most of its functions – apart from that of management – passed to the Ministry of Defence. The 600-year-old office of Lord High Admiral reverted to the sovereign.

Admiralty Islands group of small islands in the southwest Pacific, part of Papua New Guinea; area 2,071 sq km/800 sq mi; population (1995 est) 35,200. The islands form part of the ▷Bismarck Archipelago and constitute with the North Western Islands the Manus district of Papua New Guinea. The largest island (about 80 km/50 mi long) is Manus of which Lorengau is the chief town. Exports are copra and pearls. The islands became a German protectorate in 1884 and an Australian mandate in 1920.

adobe in architecture, a building method employing sun-dried earth bricks; also the individual bricks. The use of earth bricks and the construction of walls by enclosing earth within moulds (*pisé de terre*) are the two principal methods of raw-earth building. The techniques are commonly found in Spain, Latin America, and the southwestern USA.

adolescence in the human life cycle, the period between the beginning of puberty and adulthood.

Adonis (Semitic *Adon* 'the Lord') in Greek mythology, a beautiful youth loved by the goddess ▷Aphrodite. He was killed while boar-hunting but was allowed to return from the underworld for a period every year to rejoin her. The anemone sprang from his blood.

adoption permanent legal transfer of parental rights and duties from one person to another, usually to provide care for children who would otherwise lack family upbringing.

Adorno, Theodor Wiesengrund (1903–1969) German philosopher, social theorist, and musicologist. Deeply influenced by the thought of Karl Marx, Adorno joined the influential Institut für Sozialforschung (Institute for Social Research) in Frankfurt in 1931, becoming known as a member of the 'Frankfurt School' of sociologists. At the rise of fascism he fled first to Oxford (1935–38) and then to the USA, acquiring US citizenship, eventually returning to Frankfurt as professor of philosophy in 1949. With Max Horkheimer, the director of the Institute, he published the *Dialectic of Enlightenment* (1947), which argued that rationality had not been an emancipatory force, but that modern science was an instrument of dehumanization. He was also the main contributor to *The Authoritarian Personality* (1950), which analysed the psychological origins of fascism within a broadly Freudian framework.

ADP abbreviation for adenosine diphosphate, the chemical product formed in cells when ▷ATP breaks down to release energy.

adrenal gland (or **suprarenal gland**) triangular endocrine gland situated on top of the ▷kidney. The adrenals are soft and yellow, and consist of two parts: the cortex and medulla. The **cortex** (outer part) secretes various steroid hormones and other hormones that control salt and water metabolism and regulate the use of carbohydrates, proteins, and fats. The **medulla** (inner part) secretes the hormones adrenaline and noradrenaline which, during times of stress, cause the heart to beat faster and harder, increase blood flow to the heart and muscle cells, and dilate airways in the lungs, thereby delivering more oxygen to cells throughout the body and in general preparing the body for 'fight or flight'.

adrenaline (or **epinephrine**) hormone secreted by the medulla of the ▷adrenal glands. Adrenaline is synthesized from a closely related substance, noradrenaline, and the two hormones are released into the bloodstream in situations of fear or stress.

Adrian IV (c. 1100–1159) Born Nicholas Breakspear. Pope 1154–59, the only English pope. He secured the execution of Arnold of Brescia and crowned Frederick I Barbarossa as German emperor. When he died, Adrian IV was at the height of a quarrel with Barbarossa over papal supremacy. He allegedly issued the controversial bull giving Ireland to Henry II of England in 1154. He was attacked for false representation, and the bull was subsequently refuted.

Adriatic Sea large arm of the Mediterranean Sea, lying northwest to southeast between the Italian and the Balkan peninsulas. The western shore is Italian; the eastern includes Croatia, Montenegro, and Albania, with two small strips of coastline owned by Slovenia and Bosnia Herzogovina. The Strait of Otranto, between Italy and Albania, links the Adriatic with the Ionian Sea to the south. The chief ports are Venice, Brindisi, Trieste, Ancona, and Bari in Italy, and Rijeka in Croatia. The sea is about 805 km/500 mi long; area 135,250 sq km/52,220 sq mi.

adsorption taking up of a gas or liquid at the surface of another substance, most commonly a solid (for example, activated charcoal adsorbs gases). It involves molecular attraction at the surface, and should be distinguished from ▷absorption (in which a uniform solution results from a gas or liquid being incorporated into the bulk structure of a liquid or solid).

adult education in the UK, voluntary classes and courses for adults provided mainly in further-education colleges, adult-education institutes, and school premises. Adult education covers a range of subjects from electronics to flower arranging. Courses are either vocational, designed to fill the gaps in earlier education and leading to examinations and qualifications, or nonvocational, to aid the adult's cultural development and contribute to his or her general education. The ▷Open College, ▷Open University, and ▷Workers' Educational Association are adult-education bodies.

adultery voluntary sexual intercourse between a married person and someone other than his or her legal partner.

Advent (Latin *adventus* 'coming') in the Christian calendar, the preparatory season for Christmas, including the four Sundays preceding it. It begins with Advent Sunday, the Sunday that falls nearest (before or after) St Andrew's Day (30 November).

> **Viscount Leverhulme**
> English industrialist
>
> *Half the money I spend on advertising is wasted, and the trouble is I don't know which half.*
>
> Quoted in D Ogilvy *Confessions of an Advertising Man*

Adventist person who believes that Jesus will return to make a second appearance on Earth. Expectation of the Second Coming of Christ is found in New Testament writings generally. Adventist views are held in particular by the ▷Seventh-Day Adventists church (with 4 million members in 200 countries), the Christadelphians, the ▷Jehovah's Witnesses, the Four Square Gospel Alliance, the Advent Christian church, and the Evangelical Adventist church.

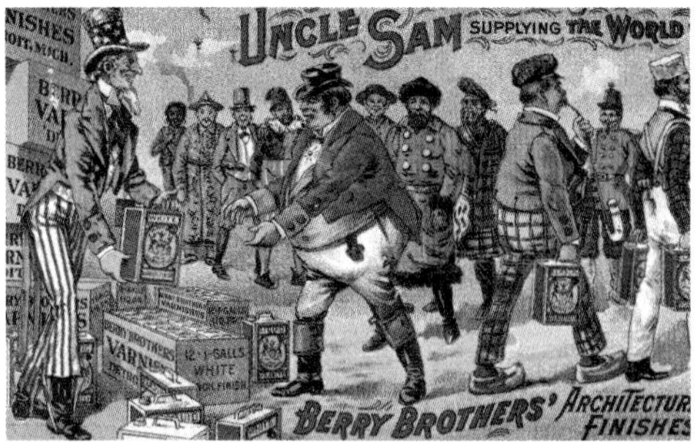

ADVERTISING A late 19th-century advertisement for US exports shows Uncle Sam 'supplying the world' with a variety of varnishes. *Archive Photos*

advertising any of various methods used by a company to increase the sales of its products or services or to promote a brand name. Advertising is also used by organizations and individuals to communicate an idea or image, to recruit staff, to publicize an event, or to locate an item or commodity.

Advisory, Conciliation, and Arbitration Service (ACAS) in the UK, government-funded independent body set up under the Employment Protection Act 1975 to improve industrial relations through its advisory, conciliation, and arbitration services. Specifically, ACAS aims to encourage the extension of collective bargaining and, wherever possible, the reform of collective-bargaining machinery. In 1998 it had more than 600 staff.

Adygeya (or **Adigey** or **Adygei**) republic surrounded by the Krasnodar krai (territory), in the southwest of the Russian Federation; area 7,600 sq km/2,934 sq mi; population (1996) 450,000 (68% Russians, 22% Adygeans). The capital is ▷Maikop. It occupied its present borders from 1936, and attained the status of a republic when the Soviet Union collapsed in 1991. It is situated on the left bank of the River Kuban, with plains in the north (providing plentiful fertile black soil called *chernozem*) and the foothills of the Caucasus Mountains in the south.

Aegean art the art of the civilizations that flourished around the Aegean (an area that included mainland Greece, the Cyclades Islands, and Crete) in the Bronze Age, about 2800–1100 BC. Despite cultural interchange by way of trade with the contemporaneous civilizations of Egypt and Mesopotamia, the Aegean cultures developed their own highly distinctive styles.

Cycladic art The art of the Bronze Age civilization in the Cyclades Islands, about 2500–1400 BC, is exemplified by pottery with incised ornament and marble statuettes, usually highly stylized female nudes representing the Mother Goddess in almost abstract simplicity, her face reduced to an elongated oval with a triangular nose. The Cycladic culture preceded the Minoan, ran concurrently with it, and eventually shared its fate, becoming assimilated into the Mycenaean culture.

Minoan art The art of Bronze Age Crete, about 2300–1100 BC, is of a high aesthetic standard, reflecting the artistic orientation and zest for life of the Minoan people. Its fine pottery, painted in a fresh, spontaneous style with plant and animal motifs curving to suit the form of the vases, comes in various styles but is best represented by 'light-on-dark' and Kamares-style ware (polychrome on a dark background). Its magnificent palaces, such as Knossos, Phaestos, and Mallia, were decorated with cheerful ▷frescoes depicting scenes from everyday life, plants, birds, leaping fish, and dolphins; fragments remain, such as the lily fresco from Ambisos (Iraklion Museum, Crete). The culture came to an end when, after the eruption of the volcano on Thera (now Santorini) and the destruction of the Minoan centre on that island, the Mycenaeans gained control in the Aegean.

Mycenaean art Mycenaean art, about 1580–1100 BC, reflects the warlike preoccupations of the mainland Mycenaean society, both in character and in the subjects portrayed. Fortified citadels were developed, such as that of Mycenae itself, which was entered through the Lion Gate, about 1330 BC, so called because of the massive lion figures, carved from stone, that adorned it. Stylized frescoes decorated its palaces and its pottery, typically dark on light, was centred on large bowls (*kraters*), depicting scenes of warfare. Perhaps its over-riding artistic contribution lies in its metalwork, principally in bronze and gold; for example, the royal funeral mask (National Museum, Athens), about 1500 BC. Many of the ideas and art forms of the Mycenaean and other early seafaring civilizations were later adapted by the Greeks (see ▷Greek art).

Aegean civilization the cultures of Bronze Age Greece, including the ▷Minoan civilization of Crete and the ▷Mycenaean civilization of the Peloponnese and mainland Greece.

Aegean Islands region of Greece comprising the Dodecanese islands, the Cyclades islands, Lesvos, Samos, and Chios; area 9,122 sq km/3,523 sq mi; population (1991) 460,800.

Aegean Sea branch of the Mediterranean between Greece and Turkey, extending as far south as Crete; the Dardanelles connect it with the Sea of Marmara, in turn linked with the Black Sea via the Bosporus. It is about 600 km/372 mi long and 290 km/180 mi wide, and covers some 214,000 sq km/82,625 sq mi, with a maximum depth of 3,540 m/11,600 ft. Tides are minimal, with a range of only about 40 cm/15 in. The numerous islands in the Aegean Sea include Crete, the Cyclades, the Sporades, and the Dodecanese. There is political tension between Greece and Turkey over sea limits claimed by Greece around such islands as Lesvos, Chios, Samos, and Kos.

Aelfric (c. 955–1020) English writer and abbot. Between 990 and 998 he wrote in vernacular ▷Old English prose two sets of sermons known as *Catholic Homilies*, and a further set known as *Lives of the Saints*, all of them largely translated from Latin. They are notable for their style and rhythm.

Aeneas in classical mythology, a Trojan prince who became the ancestral hero of the Romans. According to ▷Homer, he was the son of Anchises and the goddess Aphrodite. During the Trojan War he owed his life to the frequent intervention of the gods. The legend on which Virgil's epic poem the *Aeneid* is based describes his escape from Troy and his eventual settlement in Latium, on the Italian peninsula.

AENEAS A mural in Pompeii, Italy, dating from the 1st century, showing the Trojan hero Aeneas receiving treatment for a wound. His mother, the Greek goddess Aphrodite, looks on anxiously. *The Art Archive/Archaeological Museum Naples/Dagli Orti*

Aeolian Islands another name for the ▷Lipari Islands.

aerial (or antenna) in radio and television broadcasting, a conducting device that radiates or receives electromagnetic waves. The design of an aerial depends principally on the wavelength of the signal. Long waves (hundreds of metres in wavelength) may employ long wire aerials; short waves (several centimetres in wavelength) may employ rods and dipoles; microwaves may also use dipoles – often with reflectors arranged like a toast rack – or highly directional parabolic dish aerials. Because microwaves travel in straight lines, requiring line-of-sight communication, microwave aerials are usually located at the tops of tall masts or towers.

aerobic in biology, term used to describe those organisms that require oxygen (usually dissolved in water) for the efficient release of energy contained in food molecules, such as glucose. They include almost all organisms (plants as well as animals) with the exception of certain bacteria, yeasts, and internal parasites.

Aerobic reactions occur inside every cell and lead to the formation of energy-rich ▷ATP, subsequently used by the cell for driving its metabolic processes. Oxygen is used to convert glucose to carbon dioxide and water, thereby releasing energy.

Most aerobic organisms die in the absence of oxygen, but certain organisms and cells, such as those found in muscle tissue, can function for short periods anaerobically (without oxygen). ▷Anaerobic organisms can survive without oxygen.

aerobics (Greek 'air' and 'life') exercises to improve the performance of the heart and lungs, involving strenuous application of movement to raise the heart rate to 120 beats per minute or more for sessions of 5–20 minutes' duration, 3–5 times per week.
Related Web site: Fitness Online http://www.fitnessonline.com/

aerodynamics branch of fluid physics that studies the forces exerted by air or other gases in motion. Examples include the airflow around bodies moving at speed through the atmosphere (such as land vehicles, bullets, rockets, and aircraft), the behaviour of gas in engines and furnaces, air conditioning of buildings, the deposition of snow, the operation of air-cushion vehicles (hovercraft), wind loads on buildings and bridges, bird and insect flight, musical wind instruments, and meteorology. For maximum efficiency, the aim is usually to design the shape of an object to produce a streamlined flow, with a minimum of turbulence in the moving air. The behaviour of aerosols or the pollution of the atmosphere by foreign particles are other aspects of aerodynamics.

aerogel light, transparent, highly porous material composed of more than 90% air. Such materials are formed from silica, metal oxides, and organic chemicals, and are produced by drying gels – networks of linked molecules suspended in a liquid – so that air fills the spaces previously occupied by the liquid. They are excellent heat insulators and have unusual optical, electrical, and acoustic properties.

aeronautics science of travel through the Earth's atmosphere, including aerodynamics, aircraft structures, jet and rocket propulsion, and aerial navigation.

In **subsonic aeronautics** (below the speed of sound), aerodynamic forces increase at the rate of the square of the speed.

Transsonic aeronautics covers the speed range from just below to just above the speed of sound and is crucial to aircraft design. Ordinary sound waves move at about 1,225 kph/760 mph at sea level, and air in front of an aircraft moving slower than this is 'warned' by the waves so that it can move aside. However, as the flying speed approaches that of the sound waves, the warning is too late for the air to escape, and the aircraft pushes the air aside, creating shock waves, which absorb much power and create design problems. On the ground the shock waves give rise to a ▷sonic boom. It was once thought that the speed of sound was a speed limit to aircraft, and the term ▷sound barrier came into use.

Supersonic aeronautics concerns speeds above that of sound and in one sense may be considered a much older study than aeronautics itself, since the study of the flight of bullets, known as ▷ballistics, was undertaken soon after the introduction of firearms. **Hypersonics** is the study of airflows and forces at speeds above five times that of sound (Mach 5); for example, for guided missiles, space rockets, and advanced concepts such as HOTOL (horizontal takeoff and landing). For all flight speeds streamlining is necessary to reduce the effects of air resistance.

Aeronautics is distinguished from astronautics, which is the science of travel through space. Astronavigation (navigation by reference to the stars) is used in aircraft as well as in ships and is a part of aeronautics.
Related Web site: American Institute of Aeronautics and Astronautics Home Page http://www.aiaa.org/

aeroplane (US airplane) powered heavier-than-air craft supported in flight by fixed wings. Aeroplanes are propelled by the thrust of a jet engine, a rocket engine, or airscrew (propeller), as well as combinations of these. They must be designed aerodynamically, since streamlining ensures maximum flight efficiency. The Wright brothers flew the first powered plane (a biplane) in Kitty Hawk, North Carolina, USA, in 1903. For the history of aircraft and aviation, see ▷flight.
Design Efficient streamlining prevents the formation of shock waves over the body surface and wings, which would cause instability and power loss. The wing of an aeroplane has the cross-sectional shape of an aerofoil, being broad and curved at the front, flat underneath (sometimes slightly curved), curved on top, and tapered to a sharp point at the rear. It is so shaped that air passing above it is speeded up, reducing pressure below atmospheric pressure, and air passing below it is slower thus increasing pressure and providing a double effect. This follows from ▷Bernoulli's principle and results in a force acting vertically upwards, called lift, which counters the plane's weight. In level flight lift equals weight. The wings develop sufficient lift to support the plane when they move quickly through the air. The thrust that causes propulsion comes from the reaction to the air stream accelerated backwards by the propeller or the gases shooting backwards from the jet exhaust.

In flight the engine thrust must overcome the air resistance, or drag. Drag depends on frontal area (for example, large, airliner; small, fighter plane) and shape (drag coefficient); in level flight, drag equals thrust. The drag is reduced by streamlining the plane, resulting in higher speed and reduced fuel consumption for a given power. Less fuel need be carried for a given distance of travel, so a larger payload (cargo or passengers) can be carried.

AEROPLANE The 'Blue Angels' in FA-18 fighters are a special flight demonstration squadron of the US Navy. Their public aviation displays are known for the choreographed skills of the pilots and the acrobatic manoeuvres they perform, with up to six jets flying in formation. *Image Bank*

aerosol particles of liquid or solid suspended in a gas. Fog is a common natural example. Aerosol cans can contain a substance such as scent or cleaner packed under pressure with a device for releasing it as a fine spray. Most aerosols used chlorofluorocarbons (CFCs) as propellants until these were found to cause destruction of the ▷ozone layer in the stratosphere.

Aeschylus (c. 525–c. 456 BC) Athenian dramatist. He developed Greek tragedy by introducing the second actor, thus enabling true dialogue and dramatic action to occur independently of the chorus. Ranked with ▷Euripides and ▷Sophocles as one of the three great tragedians, Aeschylus composed some 90 plays between 500 and 456 BC, of which seven complete tragedies survive in his name: *Persians* (472 BC), *Seven Against Thebes* (467 BC), *Suppliants* (463 BC), the ▷*Oresteia* trilogy (*Agamemnon*, *Libation-Bearers*, and *Eumenides*) (458 BC), and *Prometheus Bound* (the last, although attributed to him, is of uncertain date and authorship).
Related Web site: Works By Aeschylus http://classics.mit.edu/Browse/browse-Aeschylus.html

> **Aeschylus**
> *Every ruler is harsh whose rule is new.*
> Prometheus Bound

Aesculapius in Roman mythology, the god of medicine, equivalent to the Greek ▷Asclepius.

AESOP 'The Hare and the Tortoise' from *Aesop's Fables*, illustrated by Charles Bennett, 1857. *Art Archive*

Aesop by tradition, a writer of Greek fables. According to the historian Herodotus, he lived in the mid-6th century BC and was a slave. The fables that are ascribed to him were collected at a later date and are anecdotal stories using animal characters to illustrate moral or satirical points.
Related Web site: Aesop's Fables http://www.pacificnet.net/~johnr/aesop/

Aesthetic Movement English artistic movement of the late 19th century, dedicated to the doctrine of 'art for art's sake' – that is, art as a self-sufficient entity concerned solely with beauty and not with any moral or social purpose. Associated with the movement were the artists Aubrey ▷Beardsley and James McNeill ▷Whistler and writers Walter ▷Pater and Oscar ▷Wilde .

Afghanistan

Afghanistan mountainous, landlocked country in south-central Asia, bounded north by Tajikistan, Turkmenistan, and Uzbekistan, west by Iran, and south and east by Pakistan, India, and China.

NATIONAL NAME *Dowlat-e Eslāmi-ye Afghānestān/Islamic State of Afghanistan*
AREA 652,225 sq km/251,825 sq mi
CAPITAL Kabul
MAJOR TOWNS/CITIES Kandahar, Herat, Mazar-e Sharif, Jalalabad, Kondoz, Qal'eh-ye Now
PHYSICAL FEATURES mountainous in centre and northeast (Hindu Kush mountain range; Khyber and Salang passes, Wakhan salient, and Panjshir Valley), plains in north and southwest, Amu Darya (Oxus) River, Helmand River, Lake Saberi

Government

HEAD OF STATE AND GOVERNMENT Hamid Karzai from 2001
POLITICAL SYSTEM in transition
POLITICAL EXECUTIVE in transition
ADMINISTRATIVE DIVISIONS 31 provinces
POLITICAL PARTIES in transition
ARMED FORCES 50,000; plus paramilitary forces of 70,000 (2002 est)

DEATH PENALTY retains and uses the death penalty for ordinary crimes
EDUCATION SPEND (% GDP) 1.0 (1999 est)
HEALTH SPEND (% GDP) 1.0 (2000 est)

Economy and resources

CURRENCY afgháni
GPD (US$) 21 billion (2000 est)
GNI PER CAPITA (PPP) (US$) 800 (2000 est)
CONSUMER PRICE INFLATION 2% (2003 est)
FOREIGN DEBT (US$) 5.4 billion (2001 est)
MAJOR TRADING PARTNERS Russia, Japan, Singapore, Pakistan, India, Western Europe, USA, Tajikistan, Turkmenistan, China
RESOURCES natural gas, coal, iron ore, barytes, lapis lazuli, salt, talc, copper, chrome, gold, silver, asbestos, small petroleum reserves
INDUSTRIES food products, cotton textiles, cement, coalmining, chemical fertilizers, small vehicle assembly plants, processed hides and skins, carpetmaking, sugar manufacture, leather and plastic goods

EXPORTS fruit and nuts, carpets, wool, karakul skins, cotton, natural gas, precious and semi-precious gems. Principal market: Pakistan (1999)
IMPORTS basic manufactured goods and foodstuffs (notably wheat), petroleum products, textiles, fertilizers, vehicles and spare parts. Principal source: Pakistan (1999)
ARABLE LAND 12.1% (2000 est)
AGRICULTURAL PRODUCTS wheat, barley, maize, rice, fruit and vegetables; livestock rearing (sheep, goats, cattle, and camels); world's leading opium producer (2002)

Population and society

POPULATION 23,897,000 (2003 est)
POPULATION GROWTH RATE 2.4% (2000–15)
POPULATION DENSITY (per sq km) 37 (2003 est)
URBAN POPULATION (% of total) 23 (2003 est)
AGE DISTRIBUTION (% of total population) 0–14 43%, 15–59 52%, 60+ 5% (2002 est)
ETHNIC GROUPS Pathans (or Pashtuns) comprise the largest ethnic group, 38% of the population, followed by the Tajiks (concentrated in the north, 25%), the Uzbeks (6%), and Hazaras (19%)
LANGUAGE Pashto, Dari (both official), Uzbek, Turkmen, Balochi, Pashai
RELIGION Muslim (84% Sunni, 15% Shiite), other 1%
EDUCATION (compulsory years) 6
LITERACY RATE 52% (men); 22% (women) (2000 est)
LABOUR FORCE 68% agriculture, 16% industry, 16% services (1992 est)
LIFE EXPECTANCY 43 (men); 43 (women) (2000–05)
CHILD MORTALITY RATE (under 5, per 1,000 live births) 257 (2001)
PHYSICIANS (per 1,000 people) 0.1 (1997 est)
TV SETS (per 1,000 people) 14 (2001 est)
RADIOS (per 1,000 people) 114 (2001 est)

See also ▷Afghan Wars; ▷Alexander (III) the Great; ▷Genghis Khan; ▷Tamerlane.

Chronology

6th century BC: Part of Persian Empire under Cyrus II and Darius I.

329 BC: Conquered by Alexander the Great.

323 BC: Fell to the Seleucids, who ruled from Babylon.

304 BC: Ruled by Mauryan dynasty in south and independent Bactria in north.

135 BC: Central Asian tribes established Kusana dynasty.

3rd–7th centuries AD: Decline of Kusana dynasty. Emergence of Sassanids as ruling power.

642–11th century: First Muslim invasion followed by a succession of Muslim dynasties, including Mahmud of Ghazni in 998.

1219–14th century: Mongol invasions led by Genghis Khan and Tamerlane.

16th–18th centuries: Much of Afghanistan came under the rule of the Mogul Empire.

1747: Afghanistan became an independent emirate under Dost Muhammad.

1838–42: First Afghan War, the first in a series of three wars between Britain and Afghanistan, instigated by Britain to counter the threat to British India from expanding Russian influence in Afghanistan.

1878–80: Second Afghan War.

1919: Afghanistan recovered full independence following the Third Afghan War.

1953: Lt-Gen Daud Khan became prime minister.

1963: Daud Khan forced to resign and constitutional monarchy established.

1973: Monarchy overthrown in coup by Daud Khan.

1978: Daud Khan assassinated in coup. Start of Muslim guerrilla (Mujahedin) resistance.

1979: The USSR invaded the country to prop up the pro-Soviet government.

1986: Partial Soviet troop withdrawal.

1988: New non-Marxist constitution adopted.

1989: Withdrawal of Soviet troops; Mujahedin continued resistance to communist People's Democratic Party of Afghanistan (PDPA) regime and civil war intensified.

1991: US and Soviet military aid withdrawn. Mujahedin began talks with the Russians and Kabul government.

1992: Mujahedin leader Burhanuddin Rabbani was elected president.

1993–94: There was fighting around Kabul.

1996: The Talibaan controlled two-thirds of the country, including Kabul; the country was split between the Talibaan-controlled fundamentalist south and the more liberal north; strict Islamic law was imposed.

1997: The Talibaan was recognized as the legitimate government by Pakistan and Saudi Arabia.

1998: Two earthquakes in the north killed over 8,000 people. The USA launched a missile attack on a suspected terrorist site in retaliation for bombings of US embassies in Nairobi and Dar es Salaam. Talibaan massacred 6,000 people at Mazar-I-Sharif.

1999: Intending to punish the Talibaan regime for failing to expel suspected terrorist Osama bin Laden, the United Nations (UN) imposed sanctions on Afghanistan in November.

2000: Fighting continued between the Talibaan and the opposing United Islamic Front for Salvation of Afghanistan (UIFSA), led by Ahmed Shah Masud.

2001: The US named Osama bin Laden as prime suspect in the terrorist attacks on the USA on 11 September 2001, and US and British forces launched a military offensive when the Talibaan did not hand him over. By the end of November, the allied forces together with the Afghan opposition Northern Alliance had removed the Talibaan from power.

2002: Hamid Karzai, an ethnic Pathan and leader of the US-endorsed interim administration, was elected president for 18 months.

AFGHANISTAN The great mosque Masjidi Jami in Herat. It was first built in the 12th century and has been rebuilt several times since it has been damaged by successive waves of war and conquest.

aesthetics branch of philosophy that deals with the nature of beauty, especially in art. It emerged as a distinct branch of enquiry in the mid-18th century.

aestivation in zoology, a state of inactivity and reduced metabolic activity, similar to ▷hibernation, that occurs during the dry season in species such as lungfish and snails. In botany, the term is used to describe the way in which flower petals and sepals are folded in the buds. It is an important feature in ▷plant classification.

affidavit legal document, used in court applications and proceedings, in which a person swears that certain facts are true.

affinity in chemistry, the force of attraction (see ▷bond) between atoms that helps to keep them in combination in a molecule. The term is also applied to attraction between molecules, such as those of biochemical significance (for example, between ▷enzymes and substrate molecules). This is the basis for affinity ▷chromatography, by which biologically important compounds are separated.

The atoms of a given element may have a greater affinity for the atoms of one element than for another (for example, hydrogen has a great affinity for chlorine, with which it easily and rapidly combines to form hydrochloric acid, but has little or no affinity for argon).

affinity in law, relationship by marriage not blood (for example, between a husband and his wife's blood relatives, between a wife and her husband's blood relatives, or between step-parent and stepchild), which may legally preclude their marriage. It is distinguished from consanguinity or blood relationship.

affirmative action government policy of positive discrimination by the use of legal measures and moral persuasion that favours women and members of minority ethnic groups in such areas as employment and education. It is designed to counter the effects of long-term discrimination against these groups. In Europe, Sweden, Belgium, the Netherlands, and Italy actively promote affirmative action through legal and financial incentives.

In the USA, the Equal Opportunities Act 1972 set up a Commission to enforce affirmative action as a policy in organizations receiving public funds; many private institutions and employers adopted voluntary affirmative-action programmes at that time. In the 1980s the policy was sometimes not rigorously enforced and there were allegations of 'reverse discrimination' (individuals receiving preferential treatment solely because they belonged to a particular group), nevertheless a review completed in 1995 reported that most programmes were justifiable.

Afghan people who are natives to or inhabitants of Afghanistan. The dominant group, particularly in Kabul, are the Pathans. The Tajiks, a smaller ethnic group, are predominantly traders and farmers in the province of Herat and around Kabul. The Hazaras, another farming group, are found in the southern mountain ranges of the Hindu Kush. The Uzbeks and Turkomen are farmers and speak Altaic-family languages. The smallest Altaic minority are the Kirghiz, who live in the Pamir. Baluchi nomads live in the south, and Nuristani farmers live in the mountains of the northeast.

Afghan hound breed of fast hunting dog resembling the ▷saluki in build, though slightly smaller.

Afghanistan see country box.

Afghan Wars three wars waged between Britain and Afghanistan to counter the threat to British India from expanding Russian influence in Afghanistan.

First Afghan War 1838–42, when the British garrison at Kabul was wiped out.

Second Afghan War 1878–80, when General Roberts captured Kabul and relieved Kandahar.

Third Afghan War 1919, when peace followed the dispatch by the UK of the first aeroplane ever seen in Kabul.

AFL–CIO abbreviation for ▷American Federation of Labor and Congress of Industrial Organizations.

Africa second largest of the seven continents. Africa is connected with Asia by the isthmus of Suez, and separated from Europe by the Mediterranean Sea. The name Africa was first given by the Romans to their African provinces with the city of Carthage, and it has since been extended to the whole continent.

area 30,097,000 sq km/11,620,451 sq mi (three times the area of Europe) **largest cities** (population over 2 million; given in millions, 2001 est) Abidjan (2.9), Addis Ababa (2.6), Alexandria (3.7), Algiers (3.8), Cairo (9.9), Casablanca (3.2), Johannesburg (2.2), Khartoum (2.3), Kinshasa (6.1), Lagos (10.9), Luanda (2.1), Maputo (2.1) **features** Great Rift Valley, containing most of the great lakes of East Africa (except Lake Victoria); Atlas Mountains in the northwest; Drakensberg mountain range in the southeast; Sahara Desert (world's largest desert) in the north; Namib, Kalahari, and Great Karoo deserts in the south; Nile, Congo, Niger, Zambezi, Limpopo, Volta, and Orange rivers **physical** dominated by a uniform central plateau comprising a southern tableland with a mean altitude of 1,070 m/3,000 ft that falls northwards to a lower elevated plain with a mean altitude of 400 m/1,300 ft. Although there are no great alpine regions or extensive coastal plains, Africa has a mean altitude of 610 m/2,000 ft, two times greater than Europe. The highest points are Mount Kilimanjaro 5,900 m/19,364 ft, and Mount Kenya 5,200 m/17,058 ft; the lowest point is Lac Assal in Djibouti −144 m/−471 ft. Compared with other continents, Africa has few broad estuaries or inlets and therefore has proportionately the shortest coastline (24,000 km/15,000 mi). The geographical extremities of the continental mainland are Cape Hafun in the east, Cape Almadies in the west, Ras Ben Sekka in the north, and Cape Agulhas in the south. The Sahel is a narrow belt of savannah and scrub forest which covers 700 million hectares/1.7 billion acres of west and central Africa; 75% of the continent lies within the tropics **population** (2000 est) 841.2 million; more than double the 1970 population of 364 million, and rising to an estimated 1 billion by 2010; annual growth rate 3% (10 times greater than Europe); 27% of the world's undernourished people live in sub-Saharan Africa, where an estimated 25 million are facing famine **industries** has 30% of the world's minerals including 45% of diamonds (Democratic Republic of Congo, Botswana, South Africa, Namibia, Angola) and 31% of gold (South Africa, Ghana, Zimbabwe); produces 11% of the world's crude petroleum, 51% of the world's cocoa (Côte d'Ivoire, Ghana, Cameroon, Nigeria), 19% of the world's coffee (Uganda, Côte d'Ivoire, Democratic Republic of Congo, Ethiopia, Cameroon, Madagascar, Kenya), 20% of the world's groundnuts (Senegal, Nigeria, Sudan, Democratic Republic of Congo), and 21% of the world's hardwood timber (Nigeria, Democratic Republic of Congo, Tanzania, Kenya) **language** over 1,000 languages are spoken in Africa; Niger-Kordofanian languages including Mandinke, Kwa, Lingala, Bemba, and Bantu (Zulu, Swahili, Kikuyu), spoken over half of Africa from Mauritania in the west to South Africa; Nilo-Saharan languages, including Dinka, Shilluk, Nuer, and Masai, spoken in central Africa from the bend of the Niger River to the foothills of Ethiopia; Afro-Asiatic (Hamito-Semitic) languages, including Arabic, Berber, Ethiopian, and Amharic, north of the Equator; Khoisan languages with 'click' consonants spoken in the southwest by Kung, Khoikhoi, and Nama people of Namibia **religion** Islam in the north and on the east coast as far south as northern Mozambique; animism below the Sahara, which survives alongside Christianity (both Catholic and Protestant) in many central and southern areas.

Related Web site: H-Africa http://h-net.msu.edu/~africa

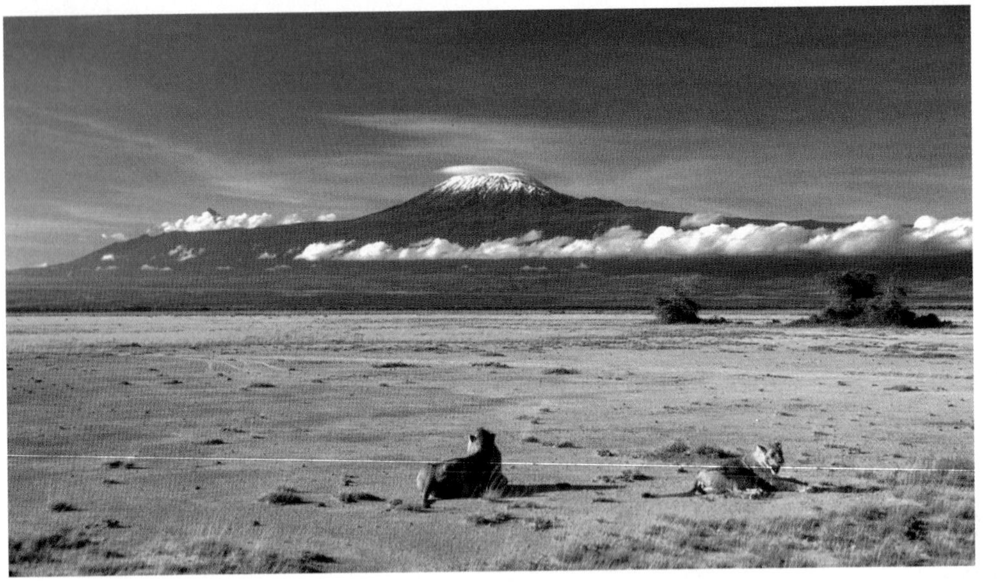

AFRICA Mount Kilimanjaro in Tanzania, East Africa. It is in the Great Rift Valley, and has two volcanic peaks: Kibo, the highest at 5,900 m/19,357 ft, and Mawenzi at 5,273 m/17,300 ft. *Corel*

Africa, Horn of projection on the east coast of Africa constituted by Somalia and adjacent territories.

African art art of sub-Saharan Africa, from prehistory onwards, ranging from the art of ancient civilizations to the new styles of post-imperialist African nations. Traditional African art forms are in the first instance functional; they embody the beliefs and values of the community. Examples of historic African art are bronze figures from the kingdoms of Benin and Ife (in Nigeria) dating from about 1500 and, also on the west coast, from the same period, bronze and brass figures for weighing gold, made by the Ashanti (Ghana).

Knowledge of African art history south of the Sahara is sketchy, partly because of the limited amount of archaeological work that has been carried out in such a huge area, and partly because humidity and termites quickly destroy perishable materials.

African literature African literature was mainly oral until the 20th century and oral traditions of proverbs, mythological narratives, and poetry persist and influence contemporary writing. There exists a wide variety of narrative, dramatic, and lyric forms. In prose narrative, the folk tale, often featuring an animal hero, is one of the most common genres; stories of a trickster-hero (in the form of a spider, a tortoise, a rabbit, a human, or a god) are particularly popular. There are also many religious myths, and stories that preserve in legendary form the history and world-view of particular groups.

Oral literature **Poetic forms** are often tied to particular occupations or cults, for example, the *ijala* performed by Yoruba hunters, or the songs of the Ewe fishing communities. Religious poetry includes hymns to the gods and allusive and highly symbolic oracular poems, such as the *Ifa* used by the Yoruba for divination; and didactic pieces in Hausa or Swahili, sometimes revealing Islamic influence. In most African languages there are numerous laments or dirges, love songs, children's chants, war poems, and poems of praise (such as the praise poem of southern Africa) and invective. Drums and horns are often used to communicate or emphasize the tonalities in some African languages, and transmission of poetry by drums is widespread in the Democratic Republic of Congo (formerly Zaire), Ghana, and Nigeria. The epic is not typical of African culture, although the Mwindo epic of the Bantu-speaking Nyanga people in the Democratic Republic of Congo (formerly Zaire), which intermingles prose and verse, has been collected and published, and the long Swahili *utenzi* have been compared to epics.

Traditional African **drama**, often associated with ritual and social events, tends to emphasize mime, dance, music, costumes, and masks rather than verbal art. Its influence on contemporary African drama is particularly significant. New oral literary forms continue to be developed for radio and popular song.

Written literature in African languages Some Swahili and Hausa literature, religious in direction and influenced by Arabic, dates from the 16th century. The didactic 18th-century *Inkeshafe*, a poem of 79 stanzas, describes ancient Swahili culture and moralizes on the transitory nature of power and riches. There are numerous narrative poems in Swahili, ranging from 100 to 6,000 four-line stanzas, generally recounting episodes from the early struggles of Islam. East Africa has been the source of much contemporary political and lyrical poetry in Swahili; Shaaban Robert (1909–1962) is a well-known Swahili poet.

In **western and southern African languages**, the first written works are associated with Christian missionary activity in the 19th and early 20th centuries. Hymns and didactic tales analogous to Bunyan's *Pilgrim's Progress* and rejecting non-Christian practices and beliefs are typical. For example, Thomas Mofolo's (1875–1948) *Chaka* (1911), written in Sotho and later translated into English, is a powerful portrayal of the Zulu leader ▷Shaka as a kind of Macbeth figure led astray by a demonic shaman. Another significant vernacular writer is the Yoruba novelist, Chief D O Fagunwa (1910–1963). The most famous of his six works, *Ogboju ode ninu igbo irunmale/The Brave Hunter in the Forest of the Four Hundred Gods* 1938, recounts the adventures of Akara-Ogun, the son of a witch and a well-known hunter, and belongs both in form and content to the traditional Yoruba folk tale.

Poetry and plays Most vernacular compositions tend to be in the form of drama or poetry rather than fiction. F Kwasi Fiawoo's (1891–1969) Ewe play, *Toko Atolia/The Fifth Landing Stage* 1937, has become a modern classic. Ghanaian poet J H Kwabena Nketia (1921–) writes in Twi, his native language. In addition to a Luo novel, Okot p'Bitek (1931–1982) from Uganda wrote three long satiric poems in Acholi, *Song of Lawino* (1966), *Song of Ocol* (1970), and *Song of a Prisoner* (1971), all translated into English by the author.

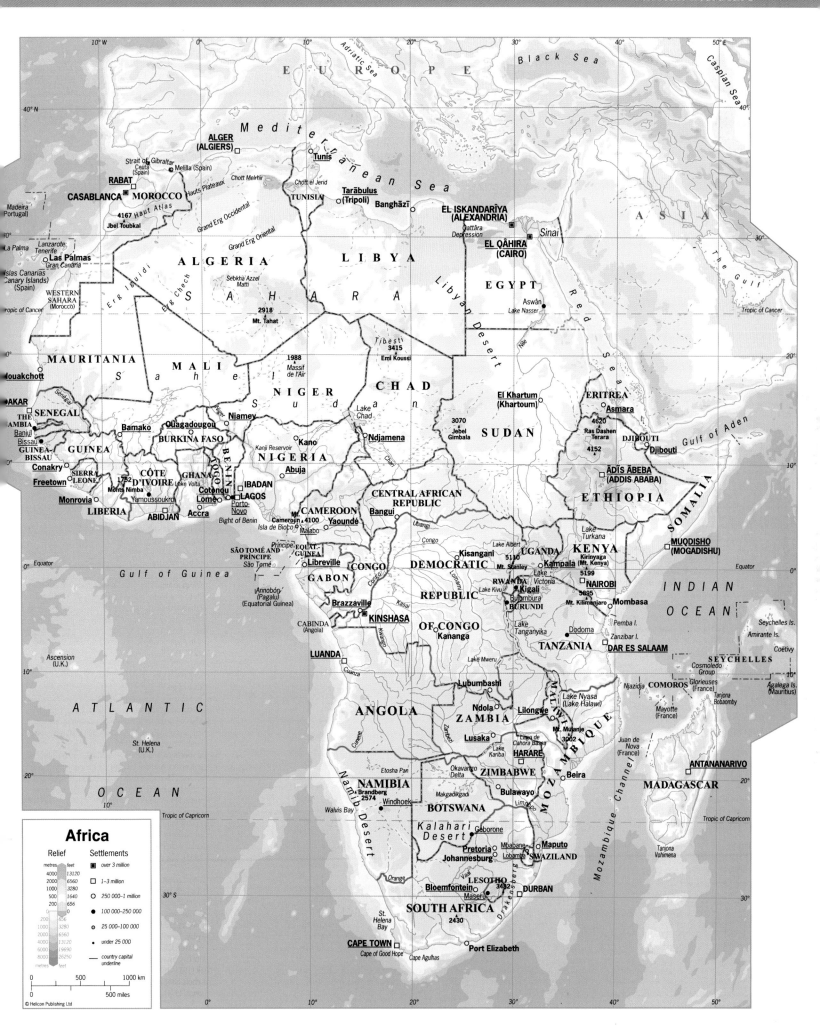

African literature in European languages Individual African-born writers have made sporadic contributions to European letters since the Renaissance, mainly in English, French, and Portuguese. Early works include those of the classical scholar Juan Latino, an enslaved African who later became a professor at the University of Granada in 1557, the 18th-century Sengalese-American poet Phyllis ▷Wheatley, and the Nigerian Olaudah Equiano, whose vivid account of his early life in Africa, his enslavement, his later adventures as a freed man, and his involvement in the abolitionist movement, went into eight editions in 18th-century England.

Among the earlier landmarks of African writing are the South African historical novel of pre-colonial times *Mhudi* (written 1917, published 1930) by Sol Plaatje (1877–1932) and the plays and poetry of H I E Dhlomo (1905–1945), recreating African landscapes and the achievements of heroes such as the Zulu leader Shaka. Later writing, including autobiographies such as that by Es'kia Mphalele (1919–), has paid more attention to the themes of urban deprivation and political oppression and violence, particularly in South Africa. This has energized the poetry of the exiled Dennis Brutus (1924–) and the novels of Alex La Guma (1925–1985), and features in the work of the Kenyan writer ▷Ngugi wa Thiong'o and the Nigerian novelist Cyprian Ekwensi (1921–). The reassertion of pre-colonial communal life, myth, and tradition, associated with condemnation of the cultural disruptions caused by colonists or Christian missionaries, has been a significant concern of the Ghanaian poet Kofi Awoonor (1935–) and of Nigerian writers such as Chinua ▷Achebe, the Ibo poet Christopher Okigbo (1932–1967), and the novelist Amos Tutuola (1920–1997), who wrote *The Palm-Wine Drunkard*.

Afro-American literature The considerable body of writing by Afro-Americans, especially in the 1920s, in turn influenced French-speaking writers from Africa and the Caribbean. Chief among these were the black American writer W E B Du Bois who became a citizen of Ghana, the Martinique poet Aimé Césaire (1913–), and Senegal's president, Léopold ▷Senghor, who were advocates of the concept of **Negritude** (blackness, belonging to a black culture), affirming a growing sense of African personality and political and cultural identity in the colonial and postcolonial period. Senghor's sonorous poems, often annotated for musical accompaniment, imitate the modes of Wolof and Serer ceremonial praise songs. Senghor's *Anthologie de la nouvelle poésie nègre et malgache* 1948, with its preface by Jean-Paul Sartre, remains a monument to the Negritude movement, which is also associated with Camera Laye's (1928–1980) autobiographical *Enfant Noir/The Dark Child* 1953 (Guinea-Bissau), Birago Diop's (1906–1989) recreations of the subject and style of griot tales in *Les Contes d'Amadou Koumba/Tales of Amadou Koumba* 1947 (Senegal), the work of the Zairean poet Tchicaya U'Tam'si (1931–1988), and the journal *Présence Africaine*. However, more recent Francophone novelists, such as Mongo Beti (1932–) and Ferdinand Oyono (1929–), while critical of colonialism, have satirized what they feel to be a tendency in Negritude to over-romanticize traditional African society.

Literature in English Africans who write in English have generally rejected Negritude as an unrealistic idealization of the African past. Chinua ▷Achebe's widely acclaimed novels *Things Fall Apart* 1958 and *Arrow of God* 1964 draw on the language and forms of oral culture to recreate the conflicts within traditional Ibo society and to show how those conflicts were exacerbated by colonialism. The plays of the Nigerian author Wole ▷Soyinka also reject attempts to glamorize the past. *The Road* 1965 interweaves Yoruba and Christian metaphysics and rituals. In South Africa, drama has been an important instrument of political protest, particularly in the work of Athol ▷Fugard.

Writing in Portuguese The struggle for independence in Angola produced revolutionary poetry, written in Portuguese, by Veriato da Cruz (1928–1973), Angostino Neto (1922–1979), and Alda do Espirito Santo (1926–). Kulungano (Marcellino dos Santos) (1929–) and Noemia de Sousa (1927–) write of despair and oppression among the poor of Mozambique. Mozambique poet José Craveirinha (1926–) has won European literary awards.

Important **women writers** include the South Africans Bessie Head (1937–1986) and Miriam Tlali (1933–), the Nigerian Flora Nwapa (1931–), and Mariama Bâ (1929–1981) from Senegal.

African National Congress (ANC) South African political party, founded in 1912 as a multiracial nationalist organization with the aim of extending the franchise to the whole population and ending all racial discrimination. Its president from 1997 is Thabo ▷Mbeki.

The ANC was banned by the government from 1960 to January 1990. Talks between the ANC and the South African government began in December 1991 and culminated in the adoption of a nonracial constitution in 1993 and the ANC's agreement to participate in a power-sharing administration, as a prelude to full majority rule. In the country's first universal suffrage elections in April 1994, the ANC won a sweeping victory, capturing 62% of the vote, and Nelson Mandela was elected president. The ANC also won

AFRIKANER An aerial view of the massacre of the Piet Retief Vortrekkers, which took place at the Kraal (settlement) of Dinizulu. *Archive Photos*

a majority in South Africa's first democratic local government elections in November 1995, when it won 66.3% of the vote.

The ANC won 66% of the vote in the country's second non-racial election in June 1999, but fell just short of a two-thirds majority in parliament. The ANC government secured the coveted two-thirds majority needed to change aspects of the South African constitution by making a deal with a small Indian-led party. Through a coalition agreement with the Minority Front, the ANC secured the single extra seat it needed after the national election, taking it to 267 seats out of 400.

Related Web site: African National Congress http://www.anc.org.za/

African nationalism political movement for the unification of Africa (Pan-Africanism) and for national self-determination. Early African political organizations included the Aborigines Rights Protection Society in the Gold Coast in 1897, the African National Congress in South Africa in 1912, and the National Congress of West Africa in 1920.

African nationalism has its roots among the educated elite (mainly 'returned' Americans of African descent and freed slaves or their descendants) in West Africa in the 19th century. Christian mission-educated, many challenged overseas mission control and founded independent churches. These were often involved in anticolonial rebellions; for example, in Natal in 1906 and Nyasaland in 1915. The Kitwala (Watchtower Movement) and Kimbanguist churches provided strong support for the nationalist cause in the 1950s.

After World War I nationalists fostered moves for self-determination. The Fourteen Points of US president Woodrow Wilson encouraged such demands in Tunisia, and delegates to London in 1919 from the Native National Congress in South Africa stressed the contribution to the war effort by the South African Native Labour Corps. Most nationalist groups functioned within the territorial boundaries of single colonies; for example, the Tanganyika African Association and the Rhodesian Bantu Voters Association. One or two groups, including the National Congress of British West Africa, had wider pan-African visions.

By 1939 African nationalist groups existed in nearly every territory of the continent. Africa's direct involvement in World War II, the weakening of the principal colonial powers, increasing anticolonialism from America (the Atlantic Charter in 1941 encouraged self-government), and Soviet criticism of imperialism inspired African nationalists.

African violet herbaceous plant from tropical central and East Africa, with velvety green leaves and scentless purple flowers. Different colours and double-flowered varieties have been bred. (*Saintpaulia ionantha*, family Gesneriaceae.)

Africa, the scramble for drive by European nations to establish colonies in Africa. It began in the 1880s, and by 1914 only two African countries remained completely independent. They were Ethiopia, which had been a kingdom for about 2,000 years, and Liberia, established in 1822 as a homeland for freed black slaves. The rest were under the control of seven European powers: Belgium, Britain, France, Germany, Italy, Portugal, and Spain. Britain and France had the most colonies. All these colonies were short-lived, and the majority attained their independence in the 1960s and 1970s.

The scramble for Africa had three main causes. The first was the work of 19th-century explorers, such as the Scottish missionary David ▷Livingstone and the French naval officer Pierre de Brazza, in opening up large areas of Africa that were previously unknown to Europeans. The second was the establishment of King Léopold II of the Belgians to set up a personal colony in the basin of the Congo River in 1885. It was later taken over by the Belgian government and named the Belgian Congo. It is now the Democratic Republic of Congo.

Bismarck intervenes Leopold's action led to the third cause of the scramble – diplomatic moves by the German Chancellor Otto von ▷Bismarck at a conference on African affairs 1884–85. Bismarck, whose interests lay mainly in Europe, encouraged other European powers, especially France, to take an active interest in acquiring land in Africa. This left Germany free to conclude alliances and increase its influence in Europe.

Afrikaans language an official language (with English) of the Republic of South Africa and Namibia. Spoken mainly by the ▷Afrikaners – descendants of Dutch and other 17th-century colonists – it is a variety of the Dutch language, modified by circumstance and the influence of German, French, and other immigrant as well as local languages. It became a standardized written language about 1875.

Afrikaner (formerly **Boer**) inhabitant of ▷South Africa descended from the original Dutch, Flemish, and ▷Huguenot settlers of the 17th century. Comprising approximately 60% of the white population in South Africa, they were originally farmers but have now become mainly urbanized. Their language is Afrikaans.

Afro-Asiatic language any of a family of languages spoken throughout the world. There are two main branches, the languages of North Africa and the languages originating in Syria, Mesopotamia, Palestine, and Arabia, but now found from Morocco in the west to the Persian Gulf in the east.

Afro-Caribbean West Indian people of African descent. Afro-Caribbeans are the descendants of West Africans captured or obtained in trade from African procurers. European slave traders then shipped them to the West Indies to English, French, Dutch, Spanish, and Portuguese colonies founded from the 16th century. Since World War II many Afro-Caribbeans have migrated to North America and to Europe, especially to the USA, the UK, and the Netherlands.

afterbirth in mammals, the placenta, umbilical cord, and ruptured membranes, which become detached from the uterus and expelled soon after birth.

afterimage persistence of an image on the retina of the eye after the object producing it has been removed. This leads to persistence of vision, a necessary phenomenon for the illusion of continuous movement in films and television. The term is also used for the persistence of sensations other than vision.

Agadir tourist resort and seaport in south Morocco, near the mouth of the River Sus; population (1993) 137,000. It was rebuilt after being destroyed by an earthquake in 1960. Agadir is one of the main fishing ports of Morocco; other industries include food processing, tourism, and crafts. The mild winter climate is suitable for the growth of citrus fruits, and cobalt, manganese, lead, and zinc are mined nearby.

Aga Khan IV, (Karim) (1936–) Spiritual head (*imam*) of the 'Ismaili' Muslim sect (see ▷Islam). He succeeded his grandfather in 1957.

Agamemnon in Greek mythology, a Greek hero of the Trojan wars, son of Atreus, king of Mycenae, and brother of ▷Menelaus. He sacrificed his daughter ▷Iphigenia in order to secure favourable winds for the Greek expedition against Troy and after a ten-year siege sacked the city, receiving Priam's daughter ▷Cassandra as a prize. On his return home, he and Cassandra were murdered by his wife ▷Clytemnestra and her lover Aegisthus.

agar jellylike carbohydrate, obtained from seaweeds. It is used mainly in microbiological experiments as a culture medium for growing bacteria and other micro-organisms. The agar is resistant to breakdown by micro-organisms, remaining a solid jelly throughout the course of the experiment.

agaric any of a group of fungi (see ▷fungus) of typical mushroom shape. Agarics include the field mushroom *Agaricus campestris* and the cultivated edible mushroom *A. brunnesiens.* Closely related is the often poisonous ▷Amanita, which includes the fly agaric *A. muscaria.* (Genus *Agaricus*, family Agaricaceae.)

Agassiz, (Jean) Louis Rodolphe (1807–1873) Swiss-born US palaeontologist and geologist who developed the idea of the ice age. He established his name through his work on the classification of fossil fishes. Unlike Charles Darwin, he did not believe that individual species themselves changed, but that new species were created from time to time.

agate cryptocrystalline (with crystals too small to be seen with an optical microscope) silica, SiO_2, composed of cloudy and banded ▷chalcedony, sometimes mixed with ▷opal, that forms in rock cavities.

AGAVE Intensive cultivation of sisal plants *Agave sisalana* near the Berenty nature reserve in Madagascar. *Premaphotos Wildlife*

agave any of several related plants with stiff, sword-shaped, spiny leaves arranged in a rosette. All species come from the warmer parts of the New World. They include *Agave sisalana*, whose fibres are used for rope making, and the Mexican century plant *A. americana*, which may take many years to mature (hence its common name). Alcoholic drinks such as tequila and pulque are made from the sap of agave plants. (Genus *Agave*, family Agavaceae.)

ageing in common usage, the period of deterioration of the physical condition of a living organism that leads to death; in biological terms, the entire life process.

ageism discrimination against older people in employment, pensions, housing, and health care.

Agent Orange selective weedkiller, notorious for its use in the 1960s during the Vietnam War by US forces to eliminate ground cover which could protect enemy forces. It was subsequently discovered to contain highly poisonous ▷dioxin. Thousands of US troops who had handled it, along with many Vietnamese people who came into contact with it, later developed cancer or produced deformed babies. In 2000 it was announced by the Pentagon that a link had been found between Agent Orange and diabetes in veterans who sprayed it during the Vietnam War.

aggression in biology, behaviour used to intimidate or injure another organism (of the same or of a different species), usually for the purposes of gaining territory, a mate, or food. Aggression often involves an escalating series of threats aimed at intimidating an opponent without having to engage in potentially dangerous physical contact. Aggressive signals include roaring by red deer, snarling by dogs, the fluffing-up of feathers by birds, and the raising of fins by some species of fish.

BATTLE OF AGINCOURT An illustration from Wavrin's *Chroniques de l'Angleterre* (around 1450, some 35 years after the event) shows the overpowering fire the English longbowmen were able to rain down upon the French infantry. *The Art Archive/British Library*

Agincourt, Battle of battle fought on 25 October 1415 at Agincourt during the Hundred Years' War, between Henry V of England and a much larger force of French under a divided command. Henry decimated the French, hastening the English conquest of Normandy. Some 6,000 French died and hundreds, including the richest nobles, were taken prisoner. Henry gained France and the French princess Catherine of Valois as his wife. The village of Agincourt (modern **Azincourt**) is south of Calais, in northern France.

agitprop (Russian 'agitation propaganda') Soviet government bureau established in September 1920 in charge of communist agitation and propaganda. The idea was later developed by left-wing groups in the West for the use of theatre and other arts to convey political messages.

agnosticism belief that the existence of God cannot be proven; that in the nature of things the individual cannot know anything of what lies behind or beyond the world of natural phenomena. The term was coined in 1869 by T H ▷Huxley.

agoraphobia ▷phobia involving fear of open spaces and public places. The anxiety produced can be so severe that some sufferers are unable to leave their homes for many years.

agouti small rodent of the genus *Dasyprocta*, family Dasyproctidae. It is found in the forests of Central and South America. The agouti is herbivorous, swift-running, and about the size of a rabbit.

Agra city in Uttar Pradesh, northern India, on the River Jumna (or Yamuna), 160 km/100 mi southeast of Delhi; population (1991) 892,000. It is a centre for commerce, tourism and industry. There are many small-scale engineering plants, and carpets, leather goods, gold and silver embroidery, and engraved marble are produced. The capital of the Mogul empire from 1566–69 and 1601–1658, it is the site of the ▷Taj Mahal, built during the latter period. Other notable buildings include the Moti Masjid (Pearl Mosque), the Jama Masjid (Great Mosque), and the Red Fort, with red sandstone walls over 20 m/65 ft high and 2.5 km/1.5 mi long. It has a university (1927). **Related Web site: AgraOnline** http://www.agraonline.com/

agrarian revolution until the 1960s historians believed that there had been an 18th-century revolution in ▷agriculture, similar to the revolution that occurred in industry.

They claimed that there had been sweeping changes, possibly in response to the increased demand for food from a rapidly expanding population. Major events included the ▷enclosure of open fields; the development of improved breeds of livestock; the introduction of four-course crop rotation; and the use of new crops such as turnips as animal fodder.

Recent research, however, has shown that these changes were only part of a much larger, slower, ongoing process of development: many were in fact underway before 1750, and other breakthroughs, such as farm mechanization, did not become common until after 1945.

Causes of improvement The main cause of change seems to have been the growing population (from around 6 million in 1700 to 11 million in 1801), particularly in the towns, which created a demand for food. This was particularly important during the Napoleonic Wars, since Napoleon's ▷Continental System prevented all trade with Europe; Britain had to produce more food, or starve. Prices rose rapidly, increasing profitability and encouraging an expansion of production; the Corn Laws also played a part in this. Villages that had been happy to be merely self-sufficient now began to look to produce for the market – so the changes involved the adoption of a new capitalist business ethic by the farmers. Better transport also played a part, for it extended the hinterland of population areas, and allowed more farmers to produce for the market.

▷Enclosure was also crucially important. In 1700 about half the arable land of England was held in open-field strips. The open-field system had some advantages, mainly social, but hampered production. Enclosure rationalized the system of land-holding, consolidated farmland, and gave improving farmers the opportunity to introduce the new methods. Agricultural propagandists such as Arthur Young and William ▷Cobbett also helped the agrarian revolution, for they helped to create a climate of improvement.

To a degree, production was increased because of technical improvements – new crops, crop rotations, selective breeding, new buildings and drainage, the use of manure, and new implements. However, change was uneven from region to region, and even farm to farm, and very gradual. The technological revolution in farming did not occur until after World War II.

New crops The introduction of new crops – such as potatoes, red clover, and turnips – into Britain in the 17th century improved farming practices, since farmers could use them to feed their livestock throughout the winter. Their use did away with the practice of slaughtering animals in the autumn and salting the meat for storage through the winter, which had been particularly detrimental to the health of the community. Also, clover replaced nutrients into the soil, and turnips allowed the land to be thoroughly weeded by hoeing.

Four-course rotation The 18th century saw the replacement of the 'three-field' system of wheat – barley – fallow by the four-course ▷crop rotation system (wheat – turnips – barley – clover), which was designed to ensure that no land would need to lie fallow between periods of cultivation and, to this end, rotated crops which absorb different kinds and quantities of nutrients from the soil. The four-course rotation system was subsequently popularized by enlightened landowners such as Viscount 'Turnip' ▷Townshend and Thomas Coke, who used it to produce greatly increased crop yields on his farmland in Norfolk, and encouraged other farmers and landowners to use the same method. Because both Coke and Townshend lived in Norfolk the system also became known as the 'Norfolk System'.

Livestock farming Other pioneers of the new farming methods developed in Britain in the latter part of the 18th century included the livestock farmer Robert ▷Bakewell, who improved the quality of horned stock and sheep, by means of selective breeding. His work resulted in a great reduction in the age at which bullocks and sheep were ready for the butcher. Other successful breeders included the Colling brothers of County Durham (Durham Shorthorns) and George Culley of Northumberland (Border Leicester sheep).

Agricola, Gnaeus Julius (40–93) Roman general and politician. Born at Forum Julii (Fréjus) in Provence, he became consul in 77, and then governor of Britain 78–85. He extended Roman rule to the Firth of Forth in Scotland and in 84 won the Battle of Mons Graupius. His fleet sailed round the north of Scotland and proved Britain an island.

agricultural revolution see ▷agrarian revolution.

agriculture (Latin *ager* 'field', *colere* 'to cultivate') the practice of farming, including the cultivation of the soil (for raising crops) and the raising of domesticated animals. The units for managing agricultural production vary from smallholdings and individually owned farms to corporate-run farms and collective farms run by entire communities or by the government.

Crops are for human or animal food, or commodities such as cotton and sisal. For successful production, the land must be prepared (ploughed, cultivated, harrowed, and rolled), seed must be planted and the growing plants nurtured. This may involve

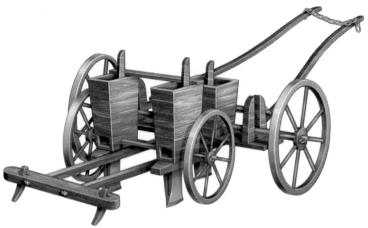

AGRARIAN REVOLUTION The seed drill, invented in about 1701 by English agriculturalist Jethro Tull, was one of many technological developments that contributed to the agrarian revolution. The sowing of seeds in uniform rows allowed weeding between the rows of seedlings during growth, so improving the yield. Previously seeds had been broadcast by hand across the land.

▷fertilizers, ▷irrigation, pest control by chemicals, and monitoring of acidity or nutrients. When the crop has grown, it must be harvested and, depending on the crop, processed in a variety of ways before it is stored or sold.

Greenhouses allow cultivation of plants that would otherwise find the climate too harsh. ▷Hydroponics allows commercial cultivation of crops using nutrient-enriched solutions instead of soil. Special methods, such as terracing, may be adopted to allow cultivation in hostile terrain and to retain topsoil in mountainous areas with heavy rainfall.

Animals are raised for wool, milk, leather, dung (as fuel), or meat. They may be semidomesticated, such as reindeer, or fully domesticated but nomadic (where naturally growing or cultivated food supplies are sparse), or kept in one location. Animal farming involves accommodation (buildings, fencing, or pasture), feeding, breeding, gathering the produce (eggs, milk, or wool), slaughtering, and further processing such as tanning.

Related Web site: Sustainable Agriculture Network http://www.sare.org/san/

agrimony herbaceous plant belonging to the rose family, with small yellow flowers on a slender spike. It grows along hedges and in fields. (*Agrimonia eupatoria*, family Rosaceae.)

Agrippa, Marcus Vipsanius (*c.* 63–12 BC) Roman general and admiral. He was instrumental in the successful campaigns and rise to power of the emperor ▷Augustus. He commanded the victorious fleet at the Battle of ▷Actium and married Augustus' daughter Julia.

agronomy study of crops and soils, a branch of agricultural science. Agronomy includes such topics as selective breeding (of plants and animals), irrigation, pest control, and soil analysis and modification.

AH in the Muslim calendar, abbreviation for ▷anno hegirae.

Ahaggar (or Hoggar) large plateau region in the central Sahara, about 1,500 km/932 mi south of Algiers. It averages about 900 m/2,953 ft above sea level, its highest point being Mount Tahat (2,918 m/9,573 ft). The plateau is the home of the formerly nomadic Tuareg.

Ahern, Bertie (1951–) Irish politician, Taoiseach (prime minister) from 1997, leader of Fianna Fáil from 1994. After the May 1997 election he formed a minority government as Ireland's youngest Taoiseach. His promotion of peace negotiations culminated in the 1998 Good Friday Agreement between Northern Ireland's contending parties, which received 94% backing in a referendum in the Irish Republic in May 1998.

ahimsa in Hinduism, Buddhism, and Jainism, the doctrine of respect for all life (including the lowest forms and even the elements themselves) and consequently an extreme form of nonviolence. It arises in part from the concept of *karma*, which holds that a person's actions (and thus any injury caused to any form of life) determine his or her experience and condition in this and future lives.

Ahmadabad (or Ahmedabad) city in Gujarat, India, situated on the Sabarmati River, 430 km/260 mi north of Mumbai (formerly Bombay); population (1991) 3,298,000. The former state capital and Gujarat's largest city, it is a major industrial centre specializing in cotton manufacturing. It has many sacred buildings of the Hindu, Muslim, and Jain faiths, as well as buildings designed by 20th-century architects, such as Le Corbusier, reflecting commercial success.

Ahmad Shah Durrani (1724–1773) founder and first ruler of Afghanistan. Elected shah in 1745, he had conquered the Punjab by 1751 and defeated the ▷Maratha people's confederacy at Panipat, Punjab, in 1761.

Ahriman in Zoroastrianism, the supreme evil spirit, lord of the darkness and death, waging war with his counterpart Ahura Mazda (Ormuzd) until a time when human beings choose to lead good lives and Ahriman is finally destroyed.

Ahura Mazda (or Ormuzd) in Zoroastrianism, the spirit of supreme good. As god of life and light he will finally prevail over his enemy, Ahriman.

Ahvaz (or Ahwaz) capital of ▷Khuzestan province, southwest Iran; population (1996 est) 805,000. Situated on the River Karun, the city is an important administrative and supply centre for the southwestern Iranian oilfields, and is connected by rail to Tehran and the Gulf. There are also textile and petrochemical industries. Ahvaz was badly damaged during the Iran–Iraq war (1980–88).

AI abbreviation for ▷artificial intelligence and ▷artificial insemination.

AI(D) abbreviation for ▷artificial insemination (by donor). AI(H) is artificial insemination by husband.

Aidan, St (*c.* 600–651) Irish monk who converted Northumbria to Christianity and founded Lindisfarne monastery on Holy Island off the northeast coast of England. His feast day is 31 August.

aid, development money given or lent on concessional terms to developing countries or spent on maintaining agencies for this purpose. In 1970, all industrialized United Nations (UN) member countries committed to giving at least 0.7% of GNP to aid. All the Scandinavian countries have met or exceeded this target, whereas the UK and the USA have not achieved it; in 1995, the UK aid budget was only 0.28% and the US figure only 0.15% of GNP. Each country spends more than half its contribution on direct bilateral assistance to countries with which they have historical or military links or hope to encourage trade. The rest goes to international organizations such as UN and ▷World Bank agencies, which distribute aid multilaterally.

Related Web site: OneWorld http://www.oneworld.org/index.html

aid, foreign financial and other assistance given by richer, usually industrialized, countries to war-damaged or developing states. See ▷aid, development

AIDS (acronym for acquired immune deficiency syndrome) the gravest of the ▷sexually transmitted diseases (STDs). It is caused by the human immunodeficiency virus (▷HIV), now known to be a ▷retrovirus, an organism first identified in 1983. HIV is transmitted in body fluids, mainly blood and genital secretions.

Diagnosis of AIDS The virus destroys the immune system, leaving the victim susceptible to diseases that would not otherwise develop. Diagnosis of AIDS is based on the appearance of rare tumours or infections in people not expected to suffer from such illness. *Pneumocystis carinii* pneumonia, for instance, normally seen only in the malnourished or those whose immune systems have been deliberately suppressed, is common among AIDS victims and, for them, a leading cause of death. Unlike other diseases, which typically claim most lives among young children and the elderly, AIDS particularly hits those of working age, dramatically changing the age structures of populations, causing widespread hardship.

Treatment In the West the time-lag between infection with HIV and the development of AIDS seems to be about ten years, but progression is far more rapid in developing countries. Roughly 50% of AIDS victims die within three years. There is no cure for the disease. It was discovered in 1995 that using a recently developed AIDS drug called 3TC in conjunction with ▷zidovudine (formerly ▷AZT) reduced levels of virus in the blood by ten times. In the West, the use of a three-drug cocktail has had dramatic effects, suppressing levels of the virus to a point where infected people can lead normal lives. Key factors in the success of this treatment are the prescription of adequate doses of drugs and patient compliance, as the drugs can have unpleasant side effects. In Africa, triple therapy drug treatment is so expensive that it is not widely used. Fears have recently been raised that the HIV virus has begun to mutate to become resistant to the current drug cocktail. Research in 1999 on 11,990 HIV patients in the USA found more than a quarter to be resistant to all three classes of HIV drugs. Likewise, in the UK, 30% of new HIV infections in 2000 were found to be caused by viruses that are resistant to at least one of the currently available treatment drugs.

Worldwide statistics Allowing for under-diagnosis, incomplete reporting, and reporting delay, it can be estimated that almost 22 million adults and children have been killed by AIDS since the 1970s. More than 75% of the cases have been in Africa, with about 7% in Asia, 4% in the USA, 7% in the rest of the Americas, and 3% in Europe. The United Nations (UN) estimated that, in January 2000, 34 million people were living with HIV or AIDS.

> **Alan Patrick Herbert**
> English writer and politician
>
> *The Farmer will never be happy again; / He carries his heart in his boots; / For either the rain is destroying his grain / Or the drought is destroying his roots.*
>
> 'The Farmer'

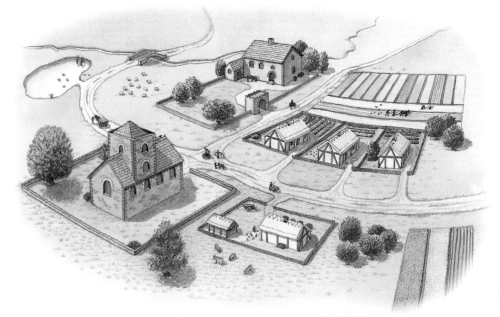

AGRICULTURE Before the agrarian revolution, land was farmed in strips separated by ditches, and livestock was grazed on common land.

Agriculture: Key Events

10 000–8000 BC	Holocene (post-glacial) period of hunters and gatherers. Harvesting and storage of wild grains in southwest Asia. Herding of reindeer in northern Eurasia. Domestic sheep in northern Iraq.
8000	Neolithic revolution with cultivation of domesticated wheats and barleys, sheep, and goats in southwest Asia. Domestication of pigs and cultivation of sugarcane in New Guinea. Wild maize (Indian corn) used as food in central America.
7000–6000	Domestic goats, sheep, and cattle in Anatolia, Greece, Persia, and the Caspian basin. Planting and harvesting techniques are transferred from Asia Minor to Europe.
5000	Beginning of Nile valley civilization. Millet is cultivated in China.
3400	Flax used for textiles in Egypt. Widespread corn production in the Americas.
c. 3100	River Nile dammed during the rule of King Menes.
3000	First record of asses used as beasts of burden in Egypt. Sumerian civilization uses barley as main crop with wheat, dates, flax, apples, plums, and grapes.
2900	Domestication of pigs in eastern Asia.
2640	Reputed start of Chinese silk industry.
2350	Wine-making in Egypt.
2250	First known irrigation dam.
1600	Important advances are made in the cultivation of vines and olives in Crete.
1500	*Shadoof* (mechanism for raising water) is used for irrigation in Egypt.
1400	Iron ploughshares are in use in India.
1300	Aqueducts and reservoirs are used for irrigation in Egypt.
1000–500	Evidence of crop rotation, manuring, and irrigation in India.
600	First windmills are used for corn grinding in Persia.
350	Rice cultivation is well established in parts of western Africa. Hunting and gathering take place in the east, central, and south parts of the continent.
c. 200	Use of gears to create ox-driven water wheel for irrigation. Archimedes screw used for irrigation.
100	Cattle-drawn iron ploughs are in use in China.
AD 65	Publication of *De Re Rustica/On Rural Things*, Latin treatise on agriculture and irrigation by the Spanish-born writer Columella.
500	'Three fields in two years' rotation used in China.
630	Cotton is introduced into Arabia.
800	Origins of the 'open field' system in northern Europe.
900	Wheeled ploughs are in use in Western Europe.
1000	Frisians (NW Netherlanders) begin to build dykes and reclaim land.
11th century	Three-field system replaces the two-field system in Western Europe. Concentration on crop growing.
12th century	Increasing use of watermills and windmills. Horses replace oxen for pulling work in many areas.
12th–14th centuries	Expansion of European population brings more land into cultivation. Crop rotations, manuring, and new crops such as beans and peas help increase productivity. Feudal system at its height.
13th–14th centuries	Agricultural recession in Western Europe with a series of bad harvests, famines, and pestilence.
1347	Black Death (plague) kills about a third of the European population.
16th century	Decline of the feudal system in Western Europe. More specialist forms of production are now possible with urban markets. Manorial estates and serfdom remain in eastern Europe. Spaniards introduce maize from North, Central, and South America into Europe. Chinese begin cultivation of non-indigenous crops such as corn, sweet potatoes, potatoes, and peanuts.
17th century	The potato is introduced into Europe. Norfolk crop rotation becomes widespread in England, involving wheat, turnips, barley, and then ryegrass/clover.
1620	Native American peoples teach the first English colonists how to cultivate maize (Indian Corn).
1700–1845	Agrarian revolution begins in England. Two million hectares of farmland in England enclosed. The removal of open fields in other parts of Europe follows.
c. 1701	Jethro Tull develops the seed drill and the horse-drawn hoe.
1783	First plough factory established in England.
1793	Invention of the cotton gin, a machine for separating cotton fibres from the seed boll (pod).
1800	Early threshing machines developed in England.
1820s	First nitrates for fertilizer imported from South America.
1840s	Extensive potato blight in Europe, failure of potato crop contributes to the Great Famine in Ireland.
1850s	Use of clay pipes for drainage well established throughout Europe.
1862	First steam plough used in the Netherlands.
1850s–90s	Major developments in transport and refrigeration technology alter the nature of agricultural markets with crops, dairy products, and wheat being shipped internationally.
1921	First attempt at crop dusting with pesticides from an aeroplane near Dayton, Ohio, USA.
1938	First self-propelled grain combine harvester used in the USA.
1942–62	Huge increase in the use of pesticides, later curbed by disquiet about their effects and increasing resistance of pests to standard controls such as DDT.
1943	*The Living Soil* by Lady Eve Balfour, one of the most important figures in the development of organic farming in the UK, is published. She begins the 'Haughley Experiment' – a long-term (30 years) trial comparing the new intensive farming regime, reliant on chemicals, with alternative organic methods.
1945 onwards	Increasing use of scientific techniques, crop specialization, and large-scale farm enterprises.
1985	First cases of bovine spongiform encephalopathy (BSE) recorded by UK vets.
1992	Number of cases of BSE in cattle in the UK is at its peak (700 cases per week).
1995	Increase in the use of genetic engineering with nearly 3,000 transgenic crops being field-tested.
1996	A global ban on UK beef exports follows the government announcement that BSE may have been transmitted to humans in the form of a variant strain of Creutzfeldt-Jakob disease (CJD) through the eating of contaminated beef. The ban seriously depresses the UK livestock market.
1996	Organic farming is on the increase in EU countries. The rise is 11% per year in the UK, 50% in Germany, and 40% in Italy.
1997	The UK government bans the sale of beef on the bone because of fears it is more likely to be contaminated with BSE than other cuts.
1998	According to the results of a survey by a team of UK psychiatrists, one in ten farmers regularly exposed to organophosphates will suffer irreversible physical and mental damage. Fears grow that genetically modified (GM) crops may have unpredictable harmful biological and environmental effects.
1999	The worldwide ban on UK beef is lifted, but France continues to prohibit beef imports from the UK. The sale of beef on the bone resumes after a UK government ban lasting two years.
2000	An outbreak of swine fever in East Anglia leads to the slaughter of thousands of pigs throughout the UK. A Dutch-based seed company compensates farmers for selling them GM-contaminated oilseed rape seeds. The official BSE enquiry publishes its 16-volume report on the crisis, blaming the government for failing to act in the interests of consumers. Cases of BSE increase in France.
2001	In February an outbreak of foot-and-mouth disease spread rapidly across the UK, and then Europe. Severe restrictions on the movement of livestock were imposed across Europe. By the end of June over 5 million animals had been slaughtered.

According to a World Health Organization (WHO) report released in May 1999, AIDS is the world's most deadly infectious disease, and the fourth leading global cause of death. Three million people died from AIDS during 2000, 80% of whom were in Africa. The United Nations (UN) Programme on HIV and AIDS estimated that, in January 2000, 34 million people were living with HIV or AIDS, 95% of which were in less developed countries, and 75% in Africa. More than 15,000 new HIV cases are revealed each day (or 5.4 million each year), with half of the people infected aged between 15 and 24.

Related Web site: AIDS and HIV Information http://www.thebody. com/index.shtml

Aiken, Howard Hathaway (1900–1973) US mathematician and computer pioneer. In 1939, in conjunction with engineers from IBM, he started work on the design of an automatic calculator using standard business-machine components. In 1944 the team completed one of the first computers, the Automatic Sequence Controlled Calculator (known as the Harvard Mark I), a programmable computer controlled by punched paper tape and using punched cards.

ailanthus any of several trees or shrubs with compound leaves made up of pointed leaflets and clusters of small greenish flowers with an unpleasant smell. The tree of heaven (*Ailanthus altissima*), native to East Asia, is grown worldwide as an ornamental; it can grow to 30 m/100 ft in height and the trunk can reach 1 m/3 ft in diameter. (Genus *Ailanthus*, family Simaroubaceae.)

Aintree racecourse situated on the outskirts of Liverpool, northwest England. The Grand National steeplechase (established in 1839) is held here every spring.

Ainu aboriginal people of Japan, driven north in the 4th century AD by ancestors of the Japanese. They now number about 25,000, inhabiting Japanese and Russian territory on Sakhalin, Hokkaido, and the Kuril Islands. Their language has no written form, and is unrelated to any other. The Ainu were recognized by the Japanese government as a minority people in 1991.

air the mixture of gases making up the Earth's ▷atmosphere.

aircraft any aeronautical vehicle capable of flying through the air. It may be lighter than air (supported by buoyancy) or heavier than air (supported by the dynamic action of air on its surfaces). ▷Balloons and ▷airships are lighter-than-air craft. Heavier-than-air craft include the ▷aeroplane, glider, autogiro, and helicopter.

AIRCRAFT The Avro Lancaster B2 on a Battle of Britain Memorial flight. *Corel*

aircraft carrier ocean-going naval vessel with a broad, flat-topped deck for launching and landing military aircraft; a floating military base for warplanes too far from home for refuelling, repairing, reconnaissance, escorting, and attack and defence operations. Aircraft are catapult-launched or take off and land on the flight-deck, a large expanse of unobstructed deck, often fitted with barriers and restraining devices to halt the landing aircraft.

The role of the carrier and its aircraft has included reconnaissance, torpedo, and bomb operations against hostile shipping, anti-submarine warfare, and air support of naval and amphibious operations. Aircraft carriers of the US Navy have formed the equivalent of mobile airfields, replacing fixed, shore-based fields for tactical and strategic attacks against land targets. The trend now seems to be towards anti-submarine warfare, although critics of the carrier emphasize how vulnerable carriers are against submarine and missile attack.

Despite their cost, aircraft carriers have always remained popular with major powers, such as the USA and the former USSR. Examples include the USSR's *Komsomolsk* (1979) (40,000 tonnes, 15 fixed-wing aircraft, 20 helicopters), the USA's *Eisenhower* (1979) (81,600 tonnes, 95 aircraft), and the British *Invincible* (1980) (19,500 tonnes). Modern aircraft carriers are equipped with combinations of fixed-wing aircraft, helicopters, missile launchers, and anti-aircraft guns.

The first purpose-designed aircraft carrier was the British HMS *Hermes*, completed in 1913. Carriers played a major role in World War II, but in post-war years the cost and vulnerability of such large vessels were thought to have outweighed their advantages. However, by 1980 the desire to have a means of destroying enemy aircraft beyond the range of a ship's own weapons – for instance, when on convoy duty – led to a widespread revival of aircraft carriers of 20,000–30,000 tonnes.

Airedale terrier breed of large terrier, about 60 cm/24 in tall, with a wiry red-brown coat and black saddle patch. It originated about 1850 in England, as a cross between the otterhound and Irish and Welsh terriers.

air force a nation's fleet of fighting aircraft and the organization that maintains them.
History The emergence of the aeroplane at first brought only limited recognition of its potential value as a means of waging war. Like the balloon, used since the American Civil War, it was considered a way of extending the vision of ground forces.

A unified air force was established in the UK 1918, Italy 1923, France 1928, Germany 1935 (after repudiating the arms limitations of the Versailles treaty), and the USA 1947 (it began as the Aeronautical Division of the Army Signal Corps 1907, and evolved into the Army's Air Service Division by 1918; by 1926 it was the Air Corps and in World War II the Army Air Force). The main specialized groupings formed during World War I – such as combat, bombing (see ▷bomb), reconnaissance, and transport – were adapted and modified in World War II; activity was extended, with self-contained tactical air forces to meet the needs of ground commanders in the main theatres of land operations and for the attack on and defence of shipping over narrow seas.

From 1945 to 1960 piston-engine aircraft were superseded by jet aircraft. Computerized guidance systems lessened the difference between missile and aircraft, and flights of unlimited duration became possible with air-to-air refuelling.

The US Strategic Air Command's bombers, for example, were capable of patrolling 24 hours a day armed with thermonuclear weapons. For some years it was anticipated that the pilot might become obsolete, but the continuation of conventional warfare and the evolution of tactical nuclear weapons led in the 1970s and 1980s to the development of advanced combat aircraft able to fly supersonically beneath an enemy's radar on strike and reconnaissance missions, as well as so-called stealth aircraft that cannot be detected by radar. See also ▷services, armed and ▷Royal Air Force.

airlock airtight chamber that allows people to pass between areas of different pressure; also an air bubble in a pipe that impedes fluid flow. An airlock may connect an environment at ordinary pressure and an environment that has high air pressure (such as a submerged caisson used for tunnelling or building dams or bridge foundations).

air pollution contamination of the atmosphere caused by the discharge, accidental or deliberate, of a wide range of toxic airborne substances. Often the amount of the released substance is relatively high in a certain locality, so the harmful effects become more noticeable. The cost of preventing any discharge of pollutants into the air is prohibitive, so attempts are more usually made to reduce the amount of discharge gradually and to disperse it as quickly as possible by using a very tall chimney, or by intermittent release.

air sac in birds, a thin-walled extension of the lungs. There are nine of these and they extend into the abdomen and bones, effectively increasing lung capacity. In mammals, it is another name for the alveoli in the lungs, and in some insects, for widenings of the trachea.

The sacs subdivide into further air spaces which partially replace the marrow in many of the bird's bones. The air space in these bones assists flight by making them lighter.

airship (or **dirigible**) any aircraft that is lighter than air and power-driven, consisting of an ellipsoidal balloon that forms the streamlined envelope or hull and has below it the propulsion system (propellers), steering mechanism, and space for crew, passengers, and/or cargo. The balloon section is filled with lighter-than-air gas, either the nonflammable helium or, before helium was industrially available in large enough quantities, the easily ignited and flammable hydrogen. The envelope's form is maintained by internal pressure in the nonrigid (blimp) and semirigid (in which the nose and tail sections have a metal framework connected by a rigid keel) types. The rigid type (zeppelin) maintains its form using an internal metal framework. Airships have been used for luxury travel, polar exploration, warfare, and advertising.

Rigid airships predominated from about 1900 until 1940. As the technology developed, the size of the envelope was increased from about 45 m/150 ft to more than 245 m/800 ft for the last two zeppelins built. In 1852 the first successful airship was designed and flown by Henri ▷Giffard of France. In 1900 the first rigid type was designed by Count (*Graf*) Ferdinand von ▷Zeppelin of Germany (though he did not produce a successful model till his L-24 in 1908). Airships were used by both sides during World War I, but they were not seriously used for military purposes after that as they were largely replaced by aeroplanes. The British mainly used small machines for naval reconnaissance and patrolling the North Sea; Germany used Schutte-Lanz and Zeppelin machines for similar patrol work and also for long-range bombing attacks against English and French cities, mainly Paris and London.
Related Web site: Airship and Blimp Resources http://www.hotairship.com/index.html

AIRSHIP A uniformed guard watches over the skeletal remains of the German airship *Hindenburg*, Lakehurst, New Jersey, USA, 1937. The airship exploded in a ball of flames while attempting to land after a transatlantic flight. The death of all 36 passengers and crew ended the development of the airship as a commercial proposition. *Archive Photos*

Aix-en-Provence city and spa in the *département* of Bouches-du-Rhône, southeast France, 29 km/18 mi north of Marseille; population (1990) 126,800. The town dates from Roman times and was the capital of the former province of Provence. The city still maintains some of its important traditional functions, namely the courts, university, and spas. These activities are now undergoing regeneration.

Aix-la-Chapelle French name of ▷Aachen, an ancient city in Germany.

Ajaccio capital and second-largest port of Corsica; population (1990) 59,300. Founded by the Genoese in 1492, it was the birthplace of Napoleon; it has been French since 1768.

Ajax Greek hero in Homer's *Iliad*. Son of Telamon, King of Salamis, he was second only to Achilles among the Greek heroes in the Trojan War. He fought ▷Hector single-handed, defended the ships, and killed many Trojans. According to subsequent Greek legends, Ajax went mad with jealousy when ▷Agamemnon awarded the armour of the dead Achilles to ▷Odysseus. He later committed suicide in shame.

Ajman smallest of the seven states making up the ▷United Arab Emirates; area 250 sq km/96 sq mi; population (1995 est) 118,800.
Related Web site: Ajman http://www.uaeforever.com/Ajman/

Ajmer city in Rajasthan, India, 350 km/220 mi southwest of Delhi; population (1991) 402,000. It is a commercial and industrial centre, with textile and leather manufacturing, railway workshops,

---

Air Pollution

The greatest single cause of air pollution in the UK is the car, which is responsible for 85% of the carbon monoxide and 45% of the oxides of nitrogen present in the atmosphere. According to a UK government report in 1998, air pollution causes up to 24,000 deaths in Britain per year.

Possibly the world's worst ever human-made air pollution disaster occurred in Indonesia in September 1997. Caused by forest clearance fires, the smoke pollution spread to other countries of the region as far as the Philippines, Thailand, and Australia.

The 1997 Kyoto protocol committed the industrialized nations of the world to cutting their levels of harmful gas emissions to 5.2% by 2012. Europe is expected to take the biggest cut of 8%, the USA 7%, and Japan 6%. The agreement covers Russia and eastern Europe as well.

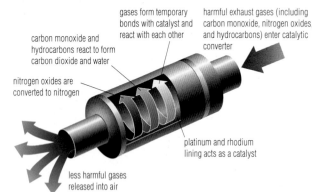

gases form temporary bonds with catalyst and react with each other

harmful exhaust gases (including carbon monoxide, nitrogen oxides, and hydrocarbons) enter catalytic converter

carbon monoxide and hydrocarbons react to form carbon dioxide and water

nitrogen oxides are converted to nitrogen

platinum and rhodium lining acts as a catalyst

less harmful gases released into air

AIR POLLUTION The diagram shows a cross section of a car's catalytic converter. Catalytic converters convert harmful exhaust gases (including carbon monoxide, nitrogen oxide, and hydrocarbons) into less harmful gases for release back into the air.

Indoor air pollution

The issue of pollution in offices and homes has become more recognized in recent years. Typically, people living in urban surroundings spend 90% of their time indoors, particularly those most at risk from the effects of pollution – the young, the old, and the infirm. Modern buildings, designed to be more energy-efficient and insulate more, tend to have greatly reduced ventilation rates. Sources of indoor air pollution include tobacco smoke, furnishings and building materials, computing equipment, and gas appliances.

JALAL UD-DIN MUHAMMAD AKBAR Mogul emperor Jalal ud-Din Muhammad Akbar leading the Mogul army about 1580. *Philip Sauvain Picture Collection*

and grain processing. Situated in a deep valley in the Aravalli Mountains at the foot of Mount Taragarh (870 m/2,800 ft), it is surrounded by a stone wall and dominated by the Taragarh fort built by the emperor ▷Akbar.

ajolote Mexican reptile of the genus *Bipes*. It and several other tropical burrowing species are placed in the Amphisbaenia, a group separate from lizards and snakes among the Squamata. Unlike the others, however, which have no legs, it has a pair of short but well-developed front legs. In line with its burrowing habits, the skull is very solid, the eyes small, and external ears absent.

The scales are arranged in rings, giving the body a wormlike appearance.

AK abbreviation for the state of ▷Alaska, USA.

Akbar, Jalal ud-Din Muhammad (1542–1605) Mogul emperor of North India from 1556, when he succeeded his father Humayun. He gradually established his rule throughout North India. He is considered the greatest of the Mogul emperors, and the firmness and wisdom of his rule won him the title 'Guardian of Mankind'; he was a patron of the arts.

à Kempis, Thomas German religious writer; see ▷Thomas à Kempis.

AKHENATON A relief depicting the Egyptian pharaoh Akhenaton with his wife Nefertiti. *Philip Sauvain Picture Collection*

Akhenaton (or Ikhnaton) King (pharaoh) of ancient Egypt of the 18th dynasty (*c.* 1353–1335 BC), who may have ruled jointly for a time with his father Amenhotep III. He developed the cult of the Sun, ▷Aton, rather than the rival cult of Amen, and removed his capital to ▷Akhetaton.

Akhetaton capital of ancient Egypt established by the monotheistic pharaoh ▷Akhenaton as the centre for his cult of the Aton, the Sun's disc; it is the modern Tell el Amarna 300 km/190 mi south of Cairo. Akhenaton's palace had formal enclosed gardens. After his death it was abandoned, and the **Amarna tablets**, found in the ruins, were probably discarded by his officials.

Akhmatova, Anna (1889–1966) Pen-name of Anna Andreevna Gorenko. Russian poet. She was a leading member of the Acmeist movement. Among her works are the cycle *Requiem* (1963), written in the 1930s and dealing with the Stalinist terror, and *Poem Without a Hero* (1962, begun 1940).

In the 1920s she published several collections of poetry in the realist style of Osip ▷Mandelshtam, but her lack of sympathy with the post-revolutionary regimes inhibited her writing, and her work was banned 1922–40 and again from 1946. From the mid-1950s her work was gradually rehabilitated in the USSR. In 1989 an Akhmatova Museum was opened in Leningrad (now St Petersburg).

Akihito (1933–) Emperor of Japan from 1989, succeeding his father Hirohito (Shōwa). His reign is called the Heisei ('achievement of universal peace') era.

Unlike previous crown princes, Akihito was educated alongside commoners at the elite Gakushuin school and in 1959 he married Michiko Shoda (1934–), the daughter of a flour-company president. Their three children, the Oxford University-educated Crown Prince Hiro, Prince Aya, and Princess Nori, were raised at Akihito's home instead of being reared by tutors and chamberlains in a separate imperial dormitory.

Akkad northern Semitic people who conquered the Sumerians 2350 BC and ruled Mesopotamia. Their language was Semitic (old Akkadian). Akkad was also the northern of the two provinces into which Babylonia was divided. The ancient city of Akkad in central Mesopotamia, founded by ▷Sargon I, was an imperial centre in the late third millennium BC; the site is unidentified, but it was on the River Euphrates somewhere near Babylon.

Akko (formerly Acre; New Testament **Ptolemais**) seaport in northwest Israel, situated on the Mediterranean Sea; population (1995 est) 48,300. The city was built on a small promontory which, with Mount Carmel to the south, forms a semicircular bay. From being part of British-mandated Palestine, it became part of Israel in 1948. Industries include tourism, fishing, and light manufactures.

Akram, Wasim (1966–) Pakistani cricketer. A left-arm fast bowler and hard-hitting batsman who made his Test debut in 1985 at the age of 18 and soon established himself as one of the world's leading players. He was the first player to take more than 400 wickets in both Test and One-day internationals, and has taken more wickets in One-day internationals than any other player, surpassing the 500-wicket mark during the 2003 World Cup in South Africa. He played county cricket for Lancashire 1988–98, and in September 1998 captained the team to victory in the Natwest Trophy and helped them clinch the AXA League title. He led Pakistan to the final of the 1999 World Cup where they were defeated by Australia. He was replaced as Pakistan captain in January 2000 and in November 2000 played his 100th Test Match, becoming just the fourth regular bowler to do so in Test history. He announced his intention to retire after the 2003 World Cup.

Akron (Greek 'summit') city in northeastern Ohio, USA, on the Cuyahoga River, 56 km/35 mi southeast of Cleveland; population (2000 est) 217,100. Industries include chemical, plastic, and aerospace products. Known as the 'Rubber Capital of the World', it is home to the headquarters of several tyre and rubber companies, although tyre production had ended here by 1982.

Aksum (or **Axum**) ancient Greek-influenced Semitic kingdom that flourished in the 1st–6th centuries AD and covered a large part of modern Ethiopia as well as the Sudan. The ruins of its capital, also called Aksum, lie northwest of ādwa, but the site has been developed as a modern city.

AL abbreviation for the state of ▷Alabama, USA.

al- for Arabic names beginning *al-*, see rest of name; for example, for 'al-Fatah', see ▷Fatah, al-.

Alabama state in southern USA. It is nicknamed Heart of Dixie or the Camellia State. Alabama was admitted to the Union in 1819 as the 22nd US state. Historically it was a plantation state associated with slavery and, in the 20th century, the civil-rights movement. It is bordered to the east by Georgia, with the Chattahoochee River forming the lower half of the boundary, to the north by Tennessee, and to the west by Mississippi, with the Tennessee River forming a small part of the boundary in the northwest. To the south is the Florida panhandle and a 100km-/60 mi-long stretch of coast on the Gulf of Mexico, bisected by Mobile Bay.

population (1996 est) 4,273,100 **area** 134,700 sq km/52,000 sq mi **capital** Montgomery **towns and cities** Birmingham, Mobile, Huntsville, Tuscaloosa **industries and products** cotton (still important though no longer prime crop), soybeans, peanuts, wood products, marble, coal, oil, natural gas, livestock, poultry, fishing, iron, steel, aluminium, chemicals, textiles, paper, power generation, aerospace industry

alabaster naturally occurring fine-grained white or light-coloured translucent form of gypsum, often streaked or mottled. A soft material, it is easily carved.

Alamein, El, Battles of two decisive battles of World War II in the western desert of northern Egypt. In the first (1–27 July 1942), the British 8th Army under ▷Auchinleck held off the German and Italian forces under ▷Rommel; in the second (23 October–4 November 1942), ▷Montgomery defeated Rommel.

ALABASTER The working of alabaster in Egypt. *Image Bank*

Alamo, the mission fortress in San Antonio, Texas, USA. During the War of Texan Independence from Mexico, it was besieged 23 February–6 March 1836 by ▷Santa Anna and 4,000 Mexicans. They killed the garrison of about 180 Texans, including Davy ▷Crockett and Jim Bowie.

THE ALAMO Last stand at the Alamo in San Antonio, Texas, USA. *Art Archive*

Alanbrooke, Alan Francis Brooke (1883–1963) 1st Viscount Alanbrooke. British army officer. He was Chief of Staff in World War II and largely responsible for the strategy that led to the German defeat.

Åland Islands (Finnish **Ahvenanmaa** 'land of waters') group of some 6,000 islands in the Baltic Sea, at the southern extremity of the Gulf of Bothnia; area 1,481 sq km/572 sq mi; population (1992) 25,000. Only 80 are inhabited; the largest island, Åland, has a small town, Mariehamn. The main sectors of the island economy are tourism, agriculture, and shipping.

Alani (or **Alans**) a nomadic pastoral people in the ancient world, speaking an Iranian language and occupying steppe land to the northeast of the Black Sea. The Alani migrated into the eastern provinces of the Roman Empire and were mentioned in Latin literature in the 1st century. They had the reputation of being a warlike people, specializing in horse breeding, and they eventually split into two groups.

Alania (formerly **North Ossetia**) autonomous republic in the south of the Russian Federation, on the border with Georgia; area 8,000 sq km/3,088 sq mi; population (1992) 695,000. A new constitution was adopted in 1994 and the republic took its former name of Alania. The capital is Vladikavkaz (formerly Ordzhonikidze). Alania lies on the northern slopes of the central Caucasus, and its main rivers are the Terek, the Gizeldon, and the

Ardon. Its industries include mining and metallurgy (lead, zinc, silver), maize processing, timber and woodwork, textiles, building materials, distilleries, food processing, and hydroelectric power generation.

Alaric (c. 370–410) Visigothic king 395–410 who campaigned against the Romans in the Balkans and Italy. On 24 August 410 he captured and sacked Rome. After three days he led the Goths south, intending to invade Sicily and then Africa, but died of a sudden illness.

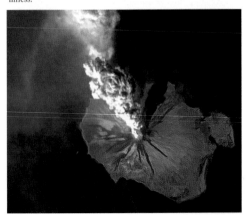

ALASKA A satellite photograph showing the Augustine volcano in Cook Inlet, south of Anchorage, Alaska. *Image Bank*

Alaska largest state of the USA, located on the northwest extremity of North America, and separated from the lower 48 states by British Columbia. It is nicknamed Last Frontier. Alaska was admitted to the Union in 1959 as the 49th US state. Historically and commercially the state has been associated with mineral exploitation. It is bordered to the east by the Yukon Territory, Canada, and to the southeast, along its panhandle, by the Yukon Territory and British Columbia, Canada. Northern Alaska lies on the Beaufort Sea, part of the Arctic Ocean. To the northwest is the Chukchi Sea, narrowing to about 80 km/50 mi at the Bering Strait, which separates the Alaskan Seward Peninsula from Russian East Asia. The Bering Sea is bounded to the south by Alaska's long ▷Aleutian Islandchain, extending in an east–west arc across the North Pacific Ocean from the Alaska Peninsula. To the peninsula's east is the Gulf of Alaska.

> **population** (2000) 626,900; including 15% American Indians, Aleuts, and Inuit **total area** 1,530,700 sq km/591,004 sq mi
> **land area** 1,478,457 sq km/570,833 sq mi **capital** Juneau
> **towns and cities** Anchorage, Fairbanks, Fort Yukon, Holy Cross, Nome, College, Sitka **industries and products** oil, natural gas, coal, copper, iron, gold, tin, fur, salmon fisheries and canneries, lumber; tourism is a large and growing industry (tourists outnumber residents each year)
> **Related Web site:** Alaska OnLine http://www.alaskanet.com/index.html

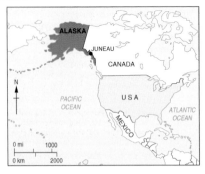

Alaskan malamute breed of dog. It is a type of ▷husky.

Alba Gaelic name for ▷Scotland; also an alternative spelling for ▷Alva, Ferdinand Alvarez de Toledo, Duke of Alva, Spanish politician and general.

albacore name loosely applied to several species of fishes found in warm regions of the Atlantic and Pacific oceans, in particular to a large tuna, *Thunnus alalunga*, and to several other species of the mackerel family.

Alban, St (lived 3rd century) First Christian martyr in England. In 793 King Offa founded a monastery on the site of Alban's martyrdom, around which the city of St Albans grew up. His feast day is 20 June.

Albania see country box.

Albany capital of ▷New York State, USA, situated on the west bank of the Hudson River, about 225 km/140 mi north of New York City; population (1994 est) 105,000. Albany is an important deep-water port and state administrative centre; its chief industries include clothing, brewing, and engineering. Albany was originally a Dutch trading post called Fort Nassau (1614). It was renamed Albany in 1664 when the English took control. The completion of the Champlain Canal (1822) and the Erie Canal (1825), as well as the Hudson Railroad (1831), helped to foster its subsequent economic development.

ALBATROSS The wandering albatross *Diomedea exulans*. Courtship involves elaborate displays of dancing, bill-rubbing, and wing-spreading.

albatross large seabird, genus *Diomedea*, with long narrow wings adapted for gliding and a wingspan of up to 3 m/10 ft, mainly found in the southern hemisphere. It belongs to the family Diomedeidae, order Procellariiformes, the same group as petrels and shearwaters. The external nostrils of birds in this order are more or less tubular, and the bills are hooked.

Albatrosses feed mainly on squid and fish, and nest on remote oceanic islands. Albatrosses can cover enormous distances, flying as far as 16,100 km/10,000 mi in 33 days, or up to 640 km/600 mi in one day. They continue flying even after dark, at speeds of up to 53.5 kph/50 mph, though they may stop for an hour's rest and to feed during the night. They are sometimes called 'gooney birds', probably because of their clumsy way of landing. Albatrosses are becoming increasingly rare, and are in danger of extinction. In the southern hemisphere, more than 40,000 albatrosses drown each year as a result of catching squid attached to bait lines.

The Diomedeidae family contains 14 species of albatross found in the South Atlantic and the Pacific oceans. The **wandering albatross** *D. exulans*, which has a wingspan of up to 3.4 m/11 ft, is the largest oceanic bird and can live for up to 80 years. Its huge wingspan means that it has difficulty in taking off unless there are strong winds. For this reason it nests on cliffs on islands. A single white egg is laid. The chick's full weight is 12 kg/26 lb, heavier than the parents, which typically weigh around 9 kg/20 lb. The chick needs this extra body weight to survive the Antarctic winter; the parents only return to the chick if and when they can find food for it.

albedo fraction of the incoming light reflected by a body such as a planet. A body with a high albedo, near 1, is very bright, while a body with a low albedo, near 0, is dark. The Moon has an average albedo of 0.12, Venus 0.76, Earth 0.37.

Albee, Edward Franklin (1928–) US dramatist. His internationally performed plays are associated with the Theatre of the ▷Absurd and include *The Zoo Story* (1960), *The American Dream* (1961), *Who's Afraid of Virginia Woolf?* (1962) (his most successful play; also filmed (1966), with Elizabeth Taylor and Richard Burton as the quarrelling, alcoholic, academic couple), and *Tiny Alice* (1965). *A Delicate Balance* (1966) and *Seascape* (1975) both won Pulitzer prizes, and *Three Tall Women* (1994) marked his return to critical acclaim.

Alberta province of western Canada; area 661,200 sq km/255,223 sq mi; population (2001 est) 2,974,800. Its capital is ▷Edmonton, and the main towns and cities include Calgary, Lethbridge, Medicine Hat, and Red Deer. Oil extraction is the most important economic activity in Alberta, with the province accounting for most of the country's oil production. It became a province in 1905.

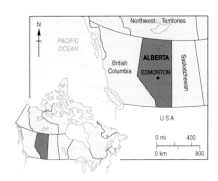

The region now occupied by Alberta lay largely within Rupert's Land, the area granted in 1670 to the ▷Hudson's Bay Company (HBC) to pursue their commerce in furs. In the 18th century, French traders from Montréal also began to operate here; organized by the North West Company from the 1780s, they regularly clashed with HBC traders until the two companies merged in 1821. Rocky Mountain House, Edmonton, and Fort Chipewyan were among the centres of the fur trade.

In 1870, the HBC sold its claims to the newly created Dominion of Canada, and the region became part of the Northwest Territories. The construction of the transcontinental Canadian Pacific Railway (1881–85) through Medicine Hat, Calgary, and the Kicking Horse Pass brought rapid settlement to the south. A further influx of immigrants arrived in the 1890s, when the Canadian Pacific Railway company built a second line through Lethbridge and the Crowsnest Pass. Activity throughout the region was stimulated by the ▷Klondike gold rush of 1896, and in 1905 Alberta became a province. Created out of a southwestern area of Northwest Territories, it was named after one of Queen Victoria's daughters. At first, Alberta was primarily an agricultural province, with cattle and lumber as its main products. Its people suffered great hardship during the 1930s as a result of the Great Depression and periods of severe drought. However, the building of Canadian National Railway lines through Edmonton and the Yellowhead Pass in the 1910s, and the province's contribution to the Allied war effort during World War II (notably, military aviation and related activities) helped alleviate periods of economic depression.

After World War II, the discovery of huge mineral deposits, such as the major oil strike at Leduc and the exploitation of vast tar sands along the Athabasca River near Fort McMurray, brought new prosperity to the province. Edmonton and Calgary developed into financial, commercial, and cultural centres that numbered among Canada's most populous and affluent cities.

> **Edward Albee**
> *I have a fine sense of the ridiculous, but no sense of humour.*
> *Who's Afraid of Virginia Woolf?*

Alberti, Leon Battista (1404–1472) Italian Renaissance architect and theorist. He set out the principles of classical architecture, and covered their modification for Renaissance practice, in *De re aedificatoria/ On Architecture*, which he started in 1452 and worked on until his death (published in 1485; translated as *Ten Books on Architecture* in 1955).

EDWARD ALBEE US dramatist Edward Albee, famous for writing *Who's Afraid of Virginia Woolf?* in 1962. *Archive Photos*

Albert, Lake lake on the border of Uganda and the Democratic Republic of Congo in the Great ▷Rift Valley; area 5,600 sq km/2,162 sq mi. The first European to see it was the British explorer Samuel ▷Baker, who named it Lake Albert after the Prince Consort. From 1973 to 1997 it was called Lake Mobutu after President Mobutu of Zaire (now Democratic Republic of Congo).

Albert, Prince Consort (1819–1861) Husband of British Queen ▷Victoria from 1840. A patron of the arts, science, and industry, Albert was the second son of the Duke of Saxe Coburg-Gotha and first cousin to Queen Victoria, whose chief adviser he became. He planned the Great Exhibition of 1851, the profits from which were used to buy the sites in London of all the South Kensington museums and colleges and the Royal Albert Hall, built in 1871. He died of typhoid. The Queen never fully recovered from his premature death, and remained in mourning for him for the rest of her life.

Albert also popularized the Christmas tree in England. He was regarded by the British people with groundless suspicion because of his German connections.

The **Albert Memorial** 1872, designed by Gilbert Scott, in Kensington Gardens, London, is a typical example of Victorian decorative art.

Albigenses heretical sect of Christians (also known as the Cathars) who flourished in southern France near Albi and Toulouse during the 11th–13th centuries. They adopted the Manichean belief in the duality of good and evil and pictured Jesus as being a rebel against the cruelty of an omnipotent God.

albinism rare hereditary condition in which the body has no tyrosinase, one of the enzymes that form the pigment ▷melanin, normally found in the skin, hair, and eyes. As a result, the hair is white and the skin and eyes are pink. The skin and eyes are abnormally sensitive to light, and vision is often impaired. The condition occurs among all human and animal groups.

Albion name for Britain used by the ancient Greeks and Romans. It was mentioned by Pytheas of Massilia (4th century BC), and is probably of Celtic origin, but the Romans, having in mind the white cliffs of Dover, assumed it to be derived from the word *albus* (white).

Ålborg port in Denmark 32 km/20 mi inland from the Kattegat, on the south shore of the Limfjord; population (1995) 159,000. One of Denmark's oldest cities, it has a castle and the Budolfi cathedral (named after the English St Botolph), dating mainly from about 1400. It is the capital of Nordjylland county in Jylland (Jutland); the port is linked to Nørresundby on the north side of the fjord by a tunnel built in 1969. Major industries include shipbuilding, cement, and textiles.

albumin any of a group of sulphur-containing ▷proteins. The best known is in the form of egg white (albumen); others occur in milk, and as a major component of serum. Many vegetables and fluids also contain albumins. They are soluble in water and dilute salt solutions, and are coagulated by heat.

Albuquerque largest city of New Mexico, USA, situated east of the Rio Grande, in the Pueblo district; seat of Bernalillo County;

population (1994 est) 412,000. Albuquerque is a resort and industrial centre specializing in electronic products and aerospace equipment, and is a centre for livestock rearing. Founded in 1706, it was named after the viceroy of New Spain, Afonso de ▷Albuquerque, and was incorporated as a city in 1891.

Albuquerque, Afonso de (1453–1515) Viceroy and founder of the Portuguese East Indies with strongholds in Ceylon, Goa, and Malacca 1508–15. In 1515 the king of Portugal recalled him, putting Albuquerque's personal enemy Lopes Soares in his place. He died at sea on the way home when his ship *Flor del Mar* was lost between Malaysia and India.

alchemy (Arabic *al-Kimya*) supposed technique of transmuting base metals, such as lead and mercury, into silver and gold by the philosopher's stone, a hypothetical substance, to which was also attributed the power to give eternal life.

Related Web site: Alchemy Virtual Library http://www.levity.com/alchemy/home.html

Alcibiades (451/0–404/3 BC) Athenian politician and general during the Peloponnesian War. In 415 BC Alcibiades was appointed one of the commanders of an Athenian expedition against Sicily, but was recalled to answer charges of sacrilege and fled to Sparta. Further scandal led to his flight to Persia, but he rehabilitated himself with the Athenians and played a leading part at Cyzicus in 410 BC. He was given command of Athenian forces in Asia Minor but was replaced after his lieutenant's defeat off Notium in 407 BC. He was murdered shortly after the war.

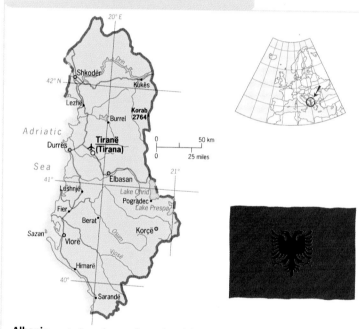

Albania country in southeastern Europe, bounded north by Serbia and Montenegro, east by Macedonia, south by Greece, and west and southwest by the Adriatic Sea.

NATIONAL NAME *Republika e Shqipërisë/Republic of Albania*
AREA 28,748 sq km/11,099 sq mi
CAPITAL Tirana
MAJOR TOWNS/CITIES Durrës, Shkodër, Elbasan, Vlorë, Korçë
MAJOR PORTS Durrës
PHYSICAL FEATURES mainly mountainous, with rivers flowing east–west, and a narrow coastal plain

Government

HEAD OF STATE Alfred Moisiu from 2002
HEAD OF GOVERNMENT Fatos Nano from 2002
POLITICAL SYSTEM emergent democracy
POLITICAL EXECUTIVE limited presidency
ADMINISTRATIVE DIVISIONS 36 districts and one municipality
ARMED FORCES 27,000 (2002 est)
CONSCRIPTION compulsory for 12 months
DEATH PENALTY abolished for ordinary crimes in 2000; laws provide for the death penalty for exceptional crimes, such as crimes committed in wartime
DEFENCE SPEND (% GDP) 2.5 (2002 est)

EDUCATION SPEND (% GDP) 3.4 (2000 est)
HEALTH SPEND (% GDP) 3.4 (2000 est)

Economy and resources

CURRENCY lek
GPD (US$) 4.7 billion (2002 est)
REAL GDP GROWTH (% change on previous year) 7.3 (2001)
GNI (US$) 4.4 billion (2002 est)
GNI PER CAPITA (PPP) (US$) 4,040 (2002 est)
CONSUMER PRICE INFLATION 5.3% (2002 est)
UNEMPLOYMENT 18% (2000)
FOREIGN DEBT (US$) 901 million (2001 est)
MAJOR TRADING PARTNERS Italy, Greece, Germany, Bulgaria, Austria, Turkey, Slovenia
RESOURCES chromite (one of world's largest producers), copper, coal, nickel, petroleum and natural gas
INDUSTRIES food processing, mineral and oil extraction, textiles, oil products, cement, energy generation
EXPORTS textiles and footwear, mineral products, base metals, food and live animals, beverages and tobacco, vegetable products. Principal market: Italy 70.3% (2000)
IMPORTS textiles and footwear, machinery and transport equipment, fuels and minerals,

plant and animal raw materials, chemical products. Principal source: Italy 36.2% (2000)
ARABLE LAND 21.1% (2000 est)
AGRICULTURAL PRODUCTS wheat, sugar beet, maize, potatoes, barley, sorghum, cotton, tobacco, vegetables

Population and society

POPULATION 3,166,000 (2003 est)
POPULATION GROWTH RATE 1% (2000–15)
POPULATION DENSITY (per sq km) 110 (2003 est)
URBAN POPULATION (% of total) 44 (2003 est)
AGE DISTRIBUTION (% of total population) 0–14 29%, 15–59 62%, 60+ 9% (2002 est)
ETHNIC GROUPS 95% of Albanian, non-Slavic, descent; 3% ethnic Greek (concentrated in south)
LANGUAGE Albanian (official), Greek
RELIGION Muslim, Albanian Orthodox, Roman Catholic
EDUCATION (compulsory years) 8
LITERACY RATE 93% (men); 79% (women) (2003 est)
LABOUR FORCE 24% agriculture, 45% industry, 31% services (1991)
LIFE EXPECTANCY 71 (men); 77 (women) (2000–05)
CHILD MORTALITY RATE (under 5, per 1,000 live births) 30 (2001)
PHYSICIANS (per 1,000 people) 1.3 (1998 est)
HOSPITAL BEDS (per 1,000 people) 3.2 (1998 est)
TV SETS (per 1,000 people) 123 (2001 est)
RADIOS (per 1,000 people) 260 (2001 est)
INTERNET USERS (per 10,000 people) 29.8 (2002 est)
PERSONAL COMPUTER USERS (per 100 people) 0.9 (2002 est)

ALBANIA A stamp produced in 1964, celebrating 20 years of Albanian independence. In 1944 German occupying forces withdrew and a Communist provisional government was established. *Stanley Gibbons*

See also ▷Byzantine Empire; ▷Ottoman Empire.

Chronology

2000 BC: Albania was part of Illyria.

168 BC: Illyria was conquered by the Romans.

AD 395: Became part of Byzantine Empire.

6th–14th centuries: Byzantine decline exploited by Serbs, Normans, Slavs, Bulgarians, and Venetians.

1381: Ottoman invasion of Albania followed by years of resistance to Turkish rule.

1468: Resistance led by national hero Skanderbeg (George Kastrioti) largely collapsed, and Albania passed to Ottoman Empire.

15th–16th centuries: Thousands fled to southern Italy to escape Ottoman rule; over half of the rest of the population converted to Islam.

1878: Foundation of Albanian League promoted emergence of nationalism.

1912: Achieved independence from Turkey as a result of First Balkan War and end of Ottoman Empire in Europe.

1914–20: Occupied by Italy.

1925: Declared itself a republic.

1928–39: Monarchy of King Zog.

1939: Italian occupation led by Benito Mussolini.

1943–44: Under German rule following Italian surrender.

1946: Proclaimed Communist People's Republic of Albania, with Enver Hoxha as premier.

1949: Developed close links with Joseph Stalin in USSR and entered Comecon (Council for Mutual Economic Assistance).

1961: Broke with USSR in wake of Nikita Khrushchev's denunciation of Stalin, and withdrew from Comecon. In 1978 Albania also severed diplomatic links with China.

1987: Normal diplomatic relations restored with Canada, Greece, and West Germany.

1990–91: The one-party system was abandoned in the face of popular protest; the first opposition party was formed, and the first multiparty elections were held.

1992: Former communist officials were charged with corruption and abuse of power. Totalitarian and communist parties were banned.

1993: Conflict began between ethnic Greeks and Albanians, followed by a purge of ethnic Greeks from the civil service and army.

1997: Antigovernment riots; police killed demonstrators in the southern port of Vlorë. Southern Albania fell under rebel control. The government signed a World Bank and IMF rescue package to salvage the economy.

1998: A new constitution came into effect.

1999: Ilir Meta, a socialist, became prime minister.

Alcock, John William (1892–1919) British aviator. On 14 June 1919, he and Arthur Whitten Brown (1886–1948) made the first non-stop transatlantic flight, from Newfoundland to Ireland. Awarded the KBE in 1919.

alcohol any member of a group of organic chemical compounds characterized by the presence of one or more aliphatic OH (hydroxyl) groups in the molecule, and which form ▷esters with acids. The main uses of alcohols are as solvents for gums, resins, lacquers, and varnishes; in the making of dyes; for essential oils in perfumery; and for medical substances in pharmacy. The alcohol produced naturally in the ▷fermentation process and consumed as part of alcoholic beverages is called ▷ethanol.

Alcohols may be liquids or solids, according to the size and complexity of the molecule. The five simplest alcohols form a series in which the number of carbon and hydrogen atoms increases progressively, each one having an extra CH_2 (methylene) group in the molecule: methanol or wood spirit (methyl alcohol, CH_3OH); ethanol (ethyl alcohol, C_2H_5OH); propanol (propyl alcohol, C_3H_7OH); butanol (butyl alcohol, C_4H_9OH); and pentanol (amyl alcohol, $C_5H_{11}OH$). The lower alcohols are liquids that mix with water; the higher alcohols, such as pentanol, are oily liquids immiscible with water; and the highest are waxy solids – for example, hexadecanol (cetyl alcohol, $C_{16}H_{33}OH$) and melissyl alcohol ($C_{30}H_{61}OH$), which occur in sperm-whale oil and beeswax respectively. Alcohols containing the CH_2OH group are primary; those containing CHOH are secondary; while those containing COH are tertiary.

alcoholic beverage any drink containing alcohol, often used for its intoxicating effects. ▷Ethanol (ethyl alcohol), a colourless liquid (C_2H_5OH) is the basis of all common intoxicants. Foods rich in sugars, such as grapes, produce this alcohol as a natural product of decay, called fermentation.

Alcoholics Anonymous (AA) voluntary self-help organization established in 1934 in the USA to combat alcoholism; branches now exist in many other countries.

alcoholism dependence on alcohol. It is characterized as an illness when consumption of alcohol interferes with normal physical or emotional health. Excessive alcohol consumption, whether through sustained ingestion or irregular drinking bouts or binges, may produce physical and psychological addiction and lead to nutritional and emotional disorders. Long-term heavy consumption of alcohol leads to diseases of the heart, liver, and peripheral nerves. Support groups such as Alcoholics Anonymous are helpful.

Alcott, Louisa May (1832–1888) US author. Her children's classic *Little Women* (1869) drew on her own home circumstances; the principal character Jo was a partial self-portrait. Sequels to *Little Women* were *Good Wives* (1869), *Little Men* (1871), and *Jo's Boys* (1886).

> **Louisa May Alcott**
> *I don't believe fine young ladies enjoy themselves a bit more than we do, in spite of our burnt hair, old gowns, one glove apiece and tight slippers.*
> Little Women ch. 3

LOUISA MAY ALCOTT The author of *Little Women* and other US classics. *Archive Photos*

Alcuin (735–804) Born Flaccus Albinus Alcuinus. English scholar. Born in York, he went to Rome in 780, and in 782 took up residence at Charlemagne's court in Aachen. From 796 he was abbot at St Martin's in Tours. He disseminated Anglo-Saxon scholarship. Alcuin organized education and learning in the Frankish empire and was a prominent member of Charlemagne's academy, providing a strong impulse to the Carolingian Renaissance.

> **Alcuin**
> *Vox populi, vox dei.*
> *The voice of the people is the voice of God.*
> Letter to the Emperor Charlemagne (800)

Aldebaran (or **Alpha Tauri**) brightest star in the constellation Taurus and the 14th-brightest star in the night sky; it marks the eye of the 'bull'. Aldebaran is a red giant 65 light years away from the Sun, shining with a true luminosity of about 100 times that of the Sun.

Aldeburgh small town and coastal resort in Suffolk, eastern England, 33 km/20 mi from Ipswich; population (1991) 2,700. It maintains a small fishing fleet, serving the local market. The Aldeburgh Festival, founded in 1948 by the English composer Benjamin Britten, is held annually at the Snape Maltings, 8 km/5 mi west of the town. It is the home of the Britten–Pears School for Advanced Musical Studies.

aldehyde any of a group of organic chemical compounds prepared by oxidation of primary alcohols, so that the OH (hydroxyl) group loses its hydrogen to give an oxygen joined by a double bond to a carbon atom (the aldehyde group, with the formula CHO).

The name is made up from **al**cohol **dehyd**rogenation – that is, alcohol from which hydrogen has been removed. Aldehydes are usually liquids and include methanal (formaldehyde), ethanal (acetaldehyde), and benzaldehyde.

alder any of a group of trees or shrubs belonging to the birch family, found mainly in cooler parts of the northern hemisphere and characterized by toothed leaves and catkins. (Genus *Alnus*, family Betulaceae.)

Related Web site: Alder, Common http://www.botanical.com/botanical/mgmh/a/alder019.html

alder fly member of the family Sialidae of the insect order Neuroptera (suborder Megaloptera). The alder flies are around 20 mm/0.8 in long and dark, with the general features typical of the order Neuroptera. Although they have an almost worldwide distribution, their numbers in terms of genera and species are very limited.

Aldermaston village in west Berkshire, England, and site of an atomic and biological weapons research establishment, which employs some 5,000 people working on the production of nuclear warheads. During 1958–63 the Campaign for Nuclear Disarmament (CND) made it the focus of an annual Easter protest march.

Alderney third largest of the ▷Channel Islands, with its capital at St Anne's; area 8 sq km/3 sq mi; population (1991) 2,300. Tourism flourished on Alderney from the early 20th century. The main employers are now tourist-related businesses and services providing building and maintenance work for locals and immigrants. There is also a small finance industry.

Aldershot town in Hampshire, southern England, 56 km/35 mi southwest of London; population (1991) 51,400. Industrial products include electronics, and vehicle components for cars and tankers. It contains the largest permanent military training camp in the UK, dating from 1854. The Ministry of Defence owns over 850 ha/2,100 acres here, mainly north of the town centre.

Aldiss, Brian Wilson (1925–) English novelist, science-fiction writer, anthologist, and critic. His futuristic novels include *Non-Stop* (1958), *Barefoot in the Head* (1969), the 'Helliconia' trilogy (1982–85), and *Somewhere East of Life* (1994). He has also published several volumes of short stories, including *Seasons in Flight* (1984). *Trillion Year Spree* (1986) is a revised edition of his history of science fiction, *Billion Year Spree* (1973).

Aldrin, Edwin Eugene ('Buzz') (1930–) US astronaut who landed on the Moon with Neil ▷Armstrong during the *Apollo 11* mission in July 1969, becoming the second person to set foot on the Moon.

> **Alexander I**
> *Napoleon thinks I am a fool, but he who laughs last laughs longest.*
> Letter from Alexander I to his sister Catherine 8 October 1808, after meeting Napoleon at Erfurt

aleatory music (Latin *alea* 'dice') method of composition practised by post-war avant-garde composers in which the performer or conductor chooses the order of succession of the composed pieces. Examples of aleatory music include Pierre Boulez's *Piano Sonata No 3* (1956–57), Earle Brown's *Available Forms I* (1961), and Stockhausen's *Momente/Moments* (1961–72). Another term for aleatory music is 'mobile form'.

Aleatory music is distantly related to the 18th-century 'musical dice game' and to the freely assembled music for silent movies using theme catalogues by Giuseppe Becce and others. The use by John ▷Cage of dice and the I Ching differs in that it intervenes in the actual process of composition.

Alemanni (or **Alamanni**; Gothic 'united men' or 'men from all parts') Germanic people who from the 2nd century occupied an area bounded by the rivers Rhine, Danube, and Main. They were part of the medieval western German grouping of peoples that also included Franks, Saxons, Frisians, and Thuringians. Late in the 5th century they crossed the Rhine and Danube and settled in what is now Alsace and northern Switzerland, where they introduced the German language. They were fully absorbed into the East Frankish kingdom in the 9th century. Their name survives through the French and Spanish words for German (*Allemagne, Alemania*).

Aleppo (Arabic **Halab**) ancient city in northwest Syria, situated on the River Kuweik on the edge of the Syrian Desert; population (1993) 1,494,000. It is the administrative centre of the governorate of Aleppo; population (1996 est) 3,694,000. Silk and cotton goods, leather, grain, carpets, tobacco, and metalwork are produced. Chief industries are cotton and wool textile manufacturing. There has been a settlement on the site for at least 4,000 years.

Aletsch most extensive glacier in Europe, 23.6 km/14.7 mi long, beginning on the southern slopes of the Jungfrau in the Bernese Alps, Switzerland.

Aleut a people who are indigenous to the Aleutian Islands; a few thousand remain worldwide, most in the Aleutian Islands and mainland Alaska. They were exploited by Russian fur traders in the 18th and 19th centuries, and their forced evacuation 1942–45 earned the USA a United Nations reprimand in 1959; compensation was paid in 1990. From the 1980s concern for wildlife and diminishing demand for furs threatened their traditional livelihood of seal trapping.

Aleutian Islands volcanic island chain in the North Pacific, stretching 1,900 km/1,200 mi southwest of Alaska, of which it forms part, towards Kamchatka; population in Aleutians East Borough (2000 est) 2,700; in West Census Area (2000 est) 5,500. There are 14 large and more than 100 small islands running along the Aleutian Trench; the largest island is Unimak (with an area of 3,500 sq km/1,360 sq mi), which contains two active volcanoes. The islands are mountainous, barren, and treeless; they are ice-free all year but are often foggy, with only about 25 days of sunshine recorded annually. The only industries are fishing, seal hunting, and sheep farming; the main exports are fish and furs.

A level (or **Advanced level**) in England, Wales, and Northern Ireland, examinations taken by students usually at the age of 18, after two years' study, in no more than four subjects at one time. Two A-level passes are normally required for entry to a university degree course. Scottish students sit Highers.

Alexander eight popes, including:

Alexander III (died 1181) Born Orlando Bandinelli. Pope 1159–81. His authority was opposed by Frederick I Barbarossa, but Alexander eventually compelled him to render homage in 1178. He held the third Lateran Council in 1179. He supported Henry II of England in his invasion of Ireland, but imposed penance on him after the murder of Thomas à ▷Becket.

Alexander VI (1430 or 1432–1503) Born Rodrigo Borgia or Rodrigo Borja. Pope 1492–1503. Of Spanish origin, he bribed his way to the papacy, where he furthered the advancement of his illegitimate children, who included Cesare and Lucrezia ▷Borgia. When ▷Savonarola preached against his corrupt practices Alexander had him executed.

Alexander three tsars of Russia:

Alexander I (1777–1825) Tsar of Russia from 1801. Defeated by Napoleon at Austerlitz in 1805, he made peace at Tilsit in 1807, but economic crisis led to a break with Napoleon's ▷Continental System and the opening of Russian ports to British trade; this led to Napoleon's ill-fated invasion of Russia in 1812. After the Congress of Vienna in 1815, Alexander hoped through the Holy Alliance with Austria and Prussia to establish a new Christian order in Europe.

Alexander II (1818–1881) Tsar of Russia from 1855. He embarked on reforms of the army, the government, and education, and is remembered as 'the Liberator' for his emancipation of the serfs in 1861, but he lacked the personnel to implement his reforms.

ALEXANDER II Tsar of Russia Alexander II. *Philip Sauvain Picture Collection*

However, the revolutionary element remained unsatisfied, and Alexander became increasingly autocratic and reactionary. He was assassinated by an anarchistic terrorist group, the ▷Nihilists.

Alexander III (1845–1894) Tsar of Russia from 1881, when he succeeded his father, Alexander II. He pursued a reactionary policy, promoting Russification and persecuting the Jews. He married Dagmar (1847–1928), daughter of Christian IX of Denmark and sister of Queen Alexandra of Britain, in 1866.

Alexander three kings of Scotland:

Alexander I (c. 1078–1124) King of Scotland from 1107, known as 'the Fierce'. He ruled over the area to the north of the rivers Forth and Clyde, while his brother and successor ▷David ruled over the area to the south. He assisted Henry I of England in his campaign against Wales in 1114, but defended the independence of the church in Scotland. Several monasteries, including the abbeys of Inchcolm and Scone, were established by him.

Alexander II (1198–1249) King of Scotland from 1214, when he succeeded his father, William the Lion. Alexander supported the English barons in their struggle with King John after ▷Magna Carta. The accession of Henry III of England allowed a *rapprochement* between the two countries, and the boundaries between England and Scotland were agreed by the Treaty of York in 1237. By the Treaty of Newcastle in 1244 he pledged allegiance to Henry III. Alexander consolidated royal authority in Scotland and was a generous patron of the church.

In 1221 he married Joanna, the sister of Henry III. In 1239, after her death he married Marie de Coucy, with whom he had a son, Alexander III.

Alexander III (1241–1286) King of Scotland from 1249, son of Alexander II. After defeating the Norwegian forces in 1263, he was able to extend his authority over the Western Isles, which had been dependent on Norway. The later period of his reign was devoted to administrative reforms, which limited the power of the barons and brought a period of peace and prosperity to Scotland.

He died as the result of a fall from his horse, leaving his granddaughter Margaret, the Maid of Norway, to become queen of Scotland.

Alexander I, Karageorgevich (1888–1934) Regent of Serbia 1912–21 and king of Yugoslavia 1921–34, as dictator from 1929. The second son of Peter I, King of Serbia, he was declared regent for his father in 1912 and on his father's death became king of the state of South Slavs – Yugoslavia – that had come into being in 1918.

Rivalries with neighbouring powers and among the Croats, Serbs, and Slovenes within the country led Alexander to establish a personal dictatorship. He was assassinated on a state visit to France, and Mussolini's government was later declared to have instigated the crime.

Alexander, Harold Rupert Leofric George (1891–1969) 1st Earl Alexander of Tunis. British field marshal, a commander in World War II in France, Burma (now Myanmar), North Africa, and the Mediterranean. He was governor general of Canada 1946–52 and UK minister of defence 1952–54. He was appointed KCB in 1942, Viscount in 1946, and Earl Alexander of Tunis in 1952, and was awarded the OM in 1959.

Alexander Nevski, St (1220–1263) Russian military leader, ruler of Novgorod in 1236, and Grand Prince of Vladimir in 1252. He survived Mongol attacks in 1237–40, which enabled him to defeat the Swedes in 1240 and the Germans in 1242.

alexanders strong-smelling tall ▷herbaceous plant belonging to the carrot family. It is found along hedgerows and on cliffs throughout southern Europe. Its yellow flowers appear in spring and early summer. (*Smyrnium olusatrum*, family Umbelliferae.)

Alexander Severus (AD 208–235) Born Marcus Aurelius Severus Alexander. Roman emperor from 222, when he succeeded his cousin Heliogabalus. He attempted to involve the Senate more closely in administration, and was the patron of the jurists Ulpian and Paulus, and the historian Cassius Dio. His campaign against the Persians in 232 achieved some success, but in 235, on his way to defend Gaul against German invaders, he was killed in a mutiny.

Alexander technique in alternative medicine, a method of correcting bad habits of posture, breathing, and muscular tension, which Australian therapist F M Alexander maintained cause many ailments. The technique is also used to promote general health and relaxation and enhance vitality.

Alexander (III) the Great (356–323 BC) King of Macedon 336–323 BC and conqueror of the Persian Empire. As commander of the powerful Macedonian army he conquered Greece in 336 BC, defeated the Persian king Darius III in Asia Minor in 333 BC, then moved on to Egypt where he founded Alexandria. He defeated the Persians again in Assyria in 331 BC, then advanced further east, invading India in 327 BC. He conquered the Punjab before mutinous troops forced his retreat.

The son of King Philip II of Macedon and Queen Olympias, Alexander was educated by the philosopher Aristotle. He won his spurs in 338 BC, commanding the cavalry at the Battle of Chaeronea. At the age of 20 he succeeded to the throne after the assassination of his father Philip (II) of Macedon in 336 BC. Though Thebes seized the opportunity to revolt while he was absent campaigning in the northwest, he rapidly reimposed his authority by destroying the city in 335 BC. Alexander inherited not only a magnificent army from his father but also plans to invade the Persian Empire, and in 334 BC he crossed the Hellespont (now the Dardanelles), never to return. Victory at the river Granicus that year gave him control of western Asia Minor, and then, ignoring Persian superiority at sea, he turned east, winning his second victory at Issus in the autumn of 333 BC, this time over the Persian king Darius himself. After taking Tyre and Gaza in epic sieges, he next invaded Egypt, where he spent the winter of 332/1 BC. Meanwhile, Darius assembled an army of half a million men for a final battle at Gaugamela on 1 October 331 BC, but Alexander, with 47,000 men, drove the Persians into retreat. This victory laid open the heartland of the Persian Empire and Babylon, Susa, and Persepolis were occupied in turn. The murder of Darius by his own entourage in the summer of 330 BC enabled Alexander to pose as his rightful successor. Widespread revolts in the northeast, however, took some three years of marching, sieges, and savage fighting to subdue. This was followed by the invasion of India in 327 BC, victory at the river Hydaspes (now Jhelum), and a further march eastwards until, at the river Hyphasis (now Beas), the army refused to go any further. Turning back, Alexander descended the river Indus, subduing any tribe which refused to submit, and reached the delta in July 325 BC. He then sent his fleet westwards, while he marched through the deserts of southern Baluchistan to rendezvous with it in southeast Iran in December, and to return to Susa early in 324 BC. In Susa, he made Darius's daughter his second wife. Further plans of conquest were cut short by his death in June 323 BC.

Alexandra Feodorovna (1872–1918) Last tsarina of Russia 1894–1917. She was the former Princess Alix of Hessen and granddaughter of Britain's Queen Victoria. She married ▷Nicholas II and, from 1907, fell under the spell of ▷Rasputin, a 'holy man' brought to the palace to try to cure her son of haemophilia. She was shot with the rest of her family by the Bolsheviks in the Russian Revolution.

Alexandria (or Al Iskandariya) city, chief port, and second-largest city of Egypt, situated between the Mediterranean and Lake Maryut; population (1992) 3,380,000. It is linked by canal with the Nile. There is oil refining, gas processing, and trade in cotton and grain. Founded in 331 BC by Alexander the Great, Alexandria was the capital of Egypt for over 1,000 years.

Related Web site: Alexandria, Egypt http://ce.eng.usf.edu/pharos/alexandria/

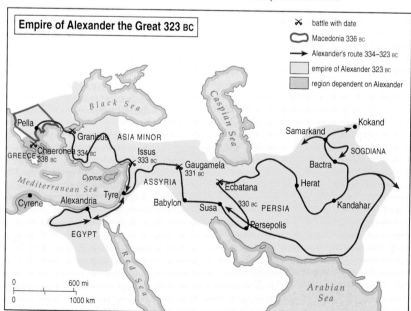

Empire of Alexander the Great 323 BC

✖ battle with date
Macedonia 336 BC
→ Alexander's route 334–323 BC
empire of Alexander 323 BC
region dependent on Alexander

ALEXANDER (III) THE GREAT Alexander the Great, king of Macedon, portrayed on a throne, receiving tribute from his new Persian subjects, as featured in a 14th-century Armenian copy of an Ancient Greek Alexander Romance dating from the 5th century AD. *The Art Archive/Mechitarista Congregation Venice/Dagli Orti*

Alexandria, Library of the world's first state-funded scientific institution, founded in 330 BC in Alexandria, Egypt, by Ptolemy I and further expanded by Ptolemy II. It comprised a museum, teaching facilities, and a library that contained up to 700,000 scrolls, including much ancient Greek literature. It sustained significant damage in AD 391, when the Roman emperor Theodosius I ordered its destruction. It was burned down in 640 AD at the time of the Arab conquest.

Related Web site: Library of Alexandria http://www.perseus.tufts.edu/GreekScience/Students/Ellen/Museum.html

ALEXANDRIA View inside the catacombs of Kom esh-Shuqafa, in Alexandria, Egypt. This funerary complex is Roman in origin, dating from the 2nd century AD. *The Art Archive/Komesh Shawqafa Egypt/Dagli Orti*

Alexandria, school of group of writers and scholars of Alexandria, Egypt, who made the city the chief centre of culture in the Western world from about 331 BC to AD 642. They include the poets Callimachus, Apollonius of Rhodes, and Theocritus; ▷Euclid, pioneer of geometry; ▷Eratosthenes, a geographer; Hipparchus, who developed a system of trigonometry; Ptolemy, whose system of astronomy endured for over 1,000 years; and the Jewish philosopher Philo. The Gnostics and Neo-Platonists also flourished in Alexandria.

Alexius five emperors of Byzantium, including:

Alexius I (1048–1118) (**Comnenus**) Byzantine emperor 1081–1118. With meagre resources, he dealt successfully with internal dissent and a series of external threats from the Turks and Normans. He managed the difficult passage of the First Crusade through Byzantine territory on its way to Jerusalem, and by the end of his reign he had, with the help of the Crusaders, restored much of Byzantine control over Anatolia. His daughter ▷Anna Comnena chronicled his reign.

Alexius III (died 1210) (**Angelos**) Byzantine emperor 1195–1203. He gained power by deposing and blinding his brother Isaac II, but Isaac's Venetian allies enabled him and his son Alexius IV to regain power as coemperors.

Alexius IV (1182–1204) (**Angelos**) Byzantine emperor from 1203, when, with the aid of the army of the Fourth Crusade, he deposed his uncle Alexius III. He soon lost the support of the Crusaders (by that time occupying Constantinople), and was overthrown and murdered by another Alexius, Alexius Mourtzouphlus (son-in-law of Alexius III) in 1204, an act which the Crusaders used as a pretext to sack the city the same year.

alfalfa (or **lucerne**) perennial tall ▷herbaceous plant belonging to the pea family. It is native to Europe and Asia and has spikes of small purple flowers in late summer. It is now a major fodder crop, commonly processed into hay, meal, or silage. Alfalfa sprouts, the sprouted seeds, have become a popular salad ingredient. (*Medicago sativa*, family Leguminosae.)

Alfonsín Foulkes, Raúl Ricardo (1927–) Argentine politician and president 1983–89. Becoming president at the time of the country's return to civilian government, he set up an investigation of the army's human-rights violations, with the subsequent trial and detention of many former military and political leaders. Economic problems caused him to seek help from the International Monetary Fund and introduce austerity measures, leading to debt restructuring and fiscal reform.

Alfonso thirteen kings of León, Castile, and Spain, including:

Alfonso VII (*c.* 1107–1157) King of León and Castile from 1126 who attempted to unite Spain. Although he protected the Moors, he was killed trying to check a Moorish rising.

Alfonso (X) the Wise (1221–1284) King of Castile from 1252. His reign was politically unsuccessful but he contributed to learning: he made Castilian the official language of the country and commissioned a history of Spain and an encyclopedia, as well as several translations from Arabic concerning, among other subjects, astronomy and games.

Alfonso (XI) the Avenger (1311–1350) King of Castile and León from 1312. He ruled cruelly, repressed a rebellion by his nobles, and defeated the last Moorish invasion in 1340.

Alfonso XII (1857–1885) King of Spain from 1875, son of ▷Isabella II. He assumed the throne after a period of republican government following his mother's flight and effective abdication in 1868. His rule was peaceful. He ended the civil war started by the Carlists and drafted a constitution, both in 1876.

Alfonso XIII (1886–1941) King of Spain 1886–1931. He assumed power in 1906 and married Princess Ena, granddaughter of Queen Victoria of Great Britain, in the same year. He abdicated in 1931 soon after the fall of the Primo de Rivera dictatorship 1923–30 (which he supported), and Spain became a republic. His assassination was attempted several times.

Alfred the Great (*c.* 849–*c.* 901) Anglo-Saxon king 871–899 who defended England against Danish invasion and founded the first English navy. He succeeded his brother Aethelred to the throne of Wessex in 871, and a new legal code came into force during his reign. He encouraged the translation of scholarly works from Latin (some he translated himself), and promoted the development of the ▷Anglo-Saxon Chronicle.

Through a combination of hard fighting and diplomacy Alfred managed to keep Wessex free of Danish control after the other Anglo-Saxon kingdoms had succumbed. His skill as a military commander first came to light at the Battle of Ashdown in 871 when he led the Saxon army to victory against the Danes. Not all his campaigns were so successful; on a number of occasions he had to resort to buying off the Danes for a brief respite. His great victory at Edington in 878 secured the survival of Wessex, and his peace treaty with the Danish king Guthrum in 886 established a boundary between the Danelaw, east of Watling Street, and the Saxons to the west. The *Anglo-Saxon Chronicle* says that following his capture of London in 866 'all the English people submitted to him, except those who were in captivity to the Danes'. In some respects, therefore, Alfred could be considered the first king of England.

ALFRED THE GREAT 'The Alfred Jewel', in the Ashmolean Museum, Oxford, England. This cloisonné enamel portrait, mounted in crystal, is believed to be part of the treasure of Alfred the Great. *The Art Archive/Ashmolean Museum Oxford/Eileen Tweedy*

algae (singular **alga**) highly varied group of plants, ranging from single-celled forms to large and complex seaweeds. They live in both fresh and salt water, and in damp soil. Algae do not have true roots, stems, or leaves.

Marine algae help combat ▷global warming by removing carbon dioxide from the atmosphere during ▷photosynthesis.

Algarve (Arabic *al-gharb* 'the west') ancient kingdom in southern Portugal, bordered on the east by Spain, and on the west and south by the Atlantic Ocean; it is co-extensive with the modern district of Faro, the provincial capital of the Algarve; area 5,071 sq km/1,958 sq mi; population (1995 est) 346,000. The population increased during the 1980s and 1990s as a result of inward migration. Tourism is the largest employer in the area. It is based mainly on beach resorts although there has been a shift towards cultural and golfing tourism. Regional agriculture is mainly citrus fruits, due to the use of modern irrigation methods, although traditional crops of grapes, olives, figs, almonds, and carobs are still grown. The hilly areas are heavily forested with pine and eucalyptus trees.

Related Web site: Welcome to the Algarve http://www.nexus-pt.com/algarve.htm

algebra branch of mathematics in which the general properties of numbers are studied by using symbols, usually letters, to represent variables and unknown quantities. For example, the algebraic statement

$$(x+y)^2 = x^2 + 2xy + y^2$$

is true for all values of x and y. If $x = 7$ and $y = 3$, for instance:

$$(7+3)^2 = 7^2 + 2(7 \times 3) + 3^2 = 100$$

An algebraic expression that has one or more variables (denoted by letters) is a ▷polynomial equation. Algebra is used in many areas of mathematics – for example, matrix algebra and Boolean algebra (the latter is used in working out the logic for computers).

In ordinary algebra the same operations are carried on as in arithmetic, but, as the symbols are capable of a more generalized and extended meaning than the figures used in arithmetic, it facilitates calculation where the numerical values are not known, or are inconveniently large or small, or where it is desirable to keep them in an analysed form.

Within an algebraic equation the separate calculations involved must be completed in a set order. Any elements in brackets should always be calculated first, followed by multiplication, division, addition, and subtraction.

Quadratic equation This is a polynomial equation of second degree (that is, an equation containing as its highest power the square of a variable, such as x^2). The general formula of such equations is:

$$ax^2 + bx + c = 0$$

in which a, b, and c are real numbers, and only the coefficient a cannot equal 0.

Some quadratic equations can be solved by factorization, or the values of x can be found by using the formula for the general solution

$$x = \frac{[-b \pm \sqrt{b^2 - 4ac}]}{2a}$$

Depending on the value of the discriminant $b^2 - 4ac$, a quadratic equation has two real, two equal, or two complex roots (solutions). When

$$b^2 - 4ac > 0$$

there are two distinct real roots. When

$$b^2 - 4ac = 0$$

there are two equal real roots. When

$$b^2 - 4ac < 0$$

there are two distinct complex roots.

Simultaneous equations If there are two or more algebraic equations that contain two or more unknown quantities that may have a unique solution they can be solved simultaneously. For example, in the case of two linear equations with two unknown variables, such as:

(i) $x + 3y = 6$ and

(ii) $3y - 2x = 4$

the solution will be those unique values of x and y that are valid for both equations. Linear simultaneous equations can be solved by using algebraic manipulation to eliminate one of the variables. For example, both sides of equation (i) could be multiplied by 2, which gives $2x + 6y = 12$. This can be added to equation (ii) to get $9y = 16$, which is easily solved: $y = \frac{16}{9}$. The variable x can now be found by inserting the known y value into either original equation and solving for x.

'Algebra' was originally the name given to the study of equations. In the 9th century, the Arab mathematician Muhammad ibn-Mūsā al-▷Khwārizmī used the term *al-jabr* for the process of adding equal quantities to both sides of an equation. When his treatise was later translated into Latin, *al-jabr* became 'algebra' and the word was adopted as the name for the whole subject.

Related Web site: Fundamental Theorem of Algebra http://www-history.mcs.st-and.ac.uk/~history/HistTopics/Fund_theorem_of_algebra.html

Algeciras port in Cádiz province, southern Spain, situated to the west of Gibraltar across the Bay of Algeciras; population (1994) 104,000. An industrial complex, built around a petrol refinery, was established in the Bay of Algeciras in the 1970s. Algeciras was originally founded by the ▷Moors in 713; it was taken from them by Alfonso XI of Castile in 1344.

Algeria see country box.

Algiers (Arabic **al-Jazair**; French **Alger**) capital of Algeria, situated on the narrow coastal plain between the Atlas Mountains and the Mediterranean; population (1995) 2,168,000. It distributes grain, iron, phosphates, wines, and oil from central Algeria. The main industries are oil refining, petrochemicals, and metal working. The city is a popular winter resort.

History Algiers was founded by the Arabs in 935. The old town is dominated by the Kasbah, the palace and prison of the Turkish rulers who took the town in the early 16th century. The new town, constructed under French rule after 1830, is in European style. The Battle of Algiers, between the Algerian nationalist population and the French army and settlers, took place here during the Algerian War of Independence 1954–62.

Algiers, Battle of
bitter conflict in Algiers 1954–62 between the Algerian nationalist population and the French colonial army and French settlers. The conflict ended with Algerian independence in 1962.

ALGOL
(contraction of algorithmic language) in computing, an early high-level programming language, developed in the 1950s and 1960s for scientific applications. A general-purpose language, ALGOL is best suited to mathematical work and has an algebraic

style. Although no longer in common use, it has greatly influenced more recent languages, such as Ada and Pascal.

Algol
(or Beta Persei) ▷eclipsing binary, a pair of orbiting stars in the constellation Perseus, one of which eclipses the other every 69 hours, causing its brightness to drop by two-thirds.

Algonquin
the Algonquian-speaking hunting and fishing people who once lived around the Ottawa River in eastern Canada. Many now live on reservations in northeastern USA, eastern Ontario, and western Québec; others have chosen to live among the general populations of Canada and the USA.

algorithm
procedure or series of steps that can be used to solve a problem.

In computer science, it describes the logical sequence of operations to be performed by a program. A ▷flow chart is a visual representation of an algorithm.

The word derives from the name of 9th-century Arab mathematician Muhammad ibn-Mūsā al-▷Khwārizmī.

Alhambra
fortified palace in Granada, Spain, built by Moorish kings, mainly between 1248 and 1354. It stands on a rocky hill and is a fine example of Moorish architecture.

Ali
(c. 598–661) 4th ▷caliph of ▷Islam. He was born in Mecca, the son of Abu Talib, and was the cousin and close friend and supporter of the prophet Muhammad, who gave him his daughter Fatima in marriage. He was one of the first to believe in Islam. On Muhammad's death in 632, Ali had a claim to succeed him, but this was not conceded until 656, following the murder of the third caliph, Uthman. After a brief and stormy reign, Ali was assassinated. Controversy has raged around Ali's name between the Sunni Muslims and the Shiites, the former denying his right to the caliphate and the latter supporting it.

Ali, Muhammad
(1942–) Adopted name of Cassius Marcellus Clay, Jr. US boxer. Olympic light-heavyweight champion in 1960, he went on to become world professional heavyweight champion in 1964, and was the only man to regain the title twice.

Algeria

MAJOR TRADING PARTNERS France, Italy, Germany, USA, Canada, Spain, Turkey
RESOURCES natural gas and petroleum, iron ore, phosphates, lead, zinc, mercury, silver, salt, antimony, copper
INDUSTRIES food processing, machinery and transport equipment, textiles, cement, tobacco, consumer goods
EXPORTS crude oil, gas, vegetables, tobacco, hides, dates. Principal market: Italy 22.8% (2001)
IMPORTS machinery and transportation equipment, food and basic manufactures. Principal source: France 37.3% (2001)
ARABLE LAND 3.2% (2000 est)
AGRICULTURAL PRODUCTS wheat, barley, potatoes, citrus fruits, olives, grapes; livestock rearing (sheep and cattle)

Population and society

POPULATION 31,800,000 (2003 est)
POPULATION GROWTH RATE 1.7% (2000–15)
POPULATION DENSITY (per sq km) 13 (2003 est)
urban population (% of total) 59 (2003 est)
AGE DISTRIBUTION (% of total population) 0–14 34%, 15–59 61%, 60+ 5% (2002 est)
ETHNIC GROUPS 99% of Arab Berber origin, the remainder of European descent, mainly French
LANGUAGE Arabic (official), Berber, French
RELIGION Sunni Muslim (state religion) 99%, Christian and Jewish 1%
EDUCATION (compulsory years) 9
LITERACY RATE 79% (men); 61% (women) (2003 est)
LABOUR FORCE 29% of population: 24% agriculture, 32% industry, 44% services (2000)
LIFE EXPECTANCY 68 (men); 71 (women) (2000–05)
CHILD MORTALITY RATE (under 5, per 1,000 live births) 49 (2001)
PHYSICIANS (per 1,000 people) 0.8 (1995 est)
HOSPITAL BEDS (per 1,000 people) 2.1 (1995 est)
TV SETS (per 1,000 people) 114 (2001 est)
RADIOS (per 1,000 people) 244 (2001 est)
INTERNET USERS (per 10,000 people) 159.8 (2002 est)
PERSONAL COMPUTER USERS (per 100 people) 0.8 (2002 est)

See also ▷Berber.

Algeria country in North Africa, bounded east by Tunisia and Libya, southeast by Niger, southwest by Mali and Mauritania, northwest by Morocco, and north by the Mediterranean Sea.

NATIONAL NAME *Al-Jumhuriyyat al-Jaza'iriyya ad-Dimuqratiyya ash-Sha'biyya/Democratic People's Republic of Algeria*
AREA 2,381,741 sq km/919,590 sq mi
CAPITAL Algiers (Arabic al-Jaza'ir)
MAJOR TOWNS/CITIES Oran, Annaba, Blida, Sétif, Constantine
MAJOR PORTS Oran (Ouahran), Annaba (Bône)
PHYSICAL FEATURES coastal plains backed by mountains in north, Sahara desert in south; Atlas mountains, Barbary Coast, Chott Melrhir depression, Hoggar mountains

Government

HEAD OF STATE Abdelaziz Bouteflika from 1999
HEAD OF GOVERNMENT Ahmed Ouyahia from 2003

POLITICAL SYSTEM military
POLITICAL EXECUTIVE military
ADMINISTRATIVE DIVISIONS 48 departments
ARMED FORCES 136,700 (2002 est)
CONSCRIPTION compulsory for 18 months
DEATH PENALTY retained and used for ordinary crimes
DEFENCE SPEND (% GDP) 5.9 (2002 est)
EDUCATION SPEND (% GDP) 4.3 (1999)
HEALTH SPEND (% GDP) 3.6 (2000 est)

Economy and resources

CURRENCY Algerian dinar
GPD (US$) 55.7 billion (2002 est)
REAL GDP GROWTH (% change on previous year) 1.9 (2001)
GNI (US$) 53.8 billion (2002 est)
GNI PER CAPITA (PPP) (US$) 5,330 (2002 est)
CONSUMER PRICE INFLATION 1.4% (2002 est)
UNEMPLOYMENT 29.8% (2000)
FOREIGN DEBT (US$) 22 billion (2001 est)

Chronology

9th century BC: Part of Carthaginian Empire.

146 BC: Conquered by Romans, who called the area Numidia.

6th century: Part of the Byzantine Empire.

late 7th century: Conquered by Muslim Arabs, who spread Islam as the basis of a new Berberized Arab-Islamic civilization.

1516: Ottoman Turks expelled recent Christian Spanish invaders.

1816: Anglo-Dutch forces bombarded Algiers as a reprisal against the Barbary pirates' attacks on Mediterranean shipping.

1830–47: French occupation of Algiers, followed by extension of control to the north, overcoming fierce resistance from Amir Abd al-Qadir, a champion of Arab Algerian nationalism, and from Morocco.

1850–70: The mountainous inland region, inhabited by the Kabyles, was occupied by the French.

1871: There was a major rebellion against French rule as French settlers began to take over the land.

1900–09: The Sahara region was subdued by France, who kept it under military rule.

1940: Following France's defeat by Nazi Germany, Algeria became allied to the pro-Nazi Vichy regime during World War II.

1945: 8,000 died following the ruthless suppression of an abortive uprising against French rule.

1954–62: Battle of Algiers: bitter war of independence fought between the National Liberation Front (FLN) and the French colonial army.

1958: French inability to resolve the civil war in Algeria, toppled the Fourth Republic and brought to power, in Paris, Gen Charles de Gaulle, who accepted the principle of national self-determination.

1962: Independence from France was achieved and a republic declared. Many French settlers fled.

1963: A one-party state was established.

1976: New Islamic-socialist constitution approved.

1988: Riots took place in protest at austerity policies; 170 people were killed. A reform programme was introduced.

1989: Constitutional changes introduced limited political pluralism.

1992: The military took control of the government and a state of emergency was declared.

1993: The civil strife worsened, with assassinations of politicians and other public figures.

1994: The fundamentalists' campaign of violence intensified.

1996: The constitution was amended to increase the president's powers and counter religious fundamentalism. Arabic was declared the official public language.

1998: The violence continued.

1999: Abdel Aziz Bouteflika was elected president.

2000: Ali Benflis was appointed prime minister. The violence continued, averaging 200 deaths a month.

ALGERIA Late afternoon in Tassili-N-Ajjer in southeastern Algeria, and two Bedouin enjoy an animated discussion. *Image Bank*

MUHAMMAD ALI US boxer Muhammad Ali, three times world heavyweight champion. *Archive Photos*

He was known for his fast footwork and extrovert nature. In December 1999 he was voted the British Broadcasting Corporation (BBC) Sports Personality of the Century and the US magazine *Sports Illustrated* and the US newspaper *USA Today* both named him Sportsman of the Century.

He had his title stripped from him in 1967 for refusing to be drafted into the US Army. He regained his title in 1974, lost it in February 1978, and regained it seven months later.

Related Web site: Ali – A Brief History http://www.webgalleria.com/alibio.html

alibi (Latin 'elsewhere') in law, a provable assertion that the accused was at some other place when a crime was committed.

Alicante seaport and administrative capital of Alicante province, southeast Spain, situated on the Mediterranean coast, 123 km/77 mi south of Valencia; population (1991) 261,300. It exports wine, olive oil, and fruit, and has ferry services to the Balearic Islands. There is food-processing and other light industry; products include leather, textiles, and pottery. Almond paste sweetmeats (*turrones*) are a local speciality.

alien (Latin *alienus* 'foreign') in law, a person who is not a citizen of a particular nation.

alienation sense of isolation, powerlessness, and therefore frustration; a feeling of loss of control over one's life; a sense of estrangement from society or even from oneself. As a concept it was developed by German philosophers G W F Hegel and Karl Marx; the latter used it as a description and criticism of the condition that developed among workers in capitalist society.

alimentary canal in animals, the tube through which food passes; it extends from the mouth to the anus. It is a complex organ, adapted for ▷digestion. In human adults, it is about 9 m/30 ft long, consisting of the mouth cavity, pharynx, oesophagus, stomach, and the small and large intestines.

alimony in the USA, money allowance given by court order to a former spouse after separation or ▷divorce. The right has been extended to relationships outside marriage and is colloquially termed palimony. Alimony is separate and distinct from court orders for child support.

Ali Pasha, Mehmed Emin (1815–1871) Grand vizier (chief minister) of the Ottoman Empire 1855–56, 1858–59, 1861, and 1867–71, noted for his attempts to Westernize the Ottoman Empire.

aliphatic compound any organic chemical compound in which the carbon atoms are joined in straight chains, as in hexane (C_6H_{14}), or in branched chains, as in 2-methylpentane ($CH_3CH(CH_3)CH_2CH_2CH_3$).

Aliphatic compounds have bonding electrons localized within the vicinity of the bonded atoms. ▷Cyclic compounds that do not have delocalized electrons are also aliphatic, as in the alicyclic compound cyclohexane (C_6H_{12}) or the heterocyclic piperidine ($C_5H_{11}N$). Compare ▷aromatic compound.

alkali in chemistry, a ▷base that is soluble in water. Alkalis neutralize acids and are soapy to the touch. The strength of an alkali is measured by its hydrogen-ion concentration, indicated by the ▷pH value. They may be divided into strong and weak alkalis: a strong alkali (for example, potassium hydroxide, KOH) ionizes completely when disssolved in water, whereas a weak alkali (for example, ammonium hydroxide, NH_4OH) exists in a partially ionized state in solution. All alkalis have a pH above 7.0.

The hydroxides of metals are alkalis. Those of sodium and potassium are chemically powerful; both were historically derived from the ashes of plants.

The four main alkalis are sodium hydroxide (caustic soda, NaOH); potassium hydroxide (caustic potash, KOH); calcium hydroxide (slaked lime or limewater, $Ca(OH)_2$); and aqueous ammonia ($NH_{3\,(aq)}$). Their solutions all contain the hydroxide ion OH^-, which gives them a characteristic set of properties.

alkali metal any of a group of six metallic elements with similar chemical properties: lithium, sodium, potassium, rubidium, caesium, and francium. They form a linked group (Group One) in the ▷periodic table of the elements. They are univalent (have a valency of one) and of very low density (lithium, sodium, and potassium float on water); in general they are reactive, soft, low-melting-point metals. Because of their reactivity they are only found as compounds in nature.

alkaline-earth metal any of a group of six metallic elements with similar bonding properties: beryllium, magnesium, calcium, strontium, barium, and radium. They form a linked group in the ▷periodic table of the elements. They are strongly basic, bivalent (have a valency of two), and occur in nature only in compounds.

They and their compounds are used to make alloys, oxidizers, and drying agents.

alkaloid any of a number of physiologically active and frequently poisonous substances contained in some plants. They are usually organic bases and contain nitrogen. They form salts with acids and, when soluble, give alkaline solutions.

alkane member of a group of ▷hydrocarbons having the general formula C_nH_{2n+2}, commonly known as **paraffins**. As they contain only single ▷covalent bonds, alkanes are said to be saturated. Lighter alkanes, such as methane, ethane, propane, and butane, are colourless gases; heavier ones are liquids or solids. In nature they are found in natural gas and petroleum.

Related Web site: Properties and Reactions of Alkanes http://mychemistrypage.future.easyspace.com/Organic/Alkanes_and_Alkenes/Properties_of_Alkanes.htm

alkene member of the group of ▷hydrocarbons having the general formula C_nH_{2n}, formerly known as **olefins**. Alkenes are unsaturated compounds, characterized by one or more double bonds between adjacent carbon atoms. Lighter alkenes, such as ethene and propene, are gases, obtained from the ▷cracking of oil fractions. Alkenes react by addition, and many useful compounds, such as poly(ethene) and bromoethane, are made from them.

alkyne member of the group of ▷hydrocarbons with the general formula C_nH_{2n-2}, formerly known as the **acetylenes**. They are unsaturated compounds, characterized by one or more triple bonds between adjacent carbon atoms. Lighter alkynes, such as ethyne, are gases; heavier ones are liquids or solids.

Allah (Arabic *al-Ilah* 'the God') Islamic name for God.

Allahabad ('city of god') historic city in Uttar Pradesh state, India, 580 km/360 mi southeast of Delhi, on the Yamuna River where it meets the Ganges and the mythical underground Seraswati River; population (1991) 806,000. A growing commercial centre, its main industries are textiles and food processing. A Hindu religious event, the festival of the jar of nectar of immortality (Kumbh Mela), is held here every 12 years with the participants washing away sin

> **Muhammad Ali**
> *Float like a butterfly,*
> *sting like a bee.*
> Catchphrase

SALVADOR ALLENDE Chilean political leader Salvador Allende, seen here in 1970. He died during a US-supported coup led by General Pinochet. *Archive Photos*

and sickness by bathing in the rivers; in 1989 15 million pilgrims attended. It is also the site of the Asoka Pillar, dating from 232 BC, on which are carved edicts of the Emperor ▷Asoka.

Allegheny Mountains (or the Alleghenies) mountain range over 800 km/500 mi long extending from Pennsylvania to Virginia, rising to more than 1,500 m/4,900 ft and averaging 750 m/2,500 ft. The Alleghenies are rich in hardwood timber and bituminous coal, and also contain iron ore, natural gas, clay, and petroleum. The mountains initially hindered western migration, with the first settlement to the west being Marietta in 1788.

allegory in literature, the description or illustration of one thing in terms of another, or the personification of abstract ideas. The term is also used for a work of poetry or prose in the form of an extended metaphor or parable that makes use of symbolic fictional characters.

allegro (Italian 'merry, lively') in music, a lively or quick passage, movement, or composition.

allele one of two or more alternative forms of a ▷gene at a given position (locus) on a chromosome, caused by a difference in the sequence of ▷DNA. Blue and brown eyes in humans are determined by different alleles of the gene for eye colour.

Allen, Bog of wetland east of the River Shannon in the Republic of Ireland, comprising some 958 sq km/370 sq mi of the counties of Offaly, Laois, and Kildare. It is the country's main source of ▷peat fuel.

Allen, Woody (1935–) Adopted name of Allen Stewart Konigsberg. US film writer, director, and actor. One of the true auteurs of contemporary American cinema, Allen has written, directed, and frequently acted in a number of comic and dramatic works which are informed by his personal aesthetic, religious, and sexual preoccupations. Allen's filmography includes such critically acclaimed works as *Annie Hall* (1977), which won an Academy Award for Best Picture in 1977, *Manhattan* (1979), *Hannah and Her Sisters* (1986), *Radio Days* (1987), *Crimes and Misdemeanours* (1989), *Bullets Over Broadway* (1994), and *Deconstructing Harry* (1997). In 2000 he directed and acted in *Small Time Crooks*.

Allenby, Edmund Henry Hynman (1861–1936) 1st Viscount Allenby. British field marshal. In World War I he served in France before taking command 1917–19 of the British forces in the Middle East. After preparations in Egypt, he captured Gaza, Beersheba and, in 1917, Jerusalem. His defeat of the Turkish forces at Megiddo in Palestine in September 1918 was followed almost at once by the capitulation of Turkey. He was high commissioner in Egypt 1919–35. KCB 1915, Viscount 1919.

Allende (Gossens), Salvador (1908–1973) Chilean left-wing politician, president 1970–73. Elected president as the candidate of the Popular Front alliance, Allende never succeeded in keeping the electoral alliance together in government. His failure to solve the country's economic problems or to deal with political subversion allowed the army, backed by the Central Intelligence Agency (CIA), to stage the 1973 coup that brought about the death of Allende and many of his supporters.

ethene   propene   butene

— single bond
= double bond
H hydrogen
C carbon

ALKENE The alkene series of hydrocarbons ethene (C_2H_4), propene ($CH_3CH=CH_2$), and butene (C_4H_8). Alkenes all have the general formula C_nH_{2n}.

allergy special sensitivity of the body that makes it react with an exaggerated response of the natural immune defence mechanism to the introduction of an otherwise harmless foreign substance (allergen).

Alliance, the in UK politics, a loose union (1981–87) formed by the ▷Liberal Party and ▷Social Democratic Party (SDP) for electoral purposes.

Allied Coordination Committee (or Operation Stay Behind or **Gladio**) secret right-wing paramilitary network in Western Europe, set up in the 1950s to arm guerrillas chosen from the civilian population in the event of Soviet invasion or communist takeover. Initiated and partly funded by the US ▷Central Intelligence Agency (CIA), it was linked to the ▷North Atlantic Treaty Organization.

Its past or present existence was officially acknowledged in 1990 by Belgium, France, (West) Germany, Greece, Italy, the Netherlands, Norway, and Portugal; in the UK the matter is covered by the ▷Official Secrets Act. In 1990 those governments that confirmed their countries' participation said that the branches had been or would be closed down.

Allies, the in World War I, the 23 countries allied against the Central Powers (Germany, Austro-Hungary, Turkey, and Bulgaria), including France, Italy, Russia, the UK, Australia and other Commonwealth nations, and, in the latter part of the war, the USA. In World War II the Allies were the 49 countries allied against the ▷Axis Powers (Germany, Italy, and Japan), including France, the UK, Australia and other Commonwealth nations, the USA, and the former Soviet Union.

alligator (Spanish *el lagarto* 'the lizard') reptile of the genus *Alligator*, related to the crocodile. There are only two living species: *A. mississipiensis*, the Mississippi alligator of the southern states of the USA, and *A. sinensis* from the swamps of the lower Chang Jiang River in China. The former grows to about 4 m/12 ft, but the latter only to 1.5 m/5 ft. Alligators lay their eggs in waterside nests of mud and vegetation and are good mothers. They swim well with lashing movements of the tail and feed on fish and mammals but seldom attack people.

The skin is of value for fancy leather, and alligator farms have been established in the USA. Closely related are the caymans of South America; these belong to the genus *Caiman*. Alligators ranged across northern Europe from the Upper Cretaceous to the Pliocene period.

Related Web site: American Alligator http://www.seaworld.org/animal_bytes/alligatorab.html

alliteration in poetry and prose, the use, within a line or phrase, of words beginning with the same sound, as in 'Two tired toads trotting to Tewkesbury'. It was a common device in Old English poetry, and its use survives in many traditional phrases, such as *dead as a doornail* and *pretty as a picture*.

allium any of a group of plants of the lily family, usually strong-smelling with a sharp taste; they form bulbs in which sugar is stored. Cultivated species include onion, garlic, chive, and leek. Some species are grown in gardens for their decorative globular heads of white, pink, or purple flowers. (Genus *Allium*, family Liliaceae.)

allopathy (Greek *allos* 'other', *pathos* 'suffering') in ▷homeopathy, a term used for orthodox medicine, using therapies designed to counteract the manifestations of the disease. In strict usage, allopathy is the opposite of homeopathy.

allotropy property whereby an element can exist in two or more forms (allotropes), each possessing different physical properties but the same state of matter (gas, liquid, or solid). The allotropes of carbon are diamond, fullerene, and graphite. Sulphur has several allotropes (flowers of sulphur, plastic, rhombic, and monoclinic). These solids have different crystal structures, as do the white and grey forms of tin and the black, red, and white forms of phosphorus.

Oxygen exists as two gaseous allotropes: one used by organisms for respiration (O_2), and the other a poisonous pollutant, ozone (O_3).

alloy metal blended with some other metallic or nonmetallic substance to give it special qualities, such as resistance to corrosion, greater hardness, or tensile strength. Useful alloys include bronze, brass, cupronickel, duralumin, German silver, gunmetal, pewter, solder, steel, and stainless steel.

Among the oldest alloys is bronze (mainly an alloy of copper and tin), the widespread use of which ushered in the Bronze Age. Complex alloys are now common; for example, in dentistry, where a cheaper alternative to gold is made of chromium, cobalt, molybdenum, and titanium. Among the most recent alloys are superplastics: alloys that can stretch to double their length at specific temperatures, permitting, for example, their injection into moulds as easily as plastic.

All Saints' Day (or All-Hallows; or **Hallowmas**) festival on 1 November for all Christian saints and martyrs who have no special day of their own. It was instituted in 835.

All Souls' Day festival in the Roman Catholic Church, held on 2 November (following All Saints' Day) in the conviction that through prayer and self-denial the faithful can hasten the deliverance of souls expiating their sins in purgatory.

allspice spice prepared from the dried berries of the evergreen pimento tree, also known as the West Indian pepper tree, (*Pimenta dioica*) of the myrtle family, cultivated chiefly in Jamaica. It has an aroma similar to that of a mixture of cinnamon, cloves, and nutmeg.

alluvial deposit layer of broken rocky matter, or sediment, formed from material that has been carried in suspension by a river or stream and dropped as the velocity of the current decreases. River plains and deltas are made entirely of alluvial deposits, but smaller pockets can be found in the beds of upland torrents.

Al Manamah capital and free trade port of Bahrain, on Bahrain Island; population (1991) 137,000. It handles oil and entrepôt trade.

Alma-Tadema, Lawrence (1836–1912) Dutch artist who worked in England from 1870. He painted romantic, idealized scenes from ancient Greek, Roman, and Egyptian life, which combined Victorian sentiment with detailed historical accuracy.

Almaty (formerly Vernyi (1854–1921), Alma-Ata (1921–94)) former capital of ▷Kazakhstan to 1998, in the southeast of the country on the Almaatinka River, and capital of Almaty oblast; population (1996) 1,500,000. Its industries include engineering, printing, tobacco processing, textile manufacturing, and the production of leather goods. The city is at the centre of a large fruit-growing region, and food processing (meat packing, flour milling, wine bottling) is also a major source of employment in the city.

Almería Spanish city, chief town of a province of the same name on the Mediterranean; population (1994) 167,000. The province is famous for its white grapes, and in the Sierra Nevada are rich mineral deposits.

Almohad Berber dynasty 1130–1269 founded by the Berber prophet Muhammad ibn Tumart (*c.* 1080–1130). The Almohads ruled much of Morocco and Spain, which they took by defeating the ▷Almoravids; they later took the area that today forms Algeria and Tunis. Their policy of religious 'purity' involved the forced conversion and massacre of the Jewish population of Spain. The Almohads were themselves defeated by the Christian kings of Spain in 1212, and in Morocco in 1269.

almond tree related to the peach and apricot. Dessert almonds, which can be eaten whole, are the kernels of the fruit of the sweet variety *Prunus amygdalus dulcis*, which is also used to produce a low-cholesterol cooking oil. Oil of bitter almonds, from the variety *P. amygdalus amara*, is used in flavouring. Bitter almonds contain hydrocyanic acid, which is poisonous and must be extracted before the oil can be processed. Almond oil is also used for cosmetics, perfumes, and fine lubricants. (*Prunus amygdalus*, family Rosaceae.)

Related Web site: Almonds http://www.botanical.com/botanical/mgmh/a/almon026.html

ALMOND Almond trees in bloom in France. *Image Bank*

Almoravid Berber dynasty 1056–1147 founded by the prophet Abdullah ibn Tashfin, ruling much of Morocco and Spain in the 11th–12th centuries. The Almoravids came from the Sahara and in the 11th century began laying the foundations of an empire covering the whole of Morocco and parts of Algeria; their capital was the newly founded Marrakesh. In 1086 they defeated Alfonso VI of Castile to gain much of Spain. They were later overthrown by the ▷Almohads.

Al Mukalla seaport capital of the Hadhramaut coastal region of Yemen, on the Gulf of Aden 480 km/300 mi east of Aden; population (1995 est) 154,400.

aloe one of a group of plants native to southern Africa, with long, fleshy, spiny-edged leaves. The drug usually referred to as 'bitter aloes' is a powerful purgative (agent that causes the body to expel impurities) prepared from the juice of the leaves of several of the species. (Genus *Aloe*, family Liliaceae.)

Related Web site: Aloes http://www.botanical.com/botanical/mgmh/a/aloes027.html

alpaca domesticated South American hoofed mammal *Lama pacos* of the camel family, found in Chile, Peru, and Bolivia, and herded at high elevations in the Andes. It is bred mainly for its long, fine, silky wool, and stands about 1 m/3 ft tall at the shoulder with neck and head another 60 cm/2 ft.

ALPACA An alpaca breeding farm in Ecuador. *Image Bank*

alphabet set of conventional symbols used for writing, based on a correlation between individual symbols and spoken sounds, so called from *alpha* (α) and *beta* (β), the names of the first two letters of the classical Greek alphabet. The earliest known alphabet is from

ALLIGATOR These alligators live in the Everglades, Florida, USA. The alligator is related to the crocodile, but is smaller and less likely to attack people. *Image Bank*

Palestine, about 1700 BC. Alphabetic writing now takes many forms – for example, the Hebrew *aleph-beth* and the Arabic script, both written from right to left; the Devanagari script of the Hindus, in which the symbols 'hang' from a line common to all the symbols; and the Greek alphabet, with the first clearly delineated vowel symbols.

Alpha Centauri brightest star in the constellation Centaurus; see ▷Rigil Kent.

alpha particle positively charged, high-energy particle emitted from the nucleus of a radioactive atom. It is one of the products of the spontaneous disintegration of radioactive elements (see ▷radioactivity) such as radium and thorium, and is identical with the nucleus of a helium atom – that is, it consists of two protons and two neutrons. The process of emission, **alpha decay**, transforms one element into another, decreasing the atomic (or proton) number by two and the atomic mass (or nucleon number) by four.

Alps the highest and most extensive mountain range in Europe. The Alps run in an arc from the Mediterranean coast of France in the west through northern Italy, Switzerland, southern Germany, and Austria to the outskirts of Vienna and the River Danube in the east – a total distance of some 960 km/597 mi. Alpine ranges also extend down the Adriatic coast into Slovenia and Croatia. The Alps form a natural frontier between several countries in south-central Europe. The highest peak, at 4,808 m/15,774 ft, is ▷Mont Blanc, on the Franco-Italian border. The Alps are the source of many of Europe's major rivers – or their tributaries – including the Rhine, the Rhône, the Po, and the Danube. As well as agriculture, an important economic activity in the Alps is tourism.

Alps, Australian see ▷Australian Alps.

Alps, Southern see ▷Southern Alps.

al-Qaeda Islamic-extremist international terrorist organization, controlled by Osama ▷bin Laden. It was responsible on 11 September 2001 for the world's single worst terrorist atrocity, with the suicide hijackings of airliners that crashed into the World Trade Center in New York City and other targets, including the Pentagon, at the cost of over 3,000 lives. Al-Qaeda is not a unified organization with an identifiable structure, but has links with Islamic fundamentalist terrorist groups in over 40 countries who share its ideology of global jihad (holy war). Its key targets are the US (who they regard as the 'Great Satan'), Israel and their allies, and its aim is to 'liberate' Islam's three holiest places – Mecca, Medina and Jerusalem – and remove US troops from Saudi Arabia.

Alsace region of France; area 8,300 sq km/3,204 sq mi; population (1999 est) 1,734,100. It consists of the *départements* of Bas-Rhin and Haut-Rhin; its administrative centre is ▷Strasbourg. Alsace has much rich agricultural land, and is noted for its white wines.

Alsace-Lorraine area of northeast France, lying west of the River Rhine. It forms the French regions of ▷Alsace and ▷Lorraine. The former iron and steel industries are being replaced by electronics, chemicals, and precision engineering.

Alsatian another name for the ▷German shepherd dog.

Altai (or Altay; formerly **Oirot Autonomous Oblast** (1922–48)) republic of the Russian Federation, within the Altai krai (territory) of southern Siberia; area 92,600 sq km/35,752 sq mi; population (1996) 202,000 (24% urban). The oblast was formed in 1922, and Altai was formed after the break-up of the Soviet Union in 1992. Its capital is Gorno-Altaisk.

Altai Mountains (or **Altay Mountains**) mountain system running through ▷Kazakhstan, the ▷Altai Republic of the Russian Federation, western ▷Mongolia, and northern ▷China. It is divided into two parts: the Russian Altai, which includes the highest peak, Mount Belukha, 4,506 m/14,783 ft, on the border with Kazakhstan; and the Mongolian or Great Altai. Alpine pastureland is found on the upper slopes below the snowline, while the lower slopes are heavily wooded with a variety of conifer and birch trees.

Altair (or **Alpha Aquilae**) brightest star in the constellation Aquila and the 13th-brightest star in the night sky. It is a white star about 16 light years away from the Sun and forms the Summer Triangle with the stars Deneb (in the constellation Cygnus) and Vega (in Lyra).

Altamira cave decorated with Palaeolithic wall paintings, the first such to be discovered, in 1879. The paintings are realistic depictions of bison, deer, and horses in polychrome (several colours). The cave is near the village of Santillana del Mar in Santander province, northern Spain; other well-known Palaeolithic cave paintings are in ▷Lascaux, southwestern France.

Altamira Amazonian city in the state of Pará, northeastern Brazil, situated at the junction of the Trans-Amazonian Highway with the Xingu River, 700 km/400 mi southwest of Belém; population (1991) 157,900.

altarpiece a painting (more rarely a sculpture) placed on, behind, or above an altar in a Christian church. Altarpieces vary greatly in size, construction, and number of images (diptych, triptych, and polyptych). Some are small and portable; some (known as a **retable** or **reredos** – there is no clear distinction) are fixed.

Altay alternative spelling for ▷Altai in Russia.

Altdorfer, Albrecht (*c.* 1480–1538) German painter, architect, and printmaker. He was active in Regensburg, Bavaria. He is best known for his vast panoramic battle scenes in which his use of light creates movement and drama. On a smaller scale, he also painted some of the first true landscapes (see ▷landscape painting).

alternate angles a pair of angles that lie on opposite sides and at opposite ends of a transversal (a line that cuts two or more lines in the same plane). The alternate angles formed by a transversal of two parallel lines are equal.

alternating current (AC) electric current that flows for an interval of time in one direction and then in the opposite direction, that is, a current that flows in alternately reversed directions through or around a circuit. Electric energy is usually generated as alternating current in a power station, and alternating currents may be used for both power and lighting.

The advantage of alternating current over direct current (DC), as from a battery, is that its voltage can be raised or lowered economically by a transformer: high voltage for generation and transmission, and low voltage for safe utilization. Railways, factories, and domestic appliances, for example, use alternating current.

alternation of generations typical life cycle of terrestrial plants and some seaweeds, in which there are two distinct forms occurring alternately: **diploid** (having two sets of chromosomes) and **haploid** (one set of chromosomes). The diploid generation produces haploid spores by ▷meiosis, and is called the sporophyte, while the haploid generation produces gametes (sex cells), and is called the gametophyte. The gametes fuse to form a diploid ▷zygote which develops into a new sporophyte; thus the sporophyte and gametophyte alternate.

ALPS The Alpine peaks, as seen in this photograph of the French Alps, are snow-covered and often lost in cloud. *Image Bank*

alternative medicine see ▷medicine, alternative.

alternator electricity ▷generator that produces an alternating current.

Althing parliament of Iceland, established in about 930, the oldest in the world. It was dissolved in 1800, revived in 1843 as an advisory body, and became a legislative body again in 1874. It has 63 members who serve a four-year term.

altiplano sparsely populated upland plateau of the Andes of South America, stretching from southern Peru to northwestern Argentina. The height of the altiplano is 3,000–4,000 m/ 10,000–13,000 ft.

Altman, Robert (1925–) US film director and producer. His films vary in tone from the comic to the elegiac, but are frequently ambitious in both content and form, utilizing a complex and sometimes fragmentary style. His antiwar comedy *M*A*S*H* (1970) was a critical and commercial success, as were *Nashville* (1975) and *The Player* (1992).

alto (Italian 'high') voice or musical instrument between tenor and soprano, of approximate range G3–D5. As a prefix to the name of an instrument, for example alto saxophone, it denotes a size larger than soprano.

altruism in biology, helping another individual of the same species to reproduce more effectively, as a direct result of which the altruist may leave fewer offspring itself. Female honey bees (workers) behave altruistically by rearing sisters in order to help their mother, the queen bee, reproduce, and forgo any possibility of reproducing themselves.

ALU abbreviation for ▷arithmetic and logic unit.

alum any double sulphate of a monovalent metal or radical (such as sodium, potassium, or ammonium) and a trivalent metal (such as aluminium, chromium, or iron). The commonest alum is the double sulphate of potassium and aluminium, $K_2Al_2(SO_4)_4.24H_2O$, a white crystalline powder that is readily soluble in water. It is used in curing animal skins. Other alums are used in papermaking and to fix dye in the textile industry.

alumina (or **corundum**) Al_2O_3 oxide of aluminium, widely distributed in clays, slates, and shales. It is formed by the decomposition of the feldspars in granite and used as an abrasive. Typically it is a white powder, soluble in most strong acids or caustic alkalis but not in water. Impure alumina is called 'emery'. Rubies, sapphires, and topaz are corundum gemstones.

aluminium lightweight, silver-white, ductile and malleable, metallic element, symbol Al, atomic number 13, relative atomic mass 26.9815, melting point 658°C/1,216°F. It is the third most abundant element (and the most abundant metal) in the Earth's crust, of which it makes up about 8.1% by mass. It is non-magnetic, an excellent conductor of electricity, and oxidizes easily, the layer of oxide on its surface making it highly resistant to tarnish.

Alva, Ferdinand Alvarez de Toledo (1508–1582) Duke of Alva or Alba. Spanish politician and general. He successfully commanded the Spanish armies of the Holy Roman Emperor Charles V and his son Philip II of Spain. In 1567 he was appointed governor of the Netherlands, where he set up a reign of terror to suppress Protestantism and the revolt of the Netherlands. In 1573 he was recalled at his own request. He later led a successful expedition against Portugal 1580–81.

Alvarez Quintero, Serafin (1871–1938) Spanish dramatist. One of two brothers (the other was Joaquin, 1873–1944). Born near Seville, from 1897 he produced about 200 comedies, principally dealing with local life in Andalusia. Among them are *Papá Juan: centenario* (1909) and *Los mosquitos* (1928).

Alzheimer's disease common manifestation of ▷dementia, thought to afflict 1 in 20 people over 65. After heart disease, cancer, and strokes it is the most common cause of death in the Western world. Attacking the brain's 'grey matter', it is a disease of mental processes rather than physical function, characterized by memory loss and progressive intellectual impairment. It was first described by Alois Alzheimer in 1906. Dementia affects nearly 18 million people worldwide and numbers are expected to rise.

Amal radical Lebanese ▷Shiite military force, established by Musa Sadr in the 1970s; its headquarters are in Borj al-Barajneh. The movement split into extremist and moderate groups in 1982, but both sides agreed on the aim of increasing Shiite political representation in Lebanon.

Amalfi seaport and resort in Campania, Italy, situated at the foot of Monte Cerrato, on the Gulf of Salerno, 39 km/24 mi southeast of Naples; population (1990) 5,900. For 700 years it was an independent republic. It is an ancient archiepiscopal see (seat of an archbishop) and has a Romanesque cathedral.

amalgam any alloy of mercury with other metals. Most metals will form amalgams, except iron and platinum. Amalgam is used in dentistry for filling teeth, and usually contains copper, silver, and zinc as the main alloying ingredients. This amalgam is pliable when first mixed and then sets hard, but the mercury leaches out and may cause a type of heavy-metal poisoning.

amanita any of a group of fungi (see ▷fungus) distinguished by a ring (or volva) around the base of the stalk, warty patches on the cap, and the clear white colour of the gills. Many of the species are brightly coloured and highly poisonous. (Genus *Amanita*, family Agaricaceae.)

Amarillo city in the panhandle of northern Texas, USA, situated on the high plains, west of the Canadian and Red rivers; population (1994 est) 165,000. The centre of the world's largest cattle-

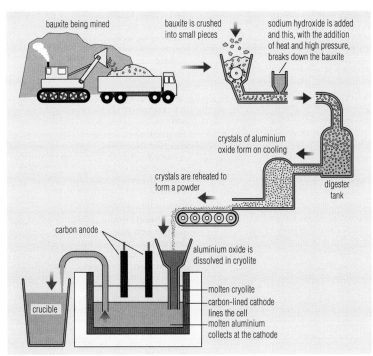

ALUMINIUM The extraction of aluminium is a two-stage process. In the first stage bauxite is crushed to extract aluminium oxide (alumina). In the second stage pure aluminium is extracted from the alumina by electrolysis.

American Indians: Major Cultural Groups	
North America	
Arctic	Inuit, Aleut
Subarctic	Algonquin, Cree, Ottawa
northeast woodlands	Huron, Iroquois, Mohican, Shawnee (Tecumseh)
southeast woodlands	Cherokee, Choctaw, Creek, Hopewell, Natchez, Seminole
Great Plains	Blackfoot, Cheyenne, Comanche, Pawnee, Sioux
northwest coast	Chinook, Tlingit, Tsimshian
Desert West	Apache, Navajo, Pueblo, Hopi, Mojave, Shoshone
Central America	
	Maya, Toltec, Aztec, Mexican
South America	
eastern	Carib, Xingu
central	Guaraní, Miskito
western	Araucanian, Aymara, Chimú, Inca, Jivaro, Quechua

producing area, it processes the live animal into frozen supermarket packets in a single continuous operation on an assembly line. Other industries include oil, farming, copper and zinc refining, and the manufacture of helicopters. There is a large helium plant here, and the city is also a centre for the assembly of nuclear warheads.

Amazon (Portuguese and Spanish **Rio Amazonas**; Indian Amossona 'destroyer of boats') river in South America, the second longest in the world; length 6,516 km/4,050 mi. The Amazon ranks as the largest river in the world in terms of the volume of water it discharges (around 95,000 cu m/3.3 million cu ft every second), its number of tributaries (over 500), and the total basin area that it drains (7 million sq km/2.7 million sq mi – almost half the landmass of South America). It has 48,280 km/30,000 mi of navigable waterways. The river empties into the Atlantic Ocean on the Equator, through an estuary 80 km/50 mi wide. Over 5 million sq km/ 2 million sq mi of the Amazon basin is virgin rainforest, containing 30% of all known plant and animal species. This is the wettest region on Earth, with an average annual rainfall of 2.54 m/8.3 ft.

The Amazon's principal headstreams, the Marañón and the Ucayali, rise in the Andean highlands of central Peru, and unite to flow in a general easterly direction for about 4,000 km/2,500 mi across northern Brazil.

Loss of tropical forest The opening up of the Amazon River basin to settlers from the overpopulated northeast region or coast of Brazil has resulted in a massive burning of tropical forest to create both arable and pastoral land. The problems of soil erosion, the disappearance of potentially useful plant and animal species, and the possible impact of large-scale forest clearance on global warming of the atmosphere have become environmental issues of international concern. In June 1990 the Instituto Nacional de Pesquisas Espacias (INPE)(National Space Research Institute) announced that 8% of the rainforest in the area had been destroyed by deforestation, amounting to 404,000 sq km/155,944 sq mi – an area almost the size of Sweden. More recent data from INPE has highlighted continued increases in the rate of deforestation throughout the 1990s.

Related Web site: Amazon Interactive http://www.eduweb.com/ amazon.html

Amazon in Greek mythology, a member of a group of female warriors living near the Black Sea, who cut off their right breasts to use the bow more easily. Their queen Penthesilea was killed by ▷Achilles at the siege of Troy. The term Amazon has come to mean a large, strong woman.

Related Web site: Amazons http://www.net4you.co.at/users/ poellauerg/Amazons/index.html

Amazonia those regions of Brazil, Colombia, Ecuador, Peru, and Bolivia lying within the basin of the Amazon River.

Amazonian Indian indigenous inhabitants of the Amazon River Basin in South America. The majority of the societies are kin-based; traditional livelihood includes hunting and gathering, fishing, and shifting cultivation. A wide range of indigenous

languages are spoken. Numbering perhaps 2.5 million in the 16th century, they had been reduced to perhaps one-tenth of that number by the 1820s. Their rainforests are being destroyed for mining and ranching, and they are being killed, transported, or assimilated. In June 1998 a previously unknown tribe of about 200 hunters and gatherers was discovered in Brazil's Amazon rainforest.

amber fossilized ▷resin from coniferous trees of the Middle ▷Tertiary period. It is often washed ashore on the Baltic coast with plant and animal specimens preserved in it; many extinct species have been found preserved in this way. It ranges in colour from red to yellow, and is used to make jewellery.

ambergris fatty substance, resembling wax, found in the stomach and intestines of the sperm ▷whale. It is found floating in warm seas, and is used in perfumery as a fixative.

Ambrose, Curtly Elconn Lynwall (1963–) West Indies cricketer, born in Antigua. He was a very tall right-arm opening bowler, whose ability to bowl fast and accurately whilst extracting bounce and movement from even the most benign pitches made him the world's most feared pace bowler in the 1990s. In 2000 he became only the fifth player to take 400 or more Test wickets. He played county cricket for Northamptonshire between 1989 and 1996. He retired from Test cricket after the 2000 West Indies tour of England.

Amenhotep III (1391–1353 BC) King (pharaoh) of ancient Egypt. He built great monuments at Thebes, including the temples at Luxor. Two portrait statues at his mortuary temple were known to the Greeks as the colossi of Memnon; one was cracked, and when the temperature changed at dawn it gave out an eerie sound, then thought supernatural. His son **Amenhotep IV** changed his name to ▷Akhenaton.

America landmass in the Western hemisphere of the Earth, comprising the continents of ▷North America and ▷South America, with ▷Central America in between. This great landmass extends from the Arctic to the Antarctic, from beyond 75° N to past 55° S. The area is about 42,000,000 sq km/16,000,000 sq mi, and the estimated population is over 832 million (2000 est). Politically, it consists of 36 nations and US, British, French, and Dutch dependencies.

The name America is derived from Amerigo Vespucci, the Florentine navigator who was falsely supposed to have been the first European to reach the American mainland in 1497. The name is also popularly used to refer to the USA, a usage which many Canadians, South Americans, and other non-US Americans dislike.

Related Web site: Old Sturbridge Village – Where Early America Comes Alive http://www.osv.org/

American Civil War 1861–65; see ▷Civil War, American.

American Federation of Labor (and Congress of Industrial Organizations (AFL–CIO)) federation of North American trade unions, representing through 68 affiliated unions, 13 million workers, or about 14% of the workforce in North America (2000).

American football see ▷football, American.

American Independence, War of alternative name of the ▷American Revolution, the revolt 1775–83 of the British North American colonies that resulted in the establishment of the United States of America.

Related Web site: From Revolution to Reconstruction http://grid. let.rug.nl/~welling/usa/revolution.html

American Indian (or **Native American**) member of one of the aboriginal peoples of the Americas; the Arctic peoples (Inuit and Aleut) are often included, especially by the Bureau of Indian Affairs (BIA) of the US Department of the Interior, responsible for overseeing policy on US American Indian life, their reservations, education, and social welfare. The first American Indians arrived during the last ice age, approximately 20,000–30,000 years ago, passing from northeastern Siberia into Alaska over a land-bridge across the Bering Strait. The earliest reliably dated archaeological sites in North America are about 13,000–14,000 years old. In South America they are generally dated at about 12,000–13,000 years old, but discoveries made in 1989 suggest an even earlier date, perhaps 35,000–40,000 years ago. There are about 1.9 million (1995) American Indians in the USA and Canada.

Related Web site: First Nations Histories http://www.dickshovel.com/ Compacts.html

American Indian and Inuit art the art of the North American indigenous peoples. Weaving and beadwork feature prominently in the art of several peoples; the totem poles of the peoples of the North Pacific coast and the ivory carvings of the Inuit are highly distinctive.

American literature see ▷United States literature.

American Revolution revolt 1775–83 of the British North American colonies, resulting in the establishment of the United States of America. It was caused by colonial opposition to British economic exploitation and by the unwillingness of the colonists to pay for a standing army. It was also fuelled by the colonists' antimonarchist sentiment and their desire to participate in the policies affecting them.

Resentment had been growing in the American colonies from 1763 onward as a result of high-handed British legislation, like the ▷Stamp Act of 1765, and the Townshend Acts of 1767, which

AMERICAN INDIAN A reproduction of a wooden tablet inscribed with the symbolic picture-writing of the Ojibbeway Indians. *Philip Sauvain Picture Collection*

in ▷pitchblende and other uranium ores, where it is produced from the decay of neutron-bombarded plutonium, and is the element with the highest atomic number that occurs in nature. It is synthesized in quantity only in nuclear reactors by the bombardment of plutonium with neutrons. Its longest-lived isotope is Am-243, with a half-life of 7,650 years.

The element was named by Glenn Seaborg, one of the team who first synthesized it in 1944. Ten isotopes are known.

amethyst variety of ▷quartz, SiO_2, coloured violet by the presence of small quantities of impurities such as manganese or iron; used as a semiprecious stone. Amethysts are found chiefly in the Ural Mountains, India, the USA, Uruguay, and Brazil.

Amhara an ethnic group comprising approximately 25% of the population of Ethiopia; 13 million (1987). The Amhara are traditionally farmers. They speak Amharic, a language of the Semitic branch of the Hamito-Semitic (Afro-Asiatic) family. Most are members of the Ethiopian Christian Church.

amide any organic chemical derived from a fatty acid by the replacement of the hydroxyl group (–OH) by an amino group (–NH$_2$).

One of the simplest amides is ethanamide (acetamide, CH_3CONH_2), which has a strong odour.

Amiens administrative centre of Somme *département* and the major town in the ▷Picardy region of northeast France, 130 km/81 mi north of Paris at the confluence of the rivers ▷Somme and Avre; population (1999 est) 135,500. Situated in an area irrigated by canals, it has been a market-gardening region and textile centre since the Middle Ages, and has produced velvet since the 16th century. Other industries include clothing, tyres, chemicals, and machinery. Amiens is the seat of the University of Picardy. Amiens gave its name to the battles of August 1918, when British field marshal Douglas Haig launched his victorious offensive in World War I.

Amies, (Edwin) Hardy (1909–) English couturier. He is noted for his tailored clothes for women and menswear designs. From 1948, he was one of Queen Elizabeth II's dressmakers.

Amin (Dada), Idi (1925–2003) Ugandan politician, president 1971–79. He led the coup that deposed Milton Obote in 1971, expelled the Asian community in 1972, and exercised a reign of terror over his people during which an estimated 300,000 people were killed. After he invaded Tanzania in 1978, the Tanzanian army combined with dissident Ugandans to counter-attack. Despite assistance from Libya, Amin's forces collapsed and he fled in 1979. Latterly he lived in Saudi Arabia.

Amin was commissioned into the new Ugandan army in 1962 and an alliance with President Obote led to rapid promotion; by 1966 he was commander of the armed forces. Mounting evidence of Amin's corruption and brutality had convinced Obote to replace him at the end of 1970, but Amin seized power before he could do so. He suspended the constitution and all political activity and took legislative and executive powers into his own hands. During his brutal regime a large proportion of the educated elite were killed or fled into exile, as well as significant numbers of the Acholi and Langi peoples and Christians. His so-called 'economic war' against foreign domination resulted in the mass expulsion of the Asian population in 1972, appropriation of their assets promoting further collapse in the economy.

amine any of a class of organic chemical compounds in which one or more of the hydrogen atoms of ammonia (NH$_3$) have been replaced by other groups of atoms.

Methyl **amines** have unpleasant ammonia odours and occur in decomposing fish. They are all gases at ordinary temperature.

Aromatic **amine compounds** include aniline, which is used in dyeing.

amino acid water-soluble organic ▷molecule, mainly composed of carbon, oxygen, hydrogen, and nitrogen, containing both a basic amino group (NH$_2$) and an acidic carboxyl (COOH) group. They are small molecules able to pass through membranes. When two or more amino acids are joined together, they are known as ▷peptides; ▷proteins are made up of peptide chains folded or twisted in characteristic shapes.

Many different proteins are found in the cells of living organisms, but they are all made up of the same 20 amino acids, joined together in varying combinations (although other types of amino acid do occur infrequently in nature). Eight of these, the **essential amino acids**, cannot be synthesized by humans and must be obtained from the diet. Children need a further two amino acids that are not essential for adults. Other animals also need some preformed amino acids in their diet, but green plants can manufacture all the amino acids they need from simpler molecules, relying on energy from the Sun and minerals (including nitrates) from the soil.

Related Web sites: Amino Acids http://www.chemie.fu-berlin.de/chemistry/bio/amino-acids_en.html
Molecular Expressions: The Amino Acid Collection http://micro.magnet.fsu.edu/aminoacids/index.html

Amis, Kingsley (William) (1922–1995) English novelist and poet. He was associated early on with the ▷Angry Young Men group of writers. His sharply ironic works include the best-selling *Lucky Jim* (1954; his first novel), a comic portrayal of life at a provincial university. His later novels include the satiric comedy *The Old Devils* (1986), for which he won the Booker Prize.

His other novels, written in a variety of genres, include the spy story *The Anti-Death League* (1966), the ghost story *The Green Man* (1969), *The Riverside Villas Murder* (1973), which imitates a classic detective story, and *The Alteration* (1976), which imagines a 20th-century society dominated by the Catholic Church. He was the father of writer Martin Amis. He was knighted in 1990.

Amis, Martin Louis (1949–) English novelist and journalist, the son of novelist and poet Kingsley Amis. His works are characterized by their acerbic black humour and include *The Rachel Papers* (1973), a memoir of adolescence told through flashbacks, *Dead Babies* (1975), which addresses decadence and sadism, *Money* (1984), *London Fields* (1989), and *Time's Arrow* (1991). Later works include *Night Train* (1997), *Heavy Water and Other Stories* (1998), *Yellow Dog* (2003), and his memoir *Experience* (2000).

Amman capital and chief industrial centre of Jordan, 80 km/50 mi northeast of Jerusalem; population (1994 est) 1,300,000. It is a major communications centre, linking historic trade routes across the Middle East.

Features Amman is built on the site of the Old Testament Rabbath-Ammon (Philadelphia), capital of the Ammonites. It has a well-preserved Roman amphitheatre.

History The population was swollen by waves of refugees following upheavals in Palestine in 1948, 1967, and 1973. The modern city has developed since the turn of the century from a small Circassian village sited among the old city ruins to a large urban centre. Amman was the scene of most of the fighting between Palestinians and the Jordanian army in 1970.

ammeter instrument that measures electric current (flow of charge per unit time), usually in ▷amperes, through a conductor. It should not to be confused with a ▷voltmeter, which measures potential difference between two points in a circuit. The ammeter is placed in series (see ▷series circuit) with the component through which current is to be measured, and is constructed with a low internal resistance in order to prevent the reduction of that current as it flows through the instrument itself. A common type is the ▷moving-coil meter, which measures direct current (DC), but can, in the presence of a rectifier, measure alternating current (AC) also. Hot-wire, moving-iron, and dynamometer ammeters can be used for both DC and AC.

Ammon (or Amen or Amun) in Egyptian mythology, king of the gods; the equivalent of the Greek Zeus (Roman Jupiter). The Egyptian pharaohs identified themselves with his supremacy, adopting his name as in Tutankh*amen*. In art he is represented as a ram or goose, as a man with a ram's head, or as a man crowned with two tall feathers. He had temples at Siwa oasis, Libya, and at Napata and ▷Thebes, Egypt; his oracle at Siwa was patronized by the classical Greeks.

ammonia NH$_3$ colourless pungent-smelling gas, lighter than air and very soluble in water. It is made on an industrial scale by the

AMERICAN REVOLUTION American general Horatio Gates was appointed brigadier general of the Continental Army by George Washington in 1775. He won a major victory over the British at the Battle of Saratoga Springs in 1777. *Archive Photos*

imposed taxes on various goods, including tea. The first casualties of the revolution occurred in the Boston Massacre of 1770, when British troops opened fire on protesters. In the Boston Tea Party of 1773, protesters disguised as Indians emptied 342 chests of cheap imported tea into the harbour. In 1775 fighting broke out at Lexington and Concord, and in the same year the Americans invaded Canada and George Washington was appointed commander-in-chief of the America forces. The Declaration of Independence was issued in 1776, but Washington's troops suffered a series of defeats at the hands of General Howe.

The turning point in the war came with the decisive American victory at the Battle of Saratoga Springs in 1777, which prompted the French to enter the war on the American side. American military success culminated in British defeat and surrender at Yorktown in 1781. The defeat forced the resignation of the prime minister Lord ▷North, one of the war's main advocates. Under the Peace of Versailles, on 3 September 1783 Britain recognized the independence of the USA, and in return was allowed to retain Canada and recovered its West Indian territories.

Related Web site: Liberty! The American Revolution http://www.pbs.org/ktca/liberty/index.html

American Samoa see ▷Samoa, American.

americium radioactive metallic element of the ▷actinide series, symbol Am, atomic number 95, relative atomic mass 243.13; it was first synthesized in 1944. It occurs in nature in minute quantities

IDI AMIN Idi Amin, Ugandan president 1971–79. His regime became notorious as one of modern Africa's harshest dictatorships. *Archive Photos*

AMHARA The Amharic script is an offshoot of the Ethiopic alphabet, itself a descendant of the South Semitic branch of languages, and the only South Semitic script still in use. *Art Archive*

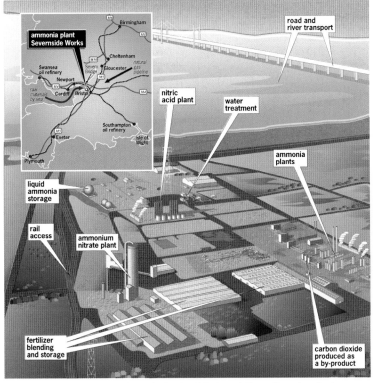

AMMONIA The Severnside Works on the banks of the Bristol Channel is a plant for the manufacture of ammonia and ammonia products.

▷Haber (or Haber–Bosch) process, and used mainly to produce nitrogenous fertilizers, nitric acid, and some explosives.

In aquatic organisms and some insects, nitrogenous waste (from the breakdown of amino acids) is excreted in the form of ammonia, rather than as urea in mammals.

ammonite extinct marine ▷cephalopod mollusc of the order Ammonoidea, related to the modern nautilus. The shell was curled in a plane spiral and made up of numerous gas-filled chambers, the outermost containing the body of the animal. Many species flourished between 200 million and 65 million years ago, ranging in size from that of a small coin to 2 m/6 ft across.

amnesia loss or impairment of memory. As a clinical condition it may be caused by disease or injury to the brain, by some drugs, or by shock; in some cases it may be a symptom of an emotional disorder.

amnesty act of state granted by a government by which pardon of certain past offences is accorded . This may be in the form of the release of political prisoners under a general pardon, or of the release of a person or group of people from criminal liability for a particular action. In addition, there are occasional amnesties for those who surrender firearms or other items that they hold illegally.

Amnesty International human-rights organization established in the UK in 1961 to campaign for the release of prisoners of conscience worldwide; fair trials for all political prisoners; an end to the death penalty, torture, and other inhuman treatment of all prisoners; and the cessation of extrajudicial executions and 'disappearances'. It is politically and economically unaligned.

The organization was awarded the Nobel Prize for Peace in 1977 for its work to secure the release of political prisoners. It is based in London.

amniocentesis sampling the amniotic fluid surrounding a fetus in the womb for diagnostic purposes. It is used to detect Down's Syndrome and other genetic abnormalities. The procedure carries a 1 in 200 risk of miscarriage.

amoeba (plural **amoebae**) one of the simplest living animals, consisting of a single cell and belonging to the ▷protozoa group. The body consists of colourless protoplasm. Its activities are controlled by the nucleus, and it feeds by flowing round and engulfing organic debris. It reproduces by ▷binary fission. Some species of amoeba are harmful parasites.

ampere SI unit (symbol A) of electrical current. Electrical current is measured in a similar way to water current, in terms of an amount per unit time; one ampere (amp) represents a flow of one coulomb per second, which is about 6.28×10^{18} ▷electrons per second.

The ampere is defined as the current that produces a specific magnetic force between two long, straight, parallel conductors

placed 1 m/3.3 ft apart in a vacuum. It is named after the French scientist André Ampère.

amphetamine (or **speed**) powerful synthetic ▷stimulant. Benzedrine was the earliest amphetamine marketed, used as a 'pep pill' in World War II to help soldiers overcome fatigue, and until the 1970s amphetamines were prescribed by doctors as an appetite suppressant for weight loss; as an anti-depressant, to induce euphoria; and as a stimulant, to increase alertness. Indications for its use today are very restricted because of severe side effects, including addiction. It is a sulphate or phosphate form of $C_9H_{13}N$.

amphibian (Greek 'double life') member of the vertebrate class Amphibia, which generally spend their larval (tadpole) stage in fresh water, transferring to land at maturity (after ▷metamorphosis) and generally returning to water to breed. Like fish and reptiles, they continue to grow throughout life, and cannot maintain a temperature greatly differing from that of their environment. The class contains 4,553 known species, 4,000 of which are frogs and toads, 390 salamanders, and 163 caecilians (wormlike in appearance).

According to analysis of statistics from over 900 amphibian populations taken 1950–97, by Canadian and Swiss researchers, and published in 2000, amphibian populations have been declining at a rate of about 4% per year. US biologists concluded that the marked worldwide decline in amphibian populations is unlikely to have a single cause. Possible causes have been cited as increased ultraviolet radiation exposure, pollution, global climate change, and infection.

amphitheatre (Greek *amphi* 'around') large oval or circular building used by the Romans for gladiatorial contests, fights of wild animals, and other similar events. It is an open structure with a central arena surrounded by rising rows of seats. The ▷Colosseum in Rome, completed in AD 80, held 50,000 spectators.

amplifier electronic device that magnifies the strength of a signal, such as a radio signal. The ratio of output signal strength to input signal strength is called the gain of the amplifier. As well as achieving high gain, an amplifier should be free from distortion and able to operate over a range of frequencies. Practical amplifiers are usually complex circuits, although simple amplifiers can be built from single transistors or valves.

amplitude modulation (AM) method by which radio waves are altered for the transmission of broadcasting signals. AM waves are constant in frequency, but the amplitude of the transmitting wave varies in accordance with the signal being broadcast.

Amritsar industrial city in the Punjab, India; population (1991) 709,000. It is the holy city of ▷Sikhism, with the Guru Nanak University (named after the first Sikh guru), and the Golden Temple, surrounded by the sacred pool Amrita Saras. The Jallianwalah Bagh area of the city was the scene of the ▷Amritsar Massacre in 1919. In 1984, armed Sikh demonstrators were evicted from the Golden Temple by the Indian army, in Operation Bluestar, led by Gen Dayal. Over 300 were killed. Later in 1984, Indian prime minister Indira Gandhi was assassinated in reprisal by Sikh extremists wanting an independent Sikh state in Punjab. The whole of Punjab was put under presidential control in 1987 following riots. Rajiv Gandhi ordered further attacks on the Golden Temple in 1988.

Amritsar Massacre (or **Jallianwalah Bagh massacre**) the killing of 379 Indians (and wounding of 1,200) in ▷Amritsar, at the site of a Sikh religious shrine in the Punjab in 1919. British troops under Gen Edward Dyer opened fire without warning on a crowd of some 10,000, assembled to protest against the arrest of two Indian National Congress leaders (see ▷Congress Party).

Amsterdam official capital of the Netherlands; population (1999 est) 727,000. The Netherlands' second most important port after Rotterdam, Amsterdam is connected to the North Sea by the North Sea Canal, completed in 1876. A new canal leading to the

River Waal, south of Utrecht, was completed in 1952 to improve the connection between Amsterdam and the River Rhine. Industries include diamond cutting and polishing, sugar refining, clothes manufacture, printing, chemicals, shipbuilding, brewing, and distilling. Amsterdam is also an international centre of banking and insurance. The city's rich cultural heritage, including several notable architectural features such as the Royal Palace, completed in 1655, and a number of art galleries and museums, among them the Rijksmuseum, the Vincent Van Gogh Museum, and the Anne Frank house, make it a popular tourist destination. Amsterdam has two universities, the Municipal University and the Free University. An international airport lies to the southwest at Schipol. An underground railway system now extends above ground to Bijlmermeer, a suburban development to the south of the city.

At the beginning of the 13th century, when Giesebrecht II of Amstel built a castle at Amsterdam (which means dam on the Amstel), it was no more than a fishing village. The city became part of Holland in 1317, and passed to the control of the Duke of Burgundy in 1428. It was freed from Spanish domination in 1579. After the golden age of the 17th century it declined in maritime importance. The Prussians occupied the city in 1787, and it was taken by the French in 1795. Louis Bonaparte chose the city as capital of the Netherlands in 1808. Amsterdam was occupied by the Germans during World War II.

Related Web site: Internet Guide to Amsterdam http://www.cwi.nl/~steven/amsterdam.html

AMSTERDAM Aerial view of one of the oldest parts of the city of Amsterdam, Netherlands, near the harbour. *Image Bank*

Amu Darya (or **Amudar'ya**; formerly **Oxus**) river in central Asia, flowing 2,530 km/1,578 mi from the ▷Pamirs to the ▷Aral Sea.

Amundsen, Roald Engelbrecht Gravning (1872–1928) Norwegian explorer who in 1903–06 became the first person to navigate the ▷Northwest Passage. Beaten to the North Pole by US explorer Robert Peary in 1910, he reached the South Pole ahead of Captain Scott in 1911.

In 1918, Amundsen made an unsuccessful attempt to drift across the North Pole in the ship *Maud* and in 1925 tried unsuccessfully to fly from Spitsbergen, in the Arctic Ocean north of Norway, to the Pole by aeroplane. The following year he joined the Italian explorer Umberto Nobile (1885–1978) in the airship *Norge*, which circled the North Pole twice and landed in Alaska. Amundsen was killed in a plane crash over the Arctic Ocean while searching for Nobile and his airship *Italia*.

Related Web site: Amundsen, Roald http://www.south-pole.com/p0000101.htm

Amur river in east Asia, which with its tributary, the Ussuri, forms the boundary between Russia and China for much of its course. Formed by the Argun and Shilka rivers, the Amur flows for over 4,400 km/2,730 mi and enters the Sea of Okhotsk. At its mouth at Nikolevsk it is 16 km/10 mi wide.

amyl alcohol former name for ▷pentanol.

amylase one of a group of ▷enzymes that break down starches into their component molecules (sugars) for use in the body. It occurs widely in both plants and animals. In humans, it is found in saliva and in pancreatic juices.

Human amylase has an optimum pH of 7.2–7.4. Like most enzymes amylase is denatured by temperatures above 60°C.

Anabaptist (Greek 'baptize again') member of any of various 16th-century radical Protestant sects. They believed in adult rather than child baptism, and sought to establish utopian communities. Anabaptist groups spread rapidly in northern Europe, particularly in Germany, and were widely persecuted.

Related Web site: Anabaptist-Mennonite History http://www.anabaptists.org/history/

anabolic steroid any ▷hormone of the ▷steroid group that stimulates tissue growth. Its use in medicine is limited to the treatment of some anaemias and breast cancers; it may help to break up blood clots. Side effects include aggressive behaviour, masculinization in women, and, in children, reduced height.

It is used in sports, such as weightlifting and athletics, to increase muscle bulk for greater strength and stamina, but it is widely condemned because of the side effects. In 1988 the Canadian sprinter Ben Johnson was stripped of an Olympic gold medal for having taken anabolic steroids.

anabolism process of building up body tissue, promoted by the influence of certain hormones. It is the constructive side of ▷metabolism, as opposed to ▷catabolism.

anaconda South American snake *Eunectes murinus*, a member of the python and boa family, the Boidae. One of the largest snakes, growing to 9 m/30 ft or more, it is found in and near water, where it lies in wait for the birds and animals on which it feeds. The anaconda is not venomous, but kills its prey by coiling round it and squeezing until the creature suffocates.

Females are up to 5 times larger than males. They have litters of up to 80 young, born live, and each weighing only 250–300 g. The gestation period last six to eight months, during which time the female will not eat at all.

ANACONDA The anaconda is a climber as well as a swimmer, and may be found in trees along river banks.

anaemia condition caused by a shortage of haemoglobin, the oxygen-carrying component of red blood cells. The main symptoms are fatigue, pallor, breathlessness, palpitations, and poor resistance to infection. Treatment depends on the cause.

Anaemia arises either from abnormal loss or defective production of haemoglobin. Excessive loss occurs, for instance, with chronic slow bleeding or with accelerated destruction (haemolysis) of red blood cells. Defective production may be due to iron deficiency, vitamin B_{12} deficiency (pernicious anaemia), certain blood diseases (sickle-cell disease and thalassaemia), chronic infection, kidney disease, or certain kinds of poisoning. Untreated anaemia taxes the heart and may prove fatal.

anaerobic not requiring oxygen for the release of energy from food molecules such as glucose. Anaerobic organisms include many bacteria, yeasts, and internal parasites. Anaerobic respiration in humans is less efficient than aerobic respiration at releasing energy, but releases energy faster: see ▷respiration.

Obligate anaerobes, such as certain primitive bacteria, cannot function in the presence of oxygen; but **facultative anaerobes**, like the fermenting yeasts and most bacteria, can function with or without oxygen. Anaerobic organisms release much less

of the available energy from their food than do ▷aerobic organisms.

In plants, yeasts, and bacteria, anaerobic respiration results in the production of alcohol and carbon dioxide, a process that is exploited by both the brewing and the baking industries (see ▷fermentation). Normally aerobic animal cells can respire anaerobically for short periods of time when oxygen levels are low, but are ultimately fatigued by the build-up of the lactic acid produced in the process. This is seen particularly in muscle cells during intense activity, when the demand for oxygen can outstrip supply (see ▷oxygen debt).

Although anaerobic respiration is a primitive and inefficient form of energy release, deriving from the period when oxygen was missing from the atmosphere, it can also be seen as an ▷adaptation. To survive in some habitats, such as the muddy bottom of a polluted river, an organism must be to a large extent independent of oxygen; such habitats are said to be **anoxic**.

anaesthetic drug that produces loss of sensation or consciousness; the resulting state is **anaesthesia**, in which the patient is insensitive to stimuli. Anaesthesia may also happen as a result of nerve disorder.

Ever since the first successful operation in 1846 on a patient rendered unconscious by ether, advances have been aimed at increasing safety and control. Sedatives may be given before the anaesthetic to make the process easier. The level and duration of unconsciousness are managed precisely. Where general anaesthesia may be inappropriate (for example, in childbirth, for a small procedure, or in the elderly), many other techniques are available. A topical substance may be applied to the skin or tissue surface; a local agent may be injected into the tissues under the skin in the area to be treated; or a regional block of sensation may be achieved by injection into a nerve. Spinal anaesthetic, such as epidural, is injected into the tissues surrounding the spinal cord, producing loss of feeling in the lower part of the body.

analgesic agent for relieving ▷pain. ▷Opiates alter the perception or appreciation of pain and are effective in controlling 'deep' visceral (internal) pain. Non-opiates, such as ▷aspirin, ▷paracetamol, and NSAIDs (nonsteroidal anti-inflammatory drugs), relieve musculoskeletal pain and reduce inflammation in soft tissues.

Pain is felt when electrical stimuli travel along a nerve pathway, from peripheral nerve fibres to the brain via the spinal cord.

An anaesthetic agent acts either by preventing stimuli from being sent (local), or by removing awareness of them (general). Analgesic drugs act on both.

Temporary or permanent analgesia may be achieved by injection of an anaesthetic agent into, or the severing of, a nerve. Implanted devices enable patients to deliver controlled electrical stimulation to block pain impulses. Production of the body's natural opiates, ▷endorphins, can be manipulated by techniques such as relaxation and biofeedback. However, for the severe pain of, for example, terminal cancer, opiate analgesics are required.

US researchers found in 1996 that some painkillers were more effective and provided longer-lasting relief for women than men.

analogous in biology, term describing a structure that has a similar function to a structure in another organism, but not a similar evolutionary path. For example, the wings of bees and of birds have the same purpose – to give powered flight – but have different origins. Compare ▷homologous.

analogue (of a quantity or device) changing continuously; by contrast, a ▷digital quantity or device varies in series of distinct steps. For example, an analogue clock measures time by means of a continuous movement of hands around a dial, whereas a digital clock measures time with a numerical display that changes in a series of discrete steps.

Most computers are digital devices. Therefore, any signals and data from an analogue device must be passed through a suitable ▷analogue-to-digital converter before they can be received and processed by computer. Similarly, output signals from digital computers must be passed through a ▷digital-to-analogue converter before they can be received by an analogue device.

analogue computer computing device that performs calculations through the interaction of continuously varying physical quantities, such as voltages (as distinct from the more common ▷digital computer, which works with discrete quantities). An analogue computer is said to operate in real time (corresponding to time in the real world), and can therefore be used to monitor and control other events as they happen.

analogue signal in electronics, current or voltage that conveys or stores information, and varies continuously in the same way as the information it represents (compare ▷digital signal). Analogue signals are prone to interference and distortion.

analysis branch of mathematics concerned with limiting processes on axiomatic number systems; ▷calculus of variations and infinitesimal calculus is now called analysis.

analytical chemistry branch of chemistry that deals with the determination of the chemical composition of substances. **Qualitative analysis** determines the identities of the substances in a given sample; **quantitative analysis** determines how much of a particular substance is present.

Simple qualitative techniques exploit the specific, easily observable properties of elements or compounds – for example, the flame test makes use of the different flame colours produced by metal cations when their compounds are held in a hot flame. More sophisticated methods, such as those of ▷spectroscopy, are required where substances are present in very low concentrations or where several substances have similar properties.

Most quantitative analyses involve initial stages in which the substance to be measured is extracted from the test sample, and purified. The final analytical stages (or 'finishes') may involve measurement of the substance's mass (gravimetry) or volume (volumetry, titrimetry), or a number of techniques initially developed for qualitative analysis, such as fluorescence and absorption spectroscopy, chromatography, electrophoresis, and polarography. Many modern methods enable quantification by means of a detecting device that is integrated into the extraction procedure (as in gas–liquid chromatography).

Related Web site: Analytical Chemistry Basics http://www.chem.vt.edu/chem-ed/ac-basic.html

analytical geometry another name for ▷coordinate geometry.

anarchism (Greek *anarkhos* 'without ruler') political belief that society should have no government, laws, police, or other authority, but should be a free association of all its members. It does not mean 'without order'; most theories of anarchism imply an order of a very strict and symmetrical kind, but they maintain that such order can be achieved by cooperation. Anarchism must not be confused with nihilism (a purely negative and destructive activity directed against society); anarchism is essentially a pacifist movement.

Anatolia (Turkish **Anadolu**) Asian part of Turkey, consisting of a mountainous peninsula with the Black Sea to the north, the Aegean Sea to the west, and the Mediterranean Sea to the south.

ANATOLIA Nemrut Dagi in eastern Anatolia, Turkey. Situated on the peak of Nemrut Dagi, at a height of 2,100 m/6,890 ft, are the gigantic mausoleum and stone statues built by Commagene King Antiochus I in the 1st century BC. *Image Bank*

anatomy study of the structure of the body and its component parts, especially the ▷human body, as distinguished from physiology, which is the study of bodily functions.

Herophilus of Chalcedon (*c.* 330–*c.* 260 BC) is regarded as the founder of anatomy. In the 2nd century AD, the Graeco-Roman physician Galen produced an account of anatomy that was the only source of anatomical knowledge until *On the Working of the Human Body* (1543) by Belgian physician Andreas Vesalius. In 1628, English physician William Harvey published his demonstration of the circulation of the blood. With the invention of the microscope, Italian physiologist Marcello Malpighi and Dutch microscopist Anton van Leeuwenhoek were able to found the study of histology. In 1747, Albinus, with the help of the artist Wandelaar, produced the most exact account of the bones and muscles, and in 1757–65 Swiss biologist Albrecht von Haller gave the most complete and exact description of the organs that had yet appeared. Among the anatomical writers of the early 19th century are the surgeon Charles Bell, Jonas Quain, and Henry Gray. Radiographic anatomy (using X-rays; see ▷radiography) has been one of the triumphs of the 20th century, which has also been marked by immense activity in embryological investigation.

Related Web site: Visible Human Project http://www.nlm.nih.gov/research/visible/visible_gallery.html

ANC abbreviation for ▷African National Congress, a South African political party and former nationalist organization.

ancestor worship religious rituals and beliefs oriented towards deceased members of a family or group as a symbolic expression of values or in the belief that the souls of the dead remain involved in this world and are capable of influencing current events.

Anchorage port and largest city in Alaska, USA, at the head of Cook Inlet; population (2000 est) 260,300. It is an important centre of administration, communication, and commerce for much of central and western Alaska. Local industries include oil and gas extraction, tourism, and fish canning.

Anchorage was established in 1914 as the main supply base for the construction of the Alaska railroad to Fairbanks, and during World War II it became the headquarters for the US Alaska Defense Command. Two nearby US military bases, Fort Richardson and Elmendorf Air Force Base, remain important local employers. The Trans-Alaska Oil Pipeline passes through the city.

Related Web site: Anchorage, Alaska http://www.ci.anchorage.ak.us/Anchorage/index.html

anchovy small fish *Engraulis encrasicholus* of the ▷herring family. It is fished extensively, being abundant in the Mediterranean, and is also found on the Atlantic coast of Europe and in the Black Sea. It grows to 20 cm/8 in.

ancien régime the old order; the feudal, absolute monarchy in France before the French Revolution of 1789.

Ancona (Greek *angkon* 'elbow', referring to the town's position on a promontory) Italian city, naval base and ferry port; capital of Marche region, situated on the Adriatic Sea 140 km/87 mi northeast of Rome; population (1992) 100,700. There are shipbuilding, chemical, fishing, and engineering industries here. Ancona has a Romanesque cathedral and a former palace of the popes.

Andalusia (Spanish **Andalucía**) autonomous community of southern Spain, including the provinces of Almería, Cádiz, Córdoba, Granada, Huelva, Jaén, Málaga, and Seville; area 87,300 sq km/33,698 sq mi; population (1996 est) 7,234,900. The Guadalquivir River flows through Andalusia, which is bounded on the north by the Sierra Morena mountain range. The region is fertile, and produces oranges and wine (especially sherry); horses are bred here also, and copper is mined at Rio Tinto. ▷Seville, an inland port, is the administrative capital and the largest industrial centre; Málaga, Cádiz, and Algeciras are the chief ports and also important industrial centres. The Costa del Sol on the south coast has many tourist resorts, including Marbella and Torremolinos; the Sierra Nevada mountain range in the southeast is a winter ski destination.

Andaman and Nicobar Islands two groups of islands in the Bay of Bengal, 1,200 km/745 mi off the east coast of India, forming a Union Territory of the Republic of India; capital Port Blair; area 8,300 sq km/3,204 sq mi; population (2001 est) 381,000. Much of the islands is densely forested and the economy is based on fishing, timber, rubber, fruit, nuts, coffee, and rice.

Andaman Islands group of Indian islands, part of the Union Territory of ▷Andaman and Nicobar Islands.

Andean Indian any indigenous inhabitant of the Andes range in South America, stretching from Ecuador to Peru to Chile, and including both the coast and the highlands. Many Andean civilizations developed in this region from local fishing-hunting-farming societies, all of which predated the ▷Inca, who consolidated the entire region and ruled from about 1200.

The earliest pan-Andean civilization was the Chavin, about 1200–300 BC, which was followed by large and important coastal city-states, such as the Mochica, the Chimú, the Nazca, and the Paracas. The region was dominated by the Tiahuanaco when the Inca started to expand, who took them and outlying peoples into their empire, and imposed the Quechua language on all. It is now spoken by over 10 million people and is a member of the Andean-Equatorial family.

Andersen, Hans Christian (1805–1875) Danish writer of fairy tales. Examples include 'The Ugly Duckling', 'The Snow Queen', 'The Little Mermaid', and 'The Emperor's New Clothes'. Their inventiveness, sensitivity, and strong sense of wonder have given these stories perennial and universal appeal; they have been translated into many languages. He also wrote adult novels and travel books.

Related Web site: Andersen, Hans Christian http://www.math.technion.ac.il/~rl/Andersen/

Anderson, Elizabeth Garrett (1836–1917) English physician, the first English woman to qualify in medicine. Unable to attend medical school, Anderson studied privately and was licensed by the Society of Apothecaries in London in 1865. She was physician to the Marylebone Dispensary for Women and Children (later renamed the Elizabeth Garrett Anderson Hospital).

Andes great mountain system or cordillera that forms the western fringe of South America, extending through some 67° of latitude and the republics of Colombia, Venezuela, Ecuador, Peru, Bolivia, Chile, and Argentina. It is the longest mountain range in the world, 8,000 km/5,000 mi, and its peaks exceed 3,600 m/12,000 ft in height for half that length.

Formation Geologically speaking, the Andes are new mountains, having attained their present height by vertical upheaval of the entire strip of the Earth's crust as recently as the latter part of the Tertiary era and the Quaternary. They have been greatly affected by weathering; rivers have cut deep gorges, and glaciers have produced characteristic valleys. The majority of the individual mountains are volcanic; some are still active.

Peaks The whole system may be divided into two almost parallel ranges. The southernmost extremity is Cape Horn, but the range extends into the sea and forms islands. Among the highest peaks are Cotopaxi (5,897 m/19,347 ft) and Chimborazo (6,310 m/20,702 ft) in Ecuador, Cerro de Pasco (4,602 m/15,098 ft) and El Misti (5,822 m/19,101 ft) in Peru, Illampu (6,450 m/21,161 ft) and Illimani (6,451 m/21,164 ft) in Bolivia, Cerro Aconcagua (6,960 m/22,834 ft) (the highest mountain in the Western hemisphere) in Argentina, and Ojos del Salado (6,908 m/22,664 ft) in Chile.

Conditions Andean mineral resources include gold, silver, tin, tungsten, bismuth, vanadium, copper, and lead. Difficult communications make mining expensive, and for a long time pack animals were the chief form of transport, but air transport has since greatly reduced the difficulties. Three railways cross the Andes: from Valparaíso (Chile) to Buenos Aires (Argentina), from Antofagasta (Chile) to Salta (Argentina), and Antofagasta via Uyuni (Bolivia) to Asunción (Paraguay).

The majority of the sparse population is dependent on agriculture, the nature and products of which vary with the natural environment. Latitudinal and altitudinal influences, topography and ocean currents play an important role in controlling local climate. For example, the cold ▷Peru Current creates cloudy, but dry conditions forming the characteristic arid/desert areas off the west coast. Oscillations in the Pacific Ocean circulation, however, bring heavy rains and floods to these areas – the ▷*El Niño* effect occurs about every 5–8 years. Given the variability of the climate, agricultural conditions have been adapted to suit local conditions and irrigation is common. Potatoes are cultivated often up to altitudes of 4,000 m/13,120 ft on impressive terraces. In the higher regions llamas and alpacas are herded. On the coast fish and cotton are the dominant agricultural products. Wine production is becoming increasingly important for many countries and regions, most especially Chile.

Newcomers to the Andean plateau, which includes Lake ▷Titicaca, suffer from *puna*, mountain sickness, but indigenous peoples have hearts and lungs adapted to altitude. The main headstreams of the River Amazon rise in the Peruvian Andes.

Roads and national parks The Pan-American Highway ends at Yaviza, southeastern Panama – the Darién Gap section is not yet complete. The section remaining passes through dense tropical rainforest, which since 1980 has been declared a World Heritage site and international biosphere reserve by the United Nations Educational, Scientific, and Cultural Organization. The Darién National Park (the Parque Nacional del Darién) established by Panama covers 90% of the frontier region with Colombia. Colombia has established an equivalent park/reserve called 'Parque Nacional Los Katiós'. Together they form the largest national park in Central America.

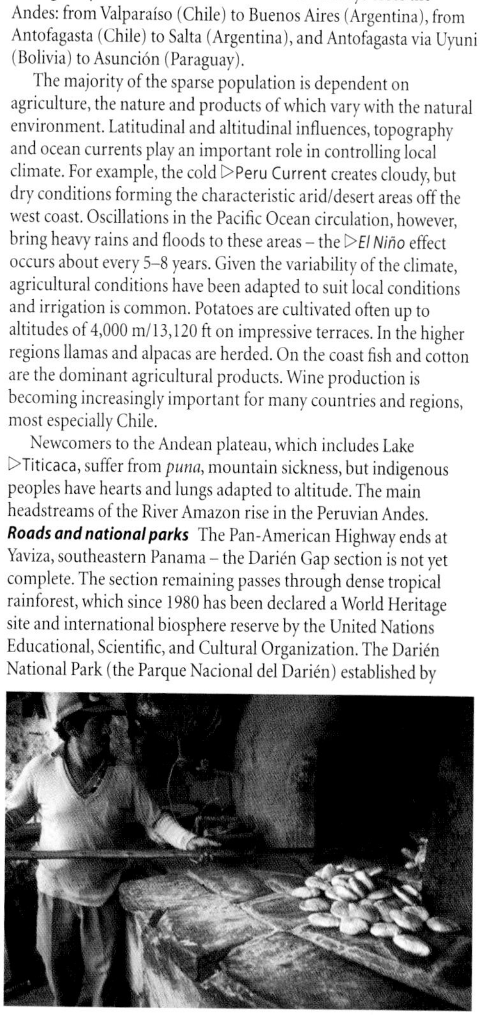

ANDES A baker in the mountainous Andes region of Peru, baking the traditional *oropesa* bread. *Image Bank*

Related Web site: Andean History http://www.ddg.com/LIS/aurelia/andhis.htm

andesite volcanic igneous rock, intermediate in silica content between rhyolite and basalt. It is characterized by a large quantity of feldspar ▷minerals, giving it a light colour. Andesite erupts from volcanoes at destructive plate margins (where one plate of the Earth's surface moves beneath another; see ▷plate tectonics), including the Andes, from which it gets its name.

Andhra Pradesh state in east central India; area 275,100 sq km/106,216 sq mi; population (2001 est) 81,293,000. The main cities and towns are ▷Hyderabad (capital), Secunderabad, Visakhapatnam, Vijayawada, Kakinda, Guntur, and Nellore. The state is situated on coastal plains with extensive river valleys (Krishna and Godavari) reaching into the Eastern Ghats; smaller rivers are the Pennar and Cheyyar; the Deccan plateau lies inland. The main industries are mica, coal, iron ore, oil refining, shipbuilding, and fertilizers; the main agricultural products are rice, millet, sugar cane, tobacco, groundnuts, sorghum, and cotton. The languages spoken are Telugu, Urdu, and Tamil.

Ando, Tadao (1941–) Japanese architect. His work employs vernacular materials and styles alongside modernist techniques. His design for Azuma House in Osaka, Japan, in 1975, one in a series of private houses, combines an austere, fortresslike facade with a minutely detailed interior. Materials such as timber and concrete are sensitively used, continuing the traditions of Japanese domestic architecture.

Andorra see country box.

Andrea del Sarto (1486–1530) Born Andrea d'Agnolo di Francesco. Italian Renaissance painter. Active in Florence, he was one of the finest portraitists and religious painters of his time. His frescoes in Florence, such as the *Birth of the Virgin* (1514; Sta Annunziata), rank among the greatest of the Renaissance. His style is serene and noble, characteristic of High Renaissance art.

Andreotti, Giulio (1919–) Italian Christian Democrat politician, a fervent European. He headed seven post-war governments: 1972–73, 1976–79 (four successive terms), and 1989–92 (two terms). In addition he was defence minister eight times, and foreign minister five times. In 1993 Andreotti was among several high-ranking politicians accused of possible involvement in Italy's corruption network; he went on trial in September 1995 charged with using his influence to protect Mafia leaders in exchange for political support. He was acquitted in October 1999.

Andrew, St (lived 1st century AD) New Testament apostle and patron saint of Scotland and Greece. According to tradition, he went with John to Ephesus, preached in Scythia, and was martyred at Patrai in Greece on an X-shaped cross (St Andrew's cross). Feast day 30 November.

A native of Bethsaida, he was Simon Peter's brother. With Peter, James, and John, who worked with him as fishers at Capernaum, he formed the inner circle of Jesus' 12 disciples.

Some time before the 8th century bones claimed to be his were brought to St Andrews in Scotland. The X-shaped cross represents Scotland in the Union Jack.

Andrew (Andrew Albert Christian Edward) (1960–) Prince of the UK, Duke of York, second son of Queen Elizabeth II. He married Sarah Ferguson in 1986; their first daughter, Princess Beatrice, was born in 1988, and their second daughter, Princess Eugenie, was born in 1990. The couple separated in 1992 and were officially divorced in May 1996. Prince Andrew was a naval helicopter pilot and served during the Falklands War, and in 1999 accepted a naval post in international relations.

Andrew, Rob (Christopher Robert) (1963–) English rugby union player. He was England's record points scorer with 396 points in 71 internationals between 1985 and 1997, until he was surpassed by Jonny Wilkinson, but he remains second in the all-time points list. He also played five times for the British Lions, and is the most capped stand-off in international rugby. Renowned for his all-round kicking skills, his 23 drop goals are an international record.

Related Web site: Andrew, Rob http://web.onyxnet.co.uk/Tony Kirlew-onyxnet.co.uk/playerRobAndrew.htm

Andrews, Julie (1935–) Stage name of Julia Elizabeth Wells. English-born US actor and singer. She was the original Eliza Doolittle in the Broadway production of Lerner and Loewe's musical *My Fair Lady* (1956), and also appeared in their *Camelot* (1960). She is particularly associated with the hit film *The Sound of Music* (1965).

androecium male part of a flower, comprising a number of ▷stamens.

androgen general name for any male sex hormone, of which ▷testosterone is the most important.

They are all ▷steroids and are principally involved in the production of male ▷secondary sexual characteristics (such as beard growth).

Andromache in Greek mythology, the loyal wife of ▷Hector and mother of Astyanax. After the fall of Troy she was awarded to Neoptolemus, Achilles' son; she later married a Trojan seer called Helenus. Andromache is the heroine of Homer's *Iliad* and the subject of a play by ▷Euripides.

Andromeda major constellation of the northern hemisphere, visible in autumn. Its main feature is the Andromeda galaxy. The star Alpha Andromedae forms one corner of the Square of Pegasus. It is named after the princess of Greek mythology.

Andromeda galaxy galaxy 2.2 million light years away from Earth in the constellation Andromeda, and the most distant object visible to the naked eye. It is the largest member of the Local Group of galaxies.

Like the Milky Way, it is a spiral orbited by several companion galaxies but contains about twice as many stars as the Milky Way. It is about 200,000 light years across.

Andropov, Yuri (1914–1984) Soviet communist politician, president of the USSR 1983–84. As chief of the KGB 1967–82, he established a reputation for efficiently suppressing dissent.

anemometer device for measuring wind speed and liquid flow. The most basic form, the **cup-type anemometer**, consists of cups at the ends of arms, which rotate when the wind blows. The speed of rotation indicates the wind speed.

Vane-type anemometers have vanes, like a small windmill or propeller, that rotate when the wind blows. **Pressure-tube anemometers** use the pressure generated by the wind to indicate speed. The wind blowing into or across a tube develops a pressure, proportional to the wind speed, that is measured by a manometer or pressure gauge. **Hot-wire anemometers** work on the principle that the rate at which heat is transferred from a hot wire to the surrounding air is a measure of the air speed. Wind speed is determined by measuring either the electric current required to maintain a hot wire at a constant temperature, or the variation of resistance while a constant current is maintained.

anemone flowering plant belonging to the buttercup family, found in northern temperate regions, mainly in woodland. It has ▷sepals which are coloured to attract insects. (Genus *Anemone*, family Ranunculaceae.)

anemophily type of ▷pollination in which the pollen is carried on the wind. Anemophilous flowers are usually unscented, have either very reduced petals and sepals or lack them altogether, and do not produce nectar. In some species they are borne in ▷catkins. Male and female reproductive structures are commonly found in separate flowers. The male flowers have numerous exposed stamens, often on long filaments; the female flowers have long, often branched, feathery stigmas.

aneroid barometer kind of ▷barometer.

aneurysm weakening in the wall of an artery, causing it to balloon outwards with the risk of rupture and serious, often fatal, blood loss. If detected in time, some accessible aneurysms can be repaired by bypass surgery, but such major surgery carries a high risk for patients in poor health.

Angad (1504–1552) Indian religious leader, second guru (teacher) of Sikhism 1539–52, succeeding Nanak. He popularized the alphabet known as Gurmukhi, in which the Sikh scriptures are written.

angel (Greek *angelos* 'messenger') in Jewish, Christian, and Muslim belief, a supernatural being intermediate between God and humans. The Christian hierarchy has nine orders, from the top down: Seraphim, Cherubim, Thrones (who contemplate God and reflect his glory), Dominations, Virtues, Powers (who regulate the stars and the universe), Principalities, Archangels, and Angels (who minister to humanity). In traditional Catholic belief every human being has a guardian angel. The existence of angels was reasserted by Pope John Paul II in 1986.

> ### G C Lichtenberg
> German physicist and philosopher
>
> *If an angel were ever to tell us anything of his philosophy I believe many propositions would sound like 2 times 2 equals 13.*
>
> Aphorisms, 'Notebook B' 44

Angel Falls waterfall on the River Caroní in the tropical rainforest of Bolívar Region, southeast Venezuela. It is the highest cataract in the world with a total height of 978 m/ 3,210 ft. The falls plunge from the lip of the Auyán–Tepúplateau (Guinana Highlands). They were named after the aviator and prospector James Angel who flew over the falls and crash-landed nearby in 1935.

angelfish any of a number of unrelated fishes. The freshwater angelfish, genus *Pterophyllum*, of South America, is a tall, side-to-side flattened fish with a striped body, up to 26 cm/10 in long, but usually smaller in captivity. The angelfish or monkfish of the genus *Squatina* is a bottom-living shark up to 1.8 m/6 ft long with a body flattened from top to bottom. The marine angelfishes, *Pomacanthus* and others, are long narrow-bodied fish with spiny fins, often brilliantly coloured, up to 60 cm/2 ft long, living around coral reefs in the tropics.

    Related Web site: Angelfish http://www.actwin.com/fish/species/ angelfish.html

angelica any of a group of tall, perennial herbs with divided leaves and clusters of white or greenish flowers, belonging to the carrot family. Most are found in Europe and Asia. The roots and fruits have long been used in cooking and in medicine. (Genus *Angelica*, family Umbelliferae.)

Angelico, Fra (c. 1400–1455) Born Guido di Pietro. Italian painter. He was a monk, active in Florence, and painted religious scenes. His series of frescoes at the monastery of San Marco, Florence, was begun after 1436. He also produced several altarpieces in a style characterized by a delicacy of line and colour.

Andorra

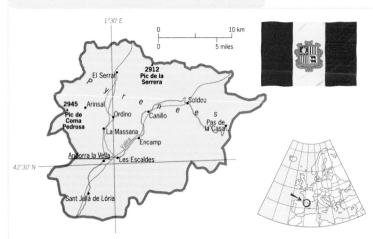

NATIONAL NAME *Principat d'Andorra/Principality of Andorra*
AREA 468 sq km/181 sq mi
CAPITAL Andorra la Vella
MAJOR TOWNS/CITIES Les Escaldes, Escaldes-Engordany (a suburb of the capital)
PHYSICAL FEATURES mountainous, with narrow valleys; the eastern Pyrenees, Valira River

ANDORRA Andorra is one of the smallest independent countries. Tobacco is the most important industry, both in the growing of tobacco and the manufacture of cigarettes. Its capital, Andorra la Vella, shown here, has also become an important tourist centre. *Andorra Tourist Board*

Government

HEADS OF STATE Joan Enric Vivez i Sicilia (bishop of Urgel, Spain; from 2003) and Jacques Chirac (president of France; from 1995)
HEAD OF GOVERNMENT Marc Forné Molné from 1994
POLITICAL SYSTEM emergent democracy
POLITICAL EXECUTIVE parliamentary
ADMINISTRATIVE DIVISIONS seven parishes
ARMED FORCES no standing army
DEATH PENALTY abolished in 1990
HEALTH SPEND (% GDP) 7.9 (2000 est)

Andorra landlocked country in the east Pyrenees, bounded north by France and south by Spain.

Economy and resources

CURRENCY euro
GPD (US$) 1.3 billion (2000)
REAL GDP GROWTH (% change on previous year) 3.7 (1999)
GNI (US$) 1.2 billion (2000)
GNI PER CAPITA (PPP) (US$) 19,370 (2000)
CONSUMER PRICE INFLATION 3.4% (2002 est)
UNEMPLOYMENT 0% (1997 est).
MAJOR TRADING PARTNERS Spain, France, USA
RESOURCES iron, lead, aluminium, hydroelectric power
INDUSTRIES cigar and cigarette manufacturing, textiles, leather goods, wood products, processed foodstuffs, furniture, tourism, banking and financial services
EXPORTS cigars and cigarettes, furniture, electricity. Principal market: Spain 60.9% (2000)
IMPORTS foodstuffs, electricity, mineral fuels. Principal source: Spain 48.6% (2000)
ARABLE LAND 2.3% (2000 est)
AGRICULTURAL PRODUCTS tobacco, potatoes, rye, barley, oats, vegetables; livestock rearing (mainly sheep) and timber production

Population and society

POPULATION 71,000 (2003 est)
POPULATION GROWTH RATE 34.1% (2000–05)
POPULATION DENSITY (per sq km) 157 (2003 est)
URBAN POPULATION (% of total) 92 (2003 est)
AGE DISTRIBUTION (% of total population) 0–14 16%, 15–59 70%, 60+ 14% (2001 est)
ETHNIC GROUPS 20% Andorrans, 44% Spanish, 11% Portuguese, 7% French, 18% other
LANGUAGE Catalan (official), Spanish, French
RELIGION Roman Catholic (92%)
EDUCATION (compulsory years) 10
LITERACY RATE 99% (men); 99% (women) (2003 est)
LABOUR FORCE 1% agriculture, 21% industry, 78% services (1998)
LIFE EXPECTANCY 81 (men); 87 (women) (2001 est)
CHILD MORTALITY RATE (under 5, per 1,000 live births) 7 (2001)
PHYSICIANS (per 1,000 people) 2.5 (1998 est)
TV SETS (per 1,000 people) 440 (1999 est)
RADIOS (per 1,000 people) 238 (1997)
INTERNET USERS (per 10,000 people) 897.4 (2000)

Chronology

AD 803: Holy Roman Emperor Charlemagne liberated Andorra from Muslim control.

819: Louis I 'the Pious' the son of Charlemagne, granted control over the area to the Spanish bishop of Urgel.

1278: A treaty was signed making Spanish bishop and French count joint rulers of Andorra. Through marriage the king of France later inherited the count's right.

1806: After a temporary suspension during the French Revolution, from 1789 the feudal arrangement of dual allegiance to the French and Spanish rulers was re-established by Napoleon Bonaparte.

1976: The first political organization, the Democratic Party of Andorra, was formed.

1981: The first prime minister was appointed by the General Council.

1991: Links with the European Community (EC) were formalized.

1993: A new constitution legalized political parties and introduced the first direct elections. Andorra became a member of the United Nations (UN).

1994: Andorra joined the Council of Europe.

1997: The 'Partit Liberal Andorra' (PLA; Liberal Party of Andorra) won an assembly majority in a general election.

2001: In general elections, PLA retained power.

Fra Angelico joined the Dominican order in about 1420. After his novitiate, he resumed a career as a painter of religious images and altarpieces, many of which have small predella scenes beneath them, depicting events in the life of a saint. The central images of the paintings are highly decorated with pure, bright colours and gold-leaf designs, while the predella scenes are often lively and relatively unsophisticated. There is a similar simplicity to his frescoes in the cells at San Marco, which are principally devotional works. Fra Angelico's later fresco sequences, *Scenes from the Life of Christ* (Orvieto Cathedral) and *Scenes from the Lives of SS Stephen and Lawrence* (1440s; chapel of Nicholas V, Vatican Palace), are more elaborate.

Angelou, Maya (1928–) Born Marguerite Annie Johnson. US writer and black activist. She became noted for her powerful autobiographical works, *I Know Why the Caged Bird Sings* (1970) and its four sequels up to *All God's Children Need Travelling Shoes* (1986). Based on her traumatic childhood, they tell of the struggles towards physical and spiritual liberation of a black woman from growing up in the South to emigrating to Ghana.

Maya Angelou
Children's talent to endure stems from their ignorance of alternatives.
I Know Why the Caged Bird Sings ch. 17 (1969)

Angers ancient French city and administrative centre of Maine-et-Loire *département*, situated on the River Maine just north of its conjunction with the Loire and just south of its conjunction with the Mayenne; population (1990) 146,100. Its main products include electrical machinery, wine, and Cointreau liqueur. It is a bishopric with a 12th–13th-century Gothic cathedral. The 12th–13th-century castle is a tourist attraction.

Angevin term used to describe the English kings Henry II and Richard I (also known, with the later English kings up to Richard III, as the Plantagenets). Angevin derives from Anjou, a region in northwestern France. The Angevin Empire comprised the territories (including England) that belonged to the Anjou dynasty.

angina (or **angina pectoris**) severe pain in the chest due to impaired blood supply to the heart muscle because a coronary artery is narrowed. Faintness and difficulty in breathing accompany the pain. Treatment is by drugs or bypass surgery.

angiosperm flowering plant in which the seeds are enclosed within an ovary, which ripens into a fruit. Angiosperms are divided into ▷monocotyledons (single seed leaf in the embryo) and ▷dicotyledons (two seed leaves in the embryo). They include the majority of flowers, herbs, grasses, and trees except conifers.

ANGLING Trout fishing is a popular form of recreational fishing. In the UK, some of the best wild brown trout fishing is to be found in the lochs of north and northwest Scotland, with the optimum period being May to July. Some of the best rivers for brown trout fishing are the Don, the Tay, and the Tweed, all of which also have salmon runs. *Image Bank*

Ang Lee (1954–) Taiwanese film director, screenwriter, and producer. He has enjoyed critical and commercial success with his comedies of manners *The Wedding Banquet* (1993) and *Eat Drink Man Woman* (1994), and subsequently the English-language *Sense and Sensibility* (1995), based on the actor Emma Thompson's adaptation of the Jane Austen novel. In 1997 he directed *The Ice Storm*. In 2000 he directed the Oscar-winning *Crouching Tiger, Hidden Dragon*.

Angle member of the Germanic tribe that occupied the Schleswig-Holstein district of North Germany known as Angeln. The Angles, or Angli, invaded Britain after the Roman withdrawal in the 5th century and settled in East Anglia, Mercia, and Northumbria. The name 'England' (Angleland) is derived from this tribe. See ▷Anglo-Saxon.

angle in mathematics, the amount of turn or rotation; it may be defined by a pair of rays (half-lines) that share a common endpoint but do not lie on the same line. Angles are measured in ▷degrees (°) or ▷radians (rads) – a complete turn or circle being 360° or 2π rads.

Angles are classified generally by their degree measures: **acute angles** are less than 90°; **right angles** are exactly 90° (a quarter turn); **obtuse angles** are greater than 90° but less than 180° (a straight line); **reflex angles** are greater than 180° but less than 360°. Angles that add up to 180° are called **supplementary angles**.

Angles in triangles A triangle has three interior angles which together add up to 180°. In an equilateral triangle these angles are equal (60°). The exterior angles of a triangle (those produced if one side is extended beyond the triangle) are equal to the sum of the opposite internal angles. Unknown angles in a right-angled triangle can be worked out using ▷trigonometry.

Angles in polygons Regular polygons have three types of angle: interior, exterior, and the angle at the centre (produced when a triangle is drawn inside the polygon, with the centre as its apex and one side of the polygon as its base). The angle at the centre is equal to the exterior angle and it is found by dividing 360° by the number of sides in the polygon. For example, the angle at the centre of an octagon is 45° (360 ÷ 8).

angle of declination angle at a particular point on the Earth's surface between the direction of the true or geographic North Pole and the magnetic north pole. The angle of declination has varied over time because of the slow drift in the position of the magnetic north pole.

angler any of an order of fishes Lophiiformes, with flattened body and broad head and jaws. Many species have small, plantlike tufts on their skin. These act as camouflage for the fish as it waits, either floating among seaweed or lying on the sea bottom, twitching the enlarged tip of the threadlike first ray of its dorsal fin to entice prey.

Anglesey (Welsh Ynys Môn (island); **Sir Ynys Môn** (authority)) island and unitary authority off the northwest coast of Wales.

area 720 sq km/278 sq mi (34 km/21 mi long and 31 km/19 mi broad) **towns** Llangefni (administrative headquarters), Holyhead, Beaumaris, Amlwch **features** separated from the mainland by the Menai Strait, which is crossed by the Britannia tubular railway bridge and Telford's suspension bridge, originally built between 1819 and 1826 but rebuilt since; rich fauna, notably bird life, and flora; many buildings and relics of historic interest **industries** manufacture of toys and electrical goods; bromine extraction from the sea **agriculture** sheep farming, varied agriculture **population** (1996) 71,100

The port of Holyhead, on the adjoining Holy Island, has an aluminium smelting plant and a ferry service to Ireland. The Wylfa nuclear power station is located 10 km/6 mi west of Amlwch. Lead, copper, and zinc were once mined here. Anglesey was the ancient granary of Wales.

Anglican Communion family of Christian churches including the ▷Church of England, the US Episcopal Church, and those holding the same essential doctrines, that is the Lambeth Quadrilateral 1888 Holy Scripture as the basis of all doctrine, the Nicene and Apostles' Creeds, Holy Baptism and Holy Communion, and the historic episcopate.

Anglicanism see ▷Anglican Communion.

angling fishing with rod and line. It is widespread and ancient in origin, fish hooks having been found in prehistoric cave dwellings. Competition angling exists and world championships take place for most branches of the sport.

The oldest is the World Freshwater Championship, inaugurated in 1957.

Related Web site: Fishing.co.uk http://www.fishing.co.uk/

Anglo-American War war between the USA and Britain 1812–1814; see ▷War of 1812.

Anglo-Catholicism in the Anglican Church, the Catholic heritage of faith and liturgical practice which was stressed by the founders of the ▷Oxford Movement. The term was first used in 1838 to describe the movement, which began in the wake of pressure from the more Protestant wing of the Church of England. Since the Church of England voted in 1992 to ordain women as priests, some Anglo-Catholics have found it difficult to remain within the Church of England.

Anglo-Irish Agreement (or **Hillsborough Agreement**) concord reached in 1985 between the UK prime minister Margaret Thatcher and Irish prime minister Garret FitzGerald. One sign of the improved relations between the two countries was increased cooperation between police and security forces across the border between Northern Ireland and the Republic of Ireland.

The pact also gave the Irish Republic a greater voice in the conduct of Northern Ireland's affairs. However, the agreement was rejected by Northern Ireland Unionists as a step towards renunciation of British sovereignty. Following further talks in March 1988, the UK and Irish prime ministers issued a joint statement in Northern Ireland. The statement did not envisage any particular outcome, but specified that the consent of the majority of the people of Northern Ireland was required before there could be any constitutional change.

All-party peace talks were planned during the IRA ceasefire from 1994 to 1996, but were delayed by the IRA's unwillingness to decommission its arms prior to full British troop withdrawal from Northern Ireland. After the ceasefire was restored in July 1997, multiparty peace talks on the future of Northern Ireland started in September 1997.

Anglo-Saxon one of several groups of Germanic invaders (including Angles, Saxons, and Jutes) that conquered much of Britain between the 5th and 7th centuries. Initially they established conquest kingdoms, commonly referred to as the Heptarchy; these were united in the early 9th century under the overlordship of Wessex. The Norman invasion in 1066 brought Anglo-Saxon rule to an end.

The Jutes probably came from the Rhineland and not, as was formerly believed, from Jutland. The Angles and Saxons came from Schleswig-Holstein, and may have united before invading. The Angles settled largely in East Anglia, Mercia, and Northumbria; the Saxons in Essex, Sussex, and Wessex; and the Jutes in Kent and southern Hampshire.

There was probably considerable intermarriage with the Romanized Celts of ancient Britain, although the latter's language and civilization almost disappeared. The English-speaking peoples of Britain, the Commonwealth, and the USA are often referred to today as Anglo-Saxons, but the term is inaccurate, as the Welsh, Scots, and Irish are mainly of Celtic or Norse descent, and by the 1980s fewer than 15% of US citizens were of British descent.

Anglo-Saxon art English art from the late 5th century to the 11th century. Sculpted crosses and ivories, manuscript painting, and gold and enamel jewellery survive, demonstrating a love of intricate, interwoven designs. The relics of the ▷Sutton Hoo ship burial (7th century) and the *Lindisfarne Gospels* (about 690; British Museum, London) have typical Celtic ornamental patterns. In the manuscripts of southern England, in particular those produced at Winchester and Canterbury, a different style emerged in the 9th century, with delicate, lively pen-and-ink figures and heavily decorative foliage borders.

Anglo-Saxon Chronicle a history of England from the Roman invasion to the 11th century, consisting of a series of chronicles written in Old English by monks, begun in the 9th century (during the reign of King Alfred), and continuing until 1154.

The Chronicle, comprising seven different manuscripts, forms a unique record of early English history and also of the development of Old English prose up to its final stages. By 1154 Old English had been superseded by Middle English.

Related Web site: Anglo-Saxon Chronicle http://sunsite.berkeley.edu/OMACL/Anglo/

Anglo-Saxon language group of dialects, also known as Old English, spoken between the 5th and 12th centuries by peoples of Saxon origin who invaded and settled in central and southern England in the 5th–7th centuries; thus the term properly does not include the language of the Angles who settled in the areas to the north. See ▷Old English; ▷Old English literature; and ▷English language.

Anglo-Saxon literature another name for ▷Old English literature.

Angola see country box.

Angora earlier form of ▷Ankara, Turkey, which gave its name to the Angora goat (see ▷mohair), and hence to other species of long-haired animal, such as the Angora rabbit (a native of the island of Madeira) and the Angora cat. Angora 'wool' from these animals has long, smooth fibres, and the demand for the fibre has led to wool farming in Europe, Japan, and the USA.

Angry Young Men journalistic term applied to a loose group of British writers who emerged in the 1950s after the creative hiatus that followed World War II. They revolted against the prevailing social mores, class distinction, and 'good taste'. Their dissatisfaction was expressed in works such as Kingsley Amis's *Lucky Jim* (1954), John ▷Osborne's *Look Back in Anger* (1956), Colin Wilson's *The Outsider* (1956), John Braine's *Room at the Top* (1957), and John Wain's *Hurry on Down* (1953).

angstrom unit (symbol Å) of length equal to 10^{-10} metres or one-ten-millionth of a millimetre, used for atomic measurements and the wavelengths of electromagnetic radiation. It is named after the Swedish scientist A J Ångström.

Ångström, Anders Jonas (1814–1874) Swedish astrophysicist who worked in spectroscopy and solar physics. In 1861 he identified the presence of hydrogen in the Sun. His outstanding *Recherches sur le spectre solaire* (1868) presented an atlas of the solar spectrum with measurements of 1,000 spectral lines expressed in units of one-ten-millionth of a millimetre, the unit which later became the angstrom.

Anguilla island in the eastern Caribbean; area 160 sq km/62 sq mi; population (2000) 11,800. Anguilla is a popular tourist destination because of its white coral-sand beaches. However, 80% of its coral reef has been lost through tourism (pollution and souvenir sales). Its main exports include lobster and salt. The currency used is the East Caribbean dollar. It has been a separate dependency of the UK since 1980, with its capital being The Valley. Both English and Creole languages are spoken.

A British colony from 1650, Anguilla was long associated with St Christopher–Nevis but revolted against alleged domination by the larger island and seceded in 1967. A small British force restored order in 1969, and Anguilla retained a special position at its own request; since 1980 it has been a separate dependency of the UK. From 1982, the government has consisted of the governor, executive council, and legislative house of assembly.

Related Web site: Anguilla http://www.umsl.edu/services/govdocs/wofact96/16.htm

Angus unitary authority on the east coast of Scotland. A former county, it was part of Tayside region 1975–96.

area 2,187 sq km/844 sq mi **towns** Arbroath, Brechin, Carnoustie, Forfar (administrative headquarters), Kirriemuir, and Montrose **physical** the ▷Grampian Mountains in the north are dissected by the fertile valleys of the rivers Isla, Clova, Prosen, Water of Saughs, and North Esk; the wide Vale of Strathmore separates the Grampian Mountains from the low-lying Sidlaw Hills in the south **features** Pictish and Iron Age remains **industries** textiles, light engineering (declining), fish processing **agriculture** some fishing (mainly in Arbroath), cereal production **population** (1996) 111,300

Anhui (or Anhwei) province of eastern China, bounded to the north by Shandong, to the east by Jiangsu, to the southeast by Zhejiang, to the south by Jiangxi, to the southwest by Hubei, and to the northwest by Henan provinces; area 139,900 sq km/54,000 sq mi; population (1996) 60,700,000. Anhui is an intensively cultivated province, with grain the most important crop. Its capital is ▷Hefei, while important towns and cities include Anqing, Bengbu, Huainan, and Wuhu.

Related Web site: Brief Introduction to Anhui Province http://www.wtci.org/mdsisters/province_of_anhui.htm

anhydride chemical compound obtained by the removal of water from another compound; usually a dehydrated acid. For example, sulphur(VI) oxide (sulphur trioxide, SO_3) is the anhydride of sulphuric acid (H_2SO_4).

aniline (Portuguese *anil* 'indigo') $C_6H_5NH_2$ or phenylamine one of the simplest aromatic chemicals (a substance related to benzene, with its carbon atoms joined in a ring). When pure, it is a colourless

Angola

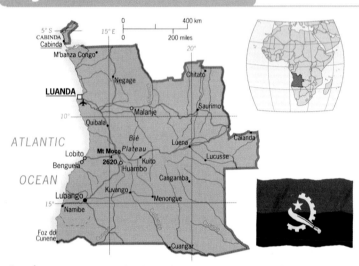

Angola country in southwest Africa, bounded west by the Atlantic ocean, north and northeast by Congo (formerly Zaire), east by Zambia, and south by Namibia. The Cabinda enclave, a district of Angola, is bounded west by the Atlantic Ocean, north by the Congo River, and east and south by Congo.

NATIONAL NAME *República de Angola*/Republic of Angola
AREA 1,246,700 sq km/481,350 sq mi
CAPITAL Luanda (and chief port)
MAJOR TOWNS/CITIES Lobito, Benguela, Huambo, Lubango, Malanje, Namibe, Kuito
MAJOR PORTS Huambo, Lubango, Malanje
PHYSICAL FEATURES narrow coastal plain rises to vast interior plateau with rainforest in northwest; desert in south; Cuanza, Cuito, Cubango, and Cunene rivers

Government

HEAD OF STATE José Eduardo dos Santos from 1979
HEAD OF GOVERNMENT Fernando da Piedade Dias dos Santos from 2002
POLITICAL SYSTEM emergent democracy
POLITICAL EXECUTIVE limited presidency
ADMINISTRATIVE DIVISIONS 18 provinces
ARMED FORCES 100,000; plus paramilitary forces of 10,000 (2002 est)

ANGOLA A stamp from Angola. With its long Atlantic coastline, Angola has several major ports, which play an important part in international trade. *Stanley Gibbons*

CONSCRIPTION military service is compulsory for two years
DEATH PENALTY abolished in 1992
DEFENCE SPEND (% GDP) 9.8 (2002 est)
EDUCATION SPEND (% GDP) 2.7 (2001 est)
HEALTH SPEND (% GDP) 3.6 (2000 est)

Economy and resources

CURRENCY kwanza
GPD (US$) 11.4 billion (2002 est)
REAL GDP GROWTH (% change on previous year) 3.3 (2001)
GNI (US$) 9.2 billion (2002 est)
GNI PER CAPITA (PPP) (US$) 1,730 (2002 est)
CONSUMER PRICE INFLATION 109% (2002 est)
UNEMPLOYMENT 55% (2001)
FOREIGN DEBT (US$) 8.1 billion (2001 est)
MAJOR TRADING PARTNERS Portugal, USA, South Africa, Germany, France, Brazil, the Netherlands, China, Taiwan
RESOURCES petroleum, diamonds, granite, iron ore, marble, salt, phosphates, manganese, copper
INDUSTRIES mining, petroleum refining, food processing, textiles, construction materials
EXPORTS petroleum and petroleum products, diamonds, gas. Principal market: USA 60% (1999)
IMPORTS foodstuffs, transport equipment, base metals, electrical equipment. Principal source: Portugal 19% (1999)
ARABLE LAND 2.4% (2000 est)

AGRICULTURAL PRODUCTS coffee, sugar cane, bananas, cassava, maize, sweet potatoes

Population and society

POPULATION 13,625,000 (2003 est)
POPULATION GROWTH RATE 2.7% (2000–15)
POPULATION DENSITY (per sq km) 11 (2003 est)
URBAN POPULATION (% of total) 36 (2003 est)
AGE DISTRIBUTION (% of total population) 0–14 48%, 15–59 48%, 60+ 4% (2002 est)
ETHNIC GROUPS nine main ethnic groups (Bakongo, Quimbundo, Lunda-Quioco (or Tchokwe), Ovimnundo, Ganguela, Nhaneca-Huambe, Ambo, Herero and the Xindonga), and about 100 subgroups. A major exodus of Europeans in the 1970s left around 30,000, mainly Portuguese. 2% mestizo (mixed European and Native American), 1% European

LANGUAGE Portuguese (official), Bantu, other native dialects
RELIGION Roman Catholic 38%, Protestant 15%, animist 47%
EDUCATION (compulsory years) 8
LITERACY RATE 56% (men); 28% (women) (1998 est)
LABOUR FORCE 71.8% agriculture, 7.1% industry, 21.1% services (2000)
LIFE EXPECTANCY 37 (men); 42 (women) (2000–05)
CHILD MORTALITY RATE (under 5, per 1,000 live births) 260 (2001)
PHYSICIANS (per 1,000 people) 0.08 (1997 est)
TV SETS (per 1,000 people) 19 (2001 est)
RADIOS (per 1,000 people) 74 (2001 est)
INTERNET USERS (per 10,000 people) 29.4 (2002 est)
PERSONAL COMPUTER USERS (per 100 people) 0.2 (2002 est)

See also ▷UNITA.

Chronology

14th century: The powerful Kongo kingdom controlled much of northern Angola.

early 16th century: The Kongo ruler King Afonso I adopted Christianity and sought relations with Portuguese traders.

1575 and 1617: Portugal secured control over the ports of Luanda and Benguela and began to penetrate inland, meeting resistance from Queen Nzinga, the Ndonga ruler.

17th–18th centuries: Inland, the Lunda peoples established powerful kingdoms that stretched into southern Congo. The Portuguese made Angola a key centre for the export of slaves; over 1 million were shipped to Brazil 1580–1680.

1836: The slave trade was officially abolished.

1885–1915: Military campaigns were waged by Portugal to conquer the interior.

1951: Angola became an overseas territory of Portugal.

1956: The People's Movement for the Liberation of Angola (MPLA), a socialist guerrilla independence movement based in the Congo, was formed.

1961: 50,000 people were massacred in rebellions on coffee plantations. Forced labour was abolished. There was an armed struggle for independence.

1962: The National Front for the Liberation of Angola (FNLA), a nationalist guerrilla movement, was formed.

1966: The National Union for the Total Independence of Angola (UNITA) was formed in southeastern Angola as a breakaway from the FNLA.

1975: Independence from Portugal was achieved. The MPLA (backed by Cuba) proclaimed the People's Republic of Angola. The FNLA and UNITA (backed by South Africa and the USA) proclaimed the People's Democratic Republic of Angola.

1976: The MPLA gained control of most of the country. South African troops withdrew, but Cuban units remained as the civil war continued.

1980: UNITA guerrillas, aided by South Africa, continued raids against the government and bases of the Namibian South West Africa People's Organization (SWAPO) in Angola.

1988: A peace treaty providing for the withdrawal of all foreign troops was signed with South Africa and Cuba.

1989: A ceasefire agreed with UNITA broke down and guerrilla activity resumed.

1991: A peace agreement ended the civil war. An amnesty was declared for all political prisoners, and there was a new multiparty constitution.

1992: A MPLA general election victory was fiercely disputed by UNITA, and plunged the country into renewed civil war.

1993: The MPLA government was recognized by the USA. United Nations (UN) sanctions were imposed against UNITA.

1994: A peace treaty was signed by the government and UNITA representatives.

1995: UN peacekeepers were drafted in.

1996: UNITA leader Jonas Savimbi rejected an offer of the vice presidency.

1997: A national unity government was eventually sworn in but was boycotted by Savimbi.

1998: UNITA was demilitarized and transformed into a political party, but after UNITA was accused of massacres, UNITA ministers were suspended and the peace process threatened.

2000: Fighting between government forces and UNITA rebels continued in the south and east.

2002: UNITA leader Jonas Savimbi was killed in combat. The government signed a ceasefire agreement with UNITA, which reorganized itself as a political party.

oily liquid; it has a characteristic odour, and turns brown on contact with air. It occurs in coal tar, and is used in the rubber industry and to make drugs and dyes. It is highly poisonous.

Aniline was discovered in 1826, and was originally prepared by the dry distillation of ▷indigo, hence its name.

animal (or **metazoan**; Latin *anima* 'breath', 'life') member of the ▷kingdom Animalia, one of the major categories of living things, the science of which is **zoology**. Animals are all multi-cellular ▷heterotrophs (they obtain their energy from organic substances produced by other organisms); they have eukaryotic cells (the genetic material is contained within a distinct nucleus) which are bounded by a thin cell membrane rather than the thick cell wall of plants. Most animals are capable of moving around for at least part of their life cycle.

In the past, it was common to include the single-celled ▷protozoa with the animals, but these are now classified as protists, together with single-celled plants. Thus all animals are multicellular. The oldest land animals known date back 440 million years. Their remains were found 1990 in a sandstone deposit near Ludlow, Shropshire, UK, and included fragments of two centipedes a few centimetres long and a primitive spider measuring about 1 mm.

Related Web site: Electronic Zoo http://netvet.wustl.edu/e-zoo.htm

animal liberation loose international movement against the infliction of suffering on animals, whether for scientific, military, or commercial research, or in being raised for food. The movement was sparked by the book *Animal Liberation* (1975) by Australian philosopher Peter Singer (1946–) and encompasses many different organizations.

animism in anthropology, the belief that everything, whether animate or inanimate, possesses a soul or spirit. It is a fundamental system of belief in certain religions, particularly those of some pre-industrial societies. Linked with this is the worship of natural objects such as stones and trees, thought to harbour spirits (naturism); fetishism; and ancestor worship.

anion ion carrying a negative charge. During electrolysis, anions in the electrolyte move towards the anode (positive electrode).

An electrolyte, such as the salt zinc chloride ($ZnCl_2$), is dissociated in aqueous solution or in the molten state into doubly charged Zn^{2+} zinc ▷cations and singly-charged Cl^- anions. During electrolysis, the zinc cations flow to the cathode (to become discharged and liberate zinc metal) and the chloride anions flow to the anode (to become discharged and form chlorine gas).

anise Mediterranean plant belonging to the carrot family, with small creamy-white flowers in clusters; its fragrant seeds, similar to liquorice in taste, are used to flavour foods. Aniseed oil is used in cough medicines. (*Pimpinella anisum*, family Umbelliferae.)

Anjou former province of northern France. Its capital was ▷Angers, and it is now covered by the *département* of Maine-et-Loire and parts of Indre-et-Loire, Mayenne, and Sarthe. In 1154 the count of Anjou became king of England as Henry II, but in 1204 the territory was lost by King John to Philip Augustus of France. In 1480 Anjou was annexed to the French crown. The people are called ▷Angevins, a name also applied by the English to the first three ▷Plantagenet kings.

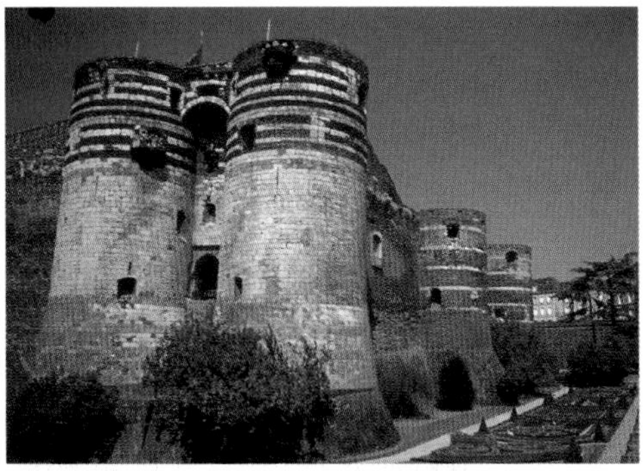

ANJOU The 13th-century moated castle of Angers, in Anjou, western France. *Corel*

Ankara (formerly **Angora**) capital of Turkey; population (1990) 2,559,500. Industries include cement, textiles, and leather products. It replaced Istanbul (then in Allied occupation) as capital in 1923.

Anna Comnena (1083–after 1148) Byzantine historian, daughter of the emperor ▷Alexius I. After a number of abortive attempts to alter the imperial succession in favour of her husband, Nicephorus Bryennius (*c.* 1062–1137), she retired to a convent to write her major work, the *Alexiad*, the history of her father's reign. It describes the Byzantine view of public office, as well as the religious and intellectual life of the period.

Annaba (formerly **Bône**; 'city of jujube trees') seaport in Algeria; population (1991 est) 343,000. It is situated in Annaba department close to the Tunisian border. Major industries include an iron and steel complex, railway workshops, and aluminium and chemical works. Iron ore, phosphates, and other minerals, extracted in Tébessa to the southeast, are exported, as are wine and cork.

Annam former country of Southeast Asia, incorporated in Vietnam in 1946 as Central Vietnam. Its capital was Hué. A Bronze Age civilization was flourishing in the area when China conquered it in about 111 BC. The Chinese named their conquest An-Nam, 'peaceful south'. Independent from 1428, Annam signed a treaty with France in 1787 and became a French protectorate, part of Indochina in 1884. During World War II, Annam was occupied by Japan.

Annamese the majority ethnic group in Vietnam, comprising 90% of the population. The Annamese language is distinct from Vietnamese, though it has been influenced by Chinese and has loan words from Khmer. Their religion combines elements of Buddhism, Confucianism, and Taoism, as well as ancestor worship.

Annan, Kofi (1938–) Ghanaian diplomat, secretary general of the United Nations (UN) from 1997. Heading the peacekeeping department of the UN from 1993, he oversaw its peacekeeping operations in Somalia from 1993 and in Bosnia-Herzegovina from 1995. He was re-elected in 2001, and in the same year shared the Nobel Prize for peacekeeping with the UN itself.

Annan was the son of a Fante tribal chief. He gained a management degree from the Massachusetts Institute of Technology (MIT), USA, and went on to become a diplomat after joining the World Health Organization (WHO) in 1962. He was elected secretary general of the UN after the USA vetoed the re-election of Boutros Boutros-Ghali. In February 1998 he negotiated an agreement with Iraq to allow UN inspectors unrestricted access to supposed chemical and biological weapon sites. In December 1999 an independent UN inquiry published a report into Annan's failure as head of peacekeeping to stop the genocide in Rwanda in 1994.

Kofi Annan

I am a cheerleader, I am a promoter, I am a salesman, I am a debt collector, I am a father confessor, and there are aspects I still have to discover.

On his first 13 months in the job, *Time*, 9 March 1998

Annapolis seaport and capital of ▷Maryland, USA, near the mouth of the River Severn on Chesapeake Bay; seat of Anne Arundel County; population (1996) 33,200. Annapolis, whose industries include radar equipment, is a commercial centre for the surrounding agricultural area, and its waterside setting and historic buildings make it a popular recreational and tourist area, lying as it does only 40 km/25 mi from both Washington and Baltimore. Founded in 1694 as the capital of colonial Maryland, Annapolis was named after Princess (later Queen) Anne in 1697, and incorporated as a city in 1796.

Annapurna mountain 8,075 m/26,502 ft in the Himalayas, Nepal. The north face was first climbed by a French expedition (Maurice Herzog) in 1950 and the south by a British team in 1970.

Anne (1665–1714) Queen of Great Britain and Ireland 1702–14. She was the second daughter of James, Duke of York, who became James II, and his first wife, Anne Hyde, daughter of Edward Hyde, Earl of Clarendon. She succeeded William III in 1702. Events of her reign include the War of the ▷Spanish Succession, Marlborough's victories at Blenheim, Ramillies, Oudenarde, and Malplaquet, and the union of the English and Scottish parliaments in the 1707 Act of ▷Union.

Anne received a Protestant upbringing, and in 1683 married Prince George of Denmark (1653–1708). Of their many children only one survived infancy: William, Duke of Gloucester (1689–1700). For the greater part of her life Anne was a close friend of Sarah Churchill (1650–1744), the wife of John Churchill (1650–1722), afterwards created 1st Duke of ▷Marlborough in 1702. The Churchills' influence was partly responsible for her desertion of her father for William of Orange, her brother-in-law, later William III, during the ▷Glorious Revolution of 1688. The Churchills' influence later also led her to engage in Jacobite intrigues. Although her sympathies were Tory, she accepted a predominantly Whig government 1704–10. The influence of the Churchills began to decline from 1707. After a violent quarrel in 1710, Sarah Churchill was dismissed from court, and Abigail Masham succeeded the duchess as Anne's favourite, using her influence to further the Tories.

Anne (Anne Elizabeth Alice Louise) (1950–) Princess of the UK, second child of Queen Elizabeth II, declared Princess Royal in 1987. She is actively involved in global charity work, especially for children. An excellent horse rider, she won silver medals in both individual and team events in the 1975 European Championships, and competed in the 1976 Olympics.

In 1973 she married Capt Mark Phillips (1949–); they separated in 1989 and were divorced in 1992. In December 1992 she married Commander Timothy Laurence. Her son Peter (1977–) was the first direct descendant of the Queen not to bear a title. She also has a daughter, Zara (1981–).

annealing controlled cooling of a material to increase ductility and strength. The process involves first heating a material (usually glass or metal) for a given time at a given temperature, followed by slow cooling. It is a common form of ▷heat treatment.

annelid any segmented worm of the phylum Annelida. Annelids include earthworms, leeches, and marine worms such as lugworms.

They have a distinct head and soft body, which is divided into a number of similar segments shut off from one another internally by membranous partitions, but there are no jointed appendages.

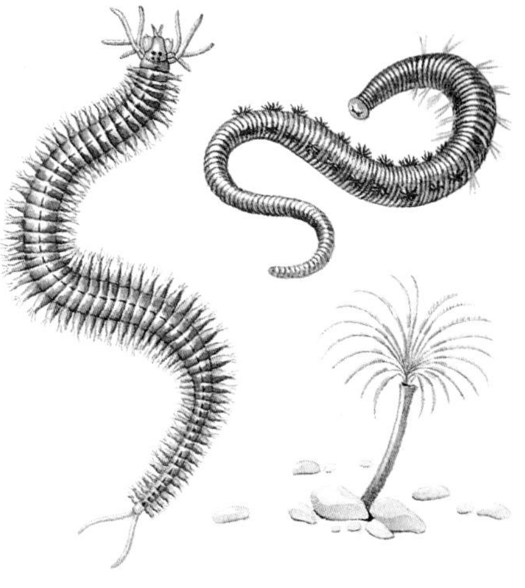

ANNELID The ragworm, lugworm, and peacock worm shown here are all marine species of annelids (segmented worms).

Annelids are noted for their ability to regenerate missing parts of their bodies.

Anne of Austria (1601–1666) Queen of France from 1615 and regent 1643–61. Daughter of Philip III of Spain, she married Louis XIII of France (whose chief minister, Cardinal Richelieu, worked against her). On her husband's death she became regent for their son, Louis XIV, until his majority.

Anne of Cleves (1515–1557) Fourth wife of ▷Henry VIII of England, whom she married in 1540. She was the daughter of the Duke of Cleves, and was recommended to Henry as a wife by Thomas ▷Cromwell, who wanted an alliance with German Protestantism against the Holy Roman Empire. Henry did not like her looks, had the marriage declared void after six months, pensioned her, and had Cromwell beheaded.

Anne of Denmark (1574–1619) Queen consort of James VI of Scotland (from 1603 ▷James I of England). She was the daughter of Frederick II of Denmark and Norway, and married James in 1589. She bore him five children, two of whom survived: Charles I and Elizabeth of Bohemia. Anne was suspected of Catholic leanings and was notably extravagant but seems to have had little influence on state affairs.

annihilation in nuclear physics, a process in which a particle and its 'mirror image' particle called an antiparticle collide and disappear, with the creation of a burst of energy. The energy created is equivalent to the mass of the colliding particles in accordance with the ▷mass–energy equation. For example, an electron and a positron annihilate to produce a burst of high-energy X-rays. Not all particle–antiparticle interactions result in annihilation; the exception concerns the group called ▷mesons, which belong to the class of particles that are composed of ▷quarks and their antiquarks. See ▷antimatter.

anno Domini (Latin 'in the year of our Lord') in the Christian chronological system, refers to dates since the birth of Jesus, denoted by the letters AD. There is no year 0, so AD 1 follows immediately after the year 1 BC (before Christ). The system became the standard reckoning in the Western world after being adopted by English historian Bede in the 8th century. The abbreviations CE (Common Era) and BCE (before Common Era) are often used instead by scholars and writers as objective, rather than religious, terms.

anno hegirae (Latin 'year of the flight') first year of the Muslim calendar, the year of the flight of Muhammad from Mecca to Medina in 622. In dates it is often abbreviated to AH.

annual percentage rate (APR) the true annual rate of ▷interest charged for a loan. Lenders usually increase the return on their money by compounding the interest payable on a loan to that loan on a monthly or even daily basis. This means that each time that interest is payable on a loan it is charged not only on the initial sum (principal) but also on the interest previously added to that principal. As a result, APR is usually approximately double the flat rate of interest, or simple interest.

annual plant plant that completes its life cycle within one year, during which time it germinates, grows to maturity, bears flowers, produces seed, and then dies.

annual rings (or **growth rings**) concentric rings visible on the wood of a cut tree trunk or other woody stem. Each ring represents a period of growth when new ▷xylem is laid down to replace tissue being converted into wood (secondary xylem). The wood formed from xylem produced in the spring and early summer has larger and more numerous vessels than the wood formed from xylem produced in autumn when growth is slowing down. The result is a clear boundary between the pale spring wood and the denser, darker autumn wood. Annual rings may be used to estimate the age of the plant (see ▷dendrochronology), although occasionally more than one growth ring is produced in a given year.

Annunciation in the New Testament, the announcement to Mary by the archangel Gabriel that she was to be the mother of Christ; the feast of the Annunciation is 25 March (also known as Lady Day).

anode in chemistry, the positive electrode of an electrolytic ▷cell, towards which negative particles (anions), usually in solution, are attracted. See ▷electrolysis.

anodizing process that increases the resistance to ▷corrosion of a metal, such as aluminium, by building up a protective oxide layer on the surface. The natural corrosion resistance of aluminium is provided by a thin film of aluminium oxide; anodizing increases the thickness of this film and thus the corrosion protection.

anorexia lack of desire to eat, or refusal to eat, especially the pathological condition of anorexia nervosa, most often found in adolescent girls and young women. Compulsive eating, or ▷bulimia, distortions of body image, and depression often accompany anorexia.

Anorexia nervosa is characterized by severe self-imposed restriction of food intake. The consequent weight loss may lead, in women, to absence of menstruation. Anorexic patients sometimes commit suicide. Anorexia nervosa is often associated with increased physical activity and symptoms of mental disorders. Psychotherapy is an important part of the treatment.

Anouilh, Jean (1910–1987) French dramatist. His plays, which are often studies in the contrast between purity and cynical worldliness, include *Antigone* (1944), *L'Invitation au château/Ring Round the Moon* (1947), *Colombe* (1950), and *Becket* (1959), about St Thomas à Becket and Henry II.

Jean Anouilh
Beauty is one of the rare things that do not lead to doubt of God.
Becket Act 1

Anselm, St (*c.* 1033–1109) Italian priest and philosopher. He was born in Piedmont and educated at the abbey of Bec in Normandy, which, as abbot from 1078, he made a centre of scholarship in Europe. He was appointed archbishop of Canterbury by William II of England in 1093, but was later forced into exile. He holds an important place in the development of ▷scholasticism. Feast day 21 April.

Anshan (or **An-shan**) city in Liaoning province, 89 km/55 mi southeast of Shenyang; population (1994) 1,430,000. The iron and steel centre started here in 1918 was expanded by the Japanese, dismantled by the Russians, and restored by the communist government of China. It produces some 8 million tonnes of steel annually. Other products include chemicals, tractors, and machinery.

ant insect belonging to the family Formicidae, and to the same order (Hymenoptera) as bees and wasps. Ants are characterized by a conspicuous waist and elbowed antennae. About 10,000 different species are known; all are social in habit, and all construct nests of various kinds. Ants are found in all parts of the world, except the polar regions. It is estimated that there are about 10 million billion ants.

Ant behaviour is complex, and serves the colony rather than the individual. Ants find their way by light patterns, gravity (special sense organs are located in the joints of their legs), and chemical trails between food areas and the nest.

Specialized roles Communities include **workers**, sterile, wingless females, often all alike, although in some species large-headed 'soldiers' are differentiated; **fertile females**, fewer in number and usually winged; and **males**, also winged and smaller than their consorts, with whom they leave the nest on a nuptial flight at certain times of the year. After aerial mating, the males die, and the fertilized queens lose their wings when they settle, laying eggs to found their own new colonies. The eggs hatch into wormlike larvae, which then pupate in silk cocoons before emerging as adults.

Remarkable species Some species conduct warfare. Others are pastoralists, tending herds of ▷aphids and collecting a sweet secretion ('honeydew') from them. Army (South American) and driver (African) ants march nomadically in huge columns, devouring even tethered animals in their path. Leaf-cutter ants, genus *Atta*, use pieces of leaf to grow edible fungus in underground 'gardens' which can be up to 5 m/16 ft deep and cover hundreds of square metres. Weaver ants, genus *Oecophylla*, use their silk-producing larvae as living shuttles to bind the edges of leaves together to form the nest. Eurasian robber ants *Formica sanguinea* raid the nests of another ant species, *Formica fusca*, for pupae, then use the adults as 'slaves' when they hatch. Among honey ants, some workers serve as distended honey stores.

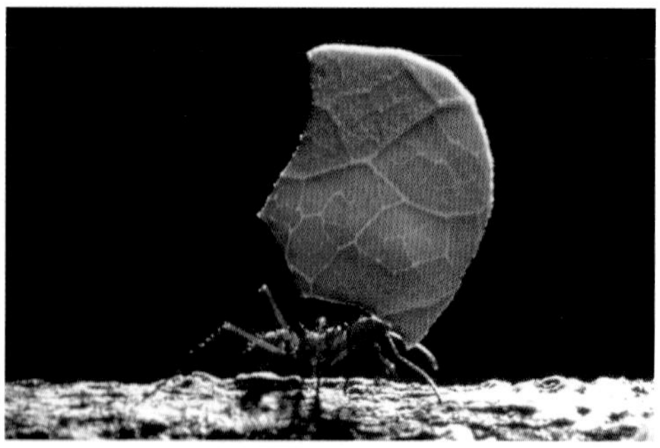

ANT This leaf-cutter ant is at work in Costa Rica, carrying a piece of leaf. Leaf-cutter ants store the pieces underground, where an edible fungus grows upon them. These so-called 'gardens' can cover hundreds of square metres.
Image Bank

antacid any substance that neutralizes stomach acid, such as sodium bicarbonate or magnesium hydroxide ('milk of magnesia'). Antacids are weak ▷bases, swallowed as solids or emulsions. They may be taken between meals to relieve symptoms of hyperacidity, such as pain, bloating, nausea, and 'heartburn'. Excessive or prolonged need for antacids should be investigated medically.

Antall, József (1932–1993) Hungarian politician, prime minister 1990–93. He led the centre-right Hungarian Democratic Forum (MDF) to electoral victory in April 1990, becoming Hungary's first post-communist prime minister. He promoted gradual, and successful, privatization and encouraged inward foreign investment.

Antalya Mediterranean port on the west coast of Turkey and capital of a province of the same name; population (1990) 378,200. The port trades in grain and timber. Industries include canning and flour milling. It is a popular coastal resort.

Antananarivo (formerly **Tananarive**) capital and administrative centre of Madagascar, on the interior plateau, with a rail link to Tamatave; population (1993) 1,052,800. Industries include food processing, leather goods, clothing, wood pulp and paper manufacturing, and brewing.

Antarctica continent surrounding the South Pole, arbitrarily defined as the region lying south of the Antarctic Circle. Occupying 10% of the world's surface, it is almost one-and-a-half times the size of the USA. Antarctica contains 90% of the world's ice, representing nearly three-quarters of its fresh water. It is thought that if all the ice suddenly melted, the world sea level would rise by 60 m/197 ft.

area 13,000,000 sq km/5,019,300 sq mi; ice shelves which fill the surrounding seas add a further 1,300,000 sq km/501,930 sq mi to this figure **features** Mount Erebus on Ross Island is the world's southernmost active volcano; the Ross Ice Shelf is formed by several glaciers coalescing in the Ross Sea **physical** Antarctica can be divided into two regions, separated by the Transantarctic Mountains, which extend for 3,500 km/2,175 mi and whose peaks, many of them exceeding 3,000 m/9,850 ft in height, protrude through the ice. The larger region, known as Greater or East Antarctica, is comprised of ancient rocks lying mostly at sea level, which are approximately 3,800 million years old. In contrast, Lesser or West Antarctica is 150–200 million years old and has mountain ranges buried under the ice. These include the Antarctic Peninsular and the Ellsworth Mountains, in which the highest peak in Antarctica, the Vinson Massif, is located; height 5,140 m/16,863 ft. The few peaks that are visible above the ice are known as nunataks. Two vast seas, the Ross Sea and the Weddell Sea, cut into the continent. Between them lies the mountainous Antarctic Peninsula, which was originally connected to South America before continental drift **population** no permanent residents and no indigenous inhabitants; settlement limited to scientific research stations with maximum population of 10,000 (including 3,000 tourists) during the summer months. Sectors of Antarctica are claimed by Argentina, Australia, Chile, France, the UK, Norway, and New Zealand **Antarctic ice** Around 2% of the land is ice free. With an estimated volume of 30 million cu km/7.2 million cu mi, the ice-cap has an average thickness of approximately 2,000 m/6,600 ft, in places reaching depths of 4,000 m/13,000 ft or more. Each annual layer of snow preserves a record of global conditions, and where no melting at the surface of the bedrock has occurred the ice can be a million years old. The snow in the Antarctic rarely melts but accumulates into massive ice caps. As the ice caps grow, the weight of the ice squeezes the ice cap sideways towards the coast, where ice shelves extend out into the surrounding seas. These fringing ice shelves are broken up by ocean tides and waves, creating icebergs. Solid ice attached to the Antarctic landmass is known as fast ice. If the ice forms a ridge more than 2 m/6.6 ft above sea level, it is known as an ice shelf. Pack ice is a mixture of ice floes in water. A lead is a navigable passage through pack ice. A polyna is a small area of open water surrounded by ice. The Antarctic Convergence is the point at which colder water from Antarctica meets and flows beneath warmer subantarctic water. The position of the Convergence may vary by up to 100 km/62 mi **climate** The combination of cold air, high winds, and blowing snow makes Antarctica's climate the severest in the world. The location of Antarctica at the south pole results in only small amounts of energy being received from the sun. The temperatures are consequently very low. The Antarctic continent is surrounded by the Southern Ocean, which creates a physical barrier between Antarctica and the warmer seas and lands to the north. This creates a refrigeration of the Antarctic. It is the coldest continent on Earth, with a mean annual temperature at the South Pole of −49°C/−56°F. In 1983 a temperature of −89°C/−128°F was recorded in Antarctica at the Russian base Vostok, the lowest ever in the world. Precipitation is largely in the form of snow or hoar-frost rather than rain, which rarely exceeds 50 mm/2 in per year (less than the Sahara Desert). The minimal snow fall makes Antarctica one of the most arid deserts on Earth. Dry valleys are unique areas that remain snow-free all the year round because of the katabatic winds that remove moisture. The Antarctic summer (the period during which the ice melts) has lengthened from 60 to 90 days since the 1970s. The average temperature on the Antarctic Peninsula has risen by approximately 2.5°C/4.5°F since monitoring started in the 1950s, a result of the ▷greenhouse effect **flora and fauna** The Antarctic ecosystem is characterized by large numbers of relatively few species of higher plants and animals, and a short food chain from tiny marine plants to whales, seals, penguins, and other sea birds. Plant life is rich in the Sub-Antarctic islands but is practically nonexistent in continental Antarctica. Only two species of flowering plant are known: the Antarctic pearlwort and the Antarctic hairgrass, both of which are rapidly increasing. There are about 85 species of moss, 200 species of lichen, and over 400 species of algae. As the Antarctic ice shelves disintegrate with the lengthening summers, new lichens are appearing in soil uncovered by the retreating glaciers. There are five animal species which breed ashore during the winter months: emperor penguins, king penguins, wandering albatross, grey petrel, and the grey-winged petrel. The emperor penguin breeds under the most extreme environmental conditions of any vertebrate animal. There are only 67 species of insect; the largest in Antarctica is a midge measuring 12 mm/0.5 in. There are no native land mammals (the Arctic has 40); no resident land birds (the Arctic has 8); and fewer than 50 species of seabirds, only 13 of which breed in Antarctica. Because of the cold conditions, animals live longer, produce fewer eggs, and protect them for longer. The oceans around the Antarctic contain relatively few fish; it is estimated that there are six times as many squid by weight in Antarctic seas as fish. Three-quarters of the Antarctic fish belong to the order *Nototheniidae*, comprising five families, of which four are found only in Antarctica, reflecting the need for specialization to survive in such hostile conditions. Most of them are deepwater fish. There is a high level of parental care, unusual in fish. Fish have low levels of haemoglobin, and some have a specialized 'antifreeze' glycoprotein in their blood, which lowers its freezing point, enabling them to survive without freezing in the sea at −1.9°C/28.6°F. Large creatures on the Antarctic seabed, discovered in the late 1990s, include: isopods up to 17 cm/7 in long; sea spiders up to 33 cm/13 in (1,000 times larger than European sea spiders); ribbon worms 3 m/10 ft long; and a sponge 3 m/10 ft tall **products** Cod, Antarctic icefish, and krill are fished in Antarctic waters. Whaling, which began in the early 20th century, ceased during the 1960s as a result of overfishing, although Norway and Iceland defied the ban in 1992 and recommenced whaling. Petroleum, coal, and minerals such as palladium and platinum exist, but their exploitation is prevented by a 50-year ban on commercial mining, agreed by 39 nations in 1991. **exploration** The first person to explore Antarctica was Captain James Cook, who reached 70° 10′ South in 1774; the most southerly point to which a ship had ever sailed. In 1775 Cook took possession of the Isle of Georgia and reached the ▷South Sandwich Islands. In 1819 William Smith landed on and claimed for the UK the ▷South Shetland Islands.

Related Web site: Antarctica http://www.umsl.edu/services/govdocs/wofact96/17.htm

Antarctic Circle imaginary line that encircles the South Pole at latitude 66° 32′ S. The line encompasses the continent of Antarctica and the Antarctic Ocean.

Antarctic Ocean popular name for the reaches of the Atlantic, Indian, and Pacific oceans extending south of the Antarctic Circle (66° 32′S). The term is not used by the International Hydrographic Bureau.

Antarctic Territory, Australian islands and territories south of 60° south, between 160° and 45° east longitude, excluding Adélie Land; area 6,044,000 sq km/2,333,600 sq mi of land and 75,800 sq km/29,259 sq mi of ice shelf. The population on the Antarctic continent is limited to scientific personnel.

Antarctic Territory, British British dependent territory created in 1961 and comprising all British territories south of latitude 60° south and between 20° and 80° west longitude, including the South Orkney Islands, the South Shetland Islands, the Antarctic Peninsula and all adjacent lands, and Coats Land, extending to the South Pole; total land area 1,810,000 sq km/700,000 sq mi; population (exclusively scientific personnel) *c.* 300.

Antarctic Treaty international agreement between 13 nations aiming to promote scientific research and keep Antarctica free from conflict, dating from 1961. In 1991 a 50-year ban on mining activity was secured. An environmental protection protocol, addressing the issues of wildlife conservation, mineral exploitation, and marine pollution, came into effect in January 1998 after it was ratified by Japan. Antarctica is now a designated 'natural reserve devoted to peace and science'.

Antares (or Alpha Scorpii) brightest star in the constellation Scorpius and the 15th-brightest star in the night sky. It is a red supergiant several hundred times larger than the Sun and perhaps 10,000 times as luminous. It lies about 420 light years away from the Sun, and varies in brightness.

anteater mammal of the family Myrmecophagidae, order Edentata, native to Mexico, Central America, and tropical South America. The anteater lives almost entirely on ants and termites. It has toothless jaws, an extensile tongue, and claws for breaking into the nests of its prey.

Species include the giant anteater *Myrmecophaga tridactyla*, about 1.8 m/6 ft long including the tail, the tamandua or collared anteater *Tamandua tetradactyla*, about 90 cm/3.5 ft long, and the silky anteater *Cyclopes didactyla*, about 35 cm/14 in long. The name is also incorrectly applied to the aardvark, the echidna, and the pangolin.

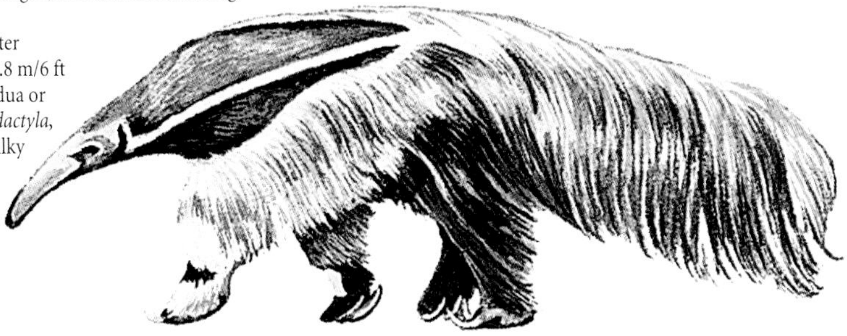

ANTEATER The anteater is a relative of the sloths, armadillos, and pangolins. There are four species, native to South and Central America. The giant anteater *Myrmecophaga tridactyla* is 1.8 m/6 ft long with an elongated face, hairy coat, and bushy tail.

antebellum (Latin *ante bellum* 'before the war') in US usage, an adjective referring to the period just before the Civil War (1861–65).

antelope any of numerous kinds of even-toed, hoofed mammals belonging to the cow family, Bovidae. Most antelopes are lightly built and good runners. They are grazers or browsers, and chew the cud. They range in size from the dik-diks and duikers, only 30 cm/1 ft high, to the eland, which can be 1.8 m/6 ft at the shoulder.

The majority of antelopes are African, including the eland, wildebeest, kudu, springbok, and waterbuck, although other species live in parts of Asia, including the deserts of Arabia and the Middle East. The pronghorn antelope *Antilocapra americana* of North America belongs to a different family, the Antilocapridae.

antenatal in medicine, before birth. Antenatal care refers to health services provided to ensure the health of pregnant women and their babies.

antenna in radio and television, another name for ▷aerial.

antenna in zoology, an appendage ('feeler') on the head. Insects, centipedes, and millipedes each have one pair of antennae but there are two pairs in crustaceans, such as shrimps. In insects, the antennae are involved with the senses of smell and touch; they are frequently complex structures with large surface areas that increase the ability to detect scents.

anthem in music, a short, usually elaborate, religious choral composition, sometimes accompanied by the organ; also a song of loyalty and devotion.

anther in a flower, the terminal part of a stamen in which the ▷pollen grains are produced. It is usually borne on a slender stalk or filament, and has two lobes, each containing two chambers, or pollen sacs, within which the pollen is formed.

antheridium organ producing the male gametes, ▷antherozoids, in algae, bryophytes (mosses and liverworts), and pteridophytes (ferns, club mosses, and horsetails). It may be either single-celled, as in most algae, or multicellular, as in bryophytes and pteridophytes.

antherozoid motile (or independently moving) male gamete produced by algae, bryophytes (mosses and liverworts), pteridophytes (ferns, club mosses, and horsetails), and some gymnosperms (notably the cycads). Antherozoids are formed in an antheridium and, after being released, swim by means of one or more flagella, to the female gametes. Higher plants have nonmotile male gametes contained within ▷pollen grains.

Anthony, St (*c.* 251–356) Also known as Anthony of Thebes. Egyptian founder of Christian monasticism. At the age of 20, he renounced all his possessions and began a hermetic life of study and prayer, later seeking further solitude in a cave in the desert.

Anthony, Susan B(rownell) (1820–1906) US pioneering campaigner for women's rights who also worked for the antislavery and temperance movements. Her causes included equality of pay for women teachers, married women's property rights, and women's suffrage. In 1869, with Elizabeth Cady ▷Stanton, she founded the National Woman Suffrage Association.

> **Susan Anthony**
> *The true Republic: men, their rights and nothing more; women, their rights and nothing less.*
> Motto of her newspaper *Revolution*

anthracite (from Greek *anthrax* 'coal') hard, dense, shiny variety of ▷coal, containing over 90% carbon and a low percentage of ash and impurities, which causes it to burn without flame, smoke, or smell, and giving off relatively little sulphur dioxide.

anthrax disease of livestock, occasionally transmitted to humans, usually via infected hides and fleeces. It may also be used as a weapon in biological warfare. It may develop as black skin pustules or severe pneumonia. Treatment is with antibiotics. Vaccination is effective.

anthropoid (Greek *anthropos* 'man', *eidos* 'resemblance') any primate belonging to the suborder Anthropoidea, including monkeys, apes, and humans.

anthropology (Greek *anthropos* 'man', *logos* 'discourse') the study of humankind. It investigates the cultural, social, and physical diversity of the human species, both past and present. It is divided into two broad categories: biological or physical anthropology, which attempts to explain human biological variation from an evolutionary perspective; and the larger field of social or cultural anthropology, which attempts to explain the variety of human cultures. This differs from sociology in that anthropologists are concerned with cultures and societies other than their own.

Biological anthropology Biological anthropology is concerned with human ▷palaeontology, primatology, human adaptation, ▷demography, population genetics, and human growth and development.

Social anthropology Social or cultural anthropology is divided into three subfields: social or cultural anthropology proper, ▷prehistory or prehistoric archaelogy, and anthropological linguistics. The term 'anthropology' is frequently used to refer solely to social anthropology. With a wide range of theoretical perspectives and topical interests, it overlaps with many other disciplines. It is a uniquely Western social science.

Participant observation Anthropology's primary method involves the researcher living for a year or more in another culture, speaking the local language and participating in all aspects of everyday life; and writing about it afterwards. By comparing these accounts, anthropologists hope to understand who we are.

anthropomorphism (Greek *anthropos* 'man', *morphe* 'shape') the attribution of human characteristics to animals, inanimate objects, or deities. It appears in the mythologies of many cultures and as a literary device in fables and allegories.

antibiotic drug that kills or inhibits the growth of bacteria and fungi. It is derived from living organisms such as fungi or bacteria, which distinguishes it from synthetic antimicrobials.

The earliest antibiotics, the ▷penicillins, came into use from 1941 and were quickly joined by chloramphenicol, the ▷cephalosporins, erythromycins, tetracyclines, and aminoglycosides. A range of broad-spectrum antibiotics, the 4-quinolones, was developed in 1989, of which ciprofloxacin was the first. Each class and individual antibiotic acts in a different way and may be effective against either a broad spectrum or a specific type of disease-causing agent. Use of antibiotics has become more selective as side effects, such as toxicity, allergy, and resistance, have become better understood. Bacteria have the ability to develop resistance following repeated or subclinical (insufficient) doses, so more advanced and synthetic antibiotics are continually required to overcome them.

antibody protein molecule produced in the blood by ▷lymphocytes in response to the presence of foreign or invading substances (▷antigens); such substances include the proteins carried on the surface of infecting micro-organisms. Antibody production is only one aspect of ▷immunity in vertebrates.

Each antibody acts against only one kind of antigen, and combines with it to form a 'complex'. This action may render antigens harmless, or it may destroy micro-organisms by setting off chemical changes that cause them to self-destruct.

In other cases, the formation of a complex will cause antigens to form clumps that can then be detected and engulfed by white blood cells, such as ▷macrophages and ▷phagocytes.

Each bacterial or viral infection will bring about the manufacture of a specific antibody, which will then fight the disease. Many diseases can only be contracted once because antibodies remain in the blood after the infection has passed, preventing any further invasion. Vaccination boosts a person's resistance by causing the production of antibodies specific to particular infections.

Antibodies were discovered in 1890 by the German physician Emil von ▷Behring and the Japanese bacteriologist Shibasaburo ▷Kitasato.

Large quantities of specific antibodies can now be obtained by the monoclonal technique (see ▷monoclonal antibody).

Related Web site: Antibody Resource Page http://www.antibodyresource.com/

Antichrist in Christian theology, the opponent of Christ. The appearance of the Antichrist was believed to signal the Second Coming, at which Christ would conquer his opponent. The concept may stem from the idea of conflict between Light and Darkness, present in Persian, Babylonian, and Jewish literature, which influenced early Christian thought.

anticoagulant substance that inhibits the formation of blood clots. Common anticoagulants are heparin, produced by the liver and some white blood cells, and derivatives of coumarin. Anticoagulants are used medically in the prevention and treatment of thrombosis and heart attacks. Anticoagulant substances are also produced by blood-feeding animals, such as mosquitoes, leeches, and vampire bats, to keep the victim's blood flowing.

Anti-Corn Law League an extra-parliamentary pressure group formed in the UK in September 1838 by Manchester industrialists, and led by Liberals Richard ▷Cobden and John ▷Bright. It argued for free trade and campaigned successfully against duties on the import of foreign corn to Britain imposed by the ▷Corn Laws, which were repealed in 1846.

Campaigning on a single issue, the league initiated strategies for popular mobilization and agitation including mass meetings, lecture tours, pamphleteering, opinion polls, and parliamentary lobbying. Reaction by the conservative landed interests was organized with the establishment of the Central Agricultural Protection Society, nicknamed the Anti-League. In June 1846 political pressure, the state of the economy, and the Irish situation prompted Prime Minister ▷Peel to repeal the Corn Laws.

anticyclone area of high atmospheric pressure caused by descending air, which becomes warm and dry. Winds radiate from a calm centre, taking a clockwise direction in the northern hemisphere and an anticlockwise direction in the southern hemisphere. Anticyclones are characterized by clear weather and the absence of rain and violent winds. In summer they bring hot, sunny days and in winter they bring fine, frosty spells, although fog and low cloud are not uncommon in the UK. Blocking anticyclones, which prevent the normal air circulation of an area, can cause summer droughts and severe winters.

For example, the summer drought in Britain in 1976, and the severe winters of 1947 and 1963 were caused by blocking anticyclones.

antidepressant any drug used to relieve symptoms in depressive illness. The main groups are the selective serotonin-reuptake inhibitors (SSRIs), the tricyclic antidepressants (TCADs), and the monoamine oxidase inhibitors (MAOIs). They all act by altering chemicals available to the central nervous system. All may produce serious side effects.

antigen any substance that causes the production of ▷antibodies by the body's immune system. Common antigens include the proteins carried on the surface of bacteria, viruses, and pollen grains. The proteins of incompatible blood groups or tissues also act as antigens, which has to be taken into account in medical procedures such as blood transfusions and organ transplants.

Antigone in Greek mythology, the daughter of Jocasta by her son ▷Oedipus. She is the subject of a tragedy by ▷Sophocles.

Antigua and Barbuda see country box.

antihistamine any substance that counteracts the effects of ▷histamine. Antihistamines may occur naturally or they may be synthesized.

Antilles group of West Indian islands, divided N–S into the **Greater Antilles** (Cuba, Jamaica, Haiti–Dominican Republic, Puerto Rico) and **Lesser Antilles**, subdivided into the Leeward Islands (Virgin Islands, St Kitts and Nevis, Antigua and Barbuda, Anguilla, Montserrat, and Guadeloupe) and the Windward Islands (Dominica, Martinique, St Lucia, St Vincent and the Grenadines, Barbados, and Grenada).

antimatter in physics, a form of matter in which most of the attributes (such as electrical charge, magnetic moment, and spin) of ▷elementary particles are reversed. Such particles (▷antiparticles) can be created in particle accelerators, such as those at ▷CERN in Geneva, Switzerland, and at ▷Fermilab in the USA. In 1996 physicists at CERN created the first atoms of antimatter: nine atoms of antihydrogen survived for 40 nanoseconds.

antimony silver-white, brittle, semimetallic element (a metalloid), symbol Sb (from Latin *stibium*), atomic number 51, relative atomic mass 121.75. It occurs chiefly as the ore stibnite, and is used to make alloys harder; it is also used in photosensitive substances in colour photography, optical electronics, fireproofing, pigments, and medicine. It was employed by the ancient Egyptians in a mixture to protect the eyes from flies.

antinuclear movement organization or mass movement opposed to the proliferation of nuclear weapons and/or the use of nuclear energy. It overlaps with the ▷peace movement and the ▷green movement.

Antioch ancient capital of the Greek kingdom of Syria, founded 300 BC by Seleucus I in memory of his father Antiochus, and famed for its splendour and luxury. Under the Romans it was an early centre of Christianity. St Paul set off on his missionary journeys from here. It was captured by the Arabs in AD 637. After a five-month siege in 1098 Antioch was taken by the crusaders, who held it until 1268. The site is now occupied by the Turkish town of Antakya.

Antiochus thirteen kings of Syria of the Seleucid dynasty, including:

Antiochus I (*c.* 324–*c.* 261 BC) King of Syria from 281 BC, son of Seleucus I, one of the generals of Alexander the Great. He earned the title of Antiochus Soter, or Saviour, by his defeat of the Gauls in Galatia in 276 BC.

Antiochus (III) the Great (*c.* 241–187 BC) King of Syria 223–187 BC. He earned his title 'the Great' by restoring the Seleucid empire in 25 years of continuous campaigning from western Asia Minor to Afghanistan. He also finally wrested the Lebanon and Palestine from Egypt, despite defeat at Raphia in 201 BC.

Antiochus IV (*c.* 215–164 BC) King of Syria from 175 BC, known as Antiochus Epiphanes, the Illustrious, son of Antiochus III. He occupied Jerusalem about 170 BC, seizing much of the Temple treasure, and instituted worship of the Greek type in the Temple in an attempt to eradicate Judaism. This produced the revolt of the Hebrews under the Maccabees; Antiochus died before he could suppress it.

Antiochus VII (*c.* 159–129 BC) King of Syria from 138 BC. The last strong ruler of the Seleucid dynasty, he took Jerusalem in 134 BC, reducing the Maccabees to subjection. He was defeated and killed in battle against the ▷Parthians.

Antiochus XIII (lived 1st century BC) King of Syria 69–65 BC, the last of the Seleucid dynasty. During his reign Syria was made a Roman province by Pompey the Great.

antiparticle in nuclear physics, a particle corresponding in mass and properties to a given ▷elementary particle but with the opposite electrical charge, magnetic charge, or coupling to other fundamental forces. For example, an electron carries a negative charge whereas its antiparticle, the positron, carries a positive one. When a particle and its antiparticle collide, they destroy each other, in the process called 'annihilation', their total energy being converted to lighter particles and/or photons. A substance consisting entirely of antiparticles is known as ▷antimatter.

Other antiparticles include the negatively charged antiproton and the antineutron.

antiphony music exploiting directional and canonic opposition of widely spaced choirs or groups of instruments to create perspectives in sound. It was developed in 17th-century Venice by Giovanni Gabrieli and in Germany by his pupil Heinrich Schütz and Roland de Lassus; an example is the double-choir motet *Alma Redemptoris Mater* (1604). The practice was revived in the 20th century by Béla Bartók, Karlheinz Stockhausen, and Luciano Berio.

antipodes (Greek 'opposite feet') places at opposite points on the globe.

In the UK, Australia and New Zealand are called the Antipodes.

antipope rival claimant to the elected pope for the leadership of the Roman Catholic Church, for instance in the Great Schism 1378–1417 when there were rival popes in Rome and Avignon.

antirrhinum any of several plants in the figwort family, including the snapdragon (*Antirrhinum majus*). Foxgloves and toadflax are relatives. Antirrhinums are native to the Mediterranean region and western North America. (Genus *Antirrhinum*, family Scrophulariaceae.)

anti-Semitism prejudice or discrimination against, and persecution of, the Jews as an ethnic group. Historically this has

Antigua and Barbuda

Antigua and Barbuda country comprising three islands in the eastern Caribbean (Antigua, Barbuda, and uninhabited Redonda).

AREA 440 sq km/169 sq mi (Antigua 280 sq km/108 sq mi, Barbuda 161 sq km/62 sq mi, plus Redonda 1 sq km/0.4 sq mi)
CAPITAL St John's (on Antigua) (and chief port)
MAJOR TOWNS/CITIES Codrington (on Barbuda)
PHYSICAL FEATURES low-lying tropical islands of limestone and coral with some higher volcanic outcrops; no rivers and low rainfall result in frequent droughts and deforestation. Antigua is the largest of the Leeward Islands; Redonda is an uninhabited island of volcanic rock rising to 305 m/1,000 ft

Government
HEAD OF STATE Queen Elizabeth II from 1981, represented by Governor General James B Carlisle from 1993
HEAD OF GOVERNMENT Lester Bird from 1994

POLITICAL SYSTEM liberal democracy
POLITICAL EXECUTIVE parliamentary
ADMINISTRATIVE DIVISIONS six parishes and two dependencies
ARMED FORCES 200 (2002 est); US government leases two military bases on Antigua
DEATH PENALTY retained and used for ordinary crimes

Economy and resources
CURRENCY East Caribbean dollar
GPD (US$) 710 million (2002 est)
REAL GDP GROWTH (% change on previous year) 24.5 (2000 est)
GNI (US$) 647 million (2002 est)
GNI PER CAPITA (PPP) (US$) 9,960 (2002 est)
CONSUMER PRICE INFLATION 1% (2002 est)
UNEMPLOYMENT 4.5% (2000)
FOREIGN DEBT (US$) 717 million (2001 est)
MAJOR TRADING PARTNERS Barbados, USA, UK, Canada, Trinidad and Tobago, Guyana
INDUSTRIES oil refining, food and beverage products, paint, bedding, furniture, electrical components. Tourism is the main economic activity.

EXPORTS petroleum products, food, manufactures, machinery and transport equipment. Principal market: Barbados 15% (1999 est)
IMPORTS petroleum, food and live animals, machinery and transport equipment, manufactures, chemicals. Principal source: USA 27% (1998 est)
ARABLE LAND 18% (2000 est)
AGRICULTURAL PRODUCTS cucumbers, pumpkins, mangoes, coconuts, limes, melons, pineapples, cotton; fishing

Population and society
POPULATION 73,000 (2003 est)
POPULATION GROWTH RATE 0.3% (2000–05)
POPULATION DENSITY (per sq km) 166 (2003 est)
URBAN POPULATION (% of total) 38 (2003 est)
AGE DISTRIBUTION (% of total population) 0–14 28%, 15–59 63%, 60+ 9% (2002 est)

ETHNIC GROUPS population almost entirely of black African descent, British, Portuguese, Lebanese, Syrian
LANGUAGE English (official), local dialects
RELIGION Christian (mostly Anglican)
EDUCATION (compulsory years) 11
LITERACY RATE 90% (men); 87% (women) (2001 est)
LABOUR FORCE 11% agriculture, 19.7% industry, 69.3% services (1991)
LIFE EXPECTANCY 69 (men); 74 (women) (2000–05)
PHYSICIANS (per 1,000 people) 1.1 (1996 est)
HOSPITAL BEDS (per 1,000 people) 3.9 (1998 est)
TV SETS (per 1,000 people) 493 (1999 est)
INTERNET USERS (per 10,000 people) 904.1 (2002 est)

Chronology
1493: Antigua, peopled by American Indian Caribs, was visited by Christopher Columbus.
1632: Antigua was colonized by British settlers from St Kitts.
1667: The Treaty of Breda ceded Antigua to Britain.
1674: Christopher Codrington, a sugar planter from Barbados, established sugar plantations and acquired Barbuda island on lease from the British monarch in 1685; Africans were brought in as slaves.
1834: Antigua's slaves were freed.
1860: Barbuda was annexed.
1871–1956: Antigua and Barbuda were administered as part of the Leeward Islands federation.
1958–62: Antigua and Barbuda became part of the West Indies Federation.
1967: Antigua and Barbuda became an associated state within the Commonwealth.
1969: A separatist movement developed on Barbuda.
1981: Independence from Britain was achieved.
1983: Antigua and Barbuda assisted in the US invasion of Grenada.
1994: General elections were won by the ALP, with Lester Bird becoming prime minister.

ANTIGUA AND BARBUDA The Caribbean islands of Antigua and Barbuda are volcanic in origin. There are no rivers on the islands, and all water supplies come from stored rainwater. British influence from colonial days is evident in this Anglican cathedral. *Leonardo.com*

been practised for almost 2,000 years by European Christians. Anti-Semitism was a tenet of Nazi Germany, and in the ▷Holocaust 1933–45 about 6 million Jews died in concentration camps and in local extermination ▷pogroms, such as the siege of the Warsaw ghetto. In eastern Europe, as well as in Islamic nations, anti-Semitism exists and is promoted by neofascist groups. It is a form of ▷racism.

antiseptic any substance that kills or inhibits the growth of micro-organisms. The use of antiseptics was pioneered by Joseph ▷Lister. He used carbolic acid (▷phenol), which is a weak antiseptic; antiseptics such as TCP are derived from this.

antivivisection opposition to vivisection, that is, experiments on living animals, which is practised in the pharmaceutical and cosmetics industries on the grounds that it may result in discoveries of importance to medical science. Antivivisectionists argue that it is immoral to inflict pain on helpless creatures, and that it is unscientific because results achieved with animals may not be paralleled with human beings.

antler 'horn' of a deer, often branched, and made of bone rather than horn. Antlers, unlike true horns, are shed and regrown each year. Reindeer of both sexes grow them, but in all other types of deer, only the males have antlers.

ant lion larva of one of the insects of the family Myrmeleontidae, order Neuroptera, which traps ants by waiting at the bottom of a pit dug in loose, sandy soil. Ant lions are mainly tropical, but also occur in parts of Europe, where there are more than 40 species, and in the USA, where they are called doodlebugs.

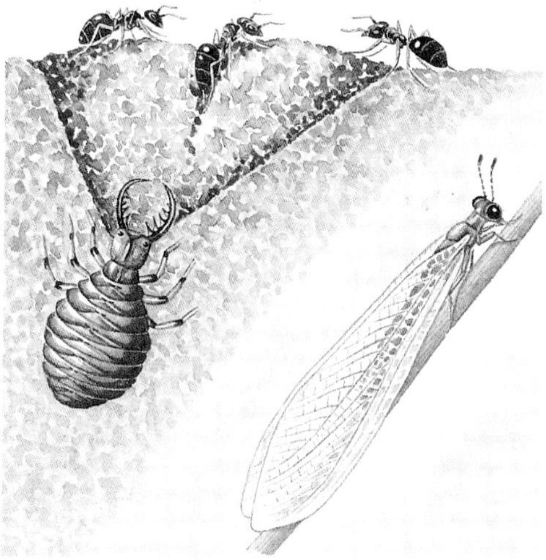

ANT LION There are about 1,000 species of ant lion; all larvae, and many adults, are carnivorous, feeding on insects and spiders. They lay their eggs singly in sand or dry soil. Larvae of the genus *Myrmeleon* live in funnel-shaped sandy pits, with their strong, toothed jaws ready to trap any insect that stumbles in.

Antonello da Messina (*c.* 1430–1479) Italian painter. He was a pioneer in his country of the technique of oil painting developed by Flemish artists; he acquired his knowledge of it in Naples, or, if the historian Vasari is to be believed, he may have learnt it from Jan van ▷Eyck himself. Flemish influence is reflected in his brushwork, his use of light, and sometimes in his imagery. Surviving works include bust-length portraits and sombre religious paintings.

Antonine Wall Roman line of fortification built in Scotland in 142 in the reign of Antoninus Pius (ruled 138–61). It was the Roman empire's furthest northwest frontier, between the Clyde and Forth rivers in Scotland. It was defended until about 200, after which the frontier returned to ▷Hadrian's Wall.

Antoninus Pius, Titus Aurelius Fulvus (AD 86–161) Roman emperor. He was adopted in 138 as Hadrian's heir, and succeeded him later that year. He enjoyed a prosperous reign, during which the ▷Antonine Wall was built. His daughter Faustina the Younger married his successor ▷Marcus Aurelius.

Antonioni, Michelangelo (1912–) Italian film director. He specialized in subtle presentations of neuroses and personal relationships among the leisured classes, with an elliptical approach to film narrative. His directorial credits include *L'Avventura* (1960), *L'Eclisse/Eclipse* (1962), *Il Deserto Rosso/Red Desert* (1964), and *Blow-Up* (1966).

Having studied film direction at the Centro Sperimentale in Rome, Antonioni went on to become a screenwriter and documentarist. He made his feature-film directorial debut with *Cronaca di un amore/Story of a Love Affair* (1950). His other films include *La Notte/The Night* (1961), *Zabriskie Point* (1970), and *The Passenger* (1975). In 1995, with the aid of the German film-maker Wim Wenders, he completed *Par-delà les nuages/Beyond the Clouds.*

Antrim county of Northern Ireland.

area 2,830 sq km/1,092 sq mi **towns and cities** ▷Belfast (county town), Larne (port), Antrim, Ballymena, Lisburn, Carrickfergus **physical** peat bogs; Antrim borders Lough Neagh, and is separated from Scotland by the North Channel, which is only 21 km/13 mi wide at Torr Head, the narrowest point; the main rivers are the Bann and the Lagan **features** ▷Giant's Causeway, a World Heritage Site, consisting of natural polygonal, mainly hexagonal, basalt columns on the north coast; Antrim Mountains (highest point Trostan 554 m/1,817 ft) and the Glens of Antrim (an area of outstanding natural beauty, dominated by a high plateau cut by deep glens which sweep eastward to the sea); Kebble National Nature Reserve on Rathlin Island, off the coast near Ballycastle; Bushmills Distillery, in the village of Bushmills, has the oldest known licence for distilling whiskey; there are a number of early fortifications, castles, and medieval ecclesiastical remains in the county; the village of Cushendun was built by Clough Williams-Ellis; Carnfunnock Country Park **industries** shipbuilding; traditional linen production was largely replaced by the manufacture of artificial fibres, in turn now mostly closed down, whiskey, agriculture (the Bann Valley is particularly fertile) **agriculture** potatoes, oats, livestock **population** (1991) 655,000

Related Web site: County Antrim http://www.interknowledge.com/northern-ireland/ukiant00.htm

Antwerp (Flemish **Antwerpen**; French **Anvers**) port in Belgium on the River Schelde, capital of the province of Antwerp, 43 km/27 mi north of Brussels; population (1997) 453,000. It is Belgium's second city and is also the largest town in Flanders, the Flemish-speaking part of Belgium. One of the world's busiest ports, it claims to be the world's leading centre for diamond cutting and dealing. Other industries include shipbuilding, oil refining, petrochemicals, and textiles. The home of the artist ▷Rubens is preserved, and several of his works are in the Gothic cathedral.

Related Web site: Antwerp http://users.pandora.be/eric.kumiko/

Anubis in Egyptian mythology, the jackal-headed god of the dead, son of Osiris. Anubis presided over the funeral cult, including the weighing of the heart and embalming, and led the dead to judgement.

anus (or **anal canal**) the opening at the end of the alimentary canal that allows undigested food and other waste materials to pass out of the body, in the form of faeces. In humans, the term is also used to describe the last 4 cm/1.5 in of the alimentary canal. The anus is found in all types of multicellular animal except the coelenterates (sponges) and the platyhelminths (flatworms), which have a mouth only.

anxiety unpleasant, distressing emotion usually to be distinguished from fear. Fear is aroused by the perception of actual or threatened danger; anxiety arises when the danger is imagined or cannot be identified or clearly perceived. It is a normal response in stressful situations, but is frequently experienced in many mental disorders.

Anyang (ancient **Yin**; later **Changteh** or **Zhangde**) city in Henan province, east China; population (1994) 1,038,000. It lies on the Beijing–Guangzhou railway. Iron- and steel-smelting are the principal industries, using local coal and iron ore from the nearby Hanxing mining area, and the Hebi coalmining complex. Engineering and the manufacture of textiles are also important.

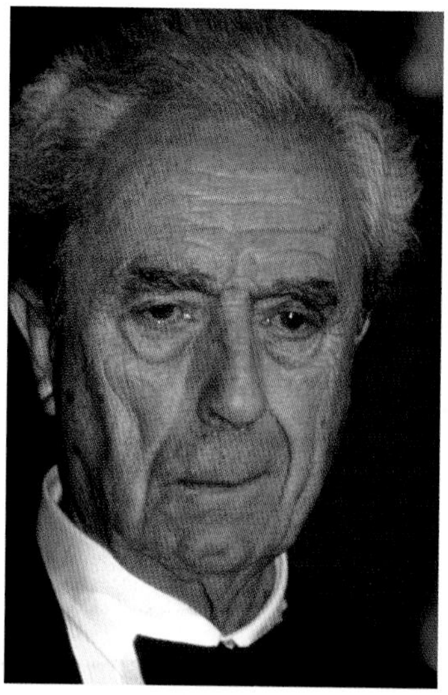

MICHELANGELO ANTONIONI Italian film director Michelangelo Antonioni, who reached almost cult status with the films he directed, produced and/or wrote during the 1960s. *Image Bank*

The city was a capital of the Shang dynasty (16th–11th centuries BC). Rich archaeological remains have been uncovered since the 1920s.

Anzac (acronym for Australian and New Zealand Army Corps) general term for all troops of both countries serving in World War I, particularly one who fought at ▷Gallipoli, and to some extent in World War II. It began as a code name based on the initials of the Corps in January 1915. The term may also be used generally of any Australian or New Zealand soldier, though 'digger' is more usual.

Anzio, Battle of in World War II, the beachhead invasion of Italy 22 Jan–23 May 1944 by Allied troops; failure to use information gained by deciphering German codes (see ▷Ultra) led to Allied troops being stranded temporarily after German attacks.

Aoraki (formerly **Mount Cook**) highest point, 3,764 m/12,349 ft, of the ▷Southern Alps, a range of mountains running through New Zealand.

aorta the body's main ▷artery, arising from the left ventricle of the heart in birds and mammals. Carrying freshly oxygenated blood, it arches over the top of the heart and descends through the trunk, finally splitting in the lower abdomen to form the two iliac arteries. Loss of elasticity in the aorta provides evidence of atherosclerosis, which may lead to heart disease.

Apache (Apache 'fighting men') member of an ▷American Indian people numbering about 11,000 in the late 20th century and who traditionally lived by hunting bison, gathering wild plant foods, farming maize, and raiding other tribes in what is now Arizona, and parts of Colorado, New Mexico, Texas, and north Mexico. Culturally divided into the Western and Eastern Apache, they and their neighbours the ▷Navajo are descendants of Athabaskan-speaking Indians who migrated to the southwest from Canada about AD 1000. They were known as fierce raiders and horse warriors in the 18th and 19th centuries. They now live on reservations in Arizona, southwest Oklahoma, and New Mexico. Apache also refers to any of several southern Athabaskan languages and dialects spoken by these people.

apartheid (Afrikaans 'apartness') racial-segregation policy of the government of South Africa from 1948 to 1994. Under the apartheid system, nonwhites – classified as Bantu (black), coloured (mixed), or Indian – did not share full rights of citizenship with the white minority. For example, black people could not vote in parliamentary elections, and until 1990 many public facilities and institutions were restricted to the use of one race only. The establishment of ▷Black National States was another manifestation of apartheid. In 1991, after years of internal dissent and violence and the boycott of South Africa, including the imposition of international trade sanctions by the United Nations (UN) and other organizations, President F W ▷de Klerk repealed the key elements of apartheid legislation and by 1994 apartheid had ceased to exist.

The term apartheid has also been loosely applied to similar movements and other forms of racial separation, for example social or educational, in other parts of the world.

apatite common calcium phosphate mineral, $Ca_5(PO_4)_3(F,OH,Cl)$. Apatite has a hexagonal structure and occurs widely in igneous rocks, such as pegmatite, and in contact metamorphic rocks, such as marbles. It is used in the manufacture of fertilizer and as a source of phosphorus. Carbonate hydroxylapatite, $Ca_5(PO_4CO_3)_3(OH)_2$, is the chief constituent of tooth enamel and, together with other related phosphate minerals, is the inorganic constituent of bone. Apatite ranks 5 on the ▷Mohs scale of hardness.

apatosaurus large plant-eating dinosaur, formerly called brontosaurus, which flourished about 145 million years ago. Up to 21 m/69 ft long and 30 tonnes in weight, it stood on four elephant-like legs and had a long tail, long neck, and small head. It probably snipped off low-growing vegetation with peglike front teeth, and swallowed it whole to be ground by pebbles in the stomach.

ape ▷primate of the family Pongidae, closely related to humans, including gibbon, orang-utan, chimpanzee, and gorilla.

The earliest known ape is believed by US researchers to have lived 20 million yeas ago in Uganda. *Morotopithecus* was about the size of a modern chimpanzee.

Apelles (lived 4th century BC) Greek painter, one of the most celebrated of antiquity. No trace of his work, which was praised for its startling realism, now remains. He was court artist to Philip II of Macedon and then to Alexander the Great, whose portrait Apelles alone was allowed to paint.

Apennines chain of mountains stretching the length of the Italian peninsula. An older and more weathered continuation of the Maritime Alps, from Genoa the Apennines swing across the peninsula to Ancona on the east coast, and then back to the west coast and into the 'toe' of Italy. The system is continued over the Strait of Messina along the north Sicilian coast, then across the

Mediterranean Sea in a series of islands to the Atlas Mountains of North Africa. The highest peak is Monte Corno in Gran Sasso d'Italia at 2,914 m/9,560 ft.

aperture in photography, an opening in the camera that allows light to pass through the lens to strike the film. Controlled by the iris diaphragm, it can be set mechanically or electronically at various diameters.

aphasia general term for the many types of disturbance in language that are due to brain damage, especially in the speech areas of the dominant hemisphere.

aphid any of the family of small insects, Aphididae, in the order Hemiptera, suborder Homoptera, that live by sucking sap from plants. There are many species, often adapted to particular plants; some are agricultural pests.

In some stages of their life cycle, wingless females rapidly produce large numbers of live young by ▷parthenogenesis, leading to enormous infestations, and numbers can approach 2 billion per hectare/1 billion per acre. They can also cause damage by transmitting viral diseases. An aphid that damages cypress and cedar trees appeared in Malawi in 1985 and by 1991 was attacking millions of trees in central and East Africa. Some research suggests, however, that aphids may help promote fertility in the soil through the waste they secrete, which is termed honeydew. Aphids are also known as plant lice, greenflies, or blackflies.

APHID A colony of aphids *Cavariella konoi*, feeding on green stems of the almond willow. *Premaphotos Wildlife*

Aphrodite in Greek mythology, the goddess of love (Roman Venus, Phoenician Astarte, Babylonian Ishtar). She is said to be either a daughter of ▷Zeus (in Homer) or sprung from the foam of the sea (in Hesiod). She was the unfaithful wife of Hephaestus, the god of fire, and the mother of Eros.

Apis ancient Egyptian deity, a manifestation of the creator god Ptah of Memphis, in the form of a black bull with a small white triangle on the forehead, often bearing a Sun-disc between its horns.

Apocrypha (Greek *apokryptein* 'to hide away') appendix to the Old Testament of the Bible, 14 books not included in the final Hebrew canon but recognized by Roman Catholics. There are also disputed New Testament texts known as Apocrypha.

Apollinaire, Guillaume (1880–1918) Pen-name of Guillaume Apollinaire de Kostrowitsky. French poet of aristocratic Polish descent. He was a leader of the avant-garde in Parisian literary and artistic circles. His novel *Le Poète assassiné/The Poet Assassinated* (1916), followed by the experimental poems *Alcools/Alcohols* (1913) and *Calligrammes/Word Pictures* (1918), show him as a representative of the Cubist and Futurist movements.

Apollo in Greek and Roman mythology, the god of sun, music, poetry, prophecy, agriculture, and pastoral life, and leader of the Muses. He was the twin child (with ▷Artemis) of Zeus and Leto. Ancient statues show Apollo as the embodiment of the Greek ideal of male beauty. His chief cult centres were his supposed birthplace on the island of Delos, in the Cyclades, and Delphi.

Apollonius of Perga (*c.* 262–*c.* 190 BC) Greek mathematician, called 'the Great Geometer'. In his work *Konica/The Conics* he showed that a plane intersecting a cone will generate an ellipse, a parabola, or a hyperbola, depending on the angle of intersection. In astronomy, he used a system of circles called epicycles and deferents to explain the motion of the planets; this system, as refined by Ptolemy, was used until the Renaissance.

Apollonius of Rhodes (or Apollonius Rhodius) (lived 3rd century BC) Greek poet. He was the author of the epic *Argonautica*,

which tells the story of Jason and the Argonauts and their quest for the Golden Fleece. A pupil of Callimachus, he was for a time head of the library at Alexandria.

Apollo project US space project to land a person on the Moon, achieved on 20 July 1969, when Neil ▷Armstrong was the first to set foot there. He was accompanied on the Moon's surface by 'Buzz' ▷Aldrin; Michael Collins remained in the orbiting command module.

The programme was announced in 1961 by President Kennedy. The world's most powerful rocket, *Saturn V*, was built to launch the Apollo spacecraft, which carried three astronauts. When the spacecraft was in orbit around the Moon, two astronauts would descend to the surface in a lunar module to take samples of rock and set up experiments that would send data back to Earth. After three other preparatory flights, *Apollo 11* made the first lunar landing. Five more crewed landings followed, the last in 1972. The total cost of the programme was over US$24 billion.

Related Web site: Apollo 11 http://www.hq.nasa.gov/alsj/a11/a11.html

Apo, Mount active volcano and highest peak in the Philippines, rising to 2,954 m/9,692 ft on the island of Mindanao.

aposematic coloration in biology, the technical name for warning coloration markings that make a dangerous, poisonous, or foul-tasting animal particularly conspicuous and recognizable to a predator. Examples include the yellow and black stripes of bees and wasps, and the bright red or yellow colours of many poisonous frogs and snakes. See also ▷mimicry.

a posteriori (Latin 'from the latter') in logic, an argument that deduces causes from their effects; inductive reasoning; the converse of ▷a priori.

apostle (Greek 'messenger') in the New Testament, any of the chosen 12 ▷disciples sent out by Jesus after his resurrection to preach the Gospel.

In the earliest days of Christianity the term was extended to include some who had never known Jesus in the flesh, notably St Paul.

Apostles' creed one of the three ancient ▷creeds of the Christian church. It probably dates from the 2nd century.

apostolic succession doctrine in the Christian church that certain spiritual powers were received by the first apostles directly from Jesus, and have been handed down in the ceremony of 'laying on of hands' from generation to generation of bishops.

apothecaries' weights obsolete units of mass, formerly used in pharmacy: 20 grains equal one scruple; three scruples equal one dram; eight drams equal an apothecary's ounce (oz apoth.), and 12 such ounces equal an apothecary's pound (lb apoth.). There are 7,000 grains in one pound avoirdupois (0.454 kg).

Appalachian Mountains mountain system in eastern North America, stretching about 2,400 km/1,500 mi from Alabama to Québec. The chain, composed of ancient eroded rocks and rounded peaks, includes the Allegheny, Catskill, and Blue Ridge Mountains. Its width in some parts reaches 500 km/311 mi. Mount Mitchell, in the Blue Ridge Mountains, is the highest peak at 2,037 m/6,684 ft. The eastern edge has a fall line to the coastal plain where Philadelphia, Baltimore, and Washington stand. The Appalachians are heavily forested and contain deposits of coal and other minerals.

apparent depth depth that a transparent material such as water or glass appears to have when viewed from above. This is less than its real depth because of the ▷refraction that takes place when light passes into a less dense medium. The ratio of the real depth to the apparent depth of a transparent material is equal to its ▷refractive index.

appeal in law, an application for a rehearing of all or part of an issue that has already been dealt with by a lower court or tribunal.

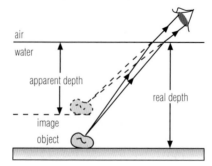

APPARENT DEPTH The diagram shows the apparent depth of an object in water when viewed from above. This is less than the object's real depth because of refractive effects: the light wave bends as it passes from the denser water into the less dense air.

APPLE A Polish farmer harvesting apples. Eastern Europe is a major apple producer and has been for many thousands of years. *Image Bank*

The outcome can be a new decision on all or part of the points raised, or the previous decision may be upheld. In criminal cases, an appeal may be against conviction and either the prosecution or the defence may appeal against sentence.

appeasement historically, the conciliatory policy adopted by the British government, in particular under Neville Chamberlain, towards the Nazi and fascist dictators in Europe in the 1930s in an effort to maintain peace. It was strongly opposed by Winston Churchill, but the ▷Munich Agreement of 1938 was almost universally hailed as its justification. Appeasement ended when Germany occupied Bohemia–Moravia in March 1939.

appendicitis inflammation of the appendix, a small, blind extension of the bowel in the lower right abdomen. In an acute attack, the pus-filled appendix may burst, causing a potentially lethal spread of infection. Treatment is by removal (appendicectomy).

There are 50,000 appendicectomies per year in Britain (1998).

appendix a short, blind-ended tube attached to the caecum. It has no known function in humans, but in herbivores it may be large, containing millions of bacteria that secrete enzymes to digest grass (as no vertebrate can secrete enzymes that will digest cellulose, the main constituent of plant cell walls).

apple fruit of several species of apple tree. There are several hundred varieties of cultivated apples, grown all over the world, which may be divided into eating, cooking, and cider apples. All are derived from the wild ▷crab apple. (Genus *Malus*, family Rosaceae.)

Related Web site: Apple http://www.botanical.com/botanical/mgmh/a/apple044.html

Appleton layer (or F layer) band containing ionized gases in the Earth's upper atmosphere, at a height of 150–1,000 km/ 94–625 mi, above the ▷E layer (formerly the Kennelly–Heaviside layer). It acts as a dependable reflector of radio signals as it is not affected by atmospheric conditions, although its ionic composition varies with the sunspot cycle.

The Appleton layer has the highest concentration of free electrons and ions of the atmospheric layers. It is named after the English physicist Edward Appleton.

application in computing, program or job designed for the benefit of the end user. Examples of **general purpose** application programs include ▷word processors, ▷desktop publishing programs, ▷databases, ▷spreadsheet packages, and graphics programs (see ▷CAD and ▷CAM). **Application-specific** programs include payroll and stock control systems. Applications may also be **custom designed** to solve a specific problem, not catered for in other types of application.

The term is used to distinguish such programs from those that control the computer (▷systems programs) or assist the programmer, such as a ▷compiler.

Appomattox Court House former village in Virginia, USA, scene of the surrender on 9 April 1865 of the Confederate army under Robert E Lee to the Union army under Ulysses S Grant, which ended the American Civil War.

The house where the surrender was signed is now a museum, 5 km/3 mi from the modern village of Appomattox.

Related Web site: Surrender at Appomattox, 1865 http://www.ibiscom.com/appomatx.htm

APR abbreviation for ▷annual percentage rate.

apricot yellow-fleshed fruit of the apricot tree, which is closely related to the almond, peach, plum, and cherry. Although native to the Far East, it has long been cultivated in Armenia, from where it was introduced into Europe and the USA. (Genus *Prunus armeniaca*, family Rosaceae.)

Related Web site: Apricot http://www.botanical.com/botanical/mgmh/a/apric050.html

a priori (Latin 'from what comes before') in logic, an argument that is known to be true, or false, without reference to experience; the converse of ▷a posteriori.

Apuleius, Lucius (lived 2nd century AD) Roman lawyer, philosopher, and writer. He was the author of *The Golden Ass*, or *Metamorphoses*, a prose fantasy.

Apulia (Italian **Puglia**) region of Italy, the southeast 'heel', comprising the provinces of Bari, Brindisi, Foggia, Lecce, and Taranto; area 19,362 sq km/7,476 sq mi; population (1999 est) 4,090,000. The capital is ▷Bari, and the main industrial centre Taranto. Agriculture is the most important sector, in terms of employment and of production.

Aqaba, Gulf of gulf extending northwards from the Red Sea for 160 km/100 mi to the Negev; its coastline is uninhabited except at its head, where the frontiers of Israel, Egypt, Jordan, and Saudi Arabia converge. The two ports of Elat (Israeli **Elath**) and Aqaba, Jordan's only port, are situated here. A border crossing near the two ports was opened in 1994, for non-Israelis and non-Jordanians, to encourage the eastern Mediterranean tourist industry.

Aqtöbe (formerly Russian **Aktyubinsk** (1869–1993)) industrial city on the River Ilek, in northwestern Kazakhstan, 100 km/62 mi south of the border with the Russian Federation, capital of Aqtöbe oblast (region); population (1995) 260,000. Chemicals, metals, electrical equipment are among the goods manufactured here. Aqtöbe stands on the main Moscow–Tashkent railway line; it is also located near to a large natural-gas field at Karachaganak.

aquaculture the cultivation of fish and shellfish for human consumption; see ▷fish farming.

aqualung (or **scuba**) underwater breathing apparatus worn by divers, developed in the early 1940s by French diver Jacques Cousteau. Compressed-air cylinders strapped to the diver's back are regulated by a valve system and by a mouth tube to provide air to the diver at the same pressure as that of the surrounding water (which increases with the depth).

Related Web site: DiverNet http://www.divernet.com/

aquamarine blue variety of the mineral ▷beryl. A semiprecious gemstone, it is used in jewellery.

aquarium tank or similar container used for the study and display of living aquatic plants and animals. The same name is used for institutions that exhibit aquatic life. These have been common since Roman times, but the first modern public aquarium was opened in Regent's Park, London in 1853. A recent development is the oceanarium or seaquarium, a large display of marine life forms.

Aquarius zodiacal constellation a little south of the celestial equator near Pegasus. Aquarius is represented as a man pouring water from a jar. The Sun passes through Aquarius from late February to early March. In astrology, the dates for Aquarius, the 11th sign of the zodiac, are between about 20 January and 18 February (see ▷precession).

aquatic insect insect that spends all or part of its life in water. Of the 29 insect orders, 11 members have some aquatic stages. Most of these have aquatic, immature stages, which usually take place in fresh water, sometimes in brackish water (very few species are truly marine); the adults are terrestrial, but in some orders there are species where all stages (egg, larva, and adult) live in the water.

aquatint printmaking technique. When combined with ▷etching it produces areas of subtle tone as well as more precisely etched lines. Aquatint became common in the late 18th century.

aqueduct any artificial channel or conduit for water, originally applied to water supply tunnels, but later used to refer to elevated structures of stone, wood, or iron carrying navigable canals across valleys. One of the first great aqueducts was built in 691 BC, carrying water for 80 km/50 mi to Ninevah, capital of the ancient Assyrian Empire. Many Roman aqueducts are still standing, for example the one carried by the Pont du Gard at Nîmes in southern France, built about 8 BC (48 m/160 ft high).

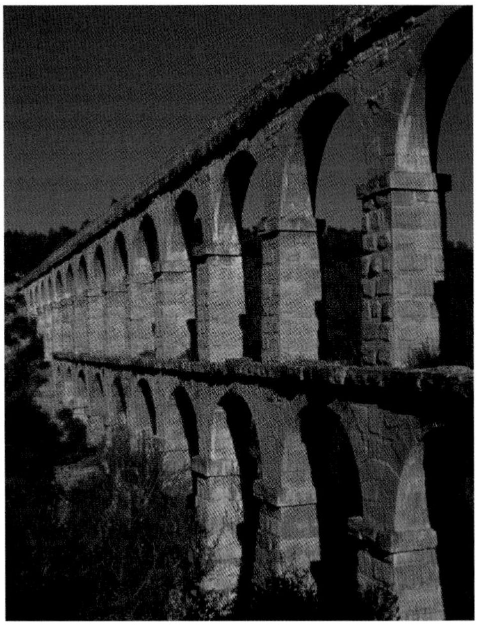

AQUEDUCT The Aqueducte de les Farreres near Tarragona, in Catalonia, Spain. It is named after the local rust-red water, and is also known as the Ponte del Diable ('Devil's Bridge'). *Image Bank*

aqueous humour watery fluid found in the chamber between the cornea and lens of the vertebrate eye. Similar to blood serum in composition, it is constantly renewed.

aquifer a body of rock through which appreciable amounts of water can flow. The rock of an aquifer must be porous and permeable (full of interconnected holes) so that it can conduct water. Aquifers are an important source of fresh water, for example, for drinking and irrigation, in many arid areas of the world, and are exploited by the use of ▷artesian wells.

An aquifer may be underlain, overlain, or sandwiched between less permeable layers, called aquicludes or **aquitards**, which impede water movement. Sandstones and porous limestones make the best aquifers.

Aquila constellation on the celestial equator (see ▷celestial sphere). Its brightest star is first-magnitude ▷Altair, flanked by the stars Beta and Gamma Aquilae. It is represented by an eagle.

Aquileia ancient town in northeastern Italy, at the head of the Adriatic Sea. It was founded in 181 BC by the Romans, who were attracted both by its strategic position (it controlled routes across the Alps) and by the gold mines in the area. It became a colony of great military and commercial importance, and was known especially for its amber trade; it was also a centre of Mithraism. In AD 452 ▷Attila destroyed the town and its inhabitants took refuge in the lagoons of Venice.

Aquinas, St Thomas (1225–1274) Italian philosopher and theologian, the greatest figure of the school of ▷scholasticism. He was a Dominican monk, known as the 'Angelic Doctor'. In 1879 his works were recognized as the basis of Catholic theology. His *Summa contra Gentiles/Against the Errors of the Infidels* (1259–64) argues that reason and faith are compatible. He assimilated the philosophy of Aristotle into Christian doctrine. He was canonized in 1323.

His unfinished *Summa Theologica*, begun 1265, deals with the nature of God, morality, and the work of Jesus.

His works embodied the world view taught in universities until the mid-17th century, and include scientific ideas derived from Aristotle. The philosophy of Aquinas is known as **Thomism**.

Related Web site: Summa Theologica of St Thomas Aquinas http://www.newadvent.org/summa/

Aquino, (Maria) Corazon (1933–) Called 'Cory'; born Maria Corazon Cojuangco. Filipino centrist politician, president 1986–92. She was instrumental in the nonviolent overthrow of President Ferdinand ▷Marcos in 1986. As president, she sought to rule in a conciliatory manner, but encountered opposition from the left (communist guerrillas) and the right (army coup attempts), and her land reforms were seen as inadequate.

Aquitaine region of southwest France; administrative capital ▷Bordeaux; area 41,308 sq km/15,949 sq mi; population (1999) 2,908,400. It comprises the *départements* of Dordogne, Gironde, Landes, Lot-et-Garonne, and Pyrénées-Atlantiques. Red wines (Margaux, St Julien) are produced in the ▷Médoc district, bordering the Gironde. Aquitaine was an English possession 1152–1453.

AR abbreviation for the state of ▷Arkansas, USA.

Arab any of the Semitic (see ▷Semite) people native to the Arabian peninsula, but now settled throughout North Africa and the nations of the Middle East.

Arab Common Market organization providing for the abolition of customs duties on agricultural products, and reductions on other items, between the member states: Egypt, Iraq, Jordan, Libya, Mauritania, Syria, and Yemen. It was founded in 1964.

Arab Emirates see ▷United Arab Emirates.

arabesque in the visual arts, a linear decoration based on plant forms. It is a feature of ancient Greek and Roman art and is particularly common in Islamic art (hence the term).

arabesque in ballet, a pose in which the dancer stands on one leg, straight or bent, with the other leg raised behind, fully extended. The arms are held in a harmonious position to give the longest possible line from fingertips to toes. It is one of the fundamental positions in ballet.

Arabia (or Arabian Peninsula; Arabic **Jazirat al-Arab**, the 'peninsula of the Arabs') peninsula between the Gulf and the Red Sea, in southwest Asia; area 2,600,000 sq km/1,000,000 sq mi. The length from north to south is about 2,400 km/1,490 mi and the greatest width about 1,600 km/994 mi. The peninsula contains the world's richest gas reserves and half the world's oil reserves. It comprises the states of Bahrain, Kuwait, Oman, Qatar, Saudi Arabia, the United Arab Emirates, and Yemen.

Related Web site: Lost City of Arabia http://www.pbs.org/wgbh/nova/ubar/

Arabian Gulf another name for the ▷Persian Gulf.

Arabian Sea northwestern branch of the ▷Indian Ocean, covering 3,859,000 sq km/1,489,970 sq mi, with India to the east, Pakistan and Iran to the north, and the Arabian Peninsula and Somalia to the west. It is linked with the Red Sea via the Gulf of Aden, and with the Persian Gulf via the Gulf of Oman. Its mean depth is 2,730 m/8,956 ft. The chief river flowing into the Arabian Sea is the Indus, which is linked with a large submarine canyon in the continental shelf. The sea is rich in fish.

Arabic language major Semitic language of the Hamito-Semitic family of West Asia and North Africa, originating among the Arabs of the Arabian peninsula. It is spoken today by about 120 million people in the Middle East and North Africa. Arabic script is written from right to left.

Related Web site: Arabic Writing http://www.islam.org/Mosque/ihame/Ref3.htm

Arab–Israeli Wars series of wars and territorial conflicts between Israel and various Arab states in the Middle East since the founding of the state of Israel in May 1948. These include the war of 1948–49; the 1956 Suez War between Israel and Egypt; the Six-Day War of 1967, in which Israel captured territory from Syria and Jordan; the October War of 1973; and the 1982–85 war between Israel and Lebanon. In the times between the wars tension has remained high in the area, and has resulted in skirmishes and terrorist activity taking place on both sides. See also the History of the Conflict in the Middle East Focus Feature on pp. 628–629.

Arab League (or League of Arab States) organization of Arab states established in Cairo in 1945 to promote Arab unity, primarily in opposition to Israel. The original members were Egypt, Syria, Iraq, Lebanon, Transjordan (Jordan 1949), Saudi Arabia, and Yemen. They were later joined by Algeria, Bahrain, Comoros, Djibouti, Kuwait, Libya, Mauritania, Morocco, Oman, Palestine, the PLO, Qatar, Somalia, Sudan, Tunisia, and the United Arab Emirates. In 1979 Egypt was suspended and the league's headquarters transferred to Tunis in protest against the Egypt–Israeli peace, but

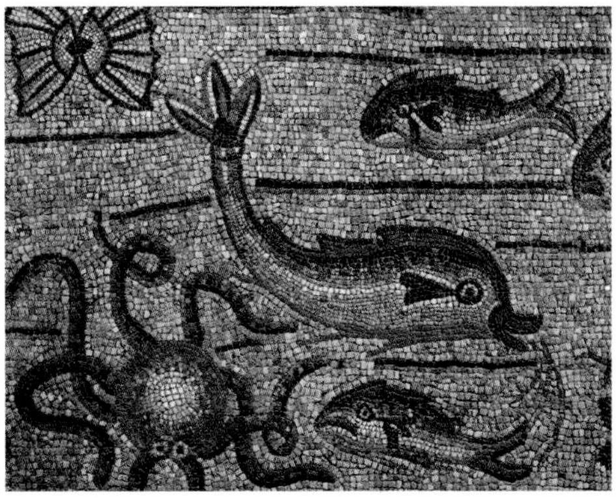

AQUILEIA A detail from a mosaic of fish in the sea from the basilica of Aquileia, Italy, dating from the 4th century AD. *The Art Archive/Anthropological Institute Turin/Dagli Orti*

Egypt was readmitted as a full member in May 1989, and in March 1990 its headquarters returned to Cairo. Despite the strains imposed on it by the 1990–91 Gulf War, the alliance survived.

Arab Maghreb Union (AMU) association formed in 1989 by Algeria, Libya, Mauritania, Morocco, and Tunisia to formulate common policies on military, economic, international, and cultural issues.

Arab Monetary Fund (AMF) money reserve established in 1976 by many Arab states plus the Palestine Liberation Organization (PLO) to provide a mechanism for promoting greater stability in exchange rates and to coordinate Arab economic and monetary policies. It operates mainly by regulating petrodollars within the Arab community to make member countries less dependent on the West for the handling of their surplus money. The fund's headquarters are in Abu Dhabi in the United Arab Emirates.

arachnid (or **arachnoid**) type of arthropod of the class Arachnida, including spiders, scorpions, ticks, and mites. They differ from insects in possessing only two main body regions, the cephalothorax and the abdomen, and in having eight legs.

Related Web site: Arachnology http://www.ufsia.ac.be/Arachnology/Arachnology.html

Arafat, Yassir (1929–) Born Muhammad Abed Ar'ouf Arafat. Palestinian nationalist politician, cofounder of al-▷Fatah in 1957, president of the Palestinian National Authority from 1994, and leader of the ▷Palestine Liberation Organization (PLO) from 1969. His support for Saddam Hussein after Iraq's invasion of Kuwait in 1990 weakened his international standing, but he was subsequently influential in the Middle East peace talks and in 1993 reached a historic peace accord of mutual recognition with Israel, under which the Gaza Strip and Jericho were transferred to PLO control. He returned to the former occupied territories in 1994 as head of an embryonic Palestinian state, and he shared the Nobel Prize for Peace in 1994 with Yitzhak ▷Rabin and Israeli foreign minister Shimon ▷Peres for their agreement of an accord on Palestinian self-rule. In 1995 an agreement was reached on further Israeli troop withdrawals from areas in the West Bank, and Arafat took the unprecedented step in October 1995 of inviting the terrorist organization Hamas to talks on Palestinian self-rule.

In November 1995 the Israeli prime minister, Yitzhak Rabin, was assassinated by an Israeli extremist and the peace process appeared to be threatened. Rabin was succeeded by the moderate Shimon Peres but he lost the 1996 general election and was replaced by the hard-line Likud leader Binjamin Netanyahu. Despite this, Arafat continued his efforts for a lasting peace. He was elected president, with almost 90% of the popular vote, of the self-governing Palestinian National Council in 1996. In October 1998, the 'Wye agreement' was signed, providing for a further 13% withdrawal of Israeli forces from the West Bank.

In May 1999 Labour candidate Ehud Barak was elected as Israel's prime minister, and Arafat announced that an independent Palestine state would be declared by the end of the year. Later that month Arafat met with King Abdullah of Jordan prior to the reopening of peace talks with Israel.

Arafura Sea area of the Pacific Ocean between northern Australia and Indonesia, bounded by the Timor Sea in the west and the Coral Sea, via the Torres Strait, in the east; 1,290 km/800 mi long and 560 km/350 mi wide. It lies on the Arafura Shelf, and is 50–80 m/165–265 ft deep. The Indonesian Aru islands lie to the north. To the northwest, the Aru Trough (3,650 m/12,000 ft deep) separates the Arafura Sea from the Banda Sea.

Aragón autonomous community and former kingdom of northeast Spain, including the provinces of Huesca, Teruel, and Zaragoza; area 47,700 sq km/18,420 sq mi; population (1994) 1,183,600. Products include cereals, rice, olive oil, almonds, figs, grapes, and olives; merino wool is a major export. The principal river of Aragón is the Ebro, which receives numerous tributaries both from the mountains of the south and from the Pyrenees in the north. Aragón was an independent kingdom from 1035 to 1479. The capital of modern Aragón is ▷Zaragoza.

Aragon, Louis (1897–1982) French poet and novelist. Beginning as a Dadaist, he became one of the leaders of Surrealism, published volumes of verse, and in 1930 joined the Communist Party. Taken prisoner in World War II, he escaped to join the Resistance; his experiences are reflected in the poetry of *Le Crève-coeur/Heart-break* (1941) and *Les Yeux d'Elsa/Elsa's Eyes* (1942).

Arakan (or **Rakhine**) state of ▷Myanmar (formerly Burma) on the Bay of Bengal coast, some 645 km/400 mi long and strewn with islands; population (1994 est) 2,482,000. Most of Arakan is mountainous or hilly land, originally covered with tropical forest, though this has now mainly been destroyed by shifting cultivation and has been replaced by a dense growth of bamboo. Only 10% of the area, mainly in river deltas, is cultivated, with rice and tobacco being leading crops. The chief town is Sittwe. It is bounded along its eastern side by the Arakan Yoma, a mountain range rising to 3,000 m/10,000 ft. It shares a short border with Bangladesh to the north. The ancient kingdom of Arakan was conquered by Burma in 1785.

Aral Sea (Russian **Aralskoye More**) inland sea divided between Kazakhstan and Uzbekistan, the world's fourth-largest lake; former area 62,000 sq km/24,000 sq mi, but decreasing. Water from its tributaries, the Amu Darya and Syr Darya, has been diverted for irrigation and city use, and the sea is disappearing, with long-term consequences for the climate.

Aramaic language Semitic language of the Hamito-Semitic family of western Asia, the everyday language of Palestine 2,000 years ago, during the Roman occupation and the time of Jesus.

Aran Islands group of three limestone islands in the mouth of Galway Bay, which is about 32 km/20 mi wide. They lie 48 km/30 mi from Galway, on the west coast of the Republic of Ireland; the principal town is Kilronan on Inishmore. The islands form a natural breakwater, and comprise Inishmore (Irish Inis Mór), area 3,092 ha/7,637 acres, population (1996) 838; Inishmaan (Irish Inis Meáin), area 912 ha/2,253 acres, population (1996) 191; and Inisheer (Irish Inis Óirr), area 567 ha/1,400 acres, population (1996) 274. The chief industries are tourism, fishing, and agriculture.

Arapaho (Arapaho 'trader') member of an ▷American Indian people numbering about 5,000 (1990) and living on a reservations in Wyoming and Oklahoma and whose language belongs to the Algonquian family.

Ararat, Mount double-peaked mountain in Turkey near the Iranian border; Great Ararat, at 5,137 m/16,854 ft, is the highest mountain in Turkey. It was the reputed resting place of Noah's Ark after the Flood.

Araucanian Indian (or **Araucanian Mapuche**) member of a group of South American peoples native to central Chile and the Argentine pampas. They were agriculturalists and hunters, as well as renowned warriors, defeating the Incas and resisting the Spanish for 200 years. Originally, they lived in small villages; some 200,000 still survive in reserves. Scholars are divided over whether the Araucanian language belongs to the Penutian or the Andean-Equatorial family.

araucaria coniferous tree related to the firs, with flat, scalelike needles. Once widespread, it is now native only to the southern hemisphere. Some grow to gigantic size. Araucarias include the monkey-puzzle tree (*Araucaria araucana*), the Australian bunya bunya pine (*A. bidwillii*), and the Norfolk Island pine (*A. heterophylla*). (Genus *Araucaria*, family Araucariaceae.)

Arawak indigenous American people of the Caribbean and northeastern Amazon Basin. Arawaks lived mainly by shifting cultivation in tropical forests. They were driven out of many West Indian islands by another American Indian people, the Caribs, shortly before the arrival of the Spanish in the 16th century. Subsequently, their numbers on ▷Hispaniola declined from some 4 million in 1492 to a few thousand after their exploitation by the Spanish in their search for gold; the remaining few were eradicated by disease (smallpox was introduced in 1518). Arawakan languages belong to the Andean-Equatorial group.

arbitration submission of a dispute to a third, unbiased party for settlement. It may be personal litigation, a trade-union issue, or an international dispute.

arbor vitae any of several coniferous trees or shrubs belonging to the cypress family, with flattened branchlets covered in overlapping aromatic green scales. The northern white cedar (*Thuja occidentalis*) and the western red cedar (*T. plicata*) are found in North America. The Chinese or oriental species *T. orientalis*, reaching 18 m/60 ft in height, is widely grown as an ornamental. (Genus *Thuja*, family Cupressaceae.)

Arbroath fishing town in Angus, on the east coast of Scotland, 26 km/16 mi northeast of Dundee, at the mouth of Brothock Water; population (1991) 23,500. In 1320 the Declaration of Arbroath was signed by the Scottish Parliament in Arbroath Abbey, proclaiming Scotland's independence to the pope. The town has a number of oil-related firms, a fishing industry and produces smoked haddock (Arbroath smokies). The harbour at Arbroath has been working for many years. Although not as busy as in past times, many fishing boats still sail from Arbroath.

Arbuthnot, John (1667–1735) Scottish writer and physician. He attended Prince George and then Queen Anne from 1705 to 1714. He was a friend of Alexander Pope, Thomas Gray, and Jonathan Swift and was the chief author of the satiric *Memoirs of Martinus Scriblerus* (1741). He created the English national character of ▷John Bull, a prosperous farmer, in his 'History of John Bull' (1712) pamphlets advocating peace with France.

arbutus any of a group of evergreen shrubs belonging to the heath family, found in temperate regions. The strawberry tree (*Arbutus unedo*) is grown for its ornamental, strawberrylike fruit. (Genus *Arbutus*, family Ericaceae.)

arc in geometry, a section of a curved line or circle. A circle has three types of arc: a **semicircle**, which is exactly half of the circle; **minor arcs**, which are less than the semicircle; and **major arcs**, which are greater than the semicircle.

An arc of a circle is measured in degrees, according to the angle formed by joining its two ends to the centre of that circle. A semicircle is therefore 180°, whereas a minor arc will always be less than 180° (acute or obtuse) and a major arc will always be greater than 180° but less than 360° (reflex).

Arcadia (Greek **Arkadhia**) central plateau and department of southern Greece; area 4,419 sq km/1,706 sq mi; population (1991) 103,800. Tripolis is the capital town.

Arc de Triomphe arch at the head of the Champs Elysées in the Place de l'Etoile, Paris, France, begun by Napoleon in 1806 and completed in 1836. It was intended to commemorate Napoleon's victories of 1805–06 and commissioned from Jean Chalgrin. Beneath it rests France's 'Unknown Soldier'.

arch in masonry, a curved structure that supports the weight of material over an open space, as in a bridge or doorway. The first arches consisted of several wedge-shaped stones supported by their mutual pressure. The term is also applied to any curved structure that is an arch in form only, such as the Arc de Triomphe, Paris, 1806–36.

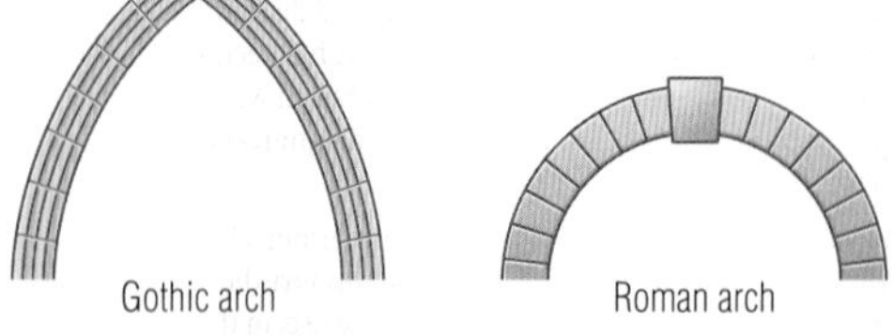

ARCH A Gothic arch and a Roman arch.

Ancient Microbes (Archaea)

The micro-organisms known as Archaea were originally classified as bacterial, but in 1996 when the genome of *Methanococcus jannaschii* (an archaeaon that lives in undersea volcanic vents at temperatures around 100°C/212°F) was sequenced, US geneticists found that 56% of its genes were unlike those of any other organism, making Archaea unique.

Micro-organisms that thrive in extreme environments like undersea vents, at very low temperatures, or in highly acidic or highly alkaline conditions are known as extremophiles. Such environments also include the Dead Sea, salt pans, hot springs, and even refuse tips.

It is likely that the environment around undersea volcanic vents, often referred to as **superheated chemical soup**, reproduces conditions on Earth when the first forms of life emerged, about 4 billion years ago. If so, the Archaea that are found here may be more closely related to the earliest organisms on Earth than any other present-day species.

Extremophiles have special enzymes (biological catalysts) that are highly stable and the properties of these enzymes makes them useful for industrial applications. An enzyme from a hot-spring organism (*Thermus aquaticus*) is used in DNA fingerprinting and gene analysis, a process which requires a version of a particular enzyme that can withstand high temperatures. Other properties of enzymes from newly discovered extremophiles are likely to have further industrial uses. Cold-tolerant enzymes may be used in food processing and for detergents; acid tolerance is important in the chemical industry; and alkali tolerance is also likely to improve detergents.

Archaea group of micro-organisms that are without a nucleus and have a single chromosome. Most taxonomists now classify these bacteria in their own kingdom, separate from other bacteria. All are strict anaerobes, that is, they are killed by oxygen.

Related Web site: Life in Extreme Environments http://www.reston.com/astro/extreme.html

Archaean (or Archaeozoic) widely used term for the earliest era of geological time; the first part of the Precambrian **Eon**, spanning the interval from the formation of Earth to about 2,500 million years ago.

archaeology (Greek *archaia* 'ancient things', *logos* 'study') study of prehistory and history, based on the examination of physical remains. Principal activities include preliminary field (or site) surveys, excavation (where necessary), and the classification, ▷dating, and interpretation of finds.

History A museum found at the ancient Sumerian city of Ur indicates that interest in the physical remains of the past stretches back into prehistory. In the Renaissance this interest gained momentum among dealers in and collectors of ancient art and was further stimulated by discoveries made in Africa, the Americas, and Asia by Europeans during the period of imperialist colonization in the 16th–19th centuries, such as the antiquities discovered during Napoleon's Egyptian campaign in the 1790s. ▷Romanticism in Europe stimulated an enthusiasm for the mouldering skull, the ancient potsherds, ruins, and dolmens; relating archaeology to a wider context of art and literature.

Towards the end of the 19th century archaeology became an academic study, making increasing use of scientific techniques and systematic methodologies such as aerial photography. Since World War II new developments within the discipline include medieval, postmedieval, landscape, and industrial archaeology; underwater reconnaissance enabling the excavation of underwater sites; and rescue archaeology (excavation of sites risking destruction).

Related disciplines Useful in archaeological studies are ▷dendrochronology (tree-ring dating), ▷geochronology (science of measuring geological time), stratigraphy (study of geological strata), palaeobotany (study of ancient pollens, seeds, and grains), archaeozoology (analysis of animal remains), epigraphy (study of inscriptions), and numismatics (study of coins).

Related Web sites: Archaeology http://www.archaeology.org/
Glossary of Archaeological Terms http://www.smu.edu/~anthrop/glossary.html

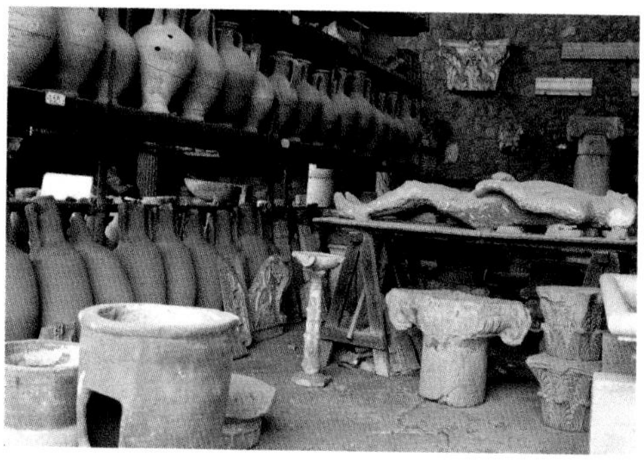

ARCHAEOLOGY Palaeolithic and Neolithic remains, including rock paintings and carvings, indicate the presence of ancient communities in what is now part of the West African republic of Mali. They are now covered by the Sahara Desert. *Image Bank*

Archaeology: Key Dates

14th–16th centuries	There is renewed interest in Europe in classical Greek and Roman art and architecture, including ruins and buried art and artefacts.
1748	The Roman city of Pompeii is discovered buried under volcanic ash from Vesuvius.
1784	Thomas Jefferson excavates an Indian burial mound on the Rivanna River in Virginia, USA, and writes a report on his finds.
1790	John Frere identifies Old Stone Age (Palaeolithic) tools together with large extinct animals.
1822	Jean François Champollion deciphers Egyptian hieroglyphics.
1836	Christian Thomsen devises the Stone, Bronze, and Iron Age classification (Three Age System).
1840s	Austen Layard excavates the Assyrian capital of Nineveh.
1868	The Great Zimbabwe ruins in southern Africa are first seen by Europeans.
1871	Heinrich Schliemann begins excavations at Troy.
1879	Ice Age paintings are first discovered at Altamira, Spain.
1880s	Augustus Pitt-Rivers develops the concept of stratigraphy (identification of successive layers of soil within a site with successive archaeological stages, the most recent being at the top).
1891	Flinders Petrie begins excavating Akhetaton in Egypt.
1899–1935	Arthur Evans excavates Minoan Knossos in Crete.
1900–44	Max Uhle begins the systematic study of the civilizations of Peru.
1911	The Inca city of Machu Picchu is discovered by Hiram Bingham in the Andes.
1911–12	The Piltdown skull is 'discovered'; it is proved to be a fake in 1949.
1914–18	Osbert Crawford develops the technique of aerial survey of sites.
1917–27	John Eric Thompson (1898–1975) investigates the great Maya sites in Yucatán, Mexico.
1922	Tutankhamen's tomb in Egypt is opened by Howard Carter.
1935	Dendrochronology (dating events in the distant past by counting tree rings) is developed by A E Douglass.
1939	An Anglo-Saxon ship-burial treasure is found at Sutton Hoo, England.
1947	The first of the Dead Sea Scrolls is discovered.
1948	The 'Proconsul' prehistoric ape is discovered by Mary Leakey in Kenya.
1950s–1970s	Several early hominid fossils are found by Louis and Mary Leakey in Olduvai Gorge, Tanzania.
1953	Michael Ventris deciphers Linear B, a forerunner of ancient Greek used by the Mycenaeans.
1960s	Radiocarbon and thermoluminescence measurement techniques are developed as aids for dating remains.
1961	The Swedish warship *Wasa* is raised at Stockholm, Sweden.
1963	Walter Emery pioneers rescue archaeology at Abu Simbel, Egypt, before the site is flooded by the Aswan Dam.
1969	Human remains found at Lake Mungo, Australia, are dated at 26,000 years; earliest evidence of ritual cremation.
1974	The tomb of Shi Huangdi, with its terracotta army, is discovered in China; the partial skeleton of a 3.18 million year old hominid nicknamed 'Lucy' is found in Ethiopia, and hominid footprints, 3.8 million years old, at Laetoli in Tanzania.
1978	The tomb of Philip II of Macedon (Alexander the Great's father) is discovered in Greece.
1979	The Aztec capital Tenochtitlán is excavated beneath a zone of Mexico City.
1982	Henry VIII's warship *Mary Rose* of 1545 is raised and studied using new techniques in underwater archaeology.
1985	The tomb of Maya, Tutankhamen's treasurer, is discovered at Sakkara, Egypt.
1988	The Turin Shroud is established as being of medieval origin by radiocarbon dating.
1989	The remains of the Globe and Rose Theatres, where many of Shakespeare's plays were originally performed, are discovered in London.
1991	The clothed body of man from 5,300 years ago, with bow, arrows, copper axe, and other implements, is found preserved in ice in the Italian Alps.
1992	The world's oldest surviving wooden structure, a well 15 m/49 ft deep made of huge oak timbers at Kückhoven, Germany, is dated using dendrochronology to 5090 BC. The world's oldest sea-going vessel, dating from about 1400 BC, is discovered at Dover, England.
1993	Drawings in charcoal on the walls of the Cosquer Cave (near Marseille, France, discovered 1991) were radiocarbon-dated to be 27,110 and *c.* 19,000 years old; a fragment of cloth found on a tool handle unearthed in Çayönü, southeast Turkey in 1988 is radiocarbon-dated at 9,000 years old, making it the oldest cloth ever found.
1994	The discovery in Ethiopia of fossils of one of the earliest known ancestral humans, *Ardipithecus ramidus*, (about 4.4 million years old) is announced; a major new Ice Age cave, the Grotte Chauvet, is found in southeast France, containing a network of hundreds of Palaeolithic cave drawings, dating from 30,000 years ago. Rivalling those of Lascaux and Altamira, they include depictions of a panther and an owl – previously unknown in Palaeolithic art.
1995	A vast underground tomb, believed to be the burial site of 50 of the sons of Ramses II, is discovered. It is the largest yet found in the Valley of the Kings. Researchers in Spain find human remains dating back more than 780,000 years, in a cave site at Gran Dolina at Atapuerca in northern central Spain. Previously it was thought humans reached Europe around 300,000 years later than this. Scientific tests reveal that certain of the paintings within the Chauvet complex, discovered in 1994, are between 30,340 and 32,410 years old, making them the world's oldest known paintings.
1997	Spanish palaeontologists, studying 8,000-year-old fossilized bones in northern Spain, claim to have discovered a new human species *Homo antecessor*.
1998	Stone tools, belonging to *Homo erectus* and dated at about 8,000 years old, are discoverd by Australian palaeontologists on Flores, an island near Bali. The discovery provides strong evidence that *Homo erectus* were seafarers and had the language abilities and social structure to organize the colonization of new islands.
1999	The earliest playable wind instruments are excavated from a Neolithic site in Henan Province, China. The six bone flutes date from between 7000 and 5700 BC.

archaeopteryx (Greek *archaios* 'ancient', *pterux* 'wing') extinct primitive bird, known from fossilized remains, about 160 million years old, found in limestone deposits in Bavaria, Germany. It is popularly known as 'the first bird', although some earlier bird ancestors are now known. It was about the size of a crow and had feathers and wings, with three clawlike digits at the end of each wing, but in many respects its skeleton is reptilian (teeth and a long, bony tail) and very like some small meat-eating dinosaurs of the time.

Archangel (Russian **Arkhangelsk**) port in the north of the Russian Federation, capital of Archangelsk Oblast; population (1990) 419,000. Situated on the Northern Dvina River, it is Russia's chief timber-exporting port, and the centre of a rapidly growing mineral extraction industry (oil drilling and diamond mining). Formerly blocked by ice for half the year, it has been kept open constantly since 1979 by icebreakers. Archangel was made an open port by Boris ▷Godunov and was of vital significance for trade until Peter the Great built St Petersburg.

archbishop in the Christian church, a bishop of superior rank who has authority over other bishops in his jurisdiction and often over an ecclesiastical province. The office exists in the Roman Catholic, Eastern Orthodox, and Anglican churches.

archdeacon originally an ordained dignitary of the Christian church charged with the supervision of the deacons attached to a cathedral. Today in the Roman Catholic Church the office is purely titular; in the Anglican Church an archdeacon, directly subordinate to the bishop, still has many business duties, such as the periodic inspection of churches. The office is not found in other Protestant churches.

Archer, Thomas (1668–1743) English architect. He is noted for his interpretations of Italian baroque, which he studied at first hand during a continental Grand Tour 1691–95. He was active 1703–15, after which he took up the post of Controller of Customs at Newcastle. Notable among his designs are the north front of Chatsworth House 1704–05, the church of St John, Smith Square, London, 1714–28, and the Cathedral of St Philip, Birmingham, 1710–15.

archerfish surface-living fish of the family Toxotidae, such as the genus *Toxotes*, native to Southeast Asia and Australia. The archerfish grows to about 25 cm/10 in and is able to shoot down insects up to 1.5 m/5 ft above the water by spitting a jet of water from its mouth.

archery use of the bow and arrow, originally in hunting and warfare, now as a competitive sport. The world governing body is the Fédération Internationale de Tir à l'Arc (FITA) founded in 1931. In competitions, results are based on double FITA rounds;

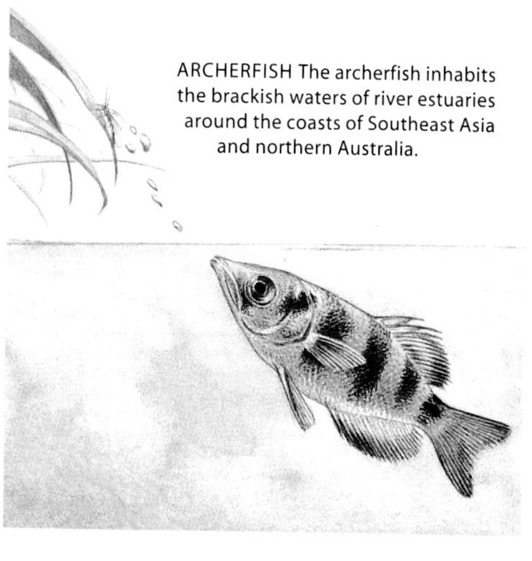

ARCHERFISH The archerfish inhabits the brackish waters of river estuaries around the coasts of Southeast Asia and northern Australia.

that is, 72 arrows at each of four targets at 90, 70, 50, and 30 metres (70, 60, 50, and 30 for women). The best possible score is 2,880. Archery was reintroduced to the Olympic Games in 1972.

Related Web site: Archery Index http://atschool.eduweb.co.uk/splomas/myarch/archy1.html#British

Archimedes (*c*. 287–212 BC) Greek mathematician who made major discoveries in geometry, hydrostatics, and mechanics, and established the sciences of statics and hydrostatics. He formulated a law of fluid displacement (Archimedes' principle), and is credited with the invention of the Archimedes screw, a cylindrical device for raising water. His method of finding mathematical proof to substantiate experiment and observation became the method of modern science in the High Renaissance.

Hydrostatics and Archimedes' principle The best-known result of Archimedes' work on hydrostatics is ▷Archimedes' principle, which states that a body immersed in water will displace a volume of fluid that weighs as much as the body would weigh in air. It is alleged that Archimedes' principle was discovered when he stepped into the public bath and saw the water overflow. He was so delighted that he rushed home naked, crying 'Eureka! Eureka!' ('I have found it! I have found it!').

He used his discovery to prove that the goldsmith of Hieron II, King of Syracuse, had adulterated a gold crown with silver. Archimedes realized that if the gold had been mixed with silver (which is less dense than gold), the crown would have a greater volume and therefore displace more water than an equal weight of pure gold. The story goes that the crown was found to be impure, and that the unfortunate goldsmith was executed.

Statics and the lever In the field of statics, he is credited with working out the rigorous mathematical proofs behind the law of the lever. The lever had been used by other scientists, but it was Archimedes who demonstrated mathematically that the ratio of the effort applied to the load raised is equal to the inverse ratio of the distances of the effort and load from the pivot or fulcrum of the lever. Archimedes is credited with having claimed that if he had a sufficiently distant place to stand, he could use a lever to move the world.

This claim is said to have given rise to a challenge from King Hieron to Archimedes to show how he could move a truly heavy object with ease, even if he could not move the world. In answer to this, Archimedes developed a system of compound pulleys. According to Plutarch's *Life of Marcellus* (who sacked Syracuse), Archimedes used this to move with ease a ship that had been lifted with great effort by many men out of the harbour on to dry land. The ship was laden with passengers, crew and freight, but Archimedes – sitting at a distance from the ship – was reportedly able to pull it over the land as though it were gliding through water.

Mathematics Archimedes wrote many mathematical treatises, some of which still exist in altered forms in Arabic. Archimedes' approximation for the value for π was more accurate than any previous estimate – the value lying between $\frac{223}{71}$ and $\frac{220}{70}$. The average of these two numbers is less than 0.0003 different from the modern approximation for π. He also examined the expression of very large numbers, using a special notation to estimate the number of grains of sand in the Universe. Although the result, 10^{63}, was far from accurate, Archimedes demonstrated that large numbers could be considered and handled effectively.

Archimedes also evolved methods to solve cubic equations and to determine square roots by approximation. His formulae for the determination of the surface areas and volumes of curved surfaces and solids anticipated the development of integral calculus, which did not come for another 2,000 years. Archimedes had decreed that his gravestone be inscribed with a cylinder enclosing a sphere together with the formula for the ratio of their volumes – a discovery that he regarded as his greatest achievement.

Related Web site: Archimedes Home Page http://www.mcs.drexel.edu/~crorres/Archimedes/contents.html

Archimedes

Give me but one firm place on which to stand, and I will move the earth.

On the lever, quoted in *Pappus Alexander*

Archimedes' principle in physics, the principle that the weight of the liquid displaced by a floating body is equal to the weight of the body. The principle is often stated in the form: 'an object totally or partially submerged in a fluid displaces a volume of fluid that weighs the same as the apparent loss in weight of the object (which, in turn, equals the upwards force, or upthrust, experienced by that object).' It was discovered by the Greek mathematician Archimedes.

Archimedes screw one of the earliest kinds of pump, associated with the Greek mathematician Archimedes. It consists of an enormous spiral screw revolving inside a close-fitting cylinder. It is used, for example, to raise water for irrigation.

archipelago group of islands, or an area of sea containing a group of islands. The islands of an archipelago are usually volcanic in origin, and they sometimes represent the tops of peaks in areas around continental margins flooded by the sea.

Volcanic islands are formed either when a hot spot within the Earth's mantle produces a chain of volcanoes on the surface, such as the Hawaiian Archipelago or at a destructive plate margin (see ▷plate tectonics) where the subduction of one plate beneath another produces an arc-shaped island group called an 'island arc', such as the Aleutian Archipelago. Novaya Zemlya in the Arctic Ocean, the northern extension of the Ural Mountains, resulted from continental flooding.

Archipelago de las Perlas (or **Pearl Islands**) group of 227 largely uninhabited islands in the Gulf of Panama, Central America, 64 km/40 mi southeast of Panama, to which republic the islands belong. The main islands are San Miguel (the largest), San José, and Pedro González. The main industries are deep-sea fishing, and sea angling by tourists.

Archipenko, Alexander (1887–1964) Ukrainian-born abstract sculptor. He pioneered cubist sculpture, producing geometrically stylized forms, as in *Woman Combing Her Hair* (1915; Tate Gallery, London). He also experimented with polychrome reliefs (which he called 'sculpto-paintings'), with clear plastics and other materials, and sculptures incorporating lights. These experiments with form, colours, and materials had a profound influence on the development of 20th-century sculpture.

architecture art of designing structures. The term covers the design of the visual appearance of structures; their internal arrangements of space; selection of external and internal building materials; design or selection of natural and artificial lighting systems, as well as mechanical, electrical, and plumbing systems; and design or selection of decorations and furnishings. Architectural style may emerge from evolution of techniques and styles particular to a culture in a given time period with or without identifiable individuals as architects, or may be attributed to specific individuals or groups of architects working together on a project.

Related Web site: Architecture: A Virtual Tour http://archpropplan.auckland.ac.nz/virtualtour/

Arcimboldo, Giuseppe (1527–1593) Milanese painter and designer. His trademark was the composing of fantastical portraits from fruit, plant, and animal details; he also designed tapestries. Much of his career (1562–1587) was spent as portrait painter at the court of Rudolf II in Prague.

arc lamp (or **arc light**) electric light that uses the illumination of an electric arc maintained between two electrodes. The English chemist Humphry Davy demonstrated the electric arc in 1802 and electric arc lighting was first introduced by English electrical engineer W E Staite in 1846. The lamp consists of two carbon electrodes, between which a very high voltage is maintained. Electric current arcs (jumps) between the two electrodes, creating a brilliant light. Its main use in recent years has been in cinema projectors.

arc minute, arc second units for measuring small angles, used in geometry, surveying, map-making, and astronomy. An arc minute (symbol ′) is one-sixtieth of a degree, and an arc second (symbol ″) is one-sixtieth of an arc minute. Small distances in the sky, as between two close stars or the apparent width of a planet's disc, are expressed in minutes and seconds of arc.

Ernest Dimnet

French churchman and writer

Architecture, of all the arts, is the one which acts the most slowly, but the most surely, on the soul.

What We Live By pt 2, ch. 12

arctic animals animals inhabiting the ▷Arctic. The birds are chiefly sea birds, such as petrels, eider ducks, cormorants, auks, gulls, puffins, and guillemots; all are migratory. The mammals include the walrus, seals, and several varieties of whale; the polar bear, reindeer, elk, fox, wolf, ermine, and musk ox are the principal terrestrial mammals.

Arctic Circle imaginary line that encircles the North Pole at latitude 66° 30′ north. Within this line there is at least one day in the summer during which the Sun never sets, and at least one day in the winter during which the Sun never rises.

Arctic Ocean ocean surrounding the North Pole; area 14,000,000 sq km/5,405,400 sq mi. Because of the Siberian and North American rivers flowing into it, it has comparatively low salinity and freezes readily.

Related Web site: Arctic Ocean http://www.umsl.edu/services/govdocs/wofact96/19.htm

Arctic, the that part of the northern hemisphere surrounding the North Pole; arbitrarily defined as the region lying north of the Arctic Circle (66° 30′ north) or north of the treeline; area 36,000,000 sq km/14,000,000 sq mi; population around 1 million.

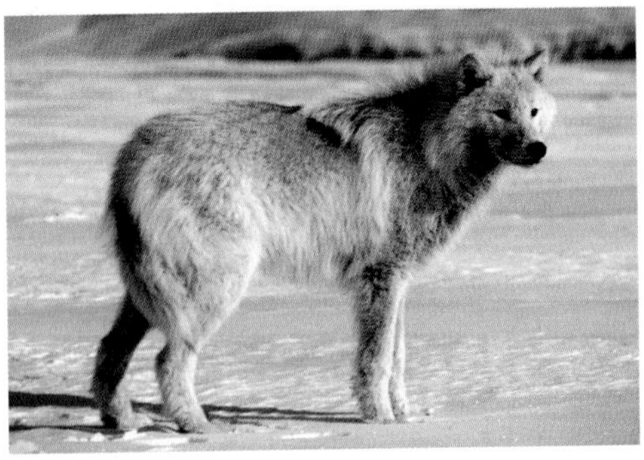

THE ARCTIC An Arctic wolf in its camouflage winter coat. *Corel*

There is no Arctic continent; the greater part of the region comprises the Arctic Ocean, which is the world's smallest ocean. Arctic climate, fauna, and flora extend over the islands and northern edges of continental land masses that surround the Arctic Ocean (Svalbard, Iceland, Greenland, Siberia, Scandinavia, Alaska, and Canada).

Related Web site: Arctic Circle http://arcticcircle.uconn.edu/

Arcturus (or **Alpha Boötis**) brightest star in the constellation Boötes and the fourth-brightest star in the night sky. Arcturus is a red giant about 28 times larger than the Sun and 70 times more luminous, 36 light years away from the Sun.

Ardennes hilly, wooded plateau in northeast France, southeast Belgium, and northern Luxembourg, cut through by the River ▷Meuse. The area gives its name to the region of ▷Champagne-Ardenne and the *département* of the Ardennes in France. The highest hills are about 590 m/1,936 ft. Cattle and sheep are raised and the area is rich in timber and minerals. There was heavy fighting here in both world wars, notably in the Battle of the ▷Bulge (1944–1945, also known as the Ardennes offensive). In World War I it was the route of the main German advance in 1914.

are metric unit of area, equal to 100 square metres (119.6 sq yd); 100 ares make one ▷hectare.

area the size of a surface. It is measured in square units, usually square centimetres (cm^2), square metres (m^2), or square kilometres (km^2). Surface area is the area of the outer surface of a solid.

areca any of a group of palm trees native to Asia and Australia. The ▷betel nut comes from the species *Areca catechu*. (Genus *Areca*.)

Arecibo town in northwest Puerto Rico. It is located on the Atlantic Ocean at the mouth of the Arecibo River, 77 km/48 mi to the west of San Juan. This colonial centre was originally settled in the mid-16th century. A port with some light manufacturing facilities and the site of a college of the University of Puerto Rico, it is also a trade, processing, and distribution hub for an agricultural region producing sugar cane, coffee, fruit, and tobacco. The rum and pharmaceutical industries are also important. The Cueva del Indio caves and the Río Camuy Cave Park are nearby, and 19 km/12 mi to the south is Cornell University's Arecibo Observatory, the site of the world's largest single-dish ▷radio telescope.

Arendt, Hannah (1906–1975) German-born US political philosopher. Her concerns included totalitarianism, the nature of evil, and the erosion of public participation in the political process. Her works include *Eichmann in Jerusalem* (1963) and *On Violence* (1972).

Arequipa capital of Arequipa department in the western Andes of southern Peru; it stands at a height of 2,363 m/7,753 ft in a fertile valley at the base of the dormant volcano El Misti (5,822 m/19,100 ft); industries include textiles, soap, and leather goods; population (1993) 619,200. It is the second-largest city of Peru and the cultural focus of southern Peru. Arequipa was founded by Pizarro in 1540 on the site of an ancient Inca city, and has a cathedral, founded in 1621, and a university.

Ares in Greek mythology, the god of war, equivalent to the Roman ▷Mars. The son of Zeus and Hera, he was worshipped chiefly in Thrace.

arête (German **grat**; North American **combe-ridge**) sharp narrow ridge separating two ▷glacial troughs (valleys), or ▷corries. The typical U-shaped cross sections of glacial troughs give arêtes very steep sides. Arêtes are common in glaciated mountain regions such as the Rockies, the Himalayas, and the Alps.

Arezzo (ancient **Arretium**) town in Tuscany, Italy, 80 km/50 mi southeast of Florence; population (1999) 91,300. Originally an ▷Etruscan settlement, Arezzo is an important market for agricultural and animal products from the fertile surrounding districts, and trades in textiles and clothing, shoes, olive oil, antiques, and gold and jewellery crafts. There is a fresco series by the Renaissance painter ▷Piero della Francesca.

argali wild sheep from the mountains of Central Asia. It is the largest species of sheep with a shoulder height of up to 1.2 m/4 ft. Argali *Ovis ammon* is in family Bovidae, order Artiodactyla.

Argand diagram in mathematics, a method for representing complex numbers by Cartesian coordinates (x, y). Along the x-axis (horizontal axis) are plotted the real numbers, and along the y-axis (vertical axis) the nonreal, or ▷imaginary, numbers.

Argentina see country box.

argon (Greek *argos* 'idle') colourless, odourless, nonmetallic, gaseous element, symbol Ar, atomic number 18, relative atomic mass 39.948. It is grouped with the ▷inert gases, since it was long believed not to react with other substances, but observations now indicate that it can be made to combine with boron fluoride to form compounds. It constitutes almost 1% of the Earth's atmosphere, and was discovered in 1894 by British chemists John Rayleigh and William Ramsay after all oxygen and nitrogen had been removed chemically from a sample of air. It is used in electric discharge tubes and argon lasers.

argonaut (or **paper nautilus**) octopus living in the open sea, genus *Argonauta*. The female of the common paper nautilus, *A. argo*, is 20 cm/8 in across, and secretes a spiralled papery shell for her eggs from the web of the first pair of arms. The male is a shell-less dwarf, 1 cm/0.4 in across.

Argonauts in Greek mythology, the band of heroes who accompanied ▷Jason when he set sail in the *Argo* to find the ▷Golden Fleece.

Related Web site: Jason and the Argonauts http://www.greece.org/poseidon/work/argonautika/argo.html

Argos city in ancient Greece, at the head of the Gulf of Nauplia, which was once a cult centre of the goddess Hera; her celebrated sanctuary lay outside the city. In the Homeric age the name 'Argives' was sometimes used instead of 'Greeks'. Although one of the most important cities in the Peloponnese, Argos was dominated by ▷Corinth and ▷Sparta. During the classical period the city repeatedly, but unsuccessfully, contested supremacy in southern Greece with Sparta.

Argus in Greek mythology, a giant with 100 eyes. When he was killed by Hermes, Hera transplanted his eyes into the tail of her favourite bird, the peacock.

Argyll and Bute unitary authority in western Scotland, created in 1996 from the district of the same name and part of Dumbarton district, which were both parts of Strathclyde region; it includes the islands of Gigha, Bute, Mull, Islay, Jura, Tiree, Coll, Colonsay, Iona, and Staffa.

area 7,016 sq km/2,709 sq mi **towns** Campbeltown, Dunoon, Helensburgh, Inveraray, Lochgilphead (administrative headquarters), Oban, Rothesay **physical** rural area consisting of mainland and islands; the coast is heavily indented. Inland the area is mountainous; highest peak, Ben Cruachan (1,126 m/3,693 ft). Lochs Fyne and Long are the largest sea lochs; freshwater lochs include Loch Awe and Loch Lomond; Fingal's Cave (Staffa); Corryvrekan Whirlpool (Jura-Scarba); Ben Arthur (The Cobbler), 884 m/2,900 ft **features** Bronze, Stone, and Iron Age remains **industries** limited manufacture, seaweed processing, fish, timber harvesting **agriculture** sheep, forestry **population** (1996) 89,300

Related Web site: Argyll and Bute Council http://www.argyll-bute.gov.uk/

Argyll, Archibald Campbell, 5th Earl of Argyll (1530–1573) adherent of the Scottish presbyterian John ▷Knox. A supporter of Mary Queen of Scots from 1561, he commanded her forces after her escape from Lochleven Castle in 1568. Following her defeat at Langside, he revised his position, made peace with the regent, James Stuart, Earl of Murray, and became Lord High Chancellor of Scotland in 1572. He succeeded to the earldom in 1558.

Argyllshire former county on the west coast of Scotland, including the Inner Hebridean Islands, which was for the most part merged into Argyll and Bute district in Strathclyde region in 1975.

Århus (or **Aarhus**) second-largest city of Denmark, on the east coast overlooking the Kattegat; population (1995) 277,500. It is the capital of Århus county in Jylland (Jutland) and a shipping and commercial centre.

Ariadne in Greek mythology, the daughter of Minos, King of Crete. When ▷Theseus came from Athens as one of the sacrificial victims offered to the ▷Minotaur, she fell in love with him and gave him a ball of thread, which enabled him to find his way out of the labyrinth. When Theseus abandoned her on the island of Naxos, she married ▷Dionysus.

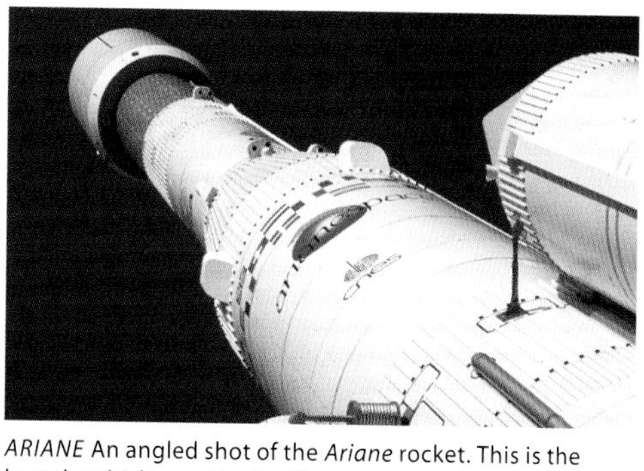

ARIANE An angled shot of the *Ariane* rocket. This is the launch vehicle used by the European Space Agency (ESA), a consortium of 14 European countries dedicated to space research and its related technology. *Image Bank*

Ariane launch vehicle built in a series by the European Space Agency (first flight in 1979). The launch site is at Kourou in French Guiana. Ariane is a three-stage rocket using liquid fuels. Small solid-fuel and liquid-fuel boosters can be attached to its first stage to increase carrying power.

> **John Collins Bossidy**
> US writer
>
> *And this is good old Boston, / The home of the bean and the cod, / Where the Lowells talk to the Cabots, / And the Cabots talk only to God.*
>
> *On the Aristocracy of Harvard*

Arianism system of Christian theology that denied the complete divinity of Jesus, giving God the Father primacy over the created son Jesus. It was founded about 310 by Arius, and condemned as heretical at the Council of Nicaea in 325.

Arica port and northernmost city of Chile, in Tarapacá region 20 km/12 mi from the Peruvian border; it is situated in a rainless district north of the Atacama Desert; population (1992) 169,200. The city is linked by railway to La Paz, Bolivia, and much of Bolivia's foreign trade is shipped via Arica. Fishmeal is an important industry. Tourism and the creation of a duty-free zone have boosted the local population. There is an increasing international trade in minerals. The world's largest open-pit copper mine at nearby Chuquicamata dominates the country's mining sector.

arid region in earth science, a region that is very dry and has little vegetation. Aridity depends on temperature, rainfall, and evaporation, and so is difficult to quantify, but an arid area is usually defined as one that receives less than 250 mm/10 in of rainfall each year. (By comparison, New York City receives 1,120 mm/44 in per year.) There are arid regions in North Africa, Pakistan, Australia, the USA, and elsewhere. Very arid regions are ▷deserts.

Ariège river in southern France, which rises in the Pyrenees and flows north to join the Garonne 10 km/6 mi south of Toulouse; length 170 km/106 mi. It gives its name to the *département* of Ariège.

> **Aristophanes**
>
> *Our poet says that he deserves a rich reward at your hands for having stopped you being too easily deceived by the words of foreigners, taking pleasure in flattery, being citizens of Emptyhead.*
>
> Autobiographical comment put into the mouths of the chorus in *Acharnians* 633

Aries zodiacal constellation in the northern hemisphere between Pisces and Taurus, near Auriga, represented as the legendary ram whose golden fleece was sought by Jason and the Argonauts.

Its most distinctive feature is a curve of three stars of decreasing brightness. The brightest of these is Hamal or Alpha Arietis, 65 light years from Earth.

The Sun passes through Aries from late April to mid-May. In astrology, the dates for Aries, the first sign of the zodiac, are between about 21 March and 19 April (see ▷precession). The spring ▷equinox once lay in Aries, but has now moved into Pisces through the effect of the Earth's precession (wobble).

Ariosto, Ludovico (1474–1533) Italian poet. He wrote Latin poems and comedies on classical lines. His major work is the poem *Orlando furioso* (1516, published in 1532), an epic treatment of the ▷Roland story, the perfect poetic expression of the Italian Renaissance.

Aristarchus of Samos (*c.* 320–*c.* 250 BC) Greek astronomer. The first to argue that the Earth moves around the Sun, he was ridiculed for his beliefs. He was also the first astronomer to estimate (quite inaccurately) the sizes of the Sun and Moon and their distances from the Earth.

Aristide, Jean-Bertrand (1953–) President of Haiti 1990–91, 1994–95, and from 2001. A left-wing Catholic priest opposed to the right-wing regime of the Duvalier family, he relinquished his priesthood to concentrate on the presidency. He campaigned for the National Front for Change and Democracy, representing a loose coalition of peasants, trade unionists, and clerics, and won 70% of the vote. He was deposed by the military in September 1991 and took refuge in the USA. In September 1994, under an agreement brokered by former US president Jimmy Carter, the military stepped down and allowed Aristide to return. Constitutionally barred from seeking a second term in December 1995, he was succeeded by his preferred candidate René Préval. After Préval dissolved parliament in 1999, elections in 2000 returned Aristide to the presidency.

Aristides (*c.* 530–468 BC) Athenian politician. He was one of the ten Athenian generals at the Battle of ▷Marathon in 490 BC and was elected chief archon, or magistrate. Later he came into conflict with the democratic leader Themistocles, and was exiled in about 483 BC. He returned to fight against the Persians at Salamis in 480 BC and in the following year commanded the Athenians at Plataea. As commander of the Athenian fleet he established the alliance of Ionian states known as the Delian League.

aristocracy (Greek *aristos* 'best', *kratos* 'power') social elite or system of political power associated with landed wealth, as in Western Europe; with monetary wealth, as in Carthage and Venice; or with religious superiority, as were the Brahmans in India. Aristocracies are also usually associated with monarchy but have frequently been in conflict with the sovereign over their respective rights and privileges. In Europe, their economic base was undermined during the 19th century by inflation and falling agricultural prices, leading to their demise as a political force after 1914.

The Prussian (Junker) aristocracy based its legitimacy not only on landed wealth but also on service to the state.

Aristophanes (*c.* 445–*c.* 380 BC) Greek comedy dramatist. Of his 11 extant plays (of a total of over 40), the early comedies are remarkable for the violent satire with which he ridiculed the democratic war leaders. He also satirized contemporary issues such as the new learning of Socrates in *The Clouds* (423 BC) and the obsession with war, with the sex-strike of women in *Lysistrata* (411 BC). The chorus plays a prominent role, frequently giving the play its title, as in *The Wasps* (422 BC), *The Birds* (414 BC), and *The Frogs* (405 BC).

Related Web site: Works by Aristophanes http://classics.mit.edu/Browse/browse-Aristophanes.html

Aristotle (384–322 BC) Greek philosopher who advocated reason and moderation. He maintained that sense experience is our only source of knowledge, and that by reasoning we can discover the essences of things, that is, their distinguishing qualities. In his works on ethics and politics, he suggested that human happiness consists in living in conformity with nature. He derived his political theory from the recognition that mutual aid is natural to humankind, and refused to set up any one constitution as universally ideal. Of Aristotle's works, around 22 treatises survive, dealing with logic, metaphysics, physics, astronomy, meteorology, biology, psychology, ethics, politics, and literary criticism.

Aristotle was born in Stagira in Thrace and studied in Athens, where he became a distinguished member of the Academy founded by Plato. He then opened a school at Assos. At this time he regarded himself as a Platonist, but his subsequent thought led him further from the traditions that had formed his early background and he was later critical of Plato. In about 344 BC he moved to Mytilene in Lesvos, and devoted the next two years to the study of natural history. Meanwhile, during his residence at Assos, he had married Pythias, niece and adopted daughter of Hermeias, ruler of Atarneus.

In 342 BC he accepted an invitation from Philip II of Macedon to go to Pella as tutor to Philip's son Alexander the Great. In 335 BC he opened a school in the Lyceum (grove sacred to Apollo) in Athens. It became known as the 'peripatetic school' because he walked up and down as he talked, and his works are a collection of his lecture notes. When Alexander died in 323 BC, Aristotle was forced to flee to Chalcis, where he died.

Among his many contributions to political thought were the first systematic attempts to distinguish between different forms of government, ideas about the role of law in the state, and the conception of a science of politics.

In the *Poetics*, Aristotle defines tragic drama as an imitation (mimesis) of the actions of human beings, with character

Argentina

Argentina country in South America, bounded west and south by Chile, north by Bolivia, and east by Paraguay, Brazil, Uruguay, and the Atlantic Ocean.

NATIONAL NAME *República Argentina/Argentine Republic*
AREA 2,780,400 sq km/1,073,518 sq mi
CAPITAL Buenos Aires
MAJOR TOWNS/CITIES Rosario, Córdoba, San Miguel de Tucumán, Mendoza, Santa Fé, La Plata
MAJOR PORTS La Plata and Bahía Blanca
PHYSICAL FEATURES mountains in west, forest and savannah in north, pampas (treeless plains) in east-central area, Patagonian plateau in south; rivers Colorado, Salado, Paraná, Uruguay, Río de La Plata estuary; Andes mountains, with Aconcagua the highest peak in western hemisphere; Iguaçu Falls
TERRITORIES disputed claim to the Falkland Islands (*Islas Malvinas*), and part of Antarctica

Government

HEAD OF STATE AND GOVERNMENT Néstor Kirchner Ostoic from 2003
POLITICAL SYSTEM liberal democracy
POLITICAL EXECUTIVE limited presidency
ADMINISTRATIVE DIVISIONS 23 provinces and one federal district (Buenos Aires)
ARMED FORCES 69,900; plus paramilitary gendarmerie of 31,200 (2002 est)
CONSCRIPTION abolished in 1995
DEATH PENALTY abolished for ordinary crimes in 1984; laws provide for the death penalty for exceptional crimes, such as crimes committed in wartime
EDUCATION SPEND (% GDP) 4.6 (2001 est)
HEALTH SPEND (% GDP) 8.6 (2000 est)

Economy and resources

CURRENCY peso (= 10,000 australs, which it replaced in 1992)
GPD (US$) 102.2 billion (2002 est)
REAL GDP GROWTH (% change on previous year) –4.6 (2001)
GNI (US$) 152.1 billion (2002 est)
GNI PER CAPITA (PPP) (US$) 9,930 (2002 est)
CONSUMER PRICE INFLATION 22.3% (2003 est)
UNEMPLOYMENT 16.4% (2001)
FOREIGN DEBT (US$) 171.4 billion (2001 est)
MAJOR TRADING PARTNERS Brazil, Chile, China, USA, Germany, France, Italy
RESOURCES coal, crude oil, natural gas, iron ore, lead ore, zinc ore, tin, gold, silver, uranium ore, marble, borates, granite
INDUSTRIES petroleum and petroleum products, primary iron, crude steel, sulphuric acid, synthetic rubber, paper and paper products, crude oil, cement, cigarettes, motor vehicles
EXPORTS meat and meat products, prepared animal fodder, cereals, petroleum and petroleum products, soybeans, vegetable oils and fats. Principal market: Brazil 27% (2000)
IMPORTS machinery and transport equipment, chemicals and mineral products. Principal sources: Brazil 26% (2000)
ARABLE LAND 9.1% (2000 est)
AGRICULTURAL PRODUCTS wheat, maize, soybeans, sugar cane, rice, sorghum, potatoes, tobacco, sunflowers, cotton, vine fruits, citrus fruit; livestock production (chiefly cattle)

Population and society

POPULATION 38,428,000 (2003 est)
POPULATION GROWTH RATE 1% (2000–15)
POPULATION DENSITY (per sq km) 14 (2003 est)
URBAN POPULATION (% of total) 89 (2003 est)
AGE DISTRIBUTION (% of total population) 0–14 27%, 15–59 60%, 60+ 13% (2002 est)
ETHNIC GROUPS 85% of European descent, mainly Spanish; 15% mestizo (offspring of Spanish–American and American Indian parents)
LANGUAGE Spanish (official) (95%), Italian (3%), English, German, French
RELIGION predominantly Roman Catholic (state-supported), 2% protestant, 2% Jewish
EDUCATION (compulsory years) 7; age limits 7–16
LITERACY RATE 97% (men); 97% (women) (2003 est)
LABOUR FORCE 1% agriculture, 25% industry, 74% services (1998)
LIFE EXPECTANCY 71 (men); 78 (women) (2000–05)
CHILD MORTALITY RATE (under 5, per 1,000 live births) 19 (2001)
PHYSICIANS (per 1,000 people) 2.7 (1998 est)
HOSPITAL BEDS (per 1,000 people) 3.3 (1998 est)
TV SETS (per 1,000 people) 326 (2001 est)
RADIOS (per 1,000 people) 681 (1997)
INTERNET USERS (per 10,000 people) 1,120.2 (2002 est)
PERSONAL COMPUTER USERS (per 100 people) 8.2 (2002 est)

See also ▷Falkland Islands; ▷Perón, Eva; ▷Perón, Isabel; ▷Perón, Juan.

Chronology

1516: The Spanish navigator Juan Díaz de Solis discovered Río de La Plata.

1536: Buenos Aires was founded, but was soon abandoned because of attacks by American Indians.

1580: Buenos Aires was re-established as part of the Spanish province of Asunción.

1617: Buenos Aires became a separate province within the Spanish viceroyalty of Lima.

1776: The Spanish South American Empire was reorganized: Atlantic regions became viceroyalty of La Plata, with Buenos Aires as capital.

1810: After the French conquest of Spain, Buenos Aires junta took over government of viceroyalty.

1816: Independence was proclaimed, as the United Provinces of Río de La Plata, but Bolivia and Uruguay soon seceded; civil war followed between federalists and those who wanted a unitary state.

1835–52: Dictatorship of Gen Juan Manuel Rosas.

1853: Adoption of federal constitution based on US model; Buenos Aires refused to join confederation.

1861: Buenos Aires was incorporated into the Argentine confederation by force.

1865–70: Argentina took part in the War of Triple Alliance against Paraguay.

late 19th century: Large-scale European immigration and economic development.

1880: Buenos Aires became the national capital.

1880–1916: The government was dominated by an oligarchy of conservative landowners.

1916: The secret ballot was introduced and the Radical Party of Hipólito Irigoyen won elections, beginning a period of 14 years in government.

1930: A military coup ushered in a series of conservative governments sustained by violence and fraud.

1946: Col Juan Perón won presidential elections; he secured working-class support through welfare measures, trade unionism, and the popularity of his wife, Eva Perón (Evita).

1949: A new constitution abolished federalism and increased powers of president.

1952: Death of Evita. Support for Perón began to decline.

1955: Perón was overthrown; the constitution of 1853 was restored.

1966–70: Dictatorship of Gen Juan Carlos Ongania.

1973: Perónist Party won free elections; Perón returned from exile in Spain to become president.

1974: Perón died and was succeeded by his third wife, Isabel Perón.

1976: A coup resulted in rule by a military junta.

1976–83: The military regime conducted murderous campaign ('Dirty War') against left-wing elements. More than 8,000 people disappeared.

1982: Argentina invaded the Falkland Islands but was defeated by the UK.

1983: Return to civilian rule; an investigation into the 'Dirty War' was launched.

1989: Annual inflation reached 12,000%.

1990: Full diplomatic relations with the UK restored.

1999: Fernando de la Rua won presidential elections

2000: Spending cuts aimed to bring the economy into line with targets set by the International Monetary Fund (IMF).

2001: Congress granted President de la Rúa emergency powers to implement his economic programme.

2002: Eduardo Duhalde took office in January as Argentina's fifth president in two weeks. In the wake of continuing financial upheaval the government devalued the peso.

ARGENTINA Eroded desert slopes near Tres Cruces in the Quebrada da Humahuaca in Jujuy province, Argentina. *K G Preston-Mafham/Premaphotos Wildlife*

ARISTOTLE A 14th-century manuscript showing Aristotle teaching the young Alexander, later Alexander the Great, king of Macedon. Typically, the illustration uses medieval dress and architecture to show a scene from many centuries earlier. *The Art Archive/British Library*

subordinated to plot. The audience is affected by pity and fear, but experiences a purgation (catharsis) of these emotions through watching the play. The second book of the *Poetics*, on comedy, is lost. The three books of the *Rhetoric* form the earliest analytical discussion of the techniques of persuasion, and the last presents a theory of the emotions to which a speaker must appeal.

In the Middle Ages, Aristotle's philosophy first became the foundation of Islamic philosophy, and was then incorporated into Christian theology; medieval scholars tended to accept his vast output without question. Aristotle held that all matter consisted of a single 'prime matter', which was always determined by some form. The simplest kinds of matter were the four elements – earth, water, air, and fire – which in varying proportions constituted all things. According to Aristotle's laws of motion, bodies moved upwards or downwards in straight lines. Earth and water fell, air and fire rose. To explain the motion of the heavenly spheres, Aristotle introduced a fifth element, ether, whose natural movement was circular.

Related Web site: Aristotle http://www-history.mcs.st-and.ac.uk/history/Mathematicians/Aristotle.html

Aristotle
What we have to learn to do, we learn by doing.
Nicomachean Ethics Book II

arithmetic branch of mathematics concerned with the study of numbers and their properties. The fundamental operations of arithmetic are addition, subtraction, multiplication, and division. Raising to powers (for example, squaring or cubing a number), the extraction of roots (for example, square roots), percentages, fractions, and ratios are developed from these operations.

Forms of simple arithmetic existed in prehistoric times. In China, Egypt, Babylon, and early civilizations generally, arithmetic was used for commercial purposes, records of taxation, and astronomy. During the Dark Ages in Europe, knowledge of arithmetic was preserved in India and later among the Arabs. European mathematics revived with the development of trade and overseas exploration. Hindu-Arabic numerals replaced Roman numerals, allowing calculations to be made on paper, instead of by the ▷abacus.

The essential feature of this number system was the introduction of zero, which allows us to have a **place–value** system. The decimal numeral system employs ten numerals (0,1,2,3,4,5,6,7,8,9) and is said to operate in 'base ten'. In a base-ten number, each position has a value ten times that of the position to its immediate right; for example, in the number 23 the numeral 3 represents three units (ones), and the numeral 2 represents two tens. The Babylonians, however, used a complex base-sixty system, residues of which are found today in the number of minutes in each hour and in angular measurement (6×60 degrees). The Mayas used a base-twenty system.

There have been many inventions and developments to make the manipulation of the arithmetic processes easier, such as the invention of ▷logarithms by Scottish mathematician John ▷Napier in 1614 and of the slide rule in the period 1620–30. Since then, many forms of ready reckoners, mechanical and electronic calculators, and computers have been invented.

Modern computers fundamentally operate in base two, using only two numerals (0,1), known as a **binary** system. In binary, each position has a value twice as great as the position to its immediate right, so that for example binary 111 (or 111_2) is equal to 7 in the decimal system, and binary 1111 (or 1111_2) is equal to 15. Because the main operations of subtraction, multiplication, and division can be reduced mathematically to addition, digital computers carry out calculations by adding, usually in binary numbers in which the numerals 0 and 1 can be represented by off and on pulses of electric current.

Modular or modulo **arithmetic**, sometimes known as residue arithmetic or clock arithmetic, can take only a specific number of digits, whatever the value. For example, in modulo 4 (mod 4) the only values any number can take are 0, 1, 2, or 3. In this system, 7 is written as 3 mod 4, and 35 is also 3 mod 4. Notice 3 is the residue, or remainder, when 7 or 35 is divided by 4. This form of arithmetic is often illustrated on a circle. It deals with events recurring in regular cycles, and is used in describing the functioning of petrol engines, electrical generators, and so on. For example, in the mod 12, the answer to a question as to what time it will be in five hours if it is now ten o'clock can be expressed 10 + 5 = 3.

arithmetic and logic unit (ALU) in a computer, the part of the ▷central processing unit (CPU) that performs the basic arithmetic and logic operations on data.

arithmetic mean the average of a set of n numbers, obtained by adding the numbers and dividing by n. For example, the arithmetic mean of the set of 5 numbers 1, 3, 6, 8, and 12 is
$$(1 + 3 + 6 + 8 + 12)/5 = 30/5 = 6.$$
The term 'average' is often used to refer only to the arithmetic mean, even though the mean is in fact only one form of average (the others include ▷median and ▷mode).

arithmetic progression (or **arithmetic sequence**) sequence of numbers or terms that have a common difference between any one term and the next in the sequence. For example, 2, 7, 12, 17, 22, 27, … is an arithmetic sequence with a common difference of 5.

The nth term in any arithmetic progression can be found using the formula:
$$n\text{th term} = a + (n-1)d$$
where a is the first term and d is the common difference.

An **arithmetic series** is the sum of the terms in an arithmetic sequence. The sum S of n terms is given by:
$$S = \frac{n}{2}[2a + (n-1)d]$$

Arizona state in southwestern USA. It is nicknamed Grand Canyon State. Arizona was admitted to the Union in 1912 as the 48th US state. The state is renowned for its natural wonders, including Monument Valley and the Grand Canyon, and is strongly associated with such indigenous peoples as the Navajo and Hopi. It is bordered to the east by New Mexico, to the south by the Mexican state of Sonora, to the west by the Mexican state of Baja California and the US states of California and Nevada, and to the north by Utah, and at the 'Four Corners' to the northeast, Colorado.

population (1996 est) 4,428,100; including 5.6% American Indians (Navajo, Hopi, Apache), who by treaty own 25% of the state **area** 294,100 sq mi/113,500 sq km **capital** Phoenix **towns and cities** Tucson, Scottsdale, Tempe, Mesa, Glendale, Flagstaff **industries and products** cotton under irrigation, livestock ranching, copper (more than half of US annual output), silver, uranium mining, molybdenum, electronics, aircraft

Related Web site: Palatki – 6,000 Years of Arizona Rock Art http://aztec.asu.edu/azrha/palatki/palatki.html

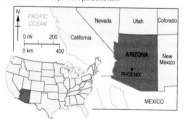

Arjan Indian religious leader, fifth guru (teacher) of Sikhism 1581–1606. He built the Golden Temple in ▷Amritsar and compiled the *Adi Granth*, the first volume of Sikh scriptures. He died in Muslim custody.

Arkansas state in southern central USA. It is nicknamed Land of Opportunity. Arkansas was admitted to the Union in 1836 as the 25th US state. Historically it was a cotton plantation state,

dependent on slavery. It was the site of civil-rights struggles in the 1950s and 1960s and became closely associated with the political intrigues surrounding Bill Clinton during his presidential tenure in the 1990s. Arkansas is bordered to the south by Louisiana, to the southwest by Texas, to the west by Oklahoma, to the north by Missouri, and to the east by Tennessee and Mississippi; the Red, St Francis, and Mississippi rivers form part of its natural borders.

population (1996 est) 2,510,000 **area** 137,800 sq km/53,191 sq mi **capital** Little Rock **towns and cities** Fort Smith, Pine Bluff, Fayetteville, North Little Rock **industries and products** cotton, soybeans, rice, oil, natural gas, timber, processed foods, electronics, financial sector, military bases

Related Web site: Welcome to Arkansas USA http://www.arkansasUSA.com/

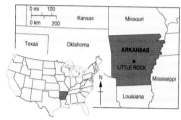

Arkwright, Richard (1732–1792) English inventor and manufacturing pioneer who in 1768 developed a machine for spinning cotton (he called it a 'water frame'). In 1771 he set up a water-powered spinning factory and in 1790 he installed steam power in a Nottingham factory. He was knighted in 1786.

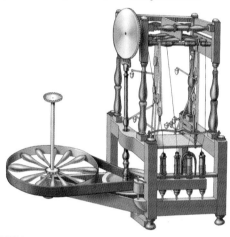

RICHARD ARKWRIGHT English inventor Richard Arkwright devised his 'water frame', for spinning cotton, in 1768.

Arles town in Bouches-du-Rhône *département*, southwest France, on the Arles canal and the left bank of the Rhône, at the head of the Camargue delta; population (1990) 52,600. Its main economic activities are tourism and agriculture, and it is in an important fruit- and vine-growing district. Roman relics include an aqueduct, baths, and a 21,000-spectator amphitheatre now used for bullfighting and plays. The Romanesque-Provençal church of St Trophime, formerly an archiepiscopal cathedral, has fine cloisters and a notable 12th-century portal. The painter Vincent ▷van Gogh lived here 1888–89, during which time he painted some of his major works.

Arlington county in Virginia, and a suburb of Washington, DC, which it faces across the Potomac River; area 67 sq km/26 sq mi; population (1994 est) 175,000. Arlington is a busy residential community with clusters of modern high-rise buildings and some light manufacturing (electrical components, scientific instruments, machinery). It is home to Strayer College (1892) and Marymount University (1950), as well as numerous federal buildings.

Armada fleet sent by Philip II of Spain against England in 1588. See ▷Spanish Armada.

armadillo mammal of the family Dasypodidae, with an armour of bony plates along its back or, in some species, almost covering the entire body. Around 20 species live between Texas and Patagonia and range in size from the fairy armadillo, or pichiciego, *Chlamyphorus truncatus*, at 13 cm/5 in, to the giant armadillo *Priodontes giganteus*, 1.5 m/4.5 ft long. Armadillos feed on insects, snakes, fruit, and carrion. Some can roll into an armoured ball if attacked; others defend themselves with their claws or rely on rapid burrowing for protection.

They belong to the order Edentata ('without teeth') which also includes sloths and anteaters. However, only the latter are toothless. Some species of armadillos can have up to 90 peglike teeth.

Armageddon in the New Testament (Revelation 16:16), the site of the final battle between the nations that will end the world; it has been identified with ▷Megiddo in Israel.

Armagh (Irish **Ard Mhacha**; 'the height of Mhacha' (a legendary queen) county of Northern Ireland.

area 1,250 sq km/483 sq mi **towns and cities** ▷Armagh (county town), Lurgan and Portadown (merged to form Craigavon), Keady **physical** smallest county of Northern Ireland; flat in the north, with many bogs and mounds formed from glacial deposits; low hills in the south, the highest of which is Slieve Gullion (577 m/1,893 ft); principal rivers are the Bann, the Blackwater and its tributary, the Callan **features** Blackwater River Park; the 17th-century manor Ardress House; Camagh Forest; Oxford Island Nature Reserve; Gosford Forest Park **agriculture** good farmland (apart from the marshy areas by Lough Neagh) with apple orchards; potatoes; flax; emphasis on livestock rearing in the south; fruit growing and market gardening in the north **industries** linen manufacture (Portadown and Lurgan were the principal centres of the linen industry); milling; light engineering; concrete; potato crisps **population** (1981) 119,000 **borders** The River Blackwater, which flows into Lough Neagh, forms the western boundary with County Tyrone; County Down lies to the east. The hills of igneous rock encircling Slieve Gullion form part of the border with County Louth in the Republic of Ireland. **history** Armagh is noted for its rich archaeological remains, including those at Emain Macha, a large earthwork 4 km/2.5 mi west of the city of Armagh, reputed to have been built by Queen Mhacha in 300 BC. Eamhain Macha was the seat of the kings of Ulster until AD 332, and the county of Armagh has been significant in many conflicts over territory, including battles over Ulster between the British and Irish during the 17th–19th centuries.

Related Web site: County Armagh http://www.interknowledge.com/northern-ireland/ukiarm00.htm

Armagh city and county town of County ▷Armagh, Northern Ireland; population (1991) 14,300. Industries include textiles, including linen; the manufacture of shoes, optical instruments, and chemicals; and engineering and food processing. The city became the religious centre of Ireland in the 5th century when ▷St Patrick was made archbishop.

Armani, Giorgio (1935–) Italian fashion designer. He launched his first menswear collection in 1974 and the following year started designing women's clothing. His work is known for understated styles, and fine fabrics. He pioneered the 'unstructured jacket' and his designs are marketed under different labels, from exclusive models to the less expensive diffusion range.

armature in a motor or generator, the wire-wound coil that carries the current and rotates in a magnetic field. (In alternating-current machines, the armature is sometimes stationary.) The pole piece of a permanent magnet or electromagnet and the moving, iron part of a ▷solenoid, especially if the latter acts as a switch, may also be referred to as armatures.

armed forces state military organizations; the ▷army, ▷navy, and ▷air force.

Armenia see country box.

Armenian member of the largest ethnic group inhabiting Armenia. There are Armenian minorities in Azerbaijan (see ▷Nagorno-Karabakh), as well as in Syria, Lebanon, Turkey, and Iran. Christianity was introduced to the ancient Armenian kingdom in the 3rd century. There are 4–5 million speakers of Armenian, which belongs to the Indo-European family of languages.

Armenian Church form of Christianity adopted in Armenia in the 3rd century. The Catholicos, or exarch, is the supreme head, and Echmiadzin (near Yerevan) is his traditional seat. Believers number about 2 million.

Armenian language one of the main divisions of the Indo-European language family. Old Armenian, the classical literary language, is still used in the liturgy of the Armenian Church. Armenian was not written down until the 5th century AD, when an alphabet of 36 (now 38) letters was evolved. Literature flourished in the 4th to 14th centuries, revived in the 18th, and continued throughout the 20th.

Armenian massacres series of massacres of Armenians by Turkish soldiers between 1895 and 1915. In 1894–96 demands for better treatment led to massacres of Armenians in eastern Asia Minor. Over 50,000 Armenians were killed by Kurdish irregulars and Ottoman troops. The killing was stopped by the major European powers, but in 1915 Ottoman suspicions of Armenian loyalty led to further massacres and deportations. The Turks deported 1.75 million Armenians to Syria and Palestine; 600,000 to 1 million were either killed or died of starvation during the journey.

Arminius (*c.* 18 BC–19 AD) German **Hermann**. German chieftain of the Cherusci tribe. An ex-soldier of the Roman army, he annihilated a Roman force led by Quintilius Varus in the Teutoburger Forest area in AD 9, and saved Germany from becoming a Roman province. He survived an assassination attempt by Tiberius in AD 19, but was treacherously killed by some of his kinsmen in the same year.

Arminius, Jacobus (1560–1609) Dutch **Jakob Harmensen**. Dutch Protestant priest who founded Arminianism, a school of Christian theology opposed to John Calvin's doctrine of predestination. His views were developed by Simon Episcopius (1583–1643). Arminianism is the basis of Wesleyan ▷Methodism.

armistice cessation of hostilities while awaiting a peace settlement. **The Armistice** refers specifically to the end of World War I between Germany and the Allies on 11 November 1918. On 22 June 1940, following the German invasion of France, French representatives signed an armistice with Germany in the same railway carriage at Compiègne as in 1918. No armistice was signed with either Germany or Japan in 1945; both nations surrendered and there was no provision for the suspension of fighting. The Korean armistice, signed at Panmunjom on 27 July 1953, terminated the Korean War 1950–53.

Armistice Day anniversary of the armistice signed 11 November 1918, ending World War I.

ARMISTICE DAY On 11 November 1918, the people of London went out onto the streets to celebrate the end of the 'war to end war'. In this photograph, servicemen and women, carrying flags, celebrate in the Strand, a street in central London. *Archive Photos*

armour body protection worn in battle. Body armour is depicted in Greek and Roman art. Chain mail was developed in the Middle Ages but the craft of the armourer in Europe reached its height in design in the 15th century, when knights were completely encased in plate armour that still allowed freedom of movement. Medieval Japanese armour was articulated, made of iron, gilded metal, leather, and silk. Contemporary bulletproof vests and riot gear are forms of armour. The term is used in a modern context to refer to a mechanized armoured vehicle, such as a tank.

Since World War II armour for tanks and ships has been developed beyond an increasing thickness of steel plate, becoming an increasingly light, layered composite, including materials such as ceramics. More controversial is 'reactive' armour, consisting of 'shoeboxes' made of armour containing small, quick-acting explosive charges, which are attached at the most vulnerable points of a tank, in order to break up the force of entry of an enemy warhead. This type is used by, for example, Israel, but the incorporation of explosive material in a tank has potential drawbacks.

The invention of gunpowder led, by degrees, to the virtual abandonment of armour until World War I, when the helmet reappeared as a defence against shrapnel. Suits of armour in the Tower of London were studied by US designers of astronaut wear.

ARMOUR An example of a knight's armour, San Gimignano, Italy. *Image Bank*

Modern armour, used by the army, police, security guards, and people at risk from assassination, uses nylon and fibreglass and is often worn beneath their clothing.

arms control attempts to limit the arms race between the superpowers by reaching agreements to restrict the production of certain weapons; see ▷disarmament.

arms trade sale of conventional weapons, such as tanks, combat aircraft, and related technology, from a manufacturing country to another nation. Arms exports are known in the trade as 'arms transfers'. Most transfers take place between governments and can be accompanied by training and maintenance agreements. International agreements, such as the Nuclear Non-Proliferation Treaty, outlaw the transfer of nuclear weapons and weapons of biological or chemical warfare. There are also agreements not to supply certain countries with conventional weapons, such as Iraq, Libya, and Yugoslavia, which may use weapons for internal repression or neighbour disputes. However, an active black market means that these arms embargoes are typically overcome. Around a half of the world's arms exports end up in Third World countries. Iraq, for instance, was armed in the years leading up to the 1991 Gulf War mainly by the USSR but also by France, Brazil, and South Africa.

Related Web site: Campaign Against Arms Trade http://www.caat.demon.co.uk/

Armstrong, Louis (1901–1971) Called 'Satchmo'. US jazz cornet and trumpet player and singer. His Chicago recordings in the 1920s with the Hot Five and Hot Seven brought him recognition for his warm and pure trumpet tone, his skill at improvisation, and his quirky, gravelly voice. From the 1930s he also appeared in films.

Armstrong was born in New Orleans. In 1923 he joined the Creole Jazz Band led by the cornet player Joe 'King' Oliver in Chicago, but soon broke away and fronted various bands of his own. In 1947 he formed the Louis Armstrong All-Stars. He firmly established the pre-eminence of the virtuoso jazz soloist. He is also credited with the invention of scat singing.

Related Web site: Louis Armstrong: Satchography http://www.satchography.com/home.html

Armstrong, Neil Alden (1930–) US astronaut. In 1969, he became the first person to set foot on the Moon, and said, 'That's one small step for a man, one giant leap for mankind.' The Moon landing was part of the ▷Apollo project.

Born in Ohio, Armstrong gained his pilot's licence at 16, studied aeronautics at Purdue University, and served as a naval pilot in Korea 1949–52 before joining NASA as a test pilot. He joined the US National Aerospace Program in 1962, and commanded *Gemini 8* in March 1966, linking with an unmanned *Agena* rocket. With Edwin 'Buzz' ▷Aldrin and Michael Collins (1930–) in *Apollo 11* on 16 July 1969, he lifted off from Cape Kennedy to land, four days later, on the Moon.

army organized military force for fighting on the ground. A national army is used to further a political policy by force either within the state or on the territory of another state. Most countries have a national army, maintained by taxation, and raised either by conscription (compulsory military service) or voluntarily (paid professionals). Private armies may be employed by individuals and groups.

Ancient armies (to 1066) Armies were common to all ancient civilizations. The first identifiable regular army occurred in about 1600 BC, when the Egyptian ruler, Amosis, formed an integral force of infantry, archers, and chariot-borne troops to expel the Hyksos invaders. The method of raising an army on a system of quasi-conscription was introduced by the Egyptians. In the latter days of Greek history conscription was normal. The Spartans trained from childhood for service from the age of 21 to 26 in a full-time regular force as a heavily armed infantryman, or **hoplite**. Roman armies subjected all male citizens to military service in **legions** of 6,000 men divided into **cohorts** of 600 men. Cohorts were similarly divided into six **centuries** of 100 men. The concept of duty to military service continued following the collapse of the Roman Empire. For example, the Anglo-Saxon **fyrd** obliged all able-bodied men to serve in defence of Britain against Danish and then Norman invasion.

Armies of knights and mercenaries (1066–1648) Medieval monarchs relied upon mounted men-at-arms, or **chevaliers**, who in turn called on serfs from the land. Feudal armies were thus inherently limited in size and could only fight for limited periods. Free **yeomen** armed with longbows were required by law to practise at the **butts** and provided an early form of indirect fire as **artillery**. In Europe paid troops, or **soldi**, and mounted troops, or **serviertes** (sergeants), made themselves available as **freelances**. By the end of the 15th century, **battles** or **battalions** of pikemen provided defence against the mounted knight. The hard gun, or **arquebus**, heralded the coming of infantrymen as known today. Those who wished to avoid military service could do so by paying **scutage**. For the majority the **conpane**, or **company**, was their home; they were placed under royal command by **ordonnances** and led by crown office holders, or **officiers**. Increased costs led to the formation of the first mercenary armies. For example, the **Great Company** of 10,000 men acted as an international force, employing contractors, or **condottieri**, to serve the highest bidder. By the 16th century the long musket, pikemen, and the use of fortifications combined against the knight. **Sappers** became increasingly important in the creation and breaking of obstacles such as at Metz, a forerunner of the Maginot Line.

Professional armies (1648–1792) The emergence of the European nation-state saw the growth of more professional standing armies which trained in drills, used formations to maximize firepower, and introduced service discipline. The invention of the ring bayonet and the flintlock saw the demise of pikemen and the increased capability to fire from three ranks (today still the standard drill formation in the British Army). Artillery was now mobile and fully integrated into the army structure. The defects of raw levies, noble amateurs, and mercenaries led Oliver Cromwell to create the New Model Army for the larger campaigns of the English Civil War. After the Restoration, Charles II established a small standing army, which was expanded under James II and William III. In France, a model regiment was set up under de Martinet which set standards of uniformity for all to follow. State taxation provided for a formal system of army administration (uniforms, pay, ammunition). Nevertheless, recruits remained mainly society's misfits and delinquents. Collectively termed **other ranks**, they were divided from commissioned officers by a rigid hierarchical structure. The sheer cost of such armies forced wars to be fought by manoeuvre rather than by pitched battle, aiming to starve one's opponent into defeat while protecting one's own logistic chain.

Armies of the revolution (1792–1819) Napoleon's organization of his army into autonomous **corps** of two to three **divisions**, in turn comprising two **brigades** of two **regiments** of two **battalions**, was a major step forward in allowing a rapid and flexible deployment of forces.

Small-scale skirmishing by **light infantry**, coupled with the increasing devastation created by artillery or densely packed formations, saw the beginnings of the **dispersed battlefield**. Victory in war was now synonymous with the complete destruction of the enemy in battle. Reservists were conscripted to allow the mass army to fight wars through to the bitter end. (Only Britain, by virtue of the English Channel and the Royal Navy, was able to avoid the need to provide such large land forces.) Officers were now required to be professionally trained; the Royal Military College was set up in Britain in 1802, St Cyr in France in 1808, the Kriegsakademie in Berlin in 1810, and the Russian Imperial Military Academy in 1832.

Armenia

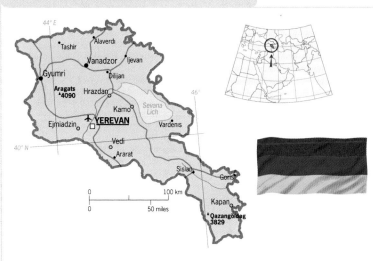

Armenia country in western Asia, bounded east by Azerbaijan, north by Georgia, west by Turkey, and south by Iran.

NATIONAL NAME *Hayastani Hanrapetoutioun/Republic of Armenia*
AREA 29,800 sq km/11,505 sq mi
CAPITAL Yerevan
MAJOR TOWNS/CITIES Gyumri (formerly Leninakan), Vanadzor (formerly Kirovakan), Hrazdan, Aboyvan
PHYSICAL FEATURES mainly mountainous (including Mount Ararat), wooded

Government

HEAD OF STATE Robert Kocharian from 1998
HEAD OF GOVERNMENT Andranik Markaryan from 2000
POLITICAL SYSTEM authoritarian nationalist
POLITICAL EXECUTIVE unlimited presidency
ADMINISTRATIVE DIVISIONS 11 provinces, including the capital, Yerevan
ARMED FORCES 44,600 (2002 est)
CONSCRIPTION compulsory for 24 months
DEATH PENALTY retained and used for ordinary crimes
DEFENCE SPEND (% GDP) 6.4 (2002 est)
EDUCATION SPEND (% GDP) 2.9 (2001 est)
HEALTH SPEND (% GDP) 7.5 (2000 est)

Economy and resources

CURRENCY dram (replaced Russian rouble in 1993)
GPD (US$) 2.4 billion (2002 est)
REAL GDP GROWTH (% change on previous year) 9.6 (2001)
GNI (US$) 2.4 billion (2002 est)
GNI PER CAPITA (PPP) (US$) 2,880 (2001)
CONSUMER PRICE INFLATION 2.2% (2003 est)
UNEMPLOYMENT 10.3% (2001)
FOREIGN DEBT (US$) 1 billion (2001 est)
MAJOR TRADING PARTNERS Russia, USA, UK, Belgium, Israel, Iran
RESOURCES copper, zinc, molybdenum, iron, silver, marble, granite
INDUSTRIES food processing and beverages, fertilizers, synthetic rubber, machinery and metal products, textiles, garments
EXPORTS precious or semi-precious metals and stones, machinery and metalworking products, chemical and petroleum products, base metals, equipment. Principal market: Russia 17.7% (2001)
IMPORTS light industrial products, petroleum and derivatives, industrial raw materials, vegetable products. Principal source: Russia 19.5% (2001)
ARABLE LAND 17.6% (2000 est)
AGRICULTURAL PRODUCTS potatoes, vegetables, fruits, cotton, almonds, olives, figs, cereals; livestock rearing (sheep and cattle)

Population and society

POPULATION 3,061,000 (2003 est)
POPULATION GROWTH RATE 0.4% (2000–15)
POPULATION DENSITY (per sq km) 103 (2003 est)
URBAN POPULATION (% of total) 67 (2003 est)
AGE DISTRIBUTION (% of total population) 0–14 21%, 15–59 66%, 60+ 13% (2002 est)
ETHNIC GROUPS 93% of Armenian ethnic descent, 3% Azeri, 2% Russian, and 2% Kurdish
LANGUAGE Armenian (official)
RELIGION Armenian Orthodox
EDUCATION (compulsory years) 9
LITERACY RATE 99% (men); 98% (women) (2003 est)
LABOUR FORCE 32.2% agriculture, 32.8% industry, 35% services (1993)
LIFE EXPECTANCY 69 (men); 76 (women) (2000–05)
CHILD MORTALITY RATE (under 5, per 1,000 live births) 35 (2001)
PHYSICIANS (per 1,000 people) 3.2 (1998 est)
HOSPITAL BEDS (per 1,000 people) 0.7 (1998 est)
TV SETS (per 1,000 people) 230 (2001 est)
RADIOS (per 1,000 people) 225 (2001 est)
INTERNET USERS (per 10,000 people) 157.9 (2002 est)
PERSONAL COMPUTER USERS (per 100 people) 1.6 (2002 est)

See also ▷Armenian massacres; ▷Azerbaijan; ▷Nagorno-Karabakh.

Chronology

6th century BC: Armenian peoples moved into the area, which was then part of the Persian Empire.

c. 94–56 BC: Under King Tigranes II 'the Great', Armenia reached the height of its power, becoming the strongest state in the eastern Roman empire.

c. AD 300: Christianity became the state religion when the local ruler was converted by St Gregory the Illuminator.

c. AD 390: Armenia was divided between Byzantine Armenia, which became part of the Byzantine Empire, and Persarmenia, under Persian control.

886–1045: Became independent under the Bagratid monarchy.

13th century: After being overrun by the Mongols, a substantially independent Little Armenia survived until 1375.

early 16th century: Conquered by Muslim Ottoman Turks.

1813–28: Russia took control of eastern Armenia.

late 19th century: Revival in Armenian culture and national spirit, provoking Ottoman backlash in western Armenia and international concern at Armenian maltreatment: the 'Armenian Question'.

1894–96: Armenians were massacred by Turkish soldiers in an attempt to suppress unrest.

1915: Suspected of pro-Russian sympathies, two-thirds of Armenia's population of 2 million were deported to Syria and Palestine. Around 600,000 to 1 million died en route: the survivors contributed towards an Armenian diaspora in Europe and North America.

1916: Armenia was conquered by tsarist Russia and became part of a brief 'Transcaucasian Alliance' with Georgia and Azerbaijan.

1918: Armenia became an independent republic.

1920: Occupied by Red Army of Soviet Union (USSR), but western Armenia remained part of Turkey and northwest Iran.

1936: Became constituent republic of USSR; rapid industrial development.

late 1980s: Armenian 'national reawakening', encouraged by *glasnost* (openness) initiative of Soviet leader Mikhail Gorbachev.

1988: Around 20,000 people died in an earthquake.

1989: Strife-torn Nagorno-Karabakh was placed under direct rule from Moscow; civil war erupted with Azerbaijan over Nagorno-Karabakh and Nakhichevan, an Azerbaijani-peopled enclave in Armenia.

1990: Independence was declared, but ignored by Moscow and the international community.

1991: After the collapse of the USSR, Armenia joined the new Commonwealth of Independent States. Nagorno-Karabakh declared its independence.

1992: Armenia was recognized as an independent state by the USA and admitted into the United Nations (UN).

1993: Armenian forces gained control of more than a fifth of Azerbaijan.

1994: A Nagorno-Karabakh ceasefire ended the conflict.

1997: There was border fighting with Azerbaijan.

1999: Prime Minister Vazgen Sarkisian was assassinated in October. He was replaced by his brother, Amen Sarkisian.

2000: President Robert Kocharian dismissed Amen Sarkisian as prime minister and replaced him with Andranik Markaryan.

2001: Armenia was admitted to the Council of Europe.

ARMENIA Armenia is a land of mountains and deep valleys, surrounding a high plateau. Industries such as copper mining are important to the economy, though the country is also agriculturally rich. This market hall in the capital, Yerevan, has apricots, peaches and grapes. *Corel*

Semaphore telegraph and **observation balloons** were first steps to increasing the commander's ability to observe enemy movements. The British army, under Wellington, was very strong, but afterwards decreased in numbers and efficiency.

National armies (1819–1914) The defeat of Revolutionary France saw a return to the traditions of the 18th century and a reduction in conscription. Meanwhile the railway revolutionized the deployment of forces, permitting quick mobilization, continuous resupply to the front, and rapid evacuation of casualties to the rear. The US Civil War has been called the Railway War. By 1870, the limitation of supply inherent to the Napoleonic army had been overcome and once again armies of over 1 million could be deployed. By 1914, continental armies numbered as many as 3 million and were based on conscription. A general staff was now required to manage these. **Breech-loading rifles** and **machine guns** ensured a higher casualty rate.

19th-century armies The 19th century saw the great development of rapidly produced missile weapons and the use of railways to move troops and materials.

Technological armies (1918–45) The advent of the internal combustion engine allowed new advances in mobility to overcome the supremacy of the defensive over the offensive. The **tank** and the **radio** were vital to the evolution of armoured warfare or **Blitzkrieg**. Armies were able to reorganize into highly mobile formations, such as the German **Panzer Divisions**, which utilized speed, firepower, and surprise to overwhelm static defences and thereby dislocate the army's rear.

The armies of World War II were very mobile, and were closely coordinated with the navy and air force. The requirement to fuel and maintain such huge fleets of vehicles again increased the need to maintain supplies. The complexity of the mechanized army demanded a wide range of skills not easily found through conscription.

Armies of the nuclear age (1945–) The advent of tactical nuclear weapons severely compounded the problems of mass concentration and thus protected mobility assumed greater importance to allow rapid concentration and dispersal of forces in what could be a high chemical threat zone. From the 1960s there were sophisticated developments in tanks and antitank weapons, mortar-locating radar, and heat-seeking missiles.

As a result of the ending of the Cold War, the US and the former Soviet and European armies are being substantially cut in the 1990s. The UK army will be cut from 155,000 to 119,000. The US army announced in February 1999 that it was creating new units called Strike Forces. These will combine elements of light and heavy divisions to allow the army to respond better to sudden crises, and are expected to be operational within a year.

Arnhem, Battle of in World War II, airborne operation by the Allies, 17–26 September 1944, to secure a bridgehead over the Rhine, thereby opening the way for a thrust towards the Ruhr and a possible early end to the war. It was only partially successful, with 7,600 casualties.

Arnhem Land plateau of the central peninsula in northeast Northern Territory, Australia, west of the Gulf of Carpentaria; approximate area 80,776 sq km/31,188 sq mi. Arnhem Land was named after a Dutch ship which dropped anchor here in 1618. The chief town is Nhulunbuy; population (1996) 3,695. It is the largest of the Aboriginal reserves, and was declared Aboriginal land in 1976. Many of the inhabitants live in small settlements and maintain a traditional way of life. Bauxite and uranium mining and the supporting industries provide the main economic base of the area.

Arnim, Ludwig Achim von (1781–1831) German Romantic poet and novelist. He wrote short stories, a romance *Armut, Schuld und Busse der Gräfin Dolores/Countess Dolores* (1810), and plays, but left the historical novel *Die Kronenwächter* (1817) unfinished. With Clemens Brentano he collected the German folk songs in *Des Knaben Wunderhorn/The Boy's Magic Horn* (1805–08), several of which were set to music by Mahler.

Arno Italian river 240 km/150 mi long, rising in the Apennines, and flowing westwards to the Mediterranean Sea. Florence and Pisa stand on its banks. A flood in 1966 damaged virtually every Renaissance landmark in Florence.

Arnold, Benedict (1741–1801) US soldier and military strategist who, during the American Revolution, won the turning-point battle at Saratoga in 1777 for the Americans. He is chiefly remembered as a traitor to the American side, having plotted to betray the strategic post at West Point to the British.

Arnold, Malcolm Henry (1921–) English composer. His work is tonal and includes a large amount of orchestral, chamber, ballet, and vocal music. His overtures *Beckus the Dandipratt* (1948), *A Sussex Overture* (1951), and *Tam O'Shanter* (1955) are well known. His operas include *The Dancing Master* (1951), and he has written music for more than 80 films, including *The Bridge on the River Kwai* (1957), for which he won an Academy Award.

Arnold, Matthew (1822–1888) English poet and critic. His poem 'Dover Beach' (1867) was widely regarded as one of the most eloquent expressions of the spiritual anxieties of Victorian England. In his highly influential critical essays collected in *Culture and Anarchy* (1869), he attacked the smugness and philistinism of the Victorian middle classes, and argued for a new culture based on the pursuit of artistic and intellectual values. He was the son of Thomas Arnold, headmaster of Rugby school.

Related Web site: Selected Poetry and Prose of Matthew Arnold (1822–1888) http://www.library.utoronto.ca/utel/rp/authors/arnold.html

> **Matthew Arnold**
> *Culture, the acquainting ourselves with the best that has been known and said in the world, and thus with the history of the human spirit.*
> Literature and Dogma, preface to 1873 edition

Arnold, Thomas (1795–1842) English schoolmaster, father of the poet and critic Matthew ▷Arnold. He was headmaster of Rugby School 1828–42. His regime has been graphically described in Thomas Hughes's *Tom Brown's Schooldays* (1857). He emphasized training of character, and had a profound influence on public school education.

aromatherapy in alternative medicine, use of oils and essences derived from plants, flowers, and wood resins. Bactericidal properties and beneficial effects upon physiological functions are attributed to the oils, which are sometimes ingested but generally massaged into the skin.

aromatic compound organic chemical compound in which some of the bonding electrons are delocalized (shared among several atoms within the molecule and not localized in the vicinity of the atoms involved in bonding). The commonest aromatic compounds have ring structures, the atoms comprising the ring being either all carbon or containing one or more different atoms (usually nitrogen, sulphur, or oxygen). Typical examples are benzene (C_6H_6) and pyridine (C_5H_5N).

Arp, Hans (or **Jean**) (1887–1966) French abstract painter, sculptor, and poet. He was one of the founders of the ▷Dada movement in 1916, and was later associated with the Surrealists. Using chance and automatism, Arp developed an abstract sculpture whose sensuous shapes suggest organic forms. In many of his works, in particular his early collages, he collaborated with his wife **Sophie Taeuber-Arp** (1889–1943).

Arran large island in the Firth of Clyde, lying between the Kintyre peninsula and the mainland of North Ayrshire, Scotland; area 427 sq km/165 sq mi; population (1991) 4,500. The economy is largely based on tourism and craft industries, though other industries include whisky distilling and food processing. The island, which is mountainous to the north and undulating to the south, is a popular holiday resort. The chief town is Brodick.

Arras French town on the Scarpe River northeast of Paris; population (1990) 42,700. It is the capital of Pas-de-Calais *département*, and was formerly known for tapestry. It was the birthplace of the French revolutionary leader Robespierre.

arrest apprehension and detention of a person suspected of a crime. In Britain, an arrest may be made on a magistrate's warrant, but a police constable is empowered to arrest without warrant in all cases where he or she has reasonable ground for thinking a serious offence has been committed.

Arrhenius, Svante August (1859–1927) Swedish scientist, the founder of physical chemistry. He was awarded the Nobel Prize for Chemistry in 1903 for his study of electrolysis. In 1905 he predicted global warming as a result of carbon dioxide emission from burning fossil fuels.

Arrhenius explained that in an ▷electrolyte the dissolved substance is dissociated into electrically charged ions. The electrolyte conducts electricity because the ions migrate through the solution.

arrhythmia disturbance of the normal rhythm of the heart. There are various kinds of arrhythmia, some benign, some indicative of heart disease. In extreme cases, the heart may beat so fast as to be potentially lethal and surgery may be used to correct the condition.

arrowroot starchy substance used as a thickener in cooking, produced from the clumpy roots of various tropical plants. The true arrowroot (*Maranta arundinacea*) was used by native South Americans as an antidote against the effects of poisoned arrows.

Related Web site: Arrowroot http://www.botanical.com/botanical/mgmh/a/arrow064.html

Arsacid dynasty Rulers of ancient Parthia *c.* 250 BC–AD 226, who took their titles from their founder Arsaces. At its peak the dynasty controlled a territory from eastern India to western Mesopotamia, with a summer capital at Ecbatana and a winter palace at ▷Ctesiphon. Claiming descent from the Persian Achaemenids, but adopting Hellenistic Greek methods of administration, they successfully challenged Roman expansion, defeating the Roman general Crassus at the battle of Carrhae in 53 BC. The Arsacid dynasty came to an end with the overthrow of Parthia by Ardashir in AD 226; it was succeeded by the ▷Sassanian Empire.

arsenic brittle, greyish-white, semimetallic element (a metalloid), symbol As, atomic number 33, relative atomic mass 74.92. It occurs in many ores and occasionally in its elemental state, and is widely distributed, being present in minute quantities in the soil, the sea, and the human body. In larger quantities, it is poisonous. The chief source of arsenic compounds is as a by-product from metallurgical processes. It is used in making semiconductors, alloys, and solders.

Arsenic poisoning As it is a cumulative poison, its presence in food and drugs is very dangerous. The symptoms of arsenic poisoning are vomiting, diarrhoea, tingling and possibly numbness in the limbs, and collapse. It featured in some drugs, including Salvarsan, the first specific treatment for syphilis. Its name derives from the Latin *arsenicum*. The safe level for arsenic in drinking water, as recommended by the World Health Organization, is 10 micrograms per litre.

art in the broadest sense, all the processes and products of human skill, imagination, and invention; the opposite of nature. In contemporary usage, definitions of art usually reflect aesthetic criteria, and the term may encompass literature, music, drama, painting, and sculpture. Popularly, the term is most commonly used to refer to the visual arts. In Western culture, aesthetic criteria introduced by the ancient Greeks still influence our perceptions and judgements of art.

Representation and inspiration Two currents of thought run through our ideas about art. In one, derived from Aristotle, art is concerned with mimesis (imitation), the representation of appearances, and gives pleasure through the accuracy and skill with which it depicts the real world. The other view, derived from Plato, holds that the artist is inspired by the Muses (or by God, or by the inner impulses, or by the collective unconscious) to express that which is beyond appearances – inner feelings, eternal truths, or the essence of the age.

Art forms In the visual arts of Western civilizations, painting and sculpture have been the dominant forms for many centuries.

ART Dating from the 6th century BC, these Etruscan tombs in Tarquinia, Italy are among the earliest surviving examples of Italian art. *The Art Archive/Dagli Orti*

This has not always been the case in other cultures. ▷Islamic art, for example, is one of ornament, for under the Muslim religion artists were forbidden to usurp the divine right of creation by portraying living creatures. In some cultures masks, tattoos, pottery, and metalwork have been the main forms of visual art. Recent technology has made new art forms possible, such as photography and cinema, and today electronic media have led to entirely new ways of creating and presenting visual images. See also ▷Egyptian art; indigenous art traditions, for example ▷Oceanic art; ▷medieval art; the arts of individual countries, such as ▷French art; individual movements, such as ▷Romanticism, ▷Cubism, and ▷Impressionism; and ▷painting and ▷sculpture. See also Using Computers in Art and Design Focus Feature on pp. 52–53.

Related Web site: Art Room http://www.arts.ufl.edu/art/rt_room/index.html

Artaud, Antonin (1896–1948) French actor, theatre director, and theorist. Although his play *Les Cenci/The Cenci* (1935) was a failure, his passionate manifestos in *Theatre of* ▷*Cruelty* (1931–36), advocating the release of feelings usually repressed in the unconscious, have been an important influence on modern dramatists and directors, such as Brook and Grotowski.

art deco style in the decorative arts which influenced design and architecture. It emerged in Europe in the 1920s and continued through the 1930s, becoming particularly popular in the USA and France. A self-consciously modern style, originally called 'Jazz Modern', it is characterized by angular, geometrical patterns and bright colours, and by the use of materials such as enamel, chrome, glass, and plastic. The graphic artist Erté was a fashionable exponent.

Related Web site: Art Deco http://www.arts.ilstu.edu/exhibits/pcfare/deco.html

ART DECO A plate from an art deco fashion magazine of October 1921, showing a two-piece outfit with a stylish V-banded front (the 'Banjo') and a large floppy hat (by Antinéa) with crepe around and flowing from it. *The Art Archive/Victoria and Albert Museum London/Graham Brandon*

Artemis in Greek mythology, the goddess of chastity, all young creatures, the Moon, and the hunt (Roman Diana). She was the daughter of Zeus and the Titaness Leto, and the twin sister of ▷Apollo. She was worshipped at cult centres throughout the Greek world; one of the largest was at Ephesus where her great temple, reconstructed several times in antiquity, was one of the ▷Seven Wonders of the World.

arteriosclerosis hardening of the arteries, with thickening and loss of elasticity. It is associated with smoking, ageing, and a diet high in saturated fats. The term is used loosely as a synonym for atherosclerosis.

artery vessel that carries blood from the heart to the rest of the body. It is built to withstand considerable pressure, having thick walls which contain smooth muscle fibres. During contraction of the heart muscle, arteries expand in diameter to allow for the sudden increase in pressure that occurs; the resulting ▷pulse or pressure wave can be felt at the wrist. Not all arteries carry oxygenated (oxygen-rich) blood; the pulmonary arteries convey deoxygenated (oxygen-poor) blood from the heart to the lungs.

artesian well well that is supplied with water rising naturally from an underground water-saturated rock layer (▷aquifer). The water rises from the aquifer under its own pressure. Such a well may be drilled into an aquifer that is confined by impermeable rocks both above and below. If the water table (the top of the region of water saturation) in that aquifer is above the level of the well head, hydrostatic pressure will force the water to the surface.

Artesian wells are often overexploited because their water is fresh and easily available, and they eventually become unreliable. There is also some concern that pollutants such as pesticides or nitrates can seep into the aquifers.

Much use is made of artesian wells in eastern Australia, where aquifers filled by water in the Great Dividing Range run beneath the arid surface of the Simpson Desert. The artesian well is named after Artois, a French province, where the phenomenon was first observed.

art history the study of works of art. German archaeologist Johann Winckelmann laid the foundations for a systematic study of art history as early as the mid-18th century, but it did not become an academic discipline until 1844 when a chair was established at Berlin University. Two basic approaches had emerged by the end of the 19th century: the first considered art in relation to its cultural or social context (Jacob ▷Burckhardt, Hippolyte Taine); the second sought to analyse works of art in terms of such 'formal' properties as colour, line, and form (Heinrich Wölfflin). A later approach, rejecting the formalism of Wölfflin, concentrated on ▷iconography, the study of the meaning of works of art (Erwin Panofsky, Emille Mâle).

arthritis inflammation of the joints, with pain, swelling, and restricted motion. Many conditions may cause arthritis, including gout, infection, and trauma to the joint. There are three main forms of arthritis: ▷rheumatoid arthritis; osteoarthritis; and septic arthritis.

arthropod member of the phylum Arthropoda; an invertebrate animal with jointed legs and a segmented body with a horny or chitinous casing (exoskeleton), which is shed periodically and replaced as the animal grows. Included are arachnids such as spiders and mites, as well as crustaceans, millipedes, centipedes, and insects.

Arthur (lived 6th century) semi-legendary Romano-British warleader who led British resistance against the Saxons, Picts, and Scots in the first half of the 6th century. He was probably a warlord rather than a king. He operated throughout Britain, commanding a small force of mobile warriors, reminiscent of the late Roman *comitatenses* (line units). Arthur is credited with a great victory over the Saxons at Mount Badon, possibly in Dorset.

Arthur is said to have been born in Tintagel, Cornwall, and buried in Glastonbury, Somerset, although his life is too shrouded in legend for any of the details to be certain. His legendary base, 'Camelot', has been tentatively identified as a hill fort at South Cadbury in Somerset.

Arthur, Chester Alan (1830–1886) 21st president of the USA 1881–85, a Republican. In 1880 he was chosen as James ▷Garfield's vice-president, and was his successor when Garfield was assassinated the following year.

artichoke either of two plants belonging to the sunflower family, parts of which are eaten as vegetables. The common or globe artichoke (*Cynara scolymus*) is a form of thistle native to the Mediterranean. It is tall, with purplish-blue flowers; the leaflike structures (bracts) around the unopened flower are eaten. The Jerusalem artichoke (*Helianthus tuberosus*), which has edible tubers, is a native of North America (its common name is a corruption of the Italian for sunflower, *girasole*). (Family Compositae.)

Related Web site: Artichoke, Globe http://www.botanical.com/botanical/mgmh/a/artic066.html

artificial insemination (AI) introduction by instrument of semen from a sperm bank or donor into the female reproductive tract to bring about fertilization. Originally used by animal breeders to improve stock with sperm from high-quality males, in the 20th century it has been developed for use in humans, to help the infertile. See ▷in vitro fertilization.

artificial intelligence (AI) branch of science concerned with creating computer programs that can perform actions comparable with those of an intelligent human. Current AI research covers such areas as planning (for robot behaviour), language understanding, pattern recognition, and knowledge representation.

The possibility of artificial intelligence was first proposed by the English mathematician Alan ▷Turing in 1950. Early AI programs, developed in the 1960s, attempted simulations of human intelligence or were aimed at general problem-solving techniques. By the mid-1990s, scientists were concluding that AI was more difficult to create than they had imagined. It is now thought that intelligent behaviour depends as much on the knowledge a system possesses as on its reasoning power. Present emphasis is on ▷knowledge-based systems, such as expert systems, while research projects focus on ▷neural networks, which attempt to mimic the structure of the human brain.

On the ▷Internet, small bits of software that automate common routines or attempt to predict human likes or behaviour based on past experience are called intelligent agents or bots.

artificial respiration emergency procedure to restart breathing once it has stopped; in cases of electric shock or apparent drowning, for example, the first choice is the expired-air method, the kiss of life by mouth-to-mouth breathing until natural breathing is restored.

artificial selection in biology, selective breeding of individuals that exhibit the particular characteristics that a plant or animal breeder wishes to develop. In plants, desirable features might include resistance to disease, high yield (in crop plants), or attractive appearance. In animal breeding, selection has led to the development of particular breeds of cattle for improved meat production (such as the Aberdeen Angus) or milk production (such as Jersey cows).

Artificial selection was practised by the Sumerians at least 5,500 years ago and carried on through the succeeding ages, with the result that all common vegetables, fruit, and livestock are long modified by selective breeding. Artificial selection, particularly of pigeons, was studied by the English evolutionist Charles Darwin who saw a similarity between this phenomenon and the processes of natural selection.

artillery collective term for military ▷firearms too heavy to be carried. Artillery can be mounted on tracks, wheels, ships, or aeroplanes and includes cannons and rocket launchers.

art nouveau in the visual arts, interior design, and architecture, a decorative style flourishing from 1890 to 1910 and characterized by organic, sinuous patterns and ornamentations based on plant forms. In England, it appears in the illustrations of Aubrey Beardsley; in Scotland, in the interior and exterior designs of Charles Rennie Mackintosh; in France, in the glass of René Lalique and the posters of Alphonse Mucha; and in the USA, in the lamps and metalwork of Louis Comfort Tiffany. It was known as Jugendstil in Germany and Stile Liberty in Italy, after a fashionable London department store.

Arts and Crafts Movement English social and aesthetic movement of the late 19th century which stressed the importance of manual skills and the dignity of labour. It expressed a rejection of Victorian industrialization and mass production, and a nostalgic desire to return to a medieval way of life. The movement influenced art nouveau and, less directly, the Bauhaus school of design.

Related Web site: Arts and Crafts Society http://www.arts-crafts.com/

Arts Councils UK organizations that aid music, drama, opera, and visual arts with government funds. They came into being in April 1994 when the Arts Council of Great Britain was divided into the separate and independent Arts Councils of England, Scotland, Wales, and Northern Ireland.

Aruba island in the Caribbean, the westernmost of the Lesser Antilles, 30 km/19 mi north of the Paraguana Peninsula in Venezuela; area 193 sq km/75 sq mi; population (1996) 66,687 (half of Indian descent). The chief town is Oranjestad. Aruba is an overseas territory of the Netherlands. Languages spoken are Dutch (official) and Papiamento (a Creole language). Tourism is a mainstay of the economy.

First inhabited by Arawak peoples, Aruba came under the control of a number of colonial powers. In 1494, the Spanish arrived on the island, claiming it as Spanish territory in 1499. The Dutch gained control in 1636 and the British occupied the island 1805–16 during the Napoleonic Wars. Part of the Dutch West Indies from 1828, and part of the Netherlands Antilles from 1845, Aruba obtained separate status from the other Netherlands Antilles in 1986 and has full internal autonomy under a political arrangement called 'status aparte'. It was due to become fully independent in 1996, but a 1990 agreement deleted references to eventual independence.

Related Web site: Aruba http://www.umsl.edu/services/govdocs/wofact96/22.htm

arum any of a group of mainly European plants with narrow leaves and a single, usually white, special leaf (spathe) surrounding the spike of tiny flowers. The ornamental arum called the trumpet lily (*Zantedeschia aethiopica*) is a native of South Africa. (Genus *Arum*, family Araceae.)

Arunachal Pradesh state of India, in the Himalayas on the borders of Tibet and Myanmar; area 83,700 sq km/32,316 sq mi; population (2001 est) 1,163,000 (over 80 ethnic groups). Formerly

(*continued on p. 54.*)

Using Computers in Art and Design

by Clive Gillman

The process of making art has always been one in which technology and individual creativity have worked together. This has been true from earliest times when painters had a sorcerer-like knowledge of how to create vivid colours, and sculptors transformed the materials they had around them into representations of the world.

DIGITALLY ALTERED PHOTOGRAPHS created by manipulating images taken with a digital camera. The effects used in the portrait (*above*) included increasing the colour saturation and hue (to make the colours stronger), exaggerating the shadows, and recolouring by hand. The figures in the street scene (*above right*) were masked so that different treatments could be applied to the background and the figures. The swirling pattern was created by using a zoom effect. *Mark Salad*

art and technology

The development of the computer has been the latest in a long line of more recent technological advances that have brought us new ways of seeing. Photography, cinema, radio, and television have become the key media through which we view and understand the world around us, and it is the art and culture of these forms that defined the 20th century. The computer, the most recent arrival, is still in its infancy as a creative tool, but it is clear that its influence has already been felt in most forms of art and culture.

history

Early computers, although useful in other ways, were not immediately identified as machines through which art might be made. However, technology developed rapidly and useful design tools began to appear throughout the 1950s and 1960s. The **flat-image scanner** (for digitizing photographs and other images) was invented in 1957, closely followed by the **image plotter** (a form of printer) in 1959. In 1960 the term '**computer graphics**' was coined by William A Fetter, who was working for US military and commercial aircraft manufacturer Boeing. He used

the term to describe a process of visualizing cockpit designs. In 1962, Sketchpad, an interactive graphics system for drawing directly onto a computer screen, was developed by US electronics engineer Ivan Sutherland, and a year later US computer scientist Douglas Engelbart patented the first computer mouse prototype.

Computers slowly began to appear in new settings. One of the first artists to explore the potential of electronic technology was the US pop artist Robert Rauschenberg. In 1963 he formed a partnership with US technologist Billy Klüver and they began to produce collaborative performance works under the name 'Experiments in Art and Technology'. Five years later, in 1968, one of the first major art exhibitions to be based around computer technology took place at the Institute of Contemporary Arts in London. This exhibition, entitled 'Cybernetic Serendipity', was curated by Polish-born English art expert Jasia Reichardt and featured computer-generated paintings, sculptures, films, music, and poetry. This landmark show was hugely influential in highlighting the significance of computer technology as a creative tool.

key tools

As computers continued to become smaller and cheaper, and therefore more widespread, the emphasis continued to shift from engineers and technologists to a wider, more diverse group of users. The first **mass-market computers** such as the Apple II, the Commodore Amiga, and the IBM PC introduced a wide range of people to computers for the first time, and artists were quick to explore the creative possibilities of these new tools. Although by today's standards these computers were expensive and low powered, newer models were developed and an increasing range of application software for graphics began to appear.

One of the most important tools that emerged at this time was a software application called **Aldus Pagemaker**. This tool was created in 1985 to allow designers to use computers for the layout and typesetting of print. It very quickly became the most popular way to produce publications and spawned a whole new industry called 'desktop publishing' or DTP. The success of Pagemaker and the introduction of affordable colour graphics systems led to the development of a number of other tools aimed at supporting the publishing industry, most notably **Adobe Photoshop**, which, for many aspiring computer artists, has provided the canvas for their first explorations of the medium.

High-end graphics tools were also developed through the 1970s and 1980s, many of which have specialist applications such as television graphics, computer-aided design (CAD), or virtual reality simulators. One ground-breaking tool used by artists in the 1980s was the Quantel Paintbox system, a complete graphics suite that used a pressure-sensitive pen and tablet device with which artists could paint intuitively. This was used by the English painters Howard Hodgkin and David Hockney, but probably was seen by most people in television advertising and news graphics.

As these tools grew in sophistication, two distinct forms of computer graphics emerged: **bitmap editors** and **vector graphics**. Bitmap editors allow the user to change and edit the individual pixels (picture elements) of an image, and are normally used for manipulating photographs or for graphics that will only be displayed on a computer screen or television. Adobe Photoshop is an example of this kind of tool. In vector graphics, the computer uses a special language to describe the shape and form of a computer graphic object. This object can then be rendered into a bitmap for screen display or for printing. This form of tool is mainly used for the creation of 3-D graphics or for architectural or product design. Many of these tools use a software technology called PostScript to create the image. Vector graphics tools include Illustrator, Freehand, and AutoCAD.

work or play?

While computer graphics often produce results that are indiscernible from conventional media such as photography or painting, this may not always be the case. Many artists regard digital art as something unique to the computer rather than an emulation of an existing art form. Like cinema, which developed as an art form in its own right out of a hybrid of photography and theatre, digital art will define its own language and codes. But this will take time.

US computer scientist Ted Nelson, one of the key proponents of the new technology, believes that many of us are only 'using the computer as a paper simulator'. He coined the term '**hypertext**' to describe the links between items that mean information can be found by following many different paths, rather than following one line from start to finish. In other words, just as this encyclopedia can be read by following cross references from one article to another, rather than starting on page one and reading the pages in order to the end, so the Internet allows many different

COMPUTER-AIDED DESIGN (CAD) Image of a gas turbine, showing three-dimensional modeling. CAD systems are widely used in architecture, electronics, and engineering, for example in the motor-vehicle industry, where cars designed with the assistance of computers are now commonplace. With a CAD system, picture components are accurately positioned using grid lines. Pictures can be resized, rotated, or mirrored without loss of quality or proportion. © Jonathan Jones

pieces of information to be accessed from many different starting points. Nelson has been a champion of the development of this form of creativity.

Today the term hypertext has to some extent been displaced by the more popular, but less specific, notion of '**multimedia**', text accompanied by sound and images, for example. We are still some way away from Nelson's vision of an active virtual world. But while the idea that computer art is a distinct form of creative practice has still to gain wider acceptance, it is clear that some artists are beginning to define a new canon.

Among those who have been significant in defining this new ground, several have chosen to explore games and gameplay, an area that seems to present particularly fertile ground for the interactive potential of the computer. Japanese artist Toshio Iwai, who has created elegant interactive sound games, is one of the foremost exponents of this way of working. His work has been shown in art galleries, museums, and in the Play Zone at the Millennium Dome in London. English artist Susan Collins has also created interactive projections that allow Internet users to view and influence images being projected onto pedestrians in city centres around the globe and, at the same time, to enter into dialogue with them. Australian artist Jeffrey Shaw, who is based at the ZKM Institute at Karlsruhe, Germany, has created a number of works, one of which is an interactive piece called 'The Legible City'. In this work, the viewer explores a huge projected map of New York City by pedalling and steering a bicycle which controls the projected image. The streets are made up of enormous texts which the user reads by exploring the complex urban street patterns.

centre stage

While some artists produce digital work for the art gallery, others are experimenting with the rapidly growing world of the **Internet**, exploring ideas of connectivity, distance, and simultaneity.

However, the first areas to have achieved broad popular success are those in which digital technology has been used to enhance traditional media forms: in music, in photography, and in design, but probably most visibly in Hollywood cinema, where **digital special effects** have become the stars of many films. Organizations like the US digital entertainment company Industrial Light and Magic have specialized in pushing the boundaries of computer-assisted special effects, while US animator John Lasseter has achieved worldwide success with the **Toy Story** movies, in which high-level technical skill has been married with the animator's craft to produce hugely entertaining results.

the future for digital art

Whatever the precise form that digital art will take, it seems that the art of the digital age will emerge in ways that will surround us and define our world view. This may well happen in ways that we cannot yet predict, although many believe that the realm of computer games will mature and produce works that have the resonance of novels or the involvement of cinema. Computer games such as **Myst**, released in 1992 by the Miller Brothers, or **Ceremony of Innocence**, directed by English artist Alex Mayhew, suggest future directions and ways in which the computer can become as challenging and engaging as the best linear media.

However, what will always remain important is what we choose to say within the media forms available to us. It seems likely that, for the next few years at least, digital media will increasingly provide a window on the world and will be the vehicle for much new creativity.

(*continued from p. 51.*)
part of the state of Assam, Arunachal Pradesh became a state of India in 1987. The main towns include Bomdila and Ziro, while its capital is Itanagar.

Arundel market town in West Sussex, southern England, on the River Arun; population (1991) 3,300. Tourism is an important summer industry. Its Norman castle, much restored, is the seat of the Duke of Norfolk and Earl of Arundel, Earl Marshal of England.

Arup, Ove (1895–1988) Danish civil engineer. He founded the British-based architectural practice, Arup Associates, a firm noted for the considered and elegant manner in which modern materials, especially concrete, are employed in its designs. Set up in 1963, the practice represented Arup's ideal of interdisciplinary cooperation. Examples of its work are at Somerville College, Oxford (1958–62), and Corpus Christi, Cambridge (1961–64).

Arvand Iranian name for the ▷Shatt-al-Arab waterway.

Aryan the hypothetical parent language of an ancient people believed to have lived between Central Asia and Eastern Europe and to have reached Persia and India in one direction and Europe in another, some time in the 2nd century BC, diversifying into the various ▷Indo-European language speakers of later times.

Aryan languages 19th-century name for the ▷Indo-European languages; the languages of the Aryan peoples of India. The name Aryan is no longer used by language scholars because of its association with the Nazi concept of white supremacy.

Asante alternative form of ▷Ashanti, a region of Ghana.

asbestos any of several related minerals of fibrous structure that offer great heat resistance because of their nonflammability and poor conductivity. Commercial asbestos is generally either made from serpentine ('white' asbestos) or from sodium iron silicate ('blue' asbestos). The fibres are woven together or bound by an inert material. Over time the fibres can work loose and, because they are small enough to float freely in the air or be inhaled, asbestos usage is now strictly controlled; exposure to its dust can cause cancer.

Ascension British island of volcanic origin in the South Atlantic, a dependency of ▷St Helena since 1922; area 88 sq km/34 sq mi; population (2001 est) 1,100 (excluding military personnel). The chief settlement is Georgetown.

Ascension Day (or **Holy Thursday**) in the Christian calendar, the feast day commemorating Jesus' ascension into heaven. It is the 40th day after Easter.

Ascham, Roger (c. 1515–1568) English scholar and royal tutor. His writings include *Toxophilus* (1545), a treatise on archery written in dialogue form, and an educational treatise *The Scholemaster*, published by his widow in 1570. His works could be taken as exemplary of an English Protestant schizophrenia: on the one hand, a mastery of the skills pioneered by the humanists, on the other, a distrust of Italy and all things Italian.

In 1548 Ascham was appointed tutor to Princess Elizabeth. He retained favour under Edward VI and Queen Mary (despite his Protestant views), and returned to Elizabeth's service as her secretary after she became queen.

ASCII (acronym for American Standard Code for Information Interchange) in computing, coding system in which numbers are assigned to letters, digits, and punctuation symbols. Although computers work in code based on the ▷binary number system, ASCII numbers are usually quoted as decimal or ▷hexadecimal numbers. For example, the decimal number 45 (binary 0101101) represents a hyphen, and 65 (binary 1000001) a capital A. The first 32 codes are used for control functions, such as carriage return and backspace.

Strictly speaking, ASCII is a 7-bit binary code, allowing 128 different characters to be represented, but an eighth bit is often used to provide ▷parity or to allow for extra characters. The system is widely used for the storage of text and for the transmission of data between computers.

Related Web site: ASCII Chart and Other Resources http://www.jimprice.com/jim-asc.htm

Asclepius in Greek mythology, the god of medicine (Roman Aesculapius); son of ▷Apollo; father of Panacea and ▷Hygieia, goddess of health. His emblem was the caduceus, a winged staff encoiled by two snakes; the creatures appear to renew life by shedding their skin. His worship originated in Thessaly in northern Greece, but the major sanctuary of the classical period was at ▷Epidaurus. Patients slept in his temple overnight, and treatment was based on their dreams. The cult spread to Rome in 293 BC.

ascorbic acid (or $C_6H_8O_6$ or **vitamin C**) a relatively simple organic acid found in citrus fruits and vegetables. It is soluble in water and destroyed by prolonged boiling, so soaking or overcooking of vegetables reduces their vitamin C content. Lack of ascorbic acid results in scurvy.

ASEAN acronym for ▷Association of South East Asian Nations.

asepsis practice of ensuring that bacteria are excluded from open sites during surgery, wound dressing, blood sampling, and other medical procedures. Aseptic technique is a first line of defence against infection.

asexual reproduction in biology, reproduction that does not involve the manufacture and fusion of sex cells (gametes). The process carries a clear advantage in that there is no need to search for a mate nor to develop complex pollinating mechanisms; every asexual organism can reproduce on its own. Asexual reproduction can therefore lead to a rapid population build-up. However, there is little genetic variation because the progeny are identical to the parent.

In evolutionary terms, the disadvantage of asexual reproduction arises from the fact that only identical individuals, or clones, are produced – there is no variation.

In the field of horticulture, where standardized production is needed, this is useful, but in the wild, an asexual population that cannot adapt to a changing environment or evolve defences against a new disease is at risk of extinction. Many asexually reproducing organisms are therefore capable of reproducing sexually as well.

Asexual processes include ▷binary fission, in which the parent organism splits into two or more 'daughter' organisms, and budding, in which a new organism is formed initially as an outgrowth of the parent organism. The asexual reproduction of spores, as in ferns and mosses, is also common and many plants reproduce asexually by means of runners, rhizomes, bulbs, and corms; see also ▷vegetative reproduction.

ash any tree of a worldwide group belonging to the olive family, with winged fruits. The ▷mountain ash or rowan, which resembles the ash, belongs to the family Rosaceae. (Genus *Fraxinus*, family Oleaceae.)

Related Web site: Ash Trees http://www.botanical.com/botanical/mgmh/a/ash--073.html

Ashanti (or **Asante**) region of Ghana, western Africa; area 25,100 sq km/9,700 sq mi; population (1990 est) 2,487,300. Kumasi is the capital. It is the most densely populated region in Ghana, and most of the people are Ashanti. Most are cultivators and the main crop is cocoa, but the region is also noted for its forestry, mining of bauxite, metalwork, and textiles. For more than 200 years Ashanti was an independent kingdom.

Ashcan School group of US realist painters active about 1908–14. The School's central figures were Robert Henri, George Luks, William Glackens, Everett Shinn, and John Sloan, all former members of The Eight (a group of realist painters who exhibited together in 1908 outside of the official circuit). Their subjects were taken from city life, depicting in particular the poor and the outcast. They organized the Armory Show of 1913, which introduced modern European art to the USA.

Ashcroft, Peggy (1907–1991) English actor. Her Shakespearean roles included Desdemona in *Othello* (1930) (with Paul Robeson) and Juliet in *Romeo and Juliet* (1935) (with Laurence Olivier and John Gielgud), and she appeared in the British TV play *Caught on a Train* (1980; BAFTA award), the series *The Jewel in the Crown* (1984), and the film *A Passage to India* (1984).

> **Roger Ascham**
> *He that will write well in any tongue must follow the counsel of Aristotle: to speak as the common people do, to think as wise men do.*
> *Toxophilus*

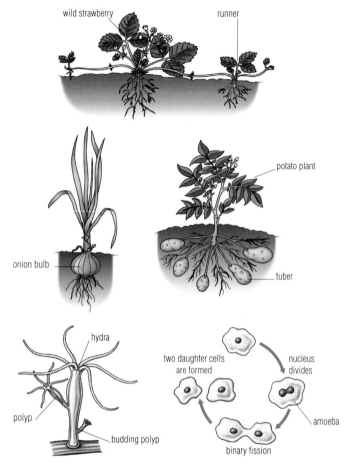

Asexual reproduction

wild strawberry · runner · potato plant · onion bulb · tuber · hydra · polyp · budding polyp · two daughter cells are formed · nucleus divides · amoeba · binary fission

ASEXUAL REPRODUCTION Asexual reproduction is the simplest form of reproduction, occurring in many plants and simple animals. Strawberry plants can reproduce by sending out runners; onion plants form bulbs; and potato plants form tubers. Amoebas divide into two (binary fission) and hydra form new hydra by budding. The offspring are always genetically identical to the parent.

Ashdod (Hebrew **Isdud** or **Esdud**) deep-water port of Israel, on the Mediterranean 32 km/20 mi south of Tel Aviv; population (1994) 120,100. It is 3 km/1.9 mi from the ancient city of the same name.

Ashdown, Paddy (Jeremy John Durham) (1941–) British politician, leader of the merged Social and Liberal Democrats 1988–99. His party significantly increased its seat holding in the 1997 general election, winning more seats than it had had since the 1920s, and cooperated in areas such as constitutional reform with the new Labour government of Tony Blair. From 1997 Ashdown sat with Blair on a joint cabinet committee, whose scope was extended from constitutional issues in November 1998 to cover areas such as health, education, and Europe. Ashdown announced in late January 1999 that he would stand down as Liberal Democrat leader in the summer of that year after holding the position for 11 years. He was replaced by Charles Kennedy, elected in August 1999.

Ashe, Arthur (Robert, Jr) (1943–1993) US tennis player and coach. He won the US national men's singles title at Forest Hills and the first US Open in 1968. Known for his exceptionally strong

ASHANTI 'First day of the yam custom, with king of the Ashanti and British troops', from Thomas Bowdich's *Mission from Cape Coast Castle to Ashantee* (1819). *Art Archive*

serve, Ashe turned professional in 1969. He won the Australian men's title in 1970 and Wimbledon in 1975. Cardiac problems ended his playing career in 1979, but he continued his involvement with the sport as captain of the US Davis Cup team. In 1992 he launched a fund-raising campaign to combat AIDS.

Related Web site: Ashe, Arthur http://www.cmgww.com/sports/ashe/ashe.html

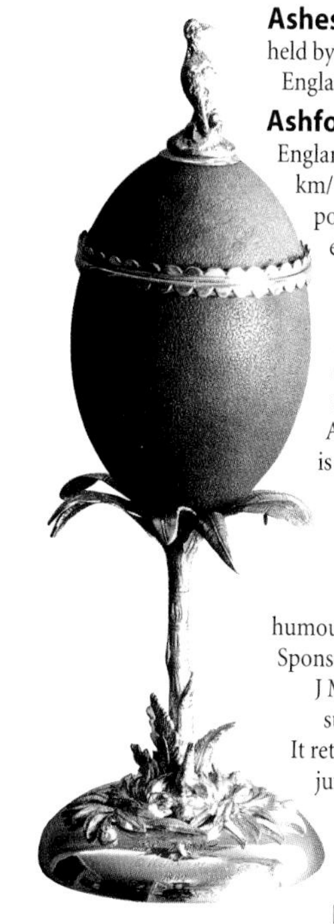

THE ASHES The urn containing the Ashes, a cremated cricket bail. *The Art Archive/Marylebone Cricket Ground*

Ashes, the cricket trophy theoretically held by the winning team in the England–Australia test series.

Ashford market town in Kent, southeast England, on the Great Stour River, 22 km/14 mi southwest of Canterbury; population (1991) 52,000. It expanded in the 1980s as a new commercial and industrial centre for the southeast. Industries include a railway works, light engineering, brewing, and the manufacture of agricultural goods. A terminus of the ▷Channel Tunnel is sited here.

Ashford, Daisy (Margaret Mary Julia) (1881–1972) English writer. *The Young Visiters* (1919), a novel of unconscious humour, was written when she was nine. Sponsored by the novelist and playwright J M Barrie, the book won instant success by its artless charm. It retained its popularity and became a juvenile classic.

Ashgabat (formerly **Poltoratsk** (1919–27); **Ashkhabad** (1927–92)) capital of ▷Turkmenistan; population (1996) 450,000. Industries include the manufacture of glass, carpets (handwoven 'Bukhara' carpets and rugs are made here), and cotton. The city is in a spectacular natural setting, between the ▷Kara-Kum Desert and the Kopet-Dag mountain range.

Ashikaga in Japanese history, the family who held the office of ▷shogun 1338–1573, a period of civil wars. Nō drama evolved under the patronage of Ashikaga shoguns. Relations with China improved intermittently and there was trade with Korea. The last (15th) Ashikaga shogun was ousted by Oda Nobunaga at the start of the Momoyama period. The Ashikaga belonged to the Minamoto clan.

Ashkenazi (plural **Ashkenazim**) any Jew of German or Eastern European descent, as opposed to a Sephardi, of Spanish, Portuguese, or North African descent.

Ashkenazy, Vladimir (1937–) Russian-born pianist and conductor. He was music director of the Royal Philharmonic, London, from 1987 and of the Berlin Radio Symphony Orchestra from 1989. He excels in Rachmaninov, Prokofiev, and Liszt.

After studying in Moscow, he toured the USA in 1958. In 1962 he was joint winner of the Tchaikovsky Competition with John Ogdon. He settled in England in 1963 and moved to Iceland in 1968.

Ashkhabad former name (to 1992) of ▷Ashgabat.

Ashley, Laura (1925–1985) Born Laura Mountney. Welsh designer. She established and gave her name to a Neo-Victorian country style in clothes and furnishings manufactured by her company from 1953. She founded a highly successful international chain of shops.

Ashmore and Cartier Islands group of uninhabited Australian islands comprising Middle, East, and West Islands (the Ashmores), and Cartier Island, in the Indian Ocean, about 190 km/120 mi off the northwest coast of Australia; area 5 sq km/2 sq mi. They were transferred to the authority of Australia by Britain in 1931. Formerly administered as part of the Northern Territory, they became a separate territory in 1978. West Ashmore has an automated weather station. Ashmore reef was declared a national nature reserve in 1983.

ashram Indian community whose members lead a simple life of discipline and self-denial and devote themselves to social service. Noted ashrams are those founded by Mahatma Gandhi at Wardha (near Nagpur, Maharashtra state) and poet Rabindranath Tagore at Santiniketan.

Ashton, Frederick William Mallandaine (1904–1988) English choreographer and dancer. He was director of the Royal Ballet, London 1963–70. He studied with Marie Rambert before joining the Sadler's Wells (now Royal) Ballet in 1935 as chief choreographer. His choreography is marked by a soft, pliant, classical lyricism. His many works and long association with Margot Fonteyn, for whom he created her most famous roles, contributed to the worldwide reputation of British ballet and to the popularity of ballet in the mid-20th century. He was knighted in 1962.

Ash Wednesday first day of Lent, the period in the Christian calendar leading up to Easter; in the Roman Catholic Church the foreheads of the congregation are marked with a cross in ash, as a sign of penitence.

Asia largest of the continents, occupying one-third of the total land surface of the world. The origin of the name is unknown, though it seems probable that it was at first used with a restricted local application, gradually extended to the whole continent.

area 44,000,000 sq km/17,000,000 sq mi **largest cities** (population over 5 million) Bangkok, Beijing, Calcutta, Chennai (formerly Madras), Delhi, Dhaka, Hong Kong, Hyderabad, Istanbul, Jakarta, Karachi, Lahore, Manila, Mumbai (formerly Bombay), Osaka, Seoul, Shanghai, Shenyang, Tehran, Tianjin, Tokyo **features** Mount Everest, at 8,872 m/29,118 ft is the world's highest mountain; the Dead Sea at −394 m/−1,293 ft is the world's lowest point below sea level; rivers (over 3,200 km/2,000 mi) include Chang Jiang (Yangtze), Huang He (Yellow River), Ob-Irtysh, Amur, Lena, Mekong, Yenisey; lakes (over 18,000 sq km/7,000 sq mi) include the Caspian Sea (the largest lake in the world), the Aral Sea, Lake Baikal (largest freshwater lake in Eurasia), Balkhash; deserts include the Gobi, Takla Makan, Syrian Desert, Arabian Desert, Negev **physical** lying in the eastern hemisphere, Asia extends from the Arctic Circle to just over 10° south of the Equator. The Asian mainland, which forms the greater part of the Eurasian continent, lies entirely in the northern hemisphere and stretches from Cape Chelyubinsk at its northern extremity to Cape Piai at the southern tip of the Malay Peninsula. From Dezhneva Cape in the east, the mainland extends west over more than 165° longitude to Cape Baba in Turkey **climate** showing great extremes and contrasts, the heart of the continent becomes bitterly cold in winter and extremely hot in summer. When the heated air over land rises, moisture-laden air from the surrounding seas flows in, bringing heavy monsoon rains to all Southeast Asia, China, and Japan between May and October **industries** 62% of the population are employed in agriculture; Asia produces 46% of the world's cereal crops (91% of the world's rice); other crops include mangoes (India), groundnuts (India, China), 84% of the world's copra (Philippines, Indonesia), 93% of the world's rubber (Indonesia, Malaysia, Thailand), tobacco (China), flax (China, Russia), 95% of the world's jute (India, Bangladesh, China), cotton (China, India, Pakistan), silk (China, India), fish (Japan, China, Korea, Thailand); China produces 55% of the world's tungsten; 45% of the world's tin is produced by Malaysia, China, and Indonesia; Saudi Arabia is the world's largest producer of oil **population** (2000 est) 3,672 million; the world's largest population, amounting to more than half the total number of people in the world; between 1950 and 1990 the death rate and infant mortality were reduced by more than 60%; annual growth rate 1.6%; exceeded only by Africa **language** predominantly tonal languages (Chinese) and Japanese in the east, Indo-Iranian languages (Hindi, Urdu, Persian) in South Asia, Altaic languages (Mongolian, Turkish) in West and Central Asia, Semitic languages (Arabic, Hebrew) in the southwest **religion** the major religions of the world had their origins in Asia – Judaism and Christianity in the Middle East; Islam in Arabia; Buddhism, Hinduism, and Sikhism in India; Confucianism in China; and Shintoism in Japan

Asia Minor historical name for ▷Anatolia, the Asian part of Turkey.

Asian the native peoples and inhabitants of the continent of Asia, which is the contiguous land mass east of the Ural Mountains, the traditional boundary between Europe and Asia. The region is culturally heterogenous with numerous distinctive ethnic and sociolinguistic groups, totalling over half the Earth's human population (including China, India, and Japan). The American Indians were Asian migrants to the New World during the last Ice Age.

Asian Republics, Central see ▷Central Asian Republics.

Asiatic wild ass alternative name for both the kiang and the ▷onager.

Asimov, Isaac (1920–1992) Russian-born US author and editor of science fiction and nonfiction. He published more than 400 books, including his science fiction novels *I, Robot* (1950) and the *Foundation* trilogy (1951–53), continued in *Foundation's Edge* (1983). His two-volume work *The Intelligent Man's Guide to Science* (1960) gained critical acclaim.

AS level (or **Advanced Supplementary level**) examinations introduced in the UK in 1988 as the equivalent to 'half an ▷A level' as a means of broadening the sixth-form (age 16–18) curriculum and including more students in the examination system.

Asmara (or **Asmera**) capital of Eritrea, 64 km/40 mi southwest of Massawa on the Red Sea and 2,300 m/7,546 ft above sea level; population (1991) 367,300. Products include beer, clothes, and textiles. The University of Asmara is here, together with a naval school, a cathedral and many modern buildings. The population is half Christian and half Muslim.

Asoka (or **Ashoka**) (lived *c.* 272–228 BC) ▷Mauryan emperor of India *c.* 268–232 BC, the greatest of the Mauryan rulers. He inherited an empire covering most of north and south-central India which, at its height, had a population of at least 30 million, with its capital at ▷Pataliputra. A devout Buddhist, he renounced militarism and concentrated on establishing an efficient administration with a large standing army and a secret police.

asp any of several venomous snakes, including *Vipera aspis* of southern Europe, allied to the adder, and the Egyptian cobra *Naja haje*, reputed to have been used by the Egyptian queen Cleopatra for her suicide.

asparagus any of a group of plants with small scalelike leaves and many fine, feathery branches. Native to Europe and Asia, *Asparagus officinalis* is cultivated and the tender young shoots (spears) are greatly prized as a vegetable. (Genus *Asparagus*, family Liliaceae.)

Related Web site: Asparagus http://www.ext.vt.edu/pubs/envirohort/426-401/426-401.html

aspartame noncarbohydrate sweetener used in foods under the tradename Nutrasweet. It is about 200 times as sweet as sugar and, unlike saccharine, has no aftertaste.

The aspartame molecule consists of two amino acids (aspartic acid and phenylalanine) linked by a methylene ($-CH_2-$) group. It breaks down slowly at room temperature and rapidly at higher temperatures. It is not suitable for people who suffer from phenylketonuria.

Aspen resort town in central Colorado, on the Roaring Fork River, lying at an altitude of 2,417 m/7,930 ft; seat of Pitkin County; population (1991) 3,700. Aspen offers winter skiing and summer river rafting, and is a cultural centre with an annual music festival.

aspen any of several species of ▷poplar tree. The European quaking aspen (*Populus tremula*) has flattened leafstalks that cause the leaves to flutter in the slightest breeze. The soft, light-coloured wood is used for matches and paper pulp. (Genus *Populus*.)

asphalt mineral mixture containing semisolid brown or black ▷bitumen, used in the construction industry. Asphalt is mixed with rock chips to form paving material, and the purer varieties are used for insulating material and for waterproofing masonry. It can be produced artificially by the distillation of ▷petroleum.

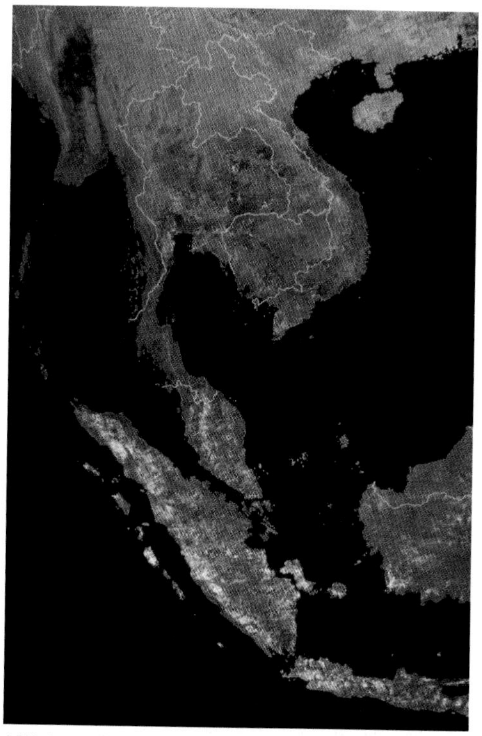

ASIA A map-like satellite photograph showing Malaysia, Thailand, Cambodia, and Vietnam. *Image Bank*

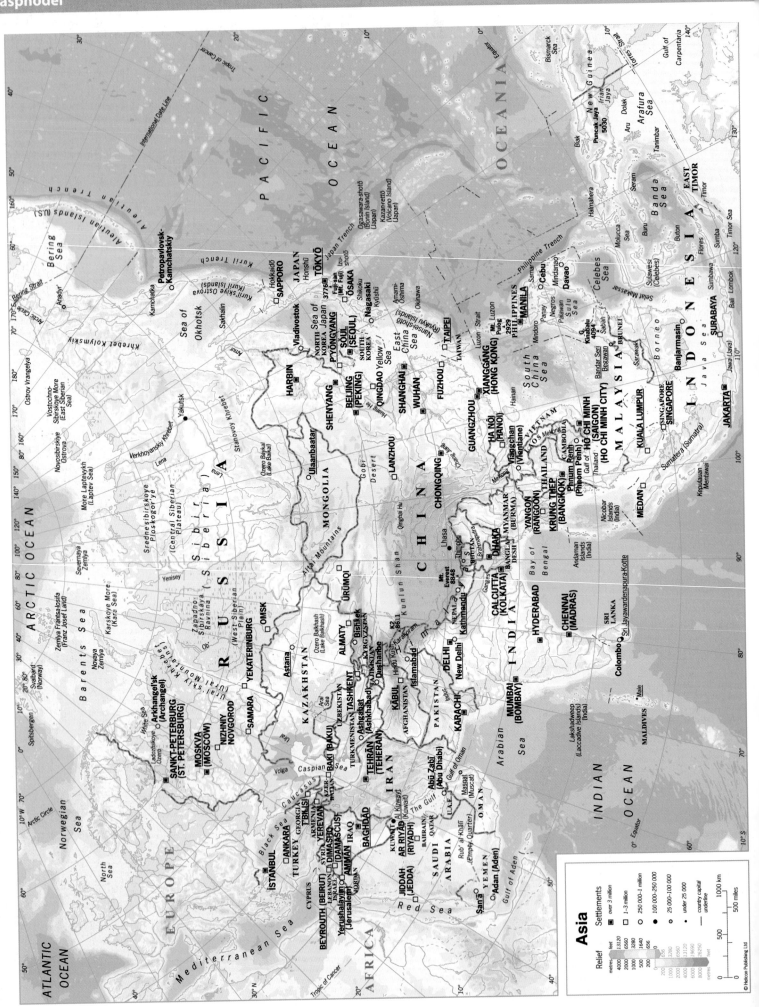

Asia

Relief

metres	feet
4000	13120
2000	6560
1000	3280
500	1640
200	656
200	656
2000	6560
4000	13120
6000	19690
8000	26250
metres	feet

Settlements

- ■ over 3 million
- ■ 1–3 million
- ● 250 000–1 million
- ○ 100 000–250 000
- ○ 25 000–100 000
- · under 25 000
- — country capital
- underline

0   500   1000 km
0   500   1000 miles

© Helicon Publishing Ltd

asphodel either of two related Old World plants of the lily family. The white asphodel or king's spear (*Asphodelus albus*) is found in Italy and Greece, sometimes covering large areas, and providing grazing for sheep. The other asphodel is the yellow asphodel (*Asphodeline lutea*). (Genera *Asphodelus* and *Asphodeline*, family Liliaceae.)

Related Web site: Asphodel http://www.botanical.com/botanical/mgmh/a/aspho080.html

asphyxia suffocation; a lack of oxygen that produces a potentially lethal build-up of carbon dioxide waste in the tissues.

aspidistra any of several Asiatic plants of the lily family. The Chinese *Aspidistra elatior* has broad leaves which taper to a point and, like all aspidistras, grows well in warm indoor conditions. (Genus *Aspidistra*, family Liliaceae.)

aspirin acetylsalicylic acid, a popular pain-relieving drug (▷analgesic) developed in the late 19th century as a household remedy for aches and pains. It relieves pain and reduces inflammation and fever. It is derived from the white willow tree *Salix alba*, and is the world's most widely used drug.

Aspirin was first refined from salicylic acid by German chemist Felix Hoffman, and marketed in 1899. Although salicylic acid occurs naturally in willow bark (and has been used for pain relief since 1763) the acetyl derivative is less bitter and less likely to cause vomiting.

Regular use of aspirin is recommended for people at increased risk of heart attack, thrombosis, and some kinds of stroke. However, aspirin may cause stomach bleeding, kidney damage, and hearing defects. It is no longer considered suitable for children under 12 because of a suspected link with a rare disease, Reye's syndrome (consequently, acetaminophen is often substituted).

Asquith, Herbert Henry (1852–1928) 1st Earl of Oxford and Asquith. British Liberal politician, prime minister 1908–16. As chancellor of the Exchequer, he introduced old-age pensions in 1908. He limited the powers of the House of Lords and attempted to give Ireland ▷home rule.

Asquith was born in Yorkshire, and on completing his education became a barrister, achieving prominence in 1889 as junior counsel for the Irish Nationalist members in a case involving Charles ▷Parnell. Asquith was first elected Liberal member of Parliament for East Fife in 1886 and held the seat until 1918. He was home secretary in William Gladstone's 1892–95 government. When Henry Campbell-Bannerman formed his government in 1905, Asquith was made chancellor of the Exchequer, becoming prime minister on Campbell-Bannerman's resignation in 1908.

Forcing through the radical budget of his chancellor David ▷Lloyd George led Asquith into two elections in 1910; this resulted in the Parliament Act of 1911, which limited the right of the Lords to veto legislation. His endeavours to pass the home rule for Ireland Bill led to the Curragh 'Mutiny' and incipient civil war. Unity was re-established by the outbreak of World War I in 1914, and a coalition government was formed in May 1915. However, Asquith's attitude of 'wait and see' was not suitable to all-out war. In December 1916 he was driven to resign and was replaced by Lloyd George. This event caused a disastrous split in the Liberal Party, which went into eclipse after 1918, though Asquith remained its official leader until 1926.

ass any of several horselike, odd-toed, hoofed mammals of the genus *Equus*, family Equidae. Species include the African wild ass *E. asinus*, and the Asian wild ass *E. hemionus*. They differ from horses in their smaller size, larger ears, tufted tail, and characteristic bray. Donkeys and burros are domesticated asses.

Assad, Hafez al (1930–2000) Syrian Ba'athist politician, president 1971–2000. He became prime minister after a bloodless military coup in 1970. The following year he became the first president to be elected by popular vote. Having suppressed dissent, he was re-elected in 1978, 1985, 1991, and 1999. He was a Shia (Alawite) Muslim.

He ruthlessly suppressed domestic opposition, and was Iran's only major Arab ally in its war against Iraq. He steadfastly pursued military parity with Israel, and made himself a key player in any settlement of the Lebanese civil war or Middle East conflict generally. His support for United Nations action against Iraq following its invasion of Kuwait in 1990 raised his international standing. In 1995, following intense US diplomatic pressure, he was close to reaching a mutual peace agreement with Israel. However, the assassination of Yitzhak ▷Rabin in November 1995 and the return of a Likud-led government in Israel seriously threatened the peace process. Upon his death in June 2000 he was succeeded by his son, Bashar.

Assam state of northeast India; area 78,400 sq km/30,270 sq mi; population (2001 est) 27,428,000. The state includes 12 million Assamese (Hindus), 5 million Bengalis (chiefly Muslim immigrants from Bangladesh), Nepalis, and 2 million indigenous people (Christian and traditional religions). Assamese is the official language. Half of India's oil is produced here, while coal, petrochemicals, paper, and cement are the other main industries. Half of India's tea is grown here, with rice, jute, sugar, and cotton also being popular crops. Its main towns and cities are Guwahati, Dibrugarh, Silchar, while the capital is Dispur, a suburb of Guwahati.

assassination murder, usually of a political, royal, or public person. The term derives from the order of the Assassins, a Muslim sect that, in the 11th and 12th centuries, murdered officials to further its political ends.

assassin bug member of a family of blood-sucking bugs that contains about 4,000 species. Assassin bugs are mainly predators, feeding on other insects, but some species feed on birds and mammals, including humans. They are found, mainly in tropical regions, although some have established themselves in Europe and North America.

Classification Assassin bugs are in the family Reduviidae, suborder Heteroptera, order Hemiptera (true bugs), class Insecta, phylum Arthropoda.

assault intentional act or threat of physical violence against a person. In English law it is both a crime and a ▷tort (a civil wrong). The kinds of criminal assault are common (ordinary); aggravated (more serious, such as causing actual bodily harm); or indecent (of a sexual nature).

assay in chemistry, the determination of the quantity of a given substance present in a sample. Usually it refers to determining the purity of precious metals.

The assay may be carried out by 'wet' methods, when the sample is wholly or partially dissolved in some reagent (often an acid), or by 'dry' or 'fire' methods, in which the compounds present in the sample are combined with other substances.

assembly language low-level computer-programming language closely related to a computer's internal codes. It consists chiefly of a set of short sequences of letters (mnemonics), which are translated, by a program called an assembler, into ▷machine code for the computer's ▷central processing unit (CPU) to follow directly. In assembly language, for example, 'JMP' means 'jump' and 'LDA' means 'load accumulator'. Assembly code is used by programmers who need to write very fast or efficient programs.

Because they are much easier to use, high-level languages are normally used in preference to assembly languages. An assembly language may still be used in some cases, however, particularly when no suitable high-level language exists or where a very efficient machine-code program is required.

asset in accounting, anything owned by or owed to the company that is either cash or can be turned into cash. The term covers physical assets such as land or property of a company or individual, as well as financial assets such as cash, payments due from bills, and investments. Assets are divided into fixed assets and current assets. On a company's balance sheet, total assets must be equal to total liabilities (money and services owed).

asset stripping sale or exploitation by other means of the assets of a business, often one that has been taken over for that very purpose. The parts of the business may be potentially more valuable separately than together. Asset stripping is a major force for the more efficient use of assets.

assimilation in animals, the process by which absorbed food molecules, circulating in the blood, pass into the cells and are used for growth, tissue repair, and other metabolic activities. The actual destiny of each food molecule depends not only on its type, but also on the body requirements at that time.

Assisi (ancient **Asisium**) medieval town in Umbria, Italy, 19 km/12 mi southeast of Perugia, in the foothills of the Apennines overlooking the Tiber Valley; population (1990) 24,800. It is a long-established place of pilgrimage. St Francis was born here and is buried in the Franciscan monastery, completed in 1253. Its basilica was adorned with frescoes by Giotto, Cimabue, Cavallini, and others. Assisi was severely damaged by two earthquakes which hit central Italy in late September 1997, crippling the town's economy which had been dependent on tourism.

Assisted Places Scheme in UK education, a scheme established in 1980 by which the government assisted parents with the cost of fees at ▷independent schools on a means-tested basis. The scheme was abolished in 1997.

Assiut alternative transliteration of ▷Asyut, a city in Egypt.

assize in medieval Europe, the passing of laws, either by the king with the consent of nobles, as in the Constitutions of ▷Clarendon passed by Henry II of England in 1164; or as a complete system, such as the Assizes of Jerusalem, a compilation of the law of the feudal kingdom of Jerusalem in the 13th century.

Association of Caribbean States (ACS) association of 25 states in the Caribbean region, formed in 1994 in Colombia to promote social, political, and economic cooperation and eventual integration. Its members include the states of the Caribbean and Central America plus Colombia, Suriname, and Venezuela. Associate membership has been adopted by 12 dependent territories in the region. Its creation was seen largely as a reaction to the ▷North American Free Trade Agreement between the USA, Canada, and Mexico, although its far smaller market raised doubts about its vitality.

Association of South East Asian Nations (ASEAN) regional alliance formed in Bangkok in 1967; it took over the nonmilitary role of the Southeast Asia Treaty Organization in 1975. Its members are Indonesia, Malaysia, the Philippines, Singapore, Thailand, (from 1984) Brunei, (from 1995) Vietnam, (from 1997) Laos and Myanmar, and (from 1999) Cambodia; its headquarters are in Jakarta, Indonesia. North Korea took part in the organization for the first time at the 2000 annual meeting of foreign ministers.

associative operation in mathematics, an operation in which the outcome is independent of the grouping of the numbers or symbols concerned. For example, multiplication is associative, as $4 \times (3 \times 2) = (4 \times 3) \times 2 = 24$; however, division is not, as $12 \div (4 \div 2) = 6$, but $(12 \div 4) \div 2 = 1.5$. Compare ▷commutative operation and ▷distributive operation.

assonance the matching of vowel (or, sometimes, consonant) sounds in a line, generally in poetry. 'Load' and 'moat', 'farther' and 'harder' are examples of assonance, since they match in vowel sounds and stress pattern, but do not ▷rhyme.

assortative mating in population genetics, selective mating in a population between individuals that are genetically related or have similar characteristics. If sufficiently consistent, assortative mating can theoretically result in the evolution of new species without geographical isolation (see ▷speciation).

assurance form of long-term saving where individuals pay monthly premiums, typically over 10 or 25 years, and at the end receive a large lump sum. For example, a person may save £50 a month and at the end of 25 years receive a lump sum of £40,000. Assurance policies are offered by assurance companies which invest savers' monthly premiums, typically in stocks, shares, and property.

Assyria empire in the Middle East *c.* 2500–612 BC, in northern Mesopotamia (now Iraq); early capital Ashur, later Nineveh. It was initially subject to Sumer and intermittently to Babylon. The Assyrians adopted largely the Sumerian religion and structure of society. At its greatest extent the empire included Egypt and stretched from the eastern Mediterranean coast to the head of the Persian Gulf. Much of Assyrian religion, law, social structure, and artistic achievement was derived from neighbouring sources. The Assyrians adopted the cuneiform script (invented by the Sumerians in 3500 BC) and took over the Sumerian pantheon, although the Assyrian god, Ashur, assumed the chief place in the cult. The library of Ashurbanipal excavated at Nineveh is evidence of the thoroughness with which Babylonian culture had been assimilated. See Assyrian empire map on p. 58.

Astaire, Fred (1899–1987) Adopted name of Frederick Austerlitz. US dancer, actor, singer, and choreographer. The greatest popular dancer of his time, he starred in numerous films, including *Top Hat* (1935), *Easter Parade* (1948), and *Funny Face* (1957), many containing inventive sequences that he designed and choreographed himself. He made ten classic films with the most popular of his dancing partners, Ginger ▷Rogers.

> **Fred Astaire**
> *I have no desire to prove anything by dancing . . . I just dance.*
> Remark

Astaire was born in Omaha, Nebraska, and taken to New York in 1904. He danced in partnership with his sister **Adele Astaire** (1897–1981) from 1906 until her marriage in 1932, and they became public favourites on Broadway and in London. He entered films in 1933. Among his many other films are *Roberta* (1935), *Follow the Fleet* (1936), *Swing Time* (1936), and *The Band Wagon* (1953). He later played straight dramatic roles in such films as *On the Beach* (1959). He was the recipient of the American Film Institute's Life Achievement Award in 1981.

Astaire was a virtuoso dancer and a perfectionist known for his elegant style. As a singer, he used first-rate material (some of which he wrote himself) and interpreted it intelligently; songs he recorded include 'Isn't This a Lovely Day?' (1935), 'I'm Building Up to an Awful Letdown' (1936), and 'A Fine Romance' (1937).

Related Web site: Astaire, Fred http://www.reelclassics.com/Actors/Astaire/astaire.htm

Astarte (or **Ashtoreth**) in Canaanite and Syrian mythology, a goddess of sexual passion (equivalent to the Babylonian and Assyrian goddess ▷Ishtar). As goddess of maternity and fertility, she was associated with ▷Tammuz or ▷Adonis, who represented the passage of the seasons. She was also a warrior goddess.

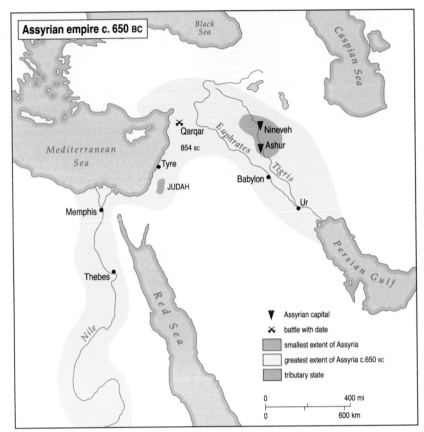

ASSYRIAN EMPIRE See Assyria entry on p. 57.

Assyrian empire c. 650 BC

▼ Assyrian capital
✕ battle with date
　smallest extent of Assyria
　greatest extent of Assyria c.650 BC
　tributary state

| 0 | 400 mi |
| 0 | 600 km |

astatine (Greek *astatos* 'unstable') nonmetallic, radioactive element, symbol At, atomic number 85, relative atomic mass 210. It is a member of the ▷halogen group, and is very rare in nature. Astatine is highly unstable, with at least 19 isotopes; the longest lived has a half-life of about eight hours.

aster any plant of a large group belonging to the same subfamily as the daisy. All asters have starlike flowers with yellow centres and outer rays (not petals) varying from blue and purple to white. Asters come in many sizes. Many are cultivated as garden flowers, including the Michaelmas daisy (*Aster nova-belgii*). (Genus *Aster*, family Compositae.)

asteroid any of many thousands of small bodies, composed of rock and iron, that orbit the Sun. Most lie in a belt between the orbits of Mars and Jupiter, and are thought to be fragments left over from the formation of the ▷Solar System. About 100,000 may exist, but their total mass is only a few hundredths the mass of the Moon.

The largest asteroids are sometimes called minor planets; these include ▷Ceres (the largest asteroid, 940 km/584 mi in diameter) and Vesta (which has a light-coloured surface, and is the brightest as seen from Earth). Some asteroids are in orbits that bring them close to Earth, and some, such as the ▷Apollo asteroids, which include ▷Eros, and ▷Icarus, even cross Earth's orbit; and may be remnants of former comets.

The first asteroid was discovered by the Italian astronomer Giuseppe Piazzi at the Palermo Observatory, Sicily, on 1 January 1801. The first asteroid moon was observed by the space probe ▷Galileo in 1993 orbiting asteroid Ida.

Recent research NASA's Near Earth Asteroid Rendezvous (NEAR) was launched in 1996 and since February 2000, it has been orbiting the asteroid Eros at a distance that has been gradually reduced to a few tens of kilometres, to collect data on asteroid composition.

NASA's Near Earth Asteroid Tracking (NEAT) system had detected more than 11,000 asteroids by August 2000. There are an estimated 1,000–2,000 near-Earth asteroids (NEAs) with a diameter greater than 1 km/0.62 mi, according to research released by US astronomers in January 2000.

asthenosphere a layer within Earth's ▷mantle lying beneath the ▷lithosphere, typically beginning at a depth of approximately 100 km/63 mi and extending to depths of approximately 260 km/160 mi. Sometimes referred to as the 'weak sphere', it is characterized by being weaker and more elastic than the surrounding mantle.

The asthenosphere's elastic behaviour and low viscosity allow the overlying, more rigid plates of lithosphere to move laterally in a process known as ▷plate tectonics. Its elasticity and viscosity also allow overlying crust and mantle to move vertically in response to gravity to achieve isostatic equilibrium (see ▷isostasy).

asthma chronic condition characterized by difficulty in breathing due to spasm of the bronchi (air passages) in the lungs. Attacks may be provoked by allergy, infection, and stress. The incidence of asthma may be increasing as a result of air pollution and occupational hazard. Treatment is with ▷bronchodilators to relax the bronchial muscles and thereby ease the breathing, and in severe cases by inhaled ▷steroids that reduce inflammation of the bronchi.

Extrinsic asthma, which is triggered by exposure to irritants such as pollen and dust, is more common in children and young adults. In February 1997 Brazilian researchers reported two species of dust mite actually living on children's scalps. This explains why vacuuming of bedding sometimes fails to prevent asthma attacks. The use of antidandruff shampoo should keep numbers of mites down by reducing their food supply. Less common, intrinsic asthma tends to start in the middle years.

Approximately 5–10% of children suffer from asthma, but about a third of these will show no symptoms after adolescence, while another 5–10% of people develop the condition as adults. Growing evidence that the immune system is involved in both forms of asthma has raised the possibility of a new approach to treatment.

Although the symptoms are similar to those of bronchial asthma, **cardiac asthma** is an unrelated condition and is a symptom of heart deterioration.

The British National Asthma Campaign estimated in 1998 that 3.4 million people suffered from asthma in the UK. It causes about 2,000 deaths per year. Asthmatics may monitor their own status by use of a peak-flow meter, a device that measures how rapidly air is breathed out. Peak-flow meters are available on prescription in the UK.

Asti town in Piedmont, southeast of Turin, Italy; population (1990) 74,500. Asti province is famed for its sparkling wine. Other products include chemicals, textiles, and glass. The town has annual jousting and gastronomic festivals.

astigmatism aberration occurring in the lens of the eye. It results when the curvature of the lens differs in two perpendicular planes, so that rays in one plane may be in focus while rays in the other are not. With astigmatic eyesight, the vertical and horizontal cannot be in focus at the same time; correction is by the use of a cylindrical lens that reduces the overall focal length of one plane so that both planes are seen in sharp focus.

Astor Prominent US and British family. John Jacob Astor (1763–1848) emigrated from Germany to the USA in 1783, and became a millionaire. His great-grandson Waldorf Astor,

2nd Viscount Astor (1879–1952), was a British politician, and served as Conservative member of Parliament for Plymouth from 1910 to 1919, when he succeeded to the peerage. His US-born wife Nancy Witcher Langhorne, **Lady Astor** (1879–1964), was the first woman member of Parliament to take a seat in the House of Commons, when she succeeded her husband in the constituency of Plymouth in November 1919. She remained in parliament until 1945, as an active champion of women's rights, educational issues, and temperance.

William Backhouse Astor (1792–1875) was known as the 'landlord of New York'. John Jacob Astor's grandson **William Waldorf Astor** (1848–1919), was a US diplomat and writer. In 1893 he bought the *Pall Mall Gazette*, and founded the *Pall Mall Magazine*. He became naturalized British in 1899.

Astrakhan capital city, economic and cultural centre of Astrakhan oblast (region), southwestern Russian Federation; population (1996 est) 488,000. Astrakhan is sited in the Volga delta on the northeastern shore of the Caspian Sea. It is one of the Russian Federation's principal ports, which developed rapidly in the 1870s with the growth of the oil industry at Baku (now in Azerbaijan). There is a major fishing and canning industry here, together with shipbuilding and cotton manufacturing.

astrolabe ancient navigational instrument, forerunner of the sextant. Astrolabes usually consisted of a flat disc with a sighting rod that could be pivoted to point at the Sun or bright stars.

From the altitude of the Sun or star above the horizon, the local time could be estimated.

astrology (Greek *astron* 'star', *legein* 'speak') study of the relative position of the planets and stars in the belief that they influence events on Earth. The astrologer casts a ▷horoscope based on the time and place of the subject's birth. Astrology has no proven scientific basis, but has been widespread since ancient times. Western astrology is based on the 12 signs of the zodiac; Chinese astrology is based on a 60-year cycle and lunar calendar.

astrometry measurement of the precise positions of stars, planets, and other bodies in space. Such information is needed for practical purposes including accurate timekeeping, surveying and navigation, and calculating orbits and measuring distances in space. Astrometry is not concerned with the surface features or the physical nature of the body under study.

astronomical unit unit (symbol AU) equal to the mean distance of the Earth from the Sun: 149.6 million km/92.96 million mi. It is used to describe planetary distances. Light travels this distance in approximately 8.3 minutes.

astronomy science of the celestial bodies: the Sun, the Moon, and the planets; the stars and galaxies; and all other objects in the universe. It is concerned with their positions, motions, distances, and physical conditions and with their origins and evolution. Astronomy thus divides into fields such as astrophysics, celestial mechanics, and ▷cosmology. See also ▷gamma-ray astronomy, ▷infrared astronomy, ▷radio astronomy, ▷ultraviolet astronomy, and ▷X-ray astronomy.

Greek astronomers Astronomy is perhaps the oldest recorded science; there are observational records from ancient Babylonia, China, Egypt, and Mexico. The first true astronomers, however, were the Greeks, who deduced the Earth to be a sphere and attempted to measure its size. Ancient Greek astronomers included ▷Thales and ▷Pythagoras. ▷Eratosthenes of Cyrene measured the size of the Earth with considerable accuracy. Star catalogues were drawn up, the most celebrated being that of Hipparchus. The *Almagest*, by ▷Ptolemy of Alexandria, summarized Greek astronomy and survived in its Arabic translation. The Greeks still regarded the Earth as the centre of the universe, although this was doubted by some philosophers, notably ▷Aristarchus of Samos, who maintained that the Earth moves around the Sun.

Ptolemy, the last famous astronomer of the Greek school, died in about AD 180, and little progress was made for some centuries. *Arab revival* The Arabs revived the science, developing the astrolabe and producing good star catalogues. Unfortunately, a general belief in the pseudoscience of astrology continued until the end of the Middle Ages (and has been revived from time to time). *The Sun at the centre* The dawn of a new era came in 1543, when a Polish canon, ▷Copernicus, published a work entitled *De revolutionibus orbium coelestium/On the Revolutions of the Heavenly Spheres*, in which he demonstrated that the Sun, not the Earth, is the centre of our planetary system. (Copernicus was wrong in many respects – for instance, he still believed that all celestial orbits must be perfectly circular.) Tycho ▷Brahe, a Dane, increased the accuracy of observations by means of improved instruments allied to his own personal skill, and his observations were used by German mathematician Johannes ▷Kepler to prove the validity of the Copernican system. Considerable opposition existed, however, for removing the Earth from its central position in the universe; the Catholic Church was openly hostile to the idea, and, ironically,

Brahe never accepted the idea that the Earth could move around the Sun. Yet before the end of the 17th century, the theoretical work of Isaac ▷Newton had established celestial mechanics.

Galileo and the telescope The refracting telescope was invented about 1608, by Hans ▷Lippershey in Holland, and was first applied to astronomy by Italian scientist ▷Galileo in the winter of 1609–10. Immediately, Galileo made a series of spectacular discoveries. He found the four largest satellites of Jupiter, which gave strong support to the Copernican theory; he saw the craters of the Moon, the phases of Venus, and the myriad faint stars of our ▷Galaxy, the Milky Way.

Galileo's most powerful telescope magnified only 30 times, but it was not long before larger telescopes were built and official observatories were established.

Galileo's telescope was a refractor; that is to say, it collected its light by means of a glass lens or object glass. Difficulties with his design led Newton, in 1671, to construct a reflector, in which the light is collected by means of a curved mirror.

Further discoveries In the 17th and 18th centuries astronomers were mostly concerned with positional measurements. Uranus was discovered in 1781 by William ▷Herschel, and this was soon followed by the discovery of the first four asteroids, Ceres in 1801, Pallas in 1802, Juno in 1804, and Vesta in 1807. In 1846 Neptune was located by Johann Galle, following calculations by British astronomer John Couch ▷Adams and French astronomer Urbain Jean Joseph Leverrier. Also significant was the first measurement of the distance of a star, when in 1838 the German astronomer Friedrich ▷Bessel measured the ▷parallax of the star 61 Cygni, and calculated that it lies at a distance of about 6 light years (about half the correct value).

Astronomical spectroscopy was developed, first by Fraunhofer in Germany and then by people such as Pietro Angelo Secchi and William Huggins, while Gustav ▷Kirchhoff successfully interpreted the spectra of the Sun and stars. By the 1860s good photographs of the Moon had been obtained, and by the end of the century photographic methods had started to play a leading role in research.

A growing universe This concept of an expanding and evolving universe at first rested largely on ▷Hubble's law, relating the distance of objects to the amount their spectra shift towards red – the ▷red shift. Subsequent evidence derived from objects studied in other parts of the ▷electromagnetic spectrum, at radio and X-ray wavelengths, has provided confirmation. ▷Radio astronomy established its place in probing the structure of the universe by demonstrating in 1954 that an optically visible distant galaxy was identical with a powerful radio source known as Cygnus A. Later analysis of the comparative number, strength, and distance of radio sources suggested that in the distant past these, including the ▷quasars discovered in 1963, had been much more powerful and numerous than today. This fact suggested that the universe has been evolving from an origin, and is not of infinite age as expected under a ▷steady-state theory.

The discovery in 1965 of microwave background radiation was evidence for the enormous temperature of the giant explosion, or Big Bang, that brought the universe into existence.

Further exploration Although the practical limit in size and efficiency of optical telescopes has apparently been reached, the siting of these and other types of telescope at new observatories in the previously neglected southern hemisphere has opened fresh areas of the sky to search. Australia has been in the forefront of these developments. The most remarkable recent extension of the powers of astronomy to explore the universe is in the use of rockets, satellites, space stations, and space probes. Even the range and accuracy of the conventional telescope may be greatly improved free from the Earth's atmosphere. When the USA launched the Hubble Space Telescope into permanent orbit in 1990, it was the most powerful optical telescope yet constructed, with a 2.4 m/94.5 in mirror. It detects celestial phenomena seven times more distant (up to 14 billion light years) than any Earth-based telescope. See also ▷black hole; ▷infrared radiation.

astrophotography use of photography in astronomical research. Modern-day astrophotography uses techniques such as ▷charge-coupled devices (CCDs).

astrophysics study of the physical nature of stars, galaxies, and the universe. It began with the development of spectroscopy in the 19th century, which allowed astronomers to analyse the composition of stars from their light. Astrophysicists view the universe as a vast natural laboratory in which they can study matter under conditions of temperature, pressure, and density that are unattainable on Earth.

Asturias autonomous community of northern Spain; area 10,600 sq km/4,092 sq mi; population (1991) 1,091,100. Agricultural products include maize, fruit, cider, and dairy products, and sheep and other livestock are reared. In the past Asturias produced half of Spain's coal; most of the coal mines have since closed down. Oviedo (the capital) and Gijón are the main industrial towns.

Related Web site: Principality of Asturias http://www.DocuWeb.ca/SiSpain/english/politics/autonomo/asturias/index.html

ATACAMA DESERT Although the Atacama region of Chile is mostly arid, in the Pan de Azúcar National Park, high cliffs produce dense coastal fogs that support a rich flora and fauna, especially cacti. *Premaphotos Wildlife*

Asturias, Miguel Ángel (1899–1974) Guatemalan author and diplomat. He published poetry, Guatemalan legends, and novels, such as *El señor presidente/The President* (1946), *Men of Corn* (1949), and *Strong Wind* (1950), attacking Latin-American dictatorships and 'Yankee imperialism'. He was awarded the Nobel Prize for Literature in 1967.

Asunción capital and chief port of Paraguay, situated on the east bank of the Paraguay River, near its confluence with the River Pilcomayo; population (1992) 502,400 (metropolitan area 637,700); there are textile, footwear, and food processing industries. The climate is subtropical, and cattle are raised in the surrounding area, and maize, cotton, sugar, fruit, and tobacco are grown.

asylum, political in international law, refuge granted in another country to a person who, for political reasons, cannot return to his or her own country without putting himself or herself in danger. A person seeking asylum is a type of ▷refugee, someone who has fled their own country because of a well-founded fear of persecution for reasons of race, religion, nationality, political opinion, or membership in a particular social group, and who cannot or does not want to return.

asymptote in ▷coordinate geometry, a straight line that a curve approaches progressively more closely but never reaches. The *x* and *y* axes are asymptotes to the graph of xy = constant (a rectangular ▷hyperbola).

If a point on a curve approaches a straight line such that its distance from the straight line is *d*, then the line is an asymptote to the curve if limit *d* tends to zero as the point moves towards infinity. Among ▷conic sections (curves obtained by the intersection of a plane and a double cone), a hyperbola has two asymptotes, which in the case of a rectangular hyperbola are at right angles to each other.

Asyut commercial centre in southern Egypt, near the west bank of the Nile, 322 km/200 mi south of Cairo; population (1992) 321,000. It is the capital of the governorate (area 1,600 sq km/618 sq mi; population (1996) 2,802,185) of the same name. One of the Nile dams is located here. An ancient Graeco-Egyptian city, it has many rock tombs of 11th and 12th-dynasty nobles.

Atacama Desert arid coastal region of northern Chile, with an area of about 80,000 sq km/31,000 sq mi, and extending south from the Peruvian border for 965 km/600 mi. It consists of a series of salt pans within a plateau region. Its rainless condition is caused by the ▷Peru Current offshore; any moist airstreams from the Amazon basin are blocked by the Andean Mountains. The desert has silver and copper mines, and extensive nitrate and iodine deposits. The main population centres are the ports of Antofagasta and Iquique.

Atahualpa (*c.* 1502–1533) Last emperor of the Incas of Peru. He was taken prisoner in 1532 when the Spaniards arrived and agreed to pay a substantial ransom, but he was accused of plotting against the conquistador Pizarro and was sentenced to be burned. On his consenting to Christian baptism, the sentence was commuted to strangulation.

Atatürk, Kemal (1881–1938) Born Musata Kemal Pasha. (Turkish 'Father of the Turks') Turkish politician and general, first president of Turkey from 1923. After World War I he established a provisional rebel government and in 1921–22 the Turkish armies under his leadership expelled the Greeks who were occupying Turkey. He was the founder of the modern republic, which he ruled as a virtual dictator, with a policy of consistent and radical Westernization.

Kemal, born in Thessaloniki, was banished in 1904 for joining a revolutionary society. Later he was pardoned and promoted in the army and was largely responsible for the successful defence of the Dardanelles against the British in 1915. In 1918, after Turkey had been defeated, he was sent into Anatolia to implement the demobilization of the Turkish forces in accordance with the armistice terms, but instead he established a provisional government opposed to that of Constantinople (modern Isanbul, then under Allied control) and in 1921 led the Turkish armies against the Greeks, who had occupied a large part of Anatolia. He checked them at the Battle of the Sakaria, 23 August–13 September 1921, for which he was granted the title of Ghazi ('the Victorious'), and within a year had expelled the Greeks from Turkish soil. War with the British was averted by his diplomacy, and Turkey in Europe passed under Kemal's control. On 29 October 1923 Turkey was proclaimed a republic with Kemal as first president.

KEMAL ATATÜRK As president from 1923–38, the Turkish soldier and politician pursued a programme of Westernization that affected all aspects of Turkish life – women were given the vote, the traditional Turkish fez was prohibited, and Roman lettering replaced Arabic. *Archive Photos*

Atatürk Dam dam on the River Euphrates, in the province of Gaziantep, southern Turkey, completed in 1989. The lake, 550 km/340 mi southeast of Ankara, covers 815 sq km/315 sq mi (when full, it holds four times the annual flow of the Euphrates). In 1990 it was filled for the first time, submerging 25 villages, all of whose 55,000 inhabitants were relocated.

atavism (Latin *atavus* 'ancestor') in genetics, the reappearance of a characteristic not apparent in the immediately preceding generations; in psychology, the manifestation of primitive forms of behaviour.

Athanasian creed one of the three ancient ▷creeds of the Christian church. Mainly a definition of the Trinity and Incarnation, it was written many years after the death of Athanasius, but was attributed to him as the chief upholder of Trinitarian doctrine.

Athanasius, St (296–373) Bishop of Alexandria, Egypt, supporter of the doctrines of the Trinity and Incarnation. He was a disciple of St Anthony the hermit, and an opponent of ▷Arianism in the great Arian controversy. Following the official condemnation of Arianism at the Council of Nicaea in 325, Athanasius was appointed bishop of Alexandria in 328. The Athanasian creed was not actually written by him, although it reflects his views.

atheism nonbelief in, or the positive denial of, the existence of a God or gods. A related concept is ▷agnosticism. Like theism, its opposite, atheism cannot be proved or disproved conclusively.

Related Web site: Atheist Express http://www.hti.net/www/atheism/

Athelstan (895–939) King of England 924–39. The son of ▷Edward the Elder, Athelstan brought about English unity by ruling both Mercia and Wessex. He defeated an invasion by Scots, Irish, and the men of Strathclyde at Brunanburh in 937. He overcame the Scandinavian kingdom based in York and increased English power on the Welsh and Scottish borders.

Athena (or Athene; or Pallas Athena) in Greek mythology, the goddess of war, wisdom, and the arts and crafts (Roman **Minerva**). She was reputed to have sprung fully-armed and grown from the head of Zeus, after he had swallowed her mother Metis, the Titaness of wisdom. In Homer's *Odyssey*, Athena is the protector of ▷Odysseus and his son Telemachus. Her chief cult centre was the ▷Parthenon in Athens, and her principal festival was the Panathenaea, held every fourth year in August.

Athens (Greek **Athinai**) capital city of Greece and of ancient Attica; population (1991) 784,100, metropolitan area (1991) 3,096,800. Situated 8 km/5 mi northeast of its port of Piraeus on the Gulf of Aegina, it is built around the rocky hills of the Acropolis 169 m/555 ft and the Areopagus 112 m/368 ft, and is overlooked from the northeast by the hill of Lycabettus, 277 m/909 ft high. It lies in the south of the central plain of Attica, watered by the mountain streams of Cephissus and Ilissus. It has less green space than any other European capital (4%) and severe air and noise pollution. Athens was scheduled to host the Olympic Games in 2004.

Features The Acropolis dominates the city. Remains of ancient Greece include the Parthenon, the Erechtheum, and the temple of Athena Nike. Near the site of the ancient Agora (marketplace) stands the Theseum, and south of the Acropolis is the theatre of Dionysus. To the southeast stand the gate of Hadrian and the columns of the temple of Olympian Zeus. Nearby is the marble stadium built about 330 BC and restored in 1896.

History The site was first inhabited about 3000 BC with Athens as the capital of a united Attica before 700 BC. Captured and sacked by the Persians in 480 BC, it became the first city of Greece in power and culture under ▷Pericles. After the death of Alexander the Great the city fell into comparative decline, but it flourished as an intellectual centre until AD 529 when the philosophical schools were closed by Justinian. In 1458 it was captured by the Turks, who held it until 1833; it was chosen as the capital of Greece in 1834. During World War II, it was occupied by the Germans April 1941–October 1944 and was then the scene of fierce street fighting between monarchist and communist partisan factions until January 1945.

Related Web sites: Ancient City of Athens http://www.indiana.edu/~kglowack/athens/

Welcome to Athens http://agn.hol.gr/hellas/attica/athens.htm

ATHENS A guard in full ceremonial uniform outside government buildings in Athens, Greece. *Image Bank*

Atherton, Michael Andrew (1968–) English cricketer. A right-handed opening batsman from Lancashire who captained England in a record 52 Tests from 1993 to 1998. He made his Test debut in 1989.

Related Web site: Michael Atherton Factfile http://www-usa8.cricket.org/link_to_database/ARCHIVE/CRICKET_NEWS/1999/MAR/ATHERS_ET_FACTFILE_31MAR1999.html

athletics competitive track and field events consisting of running, throwing, and jumping disciplines. Running events range from sprint races (100 metres) and hurdles to cross-country running and the ▷marathon (26 miles 385 yards). Jumping events are the high jump, long jump, triple jump, and pole vault. Throwing events are javelin, discus, shot put, and hammer throw.

Related Web site: International Amateur Athletics Federation http://www.iaaf.org/

Athos mountainous peninsula on the Macedonian coast of Greece. Its peak is 2,033 m/6,672 ft high. The promontory is occupied by a group of 20 Orthodox monasteries, inhabited by some 3,000 monks and lay brothers. A council of representatives from the monasteries runs the affairs of the peninsula as a self-governing republic under the protection of the Greek government.

Atlanta capital and largest city of ▷Georgia, USA, situated 300 m/984 ft above sea level in the foothills of the Blue Ridge Mountains; seat of Fulton County; population (2000 est) 416,500, metropolitan area (1992) 3,143,000. It is the headquarters of Coca-Cola and since 1994 EarthLink, an Internet service provider; there are also Ford and Lockheed motor-vehicle and aircraft assembly plants. Atlanta hosted the 1996 Olympic Games.

History Originally named Terminus, Atlanta was settled in 1837 (the site was chosen as the southern terminus of the Western and Atlantic Railroad); the name was changed to Atlanta in 1845. During the American Civil War the city was captured and partly destroyed by Gen ▷Sherman in 1864; it became the state capital in 1868. The city grew in importance after 1900 and became the financial, trade, and convention centre for the southeastern USA. Atlanta was the first large city in the South to elect a black mayor, Maynard Jackson, in 1973.

Features A few sites from the earliest settlement are preserved in the Underground Atlanta complex. Historic buildings include the State Capitol (1889), with its dome gilded with gold leaf mined nearby during the first gold rush; Wren's Nest (the home of Joel Chandler Harris, creator of Uncle Remus); the Georgia Governors' Mansion; and the Atlanta History Center, which includes Tullis Smith Farm plantation house (1845), and Palladian Swan House Mansion. The High Museum of Art, in the Georgia-Pacific Building, has an important collection of American contemporary and decorative art. Educational institutions include Atlanta University, Emory University, and the Georgia Institute of Technology.

Atlantic, Battle of the German campaign during World War I to prevent merchant shipping from delivering food supplies from the USA to the Allies, chiefly the UK. By 1917, some 875,000 tons of shipping had been lost. The odds were only turned by the belated use of naval convoys and depth charges to deter submarine attack.

Atlantic, Battle of the during World War II, continuous battle fought in the Atlantic Ocean by the sea and air forces of the Allies and Germany, to control the supply routes to the UK. The Allies destroyed nearly 800 U-boats during the war and at least 2,200 convoys of 75,000 merchant ships crossed the Atlantic, protected by Allied naval forces.

Atlantic City seaside resort on Absecon Island, southeastern New Jersey, USA; population (1990) 38,000. Formerly a family resort, Atlantic City is now a centre for casino gambling, which was legalized here in 1978. Other industries include shell fishing.

Features The city's first 'boardwalk' (a wooden pavement along the beach) was built in 1870; it is about 10 km/6 mi long and is lined with skyscrapers with hotels, shops, and theatres, and has five amusement piers which project out into the ocean.

Atlantic Ocean ocean lying between Europe and Africa to the east and the Americas to the west; area of basin 81,500,000 sq km/31,500,000 sq mi; including the Arctic Ocean and Antarctic seas, 106,200,000 sq km/41,000,000 sq mi. It is generally divided by the equator into the North Atlantic and South Atlantic. It was probably named after the legendary island continent of ▷Atlantis. The average depth is 3 km/2 mi; greatest depth is at the Milwaukee Depth in the Puerto Rico Trench 8,648 m/28,374 ft. The ▷Mid-Atlantic Ridge, of which the Azores, Ascension, St Helena, and Tristan da Cunha form part, divides it from north to south. Lava welling up from this central area annually increases the distance between South America and Africa. The North Atlantic is the saltiest of the main oceans and has the largest tidal range.

Related Web site: Atlantic Ocean http://www.umsl.edu/services/govdocs/wofact96/24.htm

Atlantis in Greek mythology, an island continent west of the Straits of Gibraltar, said to have sunk following an earthquake. Although the Atlantic Ocean is probably named after it, the structure of the sea bed rules out its former existence in the Atlantic region. Derived from an Egyptian priest's account, the Greek philosopher Plato created an imaginary early history for the island in *Timaeus and Critias*, describing it as a utopia (perfect place) submerged 9,000 years previously as punishment for waging war against Athens; an act deemed impious.

Atlas in Greek mythology, one of the ▷Titans who revolted against the gods; as punishment, he was compelled to support the heavens on his head and shoulders. Growing weary, he asked ▷Perseus to turn him into stone by showing him the ▷Medusa's head, and was transformed into Mount Atlas.

atlas book of maps. The atlas was introduced in the 16th century by ▷Mercator, who began work on it in 1585; it was completed by his son in 1594. Early atlases had a frontispiece showing ▷Atlas supporting the globe.

Atlas Mountains mountain system of northwest Africa, stretching 2,400 km/1,500 mi from the Atlantic coast of Morocco to the Gulf of Gabes, Tunisia, and lying between the Mediterranean on the north and the Sahara on the south. The highest peak is Mount Toubkal 4,165 m/13,665 ft.

atman in Hinduism, the individual soul or the eternal essential self.

atmosphere mixture of gases surrounding a planet. Planetary atmospheres are prevented from escaping by the pull of gravity. Atmospheric pressure, the density of gases in the atmosphere, decreases with altitude. In its lowest layer, the Earth's atmosphere consists of nitrogen (78%) and oxygen (21%), both in molecular form (two atoms bonded together) and 1% argon. Small quantities of other gases are important to the chemistry and physics of the Earth's atmosphere, including water, carbon dioxide, and ozone. The atmosphere plays a major part in the various cycles of nature (the ▷water cycle, the ▷carbon cycle, and the ▷nitrogen cycle). It is the principal industrial source of nitrogen, oxygen, and argon, which are obtained by fractional distillation of liquid air.

The Earth's atmosphere is divided into four regions of atmosphere classified by temperature.

Troposphere This is the lowest level of the atmosphere (altitudes from 0 to 10 km/6 mi) and it is heated to an average temperature of 15°C/59°F by the Earth, which in turn is warmed by infrared and visible radiation from the Sun. Warm air cools as it rises in the troposphere and this rising of warm air causes rain and most other weather phenomena. The top of the troposphere is approximately −60°C/−76°F.

Stratosphere Temperature increases with altitude in this next layer (from 10 km/6 mi to 50 km/31 mi), from −60°C/−76°F to near 0°C/32°F.

Mesosphere Temperature decreases with altitude through the mesosphere (50 km/31 mi to 80 km/50 mi), from 0°C/32°F to below −100°C/−148°F.

Thermosphere In the highest layer (80 km/50mi to about 700 km/450 mi), temperature rises with altitude to extreme values of thousands of degrees. The meaning of these extreme temperatures can be misleading. High thermosphere temperatures represent little heat because they are defined by motions among so few atoms and molecules spaced widely apart from one another.

atmosphere (or **standard atmosphere**) in physics, a unit (symbol atm) of pressure equal to 760 torr, 1013.25 millibars, or 1.01325×10^5 pascals, or newtons per square metre. The actual pressure exerted by the atmosphere fluctuates around this value, which is assumed to be standard at sea level and 0°C/32°F, and is used when dealing with very high pressures.

atmospheric pressure pressure at any point on the Earth's surface that is due to the weight of the column of air above it; it therefore decreases as altitude increases, simply because there is less air above. At sea level the average pressure is 101 kilopascals (1,013 millibars, 760 mmHg, or 14.7 lb per sq in, or 1 atmosphere). Changes in atmospheric pressure, measured with a barometer, are used in weather forecasting. Areas of relatively high pressure are called ▷anticyclones; areas of low pressure are called ▷depressions.

atoll continuous or broken circle of ▷coral reef and low coral islands surrounding a lagoon.

atom (Greek *atomos* 'undivided') smallest unit of matter that can take part in a chemical reaction, and which cannot be broken down chemically into anything simpler. An atom is made up of protons and neutrons in a central nucleus surrounded by electrons (see ▷atomic structure). The atoms of the various elements differ in atomic number, relative atomic mass, and chemical behaviour.

Atoms are much too small to be seen by even the most powerful optical microscope (the largest, caesium, has a diameter of 0.0000005 mm/0.00000002 in), and they are in constant motion.

However, modern electron microscopes, such as the ▷scanning tunnelling microscope (STM) and the ▷atomic force microscope (AFM), can produce images of individual atoms and molecules.

Related Web sites: Elementary Particles http://www.neutron.anl.gov/Particles.htm

Theory of Atoms in Molecules http://www.chemistry.mcmaster.ca/faculty/bader/aim/

atom, electronic structure of the arrangement of electrons around the nucleus of an atom, in distinct energy levels, also called orbitals or shells (see ▷orbital, atomic). These shells can be regarded as a series of concentric spheres, each of which can contain a certain maximum number of electrons; the noble gases have an arrangement in which every shell contains this number (see ▷noble gas structure). The energy levels are usually numbered beginning with the shell nearest to the nucleus. The outermost shell is known as the ▷valency shell as it contains the valence electrons.

The lowest energy level, or innermost shell, can contain no more than two electrons. Outer shells are considered to be stable when they contain eight electrons but additional electrons can sometimes be accommodated provided that the outermost shell has a stable configuration. Electrons in unfilled shells are available to take part in chemical bonding, giving rise to the concept of valency. In ions, the electron shells contain more or fewer electrons than are required for a neutral atom, generating negative or positive charges.

The atomic number of an element indicates the number of electrons in a neutral atom. From this it is possible to deduce its electronic structure. For example, sodium has atomic number 11 ($Z = 11$) and its electronic arrangement (configuration) is two electrons in the first energy level, eight electrons in the second energy level and one electron in the third energy level – generally written as 2.8.1. Similarly for sulphur ($Z = 16$), the electron arrangement will be 2.8.6. The electronic structure dictates whether two elements will combine by ionic or covalent bonding (see ▷bond) or not at all.

atomic bomb (or **atom bomb**) bomb deriving its explosive force from nuclear fission (see ▷nuclear energy) as a result of a neutron chain reaction, developed in the 1940s in the USA into a usable weapon.

Research began in the UK in 1940 and was transferred to the USA after its entry into World War II the following year. Known as the **Manhattan Project**, the work was carried out under the direction of the US physicist J Robert Oppenheimer at Los Alamos, New Mexico.

After one test explosion, two atomic bombs were dropped on the Japanese cities of ▷Hiroshima (6 August 1945) and ▷Nagasaki (9 August 1945); the bomb dropped on Hiroshima was as powerful as 12,700 tonnes of TNT, that on Nagaskai was equivalent to 22,000 tonnes of TNT. The USSR first detonated an atomic bomb in 1949 and the UK in 1952.

The test site used by the UK was in the Monte Bello Islands off Australia. The development of the hydrogen bomb in the 1950s rendered the early atomic bomb obsolete. See ▷nuclear warfare.

Related Web site: Atomic Bomb: Decision http://www.dannen.com/decision/index.html

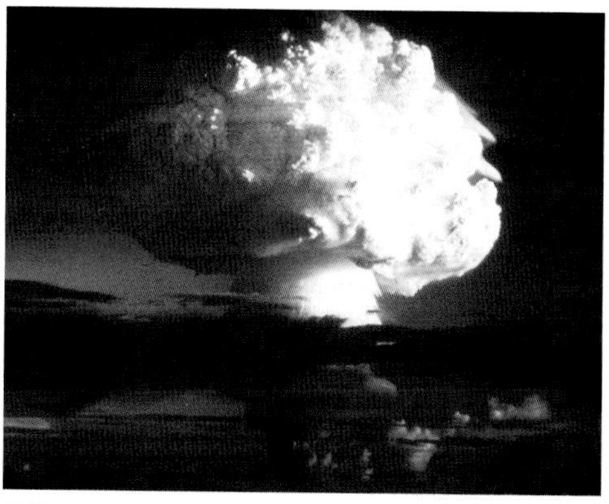

ATOMIC BOMB A test explosion of an atomic bomb in the 1950s. *Archive Photos*

atomic clock timekeeping device regulated by various periodic processes occurring in atoms and molecules, such as atomic vibration or the frequency of absorbed or emitted radiation.

atomic energy another name for ▷nuclear energy.

atomicity number of atoms of an ▷element that combine together to form a molecule. A molecule of oxygen (O_2) has atomicity 2; sulphur (S_8) has atomicity 8.

atomic mass see ▷relative atomic mass.

atomic mass unit (or **dalton**; symbol u) unit of mass that is used to measure the relative mass of atoms and molecules. It is equal to one-twelfth of the mass of a carbon-12 atom, which is approximately the mass of a proton or 1.66×10^{-27} kg. The ▷relative atomic mass of an atom has no units; thus oxygen-16 has an atomic mass of 16 daltons but a relative atomic mass of 16.

atomic number (or **proton number**) the number (symbol Z) of protons in the nucleus of an atom. It is equal to the positive charge on the nucleus. In a neutral atom, it is also equal to the number of electrons surrounding the nucleus. The chemical elements are arranged in the ▷periodic table of the elements according to their atomic number. See also ▷nuclear notation.

atomic radiation energy given out by disintegrating atoms during ▷radioactive decay, whether natural or synthesized. The energy may be in the form of fast-moving particles, known as ▷alpha particles and ▷beta particles, or in the form of high-energy electromagnetic waves known as ▷gamma radiation. Overlong exposure to atomic radiation can lead to ▷radiation sickness.

Radiation biology studies the effect of radiation on living organisms. Exposure to atomic radiation is linked to chromosomal damage, cancer, and, in laboratory animals at least, hereditary disease.

atomic structure internal structure of an ▷atom.

The nucleus The core of the atom is the **nucleus**, a dense body only one ten-thousandth the diameter of the atom itself. The simplest nucleus, that of hydrogen, comprises a single stable positively charged particle, the **proton**. Nuclei of other elements contain more protons and additional particles, called **neutrons**, of about the same mass as the proton but with no electrical charge. Each element has its own characteristic nucleus with a unique number of protons, the atomic number. The number of neutrons may vary. Where atoms of a single element have different numbers of neutrons, they are called ▷isotopes. Although some isotopes tend to be unstable and exhibit ▷radioactivity, they all have identical chemical properties.

Electrons The nucleus is surrounded by a number of moving **electrons**, each of which has a negative charge equal to the positive charge on a proton, but which weighs only $\frac{1}{1836}$ times as much. In a neutral atom, the nucleus is surrounded by the same number of electrons as it contains protons. According to ▷quantum theory, the position of an electron is uncertain; it may be found at any point. However, it is more likely to be found in some places than others. The region of space in which an electron is most likely to be found is called an orbital (see ▷orbital, atomic). The chemical properties of an element are determined by the ease with which its atoms can gain or lose electrons.

Attraction and repulsion Atoms are held together by the electrical forces of attraction between each negative electron and the positive protons within the nucleus. The latter repel one another with enormous forces; a nucleus holds together only because an even stronger force, called the **strong nuclear force**, attracts the protons and neutrons to one another. The strong force acts over a very short range – the protons and neutrons must be in virtual contact with one another (see ▷forces, fundamental). If, therefore, a fragment of a complex nucleus, containing some protons, becomes only slightly loosened from the main group of neutrons and protons, the natural repulsion between the protons will cause this fragment to fly apart from the rest of the nucleus at high speed. It is by such fragmentation of atomic nuclei (nuclear ▷fission) that nuclear energy is released.

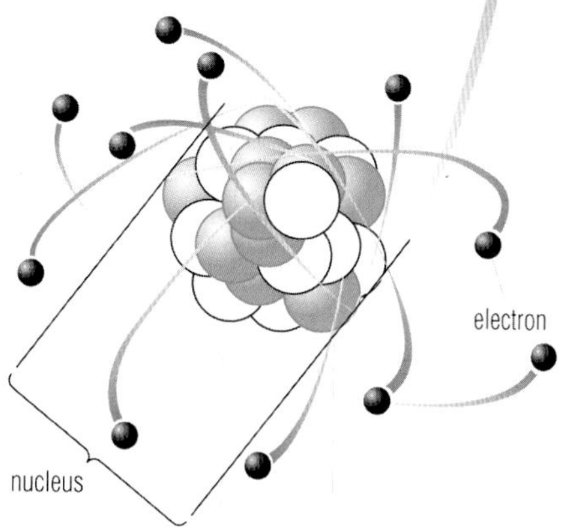

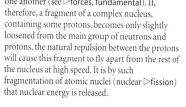

ATOMIC STRUCTURE The structure of a sodium atom. The nucleus is composed of 12 protons and 11 neutrons. Eleven electrons orbit the nucleus in 3 orbits: 2 in the inner orbit, 8 in the middle, and 1 in the outer.

atomic weight another name for ▷relative atomic mass.

atomizer device that produces a spray of fine droplets of liquid. A vertical tube connected with a horizontal tube dips into a bottle of liquid, and at one end of the horizontal tube is a nozzle, at the other a rubber bulb. When the bulb is squeezed, air rushes over the top of the vertical tube and out through the nozzle. Following ▷Bernoulli's principle, the pressure at the top of the vertical tube is reduced, allowing the liquid to rise. The air stream picks up the liquid, breaks it up into tiny drops, and carries it out of the nozzle as a spray. Scent spray, paint spray guns, and carburettors all use the principle of the atomizer.

Aton in ancient Egypt, the invisible power of the sun, represented by the Sun's disc with arms. It was an emblem of the single sun god whose worship was promoted by ▷Akhenaton in an attempt to replace the many gods of traditional devotion.

atonality music in which the sense of ▷tonality is distorted or obscured; music of no apparent key. It is used by film and television composers for situations of mystery or horror, exploiting dissonance for its power to disturb.

atonement in Christian theology, the doctrine that Jesus suffered on the cross to bring about reconciliation and forgiveness between God and humanity.

Atonement, Day of Jewish holy day (**Yom Kippur**) held on the tenth day of Tishri (Sept–Oct), the first month of the Jewish year. It is a day of fasting, penitence, and cleansing from sin, ending the Ten Days of Penitence that follow Rosh Hashanah, the Jewish New Year.

ATP (or **adenosine triphosphate**) abbreviation for a nucleotide molecule found in all cells. It can yield large amounts of energy, and is used to drive the thousands of biological processes needed to sustain life, growth, movement, and reproduction. Green plants use light energy to manufacture ATP as part of the process of ▷photosynthesis. In animals, ATP is formed by the breakdown of glucose molecules, usually obtained from the carbohydrate component of a diet, in a series of reactions termed ▷respiration. It is the driving force behind muscle contraction and the synthesis of complex molecules needed by individual cells.

atrium in architecture, an open inner courtyard. An atrium was originally the central court or main room of an ancient Roman house, open to the sky, often with a shallow pool to catch rainwater.

atrophy in medicine, a diminution in size and function, or output, of a body tissue or organ. It is usually due to nutritional impairment, disease, or disuse (muscle).

atropine alkaloid derived from ▷belladonna, a plant with toxic properties. It acts as an anticholinergic, inhibiting the passage of certain nerve impulses. It is used in premedication, to reduce bronchial and gastric secretions. It is also administered as a mild antispasmodic drug, and to dilate the pupil of the eye.

attar of roses perfume derived from the essential oil of roses (usually damask roses), obtained by crushing and distilling the petals of the flowers.

Attenborough, Richard (Samuel) (1923–) Baron Attenborough. English director, actor, and producer. He appeared in such films as *Brighton Rock* (1947) and *10 Rillington Place* (1971), and directed *Oh! What a Lovely War* (1969), and such biopics as *Gandhi* (which won eight Academy Awards) (1982) and *Cry Freedom* (1987).

He is the brother of naturalist David Attenborough.

attention-deficit hyperactivity disorder (ADHD) psychiatric condition occurring in young children characterized by impaired attention and hyperactivity. The disorder, associated with disruptive behaviour, learning difficulties, and under-achievement, is more common in boys. It is treated with methylphenidate (Ritalin). There was a 50% increase in the use of the drug in the USA 1994–96, with an estimated 5% of school-age boys diagnosed as suffering from ADHD. In 1998 the number of children and adults in the USA taking medication for ADHD (mostly Ritalin) was approximately 4 million. In the UK the prescription of Ritalin doubles each year.

Attica (Greek **Attiki**) region of Greece comprising Athens and the district around it; area 3,381 sq km/1,305 sq mi; population (1991) 3,522,800. It is renowned for its language, art, and philosophical thought in Classical times. It is a prefecture of modern Greece with Athens as its capital.

Attila (*c.* 406–453) King of the Huns in an area from the Alps to the Caspian Sea from 434, known to later Christian history as the 'Scourge of God'. He twice attacked the Eastern Roman Empire to increase the quantity of tribute paid to him, 441–443 and 447–449, and then attacked the Western Roman Empire 450–452.

Attila first ruled jointly with his brother Bleda, whom he murdered in 444. In 450 Honoria, the sister of the western emperor Valentinian III, appealed to him to rescue her from an arranged marriage, and Attila used her appeal to attack the West. He was forced back from Orléans by Aetius and Theodoric, King of the Visigoths, and defeated by them on the Catalaunian Fields 451. In 452 he led the Huns into Italy, and was induced to withdraw by Pope ▷Leo I.

He died on the night of his marriage to the German Ildico, either by poison or, as Chaucer represents it in his *Pardoner's Tale*, from a nasal haemorrhage induced by drunkenness.

Attila lived in relative simplicity in his camp close to the Danube, which was described by the Greek historian Priscus after a diplomatic mission. But his advisers included a Greek, Orestes, and his control over a large territory required administrative abilities. His conscious aims were to prevent the Huns from serving in the imperial armies and to use force to exact as much tribute or land from both parts of the empire as he could. His burial place was kept secret.

Attis (or **Atys**) in classical mythology, a Phrygian god whose death and resurrection symbolized the end of winter and the arrival of spring; also regarded as a vegetation god. Beloved by the earth goddess Cybele, who drove him mad as punishment for his infidelity, he castrated himself and bled to death. Violets sprang from his blood, and Zeus turned him into a pine tree.

Attlee, Clement (Richard) (1883–1967) 1st Earl Attlee. British Labour politician. In the coalition government during World War II he was Lord Privy Seal 1940–42, dominions secretary 1942–43, and Lord President of the Council 1943–45, as well as deputy prime minister from 1942. As prime minister 1945–51 he introduced a sweeping programme of nationalization and a whole new system of social services.

Attlee was educated at Oxford and practised as a barrister 1906–09. Social work in London's East End and cooperation in poor-law reform led him to become a socialist; he joined the Fabian Society and the Independent Labour Party in 1908. He became a lecturer in social science at the London School of Economics in 1913. After service in World War I he was mayor of Stepney in east London 1919–20, and Labour member of Parliament for Limehouse 1922–50 and for West Walthamstow 1950–55. In the first Labour government he was undersecretary for war in 1924 and in the second chancellor of the Duchy of Lancaster and postmaster general 1929–31. In 1935 he became leader of the opposition. In July 1945 he became prime minister after a Labour landslide in the general election. The government was returned to power with a much reduced majority in 1950 and was defeated in 1951. He was created 1st Earl in 1955 on his retirement as leader of the opposition.

attorney person who represents another in legal matters. In the USA, attorney is the formal title for a lawyer.

Attorney General in the UK, principal law officer of the crown and head of the English Bar; the post is one of great political importance. In the USA, it is the chief law officer of the government and head of the Department of Justice.

Atwood, Margaret Eleanor (1939–) Canadian novelist, short-story writer, and poet. Her novels, which often treat feminist themes with wit and irony, include *The Edible Woman* (1969), *Life Before Man* (1979), *Bodily Harm* (1981), *The Handmaid's Tale* (1986, filmed 1990, opera 2003), *Cat's Eye* (1989), *The Blind Assassin* (2000, Booker Prize), and *Oryx and Crake* (2003).

aubergine (or **eggplant**) plant belonging to the nightshade family, native to tropical Asia. Its purple-skinned, sometimes white, fruits are eaten as a vegetable. (*Solanum melongena*, family Solanaceae.)

Aubrey, John (1626–1697) English biographer and antiquary. He was the first to claim Stonehenge as a Druid temple. His *Lives*, begun in 1667, contains gossip, anecdotes, and valuable insights into the celebrities of his time. It was published as *Brief Lives* in 1898. *Miscellanies* (1696), a work on folklore and ghost stories, was the only work to be published during his lifetime.

aubrietia any of a group of spring-flowering dwarf perennial plants native to the Middle East. All are trailing plants with showy, purple flowers. They are widely cultivated in rock gardens. (Genus *Aubrieta*, family Cruciferae.)

Auchinleck, Claude John Eyre (1884–1981) British commander in World War II. He won the First Battle of El ▷Alamein in 1942 in northern Egypt. In 1943 he became commander-in-chief in India and founded the modern Indian and Pakistani armies. In 1946 he was promoted to field marshal; he retired in 1947.

Auckland largest city of North Island, New Zealand, in the north of the island, in an area of impressive volcanic scenery; population (1996) 997,900. It fills the isthmus that separates its two harbours (Waitemata and Manukau), and its suburbs spread north across the Harbour Bridge. It is the country's chief port and leading industrial centre, having iron and steel plants, engineering, car assembly, textiles, food processing, sugar refining, and brewing. Auckland was officially founded as New Zealand's capital in 1840, remaining so until 1865.

auction sale of goods or property in public to the highest bidder. There are usually conditions of sale by which all bidders are bound. Leading world auctioneers are Christie's and Sotheby's.

A bid may be withdrawn at any time before the auctioneer brings down the hammer, and the seller is likewise entitled to withdraw any lot before the hammer falls. In recent years, auction houses have been increasingly examined for illegal practices. It is illegal for the seller or anyone on their behalf to make a bid for their own goods unless their right to do so has been reserved and notified before the sale. Christie's New York chairman, Donald Bathurst, resigned after he was found to have falsely stated that some paintings had been sold, a practice known as 'buying-in'. 'Rings' of dealers agreeing to keep prices down are illegal. A reserve price is kept secret, but an upset price (the minimum price fixed for the property offered) is made public before the sale. An auction where property is first offered at a high price and gradually reduced until a bid is received is known as a **Dutch auction**.

Aude river in southeast France, which rises in the *département* of Pyrénées-Orientales, then flows north and east through the *département* of Aude and into the Mediterranean Sea near Narbonne; length 210 km/130 mi. ▷Carcassonne is the main town through which it passes.

Auden, W(ystan) H(ugh) (1907–1973) English-born US poet. He wrote some of his most original poetry, such as *Look, Stranger!* (1936), in the 1930s when he led the influential left-wing literary group that included Louis MacNeice, Stephen Spender, and Cecil Day-Lewis. He moved to the USA in 1939, became a US citizen in 1946, and adopted a more conservative and Christian viewpoint, for example in *The Age of Anxiety* (1947).

He also wrote verse dramas with Christopher ▷Isherwood, such as *The Dog Beneath the Skin* (1935) and *The Ascent of F6* (1936), and opera librettos, notably for Igor Stravinsky's *The Rake's Progress* (1951). Auden was professor of poetry at Oxford from 1956 to 1961. His last works, including *Academic Graffiti* (1971) and *Thank You, Fog* (1973), are light and mocking in style and tone, but are dazzling virtuoso performances by a poet who recognized his position as the leading writer in verse of his time.

Related Web site: W H Auden's Poetry http://www.sat.dundee.ac.uk/~arb/speleo/auden.html

audit official inspection of a company's accounts by a qualified accountant as required by law each year to ensure that the company balance sheet reflects the true state of its affairs.

Audubon, John James (1785–1851) US naturalist and artist. In 1827, after extensive travels and observations of birds, he published the first part of his *Birds of North America*, with a remarkable series of colour plates. Later he produced a similar work on North American quadrupeds.

Auerbach, Frank Helmuth (1931–) German-born British painter. He is best known for his portraits and views of Primrose Hill and Camden Town, London; his style, formatively influenced by David ▷Bomberg, is characterized by the heavy reworking of charcoal or thickly applied paint. In 1986 he was Britain's representative at the Venice Biennale.

Augean stables in Greek mythology, the stables of Augeas, king of Elis in southern Greece. The yards, containing 3,000 cattle, had not been swept for 30 years. ▷Heracles had to clean them as one of 12 labours set by Eurystheus, king of Argos; a feat accomplished in one day by diverting the rivers Peneius and Alpheus.

Augsburg industrial city in Bavaria, Germany, at the confluence of the Wertach and Lech rivers, 52 km/32 mi northwest of Munich; population (1995) 261,000. Products include textiles, cash registers, diesel engines, motor vehicles, electrical goods, and aircraft. It is named after the Roman emperor Augustus, who founded it in 15 BC.

Augsburg, Confession of statement of the Lutheran faith composed by Philip ▷Melanchthon. Presented to the Holy Roman Emperor Charles V, at the Diet of Augsburg in 1530, it was intended originally as a working document for the negotiations at the Diet aiming at reconciliation between Lutherans and Catholics. It came, however, to be seen as the crucial expression of Lutheran beliefs.

augur member of a college of Roman priests who interpreted the will of the gods from signs or 'auspices' such as the flight, song, or feeding of birds, the condition of the entrails of sacrificed animals, and the direction of thunder and lightning. Their advice was sought before battle and on other important occasions. Consuls and other high officials had the right to consult the auspices themselves, and a campaign was said to be conducted 'under the auspices' of the general who had consulted the gods.

Augustan Age golden age of the Roman emperor ▷Augustus (31 BC–AD 14), during which art and literature flourished. The term is also applied to later periods in which writers used classical ideals, such as in the reign of Queen Anne in England (1702–14).

Augustine, St (died 605) First archbishop of Canterbury, England. He was sent from Rome to convert England to Christianity by Pope Gregory I. He landed at Ebbsfleet in Kent in 597 and soon after baptized Ethelbert, King of Kent, along with many of his subjects. He was consecrated bishop of the English at Arles in the same year, and appointed archbishop in 601, establishing his see at Canterbury. Feast day is 26 May.

Augustine was originally prior of the Benedictine monastery of St Andrew, Rome. In 603 he attempted unsuccessfully to unite the Roman and native Celtic churches at a conference on the Severn. He founded Christ Church, Canterbury, in 603, and the abbey of Saints Peter and Paul, now the site of Saint Augustine's Missionary College.

Related Web site: Mission of St Augustine of Canterbury to the British http://users.aol.com/butrousch/augustine/index.htm

Augustine of Hippo, St (354–430) Born Aurelius Augustinus. One of the early Christian leaders and writers known as the Fathers of the Church. He was converted to Christianity by Ambrose in Milan and became bishop of Hippo (modern Annaba, Algeria) in 396. Among Augustine's many writings are his *Confessions*, a spiritual autobiography, and *De Civitate Dei/The City of God*, vindicating the Christian church and divine providence in 22 books.

Related Web site: Augustine http://ccat.sas.upenn.edu/jod/twayne/tabcont.html

Augustinian member of a religious community that follows the Rule of St ▷Augustine of Hippo. It includes the Canons of St Augustine, Augustinian Friars and Hermits, Premonstratensians, Gilbertines, and Trinitarians.

Augustus (63 BC–AD 14) Title of Octavian (born Gaius Octavius), first Roman emperor 31 BC–AD 14. He joined forces with ▷Mark Antony and Lepidus in the Second Triumvirate. Following Mark Antony's liaison with the Egyptian queen ▷Cleopatra, Augustus defeated her troops at Actium in 31 BC. As emperor he reformed the government of the empire, the army, and Rome's public services, and was a patron of the arts. The period of his rule is known as the ▷Augustan Age.

> **Suetonius**
> Roman emperor
>
> *He so improved the city that he justly boasted that he found it brick and left it marble.*
>
> *Lives of the Caesars*, 'Augustus'

Born in Rome, Octavian was the son of the senator Gaius Octavius and Atia, niece of Julius Caesar. He was elected to the college of pontiffs at the age of 15 or 16 and on Caesar's death Caesar's will declared him his adopted son and principal heir, and he took the name Gaius Julius Caesar Octavianus (though he himself preferred to omit 'Octavianus'). Octavian had one child, Julia, by his first wife, Scribonia.

The Second Triumvirate Following the murder of Caesar in 44 BC, Octavian allied himself with the senatorial party and with the consuls Hirtius and Pansa defeated Mark Antony at Mutina in 43 BC. In the same year he was made consul and formed, with Mark Antony and Lepidus, the Second Triumvirate, an agreement to divide up the Roman world between them and rule together for five years. Proscriptions followed, in which some 2,000 knights and 300 senators lost their lives. ▷Brutus and Cassius, who had control of the eastern Roman provinces and the support of the republicans, were defeated at Philippi in 42 BC, effectively bringing the Republic to an end. A fresh distribution of the provinces was made in 40 BC, Octavian taking the western provinces, Antony the eastern provinces, and Lepidus Africa. The alliance was cemented by a marriage between Mark Antony and Octavian's sister, Octavia.

With the help of his friend and exact contemporary ▷Agrippa, Octavian then defeated Sextus Pompeius in 36 BC. Lepidus was forced to retire and Octavian proceeded to establish his own authority with the help most notably of the brilliant general Agrippa. He won public confidence in his administration.

Battle of Actium While Octavian had consolidated his hold on the western part of the Roman dominion, Mark Antony had formed a liaison with the Egyptian queen ▷Cleopatra, and had spent most of his time at Alexandria. The Senate declared war against Cleopatra in 31 BC. Octavian's fleet, commanded by Agrippa, annihilated the combined fleet of Antony and Cleopatra at Actium off the northwest coast of Greece in 31 BC and Alexandria was captured in 30 BC, when Antony and Cleopatra committed suicide. Octavian's supremacy was now unchallenged.

The principate Octavian spent the next few years using his irregular and absolute power to consolidate his position. He returned to Italy in the summer of 29 BC and was hailed as the saviour of Rome and the restorer of peace after 20 years of war and civil strife. In 28/27 BC he inaugurated the system of government known as the 'principate'. He resigned his extraordinary powers and the republican constitution was in outward form restored, but Octavian had the controlling hand. He received from the Senate the title of Augustus ('venerable'), and an extended proconsular command, which gave him control of the bulk of the army. In 23 BC he resigned the consulship which he had held every year since 31 BC. In return, he received certain specific consular prerogatives, and the tribunician power to introduce legislation and veto most acts of state, and his proconsular authority (*imperium*) was made superior to that of all other proconsuls. By the end of his reign all but one of Rome's legions were under his direct control.

Foreign policy From the end of 27 BC until the autumn of 19 BC, Augustus was absent from Rome pacifying and reorganizing the provinces, first in the west and then in the east. In 18 BC his *imperium*, or supreme command, was renewed for five years. From 16 BC to 13 BC he was again absent, strengthening and extending the northern frontiers. His *imperium* was renewed for another five years when he returned.

Throughout this period, and thereafter, Gallia Comata, most of Spain, the Balkans, Syria, and Egypt were under his direct control, and administered for him by his own legates and prefects.

Augustus established a firm frontier for the empire: to the north, the friendly Batavians held the Rhine delta, and then the line followed the course of the Rhine and Danube; to the east, the Parthians were friendly, and the Euphrates gave the next line; to the south, the African colonies were protected by the desert; to the west were Spain and Gaul. The provinces were governed either by imperial legates responsible to the *princeps* or by proconsuls appointed by the Senate.

Administrative reforms An able administrator, Augustus made the army a profession, with fixed pay and length of service, and a permanent fleet was established. During his reign Rome gained an adequate water supply, a fire brigade, a police force, and a large number of public buildings. In his programme of reforms Augustus received the support of three loyal and capable helpers, Agrippa, Maecenas, and his wife Livia.

Later years of Augustus' reign After the death of Lepidus in 13/12 BC Augustus was elected *pontifex maximus*. The years after 12 BC were marked by private and public calamities: the marriage of Augustus' daughter Julia to his stepson ▷Tiberius proved disastrous; a serious revolt occurred in Pannonia in AD 6; and in Germany three legions under Varus were annihilated in the Teutoberg Forest in AD 9. Augustus died at Nola in AD 14 at the age of 76. Augustus' chosen successors, Marcellus, Agrippa, and his grandsons Gaius and Lucius Caesar, had all died before him, but he was finally able to pass on his power to his stepson and adopted son, ▷Tiberius.

The principate of Augustus saw a great flowering of architecture and literature. (Augustus boasted that he 'found Rome brick and left it marble'.) The major literary figures included ▷Livy, Virgil, Horace, and Ovid.

auk oceanic bird belonging to the family Alcidae, order Charadriiformes, consisting of 22 species of marine diving birds including razorbills, puffins, murres, and guillemots. Confined to the northern hemisphere, their range extends from well inside the Arctic Circle to the lower temperate regions. They feed on fish, and use their wings to 'fly' underwater in pursuit.

Aung San (1916–1947) Burmese (Myanmar) politician. He was a founder and leader of the Anti-Fascist People's Freedom League, which led Burma's fight for independence from the UK. During World War II he collaborated first with Japan and then with the UK. In 1947 he became head of Burma's provisional government but was assassinated the same year by political opponents. His daughter Aung San ▷Suu Kyi spearheaded a nonviolent pro-democracy movement in Myanmar from 1988.

Imprisoned for his nationalist activities while a student in Rangoon, Aung escaped to Japan in 1940. He returned to lead the Burma Independence Army, which assisted the Japanese invasion in 1942, and became defence minister in the puppet government set up by the Japanese. Before long, however, he secretly contacted the Resistance movement, and from March 1945 openly cooperated with the British in the expulsion of the Japanese. Burma became independent in 1948, after his death.

Aung San Suu Kyi Burmese (Myanmar) politician; see ▷Suu Kyi.

Aurangzeb (or **Aurungzebe**) (1618–1707) Mogul emperor of northern India from 1658. Third son of ▷Shah Jahan, he made himself master of the court by a palace revolution. His reign was the most brilliant period of the Mogul dynasty, but his despotic tendencies and Muslim fanaticism aroused much opposition. His latter years were spent in war with the princes of Rajputana and the Marathas and Sikhs. His drive south into the Deccan overextended Mogul resources.

Aurelian (*c.* AD 215–275) Born Lucius Domitius Aurelianus. Roman emperor 270–75. A successful soldier, he was proclaimed emperor by his troops on the death of Claudius II. He campaigned on the Danube and then defeated a large raid into Italy mounted by the Alamanni and Juthungi. He moved east and captured Queen Zenobia of Palmyra (now Tadmur, Syria) by the end of 272, destroying Palmyra itself in 273. He was planning a campaign against the Persians when he was murdered by a group of his own officers.

Aurelius Antoninus full name of ▷Caracalla, Roman emperor from 211.

Aurelius, Marcus Roman emperor; see ▷Marcus Aurelius Antoninus.

Auric, Georges (1899–1983) French composer. His works include a comic opera, several ballets, and incidental music to films including Jean Cocteau's *Orphée/Orpheus* (1950). He was one of the musical group called ▷Les Six, who were influenced by Erik ▷Satie.

auricula species of ▷primrose, a plant whose leaves are said to resemble a bear's ears. It grows wild in the Alps but is popular in cool-climate areas and often cultivated in gardens. (*Primula auricula.*)

Auriga constellation of the northern hemisphere, represented as a charioteer. Its brightest star is the first-magnitude ▷Capella, about 42 light years from the sun; Epsilon Aurigae is an ▷eclipsing binary star with a period of 27 years, the longest of its kind (last eclipse in 1983).

Aurignacian in archaeology, an Old Stone Age culture in Europe that came between the Mousterian and the Solutrean in the Upper Palaeolithic. The name is derived from a rock-shelter at Aurignac in the Pyrenees of France. The earliest cave paintings and figurines are attributed to the Aurignacian peoples of Western Europe about 30,000 BC.

aurochs (plural **aurochs**) extinct species of long-horned wild cattle *Bos primigenius* that formerly roamed Europe, southwestern Asia, and North Africa. It survived in Poland until 1627. Black to reddish or grey, it was up to 1.8 m/6 ft at the shoulder. It is depicted in many cave paintings, and is considered the ancestor of domestic cattle.

Aurora in Roman mythology, goddess of the dawn (Greek Eos). Preceded by her sons, the fresh morning winds, she would fly or drive a chariot across the sky to announce the approach of ▷Apollo's chariot bearing the sun.

aurora coloured light in the night sky near the Earth's magnetic poles, called **aurora borealis** ('northern lights') in the northern hemisphere and **aurora australis** in the southern hemisphere. Although aurorae are usually restricted to the polar skies, fluctuations in the ▷solar wind occasionally cause them to be visible at lower latitudes. An aurora is usually in the form of a luminous arch with its apex towards the magnetic pole followed by arcs, bands, rays, curtains, and coronas, usually green but often showing shades of blue and red, and sometimes yellow or white. Aurorae are caused at heights of over 100 km/60 mi by a fast stream of charged particles from solar flares and low-density 'holes' in the Sun's corona. These are guided by the Earth's magnetic field towards the north and south magnetic poles, where they enter the upper atmosphere and bombard the gases in the atmosphere, causing them to emit visible light.

Related Web site: Auroras: Paintings in the Sky http://www.exploratorium.edu/learning_studio/auroras/

Auschwitz (Polish **Oswięcim**) town near Kraków in Poland, the site of a notorious ▷concentration camp used by the Nazis in World War II to exterminate Jews and other political and social minorities, as part of the 'final solution'. Each of the four gas chambers could hold 6,000 people.

auscultation evaluation of internal organs by listening, usually with the aid of a stethoscope.

Austen, Jane (1775–1817) English novelist. She described her raw material as 'three or four families in a Country Village'. *Sense and Sensibility* was published in 1811, *Pride and Prejudice* in 1813, *Mansfield Park* in 1814, *Emma* in 1816, and *Northanger Abbey* and *Persuasion* together in 1818, all anonymously. She observed speech and manners with wit and precision, and her penetrating observation of human behaviour results in insights that transcend period. Many of her works have been successfully adapted for film and television.

> **Jane Austen**
>
> *There is not one in a hundred of either sex who is not taken in when they marry. Look where I will, I see that it is so; and I feel that it must be so, when I consider that it is, of all transactions, the one in which people expect most from others, and are least honest themselves.*
>
> *Mansfield Park* ch. 5

Her novels reveal Jane Austen as a scrupulous and conscious artist; absolute accuracy of information is allied to absolute precision of language. Describing individuals

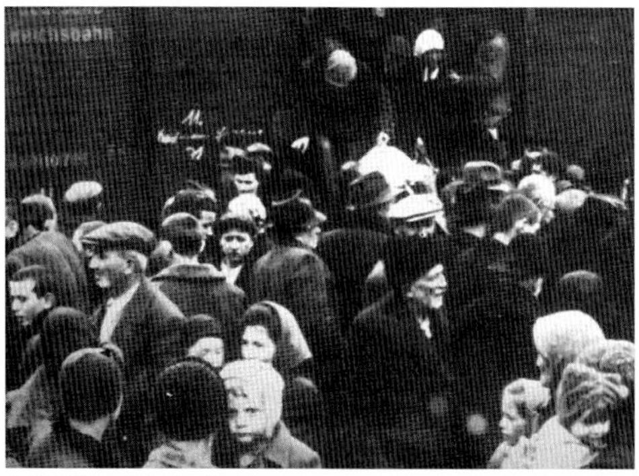

AUSCHWITZ Arrival of deportees at the concentration camp at Auschwitz in 1944, during World War II. *Archive Photos*

coping with ordinary life and social pressures, she probes the centres of human experience, using a sharp, satiric wit to expose the follies, hypocrisies, and false truths of the world.

Austen was born in Steventon, Hampshire, where her father was rector. She was sent to school in Reading with her elder sister Cassandra, who was her lifelong friend and confidante, but she was mostly taught by her father. In 1801 the family moved to Bath and after the death of her father in 1805, to Southampton, settling in 1809 with her mother and sisters in a house in Chawton, Hampshire, provided by her brother Edward (1768–1852). She died in Winchester, and is buried in the cathedral.

Austerlitz, Battle of battle on 2 December 1805, in which the French forces of Emperor Napoleon Bonaparte defeated those of Alexander I of Russia and Francis II of Austria at a small town in the Czech Republic (formerly in Austria), 19 km/12 mi east of Brno. The battle was one of Napoleon's greatest victories, resulting in the end of the coalition against France – the Austrians signed the Treaty of Pressburg and the Russians retired to their own territory.

Austin capital of ▷Texas, on the Colorado River; seat of Travis County; population (1994 est) 514,000. It is the market centre for the surrounding agricultural region, and an important centre for electronic and scientific research and the manufacture of high technology goods, including semiconductors and computers.

Austin, Alfred (1835–1913) English poet. His satirical poem *The Season* (1861) was followed by plays and volumes of poetry little read today. *The Garden that I Love* (1894) is a prose idyll. He was poet laureate 1896–1913.

Australasia and Oceania two geographical terms; **Australasia** is applied somewhat loosely to the islands of the South Pacific, including Australia, New Zealand, and their adjacent islands, while **Oceania** is a general or collective name for the groups of islands in the southern and central Pacific Ocean, comprising all those intervening between the southeastern shores of Asia and the western shores of America. The 10,000 or more Pacific Islands offer a great diversity of environments, from almost barren, waterless coral atolls to vast, continental islands.

area 8,500,000 sq km/3,300,000 sq mi (land area) **largest cities** (population over 500,000) Sydney, Melbourne, Brisbane, Perth, Adelaide, Auckland **features** the Challenger Deep in the Mariana Trench −11,034 m/−36,201 ft is the greatest known depth of sea in the world; Ayers Rock in Northern Territory, Australia, is the world's largest monolith; the Great Barrier Reef is the longest coral reef in the world; Mount Kosciusko 2,229 m/7,316 ft in New South Wales is the highest peak in Australia; Aoraki 3,764 m/12,349 ft is the highest peak in New Zealand **physical** Oceania can be broadly divided into groups of volcanic and coral islands on the basis of the ethnic origins of their inhabitants: Micronesia (Guam, Kiribati, Mariana, Marshall, Caroline Islands), Melanesia (Papua New Guinea, Vanuatu, New Caledonia, Fiji Islands, Solomon Islands), and Polynesia (Tonga, Samoa, Line Islands, Tuvalu, French Polynesia, Pitcairn); the highest point is Mount Wilhelm, Papua New Guinea 4,509 m/14,793 ft; the lowest point is Lake Eyre, South Australia −16 m/−52 ft; the longest river is the Murray in southeast Australia 2,590 km/1,609 mi; Australia is the largest island in the world. Most of the small islands are coral atolls, though some are of volcanic origin **population** (2000 est) 30.5 million, set to reach 39 million by 2025; annual growth rate from 1980 to 1985 1.5%; Australia accounts for 62% of the population **language** English, French (French Polynesia, New Caledonia, Wallis and Futuna, Vanuatu); a wide range of indigenous Aboriginal, Maori, Melanesian, Micronesian, and Polynesian languages and dialects (over 700 in Papua New Guinea) are spoken **religion** predominantly Christian; 30% of the people of Tonga adhere

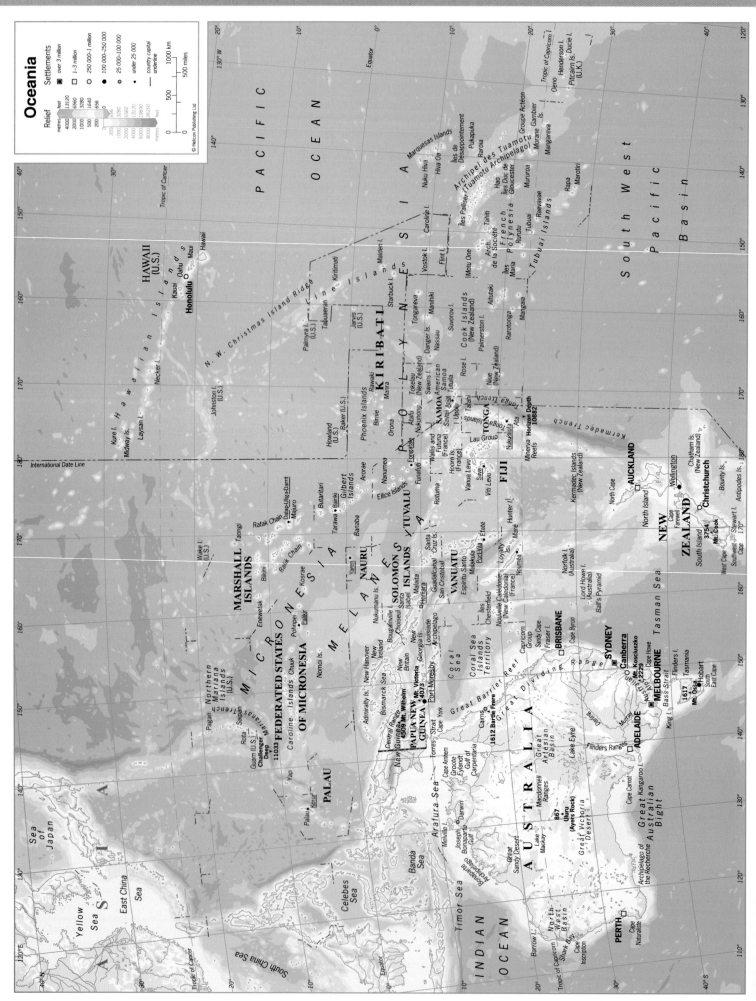

Australia

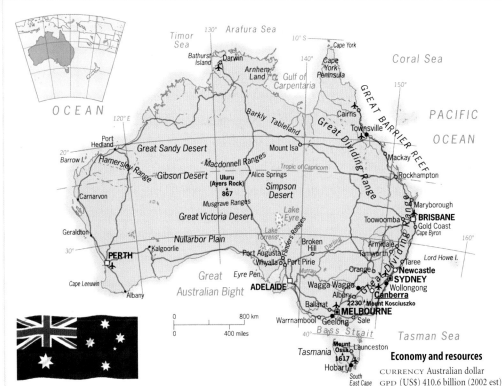

Australia country occupying all of the Earth's smallest continent, situated south of Indonesia, between the Pacific and Indian oceans.

NATIONAL NAME *Commonwealth of Australia*
AREA 7,682,850 sq km/2,966,136 sq mi
CAPITAL Canberra
MAJOR TOWNS/CITIES Adelaide, Alice Springs, Brisbane, Darwin, Melbourne, Perth, Sydney, Hobart, Newcastle, Wollongong
PHYSICAL FEATURES Uluru; Arnhem Land; Gulf of Carpentaria; Cape York Peninsula; Great Australian Bight; Great Sandy Desert; Gibson Desert; Great Victoria Desert; Simpson Desert; the Great Barrier Reef; Great Dividing Range and Australian Alps in the east (Mount Kosciusko, 2,229 m/7,136 ft, Australia's highest peak). The fertile southeast region is watered by the Darling, Lachlan, Murrumbridgee, and Murray rivers. Lake Eyre basin and Nullarbor Plain in the south
TERRITORIES Norfolk Island, Christmas Island, Cocos (Keeling) Islands, Ashmore and Cartier Islands, Coral Sea Islands, Heard Island and McDonald Islands, Australian Antarctic Territory

Government

HEAD OF STATE Queen Elizabeth II from 1952, represented by Governor General Michael Jeffery from 2003
HEAD OF GOVERNMENT John Howard from 1996
POLITICAL SYSTEM liberal democracy
POLITICAL EXECUTIVE parliamentary
ADMINISTRATIVE DIVISIONS six states and three territories
ARMED FORCES 50,900 (2002 est)
CONSCRIPTION military service is voluntary
DEATH PENALTY abolished in 1985
DEFENCE SPEND (% GDP) 2.0 (2002 est)
EDUCATION SPEND (% GDP) 5.1 (2000 est)
HEALTH SPEND (% GDP) 8.3 (2000 est)

Economy and resources

CURRENCY Australian dollar
GPD (US$) 410.6 billion (2002 est)
REAL GDP GROWTH (% change on previous year) 2.7 (2001)
GNI (US$) 386.6 billion (2002 est)
GNI PER CAPITA (PPP) (US$) 26,960 (2002 est)
CONSUMER PRICE INFLATION 2.6% (2003 est)
UNEMPLOYMENT 6.7% (2001)
MAJOR TRADING PARTNERS USA, Japan, EU, New Zealand, South Korea, China, Taiwan, Singapore
RESOURCES coal, iron ore (world's third-largest producer), bauxite, copper, zinc (world's second-largest producer), nickel (world's fifth-largest producer), uranium, gold, diamonds
INDUSTRIES mining, metal products, textiles, wood and paper products, chemical products, electrical machinery, transport equipment, printing, publishing and recording media, tourism, electronic communications
EXPORTS major world producer of raw materials: iron ore, aluminium, coal, nickel, zinc, lead, gold, tin, tungsten, uranium, crude oil; wool, meat, cereals, fruit, sugar, wine. Principal market: Japan 19.3% (2000)
IMPORTS processed industrial supplies, transport equipment and parts, road vehicles, petroleum and petroleum products, medicinal and pharmaceutical products, organic chemicals, consumer goods. Principal source: USA 21.2% (2000)
ARABLE LAND 6.5% (2000 est)
AGRICULTURAL PRODUCTS wheat, barley, oats, rice, sugar cane, fruit, grapes; livestock (cattle and sheep) and dairy products

Population and society

POPULATION 19,731,000 (2003 est)
POPULATION GROWTH RATE 0.8% (2000–15)
POPULATION DENSITY (per sq km) 3 (2003 est)
URBAN POPULATION (% of total) 92 (2003 est)
AGE DISTRIBUTION (% of total population) 0–14 20%, 15–59 63%, 60+ 17% (2002 est)
ETHNIC GROUPS 92% of European descent; 7% Asian, 1% Aborigine and other
LANGUAGE English (official), Aboriginal languages
RELIGION Anglican 26%, Roman Catholic 26%, other Christian 24%
EDUCATION (compulsory years) 10 or 11 (states vary)

Chronology

c. **40,000 BC**: Aboriginal immigration from southern India, Sri Lanka, and Southeast Asia.
AD 1606: First recorded sightings of Australia by Europeans including discovery of Cape York by Dutch explorer Willem Jansz in *Duyfken*.
1770: Capt James Cook claimed New South Wales for Britain.
1788: Sydney founded as British penal colony.
late 18th–19th centuries: Great age of exploration.
1804: Castle Hill Rising by Irish convicts in New South Wales.
1813: Crossing of Blue Mountains removed major barrier to exploration of interior.
1825: Tasmania seceded from New South Wales.
1829: Western Australia colonized.
1836: South Australia colonized.
1840–68: End of convict transportation.
1850: British Act of Parliament permitted Australian colonies to achieve virtual self-government.
1851–61: Gold rushes contributed to exploration and economic growth.
1851: Victoria seceded from New South Wales.
1855: Victoria achieved self-government.
1856: New South Wales, South Australia, and Tasmania achieved self-government.
1859: Queensland was formed from New South Wales and achieved self-government.
1890: Western Australia achieved self-government.
1891: Depression gave rise to Australian Labor Party.
1901: The Commonwealth of Australia was created.
1919: Australia was given mandates over Papua New Guinea and the Solomon Islands.
1927: The seat of federal government moved to Canberra.
1931: Statute of Westminster confirmed Australian independence.
1933: Western Australia's vote to secede was overruled.
1948–75: Influx of around 2 million new immigrants, chiefly from continental Europe.
1967: A referendum gave Australian Aborigines full citizenship rights.
1970s: Japan became Australia's chief trading partner.
1974: 'White Australia' immigration restrictions were abolished.
1975: Papua New Guinea became independent.
1978: Northern Territory achieved self-government.
1986: Australia Act passed by British Parliament, eliminating last vestiges of British legal authority.
1988: A Free Trade Agreement was signed with New Zealand.
1992: The Citizenship Act removed the oath of allegiance to the British crown.
1998: John Howard's Liberal–National coalition government was re-elected.
1999: Australians voted to keep the British queen as head of state, rather than become a republic.
2001: The ruling Liberal Party lost two state elections as the economy suffered a sharp slowdown.

LITERACY RATE 99% (men); 99% (women) (2003 est)
LABOUR FORCE 4.9% agriculture, 21.4% industry, 73.6% services (1999)
LIFE EXPECTANCY 76 (men); 82 (women) (2000–05)
CHILD MORTALITY RATE (under 5, per 1,000 live births) 6 (2001)
PHYSICIANS (per 1,000 people) 2.4 (1998 est)
HOSPITAL BEDS (per 1,000 people) 7.9 (1998 est)
TV SETS (per 1,000 people) 731 (2001 est)
RADIOS (per 1,000 people) 1,999 (2001 est)
INTERNET USERS (per 10,000 people) 4,272 (2002 est)
PERSONAL COMPUTER USERS (per 100 people) 56.5 (2002 est)

See also ▷Australian Aborigine; ▷Cook, James; ▷New South Wales.

AUSTRALIA These strange boulders make up part of the 'Devil's Marbles' granite formation at the very centre of the Northern Territory, Australia. Reminiscent in the fading sunlight of the dramatic colourations of Uluru (c. 720 km/450 mi south-southwest), the 'Marbles' are not as well known nor as easily accessible. *Image Bank*

to the Free Wesleyan Church; 70% of the people of Tokelau adhere to the Congregational Church; French overseas territories are largely Roman Catholic **industries** With a small home market, the region has a manufacturing sector dedicated to servicing domestic requirements and a large export-oriented sector, 70% of which is based on exports of primary agricultural or mineral products. Australia is a major producer of bauxite, nickel, silver, cobalt, gold, iron ore, diamonds, lead, and uranium; New Caledonia is a source of cobalt, chromite, and nickel; Papua New Guinea produces gold and copper. Agricultural products include coconuts, copra, palm oil, coffee, cocoa, phosphates (Nauru), rubber (Papua New Guinea), 40% of the world's wool (Australia, New Zealand); New Zealand and Australia are, respectively, the world's second- and third-largest producers of mutton and lamb; fishing and tourism are also major industries. **history** There is a mixed diversity of race, language, and culture. The islands of Melanesia, dominated by Papua New Guinea, were the first to be settled. Human prehistory may stretch back some 40,000 years in Papua New Guinea, and recent archaeology in the highlands suggests that agriculture was practised there as long as 9,000 years ago. But the settlement of the remainder of the Pacific occurred only during the last 6,000 years, and in Polynesia as recently as 2,000 years ago. Food crops (notably yam, taro, banana, and coconut) and domestic animals (pig, dog, chicken) are all of Southeast Asian origin, with the exception of the sweet potato (important in the Papua New Guinea highlands and Polynesia), which was probably introduced into the Pacific from America.

Australia: States and Territories *(– = not applicable.)*

State	Capital	Area sq km	Area sq mi	Population (1998)
New South Wales	Sydney	801,600	309,500	6,341,600
Queensland	Brisbane	1,727,200	666,872	3,456,300
South Australia	Adelaide	984,377	380,070	1,487,300
Tasmania	Hobart	67,800	26,177	471,900
Victoria	Melbourne	227,620	87,884	4,660,900
Western Australia	Perth	2,525,500	975,095	1,831,400
Territory				
Australian Capital Territory	Canberra	2,400	926	308,400
Northern Territory	Darwin	1,346,200	519,767	190,000
External Territory				
Ashmore and Cartier Islands	–	5	2	uninhabited
Australian Antarctic Territory	–	6,044,000	2,333,590	uninhabited except for scientific stations
Christmas Island	–	135	52	2,500[1]
Cocos (Keeling) Islands	–	14	5.5	590[2]
Coral Sea Islands[3]	–	3	3	uninhabited except for scientific stations
Heard Island and McDonald Islands	–	410	158	uninhabited
Norfolk Island	–	40	15.5	1,900[2]

[1] 1994 estimate. [2] 1993 figure. [3] Sea area of Coral Sea Islands is 780,000 sq km/301,158 sq mi; land area of the islands is approximately 2.6 sq km/1 sq mi.

Australia see country box.

Australian Aborigine member of any of the 500 groups of indigenous inhabitants of the continent of Australia, who migrated to this region from South Asia about 40,000 years ago. Traditionally hunters and gatherers, they are found throughout the continent and their languages probably belong to more than one linguistic family. They are dark-skinned, with fair hair in childhood and heavy dark beards and body hair in adult males. There are about 228,000 Aborigines in Australia, making up about 1.5% of the population of 16 million. The Aborigine rights movement campaigns against racial discrimination in housing, education, wages, and medical facilities.

Related Web site: Australian Aborigine http://aboriginalart.com.au/

Australian Alps southeastern and highest area of the Eastern Highlands of Australia, extending for about 433 km/269 mi through Victoria and New South Wales in a northeasterly direction, and forming a continuation of the ▷Great Dividing Range. They include the ▷Snowy Mountains and Mount ▷Kosciusko, Australia's highest mountain, 2,229 m/7,316 ft. The Alps are popular for winter sports.

Australian art art in Australia appears to date back at least 40,000 years, judging by radiocarbon dates obtained from organic material trapped in varnish that is covering apparently abstract rock engravings in South Australia, but may be even older, since worn crayons of ochre have been found in occupation layers of more than 50,000 years ago. Aboriginal art is closely linked with religion and mythology and includes rock and bark paintings. True Aboriginal art is now rare. European-style art developed in the 18th century, with landscape painting predominating.

Precolonial art Pictures and decorated objects were produced in nearly all settled areas. Subjects included humans, animals, and geometric ornament. The 'X-ray style', showing the inner organs in an animal portrait, is unique to Australian ▷Aboriginal art.

18th century The first European paintings were documentary, depicting the Aborigines, the flora and fauna, and topographical scenes of Sydney and the surrounding area, showing the progress of development. They were executed by immigrant artists, mostly from Britain, France, and Germany.

Late 19th–early 20th century The landscape painters of the Heidelberg School, notably Tom Roberts and later Arthur Streeton, became known outside Australia.

20th century The figurative painters William Dobell, Russell Drysdale, Sidney Nolan, and Albert Namatjira are among Australia's best-known modern artists. Sidney Nolan created a highly individual vision of the Australian landscape and of such folk heroes as Ned Kelly.

Australian Capital Territory federal territory of southeastern Australia, an enclave in the state of New South Wales; it includes Jervis Bay Territory (the site of Canberra's port on the coast) for administrative purposes; area 2,400 sq km/926 sq mi (Jervis Bay 73 sq km/28 sq mi); population (1996) 297,000. Government administration and defence employs almost half of the population of Australian Capital Territory; retail, property, and business services are also important. ▷Canberra is the main city in the territory.

Related Web site: Australian Capital Territory http://www.act.gov.au/

Australian literature Australian literature begins with the letters, journals, and memoirs of early settlers and explorers. The first poet of note was Charles Harpur (1813–1868); idioms and rhythms typical of the country were developed by, among others, Henry Kendall (1841–1882) and Andrew Barton (Banjo) Paterson. More recent poets include Christopher Brennan and Judith Wright, Kenneth Slessor, R D (Robert David) Fitzgerald (1902–1987), A D (Alec Derwent) Hope (1907–2000), James McAuley (1917–1976), and poet and novelist David ▷Malouf. Among early Australian novelists are Marcus Clarke, Rolfe Boldrewood, and Henry Handel Richardson. Striking a harsh vein in contemporary themes are the dramatist Ray Lawler and novelist Patrick ▷White; the latter received the Nobel Prize for Literature in 1973. Thomas ▷Keneally won the 1982 Booker Prize for *Schindler's Ark*.

Douglas Jerrold
English dramatist

Earth is here so kind that just tickle her with a hoe and she laughs with a harvest.

On Australia, in *A Man Made of Money*

The growth of Australian cinema in the 1970s and 1980s helped and benefited from a late flowering of Australian drama. Aboriginal culture, used as an imaginative resource by nationalist writers between the wars, has given rise both to translated collections of oral poetry, myth, and narrative, and to a modern, politically radical, tradition of Aboriginal literature in English.

Australian terrier small low-set dog with a long body and straight back. Its straight, rough coat is about 5–6.5 cm/2–2.5 in long, and blue or silver-grey, and tan or clear red or sandy in colour. It has a long head with a topknot of soft hair and ears either pricked or dropped forwards towards the front. Australian terriers are about 25 cm/10 in high and weigh 4.5–5 kg/10–11 lb.

Austral Islands alternative name for ▷Tubuai Islands, part of ▷French Polynesia.

Austria see country box.

Austrian Succession, War of the war 1740–48 between Austria (supported by England and Holland) and Prussia (supported by France and Spain). The Holy Roman Emperor Charles VI died in 1740 and the succession of his daughter Maria Theresa was disputed by a number of European powers. Frederick the Great of Prussia seized Silesia from Austria. At Dettingen in 1743 an army of British, Austrians, and Hanoverians under the command of George II was victorious over the French. In 1745 an Austro-English army was defeated at Fontenoy but British naval superiority was confirmed, and there were gains in the Americas and India. The war was ended in 1748 by the Treaty of Aix-la-Chapelle.

Quentin Crisp
English writer

An autobiography is an obituary in serial form with the last instalment missing.

The Naked Civil Servant ch. 29 (1931)

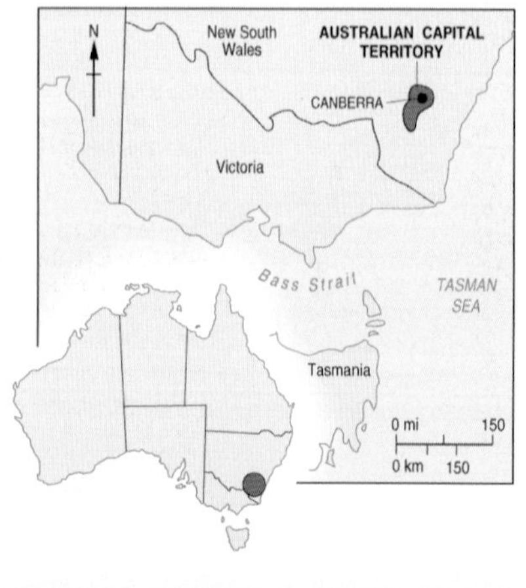

Austro-Hungarian Empire the Dual Monarchy established by the Habsburg Franz Joseph in 1867 between his empire of Austria and his kingdom of Hungary (including territory that became Czechoslovakia as well as parts of Poland, the Ukraine, Romania, Yugoslavia, and Italy).

It collapsed in the autumn of 1918 with the end of World War I. Only two king-emperors ruled: Franz Joseph and Karl.

Austronesian languages (or **Malayo-Polynesian**) family of languages spoken in Malaysia, the Indonesian archipelago, parts of the region that was formerly Indochina, Taiwan, Madagascar, Melanesia, and Polynesia (excluding Australia and most of New Guinea). The group contains some 500 distinct languages, including Malay in Malaysia, Bahasa in Indonesia, Fijian, Hawaiian, and Maori.

authenticity in music, a trend initiated in Austria and the Netherlands in the 1950s and 1960s aiming to reproduce the original conditions of early music performance and instrumentation as a means of rediscovering aesthetic terms of reference. It was pioneered by performers like Nikolaus Harnoncourt and Gustav Leonhardt. Authenticity stimulated important practical research in manuscript editing and transcription, instrument making, dance, architectural acoustics, and vocal techniques and encouraged performance of vocal works in the original language. The interest in authenticity grew rapidly; there are a number of flourishing and highly regarded 'authentic' ensembles in the USA and in every major West European country as well as in certain Central European centres.

authoritarianism rule of a country by a dominant elite who repress opponents and the press to maintain their own wealth and power. They are frequently indifferent to activities not affecting their security, and rival power centres, such as trade unions and political parties, are often allowed to exist, although under tight control. An extreme form is ▷totalitarianism.

autism, infantile rare disorder, generally present from birth, characterized by a withdrawn state and a failure to develop normally in language or social behaviour. Although the autistic child may, rarely, show signs of high intelligence (in music or with numbers, for example), many have impaired intellect. The cause is unknown, but is thought to involve a number of factors, possibly including an inherent abnormality of the child's brain. Special education may bring about some improvement.

autobiography a person's own biography, or written account of his or her life, distinguished from the journal or diary by being a connected narrative, and from memoirs by dealing less with contemporary events and personalities. *The Boke of Margery Kempe* (about 1432–36) is the oldest known autobiography in English.

autochrome in photography, a single-plate additive colour process devised by the ▷Lumière brothers in 1903. It was the first commercially available process, in use 1907–35.

autoclave pressurized vessel that uses superheated steam to sterilize materials and equipment such as surgical instruments. It is similar in principle to a pressure cooker.

autocracy form of government in which one person holds absolute power. The autocrat has uncontrolled and undisputed authority. Russian government under the tsars was an autocracy extending from the mid-16th century to the early 20th century. The title *Autocratix* (a female autocrat) was assumed by Catherine II of Russia in the 18th century.

auto-da-fé (Portuguese 'act of faith') religious ceremony, including a procession, solemn mass, and sermon, which accompanied the sentencing of heretics by the Spanish ▷Inquisition before they were handed over to the secular authorities for punishment, usually burning.

autoimmunity in medicine, condition in which the body's immune responses are mobilized not against 'foreign' matter, such

as invading germs, but against the body itself. Diseases considered to be of autoimmune origin include ▷myasthenia gravis, ▷rheumatoid arthritis, and ▷lupus erythematosus.

autolysis in biology, the destruction of a ▷cell after its death by the action of its own ▷enzymes, which break down its structural molecules.

automation widespread use of self-regulating machines in industry. Automation involves the addition of control devices, using electronic sensing and computing techniques, which often follow the pattern of human nervous and brain functions, to already

mechanized physical processes of production and distribution; for example, steel processing, mining, chemical production, and road, rail, and air control.

automatism performance of actions without awareness or conscious intent. It is seen in sleepwalking and in some (relatively rare) psychotic states.

autonomic nervous system in mammals, the part of the nervous system that controls those functions not controlled voluntarily, including the heart rate, activity of the intestines, and the production of sweat.

Austria

Austria landlocked country in central Europe, bounded east by Hungary, south by Slovenia and Italy, west by Switzerland and Liechtenstein, northwest by Germany, north by the Czech Republic, and northeast by the Slovak Republic.

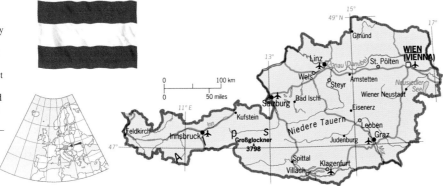

NATIONAL NAME *Republik Österreich/Republic of Austria*
AREA 83,859 sq km/32,367 sq mi
CAPITAL Vienna
MAJOR TOWNS/CITIES Graz, Linz, Salzburg, Innsbruck, Klagenfurt
PHYSICAL FEATURES landlocked mountainous state, with Alps in west and south (Austrian Alps, including Grossglockner and Brenner and Semmering passes, Lechtaler and Allgauer Alps north of River Inn, Carnic Alps on Italian border) and low relief in east where most of the population is concentrated; River Danube

Government

HEAD OF STATE Thomas Klestil from 1992
HEAD OF GOVERNMENT Wolfgang Schüssel from 2000
POLITICAL SYSTEM liberal democracy
POLITICAL EXECUTIVE parliamentary
ADMINISTRATIVE DIVISIONS nine provinces
ARMED FORCES 34,600 (2002 est)
CONSCRIPTION seven months
DEATH PENALTY abolished in 1968
DEFENCE SPEND (% GDP) 0.8 (2002 est)
EDUCATION SPEND (% GDP) 5.8 (2001 est)
HEALTH SPEND (% GDP) 8 (2000 est)

Economy and resources

CURRENCY euro (schilling until 2002)
GPD (US$) 202.9 billion (2002 est)
REAL GDP GROWTH (% change on previous year) 0.7 (2001)
GNI (US$) 190.4 billion (2002 est)

GNI PER CAPITA (PPP) (US$) 28,240 (2002 est)
CONSUMER PRICE INFLATION 1% (2003 est)
UNEMPLOYMENT 3.6% (2001)
MAJOR TRADING PARTNERS EU, Switzerland, USA, Japan, Eastern Europe
RESOURCES lignite, iron, kaolin, gypsum, talcum, magnesite, lead, zinc, forests
INDUSTRIES raw and rolled steel, machinery, cellulose, paper, cardboard, cement, fertilizers, viscose staple yarn, sawn timber, flat glass, salt, sugar, milk, margarine
EXPORTS dairy products, food products, wood and paper products, machinery and transport equipment, metal and metal products, chemical products. Principal market for exports: Germany 33% (2000)
IMPORTS petroleum and petroleum products, food and live animals, chemicals and related products, textiles, clothing. Principal source: Germany 41% (2001)
ARABLE LAND 16.9% (2000 est)
AGRICULTURAL PRODUCTS wheat, barley, rye, oats, potatoes, maize, sugar beet; dairy products

Population and society

POPULATION 8,116,000 (2003 est)
POPULATION GROWTH RATE −0.1% (2000–15)
POPULATION DENSITY (per sq km) 97 (2003 est)
URBAN POPULATION (% of total) 68 (2003 est)

AGE DISTRIBUTION (% of total population) 0–14 16%, 15–59 63%, 60+ 21% (2002 est)
ETHNIC GROUPS 99% German, 0.3% Croatian, 0.2% Slovene
LANGUAGE German (official)
RELIGION Roman Catholic 78%, Protestant 5%
EDUCATION (compulsory years) 9
LITERACY RATE 99% (men); 99% (women) (2003 est)
LABOUR FORCE 6.1% agriculture, 30.4% industry, 63.4% services (1999)
LIFE EXPECTANCY 75 (men); 82 (women) (2000–05)
CHILD MORTALITY RATE (under 5, per 1,000 live births) 5 (2001)
PHYSICIANS (per 1,000 people) 3.1 (1998 est)
HOSPITAL BEDS (per 1,000 people) 8.6 (1998 est)
TV SETS (per 1,000 people) 542 (2001 est)
RADIOS (per 1,000 people) 753 (1997)
INTERNET USERS (per 10,000 people) 4,093.6 (2002 est)
PERSONAL COMPUTER USERS (per 100 people) 36.9 (2002 est)

See also ▷Austrian Succession, War of the; ▷Austro-Hungarian Empire; ▷Metternich, Klemens, Prince von.

Chronology

14 BC: Country south of River Danube conquered by Romans.
5th century AD: The region was occupied by Vandals, Huns, Goths, Lombards, and Avars.
791: Charlemagne conquered the Avars and established East Mark, the nucleus of the future Austrian Empire.
976: Holy Roman Emperor Otto II granted East Mark to House of Babenburg, which ruled until 1246.
1282: Holy Roman Emperor Rudolf of Habsburg seized Austria and invested his son as its duke; for over 500 years most rulers of Austria were elected Holy Roman Emperor.
1453: Austria became an archduchy.
1519–56: Emperor Charles V was both archduke of Austria and king of Spain; the Habsburgs were dominant in Europe.
1526: Bohemia came under Habsburg rule.
1529: Vienna was besieged by the Ottoman Turks.
1618–48: Thirty Years' War: Habsburgs weakened by failure to secure control over Germany.
1683: Polish-Austrian force led by Jan Sobieski defeated the Turks at Vienna.

1699: Treaty of Karlowitz: Austrians expelled the Turks from Hungary, which came under Habsburg rule.
1713: By the Treaty of Utrecht, Austria obtained the Spanish Netherlands (Belgium) and political control over most of Italy.
1740–48: War of Austrian Succession: Prussia (supported by France and Spain) attacked Austria (supported by Holland and England) on the pretext of disputing rights of Maria Theresa; Austria lost Silesia to Prussia.
1772: Austria joined in partition of Poland, annexing Galicia.
1780–90: 'Enlightened despotism': Joseph II tried to impose radical reforms.
1792: Austria went to war with revolutionary France.
1804: Francis II took the title Emperor of Austria.
1806: The Holy Roman Empire was abolished.
1809–48: Austria took a leading role in resisting liberalism and nationalism throughout Europe.
1815: After the Napoleonic Wars, Austria lost its Netherlands but received Lombardy and Venetia.
1848: Outbreak of liberal-nationalist revolts throughout the Austrian Empire; Ferdinand I abdicated in favour of Franz Joseph; revolutions suppressed with difficulty.
1859: France and Sardinia expelled Austrians from Lombardy by force.
1866: Seven Weeks' War: Prussia defeated Austria, which ceded Venetia to Italy.
1867: Austria conceded equality to Hungary within the dual monarchy of Austria-Hungary.
1878: Treaty of Berlin: Austria-Hungary occupied Bosnia-Herzegovina; annexed in 1908.
1914: Archduke Franz Ferdinand, the heir to the throne, was assassinated by a Serbian nationalist; Austria-Hungary invaded Serbia, precipitating World War I.
1916: Death of Franz Joseph; succeeded by Karl I.
1918: Austria-Hungary collapsed in military defeat; empire dissolved; republic proclaimed.
1919: Treaty of St Germain reduced Austria to its present boundaries and prohibited union with Germany.
1934: Political instability culminated in brief civil war; right-wingers defeated socialists.
1938: The *Anschluss*: Nazi Germany incorporated Austria into the Third Reich.
1945: Following World War II, the victorious Allies divided Austria into four zones of occupation (US, British, French, and Soviet); the Second Republic was established under Karl Renner.
1955: Austrian State Treaty ended occupation; Austria regained independence on condition of neutrality.
1960–70s: Austria experienced rapid industrialization and prosperity.
1986: Kurt Waldheim was elected president, despite allegations of war crimes during World War II. This led to some diplomatic isolation until Waldheim's replacement by Thomas Klestil in 1992.
1995: Austria became a full member of the European Union (EU).
1998: NATO membership was ruled out.
2000: A new coalition government was elected, made up of the conservative People's Party and the far-right Freedom Party, led by Jörg Haider. Wolfgang Schüssel became prime minister, while Haider remained a senior partner in the coalition. This marked the inclusion of the far right in a West European government for the first time since World War II, and was met with protests from across Europe and the imposition of diplomatic sanctions. At the end of February, Haider resigned. In September, diplomatic sanctions lifted after favourable report on the country's human rights record.
2002: The right-wing coalition government collapsed.

AUSTRIA Summer in the Alps at Otzal, Austria. *Corel*

There are two divisions of the autonomic nervous system. The **sympathetic** system responds to stress, when it speeds the heart rate, increases blood pressure, and generally prepares the body for action. The **parasympathetic** system is more important when the body is at rest, since it slows the heart rate, decreases blood pressure, and stimulates the digestive system.

At all times, both types of autonomic nerves carry signals that bring about adjustments in visceral organs. The actual rate of heartbeat is the net outcome of opposing signals. Today, it is known that the word 'autonomic' is misleading – the reflexes managed by this system are actually integrated by commands from the brain and spinal cord (the central nervous system).

autonomy in politics, a term used to describe political self-government of a state or, more commonly, a subdivision of a state. Autonomy may be based upon cultural or ethnic differences and often leads eventually to independence.

autopsy (or **postmortem**) examination of the internal organs and tissues of a dead body, performed to try to establish the cause of death.

autoradiography in biology, a technique for following the movement of molecules within an organism, especially a plant, by labelling with a radioactive isotope that can be traced on photographs. It is commonly used to study ▷photosynthesis, where the pathway of radioactive carbon dioxide can be traced as it moves through the various chemical stages.

autosome any ▷chromosome in the cell other than a sex chromosome. Autosomes are of the same number and kind in both males and females of a given species.

autosuggestion conscious or unconscious acceptance of an idea as true, without demanding rational proof, but with potential subsequent effect for good or ill. Pioneered by French psychotherapist Emile Coué in healing, it is sometimes used in modern psychotherapy to conquer nervous habits and dependence on addictive substances such as tobacco and alcohol.

autotroph any living organism that synthesizes organic substances from inorganic molecules by using light or chemical energy. Autotrophs are the primary producers in all food chains since the materials they synthesize and store are the energy sources of all other organisms. All green plants and many planktonic organisms are autotrophs, using sunlight to convert carbon dioxide and water into sugars by ▷photosynthesis.

The total ▷biomass of autotrophs is far greater than that of animals, reflecting the dependence of animals on plants, and the ultimate dependence of all life on energy from the Sun – green plants convert light energy into a form of chemical energy (food) that animals can exploit. Some bacteria use the chemical energy of sulphur compounds to synthesize organic substances. It is estimated that 10% of the energy in autotrophs can pass into the next stage of the ▷food chain, the rest being lost as heat or indigestible matter. See also ▷heterotroph.

autumnal equinox see ▷equinox.

autumn crocus any of a group of late-flowering plants belonging to the lily family. The mauve meadow saffron (*Colchicum autumnale*) yields colchicine, which is used in treating gout and in plant breeding. (Genus *Colchicum*, family Liliaceae.)

Auvergne ancient province of central France and modern region comprising the *départements* of Allier, Cantal, Haute-Loire, and Puy-de-Dôme; administrative centre ▷Clermont-Ferrand; area 26,000 sq km/10,000 sq mi; population (1999) 1,308,900. It is a mountainous area, composed chiefly of volcanic rocks in several masses. Products include cattle, sheep, tyres, and metal goods.

Auxerre administrative centre of Yonne *département*, in France, 170 km/106 mi southeast of Paris, on the River Yonne; population (1990) 40,600. Auxerre is a market town and produces wines and metal goods.

auxin plant ▷hormone that promotes stem and root growth in plants. Auxins influence many aspects of plant growth and development, including cell enlargement, inhibition of development of axillary buds, ▷tropisms, and the initiation of roots. Synthetic auxins are used in rooting powders for cuttings, and in some weedkillers, where high auxin concentrations cause such rapid growth that the plants die. They are also used to prevent premature fruitdrop in orchards. The most common naturally occurring auxin is known as indoleacetic acid, or IAA. It is produced in the shoot apex and transported to other parts of the plant.

avalanche (from French *avaler* 'to swallow') fall or flow of a mass of snow and ice down a steep slope under the force of gravity. Avalanches occur because of the unstable nature of snow masses in mountain areas.

Avalokiteśvara in Mahāyāna Buddhism, one of the most important ▷bodhisattvas, seen as embodying compassion. He is an emanation of Amida Buddha. In China, as **Kuan Yin**, and Japan, as **Kannon**, he is confused with his female consort, becoming the popular goddess of mercy.

Avalon (or **Isle of Apples**) in Celtic mythology, the island of the blessed or paradise; one of the names of the Welsh **Otherworld**. In the legend of King Arthur, it is the land of heroes, a fruitful land of youth and health ruled over by ▷Morgan le Fay; Arthur is conveyed here to be healed of his wounds after his final battle with ▷Mordred. It has been identified since the Middle Ages with ▷Glastonbury in Somerset, southwest England.

avant-garde (French 'forward guard') in the arts, those artists or works that are in the forefront of new developments in their media. The term was introduced (as was 'reactionary') after the French Revolution, when it was used to describe any socialist political movement.

avatar in Hindu mythology, the descent of a deity to Earth in a visible form, for example the ten avatars of ▷Vishnu.

Avebury Europe's largest stone circle (diameter 412 m/1,350 ft), in Wiltshire, England. This megalithic henge monument is thought to be part of a ritual complex, and contains 650 massive blocks of stone arranged in circles and avenues. It was probably constructed around 3,500 years ago, and is linked with nearby Silbury Hill.

The henge, an earthen bank and interior ditch with entrances on opposite sides, originally rose 15 m/49 ft above the bottom of the ditch. This earthwork and an outer ring of stones surround the inner circles. The stones vary in size from 1.5 m/5 ft to 5.5 m/18 ft high and 1 m/3 ft to 3.65 m/12 ft broad. They were erected by a late Neolithic or early Bronze Age culture. The remains that can be seen today may cover an earlier site – as may be the case at a number of prehistoric sites.

When the village of Avebury developed within the circle, many of the blocks were used for building material. In the Middle Ages many of the stones were buried.

Ave Maria (Latin 'Hail, Mary') Christian prayer to the Virgin Mary, which takes its name from the archangel Gabriel's salutation to the Virgin Mary when announcing that she would be the mother of the Messiah (Luke 11:28).

avens any of several low-growing plants found throughout Europe, Asia, and North Africa. (Genus *Geum*, family Rosaceae.)

average in statistics, a term used inexactly to indicate the typical member of a set of data. It usually refers to the ▷arithmetic mean. The term is also used to refer to the middle member of the set when it is sorted in ascending or descending order (the ▷median), and the most commonly occurring item of data (the ▷mode), as in 'the average family'.

Averroës (1126–1198) Arabic **Ibn Rushd**. Arabian philosopher who argued for the eternity of matter and against the immortality of the individual soul. His philosophical writings, including commentaries on Aristotle and on Plato's *Republic*, became known to the West through Latin translations. He influenced Christian and Jewish writers into the Renaissance, and reconciled Islamic and Greek thought in asserting that philosophic truth comes through reason. St Thomas Aquinas opposed this position.

Averroës was born in Córdoba, Spain, trained in medicine, and became physician to the caliph as well as judge of Seville and Córdoba. He was accused of heresy by the Islamic authorities and banished in 1195. Later he was recalled, and died in Marrakesh, North Africa.

'Averroism' was taught in Paris and elsewhere in the 13th century by the 'Averroists', who defended a distinction between philosophical truth and revealed religion.

AVENS Water avens *Geum rivale* is a downy plant with nodding orange-pink flowers. It is an inhabitant of damp woodland, marshes, streamsides, and wet rocks. *Premaphotos Wildlife*

Avery, Milton (1893–1965) US painter. His early work was inspired by ▷Matisse, portraying subjects in thin, flat, richly coloured strokes. His later work, although still figurative, shows the influence of Mark ▷Rothko and other experimental US artists.

Avicenna (979–1037) Arabic **Ibn Sina**. Iranian philosopher and physician. He was the most renowned philosopher of medieval Islam. His *Canon Medicinae* was a standard work for many centuries. His philosophical writings were influenced by al-Farabi, Aristotle, and the neo-Platonists, and in turn influenced the scholastics of the 13th century.

Aviemore all-year sports and tourist centre, in the Highland unitary authority, Scotland, 45 km/28 mi southeast of Inverness and adjacent to the Cairngorm Mountains. The centre specializes in winter sporting activities.

Avignon city in Provence, France, administrative centre of Vaucluse *département*, on the River Rhône, 80 km/50 mi northwest of Marseille; population (1990) 89,400, conurbation 180,000. Tourism and food processing are important; other industries include the manufacture of leather, textiles, soaps, machinery, and chemicals. Avignon has a significant trade in wine. There is an atomic plant at Marcoule nearby. An important Gallic and Roman city, it has a 12th-century bridge (only half of which still stands), a 13th-century cathedral, 14th-century walls, and the Palais des Papes, the enormous fortress-palace of the popes, one of the most magnificent Gothic buildings of the 14th century.

Related Web site: Avignon http://www.avignon-et-provence.com/avi/gb/pres/p1.htm

AVIGNON The Palais des Papes, or Palace of the Popes, at Avignon, France. *Philip Sauvain Picture Collection*

Avila capital of Avila province, central Spain, situated 1,100 m/3,609 ft above sea level 90 km/56 mi northwest of Madrid, and enclosed on three sides by mountains; population (1991) 46,000. It has a Gothic cathedral and the convent and church of St Teresa, who was born here. The medieval town walls are among the best preserved in Europe.

avocado tree belonging to the laurel family, native to Central America. Its dark-green, thick-skinned, pear-shaped fruit has buttery-textured flesh and is used in salads. (*Persea americana*, family Lauraceae.)

avocet wading bird, with a characteristic long, narrow, upturned bill, which it uses to sift water as it feeds in the shallows. It is about 45 cm/18 in long, has long legs, partly webbed feet, and black and white plumage. There are four species of avocet, genus *Recurvirostra*, family Recurvirostridae, order Charadriiformes. They are found in Europe, Africa, and central and southern Asia. Stilts belong to the same family.

Avogadro's hypothesis in chemistry, the law stating that equal volumes of all gases, when at the same temperature and pressure, have the same numbers of molecules. It was first propounded by Amedeo Avogadro.

Related Web site: Avogadro's Hypothesis http://www.carlton.paschools.pa.sk.ca/chemical/molemass/avogadro.htm

Avogadro's number (or Avogadro's constant) the number of carbon atoms in 12 g of the carbon-12 isotope (6.022045×10^{23}). The relative atomic mass of any element, expressed in grams, contains this number of atoms. It is named after Amedeo Avogadro.

avoirdupois system of units of mass based on the pound (0.45 kg), which consists of 16 ounces (each of 16 drams) or 7,000 grains (each equal to 65 mg).

Avon (or **Upper Avon** or **Warwickshire Avon**; Celtic *afon* 'river') river in southern England; length 154 km/96 mi. It rises in the Northamptonshire uplands near Naseby and flows southwest through Warwick, Stratford-upon-Avon, and Evesham, before joining the River Severn near Tewkesbury, Gloucestershire.

Awash river that rises to the south of Addis Ababa in Ethiopia and flows northeast to Lake Abba on the frontier with Djibouti, ending in a chain of salt lakes; length 800 km/500 mi. Cotton is grown along the river valley and the Koka Dam (1960) supplies hydroelectric power. Although deep inside present-day Ethiopia, the Awash River was considered by Somalis to mark the eastern limit of Ethiopian sovereignty prior to the colonial division of Somaliland in the 19th century.

axil upper angle between a leaf (or bract) and the stem from which it grows. Organs developing in the axil, such as shoots and buds, are termed axillary, or lateral.

axiom in mathematics, a statement that is assumed to be true and upon which theorems are proved by using logical deduction; for example, two straight lines cannot enclose a space. The Greek mathematician Euclid used a series of axioms that he considered could not be demonstrated in terms of simpler concepts to prove his geometrical theorems.

Axis alliance of Nazi Germany and fascist Italy before and during World War II. The **Rome–Berlin Axis** was formed in 1936, when Italy was being threatened with sanctions because of its invasion of Ethiopia (Abyssinia). It became a full military and political alliance in May 1939. A ten-year alliance between Germany, Italy, and Japan (**Rome–Berlin–Tokyo Axis**) was signed in September 1940 and was subsequently joined by Hungary, Bulgaria, Romania, and the puppet states of Slovakia and Croatia. The Axis collapsed with the fall of Mussolini and the surrender of Italy in 1943 and Germany and Japan in 1945.

axis (plural **axes**) in geometry, one of the reference lines by which a point on a graph may be located. The horizontal axis is usually referred to as the *x*-axis, and the vertical axis as the *y*-axis. The term is also used to refer to the imaginary line about which an object may be said to be symmetrical (**axis of symmetry**) – for example, the diagonal of a square – or the line about which an object may revolve (**axis of rotation**).

axis deer (or **chital**) species of deer found in India and the East Indies. It is profusely spotted with white on a fawn background, shading from almost black on the back to white on the underparts.

Classification The axis deer *Axis axis* is in family Cervidae, order Artiodactyla.

axolotl (Aztec 'water monster') aquatic larval form ('tadpole') of the Mexican salamander *Ambystoma mexicanum*, belonging to the family Ambystomatidae. Axolotls may be up to 30 cm/12 in long. They are remarkable because they can breed without changing to the adult form, and will metamorphose into adults only in response to the drying-up of their ponds. The adults then migrate to another pond.

Axolotls resemble a newt in shape, having a powerful tail, two pairs of weak limbs, and three pairs of simple external gills. They lay eggs like a frog's in strings attached to water plants by a viscous substance, and the young, hatched in two to three weeks, resemble the parents.

axon long threadlike extension of a ▷nerve cell that conducts electrochemical impulses away from the cell body towards other nerve cells, or towards an effector organ such as a muscle. Axons terminate in ▷synapses, junctions with other nerve cells, muscles, or glands.

Axum variant spelling of ▷Aksum, a kingdom that flourished in the 1st–6th centuries AD.

ayatollah (Arabic 'sign of God') honorific title awarded to Shiite Muslims in Iran by popular consent, as, for example, to Ayatollah Ruhollah ▷Khomeini (1900–1989).

Ayckbourn, Alan (1939–   ) English playwright and artistic director of the Stephen Joseph Theatre, Scarborough, North Yorkshire, from 1970. His prolific output, characterized by comic dialogue and teasing experiments in dramatic structure, includes *Relatively Speaking* (1967), *Absurd Person Singular* (1972), a trilogy *The Norman Conquests* (1974), *Intimate Exchanges* (1982), *A Woman in Mind* (1986), *Haunting Julia* (1994), and *Things We Do For Love*. He has also written a number of plays for children, including *Invisible Friends* (1989) and *This Is Where We Came In* (1990).

aye-aye nocturnal tree-climbing prosimian *Daubentonia madagascariensis* of Madagascar, related to the lemurs. It is just over 1 m/3 ft long, including a tail 50 cm/20 in long.

It has an exceptionally long middle finger with which it probes for insects and their larvae under the bark of trees, and gnawing, rodentlike front teeth, with which it tears off the bark to get at its prey. The aye-aye has become rare through loss of its forest habitat, and is now classified as an endangered species.

Ayer, A(lfred) J(ules) (1910–1989) English philosopher. He wrote *Language, Truth and Logic* (1936), an exposition of the theory of 'logical positivism', presenting a criterion by which meaningful statements (essentially truths of logic, as well as statements derived from experience) could be distinguished from meaningless metaphysical utterances (for example, claims that there is a God or that the world external to our own minds is illusory). He was knighted in 1970. He was professor of logic at Oxford 1959–78. Later works include *Probability and Evidence* (1972) and *Philosophy in the Twentieth Century* (1982).

> **A J Ayer**
> *If I had been someone not very clever, I would have done an easier job like publishing. That's the easiest job I can think of.*
> Remark

Ayers Rock (Aboriginal **Uluru**) vast ovate mass of pinkish rock in Northern Territory, Australia; 335 m/1,110 ft high and 9 km/6 mi around. For the Aboriginals, whose paintings decorate its caves, it has magical significance.

It is named after Henry Ayers, a former premier of South Australia.

Ayesha (611–678) Third and favourite wife of the prophet Muhammad, who married her when she was nine. Her father, Abu Bakr, became ▷caliph on Muhammad's death in 632. She bitterly opposed the later succession to the caliphate of Ali, who had once accused her of infidelity.

Aymara the American Indian people of Bolivia and Peru, builders of a great culture, who were conquered first by the Incas and then by the Spaniards. Today 1.4 million Aymara farm and herd llamas and alpacas in the highlands; their language, belonging to the Andean-Equatorial language family, survives, and their Roman Catholicism incorporates elements of their old beliefs.

Ayr administrative headquarters of ▷South Ayrshire, southwest Scotland, at the mouth of the River Ayr; population (1991) 48,000. Ayr has strong associations with the poet Robert ▷Burns.

Industries include fishing, electronics, shipbuilding in Troon, and aircraft parts.

Ayrshire former county of southwest Scotland, on the Firth of Clyde, which was merged to form the greater part of four districts in Strathclyde region in 1975.

Aytoun (or **Ayton**), **Robert** (1569–1638) Scottish poet. He was employed by James VI and I and wrote songs and courtly verse. Aytoun is the reputed author of the lines on which Robert ▷Burns based 'Auld Lang Syne'. Aytoun was one of the first Scottish poets to write in English rather than in Scots; he also wrote in Latin, Greek, and French.

Aytoun, W(illiam) E(dmonstoune) (1813–1865) Scottish poet and satirist. He is remembered for *A Book of Ballads* 1845, written under the pseudonym Bon Gaultier with the Scottish nationalist Theodore Martin (1816–1909); for *Lays of the Scottish Cavaliers* (1849); and for inventing the 'Spasmodic School' of poetry, parodying contemporary poets who were attempting to write romantic verse.

Ayurveda basically naturopathic system of medicine widely practised in India and based on principles derived from the ancient Hindu scriptures, the ▷Vedas. Hospital treatments and remedial prescriptions tend to be nonspecific and to coordinate holistic therapies for body, mind, and spirit.

AZ abbreviation for the state of ▷Arizona, USA.

azalea any of a group of deciduous flowering shrubs belonging to the heath family. Several species are native to Asia and North America, and many cultivated varieties have been derived from these. Azaleas are closely related to the mostly evergreen ▷rhododendrons. (Genus *Rhododendron*, family Ericaceae.)

Azerbaijan see country box, p 70.

Azerbaijan, Iranian (ancient Atropatene) two provinces of northwest Iran: **Eastern Azerbaijan** (population (1996 est) 3,325,500, capital Tabriz); and **Western Azerbaijan** (population (1996 est) 2,496,300, capital Orumiyeh). Azerbaijanis in Iran, as in the Republic of Azerbaijan, are mainly Shiite Muslim ethnic Turks, descendants of followers of the Khans from the Mongol Empire.

Azeri (or **Azerbaijani**) native of the Azerbaijan region of Iran (population 5,500,000) or of the Republic of Azerbaijan (formerly a Soviet republic) (population 7,145,600). Azeri is a Turkic language belonging to the Altaic family. Of the total population of Azeris, 70% are Shiite Muslims and 30% Sunni Muslims.

azimuth in astronomy, the angular distance of an object eastwards along the horizon, measured from due north, between the astronomical ▷meridian (the vertical circle passing through the centre of the sky and the north and south points on the horizon) and the vertical circle containing the celestial body whose position is to be measured.

azo dye synthetic dye containing the azo group of two nitrogen atoms (N=N) connecting aromatic ring compounds. Azo dyes are usually red, brown, or yellow, and make up about half the dyes produced. They are manufactured from aromatic ▷amines.

Azores group of nine islands in the north Atlantic, forming an autonomous region belonging to Portugal; area 2,247 sq km/867 sq mi; population (1991) 237,800. The islands are outlying peaks of the Mid-Atlantic Ridge and are volcanic in origin. Products include sugar cane, coffee, tobacco, fruit, and wine. There

AXOLOTL The rare axolotl *Ambystoma mexicanum* lives in mountain lakes in Mexico.

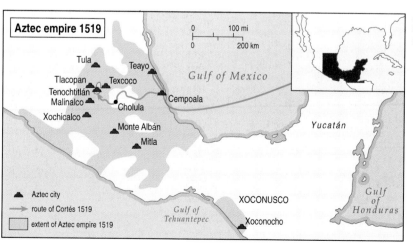

AZTEC EMPIRE See Aztec entry on p. 70.

Aztec empire 1519

0   100 mi
0   200 km

Gulf of Mexico

Tula
Teayo
Tlacopan   Texcoco
Tenochtitlán
Malinalco   Cholula   Cempoala
Xochicalco
Monte Albán
Mitla

Yucatán

XOCONUSCO
Xoconocho

Gulf of Tehuantepec

Gulf of Honduras

▲ Aztec city
→ route of Cortés 1519
☐ extent of Aztec empire 1519

are many hot springs, and the countryside is mountainous and rugged. The climate is moist but mild, and some of the islands are used as winter resorts. The administrative capital is Ponta Delgada on the main island, São Miguel; the other islands are Santa Maria, Terceira, Graciosa, São Jorge, Pico, Faial, Flores, and Corvo.

Related Web site: Azores Island Web Page http://www.geocities. com/TheTropics/2140/azores.html

Azov, Sea of (Russian *Azovskoye More*, Latin *Palus Maeotis*) inland sea between Ukraine and Russia, forming a gulf in the northeast of the Black Sea, to which it is connected by the narrow Kerch Strait. It has an area of 37,555 sq km/14,500 sq mi, and is extremely shallow, with an average depth of only 8 m/26 ft, and nowhere exceeding 16 m/52 ft. The sea is frozen for four to six months every year. Principal ports include Rostov-na-Donu, Mariupol, Kerch', and Taganrog. The main rivers flowing into the Sea of Azov are the ▷Don, and the ▷Kuban.

AZT drug used in the treatment of AIDS; see ▷zidovudine.

Aztec member of an American Indian people who migrated south into the valley of Mexico in the 1100s, and in 1325 began reclaiming lake marshland to build their capital, Tenochtitlán, on the site now occupied by Mexico City. Under their emperor Montezuma I, who reigned from 1440, the Aztecs created an empire in central Mexico.

After the Spanish conquistador Hernán ▷Cortés landed in 1519, ▷Montezuma II, who reigned from 1502, was killed and Tenochtitlán was destroyed. ▷Nahuatl is the Aztec language; it belongs to the Uto-Aztecan family of languages, and is still spoken by some Mexicans. See Aztec empire map on p. 69.

Azerbaijan

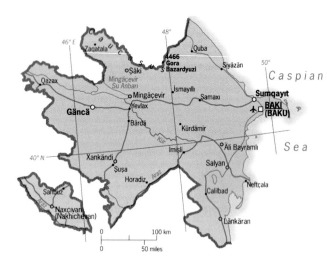

Azerbaijan country in western Asia, bounded south by Iran, east by the Caspian Sea, west by Armenia and Georgia, and north by Russia.

NATIONAL NAME *Azärbaycan Respublikasi/Republic of Azerbaijan*
AREA 86,600 sq km/33,436 sq mi
CAPITAL Baku
MAJOR TOWNS/CITIES Gäncä, Sumqayit, Nakhichevan, Xankändi, Mingechaur
PHYSICAL FEATURES Caspian Sea with rich oil reserves; the country ranges from semidesert to the Caucasus Mountains

Government

HEAD OF STATE AND GOVERNMENT Ilham Aliyev from 2003
POLITICAL SYSTEM authoritarian nationalist
POLITICAL EXECUTIVE unlimited presidency
ADMINISTRATIVE DIVISIONS 64 administrative districts, one autonomous

AZERBAIJAN The Taza Pir Mosque in Baku is depicted on this stamp from Azerbaijan. Like many mosques in the city, it serves both Sunni and Shia Muslims. *Stanley Gibbons*

republic (Nakhichevan), and an autonomous oblast (Nagorno-Karabakh)
ARMED FORCES 72,100 (2002 est)
CONSCRIPTION military service is for 17 months
DEATH PENALTY abolished in 1998
DEFENCE SPEND (% GDP) 3.3 (2002 est)
EDUCATION SPEND (% GDP) 13.4 (2001 est)
HEALTH SPEND (% GDP) 2.11 (2000 est)

Economy and resources

CURRENCY manat (replaced Russian rouble in 1993)
GPD (US$) 6.1 billion (2002 est)
REAL GDP GROWTH (% change on previous year) 9.9 (2001)
GNI (US$) 5.8 billion (2002 est)
GNI PER CAPITA (PPP) (US$) 2,920 (2002 est)
CONSUMER PRICE INFLATION 2.7% (2003 est)
UNEMPLOYMENT 1% (2001)
FOREIGN DEBT (US$) 1.6 billion (2001 est)
MAJOR TRADING PARTNERS Italy, Russia, Israel, Turkey, Georgia, USA, Iran, Germany
RESOURCES petroleum, natural gas, iron ore, aluminium, copper, barytes, cobalt, precious metals, limestone, salt
INDUSTRIES petroleum extraction and refining, chemicals, petrochemicals, construction, machinery, food processing, textiles, timber
EXPORTS refined petroleum products, machinery, food products, textiles, chemicals. Principal market: Italy 57.2% (2001)
IMPORTS industrial raw materials, processed food, machinery. Principal source: USA 16.1% (2001)
ARABLE LAND 19% (2000 est)

AGRICULTURAL PRODUCTS grain, grapes and other fruit, vegetables, cotton, silk, tobacco; livestock rearing (cattle, sheep, and goats); fisheries (about 10 tonnes of caviar are produced annually); silkworm breeding

Population and society

POPULATION 8,370,000 (2003 est)
POPULATION GROWTH RATE 0.9% (2000–15)
POPULATION DENSITY (per sq km) 97 (2003 est)
URBAN POPULATION (% of total) 52 (2003 est)
AGE DISTRIBUTION (% of total population) 0–14 27%, 15–59 62%, 60+ 11% (2002 est)
ETHNIC GROUPS 83% of Azeri descent, 6% Russian, 6% Armenian
LANGUAGE Azeri (official), Russian
RELIGION Shiite Muslim 68%, Sunni Muslim 27%, Russian Orthodox 3%, Armenian Orthodox 2%
EDUCATION (compulsory years) 11
LITERACY RATE 99% (men); 99% (women) (2003 est)
LABOUR FORCE 42.3% agriculture, 11.7% industry, 46.1% services (1999)
LIFE EXPECTANCY 69 (men); 76 (women) (2000–05)
CHILD MORTALITY RATE (under 5, per 1,000 live births) 105 (2001)
PHYSICIANS (per 1,000 people) 3.6 (1999 est)
HOSPITAL BEDS (per 1,000 people) 9.7 (1999 est)
TV SETS (per 1,000 people) 321 (2001 est)
RADIOS (per 1,000 people) 25 (2001 est)
INTERNET USERS (per 10,000 people) 368.5 (2002 est)

See also ▷Armenia; ▷Nagorno-Karabakh.

Chronology

4th century BC: Established as an independent state for the first time by Atrophates, a vassal of Alexander III of Macedon.

7th century AD: Spread of Islam.

11th century: Immigration by Oghuz Seljuk peoples, from the steppes to the northeast.

13th–14th centuries: Incorporated within Mongol Empire; the Mongol ruler Tamerlane had his capital at Samarkand.

16th century: Baku besieged and incorporated within Ottoman Empire, before falling under Persian dominance.

1805: Khanates (chieftaincies), including Karabakh and Shirvan, which had won independence from Persia, gradually became Russian protectorates, being confirmed by the Treaty of Gulistan, which concluded the 1804–13 First Russo-Iranian War.

1828: Under the Treaty of Turkmenchai, which concluded the Second Russo-Iranian War begun in 1826, Persia was granted control over southern and Russia over northern Azerbaijan.

late 19th century: The petroleum industry developed, resulting in a large influx of Slav immigrants to Baku.

1917–18: Member of anti-Bolshevik Transcaucasian Federation.

1918: Became an independent republic.

1920: Occupied by Red Army and subsequently forcibly secularized.

1922–36: Became part of the Transcaucasian Federal Republic with Georgia and Armenia.

early 1930s: Peasant uprisings against agricultural collectivization and Stalinist purges of the local Communist Party.

1936: Became a constituent republic of the USSR.

late 1980s: Growth in nationalist sentiment, taking advantage of the *glasnost* initiative of the reformist Soviet leader Mikhail Gorbachev.

1988: Riots followed the request of Nagorno-Karabakh, an Armenian-peopled enclave within Azerbaijan, for transfer to Armenia.

1989: Nagorno-Karabakh was placed under direct rule from Moscow; civil war broke out with Armenia over Nagorno-Karabakh.

1990: Soviet troops were dispatched to Baku to restore order amid calls for secession from the USSR.

1991: Independence was declared after the collapse of an anti-Gorbachev coup in Moscow, which had been supported by the Azeri communist leadership. Azerbaijan joined the new Commonwealth of Independent States (CIS); Nagorno-Karabakh declared independence.

1992: Azerbaijan admitted into the United Nations (UN).

1993: Nagorno-Karabakh was overtaken by Armenian forces.

1995: An attempted coup was foiled. A market-centred economic reform programme was introduced.

1997: There was border fighting with Armenia.

1998: A new pro-government grouping, Democratic Azerbaijan, was formed. Heidar Aliyev was re-elected president in a disputed poll.

2000: Heidar Aliyev was re-elected, although foreign observers denounced the election as deeply flawed.

2001: Azerbaijan was admitted into the Council of Europe. A declaration was signed with Russia, agreeing on political, economic and military cooperation.

BA in education, abbreviation for the degree of **Bachelor of Arts**.

Baader–Meinhof gang popular name for the West German left-wing guerrilla group the *Rote Armee Fraktion/Red Army Faction*, active from 1968 against what it perceived as US imperialism. The three main founding members were Andreas Baader, Gudrun Ensslin, and Ulrike Meinhof.

Baal (Semitic 'lord' or 'owner') divine title given to their chief male gods by the Phoenicians, or Canaanites, of the eastern Mediterranean coast about 1200–332 BC. Their worship as fertility gods, often orgiastic and of a phallic character, was strongly denounced by the Hebrew prophets.

    Related Web site: Baal http://www.newadvent.org/cathen/02175a.htm

Baalbek city of ancient Syria, now in Lebanon, 60 km/36 mi northeast of Beirut. It was originally a centre of Baal worship. The Greeks identified Baal with Helios, the Sun, and renamed Baalbek **Heliopolis**. Its ruins, including Roman temples, survive, notably the Temple of Jupiter Heliopolitanus and the Temple of Bacchus, built in the 2nd century AD, which is still almost intact.

BAALBEK Roman ruins of a temple complex at Baalbek, in the Bekaa, Lebanon. *Image Bank*

Ba'ath Party (anglicized **Party of Arab Renaissance**) ruling political party in Iraq and Syria. Despite public support of pan-Arab unity and its foundation in 1943 as a party of Arab nationalism, its ideology has been so vague that it has fostered widely differing (and often opposing) parties in Syria and Iraq.

Babbage, Charles (1792–1871) English mathematician who devised a precursor of the computer. He designed an analytical engine, a general-purpose mechanical computing device for performing different calculations according to a program input on punched cards (an idea borrowed from the ▷Jacquard loom). This device was never built, but it embodied many of the principles on which digital computers are based.

Babbage was born in Totnes, Devon. As a student at Cambridge, he assisted John ▷Herschel with his astronomical calculations and thought they could be better done by machines. His mechanical calculator, or ▷difference engine, begun in 1822, which could compute squares to six places of decimals, got him a commission from the British Admiralty for an expanded version. But this project was abandoned in favour of the analytical engine, on which he worked for the rest of his life. The difference engine could perform only one function, once it was set up. The analytical engine was intended to perform many functions; it was to store numbers and be capable of working to a program. The first computer printer, also designed but never built by Charles Babbage, was completed and put on show at London's Science Museum in April 2000.

Babbit metal soft, white metal, an ▷alloy of tin, lead, copper, and antimony, used to reduce friction in bearings, developed by the US inventor Isaac Babbit in 1839.

Babbitt, Milton (1916–) US composer and theorist. He pioneered the application of information theory to music in the 1950s, introducing set theory to series manipulations and the term 'pitch class' to define every octave identity of a note name. His works include four string quartets, works for orchestra, *Philomel* for soprano and electronic tape (1963–64), and *Ensembles for Synthesizer* (1967), both composed using the 1960 RCA Princeton-Columbia Mark II Synthesizer, which he helped to design.

babbler bird of the thrush family Muscicapidae with a loud babbling cry. Babblers, subfamily Timaliinae, are found in the Old World, and there are some 250 species in the group.

Babel Hebrew name for the city of ▷Babylon, chiefly associated with the **Tower of Babel** which, in the Genesis story in the Old Testament, was erected in the plain of Shinar by the descendants of Noah. It was a ziggurat, or staged temple, seven storeys high (100 m/328 ft) with a shrine of Marduk on the summit. It was built by Nabopolassar, father of Nebuchadnezzar, and was destroyed when Sennacherib sacked the city in 689 BC.

Babel, Isaak Emmanuilovich (1894–1940) Russian writer. Born in Odessa, he was an ardent supporter of the Revolution and fought with Budyenny's cavalry in the Polish campaign of 1921–22, an experience which inspired *Red Cavalry* (1926). His other works include *Stories from Odessa* (1924), which portrays the life of the Odessa Jews.

Babeuf, François-Noël (1760–1797) French revolutionary journalist, a pioneer of practical socialism. In 1794 he founded a newspaper in Paris, later known as the *Tribune of the People*, in which he demanded the equality of all people. He was guillotined for conspiring against the ruling Directory during the French Revolution.

Babi faith faith from which the ▷Baha'i faith grew.

babirusa wild pig *Babirousa babyrussa*, becoming increasingly rare, found in the moist forests and by the water of Sulawesi, Buru, and nearby Indonesian islands. The male has large upper tusks which grow upwards through the skin of the snout and curve back towards the forehead. The babirusa is up to 80 cm/2.5 ft at the shoulder. It is nocturnal, and swims well.

Babism religious movement founded during the 1840s by Mirza Ali Muhammad ('the ▷Bab'). An offshoot of Islam, it differs mainly in the belief that Muhammad was not the last of the prophets. The movement split into two groups after the death of the Bab; Baha'u'llah, the leader of one of these groups, founded the ▷Baha'i faith.

Babi Yar ravine near Kiev, Ukraine, where more than 100,000 people (80,000 of whom were Jews, the remainder being Poles, Russians, and Ukrainians) were murdered by the Nazis in 1941. The site was ignored until the Soviet poet Yevgeny ▷Yevtushenko wrote a poem called 'Babi Yar' (1961) in protest at plans for a sports centre on the site.

> ## Charles Babbage
> *The whole of the developments and operations of analysis are now capable of being executed by machinery. . . . As soon as an Analytical Engine exists, it will necessarily guide the future course of science.*
>
> Passages from the Life of a Philosopher
> 1864

baboon large monkey of the genus *Papio*, with a long doglike muzzle and large canine teeth, spending much of its time on the ground in open country. Males, with head and body up to 1.1 m/3.5 ft long, are larger than females, and dominant males rule the 'troops' in which baboons live. They inhabit Africa and southwestern Arabia.

    Species include the **olive baboon** *P. anubis* from West Africa to Kenya, the **chacma** *P. ursinus* from South Africa, and the **sacred baboon** *P. hamadryas* from northeastern Africa and southwestern Arabia. The male sacred baboon has a 'cape' of long hair.

Bab, the (1819–1850) Adopted name of Mirza Ali Muhammad. (Arabic 'gate') Persian religious leader, born in Shiraz, founder of ▷Babism, an offshoot of Islam. In 1844 he proclaimed that he was a gateway to the Hidden Imam, a new messenger of Allah who was to come. He gained a large following whose activities caused the Persian authorities to fear a rebellion, and who were therefore persecuted. The Bab was executed for heresy.

THE BAB The Shrine of the Bab on Mount Carmel, Haifa, Israel. *Image Bank*

Babur (1483–1530) Born Zahir ud-Din Muhammad. (Arabic 'lion') First Great Mogul of India from 1526. He was the great-grandson of the Mogul conqueror Tamerlane and, at the age of 11, succeeded his father, Omar Sheikh Mirza, as ruler of Fergana (Turkestan). In 1526 he defeated the emperor of Delhi at Panipat in the Punjab, captured Delhi and ▷Agra (the site of the Taj Mahal), and established a dynasty that lasted until 1858.

Babylon capital of ancient Babylonia, on the bank of the lower Euphrates River. The site is now in Iraq, 88 km/55 mi south of Baghdad and 8 km/5 mi north of Hillah, which is built chiefly of bricks from the ruins of Babylon. The Hanging Gardens of Babylon, one of the ▷Seven Wonders of the World, were probably erected on a vaulted stone base, the only stone construction in the mud-brick city. They formed a series of terraces, irrigated by a hydraulic system. In 1986–89 Iraqi President Saddam Hussein constructed a replica of the Southern Palace and citadel of Nebuchadnezzar II, based on the plans of the German archaeologist Robert Koldeway. It was bombed in the Iraq war. In ▷Rastafarianism, Babylon is the non-African world.

BABYLON A mythical lion of Babylon, depicted on coloured glazed bricks. *Philip Sauvain Picture Collection*

Babylonian captivity exile of Jewish deportees to Babylon after Nebuchadnezzar II's capture of Jerusalem in 586 BC. According to tradition, the captivity lasted 70 years, but Cyrus of Persia, who conquered Babylon, actually allowed them to go home in 536 BC. By analogy, the name has also been applied to the papal exile to Avignon, France, AD 1309–77.

Bacall, Lauren (1924–) Stage name of Betty Joan Perske. US actor. She became an overnight star when cast by Howard Hawks opposite Humphrey Bogart in *To Have and Have Not* (1944). She and Bogart went on to star together in *The Big Sleep* (1946), *The Dark Passage* (1947), and *Key Largo* (1948). They married in 1945.

Bacchus in Greek and Roman mythology, the god of fertility (see ▷Dionysus) and of wine; his rites (the **Bacchanalia**) were orgiastic.

Bach, Carl Philip Emanuel (1714–1788) German composer. He was the third son of Johann Sebastian Bach. He introduced a new 'homophonic' style, light and easy to follow, which influenced Mozart, Haydn, and Beethoven.

In the service of Frederick the Great 1740–67, he left to become master of church music at Hamburg in 1768. He wrote over 200 pieces for keyboard instruments, and published a guide to playing the piano. Through his music and concert performances he helped to establish a leading solo role for the piano in Western music.

Bach, Johann Christian (1735–1782) German composer. The eleventh son of Johann Sebastian Bach, he became celebrated in Italy as a composer of operas. In 1762 he was invited to London, where he became music master to the royal family. He remained in England until his death; his great popularity both as a composer and a performer declined in his last years for political and medical reasons.

Bach, Johann Sebastian (1685–1750) German composer. A master of ▷counterpoint, his music epitomizes the baroque polyphonic style. His orchestral music includes the six *Brandenburg Concertos* (1721), other concertos for keyboard instrument and violin, four orchestral suites, sonatas for various instruments, three partitas and three sonatas for violin solo, and six unaccompanied cello suites. Bach's keyboard music, for clavier and organ, his fugues, and his choral music are of equal importance. He also wrote chamber music and songs.

His appointments included positions at the courts of Weimar and Anhalt-Cöthen, and from 1723 until his death he was musical director at St Thomas's choir school in Leipzig.

He married twice and had over 20 children (although several died in infancy). His second wife, Anna Magdalena Wilcken, was a soprano; she also worked for him when his sight failed in later years.

Although he was not always appreciated by his contemporaries, Bach's place in music history was aptly summed up by his first major biographer, Johann Nikolaus Forkel (1749–1818; *Über Johann Sebastian Bachs Leben, Kunst, und Kunstwerke* (1802), English translation 1820 and 1920): 'He is the river, to which all other composers are tributaries'.

Related Web site: JS Bach Archive and Bibliography http://www.let.rug.nl/Linguistics/diversen/bach/intro.html

Bach, Wilhelm Friedemann (1710–1784) German composer. The eldest son of Johann Sebastian Bach, he was also an organist, improviser, and master of ▷counterpoint.

bacille Calmette-Guérin tuberculosis vaccine ▷BCG.

bacillus a genus of rod-shaped ▷bacteria that occur everywhere in the soil and air. Some are responsible for diseases such as ▷anthrax, or for causing food spoilage.

backgammon board game for two players, often used in gambling. It was known in Mesopotamia, Greece, Rome, and in medieval England.

background radiation radiation that is always present in the environment. By far the greater proportion (87%) of it is emitted from natural sources. Alpha and beta particles, and gamma radiation are radiated by the traces of radioactive minerals that occur naturally in the environment and even in the human body, and by radioactive gases such as ▷radon, which are found in soil and may seep upwards into buildings. Radiation from space (▷cosmic radiation) also contributes to the background level.

The **background count** is the count registered on a ▷Gieger counter when no other radioactive source is nearby.

back pain aches in the region of the spine. Low back pain can be caused by a very wide range of medical conditions. About half of all episodes of back pain will resolve within a week, but severe back pain can be chronic and disabling. The causes include muscle sprain, a prolapsed intervertebral disc, and vertebral collapse due to ▷osteoporosis or cancer. Treatment methods include rest, analgesics, physiotherapy, osteopathy, and exercises.

backswimmer (or **water boatman**) aquatic predatory bug living mostly in fresh water. The adults are about 15 mm/0.5 in long and rest upside down at the water surface to breathe. When disturbed they dive, carrying with them a supply of air trapped under the wings. They have piercing beaks, used in feeding on tadpoles and small fish.

Classification Backswimmers belong to the genus *Notonecta*, family Notonectidae in suborder Heteroptera, order Hemiptera (true bugs), class Insecta, phylum Arthropoda.

Females have a sharp ovipositor to pierce the stems of aquatic plants. In each notch one egg is laid; each female lays a total of approximately 60 eggs over a period of a few weeks. Backswimmers fly readily from pond to pond.

Four species of backswimmer are found in Britain. The most common is *Notonecta glauca* found in most British ponds and lakes. The others are: *N. obliqua*; *N. maculata*, with mottled elytra (wing cases), often found in freshwater habitats in southern England; *N. viridis*, found mainly in brackish waters.

backup system in computing, duplicate computer system that can take over the operation of a main computer system in the event of equipment failure. A large interactive system, such as an airline's ticket-booking system, cannot be out of action for even a few hours without causing considerable disruption. In such cases a complete duplicate computer system may be provided to take over and run the system should the main computer develop a fault or need maintenance.

Bacon, Francis (1909–1992) Irish painter. Self-taught, he practised abstract art, then developed a stark Expressionist style characterized by distorted, blurred figures enclosed in loosely defined space. He aimed to 'bring the figurative thing up onto the nervous system more violently and more poignantly'. One of his best-known works is *Study after Velázquez's Portrait of Pope Innocent X* (1953; Museum of Modern Art, New York).

Bacon moved to London in 1925, began to paint in about 1930, and held his first show in London in 1949. He destroyed much of his early work. *Three Studies for Figures at the Base of a Crucifixion* (about 1944; Tate Gallery, London) is an early example of his mature style, which is often seen as a powerful expression of the existential anxiety and nihilism of 20th-century life.

Bacon, Francis (1561–1626) 1st Baron Verulam and Viscount St Albans. English philosopher, politician, and writer, a founder of modern scientific research. His works include *Essays* (1597, revised and augmented 1612 and 1625), characterized by pith and brevity; *The Advancement of Learning* (1605), a seminal work discussing scientific method; *Novum Organum* (1620), in which he redefined the task of natural science, seeing it as a means of empirical discovery and a method of increasing human power over nature; and *The New Atlantis* (1626), describing a utopian state in which scientific knowledge is systematically sought and exploited. He was briefly Lord Chancellor in 1618 but lost his post through corruption.

> **Francis Bacon**
> *A little philosophy inclineth man's mind to atheism, but depth in philosophy bringeth men's minds about to religion.*
> Essays, 'Atheism' 1597

Bacon was born in London, studied law at Cambridge from 1573, was part of the embassy in France until 1579, and became a member of Parliament in 1584. In 1596 he became a Queen's Counsel. He was the nephew of Queen Elizabeth's adviser Lord ▷Burghley, but turned against him when he failed to provide Bacon with patronage and attached himself to Burghley's rival, the Earl of Essex. He subsequently helped secure the execution of the Earl of Essex as a traitor in 1601. Bacon was accused of ingratitude to his patron, but he defended himself in *Apology* (1604), arguing that his first loyalty was to his sovereign. In 1618, having risen to Lord Chancellor, he confessed to bribe-taking, was fined £40,000 (which was later remitted by the king), and spent four days in the Tower of London. From then on he devoted himself to science and writing, in both Latin and English.

Satirist Alexander Pope called Bacon 'the wisest, brightest, and meanest of mankind'. Knighted on the accession of James I in 1603, he became Baron Verulam in 1618 and Viscount St Albans in 1621. His writings helped to inspire the founding of the ▷Royal Society. The **Baconian theory**, originated by James Willmot in 1785, suggesting that the works of Shakespeare were written by Bacon, is not taken seriously by scholars.

He died after catching a cold while stuffing a chicken with snow in an early experiment in refrigeration.

Related Web site: Bacon, Francis (philosopher) http://www.luminarium.org/sevenlit/bacon/index.html

Bacon, Roger (*c.* 1214–1294) English philosopher and scientist. He was interested in alchemy, the biological and physical sciences, and magic. Many discoveries have been credited to him, including the magnifying lens. He foresaw the extensive use of gunpowder and mechanical cars, boats, and planes. Bacon was known as *Doctor Mirabilis* (Wonderful Teacher).

In 1266, at the invitation of his friend Pope Clement IV, he began his *Opus majus/Great Work*, a compendium of all branches of knowledge. In 1268 he sent this with his *Opus minus/Lesser Work* and other writings to the pope. In 1277 Bacon was condemned and imprisoned by the Christian church for 'certain novelties' (heresy) and not released until 1292.

Bacon wrote in Latin and his works include *On Mirrors*, *Metaphysical*, and *On the Multiplication of Species*. He followed the maxim 'Cease to be ruled by dogmas and authorities; look at the world!'

Related Web site: Bacon, Roger http://www-groups.dcs.st-and.ac.uk/history/Mathematicians/Bacon.html

bacteria (singular **bacterium**) microscopic single-celled organisms lacking a nucleus. Bacteria are widespread, being present in soil, air, and water, and as parasites on and in other living things. Some parasitic bacteria cause disease by producing toxins, but others are harmless and can even benefit their hosts. Bacteria usually reproduce by ▷binary fission (dividing into two equal parts), and, on average, this occurs every 20 minutes. Only 4,000 species of bacteria are known (in 1998), although bacteriologists believe that around 3 million species may actually exist. Certain types of bacteria are vital in many food and industrial processes, while others play an essential role in the ▷nitrogen cycle, which maintains soil fertility.

Bacteria have a large loop of ▷DNA, sometimes called a bacterial chromosome. In addition there are often small, circular pieces of DNA known as ▷plasmids that carry spare genetic information. These plasmids can readily move from one bacterium to another, even though the bacteria may be of different species. In a sense, they are parasites within the bacterial cell, but they survive by coding characteristics that promote the survival of their hosts. For example, some plasmids confer antibiotic resistance on the bacteria they inhabit. The rapid and problematic spread of antibiotic resistance among bacteria is due to these plasmids.

Classification Bacteria are now classified biochemically, but their varying shapes provide a rough classification; for example, **cocci** are round or oval, **bacilli** are rodlike, **spirilla** are spiral, and **vibrios** are shaped like commas. Exceptionally, one bacterium has been found, *Gemmata obscuriglobus*, that does have a nucleus. Bacteria can also be classified into two broad classes (called Gram positive and Gram negative) according to their reactions to certain stains, or dyes, used in microscopy. The staining technique, called the Gram test after Danish bacteriologist Hans Gram, allows doctors to identify many bacteria quickly.

bacteriology the study of ▷bacteria.

bacteriophage virus that attacks ▷bacteria, commonly called a phage. Such viruses are now of use in genetic engineering.

Bactria province of the ancient Persian empire (now divided between Afghanistan, Pakistan, and Tajikistan) which was partly conquered by Alexander the Great. During the 6th–3rd centuries BC it was a centre of east–west trade and cultural exchange.

Bactrian species of ▷camel *Camelus bactrianus* found in the Gobi Desert in Central Asia. Body fat is stored in two humps on the back. It has very long winter fur which is shed in ragged lumps. The head and body length is about 3 m/10 ft, and the camel is up to 2.1 m/6.8 ft tall at the shoulder. Most Bactrian camels are domesticated and are used as beasts of burden in western Asia.

Badajoz capital of Badajoz province in Extremadura, southwest Spain, situated on the River Guadiana at the Portuguese frontier; population (1991) 121,900. Textiles, pottery, leather, and soap are manufactured. Badajoz has a 16th-century bridge and a 13th-century cathedral.

bad debt bill or debt which has not been paid and is most unlikely to be paid. Bad debts eventually have to be 'written off' on the profit and loss account. They are counted as a provision and are deducted from the account.

Baden former state of southwestern Germany, which had Karlsruhe as its capital. Baden was captured from the Romans in 282 by the Alemanni; later it became a margravate and, in 1806, a grand duchy. A state of the German empire 1871–1918, then a republic, and under Hitler a *Gau* (province), it was divided between the *Länder* of Württemberg-Baden and Baden in 1945 and in 1952 made part of ▷Baden-Württemberg.

Baden town in Aargau canton, Switzerland, near Zürich, at an altitude of 388 m/1,273 ft; population (1990) 14,800. Its hot sulphur springs and mineral waters have been visited since Roman times.

Baden-Baden Black Forest spa town in Baden-Württemberg, southwestern Germany, in the Oos valley, 68 km/42 mi west of Stuttgart; population (1995) 52,600. Its mineral springs have been known since Roman times, and it became a fashionable spa in the 19th century. The town has a conference centre, the Kongresshaus (1968).

Baden-Powell, Robert Stephenson Smyth (1857–1941) 1st Baron Baden-Powell. British general, founder of the ▷Scout Association. He was commander of the garrison during the 217-day siege of Mafeking (now Mafikeng) in the Second South African War (1899–1900). After 1907 he devoted his time to developing the Scout movement, which rapidly spread throughout the world.

Baden-Powell began the Scout movement in 1907 with a camp for 20 boys on Brownsea Island, Poole Harbour, Dorset. He published *Scouting for Boys* (1908) and about 30 other books. He was World Chief Scout from 1920. With his sister Agnes (1858–1945) he founded the Girl Guides in 1910. Knighted 1909, Baron 1929.

Born in London, he was educated at Charterhouse. After failing to gain a place at Oxford University he joined the Indian Army, being commissioned in the Hussars in 1876; he became its youngest colonel by the age of 40. His defence of Mafikeng brought him worldwide fame.

Baden-Württemberg administrative region (German *Land*) of Germany, bounded to the west by France, to the south by Switzerland, to the east by Bavaria, and to the west by the Rhine valley. area 35,800 sq km/13,820 sq mi; population (1995) 10,350,000. The capital is ▷Stuttgart; main cities and towns are Mannheim, Karlsruhe, Freiburg im Breisgau, Heidelberg, Heilbronn, Pforzheim, and Ulm. The area has the Rhine as boundary to the south and west and it contains the ▷Black Forest; the source of the River Danube is at Donaueschingen in the Black Forest mountains. Principal industries are luxury motor vehicles, jewellery, watches, clocks, musical instruments, textiles, chemicals, iron, steel, electrical equipment, surgical instruments, and precision engineering. Agricultural activities centre on wine production, animal husbandry, and fruit growing.

BADGER The American badger is slightly smaller than its Eurasian cousin. Unlike the Eurasian badger, it is a solitary creature, and lives mainly on small rodents.

badger large mammal of the weasel family with molar teeth of a crushing type adapted to a partly vegetable diet, and short strong legs with long claws suitable for digging. The Eurasian **common badger** *Meles meles* is about 1 m/3 ft long, with long, coarse, greyish hair on the back, and a white face with a broad black stripe along each side. Mainly a woodland animal, it is harmless and nocturnal, and spends the day in a system of burrows called a 'sett'. It feeds on roots, a variety of fruits and nuts, insects, worms, mice, and young rabbits.

The Eurasian badger lives for up to 15 years. It mates February to March, and again July to September if the earlier mating has not resulted in fertilization. Implantation of the ▷blastocyst (early embryo) is however delayed until December. Cubs are born January to March, and remain below ground for eight weeks. They remain with the sow at least until autumn.

The **American badger** *Taxidea taxus* is slightly smaller than the Eurasian badger, and lives in open country in North America. Various species of hog badger, ferret badger, and stink badger occur in South and East Asia, the last having the well-developed anal scent glands characteristic of the weasel family.

Between 1989 and 1997 the British badger population increased by 70%. In 1998 the Ministry of Agriculture, Fisheries and Food (MAFF) announced approval of an experiment suggested by the Krebs report *Bovine Tuberculosis in Badgers*, in which an estimated 10,000 badgers will be culled in an attempt to establish once and for all if badgers do transmit bovine TB to cattle. In designated areas where TB incidence is highest all badgers will be culled; in other selected areas badgers will be culled only if an outbreak of TB occurs; and in control areas there will be no culling even if there is an outbreak. All other culling should cease during the experimental period.

The MAFF badger culling experiment began in autumn 1998. The experiment will take place over six or seven years and an estimated 12,000 badgers will be killed as a consequence.

There are approximately 50,000 badgers killed in road accidents each year in Britain (1998).

Related Web site: Badgers.org.uk http://www.badgers.org.uk/

badlands barren landscape cut by erosion into a maze of ravines, pinnacles, gullies, and sharp-edged ridges. Areas in South Dakota and Nebraska, USA, are examples.

badminton racket game similar to lawn ▷tennis but played on a smaller court and with a shuttlecock (a half sphere of cork or plastic with a feather or nylon skirt) instead of a ball. The object of the game is to prevent the opponent from being able to return the shuttlecock.

Badoglio, Pietro (1871–1956) Italian soldier and fascist politician. He served as a general in World War I and subsequently in the campaigns against the peoples of Tripoli and Cyrenaica. In 1935 he became commander-in-chief in Ethiopia, adopting ruthless measures to break patriot resistance. He was created viceroy of Ethiopia and duke of Addis Ababa in 1936. He resigned during the disastrous campaign into Greece in 1940 and succeeded Mussolini as prime minister of Italy from July 1943 to June 1944, negotiating the armistice with the Allies.

Baffin, William (1584–1622) English explorer and navigator. In 1616 he and Robert Bylot explored Baffin Bay, northeastern Canada, and reached latitude 77° 45′ N, which for 236 years remained the 'furthest north'.

Baffin Island island in the Canadian territory of ▷Nunavut, Canada, situated across the entrance to ▷Hudson Bay; area 507,450 sq km/ 195,930 sq mi; population (2001 est) 14,400.

Features Baffin Island is the largest island in the Canadian Arctic; the mountains here rise above 2,000 m/6,000 ft, and there are several large lakes. The northernmost part of the strait separating Baffin Island from Greenland forms Baffin Bay; the southern end is Davis Strait. The predominantly Inuit population is settled mainly around Lake Harbour and Frobisher Bay in the south.

It is named after William Baffin, who carried out research here in 1616 during his search for the ▷Northwest Passage. Sir Martin ▷Frobisher, who landed here in 1576, discovered gold, and there are coal and iron-ore deposits.

BAFTA acronym for **British Academy of Film and Television Arts**, formed in 1959 as a result of the amalgamation of the British Film Academy (founded in 1948) and the Guild of Television Producers (founded in 1954).

bagatelle (French 'trifle') in music, a short character piece, often for piano.

Bagehot, Walter (1826–1877) British writer and economist. His *English Constitution* published in 1867, a classic analysis of the British political system, is still a standard work.

> **Beryl Bainbridge**
> *There are so many ways of dying it's astonishing any of us choose old age.*
> *Young Adolf* ch. 12

Baggara members of the nomadic Bedouin people of the Nile Basin, principally in Kordofan, Sudan, west of the White Nile. They are Muslims, traditionally occupied in cattle herding and big-game hunting. Their language is probably Hamito-Semitic (Afro-Asiatic).

Baghdad historic city and capital of Iraq, and capital of the governorate of Baghdad, on the River Tigris; population (1995 est) 5,385,000. Industries include oil refining, distilling, tanning, tobacco processing, and the manufacture of textiles and cement. Founded in 762, it became Iraq's capital in 1921. During the Gulf War in 1991 and the Iraq War in 2003, US- and UK-led coalition forces bombed it in repeated air raids.

Features Bridges connect the east and west banks of the River Tigris. To the southeast, on the river, are the ruins of **Ctesiphon**, capital of Parthia from about 250 BC–AD 226 and of the ▷Sassanian Empire from about 226–641. The Kadhimain Mosque (1515) is one of the most important in Iraq. The Iraqi Museum has collections of ancient artefacts. Baghdad's university was established in 1858.

History A transportation hub from the earliest times, it was developed by the 8th-century caliph Harun al-Rashid, although little of the *Arabian Nights* city remains. It was overrun in 1258 by the Mongols, who destroyed the irrigation system. In 1639 it was taken by the Turks. During World War I it was part of the Turkish Empire until it was captured in March 1917 by General Sir Frederick Maude (1864–1917).

BADLANDS Hoodoos, east of Drumheller in Alberta Province, Canada. Sandstone rock has eroded into curious columns in the badlands of southern Alberta. *Corel*

Bagnold, Enid (Algerine) (1889–1981) English novelist and dramatist. Her novel *National Velvet* (1935), about a girl who wins the Grand National on a horse won in a raffle, was made into a film in 1944 starring Elizabeth Taylor. Her most notable play was *The Chalk Garden* (1954).

Bago (or **Pegu**) city in southern Myanmar on the River Pegu, 76 km/47 mi northeast of Yangon; population (1998 est) 198,900. It was founded in 573 and was once an important seaport, and now lies on the Yangon–Mandalay railway. Bago has many rice and saw mills, as it is surrounded by an area of rice production and the forested slopes of the Pegu Yoma. It has long been a centre of Buddhist culture.

bagpipes any of an ancient family of double-reed folk woodwind instruments employing a bladder, filled by the player through a mouthpiece, or bellows as an air reservoir to a 'chanter' or fingered melody pipe, and two or three optional drone pipes providing a continuous accompanying harmony.

Related Web site: Bagpipes of the World http://www.rootsworld.com/rw/feature/gaida.html

Bahadur Shah II (1775–1862) Last of the Mogul emperors of India. He reigned, though in name only, as king of Delhi 1837–57, when he was hailed by the mutineers of the ▷Indian Mutiny as an independent emperor at Delhi. After the rebellion he was exiled to Burma (now Myanmar) with his family.

Baha'i Faith religion founded in the 19th century from a Muslim splinter group, ▷Babism, by the Persian ▷Baha'u'llah. His message in essence was that all great religious leaders are manifestations of the unknowable God and all scriptures are sacred. There is no priesthood: all Baha'is are expected to teach, and to work towards world unification. There are about 6 million Baha'is worldwide.

Related Web site: Bahá'í Faith Page http://www.bcca.org/bahaivision/

Bahamas see country box.

Baha'u'llah (1817–1892) Born Mirza Hosein Ali. Persian founder of the ▷Baha'i religion. Baha'u'llah, 'God's Glory', proclaimed himself as the prophet the Bab (see ▷Babism) had foretold.

Bahawalpur (or **Bhawalpur**) city in Punjab, Pakistan, situated on the Sutlej River 350 km/220 mi southwest of Lahore; population (1998 est) 403,400. Once the capital of the former Indian princely state of Bahawalpur, it is now an industrial city relying on cotton ginning, rice and flour milling, and the production of hand-woven textiles. A rich agricultural area surrounds the city, irrigated by canals. The Islamia University was established in 1975.

Bahrain see country box.

Baikal, Lake (Russian **Baykal Ozero**) freshwater lake in southern Siberia, Russia, the largest in Asia, and the eighth largest in the world (area 31,500 sq km/12,150 sq mi). Lake Baikal is also the world's deepest lake (up to 1,640 m/5,700 ft) and its oldest, having existed for over 25 million years. It extends for some 636 km/395 mi, and has an average width of 48 km/30 mi. Fed by more than 300 rivers, the main one of which is the Selenga, it is drained only by the Lower Angara. Lake Baikal is famous for its great clarity and the diversity of its fauna.

Related Web site: Natural World Heritage Properties – Lake Baikal http://www.wcmc.org.uk/protected_areas/data/wh/baikal.htm

bail the temporary setting at liberty of a person in legal custody on an undertaking (usually backed by some security, bonds or money, given either by that person or by someone else) to attend at a court at a stated time and place. If the person does not attend, the bail may be forfeited.

Baile Átha Cliath (Irish 'the town of the ford of the hurdles') official Irish name of ▷Dublin, capital of the Republic of Ireland, from 1922.

bailey an open space or court of a stone-built castle.

Bailey, Donovan (1967–) Jamaican-born Canadian athlete. At the 1996 Olympic Games held in Atlanta he won the men's 100 metres gold medal in a world record time of 9.84 seconds, going on to lead Canada to gold in the men's 4 × 100 metre relay. In June 1999 his 100 metres world record of 9.84 seconds was broken by Maurice Greene of the USA who ran 9.79 seconds at a meeting in Athens, Greece. Injuries hampered his attempt to defend his Olympic title in 2000. He retired in 2001.

bailiff officer of the court whose job, usually in the county courts, is to serve notices and enforce the court's orders involving seizure of the goods of a debtor.

Bainbridge, Beryl (1934–) English novelist. Her writing has dramatic economy and pace, it is acutely observed, peppered with ironic black humour, and often deals with the tragedy and comedy of human self-delusion. She achieved critical acclaim with *The Dressmaker* (1973), set in wartime England. *Birthday Boys* (1991), *Every Man for Himself* (1996), and *Master Georgie* (1998) are novels of historical realism centring respectively on R F Scott's expedition to the South Pole, the sinking of the Titanic, and the Crimean War. *Master Georgie* was shortlisted for the 1998 Booker Prize.

Baird, John Logie (1888–1946) Scottish electrical engineer who pioneered television. In 1925 he gave the first public demonstration of television, transmitting an image of a recognizable human face. The following year, he gave the world's first demonstration of true television before an audience of about 50 scientists at the Royal Institution, London. By 1928 Baird had succeeded in demonstrating colour television.

Baird used a mechanical scanner which temporarily changed an image into a sequence of electronic signals that could then be reconstructed on a screen as a pattern of half-tones. The neon discharge lamp Baird used offered a simple means for the electrical modulation of light at the receiver. His first pictures were formed of

JOHN LOGIE BAIRD A 1920s photograph of the Baird television machine, first demonstrated in England in 1925. *Archive Photos*

only 30 lines repeated approximately 10 times a second. The results were crude but it was the start of television as a practical technology.

By 1927, Baird had transmitted television over 700 km/435 mi of telephone line between London and Glasgow and soon after made the first television broadcast using radio, between London and the SS *Berengaria* , halfway across the Atlantic Ocean. He also made the first transatlantic television broadcast between Britain and the USA when signals transmitted from the Baird station in Coulson, Kent, were picked up by a receiver in Hartsdale, New York.

Baird's black-and-white system was used by the BBC in an experimental television service in 1929. In 1936, when the public television service was started, his system was threatened by one promoted by Marconi-EMI. The following year the Baird system was dropped in favour of the Marconi electronic system, which gave a better definition.

Bairiki port and capital of Kiribati on Tarawa atoll; population (1998 est) 2,565. Mother-of-pearl and copra are exported.

Baja California mountainous peninsula that forms the twin northwestern states of Lower (Spanish *baja*) California, Mexico; Baja California Norte in the north, and Baja California Sur in the south.

Bakelite first synthetic ▷plastic, created by Leo ▷Baekeland in 1909. Bakelite is hard, tough, and heatproof, and is used as an electrical insulator. It is made by the reaction of phenol with formaldehyde, producing a powdery resin that sets solid when heated. Objects are made by subjecting the resin to compression moulding (simultaneous heat and pressure in a mould).

Baker, Josephine (1906–1975) Born Freda Josephine McDonald. US-born dancer and entertainer. Baker achieved international fame for her daring stage act which involved lively dancing, scat singing, and scanty costume. After appearing in the Paris Folies Bergère in 1925, she became enormously successful in France, becoming a French citizen in 1937. Baker boycotted the USA for many years, refusing to accept the secondary status afforded to

African-American citizens. On her return to the USA in the 1950s, she campaigned for racial equality, forcing the integration of several theatres and night-clubs. She addressed the crowds before the Lincoln Memorial at the 1963 march on Washington.

Baker, Norma Jean US film actor; see Marilyn ▷Monroe.

Baker, Samuel White (1821–1893) English explorer, in 1864 the first European to sight Lake Albert Nyanza in central Africa, and discover that the River Nile flowed through it.

baking powder mixture of ▷bicarbonate of soda, an acidic compound, and a nonreactive filler (usually starch or calcium sulphate), used in baking as a raising agent. It gives a light open texture to cakes and scones, and is used as a substitute for yeast in making soda bread.

Bakst, Leon (1866–1924) Adopted name of Leon Rosenberg. Russian painter and theatrical designer. He combined intense colours and fantastic images adapted from Oriental and folk art with an art nouveau tendency toward graceful surface pattern. His designs for Diaghilev's touring Ballets Russes made a deep impression in Paris from 1909 to 1914.

Baku capital city of the republic of ▷Azerbaijan, located on the Apsheron Peninsula on the western shore of the Caspian Sea. Baku is an important industrial city and port. It has been a major centre of oil extraction and refining since the 1870s; the oilfields here are linked by pipelines with the Georgian Black Sea port of Batumi, while petroleum exports to Russia are shipped across the Caspian to Astrakhan. Heavy engineering enterprises in the city produce equipment for the oil industry and ships; light industries include leather tanning and food processing. Baku has a hot climate and is subject to strong northwest winds.

Bakunin, Mikhail (1814–1876) Russian anarchist, active in Europe. In 1848 he was expelled from France as a revolutionary agitator. In Switzerland in the 1860s he became recognized as the leader of the anarchist movement. In 1869 he joined the First International (a coordinating socialist body) but, after stormy conflicts with Karl Marx, was expelled in 1872.

Bahamas

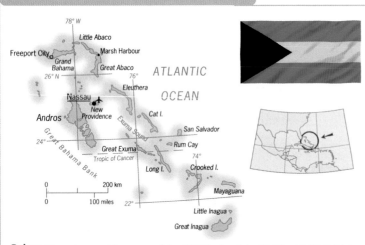

Bahamas country comprising a group of about 700 islands and about 2,400 uninhabited islets in the Caribbean, 80 km/50 mi from the southeast coast of Florida. They extend for about 1,223 km/760 mi from northwest to southeast, but only 22 of the islands are inhabited.

Government

NATIONAL NAME *Commonwealth of the Bahamas*
AREA 13,880 sq km/5,383 sq mi
CAPITAL Nassau (on New Providence island)
MAJOR TOWNS/CITIES Freeport (on Grand Bahama)
PHYSICAL FEATURES comprises 700 tropical coral islands and about 1,000 cays; the Exumas are a narrow spine of 365 islands; only 30 of the desert islands are inhabited; Blue Holes of Andros, the world's longest and deepest submarine caves
PRINCIPAL ISLANDS Andros, Grand Bahama, Abaco, Eleuthera, New Providence, Berry Islands, Bimini Islands, Great Inagua, Acklins Island, Exuma Islands, Mayguana, Crooked Island, Long Island, Cat Islands, Rum Cay, Watling (San Salvador) Island, Inagua Islands

Government

HEAD OF STATE Queen Elizabeth II from 1973, represented by Governor General Ivy Dumont from 2001

HEAD OF GOVERNMENT Perry Christie from 2002
POLITICAL SYSTEM liberal democracy
POLITICAL EXECUTIVE parliamentary
ADMINISTRATIVE DIVISIONS 21 districts
ARMED FORCES 900 (2002 est)
DEATH PENALTY retained and used for ordinary crimes

Economy and resources

CURRENCY Bahamian dollar
GPD (US$) 4.8 billion (2002 est)
REAL GDP GROWTH (% change on previous year) –0.5 (2001)
GNI (US$) 4.53 billion (2000)
GNI PER CAPITA (PPP) (US$) 16,500 (2001)
CONSUMER PRICE INFLATION 1.22% (2003 est)
UNEMPLOYMENT 7.8% (1999)
FOREIGN DEBT (US$) 613 million (2001 est)
MAJOR TRADING PARTNERS USA, Italy, UK, Japan, France, South Korea, Germany

RESOURCES aragonite (extracted from seabed), chalk, salt
INDUSTRIES pharmaceutical chemicals, salt, rum, beer, cement, shipping, financial services, tourism
EXPORTS fish and crawfish, oil products and transhipments, chemicals, rum, aragonite, fruit and vegetables. Principal market: USA 28.2% (2000)
IMPORTS machinery and transport equipment, basic manufactures, petroleum and products, chemicals. Principal source: USA 31.6% (2000)
ARABLE LAND 1% (2002 est)
AGRICULTURAL PRODUCTS sugar cane, cucumbers, tomatoes, pineapples, papayas, mangoes, avocados, limes and other citrus fruit; commercial fishing (conches and crustaceans)

Population and society

POPULATION 314,000 (2003 est)
POPULATION GROWTH RATE 1.3% (2000–05)
POPULATION DENSITY (per sq km) 23 (2003 est)

BAHAMAS The pier at Nassau, on the northeastern coast of New Providence Island. Nassau was founded as Charles Towne in 1656, destroyed by Spanish forces in 1694, then rebuilt and renamed Nassau after the family name of William (III) of Orange, King of Great Britain and Ireland. *Photodisk*

URBAN POPULATION (% of total) 89 (2003 est)
AGE DISTRIBUTION (% of total population) 0–14 29%, 15–59 63%, 60+ 8% (2002 est)
ETHNIC GROUPS about 85% of the population is of African origin, remainder mainly British, American, and Canadian
LANGUAGE English (official), Creole
RELIGION Christian 94% (Baptist 32%, Roman Catholic 19%, Anglican 20%, other Protestant 23%)
EDUCATION (compulsory years) 10
LITERACY RATE 95% (men); 96% (women) (2003 est)
LABOUR FORCE 3.7% agriculture, 15.4% industry, 80.9% services (1998)
LIFE EXPECTANCY 64 (men); 70 (women) (2000–05)
TV SETS (per 1,000 people) 243 (1999 est)
INTERNET USERS (per 10,000 people) 679.7 (2002 est)

See also ▷Arawak; ▷Carib.

Chronology

8th–9th centuries AD: Arawak Indians driven northwards to the islands by the Caribs.

1492: Visited by Christopher Columbus; Arawaks deported to provide cheap labour for the gold and silver mines of Cuba and Hispaniola (Haiti).

1629: King Charles I of England granted the islands to Robert Heath.

1666: The colonization of New Providence island began.

1783: Recovered after brief Spanish occupation and became a British colony, being settled during the American War of Independence by American loyalists, who brought with them black slaves.

1838: Slaves were emancipated.

from 1950s: Major development of the tourist trade.

1964: Became internally self-governing.

1967: First national assembly elections.

1973: Full independence was achieved within the British Commonwealth.

1992: A centre-left Free National Movement (FNM) led by Hubert Ingraham won an absolute majority in elections.

Balaclava, Battle of a Russian attack on 25 October 1854, during the Crimean War, on British positions, near a town in Ukraine, 10 km/6 mi southeast of Sevastopol. It was the scene of the ill-timed **Charge of the Light Brigade** of British cavalry against the Russian entrenched artillery. Of the 673 soldiers who took part, there were 272 casualties. **Balaclava helmets** were knitted hoods worn here by soldiers in the bitter weather.

Balakirev, Mily Alexeyevich (1837–1910) Russian composer. He wrote piano music including the fantasy *Islamey* (1869/1902), orchestral works, songs, and a symphonic poem *Tamara*, all imbued with the Russian national character and spirit. He was leader of the group known as 'The Five' and taught its members, Mussorgsky, Cui, Rimsky-Korsakov, and Borodin.

balalaika Russian musical instrument, resembling a guitar. It has a triangular soundbox, frets, and two, three, or four strings played by strumming with the fingers. A range of instruments is made, from treble to bass, and orchestras of balalaikas are popular in Russia.

balance apparatus for weighing or measuring mass. The various types include the **beam balance**, consisting of a centrally pivoted lever with pans hanging from each end, and the **spring balance**, in which the object to be weighed stretches (or compresses) a vertical coil spring fitted with a pointer that indicates the weight on a scale. Kitchen and bathroom scales are balances.

balance of nature in ecology, the idea that there is an inherent equilibrium in most ▷ecosystems, with plants and animals interacting so as to produce a stable, continuing system of life on Earth. The activities of human beings can, and frequently do, disrupt the balance of nature.

balance of payments in economics, an account of a country's debit and credit transactions with other countries. Items are divided into the **current account**, which includes both visible trade (imports and exports of goods) and invisible trade (services such as transport, tourism, interest, and dividends), and the **capital account**, which includes investment in and out of the country, international grants, and loans. Deficits or surpluses on these accounts are brought into balance by buying and selling reserves of foreign currencies.

A **balance of payments crisis** arises when a country's current account deteriorates because the cost of imports exceeds income from exports. In developing countries persistent trade deficits often result in heavy government borrowing overseas, which in turn leads to a ▷debt crisis.

balance of power in politics, the theory that the best way of ensuring international order is to have power so distributed among states that no single state is able to achieve a dominant position. The term, which may also refer more simply to the actual distribution of power, is one of the most enduring concepts in international relations. Since the development of nuclear weapons, it has been asserted that the balance of power has been replaced by a 'balance of terror'.

balance of trade the balance of trade transactions of a country recorded in its current account; it forms one component of the country's ▷balance of payments.

Balanchine, George (1904–1983) Born Georgi Melitonovich Balanchivadze. Russian-born US choreographer. After leaving the USSR in 1924, he worked with ▷Diaghilev in France. Moving to the USA in 1933, he became a major influence on dance, starting the New York City Ballet in 1948. He was the most influential 20th-century choreographer of ballet in the USA. He developed an 'American Neoclassic' dance style and made the New York City Ballet one of the world's great companies. His ballets are usually plotless and are performed in practice clothes to modern music. He also choreographed dances for five Hollywood films.

His many works include *Apollon Musagète* (1928) and *The Prodigal Son* (1929) for Diaghilev; *Serenade* (1934); several works with music by Stravinsky, such as *Agon* (1957) and *Duo Concertante* (1972); and Broadway musicals, such as *On Your Toes* (1936) and *The Boys from Syracuse* (1938).

Balboa, Vasco Núñez de (1475–1519) Spanish ▷conquistador. He founded a settlement at Darien (now Panama) in 1511 and crossed the Isthmus in search of gold, reaching the Pacific Ocean (which he called the South Sea) on 25 September 1513, after a 25-day expedition. He was made admiral of the Pacific and governor of Panama but was removed by Spanish court intrigue, imprisoned, and executed.

Balder (called 'the Good') in Norse mythology, the best, wisest, and most loved of all the gods; son of Odin and Frigga; husband of Nanna. He was one of the Aesir (principal gods), but was killed unwittingly with a twig of mistletoe shot by Hodur, his blind brother; the tragedy was engineered by the god-giant ▷Loki.

Bahrain

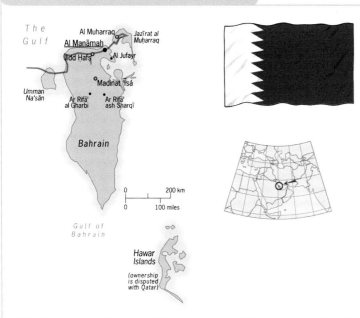

Bahrain country comprising a group of islands in the Persian Gulf, between Saudi Arabia and Iran.

NATIONAL NAME *Mamlakat al-Bahrayn/ Kingdom of Bahrain*
AREA 688 sq km/266 sq mi
CAPITAL Al Manamah (on Bahrain island)
MAJOR TOWNS/CITIES Al Muharraq, Jidd Hafs, Isa Town, Rifa'a, Sitra
MAJOR PORTS Mina Sulman
PHYSICAL FEATURES archipelago of 35 islands in Arabian Gulf, composed largely of sand-covered limestone; generally poor and infertile soil; flat and hot; causeway linking Bahrain to mainland Saudi Arabia

Government

HEAD OF STATE Sheikh Hamad bin Isa al-Khalifa from 1999
HEAD OF GOVERNMENT Sheikh Khalifa bin Salman al-Khalifa from 1970
POLITICAL SYSTEM monarchy
POLITICAL EXECUTIVE absolute
ADMINISTRATIVE DIVISIONS 12 municipalities
ARMED FORCES 10,700 (2002 est)
DEATH PENALTY retained and used for ordinary crimes

Economy and resources

CURRENCY Bahraini dinar
GPD (US$) 7.9 billion (2002 est)
REAL GDP GROWTH (% change on previous year) 4.8 (2001)
GNI (US$) 7.2 billion (2002 est)
GNI PER CAPITA (PPP) (US$) 15,900 (2002 est)
CONSUMER PRICE INFLATION –1.3% (2003 est)
UNEMPLOYMENT 15% (1999)
FOREIGN DEBT (US$) 2.5 billion (2001 est)
MAJOR TRADING PARTNERS India, Saudi Arabia, Japan, South Korea, Australia, USA, UK, France
RESOURCES petroleum and natural gas
INDUSTRIES petroleum refining, aluminium smelting, petrochemicals, shipbuilding and repairs, electronics assembly, banking
EXPORTS petroleum and petroleum products, aluminium, chemicals, textiles. Principal market: India 8.4% (2000)
IMPORTS crude petroleum, machinery and transport equipment, chemicals. Principal source: Saudi Arabia 28.7% (2000)
ARABLE LAND 1% (2000 est)

AGRICULTURAL PRODUCTS dates, tomatoes, melons, vegetables; poultry, fishing

Population and society

POPULATION 724,000 (2003 est)
POPULATION GROWTH RATE 1.7% (2000–05)
POPULATION DENSITY (per sq km) 1,068 (2003 est)
URBAN POPULATION (% of total) 93 (2003 est)
AGE DISTRIBUTION (% of total population) 0–14 27%, 15–59 68%, 60+ 5% (2002 est)
ETHNIC GROUPS 63% Bahraini, 13% Asian, 10% other Arab, 8% Iranian
LANGUAGE Arabic (official), Farsi, English, Urdu
RELIGION 85% Muslim (Shiite 60%, Sunni 40%), Christian; Islam is the state religion
EDUCATION (compulsory years) 12
LITERACY RATE 92% (men); 85% (women) (2003 est)
LABOUR FORCE 0.8% agriculture, 54.7% industry, 44.5% services (1994)

Chronology

4th century AD: Became part of Persian (Iranian) Sassanian Empire.

7th century: Adopted Islam.

8th century: Came under Arab Abbasid control.

1521: Seized by Portugal and held for eight decades, despite local unrest.

1602: Fell under the control of a Persian Shiite dynasty.

1783: Persian rule was overthrown and Bahrain became a sheikdom under the Sunni Muslim al-Khalifa dynasty, which originate from the same tribal federation, the Anaza, as the al-Saud family who now rule Saudi Arabia.

1816–20: Friendship and peace treaties were signed with Britain, which sought to end piracy in the Gulf.

1861: Became British protectorate; government shared between the ruling sheikh (Arab leader) and a British adviser.

1923: British influence increased when Sheikh Isa al-Khalifa was deposed and Charles Belgrave was appointed as the dominating 'adviser' to the new ruler.

1928: Sovereignty was claimed by Persia (Iran).

1930s: Oil was discovered, providing the backbone for the country's wealth.

1953–56: Council for National Unity was formed by Arab nationalists, but was suppressed after large demonstrations against British participation in the Suez War.

LIFE EXPECTANCY 72 (men); 76 (women) (2000–05)
TV SETS (per 1,000 people) 446 (1999 est)
INTERNET USERS (per 10,000 people) 2,474.7 (2002 est)
PERSONAL COMPUTER USERS (per 100 people) 16 (2002 est)

BAHRAIN Oil and its related industries are vital to Bahrain's wealth. *Stanley Gibbons*

1968: Britain announced its intention to withdraw its forces. Bahrain formed, with Qatar and the Trucial States of the United Arab Emirates, the Federation of Arab Emirates.

1970: Iran accepted a United Nations (UN) report showing that Bahrain's inhabitants preferred independence to Iranian control.

1971: Qatar and the Trucial States withdrew from the federation; Bahrain became an independent state under Sheikh Isa bin Sulman al-Khalifa as emir.

1973: A new constitution was adopted.

1975: The national assembly was dissolved and political activists driven underground. The emir and his family assumed virtually absolute power.

early 1980s: Tensions between the Sunni and Shiite Muslim communities were heightened by the Iranian Shiite Revolution of 1979.

1986: A causeway opened linking the island with Saudi Arabia.

1991: Bahrain joined a UN coalition that ousted Iraq from its occupation of Kuwait, and signed a defence cooperation agreement with the USA.

1995: Prodemocracy demonstrations were violently suppressed, with 11 deaths.

1999: Sheikh Hamad became Emir and head of state.

2001: Bahrain and Qatar accepted the ruling of the International Court of Justice on a long-standing territorial dispute. Women were given the vote for the first time.

2002: Sheikh Hamad bin Isaal Khalifa proclaimed himself king.

baldness loss of hair from the scalp, common in older men. Its onset and extent are influenced by genetic make-up and the level of male sex ▷hormones. There is no cure, and expedients such as hair implants may have no lasting effect. Hair loss in both sexes may also occur as a result of ill health or radiation treatment, such as for cancer. Alopecia, a condition in which the hair falls out in patches, is different from the 'male-pattern baldness' described above.

Baldwin, James Arthur (1924–1987) US writer and civil-rights activist. He portrayed with vivid intensity the suffering and despair of African-Americans in contemporary society. After his first novel, *Go Tell It on the Mountain* (1953), set in Harlem, and *Giovanni's Room* (1956), about a homosexual relationship in Paris, his writing became more politically indignant with *Another Country* (1962) and *The Fire Next Time* (1963), a collection of essays.

Other works include his play *The Amen Corner* (1955), the autobiographical essays 'Notes of a Native Son' (1955), and the novel *Just Above My Head* (1979).

Baldwin, Stanley (1867–1947) 1st Earl Baldwin of Bewdley. British Conservative politician, prime minister 1923–24, 1924–29, and 1935–37. He weathered the general strike of 1926, secured complete adult suffrage in 1928, and handled the ▷abdication crisis of Edward VIII in 1936, but failed to prepare Britain for World War II.

Baldwin was born in Bewdley, Worcestershire, the son of an iron and steel magnate. In 1908 he became Unionist member of Parliament for Bewdley, and in 1916 he was made parliamentary private secretary to Andrew Bonar ▷Law. Baldwin was financial secretary to the Treasury 1917–21, and then appointed to the presidency of the Board of Trade. In 1919 he anonymously gave the Treasury £50,000 of War Loan for cancellation, representing about 20% of his fortune. He was a leader in the disruption of the David ▷Lloyd George coalition in 1922, and, as chancellor under Bonar Law, achieved a settlement of war debts with the USA.

As prime minister 1923–24 and again 1924–29, Baldwin passed the Trades Disputes Act of 1927 after the general strike, granted widows' and orphans' pensions, and equal voting rights for women in 1928. He joined the national government of Ramsay ▷MacDonald in 1931 as Lord President of the Council. He handled the abdication crisis during his third premiership 1935–37, after the resignation of MacDonald, but was later much criticized for his failures both to resist popular desire for an accommodation with the dictators Hitler and Mussolini and to rearm more effectively.

James Baldwin

It comes as a great shock to see Gary Cooper killing off the Indians and, although you are rooting for Gary Cooper, that the Indians are you.

Speech at Cambridge University 17 February 1965

Stanley Baldwin

The gift of rhetoric has been responsible for more bloodshed on this earth than all the guns and explosives that were ever invented.

The Observer 16 March 1924

Bâle French form of Basle or ▷Basel, a city in Switzerland.

Balearic Islands (Spanish Baleares) group of Mediterranean islands forming an autonomous region of Spain, comprising ▷Mallorca, ▷Menorca, ▷Ibiza, Cabrera, and ▷Formentera; area 5,014 sq km/1,936 sq mi; population (1991) 709,100. The capital is ▷Palma de Mallorca. Tourism is a mainstay of the economy; other industries include figs, olives, oranges, wine, brandy, coal, iron, and slate.

Balenciaga, Cristóbal (1895–1972) Spanish couturier. His influential innovations in women's clothing included drop shoulder lines, nipped-in waists, and rounded hips, followed by three-quarter length sleeves and the pillbox hat. During the 1950s–1960s he moved away from fitted outfits to show loose designs such as a dress known as the 'sack' (cut full around the body and gathered or tapered into a narrow hem-band just below the knees) in 1956 and loose full jackets in the 1960s. He retired in 1968.

Balfour, Arthur James (1848–1930) 1st Earl of Balfour. British Conservative politician, born in Scotland, prime minister 1902–05, and foreign secretary 1916–19. He issued the Balfour Declaration in 1917 and was involved in peace negotiations after World War I, signing the Treaty of Versailles.

The son of a Scottish landowner, Balfour was educated at Eton and Cambridge and was elected a Conservative member of Parliament in 1874. In Lord Salisbury's ministry he was made chief secretary for Ireland in 1887, and for his ruthless vigour was called 'Bloody Balfour' by Irish nationalists. In 1891 and again in 1895 he became First Lord of the Treasury and leader of the Commons, and in 1902 he succeeded Salisbury as prime minister. His cabinet was divided over Joseph Chamberlain's tariff-reform proposals, and in the 1906 elections suffered a crushing defeat.

BALI A ruined gateway to a traditional village temple in Bali. The temple walls usually enclose a number of gilded shrines, flowering trees, pavilions, and courtyards. There is a bell to summon villagers to meetings or feasts. *Corel*

Balfour retired from the party leadership in 1911. In 1915 he joined the Asquith coalition as First Lord of the Admiralty. As foreign secretary 1916–19 he issued the ▷Balfour Declaration in favour of a national home in Palestine for the Jews.

Balfour Declaration letter, dated 2 November 1917, from British foreign secretary A J Balfour to Lord Rothschild (chair, British Zionist Federation) stating: 'HM government view with favour the establishment in Palestine of a national home for the Jewish people.' It helped form the basis for the foundation of ▷Israel in 1948.

Bali island of Indonesia, east of Java, one of the Sunda Islands; area 5,800 sq km/2,240 sq mi; population (1995 est) 3,037,000. The capital is Denpasar. The island features volcanic mountains, the highest peak is Gunung Agaung (3,142 m/10,308 ft). Industries include gold and silver work, woodcarving, weaving, copra, salt, coffee, and tourism; arts include Balinese dancing, music (the Gamelan), and drama. Bali's Hindu culture goes back to the 7th century; the Dutch gained control of the island by 1908. In October 2002 a car bomb exploded at a nightclub in the tourist centre of Kuta, killing about 200 people, mostly Australians. The Indonesian authorities blamed Islamic extremists belonging to Jemaah Islamiah, thought to be linked to the al-Qaeda terrorist network.

Baliol (or Balliol), **John de** (*c.* 1249–1315) King of Scotland 1292–96. As an heir to the Scottish throne on the death of ▷Margaret, the Maid of Norway, he had the support of the English king, Edward I, against 12 other claimants. Baliol was proclaimed king, having paid homage to Edward. When English forces attacked Scotland, Baliol rebelled against England and gave up the kingdom.

Balkans (Turkish 'mountains') peninsula of southeastern Europe, stretching into Slovenia between the Adriatic and Aegean seas, comprising Albania, Bosnia-Herzegovina, Bulgaria, Croatia, Greece, Romania, the part of Turkey in Europe, Slovenia, Serbia and Montenegro, Kosovo, and Macedonia. It is joined to the rest of Europe by an isthmus 1,200 km/750 mi wide between Rijeka on the west and the mouth of the Danube on the Black Sea to the east.

John Ball

From the beginning all were created equal by nature, slavery was introduced through the unjust oppression of worthless men, against the will of God; for, if God had wanted to create slaves, he would surely have decided at the beginning of the world who was to be slave and who master.

Sermon at Blackheath, 1381

Balkan Wars two wars 1912–13 and 1913 (preceding World War I) which resulted in the expulsion by the Balkan states of Ottoman Turkey from Europe, except for a small area around Istanbul.

The **First Balkan War**, 1912, of Bulgaria, Serbia, Greece, and Montenegro against Turkey, forced the Turks to ask for an armistice, but the London-held peace negotiations broke down when the Turks, while agreeing to surrender all Turkey-in-Europe west of the city of Edirne (formerly Adrianople), refused to give up the city itself. In February 1913 hostilities were resumed. Edirne fell on 26 March, and on 30 May, by the Treaty of London, Turkey retained in Europe only a small piece of eastern Thrace and the Gallipoli peninsula.

The **Second Balkan War**, June–July 1913, took place when the victors fought over acquisitions in Macedonia, from most of which Bulgaria was excluded. Bulgaria attacked Greece and Serbia, which were joined by Romania. Bulgaria was defeated, and Turkey retained Thrace.

Balkhash, Lake lake in eastern ▷Kazakhstan, the eastern half of which is salty, and the western half fresh; area 17,400 sq km/6,715 sq mi. Lake Balkhash is 600 km/375 mi long and is fed by several rivers, including the Karatal, Lepsy and Ili, but has no outlet. It is very shallow, especially in the east, and is frozen throughout the winter (November–mid-April).

Ball, John (died *c.* 1381) English priest. He was one of the leaders of the ▷Peasants' Revolt of 1381, known as 'the mad priest of Kent'. A follower of John Wycliffe and a believer in social equality, he was imprisoned for disagreeing with the archbishop of Canterbury. During the revolt he was released from prison, and when in Blackheath, London, incited people against the ruling classes by preaching from the text 'When Adam delved and Eve span, who was then the gentleman?' When the revolt collapsed he escaped but was captured near Coventry and executed.

Ball, Lucille (Desirée) (1911–1989) US comedy actor. From 1951 to 1957 she starred with her husband, the Cuban bandleader Desi Arnaz (1917–1986), in the television sitcom *I Love Lucy*, the first US television show filmed before an audience. It was followed by *The Lucy Show* (1962–68) and *Here's Lucy* (1968–74).

ballad (Latin *ballare* 'to dance') form of traditional narrative poetry, widespread in Europe and the USA. Ballads are metrically simple, sometimes (as in Russia) unstrophic and unrhymed or (as in Denmark) dependent on assonance. Concerned with some strongly emotional event, the ballad is halfway between the lyric and the epic. Most English ballads date from the 15th century but may describe earlier events. Poets of the Romantic movement both in England and in Germany were greatly influenced by the ballad revival, as seen in, for example, the *Lyrical Ballads* (1798) of ▷Wordsworth and ▷Coleridge. *Des Knaben Wunderhorn/The Boy's Magic Horn* (1805–08), a collection edited by Clemens Brentano and Achim von ▷Arnim, was a major influence on 19th-century German poetry. The ballad form was adapted in 'broadsheets', with a satirical or political motive, and in the 'hanging' ballads purporting to come from condemned criminals.

ballade in literature, a poetic form developed in France in the later Middle Ages from the ballad, generally consisting of one or more groups of three stanzas of seven or eight lines each, followed by a shorter stanza or envoy, the last line being repeated as a chorus. In music, a ballade is an instrumental piece based on a story; a form used in piano works by Chopin and Liszt.

Balladur, Edouard (1929–) French Conservative politician, prime minister 1993–95. During his first year of 'co-habitation' with socialist president François Mitterrand he demonstrated the sureness of his political touch, retaining popular support despite active opposition to some of his more right-wing policies. He unsuccessfully contested the presidency in 1995. He is a supporter of the European Union and of the maintainance of close relations between France and Germany.

ball-and-socket joint joint between bones that allows considerable movement in three dimensions, for instance the joint between the pelvis and the femur. To facilitate movement, such joints are rimmed with cartilage and lubricated by synovial fluid. The bones are kept in place by ligaments and moved by muscles.

Ballarat city in Victoria, Australia, 112 km/70 mi northwest of Melbourne; population (1996) 64,831. It is Victoria's largest inland city, the third-largest city of the state, and is an important railway junction. Industries include the manufacture of agricultural machinery, fibreglass, and paper; champagne, cheese, and lavender are

BALLET Classical ballet, with its origins in 16th-century French court ballet, emerged as an art form in its own right during the 18th century. *Image Bank*

produced in the area and tourism is important. Ballarat was founded in the 1851 gold rush, after the discovery of the largest gold reserves in Australia.

Ballard, J(ames) G(raham) (1930–) English novelist.
He became prominent in the 1960s for his science fiction works on the theme of catastrophe and collapse of the urban landscape. His first novel was *The Drowned World* (1962), and later works include *Crash!* (1973), *High-Rise* (1975), the partly autobiographical *Empire of the Sun* (1984), dealing with his internment in China during World War II, and the autobiographical novel *The Kindness of Women* (1991). His fundamentally moral vision is expressed with an untrammelled imagination and pessimistic irony.

Ballesteros, Seve(riano) (1957–) Spanish golfer. He came
to prominence in 1976 and has won
several leading tournaments in the USA, including the Masters Tournament in 1980 and 1983. He has also won the British Open three times: in 1979, 1984, and 1988.

Related Web site: Ballesteros, Severiano http://golfeurope.com/almanac/players/ballesteros.htm

ballet (Italian *balletto* 'a little dance') theatrical representation in ▷dance form in which music also plays a major part in telling a story or conveying a mood. Some such form of entertainment existed in ancient Greece, but Western ballet as we know it today first appeared in Renaissance Italy, where it was a court entertainment. From there it was brought by Catherine de' Medici to France in the form of a spectacle combining singing, dancing, and declamation. During the 18th century there were major developments in technique and ballet gradually became divorced from opera, emerging as an art form in its own right.

In the 20th century Russian ballet had a vital influence on the classical tradition in the West, and ballet developed further in the USA through the work of George Balanchine and the American Ballet Theater, and in the UK through the influence of Marie Rambert.

▷Modern dance is a separate development.

History The first important dramatic ballet, the *Ballet comique de la reine*, was produced in 1581 by the Italian Balthasar de Beaujoyeux at the French court and was performed by male courtiers, with ladies of the court forming the *corps de ballet*. In 1661 Louis XIV founded the Académie Royale de Danse, to which all subsequent ballet activities throughout the world can be traced. Long, flowing court dress was worn by the dancers until the 1720s when Marie-Anne Camargo, the first great ballerina, shortened her skirt to reveal her ankles, thus allowing greater movement *à terre* and the development of dancing *en l'air*.

During the 18th century ballet spread to virtually every major capital in Europe. Vienna became an important centre and was instrumental in developing the dramatic aspect of the art as opposed to the athletic qualities, which also evolved considerably

during this century, particularly among male dancers. In the early 19th century a Paris costumier, Maillot, invented tights, which allowed complete muscular freedom. The first of the great ballet masters was Jean-Georges ▷Noverre, and great contemporary dancers were Teresa Vestris, Anna Friedrike Heinel, Jean Dauberval, and Maximilien Gardel.

Carlo Blasis is regarded as the founder of classical ballet, since he defined the standard conventional steps and accompanying gestures.
Romantic ballet The great Romantic era of the dancers Marie Taglioni, Fanny Elssler, Carlotta Grisi, Lucile Grahn, and Fanny Cerrito began about 1830 but survives today only in the ballets *Giselle* (1841) and *Les Sylphides* (1832). Characteristics of this era were the new calf-length white dress and the introduction of dancing on the toes, *sur les pointes*. The technique of the female dancer was developed, but the role of the male dancer was reduced to that of being her partner. Important choreographers of the period were Jules Joseph Perrot, Arthur Saint-Léon, and August Bournonville. From 1860 ballet declined rapidly in popular favour in Europe, but its importance was maintained in St Petersburg under Marius Petipa.
Russian ballet Russian ballet was introduced to the West by Sergei ▷Diaghilev, who set out for Paris in 1909 and founded the Ballets Russes (Russian Ballet), at about the same time that Isadora ▷Duncan, a fervent opponent of classical ballet, was touring Europe. Associated with Diaghilev were Mikhail Fokine, Enrico Cecchetti, Vaslav ▷Nijinsky, Anna Pavlova, Tamara Karsavina, Léonide Massine, Bronislava Nijinska, George Balanchine, and Serge Lifar. Ballets presented by his company, before its break-up after his death in 1929, included *Les Sylphides*, *Schéhérazade*, *Petrouchka*, *Le Sacre du printemps/The Rite of Spring*, and *Les Noces*.

Diaghilev and Fokine pioneered a new and exciting combination of the perfect technique of imperial Russian dancers and the appealing naturalism favoured by Isadora Duncan. In Russia ballet continues to flourish, the two chief companies being the Kirov and the Bolshoi. Best-known ballerinas have been Galina Ulanova and Maya ▷Plisetskaya, and male dancers have included Mikhail ▷Baryshnikov, Irek Mukhamedov, and Alexander Godunov, now dancing in the West.
American ballet American ballet was firmly established by the founding of Balanchine's School of American Ballet in 1934, and by de Basil and René Blum's Ballets Russes de Monte Carlo and Massine's Ballets Russes de Monte Carlo, which also carried on the Diaghilev tradition. In 1939 the dancer Lucia Chase and ballet director Richard Pleasant founded the American Ballet Theater. From 1948 the New York City Ballet, under the guiding influence of Balanchine, developed a genuine American neoclassic style.
British ballet Marie Rambert initiated in 1926 the company that developed into the Ballet Rambert, and launched the careers of choreographers such as Frederick Ashton and Anthony Tudor. The national company, the ▷Royal Ballet

(so named in 1956), grew from foundations laid by Ninette de Valois and Frederick Ashton in 1928. British dancers include Alicia Markova, Anton Dolin, Margot ▷Fonteyn, Antoinette Sibley, Lynn Seymour, Beryl Grey, Anthony Dowell, David Wall, Merle Park, and Lesley Collier; choreographers include Kenneth MacMillan. Fonteyn's partners included Robert Helpmann and Rudolf ▷Nureyev.
Ballet music During the 16th and 17th centuries there was not always a clear distinction between opera and ballet, since ballet during this period often included singing, and operas often included dance. The influence of the court composer Jean-Baptiste Lully on the development of ballet under Louis XIV in France was significant (Lully was a dancer himself, as was the king). During this period many courtly dances originated, including the gavotte, passepied, bourrée, and ▷minuet. In the 19th century, as public interest in ballet increased, Russia produced composers of international reputation such as Pyotr Il'yich Tchaikovsky, whose ballet scores include *Swan Lake* (1876), *Sleeping Beauty* (1890), and *The Nutcracker* (1892).

With the modern era of ballet which began in 1909 with the founding of the Ballets Russes, innovative choreography transformed the visual aspects of ballet and striking new compositions by Achille Claude Debussy, Maurice Ravel, and especially Igor Stravinsky (in, for example, *The Rite of Spring*, 1913) left their mark not only on the ballet composers who followed, but on the course of music history itself. Later in the century, the formal tradition of ballet was upset by the influence of jazz, jazz rhythms, and modern dance originating in the USA, which introduced greater freedom of bodily expression.

Today there exists a wide range of musical and choreographic styles, ranging from the classical to the popular. Many full ballet scores have been reduced by composers to ballet ▷suites or purely orchestral works, which incorporate the essential musical elements, tending to omit musically nonthematic and transitional passages which may be, nevertheless, essential to the choreography and visual narration. Examples include Stravinsky's *The Firebird* (1910) and Ravel's *Boléro* (1928).

Related Web site: BalletWeb http://www.novia.net/~jlw/index.html

ballistics study of the motion and impact of projectiles such as bullets, bombs, and missiles. For projectiles from a gun, relevant exterior factors include temperature, barometric pressure, and wind strength; and for nuclear missiles these extend to such factors as the speed at which the Earth turns.

balloon lighter-than-air craft that consists of a gasbag filled with gas lighter than the surrounding air and an attached basket, or gondola, for carrying passengers and/or instruments. In 1783, the first successful human ascent was in Paris, in a hot-air balloon designed by the ▷Montgolfier brothers Joseph Michel and Jacques Etienne. In 1785, a hydrogen-filled balloon designed by French physicist Jacques Charles travelled across the English Channel.

> **Bob Walingunda**
> Balloonist
>
> *Flying in a balloon is so totally irrelevant and beautiful. You don't know where you're going until you get there.*
>
> 1973

BALLOON The first non-stop trip around the world in a balloon was completed on 20 March 1999 by Bertrand Piccard and Brian Jones. They started their journey in Switzerland and landed in Egypt 46,000 km/29,000 mi later. *Image Bank*

ballot (Italian *ballotta*, diminutive of *balla*, 'a ball') the process of voting in an election. In political elections in democracies ballots are usually secret: voters indicate their choice of candidate on a voting slip that is placed in a sealed ballot box. **Ballot rigging** is a term used to describe elections that are fraudulent because of interference with the voting process or the counting of ▷votes.

ballroom dancing collective term for social dances such as the ▷foxtrot, quickstep, ▷tango, and ▷waltz.

ball valve valve that works by the action of external pressure raising a ball and thereby opening a hole.

Balmaceda, José Manuel (1840–1891) Chilean president 1886–91. He inaugurated a vast reform programme including education, railways, communications, and public utilities, and invested revenue from Chile's nitrate fields in public works. The volatility of this key market led him to denounce foreign interests in Chile.

balm, lemon garden herb, see ▷lemon balm.

Balmoral Castle residence of the British royal family in Scotland on the River Dee, 10 km/6 mi northeast of Braemar, Aberdeenshire. It was purchased for Queen Victoria by her husband, Prince Albert, in 1852. King Robert II of Scotland (1316–1390) held a hunting seat in the grounds, and by 1390 a stone castle was built. Prince Albert bought the estate from the owners, the Farquarson family of Inverey, who acquired it in 1662. The present castle was built from 1853 to 1856, planned by William Smith, the City Architect of Aberdeen, under the supervision of Prince Albert. The stone was taken from the quarries of Glen Gelder, which produced the light-coloured granite. Upon the death of Queen Victoria, the estate passed to her descendants, and subsequent generations have made changes, the Duke of Edinburgh, for example, enlarging the flower garden and creating a water garden.

balsam any of various garden plants belonging to the balsam family. They are usually annuals with spurred red or white flowers and pods that burst and scatter their seeds when ripe. (Genus *Impatiens*, family Balsaminaceae.)

In medicine and perfumery, balsam refers to various oily or gummy aromatic plant ▷resins, such as balsam of Peru from the Central American tree *Myroxylon pereirae*.

Balthus (1908–) Pseudonym of Balthazar Klossowksi de Rola. Polish-born French painter. He is famed for his enigmatic paintings of interiors featuring languid, pubescent girls, both clothed and nude, for example *Nude with Cat* (*c.* 1954; National Gallery of Victoria, Melbourne). The studied, intense realism with which his self-absorbed figures are depicted lends his pictures a dreamlike quality.

Baltic, Battle of the naval battle fought off Copenhagen on 2 April 1801, in which a British fleet under Sir Hyde Parker, with ▷Nelson as second-in-command, annihilated the Danish navy.

Baltic Sea shallow sea, extending northeast from the narrow Skagerrak and Kattegat, between Sweden and Denmark, to the Gulf of Bothnia between Sweden and Finland. Its coastline is 8,000 km/5,000 mi long; the sea is 1,500 km/930 mi long and 650 km/404 mi wide, and its area, including the gulfs of Riga, Finland, and Bothnia, is 422,300 sq km/163,000 sq mi. Its average depth is 65 m/213 ft, but it is 460 m/1,500 ft at its deepest.

Its shoreline is shared by Denmark, Germany, Poland, the Baltic States, Russia, Finland, and Sweden.

Baltic States collective name for the states of ▷Estonia, ▷Latvia, and ▷Lithuania. They were formed as independent states after World War I out of former territories of the Russian Empire. The government of the USSR recognized their independence in peace treaties signed in 1920, but in 1939 forced them to allow occupation of important military bases by Soviet troops. In the following year, the Baltic states were absorbed into the Soviet Union as constituent republics. They regained their independence in September 1991 after the collapse of the Soviet Union.

Related Web site: Baltic Assembly, Baltic Council of Ministers, and Nordic Council http://www.lrs.lt/baltasm/indexa.htm

Baltimore industrial port and largest city in Maryland, USA, on the western shore of Chesapeake Bay, 50 km/31 mi northeast of Washington, DC; population (1994 est) 703,000; metropolitan area (1992 est) 2,434,000. Industries include shipbuilding, oil refining, food processing, and the manufacture of steel, chemicals, and aerospace equipment. The city was named after the founder of Maryland, Lord Baltimore (1579–1632). Baltimore dates from 1729 and was incorporated as a city in 1797.

Baltistan region in the ▷Karakoram range of northeast Kashmir, western ▷Ladakh, held by Pakistan since 1949. The region lies to the south of K2, the world's second highest mountain (8,611 m/28,2161 ft); the average elevation is 3,350 m/11,000 ft. It contains the upper reaches of the Indus River. It is the home of Balti Muslims of Tibetan origin.

Baluchistan mountainous desert area, comprising a province of Pakistan, part of the Iranian province of Sistán and Balúchestan, and a small area of Afghanistan. The Pakistani province has an area of 347,200 sq km/134,050 sq mi and a population (2002 est) of 7,215,700; its capital is Quetta. Sistán and Balúchestan has an area of 181,600 sq km/70,098 sq mi and a population (2002 est) of 2,093,600; its capital is Zahedan. The Quetta region has become important for fruit-growing. Coal, natural gas, chrome and other minerals have been discovered and exploited. The 1,600 km/1,000 mi rail network has strategic as well as economic significance. Much of Baluchistan consists of dry and rocky plateau areas with a rainfall of less than 13 cm/5 in a year and therefore little plant life.

Balzac, Honoré de (1799–1850) French writer. He was one of the major novelists of the 19th century. His first success was *Les Chouans/The Chouans*, inspired by Walter Scott. This was the beginning of the long series of novels *La Comédie humaine/The Human Comedy* which includes *Eugénie Grandet* (1833), *Le Père Goriot* (1834), and *Cousine Bette* (1846). He also wrote the Rabelaisian *Contes drolatiques/Ribald Tales* (1833).

Born in Tours, Balzac studied law and worked as a notary's clerk in Paris before turning to literature. His first attempts included tragedies such as *Cromwell* and novels published under a pseudonym with no great success. A venture in printing and publishing 1825–28 involved him in a lifelong web of debt. His patroness, Madame de Berny, figures in *Le Lys dans la vallée/The Lily in the Valley* (1836). Balzac intended his major work *La Comédie humaine* to comprise 143 volumes, depicting every aspect of society in 19th-century France, of which he completed 80. Titles and characters include *Cousin Pons* (1847); and the doctor of *Le Médicin de la campagne/The Country Doctor* (1833), the great businessman of *La Maison de Nucingen/The House of Nucingen* (1838), and the cleric of *Le Curé de village/The Village Parson* (1839). Balzac corresponded constantly with the Polish countess Evelina Hanska after meeting her 1833, and they married four months before his death in Paris. He was buried in Père Lachaise cemetery, Paris.

Bamako capital and port of ▷Mali on the upper Niger river; population (2001 est) 947,100. It produces pharmaceuticals, chemicals, textiles, food products, beer, tobacco, and metal products. The Grand Mosque, Malian Museum, and BCEAO Tower are situated here.

bamboo any of a large group of giant grass plants, found mainly in tropical and subtropical regions. Some species grow as tall as 36 m/120 ft. The stems are hollow and jointed and can be used in furniture, house, and boat construction. The young shoots are edible; paper is made from the stems. (Genus *Bambusa*, family Gramineae.)

banana any of several treelike tropical plants which grow up to 8 m/25 ft high. The edible banana is the fruit of a sterile hybrid form. (Genus *Musa*, family Musaceae.)

Banbury market town in Oxfordshire, central England, on the River Cherwell, 40 km/25 mi north of Oxford, and administrative centre for Cherwell District Council; population (1991) 39,900. Industries include food processing (Kraft Jacobs Suchard), traditional brewing (Hook Norton, Merivales), printing, and the manufacture of car components, electrical goods, and aluminium. The **Banbury Cross** of the nursery rhyme 'Ride a Cock Horse to Banbury Cross' was destroyed by the Puritans in 1602, but replaced in 1859.

BANANA A truck laden with bananas near Havana, Cuba. The demand for bananas in Western countries is huge, creating a great revenue-earner for countries that produce them. *Image Bank*

Banca alternative form of the Indonesian island ▷Bangka.

Bancroft, George (1800–1891) US diplomat and historian. A Democrat, he was secretary of the navy in 1845 when he established the US Naval Academy at Annapolis, Maryland, and as acting secretary of war (May 1846) was instrumental in bringing about the occupation of California and the ▷Mexican War. He wrote a *History of the United States* (1834–76).

Banda, Hastings Kamuzu (1905–1997) Malawi politician, physician, and president (1966–94). He led his country's independence movement and was prime minister of Nyasaland (the former name of Malawi) from 1964. He became Malawi's first president in 1966 and was named president for life in 1971; his rule was authoritarian. Having bowed to opposition pressure and opened the way for a pluralist system, Banda stood in the first free presidential elections for 30 years in 1994, but was defeated by Bakili Muluzi. In January 1996 he and his former aide, John Tembo, were acquitted of the murders of three senior politicians and a lawyer in 1983.

At an early age Banda left Nyasaland for neighbouring Rhodesia, and then South Africa, where he worked in the gold mines. By 1925 he had saved enough money to buy a ticket to the USA to take up a scholarship at the Wilberforce Institute, Ohio. From there he went to Chicago University and then a medical college in Nashville, Tennessee, where he qualified as a doctor in 1937. To fulfil his ambition to practise in the UK he needed more qualifications, which he acquired in Edinburgh. He then went into general practice in the north of England and London until 1953; he subsequently established a practice on the Gold Coast (now Ghana).

In 1958 he returned to his native country and in the following year founded the Malawi Congress Party (MCP), to lead the fight for independence. The MCP was to become his personal political machine. He was arrested in Rhodesia for subversion and imprisoned for nearly a year before being deported to Nyasaland.

In October 1993 he underwent brain surgery, temporarily handing power to a presidential council. He announced his retirement from active politics in August 1994.

Related Web site: Banda, Hastings http://www.africanews.org/south/malawi/stories/19971201_feat2.html

Bandaranaike, Sirimavo (1916–2000) Born Sirimavo Ratwatte Dias Bandaranaike. Sri Lankan politician, prime minister 1994–2000. She succeeded her husband Solomon ▷Bandaranaike to become the world's first female prime minister, 1960–65 and 1970–77, but was expelled from parliament in 1980 for abuse of her powers while in office. Her daughter Chandrika Bandaranaike ▷Kumaratunga was elected president in 1994. She resigned her position on 10 August 2000 because of poor health, and was replaced by Ratnasiri Wickremanayake.

Bandaranaike, Solomon West Ridgeway Dias (1899–1959) Sri Lankan nationalist politician. In 1952 he founded the Sri Lanka Freedom Party and in 1956 became prime minister, pledged to a socialist programme and a neutral foreign policy. He failed to satisfy extremists and was assassinated by a Buddhist monk.

Bandar Seri Begawan (formerly **Brunei Town** (until 1970)) capital and largest town of Brunei, 14 km/9 mi from the mouth of the Brunei River; population (1992) 55,000. Industries include oil refining and construction.

bandicoot small marsupial mammal inhabiting Australia and New Guinea. There are about 11 species, family Peramelidae. Bandicoots are rat- or rabbit-sized and live in burrows. They have long snouts, eat insects, and are nocturnal. A related group, the rabbit bandicoots or bilbies, is reduced to a single species that is now endangered and protected by law.

banding in UK education, the division of school pupils into broad streams by ability. Banding is used by some local authorities to ensure that comprehensive schools receive an intake of children spread right across the ability range. It is used internally by some schools as a means of avoiding groups of widely mixed ability.

Bandung commercial city and capital of Jawa Barat (West Java) province on the island of Java, Indonesia; population (1997 est) 2,429,000. Bandung is the third-largest city in Indonesia and was the administrative centre when the country was the Netherlands East Indies. It lies 180 km/112 mi southeast of Jakarta, the capital, and has an airport, two universities (established in 1955 and 1957), and a centre for nuclear research (established in 1964). Industries include textiles, chemicals, and plastics.

Bandung Conference first conference, in 1955, of the Afro-Asian nations, proclaiming anticolonialism and neutrality between East and West. It was organized by Indonesia, Myanmar, Sri Lanka, India, and Pakistan.

bandy-bandy venomous Australian snake *Vermicella annulata* of the cobra family, which grows to about 75 cm/2.5 ft. It is banded in black and white. It is not aggressive toward humans.

Bangalore capital of ▷Karnataka state, southern India, lying 950 m/3,000 ft above sea level; population (1991) 4,087,000. Industries include electronics, aircraft and machine-tools construction, and coffee. Bangalore University and the University of Agriculture Sciences were founded in 1964, and the National Aeronautical Institute in 1960.

Bangka (or **Banka** or **Banca**) Indonesian island off the east coast of Sumatra; area 12,000 sq km/4,600 sq mi. The capital is Pangkalpinang. It is one of the world's largest producers of tin.

Bangkok (Thai *Krung Thep* 'City of Angels') capital and port of Thailand, on the River Chao Phraya; population (2000 est) 6,320,200. Products include paper, ceramics, cement, textiles, aircraft, and silk. It is the headquarters of the Southeast Asia Treaty Organization (SEATO).
    Related Web site: Bangkok http://www.bu.ac.th/thailand/bangkok.html

Bangladesh see country box.

Bangor cathedral, university, and market town in Gwynedd, north Wales, on the Menai Strait 15 km/9 mi northeast of Caernarfon; population (1991 est) 12,338. Industries include chemicals, electrical goods, and engineering. Trade in slate from Penrhyn quarries was at one time very important, but has declined

in recent decades. Bangor is set in a region of outstanding natural beauty, with Snowdonia National Park and the Gwynedd coastline on its doorstep.

Bangui capital and main river port of the ▷Central African Republic, on the River Ubangi; population (1995 est) 698,000. The city is the centre for the country's light industries, including beer, cigarettes, office machinery, and timber and metal products. Bangui has an airport and contains the main depot for the storage and transportation of imported petroleum products. The city, which also serves as an outlet for the Republic of Chad, has a considerable trade in cotton and coffee.

Banjarmasin river port in Indonesia, on the island of Borneo;

Bangladesh

Bangladesh formerly East Bengal (until 1955), East Pakistan (1955–71) country in southern Asia, bounded north, west, and east by India, southeast by Myanmar, and south by the Bay of Bengal.

NATIONAL NAME *Gana Prajatantri Bangladesh/People's Republic of Bangladesh*
AREA 144,000 sq km/55,598 sq mi
CAPITAL Dhaka
MAJOR TOWNS/CITIES Rajshahi, Khulna, Chittagong, Sylhet, Rangpur, Narayanganj
MAJOR PORTS Chittagong, Khulna
PHYSICAL FEATURES flat delta of rivers Ganges (Padma) and Brahmaputra (Jamuna), the largest estuarine delta in the world; annual

rainfall of 2,540 mm/100 in; some 75% of the land is less than 3 m/10 ft above sea level; hilly in extreme southeast and northeast

Government
HEAD OF STATE Iajuddin Ahmed from 2002
HEAD OF GOVERNMENT Khaleda Zia from 2001
POLITICAL SYSTEM emergent democracy
POLITICAL EXECUTIVE parliamentary

ADMINISTRATIVE DIVISIONS 64 districts within four divisions
ARMED FORCES 137,000 (2002 est)
DEATH PENALTY retained and used for ordinary crimes

Economy and resources
CURRENCY taka
GPD (US$) 47.3 billion (2002 est)
REAL GDP GROWTH (% change on previous year) 5.2 (2001)
GNI (US$) 48.5 billion (2002 est)
GNI PER CAPITA (PPP) (US$) 1,720 (2002 est)
CONSUMER PRICE INFLATION 5.2% (2003 est)
UNEMPLOYMENT 2.5% (2001)
FOREIGN DEBT (US$) 15.8 billion (2001 est)
MAJOR TRADING PARTNERS USA, India, Germany, China, Japan, Singapore, UK, Italy, France, the Netherlands, South Korea, Belgium
RESOURCES natural gas, coal, limestone, china clay, glass sand
INDUSTRIES textiles, food processing, industrial chemicals, petroleum refineries, cement
EXPORTS clothing, raw jute and jute goods, tea, leather and leather products, shrimps and frogs' legs. Principal market: USA 29.6% (2001)
IMPORTS wheat, crude petroleum and petroleum products, pharmaceuticals, cement, raw cotton, machinery and transport equipment. Principal source: India 13.1% (2001)
ARABLE LAND 62.5% (2000 est)
AGRICULTURAL PRODUCTS rice, jute, wheat, tobacco, tea; fishing and fish products

Population and society
POPULATION 146,736,000 (2003 est)
POPULATION GROWTH RATE 1.6% (2000–15)
POPULATION DENSITY (per sq km) 1,019 (2003 est)
URBAN POPULATION (% of total) 27 (2003 est)
AGE DISTRIBUTION (% of total population) 0–14 38%, 15–59 57%, 60+ 5% (2002 est)
ETHNIC GROUPS 98% of Bengali descent, quarter of a million Bihari, and around 1 million belonging to 'tribal' communities
LANGUAGE Bengali (official), English
RELIGION Muslim 88%, Hindu 11%; Islam is the state religion EDUCATION (compulsory years) 5
LITERACY RATE 51% (men); 32% (women) (2003 est)
LABOUR FORCE 59.1% agriculture, 9.5% industry, 31.4% services (1997)
LIFE EXPECTANCY 61 (men); 62 (women) (2000–05)
CHILD MORTALITY RATE (under 5, per 1,000 live births) 77 (2001)
PHYSICIANS (per 1,000 people) 0.2 (1997 est)
TV SETS (per 1,000 people) 17 (2001 est)
RADIOS (per 1,000 people) 49 (2001 est)
INTERNET USERS (per 10,000 people) 15.3 (2002 est)
PERSONAL COMPUTER USERS (per 100 people) 0.3 (2002 est)

See also ▷British East India Company; ▷Pakistan.

Chronology

c. **1000 BC**: Arrival of Bang tribe in lower Ganges valley, establishing the kingdom of Banga (Bengal).

8th–12th centuries AD: Bengal was ruled successively by the Buddhist Pala and Hindu Senha dynasties.

1199: Bengal was invaded and briefly ruled by the Muslim Khiljis from Central Asia.

1576: Bengal was conquered by the Muslim Mogul emperor Akbar.

1651: The British East India Company established a commercial factory in Bengal.

1757: Bengal came under de facto British rule after Robert Clive defeated the nawab (ruler) of Bengal at Battle of Plassey.

1905–12: Bengal was briefly partitioned by the British Raj into a Muslim-dominated east and Hindu-dominated west.

1906: The Muslim League (ML) was founded in Dhaka.

1947: Bengal was formed into an eastern province of Pakistan on the partition of British India, with the ML administration in power.

1954: The opposition United Front, dominated by the Awami League (AL) and campaigning for East Bengal's autonomy, trounced the ML in elections.

1955: East Bengal was renamed East Pakistan.

1966: Sheikh Mujibur Rahman of AL announced a Six-Point Programme of autonomy for East Pakistan.

1970: 500,000 people were killed in a cyclone. The pro-autonomy AL secured an electoral victory in East Pakistan.

1971: Bangladesh ('land of the Bangla speakers') emerged as an independent nation after a bloody civil war with Indian military intervention on the side of East Pakistan; 10 million refugees fled to India.

1974: Hundreds of thousands died in a famine; a state of emergency was declared.

1975: Martial law was imposed.

1978–79: Elections were held and civilian rule restored.

1982: Martial law was reimposed after a military coup.

1986: Elections were held but disputed. Martial law ended.

1987: A state of emergency was declared in response to demonstrations and violent strikes.

1988: Assembly elections were boycotted by the main opposition parties. The state of emergency was lifted. Islam was made the state religion. Monsoon floods left 30 million people homeless and thousands dead.

1991: A cyclone killed around 139,000 people and left up to 10 million homeless. Parliamentary government was restored.

1996: Power was handed to a neutral caretaker government. A general election was won by the AL, led by Sheikh Hasina Wazed, and Shahabuddin Ahmed was appointed president. The BNP boycotted parliament. An agreement was made with India on the sharing of River Ganges water.

1998: The BNP ended its boycott of parliament. Two-thirds of Bangladesh was devastated by floods; 1,300 people were killed. Opposition-supported general strikes sought the removal of Sheikh Hasina's government.

2000: Ex-president Hussain Mohammad Ershad was fined US$1 million and sentenced to five-years' imprisonment for corruption by the Dhaka high court.

BANGLADESH The Bangladesh countryside is typified by extensive flood plains cultivated with rice, but with a rising population density the pressure on limited land resources is high. *Corel*

capital of Kalimantan Selatan province; population (1995 est) 534,600. It exports rubber, timber, and precious stones.

banjo resonant stringed musical instrument with a long fretted neck and circular drum-type soundbox covered on the topside only by stretched skin (now usually plastic). It is played with a plectrum. Modern banjos normally have five strings.

Related Web site: 5-String Banjo http://www.trussel.com/f_banj.htm

Banjul capital and chief port of Gambia, on an island at the mouth of the River Gambia; population of urban area (1995 est) 186,000; city 58,700 (1995 est). It is located 195 km/121 mi southeast of Dakar (capital of Senegal). Established in 1816 as a settlement for freed slaves, it was known as Bathurst until 1973. The city has an airport and industries include peanut processing and exporting, brewing, and tourism (centred at the nearby resorts of Bakau, Fajara, Kotu, and Kololi).

bank financial institution that uses funds deposited with it to lend money to companies or individuals, and also provides financial services to its customers. The first banks opened in Italy and Cataluña around 1400.

In 1900 half the world's top ten banks were British; by 1950, the dominant banking nation had become the USA, with half of the world's top ten banks based there. In terms of assets, seven of the world's top ten banks were Japanese in 1988.

A **central bank** (in the UK, the Bank of England) issues currency for the government, in order to provide cash for circulation and exchange. Commercial banks in the UK attract customers to deposit money with them mainly by offering either money transmission services, such as a cheque service, or ▷interest on the money deposited, or some combination of the two. Banks are the single most important source of ▷loans and ▷overdrafts for companies.

Banka alternative form of ▷Bangka, an Indonesian island.

Bankhead, Tallulah (1903–1968) US actor. She was renowned for her wit and flamboyant lifestyle. Her stage appearances include *Dark Victory* (1934), Lillian Hellman's *The Little Foxes* (1939), and Thornton Wilder's *The Skin of Our Teeth* (1942). Her films include Alfred Hitchcock's *Lifeboat* (1943).

bank holiday in the UK, a public holiday, when banks are closed by law. Bank holidays were instituted by the Bank Holiday Acts 1871 and 1875.

Bank of England UK central bank founded by act of Parliament in 1694. It was entrusted with issuing bank notes in 1844 and nationalized in 1946. It is banker to the clearing banks and the UK government.

Related Web site: Bank of England – Banknote Printing http://www.bankofengland.co.uk/banknotes/index.htm

bankruptcy process by which the property of a person (in legal terms, an individual or corporation) unable to pay debts is taken away under a court order and divided fairly among the person's creditors, after preferential payments such as taxes and wages. Proceedings may be instituted either by the debtor (voluntary bankruptcy) or by any creditor for a substantial sum (involuntary bankruptcy). Until 'discharged', a bankrupt is severely restricted in financial activities.

Banks, Joseph (1743–1820) English naturalist and explorer. In the position of naturalist, he accompanied Captain James ▷Cook on an expedition from 1768 to 1771 to the southern hemisphere in the *Endeavour*, and brought back 3,600 plants, a large proportion of which had not been classified previously. The *Banksia* genus of shrubs is named after him.

Banks was born in London and educated at Oxford. Inheriting a fortune, he made his first voyage in 1766, to Labrador and Newfoundland. The expedition in the *Endeavour* explored the coasts of New Zealand and Australia. Banks' plant-collecting activities at the first landing place in Australia (near present-day Sydney) gave rise to the name of the area – Botany Bay. He also studied the Australian fauna. In 1772 Banks went on his last expedition, to Iceland, where he studied geysers. He was instrumental in establishing the first colony at Botany Bay in 1788.

As a result of the friendship between Banks and George III, the Royal Botanic Gardens at Kew – of which Banks was the honorary director – became a focus of botanical research.

banksia any shrub or tree of a group native to Australia, including the honeysuckle tree. They are named after the English naturalist and explorer Joseph ▷Banks. (Genus *Banksia*, family Proteaceae.)

Bannister, Roger Gilbert (1929–) English track and field athlete. He was the first person to run a mile in under four minutes. He achieved this feat at Oxford, England, on 6 May 1954, in a time of 3 min 59.4 sec.

Bannister broke the four-minute barrier on one more occasion: at the 1954 Commonwealth Games in Vancouver, Canada, when he was involved with John Landy from Australia, in the 'Mile of the Century', so called because it was a clash between the only two

BANTENG As it is mainly an animal of tropical forests, the banteng ox is usually difficult to observe except when it wanders into a forest clearing, as in this nature reserve in Java. *Premaphotos Wildlife*

people to have broken the four-minute barrier for the mile at that time. An eminent neurologist, he was knighted in 1975.

Related Web site: Bannister, Roger http://cgi.cnnsi.com/features/1998/sportsman/1954/

Bannockburn, Battle of battle fought on 23–24 June 1314 at Bannockburn, Scotland, between Robert (I) the Bruce, King of Scotland, and Edward II of England. The defeat of the English led to the independence of Scotland.

Edward II, attempting to relieve Stirling castle, led over 2,000 knights and 15,000 foot soldiers, including about 5,000 archers. Bruce had only 500 light cavalry and some 7,000 foot soldiers. He took up a defensive position behind a stream and dug pits to hamper the English cavalry. An English attack was repulsed, so Edward's forces made a night march to outflank the obstacles. This manoeuvre was badly executed, leaving Edward's knights in boggy ground and the archers out of position in the rear. Bruce blocked the English advance with schiltrons (tightly packed formations) of pikemen, then, as the archers tried to deploy, charged with his cavalry and routed them. The English knights' charges against the Scottish schiltrons suffered heavy casualties, and 500 noblemen were taken for ransom.

bantam small ornamental variety of domestic chicken weighing about 0.5–1 kg/1–2 lb. Bantams can either be a small version of one of the larger breeds, or a separate type. Some are prolific egg layers. Bantam cocks have a reputation as spirited fighters.

banteng wild species of cattle *Bos banteng*, now scarce, but formerly ranging from Myanmar (Burma) through Southeast Asia to Malaysia and Java, inhabiting hilly forests. Its colour varies from

BANKSIA A drawing by Sydney Parkinson of *Banksia serrata* or 'saw banksias', an Australian tree that can grow to 20 m/70 ft high, with a corresponding spread of 8 m/25 ft. *The Art Archive/British Museum*

pale brown to blue-black, usually with white stockings and rump patch, and it is up to 1.5 m/5 ft at the shoulder.

Banting, Frederick Grant (1891–1941) Canadian physician who was awarded a Nobel Prize for Physiology or Medicine in 1923 for his discovery, in 1921, of a technique for isolating the hormone insulin. Banting and his colleague Charles ▷Best tied off the ducts of the ▷pancreas to determine the function of the cells known as the ▷islets of Langerhans and thus made possible the treatment of diabetes. John J R Macleod, Banting's mentor, shared the prize, and Banting divided his prize with Best.

Bantu languages group of related languages belonging to the Niger-Congo family, spoken widely over the greater part of Africa south of the Sahara, including Swahili, Xhosa, and Zulu. Meaning 'people' in Zulu, the word Bantu itself illustrates a characteristic use of prefixes: *mu-ntu* 'man', *ba-ntu* 'people'.

Bantustan (or homeland) name until 1978 for a ▷Black National State in the Republic of South Africa.

banyan tropical Asian fig tree. It produces aerial roots that grow down from its spreading branches, forming supporting pillars that look like separate trunks. (*Ficus benghalensis*, family Moraceae.)

baobab tree with rootlike branches, hence the nickname 'upside-down tree', and a disproportionately thick girth, up to 9 m/30 ft in diameter. The pulp of its fruit is edible and is known as monkey bread. (Genus *Adansonia*, family Bombacaceae.)

baptism (Greek 'to dip') immersion in or sprinkling with water as a religious rite of initiation. It was practised long before the beginning of Christianity. In the Christian baptism ceremony, sponsors or godparents make vows on behalf of the child, which are renewed by the child at confirmation. It is one of the seven sacraments. The *amrit* ceremony in Sikhism is sometimes referred to as baptism.

Baptist member of any of several Protestant and evangelical Christian sects that practise baptism by immersion only upon profession of faith. Baptists seek their authority in the Bible. They originated among English Dissenters who took refuge in the Netherlands in the early 17th century, and spread by emigration and, later, missionary activity. Of the world total of approximately 31 million, some 26.5 million are in the USA and 265,000 in the UK.

bar unit of pressure equal to 10^5 pascals or 10^6 dynes/cm^2, approximately 750 mm Hg or 0.987 atm. Its diminutive, the **millibar** (one-thousandth of a bar), is commonly used by meteorologists.

Barabbas In the New Testament, a condemned robber released by Pilate at Passover instead of Jesus to appease a mob.

Barak, Ehud (1942–) Born Ehud Brog. Israeli Labour politician, prime minister 1999–2001, former chief of staff of the Israeli army, and the most decorated soldier in the nation's history. As prime minister, Barak formed a government consisting of seven parties, the 'One Israel' alliance. Bringing together several different political views, Barak faced a continuous struggle to keep them together. A protégé of the late prime minister Yitzhak ▷Rabin, Barak's policies follow his belief that Israel has to be strong in order to enjoy peace and security. His campaign emphasized progress in the Middle East peace process, and he withdrew Israeli forces from Lebanon, the Golan Heights (Syria), and much of the West Bank. Talks stalled in May 2000 over the future of Jerusalem and violence from October led to Barak's resignation in December and subsequent defeat in prime ministerial elections in February 2001.

barb general name for fish of the genus *Barbus* and some related genera of the family Cyprinidae. As well as the ▷barbel, barbs include many small tropical Old World species, some of which are familiar aquarium species. They are active egg-laying species, usually of 'typical' fish shape and with barbels at the corner of the mouth.

Barbados see country box.

Barbary ape tailless, yellowish-brown macaque monkey *Macaca sylvanus*, 55–75 cm/20–30 in long. Barbary apes are found in the mountains and wilds of Algeria and Morocco, especially in the forests of the Atlas Mountains. They were introduced to Gibraltar, where legend has it that the British will leave if the ape colony dies out.

The macaque is threatened by illegal logging, which is devastating some of the ancient forests in the area. Although it is breeding well in captivity, forest loss may confound attempts to reintroduce this species into the wild.

Barbary sheep (or **aoudad** or **udad**) species of bovid related to the goat and sheep. It has powerful horns and a goatlike odour, but is distinguished from goats by its longer tail and the mane of long hair on the throat and upper parts of the forelegs. It is found in North Africa and parts of the Sudan. The Barbary sheep *Ammotragus lervia* is in family Bovidae, order Artiodactyla.

barbastelle insect-eating bat *Barbastella barbastellus* with hairy cheeks and lips, 'frosted' black fur, and a wingspan of about 25 cm/10 in. It lives in hollow trees and under roofs, and is occasionally found in the UK but more commonly in Europe.

barbel freshwater fish *Barbus barbus* found in fast-flowing rivers with sand or gravel bottoms in Britain and Europe. Long-bodied, and up to 1 m/3 ft long in total, the barbel has four **barbels** ('little beards' – sensory fleshy filaments) near the mouth.

BARBERRY Creeping barberry *Berberis repens* is native to North America. *Premaphotos Wildlife*

Barber, Samuel (1910–1981) US composer. He worked in a neoclassical, astringent style. Compositions include *Adagio for Strings* (1936) and the opera *Vanessa* (1958), which won one of his two Pulitzer prizes. Another opera, *Antony and Cleopatra* (1966), was commissioned for the opening of the new Metropolitan Opera House at the Lincoln Center, New York City. Owing to an over-elaborate staging the opera was a failure at its premiere, although it had some success in a revised version in 1974. Barber's music is lyrical and fastidiously worked. His later works include *The Lovers* (1971).

barberry any spiny shrub belonging to the barberry family, with sour red berries and yellow flowers. These shrubs are often used as hedges. (Genus *Berberis*, family Berberidaceae.)

barbershop in music, a style of unaccompanied close-harmony singing of sentimental ballads, revived in the USA during the 19th century. Traditionally sung by four male voices, since the 1970s it has developed as a style of ▷a cappella choral singing for both male and female voices.

barbet (Latin *barbatus*, 'bearded') small, tropical bird, often brightly coloured. There are about 78 species of barbet in the family Capitonidae, order Piciformes, common to tropical Africa, Asia,

BARBET The barbet digs nest holes in termite mounds and rotten tree-stumps with its large and often sharp-toothed beak. It may also take up residence in old woodpecker holes.

Barbados

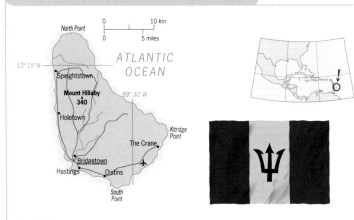

Barbados island country in the Caribbean, one of the Lesser Antilles. It is about 483 km/300 mi north of Venezuela.

AREA 430 sq km/166 sq mi
CAPITAL Bridgetown
MAJOR TOWNS/CITIES Speightstown, Holetown, Oistins
PHYSICAL FEATURES most easterly island of the West Indies; surrounded by coral reefs; subject to hurricanes June–November; highest point Mount Hillaby 340 m/1,115 ft

Government

HEAD OF STATE Queen Elizabeth II from 1966, represented by Governor General Sir Clifford Straughn Husbands from 1996
HEAD OF GOVERNMENT Owen Arthur from 1994
POLITICAL SYSTEM liberal democracy
POLITICAL EXECUTIVE parliamentary
ADMINISTRATIVE DIVISIONS 11 parishes
ARMED FORCES 600 (2002 est)
DEATH PENALTY retained and used for ordinary crimes

Economy and resources

CURRENCY Barbados dollar
GPD (US$) 2.8 billion (2002 est)
REAL GDP GROWTH (% change on previous year) –2.8 (2001)
GNI (US$) 2.6 billion (2002 est)
GNI PER CAPITA (PPP) (US$) 15,560 (2002 est)

CONSUMER PRICE INFLATION 1.5% (2003 est)
UNEMPLOYMENT 10.1% (2001)
FOREIGN DEBT (US$) 1.3 billion (2001 est)
MAJOR TRADING PARTNERS UK, USA, Trinidad and Tobago, Japan, Canada, Jamaica
RESOURCES petroleum and natural gas
INDUSTRIES sugar refining, food processing, industrial chemicals, beverages, tobacco, household appliances, electrical components, plastic products, electronic parts, tourism
EXPORTS sugar, molasses, syrup-rum, chemicals, electrical components. Principal market: USA 15.3% (2000)
IMPORTS machinery, foodstuffs, motor cars, construction materials, basic manufactures. Principal source: USA 40.8% (2000)
ARABLE LAND 37% (2000 est)
AGRICULTURAL PRODUCTS sugar cane, cotton, sweet potatoes, yams, carrots, and other vegetables; fishing (740 fishing vessels employed in 1994)

Population and society

POPULATION 270,000 (2003 est)
POPULATION GROWTH RATE 0.4% (2000–05)

POPULATION DENSITY (per sq km) 629 (2003 est)
URBAN POPULATION (% of total) 52 (2003 est)
AGE DISTRIBUTION (% of total population) 0–14 20%, 15–59 67%, 60+ 13% (2002 est)
ETHNIC GROUPS about 80% of African descent, about 16% mixed ethnicity, and 4% of European origin (mostly British)
LANGUAGE English (official), Bajan (a Barbadian English dialect)
RELIGION 40% Anglican, 8% Pentecostal, 6% Methodist, 4% Roman Catholic
EDUCATION (compulsory years) 12
LITERACY RATE 99% (men); 99% (women) (2003 est)
LABOUR FORCE 4.2% agriculture, 21.5% industry, 74.1% services (1999)
LIFE EXPECTANCY 75 (men); 80 (women) (2000–05)
CHILD MORTALITY RATE (under 5, per 1,000 live births) 14 (2001)
PHYSICIANS (per 1,000 people) 1.3 (1994 est)
HOSPITAL BEDS (per 1,000 people) 7.6 (1996 est)
TV SETS (per 1,000 people) 290 (1999 est)
RADIOS (per 1,000 people) 651 (1999 est)
INTERNET USERS (per 10,000 people) 559.1 (2002 est)
PERSONAL COMPUTER USERS (per 100 people) 10.4 (2002 est)

Chronology

1536: Visited by Portuguese explorer Pedro a Campos and the name Los Barbados ('The Bearded Ones') given in reference to its 'bearded' fig trees. Indigenous Arawak people were virtually wiped out, via epidemics, after contact with Europeans.

1627: British colony established; developed as a sugar-plantation economy, initially on basis of black slaves brought in from West Africa.

1639: The island's first parliament, the House of Assembly, was established.

1834: The island's slaves were freed.

1937: There was an outbreak of riots, followed by establishment of the Barbados Labour Party (BLP) by Grantley Adams, and moves towards a more independent political system.

See also ▷Arawak; ▷West Indies, Federation of the.

BARBADOS Ragged Point lighthouse. It is situated on the Atlantic coast at the most easterly point of the island. *Corel*

1951: Universal adult suffrage was introduced. The BLP won a general election.

1954: Ministerial government was established, with BLP leader Adams as the first prime minister.

1955: A group broke away from the BLP and formed the Democratic Labour Party (DLP).

1961: Independence was achieved from Britain.

1966: Barbados achieved full independence within the Commonwealth.

1967: Barbados became a member of the United Nations (UN).

1972: Diplomatic relations with Cuba were established.

1983: Barbados supported the US invasion of Grenada.

1999: The BLP gained a landslide victory in general elections, securing 26 of the 28 House of Assembly seats.

and America. Barbets eat insects and fruit and, being distant relations of woodpeckers, drill nest holes with their beaks. The name comes from the 'little beard' of bristles about the mouth that assists them in catching insects.

Barbican, the arts and residential complex in the City of London. The Barbican Arts Centre (1982) contains theatres, cinemas, and exhibition and concert halls. The architects were Powell, Chamberlin, and Bon.

Barbie, Klaus (1913–1991) German Nazi, a member of the ▷SS paramilitary organization from 1936. During World War II he was involved in the deportation of Jews from the occupied Netherlands from 1940 to 1942 and in tracking down Jews and Resistance workers in France from 1942 to 1945. He was arrested in 1983 and convicted of crimes against humanity in France in 1987.

His work as an SS commander, based in Lyon, included the rounding-up of Jewish children from an orphanage at Izieu and the torture of the Resistance leader Jean Moulin. His ruthlessness during this time earned him the epithet the 'Butcher of Lyon'. Having escaped capture in 1945, Barbie was employed by the US intelligence services in Germany before moving to Bolivia in 1951. Expelled from there in 1983, he was returned to France, where he was tried by a court in Lyon. He died in prison.

Barbirolli, John (Giovanni Battista) (1899–1970) English conductor. He excelled in the Romantic repertory, especially the symphonies of Elgar, Sibelius, Mahler, and Vaughan Williams. Trained as a cellist, he succeeded Arturo Toscanini as conductor of the New York Philharmonic Orchestra from 1937 to 1943 and was conductor of the Hallé Orchestra, Manchester, England from 1943 to 1970.

barbiturate hypnosedative drug, commonly known as a 'sleeping pill', consisting of any salt or ester of barbituric acid $C_4H_4O_3N_2$. It works by depressing brain activity. Most barbiturates, being highly addictive, are no longer prescribed and are listed as controlled substances.

Barbizon School French school of landscape painters of the mid-19th century, based at Barbizon in the forest of Fontainebleau. They aimed to paint fresh, realistic scenes, sketching and painting their subjects in the open air. Members included Jean François Millet, Théodore Rousseau, and Charles Daubigny.

Barbour, John (*c.* 1320–1395) Scottish poet. His epic 13,000-line poem *The Brus* (written 1374–75, printed 1571) chronicles the war of Scottish independence and includes a vivid account of Robert Bruce's victory over the English at Bannockburn in 1314. It is among the earliest known works of Scottish poetry.

Barbuda one of the islands that form the state of ▷Antigua and Barbuda.

Barcelona port and capital of Barcelona province and of the autonomous community of ▷Cataluña, northeast Spain; population (1994) 1,631,000. Industries include textiles, engineering, and chemicals. As the chief centre of Catalan nationalism, Barcelona was prominent in the overthrow of the monarchy in 1931 and was the last city of the republic to surrender to Franco in 1939. The city hosted the Summer Olympics in 1992.

Features The Ramblas, tree-lined promenades leading from the Plaza de Cataluña, the largest square in Spain; ▷Gaudí's unfinished church of the Holy Family (1883); the Pueblo Español (1929), with specimens of Spanish architecture; a replica of Columbus's flagship the *Santa Maria*, in the Maritime Museum; a large collection of art by Picasso.

History Founded in the 3rd century BC, Barcelona was ruled independently by the Counts of Barcelona from the 9th century AD, becoming a commercial centre for Aragón and Cataluña in the 13th–14th centuries and one of the leading ports of the Mediterranean. The city was devastated in the Catalan Revolt of 1652 and again during the War of Spanish Succession in 1714. At the forefront of the fight for regional autonomy during the Spanish Civil War, Barcelona suffered as a result of insurrections in 1835, 1856, 1874, and 1909. In 1923 there was a general strike, and in 1925 the city was for a time under martial law. Barcelona was held by the Republicans during the Spanish Civil War of 1936–39, and towards the end of 1937 it replaced Valencia as the capital of the Republican government.

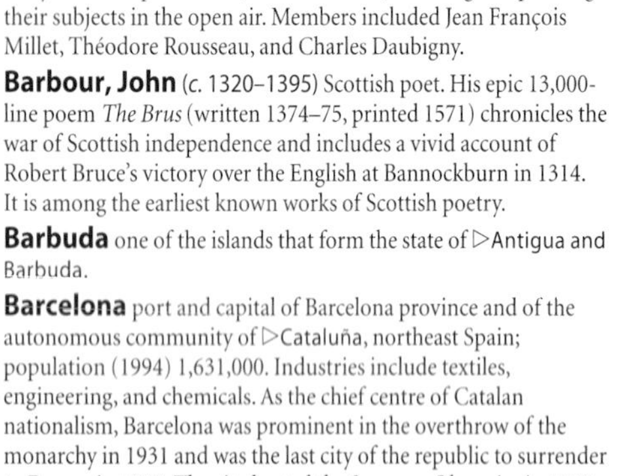

BARCELONA The container harbour at Barcelona, Spain.
Image Bank

Industrial development Barcelona was the centre of early industrialization in Spain, with a textile industry developing towards the end of the 18th century, using the spinning jenny less than ten years after it had been invented. This development was interrupted by the Napoleonic Wars (1808–14), but resumed with the introduction of steam-powered machinery in the Barcelona textile industry by José Bonaplata in 1832, and with the founding of the engineering company, La Máquina Terrestre y Marítima, in 1855.

bar code pattern of bars and spaces that can be read by a computer. Bar codes are widely used in retailing, industrial distribution, and libraries. The code is read by a scanning device; the computer determines the code from the widths of the bars and spaces.

bard Celtic minstrel who, in addition to composing songs, usually at a court, often held important political posts. Originating in the pre-Christian era, bards were persecuted in Wales during the 13th century on political grounds. Since the 19th century annual meetings and competitions in Wales – known as ▷eisteddfod – have attempted to revive the musical tradition of the bard.

Bardeen, John (1908–1991) US physicist. He was awarded the Nobel Prize for Physics in 1956, with Walter Brattain and William Shockley, for the development of the ▷transistor in 1948 and he became the first double winner of the Nobel Prize for Physics in 1972 (with Leon ▷Cooper and Robert Schrieffer) for his work on ▷superconductivity.

Bardot, Brigitte (1934–) Adopted name of Camille Javal. French film actor. A celebrated sex symbol of the 1950s and 1960s, she did much to popularize French cinema internationally. Her films include *Et Dieu créa la femme/And God Created Woman* (1956) directed by Roger Vadim (1928–), Jean-Luc Godard's *Le Mépris* (1963), Louis Malle's *Viva Maria!* (1965), and *Shalako* (1968).

Bardot studied at the Paris Conservatoire and made her film debut in 1952. Since retiring from acting in 1973, she has devoted herself to animal welfare.

Related Web site: Bardot, Brigitte http://www.xs4all.nl/~robinw/brigitte/index.htm

Barebones Parliament English assembly called by Oliver ▷Cromwell to replace the ▷Rump Parliament in July 1653. Although its members attempted to pass sensible legislation (civil marriage; registration of births, deaths, and marriages; custody of lunatics), their attempts to abolish tithes, patronage, and the court of chancery, and to codify the law, led to the resignation of the moderates and its dissolution in December 1653.

The assembly consisted of 140 members selected by the army and derived its name from one of its members, Praise-God Barbon.

Daniel Barenboim
Today, conducting is a question of ego: a lot of people believe they are actually playing the music.
Quoted in Jacobson *Reverberations* 1975

Bareilly industrial city in Uttar Pradesh, northern India; population (1991) 591,000. Its industries include sugar production, and furniture and rope manufacture. Founded in 1537, it was a Mogul capital in 1657 and ceded to the British in 1801. In 1857 it was a centre of the Indian Mutiny. Bareilly College was founded in 1837. The Indian Veterinary Research Institute is at Izatnagar, part of the Bareilly urban area.

Barenboim, Daniel (1942–) Israeli pianist and conductor. Pianist/conductor with the English Chamber Orchestra from 1964, he became conductor of the New York Philharmonic Orchestra in 1970, musical director of the Orchestre de Paris in 1975, and director of the Chicago Symphony Orchestra in 1991. As a pianist he specialized in the German classic and romantic repertoire; as a conductor he has extended into 19th- and 20th-century French music, including Boulez. He was married to the cellist Jacqueline Du Pré.

Barents, Willem (*c.* 1550–1597) Dutch explorer and navigator. He made three expeditions to seek the ▷Northeast Passage; he died on the last voyage. The Barents Sea, part of the Arctic Ocean north of Norway, is named after him.

Bari (ancient Barium) capital of Apulia region, southern Italy, and industrial and ferry port on the Adriatic Sea; population (1992) 342,100. It is the site of Italy's first nuclear power station. Part of the town is known as Tecnopolis, the Italian equivalent of ▷Silicon Valley.

WILLEM BARENTS An illustration from Gerrit de Veer's *Narrative of Barents' Last Voyage* (1598). The ship is caught in the Arctic ice, and is being piloted by a tender.
The Art Archive

Baring-Gould, Sabine (1834–1924) English writer and cleric. His work includes novels and books of travel, mythology, and folklore; he also wrote the words of the hymn 'Onward, Christian Soldiers'.

baritone male voice pitched between bass and tenor, of approximate range G2–F4. As a prefix to the name of an instrument, for example baritone saxophone, it indicates that the instrument sounds in approximately the same range.

barium (Greek *barytes* 'heavy') soft, silver-white, metallic element, symbol Ba, atomic number 56, relative atomic mass 137.33. It is one of the alkaline-earth metals, found in nature as barium carbonate and barium sulphate. As the sulphate it is used in medicine: taken as a suspension (a 'barium meal'), its movement along the gut is followed using X-rays. The barium sulphate, which is opaque to X-rays, shows the shape of the gut, revealing any abnormalities of the alimentary canal. Barium is also used in alloys, pigments, and safety matches and, with strontium, forms the emissive surface in cathode-ray tubes. It was first discovered in barytes or heavy spar.

bark protective outer layer on the stems and roots of woody plants, composed mainly of dead cells. To allow for expansion of the stem, the bark is continually added to from within, and the outer surface often becomes cracked or is shed as scales. Trees deposit a variety of chemicals in their bark, including poisons. Many of these chemical substances have economic value because they can be used in the manufacture of drugs. Quinine, derived from the bark of the *Cinchona* tree, is used to fight malarial infections; curare, an anaesthetic used in medicine, comes from the *Strychnus toxifera* tree in the Amazonian rainforest.

Bark technically includes all the tissues external to the vascular ▷cambium (the ▷phloem, cortex, and periderm), and its thickness may vary from 2.5 mm/0.1 in to 30 cm/12 in or more, as in the giant redwood *Sequoia* where it forms a thick, spongy layer.

bark beetle any one of a number of species of mainly wood-boring beetles. Bark beetles are cylindrical, brown or black, and 1–9 mm/0.04–0.4 in long. Some live just under the bark and others bore deeper into the hardwood. The detailed tunnelling pattern that they make within the trunk varies with the species concerned, and is used for identification.

Barking and Dagenham outer London borough of east Greater London, England

Population (1991) 143,700

Industries cars; paint; telephone cables; pharmaceuticals

History There is evidence of Bronze Age and Iron Age settlement in the area. From the 14th to the 19th century, fishing was the most important industry in the Barking area, supplying local as well as London markets. In 1887 the riverfront at Dagenham was turned into a major dock, marking the beginning of industrialisation in the area. Major industry became increasingly prominent when, in 1924, the Ford Motor Company bought land in Dagenham. Between 1929 and 1931 a Ford factory was built, and for 71 years was a major employer. In 2002 the car production plant was closed and diesel engines are now manufactured there.

Features There are many historical churches in the area: Barking Abbey is the second oldest Saxon Abbey in the country, the Parish Church of St Peter and St Paul in Dagenham Village dates from the 13th Century, and St Margaret's Church from the 15th century. Other historical buildings include the Cross Keys Inn at Dagenham

(c.1500), and Eastbury Manor house (16th century). The main municipal office at the Civic Centre, Dagenham, is also of interest with 1930s art deco features.

barley cereal belonging to a family of grasses. It resembles wheat but is more tolerant of cold and draughts. Cultivated barley (*Hordeum vulgare*) comes in three main varieties – six-rowed, four-rowed, and two-rowed. (Family Gramineae.)

bar mitzvah (Hebrew 'son of the commandment') in Judaism, initiation of a boy, which takes place at the age of 13, into the adult Jewish community; less common is the **bat mitzvah** or **bat** for girls aged 12. The child reads a passage from the Torah in the synagogue on the Sabbath and is subsequently regarded as a full member of the congregation.

Barnabas, St (lived 1st century AD) In the New Testament, a 'fellow labourer' with St Paul; he went with St Mark on a missionary journey to Cyprus, his birthplace. Feast day 11 June.

barnacle marine crustacean of the subclass Cirripedia. The larval form is free-swimming, but when mature, it fixes itself by the head to rock or floating wood. The animal then remains attached, enclosed in a shell through which the cirri (modified legs) protrude to sweep food into the mouth. Barnacles include the stalked **goose barnacle** *Lepas anatifera* found on ships' bottoms, and the **acorn barnacles**, such as *Balanus balanoides*, common on rocks.

BARNACLE A colony of acorn barnacles exposed at low tide, on a rock surface. The larger barnacles are the most advanced in age. *Dr Rod Preston-Mafham/Premaphotos Wildlife*

Barnard, Christiaan Neethling (1922–) South African surgeon who performed the first human heart transplant in 1967 at Groote Schuur Hospital in Cape Town. The 54-year-old patient lived for 18 days.

Barnardo, Thomas John (1845–1905) British philanthropist. He was known as Dr Barnardo, although he was not medically qualified. He opened the first of a series of homes for destitute children in 1867 in Stepney, East London.

Barnard's star star, 6 light years away from the Sun, in the constellation Ophiuchus. It is the second-closest star to the Sun, after Alpha Centauri, a triple star, the closest component of which, Proxima Centauri, is 4.2 light years away from the Sun. It is a faint red dwarf of 10th magnitude, visible only through a telescope. It is named after the US astronomer Edward E Barnard (1857–1923), who discovered in 1916 that it has the fastest proper motion of any star, 10.3 arc seconds per year.

Barnes, Julian (Patrick) (1946–) English novelist. His first novel, *Metroland*, was published in 1981, followed by *Before She Met Me* in 1982. It was his third novel, *Flaubert's Parrot* (1984) – skilfully combining fiction, biography, and essay – that brought him an international reputation, winning the French *Prix Medicis Etrangère* (the first British book to do so). Later works include a political parable, *The Porcupine* (1992), *Cross Channel* (1996), a collection of stories about the British in France, *England, England* (1998), a futuristic comedy (shortlisted for the Booker Prize in 1998), and *Love, Etc* (2000), a novel.

Barnet outer London borough of northwest Greater London, including the district of Hendon
Population (1991) 293,600
Industries Barnet has the highest level of self-employment in Greater London, and a low rate of unemployment. The main economic sectors are the retail and service sectors. Industries in Barnet include the UK headquarters of multinational companies such as McDonalds, Demon Internet and Pentland.
History During the Wars of the ▷Roses, it was the site of the Battle of Barnet (1471). Suburban development from London reached Barnet early in the 20th century with the opening of an underground line to Golders Green in 1907. Hampstead Garden Suburb was also started in 1907, and extended in the interwar years. It was an important part of the ▷Garden City movement. Barnet's

population is expanding, and approximately 20% (2000) of the population are from ethnic minority groups. Over 120 languages are spoken in the borough.
Features The Metropolitan Police Training Centre, Royal Air Force Battle of Britain, and Bomber Command museums are all situated in Hendon. Barnet College, a new further education college, the result of a merger between two existing colleges, was founded in August 2000.

Barnet, Battle of in the Wars of the ▷Roses, the defeat of Lancaster by York on 14 April 1471 in Barnet (now in northwest London).

Barnsley town and administrative headquarters of Barnsley metropolitan borough, South Yorkshire, England, on the River Dearne, 26 km/16 mi north of Sheffield; population (1991) Barnsley 75,100; Dearne Valley urban area 211,500. It lies on one of Britain's richest coal fields, although the industry is in decline. Manufactured products include steel, glass, paper, carpets, cakes (Lyons), sports equipment (Dunlop-Slazenger), and clothing. The headquarters of the National Union of Mineworkers are sited here.
Barnsley was mentioned in the Domesday Book of 1086. The town received the right to hold a market in 1249, and open-air and covered markets are still held, with over 1,000 stalls each week. Cannon Hall, built in about 1765, is now a country-house museum. The classical-style town hall, built in 1933, is faced in Portland stone and has a central tower rising to a height of 145ft.

Barnum, P(hineas) T(aylor) (1810–1891) US showman. In 1871 he established the 'Greatest Show on Earth', which included the midget 'Tom Thumb', a circus, a menagerie, and an exhibition of 'freaks', conveyed in 100 railway carriages. In 1881, it merged with its chief competitor and has continued to this day as the Ringling Brothers and Barnum and Bailey Circus.

TOM THUMB
"He is smaller than any infant that ever walked alone, is 25 inches in height and weighs only 15 pounds"
Coloured lithograph by Day & Haghe

P T BARNUM A photograph of Charles Sherwood Stratton, who was employed by P T Barnum, the US circus proprietor. Stratton was only 64 cm/25 in tall when first found by Barnum, and was exhibited in Europe in 1844 at the age of six years. It was Barnum who gave him the circus name of 'General Tom Thumb'. *The Art Archive*

barograph device for recording variations in atmospheric pressure. A pen, governed by the movements of an aneroid ▷barometer, makes a continuous line on a paper strip on a cylinder that rotates over a day or week to create a **barogram**, or permanent record of variations in atmospheric pressure.

barometer instrument that measures atmospheric pressure as an indication of weather. Most often used are the **mercury barometer** and the **aneroid barometer**.
In a mercury barometer a column of mercury in a glass tube, roughly 0.75 m/2.5 ft high (closed at one end, curved upwards at the other), is balanced by the pressure of the atmosphere on the open end; any change in the height of the column reflects a change in pressure. In an aneroid barometer, a shallow cylindrical metal box containing a partial vacuum expands or contracts in response to changes in pressure.

BARONS' WARS At the Battle of Lincoln in 1217, during the first Barons' War, the followers of King John I of England defeated the barons who had offered the English crown to Prince Louis of France (the dauphin). *Art Archive*

baron rank in the ▷peerage of the UK, above a baronet and below a viscount. Historically, any member of the higher nobility, a direct vassal (feudal servant) of the king, not bearing other titles such as duke or count. The term originally meant the vassal of a lord, but acquired its present meaning in the 12th century.

baronet British order of chivalry below the rank of baron, but above that of knight, created in 1611 by James I to finance the settlement of Ulster. It is a hereditary honour, although women cannot succeed to a baronetcy. A baronet does not have a seat in the House of Lords but is entitled to the style *Sir* before his name. The sale of baronetcies was made illegal in 1937.

Barons' Wars civil wars in England: 1215–17 between King ▷John and his barons, over his failure to honour ▷Magna Carta; 1264–67 between ▷Henry III (and the future Edward I) and his barons (led by Simon de ▷Montfort); 1264 14 May Battle of Lewes at which Henry III was defeated and captured; 1265 4 August Simon de Montfort was defeated by Edward at Evesham and killed.

baroque in the visual arts, architecture, and music, a style flourishing in Europe 1600–1750, broadly characterized as expressive, flamboyant, and dynamic. Playing a central role in the crusading work of the Catholic Counter-Reformation, the baroque used elaborate effects to appeal directly to the emotions. In some of its most characteristic works – such as Giovanni Bernini's Cornaro Chapel (Sta Maria della Vittoria, Rome), containing his sculpture

BAROQUE *The Four Rivers Fountain* (1648–51), designed by Italian painter and architect Gianlorenzo Bernini, in Piazza Navona, Rome, in front of the church of Sant'Agnese in Agone (begun in 1652), which was designed by Italian baroque architect Francesco Borromini. *The Art Archive/RAMC Historical Museum/Harper Collins Publishers*

Ecstasy of St Theresa (1645–52) – painting, sculpture, decoration, and architecture were designed to create a single, dramatic effect. Many masterpieces of the baroque emerged in churches and palaces in Rome, but the style soon spread throughout Europe, changing in character as it did so. The term baroque has also by extension been used to describe the music and literature of the period, but it has a much less clear meaning in these fields, and is more a convenient label than a stylistic description.

Barra southern island of the larger Outer ▷Hebrides, Scotland, part of the Western Isles unitary council area; area 90 sq km/ 35 sq mi; population (1991) 1,280. It is separated from South Uist by the Sound of Barra. The principal town is Castlebay. The main industries are fishing and tourism.

barracuda large predatory fish *Sphyraena barracuda* found in the warmer seas of the world. It can grow over 2 m/6 ft long and has a superficial resemblance to a pike. Young fish shoal, but the older ones are solitary. The barracuda has very sharp shearing teeth and may attack people.

Barranquilla major port and capital of Atlántico department on the Caribbean coast of northern Colombia, founded in 1629, on the western bank of the Magdalena River; population (1994) 1,049,000. Industries include chemicals, tobacco, food-processing, textiles, furniture, and footwear. Coffee, coal, oil and nickel are exported. It is a commercial centre and a terminal for river traffic.

Barras, Paul François Jean Nicolas, Count (1755–1829) French revolutionary. He was elected to the National Convention in 1792 and helped to overthrow Robespierre in 1794. In 1795 he became a member of the ruling Directory (see ▷French Revolution). In 1796 he brought about the marriage of his former mistress, Joséphine de Beauharnais, with Napoleon and assumed dictatorial powers. After Napoleon's coup d'état on 19 November 1799, Barras fell into disgrace.

Barrault, Jean-Louis (1910–1994) French actor and stage director. He appeared in such films as *La Symphonie fantastique* (1942) and *La Ronde* (1950), and as the mime Baptiste in Marcel Carné's cinema classic *Les Enfants du Paradis* (1945).

Barre, Raymond Octave Joseph (1924–) French centre-right politician, prime minister 1976–81 under President Valéry ▷Giscard d'Estaing, when he gained a reputation as a tough and determined budget-cutter.

barrel unit of liquid capacity, the value of which depends on the liquid being measured. It is used for petroleum, a barrel of which contains 159 litres/35 imperial gallons; a barrel of alcohol contains 189 litres/41.5 imperial gallons.

barrel organ portable pipe organ, played by turning a handle, or occasionally by a clockwork mechanism. The handle works a pump and drives a replaceable cylinder upon which music is embossed as a pattern of ridges controlling the passage of air to the pipes. It is often confused with the barrel or street piano used by buskers, which employed a barrel-and-pin mechanism to control a piano hammer action.

Barrett Browning, Elizabeth English poet; see ▷Browning, Elizabeth Barrett.

Barrie, J(ames) M(atthew) (1860–1937) Scottish dramatist and novelist. His work includes *The Admirable Crichton* (1902) and the children's fantasy *Peter Pan* (1904).

barrier island long island of sand, lying offshore and parallel to the coast.

Some are over 100 km/60 mi in length. Most barrier islands are derived from marine sands piled up by shallow longshore currents that sweep sand parallel to the seashore. Others are derived from former spits, connected to land and built up by drifted sand, that were later severed from the mainland.

barrier reef ▷coral reef that lies offshore, separated from the mainland by a shallow lagoon.

Barrios de Chamorro, Violeta (*c.* 1939–) Nicaraguan newspaper publisher and politician, president 1990–96. With strong US support, she was elected to be the candidate for the National Opposition Union (UNO) in 1989, winning the presidency from David ▷Ortega Saavedra in February 1990 and thus ending the period of ▷Sandinista rule and the decade-long ▷Contra war. She did not contest the 1996 presidential election.

barrister in the UK, a lawyer qualified by study at the ▷Inns of Court to plead for a client in court. In Scotland such lawyers are called advocates. Barristers also undertake the writing of opinions on the prospects of a case before trial. They act for clients through the intermediary of ▷solicitors. In the USA an attorney may serve the functions of barrister and solicitor.

barrow (Old English *beorgh* 'hill or mound') burial mound, usually composed of earth but sometimes of stones. Examples are found in many parts of the world. The two main types are **long**, dating from the Neolithic period (New Stone Age), and **round**, dating from the Mesolithic period (early Bronze Age). Barrows made entirely of stones are known as cairns.

Barrow town and administrative headquarters of North Slope Borough, north-central Alaska; population (1990) 3,500. It is situated on the Arctic Ocean, 18 km/11 mi southwest of the northernmost point in the USA, Point Barrow (71° 23′ N). It lies 820 km/510 mi north-northwest of Fairbanks. Barrow is the northernmost town in the USA, and is home to the world's largest Inuit settlement. The town serves as a regional trading centre. Whaling, trapping, crafts, government work, and the oil industry have all been important to the local economy.

Barrow, Clyde US criminal; see ▷Bonnie and Clyde.

Barry, Charles (1795–1860) English architect. He designed the neo-Gothic new Palace of Westminster, London (the Houses of Parliament; 1840–60), in collaboration with A W N ▷Pugin. His early designs for the Travellers Club (1829–32) and for the Reform Club (1837), both in London, were in Renaissance style.

Barry, comtesse du mistress of Louis XV of France; see ▷du Barry.

Roland Barthes
Through the mythology of Einstein, the world blissfully regained the image of knowledge reduced to a formula.
On Albert Einstein, in *Mythologies*

Barstow, Stan (1928–) English novelist. His realist novels describe northern working-class life and include *A Kind of Loving* (1960) (filmed in 1962), a first-person, present-tense narrative of a young man trapped into marriage. He ranks with John ▷Braine, Alan Sillitoe, David Storey, and Keith Waterhouse as a contributor to the modern regional novel.

Barth, Heinrich (1821–1865) German geographer and explorer who in explorations of North Africa between 1844 and 1855 established the exact course of the River Niger.

Barth, Karl (1886–1968) Swiss Protestant theologian. A socialist in his political views, he attacked the Nazis. His *Church Dogmatics* (1932–62) makes the resurrection of Jesus the focal point of Christianity.

Barthes, Roland (1915–1980) French critic and theorist of ▷semiology, the science of signs and symbols. One of the French 'new critics' and an exponent of ▷structuralism, he attacked traditional literary criticism in his first collection of essays, *Le Degré zéro de l'écriture/Writing Degree Zero* (1953).

Bartholomew, St In the New Testament, one of the apostles. Some legends relate that after the Crucifixion he took Christianity to India; others that he was a missionary in Anatolia and Armenia, where he suffered martyrdom by being flayed alive. Feast day 24 August.

Bartholomew, Massacre of St slaughter of Huguenots (Protestants) in Paris in 1572; see ▷St Bartholomew, Massacre of.

Bartók, Béla (1881–1945) Hungarian composer. His works combine folk elements with mathematical concepts of tonal and rhythmic proportion. His large output includes six string quartets, a *Divertimento* for string orchestra (1939), concertos for piano, violin, and viola, the *Concerto for Orchestra* (1943–44), a one-act opera *Duke Bluebeard's Castle* (1911), and graded teaching pieces for piano.

A child prodigy, Bartók studied music at the Budapest Conservatory, later working with Zoltán ▷Kodály in recording and transcribing the folk music of Hungary and adjoining countries. His ballet *The Miraculous Mandarin* (1918–19) was banned because of its subject matter (it was set in a brothel). Bartók died in the USA, having fled from Hungary in 1940.

Bartolommeo, Fra (*c.* 1472–1517) Also known as **Baccio della Porta**. Italian religious painter of the High Renaissance, active in Florence. He introduced Venetian artists to the Florentine High Renaissance style during a visit to Venice in 1508, and took back with him to Florence a Venetian sense of colour. His style is one of classic simplicity and order, as in *The Mystical Marriage of St Catherine* (1511; Louvre, Paris).

Barton, Edmund (1849–1920) Australian politician. He was leader of the Federation Movement from 1896 and first prime minister of Australia 1901–03.

baryon in nuclear physics, a heavy subatomic particle made up of three indivisible elementary particles called quarks. The baryons form a subclass of the ▷hadrons and comprise the nucleons (protons and neutrons) and hyperons.

Baryshnikov, Mikhail Nikolayevich (1948–) Latvian-born dancer, now based in the USA. He joined the Kirov Ballet in 1967 and, after defecting from the USSR in 1974, joined the American Ballet Theater (ABT) as principal dancer, partnering Gelsey Kirkland. He left to join the New York City Ballet (1978–80), but rejoined ABT as director 1980–90. From 1990 he has danced for various companies including his own modern dance company, White Oak Project. His physical prowess and amazing aerial feats have combined with an impish sense of humour and dash to make him one of the most accessible of dancers.

basal metabolic rate (BMR) minimum amount of energy needed by the body to maintain life. It is measured when the subject is awake but resting, and includes the energy required to keep the heart beating, sustain breathing, repair tissues, and keep the brain and nerves functioning. Measuring the subject's consumption of oxygen gives an accurate value for BMR, because oxygen is needed to release energy from food.

basalt commonest volcanic ▷igneous rock in the solar system. Much of the surfaces of the terrestrial planets Mercury, Venus, Earth, and Mars, as well as the Moon, are composed of basalt. Earth's ocean floor is virtually entirely made of basalt. Basalt is mafic, that is, it contains relatively little ▷silica: about 50% by weight. It is usually dark grey but can also be green, brown, or black. Its essential constituent minerals are calcium-rich ▷feldspar, and calcium-rich and magnesium-rich ▷pyroxene.

BASALT A basalt outcrop in the French Auvergne. Basalt is a volcanic rock that, when it cools, sometimes cracks along its natural planes of cleavage to produce distinctive hexagonal columns. *Premaphotos Wildlife*

bascule bridge type of drawbridge in which one or two counterweighted deck members pivot upwards to allow shipping to pass underneath. One example is the double bascule Tower Bridge, London.

base in chemistry, a substance that accepts protons. Bases can contain negative ions such as the hydroxide ion (OH^-), which is the strongest base, or be molecules such as ammonia (NH_3). Ammonia is a weak base, as only some of its molecules accept protons.

$$OH^- + H^+_{(aq)} \rightarrow H_2O_{(l)}$$

$$NH_3 + H_2O \leftrightarrow NH_4^+ + OH^-$$

Bases that dissolve in water are called alkalis. Inorganic bases are usually oxides or hydroxides of metals, which react with dilute acids to form a salt and water. Many carbonates also react with dilute acids, additionally giving off carbon dioxide.

base in mathematics, the number of different single-digit symbols used in a particular number system. In our usual (decimal) counting system of numbers (with symbols 0, 1, 2, 3, 4, 5, 6, 7, 8, 9) the base is 10. In the ▷binary number system, which has only the symbols 1 and 0, the base is two. A base is also a number that, when raised to a particular power (that is, when multiplied by itself a particular number of times as in $10^2 = 10 \times 10 = 100$), has a ▷logarithm equal to the power. For example, the logarithm of 100 to the base ten is 2.

In geometry, the term is used to denote the line or area on which a polygon or solid stands.

In general, any number system subscribing to a place-value system with base value b may be represented by $\ldots b^4, b^3, b^2, b^1, b^0, b^{-1}, b^{-2}, b^{-3}, \ldots$.

Hence in base ten the columns represent $\ldots 10^4, 10^3, 10^2, 10^1, 10^0, 10^{-1}, 10^{-2}, 10^{-3} \ldots$, in base two $\ldots 2^4, 2^3, 2^2, 2^1, 2^0, 2^{-1}, 2^{-2}, 2^{-3} \ldots$, and in base eight $\ldots 8^4, 8^3, 8^2, 8^1, 8^0, 8^{-1}, 8^{-2}, 8^{-3} \ldots$. For bases beyond 10, the denary numbers 10, 11, 12, and so on must be replaced by a single digit. Thus in base 16, all numbers up to 15 must be represented by single-digit 'numbers', since 10 in hexadecimal would mean 16 in decimal. Hence decimal 10, 11, 12, 13, 14, 15 are represented in hexadecimal by letters A, B, C, D, E, F.

BASEBALL The view from high up in the Shea Stadium, New York, USA, showing the layout of the field, or pitch. *Image Bank*

baseball national summer game of the USA, derived in the 19th century from the English game of ▷rounders. Baseball is a bat-and-ball game played between two teams, each of nine players, on a pitch ('field') marked out in the form of a diamond, with a base at each corner. The ball is struck with a cylindrical bat, and the players try to score ('make a run') by circuiting the bases. A 'home run' is a circuit on one hit.

Related Web sites: Major League Baseball http://www. majorleaguebaseball.com/

Basel (or **Basle**; French **Bâle**) commercial and industrial city, capital of Basel-Stadt demi-canton, Switzerland, situated on the Rhine at the point where the French, German, and Swiss borders meet; population (2003 est) 162,800. Manufactured goods include dyes, textiles, vitamins, agrochemicals, dietary products, and genetic products.

Basel was a strong military station under the Romans. In 1501 it joined the Swiss confederation and later developed as a centre for the Reformation.

Related Web site: Basel Online http://www.bsonline.ch/english/index.cfm

basenji breed of dog originating in Central Africa, where it is used for hunting. About 41 cm/16 in tall, it has pointed ears, curled tail, and short glossy coat of black or red, often with white markings. It is remarkable because it has no true bark.

base pair in biochemistry, the linkage of two base (purine or pyrimidine) molecules that join the complementary strands of ▷DNA. Adenine forms a base pair with thymine (or uracil in RNA) and cytosine pairs with guanine in a double stranded nucleic acid molecule.

One base lies on one strand of the DNA double helix, and one on the other, so that the base pairs link the two strands like the rungs of a ladder. In DNA, there are four bases: adenine and guanine (purines) and cytosine and thymine (pyrimidines). Adenine always pairs with thymine, and cytosine with guanine.

Bashkir the majority ethnic group of the autonomous republic of Bashkir in Russia. The Bashkirs are agriculturalists and have been Muslims since the 13th century. The Bashkir language belongs to the Turkic branch of the Altaic family, and has about 1 million speakers.

Bashkortostan (formerly **Bashkiria** or **Bashkir Autonomous SSR**) autonomous republic of the Russian Federation; area 143,600 sq km/55,444 sq mi; population (1990) 3,964,000 (40% Russian, 30% Tatar, 25% Bashkir). The capital is ▷Ufa. The Ural Mountains are in the east and River Kama in the northwest; other rivers are Belaya, Ufa, Dema, and Zilim. Chief industries are oil, natural gas, minerals (gold and iron ore), chemicals, engineering, timber, and paper. The languages Russian and Bashkir are spoken.

Bashō (1644–1694) Pen-name of Matsuo Munefusa. Japanese poet. He was a master of the **haiku**, a 17-syllable poetic form with lines of 5, 7, and 5 syllables, which he infused with subtle allusiveness. His *Oku-no-hosomichi/The Narrow Road to the Deep North* (1694), an account of a visit to northern and western Honshū, consists of haiku interspersed with prose passages.

BASIC (acronym for beginner's all-purpose symbolic instruction code) high-level computer-programming language, developed in 1964, originally designed to take advantage of ▷multiuser systems (which can be used by many people at the same time). The language is relatively easy to learn and is popular among microcomputer users.

Basic English simplified form of English devised and promoted by the writer and scholar C K Ogden and the literary critic I A Richards in the 1920s and 1930s as an international auxiliary language; as a route into ▷Standard English for foreign learners (little used now); and as a reminder to the English-speaking world of the virtues of plain language. Its name derives from the initial

letters of British, American, scientific, international, and commercial.

basic–oxygen process most widely used method of steelmaking, involving the blasting of oxygen at high pressure into molten pig iron.

basidiocarp spore-bearing body, or 'fruiting body', of all basidiomycete fungi (see ▷fungus), except the rusts and smuts. A well known example is the edible mushroom *Agaricus brunnescens*. Other types include globular basidiocarps (puffballs) or flat ones that project from tree trunks (brackets). They are made up of a mass of tightly packed, intermeshed hyphae.

Basie, Count (William) (1904–1984) US jazz band leader and pianist. He developed the big-band jazz sound and a simplified, swinging style of music. He led impressive groups of musicians in a career spanning more than 50 years. Basie's compositions include 'One O'Clock Jump' and 'Jumpin' at the Woodside'.

His solo piano technique was influenced by the style of Fats Waller. Some consider his the definitive dance band.

Basil II (c. 958–1025) Byzantine emperor 976–1025. He completed the work of his predecessors Nicephorus (II) Phocas and John Zimisces and expanded the borders of the Byzantine Empire to their greatest extent since the 5th century. He eliminated political rivals, drove the Muslims from Syria, and destroyed the power of the Bulgars.

Basil, St (c. 330–379) Cappadocian monk, known as 'the Great', founder of the Basilian monks. Elected bishop of Caesarea 370, Basil opposed the heresy of ▷Arianism. He wrote many theological works and composed the *Liturgy of St Basil*, in use in the Eastern Orthodox Church. Feast day 2 January.

basil (or **sweet basil**) plant with aromatic leaves, belonging to the mint family. A native of the tropics, it is cultivated in Europe as a herb and used to flavour food. Its small white flowers appear on spikes. (Genus *Ocimum basilicum*, family Labiatae.)

Basildon industrial town in Essex, eastern England, 19 km/12 mi southwest of Chelmsford; population (1994 est) 101,000. It was designated a ▷new town in 1949 to accommodate overspill population from London. Industries include printing, engineering, and the manufacture of chemicals and clothing.

basilica Roman public building; a large roofed hall flanked by columns, generally with an aisle on each side, used for judicial or other public business. The earliest known basilica, at Pompeii, dates from the 2nd century BC. This architectural form was adopted by the early Christians for their churches.

Basilicata (Roman **Lucania**) mountainous region of southern Italy, comprising the provinces of Potenza and Matera; area 10,000 sq km/3,860 sq mi; population (1992 est) 610,800. Its capital is Potenza. Agriculture is important; durum wheat, olives, and grapes are cultivated, and sheep and goats raised.

basilisk Central and South American lizard, genus *Basiliscus*. It is about 50 cm/20 in long and weighs about 90 g/0.2 lb. Its rapid speed (more than 2 m/6.6 ft per second) and the formation of air pockets around the feet enable it to run short distances across the surface of water. The male has a well-developed crest on the head, body, and tail.

BASILISK The double-crested basilisk. *Image Bank*

Basingstoke town in Hampshire, England, 72 km/45 mi west-southwest of London; population (1998) 90,000. It is a financial centre, containing the headquarters of the Automobile Association and Sun Life Insurance. Industries include light engineering, food processing, printing, publishing, and the manufacture of cosmetics (Wella, Alberto-Culver), scientific instruments, medical equipment, agricultural machinery, and electronics.

> **Count Basie**
> *I just sit, wink and play.*
> The Sunday Times April 1984

basketball ball game between two teams of five players on an indoor enclosed court. The object is, via a series of passing moves, to throw the large inflated ball through a circular hoop and net positioned at each end of the court, 3.05 m/10 ft above the in ground. The first world championship for men was held in 1950, and 1953 for women. They are now held every four years.

basketry ancient craft (Mesolithic–Neolithic) used to make a wide range of objects (from baskets to furniture) by interweaving or braiding rushes, cane, or other equally strong and supple natural fibres. Wickerwork is a more rigid type of basketry worked onto a sturdy frame, usually made from strips of willow.

Basle alternative form of ▷Basel, a city in Switzerland.

Basque the people inhabiting the ▷Basque Country of central northern Spain and the extreme southwest of France. The Basques are a pre-Indo-European people whose language (**Euskara**) is unrelated to any other language. Although both the Romans and, later, the Visigoths conquered them, they largely maintained their independence until the 19th century. During the Spanish Civil War (1936–39), they were on the republican side defeated by Franco. The Basque separatist movement ▷Euskadi ta Askatasuna (ETA; 'Basque Nation and Liberty') and the French organization Iparretarrak ('ETA fighters from the North Side') have engaged in guerrilla activity from 1968 in an attempt to secure a united Basque state.

Basque Country (Basque **Euskal Herria**) homeland of the ▷Basque people in the western Pyrenees, divided by the Franco-Spanish border.

The Spanish Basque Country (Spanish *País Vasco*) is an autonomous region (created in 1979) of central northern Spain, comprising the provinces of Vizcaya, Alava, and Guipúzcoa (Basque *Bizkaia*, *Araba*, and *Gipuzkoa*); area 7,300 sq km/2,818 sq mi; population (1991) 2,104,000.

The French Basque Country (French *Pays Basque*) is the area occupied by Basques in the *département* of Pyrénées-Atlantiques. It is estimated that there are about 170,000 Basques in France.

Basque language language of Western Europe known to its speakers, the Basques, as *Euskara*, and apparently unrelated to any other language on Earth. It is spoken by some half a million people in central northern Spain and southwestern France, around the Bay of Biscay, as well as by emigrants in both

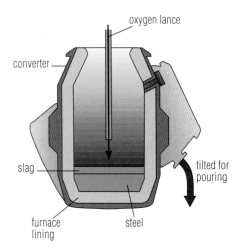
BASIC–OXYGEN PROCESS In the basic–oxygen process oxygen is blown at high pressure through molten pig iron and scrap steel in a converter lined with basic refractory materials. The impurities, principally carbon, quickly burn out, producing steel.

Europe and the Americas. The language is of central importance to the Basque nationalist movement.

Basra (Arabic **al-Basrah**) principal city in southeast Iraq, 97 km/60 mi from the Gulf; population (2002 est) 1,337,600. Basra lies at the head of the tidal Shatt al-Arab waterway (formed by the confluence of the Tigris and Euphrates rivers). Founded in the 7th century and now Iraq's main port on the Shatt-al-Arab River, exports include wool, oil, cereal, and dates. It can be reached by large ocean-going vessels, though it lies 120 km/75 mi from the Persian Gulf. Aerial bombing by US- and UK-led forces in the 1991 Gulf War and the 2003 Iraq War severely damaged the city's infrastructure.

bas relief see ▷relief.

bass long-bodied scaly sea fish *Morone labrax* found in the North Atlantic and Mediterranean. They grow to 1 m/3 ft, and are often seen in shoals.

bass the lowest male voice, of approximate range C2–D4. As the prefix to the name of an instrument, it indicates that the instrument sounds in approximately the same range.

Basse-Normandie (English **Lower Normandy**) coastal region of northwest France lying between Haute-Normandie and Brittany (Bretagne). It includes the *départements* of Calvados, Manche, and Orne; area 17,600 sq km/6,794 sq mi; population (1999 est) 1,422,200. Its administrative centre is ▷Caen. Apart from stock farming, dairy farming, and textiles, the area produces apples, cider, and Calvados apple brandy. Tourism is important.

basset any of several breeds of hound with a long low body and long pendulous ears, of a type originally bred in France for hunting hares by scent.

Basse-Terre one of two main islands of the French overseas *département* of Guadeloupe in the Leeward Islands, West Indies; area 848 sq km/327 sq mi; population (1995 est) 169,000. A narrow stretch of water, the Rivière Salée, divides it from Grande-Terre, the other main island. It has an active volcano, Grande Soufrière, rising to 1,484 m/4,870 ft.

Basseterre capital and port of St Kitts and Nevis, in the Leeward Islands; population (1990 est) 15,000. Industries include data processing, rum, clothes, and electrical components.

basset horn musical woodwind instrument, a wide-bore alto clarinet pitched in F, invented about 1765 and used by Mozart in his *Masonic Funeral Music* (1785), for example, and by Richard Strauss. It was revived in 1981 by Karlheinz Stockhausen and features prominently as a solo in his opera cycle *LICHT*. Performers include Alan Hacker and Suzanne Stephens.

bassoon double-reed woodwind instrument in C, the bass of the oboe family. It doubles back on itself in a tube about 2.5 m/7.5 ft long and has a rich and deep tone. The bassoon concert repertoire extends from the early baroque via Vivaldi, Mozart, and Dukas to Stockhausen.

Bass Strait sea channel separating the mainland of Australia from Tasmania. The strait is 322 km/200 mi long, with an average width of 255 km/158 mi. Oil was discovered here in 1965 and first extracted in 1969. The region now has 18 oil and gas fields.

Bastia (Italian *bastiglia* 'fortress') port and commercial centre on the northeast coast of Corsica, France, administrative centre of the *département* of Haute-Corse, 96 km/60 mi northeast of Ajaccio; population (1990) 52,390. Industries include the manufacture of processed foods. Founded in 1380 by the Genoese, who built a fortress to protect it, Bastia was the capital of Corsica until 1791. The town has several fine churches, notably San Giovanni Battiste with its classical facades.

Bastille castle of St Antoine, built about 1370 as part of the fortifications of Paris. It was made a state prison by Cardinal ▷Richelieu and was stormed by the mob that set the French Revolution in motion on 14 July 1789. Only seven prisoners were found in the castle when it was stormed; the governor and most of the garrison were killed, and the Bastille was razed.

bat any mammal of the order Chiroptera, related to the Insectivora (hedgehogs and shrews), but differing from them in being able to fly. Bats are the only true flying mammals. Their forelimbs are developed as wings capable of rapid and sustained flight. There are two main groups of bats: **megabats**, which eat fruit, and **microbats**, which mainly eat insects. Many microbats rely largely on ▷echolocation for navigation and finding prey, sending out pulses of high-pitched sound and listening for the echo.

Bats are nocturnal, and those native to temperate countries hibernate in winter. There are about 977 species forming the order Chiroptera, making this the second-largest mammalian order; bats make up nearly one-quarter of the world's mammals. Although bats are widely distributed, populations have declined alarmingly and many species are now endangered.

Megabats The Megachiroptera live in the tropical regions of the Old World, Australia, and the Pacific, and feed on fruit, nectar, and pollen. The hind feet have five toes with sharp hooked claws from which the animal suspends, head downwards, when resting. There are 162 species of Megachiroptera. Relatively large, weighing up to 900 g/2 lb and with a wingspan as great as 1.5 m/5 ft, they have large eyes and a long face, earning them the name 'flying fox'. Most orient by sight.

Many rainforest trees depend on bats for pollination and seed dispersal, and around 300 bat-dependent plant species yield more than 450 economically valuable products. Some bats are keystone species on whose survival whole ecosystems may depend. Bat-pollinated flowers tend to smell of garlic, rotting vegetation, or fungus.

Microbats Most bats are Microchiroptera: small and insect-eating. Some eat fish as well as insects; others consume small rodents, frogs, lizards, or birds; a few, ▷vampire bats, feed on the blood of mammals. A single bat may eat 3,000 insects in one night. There are about 750 species. They roost in caves, crevices, and hollow trees. The bumblebee bat, inhabiting Southeast Asian rainforests, is the smallest mammal in the world. A new species of bat, *Rhinolophus convexus*, was discovered in Malaysia, at an altitude of 1,600 m in the Cameron Highlands, in 1997. It is related to the tropical horseshoe bats.

Many microbats have poor sight and orientation and hunt their prey principally by echolocation. They have relatively large ears and many have nose-leaves, fleshy appendages around the nose and mouth, that probably help in sending or receiving the signals, which are squeaks pitched so high as to be inaudible to the human ear.

Ancestors The difference in the two bat groups is so marked that many biologists believed that they must have had different ancestors: microbats descending from insectivores and megabats descending from primates. However, analysis of the proteins in blood serum from megabats and primates by German biologists in 1994 showed enough similarities to suggest a close taxonomic relationship between the two groups. In 2000 Japanese researchers analysing mitochondrial DNA concluded that megabats and microbats do share a common origin. They proposed that the bat order evolved 83 million years ago, and that the two groups diverged around 58 million years ago.

Biology A bat's wings consist of a thin hairless skin expansion, stretched between the four fingers of the hand, from the last finger down to the hindlimb, and from the hindlimb to the tail. The thumb is free and has a sharp claw to help in climbing. The shoulder girdle and breastbone are large, the latter being keeled, and the pelvic girdle is small. The bones of the limbs are hollow, other bones are slight, and the ribs are flattened.

An adult female bat usually rears only one pup a year, which she carries with her during flight. In species that hibernate, mating may take place before hibernation, the female storing the sperm in the genital tract throughout the winter and using it to fertilize her egg on awakening in spring.

In Britain, there are about 12 species of bat belonging to the families Rhinolophidae (the horseshoe bats, with nose-leaves) and Vespertilionidae (small bats, about 6 cm/2½ in long, with plain noses). Since 1981 bats have been protected by law in Britain.

Related Web site: Bat Conservation International http://www.batcon.org/

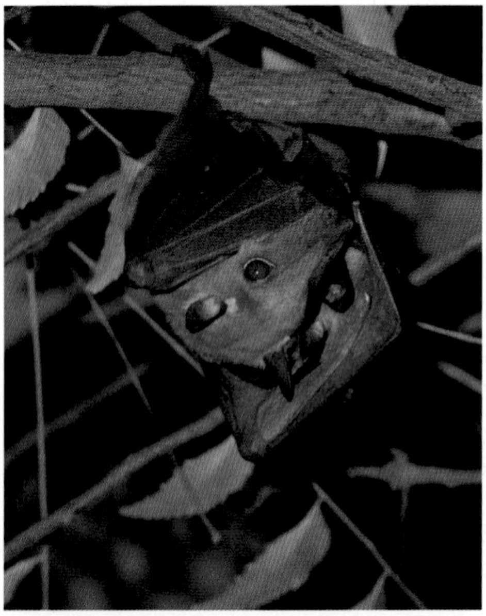

BAT The Gambian epauletted bat *Epomophorus gambianus* is a common species in West Africa. A young bat is visible tucked under the wing of one of the females pictured.
Premaphotos Wildlife

Bataan peninsula in Luzon, the Philippines, which was defended against the Japanese in World War II by US and Filipino troops under Gen MacArthur from 1 January to 9 April 1942. MacArthur was evacuated, but some 67,000 Allied prisoners died on the **Bataan Death March** to camps in the interior.

Batak several distinct but related peoples of northern Sumatra in Indonesia. Numbering approximately 2.5 million, the Batak speak languages belonging to the Austronesian family.

batch processing in computing, system for processing data with little or no operator intervention. Batches of data are prepared in advance to be processed during regular 'runs' (for example, each night). This allows efficient use of the computer and is well suited to applications of a repetitive nature, such as a company payroll, or the production of utility bills.

bat-eared fox small African fox *Otocyon megalotis*, with huge ears, sandy or greyish coat, black legs, and black-tipped bushy tail. They measure about 80 cm/31.5 in in length, including tail, and are 30 cm/12 in at the shoulder; weight 3–5 kg/6.5–11 lb. Bat-eared foxes feed on insects, particularly termites. There are East African and South African subspecies.

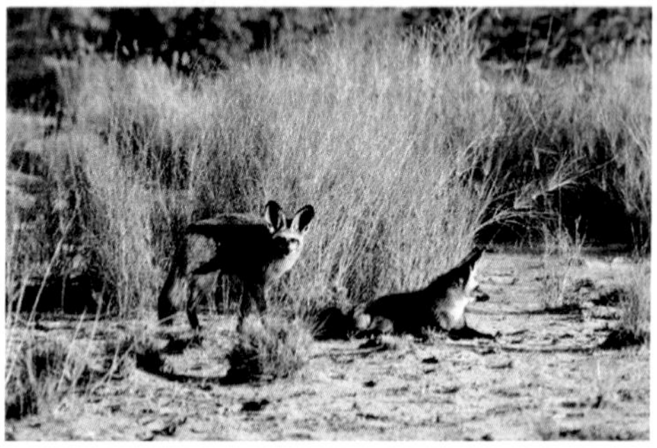

BAT-EARED FOX A pair of bat-eared foxes *Otocyon megalotis* in the Kalahari Desert, southern Africa.
K G Preston-Mafham/Premaphotos Wildlife

Bates, H(erbert) E(rnest) (1905–1974) English writer. Of his many novels and short stories, *The Jacaranda Tree* (1949) and *The Darling Buds of May* (1958) particularly demonstrate the fineness of his natural observation and compassionate portrayal of character. His work captures the feeling of life in the changing countryside of England in a simple, direct manner.

Bates was born in Rushden, Northamptonshire, and educated at Kettering Grammar School. He worked as a reporter and warehouse clerk before publishing *The Two Sisters* at the age of 21. From that time he published almost one book a year; in all about 30 novels and as many volumes of short stories. *Fair Stood the Wind for France* (1944) was based on his experience as a squadron leader in World War II, during which time he also wrote stories under the pseudonym Flying Officer X. His five novels featuring the Larkin family began with *The Darling Buds of May*, which was followed by *A Breath of French Air* (1959), *When the Green Woods Laugh* (1960), *Oh! To be in England* (1963), and *A Little of What You Fancy* (1970). The novels were filmed as a television series in the 1990s.

His other novels include *The Fallow Land* (1932), *A House of Women* (1936), *The Purple Plain* (1947), *Love for Lydia* (1952), and *The Feast of July* (1954). His collections of short stories include *The Woman Who Had Imagination* (1934), *The Flying Goat* (1939), *The Beauty of the Dead* (1940), *My Uncle Silas* (1940), *The Bride Comes to Evensford* (1949), and *The Four Beauties* (1968).

Bates, H(enry) W(alter) (1825–1892) English naturalist and explorer. He spent 11 years collecting animals and plants in South America and identified 8,000 new species of insects. He made a special study of ▷camouflage in animals, and his observation of insect imitation of species that are unpleasant to predators is known as 'Batesian mimicry'.

Bates eyesight training method developed by US ophthalmologist William Bates (1860–1931) to enable people to correct problems of vision without wearing glasses. The method is of proven effectiveness in relieving all refractive conditions, correcting squints, lazy eyes, and similar problems, but does not claim to treat eye disease.

Bath historic city and administrative headquarters of ▷Bath and North East Somerset unitary authority, southwest England, 171 km/106 mi west of London; population (1991 est) 78,700. Industries include printing, plastics, engineering, and tourism.

Bath was the site of the Roman town of Aquae Sulis, and in the 18th century flourished as a fashionable spa, with the only naturally occurring hot mineral springs in Britain. Although the baths were closed to the public in 1977, a Millennium Spa Project, due to open in summer 2002, is intended to bring back public bathing to Bath's hot springs.

Features The remains of the Roman baths and adjacent temple are among the finest Roman remains in Britain. The Gothic Bath Abbey has an unusually decorated west front and fine fan-vaulting. The city has much 18th-century architecture, including Queen Square (1736) and the Circus (1754), designed by John Wood the Elder; the Assembly Rooms (1771) and the Royal Crescent (1775) were designed by the younger John Wood. The Bath Festival Orchestra is based here and the University of Bath was established in 1966. The city of Bath is a World Heritage site.

History The Roman town of Aquae Sulis ('waters of Sul' – the British goddess of wisdom) was established in the first 20 years after the Roman invasion of AD 43. In medieval times the springs were crown property, administered by the church, but the city was transformed in the 18th century to a fashionable spa, presided over by the Welsh dandy 'Beau' Nash.

Economy Tourism and retail are the growth industries in Bath. In 1999 there were 5,224 people employed in positions directly relating to tourism, with an additional 1,412 employed indirectly. The total value of tourism (excluding regional shoppers) to Bath in 1999 was estimated to be £184.1 million.

Bath and North East Somerset
unitary authority in southwest England created in 1996 from part of the former county of Avon.

area 351 sq km/136 sq mi towns and cities ▷Bath (administrative headquarters), Keynsham, Chew Magna, Paulton, Radstock, Peasedown St John, Midsomer Norton features River Avon and tributaries; Chew Valley Lake; Beckford's Tower (Bath) built in 1827 for William Beckford; Roman baths with hot springs (Bath); Regency architecture including Royal Crescent, The Circus, and Assembly Rooms designed by John Wood (1700–1854) and his son John Wood; Pulteney Bridge, 18th century shop-lined Italianate bridge designed by Robert Adam; Stanton Drew bronze age stone circles including second largest in Great Britain. industries tourism, central government administration, clothing manufacture population (1996) 158,700 famous people Thomas Bowdler, John Wood

batholith
large, irregular, deep-seated mass of intrusive ▷igneous rock, usually granite, with an exposed surface of more than 100 sq km/40 sq mi. The mass forms by the intrusion or upswelling of magma (molten rock) through the surrounding rock. Batholiths form the core of some large mountain ranges like the Sierra Nevada of western North America.

Bath, Order of the
British order of knighthood (see ▷knighthood, orders of), believed to have been founded in 1399 by Henry IV. The order now consists of three classes: Knights of the Grand Cross (GCB), Knights Commanders (KCB), and Knights Companions (CB).

Báthory, Stephen
(1533–1586) King of Poland, elected by a diet convened in 1575 and crowned in 1576. Báthory succeeded in driving the Russian troops of Ivan the Terrible out of his country. His military successes brought potential conflicts with Sweden, but he died before these developed.

batik
Javanese technique of dyeing fabrics in which areas to be left undyed are sealed with wax. Practised throughout Indonesia, the craft was introduced to the West by Dutch traders.

Batista (y Zaldívar), Fulgencio
(1901–1973) Cuban right-wing dictator, dictator-president 1934–44 and 1952–59. Having led the September 1933 coup to install Ramón Grau San Martín in power, he forced Grau's resignation in 1934 to become Cuba's effective ruler, as formal president from 1940. Exiled in the USA 1944–49, he ousted President Carlos Prío Socarrás in a military coup in 1952. His authoritarian methods enabled him to jail his opponents and amass a large personal fortune. He was overthrown by rebel forces led by Fidel ▷Castro in 1959. Batista fled to the Dominican Republic and later to Portugal. He died in Spain.

Baton Rouge
deep-water port on the Mississippi River, USA, the capital of ▷Louisiana; population (2000 est) 227,800. Industries include oil refining, petrochemicals, and iron; the port has become one of the largest in the country.

Battersea
district of the inner London borough of Wandsworth, London, England; on the south bank of the Thames. It has a park (including a funfair 1951–74), Battersea Dogs' Home (opened 1860) for strays, and is the site of Battersea Power Station (designed by Giles Gilbert Scott in 1937, with an art deco interior), which closed in 1983. In August 2000, detailed planning consent for conversion of the power station to a leisure and entertainment

complex was granted to developers, and work is scheduled to begin in 2001.

battery
any energy-storage device allowing release of electricity on demand. It is made up of one or more electrical ▷cells. Primary-cell batteries are disposable; secondary-cell batteries, or ▷accumulators, are rechargeable. Primary-cell batteries are an extremely uneconomical form of energy, since they produce only 2% of the power used in their manufacture. It is dangerous to try to recharge a primary-cell battery.

The first electric battery (and current) was produced by an Italian, Alessandro Volta, who tested various combinations of metals connected by salt solution. Volta had seen Luigi Galvani's experiment with a dead frog after accidentally discovering that he could make its leg twitch by touching it with two different metals.

Batumi
(or Batum) Black Sea port and capital of the autonomous republic of Adjaria, in southwestern Georgia. Key industries include oil refining and manufacture of clothing and pharmaceuticals. Batumi receives its crude oil via a pipeline running from the oilfields at Baku in Azerbaijan. Tea and citrus fruits are grown in the region around the city.

baud
in engineering, a unit of electrical signalling speed equal to one pulse per second, measuring the rate at which signals are sent between electronic devices such as telegraphs and computers.

Bauds were used as a measure to identify the speed of ▷modems until the early 1990s because at the lower modem speeds available then the baud rate generally equalled the rate of transmission measured in bps (bits per second). At higher speeds, this is not the case, and modem speeds now are generally quoted in bps.

Baudelaire, Charles Pierre
(1821–1867) French poet. His immensely influential work combined rhythmical and musical perfection with a morbid romanticism and eroticism, finding beauty in decadence and evil. His first and best-known book of verse was *Les Fleurs du mal/Flowers of Evil* (1857). He was one of the main figures in the development of ▷Symbolism.

Related Web site: Baudelaire, Charles http://www.geocities.com/Paris/Metro/1301/

Baudouin
(1930–1993) King of the Belgians 1951–93. In 1950 his father, ▷Leopold III, abdicated and Baudouin was known until his succession in 1951 as *Le Prince Royal*. During his reign he succeeded in holding together a country divided by religion and language, while presiding over the dismemberment of Belgium's imperial past. In 1960 he married Fabiola de Mora y Aragón (1928–), member of a Spanish noble family. They were unable to have any children, and he was succeeded by his brother, Albert, in 1993.

Bauhaus
German school of art and design founded in 1919 in Weimar by the architect Walter ▷Gropius in an attempt to fuse art, design, architecture, and crafts into a unified whole. In 1925, under political pressure, it moved to Dessau (where it was housed in a

CHARLES BAUDELAIRE A portrait of the French poet Charles Baudelaire, by Etienne Carjat. *The Art Archive/ Eileen Tweedy*

building designed by Gropius), and in 1932 it made another forced move to Berlin, where it was closed by the Nazis the following year. In spite of its short life and troubled existence, the Bauhaus is regarded as the most important art school of the 20th century, and it exercised a huge influence on the world of design and methods of art education. The teachers at the school included some of the outstanding artists of the time, among them the painters Paul Klee and Wassily Kandinsky and the architect Ludwig Mies van der Rohe.

Baum, L(yman) Frank
(1856–1919) US writer. He was the author of the children's fantasy *The Wonderful Wizard of Oz* (1900) and its 13 sequels. The series was continued by another author after his death. The film *The Wizard of Oz* (1939) with Judy ▷Garland became a US classic.

bauxite
principal ore of ▷aluminium, consisting of a mixture of hydrated aluminium oxides and hydroxides, generally contaminated with compounds of iron, which give it a red colour. It is formed by the ▷chemical weathering of rocks in tropical climates. Chief producers of bauxite are Australia, Guinea, Jamaica, Russia, Kazakhstan, Suriname, and Brazil.

Bavaria
(German *Bayern*) administrative region (German *Land*) in southeast Germany; bordered on the west by Hesse and Baden Württemberg, on the north by Thuringia and Saxony, on the northeast by the Czech Republic, and on the south and southeast by Austria; area 70,600 sq km/27,252 sq mi; population (1999 est) 12,155,000. Bavaria is the largest of the German *Länder*. The capital is ▷Munich; main cities and towns are Nuremberg, Augsburg, Würzburg, Regensburg, Passau, Fürth, and Ingolstadt. Bavaria's main industries are electronics, electrical engineering, optics, automobile assembly, aerospace, brewing, chemicals, plastics, oil

FULGENCIO BATISTA This photograph of the former dictator-president of Cuba, Fulgencio Batista was taken in 1959, after the Castro-led rebellion had ousted Batista on 1 January of that year. *Archive Photos*

BAUXITE The conveyor belt at a bauxite mine in Australia. Bauxite (the chief ore of aluminium) is so called because it was first discovered at Les Baux, in France. *Image Bank*

refining, textiles, and glass. In the agricultural sector the main products are wheat, rye, barley, oats, potatoes, and sugar beet; there is also livestock farming, forestry, and wine growing.

Related Web site: Bavaria Online http://www.bavaria.com/

Bax, Arnold Edward Trevor (1883–1953) English composer. His works, often based on Celtic legends, include seven symphonies, *The Garden of Fand* (1913–16), and *Tintagel* (1917–19) (both tone poems). He was Master of the King's Musick 1942–53.

bay any of various species of ▷laurel tree. The aromatic evergreen leaves are used for flavouring in cookery. There is also a golden-leaved variety. (Genus *Laurus*, family Lauraceae.)

Bayern German name for ▷Bavaria, a region of Germany.

Bayeux town in the *département* of Calvados, northern France, on the River Aure, 27 km/17 mi northwest of Caen; population (1990) 14,700. The town has an agricultural market, and industries include the production of pottery, lace, and processed foods. Its museum houses the 11th-century ▷Bayeux Tapestry. There is a 13th-century Gothic cathedral.

Bayeux Tapestry linen hanging made about 1067–70 that gives a vivid pictorial record of the invasion of England by William I (the Conqueror) in 1066. It is an embroidery rather than a true tapestry, sewn with woollen threads in blue, green, red, and yellow, 70 m/231 ft long and 50 cm/20 in wide, and containing 72 separate scenes with descriptive wording in Latin. It is exhibited at the museum of Bayeux in Normandy, France.

Bayliss, William Maddock (1860–1924) English physiologist who discovered the digestive hormone secretin, the first hormone to be found, with Ernest Starling in 1902. During World War I, Bayliss introduced the use of saline (salt water) injections to help the injured recover from ▷shock. He was knighted in 1922.

bayonet short sword attached to the muzzle of a firearm. The bayonet was placed inside the barrel of the muzzleloading muskets of the late 17th century. The **sock** or ring bayonet, invented in 1700, allowed a weapon to be fired without interruption, leading to the demise of the pike.

Bayonne river port in the French *département* of Pyrénées-Atlantique in southwest France, situated at the confluence of the Adour and Nive rivers, 5 km/3 mi from the sea; population (1990) 41,800. Historically a centre for the making of swords and knives, the town claims the invention of the bayonet. Bayonne is a centre of ▷Basque culture, and lies in an important tourist area. Industries include the manufacture of leather, fertilizers, steel, and aircraft. It also has distilleries and ham-curing factories, and trades in timber.

Bayreuth town in Bavaria, south Germany, on the Red Main River, 65 km/40 mi northeast of Nuremberg; population (1995) 72,700. There are cotton textile, porcelain, cigarette, and optical industries. Bayreuth was the home of the composer Richard Wagner, and the Wagner theatre was established in 1876 as a performing centre for his operas. Opera festivals are held here every summer.

Bazalgette, Joseph William (1819–1890) British civil engineer who, as chief engineer to the London Board of Works, designed London's sewer system, a total of 155 km/83 mi of sewers, covering an area of 256 sq km/100 sq mi. It was completed in 1865.

BBC abbreviation for ▷British Broadcasting Corporation.

BC in the Christian calendar, abbreviation for **before Christ**, used with dates.

BCG abbreviation for **bacille Calmette-Guérin**, bacillus injected as a vaccine to confer active immunity to ▷tuberculosis (TB).

beach strip of land bordering the sea, normally consisting of boulders and pebbles on exposed coasts or ▷sand on sheltered coasts. It is usually defined by the high- and low-water marks. A berm, a ridge of sand and pebbles, may be found at the farthest point that the water reaches.

Beach Boys, the US pop group. Their first hit was 'Surfin' USA' (1963); this was followed by 'I Get Around' (1964), and 'California Girls' (1965).

The band was formed in Los Angeles in 1961 by the brothers Brian, Carl, and Dennis Wilson. They began as exponents of vocal-harmony surf music with Chuck Berry guitar riffs, but the compositions, arrangements, and production by Brian Wilson became highly complex under the influence of psychedelic rock, as in 'Good Vibrations' (1966) and the album *Pet Sounds* (1966).

Related Web site: Beach Boys Web Sounds http://www.personal. u-net.com/~pcworld5/index.htm

Beachy Head (French *beau chef*, 'beautiful head') chalk headland on the south coast of England, between Seaford and Eastbourne in East Sussex. Rising to 163 m/535 ft, it is the eastern end of the South Downs. The lighthouse at the foot of the cliff is 38 m/125 ft high.

Beaconsfield title taken by Benjamin ▷Disraeli, prime minister of Britain in 1868 and 1874–80.

beagle short-haired hound with pendant ears, sickle tail, and a bell-like voice for hunting hares on foot ('beagling').

Beagle Channel channel to the south of Tierra del Fuego, South America, named after the ship of Charles ▷Darwin's voyage. Three islands at its eastern end, with krill and oil reserves within their 322 km/200 mi territorial waters, and the dependent sector of the Antarctic with its resources, were disputed between Argentina and Chile and awarded to Chile in 1985.

beak horn-covered projecting jaws of a bird (see ▷bill), or other horny jaws such as those of the octopus, platypus, or tortoise.

Beaker people prehistoric people thought to have been of Iberian origin, who spread out over Europe from the 3rd millennium BC. They were skilled in metalworking, and are associated with distinctive earthenware drinking vessels with various designs, in particular, a type of beaker with a bell-shaped profile, widely distributed throughout Europe.

bean seed of a large number of leguminous plants (see ▷legume). Beans are rich in nitrogen compounds and proteins and are grown both for human consumption and as food for cattle and

BEAN The green snap bean harvest in Wisconsin, USA. *Image Bank*

horses. Varieties of bean are grown throughout Europe, the USA, South America, China, Japan, Southeast Asia, and Australia.

Related Web site: Beans http://www.ext.vt.edu/pubs/envirohort/ 426-402/426-402.html

bear in business, a speculator who sells stocks or shares on the stock exchange expecting a fall in the price in order to buy them back at a profit, the opposite of a ▷bull.

In a bear market, prices fall, and bears prosper.

bear large mammal with a heavily built body, short powerful limbs, and a very short tail. Bears breed once a year, producing one to four cubs. In northern regions they hibernate, and the young are born in the winter den. They are found mainly in North America and northern Asia. The skin of the polar bear is black to conserve 80–90% of the solar energy trapped and channelled down the hollow hairs of its fur.

Bears walk on the soles of the feet and have long, nonretractable claws. The bear family, Ursidae, is related to carnivores such as dogs and weasels, and all are capable of killing prey. (The panda is probably related to both bears and raccoons.)

Species There are seven species of bear. The **brown bear** *Ursus arctos* formerly ranged across most of Europe, northern Asia, and North America, but is now reduced in number. It varies in size from under 2 m/7 ft long in parts of the Old World to 2.8 m/9 ft long and 780 kg/1,700 lb in Alaska. The **grizzly bear** is a North American variety of this species, and another subspecies, the **Kodiak bear** of Alaska, is the largest living land carnivore.

The white **polar bear** *Thalarctos maritimus* is up to 2.5 m/8 ft long, has furry undersides to the feet, and feeds mainly on seals. It is found in the north polar region. The North American **black bear** *Euarctos americanus* and the **Asian black bear** *Selenarctos thibetanus* are smaller, only about 1.6 m/5 ft long. The latter has a white V-mark on its chest.

The **spectacled bear** *Tremarctos ornatus* of the Andes is similarly sized, as is the **sloth bear** *Melursus ursinus* of India and Sri Lanka, which has a shaggy coat and uses its claws and protrusile lips to obtain termites, one of its preferred foods. The smallest bear is the Malaysian **sun bear** *Helarctos malayanus*, rarely more than 1.2 m/4 ft long, a good climber, whose favourite food is honey.

Threat of extinction Of the seven species of bear, five are currently reckoned to be endangered and all apart from the polar bear and the American black bear are in decline. The population of brown bears in the Pyrenees was estimated at eight in 1994, and it was feared they would be extinct in 20 years unless new bears are introduced. In May 1996 two female Slovenian brown bears were released into the central Pyrenees; the Slovenian brown bear is closest genetically to the Pyrenean one. In 1998 the bear population in the Pyrenees totalled six.

In 1992, American black bears were upgraded to Appendix 2 of CITES (Convention on International Trade in Endangered Species) to stem the trade in their gall bladders, which are used in Asian

BAYEUX TAPESTRY A replica of the Bayeux Tapestry, one of the earliest examples of European embroidery. *The Art Archive/ Eileen Tweedy*

BEAR Grizzly bears *Ursus arctos* will hunt for fish in rivers or lakes. They can grow up to 2.5 m/8.3 ft in length. *Corel*

Beat Generation (or Beat movement) US social and literary movement of the 1950s and early 1960s. Members of the Beat Generation, called beatniks, responded to the conformist materialism of the period by adopting lifestyles derived from Henry David Thoreau's social disobedience and Walt Whitman's poetry of the open road. The most influential writers were Jack ▷Kerouac (who is credited with coining the term), Allen ▷Ginsberg, and William ▷Burroughs.

Related Web site: Beat Generation http://www.charm.net/~brooklyn/Topics/BeatGen.html

beatification in the Catholic Church, the first step towards ▷canonization. Persons who have been beatified can be prayed to, and the title 'Blessed' can be put before their names.

Beatitudes in the New Testament, the sayings of Jesus reported in Matthew 5: 3–11 and Luke 6: 20–22, depicting the spiritual qualities that characterize members of the Kingdom of God.

Beatles, the English pop group 1960–70. The members, all born in Liverpool, were John ▷Lennon (1940–1980, rhythm guitar, vocals), Paul ▷McCartney (1942–, bass, vocals), George Harrison (1943–2001, lead guitar, vocals), and Ringo Starr (formerly Richard Starkey, 1940–, drums). Using songs written largely by Lennon and McCartney, the Beatles dominated rock music and pop culture in the 1960s.

The Beatles gained early experience in Liverpool and Hamburg, West Germany. They had a top-30 hit with their first record, 'Love Me Do' (1962), followed by 'Please Please Me' which reached number one. Every subsequent single and album released until 1967 reached number one in the UK charts.

At the peak of Beatlemania they starred in two films, *A Hard Day's Night* (1964) and *Help!* (1965), and provided songs for the animated film *Yellow Submarine* (1968). Their ballad 'Yesterday' (1965) was covered by 1,186 different performers in the first ten years. The album *Sgt Pepper's Lonely Hearts Club Band* (1967), recorded on two four-track machines, anticipated subsequent technological developments.

The Beatles were the first British group to challenge the US dominance of rock and roll, and continued to influence popular music beyond their break-up in 1970. Of the 30 songs most frequently broadcast in the USA between 1955 and 1991, 13 were written by members of the Beatles. They pursued separate careers with varying success. George Harrison's biggest hit, 'My Sweet Lord' (1970), fell victim to a plagiarism suit. His album *Cloud Nine* (1987) was particularly well received, and in 1988 he became a member of the Traveling Wilburys, a group that also includes Bob Dylan. Ringo Starr has appeared in a number of films, released an album, *Ringo* (1973), and later formed his All-Starr band.

Related Web site: Internet Beatles Album http://www.getback.org/

beat music pop music that evolved in the UK in the early 1960s, known in its purest form as ▷Mersey beat, and as British Invasion in the USA. The beat groups characteristically had a simple, guitar-dominated line-up, vocal harmonies, and catchy tunes. They included the Beatles (1960–70), the Hollies (1962–), and the Zombies (1962–67).

Beaton, Cecil Walter Hardy (1904–1980) English photographer. His elegant and sophisticated fashion pictures and society portraits often employed exotic props and settings. He adopted a more simple style for his wartime photographs of bomb-damaged London. He also worked as a stage and film designer, notably for the musicals *Gigi* (1959) and *My Fair Lady* (1965). He was knighted in 1972.

Beatrix, (Wilhelmina Armgard) (1938–) Queen of the Netherlands. The eldest daughter of Queen ▷Juliana, she succeeded to the throne on her mother's abdication in 1980. In 1966 she married West German diplomat Claus von Amsberg, who was created Prince of the Netherlands. Her heir is Prince Willem Alexander.

Beatty, David (1871–1936) 1st Earl Beatty. British admiral in World War I. He commanded the cruiser squadron 1912–16 and bore the brunt of the Battle of ▷Jutland in 1916.

Beaufort, Francis (1774–1857) British admiral, hydrographer to the Royal Navy from 1829; the Beaufort scale and the Beaufort Sea in the Arctic Ocean are named after him. Made Knight Commander of the Bath (KCB) in 1848.

Beaufort, Henry (1375–1447) English politician and cleric. As chancellor of England, he supported his half-brother ▷Henry IV and made enormous personal loans to Henry V to finance war against France. As a guardian of Henry VI during his minority, from 1421 he was in effective control of the country until 1426. In the same year he was created a cardinal.

Beaufort scale system of recording wind velocity, devised by Francis Beaufort in 1806. It is a numerical scale ranging from 0 to 17, calm being indicated by 0 and a hurricane by 12; 13–17 indicate degrees of hurricane force.

In 1874 the scale received international recognition; it was modified in 1926. Measurements are made at 10 m/33 ft above ground level.

Beaufort Sea section of the Arctic Ocean off Alaska and Canada, named after the British admiral Francis ▷Beaufort. Oil drilling is allowed only in the winter months because the sea is the breeding and migration route of bowhead whales, the staple diet of the local Inuit people.

Beaumarchais, Pierre Augustin Caron de (1732–1799) French dramatist. His great comedies, *Le Barbier de Seville/The Barber of Seville* (1775) and *Le Mariage de Figaro/The Marriage of Figaro* (1778, but prohibited until 1784), form the basis of operas by ▷Rossini and ▷Mozart, with their blend of social criticism and sharp humour.

Beaumont, Francis (1584–1616) English dramatist and poet. From about 1606 to 1613 he collaborated with John ▷Fletcher. Their joint plays include the tragicomedies *Philaster* (1610), *A King and No King* (c. 1611), and *The Maid's Tragedy* (c. 1611). *The Woman Hater* (about c. 1606) and *The Knight of the Burning Pestle* (c. 1607), which is a satire on the audience, are ascribed to Beaumont alone.

> ### Francis Beaumont and John Fletcher
> *Death hath so many doors to let out life.*
> The Customs of the Country

Beaune city in the *département* of Côte-d'Or, France, 35 km/22 mi southwest of Dijon; population (1990) 22,100. It is the centre of the Burgundy wine trade, and has a wine museum, the Musée du Vin de Bourgogne. Industries include the production of agricultural equipment, casks, oil, white metal, and mustard. Notable buildings in the town include two 12th-century churches and a hospital, St Etienne, founded in 1443.

Beauregard, Pierre Gustave Toutant (1818–1893) US military leader and Confederate general. Opening fire on ▷Fort Sumter, South Carolina, he started the American Civil War in 1861. His military successes were clouded by his conflicts with Confederate president Jefferson Davis.

Beauvais (Latin Bellovacum or Caesaromagus) administrative centre of the Oise *département* in the ▷Picardy region of north-central France, situated 76 km/47 mi northwest of Paris at the confluence of the Thérain and Avelon rivers; population (1999 est) 57,400. It is a trading centre for fruit, dairy produce, and agricultural machinery. Beauvais is the seat of a bishopric, has the tallest Gothic cathedral in France (St Pierre, 68 m/223 ft), and was renowned for tapestries. The town centre suffered serious bomb damage in 1940, and was rebuilt in a modern style.

> ### Simone de Beauvoir
> *One is not born a woman. One becomes one.*
> The Second Sex

Beauvoir, Simone de (1908–1986) French socialist, feminist, and writer. She played a large role in French intellectual life from the 1940s to the 1980s. Her book *Le Deuxième Sexe/The Second Sex* (1949), one of the first major feminist texts, is an encyclopedic study of the role of women in society, drawing on literature, myth, and history. In this work she argues that the subservient position of women is the result of their systematic repression by a male-dominated society that denies their independence, identity, and sexuality.

She also published novels, including *Les Mandarins/The Mandarins* (1954; winner of the Prix Goncourt), and many autobiographical volumes. She taught philosophy at the University of Paris 1931–43 and was a lifelong companion of the philosopher

traditional medicine to treat liver disease. The gall bladders contain an active substance, ursodiol, which is tapped through surgically-implanted tubes. Although an inexpensive synthetic version of ursodiol is available, in 1995 there were at least 10,000 bears being kept in farms in China for their gall bladders, for which many people still prefer to pay thousands of dollars. Trade in Asian black bears and their parts is illegal.

The brown bear is thought to have become extinct in Britain around AD 900. Its elimination was caused by loss of habitat (it requires a very large area of undisturbed woodland) but was also related to its highly territorial habit; brown bears return repeatedly to fruits and berries within their home territory, making them an easy prey for hunters.

bearberry any of a group of evergreen trailing shrubs belonging to the heath family, found in high and rocky places. Most bearberries are North American but *Arctostaphylos uva-ursi* is also found in Asia and Europe in northern mountainous regions. It has small pink flowers in spring, followed by red berries that are dry but edible. (Genus *Arctostaphylos*, family Ericaceae.)

Beardsley, Aubrey Vincent (1872–1898) English illustrator and leading member of the ▷Aesthetic Movement. His meticulously executed black-and-white drawings show the influence of Japanese prints and French rococo, and also display the sinuous line, asymmetry, and decorative mannerisms of art nouveau. His work was often charged with being grotesque and decadent. He became known through *The Yellow Book* magazine, for which he was the art editor, and through his drawings for Oscar Wilde's *Salome* (1893). He became a Roman Catholic in 1897. He died of tuberculosis.

Bear, Great and Little common names (and translations of the Latin) for the constellations ▷Ursa Major and ▷Ursa Minor respectively.

bearing device used in a machine to allow free movement between two parts, typically the rotation of a shaft in a housing. **Ball bearings** consist of two rings, one fixed to a housing, one to the rotating shaft. Between them is a set, or race, of steel balls. They are widely used to support shafts, as in the spindle in the hub of a bicycle wheel.

bearing the direction of a fixed point, or the path of a moving object, from a point of observation on the Earth's surface, expressed as an angle from the north. Bearings are taken by ▷compass and are measured in degrees (°), given as three-digit numbers increasing clockwise. For instance, north is 000°, northeast is 045°, south is 180°, and southwest is 225°.

True north differs slightly from magnetic north (the direction in which a compass needle points), hence northeast may be denoted as 045M or 045T, depending on whether the reference line is magnetic (M) or true (T) north. True north also differs slightly from grid north since it is impossible to show a spherical Earth on a flat map.

beat frequency in musical acoustics, fluctuation produced when two notes of nearly equal pitch or ▷frequency are heard together. Beats result from the ▷interference between the sound waves of the notes. The frequency of the beats equals the difference in frequency of the notes.

Musicians use the effect when tuning their instruments. A similar effect can occur in electrical circuits when two alternating currents are present, producing regular variations in the overall current.

Jean-Paul ▷Sartre; *La Cérémonie des Adieux/Adieux: A Farewell to Sartre* (1981) gives an intimate insight into their relationship.

Related Web site: Beauvoir, Simone de http://people.delphi.com/gkemerling/ph/beav.htm

beaver aquatic rodent with webbed hind feet, a broad flat scaly tail, and thick waterproof fur. It has very large incisor teeth and fells trees to feed on the bark and to use the logs to construct the 'lodge', in which the young are reared, food is stored, and much of the winter is spent. There are two species, the Canadian *Castor canadensis* and the European *C. fiber*. They grow up to 1.4 m/4.6 ft in length and weigh about 20 kg/44 lb.

Beavers are monogamous and a pair will produce a litter of twins each year. Their territory consists of about 3 km/2 mi of river. Beavers can construct dams on streams, and thus modify the environment considerably; beaver ponds act as traps for minerals and provide fertile living conditions for other species – zooplankton biomass may be 1,000 times greater within a beaver pond than elsewhere. Beavers once ranged across Europe, northern Asia, and North America, but in Europe now only survive where they are protected, and are reduced elsewhere, partly through trapping for their fur.

Beavers became extinct in Britain in *c.* 1550. It was highly prized for its meat, its fur, and for secretions from its glands which were used for medicinal purposes, and was over-hunted. Victorian naturalists tried and failed to reintroduce it, and a colony released on the Isle of Bute in 1875 grew to 27 before dying out in *c.* 1890. Beavers are to be reintroduced into Scotland in early 2001. A seven-year pilot project was given the go-ahead in April 2000 by the Scottish Natural Heritage. The first release will comprise 12 animals, and will represent the first native animals to be reintroduced to Britain.

Beaverbrook, (William) Max(well) Aitken, 1st Baron Beaverbrook (1879–1964) Canadian-born British financier, newspaper proprietor, and politician. He bought a majority interest in the *Daily Express* in 1919, founded the *Sunday Express* in 1921, and bought the London *Evening Standard* in 1923. He served in David Lloyd George's World War I cabinet and Winston Churchill's World War II cabinet. He received a knighthood in 1911 and was made a baronet in 1916.

Having made a fortune in cement in Canada, he entered British politics, first in support of Andrew Bonar Law, then of Lloyd George, becoming minister of information 1918–19. In World War II he was minister of supply 1940–41.

Between the wars he used his newspapers, in particular the *Daily Express*, to campaign for empire free trade, against Prime Minister Stanley Baldwin. Later he opposed British entry to the European Economic Community (EEC).

Beaverbrook was born in Maple, Ontario, the son of an immigrant Presbyterian minister. After studying law at the University of New Brunswick he became a life insurance salesman, going on to deal in bonds, and then made a fortune out of a controversial merger of three companies into the Canadian Cement Company. He resigned from the Conservative Party in 1949 and his newspapers became politically independent. His other memoirs include *Politicians and the Press* (1925), *Men and Power: 1917–18* (1936), and *The Decline and Fall of Lloyd George* (1963).

bebop (or **bop**) hot jazz style, rhythmically complex, virtuosic, and highly improvisational. It was developed in New York in the 1940s and 1950s by Charlie Parker, Dizzy Gillespie, Thelonius Monk, and other black musicians reacting against swing music.

Bechet, Sidney Joseph (1897–1959) US jazz musician. He played clarinet and was the first to forge an individual style on soprano saxophone. Bechet was based in Paris in the late 1920s and the 1950s, where he was recognized by classical musicians as a serious artist.

Bechuanaland former name (to 1966) of ▷Botswana.

Becker, Boris (1967–) German tennis player. In 1985, at the age of 17, he became the youngest winner of a singles title at Wimbledon. He won the title three times and helped West Germany to win the Davis Cup in 1988 and 1989. He also won the US Open in 1989 and the Grand Prix Masters/ATP Tour World Championship in 1992.

Related Web site: Boris Becker Profile http://www.sportsline.com/u/tennis/players/Becker.htm

Becket, St Thomas à (1118–1170) English archbishop and politician. He was chancellor to Henry II from 1155 to 1162, when he was appointed Archbishop of Canterbury. The interests of the Roman Catholic medieval church soon conflicted with those of the crown and Becket was assassinated; he was canonized in 1172.

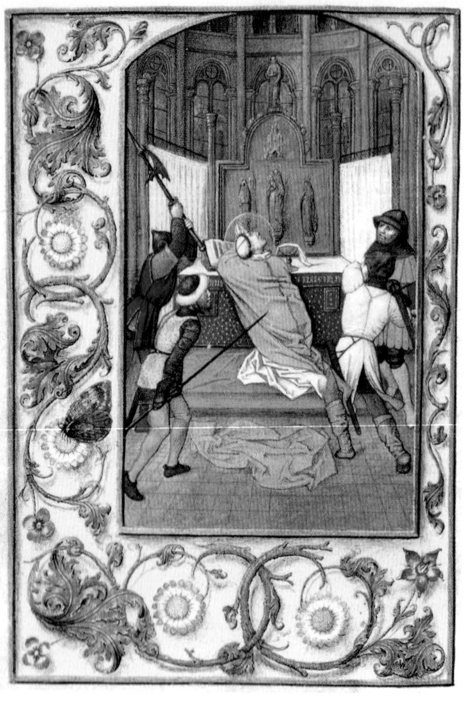

ST THOMAS À BECKET A medieval, illustrated-manuscript page depicting the murder of Thomas à Becket. *The Art Archive/British Library/British Library*

A friend of Henry II, Becket was a loyal chancellor, but on becoming archbishop of Canterbury he changed his lifestyle and fiercely defended the rights of the church. In 1164 he opposed Henry's attempt to increase the power of the crown over the church courts, and had to flee the country; he returned in 1170, but the reconciliation soon broke down. Some historians suggest that Becket consciously engineered his own martyrdom. Encouraged by a hasty outburst from the king, who shouted out angrily: "Who will rid me of this turbulent priest?", four knights burst into Canterbury Cathedral and murdered Becket in front of the altar, the last blow taking off the crown of his head and scattering his brains over the floor. His death ended Henry's attempt to dominate the church; in 1174 the king had to do penance for the murder, walking barefoot through Canterbury, and allowing the monks to whip him. Becket was declared a saint, and his shrine became the busiest centre of ▷pilgrimage in England until the Reformation. His martyrdom was the subject of T S Eliot's play *Murder in the Cathedral* (1935).

Related Web site: Murder of Thomas Becket, 1170 http://www.ibiscom.com/becket.htm#TOP

> **Bede**
> *. . . as if, when you are sitting at dinner with your chiefs and ministers in wintertime . . . a sparrow from outside flew quickly through the hall . . . having come out of the winter it returns to the winter. Man's life appears like this: of what came before, and what follows, we are ignorant.*
> *Ecclesiastical History of the English People* early 8th century

> **Samuel Beckett**
> *To find a form that accommodates the mess, that is the task of the artist now.*
> Quoted in Bair, *Samuel Beckett, a Biography* ch. 21

Beckett, Samuel Barclay (1906–1989) Irish dramatist, novelist, and poet, who wrote in both French and English. His play *En attendant Godot* – first performed in Paris in 1952, and then in his own translation as *Waiting for Godot* in London in 1955 and New York in 1956 – and his later dramas, such as *Fin de partie/Endgame* (1957–58) and *Happy Days* (1961), won him international acclaim. He was awarded the Nobel Prize for Literature in 1969. As well as paring character to the grimmest essentials, Beckett honed his prose with meticulous precision to a painful articulateness, scrupulously cautious of redundancy. Composition in French, before translating into English, helped towards this distillation of style.

Related Web site: Samuel Beckett End Page http://beckett.english.ucsb.edu/

Beckham, David Robert Joseph (1975–) English footballer. A midfielder with great passing ability, he was a member of the highly succesful Manchester United sides in the late 1990s and early 2000s, and also played for Real Madrid; he was regarded as one of the world's best players. He helped Manchester United to win the FA Premier League in the 1995–96, 1996–97, 1998–99, and 1999–2000 seasons, and also won an FA Cup-winner's medal with Manchester United in 1996 and 1999. By 18 September 2000 he had made 35 international appearances for England. He became captain of England in November 2000. In 1999 he married Victoria Adams.

Beckmann, Max (1884–1950) German expressionist painter and graphic artist. He was influenced both by medieval art and by the *Neue Sachlichkeit* movement and after World War I his art concentrated on themes of cruelty in human society, as in *Night* (1918–19; Kunstsammlung Nardrheim-Westfalen, Düsseldorf).

becquerel SI unit (symbol Bq) of ▷radioactivity, equal to one radioactive disintegration (change in the nucleus of an atom when a particle or ray is given off) per second.

The becquerel is much smaller than the previous standard unit, the curie (3.7×10^{10} Bq). It is named after French physicist Henri Becquerel.

Becquerel, (Antoine) Henri (1852–1908) French physicist. He was awarded the Nobel Prize for Physics in 1903 for his discovery of penetrating radiation coming from uranium salts, the first indication of spontaneous ▷radioactivity. He shared the award with Marie and Pierre ▷Curie.

Related Web site: Biography of A H Becquerel http://www.nobel.se/physics/laureates/1903/becquerel-bio.html

bed in geology, a single ▷sedimentary rock unit with a distinct set of physical characteristics or contained fossils, readily distinguishable from those of beds above and below. Well-defined partings called bedding planes separate successive beds or strata.

The depth of a bed can vary from a fraction of a centimetre to several metres or yards, and can extend over any area. The term is also used to indicate the floor beneath a body of water (lake bed) and a layer formed by a fall of particles (ash bed).

bedbug flattened wingless red-brown insect *Cimex lectularius* with piercing mouthparts. Bed bugs live in bedlinen crevices during the day and feed on human blood at night. They lay their eggs in the crevices and these hatch in a few days into nymphs (miniature versions of the adults) that take ten weeks and five skin moults to reach adult size. Adults can live for several years if undisturbed.

Bede (*c.* 673–735) English theologian and historian, known as the Venerable Bede. Active in Durham and Northumbria, he wrote many scientific, theological, and historical works. His *Historia Ecclesiastica Gentis Anglorum* (*Ecclesiastical History of the English People*) of 731 is a primary source for early English history, and was translated into the vernacular by King Alfred.

Born at Monkwearmouth, Durham, Bede entered the local monastery at the age of seven, later transferring to Jarrow, where he became a priest in about 703. He devoted his life to writing and teaching; among his pupils was Egbert, archbishop of York. He was canonized in 1899. Much of our knowledge of England in the Dark Ages prior to the 8th century depends on Bede's historical works and his painstaking efforts to research and validate original sources, both documentary and oral testimony. He popularized the system of dating events from the birth of Christ.

Bedford town and administrative headquarters of ▷Bedfordshire, southern England, on the River Ouse, about 80 km/50 mi north of London; population (1991 est) 73,900. Industries include light engineering, food-processing, aircraft services, and the manufacture of agricultural machinery, diesel engines, pumps, bricks, communications systems, and electronic components. The writer John ▷Bunyan is said to have written part of *The Pilgrim's Progress* (1678) while imprisoned in the town.

Bedfordshire county of south central England (since April 1997 Luton has been a separate unitary authority).

area 1,192 sq km/460 sq mi **towns and cities** ▷Bedford (administrative headquarters), Dunstable **physical** the Great Ouse River and its tributary, the Ivel; the county is low lying with the Chiltern Hills in the southwest **features** Whipsnade Wild Animal Park, near Dunstable (200 ha/494 acres), belonging to the London Zoological Society; Woburn Abbey, seat of the duke of Bedford; Cranfield Institute of Technology **agriculture** cereals (especially wheat and barley); vegetables **industries** agricultural machinery; cement manufacture (using local chalk); clay; electrical goods; gravel; motor vehicles and parts; packaging; sand; brickworks at Stewartby **population** (1996) 548,800 **famous people** John Bunyan, John Howard, Joseph Paxton

BEDLAM A scene from Hogarth's *A Rake's Progress* (1735), set in Bedlam, London's main hospital for the insane at the time. Sightseers, such as the two women in the background, could pay to look at the inmates chained up in their cells. *Philip Sauvain Picture Collection*

Bedlam popular name for Bethlem Royal Hospital, the earliest mental hospital in Europe. The Priory of St Mary of Bethlehem was founded in Bishopsgate, London, in 1247 and was used as a hospice by the 14th century. It has been sited in West Wickham, Kent, since 1930. It is now used as a slang word meaning chaos.

Bedlington breed of ▷terrier with a short body, long legs, and curly hair, usually grey, named after a district of Northumberland, England.

Bedouin (Arabic 'desert dweller') member of any of the nomadic, Arabic-speaking peoples occupying the desert regions of Arabia and North Africa. Originating in Arabia, they spread to Syria and Mesopotamia, and later to Egypt and Tunisia.

bee four-winged insect of the superfamily Apoidea in the order Hymenoptera, usually with a sting. There are over 12,000 species, of which fewer than 1 in 20 are social in habit. The **hive bee** or **honeybee** *Apis mellifera* establishes perennial colonies of about 80,000, the majority being infertile females (workers), with a few larger fertile males (drones), and a single very large fertile female (the queen). Worker bees live for no more than a few weeks, while a drone may live a few months, and a queen several years. Queen honeybees lay two kinds of eggs: fertilized, female eggs, which have two sets of chromosomes and develop into workers or queens, and unfertilized, male eggs, which have only one set of chromosomes and develop into drones.

Bees transmit information to each other about food sources by 'dances', each movement giving rise to sound impulses which are

BEE The multiple storey box hive shown here was invented by Moses Quinby of New York, USA, who also invented the smoker used to pacify the bees. *Image Bank*

picked up by tiny hairs on the back of the bee's head, the orientation of the dance also having significance. They use the Sun in navigation (see ▷migration) in their navigation. Besides their use in crop pollination and production of honey and wax, bees (by a measure of contaminants brought back to their hives) can provide an inexpensive and effective monitor of industrial and other pollution of the atmosphere and soil.

The most familiar species is the ▷bumblebee, genus *Bombus*, which is larger and stronger than the hive bee and so is adapted to fertilize plants in which the pollen and nectar lie deep, as in red clover; they can work in colder weather than the hive bee.

Social bees, apart from the bumblebee and the hive bee, include the stingless South American **vulture bee** *Trigona hypogea*, discovered in 1982, which is solely carnivorous.

Solitary bees include species useful in pollinating orchards in spring, and may make their nests in tunnels under the ground or in hollow plant stems; 'cuckoo' bees lay their eggs in the nests of bumblebees, which they closely resemble.

The killer bees of South America are a hybrid type, created when an African subspecies of honeybee escaped from a research establishment in Brazil in 1957. They mated with, and supplanted, the honeybees of European origin in most of South and Central America, and by 1990 had spread as far north as Texas, USA. As well as being more productive and resistant to disease than European honeybees, they also defend their hives more aggressively, in larger numbers, and for a greater length of time than other honeybees. However, their stings are no more venomous, and although they have killed hundreds of thousands of animals and probably more than 1,000 people, most individuals survive an attack, and almost all deaths have occurred where the victim has somehow been prevented from fleeing.

Most bees are passive unless disturbed, but some species are aggressive. One bee sting may be fatal to a person who is allergic to them, but this is comparatively rare (about 1.5% of the population), and most adults can survive 300–500 stings without treatment. A vaccine treatment against bee stings, which uses concentrated venom (melitin), has been developed.

Britain saw its first outbreak of the bee disease varroasis in 1992. It is spread by mites. By 1998, 25% of Britain's 250 native species of bee were classified as threatened.

beech one of several European hardwood trees or related trees growing in Australasia and South America. The common beech (*Fagus sylvaticus*), found in European forests, has a smooth grey trunk and edible nuts, or 'mast', which are used as animal feed or processed for oil. The timber is used in furniture. (Genera *Fagus* and *Nothofagus*, family Fagaceae.)

Related Web site: Beech http://www.botanical.com/botanical/mgmh/b/beech-27.html

Beecham, Thomas (1879–1961) English conductor and impresario. He established the Royal Philharmonic Orchestra in 1946 and fostered the works of composers such as Delius, Sibelius, and Richard Strauss. He was knighted and succeeded to the baronetcy in 1916.

Beecher, Harriet unmarried name of US author Harriet Beecher ▷Stowe who wrote *Uncle Tom's Cabin*.

Beecher, Henry Ward (1813–1887) US Congregational minister and militant opponent of slavery, son of the pulpit orator Lyman ▷Beecher and brother of the writer Harriet Beecher ▷Stowe.

Beecher, Lyman (1775–1863) US Congregational and Presbyterian minister, one of the most popular pulpit orators of his time. He was the father of Harriet Beecher ▷Stowe and Henry Ward Beecher.

bee-eater brightly-coloured bird *Merops apiaster*, family Meropidae, order Coraciiformes, found in Africa, southern Europe, and Asia. Bee-eaters are slender, with chestnut, yellow, and blue-green plumage, a long bill and pointed wings, and a flight like that of the swallow, which they resemble in shape. They feed on bees, wasps, and other insects, and nest in colonies in holes dug out with their long bills in sandy river banks.

The European bee-eater migrates from Africa, where it also breeds, to southern and central Europe. It is a rare visitor to the UK.

Beelzebub (Hebrew 'lord of the flies') in the New Testament, the leader of the devils, sometimes identified with Satan

and sometimes with his chief assistant (see ▷devil). In the Old Testament Beelzebub was a fertility god worshipped by the Philistines and other Semitic groups (▷Baal).

Beerbohm, (Henry) Max(imilian) (1872–1956) English caricaturist and author. A perfectionist in style, he contributed to *The Yellow Book* (1894); wrote a novel of Oxford undergraduate life, *Zuleika Dobson* (1911); and published volumes of caricature, including *Rossetti and His Circle* (1922). He succeeded George Bernard Shaw as critic to the *Saturday Review* in 1898.

Beersheba (Arabic *Bir-es-Saba*, 'seven wells') industrial city in the south of Israel, 80 km/50 mi from Jerusalem; population (1997) 160,364. It is the chief centre of the Negev Desert and has been a settlement from the Stone Age.

beet any of several plants belonging to the goosefoot family, used as food crops. One variety of the common beet (*Beta vulgaris*) is used to produce sugar and another, the mangelwurzel, is grown as a cattle feed. The beetroot, or red beet (*B. rubra*), is a salad plant. (Genus *Beta*, family Chenopodiaceae.)

Beethoven, Ludwig van (1770–1827) German composer and pianist. His mastery of musical expression in every genre made him the dominant influence on 19th-century music. Beethoven's repertoire includes concert overtures; the opera *Fidelio* (1805, revised 1806 and 1814); 5 piano concertos and 2 for violin (one unfinished); 32 piano sonatas, including the *Moonlight* (1801) and *Appassionata* (1804–05); 17 string quartets; the Mass in D (*Missa solemnis*) (1819–22); and 9 symphonies, as well as many youthful works. He usually played his own piano pieces and conducted his orchestral works until he was hampered by deafness in 1801; nevertheless he continued to compose.

Born in Bonn, the son and grandson of musicians in the service of the Elector of Cologne in Bonn, Beethoven became deputy organist at the court of the Elector of Cologne at Bonn before he was 12; later he studied under Haydn and possibly Mozart, whose influence dominated his early work. From 1808 he received a small allowance from aristocratic patrons.

Beethoven's career spanned the transition from classicism to Romanticism. He was aware of the problems his music created for listeners and performers alike (part of the slow movement of the Choral Symphony had to be cut at its premiere), but although contemporary audiences found his visionary late music difficult, Beethoven's reputation was well established throughout Europe.

Of his symphonies the best known are the Third (*Eroica*) (1803), originally intended to be dedicated to Napoleon, with whom Beethoven became disillusioned, the Fifth (1807–08), the Sixth (*Pastoral*) (1808), and the Ninth (*Choral*) (1817–24), which includes the passage from Schiller's 'Ode to Joy' chosen as the anthem of Europe.

Related Web site: Beethoven, Ludwig http://www.geocities.com/Paris/3486/beetfi.html

beetle common name of insects in the order Coleoptera (Greek 'sheath-winged') with leathery forewings folding down in a protective sheath over the membranous hindwings, which are those used for flight. They pass through a complete metamorphosis. They include some of the largest and smallest

BEETLE The *Tragocephala juncunda* is a Madagascan member of the family Cerambycidae, which contains some of the most striking of all beetles. The antennae are usually long, especially in the males, giving rise to the common name of longhorn beetles. Most cerambycid larvae develop within timber. *Premaphotos Wildlife*

of all insects: the largest is the **Hercules beetle** *Dynastes hercules* of the South American rainforests, 15 cm/6 in long; the smallest is only 0.05 cm/0.02 in long. Comprising more than 50% of the animal kingdom, beetles number some 370,000 named species, with many not yet described.

Beetles are found in almost every land and freshwater habitat, and feed on almost anything edible. Examples include **click beetle** or **skipjack** species of the family Elateridae, so called because if they fall on their backs they right themselves with a jump and a loud click; the larvae, known as **wireworms**, feed on the roots of crops. In some tropical species of Elateridae the beetles have luminous organs between the head and abdomen and are known as **fireflies**. The potato pest **Colorado beetle** *Leptinotarsa decemlineata* is striped in black and yellow. The **blister beetle** *Lytta vesicatoriaf*, a shiny green species from southern Europe, was once sold pulverized as an aphrodisiac and contains the toxin cantharidin. The larvae of the **furniture beetle** *Anobium punctatum* and the **deathwatch beetle** *Xestobium rufovillosum* and their relatives are serious pests of structural timbers and furniture (see ▷woodworm).

Related Web site: Beetles http://www.ent.iastate.edu/imagegal/coleoptera/

Begin, Menachem (1913–1992) Israeli politician. He was leader of the extremist Irgun Zvai Leumi organization in Palestine from 1942 and prime minister of Israel 1977–83, as head of the right-wing Likud party. Following strong encouragement from US president Jimmy ▷Carter, he entered into negotiations with President Anwar ▷Sadat of Egypt, which resulted in the Camp David Agreements. He shared the Nobel Prize for Peace in 1978 with Anwar Sadat for their efforts towards the Israel-Egypt peace treaty of 1979. In 1981 Begin won a new term of office but his health was failing. The death of his wife in 1982 was a grave blow, resulting in his retirement in September 1983. For the rest of his life he was a virtual recluse.

Begin was born in Brest-Litovsk, Russia (now Brest, in Belarus), studied law in Warsaw, and fled to the USSR in 1939. As leader of the Irgun group, he was responsible in 1946 for a bomb attack at the King David Hotel, Jerusalem, which killed over 100 people.

Related Web site: Begin, Menachem http://www.nobel.se/peace/laureates/1978/begin-bio.html

begonia any of a group of tropical and subtropical plants. They have fleshy and succulent leaves, and some have large, brilliant flowers. There are numerous species in the tropics, especially in South America and India. (Genus *Begonia*, family Begoniaceae.)

Behan, Brendan Francis (1923–1964) Irish writer and dramatist, born in Dublin and educated by the Christian Brothers until the age of 14. Behan's extended family included many talented musicians and writers as well as Republican activists. An important figure of both controversy and literary brilliance, Behan is best known for his autobiography *Borstal Boy* (1958), based on his experiences of prison and knowledge of the workings of the ▷IRA. These themes are revisited in his play *The Quare Fellow* (1954), and tragicomedy *The Hostage* (1958), first written in Gaelic as *An Giall*. Behan's other output included poetry in Gaelic, radio plays, and some late volumes of reminiscence and anecdote, notably *Brendan Behan's New York* (1964).

Brendan Behan
There's no such thing as bad publicity except your own obituary.
Remark quoted in Dominic Behan *My Brother Brendan*

behaviourism school of psychology originating in the USA, of which the leading exponent was John B ▷Watson.

Behaviourists maintain that all human activity can ultimately be explained in terms of conditioned reactions or reflexes and habits formed in consequence. Leading behaviourists include Ivan ▷Pavlov and B F ▷Skinner.

behaviour therapy in psychology, the application of behavioural principles, derived from learning theories, to the treatment of clinical conditions such as ▷phobias, ▷obsessions, and sexual and interpersonal problems.

behemoth (Hebrew 'beasts') in the Old Testament (Job 40), an animal cited by God as evidence of his power; usually thought to refer to the hippopotamus. It is used proverbially to mean any giant and powerful creature.

Behn, Aphra (1640–1689) English novelist and dramatist. She was the first woman in England to earn her living as a writer. Her works were criticized for their explicitness; they frequently present events from a woman's point of view. Her novel *Oroonoko* (1688), based on her visit to Suriname, is an attack on slavery.

Between 1670 and 1687 fifteen of her plays were produced, including *The Forced Marriage* (1670) and *The Rover* (1677). As in *The Lucky Chance* (1686), condemnation of forced and mercenary marriages was a recurring theme in her work. She had the patronage of James I and was employed as a government spy in Holland in 1666.

Related Web site: Aphra Behn Page http://lit-arts.com/rmn/behn/index-ab.htm

Behrens, Peter (1868–1940) German architect. A pioneer of the ▷Modern Movement and of the adaptation of architecture to industry. He designed the AEG turbine factory in Berlin (1909), a landmark in industrial architecture, and taught Le Corbusier, Walter Gropius, and Mies van der Rohe.

Behring, Emil (Adolph von) (1854–1917) German physician who was awarded the first Nobel Prize for Physiology or Medicine, in 1901, for his discovery that the body produces antitoxins, substances able to counteract poisons released by bacteria. Using this knowledge, he developed new treatments for diseases such as ▷diphtheria.

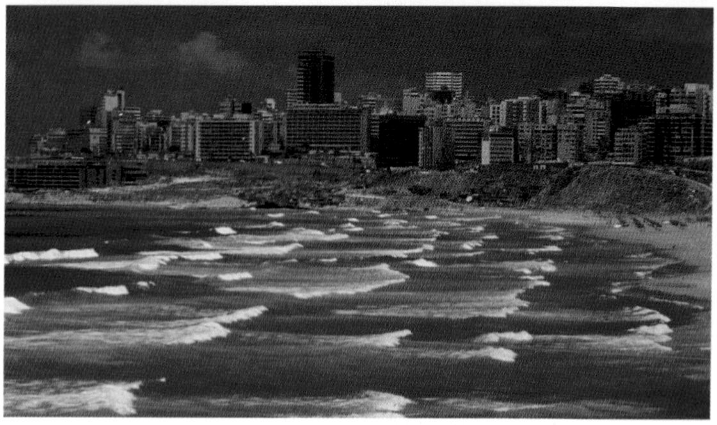

BEIRUT Beirut was once the Lebanese centre of trade in the Mediterranean Sea. The city was crippled by the civil wars of the 1970s and 1980s, and the business district was destroyed. *Image Bank*

Beiderbecke, Bix (Leon Bismarck) (1903–1931) US jazz cornetist, composer, and pianist. A romantic soloist with the bands of King Oliver, Louis Armstrong, and Paul Whiteman, Beiderbecke was the first acknowledged white jazz innovator. He was influenced by the classical composers Debussy, Ravel, and Stravinsky.

His reputation grew after his early death with the publication of Dorothy Baker's novel *Young Man with a Horn* (1938), based on his life.

Related Web site: Bix Beiderbecke Resources http://ms.cc.sunysb.edu/~alhaim/index.html

Beijing (or Peking; 'northern capital') capital of ▷China; parts of the northeast municipal boundary coincide with sections of the ▷Great Wall of China; population (1994) 7,084,000. The municipality of Beijing has an area of 17,800 sq km/6,871 sq mi and a population (1996) of 12,590,000. Industries include engineering and the production of steel, vehicles, textiles, and petrochemicals.

Features Tiananmen Gate (Gate of Heavenly Peace) and Tiananmen Square (in 1989 the site of student protest violently suppressed by the army) ; the Forbidden City (the Imperial Palace known as the **Gu Gong**), built between 1406 and 1420 by the Ming emperor Yong Le; the Great Hall of the People (1959), seat of the National People's Congress; the Museum of China's History and Revolution; the Chairman Mao Memorial Hall (1977); the Summer Palace built by the Empress Dowager Ci Xi (damaged by European powers in 1900, but restored in 1903 and after 1949); the Old Summer Palace (original Summer Palace destroyed by French and British troops during the Second Opium War, 1856–60); the Temple of Heaven (Tiantan); and the Ming tombs 50 km/30 mi to the northwest.

History Records of earliest settlements date back to 1000 BC. Beijing developed substantially as the 13th-century capital (known as **Dadu**) of the Mongol emperor Kublai Khan. During the Ming dynasty (1368–1644) the capital was moved to Nanjing for 35 years, and Beijing was renamed **Beiping** (Northern Peace). It was called Beijing (Northern Capital) when it became capital again from 1421.

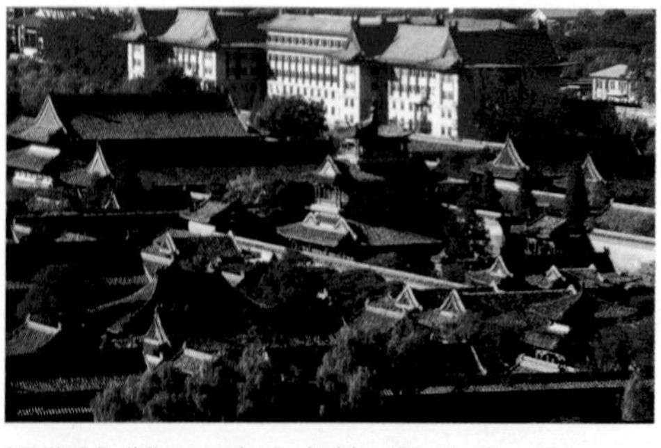

BEIJING Buildings in the Forbidden City, Beijing, China. Built in 1406–20 as the palace for emperors of the Ming dynasty, the walled city contains many temples, halls, palace rooms, and living-quarters. Now open to the public, it was once forbidden for an ordinary person to enter the palaces. *Image Bank*

In 1928 the nationalist Guomindang returned the capital to Nanjing and gave Beijing its former name of Beiping. It was held by Japan from 1937 to 1945. In 1949 the new communist government shifted the capital back to the city and renamed it Beijing.

Related Web site: Beijing Pages http://www.flashpaper.com/beijing/

Beirut (or Beyrouth) capital and port of ▷Lebanon, 90 km/60 mi northwest of Damascus, situated on a promontory into the eastern Mediterranean with the Lebanon Mountains behind it; population (1993) 1,200,000. It was devastated by civil war in the 1970s and 1980s. The city dates back to at least 1400 BC.

Recent history Before the civil war of 1975–90, Beirut was an international financial and educational centre, with four universities (Lebanese, Arab, French, and US); it was also a centre of espionage. Subsequent struggles for power among Christian and Muslim factions caused widespread destruction. From July to September 1982 the city was besieged and sections virtually destroyed by the Israeli army to enforce the withdrawal of the forces of the Palestinian Liberation Organization (PLO). After the ceasefire, 500 Palestinians were massacred in the Sabra–Shatila camps on 16–18 September 1982 by dissident ▷Phalangist and ▷Maronite troops, with alleged Israeli complicity. Civil disturbances continued, characterized by sporadic street fighting and hostage taking. In 1987 Syrian troops entered the city and have remained. Intensive fighting broke out between Christian and Syrian troops in Beirut, and by 1990 the strength of Syrian military forces in greater Beirut and east Lebanon was estimated at 42,000. In October 1990 President Elias Hwari formally invited Syrian troops to remove the Maronite Christian leader General Michel Aoun from his east Beirut stronghold; the troops then went on to dismantle the 'Green Line' separating Muslim western and Christian eastern Beirut. The Syrian-backed 'Greater Beirut Security Plan' was subsequently implemented by the Lebanese government, enforcing the withdrawal of all militias from greater Beirut. A controversial plan for the complete reconstruction of central Beirut, put forward by the Lebanese Prime Minister Rafiq al Hariri, is now being implemented.

Bejaia (French **Bougie**) port in Algeria, 193 km/120 mi east of Algiers; population (1998 est) 165,800. The town lies on the edge of a fertile plain, with an annual rainfall of 1,000 mm/40 in at the mouth of the Wadi Soummam and near Mount Gouraya (660 m/2,165 ft). Trade includes exports in wood, hides, iron ore, phosphates, tobacco, hydrocarbons, and liqueurs. Bejaia dates from Roman times, and has also been controlled by pirates, by the Spanish and by the Turks. It grew to greater importance from 1833 after French occupation, and especially after the improvement of the harbour between 1905 and 1909. The installation of the oil pipeline from Hassi Messaoud in 1959 brought a further boost to its prosperity as it became a major exporting port for Saharan oil, and exports now also include olive oil, wine and cork.

Bekaa, the (or El Beqa'a) valley in central Lebanon, situated between the Lebanon and Anti-Lebanon mountain ranges; length 130 km/80 mi, width 20 km/12 mi. It is also a governorate, its main population centres being the city of Zahle and the ancient town of ▷Baalbek. The Orontes and Litani rivers rise in the Bekaa. The southern part of the valley is particularly fertile with significant production of wheat, maize, cotton, fruit, and, in recent years, hashish and opium. Of strategic importance, the Bekaa was occupied by Syrian troops following the outbreak of the Lebanese civil war in the mid-1970s and has been a centre of operations for the radical Islamic Hezbollah organization.

Belarus (or **Byelorussia** or **Belorussia**) see country box.

Belau former name for the Republic of ▷Palau.

bel canto (Italian 'beautiful song') in music, an 18th-century Italian style of singing with emphasis on perfect technique and beautiful tone. The style reached its peak in the operas of Gioacchino ▷Rossini, Gaetano ▷Donizetti, and Vincenzo ▷Bellini.

Belém (or Belém do Pará) port and capital of Pará federal unit (state) in northern Brazil, on the River Pará near the mouth of the River Tocantins and River Amazon, 144 km/89 mi from the Atlantic; population (1991) 1,235,600 (metropolitan area 1,620,600). Belém lies just 161 km/100 mi south of the Equator, and is hot (mean temperature 27°C/80°F) and humid with a high rainfall. It is the chief trade and distribution centre of northern Brazil, and main exports include rubber, nuts, tropical hardwoods, and jute.

Belfast (Irish *Beal Feirste* 'the mouth of the Farset') city and industrial port in County Antrim and County Down, Northern Ireland, at the mouth of the River Lagan on Belfast Lough; county town of County ▷Antrim, and capital of Northern Ireland since 1920.

Population (2001 est) 257,400 (Protestants form the majority in east Belfast, Catholics in the west)

Industries Employment in Belfast is now heavily geared towards the public sector, which has replaced jobs lost in traditional local industries such as shipbuilding (although the Harland and Wolff shipyard is still active), textiles, and engineering. The Titanic was built here in 1912. The city is currently undergoing major redevelopment, both in terms of physical infrastructure (particularly along the River Lagan) and industrial investment, which is partly funded by the EU

Features City Hall (1906); Stormont (the former parliament buildings and from 1998 the seat of the Northern Ireland Assembly); Waterfront Hall, opened in 1997; the Linen Hall Library (1788); Belfast Castle (built 1870; former home of the Donegall family); Queen's University (1849, 1909); Botanic Gardens; Cave Hill Country Park; Ulster Museum.

History Belfast had a castle built in 1177 by the Anglo-Norman John de Courcy, but did not grow much until after 1603 when the land was granted to Sir Arthur Chichester who built a 'towne of good forme'; it was incorporated in 1613. With the settlement of English and Scots, Belfast became a centre of Irish Protestantism in the 17th century. An influx of Huguenots after 1685 extended the linen industry, and the 1800 Act of Union with England resulted in the promotion of Belfast as an industrial centre. It was created a city in 1888, with a lord mayor from 1892. During the 19th century, Belfast experienced significant immigration from surrounding rural counties, leading to an increase in the Catholic proportion of the population, to about 30% by 1850. By 1991, the Catholic proportion had reached 42%. Residential segregation of Catholics and Protestants continues to be marked. From 1968 onwards the city was heavily damaged by civil disturbances and terrorist activity until the first ceasefires in 1994.

Belfort administrative centre of the *département* of the Territoire de Belfort in the Franche-Comté region of northeast France, situated on the River Savoureuse, in the Trouée de Belfort (**Belfort Gap**), a 24 km/15 mi pass between the Vosges and Jura mountains; population (1990) 51,900. The town is the centre of a trade in wine and grain, and its industries include chemicals, engineering, plastics, and textiles.

Belarus

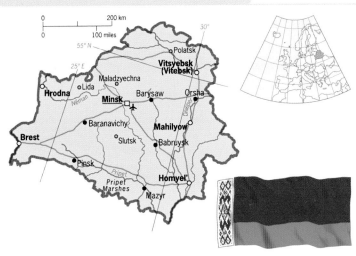

Belarus or Byelorussia or Belorussia country in east-central Europe, bounded south by Ukraine, east by Russia, west by Poland, and north by Latvia and Lithuania.

NATIONAL NAME *Respublika Belarus/Republic of Belarus*
AREA 207,600 sq km/80,154 sq mi
CAPITAL Minsk (Belorussian Mensk)
MAJOR TOWNS/CITIES Gomel, Vitsebsk, Mahilyow, Bobruisk, Hrodna, Brest
PHYSICAL FEATURES more than 25% forested; rivers Dvina, Dnieper and its tributaries, including the Pripet and Beresina; the Pripet Marshes in the east; mild and damp climate

Government

HEAD OF STATE Alexandr Lukashenko from 1994
HEAD OF GOVERNMENT Sjarhej Sidorski from 2003
POLITICAL SYSTEM authoritarian nationalist
POLITICAL EXECUTIVE unlimited presidency
ADMINISTRATIVE DIVISIONS six regions (oblasts)
ARMED FORCES 70,800 (2002 est)
DEATH PENALTY retained and used for ordinary crimes

Economy and resources

CURRENCY Belarus rouble, or zaichik
GPD (US$) 14.3 billion (2002 est)
REAL GDP GROWTH (% change on previous year) 4.1 (2001)
GNI (US$) 13.5 billion (2002 est)
GNI PER CAPITA (PPP) (US$) 5,330 (2002 est)
CONSUMER PRICE INFLATION 28.6% (2003 est)
UNEMPLOYMENT 2.9% (2000)
FOREIGN DEBT (US$) 929 million (2001 est)

MAJOR TRADING PARTNERS Russia, Ukraine, Kazakhstan, Germany, Poland, Latvia, Lithuania
RESOURCES petroleum, natural gas, peat, salt, coal, lignite
INDUSTRIES machine building, metalworking, electronics, chemicals, construction materials, food processing, textiles
EXPORTS machinery, petroleum and gas, chemicals and petrochemicals, iron and steel, light industrial goods, textiles. Principal market: Russia 53.7% (2001)
IMPORTS petroleum, natural gas, chemicals and rubber, machinery, processed foods, agricultural raw materials. Principal source: Russia 65% (2001)
ARABLE LAND 29.6% (2000 est)
AGRICULTURAL PRODUCTS potatoes, grain, sugar beet; livestock rearing (cattle and pigs) and dairy products. Livestock sector accounts for approximately 60% of agricultural output

Population and society

POPULATION 9,895,000 (2003 est)
POPULATION GROWTH RATE –0.4% (2000–15)
POPULATION DENSITY (per sq km) 48 (2003 est)
URBAN POPULATION (% of total) 70 (2003 est)
AGE DISTRIBUTION (% of total population) 0–14 17%, 15–59 64%, 60+ 19% (2002 est)

ETHNIC GROUPS 78% of Belorussian ('eastern Slav') descent, 13% ethnic Russian, 4% Polish, 3% Ukranian, 1% Jewish
LANGUAGE Belorussian (official), Russian, Polish
RELIGION 80% Eastern Orthodox; Baptist, Roman Catholic Muslim, and Jewish minorities
EDUCATION (compulsory years) 11
LITERACY RATE 99% (men); 99% (women) (2003 est)
LABOUR FORCE 17.4% agriculture, 34.7% industry, 47.9% services (1997)
LIFE EXPECTANCY 65 (men); 75 (women) (2000–05)
CHILD MORTALITY RATE (under 5, per 1,000 live births) 20 (2001)
PHYSICIANS (per 1,000 people) 4.4 (1998 est)
HOSPITAL BEDS (per 1,000 people) 12.2 (1998 est)
TV SETS (per 1,000 people) 342 (2001 est)
RADIOS (per 1,000 people) 199 (2001 est)
INTERNET USERS (per 10,000 people) 815.8 (2002 est)

Chronology

5th–8th centuries: Settled by East Slavic tribes, ancestors of present-day Belorussians.
11th century: Minsk was founded.
12th century: Part of Kievan Russia, to the south, with independent Belarus state developing around Polotsk, on River Dvina.
14th century: Incorporated within Slavonic Grand Duchy of Lithuania, to the west.
1569: Union with Poland.
late 18th century: Came under control of tsarist Russia as Belarussia ('White Russia'), following three partitions of Poland in 1772, 1793, and 1795.
1812: Minsk was destroyed by French emperor Napoleon Bonaparte during his campaign against Russia.
1839: The Belorussian Catholic Church was abolished.
1914–18: Belarus was the site of fierce fighting between Germany and Russia during World War I.
1918–19: Belarus was briefly independent from Russia.
1919–20: Wars between Poland and Soviet Russia over control of Belarus.
1921: West Belarus was ruled by Poland; East Belarus became a Soviet republic.
1930s: Agriculture was collectivized despite peasant resistance; over 100,000 people, chiefly writers and intellectuals, shot in mass executions ordered by the Soviet dictator Joseph Stalin.
1939: West Belarus was occupied by Soviet troops.
1941–44: The Nazi occupation resulted in the death of 1.3 million people, including many Jews; Minsk was destroyed.

1945: Belarus became a founding member of the United Nations (UN); much of West Belarus was incorporated into Soviet republic.
1950s–60s: Large-scale immigration of ethnic Russians and 'Russification'.
1986: Fallout from the nearby Chernobyl nuclear reactor in Ukraine rendered 20% of agricultural land unusable.
1989: The Belorussian Popular Front was established as national identity was revived under the *glasnost* initiative of Soviet leader Mikhail Gorbachev.
1990: Belorussian was established as the state language and republican sovereignty declared.
1991: Independence was recognized by the USA; the Commonwealth of Independent States (CIS) was formed in Minsk.
1996: An agreement on economic union was signed with Russia. Syargey Ling became prime minister.
1997: There were prodemocracy demonstrations.
1998: The Belarus rouble was devalued. A new left-wing and centrist political coalition was created. Food rationing was imposed as the economy deteriorated. Belarus signed a common policy with Russia on economic, foreign, and military matters.
2000: President Lukashenka dismissed Prime Minister Syargey Ling and named the Russian-born mayor of Minsk, Uladzimir Yarmoshyn as acting prime minister. Elections in October maintained Lukashenka in power, although foreign observers described the election as below international standards for fairness and opposition leaders led popular protests.

BELARUS In traditional Belorussian costumes, the colours red and white predominate; white is a reference to the name of the country, 'White Russia', and red symbolizes national freedom. *Stanley Gibbons*

Belgium

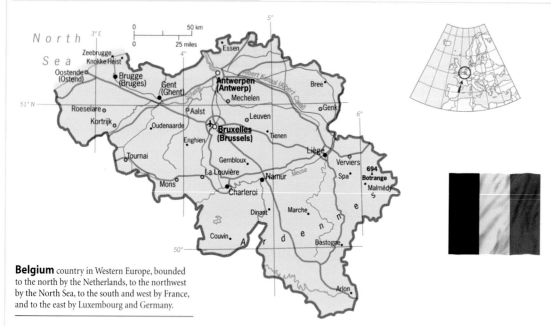

Belgium country in Western Europe, bounded to the north by the Netherlands, to the northwest by the North Sea, to the south and west by France, and to the east by Luxembourg and Germany.

NATIONAL NAME *Royaume de Belgique* (French), *Koninkrijk België* (Flemish)/*Kingdom of Belgium*
AREA 30,510 sq km/11,779 sq mi
CAPITAL Brussels
MAJOR TOWNS/CITIES Antwerp, Ghent, Liège, Charleroi, Bruges, Mons, Namur, Louvain
MAJOR PORTS Antwerp, Ostend, Zeebrugge
PHYSICAL FEATURES fertile coastal plain in northwest, central rolling hills rise eastwards, hills and forest in southeast; Ardennes Forest; rivers Schelde and Meuse

Government

HEAD OF STATE King Albert II from 1993
HEAD OF GOVERNMENT Guy Verhofstadt from 1999
POLITICAL SYSTEM liberal democracy
POLITICAL EXECUTIVE parliamentary
ADMINISTRATIVE DIVISIONS ten provinces within two regions, and the capital, Brussels
ARMED FORCES 39,200 (2002 est)
CONSCRIPTION military service is voluntary
DEATH PENALTY abolished in 1996
DEFENCE SPEND (% GDP) 1.3 (2002 est)
EDUCATION SPEND (% GDP) 5.9 (2000 est)
HEALTH SPEND (% GDP) 8.7 (2000 est)

Economy and resources

CURRENCY euro (Belgian franc until 2002)
GPD (US$) 247.6 billion (2002 est)
REAL GDP GROWTH (% change on previous year) 0.8 (2001)
GNI (US$) 239.9 billion (2002 est)
GNI PER CAPITA (PPP) (US$) 27,350 (2002 est)
CONSUMER PRICE INFLATION 1.6% (2003 est)
UNEMPLOYMENT 7.2% (2002)
MAJOR TRADING PARTNERS Germany, the Netherlands, France, UK, Belgium, Luxembourg, USA
RESOURCES coal, coke, natural gas, iron
INDUSTRIES wrought and finished steel, cast iron, sugar refining, glassware, chemicals and related products, beer, textiles, rubber and plastic products
EXPORTS food, livestock and livestock products, gem diamonds, iron and steel manufacturers, machinery and transport equipment, chemicals and related products. Principal market: France 17.6% (2000)
IMPORTS food and live animals, beverages and tobacco, machinery and transport equipment, precious metals and stones, mineral fuels and lubricants, chemicals and related products. Principal source: the Netherlands 17.5% (2000)
ARABLE LAND 24.8% (2000 est)
AGRICULTURAL PRODUCTS wheat, barley, potatoes, beet (sugar and fodder), fruit, tobacco; livestock (pigs and cattle) and dairy products

Population and society

POPULATION 10,318,000 (2003 est)
POPULATION GROWTH RATE 0.0% (2000–15)

POPULATION DENSITY (per sq km) 338 (2003 est)
URBAN POPULATION (% of total) 98 (2003 est)
AGE DISTRIBUTION (% of total population) 0–14 17%, 15–59 61%, 60+ 22% (2002 est)
ETHNIC GROUPS mainly Flemings in north, Walloons in south
LANGUAGE Flemish (a Dutch dialect, known as *Vlaams*; official) (spoken by 56%, mainly in Flanders, in the north), French (especially the dialect Walloon; official) (spoken by 32%, mainly in Wallonia, in the south), German (0.6%; mainly near the eastern border)
RELIGION Roman Catholic 75%, various Protestant denominations
EDUCATION (compulsory years) 12
LITERACY RATE 99% (men); 99% (women) (2003 est)
LABOUR FORCE 2.2% agriculture, 27.2% industry, 70.5% services (1998)
LIFE EXPECTANCY 76 (men); 82 (women) (2000–05)
CHILD MORTALITY RATE (under 5, per 1,000 live births) 6 (2001)
PHYSICIANS (per 1,000 people) 3.9 (1998 est)
HOSPITAL BEDS (per 1,000 people) 7.3 (1998 est)
TV SETS (per 1,000 people) 543 (2001 est)
RADIOS (per 1,000 people) 793 (1997)
INTERNET USERS (per 10,000 people) 3,286.3 (2002 est)
PERSONAL COMPUTER USERS (per 100 people) 24.2 (2002 est)

See also ▷Charlemagne; ▷Flanders; ▷Netherlands, The.

See also ▷Charlemagne; ▷Flanders; ▷Netherlands, The.

Chronology

57 BC: Romans conquered the Belgae (the indigenous Celtic people), and formed the province of Belgica.
3rd–4th centuries AD: The region was overrun by Franks and Saxons.
8th–9th centuries: Part of Frankish Empire; peace and order fostered growth of Ghent, Bruges, and Brussels.
843: Division of Holy Roman Empire; became part of Lotharingia, but frequent repartitioning followed.
10th–11th centuries: Several feudal states emerged: Flanders, Hainaut, Namur, Brabant, Limburg, and Luxembourg, all nominally subject to French king or Holy Roman Emperor, but in practice independent.
12th century: The economy began to flourish.
15th century: One by one, the states came under rule of the dukes of Burgundy.
1477: Passed into Habsburg dominions through the marriage of Mary of Burgundy to Maximilian, archduke of Austria.
1555: Division of Habsburg dominions; Low Countries allotted to Spain.
1648: Independence of Dutch Republic recognized; south retained by Spain.
1713: Treaty of Utrecht transferred Spanish Netherlands to Austrian rule.
1792–97: Austrian Netherlands invaded by revolutionary France and finally annexed.
1815: The Congress of Vienna reunited north and south Netherlands as one kingdom under the House of Orange.
1830: The largely French-speaking people in south rebelled against union with Holland and declared Belgian independence.
1831: Leopold of Saxe-Coburg-Gotha became the first king of Belgium.

1839: The Treaty of London recognized the independence of Belgium and guaranteed its neutrality.
1914–18: Belgium was invaded and occupied by Germany. Belgian forces under King Albert I fought in conjunction with the Allies.
1919: Belgium acquired the Eupen-Malmédy region from Germany.
1940: Second invasion by Germany; King Leopold III ordered the Belgian army to capitulate.
1944–45: Belgium was liberated.
1948: Belgium formed the Benelux customs union with Luxembourg and the Netherlands.
1949: Belgium was a founding member of the North Atlantic Treaty Organization (NATO). Brussels became its headquarters in 1967.
1958: Belgium was a founding member of the European Economic Community (EEC), which made Brussels its headquarters.
1971: The constitution was amended to safeguard cultural rights of Flemish- (Flanders in north) and French-speaking communities (Walloons in southeast).
1974: Separate regional councils and ministerial committees were established for Flemings and Walloons.
1980: There was violence over language divisions; regional assemblies for Flanders and Wallonia and a three-member executive for Brussels were created.
1999: In the general election, Guy Verhofstadt became liberal prime minister of a coalition government together with socialists and Greens.
2000: Local elections were marked by the rise of the far-right party Vlaams Blok, which campaigned against immigration.

BELGIUM The view across the old harbour, Ostend, Belgium. *Corel*

Belgian Congo former name (1908–60) of the Democratic Republic of ▷Congo; known 1960–97 as Zaire.

Belgium see country box.

Belgrade (Serbo-Croat *Beograd*, 'white fortress') port and capital of the Federal Republic of Yugoslavia, and of its constituent republic of Serbia, at the confluence of the Danube and Sava rivers: population (1991) 1,168,500. It is linked to the port of Bar on the Adriatic Sea. Industries include light engineering, food processing, textiles, pharmaceuticals, and electrical goods.

Belgravia residential district of west central London, laid out in squares by Thomas Cubitt (1788–1855) between 1825 and 1830, and bounded to the north by Knightsbridge.

Belisarius (*c.* 505–565) East Roman general who led Rome's reconquest of the West. Though given inadequate resources by the jealous emperor Justinian I, Belisarius achieved notable victories against the Persians, Huns, Vandals, and Goths.

Belize see country box.

Belize City former capital (until 1970) and chief port of Belize, situated at the mouth of the Belize River on the Caribbean coast; population (2000 est) 49,100. It is Belize's largest city and capital of Belize district. Exports include sugar, timber, citrus fruits, coconuts, and maize. The port also serves parts of Mexico. The city was severely damaged by hurricanes in September 1931 and in October 1961, after which it was decided to move the capital inland, to Belmopan.

Many of the houses in Belize City are built of wood, and stand on piles above the mangrove swamp on both banks of Haulover Creek. The harbour is shallow, and navigation is impaired by sand bars. The river, which divides the city, is spanned by a swing bridge, which is opened to allow the river traffic through.

bell musical instrument, made in many sizes, comprising a suspended resonating vessel swung by a handle or from a pivoted frame to make contact with a beater which hangs inside the bell. Church bells are among the most massive structures to be cast in bronze in one piece; from high up in a steeple they can be heard for many miles. Their shape, a flared bowl with a thickened rim, is engineered to produce a clangorous mixture of tones. Miniature **handbells** are tuned to resonate harmoniously. Orchestral **tubular bells**, of brass or steel, are tuned to a chromatic scale of pitches and are played by striking with a wooden mallet. A set of steeple bells played from a keyboard is called a **carillon**.

Bell, Alexander Graham (1847–1922) Scottish-born US scientist and inventor. He was the first person ever to transmit speech from one point to another by electrical means. This invention – the telephone – was made in 1876, when Bell transmitted speech from Paris, Ontario, to Brantford, Ontario (a distance of 13 km/8 mi). Later Bell experimented with a type of phonograph and, in aeronautics, invented the tricycle undercarriage.

Bell also invented a photophone, which used selenium crystals to apply the telephone principle to transmitting words in a beam of light. He thus achieved the first wireless transmission of speech.
Related Web site: Alexander Graham Bell's Path to the Telephone
http://jefferson.village.virginia.edu/albell/homepage.html

> **Alexander Graham Bell**
> *Mr Watson, come here;*
> *I want you.*
>
> First complete sentence spoken over the telephone in March 1876

belladonna (or **deadly nightshade**) poisonous plant belonging to the nightshade family, found in Europe and Asia. It grows to 1.5 m/5 ft in height, with dull green leaves growing in unequal pairs, up to 20 cm/8 in long, and single purplish flowers that produce deadly black berries. Drugs are made from the leaves. (*Atropa belladonna*, family Solanaceae.)
Related Web site: Nightshade, Deadly http://www.botanical.com/botanical/mgmh/n/nighde05.html

Bell Burnell, (Susan) Jocelyn (1943–) Northern Irish astronomer. In 1967 she discovered the first ▷pulsar (rapidly flashing star) with British radio astronomer Antony ▷Hewish and colleagues at the Mullard Radio Astronomy Observatory, Cambridge, England.

belles lettres (French 'fine letters') literature that is appreciated more for its aesthetic qualities than for its content.

bellflower general name for many plants with bell-shaped flowers. The ▷harebell (*Campanula rotundifolia*) is a wild bellflower. The Canterbury bell (*C. medium*) is the garden variety, originally from southern Europe. (Genus *Campanula*, family Campanulaceae.)

Bellingshausen, Fabian Gottlieb von (1778–1852) Russian Antarctic explorer, the first to sight and circumnavigate the Antarctic continent 1819–21, although he did not realize what it was.

Bellini Venetian family of artists, founders of the Venetian School in the 15th and early 16th centuries. Jacopo Bellini

---

Belize

Belize formerly British Honduras (until 1973) country in Central America, bounded north by Mexico, west and south by Guatemala, and east by the Caribbean Sea.

AREA 22,963 sq km/8,866 sq mi
CAPITAL Belmopan
MAJOR TOWNS/CITIES Belize City, Dangriga, Orange Walk, Corozal, San Ignacio de Agana
MAJOR PORTS Belize City, Dangriga, Punta Gorda
PHYSICAL FEATURES tropical swampy coastal plain, Maya Mountains in south; over 90% forested

Government
HEAD OF STATE Queen Elizabeth II from 1981, represented by Governor General Dr Colville Young from 1993
HEAD OF GOVERNMENT Said Musa from 1998
POLITICAL SYSTEM liberal democracy
POLITICAL EXECUTIVE parliamentary
ADMINISTRATIVE DIVISIONS six districts
ARMED FORCES 1,100; plus 700 militia reserves (2002 est)
CONSCRIPTION military service is voluntary
DEATH PENALTY retained and used for ordinary crimes

Economy and resources
CURRENCY Belize dollar
GPD (US$) 843 million (2002 est)
REAL GDP GROWTH (% change on previous year) 4.6 (2001)
GNI (US$) 750 million (2002 est)
GNI PER CAPITA (PPP) (US$) 5,340 (2002 est)
CONSUMER PRICE INFLATION 1.5% (2003 est)
UNEMPLOYMENT 12.8% (2000)
FOREIGN DEBT (US$) 988 million (2001 est)
MAJOR TRADING PARTNERS USA, UK, Mexico, Canada, EU, Caricom
INDUSTRIES clothing, agricultural products (particularly sugar cane for sugar and rum), timber, tobacco
EXPORTS sugar, clothes, citrus products, forestry and fish products, bananas. Principal market: USA 53.8% (2001)
IMPORTS foodstuffs, machinery and transport equipment, mineral fuels, chemicals, basic manufactures. Principal source: USA 47.2% (2001)
ARABLE LAND 2.8% (2000 est)

AGRICULTURAL PRODUCTS sugar cane, citrus fruits, bananas, maize, red kidney beans, rice; livestock rearing (cattle, pigs, and poultry); fishing; timber reserves

Population and society
POPULATION 256,000 (2003 est)
POPULATION GROWTH RATE 1.9% (2000–05)
POPULATION DENSITY (per sq km) 11 (2003 est)
URBAN POPULATION (% of total) 48 (2003 est)
AGE DISTRIBUTION (% of total population) 0–14 37%, 15–59 57%, 60+ 6% (2002 est)
ETHNIC GROUPS 44% mestizos, 30% Creoles, Maya 11%, Garifuna 7%, East Indians, Mennonites, Canadians and Europeans, including Spanish and British
LANGUAGE English (official), Spanish (widely spoken), Creole dialects
RELIGION Roman Catholic 62%, Protestant 30%
EDUCATION (compulsory years) 10

LITERACY RATE 94% (men); 94% (women) (2003 est)
LABOUR FORCE 27.5% agriculture, 17.2% industry, 55.3% services (1999)
LIFE EXPECTANCY 70 (men); 73 (women) (2000–05)
CHILD MORTALITY RATE (under 5, per 1,000 live births) 40 (2001)
PHYSICIANS (per 1,000 people) 0.6 (1996 est)
HOSPITAL BEDS (per 1,000 people) 2.1 (1996 est)
TV SETS (per 1,000 people) 183 (1999 est)
RADIOS (per 1,000 people) 578 (1997)
INTERNET USERS (per 10,000 people) 896.6 (2002 est)
PERSONAL COMPUTER USERS (per 100 people) 13.8 (2002 est)

See also ▷Guatemala; ▷Maya.

Chronology
325–925 AD: Part of American Indian Maya civilization.
1600s: Colonized by British buccaneers and log-cutters.
1862: Formally declared a British colony, known as British Honduras.
1893: Mexico renounced its longstanding claim to the territory.
1954: Constitution adopted, providing for limited internal self-government.
1964: Self-government was achieved. Universal adult suffrage and a two-chamber legislature were introduced.
1970: The capital was moved from Belize City to the new town of Belmopan.
1973: Name changed to Belize.
1975: British troops sent to defend the long-disputed frontier with Guatemala.
1980: The United Nations (UN) called for full independence.
1981: Full independence was achieved.
1991: Diplomatic relations were re-established with Guatemala, which finally recognized Belize's sovereignty.
1993: The UK announced its intention to withdraw troops following the resolution of the border dispute with Guatemala.
1998: The PUP won a sweeping victory in assembly elections, with Said Musa as prime minister.

BELIZE A slate carving of a Mayan Indian. The Maya spread into Belize and other tropical lowland areas in around 2000 BC. *Corel*

(*c.* 1400–1470/71) worked in Venice, Padua, Verona, and Ferrara. **Gentile Bellini** (*c.* 1429–1507) was probably the elder son of Jacopo and was trained by him. Although now overshadowed by his brother, he was no less famous in his own day. **Giovanni Bellini** (*c.* 1430–1516) contributed more than any other painter of his time to the creation of the great Venetian School.

Bellini, Vincenzo (1801–1835) Italian composer of operas. He collaborated with the tenor Giovanni Battista Rubini (1794–1854) to develop a new simplicity of melodic expression in romantic evocations of classic themes, as in *La sonnambula/The Sleepwalker* and *Norma* (both 1831). In *I puritani/The Puritans* (1835), his last work, he discovered a new boldness and vigour of orchestral effect.

His popularity after his death was enormous, but his operas later fell into neglect. Since World War II, however, singers including Maria Callas, Joan Sutherland, and Montserrat Caballé, have helped to restore their popularity.

VINCENZO BELLINI A lithograph of the Italian composer Vincenzo Bellini, by French painter Jean François Millet. *The Art Archive/La Scala Milan/Dagli Orti*

Belloc, (Joseph) Hilaire (René Pierre) (1870–1953) French-born British writer. He wrote nonsense verse for children, including *The Bad Child's Book of Beasts* (1896) and *Cautionary Tales for Children* (1907). Belloc also wrote historical, biographical, travel, and religious books (he was a devout Catholic). With G K ▷Chesterton, he advocated a return to the late medieval ▷guild system of commercial association in place of capitalism or socialism.

> **Hilaire Belloc**
> *When I am dead,*
> *I hope it may be said: /*
> *'His sins were scarlet, but*
> *his books were read.'*
> 'On His Books'

Bellona in Roman mythology, the goddess of war; wife or sister of ▷Mars, god of war. During the Third Samnite War between Rome and the Samnites of northern Italy in 296 BC, the Sabine aristocrat Appius Claudius of Rome vowed to dedicate a temple to her. The building was eventually erected in the Campus Martius in 293 BC, near the altar of Mars.

Bellow, Saul (1915–) Canadian-born US novelist. From his first novel, *Dangling Man* (1944), Bellow typically set his naturalistic narratives in Chicago and made his central character an anxious, Jewish-American intellectual. In *The Adventures of Augie March* (1953) and *Henderson the Rain King* (1959), he created confident and comic picaresque heroes, before *Herzog* (1964), which pitches a comic but distressed scholar into a world of darkening humanism. Later works, developing Bellow's depiction of an age of urban disorder and indifference, include the near-apocalyptic *Mr Sammler's Planet* (1970), *Humboldt's Gift* (1975), *The Dean's December* (1982), *More Die of Heartbreak* (1987), and the novella *A Theft* (1989). He was awarded the Nobel Prize for Literature in 1976 for his finely styled works and skilled characterizations. Other works include *Him with His Foot in His Mouth* (1984), *Something to Remember Me By* (1992), *The Actual* (1997), and *Ravelstein* (2000).

Related Web site: Bellow, Saul http://www.emanuelnyc.org/bulletin/archive/36.html

> **Saul Bellow**
> *Death is the dark backing a mirror needs if we are to see anything.*
> *The Observer* December 1983

bell ringing (or **campanology**) the art of ringing church bells individually or in sequence by rhythmically drawing on a rope fastened to a wheel rotating the bell, so that it falls back and strikes in time. **Change ringing** is an English art, dating from the 17th century, of ringing a patterned sequence of permutations of 5–12 church bells, using one player to each bell.

belly dancing dance of the Middle East. It is characterized by the use of the hips, spine, shoulders, and stomach muscles rather than the legs. The dance is performed by women and is accompanied by varying rhythms. Traditionally, belly dance was performed only among women as a celebration of birth.

Belmondo, Jean-Paul (1933–) French film actor. He gained international celebrity in Jean-Luc Godard's seminal French New Wave film *A bout de souffle/Breathless* (1959). His other films include *Cartouche* (1961), *L'Homme de Rio/That Man from Rio* (1964), Godard's *Pierrot le fou* (1965), *Borsalino* (1970), *Stavisky* (1974), and *Les Misérables* (1995).

Belmopan capital of ▷Belize from 1970; situated in central Belize, 80 km/50 mi inland in Central America, between the Belize and Sibun Rivers. It is 80 km/50 mi southwest of Belize City, near the junction of the Western Highway and the Hummingbird Highway to Dangriga; population (2000 est) 8,100. Principal exports from the region are sugar cane, citrus fruits, bananas, and coconuts. Belmopan was established in 1970 in the mountainous interior to replace Belize City as the administrative centre of the country following hurricane damage to the latter in 1961. The traditional Maya-style architecture prevails.

In 1985 in the nearby Valley of Peace, a new camp for refugees from El Salvador and Guatemala was made a permanent settlement.

Belorussia see ▷Belarus.

Belorussian (or **Byelorussian** 'White Russian') member of an eastern Slav people closely related to the Russians (Great Russians) and Ukrainians, who live in Belarus and the surrounding area. Belorussian, a Balto-Slavic language belonging to the Indo-European family, is spoken by about 10 million people, including some in Poland. It is written in the Cyrillic script. Belorussian literature dates from the 11th century.

Belshazzar In the Old Testament, the last king of Babylon, son of Nebuchadnezzar. During a feast (known as **Belshazzar's Feast**) he saw a message, interpreted by ▷Daniel as prophesying the fall of Babylon and death of Belshazzar.

Bemba a people native to northeastern Zambia and neighbouring areas of the Democratic Republic of Congo (formerly Zaire) and Zimbabwe. They number about 3 million, many residing in urban areas such as Lusaka and Copperbelt. The Bemba language belongs to the Bantu branch of the Niger–Congo family.

Ben Ali, Zine el Abidine (1936–) Tunisian politician, president from 1987. After training in France and the USA, he returned to Tunisia and became director general of national security. He was made minister of the interior and then prime minister under the ageing president for life Habib ▷Bourguiba, whom he deposed in 1987 in a bloodless coup with the aid of ministerial colleagues. He ended the personality cult established by Bourguiba and moved towards a pluralist political system. He was re-elected in 1994, with 99% of the popular vote.

Benares alternative transliteration of ▷Varanasi, a holy Hindu city in Uttar Pradesh, India.

Ben Bella, Muhammad Ahmed (1916–) Algerian politician. He was among the leaders of the Front de Libération Nationale (FLN), the first prime minister of independent Algeria 1962–63, and its first president 1963–65. His centralization of power and systematic purges were among the reasons behind his overthrow in 1965 by Houari ▷Boumédienne. He was detained until 1979. In 1985 he founded a new party, Mouvement pour la Démocratie en Algérie (MDA), and returned to Algeria in 1990 after nine years in exile. The cancellation of the 1991 legislative elections led to his exile for the second time, and his party was banned in 1997.

bends (or **compressed-air sickness** or **caisson disease**) popular name for a syndrome seen in deep-sea divers, arising from too rapid a release of nitrogen from solution in their blood. If a diver surfaces too quickly, nitrogen that had dissolved in the blood under increasing water pressure is suddenly released, forming bubbles in the bloodstream and causing pain (the 'bends') and paralysis. Immediate treatment is gradual decompression in a decompression chamber, whilst breathing pure oxygen.

Benedict, St (*c.* 480–*c.* 547) founder of Christian monasticism in the West and of the ▷Benedictine order. He founded the monastery of Monte Cassino and others in Italy. His feast day is 11 July.

Related Web site: St Benedict of Nursia http://www.osb.org/gen/bendct.html

Benedictine order religious order of monks and nuns in the Roman Catholic Church, founded by St ▷Benedict at Subiaco, Italy, in the 6th century. It had a strong influence on medieval learning and reached the height of its prosperity early in the 14th century.

benediction blessing recited at the end of a Christian service, particularly the Mass.

benefice in the early Middle Ages, a donation of land or money to the Christian church as an act of devotion; from the 12th century, the term came to mean the income enjoyed by clergy.

Benelux (acronym for Belgium, the Netherlands, and Luxembourg) customs union of Belgium, the Netherlands, and Luxembourg, an agreement for which was signed in London by the three governments in exile in 1944, and ratified in 1947. It came into force in 1948 and was further extended and strengthened by the Benelux Economic Union Treaty in 1958. The full economic union between the three countries came into operation in 1960. The three Benelux countries were founder-members of the European Economic Community (now the ▷European Union), for which the Benelux union was an important stimulus.

Beneš, Edvard (1884–1948) Czechoslovak politician. He worked with Tomáš ▷Masaryk towards Czechoslovak nationalism from 1918 and was foreign minister and representative at the League of Nations. He was president of the republic from 1935 until forced to resign by the Germans and headed a government in exile in London during World War II. He personally gave the order for the assassination of Reinhard ▷Heydrich in Prague in 1942. Having signed an agreement with Joseph Stalin, he returned home as president in 1945 but resigned again after the communist coup in 1948.

Bengal former province of British India, in the northeast of the subcontinent. It was the first major part of India to come under the control of the British ▷East India Company (the 'Bengal Presidency'). When India gained independence in 1947, Bengal was divided into ▷West Bengal, a state of India, and East Bengal, which from 1972 onwards became part of the newly independent state of ▷Bangladesh.

Bengal was first partitioned in 1905, when the viceroy, Lord Curzon, decided to divide the huge single province of Bengal, Bihar, and Orissa in two to simplify administration. The mainly Muslim East Bengal, which incorporated the Assam region, was centred around Dhaka (Dacca), while Hindu West Bengal had its capital at Calcutta. Many Bengalis saw the partition as an attempt to stifle the strong independence movement in the province, and the change was bitterly resented. The strength of opposition led the British to reunite East and West Bengal in 1911, with Assam and Orissa–Bihar as two new administrative regions. In 1943 a devastating famine, caused by a slump in demand for jute and a bad harvest, resulted in the death of over 3 million of Bengal's inhabitants.

Bengal, Bay of part of the Indian Ocean lying between the east coast of India and the west coast of Myanmar (Burma) and the Malay Peninsula.

The Irrawaddy, Ganges, and Brahmaputra rivers flow into the bay. The principal islands are to be found in the Andaman and Nicobar groups.

Bengali people of Bengali culture from Bangladesh and India (West Bengal, Tripura). There are 80–150 million speakers of Bengali, an Indo-Iranian language belonging to the Indo-European family. It is the official language of Bangladesh and of the state of Bengal and is also used by emigrant Bangladeshi and Bengali communities in such countries as the UK and the USA. Bengalis in Bangladesh are predominantly Muslim, whereas those in India are mainly Hindu.

Benghazi (or **Banghazi**) historic city and industrial port in northern Libya on the Gulf of Sirte; population (1995 est) 545,000. It is the second largest Libyan city and lies 645 km/400 mi east of the largest, Tripoli. There are oil refining and engineering industries. It was controlled by Turkey between the 16th century and 1911, and by Italy from 1911 to 1942; it was a major naval supply base during World War II. The university was founded in 1955.

Ben-Gurion, David (1886–1973) Adopted name of David Gruen. Israeli statesman and socialist politician. He was one of the founders of the state of Israel, the country's first prime minister 1948–53, and again 1955–63. He retired from politics in 1970, but remained a lasting symbol of the Israeli state.

He was born in Poland and went to Palestine in 1906 to farm. He was a leader of the Zionist movement, and as defence minister he presided over the development of Israel's armed forces into one of the strongest armies in the Middle East.

Benin see country box.

Benin former African kingdom 1200–1897, now a province of Nigeria. It reached the

> ## David Ben-Gurion
> *Ours is a country built more on people than on territory. The Jews will come from everywhere: from France, from Russia, from America, from Yemen . . . Their faith is their passport.*
>
> Recalled by Shimon Peres *The New York Times* 5 October 1986

height of its power in the 14th–17th centuries when it ruled the area between the Niger Delta and Lagos. The province trades in timber and rubber.

Benn, Tony (Anthony Neil Wedgwood) (1925–   ) British Labour politician, formerly the leading figure on the party's left wing. He was minister of technology 1966–70 and secretary of state for industry 1974–75, but his campaign against entry to the European Community (EC; now the European Union) led to his transfer to the Department of Energy 1975–79. A skilled parliamentary orator, he twice unsuccessfully contested the Labour Party leadership. Benn announced in June 1999 that he would stand down as an MP after

nearly half a century in Parliament. He would, however, continue to be politically active.

Born the son of the 1st Viscount Stansgate, a Labour peer, Benn was educated at Oxford. He was member of Parliament for Bristol Southeast 1950–60, when he succeeded to his father's title. Despite refusing to accept the title and being re-elected in Bristol in 1961, he was debarred from sitting in the House of Commons by a judgement of the Electoral Court. His subsequent campaign to disclaim those inheriting titles to disclaim them led to the passing of the Peerage Act in 1963; Benn was the first person to disclaim a title under this act.

He was again MP for Bristol Southeast 1963–83 and was postmaster general in the 1964 Labour government, becoming a member of the cabinet in 1966 as minister of technology. After Labour's defeat in 1970, he was the opposition spokesperson on trade and industry 1970–74 and a leading campaigner against

Benin

Bight of Benin

Benin formerly Dahomey (1899–1975) country in west Africa, bounded east by Nigeria, north by Niger and Burkina Faso, west by Togo, and south by the Gulf of Guinea.

NATIONAL NAME *République du Bénin/Republic of Benin*
AREA 112,622 sq km/43,483 sq mi
CAPITAL Porto-Novo (official), Cotonou (de facto)
MAJOR TOWNS/CITIES Abomey, Natitingou, Parakou, Kandi, Ouidah, Djougou, Bohicon, Cotonou
MAJOR PORTS Cotonou
PHYSICAL FEATURES flat to undulating terrain; hot and humid in south; semiarid in north; coastal lagoons with fishing villages on stilts; Niger River in northeast

Government

HEAD OF STATE AND GOVERNMENT Mathieu Kerekou from 1996
POLITICAL SYSTEM emergent democracy
POLITICAL EXECUTIVE limited presidency
ADMINISTRATIVE DIVISIONS twelve departments
ARMED FORCES 4,600 (2002 est)
CONSCRIPTION by selective conscription for 18 months
DEATH PENALTY retained and used for ordinary crimes
DEFENCE SPEND (% GDP) 1.8 (2002 est)
EDUCATION SPEND (% GDP) 3.2 (2001 est)
HEALTH SPEND (% GDP) 3.2 (2000 est)

Economy and resources

CURRENCY franc CFA
GPD (US$) 2.7 billion (2002 est)
REAL GDP GROWTH (% change on previous year) 5.0 (2001)

GNI (US$) 2.5 billion (2002 est)
GNI PER CAPITA (PPP) (US$) 1,020 (2002 est)
CONSUMER PRICE INFLATION 2.4% (2003 est)
FOREIGN DEBT (US$) 1.6 billion (2001 est)
MAJOR TRADING PARTNERS India, France, Brazil, Libya, China, Indonesia, UK, Italy, Côte d'Ivoire
RESOURCES petroleum, limestone, marble
INDUSTRIES palm-oil processing, brewing, cement, cotton ginning, sugar refining, textiles
EXPORTS cotton and textiles, crude petroleum, palm oil and other palm products. Principal market: India 21% (2001)
IMPORTS oil, foodstuffs (particularly cereals), miscellaneous manufactured articles (notably cotton yarn and fabrics), machinery and transport equipment, beverages, tobacco. Principal source: China 35% (2001)
ARABLE LAND 17.6% (2000 est)
AGRICULTURAL PRODUCTS cotton, maize, yarns, cassava, sorghum, millet; fishing

Population and society

POPULATION 6,736,000 (2003 est)
POPULATION GROWTH RATE 2.4% (2000–15)
POPULATION DENSITY (per sq km) 60 (2003 est)
URBAN POPULATION (% of total) 45 (2003 est)

AGE DISTRIBUTION (% of total population) 0–14 46%, 15–59 50%, 60+ 4% (2002 est)
ETHNIC GROUPS 99% indigenous African, distributed among 42 ethnic groups, the largest being the Fon, Adja, Yoruba, and Braiba; small European (mainly French) community
LANGUAGE French (official), Fon (47%), Yoruba (9%) (both in the south), six major tribal languages in the north
RELIGION animist 70%, Muslim 15%, Christian 15%
EDUCATION (compulsory years) 6
LITERACY RATE 56% (men); 26% (women) (2003 est)

LABOUR FORCE 46% of population: 64% agriculture, 8% industry, 28% services (1990)
LIFE EXPECTANCY 48 (men); 53 (women) (2000–05)
CHILD MORTALITY RATE (under 5, per 1,000 live births) 158 (2001)
PHYSICIANS (per 1,000 people) 0.1 (1998 est)
TV SETS (per 1,000 people) 44 (2001 est)
RADIOS (per 1,000 people) 441 (2001 est)
INTERNET USERS (per 10,000 people) 38.8 (2002 est)
PERSONAL COMPUTER USERS (per 100 people) 0.2 (2002 est)

See also ▷Fon.

BENIN Waterways flow through the village of Ganive. Benin has an extensive network of permanent waterways, which flow north towards the Niger River and south towards the Atlantic Ocean. *Corel*

Chronology

12th–13th centuries: The area was settled by a Ewe-speaking people called the Aja, who mixed with local peoples and gradually formed the Fon ethnic group.

16th century: The Aja kingdom, called Great Ardha, was at its peak.

early 17th century: The Kingdom of Dahomey was established in the south by Fon peoples, who defeated the neighbouring Dan; following contact with European traders, the kingdom became an intermediary in the slave trade.

1800–50: King Dezo of Dahomey raised regiments of female soldiers to attack the Yoruba ('land of the big cities') kingdom of eastern Benin and southwest Nigeria in order to obtain slaves.

1857: A French base was established at Grand-Popo.

1892–94: War broke out between the French and Dahomey, after which the victorious French established a protectorate.

1899: Incorporated in federation of French West Africa as Dahomey.

1914: During World War I French troops from Dahomey participated in conquest of German-ruled Togoland to the west.

1940–44: During World War II, along with the rest of French West Africa, the country supported the 'Free French' anti-Nazi resistance cause.

1960: Independence achieved from France.

1960–77: Acute political instability, with frequent switches from civilian to military rule, and regional ethnic disputes.

1975: The name of the country was changed from Dahomey to Benin.

1989: The army was deployed against antigovernment strikers and protesters, inspired by Eastern European revolutions; Marxist-Leninism was dropped as the official ideology and a market-centred economic reform programme adopted.

1990: A referendum backed the establishment of multiparty politics.

1991: In multiparty elections, the leader of the new Benin Renaissance Party (PRB), Nicéphore Soglo, became president and formed a ten-party coalition government.

1996: Major Mathieu Kerekou became president.

1998: Prime Minister Adrien Houngbedji resigned; no immediate successor was appointed.

2001: President Kerekou was re-elected amidst allegations of electoral fraud.

Britain's entry into the EC. He was chair of the Labour Party 1971–72. In March 1974 he became secretary of state for industry. At the time of the 1975 referendum he campaigned against the renegotiated terms of British membership of the EC (now the EU), and in June 1975 was appointed secretary of state for energy.

He unsuccessfully contested the Labour Party leadership in 1976, defeated by James Callaghan. In 1981 he challenged Denis Healey for the deputy leadership of the party and was so narrowly defeated that he established himself as the acknowledged leader of the left. In 1984 he became MP for Chesterfield and in 1988 he made another unsuccessful bid for the Labour leadership against Neil Kinnock. Though marginalized on the party's left wing, he remained an outspoken backbench critic of the centralization of party control that has been exercised under the leadership of Tony Blair.

Bennett, Alan (1934–) English dramatist and screenwriter. His works (often set in his native north of England) treat such subjects as class, senility, illness, and death with macabre comedy. They include the series of monologues for television *Talking Heads* (1988) and *Talking Heads 2* (1998), and the play *The Madness of George III* (1991), made into the critically acclaimed film *The Madness of King George* (1995; Academy Award for best adapted screenplay).

His other screenwriting credits include *A Private Function* (1985) and *Prick Up Your Ears* (1987), based on the relationship between the dramatist Joe Orton and his lover Kenneth Halliwell.

> **Alan Bennett**
> *Life is rather like a tin of sardines – we're all of us looking for the key.*
> Beyond the Fringe

Bennett, (Enoch) Arnold (1867–1931) English novelist, playwright, and journalist. His major works are set in the industrial 'five towns' of the Potteries in Staffordshire (now Stoke-on-Trent) and are concerned with the manner in which the environment dictates the pattern of his characters' lives. They include *Anna of the Five Towns* (1902), *The Old Wives' Tale* (1908), and the trilogy *Clayhanger, Hilda Lessways*, and *These Twain* (1910–15).

Bennett often describes working-class life in great detail but rarely offers any comments or judgements on it. He also wrote a number of successful plays including *Milestones* (with Edward Knoblock; 1912).

Bennett, Richard Rodney (1936–) English composer of jazz, film music, symphonies, and operas. His film scores for *Far from the Madding Crowd* (1967), *Nicholas and Alexandra* (1971), and *Murder on the Orient Express* (1974) all received Academy Award nominations. His operas include *The Mines of Sulphur* (1963) and *Victory* (1970).

Ben Nevis highest mountain in the British Isles (1,344 m/ 4,409 ft), 7 km/4 mi southeast of Fort William, Scotland.

bent (or bent grass) any of a group of grasses. Creeping bent grass (*Agrostis stolonifera*), also known as fiorin, is common in northern North America, Europe, and Asia, including lowland Britain. It spreads by ▷runners and has large attractive clusters (panicles) of yellow or purple flowers on thin stalks, like oats. It is often used on lawns and golf courses. (Genus *Agrostris*, family Gramineae.)

Bentham, Jeremy (1748–1832) English philosopher, legal and social reformer, and founder of ▷utilitarianism. The essence of his moral philosophy is found in the pronouncement of his *Principles of Morals and Legislation* (written in 1780, published in 1789): that the object of all legislation should be 'the greatest happiness for the greatest number'.

Bentham declared that the 'utility' of any law is to be measured by the extent to which it promotes the pleasure, good, and happiness of the people concerned. In 1776 he published *Fragments on Government*. He made suggestions for the reform of the poor law in 1798, which formed the basis of the reforms enacted in 1834, and in his *Catechism of Parliamentary Reform*, published in 1817, he proposed annual elections, the secret ballot, and universal male suffrage. He was also a pioneer of prison reform.

In economics he was an apostle of *laissez-faire*, and in his *Defence of Usury* (1787) and *Manual of Political Economy* (1798) he contended that his principle of 'utility' was best served by allowing every man (sic) to pursue his own interests unhindered by restrictive legislation. He was made a citizen of the French Republic in 1792.

Related Web site: Bentham, Jeremy http://socserv2.socsci.mcmaster.ca/~econ/ugcm/3ll3/bentham/index.html

> **Edmund Clerihew Bentley**
> *Sir Christopher Wren / Said, 'I am going to dine with some men. / If anybody calls / Say I am designing St Paul's.'*
> Biography for Beginners, 'Sir Christopher Wren'

Bentley, Edmund Clerihew (1875–1956) English writer. He invented the four-line humorous verse form known as the clerihew, first collected in *Biography for Beginners* (1905) and then in *More Biography* (1929). He was also the author of the classic detective story *Trent's Last Case* (1913), introducing a new naturalistic style that replaced Sherlock Holmesian romanticism.

Bentley, John Francis (1839–1902) English architect, born at Doncaster. In 1894 he was appointed architect for the new Roman Catholic Cathedral at Westminster, London (1895–1903). The Byzantine style was chosen for the cathedral, and Bentley made an extensive tour of southeastern Europe in order to study Byzantine architecture. His design shows an original treatment of the style; but he did not live to see the completion of the building.

bentwood type of furniture, originally made by steam-heating and then bending rods of wood to form panels. Initially a country style, it was patented in the early 19th century in the USA. Twentieth-century designers such as Marcel ▷Breuer and Alvar ▷Aalto have developed a different form by bending sheets of plywood.

Benz, Karl (Friedrich) (1844–1929) German automobile engineer. He produced the world's first petrol-driven motor vehicle. He built his first model engine in 1878 and the petrol-driven car in 1885.

Benz made his first four-wheeled prototype in 1891 and by 1895 he was building a range of four-wheeled vehicles that were light, strong, inexpensive, and simple to operate. These vehicles ran at speeds of about 24 kph/15 mph. In 1926, the thriving company merged with the German firm of Daimler to form Daimler-Benz.

Related Web site: Benz, Karl http://www.specialcar.com/test/demo/p6a_e.htm

benzaldehyde C_6H_5CHO colourless liquid with the characteristic odour of almonds. It is used as a solvent and in the making of perfumes and dyes. It occurs in certain leaves, such as the cherry, laurel, and peach, and in a combined form in certain nuts and kernels. It can be extracted from such natural sources, but is usually made from ▷toluene.

Benzedrine trade name for ▷amphetamine, a stimulant drug.

benzene C_6H_6 clear liquid hydrocarbon of characteristic odour, occurring in coal tar. It is used as a solvent and in the synthesis of many chemicals.

The benzene molecule consists of a ring of six carbon atoms, all of which are in a single plane, and it is one of the simplest ▷cyclic compounds. Benzene is the simplest of a class of compounds collectively known as **aromatic compounds**. Some are considered carcinogenic (cancer-inducing).

In the UK levels of airborne benzene in urban areas were declared a health risk in 1994. Benzene pollution comes from combustion of petrol (80%), diesel exhausts, and evaporation from petrol pumps. One part per billion was recommended as a safe level; 13 parts per billion was recorded in London in 1991. According to the World Health Organization, there is no safe level.

benzodiazepine any of a group of mood-altering drugs (tranquillizers), for example Librium and Valium. They are addictive and interfere with the process by which information is transmitted between brain cells, and various side effects arise from continued use. They were originally developed as muscle relaxants, and then excessively prescribed in the West as anxiety-relieving drugs.

benzoic acid C_6H_5COOH white crystalline solid, sparingly soluble in water, that is used as a preservative for certain foods and as an antiseptic. It is obtained chemically by the direct oxidation of benzaldehyde and occurs in certain natural resins, some essential oils, and as hippuric acid.

benzoin resin (thick liquid that hardens in the air) obtained by making cuts in the bark of the tree *Styrax benzoin*, which grows in the East Indies. Benzoin is used in cosmetics, perfumes, and incense.

Beograd Serbo-Croatian form of ▷Belgrade, the capital of Yugoslavia.

Berber the non-Semitic Caucasoid people of North Africa who since prehistoric times have inhabited Barbary – the Mediterranean coastlands from Egypt to the Atlantic. Their language, present-day Berber (a member of the Hamito-Semitic or Afro-Asiatic language family), is written in both Arabic and Berber characters and is spoken by about 10 million people: about one-third of Algerians and nearly two-thirds of Moroccans. Berbers are mainly agricultural, but some are still nomadic.

Berbera seaport in Somalia, with the only sheltered harbour on the south side of the Gulf of Aden; population (1990) 70,000. It is in a strategic position on the oil route and has a deep-sea port completed in 1969. The port, which was the capital of ▷British Somaliland until 1941, is the terminus of roads from Hargeysa and Burko, and an airport now adds to its accessibility. Berbera exports sheep, gum arabic, frankincense, and myrrh. Its seaborne trade is chiefly with Aden which lies in Yemen 240 km/150 mi to the north.

Berdyaev, Nikolai Alexandrovich (1874–1948) Russian philosopher who often challenged official Soviet viewpoints after the Revolution of 1917. Although appointed professor of philosophy in 1919 at Moscow University, he was exiled in 1922 for defending Orthodox Christian religion. His books include *The Meaning of History* (1923) and *The Destiny of Man* (1935).

Bérégovoy, Pierre (Eugène) (1925–1993) French socialist politician, prime minister 1992–93. A close ally of François ▷Mitterrand, he was named chief of staff in 1981 after managing the successful presidential campaign. He was social affairs minister 1982–84 and finance minister 1984–86 and 1988–92. He resigned as premier after the socialists' defeat in the March 1993 general election, and shortly afterwards committed suicide.

Berengaria of Navarre (1165–*c.* 1230) Queen of England. The only English queen never to set foot in England, she was the daughter of King Sancho VI of Navarre. She married Richard I of England in Cyprus 1191, and accompanied him on his crusade to the Holy Land.

Berg, Alban (1885–1935) Austrian composer. He studied under Arnold Schoenberg and developed a personal 12-tone idiom of great emotional and stylistic versatility. His relatively small output includes two operas – *Wozzeck* (1914–20), a grim story of working-class life, and the unfinished *Lulu* (1929–35) – and chamber music incorporating coded references to friends and family.

His music is emotionally expressive, and sometimes anguished, but it can also be lyrical, as in the violin concerto (1935).

Berg, Paul (1926–) US molecular biologist. In 1972, using gene-splicing techniques developed by others, Berg spliced and combined into a single hybrid the ▷DNA from an animal tumour virus (SV40) and the DNA from a bacterial virus. He shared the Nobel Prize for Chemistry in 1980 for his work on the biochemistry of nucleic acids, especially recombinant DNA.

Bergamo town in Lombardy, Italy, 48 km/30 mi northeast of Milan, at the foot of the Alps between the rivers Brembo and Serio; population (1992) 115,100. Industries include printing, engineering, and the manufacture of cement, textiles (silk), and electrical goods. The Academia Carrara holds a collection of paintings.

bergamot small evergreen tree belonging to the rue family. A fragrant citrus-scented essence is obtained from the rind of its fruit and used as a perfume and food flavouring, for example in Earl Grey tea. The sole source of supply is southern Calabria, Italy, but the name comes from the town of Bergamo, in Lombardy. (*Citrus bergamia*, family Rutaceae.)

Bergen industrial port and capital of Hordaland county on the southwest coast of Norway; population (1994) 195,000. Industries include shipbuilding, engineering, and fishing. Often called the 'gateway to the fjords', Bergen is a major centre for tours of the fjords of Norway's west coast. Founded in 1070, Bergen was a member of the ▷Hanseatic League.

Related Web site: Welcome to Bergen – The Gateway to the Fjords of Norway http://www.vib.no/Bergen/reiseliv/tourist/index.html

Bergius, Friedrich Karl Rudolf (1884–1949) German research chemist who invented processes for converting coal into oil and wood into sugar. He shared the Nobel Prize for Chemistry in 1931 with Carl Bosch for his part in inventing and developing high-pressure industrial methods.

Bergman, (Ernst) Ingmar (1918–) Swedish stage and film director. He is regarded by many as a unique auteur and one of the masters of modern cinema. His work deals with complex moral, psychological, and metaphysical problems and is often strongly pessimistic. Bergman gained an international reputation with *Det sjunde inseglet/The Seventh Seal* and *Smultronstället/Wild Strawberries* (both 1957). He has also directed *Junfrukällan/The Virgin Spring* (1959), *Tystnaden/The Silence* (1963), *Persona* (1966), *Viskningar och rop/Cries and Whispers* (1972), and *Fanny och Alexander/Fanny and Alexander* (1982).

His understanding portrayal of women was already evident in his early films, including *Sommarnattens Leende/Smiles of a Summer Night* (1955). His tormented search for spiritual truth was given increasingly stark expression. His work has had a profound influence on many subsequent film-makers, most notably Woody Allen.

Bergman, Ingrid (1915–1982) Swedish-born actor. Having moved to the USA in 1939 to appear in David O Selznick's remake of the Swedish film *Intermezzo* (1936) in which she had first come to prominence, she went on to appear in such Hollywood classics as *Casablanca* (1942), *For Whom the Bell Tolls* (1943), *Gaslight* (1944; for which she won an Academy Award), and *Notorious* (1946). On screen she projected a combination of radiance, refined beauty, and fortitude.

By leaving her husband to have a child with director Roberto Rossellini, she broke an unofficial code of Hollywood star behaviour and was ostracized for many years. During her 'exile', she made films in Europe; *Stromboli* (1949) was directed by Rossellini. Returning to the USA, she made such films as *Anastasia* (1956) and *Murder on the Orient Express* (1974), winning Academy Awards for both.

Bergson, Henri Louis (1859–1941) French philosopher. He believed that time, change, and development were the essence of reality. He thought that time was a continuous process in which one period merged imperceptibly into the next. In *Creative Evolution* (1907) he attempted to prove that all evolution and progress are due to the working of the *élan vital*, or life force. He was awarded the Nobel Prize for Literature in 1927.

beriberi nutritional disorder occurring mostly in the tropics and resulting from a deficiency of vitamin B₁ (▷thiamine). The disease takes two forms: in one ▷oedema (waterlogging of the tissues) occurs; in the other there is severe emaciation. There is nerve degeneration in both forms and many victims succumb to heart failure.

Beringia (or Bering Land Bridge) former land bridge 1,600 km/1,000 mi wide between Asia and North America; it existed during the ice ages that occurred before 35,000 BC and during the period 24,000–9000 BC. As the climate warmed and the ice sheets melted, Beringia flooded. It is now covered by the Bering Strait and Chukchi Sea.

Bering, Vitus Jonassen (1681–1741) Danish explorer. He was the first European to sight Alaska. He died on Bering Island in the Bering Sea, both named after him, as is the Bering Strait, which separates Asia (Russia) from North America (Alaska).

Bering Sea section of the Pacific Ocean north of the Aleutian Islands, between Siberia and Alaska; area 2.28 million sq km/880,000 sq mi. It connects with the Chukchi Sea, to the north, via the Bering Strait, extending for 87 km/54 mi from east–west, between the Chukchi Peninsula of Siberia and the Seward Peninsula of Alaska. It is named after the Danish explorer Vitus ▷Bering, who explored the Bering Strait.

Bering Strait strait between Alaska and Siberia, linking the North Pacific and Arctic oceans.

Berio, Luciano (1925–2003) Italian composer. His work combines serial techniques with commedia dell'arte and antiphonal practices, as in *Alleluiah II* (1958), for five instrumental groups. His prolific output includes 11 *Sequenzas/Sequences* (1958–85) for various solo instruments or voice, *Sinfonia* (1968–69) for voices and orchestra, *Formazioni/Formations* (1987) for orchestra, and the opera *Un re in ascolto/A King Listens* (1984).

Berkeley city in central California, USA, 10 km/6 mi north of Oakland, on the northeastern side of San Francisco Bay; population (1992) 101,100. It has an industrial waterfront, but is best known as the main campus of the University of California and for nuclear research at the Lawrence Berkeley Laboratory. During the 1960s, the campus was the site of major political demonstrations against US military involvement in Vietnam.

Berkeley, Busby (1895–1976) Stage name of William Berkeley Enos. US choreographer and film director. He used ingenious and extravagant sets and teams of female dancers to create song and dance sequences that formed large-scale kaleidoscopic patterns when filmed from above, as in *Gold Diggers of 1933* and *Footlight Parade* (1933).

Berkeley, George (1685–1753) Irish philosopher and cleric who believed that nothing exists apart from perception, and that the all-seeing mind of God makes possible the continued apparent existence of things. For Berkeley, everyday objects are collections of

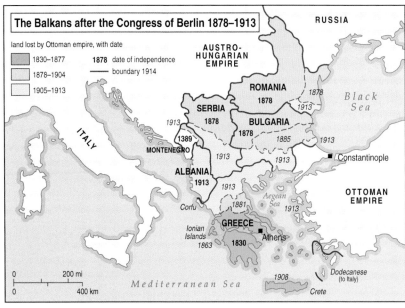

The Balkans after the Congress of Berlin 1878–1913

land lost by Ottoman empire, with date
- 1830–1877
- 1878–1904
- 1905–1913

1878 date of independence
—— boundary 1914

RUSSIA
AUSTRO-HUNGARIAN EMPIRE
ITALY
ROMANIA 1878
SERBIA 1878
BULGARIA 1878
MONTENEGRO 1389
ALBANIA 1913
GREECE 1830
Athens
Corfu
Ionian Islands 1863
Aegean Sea
Black Sea
Constantinople
OTTOMAN EMPIRE
Dodecanese (to Italy)
Crete
Mediterranean Sea

0   200 mi
0   400 km

See entry on page 100.

ideas or sensations, hence the dictum *esse est percipi* ('to exist is to be perceived'). He became bishop of Cloyne in 1734.

Berkeley, Lennox Randal Francis (1903–1989) English composer. His works for the voice include *The Hill of the Graces* (1975), verses from Spenser's *Faerie Queene* set for eight-part unaccompanied chorus; and his operas *Nelson* (1954) and *Ruth* (1956).

berkelium synthesized, radioactive, metallic element of the actinide series, symbol Bk, atomic number 97, relative atomic mass 247.

It was first produced in 1949 by Glenn Seaborg and his team, at the University of California at Berkeley, USA, after which it is named.

Berkoff, Steven (1937–) English dramatist and actor. His abrasive and satirical plays include *East* (1975), *Greek* (1979), and *West* (1983). Berkoff's production of Oscar Wilde's *Salome* was staged in 1991. His *Collected Plays* (2 vols) were published in 1994.

Berkshire (or Royal Berkshire) former county of south-central England; from April 1998 split into six unitary authorities: ▷West Berkshire, ▷Reading, ▷Slough, ▷Windsor and Maidenhead, ▷Wokingham and ▷Bracknell Forest.

Berlin industrial city and capital of the Federal Republic of ▷Germany, lying on the River Spree; population (2001 est) 3,317,000. Products include machine tools, engineering goods (including cars), electrical goods, paper, food and drink, and printed works. After the division of Germany in 1949, East Berlin became the capital of East Germany and Bonn was made the provisional capital of West Germany. The ▷Berlin Wall divided the city from 1961 until 1989. Following the reunification of Germany on 3 October 1990, East and West Berlin were once more reunited as the 16th *Land* (state) of the Federal Republic.

Features Unter den Linden, the tree-lined avenue that was once the whole city's focal point, has been restored in what was formerly East Berlin. The fashionable Kurfürstendamm and the residential Hansa quarter (1957) form part of the former West Berlin. Prominent buildings include the Reichstag (parliament building); Schloss Bellevue (Berlin residence of the president); Schloss Charlottenburg (housing several museums); the ruined Kaiser-Wilhelm-Kirche; Congress Hall ('the pregnant oyster'); the restored 18th-century State Opera; the National Gallery (1968), designed by Mies van der Rohe; and the Dahlem Picture Gallery. It is also the home of the Berlin Philharmonic Orchestra (established in 1867).

The Reichstag (burned down in 1933) is to be rebuilt under the direction of Sir Norman Foster. In 1995 the *Wrapping of the Reichstag* by the artist Christo Javacheff attracted 5 million tourists. Friedrichstrasse, the Alexanderplatz, and No Man's Land are being redeveloped. The Tiergarten (250 ha/618 acres) park includes a zoo. The environs of Berlin include the Grünewald forest and the Wannsee and Havel lakes. In the Grünewald is the Trümmerberg, a hill 130 m/427 ft high, formed out of 18 million cubic metres/70 million cubic feet of war debris, and now used as an artificial ski slope.

The city contains several research institutes including the Hahn-Meitner Institute for Nuclear Research, the Max Planck Institute, and the Research Institute for Marine Engineering and Shipbuilding. Berlin, with three universities and other institutions, is also a major centre of higher education.

History First mentioned in about 1230, the city grew out of a fishing village, joined the ▷Hanseatic League trade federation in the 15th century. Berlin's growth and importance was closely tied to the rise of the ▷Hohenzollern family, and it became their capital in the 16th century. From the middle of the 18th century Berlin developed into a commercial and cultural centre. After the Napoleonic Wars, Friedrich Wilhelm III was responsible for the squares, avenues, and Neo-Classical buildings, many designed by Karl Friedrich Schinkel, including the Altes Museum and the Schauspielhaus.

In World War II air raids and conquest by the Soviet army (23 April–2 May 1945), destroyed much of the city. After the war, Berlin was divided into four sectors – British, US, French, and Soviet – and until 1948 was under quadripartite government by the Allies. Following the ▷Berlin blockade the city was divided, with the USSR maintaining a separate municipal government in

BERLIN The ruined Kaiser Wilhelm Church, Berlin, Germany, is seen through a modern sculpture in the Europa Centre.
Image Bank

its sector. The other three sectors (West Berlin) were made a *Land* of the Federal Republic in May 1949 and Bonn became the provisional capital; in October 1949 East Berlin was proclaimed capital of East Germany. On 13 August 1961 the Soviet zone was sealed off by the Russians, and the Berlin Wall was built along the zonal boundary. Access to East Berlin was severely restricted, although restrictions were lifted occasionally, and a pass system was introduced in 1964.

In June 1991 the Bundestag (the lower chamber of government) voted to restore Berlin as the capital of a unified Germany (by 337 votes to 320 votes). The move of the Bundestag offices went ahead despite a campaign by some politicians to delay it until 2010 or stop it altogether.

Related Web site: Berlin http://userpage.chemie.fu-berlin.de/adressen/berlin.html

Berlin, Irving (1888–1989) Adopted name of Israel Baline. Belorussian-born US songwriter. His songs include hits such as 'Alexander's Ragtime Band' (1911), 'Always' (1925), 'God Bless America' (1917, published 1939), and 'White Christmas' (1942), and the musicals *Top Hat* (1935), *Annie Get Your Gun* (1946), and *Call Me Madam* (1950). He also provided songs for films like *Blue Skies* (1946) and *Easter Parade* (1948). His 'White Christmas' has been the most performed Christmas song in history, with more than 500 versions recorded.

Born in Belarus, Berlin grew up in New York and had his first song published in 1907. He began providing songs for vaudeville and revues and went on to own a theatre, the Music Box, where he appeared in his own revues in 1921 and 1923. Generally writing both lyrics and music, he was instrumental in the development of the popular song, taking it from jazz and ragtime to swing and romantic ballads.

IRVING BERLIN US composer Irving Berlin singing with soldiers at an army camp in the 1940s. *Archive Photos*

Berlin blockade the closing of entry to Berlin from the west by Soviet Forces from June 1948 to May 1949. It was an attempt to prevent the other Allies (the USA, France, and the UK) unifying the western part of Germany. The British and US forces responded by sending supplies to the city by air for over a year (the **Berlin airlift**). In May 1949 the blockade was lifted; the airlift continued until September. The blockade marked the formal division of the city into Eastern and Western sectors. In 1961 East Berlin was sealed off with the construction of the ▷Berlin Wall.

Berlin, Conference of conference 1884–85 of the major European powers (France, Germany, the UK, Belgium, and Portugal) called by Chancellor Otto von Bismarck to decide on the colonial partition of Africa.

Berlin, Congress of congress of the European powers (Russia, Turkey, Austria-Hungary, the UK, France, Italy, and Germany) held in Berlin in 1878 to determine the boundaries of the Balkan states after the Russo-Turkish war of 1877–78.

Prime Minister Disraeli attended as the UK's chief envoy, and declared on his return to England that he had brought back 'peace with honour'. See map on p. 99.

Berlin Wall dividing barrier between East and West Berlin from 1961 to 1989, erected by East Germany to prevent East Germans from leaving for West Germany. Escapers were shot on sight.

Berlin had been formally divided into East and West sectors following the ▷Berlin blockade by Soviet forces during June 1948–May 1949. From 13 August 1961 the East German security forces sealed off all but 12 of the 80 crossing points to West Berlin with a barbed wire barrier. It was reinforced with concrete by the Russians to prevent the escape of unwilling inhabitants of East Berlin to the rival political and economic system of West Berlin. The interconnecting link between East and West Berlin was **Checkpoint Charlie**, where both sides exchanged captured spies. On 9 November 1989 the East German government opened its borders to try to halt the mass exodus of its citizens to the West via other Eastern bloc countries, and the wall was gradually dismantled, with portions of it sold off as souvenirs. See ▷Germany, **reform in East Germany**.

Related Web site: Chris De Witt's Berlin Wall Website http://www.appropriatesoftware.com/BerlinWall/welcome.html

Berlioz, (Louis) Hector (1803–1869) French Romantic composer. He is noted as the founder of modern orchestration. Much of his music was inspired by drama and literature and has a theatrical quality. He wrote symphonic works, such as *Symphonie fantastique* (1830–31) and *Roméo et Juliette* (1839); dramatic cantatas including *La Damnation de Faust* (1846) and *L'Enfance du Christ* (1850–54); sacred music; and three operas: *Benvenuto Cellini* (1838), *Les Troyens* (1856–58), and *Béatrice et Bénédict* (1860–62).

Berlioz studied music at the Paris Conservatoire. He won the Prix de Rome in 1830, and spent two years in Italy. In 1833 he married Harriet Smithson, an Irish actor playing Shakespearean parts in Paris, but they separated in 1842. After some years of poverty and public neglect, he went to Germany in 1842, where he conducted his own works. He subsequently visited Russia and England. In 1854 he married Marie Recio, a singer.

Related Web site: Berlioz, Hector http://w3.rz-berlin.mpg.de/cmp/berlioz.html

Bermuda British colony in the Northwest Atlantic Ocean; area 54 sq km/21 sq mi; population (1994) 60,500. The colony consists of about 150 small islands, of which 20 are inhabited, linked by bridges and causeways. The capital and chief port is ▷Hamilton. Bermuda is Britain's oldest colony, officially taken by the crown in 1684. Under the constitution of 1968, it is fully self-governing, with a governor (Thorold Masefield from 1997), senate, and elected House of Assembly (premier from 1998 Jennifer Smith, Progressive Labour Party). Industries include growing Easter lilies and pharmaceuticals; tourism, banking, and insurance are also important. The currency used in the colony is the Bermuda dollar, the main language spoken is English, and the main religion is Christianity.

Related Web site: Bermuda http://www.umsl.edu/services/govdocs/wofact96/38.htm

Bermuda Triangle sea area bounded by Bermuda, Florida, and Puerto Rico, which gained the nickname 'Deadly Bermuda Triangle' in 1964 when it was suggested that unexplained disappearances of ships and aircraft were exceptionally frequent there. Analysis of the data has not confirmed the idea.

Bern (French **Berne**) capital of ▷Switzerland and of Bern canton, in the west of the country on the River Aare; population (1994) 134,100. Industries include the manufacture of textiles, chocolate, pharmaceuticals, and light metal and electrical goods. There is a magnificent Gothic cathedral, dating from the 15th century. Bern joined the Swiss confederation in 1353 as its eighth member, and became the capital in 1848.

Bern was founded in 1191 and made a free imperial city by Frederick II in 1218. Its name is derived from the bear on its coat of arms, and there has been a bear pit in the city since the 16th century. The minster was begun in 1421, the town hall in 1406, and the university in 1834. It is the seat of the Universal Postal Union.

Related Web site: Welcome to Berne http://www.berntourismus.ch/

Bernadette of Lourdes, St (originally Maries Bernard Soubirous) (1844–1879) French saint, born in Lourdes in the French Pyrenees. In February 1858 she had a vision of the Virgin Mary in a grotto, and it became a centre of pilgrimage. Many sick people who were dipped in the water of a spring there were said to have been cured. Canonized in 1933. Her feast day is 16 April.

Bernadotte, Count Folke (1895–1948) Swedish diplomat and president of the Swedish Red Cross. In 1945 he conveyed Nazi commander Heinrich Himmler's offer of capitulation to the British and US governments, and in 1948 was United Nations mediator in Palestine, where he was assassinated by Israeli Stern Gang guerrillas. He was a nephew of Gustaf VI of Sweden.

Bernadotte, Jean-Baptiste Jules (1763–1844) Marshal in Napoleon's army who in 1818 became ▷Charles XIV of Sweden. Hence, Bernadotte is the family name of the present royal house of Sweden.

Bernard, Claude (1813–1878) French physiologist and founder of experimental medicine. Bernard first demonstrated that digestion is not restricted to the stomach, but takes place throughout the small intestine. He discovered the digestive input of the pancreas, several functions of the liver, and the vasomotor nerves which dilate and contract the blood vessels and thus regulate body temperature. This led him to the concept of the *milieu intérieur* ('internal environment') whose stability is essential to good health.

Bernard of Clairvaux, St (1090–1153) Christian founder in 1115 of Clairvaux monastery in Champagne, France. He reinvigorated the ▷Cistercian order, preached in support of the Second Crusade in 1146, and had the scholastic philosopher Abelard condemned for heresy. He is often depicted with a beehive. Canonized in 1174. His feast day is 20 August.

Bernard of Menthon, St (923–1008) Also known as **Bernard of Montjoux**. Christian priest, founder of the hospices for travellers on the Alpine passes that bear his name. The large, heavily built **St Bernard** dogs, formerly employed to find travellers lost in the snow, were also named after him. He is the patron saint of mountaineers. Canonized in 1115. His feast day is 28 May.

Bernese Alps mountainous area in the south of Bern canton. It includes the Jungfrau, Eiger, and Finsteraarhorn peaks. Interlaken is the chief town.

Bernhardt, Sarah (1844–1923) Stage name of Henriette Rosine Bernard. French actor. She dominated the stage in her day, frequently performing at the Comédie Française in Paris. She excelled in tragic roles, including Cordelia in Shakespeare's *King Lear*, the title role in Racine's *Phèdre*, and the male roles of Hamlet and of Napoleon's son in Edmond Rostand's *L'Aiglon*.

Bernoulli's principle law stating that the pressure of a fluid varies inversely with speed, an increase in speed producing a decrease in pressure (such as a drop in hydraulic pressure as the fluid speeds up flowing through a constriction in a pipe) and vice versa. The principle also explains the pressure differences on each surface of an aerofoil, which gives lift to the wing of an aircraft. The principle was named after Swiss mathematician and physicist Daniel Bernoulli.

Related Web site: Bernoulli's Equation http://www.grc.nasa.gov/WWW/K-12/airplane/bern.html

Bernstein, Leonard (1918–1990) US composer, conductor, and pianist. He was one of the most energetic and versatile 20th-century US musicians. His works, which established a vogue for realistic, contemporary themes, include symphonies such as *The Age of Anxiety* (1949), ballets such as *Fancy Free* (1944), and scores for musicals, including *Wonderful Town* (1953), *West Side Story* (1957), and *Mass* (1971) in memory of President J F Kennedy.

Related Web site: Bernstein, Leonard http://www.leonardbernstein.com

LEONARD BERNSTEIN US composer and conductor Leonard Bernstein. One of Bernstein's greatest achievements was his series of Young People's Concerts with the New York Philharmonic, televised programs that introduced a whole generation to classical music. He conducted these concerts from 1958 to 1972, and referred to them as being 'among my favourite, most highly prized activities of my life.' *Art Archive*

berry fleshy, many-seeded ▷fruit that does not split open to release the seeds. The outer layer of tissue, the exocarp, forms an outer skin that is often brightly coloured to attract birds to eat the fruit and thus disperse the seeds. Examples of berries are the tomato and the grape.

Berry, Chuck (1926–) Born Charles Edward Anderson Berry. US rock-and-roll singer, songwriter, and guitarist. His characteristic guitar riffs became staples of rock music, and his humorous storytelling lyrics were also emulated. He had a string of hits in the 1950s and 1960s beginning with 'Maybellene' (1955), which became an early rock-and-roll classic. He enjoyed a revival of popularity in the 1970s and 1980s. In 1986 he was an inaugural member of the Rock 'n' Roll Hall of Fame.

Born in St Louis, Missouri, Berry began as a blues guitarist in local clubs. Early songs like 'Roll Over Beethoven' (1956), 'Rock 'n'

Roll Music' (1957), 'Sweet Little Sixteen' (1958), and 'Johnny B Goode' (1958) are classics of the genre, and one of them was chosen as a sample of Earth music for the *Voyager* space probes. Berry's biggest hit was provided by the 1972 song, 'My Ding A Ling', which saw him reach a new generation of teenagers. Berry's later career was marred by trouble with the law, and he often seemed to have lost respect for his own work. He was the subject of a film tribute, *Hail! Hail! Rock 'n' Roll* (1987).

Berthollet, Claude Louis (1748–1822) Count. French chemist who carried out research into dyes and bleaches (introducing the use of ▷chlorine as a bleach) and determined the composition of ▷ammonia. Modern chemical nomenclature is based on a system worked out by Berthollet and Antoine ▷Lavoisier.

Bertolucci, Bernardo (1940–) Italian film director. His work combines political and historical perspectives with an elegant and lyrical visual appeal. Such films as *Strategia del ragno/The Spider's Stratagem* (1970), *Il conformista/The Conformist* (1970), and *The Last Emperor* (1987) (which won nine Academy Awards) have demonstrated his philosophical complexity and visual sophistication.

Bertolucci made his feature-film debut with *Prima della rivoluzione/Before the Revolution* (1964), revealing a politically committed sensibility and an indebtedness to the work of Jean-Luc Godard. In 1998 he received the Freedom of Expression award in the National Board of Review of Motion Pictures Awards.

beryl mineral, beryllium aluminium silicate, $3BeO.Al_2O_3.6SiO_2$, which forms crystals chiefly in granite. It is the chief ore of beryllium. Two of its gem forms are aquamarine (light-blue crystals) and emerald (dark-green crystals).

beryllium hard, light-weight, silver-white, metallic element, symbol Be, atomic number 4, relative atomic mass 9.012. It is one of the ▷alkaline-earth metals, with chemical properties similar to those of magnesium. In nature it is found only in combination with other elements and occurs mainly as beryl ($3BeO.Al_2O_3.6SiO_2$). It is used to make sturdy, light alloys and to control the speed of neutrons in nuclear reactors. Beryllium oxide was discovered in 1798 by French chemist Louis-Nicolas Vauquelin (1763–1829), but the element was not isolated until 1828, by Friedrich Wöhler and Antoine-Alexandre-Brutus Bussy independently.

Berzelius, Jöns Jakob (1779–1848) Swedish chemist. He accurately determined more than 2,000 relative atomic and molecular masses. In 1813–14, he devised the system of chemical symbols and formulae now in use and proposed oxygen as a reference standard for atomic masses. His discoveries include the elements cerium in 1804, selenium in 1817, and thorium in 1828; he was the first to prepare silicon in its amorphous form and to isolate zirconium. The words 'isomerism', 'allotropy', and 'protein' were coined by him.

Berzelius noted that some reactions appeared to work faster in the presence of another substance which itself did not appear to change, and postulated that such a substance contained a **catalytic force**. Platinum, for example, was capable of speeding up reactions between gases. Although he appreciated the nature of catalysis, he was unable to give any real explanation of the mechanism.

Besançon administrative centre of the *département* of Doubs and of the ▷Franche-Comté region of France, situated on the River Doubs 75 km/47 mi east of Dijon; population (1990) 119,200. It is an agricultural trading centre and industries include the manufacture of textiles, processed foods, cars, and paper. It is the principal French centre for the manufacture of watches and clocks, and has a school of watch-making. It also has a university. The first factory to produce artificial fibres was established here in 1890.

The writer Victor Hugo (1802–1885) and the Lumière brothers (1862–1954, 1864–1885), inventors of cinematography, were born here.

Besant, Walter (1836–1901) English writer. He wrote novels in partnership with James Rice (1843–1882), and produced an attack on the social evils of the East End of London, *All Sorts and Conditions of Men* (1882), and an unfinished *Survey of London* (1902–12). He was the brother-in-law of the feminist activist Annie Besant. He was knighted in 1895.

Bessarabia former region in southeastern Europe, bordering on the Black Sea and standing between the Prut and Dniester rivers. Its capital was at Kishinev. The region is now divided between the states of Moldova and Ukraine.

Bessel, Friedrich Wilhelm (1784–1846) German astronomer and mathematician. He was the first person to find the approximate distance to a star by direct methods when he measured the ▷parallax (annual displacement) of the star 61 Cygni in 1838. In mathematics, he introduced the series of functions now known as Bessel functions.

Bessemer process first cheap method of making ▷steel, invented by Henry Bessemer in England 1856. It has since been superseded by more efficient steel-making processes, such as the ▷basic-oxygen process. In the Bessemer process compressed air is blown into the bottom of a converter, a furnace shaped like a cement mixer, containing molten pig iron. The excess carbon in the iron burns out, other impurities form a slag, and the furnace is emptied by tilting.

Best, Charles H(erbert) (1899–1978) Canadian physiologist. He was one of the team of Canadian scientists including Frederick ▷Banting whose research resulted in 1922 in the discovery of insulin as a treatment for diabetes.

Best also discovered the vitamin choline and the enzyme histaminase, and introduced the use of the anticoagulant heparin.

Best, George (1946–) Northern Irish footballer. One of football's greatest talents, he was a vital member of the Manchester United side that won the league championship in 1965 and 1967, and the European Cup in 1968, when he was voted both English and European footballer of the year. A goal provider as much as a goal scorer, he scored 134 goals in his 349 appearances for the club from 1963 to 1973.

Related Web site: Best, George http://dnausers.d-n-a.net/dnetmQXk/legends/georgebest.htm

bestiary in medieval times, a book with stories and illustrations which depicted real and mythical animals or plants to illustrate a (usually Christian) moral. The stories were initially derived from the Greek *Physiologus*, a collection of 48 such stories, written in Alexandria around the 2nd century.

beta-blocker any of a class of drugs that block impulses that stimulate certain nerve endings (beta receptors) serving the heart muscle. This reduces the heart rate and the force of contraction, which in turn reduces the amount of oxygen (and therefore the blood supply) required by the heart. Beta-blockers may be useful in the treatment of angina, arrhythmia (abnormal heart rhythms), and raised blood pressure, and following heart attacks. They must be withdrawn from use gradually.

beta decay disintegration of the nucleus of an atom to produce a beta particle, or high-speed electron, and an electron antineutrino. During beta decay, a neutron in the nucleus changes into a proton, thereby increasing the atomic number by one while the mass number stays the same. The mass lost in the change is converted into kinetic (movement) energy of the beta particle. Beta decay is caused by the weak nuclear force, one of the fundamental ▷forces of nature operating inside the nucleus.

beta particle electron ejected with great velocity from a radioactive atom that is undergoing spontaneous disintegration. Beta particles do not exist in the nucleus but are created on disintegration, beta decay, when a neutron converts to a proton by emitting an electron.

Beta particles are more penetrating than ▷alpha particles, but less so than ▷gamma radiation; they can travel several metres in air, but are stopped by 2–3 mm of aluminium. They are less strongly ionizing than alpha particles and, like cathode rays, are easily deflected by magnetic and electric fields.

Betelgeuse (or **Alpha Orionis**) red supergiant star in the constellation of ▷Orion. It is the tenth-brightest star in the night sky, although its brightness varies. It is 1,100 million km/700 million mi across, about 800 times larger than the Sun, roughly the same size as the orbit of Mars. It is over 10,000 times as luminous as the Sun, and lies 310 light years from the Sun. Light takes 60 minutes to travel across the giant star.

It was the first star whose angular diameter was measured with the Mount Wilson ▷interferometer in 1920.

betel nut fruit of the areca palm (*Areca catechu*), which is chewed together with lime and betel pepper as a stimulant by peoples of the East and Papua New Guinea. Chewing it blackens the teeth and stains the mouth deep red.

Bethlehem (Arabic **Beit-Lahm**) city on the west bank of the River Jordan, 8 km/5 mi south of Jerusalem; population (1997 est) 135,000. It was occupied by Israel in 1967 and came under control of the Palestinian Authority in December 1995. In the Bible it is mentioned as the birthplace of King David and Jesus, and in 326 the Church of the Nativity was built over the grotto said to be the birthplace of Jesus.

Related Web site: Bethlehem University http://www.bethlehem.edu/

> **John Betjeman**
> *Poetry is the shortest way of saying things.*
> Quoted in postscript to Michael Harrison and Christopher Stuart-Clark (ed) *New Dragon Book of Verse* 1977

Betjeman, John (1906–1984) English poet and essayist. He was the originator of a peculiarly English light verse, nostalgic, and delighting in Victorian and Edwardian architecture. He also wrote prose works on architecture and social history which reflect his interest in the Gothic Revival. His *Collected Poems* appeared in 1958 and a verse autobiography, *Summoned by Bells*, in 1960.

Betjeman's verse, seen by some as facile, has been much enjoyed for its compassion and wit, and its evocation of places and situations. His letters, edited by his daughter, Candida Lycett Green, were published in two volumes (1994 and 1995). He was knighted in 1969 and became poet laureate in 1972.

Related Web site: Betjeman, John http://www.johnbetjeman.com/

betony plant belonging to the mint family, formerly used in medicine and dyeing. It has a hairy stem and leaves, and dense heads of reddish-purple flowers. (*Stachys* (formerly *Betonica*) *officinalis*, family Labiatae.)

Bettelheim, Bruno (1903–1990) Austrian-born US child psychologist. At the University of Chicago he founded a treatment centre for emotionally disturbed children based on the principle of a supportive home environment. Among his books are *Love Is Not Enough* (1950) and *The Uses of Enchantment: The Meaning and Importance of Fairy Tales* (1976).

betting wagering money on the outcome of a game, race, or other event, not necessarily a sporting event.

Beuys, Joseph (1921–1986) German sculptor and performance artist. He was one of the leaders of the European avant-garde during the 1970s and 1980s. An exponent of Arte Povera, he made use of so-called 'worthless', unusual materials such as felt and fat. His best-known performance was *How to Explain Pictures to a Dead Hare* (1965). He was also an influential exponent of video art, for example, *Felt TV* (1968).

Bevan, Aneurin (Nye) (1897–1960) British Labour politician. Son of a Welsh miner, and himself a miner at 13, he was member of Parliament for Ebbw Vale 1929–60. As minister of health 1945–51, he inaugurated the National ▷Health Service (NHS); he was minister of labour from January to April 1951, when he resigned (with Harold Wilson) on the introduction of NHS charges and led a Bevanite faction against the government. In 1956 he became chief Labour spokesperson on foreign affairs, and deputy leader of the Labour party in 1959. He was an outstanding speaker.

Beveridge Report, the in Britain, popular name of *Social Insurance and Allied Services*, a report written by William Beveridge in 1942 that formed the basis for the social-reform legislation of the Labour government of 1945–50.

Beveridge, William Henry (1879–1963) 1st Baron Beveridge. British economist. A civil servant, he acted as Lloyd George's lieutenant in the social legislation of the Liberal government before World War I. His *Report on Social Insurance and Allied Services* (1942), known as the **Beveridge Report**, formed the basis of the welfare state in Britain.

Beverly Hills residential city and a part of greater Los Angeles, southwest California, USA; population (1990) 31,900. It is located 16 km/10 mi northwest of Los Angeles city centre, and extends up the Santa Monica Mountains to the north. It is entirely surrounded by the city of Los Angeles. There is some light manufacturing, chiefly of electronic equipment, and a number of corporate and financial offices. Rodeo Drive is a popular shopping area for prestige goods.

Bevin, Ernest (1881–1951) British Labour politician. Chief creator of the Transport and General Workers' Union, he was its general secretary 1921–40. He served as minister of labour and national service 1940–45 in Winston Churchill's wartime coalition government, and organized the 'Bevin boys', chosen by ballot to work in the coalmines as war service. As foreign secretary in the Labour government 1945–51, he played a leading part in the creation of ▷NATO.

Bewick, Thomas (1753–1828) English wood engraver. He excelled in animal subjects, some of his finest works appearing in his illustrated *A General History of Quadrupeds* (1790) and *A History of British Birds* (1797–1804).

Bexley outer borough of southeast Greater London, including the suburbs of Crayford, Erith, and Sidcup; population (1996 est) 219,300. Local industries include armaments manufacture at Crayford, site of the Vickers Factory, since the 19th century.

Beza, Théodore (1519–1605) French Théodore De Bèsze. French church reformer. He settled in Geneva, Switzerland, where he worked with the Protestant leader John Calvin and succeeded him as head of the reformed church there in 1564. He wrote in defence of the burning of Spanish theologian Michael ▷Servetus (1554) and produced a Latin translation of the New Testament.

Béziers town in the Hérault *département* in southern France, situated at the crossing of the River Orb and the Canal du Midi, 60 km/37 mi southwest of Montpellier; population (1990) 72,300. It is a centre of the wine and spirit trade. Other industries include the manufacture of textiles, chemicals, and confectionery. Features include pre-Roman and Roman remains, the Gothic church of St-Nazaire, formerly a cathedral, and ancient city walls.

BFI abbreviation for ▷British Film Institute.

BFPO abbreviation for **British Forces Post Office**.

bhakti (Sanskrit 'devotion') in Hinduism, a tradition of worship that emphasizes devotion to a personal god as the sole necessary means for achieving salvation. It developed in southern India in the 6th–8th centuries and in northern India from the 14th century.

bhang name for a weak form of the drug ▷cannabis used in India.

Bharat Hindi name for ▷India.

Bhopal industrial city and capital of ▷Madhya Pradesh, central India, 525 km/326 mi southwest of Allahabad; population (1991) 1,064,000. Textiles, chemicals, electrical goods, and jewellery are manufactured. Nearby Bhimbetka Caves, discovered in 1973, have the world's largest collection of prehistoric paintings, about 10,000 years old. In 1984 some 2,600 people died from an escape of the poisonous gas methyl isocyanate from a factory owned by US company Union Carbide; another 300,000 suffer from long-term health problems.

Bhumibol Adulyadej (1927–   ) King of Thailand from 1946. Born in the USA and educated in Bangkok and Switzerland, he succeeded to the throne on the assassination of his brother. In 1973 he was active, with popular support, in overthrowing the military government of Marshal Thanom Kittikachorn and thus ended a sequence of army-dominated regimes in power from 1932.

Bhutan see country box.

Bhutto, Benazir (1953–   ) Pakistani politician. She was leader of the Pakistan People's Party (PPP) from 1984, a position she held in exile until 1986. Bhutto became prime minister of Pakistan from 1988 until 1990, when the opposition manoeuvred her from office and charged her with corruption. She again rose to the office of prime minister (1993–96), only to be removed for a second time under suspicion of corruption. In 1999, while living in self-imposed exile in London, Bhutto was found guilty of corruption and given a five-year prison sentence.

Born into a wealthy, feudal, land-owning family, Benazir Bhutto was educated at Harvard and Oxford universities. She returned to Pakistan in 1977 but was placed under house arrest after General ▷Zia ul-Haq seized power from her father, Prime Minister Zulfikar Ali Bhutto, who was hanged in 1979. On her release she moved to the UK and became, with her mother Nusrat, the joint leader in exile of the opposition PPP.

When martial law had been lifted, she returned to Pakistan in April 1986 and became the first female leader of a Muslim state in November 1988. In August 1990, she was removed from office by presidential decree on charges of corruption and abuse of power. Bhutto returned to office in 1993 following a power struggle between President Ghulam Ishaq Khan and Prime Minister Nawaz Sharif. She was removed from office in November 1996 amidst increasing concern over government corruption. In January 1998, 12 charges were filed against the Bhutto family by the government and she and her husband were found guilty of corruption in April 1999. However, in April 2001, Pakistan's Supreme Court quashed the convictions and ordered a retrial.

Related Web site: Bhutto, Benazir http://www.wic.org/bio/bbhutto.htm

Bhutto, Zulfikar Ali (1928–1979) Pakistani politician, president 1971–73, and prime minister from 1973 until the 1977 military coup led by General ▷Zia ul-Haq. In 1978 Bhutto was

> ### Bible
> *In the beginning was the Word, and the Word was with God, and the Word was God.*
>
> John 1:1

Bhutan

Bhutan mountainous, landlocked country in the eastern Himalayas (southeast Asia), bounded north and west by Tibet (China) and to the south and east by India.

NATIONAL NAME *Druk-yul/Kingdom of Bhutan*
AREA 47,500 sq km/18,147 sq mi
CAPITAL Thimphu
MAJOR TOWNS/CITIES Paro, Punakha, Mongar, Phuntsholing, Wangdiphodrang, Tashigang
PHYSICAL FEATURES occupies southern slopes of the Himalayas; Gangkar Punsum (7,529 m/24,700 ft) is one of the world's highest unclimbed peaks; cut by valleys formed by tributaries of the Brahmaputra; thick forests in south

Government

HEAD OF STATE Jigme Singye Wangchuk from 1972
HEAD OF GOVERNMENT Lyompo Kinzang Dorji from 2002
POLITICAL SYSTEM absolutist
POLITICAL EXECUTIVE absolute
ADMINISTRATIVE DIVISIONS 20 districts
ARMED FORCES 6,000 (2000)
DEATH PENALTY retains the death penalty for ordinary crimes but can be considered abolitionist in practice; date of last known execution 1964

Economy and resources

CURRENCY ngultrum, although the Indian rupee is also accepted
GPD (US$) 594 million (2002 est)
REAL GDP GROWTH (% change on previous year) 7.0 (2001)
GNI (US$) 505 million (2002 est)
GNI PER CAPITA (PPP) (US$) 1,530 (2002 est)
CONSUMER PRICE INFLATION 5% (2003 est)
FOREIGN DEBT (US$) 225 million (2001 est)
MAJOR TRADING PARTNERS India, Bangladesh, Singapore, Europe
RESOURCES limestone, gypsum, coal, slate, dolomite, lead, talc, copper
INDUSTRIES food processing, cement, calcium carbide, textiles, tourism, cardamon, gypsum, timber, handicrafts, cement, fruit, electricity, precious stones, spices
EXPORTS cardamom, cement, timber, fruit, electricity, precious stones, spices. Principal market: India 94% (1998)
IMPORTS aircraft, mineral fuels, machinery and transport equipment, rice. Principal source: India 77% (1998)
ARABLE LAND 2.8% (2000 est)
AGRICULTURAL PRODUCTS potatoes, rice, apples, oranges, cardamoms; timber production

Population and society

POPULATION 2,257,000 (2003 est)
POPULATION GROWTH RATE 2.6% (2000–05)
POPULATION DENSITY (per sq km) 48 (2003 est)
URBAN POPULATION (% of total) 8 (2003 est)
AGE DISTRIBUTION (% of total population) 0–14 42%, 15–59 51%, 60+ 7% (2002 est)
ETHNIC GROUPS 60% Bhotia, living principally in north and east (Tibetan descent), 32%; a substantial Nepali minority (about 30%) lives in the south – they are prohibited from moving into the Bhotia-dominated north; 10% indigenous or migrant tribes
LANGUAGE Dzongkha (a Tibetan dialect; official), Tibetan, Sharchop, Bumthap, Nepali, English
RELIGION 70% Mahayana Buddhist (state religion), 25% Hindu
EDUCATION not compulsory
LITERACY RATE 61% (men); 34% (women) (2000 est)

LABOUR FORCE 93% agriculture, 2% industry, 5% services (2000)
LIFE EXPECTANCY 62 (men); 65 (women) (2000–05)
CHILD MORTALITY RATE (under 5, per 1,000 live births) 95 (2001)
PHYSICIANS (per 1,000 people) 1.6 (1998 est)
HOSPITAL BEDS (per 1,000 people) 1.8 (1998 est)
TV SETS (per 1,000 people) 6 (1999 est)
RADIOS (per 1,000 people) 18 (1997)
INTERNET USERS (per 10,000 people) 144.8 (2002 est)

See also ▷British East India Company.

Chronology

to 8th century: Under effective Indian control.

16th century: Came under Tibetan rule.

1616–51: Unified by Ngawang Namgyal, leader of the Drukpa Kagyu (Thunder Dragon) Tibetan Buddhist branch.

1720: Came under Chinese rule.

1774: Treaty signed with East India Company.

1865: Trade treaty with Britain signed after invasion.

1907: Ugyen Wangchuk, governor of Tongsa, became Bhutan's first hereditary monarch.

1910: Anglo-Bhutanese Treaty signed, placing foreign relations under the 'guidance' of the British government in India.

1949: Indo-Bhutan Treaty of Friendship signed, giving India continued influence over Bhutan's foreign relations, but returning territory annexed in 1865.

1953: The national assembly (Tshogdu) was established.

1958: Slavery was abolished.

1959: 4,000 Tibetan refugees were given asylum after Chinese annexation of Tibet.

1968: The first cabinet was established.

1973: Bhutan joined the nonaligned movement.

1979: Tibetan refugees were told to take Bhutanese citizenship or leave; most stayed.

1983: Bhutan became a founding member of the South Asian Regional Association for Cooperation.

1988: The Buddhist Dzongkha king imposed a 'code of conduct' suppressing the customs of the large Hindu-Nepali community in the south.

1990: Hundreds of people were allegedly killed during prodemocracy demonstrations.

1998: Political powers were ceded from the monarchy to the National Assembly. Lyonpo Jigme Thimley became prime minister.

BHUTAN Education in Bhutan is conducted in Dzongkha, the national language and a Tibetan dialect, so much of the teaching beyond a primary level is by Buddhist monks. The Nepalese Hindu minority must rely on state colleges, such as this one at Tashigang in the eastern part of the country. *Corel*

Books of the Bible

Name of book	Chapters	Date written
Books of the Old Testament		
Genesis	50	mid-8th century BC
Exodus	40	950–586 BC
Leviticus	27	mid-7th century BC
Numbers	36	850–650 BC
Deuteronomy	34	mid-7th century BC
Joshua	24	c. 550 BC
Judges	21	c. 550 BC
Ruth	4	late 3rd century BC
1 Samuel	31	c. 900 BC
2 Samuel	24	c. 900 BC
1 Kings	22	550–600 BC
2 Kings	25	550–600 BC
1 Chronicles	29	c. 300 BC
2 Chronicles	36	c. 300 BC
Ezra	10	c. 450 BC
Nehemiah	13	c. 450 BC
Esther	10	c. 200 BC
Job	42	600–400 BC
Psalms	150	6th–2nd century BC
Proverbs	31	350–150 BC
Ecclesiastes	12	c. 200 BC
Song of Solomon	8	3rd century BC
Isaiah	66	late 3rd century BC
Jeremiah	52	604 BC
Lamentations	5	586–536 BC
Ezekiel	48	6th century BC
Daniel	12	c. 166 BC
Hosea	14	c. 732 BC
Joel	3	c. 500 BC
Amos	9	775–750 BC
Obadiah	1	6th–3rd century BC
Jonah	4	600–200 BC
Micah	7	late 3rd century BC
Nahum	3	c. 626 BC
Habakkuk	3	c. 600 BC
Zephaniah	3	3rd century BC
Haggai	2	c. 520 BC
Zechariah	14	c. 520 BC
Malachi	4	c. 430 BC
Books of the New Testament		
Matthew	28	before AD 70
Mark	16	before AD 70
Luke	24	AD 70–80
John	21	AD 90–100
Acts	28	AD 70–80
Romans	16	AD 355–358
1 Corinthians	16	AD 57
2 Corinthians	13	AD 57
Galatians	6	AD 53
Ephesians	6	AD 140
Philippians	4	AD 63
Colossians	4	AD 140
1 Thessalonians	5	AD 50–54
2 Thessalonians	3	AD 50–54
1 Timothy	6	before AD 64
2 Timothy	4	before AD 64
Titus	3	before AD 64
Philemon	1	AD 60–62
Hebrews	13	AD 80–90
James	5	before AD 52
1 Peter	5	before AD 64
2 Peter	3	before AD 64
1 John	5	AD 90–100
2 John	1	AD 90–100
3 John	1	AD 90–100
Jude	1	AD 75–80
Revelation	22	AD 81–96

sentenced to death for conspiring to murder a political opponent and was hanged the following year. He was the father of Benazir Bhutto.

Biafra, Bight of (or Bonny, Bight of) area of sea off the coasts of Nigeria and Cameroon.

Biafra, Republic of African state proclaimed 1967 when fears that Nigerian central government was increasingly in the hands of the rival Hausa tribe led the predominantly Ibo Eastern Region of Nigeria to secede under Lt-Col Odumegwu Ojukwu. On the proclamation of Biafra, civil war ensued with the rest of the federation. In a bitterly fought campaign federal forces confined the Biafrans to a shrinking area of the interior by 1968, and by 1970

Biafra ceased to exist. Around 1 million Biafrans died in the famine caused by the civil war.

Bible (Greek *ta biblia* 'the books') the sacred book of the Jewish and Christian religions. The Hebrew Bible, recognized by both Jews and Christians, is called the ▷Old Testament by Christians. The ▷New Testament comprises books recognized by the Christian church from the 4th century as canonical. The Roman Catholic Bible also includes the ▷Apocrypha.

Related Web site: Bible Gateway http://bible.gospelcom.net/

bicarbonate of soda (or baking soda) (technical name sodium hydrogencarbonate) $NaHCO_3$ white crystalline solid that neutralizes acids and is used in medicine to treat acid indigestion. It is also used in baking powders and effervescent drinks.

bichir African fish, genus *Polypterus*, found in tropical swamps and rivers. Cylindrical in shape, some species grow to 70 cm/2.3 ft or more. They show many 'primitive' features, such as breathing air by using the swimbladder, having a spiral valve in the intestine, having heavy bony scales, and having larvae with external gills. These, and the fleshy fins, lead some scientists to think they are related to lungfish and coelacanths.

bicycle pedal-driven two-wheeled vehicle used in ▷cycling. It consists of a metal frame mounted on two large wire-spoked wheels, with handlebars in front and a seat between the front and back wheels. The bicycle is an energy-efficient, nonpolluting form of transport, and it is estimated that 800 million bicycles are in use throughout the world – outnumbering cars three to one. China, India, Denmark, and the Netherlands are countries with a high use of bicycles. More than 10% of road spending in the Netherlands is on cycleways and bicycle parking.

BICYCLE The 'hobby horse' and the 'bone-shaker' were two of the earliest bicycles designed. From pre-pedal machines such as the 'hobby horse' (designed in the late 18th century) came the introduction of the pedal with the 'bone-shaker' bicycle. *Archive Photos*

Bidault, Georges Augustin (1899–1983) French Christian Democrat politician, cofounder of the Mouvement Républicain Populaire (MRP) and prime minister 1946 and 1949–50.

Bienne French form of Biel, a town in Switzerland.

biennial plant plant that completes its life cycle in two years. During the first year it grows vegetatively and the surplus food produced is stored in its ▷perennating organ, usually the root. In the following year these food reserves are used for the production of leaves, flowers, and seeds, after which the plant dies. Many root vegetables are biennials, including the carrot *Daucus carota* and parsnip *Pastinaca sativa*. Some garden plants that are grown as biennials are actually perennials, for example, the wallflower *Cheiranthus cheiri*.

Bierce, Ambrose Gwinnett (1842–c. 1914) US author. After service in the American Civil War, he established his reputation as a master of the short story, his themes being war and the supernatural, as in *Tales of Soldiers and Civilians* (1891) and *Can Such Things Be?* (1893). He also wrote *The Devil's Dictionary* (1911; first published as *The Cynic's Word Book* in 1906), a collection of ironic definitions showing his sardonic humour. He disappeared in Mexico in 1913.

Bierstadt, Albert (1830–1902) German-born US landscape painter. His spectacular panoramas of the American wilderness fell out of favour after his death until interest in the ▷Hudson River School was rekindled in the late 20th century. A classic work is *Thunderstorm in the Rocky Mountains* (1859; Museum of Fine Arts, Boston).

> ### Georges Bidault
> *Freedom is when one hears the bell at 7 o'clock in the morning and knows it is the milkman and not the Gestapo.*
> *The Observer* 23 April 1950

> ### Ambrose Bierce
> *Education, n. That which discloses to the wise and disguises from the foolish their lack of understanding.*
> *The Devil's Dictionary* (1911)

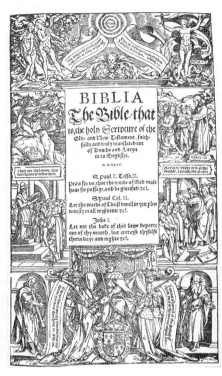

BIBLE Title page of the first complete English Bible, printed in Zurich in 1535. *Philip Sauvain Picture Collection*

bigamy in law, the offence of marrying a person while already lawfully married to another. In some countries marriage to more than one wife or husband is lawful; see also ▷polygamy.

big-band jazz swing music created in the late 1930s and 1940s by bands of 13 or more players, such as those of Duke ▷Ellington and Benny Goodman. Big-band jazz relied on fixed arrangements, where there is more than one instrument to some of the parts, rather than improvisation. Big bands were mainly dance bands, and they ceased to be economically viable in the 1950s.

Big Bang in astronomy, the hypothetical 'explosive' event that marked the origin of the universe as we know it. At the time of the Big Bang, the entire universe was squeezed into a hot, superdense state. The Big Bang explosion threw this compact material outwards, producing the expanding universe (see ▷red shift). The cause of the Big Bang is unknown; observations of the current rate of expansion of the universe suggest that it took place about 10–20 billion years ago. The Big Bang theory began modern ▷cosmology.

According to a modified version of the Big Bang, called the **inflationary theory**, the universe underwent a rapid period of expansion shortly after the Big Bang, which accounts for its current large size and uniform nature. The inflationary theory is supported by the most recent observations of the ▷cosmic background radiation.

Scientists have calculated that one 10^{-36} second (equivalent to one million-million-million-million-million-millionth of a second) before the Big Bang, the universe was the size of a pea, and the temperature was 10 billion million million million°C (18 million million million°F). One second after the Big Bang, the temperature was about 10 billion°C (18 billion°F).

The first detailed images of the universe as it existed 300,000 years after the Big Bang were released by the US National Aeronautics and Space Administration (NASA) in April 2000. The images were created by mapping cosmic background radiation.

Big Bang in economics, popular term for the changes instituted in late 1986 to the organization and practices of the City of London as Britain's financial centre, including the liberalization of the London ▷stock exchange. This involved merging the functions of jobber (dealer in stocks and shares) and broker (who mediates between the jobber and the public), introducing negotiated commission rates, and allowing foreign banks and financial companies to own British brokers/jobbers, or themselves to join the London Stock Exchange.

Big Ben popular name for the bell in the clock tower of the Houses of Parliament in London, cast at the Whitechapel Bell Foundry in 1858, and known as 'Big Ben' after Benjamin Hall, First Commissioner of Works at the time. It weighs 13.7 tonnes. The name is often used to mean the tower as well.

bight coastal indentation, crescent-shaped or gently curving, such as the Bight of ▷Biafra in West Africa and the Great Australian Bight.

Bihar (or **Behar**) state of northeast India; area 173,900 sq km/ 67,125 sq mi; population (2001 est) 77,633,000 (75% living in northern plains). The capital is ▷Patna. The River Ganges runs west–east in the north of the state, through intensely cultivated alluvial plains which are prone to drought and floods. In the largely forested south are the Rajmahal Hills and Chota Nagpur plateau. The chief industries are copper, iron, and coal; Bihar accounts for 40% of India's mineral production. Important agricultural products are rice, jute, sugar cane, cereals, oilseed, tobacco, and potatoes. The languages spoken are Hindi and Bihari.

Bihari a northern Indian people, also living in Bangladesh, Nepal, and Pakistan, and numbering over 40 million. The Bihari are mainly Muslim. The Bihari language is related to Hindi and has several widely varying dialects. It belongs to the Indic branch of the Indo-European family. Many Bihari were massacred during the formation of Bangladesh, which they opposed.

Bikini Atoll atoll in the ▷Marshall Islands, western Pacific, where the USA carried out 23 atomic- and hydrogen-bomb tests (some underwater) from 1946 to 1958. The islanders were relocated by the USA before 1946. Some returned after Bikini was declared safe for habitation 1969, but they were again removed in the late 1970s because of continuing harmful levels of radiation. In 1990 a US plan was announced to remove radioactive topsoil, allowing 800 islanders to return home.
   Related Web site: Bikini Atoll http://www.bikiniatoll.com/

Biko, Steve (1946–1977) Born Bantu Stephen Biko. South African civil-rights leader. An active opponent of ▷apartheid, he was arrested in September 1977; he died in detention six days later. Following his death in the custody of South African police, he became a symbol of the anti-apartheid movement. An inquest in the late 1980s found no-one was to blame for Biko's death.

Five former security policemen confessed to being involved in Biko's murder in January 1997. They applied for an amnesty to the Truth and Reconciliation Commission (TRC), the body charged with healing South Africa by exposing its past and laying foundations for a more peaceful future. The amnesty application angered Biko's family, and his widow challenged the legitimacy of the TRC in the Constitutional Court.

Biko founded the South African Students Organization (SASO) in 1968 and was cofounder in 1972 of the Black People's Convention, also called the Black Consciousness movement, a radical association of South African students that aimed to develop black pride.

Bilbao industrial port and capital of Vizcaya province in the Basque Country, northern Spain; it is surrounded by mountains,

BILBAO The Guggenheim Art Museum in Bilbao, Spain, one of several art museums patronized by the US philanthropist Peggy Guggenheim. *Image Bank*

and situated on an inlet of the Bay of Biscay, and on the Nervion River; population (1994) 372,000. Bilbao is a commercial centre and one of the chief ports in Spain; industries include iron and steel production, shipbuilding, chemicals, cement, and food-processing.

bilberry any of several shrubs belonging to the heath family, closely related to North American blueberries. Bilberries are sometimes referred to as blaeberries, whortleberries, or huckleberries. They have blue or black edible berries. (Genus *Vaccinium*, family Ericaceae.)
   Related Web site: Bilberry
   http://www.botanical.com/botanical/
   mgmh/b/bilber37.html

BILBERRY The common bilberry *Vaccinium myrtillus*, shown here, is found across Europe and northern Asia. *Premaphotos Wildlife*

bilby rabbit-eared bandicoot *Macrotis lagotis*, a lightly built marsupial with big ears and long nose. This burrowing animal is mainly carnivorous, and its pouch opens backwards.

Bildungsroman (German 'education novel') novel that deals with the psychological and emotional development of its protagonist, tracing his or her life from inexperienced youth to maturity. The first example of the type is generally considered to be C M Wieland's *Agathon* (1765–66), but it was ▷Goethe's *Wilhelm Meisters Lehrjahre/Wilhelm Meister's Apprenticeship* (1795–96) that established the genre. Although taken up by writers in other languages, it remained chiefly a German form; later examples include Thomas ▷Mann's *Der Zauberberg/The Magic Mountain* (1924).

bile brownish alkaline fluid produced by the liver. Bile is stored in the gall bladder and is intermittently released into the duodenum (small intestine) to aid digestion. Bile consists of bile salts, bile pigments, cholesterol, and lecithin. Bile salts assist in the breakdown and absorption of fats; bile pigments are the breakdown products of old red blood cells that are passed into the gut to be eliminated with the faeces.

bilharzia (or **schistosomiasis**) disease that causes anaemia, inflammation, formation of scar tissue, dysentery, enlargement of the spleen and liver, cancer of the bladder, and cirrhosis of the liver. It is contracted by bathing in water contaminated with human sewage. Some 200 million people are thought to suffer from this disease in the tropics, and 750,000 people a year die.

Freshwater snails act as host to the first larval stage of blood flukes of the genus *Schistosoma*; when these larvae leave the snail in their second stage of development, they are able to pass through human skin, become sexually mature, and produce quantities of eggs, which pass to the intestine or bladder. Numerous eggs are excreted from the body in urine or faeces to continue the cycle. Treatment is by means of drugs, usually containing antimony, to kill the parasites.

bill in birds, the projection of the skull bones covered with a horny sheath. It is not normally sensitive, except in some aquatic birds, rooks, and woodpeckers, where the bill is used to locate food that is not visible. The bills of birds are adapted by shape and size to specific diets, for example, shovellers use their bills to sieve mud in order to extract food; birds of prey have hooked bills adapted to tearing flesh; the bills of the avocet and the curlew are long and narrow for picking tiny invertebrates out of the mud; and those of woodpeckers are sharp for pecking holes in trees and plucking out insects. The bill is also used by birds for preening, fighting, display, and nest-building.

billet doux (French 'sweet note') a letter to or from one's lover.

billiards indoor game played, normally by two players, with tapered poles (cues) and composition balls (one red, two white) on a rectangular table covered with a green, feltlike cloth (baize). The table has six pockets, one at each corner and in each of the long sides at the middle. Scoring strokes are made by potting the red ball, potting the opponent's ball, or potting another ball off one of these two. The cannon (when the cue ball hits the two other balls on the table) is another scoring stroke. In 1998 billiards received recognition from the International Olympic Committee as an Olympic sport, along with snooker, pool, and carom (or French) billiards.

billion the cardinal number represented by a 1 followed by nine zeros (1,000,000,000 or 10^9), equivalent to a thousand million.

Bill of Rights in the USA, the first ten amendments to the US ▷Constitution, incorporated in 1791:
1 guarantees freedom of worship, of speech, of the press, of assembly, and to petition the government;
2 grants the right to keep and bear arms;
3 prohibits billeting of soldiers in private homes in peacetime;
4 forbids unreasonable search and seizure;
5 guarantees none be 'deprived of life, liberty or property without due process of law' or compelled in any criminal case to be a witness against himself or herself;
6 grants the right to speedy trial, to call witnesses, and to have defence counsel;
7 grants the right to trial by jury of one's peers;
8 prevents the infliction of excessive bail or fines, or 'cruel and unusual punishment';
9, 10 provide a safeguard to the states and people for all rights not specifically delegated to the central government.
   Related Web site: Bill of Rights http://earlyamerica.com/
   earlyamerica/freedom/bill/index.html

Bill of Rights in Britain, an act of Parliament of 1689 which established Parliament as the primary governing body of the country. It made provisions limiting ▷royal prerogative with respect to legislation, executive power, money levies, courts, and the army, and stipulated Parliament's consent to many government functions.

The Bill of Rights embodied the Declaration of Rights which contained the conditions on which William and Mary were offered the throne in the ▷Glorious Revolution. The act made illegal the suspension of laws by royal authority without Parliament's consent; the power to dispense with laws; the establishment of special courts of law; levying money by royal prerogative without Parliament's consent; and the maintenance of a standing army in peacetime without Parliament's consent. It also asserted a right to petition the sovereign, freedom of parliamentary elections, freedom of speech in parliamentary debates, and the necessity of frequent parliaments.

The Bill of Rights is the nearest approach to a written constitution that the United Kingdom possesses. Its provisions, where applicable, were incorporated in the US constitution ratified in 1788.

Billy the Kid (1859–1881) Born William H Bonney. US outlaw. A leader in the 1878 Lincoln County cattle war in New Mexico, he allegedly killed his first victim at 12 and was reputed to have killed 21 men by age 18.

Born in Brooklyn, New York, Bonney moved west with his family to Kansas and then New Mexico. He was sentenced to death for murdering a sheriff, but escaped (killing two guards), and was finally shot by Sheriff Pat Garrett while trying to avoid recapture.

binary fission in biology, a form of ▷asexual reproduction, whereby a single-celled organism, such as a bacterium or the amoeba, divides into two smaller 'daughter' cells.

binary number system system of numbers to ▷base two, using combinations of the digits 1 and 0. Codes based on binary numbers are used to represent instructions and data in all modern digital computers, the values of the binary digits (contracted to 'bits') being stored or transmitted as, for example, open/closed switches, magnetized/unmagnetized disks and tapes, and high/low voltages in circuits.

binary number code

data	A
binary code	0 1 0 0 0 0 0 1
digital signal in the computer	⎍_⎍_ →

BINARY NUMBER SYSTEM The capital letter A represented in binary form.

The value of any position in a binary number increases by powers of 2 (doubles) with each move from right to left (1, 2, 4, 8, 16, and so on). For example, 1011 in the binary number system represents $(1 \times 8) + (0 \times 4) + (1 \times 2) + (1 \times 1)$, which adds up to 11 in the decimal system.

The value of any position in a normal decimal, or base-10, number increases by powers of 10 with each move from right to left (1, 10, 100, 1,000, 10,000, and so on). For example, the decimal number 2,567 stands for:

$(2 \times 1,000) + (5 \times 100) + (6 \times 10) + (7 \times 1)$.

binary search in computing, rapid technique used to find any particular record in a list of records held in sequential order. The computer is programmed to compare the record sought with the record in the middle of the ordered list. This being done, the computer discards the half of the list in which the record does not appear, thereby reducing the number of records left to search by half. This process of selecting the middle record and discarding the unwanted half of the list is repeated until the required record is found.

binary star pair of stars moving in orbit around their common centre of mass. Observations show that most stars are binary, or even multiple – for example, the nearest star system to the Sun, ▷Rigil Kent (Alpha Centauri).

One of the stars in the binary system Epsilon Aurigae may be the largest star known. Its diameter is 2,800 times that of the Sun. If it were in the position of the Sun, it would engulf Mercury, Venus, Earth, Mars, Jupiter, and Saturn. A spectroscopic binary is a binary in which two stars are so close together that they cannot be seen separately, but their separate light spectra can be distinguished by a spectroscope.

Another type is the ▷eclipsing binary, A double star in which the two stars periodically pass in front of each other as seen from Earth. When one star crosses in front of the other, the total light received on Earth from the two stars declines. The first eclipsing binary to be noticed was Algol, in 1670, by Italian astronomer Germniano Montanari.

binary weapon in chemical warfare, weapon consisting of two substances that in isolation are harmless but when mixed together form a poisonous nerve gas. They are loaded into the delivery system separately and combine after launch.

binding energy in physics, the amount of energy needed to break the nucleus of an atom into the neutrons and protons of which it is made.

bind over in law, a UK court order that requires a person to carry out some act, usually by an order given in a magistrates' court. A person may be bound over to appear in court at a particular time if bail has been granted or, most commonly, be bound over not to commit some offence; for example, causing a breach of the peace.

binoculars optical instrument for viewing an object in magnification with both eyes; for example, field glasses and opera glasses. Binoculars consist of two telescopes containing lenses and prisms, which produce a stereoscopic effect as well as magnifying the image.

Use of prisms has the effect of 'folding' the light path, allowing for a compact design.

binomial in mathematics, an expression consisting of two terms, such as $a + b$ or $a - b$.

binomial system of nomenclature in biology, the system in which all organisms are identified by a two-part Latinized name. Devised by the biologist ▷Linnaeus, it is also known as the Linnaean system. The first name is capitalized and identifies the ▷genus; the second identifies the ▷species within that genus, for example *Homo Sapiens* for humans means 'wise man'.

binturong shaggy-coated mammal *Arctitis binturong*, the largest member of the mongoose family, nearly 1 m/3 ft long excluding a long muscular tail with a prehensile tip. Mainly nocturnal and tree-dwelling, the binturong is found in the forests of Southeast Asia, feeding on fruit, eggs, and small animals.

Binyon, (Robert) Laurence (1869–1943) English poet. His ode 'For the Fallen' (1914) is frequently quoted in war memorial services and was set to music by English composer Edward ▷Elgar. Binyon's verse volumes include *London Visions* (1896); his art criticism includes *Painting in the Far East* (1908).

> ### Laurence Binyon
> *They shall grow not old, as we that are left grow old: / Age shall not weary them, nor the years condemn. / At the going down of the sun and in the morning / We will remember them.*
>
> 'Poem For the Fallen'

Bío-Bío longest river in Chile; length 370 km/230 mi. It rises in the southern Andes, on the border with Argentina, and flows northwest to the Pacific Ocean near Concepción. The name is an ▷Araucanian term meaning 'much water'. Orchards, cereal crops and Chile's main vineyards are located in the Bío-Bío river valley.

biochemical oxygen demand (**BOD**) the amount of dissolved oxygen taken up by micro-organisms in a sample of water. Since these micro-organisms live by decomposing organic matter, and the amount of oxygen used is proportional to their number and metabolic rate, BOD can be used as a measure of the extent to which the water is polluted with organic compounds.

biochemistry science concerned with the chemistry of living organisms: the structure and reactions of proteins (such as enzymes), nucleic acids, carbohydrates, and lipids.

Its study has led to an increased understanding of life processes, such as those by which organisms synthesize essential chemicals from food materials, store and generate energy, and pass on their characteristics through their genetic material. A great deal of medical research is concerned with the ways in which these processes are disrupted. Biochemistry also has applications in agriculture and in the food industry (for instance, in the use of enzymes).

biodegradable capable of being broken down by living organisms, principally bacteria and fungi. In biodegradable substances, such as food and sewage, the natural processes of decay lead to compaction and liquefaction, and to the release of nutrients that are then recycled by the ecosystem.

This process can have some disadvantageous side effects, such as the release of methane, an explosive greenhouse gas. However, the technology now exists for waste tips to collect methane in underground pipes, drawing it off and using it as a cheap source of energy. Nonbiodegradable substances, such as glass, heavy metals, and most types of plastic, present serious problems of disposal.

biodiversity (contraction of biological diversity) measure of the variety of the Earth's animal, plant, and microbial species, of genetic differences within species, and of the ecosystems that support those species. Its maintenance is important for ecological stability and as a resource for research into, for example, discovering new drugs and crops.

biodynamic farming agricultural practice based on the principle of ▷homeopathy: tiny quantities of a substance are applied to transmit vital qualities to the soil. It is a form of ▷organic farming, and was developed by the Austrian holistic mystic Rudolf ▷Steiner and Ehrenfried Pfiffer.

bioengineering the application of engineering to biology and medicine. Common applications include the design and use of artificial limbs, joints, and organs, including hip joints and heart valves.

biofeedback in medicine, the use of electrophysiological monitoring devices to 'feed back' information about internal processes and thus facilitate conscious control. Developed in the USA in the 1960s, independently by neurophysiologist Barbara Brown and neuropsychiatrist Joseph Kamiya, the technique is effective in alleviating hypertension and preventing associated organic and physiological dysfunctions.

biofuel any solid, liquid, or gaseous fuel produced from organic (once living) matter, either directly from plants or indirectly from industrial, commercial, domestic, or agricultural wastes. There are three main methods for the development of biofuels: the burning of dry organic wastes (such as household refuse, industrial and agricultural wastes, straw, wood, and peat); the fermentation of

Biochemistry: Key Dates

c. 1830	Johannes Müller discovers proteins.
1833	Anselme Payen and J F Persoz first isolate an enzyme.
1862	Haemoglobin is first crystallized.
1869	The genetic material DNA (deoxyribonucleic acid) is discovered by Friedrich Mieschler.
1899	Emil Fischer postulates the 'lock-and-key' hypothesis to explain the specificity of enzyme action.
1913	Leonor Michaelis and M L Menten develop a mathematical equation describing the rate of enzyme-catalysed reactions.
1920	The chromosome theory of heredity is postulated by Thomas H Morgan; growth hormone is discovered by Herbert McLean Evans and J A Long.
1921	Insulin is first isolated from the pancreas by Frederick Banting and Charles Best.
1928	Alexander Fleming discovers penicillin.
1930s	The structures of the vitamins are identified, allowing them to be isolated and synthesized, and paving the way for similar work with other substances.
1940	Hans Krebs proposes the Krebs (citric acid) cycle describing the chemical reactions in cells that underly the metabolism of living organisms.
1943	The role of DNA in genetic inheritance is first demonstrated by Oswald Avery, Colin MacLeod, and Maclyn McCarty.
1953	James Watson and Francis Crick determine the molecular structure of DNA.
1956	Mahlon Hoagland and Paul Zamecnick discover transfer RNA (ribonucleic acid); mechanisms for the biosynthesis of RNA and DNA are discovered by Arthur Kornberg and Severo Ochoa.
1960	Messenger RNA is discovered by Sidney Brenner and François Jacob.
1961	Marshall Nirenberg and Severo Ochoa determine the chemical nature of the genetic code.
1982	Louis Chedid and Michael Sela develop the first synthesized vaccine.
1983	The first commercially available product of genetic engineering (Humulin) is launched.
1985	Alec Jeffreys devises genetic fingerprinting.
1993	Experimental gene therapy cures cystic fibrosis in mice.
1997	US geneticists construct the first artificial human chromosome.
1999	US geneticists in Boston create a human cancer tumour in a laboratory culture dish and describe three genetic changes needed to turn a normal human cell into a cancer cell. One change activates the gene that produces the enzyme telomerase, which causes the cell to multiply without limit.
2000	US researchers make discoveries that improve the scientific understanding of genetic factors in the causes of obesity.

BINOCULARS The essential components of binoculars are objective lenses, eyepieces, and a system of prisms to invert and reverse the image. A focusing system provides a sharp image by adjusting the relative positions of these components.

(labels: focusing/adjustment, eyepiece, eyepiece lenses, prisms, light path, objective lens)

wet wastes (such as animal dung) in the absence of oxygen to produce biogas (containing up to 60% methane), or the fermentation of sugar cane or corn to produce alcohol and esters; and energy forestry (producing fast-growing wood for fuel).

biogeography study of how and why plants and animals are distributed around the world, in the past as well as in the present; more specifically, a theory describing the geographical distribution of ▷species developed by Robert MacArthur and US zoologist Edward O ▷Wilson. The theory argues that, for many species, ecological specializations mean that suitable habitats are patchy in their occurrence. For example, for a dragonfly, ponds in which to breed are separated by large tracts of land, and for edelweiss adapted to alpine peaks the deep valleys between cannot be colonized.

biography account of a person's life. When it is written by that person, it is an ▷autobiography. Biography may consist simply of the factual details of a person's life told in chronological order, but has generally become a matter of interpretation as well as historical accuracy. Unofficial biographies (not sanctioned by the subject) have frequently led to legal disputes over both interpretation and facts.

biological clock regular internal rhythm of activity, produced by unknown mechanisms, and not dependent on external time signals. Such clocks are known to exist in almost all animals, and also in many plants, fungi, and unicellular organisms; the first biological clock gene in plants was isolated in 1995 by a US team of researchers. In higher organisms, there appears to be a series of clocks of graded importance. For example, although body temperature and activity cycles in human beings are normally 'set' to 24 hours, the two cycles may vary independently, showing that two clock mechanisms are involved.

biological control control of pests such as insects and fungi through biological means, rather than the use of chemicals. This can include breeding resistant crop strains; inducing sterility in the pest; infecting the pest species with disease organisms; or introducing the pest's natural predator. Biological control tends to be naturally self-regulating, but as ecosystems are so complex, it is difficult to predict all the consequences of introducing a biological controlling agent.

Ladybirds are sometimes used to control aphids as both adults and larvae feed on them. In 1998, French researchers patented a method of selective breeding to produce hardy flightless ladybirds for use in biological control, as captive populations are far more effective than mobile ones.

The introduction of the cane toad to Australia 50 years ago to eradicate a beetle that was destroying sugar beet provides an example of the unpredictability of biological control. Since the cane toad is poisonous it has few Australian predators and it is now a pest, spreading throughout eastern and northern Australia at a rate of 35 km/22 mi a year.

biological shield shield around a nuclear reactor that is intended to protect personnel from the effects of ▷radiation. It usually consists of a thick wall of steel and concrete.

biological warfare the use of living organisms, or of infectious material derived from them, to bring about death or disease in humans, animals, or plants. At least ten countries have this capability. Advances in ▷genetic engineering make the development of new varieties of potentially offensive biological weapons more likely.

biological weathering (or **organic weathering**) form of ▷weathering caused by the activities of living organisms – for example, the growth of roots or the burrowing of animals. Tree roots are probably the most significant agents of biological weathering as they are capable of prising apart rocks by growing into cracks and joints.

biology (Greek *bios* 'life', *logos* 'discourse') science of life. Biology includes all the life sciences – for example, anatomy and physiology (the study of the structure of living things), cytology (the study of cells), zoology (the study of animals) and botany (the study of plants), ecology (the study of habitats and the interaction of living species), animal behaviour, embryology, and taxonomy, and plant breeding. Increasingly in the 20th century biologists have concentrated on molecular structures: biochemistry, biophysics, 2003 and genetics (the study of inheritance and variation).

Biological research has come a long way towards understanding the nature of life, and by 2003 our knowledge was further extended as the international ▷Human Genome Project mapped the entire genetic code contained in the 23 pairs of human chromosomes. See the feature essay *The Human Genome Project*.

bioluminescence production of light by living organisms. It is a feature of many deep-sea fishes, crustaceans, and other marine animals. On land, bioluminescence is seen in some nocturnal insects such as glow-worms and fireflies, and in certain bacteria and fungi. Light is usually produced by the oxidation of luciferin, a reaction catalysed by the ▷enzyme luciferase. This reaction is unique, being the only known biological oxidation that does not produce heat. Animal luminescence is involved in communication, camouflage, and the luring of prey.

biomass the total mass of living organisms present in a given area. It may be specified for a particular species (such as earthworm biomass) or for a general category (such as herbivore biomass). Estimates also exist for the entire global plant biomass. Measurements of biomass can be used to study interactions between organisms, the stability of those interactions, and variations in population numbers. Where dry biomass is measured, the material is dried to remove all water before weighing.

Some two-thirds of the world's population cooks and heats water by burning biomass, usually wood. Plant biomass can be a renewable source of energy as replacement supplies can be grown relatively quickly. Fossil fuels however, originally formed from biomass, accumulate so slowly that they cannot be considered renewable. The burning of biomass (defined either as natural areas of the ecosystem or as forest, grasslands, and fuelwoods) produces 3.5 million tonnes of carbon in the form of carbon dioxide each year, accounting for up to 40% of the world's annual carbon dioxide production.

Related Web site: Bioenergy Information Network http://bioenergy.ornl.gov/

biome broad natural assemblage of plants and animals shaped by common patterns of vegetation and climate. Examples include the tundra biome, the rainforest biome, and the desert biome.

biomechanics application of mechanical engineering principles and techniques in the field of medicine and surgery, studying natural structures to improve those produced by humans. For example, mother-of-pearl is structurally superior to glass fibre, and deer antlers have outstanding durability because they are composed of microscopic fibres. Such natural structures may form the basis of high-tech composites. Biomechanics has been responsible for many recent advances in ▷orthopaedics, anaesthesia, and intensive care. Biomechanical assessment of the requirements for replacement of joints, including evaluation of the stresses and strains between parts, and their reliability, has allowed development of implants with very low friction and long life.

bionics (from 'biological electronics') design and development of electronic or mechanical artificial systems that imitate those of living things. The bionic arm, for example, is an artificial limb (▷prosthesis) that uses electronics to amplify minute electrical signals generated in body muscles to work electric motors, which operate the joints of the fingers and wrist.

biophysics application of physical laws to the properties of living organisms. Examples include using the principles of ▷mechanics to calculate the strength of bones and muscles, and ▷thermodynamics to study plant and animal energetics.

biopsy removal of a living tissue sample from the body for diagnostic examination.

biosphere the narrow zone that supports life on our planet. It is limited to the waters of the Earth, a fraction of its crust, and the lower regions of the atmosphere. The biosphere is made up of all the Earth's ▷ecosystems. It is affected by external forces such as the Sun's rays, which provide energy, the gravitational effects of the Sun and Moon, and cosmic radiations.

biosynthesis synthesis of organic chemicals from simple inorganic ones by living cells – for example, the conversion of carbon dioxide and water to glucose by plants during ▷photosynthesis.

Other biosynthetic reactions produce cell constituents including proteins and fats.

Biosynthesis requires energy; in the initial stages of photosynthesis this is obtained from sunlight, but more often it is supplied by the ▷ATP molecule. The term is also used in connection with biotechnology processes.

Biosynthesis requires energy; in the initial or light-dependent stages of photosynthesis this is obtained from sunlight, but in all other instances, it is supplied chemically by ▷ATP and NADPH. The term is also used in connection with the products achieved through biotechnology processes.

biotechnology industrial use of living organisms to manufacture food, drugs, or other products. The brewing and baking industries have long relied on the yeast micro-organism for ▷fermentation purposes, while the dairy industry employs a range of bacteria and fungi to convert milk into cheeses and yoghurts. ▷Enzymes, whether extracted from cells or produced artificially, are central to most biotechnological applications.

Recent advances include ▷genetic engineering, in which single-celled organisms with modified ▷DNA are used to produce insulin and other drugs.

In 1993 two-thirds of biotechnology companies were concentrating on human health developments, whilst only 1 in 10 were concerned with applications for food and agriculture.

biotin (or **vitamin H**) vitamin of the B complex, found in many different kinds of food; egg yolk, liver, legumes, and yeast contain large amounts. Biotin is essential to the metabolism of fats. Its absence from the diet may lead to dermatitis.

birch any of a group of slender trees with small leaves and fine, peeling bark. About 40 species are found in cool temperate parts of the northern hemisphere. Birches grow rapidly, and their hard, beautiful wood is used for veneers and cabinet work. (Genus *Betula*, family Betulaceae.)

Related Web site: Birch, Common http://www.botanical.com/botanical/mgmh/b/bircom43.html

bird backboned animal of the class Aves, the biggest group of land vertebrates, characterized by warm blood, feathers, wings, breathing through lungs, and egg-laying by the female. Birds are bipedal; feet are usually adapted for perching and never have more than four toes. Hearing and eyesight are well developed, but the sense of smell is usually poor. No existing species of bird possesses teeth.

Most birds fly, but some groups (such as ostriches) are flightless, and others include flightless members. Many communicate by sounds (nearly half of all known species are songbirds) or by visual displays, in connection with which many species are brightly coloured, usually the males. Birds have highly developed patterns of instinctive behaviour. There are nearly 8,500 species of birds.

According to the Red List of endangered species published by the World Conservation Union for 1996, 11% of bird species are threatened with extinction.

Wing structure The wing consists of the typical bones of a forelimb, the humerus, radius and ulna, carpus, metacarpus, and digits. The first digit is the pollex, or thumb, to which some feathers, known as ala spuria, or bastard wing, are attached; the

Biological Weapons

Biological weapons use disease-causing organisms to injure or kill, delivering such organisms in bombs or missiles. Biological agents come in many different forms, the simplest being 'spores', microscopic life forms that induce fatal illnesses. Some, such as anthrax, occur naturally. Biological weapons are extremely powerful; in an attack on a typical city a nuclear bomb weighing 181 kg/400 lbs could kill up to 40,000 people, but a device containing just 32 kg/70 lbs of deadly anthrax could kill twice that number.

The use of biological weapons is banned by the major powers, but research and development continues. Many countries, particularly in the developing world, do not want to give up such weapons because they are simple and cheap to produce. The weapons can be produced in inconspicuous places such as laboratories, factories, and hospitals. They can be made secretly – hidden stockpiles of anthrax were discovered in Iraq by Western intelligence agents. Existing military lines of defence offer little protection, for example, there is no system that can warn of a biological attack.

The potential for the use of genetic engineering in the production of biological weapons is a major concern. Russian researchers have managed to combine the genes of the disease smallpox with those of the killer virus Ebola to produce a new biological weapon. It may also be possible to disguise the microscopic 'appearance' of a biological weapon such as anthrax to look like a harmless organism to evade detection.

Biology: Key Dates

c. 500 BC	First studies of the structure and behaviour of animals, by the Alcmaeon of Croton.
c. 450	Hippocrates of Kos undertakes the first detailed studies of human anatomy.
c. 350	Aristotle lays down the basic philosophy of the biological sciences and outlines a theory of evolution.
c. 300	Theophrastus carries out the first detailed studies of plants.
c. AD 175	Galen establishes the basic principles of anatomy and physiology.
c. 1500	Leonardo da Vinci studies human anatomy to improve his drawing ability and produces detailed anatomical drawings.
1628	William Harvey describes the circulation of the blood and the function of the heart as a pump.
1665	Robert Hooke uses a microscope to describe the cellular structure of plants. This is the first description of cells.
1672	Marcello Malpighi undertakes the first studies in embryology by describing the development of a chicken egg.
1677	Anton van Leeuwenhoek greatly improves the microscope and uses it to describe spermatozoa as well as many micro-organisms.
1736	Carolus Linnaeus (Carl von Linné) publishes his systematic classification of plants, so establishing taxonomy.
1768–79	James Cook's voyages of discovery in the Pacific reveal a great diversity of living species, prompting the development of theories to explain their origin.
1796	Edward Jenner establishes the practice of vaccination against smallpox, laying the foundations for theories of antibodies and immune reactions.
1809	Jean-Baptiste Lamarck advocates a theory of evolution through inheritance of acquired characteristics.
1812	Mary Anning discovers the fossilized skeleton of an ichthyosaurus, one of the first finds proving that huge reptiles once dominated the Earth. The discovery paves the way for a new understanding of the Earth's remote past, challenging the Biblical account of creation.
1822	Gideon and Anne Mantell discover the fossil of an iguanadon.
1839	Theodor Schwann proposes that all living matter is made up of cells.
1842	Richard Owen coins the word 'dinosaur' (from the Greek for terrible lizard) to describe the animals belonging to what we now know as two groups of reptiles that dominated the Earth for 175 million years during the Triassic, Jurassic and Cretaceous periods.
1857	Louis Pasteur establishes that micro-organisms are responsible for fermentation, creating the discipline of microbiology.
1859	Charles Darwin publishes 'On the Origin of Species', expounding his theory of the evolution of species by natural selection.
1865	Gregor Mendel pioneers the study of inheritance with his experiments on peas, but achieves little recognition.
1869	Alfred Russell Wallace, who arrived at a theory of the origin of species independently of Darwin, describes the differences between the flora and fauna in the western and eastern parts of the Malay archpelago. Those in the west are related to plants and animals in Asia, those of the east are related to species found in Australia. An imaginary line, called Wallace's Line, divides the two populations.
1883	August Weismann proposes his theory of the continuity of the germ plasm.
1900	Mendel's work is rediscovered and the science of genetics founded.
1910	T H Morgan discovers that genes are physically located on chromosomes within cell nuclei.
1935	Konrad Lorenz publishes the first of many major studies of animal behaviour, creating the discipline of ethology.
1944	Oswald Avery and co-workers discover that genes consist of DNA.
1953	James Watson and Francis Crick describe the molecular structure of DNA.
1964	William Hamilton recognizes the importance of inclusive fitness, so paving the way for the development of sociobiology.
1969	Jonathan Beckwith and co-workers isolate a single gene for the first time.
1973	Stanley H Cohen and Herbert W Boyer demonstrate the use of restrictive enzymes for slicing up DNA.
1975	Discovery of endogenous opiates (the brain's own painkillers) opens up a new phase in the study of brain chemistry.
1976	Har Gobind Khorana and his colleagues construct the first artificial gene to function naturally when inserted into a bacterial cell, a major step in genetic engineering.
1982	Gene databases are established at Heidelberg, Germany, for the European Molecular Biology Laboratory, and at Los Alamos, USA, for the US National Laboratories.
1985	The first human cancer gene, retinoblastoma, is isolated by researchers at the Massachusetts Eye and Ear Infirmary and the Whitehead Institute, Massachusetts, USA.
1988	The Human Genome Organization (HUGO) is established in Washington, DC, USA, with the aim of mapping the complete sequence of human DNA.
1991	Biosphere 2, an experiment that attempts to reproduce the world's biosphere in miniature within a sealed glass dome, is launched in Arizona, USA.
1992	Researchers at the University of California, USA, stimulate the multiplication of isolated brain cells of mice, overturning the axiom that mammalian brains cannot produce replacement cells once birth has taken place. The world's largest organism, a honey fungus with underground hyphae (filaments) spreading across 600 hectares/1,480 acres, is discovered in Washington State, USA.
1994	Scientists from Pakistan and the USA unearth a 50-million-year-old fossil whale with hind legs that would have enabled it to walk on land.
1996	The sequencing of the genome of brewer's yeast Saccharomyces cerevisiae is completed, the first time this has been achieved for an organism more complex than a bacterium. The 12 million base pairs of genes took 300 scientists six years to map.
	A new muscle is discovered by two US dentists. It is 3 cm/1 in long, and runs from the jaw to behind the eye socket.
1997	The first mammal to be cloned from a nonreproductive cell is born. The lamb (named Dolly) has been cloned from an udder cell from a six-year-old ewe.
1999	Canadian researchers engineer an artificial chromosome that can be inserted into mammal cells and then transmitted from one generation to the next. The development has important implications towards germ-line therapy where a defect is corrected in the gametes and the change passed on to future generations.
2000	Scientists complete a rough working draft of the map of the entire human genome.

second digit is the index, which bears the large feathers known as the primaries or manuals, usually ten in number. The primary feathers, with the secondaries or cubitals, which are attached to the ulna, form the large wing-quills, called remiges, which are used in flight.

Anatomy The sternum, or breastbone, of birds is affected by their powers of flight: those birds which are able to fly have a keel projecting from the sternum and serving as the basis of attachment of the great pectoral muscles which move the wings. In birds that do not fly the keel is absent or greatly reduced. The vertebral column is completed in the tail region by a flat plate known as the pygostyle, which forms a support for the rectrices, or steering tailfeathers.

The legs are composed of the femur, tibia and fibula, and the bones of the foot; the feet usually have four toes, but in many cases there are only three. In swimming birds the legs are placed well back.

The uropygial gland on the pygostyle (bone in the tail) is an oil gland used by birds in preening their feathers, as their skin contains no sebaceous glands. The eyes have an upper and a lower eyelid and a semitransparent nictitating membrane with which the bird can cover its eyes at will.

The **vascular system** contains warm blood, which is kept usually at a higher temperature (about 41°C/106°F) than that of mammals; death from cold is rare unless the bird is starving or ill. The aortic arch (main blood vessel leaving the heart) is on the right side of a bird, whereas it is on the left in a mammal. The heart of a bird consists of a right and a left half with four chambers.

The **lungs** are small and prolonged into air-sacs connected to a number of air-spaces in the bones. These air-spaces are largest in powerful fliers, but they are not so highly developed in young, small, aquatic, and terrestrial birds. These air-spaces increase the efficiency of the respiratory system and reduce the weight of the bones. The lungs themselves are more efficient than those of mammals; the air is circulated through a system of fine capillary tubes, allowing continuous gas exchange to take place, whereas in mammals the air comes to rest in blind air sacs.

The organ of voice is not the larynx, but usually the syrinx, a peculiarity of this class formed at the bifurcation of the trachea (windpipe) and the modulations are effected by movements of the adjoining muscles.

Digestion Digestion takes place in the oesophagus, stomach, and intestines in a manner basically similar to mammals. The tongue aids in feeding, and there is frequently a **crop**, a dilation of the oesophagus, where food is stored and softened. The stomach is small with little storage capacity and usually consists of the proventriculus, which secretes digestive juices, and the gizzard, which is tough and muscular and grinds the food, sometimes with the aid of grit and stones retained within it. Digestion is completed, and absorption occurs, in the intestine and the digestive caeca. The intestine ends in a cloaca through which both urine and faeces are excreted.

Nesting and eggs Typically eggs are brooded in a nest and, on hatching, the young receive a period of parental care. The collection of nest material, nest building, and incubation may be carried out by the male, female, or both. The cuckoo neither builds a nest nor rears its own young, but places the eggs in the nest of another bird and leaves the foster parents to care for them.

Hatching Just before hatching the chick's head breaks through the egg membrane so that it is now breathing air in the air space between membrane and shell. Chicks in a clutch may make a clicking noise (sometimes clicking at a rate of over a hundred clicks per second) that enables them to communicate with the other chicks that are hatching, so that they can synchronize hatching. This is often that case with ground hatching birds that will usually abandon the nest site once chicks are hatched, to help avoid detection by predators by not staying too long in one

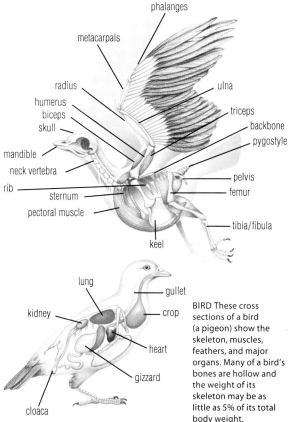

BIRD These cross sections of a bird (a pigeon) show the skeleton, muscles, feathers, and major organs. Many of a bird's bones are hollow and the weight of its skeleton may be as little as 5% of its total body weight.

place. For example, the female quail lays her eggs over two weeks, and yet the eggs will hatch together.

To escape from the egg, the chick must force its way through the shell. Its beak is still very soft but it has upon it a beak tooth or egg tooth, a small spike, usually on top of the beak, with which it pushes against the shell. There is a special muscle at the back of its neck that gives the chick extra strength to hammer against the shell. It may also kick with its legs.

The study of birds is called ▷ornithology.

Conservation measures In most countries today official protection is given to birds, especially those that counteract the spread of injurious insects, slugs, snails, mice, and voles, and are therefore useful to agriculture. Bird sanctuaries exist in most countries of Europe and in the USA, and the recent increase in their numbers reflects an upsurge of popular interest in birds. In Britain, the growth of the Royal Society for the Protection of Birds is evidence of this.

Related Web site: Bird On! http://birdcare.com/birdon/welcome_text.html

Bird, Isabella Lucy (1831–1904) Married name Isabella Bishop. British traveller and writer who wrote extensively of her journeys in the USA, Persia, Tibet, Kurdistan, China, Japan, and Korea. A fearless horsewoman, she generally travelled alone and in later life undertook medical missionary work.

bird louse parasitic biting louse, found mainly on birds, less frequently on mammals. Bird lice are wingless ectoparasites (living on the skin of their hosts), have biting mouthparts (as opposed to true lice which have sucking mouthparts), and reduced eyes. Bird lice are in the order Mallophaga, class Insecta, phylum Arthropoda.

bird of paradise one of 40 species of crowlike birds in the family Paradiseidae, native to New Guinea and neighbouring islands. Females are generally drably coloured, but the males have bright and elaborate plumage used in courtship display. Hunted almost to extinction for their plumage, they are now subject to conservation.

They are smallish birds, extremely active, and have compressed beaks, large toes, and strong feet. Their food consists chiefly of fruits, seeds, and nectar, but it may also include insects and small animals, such as worms. The Australian ▷bowerbirds are closely related.

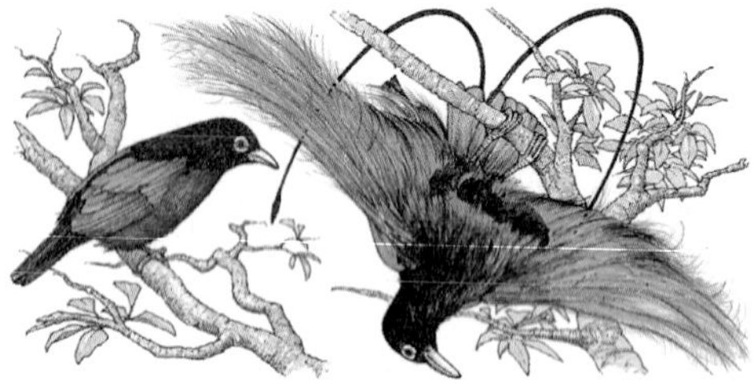

BIRD OF PARADISE The male blue bird of paradise displays to the female high up in the tree canopy.

Birendra, Bir Bikram Shah Dev (1945–) King of Nepal from 1972, when he succeeded his father Mahendra; he was formally crowned in 1975. King Birendra oversaw Nepal's return to multiparty politics and introduced a new constitution in 1990.

Birkenhead seaport and industrial town in Wirral, Merseyside, England, opposite Liverpool on the Wirral peninsula, on the west bank of the Mersey estuary; population (1994 est) 93,100; Birkenhead urban area 270,200. It developed as a shipbuilding town with important dock facilities, but other principal industries now include engineering and flour-milling. The Mersey rail tunnel (1886), the Queensway road tunnel (1934), and a passenger ferry service link Birkenhead with Liverpool.

Birkenhead, F(rederick) E(dwin) Smith (1872–1930) 1st Earl of Birkenhead. British lawyer and Conservative politician. He was a flamboyant and ambitious character, and played a major role in securing the Anglo-Irish Treaty in 1921, which created the Irish Free State (now the Republic of Ireland). As a lawyer, his greatest achievement was the Law of Property Act of 1922, which forms the basis of current English land law.

Birmingham industrial city and administrative headquarters of ▷West Midlands metropolitan county, central England, second-largest city in the UK, 177 km/110 mi northwest of London; population (1994 est) 1,220,000, metropolitan area 2,632,000. It is a major manufacturing, engineering, commercial, and service centre. The city's concert halls, theatres, and three universities also make it an important cultural and educational centre. Its chief products are motor vehicles, vehicle components and accessories, machine tools, aerospace control systems, electrical equipment, plastics, chemicals, food, chocolate (Cadbury), jewellery, tyres, glass, cars, and guns.

Features National Exhibition Centre and National Indoor Arena; International Convention Centre; Birmingham International Airport; the Bull Ring shopping and office complex; restored canal walks ('Britain's Canal City'); Millennium Point science, technology, and entertainment complex, a Millennium Commission Landmark Project, due for completion in 2001.

Music and theatre Symphony Hall (opened 1991), within the International Convention Centre, home to the City of Birmingham Symphony Orchestra, with a capacity of over 4,000; Birmingham ▷Royal Ballet (based in London until 1990); Birmingham Conservatoire, now part of the University of Central England; the repertory theatre founded in 1913 by Barry Jackson (1879–1961); D'Oyly Carte Opera Company.

Museums and galleries Barber Institute of Fine Arts (Birmingham University, Edgbaston); the City Museum and Art Gallery (1864–81), containing a fine Pre-Raphaelite collection; the Museum of Science and Industry; Gas Hall, displaying temporary art exhibitions.

Educational institutions University of Birmingham (1900); Aston University (1966), and University of Central England (formerly Birmingham Polytechnic), established in 1992.

Industrial history Birmingham supplied large quantities of weapons to the Parliamentary forces of Oliver Cromwell during the English Civil War. Its location on the edge of the south Staffordshire coalfields, its skilled workforce, and its reputation for producing small arms allowed it to develop rapidly during the 18th and 19th centuries – much of the city was rebuilt between 1875 and 1882. It was a centre for munitions manufacture during both world wars. High-tech and service industries have gradually overtaken the city's traditional but declining large-scale metal industry.

Otto von Bismarck

Die Politik ist keine exakte Wissenschaft.

Politics is not an exact science.

Speech in Prussian Chamber 18 December 1863

Birmingham city in north-central Alabama, USA, situated in the Jones Valley, at the southern end of the Appalachian Mountains; seat of Jefferson County; population (1994 est) 265,000. It is the largest city in ▷Alabama and is an industrial centre for iron, steel (Birmingham was once the steelmaking centre of the South), chemicals, building materials, railroad and aircraft equipment, computers, and cotton textiles; its port is connected to the Gulf of Mexico via the Black Warrior River.

Related Web site: Birmingham http://www.bcvb.org/

Birmingham Royal Ballet formerly the **Sadler's Wells Royal Ballet**. The company relocated to new purpose-built facilities at the Birmingham Hippodrome in 1990, when it was renamed the Birmingham Royal Ballet. David Bintley became artistic director in 1995.

Biró, Lazlo (1900–1985) Hungarian-born Argentine who invented a ballpoint pen in 1944. His name became generic for ballpoint pens in the UK.

birth act of producing live young from within the body of female animals. Both viviparous and ovoviviparous animals give birth to young. In viviparous animals, embryos obtain nourishment from the mother via a ▷placenta or other means.

In ovoviviparous animals, fertilized eggs develop and hatch in the oviduct of the mother and gain little or no nourishment from maternal tissues. See also ▷pregnancy.

birth control another name for ▷family planning; see also ▷contraceptive.

birth rate the number of live births per thousand of the population over a period of time, usually a year (sometimes it is also expressed as a percentage). For example, a birth rate of 20 per thousand (or 2%) would mean that 20 babies were being born per thousand of the population. It is sometimes called **crude birth rate** because it takes in the whole population, including men and women who are too old to bear children.

Birtwistle, Harrison (1934–) English avant-garde composer. He has specialized in chamber music, for example, his chamber opera *Punch and Judy* (1967) and *Down by the Greenwood Side* (1969). Birtwistle's early music was influenced by the US composer Igor Stravinsky and by the medieval and Renaissance masters, and for many years he worked alongside Peter Maxwell ▷Davies.

Biscay, Bay of bay of the Atlantic Ocean between northern Spain and western France, known for rough seas and high tides. It is traditionally a rich fishing area.

Bishkek (formerly **Pishpek** (1878–1926); **Frunze** (1926–92)) capital of ▷Kyrgyzstan; population (1996) 670,000. Bishkek is situated in the valley of the River Chu north of the Kyrgyz Alatau mountain range, 180 km/112 mi west of Almaty in Kazakhstan. Among the goods produced here are textiles, agricultural machinery, and electrical goods. Food industries include meat-packing and tobacco production.

bishop (Greek 'overseer') priest next in rank to an archbishop in the Roman Catholic, Eastern Orthodox, Anglican churches. A bishop has charge of a district called a **diocese**.

Bishop, Isabella married name of the travel writer Isabella ▷Bird.

Bismarck capital of ▷North Dakota, USA, situated on the east bank of the Missouri in the south-central part of the state; seat of Burleigh County; population (2000 est) 55,500. It is a shipping point for the region's agricultural and livestock products, and for oil products from nearby oil wells. Originally an American Indian site, Bismarck was first settled by Europeans in 1872 and was incorporated in 1875.

Bismarck, Otto Eduard Leopold von (1815–1898) German politician, prime minister of Prussia 1862–90 and chancellor of the German Empire 1871–90. He pursued an aggressively expansionist policy, waging wars against Denmark (1863–64), Austria (1866), and France (1870–71), which brought about the unification of Germany. He became Prince in 1871.

Bismarck was ambitious to establish Prussia's leadership within Germany and eliminate the influence of Austria. He secured Austria's support for his successful war against Denmark then, in 1866, went to war against Austria and its allies (the ▷Seven Weeks' War), his victory forcing Austria out of the German Bund and unifying the northern German states into the North German Confederation under his own chancellorship in 1867. He then defeated France, under Napoleon III, in the Franco-Prussian War 1870–71, proclaimed the German Empire in 1871, and annexed Alsace-Lorraine. He tried to secure his work by the ▷Triple Alliance in 1881 with Austria and Italy but ran into difficulties at home with the Roman Catholic Church and the socialist movement and was forced to resign by Wilhelm II on 18 March 1890.

Related Web site: Bismarck Memorial http://sangha.net/messengers/bismark.htm

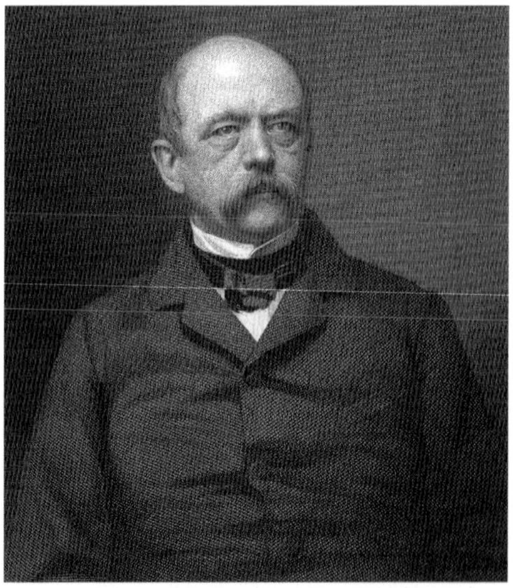

OTTO VON BISMARCK A Prussian statesman and first chancellor of a united Germany, Bismarck believed that German problems must be solved by 'blood and iron' rather than by words. *Archive Photos*

Bismarck Archipelago group of over 200 islands in the southwest Pacific Ocean, part of ▷Papua New Guinea; area 49,660 sq km/19,200 sq mi. The largest island is New Britain. Coconut fibre, copra, cotton, rubber, coffee, tortoiseshell, trepang (sea cucumbers), mother-of-pearl, and fruit are the chief products. The population is mostly Papuan.

bismuth hard, brittle, pinkish-white, metallic element, symbol Bi, atomic number 83, relative atomic mass 208.98. It has the highest atomic number of all the stable elements (the elements from atomic number 84 up are radioactive). Bismuth occurs in ores and occasionally as a free metal (▷native metal). It is a poor conductor of heat and electricity, and is used in alloys of low melting point and in medical compounds to soothe gastric ulcers. The name comes from the Latin *besemutum*, from the earlier German *Wismut*.

bison large, hoofed mammal of the bovine family. There are two species, both brown. The **European bison** or **wisent** *Bison bonasus*, of which only a few protected herds survive, is about 2 m/7 ft high and weighs up to 1,100 kg/2,500 lb. The **North American bison**

(also known historically as the North American buffalo) *Bison bison* is slightly smaller, with a heavier mane and more sloping hindquarters. Formerly roaming the prairies in vast numbers, it was almost exterminated in the 19th century, but survives in protected areas. There were about 14,000 bison in North American reserves in 1994.

Crossed with domestic cattle, the North American bison has produced a hardy hybrid, the 'beefalo', producing a lean carcass on an economical grass diet.

Bissau capital and chief port of ▷Guinea-Bissau, on an island at the mouth of the Geba River; population (1992) 145,000. Originally a Portuguese fortified slave-trading centre (1687), Bissau became a free port in 1869. Industries include agricultural processing, fishing, textiles, and crafts. There are refrigeration units at the port, and there is an international airport and a university. Bissau replaced Bolama as the capital in 1941.

bit (contraction of binary digit) in computing, a single binary digit, either 0 or 1. A bit is the smallest unit of data stored in a computer; all other data must be coded into a pattern of individual bits. A ▷byte represents sufficient computer memory to store a single character of data, and usually contains eight bits. For example, in the ▷ASCII code system used by most microcomputers the capital letter A would be stored in a single byte of memory as the bit pattern 01000001.

bittern any of several species of small herons, in particular the common bittern *Botaurus stellaris* of Europe and Asia. It is shy, stoutly built, buff-coloured, speckled with black and tawny brown, with a long bill and a loud, booming call. Its habit of holding its neck and bill in a vertical position conceals it among the reeds, where it rests by day, hunting for frogs, reptiles, and fish towards nightfall. An inhabitant of marshy country, it is now extremely rare in Britain. In 2000 there were only an estimated 20 pairs of bitterns breeding in the British Isles.

bittersweet alternative name for the woody ▷nightshade plant.

bitumen impure mixture of hydrocarbons, including such deposits as petroleum, asphalt, and natural gas, although sometimes the term is restricted to a soft pitch resembling asphalt.

bivalve marine or freshwater mollusc whose body is enclosed between two shells hinged together by a ligament on the dorsal side of the body.

Bizet, Georges (Alexandre César Léopold) (1838–1875) French composer of operas. Among his works are *Les Pêcheurs de perles/The Pearl Fishers* (1863) and *La Jolie Fille de Perth/The Fair Maid of Perth* (1866). He also wrote the concert overture *Patrie* and incidental music to Alphonse Daudet's play *L'Arlésienne* (1872), which has remained a standard work in the form of two suites for orchestra. His operatic masterpiece *Carmen* was produced a few months before his death. His Symphony in C, written when he was 17, is now frequently performed.

Related Web site: Bizet, Georges http://w3.rz-berlin.mpg.de/cmp/bizet.html

Black, Conrad Moffat (1940–) Canadian newspaper publisher. Between 1985 and 1990 he gained control of the right-wing *Daily Telegraph*, *Sunday Telegraph*, and *Spectator* weekly magazine in the UK, and he owns a number of Canadian newspapers.

Black and Tans nickname of a special auxiliary force of the Royal Irish Constabulary formed from British ex-soldiers on 2 January 1920 and in action in Ireland March 1920–December 1921. They were employed by the British government to combat the killing of policemen by the Irish Republican Army (IRA), the military wing of the Irish nationalist ▷Sinn Fein government, during the Anglo-Irish War, or War of Independence (1919–21). The name derives from the colours of their improvised khaki and black uniforms, and was also the name of a famous pack of hounds.

black beetle another name for ▷cockroach, although cockroaches belong to an entirely different order of insects (Dictyoptera) from the beetles (Coleoptera).

blackberry prickly shrub, closely related to raspberries and dewberries. Native to northern parts of Europe, it produces pink or white blossom and edible black compound fruits. (*Rubus fruticosus*, family Rosaceae.)

Related Web site: Blackberry http://www.botanical.com/botanical/mgmh/b/blaber49.html

blackbird bird *Turdus merula* of the thrush family, Muscicapidae, order Passeriformes, about 25 cm/10 in long. The male is black with a yellow bill and eyelids, the female dark brown with a dark beak. It lays three to five blue-green eggs with brown spots in a nest of grass and moss, plastered with mud, built in thickets or creeper-clad trees. The blackbird feeds on fruit, seeds, worms, grubs, and snails. Its song is rich and flutelike.

Found across Europe, Asia, and North Africa, the blackbird adapts well to human presence and gardens, and is one of the most common British birds. North American 'blackbirds' belong to a different family of birds, the Icteridae.

There were approximately 4 million breeding pairs in Britain in 1997.

black box popular name for the unit containing an aeroplane's flight and voice recorders. These monitor the plane's behaviour and the crew's conversation, thus providing valuable clues to the cause of a disaster. The box is nearly indestructible and usually painted orange for easy recovery. The name also refers to any compact electronic device that can be quickly connected or disconnected as a unit.

The voice recorder records in a 30-minute loop, so that the last minutes of a flight can be listened to if there has been an accident. The flight data recorder functions on a 25-hour loop. Neither recorder is battery operated so, as happened in the 1998 Swissair crash that killed 229 people, the final data may be missing as power gets cut off. The only part of a blackbox that is battery operated is its underwater locator, that will transmit a signal for 35 days after the crash to aid its location.

The maritime equivalent is the **voyage recorder**, installed in ships from 1989. It has 350 sensors to record the performance of engines, pumps, navigation lights, alarms, radar, and hull stress.

blackbuck antelope *Antilope cervicapra* found in central and northwestern India. It is related to the gazelle, from which it differs in having spirally-twisted horns. The male is black above and white beneath, whereas the female and young are fawn-coloured above. It is about 76 cm/2.5 ft in height.

Blackburn industrial city and administrative headquarters of ▷Blackburn and Darwen unitary authority, northwest England, on the Leeds–Liverpool canal, 32 km/20 mi northwest of Manchester; population (1991) 106,000. Until April 1998 it was part of the county of Lancashire. Historically the city was a centre of the cotton-weaving industry, but other important industries now include engineering, brewing, and high-tech industries. Textiles, electronics, radio and television components, leather, chemicals, paper, tufted carpets, and compact discs (Polygram) are produced.

Blackburn with Darwen unitary authority (borough status) in northwest England created in 1998, formerly part of Lancashire.
area 136 sq km/53 sq mi **towns and cities** ▷Blackburn (administrative headquarters), Darwen **features** Leeds–Liverpool canal; River Darwen; Darwen Hill and Tower (372 m/1,220 ft); western foothills of Rossendale uplands; Lewis Textile Museum (Blackburn) includes working model of spinning jenny; Blackburn Museum and Art Gallery has largest display of European icons in Britain **industries** engineering, brewing, chemicals, high technology industries, textiles, leather, electronics, paint, paper, carpets, compact discs **population** (1996) 139,400 **famous people** James Hargreaves

blackcap ▷warbler *Sylvia atricapilla*, family Muscicapidae, order Passeriformes. The male has a black cap, the female a reddish-brown one. The general colour of the bird is an ashen-grey, turning to an olive-brown above and pale or whitish-grey below. About 14 cm/5.5 in long, the blackcap likes wooded areas, and is a summer visitor to northern Europe, wintering in Africa.

blackcock (or heathcock) large grouse *Lyrurus tetrix* found on moors and in open woods in northern Europe and Asia. The male is mainly black with a lyre-shaped tail, and grows up to 54 cm/1.7 ft in height. The female is speckled brown and only 40 cm/1.3 ft tall. Their food consists of buds, young shoots, berries, and insects.

Black Country central area of England, to the west and north of Birmingham, incorporating the towns of Dudley, ▷Walsall, ▷Wolverhampton, and Sandwell. Heavily industrialized, it gained its name in the 19th century from its belching chimneys and mining spoil. Anti-pollution laws and the decline of heavy industry have changed the region's landscape. Coalmining in the area ceased in 1968.

blackcurrant variety of ▷currant.

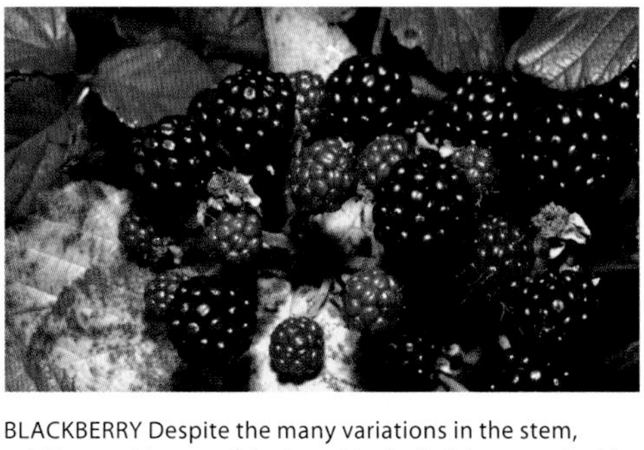

BLACKBERRY Despite the many variations in the stem, prickles, and leaves of the bramble, its fruit is recognizable as the familiar edible blackberry. *Premaphotos Wildlife*

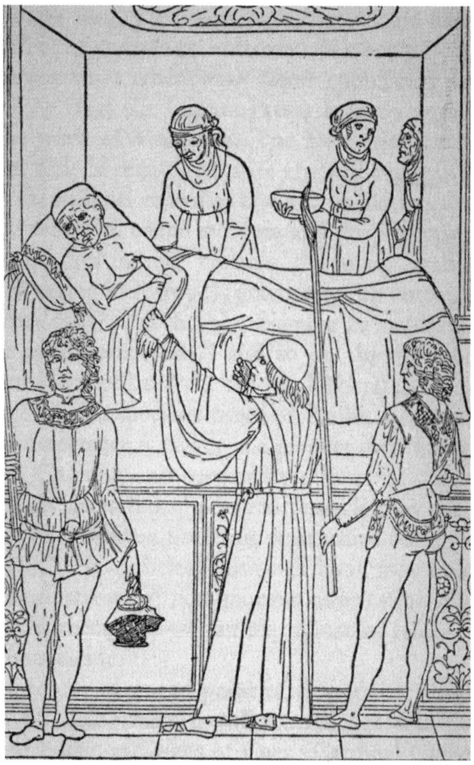

BLACK DEATH An illustration of a visit to a plague-stricken patient, from *Fasciculus Medicinae*, Venice, *c.* 1500. In this picture, the physician takes the pulse of the patient while holding a sponge to his nose. His assistants hold incense burners and torches. *Archive Photos*

Black Death great epidemic of ▷plague, mainly the bubonic variant, that ravaged Europe in the mid-14th century. Contemporary estimates that it killed between one-third and half of the population (about 75 million people) are probably accurate. The cause of the plague was the bacterium *Yersinia pestis*, transmitted by fleas that infested migrating Asian black rats. Originating in China, the disease followed the trade routes through India into Europe. The name Black Death was first used in England in the early 19th century.

black earth exceedingly fertile soil that covers a belt of land in northeastern North America, Europe, and Asia.

black economy unofficial economy of a country, which includes undeclared earnings from a second job ('moonlighting'), and enjoyment of undervalued goods and services (such as company 'perks'), designed for tax evasion purposes. In industrialized countries, it has been estimated to equal about 10% of ▷gross domestic product.

In the UK, the black economy was estimated in 1993 at £36–50 billion a year.

blackfly small but stoutly built blood-sucking flies with short antennae. Blackflies have broad wings with all the obvious veins in the anterior part of the wing. The family is widely distributed, the adults often occurring in such large numbers as to make them a nuisance. They are most abundant in north temperate and subarctic regions.

Classification Blackflies are in family Simuliidae, order Diptera, class Insecta, phylum Arthropoda.

blackfly plant-sucking insect, a type of ▷aphid.

Blackfoot member of an ▷American Indian people who live in Montana, USA, and Saskatchewan and Alberta, Canada. They number about 32,000 (1990) and consist of three subtribes: the Blackfoot proper, the Blood, and the Piegan. They were skilled horse-riding buffalo hunters until their territories were settled by Europeans. Their name derives from their black moccasins. Their language belongs to the Algonquian family.

Black Forest (German **Schwarzwald**) mountainous region of coniferous forest in Baden-Württemberg, western Germany; length 160 km/100 mi, greatest breadth 57 km/35 mi. Bounded to the west and south by the Rhine, which separates it from the Vosges, it rises to 1,493 m/4,898 ft in the Feldberg. It extends to the Swiss border in the south and to the Neckar valley in the north. Parts of the forest have recently been affected by ▷acid rain. The region is a popular tourist destination and lumbering is an important industry.

Black Friday 24 September 1869, a day on which Jay Gould (1836–1892) and James Fisk (1834–1872), stock manipulators, attempted to corner the gold market by trying to prevent the government from selling gold. President Grant refused to agree, but they spread the rumour that the president was opposed to the sales.

George S Boutweel (1818–1905), with Grant's approval, ordered the sale of $4 million in gold. The gold price plunged and many speculators were ruined. Gould and Fisk made about $11 million out of their manipulation of the market.

Black Hills mountains in western South Dakota and northeastern Wyoming, USA. They rise out of the Great Plains, 300–400 km/186–248 mi east of the Rocky Mountains front. The Black Hills occupy about 15,500 sq km/6,000 sq mi and rise to 2,207 m/7,242 ft at Harney Peak, South Dakota. The region includes a national forest (area 4,921 sq km/1,900 sq mi) and Mount ▷Rushmore, which has the face of four former presidents carved into a granite cliff (height 1,745 m/5,725 ft).

black hole object in space whose gravity is so great that nothing can escape from it, not even light. Thought to form when massive stars shrink at the end of their lives, a black hole sucks in more matter, including other stars, from the space around it. Matter that falls into a black hole is squeezed to infinite density at the centre of the hole. Black holes can be detected because gas falling towards them becomes so hot that it emits X-rays.

Black holes containing the mass of millions of stars are thought to lie at the centres of ▷quasars. Satellites have detected X-rays from a number of objects that may be black holes, but only a small number of likely black holes in our Galaxy have been identified.

Black Hole of Calcutta incident in Anglo-Indian history: according to tradition, the nawab (ruler) of Bengal confined 146 British prisoners on the night of 20 June 1756 in one small room, of whom only 23 allegedly survived. Later research reduced the death count to 43, assigning negligence rather than intention.

Blacking, John Anthony Randoll (1928–1990) British anthropologist and ethnomusicologist who researched the relationship between music and body movement, and the patterns of social and musical organization. His most widely read book is *How Musical is Man?* (1973).

blackmail criminal offence of extorting money with menaces or threats of detrimental action, such as exposure of some misconduct on the part of the victim.

Black Monday worldwide stockmarket crash that began 19 October 1987, prompted by the announcement of worse-than-expected US trade figures and the response by US Secretary of the Treasury, James Baker, who indicated that the sliding dollar needed to decline further. This caused a world panic as fears of the likely impact of a US recession were voiced by the major industrialized countries. The expected world recession did not occur; by the end of 1988 it was clear that the main effect had been a steadying in stock market activity and only a slight slowdown in world economic growth.

Blackmore, R(ichard) D(oddridge) (1825–1900) English novelist. His romance *Lorna Doone* (1869), set on Exmoor, southwest England, in the late 17th century, won him lasting popularity.

Black Muslims religious group founded in 1930 in the USA. Members adhere to Muslim values and believe in economic independence for black Americans. Under the leadership of Louis ▷Farrakhan and the group's original name of the ▷Nation of Islam, the movement has undergone a resurgence of popularity in recent years. In October 1995 more than 400,000 black males attended a 'Million Man March' to Washington DC. Organized by the Nation of Islam, it was the largest ever civil-rights demonstration in US history.

black nationalism movement towards black separatism in the USA during the 1960s; see ▷Black Power.

Black National State area in the Republic of South Africa set aside from 1971 to 1994 for development towards self-government by black Africans, in accordance with ▷apartheid. Before 1980 these areas were known as **black homelands** or **bantustans**. Making up less than 14% of the country, they tended to be situated in arid areas (though some had mineral wealth), often in scattered blocks. This meant that they were unsuitable for agriculture and unlikely to be profitable economic units. Those that achieved nominal independence were Transkei in 1976, Bophuthatswana in 1977, Venda in 1979, and Ciskei in 1981. They were not recognized outside South Africa because of their racial basis.

Blackpool seaside resort and unitary authority in northwest England, 45 km/28 mi north of Liverpool; part of the county of Lancashire until April 1998.

area 35 sq km/14 sq mi **physical** with its neighbours Lytham St Annes to the south and Fleetwood to the north, Blackpool is part of an urban ribbon between the Ribble estuary and Morecambe Bay **features** 11 km/7 mi of promenades, known for their autumn 'illuminations' of coloured lights; Blackpool Tower (built in 1894 and modelled on the Eiffel Tower in Paris), 157 m/518 ft high; the Pleasure Beach, an amusement park that includes one of Europe's largest and fastest roller-coasters, 75 m/235 ft high and 1.5 km/1 mi long (opened in 1994); three 19th-century piers; the Wintergardens, Grand Theatre, and Sealife Centre; a tram, which first operated in 1885, transports visitors along the promenade **industries** Blackpool is the largest holiday resort in northern England, and provides important conference business facilities. Other industries include light engineering and the production of confectionery and biscuits **population** (1997) 151,200; Blackpool urban area (1991) 261,400
Related Web site: Welcome to Blackpool – Entertainment Capital of the North http://www.blackpool.gov.uk/

Black Power movement towards black separatism in the USA during the 1960s, embodied in the **Black Panther Party** founded in 1966 by Huey Newton and Bobby Seale. Its declared aim was the creation of a separate black state in the USA to be established by a black plebiscite under the aegis of the United Nations. Following a National Black Political Convention in 1972, a National Black Assembly was established to exercise pressure on the Democratic and Republican parties.

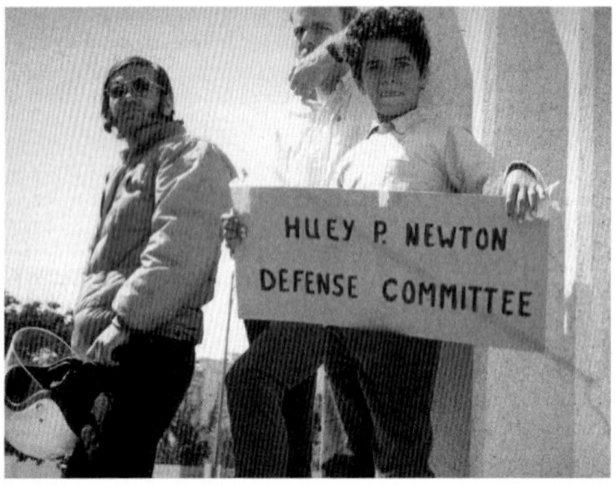

BLACK POWER A boy standing with adult protesters displays a sign on the opening day of Huey Newton's trial in Oakland, California, USA. *Archive Photos*

Black Prince nickname of ▷Edward, Prince of Wales, eldest son of Edward III of England.

Black Sea (Russian **Chernoye More**) inland sea in southeast Europe, linked with the seas of Azov and Marmara, and via the Dardanelles strait with the Mediterranean; area 423,000 sq km/163,320 sq mi; maximum depth 2,245 m/7,365 ft, decreasing in the Sea of Azov to only 13.5 m/44 ft. It is bounded by Ukraine, Russia, Georgia, Turkey, Bulgaria, and Romania, and the rivers Danube, Volga, Bug, Dniester and Dnieper flow into it, keeping salinity levels low. Uranium deposits beneath it are among the world's largest. About 90% of the water is polluted, mainly by agricultural fertilizers.

Blackshirts term widely used to describe fascist paramilitary organizations. Originating with Mussolini's fascist Squadristi in the 1920s, it was also applied to the Nazi SS (*Schutzstaffel*) and to the followers of Oswald Mosley's British Union of Fascists.

blacksnake any of several species of snake. The blacksnake *Pseudechis porphyriacus* is a venomous snake of the cobra family found in damp forests and swamps in eastern Australia. The blacksnake, *Coluber constrictor* from the eastern USA, is a relative of the European grass snake, growing up to 1.2 m/4 ft long, and without venom.

Black Stone in Islam, the sacred stone built into the east corner of the ▷Kaaba which is a focal point of the *hajj*, or pilgrimage, to Mecca.

blackthorn densely branched spiny European bush. It produces white blossom on bare black branches in early spring. Its sour plumlike blue-black fruit, the sloe, is used to make sloe gin. (*Prunus spinosa*, family Rosaceae.)

Black Thursday day of the Wall Street stock market crash on 24 October 1929, which precipitated the ▷Depression in the USA and throughout the world.

black widow North American spider *Latrodectus mactans*. The male is small and harmless, but the female is 1.3 cm/0.5 in long

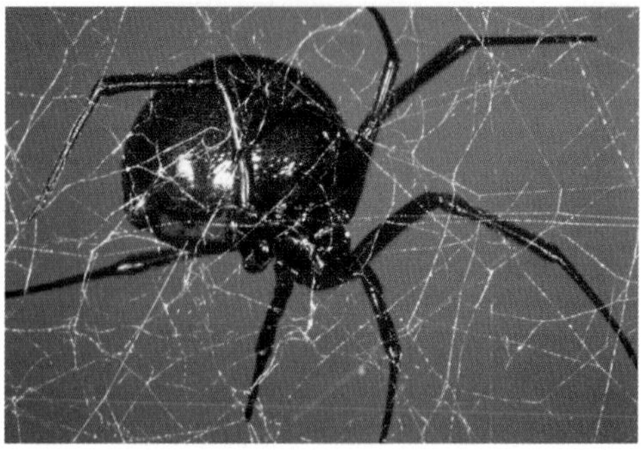
BLACK WIDOW A black widow spider weaving a web. Webs of widow spiders are poorly defined, amorphous sheetings of very strong, fine silk. *Archive Photos*

with a red patch below the abdomen and a powerful venomous bite. The bite causes pain and fever in human victims, but they usually recover.

bladder hollow elastic-walled organ which stores the urine produced in the kidneys. It is present in the ▷urinary systems of some fishes, most amphibians, some reptiles, and all mammals. Urine enters the bladder through two ureters, one leading from each kidney, and leaves it through the urethra.

Blaenau Gwent unitary authority in south Wales, created in 1996 from part of the former county of Gwent.

area 109 sq km/42 sq mi **towns** Ebbw Vale (administrative headquarters), Tredegar, Abertillery **features** Mynydd Carn-y-Cefn (550 m/1,800 ft); rivers Sirhowy and Ebbw; part of the Brecon Beacons National Park is here **population** (1996) 73,000

Blair, Tony (Anthony Charles Lynton) (1953–) British politician, born in Edinburgh, Scotland, leader of the Labour Party from 1994, prime minister from 1997. A centrist in the manner of his predecessor John Smith, he became Labour's youngest leader by a large majority in the first fully democratic elections to the post in July 1994. In 1995 he won approval of a new Labour Party charter, intended to distance the party from its traditional socialist base and promote 'social market' values. He and his party secured a landslide victory in the 1997 general election with a 179-seat majority. He retained a high public approval rating of 60% in February 1998.

Blair retained a remarkably high level of public approval throughout his first year as prime minister, which included the key initiatives of Scottish and Welsh devolution and a peace agreement in Northern Ireland. Along with the creation of an elected mayor for London, they were approved in 1997–98 referenda. The economic strategy of the Blair government differed little from that of the preceding Conservative administrations, involving tight control over public expenditure and the promotion, in the Private Finance Initiative, of 'public–private partnerships'. In 2003 Blair was widely criticised for his perceived militarism, which resulted in the deployment of UK forces in the ▷Iraq War, and faced rebellion from 139 Labour MPs in the parliamentary vote on military action. Later there were accusations that his government had overstated the threat posed by Saddam Hussein.

Blair governed in presidential style, delegating much to individual ministers, but intervening in key areas, such as welfare reform.

Tony Blair

There's only one thing the public dislikes more than a leader in control of his party, and that's a leader not in control of his party.

Speaking at the Old Vic celebrations of the Labour Party's 100th birthday. *Daily Telegraph*, 28 February 2000

Blake, George (1922–1994) British double agent who worked for MI6 (see ▷intelligence) and also for the USSR. Blake was unmasked by a Polish defector in 1961 and imprisoned, but escaped to the Eastern bloc in 1966. He is said to have betrayed at least 42 British agents to the Soviet side.

Blake, Quentin Saxby (1932–) English book illustrator and author of books for children. His animated pen-and-ink drawings are instantly recognizable. A prolific illustrator of children's books written by others, including Roald Dahl, Stella Gibbons, George Orwell, and Evelyn Waugh, he has also written and illustrated his own books, including *Mr Magnolia* (1980) (Kate Greenaway Medal) and *Mrs Armitage and the Big Wave* (1997).

Blake, Robert (1599–1657) British admiral of the Parliamentary forces during the English ▷Civil War. Appointed 'general-at-sea' in 1649, the following year he destroyed Prince Rupert's privateering Royalist fleet off Cartagena, Spain. In 1652 he won several engagements against the Dutch navy. In 1654 he bombarded Tunis, the stronghold of the Barbary corsairs, and in 1657 captured the Spanish treasure fleet in Santa Cruz.

WILLIAM BLAKE A watercolour by the English poet and painter William Blake. *The Art Archive/Cairo Museum/Dagli Orti*

Blake, William (1757–1827) English poet, artist, engraver, and visionary, and one of the most important figures of English ▷Romanticism. His lyrics, often written with a childlike simplicity, as in *Songs of Innocence* (1789) and *Songs of Experience* (1794), express a unique spiritual vision. In his 'prophetic books', including *The Marriage of Heaven and Hell* (1790), he created a vast personal mythology. He illustrated his own works with hand-coloured engravings.

Blake was born in London and, at the age of 14, he was apprenticed to an engraver before entering the Royal Academy in 1778. He then became an independent engraver and in 1782 married Catherine Boucher, who collaborated with him on many of his projects. *Songs of Innocence* was the first of his own poetic works that he illustrated and engraved, his highly individual style ultimately based on Michelangelo and Raphael. The complementary volume, *Songs of Experience*, which contains the poems 'Tyger! Tyger! burning bright' and 'London', expresses Blake's keen awareness of cruelty and injustice. After 1804 he devoted himself to illustrative work and to large watercolour designs for the biblical *Book of Job* (1821), John Milton's *Paradise Lost* (1822), and Dante's *Divina commedia* (1825). Blake's poem 'Jerusalem' (1820) was set to music by Charles Parry.

Blamey, Thomas Albert (1884–1951) Australian field marshal. Born in New South Wales, he served at Gallipoli, Turkey, and on the Western Front in World War I. After his recall to Australia in 1942 and appointment as commander-in-chief, Allied Land Forces, he commanded operations on the Kokoda Trail and the recapture of Papua.

Blanc, (Jean Joseph Charles) Louis (1811–1882) French socialist and journalist. In 1839 he founded the *Revue du progrès*, in which he published his *Organisation du travail*, advocating the establishment of cooperative workshops and other socialist schemes. He was a member of the provisional government of 1848 (see ▷revolutions of 1848) and from its fall lived in the UK until 1871.

blank verse in literature, the unrhymed iambic pentameter or ten-syllable line of five stresses. First used by the Italian Gian Giorgio Trissino in his tragedy *Sofonisba* (1514–15), it was introduced to England about 1540 by the Earl of Surrey, who used it in his translation of Virgil's *Aeneid*. It was developed by Christopher Marlowe and Shakespeare, quickly becoming the distinctive verse form of Elizabethan and Jacobean drama. It was later used by Milton in *Paradise Lost* (1667) and by Wordsworth in *The Prelude* (1805). More recent exponents of blank verse in English include Thomas Hardy, T S Eliot, and Robert Frost.

Blanqui, (Louis) Auguste (1805–1881) French revolutionary politician. He formulated the theory of the 'dictatorship of the proletariat', used by Karl Marx, and spent a total of 33 years in prison for insurrection. Although in prison, he was elected president of the Commune of Paris in 1871. His followers, the Blanquists, joined with the Marxists in 1881.

Blantyre chief industrial and commercial centre of Malawi, in the Shire highlands at the foot of Mchiru Mountain; population (1993) 399,000. The largest city in Malawi, it produces tea, coffee, rubber, tobacco, textiles, and wood products.

Blashford-Snell, John (1936–   ) English explorer and soldier. His expeditions have included the first descent and

---

BLAST FURNACE The blast furnace is used to extract iron from a mixture of iron ore, coke, and limestone. The less dense impurities float above the molten iron and are tapped off as slag. The molten iron sinks to the bottom of the furnace and is tapped off into moulds referred to as pigs. The iron extracted this way is also known as pig iron.

firebrick lining

waste gases (mainly nitrogen, carbon monoxide, and carbon dioxide)

iron ore, coke, and limestone

loading skip

air heater

1,900°C

hot air (850°C)

slag

molten slag

molten iron out

---

exploration of the Blue Nile (1968); the journey north to south from Alaska to Cape Horn, crossing the Darien Gap between Panama and Colombia for the first time (1971–72); and the first complete navigation of the Congo River, Africa (1974–75).

blasphemy (Greek 'evil-speaking') written or spoken insult directed against religious belief or sacred things with deliberate intent to outrage believers.

blast furnace smelting furnace used to extract metals from their ores, chiefly pig iron from iron ore. The temperature is raised by the injection of an air blast.

blastocyst in mammals, the hollow ball of cells which is an early stage in the development of the ▷embryo, roughly equivalent to the ▷blastula of other animal groups.

blastomere in biology, a cell formed in the first stages of embryonic development, after the splitting of the fertilized ovum, but before the formation of the ▷blastula or blastocyst.

blastula early stage in the development of a fertilized egg, when the egg changes from a solid mass of cells (the morula) to a hollow ball of cells (the blastula), containing a fluid-filled cavity (the blastocoel). See also ▷embryology.

Blaue Reiter, der (German the Blue Rider) loose association of German expressionist painters formed in 1911 in Munich. They were united by an interest in the expressive qualities of colour, in primitive and folk art, and in the necessity of painting 'the inner, spiritual side of nature', though their individual styles varied greatly. Two central figures were ▷Kandinsky and Franz ▷Marc.

bleaching decolorization of coloured materials. The two main types of bleaching agent are the **oxidizing bleaches**, which bring about the ▷oxidation of pigments and include the ultraviolet rays in sunshine, hydrogen peroxide, and chlorine in household bleaches, and the **reducing bleaches**, which bring about ▷reduction and include sulphur dioxide.

Bleaching processes have been known from antiquity, mainly those acting through sunlight. Both natural and synthetic pigments usually possess highly complex molecules, the colour property often being due only to a part of the molecule. Bleaches usually attack only that small part, yielding another substance similar in chemical structure but colourless.

bleak freshwater fish *Alburnus alburnus* of the carp family. It is up to to 20 cm/8 in long, and lives in still or slow-running clear water in Britain and Europe.

bleeding loss of blood from the circulation; see ▷haemorrhage.

blenny any fish of the family Blenniidae, mostly small fishes found near rocky shores, with elongated slimy bodies tapering from head to tail, no scales, and long pelvic fins set far forward.

Blériot, Louis (1872–1936) French aviator. In a 24-horsepower monoplane of his own construction, he made the first flight across the English Channel on 25 July 1909.

blesbok African antelope *Damaliscus albifrons*, about 1 m/3 ft high, with curved horns, brownish body, and a white blaze on the face. It was seriously depleted in the wild at the end of the 19th century. A few protected herds survive in South Africa. It is farmed for meat.

Bligh, William (1754–1817) English sailor. He accompanied Captain James ▷Cook on his second voyage around the world (1772–74), and in 1787 commanded HMS *Bounty* on an expedition to the Pacific. On the return voyage, in protest against harsh treatment, the crew mutinied. Bligh was sent to Australia as governor of New South Wales in 1805, where his discipline again provoked a mutiny in 1808 (the Rum Rebellion).

Bligh went to Tahiti with the *Bounty* to collect breadfruit-tree specimens, and gained the nickname 'Breadfruit Bligh'. In the mutiny, he and those of the crew who supported him were cast adrift in a boat with no map and few provisions. They survived, after many weeks reaching Timor, near Java, having drifted 5,822 km/3,618 mi. Many of the crew settled in the ▷Pitcairn Islands. On his return to England in 1790, Bligh was exonerated for his conduct.

In the Revolutionary Wars, Bligh took part in several naval battles: he was present at the Nore in 1797, later fought at Camperdown, and was specially mentioned at the battle of Copenhagen in 1801. After the failure of his Australian appointment, he returned to Britain, and was made an admiral in 1811.

blight any of a number of plant diseases caused mainly by parasitic species of ▷fungus, which produce a whitish appearance on leaf and stem surfaces; for example, **potato blight** *Phytophthora infestans*. General damage caused by aphids or pollution is sometimes known as blight.

blimp airship; any self-propelled, lighter-than-air craft that can be steered. A blimp with a soft frame is also called a **dirigible**; a ▷zeppelin is rigid-framed.

blindness complete absence or impairment of sight. It may be caused by heredity, accident, disease, or deterioration with age.

blind spot area where the optic nerve and blood vessels pass through the retina of the ▷eye. No visual image can be formed as there are no light-sensitive cells in this part of the retina.

Thus the organism is blind to objects that fall in this part of the visual field.

Bliss, Arthur Edward Drummond (1891–1975) English composer and conductor. He became Master of the Queen's Musick in 1953. Among his works are *A Colour Symphony* (1922); music for

WILLIAM BLIGH An aquatint by Robert Dodd, showing William Bligh and others being cast adrift, with his ship, *HMS Bounty*, in the background. *The Art Archive*

---

the ballets *Checkmate* (1937), *Miracle in the Gorbals* (1944), and *Adam Zero* (1946); an opera *The Olympians* (1949); and dramatic film music, including *Things to Come* (1935). He conducted the first performance of US composer Igor Stravinsky's *Ragtime* for 11 instruments in 1918.

blister beetle (or **oil beetle**) any of a small group of medium sized (3–20 mm/0.1–0.8 in) often brightly coloured beetles. Most give off an evil-smelling liquid, containing the irritant cantharidin, from the joints of their legs as a defence mechanism. When in contact with human skin, the liquid causes inflammation and blisters. Blister beetles are members of the family Meloidae, order Coleoptera, class Insecta, phylum Arthropoda.

Blitzkrieg (German 'lightning war') swift military campaign, as used by Germany at the beginning of World War II (1939–41). It was characterized by rapid movement by mechanized forces, supported by tactical air forces acting as 'flying artillery' and is best exemplified by the campaigns in Poland in 1939 and France in 1940.

Blixen, Karen (1885–1962) Baroness Blixen; born Karen Christentze Dinesen. Danish writer. She wrote mainly in English and is best known for her short stories, Gothic fantasies with a haunting, often mythic quality, published in such collections as *Seven Gothic Tales* (1934) and *Winter's Tales* (1942) under the pen-name **Isak Dinesen**. Her autobiography *Out of Africa* (1937; filmed 1985) is based on her experience of running a coffee plantation in Kenya.

Bloch, Marc (1886–1944) French historian, leading member of the Annales school. Most of his research was into medieval European history. He held that economic structures and systems of belief were just as important to the study of history as legal norms and institutional practices, and pioneered the use of comparative history.

blockade cutting-off of a place by hostile forces by land, sea, or air so as to prevent any movement to or fro, in order to compel a surrender without attack or to achieve some other political aim (for example, the ▷Berlin blockade (1948) and Union blockade of Confederate ports during the American Civil War). Economic sanctions are sometimes used in an attempt to achieve the same effect.

Bloemfontein (Afrikaans 'fountain of flowers') capital of the ▷Free State (formerly Orange Free State) and judicial capital of the Republic of South Africa; population (1991) 300,150. Founded in 1846 and declared a municipality in 1880, the city produces canned fruit, glassware, furniture, plastics, and railway engineering. The city's climate makes it a popular health resort.

blood fluid circulating in the arteries, veins, and capillaries of vertebrate animals; the term also refers to the corresponding fluid in those invertebrates that possess a closed ▷circulatory system. Blood carries nutrients and oxygen to each body cell and removes waste products, such as carbon dioxide. It is also important in the immune response and, in many animals, in the distribution of heat throughout the body.

In humans blood makes up 5% of the body weight, occupying a volume of 5.5 l/10 pt in the average adult. It is composed of a fluid called ▷plasma, in which are suspended microscopic cells of three main varieties:

Red cells (erythrocytes) form nearly half the volume of the blood, with about 6 million red cells in every millilitre of an adult's blood. They transport oxygen around the body. Their red colour is caused by ▷haemoglobin.

White cells (leucocytes) are of various kinds. Some (phagocytes) ingest invading bacteria and so protect the body from disease; these also help to repair injured tissues. Others (lymphocytes) produce antibodies, which help provide immunity.

Blood **platelets** (thrombocytes) assist in the clotting of blood.

Blood cells constantly wear out and die and are replaced from the bone marrow. Red blood cells die at the rate of 200 billion per day but the body produces new cells at an average rate of 9,000 million per hour.

Blood, Thomas (1618–1680) Irish adventurer, known as Colonel Blood. In 1663 he tried to seize the Lord Lieutenant of Ireland at Dublin Castle, and in 1670 he attempted to assassinate the Duke of Ormond in 1670, possibly on instructions from the Duke of ▷Buckingham. In 1671 he and three accomplices succeeded in stealing the crown and orb from the Tower of London, but were captured soon afterwards.

Blood received estates in Ireland in return for military services rendered to the Parliamentary party during the English Civil War. These were forfeited at the Restoration of the monarchy but were later returned by Charles II. In 1671 Charles II visited him in prison, and through his favour Blood obtained his release.

blood clotting complex series of events (known as the blood clotting cascade) resulting from a series of enzymatic reactions in the blood that prevents excessive bleeding after injury. The result is the formation of a meshwork of protein fibres (fibrin) and trapped blood cells over the cut blood vessels.

When platelets (cell fragments) in the bloodstream come into contact with a damaged blood vessel, they and the vessel wall itself release the enzyme **thrombokinase**, which brings about the conversion of the inactive enzyme **prothrombin** into the active **thrombin**. Thrombin in turn catalyses the conversion of the soluble protein **fibrinogen**, present in blood plasma, to the insoluble **fibrin**. This fibrous protein forms a net over the wound that traps red blood cells and seals the wound; the resulting jellylike clot hardens on exposure to air to form a scab. Calcium, vitamin K, and a variety of enzymes called factors are also necessary for efficient blood clotting. ▷Haemophilia is one of several diseases in which the clotting mechanism is impaired.

blood group any of the types into which blood is classified according to the presence or otherwise of certain ▷antigens on the surface of its red cells. Red blood cells of one individual may carry molecules on their surface that act as antigens in another individual whose red blood cells lack these molecules. The two main antigens are designated A and B. These give rise to four blood groups: having A only (A), having B only (B), having both (AB), and having neither (O). Each of these groups may or may not contain the ▷rhesus factor. Correct typing of blood groups is vital in transfusion, since incompatible types of donor and recipient blood will result in coagulation, with possible death of the recipient.

The ABO system was first described by Austrian scientist Karl ▷Landsteiner in 1902. Subsequent research revealed at least 14 main types of blood group systems, 11 of which are involved with induced ▷antibody production. Blood typing is also of importance in forensic medicine, cases of disputed paternity, and in anthropological studies.

In the UK, 44% of people are blood group O, 45% blood group A, 8% group B, and 3% group AB.

Amelia Jenks Bloomer

The costume of woman . . . should conduce at once to her health, comfort, and usefulness . . . while it should not fail also to conduce to her personal adornment, it should make that end of secondary importance.

Letter, June 1857

bloodhound breed of dog that originated as a hunting dog in Belgium in the Middle Ages. Black and tan in colour, it has long, pendulous ears and distinctive wrinkled head and face. It grows to a height of about 65 cm/26 in. Its excellent powers of scent have been employed in tracking and criminal detection from very early times.

blood poisoning presence in the bloodstream of quantities of bacteria or bacterial toxins sufficient to cause serious illness.

blood pressure pressure, or tension, of the blood against the inner walls of blood vessels, especially the arteries, due to the muscular pumping activity of the heart. Abnormally high blood pressure (▷hypertension) may be associated with various conditions or arise with no obvious cause; abnormally low blood pressure (hypotension) occurs in ▷shock and after excessive fluid or blood loss from any cause.

In mammals, the left ventricle of the ▷heart pumps blood into the arterial system. This pumping is assisted by waves of muscular contraction by the arteries themselves, but resisted by the elasticity of the inner and outer walls of the same arteries. Pressure is greatest when the heart ventricle contracts (**systole**) and lowest when the ventricle relaxes (**diastole**), and pressure is solely maintained by the elasticity of the arteries. Blood pressure is measured in millimetres of mercury (the height of a column on the measuring instrument, a sphygmomanometer). Normal human blood pressure varies with age, but in a young healthy adult it is around 120/80 mm Hg; the first number represents the systolic pressure and the second the diastolic. Large deviations from this reading usually indicate ill health.

blood test laboratory evaluation of a blood sample. There are numerous blood tests, from simple typing to establish the ▷blood group to sophisticated biochemical assays of substances, such as hormones, present in the blood only in minute quantities.

blood transfusion see ▷transfusion.

bloodworm larvae of the ▷midge. They are red because their blood plasma contains haemoglobin like human blood, which increases its ability to take up oxygen. This is of value to the larvae, which commonly burrow in the oxygen-poor mud bottom of pools and rivers. They feed on algae and detritus.

Bloodworms are long, with a distinct head, and segmentation of the abdomen. Prolegs (leglike projections) are found on the first thoracic and last abdominal segments. Gills are present on the last abdominal segment, and often on the segment preceding it. On average they measure 6 mm/0.2 in in length.

Bloodworms frequently build tubes of mud around themselves, which may be attached to stones. They constitute a major part of the diet of fish, hence they are often used as bait by anglers.

Not all bloodworms are red. Those that do not live in mud tubes, but frequent the surface waters, are green, and some species have blue bands.

bloom whitish powdery or waxlike coating over the surface of certain fruits that easily rubs off when handled. It often contains ▷yeasts that live on the sugars in the fruit. The term bloom is also used to describe a rapid increase in number of certain species of algae found in lakes, ponds, and oceans.

Bloomer, Amelia (1818–1894) Born Amelia Jenks. US campaigner for women's rights. In 1849, when unwieldy crinolines were the fashion, she introduced a knee-length skirt combined with loose trousers gathered at the ankles, which became known as **bloomers** (also called 'rational dress'). She published the magazine *The Lily* (1849–54), which campaigned for women's rights and dress reform, and lectured with Susan B ▷Anthony in New York, USA.

Bloomsbury Group intellectual circle of writers and artists based in Bloomsbury, London, which flourished in the 1920s. It centred on the house of publisher Leonard Woolf and his wife, novelist Virginia ▷Woolf. Typically modernist, their innovative artistic contributions represented an important section of the English avant-garde.

The circle included the artists Duncan ▷Grant and Vanessa Bell, the biographer Lytton ▷Strachey, art critics Roger Fry and Clive Bell, and the economist John Maynard ▷Keynes. From their emphasis on close interpersonal relationships and their fastidious attitude towards contemporary culture arose many accusations of elitism. They also held sceptical views on social and political conventions and religious practices.

blowfly any fly of the genus *Calliphora*, also known as bluebottle, or of the related genus *Lucilia*, when it is greenbottle. It lays its eggs in dead flesh, on which the maggots feed.

blubber thick layer of ▷fat under the skin of marine mammals, which provides an energy store and an effective insulating layer, preventing the loss of body heat to the surrounding water. Blubber has been used (when boiled down) in engineering, food processing, cosmetics, and printing, but all of these products can now be produced synthetically.

Blücher, Gebhard Leberecht von (1742–1819) Prussian general and field marshal, popularly known as 'Marshal Forward'. He took an active part in the patriotic movement, and in the War of German Liberation defeated the French as commander-in-chief at Leipzig in 1813, crossed the Rhine to Paris in 1814, and was made prince of Wahlstadt (Silesia).

In 1815 he was defeated by Napoleon at Ligny but came to the aid of British commander Wellington at ▷Waterloo.

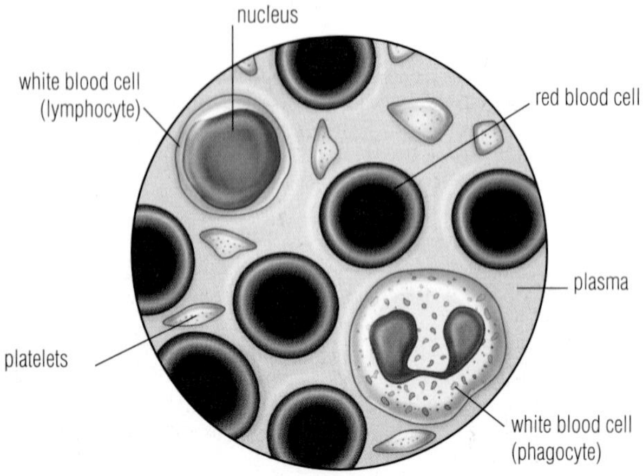

BLOOD Human blood contains red blood cells, white blood cells (phagocytes and lymphocytes), and platelets, suspended in plasma.

BLUEBELL The bluebell is a bulbous plant abundant in woods, hedgerows, and meadows adjoining woods. It thrives in good soil with partial shade.

bluebell name given in Scotland to the ▷harebell (*Campanula rotundifolia*), and in England to the wild hyacinth (*Endymion nonscriptus*), belonging to the lily family (Liliaceae).
    Related Web site: Bluebell http://www.botanical.com/botanical/mgmh/b/bluebe60.html

blueberry any of various North American shrubs belonging to the heath family, growing in acid soil. The genus also includes huckleberries, bilberries, deerberries, and cranberries, many of which resemble each other and are difficult to tell apart from blueberries. All have small oval short-stalked leaves, slender green or reddish twigs, and whitish bell-like blossoms. Only true blueberries, however, have tiny granular speckles on their twigs. Blueberries have black or blue edible fruits, often covered with a white bloom. (Genus *Vaccinium*, family Ericaceae.)

bluebird (or **blue robin** or **blue warbler**) three species of a North American bird, genus *Sialia*, belonging to the thrush subfamily, Turdinae, order Passeriformes. The eastern bluebird *Sialia sialis* is regarded as the herald of spring as it returns from migration. About 18 cm/7 in long, it has a reddish breast, the upper plumage being sky-blue, and a distinctive song. It lays about six pale-blue eggs.

bluebottle another name for ▷blowfly.

bluebuck any of several species of antelope, including the blue ▷duiker *Cephalophus monticola* of South Africa, about 33 cm/13 in high. The male of the Indian nilgai antelope is also known as the bluebuck.

blue chip in business and finance, a stock that is considered strong and reliable in terms of the dividend yield and capital value. Blue-chip companies are favoured by stock-market investors more interested in security than risk taking.

bluegrass dense spreading grass, which is blue-tinted and grows in clumps. Various species are known from the northern hemisphere. Kentucky bluegrass (*Poa pratensis*), introduced to the USA from Europe, provides pasture for horses. (Genus *Poa*, family Gramineae.)

blue-green algae (or **cyanobacteria**) single-celled, primitive organisms that resemble bacteria in their internal cell organization, sometimes joined together in colonies or filaments. Blue-green algae are among the oldest known living organisms and, with bacteria, belong to the kingdom Monera; remains have been found in rocks up to 3.5 billion years old. They are widely distributed in aquatic habitats, on the damp surfaces of rocks and trees, and in the soil.
    Blue-green algae and bacteria are prokaryotic organisms. Some can fix nitrogen and thus are necessary to the nitrogen cycle, while others follow a symbiotic existence – for example, living in association with fungi to form lichens. Fresh water can become polluted by nitrates and phosphates from fertilizers and detergents. This eutrophication, or overenrichment, of the water causes multiplication of the algae in the form of algae blooms. The algae multiply and cover the water's surface, remaining harmless until they give off toxins as they decay. These toxins kill fish and other wildlife and can be harmful to domestic animals, cattle, and people.

blue gum either of two Australian trees: Tasmanian blue gum (*Eucalyptus globulus*) of the myrtle family, with bluish bark, a chief source of eucalyptus oil; or the tall, straight Sydney blue gum (*E. saligna*). The former is widely cultivated in California and has also been planted in South America, India, parts of Africa, and southern Europe.

Blue Mountains part of the ▷Great Dividing Range, New South Wales, Australia, running almost parallel with the coast, 80–100 km/50–62 mi west of Sydney. The highest peak is Mount Beemarang (1,247 m/4,091 ft). The mountains are popular with tourists, attracted by the fine scenery.

Blue Nile (Arabic **Al Bahr al-Azraq**) river rising at a spring site upstream of Lake Tana in Ethiopia, 2,150 m/7,054 ft above sea level. Flowing west then north for 1,460 km/907 mi, it eventually meets the White Nile at Khartoum. A length of 800 km/500 mi is navigable at high water. Some 80% of Sudan's electricity is provided by hydroelectric schemes at Roseires and Sennar, and these dams provide irrigation water for over 10,000 sq km/3,860 sq mi of the Gezira Plain.

blueprint photographic process used for copying engineering drawings and architectural plans, so called because it produces a white copy of the original against a blue background.

Blue Ridge Mountains mountain range in southeastern USA, and part of the ▷Appalachian Mountains system. The Blue Ridge Mountains run from northwest Georgia to West Virginia. The highest summit (and also the highest point in eastern USA) is Mount Mitchell; height 2,037 m/6,684 ft.

blues African-American music that originated in the work songs and Negro spirituals of the rural American South in the late 19th century. It is characterized by a 12-bar, or occasionally 16-bar, construction and melancholy lyrics which relate tales of woe or unhappy love. The guitar has been the dominant instrument; harmonica and piano are also common. Blues guitar and vocal styles have played a vital part in the development of jazz, rock, and pop music in general.
    Related Web site: Blues Access Online http://www.he.net/~blues/

blue shift in astronomy, a manifestation of the ▷Doppler effect in which an object appears bluer when it is moving towards the observer or the observer is moving towards it (blue light is of a higher frequency than other colours in the spectrum). The blue shift is the opposite of the ▷red shift.

Blum, Léon (1872–1950) French socialist politician, parliamentary leader of the Section Française de l'Internationale Ouvrière (SFIO) in the inter-war period and the first socialist prime minister of France 1936–37, when his Popular Front government introduced paid holidays and the 40-hour working week in France. He was prime minister again in 1938 and 1946.

Blunden, Edmund (Charles) (1896–1974) English poet and critic. He served in World War I and published the prose work *Undertones of War* (1928). His poetry is mainly about rural life. Among his scholarly contributions was the discovery and publication of some poems by the 19th-century poet John ▷Clare.

Blunt, Anthony Frederick (1907–1983) English art historian and double agent. As a Cambridge lecturer, he recruited for the Soviet secret service and, as a member of the British Secret Service 1940–45, passed information to the USSR. In 1951 he assisted the defection to the USSR of the British agents Guy Burgess and Donald Maclean (1913–1983). He was the author of many respected works on Italian and French art, including a study of Poussin 1966–67. Unmasked in 1964, he was given immunity after his confession.

Blunt, Wilfrid Scawen (1840–1922) English poet. He travelled in the Middle East, becoming a supporter of Arab nationalism. He also supported Irish home rule (he was imprisoned 1887–88), and wrote anti-imperialist books as well as poetry and diaries.

Blyton, Enid Mary (1897–1968) English writer of children's books. She used her abilities as a trained teacher of young children and a journalist, coupled with her ability to think like a child, to produce books at all levels which, though criticized for their predictability and lack of characterization, and more recently for social, racial, and sexual stereotyping, satisfy the reader's need for security. Her best-selling series were, the *Famous Five* series, the 'Secret Seven', and 'Noddy'.

boa any of various nonvenomous snakes of the family Boidae, found mainly in tropical and subtropical parts of the New World. Boas feed mainly on small mammals and birds. They catch these in their teeth or kill them by constriction (crushing the creature within their coils until it suffocates). The boa constrictor *Constrictor constrictor* can grow up to 5.5 m/18.5 ft long, but rarely reaches more than 4 m/12 ft. Other boas include the anaconda and the emerald tree boa *Boa canina*, about 2 m/6 ft long and bright green.
    Some small burrowing boas live in North Africa and western Asia, while other species live on Madagascar and some Pacific islands, but the majority of boas live in South and Central America. The name boa is sometimes used loosely to include the pythons of the Old World, which also belong to the Boidae family, and which share with boas vestiges of hind limbs and constricting habits.

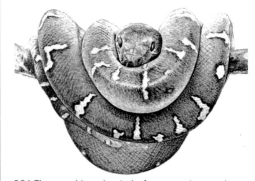

BOA The emerald tree boa is the fastest-moving member of the boa family.

Boadicea alternative (Latin) spelling of British queen ▷Boudicca.

boar wild member of the pig family, such as the Eurasian wild boar *Sus scrofa*, from which domestic pig breeds derive. The wild boar is sturdily built, being 1.5 m/4.5 ft long and 1 m/3 ft high,

BLUEBUCK The Indian bluebuck, or nilgai, *Boselaphus tragocamelus* is the largest of all Asiatic antelopes. In areas where the Hindu religion predominates, the bluebuck's resemblance to a cow has earned it a large degree of protection.
Premaphotos Wildlife

and possesses formidable tusks. Of gregarious nature and mainly woodland-dwelling, it feeds on roots, nuts, insects, and some carrion.

The dark coat of the adult boar is made up of coarse bristles with varying amounts of underfur, but the young are striped. The male domestic pig is also known as a boar, the female as a sow.

Interest in wild-boar farming is reviving in Britain because of the meat's gamelike taste, low fat, and free-range associations.

board of visitors in the UK penal system, a body of people independent of the government who supervise the state of prison premises, the administration of prisons, and the treatment of the prisoners.

Boards of visitors also serve as disciplinary tribunals. Research has indicated that about 40% of members are magistrates.

boarfish marine bony fish found chiefly in the Mediterranean and northeast Atlantic. It has a flat oval body that is reddish coloured with seven transverse orange bands on the back. Boarfish are related to the dory.

Classification Boarfish *Capros aper* belongs to the order Zeiformes, class Osteichthyes.

Boas, Franz (1858–1942) German-born US anthropologist. He stressed the need to study 'four fields' – ethnology, linguistics, physical anthropology, and archaeology – before generalizations might be made about any one culture or comparisons about any number of cultures.

boat people illegal emigrants travelling by sea, especially those Vietnamese who left their country after the takeover of South Vietnam in 1975 by North Vietnam. In 1979, almost 69,000 boat people landed in Hong Kong in a single year. By 1988, it was decided to treat all boat people as illegal immigrants unless they could prove they qualified for refugee status. In all, some 160,000 Vietnamese fled to Hong Kong, many being attacked at sea by Thai pirates, and in 1989 50,000 remained there in cramped, squalid refugee camps. The UK government began forced repatriation in 1989, leaving only 18,000 in Hong Kong by 1996. Before taking over Hong Kong in 1997, the Chinese authorities made it clear that they wanted all the Vietnamese cleared out of the territory. At the end of 1997, 3,364 refugees were still living in Hong Kong. In January 1998, the Hong Kong Executive Council ended the policy of granting asylum to the boat people. A UN-backed plan to accelerate the repatriation of around 38,000 boat people living in Southeast Asia was announced in January 1996. Hong Kong closed its last camp for boat people in May 2000, after a decision made in February of that year to give the Vietnamese refugees residency in Hong Kong.

Boat Race, the annual UK ▷rowing race between the crews of Oxford and Cambridge universities. It is held during the Easter vacation over a 6.8 km/4.25 mi course on the River Thames between Putney and Mortlake, southwest London.

bobcat wild cat *Lynx rufus* living in a variety of habitats from southern Canada through to southern Mexico. It is similar to the lynx, but only 75 cm/2.5 ft long, with reddish fur and less well-developed ear tufts.
> Related Web site: Lynx Rufus – Bobcat http://www.sbceo. k12.ca.us/~mcssb/sbpanda/bobcat.html

bobolink North American songbird *Dolichonyx oryzivorus*, family Icteridae, order Passeriformes, that takes its common name from the distinctive call of the male. It has a long middle toe and pointed tailfeathers. Breeding males are mostly black, with a white rump; females are buff-coloured with dark streaks. Bobolinks are about 18 cm/7 in long and build their nests on the ground in hayfields and weedy meadows.

bobsleighing (or bobsledding) sport of racing steel-bodied, steerable toboggans, crewed by two or four people, down mountain ice chutes at speeds of up to 130 kph/80 mph. It was introduced as a men's Olympic event in 1924 (the four-crew event was introduced at the 1924 Winter Olympics and the two-crew in 1932). Women's Olympic bobsleighing will be introduced at the 2002 Winter Games. Men's world championships have been held every year since 1931. Included among the major bobsleighing events are the Olympic Championships and the World Championships. In Olympic years winners automatically become world champions.
> Related Web site: International Bobsled and Skeleton Federation http://www.bobsleigh.com/

Boccaccio, Giovanni (1313–1375) Italian writer and poet. He is chiefly known for the collection of tales called the *Decameron* (1348–53). Equally at home with tragic and comic narrative, he laid the foundations for the humanism of the Renaissance and raised vernacular literature to the status enjoyed by the ancient classics.

He was born in Florence but lived in Naples 1328–41, where he fell in love with the unfaithful 'Fiammetta' who inspired his early poetry. Before returning to Florence in 1341 he had written the romance *Filostrato* and the verse narrative *Teseide* (used by Chaucer in his *Troilus and Criseyde* and 'The Knight's Tale'). *Teseide* is the first romantic narrative to appear in the Italian language in *ottava rima*, the metre adopted by ▷Ariosto and ▷Tasso. The narrative poem *Filostrato* is also written in *ottava rima*. Boccaccio was much influenced by the poet ▷Petrarch, whom he met in 1350.

Bodensee German name for Lake ▷Constance, north of the Alps.

Bode's law (or Titius-Bode law) numerical sequence that gives the approximate distances, in astronomical units (distance between Earth and Sun = one astronomical unit), of the planets from the Sun by adding 4 to each term of the series 0, 3, 6, 12, 24, ... and then dividing by 10. Bode's law predicted the existence of a planet between ▷Mars and ▷Jupiter, which led to the discovery of the asteroids.

Bodhidharma (lived 6th century) Indian Buddhist and teacher. He entered China from southern India about 520 and was the founder of the Ch'an school. Ch'an focuses on contemplation leading to intuitive meditation, a direct pointing to and stilling of the human mind. In the 20th century, the Japanese variation, ▷Zen, has attracted many followers in the West.

bodhisattva in Mahāyāna Buddhism, someone who seeks ▷enlightenment in order to help other living beings. A bodhisattva is free to enter ▷nirvana but voluntarily chooses to be reborn until all other beings have attained that state. Bodhisattvas are seen as intercessors to whom believers may pray for help.

Bodmin market town in Cornwall, southwest England, 48 km/ 30 mi northwest of Plymouth; population (1991) 13,100. It is the commercial centre of a farming area. Other activites include some light industry and the provision of tourist services. Bodmin Moor, to the northeast, is a granite upland culminating in Brown Willy, the highest point in Cornwall at 419 m/1,375 ft.

Boeing Company, the US military and commercial aircraft manufacturer. Among the models Boeing has produced are the B-17 Flying Fortress, 1935; the B-52 Stratofortress, 1952; the Chinook helicopter, 1961; the first jetliner, the Boeing 707, 1957; the ▷jumbo jet or Boeing 747, 1969; the jetfoil, 1975; and the 777-300 jetliner, 1997.

John Snagge
British sports commentator

It's Oxford! No, it's Cambridge! I can't see. It's Oxford . . . no . . . well, one of them must be winning!

Commenting on the 1954 Oxford versus Cambridge boat race

Boeotia ancient and modern district of central Greece, of which ▷Thebes was and remains the chief city. The **Boeotian League** (formed by ten city-states in the 6th century BC) was brought under strong central Theban control in the later 5th century BC. It superseded ▷Sparta as the leading military power in Greece in the 4th century BC until the rise of ▷Philip II of Macedon.

Boer Dutch settler or descendant of Dutch and Huguenot settlers in South Africa; see also ▷Afrikaner.

Boer War the second of the ▷South African Wars 1899–1902, waged between Dutch settlers in South Africa and the British.

BOBSLEIGHING A four-crew bobsleigh team steer their way through a race. *Corel*

Boethius, Anicius Manlius Severinus (AD 480–524) Roman philosopher. He wrote treatises on music and mathematics and *De Consolatione Philosophiae/The Consolation of Philosophy*, a dialogue in prose. It was translated into European languages during the Middle Ages.
> Related Web site: Boethius: Consolation of Philosophy http:// etext.lib.virginia.edu/latin/boethius/consolatio.html

bog type of wetland where decomposition is slowed down and dead plant matter accumulates as ▷peat. Bogs develop under conditions of low temperature, high acidity, low nutrient supply, stagnant water, and oxygen deficiency. Typical bog plants are sphagnum moss, rushes, and cotton grass; insectivorous plants such as sundews and bladderworts are common in bogs (insect prey make up for the lack of nutrients).

Large bogs are found in Ireland and northern Scotland. They are dominated by heather, cotton grass, and over 30 species of sphagnum mosses which make up the general bog matrix. The rolling blanket bogs of Scotland are a southern outcrop of the arctic tundra ecosystem, and have taken thousands of years to develop.

According to government figures November 1994, Scotland's peat bogs contain three-quarters of all carbon locked up in organic material in Britain.

Bogarde, Dirk (1921–1999) Stage name of Derek Niven van den Bogaerde. English actor. He appeared in comedies and adventure films such as *Doctor in the House* (1954) and *Campbell's Kingdom* (1957), before acquiring international recognition for complex roles in Joseph Losey's *The Servant* (1963) and *Accident* (1967), and Luchino Visconti's *Death in Venice* (1971). As a writer he was best known for his volumes of autobiography. He was knighted in 1992.

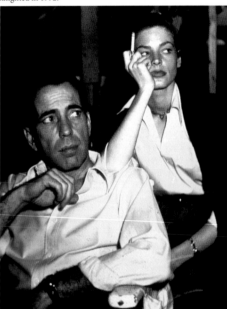

HUMPHREY BOGART US actors Humphrey Bogart and Lauren Bacall, in a picture from the 1940s. *Archive Photos*

Bogart, Humphrey (DeForest) (1899–1957) US film actor. He became an international cult figure through roles as a tough, romantic loner in such films as *High Sierra* (1941), *The Maltese Falcon* (1941), *Casablanca* (1942), *To Have and Have Not* (1944), *The Big Sleep* (1946), and *In a Lonely Place* (1950). He won an Academy Award for his role in *The African Queen* (1952).

After a short stage career, Bogart spent much of the 1930s playing secondary roles to the likes of James Cagney and George Raft. He achieved fame as a gangster in *The Petrified Forest* (1936). Bogart's other films include *Dead Reckoning* (1947), *The Dark Passage* (1947), *Key Largo* (1948), *The Treasure of the Sierra Madre* (1948), *The Enforcer* (1951), *The Barefoot Contessa* (1954), *Beat the Devil* (1954), *The Caine Mutiny* (1954), and *The Harder They Fall* (1956). He was married to Lauren Bacall, his frequent co-star, from 1945 until his death.

Bogart was named the top male screen legend in an American Film Institute poll in 1999.
> Related Web site: Tribute to Humphrey Bogart http://www. macconsult.com/bogart/

bogbean (or buckbean) aquatic or bog plant belonging to the gentian family, with a creeping rhizome (underground stem) and leaves and pink flower spikes held above water. It is found over much of the northern hemisphere. (*Menyanthes trifoliata*, family Gentianaceae.)

Bogotá (officially **Santa Fé de Bogotá**) capital of ▷Colombia, and of Cundinamarca department, situated at 2,640 m/8,660 ft above sea level, on the edge of the Eastern Cordillera plateau of the Andes; population (1999) 6,260,900. Main industries include textiles, chemicals, food processing, and tobacco. Bogotá is Colombia's largest city, and the financial, commercial, and cultural centre of the country. It has several universities and museums.
Features Home of Simon Bolívar; world's largest collection of pre-Columbian gold objects in its Gold Museum; its two oldest universities were founded in 1580 and 1622.
History It was founded by the Spaniard Gonzalo Jiménez de Quesada in 1538 on the site of the Chibcha Indian settlement of Bacatá, and orginally named 'Santa Fé de Bogotá'. In 1598 Bogotá became the capital of the viceroyalty of New Granada, which became the republic of Columbia in 1718.

Bohemia area of the Czech Republic, a fertile plateau drained by the Elbe and Vltava rivers. It is rich in mineral resources, including uranium, coal, lignite, iron ore, silver, and graphite. The main cities are Prague and Plzeň. The name Bohemia derives from the Celtic Boii, its earliest known inhabitants.

Bohr, Niels Henrik David (1885–1962) Danish physicist who was awarded the Nobel Prize for Physics in 1922 for his discovery of the structure of atoms and the radiation emanating from them. He pioneered ▷quantum theory by showing that the nuclei of atoms are surrounded by shells of electrons, each assigned particular sets of quantum numbers according to their orbits. He explained the structure and behaviour of the nucleus, as well as the process of nuclear ▷fission. Bohr also proposed the doctrine of **complementarity**, the theory that a fundamental particle is neither a wave nor a particle, because these are complementary modes of description.

Related Web site: Niels Bohr Institute History http://www.nbi.dk/nbi-history.html

bohrium synthesized, radioactive element of the ▷transactinide series, symbol Bh, atomic number 107, relative atomic mass 262. It was first synthesized by the Joint Institute for Nuclear Research in Dubna, Russia, in 1976; in 1981 the Laboratory for Heavy Ion Research in Darmstadt, Germany, confirmed its existence. It was named in 1997 after Danish physicist Niels ▷Bohr. Its temporary name was unnilseptium.

The first chemical study of bohrium was published in 2000, after experiments by Swiss researchers produced six atoms of bohrium-267 (half-life 17 seconds). It behaved like a typical group VII element, with chemical similarities to technetium and rhenium.

Boileau Despréaux, Nicolas (1636–1711) French poet and critic. After a series of contemporary satires, his 'Epîtres/Epistles' (1669–77) led to his joint appointment with the dramatist Jean Racine as royal historiographer in 1677. Later works include *L'Art poétique/The Art of Poetry* (1674) and the mock-heroic *Le Lutrin/The Lectern* (1674–83).

boiler any vessel that converts water into steam. Boilers are used in conventional power stations to generate steam to feed steam ▷turbines, which drive the electricity generators. They are also used in steamships, which are propelled by steam turbines, and in steam locomotives. Every boiler has a furnace in which fuel (coal, oil, or gas) is burned to produce hot gases, and a system of tubes in which heat is transferred from the gases to the water.

boiling point for any given liquid, the temperature at which the application of heat raises the temperature of the liquid no further, but converts it into vapour.

The boiling point of water under normal pressure is 100°C/212°F. The lower the pressure, the lower the boiling point and vice versa.

Boiling Points of Selected Liquids

Liquid	Boiling point	
	°C	°F
Methanol	64.7	148.5
Ethanol	78.2	172.8
Benzene	80.1	176.2
Water	100.0	212.0
Octane	125.6	258.1
Turpentine	156.0	312.8
Glycerol	290.0	554.0
Mercury	356.9	674.4

Bokassa, Jean-Bédel (1921–1996) Central African Republic president 1966–79 and self-proclaimed emperor 1977–79. Commander-in-chief from 1963, in December 1965 he led the military coup that gave him the presidency. On 4 December 1976 he proclaimed the Central African Empire and one year later crowned himself emperor for life.

His regime was characterized by arbitrary state violence and cruelty. Overthrown in 1979, Bokassa was in exile in the Côte d'Ivoire until 1986. Upon his return he was sentenced to death, but this was commuted to life imprisonment in 1988.

Bokassa, born at Bobangui, joined the French army in 1939 and was awarded the Croix de Guerre for his service with the French colonial forces in Indochina. When the Central African Republic achieved independence in 1960, he was invited to establish an army. After seizing power, he annulled the constitution and made himself president for life in 1972, and marshal of the republic in 1974. In 1976 he called in former president David Dacko (1930–), whom he had overthrown, as his adviser. Backed by France, Dacko deposed him in a coup while Bokassa was visiting Libya during 1979.

Bokhara variant spelling of ▷Bukhara, a city in Uzbekistan.

bolero Spanish dance in moderate triple time (3/4), invented in the late 18th century. It is performed by a solo dancer or a couple, usually with castanet accompaniment, and is still a contemporary form of dance in Caribbean countries. In music, Maurice Ravel's one-act ballet score *Boléro* (1928) is the most famous example.

boletus any of several fleshy fungi (see ▷fungus) with thick stems and caps of various colours. The European *Boletus edulis* is edible, but some species are poisonous. (Genus *Boletus*, class Basidiomycetes.)

Boleyn, Anne (*c.* 1507–1536) Queen of England 1533–36 as the second wife of Henry VIII. She gave birth to the future Queen Elizabeth I in 1533, but was unable to produce a male heir to the throne, and was executed on a false charge.

Having no male heir by his first wife, Catherine of Aragon, Henry broke from Rome and the pope (starting the ▷Reformation) in order to divorce Catherine and marry Anne. She was married to him in 1533, but three years later was accused of adultery and incest with her half-brother (a charge invented by Thomas ▷Cromwell), and sent to the Tower of London. She was declared guilty, and was beheaded on 19 May 1536 at Tower Green.

ANNE BOLEYN A portrait of Anne Boleyn, second wife of King Henry VIII of England, by Flemish artist Frans Pourbus.
The Art Archive/Civiche Race d'Arte Pavia Italy/Dagli Orti

Bolger, Jim (1935–) Born James Brendan Bolger. New Zealand National Party centre-right politician, prime minister 1990–97. His government improved relations with the USA, which had deteriorated sharply when the preceding Labour governments had banned nuclear-powered and nuclear-armed ships from entering New Zealand's harbours. It also oversaw an upturn in the economy. However, the failure to honour election pledges, particularly in the welfare area, where there were cuts in provision, meant that National Party support slipped in the November 1993 general election and the government was only re-elected with a majority of one. The October 1996 general election, held for the first time under a mixed-member system of proportional representation, was inconclusive and Bolger was forced to form a coalition government, with the New Zealand First Party leader, Winston Peters, as his deputy. In November 1997 he resigned and was replaced as prime minister by his transport minister, Jenny ▷Shipley, who had led a right-wing revolt against his leadership.

Bolingbroke title of Henry of Bolingbroke, ▷Henry IV of England.

Bolingbroke, Henry St John 1st Viscount Bolingbroke (1678–1751) British Tory politician and political philosopher. He was foreign secretary 1710–14 and a Jacobite conspirator. His books, such as *Idea of a Patriot King* (1738) and *The Dissertation upon Parties* (1735), laid the foundations for 19th-century Toryism.

Secretary of war 1704–08, he became foreign secretary in Robert Harley's ministry in 1710, and in 1713 negotiated the Treaty of Utrecht. His plans to restore the 'Old Pretender' James Francis Edward Stuart were ruined by Queen Anne's death only five days after he had secured the dismissal of Harley in 1714. He fled abroad, returning in 1723, when he worked to overthrow Robert Walpole.

Related Web site: Bolingbroke, Henry St John http://socserv2.socsci.mcmaster.ca/~econ/ugcm/3ll3/bolingbroke/index.html

Bolívar, Simón (1783–1830) South American nationalist, leader of revolutionary armies, known as **the Liberator**. He fought the Spanish colonial forces in several uprisings and eventually liberated Colombia in 1819, his native Venezuela in 1821, Ecuador in 1822, Peru in 1824, and Bolivia (a new state named after him, formerly Upper Peru) in 1825.

Born in Venezuela, he joined that country's revolution against Spain in 1810, and in the following year he declared Venezuela independent. His army was soon defeated by the Spanish, however, and he was forced to flee. Many battles and defeats followed, and it was not until 1819 that Bolívar won his first major victory, defeating the Spanish in Colombia and winning independence for that country. He went on to liberate Venezuela in 1821 and (along with Antonio ▷Sucre) Ecuador in 1822. These three countries were united into the republic of Gran Colombia with Bolívar as its president. In 1824 Bolívar helped bring about the defeat of Spanish forces in Peru, and the area known as Upper Peru was renamed 'Bolivia' in Bolívar's honour. Within the next few years, Venezuela and Ecuador seceded from the union, and in 1830 Bolívar resigned as president. He died the same year, despised by many for his dictatorial ways but since revered as South America's greatest liberator.

Bolivia see country box.

Böll, Heinrich (Theodor) (1917–1985) German novelist. A radical Catholic and anti-Nazi, he attacked Germany's political past and the materialism of its contemporary society. His many publications include poems, short stories, and novels which satirized West German society, for example *Billard um Halbzehn/Billiards at Half-Past Nine* (1959) and *Gruppenbild mit Dame/Group Portrait with Lady* (1971). He was awarded the Nobel Prize for Literature in 1972.

boll weevil small American beetle *Anthonomus grandis* of the weevil group. The female lays her eggs in the unripe pods or 'bolls' of the cotton plant, and on these the larvae feed, causing great destruction.

Bologna (Etruscan **Felsina**; Roman **Bononia**) industrial town and capital of Emilia-Romagna, Italy, at the foot of the Apennines, 80 km/50 mi north of Florence; population (1992) 401,300. It is a major rail hub. Industries include engineering, food-processing, and the manufacture of electrical components and chemicals. An important venue for specialist trade fairs (perfume, camping), it also hosts an annual international children's book fair.

Related Web site: Welcome to the City of Bologna http://www.comune.bologna.it/TouringBologna/

Bolshevik (from Russian *bolshinstvo* 'a majority') member of the majority of the Russian Social Democratic Party who split from the ▷Mensheviks in 1903. The Bolsheviks, under ▷Lenin, advocated the destruction of capitalist political and economic institutions, and the setting up of a socialist state with power in the hands of the workers. The Bolsheviks set the ▷Russian Revolution of 1917 in motion. They changed their name to the Russian Communist Party in 1918.

Bolt, Robert (Oxton) (1924–1995) English dramatist and screenwriter. He wrote historical plays, such as *A Man for All Seasons* (1960; filmed 1966); his screenplays include *Lawrence of Arabia* (1962), *Dr Zhivago* (1965) (both Academy Awards), *Ryan's Daughter* (1970), *Lady Caroline Lamb* (1972), which he also directed, *The Bounty* (1984), and *The Mission* (1986).

Bolton town and administrative headquarters of Bolton metropolitan borough, Greater Manchester, northwest England, on the River Croal, 18 km/11 mi northwest of Manchester; population (2001 est) 138,600. Industries include engineering and the manufacture of chemicals, paper, and textiles. Bolton developed rapidly in the 18th century as a cotton-spinning town. Samuel Crompton, inventor of the spinning mule in 1779, was born nearby.

Boltzmann constant in physics, the constant (symbol k) that relates the kinetic energy (energy of motion) of a gas atom or molecule to temperature. Its value is 1.38066×10^{-23} joules per kelvin. It is equal to the gas constant R, divided by ▷Avogadro's number.

bomb container filled with explosive or chemical material and generally used in warfare. There are also ▷incendiary bombs and nuclear bombs and missiles (see ▷nuclear warfare). Any object designed to cause damage by explosion can be called a bomb (car bombs, letter bombs). Initially dropped from aeroplanes (from World War I), bombs were in World War II also launched by rocket (▷V1, V2). The 1960s saw the development of missiles that could be launched from aircraft, land sites, or submarines. In the 1970s laser guidance systems were developed to hit small targets with accuracy.
Related Web site: Bomb Squad http://www.pbs.org/wgbh/nova/robots/

bombardier beetle beetle that emits an evil-smelling fluid from its abdomen, as a defence mechanism. This fluid rapidly evaporates into a gas, which appears like a minute jet of smoke when in contact with air, and blinds the predator about to attack.
Classification Bombardier beetles in genus *Brachinus*, family Carabidae, order Coleoptera, class Insecta, phylum Arthropoda.

bombast inflated or high-sounding language. Pistol, from Shakespeare's play *Henry V*, is characterized by his use of bombastic language: 'Let gallows gape for dog; let man go free,/And let not hemp his windpipe suffocate.' can be expressed simply as 'Hang dogs but not men'.

Bombay former name (until 1995) of ▷Mumbai, capital of Maharashtra state in west central India. The city's name was officially changed in July 1995, and was renamed Mumbai after the goddess Mumba, the name in the local Marathi language for Parvati, the wife of the Hindu god Shiva.

Bombay former province of British India; the capital was the city of Bombay (now Mumbai). In 1960 the major part became the two new states of ▷Gujarat and ▷Maharashtra.

Bombay duck (or **bummalow**) small fish *Harpodon nehereus* found in the Indian Ocean. It has a thin body, up to 40 cm/16 in long, and sharp, pointed teeth. It feeds on shellfish and other small fish. It is valuable as a food fish, and is eaten, salted and dried, with dishes such as curry.

Bomberg, David (Garshen) (1890–1957) English painter and founder member of the London Group. He applied forms inspired by cubism and Vorticism to figurative subjects, treating them as patterns of brightly coloured interlocking planes in such early works as *The Mud Bath* (1914; Tate Gallery, London). After

---

Bolivia

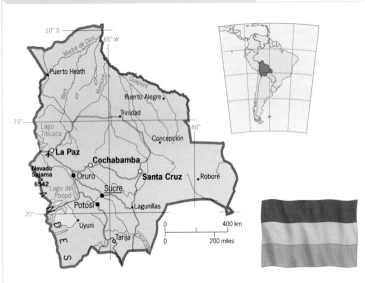

Bolivia landlocked country in central Andes mountains in South America, bounded north and east by Brazil, southeast by Paraguay, south by Argentina, and west by Chile and Peru.

NATIONAL NAME *República de Bolivia/Republic of Bolivia*
AREA 1,098,581 sq km/424,162 sq mi
CAPITAL La Paz (seat of government), Sucre (legal capital and seat of the judiciary)
MAJOR TOWNS/CITIES Santa Cruz, Cochabamba, Oruro, El Alto, Potosí, Tarija
PHYSICAL FEATURES high plateau (Altiplano) between mountain ridges (cordilleras); forest and lowlands (llano) in east; Andes; lakes Titicaca (the world's highest navigable lake, 3,800 m/12,500 ft) and Poopó

Government

HEAD OF STATE AND GOVERNMENT Carlos Mesa Gisbert from 2003
POLITICAL SYSTEM liberal democracy
POLITICAL EXECUTIVE limited presidency
ADMINISTRATIVE DIVISIONS nine departments
ARMED FORCES 31,500 (2002 est)
CONSCRIPTION selective conscription for 12 months at the age of 18
DEATH PENALTY abolished for ordinary crimes in 1997; laws provide for the death penalty for exceptional crimes, such as crimes committed in wartime
DEFENCE SPEND (% GDP) 1.6 (2002 est)
EDUCATION SPEND (% GDP) 5.5 (2001 est)
HEALTH SPEND (% GDP) 6.7 (2000 est)

Economy and resources

CURRENCY boliviano
GPD (US$) 7.7 billion (2002 est)
REAL GDP GROWTH (% change on previous year) 1.2 (2001)
GNI (US$) 7.9 billion (2002 est)

GNI PER CAPITA (PPP) (US$) 2,300 (2002 est)
CONSUMER PRICE INFLATION 2.6% (2003 est)
UNEMPLOYMENT 7.6% (2000)
FOREIGN DEBT (US$) 4.7 billion (2001 est)
MAJOR TRADING PARTNERS USA, Brazil, Argentina, Peru, Colombia, Chile, UK, Ecuador, Sweden, Uruguay
RESOURCES petroleum, natural gas, tin (world's fifth-largest producer), zinc, silver, gold, lead, antimony, tungsten, copper
INDUSTRIES mining, food products, petroleum refining, tobacco, textiles
EXPORTS metallic minerals, natural gas, jewellery, soybeans, wood. Principal market: USA 24.2% (2000). Illegal trade in coca and its derivatives (mainly cocaine) constituted more than 50% of Bolivia's export earnings in 1997 according to the UN.

BOLIVIA A llama at a waterhole. *Image Bank*

IMPORTS industrial materials, machinery and transport equipment, consumer goods. Principal source: USA 21.8% (2000)
ARABLE LAND 1.8% (2000 est)
AGRICULTURAL PRODUCTS coffee, coca, soybeans, sugar cane, rice, chestnuts, maize, potatoes; livestock products (beef and hides); forest resources

Population and society

POPULATION 8,808,000 (2003 est)
POPULATION GROWTH RATE 1.8% (2000–15)
POPULATION DENSITY (per sq km) 8 (2003 est)
URBAN POPULATION (% of total) 64 (2003 est)
AGE DISTRIBUTION (% of total population) 0–14 39%, 15–59 55%, 60+ 6% (2002 est)
ETHNIC GROUPS 30% Quechua Indians, 25% Aymara Indians, 25–30% mixed, 5–15% of European descent
LANGUAGE Spanish (official) (4%), Aymara, Quechua
RELIGION Roman Catholic 90% (state-recognized)
EDUCATION (compulsory years) 8
LITERACY RATE 92% (men); 79% (women) (2003 est)
LABOUR FORCE 2.1% agriculture, 28.8% industry, 69% services (1996)
LIFE EXPECTANCY 62 (men); 66 (women) (2000–05)
CHILD MORTALITY RATE (under 5, per 1,000 live births) 77 (2001)
PHYSICIANS (per 1,000 people) 1.3 (1998 est)
HOSPITAL BEDS (per 1,000 people) 1.7 (1998 est)
TV SETS (per 1,000 people) 121 (2001 est)
RADIOS (per 1,000 people) 676 (1998)
INTERNET USERS (per 10,000 people) 323.7 (2002 est)
PERSONAL COMPUTER USERS (per 100 people) 2.3 (2002 est)

See also ▷Bolívar, Simón; ▷Inca.

Chronology

c. AD 600: Development of sophisticated civilization at Tiahuanaco, south of Lake Titicaca.

c. 1200: Tiahuanaco culture was succeeded by smaller Aymara-speaking kingdoms.

16th century: Became incorporated within westerly Quechua-speaking Inca civilization, centred in Peru.

1538: Conquered by Spanish and, known as 'Upper Peru', became part of the Viceroyalty of Peru, whose capital was at Lima (Peru); Charcas (now Sucre) became the local capital.

1545: Silver was discovered at Potosí in the southwest, which developed into chief silver-mining town and most important city in South America in the 17th and 18th centuries.

1776: Transferred to the Viceroyalty of La Plata, with its capital in Buenos Aires.

late 18th century: Increasing resistance of American Indians and mestizos to Spanish rule; silver production slumped.

1825: Liberated from Spanish rule by the Venezuelan freedom fighter Simón Bolívar, after whom the country was named, and his general, Antonio José de Sucre; Sucre became Bolivia's first president.

1836–39: Bolivia became part of a federation with Peru, headed by Bolivian president Andres Santa Cruz, but it dissolved following defeat in war with Chile.

1879–84: Coastal territory in the Atacama, containing valuable minerals, was lost after defeat in war with Chile.

1903: Territory was lost to Brazil.

1932–35: Further territory was lost after defeat by Paraguay in the Chaco War, fought over control of the Chaco Boreal.

1952: After the military regime was overthrown in the Bolivian National Revolution, Dr Victor Paz Estenssoro of the centrist National Revolutionary Movement (MNR) became president and introduced social reforms.

1964: An army coup was led by Vice-President Gen René Barrientos.

1967: There was a peasant uprising, led by Ernesto 'Che' Guevara. The uprising was put down with US help, and Guevara was killed.

1969: Barrientos was killed in a plane crash, and replaced by Siles Salinas, who was soon deposed in an army coup.

1971: Col Hugo Banzer Suárez came to power after a military coup.

1974: An attempted coup prompted Banzer to postpone promised elections and ban political and trade-union activity.

1980: Inconclusive elections were followed by the country's 189th coup. Allegations of corruption and drug trafficking led to the cancellation of US and European Community (EC) aid.

1982: With the economy worsening, the military junta handed power over to a civilian administration headed by Siles Zuazo.

1983: US and EC economic aid resumed as austerity measures were introduced.

1985: The inflation rate was 23,000%.

1993: Foreign investment was encouraged as inflation fell to single figures.

1997: Hugo Banzer was elected president.

2000: The government lost support due to widespread poverty and the stagnation of the economy. There were violent clashes between security forces and protestors, who called for the resignation of President Banzer.

World War I he turned to landscape painting. Moving away from semi-abstraction in the mid-1920s, his work became more representational. He gained recognition only towards the end of his life.

bona fide (Latin 'in good faith') legal phrase used to signify that a contract is undertaken without intentional misrepresentation.

Bonaparte Corsican family of Italian origin that gave rise to the Napoleonic dynasty: see ▷Napoleon I, ▷Napoleon II, and ▷Napoleon III. Others were the brothers and sister of Napoleon I:

Joseph (1768–1844) whom Napoleon made king of Naples in 1806 and of Spain in 1808;

Lucien (1775–1840) whose handling of the Council of Five Hundred on 10 November 1799 ensured Napoleon's future;

Louis (1778–1846) the father of Napoleon III, who was made king of Holland 1806–10; also called (from 1810) comte de Saint Leu;

Caroline (1782–1839) who married Joachim ▷Murat in 1800; full name Maria Annunciata Caroline;

Jerome (1784–1860) made king of Westphalia in 1807.

Bonar Law British Conservative politician; see ▷Law, Andrew Bonar.

Bonaventura, St (1221–1274) Born Giovanni di Fidanza. Italian Roman Catholic theologian. He entered the Franciscan order in 1243, became professor of theology in Paris, and in 1256 general of his order. In 1273 he was created cardinal and bishop of Albano. He was canonized in 1482. His feast day is 15 July.

bond in chemistry, the result of the forces of attraction that hold together atoms of an element or elements to form a molecule. The principal types of bonding are ▷ionic, ▷covalent, ▷metallic, and ▷intermolecular (such as hydrogen bonding).

The type of bond formed depends on the elements concerned and their electronic structure. In an ionic or electrovalent bond, common in inorganic compounds, the combining atoms gain or lose electrons to become ions; for example, sodium (Na) loses an electron to form a sodium ion (Na^+) while chlorine (Cl) gains an electron to form a chloride ion (Cl^-) in the ionic bond of sodium chloride (NaCl).

In a covalent bond, the atomic orbitals of two atoms overlap to form a molecular orbital containing two electrons, which are thus effectively shared between the two atoms. Covalent bonds are common in organic compounds, such as the four carbon–hydrogen bonds in methane (CH_4). In a dative covalent or coordinate bond, one of the combining atoms supplies both of the valence electrons in the bond.

A metallic bond joins metals in a crystal lattice, the atoms occupy lattice positions as positive ions, and valence electrons are shared between all the ions in an 'electron gas'.

In a hydrogen bond, a hydrogen atom joined to an electronegative atom, such as nitrogen or oxygen, becomes partially positively charged, and is weakly attracted to another electronegative atom on a neighbouring molecule.

bond in commerce, a security issued by a government, local authority, company, bank, or other institution on fixed interest. Usually a long-term security, a bond may be irredeemable (with no date of redemption), secured (giving the investor a claim on the company's property or on a part of its assets), or unsecured (not protected by a lien). Property bonds are nonfixed securities with the yield fixed to property investment. See also ▷Eurobond.

Bond, Edward (1934–) English dramatist. His early work aroused controversy because of the savagery of some of his imagery, for example, the brutal stoning of a baby by bored youths in *Saved* (1965). Other works include *Early Morning* (1968); *Lear* (1972), a reworking of Shakespeare's play; *Bingo* (1973), an account of Shakespeare's last days; *The War Plays* (1985); and *Jackets 2/Sugawara* and *In the Company of Men* (both 1990).

For television he wrote *Olly's Prison* (1991) and *Tuesday* (1993). *Early Morning* was the last play to be banned in the UK by the Lord Chamberlain.

> **Edward Bond**
> *We have only one thing to keep us sane, pity; and the man without pity is mad.*
> Lear

bone hard connective tissue comprising the ▷skeleton of most vertebrate animals. Bone is composed of a network of collagen fibres impregnated with mineral salts (largely calcium phosphate and calcium carbonate), a combination that gives it great density and strength, comparable in some cases with that of reinforced concrete. Enclosed within this solid matrix are bone cells, blood vessels, and nerves. The interior of the long bones of the limbs consists of a spongy matrix filled with a soft marrow that produces blood cells.

There are two types of bone: those that develop by replacing ▷cartilage and those that form directly from connective tissue.

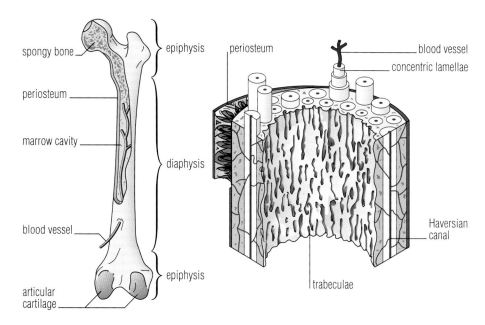

BONE The upper end of the thighbone, or femur, is made up of spongy bone, which has a fine lacework structure designed to transmit the weight of the body. The shaft of the femur consists of hard compact bone designed to resist bending. Fine channels carrying blood vessels, nerves, and lymphatics interweave even the densest bone.

The latter, which includes the bones of the cranium, are usually platelike in shape and form in the skin of the developing embryo. Humans have 206 distinct bones in the skeleton (see ▷human body), of which the smallest are the three ossicles in the middle ear. However, a different total is sometimes given, because of a number of fused pairs of bones in the skull that may be counted as one or two bones.

bone china (or **softpaste**) semiporcelain made of 5% bone ash added to 95% kaolin. It was first made in the West in imitation of Chinese porcelain, whose formula was kept secret by the Chinese.

bone marrow substance found inside the cavity of bones. In early life it produces red blood cells but later on lipids (fat) accumulate and its colour changes from red to yellow.

bongo Central African antelope *Boocercus eurycerus*, living in dense humid forests. Up to 1.4 m/4.5 ft at the shoulder, it has spiral horns which may be 80 cm/2.6 ft or more in length. The body is rich chestnut, with narrow white stripes running vertically down the sides, and a black belly.

Boniface name of nine popes, including:

Boniface VIII (*c.* 1235–1303) Born Benedict Caetani. Pope from 1294. He clashed unsuccessfully with Philip IV of France over his taxation of the clergy, and also with Henry III of England.

Boniface, St (680–754) English Benedictine monk, known as the 'Apostle of Germany'; originally named Wynfrith. After a missionary journey to Frisia in 716, he was given the task of bringing Christianity to Germany in 718 by Pope Gregory II, and was appointed archbishop of Mainz in 746. He returned to Frisia in 754 and was martyred near Dockum. His feast day is 5 June.

Bonin and Volcano islands Japanese islands in the Pacific, north of the Marianas and 1,300 km/800 mi east of the Ryukyu Islands. They were under US control from 1945 to 1968. The **Bonin Islands** (Japanese *Ogasawara Gunto*) number 27 (in three groups), the largest being Chichijima: area 104 sq km/40 sq mi, population (1991) 2,430. The **Volcano Islands** (Japanese *Kazan Retto*) number three, including Iwo Jima, scene of some of the fiercest fighting of World War II; total area 28 sq km/ 11 sq mi. They have no civilian population, but a 200-strong maritime self-defence force and a 100-strong air self-defence force are stationed there.

Bonington, Chris(tian John Storey) (1934–) English mountaineer. He took part in the first ascent of Annapurna II in 1960, Nuptse in 1961, and the first British ascent of the north face of the Eiger in 1962, climbed the central Tower of Paine in Patagonia in 1963, and was the leader of an Everest expedition in 1975 and again in 1985, reaching the summit.

bonito any of various species of medium-sized tuna, predatory fish of the genus *Sarda*, in the mackerel family. The ocean bonito *Katsuwonus pelamis* grows to 1 m/3 ft and is common in tropical seas. The Atlantic bonito *Sarda sarda* is found in the Mediterranean and tropical Atlantic and grows to the same length but has a narrower body.

bon mot (French 'good word') witty remark.

Bonn industrial city in North Rhine-Westphalia, Germany, 18 km/15 mi southeast of Cologne, on the left bank of the Rhine; population (1995) 291,700. Industries include the manufacture of chemicals, textiles, plastics, and aluminium. Bonn was the seat of government of West Germany 1949–90 and of the Federal Republic of Germany from 1990. In 1991 the Bundestag voted to move the capital to Berlin. This has taken place in phases, with the major phase in 1998.

Bonnard, Pierre (1867–1947) French painter, designer, and graphic artist. Influenced by Gauguin and Japanese prints, he specialized in intimate domestic scenes and landscapes, his paintings shimmering with colour and light. With other members of *les Nabis*, he explored the decorative arts (posters, stained glass, furniture), but is most widely known for his series of nudes, for example, *Nude in the Bath* (1938; Petit Palais, Paris).

BONNIE AND CLYDE Clyde Barrow and Bonnie Parker, US criminals who became infamous for a series of robberies in the 1930s. See entry overleaf. *Archive Photos*

Bonney, William H US outlaw known by the name of ▷Billy the Kid.

Bonnie and Clyde Bonnie Parker (1911–1934) and Clyde Barrow (1909–1934). Infamous US criminals who carried out a series of small-scale robberies in Texas, Oklahoma, New Mexico, and Missouri between August 1932 and May 1934. They were eventually betrayed and then killed in a police ambush.

Much of their fame emanated from encounters with the police and their coverage by the press. Their story was filmed as *Bonnie and Clyde* (1967) by the US director Arthur Penn. See picture on p. 117.

Bonnie Prince Charlie Scottish name for ▷Charles Edward Stuart, pretender to the throne.

Bonny, Bight of alternative name for the Bight of ▷Biafra.

bonsai (Japanese 'bowl cultivation') art of producing miniature trees by selective pruning. It originated in China many centuries ago and later spread to Japan.

Bonus Army (or **Bonus Expeditionary Force**) in US history, a march on Washington, DC, by unemployed ex-servicemen during the great ▷Depression to lobby Congress for immediate cash payment of a promised war veterans' bonus.

bony fish fish of the class Osteichthyes, the largest and most important class of fish. The head covering and the scales are based on bone. Bony fish have a swimbladder, which may be modified into lungs and the gills are covered by a flap, the operculum.

boobook owl *Ninox novaeseelandiae* found in Australia, so named because of its call.

booby tropical seabird of the genus *Sula*, in the same family, Sulidae, as the northern ▷gannet, order Pelicaniformes. There are six species, including the circumtropical brown booby *S. leucogaster*. Plumage is white and black or brown, with no feathers on the throat and lower jaw. They inhabit coastal waters, and dive to catch fish. The name was given by sailors who saw the bird's tameness as stupidity.

One species, **Abbott's booby**, breeds only on Christmas Island, in the western Indian Ocean. Unlike most boobies and gannets, it nests high up in trees. Large parts of its breeding ground have been destroyed by phosphate mining, but conservation measures now protect the site.

BOOBY An Abbott's booby. Like the closely related gannet, boobies plunge into the sea to catch fish and squid.

boogie-woogie jazz played on the piano, using a repeated motif for the left hand. It was common in the USA from around 1900 to the 1950s.

Boogie-woogie players included Pinetop Smith, Meade 'Lux' Lewis, and Jimmy Yancey. Rock-and-roll pianist Jerry Lee Lewis adapted the style.

bookbinding securing of the pages of a book between protective covers by sewing and/or gluing. Cloth binding was first introduced in 1822, but from the mid-20th century synthetic bindings were increasingly employed, and most hardback books are bound by machine.

Booker Prize for Fiction British literary prize of £50,000 awarded annually (from 1969) to a Commonwealth writer by the Man group (formerly Booker and Booker McConnell) for a novel written in English by a citizen of the Commonwealth or Republic of Ireland, and published in the UK during the previous year.

book-keeping process of recording commercial transactions in a systematic and established procedure. These records provide the basis for the preparation of accounts.

booklouse any of numerous species of tiny wingless insects of the order Psocoptera, especially *Atropus pulsatoria*, which lives in books and papers, feeding on starches and moulds.

Book of the Dead ancient Egyptian book of magic spells, known as the *Book of Coming Forth by Day*, buried with the dead as a guide to reaching the kingdom of ▷Osiris, the god of the underworld.

BOOK OF THE DEAD Two pictures from the Heruben papyrus of the *Book of the Dead*, a script that was found in most Egyptian burials. *The Art Archive/Egyptian Museum Cairo/Dagli Orti*

Boole, George (1815–1864) English mathematician. His work *The Mathematical Analysis of Logic* (1847) established the basis of modern mathematical logic, and his **Boolean algebra** can be used in designing computers.

Boole's system is essentially two-valued. By subdividing objects into separate classes, each with a given property, his algebra makes it possible to treat different classes according to the presence or absence of the same property. Hence it involves just two numbers, 0 and 1 – the binary system used in the computer.

Related Web site: Boole, George http://www-history.mcs.st-and.ac.uk/history/Mathematicians/Boole.html

boomerang hand-thrown, flat wooden hunting missile shaped in a curved angle, formerly used throughout the world but developed by the Australian Aborigines to a great degree of diversity and elaboration. It is used to kill game and as a weapon or, in the case of the returning boomerang, for recreation.

boomslang rear-fanged venomous African snake *Dispholidus typus*, often green but sometimes brown or blackish, and growing to a length of 2 m/6 ft. It lives in trees, and feeds on tree-dwelling lizards such as chameleons. Its venom can be fatal to humans; however, boomslangs rarely attack people.

Boone, Daniel (1734–1820) US pioneer. He cleared a forest path called the Wilderness Road (East Virginia–Kentucky) in 1775 and for the first westward migration of settlers.

Related Web site: Daniel Boone: Myth and Reality http://xroads.virginia.edu/~HYPER/HNS/Boone/smithhome.html

boot (or **bootstrap**) in computing, the process of starting up a computer. Most computers have a small, built-in boot program that starts automatically when the computer is switched on – its only task is to load a slightly larger program, usually from a hard disk, which in turn loads the main ▷operating system.

Boötes constellation of the northern hemisphere represented by a herdsman driving a bear (▷Ursa Major) around the pole. Its brightest star is ▷Arcturus (or Alpha Boötis), which is 36 light years from Earth. The herdsman is assisted by the neighbouring ▷Canes Venatici, 'the Hunting Dogs'.

Booth, John Wilkes (1838–1865) US actor and Confederate sympathizer who assassinated President Abraham ▷Lincoln 14 April 1865.

Booth, William (1829–1912) English founder of the ▷Salvation Army (1878), and its first 'general'.

Boothe, Clare US journalist, playwright, and politician; see Clare Boothe ▷Luce.

BOOKLOUSE Some of the booklice inhabiting tropical rainforests graze openly on the surface cuticle of leaves, rather than lurking in dark nooks and crannies. *Premaphotos Wildlife*

bootlegging illegal manufacture, distribution, or sale of a product. The term originated in the USA, when the sale of alcohol to American Indians was illegal and bottles were hidden for sale in the legs of the jackboots of unscrupulous traders. The term was later used for all illegal liquor sales during the period of ▷Prohibition in the USA 1919–33. More recently it has been applied to unauthorized commercial tape recordings and the copying of computer software.

Bophuthatswana, Republic of former ▷Black National State within South Africa, independent from 1977 (although not recognized by the United Nations) until 1994 when it was re-integrated into South Africa (in North West Province, Free State (formerly Orange Free State), and Mpumalanga (formerly Eastern Transvaal)) after rioting broke out in the run-up to the first multiracial elections.

borage plant native to southern Europe, used in salads and in medicine. It has small blue flowers and hairy leaves. (*Borago officinalis*, family Boraginaceae.)

Related Web site: Borage http://www.botanical.com/botanical/mgmh/b/borage66.html

BORAGE Borage is an annual plant, growing between 90 cm/3 ft and 120 cm/4 ft high.

borax hydrous sodium borate, $Na_2B_4O_7.10H_2O$, found as soft, whitish crystals or encrustations on the shores of hot springs and in the dry beds of salt lakes in arid regions, where it occurs with other borates, halite, and gypsum. It is used in bleaches and washing powders.

Bordeaux administrative centre of the *département* of Gironde and of the ▷Aquitaine region, southwest France, situated on the River Garonne, 100 km/62 mi from the Atlantic; population (1990) 213,300, conurbation 685,000. Bordeaux is accessible to seagoing ships and is a major port; it is a centre for the wine trade, oil refining, chemicals, and the aircraft and aeronautics industries. Other industries include shipbuilding, sugar refining, and the manufacture of electrical goods, motor vehicles, and processed foods. Bordeaux was under the English crown for three centuries until 1453. In 1870, 1914, and 1940 the French government was moved here because of German invasions.

Border, Allan Robert (1955–) Australian cricketer, left-handed batsman, and captain of Australia 1985–94. He retired from international cricket in 1994 as holder of world records for most test runs (11,174), most test matches as captain (93), most appearances in test matches (156), most consecutive appearances in test matches (153), most catches in test matches by an outfielder (156), and most appearances in one-day internationals (263). Border played for Queensland after starting his career with New South Wales and has played in England for Gloucestershire and Essex.

Related Web site: Border, Allan http://www.q-net.net.au/~gihan/border/index.html

border terrier small, hardy, short-tailed dog with an otterlike head, moderately broad skull and short, strong muzzle. Its small, V-shaped ears drop forward. The coat is hard and dense with a close undercoat and is red, beige, and tan, or blue and tan. Dogs weigh 6–7 kg/13–15.5 lb; bitches 5–6.5 kg/ 11–14.5 lb.

Bordet, Jules Jean Baptiste Vincent (1870–1961) Belgian bacteriologist and immunologist who was awarded a Nobel Prize for Physiology or Medicine in 1919 for his work on immunity. He researched the role of blood serum in the human immune response, and was the first to isolate the whooping-cough bacillus, in 1906.

bore surge of tidal water up an estuary or a river, caused by the funnelling of the rising tide by a narrowing river mouth. A very high tide, possibly fanned by wind, may build up when it is held back by a river current in the river mouth. The result is a broken wave, a metre or a few feet high, that rushes upstream.

Borelli, Giovanni Alfonso (1608–1679) Italian scientist who explored the links between physics and medicine and showed how mechanical principles could be applied to animal ▷physiology. This approach, known as iatrophysics, has proved basic to understanding how the mammalian body works.

Borg, Björn Rune (1956–) Swedish tennis player. He won the men's singles title at Wimbledon five times 1976–80, a record since the abolition of the challenge system in 1922. He also won six French Open singles titles 1974–75 and 1978–81 inclusive.

Related Web site: Borg, Björn http://www.springhill7.freeserve.co.uk/borg.htm

Borges, Jorge Luis (1899–1986) Argentine poet and short-story writer. He was an exponent of ▷magic realism. In 1961 he became director of the National Library, Buenos Aires, and was professor of English literature at the university there. He is known for his fantastic and paradoxical work *Ficciones/Fictions* (1944). He became blind in later life, but continued to write.

Borges explored metaphysical themes in early works such as *Ficciones* and *El Aleph/The Aleph, and other Stories* (1949). In a later collection of tales *El informe de Brodie/Dr Brodie's Report* (1972) he adopted a more realistic style, reminiscent of the work of the young Rudyard ▷Kipling, of whom he was a great admirer. *El libro de arena/The Book of Sand* (1975) marked a return to more fantastic themes.

> **Jorge Luis Borges**
> *Writing is nothing more than a guided dream.*
> *Dr Brodie's Report*

Borgia, Cesare (*c.* 1475–1507) Italian general, illegitimate son of Pope ▷Alexander VI. Made a cardinal at 17 by his father, he resigned to become captain-general of the papacy, campaigning successfully against the city republics of Italy. Ruthless and treacherous in war, he was an able ruler (a model for Machiavelli's *The Prince*), but his power crumbled on the death of his father. He was a patron of artists, including Leonardo da Vinci.

CESARE BORGIA A portrait of the Italian general Cesare Borgia by Italian painter Altobello Meloni. *The Art Archive/Accademia Carrara Bergamo Italy/Dagli Orti*

Borgia, Lucrezia (1480–1519) Duchess of Ferrara from 1501. She was the illegitimate daughter of Pope ▷Alexander VI and sister of Cesare ▷Borgia. She was married at 12 and again at 13 to further her father's ambitions, both marriages being annulled by him. At 18 she was married again, but her husband was murdered in 1500 on the order of her brother, with whom (as well as with her father) she was said to have committed incest. Her final marriage was to the Alfonso d'Este, the heir to the duchy of Ferrara. She made the court a centre of culture and was a patron of authors and artists such as Ariosto and Titian.

boric acid (or **boracic acid**) $B(OH)_3$ acid formed by the combination of hydrogen and oxygen with nonmetallic boron. It is a weak antiseptic and is used in the manufacture of glass and enamels. It is also an efficient insecticide against ants and cockroaches.

Boris III (1894–1943) Tsar of Bulgaria from 1918, when he succeeded his father, Ferdinand I. From 1934 he was a virtual dictator until his sudden and mysterious death following a visit to Hitler. His son Simeon II was tsar until deposed in 1946.

Boris Godunov tsar of Russia from 1598; see Boris ▷Godunov.

Bormann, Martin (1900–1945) German Nazi leader. He took part in the abortive Munich beer-hall putsch (uprising) in 1923 and rose to high positions in the Nazi Party, becoming deputy party leader in May 1941 following the flight of Rudolf Hess to Britain.

Born, Max (1882–1970) German-born British physicist. He was awarded the Nobel Prize for Physics in 1954 for fundamental work on the ▷quantum theory, especially his 1926 discovery that the wave function of an electron is linked to the probability that the electron is to be found at any point.

In 1924 Born coined the term 'quantum mechanics'. He made Göttingen a leading centre for theoretical physics and together with his students and collaborators – notably Werner ▷Heisenberg – he devised in 1925 a system called matrix mechanics that accounted mathematically for the position and momentum of the electron in the atom. He also devised a technique, called the Born approximation method, for computing the behaviour of subatomic particles, which is of great use in high-energy physics.

Related Web site: Born, Max http://www-history.mcs.st-and.ac.uk/history/Mathematicians/Born.html

Borneo third-largest island in the world, one of the Sunda Islands in the West Pacific; area 754,000 sq km/290,000 sq mi; population 15,969,500. It comprises the Malaysian territories of ▷Sabah and ▷Sarawak; ▷Brunei; and, occupying by far the largest part, the Indonesian territory of ▷Kalimantan. It is mountainous and densely forested.

In coastal areas the people of Borneo are mainly of Malaysian origin, with a few Chinese, and the interior is inhabited by the indigenous Dyaks. It was formerly under both Dutch and British colonial influence until Sarawak was formed in 1841.

Bornu kingdom of the 9th–19th centuries to the west and south of Lake Chad, western central Africa. Converted to Islam in the 11th century, Bornu reached its greatest strength in the 15th–18th centuries. From 1901 it was absorbed in the British, French, and German colonies in this area, which became the states of Niger, Cameroon, and Nigeria. The largest section of ancient Bornu is now the **state of Bornu** in Nigeria.

Borodin, Aleksandr Porfirevich (1833–1887) Russian composer. Born in St Petersburg, the illegitimate son of a Russian prince, he became by profession an expert in medical chemistry, but in his spare time devoted himself to writing music. His principal work is the opera *Prince Igor*, left unfinished; it was completed by Nikolai Rimsky-Korsakov and Aleksandr Glazunov and includes the Polovtsian Dances. His other works include symphonies, songs, and chamber music, using traditional Russian themes.

> **Aleksandr Borodin**
> *Music is a pastime, a relaxation from more serious occupations.*
> In a letter to Krylov 1867

Borodino, Battle of French victory over Russian forces under Kutusov on 7 September 1812 near the village of Borodino, 110km/70 mi northwest of Moscow, during Napoleon Bonaparte's invasion of Russia. This was one of the bloodiest battles of the Napoleonic years: the Russians lost 15,000 dead and 25,000 wounded; the French lost about 28,000, including 12 generals.

boron nonmetallic element, symbol B, atomic number 5, relative atomic mass 10.811. In nature it is found only in compounds, as with sodium and oxygen in borax. It exists in two allotropic forms (see ▷allotropy): brown amorphous powder and very hard, brilliant crystals. Its compounds are used in the preparation of boric acid, water softeners, soaps, enamels, glass, and pottery glazes. In alloys it is used to harden steel. Because it absorbs slow neutrons, it is used to make boron carbide control rods for nuclear reactors. It is a necessary trace element in the human diet.

Boross, Peter (1928–) Hungarian politician, prime minister 1993–94. Brought into Joszef ▷Antall's government as a nonpolitical technocrat, he became deputy chair of the ruling Hungarian Democratic Forum in 1991 and acting prime minister during Antall's recurring bouts of illness. When Antall died in December 1993, Boross succeeded him, but lost office to Gyula Horn, of the ex-communist Hungarian Socialist Party, in the July 1994 elections.

borough (Old English burg, 'a walled or fortified place') urban-based unit of local government in the UK and USA. It existed in the UK from the 8th century until 1974, when it continued as an honorary status granted by royal charter to a district council, entitling its leader to the title of mayor. In England in 1998 there were 32 London borough councils and 36 metropolitan borough councils. The name is sometimes encountered in the USA: New York City has five administrative boroughs, Alaska has local government boroughs, and in other states some smaller towns use the name.

Borromini, Francesco, originally Francesco Castelli (1599–1667) Swiss-born Italian baroque architect. He was one of the two most important architects (with Bernini, his main rival) in 17th-century Rome. Whereas Bernini designed in a florid, expansive style, his pupil Borromini developed a highly idiosyncratic and austere use of the classical language of architecture. His genius may be seen in the cathedrals of San Carlo alle Quattro Fontane (1637–41), Sant' Ivo della Sapienza (1643–60), and the Oratory of San Filippo Neri (1638–50).

borrowing (or **loan word**) word derived from another language. English has borrowed thousands of words from other languages over the centuries. Some are used without adaptation, but others have been changed slightly to fit in with the patterns of English.

For example, *banana* is from Spanish or Portuguese, *marmalade* is from Portuguese, *thug* is from Hindi, and *slim* is from Dutch. *Telephone* is formed from two Greek roots, *tele* meaning 'far off' and *phone* meaning 'sound'; *debt* is from the Latin word *debitum*; *awkward* has its origins in the Old Norse word *öfugr* meaning 'turned the wrong way round.'

borstal in the UK, formerly a place of detention for offenders aged 15–21, first introduced in 1908. From 1983 borstal institutions were officially known as youth custody centres, and have been replaced by **young offender institutions**.

borzoi (Russian 'swift') breed of large dog originating in Russia. It is of the greyhound type, white with darker markings, with a thick, silky coat, and stands 75 cm/30 in or more at the shoulder.

Bosch, Hieronymus (*c.* 1460–1516) Born Jeroen van Aken. Early Dutch painter. His fantastic visions, often filled with bizarre and cruel images, depict a sinful world in which people are tormented by demons and weird creatures, as in *Hell*, a panel from the triptych *The Garden of Earthly Delights* (*c.* 1505–10; Prado, Madrid). In their richness, complexity, and sheer strangeness, his pictures foreshadow surrealism.

Bosnia-Herzegovina see country box.

Bosnian Crisis period of international tension in 1908 when Austria attempted to capitalize on Turkish weakness after the ▷Young Turk revolt by annexing the provinces of Bosnia and Herzegovina. Austria obtained Russian approval in exchange for conceding Russian access to the Bosporus straits.

boson in physics, an elementary particle whose spin can only take values that are whole numbers or zero. Bosons may be classified as ▷gauge bosons (carriers of the four fundamental forces) or ▷mesons. All elementary particles are either bosons or ▷fermions.

Unlike fermions, more than one boson in a system (such as an atom) can possess the same energy state. When developed mathematically, this statement is known as the Bose–Einstein law, after its discoverers Indian physicist Satyendra Bose and Albert Einstein.

Bosporus (Turkish **Karadeniz Boğazi**) strait 27 km/17 mi long, joining the Black Sea with the Sea of Marmara and forming part of the water division between Europe and Asia; its name may be derived from the Greek legend of Io. Istanbul stands on its west side. The **Bosporus Bridge** (1973), 1,621 m/5,320 ft, links Istanbul and Anatolia (the Asian part of Turkey). In 1988 a second bridge across the straits was opened, linking Asia and Europe.

bossa nova Brazilian dance rhythm of the 1950s, combining samba and cool jazz. It became internationally popular in songs like 'The Girl From Ipanema' (1964).

Boston port and market town in Lincolnshire, eastern England, on the River Witham, 50 km/31 mi southeast of Lincoln; population (1991) 34,600. Industries include food-processing and shell-fishing, and the manufacture of labels and tags. Trade is conducted particularly with Scandinavia and the Baltic countries, agricultural products forming the bulk of the traffic.

Boston industrial port and commercial centre, capital of Massachusetts, USA, on Massachusetts Bay; population (1998 est) 555,400; metropolitan area (1992) 5,439,000. Its economy is dominated by financial and health services and government. It is also a publishing and academic centre. The subway system, begun in 1897, was the first in the USA. Boston's baseball team, the Red Sox, is based at Fenway Park. Boston was founded by Puritans in 1630 and has played an important role in American history.

Related Web site: Boston Online http://www.boston-online.com/

Boston Tea Party protest in 1773 by colonists in Massachusetts, USA, against the tea tax imposed on them by the British government before the ▷American Revolution.

When a valuable consignment of tea (belonging to the East India Company and intended for sale in the American colonies) arrived in Boston Harbor, it was thrown overboard by a group of Bostonians disguised as American Indians during the night of 16 December 1773. The British government, angered by this and other colonial protests against British policy, took retaliatory measures in 1774, including the closing of the port of Boston.

The consignment, brought on three ships from England, was valued at £15,000.

Boswell, James (1740–1795) Scottish biographer and diarist. He was a member of Samuel ▷Johnson's Literary Club and the two men travelled to Scotland together in 1773, as recorded in Boswell's *Journal of a Tour to the Hebrides* (1785). His *Life of Samuel Johnson* was published in 1791. Boswell's ability to record Johnson's pithy conversation verbatim makes this a classic of English biography.

Boswell was born in Edinburgh. He qualified as a lawyer in 1766 but centred his ambitions on literature and politics. He first met Johnson in 1763, and following a European tour, established a place in his intimate circle, becoming a member of the Literary Club in 1773.

On his succession to his father's estate in 1782, Boswell made further attempts to enter Parliament, qualified to practise as a barrister in England in 1786, and was recorder of Carlisle from 1788–90. In 1789 he settled in London.

Bosnia-Herzegovina

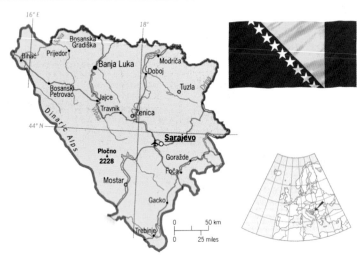

Bosnia-Herzegovina country in central Europe, bounded north and west by Croatia, east and south by Serbia and Montenegro.

NATIONAL NAME *Bosna i Hercegovina/Bosnia-Herzegovina*
AREA 51,129 sq km/19,740 sq mi
CAPITAL Sarajevo
MAJOR TOWNS/CITIES Banja Luka, Mostar, Prijedor, Tuzla, Zenica, Bihac, Gorazde
PHYSICAL FEATURES barren, mountainous country, part of the Dinaric Alps; limestone gorges; 20 km/12 mi of coastline with no harbour

Government

HEAD OF STATE Borislav Paravac, Sulejman Tihic, and Dragan Covic from 2003
HEAD OF GOVERNMENT Adnan Terzic from 2003
POLITICAL SYSTEM emergent democracy
POLITICAL EXECUTIVE limited presidency
ADMINISTRATIVE DIVISIONS ten cantons
ARMED FORCES 19,800 (2002 est)
DEATH PENALTY abolished for ordinary crimes in 1997; laws provide for the death penalty for exceptional crimes, such as crimes committed in wartime

Economy and resources

CURRENCY dinar
GPD (US$) 5.2 billion (2002 est)
REAL GDP GROWTH (% change on previous year) 5.6 (2001)
GNI (US$) 5.2 billion (2002 est)
GNI PER CAPITA (PPP) (US$) 5,800 (2002 est)
CONSUMER PRICE INFLATION 0.5% (2003 est)
UNEMPLOYMENT 40.1% (2000)
FOREIGN DEBT (US$) 2 billion (2001)
MAJOR TRADING PARTNERS Croatia, Serbia and Montenegro, Italy, Slovenia, Germany, Hungary, Switzerland
RESOURCES copper, lead, zinc, iron ore, coal, bauxite, manganese
INDUSTRIES iron and crude steel, armaments, cement, textiles, vehicle assembly, wood products, oil refining, electrical appliances, cigarettes; industrial infrastructure virtually destroyed by war
EXPORTS coal, base metals, domestic appliances (industrial production and mining remain low). Principal market: Italy 27% (2000)
IMPORTS foodstuffs, basic manufactured goods, processed and semiprocessed goods. Principal source: Croatia 24.5% (2000)
ARABLE LAND 9.8% (2000 est)
AGRICULTURAL PRODUCTS maize, wheat, potatoes, vegetables, rice, tobacco, fruit, olives, grapes; livestock rearing (sheep and cattle); timber reserves

Population and society

POPULATION 4,161,000 (2003 est)
POPULATION GROWTH RATE 0.6% (2000–15)

POPULATION DENSITY (per sq km) 81 (2003 est)
URBAN POPULATION (% of total) 44 (2003 est)
AGE DISTRIBUTION (% of total population) 0–14 18%, 15–59 67%, 60+ 15% (2002 est)
ETHNIC GROUPS 40% ethnic Muslim, 38% Serb, 22% Croat. Croats are most thickly settled in southwest Bosnia and western Herzegovina, Serbs in eastern and western Bosnia. Since the start of the civil war in 1992 many Croats and Muslims have fled as refugees to neighbouring states
LANGUAGE Serbian, Croat, Bosnian
RELIGION 40% Muslim, 31% Serbian Orthodox, 15% Roman Catholic
EDUCATION (compulsory years) 8

LITERACY RATE 94% (men); 93% (women) (2001 est)
LABOUR FORCE 11.3% agriculture, 47.5% industry, 41.2% services (1990)
LIFE EXPECTANCY 71 (men); 77 (women) (2000–05)
CHILD MORTALITY RATE (under 5, per 1,000 live births) 18 (2001)
PHYSICIANS (per 1,000 people) 1.4 (1998 est)
HOSPITAL BEDS (per 1,000 people) 1.8 (1998 est)
TV SETS (per 1,000 people) 112 (1999)
RADIOS (per 1,000 people) 245 (1999)
INTERNET USERS (per 10,000 people) 243.9 (2002 est)

See also ▷Habsburg; ▷Ottoman Empire; ▷Serbia and Montenegro.

See also ▷Habsburg; ▷Ottoman Empire; ▷Serbia and Montenegro.

Chronology

1st century AD: Part of Roman province of Illyricum.

395: On division of Roman Empire, stayed in west, along with Croatia and Slovenia, while Serbia to the east became part of the Byzantine Empire.

7th century: Settled by Slav tribes.

12–15th centuries: Independent state.

1463 and 1482: Bosnia and Herzegovina, in south, successively conquered by Ottoman Turks; many Slavs were converted to Sunni Islam.

1878: Became an Austrian protectorate, following Bosnian revolt against Turkish rule in 1875–76.

1908: Annexed by Austrian Habsburgs in wake of Turkish Revolution.

1914: Archduke Franz Ferdinand, the Habsburg heir, was assassinated in Sarajevo by a Bosnian-Serb extremist, precipitating World War I.

1918: On the collapse of the Habsburg Empire, the region became part of the Serb-dominated 'Kingdom of Serbs, Croats, and Slovenes', known as Yugoslavia from 1929.

1941: The region was occupied by Nazi Germany and became 'Greater Croatia' fascist puppet state and the scene of fierce fighting.

1943–44: Bosnia was liberated by communist Partisans, led by Marshal Tito.

1945: The region became a republic within the Yugoslav Socialist Federation.

1980: There was an upsurge in Islamic nationalism.

1990: Ethnic violence erupted between Muslims and Serbs. Communists were defeated in multiparty elections; a coalition was formed by Serb, Muslim, and Croatian parties.

1991: The Serb–Croat civil war in Croatia spread unrest into Bosnia. Fears that Serbia planned to annex Serb-dominated parts of the republic led to a declaration of sovereignty by parliament. Serbs within Bosnia established autonomous enclaves.

1992: Bosnia was admitted into the United Nations (UN). Violent civil war broke out, as an independent 'Serbian Republic of Bosnia-Herzegovina', comprising parts of the east and the west, was proclaimed by Bosnian-Serb militia leader Radovan Karadzic, with Serbian backing. UN forces were drafted into Sarajevo to break the Serb siege of the city; Bosnian Serbs were accused of 'ethnic cleansing', particularly of Muslims.

1993: A UN–EC peace plan failed. The USA began airdrops of food and medical supplies. Six UN

'safe areas' were created, intended as havens for Muslim civilians. A Croat–Serb partition plan was rejected by Muslims.

1994: The Serb siege of Sarajevo was lifted after a UN–NATO ultimatum and Russian diplomatic intervention. A Croat–Muslim federation was formed.

1995: Hostilities resumed. A US-sponsored peace accord, providing for two sovereign states (a Muslim–Croat federation and a Bosnian Serb Republic, the Republika Srpska) as well as a central legislature (House of Representatives, House of Peoples, and three-person presidency), was agreed at Dayton, Ohio. A 60,000-strong NATO peacekeeping force was deployed.

1996: An International Criminal Tribunal for Former Yugoslavia began in the Hague and an arms-control accord was signed. Full diplomatic relations were established with Yugoslavia. The collective presidency was elected, consisting of Alija Izetbegovic (Muslim), Momcilo Krajisnik (Serb), and Kresimir Zubak (Croat); Izetbegovic was elected overall president. Biljana Plavsic was elected president of the Serb Republic and Gojko Klickovic its prime minister. Edhem Bicakcic became prime minister of the Muslim–Croat Federation.

1997: Vladimir Soljic was elected president of the Muslim–Croat Federation. The Serb part of Bosnia signed a customs agreement with Yugoslavia.

1998: A moderate, pro-western government was formed in the Bosnian Serb republic, headed by Milorad Dodik; Nikola Poplasen became president. The first Muslims and Croats were convicted in The Hague for war crimes during 1992. Zivko Radisic and Ante Jelavic replaced Krajisnik and Zubak respectively on the rotating presidency.

2000: In January, Ejup Ganic became president of the Muslim–Croat federation. Mirko Sarovic became president of the Bosnian Serb republic. Izbetgovic was replaced by Halid Genjac as the Muslim member of the rotating presidency. The northeastern town of Brcko, the only territorial dispute outstanding from the Dayton peace accord, was established as a self-governing neutral district in March, to be ruled by an elected alliance. The year saw three changes of prime minister, with Martin Raguz elected in October.

2001: Biljana Plavsic gave herself up to the war crimes tribunal, but pleaded 'not guilty' to nine counts of war crimes.

BOSNIA-HERZEGOVINA The medieval fortress of Bobovac is shown on this Bosnian stamp. *Stanley Gibbons*

Bosworth, Battle of battle fought on 22 August 1485, during the English Wars of the Roses (see ▷Roses, Wars of the). Richard III, the Yorkist king, was defeated and killed by Henry Tudor, who became Henry VII. The battlefield is near the village of Market Bosworth, 19 km/12 mi west of Leicester, England.

Henry Tudor inherited the Lancastrian claim and invaded England through Wales, landing at Milford Haven on 7 August. Richard had 11,000–12,000 men and a strong position on Ambion Hill. Henry had 5,000–7,000 troops, but Lord Stanley and his brother commanded 5,000 and 3,000 men to the north and south of the royalists, respectively. Accounts of the battle are unclear, but it is possible that the Lancastrian Earl of Oxford was able to swing around the right flank of the royal army. This enabled a better concentration of force, left Northumberland unengaged on the royalist left, and brought Henry closer to Lord Stanley. After some fierce fighting, Richard saw Henry's banner moving northwards. Richard charged with his cavalry and almost cut his way through to Henry before he was killed as the Stanley troops joined the fray.

Related Web site: Battle of Bosworth http://www.r3.org/bosworth/index.html

BOT abbreviation for **Board of Trade**.

botanical garden place where a wide range of plants is grown, providing the opportunity to see a botanical diversity not likely to be encountered naturally. Among the earliest forms of botanical garden was the **physic garden**, devoted to the study and growth of medicinal plants; an example is the Chelsea Physic Garden in London, established in 1673 and still in existence. Following increased botanical exploration, botanical gardens were used to test the commercial potential of new plants being sent back from all parts of the world.

botany (Greek *botane* 'herb') the study of living and fossil ▷plants, including form, function, interaction with the environment, and classification.

Botany is subdivided into a number of specialized studies, such as the identification and classification of plants (taxonomy), their external formation (plant morphology), their internal arrangement (plant anatomy), their microscopic examination (plant histology), their functioning and life history (plant physiology), and their distribution over the Earth's surface in relation to their surroundings (plant ecology). Palaeobotany concerns the study of fossil plants, while economic botany deals with the utility of plants. ▷Horticulture, ▷agriculture, and ▷forestry are branches of botany.

Related Web site: GardenWeb Glossary of Botanical Terms http://www.gardenweb.com/glossary/

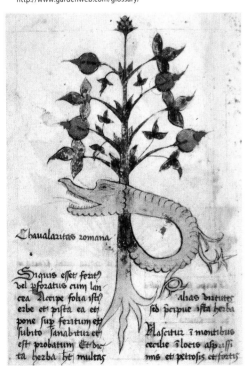

BOTANY A herbal from Trento, Italy, from the 14th century, showing the *Chavalaritas Roma* plant, which was used for sutures and to stop haemorrhages. Herbals were ancient manuals to aid in the identification of plants for medicinal purposes; many manuscript herbals were published in medieval Europe, drawing largely on the herbals compiled by the ancient Greeks. *Art Archive*

Botany Bay inlet on the east coast of New South Wales, Australia, 8 km/5 mi south of Sydney. It is the outlet of the River Georges. The English explorer Captain James ▷Cook landed here in 1770. In 1787 the bay was chosen as the site for a British penal colony, but proved unsuitable, and the colony was located at Port Jackson.

botfly any fly of the family Oestridae. The larvae are parasites that feed on the skin (warblefly of cattle) or in the nasal cavity (nostrilflies of sheep and deer). The horse botfly belongs to another family, the Gasterophilidae. It has a parasitic larva that feeds in the horse's stomach.

Botha, Louis (1862–1919) South African soldier and politician. He was a commander in the Second South African War (Boer War). In 1907 he became premier of the Transvaal and in 1910 of the first Union South African government. On the outbreak of World War I in 1914 he rallied South Africa to the Commonwealth, suppressed a Boer revolt, and conquered German South West Africa.

Botha was born in Natal. Elected a member of the Volksraad (parliament) in 1897, he supported the more moderate Piet Joubert (1834–1900) against Paul Kruger (1825–1904). On the outbreak of the Second South African War he commanded the Boers besieging Ladysmith, and in 1900 succeeded Joubert in command Of the Transvaal forces. When the Union of South Africa was formed in 1910, Botha became prime minister, and at the Versailles peace conference in 1919 he represented South Africa.

Botha, P(ieter) W(illem) (1916–) South African politician, prime minister 1978–89. He initiated a modification of ▷apartheid, which later slowed down in the face of ▷Afrikaner (Boer) opposition, and made use of force both inside and outside South Africa to stifle ▷African National Congress (ANC) party activity. In 1984 he became the first executive state president. After suffering a stroke in 1989, he unwillingly resigned both party leadership and presidency and was succeeded by F W ▷de Klerk.

Botham, Ian Terence (1955–) English cricketer. One of the world's greatest all-rounders, in 102 Tests for England between 1977 and 1992 he became the first player in Test cricket to score over 5,000 runs as well as take over 300 wickets. He played county cricket for Somerset, Worcestershire, and Durham, and briefly represented Queensland in the Sheffield Shield.

Bothwell, James Hepburn, 4th Earl of Bothwell (c. 1536–1578) Scottish nobleman. The third husband of ▷Mary Queen of Scots, 1567–70, he was alleged to have arranged the explosion that killed Darnley, her previous husband, in 1567. He succeeded as Earl in 1556 and became Duke in 1567.

Tried and acquitted a few weeks after the assassination, he abducted Mary and married her on 15 May 1567. A revolt ensued, and Bothwell was forced to flee. In 1570 Mary obtained a divorce, and Bothwell was confined in a castle in the Netherlands where he died insane.

bo tree (or peepul) Indian ▷fig tree, said to be the tree under which the Buddha became enlightened. (*Ficus religiosa*, family Moraceae.)

Botswana see country box.

Botticelli, Sandro (1445–1510) Born Alessandro Filipepi. Florentine painter. He depicted religious and mythological subjects. He was patronized by the ruling ▷Medici family and was deeply influenced by their Neo-Platonic circle. It was for the Medicis that he painted *Primavera* (1478) and *The Birth of Venus* (c. 1482–84). From the

SANDRO BOTTICELLI *The Adoration of the Magi* (c. 1476) by Italian artist Sandro Botticelli, depicting the arrival of the three kings at Christ's birthplace. *The Art Archive/San Angelo in Formis Capua Italy/Dagli Orti*

1490s he was influenced by the religious fanatic ▷Savonarola, and developed a harshly expressive and emotional style, as seen in his *Mystic Nativity* (1500).

His work for the Medicis was designed to cater to the educated classical tastes of the day. As well as his sentimental and beautiful young Madonnas, he produced a series of inventive compositions, including *tondi* (circular paintings) and illustrations for Dante's ▷*Divine Comedy*. He broke with the Medicis after their execution of Savonarola.

bottlebrush any of several trees or shrubs common in Australia, belonging to the myrtle family. They have cylindrical, composite flower heads in green, yellow, white, various shades of red, and violet. (Genus *Callistemon*, family Myrtaceae.)

BOTTLEBRUSH The bottlebrush *Callistemon macro-ponctatus* is speckled yellow by its elongated stamens. *K G Preston-Mafham/Premaphotos Wildlife*

botulism rare, often fatal type of ▷food poisoning. Symptoms include vomiting, diarrhoea, muscular paralysis, breathing difficulties and disturbed vision.

It is caused by a toxin produced by the bacterium *Clostridium botulinum*, found in soil and sometimes in improperly canned foods.

Boucher, François (1703–1770) French rococo painter. He was court painter to Louis XV from 1765, and was popular for his light-hearted, decorative scenes which often convey a playful eroticism, as in *Diana Bathing* (1742; Louvre, Paris).

Boudicca (died AD 61) Queen of the Iceni (native Britons), often referred to by the Latin form of her name, **Boadicea**.

Her husband, King Prasutagus, had been a tributary of the Romans, but on his death in AD 60 the territory of the Iceni was violently annexed. Boudicca was scourged and her daughters raped. Boudicca raised the whole of southeastern England in revolt, and before the main Roman armies could return from campaigning in Wales she burned Londinium (London), Verulamium (St Albans), and Camulodunum (Colchester). Later the Romans under governor Suetonius Paulinus defeated the British between London and Chester; they were virtually annihilated and Boudicca poisoned herself.

> **Boudicca**
> *I am not fighting for my kingdom and wealth now. I am fighting as an ordinary person for my lost freedom, my bruised body, and my outraged daughters.*
> Address to her army before the Icenian revolt in AD 61, quoted by Tacitus

Related Web site: Boudicca, Queen of the Iceni http://www.athenapub.com/boudicca.htm

Boudin, (Louis) Eugène (1824–1898) French artist. A forerunner of the Impressionists, he is known for his luminous seaside scenes painted in the open air, such as *Beach at Trouville* (1873; National Gallery, London).

Bougainville autonomous island, formerly of Papua New Guinea, which with Buka Island and other smaller islands forms the province of North Solomon; area 10,620 sq km/4,100 sq mi; population (1994) 160,000. It is the largest of the Solomon Islands archipelago. The capital is Arawa. The land is volcanic and mountainous, with the Emperor Range in the north and Crown Prince Range in the south; the highest peak is the active volcano Mount Balbi, 3,110 m/10,205 ft. The chief industries are copper, gold, and silver; copra, ivory nuts, and tortoiseshell are exported.

Bougainville, Louis Antoine de (1729–1811) French navigator. After service with the French in Canada during the Seven Years' War, he made the first French circumnavigation of the world in 1766–69 and the first systematic observations of longitude.

bougainvillea any plant of a group of South American tropical vines of the four o'clock family, now cultivated in warm countries around the world for the colourful red and purple bracts (leaflike structures) that cover the flowers. They are named after the French navigator Louis de ▷Bougainville. (Genus *Bougainvillea*, family Nyctaginaceae.)

Bouguer anomaly an anomaly in the local gravitational force that is due to the density of rocks rather than local topography, elevation, or latitude. A positive anomaly, for instance, is generally indicative of denser and therefore more massive rocks at or below the surface. A negative anomaly indicates less massive materials. Calculations of bouguer anomalies are used for mineral prospecting and for understanding the structure beneath the Earth's surface. The Bouguer anomaly is named after its discoverer, the French mathematician Pierre Bouguer, who first observed it in 1735.

Boulanger, Nadia Juliette (1887–1979) French music teacher and conductor. She studied under Gabriel Fauré at the Paris Conservatory, where she later taught, as well as at the École Normale de Musique and the American Conservatory at Fontainebleau. Many distinguished composers were her pupils, including her sister, Lili Boulanger, Lennox Berkeley, Aaron Copland, Jean Françaix, Roy Harris, Walter Piston, and Philip Glass.

boulder clay another name for ▷till, a type of glacial deposit.

Boulez, Pierre (1925–   ) French composer and conductor. He is the founder and director of IRCAM, a music research studio in Paris opened in 1977. His music, strictly adhering to ideas of serialism and and expressionistic in style, includes the cantatas *Le Visage Nuptial* (1946–52) and *Le Marteau sans maître* (1953–55), both to texts by René Char; *Pli selon pli* (1962) for soprano and orchestra; and *Répons* (1981) for soloists, orchestra, tapes, and computer-generated sounds.

Boullée, Etienne-Louis (1728–1799) French neoclassical architect. Although he built very little, he was a major influence on the architecture of his day, and his austere, visionary works have influenced late 20th-century architects such as the Italian Aldo Rossi. Boullée's abstract, geometric style is exemplified in his design for a spherical monument to the scientist Isaac Newton, 150 m/ 500 ft high.

Boulogne-sur-Mer port on the English Channel in the *département* of Pas-de-Calais, northern France, situated at the mouth of the River Liane; population (1990) 44,200, conurbation 95,000. The city is a ferry port (connecting with the English ports of Dover and Folkestone) and seaside resort. Industries include oil refining, food processing, boatbuilding and the manufacture of

textiles, It is the chief fishing port of France and carries an important import/export trade. Boulogne was a medieval countship, but was united with the French crown by Louis XI in 1477.

Boulting John Edward (1913–1985) and Roy (1913–2001). English director–producer team that was successful in the years after World War II. Their films include *Brighton Rock* (1947), *Lucky Jim* (1957), and *I'm All Right Jack* (1959). They were twins.

Boumédienne, Houari (1925–1978) Adopted name of Muhammad Boukharouba. Algerian politician who brought the nationalist leader Mohammed ▷Ben Bella to power by a revolt in 1962 and superseded him as president in 1965 by a further coup. During his 13 years in office, he presided over an ambitious programme of economic development and promoted Algeria as an active champion of the Third World cause. In late 1978 he died of a rare blood disease.

Boundary Peak mountain in Esmeralda County, southwest Nevada; height 4,006 m/13,143 ft. It is located 105 km/65 mi north-northwest of Tonopah, in the Toiyabe National Forest. The northernmost peak of the White Mountains, it is the highest point in Nevada and lies immediately northeast of the California– Nevada border.

Botswana

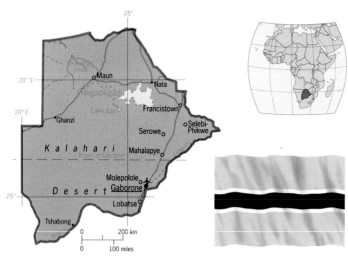

BOTSWANA Short-nosed, with long, splayed hooves and long tails, red lechwe are found in northern Botswana, particularly in the swampland of the Okavango delta. *Photodisk*

See also ▷Kung; ▷Tswana.

Botswana formerly Bechuanaland (until 1966) landlocked country in central southern Africa, bounded south and southeast by South Africa, west and north by Namibia, and northeast by Zimbabwe.

NATIONAL NAME *Republic of Botswana*
AREA 582,000 sq km/224,710 sq mi
CAPITAL Gaborone
MAJOR TOWNS/CITIES Mahalapye, Serowe, Francistown, Selebi-Phikwe, Molepoloe, Kange, Maun
PHYSICAL FEATURES Kalahari Desert in southwest (70–80% of national territory is desert), plains (Makgadikgadi salt pans) in east, fertile lands and Okavango Delta in north

Government

HEAD OF STATE AND GOVERNMENT Festus Mogae from 1998
POLITICAL SYSTEM liberal democracy
POLITICAL EXECUTIVE limited presidency
ADMINISTRATIVE DIVISIONS nine district councils and four town councils
ARMED FORCES 9,000 (2002 est)
DEATH PENALTY retained and used for ordinary crimes

Economy and resources

CURRENCY pula
GPD (US$) 5.2 billion (2002 est)
REAL GDP GROWTH (% change on previous year) 1.5 (2001)
GNI (US$) 5.1 billion (2002 est)
GNI PER CAPITA (PPP) (US$) 7,770 (2002 est)
CONSUMER PRICE INFLATION 4.7% (2003 est)

UNEMPLOYMENT 19% (2000)
FOREIGN DEBT (US$) 481 million (2001 est)
MAJOR TRADING PARTNERS Lesotho, Namibia, South Africa, Swaziland – all fellow SACU (Southern African Customs Union) members; UK and other European countries, USA
RESOURCES diamonds (world's third-largest producer), copper-nickel ore, coal, soda ash, gold, cobalt, salt, plutonium, asbestos, chromite, iron, silver, manganese, talc, uranium
INDUSTRIES mining, food processing, textiles and clothing, beverages, soap, chemicals, paper, plastics, electrical goods
EXPORTS diamonds, copper and nickel, beef. Principal market: UK 70% (2000)
IMPORTS machinery and transport equipment, food, beverages, tobacco, chemicals and rubber products, textiles and footwear, fuels, wood and paper products. Principal source: SACU 77.4% (2000)
ARABLE LAND 0.7% (2000 est)
AGRICULTURAL PRODUCTS sorghum, vegetables, pulses; cattle raising (principally for beef production) is main agricultural activity

Population and society

POPULATION 1,785,000 (2003 est)
POPULATION GROWTH RATE 0.6% (2000–15)

POPULATION DENSITY (per sq km) 3 (2003 est)
URBAN POPULATION (% of total) 50 (2003 est)
AGE DISTRIBUTION (% of total population) 0–14 42%, 15–59 53%, 60+ 5% (2002 est)
ETHNIC GROUPS about 95% Tswana (Butswana) and 4% Kalanga, Basarwa, and Kgalagadi; 1% European
LANGUAGE English (official), Setswana (national)
RELIGION Christian 50%, animist 50%
EDUCATION not compulsory
LITERACY RATE 77% (men); 82% (women) (2003 est)
LABOUR FORCE 15.6% agriculture, 25.6% industry, 58.7% services (1996)
LIFE EXPECTANCY 39 (men); 41 (women) (2000–05)
CHILD MORTALITY RATE (under 5, per 1,000 live births) 110 (2001)
PHYSICIANS (per 1,000 people) 0.2 (1995 est)
HOSPITAL BEDS (per 1,000 people) 1.6 (1994 est)
TV SETS (per 1,000 people) 30 (2001 est)
RADIOS (per 1,000 people) 156 (1997)
INTERNET USERS (per 10,000 people) 297.5 (2002 est)
PERSONAL COMPUTER USERS (per 100 people) 4.1 (2002 est)

Chronology

18th century: Formerly inhabited by nomadic hunter-gatherer groups, including the Kung, the area was settled by the Tswana people, from whose eight branches the majority of the people are descended.

1872: Khama III the Great, a converted Christian, became chief of the Bamangwato, the largest Tswana group. He developed a strong army and greater unity among the Botswana peoples.

1885: Became the British protectorate of Bechuanaland at the request of Chief Khama, who feared invasion by Boers from the Transvaal (South Africa) following the discovery of gold.

1895: The southern part of the Bechuanaland Protectorate was annexed by Cape Colony (South Africa).

1960: A new constitution created a legislative council controlled (until 1963) by a British High Commissioner.

1965: The capital was transferred from Mafeking to Gaborone. Internal self-government was achieved.

1966: Independence was achieved from Britain. Name changed to Botswana.

mid-1970s: The economy grew rapidly as diamond mining expanded.

1985: South African raid on Gaborone, allegedly in search of African National Congress (ANC) guerrillas.

1993: Relations with South Africa were fully normalized following the end of apartheid and the establishment of a multiracial government.

1997: Major constitutional changes reduced the voting age to 18.

1998: Festus Mogae (BDP) became president.

Bourbon, Charles 8th Duke of Bourbon (1490–1527) Constable of France, honoured for his courage at the Battle of Marignano in 1515. Later he served the Holy Roman Emperor Charles V, and helped to drive the French from Italy. In 1526 he was made duke of Milan, and in 1527 he marched on Rome but was killed in the assault (by a shot the artist Benvenuto ▷Cellini claimed to have fired). His troops proceeded to sack the city.

Bourbon, duchy of originally a seigneury (feudal domain) created in the 10th century in the county of Bourges, central France, held by the Bourbon family. It became a duchy in 1327.

Bourbon dynasty French royal house (succeeding that of ▷Valois), beginning with Henry IV and ending with Louis XVI, with a brief revival under Louis XVIII, Charles X, and Louis Philippe. The Bourbons also ruled Spain almost uninterruptedly from Philip V to Alfonso XIII and were restored in 1975 (▷Juan Carlos); at one point they also ruled Naples and several Italian duchies. The Grand Duke of Luxembourg is also a Bourbon by male descent.

Bourdon gauge instrument for measuring pressure, patented by French watchmaker Eugène Bourdon in 1849. The gauge contains a C-shaped tube, closed at one end. When the pressure inside the tube increases, the tube uncurls slightly causing a small movement at its closed end. A system of levers and gears magnifies this movement and turns a pointer, which indicates the pressure on a circular scale. Bourdon gauges are often fitted to cylinders of compressed gas used in industry and hospitals.

BOURDON GAUGE The dial of a Bourdon gauge. The gauge may be used to measure the pressure of all types of liquids and gases, up to pressures of 70,000 newtons per sq cm/100,000 pounds-force per sq in. *Image Bank*

Bourgeois, Léon Victor Auguste (1851–1925) French politician. Entering politics as a Radical, he was prime minister in 1895, and later served in many cabinets. He was awarded the Nobel Prize for Peace in 1920 for his pioneering advocacy of the League of Nations and international cooperation.

bourgeoisie (French 'the freemen of a borough') the social class above the workers and peasants, and below the nobility; the middle class. 'Bourgeoisie' (and **bourgeois**) has also acquired a contemptuous sense, implying commonplace, philistine respectability. By socialists it is applied to the whole propertied class, as distinct from the proletariat.

Bourgogne French name of ▷Burgundy, a region of eastern France.

Bourguiba, Habib ben Ali (1903–2000) Tunisian politician, first president of Tunisia 1957–87. He became prime minister in 1956 and president (for life from 1975) and prime minister of the Tunisian republic in 1957; he was overthrown in a bloodless coup in 1987.

Bournemouth seaside resort and unitary authority in southern England. The town lies on Poole Bay, 40 km/25 mi southwest of Southampton, and was part of the county of Dorset until 1997.
   area 46 sq km/18 sq mi   **features** a 10 km/6 mi stretch of sands, as well as parks, winter gardens, and two piers, one of which is 305 m/1,000 ft long. The Bourne stream, bordered by gardens, runs through the town centre. The Russell-Cotes Museum and Art Gallery houses a collection of Japanese art and 17th–20th century paintings. The Pavilion, opened in 1929, includes a theatre. The Bournemouth International Centre (BIC) has sports, entertainment, and conference facilities. Bournemouth University was founded in 1992 (formerly Bournemouth Polytechnic). Bournemouth Airport is at Hurn to the north of the town.   **industries** tourism, the provision of insurance, banking, and financial services, and the manufacture of communications systems (Siemens); an International Conference Centre is situated here   **population** (2000 est) 161,300   **famous people** Charles Parry, Mary Shelley, Percy Bysshe Shelley, Robert Louis Stevenson
   Related Web site: It's Better in Bournemouth http://www.bournemouth.gov.uk/

Bournonville, August (1805–1879) Danish dancer and choreographer. In 1830 he was appointed director of the Royal Danish Ballet, the company for which he both danced and created his ballets. His works, unlike that of the then prevalent Romantic era, are ebullient, warmly good-humoured, and give equal importance to both male and female dancers. His style is marked by swift, fluid footwork accompanied by patterns of arcing leaps. His works, of which only a dozen survive, include a version of *La Sylphide* (1836) and *Napoli* (1842).

Boutros-Ghali, Boutros (1922–) Egyptian diplomat and politician, deputy prime minister 1991–92, secretary general of the United Nations (UN) 1992–96. He worked towards peace in the Middle East in the foreign ministry posts he held from 1977 to 1991. After taking office at the UN he encountered a succession of challenges regarding the organization's role in conflict areas such as Bosnia-Herzegovina, Somalia, Haiti, and Rwanda, with which he dealt with varying degrees of success. In June 1996 the US government signified its intention to veto his re-election for a second term, and in December 1996 he was replaced by Kofi Annan.

Bouts, Dirk (or Dierick) (c. 1420–1475) Dutch painter. Born in Haarlem, he settled in Louvain, painting portraits and religious scenes influenced by Rogier van der Weyden, Albert van Ouwater, and Petrus Christus. *The Last Supper* (1464–68; St Pierre, Louvain) is one of his finest works.

Bouvines, Battle of decisive victory for Philip II (Philip Augustus) of France on 27 July 1214, near the village of Bouvines in Flanders, over the Holy Roman Emperor Otto IV and his allies, including King John of England. The battle, one of the most decisive in medieval Europe, so weakened Otto that it ensured the succession of Frederick II as Holy Roman Emperor and confirmed Philip as ruler of the whole of northern France and Flanders; it led to the renunciation of all English claims to the region.

bovine spongiform encephalopathy (BSE or mad cow disease) disease of cattle, related to ▷scrapie in sheep, which attacks the nervous system, causing aggression, lack of coordination, and collapse. First identified in 1985, by 1996 it had claimed 158,000 British cattle. After safety measures were put in place, British beef was declared safe (by the British government) in 1999. Following outbreaks of BSE in French, German, and Spanish cattle in late 2000, European Union (EU) agriculture ministers agreed to ban, as of 1 January 2001, the use of meat and bone meal from animal feed and to ban all cattle over 30 months old from the food chain unless tested for BSE.

BSE is one of a group of diseases known as the transmissible spongiform encephalopathies, since they are characterized by the appearance of spongy changes in brain tissue. Some scientists believe that all these conditions, including Creutzfeldt–Jakob disease (CJD) in humans, are in effect the same disease, and in 1996 a link was established between the deaths of 10 young people from CJD and the consumption of beef products.

The cause of these universally fatal diseases is not fully understood, but they may be the result of a rogue protein called a ▷prion. A prion may be inborn or it may be transmitted in contaminated tissue.

An official European Commission Report released in March 1997 suggested the extent of BSE throughout the EU was much wider than governments were prepared to admit. The first cases of BSE in Denmark, France, Germany, and Spain were reported in 2000. In January 2001, the United Nations Food and Agriculture Organization (FAO) warned developing nations to take action to prevent BSE becoming a worldwide problem, as potentially contaminated meat and bone-meal had been exported to the developing world after the BSE outbreak in Britain.
BSE in Britain The source of the disease has been traced to manufactured protein feed incorporating the rendered brains of scrapie-infected sheep. Following the British government's ban on the use of offal in feed in 1988, the epidemic continued, indicating that the disease could be transmitted from cows to their calves. It was not until 1996 that government scientists admitted that this was so.

In 1996, when links between BSE and CJD were demonstrated, export of British beef was prohibited and consumption of beef in Britain fell 15–20% compared with 1995. The price fell 14% in the same period. Support for the beef industry amounting to £1,370 million came from the British government and the EU. In 1997, it emerged that the British government had allowed more than 6,000 carcasses suspected of having BSE to be buried in landfill sites across Britain – in direct contravention of its own regulations. Because of fears that BSE could get into drinking water, or the food chain, both the British government and the EU have insisted the carcasses should be incinerated.

In November 1998, the British government announced a £120 million emergency aid package for Britain's farmers, partly to compensate for the effects of the BSE crisis. By the end of 1999, beef exports had been resumed to all European countries except France, who despite legal threats, refused to accept that British beef no longer posed a risk of human infection.

In October 2000, the results of the government's BSE inquiry, the Phillips report, were published.

Bow, Clara (1905–1965) US film actor. She was known as a 'Jazz Baby' and the 'It Girl' after her portrayal of a glamorous flapper in the silent film *It* (1927).

Bow Bells the bells of St Mary-le-Bow church, Cheapside, London; a person born within the sound of Bow Bells is traditionally considered a true Cockney. The bells also feature in the legend of Dick ▷Whittington.

Bowdler, Thomas (1754–1825) English editor. His expurgated versions of Shakespeare and other authors gave rise to the verb bowdlerize.

bower bird New Guinean and northern Australian bird of the family Ptilonorhynchidae, order Passeriformes, related to the ▷bird of paradise. The males are dull-coloured, and build elaborate bowers of sticks and grass, decorated with shells, feathers, or flowers, and even painted with the juice of berries, to attract the females. There are 17 species.

BOWER BIRD The regent bower bird *Sericulus chrysocephalus* is found in the rainforests of northeast Australia and New Guinea.

bowfin North American fish *Amia calva* with a swim bladder highly developed as an air sac, enabling it to breathe air. It is the only surviving member of a primitive group of bony fishes.

bowhead Arctic whale *Balaena mysticetus* with strongly curving upper jawbones supporting the plates of baleen with which it sifts planktonic crustaceans from the water. Averaging 15 m/50 ft long and 90 tonnes/100 tons in weight, these slow-moving, placid whales were once extremely common, but by the 17th century were already becoming scarce through hunting. In 2000 it was believed that only 700–1,000 bowhead whales remained in existence.

Bowie, David (1947–) Stage name of David Robert Jones. English pop singer, songwriter, and actor. His career has been a series of image changes. His hits include 'Jean Genie' (1973), 'Rebel, Rebel' (1974), 'Golden Years' (1975), and 'Underground' (1986). He has acted in plays and films, including Nicolas Roeg's *The Man Who Fell to Earth* (1976).

In October 1998, *Time Out* magazine named him the most influential pop star of the last 30 years.
   Related Web site: David Bowie: Teenage Wildlife http://www.etete.com/Bowie/

Bowles, Paul (1910–1999) US writer and composer. Born in New York City, he studied music composition with Aaron Copland and Virgil Thomson, writing scores for ballets, films, and an opera, *The Wind Remains* (1943), as well as incidental music for plays. He settled in Morocco, the setting of his novels *The Sheltering Sky* (1949, filmed 1990) and *Let It Come Down* (1952), which chillingly depict the existential breakdown of Westerners unable to survive self-exposure in an alien culture. Other works include *A Thousand Days for Mokhtar* (1989) and *Too Far from Home* (1994). His autobiography, *Without Stopping*, was published in 1972.

bowling indoor sport; see ▷tenpin bowling.

bowls outdoor and indoor game popular in Commonwealth countries. It has been played in Britain since the 13th century and was popularized by Francis Drake, who is reputed to have played bowls on Plymouth Hoe as the Spanish Armada approached in 1588.

Related Web site: Lawn Bowling http://www.tcn.net/~jdevons/test1.html

box any of several small evergreen trees and shrubs, with small, leathery leaves. Some species are used as hedging plants and for shaping into garden ornaments. (Genus *Buxus*, family Buxaceae.)

Related Web site: Box http://www.botanical.com/botanical/mgmh/b/box—67.html

Boxer member of the *I ho ch'üan* ('Righteous Harmonious Fists'), a society of Chinese nationalists dedicated to fighting Western influence in China. They were known as Boxers by Westerners as they practised boxing training which they believed made them impervious to bullets. In 1898 the Chinese government persuaded the Boxers to join forces to oppose foreigners. In 1900 the ▷Boxer Rebellion was instigated by the empress ▷Zi Xi and thousands of Chinese Christian converts and missionaries were murdered.

boxer breed of dog, about 60 cm/24 in tall, with a smooth coat and a set-back nose. The tail is usually docked. A boxer is usually brown, often with white markings, but may be fawn or brindled.

Boxer Rebellion (or Boxer Uprising) rebellion of 1900 by the Chinese nationalist ▷Boxer society against Western influence. European and US legations in Beijing (Peking) were besieged and many missionaries and Europeans were killed. An international punitive force was dispatched and Beijing was captured on 14 August 1900. In September 1901 China agreed to pay reperations.

boxfish (or **trunkfish**) any fish of the family Ostraciodontidae, with scales that are hexagonal bony plates fused to form a box covering the body, only the mouth and fins being free of the armour. Boxfishes swim slowly. The cowfish, genus *Lactophrys*, with two 'horns' above the eyes, is a member of this group.

boxing fighting with gloved fists, almost entirely a male sport. The sport dates from the 18th century, when fights were fought with bare knuckles and untimed rounds. Each round ended with a knockdown. Fighting with gloves became the accepted form in the latter part of the 19th century after the formulation of the Queensberry Rules in 1867.

Jack Broughton was one of the early champions and in 1743 drew up the first set of boxing rules. Fights continued until one boxer was unable to continue. Later, the London Prize Ring Rules (1838) gave fighters that had been knocked down 30 seconds to return to a mark scratched in the middle of the ring (the origin of the phrase 'coming up to scratch') or lose the bout.

The last bare-knuckle championship fight was between John L Sullivan and Jake Kilrain in 1899. Today all boxing follows the original Queensberry Rules, but with modifications. Contests take place in a roped ring 4.3–6.1 m/14–20 ft square. All rounds last three minutes. Amateur bouts last three rounds; professional championship bouts last as many as 12 or 15 rounds. Boxers are classified according to weight and may not fight in a division lighter than their own. The weight divisions in professional boxing range from **strawweight** (also known as paperweight and mini-flyweight), under 49 kg/108 lb, to **heavyweight**, over 88 kg/195 lb.

BOXING After being banned in 1997, US boxer Mike Tyson began an attempted comeback in January 2000. *Archive Photos*

The Amateur Boxing Association of England agreed 1996 to allow women to train and fight under its rules from October 1997. At the time of the ABA decision there were no recognized professional women boxers.

Related Web site: Boxing Monthly Online http://www.boxing-monthly.co.uk/

Boycott, Charles Cunningham (1832–1897) English ex-serviceman and land agent in County Mayo, Ireland, 1873–86. He strongly opposed the demands for agrarian reform by the Irish Land League, 1879–81, with the result that the peasants refused to work for him; hence the word **boycott**, meaning to isolate an individual, organization, or country, socially or commercially.

Boycott, Geoffrey (1940–) English cricketer. A prolific right-handed opening batsman for Yorkshire and England, he made 8,114 Test runs in 108 matches between 1964 and 1982 at an average of 47.72. He is one of only six players to have hit over 150 first-class centuries.

Related Web site: Boycott, Geoffrey http://www-uk3.cricket.org/link_to_database/PLAYERS/ENG/B/BOYCOTT_G_01001228/

Boyle's law law stating that the volume of a given mass of gas at a constant temperature is inversely proportional to its pressure. For example, if the pressure on a gas doubles, its volume will be reduced by a half, and vice versa. The law was discovered in 1662 by Irish physicist and chemist Robert Boyle. See also ▷gas laws.

Boyne river in the Republic of Ireland, rising in the Bog of Allen in County Kildare, and flowing 110 km/69 mi northeastwards through Trim, Navan, and Drogheda to the Irish Sea. An obelisk marks the site of the Battle of the ▷Boyne, fought at Oldbridge near the mouth of the river on 1 July 1690.

Boyne, Battle of the battle fought on 1 July 1690 in eastern Ireland, in which the exiled King James II was defeated by William III and fled to France. It was the decisive battle of the War of English Succession, confirming a Protestant monarch, and has become the most commemorated battle in modern Irish history. It took its name from the River Boyne which rises in County Kildare and flows 110 km/69 mi northeast to the Irish Sea.

Bozen German form of Bolzano, a town in Italy.

Brabant (Flemish **Braband**) former duchy of Western Europe, comprising the Dutch province of ▷North Brabant and the Belgian provinces of Brabant and Antwerp. They were divided when Belgium became independent in 1830. The present-day Belgian Brabant comprises two provinces: Flemish Brabant (area 2,106 sq km/813 sq mi; population (1997) 1,004,700) and Walloon Brabant (area 1,091 sq km/421 sq mi; population (1997) 341,600). Belgian Brabant is very densely populated, and rich both in agriculture and industry. The principal towns are Louvain in Flemish Brabant, Nivelles in Walloon Brabant, and the Belgian capital, Brussels.

brachiopod (or **lamp shell**) any member of the phylum Brachiopoda, marine invertebrates with two shells, resembling but totally unrelated to bivalves.

There are about 300 living species; they were much more numerous in past geological ages. They are suspension feeders, ingesting minute food particles from water. A single internal organ, the lophophore, handles feeding, aspiration, and excretion.

bracken any of several large ferns (especially *Pteridium aquilinum*) which grow abundantly in the northern hemisphere. The rootstock produces coarse fronds each year, which die down in autumn.

bracket fungus any of a group of fungi (see ▷fungus) with fruiting bodies that grow like shelves from the trunks and branches of trees. (Class Basidiomycetes.)

brackets pairs of signs that show which part of a calculation should be worked out first.

For example, 4(7+3) indicates that 4 is to be multiplied by the result obtained from adding 7 and 3. The mnemonic BODMAS can help you to remember the order in which an arithmetical expression should be calculated. Brackets may be nested, for example, 4(20−(7+3)), in which case the expression 7+3 within the innermost pair of brackets is evaluated first, the result subtracted from 20 and that result multiplied by 4.

Bracknell town and administrative headquarters of ▷Bracknell Forest unitary authority in southern England, 16 km/10 mi southeast of Reading; population (1996 est) 52,100. It was designated a ▷new town in 1949; before 1998 it was part of the county of Berkshire.

The headquarters of the Meteorological Office are here. Bracknell is one of the world's two global area forecasting centres which monitor upper-level winds and temperatures for all air traffic. Industries include engineering, electronics, and the manufacture of biscuits (Burtons).

Bracknell Forest unitary authority (borough status) in central south England, created in 1998 from part of the former county of Berkshire.

area 109 sq km/42 sq mi **towns** ▷Bracknell (administrative headquarters), Sandhurst, Crowthorne **features** Royal Military Academy at Sandhurst (established in 1799 for officer training); the Meteorological Office at Bracknell (one of two global forecasting centres for the world's airlines); Transport Research Laboratory, Broadmoor Hospital **industries** high technology industries, engineering, electronics, manufacture of clothing and furniture, bakery products **population** (1997) 109,600

bract leaflike structure in whose ▷axil a flower or inflorescence develops. Bracts are generally green and smaller than the true leaves. However, in some plants they may be brightly coloured and conspicuous, taking over the role of attracting pollinating insects to the flowers, whose own petals are small; examples include poinsettia *Euphorbia pulcherrima* and bougainvillea.

Bradbury, Malcolm (Stanley) (1932–2000) English novelist and critic. His fiction includes comic and satiric portrayals of provincial British and US campus life: *Eating People is Wrong* (1959) (his first novel), *Stepping Westward* (1965), and *The History Man* (1975). *Dr Criminale* (1992) is an academic satire with a 1990s setting. His critical works include *The Modern American Novel* (1983) and *The Modern British Novel* (1993). He was knighted in 1999.

Bradford industrial city and metropolitan borough in West Yorkshire, England, 14 km/9 mi west of Leeds; population (1994 est) 357,000. The manufacture of wool textiles, traditionally the base of Bradford's prosperity, declined in the 1970s but remains important. Other principal industries now include printing, precision and construction engineering, and the manufacture of chemicals and electronics. Stone-quarrying, brewing, photo-engraving, and publishing make a notable contribution to the city's economy. Bradford is also a major centre for financial services.

Related Web site: City of Bradford http://www.bradford.gov.uk/

Bradlaugh, Charles (1833–1891) British freethinker and radical politician. In 1880 he was elected Liberal member of Parliament for Northampton, but was not allowed to take his seat until 1886 because, as an atheist, he claimed the right (unsuccessfully) to affirm instead of taking the oath. He was associated with the feminist Annie Besant.

Bradley, Omar Nelson (1893–1981) US general in World War II. In 1943 he commanded the 2nd US Corps in their victories in Tunisia and Sicily, leading to the surrender of 250,000 Axis troops, and in 1944 led the US troops in the invasion of France. His command, as the 12th Army Group, grew to 1.3 million troops, the largest US force ever assembled.

Bradman, Don(ald George) (1908–2001) Australian Test cricketer. From 52 Test matches he averaged 99.94 runs per innings, the highest average in Test history. He only needed four runs from his final Test innings to average 100 but was dismissed second ball. In April 2000 he was unanimously voted to be the greatest cricketer of the 20th century by the Wisden Cricketers' Almanack.

Related Web site: The Legend of Sir Donald Bradman http://www.pnc.com.au/~scurry/

Braganza the royal house of Portugal whose members reigned from 1640 until 1910; members of another branch were emperors of Brazil from 1822 to 1889.

Brahe, Tycho (1546–1601) Danish astronomer. His accurate observations of the planets enabled German astronomer and mathematician Johannes ▷Kepler to prove that planets orbit the Sun in ellipses. Brahe's discovery and report of the 1572 supernova brought him recognition, and his observations of the comet of 1577 proved that it moved in an orbit among the planets, thus disproving Aristotle's view that comets were in the Earth's atmosphere.

BRACKET FUNGUS Bracket fungus *Trametes* growing on a fallen log in the Ugandan rainforest. *Ken Preston-Mafham/Premaphotos Wildlife*

Brahe was a colourful figure who wore a silver nose after his own was cut off in a duel, and who took an interest in alchemy. In 1576 Frederick II of Denmark gave him the island of Hven, where he set up an observatory. Brahe was the greatest observer in the days before telescopes, making the most accurate measurements of the positions of stars and planets. He moved to Prague as imperial mathematician in 1599, where he was joined by Kepler, who inherited his observations when he died.

Related Web site: Brahe, Tycho
http://es.rice.edu/ES/humsoc/
Galileo/People/tycho_brahe.html

Brahma in Hinduism, the creator of the cosmos, who forms with Vishnu and Siva the Trimurti, or three aspects of the absolute spirit.

Brahman in Hinduism, the supreme being, an abstract, impersonal world soul into whom the *atman*, or individual soul, will eventually be absorbed when its cycle of rebirth is ended.

Brahmanism earliest stage in the development of ▷Hinduism.

Its sacred scriptures are the ▷Vedas, with their accompanying literature of comment and explanation known as Brahmanas, Aranyakas, and Upanishads.

Brahmaputra river in Asia 2,900 km/1,800 mi long, a tributary of the ▷Ganges, rising in the ▷Himalayas range, and flowing through Tibet, India, and Bangladesh.

Brahms, Johannes (1833–1897) German composer, pianist, and conductor. He is considered one of the greatest composers of symphonic music and of songs. His works include four symphonies, lieder (songs), concertos for piano and for violin, chamber music, sonatas, and the choral *Ein Deutsches Requiem/A German Requiem* (1868). He performed and conducted his own works.

In 1853 the violinist Joseph Joachim introduced him to the composers Liszt and Schumann, who encouraged his work. From 1868 Brahms made his home in Vienna, Austria. Although his music belongs to a reflective strain of Romanticism, similar to Wordsworth in poetry, Brahms saw himself as continuing the classical tradition from the point to which Beethoven had brought it. To his contemporaries, he was a strict formalist, in opposition to the Romantic sensuality of Wagner. His influence on Mahler and Schoenberg was profound.

Related Web site: Welcome to the Johannes Brahms WebSource
http://www.mjq.net/brahms/

Braille system of writing for the blind. Letters are represented by a combination of raised dots on paper or other materials, which are then read by touch. It was invented in 1829 by **Louis Braille**, who became blind at the age of three.

brain in higher animals, a mass of interconnected ▷nerve cells forming the anterior part of the ▷central nervous system, whose activities it coordinates and controls. In ▷vertebrates, the brain is contained by the skull. At the base of the ▷brainstem, the **medulla oblongata** contains centres for the control of respiration, heartbeat rate and strength, and blood pressure. Overlying this is the cerebellum, which is concerned with coordinating complex muscular processes such as maintaining posture and moving limbs.

The cerebral hemispheres (**cerebrum**) are paired outgrowths of the front end of the forebrain, in early vertebrates mainly concerned with the senses, but in higher vertebrates greatly developed and involved in the integration of all sensory input and motor output, and in thought, emotions, memory, and behaviour.

In vertebrates, many of the nerve fibres from the two sides of the body cross over as they enter the brain, so that the left cerebral hemisphere is associated with the right side of the body and vice versa. In humans, a certain asymmetry develops in the two halves of the cerebrum. In right-handed people, the left hemisphere seems to play a greater role in controlling verbal and some mathematical skills, whereas the right hemisphere is more involved in spatial perception. In general, however, skills and abilities are not closely localized. In the brain, nerve impulses are passed across ▷synapses by neurotransmitters, in the same way as in other parts of the nervous system.

In mammals the cerebrum is the largest part of the brain, carrying the **cerebral cortex**. This consists of a thick surface layer of cell bodies (grey matter), below which fibre tracts (white matter) connect various parts of the cortex to each other and to other points in the central nervous system. As cerebral complexity grows, the surface of the brain becomes convoluted into deep folds. In higher mammals, there are large unassigned areas of the brain that seem to be connected with intelligence, personality, and higher

mental faculties. Language is controlled in two special regions usually in the left side of the brain: **Broca's area** governs the ability to talk, and **Wernicke's area** is responsible for the comprehension of spoken and written words. In 1990, scientists at Johns Hopkins University, Baltimore, succeeded in culturing human brain cells.

See also The Human Brain Focus Feature on pp. 126–127.

Related Web site: Virtual Body
http://www.ehc.com/vbody.asp

brain damage impairment which can be caused by trauma (for example, accidents) or disease (such as encephalitis), or which may be present at birth. Depending on the area of the brain that is affected, language, movement, sensation, judgement, or other abilities may be impaired.

Braine, John (Gerard) (1922–1986) English novelist. His novel *Room at the Top* (1957) cast Braine as one of the leading ▷Angry Young Men of the period. It created the character of Joe Lampton, one of the first of the northern working-class antiheroes, who reappears in *Life at the Top* (1962).

brainstem region where the top of the spinal cord merges with the undersurface of the brain, consisting largely of the medulla oblongata and midbrain.

brake device used to slow down or stop the movement of a moving body or vehicle. The mechanically applied calliper brake used on bicycles uses a scissor action to press hard rubber blocks against the wheel rim. The main braking system of a car works

disc brake

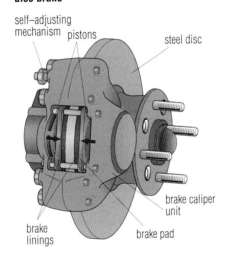

self–adjusting mechanism
pistons
steel disc
brake linings
brake caliper unit
brake pad

drum brake

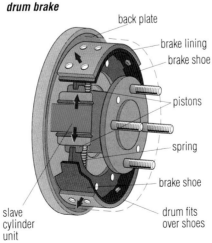

back plate
brake lining
brake shoe
pistons
spring
brake shoe
slave cylinder unit
drum fits over shoes

BRAKE Two common braking systems: the disc brake (top) and the drum brake (bottom). In the disc brake, increased hydraulic pressure of the brake fluid in the pistons forces the brake pads against the steel disc attached to the wheel. A self-adjusting mechanism balances the force on each pad. In the drum brake, increased pressure of the brake fluid within the slave cylinder forces the brake pad against the brake drum attached to the wheel.

hydraulically: when the driver depresses the brake pedal, liquid pressure forces pistons to apply brakes on each wheel.

Bramah, Joseph (1748–1814) English inventor of a flushing water closet (1778), an 'unpickable' lock (1784), and the hydraulic press (1795). The press made use of Blaise Pascal's regulation (that pressure in fluid contained in a vessel is evenly distributed) and employed water as the hydraulic fluid; it was used in cotton baling and in forging.

Bramante (1444–1514) Adopted name of Donato di Pascuccio. Italian High Renaissance architect and artist. Inspired by classical designs and by the work of Leonardo da Vinci, he was employed by Pope Julius II in rebuilding part of the Vatican and St Peter's in Rome. The circular Tempietto of San Pietro in Montorio, Rome (commissioned in 1502, built about 1510), is possibly his most important completed work. Though small in size, this circular colonnaded building possesses much of the grandeur of ancient Roman buildings.

bramble any of a group of prickly bushes belonging to the rose family. Examples are ▷blackberry, raspberry, and dewberry. (Genus *Rubus*, family Rosaceae.)

brambling (or bramble finch) bird *Fringilla montifringilla* belonging to the finch family Fringillidae, order Passeriformes. It is about 15 cm/6 in long, and breeds in northern Europe and Asia.

Branagh, Kenneth (Charles) (1960–) Northern Irish stage and film actor, director, and producer. He co-founded the Renaissance Theatre Company in 1987. His first film as both actor and director was *Henry V* (1989); he returned to Shakespeare with lavish film versions of *Much Ado About Nothing* (1993), *Hamlet* (1996), and *Love's Labours Lost* (2000).

Branagh's first Hollywood film was *Dead Again* (1992), a stylish film noir. He also demonstrated a deft comic touch with *Peter's Friends* (1992) and *In the Bleak Midwinter* (1995), although his interpretation of *Mary Shelley's Frankenstein* (1994) was coolly received. His return to theatre direction in 2001 with *The Play What I Wrote*, was widely acclaimed. He married the actor and scriptwriter Emma ▷Thompson in 1989; they separated in 1995.

Brancusi, Constantin (1876–1957) Romanian sculptor. One of the main figures of 20th-century art, he revolutionized modern sculpture. Active in Paris from 1904, he was a pioneer of abstract sculpture, reducing a few basic themes such as birds, fishes, and the human head to simple essential forms appropriate to the special quality of his material, whether stone, bronze, or wood. His works include *Sleeping Muse* (1910; Musée National d'Art Moderne, Paris) and *Bird in Space* (1928; Museum of Modern Art, New York).

Brandenburg administrative *Land* (state) of Germany; area 25,000 sq km/10,000 sq mi; population (1995) 2,500,000. The capital is ▷Potsdam; other main cities and towns are Cottbus, Brandenburg, and Frankfurt-an-der-Oder. The main industries are iron and steel, paper, pulp, metal products, and semiconductors.

Brando, Marlon (1924–) US actor. One of the great exponents of ▷method acting, he cultivated a mumbling speech and had a powerful presence on both stage and screen. He won Best Actor Academy Awards for *On the Waterfront* (1954) and *The Godfather* (1972), although he

CONSTANTIN BRANCUSI The Maiastra bronze, produced in 1911 by the Romanian sculptor Constantin Brancusi, and now in the Tate Gallery, London, England. *The Art Archive/Tate Gallery London/Eileen Tweedy*

declined the second award to protest against the way Hollywood portrayed American Indians. Brando directed one film, the camp psychological Western *One Eyed Jacks* (1961).

Brando was born in Omaha, Nebraska, and began his career in New York, New York. He made his Broadway debut in *I Remember Mama* (1944) and achieved fame in the play *A Streetcar Named Desire* (1947), dazzling critics and changing the way the play was perceived. His subsequent films include
cont'd on p. 128

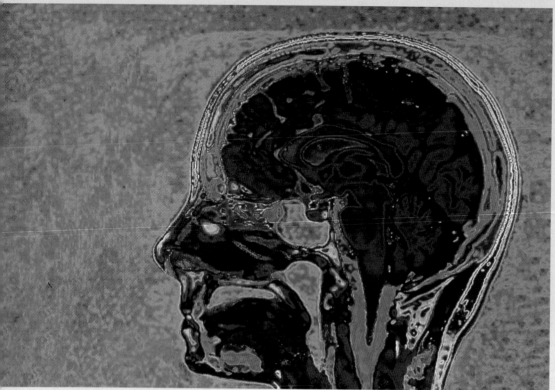

BRAIN SCAN A magnetic resonance imaging (MRI) scan of a human brain. © Image Bank

The Human Brain

by Matthew Walker

The brain is the most complex organ in the human body. It is the controller of all that we do and achieve. Yet despite the wealth of research that has been carried out on the brain, our knowledge of how it works is very limited.

the composition of the brain

It would be reasonable to assume that the intelligence of an animal related directly to the size of the brain, but this is not the case. Intelligence more directly relates to the relative size of the brain compared to body weight. Thus, blue whales, as the largest mammal, have the largest brain (weighing about 8 kg/17.6 lb), but relative to body size humans have the largest brain (weighing about 1.4 kg/3.1 lb).

The human brain contains approximately 100 billion nerve cells. These cells can only be seen under a microscope. Each nerve cell is connected to, on average, over 1,000 other nerve cells, making over 100 trillion connections in all. The nerve cells consist of a body with finger-like extensions and a long arm called an **axon**. Electrical impulses travel down the

axon from the cell body. When the impulses reach the end of the axon, they cause the release of a chemical (called a **neurotransmitter**) that travels across a small gap (the synaptic cleft) to act on 'receivers' termed **receptors** on the connected nerve cell. This is how nerve cells communicate with one another. Some of these chemicals 'excite' connected nerve cells, and if these nerve cells are sufficiently excited they fire (that is, they send an electrical impulse down their axons). If only excitation were present, then eventually all the nerve cells in the brain would be firing together; this is what happens in epileptic fits. To avoid this happening, some nerve cells release a chemical that prevents connected nerves from firing (it 'inhibits' connected nerve cells). The proper operation of the brain is dependent on this balance of excitation and inhibition.

A collection of nerve cells appears grey in colour, and thus areas of the brain in which there are mainly nerve cells are termed **grey matter**. The axons, on the other hand, often have an insulating coat that makes a collection of them appear white, and thus areas in which there are mainly axons are called **white matter**. The bulk of the human brain consists of white matter, surrounded by a rim of grey matter. The axons can

travel great distances in the brain and can connect a nerve cell on one side of the brain to a nerve cell on the other side. The brain is surprisingly soft, having the consistency of crème caramel, and thus the skull is critical in protecting it. In addition, tough coverings, the **meninges** (it is these which are infected in patients suffering from meningitis), also protect the brain. Within the meninges, the brain is surrounded by fluid that both protects and provides nutrients; this fluid is termed **cerebrospinal fluid** as it covers the brain and spinal cord. Cerebrospinal fluid not only surrounds the brain, but is also contained within the brain in spaces called **ventricles**.

the structure of the brain

The brain can be divided into three parts: the brainstem, cerebellum, and forebrain.

The **brainstem** is the continuation of the spinal cord. It receives sensory inputs from the face, and from hearing and balance organs in the inner ear, and also sends nerve signals to facial muscles, including those that move the eyes and determine the size of the pupil. The base of the brainstem, called the **medulla oblongata**, has a vital function in controlling breathing and heart rate; people cannot live with significant damage to this area.

The **cerebellum** is involved in balance and coordination. It looks like a cauliflower and lies at the back of the brain. The cerebellum also provides a motor memory so that rapid repetitive movements such as typing or piano playing can be controlled without conscious attention.

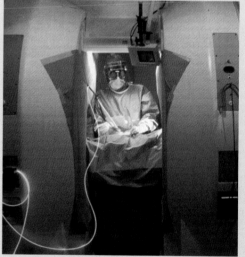

THE BRAIN of a patient is scanned using magnetic resonance imaging (MRI). MRI scanning is very useful in diagnosing disease in soft tissue such as the brain and spinal cord. The patient is not exposed to harmful radiation. © Image Bank

The **forebrain** can be further divided into the diencephalon, which includes the thalamus, hypothalamus, and pituitary gland, and the telencephalon, consisting of the corpus striatum and the cerebral cortex.

The **thalamus** is like a telephone exchange, transmitting information from the sensory organs to specific areas of the cortex, where it is analysed. The thalamus also plays a role in memory formation and emotional response.

The **hypothalamus** controls functions necessary for survival, such as hunger and thirst. Close by is the pituitary gland which, in response to signals from the hypothalamus, releases hormones that control many sexual functions (such as menstruation and sperm production). Importantly, in addition, the hypothalamus and pituitary, through the release of hormones, control the internal environment of the body, for example by regulating body temperature and fluid balance.

The **corpus striatum**, along with the **substantia nigra**, form the basal ganglia. These help start and control movements. Degeneration of the substantia nigra is associated with Parkinson's disease, in which people have problems initiating movements, and degeneration of the corpus striatum is seen in Huntingdon's disease, which is characterized by an inability to stop moving.

The **cerebral cortex** provides the link between the appreciation of sensory inputs, the control of movement, and conscious thought. It also selects and stores memories and forms emotions. The cortex makes up 90% of the volume of the brain. It is divided into two halves (hemispheres) joined in the middle by the corpus callosum so that each half 'knows' what the other half is doing. The right half controls the left-hand side of the body, and the left half controls the right-hand side of the body. For most of us, the left half is dominant. To a certain extent, the dominant side determines handedness. Right-handed people are left-hemisphere dominant. However, only about half the people who are left-handed are right-hemisphere dominant. The dominant hemisphere is largely responsible for linguistic and logical ability. Recognizing where things are in space and recognizing faces depends on the non-dominant hemisphere. Although much has been made of the right hemisphere being the 'artistic' hemisphere, this is largely untrue (for example, music appreciation and musicianship rely on both hemispheres). Indeed, studies of people who have the corpus callosum cut have revealed that many functions are shared between the hemispheres.

localization of function

Each hemisphere is further divided into four lobes: frontal (at the front), parietal (in the middle), temporal (at the sides), and occipital (at the back).

Certain functions of the brain are localized to specific regions of the cortex. The **frontal lobe** is involved in planning, reasoning, problem solving, speech, and controlling movement. The **parietal lobe** enables the perception of touch. The **temporal lobe** is involved in the perception of sound and smell, and plays a role in memory, emotion, and language. The **occipital lobe** processes visual information.

The inner part of the temporal lobe consists of a curved structure called the **hippocampus** (literally

'sea horse' because of its shape). The hippocampus is critical for memory formation, and damage to the hippocampus can result in problems forming new memories. The hippocampus connects to a variety of structures, including the amygdala (literally 'almond' because of its shape; which generates our response to fear), the hypothalamus, the thalamus, and other parts of the cortex that together make up the 'limbic' system. This system is essential for emotional response, memory formation, and the association of emotions with memories.

An area in the dominant temporal lobe first described in the late 19th century by German neurologist and psychiatrist Carl Wernicke (Wernicke's area) is necessary for understanding and recognizing language. People who have strokes affecting this area cannot understand what is said and tend to speak fluently using nonsense words.

This area, which generates language, sends a signal to an area in the frontal lobe called Broca's area, which generates speech. People who have strokes affecting Broca's area cannot talk fluently and have problems naming objects but can understand what is said to them.

developments in research

Although there have been great advances in understanding the brain and the localization of various functions, much is still not understood. In the 19th century, localization of function was largely

determined by studying people who had suffered injuries to the brain (often following strokes) and identifying where the defect was (usually after the person had died) and what the person could not do. More recently, advanced techniques have involved imaging people's brains using **special scans** such as magnetic resonance imaging (MRI) and positron emission tomography (PET). These techniques can look in detail at the brain, and can determine which parts are active when someone carries out a particular task.

Brain repair has also become the subject of much recent medical research, both by stimulating nerve cell production in the brain with drugs and by transplanting primitive nerve cells into the brain. Although this research is still in its early stages, it may be possible to repair parts of the brain that become damaged by strokes and head injuries,

or that degenerate in Parkinson's or other similar diseases.

On a smaller scale, it is not clear how the working of nerve cells relates to the function of the brain. Techniques are now available to keep small pieces of tissue removed from the brain alive and to record the electrical activity of single nerve cells. This has given us a considerable insight into how nerve cells communicate with one another, and how drugs that act on the brain produce their effect. We are still, however, a long way from understanding how the brain works.

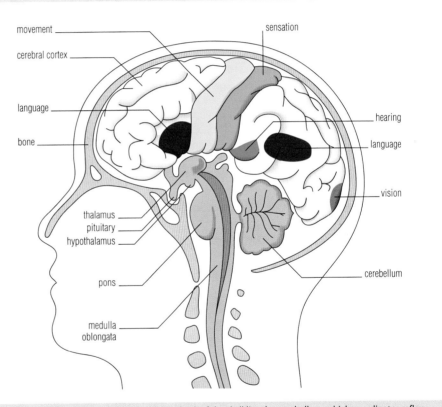

THE BRAIN The structure of the human brain. At the back of the skull lies the cerebellum, which coordinates reflex actions that control muscular activity. The medulla controls respiration, heartbeat, and blood pressure. The hypothalamus is concerned with instinctive drives and emotions. The thalamus relays signals to and from various parts of the brain. The pituitary gland controls the body's hormones. Distinct areas of the large convoluted cerebral hemispheres that fill most of the skull are linked to sensations, such as hearing and sight, and voluntary activities, such as movement.

MARLON BRANDO A studio picture of the US actor Marlon Brando during the 1960s. *Image Bank*

The Men (1950), *A Streetcar Named Desire* (1951), and *The Wild One* (1954). In 1959 he formed Pennebar Productions to make *One Eyed Jacks*. Later films include *Last Tango in Paris* (1973), *Apocalypse Now* (1979), *The Freshman* (1990), *Don Juan DeMarco* (1995), and *The Score* (2001). His influence has been evident in the work of more recent actors, including Robert De Niro.

> **Marlon Brando**
> *An actor is a guy who, if you aren't talking about him, isn't listening.*
> The Observer January 1956

Brandt, Willy (1913–1992) Adopted name of Karl Herbert Frahm. German socialist politician, federal chancellor (premier) of West Germany 1969–74. He played a key role in the remoulding of the Social Democratic Party (SPD) as a moderate socialist force (leader 1964–87). As mayor of West Berlin 1957–66, Brandt became internationally known during the Berlin Wall crisis of 1961. He was awarded the Nobel Prize for Peace in 1971 for his contribution towards reconciliation between West and East Germany.

In the 'grand coalition' 1966–69, Brandt served as foreign minister and introduced Ostpolitik, a policy of reconciliation between East and West Europe, which was continued when he became federal chancellor in 1969 and culminated in the 1972 signing of the Basic Treaty with East Germany. He chaired the Brandt Commission on Third World problems 1977–83 and was a member of the European Parliament 1979–83.

Branson, Richard (1950–) English entrepreneur whose Virgin company developed quickly, diversifying from retailing records to the airline business and Virgin trains.

He was born in Surrey, England, and the 1968 launch of *Student* magazine proved to be the first of his many successful business ventures.

Braque, Georges (1882–1963) French painter. With Picasso, he played a decisive role in the development of cubism (1907–1910). It was during this period that he began to experiment with collage and invented the technique of gluing paper, wood, and other materials to canvas.

Braque was the first to exhibit a cubist work, at the Salon des Indépendants in 1908. The idea behind cubism led logically to abstraction, a path that Braque pursued without losing a sense of pictorial beauty. In his many still lifes he shows how from some quite simple object, such as a dish of fruit, a whole set of novel relationships and harmonies can be derived. Still active in his last years, he produced a series of studio interiors which are among the finest of his works in their highly original conception of space.

> **Georges Braque**
> *Art is meant to disturb, science reassures.*
> Pensées sur l'Art

Brasília capital of Brazil from 1960, situated on the central plateau 1,150 m/3,773 ft above sea level; population (2000 est) 2,043,200. The main area of employment is in government service; only light industry is allowed within the city. Brasília is also capital of the Federal District, which has an area of 5,794 sq km/2,317 sq mi. The city was designed to accommodate up to 500,000 people, which has now been considerably exceeded, and many people live in shanty towns located outside the main city.

Features Palácio da Alvorada (official residence of the president); National Congress building; the striking cathedral where the city was inaugurated; Central Square of Three Powers; the University of Brasília, founded in 1962; Parque Nacional de Brasília, founded in 1961; the city is surrounded by an artificial lake (Lago do Paranoá) created to assist in maintaining higher relative humidity as the city is located in a very hot and dry region.

History It was planned by Lúcio Costa (1902–98), with Oscar Niemeyer as chief architect, as a completely new city. The idea of a capital city in the interior was first discussed in 1789, but the present site was not chosen until 1956, when it was selected by the then president Juscelino Kubitschek. It was inaugurated in 1960.

Related Web site: Brasília's Home Page http://www.geocities.com/TheTropics/3416/

brass metal ▷alloy of copper and zinc, with not more than 5% or 6% of other metals. The zinc content ranges from 20% to 45%, and the colour of brass varies accordingly from coppery to whitish yellow. Brasses are characterized by the ease with which they may be shaped and machined; they are strong and ductile, resist many forms of corrosion, and are used for electrical fittings, ammunition cases, screws, household fittings, and ornaments.

brassica any of a group of plants, many of which are cultivated as vegetables. The most familiar is the common cabbage (*Brassica oleracea*), with its varieties broccoli, cauliflower, kale, and Brussels sprouts. (Genus *Brassica*, family Cruciferae.)

brass instrument any of a class of musical instruments made of brass or other metal, including trumpets, bugles, trombones, and horns. The function of a reed is served by the lips, shaped and tensed by the mouthpiece, acting as a valve releasing periodic pulses of pressurized air into the tube. Orchestral brass instruments are derived from signalling instruments that in their natural or valveless form produce a directionally focused range of tones from the harmonic series by overblowing to as high as the 16th harmonic. They are powerful and efficient generators, and produce tones of great depth and resonance.

Bratislava (German **Pressburg**) industrial port (engineering, chemicals, oil refining) and capital of the Slovak Republic, on the River Danube; population (1991) 441,500. It was the capital of Hungary from 1526 to 1784 and capital of Slovakia (within Czechoslovakia) until 1993.

Braun, Eva (1912–1945) German mistress of Adolf Hitler. Secretary to Hitler's photographer and personal friend, Heinrich Hoffmann, she became Hitler's mistress in the 1930s and married him in the air-raid shelter of the Chancellery in Berlin on 29 April 1945. The next day they committed suicide together.

Braun, Wernher von German rocket engineer; see ▷von Braun.

Braunschweig German form of ▷Brunswick, a city in Lower Saxony, Germany.

Brazil see country box.

Brazil nut gigantic South American tree; also its seed, which is rich in oil and highly nutritious. The seeds (nuts) are enclosed in a hard outer casing, each fruit containing 10–20 seeds arranged like the segments of an orange. The timber of the tree is also valuable. (*Bertholletia excelsa*, family Lecythidaceae.)

brazing method of joining two metals by melting an ▷alloy or metal into the joint. It is similar to soldering (see ▷solder) but takes place at a much higher temperature. Copper and silver alloys are widely used for brazing, at temperatures up to about 900°C/1,650°F.

Brazzaville river port and capital of the Republic of the Congo (Congo-Brazzaville), on the west bank of the Congo River, opposite Kinshasa; population (1995 est) 937,600. Industries include foundries, railway repairs, shipbuilding, beverages, textiles, food processing, shoes, soap, furniture, and bricks. Tourism is important, with arts and crafts markets in the Plateau district of the city. There is a cathedral built in 1892 and the Pasteur Institute founded in 1908. The city stands on Malebo Pool (Stanley Pool).

Brazzaville was founded in 1884 by the French explorer Count Pierre Savorgnan de Brazza (1852–1905). From 1882 to 1960 it was under French rule. It was the African headquarters of the Free (later Fighting) French during World War II. It is an important transhipment point between river transport and the railway to Pointe-Noire on the Atlantic coast.

BRASSICA The wild cabbage *Brassica oleracea*, the ancestor of the familiar edible brassicas (such as cabbages and Brussels sprouts), grows along the maritime cliffs of the Atlantic coast of Europe and along the Mediterranean. *Premaphotos Wildlife*

breadfruit fruit of two tropical trees belonging to the mulberry family. It is highly nutritious and when baked is said to taste like bread. It is native to many South Pacific islands. (*Artocarpus communis* and *A. altilis*, family Moraceae.)

Breakspear, Nicholas original name of ▷Adrian IV, the only English pope.

bream deep-bodied, flattened fish *Abramis brama* of the carp family, growing to about 50 cm/1.6 ft, typically found in lowland rivers across Europe.

breast one of a pair of organs on the chest of the human female, also known as a ▷mammary gland. Each of the two breasts contains milk-producing cells and a network of tubes or ducts that lead to openings in the nipple.

Milk-producing cells in the breast do not become active until a woman has given birth to a baby. Breast milk is made from substances extracted from the mother's blood as it passes through the breasts, and contains all the nourishment a baby needs. Breast-fed newborns develop fewer infections than bottle-fed babies because of the antibodies and white blood cells contained in breast milk. These are particularly abundant in the colostrum produced in the first few days of breast-feeding.

breast cancer in medicine, ▷cancer of the ▷breast. It is usually diagnosed following the detection of a painless lump in the breast (either through self-examination or ▷mammography). Other, less common symptoms, include changes in the shape or texture of the breast and discharge from the nipple. It is the commonest cancer amongst women: there are 28,000 new cases of breast cancer in Britain each year and 185,700 in the USA.

breast screening in medicine, examination of the breast to detect the presence of breast cancer at an early stage. Screening methods include self-screening by monthly examination of the breasts and formal programmes of screening by palpation (physical examination) and mammography in special clinics. Screening may be offered to older women on a routine basis and it is important in women with a family history of breast cancer.

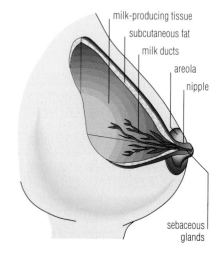

milk-producing tissue
subcutaneous fat
milk ducts
areola
nipple
sebaceous glands

BREAST Milk produced in the tissue of the human breast to feed a baby after a woman has given birth passes along ducts which lead to openings in the nipple.

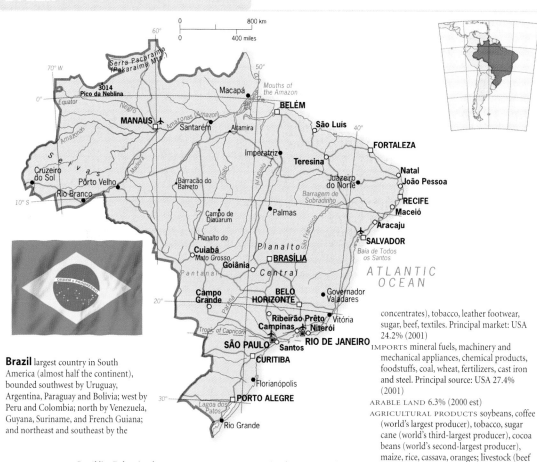

Brazil largest country in South America (almost half the continent), bounded southwest by Uruguay, Argentina, Paraguay and Bolivia; west by Peru and Colombia; north by Venezuela, Guyana, Suriname, and French Guiana; and northeast and southeast by the

NATIONAL NAME *República Federativa do Brasil/Federative Republic of Brazil*

AREA 8,511,965 sq km/3,286,469 sq mi

CAPITAL Brasilia

MAJOR TOWNS/CITIES São Paulo, Belo Horizonte, Nova Iguaçu, Rio de Janeiro, Belém, Recife, Porto Alegre, Salvador, Curitiba, Manaus, Fortaleza

MAJOR PORTS Rio de Janeiro, Belém, Recife, Porto Alegre, Salvador

PHYSICAL FEATURES the densely forested Amazon basin covers the northern half of the country with a network of rivers; south is fertile; enormous energy resources, both hydroelectric (Itaipú Reservoir on the Paraná, and Tucuruí on the Tocantins) and nuclear (uranium ores); mostly tropical climate

Government

HEAD OF STATE AND GOVERNMENT Luiz Inácio da Silva from 2003

POLITICAL SYSTEM liberal democracy

POLITICAL EXECUTIVE limited presidency

ADMINISTRATIVE DIVISIONS 26 states and one federal district

ARMED FORCES 287,600; plus public security forces under army control of 385,600 (2002 est)

CONSCRIPTION 12 months

DEATH PENALTY abolished for ordinary crimes in 1979; laws provide for the death penalty for exceptional crimes, such as crimes committed in wartime

DEFENCE SPEND (% GDP) 2.3 (2002 est)

EDUCATION SPEND (% GDP) 3.8 (2001 est)

HEALTH SPEND (% GDP) 8.3 (2000 est)

Economy and resources

CURRENCY real

GPD (US$) 452.4 billion (2002 est)

REAL GDP GROWTH (% change on previous year) 1.5 (2001)

GNI (US$) 497.4 billion (2002 est)

GNI PER CAPITA (PPP) (US$) 7,250 (2002)

CONSUMER PRICE INFLATION 14% (2003 est)

UNEMPLOYMENT 7.6% (1998)

FOREIGN DEBT (US$) 185.2 billion (2001 est)

MAJOR TRADING PARTNERS USA, Argentina, Germany, Japan, the Netherlands

RESOURCES iron ore (world's second-largest producer), tin (world's fourth-largest producer), aluminium (world's fourth-largest producer), gold, phosphates, platinum, bauxite, uranium, manganese, coal, copper, petroleum, natural gas, hydroelectric power, forests

INDUSTRIES mining, steel, machinery and transport equipment, food processing, textiles and clothing, chemicals, petrochemicals, cement, lumber

EXPORTS steel products, transport equipment, coffee, iron ore and concentrates, aluminium, iron, tin, soybeans, meal and oils, orange juice (85% of world's concentrates), tobacco, leather footwear, sugar, beef, textiles. Principal market: USA 24.2% (2001)

IMPORTS mineral fuels, machinery and mechanical appliances, chemical products, foodstuffs, coal, wheat, fertilizers, cast iron and steel. Principal source: USA 27.4% (2001)

ARABLE LAND 6.3% (2000 est)

AGRICULTURAL PRODUCTS soybeans, coffee (world's largest producer), tobacco, sugar cane (world's third-largest producer), cocoa beans (world's second-largest producer), maize, rice, cassava, oranges; livestock (beef and poultry)

Chronology

1500: Originally inhabited by South American Indians. Portuguese explorer Pedro Alvares Cabral sighted and claimed Brazil for Portugal.

1580–1640: Brazil came under Spanish rule along with Portugal.

17th century: Sugar-cane plantations were established with slave labour in coastal regions, making Brazil the world's largest supplier of sugar; cattle ranching was developed inland.

1695: Gold was discovered in the central highlands.

1763: The colonial capital moved from Bahía to Rio de Janeiro.

1770: Brazil's first coffee plantations were established in Rio de Janeiro.

18th century: Population in 1798 totalled 3.3 million, of which around 1.9 million were slaves, mainly of African origin; significant growth of gold-mining industry.

1808: The Portuguese regent, Prince John, arrived in Brazil and established his court at Rio de Janeiro; Brazilian trade opened to foreign merchants.

1815: The United Kingdom of Portugal, Brazil, and Algarve made Brazil co-equal with Portugal.

1821: Crown Prince Pedro took over the government of Brazil.

1822: Pedro defied orders to return to Portugal; he declared Brazil's independence to avoid reversion to colonial status.

1825: King John VI recognized his son as Emperor Pedro I of Brazil.

1831: Pedro I abdicated in favour of his infant son, Pedro II.

1847: The first prime minister was appointed, but the emperor retained many powers.

1865–70: Brazilian efforts to control Uruguay led to the War of the Triple Alliance with Paraguay.

1888: Slavery was abolished in Brazil.

Population and society

POPULATION 178,470,000 (2003 est)

POPULATION GROWTH RATE 1.1% (2000–15)

POPULATION DENSITY (per sq km) 21 (2003 est)

URBAN POPULATION (% of total) 83 (2003 est)

AGE DISTRIBUTION (% of total population) 0–14 28%, 15–59 64%, 60+ 8% (2002 est)

ETHNIC GROUPS wide range of ethnic groups, including 55% of European origin (mainly Portuguese, Italian, and German), 38% of mixed parentage, 6% of African origin, as well as American Indians and Japanese

LANGUAGE Portuguese (official), Spanish, English, French, 120 Indian languages

RELIGION Roman Catholic 70%; Indian faiths

EDUCATION (compulsory years) 8

LITERACY RATE 93% (men); 82% (women) (2003 est)

LABOUR FORCE 23.4% agriculture, 20.1% industry, 56.5% services (1998)

LIFE EXPECTANCY 64 (men); 73 (women) (2000–05)

CHILD MORTALITY RATE (under 5, per 1,000 live births) 36 (2001)

PHYSICIANS (per 1,000 people) 1.3 (1998 est)

HOSPITAL BEDS (per 1,000 people) 3.1 (1998 est)

TV SETS (per 1,000 people) 349 (2001 est)

RADIOS (per 1,000 people) 444 (1997)

INTERNET USERS (per 10,000 people) 822.4 (2002 est)

PERSONAL COMPUTER USERS (per 100 people) 7.5 (2002 est)

See also ▷Amazon; ▷Amazonian Indian; ▷slavery.

1889: The monarch was overthrown by a liberal revolt; a federal republic was established, with a central government by the coffee planters.

1902: Brazil produced 65% of the world's coffee.

1915–19: Lack of European imports during World War I led to rapid industrialization.

1930: A revolution against the coffee planter oligarchy placed Getúlio Vargas in power; he introduced social reforms.

1937: Vargas established an authoritarian corporate state.

1942: Brazil entered World War II as an ally of USA.

1945–54: Vargas was ousted by a military coup. In 1951 he was elected president and continued to extend the state control of the economy. In 1954 he committed suicide.

1960: The capital moved to Brasília.

1964: A bloodless coup established a technocratic military regime; free political parties were abolished; concentration on industrial growth.

1985: Tancredo Neves became the first civilian president in 21 years.

1989: Fernando Collor (PRN) was elected president. Brazil suspended its foreign debt payments.

1992: Collor was charged with corruption and replaced by Vice-President Itamar Franco.

1994: A new currency was introduced, the third in eight years. Fernando Henrique Cardoso (PSDB) won presidential elections. Collor was cleared of corruption charges.

1997: The constitution was amended to allow the president to seek a second term of office.

1998: President Cardoso was re-elected. An IMF rescue package was announced.

2002: The IMF granted the government a US$30 million loan. With a comprehensive victory in presidential elections, Luiz Inacio Lula da Silva ('Lula') of the left-wing Partido dos Trabalhadores (PT; Workers' Party) was able to put a left-wing government in power for the first time in 40 years.

BRAZIL A soybean field in Brazil, a principal producer of soybeans. *Image Bank*

Breathalyzer trademark for an instrument for on-the-spot checking by police of the amount of alcohol consumed by a suspect driver. The driver breathes into a plastic bag connected to a tube containing a chemical (such as a diluted solution of potassium dichromate in 50% sulphuric acid) that changes colour in the presence of alcohol. Another method is to use a gas chromatograph, again from a breath sample.

breathing in terrestrial animals, the muscular movements whereby air is taken into the lungs and then expelled, a form of gas exchange. Breathing is sometimes referred to as external respiration, for true respiration is a cellular (internal) process.

Lungs are specialized for gas exchange but are not themselves muscular, consisting of spongy material. In order for oxygen to be passed to the blood and carbon dioxide removed, air is drawn into the lungs (inhaled) by the contraction of the diaphragm and intercostal muscles; relaxation of these muscles enables air to be breathed out (exhaled). The rate of breathing is controlled by the brain. High levels of activity lead to a greater demand for oxygen and an increased rate of breathing.

breccia coarse-grained clastic ▷sedimentary rock, made up of broken fragments (clasts) of pre-existing rocks held together in a fine-grained matrix. It is similar to ▷conglomerate but the fragments in breccia are jagged in shape.

Brecht, Bertolt (Eugen Berthold Friedrich) (1898–1956) German dramatist and poet. He was one of the most influential figures in 20th-century theatre. A committed Marxist, he sought to develop an 'epic theatre' which aimed to destroy the 'suspension of disbelief' usual in the theatre and so encourage audiences to develop an active and critical attitude to a play's subject. He adapted John Gay's *The Beggar's Opera* as *Die Dreigroschenoper/The Threepenny Opera* (1928), set to music by Kurt Weill. Later plays include *Mutter Courage und ihre Kinder/Mother Courage and her Children* (1941), set during the Thirty Years' War, and *Der kaukasische Kreidekreis/The Caucasian Chalk Circle* (1945).

As an anti-Nazi, Brecht left Germany in 1933 for Scandinavia and the USA; he became an Austrian citizen after World War II. He established the Berliner Ensemble theatre group in East Germany in 1949, and in the same year published *Kleines Organon für das Theater/Little Treatise on the Theatre*, a concise expression of his theatrical philosophy. His other works include *Leben des Galilei/The Life of Galileo* (1938), *Der gute Mensch von Setzuan/The Good Woman of Setzuan* (1943), and *Der aufhaltsame Aufstieg der Arturo Ui/The Resistible Rise of Arturo Ui* (1958).

Related Web site: Bertolt Brecht Home Page http://www.geocities.com/Broadway/Stage/1052/brecht1.htm

> **Bertolt Brecht**
> *Erst kommt das Fressen, dann kommt die Moral.*
> *Food comes first, then morals.*
> Die Dreigroschenoper/ The Threepenny Opera

Brecknockshire (or Breconshire; Welsh **Sir Frycheiniog**) former county of Wales. It became a district of Powys between 1974 and 1996, and is now part of ▷Powys unitary authority.

breed recognizable group of domestic animals, within a species, with distinctive characteristics that have been produced by ▷artificial selection.

breeder reactor (or **fast breeder**) alternative names for ▷fast reactor, a type of nuclear reactor.

breeding in biology, the crossing and selection of animals and plants to change the characteristics of an existing ▷breed or cultivar (variety), or to produce a new one.

breeding in nuclear physics, a process in a reactor in which more fissionable material is produced than is consumed in running the reactor.

Brel, Jacques (1929–1978) Belgian singer and songwriter. He was active in France from 1953, where his fatalistic ballads made him a star. Of his more than 400 songs, many have been recorded in translation by singers as diverse as Frank Sinatra and David Bowie. 'Ne me quitte pas/If You Go Away' (1964) is one of his best-known songs.

Bremen industrial port and capital of the *Land* (state) of ▷Bremen, Germany, on the River Weser 69 km/43 mi from the open sea; population (1995) 549,000. Industries include iron, steel, oil refining, the manufacture of chemicals, aircraft, and cars, ship repairing, marine engineering, and electronics. The Bremer Vulkan Shipyards closed in 1996. Nearby Bremerhaven serves as an outport.

Bremen administrative region (German *Land*) of Germany, consisting of the cities of Bremen and Bremerhaven; area 400 sq km/154 sq mi; population (1999 est) 663,100.

Brenner Pass lowest of the Alpine passes, 1,370 m/4,495 ft; it leads from Trentino–Alto Adige, Italy, to the Austrian Tirol, and is 19 km/12 mi long.

Brent outer borough of northwest Greater London. It includes the suburbs of Wembley and Willesden.

Features Wembley Stadium (1923); the Kilburn State Cinema (1937), the largest cinema in Europe when built; Brent Cross shopping centre (1976), first regional shopping centre in Europe; Neasden Temple (1995), the largest Hindu temple outside India; population (1991) 243,000.

Brenton, Howard (1942–) English dramatist. His political theatre, deliberately provocative, includes *The Churchill Play* (1974) and *The Romans in Britain* (1980).

Brescia (ancient **Brixia**) town in Lombardy, northern Italy, 84 km/52 mi east of Milan; population (1992) 192,900. Industries include precision engineering, brewing, and the manufacture of iron, steel, machine tools, transport equipment, firearms, metal products, and textiles. It has medieval walls and two cathedrals (12th and 17th century).

Breslau German name of ▷Wrocław, a city in Poland.

Brest city and river port in Belarus, capital and economic and cultural centre of Brest oblast, at the junction of the Western Bug and Mukhavets rivers and near the Polish frontier; population (1990) 268,800. Situated 346 km/215 mi southwest of Minsk, it is a busy centre of rail and road communications, and its industries include engineering and textile manufature. Brest was a Polish town until 1795 when it was acquired by Russia, and reverted to Poland (1919–39). In World War I, the Russian truce with the Central Powers, the Treaty of ▷Brest-Litovsk (an older Russian name for the city), was signed here in March 1918.

Brest naval base and industrial port in the *département* of Finistère, situated on two hills separated by the River Penfeld at **Rade de Brest** (Brest Roads), a great bay whose only entrance is a narrow channel, at the western extremity of Brittany in northwest France; population (1990) 201,500. The town has a naval academy, several schools of nautical science, a university and an oceanographic research centre. Industries include electronics, shipbuilding and the manufacture of chemicals and paper. Occupied as a U-boat base by the Germans from 1940 to 1944, part of the old city was destroyed by Allied bombing and the retreating Germans.

Brest-Litovsk, Treaty of bilateral treaty signed on 3 March 1918 between Russia and Germany, Austria-Hungary, and their allies. Under its terms, Russia agreed to recognize the independence of Georgia, Ukraine, Poland, and the Baltic States, and to pay heavy compensation. Under the November 1918 armistice that ended World War I, it was annulled, since Russia was one of the winning allies.

Bretagne French form of ▷Brittany, a region of northwest France.

Brétigny, Treaty of treaty made between Edward III of England and John II of France in 1360 at the end of the first phase of the Hundred Years' War, under which Edward received Aquitaine and its dependencies in exchange for renunciation of his claim to the French throne.

Breton, André (1896–1966) French writer and poet. He was among the leaders of the ▷Dada art movement and was also a founder of surrealism, publishing *Le Manifeste de surréalisme/Surrealist Manifesto* (1924).

Les Champs magnétiques/Magnetic Fields (1921), written with fellow Dadaist Philippe Soupault, was an experiment in automatic writing. Breton soon turned to surrealism. Influenced by communism and the theories of psychoanalyst Sigmund Freud, he believed that on both a personal and a political level surrealist techniques could shatter the inhibiting order and propriety of the conscious mind (bourgeois society) and release deep reserves of creative energy.

Related Web site: 'André Breton and Problems of 20th-Century Culture' http://www.wsws.org/arts/1997/jun1997/breton1.shtml

Breton language member of the Celtic branch of the Indo-European language family; the language of Brittany in France, related to Welsh and Cornish, and descended from the speech of Celts who left Britain as a consequence of the Anglo-Saxon invasions of the 5th and 6th centuries. Officially neglected for centuries, Breton is now a recognized language of France.

Bretton Woods township in New Hampshire, USA, where the United Nations Monetary and Financial Conference was held in 1944 to discuss post-war international payments problems. The agreements reached on financial assistance and measures to stabilize exchange rates led to the creation of the International Bank for Reconstruction and Development in 1945 and the International Monetary Fund (IMF).

Breuer, Josef (1842–1925) Viennese physician, one of the pioneers of psychoanalysis. He applied it successfully to cases of hysteria, and collaborated with ▷Freud on *Studien über Hysterie/Studies in Hysteria* (1895).

Breuer, Marcel (Lajos) (1902–1981) Hungarian-born US architect and designer. He studied and taught at the ▷Bauhaus school in Germany. His tubular steel chair, known as the Wassily chair (1925), was the first of its kind. He moved to England, then to the USA, where he was in partnership with Walter ▷Gropius (1937–40). His buildings show an affinity with natural materials, as exemplified in the Bijenkorf, Rotterdam, the Netherlands (with Elzas; 1953).

brewing making of beer, ale, or other alcoholic beverage, from ▷malt and ▷barley by steeping (mashing), boiling, and fermenting. Mashing the barley releases its sugars. Yeast is then added, which contains the enzymes needed to convert the sugars into ethanol (alcohol) and carbon dioxide. Hops are added to give a bitter taste.

BREWING A brewery in Venezuela. After mashing (steeping) the barley, the resultant liquid, wort, is boiled in large copper vats to sterilize and concentrate it before the addition of hops. *Image Bank*

Brewster, David (1781–1868) Scottish physicist who made discoveries about the diffraction and polarization of light, and invented the kaleidoscope in 1816. He was knighted in 1831.

Brezhnev, Leonid Ilyich (1906–1982) Soviet leader. A protégé of Joseph Stalin and Nikita Khrushchev, he came to power (after he and Aleksei ▷Kosygin forced Khrushchev to resign) as general secretary of the Communist Party of the Soviet Union (CPSU) 1964–82 and was president 1977–82. Domestically he was conservative; abroad the USSR was established as a military and political superpower during the Brezhnev era, extending its influence in Africa and Asia.

Brezhnev, born in the Ukraine, joined the CPSU in the 1920s. In 1938 he was made head of propaganda by the new Ukrainian party chief, Khrushchev, and ascended in the local party hierarchy. After World War II he caught the attention of the CPSU leader Stalin, who inducted Brezhnev into the secretariat and Politburo in 1952. Brezhnev was removed from these posts after Stalin's death in 1953, but returned in 1956 with Khrushchev's patronage. In 1960, as criticism of Khrushchev mounted, Brezhnev was moved to the ceremonial post of state president and began to criticize Khrushchev's policies openly.

Brezhnev stepped down as president in 1963 and returned to the Politburo and secretariat. He was elected CPSU general secretary in 1964, when Khrushchev was ousted, and gradually came to dominate the conservative and consensual coalition. In 1977 he regained the additional title of state president under the new constitution.

He suffered an illness (thought to have been a stroke or heart attack) March–April 1976 that was believed to have affected his thought and speech so severely that he was not able to make decisions. These were made by his entourage, for example, committing troops to Afghanistan to prop up the government. Within the USSR, economic difficulties mounted; the Brezhnev era was a period of caution and stagnation, although outwardly imperialist.

Brian Bóruma (or Brian Boru) (*c*. 941–1014) King of Munster from 976 and high king of Ireland from 999. His campaigns represent the rise of Munster as a power in Ireland, symbolized by his victory over Leinster and the Dublin Norse at Glen Mama in 999. He was renowned as a builder of forts, and this may have been his most significant military legacy. He died in victory over the Vikings at Clontarf in Dublin.

Briand, Aristide (1862–1932) French republican politician, 11 times prime minister 1909–29. A skilful parliamentary tactician and orator, he was seldom out of ministerial office between 1906 and 1932. As foreign minister 1925–32, he was the architect, with the German chancellor Gustav Stresemann, of the 1925 Locarno Pact (settling Germany's western frontier) and the 1928 Kellogg–Briand Pact (renouncing war). In 1930 he outlined an early scheme for the political and economic unification of Europe. He shared the Nobel Prize for Peace in 1926 with Stresemann for their work for European reconciliation.

bribery corruptly receiving or agreeing to receive, giving or promising to give, any gift, loan, fee, reward, or advantage as an inducement or reward to persons in certain positions of trust. For example, it is an offence to improperly influence in this way judges or other judicial officers, members and officers of public bodies, or voters at public elections.

brick common block-shaped building material, with all opposite sides parallel. It is made of clay that has been fired in a kiln. Bricks are made by kneading a mixture of crushed clay and other materials into a stiff mud and extruding it into a ribbon. The ribbon is cut into individual bricks, which are fired at a temperature of up to about 1,000°C/1,800°F. Bricks may alternatively be pressed into shape in moulds.

bridewealth (or bride price) goods or property presented by a man's family to his prospective wife's family as part of the marriage agreement. It is common practice among many societies in Africa, Asia, and the Pacific, and some American Indian groups. In most European and South Asian countries the alternative custom is ▷dowry.

bridge structure that provides a continuous path or road over water, valleys, ravines, or above other roads. The basic designs and composites of these are based on the way they bear the weight of the structure and its load. **Beam**, or **girder**, bridges are supported at each end by the ground with the weight thrusting downwards. **Cantilever** bridges are a complex form of girder in which only one end is supported. **Arch** bridges thrust outwards and downwards at their ends. **Suspension** bridges use cables under tension to pull inwards against anchorages on either side of the span, so that the roadway hangs from the main cables by the network of vertical cables. The **cable-stayed** bridge relies on diagonal cables connected directly between the bridge deck and supporting towers at each end. Some bridges are too low to allow traffic to pass beneath easily, so they are designed with movable parts, like swing and draw bridges.
Related Web site: Bridges: Panoramic Photographs, 1851–1991 http://lcweb2.loc.gov/cgi-bin/query/r?ammem/pan:FIELD(SUBJ+band(+Bridges+))

bridge card game derived from whist. First played among members of the Indian Civil Service about 1900, bridge was brought to England in 1903 and played at the Portland Club in 1908. It is played in two forms: auction bridge and contract bridge.

Bridgend unitary authority in south Wales created in 1996 from part of the former county of Mid Glamorgan.
area 40 sq km/15 sq mi **towns** Bridgend (administrative headquarters), Porthcawl (resort and residential area), Maesteg

physical most of the authority consists of the western end of a lowland plateau, Bro Morgannwg, a rich agricultural area of mixed farming and large villages; in the north is the Cymer Forest and Mynydd Caerau (556 m/1,824 ft) **industries** civil engineering; chocolate manufacture **population** (1996) 128,300

Bridges, Robert Seymour (1844–1930) English poet and critic. He was poet laureate from 1913 to 1930. His topographical poems and lyrics, which he began to publish in 1873, demonstrate a great command of rhythm and melody. He wrote *The Testament of Beauty* (1929), a long philosophical poem. In 1918 he edited and published posthumously the poems of Gerard Manley ▷Hopkins.

Bridgetown port and capital of Barbados; population (1995 est) 6,100. It lies in the southwest of the island on Carlisle Bay and to the northwest includes a recently built deep water harbour, through which the products of traditional sugar manufacturing are exported. Tourism is also an important industry, and to the north

cantilever bridge

arch bridge

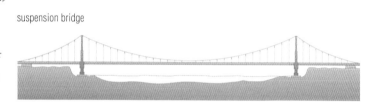

suspension bridge

cable-stayed bridge

truss girder bridge

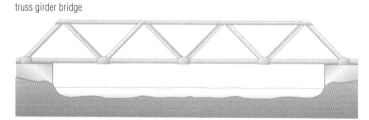

clapper bridge

BRIDGE Clapper bridges were some of the earliest bridges. Bridges need to be designed to support their own weight and the weight of traffic over them, so upward forces must considerably outweigh downward forces. They also have to resist torsion (twisting force) and withstand strong winds and the movement of traffic crossing.

of Bridgetown is the resort of Paradise Beach. Bridgetown was founded in 1628.

A campus of the University of the West Indies in the town dates from 1963. Bridgetown was the birthplace of Edward Braithwaite, the poet and historian, and of the cricketers Clyde Walcott and Sir Frank Worrell.

Bright, John (1811–1889) British Liberal politician. He was a campaigner for free trade, peace, and social reform. A Quaker mill-owner, he was among the founders of the Anti-Corn Law League in 1839, and was largely instrumental in securing the passage of the Reform Bill of 1867.

He sat in Gladstone's cabinets as president of the Board of Trade 1868–70 and chancellor of the Duchy of Lancaster 1873–74 and 1880–82, but broke with him over the Irish Home Rule Bill.

After entering Parliament in 1843 Bright led the struggle there for free trade, together with Richard ▷Cobden, which achieved success in 1846. His *laissez-faire* principles also made him a prominent opponent of factory reform. His influence was constantly exerted on behalf of peace, as when he opposed the Crimean War, Palmerston's aggressive policy in China, Disraeli's anti-Russian policy, and the bombardment of Alexandria. During the American Civil War he was outspoken in support of the North. Bright owed much of his influence to his skill as a speaker.

Brighton seaside resort in ▷Brighton and Hove unitary authority, on the south coast of England; population (1994 est) 155,000. The city was part of the county of East Sussex until 1997. It is an education and service centre with two universities, language schools, and tourist and conference business facilities.

The city developed in the 18th century as a fashionable health resort patronized, from 1783, by the Prince of Wales (later George IV). The Royal Pavilion, extensively remodelled by John Nash between 1815 and 1822 in a mixture of classical and oriental styles, reopened in 1990 after nine years of restoration. Other features include the Palace Pier and an aquarium.

BRIGHTON The Royal Pavilion, Brighton, rebuilt by John Nash for the pleasure-loving Prince of Wales (later George IV). Nash was the Prince's favourite architect. The exotic hybrid of classical and oriental styles that he employed has been called 'Hindoo-Gothic'. *Philip Sauvain Picture Collection*

Brighton and Hove unitary authority in southern England, created in 1997.
area 84 sq km/32 sq mi **towns** Brighton, Hove (administrative headquarters), Woodingdean, Rottingdean, Portslade-by-Sea **features** English Channel; South Downs; Royal Pavilion (Brighton) redesigned and enlarged by John Nash in the 19th century; Palace Pier and West Pier (Brighton); Hollingbury Castle fort; Booth Museum of Natural History (Brighton); British Engineerium (Hove) **industries** financial services (including American Express), tourism, conference facilities, language schools **population** (2000) 258,100 **famous people** Martin Ryle
Related Web site: Virtual Brighton and Hove http://www.brighton.co.uk/

brill flatfish *Scophthalmus laevis*, living in shallow water over sandy bottoms in the northeastern Atlantic and Mediterranean. It is a freckled sandy brown, and grows to 60 cm/2 ft.

Brisbane capital and chief port of the state of ▷Queensland, Australia; population (1996) 1,291,157. Brisbane is situated on the east coast of Australia, 14 km/9 mi inland of the mouth of the River Brisbane, about 29 km/18 mi south of Moreton Bay. It is the third-largest city in Australia, and the financial and commercial centre for Queensland; it has diverse industries including shipbuilding, engineering, brewing, food processing, tobacco production, tanning, the manufacture of agricultural machinery, shoes, and clothing. Tourism is also important. A pipeline from Moonie carries oil for refining. Brisbane has three universities, Queensland University (1909), Griffith University (1975), and Queensland University of Technology (1989).

BRISBANE A view of Brisbane, on the coast of eastern Australia. *Image Bank*

Brisbane was founded as a penal colony (moved from its original site at Moreton Bay in 1825), and named after the Scottish astronomer Sir Thomas Brisbane, governor of New South Wales 1821–5. Notable buildings include Parliament House, City Hall, and the Windmill, Brisbane's oldest building.

Related Web site: Brisbane City Life http://www.maxlink.com.au/bcl/

Brissot, Jacques Pierre (1754–1793) French revolutionary leader, born in Chartres. He became a member of the legislative assembly and the National Convention, but his party of moderate republicans, the ▷Girondins, or Brissotins, fell foul of Robespierre, and Brissot was guillotined.

bristlecone pine the oldest living species of ▷pine tree.

bristletail primitive wingless insect of the order Thysanura. Up to 2 cm/0.8 in long, bristletails have a body tapering from front to back, two long antennae, and three 'tails' at the rear end. They include the **silverfish** *Lepisma saccharina* and the **firebrat** *Thermobia domestica*. Two-tailed bristletails constitute another insect order, the Diplura. They live under stones and fallen branches, feeding on decaying material.

BRISTLETAIL Silverfish *Lepisma saccharina* on a household rug feeding on food scraps and other bits of domestic detritus. *Dr Rod Preston-Mafham/Premaphotos Wildlife*

bristle-worm (or polychaete) segmented worm of the class Polychaeta, characterized by having a pair of fleshy paddles (parapodia) on each segment, together with prominent bristles (setae), and a well-developed head with a pair each of eyes, antennae, and palps. Most bristle-worms are marine, and live in burrows in sand and mud or in rock crevices and under stones. More than 5,300 species are recognized.

Bristol industrial port and unitary authority in southwest England, at the junction of the rivers Avon and Frome; it was part of the former county of Avon to 1996.

area 109 sq km/42 sq mi **features** new city centre, with British engineer and inventor Isambard Kingdom ▷Brunel's Temple Meads railway station as its focus; old docks have been redeveloped for housing and industry; there is a 12th-century cathedral and 13th–14th-century St Mary Redcliffe church; National Lifeboat Museum; Clifton Suspension Bridge (completed in 1864), designed by Brunel; aerospace complex in the suburb of Filton; University of Bristol (founded in 1909) and University of the West of England (established in 1992), formerly the Bristol Polytechnic; Ashton Court mansion, which hosts the annual International Balloon Fiesta and North Somerset show; Bristol 2000, a Millennium Commission Landmark Project in the city's harbour area, includes Wildscreen

World, the world's first electronic zoo **industries** engineering, microelectronics, tobacco, printing, metal refining, banking, insurance, sugar refining, and the manufacture of aircraft engines, chemicals, paper, soap, Bristol 'blue' glass, and chocolate **population** (1996) 374,300, urban area (1991) 516,500 **famous people** Thomas Chatterton, W G Grace, Cary Grant **Related Web site: Bristol City Council** http://www.bristol-city.gov.uk/

Britain island off the north-west coast of Europe, one of the British Isles. It comprises England, Scotland, and Wales (together officially known as ▷Great Britain), and is part of the ▷United Kingdom. The name is also sometimes used loosely to denote the United Kingdom. It is derived from the Roman name for the island **Britannia**, which in turn is derived from the ancient Celtic name for the inhabitants, *Bryttas*.

Britain, ancient period in the British Isles (excluding Ireland) extending through prehistory to the Roman occupation (1st century AD). Settled agricultural life evolved in Britain during the 3rd millennium BC. A peak was reached in Neolithic society in southern England early in the 2nd millennium BC, with the construction of the great stone circles of Avebury and Stonehenge. It was succeeded in central southern Britain by the Early Bronze Age Wessex culture, with strong trade links across Europe. The Iron Age culture of the Celts was predominant in the last few centuries BC, and the Belgae (of mixed Germanic and Celtic stock) were partially Romanized in the century between the first Roman invasion of Britain under Julius Caesar (54 BC) and the Roman conquest (AD 43). For later history, see ▷Roman Britain; ▷United Kingdom.

At the end of the last Ice Age, Britain had a cave-dwelling population of Palaeolithic hunter-gatherers, whose culture was called Creswellian, after Creswell Crags, Derbyshire, where remains of flint tools were found. Throughout prehistory successive waves of migrants from continental Europe accelerated or introduced cultural innovations. Important Neolithic remains include: the stone houses of Skara Brae, Orkney; so-called causewayed camps in which hilltops such as Windmill Hill, Wiltshire, were enclosed by concentric fortifications of ditches and banks; the first stages of the construction of the ritual monuments known as henges (for example, Stonehenge, Woodhenge); and the flint mines at Grimes Graves, Norfolk. Burial of the dead was in elongated earth mounds (long barrows).

The ▷Beaker people probably introduced copper working to the British Isles. The aristocratic society of the Bronze Age Wessex culture of southern England is characterized by its circular burial mounds (round barrows); the dead were either buried or cremated, and cremated remains were placed in pottery urns. Later invaders were the ▷Celts, a warrior aristocracy with an Iron Age technology; they introduced horse-drawn chariots, had their own distinctive art forms (see ▷Celtic art), and occupied fortified hilltops. The Belgae, who buried the ashes of their dead in richly furnished flat graves, were responsible for the earliest British sites large and complex enough to be called towns; settled in southern Britain, the Belgae resisted the Romans from centres such as Maiden Castle, Dorset.

Britain, Battle of World War II air battle between German and British air forces over Britain from 10 July to 31 October 1940.

Related Web site: Battle of Britain http://www.geocities.com/Pentagon/4143/

Britannicus, Tiberius Claudius Caesar (*c.* AD 41–55) Roman prince, son of the Emperor Claudius and Messalina; so-called from his father's conquest of Britain. He was poisoned by Nero.

British Broadcasting Corporation (BBC) the UK state-owned broadcasting network. It operates television and national and local radio stations, and is financed by the sale of television (originally radio) licences. It is not permitted to carry advertisements

but it has an additional source of income through its publishing interests and the sales of its programmes. The BBC is controlled by a board of governors, each appointed by the government for five years. The BBC was converted from a private company (established in 1922) to a public corporation under royal charter in 1927. Under the charter, news programmes were required to be politically impartial. The first director-general was John Reith from 1922 to 1938.

Related Web site: BBC Online http://www.bbc.co.uk

British Columbia most westerly, and only Pacific, province of Canada. It is bordered on the east by Alberta, with the Continental Divide in the Rocky Mountains forming its southeastern boundary. To the south, it has a frontier along the 49th Parallel with the US states of Montana, Idaho, and Washington. To the north, along the 60th Parallel, lie the Northwest Territories and Yukon Territory. British Columbia borders in the northwest on the panhandle of Alaska for about half its length (the other half forming the frontier with Yukon Territory); area 947,800 sq km/365,851 sq mi; population (2001 est) 3,907,700. The capital is ▷Victoria; other main cities and towns are Vancouver, Prince George, Kamloops, Kelowna, Surrey, Richmond, and Nanaimo. British Columbia is mostly mountainous and over half the land is forested; it has a deeply indented coastline, over 80 major lakes, and numerous rivers, including the Fraser and Columbia. Chief industries are lumbering and the manufacture of finished wood products, fishing, mining (coal, copper, iron, lead), extraction of oil and natural gas, and hydroelectric power generation; there is also fruit and vegetable growing.

The region that is now British Columbia was originally home to numerous small Salishan- and Wakashan-speaking groups, chiefly resident along the coast. Europeans (the Spanish and English) first sighted the area in the 1770s. While searching for the Northwest Passage, Captain James Cook explored the coast in 1778 and, after some conflict with the Spanish around Nootka Sound, the region was brought under British control by a 1790 convention. Operatives of both the North West Company (NWC; including Alexander Mackenzie and Simon Fraser) and the Hudson's Bay Company (HBC) were soon exploring its rivers and coastline. In 1821, the two trading concerns combined under the HBC banner.

As part of the huge Oregon Country, the lower coast was the subject of disputes with US interests until the 1846 treaty that established the 49th Parallel as British Columbia's southern boundary. Vancouver Island formally became the first British colony in the region, with Victoria as its capital, in 1849. In 1858 the Cariboo gold rush brought an new influx of settlers to the mainland, which, together with the Queen Charlotte Islands, became a second colony, briefly known as New Caledonia. In 1866 Vancouver Island and the mainland colony were united; New Westminster was the first capital, but was replaced by Victoria in 1868.

In 1871, the HBC relinquished its rights over the area, and British Columbia joined the Confederation. Eager to reinforce its sovereignty in the face of possible US encroachment, the new Dominion of Canada had announced that it would build an intercontinental railway to connect British Columbia with the east. Accordingly, in 1885 the 'last spike' was driven at Craigellachie on the Canadian Pacific Railway line through Kicking Horse Pass in the Rockies. Initially, this line terminated at Port Moody, but was quickly extended (by 1887) to the infant city of Vancouver, a lumbering settlement that immediately boomed, becoming Canada's – and by the mid-20th century, North America's – chief Pacific port. The CPR subsequently opened a second, southern line

BRITISH COLUMBIA Herding horses at Douglas Lake ranch in British Columbia, Canada. *Image Bank*

through Crowsnest Pass, an important coal-mining district. In 1915 lines that were later to become part of the Canadian National Railway network were opened through Yellowhead Pass, continuing on to Prince George and the north coast port of Prince Rupert. British Columbia now had connections that allowed it to ship out local and Prairie Province wheat and other products, and to send its own fruits, fish, and minerals east. The opening of the Panama Canal (also in 1915) enhanced the role of Pacific ports. The CPR developed steamship lines that made Vancouver a leading port in Far Eastern trade.

British Council semi-official organization set up in 1934 (royal charter 1940) to promote a wider knowledge of the UK, excluding politics and commerce, and to develop cultural relations with other countries. It employs more than 6,000 people and is represented in 109 countries, running libraries, English-teaching operations, and resource centres.

British East India Company commercial company (1600–1858) chartered by Queen Elizabeth I and given a monopoly of trade between England and the Far East. In the 18th century, the company became, in effect, the ruler of a large part of India, and a form of dual control by the company and a committee responsible to Parliament in London was introduced by Pitt's India Act 1784. The end of the monopoly of China trade came in 1834, and after the ▷Indian Mutiny of 1857–58 the crown took complete control of the government of British India. The India Act 1858 abolished the company.

British Empire empire covering, at its height in the 1920s, about a sixth of the landmass of the Earth, all of its lands recognizing the ▷United Kingdom (UK) as their leader. It consisted of the Empire of India, four self-governing countries known as dominions, and dozens of colonies and territories. The Empire was a source of great pride to the British, who believed that it was an institution for civilizing the world, and for many years Empire Day (24 May) saw celebration throughout the UK. After World War II it

BRITISH EMPIRE A scene from the Indian Mutiny of 1857–58, in a painting by the Scottish painter Orlando Norie. *The Art Archive/Harper Collins Publishers*

began to dissolve as colony after colony became independent, and today the UK has only 13 small dependent territories. With 52 other independent countries, it forms the ▷Commonwealth. Although Britain's monarch is accepted as head of the Commonwealth, most of its member states are republics.

British Empire, Order of the British order of knighthood (see ▷knighthood, orders of) instituted in 1917 by George V. There are military and civil divisions, and the ranks are GBE, Knight Grand Cross or Dame Grand Cross; KBE, Knight Commander; DBE, Dame Commander; CBE, Commander; OBE, Officer; MBE, Member.

British Expeditionary Force (BEF) during World War I (1914–18) the term commonly referred to the British army serving in France and Flanders, although strictly speaking it referred only to the forces sent to France in 1914; during World War II it was also the army in Europe, which was evacuated from Dunkirk, France in 1940.

British Honduras former name (to 1973) of ▷Belize.

British Indian Ocean Territory British colony in the Indian Ocean directly administered by the Foreign and Commonwealth Office, consisting of the Chagos Archipelago some 1,900 km/ 1,200 mi northeast of Mauritius; area 60 sq km/23 sq mi. Copra, salted fish, and tortoiseshell are produced. There is a US naval and air base on Diego Garcia. In 2000 a number of Ilois, British subjects

who had lived on the Chagos islands, claimed that the British government had unlawfully removed them from the islands during the period 1967–73 to allow the US military base to be built. The High Court ruled that they had been unlawfully ejected, and the remaining Ilois, many in exile in Mauritius, began planning to return to the islands.
Related Web site: British Indian Ocean Territory http://www.umsl.edu/services/govdocs/wofact96/45.htm

British Isles group of islands off the northwest coast of Europe, consisting of Great Britain (England, Wales, and Scotland), Ireland, the Channel Islands, the Orkney and Shetland islands, the Isle of Man, and many other islands that are included in various counties, such as the Isle of Wight, Scilly Isles, Lundy Island, and the Inner and Outer Hebrides. The islands are divided from Europe by the North Sea, Strait of Dover, and the English Channel, and face the Atlantic to the west.

British Legion organization to promote the welfare of British veterans of war service and their dependants. Established under the leadership of Douglas Haig in 1921 (royal charter 1925) it became the Royal British Legion in 1971; it is nonpolitical.

British Library national library of the UK. Created in 1973, it comprises the reference division (the former library departments of the British Museum, rehoused in Euston Road, St Pancras, London); lending division at Boston Spa, Yorkshire, from which full text documents and graphics can be sent by satellite link to other countries; bibliographic services division (incorporating the British National Bibliography); and the National Sound Archive in South Kensington, London.

British Museum largest museum of the UK. Founded in 1753, it opened in London in 1759. Rapid additions led to the construction of the present buildings (1823–47). In 1881 the Natural History Museum was transferred to South Kensington.

British Somaliland British protectorate comprising over 176,000 sq km/67,980 sq mi of territory on the Somali coast of East Africa from 1884 until the independence of Somalia in 1960. British authorities were harassed by Somali nationalists under the leadership of Muhammad bin Abdullah Hassan.

British Standards Institution (BSI) UK national standards body. Although government funded, the institution is independent. The BSI interprets international technical standards for the UK, and also sets its own.

British Virgin Islands part of the ▷Virgin Islands group in the West Indies.
Related Web site: British Virgin Islands http://www.umsl.edu/services/govdocs/wofact96/46.htm

Brittain, Vera (Mary) (1893–1970) English socialist writer. She was a nurse to the troops overseas from 1915 to 1919, as told in her book *Testament of Youth* (1933); *Testament of Friendship* (1940) commemorates English novelist Winifred Holtby.

Brittany (French **Bretagne**; Breton **Breiz**) modern region of northwest France and former province, on the Breton peninsula between the Bay of Biscay and the English Channel; area 27,200 sq km/10,499 sq mi; population (1999 est) 2,906,200. A farming region, it includes the *départements* of Côtes-d'Armor, Finistère, Ille-et-Vilaine, and Morbihan. The administrative centre is ▷Rennes, and other towns include Brest, Lorient, Nantes, St-Brieuc, Vannes, and Quimper.

Britten, (Edward) Benjamin, Baron Britten (1913–1976) English composer. He often wrote for the individual voice; for example, the role in the opera *Peter Grimes* (1945), based on verses by George Crabbe, was written for his life companion, the tenor Peter ▷Pears. Among his many works are the *Young Person's Guide to the Orchestra* (1946); the chamber opera *The Rape of Lucretia* (1946); *Billy Budd* (1951); *A Midsummer Night's Dream* (Shakespeare; 1960); and *Death in Venice* (after Thomas Mann; 1973).

Born in Lowestoft, Suffolk, Britten was educated at Gresham's School, Holt, Norfolk. He studied piano with Harold Samuel and composition with Frank Bridge. Later, with a scholarship, he studied under Arthur Benjamin and John Ireland at the Royal College of Music, London. He worked in the USA 1939–42, then returned to England and devoted himself to composing at his home in Aldeburgh, Suffolk, where he and Pears established an annual music festival in 1948. His oratorio *War Requiem* (1961) combines

current name	colonial names and history	colonized	independent
India	British East India Company	18th century–1858	1947
Pakistan	British East India Company	18th century–1858	1947
Myanmar	Burma	1866	1948
Sri Lanka	Portuguese, Dutch 1602–1796; Ceylon 1802–1972	16th century	1948
Ghana	Gold Coast; British Togoland integrated 1956	18th–19th centuries	1957
Nigeria		1861	1960
Cyprus	Turkish to 1878, then British rule	1878	1960
Sierra Leone	British protectorate	1788	1961
Tanzania	German East Africa to 1921; British mandate from League of Nations/UN as Tanganyika	19th century	1961
Jamaica	Spanish to 1655	16th century	1962
Trinidad & Tobago	Spanish 1532–1797; British 1797–1962	1532	1962
Uganda	British protectorate	1894	1962
Kenya	British colony from 1920	1895	1963
Malaysia	British interests from 1786; Federation of Malaya 1957–63	1874	1963
Malawi	British protectorate of Nyasaland 1907–53; Federation of Rhodesia & Nyasaland 1953–64	1891	1964
Malta	French 1798–1814	1798	1964
Zambia	Northern Rhodesia – British protectorate; Federation of Rhodesia & Nyasaland 1953–64	1924	1964
The Gambia		1888	1965
Singapore	Federation of Malaya 1963–65	1858	1965
Guyana	Dutch to 1796; British Guiana 1796–1966	1620	1966
Botswana	Bechuanaland – British protectorate	1885	1966
Lesotho	Basutoland	1868	1966
Bangladesh	British East India Company 18th century–1858; British India 1858–1947; eastern Pakistan 1947–71	18th century	1971
Zimbabwe	Southern Rhodesia from 1923; UDI under Ian Smith 1965–79	1895	1980
Belize	British Honduras	17th century	1981
Hong Kong	Hong Kong	1841	1997 (returned to China)

the liturgical text with poems by Wilfred Owen, and was written for the rededication of Coventry Cathedral in 1962.

Related Web site: Britten, Benjamin http://www.geocities.com/Vienna/Strasse/1523/britten.htm

brittle-star any member of the echinoderm class Ophiuroidea. A brittle-star resembles a starfish, and has a small, central, rounded body and long, flexible, spiny arms used for walking. The small brittle-star *Amphipholis squamata* is greyish, about 4.5 cm/2 in across, and found on sea bottoms worldwide. It broods its young, and its arms can be luminous.

About 2,000 species of brittle-stars and basket-stars, whose arms are tangled and rootlike, are included in this group.

Brno industrial city (chemicals, arms, textiles, machinery) in the Czech Republic; population (1993) 390,000. Now the second-largest city in the Czech Republic, Brno was formerly the capital of the Austrian crown land of Moravia.

broadbill primitive perching bird of the family Eurylaimidae, found in Africa and South Asia. Broadbills are forest birds and are often found near water. They are gregarious and noisy, have brilliant coloration and wide bills, and feed largely on insects.

broadcasting the transmission of sound and vision programmes by ▷radio and ▷television. Broadcasting may be organized under private enterprise, as in the USA, or may operate under a compromise system, as in Britain, where a television and radio service controlled by the state-regulated ▷British Broadcasting Corporation (BBC) operates alongside commercial channels operating under franchises granted by the Independent Television Commission (known as the Independent Broadcasting Authority before 1991) and the Radio Authority.

broad-leaved tree another name for a tree belonging to the ▷angiosperms, such as ash, beech, oak, maple, or birch. The leaves are generally broad and flat, in contrast to the needlelike leaves of most ▷conifers. See also ▷deciduous tree.

Broadmoor special hospital (established in 1863) in Crowthorne, England, for those formerly described as 'criminally insane'. Patients are admitted if considered by a psychiatrist to be both mentally disordered and potentially dangerous.

Broads, Norfolk area of navigable lakes and rivers in England; see ▷Norfolk Broads.

Broadway major avenue in New York running northwest from the tip of Manhattan and crossing Times Square at 42nd Street, at the heart of the theatre district, where Broadway is known as 'the Great White Way'. New York theatres situated outside this area are described as **off-Broadway**; those even smaller and farther away are **off-off-Broadway**, the home of avant-garde and experimental works.

brocade rich woven fabric, produced on a Jacquard loom. It is patterned, normally with more than two colours. Today brocade may be produced from artificial fibres, but it was traditionally made from silk, sometimes with highlights in metal thread.

broccoli variety of ▷cabbage. It contains high levels of the glucosinolate compound glucoraphanin. A breakdown product of this was found to neutralize damage to cells and so help to prevent cancer.

broderie anglaise (French 'English embroidery') embroidered fabric, usually white cotton, in which holes are cut in patterns and oversewn, often to decorate lingerie, shirts, and skirts.

Brodsky, Joseph Alexandrovich (1940–1996) Russian poet. He emigrated to the USA in 1972. His work, often dealing with themes of exile, is admired for its wit and economy of language, particularly in its use of understatement. Many of his poems, written in Russian, have been translated into English (*A Part of Speech* (1980)). Later in his career he also wrote in English. He was awarded the Nobel Prize for Literature in 1987 and became US poet laureate in 1991.

Broglie, Louis Victor Pierre Raymond de (1892–1987) 7th duc de Broglie. French theoretical physicist. He established that all subatomic particles can be described either by particle equations or by wave equations, thus laying the foundations of wave mechanics. He was awarded the Nobel Prize for Physics in 1929 for his discovery of the wavelike nature of electrons. Succeeded as Duke in 1960.

De Broglie's discovery of wave–particle duality enabled physicists to view Einstein's conviction that matter and energy are interconvertible as being fundamental to the structure of matter. The study of matter waves led not only to a much deeper understanding of the nature of the atom but also to explanations of chemical bonds and the practical application of electron waves in electron microscopes.

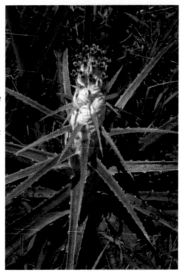

BROMELIAD The large *Bromelia balansae* is one of numerous terrestrial bromeliads present on the sand dunes of the Brazilian coast near Rio; it is also widespread in dry areas inland. *Premaphotos Wildlife*

Broglie, (Louis César Victor) Maurice de (1875–1960) 6th duc de Broglie. French physicist. He worked on X-rays and gamma rays, and helped to establish the Einsteinian description of light in terms of photons. He was the brother of Louis de Broglie.

brolga or **native companion**, Australian crane *Grus rubicunda*, about 1.5 m/5 ft tall, mainly grey with a red patch on the head.

brome grass any of several annual grasses found in temperate regions; some are used as food for horses and cattle, but many are weeds. (Genus *Bromus*, family Gramineae.)

bromeliad any tropical or subtropical plant belonging to the pineapple family, usually with stiff leathery leaves, which are often coloured and patterned, and bright, attractive flower spikes. There are about 1,400 species in tropical America; several are cultivated as greenhouse plants. (Family Bromeliaceae.)

bromine (Greek *bromos* 'stench') dark, reddish-brown, nonmetallic element, a volatile liquid at room temperature, symbol Br, atomic number 35, relative atomic mass 79.904. It is a member of the ▷halogen group, has an unpleasant odour, and is very irritating to mucous membranes. Its salts are known as bromides.

Bromine was formerly extracted from salt beds but is now mostly obtained from sea water, where it occurs in small quantities. Its compounds are used in photography and in the chemical and pharmaceutical industries.

Bromley outer borough of southeast Greater London
Features Crystal Palace, re-erected at Sydenham in 1854 and burned down in 1936, site now partly occupied by the National Sports Centre; 13th-century parish church of SS Peter and Paul; 17th-century Bromley College; chalk caves and tunnels at Chislehurst; Keston Common has a Roman cemetery and traces of a Roman villa; Holwood Park contains 'Caesar's Camp', the site of a British encampment with earthworks dating from *c.* 200 BC. It is the best surviving field monument in Greater London.
Population (1991) 290,600
Famous people William Pitt, H G Wells, W G Grace

JOSEPH BRODSKY A photograph of Joseph Brodsky, the Nobel Prize winner, in 1995, a year before his death. *Archive Photos*

bronchitis inflammation of the bronchi (air passages) of the lungs, usually caused initially by a viral infection, such as a cold or flu. It is aggravated by environmental pollutants, especially smoking, and results in a persistent cough, irritated mucus-secreting glands, and large amounts of sputum.

bronchodilator drug that relieves obstruction of the airways by causing the bronchi and bronchioles to relax and widen. It is most useful in the treatment of ▷asthma.

Bronson, Charles (1922–2003) Stage name of Charles Buchinsky. US film actor. He developed the screen persona of a hard-bitten loner over the years, working in both Hollywood and Europe. His films include *The Magnificent Seven* (1960), *The Great Escape* (1963), *The Dirty Dozen* (1967), Sergio Leone's epic *C'era una volta il West/Once Upon a Time in the West* (1968), and Sean Penn's directorial debut *The Indian Runner* (1991).

Brontë Three English novelists, daughters of a Yorkshire parson. Charlotte (1816–1855), notably with *Jane Eyre* (1847) and *Villette* (1853), reshaped autobiographical material into vivid narrative. Emily (1818–1848) in *Wuthering Heights* (1847) expressed the intensity and nature mysticism which also pervades her poetry (*Poems*, 1846). The more modest talent of Anne (1820–1849) produced *Agnes Grey* (1847) and *The Tenant of Wildfell Hall* (1848).

The Brontës were brought up by an aunt in their father's rectory (now a museum) at Haworth in Yorkshire. In 1846 the sisters published a volume of poems under the pen-names Currer (Charlotte), Ellis (Emily), and Acton (Anne) Bell. In 1847 (using the same names), they published the novels *Jane Eyre*, *Wuthering Heights*, and *Agnes Grey*. During 1848–49 Emily, Anne, and their brother Patrick Branwell (1817–1848) all died of tuberculosis, aided in Branwell's case by alcohol and opium addiction; his portrait of the sisters survives. Charlotte married her father's curate, A B Nicholls, in 1854, and died during pregnancy. The sisters share a memorial in Westminster Abbey, London.

Related Web site: Brontë Sisters http://www2.sbbs.se/hp/cfalk/bronteng.htm

brontosaurus former name of a type of large, plant-eating dinosaur, now better known as ▷apatosaurus.

Bronx, the northernmost borough of ▷New York City, USA, northeast of the Harlem River; area 109 sq km/42 sq mi; population (1990) 1,169,000. The Bronx is bounded on the north by Westchester County, on the east by Long Island Sound, on the south by the East River, and on the west by the Harlem and Hudson rivers; it is largely a residential area. The New York Zoological Society and Gardens are here, popularly called the Bronx Zoo and the Bronx Botanical Gardens. Yankee Stadium, home of the New York Yankees baseball team, is also located here.

bronze alloy of copper and tin, yellow or brown in colour. It is harder than pure copper, more suitable for ▷casting, and also resists ▷corrosion. Bronze may contain as much as 25% tin, together with small amounts of other metals, mainly lead.

Bronze Age stage of prehistory and early history when copper and bronze (an alloy of tin and copper) became the first metals worked extensively and used for tools and weapons. One of the classifications of the Danish archaeologist Christian Thomsen's Three Age System, it developed out of the Stone Age and generally preceded the Iron Age. It first began in the Far East and may be dated 5000–1200 BC in the Middle East and about 2000–500 BC in Europe. Mining and metalworking were the first specialized industries, and the invention of the wheel during this time revolutionized transport. Agricultural productivity (which began during the New Stone Age, or Neolithic period, about 6000 BC) was transformed by the ox-drawn plough, increasing the size of the population that could be supported by farming.

BRONZE AGE A bronze dagger from Bush Barrow, near Stonehenge, Wiltshire, England. Dating to the mid-2nd millennium BC, the dagger is believed to have been imported from Brittany, and therefore attests to the existence of links with Europe in the Bronze Age. *The Art Archive/Musée du Louvre Paris/Dagli Orti*

In some areas, including most of Africa, there was no Bronze Age, and ironworking was introduced directly into the Stone Age economy.

Bronzino, Agnolo (1503–1572) Italian Mannerist painter. He is known for his cool, elegant portraits – *Lucrezia Panciatichi* (*c.* 1540; Uffizi, Florence) is typical – and for the allegory *Venus, Cupid, Folly and Time* (*c.* 1545; National Gallery, London).

Brook, Peter Stephen Paul (1925–) English theatre director with a particularly innovative style. His work with the Royal Shakespeare Company (which he joined in 1962) included a production of Shakespeare's *A Midsummer Night's Dream* (1970), set in a white gymnasium and combining elements of circus and commedia dell'arte. In the same year he founded an independent initiative, Le Centre International de Créations Théâtrales/The International Centre for Theatre Research in Paris. Brook's later productions aim to combine elements from different cultures and include *The Conference of the Birds* (1973), based on a Persian story, and *The Mahabarata* (1985–88), a cycle of three plays based on the Hindu epic.

Brooke, Rupert (Chawner) (1887–1915) English poet. He stands as a symbol of the World War I 'lost generation'. His five war sonnets, including 'The Soldier', were published posthumously. Other notable poems are 'Grantchester' (1912) and 'The Great Lover', written in 1914. Brooke's war sonnets were published in *1914 and Other Poems* (1915); they caught the prevailing early wartime spirit of selfless patriotism.

Brooke was born in Rugby, Warwickshire. He was awarded a fellowship at King's, his own college at Cambridge University, in 1913, but having had a nervous breakdown he travelled abroad. He toured America (*Letters from America*, 1916), New Zealand, and the South Seas, and in 1914 became an officer in the Royal Naval Volunteer Reserve. After fighting at Antwerp, Belgium, he sailed for the Dardanelles, but died of blood poisoning on the Greek island of Skyros, where he is buried.

Related Web site: Collected Poems of Rupert Brooke http://digital.library.upenn.edu/webbin/gutbook/lookup?num=262

Brookeborough, Basil Stanlake Brooke (1888–1973) Viscount Brookeborough. Northern Irish Unionist politician and prime minister 1943–63. He was born in Colebrook, County Fermanagh, and educated at Winchester and Sandhurst. A conservative unionist and staunch advocate of strong links with Britain, he entered the Northern Ireland House of Commons in 1929 and held ministerial posts 1933–45. His regime, particularly in the 1950s and 1960s, saw moderate improvements in economic prosperity and community relations but maintained an illiberal stance towards Northern Ireland's Catholic minority, and made no real attempt at significant political or economic reform.

Brooklyn borough of New York City, USA, occupying the southwestern end of Long Island; area 184 sq km/71 sq mi; population (1990) 2,300,700. It is linked to Manhattan Island by the Brooklyn Bridge (1883), the Williamsburg Bridge (1903), the Manhattan Bridge (1909), and the Brooklyn–Battery Tunnel (1950); and to Staten Island by the Verrazano-Narrows Bridge (1964). Brooklyn is a densely populated residential area, and its waterfront is highly industrialized. There are more than 60 parks here, of which Prospect Park is the largest. There is also a museum, a botanical garden, and a beach and amusement area at Coney Island.

BROOKLYN Pedestrians walking across the Brooklyn Bridge, the suspension bridge between lower Manhattan and Brooklyn Heights, New York, USA. *Archive Photos*

Brookner, Anita (1928–) English novelist and art historian. Her novels include *Hotel du Lac* (1984; Booker Prize), *A Misalliance* (1986), *Latecomers* (1988), *A Closed Eye* (1991), *Family Romance* (1993), *A Private View* (1994), *Incidents in the rue Laugier* (1995), *Altered States* (1996), *Falling Slowly* (1998), and *Undue Influence* (1999). She was Reader at the Courtauld Institute 1977–88, and Slade Professor of Fine Art at Cambridge 1967–68, the first woman to hold the post. In 2000 she published *Romanticism and its Discontents*, a historical survey about the romantic hero in writing and painting.

Brooks, Louise (1906–1985) US actor. Her dark, enigmatic beauty can be seen in silent films such as *A Girl in Every Port* (1928) and *Die Büchse der Pandora/Pandora's Box* and *Das Tagebuch einer Verlorenen/The Diary of a Lost Girl* (both 1929), both directed by G W Pabst. At 25 she had appeared in 17 films. She retired from the screen in 1938.

Brooks, Mel (1926–) Stage name of Melvin Kaminsky. US film director and comedian. His films, known for their madcap slapstick and verbal humour, include *The Producers* (1968), which won an Academy Award for Best Screenplay, *Blazing Saddles* (1974), and *Dracula: Dead and Loving It* (1995).

broom any of a group of shrubs (especially species of *Cytisus* and *Spartium*), often cultivated for their bright yellow flowers. (Family Leguminosae.)

Related Web site: Broom http://www.botanical.com/botanical/mgmh/b/broom-70.html

Brown, Capability (Lancelot) (1716–1783) English landscape gardener and architect. He acquired his nickname because of his continual enthusiasm for the 'capabilities' of natural landscapes. He worked on or improved the gardens of many great houses and estates, including Hampton Court; Kew; Blenheim, Oxfordshire; Stowe, Buckinghamshire; and Petworth, West Sussex, occasionally contributing to the architectural designs.

Brown, Earle (1926–2002) US composer. He pioneered ▷graph notation (a method of notating controlled improvisation by graphical means) and mobile form during the 1950s, as in *Available Forms II* (1962) for ensemble and two conductors. He was an associate of John ▷Cage and was influenced by the visual arts, especially the work of Alexander Calder and Jackson Pollock.

Brown, Ford Madox (1821–1893) English painter, associated with the ▷Pre-Raphaelite Brotherhood through his pupil Dante Gabriel Rossetti. His pictures, which include *The Last of England* (1855; City Art Gallery, Birmingham) and *Work* (1852–65; City Art Gallery, Manchester), are characterized by elaborate symbolism and abundance of realistic detail.

He studied under the Belgian painter and engraver Baron Gustaf Wappers (1803–1874) at Antwerp, Belgium, worked for three years in Paris, and was influenced by the German Nazarenes, a group of painters whom he met when visiting Rome in 1845. He settled in London and Rossetti became his pupil in 1848. Although not a member of the English Pre-Raphaelite Brotherhood, he was drawn by Rossetti into its orbit and his works clearly reflect Pre-Raphaelite enthusiasms. His paintings for the town hall in Manchester (1878–93) were a notable effort to interpret local and social history. His later subject pictures, romantic treatments of scenes from history and literature such as *Christ Washing St Peter's Feet* (Tate Gallery, London), are not always harmonious in design and colour, but as a colourist he excels in some small landscapes.

Related Web site: Brown, Ford Madox http://www.oir.ucf.edu/wm/paint/auth/brown/

Brown, (James) Gordon (1951–) British Labour politician, born in Scotland, chancellor of the Exchequer from 1997. He entered Parliament in 1983, rising quickly to the opposition front bench, with a reputation as an outstanding debater. He took over from John Smith as shadow chancellor in 1992. After Smith's death in May 1994, he declined to challenge his close ally Tony Blair for the leadership, retaining his post as shadow chancellor, and assuming the chancellorship after the 1997 general election.

Brown, James (1928–) US rhythm-and-blues and soul singer. He was a pioneer of ▷funk. Staccato horn arrangements and shouted vocals characterize his hits, which include 'Please, Please, Please' (1956), 'Papa's Got a Brand New Bag' (1965), 'Say It Loud, I'm Black and I'm Proud' (1968), 'Sex Machine' (1975), and 'Living In America' (1995). Among Brown's best-loved records is the album, *Live at the Apollo* (1963); an enduring testament to the concert that launched him to celebrity.

Brown, John (1800–1859) US slavery abolitionist. With 18 men, on the night of 16 October 1859, he seized the government arsenal at Harper's Ferry in West Virginia, apparently intending to distribute weapons to runaway slaves who would then defend a mountain stronghold, which Brown hoped would become a republic of former slaves. On 18 October the arsenal was stormed by US Marines under Col Robert E ▷Lee. Brown was tried and hanged at Charlestown on 2 December, becoming a martyr and the hero of the popular song 'John Brown's Body'.

Brown, Robert (1773–1858) Scottish botanist who in 1827 discovered ▷Brownian motion. As a botanist, his more lasting work was in the field of plant morphology. He was the first to establish the real basis for the distinction between gymnosperms (pines) and angiosperms (flowering plants).

brown dwarf in astronomy, an object less massive than a star, but heavier than a planet. Brown dwarfs do not have enough mass to ignite nuclear reactions at their centres, but shine by heat released during their contraction from a gas cloud. Groups of brown dwarfs have been discovered recently, and some astronomers believe that vast numbers of them exist throughout the Galaxy.

The first brown dwarf to be positively identified was Gliese 229B (GI229B), in the constellation Lepus, by US astonomers using images from the Hubble Space Telescope. It is about 50 times as massive as Jupiter but emits only 1% of the radiation of the smallest known star and has a surface temperature of 650°C.

Browne, Thomas (1605–1682) English writer and physician. His works display a richness of style and an enquiring mind. They include *Religio medici/The Religion of a Doctor* (1643), a justification of his profession; 'Vulgar Errors' (1646), an examination of popular legend and superstition; and *Urn Burial* and *The Garden of Cyrus* (both 1658).

Thomas Browne
No man can justly censure or condemn another, because indeed no man truly knows another.
Religio Medici

On becoming chancellor in 1997, he ceded to the Bank of England full control of interest rates. He used his position as chancellor to promote key initiatives, notably the 'welfare to work' programme directed against unemployment and funded by a windfall tax imposed on privatized utilities. He gained the reputation of being an 'iron chancellor', maintaining firm control over public expenditure. This led to criticisms within his party from those seeking more funds for welfare reform and the National Health Service.

Brown was born in Kirkcaldy, Fife, the son of a Church of Scotland minister. He won a first in history at Edinburgh University before he was 20. After four years as a college lecturer and three as a television journalist, he entered the House of Commons as MP for Dunfermline East in 1983.

Despite losing the sight of one eye in a sporting accident, he is an avid reader and meticulous researcher and this, with his formidable debating skills, made his rise within the Labour Party unusually swift.

Brownian movement the continuous random motion of particles in a fluid medium (gas or liquid) as they are subjected to impact from the molecules of the medium. The phenomenon was explained by German physicist Albert Einstein in 1905 but was observed as long ago as 1827 by the Scottish botanist Robert Brown. Brown was looking at pollen grains in water under a microscope when he noticed the pollen grains were in constant, haphazard motion. The motion of these particles was due to the impact of moving water molecules. It provides evidence for the ▷kinetic theory of matter. See diagram on p. 136.

Browning, Elizabeth (Moulton) Barrett (1806–1861) English poet. In 1844 she published *Poems* (including 'The Cry of the Children'), which led to her friendship with and secret marriage to Robert ▷Browning in 1846. She wrote *Sonnets from the Portuguese* (1850), a collection of love lyrics, during their courtship. She wrote strong verse about social injustice and oppression in Victorian England, and she was a learned, fiery, and metrically experimental poet.

Anita Brookner
No blame should attach to telling the truth. But it does, it does.
A Friend from England ch. 10

Elizabeth Barrett was born near Durham. She suffered illness as a child, led a sheltered and restricted life, and was from the age of 13 regarded by her father as an invalid. She was freed from her father's oppressive influence by her marriage and move to Italy, where her health improved and she produced her mature works. See picture on p. 136.

Related Web site: Elizabeth Barrett Browning: An Overview http://landow.stg.brown.edu/victorian/ebb/browningov.html

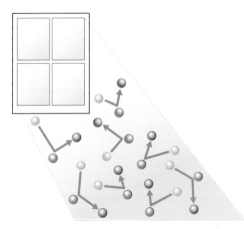

BROWNIAN MOVEMENT The irregular movement of dust particles becomes visible in the air when the particles are caught in a ray of sunlight. The tiny dust particles move randomly as they are buffeted by gas molecules in the atmosphere, which are too small to be seen with the naked eye. See entry on p. 135.

Browning, Robert (1812–1889) English poet. His work is characterized by the accomplished use of dramatic monologue (in which a single imaginary speaker reveals his or her character, thoughts, and situation) and an interest in obscure literary and historical figures. It includes *Pippa Passes* (1841) (written in dramatic form) and the poems 'The Pied Piper of Hamelin' (1842), 'My Last Duchess' (1842), 'Home Thoughts from Abroad' (1845), and 'Rabbi Ben Ezra' (1864). He was married to Elizabeth Barrett ▷Browning.

From 1837 Browning achieved moderate success with his play *Strafford* and several other works, though the narrative poem *Sordello* (1840) was initially criticized. In the pamphlet series *Bells and Pomegranates* (1841–46), which contained *Pippa Passes*, *Dramatic Lyrics* (1842), and *Dramatic Romances* (1845), he included the dramas *King Victor and King Charles* (1842), *Return of the Druses* (1843), and *Colombe's Birthday* (1844).

In 1845 he met Elizabeth Barrett; they eloped the following year and went to Italy. There he wrote *Christmas Eve and Easter Day* (1850) and much of *Men and Women* (1855), the latter containing some of his finest

> ### Robert Browning
> *That's the wise thrush; he sings each song twice over, / Lest you should think he never could recapture / The first fine careless rapture!*
>
> 'Home Thoughts from Abroad'

love poems and dramatic monologues. He published no further collection of verse until *Dramatis Personae* (1864), which was followed by *The Ring and the Book* (1868–69), based on an Italian murder story.

After his wife's death in 1861 Browning settled in England and enjoyed an established reputation, although his later works, such as *Red-Cotton Night-Cap Country* (1873), *Dramatic Idylls* (1879–80), and *Asolando* (1889), prompted opposition by their rugged obscurity of style.

Brownshirts the SA (*Sturmabteilung*) or Storm Troops, the private army of the German Nazi party, who derived their name from the colour of their uniform.

browser in computing, any program that allows the user to search for and view data. Browsers are usually limited to a particular type of data, so, for example, a graphics browser will display graphics files stored in many different file formats. Browsers usually do not permit the user to edit data, but are sometimes able to convert data from one file format to another.

Web browsers allow access to the World Wide Web. Netscape Navigator and Microsoft's Internet Explorer were the leading Web browsers in 2000. They act as a graphical user interface to information available on the Internet – reading HTML (hypertext markup language) documents and displaying them as graphical documents which may include images, video, sound, and ▷hypertext links to other documents.

Bruce one of the chief Scottish noble houses. ▷Robert (I) the Bruce and his son, David II, were both kings of Scotland descended from Robert de Bruis (died 1094), a Norman knight who arrived in England with William the Conqueror in 1066.

Bruce, Christopher (1945–) English choreographer and dancer. He became artistic director of the Rambert Dance Company in 1994. His work integrates modern and classical idioms and often chooses political or socially conscious themes, as in *Ghost Dances* (1981), which treats the theme of political oppression. Other works include *Cruel Garden* (1977), *Sergeant Early's Dream* (1984), *The Dream is Over* (1987) – a tribute to John Lennon, *Swansong* (1987), *Rooster* (1991), *Moonshine* (1993), *Quicksilver* (1996) – a tribute to Marie Rambert, and *Four Scenes* (1998), created for the opening of the new Sadler's Wells theatre in October 1998.

Bruce, James (1730–1794) Scottish explorer who, in 1770, was the first European to reach the source of the Blue Nile and, in 1773, to follow the river downstream to Cairo.

Bruce, Robert King of Scotland; see ▷Robert (I) the Bruce.

brucellosis disease of cattle, goats, and pigs, also known when transmitted to humans as **undulant fever** since it remains in the body and recurs. It was named after Australian doctor David Bruce (1855–1931), and is caused by bacteria (genus *Brucella*). It is transmitted by contact with an infected animal or by drinking contaminated milk.

Brücke, die (German 'the bridge') group of German expressionist artists (see ▷expressionism) active from 1905 to 1913, originally in Dresden, and later in Berlin. The members chose the name because they wanted to create a bridge to a new, creative future, and their work represented a rebellion against middle-class conventions and an attempt to create art that was in tune with modern life. They formed the first conscious modern movement in German art and were very influential.

Bruckner, (Josef) Anton (1824–1896) Austrian Romantic composer. He was cathedral organist at Linz 1856–68, and professor at the Vienna Conservatory from 1868. His works include many choral pieces and 11 symphonies, the last unfinished. His compositions were influenced by Wagner and Beethoven.

Brüderhof (German 'Society of Brothers') Christian Protestant sect with beliefs similar to the ▷Mennonites. They live in groups of families (single persons are assigned to a family), marry only within the sect (divorce is not allowed), and retain a 'modest' dress for women (cap or headscarf, and long skirts). In the USA they are known as Hutterites.

Brueghel (or Bruegel) Family of Flemish painters. Pieter Brueghel the Elder (*c*. 1525–1569) was one of the greatest artists of his time. His pictures of peasant life helped to establish genre painting, and he also popularized works illustrating proverbs, such as *The Blind Leading the Blind* (1568; Museo di Capodimonte, Naples). A contemporary taste for the macabre can be seen in *The Triumph of Death* (1562; Prado, Madrid), which clearly shows the influence of Hieronymus Bosch. One of his best-known works is *Hunters in the Snow* (1565; Kunsthistorisches Museum, Vienna).

ANTON BRUCKNER Success came late in Austrian composer Anton Bruckner's life, but since his death he has been increasingly admired for his intricate counterpoint and expressive orchestration. *The Art Archive/Society Friends Music Vienna/Dagli Orti*

The elder Pieter was nicknamed 'Peasant' Brueghel, referring to the subjects of his paintings. Two of his sons were also painters. Pieter Brueghel the Younger (1564–1638), called 'Hell' Brueghel, specialized in religious subjects, and another son, Jan Brueghel (1568–1625), called 'Velvet' Brueghel, painted flowers, landscapes, and seascapes.

Related Web site: Brueghel, Pieter the Elder http://mexplaza.udg.mx/wm/paint/auth/bruegel/

Bruges (Flemish **Brugge**) historic city in northwest Belgium; capital of West Flanders province, about 96 km/60 mi northwest of Brussels and 16 km/10 mi from the North Sea, to which it is connected by canal; population (1997) 115,500. The port handles coal, iron ore, oil, and fish; local industries include lace, textiles, paint, steel, beer, furniture, motors, and tourism. Bruges was the capital of medieval ▷Flanders and was mainland Europe's major wool producing town as well as its chief market town.

Related Web site: Staad Brugge http://www.brugge.be/toerisme/en/index.htm

Brugge Flemish form of ▷Bruges, a city in Belgium.

Brundtland, Gro Harlem (1939–) Norwegian Labour politician, head of the World Health Organization (WHO) from 1998. Environment minister 1974–76, she briefly took over as prime minister in 1981, a post to which she was re-elected in 1986, in 1990, and again held 1993–96, when she resigned. Leader of the Norwegian Labour Party from 1981, she resigned the post in 1992 but continued as prime minister. Retaining her seat count in the 1993 general election, she led a minority Labour government committed to European Union membership, but failed to secure backing for the membership application in a 1994 national referendum. She was chosen as the new leader of the WHO in 1998.

Brunei see country box.

Brunel, Isambard Kingdom (1806–1859) English engineer and inventor. In 1833 he became engineer to the Great Western Railway, which adopted the 2.1-m/7-ft gauge on his advice. He built the Clifton Suspension Bridge over the River Avon at Bristol and the Saltash Bridge over the River Tamar near Plymouth. His shipbuilding designs include the *Great Western* (1837), the first steamship to cross the Atlantic regularly; the *Great Britain* (1843), the first large iron ship to have a screw propeller; and the *Great Eastern* (1858), which laid the first transatlantic telegraph cable.

The son of Marc Brunel, he made major contributions in shipbuilding and bridge construction, and assisted his father in the Thames tunnel project. Brunel University in Uxbridge, London, is named after both father and son.

Brunelleschi, Filippo (1377–1446) Italian Renaissance architect. The first and one of the greatest of the Renaissance architects, he pioneered the scientific use of perspective. He was responsible for the construction of the dome of Florence Cathedral (completed 1436), a feat deemed impossible by many of his contemporaries.

ELIZABETH BARRETT BROWNING Elizabeth Barrett Browning was a Victorian poet whose works are now overshadowed by her more famous husband, Robert Browning. His nickname for her, 'my little Portuguese', reflected her dark, foreign-looking complexion and explains the title of her collection of sonnets, *Sonnets from the Portuguese*. See entry on p. 135. *Archive Photos*

His use of simple geometries and a modified classical language lend his buildings a feeling of tranquillity, to which many other early Renaissance architects aspired. His other works include the Ospedale degli Innocenti (1419) and the Pazzi Chapel (1429), both in Florence.

Brunel, Marc Isambard (1769–1849)

French-born British engineer and inventor, father of Isambard Kingdom Brunel. He constructed the tunnel under the River Thames in London from Wapping to Rotherhithe (1825–43). He was knighted in 1841.

Brunel fled to the USA in 1793 to escape the French Revolution. He became Chief Engineer of New York advising on defence. In 1799 he moved to England to mass-produce marine blocks, which were needed by the navy. Brunel demonstrated that with specially designed machine tools 10 men could do the work of 100, more quickly, more cheaply, and yield a better product. He made a large profit and invested it in sawmills in Battersea, London. Cheating partners and fire damage to the sawmills caused the business to fail and Brunel was imprisoned for debt in 1821. He spent the latter part of his life working on the Rotherhithe tunnel.

Brünn German form of ▷Brno, a city in the Czech Republic.

Bruno, St (c. 1030–1101) German founder of the monastic Catholic ▷Carthusian order. He was born in Cologne, became a priest, and controlled the cathedral school of Rheims from 1057

Filippo Brunelleschi

I wonder, if even the ancients ever raised a vault as daunting as this will be.

On vaulting a church, quoted in Vasari *Lives of the Artists* 1568

---

to 1076. Withdrawing to the mountains near Grenoble after an ecclesiastical controversy, he founded the monastery at Chartreuse in 1084. He was canonized in 1514. His feast day is 6 October.

Bruno, Giordano (1548–1600)

Born Filippo Bruno. Italian philosopher. He entered the Dominican order of monks in 1563, but his sceptical attitude to Catholic doctrines forced him to flee Italy in 1577. He was arrested by the ▷Inquisition in 1593 in Venice and burned at the stake for his adoption of Copernican astronomy and his heretical religious views.

Brunswick

(German **Braunschweig**) former independent duchy, a republic from 1918, which is now part of ▷Lower Saxony, Germany.

Brusa

alternative form of ▷Bursa, a city in Turkey.

Brussels

(Flemish **Brussel**; French **Bruxelles**) city and capital of Belgium and the province of Brabant, situated almost in the centre of the country in the Senne river valley; city population (1997) 133,800; metropolitan/capital region population (1997) 950,600.

FILIPPO BRUNELLESCHI Interior photograph of the dome of the Pazzi chapel in Santa Croce Church, Florence, Italy, designed and built by the architect Filippo Brunelleschi in 1429. *The Art Archive/Santa Croce Florence/Dagli Orti*

Brunei

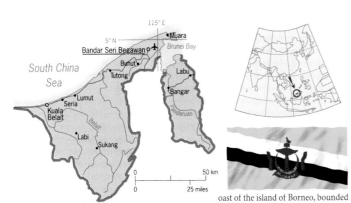

to the landward side by Sarawak and to the northwest by the South China Sea.

oast of the island of Borneo, bounded

NATIONAL NAME *Negara Brunei Darussalam/State of Brunei*
AREA 5,765 sq km/2,225 sq mi
CAPITAL Bandar Seri Begawan (and chief port)
MAJOR TOWNS/CITIES Seria, Kuala Belait
PHYSICAL FEATURES flat coastal plain with hilly lowland in west and mountains in east (Mount Pagon 1,850 m/6,070 ft); 75% of the area is forested; the Limbang valley splits Brunei in two, and its cession to Sarawak in 1890 is disputed by Brunei; tropical climate; Temburong, Tutong, and Belait rivers

Government

HEAD OF STATE AND GOVERNMENT Sultan Muda Hassanal Bolkiah from 1967
POLITICAL SYSTEM absolutist
POLITICAL EXECUTIVE absolute
ADMINISTRATIVE DIVISIONS four districts
ARMED FORCES 7,000; plus paramilitary forces of 3,400 (2002 est)
DEATH PENALTY retains the death penalty for ordinary crimes but can be considered abolitionist in practice; date of last known execution 1957

Economy and resources

CURRENCY Bruneian dollar, although the Singapore dollar is also accepted
GPD (US$) 4.8 billion (2000 est)
REAL GDP GROWTH (% change on previous year) 3.5 (2001)
GNI (US$) 7.6 billion (2000 est)
GNI PER CAPITA (PPP) (US$) 25,320 (2000 est)

CONSUMER PRICE INFLATION 1% (2003 est)
UNEMPLOYMENT 4.6% (1999)
FOREIGN DEBT (US$) 544 million (2001 est)
MAJOR TRADING PARTNERS Singapore, Japan, USA, EU countries, Malaysia, South Korea, Thailand
RESOURCES petroleum, natural gas
INDUSTRIES petroleum refining, textiles, cement, mineral water, canned foods, rubber
EXPORTS crude petroleum, natural gas and refined products, textiles. Principal market: Japan 43.6% (2001)
IMPORTS machinery and transport equipment, basic manufactures, food and live animals, chemicals. Principal source: ASEAN 52.6% (2001)
ARABLE LAND 1% (2000 est)
AGRICULTURAL PRODUCTS rice, cassava, bananas, pineapples, vegetables; fishing; forest resources

Population and society

POPULATION 358,000 (2003 est)
POPULATION GROWTH RATE 1.8% (2000–05)
POPULATION DENSITY (per sq km) 62 (2003 est)
URBAN POPULATION (% of total) 74 (2003 est)
AGE DISTRIBUTION (% of total population) 0–14 31%, 15–59 64%, 60+ 5% (2002 est)
ETHNIC GROUPS 73% indigenous Malays, predominating in government service and agriculture; more than 15% Chinese, predominating in the commercial sphere

LANGUAGE Malay (official), Chinese (Hokkien), English
RELIGION Muslim 66%, Buddhist 14%, Christian 10%
EDUCATION (compulsory years) 12
LITERACY RATE 95% (men); 88% (women) (2003 est)
LABOUR FORCE 1% agriculture, 25% industry, 74% services (1997)
LIFE EXPECTANCY 74 (men); 79 (women) (2000–05)

Chronology

15th century: An Islamic monarchy was established, ruling Brunei and north Borneo, including the Sabah and Sarawak states of Malaysia.
1841: Control of Sarawak was lost.
1888: Brunei became a British protectorate.
1906: Brunei became a British dependency.
1929: Oil was discovered.
1941–45: Brunei was occupied by Japan.
1959: A written constitution made Britain responsible for defence and external affairs.
1962: The sultan began rule by decree after a plan to join the Federation of Malaysia was opposed by a rebellion organized by the Brunei People's Party (BPP).

CHILD MORTALITY RATE (under 5, per 1,000 live births) 6 (2001)
PHYSICIANS (per 1,000 people) 0.8 (1996 est)
TV SETS (per 1,000 people) 637 (1999 est)
RADIOS (per 1,000 people) 302 (1997)
INTERNET USERS (per 10,000 people) 1,023.4 (2002 est)
PERSONAL COMPUTER USERS (per 100 people) 7.7 (2002 est)

See also ▷Borneo.

1967: Hassanal Bolkiah became sultan.
1971: Brunei was given full internal self-government.
1975: A United Nations (UN) resolution called for independence for Brunei.
1984: Independence from Britain was achieved, with Britain maintaining a small force to protect the oil and gas fields.
1985: The Brunei National Democratic Party (BNDP) was legalized.
1986: The multiethnic Brunei National United Party (BNUP) was formed; nonroyals were given key cabinet posts for the first time.
1988: The BNDP and the BNUP were banned.
1991: Brunei joined the nonaligned movement.
1998: Prince Billah was proclaimed heir to the throne.

BRUNEI The Omar Ali Saifuddin Mosque in Bandar Seri Begawan, named after the 28th Sultan of Brunei. With its high, golden dome reaching 52 m/171 ft, it is the tallest building in the capital city. In front of the mosque, in the Brunei River, lies a stone replica of a 16th-century barge. *Photodisk*

Industries include lace, textiles, machinery, and chemicals. It is the headquarters of the European Union (EU) and, since 1967, of the international secretariat of ▷NATO. It contains the Belgian royal seat, the chief courts, the chamber of commerce, and is the centre of the principal banks of the country. Founded on an island in the River Senne *c.* 580, Brussels became a city in 1312, and was declared capital of the Spanish Netherlands in 1530 and of Belgium in 1830.

Features The city has many fine buildings including the 13th-century church of Sainte Gudule; the Hôtel de Ville and Maison du Roi in the Grande Place; and the royal palace. The Musées Royaux des Beaux-Arts de Belgique hold a large art collection. The bronze fountain statue of a tiny naked boy urinating, the *Manneken Pis* (1388), is to be found here. Brussels is also the site of the world's largest cinema complex, with 24 film theatres.

Related Web site: Things to see in Brussels http://pespmc1.vub.ac.be/BRUSSEL.html

Brussels sprout one of the small edible buds along the stem of a variety of ▷cabbage. (*Brassica oleracea* var. *gemmifera.*) They are high in the glucosinolate compound sinigrin. Sinigrin was found to destroy precancerous cells in laboratory rats in 1996.

Brussels, Treaty of pact of an economic, political, cultural, and military alliance established in 17 March 1948, for 50 years, by the UK, France, and the Benelux countries, joined by West Germany and Italy in 1955. It was the forerunner of the North Atlantic Treaty Organization and the European Community (now the European Union).

Bruton, John (1947–) Irish politician, leader of Fine Gael (United Ireland Party) 1990–2001 and prime minister 1994–97. The collapse of Albert ▷Reynolds's Fianna Fáil–Labour government in November 1994 thrust Bruton, as a leader of a new coalition with Labour, into the prime ministerial vacancy. He pledged himself to the continuation of the Anglo-Irish peace process as pursued by his predecessor; in 1995 he pressed for greater urgency in negotiations for a permanent peace agreement. However, his alleged over-willingness to support the British government's cautious approach to the peace process produced strong criticism in April 1995 from the Sinn Fein leader, Gerry Adams.

Brutus, Marcus Junius (*c.* 85 BC–42 BC) Roman senator and general who conspired with ▷Cassius to assassinate Julius ▷Caesar in order to restore the purity of the Republic. He and Cassius were defeated by the united forces of ▷Mark Antony and Octavian at Philippi in 42 BC, and Brutus committed suicide.

Brutus joined the *optimates* (who aimed to increase the authority of the Senate) on the outbreak of civil war in 49 BC, but Caesar pardoned him after the Battle of Pharsalus and made him governor of Cisalpine Gaul in 46 BC and praetor in 44 BC. After Caesar's murder, Brutus spent a short time in Italy before taking possession of his province of Macedonia. He and Cassius raised an army to fight Mark Antony and Octavian, persuading most of the Macedonian forces to join them. In 42 BC they met Antony and Octavian at Philippi. Brutus inflicted a sharp reverse on Octavian's soldiers in the first battle, but could not prevent the defeat and suicide of Cassius. He was defeated in the second battle and killed himself to avoid capture.

Bruxelles French form of ▷Brussels, the capital of Belgium.

bryony either of two climbing hedgerow plants found in Britain: **white bryony** (*Bryonia dioca*) belonging to the gourd family (Cucurbitaceae), and **black bryony** (*Tamus communis*) of the yam family (Dioscoreaceae).

bryophyte member of the Bryophyta, a division of the plant kingdom containing three classes: the Hepaticae (▷liverwort), Musci (▷moss), and Anthocerotae (▷hornwort). Bryophytes are generally small, low-growing, terrestrial plants with no vascular (water-conducting) system as in higher plants. Their life cycle shows a marked ▷alternation of generations. Bryophytes chiefly occur in damp habitats and require water for the dispersal of the male gametes (▷antherozoids).

Brześć nad Bugiem Polish name of ▷Brest, a city in ▷Belarus.

BSE abbreviation for ▷bovine spongiform encephalopathy.

bubble chamber in physics, a device for observing the nature and movement of atomic particles, and their interaction with radiation. It is a vessel filled with a superheated liquid through which ionizing particles move and collide. The paths of these particles are shown by strings of bubbles, which can be photographed and studied. By using a pressurized liquid medium instead of a gas, it overcomes drawbacks inherent in the earlier ▷cloud chamber. It was invented by US physicist Donald Glaser in 1952. See ▷particle detector.

bubble memory in computing, a memory device based on the creation of small 'bubbles' on a magnetic surface. Bubble memories typically store up to 4 megabits (4 million ▷bits) of information. They are not sensitive to shock and vibration, unlike other memory devices such as disk drives, yet, like magnetic disks, they are nonvolatile and do not lose their information when the computer is switched off.

bubonic plague epidemic disease of the Middle Ages; see ▷plague and ▷Black Death.

buccaneer member of any of various groups of seafarers who plundered Spanish ships and colonies on the Spanish American coast in the 17th century. Unlike true pirates, they were acting on (sometimes spurious) commission.

Buchan, John (1875–1940) 1st Baron Tweedsmuir. Scottish writer and politician. His popular adventure stories, today sometimes criticized for their alleged snobbery, sexism, and anti-Semitism, include *The Thirty-Nine Steps*, a tale of espionage published in 1915, *Greenmantle* (1916), and *The Three Hostages* (1924).

He was Conservative member of Parliament for the Scottish universities 1927–35, and governor general of Canada 1935–40. He also wrote historical and biographical works, literary criticism, and poetry. He was created baron in 1935.

Bucharest (Romanian **București**) capital and largest city of Romania; population (1993) 2,343,800. The conurbation of Bucharest district has an area of 1,520 sq km/587 sq mi. It was originally a citadel built by Vlad the Impaler (see ▷Dracula) to stop the advance of the Ottoman invasion in the 14th century. Bucharest became the capital of the princes of Wallachia in 1698 and of Romania in 1861. Savage fighting took place in the city during Romania's 1989 revolution.

Buchenwald site of a Nazi ▷concentration camp from 1937 to 1945 at a village northeast of Weimar, eastern Germany.

Buck, Pearl S(ydenstricker) (1892–1973) US novelist. Daughter of missionaries to China, she spent much of her life there and wrote novels about Chinese life, such as *East Wind–West Wind* (1930) and *The Good Earth* (1931), for which she received a Pulitzer prize in 1932. She was awarded the Nobel Prize for Literature in 1938.

> **Pearl S Buck**
> *It is better to be first with an ugly woman than the hundredth with a beauty.*
> *The Good Earth* ch. 1

Buckingham, George Villiers 1st Duke of Buckingham (1592–1628) English courtier, adviser to James I and later Charles I. After Charles's accession, Buckingham attempted to form a Protestant coalition in Europe, which led to war with France; however, he failed to relieve the Protestants (▷Huguenots) besieged in La Rochelle in 1627. His policy on the French Protestants was attacked in Parliament, and when about to sail for La Rochelle for a second time, he was assassinated in Portsmouth.

He was introduced to the court of James I in 1614 and soon became his favourite. He failed to cement the marriage of Prince Charles and the Infanta of Spain in 1623, but on returning to England negotiated Charles's alliance with Henrietta Maria, sister of the French king. Earl from 1617, Duke from 1623.

Buckingham, George Villiers 2nd Duke of Buckingham (1628–1687) English politician, a member of the ▷Cabal under Charles II. A dissolute son of the first duke, he was brought up with the royal children. His play *The Rehearsal* satirized the style of the poet Dryden, who portrayed him as Zimri in *Absalom and Achitophel*. He succeeded to the dukedom in 1628.

Buckingham Palace London home of the British sovereign, it stands at the west end of St James's Park. The original Buckingham House, begun in 1703 for the 1st Duke of Buckingham, was sold to George III in 1761. George IV obtained a parliamentary grant for its repair and enlargement, but instead he and the architect, John ▷Nash, began a new building (1821–26). The palace was incomplete at George IV's death in 1830, when Nash was displaced by Edward Blore, who reputedly covered most of Nash's work. The Queen's Gallery presents exhibitions of portions of the royal collections, and the state rooms and Royal Mews are also open to visitors.

BUCKINGHAM PALACE The Royal Guard on parade in London, England. In 1689, the court moved to St James's Palace, which was guarded by the Foot Guards. When Queen Victoria moved into Buckingham Palace in 1837, the Queen's Guard remained at St James's Palace, with a detachment guarding Buckingham Palace, as it still does today. *Image Bank*

Buckinghamshire county of southeast central England.

area 1,565 sq km/604 sq mi **towns** Aylesbury (administrative headquarters), Beaconsfield, Buckingham, High Wycombe, Olney **physical** Chiltern Hills; Vale of Aylesbury **features** Chequers (country seat of the prime minister); Burnham Beeches; the church of the poet Gray's 'Elegy' at Stoke Poges; Cliveden, a country house designed by Charles Barry (now a hotel; it was once the home of Nancy, Lady Astor); Bletchley Park, home of World War II code-breaking activities, now used as a training post for GCHQ (Britain's electronic surveillance centre); homes of the poets William Cowper at Olney and John Milton at Chalfont St Giles, and of the Tory prime minister Disraeli at Hughenden; grave of William Penn, Quaker founder of Pennsylvania, at Jordans, near Chalfont St Giles; Stowe landscape gardens **industries** engineering; furniture (chiefly beech); paper; printing; railway workshops; motor cars **agriculture** about 75% of the land under cultivation, fertile soil; cereals (barley, wheat, oats); cattle, pigs, poultry, sheep **population** (1996) 671,700 **famous people** John Hampden, William Herschel, Ben Nicholson, George Gilbert Scott, Edmund Waller

buckminsterfullerene form of carbon, made up of molecules (buckyballs) consisting of 60 carbon atoms arranged in 12 pentagons and 20 hexagons to form a perfect sphere. It was named after the US architect and engineer Richard Buckminster Fuller because of its structural similarity to the geodesic dome that he designed. See ▷fullerene.

buckthorn any of several thorny shrubs. The buckthorn (*Rhamnus catharticus*) is native to Britain, but is also found throughout Europe, West Asia, and North Africa. Its berries were formerly used in medicine as a purgative, to clean out the bowels. (Genus *Rhamnus*, family Rhamnaceae.)

Related Web site: Buckthorns http://www.botanical.com/botanical/mgmh/b/buckth80.html

buckwheat any of a group of cereal plants. The name usually refers to *Fagopyrum esculentum*, which reaches about 1 m/3 ft in height and can grow on poor soil in a short summer. The highly nutritious black triangular seeds (groats) are eaten by both animals and humans. They can be cooked and eaten whole or as a cracked meal (kasha), or ground into flour, often made into pancakes. (Genus *Fagopyrum*, family Polygonaceae.)

buckyballs popular name for molecules of ▷buckminsterfullerene.

bud undeveloped shoot usually enclosed by protective scales; inside is a very short stem and numerous undeveloped leaves, or flower parts, or both. Terminal buds are found at the tips of shoots, while axillary buds develop in the ▷axils of the leaves, often remaining dormant unless the terminal bud is removed or damaged. Adventitious buds may be produced anywhere on the plant, their formation sometimes stimulated by an injury, such as that caused by pruning.

Budapest capital of Hungary, industrial city (chemicals, textiles) on the River Danube; population (1993 est) 2,009,000. Buda, on the right bank of the Danube, became the Hungarian capital in 1867 and was joined with Pest, on the left bank, in 1872.

History The site of a Roman outpost in the 1st century, Buda was the seat of the Magyar kings from the 14th century. It was later occupied by the Turks, and was under Hapsburg rule from the end of the 17th century. In 1867 Hungary was given self-government, and the city of Budapest was created in 1872 when the towns of Buda and Pest were joined. Hungary became independent in 1918,

with Budapest as capital. The city was occupied by German troops in World War II, and was the site of a seven-week siege by Soviet troops, finally being liberated in February 1945. It was also the scene of fighting between the Hungarians and Soviet troops in the uprising of 1956.

Related Web site: Budapest: A Little Tour http://www.fsz.bme.hu/hungary/budapest/budapest.html

Buddha (c. 563–483 BC) Born Prince Gautama Siddhārtha. (Sanskrit 'enlightened one') Religious leader, founder of ▷Buddhism, born at Lumbini in Nepal. At the age of 29 he left his wife and son and a life of luxury, to resolve the problems of existence. After six years of austerity he realized that asceticism, like overindulgence, was futile, and chose the middle way of meditation. He became enlightened under a bo, or bodhi, tree near Bodhgaya in Bihar, India. He began teaching at Varanasi, and founded the Sangha, or order of monks. He spent the rest of his life travelling around northern India, and died at Kusinagara in Uttar Pradesh. He is not a god.

The Buddha's teaching is summarized as the Four Noble Truths: the fact of frustration or suffering; that suffering has a cause; that it can be ended; and that it can be ended by following the Noble Eightfold Path – right views, right intention, right speech, right action, right livelihood, right effort, right mindfulness, and right concentration – eventually arriving at nirvana, the extinction of all craving for things of the senses and release from the cycle of rebirth.

Buddhism one of the great world religions, which originated in India in the 5th century BC. It derives from the teaching of the ▷Buddha, who is regarded as one of a series of such enlightened beings. The chief doctrine is that all phenomena share three characteristics: they are impermanent, unsatisfactory, and lack a permanent essence (such as a soul). All beings, including gods, are subject to these characteristics, but can achieve freedom through enlightenment. The main forms of Buddhism are **Theravāda** (or **Hīnayāna**) in Southeast Asia and **Mahāyāna** in North and East Asia; **Lamaism** in Tibet and **Zen** in Japan are among the many Mahāyāna forms of Buddhism. There are over 300 million Buddhists worldwide (1994).

Scriptures The only surviving complete canon of the Buddhist scriptures is that of the Sinhalese (Sri Lanka) Buddhists, in Pāli, but other schools have essentially the same canon in Sanskrit. The scriptures are divided into three groups, known as *pitaka*s (baskets): **vinaya** (discipline), listing offences and rules of life; the **sūtras** (discourse), or **dharma** (doctrine), the exposition of Buddhism by the Buddha and his disciples; and **abhidharma** (further doctrine), later discussions on doctrine.

Beliefs The self is not regarded as permanent, as it is subject to change and decay. It is attachment to the things that are essentially impermanent that causes delusion, suffering, greed, and aversion, and reinforces the sense of self. Actions which incline towards selflessness are called 'skilful' and constitute the path leading to enlightenment. In the ▷Four Noble Truths the Buddha acknowledged the existence and source of suffering and showed the way of deliverance from it through the **Eightfold Path**. The aim of following the Eightfold Path is to attain **nirvana** ('blowing out') – the eradication of all desires. Supreme reverence is accorded to the historical Buddha (Sakyamuni, or, when referred to by his clan name, Gautama), who is seen as one in a long and ongoing line of Buddhas, the next one (Maitreya) being due c. AD 3000.

Theravāda Buddhism, the School of the Elders, also known as **Hīnayāna** or Lesser Vehicle, prevails in Southeast Asia (Sri Lanka, Thailand, and Myanmar), and emphasizes the mendicant, meditative life as the way to break the cycle of **samsāra**, or death and rebirth. Its three possible goals are *arahat*: one who, under the guidance of a Buddha, has gained insight into the true nature of things; *Paccekabuddha*: an enlightened one who lives alone and does not teach; and fully awakened *Buddha*. Its scriptures are written in Pāli, an Indo-Aryan language with its roots in northern India. In India itself Buddhism had virtually died out by the 13th century, under pressure from Islam and Hinduism. However, it has 5 million devotees in the 20th century and is growing.

Mahāyāna Buddhism, or Greater Vehicle, arose at the beginning of the Christian era. It exhorts the individual not merely to attain personal nirvana, but to become a trainee Buddha, or **bodhisattva**, and so save others. Cults of various Buddhas and bodhisattvas arose. Mahāyāna Buddhism also emphasizes **śunyata**, or the experiential understanding of the emptiness of all things, even Buddhist doctrine.

Mahāyāna Buddhism prevails in China, Korea, Japan, and Tibet. In the 6th century AD Mahāyāna spread to China with the teachings of Bodhidharma and formed Ch'an, which became established in Japan from the 12th century as **Zen Buddhism**. Zen emphasizes silent meditation with sudden interruptions from a master to encourage awakening of the mind. Japan also has the lay organization **Sōka Gakkai** (Value Creation Society), founded in

Buddhism: Key Events

5th century BC	Siddhartha Gautama, the Buddha, is born as a wealthy prince. At the age of about 35 he receives enlightenment and delivers his first sermon, and the remaining 45 years of his life are spent teaching in northern India.
5th century–1st century BC	The Buddha's teachings survive orally in Middle Indian languages, and are gradually divided into the Tripitaka.
c. 300 BC	The Sangha meet in council at Vesāli to discuss allegations of misconduct on the part of certain factions. The council ends in a schism between the minority Sthaviravada and majority Mahasangha groups. The roots of the division between the two major schools of Buddhism – the Theravāda and the Mahāyāna – are sometimes traced back to the council of Vesali.
3rd century BC	Emperor Aśoka, ruler of much of South Asia, embraces Buddhism as his state religion. Buddhism is introduced in Burma and Afghanistan at this time by missionaries sent by Aśoka.
1st century BC	The Buddha's teachings are first committed to writing, in the Pāli language, in Sri Lanka. Buddhism begins to spread along trading routes through central Asia. In India, the first versions of the Astasāhasrikā Prajñāpāramitā Sūtra, considered the first Mahāyāna sūtra, are written.
1st century AD	Buddhism is taken to central Asia and China. In India Buddhism is patronized by the king Kanishka.
2nd century	Nāgārjuna, a south Indian monastic philospher and mystic, puts forward the Sūnyatāvāda or 'Way of Emptiness', which later becomes one of the central Mahāyāna doctrines.
3rd century	Buddhism expands into Southeast Asia.
399–413	The Chinese pilgrim Fa-hsien makes his famous journey from China to India to obtain Indian sūtras.
4th century	Buddhism reaches Korea and Indonesia, and is officially recognized in China. In India, a new wave of Mahāyāna sutras leads the philosophers Asanga and Vasubandhu to propound the Vijñānavāda or 'Mind-Only' school, further developing Mahāyāna philosophy.
c. 520	According to tradition, Bodhidharma, founder of the Ch'an school, arrives in China.
6th century	Buddhism is introduced to Japan as the state religion, during the regency of Prince Shotoku Taishi.
618–907	During the T'ang dynasty Buddhism enjoys a high level of importance in China and also in Korea and Japan. This period sees the beginnings of the Chinese form of Pure Land Buddhism, as well as the T'ien-t'ai, Hua-yen, and Ch'an schools.
early 7th century	Buddhism is first established in Tibet during the reign of Srong btsan sam po.
756–97	Buddhism in Tibet makes significant advances during the reign of Khri srong lde brtsan, culminating in the founding of the first Tibetan monastery, called bSam yas.
842	On the death of King gLang dar ma, Tibet loses control of central Asia and northern Buddhism temporarily loses its political influence.
842–845	Towards the end of the T'ang dynasty, Buddhism is persecuted in China, signalling a decline in its importance and a revival of Confucian and Taoist belief.
971–983	The canon of Chinese Buddhism is first established.
11th century	Buddhism in Tibet is rejuvenated by the arrival from India of the teacher Atiśa, and also by the contemporary Tibetan religious teacher Milaraspa. Many of Tibet's most important Buddhist schools are founded.
11th–15th centuries	Sri Lankan monarchs unify the Theravadin Sangha monastic orders, leading to a period of great prosperity for Theravāda, in both Sri Lanka and Southeast Asia.
12th century	Pure Land Buddhism is established in Japan by Hōnen.
1190s	Muslim Turkish invaders establish control of northern India, destroying the Buddhist university at Nalanda and imposing forced conversions to Islam. Within two centuries, Buddhism is driven out of northern India.
13th century	Efforts towards unification of the Sangha by the Buddhist monarchs of Southeast Asia lead to a consolidation of Southeast Asian Buddhism.
11th–15th centuries	Sri Lankan monarchs unify the Theravadin Sangha under orthodox Mahavihara rules, leading to a period of great prosperity for Theravāda, both in Sri Lanka and in Southeast Asia.
14th century	The scholar Bu-ston collects together the Tibetan canon.
1357–1419	Tsong-kha pa reforms Tibetan Buddhism and founds the Gelug-pa school. The heads of this school later rule Tibet under the title of Dalai Lama.
16th–17th centuries	Explorers, merchants, and military expeditions begin to bring knowledge of Buddhism to the West. Tibetan scholar Tārānātha writes a history of Buddhism in India.
19th century	The end of the Sri Lankan and Burmese monarchies, and their replacement by foreign powers, weakens the southern Buddhist Sangha considerably.
1839–1949	The Opium Wars and subsequent conflicts generally weaken the position of Buddhism in Chinese society – in particular, the T'ai-P'ing rebellion leaves many temples and monasteries destroyed.
1950s	Tibet is invaded by communist China. By 1959 all Tibetan self-rule is abolished, and the Dalai Lama flees to India along with thousands of refugees. In Tibet, the Chinese authorities attempt to eradicate Tibetan religious culture.
1960s and 1970s	The Chinese Cultural Revolution prohibits Buddhist practice in China, and many monasteries are damaged or destroyed. Conflicts in Southeast Asia result in a decline in the strength of the Southeast Asian Sangha.
1980s	The communist authorities of China and Southeast Asia gradually become more tolerant of Buddhist practice. Meanwhile in Europe and the USA Buddhism, particularly of the Theravāda, Tibetan, and Zen schools, becomes established as a significant minority religion.
1990s	China attempts to marginalize the Dalai Lama by setting up a puppet rival in Tibet. The Dalai Lama flees to India. In the Far East forms of Zen that incorporate aspects of astrological spiritism become increasingly popular.

BUDDHISM The Nayaja Buddhist temple in Sri Lanka. Every Buddhist temple has objects to remind worshippers of the Buddha's teaching: in addition to images of the Buddha himself, there is the dagoba, which preserves relics of his body or possessions, and the bo tree (a direct descendant of the tree under which the Buddha attained enlightenment). *Image Bank*

1930, which equates absolute faith with immediate material benefit; by the 1980s it was followed by more than seven million households.

Esoteric, **Tantric**, or **Diamond Buddhism** became popular in Tibet and Japan, and holds that enlightenment is already within the disciple and with the proper guidance (that is privately passed on by a master) can be realized.

buddleia any of a group of ornamental shrubs or trees with spikes of fragrant flowers. The purple or white flower heads of the butterfly bush (*Buddleia davidii*) attract large numbers of butterflies. (Genus *Buddleia*, family Buddleiaceae.)

budgerigar small Australian parakeet *Melopsittacus undulatus* of the parrot family, Psittacidae, order Psittaciformes, that feeds mainly on grass seeds. In the wild, it has a bright green body and a blue tail with yellow flares; yellow, white, blue, and mauve varieties have been bred for the pet market. Budgerigars breed freely in captivity.

Budgerigars are well adapted to their desert habitat and can survive for a month without drinking. They make the most out of the unyielding terrain by living a nomadic lifestyle, but if drought is particularly severe and they are unable to locate areas of recent rain then they refrain from breeding, as the chicks would simply not survive. Normally females lay a clutch of four to six eggs, each egg being laid a day apart, with each egg hatching after 19 days.

Related Web site: Welcome to the World of Budgerigars and Parakeets http://www.upatsix.com/

Buenos Aires industrial city, chief port, and capital of ▷Argentina, situated in the 'Capital Federal' – a separate federal district, on the south bank of the Río de la Plata, at its estuary; population (2001 est) 13,756,000. Industries include motor vehicles, engineering, oil, chemicals, textiles, paper, and food processing. Main exports are grain, beef, and wool, which are produced in the surrounding pampas. The administrative Federal District of Buenos Aires has an area of 200 sq km/77 sq mi, with a population of (2001 est) 2,729,500. Buenos Aires is the financial and cultural centre of Argentina, and has many museums and libraries. It is a major railway terminus, and has an international airport 35 km/22 mi southwest of the city centre.

Features Congress building (1906); town hall, the Cabildo; cathedral (1804); presidential palace, the Casa Rosada (the Pink House) on the Plaza de Mayo; University of Buenos Aires, founded in 1821; opera house, the Teatro Colón; avenues built in the early 20th century, modelled on those in Paris, including 9 de Julio, which was built in 1937 and was modelled on the Champs Elysées.

History Founded in 1536 by the Spaniard Pedro de Mendoza as Puerto de Santa Mariá del Buen Aire, it was abandoned after attacks by American Indians (Querandi), and refounded in 1580. It became the capital of the viceroyalty of Rió de la Plata in 1776, and federal capital of Argentina in 1880.

buffalo either of two species of wild cattle. The Asiatic water buffalo *Bubalis bubalis* is found domesticated throughout South Asia and wild in parts of India and Nepal. It likes moist conditions. Usually grey or black, up to 1.8 m/6 ft tall, both sexes carry large horns. The African buffalo *Syncerus caffer* is found in Africa, south of the Sahara, where there is grass, water, and cover in which to retreat. There are a number of subspecies, the biggest up to 1.6 m/5 ft tall, and black, with massive horns set close together over the head. The name is also commonly applied to the North American ▷bison.

bug in computing, an ▷error in a program. It can be an error in the logical structure of a program or a syntax error, such as a spelling mistake. Some bugs cause a program to fail immediately; others remain dormant, causing problems only when a particular combination of events occurs. The process of finding and removing errors from a program is called **debugging**.

bug in entomology, an insect belonging to the order Hemiptera. All these have two pairs of wings with forewings partly thickened.

They also have piercing mouthparts adapted for sucking the juices of plants or animals, the 'beak' being tucked under the body when not in use.

Bugatti racing and sports-car company, founded by the Italian Ettore Bugatti. The first car was produced in 1908, but it was not until 1924 that one of the great Bugattis, the Type 35, was produced. Bugatti cars are credited with more race wins than any others. The company was taken over by Hispano Suiza after Bugatti's death.

bugle compact valveless treble brass instrument with a shorter tube and less flared bell than the trumpet. Constructed of copper plated with brass, it has long been used as a military instrument for giving a range of signals based on the tones of a harmonic series. The bugle has a conical bore whereas the trumpet is cylindrical.

bugle any of a group of low-growing plants belonging to the mint family, with spikes of white, pink, or blue flowers. The leaves may be smooth-edged or slightly toothed, the lower ones with a long stalk. They are often grown as ground cover. (Genus *Ajuga*, family Labiatae.)

bugloss any of several plants native to Europe and Asia, distinguished by their rough, bristly leaves and small blue flowers. (Genera *Anchusa*, *Lycopsis*, and *Echium*, family Boraginaceae.)

Bujumbura (formerly **Usumbura** (until 1962)) capital of Burundi, located at the northeastern end of Lake Tanganyika; population (1996 est) 300,000. Bujumbura is the main banking and financial centre of Burundi; industries include food processing and paint manufacture. It was founded in 1899 by German colonists, and a university was established in 1960.

BULLFIGHTING A matador tests the bravery of his bull with movements of the *capote*, a red and yellow cape. *Image Bank*

Bukhara (or **Bokhara** or **Bukhoro**) city in south-central ▷Uzbekistan, on the Zerevshan River 220 km/137 mi east of Samarkand; population (1995) 250,000. A historic city with over 140 protected buildings, it was once the heart of Muslim Central Asia, and second only to Mecca as an Islamic holy site. It is the capital of the Bukhara region of Turkestan, which has given its name to a type of handwoven carpet. Textiles, including rugs and carpets, are manufactured here (though 'Bukhara' carpets are now principally made in ▷Ashgabat, in Turkmenistan). Natural gas is extracted in the surrounding region, and cotton is grown extensively.

Bukharest alternative form of ▷Bucharest, the capital of Romania.

Bukharin, Nikolai Ivanovich (1888–1938) Soviet politician and theorist. A moderate, he was the chief Bolshevik thinker after Lenin. Executed on Stalin's orders for treason in 1938, he was posthumously rehabilitated in 1988.

Bulawayo (Ndebele 'place of slaughter') industrial city and railway junction in Zimbabwe; population (1992) 620,900. The city lies at an altitude of 1,355 m/4,450 ft on the River Matsheumlope, a tributary of the Zambezi, and was founded on the site of the kraal (enclosed village), burned down in 1893, of the Matabele chief Lobengula. It produces cement and agricultural and electrical equipment. The former capital of Matabeleland, Bulawayo developed with the exploitation of gold mines in the neighbourhood. It is the second-largest city in Zimbabwe.

bulb underground bud with fleshy leaves containing a reserve food supply and with roots growing from its base. Bulbs function in vegetative reproduction and are characteristic of many monocotyledonous plants such as the daffodil, snowdrop, and onion. Bulbs are grown on a commercial scale in temperate countries, such as England and the Netherlands.

bulbil small bulb that develops above ground from a bud. Bulbils may be formed on the stem from axillary buds, as in members of the saxifrage family, or in the place of flowers, as seen in many species of onion *Allium*. They drop off the parent plant and develop into new individuals, providing a means of ▷vegetative reproduction and dispersal.

bulbul fruit-eating bird of the family Pycnonotidae, order Passeriformes, that ranges in size from that of a sparrow to a blackbird. They are mostly rather dull coloured and very secretive, living in dense forests. They are widely distributed throughout Africa and Asia; there are about 120 species.

Bulganin, Nikolai Aleksandrovich (1895–1975) Soviet politician and military leader. His career began in 1918 when he joined the Cheka, the Soviet secret police. He helped to organize Moscow's defences in World War II, became a marshal of the USSR in 1947, and was minister of defence 1947–49 and 1953–55. On the fall of Georgi Malenkov he became prime minister (chair of the council of ministers) 1955–58 until ousted by Nikita Khrushchev.

Bulgaria see country box.

Bulgarian an ethnic group living mainly in Bulgaria. There are 8–8.5 million speakers of Bulgarian, a Slavic language belonging to the Indo-European family. The Bulgarians use the Cyrillic alphabet.

Bulge, Battle of the (or **Ardennes offensive**) in World War II, Hitler's plan (code-named 'Watch on the Rhine') for a breakthrough by his field marshal Gerd von ▷Rundstedt, aimed at the US line in the Ardennes from 16 December 1944 to 28 January 1945. Hitler aimed to isolate the Allied forces north of the corridor which would be created by a drive through the Ardennes, creating a German salient (prominent part of a line of attack, also known as a 'bulge'). There were 77,000 Allied casualties and 130,000 German, including Hitler's last powerful reserve of elite Panzer units. Although US troops were encircled for some weeks at Bastogne, the German counteroffensive failed.

bulimia (Greek 'ox hunger') eating disorder in which large amounts of food are consumed in a short time ('binge'), usually followed by depression and self-criticism. The term is often used for **bulimia nervosa**, an emotional disorder in which eating is followed by deliberate vomiting and purging. This may be a chronic stage in ▷anorexia nervosa.

bull speculator who buys stocks or shares on the stock exchange expecting a rise in the price in order to sell them later at a profit, the opposite of a ▷bear. In a bull market, prices rise and bulls profit.

bull (or **papal bull**) document or edict issued by the pope; so called from the circular seals (medieval Latin *bulla*) attached to them. Some of the most celebrated bulls include Leo X's condemnation of Luther in 1520 and Pius IX's proclamation of papal infallibility in 1870.

Bull, John imaginary figure personifying England; see ▷John Bull.

bulldog British breed of dog of ancient but uncertain origin, formerly bred for bull-baiting. The head is broad and square, with deeply wrinkled cheeks, small folded ears, very short muzzle, and massive jaws, the peculiar set of the lower jaw making it difficult for the dog to release its grip. Thickset in build, the bulldog grows to about 45 cm/18 in and has a smooth beige, tawny, or brindle coat. The French bulldog is much lighter in build and has large upright ears.

bullfighting the national sport of Spain (where there are more than 400 bullrings), which is also popular in Mexico, Portugal, and much of Latin America. It involves the ritualized taunting of a bull in a circular ring, until its eventual death at the hands of the matador. Originally popular in Greece and Rome, it was introduced into Spain by the Moors in the 11th century.

bullfinch Eurasian finch with a thick head and neck and short heavy bill, genus *Pyrrhula pyrrhula*, family Fringillidae, order Passeriformes. It is small and blue-grey or black in colour, the males being reddish and the females brown on the breast. Bullfinches are 15 cm/6 in long, and usually seen in pairs. They feed on tree buds as well as seeds and berries, and are usually seen in woodland. They also live in the Aleutians and on the Alaska mainland.

BULLFINCH The bullfinch *Pyrrhula pyrrhula* is notorious for the damage it does by eating the buds of fruit trees and flowering shrubs in spring.

Bullfinches have declined in Britain by 76% since the late 1960s.

Bulgaria

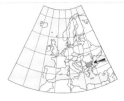

Bulgaria country in southeast Europe, bounded north by Romania, west by Serbia and Montenegro, and Macedonia, south by Greece, southeast by Turkey, and east by the Black Sea.

NATIONAL NAME *Republika Bulgaria/Republic of Bulgaria*
AREA 110,912 sq km/42,823 sq mi
CAPITAL Sofia
MAJOR TOWNS/CITIES Plovdiv, Varna, Ruse, Burgas, Stara Zagora, Pleven
MAJOR PORTS Burgas, Varna
PHYSICAL FEATURES lowland plains in north and southeast separated by mountains (Balkan and Rhodope) that cover three-quarters of the country; River Danube in north

Government

HEAD OF STATE Georgi Parvanov from 2001
HEAD OF GOVERNMENT Simeon Koburgotski from 2001
POLITICAL SYSTEM emergent democracy
POLITICAL EXECUTIVE parliamentary
ADMINISTRATIVE DIVISIONS 28 regions divided into 278 municipalities
ARMED FORCES 68,400 (2002 est)
CONSCRIPTION compulsory for nine months
DEATH PENALTY abolished in 1998
DEFENCE SPEND (% GDP) 2.5 (2002 est)
EDUCATION SPEND (% GDP) 3.2 (1999)
HEALTH SPEND (% GDP) 3.9 (2000 est)

Economy and resources

CURRENCY lev
GPD (US$) 15.6 billion (2002 est)
REAL GDP GROWTH (% change on previous year) 4 (2001)
GNI (US$) 14.1 billion (2002 est)
GNI PER CAPITA (PPP) (US$) 6,840 (2002 est)
CONSUMER PRICE INFLATION 3% (2003 est)
UNEMPLOYMENT 18.3% (2000)
FOREIGN DEBT (US$) 9 billion (2001 est)
MAJOR TRADING PARTNERS EU countries (principally Germany, Greece, Italy, Turkey, France), former USSR (principally Russia), Macedonia, USA
RESOURCES coal, iron ore, manganese, copper, lead, zinc, petroleum
INDUSTRIES food products, petroleum and coal products, metals, mining, plastics, paints, paper, beverages and tobacco, electrical machinery, textiles
EXPORTS base metals, chemical and rubber products, processed food, beverages, tobacco, chemicals, textiles, footwear. Principal market: Italy 15% (2001)
IMPORTS mineral products and fuels, chemical and rubber products, textiles, footwear, machinery and transport equipment, medicines. Principal source: Russia 19.9% (2001)

ARABLE LAND 40% (2000 est)
AGRICULTURAL PRODUCTS wheat, maize, barley, sunflower seeds, grapes, potatoes, tobacco, roses; viticulture (Bulgaria is a major exporter of wine; forest resources

Population and society

POPULATION 7,897,000 (2003 est)
POPULATION GROWTH RATE –0.6% (2000–15)
POPULATION DENSITY (per sq km) 71 (2003 est)
URBAN POPULATION (% of total) 67 (2003 est)

Chronology

c. 3500 BC onwards: Semi-nomadic pastoralists from the central Asian steppes settled in the area and formed the Thracian community.

mid-5th century BC: The Thracian state was formed; it was to extend over Bulgaria, northern Greece, and northern Turkey.

4th century BC: Phillip II and Alexander the Great of Macedonia waged largely unsuccessful campaigns against the Thracian Empire.

AD 50: The Thracians were subdued and incorporated within the Roman Empire as the province of Moesia Inferior.

3rd–6th centuries: The Thracian Empire was successively invaded and devastated by the Goths, Huns, Bulgars, and Avars.

681: The Bulgars, an originally Turkic group that had merged with earlier Slav settlers, revolted against the Avars and established, south of the River Danube, the first Bulgarian kingdom, with its capital at Pliska.

864: Orthodox Christianity was adopted by Boris I.

1018: Subjugated by the Byzantines, whose empire had its capital at Constantinople; led to Bulgarian Church breaking with Rome in 1054.

1185: Second independent Bulgarian Kingdom formed.

mid-13th century: Bulgarian state destroyed by Mongol incursions.

1396: Bulgaria became the first European state to be absorbed into the Turkish Ottoman Empire; the imposition of a harsh feudal system and the sacking of the monasteries followed.

1859: The Bulgarian Catholic Church re-established links with Rome.

1876: A Bulgarian nationalist revolt against Ottoman rule was crushed brutally by Ottomans, with 15,000 massacred at Plovdiv ('Bulgarian Atrocities').

1878: At the Congress of Berlin, concluding a Russo-Turkish war in which Bulgarian volunteers had fought alongside the Russians, the area south of the Balkans, Eastern Rumelia, remained an Ottoman province, but the area to the north became the autonomous Principality of Bulgaria, with a liberal constitution and Alexander Battenberg as prince.

1885: Eastern Rumelia annexed by the Principality; Serbia defeated in war.

AGE DISTRIBUTION (% of total population) 0–14 15%, 15–59 63%, 60+ 22% (2002 est)
ETHNIC GROUPS Southern Slavic Bulgarians constitute around 85% of the population; 9% are ethnic Turks, who during the later 1980s were subjected to government pressure to adopt Slavic names and to resettle elsewhere; 3% Gypsy, 3% Macedonian
LANGUAGE Bulgarian (official), Turkish
RELIGION Eastern Orthodox Christian, Muslim, Jewish, Roman Catholic, Protestant
EDUCATION (compulsory years) 8
LITERACY RATE 99% (men); 98% (women) (2003 est)
LABOUR FORCE 26.6% agriculture, 29.1% industry, 44.3% services (1999)
LIFE EXPECTANCY 67 (men); 75 (women) (2000–05)
CHILD MORTALITY RATE (under 5, per 1,000 live births) 16 (2001)
PHYSICIANS (per 1,000 people) 3.5 (2000 est)
HOSPITAL BEDS (per 1,000 people) 7.4 (2000 est)
TV SETS (per 1,000 people) 453 (2001)
RADIOS (per 1,000 people) 543 (1997)
INTERNET USERS (per 10,000 people) 897.3 (2002 est)
PERSONAL COMPUTER USERS (per 100 people) 5.2 (2002 est)

See also ▷Balkan Wars; ▷Byzantine Empire; ▷Ottoman Empire; ▷Thrace.

1908: Full independence proclaimed from Turkish rule, with Ferdinand I as tsar.

1913: Following defeat in the Second Balkan War, King Ferdinand I abdicated and was replaced by his son Boris III.

1919: Bulgarian Agrarian Union government, led by Alexander Stamboliiski, came to power and redistributed land to poor peasants.

1923: Agrarian government was overthrown in right-wing coup and Stamboliiski murdered.

1934: A semifascist dictatorship was established by King Boris III.

1944: Soviet invasion of German-occupied Bulgaria.

1946: The monarchy was abolished and a communist-dominated people's republic proclaimed following a plebiscite.

1947: Gained South Dobruja in the northeast, along the Black Sea, from Romania; Soviet-style constitution established a one-party state; industries and financial institutions were nationalized and cooperative farming introduced.

1954: Bulgaria became a loyal and cautious satellite of the USSR.

1968: Bulgaria participated in the Soviet-led invasion of Czechoslovakia.

1971: A new constitution was introduced.

1985–89: Haphazard administrative and economic reforms, known as *preustroistvo* ('restructuring'), were introduced under the stimulus of the reformist Soviet leader Mikhail Gorbachev.

1989: A programme of enforced 'Bulgarianization' resulted in a mass exodus of ethnic Turks to Turkey. Opposition parties were tolerated.

1991: A new liberal-democratic constitution was adopted. The first noncommunist government was formed.

1993: A voucher-based 'mass privatization' programme was launched.

1996: Radical economic and industrial reforms were imposed. There was mounting inflation and public protest at the state of the economy.

1997: There was a general strike. The UDF leader Ivan Kostov became prime minister. The Bulgarian currency was pegged to the Deutschmark in return for support from the International Monetary Fund. A new political group, the Real Reform Movement (DESIR), was formed.

1999: Bulgaria joined the Central European Free Trade Agreement (CEFTA).

BULGARIA Rila Monastery in the Rila Mountains of the southwest region of Bulgaria. Founded in the 10th century by the hermit saint Ivan Rilski, the original monastery was 4 km/2.5 mi to the east of this site. It was rebuilt here in the 14th century by the local ruler Hrelyo Dragovol, but had to be completely reconstructed after a devastating fire in 1833. *Photodisk*

BULLFROG The South African bullfrog *Pyxicephalus adspersus* is the largest South African frog, growing up to 20 cm/8 in, and feeds on mice, lizards, and other frogs.
K G Preston-Mafham/Premaphotos Wildlife

bullfrog large ▷frog of the genera *Rana* or *Pyxicephalus*, family Ranidae. The North American bullfrog is *R. catesbiane*, the Asian bullfrog *R. tigrina*, and the African bullfrog *P. adspersus*.

bullhead (or miller's thumb) small fish *Cottus gobio* found in fresh water in the northern hemisphere, often under stones. It has a large head, a spine on the gill cover, and grows to 10 cm/4 in.

bullroarer (or whizzer or whizzing stick or lightning stick) musical instrument used by Australian Aborigines for communication and during religious rites. It consists of a weighted aerofoil (a rectangular slat of wood about 15 cm/6 in to 60 cm/24 in long and about 1.25 cm/0.5 in to 5 cm/2 in wide) whirled rapidly about the head on a long cord to make a deep whirring noise. It is also used in many other parts of the world, including Britain.

Bull Run, Battles of in the American Civil War, two victories for the Confederate army under General Robert E Lee at **Manassas** Junction, northeastern Virginia, named after the stream where they took place: **First Battle of Bull Run** 21 July 1861; **Second Battle of Bull Run** 29–30 August 1862. The battles are known as the Battle of Manassas in the southern states.

bull terrier breed of dog, originating as a cross between a terrier and a bulldog. Very powerfully built, it grows to about 40 cm/16 in tall, and has a short, usually white, coat, narrow eyes, and distinctive egg-shaped head. It was formerly used in bull-baiting. Pit bull terriers are used in illegal dog fights. The Staffordshire bull terrier is a distinct breed.

Bülow, Bernhard Heinrich Martin Karl, Prince von Bülow (1849–1929) German diplomat and politician. He was chancellor of the German Empire 1900–09 under Kaiser Wilhelm II and, holding that self-interest was the only rule for any state, adopted attitudes to France and Russia that unintentionally reinforced the trend towards opposing European power groups: the ▷Triple Entente (Britain, France, Russia) and the ▷Triple Alliance (Germany, Austria-Hungary, Italy).

bulrush either of two plants: the great reed mace or cat's tail (*Typha latifolia*) with velvety chocolate-brown spikes of tightly packed flowers reaching up to 15 cm/6 in long; and a type of sedge (*Scirpus lacustris*) with tufts of reddish-brown flowers at the top of a rounded, rushlike stem.

Bulwer-Lytton, Edward George Earle 1st Baron Lytton. English writer; see Edward ▷Lytton.

bumblebee any large ▷bee, 2–5 cm/1–2 in, usually dark-coloured but banded with yellow, orange, or white, belonging to the genus *Bombus*.

Most species live in small colonies, usually underground, often in an old mousehole. The queen lays her eggs in a hollow nest of moss or grass at the beginning of the season. The larvae are fed on pollen and honey, and develop into workers. All the bees die at the end of the season except fertilized females, which hibernate and produce fresh colonies in the spring. Bumblebees are found naturally all over the world, with the exception of Australia, where they have been introduced to facilitate the pollination of some cultivated varieties of clover.

Bumblebees in the UK are in decline. In 1997, of the 19 native species 13 were failing to thrive. In 1999 only 16 species remained, out of which three were close to extinction, six were threatened, and one may already have been extinct. This is due to a number of factors, including intensive agriculture, reduction in hedgerows, and competition from honeybees.

Bunche, Ralph Johnson (1904–1971) US diplomat. He was principal director of the United Nations Department of Trusteeship 1948–54 and UN undersecretary 1955–67, acting as mediator in Palestine 1948–49 and as special representative in the Congo in 1960. He became UN undersecretary general in 1968. He was awarded the Nobel Prize for Peace in 1950 for negotiating the Arab-Israel truce of 1949.

Bunker Hill, Battle of the first significant engagement in the ▷American Revolution, on 17 June 1775, near a small hill in Charlestown (now part of Boston), Massachusetts; the battle actually took place on Breed's Hill, but is named after Bunker Hill as this was the more significant of the two. Although the colonists were defeated, they were able to retreat to Boston in good order.

Bunsen burner gas burner used in laboratories, consisting of a vertical metal tube through which a fine jet of fuel gas is directed. Air is drawn in through airholes near the base of the tube and the mixture is ignited and burns at the tube's upper opening.

The invention of the burner is attributed to German chemist Robert von Bunsen in 1855, but English chemist and physicist Michael Faraday is known to have produced a similar device at an earlier date. A later refinement was the metal collar that can be turned to close or partially close the airholes, thereby regulating the amount of air sucked in and hence the heat of the burner's flame.

bunting any of a number of sturdy, finchlike birds with short, thick bills, of the family Emberizidae, order Passeriformes, especially the genera *Passerim* and *Emberiza*. Most of these brightly coloured birds are native to the New World.

Corn buntings have declined in Britain by 80% since the late 1960s. The commonest British species are the ▷yellowhammer *Emberiza citrinella*, the reed bunting *E. schoeniclus*, and the corn bunting *E. calandra*. Also found are the snow bunting *Plectrophenax nivalis* of the far north, which is largely white-plumaged and migrates to temperate Europe in the winter; the cirl bunting *E. cirlus*; the Lapland bunting *Calcarius lapponicus*; and the ▷ortolan.

Buñuel, Luis (1900–1983) Spanish-born film director. He is widely considered one of the giants of European art cinema, responsible for such enduring classics as *Los Olvidados/The Young and the Damned* (1950), *Viridiana* (1961), *Belle de Jour* (1966), and *Le Charme discret de la bourgeoisie/The Discreet Charm of the Bourgeoisie* (1972).

Related Web site: Buñuel – A Centenary Conference http://www.bunuel2000.freeuk.com/

Bunyan, John (1628–1688) English writer, author of *The Pilgrim's Progress* (first part 1678, second part 1684), one of the best-known religious allegories in English. A Baptist, he was imprisoned in Bedford from 1660 until 1672 for unlicensed preaching and wrote *Grace Abounding* in 1666, which describes his early spiritual life. He started to write *The Pilgrim's Progress* during a second jail sentence from 1676 until 1677. Written in straightforward language with fervour and imagination, it achieved immediate popularity and was highly influential.

buoyancy lifting effect of a fluid on a body wholly or partly immersed in it. This was studied by ▷Archimedes in the 3rd century BC.

bur (or burr) in botany, a type of 'false fruit' or ▷pseudocarp, surrounded by numerous hooks; for instance, that of burdock *Arctium*, where the hooks are formed from bracts surrounding the flowerhead. Burs catch in the feathers or fur of passing animals, and thus may be dispersed over considerable distances.

BUR A bur entangled in a fox's fur. By the time the animal grooms itself and discards the bur it will probably have transported it some distance. A number of plants, including the burdock (shown here), disperse their seeds in this way.

Burbage, Richard (*c.* 1567–1619) English actor. He is thought to have been Shakespeare's original Hamlet, Othello, and Lear. He also appeared in first productions of works by Ben Jonson, Thomas Kyd, and John Webster. His father **James Burbage** (*c.* 1530–1597) built the first English playhouse, known as 'the Theatre'; his brother **Cuthbert Burbage** (*c.* 1566–1636) built the original Globe Theatre in London in 1599.

burbot (or eelpout) long, rounded fish *Lota lota* of the cod family, the only one living entirely in fresh water. Up to 1 m/3 ft long, it lives on the bottom of clear lakes and rivers, often in holes or under rocks, throughout Europe, Asia, and North America.

Burckhardt, Jacob Christoph (1818–1897) Swiss art historian, one of the founders of cultural history as a discipline. His *The Civilization of the Renaissance in Italy* (1860), intended as part of a study of world cultural history, profoundly influenced thought on the Renaissance.

burdock any of several bushy herbs characterized by hairy leaves and ripe fruit enclosed in ▷burs with strong hooks. (Genus *Arctium*, family Compositae.)

Related Web site: Burdock http://www.botanical.com/botanical/mgmh/b/burdoc87.html

bureaucracy organization whose structure and operations are governed to a high degree by written rules and a hierarchy of offices; in its broadest sense, all forms of administration, and in its narrowest, rule by officials.

Bureau of Indian Affairs bureau within the US Department of the Interior responsible for administering federal programmes for recognized American Indian ethnic groups, and for promoting American Indian self-determination. Created on 11 March 1824, its primary responsibility has been to 'civilize' and educate American Indians, although it has also administered treaty negotiations, regulated and licensed trade with American Indians, controlled liquor in Native areas, settled land disputes, and implemented the allotment system of the Dawes Act of 1887 and the Indian Reorganization Act of 1934. The Bureau of Indian Affairs (BIA) has a responsibility to enhance the quality of life, promote economic opportunities, and protect assets of American Indians and Alaskan Natives. It does so by providing law enforcement, social services, health care facilities, education, housing, and business loans.

Burgenland federal state of southeast Austria, extending south from the Danube along the western border of the Hungarian plain;

BUMBLEBEE The bumblebee *Bombus dahlbomi* on a legume flower in a southern beech forest in Argentina. *Premaphotos Wildlife*

area 4,000 sq km/1,544 sq mi; population (1994) 273,600. It is a largely agricultural region adjoining the Neusiedler See, and produces timber, fruit, sugar, wine, lignite, antimony, and limestone. Its capital is Eisenstadt. In the north it is generally flat, but in the south are spurs of the Alps, with the valleys of the River Raab and its tributaries.

Related Web site: Burgenland http://www.tourist-net.co.at/ burgl1e.htm

Burges, William (1827–1881) English Gothic Revival architect and designer. His style is characterized by sumptuous interiors with carving, painting, and gilding. His chief works are St Finbarr's Cathedral in Cork (1862–76), the Speech Room at Harrow School (1872), and additions to and the remodelling of Cardiff Castle (1868–85) and Castle Coch near Cardiff (1875–91).

Burgess, Anthony (1917–1993) Pen-name of John Anthony Burgess Wilson. English novelist, critic, and composer. A prolific and versatile writer, Burgess wrote about 60 books as well as screenplays, television scripts, and reviews. His work includes *A Clockwork Orange* (1962) (made into a film by Stanley Kubrick in 1971), a despairing depiction of high technology and violence set in a future London terrorized by teenage gangs, and the panoramic *Earthly Powers* (1980).

Style Burgess's works often show an experimental approach to language – *A Clockwork Orange* is written in 'nadsat', the imaginary argot of the teenage narrator, and his fictional biography of Shakespeare, *Nothing Like the Sun* (1964), is written in a mock-Elizabethan dialect. His vision has been described as bleak and pessimistic, but his work is also comic and satiric, as in his novels featuring the poet Enderby.

Related Web site: Stanley Kubrick's A Clockwork Orange http://www.clockworkorange.com

burgh (or **burh** or **borough**) archaic form of ▷borough.

burgh former unit of Scottish local government, referring to a town enjoying a degree of self-government. Burghs were abolished in 1975; the terms **burgh** and **royal burgh** once gave mercantile privilege but are now only an honorary distinction.

Burgh, Hubert de (died 1243) English ▷justiciar and regent of England. He began his career in the administration of Richard I, and was promoted to the justiciarship by King John; he remained in that position under Henry III from 1216 until his dismissal in 1232. He was a supporter of King John against the barons, and ended French intervention in England by his defeat of the French fleet in the Strait of Dover in 1217. He became the most powerful figure in Henry III's minority following the death of the regent, William Marshall, in 1219. He reorganized royal administration and the Common Law.

Burghley, William Cecil 1st Baron Burghley (1520–1598) English politician, chief adviser to Elizabeth I as secretary of state from 1558 and Lord High Treasurer from 1572. He was largely responsible for the religious settlement of 1559, and took a leading role in the events preceding the execution of Mary Queen of Scots in 1587.

burglary offence committed when a trespasser enters a building intending to steal, do damage to property, grievously harm any person, or rape a woman. Entry needs only be effective so, for example, a person who puts their hand through a broken shop window to steal something may be guilty of burglary.

Burgundy ancient kingdom in the valleys of the rivers Rhône and Saône in eastern France and southwestern Germany, partly corresponding with modern-day Burgundy. Settled by the Teutonic Burgundi around AD 443, and brought under Frankish control in AD 534, Burgundy played a central role in the medieval history of northwestern Europe.

Burgundy (French **Bourgogne**) modern region and former duchy of east-central France that includes the *départements* of Ain, Côte-d'Or, Nièvre, Saône-et-Loire, and Yonne; area 31,600 sq km/ 12,198 sq mi; population (1990) 1,609,700. Its administrative centre is ▷Dijon.

Burke, Edmund (1729–1797) British Whig politician and political theorist, born in Dublin, Ireland. During a parliamentary career spanning more than 30 years, he was famous for opposing the government's attempts to coerce the American colonists, for example in *Thoughts on the Present Discontents* (1770), and for supporting the emancipation of Ireland. However, he was a vehement opponent of the French Revolution, which he denounced in *Reflections on the Revolution in France* (1790), and attacked the suggestion of peace with France in *Letters on a Regicide Peace* (1795–97).

Burke was also the author of *A Philosophical Inquiry into the Origin of our Ideas on the Sublime and Beautiful* (1756), on aesthetics. He was a leading figure in the impeachment of the British colonial administrator Warren ▷Hastings. Burke's basic political credo – that liberty is only possible within the strict framework of law and order – ensured that he was subsequently revered by British Conservatives as one of their main inspirational figures.

Burke, Robert O'Hara (1821–1861) Irish-born Australian explorer who in 1860–61 made the first south–north crossing of Australia (from Victoria to the Gulf of Carpentaria), with William Wills (1834–1861). Both died on the return journey, and only one of their party survived.

Burkina Faso (formerly **Upper Volta**) see country box.

burlesque in the 17th and 18th centuries, a form of satirical comedy parodying a particular play or dramatic genre. For example, John ▷Gay's *The Beggar's Opera* (1728) is a burlesque of 18th-century opera, and Richard Brinsley ▷Sheridan's *The Critic* (1777) satirizes the sentimentality in contemporary drama. In the USA from the mid-19th century, burlesque referred to a sex-and-comedy show invented by Michael Bennett Leavitt in 1866 with acts including acrobats, singers, and comedians. During the 1920s striptease was introduced in order to counteract the growing popularity of the movies; Gypsy Rose Lee was the most famous stripper. Burlesque was frequently banned in the USA.

Burlington, Richard Boyle 3rd Earl of Burlington (1695–1753) Anglo-Irish architectural patron and architect. He was one of the premier exponents of the Palladian style in Britain. His buildings are characterized by absolute adherence to the classical rules. William ▷Kent was his major protégé.

Burma former name (to 1989) of ▷Myanmar.

Related Web site: Burma http://www.umsl.edu/services/govdocs/ wofact96/50.htm

Burman the largest ethnic group in Myanmar (formerly Burma). The Burmans, speakers of a Sino-Tibetan language, migrated from the hills of Tibet, settling in the areas around Mandalay by the 11th century.

burn in medicine, destruction of body tissue by extremes of temperature, corrosive chemicals, electricity, or radiation. **First-degree burns** may cause reddening; **second-degree burns** cause blistering and irritation but usually heal spontaneously; **third-degree burns** are disfiguring and may be life-threatening.

Burns cause plasma, the fluid component of the blood, to leak from the blood vessels, and it is this loss of circulating fluid that engenders ▷shock. Emergency treatment is needed for third-degree burns in order to replace the fluid volume, prevent infection (a serious threat to the severely burned), and reduce the pain. Plastic, or reconstructive, surgery, including skin grafting, may be required to compensate for damaged tissue and minimize disfigurement. If a skin graft is necessary, dead tissue must be removed from a burn (a process known as debridement) so that the patient's blood supply can nourish the graft.

Burne-Jones, Edward Coley (1833–1898) English painter. In 1856 he was apprenticed to the Pre-Raphaelite painter and poet Dante Gabriel ▷Rossetti, who remained a dominant influence. His paintings, inspired by legend and myth, were characterized by elongated forms and subdued tones, as in *King Cophetua and the Beggar Maid* (1880–84; Tate Gallery, London). He also collaborated with William ▷Morris in designing stained-glass windows, tapestries, and book decorations for the Kelmscott Press. His work influenced both ▷Symbolism and ▷art nouveau. He was created a baronet in 1894.

Related Web site: Burne-Jones, Sir Edward Coley http://sunsite.unc.edu/wm/paint/auth/burne-jones/

Burnell, Jocelyn Bell Northern Irish astronomer. See ▷Bell-Burnell.

burnet herb belonging to the rose family, also known as **salad burnet**. It smells of cucumber and can be used in salads. The name is also used for other members of the genus. (*Sanguisorba minor*, family Rosaceae.)

Burnett, Frances Eliza Hodgson (1849–1924) English writer. She emigrated with her family to the USA in 1865. Her novels for children include the rags-to-riches tale *Little Lord Fauntleroy* (1886) and *The Secret Garden* (1911), which has its values anchored in nature mysticism.

Burney, Fanny (Frances) (1752–1840) English novelist and diarist. She achieved success with *Evelina*, an epistolary novel published in 1778, became a member of Samuel ▷Johnson's circle,

and received a post at court from Queen Charlotte. She published three further novels, *Cecilia* (1782), *Camilla* (1796), and *The Wanderer* (1814).

Burns, Robert (1759–1796) Scottish poet. He used a form of Scots dialect at a time when it was not considered suitably 'elevated' for literature. Burns's first volume, *Poems, Chiefly in the Scottish Dialect*, appeared in 1786. In addition to his poetry (such as 'To a Mouse'), Burns wrote or adapted many songs, including 'Auld Lang Syne'. **Burns Night** is celebrated on 25 January, his birthday.

Burns, who wrote as well in English as he did in Scots, is recognized as the culminating figure in two centuries' tradition of folk song and genre poetry and one of the greatest of all writers of love songs. Although not a Romantic himself, the example of his work was one of the vital influences in the coming Romantic movement. He contributed some 300 songs to James Johnson's *Scots Musical Museum* (1787–1803) and Thomson's *Select Collection of Original Scottish Airs* (1793–1841). Whether composing original pieces or, as in the case of 'Auld Lang Syne', revitalizing a song which had already passed through more than one version, he had the touch of lyric genius. To this he added a power of vitriolic satire, shown in such poems as 'Holy Willie's Prayer', and a command of vivid description that appears at its best in 'Tam o' Shanter' and 'The Jolly Beggars'.

Related Web site: Selected Poetry of Robert Burns http://www.library.utoronto.ca/utel/ rp/authors/burns.html

Burr, Aaron (1756–1836) US politician, Republican vice-president 1801–05. In 1804 he killed his political rival Alexander ▷Hamilton in a duel. In 1807 Burr was tried and acquitted of treason charges, which implicated him variously in a scheme to conquer Mexico, or part of Florida, or to rule over a seceded Louisiana.

Burroughs, Edgar Rice (1875–1950) US novelist. He wrote *Tarzan of the Apes* (1914; filmed 1918), the story of an aristocratic child lost in the jungle and reared by apes, and followed it with over 20 more books about the Tarzan character. He also wrote a series of novels about life on Mars, including *A Princess of Mars* (1917) and *Synthetic Men of Mars* (1940).

Related Web site: Tarzan of the Apes by Edgar Rice Burroughs http://www.cs.cmu.edu/People/rgs/tarz-ftitle.html

EDWARD BURNE-JONES A portrait by English Pre-Raphaelite painter Edward Burne-Jones of Sidonia von Borke, painted in 1860. *The Art Archive/San Angelo in Formis Capua Italy/Dagli Orti*

Burroughs, William S(eward) (1914–1997) US author.
One of the most culturally influential post-war writers, his work is noted for its experimental methods, black humour, explicit homo-eroticism, and apocalyptic vision. In 1944 he met Allen Ginsberg and Jack Kerouac, all three becoming leading members of the ▷Beat Generation. His first novel, *Junkie* (1953), documented his heroin addiction and expatriation to Mexico, where in 1951 he accidentally killed his common-law wife. He settled in Tangier in 1954 and wrote his celebrated anti-novel *Naked Lunch* (1959). A landmark federal court case deemed *Naked Lunch* not obscene; this broke the ground for other books, helping to eliminate censorship of the printed word in the USA.

Bursa
city in northwestern Turkey, with a port at Mudania; population (1990) 834,600. It was the capital of the Ottoman Empire from 1326 until 1423.

Burton, Richard (1925–1984)
Stage name of Richard Walter Jenkins. Welsh stage and screen actor. He had a rich, dramatic voice but his career was dogged by personal problems and an often poor choice of roles. Films in which he appeared with his wife Elizabeth ▷Taylor include *Cleopatra* (1963) and *Who's Afraid of Virginia Woolf?* (1966). Among his later films are *Equus* (1977) and *Nineteen Eighty-Four* (1984).

Burton, Richard Francis (1821–1890)
English explorer and translator (he knew 35 oriental languages). He travelled mainly in the Middle East and northeast Africa, often disguised as a Muslim. He made two attempts to find the source of the White Nile, in 1855 and 1857–58 (on the second, with John ▷Speke, he reached Lake Tanganyika), and wrote many travel books. He translated oriental erotica and the *Arabian Nights* (1885–88).

After military service in India, Burton explored the Arabian peninsula and Somaliland. In 1853 he visited Mecca and Medina disguised as an Afghan pilgrim; he was then commissioned by the Foreign Office to explore the sources of the Nile. Later travels took him to North and South America. His translations include the *Kama Sutra of Vatsyayana* 1883 and *The Perfumed Garden* 1886. His wife, who had accompanied him on some journeys, burned his unpublished manuscripts and diaries after his death.

Burton upon Trent
town in Staffordshire, central England, on the River Trent, northeast of Birmingham; population (2001 est) 60,500. It is a former cotton-spinning town. Brewing is the principal industry, with five major breweries in operation; Marmite savoury spread is produced from the yeast by-products.

RICHARD BURTON Welsh actor Richard Burton who married and divorced, then remarried film star Elizabeth Taylor, with whom he is pictured here. *Archive Photos*

Burkina Faso

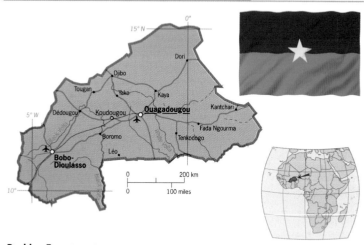

Burkina Faso formerly Upper Volta (until 1984) landlocked country in west Africa, bounded east by Niger, northwest and west by Mali, and south by Côte d'Ivoire, Ghana, Togo, and Benin.

AREA 274,122 sq km/105,838 sq mi
CAPITAL Ouagadougou
MAJOR TOWNS/CITIES Bobo-Dioulasso, Koudougou, Banfora, Ouahigouya, Tenkodogo
PHYSICAL FEATURES landlocked plateau with hills in west and southeast; headwaters of the River Volta; semiarid in north, forest and farmland in south; linked by rail to Abidjan in Côte d'Ivoire, Burkina Faso's only outlet to the sea

Government

HEAD OF STATE Blaise Compaoré from 1987
HEAD OF GOVERNMENT Paramanga Ernest Yonli from 2000
POLITICAL SYSTEM emergent democracy
POLITICAL EXECUTIVE limited presidency
ADMINISTRATIVE DIVISIONS 45 provinces
ARMED FORCES 10,200 (2002 est)
CONSCRIPTION military service is voluntary
DEATH PENALTY retains the death penalty for ordinary crimes but can be considered abolitionist in practice
DEFENCE SPEND (% GDP) 1.5 (2002 est)
EDUCATION SPEND (% GDP) 1.4 (1999)
HEALTH SPEND (% GDP) 4.2 (2000 est)

Economy and resources

CURRENCY franc CFA
GPD (US$) 2.8 billion (2002 est)
REAL GDP GROWTH (% change on previous year) 5.7 (2001)
GNI (US$) 2.6 billion (2002 est)
GNI PER CAPITA (PPP) (US$) 1,010 (2002 est)
CONSUMER PRICE INFLATION 3% (2003 est)
UNEMPLOYMENT 8.1% (1994 est)
FOREIGN DEBT (US$) 1.47 billion (2001 est)
MAJOR TRADING PARTNERS France, Italy, Singapore, Côte d'Ivoire, Portugal, USA, Thailand, Nigeria
RESOURCES manganese, zinc, limestone, phosphates, diamonds, gold, antimony, marble, silver, lead
INDUSTRIES food processing, textiles, cotton ginning, brewing, processing of hides and skins
EXPORTS cotton, gold, livestock and livestock products. Principal market: Singapore 14.9% (2001)
IMPORTS machinery and transport equipment, miscellaneous manufactured articles, food products (notably cereals), refined petroleum products, chemicals. Principal source: Côte d'Ivoire 29.6% (2001)
ARABLE LAND 13.9% (2000 est)
AGRICULTURAL PRODUCTS cotton, sesame seeds, sheanuts (karité nuts), millet, sorghum, maize, sugar cane, rice, groundnuts; livestock rearing (cattle, sheep, and goats)

Population and society

POPULATION 13,002,000 (2003 est)
POPULATION GROWTH RATE 2.2% (2000–15)
POPULATION DENSITY (per sq km) 47 (2003 est)
URBAN POPULATION (% of total) 18 (2003 est)
AGE DISTRIBUTION (% of total population) 0–14 49%, 15–59 46%, 60+ 5% (2002 est)
ETHNIC GROUPS over 50 ethnic groups, including the nomadic Mossi (48%), Fulani (8%), Gourma (7%), and Bisa-Samo (6%). Settled tribes include: in the north the Lobi-Dagari (4%) and the Mande (7%); in the southeast the Bobo (7%); and in the southwest the Senoufu (6%) and Gourounsi (6%)
LANGUAGE French (official), 50 Sudanic languages (90%)
RELIGION animist 40%, Sunni Muslim 50%, Christian (mainly Roman Catholic) 10%
EDUCATION (compulsory years) 6
LITERACY RATE 37% (men); 17% (women) (2003 est)
LABOUR FORCE 92% agriculture, 2% industry, 6% services (1996)
LIFE EXPECTANCY 45 (men); 46 (women) (2000–05)
CHILD MORTALITY RATE (under 5, per 1,000 live births) 197 (2001)
PHYSICIANS (per 1,000 people) 0.03 (1996 est)

HOSPITAL BEDS (per 1,000 people) 1.4 (1996 est)
TV SETS (per 1,000 people) 103 (2001 est)
RADIOS (per 1,000 people) 433 (2001 est)
INTERNET USERS (per 10,000 people) 20.9 (2002 est)
PERSONAL COMPUTER USERS (per 100 people) 0.2 (2002 est)

See also ▷Mossi; ▷West African Economic Community.

BURKINA FASO Crocodiles are found in several national parks in Burkino Faso. *Stanley Gibbons*

Chronology

13th–14th centuries: Formerly settled by Bobo, Lobi, and Gurunsi peoples, east and centre were conquered by Mossi and Gurma peoples, who established powerful warrior kingdoms, some of which survived until late 19th century.

1895–1903: France secured protectorates over the Mossi kingdom of Yatenga and the Gurma region, and annexed the Bobo and Lobi lands, meeting armed resistance.

1904: The French-controlled region, known as Upper Volta, was attached administratively to French Sudan; tribal chiefs were maintained in their traditional seats and the region was to serve as a labour reservoir for more developed colonies to the south.

1919: Made a separate French colony.

1932: Partitioned between French Sudan, the Côte d'Ivoire, and Niger.

1947: Became a French overseas territory.

1960: Independence was achieved, with Maurice Yaméogo as the first president.

1966: A military coup was led by Lt-Col Sangoulé Lamizana, and a supreme council of the armed forces established.

1977: The ban on political activities was removed. A referendum approved a new constitution based on civilian rule.

1978–80: Lamizana was elected president. In 1980 he was overthrown in a bloodless coup led by Col Saye Zerbo, as the economy deteriorated.

1982–83: Maj Jean-Baptiste Ouedraogo became president and Capt Thomas Sankara prime minister. In 1983 Sankara seized complete power.

1984: Upper Volta was renamed Burkina Faso ('land of upright men') to signify a break with the colonial past; literacy and afforestation campaigns were instigated by Sankara, who established links with Libya, Benin, and Ghana.

1987: Capt Blaise Compaoré became president.

1991: A new constitution was approved.

1992: Multiparty elections were won by the pro-Compaoré Popular Front (FP).

1996: Kadre Desire Ouedraogo was appointed prime minister.

1997: The CDP won assembly elections. Ouedraogo was reappointed prime minister.

1998: President Blaise Compaoré was re-elected with an overwhelming majority.

2000: Prime Minister Ouedraogo resigned and was replaced by Paramanga Ernest Yonli.

Engineering, food-processing, and the manufacture of tyres and rubber goods are also important. The Benedictine monks of Burton Abbey (founded in 1002) began the town's tradition of brewing in the 11th century.

Burundi see country box.

Bury city and administrative headquarters of Bury metropolitan borough, Greater Manchester, northwest England, on the River Irwell, 16 km/10 mi north of central Manchester; population (2001 est) 63,400. The principal industries are textiles, paper-making, and engineering. Other activities include printing and the manufacture of chemicals, textile machinery, felt, and paint.

Buryat (or Buryatiya; formerly (1923–58) **Buryat–Mongol Autonomous Soviet Socialist Republic**) republic in the eastern Siberian region of the Russian Federation; area 351,300 sq km/135,637 sq mi; population (1996) 1,053,000 (70% Russian, 24% Buryat). The main cities are Ulan-Ude (capital), Kyakhta, and Gusinoozersk. Buryat is bordered on the south by Mongolia, and occupies the eastern and northern shores of Lake ▷Baikal.

The land is largely mountainous and covered by coniferous forests; the Sayan Mountains are in the far west. Mineral deposits include rare metals (tungsten, molybdenum, gold), together with lignite (brown coal), iron ore, and graphite.

bus in computing, the electrical pathway through which a computer processor communicates with some of its parts and/or peripherals. Physically, a bus is a set of parallel tracks that can carry digital signals; it may take the form of copper tracks laid down on the computer's ▷printed circuit boards (PCBs), or of an external cable or connection.

Bush, George Herbert Walker (1924–) 41st president of the USA 1989–93, a Republican. He was director of the Central Intelligence Agency (CIA) 1976–81 and US vice-president 1981–89. As president, his response to the Soviet leader Mikhail Gorbachev's diplomatic initiatives were initially criticized as inadequate, but his sending of US troops to depose his former ally, General Manuel ▷Noriega of Panama, proved a popular move at home. Success in the 1991 Gulf War against Iraq further raised his standing. Domestic economic problems 1991–92 were followed by his defeat

in the 1992 presidential elections by the Democrat Bill Clinton. His son, George W ▷Bush, became president of the USA in 2001.

Related Web site: George Bush Presidential Library http://bushlibrary.tamu.edu/

Bush, George W(alker), Jr (1946–) 43rd president of the USA from 2001. Republican governor of Texas 1994–2000 and son of former president George ▷Bush, he was elected president after defeating Democrat Al ▷Gore in a hotly disputed contest and with a smaller share (48.1%) of the popular vote than his Democrat rival (48.3%). The presidency was conceded to Bush 36 days after the election, following a narrow decision by the divided US supreme court. Inexperienced in foreign affairs, Bush is supported in his administration by his father's former defence secretary, Dick ▷Cheney, who is vice-president, and the former head of the armed forces, Colin ▷Powell, who is secretary of state.

Bush has projected himself as a 'compassionate conservative', who combines traditional Republican values – such as support for low taxation, small but effective government, a strong military, and Christian family values – with greater concern for the underprivileged, including a larger role for churches and charities

Burundi

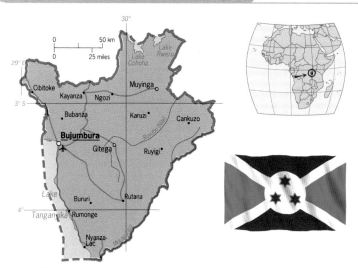

Burundi formerly Urundi (until 1962) country in east central Africa, bounded north by Rwanda, west by Congo (formerly Zaire), southwest by Lake Tanganyika, and southeast and east by Tanzania.

NATIONAL NAME *Republika y'Uburundi/République du Burundi/Republic of Burundi*
AREA 27,834 sq km/10,746 sq mi
CAPITAL Bujumbura
MAJOR TOWNS/CITIES Gitega, Bururi, Ngozi, Muyinga, Ruyigi, Kayanza
PHYSICAL FEATURES landlocked grassy highland straddling watershed of Nile and Congo; Lake Tanganyika, Great Rift Valley

Government

HEAD OF STATE AND GOVERNMENT Domitien Ndayizeye from 2003
POLITICAL SYSTEM military
POLITICAL EXECUTIVE military
ADMINISTRATIVE DIVISIONS 15 provinces
ARMED FORCES 45,500; plus paramilitary forces of 5,500 (2002 est)
CONSCRIPTION military service is voluntary
DEATH PENALTY retained and used for ordinary crimes
DEFENCE SPEND (% GDP) 5.9 (2002 est)
EDUCATION SPEND (% GDP) 3.4 (2001 est)
HEALTH SPEND (% GDP) 3.1 (2000 est)

Economy and resources

CURRENCY Burundi franc
GPD (US$) 719 million (2002 est)
REAL GDP GROWTH (% change on previous year) 2 (2001)
GNI (US$) 704 million (2002 est)
GNI PER CAPITA (PPP) (US$) 610 (2002 est)
CONSUMER PRICE INFLATION 7.1% (2003 est)
FOREIGN DEBT (US$) 1.03 billion (2001 est)

MAJOR TRADING PARTNERS Belgium, Germany, Zambia, France, Switzerland, Tanzania, Kenya, Japan, USA
RESOURCES nickel, gold, tungsten, phosphates, vanadium, uranium, peat, petroleum deposits have been detected
INDUSTRIES textiles, leather, food and agricultural products EXPORTS coffee, tea, glass products, hides and skins. Principal market: Switzerland 32.6% (2001)
IMPORTS machinery and transport equipment, petroleum and petroleum products, cement, malt (and malt flour). Principal source: Belgium 12% (2001)
ARABLE LAND 35% (2000 est)
AGRICULTURAL PRODUCTS coffee, tea, cassava, sweet potatoes, bananas, beans; cattle rearing

Population and society

POPULATION 6,825,000 (2003 est)
POPULATION GROWTH RATE 1.7% (2000–15)
POPULATION DENSITY (per sq km) 245 (2003 est)
URBAN POPULATION (% of total) 10 (2003 est)
AGE DISTRIBUTION (% of total population) 0–14 47%, 15–59 49%, 60+ 4% (2002 est)
ETHNIC GROUPS two main groups: the agriculturalist Hutu, comprising about 85% of the population, and the predominantly pastoralist Tutsi, about 14%. There is a small Pygmy (Twa) minority, comprising about 1% of the population, and a few Europeans and Asians

LANGUAGE Kirundi, French (both official), Kiswahili
RELIGION Roman Catholic 62%, Pentecostalist 5%, Anglican 1%, Muslim 1%, animist
EDUCATION (compulsory years) 6
LITERACY RATE 58% (men); 45% (women) (2003 est)
LABOUR FORCE 90.7% agriculture, 2.1% industry, 7.2% services (1997 est)
LIFE EXPECTANCY 40 (men); 41 (women) (2000–05)
CHILD MORTALITY RATE (under 5, per 1,000 live births) 190 (2001)
PHYSICIANS (per 1,000 people) 0.5 (1997 est)
HOSPITAL BEDS (per 1,000 people) 0.2 (1997 est)
TV SETS (per 1,000 people) 30 (2001 est)

RADIOS (per 1,000 people) 220 (2001 est)
INTERNET USERS (per 10,000 people) 12 (2002 est)
PERSONAL COMPUTER USERS (per 100 people) 0.1 (2002 est)

See also ▷Hutu; ▷Pygmy; ▷Rwanda; ▷Tutsi; ▷Twa.

BURUNDI These stamps reflect Burundi's Roman Catholic majority. *Stanley Gibbons*

Chronology

10th century: Originally inhabited by the hunter-gatherer Twa Pygmies. Hutu peoples settled in the region and became peasant farmers.

13th century: Taken over by Banu Hutus.

15th–17th centuries: The majority Hutu community came under the dominance of the cattle-owning Tutsi peoples, immigrants from the east, who became a semi-aristocracy; the minority Tutsis developed a feudalistic political system, organized around a nominal king, with royal princes in control of local areas.

1890: Known as Urundi, the Tutsi kingdom, along with neighbouring Rwanda, came under nominal German control as Ruanda-Urundi.

1916: Occupied by Belgium during World War I.

1923: Belgium was granted a League of Nations mandate to administer Ruanda-Urundi; it was to rule 'indirectly' through the Tutsi chiefs.

1962: Burundi was separated from Ruanda-Urundi, and given independence as a monarchy under Tutsi King Mwambutsa IV.

1965: The king refused to appoint a Hutu prime minister after an election in which Hutu candidates were victorious; an attempted coup by Hutus was brutally suppressed.

1966: The king was deposed by his teenage son Charles, who became Ntare V; he was in turn deposed by his Tutsi prime minister Col Michel Micombero, who declared Burundi a republic; the Tutsi-dominated Union for National Progress (UPRONA) was declared the only legal political party.

1972: Ntare V was killed, allegedly by Hutus, provoking a massacre of 150,000 Hutus by Tutsi soldiers; 100,000 Hutus fled to Tanzania.

1976: An army coup deposed Micombero and appointed the Tutsi Col Jean-Baptiste Bagaza as president. He launched a drive against corruption and a programme of land reforms and economic development.

1987: Bagaza was deposed in a coup by the Tutsi Maj Pierre Buyoya.

1988: About 24,000 Hutus were killed by Tutsis and 60,000 fled to Rwanda.

1992: A new multiparty constitution was adopted following a referendum.

1993: Melchior Ndadaye, a Hutu, was elected president in the first-ever democratic contest, but was killed in a coup by the Tutsi-dominated army; 100,000 people died in the massacres that followed.

1994: Cyprien Ntaryamira, a Hutu, became president but was later killed in an air crash along with the Rwandan president Juvenal Habyarimana. There was an eruption of ethnic violence; 750,000 Hutus fled to Rwanda. Hutu Sylvestre Ntibantunganya became head of state, serving with a Tutsi prime minister, as part of a four-year power-sharing agreement.

1995: Renewed ethnic violence erupted in the capital, Bujumbura, following a massacre of Hutu refugees.

1996: The former Tutsi president Pierre Buyoya seized power amid renewed ethnic violence; the coup provoked economic sanctions by other African countries. A 'government of national unity' was appointed, with Pascal-Firmin Ndimira as premier.

1998: There was renewed fighting between Tutsi-led army and Hutu rebels. A ceasefire was agreed between the warring political factions. The position of head of government was abolished, with President Buyoya assuming the role.

2000: With the civil war worsening, Nelson Mandela, the new mediator for Burundi, met government, opposition, and rebel leaders in Tanzania. A power-sharing peace agreement was reached by most political factions, though three Tutsi parties declined to sign. Despite the agreement, the war continued.

2001: A regional summit chaired by Nelson Mandela failed to bring peace.

in helping the poor. Despite his privileged upbringing, he has a populist appeal and charm, with simple tastes and a lack of curiosity in policy details. However, his mandate to govern was weakened by the nature of his presidential victory, based on a very thin plurality of counted votes in Florida, a state in which his younger brother, Jeb Bush, was governor. He is only the fourth US president to have triumphed in the electoral college despite losing the popular vote and, after John Quincy Adams, only the second son of a former president to be elected to the Oval Office. He has the shortest experience in public service of any US president since Woodrow Wilson in 1912.

Bush's administration faced its toughest challenge in the aftermath of the terrorist attacks on New York and Washington, DC, on 11 September 2001. It was the worst act of terrorism in the USA, and internal security and the fight against terrorism became the focus of the administration. Bush worked hard throughout September to build an international anti-terrorism coalition, and launched military strikes on Afghanistan in an attempt to force the Taliban regime to give up the prime suspect in the attacks, Saudi-born terrorist leader, Osama bin Laden. However, in 2003 Bush faced widespread international criticism for his administration's increasingly militaristic stance over the issue of Iraq disarmament, which resulted in the ▷Iraq War.

bushbaby small nocturnal African prosimian with long feet, long, bushy tail, and large ears. Bushbabies are active tree dwellers and feed on fruit, insects, eggs, and small birds.

bushbuck antelope *Tragelaphus scriptus* found over most of Africa south of the Sahara. Up to 1 m/3 ft tall, the males have keeled horns twisted into spirals, and are brown to blackish. The females

BUSHBUCK A male bushbuck in the Kruger National Park, South Africa. *Premaphotos Wildlife*

are generally hornless, lighter, and redder. All have white markings, including stripes or vertical rows of dots down the sides. Rarely far from water, bushbuck live in woods and thick brush.

bushel dry or liquid measure equal to eight gallons or four pecks (2,219.36 cu in/36.37 litres) in the UK; some US states have different standards according to the goods measured.

Bushmen former name for the ▷Kung, ▷San, and other hunting and gathering groups (for example, the Gikwe, Heikom, and Sekhoin) living in and around the Kalahari Desert in southern Africa. They number approximately 50,000 and speak San and other click languages of the ▷Khoisan family. They are characteristically small-statured.

bushranger Australian armed robber of the 19th century. The first bushrangers were escaped convicts. The last gang was led by Ned Kelly and his brother Dan in 1878–80. They form the subject of many Australian ballads.

Busoni, Ferruccio Dante Benvenuto (1866–1924) Italian pianist, composer, and music critic. Much of his music was for the piano, but he also composed several operas including *Doktor Faust*, completed by Philipp Jarnach after Busoni's death. His work shows the influence of Liszt and his ballet score for *Doktor Faust* shows his debt to Bizet. Specimens of his style at its best are to be found in his later sonatinas, *Sarabande und Cortège* from *Faust*, and the monumental *Fantasia contrappuntistica* for piano. An apostle of Futurism, he encouraged the French composer Edgard Varèse.

bustard bird of the family Otididae, order Gruiformes, related to ▷cranes but with a rounder body, thicker neck, and a relatively short beak. Bustards are found on the ground on open plains and fields.

The great bustard *Otis tarda* is one of the heaviest flying birds at 18 kg/40 lb, and the larger males may have a length of 1 m/3 ft and wingspan of 2.3 m/7.5 ft. It is found in northern Asia and Europe, although there are fewer than 30,000 great bustards left in Europe; two-thirds of these live on the Spanish steppes.

It has been extinct in Britain for some time. Attempts made in 1970 to naturalize it again on Salisbury Plain ended in failure but plans for another attempt were made in 2000. The little bustard *O. tetrax* is less than half the size of the great bustard, and is also found in continental Europe. The great Indian bustard is endangered because of hunting and loss of its habitat to agriculture; there are fewer than 1,000 individuals left.

butane C_4H_{10} one of two gaseous alkanes (paraffin hydrocarbons) having the same formula but differing in structure. Normal butane is derived from natural gas; isobutane is a by-product of petroleum manufacture. Liquefied under pressure, it is used as a fuel for industrial and domestic purposes (for example, in portable cookers).

Bute, John Stuart 3rd Earl of Bute (1713–1792) British Tory politician, prime minister 1762–63. On the accession of George III in 1760, he became the chief instrument in the king's policy for breaking the power of the Whigs and establishing the personal rule of the monarch through Parliament.

Buthelezi, Chief Mangosuthu Gatsha (1928–) South African Zulu leader and politician, president of the Zulu-based ▷Inkatha Freedom Party (IFP), which he founded as a paramilitary organization for attaining a nonracial democratic society in 1975. Buthelezi's threatened boycott of South Africa's first multiracial elections led to a dramatic escalation in politically motivated violence, but he eventually agreed to register his party and in May 1994 was appointed home affairs minister in the country's first post-apartheid government. In December 1995 there were unsubstantiated claims that he had colluded with the security service during the apartheid period. In June 1999 Buthelezi was offered the post of deputy president of South Africa by the new president Thabo Mbeki. Buthelezi refused the post.

Buthelezi, great-grandson of King ▷Cetewayo, became chief minister of KwaZulu, then a black ▷homeland in the Republic of South Africa, in 1970. Opposed to KwaZulu becoming a ▷Black National State, he argued instead for a confederation of black areas, with eventual majority rule over all South Africa under a one-party socialist system. He was accused of complicity in the factional violence between Inkatha and ▷African National Congress supporters that racked the townships during the early 1990s.

Butler, Richard Austen (1902–1982) Baron Butler of Saffron Walden; called 'Rab'. British Conservative politician. As minister of education 1941–45, he was responsible for the 1944 Education Act that introduced the 11-plus examination for selection of grammar school pupils; he was chancellor of the Exchequer 1951–55, Lord Privy Seal 1955–59, and foreign minister 1963–64. As a candidate for the prime ministership, he was defeated by Harold Macmillan in 1957 (under whom he was home secretary 1957–62), and by Alec Douglas Home in 1963.

Butler, Samuel (1612–1680) English satirist. His best-known poem *Hudibras*, published in three parts in 1663, 1664, and 1678, became immediately popular for its biting satire against the Puritans and on other contemporary issues.

Butler also wrote minor poetic satires, and prose 'characters' not published until 1759. He was a strong influence on the poetry of Jonathan ▷Swift.

Butler, Samuel (1835–1902) English writer. He made his name in 1872 with a satiric attack on contemporary utopianism, *Erewhon* (an anagram of *nowhere*). He is now remembered for his unfinished, semi-autobiographical discursive novel, *The Way of All Flesh*, a study of Victorian conventions, the causes and effects of the clash between generations, and religious hypocrisy (written and frequently revised 1873–84 and posthumously published in 1903).

The Fair Haven (1873) examined the miraculous element in Christianity. *Life and Habit* (1877) and other works were devoted to a criticism of the theory of natural selection. In *The Authoress of the Odyssey* (1897) he maintained that Homer's *Odyssey* was the work of a woman.

SAMUEL BUTLER After being a page in the household of Elizabeth, Countess of Kent, Samuel Butler worked as clerk to several Puritan justices of the peace. Some of the characters in his work *Hudibras* were later based on these men. *Archive Photos*

Butlin, Billy (1899–1980) Born William Heygate Edmund Colborne Butlin. British holiday-camp entrepreneur, born in South Africa. He originated a chain of camps (the first was at Skegness in 1936) that provided accommodation, meals, and amusements at an inclusive price. He was knighted in 1964.

butte steep-sided, flat-topped hill, formed in horizontally layered sedimentary rocks, largely in arid areas. A large butte with a pronounced tablelike profile is a ▷mesa.

buttercup any plant of the buttercup family with divided leaves and yellow flowers. (Genus *Ranunculus*, family Ranunculaceae.) Species include the common buttercup (*Ranunculus acris*) and the creeping buttercup (*R. repens*).

Butterfield, William (1814–1900) English Gothic Revival architect. His work is characterized by vigorous, aggressive forms and multicoloured striped and patterned brickwork. He held original views as to colour in architecture, holding that any combination of natural colours of the materials was permissible. His schools, parsonages, and cottages developed an appealing functional secular style that anticipated Philip Webb and other ▷Arts and Crafts architects.

butterfly insect belonging, like moths, to the order Lepidoptera, in which the wings are covered with tiny scales, often brightly coloured. There are some 15,000 species of butterfly, many of which

> ### Samuel Butler
> *All progress is based upon a universal innate desire on the part of every organism to live beyond its income.*
> *Notebooks, 'Life'*

BUTTE Chimney Rock near Shiprock, New Mexico, USA – a notable example of the butte geological formation. *K G Preston-Mafham/Premaphotos Wildlife*

BUTTERFLY The life cycle of a butterfly (painted lady *Vanessa cardui*). Eggs are laid on plants (usually the underside of leaves) and the larvae (caterpillars) feed on the plant, growing in size until ready to pupate. When the caterpillar is full-sized it forms a chrysalis in which it undergoes transformation from caterpillar to adult butterfly. The life cycle of moths is very similar.

are under threat throughout the world because of the destruction of habitat.

One in eight of Europe's butterfly species are under threat, according to a 1999 survey. Of the 576 European species, 71 experienced a steady decline throughout the 20th century.

In the period 1984–99, 20 of Britain's 56 resident species have declined in number.

Related Web site: Butterfly Web Site http://mgfx.com/butterfly/

butterfly fish any of several fishes, not all related. They include the freshwater butterfly fish *Pantodon buchholzi* of western Africa and the tropical marine butterfly fishes in family Chaetodontidae.

butterwort insectivorous plant belonging to the bladderwort family, with purplish flowers and a rosette of flat leaves covered with a sticky substance that traps insects. (Genus *Pinguicula*, family Lentibulariaceae.)

BUTTERWORT The tiny *Pinguicula chilensis* growing on the Cerro Cathedral in Neuquen Province, Argentina, is fairly typical of butterworts as a whole. *Premaphotos Wildlife*

buttress (from Old French *bouterez* 'to thrust'.) in architecture, a vertical mass of masonry projecting from the outer face of a wall at intervals, to resist the outward thrust of a vault, roof-truss, or girder. Buttresses were seldom used in classical architecture, and in Romanesque architecture were of slight bulk and projection; but in the Gothic period they were progressively increased in size, thus enabling the intervening wall to be reduced in thickness and to be pierced with large windows.

Buxtehude, Dietrich (1637–1707) Danish composer. In 1668 he was appointed organist at the Marienkirche, Lübeck, Germany, where his fame attracted Johann Sebastian Bach and Handel. He is remembered for his organ works and cantatas, written for his evening concerts (*Abendmusiken*); he also wrote numerous trio sonatas for two violins, viola da gamba, and harpsichord.

buyer's market market having an excess of goods and services on offer and where prices are likely to be declining. The buyer benefits from the wide choice and competition available.

buzzard species of medium-sized hawk with broad wings, often seen soaring. Buzzards are in the falcon family, Falconidae, order Falconiformes. The **common buzzard** *Buteo buteo* of Europe and Asia is about 55 cm/1.8 ft long with a wingspan of over 1.2 m/4 ft. It preys on a variety of small animals up to the size of a rabbit.

The **rough-legged buzzard** *B. lagopus* lives in the northern tundra and eats lemmings. The **honey buzzard** *Pernis apivora* feeds largely, as its name suggests, on honey and insect larvae. It spends the summer in Europe and western Asia and winters in Africa. The **red-shouldered hawk** *B. lineatus* and **red-tailed hawk** *B. jamaicensis* occur in North America.

Byatt, A(ntonia) S(usan) (1936–   ) English novelist and critic. Her fifth novel, *Possession*, won the 1990 Booker Prize. *The Virgin in the Garden* (1978) is a confident, zestfully handled account of a varied group of characters putting on a school play during the coronation year of 1953. It has a sequel, *Still Life* (1985). The third part of this projected quartet is *Babel Tower* (1996), set in the 1960s. *Angels and Insects* (1992) has twin themes of entomology and spiritualism.

Byatt was born in Sheffield and educated at a Quaker boarding school (with her sister, novelist Margaret Drabble) and at Newnham College, Cambridge. Her collection of short stories,

Elementals, was published in 1998. Other works include the novel *A Biographer's Tale* (2000).

Related Web site: A S Byatt's Possession http://www.sjsu.edu/depts/jwss.old/possession/

Byblos ancient Phoenician city (modern Jebeil), 32 km/20 mi north of Beirut, Lebanon. Known to the Assyrians and Babylonians as **Gubla**, it had a thriving export of cedar and pinewood to Egypt as early as 1500 BC. In Roman times it boasted an amphitheatre, baths, and a temple, and was known for its celebration of the resurrection of Adonis, worshipped as a god of vegetation.

Byelorussia alternative name for ▷Belarus.

Byrd, Richard Evelyn (1888–1957) US aviator and explorer. The first to fly over the North Pole (1926), he also flew over the South Pole (1929) and led five overland expeditions in Antarctica.

Related Web site: Byrd, Richard E http://www-bprc.mps.ohio-state.edu:80

Byrd, William (1543–1623) English composer. His sacred and secular choral music, including over 200 motets and Masses for three, four, and five voices, exemplifies the English polyphonic style.

Byrds, the US pioneering folk-rock group 1964–73. Emulated for their 12-string guitar sound, as on the hits 'Mr Tambourine Man' (a 1965 version of Bob Dylan's song) and 'Eight Miles High' (1966), they moved toward country rock in the late 1960s, setting another trend.

Related Web site: International Monetary Fund http://www.imf.org/external/about.htm

Byron, George Gordon (1788–1824) 6th Baron Byron. English poet. He became the symbol of ▷Romanticism and political liberalism throughout Europe in the 19th century. His reputation was established with the first two cantos of *Childe Harold* (1812). Later works include *The Prisoner of Chillon* (1816), *Beppo* (1818), *Mazeppa* (1819), and, most notably, the satirical *Don Juan* (1819–24). He left England in 1816 and spent most of his later life in Italy.

Born in London and educated at Harrow and Cambridge University, Byron published his first volume *Hours of Idleness* in 1807 and attacked its harsh critics in *English Bards and Scotch Reviewers* (1809). Overnight fame came with the first two cantos of *Childe Harold*, which romantically describes his tours in Portugal, Spain, and the Balkans (third canto 1816, fourth 1818). In 1815 he married mathematician Ann Milbanke (1792–1860), with whom he had a daughter, Augusta Ada Byron. The couple separated shortly after the birth amid much scandal. He then went to Europe and became friendly with Percy and Mary Shelley. He engaged in Italian revolutionary politics and sailed to Greece in 1823 to further the Greek struggle for independence, but died of fever at Missolonghi. He is also remembered for his lyrics and his colloquially easy *Letters* (first published in 1830).

Related Web site: Don Juan http://eserver.org/poetry/don-juan.txt

byte sufficient computer memory to store a single character of data. The character is stored in the byte of memory as a pattern of ▷bits (binary digits), using a code such as

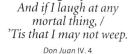

George Byron
And if I laugh at any mortal thing, /
'Tis that I may not weep.
Don Juan IV. 4

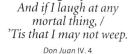

BYRON An engraving of English poet Lord Byron. *Archive Photos*

BYZANTINE A Byzantine fresco of Cain killing Abel in the basilica of Sant'Angelo in Formia, Italy. The fresco dates to the late 11th century, and is one of a number of frescos in the nave depicting Biblical scenes. *The Art Archive/ Ethnographic Museum Vinnica Ukraine/Dagli Orti*

Byzantine Empire

330	Emperor Constantine converts to Christianity and moves his capital to Constantinople.
395	The Roman Empire is divided into eastern and western halves.
476	The Western Empire is overrun by barbarian invaders.
527–565	Emperor Justinian I temporarily recovers Italy, North Africa, and parts of Spain.
7th–8th centuries	Syria, Egypt, and North Africa are lost to the Muslims, who twice besiege Constantinople (673–77, 718), but the Christian Byzantines maintain their hold on Anatolia.
8th–11th centuries	The iconoclastic controversy brings the emperors into conflict with the papacy, and in 1054 the Greek Orthodox Church breaks with the Roman.
867–1056	Under the Macedonian dynasty the Byzantine Empire reaches the height of its prosperity; the Bulgars prove a formidable danger, but after a long struggle are finally crushed in 1018 by Basil II ('the Bulgar-Slayer'). After Basil's death the Byzantine Empire declines because of internal factions.
1071–73	The Seljuk Turks conquer most of Anatolia.
1204	The Fourth Crusade sacks Constantinople and sets Baldwin of Flanders (1171–1205) on the throne of the new Latin (western European) Empire.
1261	The Greeks recapture the Latin (western European) Empire and restore the Byzantine Empire, but it maintains a precarious existence.
1453	The Turks capture Constantinople and found the Ottoman Empire.

▷ASCII. A byte usually contains eight bits – for example, the capital letter F can be stored as the bit pattern 01000110.

A single byte can specify 256 values, such as the decimal numbers from 0 to 255; in the case of a single-byte ▷pixel (picture element), it can specify 256 different colours. Three bytes (24 bits) can specify 16,777,216 values. Computer memory size is measured in **kilobytes** (1,024 bytes) or **megabytes** (1,024 kilobytes).

Byzantine style in the visual arts and architecture that originated in the 4th–5th centuries in Byzantium (the capital of the Eastern Roman Empire) and spread to Italy, throughout the Balkans, and to Russia, where it survived for many centuries. It is characterized by heavy stylization, strong linear emphasis, the use of rigid artistic stereotypes, and rich colours such as gold. Byzantine artists excelled in mosaic work, manuscript painting, and religious ▷icon painting. In architecture, the dome supported on pendentives was in widespread use.

Byzantine Empire the **Eastern Roman Empire** 395–1453, with its capital at Constantinople (formerly Byzantium, modern Istanbul). It was the direct continuation of the Roman Empire in the East, and inherited many of its traditions and institutions.

Byzantine literature literature of the Byzantine Empire, 4th–15th centuries. It was written mainly in the Greek *koinē*, a form of Greek accepted as the literary language of the 1st century and increasingly archaic and separate from the spoken tongue of the people. Byzantine literature is chiefly concerned with theology, history, and commentaries on the Greek classics. Its chief authors are the theologians Athanasius, Basil, Gregory of Nyssa, Gregory of Nazianzus, John Chrysostom, Cyril of Alexandria (all 4th century), and John of Damascus (8th century); the historians Zosimus (*c.* 500), Procopius (6th century), Psellus (1018–1097), Bryennius and his wife ▷Anna Comnena (*c.* 1100), and Georgius Acropolita (1220–1282).

The literary encyclopedia *Suda*, which provides a wealth of information on classical and Byzantine literature, was compiled in about 975. Drama was nonexistent, and poetry, apart from the hymns of the 6th–8th centuries, was scanty and stilted, but there were many popular works about the lives of the saints. The tradition ended with the fall of Constantinople in 1453.

Byzantium (modern Istanbul) ancient Greek city on the Bosporus, founded as a colony of the Greek city of Megara on an important strategic site at the entrance to the Black Sea about 660 BC. In AD 330 the capital of the Roman Empire was transferred there by Constantine the Great, who renamed it Constantinople and it became the capital of the ▷Byzantine Empire to which it gave its name.

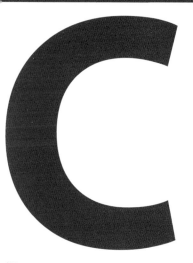

C

°**C** symbol for degrees ▷Celsius, sometimes called centigrade.

C abbreviation for **centum** (Latin 'hundred'); **century**; **centigrade**; ▷Celsius.

C in computing, a high-level, general-purpose programming language popular on minicomputers and microcomputers. Developed in the early 1970s from an earlier language called BCPL, C was first used as the language of the operating system ▷Unix, though it has since become widespread beyond Unix. It is useful for writing fast and efficient systems programs, such as operating systems (which control the operations of the computer).

c. abbreviation for **circa** (Latin 'about'), used with dates that are uncertain.

CA abbreviation for the state of ▷California, USA.

Cabal, the (from *kabbala*) group of politicians, the English king Charles II's counsellors 1667–73, whose initials made up the word by coincidence – Clifford (Thomas Clifford 1630–1673), Ashley (Anthony Ashley Cooper, 1st Earl of ▷Shaftesbury), ▷Buckingham (George Villiers, 2nd Duke of Buckingham), Arlington (Henry Bennett, 1st Earl of Arlington 1618–1685), and ▷Lauderdale (John Maitland, Duke of Lauderdale). The word cabal, meaning 'association of intriguers', is now applied to any faction that works in secret for private or political ends.

cabaret theatrical revue traditionally combining satire and song and performed in cafés or bars. Originating in Paris in the late 19th century in venues such as the Moulin Rouge, cabaret was embraced by avant-garde writers and artists. In Germany, Berlin became a centre for an increasingly political cabaret in the 1920s, which was later suppressed by the Nazis. In Britain, satirical revue was revived by the Cambridge Footlights theatre group in *Beyond the Fringe* (1961), before cabaret and alternative comedy combined to provide a new generation of stand-up entertainers during the 1980s, notably from the Comedy Store group in London.

cabbage vegetable plant related to the turnip and wild mustard, or charlock. It was cultivated as early as 2000 BC, and the many commercial varieties include kale, Brussels sprouts, common cabbage, savoy, cauliflower, sprouting broccoli, and kohlrabi. (*Brassica oleracea*, family Cruciferae.)

cabbage butterfly one of several butterfly species, the caterpillars of which feed on the leaves of members of the cabbage family, particularly as pests on cabbages. ▷Ichneumon flies parasitize the caterpillars, thereby controlling their numbers. Cabbage butterflies are in genus *Pieris* in order Lepidoptera, class Insecta, phylum Arthropoda.

cabbala alternative spelling of ▷kabbala.

Cabinda (or **Kabinda**) coastal exclave, a province of ▷Angola, bounded on the east and south by the Democratic Republic of Congo, on the north by the Republic of the Congo, and on the west by the Atlantic Ocean; area 7,770 sq km/3,000 sq mi; population (1992) 152,100. The capital is Cabinda. There are oil reserves. Products include timber and phosphates. Attached to Angola in 1886, the exclave has made claims to independence.

cabinet ('a small room, implying secrecy') in politics, the group of ministers holding a country's highest executive offices who decide government policy. In Britain the cabinet system originated under the Stuarts. Under William III it became customary for the king to select his ministers from the party with a parliamentary majority. The US cabinet, unlike the British, does not initiate legislation, and its members, appointed by the president, must not be members of Congress. The term was used in the USA from 1793.
Related Web site: Cabinet Office Home Page http://www.cabinet-office.gov.uk/

cable unit of length, used on ships, originally the length of a ship's anchor cable or 120 fathoms (219 m/720 ft), but now taken as one-tenth of a ▷nautical mile (185.3 m/608 ft).

Cable News Network (CNN) international television news channel; the 24-hour service was founded in 1980 by US entrepreneur Ted Turner (1938–) and has its headquarters in Atlanta, Georgia. It established its global reputation in 1991 with eyewitness accounts from Baghdad of the beginning of the Gulf War.

cable television distribution of broadcast signals through cable relay systems. Narrow-band systems were originally used to deliver services to areas with poor regular reception; systems with wider bands, using coaxial and fibreoptic cable, are increasingly used for distribution and development of home-based interactive services, typically telephones.

Cabot, Sebastian (1474–1557) Italian navigator and cartographer, the second son of Giovanni ▷Caboto. He explored the Brazilian coast and the Rio de la Plata for the Holy Roman Emperor Charles V 1526–30.

Cabot was also employed by Henry VIII, Edward VI, and Ferdinand of Spain. He planned a voyage to China by way of the Northeast Passage, the sea route along the north Eurasian coast, encouraged the formation of the Company of Merchant Adventurers of London in 1551, and in 1553 and 1556 directed the company's expeditions to Russia, where he opened British trade.

SEBASTIAN CABOT Italian navigator and cartographer Sebastian Cabot. *Archive Photos*

Caboto, Giovanni (c. 1450–c. 1498) English **John Cabot**. Italian navigator. Commissioned, with his three sons, by Henry VII of England to discover unknown lands, he arrived at Cape Breton Island on 24 June 1497, thus becoming the first European to reach the North American mainland (he thought he was in northeast Asia). In 1498 he sailed again, touching Greenland, and probably died on the voyage.

cactus (plural **cacti**) strictly, any plant of the family Cactaceae, although the word is commonly used to describe many different succulent and prickly plants. True cacti have a woody axis

CACTUS The strawberry cactus *Echinocereus enneacanthus*, which bears bright pink flowers and edible fruit. *Premaphotos Wildlife*

(central core) surrounded by a large fleshy stem, which takes various forms and is usually covered with spines (actually reduced leaves). They are all specially adapted to growing in dry areas.
Related Web site: Cactus and Succulent Plant Mall http://www.cactus-mall.com/index.html

CAD (acronym for computer-aided design) use of computers in creating and editing design drawings. CAD also allows such things as automatic testing of designs and multiple or animated three-dimensional views of designs. CAD systems are widely used in architecture, electronics, and engineering, for example in the motor-vehicle industry, where cars designed with the assistance of computers are now commonplace. With a CAD system, picture components are accurately positioned using grid lines. Pictures can be resized, rotated, or mirrored without loss of quality or proportion.

caddis fly insect of the order Trichoptera. Adults are generally dull brown, mothlike, with wings covered in tiny hairs. Mouthparts are poorly developed, and many caddis flies do not feed as adults. They are usually found near water.

CADDIS FLY Caddis fly adults form dense mating swarms. *Premaphotos Wildlife*

Cádiz Spanish city and naval base, capital and seaport of the province of Cádiz, sited on a peninsula on the south side of Cádiz Bay, an inlet of the Atlantic Ocean, 103 km/64 mi south of Seville; population (1991) 153,600. There are ferries to the Canary Islands and Casablanca, and shipbuilding and repairs are important, as are fishing and tourism. After the discovery of the Americas in 1492, Cádiz became one of Europe's most vital trade ports. The English adventurer Francis ▷Drake burned a Spanish fleet here in 1587 to prevent the sailing of the ▷Armada. The city has an 18th-century cathedral.

cadmium soft, silver-white, ductile, and malleable metallic element, symbol Cd, atomic number 48, relative atomic mass 112.40. Cadmium occurs in nature as a sulphide or carbonate in zinc ores. It is a toxic metal that, because of industrial dumping, has become an environmental pollutant. It is used in batteries, electroplating, and as a constituent of alloys used for bearings with low coefficients of friction; it is also a constituent of an alloy with a very low melting point.

Cadmium is also used in the control rods of nuclear reactors, because of its high absorption of neutrons. It was named in 1817 by the German chemist Friedrich Strohmeyer (1776–1835) after the Greek mythological character Cadmus.

Cadwalader (died c. 664) Semi-mythical British king, the son of Cadwallon, king of Gwynedd, North Wales, described by Geoffrey of Monmouth in his book *Historia Regum Britanniae* (*History of the Kings of Britain*).

caecilian tropical amphibian of wormlike appearance. There are about 170 species known in the family Caeciliidae, forming the amphibian order Apoda (also known as Caecilia or Gymnophiona). Caecilians have a grooved skin that gives a 'segmented' appearance; they have no trace of limbs or pelvis. The body is 20–130 cm/8–50 in long, beige to black in colour. The eyes are very small and weak or blind. They eat insects and small worms. Some species bear live young, others lay eggs.

Caecilians live in burrows in damp ground in the tropical Americas, Africa, Asia, and the Seychelles.

Caedmon (lived c. 660–670) Earliest known English Christian poet. According to the Northumbrian historian Bede, when Caedmon was a cowherd at the monastery of Whitby, he was commanded to sing by a stranger in a dream, and on waking produced a hymn on the Creation. The poem is preserved in some manuscripts. Caedmon became a monk and may have composed other religious poems.

Caen administrative centre of Calvados *département* and of the ▷Basse-Normandie region, France, on the River Orne, 200 km/124 mi from Paris; population (1990) 115,600, conurbation 189,000.

It is a busy port, connected by 11 km/7 mi of canal to the English Channel. The town is also a business centre, with ironworks, manufacturing, electrical, and electronic industries, and produces a building stone that has been used widely since the 11th century. In World War II Caen was one of the main objectives of the ▷D-Day landings and was finally captured by British forces on 9 July 1944 after five weeks' fighting, during which it was badly damaged. Despite this, the town retains many historic buildings, especially churches. The central part of the town was rebuilt in the 1950s.

Caernarfon (or Caernarvon) administrative centre of ▷Gwynedd, north Wales, situated on the southwest shore of the ▷Menai Strait; population (1991) 9,700. Formerly the Roman station of **Segontium** (Caer Seint), it is now a market town, port, and tourist centre. Industries include the manufacture of plastics and metal-working.

Caernarfonshire (Welsh **Sir Gaernarfon**) former county of north Wales, now part of ▷Gwynedd.

Caerphilly unitary authority in south Wales, created in 1996 from parts of the former counties of Mid Glamorgan and Gwent.
area 270 sq km/104 sq mi **towns** Hengoed (administrative headquarters), Caerphilly, Bargoed, Newbridge, Rhymney **physical** rivers Rhymney and Sirhowy **industries** iron and steel production and coal mining have been replaced by a wide range of light industries **population** (1996) 172,000

Caesar family name of Julius Caesar and later an imperial title. Julius Caesar's grand-nephew and adopted son Octavius became Gaius Julius Caesar Octavianus (the future emperor ▷Augustus). From his day onwards, 'Caesar' became the family name of the reigning emperor and his heirs. When the emperor ▷Nero, the last of the Julio-Claudian line, died, all his successors from Galba onwards were called 'Caesar'. What had been a family name thus became a title.

As time passed, 'Caesar' became the title of an emperor's chosen deputy and/or heir, marking him out as second only to the emperor, who had the title 'Augustus'. The titles 'tsar' in Russia and 'kaiser' in Germany were both dreived from the name Caesar.

Caesar, Gaius Julius (100–44 BC) Roman general and dictator, considered Rome's most successful military commander. He formed with Pompey the Great and Marcus Licinius ▷Crassus (the Elder) the First Triumvirate in 60 BC. He conquered Gaul 58–50 BC and invaded Britain 55–54 BC. By leading his army across the river Rubicon into Italy in 49 BC, an act of treason, he provoked a civil war which ended in 45 BC with the defeat of Pompey and his supporters. He was voted dictator for life, but was assassinated by conspirators on 15 March 44 BC. Caesar was a skilled historian whose *Commentarii*, recounting his campaigns, has had a major impact on the way military history is written up to the present day.

Caesar's early career was conventional, in marked contrast with that of his later rival Pompey. He served as a military tribune in Asia 80–78 BC where he received Rome's highest decoration, the *corona civica*, usually awarded for saving a fellow citizen's life. A patrician, Caesar allied himself with the popular party, and when elected to the office of aedile (magistrate) in 65 BC, nearly ruined himself with lavish amusements for the Roman populace. Although a free thinker, he was elected chief pontiff in 63 BC and appointed governor of Further Spain (equivalent to modern Portugal and much of western, central, and southern Spain) in 61 BC. As governor he carried out some highly successful policing actions against the tribes of the area in 61–60 BC. His political alliance with Pompey and Crassus led to a consulship in 59 BC, and in 58 BC he was given a five-year governorship, extended to ten years in 55 BC, of the provinces of Illyria on the eastern shore of the Adriatic Sea and both Transalpine and Cisalpine Gaul (corresponding to present-day northern Italy, France, Belgium, part of Germany, and the southern Netherlands). During his tenure as governor, Caesar conquered Gallic territory up to the river Rhine, suffering only two reverses in this period: a detachment of 15 cohorts was annihilated in the winter of 54 BC, and his attack on the Gallic fortress-town of Gergovia in 52 BC ended in a costly failure. When his governorship ended in 49 BC, Caesar was immensely wealthy and the leader of a highly efficient and fanatically loyal army. Pompey had become his rival after Crassus died at Carrhae in 53 BC, and sided with factions in the Senate who wished to prosecute Caesar. Caesar led his army across the river Rubicon to meet Pompey's army in Italy, provoking a civil war that lasted until 45 BC. Caesar's brilliance as a general led to his great victories at Pharsalus in 48 BC, Thapsus in 46 BC, and in 47 BC against King Pharnaces II (ruled 63–47 BC) in Asia Minor, a campaign he summarized succinctly as *veni, vidi, vici* ('I came, I saw, I conquered'). He stayed some months in Egypt, where ▷Cleopatra, queen of Egypt, gave birth to his son, Caesarion. His final victory, in 45 BC, over the sons of Pompey at Munda in Spain, ended the war. However, Caesar failed to create a permanent peace and on 15 March 44 BC was stabbed to death at the foot of Pompey's statue in the Senate (see ▷Brutus, ▷Cassius).

Caesar crossed to Britain in 55 BC to discourage British Celts from sending aid to their cousins in Gaul. He landed in Kent, but was forced to leave after a few weeks when storms threatened the safety of his fleet. He returned in 54 BC for a more substantial campaign and deafeated the Britons, who were under the leadership of Cassivelaunus. After extracting tribute and assurances that the Britons would not interfere in Gaul, he left and returned to his main business of conquering Gaul. Neither expedition was planned as an invasion: the first was a show of strength, the second a punitive expedition.

Caesarea ancient city in Palestine (now Qisarya). It was built by Herod the Great 22–12 BC, and named in honour of the Roman emperor Augustus. The constructions included an artificial harbour (*portus Augusti*). Caesarea was the administrative capital of the Roman province of Judaea.

Caesarean section surgical operation to deliver a baby by way of an incision in the mother's abdominal and uterine walls. It may be recommended for almost any obstetric complication implying a threat to mother or baby.

Caesarean section was named after the Roman emperor Julius Caesar, who was born this way. In medieval Europe, it was performed mostly in attempts to save the life of a child whose mother had died in labour. The Christian Church forbade cutting open the mother before she was dead.

Britain's Caesarean rate – around 14% of all births – is one of the highest in Europe.

Related Web site: Caesarean Section – A Brief History http://www.nlm.nih.gov/exhibition/cesarean/cesarean_1.html

caesium (Latin *caesius* 'bluish-grey') soft, silvery-white, ductile metallic element, symbol Cs, atomic number 55, relative atomic mass 132.905. It is one of the ▷alkali metals, and is the most electropositive of all the elements. In air it ignites spontaneously, and it reacts vigorously with water. It is used in the manufacture of photocells.

The rate of vibration of caesium atoms is used as the standard of measuring time. Its radioactive isotope Cs-137 (half-life 30.17 years) is a product of fission in nuclear explosions and in nuclear reactors; it is one of the most dangerous waste products of the nuclear industry, being a highly radioactive biological analogue for potassium. It was named in 1860 by Robert Bunsen, German chemist, from the blueness of its spectral line.

caffeine ▷alkaloid organic substance found in tea, coffee, and kola nuts; it stimulates the heart and central nervous system. When isolated, it is a bitter crystalline compound, $C_8H_{10}N_4O_2$. Too much caffeine (more than six average cups of tea or coffee a day) can be detrimental to health.

Related Web site: Frequently Asked Questions About Caffeine http://www.cs.unb.ca/~alopez-o/caffaq.html

Cage, John (1912–1992) US composer. His interest in Indian classical music led him to the view that the purpose of music was to change the way people listen. From 1948 he experimented with instruments, graphics, and methods of random selection in an effort to generate a music of pure incident. For example, he used 24 radios, tuned to random stations, in *Imaginary Landscape IV* (1951). His ideas profoundly influenced late 20th-century aesthetics.

Cage studied briefly with Arnold Schoenberg, also with Henry Cowell, and joined others in reacting against the European music tradition in favour of a freer idiom open to non-Western attitudes. Working in films during the 1930s, Cage assembled and toured a percussion orchestra incorporating ethnic instruments and noisemakers, for which *Double Music* (1941) was composed (with Lou Harrison). He invented the prepared piano, in which different objects are inserted between the strings, altering the tone and the sound produced, to tour as accompanist with the dancer Merce Cunningham, a lifelong collaborator.

Related Web site: Cage, John http://newalbion.com/artists/cagej/

> **John Cage**
> *Try as we might to make a silence, we cannot.*
> *Silence* (1961); 'Experimental Music' (1957)

Cage, Nicolas (1964–) Born Nicholas Coppola. US actor. He has brought an intensity and individuality to a range of films including *Birdy* (1984), *Peggy Sue Got Married* (1986), *Raising Arizona* (1987), *Wild at Heart* (1990), and *Bringing Out the Dead* (1999). He received an Academy Award for his performance as a dying alcoholic in *Leaving Las Vegas* (1995) and starred in the blockbuster *The Rock* (1996). Recent films include *City of Angels* (1998), *Gone in 60 Seconds* (2000), *The Family Man* (2000), *Captain Corelli's Mandolin* (2001), and *Matchstick Men* (2003).

Cagliari (ancient Carales) capital and port of Sardinia, Italy, on the south coast of the island on the Gulf of Cagliari; population (1992) 180,300. Industries include oil-refining and the manufacture of petrochemicals.

Cagney, James (1899–1986) US actor. His physical dynamism and staccato vocal delivery made him one of the first stars of talking pictures. Often associated with gangster roles, as in *The Public Enemy* (1931) and *White Heat* (1949), he was equally adept at playing comedy, singing, and dancing, as in *Blonde Crazy* (1931), *Footlight Parade* (1933), *A Midsummer Night's Dream* (1935), and *Yankee Doodle Dandy* (1942).

caiman (or cayman) large reptile, related to the ▷alligator.

Cain In the Old Testament, the first-born son of Adam and Eve. Motivated by jealousy, he murdered his brother Abel because the latter's sacrifice was more acceptable to God than his own.

Caine, Michael (1933–) Stage name of Maurice Joseph Micklewhite. English screen actor. He is a prolific and versatile performer with an enduring Cockney streak. Caine first rose to international prominence as the philandering leading man of the swinging London set in *Alfie* (1966)He has played historical roles in *Zulu* (1964) and *The Man Who Would Be King* (1975), hardboiled psychopaths in *Get Carter* (1971) and *Mona Lisa* (1986), and comic buffoons in *Educating Rita* (1983) and *Sweet Liberty* (1986). He won an Academy Award for his supporting role in *Hannah and Her Sisters* (1986), and won the same award in 2000 for his role in *The Cider House Rules* (1999). He received the Career Achievement award in the 1998 National Board of Review of Motion Pictures Awards and the 1999 Golden Globe for Best Actor for his role in *Little Voice* (1998). He was made a CBE in 1993, and knighted as Sir Maurice Micklewhite in 2000.

cairn Scottish breed of ▷terrier. Shaggy, short-legged, and compact, it can be sandy, greyish brindle, or red. It was formerly used for flushing out foxes and badgers.

Cairngorm Mountains granite mountain group in Scotland, northern part of the ▷Grampian Mountains, between the River Dee and the upper Spey. The central range includes four out of five of Britain's highest mountains: Ben Macdhui (1,309 m/4,296 ft), Braeriach (1,296 m/4,251 ft), Cairn Toul (1,291 m/4,235 ft), and Cairn Gorm (1,245 m/4,084 ft). Cairn Gorm can be accessed by chair-lift.

Cairo (Arabic **El Qahira**; 'the victorious') capital of Egypt, and the largest city in Africa and in the Middle East, situated on the east bank of the River Nile 13 km/8 mi above the apex of the delta and 160 km/100 mi from the Mediterranean; population (1995 est) 6,955,000. Industries include the manufacture of textiles, cement, vegetable oils, tourism and steel. At Helwan, 24 km/15 mi to the south, an industrial centre is powered by electricity from the Aswan High Dam.

Features Cairo is the site of the mosque that houses the El Azhar university (972). The Mosque of Amr dates from 643; the 12th-century Citadel contains the impressive 19th-century Muhammad Ali mosque. The city is 32 km/20 mi north of the site of the ancient Egyptian centre of ▷Memphis. The Great Pyramids and Sphinx are at nearby El ▷Giza. The government and business quarters reflect Cairo's position as a leading administrative and commercial centre, and the semi-official newspaper *al Ahram* is an influential voice in the Arab world. There are two secular universities: Cairo University (1908) and Ein Shams (1950).

History El Fustat (Old Cairo) was founded by Arabs about in about AD 642, and Al Qahira in about 1000 by the ▷Fatimid ruler Gowhar. Cairo was the capital of the Ayyubid dynasty, one of whose sultans, Saladin, built the Citadel in the late 1100s. Under the Mamelukes (1250–1517) the city prospered, but declined in the 16th century after conquest by the Turks. It became the capital of the virtually-autonomous kingdom of Egypt established by Mehmet Ali in 1805. During World War II it was the headquarters of the Allied forces in north Africa. In October 1992 an earthquake in a suburb of the city left over 500 dead. In 1994 Cairo hosted the United Nations Conference on Population and Development.

Related Web site: Cairo, the Jewel of the Orient http://ce.eng.usf.edu/pharos/cairo/

Cajun member of a French-speaking community of Louisiana, USA, descended from French-Canadians who, in the 18th century, were driven there from Nova Scotia (then known as Acadia, from which the name Cajun comes). Cajun music has a lively rhythm and features steel guitar, fiddle, and accordion.

CAL (acronym for computer-assisted learning) use of computers in education and training: the computer displays instructional material to a student and asks questions about the information given; the student's answers determine the sequence of the lessons.

calabash tropical South American evergreen tree with gourds (fruits) 50 cm/20 in across, whose dried skins are used as water containers. The Old World tropical-vine bottle gourd (*Lagenaria siceraria*, of the gourd family Cucurbitaceae) is sometimes also called a calabash, and it produces equally large gourds. (*Crescentia cujete*, family Bignoniaceae.)

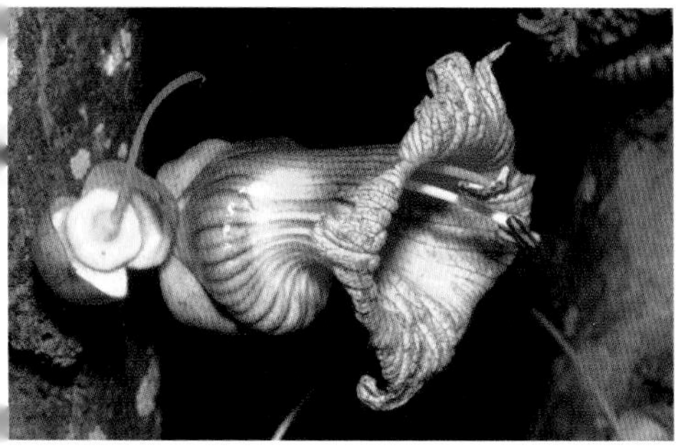

CALABASH Like many tropical trees, the flowers of the calabash tree grow directly from the wood of the trunk and branches. *Premaphotos Wildlife*

Calabria mountainous region occupying the 'toe' of Italy, comprising the provinces of Catanzaro, Cosenza, and Reggio di Calabria; area 15,100 sq km/5,800 sq mi; population (1992) 2,074,800. Its capital is Catanzaro and the principal towns are Crotone and Reggio di Calabria.

Calais port in Pas-de-Calais *département*, in northern France, 238 km/148 mi north of Paris; population (1990) 75,800, conurbation 100,000. Situated on the Strait of Dover, Calais lies on the shortest crossing of the English Channel, being just 34 km/21 mi southeast of Dover, and is a major ferry port. Its strategic position has made it the victim of several conquests from 1347, when it was conquered by the English, until 1940 when it was occupied by German forces. The entry to the ▷Channel Tunnel, completed in 1994, is at Sangatte, 6 km/3.7 mi from Calais, and the station on the new high-speed railway is at Fréthun, a similar distance from the town centre.

calceolaria plant with brilliantly coloured slipper-shaped flowers. Native to South America, calceolarias were introduced to Europe and the USA in the 1830s. (Genus *Calceolaria*, family Scrophulariaceae.)

calcite colourless, white, or light-coloured common rock-forming mineral, calcium carbonate, $CaCO_3$. It is the main constituent of ▷limestone and marble and forms many types of invertebrate shell.

calcium (Latin *calcis* 'lime') soft, silvery-white metallic element, symbol Ca, atomic number 20, relative atomic mass 40.08. It is one of the ▷alkaline-earth metals. It is the fifth most abundant element (the third most abundant metal) in the Earth's crust. It is found mainly as its carbonate $CaCO_3$, which occurs in a fairly pure condition as chalk and limestone (see ▷calcite). Calcium is an essential component of bones, teeth, shells, milk, and leaves, and it forms 1.5% of the human body by mass.

calcium carbonate ($CaCO_3$) white solid, found in nature as limestone, marble, and chalk. It is a valuable resource, used in the making of iron, steel, cement, glass, slaked lime, bleaching powder, sodium carbonate and bicarbonate, and many other industrially useful substances.

calcium hydroxide (or **slaked lime**) ($Ca(OH)_2$) white solid, slightly soluble in water. A solution of calcium hydroxide is called limewater and is used in the laboratory to test for the presence of carbon dioxide.

calculus (Latin 'pebble') branch of mathematics which uses the concept of a derivative (see ▷differentiation) to analyse the way in which the values of a ▷function vary. Calculus is probably the most widely used part of mathematics. Many real-life problems are analysed by expressing one quantity as a function of another – position of a moving object as a function of time, temperature of an object as a function of distance from a heat source, force on an object as a function of distance from the source of the force, and so on – and calculus is concerned with such functions.

There are several branches of calculus. Differential and integral calculus, both dealing with small quantities which during manipulation are made smaller and smaller, compose the **infinitesimal calculus**. **Differential equations** relate to the derivatives of a set of variables and may include the variables. Many give the mathematical models for physical phenomena such as simple harmonic motion. Differential equations are solved generally by ▷integration, depending on their degree. If no analytical processes are available, integration can be performed numerically. Other branches of calculus include calculus of variations and calculus of errors.

Related Web site: Rise of Calculus http://www-history.mcs.st-and.ac.uk/history/HistTopics/The_rise_of_calculus.html

Calcutta (or **Kolkata**) city in India, on the River Hooghly, the westernmost mouth of the River Ganges, some 130 km/80 mi north of the Bay of Bengal; population (2001 est) 4,580,500; metropolitan area (2001 est) 13,216,500. The capital of West Bengal, it is chiefly a commercial and industrial centre, its industries including engineering, shipbuilding, jute, and other textiles. It was the seat of government of British India 1773–1912.

Related Web site: Calcutta http://ezinfo.ucs.indiana.edu/~mduttara/wb/calintro.html

Calder, Alexander (Stirling) (1898–1976) US abstract sculptor. He invented **mobiles**, sculptures consisting of flat, brightly coloured shapes, suspended from wires and rods and moved by motors or currents of air. Although he was not the first sculptor to exploit real movement, no one before him had used it consistently. Huge mobiles by Calder have been installed at Kennedy Airport, New York (1957) and the UNESCO headquarters in Paris (1962).

caldera in geology, a very large basin-shaped ▷crater. Calderas are found at the tops of volcanoes, where the original peak has collapsed into an empty chamber beneath. The basin, many times larger than the original volcanic vent, may be flooded, producing a crater lake, or the flat floor may contain a number of small volcanic cones, produced by volcanic activity after the collapse.

Pedro Calderón de la Barca
Even in dreams good works are not wasted.
La vida es sueño (1635)

Calderón de la Barca, Pedro (1600–1681) Spanish dramatist and poet. After the death of Lope de Vega in 1635, he was considered to be the leading Spanish dramatist. Most celebrated of the 118 plays is the philosophical *La vida es sueño/Life is a Dream* (1635).

Caledonia Roman term for the Scottish Highlands, inhabited by the Caledoni. The tribes of the area remained outside Roman control – they were defeated but not conquered by Agricola in AD 83 to 84 and again by Septimius Severus who reached beyond modern Aberdeen in 208. Since the 18th century, the name has been revived as a romantic alternative for the whole of Scotland.

Caledonian Canal waterway in northwest Scotland, 98 km/61 mi long, linking the Atlantic and the North Sea. Situated between the Moray Firth and Loch Linnhe, the canal was constructed as a transport route to save the long sail around Scotland. It is one of Scotland's largest marina facilities. Of its total length, only a 37 km/22 mi stretch is artificial, the rest being composed of lochs Lochy, Oich, and Ness.

calendar division of the ▷year into months, weeks, and days and the method of ordering the years. From year one, an assumed date of the birth of Jesus, dates are calculated backwards (BC 'before Christ' or BCE 'before common era') and forwards (AD, Latin *anno Domini* 'in the year of the Lord', or CE 'common era'). The **lunar month** (period between one new moon and the next) naturally averages 29.5 days, but the Western calendar uses for convenience a **calendar month** with a complete number of days, 30 or 31 (February has 28). For adjustments, since there are slightly fewer than six extra hours a year left over, they are added to February as a 29th day every fourth year (**leap year**), century years being excepted unless they are divisible by 400.

The **month names** in most European languages were probably derived as follows: January from Janus, Roman god; February from *Februar*, Roman festival of purification; March from Mars, Roman god; April from Latin *aperire*, 'to open'; May from Maia, Roman goddess; June from Juno, Roman goddess; July from Julius Caesar, Roman general; August from Augustus, Roman emperor; September, October, November, December (originally the seventh to tenth months) from the Latin words meaning seventh, eighth, ninth, and tenth, respectively.

The **days of the week** are Monday named after the Moon; Tuesday from Tiu or Tyr, Anglo-Saxon and Norse god; Wednesday from Woden or Odin, Norse god; Thursday from Thor, Norse god; Friday from Freya, Norse goddess; Saturday from Saturn, Roman god; and Sunday named after the Sun.

All early calendars except the ancient Egyptian were lunar. The word calendar comes from the Latin *Kalendae* or *calendae*, the first day of each month on which, in ancient Rome, solemn proclamation was made of the appearance of the new moon.

The **Western** or **Gregorian calendar** derives from the **Julian calendar** instituted by Julius Caesar 46 BC. It was adjusted in 1582 by Pope Gregory XIII, who eliminated the accumulated error caused by a faulty calculation of the length of a year and avoided its recurrence by restricting century leap years to those divisible by 400. Other states only gradually changed from Old Style to New Style; Britain and its colonies adopted the Gregorian calendar in 1752, when the error amounted to 11 days, and 3 September 1752 became 14 September (at the same time the beginning of the year was put back from 25 March to 1 January). Russia did not adopt it until the October Revolution of 1917, so that the event (then 25 October) is currently celebrated on 7 November.

The **Jewish calendar** is a complex combination of lunar and solar cycles, varied by considerations of religious observance. A year may have 12 or 13 months, each of which normally alternates between 29 and 30 days; the New Year (Rosh Hashanah) falls between 5 September and 5 October. The calendar dates from the hypothetical creation of the world (taken as 7 October 3761 BC).

The **Chinese calendar** is lunar, with a cycle of 60 years. Both the traditional and, from 1911, the Western calendar are in use in China.

The **Muslim calendar**, also lunar, has 12 months of alternately 30 and 29 days, and a year of 354 days. This results in the calendar rotating around the seasons in a 30-year cycle. The era is counted as beginning on the day Muhammad fled from Mecca in AD 622.

Related Web site: Gregorian Calendar http://es.rice.edu/ES/humsoc/Galileo/Things/gregorian_calendar.html

California western state of the USA. It is nicknamed the Golden State, originally because of its gold mines, and more recently because of its orange groves and sunshine. California was admitted to the Union in 1850 as the 31st US state. It is bordered to the south by the Mexican state of Baja California, to the east by Arizona and Nevada, to the north by Oregon, and to the west by the Pacific Ocean.

population (2000 est) 33,871,000, the most populous state of the USA (69.9% white; 25.8% Hispanic; 9.6% Asian and Pacific islander, including many Vietnamese, 7.4% African-American; 0.8% American Indian) **area** 411,100 sq km/158,685 sq mi **capital** Sacramento **towns and cities** Los Angeles, San Diego, San Francisco, San Jose, Fresno **industries and products** leading agricultural state with fruit (peaches, citrus, grapes in the valley of the San Joaquin and Sacramento rivers), nuts, wheat, vegetables, cotton, and rice, all mostly grown by irrigation, the water being carried by concrete-lined canals to the Central and Imperial valleys; beef cattle; timber; fish; oil; natural gas; aerospace technology; electronics (Silicon Valley); financial sector; food processing; films and television programmes; tourism; leisure industry; great reserves of energy (geothermal) in the hot water that lies beneath much of the state

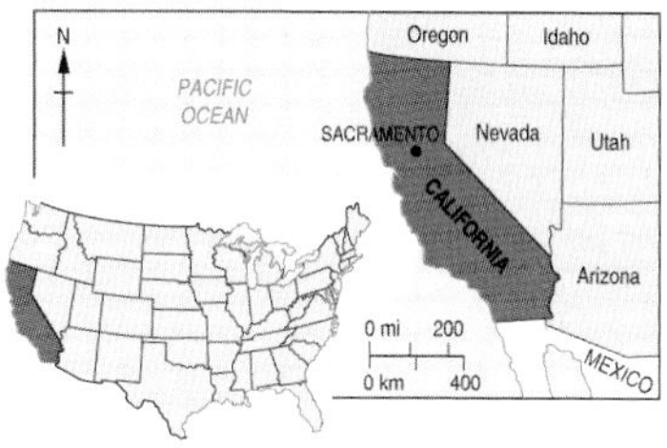

California current cold ocean ▷current in the eastern Pacific Ocean flowing southwards down the west coast of North America. It is part of the North Pacific ▷gyre (a vast, circular movement of ocean water).

californium synthesized, radioactive, metallic element of the actinide series, symbol Cf, atomic number 98, relative atomic mass 251. It is produced in very small quantities and used in nuclear reactors as a neutron source. The longest-lived isotope, Cf-251, has a half-life of 800 years.

It is named after the state of California, where it was first synthesized in 1950 by US nuclear chemist Glenn Seaborg and his team at the University of California at Berkeley.

Caligula (AD 12–41) Born Gaius Julius Caesar Germanicus. Roman emperor (AD 37–41), son of ▷Germanicus and Agrippina the Elder, and successor to ▷Tiberius. Caligula was a cruel tyrant and was assassinated by an officer of his guard. He appears to have been mentally unstable.

As a child he spent much time among the legions which his father commanded on the Rhine and was given the nickname, Caligula ('bootikins' or 'little boots'), after the small soldiers' boots *caligae* he wore. As emperor, Caligula was popular at first, thanks to his liberality and the illustrious reputation of his father. However, following a serious illness AD 37 which seemed to affect his sanity, he declared himself a god and his extravagance was a severe drain on the treasury. He built a temple to himself as *Jupiter Latiaris* and threatened to erect his own statue in the Holy of Holies at Jerusalem. In AD 39 he went to Gaul and planned an invasion of Britain, but this was abandoned and he was assassinated, together with his wife and daughter, four months after his return to Italy.

caliph title of civic and religious heads of the world of Islam. The first caliph was ▷Abu Bakr. Nominally elective, the office became hereditary, held by the Umayyad dynasty 661–750 and then by the ▷Abbasid dynasty. After the death of the last Abbasid (1258), the title was claimed by a number of Muslim chieftains in Egypt, Turkey, and India. The most powerful of these were the Turkish sultans of the Ottoman Empire.

Callaghan, (Leonard) James (1912–) Baron Callaghan of Cardiff. British Labour politician. He was home secretary 1967–70 and prime minister 1976–79 in a period of increasing economic stress. As chancellor of the Exchequer 1964–67, he introduced corporation tax, capital gains tax, and selective employment tax, and resigned following devaluation.

> **James Callaghan**
> *A lie can be half-way round the world before the truth has got its boots on.*
> Speech, 1 November 1976

Callao chief commercial port of Peru, situated 12 km/7 mi northwest of Lima on Callas Bay; sheltered by the island of San Lorenzo; population (1993) 369,800. The port handles 75% of Peru's imports and 25% of its exports. Exports include petroleum, minerals (copper, iron, silver, zinc, lead) cotton, sugar, and coffee. Manufactures include petrochemical products, fertilizers, textiles, and leather goods. It has a dockyard and an oil refinery. Callao is now contiguous with Lima and the combined metropolitan area produces 75% of Peru's manufactures.

Callas, Maria (1923–1977) Adopted name of Maria Kalogeropoulos. US lyric soprano. She was born in New York of Greek parents. With a voice of fine range and a gift for dramatic expression, she excelled in operas including *Norma*, *La sonnambula*, *Madame Butterfly*, *Aïda*, *Tosca*, and *Medea*.

She made her debut in Verona, Italy, in 1947 and at New York's Metropolitan Opera in 1956. Although her technique was not considered perfect, she helped to popularize classical coloratura roles through her expressiveness and charisma.

Related Web site: Art of Maria Callas http://welcome.to/Maria_Callas

calligraphy art of handwriting, regarded in China and Japan as the greatest of the visual arts, and playing a large part in Islamic art because the depiction of the human and animal form is forbidden.

callipers measuring instrument used, for example, to measure the internal and external diameters of pipes. Some callipers are made like a pair of compasses, having two legs, often curved, pivoting about a screw at one end. The ends of the legs are placed in contact with the object to be measured, and the gap between the ends is then measured against a rule. The slide calliper looks like an adjustable spanner, and carries a scale for direct measuring, usually with a vernier scale for accuracy.

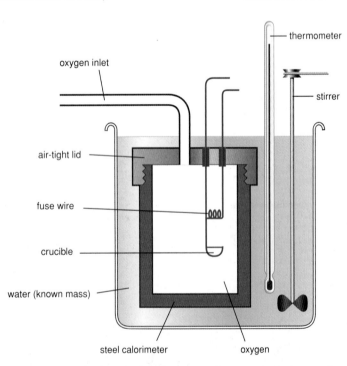

CALORIMETER A bomb calorimeter is used to measure the energy that is given out when one mole of a substance is completely burned in oxygen. A known amount of the substance is placed in the crucible, oxygen is added at 20 atmospheres pressure, and then the substance is ignited using the heated wire. As the calorimeter heats, it heats the water. The rise in water temperature is measured and from this the heat generated by the burning substance is calculated.

Callot, Jacques (*c.* 1592–1635) French engraver and painter. He was influenced by ▷Mannerism. His series of etchings *Great Miseries of War* (1633), prompted by his own experience of the Thirty Years' War, are arrestingly composed and full of horrific detail. He is regarded as one of the greatest etchers, and his enormous output includes over 1,400 prints and 1,500 drawings.

callus in botany, a tissue that forms at a damaged plant surface. Composed of large, thin-walled ▷parenchyma cells, it grows over and around the wound, eventually covering the exposed area.

In animals, a callus is a thickened pad of skin, formed where there is repeated rubbing against a hard surface. In humans, calluses often develop on the hands and feet of those involved in heavy manual work.

calorie c.g.s. unit of heat, now replaced by the ▷joule (one calorie is approximately 4.2 joules). It is the heat required to raise the temperature of one gram of water by 1°C. In dietetics, the Calorie or kilocalorie is equal to 1,000 calories.

calorific value the amount of heat generated by a given mass of fuel when it is completely burned. It is measured in joules per kilogram. Calorific values are measured experimentally with a bomb calorimeter.

calorimeter instrument used in physics to measure various thermal properties, such as heat capacity or the heat produced by fuel. A simple calorimeter consists of a heavy copper vessel that is polished (to reduce heat losses by radiation) and covered with insulating material (to reduce losses by convection and conduction).

calotype paper-based photograph using a wax paper negative, the first example of the ▷negative/positive process invented by the English photographer Fox ▷Talbot around 1834.

Calvin (or Cauvin or Chauvin), **John** (1509–1564) French-born Swiss Protestant church reformer and theologian. He was a leader of the Reformation in Geneva and set up a strict religious community there. His theological system is known as Calvinism, and his church government as ▷Presbyterianism. Calvin wrote (in Latin) *Institutes of the Christian Religion* (1536) and commentaries on the New Testament and much of the Old Testament.

Calvin, born in Noyon, Picardie, studied theology and then law, and in *c.* 1533 became prominent in Paris as an evangelical preacher. In 1534 he was obliged to leave Paris and retired to Basel, where he studied Hebrew. In 1536 he accepted an invitation to go to Geneva, Switzerland, and assist in the Reformation, but was expelled in 1538 because of public resentment against the numerous and too drastic changes he introduced. He returned to Geneva in 1541 and, in the face of strong opposition, established a rigorous theocracy (government by priests). In 1553 he had the Spanish theologian Servetus burned for heresy. He supported the ▷Huguenots in their struggle in France and the English Protestants persecuted by Queen Mary I.

Calvin, Melvin (1911–1997) US chemist awarded the Nobel Prize for Chemistry in 1961 for his study of the assimilation of carbon dioxide by plants. Using radioactive carbon-14 as a tracer, he determined the biochemical processes of ▷photosynthesis, in which green plants use ▷chlorophyll to convert carbon dioxide and water into sugar and oxygen.

Calvinism Christian doctrine as interpreted by John ▷Calvin and adopted in Scotland, parts of Switzerland, and the Netherlands; by the ▷Puritans in England and New England, USA; and by the subsequent Congregational and Presbyterian churches in the USA. Its central doctrine is predestination, under which certain souls (the elect) are predestined by God through the sacrifice of Jesus to salvation, and the rest to damnation. Although Calvinism is rarely accepted today in its strictest interpretation, the 20th century has seen a neo-Calvinist revival through the work of Karl ▷Barth.

calyx collective term for the ▷sepals of a flower, forming the outermost whorl of the ▷perianth. It surrounds the other flower parts and protects them while in bud. In some flowers, for example, the campions *Silene*, the sepals are fused along their sides, forming a tubular calyx.

CAM (acronym for computer-aided manufacturing) use of computers to control production processes; in particular, the control of machine tools and ▷robots in factories. In some factories, the whole design and production system has been automated by linking ▷CAD (computer-aided design) to CAM.

Linking flexible CAD/CAM manufacturing to computer-based sales and distribution methods makes it possible to produce semicustomized goods cheaply and in large numbers.

cam part of a machine that converts circular motion to linear motion or vice versa. The **edge cam** in a car engine is in the form of a rounded projection on a shaft, the camshaft. When the camshaft turns, the cams press against linkages (plungers or followers) that open the valves in the cylinders.

Camargue area of the ▷Rhône delta enclosed by the two principal arms of the river, south of Arles, France; area about 780 sq km/300 sq mi. One-third of the area is lake or marshland and dykes have been constructed to prevent widespread flooding. Black bulls and white horses are bred, and rice and vines are grown. A nature reserve, known for its bird life, forms the southern part.

cambium in botany, a layer of actively dividing cells (lateral ▷meristem), found within stems and roots, that gives rise to ▷secondary growth in perennial plants, causing an increase in girth. There are two main types of cambium: **vascular cambium**, which gives rise to secondary ▷xylem and ▷phloem tissues, and **cork cambium** (or phellogen), which gives rise to secondary cortex and cork tissues (see ▷bark).

Cambodia see country box.

Cambrai, Battles of two battles in World War I at Cambrai in northeastern France as British forces attempted to retake the town from the occupying Germans, eventually succeeding on 5 October 1918.

Cambrian Mountains region of hills, plateaux, and deep valleys in Wales, 175 km/110 mi long, linking Snowdonia in the northwest and the Brecon Beacons and Black Mountains in the south.

Cambrian period period of geological time roughly 570–510 million years ago; the first period of the Palaeozoic Era. All invertebrate animal life appeared, and marine algae were widespread. The **Cambrian Explosion** 530–520 million years ago saw the major radiaton in the fossil record of modern animal phyla; the earliest fossils with hard shells, such as trilobites, date from then.

The name comes from Cambria, the medieval Latin name for Wales, where Cambrian rocks are typically exposed and were first described.

JOHN CALVIN The Protestant theologian and reformer John Calvin. *Philip Sauvain Picture Collection*

Cambodia

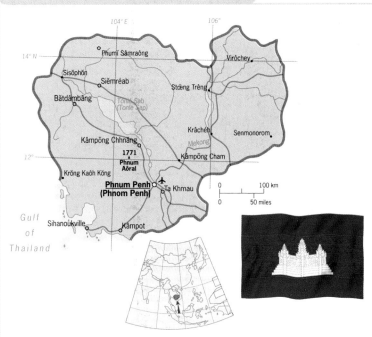

Cambodia (formerly Khmer Republic 1970–76, Kampuchea 1976–89) country in southeast Asia, bounded north and northwest by Thailand, north by Laos, east and southeast by Vietnam, and southwest by the Gulf of Thailand.

NATIONAL NAME *Preah Réaché'anachâkr Kâmpuchéa/Kingdom of Cambodia*
AREA 181,035 sq km/69,897 sq mi
CAPITAL Phnom Penh
MAJOR TOWNS/CITIES Battambang, Kompong Cham, Siem Reap, Prey Vêng, Preah Seihânu
MAJOR PORTS Kompong Cham
PHYSICAL FEATURES mostly flat, forested plains with mountains in southwest and north; Mekong River runs north–south; Lake Tonle Sap

Government

HEAD OF STATE King Norodom Sihanouk from 1991
HEAD OF GOVERNMENT Hun Sen from 1998
POLITICAL SYSTEM emergent democracy
POLITICAL EXECUTIVE dual executive
ADMINISTRATIVE DIVISIONS 20 provinces and three municipalities
ARMED FORCES 125,000 (2002 est)

CONSCRIPTION military service is compulsory for five years between ages 18 and 35; conscription authorized but not implemented since 1993
DEATH PENALTY abolished in 1989
DEFENCE SPEND (% GDP) 2.5 (2002 est)
EDUCATION SPEND (% GDP) 1.9 (2001 est)
HEALTH SPEND (% GDP) 8.1 (2000 est)

Economy and resources

CURRENCY Cambodian riel
GPD (US$) 3.7 billion (2002 est)
REAL GDP GROWTH (% change on previous year) 6.3 (2001)
GNI (US$) 3.5 billion (2002 est)
GNI PER CAPITA (PPP) (US$) 1,590 (2002 est)
CONSUMER PRICE INFLATION 3.8% (2003 est)
FOREIGN DEBT (US$) 2.4 billion (2001 est)
MAJOR TRADING PARTNERS Singapore, Thailand, Vietnam, Japan, Germany, USA, China (including Hong Kong), South Korea

RESOURCES phosphates, iron ore, gemstones, bauxite, silicon, manganese
INDUSTRIES rubber processing, seafood processing, rice milling, textiles and garments, pharmaceutical products, cigarettes
EXPORTS garments, timber, rubber, fishery products. Principal market: USA 57.9% (2001)
IMPORTS cigarettes, construction materials, petroleum products, motor vehicles, alcoholic beverages, consumer electronics. Principal source: Thailand 23.5% (2001)
ARABLE LAND 21% (2000 est)
AGRICULTURAL PRODUCTS rice, maize, sugar cane, cassava, bananas; timber and rubber (the two principal export commodities); fishing

Population and society

POPULATION 14,144,000 (2003 est)
POPULATION GROWTH RATE 1.6% (2000–15)
POPULATION DENSITY (per sq km) 78 (2003 est)
URBAN POPULATION (% of total) 19 (2003 est)
AGE DISTRIBUTION (% of total population) 0–14 43%, 15–59 53%, 60+ 4% (2002 est)

ETHNIC GROUPS 90% Khmer, 5% Vietnamese, 1% Chinese
LANGUAGE Khmer (official), French
RELIGION Theravada Buddhist 95%, Muslim, Roman Catholic
EDUCATION (compulsory years) 6
LITERACY RATE 81% (men); 60% (women) (2003 est)
LABOUR FORCE 71.2% agriculture, 7.6% industry, 21.2% services (1997 est)
LIFE EXPECTANCY 55 (men); 60 (women) (2000–05)
CHILD MORTALITY RATE (under 5, per 1,000 live births) 138 (2001)
PHYSICIANS (per 1,000 people) 0.3 (1999 est)
TV SETS (per 1,000 people) 8 (2001 est)
RADIOS (per 1,000 people) 119 (2001 est)
INTERNET USERS (per 10,000 people) 21.8 (2002 est)
PERSONAL COMPUTER USERS (per 100 people) 0.2 (2002 est)

See also ▷Buddhism; ▷Khmer Rouge; ▷Pol Pot; ▷Sihanouk, Norodom.

Chronology

1st century AD: Part of the kingdom of Hindu-Buddhist Funan (Fou Nan), centred on Mekong delta region.
6th century: Conquered by the Chenla kingdom.
9th century: Establishment by Jayavarman II of extensive and sophisticated Khmer Empire, supported by an advanced irrigation system and architectural achievements.
14th century: Theravāda Buddhism replaced Hinduism.
15th century: Came under the control of Siam (Thailand), which made Phnom Penh the capital and, later, Champa (Vietnam).
1863: Became a French protectorate.
1887: Became part of French Indo-China Union, which included Laos and Vietnam.
1941: Prince Norodom Sihanouk was elected king.
1941–45: Occupied by Japan during World War II.
1946: Recaptured by France; parliamentary constitution adopted.
1949: Guerrilla war for independence secured semi-autonomy within the French Union.
1953: Independence was achieved from France as the Kingdom of Cambodia.
1955: Norodom Sihanouk abdicated as king and became prime minister, representing the Popular Socialist Community mass movement. His father, Norodom Suramarit, became king.
1960: On the death of his father, Norodom Sihanouk became head of state.
later 1960s: There was mounting guerrilla insurgency, led by the communist Khmer Rouge, and civil war in neighbouring Vietnam.
1970: Sihanouk was overthrown by US-backed Lt-Gen Lon Nol in a right-wing coup; the new name of Khmer Republic was adopted; Sihanouk, exiled in China, formed his own guerrilla movement.
1975: Lon Nol was overthrown by the Khmer Rouge, which was backed by North Vietnam and China; Sihanouk became head of state.
1976: The Khmer Republic was renamed Democratic Kampuchea.
1976–78: The Khmer Rouge, led by Pol Pot, introduced an extreme Maoist communist programme, forcing urban groups into rural areas and resulting in over 2.5 million deaths from famine, disease, and maltreatment; Sihanouk was removed from power.
1978–79: Vietnam invaded and installed a government headed by Heng Samrin, an anti-Pol Pot communist.
1979: Democratic Kampuchea was renamed the People's Republic of Kampuchea.

1980–82: Faced by guerrilla resistance from Pol Pot's Chinese-backed Khmer Rouge and Sihanouk's Association of South East Asian Nations (ASEAN) and US-backed nationalists, more than 300,000 Cambodians fled to refugee camps in Thailand and thousands of soldiers were killed.
1985: The reformist Hun Sen was appointed prime minister and more moderate economic and cultural policies were pursued.
1987–89: Vietnamese troops were withdrawn.
1989: The People's Republic of Kampuchea was renamed the State of Cambodia and Buddhism was re-established as the state religion.
1991: There was a ceasefire, and a United Nations Transitional Authority in Cambodia (UNTAC) agreed to administer the country in conjunction with an all-party Supreme National Council; communism was abandoned. Sihanouk returned as head of state.
1992: Political prisoners were released, refugees resettled, and freedom of speech restored. However, the Khmer Rouge refused to disarm.
1993: FUNCINPEC won general elections (boycotted by the Khmer Rouge, who continued fighting); a new constitution was adopted. Sihanouk was reinstated as constitutional monarch; his son Prince Norodom Ranariddh, FUNCINPEC leader, was appointed prime minister, with CPP leader Hun Sen as deputy premier.
1994: An antigovernment coup was foiled. Seven thousand Khmer Rouge guerrillas surrendered in response to an amnesty.
1995: Prince Norodom Sirivudh, FUNCINPEC leader and half-brother of King Sihanouk, was exiled for allegedly plotting to assassinate Hun Sen and topple the government.
1996: There were heightened tensions between Hun Sen's CPP and the royalist FUNCINPEC.
1997: Pol Pot was sentenced to life imprisonment. FUNCINPEC troops were routed by the CPP, led by Hun Sen. Prime Minister Prince Norodom Ranariddh was deposed and replaced by Ung Huot. There was fighting between supporters of Hun Sen and Ranariddh.
1998: Ranariddh was found guilty of arms smuggling and colluding with the Khmer Rouge, but was pardoned by the king. Pol Pot died and thousands of Khmer Rouge guerrillas defected. The CPP won elections, and political unrest followed. A new CPP–FUNCINPEC coalition was formed, with Hun Sen as prime minister and Prince Norodom Ranariddh as president. Cambodia re-occupied its UN seat.
2002: The UN withdrew its participation from an international tribunal to try former leaders of the Khmer Rouge regime for genocide and crimes against humanity because of concerns about the independence and objectivity of the tribunal.

CAMBODIA A gathering at the Cambodian Royal Palace in Phnom Penh. Originally built in 1866 by King Norodom, it is painted in the traditional royal yellow colour. *Photodisk*

Cambridge city and administrative headquarters of ▷Cambridgeshire, eastern England, on the River Cam, 80 km/50 mi north of London; population (1997 est) 118,200. It is the seat of Cambridge University (founded in the 13th century). Industries include the manufacture of computers and electronic products, scientific instruments, and paper, printing, publishing, financial services, and insurance, as well as technological, medical, and telecommunications research. Tourism is also an important industry; there are about 3.5 million visitors each year.

Features Apart from those of Cambridge University, fine buildings include St Benet's church, with a Saxon tower (about 1000), the oldest building in Cambridge; the Holy Sepulchre or Round Church (about 1130, restored in 1841), the oldest of four round churches in England; and the Guildhall (1939). The Fitzwilliam Museum (1816) houses a fine art collection. The Backs is an ancient strip of land between the backs of the colleges and the Cam.

Colleges University colleges include Peterhouse, founded in 1284, the oldest college; King's College (1441); Queens' College (1448); Jesus College (1496); St John's College (1511); and Trinity College (1546), the largest college. Emmanuel College chapel was built by Christopher Wren in 1666. The newest college, Robinson, was founded in 1977. The collection of books in the university library (built 1931–34) includes the first book ever printed in English. Cambridge is also home to Anglia Polytechnic University.

Cambridge city in northeastern Massachusetts, on the north bank of the Charles River, just above the river's entry into Boston Harbour; seat (with Lowell) of Middlesex County; population (1998 est) 93,500. Its seaward side is industrial and includes a part of the Boston port area; industries include paper and publishing, electronic equipment and scientific instruments. Cambridge is the seat of several important colleges: Harvard University (1636), Massachusetts Institute of Technology (1861), and Radcliffe College (1879). The John F Kennedy School of Government is part of Harvard University. One quarter of the residents are students and one sixth of the workforce is employed in higher education. Although noted for its educational institutions, Cambridge used also to be an industrial town. Some of the old factories have been taken over by high tech facilities.

Cambridgeshire county of eastern England, which has contained the unitary authority Peterborough since April 1998.

area 3,410 sq km/1,316 sq mi **towns and cities** ▷Cambridge (administrative headquarters), Ely, Huntingdon, March, Wisbech, St Neots, Whittlesey **physical** county is flat with fens, whose soil is very fertile; Bedford Level (a peaty area of the fens); rivers: Nene, Ouse (with tributaries Cam, Lark, and Little Ouse), Welland **features** Cambridge University **agriculture** the county is one of the chief cereal and sugar-beet producing districts of England; fruit and vegetables are grown; there is also dairy farming and sheep-rearing **industries** brewing, paper, electronics, food processing, mechanical engineering; there are scientific and pharmaceutical research establishments **population** (1996) 703,100 **famous people** Oliver Cromwell, Octavia Hill, John Maynard Keynes
Related Web site: Cambridgeshire County Council http://www.camcnty.gov.uk/

Cambyses (lived 6th century BC) King of Persia (529–522 BC). Succeeding his father Cyrus, he assassinated his brother Smerdis and conquered Egypt in 525 BC. There he outraged many of the local religious customs and was said to have become insane. He died in Syria.

camcorder another name for a ▷video camera.

Camden Town Group school of British painters (1911–13), based in Camden, London, led by Walter ▷Sickert. The work of Spencer Gore (1878–1914) and Harold Gilman (1876–1919) is typical of the group, rendering everyday town scenes in post-Impressionist style. In 1913 they merged with another group to form the London Group.

camel large cud-chewing mammal of the even-toed hoofed order Artiodactyla. Unlike typical ruminants, it has a three-chambered stomach. It has two toes which have broad soft soles for walking on sand, and hooves resembling nails. There are two species, the single-humped **Arabian camel** *Camelus dromedarius* and the twin-humped **Bactrian camel** *C. bactrianus* from Asia. They carry a food reserve of fatty tissue in the hump, can go without drinking for long periods, can feed on salty vegetation, and withstand extremes of heat and cold, thus being well adapted to desert conditions.

The Arabian camel has long been domesticated, so that its original range is not known. It is used throughout Arabia and North Africa, and has been taken to other places such as North America and Australia, in the latter country playing a crucial part in the development of the interior. The **dromedary** is, strictly speaking, a lightly built, fast, riding variety of the Arabian camel, but often the name is applied to all one-humped camels. Arabian camels can be used as pack animals, for riding, racing, milk production, and for meat. The Bactrian camel is native to the central Asian deserts, where a small number still live wild, but most

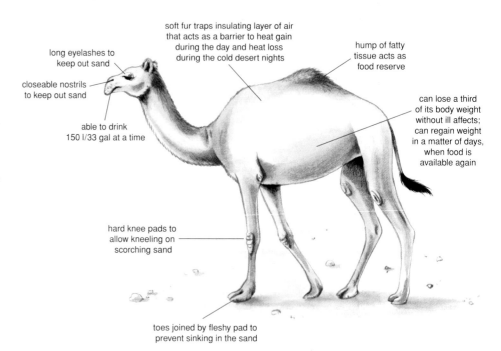

able to drink 150 l/33 gal at a time

long eyelashes to keep out sand

closeable nostrils to keep out sand

soft fur traps insulating layer of air that acts as a barrier to heat gain during the day and heat loss during the cold desert nights

hump of fatty tissue acts as food reserve

can lose a third of its body weight without ill affects; can regain weight in a matter of days, when food is available again

hard knee pads to allow kneeling on scorching sand

toes joined by fleshy pad to prevent sinking in the sand

CAMEL The Arabian camel does not actually store water in its hump, although it can do so in the lining of its stomach. During protracted periods without water, the camel can lose up to 27% of its body weight without causing harm.

are domestic animals. With a head and body length of 3 m/10 ft and shoulder height of about 2 m/6 ft, the Bactrian camel is a large animal, but not so long in the leg as the Arabian. It has a shaggy winter coat. In 1995 there were only about 730–880 Bactrian camels remaining in the wild. Smaller, flat-backed members of the camel family include the ▷alpaca, the ▷guanaco, the ▷llama, and the ▷vicuna.
Related Web site: Dromedary Camel http://www.seaworld.org/animal_bytes/dromedary_camelab.html

camellia any oriental evergreen shrub with roselike flowers belonging to the tea family. Many species, including *Camellia japonica* and *C. reticulata*, have been introduced into Europe, the USA, and Australia; they are widely cultivated as ornamental shrubs. (Genus *Camellia*, family Theaceae.)

Camelot in medieval romance, legendary seat of King Arthur. A possible site is the Iron Age hill fort of South Cadbury Castle in Somerset, England, where excavations from 1967 have revealed remains dating from 3000 BC to AD 1100, including those of a large settlement dating from the 6th century, the time ascribed to Arthur.

cameo small relief carving of semiprecious stone, shell, or glass, in which a pale-coloured surface layer is carved to reveal a darker

CAMERA A promotional picture from about 1890 of a fashionable lady holding one of George Eastman's first Kodak box cameras, the carrying-case hanging at her side. *Archive Photos*

ground. Fine cameos were produced in ancient Greece and Rome, during the Renaissance, and in the Victorian era. They were used for decorating goblets and vases, and as jewellery.

camera apparatus used in ▷photography, consisting of a lens system set in a light-proof box inside of which a sensitized film or plate can be placed. The lens collects rays of light reflected from the subject and brings them together as a sharp image on the film. The opening or hole at the front of the camera, through which light enters, is called an ▷aperture. The aperture size controls the amount of light that can enter. A shutter controls the amount of time light has to affect the film. There are small-, medium-, and large-format cameras; the format refers to the size of recorded image and the dimensions of the image obtained.
Related Web site: Cameras: The Technology of Photographic Imaging http://www.mhs.ox.ac.uk/cameras/index.htm

camera obscura darkened box with a tiny hole for projecting the inverted image of the scene outside on to a screen inside. For its development as a device for producing photographs, see ▷photography.

Cameron, Julia Margaret (1815–1879) Born Julia Margaret Pattle. British photographer. She made lively and dramatic portraits of the Victorian intelligentsia, often posed as historical or literary figures. Her sitters included her friends the English astronomer Sir John Herschel, the poet Alfred Lord Tennyson, whose *Idylls of the King* she illustrated in 1872, and Charles Darwin. She used a large camera, five-minute exposures, and wet plates.

> **Julia Margaret Cameron**
> *Whilst all that we love best in classic art / is stamped forever on the immortal face.*
> Poem 'On a Portrait' (September 1875)

Cameroon see country box.

Camoëns (or **Camões**), **Luis Vaz de** (1524–1580) Portuguese poet and soldier. He went on various military expeditions, and was shipwrecked in 1558. His poem *Os Lusiades/The Lusiads* (1572) tells the story of the explorer Vasco da Gama and incorporates much Portuguese history; it was immediately acclaimed and has become the country's national epic. His posthumously published lyric poetry is also now valued.

Camorra Italian secret society formed about 1820 by criminals in the dungeons of Naples and continued once they were freed. It dominated politics from 1848, was suppressed in 1911, but many members eventually surfaced in the US ▷Mafia. The Camorra still operates in the Naples area.

camouflage colours or structures that allow an animal to blend with its surroundings to avoid detection by other animals. Camouflage can take the form of matching the background colour, of countershading (darker on top, lighter below, to counteract natural shadows), or of irregular patterns that break up the outline of the animal's body. More elaborate camouflage involves closely resembling a feature of the natural environment, as with the stick insect; this is closely akin to ▷mimicry. Camouflage is also important as a military technique, disguising either equipment, troops, or a position in order to conceal them from an enemy.

Campaign for Nuclear Disarmament (CND)

nonparty-political British organization advocating the abolition of nuclear weapons worldwide. Since its foundation in 1958, CND has sought unilateral British initiatives to help start, and subsequently to accelerate, the multilateral process and end the arms race.

Campania

region of southern Italy, comprising the provinces of Avellino, Benevento, Caserta, Naples, and Salerno; area 13,600 sq km/5,250 sq mi; population (1992) 5,668,900. The administrative capital is ▷Naples; industrial centres include Benevento, Caserta, and Salerno. Agriculture is important; wheat, citrus fruits, wine, vegetables, tobacco, and hemp are produced. The volcano ▷Vesuvius is near Naples, and there are ancient sites at Pompeii, Herculaneum, and Paestum.

campanile (Italian, 'bell-tower', from Latin *campana* 'a bell') a term applied to towers erected in close proximity, though not attached, to many churches and town halls in Italy. The earliest examples are at Ravenna (about 9th century). Other famous examples include the campanile of St Mark's, Venice (begun 902); the leaning tower of Pisa (begun 1174); and Giotto's campanile at Florence (1334).

Campbell, Colen

(1676–1729) Scottish architect. He was one of the principal figures in British Palladian architecture. His widely influential book *Vitruvius Britannicus* was published in 1712. Among his

CAMOUFLAGE The shield (or stink) bug *Coriplatus depressus* from the rainforest of Peru represents the ultimate in camouflage. In this picture mating adults and nymphs are present, both having a coloration that matches that of the lichen-covered tree bark on which they live. *Premaphotos Wildlife*

Cameroon

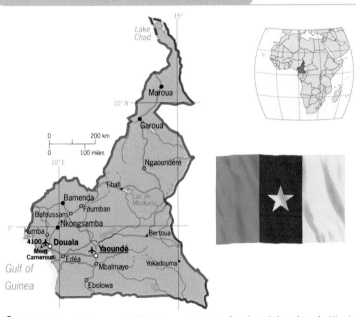

Cameroon

formerly Kamerun (until 1916) country in west Africa, bounded northwest by Nigeria, northeast by Chad, east by the Central African Republic, south by the Republic of the Congo, Gabon, and Equatorial Guinea, and west by the Atlantic.

NATIONAL NAME *République du Cameroun/Republic of Cameroon*
AREA 475,440 sq km/183,567 sq mi
CAPITAL Yaoundé
MAJOR TOWNS/CITIES Garoua, Douala, Nkongsamba, Maroua, Bamenda, Bafoussam, Ngaoundéré
MAJOR PORTS Douala
PHYSICAL FEATURES desert in far north in the Lake Chad basin, mountains in west, dry savannah plateau in the intermediate area, and dense tropical rainforest in south; Mount

CAMEROON This stamp depicts a *lamido*, a traditional provincial leader. *Stanley Gibbons*

Cameroon 4,070 m/13,358 ft, an active volcano on the coast, west of the Adamawa Mountains

Government

HEAD OF STATE Paul Biya from 1982
HEAD OF GOVERNMENT Peter Musonge Mafani from 1996
POLITICAL SYSTEM emergent democracy
POLITICAL EXECUTIVE limited presidency
ADMINISTRATIVE DIVISIONS ten provinces
ARMED FORCES 23,100; plus paramilitary forces of 9,000 (2002 est)
CONSCRIPTION military service is voluntary; paramilitary compulsory training programme in force
DEATH PENALTY retained and used for ordinary crimes
DEFENCE SPEND (% GDP) 1.2 (2002 est)
EDUCATION SPEND (% GDP) 3.2 (2001 est)
HEALTH SPEND (% GDP) 4.3 (2000 est)

Economy and resources

CURRENCY franc CFA
GPD (US$) 9.1 billion (2002 est)
REAL GDP GROWTH (% change on previous year) 4.4 (2001)
GNI (US$) 8.7 billion (2002 est)
GNI PER CAPITA (PPP) (US$) 1,640 (2002 est)

CONSUMER PRICE INFLATION 3.4% (2003 est)
UNEMPLOYMENT 30% (1998)
FOREIGN DEBT (US$) 6.8 billion (2001 est)
MAJOR TRADING PARTNERS France, Spain, Italy, the Netherlands, Nigeria, USA
RESOURCES petroleum, natural gas, tin ore, limestone, bauxite, iron ore, uranium, gold
INDUSTRIES petroleum refining, aluminium smelting, cement, food processing, footwear, beer, cigarettes
EXPORTS crude petroleum and petroleum products, timber and timber products, cocoa, coffee, aluminium, cotton, bananas. Principal market: Italy 21.7% (2000)
IMPORTS machinery and transport equipment, basic manufactures, chemicals, fuel, rice and cereals. Principal source: France 28.8% (2000)
ARABLE LAND 12.8% (2000 est)
AGRICULTURAL PRODUCTS coffee, cocoa, cotton, cassava, sorghum, millet, maize, plantains, palm (oil and kernels), rubber, bananas; livestock rearing (cattle and sheep); forestry and fishing

Population and society

POPULATION 16,018,000 (2003 est)
POPULATION GROWTH RATE 1.8% (2000–15)
POPULATION DENSITY (per sq km) 34 (2003 est)
URBAN POPULATION (% of total) 51 (2003 est)
AGE DISTRIBUTION (% of total population) 0–14 43%, 15–59 51%, 60+ 6% (2002 est)
ETHNIC GROUPS main groups include the Cameroon Highlanders (31%), Equatorial Bantu (19%), Kirdi (11%), Fulani (10%), Northwestern Bantu (8%), and Eastern Nigritic (7%)
LANGUAGE French, English (both official; often spoken in pidgin), Sudanic languages (in the north), Bantu languages (elsewhere); there has been some discontent with the emphasis on French – there are 163 indigenous peoples with their own African languages
RELIGION animist 50%, Christian 33%, Muslim 16%
EDUCATION (compulsory years) 6 in Eastern Cameroon; 7 in Western Cameroon
LITERACY RATE 81% (men); 68% (women) (2003 est)
LABOUR FORCE 62.7% agriculture, 8.7% industry, 28.6% services (1997 est)
LIFE EXPECTANCY 45 (men); 47 (women) (2000–05) CHILD MORTALITY RATE (under 5, per 1,000 live births) 155 (2001)
PHYSICIANS (per 1,000 people) 0.1 (1998 est)
TV SETS (per 1,000 people) 81 (1997)
RADIOS (per 1,000 people) 163 (1997)
INTERNET USERS (per 10,000 people) 29.2 (2002 est)

PERSONAL COMPUTER USERS (per 100 people) 0.5 (2002 est)

Chronology

1472: First visited by the Portuguese, who named it the Rio dos Camaroes ('River of Prawns') after the giant shrimps they found in the Wouri River estuary, and later introduced slave trading.

early 17th century: The Douala people migrated to the coastal region from the east and came to serve as intermediaries between Portuguese, Dutch, and English traders and interior tribes.

1809–48: The northern savannahs were conquered by the Fulani, Muslim pastoral nomads from the southern Sahara.

1856: Douala chiefs signed a commercial treaty with Britain and invited British protection.

1884: A treaty was signed establishing German rule as the protectorate of Kamerun; cocoa, coffee, and banana plantations were developed.

1916: Captured by Allied forces in World War I.

1919: Divided under League of Nations' mandates between Britain, which administered the southwest and north (adjoining Nigeria), and France, which administered the east and south.

1946: The French Cameroon and British Cameroons were made UN trust territories.

1955: The French crushed a revolt by the Union of the Cameroon Peoples (UPC), southern-based radical nationalists.

1960: French Cameroon became the independent Republic of Cameroon, with the Muslim Ahmadou Ahidjo as president; a UPC rebellion in the southwest was crushed, and a state of emergency declared.

1961: Following a UN plebiscite, the northern part of the British Cameroons merged with Nigeria, and the southern part joined the Republic of Cameroon to become the Federal Republic of Cameroon.

1966: An autocratic one-party regime was introduced; government and opposition parties merged to form the Cameroon National Union (UNC).

1970s: Petroleum exports made successful investment in education and agriculture possible.

1972: A new constitution made Cameroon a unitary state.

1982: President Ahidjo resigned; he was succeeded by his prime minister Paul Biya, a Christian.

1983–84: Biya began to remove the northern Muslim political 'barons' close to Ahidjo, who went into exile in France. Biya defeated a plot by Muslim officers from the north to overthrow him.

1985: The UNC adopted the name RDPC.

1990: There was widespread public disorder as living standards declined; Biya granted an amnesty to political prisoners.

1992: The ruling RDPC won the first multiparty elections in 28 years, with Biya as president.

1995: Cameroon was admitted to the Commonwealth.

1996: Peter Musonge Mafani became prime minister.

1997: RDPC won assembly elections; Biya was re-elected.

best-known works are Burlington House, London (1718–19); Mereworth Castle, Kent (1722–25); and Houghton Hall, Norfolk (1722–26).

Campbell, Colin (1792–1863) 1st Baron Clyde. British field marshal. He commanded the Highland Brigade at ▷Balaclava in the Crimean War and, as commander-in-chief during the Indian Mutiny, raised the siege of Lucknow and captured Cawnpore. KCB (1849), Baron (1858).

Campbell, Donald Malcolm (1921–1967) British car and speedboat enthusiast, son of Malcolm Campbell, who simultaneously held the land-speed and water-speed records. In 1964 he set the world water-speed record of 444.57 kph/276.3 mph on Lake Dumbleyung, Australia, with the turbojet hydroplane *Bluebird*, and achieved the land-speed record of 648.7 kph/403.1 mph at Lake Eyre salt flats, Australia. He was killed in 1967 in an attempt to raise his water-speed record on Coniston Water, England. In 2001 *Bluebird* was raised from Coniston Water, witnessed by Campbell's widow.

Campbell, Malcolm (1885–1948) British racing driver who once held both land- and water-speed records. He set the land-speed record nine times, pushing it up to 484.8 kph/301.1 mph at Bonneville Flats, Utah, USA, in 1935, and broke the water-speed record three times, the best being 228.2 kph/141.74 mph on Coniston Water, England, in 1939. His car and boat were both called *Bluebird*.

Campbell-Bannerman, Henry (1836–1908) British Liberal politician, prime minister 1905–08, leader of the Liberal party 1898–1908. The Entente Cordiale was broadened to embrace Russia during his premiership, which also saw the granting of 'responsible government' to the Boer republics in southern Africa. He was succeeded as prime minister and Liberal leader by H H ▷Asquith, who had effectively led the House during Campbell-Bannermann's premiership, as the latter was dogged by ill health.

Camp David official country home of US presidents, situated in the Appalachian mountains, Maryland; it was originally named Shangri-la by F D Roosevelt, but was renamed Camp David by Eisenhower (after his grandson).

Camp David Agreements two framework accords agreed in 1978 and officially signed in March 1979 by Israeli prime minister ▷Begin and Egyptian president ▷Sadat at Camp David, Maryland, USA, under the guidance of US president ▷Carter. They cover an Egypt–Israel peace treaty and phased withdrawal of Israel from Sinai, which was completed in 1982, and an overall Middle East settlement including the election by the ▷West Bank and ▷Gaza Strip Palestinians of a 'self-governing authority'. The latter issue has stalled repeatedly over questions of who should represent the Palestinians and what form the self-governing body should take.

camphor $C_{10}H_{16}O$ volatile, aromatic ▷ketone substance obtained from the camphor tree *Cinnamomum camphora*. It is distilled from chips of the wood, and is used in insect repellents and medicinal inhalants and liniments, and in the manufacture of celluloid.

Campin, Robert (c. 1378–1444) Also known as the **Master of Flémalle**. Early Netherlandish painter, active in Tournai from 1406. The few works attributed to him are almost as revolutionary in their naturalism as the van Eyck brothers' Ghent altarpiece, which they may antedate, and he ranks as one of the founders of the Netherlandish School.

campion any of several plants belonging to the pink family. They include the garden campion (*Lychnis coronaria*), the wild white and red campions (*Silene alba* and *S. dioica*), and the bladder campion (*S. vulgaris*). (Genera *Lychnis* and *Silene*, family Caryophyllaceae.)

Campion, Jane (1954–) New Zealand film director and screenwriter. She made her feature debut with *Sweetie* (1989), a dark tale of family dysfunction, then went on to make *An Angel at My Table* (1990), based on the autobiography of the writer Janet Frame, originally shown as a television miniseries. *The Piano* (1993), co-winner of the Cannes Film Festival Palme d'Or, also earned her an Academy Award for her screenplay.

Campylobacter genus of bacteria that cause serious outbreaks of gastroenteritis. They grow best at 43°C, and so are well suited to the digestive tract of birds. Poultry is therefore the most likely source of a *Campylobacter* outbreak, although the bacteria can also be transmitted via beef or milk. *Campylobacter* can survive in water for up to 15 days, so may be present in drinking water if supplies are contaminated by sewage or reservoirs are polluted by seagulls.

Camus, Albert (1913–1960) Algerian-born French writer. His works, such as the novels *L'Etranger/The Outsider* (1942) and *La Peste/The Plague* (1948), owe much to ▷existentialism in their emphasis on the absurdity and arbitrariness of life. Other works include *Le Mythe de Sisyphe/The Myth of Sisyphus* (1943) and *L'Homme révolté/The Rebel* (1951). Camus's criticism of communism in the latter book led to a protracted quarrel with the philosopher Jean-Paul Sartre. He was awarded the Nobel Prize for Literature in 1957.

The plays *Le Malentendu/Cross Purpose* and *Caligula* (both 1944), and the novel *L'Etranger* ('the study of an absurd man in an absurd world') explore various aspects of 'the Absurd', while *Le Mythe de Sisyphe* is a philosophical treatment of the same concept. With *Lettres à un ami allemand/Letters to a German Friend* (1945), *La Peste*, the play *L'Etat de siège/State of Siege* (1948), and *L'Homme révolté*, Camus moved away from metaphysical alienation and began to explore the problem of suffering in its more historical manifestations, and the concept of revolt.

Related Web site: Camus, Albert http://members.aol.com/KatharenaE/private/Philo/Camus/camus.html

> **Albert Camus**
> *What is a rebel?*
> *A man who says no.*
> The Rebel (1951)

Canaan ancient region between the Mediterranean and the Dead Sea, called in the Bible the 'Promised Land' of the Israelites. It was occupied as early as the 3rd millennium BC by the Canaanites, a Semitic-speaking people who were known to the Greeks of the 1st millennium BC as Phoenicians. The capital was Ebla (now Tell Mardikh, Syria).

Canada see country box.

Canadian art Both French and English tradition contributed to development of art in Canada from the 17th century onwards. In the colony of New France, c. 1670, Frère Luc (Claude François) transplanted the European style of religious painting. After the British conquest in 1759, contact with Europe is reflected in the work of François Beaucourt, who studied in France, and in the early 19th century in the portraits of Antoine Plamondon and Théophile Hamel. The British legacy was evident in the 18th century style of portraiture of Robert Field in Nova Scotia, and also in landscape, in which Thomas Davies was a pioneer. The Canadian scene was romantically presented by Paul Kane (1810–1871), Cornelius Krieghoff (1815–1872), and Robert Whale (1805–1887). About 1870 the romantic picturesque gave way to greater realism, as in the landscapes of John A Fraser and others and the genre paintings of Robert Harris (1849–1919), who painted the first Canadian mural in 1881, *The Fathers of the Confederation*. A poetic style of landscape was practised in the 1890s by Horatio Walker (1858–1938), Homer Watson (1885–1936) and William Brymner (1855–1925). The influence of French Impressionism seen in Maurice Cullen (1866–1934) and James Wilson Morrice (1865–1924) led eventually to a national movement exemplified by a group of painters in Montréal from 1910, who developed a powerful regional style – Tom Thomson (1877–1917) is notable among them. Recent painting shows, besides the attachment to the Canadian scene, a response to abstract art, leading abstractionists being Paul Émile Borduas, Jean Paul Riopelle and Harold Town.

Canadian literature Canadian literature in English began early in the 19th century in the Maritime Provinces with the humorous tales of T C Haliburton (1796–1865). Charles Heavysege (1816–1876) published poems combining psychological insight with Puritan values. The late 19th century brought the lyrical output of Charles G D Roberts, Bliss Carman (1861–1929), Archibald Lampman (1861–1899), and Duncan Campbell Scott (1862–1944). Realism in fiction developed with Frederick P Grove, Mazo de la Roche, creator of the 'Jalna' series, and Hugh MacLennan. Humour of worldwide appeal emerged in Stephen Leacock; Brian Moore, author of *The Luck of Ginger Coffey* (1960); and Mordecai Richler. Also widely read outside Canada was L M Montgomery (1874–1942), whose *Anne of Green Gables* (1908) became a children's classic. US novelist Saul Bellow and the communication theorist Marshall McLuhan were both Canadian-born, as were contemporary novelists Robertson Davies and Margaret ▷Atwood.

Recent poetry and fiction, stimulated by journals such as *The Canadian Forum* (founded in 1920) and *Canadian Fiction Magazine* (founded in 1971) and by a growing number of literary prizes, has become increasingly international in outlook while also drawing attention to contemporary Canadian issues such as racial and linguistic minorities and the environment.

canal artificial waterway constructed for drainage, irrigation, or navigation. **Irrigation canals** carry water for irrigation from rivers, reservoirs, or wells, and are designed to maintain an even flow of water over the whole length. **Navigation and ship canals** are constructed at one level between ▷locks, and frequently link with rivers or sea inlets to form a waterway system. The Suez Canal in 1869 and the Panama Canal in 1914 eliminated long trips around continents and dramatically shortened shipping routes.

Irrigation canals The River Nile has fed canals to maintain life in Egypt since the earliest times. The division of the waters of the Upper Indus and its tributaries, which form an extensive system in Pakistan and Punjab, India, was, for more than ten years, a major cause of dispute between India and Pakistan, settled by a treaty in 1960. The Murray basin, Victoria, Australia, and the Imperial and Central Valley projects in California, USA, are examples of 19th- and 20th-century irrigation-canal development. Excessive extraction of water for irrigation from rivers and lakes can cause environmental damage.

Canada: Provinces and Territories		Area		Population (1996)
Province	Capital	sq km	sq mi	
Alberta	Edmonton	661,190	255,285	2,696,800
British Columbia	Victoria	947,800	365,946	3,724,500
Manitoba	Winnipeg	649,950	250,946	1,113,900
New Brunswick	Fredericton	73,440	28,355	738,100
Newfoundland	St John's	405,720	156,648	551,800
Nova Scotia	Halifax	55,490	21,425	909,300
Ontario	Toronto	1,068,580	412,579	10,753,600
Prince Edward Island	Charlottetown	5,660	2,185	134,600
Québec	Québec	1,540,680	594,857	7,138,800
Saskatchewan	Regina	652,330	251,865	990,200
Territory				
Northwest Territories	Yellowknife	1,224,800	472,894	40,400
Yukon Territory	Whitehorse	483,450	186,660	30,800
Nunavut (semi-autonomous region)		2,201,500	850,000	24,000[1]

[1] 1999.

CANAL View of the Paddington Canal, London, a stretch of the Grand Junction Canal. *Philip Sauvain Picture Collection*

Canada

Inuit, and 11% other, mostly Asian
LANGUAGE English (60%), French (24%) (both official), American Indian languages, Inuktitut (Inuit)
RELIGION Roman Catholic 45%, various Protestant denominations
EDUCATION (compulsory years) 10
LITERACY RATE 99% (men); 99% (women) (2003 est)
LABOUR FORCE 3.3% agriculture, 22.6% industry, 74.1% services (2000)
LIFE EXPECTANCY 76 (men); 82 (women) (2000–05)
CHILD MORTALITY RATE (under 5, per 1,000 live births) 7 (2001)
PHYSICIANS (per 1,000 people) 2.1 (1998 est)
HOSPITAL BEDS (per 1,000 people) 3.9 (1998 est)
TV SETS (per 1,000 people) 715 (1999)
RADIOS (per 1,000 people) 1,077 (1997)
INTERNET USERS (per 10,000 people) 4,838.6 (2002 est)
PERSONAL COMPUTER USERS (per 100 people) 48.7 (2002 est)

See also ▷British Columbia; ▷Commonwealth, the (British); ▷Inuit; ▷Quebec.

Canada country occupying the northern part of the North American continent, bounded to the south by the USA, north by the Arctic Ocean, northwest by Alaska, east by the Atlantic Ocean, and west by the Pacific Ocean.

AREA 9,970,610 sq km/3,849,652 sq mi
CAPITAL Ottawa
MAJOR TOWNS/CITIES Toronto, Montréal, Vancouver, Edmonton, Calgary, Winnipeg, Québec, Hamilton, Saskatoon, Halifax, London, Kitchener, Mississauga, Laval, Surrey
PHYSICAL FEATURES mountains in west, with low-lying plains in interior and rolling hills in east; St Lawrence Seaway, Mackenzie River; Great Lakes; Arctic Archipelago; Rocky Mountains; Great Plains or Prairies; Canadian Shield; Niagara Falls; climate varies from temperate in south to arctic in north; 45% of country forested

Government

HEAD OF STATE Queen Elizabeth II from 1952, represented by Governor General Adrienne Clarkson from 1999
HEAD OF GOVERNMENT Paul Martin from 2003
POLITICAL SYSTEM liberal democracy
POLITICAL EXECUTIVE parliamentary
ADMINISTRATIVE DIVISIONS ten provinces and three territories
ARMED FORCES 52,300 (2002 est)
CONSCRIPTION military service is voluntary
DEATH PENALTY abolished in 1998
DEFENCE SPEND (% GDP) 1.1 (2002 est)

CANADA Ice in the Northwest Passage, the Atlantic–Pacific sea route around the north of Canada. *Corel*

EDUCATION SPEND (% GDP) 5.4 (2001 est)
HEALTH SPEND (% GDP) 9.1 (2000 est)

Economy and resources

CURRENCY Canadian dollar
GPD (US$) 715.7 billion (2002 est)
REAL GDP GROWTH (% change on previous year) 1.5 (2001)
GNI (US$) 700.5 billion (2002 est)
GNI PER CAPITA (PPP) (US$) 28,070 (2002 est)
CONSUMER PRICE INFLATION 2.7% (2003 est)
UNEMPLOYMENT 7.2% (2001)
MAJOR TRADING PARTNERS USA, EU countries, Japan, China, Mexico, South Korea
RESOURCES petroleum, natural gas, coal, copper (world's third-largest producer), nickel (world's second-largest producer), lead (world's fifth-largest producer), zinc (world's largest producer), iron, gold, uranium, timber
INDUSTRIES transport equipment, food products, paper and related products, wood industries, chemical products, machinery
EXPORTS motor vehicles and parts, lumber, wood pulp, paper and newsprint, crude petroleum, natural gas, aluminium and alloys, petroleum and coal products. Principal market: USA 85% (2001)
IMPORTS motor vehicle parts, passenger vehicles, computers, foodstuffs, telecommunications equipment. Principal source: USA 76% (2001)
ARABLE LAND 4.9% (2000 est)
AGRICULTURAL PRODUCTS wheat, barley, maize, oats, rapeseed, linseed; livestock production (cattle and pigs)

Population and society

POPULATION 31,510,000 (2003 est)
POPULATION GROWTH RATE 0.6% (2000–15)
POPULATION DENSITY (per sq km) 3 (2003 est)
URBAN POPULATION (% of total) 79 (2003 est)
AGE DISTRIBUTION (% of total population) 0–14 19%, 15–59 64%, 60+ 17% (2002 est)
ETHNIC GROUPS about 40% of British Irish origin, 27% French, 20% of other European descent, about 2% American Indians and

Chronology

35,000 BC: First evidence of people reaching North America from Asia by way of Beringia.

c. 2000 BC: Inuit (Eskimos) began settling the Arctic coast from Siberia eastwards to Greenland.

c. AD 1000: Vikings, including Leif Ericsson, established Vinland, a settlement in northeast America that did not survive.

1497: John Cabot, an Italian navigator in the service of English king Henry VII, landed on Cape Breton Island and claimed the area for England.

1534: French navigator Jacques Cartier reached the Gulf of St Lawrence and claimed the region for France.

1608: Samuel de Champlain, a French explorer, founded Québec; French settlers developed fur trade and fisheries.

1663: French settlements in Canada formed the colony of New France, which expanded southwards.

1670: Hudson's Bay Company established trading posts north of New France, leading to Anglo-French rivalry.

1689–97: King William's War: Anglo-French conflict in North America arising from the 'Glorious Revolution' in Europe.

1702–13: Queen Anne's War: Anglo-French conflict in North America arising from the War of the Spanish Succession in Europe; Britain gained Newfoundland.

1744–48: King George's War: Anglo-French conflict in North America arising from the War of Austrian Succession in Europe.

1756–63: Seven Years' War: James Wolfe captured Québec in 1759; France ceded Canada to Britain by the Treaty of Paris.

1775–83: American Revolution caused an influx of 40,000 United Empire Loyalists, who formed New Brunswick in 1784.

1791: Canada was divided into Upper Canada (much of modern Ontario) and Lower Canada (much of modern Québec).

1793: British explorer Alexander Mackenzie crossed the Rocky Mountains to reach the Pacific coast.

1812–14: War of 1812 between Britain and USA; US invasions repelled by both provinces.

1820s: Start of large-scale immigration from British Isles caused resentment among French Canadians.

1837: Rebellions were led by Louis Joseph Papineau in Lower Canada and William Lyon Mackenzie in Upper Canada.

1841: Upper and Lower Canada united as Province of Canada; achieved internal self-government in 1848.

1867: British North America Act united Ontario, Québec, Nova Scotia, and New Brunswick in Dominion of Canada.

1869: Red River Rebellion of Métis (people of mixed French and American Indian descent), led by Louis Riel, against British settlers in Rupert's Land.

1870: Manitoba (part of Rupert's Land) formed the fifth province of Canada; British Columbia became the sixth in 1871, and Prince Edward Island became the seventh in 1873.

1885: The Northwest Rebellion was crushed and Riel hanged. The Canadian Pacific Railway was completed.

1905: Alberta and Saskatchewan were formed from the Northwest Territories and became provinces of Canada.

1914–18: Half a million Canadian troops fought for the British Empire on the western front in World War I.

1931: The Statute of Westminster affirmed equality of status between Britain and the Dominions.

1939–45: World War II: Canadian participation in all theatres.

1949: Newfoundland became the tenth province of Canada; Canada was a founding member of the North Atlantic Treaty Organization (NATO).

1960: The Québec Liberal Party of Jean Lesage launched a 'Quiet Revolution' to re-assert French-Canadian identity.

1970: Pierre Trudeau invoked the War Measures Act to suppress separatist terrorists of the Front de Libération du Québec.

1976: The Parti Québécois won control of the Québec provincial government; a referendum rejected independence in 1980.

1982: 'Patriation' of the constitution removed Britain's last legal control over Canada.

1987: Meech Lake Accord: a constitutional amendment was proposed to increase provincial powers (to satisfy Québec); failed to be ratified in 1990.

1992: A self-governing homeland for the Inuit was approved.

1994: Canada formed the North American Free Trade Area with USA and Mexico.

1995: A Québec referendum narrowly rejected a sovereignty proposal.

1997: The Liberals were re-elected by a narrow margin.

1999: The government passed a bill making secession by Québec more difficult to achieve.

2000: The Liberals were elected for a third term.

2001: Bernard Landry replaced Lucien Bouchard as prime minister of Québec.

Ship canals Probably the oldest ship canal to be still in use, as well as the longest, is the Grand Canal in China, which links Tianjin and Hangzhou and connects the Huang He (Yellow River) and Chang Jiang. It was originally built in three stages between 485 BC and AD 283, reaching a total length of 1,780 km/1,110 mi. Large sections silted up in later years, but the entire system was dredged, widened, and rebuilt between 1958 and 1972 in conjunction with work on flood protection, irrigation, and hydroelectric schemes. It carries millions of tonnes of freight every year.

Where speed is not a prime factor, the cost-effectiveness of transporting goods by canal has encouraged a revival; Belgium, France, Germany, and the states of the former USSR are among countries that have extended and streamlined their canals. The Baltic–Volga waterway links the Lithuanian port of Klaipeda with Kahovka, at the mouth of the Dnieper on the Black Sea, a distance of 2,430 km/1,510 mi. A further canal cuts across the north Crimea, thus shortening the voyage of ships from the Dnieper through the Black Sea to the Sea of Azov. In Central America, the Panama Canal (1904–14) links the Atlantic and Pacific oceans (64 km/40 mi). In North America, the Erie Canal (1825) links the Great Lakes with the Hudson River and opened up the northeast and midwest to commerce; the St Lawrence Seaway (1954–59) extends from Montréal to Lake Ontario (290 km/180 mi) and, with the deepening of the Welland Ship Canal and some of the river channels, provides a waterway that enables ocean going vessels to travel (during the ice-free months) between the Atlantic and Duluth, Minnesota, USA, at the western end of Lake Superior, some 3,770 km/2,342 mi.

UK canals As the pace of trade increased in the UK in the 17th and 18th centuries, it was necessary to find a better way of transporting goods than by road, which was slow and subject to accidents, delays, and highway robbery. Water-borne barges could carry fifty times as much as a wagon and as much as 250 packhorses. Before the canals of the 18th century, Parliamentary legislation allowed stretches of river to be made navigable: by 1700, about 1,600 km/1,000 mi of river had been improved.

Although the first British canal was built in 1566, the first major British canal was the Bridgewater Canal 1759–61, constructed for the 3rd Duke of Bridgewater to carry coal from his collieries to Manchester. The engineer, James ▷Brindley, overcame great difficulties in the route. Thomas ▷Telford constructed the Ellesmere Canal, linking Birmingham to North Wales and Liverpool in 1795. By the 1790s, 'canal mania' had gripped the country. Between 1791 and 1794 42 canals were financed, at a total cost of £6 million. By 1830 some 6,500 km/4,000 mi of canals had been built. The canal boom was one of the causes of the ▷Industrial Revolution. Building the canals created thousands of jobs, and increased demand in the wood, brick, and clay industries. It also helped to develop civil engineering skills. The canals brought cheap coal and fresh food to the growing towns, and helped businesses by reducing transport costs. Thousands of navvies were employed in their construction, and thousands more were needed to run them. The large amounts of money raised to build the canals led to the foundation of stock exchanges, which could then be used to raise money for industry.

However, canals were slow, unsuitable for carrying passengers, and expensive to build, especially in the hill country of the north of England and Scotland, where most industrial development was taking place. After 1850 the canals were replaced by the ▷railways, as the main form of transport. Today many of Britain's canals form part of an interconnecting system of waterways some 4,000 km/2,500 mi long. Many that have become disused commercially have been restored for recreation and the use of pleasure craft.

Canaletto, Antonio (1697–1768) Adopted name of Giovanni Antonio Canal. Italian painter. He painted highly detailed views (*vedute*) of Venice (his native city), and of London and the River Thames (1746–56). Typical of his Venetian works is *Venice: Regatta on the Grand Canal* (*c.* 1735; National Gallery, London).

Canaries current cold ocean current in the North Atlantic Ocean flowing southwest from Spain along the northwest coast of Africa. It meets the northern equatorial current at a latitude of 20° N.

canary bird (*Serinus canaria*) of the finch family Fringillidae, found wild in the Canary Islands and Madeira. In its wild state the plumage is green, sometimes streaked with brown. The wild canary builds its nest of moss, feathers, and hair in thick high shrubs or trees, and produces two to four broods in a season.

Canaries have been bred as cage birds in Europe since the 15th century, and many domestic varieties are yellow or orange as a result of artificial selection.

Some canaries were used in mines as detectors of traces of poison gas in the air.

The chief varieties of the domesticated canary are the Norwich, which is the hardiest, and very rich in colour; the Belgian fancy, the most beautiful and costly; the lizard, so-called from its spotted back; the cinnamon, so named from its colour; the Yorkshire, a long, thin, closely-feathered bird; the Lancashire coppy, the largest variety, with a crest of feathers on its head; the London fancy, a little yellow or biscuit-coloured bird with black wings and tail; the Scotch fancy, a large imposing variety, bred largely in Scotland; and the roller canary, a very small bird, bred chiefly for its unusually beautiful song.

Related Web site: Canary FAQ http://www2.upatsix.com/faq/canary.htm

Canary Islands (Spanish **Islas Canarias**) group of volcanic islands and autonomous Spanish community 100 km/60 mi off the northwest coast of Africa, comprising the provinces of Las Palmas and Santa Cruz de Tenerife; area 7,300 sq km/2,818 sq mi; population (1991) 1,456,500. Products include bananas and tomatoes, both grown for export. Tourism is the major industry.

The aboriginal inhabitants of the Canary Islands were called Guanches, and the Organization of African Unity (OAU) supports the creation of an independent state, the Guanch Republic, and the revival of the Guanch language.

Canary Wharf 420 thousand-sq m/4.5 million-sq ft office development on the Isle of Dogs in London's ▷Docklands, the first phase of which was completed in 1992, along with the foundations for a further 740 thousand sq m/8 million sq ft. The complex of offices, surrounding landscaped squares, is best known for its central skyscraper, the second tallest in Europe, when built, at 244 m/800 ft. Designed by US architect Cesar Pelli (1926–), it sports a pyramid-shaped crown in stainless steel. After the collapse of the developer Olympia York in 1992, the site gained notoriety as a symbol of the economic recession in the UK, with much of its office space remaining unlet. By the end of 1995, following a rescue package, 75% had been let.

Canberra capital of ▷Australia and seat of the federal government, situated in the ▷Australian Capital Territory in southeast Australia; population (1996) 299,243. Canberra is enclosed within the state of New South Wales, 289 km/180 mi southwest of Sydney and 655 km/407 mi northeast of Melbourne, on the River Molonglo, a tributary of the Murrumbidgee. It succeeded Melbourne as capital of Australia in 1927. It is an administrative, cultural, and tourist centre. The new Parliament House (1988) is located here, as well as government offices, foreign embassies, and many buildings of national importance.

Canberra lies in a chiefly agricultural region and was built around Lake Burley Griffin, formed by the damming of the River Molonglo. The site, between Sydney and Melbourne, was chosen in 1908, and the city was named Canberra (Aboriginal 'meeting place') in 1913; it was designed by the American architect Walter Burley Griffin. Parliament first convened in Canberra in 1927 (moved from Melbourne), but the city's development was slow until after World War II.

Related Web site: Canberra's Top Secret Tour http://www.topsecret.canberra.net.au/

cancan high-kicking stage dance in fast duple time (2/4) for women (solo or line of dancers), originating in Paris, France, about 1830. The music usually associated with the cancan is the *galop* from Jacques Offenbach's *Orphée aux enfers/Orpheus in the Underworld* (1858).

Cancer faintest of the zodiacal constellations (its brightest stars are fourth magnitude). It lies in the northern hemisphere between ▷Leo and ▷Gemini, and is represented as a crab. The Sun passes through the constellation during late July and early August. In astrology, the dates for Cancer are between about 22 June and 22 July (see ▷precession).

ANTONIO CANALETTO The Bacino di San Marco – the basin in front of St Mark's, Venice, Italy – featuring the Palazzo Ducale is a scene that Italian painter Canaletto painted many times. *The Art Archive/Brera Library Milan/Dagli Orti*

Cancer's most distinctive feature is the open star cluster Praesepe, popularly known as the Beehive, visible to the naked eye as a nebulous patch.

cancer group of diseases characterized by abnormal proliferation of cells. Cancer (malignant) cells are usually degenerate, capable only of reproducing themselves (tumour formation). Malignant cells tend to spread from their site of origin by travelling through the bloodstream or lymphatic system. Cancer kills about 6 million people a year worldwide.

Causes There are more than 100 types of cancer. Some, like lung or bowel cancer, are common; others are rare. The likely causes remain unexplained. Triggering agents (▷carcinogens) include chemicals such as those found in cigarette smoke, other forms of smoke, asbestos dust, exhaust fumes, and many industrial chemicals. Some viruses can also trigger the cancerous growth of cells (see ▷oncogenes), as can X-rays and radioactivity. Dietary factors are important in some cancers; for example, lack of fibre in the diet may predispose people to bowel cancer and a diet high in animal fats and low in fresh vegetables and fruit increases the risk of breast cancer. Psychological ▷stress may increase the risk of cancer, more so if the person concerned is not able to control the source of the stress.

Philip Morris, the world's largest cigarette manufacturer acknowledged for the first time in October 1999 that scientific evidence showed smoking was addictive and could cause potentially lethal diseases such as cancer. Like its competitors, Philip Morris had for years disputed the scientific findings about the risks of smoking.

cancer genes In some families there is a genetic tendency towards a particular type of cancer. In 1993 researchers isolated the first gene that predisposes individuals to cancer. About one in 200 people in the West carry the gene. If the gene mutates, those with the altered gene have a 70% chance of developing colon cancer, and female carriers have a 50% chance of developing cancer of the uterus.

In 1994 a gene that triggers breast cancer was identified. *BRCA1* was found to be responsible for almost half the cases of inherited breast cancer, and most cases of ovarian cancer. In 1995 a link between *BRCA1* and non-inherited breast cancer was discovered. Women with the gene have an 85% chance of developing breast or ovarian cancer during their lifetime. A second breast cancer gene *BRCA2* was identified later in 1995.

The commonest cancer in young men is testicular cancer, the incidence of which has been rising by 3% a year since 1974 (1998). In February 2000, British researchers announced the discovery of a mutant gene that increases incidence of testicular cancer fiftyfold. The gene *TGCT1* is inherited from the mother and if a successful screening system is devised 95% of testicular cancer cases will be able to be predicted.

treatment Cancer is one of the leading causes of death in the industrialized world, yet it is by no means incurable, particularly in the case of certain tumours, including Hodgkin's disease, acute leukaemia, and testicular cancer. Cures are sometimes achieved with specialized treatments, such as surgery, chemotherapy with ▷cytotoxic drugs, and irradiation, or a combination of all three. ▷Monoclonal antibodies have been used therapeutically against some cancers, with limited success. There is also hope of combining a monoclonal antibody with a drug that will kill the cancer cell to produce a highly specific ▷ magic bullet drug. In 1990 it was discovered that the presence in some patients of a particular protein, *p*-glycoprotein, actively protects the cancer cells from drugs intended to destroy them. If this action can be blocked, the cancer should become far easier to treat. Public health programmes are concerned with prevention and early detection. The first of a new generation of drugs that fight all types of cancer was approved by the US Food and Drug Administration in May 2001.

A survey of skin cancer rates in the Australian town of Nambour, Queensland 1985–95 showed that 2% of the population had skin cancer. This was the highest rate ever recorded for a specific cancer. Generally, however, the incidence of cancer in Australia in the late 1990s began to fall. According to 1999 figures, Australians have a 70% risk of developing skin cancer during their lifetime; in Britain the risk is 15%.

A US trial commenced in 1995 to treat cancer patients with gene therapy. Ten women with breast cancer were injected with a virus genetically engineered to destroy tumours. Up to 1 billion viruses were injected into the chest cavity over a four-day period. Researchers are hopeful of extending life expectancy, rather than providing a total cure. UK trials began in 1995 of a drug designed to check tumour growth and prevent cancer spreading. The drug, called BB-2516, performed well in animal trials. Its manufacturer hopes it will stabilize cancer in humans, enabling sufferers to lead relatively normal lives whilst maintaining dosage.

It was announced in May 1997 at a meeting of the American Society of Clinical Oncology that scientists were in the process of developing vaccines which cause the immune system to shrink certain cancers, such as those attacking the skin, breast, prostate, and ovaries. Unlike the normal preventative vaccines, the new vaccines fight tumours that already exist. They use components of the cancer to provoke white blood cells to attack the invader.

In August 1997, US Vice-President Al Gore announced that a new technology was being used to fight and study cancer. Laser capture microdissection can take individual cells from hundreds of cell types in a tumour specimen so that scientists can determine which genes inside are active. This would eventually yield a complete inventory of genes involved in all major types of cancer. The technology was invented by Lance Liotta, chief of pathology at the National Cancer Institute.

candela SI unit (symbol cd) of luminous intensity, which replaced the old units of candle and standard candle. It measures the brightness of a light itself rather than the amount of light falling on an object, which is called **illuminance** and measured in ▷lux.

Candida albicans yeastlike fungus present in the human digestive tract and in the vagina, which causes no harm in most healthy people. However, it can cause problems if it multiplies excessively, as in vaginal candidiasis or ▷thrush, the main symptom of which is intense itching.

The most common form of thrush is oral, which often occurs in those taking steroids or prolonged courses of antibiotics.

cane reedlike stem of various plants such as the sugar cane, bamboo, and, in particular, the group of palms called rattans, consisting of the genus *Calamus* and its allies. Their slender stems are dried and used for making walking sticks, baskets, and furniture.

cane toad toad of the genus *Bufo marinus*, family Bufonidae. Also known as the giant or marine toad, the cane toad is the largest in the world. It acquired its name after being introduced to Australia during the 1930s to eradicate the cane beetle, which had become a serious pest there. However, having few natural enemies, the cane toad itself has now become a pest in Australia.

The cane toad's defence system consists of highly developed glands on each side of its neck which can squirt a poisonous fluid to a distance of around 1 m/3.3 ft.

Canes Venatici constellation of the northern hemisphere near ▷Ursa Major, identified with the hunting dogs of ▷Boötes, the herder. Its stars are faint, and it contains the Whirlpool galaxy (M51), the first spiral galaxy to be recognized.

Canetti, Elias (1905–1994) Bulgarian-born writer. He was exiled from Austria in 1937 and settled in England in 1939. His books, written in German, include *Die Blendung/Auto da Fé* (1935). He was concerned with crowd behaviour and the psychology of power, and wrote the anthropological study *Masse und Macht/Crowds and Power* (1960). He was awarded the Nobel Prize for Literature in 1981.

> ### Elias Canetti
> *When you write down your life, every page should contain something no one has ever heard about.*
>
> The Secret Heart of the Clock: notes, aphorisms, fragments (1973)

Canis Major brilliant constellation of the southern hemisphere, represented (with Canis Minor) as one of the two dogs following at the heel of ▷Orion. Its main star, ▷Sirius, is the brightest star in the night sky.

Canis Minor small constellation along the celestial equator (see ▷celestial sphere), represented as the smaller of the two dogs of ▷Orion (the other dog being ▷Canis Major). Its brightest star is the first magnitude ▷Procyon.

cannabis dried leaves and female flowers ▷marijuana and ▷resin (hashish) of certain varieties of ▷hemp, which are smoked or swallowed to produce a range of effects, including feelings of happiness and altered perception. (*Cannabis sativa*, family Cannabaceae.)

Cannes resort in Alpes-Maritimes *département* of southern France, on the Mediterranean coast and 21 km/13 mi southwest of Nice; population (1990) 69,400, Grasse-Cannes-Antibes conurbation 335,000.

Formerly a small fishing village and seaport, in 1834 Cannes attracted the patronage of the English Lord Brougham and other distinguished visitors and soon grew into a popular winter and summer holiday resort on the French ▷Riviera. The prestigious Cannes Film Festival is held here annually. The city has textile and aircraft industries, and a strong trade in olive oil, soap, fish, fruit, and flowers.

canning food preservation in hermetically sealed containers by the application of heat. Originated by Nicolas Appert in France in 1809 with glass containers, it was developed by Peter Durand in England in 1810 with cans made of sheet steel thinly coated with tin to delay corrosion. Cans for beer and soft drinks are now generally made of aluminium.

Canning, Charles John (1812–1862) 1st Earl Canning. British administrator, son of George ▷Canning and first viceroy of India from 1858. As governor general of India from 1856, he suppressed the Indian Mutiny with a fair but firm hand which earned him the nickname 'Clemency Canning'. Viscount (1837), Earl (1859).

Canning, George (1770–1827) British Tory politician, foreign secretary 1807–10 and 1822–27, and prime minister in 1827 in coalition with the Whigs. He was largely responsible, during the ▷Napoleonic Wars, for the seizure of the Danish fleet and British intervention in the Spanish peninsula.

Cannon, Annie Jump (1863–1941) US astronomer. She carried out revolutionary work on the classification of stars by examining their spectra. Her system, still used today, has spectra arranged according to temperature into categories labelled O, B, A, F, G, K, M, R, N, and S. O-type stars are the hottest, with surface temperatures ranging from 25,000 to 50,000 K (from 24,700°C/44,450°F to 49,700°C/89,500°F).

Cano, Juan Sebastian del (*c.* 1476–1526) Spanish voyager. It is claimed that he was the first sea captain to sail around the world. He sailed with Ferdinand ▷Magellan in 1519 and, after the latter's death in the Philippines, brought the *Victoria* safely home to Spain.

canoeing sport of propelling a lightweight, shallow boat, pointed at both ends, by paddles or sails. Present-day canoes are made from fibreglass, but original boats were of wooden construction covered in bark or skin. Canoeing was popularized as a sport in the 19th century.

> **Related Web site: Canoeing** http://www.canoeing.co.uk/home.html

canon in music, an echo form for two or more parts employed in classical music, for example by two solo violins in an orchestral movement by Vivaldi or Johann Sebastian Bach, as a means of generating pace and advertising professional skill.

canonical hours in the Catholic Church, seven set periods of devotion: **matins** and **lauds**, **prime**, **terce**, **sext**, **nones**, **evensong** or **vespers**, and **compline**.

canonization in the Catholic Church, the admission of one of its members to the Calendar of ▷Saints. The evidence of the candidate's exceptional piety is contested before the Congregation for the Causes of Saints by the Promotor Fidei, popularly known as the **devil's advocate**. Papal ratification of a favourable verdict results in ▷beatification, and full sainthood (conferred in St Peter's basilica, the Vatican) follows after further proof.

canon law rules and regulations of the Christian church, especially the Greek Orthodox, Roman Catholic, and Anglican churches. Its origin is sought in the declarations of Jesus and the apostles. In 1983 Pope

GEORGE CANNING The British Tory politician and prime minister for four months during 1827. *Philip Sauvain Picture Collection*

John Paul II issued a new canon law code reducing offences carrying automatic excommunication, extending the grounds for annulment of marriage, removing the ban on marriage with non-Catholics, and banning trade-union and political activity by priests.

Canopic jars in ancient Egypt, four containers for holding a dead person's embalmed organs. Each lid represented the head of one of the four sons of ▷Horus, protecting their allotted organ – the human Imset guarded the liver; Hapy the baboon, the lungs; the jackal Duamutef, the stomach; and the hawk Qebehsenuf, the intestines. Usually carved from stone, the earliest examples date from the 4th dynasty, when the lids depicted human heads.

The four sons of Horus were also associated with the four points of the compass.

Canopus (or Alpha Carinae) second-brightest star in the night sky (after Sirius), lying in the southern constellation ▷Carina. It is a yellow-white supergiant about 100 light years from the Sun, and thousands of times more luminous than the Sun.

Canova, Antonio, Marquese d'Ischia (1757–1822) Italian neoclassical sculptor. He was based in Rome from 1781. He received commissions from popes, kings, and emperors for his highly finished marble portrait busts and groups of figures. He made several portraits of Napoleon.

Cantab abbreviation for **Cantabrigiensis** (Latin 'of Cambridge').

Cantabria autonomous community of northern Spain; area 5,300 sq km/2,046 sq mi; population (1996) 527,400. From the coastline on the Bay of Biscay it rises to the Cantabrian Mountains. There is some mining here, as well as engineering and food industries, particularly dairy products. The capital is Santander.

Cantabrian Mountains (Spanish Cordillera Cantábrica) mountain range running along the north coast of Spain, continuing the line of the Pyrenees westwards for about 480 km/300 mi, parallel to the coast of the Bay of Biscay. They rise to 2,648 m/8,688 ft in the Picos de Europa massif. The mountains contain coal and iron deposits, but they are of poor quality; little is mined today.

cantata in music, an extended work for voices, from the Italian, meaning 'sung', as opposed to ▷sonata ('sounded'/'played') for instruments. A cantata can be sacred or secular, sometimes uses solo voices, and usually has orchestral accompaniment. The first printed collection of sacred cantata texts dates from 1670.

Canterbury (Old English *Cantwarabyrig* 'fortress of the men of Kent') historic cathedral city in Kent, southeast England, on the River Stour, 100 km/62 mi southeast of London; population (1991) 36,500. The city is the metropolis of the Anglican Communion and seat of the archbishop of Canterbury. It is a popular tourist destination. Paper, paper products, and electrical goods are manufactured.

Canterbury, archbishop of archbishop of the Church of England (Anglican), the primate (archbishop) of all England, and first peer of the realm, ranking next to royalty. He crowns the sovereign, has a seat in the House of Lords, and is a member of the Privy Council. He is appointed by the prime minister.

> **Related Web site: Archbishop of Canterbury** http://www.archbishopofcanterbury.org/

CANNABIS A demonstration demanding the legalization of cannabis in London, England. *Image Bank*

cantilever beam or structure that is fixed at one end only, though it may be supported at some point along its length; for example, a diving board. The cantilever principle, widely used in construction engineering, eliminates the need for a second main support at the free end of the beam, allowing for more elegant structures and reducing the amount of materials required. Many large-span bridges have been built on the cantilever principle.

Canton alternative spelling of ▷Guangzhou or Kwangchow, capital of Guangdong province in China.

canton in France, an administrative district, a subdivision of the *arrondissement*; in Switzerland, one of the 23 subdivisions forming the Confederation.

Canute (or **Cnut** or **Knut**) (*c.* 995–1035) Also known as **Canute the Great**. King of England from 1016, Denmark from 1018, and Norway from 1028. Having invaded England in 1013 with his father, Sweyn, king of Denmark, he was acclaimed king on Sweyn's death in 1014 by his ▷Viking army. Canute defeated Edmund (II) Ironside at Assandun, Essex, in 1016, and became king of all England on Edmund's death. He succeeded his brother Harold as king of Denmark in 1018, compelled King Malcolm to pay homage by invading Scotland in about 1027, and conquered Norway in 1028. He was succeeded by his illegitimate son Harold I.

Under Canute's rule English trade improved, and he gained favour with his English subjects by sending soldiers back to Denmark. The legend of Canute disenchanting his flattering courtiers by showing that the sea would not retreat at his command was first told by Henry of Huntingdon in 1130.

> ### Canute
> *Sea, I command thee that thou touch not my feet!*
> When he failed to stay the waves, quoted in William Camden *Remains Concerning Britain*

Canute VI (or **Cnut VI** or **Knut VI**) (1163–1202) King of Denmark from 1182, son and successor of Waldemar Knudsson. With his brother and successor, Waldemar II, he resisted Frederick I's northward expansion, and established Denmark as the dominant power in the Baltic.

canyon (Spanish *cañon* 'tube') deep, narrow valley or gorge running through mountains. Canyons are formed by stream down-cutting, usually in arid areas, where the rate of down-cutting is greater than the rate of weathering, and where the stream or river receives water from outside the area.

Cao Chan (or **Ts'ao Chan**) (1719–1763) Chinese novelist. His tragicomic love story *Hung Lou Meng/The Dream of the Red Chamber*, published in 1792, involves the downfall of a Manchu family and is semi-autobiographical.

cap another name for a ▷diaphragm contraceptive.

capacitance, electrical property of a capacitor that determines how much charge can be stored in it for a given potential difference between its terminals. It is equal to the ratio of the electrical charge stored to the potential difference. The SI unit of capacitance is the ▷farad, but most capacitors have much smaller capacitances, and the microfarad (a millionth of a farad) is the commonly used practical unit.

capacitor (or **condenser**) device for storing electric charge, used in electronic circuits; it consists of two or more metal plates separated by an insulating layer called a dielectric (see ▷capacitance).

Its **capacitance** is the ratio of the charge stored on either plate to the potential difference between the plates.

Cape Canaveral promontory on the Atlantic coast of Florida, USA, 367 km/228 mi north of Miami, used as a rocket launch site by ▷NASA.

It was known as Cape Kennedy 1963–73. The ▷Kennedy Space Center is nearby.

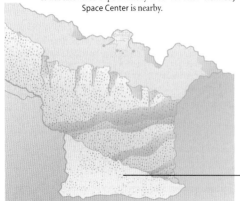

CANYON A cross section of a canyon. Canyons are formed in dry regions where rivers maintain a constant flow of water over long periods of time. The Grand Canyon, for example, was first cut around 26 million years ago, in Miocene times.

Cape Cod hook-shaped peninsula in southeastern Massachusetts, separated from the rest of the state by the Cape Cod Canal; length 100 km/62 mi; width 1.6–32 km/1–20 mi. Its beaches and woods make it a popular tourist area. The islands of ▷Martha's Vineyard and ▷Nantucket are just south of the cape.

Čapek, Karel (1890–1938) Czech writer. His works often deal with social injustice in an imaginative, satirical way. *R.U.R.* (1921) is a play in which robots (a term he coined) rebel against their controllers; the novel *War with the Newts* (1936) is a science fiction classic.

Capella (or **Alpha Aurigae**) brightest star in the constellation ▷Auriga and the sixth-brightest star in the night sky. It is a visual and spectroscopic binary that consists of a pair of yellow-giant stars 42 light years from the Sun, orbiting each other every 104 days.

Its Latin name means the 'the Little Nanny Goat': its kids are the three adjacent stars Epsilon, Eta, and Zeta Aurigae.

Cape Province (Afrikaans **Kaapprovinsie**) former province of the Republic of South Africa to 1994, now divided into Western, Eastern, and Northern Cape Provinces. It was named after the Cape of Good Hope. Dutch traders (the Dutch East India Company) established the first European settlement on the Cape in 1652, but it was taken by the British in 1795, after the French Revolutionary armies had occupied the Netherlands, and was sold to Britain for £6 million in 1814. The Cape achieved self-government in 1872. It was an original province of the Union of 1910.

caper trailing shrub native to the Mediterranean. Its flower buds are preserved in vinegar as a condiment. (*Capparis spinosa*, family Capparidaceae.)

capercaillie (or **wood-grouse** or **cock of the wood**; Gaelic *capull coille* 'cock of the wood') large bird *Tetrao urogallus* of the ▷grouse type, family Tetraonidae, order Galliformes. Found in coniferous woodland in Europe and northern Asia, it is about the size of the turkey and resembles the ▷blackcock in appearance and polygamous habit. The general colour of the male is blackish-grey above, black below, with a dark green chest, and rounded tail which is fanned out in courtship. The female is smaller, mottled, and has a reddish breast barred with black. The feathers on the legs and feet are longest in winter time, and the toes are naked. The capercaillie feeds on insects, worms, berries, and young pine-shoots. At nearly 1 m/3 ft long, the male is the biggest gamebird in Europe. The female is about 60 cm/2 ft long.

Capet, Hugh (938–996) King of France from 987, when he claimed the throne on the death of Louis V. He founded the **Capetian dynasty**, of which various branches continued to reign until the French Revolution, for example, ▷Valois and ▷Bourbon.

Cape Town (Afrikaans **Kaapstad**) port and oldest city (founded in 1652) in South Africa, situated at the northern end of the Cape Peninsula, on Table Bay; population (1991) 854, 616 (urban area); (1991) 2, 350, 200 (peninsula). Industries include horticulture and trade in wool, wine, fruit, grain, and oil. Tourism is important. It is the legislative capital of the Republic of South Africa and capital of ▷Western Cape province.

Related Web site: Cape Town http://www.toptentravel.com/capetown.html

Cape Verde see country box.

capillarity spontaneous movement of liquids up or down narrow tubes, or capillaries. The movement is due to unbalanced molecular attraction at the boundary between the liquid and the tube. If liquid molecules near the boundary are more strongly attracted to molecules in the material of the tube than to other nearby liquid molecules, the liquid will rise in the tube. If liquid molecules are less attracted to the material of the tube than to other liquid molecules, the liquid will fall.

capillary narrowest blood vessel in vertebrates, 0.008–0.02 mm in diameter, barely wider than a red blood cell. Capillaries are distributed as **beds**, complex networks connecting arteries and veins. Capillary walls are extremely thin, consisting of a single layer of cells, so that nutrients, dissolved gases, and waste products can easily pass through them. This makes the capillaries the main area of

CAPE TOWN Cape Town was the gateway for European penetration of the South African interior. *Image Bank*

exchange between the fluid (▷lymph) bathing body tissues and the blood. They provide a large surface area in order to maximize ▷diffusion.

capital in architecture, a stone placed on the top of a column, pier, or pilaster, and usually wider on the upper surface than the diameter of the supporting shaft. A capital consists of three parts: the top member, called the **abacus**, a block that acts as the supporting surface to the superstructure; the middle portion, known as the bell or **echinus**; and the lower part, called the necking or **astragal**.

capital in economics, the stock of goods used in the production of other goods. **Financial capital** is accumulated or inherited wealth held in the form of assets, such as stocks and shares, property, and bank deposits.

capitalism economic system in which the principal means of production, distribution, and exchange are in private (individual or corporate) hands and competitively operated for profit. A **mixed economy** combines the private enterprise of capitalism and a degree of state monopoly, as in nationalized industries and welfare services.

Related Web site: Capitalism.org http://www.capitalism.org/home.htm

capital punishment punishment by death. Capital punishment is retained in 87 countries and territories (2001), including the USA (38 states), China, and Islamic countries. Methods of execution include electrocution, lethal gas, hanging, shooting, lethal injection, garrotting, and decapitation. It was abolished in the UK in 1965 for all crimes except treason and piracy, and in 1998 it was entirely abolished in the UK.

Related Web site: Death Penalty Information http://sun.soci.niu.edu/%7Ecritcrim/dp/dp.html

Capone, Al(phonse) (1899–1947) Called 'Scarface'. US gangster. During the ▷Prohibition period, he built a formidable criminal organization in Chicago. He was brutal in his pursuit of dominance, killing seven members of a rival gang in the St Valentine's Day Massacre of 1929. He was imprisoned from 1931 to 1939 for income-tax evasion, the only charge that could be sustained against him.

Capote, Truman (1924–1984) Pen-name of Truman Streckfus Persons. US novelist, journalist, and playwright. After achieving early success as a writer of sparkling prose in the stories of *Other Voices, Other Rooms* (1948) and the novel *Breakfast at Tiffany's* (1958), Capote's career flagged until the sensational 'non-fiction novel' *In Cold Blood* (1965) made him a celebrity.

He was born in Louisiana and his early works, including *The Grass Harp* (1951), are about the South. He then moved to New York, where he wrote further novels and scripts for theatre and films, and produced documentary pieces for the *New Yorker* magazine. Later works included *Music for Chameleons* (1980) and the posthumously published *Answered Prayers* (1986), an unfinished novel of scandalous socialite gossip.

Related Web site: Truman Capote – A Black and White Tribute http://www.ansoniadesign.com/capote/

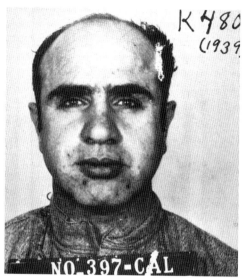

AL CAPONE US gangster Al Capone, pictured here in Alcatraz Prison, USA, in 1939. *Archive Photos*

fairy-tale comedy romance *It Happened One Night* (1934), *Mr Deeds Goes to Town* (1936), and *You Can't Take It with You* (1938). Among his other classic films are *Mr Smith Goes to Washington* (1939), and *It's a Wonderful Life* (1946).

Capri Italian island at the southern entrance of the Bay of Naples; 32 km/20 mi south of Naples; area 13 sq km/5 sq mi. It has two towns, Capri and Anacapri; the Blue Grotto on the north coast is an important tourist attraction.

Capriati, Jennifer Marie (1976–) US tennis player. A powerful right-handed player, she made history by turning professional shortly before her 14th birthday in March 1990, and ended the year ranked in the world's top 10. Off-court problems meant that she played just one professional match from September 1993 to February 1996. Her win in Strasbourg in 1999 was her first Tour title for more than six years. In 2001 she won the Austalian and French Opens and was briefly ranked as the world's number one player. In 2002 she retained her Australian Open title, beating Martina Hingis in the final for the second consecutive year.

Capricornus zodiacal constellation in the southern hemisphere next to ▷Sagittarius. It is represented as a sea-goat, and its brightest stars are third magnitude. The Sun passes through it from late January to mid-February. In astrology, the dates for Capricornus (popularly known as Capricorn) are between about 22 December and 19 January (see ▷precession).

capsicum any of a group of pepper plants belonging to the nightshade family, native to Central and South America (Genus *Capsicum*, family Solanaceae.) See picture on p. 162.

capsule in botany, a dry, usually many-seeded fruit formed from an ovary composed of two or more fused ▷carpels, which splits open to release the seeds. The same term is used for the spore-

Capra, Frank (1897–1991) Italian-born US film director. His satirical comedies, which often have the common man pitted against corrupt institutions, were hugely successful in the Depression years of the 1930s. He won Academy Awards for the

TRUMAN CAPOTE US writer Truman Capote. Capote, also a keen cook, is seen here preparing his 'chicken au chocolat'. *Archive Photos*

Cape Verde

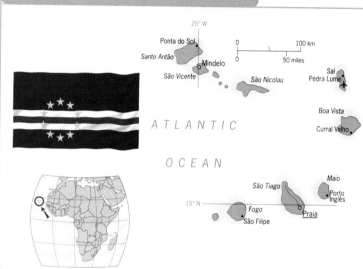

Cape Verde group of islands in the Atlantic, west of Senegal (West Africa).

NATIONAL NAME *República de Cabo Verde/Republic of Cape Verde*
AREA 4,033 sq km/1,557 sq mi
CAPITAL Praia
MAJOR TOWNS/CITIES Mindelo, Santa Maria

MAJOR PORTS Mindelo
PHYSICAL FEATURES archipelago of ten volcanic islands 565 km/350 mi west of Senegal; the windward (Barlavento) group includes Santo Antão, São Vicente, Santa Luzia (uninhabited), São Nicolau, Sal, and Boa Vista; the

CAPE VERDE
The island of Fogo is dominated by the volcano that formed it. Mount Fogo is 2,829 m/9,281 ft high and last erupted in 1995. Villages have been built upon the volcano and some inhabitants live and farm in the crater itself. *www.capeverdetravel.com*

leeward (Sotovento) group comprises Maio, São Tiago, Fogo, and Brava

Government

HEAD OF STATE Pedro Pires from 2001
HEAD OF GOVERNMENT José Maria Neves from 2001
POLITICAL SYSTEM emergent democracy
POLITICAL EXECUTIVE limited presidency
ADMINISTRATIVE DIVISIONS 18 districts
ARMED FORCES 1,200 (2002 est)

Economy and resources

CURRENCY Cape Verde escudo
GPD (US$) 631 million (2002 est)
REAL GDP GROWTH (% change on previous year) 3 (2001)
GNI (US$) 590 million (2002 est)
GNI PER CAPITA (PPP) (US$) 4,720 (2002 est)
CONSUMER PRICE INFLATION 2.5% (2003 est)
UNEMPLOYMENT 2.5% (2000)
FOREIGN DEBT (US$) 521 million (2001 est)
MAJOR TRADING PARTNERS Portugal, USA, the Netherlands, Spain, UK
RESOURCES salt, pozzolana (volcanic rock), limestone, basalt, kaolin
INDUSTRIES fish processing, machinery and electrical equipment, transport equipment, textiles, chemicals, rum
EXPORTS footwear and clothing, fish, shellfish and fish products, salt, bananas. Principal market: Portugal 89.1% (2000)
IMPORTS food and live animals, machinery and electrical equipment, transport equipment, mineral products, metals. Principal source: Portugal 52.4% (2000)
ARABLE LAND 11% (2000 est)
AGRICULTURAL PRODUCTS maize, beans, potatoes, cassava, coconuts, sugar cane, bananas, coffee, groundnuts; fishing

Population and society

POPULATION 463,000 (2003 est)
POPULATION GROWTH RATE 2.1% (2000–05)
POPULATION DENSITY (per sq km) 115 (2003 est)
URBAN POPULATION (% of total) 66 (2003 est)

AGE DISTRIBUTION (% of total population) 0–14 38%, 15–59 56%, 60+ 6% (2002 est)
ETHNIC GROUPS about 70% of mixed descent (Portuguese and African), known as mestizos or Creoles; the remainder is mainly African. The European population is very small
LANGUAGE Portuguese (official), Creole
RELIGION Roman Catholic 93%, Protestant (Nazarene Church)
EDUCATION (compulsory years) 6
LITERACY RATE 86% (men); 69% (women) (2003 est)
LABOUR FORCE 37% of population: 31% agriculture, 30% industry, 40% services (1990)
LIFE EXPECTANCY 67 (men); 73 (women) (2000–05)
CHILD MORTALITY RATE (under 5, per 1,000 live births) 38 (2001)
INTERNET USERS (per 10,000 people) 364.5 (2002)
PERSONAL COMPUTER USERS (per 100 people) 8 (2002 est)

Chronology

1462: Originally uninhabited; settled by Portuguese, who brought in slave labour from West Africa.

later 19th century: There was a decline in prosperity as slave trade ended.

1950s: A liberation movement developed on the islands and the Portuguese African mainland colony of Guinea-Bissau.

1951: Cape Verde became an overseas territory of Portugal.

1975: Independence was achieved and a national people's assembly elected, with Aristides of the PAICV as the first executive president; a policy of nonalignment followed.

1981: The goal of union with Guinea-Bissau was abandoned; Cape Verde became a one-party state.

1988: There was rising unrest and demand for political reforms.

1991: In the first multiparty elections, the new Movement for Democracy party (MPD) won a majority and Antonio Mascarenhas Monteiro became president; market-centred economic reforms were introduced.

2000: Gualberto do Rosário became prime minister.

2001: José Maria Deves became prime minister, and Pedro Pires was elected president.

CAPSICUM A capsicum, or pepper plant, at La Rioja, Spain. *Image Bank*

containing structure of mosses and liverworts; this is borne at the top of a long stalk or seta.

capuchin monkey of the genus *Cebus* found in Central and South America, so called because the hairs on the head resemble the cowl of a Capuchin monk. Capuchins live in small groups, feed on fruit and insects, and have a long tail that is semiprehensile and can give support when climbing through the trees.

Capuchin member of the Franciscan order of monks in the Roman Catholic Church, instituted by the Italian monk Matteo di Bassi (died 1552), who wished to return to the literal observance of the rule of St Francis. The Capuchin rule was drawn up in 1529 and the order recognized by the pope in 1619. The name was derived from the French term for the brown habit and pointed hood (*capuche*) that they wore. The order has been involved in missionary activity.

capybara world's largest rodent *Hydrochoerus hydrochaeris*, up to 1.3 m/4 ft long and 50 kg/110 lb in weight. It is found in South America, and belongs to the guinea-pig family. The capybara inhabits marshes and dense vegetation around water. It has thin, yellowish hair, swims well, and can rest underwater with just eyes, ears, and nose above the surface.

car small, driver-guided, passenger-carrying motor vehicle; originally the automated version of the horse-drawn carriage, meant to convey people and their goods over streets and roads.

Over 50 million motor cars are produced each year worldwide. The number of cars in the world in 1997 exceeded 500 million. Most are four-wheeled and have water-cooled, piston-type internal-combustion engines fuelled by petrol or diesel. Variations have existed for decades that use ingenious and often nonpolluting power plants, but the motor industry long ago settled on this general formula for the consumer market. Experimental and sports models are streamlined, energy-efficient, and hand-built.

CAR Production-line manufacturing was first put into effect in the car industry. The industry remains a prime example of the process. Cars in all stages of construction move slowly from stage to stage, and are progressively put together, painted, polished, and tested. *Image Bank*

Origins Although it is recorded that in 1479 Gilles de Dom was paid 25 livres (the equivalent of 25 pounds of silver) by the treasurer of Antwerp in the Low Countries for supplying a self-propelled vehicle, the ancestor of the car is generally agreed to be the cumbersome steam carriage made by Nicolas-Joseph Cugnot in 1769, still preserved in Paris. Steam was an attractive form of power to the English pioneers, and in 1803 Richard Trevithick built a working steam carriage. Later in the 19th century, practical steam coaches were used for public transport until stifled out of existence by punitive road tolls and legislation.

The first motorcars Although a Frenchman, Jean Etienne Lenoir, patented the first internal-combustion engine (gas-driven but immobile) in 1860, and an Austrian, Siegfried Marcus, built a vehicle which was shown at the Vienna Exhibition (1873), two Germans, Gottlieb Daimler and Karl Benz, are generally regarded as the creators of the motorcar. In 1885 Daimler and Benz built and ran the first petrol-driven motorcar (they worked independently with Daimler building a very efficient engine and Benz designing a car but with a poor engine). The pattern for the modern motorcar was set by Panhard in 1891 (front radiator, Daimler engine under bonnet, sliding-pinion gearbox, wooden ladder-chassis) and Mercedes in 1901 (honeycomb radiator, in-line four-cylinder engine, gate-change gearbox, pressed-steel chassis). Emerging with Haynes and Duryea in the early 1890s, US demand was so fervent that 300 makers existed by 1895; only 109 were left by 1900.

In Britain, cars were still considered to be light locomotives in the eyes of the law and, since the Red Flag Act 1865, had theoretically required someone to walk in front with a red flag (by night, a lantern). Despite these obstacles, which put UK development another ten years behind all others, in 1896 (after the Red Flag Act had been repealed) Frederick Lanchester produced an advanced and reliable vehicle, later much copied.

Motorcars as an industry The period 1905–06 inaugurated a world motorcar boom continuing to the present day. Among the legendary cars of the early 20th century are: De Dion Bouton, with the first practical high-speed engines; Mors, notable first for racing and later as a silent tourer; Napier, the 24-hour record-holder at Brooklands in 1907, unbeaten for 17 years; the incomparable Rolls-Royce Silver Ghost; the enduring Model T ▷Ford; and the many types of Bugatti and Delage, from record-breakers to luxury tourers. After World War I popular motoring began with the era of cheap, light (baby) cars made by Citroën, Peugeot, and Renault (France); Austin, Morris, Clyno, and Swift (England); Fiat (Italy); Volkswagen (Germany); and the cheap though bigger Ford, Chevrolet, and Dodge in the USA. During the interwar years a great deal of racing took place, and the experience gained benefited the everyday motorist in improved efficiency, reliability, and safety. There was a divergence between the lighter, economical European car, with its good handling, and the heavier US car, cheap, rugged, and well adapted to long distances on straight roads at speed. By this time motoring had become a universal pursuit.

After World War II small European cars tended to fall into three categories, in about equal numbers: front engine and rear drive, the classic arrangement; front engine and front-wheel drive; rear engine and rear-wheel drive. Racing cars have the engine situated in the middle for balance. From the 1950s a creative resurgence produced in practical form automatic transmission for small cars, rubber suspension, transverse engine mounting, self-levelling ride, disc brakes, and safer wet-weather tyres.

By the mid-1980s, Japan was building 8 million cars a year, on par with the USA. The largest Japanese manufacturer, Toyota, was producing 2.5 million cars per year.

caracal cat *Felis caracal* related to the ▷lynx. It has long black ear tufts, a short tail, and short reddish-fawn fur. It lives in bush and desert country in Africa, Arabia, and India, hunting birds and small mammals at night. Head and body length is about 75 cm/2.5 ft.

> ### Rootes
> English car manufacturer
>
> *No other manmade device since the shields and lances of the ancient knights fulfils a man's ego like an automobile.*
>
> Quoted in 'Who Said That?', BBC TV, 14 January 1958

Caracalla (AD *c.* 186–217) Also known as **Marcus Aurelius Severus Antoninus Augustus**; born **Septimius Bassianus**. Roman emperor from 211, son and successor of ▷Septimius Severus. He accompanied his father to Britain (208–211) and when Severus died in 211 Caracalla became joint emperor with his younger brother Geta. With the support of the army he murdered Geta in 212 and became sole ruler of the empire. During his reign in 212, Roman citizenship was extended to all the free inhabitants of the empire. He was assassinated at the instigation of his praetorian prefect Macrinus who succeeded him.

Caracas chief city and capital of ▷Venezuela, situated in the Central Highlands of the Andes Mountains 900 m/2,950 ft above sea level, 13 km/8 mi south of its port La Guaira on the Caribbean coast; population of metropolitan area (1996) 3,007,000 (Federal District 2,265,900). Main industries include oil refining, textiles, chemicals, and food processing. During the oil boom of the 1950s Caracas developed rapidly, its rate of growth greater than that of any other South American capital; much of the old colonial town was largely effaced during this period. It is now a large modern industrial and commercial centre, notably for oil companies, developed since the 1950s.

Caractacus (died *c.* 54) British chieftain who headed resistance to the Romans in southeast England from AD 43 to AD 51, but was defeated on the Welsh border. Shown in Claudius's triumphal procession, he was released in tribute to his courage and died in Rome.

carambola small evergreen tree of Southeast Asia. The fruits, called star fruit, are yellowish, about 12 cm/4 in long, with a five-pointed star-shaped cross-section. They can be eaten raw, cooked, or pickled, and are juicily acidic. The juice is also used to remove stains from hands and clothes. (*Averrhoa carambola*, family Averrhoaceae.)

carat (Arabic *quirrat* 'seed') unit for measuring the mass of precious stones; it is equal to 0.2 g/ 0.00705 oz, and is part of the troy system of weights. It is also the unit of purity in gold (US 'karat'). Pure gold is 24-carat; 22-carat (the purest used in jewellery) is 22 parts gold and two parts alloy (to give greater strength); 18-carat is 75% gold.

Caravaggio, Michelangelo Merisi da (1573–1610) Italian early baroque painter. He was active in Rome between 1592 and 1606, then in Naples, and finally in Malta. He created a forceful style, using contrasts of light and shade, dramatic foreshortening, and a meticulous attention to detail. His life was as dramatic as his art: he had to leave Rome after killing a man in a brawl.

The son of a mason in the village of Caravaggio near Milan, had some early training in Milan, but was painting in Rome before he was 20, quickly developing that famous 'naturalism' which was in strong contrast to the prevailing Mannerism of Zuccaro and the Cavaliere d'Arpino. Instead of ideal figures, he painted the types he saw and knew, delighting in plebeian traits of character, contemporary dress and carefully delineated still life. Early examples are the *Bacchus* (Uffizi), the *Fortune Teller* (Louvre), and the *Fruit Basket* (Ambrosiana, Milan). The innovation that gave him fame and made him the centre of controversy was not only that he applied this realistic method to religious painting, but also intensified its effect by combining it with a depth and drama of light and shade that he may have adapted from Tintoretto. It appears in his first commission for the Contarelli Chapel of St Luigi dei Francesi, *St Matthew and the Angel*, the *Vocation of St Matthew*, and *Martyrdom of the Apostle*. These and other works in Rome (painted 1600–07), including the *Madonna of the Serpent* (Borghese Gallery), the *Death of the Virgin* (Louvre), and the *Madonna del Rosario* (Vienna), were either refused by his patrons or were the subject of fierce argument.

caraway herb belonging to the carrot family. Native to northern temperate regions of Europe and Asia, it is grown for its spicy, aromatic seeds, which are used in cookery, medicine, and perfumery. (*Carum carvi*, family Umbelliferae.)

carbide compound of carbon and one other chemical element, usually a metal, silicon, or boron.

Calcium carbide (CaC$_2$) can be used as the starting material for many basic organic chemical syntheses, by the addition of water and generation of ethyne (acetylene). Some metallic carbides are used in engineering because of their extreme hardness and strength. Tungsten carbide is an essential ingredient of carbide tools and high-speed tools. The 'carbide process' was used during World War II to make organic chemicals from coal rather than from oil.

Car: Key Dates

1769	Nicholas-Joseph Cugnot in France builds a steam tractor.
1801	Richard Trevithick builds a steam coach.
1860	Jean Etienne Lenoir builds a gas-fuelled internal-combustion engine.
1865	The British government passes the Red Flag Act, requiring that any 'horseless carriage' be preceded by someone waving a red flag.
1876	Nikolaus August Otto improves the gas engine, making it a practical power source.
1885	Gottlieb Daimler develops a successful lightweight petrol engine and fits it to a bicycle to create the prototype of the present-day motorcycle; Karl Benz fits his lightweight petrol engine to a three-wheeled carriage to pioneer the motorcar.
1886	Gottlieb Daimler fits his engine to a four-wheeled carriage to produce a four-wheeled motorcar.
1891	René Panhard and Emile Levassor establish the present design of cars by putting the engine in front.
1896	Frederick Lanchester introduces epicyclic gearing, which foreshadows automatic transmission.
1899	C Jenatzy breaks the 100-kph barrier in an electric car *La Jamais Contente* at Achères, France, reaching 105.85 kph/65.60 mph.
1901	The first Mercedes takes to the roads; it is the direct forerunner of the present car. Ransome Olds in the USA introduces mass production on an assembly line.
1904	Louis Rigolly breaks the 100-mph barrier, reaching 166.61 kph/103.55 mph in a Gobron-Brillé at Nice, France.
1906	Rolls-Royce introduces the Silver Ghost, which establishes the company's reputation for superlatively engineered cars.
1908	Henry Ford uses assembly-line production to manufacture his celebrated Model T, nicknamed the Tin Lizzie because it uses lightweight steel sheet for the body.
1911	Cadillac introduces the electric starter and dynamo lighting.
1913	Ford introduces the moving conveyor belt to the assembly line, further accelerating production of the Model T.
1920	Duesenberg begins fitting four-wheel hydraulic brakes.
1922	The Lancia Lambda features unitary (all-in-one) construction and independent front suspension.
1927	Henry Segrave breaks the 200-mph barrier in a Sunbeam, reaching 327.89 kph/203.79 mph.
1928	Cadillac introduces the synchromesh gearbox, greatly facilitating gear changing.
1934	Citroën pioneers front-wheel drive in their 7CV model.
1936	Fiat introduces their baby car, the Topolino, with an engine capacity of 500 cc.
1938	The 'people's car', the Volkswagen Beetle, is produced in Germany.
1948	Jaguar launches the XK120 sports car; Michelin introduced the radial-ply tyre; Goodrich produces the tubeless tyre.
1950	Dunlop devises the disc brake.
1951	Buick and Chrysler introduce power steering.
1952	Rover's gas-turbine car sets a speed record of 243 kph/152 mph.
1954	Carl Bosch introduces fuel injection for cars.
1955	Citroën produces the advanced DS-19 'shark-front' car with hydropneumatic suspension.
1957	Felix Wankel builds the first rotary petrol engine.
1959	BMC (now Rover) introduces the Mini, with front-wheel drive, transverse engine, and independent rubber suspension.
1965	US car manufacturers are forced to add safety features after the publication of Ralph Nader's *Unsafe at Any Speed*.
1966	California introduces legislation limiting air pollution by cars.
1970	Gary Gabelich drives a rocket-powered car, *Blue Flame*, at a new record speed of 1,001.473 kph/622.287 mph.
1972	Dunlop introduces safety tyres, which seal themselves after a puncture.
1979	Sam Barrett exceeds the speed of sound in the rocket-engined *Budweiser Rocket*, reaching 1,190.377 kph/ 739.666 mph, a speed not officially recognized as a record because of timing difficulties.
1980	The first mass-produced car with four-wheel drive, the Audi Quattro, is introduced; Japanese car production overtakes that of the USA.
1981	BMW introduces the on-board computer, which monitors engine performance and indicates to the driver when a service is required.
1983	Richard Noble sets an official speed record in the jet-engined *Thrust 2* of 1,019.4 kph/633.5 mph; Austin Rover introduces the Maestro, the first car with a 'talking dashboard' that alerts the driver to problems.
1987	The solar-powered *Sunraycer* travels 3,000 km/1,864 mi from Darwin to Adelaide, Australia, in six days. Toyota Corona production tops 6 million in 29 years.
1988	California introduces stringent controls on car emissions, aiming for widespread use of zero emission vehicles by 1998.
1989	The first mass-produced car with four-wheel steering, the Mitsubishi Galant, is launched.
1990	Fiat and Peugeot launch electric passenger cars on the market.
1991	Satellite-based car navigation systems are launched in Japan. The European Parliament votes to adopt stringent limits on car emissions.
1992	Mazda and NEC of Japan develop an image-processing system for cars, which views the road ahead through a video camera, identifies road signs and markings, and helps the driver to avoid obstacles.
1993	A Japanese electric car, the *IZA*, built by the Tokyo Electric Power Company, reaches a speed of 176 kph/109 mph (10 kph/6 mph faster than the previous record for an electric car).
1995	Greenpeace designs an environmentally friendly car to show the industry how 'it could be done'. It produces a modified Renault Twingo with 30% less wind resistance, capable of doing 67–78 mi to the gallon (100 km per 3–3.5 litres).
1996	Daimler–Benz unveils the first fuel-cell-powered car. It is virtually pollution-free.
1997	Andy Green breaks the sound barrier in *Thrust SCC*, a car with two Rolls-Royce Spey engines (the same kind used in RAF Phantom jets), at a speed of 1,149.3 kph/714.1 mph.
2000	Production of the Mini moves from the Rover plant at Longbridge, Birmingham, to the BMW factory at Cowley, Oxfordshire, after 41 years.
2001	The first new Mini goes on sale.

CAR ASSEMBLY LINE Car engines being assembled in Detroit, Michigan, USA. *Image Bank*

carbohydrate chemical compound composed of carbon, hydrogen, and oxygen, with the basic formula $C_m(H_2O)_n$, and related compounds with the same basic structure but modified ▷functional groups. As sugar and starch, carbohydrates are an important part of a balanced human diet, providing energy for life processes including growth and movement. Excess carbohydrate intake can be converted into fat and stored in the body.

carbolic acid common name for the aromatic compound ▷phenol.

carbon (Latin *carbo, carbonaris* 'coal') non-metallic element, symbol C, atomic number 6, relative atomic mass 12.011. It occurs on its own as diamond, graphite, and as fullerenes (the allotropes), as compounds in carbonaceous rocks such as chalk and limestone, as carbon dioxide in the atmosphere, as hydrocarbons in petroleum, coal, and natural gas, and as a constituent of all organic substances.

In its amorphous form, it is familiar as coal, charcoal, and soot. The atoms of carbon can link with one another in rings or chains, giving rise to innumerable complex compounds. Of the inorganic carbon compounds, the chief ones are **carbon dioxide**(CO_2), a colourless gas formed when carbon is burned in an adequate supply of air; and **carbon monoxide** (CO), formed when carbon is oxidized in a limited supply of air. **Carbon disulphide** (CS_2) is a dense liquid with a sweetish odour. Another group of compounds is the **carbon halides**, including carbon tetrachloride (tetrachloromethane, CCl_4).

When added to steel, carbon forms a wide range of alloys with useful properties. In pure form, it is used as a moderator in nuclear reactors; as colloidal graphite it is a good lubricant and, when deposited on a surface in a vacuum, reduces photoelectric and secondary emission of electrons. Carbon is used as a fuel in the form of coal or coke. The radioactive isotope carbon-14 (half-life 5,730 years) is used as a tracer in biological research and in ▷radiocarbon dating. Analysis of interstellar dust has led to the discovery of discrete carbon molecules, each containing 60 carbon atoms. The C_{60} molecules have been named ▷buckminsterfullerene because of their structural similarity to the geodesic domes designed by US architect and engineer Buckminster Fuller.

carbonate (CO_3^{2-}) ion formed when carbon dioxide dissolves in water; any salt formed by this ion and another chemical element, usually a metal.

carbon cycle sequence by which ▷carbon circulates and is recycled through the natural world. Carbon dioxide is released into the atmosphere by

graphite

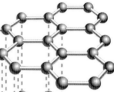

diamond

buckminsterfullerene

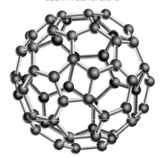

CARBON Carbon has three allotropes: diamond, graphite, and the fullerenes. Diamond is strong because each carbon atom is linked to four other carbon atoms. Graphite is made up of layers that slide across one another (giving graphite its qualities as a lubricator); each layer is a giant molecule. In the fullerenes, the carbon atoms form spherical cages. Buckminsterfullerene has 60 atoms. Other fullerenes, with 28, 32, 50, 70, and 76 carbon atoms, have also been identified.

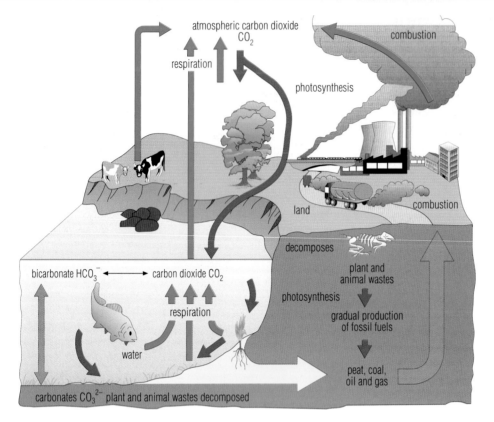

atmospheric carbon dioxide CO₂

combustion

respiration

photosynthesis

land

combustion

decomposes

bicarbonate HCO₃⁻ ← → carbon dioxide CO₂

plant and animal wastes

photosynthesis

respiration

gradual production of fossil fuels

water

peat, coal, oil and gas

carbonates CO₃²⁻ plant and animal wastes decomposed

CARBON CYCLE The carbon cycle is necessary for the continuation of life. Since there is only a limited amount of carbon in the Earth and its atmosphere, carbon must be continuously recycled if life is to continue.

living things as a result of ▷respiration. The CO_2 is taken up and converted into carbohydrates during ▷photosynthesis by plants and by organisms such as diatoms and dinoflagellates in the oceanic ▷plankton; the oxygen component is released back into the atmosphere. The carbon they accumulate is later released back into circulation in various ways. The simplest occurs when an animal eats a plant and carbon is transferred from, say, a leaf cell to the animal body. Carbon is also released through the ▷decomposition of decaying plant matter, and the burning of fossil fuels such as ▷coal (fossilized plants). The oceans absorb 25–40% of all carbon dioxide released into the atmosphere.

Today, the carbon cycle is in danger of being disrupted by the increased consumption and burning of fossil fuels, and the burning of large tracts of tropical forests, as a result of which levels of carbon dioxide are building up in the atmosphere and probably contributing to the ▷greenhouse effect.

carbon dating alternative name for ▷radiocarbon dating.

carbon dioxide (CO_2) a colourless, odourless gas, slightly soluble in water and denser than air. It is formed by the complete oxidation of carbon.

It is produced by living things during the processes of respiration and the decay of organic matter, and plays a vital role in the carbon cycle. It is used as a coolant in its solid form (known as 'dry ice'), and in the chemical industry. Its increasing density contributes to the ▷greenhouse effect and ▷global warming. Britain has 1% of the world's population, yet it produces 3% of CO_2 emissions; the USA has 5% of the world's population and produces 25% of CO_2 emissions. Annual releases of carbon dioxide reached 23 billion tonnes in 1997. According to a 1997 estimate by the World Energy council, carbon dioxide emissions rose by 7.8% between 1986 and 1996.

carbon fibre fine, black, silky filament of pure carbon produced by heat treatment from a special grade of Courtelle acrylic fibre and, used for reinforcing plastics. The resulting composite is very stiff, and, weight for weight, has four times the strength of high-tensile steel. It is used in the aerospace industry, cars, and electrical and sports equipment.

Carboniferous period period of geological time roughly 362.5 to 290 million years ago, the fifth period of the Palaeozoic Era. In the USA it is divided into two periods: the Mississippian (lower) and the Pennsylvanian (upper).

Typical of the lower-Carboniferous rocks are shallow-water ▷limestones, while upper-Carboniferous rocks have ▷delta

deposits with ▷coal (hence the name). Amphibians were abundant, and reptiles evolved during this period.

carbon monoxide (CO) colourless, odourless gas formed when carbon is oxidized in a limited supply of air. It is a poisonous constituent of car exhaust fumes, forming a stable compound with haemoglobin in the blood, thus preventing the haemoglobin from transporting oxygen to the body tissues.

In industry, carbon monoxide is used as a reducing agent in metallurgical processes – for example, in the extraction of iron in ▷blast furnaces – and is a constituent of cheap fuels such as water gas. It burns in air with a luminous blue flame to form carbon dioxide.

Carborundum trademark for a very hard, black abrasive, consisting of silicon carbide (SiC), an artificial compound of carbon and silicon. It is harder than ▷corundum but not as hard as ▷diamond.

carburation any process involving chemical combination with carbon, especially the mixing or charging of a gas, such as air, with volatile compounds of carbon (petrol, kerosene, or fuel oil) in order to increase potential heat energy during combustion. Carburation applies to combustion in the cylinders of reciprocating petrol engines of the types used in aircraft, road vehicles, or marine vessels. The device by which the liquid fuel is atomized and mixed with air is called a carburettor.

Carcassonne city in southwest France, administrative centre of Aude *département*, 100 km/62 mi southeast of Toulouse on the Canal du Midi and the River Aude, which divides it into the ancient and modern town; population (1990) 45,000. The medieval fortification, restored by Viollet-le-Duc in the 19th century, crowns a hill on the right bank of the river. Surrounded by two ramparts and 53 towers, it is the finest in France and one of the most impressive medieval fortified towns surviving.

Carchemish (now Karkamis, Turkey) historical centre of the ▷Hittite New Empire (c. 1400–1200 BC) on the River Euphrates, 80 km/50 mi northeast of Aleppo, and taken by Sargon II of Assyria in 717 BC. Nebuchadnezzar II of Babylon defeated the Egyptians here in 605 BC.

carcinogen any agent that increases the chance of a cell becoming cancerous (see ▷cancer), including various chemical

compounds, some viruses, X-rays, and other forms of ionizing radiation. The term is often used more narrowly to mean chemical carcinogens only.

carcinoma malignant ▷tumour arising from the skin, the glandular tissues, or the mucous membranes that line the gut and lungs.

Cardiff unitary authority in south Wales, created in 1996 from part of the former county of South Glamorgan; administrative headquarters is ▷Cardiff.
    area 139 sq km/54 sq mi   **population** (1996 est) 315,000

Cardiff (Welsh Caerdydd) seaport, capital of Wales (from 1955), and administrative centre of ▷Cardiff unitary authority, situated at the mouth of the Taff, Rhymney, and Ely rivers; population (1996 est) 315,000. It is the seat of government for the ▷National Assembly for Wales, which was established in 1998 following the Government of Wales Act passed by the British parliament. Industries are predominantly in the service sector, with 82% of the workforce employed in services, the largest of which are education, business services, health, and consumer services. Manufacturing has declined in importance, although electronics and motor components remain important industries.

The city dates from Roman times, the later town being built around a Norman castle. The castle was the residence of the earls and marquises of Bute from the 18th century and was given to the city in 1947 by the fifth marquis. Coal was exported until the 1920s. As the coal industry declined, iron and steel exports continued to grow, and an import trade in timber, grain and flour, tobacco, meat, and citrus fruit developed. Cardiff Airport is at Roose, 19 km/12 mi to the southwest.

A major part of the University of Wales is situated in Cardiff, including the Institute of Science and Technology, the National School of Medicine, and University College of South Wales.
    Related Web site: Cardiff, Capital City of Wales http://www.cardiff. gov.uk/

Cardiganshire (Welsh Ceredigion or Sir Aberteifi) former county of west Wales. It was merged, together with Pembrokeshire and Carmarthenshire, into Dyfed in 1974; in 1996 it became part of ▷Ceredigion.

Cardin, Pierre (1922–) French pioneering fashion designer. He was the first to launch menswear (1960) and designer ready-to-wear collections (1963) and has given his name to a perfume. Cardin has franchised his name for labelling many different accessories and household products.
    Related Web site: Cardin, Pierre http://www.pierrecardin.com/

cardinal in the Roman Catholic Church, the highest rank next to the pope. Cardinals act as an advisory body to the pope and elect him. Their red hat is the badge of office. The number of cardinals has varied; there were 151 in 1989.

cardinal number in mathematics, one of the series of numbers 0, 1, 2, 3, 4, ... Cardinal numbers relate to quantity, whereas ordinal numbers (first, second, third, fourth, …) relate to order.

cardioid heart-shaped curve traced out by a point on the circumference of a circle, resulting from the circle rolling around the edge of another circle of the same diameter.

Cardoso, Fernando Henrique (1931–) Brazilian politician and academic, leader of the moderate centre-left Social Democratic Party (PSDB), and president from 1995. As finance minister in the government of Itamar ▷Franco he had great success in masterminding a major economic restructuring programme, involving the establishment of a Social Emergency Fund (FSE) and the creation of a new accounting unit, the Unit of Real Value (URV), to replace a complex of price indices which served to fuel Brazil's runaway inflation.

care order in Britain, a court order that places a child in the care of a local authority. Surveys show that 75% of those who have been in care leave school with no qualifications. They are less likely to find employment and more likely to go to prison, and one in three was homeless in 1993. There were 63,000 children in care in the UK in 1993.

Carew, Thomas (c. 1595–c. 1640) English poet. Often associated with the ▷'Cavalier poets', he was a courtier and gentleman of the privy chamber to Charles I, for whom he wrote the spectacular masque *Coelum Britannicum* (1634). *Poems* (1640) revealed his ability to weave metaphysical wit, eroticism, and a jewelled lyricism in his work.

George Carey
People have described me as a 'management bishop' but I say to my critics: 'Jesus was a management expert too.'
Independent, July 1992

Carey, George Leonard (1935–) 103rd archbishop of Canterbury 1991–2002. A product of a liberal evangelical background, he was appointed bishop of Bath and Wells in 1987.

His support of the ▷ordination of women priests brought disagreement during his meeting with Pope John Paul II in 1992.

Carey, Mariah (1970–) US pop artist. Known for her vocal strength and range, she was the best-selling female artist of the 1990s, with 14 number one hit singles. Her Grammy award-winning first album (1990) sold more than 6 million copies. Her later albums, in which she co-wrote most of the songs, lean away from pop and more toward rhythm and blues. In 2001 she starred in, and produced the soundtrack for the film *Glitter*.

Carey, Peter Philip (1943–) Australian novelist. His works include *Bliss* (1981), *Illywhacker* (Australian slang for 'con man') (1985), and *Oscar and Lucinda* (1988), which won the Booker Prize. *The Tax Inspector* (1991) is set in modern-day Sydney, and depicts an eccentric Greek family under investigation for tax fraud. Carey won the 1998 Commonwealth Writers' Prize for his novel, *Jack Maggs* (1998). His novel *True History of the Kelly Gang* (2001), won the Booker Prize, making him only the second author to win the prize twice.

cargo cult one of a number of religious movements, chiefly in Melanesia, that first appeared in the late 19th century but were particularly prevalent during and after World War II with the apparently miraculous dropping of supplies from aeroplanes. Adherents believe in the imminent arrival of European material goods, or 'cargo', by supernatural agents such as tribal gods or ancestral spirits. In anticipation, landing strips, wharves, warehouses, and other elaborate preparations for receiving the cargo are often made, and normal activities such as gardening cease, stocks of food are destroyed, and current customs abandoned.

Carib member of a group of ▷American Indian people of the north coast of South America and the islands of the southern West Indies in the Caribbean. Those who moved north to take the islands from the Arawak Indians were alleged by the conquering Spaniards to be fierce cannibals. In 1796, the English in the West Indies deported most of them to Roatan Island, off Honduras. Carib languages belong to the Ge-Pano-Carib family.

Caribbean Community and Common Market (CARICOM) organization for economic and foreign policy coordination in the Caribbean region, established by the Treaty of Chaguaramas in 1973 to replace the former Caribbean Free Trade Association. Its members are Antigua and Barbuda, Bahamas, Barbados, Belize, Dominica, Grenada, Guyana, Haiti, Jamaica, Montserrat, St Kitts and Nevis, St Lucia, St Vincent and the Grenadines, and Trinidad and Tobago. The Bahamas is a member of the Community but not of the Common Market.

The British Virgin Islands and the Turks and Caicos Islands are associate members, and Anguilla, the Dominican Republic, Mexico, Haiti, Puerto Rico, and Venezuela are observers. CARICOM headquarters are in Georgetown, Guyana.

Caribbean Sea western part of the Atlantic Ocean between Cuba to the north and the northern coasts of South America to the south. Central America is to the west and to the east are the West Indies. The sea is about 2,740 km/1,700 mi long and 650–1,500 km/400–900 mi wide; area 2,640,000 sq km/1,019,304 sq mi. It is linked with the Gulf of Mexico via the Yucatan Strait. It is from here that the ▷Gulf Stream turns towards Europe.

caribou the ▷reindeer of North America.

caricature in the arts or literature, an exaggerated portrayal of an individual or type, aiming to ridicule or otherwise expose the subject. Classical and medieval examples of pictorial caricatures survive. Artists of the 18th, 19th, and 20th centuries have often used caricature as a way of satirizing society and politics. Notable exponents include the French artist Honoré ▷Daumier and the German George ▷Grosz. In literature, caricatures have appeared since the comedies of Aristophanes in ancient Greece. Shakespeare and Dickens were adept at creating caricatures.

CARICOM acronym for ▷Caribbean Community and Common Market.

caries decay and disintegration, usually of the substance of teeth (cavity) or bone, caused by acids produced when the bacteria that live in the mouth break down sugars in the food. Fluoride, a low sugar intake, and regular brushing are all protective. Caries form mainly in the 45 minutes following consumption of sugary food.

Carina constellation of the southern hemisphere, represented as a ship's keel. Its brightest star is ▷Canopus, the second brightest in the night sky; it also contains Eta Carinae, a massive and highly luminous star embedded in a gas cloud, perhaps 8,000 light years away from the Sun.

Carinthia (German Kärnten) federal state of alpine southeast Austria, bordering Italy and Slovenia in the south; area 9,500 sq km/3,667 sq mi; population (1994) 559,700. The capital is Klagenfurt. Mining, stock-raising and forestry are important. It was an independent duchy from 976 and a possession of the Habsburg dynasty from 1276 until 1918.

Carisbrooke village southwest of Newport, Isle of Wight, England. It was once the capital of the Isle of Wight, and remains traditionally the island's principal town. Charles I was imprisoned in its Norman castle from 1647 to 1648. The castle houses the Isle of Wight County Museum.

Carl XVI Gustavus (1946–) or Carl XVI Gustaf. King of Sweden from 1973. He succeeded his grandfather Gustavus VI, his father having been killed in an air crash 1947. Under the new Swedish constitution, which became effective on his grandfather's death, the monarchy was stripped of all power at his accession.

Carlisle city and administrative headquarters of ▷Cumbria, northwest England, on the River Eden at the western end of Hadrian's Wall, 14 km/9 mi south of the Scottish border; population (1991) 72,400. It is a leading railway and service centre. Industries include engineering and brewing (Scottish and Newcastle), and the manufacture of textiles, agricultural machinery, metal goods, confectionery, and processed foods. Carlisle was the Roman settlement of **Luguvalium**. There is a Norman cathedral and a restored castle dating from 1092.

Carlist supporter of the claims of the Spanish pretender Don Carlos de Bourbon (1788–1855), and his descendants, to the Spanish crown. The Carlist revolt continued, primarily in the Basque provinces, until 1839. In 1977 the Carlist political party was legalized and Carlos Hugo de Bourbon Parma (1930–) renounced his claim as pretender and became reconciled with King Juan Carlos. See also ▷Bourbon.

Carlow second-smallest county in the Republic of Ireland, in the province of Leinster; county town Carlow; area 900 sq km/347 sq mi; population (1996) 41,600. The land is mostly flat except for the Blackstairs mountains in the south (rising to 796 m/2,612 ft in Mount Leinster). The land in the west is fertile and well suited to dairy farming. Products include barley, wheat, and sugar beet.

Carlsson, Ingvar (Gösta) (1934–) Swedish socialist politician. Leader of the Social Democratic Labour Party (SDAP) from 1986, he was deputy prime minister 1982–86 and prime minister 1986–91 and 1994–96.

Carlyle, Thomas (1795–1881) Scottish essayist and social historian. His works include the partly autobiographical *Sartor Resartus/The Tailor Retailored* (1833–34), reflecting his loss of Christian belief; *The French Revolution* (1837); and the long essay 'Chartism' (1839), attacking the doctrine of *laissez faire*. His prose style was idiosyncratic, encompassing grand, thunderous rhetoric and deliberate obscurity.

The house in Cheyne Row, Chelsea, London, where Carlyle and his wife lived from 1834, is a museum.

THOMAS CARLYLE Thomas Carlyle, Scottish essayist and social historian. *Archive Photos*

Carmarthenshire (Welsh **Sir Gaerfyrddin**) unitary authority in south Wales; a former county, it was part of Dyfed between 1975 and 1996.

area 2,390 sq km/923 sq mi **towns** Carmarthen (administrative headquarters), Llanelli **physical** rivers ▷Tywi, Taf, Teifi; ▷Black Mountain range in the east, southern spur of the Cambrian Mountains in the north, including Mynydd Mallaen (459 m/1,1,506 ft); along the coast are extensive sands and marshes. Carmarthenshire is dominated by the Vale of Tywi, but there are numerous grassy hills, mostly under 300 m/1,000 ft; the valleys are fertile and the hillsides afford good pasturage **features** Brecon Beacons National Park on the eastern border; Museum of the Woollen Industry at DreFach-Felindre; home of Dylan ▷Thomas in the village of Laugharne, 6 km/3.7 mi southeast of St Clears; the National Botanic Garden of Wales, in the Regency park of Middleton Hall, was established in 2000 as a Millennium project **agriculture** dairy farming, stock-raising **population** (1996) 68,900

Carmelite order mendicant order of friars in the Roman Catholic Church. The order was founded on Mount Carmel in Palestine by Berthold, a crusader from Calabria, about 1155, and spread to Europe in the 13th century. The Carmelites have devoted themselves largely to missionary work and mystical theology. They are known as **White Friars** because of the white overmantle they wear (over a brown habit).

Carmichael, Hoagy (Hoagland Howard) (1899–1981) US composer, pianist, singer, and actor. His songs include 'Stardust' (1927), 'Rockin' Chair' (1930), 'Lazy River' (1931), and 'In the Cool, Cool, Cool of the Evening' (1951; Academy Award).

Carnarvon alternative spelling of ▷Caernarfon, a town in Wales.

carnation any of a large number of double-flowered cultivated varieties of a plant belonging to the ▷pink family. The flowers smell like cloves; they are divided into flake, bizarre, and picotees, according to whether the petals have one or more colours on their white base, have the colour appearing in strips, or have a coloured border to the petals. (*Dianthus caryophyllus*, family Carophyllaceae.)

carnauba palm tree native to South America, especially Brazil. It produces fine timber and a hard wax, used for polishes and lipsticks. (*Copernicia cerifera*.)

Carné, Marcel (1906–1996) French director. A romantic fatalism characterizes his films, such as *Le Quai des brumes/Port of Shadows* (1938) and *Le Jour se lève/Daybreak* (1939). His masterpiece, *Les Enfants du paradis/The Children of Paradise* (1943–45), was made with his longtime collaborator, the poet and screenwriter Jacques Prévert (1900–1977).

Carnegie, Andrew (1835–1919) US industrialist and philanthropist, born in Scotland, who developed the Pittsburgh iron and steel industries, making the USA the world's leading producer. He endowed public libraries, education, and various research trusts.

Carnegie invested successfully in railways, land, and oil. From 1873 he engaged in steelmaking, adopting new techniques. Having built up a vast empire, he disposed of it to the US Steel Trust in 1901. After his death the Carnegie trusts continued his philanthropic activities.

Carnegie Hall in New York, opened in 1891 as the Music Hall, was renamed in 1898 because of his large contribution to its construction.

carnivore an organism that eats other animals. In zoology, mammal of the order Carnivora. Although its name describes the flesh-eating ancestry of the order, it includes pandas, which are herbivorous, and civet cats, which eat fruit.

Carnivores have the greatest range of body size of any mammalian order, from the 100 g/3.5 oz weasel to the 800 kg/1,764 lb polar bear.

The characteristics of the Carnivora are sharp teeth, small incisors, a well-developed brain, a simple stomach, a reduced or absent caecum, and incomplete or absent clavicles (collarbones); there are never less than four toes on each foot; the scaphoid and lunar bones are fused in the hand; and the claws are generally sharp and powerful.

The mammalian order Carnivora includes cats, dogs, bears, badgers, and weasels.

Carnot, Lazare Nicolas Marguérite (1753–1823) French general and politician. A member of the National Convention in the French Revolution, he organized the armies of the republic. He was war minister 1800–01 and minister of the interior in 1815 under Napoleon. His work on fortification, *De la Défense de places fortes* (1810), became a military textbook. Minister of the interior during the ▷hundred days, he was proscribed at the restoration of the monarchy and retired to Germany.

Carnot joined the army as an engineer, and his transformation of French military technique in the revolutionary period earned him the title of 'Organizer of Victory'. After the coup d'état of 1797 he went abroad, but returned in 1799 when Napoleon seized power. In 1814, as governor of Antwerp, he put up a brilliant defence.

Related Web site: Carnot, Lazare Nicolas Marguérite
http://www-history.mcs.st-and.ac.uk/history/Mathematicians/Carnot.html

Carnot, (Nicolas Léonard) Sadi (1796–1832) French scientist and military engineer who founded the science of thermodynamics. His pioneering work was *Reflexions sur la puissance motrice du feu/On the Motive Power of Fire*, which considered the changes that would take place in an idealized, frictionless steam engine.

Carnot cycle series of changes in the physical condition of a gas in a reversible heat engine, necessarily in the following order: (1) isothermal expansion (without change of temperature), (2) adiabatic expansion (without change of heat content), (3) isothermal compression, and (4) adiabatic compression.

Caro, Anthony (Alfred) (1924–) English sculptor. His most typical work is large, brightly coloured abstract sculpture, horizontal in aspect, and made from prefabricated metal parts, such as I-beams, angles, and mesh visibly bolted together. An example is *Early One Morning* (1962; Tate Gallery, London). From the 1980s Caro turned to more traditional sculptural techniques and subjects; in the 1990s, for example, he made a series of bronze figures inspired by the story of the Trojan War.

carob small Mediterranean tree belonging to the ▷legume family. Its pods, 20 cm/8 in long, are used as an animal feed; they are also the source of a chocolate substitute. (*Ceratonia siliqua*, family Leguminosae.)

Carol two kings of Romania:

Carol I (1839–1914) First king of Romania (1881–1914). A prince of the house of Hohenzollern-Sigmaringen, he was invited to become prince of Romania, then part of the Ottoman Empire, in 1866. In 1877, in alliance with Russia, he declared war on Turkey, and the Congress of Berlin in 1878 recognized Romanian independence.

Carol II (1893–1953) King of Romania (1930–40). Son of King Ferdinand, he married Princess Helen of Greece and they had a son, Michael. In 1925 he renounced the succession because of his affair with Elena Lupescu and went into exile in Paris. Michael succeeded to the throne in 1927, but in 1930 Carol returned to Romania and was proclaimed king.

In 1938 he introduced a new constitution under which he practically became an absolute ruler. He was forced to abdicate by the pro-Nazi ▷Iron Guard in September 1940, went to Mexico, and married his mistress in 1947.

carol song that in medieval times was associated with a round dance; today carols are associated with festivals such as Christmas and Easter.

Carolina either of two separate states of the USA; see ▷North Carolina and ▷South Carolina.

Caroline Islands scattered archipelago in Micronesia, Pacific Ocean, consisting of over 500 coral islets; area 1,200 sq km/463 sq mi. The chief islands are Ponape, Kusai, and Truk in the eastern group, and Yap and Palau in the western group.

Caroline of Anspach (1683–1737) Queen of George II of Great Britain and Ireland. The daughter of the Margrave of Brandenburg-Anspach, she married George, Electoral Prince of Hannover, in 1705, and followed him to England in 1714 when his father became King George I.

Caroline of Brunswick (1768–1821) Queen consort of George IV of Great Britain. King George attempted to divorce her, unsuccessfully, on his accession to the throne in 1820.

> **Caroline of Brunswick**
> *The King's party and mine are like two rival inns on the road, the George and the Angel.*
> Remark made during her final attempt to be accepted as Queen (1821)

Carolingian art the art of the reign of Charlemagne, the first Holy Roman Emperor (800–814), and his descendants until about 900. In line with his revival of learning and Roman culture, Charlemagne greatly encouraged the arts, which had been in eclipse. Illuminated manuscripts, metalwork, and small-scale sculpture survive from this period. See also ▷medieval art.

Carolingian dynasty Frankish dynasty descending from ▷Pepin the Short (died 768) and named after his son Charlemagne; its last ruler was Louis V of France (reigned 966–87), who was followed by Hugh ▷Capet, first ruler of the Capetian dynasty.

carotene naturally occurring pigment of the ▷carotenoid group. Carotenes produce the orange, yellow, and red colours of carrots, tomatoes, oranges, and crustaceans.

carotenoid any of a group of yellow, orange, red, or brown pigments found in many living organisms, particularly in the ▷chloroplasts of plants. There are two main types, the **carotenes** and the **xanthophylls**. Both types are long-chain lipids (▷fats).

carp fish *Cyprinus carpio* found all over the world. It commonly grows to 50 cm/1.8 ft and 3 kg/7 lb, but may be even larger. It lives in lakes, ponds, and slow rivers. The wild form is drab, but cultivated forms may be golden, or may have few large scales (mirror carp) or be scaleless (leather carp). **Koi** carp are highly prized and can grow up to 1 m/3 ft long with a distinctive pink, red, white, or black colouring.

A large proportion of European freshwater fish belong to the carp family, Cyprinidae, and related fishes are found in Asia, Africa, and North America. The carp's fast growth, large size, and ability to live in still water with little oxygen have made it a good fish to farm, and it has been cultivated for hundreds of years and spread by human agency. Members of this family have a single non-spiny dorsal fin, pelvic fins well back on the body, and toothless jaws, although teeth in the throat form an efficient grinding apparatus. Minnows, roach, rudd, and many others, including goldfish, belong to this family. Chinese **grass carp** *Ctenopharyngodon idella* have been introduced (one sex only) to European rivers for weed control.

Related Web site: History of Koi Carp http://www.netpets.org/fish/reference/freshref/nishi.html

Carpaccio, Vittore (1450/60–1525/26) Italian painter. He is famous for scenes of his native Venice, for example, the series *The Legend of St Ursula* (1490–98; Accademia, Venice). His paintings are a graceful blend of fantasy and closely observed details from everyday life.

> **Lewis Carroll**
> *Curtsey while you're thinking what to say. It saves time.*
> Alice Through the Looking-Glass ch. 2

Carpathian Mountains central European mountain system, forming a semicircle through Slovakia–Poland–Ukraine–Moldova–Romania, 1,450 km/900 mi long. The central **Tatra Mountains** on the Slovak–Polish frontier include the highest peak, Gerlachovka, 2,663 m/8,737 ft.

carpel female reproductive unit in flowering plants (▷angiosperms). It usually comprises an ▷ovary containing one or more ovules, the stalk or style, and a ▷stigma at its top which receives the pollen. A flower may have one or more carpels, and they may be separate or fused together. Collectively the carpels of a flower are known as the ▷gynoecium.

Carpentaria, Gulf of shallow gulf opening out of the Arafura Sea, between the capes of Arnhem and York, north of Australia; 600 km/373 mi long, 490 km/304 mi wide. The first European to reach it was the Dutch navigator Abel Tasman in 1606 and it was named in 1623 in honour of Pieter Carpentier, governor general of the Dutch East Indies.

carpet thick textile fabric, generally made of wool, used for covering floors and stairs. There is a long tradition of fine handmade carpets in the Middle East, India, Pakistan, and China. Western carpets are machine-made. Carpets and rugs have also often been made in the home as a pastime, cross and tent stitch on canvas being widely used in the 18th and 19th centuries.

carpetbagger in US history, derogatory name for any of the entrepreneurs and politicians from the North who moved to the Southern states during ▷Reconstruction (1865–77) after the Civil War, to exploit the chaotic conditions for their own benefit.

carpet beetle small black or brown beetle. The larvae are covered with hairs and often known as **woolly bears**; they feed on carpets, fabrics, and hides causing damage.

Carracci three Italian painters, **Lodovico Carracci** (1555–1619) and his two cousins, the brothers **Agostino Carracci** (1557–1602) and **Annibale Carracci** (1560–1609), who founded an influential school of painting in Bologna in the late 16th century, based on close study of the Renaissance masters and also life drawing. The three played a leading role in the development of the early baroque.

carragheen species of deep-reddish branched seaweed. Named after Carragheen, near Waterford, in the Republic of Ireland, it is found on rocky shores on both sides of the Atlantic. It is exploited commercially in food and medicines and as cattle feed. (*Chondrus crispus*.)

Carrel, Alexis (1873–1944) French-born US surgeon who was awarded a Nobel Prize for Physiology or Medicine in 1912 for his work on the techniques for connecting severed blood vessels and for transplanting organs. Working at the Rockefeller Institute, New York City, he devised a way of joining blood vessels end to end (anastomosing). This was a key move in the development of transplant surgery, as was his work on keeping organs viable outside the body.

Carreras, José Maria (1947–) Spanish operatic tenor. His comprehensive repertoire includes Handel's *Samson* and his recordings include *West Side Story* (1984) under Leonard Bernstein. His vocal presence, charmingly insinuating rather than forceful, is favoured for Italian and French romantic roles.

In 1987 he became seriously ill with leukaemia, but resumed his career in 1988. Together with Placido Domingo and Luciano Pavarotti, he achieved worldwide fame in a recording of operatic hits released to coincide with the World Cup soccer series in Rome in 1990.

Carrhae, Battle of disastrous defeat in 53 BC of the invading Roman governor of Syria Marcus Licinius Crassus by the Parthians at the ancient town of Carrhae, near Haran, Turkey. All but 500 of the 6,000-strong Roman force was wiped out; the remainder, including Crassus, were captured along with their standards, a grave blow to Roman pride. Crassus himself was executed and his head delivered to the Parthian king Orontes.

carrier in medicine, anyone who harbours an infectious organism without ill effects but can pass the infection to others. The term is also applied to those who carry a recessive gene for a disease or defect without manifesting the condition.

Carroll, Lewis (1832–1898) Pen-name of Charles Lutwidge Dodgson. English author of the children's classics *Alice's Adventures in Wonderland* (1865) and its sequel *Through the Looking-Glass, and What Alice Found There* (1872). Among later works was the mock-heroic narrative poem *The Hunting of the Snark* (1876). He was a lecturer in mathematics at Oxford University from 1855 until 1881 and also published mathematical works.

Dodgson first told his fantasy stories to Alice Liddell and her sisters, daughters of the dean of Christ Church, Oxford University. His two Alice books brought 'nonsense' literature to a peak of excellence, and continue to be enjoyed by children and adults alike. Dodgson was a prolific letter writer and one of the pioneers of portrait photography (his sitters included John Ruskin, Alfred Tennyson, and D G Rossetti, as well as children). He was also responsible, in his publication of mathematical games and problems requiring the use of logic, for a general upsurge of interest in such pastimes. He is said to be, after Shakespeare, the most quoted writer in the English language.

Related Web sites: Dodgson, Charles Lutwidge http://www-groups.dcs.st-and.ac.uk/history/Mathematicians/Dodgson.html

LEWIS CARROLL An illustration by Henry Holiday (1839–1927) for English writer Lewis Carroll's poem *The Hunting of the Snark*. This mock-heroic tale, written in 1876, was one of Carroll's later works. *The Art Archive*

carrot hardy European biennial plant with feathery leaves and an orange tapering root that is eaten as a vegetable. It has been cultivated since the 16th century. The root has a high sugar content and also contains ▷carotene, which is converted into vitamin A by the human liver. (*Daucus carota*, family Umbelliferae.)

Related Web site: Root Crops http://www.ext.vt.edu/pubs/envirohort/426-422/426-422.html

Carson City capital of ▷Nevada, situated at an altitude of 1,425 m/4,674 ft near the eastern foothills of the Sierra Nevada, 48 km/30 mi south of Reno, and to the east of Lake Tahoe; population (1992) 42,800. The mainstays of the economy are tourism and legalized gambling, although mining and livestock raising are still important.

Cartagena (or Cartagena de los Indes) historic port, industrial centre, and capital of Bolívar department, on the Caribbean coast of northwest Colombia; population (1994) 726,000. There are petrochemical, textile, and pharmaceutical industries; oil and coffee are exported. The city is also a fashionable tourist resort, with beaches, lakes, and inland lagoons. There is a 16th-century cathedral, and several 16th- and 17th-century churches, and a state university, founded in 1827. The fortress 'Castillo de San Felipe de Barajas' was constructed over a period of 150 years, commencing in 1639.

Related Web site: Cartagena, Colombia http://www.liat.com/cartagena.htm

Cartagena city in the autonomous community of ▷Murcia, southeast Spain, on the Mediterranean coast; population (1994) 180,000. It is a seaport and naval base, and has metallurgical, petrochemical, and glass industries. As the naval base of the Republicans it was bombed during the Spanish Civil War (1936–39). It has a 13th-century cathedral and Roman remains.

cartel (German *Kartell* 'a group') agreement among national or international firms to fix prices for their products. A cartel may restrict supply (output) to raise prices in order to increase member profits. It therefore represents a form of ▷oligopoly. ▷OPEC, for example, is an oil cartel.

Carter, Angela (1940–1992) English writer of the ▷magic realist school. Her works are marked by elements of Gothic fantasy, a fascination with the erotic and the violent, tempered by a complex lyricism and a comic touch. Her novels include *The Magic Toyshop* (1967) (filmed in 1987) and *Nights at the Circus* (1984). She co-wrote the script for the film *The Company of Wolves* (1984), based on one of her stories. Her last novel was *Wise Children* (1991).

Carter, Jimmy (1924–) Born James Earl Carter. 39th president of the USA 1977–81, a Democrat. Features of his presidency were the return of the Panama Canal Zone to Panama, the introduction of an amnesty programme for deserters and draft dodgers of the Vietnam War, and the Camp David Agreements for peace in the Middle East. He was defeated by Ronald Reagan in 1980. During the 1990s he emerged as a mediator and peace negotiator, securing President Aristide's safe return to Haiti in 1994. He was awarded the Presidential Medal of Freedom in 1999 and the Nobel Prize for Peace in 2002.

Carter was born in Plains, Georgia, and served in the navy as a physicist until 1953, when he took over the family peanut business. He entered politics in 1962 as a Georgia state senator, and in 1970 was elected governor. In 1976 he won the Democratic presidential nomination and went on to a narrow victory over Gerald Ford. His failure to be re-elected owed much to the seizure of US embassy staff in Tehran, Iran, as hostages by a Shiite Muslim group, as well as to an economic downturn.

> **Jimmy Carter**
> *We should live our lives as though Christ were coming this afternoon.*
> Speech to Bible class in Plains, Georgia, March 1976

Related Web site: Jimmy Carter Library http://carterlibrary.galileo.peachnet.edu

Cartesian coordinates in ▷coordinate geometry, components used to define the position of a point by its perpendicular distance from a set of two or more axes, or reference lines. For a two-dimensional area defined by two axes at right angles (a horizontal x-axis and a vertical y-axis), the coordinates of a point are given by its perpendicular distances from the y-axis and x-axis, written in the form (x, y). For example, a point P that lies three units from the y-axis and four units from the x-axis has Cartesian coordinates (3, 4) (see ▷abscissa and ▷ordinate).

The Cartesian coordinate system can be extended to any finite number of dimensions (axes), and is used thus in theoretical mathematics. So coordinates can be negative numbers, or a positive and a negative, for example $(-4, -7)$, where the point would be to the left of and below zero on the axes. In three-dimensional coordinate geometry, points are located with reference to a third, z-axis, mutually at right angles to the x and y axes.

Cartesian coordinates are named after the French mathematician, René Descartes. The system is useful in creating technical drawings of machines or buildings, and in computer-aided design (▷CAD).

Carthage ancient Phoenician port in North Africa founded by colonists from Tyre in the late 9th century BC; it lay 16 km/10 mi north of Tunis, Tunisia. A leading trading centre, it was in conflict with Greece from the 6th century BC, and then with Rome, and was destroyed by Roman forces in 146 BC at the end of the **▷Punic Wars**. About 45 BC, Roman colonists settled in Carthage, and it became the wealthy capital of the province of Africa. After its capture by the Vandals in AD 439 it was little more than a pirate stronghold. From 533 it formed part of the Byzantine Empire until its final destruction by Arabs in 698, during their conquest in the name of Islam.

Carthage is said to have been founded in 814 BC by Phoenician emigrants from Tyre, led by Princess Dido. It developed an extensive commerce throughout the Mediterranean and traded with the Tin Islands, whose location is believed to have been either Cornwall, England, or southwestern Spain. After the capture of Tyre by the Babylonians in the 6th century BC, Carthage became the natural leader of the Phoenician colonies in North Africa and Spain, and there soon began a prolonged struggle with the Greeks, which centred mainly on Sicily, the east of which was dominated by Greek colonies, while the west was held by Carthaginian trading stations. About 540 BC the Carthaginians defeated a Greek attempt to land in Corsica, and in 480 BC a Carthaginian attempt to conquer the whole of Sicily was defeated by the Greeks at Himera.

The population of Carthage before its destruction by the Romans in 146 BC is said to have numbered over 700,000. The constitution was an aristocratic republic with two chief magistrates elected annually and a senate of 300 life members. One aristocratic clan, the Barcids, which included Hannibal, traced their descent from Mago in the late 6th century BC. The religion was Phoenician, including the worship of the Moon goddess Tanit, the great Sun god Baal-Hammon, and the Tyrian Meklarth; human sacrifices were not unknown. The original strength of Carthage lay in its commerce and its powerful navy; its armies were for the most part mercenaries.

Carthusian order Roman Catholic order of monks and, later, nuns, founded by St Bruno in 1084 at Chartreuse, near Grenoble, France. Living chiefly in unbroken silence, they ate one vegetarian meal a day and supported themselves by their own labours; the rule is still one of severe austerity.

Cartier, Jacques (1491–1557) French navigator who, while seeking a northwest passage to China and Japan in 1535, was the first European to sail up the St Lawrence River, Canada. On this expedition, he named the site of Montréal.

In 1534, on his first voyage from his home town of St Malo in Brittany, Cartier ventured as far as Anticosti Island off the coast of Québec. On his second voyage the following year, he landed in Pillage Bay, opposite Anticosti, which he named the Bay of St Lawrence (the name was later extended to the river). His party ventured up the river in stages until they reached the impassable rapids near the island of Montréal; they spent an extremely harsh winter there before returning home in 1536. From 1541 to 1543 Cartier led an unsuccessful attempt to find the mythical Saguenay, a kingdom rich in gold and diamonds, which, according to Native American legend, lay up the Ottawa River.

Cartier-Bresson, Henri (1908–) French photographer. He is considered one of the greatest photographic artists. His documentary work was shot in black and white, using a small-format Leica camera. His work is remarkable for its tightly structured composition and his ability to capture the decisive moment. He was a founder member of the Magnum photographic agency.

cartilage flexible bluish-white ▷connective tissue made up of the protein collagen. In cartilaginous fish it forms the skeleton; in other vertebrates it forms the greater part of the embryonic skeleton, and is replaced by ▷bone in the course of development, except in areas of wear such as bone endings, and the discs between the backbones. It also forms structural tissue in the larynx, nose, and external ear of mammals.

Cartilage does not heal itself, so where injury is severe the joint may need to be replaced surgically. In a 1994 trial, Swedish doctors repaired damaged knee joints by implanting cells cultured from the patient's own cartilage. In 1999 US chemists created an artificial liquid cartilage for use in repairing torn tissue. The cartilage is injected into a wound or damaged joint and will harden with exposure to ultraviolet light. Clinical trials commenced in 2000.

cartilaginous fish fish in which the skeleton is made of cartilage. Sharks, rays, and skates are cartilaginous. Their scales are placoid (isolated structures made of dentine resembling simple teeth) and are present all over the body surface. The scales do not continue to grow once fully formed, but are replaced by new scales as they wear out. The notochord (primitive skeletal rod) is reduced and replaced to varying degrees by cartilage.

cartography art and practice of drawing ▷maps, originally with pens and drawing boards, but now mostly with computer aided drafting programmes.

Related Web site: Mathematics of Cartography http://math.rice.edu/~lanius/pres/map/

cartoon humorous or satirical drawing or ▷caricature; a strip cartoon or ▷comic strip; traditionally, the base design for a large fresco, mosaic, or tapestry, transferred to a wall or canvas by tracing or pricking out the design on the cartoon and then dabbing with powdered charcoal to create a faint reproduction. Surviving examples include Leonardo da Vinci's *Virgin and St Anne* (National Gallery, London).

Humorous drawing Cartoons were originally drawn to encourage people to think about political or social affairs. They were also created to make people laugh, and were often accompanied by a caption. In style, cartoons are simple drawings rather than serious artworks, and are made up of basic lines, with little or no shading, giving a 'flat' image. Colour is usually simple, and flatly applied. A cartoon can be a single picture, or a series of pictures known as frames. Film ▷animations are also known as cartoons because they are made up of similar frames.

Preliminary drawing Originally a cartoon was the full size preliminary drawing made in preparation for a final work. The cartoon was either used purely as a guide for the artist, or traced or pricked out for use as an exact plan for the final piece. Michelangelo, for example, transferred the images of his cartoons directly onto the ceiling of the Sistine Chapel during the making of his fresco. Raphael's cartoons for tapestries for the Sistine Chapel are now held at the Victoria and Albert Museum, London.

Related Web site: Comics Page http://www.comicspage.com/

Cartwright, Edmund (1743–1823) English inventor. He patented the power loom (1785), built a weaving mill (1787), and patented a wool-combing machine (1789).

Caruso, Enrico (1873–1921) Italian operatic tenor. His voice was dark, with full-bodied tone and remarkable dynamic range. In 1902 he starred, with the Australian soprano Nellie Melba, in Puccini's *La Bohème/Bohemian Life*. He was among the first opera singers to achieve lasting fame through gramophone recordings.

caryatid building support or pillar in the shape of a female figure, the name deriving from the Karyatides, who were priestesses at the temple of Artemis at Karyai; the male equivalent is a **telamon** or atlas.

caryopsis dry, one-seeded ▷fruit in which the wall of the seed becomes fused to the carpel wall during its development. It is a type of ▷achene, and therefore develops from one ovary and does not split open to release the seed. Caryopses are typical of members of the grass family (Gramineae), including the cereals.

Casablanca (Arabic **Dar el-Beida**) port, commercial, and industrial centre on the Atlantic coast of Morocco; population (1993) 2,943,000. Casablanca is one of the major ports of Africa, and the industrial centre of Morocco. It trades in fish, phosphates, and manganese. The Great Hassan II Mosque, completed in 1989, is the world's largest; it is built on a platform (40,000 sq m/430,000 sq ft) jutting out over the Atlantic, with walls 60 m/200 ft high, topped by a hydraulic sliding roof, and a minaret 175 m/574 ft high.

Casals, Pablo (Pau) (1876–1973) Catalan cellist, composer, and conductor. He was largely self-taught. As a cellist, he was celebrated for his interpretations of Johann Sebastian Bach's unaccompanied suites. He wrote instrumental and choral works, including the Christmas oratorio *The Manger*.

CARYATID The caryatid porch of the Erectheum, Athens (421–406 BC). The figures have suffered badly from pollution and have now been replaced with copies. One of the originals was removed by Lord Elgin in the early 19th century, and is now in the British Museum, London, England. *Image Bank*

He was an outspoken critic of fascism who openly defied Franco, and a tireless crusader for peace.

Casanova de Seingalt, Giovanni Giacomo (1725–1798) Italian adventurer, spy, violinist, librarian, and, according to his *Memoires* (published 1826–38, although the complete text did not appear until 1960–61), one of the world's great lovers. From 1774 he was a spy in the Venetian police service. In 1782 a libel got him into trouble, and after more wanderings he was in 1785 appointed librarian to Count Waldstein at his castle of Dûx in Bohemia. It was here that Casanova wrote his *Memoires*.

CASANOVA An impression of Giovanni Casanova, the 18th-century Italian adventurer. *Archive Photos*

case in grammar, the different forms (inflections) taken by nouns, pronouns, and adjectives depending on their function in a sentence. English is a language with four inflections; most words have no more than two forms. For example, six pronouns have one form when they are the subject of the verb, and a different form when they are either objects of the verb or governed by a preposition. The six are: *I/me, he/him, she/her, we/us, they/them, who/whom*. In 'I like cats', *I* is the subject of the sentence. In 'Cats hate me', *me* is the object. Latin has six cases, and Hungarian more than 25.

casein main protein of milk, from which it can be separated by the action of acid, the enzyme rennin, or bacteria (souring); it is also the main protein in cheese. Casein is used as a protein supplement in the treatment of malnutrition. It is used commercially in cosmetics, glues, and as a sizing for coating paper.

cash crop crop grown solely for sale rather than for the farmer's own use, for example, coffee, cotton, or sugar beet. Many developing countries grow cash crops to meet their debt repayments rather than grow food for their own people. The price for these crops depends on financial interests, such as those of the multinational companies and the International Monetary Fund.

cashew tropical American tree. Widely cultivated in India and Africa, it produces poisonous kidney-shaped nuts that become edible after being roasted. (*Anacardium occidentale*, family Anacardiaceae.)

Related Web site: Cashew Nut http://www.botanical.com/botanical/mgmh/c/casnut29.html

Cash, Johnny (1932–2003) US country singer, songwriter, and guitarist. His early hits, recorded for Sun Records in Memphis, Tennessee, include the million-selling 'I Walk the Line' (1956). Many of his songs have become classics.

cash flow input of cash required to cover all expenses of a business, whether revenue or capital. Alternatively, the actual or prospective balance between the various outgoing and incoming movements which are designated in total. Cash flow is positive if receipts are greater than payments; negative if payments are greater than receipts.

cashmere natural fibre originating from the wool of the goats of Kashmir, India, used for shawls, scarves, sweaters, and coats. It can also be made artificially.

Caspian Sea world's largest inland sea, on the border between Europe and Asia east of the Black Sea, divided between Iran, Azerbaijan, Russia, Kazakhstan, and Turkmenistan. It extends north–south for 1,200 km/745 mi, and its average width is 300 km/186 mi; area about 400,000 sq km/155,000 sq mi, with a maximum depth of 1,000 m/3,250 ft. An underwater ridge divides it into two halves, of which the shallow northern half is almost salt-free. There are no tides, but violent storms make navigation hazardous. The chief ports are Astrakhan (Russia), Baku (Azerbaijan), and Bandar Shah (Iran). The River Volga supplies 80% of freshwater inflow; the Ural, Emba, Terek, Kura, and Atrek rivers also flow into the Caspian Sea. Prolonged drought, drainage in the north, and regulation of the Volga and Kura rivers reduced the area from 430,000 sq km/166,000 sq mi in 1930 to 382,000 sq km/147,000 sq mi in 1957, and left the sea approximately 28 m/90 ft below sea level. In June 1991 opening of sluices in the dams caused the water level to rise dramatically, threatening towns and industrial areas.

Cassandra in Greek mythology, Trojan daughter of Priam and Hecuba. Loved by the god ▷Apollo, she was promised the gift of prophecy in return for her favours, but rejected his advances after receiving her powers. Her thwarted lover cursed her prophecies with disbelief, including that of the fall of Troy.

Cassatt, Mary (1845–1926) US Impressionist painter and printmaker, active in France. Her colourful pictures of mothers and children show the influence of Japanese prints, as in *The Bath* (1892; Art Institute, Chicago). She excelled in etching and pastel.

cassava (or **manioc**) plant belonging to the spurge family. Native to South America, it is now widely grown throughout the tropics for its starch-containing roots, from which tapioca and bread are made. (*Manihot utilissima*, family Euphorbiaceae.)

Related Web site: Mandioca http://www.botanical.com/botanical/mgmh/m/mandio09.html

cassia bark of an aromatic Southeast Asian plant (*Cinnamomum cassia*) belonging to the laurel family (Lauraceae). It is very similar to cinnamon, and is often used as a substitute for it. *Cassia* is also a genus of pod-bearing tropical plants of the family Caesalpiniaceae, many of which have strong purgative (cleansing) properties; *C. senna* is the source of the laxative drug senna (which causes the bowels to empty).

Cassini, Giovanni Domenico (Jean Dominique) (1625–1712) Italian-born French astronomer. He discovered four moons of Saturn and the gap in the rings of Saturn now called the Cassini division.

Cassiopeia prominent constellation of the northern hemisphere, named after the mother of Andromeda. It has a distinctive W-shape, and contains one of the most powerful radio sources in the sky, Cassiopeia A. This is the remains of a ▷supernova (star explosion) that occurred *c.* AD 1702, too far away to be seen from Earth.

It was in Cassiopeia that Danish astronomer Tycho ▷Brahe observed a new star in 1572, probably a supernova, since it was visible in daylight and outshone ▷Venus for ten days.

cassiterite (or **tinstone**) mineral consisting of reddish-brown to black stannic oxide (SnO_2), usually found in granite rocks. It is the chief ore of tin. When fresh it has a bright ('adamantine') lustre. It was formerly extensively mined in Cornwall, England; today Malaysia is the world's main supplier. Other sources of cassiterite are Africa, Indonesia, and South America.

Cassius (*c.* 85 BC–42 BC) Born Gaius Cassius Longinus. Roman general and politician, one of Julius ▷Caesar's assassins. He fought with Marcus Licinius ▷Crassus (the Elder) against the Parthians in 53 BC and distinguished himself after Carrhae by defending the province of Syria. He sided with Pompey against Julius Caesar on the outbreak of the civil war in 49 BC, but was pardoned after the battle of Pharsalus in 48 BC. Nevertheless, he became a leader in the conspiracy against Caesar which resulted in the latter's murder in 44 BC.

Cassivelaunus Chieftain of the British tribe, the Catuvellauni, who led the British resistance to the Romans under Caesar in 54 BC.

Casson, Hugh Maxwell (1910–1999) English architect. He was professor at the Royal College of Art from 1953 to 1975, and president of the Royal Academy from 1976 to 1984. He was director of architecture for the Festival of Britain on the South Bank in London (1948–51), in which pavilions designed by young architects helped to popularize the ▷Modern Movement. His books include *Victorian Architecture* (1948). He was knighted in 1952.

> **Hugh Casson**
> *The British love permanence more than they love beauty.*
> The Observer 1964

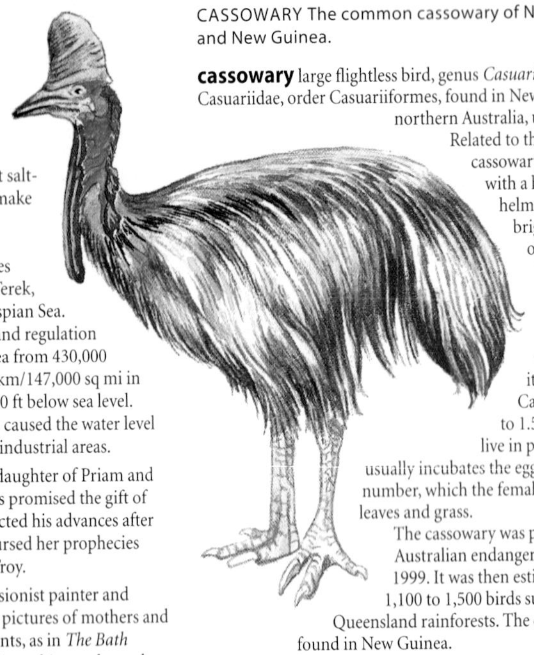

CASSOWARY The common cassowary of North Australia and New Guinea.

cassowary large flightless bird, genus *Casuarius*, of the family Casuariidae, order Casuariiformes, found in New Guinea and northern Australia, usually in forests. Related to the emu, the cassowary has a bare head with a horny casque, or helmet, on top, and brightly-coloured skin on the neck. Its loose plumage is black and its wings tiny, but it can run and leap well and defends itself by kicking. Cassowaries stand up to 1.5 m/5 ft tall. They live in pairs and the male usually incubates the eggs, about six in number, which the female lays in a nest of leaves and grass.

The cassowary was put on the Australian endangered species list in 1999. It was then estimated that only 1,100 to 1,500 birds survived in north Queensland rainforests. The cassowary is also found in New Guinea.

Related Web site: Southern Cassowary http://www.wildlife-australia.com/cass.html

Castagno, Andrea del (*c.* 1421–1457) Adopted name of Andrea di Bartolo de Bargilla. Italian Renaissance painter, active in Florence. His work, which develops from that of ▷Masaccio, is powerful and sculptural in effect, showing clear outlines and an interest in foreshortening. His *David* (*c.* 1450–57; National Gallery, Washington, DC) is typical.

castanets Spanish percussion instrument made of two hollowed wooden shells, originally chestnut wood (Spanish *castaña*). They are held in the palm and drummed together by the fingers to produce a rhythmic accompaniment to dance.

caste (Portuguese *casta* 'race') a system of stratifying a society into ranked groups defined by marriage, descent, and occupation. Most common in South Asia, caste systems are also found in other societies such as in Mali and Rwanda, and in the past, in Japan, in South Africa under apartheid, and among the ▷Natchez.

The system in Hindu society dates from ancient times and there are over 3,000 castes, known as 'jatis', which are loosely ranked into four classes known as 'varnas': **Brahmans** (priests), **Kshatriyas** (nobles and warriors), **Vaisyas** (traders and farmers), and **Sudras** (servants); plus a fifth group, **Harijan** (untouchables).

Related Web site: India's Caste System http://www.csuchico.edu/~cheinz/syllabi/asst001/spring98/india.htm

Castile kingdom founded in the 10th century, occupying the central plateau of Spain. Its union with ▷Aragón in 1479, based on the marriage of Ferdinand and Isabella, effected the foundation of the Spanish state, which at the time was occupied and ruled by the ▷Moors. Castile comprised the two great basins separated by the Sierra de Gredos and the Sierra de Guadarrama, known traditionally as Old and New Castile. The area now forms the regions of ▷Castilla–León and ▷Castilla–La Mancha.

Castilian language member of the Romance branch of the Indo-European language family, originating in northwestern Spain, in the provinces of Old and New Castile. It is the basis of present-day standard Spanish (see ▷Spanish language) and is often seen as the same language, the terms *castellano* and *español* being used interchangeably in both Spain and the Spanish-speaking countries of the Americas.

Castilla–La Mancha autonomous community of central Spain; area 79,200 sq km/30,600 sq mi; population (1991) 1,658,400. It includes the provinces of Albacete, Ciudad Real, Cuenca, Guadalajara, and Toledo. Irrigated land produces mainly cereals and vines, especially in the Valdepeñas region, and merino sheep are raised. The capital is ▷Toledo.

Castilla–León autonomous community of central Spain; area 94,100 sq km/36,300 sq mi; population (1991) 2,545,900. It includes the provinces of Avila, Burgos, León, Palencia, Salamanca, Segovia, Soria, Valladolid, and Zamora. Irrigated land produces wheat and rye; cattle, sheep, and fighting bulls are bred in the uplands. There are important food industries in Burgos, Palencia, and Segovia provinces. The capital is ▷Valladolid, which is the main manufacturing centre, particularly for engineering and the production of motor vehicles.

Related Web site: Community of Castille and Leon http://www.DocuWeb.ca/SiSpain/english/politics/autonomo/leon/index.html

casting process of producing solid objects by pouring molten material into a shaped mould and allowing it to cool. Casting is used to shape such materials as glass and plastics, as well as metals and alloys.

cast iron cheap but invaluable constructional material, most commonly used for car engine blocks. Cast iron is partly refined pig (crude) ▷iron, which is very fluid when molten and highly suitable for shaping by casting; it contains too many impurities (for example, carbon) to be readily shaped in any other way. Solid cast iron is heavy and can absorb great shock but is very brittle.

castle fortified building or group of buildings, characteristic of medieval Europe. The castle was originally designed as a defensive fortification, but it also functioned as a residence for the royalty and nobility, an administrative centre, and a place of safety for local people in times of invasion. In 13th-century Wales, Edward I built a string of castles as military centres to keep control of the country. The castle underwent many changes, its size, design, and construction being largely determined by changes in siege tactics and the development of artillery. Outstanding examples are the 12th-century Krak des Chevaliers, Syria (built by crusaders); 13th-century ▷Caernarfon Castle, Wales; and 15th-century Manzanares el Real, Spain.

Structure The main parts of a typical castle are the keep, a large central tower containing store rooms, soldiers' quarters, and a hall for the lord and his family; the inner bailey, or walled courtyard, surrounding the keep; the outer bailey, or second courtyard, separated from the inner bailey by a wall; crenellated embattlements through which missiles were discharged against an attacking enemy; rectangular or round towers projecting from the walls; the portcullis, a heavy grating which could be let down to close the main gate; and the drawbridge crossing the ditch or moat surrounding the castle. Sometimes a tower called a barbican was constructed over a gateway as an additional defensive measure.

11th century The motte-and-bailey castle appeared (the motte was a mound of earth, and the bailey a courtyard enclosed by a wall); the earliest example is on the River Loire in France, dated 1010. There were few castles in England before 1066, but the Normans, a small military army of occupation in the midst of a hostile population, built castles to defend themselves and secure the conquest – the *Anglo-Saxon Chronicle* records that they 'built castles far and wide throughout the land, oppressing the wretched people, and things went from bad to worse'. The 50 castles constructed in England between the Norman Conquest and the Domesday Book survey of 1086 were motte-and-bailey castles, because they could be built quickly by the Anglo-Saxon peasantry. At first they were made of wood, but later, because of their vulnerability to fire, they were converted to stone 'shell' keeps, such as that at Berkhamsted, Hertfordshire.

The first rectangular stone keeps date from soon after this time, such as the White Tower (*c.* 1078) in the Tower of London; Castle Hedingham, Essex; and Rochester Castle in Kent. All offer fine examples of ▷Norman architecture.

12th century More substantial defensive systems were developed, based in part on the Crusaders' experiences of sieges during the First Crusade of 1096; the first curtain walls with projecting towers were built, as at Framlingham, Suffolk.

13th century The round tower was introduced, both for curtain walls (Pembroke, Wales) and for keeps (Conisbrough, Yorkshire); concentric planning appeared in the castles of Wales, as at Harlech Castle and Beaumaris (1295; one of the finest examples in Europe, and designated a World Heritage site); fortified town walls proliferated.

14th century Gunpowder was first used, necessitating the inclusion of gunports in curtain walls, as at Bodiam, Sussex. Bamburgh Castle was the first English castle to fall to artillery.

CASTLE The castle of Beltayer sits by the Dordogne River, in southwest France. *Image Bank*

15th century Fortified manor houses were now adequate for private dwelling.

16th century Although the castle had ended as a practical means of defence, fortified coastal defences continued to be built, such as Falmouth, Cornwall.

Related Web site: Castles on the Web http://www.castlesontheweb.com/

Castlereagh, Robert Stewart (1769–1822) Viscount Castlereagh. British Tory politician. As chief secretary for Ireland 1797–1801, he suppressed the rebellion of 1798 and helped the younger Pitt secure the union of England, Scotland, and Ireland in 1801. As foreign secretary 1812–22, he coordinated European opposition to Napoleon and represented Britain at the Congress of Vienna (1814–15).

Castlereagh sat in the Irish House of Commons from 1790. When his father, an Ulster landowner, was made an earl in 1796, he took the courtesy title of Viscount Castlereagh. In Parliament he was secretary for war and the colonies 1805–06 and 1807–09, when he had to resign after a duel with foreign secretary George ▷Canning. During his time as foreign secretary, he devoted himself to the overthrow of Napoleon and subsequently to the ▷congress system. His policy abroad favoured the development of material liberalism, but at home he repressed the Reform movement, and popular opinion held him responsible for the Peterloo massacre of peaceful demonstrators in 1819.

In 1821 he succeeded his father as Marquess of Londonderry, but committed suicide the following year.

Castor and Pollux/Polydeuces (or the **Dioscuri**) in Greek mythology, the inseparable twins or sons of ▷Leda; brothers of ▷Helen and ▷Clytemnestra; protectors of sailors. Their brotherly love was symbolized in the constellation ▷Gemini. Many versions of their birth exist; in one tradition, the boys were fathered by Zeus in the form of a swan, and born from an egg.

castor-oil plant tall tropical and subtropical shrub belonging to the spurge family. The seeds, called 'castor beans' in North America, yield the purgative castor oil (which cleans out the bowels) and also ricin, one of the most powerful poisons known. Ricin can be used to destroy cancer cells, leaving normal cells untouched. (*Ricinus communis*, family Euphorbiaceae.)

Related Web site: Castor-oil Plant http://www.botanical.com/botanical/mgmh/c/casoil32.html

castration removal of the sex glands (either ovaries or testes). Male domestic animals may be castrated to prevent reproduction, to make them larger or more docile, or to eradicate disease.

Castries port and capital of St Lucia, on the northwest coast of the island in the Caribbean; population (2001 est) 59,600. It produces textiles, chemicals, tobacco, and wood and rubber products.

Castro (Ruz), Fidel (1927–) Cuban communist politician, prime minister 1959–76, and president from 1976. He led two unsuccessful coups against the right-wing regime of Fulgencio ▷Batista, and led the revolution that overthrew the dictator in 1959. He raised the standard of living for most Cubans but dealt harshly with dissenters. From 1990, deprived of the support of the USSR and experiencing the long-term effects of a US trade embargo, Castro faced increasing pressure for reform; in September 1995 he moved towards greater economic flexibility by permitting foreign ownership in major areas of commerce and industry. In January 1996 the *rapprochement* between Cuba and the USA appeared to have progressed after a visit by Democratic members of the House of Representatives, although the US embargo was not lifted. In 1998 he invited the Pope to make an unprecedented visit to Cuba. In February 1998 Castro was elected president.

> **Fidel Castro**
> *A revolution is not a bed of roses. A revolution is a struggle to the death between the future and the past.*
> Speech given on the second anniversary of the revolution, Havana, January 1961

casuarina any of a group of trees or shrubs with many species in Australia and New Guinea, also found in Africa and Asia. Commonly known as she-oaks, casuarinas have taken their Latin name from the similarity of their long, drooping branchlets to the feathers of the cassowary bird (whose genus is *Casuarius*). (Genus *Casuarina*, family Casuarinaceae.)

cat small, domesticated, carnivorous mammal *Felis catus*, often kept as a pet or for catching small pests such as rodents. Found in many colour variants, it may have short, long, or no hair, but the general shape and size is constant. Cats have short muzzles, strong limbs, and flexible spines which enable them to jump and climb. All walk on the pads of their toes (**digitigrade**) and have retractile claws, so are able to stalk their prey silently. They have large eyes and an acute sense of hearing. The canine teeth are long and well-developed, as are the shearing teeth in the side of the mouth.

CAT In some parts of its range the beautifully marked ocelot has been hunted almost to extinction for its pelt.

Origins Domestic cats have a common ancestor, the **African wild cat** *Felis libyca*, found across Africa and Arabia. This is similar to the **European wild cat** *F. silvestris*. Domestic cats can interbreed with either of these wild relatives. Various other species of small wild cat live in all continents except Antarctica and Australia. Large cats such as the lion, tiger, leopard, puma, and jaguar also belong to the cat family Felidae.

The Nature Conservancy Council for Scotland reported in 1991 that the numbers of the European wild cat *Felis silvestris* in Scotland, the purest population in Europe, had declined, particularly in the north and west, the last stronghold of the species in Britain.

catabolism in biology, the destructive part of ▷metabolism where living tissue is changed into energy and waste products.

It is the opposite of ▷anabolism. It occurs continuously in the body, but is accelerated during many disease processes, such as fever, and in starvation.

catacomb (Greek *kata* 'down'; *kumbe* 'a hollow') underground burial chambers, such as the catacombs of the early Christians. Examples include those beneath the basilica of St Sebastian in Rome, where bodies were buried in niches in the walls of the tunnels.

Catalan language member of the Romance branch of the Indo-European language family, an Iberian language closely related to Provençal in France. It is spoken in Cataluña in northeastern Spain, the Balearic Islands, Andorra, and a corner of southwestern France.

catalpa any of a group of trees belonging to the trumpet creeper family, found in North America, China, and the West Indies. The northern catalpa (*Catalpa speciosa*) of North America grows to 20 m/65 ft and has heart-shaped deciduous leaves and tubular white flowers with purple borders. (Genus *Catalpa*, family Bignoniaceae.)

Cataluña (or Catalonia; Catalan **Catalunya**) autonomous community of northeast Spain; area 31,900 sq km/12,300 sq mi; population (1991) 6,059,500. It includes the provinces of Barcelona, Girona (formerly Gerona), Lleida (formerly Lérida), and Tarragona. Olives, vines, cereals, and nuts are grown, and some livestock is raised. Cataluña is the main industrial region of Spain. Originally based on the textile industry, the region has diversified into engineering, chemicals, paper, publishing, and many service industries; hydroelectric power is also produced. The capital is ▷Barcelona.

catalyst substance that alters the speed of, or makes possible, a chemical or biochemical reaction but remains unchanged at the end of the reaction. ▷Enzymes are natural biochemical catalysts. In practice most catalysts are used to speed up reactions.

Related Web site: Catalysts http://www.purchon.co.uk/science/catalyst.html

catalytic converter device fitted to the exhaust system of a motor vehicle in order to reduce toxic emissions from the engine. It converts harmful exhaust products to relatively harmless ones by passing the exhaust gases over a mixture of catalysts coated on a metal or ceramic honeycomb (a structure that increases the surface area and therefore the amount of active catalyst with which the exhaust gases will come into contact). **Oxidation catalysts** (small

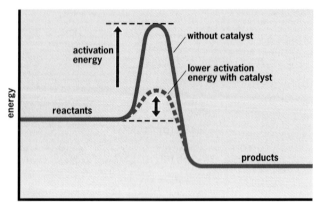

CATALYST A graph showing how a reaction speeds up with the addition of a catalyst.

amounts of precious palladium and platinum metals) convert hydrocarbons (unburnt fuel) and carbon monoxide into carbon dioxide and water, but do not affect nitrogen oxide emissions. **Three-way catalysts** (platinum and rhodium metals) convert nitrogen oxide gases into nitrogen and oxygen.

Catania industrial port in Sicily on the Gulf of Catania, just south of Mount Etna; population (1992) 329,900. It is the capital of the province of Catania. It exports local sulphur; there are also shipbuilding, textile, and light industries.

cataract eye disease in which the crystalline lens or its capsule becomes cloudy, causing blindness. Fluid accumulates between the fibres of the lens and gives place to deposits of ▷albumin. These coalesce into rounded bodies, the lens fibres break down, and areas of the lens or the lens capsule become filled with opaque products of degeneration. The condition is estimated to have blinded more than 25 million people worldwide, and 150,000 in the UK.

catarrh inflammation of any mucous membrane, especially of the nose and throat, with increased production of mucus.

catastrophe theory mathematical theory developed by René Thom in 1972, in which he showed that the growth of an organism proceeds by a series of gradual changes that are triggered by, and in turn trigger, large-scale changes or 'catastrophic' jumps. It also has applications in engineering – for example, the gradual strain on the structure of a bridge that can eventually result in a sudden collapse – and has been extended to economic and psychological events.

catchment area in earth sciences, the area from which water is collected by a river and its tributaries. In the social sciences the term may be used to denote the area from which people travel to obtain a particular service or product, such as the area from which a school draws its pupils.

catechism teaching by question and answer on the Socratic method, but chiefly as a means of instructing children in the basics of the Christian creed. A person being instructed in this way in preparation for baptism or confirmation is called a **catechumen**.

category in philosophy, a fundamental concept applied to being that cannot be reduced to anything more elementary. Aristotle listed ten categories: substance, quantity, quality, relation, place, time, position, state, action, and passion.

caterpillar larval stage of a ▷butterfly or ▷moth. Wormlike in form, the body is segmented, may be hairy, and often has scent glands. The head has strong biting mandibles, silk glands, and a spinneret.

Many caterpillars resemble the plant on which they feed, dry twigs, or rolled leaves. Others are highly coloured and rely for their protection on their irritant hairs, disagreeable smell, or on their power to eject a corrosive fluid. Yet others take up a 'threat attitude' when attacked. Caterpillars emerge from eggs that have been laid by the female insect on the food plant and feed greedily, increasing greatly in size and casting their skins several times, until the pupal stage is reached. The abdominal segments bear a varying number of 'prolegs' as well as the six true legs on the thoracic segments.

Related Web site: Rearing Caterpillars http://www.ex.ac.uk/bugclub/cater.html

catfish fish belonging to the order Siluriformes, in which barbels (feelers) on the head are well-developed, so giving a resemblance to the whiskers of a cat. Catfishes are found worldwide, mainly but not exclusively in fresh water, and are plentiful in South America.

The Eastern European **giant catfish** or **wels** *Silurus glanis* grows to 1.5 m/5 ft long or more. It has been introduced to several places in Britain. The unrelated marine **wolffish** *Anarhicas lupus*, a deep-sea relative of the blenny, growing 1.2 m/4 ft long, is sometimes called a catfish.

cathedral (Latin *cathedra* 'seat' or 'throne') principal Christian church of a bishop or archbishop, containing his throne, which is usually situated on the south side of the choir. In the Middle Ages cathedrals were used for state occasions, such as parliaments, and they are still used for royal coronations and weddings, and state funerals. Many cathedrals also house the relics of the saints, and so in the Middle Ages were centres of ▷pilgrimage. Until modern times, only a town with a cathedral could be called a city.

Catherine I (1684–1727) Empress of Russia from 1725.

A Lithuanian peasant, born Martha Skavronsky, she married a Swedish dragoon and eventually became the mistress of Peter the Great. In 1703 she was rechristened Katarina Alexeievna. The tsar divorced his wife in 1711 and married Catherine in 1712. She accompanied him on his campaigns, and showed tact and shrewdness. In 1724 she was proclaimed empress, and after Peter's death in 1725 she ruled capably with the help of her ministers. She allied Russia with Austria and Spain in an anti-English bloc.

Catherine (II) the Great (1729–1796) Empress of Russia from 1762, and daughter of the German prince of Anhalt-Zerbst. In 1745 she married the Russian grand duke Peter. Catherine dominated her husband; six months after he became Tsar Peter III in 1762, he was murdered in a coup and Catherine ruled alone. During her reign Russia extended its boundaries to include territory from wars with the Turks (1768–74), (1787–92), and from the partitions of Poland in 1772, 1793, and 1795, as well as establishing hegemony over the Black Sea.

Catherine's private life was notorious throughout Europe, but except for Grigory ▷Potemkin she did not permit her lovers to influence her policy.

She admired and aided the French ▷Encyclopédistes, including d'Alembert, and corresponded with the radical writer Voltaire.

Catherine de' Medici (1519–1589) French queen consort of Henry II, whom she married in 1533; daughter of Lorenzo de' Medici, Duke of Urbino; and mother of Francis II, Charles IX, and Henry III. At first outshone by Henry's mistress Diane de Poitiers (1490–1566), she became regent for Charles IX (1560–63) and remained in power until his death in 1574.

During the religious wars of 1562–69, she first supported the Protestant ▷Huguenots against the Roman Catholic Guises to

CATHERINE (II) THE GREAT A German by birth, Catherine the Great ruled Russia well and identified with its people throughout her life. Catherine expressed relief at Peter III's death in a coup d'etat in 1762, and took over the government of the country. *Archive Photos*

ensure her own position as ruler; she later opposed them, and has been traditionally implicated in the Massacre of ▷St Bartholomew of 1572.

> **Catherine (II) The Great**
> *I shall be an autocrat: that's my trade. And the good Lord will forgive me: that's his.*
> Attributed remark

Catherine of Alexandria, St (lived early 4th century) Christian martyr. According to legend she disputed with 50 scholars, refusing to give up her faith and marry Emperor Maxentius. Her emblem is a wheel, on which her persecutors tried to kill her (the wheel broke and she was beheaded). Her feast day is 25 November; removed from the church calendar in 1969.

Catherine of Aragón (1485–1536) First queen of Henry VIII of England, 1509–33, and mother of Mary I. Catherine had married Henry's elder brother Prince Arthur in 1501 and on his death in 1502 was betrothed to Henry, marrying him on his accession. She failed to produce a male heir and Henry divorced her without papal approval, thus creating the basis for the English ▷Reformation.

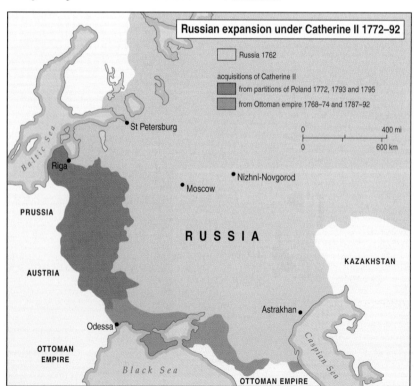

Russian expansion under Catherine II 1772–92

☐ Russia 1762

acquisitions of Catherine II

▨ from partitions of Poland 1772, 1793 and 1795

▨ from Ottoman empire 1768–74 and 1787–92

0   400 mi
0   600 km

St Petersburg

Baltic Sea

Riga

Nizhni-Novgorod

Moscow

PRUSSIA

RUSSIA

KAZAKHSTAN

AUSTRIA

Odessa

Astrakhan

Caspian Sea

OTTOMAN EMPIRE

Black Sea

OTTOMAN EMPIRE

CATHERINE OF ARAGÓN Spanish-born Catherine of Aragón, first queen of Henry VIII of England, and the mother of Mary I (Tudor) of England. *Archive Photos*

Born at Alcalá de Henares, she was the youngest daughter of Ferdinand and Isabella of Spain. After Prince Arthur's death, Catherine remained in England, virtually penniless, until her marriage to Henry in 1509. Of their six children, only Mary survived infancy. Wanting a male heir, Henry sought an annulment in 1526 when Catherine was too old to bear children. When the pope demanded that the case be referred to him, Henry married Anne Boleyn, afterwards receiving the desired decree of nullity from Thomas Cranmer, the archbishop of Canterbury, in 1533. The Reformation in England followed, and Catherine went into retirement until her death.

Catherine of Valois (1401–1437) Queen of Henry V of England, whom she married in 1420; the mother of Henry VI. After the death of Henry V, she secretly married Owen Tudor (*c.* 1400–1461) about 1425, and their son Edmund Tudor was the father of Henry VII.

catheter fine tube inserted into the body to introduce or remove fluids. The urinary catheter, passed by way of the urethra (the duct that leads urine away from the bladder) was the first to be used. In today's practice, catheters can be inserted into blood vessels, either in the limbs or trunk, to provide blood samples and local pressure measurements, and to deliver drugs and/or nutrients directly into the bloodstream.

cathode in chemistry, the negative electrode of an electrolytic ▷cell, towards which positive particles (cations), usually in solution, are attracted. See ▷electrolysis.

A cathode is given its negative charge by connecting it to the negative side of an external electrical supply. This is in contrast to the negative electrode of an electrical (battery) cell, which acquires its charge in the course of a spontaneous chemical reaction taking place within the cell.

cathode in electronics, the part of an electronic device in which electrons are generated. In a thermionic valve, electrons are produced by the heating effect of an applied current; in a photocell, they are produced by the interaction of light and a semiconducting material. The cathode is kept at a negative potential relative to the device's other electrodes (anodes) in order to ensure that the liberated electrons stream away from the cathode and towards the anodes.

cathode ray stream of fast-moving electrons that travel from a cathode (negative electrode) towards an anode (positive electrode) in a vacuum tube. They carry a negative charge and can be deflected by electric and magnetic fields. Cathode rays focused into fine beams of fast electrons are used in cathode-ray tubes, the electrons' ▷kinetic energy being converted into light energy as they collide with the tube's fluorescent screen.

cathode-ray oscilloscope (CRO) instrument used to measure electrical potentials or voltages that vary over time and to display the waveforms of electrical oscillations or signals. Readings are displayed graphically on the screen of a ▷cathode-ray tube.

cathode-ray tube (CRT) vacuum tube in which a beam of electrons is produced and focused onto a fluorescent screen. The electrons' kinetic energy is converted into light energy as they collide with the screen. It is an essential component of television

receivers, computer visual display units, and ▷oscilloscopes.

The screen of the CRT is coated on the inside with phosphor, which emits light when struck by an electron beam. The tube itself is glass and coated inside with a black graphite conducting paint, which is connected to one of three anodes. A heated filament heats a metal-oxide coated cathode that emits electrons which pass through a positively charged anode that is held at several thousand volts and accelerates the electrons to a high speed beam. The electrons accumulate on the phosphor of the screen and repel each other back to the conducting graphite paint completing a circuit.

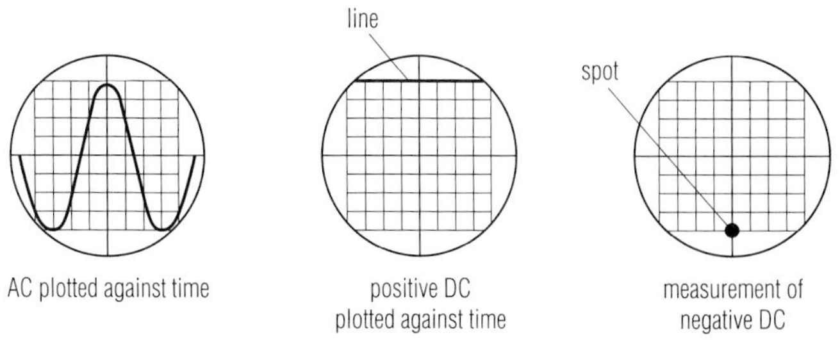

Catholic Church the whole body of the Christian church, though usually referring to the Roman Catholic Church (see ▷Roman Catholicism).

Catholic Emancipation in British history, acts of Parliament passed between 1780 and 1829 to relieve Roman Catholics of civil and political restrictions imposed from the time of Henry VIII and the Reformation.

Catiline (*c.* 108–62 BC) Born Lucius Sergius Catilina. Roman politician and conspirator. Catiline was a member of an impoverished patrician family and a former partisan of Sulla. Twice failing to be elected to the consulship in 64 BC and 63 BC, he planned a military coup, but ▷Cicero exposed his conspiracy. He died at the head of the insurgents.

cation ▷ion carrying a positive charge. During electrolysis, cations in the electrolyte move to the cathode (negative electrode).

catkin in flowering plants (▷angiosperms), a pendulous inflorescence, bearing numerous small, usually unisexual flowers. The tiny flowers are stalkless and the petals and sepals are usually absent or much reduced in size. Many types of trees bear catkins, including willows, poplars, and birches. Most plants with catkins are wind-pollinated, so the male catkins produce large quantities of pollen. Some ▷gymnosperms also have catkin-like structures that produce pollen, for example, the swamp cypress *Taxodium.*

Cato, Marcus Porcius (234–149 BC) Called 'the Censor'. Roman politician. Having significantly developed Roman rule in Spain, Cato was appointed ▷censor in 184 BC. He acted severely, taxing luxuries and heavily revising the senatorial and equestrian lists. He was violently opposed to Greek influence on Roman culture and his suspicion of the re-emergence of Carthaginian power led him to remark: 'Carthage must be destroyed.'

CAT scan (or CT scan; acronym for **computerized axial tomography scan**) sophisticated method of X-ray imaging. Quick and noninvasive, CAT scanning is used in medicine as an aid to diagnosis, helping to pinpoint problem areas without the need for exploratory surgery. It is also used in archaeology to investigate mummies.

The CAT scanner passes a narrow fan of X-rays through successive slices of the suspect body part. These slices are picked up by crystal detectors in a scintillator and converted electronically into cross-sectional images displayed on a viewing screen. Gradually, using views taken from various angles, a three-dimensional picture of the organ or tissue can be built up and irregularities analysed.

Catskill Mountains mountain range in southeastern New York State, USA, forming part of the ▷Appalachian Mountains west of the Hudson River; the highest peaks are Slide Mountain (1,281 m/4,204 ft) and Hunter Mountain (1,227 m/4,026 ft). The Catskill Mountains have long been a vacation and resort centre for residents of New York City, offering hiking, skiing, hunting and fishing. The valleys, which have been carved out by glaciation, are the chief scenic attractions; much of the mountain area is included in the Catskill Forest Preserve.

cattle any large, ruminant, even-toed, hoofed mammal of the genus *Bos*, family Bovidae, including wild species such as the yak, gaur, gayal, banteng, and kouprey, as well as domestic breeds. Asiatic water buffaloes *Bubalus*, African buffaloes *Syncerus*, and American bison *Bison* are not considered true cattle. Cattle are bred for meat (beef cattle) or milk (dairy cattle).

AC plotted against time

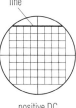
positive DC plotted against time

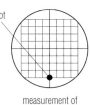
measurement of negative DC

CATHODE-RAY OSCILLOSCOPE The cathode-ray oscilloscope (CRO) is used to measure voltage and its changes over time. This is how the CRO screen would appear measuring AC and DC current.

Catullus, Gaius Valerius (*c.* 84–54 BC) Roman lyric poet. He wrote in a variety of metres and forms, from short narratives and hymns to epigrams. He moved with ease through the literary and political society of late republican Rome. His love affair with the woman he called 'Lesbia' provided the inspiration for many of his poems.

Caucasoid (or **Caucasian**) former racial classification used for any of the light-skinned peoples of the world, one of three theoretical major varieties of humans. The Caucasoid group included the indigenous peoples of Europe, the Near East, North Africa, India, and Australia. They were so named because the German anthropologist J F Blumenbach (1752–1840) theorized that they originated in the Caucasus. See ▷race.

Caucasus mountain range extending from the Taman Peninsula on the Black Sea to the Apsheron Peninsula on the Caspian Sea, a total length of 1,200 km/750 mi. The Caucasus, which form the boundary between Europe and Asia, is divided into the **Greater Caucasus** (northern) and **Little Caucasus** (southern) chains. The range crosses the territory of the Russian Federation, Georgia, Armenia, and Azerbaijan. At 5,642 m/18,510 ft, Elbrus (in the Greater Caucasus) is the highest peak in Europe. Over 40 languages are spoken by 100 ethnic groups here.

cauliflower variety of ▷cabbage, with a large edible head of fleshy, cream-coloured flowers which do not fully mature. It is similar to broccoli but less hardy. (*Brassica oleracea botrytis*, family Cruciferae.)

Related Web site: Cole Crops or Brassicas http://www.ext.vt.edu/pubs/envirohort/426-403/426-403.html

causality in philosophy, a consideration of the connection between cause and effect, usually referred to as the 'causal relationship'.

cauterization in medicine, the use of special instruments to burn or fuse small areas of body tissue to destroy dead cells, prevent the spread of infection, or seal tiny blood vessels to minimize blood loss during surgery.

caution legal term for a warning given by police questioning a suspect, which in the UK must be couched in the following terms: 'You do not have to say anything unless you wish to do so, but what you say may be given in evidence.' Persons not under arrest must also be told that they do not have to remain at the police station or with the police officer but that if they do, they may obtain legal advice if they wish. A suspect should be cautioned again after a break in questioning and upon arrest.

Cauvery (or **Kaveri**) sacred Hindu river of southern India, rising in the Western ▷Ghats and flowing 765 km/475 mi southeast through Karnataka and Tamil Nadu to meet the Bay of Bengal in a wide delta. It has been a major source of hydroelectric power since 1902 when India's first hydropower plant was built on the river. In the 1920s the river was dammed at Mettur, forming a 2,600 million cu m/91,873 million cu ft reservoir, used for irrigation and power generation.

Cavaco Silva, Anibal (1939–) Portuguese politician, finance minister 1980–81, and prime minister and Social Democratic Party (PSD) leader 1985–95. Under his leadership Portugal joined the European Community in 1985 and the Western European Union in 1988.

cavalier horseman of noble birth, but mainly used as a derogatory nickname to describe a male supporter of Charles I in the English Civil War (Cavalier), typically with courtly dress and long hair (as distinct from a Roundhead); also a supporter of Charles II after the Restoration.

Cavalier poets poets of Charles I's court, including Thomas ▷Carew, Robert ▷Herrick, Richard ▷Lovelace, and John Suckling. They wrote witty, lighthearted lyrics about love and loyalty to the monarch.

> **Marcus Porcius Cato**
> *Delenda est Carthago.*
> *Carthage must be destroyed.*
> Plutarch *Life of Cato*

Cavalli, (Pietro) Francesco (1602–1676) Italian composer. He was organist at St Mark's, Venice, and the first to make opera a popular entertainment with such works as *Equisto* (1643) and *Xerxes* (1654), later performed in honour of Louis XIV's wedding in Paris. Twenty-seven of his operas survive.

Cavan county of the Republic of Ireland, in the province of Ulster; county town Cavan; area 1,890 sq km/730 sq mi; population (1996) 52,900. The chief rivers are the Woodford, the Shannon (rising on the south slopes of Cuilcagh mountain; 667 m/2,188 ft), and the Erne, which divides Cavan into two parts: a narrow, mostly low-lying peninsula, 30 km/19 mi long, between Leitrim and Fermanagh; and an eastern section of wild and bare hill country. The chief towns are Cavan, population (1996) 3,500, and Kilmore, seat of Roman Catholic and Protestant bishoprics. The soil is generally poor and the climate moist and cold.

cave roofed-over cavity in the Earth's crust usually produced by the action of underground water or by waves on a seacoast. Caves of the former type commonly occur in areas underlain by limestone, such as Kentucky and many Balkan regions, where the rocks are soluble in water. A **pothole** is a vertical hole in rock caused by water descending a crack; it is thus open to the sky.

Limestone caves Most inland caves are found in ▷karst regions, because ▷limestone is soluble when exposed to ground water. As the water makes its way along the main joints, fissures, and bedding planes, they are constantly enlarged into potential cave passages, which ultimately join to form a complex network. ▷Stalactites and stalagmites and columns form due to water rich in calcium carbonate dripping from the roof of the cave. The collapse of the roof of a cave produces features such as **natural arches** and **steep-sided gorges**.

Limestone caves are usually found just below the water-table, wherever limestone outcrops on the surface. The biggest cave in the world is over 70 km long, at Holloch, Switzerland.

Sea caves Coastal caves are formed where relatively soft rock or rock containing definite lines of weakness, like ▷basalt at tide level, is exposed to severe wave action. The gouging process (▷corrasion) and dissolution (▷corrosion) of weaker, more soluble rock layers is exacerbated by subsidence, and the hollow in the cliff face grows still larger because of air compression in the chamber. Where the roof of a cave has fallen in, the vent up to the land surface is called a blowhole. If this grows, finally destroying the cave form, the outlying truncated 'portals' of the cave are known as stacks or columns. The Old Man of Hoy (137 m high), in the Orkney Islands, is a fine example of a stack.

CAVE Limestone formations in the Lehman Caves, Nevada, USA. As well as having such familiar cave formations as stalactites and stalagmites, the Lehman Caves feature some rarities such as shields (pictured here), which consist of two roughly circular plates fastened together, often with graceful stalactites hanging from their lower plate. *Image Bank*

cave animal animal that has adapted to life within caves. The chief characteristics of cave animals are reduced or absent eyes and consequently other well-developed sense organs, such as antennae and feelers, and their lack of colour. Most are predators, owing to the lack of vegetable matter in this dark habitat.

cavefish cave-dwelling fish, which may belong to one of several quite unrelated groups, independently adapted to life in underground waters. Cavefish have in common a tendency to blindness and atrophy of the eye, enhanced touch-sensitive organs in the skin, and loss of pigment.

Cavendish, Henry (1731–1810) English physicist and chemist. He discovered hydrogen (which he called 'inflammable air') in 1766, and determined the compositions of water and of nitric acid. The Cavendish experiment (1798) enabled him to discover the mass and density of the Earth.

Cavendish demonstrated in 1784 that water is produced when hydrogen burns in air, thus proving that water is a compound and not an element. He also worked on the production of heat and determined the freezing points for many materials, including mercury.

Cavendish, Spencer British politician; see Spencer Compton Cavendish ▷Hartington.

cavitation ▷erosion of rocks caused by the forcing of air into cracks. Cavitation results from the pounding of waves on the coast and the swirling of turbulent river currents, and exerts great pressure, eventually causing rocks to break apart.

Cavour, Camillo Benso di, Count (1810–1861) Italian nationalist politician, a leading figure in the Italian ▷*Risorgimento*. As prime minister of Piedmont 1852–59 and 1860–61, he enlisted the support of Britain and France for the concept of a united Italy, achieved in 1861; after expelling the Austrians in 1859, he assisted Garibaldi in liberating southern Italy in 1860.

Cavour was born in Turin, served in the army in early life and entered politics in 1847. From 1848 he sat in the Piedmontese parliament and held cabinet posts 1850–52. As prime minister, he sought to secure French and British sympathy for the cause of Italian unity by sending Piedmontese troops to fight in the Crimean War. In 1858 he had a secret meeting with Napoleon III at Plombières and won French support in the war of 1859 against Austria, which resulted in the union of Lombardy with Piedmont. Then the central Italian states joined the kingdom of Italy, although Savoy and Nice were to be ceded to France. With Cavour's approval Garibaldi overthrew the Neapolitan monarchy, but Cavour occupied part of the Papal States which, with Naples and Sicily, were annexed to Italy, to prevent Garibaldi from marching on Rome.

cavy short-tailed South American rodent, family Caviidae, of which the guinea-pig *Cavia porcellus* is an example. Wild cavies are greyish or brownish with rather coarse hair. They live in small groups in burrows, and have been kept for food since ancient times.

Caxton, William (*c.* 1422–1491) English printer. He learned the art of ▷printing in Cologne, Germany, in 1471 and set up a press in Belgium where he produced the first book printed in English, his own version of a French romance, *Recuyell of the Histories of Troye* (1474). Returning to England in 1476, he established himself in London, where he produced the first book printed in England, *Dictes or Sayengis of the Philosophres* (1477).

Caxton, born in Kent, was apprenticed to a London cloth dealer in 1438, and set up his own business in Bruges 1441–70; he became governor of the English merchants there, negotiating on their behalf with the dukes of Burgundy. In 1471 he went to Cologne, where he learned the art of printing, and then set up his own press in Bruges in partnership with Colard Mansion, a calligrapher. The books from Caxton's press in Westminster included editions of the poets Chaucer, John Gower, and John Lydgate (*c.* 1370–1449). He translated many texts from French and Latin and revised some English ones, such as Malory's *Morte d'Arthur*. Altogether he printed about 100 books.

Cayenne capital and chief port of the overseas *département* of ▷French Guiana in South America; situated on Cayenne Island on the Atlantic coast at the mouth of the River Cayenne; population (1995 est) 51,300. The main occupation is fishing, of which fresh and processed shrimp constitute nearly 75% of total exports by value. Rum, pineapples, hardwoods, and cayenne pepper – a main constituent of hot curries – are also exported. Many imports pass through the port as the country is very much import-dependent.

cayenne pepper (or red pepper) spice produced from the dried fruits of several species of ▷capsicum (especially *Capsicum frutescens*), a tropical American group of plants. Its origins are completely different from black or white pepper, which comes from an East Indian plant (*Piper nigrum*).

cayman another name for ▷caiman.

Cayman Islands British island group in the West Indies; area 260 sq km/100 sq mi; population (1993 est) 31,150 (mostly on Grand Cayman). The Caymans comprise three low-lying islands: Grand Cayman, Cayman Brac, and Little Cayman. The capital is ▷George Town (on Grand Cayman). The islands export seawhip coral (a source of prostaglandins), shrimps, honey, and jewellery.

The Cayman Islands were first reached by Christopher Columbus in 1503; they were acquired by Britain following the Treaty of Madrid in 1670, and became a dependency of Jamaica in 1863. In 1959 the islands became a separate crown colony, although the inhabitants chose to remain British. From that date, changes in legislation attracted foreign banks and the Caymans are now an international financial centre and tax haven as well as a tourist resort, with emphasis on scuba diving.

The Islands are governed by a governor, executive council, and legislative assembly. English is spoken; the currency is the Cayman Island dollar.

Related Web site: Cayman Islands http://www.umsl.edu/services/govdocs/wofact96/56.htm

CB abbreviation for ▷citizens' band (radio).

CD abbreviation for ▷compact disc; **Corps Diplomatique** (French 'Diplomatic Corps'); **certificate of deposit**.

CD-ROM (acronym for compact-disc read-only memory) computer storage device developed from the technology of the audio ▷compact disc. It consists of a plastic-coated metal disk, on which binary digital information is etched in the form of microscopic pits. This can then be read optically by passing a laser beam over the disk. CD-ROMs typically hold over 600 ▷megabytes of data, and are used in distributing large amounts of text, graphics, audio, and video, such as encyclopedias, catalogues, technical manuals, and games.

Standard CD-ROMs cannot have information written onto them by computer, but must be manufactured from a master, although recordable CDs, called CD-R disks, have been developed for use as computer disks. A compact disc, CD-RW, that can be overwritten repeatedly by a computer has also been developed. The compact disc, with its enormous storage capability, may eventually replace the magnetic disk as the most common form of backing store for computers.

The technology is being developed rapidly: a standard CD-ROM disk spins at between 240–1170 rpm, but faster disks have been introduced which speed up data retrieval to many times the standard speed. Research is being conducted into high-density CDs capable of storing many ▷gigabytes of data, made possible by using multiple layers on the surface of the disk, and by using double-sided disks. The first commercial examples of this research include DVD players and DVD-ROM computer disks launched in 1997.

PhotoCD, developed by Kodak and released in 1992, transfers ordinary still photographs onto CD-ROM disks.

Ceauşescu, Nicolae (1918–1989) Romanian politician, leader of the Romanian Communist Party (RCP), in power from 1965 to 1989. He pursued a policy line independent of and critical of the USSR. He appointed family members, including his wife Elena Ceauşescu (1919–1989), to senior state and party posts, and governed in an increasingly repressive manner, zealously implementing schemes that impoverished the nation. The Ceauşescus were overthrown in a bloody revolutionary coup in December 1989 and executed on Christmas Day that year.

Ceauşescu joined the underground RCP in 1933 and was imprisoned for antifascist activities 1936–38 and 1940–44. After World War II he was elected to the Grand National Assembly and was soon given ministerial posts. He was inducted into the party secretariat and Politburo in 1954–55. In 1965 he became leader of the RCP and from 1967 chair of the state council. He was elected president in 1974. As revolutionary changes rocked Eastern Europe in 1989, protests in Romania escalated until the Ceauşescu regime was toppled. After his execution, the full extent of his repressive rule and personal extravagance became public.

Cebu chief city and port of the island of Cebu in the Philippines; population (1995 est) 681,000; area of the island 5,086 sq km/1,964 sq mi. The first Spanish settlement in the Philippines, Cebu was founded as San Miguel in 1565 and became the capital of the Spanish Philippines. Industries include food processing and textiles, and there is a considerable trade in copra and tobacco.

Cecil, Robert (1563–1612) 1st Earl of Salisbury. Secretary of state to Elizabeth I of England, succeeding his father, Lord Burghley; he was afterwards chief minister to James I (James VI of Scotland) whose accession to the English throne he secured. He discovered the ▷Gunpowder Plot, the conspiracy to blow up the king and Parliament in 1605. James I created him Earl of Salisbury in 1605. He was knighted in 1591, and made a baron in 1603 and viscount in 1604.

Cecil, William see ▷Burghley, William Cecil, 1st Baron Burghley.

cedar any of an Old World group of coniferous trees belonging to the pine family. The cedar of Lebanon (*Cedrus libani*) grows to great height and age in the mountains of Syria and Asia Minor. Of the historic forests on Mount Lebanon itself, only a few groups of trees remain. (Genus *Cedrus*, family Pinaceae.)

Ceefax ('see facts') one of Britain's two ▷teletext systems (the other is Teletext), or 'magazines of the air', developed by the BBC and first broadcast on television in 1973.

celandine either of two plants belonging to different families, the only similarity being their bright yellow flowers. The **greater celandine** (*Chelidonium majus*) belongs to the poppy family and is common in hedgerows. The **lesser celandine** (*Ranunculus ficaria*) is a member of the buttercup family and is a common wayside and meadow plant in Europe.

Related Web site: Celandine, Greater http://www.botanical.com/botanical/mgmh/c/celgre43.html

Celebes English name for ▷Sulawesi, an island of Indonesia.

celery Old World plant belonging to the carrot family. It grows wild in ditches and salt marshes and has a coarse texture and sharp taste. Cultivated varieties of celery are grown under cover to make the edible stalks less bitter. (*Apium graveolens*, family Umbelliferae.)

celesta musical instrument, a keyboard ▷glockenspiel producing high-pitched sounds of glistening purity. It was invented by Auguste Mustel of Paris in 1886 and first used to effect by Tchaikovsky in *The Nutcracker* ballet (1890).

celestial mechanics branch of astronomy that deals with the calculation of the orbits of celestial bodies, their gravitational attractions (such as those that produce the Earth's tides), and also the orbits of artificial satellites and space probes. It is based on the laws of motion and gravity laid down by 17th-century English physicist and mathematician Isaac ▷Newton.

celestial sphere imaginary sphere surrounding the Earth, on which the celestial bodies seem to lie. The positions of bodies such as stars, planets, and galaxies are specified by their coordinates on

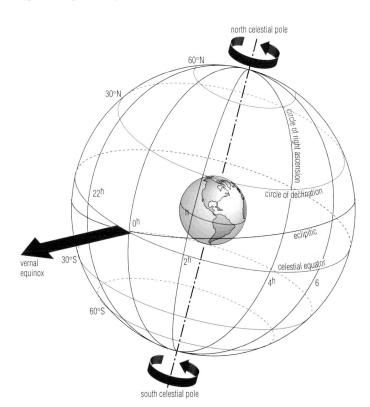

CELESTIAL SPHERE The main features of the celestial sphere. Declination runs from 0° at the celestial equator to 90° at the celestial poles. Right ascension is measured in hours eastwards from the vernal equinox, one hour corresponding to 15° of longitude.

CELL A typical plant and animal cell. Plant and animal cells share many structures, such as ribosomes, mitochondria, and chromosomes, but they also have notable differences: plant cells have chloroplasts, a large vacuole, and a cellulose cell wall. Animal cells do not have a rigid cell wall but have an outside cell membrane only.

the celestial sphere. The equivalents of latitude and longitude on the celestial sphere are called declination and right ascension (which is measured in hours from 0 to 24). The **celestial poles** lie directly above the Earth's poles, and the **celestial equator** lies over the Earth's Equator. The celestial sphere appears to rotate once around the Earth each day, actually a result of the rotation of the Earth on its axis.

cell in biology, the basic structural unit of life. It is the smallest unit capable of independent existence which can reproduce itself exactly. All living organisms – with the exception of ▷viruses – are composed of one or more cells. Single cell organisms such as bacteria, protozoa, and other micro-organisms are termed **unicellular**, while plants and animals which contain many cells are termed **multicellular** organisms. Highly complex organisms such as human beings consist of billions of cells, all of which are adapted to carry out specific functions – for instance, groups of these specialized cells are organized into tissues and organs. Although these cells may differ widely in size, appearance, and function, their essential features are similar.

Cells divide by ▷mitosis, or by ▷meiosis when ▷gametes are being formed.

The cytoplasm of all cells contains ▷ribosomes, which carry out protein synthesis, and ▷DNA, the coded instructions for the behaviour and reproduction of the cell and the chemical machinery for the translation of these instructions into the manufacture of proteins. Viruses lack this translation machinery and so have to parasitize cells in order to reproduce themselves.

Eukaryote cells In ▷eukaryote cells, found in protozoa, fungi, and higher animals and plants, DNA is organized into ▷chromosomes and is contained within a nucleus. Each eukaryote has a surrounding membrane, which is a thin layer of protein and fat that restricts the flow of substances in and out of the cell and encloses the ▷cytoplasm, a jellylike material containing the ▷nucleus and other structures (organelles) such as ▷mitochondria. The nuclei of some cells contain a dense spherical structure called the ▷nucleolus, which contains ribonucleic acid (▷RNA) for the synthesis of ribosomes. The only cells of the human body which have no nucleus are the red blood cells.

In general, plant cells differ from animal cells in that the membrane is surrounded by a ▷cell wall made of cellulose. They also have larger ▷vacuoles (fluid-filled pouches), and contain ▷chloroplasts that convert light energy to chemical energy for the synthesis of glucose.

Prokaryote cells In ▷prokaryote cells, found in bacteria and cyanobacteria, the DNA forms a simple loop and there is no nucleus. The prokaryotic cell also lacks organelles such as mitochondria, ▷chloroplasts, ▷endoplasmic reticulum, ▷Golgi apparatus, and ▷centrioles, which perform specialized tasks in eukaryotic cells.

cell, electrical (or **voltaic cell** or **galvanic cell**) device in which chemical energy is converted into electrical energy; the popular name is ▷'battery', but this strictly refers to a collection of cells in one unit. The reactive chemicals of a **primary cell** cannot be replenished, whereas **secondary cells** – such as storage batteries – are rechargeable: their chemical reactions can be reversed and the original condition restored by applying an electric current. It is dangerous to attempt to recharge a primary cell.

Each cell contains two conducting ▷electrodes immersed in an ▷electrolyte, in a container. A spontaneous chemical reaction within the cell generates a negative charge (excess of electrons) on one electrode, and a positive charge (deficiency of electrons) on the other. The accumulation of these equal but opposite charges prevents the reaction from continuing unless an outer connection (external circuit) is made between the electrodes allowing the charges to dissipate. When this occurs, electrons escape from the cell's negative terminal and are replaced at the positive, causing a current to flow. After prolonged use, the cell will become flat (ceases to supply current). The first cell was made by Italian physicist Alessandro Volta in 1800. Types of primary cells include the Daniell, Lalande, Leclanché, and so-called 'dry' cells; secondary cells include the Planté, Faure, and Edison. Newer types include the Mallory (mercury depolarizer), which has a very stable discharge curve and can be made in very small units (for example, for hearing aids), and the Venner accumulator, which can be made substantially solid for some purposes. Rechargeable nickel–cadmium dry cells are available for household use.

cell, electrolytic device to which electrical energy is applied in order to bring about a chemical reaction; see ▷electrolysis.

Cellini, Benvenuto (1500–1571) Italian Mannerist sculptor and goldsmith. Among his works are a graceful bronze *Perseus* (1545–54; Loggia dei Lanzi, Florence) and a gold salt cellar made for Francis I of France (1540–43; Kunsthistorisches Museum, Vienna), topped by nude reclining figures. He wrote a frank autobiography (begun in 1558), which gives a vivid picture both of him and his age.

Cellini was born in Florence and apprenticed to a goldsmith. In 1519 he went to Rome, later worked for the papal mint, and was once imprisoned on a charge of having embezzled pontifical jewels.

BENVENUTO CELLINI A bronze sculpture of Ganymede by Italian Mannerist sculptor and goldsmith Benvenuto Cellini. *The Art Archive/Museo del Bargello Florence/Dagli Orti*

He worked for some time in France at the court of Francis I, but finally returned to Florence in 1545.

Related Web site: Cellini, Benvenuto http://sunserv.kfki.hu/~arthp/html/c/cellini/index.html

cell membrane (or **plasma membrane**) thin layer of protein and fat surrounding cells, it controls substances passing between the cytoplasm and the intercellular space. The cell membrane is semipermeable, allowing some substances to pass through and some not.

Generally, small molecules such as water, glucose, and amino acids can penetrate the membrane, while large molecules, such as starch, cannot. Membranes also play a part in active transport, hormonal response, and cell metabolism.

cello common abbreviation for **violoncello**, bass member of the ▷violin family and lowest-pitched member of the string quartet. Its four strings are tuned C2, G2, D3, and A4. In the 17th and 18th centuries a version was made with a fifth string tuned E4. Its solo potential was recognized by Johann Sebastian Bach, and a concerto repertoire extends from Haydn (who also gave the cello a leading role in his string quartets) and Boccherini to Dvořák, Elgar, Britten, Ligeti, and Lukas Foss. The *Bachianas Brasilieras 1* by Villa-Lobos is scored for eight cellos, and Boulez's *Messagesquisse* (1977) for seven cellos.

cellophane transparent wrapping film made from wood ▷cellulose, widely used for packaging, first produced by Swiss chemist Jacques Edwin Brandenberger in 1908.

cell sap dilute fluid found in the large central vacuole of many plant cells. It is made up of water, amino acids, glucose, and salts. The sap has many functions, including storage of useful materials, and provides mechanical support for non-woody plants.

cellular phone (or **cellphone**) mobile radio telephone, one of a network connected to the telephone system by a computer-controlled communication system. Service areas are divided into small 'cells', about 5 km/3 mi across, each with a separate low-power transmitter.

cellulite fatty compound alleged by some dietitians to be produced in the body by liver disorder and to cause lumpy deposits on the hips and thighs. Medical opinion generally denies its existence, attributing the lumpy appearance to a type of subcutaneous fat deposit.

celluloid transparent or translucent, highly flammable, plastic material (a thermoplastic) made from cellulose nitrate and camphor. It was once used for toilet articles, novelties, and photographic film, but has now been replaced by the nonflammable substance ▷cellulose acetate.

cellulose complex ▷carbohydrate composed of long chains of glucose units, joined by chemical bonds called glycosidic links. It is the principal constituent of the cell wall of higher plants, and a vital ingredient in the diet of many ▷herbivores. Molecules of cellulose are organized into long, unbranched microfibrils that give support to the cell wall. No mammal produces the enzyme cellulase, necessary for digesting cellulose; mammals such as rabbits and cows are only able to digest grass because the bacteria present in their gut can manufacture it.

Cellulose is the most abundant substance found in the plant kingdom. It has numerous uses in industry: in rope-making; as a source of textiles (linen, cotton, viscose, and acetate) and plastics (cellophane and celluloid); in the manufacture of nondrip paint; and in such foods as whipped dessert toppings.

Japanese chemists produced the first synthetic cellulose in 1996 and the gene for the plant enzyme that makes cellulose was identified by Australian biologists in 1998.

cellulose nitrate (or **nitrocellulose**) series of esters of cellulose with up to three nitrate (NO_3) groups per monosaccharide unit. It is made by the action of concentrated nitric acid on cellulose (for example, cotton waste) in the presence of concentrated sulphuric acid. Fully nitrated cellulose (gun cotton) is explosive, but esters with fewer nitrate groups were once used in making lacquers, rayon, and plastics, such as coloured and photographic film, until replaced by the nonflammable cellulose acetate. ▷Celluloid is a form of cellulose nitrate.

cell wall in plants, the tough outer surface of the cell. It is constructed from a mesh of ▷cellulose and is very strong and relatively inelastic. Most living cells are turgid (swollen with water) and develop an internal hydrostatic pressure (wall pressure) that acts against the cellulose wall. The result of this turgor pressure is to give the cell, and therefore the plant, rigidity. Plants that are not woody are particularly reliant on this form of support.

Celsius scale of temperature, previously called centigrade, in which the range from freezing to boiling of water is divided into 100 degrees, freezing point being 0 degrees and boiling point 100 degrees.

The degree centigrade (°C) was officially renamed Celsius in 1948 to avoid confusion with the angular measure known as the centigrade (one hundredth of a grade). The Celsius scale is named after the Swedish astronomer Anders Celsius (1701–1744), who devised it in 1742 but in reverse (freezing point was 100°; boiling point 0°).

Celt (Greek *Keltoi*) Indo-European people that originated in Alpine Europe and spread to the Iberian peninsula and beyond. They were ironworkers and farmers. In the 1st century BC they were defeated by the Roman Empire and by Germanic tribes and confined largely to Britain, Ireland, and northern France.

The Celts' first known territory was in central Europe about 1200 BC, in the basin of the upper Danube, the Alps, and parts of France and southern Germany. In the 6th century BC they spread into Spain and Portugal. Over the next 300 years, they also spread into the British Isles (see ▷Britain, ancient), northern Italy (sacking Rome in 390 BC), Greece, the Balkans, and parts of Asia Minor, although they never established a united empire.

Between the Bronze and Iron Ages, in the 9th–5th centuries BC, they developed a transitional culture (named the **Hallstatt** culture after its archaeological site southwest of Salzburg, Austria). They farmed, raised cattle, and were pioneers of ironworking, reaching their peak in the period from the 5th century BC to the Roman conquest (the **La Tène** culture). They had pronounced musical, literary, and poetical tastes, and were distinguished for their dramatic talents. Their Druids, or priests, performed ritual-magic ceremonies which survived in the forms of ▷ordeal, augury, and exorcism. Celtic languages survive in Ireland, Wales, Scotland, the Isle of Man, and Brittany, and have been revived in Cornwall.

CELLULOSE A cellulose processing plant in Spain. Viscose, for instance, is made by treating cellulose with sodium hydroxide. *Image Bank*

Celtic art art of the Celtic peoples of Western Europe, emerging about 500 BC, probably on the Rhine. It spread to most parts of Europe, but after the 1st century BC flourished only in Britain and Ireland, its influence being felt well into the 10th century AD. Pottery, woodwork, jewellery, and weapons are among its finest products, with manuscript illumination and stone crosses featuring in late Celtic art. Typically, Celtic art is richly decorated with flowing curves which, though based on animal and plant motifs, often form semi-abstract designs. See also Celtic Art Focus Feature on pp. 176–177.

Related Web site: Ceolas Celtic Music Archive http://www.ceolas.org/ceolas.html

Celtic languages branch of the Indo-European family, divided into two groups: the **Brythonic** or **P-Celtic** (▷Welsh language, Cornish, Breton, and Gaulish) and the **Goidelic** or **Q-Celtic** (Irish, Scottish, and Manx ▷Gaelic languages). Celtic languages once stretched from the Black Sea to Britain, but have been in decline for centuries, limited to the so-called 'Celtic fringe' of western Europe.

Celtic League nationalist organization based in Ireland, aiming at an independent Celtic federation. It was founded in 1961 with representatives from Alba (Scotland), Breizh (Brittany), Eire, Kernow (Cornwall), Cymru (Wales), and Ellan Vannin (Isle of Man).

Celtic Sea sea area bounded by Wales, Ireland, and southwest England; the name is commonly used by workers in the oil industry to avoid nationalist significance. The Celtic Sea is separated from the Irish Sea by St George's Channel.

cement any bonding agent used to unite particles in a single mass or to cause one surface to adhere to another. **Portland cement** is a powder which when mixed with water and sand or gravel turns into mortar or concrete.

In geology, cement refers to a chemically precipitated material such as carbonate that occupies the interstices of clastic rocks.

cenotaph (Greek 'empty tomb') monument to commemorate a person or persons not actually buried at the site, as in the Whitehall Cenotaph, London, designed by Edwin Lutyens to commemorate the dead of both world wars.

Cenozoic Era (or **Caenozoic**) era of geological time that began 65 million years ago and continues to the present day. It is divided into the Tertiary and Quaternary periods. The Cenozoic marks the emergence of mammals as a dominant group, and the rearrangement of continental masses towards their present positions.

censor in ancient Rome, either of two senior magistrates, high officials elected every five years to hold office for 18 months. They were responsible for regulating public morality, carrying out a census of the citizens, and revising the senatorial list. The Roman censorship was instituted in 443 BC, and was last held as an independent office in 22 BC. Thereafter, the various censorial powers came to be exercised by the emperor.

censorship, film control of the content and presentation of films. Film censorship dates back almost as far as the cinema. In Britain, censorship was established in 1912, in the USA in 1922. In some countries, self-regulation of the industry has not been regarded as sufficient; in the USSR, for example, state censorship forbade the treatment of certain issues.

Censorship in Britain is the responsibility of the British Board of Film Classification (formerly the British Board of Film Censors), run by the film industry, which gives each film a rating. There is a similar body, popularly called the Hays Office (after its first president, 1922–45, Will H Hays), in the USA.

census official count of the population of a country, originally for military call-up and taxation, later for assessment of social trends as other information regarding age, sex, and occupation of each individual was included. They may become unnecessary as computerized databanks are developed. The data collected are used by government departments in planning for the future in such areas as health, education, transport, and housing.

centaur in Greek mythology, a creature half human and half horse, wild and lawless. Chiron, the mentor of the hero Heracles and tutor of the god of medicine Asclepius, was an exception. Their home was said to be on Mount Pelion, Thessaly.

Centaurus large, bright constellation of the southern hemisphere, represented as a centaur. Its brightest star, ▷Rigil Kent, is a triple star, and contains the closest star to the Sun, Proxima Centauri, which is only 4.2 light years away from the Sun, and 0.1 light years closer than its companions, Alpha Centauri A and B. Omega Centauri, which is just visible to the naked eye as a hazy patch, is the largest and brightest ▷globular cluster of stars in the sky, 16,000 light years away from the Sun.

centigrade former name for the ▷Celsius temperature scale.

CENTIPEDE A giant centipede of the species *Scolopendra*, active at night in the forests of Madagascar. *Premaphotos Wildlife*

centipede jointed-legged animal of the group Chilopoda, members of which have a distinct head and a single pair of long antennae. Their bodies are composed of segments (which may number nearly 200), each of similar form and bearing a single pair of legs. Most are small, but the tropical *Scolopendra gigantea* may reach 30 cm/1 ft in length. **Millipedes**, class Diplopoda, have fewer segments (up to 100), but have two pairs of legs on each.

Nocturnal, frequently blind, and all carnivorous, centipedes live in moist, dark places, and protect themselves by a poisonous secretion. They have a pair of poison claws, and strong jaws with poison fangs. The bite of some tropical species is dangerous to humans. Several species live in Britain, *Lithobius forficatus* being the most common.

Central African Republic see country box.

Central America the part of the Americas that links Mexico with the Isthmus of Panama, comprising ▷Belize and the republics of ▷Costa Rica, ▷El Salvador, ▷Guatemala, ▷Honduras, ▷Nicaragua, and ▷Panama.

It is also an isthmus, crossed by mountains that form part of t he Cordilleras, rising to a maximum height of 4,220 m/13,845 ft. There are numerous active volcanoes. The principal river is the Usumacinta, which rises in Guatemala and flows north for 965 km/600 mi, crossing Mexico, and empties into the Bay of Campeche in the Gulf of Mexico. Central America has an area of about 523,000 sq km/200,000 sq mi, and a population (2001 est) of 28,768,000, comprising mostly Indians or mestizos (of mixed white–Indian ancestry), with the exception of Costa Rica, which has a predominantly white population. Tropical agricultural products, raw materials, and other basic commodities are exported.

Much of Central America formed part of the ▷Maya civilization. Christopher Columbus first reached the isthmus in 1502, landing in Panama, where he founded the town of Santa María de Belén. Spanish settlers married indigenous women, and the area remained outside mainstream Spanish Empire history. When the Spanish Empire collapsed in the early 1800s, the area formed the Central American Federation, with a constitution based on that of the USA. The federation disintegrated in 1840.

Completion of the Panama Canal in 1914 enhanced the region's position as a strategic international crossroads. Demand for cash crops (bananas, coffee, cotton), especially from the USA, created a strong landowning class controlling a serf-like peasantry by military means. There has been US military intervention in the area, for example, in Nicaragua, where the dynasty of General Anastasio Somoza was founded. US President Carter reversed support for such regimes, but in the 1980s, the Reagan and Bush administrations again favoured military and financial aid to right-wing political groups, including the ▷Contras in Nicaragua. Continuing US interest was underscored by its invasion of Panama in December 1989. In 1987 President Oscar Arias Sánchez of Costa Rica formulated the Central American Peace Plan, with a view to reduce civil unrest in individual countries; it was signed by the presidents of Nicaragua, Honduras, El Salvador, Guatemala, and Costa Rica.

Central American Common Market (CACM; Mercado Común Centroamericana, MCCA) economic alliance established in 1961 by El Salvador, Guatemala, Honduras (seceded in 1970), and Nicaragua; Costa Rica joined in 1962. Formed to encourage economic development and cooperation between the smaller Central American nations and to attract industrial capital, CACM

failed to live up to early expectations: nationalist interests remained strong and by the mid-1980s political instability in the region and border conflicts between members were hindering its activities. Its offices are in Guatemala City, Guatemala.

Central Asian Republics geographical region covering the territory of five nation-states: ▷Kazakhstan, ▷Kyrgyzstan, ▷Tajikistan, ▷Turkmenistan, and ▷Uzbekistan. These republics were part of the Soviet Union before gaining their independence in 1991. Central Asia is bordered on the north by the Russian Federation, on the south by Iran and Afghanistan, and on the east by the Chinese region of Xinjiang Uygur. The western boundary of Central Asia is marked by the Caspian Sea. The topography of the region is characterized by several major mountain ranges, including the ▷Tien Shan range and the ▷Pamirs, and extensive deserts, principally the ▷Kara-Kum and ▷Kyzyl-Kum. The people of Central Asia are predominantly Muslim.

Central Command military strike force consisting of units from the US army, navy, and air force, which operates in the Middle East and North Africa. Its headquarters are in Fort McDill, Florida. It was established in 1979, following the Iranian hostage crisis and the Soviet invasion of Afghanistan, and was known as the Rapid Deployment Force until 1983. It commanded coalition forces in the Gulf War in 1991.

Central Criminal Court in the UK, crown court in the City of London, able to try all treasons and serious offences committed in the City or Greater London. First established in 1834, it is popularly known as the **Old Bailey** after part of the medieval defences of London; the present building is on the site of Newgate Prison.

central dogma in genetics and evolution, the fundamental belief that ▷genes can affect the nature of the physical body, but that changes in the body (acquired character, for example, through use or accident) cannot be translated into changes in the genes.

central heating system of heating from a central source, typically of a house, larger building, or group of buildings, as opposed to heating each room individually. Steam heat and hot-water heat are the most common systems in use. Water is heated in a furnace burning oil, gas, or solid fuel, and, as steam or hot water, is then pumped through radiators in each room. The level of temperature can be selected by adjusting a ▷thermostat on the burner or in a room.

Central Intelligence Agency (CIA) US intelligence organization established in 1947. It has actively intervened overseas, generally to undermine left-wing regimes or to protect US financial interests; for example, in the Democratic Republic of Congo (formerly Zaire) and Nicaragua. From 1980 all covert activity by the CIA had by law to be reported to Congress, preferably beforehand, and to be authorized by the president. In 1994 the CIA's estimated budget was around $3.1 billion. John M Deutsch became CIA director in 1995 after the Agency's standing was diminished by a scandal involving Aldrich Arnes, a CIA agent who had been a longtime mole for the KGB. George Tenate became director in 1997.

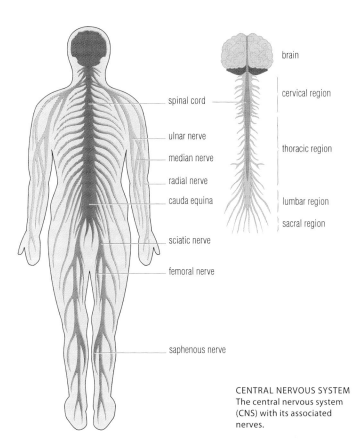

CENTRAL NERVOUS SYSTEM The central nervous system (CNS) with its associated nerves.

brain
spinal cord
cervical region
ulnar nerve
median nerve
thoracic region
radial nerve
cauda equina
lumbar region
sacral region
sciatic nerve
femoral nerve
saphenous nerve

Central Lowlands one of the three geographical divisions of Scotland, being the fertile and densely populated plain that lies between two geological fault lines, which run nearly parallel northeast–southwest across Scotland from Stonehaven to Dumbarton and from Dunbar to Girvan.

central nervous system (CNS) the brain and spinal cord, as distinct from other components of the ▷nervous system. The CNS integrates all nervous function.

In invertebrates it consists of a paired ventral nerve cord with concentrations of nerve-cell bodies, known as ▷ganglia in each segment, and a small brain in the head. Some simple invertebrates, such as sponges and jellyfishes, have no CNS but a simple network of nerve cells called a **nerve net**.

central planning alternative name for ▷command economy.

Central Powers originally the signatories of the ▷Triple Alliance of 1882: Germany, Austria-Hungary, and Italy; the name derived from the geographical position of the Germans and Austrians in Central Europe. During World War I, Italy remained neutral before joining the ▷Allies.

central processing unit (CPU) main component of a computer, the part that executes individual program instructions and controls the operation of other parts. It is sometimes called the central processor or, when contained on a single integrated circuit, a microprocessor.

The CPU has three main components: the **arithmetic and logic unit** (ALU), where all calculations and logical operations are carried out; a **control unit**, which decodes, synchronizes, and executes program instructions; and the **immediate access memory**, which stores the data and programs on which the computer is currently working. All these components contain ▷registers, which are memory locations reserved for specific purposes.

Central Treaty Organization (CENTO) military alliance that replaced the Baghdad Pact in 1959; it collapsed when the withdrawal of Iran, Pakistan, and Turkey in 1979 left the UK as the only member.

Centre region of north-central France; area 39,150 sq km/15,116 sq mi; population (1990) 2,371,000. Centre includes the *départements* of Cher, Eure-et-Loir, Indre, Indre-et-Loire, Loire-et-Cher, and Loiret. The administrative centre is ▷Orléans.

centre of mass point in or near an object at which the whole mass of the object may be considered to be concentrated. A symmetrical homogeneous object such as a sphere or cube has its centre of mass at its geometrical centre; a hollow object (such as a cup) may have its centre of mass in space inside the hollow.

Celtic Art

by Martin Henig

The *Celtae* or *Galli* were the most numerous of the peoples of prehistoric Europe, united in speaking related languages of which Welsh and Gaelic are surviving examples. Power was vested in the chieftains and a priestly caste (druids). As for the populace, most were farmers but some were skilled in metalworking. The Celts were a warlike people. The Greek geographer Strabo described them as 'mad keen on war, full of spirit, and quick to begin a fight'. They spread westwards in the 5th and 4th centuries BC into France (Gaul), Spain, and Britain, and even invaded Italy, Greece, and Asia Minor. Although ultimately subdued by the Greeks of Pergamum in the east and by the Romans in most other places, they left a remarkable artistic legacy that continues to inspire artists and writers to this day.

Celtic design and materials

Early Celtic designs were simple and linear, but around the beginning of the 5th century BC they developed into a striking abstract art of great complexity, based on an interplay of curving lines. This style, named after the site of La Tène, on Lake Neûchatel, Switzerland, drew on classical artistic prototypes such as friezes of acanthus leaves, palmettes, and stylized representations of people and animals, although Celtic artists were more interested in pattern than in representational art.

Although the Celts in the Rhineland and southern Germany produced some sculpture in stone, and pottery decorated with Celtic designs is widespread, most Celtic art is in metal. Celtic smiths were highly skilled in working their materials, notably bronze and gold, employing casting, *repoussé* (hammering sheet bronze from behind to create relief designs), and engraving. In Britain, the Celts found valuable sources of copper, lead, silver, and tin which they could mine and trade with mainland Europe for luxury goods such as gold, pottery, and wine.

Perhaps the most beautiful examples of Celtic design from before the Roman conquest are the backs of mirrors, engraved with a linear design and cross-hatched infilling, dating from the second half of the 1st century BC and the beginning of the 1st century AD. These have been found only in Britain. One of the finest comes from a grave, probably that of a woman, at Birdlip, Gloucestershire, and is displayed in Gloucester City Museum. There are other especially noteworthy examples from Holcombe in Devon, and Desborough, Northamptonshire (both displayed in the British Museum, London).

warriors and nobles

The Celtic warrior took care to look as intimidating and splendid as possible. He painted his body with blue dye made from woad plants and equipped himself with finely ornamented weapons and armour. Bronze sword-scabbards such as the one found in the River Thames at Little Wittenham, Oxfordshire, England (on display in the Ashmolean Museum, Oxford) or shields like the one found further down the Thames at Battersea, London (in the British Museum) would have looked truly magnificent, glittering in the sunlight. Horse-trappings and chariot-fittings were similarly highly decorated. In Britain, the majority of such objects have been found in rivers or peat bogs, into which they were probably thrown as lavish offerings to the gods.

Status was immensely important to the Celts, and men and women of rank wore ornamented gold neck

AN IRISH HIGH CROSS seen at dusk. Irish high crosses were the main Irish sculptural form from the 8th to 12th centuries and are widely considered to be among the most significant pieces of monumental art produced in medieval Europe. *Pascal Boret © Helicon*

torques. Those from Waldalgesheim near Mainz, Germany (displayed in the Romanisches Zentralmuseum, Mainz) date from the 4th century AD and are almost completely covered with decoration. Other examples, from what appears to be a deposit dedicated to the gods at Snettisham, Norfolk, England (in the British Museum) include many made of twisted gold wire, ornamented only at the terminals. The Roman historian Dio Cassius records that Boudicca, queen of the British tribe of the Iceni, wore such a torque in AD 60 when rousing her people in revolt against Roman rule.

feasting

Apart from fighting, feasting seems to have been the Celts' favourite activity. Sometimes Greek, Etruscan, or Roman flagons arrived in the Celtic world along with imported *amphorae* of wine. Frequently, however, such vessels were copied and adapted by Celtic artists into their own distinctive style. A pair of flagons from the 5th or 4th century BC found in Basse Yutz, Moselle, France (now in the British Museum) are based on Etruscan designs but decorated in a far richer style. Each handle is in the form of a stylized wolf, whose two cubs crouch on the rim watching a little duck on the spout; these are far from the realistic creatures of classical art, and all their features are rendered as patterned shapes. Pieces of coral set around the bases and also in the spout add to the strange beauty of the flagons.

Wine buckets were also decorated, such as those dating from perhaps the 1st century BC found at Marlborough, Wiltshire, England (in Devizes Museum, Wiltshire) and at Aylesford, Kent, England (in the British Museum). The Marlborough bucket's body is covered in sheet bronze ornamented with *repoussé* masks, dancers wearing animal skins, horses, and panels of pattern; the Aylesford example is much simpler but the escutcheons (pieces of protective metal) into which the handle fits are in the form of helmeted heads. Such objects generally come from graves, presumably placed there to ensure that their owners could enjoy the pleasures of the feast in the afterlife.

Celtic art over time

During the Roman period (in Britain, approximately AD 43–400), Celtic art did not disappear. A rich array of horse-trappings, belt-fittings, and brooches richly ornamented in enamel and embellished with curvilinear designs were used by the inhabitants of the western part of the Empire. The Celtic style also had a strong influence on the bronze smiths and sculptors working in the representational Roman manner in Gaul and Britain. This is shown, for example, in the 1st century pedimental sculpture that adorns the upper part of the front of the temple of Sulis Minerva in Bath, England. This sculpture shows the form of a Medusa mask belonging to the goddess Minerva combined with the head of Neptune in a highly inventive, abstract manner (in

A CELTIC BOWL A detail of the fertility god Cernunnos holding two figures. The Gundestrup Cauldron, a Celtic bowl of silver-plated copper which may date from the 1st century AD, is in the Danish National Museum, Copenhagen.
© *The Art Archive/Danish National Museum/Dagli Orti*

the Roman Baths Museum, Bath). A small bronze plaque from Lavington, Wiltshire, depicting Minerva herself (in the Devizes Museum), shows the goddess clad in draperies arranged in an astonishingly abstract manner.

Following the end of Roman political control in Britain, there was a revival of Celtic art, exemplified in jewellery (including so-called 'hand-pins' and brooches) and above all shown in the great hanging-bowls of the 6th and 7th centuries such as those from Lowbury Hill, Oxfordshire and Sutton Hoo, Suffolk (in the British Museum). These are typically decorated with enamelled bosses embellished with S-scrolls. The sites at which they were found suggest they were much in demand at the courts of Anglo-Saxon chieftains.

Celtic art, Ireland, and the Church

Celtic art remained largely free from direct Roman influence in Ireland. An early example of Hiberno-Celtic (Irish Celtic) art is the so-called 'Petrie crown' (in the National Museum of Ireland, Dublin), possibly from the 2nd century AD, which has horns and discs ornamented with thin, flowing trumpet curves and stylized heads of birds. After the introduction of Christianity to Ireland by St Patrick and others in the 5th century, Celtic art was employed in the service of the church, producing the most splendid metalwork of the period. It reached its peak in the late 8th or early 9th century with the superb chalice and paten (a plate or cover for the chalice) from Derrynaflan, County Tipperary, and

the Ardagh chalice, County Limerick (both in the National Museum of Ireland, Dublin), which are made of silver and embellished with gold, amber, and enamels.

The influence of Celtic art was not restricted to metalwork, however. Although they incorporate classical and Anglo-Saxon features, the finest and most accomplished examples of Celtic mastery of colour and pattern are the great illuminated Gospels from Lindisfarne, Northumberland, England (British Library), dating from the end of the 7th century, and the *Book of Kells* (Trinity College, Dublin) about a century later. These manuscripts are truly examples of what the 12th-century traveller, Gerald of Wales, called the 'the work of angels'.

CELTIC TORQUE Gold and enamel torque with horse-head decoration from Porogi Jampol Vinnica (or Vinnitsa), Ukraine, 1st century AD (Ethnographic Museum, Vinnica, Ukraine). Metal torques were a characteristic ornament of the Celts, who wore them around their necks and arms. Gold torques reflected the wearer's high status. Torques vary in design – some are completely covered in decoration while others, such as this example, are made of twisted gold wire, ornamented only at the terminals.
© *The Art Archive/Tate Gallery London*

centrifugal force in physics, apparent force arising for an observer moving with a rotating system. For an object of mass m moving with a velocity v in a circle of radius r, the centrifugal force F equals mv^2/r (outward).

centrifuge apparatus that rotates containers at high speeds, creating centrifugal forces. One use is for separating mixtures of substances of different densities.

centripetal force force that acts radially inward on an object moving in a curved path. For example, with a weight whirled in a circle at the end of a length of string, the centripetal force is the tension in the string. For an object of mass m moving with a velocity v in a circle of radius r, the centripetal force F equals mv^2/r (inward). The reaction to this force is the ▷centrifugal force.

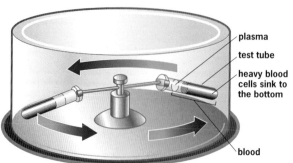

CENTRIFUGE Centrifuge being used to separate the blood plasma from blood cells. As the test tubes spin the heavier blood cells sink to the bottom. Centrifuges are useful in laboratories and on an industrial scale for separating solids in suspension in liquids.

Central African Republic

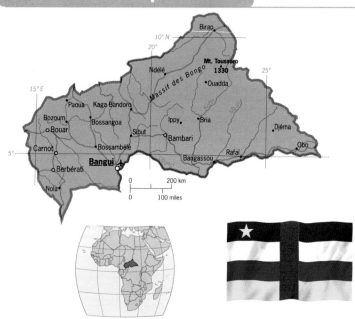

Central African Republic formerly Ubangi-Shari (until 1958), Central African Empire (1976–79) landlocked country in Central Africa, bordered northeast and east by Sudan, south by the Democratic Republic of Congo (formerly Zaire) and the Republic of the Congo, west by Cameroon, and northwest by Chad.

NATIONAL NAME *République Centrafricaine/Central African Republic*
AREA 622,436 sq km/240,322 sq mi
CAPITAL Bangui
MAJOR TOWNS/CITIES Berbérati, Bouar, Bambari, Bossangoa, Carnot, Kaga Bandoro
PHYSICAL FEATURES landlocked flat plateau, with rivers flowing north and south, and hills in northeast and southwest; dry in north, rainforest in southwest; mostly wooded; Kotto and Mbari river falls; the Ubangi River rises 6 m/20 ft at Bangui during the wet season (June–November)

CENTRAL AFRICAN REPUBLIC Music and dance flourish in the Central African Republic: for example the Aka people of the southwestern forest are internationally renowned for their performances.
Stanley Gibbons/

Government

HEAD OF STATE François Bozizé from 2003
HEAD OF GOVERNMENT Célestin Gaombalet from 2003
POLITICAL SYSTEM emergent democracy
POLITICAL EXECUTIVE limited presidency
ADMINISTRATIVE DIVISIONS 14 prefectures, two economic prefectures, and one commune (Bangui)
ARMED FORCES 2,600; plus paramilitary forces of 1,000 (2002 est)
CONSCRIPTION selective national service for two-year period
DEATH PENALTY retains the death penalty for ordinary crimes but can be considered abolitionist in practice; date of last known execution 1981
DEFENCE SPEND (% GDP) 2.1 (2002 est)
EDUCATION SPEND (% GDP) 1.6 (1999)
HEALTH SPEND (% GDP) 2.9 (2000 est)

Economy and resources

CURRENCY franc CFA
GPD (US$) 1.1 billion (2002 est)
REAL GDP GROWTH (% change on previous year) –1.5 (2001)
GNI (US$) 1.0 billion (2002 est)

GNI PER CAPITA (PPP) (US$) 1,190 (2002 est)
CONSUMER PRICE INFLATION 4.4% (2003 est)
UNEMPLOYMENT 7.6% (1996)
FOREIGN DEBT (US$) 837 million (2001 est)
MAJOR TRADING PARTNERS France, Belgium, Luxembourg, Cameroon, Spain, Pakistan, Germany
RESOURCES gem diamonds and industrial diamonds, gold, uranium, iron ore, manganese, copper
INDUSTRIES food processing, beverages, tobacco, furniture, textiles, paper, soap
EXPORTS timber, diamonds, coffee, cotton. Principal market: Belgium 53% (2001)
IMPORTS mineral fuels, machinery, road vehicles and parts, basic manufactures, food and chemical products. Principal source: France 26.5% (2001)
ARABLE LAND 3.1% (2000 est)
AGRICULTURAL PRODUCTS cassava, coffee, yams, maize, bananas, groundnuts; forestry

Population and society

POPULATION 3,865,000 (2003 est)
POPULATION GROWTH RATE 1.5% (2000–15)
POPULATION DENSITY (per sq km) 6 (2003 est)
URBAN POPULATION (% of total) 43 (2003 est)
AGE DISTRIBUTION (% of total population) 0–14 43%, 15–59 51%, 60+ 6% (2002 est)
ETHNIC GROUPS over 80 ethnic groups, but 66% of the population falls into one of six: the Baya (34%), the Banda (27%), the Mandjia (21%), the Sava (10%), the Mbimu (4%) and the Mbaka (4%). There are clearly defined ethnic zones; the forest region, inhabited by Bantu groups, the Mbaka, Lissongo, Mbimu, and Babinga; the river banks, populated by the Sango, Yakoma, Baniri, and Buraka; and the savannah region, where the Banda, Sande, Sara, Ndle, and Bizao live. Europeans number fewer than 7,000, the majority being French
LANGUAGE French (official), Sangho (national), Arabic, Hunsa, Swahili
RELIGION Protestant 25%, Roman Catholic 25%, animist 24%, Muslim 15%
EDUCATION (compulsory years) 8
LITERACY RATE 63% (men); 40% (women) (2003 est)
LABOUR FORCE 75.1% agriculture, 3.2% industry, 21.7% services (1997 est)
LIFE EXPECTANCY 39 (men); 41 (women) (2000–05)
CHILD MORTALITY RATE (under 5, per 1,000 live births) 180 (2001)
PHYSICIANS (per 1,000 people) 0.03 (1995 est)
HOSPITAL BEDS (per 1,000 people) 0.9 (1994 est)
TV SETS (per 1,000 people) 6 (2001 est)
RADIOS (per 1,000 people) 83 (1997)
INTERNET USERS (per 10,000 people) 7.9 (2002 est)

PERSONAL COMPUTER USERS (per 100 people) 0.2 (2002 est)

See also ▷Bokassa, Jean-Bédel.

Chronology

10th century: Immigration by peoples from Sudan to the east and Cameroon to the west.

16th century: Part of the Gaoga Empire.

16th–18th centuries: Population reduced greatly by slave raids both by coastal traders and Arab empires in Sudan and Chad.

19th century: The Zande nation of the Bandia peoples became powerful in the east. Bantu speakers immigrated from Zaire and the Baya from northern Cameroon.

1889–1903: The French established control over the area, quelling insurrections; a French colony known as Ubangi-Shari was formed and partitioned among commercial concessionaries.

1920–30: A series of rebellions against forced labour on coffee and cotton plantations were savagely repressed by the French.

1946: Given a territorial assembly and representation in French parliament.

1958: Achieved self-government within French Equatorial Africa, with Barthélémy Boganda, founder of the pro-independence Movement for the Social Evolution of Black Africa (MESAN), as prime minister.

1960: Achieved independence as Central African Republic; David Dacko, the nephew of the late Boganda, was elected president.

1962: The republic became a one-party state, dominated by MESAN and loyal to the French interest.

1965: Dacko was ousted in a military coup led by Col Jean-Bedel Bokassa, as the economy deteriorated.

1972: Bokassa, a violent and eccentric autocrat, declared himself president for life. In 1977 he made himself emperor of the 'Central African Empire'.

1979: Bokassa was deposed by Dacko in a French-backed bloodless coup, following violent repressive measures including the massacre of 100 children. Bokassa went into exile and the country became known as the Central African Republic again.

1981: Dacko was deposed in a bloodless coup, led by Gen André Kolingba, and a military government was established.

1983: A clandestine opposition movement was formed.

1984: Amnesty for all political party leaders was announced.

1988: Bokassa, who had returned from exile, was found guilty of murder and embezzlement; he received a death sentence, later commuted to life imprisonment.

1991: Opposition parties were allowed to form.

1992: Multiparty elections were promised, but cancelled with Kolingba in last place.

1993: Kolingba released thousands of prisoners, including Bokassa. Ange-Félix Patasse of the leftist African People's Labour Party (MLPC) was elected president, ending 12 years of military dictatorship.

1996: There was an army revolt over pay; Patasse was forced into hiding.

1999: Anicet Georges Dologuele was appointed prime minister.

cephalopod any predatory marine mollusc of the class Cephalopoda, with the mouth and head surrounded by tentacles. Cephalopods are the most intelligent, the fastest-moving, and the largest of all animals without backbones, and there are remarkable luminescent forms which swim or drift at great depths. They have the most highly developed nervous and sensory systems of all invertebrates, the eye in some closely paralleling that found in vertebrates. Examples include squid, ▷octopus, and ▷cuttlefish. Shells are rudimentary or absent in most cephalopods.

Typically, they move by swimming with the mantle (fold of outer skin) aided by the arms, but can squirt water out of the siphon (funnel) to propel themselves backwards by jet propulsion. Squid, for example, can escape predators at speeds of 11 kph/7mph. Cephalopods grow very rapidly and may be mature in a year. The female common octopus lays 150,000 eggs after copulation, and stays to brood them for as long as six weeks. After they hatch the female dies, and, although reproductive habits of many cephalopods are not known, it is thought that dying after spawning may be typical.

CEPHALOPOD An underwater photograph of squid. *Image Bank*

cephalosporin any of a class of broad-spectrum antibiotics derived from a fungus (genus *Cephalosporium*). They are similar to penicillins and are used on penicillin-resistant infections.

Cepheid variable yellow supergiant star that varies regularly in brightness every few days or weeks as a result of pulsations. The time that a Cepheid variable takes to pulsate is directly related to its average brightness; the longer the pulsation period, the brighter the star.

Cepheus constellation of the north polar region, named after King Cepheus of Greek mythology, husband of Cassiopeia and father of Andromeda. It contains the Garnet Star (Mu Cephei), a red supergiant of variable brightness that is one of the reddest-coloured stars known, and Delta Cephei, prototype of the ▷Cepheid variables, which are important both as distance indicators and for the information they give about stellar evolution.

ceramics objects made from clay, hardened into a permanent form by baking (firing) at very high temperatures in a kiln. Ceramics are used for building construction and decoration (bricks, tiles), for specialist industrial uses (linings for furnaces used to manufacture steel, fuel elements in nuclear reactors, and so on), and for plates and vessels used in the home. Different types of clay and different methods and temperatures of firing create a variety of results. Ceramics may be cast in a mould or hand-built out of slabs of clay, coiled, or thrown on a wheel. Technically, the main categories are ▷earthenware, stoneware, and hard- and softpaste porcelain (see under ▷pottery and porcelain).

Cerberus in Greek mythology, the three-headed dog which guarded the entrance to ▷Hades, the underworld.

cereal grass grown for its edible, nutrient-rich, starchy seeds. The term refers primarily to wheat, oats, rye, and barley, but may also refer to maize (corn), millet, and rice. Cereals contain about 75% complex carbohydrates and 10% protein, plus fats and fibre (roughage). They store well. If all the world's cereal crop were consumed as whole-grain products directly by humans, everyone could obtain adequate protein and carbohydrate; however, a large proportion of cereal production in affluent nations is used as animal feed to boost the production of meat, dairy products, and eggs.

The term also refers to breakfast foods prepared from the seeds of cereal crops. Some cereals require cooking (porridge oats), but most are ready to eat. Mass-marketed cereals include refined and sweetened varieties as well as whole cereals such as muesli. Whole cereals are more nutritious and provide more fibre than the refined cereals, which often have vitamins and flavourings added to replace those lost in the refining process.

cerebellum part of the brain of ▷vertebrate animals which controls muscle tone, movement, balance, and coordination. It is relatively small in lower animals such as newts and lizards, but large in birds since flight demands precise coordination. The human cerebellum is also well developed, because of the need for balance when walking or running, and for finely coordinated hand movements.

cerebral haemorrhage (or **apoplectic fit**) in medicine, a form of ▷stroke in which there is bleeding from a cerebral blood vessel into the surrounding brain tissue. It is generally caused by degenerative disease of the arteries and high blood pressure. Depending on the site and extent of bleeding, the symptoms vary from transient weakness and numbness to deep coma and death. Damage to the brain is permanent, though some recovery can be made. Strokes are likely to recur.

cerebral palsy any nonprogressive abnormality of the brain occurring during or shortly after birth. It is caused by oxygen deprivation, injury during birth, haemorrhage, meningitis, viral infection, or faulty development. Premature babies are at greater risk of being born with cerebral palsy, and in 1996 US researchers linked this to low levels of the thyroid hormone thyroxine. The condition is characterized by muscle spasm, weakness, lack of coordination, and impaired movement; or there may be spastic paralysis, with fixed deformities of the limbs. Intelligence is not always affected.

cerebrum part of the vertebrate ▷brain, formed from the two paired cerebral hemispheres, separated by a central fissure. In birds and mammals it is the largest and most developed part of the brain. It is covered with an infolded layer of grey matter, the cerebral cortex, which integrates brain functions. The cerebrum coordinates all voluntary activity.

Ceredigion unitary authority in southwest Wales, created in 1996 from part of the former county of Dyfed, of which it was a district.

    area 1,793 sq km/692 sq mi   **towns** Aberaeron (administrative headquarters), ▷Aberystwyth, Cardigan, Lampeter, Llandysul, Tregaron   **physical** part of the Cambrian Mountains, including Plynlimon Fawr (752 m/2,468 ft); rivers Teifi, Rheidol, Ystwyth, Aeron, and ▷Tywi   **features** remains of Roman roads and military stations, and inscribed stones; ruins of 12th-century Strata Florida Abbey southeast of Aberystwyth; Devil's Bridge (spanning the Rheidol Falls)   **industries** tourism, woollens production   **agriculture** sheep-rearing, dairy production   **population** (1996) 68,900

Ceres largest asteroid, 940 km/584 mi in diameter, and the first to be discovered (by Italian astronomer Giuseppe Piazzi in 1801). Ceres orbits the Sun every 4.6 years at an average distance of 414 million km/257 million mi. Its mass is about 0.014 of that of Earth's Moon.

Ceres in Roman mythology, the goddess of corn, representing the fertility of the earth as its producer; patron of the corn trade. Her cult was established in Rome by 496 BC, and showed early identification with the Greek ▷Demeter.

cerium malleable and ductile, grey, metallic element, symbol Ce, atomic number 58, relative atomic mass 140.12. It is the most abundant member of the lanthanide series, and is used in alloys, electronic components, nuclear fuels, and lighter flints. It was discovered in 1804 by the Swedish chemists Jöns Berzelius and Wilhelm Hisinger (1766–1852), and, independently, by Martin Klaproth. The element was named after the then recently discovered asteroid Ceres.

cermet (contraction of ceramics and metal) bonded material containing ceramics and metal, widely used in jet engines and nuclear reactors. Cermets behave much like metals but have the great heat resistance of ceramics. Tungsten carbide, molybdenum boride, and aluminium oxide are among the ceramics used; iron, cobalt, nickel, and chromium are among the metals.

CERN particle physics research organization founded in 1954 as a cooperative enterprise among European governments. It has laboratories at Meyrin, near Geneva, Switzerland. It houses the world's largest particle ▷accelerator, the ▷Large Electron Positron Collider (LEP), operational 1989–2000, with which notable advances were made in ▷particle physics.

certiorari in UK ▷administrative law, a remedy available by ▷judicial review whereby a superior court may quash an order or decision made by an inferior body. It has become less important in recent years following the extension of alternative remedies by judicial review. It originally took the form of a prerogative ▷writ.

MIGUEL DE CERVANTES Miguel de Cervantes, Spanish novelist, was wounded in the Battle of Lepanto in 1571, and captured and enslaved by pirates in Algeria in 1575. Once back in Spain, he began writing *Don Quixote*, considered his greatest work (part I published in 1605 and part II in 1615). *Archive Photos*

Cervantes, Saavedra, Miguel de (1547–1616) Spanish novelist, dramatist, and poet. His masterpiece ▷*Don Quixote de la Mancha* (in full *El ingenioso hidalgo Don Quixote de la Mancha*) was published in 1605. In 1613 his *Novelas ejemplares/Exemplary Novels* appeared, followed by *Viaje del Parnaso/The Voyage to Parnassus* (1614). A spurious second part of *Don Quixote* prompted Cervantes to bring out his own second part in 1615, often considered superior to the first in construction and characterization.

Cervantes entered the army in Italy, and was wounded in the sea battle of Lepanto in 1571 against the Ottoman empire. On his way back to Spain in 1575, he was captured by Barbary pirates and taken to Algiers, where he became a slave until ransomed in 1580.

Returning to Spain, he wrote several plays, and in 1585 his pastoral romance *La Galatea* was printed. *Don Quixote* was an immediate success and was soon translated into English and French.

> **Miguel de Cervantes**
> *The eyes, those silent tongues of Love.*
> *Don Quixote* pt 1 bk 2 (1605)

cervical cancer in medicine, ▷cancer of the cervix (neck of the womb). It can be detected at an early stage through screening by cervical smear.

cervical smear in medicine, removal of a small sample of tissue from the cervix (neck of the womb) to screen for changes implying a likelihood of cancer. The procedure is also known as the **Pap test** after its originator, George Papanicolau.

cervix (Latin 'neck') abbreviation for **cervix uteri**, the neck of the womb; see ▷uterus.

César (1921–1998) Adopted name of César Baldaccini. French sculptor. He created imaginary insects and animals using iron and scrap metal and, in the 1960s, crushed car bodies. From the late 1960s he experimented with works in plastic and polyurethane.

Cetewayo, (Cetshwayo) (c. 1826–1884) King of Zululand, South Africa, 1873–83, whose rule was threatened by British annexation of the Transvaal in 1877. Although he defeated the British at Isandhlwana in 1879, he was later that year defeated by them at Ulundi. Restored to his throne in 1883, he was then expelled by his subjects.

Cetus (Latin 'whale') large constellation on the celestial equator (see ▷celestial sphere), represented as a sea monster or a whale. Cetus contains the long-period variable star ▷Mira, and Tau Ceti, one of the nearest stars, which is visible with the naked eye.

Ceylon former name (to 1972) of ▷Sri Lanka.

Cézanne, Paul (1839–1906) French post-Impressionist painter. He was a leading figure in the development of modern art. He broke away from the Impressionists' concern with the ever-changing effects of light to develop a style that tried to capture the structure of natural forms, whether in landscapes, still lifes, or portraits. *Joueurs de Cartes/Cardplayers* (*c.* 1890–95; Louvre, Paris) is typical of his work.

Cézanne was educated at the Collège Bourbon of Aix, where he became a friend of French writer Emile Zola. His parents had intended him to study law, but he persuaded them to allow him to study art in Paris. He had, however, no regular training, failing in the entrance examination of the Ecole des Beaux-Arts, and his early work had an undisciplined and Romantic enthusiasm for Delacroix, Daumier and Courbet, where sensational subject matter (*L'Orgie, L'Enlèvement*) was rendered with violent and dark colour, heavily plastered on the canvas. His real apprenticeship began in the 1870s when his friendship with Camille ▷Pissarro brought him within the orbit of Impressionism. 'Never paint', Pissarro advised him, 'except with the three primary colours and their immediate derivatives', and though he did not follow this advice literally, it made him aware of the importance of pure colour. A further result of Impressionist influence was to wean him from Romantic ideas and to focus on the study of nature. *La Maison du Pendu*, which he contributed to the first Impressionist exhibition of 1874, marked this transitional stage in his art.

He found Paris generally unsympathetic, and his later life, the most creative phase, was spent largely in seclusion at Aix-en-Provence. Financially self-sufficient after the death of his wealthy father, he absorbed himself in nature and the problems of his art, which contained many interesting and fruitful contradictions. He wished to 'refashion Poussin after nature': on the other hand, the Louvre, he remarked, was 'a good book but only a means to an end'. A sense of structure, opposed to the atmospheric preoccupation of the Impressionists, dictated not only the representation of an object by planes translated into colour, but also the representation of space (as in his *Montagne St Victoire*).

The beauty of his later paintings lies in the subtle gradations of transparent colour from cold to warm, combined with and inseparable from a grand simplicity of form. In the watercolour medium itself he showed remarkable brilliance and successfully applied its transparency in oil. As in his *Joueurs de Cartes*, the human element was the result, but not the primary incentive, of his art, though he considered the study of the figure an important exercise and his many *Bathers* show a desire to achieve a great nude composition. The logic of his ideas inevitably tended towards still life, in which he excelled, and ultimately towards abstraction. In this respect he may be looked on as the progenitor of ▷cubism, which followed so soon after the retrospective exhibition of his work in 1907.

Paul Cézanne
Treat nature by the cylinder, the sphere, the cone, everything in proper perspective.
Letter to Emile Bernard, 15 April 1904

CFC abbreviation for ▷chlorofluorocarbon.

c.g.s. system system of units based on the centimetre, gram, and second, as units of length, mass, and time, respectively. It has been replaced for scientific work by the ▷SI units to avoid inconsistencies in definition of the thermal calorie and electrical quantities.

Chabrol, Claude (1930–) French film director. One of the New Wave directors, he came to the fore in the late 1950s. His works centre on murder and suspense, and include *Les Cousins/The Cousins* (1959), *Les Bonnes Femmes* (1960), *Les Biches/The Girlfriends* (1968), *Le Boucher/The Butcher* (1969), *Cop au Vin* (1984), and *L'Enfer* (1994).

Chaco province of northeast Argentina; area 99,633 sq km/ 38,469 sq mi; population (2001 est) 979,000; its capital is Resistencia, in the southeast. The province forms part of the Gran Chaco area of South America, which extends into Bolivia and Paraguay, and consists of a flat savannah lowland, mainly covered with scrub, and has many lakes and swamps. The eastern parts of the province are heavily forested, producing timber and the quebracho tree, from which tannin extract is made. The chief crop is cotton, and there is cattle-raising.

Chad see country box.

Chad, Lake lake on the northeastern boundary of Nigeria and the eastern boundary of Chad. It once varied in extent between rainy and dry seasons from 50,000 sq km/19,000 sq mi to 20,000 sq km/7,000 sq mi, but a series of droughts between 1979 and 1989 reduced its area to 2,500 sq km/965 sq mi in 1993. It is a shallow lake (depth does not exceed 5–8 m/16–26 ft), with the northern part being completely dry and the southern area being densely vegetated, with swamps and open pools. The lake was first seen by European explorers in 1823.

chafer beetle of the family Scarabeidae. The adults eat foliage or flowers, and the underground larvae feed on roots, chiefly those of grasses and cereals, and can be very destructive. Examples are the

CHAFER *Popilia bipunctata* from South Africa is one of many species of chafers which feed destructively on flowers. Species of *Popilia* often form 'mating balls' in which numerous males compete to mate with a female.
Premaphotos Wildlife

▷cockchafer and the **rose chafer** *Cetonia aurata*, about 2 cm/0.8 in long and bright green.

chaffinch bird *Fringilla coelebs* of the finch family, common throughout much of Europe and West Asia. About 15 cm/6 in long, the male is olive-brown above, with a bright chestnut breast, a bluish-grey cap, and two white bands on the upper part of the wing; the female is duller. During winter they form single-sex flocks.

Chagall, Marc (1887–1985) Belorussian-born French painter and designer. Much of his highly coloured, fantastic imagery was inspired by the village life of his boyhood and by Jewish and Belorussian folk traditions. He was an original figure, often seen as a precursor of surrealism. *I and the Village* (1911; Museum of Modern Art, New York) is characteristic.

Chagall was born in Liosno, Vitebsk, now Belarus. He studied painting under Leon Bakst in St Petersburg and then in Paris 1910–14, where, largely ignoring avant-garde movements, he concentrated on his highly personal fantasy. He worked in Russia during World War I but returned to Paris in 1922 and lived mainly in France from then on. He designed mosaics (for Israel's Knesset in the 1960s), the ceiling of the Paris Opera House in 1964, tapestries, and stage sets. Examples of his stained glass can be found in a chapel in Vence, southern France, the cathedrals of Chartres, Metz, and Reims, and in a synagogue near Jerusalem (1961). He also produced illustrated books, in particular editions of the Bible and La Fontaine's *Fables*. His autobiography, *Ma Vie/My Life*, appeared in 1933.

Chagas's disease disease common in Central and South America, infecting approximately 18 million people worldwide. It is caused by a trypanosome parasite, *Trypanosoma cruzi*, transmitted by several species of blood-sucking insect; it results in incurable damage to the heart, intestines, and brain. It is named after Brazilian doctor Carlos Chagas (1879–1934).

Chain, Ernst Boris (1906–1979) German-born British biochemist who was awarded a Nobel Prize for Physiology or Medicine in 1945, together with Alexander ▷Fleming and Howard ▷Florey (Fleming for his discovery of the bactericidal effect of penicillin, and Chain and Florey for their isolation of penicillin and its development as an antibiotic drug). Chain also discovered penicillinase, an enzyme that destroys penicillin. Chain was knighted in 1969.

chain reaction in chemistry, a succession of reactions, usually involving ▷free radicals, where the products of one stage are the reactants of the next. A chain reaction is characterized by the continual generation of reactive substances.

A chain reaction comprises three separate stages: **initiation** – the initial generation of reactive species; **propagation** – reactions that involve reactive species and generate similar or different reactive species; and **termination** – reactions that involve the reactive species but produce only stable, nonreactive substances. Chain reactions may occur slowly (for example, the oxidation of edible oils) or accelerate as the number of reactive species increases, ultimately resulting in explosion.

chain reaction in nuclear physics, a fission reaction that is maintained because neutrons released by the splitting of some atomic nuclei themselves go on to split others, releasing even more neutrons. Such a reaction can be controlled (as in a nuclear reactor) by using moderators to absorb excess neutrons. Uncontrolled, a chain reaction produces a nuclear explosion (as in an atom bomb).

Chaka alternative spelling of ▷Shaka, Zulu chief.

Chalcedon, Council of ecumenical council of the early Christian church, convoked in 451 by the Roman emperor Marcian, and held at Chalcedon (now Kadiköy, Turkey). The council, attended by over 500 bishops, resulted in the **Definition of Chalcedon**, an agreed doctrine for both the Eastern and Western churches.

chalcedony form of the mineral quartz, SiO_2, in which the crystals are so fine-grained that they are impossible to distinguish with a microscope (cryptocrystalline). Agate, onyx, and carnelian are ▷gem varieties of chalcedony.

chalcopyrite copper iron sulphide mineral, $CuFeS_2$, the most common ore of copper. It is brassy yellow in colour and may have an iridescent surface tarnish. It occurs in many different types of mineral vein, in rocks ranging from basalt to limestone.

chalice cup, usually of precious metal, used in celebrating the ▷Eucharist in the Christian church.

chalk soft, fine-grained, whitish sedimentary rock composed of calcium carbonate, $CaCO_3$, extensively quarried for use in cement, lime, and mortar, and in the manufacture of cosmetics and toothpaste. **Blackboard chalk** in fact consists of gypsum (calcium sulphate, $CaSO_4.2H_2O$).

Chalmers, Thomas (1780–1847) Scottish theologian. At the Disruption of the ▷Church of Scotland in 1843, Chalmers withdrew from the church along with a large number of other priests, and became principal of the Free Church college, thus founding the ▷Free Church of Scotland.

Châlons-sur-Marne (Latin **Catalaunum**) administrative centre of the *département* of Marne and of the ▷Champagne-Ardenne region in northeast France, 150 km/93 mi east of Paris on the right bank of the River Marne; population (1990) 51,500. Industries include champagne production, brewing, electrical engineering, and textiles manufacture. Châlons was formerly known for its worsted cloth. Tradition has it that Attila the Hun was defeated near here in his attempt to invade France at the **Battle of the Catalaunian Plains** in 451 AD by the Roman general Aëtius and the Visigoth Theodoric.

Chamberlain, (Joseph) Austen (1863–1937) British Conservative politician, elder son of Joseph ▷Chamberlain; foreign secretary 1924–29. He shared the Nobel Prize for Peace in 1925 with Charles G ▷Dawes for his work in negotiating and signing the Pact of ▷Locarno, which fixed the boundaries of Germany. In 1928 he also signed the ▷Kellogg–Briand pact to outlaw war and provide for peaceful settlement of disputes.

He was elected to Parliament in 1892 as a Liberal–Unionist, and after holding several minor posts was chancellor of the Exchequer 1903–06. During World War I he was secretary of state for India 1915–17 and member of the war cabinet in 1918. He was chancellor of the Exchequer 1919–21 and Lord Privy Seal 1921–22, but failed to secure the leadership of the party in 1922, as many Conservatives resented the part he had taken in the Irish settlement of 1921.

Related Web site: Chamberlain, Sir Joseph Austen http://www.nobel.se/peace/laureates/1925/chamberlain-bio.html

Chamberlain, Joseph (1836–1914) British politician, reformist mayor of and member of Parliament for Birmingham. In 1886 he resigned from the cabinet over William Gladstone's policy of home rule for Ireland, and led the revolt of the Liberal-Unionists that saw them merge with the Conservative Party.

Joseph Chamberlain
The day of small nations has long passed away. The day of Empires has come.
Speech in Birmingham, 12 May 1904

By 1874 Chamberlain had made a sufficient fortune in the Birmingham screw-manufacturing business to devote himself entirely to politics. He adopted radical views, and took an active part in local affairs. Three times mayor of Birmingham, he carried through many schemes of municipal development. In 1876 he was elected to Parliament and joined the republican group led by Charles Dilke, the extreme left wing of the Liberal Party. In 1880 he entered Gladstone's cabinet as president of the Board of Trade. The climax of his radical period was reached with the so-called 'unauthorized programme', which advocated, among other things, free education, graduated taxation, and smallholdings of 'three acres and a cow'.

As colonial secretary in the Marquess of Salisbury's Conservative government, Chamberlain was responsible for relations with the Boer republics up to the outbreak of war in 1899. In this position he also negotiated the Commonwealth of Australia Constitution Bill with representatives from Australia. In 1903 he resigned to

campaign for imperial preference or tariff reform as a means of consolidating the empire. In 1906, the Conservatives were routed in a general election, and Chamberlain was incapacitated by a stroke. Chamberlain was one of the most colourful figures of British politics, and his monocle and orchid made him a favourite subject for political cartoonists.

Chamberlain, Lord
in the UK, the chief officer of the royal household; see ▷Lord Chamberlain.

Chamberlain, (Arthur) Neville
(1869–1940) British Conservative politician, son of Joseph ▷Chamberlain. He was prime minister 1937–40; his policy of appeasement toward the Italian fascist dictator Benito Mussolini and German Nazi Adolf Hitler (with whom he concluded the ▷Munich Agreement in 1938) failed to prevent the outbreak of World War II. He resigned in 1940 following the defeat of the British forces in Norway.

The younger son of Joseph Chamberlain and half-brother of Austen Chamberlain, he was born in Birmingham, of which he was

> **Neville Chamberlain**
> *In war, whichever side may call itself the victor, there are no winners, but all are losers.*
> Speech at Kettering, 3 July 1938

NEVILLE CHAMBERLAIN Seen here on 30 September 1938, British prime minister Neville Chamberlain has just returned to London, England, from a meeting with German chancellor Adolf Hitler in Munich, Germany. He holds the piece of paper with which he claimed to have won 'peace in our time'. Within a year, Britain was at war with Germany. *Archive Photos*

Chad

Chad landlocked country in central North Africa, bounded north by Libya, east by Sudan, south by the Central African Republic, and west by Cameroon, Nigeria, and Niger.

NATIONAL NAME *République du Tchad/Republic of Chad*
AREA 1,284,000 sq km/495,752 sq mi
CAPITAL Ndjamena (formerly Fort Lamy)
MAJOR TOWNS/CITIES Sarh, Moundou, Abéché, Bongor, Doba, Kélo, Koumra
PHYSICAL FEATURES landlocked state with mountains (Tibetsi) and part of Sahara Desert in north; moist savannah in south; rivers in south flow northwest to Lake Chad

Government
HEAD OF STATE Idriss Deby from 1990
HEAD OF GOVERNMENT Moussa Faki from 2003
POLITICAL SYSTEM emergent democracy

CHAD A great egret on a stamp from Chad. The seasonal rivers of this country, such as the Wadi Azoum, give rise to extensive wetlands, attracting many wading birds.

POLITICAL EXECUTIVE limited presidency
ADMINISTRATIVE DIVISIONS 14 prefectures, subdivided into 28 departments
POLITICAL PARTIES Patriotic Salvation Movement (MPS), left of centre; Alliance for Democracy and Progress (RDP), left of centre; Union for Democracy and Progress (UPDT), left of centre; Action for Unity and Socialism (ACTUS), left of centre; Union for Democracy and the Republic (UDR), left of centre
ARMED FORCES 30,400; plus paramilitary forces of 4,500 (2002 est)
CONSCRIPTION conscription is for three years
DEATH PENALTY retained and used for ordinary crimes
DEFENCE SPEND (% GDP) 0.8 (2002 est)
EDUCATION SPEND (% GDP) 2 (2000 est)
HEALTH SPEND (% GDP) 3.1 (2000 est)

Economy and resources
CURRENCY franc CFA
GPD (US$) 1.9 billion (2002 est)
REAL GDP GROWTH (% change on previous year) 8.1 (2001)
GNI (US$) 1.8 billion (2002 est)
GNI PER CAPITA (PPP) (US$) 1,000 (2002 est)
CONSUMER PRICE INFLATION 4% (2003 est)
FOREIGN DEBT (US$) 1.1 billion (2001 est)
MAJOR TRADING PARTNERS France, Portugal, USA, Nigeria, Germany, Saudi Arabia, India

RESOURCES petroleum, tungsten, tin ore, bauxite, iron ore, gold, uranium, limestone, kaolin, titanium
INDUSTRIES cotton processing, sugar refinery, beer, cigarettes, soap, bicycles
EXPORTS livestock, cotton, meat, hides and skins. Principal market: Portugal 17% (2001)
IMPORTS petroleum and petroleum products, cereals, pharmaceuticals, chemicals, machinery and transport equipment, electrical equipment. Principal source: USA 46% (2001)
ARABLE LAND 2.8% (2000 est)
AGRICULTURAL PRODUCTS cotton, millet, sugar cane, sorghum, groundnuts; livestock

Population and society
POPULATION 8,598,000 (2003 est)
POPULATION GROWTH RATE 2.9% (2000–15)
POPULATION DENSITY (per sq km) 7 (2003 est)
URBAN POPULATION (% of total) 25 (2003 est)
AGE DISTRIBUTION (% of total population) 0–14 47%, 15–59 48%, 60+ 5% (2002 est)
ETHNIC GROUPS mainly Arabs in the north, and Pagan, or Kirdi, groups in the south.

There is no single dominant group in any region, the largest are the Sara, who comprise about a quarter of the total population. Europeans, mainly French, constitute a very small minority
LANGUAGE French, Arabic (both official), over 100 African languages
RELIGION Muslim 50%, Christian 25%, animist 25%
EDUCATION (compulsory years) 8
LITERACY RATE 56% (men); 39% (women) (2003 est)
LABOUR FORCE 77.8% agriculture, 6.3% industry, 15.9% services (1997 est)
LIFE EXPECTANCY 44 (men); 46 (women) (2000–05)
CHILD MORTALITY RATE (under 5, per 1,000 live births) 200 (2001)
HOSPITAL BEDS (per 1,000 people) 0.7 (1996 est)
TV SETS (per 1,000 people) 1 (2001 est)
RADIOS (per 1,000 people) 236 (2001 est)
INTERNET USERS (per 10,000 people) 19.1 (2002 est)
PERSONAL COMPUTER USERS (per 100 people) 0.2 (2002 est)

Chronology
7th–9th centuries: Berber pastoral nomads, the Zaghawa, immigrated from the north and became a ruling aristocracy, dominating the Sao people, sedentary black farmers, and establishing the Kanem state.
9th–19th centuries: The Zaghawa's Saifi dynasty formed the kingdom of Bornu, which stretched to the west and south of Lake Chad, and converted to Islam in the 11th century. At its height between the 15th and 18th centuries, it raided the south for slaves, and faced rivalry from the 16th century from the Baguirmi and Ouadai Arab kingdoms.
1820s: Visited by British explorers.
1890s–1901: Conquered by France, who ended slave raiding by Arab kingdoms.
1910: Became a colony in French Equatorial Africa. Cotton production expanded in the south.
1944: The pro-Nazi Vichy government signed an agreement giving Libya rights to the Aouzou Strip in northern Chad.
1946: Became an overseas territory of the French Republic, with its own territorial assembly and representation in the French parliament.
1960: Independence was achieved, with François Tombalbaye of the Chadian Progressive Party (CPT), dominated by Sara Christians from the south, as president.
1963: Violent opposition in the Muslim north, led by the Chadian National Liberation Front (Frolinat), backed by Libya following the banning of opposition parties.
1968: A revolt of northern militias was quelled with France's help.
1973: An Africanization campaign was launched by Tombalbaye, who changed his first name to Ngarta.

1975: Tombalbaye was killed in a military coup led by southerner Gen Félix Malloum. Frolinat continued its resistance.
1978: Malloum formed a coalition government with former Frolinat leader Hissène Habré, but it soon broke down.
1979: Malloum was forced to leave the country; an interim government was set up under Gen Goukouni Oueddei (Frolinat). Habré continued his opposition with his Army of the North (FAN), and Libya provided support for Goukouni.
1981–82: Habré gained control of half the country. Goukouni fled and set up a 'government in exile'.
1983: Habré's regime was recognized by the Organization of African Unity (OAU) and France, but in the north, Goukouni's supporters, with Libya's help, fought on. Eventually a ceasefire was agreed, with latitude 16°north dividing the country.
1987: Chad, France, and Libya agreed on an OAU ceasefire to end the civil war between the Muslim Arab north and Christian and animist black African south.
1988: Libya relinquished its claims to the Aozou Strip.
1990: President Habré was ousted after the army was defeated by Libyan-backed Patriotic Salvation Movement (MPS) rebel troops based in the Sudan and led by Habré's former ally Idriss Deby.
1991–92: Several antigovernment coups were foiled.
1993: A transitional charter was adopted, as a prelude to full democracy at a later date.
1997: A reconciliation agreement was signed with rebel forces.
1999: Nagoum Yamassoum was appointed prime minister.
2000: Former president Hissene Habré was freed after having been charged with torture and murder.

lord mayor in 1915. He was minister of health in 1923 and 1924–29, and his policies centred on slum clearance. In 1931 he was chancellor of the Exchequer in the national government, and in 1937 succeeded Stanley Baldwin as prime minister. Trying to close the old Anglo-Irish feud, he agreed to return to Ireland those ports that had been occupied by the navy.

He also attempted to appease the demands of the European dictators, particularly Mussolini. In 1938 he went to Munich and negotiated with Hitler the settlement of the Czechoslovak question. He was ecstatically received on his return, and claimed that the Munich Agreement brought 'peace in our time'. Within a year, however, the UK was at war with Germany.

Related Web site: Neville Chamberlain WAVS http://earthstation1.simplenet.com/Chamberlain.html

Chamberlin, Powell, and Bon British architectural partnership, established in 1952 by Peter Chamberlin (1919–78), Geoffrey Powell (1920–1999), and Christoph Bon (1921–). Its commissions include New Hall, Cambridge (1966), Chancellor's Court, Leeds University (1972; which features aerial walkways at right angles to elongated slabs), and the grandiose Barbican Arts Centre, London, completed in 1982.

chamber music music intended for performance in a small room or chamber, rather than in the concert hall, and usually written for instrumental combinations, played with one instrument to a part, as in the ▷string quartet.

chameleon any of 80 or so species of lizard of the family Chameleontidae. Some species have highly developed colour-changing abilities, caused by stress and changes in the intensity of light and temperature, which alter the dispersal of pigment granules in the layers of cells beneath the outer skin.

The tail is long and highly prehensile, assisting the animal when climbing. Most chameleons live in trees and move very slowly.

The tongue is very long, protrusile, and covered with a viscous secretion; it can be shot out with great rapidity to 20 cm/8 in for the capture of insects. The eyes are on 'turrets', move independently, and can swivel forward to give stereoscopic vision for 'shooting'. Most live in Africa and Madagascar, but the **common chameleon** *Chameleo chameleon* is found in Mediterranean countries; two species live in southwestern Arabia, and one species in India and Sri Lanka.

Some species of chameleon, such as the African species *C. bitaeniatus* give birth to live young; the female 'gives birth' to a fully-formed young enclosed in a membrane, which is immediately shed.

Related Web site: Chameleons http://www.skypoint.com/members/mikefry/chams.html

CHAMELEON A Madagascan chameleon. Their changes in skin colour are not solely to match the background, as the use of patchy colour and complex patterns is also an effective form of camouflage. *Image Bank*

chamois goatlike mammal *Rupicapra rupicapra* found in mountain ranges of southern Europe and Asia Minor. It is brown, with dark patches running through the eyes, and can be up to 80 cm/2.6 ft high. Chamois are very sure-footed, and live in herds of up to 30 members.

Both sexes have horns which may be 20 cm/8 in long. These are set close together and go up vertically, forming a hook at the top. Chamois skin is very soft, and excellent for cleaning glass, but the chamois is now comparatively rare and 'chamois leather' is often made from the skin of sheep and goats.

Chamorro, Barrios de, Violeta president of Nicaragua from 1990; see ▷Barrios de Chamorro.

champagne sparkling white wine invented by Dom Pérignon, a Benedictine monk, in 1668. It is made from a blend of grapes (*pinot noir* and *chardonnay*) grown in the Marne River region around Reims and Epernay, in Champagne, northeastern France. After a first fermentation, sugar and yeast are added to the still wine, which, when bottled, undergoes a second fermentation to produce the sparkle. Sugar syrup may be added to make the wine sweet (*sec*) or dry (*brut*).

Champagne-Ardenne region of northeast France; area 25,600 sq km/9,900 sq mi; population (1990) 1,347,800. Its largest town is ▷Reims, but its administrative centre is ▷Châlons-sur-Marne. It comprises the *départements* of Ardennes, Aube, Marne, and Haute-Marne. The land is fertile in the west and supports sheep and dairy farming; its vineyards produce the famous ▷champagne wines. The region also includes part of the ▷Ardennes forest.

Champaigne, Philippe de (1602–1674) French artist. He was the leading portrait painter of the court of Louis XIII. Of Flemish origin, he went to Paris in 1621 and gained the patronage of Cardinal Richelieu. His style is elegant, cool, and restrained. *Ex Voto* (1662; Louvre, Paris) is his best-known work.

champignon any of a number of edible fungi (see ▷fungus). The fairy ring champignon (*Marasmius oreades*) has this name because its fruiting bodies (mushrooms) grow in rings around the outer edge of the underground mycelium (threadlike body) of the fungus. (Family Agaricaceae.)

Champlain, Lake lake in northeastern USA (extending some 10 km/6 mi into Canada) on the New York–Vermont border, west of the Green Mountains and east of the Adirondacks; length 201 km/125 mi; area 1,116 sq km/430 sq mi. Lake Champlain is linked to the St Lawrence River via the Richelieu River, and to the Hudson River by canal; it is the fourth-largest freshwater lake in the USA.

Champlain, Samuel de (1567–1635) French pioneer, soldier, and explorer in Canada. Having served in the army of Henry IV and on an expedition to the West Indies, he began his exploration of Canada in 1603. In a third expedition in 1608 he founded and named Québec, and was appointed lieutenant governor of French Canada in 1612.

Champollion, Jean François, le Jeune (1790–1832) French Egyptologist. In 1822 he deciphered Egyptian hieroglyphics with the aid of the ▷Rosetta Stone.

chance likelihood, or ▷probability, of an event taking place, expressed as a fraction or percentage. For example, the chance that a tossed coin will land heads up is 50%.

As a science, it originated when the Chevalier de Méré consulted Blaise ▷Pascal about how to reduce his gambling losses. In 1664, in correspondence with another mathematician, Pierre de ▷Fermat, Pascal worked out the foundations of the theory of chance. This underlies the science of statistics.

chancel (from Late Latin *cancellus* 'a screen') in architecture, the eastern part of a Christian church where the choir and clergy sit, formerly kept separate from the nave by an open-work screen or rail. In some medieval churches the screen is very high, so that the congregation is completely shut off. The choir stalls and the rector's pew are in the chancel, and the altar or communion table on a raised platform at the far end.

Chancellor, Lord UK state official; see ▷Lord Chancellor.

chancellor of the Exchequer in the UK, senior cabinet minister responsible for the national economy. The office, established under Henry III, originally entailed keeping the Exchequer seal. The current chancellor of the Exchequer, from 1997, is Gordon Brown.

Chancery in the UK, a division of the High Court that deals with such matters as the administration of the estates of deceased persons, the execution of trusts, the enforcement of sales of land, and ▷foreclosure of mortgages. Before reorganization of the court system in 1875, it administered the rules of ▷equity as distinct from ▷common law.

chancroid (or **soft sore**) acute localized, sexually transmitted ulcer on or about the genitals caused by the bacterium *Haemophilus ducreyi*.

It causes painful enlargement and suppuration of lymph nodes in the groin area.

Chandigarh city of north India, in the foothills of the Himalayas; population (2001 est) 976,000. It is also a Union Territory; area 114 sq km/44 sq mi; population (1991) 640,725. Planned by the architect ▷Le Corbusier, the city was inaugurated in 1953 to replace Lahore (capital of British Punjab), which went to Pakistan at partition in 1947. Since 1966, when Chandigarh became a Union Territory, it has been the capital city of the states of both Haryana and Punjab, pending the construction of a new capital for the former.

Chandler, Raymond Thornton (1888–1959) US novelist. He turned the pulp detective mystery form into a successful genre of literature and created the quintessential private eye in the tough but chivalric loner, Philip Marlowe. Marlowe is the narrator of such books as *The Big Sleep* (1939; filmed 1946), *Farewell My Lovely* (1940; filmed 1944), *The Lady in the Lake* (1943; filmed 1947), and *The Long Goodbye* (1954; filmed 1975). He also wrote numerous screenplays, notably *Double Indemnity* (1944), *Blue Dahlia* (1946), and *Strangers on a Train* (1951).

Related Web site: Chandler Web Page http://www.geocities.com/Athens/Parthenon/3224

Chandragupta Maurya (died *c.* 297 BC) Ruler of northern India and first Indian emperor *c.* 325–296 BC, founder of the Mauryan dynasty. He overthrew the Nanda dynasty of Magadha in 325 BC and then conquered the Punjab in 322 BC after the death of ▷Alexander (III) the Great, expanding his empire west to Iran. He is credited with having united most of India.

As army commander under Danananda, the last king of the Nanda dynasty of Magadha, he made an unsuccessful attempt on the throne and fled with his wily Brahman adviser Kautilya to join the invading army of Alexander, where he was recorded as 'Sandracottos'. Having urged Alexander to press on against Danananda without success, he gathered his own army against the king and eventually became king in his place. With Kautilya's aid he established a centralized empire on the model of the Achaemenids of Iran, and defeated ▷Seleucus (I) Nicator, who had attempted to restore Macedonian rule in the east in 305 BC. Seleucus ceded India (present-day Pakistan and part of the Punjab) and eastern Afghanistan in exchange for 500 war elephants for use in his western campaigns.

Chandrasekhar, Subrahmanyan (1910–1995) Indian-born US astrophysicist who was awarded the Nobel Prize for Physics in 1983 for his theoretical studies of the physical processes in connection with the structure and evolution of stars. The Chandrasekhar limit is the maximum mass of a ▷white dwarf before it turns into a ▷neutron star.

Chanel, Coco (Gabrielle) (1883–1971) French fashion designer. She was renowned as a trendsetter and her designs have been copied worldwide. She created the 'little black dress', the informal cardigan suit, costume jewellery, and perfumes.

Her designs were inspired by her personal wish for simple, comfortable, and practical clothes. Throughout the 1920s and 1930s her look was widely influential; the basic ingredients were cardigans, woollen jersey dresses, the 'little black dress', bell-bottom trousers, and costume jewellery. Popular colours were grey, navy blue, black, and beige for the day, while for the evening she preferred white, black, and pastel shades. She closed her workshop in 1939 and did not return to fashion until 1954 when she began showing her classic suits again in soft tweed and jersey, often collarless and trimmed with braid and shown with costume jewellery such as artificial pearls or gilt chains. She continued working until her death.

Related Web site: Chanel, Coco http://www.pathfinder.com/time/time100/artists/profile/chanel.html

Chaney, Lon (Alonso) (1883–1930) US star of silent films. He often played grotesque or monstrous roles such as *The Phantom of the Opera* (1925). A master of make-up, he was nicknamed 'the Man of a Thousand Faces'. He sometimes used extremely painful devices for added effect, as in the title role in *The Hunchback of Notre Dame* (1923), when he carried over 30 kg/70 lb of costume in the form of a heavy hump and harness.

Chaney, Lon, Jr (Creighton) (1907–1973) US actor. After an acclaimed performance as Lennie in *Of Mice and Men* (1940), he went on to star in many 1940s horror films, including the title role in *The Wolf Man* (1941). His other work includes *My Favorite Brunette* (1947) and *The Haunted Palace* (1963). He was the son of the actor Lon Chaney.

COCO CHANEL French fashion designer Coco Chanel, presenting her spring–summer collection, in January 1968. *Archive Photos*

Changchiakow alternative transcription of ▷Zhangjiakou, a trading centre in Hebei province, China.

Changchun industrial city and capital of ▷Jilin province, northeast China; population (1994) 2,237,000. It is the centre of an agricultural district, and manufactures machinery, vehicles, and railway equipment.

Related Web site: Changchun City http://china.muzi.net/travel/city/changchun.htm

change of state in science, a change in the physical state (solid, liquid, or gas) of a material. For instance, melting, boiling, evaporation, and their opposites, solidification and condensation, are changes of state. The former set of changes are brought about by heating or decreased pressure; the latter by cooling or increased pressure.

Chang Jiang (or Yangtze Kiang; 'long river') longest river of China and third longest in the world, flowing about 6,300 km/3,900 mi from Qinghai to the Yellow Sea. It is a major commercial waterway. Work began on the Three Gorges Dam on the river in December 1994.

Related Web site: Yangtze River Three Gorges Tour http://www.chinavista.com/travel/yangtze/main.html

Channel, English see ▷English Channel.

Channel Islands group of islands in the English Channel, off the northwest coast of France; they are a possession of the British crown. They comprise the islands of Jersey, Guernsey, Alderney, Great and Little Sark, with the lesser Herm, Brechou, Jethou, and Lihou; area 194 sq km/75 sq mi; population (1991) 145,600. Chief industries are farming, fishing, and tourism; flowers, early potatoes, tomatoes, butterflies, and dairy cattle are exported. The official language is French (▷Norman French) but English is more widely used. The islands are a tax haven. The currency is the English pound, as well as local coinage.

Originally under the duchy of Normandy, the islands are the only part still held by the UK. The islands came under the same rule as England in 1066, and are dependent territories of the British crown. Germany occupied the islands between June 1940 and May 1945, the only British soil to be occupied by the Germans during World War II.

The main islands have their own parliaments and laws. Unless specially signified, the Channel Islands are not bound by British acts of Parliament, although the British government is responsible for defence and external relations.

Channel Tunnel tunnel built beneath the ▷English Channel, linking Britain with mainland Europe. It comprises twin rail tunnels, 50 km/31 mi long and 7.3 m/24 ft in diameter, located 40 m/130 ft beneath the seabed. Construction began in 1987, and the French and English sections were linked in December 1990. It was officially opened on 6 May 1994. The shuttle train service, Le Shuttle, opened to lorries in May 1994 and to cars in December 1994. The tunnel's high-speed train service, Eurostar, linking London to Paris and Brussels, opened in November 1994.

The final cost of the tunnel was £12 billion, and left Eurotunnel plc, the Anglo-French company that built the tunnel, £9 billion in debt. In its first year, it made a loss of £925 million. Its first net profit was announced in March 1999. Plans to build a second tunnel were being considered in January 2000.

History The idea for a tunnel goes back to Napoleonic times. In the 1880s British financier and railway promoter Edward Watkin started boring a tunnel near Dover, abandoning it in 1894 because of governmental opposition after driving 1.6 km/1 mi out to sea. In 1973 Britain and France agreed to back a tunnel, but a year later Britain pulled out following a change of government.

High-speed link The contract to build the London–Dover high-speed rail link was awarded to the London and Continental Railways Consortium in February 1996. The link, due to be completed in 2003, would allow Eurostar trains to maintain their high speeds within Britain; under existing legislation, Eurostar trains that travel at up to 300 kph/186 mph in France are forced to slow to 80 kph/50 mph once in Britain. Transit time between London and Paris is 3 hours, and 2 hours 40 minutes between London and Brussels.

> **Charlie Chaplin**
> *Life is a tragedy when seen in close-up, but a comedy in long-shot.*
> Quoted in his obituary in the *Guardian*, 28 December 1977

chanson song type common in France and Italy, often based on a folk tune that originated with the ▷troubadours. Josquin ▷Desprez was a chanson composer.

chant ritual incantation by an individual or group, for confidence or mutual support. Chants can be secular (as, for example, sports supporters' chants) or religious, both Eastern and Western. Ambrosian and ▷Gregorian chants are forms of plainsong.

chanterelle edible ▷fungus that is bright yellow and funnel-shaped. It grows in deciduous woodland. (*Cantharellus cibarius*, family Cantharellaceae.)

CHANTERELLE Like most fungi from temperate zones, the edible chanterelle *Cantharellus cibarius* is looked for in autumn, being most likely to appear when a period of warm weather is accompanied by abundant rainfall. *Premaphotos Wildlife*

chantry (from Old French *chanterie*; Latin *cantare* 'to sing') in medieval Europe, a religious foundation in which, in return for an endowment of land, the souls of the donor and the donor's family and friends would be prayed for. A chantry could be held at an existing altar, or in a specially constructed **chantry chapel** in which the donor's body was usually buried. Chantry chapels are often built off the aisle or nave of a church, and have the tomb of the founder placed in the centre. The word is also applied to the endowment intended by the founder as a perpetual stipend for masses in such a chapel.

Chao Phraya chief river (formerly Menam) of Thailand, flowing 1,200 km/750 mi into the Bight of Bangkok, an inlet of the Gulf of Thailand.

chaos theory (or chaology or **complexity theory**) branch of mathematics that attempts to describe irregular, unpredictable systems – that is, systems whose behaviour is difficult to predict because there are so many variable or unknown factors. Weather is an example of a chaotic system.

Chaos theory, which attempts to predict the *probable* behaviour of such systems, based on a rapid calculation of the impact of as wide a range of elements as possible, emerged in the 1970s with the development of sophisticated computers. First developed for use in meteorology, it has also been used in such fields as economics.

Related Web site: Chaos Club http://www.chaosclub.com/

chapel (from Latin *capella*, diminutive of *cappa* 'a cloak') a small or subordinate place of Christian worship other than a parish or cathedral church; also a church subordinate to and dependent on the principal parish church, to which it is in some way supplementary. The term can also refer to a building or part of a building or institution (for example, a palace, college, convent, hospital, or prison) erected for private devotion and often for private or semi-public religious services; also a recess in a church containing an altar that has been separately dedicated. In England the word 'chapel' is commonly applied to places of Nonconformist worship, as distinct from those of the Anglican and Roman Catholic churches.

Chapel Royal in the UK, a group of musicians and clergy serving the English monarch. Dating back at least to 1135, the Chapel Royal fostered some of England's greatest composers, especially prior to the 18th century, when many great musical works were religious in nature. Members of the Chapel Royal have included Thomas Tallis, William Byrd, and Henry Purcell.

Chaplin, Charlie (Charles Spencer) (1889–1977) English film actor and director. One of cinema's most popular stars, he made his reputation as a tramp with a smudge moustache, bowler hat, and twirling cane in silent comedies, including *The Rink* (1916), *The Kid* (1921), and *The Gold Rush* (1925). His work combines buffoonery with pathos, as in *The Great Dictator* (1940) and *Limelight* (1952).

Chaplin was born in London and first appeared on the music-hall stage at the age of five. He joined Mack Sennett's Keystone Company in Los Angeles in 1913. Along with Mary Pickford, Douglas ▷Fairbanks, and D W ▷Griffith, Chaplin formed United Artists in 1919 as an independent company to distribute their films. His other films include *City Lights* (1931), *Modern Times* (1936), and *Monsieur Verdoux* (1947). *Limelight* (1952) was awarded an Academy Award for Chaplin's musical theme. When accused of communist sympathies during the Joe McCarthy witchhunt, he left the USA in 1952 and moved to Switzerland. He received special Academy Awards in 1928 and 1972, and was knighted in 1975.

Related Web site: Charlie Chaplin Filmography http://www.cs.monash.edu.au/~pringle/silent/chaplin/filmography.html

Chapman, George (*c*. 1559–1634) English poet and dramatist. His translations of the Greek epics of Homer (completed 1616) were the earliest in England; his plays include the comedy *Eastward Ho* (with Ben ▷Jonson and John ▷Marston, 1605) and the tragedy *Bussy d'Ambois* (1607).

chapterhouse in church architecture, a building in which the canonical chapter of a monastery, cathedral, or collegiate church meets for the discussion of its affairs. It is often elaborately designed and ornamented, and usually polygonal, or octagonal, as at Lichfield and York. The position of the chapterhouse is usually to the west of the transepts of the church, to which it is connected either directly or by a passage from the cloister. Crypts are occasionally found beneath the floor.

char (or charr) fish *Salvelinus alpinus* related to the trout, living in the Arctic coastal waters, and also in Europe and North America in some upland lakes. It is one of Britain's rarest fish, and is at risk from growing acidification.

characin freshwater fish belonging to the family Characidae. There are over 1,300 species, mostly in South and Central America, but also in Africa. Most are carnivores. In typical characins, unlike the somewhat similar carp family, the mouth is toothed, and there is a small dorsal adipose fin just in front of the tail.

Characins are small fishes, often colourful, and they include ▷tetras and ▷piranhas.

charcoal black, porous form of ▷carbon, produced by heating wood or other organic materials in the absence of air. It is used as a fuel in the smelting of metals such as copper and zinc, and by artists for making black line drawings. **Activated charcoal** has been powdered and dried so that it presents a much increased surface area for adsorption; it is used for filtering and purifying liquids and gases – for example, in drinking-water filters and gas masks.

Charcoal was traditionally produced by burning dried wood in a kiln, a process lasting several days. The kiln was either a simple hole in the ground, or an earth-covered mound. Today kilns are of brick or iron, both of which allow the waste gases to be collected and used. Charcoal had many uses in earlier centuries. Because of the high temperature at which it burns (2,012°F/1,100°C), it was used in furnaces and blast furnaces before the development of ▷coke. It was also used in an industrial process for obtaining ethanoic acid (acetic acid), in producing wood tar and ▷wood pitch, and (when produced from alder or willow trees) as a component of gunpowder.

Charcot, Jean-Martin (1825–1893) French neurologist who studied hysteria, sclerosis, locomotor ataxia, and senile diseases. Among his pupils was the founder of psychiatry, Sigmund ▷Freud.

Chardin, Jean-Baptiste-Siméon (1699–1779) French painter. He took as his subjects naturalistic still lifes and quiet domestic scenes that recall the Dutch tradition. His work is a complete contrast to that of his contemporaries, the rococo painters. He developed his own technique, using successive layers

CHARGE OF THE LIGHT BRIGADE *The Charge of the Light Brigade,* an 1895 engraving by US artist Richard Caton Woodville (1825–1855). *The Art Archive/Musée du Louvre Paris/ Jacqueline Hyde*

of paint to achieve depth of tone, and is generally considered one of the finest exponents of genre painting.

Chareau, Pierre (1883–1950) French designer. He is best known for his Maison de Verre, Paris (1928–31). This predated and influenced development of the 1970s ▷high-tech approach to design in its innovative use of industrial materials, such as studded rubber flooring and glass bricks.

Charente French river, rising in the Massif Central, in Haute-Vienne *département*, 22 km/14 mi northwest of Chalus, and flowing past Angoulême and ▷Cognac into the Bay of Biscay south of Rochefort. It is 360 km/225 mi long. Its wide estuary is much silted up. It gives its name to two *départements*, Charente and Charente-Maritime.

charge see ▷electric charge.

charge-coupled device (CCD) device for forming images electronically, using a layer of silicon that releases electrons when struck by incoming light. The electrons are stored in ▷pixels and read off into a computer at the end of the exposure. CCDs are used in digital cameras, and have now almost entirely replaced photographic film for applications such as astrophotography where extreme sensitivity to light is paramount.

Charge of the Light Brigade disastrous attack by the British Light Brigade of cavalry against the Russian entrenched artillery on 25 October 1854 during the Crimean War at the Battle of ▷Balaclava. Of the 673 soldiers who took part, there were 272 casualties.

The fiasco came about as a result of a badly phrased order to 'prevent the enemy carrying away the guns'. This seems to have been intended to refer to Turkish guns captured by Russian forces in the hills above the battlefield, but the Brigade's commander assumed his target was the Russian guns about a mile away up the North Valley. He led the Brigade in a charge up the length of the valley between two rows of Russian artillery, sustaining heavy casualties. The Brigade was only saved from total destruction by French cavalry.

charismatic movement late 20th-century movement within the Christian church that emphasizes the role of the Holy Spirit in the life of the individual believer and in the life of the church. See ▷Pentecostal movement.

charity originally a Christian term meaning a selfless, disinterested form of love. This developed to include almsgiving or other actions performed by individuals to help the poor and needy. Today it refers to any independent agency (for example, Oxfam) that organizes such relief on a regular basis.

Charlemagne, Charles I the Great (742–814) King of the Franks from 768 and Holy Roman Emperor from 800. By inheritance (his father was ▷Pepin the Short) and extensive campaigns of conquest, he united most of Western Europe by 804, when after 30 years of war the Saxons came under his control.

Pepin had been mayor of the palace in Merovingian Neustria until he was crowned king by Pope Stephen II (died 757) in 754, and his sons Carl (Charlemagne) and Carloman were crowned as joint heirs. When Pepin died in 768 Charlemagne inherited the northern Frankish kingdom, and when Carloman died in 771 he also took possession of his domains. He was engaged in his first Saxon campaign when the Pope's call for help against the Lombards reached him; he crossed the Alps, captured Pavia, and took the title of king of the Lombards. The pacification and Christianizing of the Saxon peoples occupied the greater part of

Charlemagne's reign. From 792 northern Saxony was subdued, and in 804 the whole region came under his rule. In 777 the emir of Zaragoza asked for Charlemagne's help against the emir of Córdoba. Charlemagne crossed the Pyrenees in 778 and reached the Ebro but had to turn back from Zaragoza. The rearguard action of Roncesvalles, in which ▷Roland, warden of the Breton March, and other Frankish nobles were ambushed and killed by Basques, was later glorified in the *Chanson de Roland.* In 801 the district between the Pyrenees and the Llobregat was organized as the Spanish March. The independent duchy of Bavaria was incorporated in the kingdom in 788, and the Avar people were subdued 791–96. Charlemagne's last campaign was against a Danish attack on his northern frontier in 810.

The supremacy of the Frankish king in Europe found outward expression in the bestowal of the imperial title: in Rome, during Mass on Christmas Day 800, Pope Leo III crowned Charlemagne emperor. He died on 28 January 814 in Aachen, where he was buried. Soon a cycle of heroic legends and romances developed around him, including epics by Ariosto, Boiardo, and Tasso.

Charles two kings of Great Britain and Ireland:

Charles I (1600–1649) King of Great Britain and Ireland from 1625, son of James I of England (James VI of Scotland). He accepted the ▷petition of right in 1628 but then dissolved Parliament and ruled without a parliament from 1629 to 1640, a period known as the Eleven Years' Tyranny. His advisers were ▷Strafford and ▷Laud, who persecuted the ▷Puritans and provoked the Scots to revolt. The ▷Short Parliament, summoned in 1640, refused funds, and the ▷Long Parliament later that year rebelled. Charles declared war on Parliament in 1642 but surrendered in 1646 and was beheaded in 1649. He was the father of Charles II.

Charles was born in Dunfermline, Scotland, and became heir to the throne on the death of his brother Henry in 1612. He married Henrietta Maria, daughter of Henry IV of France. When he succeeded his father, friction with Parliament began at once. The parliaments of 1625 and 1626 were dissolved, and that of 1628 refused supplies until Charles had accepted the petition of right. In 1629 it attacked Charles's illegal taxation and support of Arminianism in the church, whereupon he dissolved Parliament and imprisoned its leaders.

CHARLEMAGNE A painting of Charlemagne by J P Scheuren (1825). *The Art Archive/Stadtmuseum Aachen/Dagli Orti*

For 11 years he ruled without a parliament, raising money by expedients, such as ▷ship money, which alienated the nation, while the ▷Star Chamber suppressed opposition by persecuting the Puritans. When Charles attempted to force a prayer book on the English model on Presbyterian Scotland, he found himself confronted with a nation in arms. The Short Parliament, which met in April 1640, refused to grant money until grievances were redressed, and was speedily dissolved. The Scots then advanced into England and forced their own terms on Charles. The Long Parliament met on 3 November 1640 and declared extra-parliamentary taxation illegal, abolished the Star Chamber and other prerogative courts, and voted that Parliament could not be dissolved without its own consent. Laud and other ministers were imprisoned, and Strafford condemned to death.

After the failure of his attempt to arrest the parliamentary leaders on 4 January 1642, Charles, confident that he had substantial support among those who felt that Parliament was becoming too radical and zealous, withdrew from London, and on 22 August declared war on Parliament by raising his standard at Nottingham (see ▷Civil War, English). Charles's defeat at Naseby,

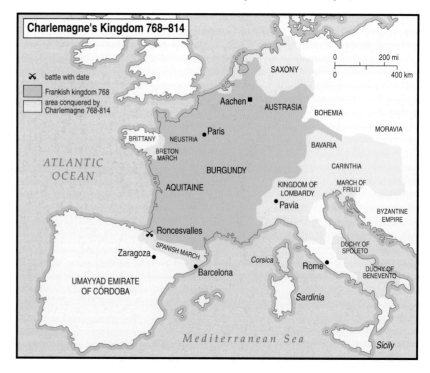

Charlemagne's Kingdom 768–814

✗ battle with date
▨ Frankish kingdom 768
☐ area conquered by Charlemagne 768-814

SAXONY
Aachen ■ AUSTRASIA
BOHEMIA
MORAVIA
Paris •
BRITTANY NEUSTRIA
BRETON MARCH
BAVARIA
ATLANTIC OCEAN
BURGUNDY
CARINTHIA
AQUITAINE
KINGDOM OF LOMBARDY
MARCH OF FRIULI
Pavia •
BYZANTINE EMPIRE
Roncesvalles ✗
SPANISH MARCH
DUCHY OF SPOLETO
Zaragoza •
Corsica
Rome •
Barcelona •
DUCHY OF BENEVENTO
UMAYYAD EMIRATE OF CÓRDOBA
Sardinia
Mediterranean Sea
Sicily

0   200 mi
0   400 km

near Leicester, in June 1645 ended all hopes of victory; in May 1646 he surrendered at Newark, Nottinghamshire, to the Scots, who handed him over to Parliament in January 1647. In June the army seized him and carried him off to Hampton Court palace, near London. While the army leaders strove to find a settlement, Charles secretly intrigued for a Scottish invasion. In November he escaped, but was recaptured and held at Carisbrooke Castle on the Isle of Wight; a Scottish invasion followed in 1648, and was shattered by Oliver ▷Cromwell at Preston, Lancashire. The army was determined 'to call Charles Stuart, that man of blood, to count'. In January 1649 the House of Commons set up a high court of justice, which tried Charles and condemned him to death. He was beheaded on 30 January in front of the Banqueting House in Whitehall, London.

Charles II (1630–1685) King of Great Britain and Ireland from 1660, when Parliament accepted the restoration of the monarchy after the collapse of Oliver Cromwell's Commonwealth; son of Charles I. His chief minister Edward ▷Clarendon, who arranged Charles's marriage in 1662 with Catherine of Braganza, was replaced in 1667 with the ▷Cabal of advisers. His plans to restore Catholicism in Britain led to war with the Netherlands (1672–74) in support of Louis XIV of France and a break with Parliament, which he dissolved in 1681. He was succeeded by James II. His mistresses included Lady Castlemaine, Nell ▷Gwyn, Lady Portsmouth, and Lucy ▷Walter.

Civil War Charles was born in St James's Palace, London. During the Civil War he lived with his father in Oxford 1642–45, and after the victory of Cromwell's Parliamentary forces he withdrew to France. Accepting the ▷Covenanters' offer to make him king, he landed in Scotland in 1650, and was crowned at Scone on 1 January 1651. An attempt to invade England was ended on 3 September by Cromwell's victory at Worcester. Charles escaped, and for nine years he wandered through France, Germany, Flanders, Spain, and Holland until the opening of negotiations by George Monk (1608–1670) in 1660.

Monarchy restored In April Charles issued the Declaration of Breda, promising a general amnesty and freedom of conscience. Parliament accepted the Declaration and he was proclaimed king on 8 May 1660. Charles landed at Dover on 26 May, and entered London three days later.

The issue of Catholicism Charles wanted to make himself absolute, and favoured Catholicism for his subjects as most consistent with absolute monarchy. The disasters of the Dutch war furnished an excuse for banishing Clarendon in 1667, and he was replaced by the Cabal of Clifford and Arlington, both secret Catholics, and ▷Buckingham, Ashley (Lord ▷Shaftesbury), and ▷Lauderdale, who had links with the ▷Dissenters.

In 1670 Charles signed the Secret Treaty of Dover, the full details of which were known only to Clifford and Arlington, whereby he promised Louis XIV of France he would declare himself a Catholic, re-establish Catholicism in England, and support the French king's projected war against the Dutch; in return Louis would finance Charles and in the event of resistance to supply him with troops. War with the Netherlands followed in 1672, and at the same time Charles issued the Declaration of Indulgence, suspending all penal laws against Catholics and Dissenters.

Opposition from Parliament In 1673, Parliament forced Charles to withdraw the Indulgence and accept a Test Act excluding all Catholics from office, and in 1674 to end the Dutch war. The Test Act broke up the Cabal, while Shaftesbury, who had learned the truth about the treaty, assumed the leadership of the opposition. Danby, the new chief minister, built up a court party in the Commons by bribery, while subsidies from Louis relieved Charles from dependence on Parliament. In 1678 Titus ▷Oates's announcement of a 'popish plot' released a general panic, which Shaftesbury exploited to introduce his Exclusion Bill, excluding James, Duke of York, from the succession as a Catholic; instead he hoped to substitute Charles's illegitimate son ▷Monmouth.

Dissolution of Parliament In 1681 Parliament was summoned to Oxford, which had been the Royalist headquarters during the Civil War. The Whigs attended armed, but when Shaftesbury rejected a last compromise, Charles dissolved Parliament and the Whigs fled in terror. Charles now ruled without a parliament, financed by Louis XIV. When the Whigs plotted a revolt, their leaders were executed, while Shaftesbury and Monmouth fled to the Netherlands.

Charles ten kings of France:

Charles I King of France, better known as the Holy Roman Emperor ▷Charlemagne.

Charles (III) the Simple (879–929) King of France (893–922), son of Louis the Stammerer. He was crowned at Reims. In 911 he ceded what later became the duchy of Normandy to the Norman chief Rollo.

CHARLES (IV) THE FAIR Charles IV, king of France, receiving envoys from England. The picture is dated 1400 and comes from the *Chroniques* of Jean Froissart, the 14th-century French historian. *The Art Archive/British Library/British Library*

Charles (IV) the Fair (1294–1328) King of France from 1322, when he succeeded Philip V as the last of the direct Capetian line.

Charles (V) the Wise (1337–1380) King of France (1364–80). He was regent during the captivity of his father John II in England from 1356 to 1360, and became king upon John's death. During the ▷Hundred Years' War he reconquered nearly all of France from England between 1369 and 1380, and diminished the power of the medieval mercenary companies in France.

Charles commanded at a distance rather than in the field, a method that had rarely succeeded in the past. He chose an excellent commander in Bertrand du Guesclin, who defeated the rebel Charles of Navarre at Cocherel in 1364.

Charles (VI) the Mad (1368–1422) (or **Charles the Well-Beloved**) King of France from 1380, succeeding his father Charles V; he was under the regency of his uncles until 1388. He became mentally unstable in 1392, and civil war broke out between the dukes of Orléans and Burgundy. ▷Henry V of England invaded France in 1415, conquering Normandy, and in 1420 forced Charles to sign the Treaty of Troyes, recognizing Henry as his successor.

Charles VII (1403–1461) King of France from 1422. Son of Charles VI, he was excluded from the succession by the Treaty of Troyes, but recognized by the south of France. In 1429 Joan of Arc raised the siege of Orléans and had him crowned at Reims. He organized France's first standing army and by 1453 had expelled the English from all of France except Calais.

Charles VIII (1470–1498) King of France from 1483, when he succeeded his father, Louis XI. In 1494 he unsuccessfully tried to claim the Neapolitan crown, and when he entered Naples in 1495 he was forced to withdraw by a coalition of Milan, Venice, Spain, and the Holy Roman Empire. He defeated them at Fornovo, but lost Naples. He died while preparing a second expedition.

Charles IX (1550–1574) King of France from 1560. Second son of Henry II and Catherine de' Medici, he succeeded his brother Francis II at the age of ten but remained under the domination of his mother's regency for ten years while France was torn by religious wars. In 1570 he fell under the influence of the ▷Huguenot leader Gaspard de Coligny; alarmed by this, Catherine instigated his order for the Massacre of ▷St Bartholomew, which led to a new religious war.

Charles X (1757–1836) King of France from 1824. Grandson of Louis XV and brother of Louis XVI and Louis XVIII, he was known as the comte d'Artois before his accession. As comte d'Artois, Charles enjoyed a notoriously dissolute life at court, and became involved in reactionary politics. Returning to France after the French Revolution, he became leader of the ultra-royalist group that put his brother Louis XVIII on the throne in 1814. He fled to England at the beginning of the French Revolution, and when he came to the throne on the death of Louis XVIII, he attempted to reverse the achievements of the Revolution. A revolt ensued in 1830, and he again fled to England.

Charles seven rulers of the Holy Roman Empire:

Charles (II) the Bald (823–877) Holy Roman Emperor from 875 and (as Charles II) king of West Francia from 843. He was the younger son of Louis (I) 'the Pious' (778–840) and warred against his brother the emperor Lothair I (*c.* 795–855). The Treaty of Verdun in 843 made him king of the West Frankish Kingdom (now France and the Spanish Marches). He entered Italy in 875 and was crowned emperor.

Charles improved Frankish defences against the Vikings, including river fortifications. His *Capitula* included military reforms on fortification, raising armies, and armaments.

Charles (III) the Fat (839–888) Holy Roman Emperor (881–87); he became king of the West Franks in 885, thus uniting for the last time the whole of Charlemagne's dominions, but was deposed.

Charles IV (1316–1378) Holy Roman Emperor from 1355 and king of Bohemia from 1346. Son of John of Luxembourg, King of Bohemia, he was elected king of Germany in 1346 and ruled all Germany from 1347. He was the founder of the first German university in Prague in 1348.

Charles V (1500–1558) Holy Roman Emperor (1519–56). Son of Philip of Burgundy and Joanna of Castile, he inherited vast possessions, which led to rivalry from Francis I of France, whose alliance with the Ottoman Empire brought Vienna under siege in 1529 and 1532. Charles was also in conflict with the Protestants in Germany until the Treaty of Passau of 1552, which allowed the Lutherans religious liberty.

CHARLES V The last Holy Roman Emperor to be crowned by the pope, Charles V, is shown here, in a 1540 fresco, with his most important rival for power in Europe, Francis I, king of France, as they enter Paris, France, together. *The Art Archive/Villa Farnese, Caprarola/Dagli Orti*

Charles VI (1685–1740) Holy Roman Emperor from 1711, father of ▷Maria Theresa, whose succession to his Austrian dominions he tried to ensure, and himself claimant to the Spanish throne in 1700, thus causing the War of the ▷Spanish Succession.

Charles VII (1697–1745) Holy Roman Emperor from 1742, opponent of ▷Maria Theresa's claim to the Austrian dominions of Charles VI.

Charles (Karl Franz Josef) (1887–1922) Emperor of Austria and king of Hungary from 1916, the last of the Habsburg emperors. He succeeded his great-uncle Franz Josef in 1916 but was forced to withdraw to Switzerland in 1918, although he refused to abdicate.

CHARLES X Charles X, King of France, pictured in his coronation robes in 1824. *The Art Archive/Album/Joseph Martin*

In 1921 he attempted unsuccessfully to regain the crown of Hungary and was deported to Madeira, where he died.

Charles (Spanish **Carlos**) Four kings of Spain; including

Charles II (1661–1700) King of Spain from 1665. The second son of Philip IV, he was the last of the Spanish Habsburg kings. Mentally disabled from birth, he bequeathed his dominions to Philip of Anjou, grandson of Louis XIV, which led to the War of the ▷Spanish Succession.

Charles III (1716–1788) King of Spain from 1759. Son of Philip V, he became duke of Parma in 1732 and conquered Naples and Sicily in 1734. On the death of his half-brother Ferdinand VI (1713–1759), he became king of Spain, handing over Naples and Sicily to his son Ferdinand (1751–1825). At home, he reformed state finances, strengthened the armed forces, and expelled the Jesuits. During his reign, Spain was involved in the Seven Years' War with France against England. This led to the loss of Florida in 1763, which was only regained when Spain and France supported the colonists during the American Revolution.

Charles IV (1748–1819) King of Spain from 1788, when he succeeded his father, Charles III; he left the government in the hands of his wife and her lover, the minister Manuel de Godoy (1767–1851). In 1808 Charles was induced to abdicate by Napoleon's machinations in favour of his son Ferdinand VII (1784–1833), who was subsequently deposed by Napoleon's brother Joseph. Charles was awarded a pension by Napoleon and died in Rome.

Charles (Swedish **Carl**) fifteen kings of Sweden (the first six were local chieftains), including:

Charles VIII (1408–1470) King of Sweden from 1448. He was elected regent of Sweden in 1438, when Sweden broke away from Denmark and Norway. He stepped down in 1441 when Christopher III of Bavaria (1418–1448) was elected king, but after his death became king. He was twice expelled by the Danes and twice restored.

Charles IX (1550–1611) King of Sweden from 1604, the youngest son of Gustavus Vasa. In 1568 he and his brother John led the rebellion against Eric XIV (1533–1577); John became king as John III and attempted to catholicize Sweden, and Charles led the opposition. John's son Sigismund, King of Poland and a Catholic, succeeded to the Swedish throne in 1592, and Charles led the Protestants. He was made regent in 1595 and deposed Sigismund in 1599. Charles was elected king of Sweden in 1604 and was involved in unsuccessful wars with Russia, Poland, and Denmark. He was the father of Gustavus Adolphus.

Charles X (1622–1660) King of Sweden from 1654, when he succeeded his cousin Christina. He waged war with Poland and Denmark and in 1657 invaded Denmark by leading his army over the frozen sea.

Charles XI (1655–1697) King of Sweden from 1660, when he succeeded his father, Charles X. His mother acted as regent until 1672 when Charles took over the government. He was a remarkable general and reformed the administration.

Charles XII (1682–1718) King of Sweden from 1697, when he succeeded his father, Charles XI. From 1700 he was involved in wars with Denmark, Poland, and Russia.

He won a succession of victories until, in 1709 while invading Russia, he was defeated at Poltava in the Ukraine, and forced to take refuge in Turkey until 1714. He was killed while besieging Fredrikshall, Norway, although it was not known whether he was murdered by his own side or by the enemy.

Charles XIII (1748–1818) King of Sweden from 1809, when he was elected; he became the first king of Sweden and Norway in 1814.

Charles XIV (1763–1844) Born Jean Baptiste Jules Bernadotte. King of Sweden and Norway from 1818. A former marshal in the French army, in 1810 he was elected crown prince of Sweden under the name of Charles John (Carl Johan). Loyal to his adopted country, he brought Sweden into the alliance against Napoleon in 1813, as a reward for which Sweden received Norway. He was the founder of the present dynasty.

Charles (Charles Philip Arthur George) (1948–) Prince of the UK, heir to the British throne, and Prince of Wales since 1958 (invested 1969). He is the first-born child of Queen Elizabeth II and the Duke of Edinburgh. He studied at Trinity College, Cambridge, (1967–70), before serving in the Royal Air Force and Royal Navy. The first royal heir since 1660 to have an English wife, he married ▷Diana, Princess of Wales (then Lady Diana Spencer), daughter of the 8th Earl Spencer, in 1981. There are two sons and heirs, William (1982–) and Henry (1984–). Amid much publicity, Charles and Diana separated in 1992 and were divorced in 1996. Following the death of Diana, Princess of Wales in 1997 Charles' popularity with the British public seemed

in some doubt; however opinion polls in 1998 indicated that public feeling had warmed towards him and to his long-standing relationship with Camilla Parker Bowles (1946–).

His concern with social issues and environmental issues has led to many projects for the young and underprivileged, of which the Prince's Trust is the best known, and he has been outspoken on the subject of the unsympathetic features of contemporary architecture.

Charles Albert (1798–1849) King of Sardinia from 1831. He showed liberal sympathies in early life, and after his accession introduced some reforms. On the outbreak of the 1848 revolution he granted a constitution and declared war on Austria. His troops were defeated at Custozza and Novara. In 1849 he abdicated in favour of his son Victor Emmanuel and retired to a monastery, where he died.

CHARLES ALBERT A contemporary painting of Charles Albert, king of Sardinia from 1831 to 1849. *The Art Archive/Cavalry Museum Pinerolo/Dagli Orti*

Charles Edward Stuart (1720–1788) Also known as **the Young Pretender** or **Bonnie Prince Charlie**. British prince, grandson of James II and son of James, the Old Pretender. In the ▷Jacobite rebellion of 1745 (the ▷Forty-Five) Charles won the support of the Scottish Highlanders; his army invaded England to claim the throne but was beaten back by the Duke of ▷Cumberland and routed at ▷Culloden on 16 April 1746. Charles fled; for five months he wandered through the Highlands with a price of £30,000 on his head before escaping to France. He visited England secretly in 1750, and may have made other visits. In later life he degenerated into a friendless drunkard. He settled in Italy in 1766.

He was born in Rome, and created Prince of Wales at birth. In July 1745 he sailed for Scotland, and landed in Inverness-shire with seven companions. On 19 August he raised his father's standard, and within a week had rallied an army of 2,000 Highlanders. He entered Edinburgh almost without resistance, won an easy victory at Prestonpans, invaded England, and by 4 December had reached Derby, where his officers insisted on a retreat. The army returned to Scotland and won a victory at Falkirk, but was forced to retire to the Highlands before Cumberland's advance.

Charles, (Mary) Eugenia (1919–) Dominican centre-right politician, prime minister 1980–95; cofounder and first leader of the cente-right Dominica Freedom Party (DFP). Two years after Dominica's independence the DFP won the 1980 general election and Charles became the Caribbean's first female prime minister. In 1993 she resigned the leadership of the DFP, but remained as prime minister until the 1995 elections, which were won by the opposition United Workers' Party (UNP). She then announced her retirement from politics.

Charles, Jacques Alexandre César (1746–1823) French physicist who studied gases and made the first ascent in a hydrogen-filled balloon in 1783. His work on the expansion of gases led to the formulation of ▷Charles's law.

Hearing of the hot-air balloons of the ▷Montgolfier brothers, Charles and his brothers began experimenting with hydrogen balloons and made their ascent only ten days after the Montgolfiers' first flight. In later flights Charles ascended to an altitude of 3,000 m/10,000 ft.

Charles Martel (c. 688–741) Frankish ruler (Mayor of the Palace) of the eastern Frankish kingdom from 717 and the whole kingdom from 731. His victory against the Moors at Moussais-la-Bataille near Tours in 732 earned him his nickname of Martel, 'the Hammer', because he halted the Islamic advance by the ▷Moors into Europe.

Charles, Ray (1930–) Adopted name of Ray Charles Robinson. US singer, songwriter, and pianist. A vastly talented musician and popular singer, he has recorded gospel, blues, rock, soul, country, and rhythm and blues. His numerous hit records include 'I've Got a Woman' (1955), 'What'd I Say' (1959), and 'Georgia on My Mind' (1960), as well as the live albums, *Ray Charles at Newport* (1958) and *Ray Charles in Person* (1960). Charles relaunched his career in the early 1980s after giving a show-stealing rendition of 'Shake Your Tailfeather' in the film *The Blues Brothers* (1980). The 1990s saw him release a much-lauded 50th anniversary anthology, *Genius & Soul* (1997), a definitive overview of his diverse recording career.

RAY CHARLES US singer, songwriter, and pianist Ray Charles, in Paris, France. *Archive Photos*

Charles's law law stating that the volume of a given mass of gas at constant pressure is directly proportional to its absolute temperature (temperature in kelvins). It was discovered by French physicist Jacques ▷Charles in 1787, and independently by French chemist Joseph Gay-Lussac in 1802.

The gas increases by 1/273 (0.003663) of its volume at 0°C for each °C rise of temperature. This means that the coefficient of expansion of all gases is the same. The law is only approximately true.

Charles the Bold, Duke of Burgundy (1433–1477) Duke of Burgundy from 1463 who fought in the French civil war at Montlhéry in 1465, then crushed Liège (1464–68). He reformed his army before engaging in an ambitious campaign for conquest, unsuccessfully besieging the imperial town of Neuss (1474–75), before being defeated in his attack on the Swiss Federation (1476–77). He died in battle near Nancy, in Lorraine.

Charleston back-kicking dance of the 1920s that originated in Charleston, South Carolina, and became a US craze following the musical *Runnin' Wild* (1923).

Charleston city and main port in southeastern South Carolina, USA, situated on a peninsula between the Ashley and Cooper rivers, at the head of a bay 11 km/7 mi from the Atlantic Ocean; seat of Charleston County; population (1992) 81,300. Industries include tourism, paper, chemicals, and petrochemicals. The original settlement dates from 1670, and Charleston was incorporated as a city in 1783; there are many historic houses and fine gardens here.

Charleston capital of ▷West Virginia and administrative headquarters of Kanawha County, situated on the Kanawha River, 85 km/53 mi upstream from its junction with the Ohio River; population (1992) 57,100. It is the commercial centre of a region that produces coal, natural gas, salt, clay, timber, and oil; it also has major chemical and glass industries.

charlock (or **wild mustard**) annual plant belonging to the cress family, found in Europe and Asia. It has hairy stems and leaves and yellow flowers. (*Sinapis arvensis*, family Cruciferae.)

Charlotte Amalie capital, tourist resort, and free port of the US Virgin Islands, on the island of St Thomas; population (1995 est) 12,600. Boat-building and rum distillation are among the economic activities. It was founded in 1672 by the Danish West India Company.

CHARLOCK Charlock, or wild mustard, *Sinapis arvensis*, growing among potatoes. *Premaphotos Wildlife*

Charlotte Augusta, Princess (1796–1817) Only child of George IV and Caroline of Brunswick, and heir to the British throne. In 1816 she married Prince Leopold of Saxe-Coburg (later Leopold I of the Belgians), but died in childbirth 18 months later.

Charlotte Sophia (1744–1818) British queen consort. The daughter of the German duke of Mecklenburg-Strelitz, she married George III of Great Britain and Ireland in 1761, and they had nine sons and six daughters.

Charlottetown capital and main port of ▷Prince Edward Island, Canada, situated on the south side of the island on Hillsborough Bay; population (1996) 32,500. Charlottetown was incorporated as a city in 1995 and serves as the administrative headquarters of Queens County. It trades in textiles, fish, timber, vegetables, and dairy produce; the main industries are food-processing, shipbuilding, and tourism.

Charlton, Bobby (Robert) (1937–) English footballer who between 1958 and 1970 scored a record 49 goals for England in 106 appearances. An elegant attacking midfield player who specialized in fierce long-range shots, he spent most of his playing career with Manchester United and played in the England team that won the World Cup in 1966. He is the younger brother of Jack ▷Charlton and the nephew of the Newcastle and England forward Jackie Milburn. Knighted in 1994.
    Related Web site: Charlton, Bobby http://dnausers.d-n-a.net/dnetmQXk/legends/bobbycharlton.htm

Charlton, Jack (John) (1935–) English footballer. A tall commanding centre-half he spent all his playing career with Leeds United and played more than 750 games for them. He appeared in the England team that won the World Cup in 1966. He is the older brother of Robert (Bobby) ▷Charlton and the nephew of the Newcastle and England forward Jackie Milburn.

charm in physics, a property possessed by one type of ▷quark (very small particles found inside protons and neutrons), called the charm quark. The effects of charm are only seen in experiments with particle ▷accelerators. See ▷elementary particles.

Charon in Greek mythology, the boatman who ferried the dead (shades) over the rivers Acheron and Styx to ▷Hades, the underworld. An *obolus* (coin) placed on the tongue of the dead paid for their passage.

Chartism radical British democratic movement, mainly of the working classes, which flourished around 1838 to 1848. It derived its name from the People's Charter, a six-point programme comprising universal male suffrage, equal electoral districts, secret ballot, annual parliaments, and abolition of the property qualification for, and payment of, members of Parliament.
    The movement grew out of the London Working Men's Association, formed in 1836 by William Lovett. Two petitions were presented to Parliament (in 1839 and 1842), and were rejected. Under the leadership of Fergus O'Connor, Chartism became a powerful expression of working class frustration, and a third petition, also rejected, was presented in 1848. The long-term failure of the movement was probably due to greater prosperity among the populace as a whole, lack of organization, and rivalry among the leadership of the movement.
    Related Web site: Chartism http://web.hist.uib.no/delfag-v97/vemund/Chartism.html

Chartres (Latin *Autricum*) administrative centre of the *département* of Eure-et-Loir in northwest France, 96 km/59 mi southwest of Paris on the River Eure; population (1990) 41,850; conurbation 84,000. The city is an agricultural centre for the fertile Plaine de la Beauce. The twin-spired cathedral of Notre Dame, completed about 1240, is a masterpiece of Gothic architecture and a world heritage monument; the city also has other medieval churches and some fine old houses, and attracts large numbers of tourists.

Charybdis in Greek mythology, a monster and the whirlpool it forms, on the Sicilian side of the northern end of the narrow Straits of Messina, opposite the sea monster Scylla.

château country house or important residence in France. The term originally applied to a French medieval castle. The château was first used as a domestic building in the late 15th century. By the reign of Louis XIII (1610–43) fortifications such as moats and keeps were no longer used for defensive purposes, but merely as decorative features. The Loire valley contains some fine examples of châteaux.

Chateaubriand, François Auguste René, Vicomte de (1768–1848) French writer. He was a founder of Romanticism. Having lived in exile from the French Revolution between 1794 and 1800, he wrote *Atala* (1801; based on his encounters with North American Indians), *Le Génie du christianisme/The Genius of Christianity* (1802) – a defence of the Christian faith in terms of social, cultural, and spiritual benefits – and the autobiographical *René* (1805).
    He visited the USA in 1791 and, on his return to France, fought for the royalist side, which was defeated at Thionville in 1792. He lived in exile in England until 1800. When he returned to France, he held diplomatic appointments under Louis XVIII, becoming ambassador to Britain in 1822. He later wrote *Mémoires d'outre-tombe/Memoirs from Beyond the Tomb* (1848–50), an account, often imaginary, of his own life.

FRANÇOIS CHATEAUBRIAND French writer François Auguste Chateaubriand, who is often credited with founding Romanticism. *Archive Photos*

Chatterton, Thomas (1752–1770) English poet. His medieval-style poems and brief life were to inspire English Romanticism. Having studied ancient documents, he composed poems he ascribed to a 15th-century monk, 'Thomas Rowley', and these were at first accepted as genuine. He committed suicide after becoming destitute.
    Seeking a patron, he sent examples to the writer Horace ▷Walpole, who, after originally being taken in, was advised that they were forgeries. In 1770 Chatterton moved to London, where during the four months until his death he contributed prose and satirical verses to various periodicals. He poisoned himself with arsenic, after having lived for weeks on the verge of starvation. His death gripped the imagination of the Romantic poets and tributes were paid to his memory by Coleridge, Shelley, Keats, and Wordsworth.
    Related Web site: Selected Poetry of Thomas Chatterton (1752–1770) http://www.library.utoronto.ca/utel/rp/authors/chattert.html

Chatwin, (Charles) Bruce (1940–1989) English writer. His works include *The Songlines* (1987), written after living with Australian Aborigines; the novel *Utz* (1988), about a manic porcelain collector in Prague; and travel pieces and journalism collected in *What Am I Doing Here* (1989).

GEOFFREY CHAUCER Author of *The Canterbury Tales*, the poet Geoffrey Chaucer was influenced by Italian writers such as Boccaccio, Dante, and Petrarch. Wise and widely travelled, his works comment on his times, on the fashion for 'courtly love', and also on the corruption of the medieval church. *Archive Photos*

Chaucer, Geoffrey (c. 1340–1400) English poet. *The Canterbury Tales*, a collection of stories told by a group of pilgrims on their way to Canterbury, reveals his knowledge of human nature and his stylistic variety, from urbane and ironic to simple and bawdy. His early work shows formal French influence, as in the dream-poem *The Book of the Duchess* and his adaptation of the French allegorical poem on courtly love, *The Romaunt of the Rose*. More mature works reflect the influence of Italian realism, as in *Troilus and Criseyde*, a substantial narrative poem about the tragic betrayal of an idealized courtly love, adapted from ▷Boccaccio. In *The Canterbury Tales* he shows his own genius for metre and characterization. Chaucer was the most influential English poet of the Middle Ages.
    He was born in London, the son of a vintner. Taken prisoner in the French wars, he had to be ransomed by Edward III in 1360. In 1366 he married Philippa Roet, sister of Katherine Swynford, the mistress and later third wife of ▷John of Gaunt, Duke of Lancaster. Payments during the period 1367 to 1374 indicate a rising fortune and show that Chaucer made several journeys abroad, both on

THOMAS CHATTERTON A picture by Henry Wallis (1830–1916) of the English poet Thomas Chatterton, painted in 1856. *The Art Archive/Tate Gallery London/Eileen Tweedy*

military service and public business. He was sent to Italy (where he may have met Boccaccio and ▷Petrarch), France, and Flanders. He was controller of wool customs (1374–86), and of petty customs (1382–86). He became justice of the peace for Kent in 1385 and knight of the shire in 1386. In 1389 he was made clerk of the king's works, and superintended undertakings at Woolwich and Smithfield. In 1391 he gave up the clerkship and accepted the position of deputy forester of North Petherton, Somerset. Late in 1399 he moved to Westminster and died the following year; he was buried in the Poets' Corner of Westminster Abbey.

> **Geoffrey Chaucer**
> *He was a verray parfit gentil knight.*
> Canterbury Tales, Prologue

chauvinism unreasonable and exaggerated patriotism and pride in one's own country, with a corresponding contempt for other nations. In the mid-20th century the expression **male chauvinism** was coined to mean an assumed superiority of the male sex over the female.

Chavez, Cesar Estrada (1927–1993) US labour organizer who founded the National Farm Workers Association in 1962 and, with the support of the AFL-CIO (Federation of North American trade unions) and other major unions, embarked on a successful campaign to unionize California grape workers. He led boycotts of citrus fruits, lettuce, and grapes in the early 1970s, but disagreement and exploitation of migrant farm labourers continued despite his successes.

Chayefsky, Paddy (Sidney) (1923–1981) US screen-writer and dramatist. A writer of great passion and insight, he established his reputation with naturalistic television plays, at least two of which – *Marty* (1955) and *Bachelor Party* (1957) – were adapted for cinema. He won Academy Awards for his screenplays for *Marty*, the bitterly satirical *The Hospital* (1971), and *Network* (1976).

Chechnya (or Chechenia or Chechen Republic) breakaway part of the former Russian autonomous republic of Checheno-Ingush, on the northern slopes of the ▷Caucasus Mountains; official name **Noxcijn Republika Ickeriy** from 1994; area 17,300 sq km/6,680 sq mi; population (1990) 1,290,000 (Chechen 90%). The capital is ▷Groznyy. Chief industries are oil extraction (at one of the largest Russian oilfields), engineering, chemicals, building materials, and timber. Most of the inhabitants are Sunni Muslim.

cheese food made from the **curds** (solids) of soured milk from cows, sheep, or goats, separated from the **whey** (liquid), then salted, put into moulds, and pressed into firm blocks. Cheese is ripened with bacteria or surface fungi, and kept for a time to mature before eating.
Related Web site: CheeseNet http://www.wgx.com/cheesenet/

CHEESE A cheese dairy in Sicily, Italy. *Image Bank*

cheetah large wild cat *Acinonyx jubatus* native to Africa, Arabia, and southwestern Asia, but now rare in some areas. Yellowish with black spots, it has a slim lithe build. It is up to 1 m/3 ft tall at the shoulder, and up to 1.5 m/5 ft long. It can reach 103 kph/64 mph, but tires after about 400 yards. Cheetahs live in open country where they hunt small antelopes, hares, and birds.

A cheetah's claws do not retract as fully as in most cats. It is the world's fastest mammal. Cheetahs face threats both from ranchers who shoot them as vermin and from general habitat destruction that is reducing the prey on which they feed, especially gazelles. As a result the wild population is thought to have fallen by over half since the 1970s; there are now thought to be no more than 5,000–12,000 left.
Related Web site: Cheetah http://dialspace.dial.pipex.com/town/plaza/abf90/cheetah.htm

Cheever, John (1912–1982) US writer. His stories and novels focus on the ironies of upper-middle-class life in suburban America. His short stories were frequently published in the *New Yorker* magazine. His first novel was *The Wapshot Chronicle* (1957),

for which he won the National Book Award. Others include *Falconer* (1977). His *Stories of John Cheever* (1978) won a Pulitzer prize.

Chekhov, Anton Pavlovich
(1860–1904) Russian dramatist and writer of short stories. His plays concentrate on the creation of atmosphere and delineation of internal development, rather than external action. His first play, *Ivanov* (1887), was a failure, as was *The Seagull* (1896) until revived by Stanislavsky in 1898 at the Moscow Art Theatre, for which Chekhov went on to write his finest plays: *Uncle Vanya* (1897), *The Three Sisters* (1901), and *The Cherry Orchard* (1904).

Chekhov was born in Taganrog, southern Russia. He qualified as a doctor in 1884, but devoted himself to writing short stories rather than practising medicine. The collection *Particoloured Stories* (1886) consolidated his reputation and gave him leisure to develop his style, as seen in *My Life* (1895), *The Lady with the Dog* (1898), and *In the Ravine* (1900).

Chekiang alternative transcription of ▷Zhejiang, a province of China.

chelate chemical compound whose molecules consist of one or more metal atoms or charged ions joined to chains of organic residues by coordinate (or dative covalent) chemical ▷bonds.

The parent organic compound is known as a **chelating agent** – for example, EDTA (ethylene-diaminetetra-acetic acid), used in chemical analysis. Chelates are used in analytical chemistry, in agriculture and horticulture as carriers of essential trace metals, in water softening, and in the treatment of thalassaemia by removing excess iron, which may build up to toxic levels in the body. Metalloproteins (natural chelates) may influence the performance of enzymes or provide a mechanism for the storage of iron in the spleen and plasma of the human body.

Cheltenham spa town at the foot of the Cotswold Hills, Gloucestershire, England, 12 km/7 mi northeast of Gloucester; population (1991) 91,300. The town has light industries including aerospace electronics and food-processing (Kraft). Tourism and the conference business are also important. Annual events include the Cheltenham Festival of Literature in October, the International Festival of Music, the National Hunt Festival in March, and the Cheltenham Cricket Festival. There is a steeplechase course in Prestbury Park, known for the annual Cheltenham Gold Cup.

Chelyabinsk capital city, economic and cultural centre of Chelyabinsk oblast (region), Russian Federation, 240 km/150 mi south of Yekaterinburg on the Miass River; population (1996 est) 1,083,000. Chelyabinsk is a major industrial centre in the Urals and an important rail centre. The main branches of industry are engineering (tractors, aircraft, machine tools), and metallurgy (steel, ferro-alloys, zinc). There is a large lignite-fired power station nearby. The important Chelyabinsk coal basin (first exploited in 1906) lies 15 km/9 mi to the east of the city. Waste from the city's plutonium plant makes it the most radioactive place in the world.

chemical change change that occurs when two or more substances (reactants) interact with each other, resulting in the production of different substances (products) with different chemical compositions. A simple example of chemical change is the burning of carbon in oxygen to produce carbon dioxide (▷combustion). Other types of chemical change include ▷decomposition, ▷oxidation, and ▷reduction.

chemical element alternative name for ▷element.

chemical equation method of indicating the reactants and products of a chemical reaction by using chemical symbols and

CHEMICAL WARFARE A man wearing an early gas mask. Its long tube and the purification system that was strapped to the chest made it very cumbersome and almost impossible to use in action during wartime. *Image Bank*

formulae. A chemical equation gives two basic pieces of information: (1) the reactants (on the left-hand side) and products (right-hand side); and (2) the reacting proportions (stoichiometry) – that is, how many units of each reactant and product are involved. The equation must balance; that is, the total number of atoms of a particular element on the left-hand side must be the same as the number of atoms of that element on the right-hand side.

$$Na_2CO_3 + 2HCl \rightarrow 2NaCl + CO_2 + H_2O$$
$$reactants \quad \rightarrow \quad products$$

This equation states that one molecule of sodium carbonate combines with two molecules of hydrochloric acid to form two molecules of sodium chloride, one of carbon dioxide, and one of water. Double arrows indicate that the reaction is reversible – in the formation of ammonia from hydrogen and nitrogen, the direction depends on the temperature and pressure of the reactants.

$$3H_2 + N_2 \leftrightarrow 2NH_3$$

Related Web site: Introduction to Chemical Equations http://www.netcomuk.co.uk/~rpeters1/aufceam.htm

chemical equilibrium condition in which the products of a reversible chemical reaction (see ▷reversible reaction) are formed at the same rate at which they decompose back into the reactants, so that the concentration of each reactant and product remains constant.

chemical warfare use in ▷war of gaseous, liquid, or solid substances intended to have a toxic effect on humans, animals, or plants. Together with ▷biological warfare, it was banned by the Geneva Protocol in 1925, and the United Nations in 1989 also voted for a ban. In June 1990 the USA and USSR agreed bilaterally to reduce their stockpile to 5,000 tonnes each by 2002. The USA began replacing its stocks with new nerve-gas ▷binary weapons. In 1993 over 120 nations, including the USA and Russian Federation, signed a treaty outlawing the manufacture, stockpiling, and use of chemical weapons. However, it was not until 1997 that the Russian parliament ratified the treaty.

chemical weathering form of ▷weathering brought about by chemical attack on rocks, usually in the presence of water. Chemical weathering involves the 'rotting', or breakdown, of the original minerals within a rock to produce new minerals (such as ▷clay minerals). Some chemicals are dissolved and carried away from the weathering source, while others are brought in.

chemiluminescence the emission of light from a substance as a result of a chemical reaction (rather than raising its temperature). See ▷luminescence.

CHEETAH A cheetah family feeding on the carcass of an impala that they have killed in a game park in Kenya. *Ken Preston-Mafham/Premaphotos Wildlife*

Chemistry: Key Events

c. 3000 BC	Egyptians begin producing bronze – an alloy of copper and tin.
c. 450 BC	Empedocles proposes that all substances are made up of a combination of four elements – earth, air, fire, and water – an idea that is developed by Plato and Aristotle and persists for over 2,000 years.
c. 400 BC	Democritus theorizes that matter consists ultimately of tiny, indivisible particles, *atomoi*. The Greek word *atomos* means uncuttable.
200	The techniques of solution, filtration, and distillation are known.
7th–17th centuries	Chemistry is dominated by alchemy, the attempt to transform nonprecious metals such as lead and copper into gold. Though misguided, it leads to the discovery of many new chemicals and techniques.
12th century	Alcohol is first distilled in Europe.
1242	Gunpowder is introduced to Europe from the Far East.
1650	Leyden University in the Netherlands sets up the first chemistry laboratory.
1661	Robert Boyle defines an element as any substance that cannot be broken down into still simpler substances and asserts that matter is composed of 'corpuscles' (atoms) of various sorts and sizes, capable of arranging themselves into groups, each of which constitutes a chemical substance.
1662	Boyle describes the inverse relationship between the volume and pressure of a fixed mass of gas (Boyle's law).
1697	Georg Stahl proposes the erroneous theory that combustible materials are rich in a substance called phlogiston, which is released when they burn.
1755	Joseph Black discovers carbon dioxide.
1774	Joseph Priestley discovers oxygen, which he calls 'dephlogisticated air'. Antoine Lavoisier demonstrates his law of conservation of mass.
1781	Henry Cavendish shows water to be a compound.
1792	Alessandro Volta demonstrates the electrochemical series.
1807	Humphry Davy passes an electric current through molten compounds (the process of electrolysis) in order to isolate elements, such as potassium, that have never been separated by chemical means. Jöns Berzelius proposes that chemicals produced by living creatures should be termed 'organic'.
1808	John Dalton publishes his atomic theory. It states that every element consists of similar indivisible particles – called atoms – which differ from the atoms of other elements in their mass. Dalton also draws up a list of relative atomic masses. Joseph Gay-Lussac announces that the volumes of gases that combine chemically with one another are in simple ratios.
1811	Amedeo Avogadro's hypothesis on the relation between the volume and number of molecules of a gas, and its temperature and pressure, is published.
1813–14	Berzelius devises the chemical symbols and formulae still used to represent elements and compounds.
1828	Franz Wöhler converts ammonium cyanate into urea – the first synthesis of an organic compound from an inorganic substance.
1832–33	Michael Faraday expounds the laws of electrolysis, and adopts the term 'ion' for the particles believed to be responsible for carrying current.
1846	Thomas Graham expounds his law of diffusion.
1853	Robert Bunsen invents the Bunsen burner.
1858	Stanislao Cannizzaro differentiates between atomic and molecular weights (masses).
1861	Organic chemistry is defined by German chemist Friedrich Kekulé as the chemistry of carbon compounds.
1864	John Newlands devises the first periodic table of the elements.
1869	Dmitri Mendeleyev expounds his periodic table of the elements (based on atomic mass), leaving gaps for elements that are predicted but have not yet been discovered.
1884	Svante Arrhenius suggests that electrolytes (solutions or molten compounds that conduct electricity) dissociate into ions, atoms, or groups of atoms that carry a positive or negative charge.
1894	William Ramsey and Lord Rayleigh discover the first inert gas, argon.
1897	The electron is discovered by J J Thomson.
1901	Mikhail Tsvet invents paper chromatography as a means of separating pigments.
1909	Sören Sörensen devises the pH scale of acidity-alkalinity.
1912	Max von Laue shows crystals to be composed of regular, repeating arrays of atoms by studying the patterns in which they diffract X-rays.
1913–14	Henry Moseley equates the atomic number of an element with the positive charge on its nuclei, and draws up the periodic table, based on atomic number, that is used today.
1916	Gilbert Newton Lewis explains covalent bonding between atoms as a sharing of electrons.
1927	Nevil Sidgwick publishes his theory of valency, based on the numbers of electrons in the outer shells of the reacting atoms.
1930	Electrophoresis, which separates particles in suspension in an electric field, is invented by Arne Tiselius.
1940	Edwin McMillan and Philip Abelson show that new elements with a higher atomic number than uranium can be formed by bombarding uranium with neutrons, and synthesize the first transuranic element, neptunium.
1950	Derek Barton deduces that some properties of organic compounds are affected by the orientation of their functional groups (the study of which becomes known as conformational analysis).
1955	Ilya Prigogine describes the thermodynamics of irreversible processes (the transformations of energy that take place in, for example, many reactions within living cells).
1962	Neil Bartlett prepares the first compound of an inert gas, xenon hexafluoroplatinate; it was previously believed that inert gases could not take part in a chemical reaction.
1965	Robert B Woodward synthesizes complex organic compounds.
1981	Quantum mechanics is applied to predict the course of chemical reactions by US chemist Roald Hoffmann and Kenichi Fukui of Japan.
1985	Fullerenes, a new class of carbon solids made up of closed cages of carbon atoms, are discovered by Harold Kroto and David Walton at the University of Sussex, England.
1987	Donald Cram, Charles Pederson, and Jean-Marie Lehn create artificial molecules that mimic the vital chemical reactions of life processes.
1990	Jean-Marie Lehn, Ulrich Koert, and Margaret Harding report the synthesis of a new class of compounds, called nucleohelicates, that mimic the double helical structure of DNA, turned inside out.
1995	German chemists build the largest ever wheel molecule, made up of 154 molybdenum atoms surrounded by oxygen atoms. It has a relative molecular mass of 24,000 and is soluble in water.
1997	The International Union of Pure and Applied Chemistry (IUPAC) officially names elements 104–109. Element 104 (discovered in Russia in 1964 and the USA in 1969) is named rutherfordium, element 105 (disovered in Russia in 1967 and the USA in 1970) is named dubnium, element 106 (discovered in 1973) is named seaborgium, element 107 (discovered in 1976) is named bohrium, element 108 (discovered in 1984) is named hassium, and element 109 (discovered in 1982) is named meitnerium.
1999	Russian scientists at the Institute of Nuclear Research at Dubna create element 114 by colliding isotopes calcium 48 and plutonium 44. Shortly afterwards, US physicists create element 118, which decays into another new element, 116, by bombarding lead with krypton.

chemisorption the attachment, by chemical means, of a single layer of molecules, atoms, or ions of gas to the surface of a solid or, less frequently, a liquid. It is the basis of catalysis (see ▷catalyst) and is of great industrial importance.

chemistry branch of science concerned with the study of the structure and composition of the different kinds of matter, the changes which matter may undergo and the phenomena which occur in the course of these changes.

Organic chemistry is the branch of chemistry that deals with carbon compounds. **Inorganic chemistry** deals with the description, properties, reactions, and preparation of all the elements and their compounds, with the exception of carbon compounds. **Physical chemistry** is concerned with the quantitative explanation of chemical phenomena and reactions, and the measurement of data required for such explanations. This branch studies in particular the movement of molecules and the effects of temperature and pressure, often with regard to gases and liquids.
Molecules, atoms, and elements All matter can exist in three states: gas, liquid, or solid. It is composed of minute particles termed **molecules**, which are constantly moving, and may be further divided into ▷atoms.

Molecules that contain atoms of one kind only are known as **elements**; those that contain atoms of different kinds are called **compounds**.
Compounds and mixtures Chemical compounds are produced by a chemical action that alters the arrangement of the atoms in the reacting molecules. Heat, light, vibration, catalytic action, radiation, or pressure, as well as moisture (for ionization), may be necessary to produce a chemical change. Examination and possible breakdown of compounds to determine their components is **analysis**, and the building up of compounds from their components is **synthesis**. When substances are brought together without changing their molecular structures they are said to be **mixtures**.
Formulas and equations Symbols are used to denote the elements. The symbol is usually the first letter or letters of the English or Latin name of the element – for example, C for carbon; Ca for calcium; Fe for iron (*ferrum*). These symbols represent one atom of the element; molecules containing more than one atom of an element are denoted by a subscript figure – for example, water is H_2O. In some substances a group of atoms acts as a single entity, and these are enclosed in parentheses in the symbol – for example $(NH_4)_2SO_4$ denotes ammonium sulphate. The symbolic representation of a molecule is known as a **formula**. A figure placed before a formula represents the number of molecules of a substance taking part in, or being produced by, a chemical reaction – for example, $2H_2O$ indicates two molecules of water. Chemical reactions are expressed by means of **equations** as in:

$$NaCl + H_2SO_4 \rightarrow NaHSO_4 + HCl$$

This equation states the fact that sodium chloride (NaCl) on being treated with sulphuric acid (H_2SO_4) is converted into sodium bisulphate (sodium hydrogensulphate, $NaHSO_4$) and hydrogen chloride (HCl). See also ▷chemical equation.
Metals, nonmetals, and the periodic system Elements are divided into **metals**, which have lustre and conduct heat and electricity, and **nonmetals**, which usually lack these properties. The **periodic system**, developed by John Newlands in 1863 and established by Dmitri ▷Mendeleyev in 1869, classified elements according to their relative atomic masses. Those elements that resemble each other in general properties were found to bear a relation to one another by weight, and these were placed in groups or families. Certain anomalies in this system were later removed by classifying the elements according to their atomic numbers. The latter is equivalent to the positive charge on the nucleus of the atom.

Related Web site: General Chemistry Online http://marie. frostburg.edu/chem/senese/101/index.shtml

Chemnitz industrial city in Saxony, Federal Republic of Germany, on the River Chemnitz, 65 km/40 mi south-southeast of Leipzig; population (1995) 271,400. Industries include engineering and the manufacture of textiles and chemicals. As a former district capital of East Germany it was named Karl-Marx-Stadt from 1953 to 1990. The city has a university (Chemnitz-Zurickan).

chemosynthesis method of making ▷protoplasm (contents of a cell) using the energy from chemical reactions, in contrast to the use of light energy employed for the same purpose in ▷photosynthesis. The process is used by certain bacteria, which can synthesize organic compounds from carbon dioxide and water using the energy from special methods of ▷respiration.

Nitrifying bacteria are a group of chemosynthetic organisms which change free nitrogen into a form that can be taken up by plants; nitrobacteria, for example, oxidize nitrites to nitrates. This is a vital part of the ▷nitrogen cycle. As chemosynthetic bacteria can survive without light energy, they can live in dark and inhospitable regions, including the hydrothermal vents of the Pacific ocean. Around these vents, where temperatures reach up to 350°C/662°F, the chemosynthetic bacteria are the basis of a food web supporting fishes and other marine life.

chemotherapy any medical treatment with chemicals. It usually refers to treatment of cancer with cytotoxic and other drugs. The term was coined by the German bacteriologist Paul Ehrlich for the use of synthetic chemicals against infectious diseases.

chemotropism movement by part of a plant in response to a chemical stimulus. The response by the plant is termed 'positive' if the growth is towards the stimulus or 'negative' if the growth is away from the stimulus.

Cheney, Dick (1941–) Born Richard Bruce Cheney. US Republican politician, vice-president from 2001. He was the youngest-ever chief-of-staff 1975–77 under President Gerald Ford, a congressman 1979–89, and defence secretary 1989–93 under President George Bush. He was selected in 2000 as the running-mate of Bush's son, George W ▷Bush, to bring experience in federal matters and foreign policy to the electoral ticket.

Chengchow alternative transcription of ▷Zhengzhou, the capital of Henan province, China.

Chengdu (or Chengtu) ancient city and capital of ▷Sichuan province, China; population (1994) 3,016,000. It is a busy rail junction and has railway workshops. Industries include food-processing, engineering, electronics, and the manufacture of textiles and petrochemicals. There are well-preserved temples of the 8th-century poet Tu Fu and other historical figures.

Chennai (formerly Madras (to 1996)) industrial port and capital of Tamil Nadu, India, on the Bay of Bengal; population (1991) 5,361,000. An all-weather artificial harbour handles cotton goods, oilseeds, hides and skins, and industrial raw materials. Main industries include cotton, cement, chemicals, railway, car and bicycle manufacture, oil refining, iron, and steel. Fort St George (1639) remains from the East India Company when Chennai was the chief port on the east coast; the fort now contains government offices and St Mary's Church, the first English church built in India (1680). Chennai was occupied by the French from 1746 to 1748 and shelled by the German ship *Emden* in 1914, the only place in India attacked in World War I. The University of Madras was founded in 1857, and there is a technical institute (1959).

CHER US singer and actor Cher's success in music, films, television, and on stage, over the course of a career which began in the 1960s, makes her one of the most enduring entertainers of our time. *Archive Photos*

Cher (1946–) Born Cherilyn Sarkasian LaPier. US singer and actor. In 1965 she had her first hit with Sonny Bono (they were the duo Sonny and Cher) with 'I Got You Babe', which topped US and UK charts. Her other top-selling singles include 'Gypsies, Tramps, and Thieves' (1971), 'Dark Lady' (1974), 'I Found Someone' (1987), 'The Shoop Shoop Song' (1991 for her film *Mermaids*), and 'Believe' (1998), which was a dance hit as well as a chart success. She has also had a successful acting career, receiving a Cannes Film Festival Best Actress award for *Mask* (1985) and an Academy Award for Best Actress in *Moonstruck* (1987).

Cher French river, rising in the Massif Central on the eastern edge of Creuse *département*, and flowing northwest to join the River ▷Loire 19 km/12 mi below Tours; length 350 km/217 mi. It is navigable from Vierzon. It gives its name to the *département* of Cher.

Cherbourg French port and naval station at the northern end of the Cotentin peninsula, in Manche *département*; population (1990) 28,800, conurbation 92,000. There is an institute for studies in nuclear warfare, and the town's dry-docks house some of the largest shipbuilding yards in France. Other industries include the manufacture of hosiery and engineering goods. Transatlantic maritime trade has declined greatly.

Cherenkov, Pavel Alexeevich (1904–1990) Soviet physicist. He was awarded the Nobel Prize for Physics in 1958 for his discovery in 1934 of *Cherenkov radiation*; this occurs as a bluish light when charged atomic particles pass through water or other media at a speed in excess of that of light. He shared the award with his colleagues Ilya Frank and Igor Tamm for work resulting in a cosmic-ray counter.

Chernobyl town in northern Ukraine, 100 km/62 mi north of Kiev; site of a former nuclear power station. On 26 April 1986, two huge explosions occurred at the plant, destroying a central reactor and breaching its 1,000-tonne roof. In the immediate vicinity of Chernobyl, 31 people died (all firemen or workers at the plant) and 135,000 were permanently evacuated. It has been estimated that there will be an additional 20,000–40,000 deaths from cancer over 60 years; 600,000 people are officially classified as at risk. According to World Health Organization (WHO) figures from 1995, the incidence of thyroid cancer in children increased 200-fold in Belarus as a result of fallout from the disaster. The last remaining nuclear reactor at Chernobyl was shut down in December 2000.

Related Web site: Chernobyl: Ten Years On http://www.nea.fr/html/rp/chernobyl/chernobyl.html

Chernomyrdin, Viktor Stepanovich (1938–) Russian politician, prime minister 1992–98. A former manager in the state gas industry and communist party apparatchik, he became prime minister in December 1992 after Russia's ex-communist-dominated parliament had ousted the market reformer Yegor Gaidar. He assumed temporary control over foreign and security policy after President Boris Yeltsin suffered a heart attack in November 1995, and again in November 1996 when Yeltsin underwent open-heart surgery. From March 1997 Chernomyrdin lost direct control over the economy to the promoted reformist ministers Anatoly Chubais and Boris Nemtsov. In March 1998 he was dismissed as prime minister, along with the entire government, by President Yeltsin.

Cherokee member of the largest group of ▷American Indian people numbering 308,000 (1990) and formerly living in the southern Appalachian Mountains of North America, in what is now Alabama, the Carolinas, Georgia, and Tennessee. The Cherokee were one of the Five Civilized Tribes and had adopted the white man's methods of farming, had a written constitution modelled on that of the USA, and a written syllabary of 85 characters invented in 1821 by their scholarly leader Sequoyah (*c*. 1770–1843). Almost the entire tribe was literate. They now live on a reservation in North Carolina and in Oklahoma.

cherry any of a group of fruit-bearing trees distinguished from plums and apricots by their fruits, which are round and smooth and not covered with a bloom. They are cultivated in temperate regions with warm summers and grow best in deep fertile soil. (Genus *Prunus*, family Rosaceae.)

chervil any of several plants belonging to the carrot family. The garden chervil (*Anthriscus cerefolium*) has leaves with a sweetish

CHERVIL Chervil is a small annual with a delicate parsley-like appearance, growing to a height of 30–45 cm/12–18 in. It has a hollow stem and its leaves are often used in cooking as a flavouring.

smell, similar to parsley. It is used as a garnish and in soups. Chervil originated on the borders of Europe and Asia and was introduced to Western Europe by the Romans. (Genus *Anthriscus*, family Umbelliferae.)

Chesapeake Bay largest of the inlets on the Atlantic coast of the USA, bordered by eastern Maryland and eastern Virginia. Chesapeake Bay extends southwards from Havre de Grace in northeast Maryland, and enters the Atlantic between Cape Charles and Cape Henry in Virginia; it is about 320 km/200 mi in length and 6–64 km/4–40 mi in width. There are several deep-water ports located on the bay: Newport News, Norfolk, Portsmouth, and Baltimore.

Cheshire county of northwest England, which has contained the unitary authorities Halton and Warrington since April 1998.
area 2,320 sq km/896 sq mi **towns and cities** ▷Chester (administrative headquarters), Crewe, Congleton, Macclesfield **physical** chiefly a fertile plain, with the Pennines in the east; rivers: Mersey, Dee, Weaver; a sandstone ridge extending south through central Cheshire together with Delamere Forest constitute a woodland and heath landscape **features** salt mines and geologically rich former copper workings at Alderley Edge (in use from Roman times until the 1920s); Little Moreton Hall; discovery of Lindow Man, the first 'bogman' to be found in mainland Britain, dating from around 500 BC; Museum of the Chemical Industry on Spike Island; Quarry Bank Mill at Styal is a cotton-industry museum **agriculture** arable farming in the north; cheese (at one time produced entirely in farmhouses) and dairy products in the centre and south of the county **industries** aerospace industry, chemicals, pharmaceuticals, salt, silk and textiles (at Congleton and Macclesfield), vehicles **famous people** Charles Dodgson (Lewis Carroll), Elizabeth Gaskell **population** (1996) 980,000

> **Bobby Fischer**
> US chess champion
>
> *I like to see my opponents squirm.*
>
> On playing chess (1972)

chess board game originating as early as the 2nd century AD. Two players use 16 pieces each, on a board of 64 squares of alternating colour, to try to force the opponent into a position where the main piece (the king) is threatened and cannot move to another position without remaining threatened. Chess originated in India and reached Britain in the 12th century via the Mediterranean.

Related Web site: Garry Kasparov's International Chess Master Academy http://www.chess.ibm.com/meet/html/d.1.html

CHESS An ivory chess piece from the Charlemagne set, which formed part of the 'Treasure of St Denis'. This horseman was made in Italy at the end of the 11th century. *The Art Archive/ Bibliothèque Nationale Paris*

Chester city and administrative headquarters of ▷Cheshire, England, on the River Dee 26 km/16 mi south of Liverpool, two miles from the border with Wales; population (1991) 80,100; Chester urban area 89,629. There are engineering, aerospace (Airbus), metallurgical, and clothing industries, and car components are manufactured. It is a centre of trade and commerce, and tourism is also important.

Chester was the site of **Deva**, a Roman legionary fortress, and remains include the largest stone-built military Roman amphitheatre to have been discovered in Britain. The town has a medieval centre and the most complete city walls in England, extending for 3 km/2 mi. Other features include the cathedral, dating from the 11th century, which is the fourth most visited cathedral in Britain, and the 'Rows', half-timbered shops with continuous galleried footwalks at first-floor level, dating from the medieval period.

Chesterfield, Philip Dormer Stanhope, 4th Earl of Chesterfield (1694–1773) English politician and writer. He was the author of *Letters to his Son* (1774), which gave voluminous instruction on aristocratic manners and morals. A member of the literary circle of Swift, Pope, and Bolingbroke, he incurred the wrath of Dr Samuel Johnson by failing to carry out an offer of patronage.

Chesterton, G(ilbert) K(eith) (1874–1936) English novelist, essayist, and poet. He wrote numerous short stories featuring a

Catholic priest, Father Brown, who solves crimes by drawing on his knowledge of human nature. Other novels include the fantasy *The Napoleon of Notting Hill* (1904) and *The Man Who Was Thursday* (1908), a deeply emotional allegory about the problem of evil.
Related Web site: American Chesterton Society http://www.chesterton.org/

chestnut any of a group of trees belonging to the beech family. The Spanish or sweet chestnut (*Castanea sativa*) produces edible nuts inside husks; its timber is also valuable. ▷Horse chestnuts are quite distinct, belonging to the genus *Aesculus*, family Hippocastanaceae. (True chestnut genus *Castanea*, family Fagaceae.)
Related Web site: Chestnut, Horse http://www.botanical.com/botanical/mgmh/c/chehor58.html

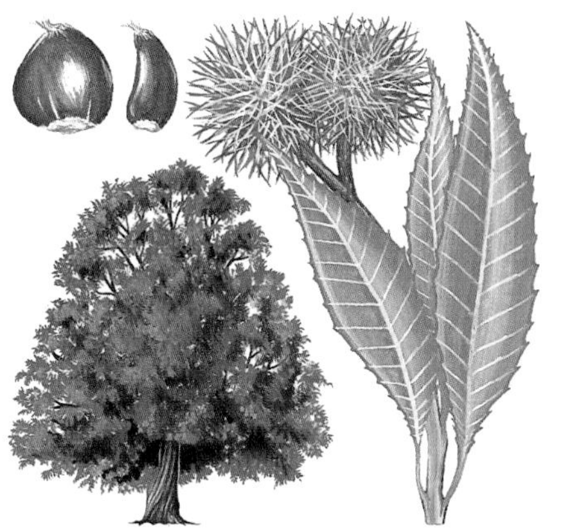

CHESTNUT There are two types of chestnut tree: the sweet or Spanish chestnut (illustrated) and the horse chestnut. The sweet chestnut, native to Southern Europe, Asia, and North America, has toothed leaves and edible seeds, and can grow to a height of 21 m/70 ft.

Chetnik member of a Serbian nationalist group that operated underground during the German occupation of Yugoslavia (today Serbia and Montenegro) in World War II. Led by Col Draza ▷Mihailovič, the Chetniks initially received aid from the Allies, but this was later transferred to the communist partisans led by Tito. The term was also popularly applied to Serb militia forces in the 1991–92 Yugoslav civil war.

Maurice Chevalier
Many a man has fallen in love with a girl in a light so dim he would not have chosen a suit by it.
Attributed remark (1955)

Chevalier, Maurice (1888–1972) French singer and actor. He began as dancing partner to the revue artiste Mistinguett at the Folies-Bergère, and made numerous films, including *Innocents of Paris* (1929), *Love Me Tonight* (1932), *The Merry Widow* (1934), and *Gigi* (1958). His signature tune was 'Louise'.

chevrotain (or **mouse deer**) small forest-dwelling mammals resembling deer. Horns are absent and they reach a maximum height at the shoulder of about 35 cm/14 in. They are active at night and feed mainly on plants and fruit.

Chhattisgarh state of central India, bordered by Maharashtra, Andhra Pradesh, Orissa, Jharkhand, Uttar Pradesh, and Madhya Pradesh; area 146,361 sq km/56,510 sq mi; population (2001 est) 17,600,000. It was carved from Madhya Pradesh and was incorporated in November 2000. The capital is Raipur. The state touches the northernmost part of the Deccan Plateau, and is crossed by the Mahandi River.

Nicknamed the 'Rice Bowl of India', Chhattisgarh provides rice to 600 rice mills within the state and Madhya Pradesh. Eighty percent of the population is involved in agricultural activities. Industries also include forest production, bauxite, limestone, iron ore, diamonds, gold, and china clay. One-third of the population is tribal, and the principal languages are Hindu and Chhattisgarhi.

Chiang Ching alternative transliteration of ▷Jiang Qing, Chinese communist politician and actor, third wife of Mao Zedong.

Chiang Kai-shek Wade-Giles transliteration of ▷Jiang Jie Shi.

chiaroscuro (Italian 'light-dark') in painting and graphic art, the balanced use of light and shade, particularly where contrasting luminous and opaque materials are represented, for example, glinting metal and dark velvet. Masters of chiaroscuro include Leonardo da Vinci, Rembrandt, and Caravaggio. The term is also used to describe a monochromatic painting employing light and dark shades only.

Chicago (Ojibway 'wild onion place') financial and industrial city in Illinois, USA, on Lake Michigan. It is the third-largest US city; population (2000 est) 2,896,000. Industries include iron, steel, chemicals, electrical goods, machinery, meatpacking and food processing, publishing, and fabricated metals. The once famous stockyards are now closed. Chicago grew from a village in the mid-19th century. The world's first skyscraper was built here in 1885 and some of the world's tallest skyscrapers, including the Sears Tower (443 m/1,454 ft high), are in Chicago.
Features The Museum of Science and Industry, opened in 1893, has 'hands-on' exhibits including a coal mine, a World War II U-boat, an Apollo spacecraft and lunar module, and exhibits by industrial firms.

The Chicago River cuts the city into three 'sides'. Chicago is known as the Windy City, so called from the breezes of Lake Michigan, as well as from its citizens' (and, allegedly, politicians') voluble talk; the lake shore ('the Gold Coast') is occupied by luxury apartment blocks. It has a symphony orchestra, an art institute, the University of Chicago (site of the first controlled nuclear reaction), DePaul and Loyola universities, a campus of the University of Illinois, and the Illinois Institute of Technology. Chicago-O'Hare International Airport was the nation's busiest between 1961 and 1998 and leading in take-offs and landings well into 1999. The Board of Trade, Mercantile Exchange, and Options Exchange are among the world's largest commodity markets.

Chicano citizens or residents of the USA who are of Mexican descent. The term was originally used for those who became US citizens after the ▷Mexican War. The word probably derives from the Spanish word *Mexicanos*.

Chichén Itzá Toltec city situated among the Maya city-states of the Yucatán peninsula, Mexico. Built on the site of an earlier Maya settlement, the city was at its height from around AD 980 to 1220 (the Classic and Post-Classic periods), after Toltec peoples from central Mexico settled here. Ruins of many important buildings remain from this time. These include a great pyramid (*Castillo*), temples with sculptures and colour reliefs, an observatory, and a sacred well (*cenote*), into which sacrifices, including human beings, were thrown.

Chichester city and market town and administrative headquarters of ▷West Sussex, southern England, 111 km/69 mi southwest of London; population (1991) 27,100. It lies in an agricultural area, and has a harbour. It was a Roman town, **Noviomagus Regnensium**, and the nearby remains of Fishbourne Palace (about AD 80) is one of the finest Roman archeological sites outside Italy.

chicken domestic fowl; see under ▷poultry.

chickenpox (or **varicella**) common, usually mild disease, caused by a virus of the ▷herpes group and transmitted by airborne droplets. Chickenpox chiefly attacks children under the age of ten. The incubation period is two to three weeks. One attack normally gives immunity for life.

The temperature rises and spots (later inflamed blisters) develop on the torso, then on the face and limbs. The sufferer recovers within a week, but remains infectious until the last scab disappears.

The US Food and Drug Administration approved a chickenpox vaccine in March 1995. Based on a weakened form of the live virus, the vaccine is expected to be 70–90% effective. A vaccine is available in Europe, but is only used in children with an impaired immune system.

chickpea annual leguminous plant (see ▷legume), grown for food in India and the Middle East. Its short hairy pods contain edible seeds similar to peas. (*Cicer arietinum*, family Leguminosae.)

chickweed any of several low-growing plants belonging to the pink family, with small white starlike flowers. (Genera *Stellaria* and *Cerastium*, family Caryophyllaceae.)

Chiclayo commercial centre and capital of Lambayeque department, northwest Peru, 640 km/400 mi northwest of Lima; population (1993) 411,500. One of Peru's fastest growing cities, it lies at the centre of an agricultural area producing rice, cotton, and sugar cane, which are all grown and processed in the region. There are tanning, distilling, and dairy industries. The city comprises a mixture of Creole, Spanish, and Indian architecture, and there is a 19th-century cathedral, designed by the English architect Andrew Townsend.

chicory plant native to Europe and West Asia, with large, usually blue, flowers. Its long taproot is used dried and roasted as a coffee substitute. As a garden vegetable, grown under cover, its blanched leaves are used in salads. It is related to ▷endive. (*Cichorium intybus*, family Compositae.)
Related Web site: Chicory http://www.botanical.com/botanical/mgmh/c/chicor61.html

Chief Dan George (1899–1981) Salish chief, actor, and writer. He first became known when he played Dustin Hoffman's American Indian grandfather in Arthur Penn's film *Little Big Man* (1970), for which he received an Academy Award nomination. He also played the Old Sioux in the epic TV miniseries 'Centennial' (1978) and Clint Eastwood's travelling companion in *The Outlaw Josey Wales* (1976). His books include *My Heart Soars* and *My Spirit Soars*.

chiffchaff small songbird *Phylloscopus collybita* of the warbler family, Muscicapidae, order Passeriformes. It is found in woodlands and thickets in Europe and northern Asia during the summer, migrating south for winter. About 11 cm/4.3 in long, olive above, greyish below, with yellow-white nether parts, an eyestripe, and usually dark legs, it looks similar to a willow warbler but has a distinctive song.

chigger (or **harvest mite**) scarlet or rusty brown ▷mite genus *Trombicula*, family Trombiculidae, in the order Acarina, common in summer and autumn. Chiggers are parasitic, and their tiny red larvae cause intensely irritating bites in places where the skin is thin, such as behind the knees or between the toes. After a time they leave their host and drop to the ground where they feed upon minute insects.

Chihuahua capital of Chihuahua state, Mexico, 1,285 km/800 mi northwest of Mexico City; population (1995 est) 589,000. It lies in the north of Mexico at an altitude of 1428 m/4685 ft, and was founded in 1707. It is the centre of both a mining district and a cattle raising area and has textile mills and smelting industries. The area is noted for breeding the small, short-haired dogs named after the town and state.

chihuahua smallest breed of dog, 15 cm/10 in high, developed in the USA from Mexican origins. It may weigh only 1 kg/2.2 lb. The domed head and wide-set ears are characteristic, and the skull is large compared to the body. It can be almost any colour, and occurs in both smooth (or even hairless) and long-coated varieties.

chilblain painful inflammation of the skin of the feet, hands, or ears, due to cold. The parts turn red, swell, itch violently, and are very tender. In bad cases, the skin cracks, blisters, or ulcerates.

child abuse the deliberate injury of a child. Child abuse can take several forms: neglect (including failure to provide adequate shelter, food, or medical treatment), physical abuse (including beating and poisoning), emotional abuse (including verbal abuse), and sexual abuse. In practice, a child is often subject to more than one form of abuse. In 1994, 1,271 children died from child abuse in the UK; over 80% were under five and nearly 50% under one. Child abuse has only been recognized as a serious problem since the 1960s but is now a major area of health, welfare, and legal practice. The protection of children from abuse ranks as a top priority in social work.

Childers, (Robert) Erskine (1870–1922) English civil servant and writer, Irish republican, author of the spy novel *The Riddle of the Sands* (1903).

Children's Crusade ▷crusade by some 10,000 children from France, the Low Countries, and Germany, in 1212, to recapture Jerusalem for Christianity. Motivated by religious piety, many of them were sold into slavery or died of disease.

CHICKWEED Alpine mouse-ear chickweed *Cerastium alpinum* growing in the French Alps. *Premaphotos Wildlife*

children's literature works specifically written for children. The earliest known illustrated children's book in English is *Goody Two Shoes* (1765), possibly written by Oliver Goldsmith. **Fairy tales** were originally part of a vast range of oral literature, credited only to the writer who first recorded them, such as Charles Perrault. During the 19th century several writers, including Hans Christian Andersen, wrote original stories in the fairy-tale genre; others, such as the Grimm brothers, collected (and sometimes adapted) existing stories.

Chile see country box.

Chilean Revolution in Chile, the presidency of Salvador ▷Allende 1970–73, the Western hemisphere's first democratically elected Marxist-oriented president of an independent state.

chilli pod, or powder made from the pod, of a variety of ▷capsicum (*Capsicum frutescens*), a small, hot, red pepper. It is widely used in cooking. The hot ingredient of chilli is capsaicin. It causes a burning sensation in the mouth by triggering nerve branches in the eyes, nose, tongue, and mouth. Capsaicin does not activate the taste buds and therefore has no flavour. It is claimed that people can become physically addicted to it.

Related Web site: Chilli! http://www.tpoint.net/~wallen/chili.html

Chiltern Hills range of chalk hills extending for some 72 km/45 mi in a curve from a point north of Reading to the Suffolk border. Coombe Hill, near Wendover, 260 m/852 ft high, is the highest point.

Chiluba, Frederick (1943–) Zambian politician and trade unionist, president from 1991. In 1993 he was forced to declare a state of emergency, following the discovery of documents suggesting an impending coup. He later carried out a major reorganization of his cabinet but failed to silence his critics. He secured re-election in November 1996.

chimaera fish of the group Holocephali. Chimaeras have thick bodies that taper to a long thin tail, large fins, smooth skin, and a cartilaginous skeleton. They can grow to 1.5 m/4.5 ft. Most chimaeras are deep-water fish, and even *Chimaera monstrosa*, a relatively shallow-living form caught around European coasts, lives at a depth of 300–500 m/1,000–1,600 ft.

Chimbote largest fishing port in Peru, situated at the mouth of the Rio Santa, 450 km/280 mi north of Lima, in the department of Ancash; population (1993) 297,000. The main industries are fishmeal and steel; fish products are exported. The port was built in the natural harbour on Ferrol Bay in the 1950s, primarily to serve the developing national steel industry.

chimera (or **chimaera**) in biology, an organism composed of tissues that are genetically different. Chimeras can develop naturally if a ▷mutation occurs in a cell of a developing embryo, but are more commonly produced artificially by implanting cells from one organism into the embryo of another.

chimera (or **chimaera**) in Greek mythology, a fire-breathing animal with a lion's head and foreparts, a goat's middle, a dragon's rear, and a tail in the form of a snake; hence any apparent hybrid of two or more creatures. The chimera was killed by the hero Bellerophon on the winged horse Pegasus.

chimpanzee highly intelligent African ape *Pan troglodytes* that lives mainly in rainforests but sometimes in wooded savannah. Chimpanzees are covered in thin but long black body hair, except for the face, hands, and feet, which may have pink or black skin. They normally walk on all fours, supporting the front of the body on the knuckles of the fingers, but can stand or walk upright for a short distance. They can grow to 1.4 m/4.5 ft tall, and weigh up to 50 kg/110 lb. They are strong and climb well, but spend time on the ground, living in loose social groups. The bulk of the diet is fruit, with some leaves, insects, and occasional meat. Females reach sexual maturity at 8–12 years of age, males at 17–18. Chimpanzees give birth to a single infant approximately every five years. Chimpanzees can use 'tools', fashioning twigs to extract termites from their nests. According to a 1998 estimate by the Worldwide Fund for Nature, the world population of chimpanzees stands at 200,000.

Chimpanzees are found in an area from West Africa to western Uganda and Tanzania in the east. There are four subspecies of common chimpanzee. The **bonobo** or pygmy chimpanzee, *Pan paniscus* is found only in a small area of rainforest in the Democratic Republic of Congo (formerly Zaire). Bonobos are a distinct species about the same height as 'common' chimpanzees, but they are of a slighter build, with less hair, and stand upright more frequently. In 1999 there were believed to be fewer than 15,000 bonobos left and these were threatened by the civil war in the Democratic Republic of Congo.

Studies of chromosomes suggest that chimpanzees are the closest apes to humans, perhaps sharing 99% of the same genes. Trained chimpanzees can learn to communicate with humans with the aid of machines or sign language, but are probably precluded from human speech by the position of the voicebox. In 1999 British researchers revealed that chimpanzees exhibit diverse cultural behaviour in different study populations, showing that behaviour is learned and passed on in chimpanzee societies. The researchers identified 39 separate behaviours, including differences in feeding techniques, courtship rituals, and domination displays.

Related Web site: Chimpanzee http://www.seaworld.org/animal_bytes/chimpanzeeab.html

Chimú South American civilization that flourished on the coast of Peru from about 1250 to about 1470, when it was conquered by the ▷Incas. The Chimú people produced fine work in gold, realistic portrait pottery, savage fanged feline images in clay, and possibly a system of writing or recording by painting patterns on beans. They built aqueducts carrying water many miles, and the huge, mazelike city of Chan Chan, 36 sq km/14 sq mi, on the coast near Trujillo.

China see country box.

china clay commercial name for ▷kaolin.

China Sea area of the Pacific Ocean bordered by China, Vietnam, Borneo, the Philippines, and Japan. Various groups of small islands and shoals, including the Paracels, 500 km/300 mi east of Vietnam, have been disputed by China and other powers because they lie in oil-rich areas. The chief rivers which flow into the South China Sea are the Red River and Mekong; the main ports include Canton, Hong Kong, Manila, Bangkok, Singapore, and Ho Chi Minh City.

Chinatown commercial section of Los Angeles, California, USA, at the northern edge of Downtown, between El Pueblo de Los Angeles to the south and Chavez Ravine to the north. Vietnamese immigrants, many of Chinese descent, now also live in the community.

Chinatown commercial and residential district in lower Manhattan, New York City, USA, on the Lower East Side, traditionally bounded to the north by Canal Street, but expanding into Little Italy in recent years. Its main commercial streets include Mott and Mulberry.

> **Bao Tong**
> Former Chinese Central Committee member and political prisoner
>
> *The history of bloodshed remains in people's hearts; they will not forget.*
>
> In a letter to President Jiang Zemin, Prime Minister Zhu Rongji, and members of the Politburo Standing Committee.

Chinatown residential and commercial section of downtown San Francisco on the east of Nob Hill, southeast of North Beach and northwest of the Financial District. It grew around Portsmouth Square, the site of the 1846 US takeover of the city; Grant Avenue is its main thoroughfare. It was the USA's first real Chinese community.

Chinatown commercial and former residential section of northern Vancouver, British Columbia, Canada, just south of Gastow, north and east of the modern Downtown and centred on Pender Street. A tourist and business zone, the Vancouver district is one of North America's oldest and largest Chinatowns.

chinchilla South American rodent *Chinchilla laniger* found in high, rather barren areas of the Andes in Bolivia and Chile. About the size of a small rabbit, it has long ears and a long bushy tail, and shelters in rock crevices. These gregarious animals have thick, soft, silver-grey fur, and were hunted almost to extinction for it. They are now farmed and protected in the wild.

Chinese the native groups or inhabitants of China and Taiwan, and those people of Chinese descent. The Chinese comprise more than 25% of the world's population, and the Chinese language (Mandarin) is the largest member of the Sino-Tibetan family.

Related Web site: Liondance http://liondance.free.fr/

Chinese art the painting and sculpture of China. From the Bronze Age to the Cultural Revolution, Chinese art shows a stylistic unity unparalleled in any other culture. From about the 1st century AD Buddhism inspired much sculpture and painting. The **Han dynasty** (206 BC–AD 220) produced outstanding metalwork, ceramics, and sculpture. The **Song dynasty** (960–1278) established standards of idyllic landscape and nature painting in a delicate calligraphic style.

Chinese language language or group of languages of the Sino-Tibetan family, spoken in China, Taiwan, Hong Kong, Singapore, and Chinese communities throughout the world. Varieties of spoken Chinese differ greatly, but all share a written form using thousands of ideographic symbols – characters – which have changed little in 2,000 years. Nowadays, *putonghua* ('common speech'), based on the educated Beijing dialect known as Mandarin Chinese, is promoted throughout China as the national spoken and written language.

Related Web site: Learn Chinese http://pasture.ecn.purdue.edu/~agenhtml/agenmc/china/ctutor.html

Chinese literature the earliest written records in Chinese date from about 1500 BC; the earliest extant literary works date from about 800 BC.

Poetry Chinese poems, often only four lines long, and written in the ancient literary language understood throughout China, consist of rhymed lines of a fixed number of syllables, ornamented by parallel phrasing and tonal pattern. The oldest poems are contained in the *Book of Songs* (800–600 BC). Some of the most celebrated Chinese poets are the nature poet T'ao Ch'ien (372–427), the master of technique Li Po, the autobiographical Bo Zhu Yi, and the wide-ranging Su Tung-p'o (1036–1101); and among the moderns using the colloquial language under European influence and experimenting in free verse are Hsu Chih-mo (1895–1931), and Pien Chih-lin (1910–).

Prose Histories are not so much literary works as collections of edited documents with moral comment, whereas the essay has long been cultivated under strict rules of form and style. An example of the latter genre is 'Upon the Original Way' by Han Yü (768–824), recalling the nation to Confucianism. Until the 16th century the short story was confined to the anecdote, startling by its strangeness and written in the literary language – for example, the stories of the poetic Tuan Ch'eng-shih (died 863); but after that time the more novelistic type of short story, written in the colloquial tongue, developed by its side. The Chinese novel evolved from the street storyteller's art and has consequently always used the popular language. The early romances *Three Kingdoms*, *All Men Are Brothers*, and *Golden Lotus* are anonymous, the earliest known author of this genre being Wu Che'ng-en (*c.* 1505–1580); the most realistic of the great novelists is Ts'ao Chan (died 1763).

Twentieth-century Chinese novels have largely adopted European form, and have been influenced by Russia, as have the realistic stories of Lu Hsün. In typical Chinese drama, the stage presentation far surpasses the text in importance (the dialogue was not even preserved in early plays), but there have been experiments in the European manner. Some recent writing such as the stories of Bai Hua (1930–) has been energized by the tension between humanist individualism and the collectivist ideology of the communist state. Personal and family experience of China's social and political upheavals in the 20th century has been recorded in some distinguished autobiographical works such as *Wild Swans: Three Daughters of China* (1991) by Jung Chang (1952–).

Chinese Revolution series of great political upheavals in China between 1911 and 1949 which eventually led to Communist Party rule and the establishment of the People's Republic of China. In 1912 a nationalist revolt overthrew the imperial Manchu dynasty. Under the leaders ▷Sun Zhong Shan (Sun Yat-sen) (1923–25) and ▷Jiang Jie Shi (Chiang Kai-shek) (1925–49), the Nationalists, or ▷Guomindang, were increasingly challenged by the growing communist movement. The 10,000-km/6,000-mi ▷Long March to the northwest, undertaken by the communists in 1934 to 1935 to escape Guomindang harassment, resulted in the emergence of ▷Mao Zedong as a communist leader. During World War II the various Chinese political groups pooled military resources against the Japanese invaders, but in 1946 the conflict reignited into open civil war. In 1949 the Guomindang were defeated at Nanjing and forced to flee to ▷Taiwan. Communist rule was established in the People's Republic of China under the leadership of Mao Zedong.

First republican government The Chinese revolution came about with the collapse of the Manchu dynasty, a result of increasing internal disorders, pressure from foreign governments, and the weakness of central government. A nationalist revolt from 1911 to 1912 led to a provisional republican constitution being proclaimed and a government established in Beijing (Peking) headed by Yuan Shihai. The Guomindang were faced with the problems of restoring the authority of central government and meeting the challenges from militaristic factions (led by ▷warlords) and the growing communist movement.

Communists retreat After 1930 Jiang launched a series of attacks that encircled the communists in southeast China and led to an attempt by communist army commander Chu Teh to break out. The resulting Long March to northwest China, from October 1934 to October 1935, reduced the communists' army from over 100,000 to little more than 8,000, mainly as a result of skirmishes with Jiang's forces and the severity of the conditions. During the march a power struggle developed between Mao Zedong and Jiang Guo T'ao which eventually split the force. Mao's group finally based itself in Yan'an, where it remained throughout the war with the Japanese, forming an uneasy alliance with the nationalists to expel the invaders.

Communist victory Mao's troops formed the basis of the Red Army that renewed the civil war against the nationalists in 1946 and emerged victorious after defeating them at Huai-Hai and Nanjing in 1949. As a result, communist rule was established in China under Mao Zedong's leadership.

chinook (American Indian 'snow-eater') warm dry wind that blows downhill on the east side of the Rocky Mountains of North America. It often occurs in winter and spring when it produces a rapid thaw, and so is important to the agriculture of the area.

Chile

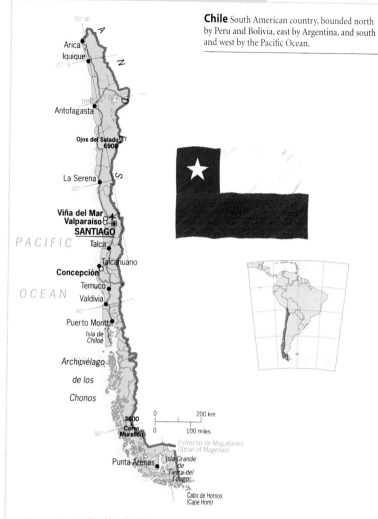

Chile South American country, bounded north by Peru and Bolivia, east by Argentina, and south and west by the Pacific Ocean.

NATIONAL NAME *República de Chile/Republic of Chile*
AREA 756,950 sq km/292,258 sq mi
CAPITAL Santiago
MAJOR TOWNS/CITIES Concepción, Viña del Mar, Valparaíso, Talcahuano, Puente Alto, Temuco, Antofagasta

MAJOR PORTS Valparaíso, Antofagasta, Arica, Iquique, Punta Arenas
PHYSICAL FEATURES Andes mountains along eastern border, Atacama Desert in north, fertile central valley, grazing land and forest in south
TERRITORIES Easter Island, Juan Fernández Islands, part of Tierra del Fuego, claim to part of Antarctica

Government

HEAD OF STATE AND GOVERNMENT Ricardo Lagos Escobar from 2000
POLITICAL SYSTEM emergent democracy
POLITICAL EXECUTIVE limited presidency
ADMINISTRATIVE DIVISIONS 12 regions and one metropolitan area
ARMED FORCES 80,500 (2002 est)
CONSCRIPTION one year (army) or two years (navy and air force); military service to be voluntary from 2005
DEATH PENALTY abolished for ordinary crimes in 2001; laws provide for the death penalty for exceptional crimes, such as crimes committed in wartime
DEFENCE SPEND (% GDP) 4.1 (2002 est)
EDUCATION SPEND (% GDP) 4.2 (2001 est)
HEALTH SPEND (% GDP) 7.2 (2000 est)

CHILE Logs stacked for export at a Chilean timber yard. The main areas of afforestation (conversion into forested land) in the country lie in the two most southerly provinces, Aisén and Magallanes. Only since the 1970s has timber become a major source of export revenue for Chile. *Image Bank*

Economy and resources

CURRENCY Chilean peso
GPD (US$) 64.2 billion (2002 est)
REAL GDP GROWTH (% change on previous year) 2.8 (2001)
GNI (US$) 66.3 billion (2002 est)
GNI PER CAPITA (PPP) (US$) 9,180 (2002 est)
CONSUMER PRICE INFLATION 3.3% (2003 est)
UNEMPLOYMENT 9.2% (2001)
FOREIGN DEBT (US$) 28.8 billion (2001 est)
MAJOR TRADING PARTNERS USA, Japan, Brazil, Germany, Argentina, UK, Mexico, China, Italy, France, South Korea
RESOURCES copper (world's largest producer), gold, silver, iron ore, molybdenum, cobalt, iodine, saltpetre, coal, natural gas, petroleum, hydroelectric power
INDUSTRIES nonferrous metals, food processing, petroleum refining, chemicals, paper products (cellulose, newsprint, paper and cardboard), motor tyres, beer, glass sheets, motor vehicles
EXPORTS copper, fruits, timber products, fishmeal, vegetables, manufactured foodstuffs and beverages. Principal market: USA 19.2% (2001)
IMPORTS machinery and transport equipment, wheat, chemical and mineral products, consumer goods, raw materials. Principal source: Argentina 17.8% (2001)
ARABLE LAND 2.6% (2000 est)
AGRICULTURAL PRODUCTS wheat, sugar beet, potatoes, maize, fruit and vegetables; livestock

Chronology

1535: The first Spanish invasion of Chile was abandoned in the face of fierce resistance from indigenous Araucanian Indians.

1541: Pedro de Valdivia began the Spanish conquest and founded Santiago.

1553: Valdivia was captured and killed by Araucanian Indians, led by Chief Lautaro.

17th century: The Spanish developed small agricultural settlements ruled by a government subordinate to the viceroy in Lima, Peru.

1778: The king of Spain appointed a captain-general to govern Chile.

1810: A Santiago junta proclaimed Chilean autonomy after Napoleon dethroned the king of Spain.

1814: The Spanish viceroy regained control of Chile.

1817: The Army of the Andes, led by José de San Martín and Bernardo O'Higgins, defeated the Spanish.

1818: Chile achieved independence from Spain with O'Higgins as supreme director.

1823–30: O'Higgins was forced to resign; a civil war between conservative centralists and liberal federalists ended with conservative victory.

1833: An autocratic republican constitution created a unitary Roman Catholic state with a strong president and limited franchise.

1851–61: President Manuel Montt bowed to pressure to liberalize the constitution and reduce privileges of landowners and the church.

1879–84: Chile defeated Peru and Bolivia in the War of the Pacific and increased its territory by a third.

late 19th century: Mining of nitrate and copper became a major industry; large-scale European immigration followed the 'pacification' of Araucanian Indians.

1891: A constitutional dispute between president and congress led to civil war; congressional victory reduced the president to figurehead status.

1925: A new constitution increased presidential powers, separated church and state, and made primary education compulsory.

1927: A military coup led to the dictatorship of Gen Carlos Ibáñez del Campo.

Population and society

POPULATION 15,805,000 (2003 est)
POPULATION GROWTH RATE 1.0% (2000–15)
POPULATION DENSITY (per sq km) 21 (2003 est)
URBAN POPULATION (% of total) 87 (2003 est)
AGE DISTRIBUTION (% of total population) 0–14 28%, 15–59 61%, 60+ 11% (2002 est)
ETHNIC GROUPS 65% mestizo (mixed American Indian and Spanish descent), 30% European, remainder mainly American Indian
LANGUAGE Spanish (official)
RELIGION Roman Catholic 80%, Protestant 13%, atheist and nonreligious 6%
EDUCATION (compulsory years) 8
LITERACY RATE 96% (men); 96% (women) (2003 est)
LABOUR FORCE 14.4% agriculture, 25.5% industry, 60.1% services (1998)
LIFE EXPECTANCY 73 (men); 79 (women) (2000–05)
CHILD MORTALITY RATE (under 5, per 1,000 live births) 12 (2001)
PHYSICIANS (per 1,000 people) 1.1 (1998 est)
HOSPITAL BEDS (per 1,000 people) 2.7 (1998 est)
TV SETS (per 1,000 people) 286 (2001 est)
RADIOS (per 1,000 people) 759 (2001 est)
INTERNET USERS (per 10,000 people) 2,375.4 (2002 est)
PERSONAL COMPUTER USERS (per 100 people) 11.9 (2002 est)

See also ▷Allende, Salvador; ▷Araucanian Indian; ▷Pinochet, Augusto.

1931: A sharp fall in price of copper and nitrate caused dramatic economic and political collapse.

1938: A Popular Front of Radicals, Socialists, and Communists took power under Pedro Aguirre Cedra, who introduced economic policies based on the US New Deal.

1948–58: The Communist Party was banned.

1970: Salvador Allende, leader of the Popular Unity coalition, became the world's first democratically elected Marxist president; he embarked on an extensive programme of nationalization and radical social reform.

1973: Allende was killed in a CIA-backed military coup; Gen Augusto Pinochet established a dictatorship combining severe political repression with free-market economics.

1981: Pinochet began an eight-year term as president under a new constitution described as a 'transition to democracy'.

1983: Economic recession provoked growing opposition to the governing regime.

1988: A referendum on whether Pinochet should serve a further term resulted in a clear 'No' vote.

1990: The military regime ended, with a Christian Democrat (Patricio Aylwin) as president, with Pinochet as commander in chief of the army. An investigation was launched into over 2,000 political executions during the military regime.

1995: Dante Cordova was appointed prime minister.

1998: Pinochet retired from the army and was made life senator. Pinochet was placed under arrest in the UK; proceedings began to extradite him to Spain on murder charges.

1999: The ruling on the extradition of Pinochet to Spain was left to the British government.

2000: Pinochet was found unfit for trial by British doctors and allowed to return to Chile. However, in Chile, Pinochet was stripped of immunity from prosecution.

2001: Pinochet was arrested and charged with organizing the killings of left-wing activists and union leaders during his time in power.

POPULATION DENSITY (per sq km) 136 (2003 est)

URBAN POPULATION (% of total) 39 (2003 est)

AGE DISTRIBUTION (% of total population) 0–14 24%, 15–59 66%, 60+ 10% (2002 est)

ETHNIC GROUPS 92% Han Chinese, the remainder being Zhuang, Uygur, Hui (Muslims), Yi, Tibetan, Miao, Manchu, Mongol, Buyi, or Korean; numerous lesser nationalities live mainly in border regions

LANGUAGE Chinese (dialects include Mandarin (official), Yue (Cantonese), Wu (Shanghaiese), Minbai, Minnah, Xiang, Gan, and Hakka)

RELIGION Taoist, Confucianist, and Buddhist; Muslim 2–3%; Christian about 1% (divided between the 'patriotic' church established in 1958 and the 'loyal' church subject to Rome); Protestant 3 million

EDUCATION (compulsory years) 9

LITERACY RATE 93% (men); 80% (women) (2003 est)

LABOUR FORCE 50% agriculture, 23% industry, 27% services (1999)

LIFE EXPECTANCY 69 (men); 73 (women) (2000–05)

CHILD MORTALITY RATE (under 5, per 1,000 live births) 39 (2001)

PHYSICIANS (per 1,000 people) 1.7 (1999 est)

HOSPITAL BEDS (per 1,000 people) 2.4 (1999 est)

TV SETS (per 1,000 people) 312 (2001 est)

RADIOS (per 1,000 people) 339 (2001 est)

INTERNET USERS (per 10,000 people) 460.1 (2002 est)

PERSONAL COMPUTER USERS (per 100 people) 2.8 (2002 est)

See also ▷Cultural Revolution; ▷Guomindang; ▷Hong Kong; ▷Mao Zedong; ▷Sino-Japanese Wars; ▷Taiwan.

Chronology

c. 3000 BC: Yangshao culture reached its peak in the Huang He Valley; displaced by Longshan culture in eastern China.

c. 1766–c. 1122 BC: First major dynasty, the Shang, arose from Longshan culture; writing and calendar developed.

c. 1122–256 BC: Zhou people of western China overthrew Shang and set up new dynasty; development of money and written laws.

c. 500 BC: Confucius expounded the philosophy that guided Chinese government and society for the next 2,000 years.

403–221 BC: 'Warring States Period': Zhou Empire broke up into small kingdoms.

221–206 BC: Qin kingdom defeated all rivals and established first empire with strong central government; emperor Shi Huangdi built the Great Wall of China.

202 BC–AD 220: Han dynasty expanded empire into central Asia; first overland trade with Europe; art and literature flourished; Buddhism introduced from India.

AD 220–581: Large-scale rebellion destroyed the Han dynasty; the empire split into three competing kingdoms; several short-lived dynasties ruled parts of China.

581–618: Sui dynasty reunified China and repelled Tatar invaders.

618–907: Tang dynasty enlarged and strengthened the empire; great revival of culture; major rebellion (875–84).

907–60: 'Five Dynasties and Ten Kingdoms': disintegration of the empire amid war and economic decline; development of printing.

960–1279: Song dynasty reunified China; civil service examinations introduced; population reached 100 million; Manchurians occupied northern China in 1127.

1279: Mongols conquered all China, which became part of the vast empire of Kublai Khan, founder of the Yuan dynasty; the Venetian traveller Marco Polo visited China (1275–92).

China the largest country in East Asia, bounded to the north by Mongolia; to the northwest by Tajikistan, Kyrgyzstan, Kazakhstan, and Afghanistan; to the southwest by India, Nepal, and Bhutan; to the south by Myanmar (Burma), Laos, and Vietnam; to the southeast by the South China Sea; to the east by the East China Sea, North Korea, and Yellow Sea; and to the northeast by Russia.

NATIONAL NAME *Zhonghua Renmin Gongheguo (Zhongguo)/People's Republic of China*

AREA 9,572,900 sq km/3,696,000 sq mi

CAPITAL Beijing (or Peking)

MAJOR TOWNS/CITIES Shanghai, Hong Kong, Chongqing, Tianjin, Guangzhou (English Canton), Shenyang (formerly Mukden), Wuhan, Nanjing, Harbin, Chengdu, Xi'an

MAJOR PORTS Tianjin, Shanghai, Hong Kong, Qingdao, Guangzhou

PHYSICAL FEATURES two-thirds of China is mountains or desert (north and west); the low-lying east is irrigated by rivers Huang He (Yellow River), Chang Jiang (Yangtze-Kiang), Xi Jiang (Si Kiang)

TERRITORIES Paracel Islands

Government

HEAD OF STATE Hu Jintao from 2003

HEAD OF GOVERNMENT Wen Jiabao from 2003

POLITICAL SYSTEM communist

POLITICAL EXECUTIVE communist

ADMINISTRATIVE DIVISIONS 23 provinces, 5 autonomous regions, 4 municipalities, and two special administrative regions

ARMED FORCES 2,270,000; plus 550,000 reserves and paramilitary forces of 1.5 million (2002 est)

CONSCRIPTION selective conscription for two years

DEATH PENALTY retained and used for ordinary crimes

DEFENCE SPEND (% GDP) 4.1 (2002 est)

EDUCATION SPEND (% GDP) 2 (1999)

HEALTH SPEND (% GDP) 5.3 (2000 est)

CHINA A bamboo forest near Huangshan, in Anhui division, China. Stretching from south of the Tropic of Cancer to north of the 50th parallel, China is a land of extremes, having areas of jungle, desert, snowy wastes, mountains, and rich farmland. Bamboo forests like this once supported significant numbers of pandas in western China. *Image Bank*

Economy and resources

CURRENCY yuan

GPD (US$) 1,237.1 billion (2002 est)

REAL GDP GROWTH (% change on previous year) 7.3 (2001)

GNI (US$) 1,209.5 billion (2002 est)

GNI PER CAPITA (PPP) (US$) 4,390 (2002 est)

CONSUMER PRICE INFLATION 0.2% (2003 est)

UNEMPLOYMENT 9.3% (2001)

FOREIGN DEBT (US$) 118.7 billion (2001 est)

MAJOR TRADING PARTNERS Japan, USA, Taiwan, South Korea, Germany, the Netherlands, UK, Singapore, Russia

RESOURCES coal, graphite, tungsten, molybdenum, antimony, tin (world's largest producer), lead (world's fifth-largest producer), mercury, bauxite, phosphate rock, iron ore (world's largest producer), diamonds, gold, manganese, zinc (world's third-largest producer), petroleum, natural gas, fish

INDUSTRIES raw cotton and cotton cloth, cement, paper, sugar, salt, plastics, aluminium ware, steel, rolled steel, chemical fertilizers, silk, woollen fabrics, bicycles, cameras, electrical appliances; tourism is growing

EXPORTS basic manufactures, miscellaneous manufactured articles (particularly clothing and toys), crude petroleum, machinery and transport equipment, fishery products, cereals, canned food, tea, raw silk, cotton cloth. Principal market: USA 20.4% (2001)

IMPORTS machinery and transport equipment, basic manufactures, chemicals, wheat, rolled steel, fertilizers. Principal source: Japan 17.6% (2001)

ARABLE LAND 13.3% (2000 est)

AGRICULTURAL PRODUCTS sweet potatoes, wheat, maize, soybeans, rice, sugar cane, tobacco, cotton, jute; world's largest fish catch

Population and society

POPULATION 1,304,196,000 (2003 est)

POPULATION GROWTH RATE 0.7% (2000–15)

China (cont.)

1368: Rebellions drove out the Mongols; Ming dynasty expanded the empire; architecture flourished in the new capital of Beijing.

1516: Portuguese explorers reached Macau.

1644: Manchurian invasion established the Qing (or Manchu) dynasty.

1796–1804: Anti-Manchu revolt weakened the Qing dynasty; a population increase in excess of food supplies led to falling living standards and cultural decline.

1839–42: First Opium War; Britain forced China to cede Hong Kong and open five ports to European trade; Second Opium War extracted further trade concessions (1856–60).

1850–64: Millions died in the Taiping Rebellion; Taipings combined Christian and Chinese beliefs and demanded land reform.

1894–95: Sino–Japanese War: Chinese driven out of Korea.

1897–98: Germany, Russia, France, and Britain leased ports in China.

1898: Hong Kong was secured by Britain on a 99-year lease.

1900: Anti-Western Boxer Rebellion crushed by foreign intervention; jealousy between the Great Powers prevented partition.

1911: Revolution broke out; Republic of China proclaimed by Sun Zhong Shan (Sun Yat-sen) of Guomindang (National People's Party).

1912: Abdication of infant emperor Pu-i; Gen Yuan Shih-K'ai became dictator.

1916: The power of the central government collapsed on the death of Yuan Shih-K'ai; northern China dominated by local warlords.

1919: Beijing students formed the 4th May movement to protest at the transfer of German possessions in China to Japan.

1921: Sun Zhong Shan elected president of nominal national government; Chinese Communist Party founded; communists worked with Guomindang to reunite China from 1923.

1925: Death of Sun Zhong Shan; leadership of Guomindang gradually passed to military commander Jiang Jie Shi (Chiang Kai-shek).

1926–28: Revolutionary Army of Jiang Jie Shi reunified China; Guomindang broke with communists and tried to suppress them in civil war.

1932: Japan invaded Manchuria and established the puppet state of Manchukuo.

1934–35: Communists undertook Long March from Jiangxi and Fujian in south to Yan'an in north to escape encirclement by Guomindang.

1937–45: Japan renewed invasion of China; Jiang Jie Shi received help from USA and Britain from 1941.

1946: Civil war resumed between Guomindang and communists led by Mao Zedong.

1949: Victorious communists proclaimed People's Republic of China under Chairman Mao; Guomindang fled to Taiwan.

1950–53: China intervened heavily in Korean War.

1958: 'Great Leap Forward': extremist five-year plan to accelerate output severely weakened the economy.

1960: Sino-Soviet split: China accused USSR of betraying communism.

1962: Economic recovery programme under Liu Shaoqi caused divisions between 'rightists' and 'leftists'; brief border war with India.

1966–69: 'Great Proletarian Cultural Revolution'; leftists overthrew Liu Shaoqi with support of Mao; Red Guards disrupted education, government, and daily life in attempt to enforce revolutionary principles.

1970: Mao supported the efforts of Prime Minister Zhou Enlai to restore order.

1971: People's Republic of China admitted to United Nations.

1976: Deaths of Zhou Enlai and Mao Zedong led to a power struggle between rightists and leftists; Hua Guofeng became leader.

1977–81: Rightist Deng Xiaoping emerged as supreme leader; pragmatic economic policies introduced market incentives and encouraged foreign trade.

1979: Full diplomatic relations with USA established

1989: Over 2,000 people were killed when the army crushed prodemocracy student demonstrations in Tiananmen Square, Beijing; international sanctions were imposed.

1993: Jiang Zemin became head of state

1996: Reunification with Taiwan was declared a priority.

1997: A border agreement was signed with Russia. Hong Kong was returned to Chinese sovereignty.

1998: Zhu Rongji became prime minister. Dissident Xu Wenli was jailed for trying to set up an opposition party.

1999: The USA and China announced a deal to allow for China's entry into the World Trade Organization (WTO), in exchange for opening China's markets to foreign firms. Macau was returned to China.

2001: Five members of the Falun Gong set themselves alight in Tiananmen Square, Beijing, in protest at the continued government crackdown on the sect. The mid-air collision of a US spy plane and a Chinese fighter jet provoked a diplomatic crisis.

2002: The country became a member of the World Trade Organization (WTO). Contact was re-established between the Dalai Lama and the Chinese government over the issue of Tibet for the first time since 1993.

chip (or **silicon chip**) another name for an ▷integrated circuit, a complete electronic circuit on a slice of silicon (or other semiconductor) crystal only a few millimetres square.

chipmunk any of several species of small ground squirrel with characteristic stripes along its side. Chipmunks live in North America and East Asia, in a variety of habitats, usually wooded, and take shelter in burrows. They have pouches in their cheeks for carrying food. They climb well but spend most of their time on or near the ground.

The **Siberian chipmunk** *Eutamias sibiricus*, about 13 cm/5 in long, is found in northern Russia, northern China, and Japan.
    Related Web site: Chipmunk Place http://www.owca.com/

Chippendale, Thomas (1718–1779) English furniture designer. He set up his workshop in St Martin's Lane, London, in 1753. His trade catalogue *The Gentleman and Cabinet Maker's Director* (1754), was a significant contribution to furniture design, and the first of its type to be published. Although many of his most characteristic designs are ▷rococo, he also employed Louis XVI, Chinese, Gothic, and neoclassical styles. He worked mainly in mahogany, newly introduced from South America.

Chippendale's work is characterized by solidity without heaviness; his ribbon-backed chairs are perhaps his most notable work, followed by his settees of two or three conjoined chairs. His business was carried on by his eldest son, Thomas (1749–1822), until 1813.

Chirac, Jacques René (1932–) French Gaullist politician and head of state, president from 1995 and prime minister 1974–76 and 1986–88, 'co-habiting' on the second occasion with the socialist president François ▷Mitterrand. Chirac led the Gaullist party 1974–95, refounding it in 1976 as the Rassemblement pour la République (RPR). He also served as the first elected mayor of Paris 1977–95.

After converting the RPR to neo-liberal economic policies and to further European integration, Chirac led the Right to electoral victory in 1986. His second government brought in major privatizations prior to the 1987 stock-market crash, but ceded ground over proposed nationality and university reforms. In 1993 he declined the premiership (which went to his former finance minister Edouard ▷Balladur).

In 1995, having twice stood unsuccessfully against Mitterrand for the presidency in 1981 and 1988, he was able to outdistance the socialist Lionel Jospin (and, on the first ballot, Balladur). Controversially, he decided temporarily to resume Pacific nuclear testing in late 1995. With his government increasingly unpopular over welfare cutbacks – linked to meeting the Maastricht criteria for European Monetary Union – Chirac miscalculated in calling early parliamentary elections in June 1997, the Left's victory forcing him into 'co-habitation' with a government led by Lionel ▷Jospin.

Chirico, Giorgio de (1888–1978) Greek-born Italian painter. He founded the school of ▷metaphysical painting, which in its enigmatic imagery and haunted, dreamlike settings presaged surrealism, as in *Nostalgia of the Infinite* (1911; Museum of Modern Art, New York).

Chiron unusual Solar-System object orbiting between Saturn and Uranus, discovered in 1977 by US astronomer Charles T Kowal (1940–).

Initially classified as an asteroid, it is now believed to be a giant cometary nucleus at least 200 km/120 mi across, composed of ice with a dark crust of carbon dust. It has a 51-year orbit and a coma (cloud of gas and dust) caused by evaporation from its surface, resembling that of a comet. It is classified as a centaur.

chiropractic in alternative medicine, technique of manipulation of the spine and other parts of the body, based on the principle that physical disorders are attributable to aberrations in the functioning of the nervous system, which manipulation can correct.

chiru Tibetan species of antelope. It is pale fawn in colour with coarse hair; the male alone has horns, and these are long, straight, ringed and gazellelike. It is nearly 1 m/3.3 ft in height.
    Classification The chiru *Pantholops hodgsoni* is in the family Bovidae (cattle and antelopes) of order Artiodactyla.

Chişinău (Russian **Kishinev**) capital of Moldova, situated in a rich agricultural area; population (1990) 676,000. It is a commercial and cultural centre; industries include cement, food processing, tobacco, and textiles.

Chissano, Joaquim (1939–) Mozambique nationalist politician, president from 1986; foreign minister 1975–86. In October 1992 he signed a peace accord with the leader of the rebel Mozambique National Resistance (MNR) party, bringing to an end 16 years of civil war, and in 1994 he won the first free presidential elections.

He was secretary to Samora ▷Machel, who led the National Front for the Liberation of Mozambique (Frelimo) during the campaign for independence in the early 1960s. When Mozambique achieved internal self-government in 1974, Chissano was appointed prime minister. After independence he served under Machel as foreign minister and on Machel's death succeeded him as president.

chitin complex long-chain compound, or ▷polymer; a nitrogenous derivative of glucose. Chitin is widely found in invertebrates. It forms the ▷exoskeleton of insects and other arthropods. It combines with protein to form a covering that can be hard and tough, as in beetles, or soft and flexible, as in caterpillars and other insect larvae. It is insoluble in water and resistant to acids, alkalis, and many organic solvents. In crustaceans such as crabs, it is impregnated with calcium carbonate for extra strength.

Chitin also occurs in some ▷protozoans and coelenterates (such as certain jellyfishes), in the jaws of annelid worms, and as the cell-wall polymer of fungi. Its uses include coating apples (still fresh after six months), coating seeds, and dressing wounds. In 1993 chemists at North Carolina State University found that it can be used to filter pollutants from industrial waste water.

Chittagong city and port in Bangladesh, 16 km/10 mi from the mouth of the Karnaphuli River, on the Bay of Bengal; population (1991) 1,364,000. Industries include steel, engineering, chemicals, and textiles.

chivalry code of gallantry and honour that medieval knights were pledged to observe. Its principal virtues were piety, honour, valour, courtesy, chastity, and loyalty. The word originally meant the knightly class of the feudal Middle Ages. Modern orders of chivalry such as the Order of the ▷Garter are awarded as a mark of royal favour or as a reward for public services; see ▷knighthood, order of.

Chivalry has its roots in the customs and outlook of the Germanic tribes; it developed in feudal France and Spain, and spread rapidly to the rest of Europe, reaching its height in the 12th and 13th centuries. It was strengthened by the ▷Crusades. The earliest orders of chivalry were the Knights Hospitallers and Knights Templars, founded to serve pilgrims to Palestine. The favourite sport of chivalry was the ▷tournament or joust. Secular literature of the period takes knighthood and chivalry as its theme.

chive (or **chives**) perennial European plant belonging to the lily family, related to onions and leeks. It has an underground bulb, long hollow tubular leaves, and globe-shaped purple flower heads. The leaves are used as a garnish for salads. (*Allium schoenoprasum*, family Liliaceae.)

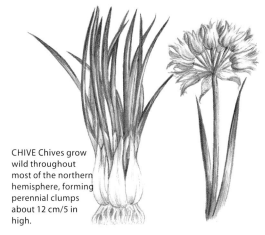

CHIVE Chives grow wild throughout most of the northern hemisphere, forming perennial clumps about 12 cm/5 in high.

chlamydia viruslike bacteria which live parasitically in animal cells, and cause disease in humans and birds. Chlamydiae are thought to be descendants of bacteria that have lost certain metabolic processes. In humans, a strain of chlamydia causes ▷trachoma, a disease found mainly in the tropics (a leading cause of blindness); venereally transmitted chlamydiae cause genital and urinary infections.

chloral (or **trichloroethanal**) (CCl_3CHO) oily, colourless liquid with a characteristic pungent smell, produced by the action of chlorine on ethanol. It is soluble in water and its compound chloral hydrate is a powerful sleep-inducing agent.

chlorate any salt derived from an acid containing both chlorine and oxygen and possessing the negative ion ClO^-, ClO_2^-, ClO_3^-, or ClO_4^-. Common chlorates are those of sodium, potassium, and barium. Certain chlorates are used in weedkillers.

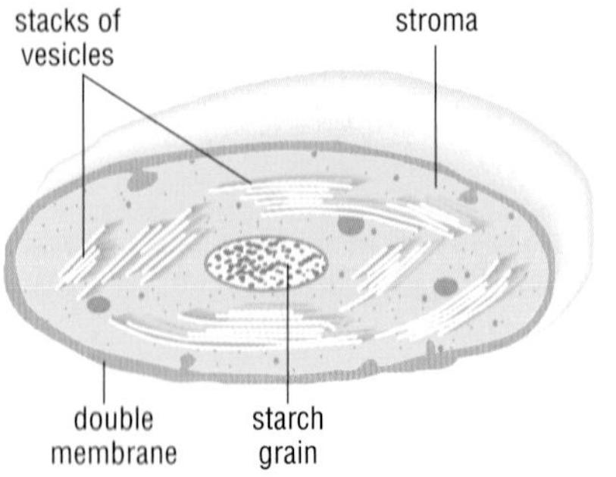

CHLOROPLAST Green chlorophyll molecules on the membranes of the vesicle stacks capture light energy to produce food by photosynthesis.

chloride Cl^- negative ion formed when hydrogen chloride dissolves in water, and any salt containing this ion, commonly formed by the action of hydrochloric acid (HCl) on various metals or by direct combination of a metal and chlorine. Sodium chloride (NaCl) is common table salt.

chlorinated solvent any liquid organic compound that contains chlorine atoms, often two or more. These compounds are very effective solvents for fats and greases, but many have toxic properties.

They include trichloromethane (chloroform, $CHCl_3$), tetrachloromethane (carbon tetrachloride, CCl_4), and trichloroethene ($CH_2ClCHCl_2$).

chlorination the treatment of water with chlorine in order to disinfect it; also, any chemical reaction in which a chlorine atom is introduced into a chemical compound.

chlorine (Greek *chloros* 'green') greenish-yellow, gaseous, nonmetallic element with a pungent odour, symbol Cl, atomic number 17, relative atomic mass 35.453. It is a member of the ▷halogen group and is widely distributed, in combination with the ▷alkali metals, as chlorates or chlorides.

Chlorine was discovered in 1774 by the German chemist Karl Scheele, but English chemist Humphry Davy first proved it to be an element in 1810 and named it after its colour. In nature it is always found in the combined form, as in hydrochloric acid, produced in the mammalian stomach for digestion. Chlorine is obtained commercially by the electrolysis of concentrated brine and is an important bleaching agent and germicide, used for sterilizing both drinking water and swimming pools. As an oxidizing agent it finds many applications in organic chemistry. The pure gas (Cl_2) is a poison and was used in gas warfare in World War I, where its release seared the membranes of the nose, throat, and lungs, producing pneumonia. Chlorine is a component of chlorofluorocarbons (CFCs) and is partially responsible for the depletion of the ▷ozone layer; it is released from the CFC molecule by the action of ultraviolet radiation in the upper atmosphere, making it available to react with and destroy the ozone. The concentration of chlorine in the atmosphere in 1997 reached just over 3 parts per billion. It is expected to reach its peak in 1999 and then start falling rapidly due to international action to curb ozone-destroying chemicals.

Related Web site: Chlorine http://c3.org/

chlorofluorocarbon (CFC) a class of synthetic chemicals that are odourless, nontoxic, nonflammable, and chemically inert. The first CFC was synthesized in 1892, but no use was found for it until the 1920s. Since then their stability and apparently harmless properties have made CFCs popular as propellants in ▷aerosol cans, as refrigerants in refrigerators and air conditioners, as degreasing agents, and in the manufacture of foam packaging. They are partly responsible for the destruction of the ▷ozone layer. In June 1990 representatives of 93 nations, including the UK and the USA, agreed to phase out production of CFCs and various other ozone-depleting chemicals by the end of the 20th century.

Related Web site: Problem of ChloroFluoroCarbons http://pooh.chem.wm.edu/chemWWW/courses/chem105/projects/group2/page5.html

chloroform (technical name **trichloromethane**) $CHCl_3$ clear, colourless, toxic, carcinogenic liquid with a characteristic pungent, sickly sweet smell and taste, formerly used as an anaesthetic (now superseded by less harmful substances).

It is used as a solvent and in the synthesis of organic chemical compounds.

chlorophyll a group of pigments including chlorophyll a and chlorophyll b, the green pigments in plants; it is responsible for the absorption of light energy during ▷photosynthesis.

The pigment absorbs the red and blue-violet parts of sunlight but reflects the green, thus giving plants their characteristic colour.

Other chlorophylls include chlorophyll c (in brown algae) and chlorophyll d (found in red algae).

chloroplast structure (▷organelle) within a plant cell containing the green pigment chlorophyll. Chloroplasts occur in most cells of the green plant that are exposed to light, often in large numbers. Typically, they are flattened and disclike, with a double membrane enclosing the stroma, a gel-like matrix. Within the stroma are stacks of fluid-containing cavities, or vesicles, where ▷photosynthesis occurs.

It is thought that the chloroplasts were originally free-living cyanobacteria (blue-green algae) which invaded larger, non-photosynthetic cells and developed a symbiotic relationship with them. Like ▷mitochondria, they contain a small amount of DNA and divide by fission. Chloroplasts are a type of ▷plastid.

chlorosis abnormal condition of green plants in which the stems and leaves turn pale green or yellow. The yellowing is due to a reduction in the levels of the green chlorophyll pigments. It may be caused by a deficiency in essential elements (such as magnesium, iron, or manganese), a lack of light, genetic factors, or viral infection.

chocolate powder, syrup, confectionery, or beverage derived from cacao seeds. See ▷cocoa and chocolate.

choir in architecture, the area of a church which is specially reserved and furnished for choristers. This is usually, but not always, in the east part of the church, occupying the west half of the chancel or sanctuary. Hence the terms 'chancel' and 'choir' have come to be almost synonymous, although sometimes this usage may be incorrect, for example at Westminster Abbey the choir is in the nave.

Noam Chomsky

If we don't believe in freedom of expression for people we despise, we don't believe in it at all.

BBC TV *The Late Show*, 25 November 1992

choir body of singers, usually of sacred music, of more than one voice to a part, whose members are able to sight read music and hold a melody. A traditional cathedral choir of male voices is required to sing responses, hymns, and psalms appropriate to the church calendar.

Related Web site: King's Singers http://www.kingssingers.com/

choke coil in physics, a coil employed to limit or suppress alternating current without stopping direct current, particularly the type used as a 'starter' in the circuit of fluorescent lighting.

Chola dynasty Southern Indian family of rulers that flourished in the 9th–13th centuries. Based on the banks of the Cauvery River, the Cholas overthrew their ▷Pallava and ▷Pandya neighbours and established themselves as the major pan-regional force. The two greatest Chola kings were Rajaraja I (reigned 985–1014) who invaded Northern Cyprus and his son Rajendra Cholavarma (reigned 1014–1044).

cholecalciferol (or **vitamin D**) fat-soluble chemical important in the uptake of calcium and phosphorous for bones. It is found in liver, fish oils and margarine. It can be produced in the skin, provided that the skin is adequately exposed to sunlight. Lack of vitamin D leads to rickets and other bone diseases.

cholecystectomy surgical removal of the ▷gall bladder. It is carried out when gallstones or infection lead to inflammation of the gall bladder, which may then be removed either by conventional surgery or by a 'keyhole' procedure (see ▷endoscopy).

cholera disease caused by infection with various strains of the bacillus *Vibrio cholerae*, transmitted in contaminated water and characterized by violent diarrhoea and vomiting. It is prevalent in many tropical areas.

The formerly high death rate during epidemics has been much reduced by treatments to prevent dehydration and loss of body salts, together with the use of antibiotics. There is an effective vaccine that must be repeated at frequent intervals for people exposed to continuous risk of infection. The worst epidemic in the Western hemisphere for 70 years occurred in Peru in 1991, with 55,000 confirmed cases and 258 deaths. It was believed to have been spread by the consumption of seafood contaminated by untreated sewage. 1991 was also the worst year on record for cholera in Africa with 13,000 deaths.

The sequencing of the complete cholera genome was completed in August 2000, revealing that many of the genes that enable cholera to attack humans are found on a single chromosome. The discovery should aid the development of a more effective vaccine and other drugs to combat the disease.

cholesterol white, crystalline ▷sterol found throughout the body, especially in fats, blood, nerve tissue, and bile; it is also provided in the diet by foods such as eggs, meat, and butter. A high level of cholesterol in the blood is thought to contribute to atherosclerosis (hardening of the arteries).

Cholesterol is an integral part of all cell membranes and the starting point for steroid hormones, including the sex hormones. It is broken down by the liver into bile salts, which are involved in fat absorption in the digestive system, and it is an essential component of **lipoproteins**, which transport fats and fatty acids in the blood. **Low-density lipoprotein cholesterol** (LDL-cholesterol), when present in excess, can enter the tissues and become deposited on the surface of the arteries, causing atherosclerosis. **High-density lipoprotein cholesterol** (HDL-cholesterol) acts as a scavenger, transporting fat and cholesterol from the tissues to the liver to be broken down. The composition of HDL-cholesterol can vary and some forms may not be as effective as others. Blood cholesterol levels can be altered by reducing the amount of alcohol and fat in the diet and by substituting some of the saturated fat for polyunsaturated fat, which gives a reduction in LDL-cholesterol. A 1999 US study of children with high levels of cholesterol found no evidence that controlling cholesterol levels through diet is harmful. Another 1999 US study suggested that cholesterol-lowering drugs are as beneficial for older men and women as they are for the middle-aged. HDL-cholesterol can be increased by exercise.

Chomsky, (Avram) Noam (1928–) US professor of linguistics and political commentator. He proposed a theory of transformational generative grammar, which attracted widespread interest because of the claims it made about the relationship between language and the mind and the universality of an underlying language structure. He has been a leading critic of the imperialist tendencies of the US government.

Chomsky distinguished between knowledge and behaviour and maintained that the focus of scientific enquiry should be on knowledge. In order to define and describe linguistic knowledge, he posited a set of abstract principles of grammar that appear to be universal and may have a biological basis.

Related Web site: Chomsky, Noam http://www.thirdworldtraveler.com/Chomsky/Noam_Chomsky.html

Chongqing (or **Chungking**, or **Pahsien**) city in Sichuan province, China, at the confluence of the Chang Jiang and Jialing Jiang rivers; population (1994) 5,408,000. It is the largest of China's four municipalities directly under the central government, with an area of 82,000 sq km/31,700 sq mi and population (1996) of 30,000,000. Industries include coalmining, food-processing, and the manufacture of iron, steel, chemicals, synthetic rubber, automobiles, electrical equipment, and textiles.

Chopin, Frédéric François (1810–1849) Polish composer and pianist. He made his debut as a pianist at the age of eight. As a performer, Chopin revolutionized the technique of pianoforte-playing, turning the hands outward and favouring a light, responsive touch. His compositions, which include two piano concertos and other orchestral works, are characterized by great volatility of mood, and rhythmic fluidity.

From 1831 he lived in Paris, France, where he became known in the fashionable salons, although he rarely performed in public. In 1836 the composer Liszt introduced him to George ▷Sand (Madame Dudevant), with whom he had a close relationship 1838–46. During this time she nursed him in Mallorca for tuberculosis, while he composed intensively and for a time regained his health. His music was used as the basis of the ballet *Les Sylphides* by Mikhail Fokine in 1909 and orchestrated by Alexander Gretchaninov (1864–1956), a pupil of Rimsky-Korsakov.

chord in geometry, a straight line joining any two points on a curve. The chord that passes through the centre of a circle (its longest chord) is the diameter. The longest and shortest chords of an ellipse (a regular oval) are called the major and minor axes, respectively.

chord in music, a group of three or more notes sounded together. The resulting combination of tones may be either harmonious or dissonant.

Related Web site: Chord Archive http://www.guitar.net/cotw/index.html

chordate animal belonging to the phylum Chordata, which includes vertebrates, sea squirts, amphioxi, and others. All these animals, at some stage of their lives, have a supporting rod of tissue (notochord or backbone) running down their bodies.

Chordates are divided into three major groups: ▷tunicates, cephalochordates (see ▷lancelet), and craniates (including all vertebrates).

chorea condition featuring involuntary movements of the face muscles and limbs. It is seen in a number of neurological diseases, including ▷Huntington's chorea.

choreography the art of creating and arranging ballet and dance for performance; originally, in the 18th century, dance notation.

chorion outermost of the three membranes enclosing the embryo of reptiles, birds, and mammals; the amnion is the innermost membrane.

chorionic villus sampling (CVS) ▷biopsy of a small sample of placental tissue, carried out in early pregnancy at 10–12 weeks' gestation. Since the placenta forms from embryonic cells, the tissue obtained can be tested to reveal genetic abnormality in the fetus. The advantage of CVS over ▷amniocentesis is that it provides an earlier diagnosis, so that if any abnormality is discovered, and the parents opt for an abortion, it can be carried out more safely.

chorus in classical Greek drama, the group of actors who jointly comment on the main action or advise the main characters. The action in Greek plays took place offstage; the chorus provided a link in the drama when the principals were offstage. The chorus did not always speak in unison; it was common for members of the chorus to show some individuality. The device of a chorus has also been used by later dramatists.

Chou En-lai alternative transliteration of ▷Zhou Enlai.

chough bird *Pyrrhocorax pyrrhocorax* of the crow family, Corvidae, order Passeriformes, about 38 cm/15 in long, black-feathered, with red bill and legs, and long hooked claws. Choughs are frugivorous and insectivorous. They make mud-walled nests and live on sea cliffs and mountains from Europe to East Asia, but are now rare.

chow chow breed of dog originating in China in ancient times. About 45 cm/1.5 ft tall, it has a broad neck and head, round catlike feet, a soft woolly undercoat with a coarse outer coat, and a mane. Its coat should be of one colour, and it has an unusual blue-black tongue.

Chrétien, (Joseph Jacques) Jean (1934–) French-Canadian politician, prime minister from 1993. He won the leadership of the Liberal Party in 1990 and defeated Kim Campbell in the October 1993 election. He was a vigorous advocate of national unity and, although himself a Québecois, consistently opposed the province's separatist ambitions. His Liberal Party won the Canadian elections of June 1997 and November 2000.

Chrétien held ministerial posts in the cabinets of Lester ▷Pearson and Pierre ▷Trudeau. After unsuccessfully contesting the Liberal Party leadership in 1984, he resigned his parliamentary seat, returning in 1990 to win the leadership on his second attempt.

Chrétien de Troyes (died *c.* 1183) French poet. His epics, which introduced the concept of the ▷Holy Grail, include *Lancelot, ou le chevalier de la charrette* (*c.* 1178), written for Marie, Countess of Champagne; *Perceval, ou le conte du Graal* (*c.* 1182), written for Philip, Count of Flanders; *Erec* (*c.* 1170); *Yvain, ou le chevalier au Lion* (*c.* 1178); and other Arthurian romances.

Christ (Greek *khristos* 'anointed one') the ▷Messiah as prophesied in the Hebrew Bible, or Old Testament.

Christchurch city on South Island, New Zealand, 11 km/7 mi from the mouth of the Avon River; population (1996) 331,400. It is the principal commercial centre of the Canterbury Plains and the seat of the University of Canterbury. Industries include fertilizers, chemicals, canning, meat processing, rail workshops, and shoes.

Christchurch uses as its port a bay in the sheltered Lyttelton Harbour on the north shore of the Banks Peninsula, which forms a denuded volcanic mass. Land has been reclaimed for service facilities, and rail and road tunnels (1867 and 1964 respectively) link Christchurch with Lyttelton.

Christchurch resort town in Dorset, southern England, at the junction of the Stour and Avon rivers, 8 km/5 mi east of Bournemouth; population (1991) 36,400. Industries include seasonal tourism, and the manufacture of plastics and electronics. The Norman and Early English Holy Trinity church is the longest parish church in England, extending for 95 m/312 ft.

christening Christian ceremony of ▷baptism of infants, including giving a name.

Christian ten kings of Denmark and Norway, including:

Christian I (1426–1481) King of Denmark from 1448, and founder of the Oldenburg dynasty. In 1450 he established the union of Denmark and Norway that lasted until 1814. He was king of Sweden 1457–64 and 1465–67.

Christian IV (1577–1648) King of Denmark and Norway from 1588. He sided with the Protestants in the Thirty Years' War (1618–48), and founded Christiania (now Oslo, capital of Norway). He was succeeded by Frederick II in 1648.

Christian IX (1818–1906) King of Denmark from 1863. His daughter Alexandra married Edward VII of the UK and another, Dagmar, married Tsar Alexander III of Russia; his second son, George, became king of Greece. In 1864 he lost the duchies of Schleswig and Holstein after a war with Austria and Prussia.

Christianity: Key Dates

1st century	The Christian Church is traditionally said to have originated at Pentecost, and separated from the parent Jewish religion by the declaration of saints Barnabas and Paul that the distinctive rites of Judaism are not necessary for entry into the Christian Church.
3rd century	Christians are persecuted under the Roman emperors Septimius Severus, Decius, and Diocletian.
312	Emperor Constantine establishes Christianity as the religion of the Roman Empire.
4th century	A settled doctrine of Christian belief evolves, with deviating beliefs condemned as heresies. Questions of discipline threaten disruption within the Church; to settle these, Constantine calls the Council of Arles in 314, followed by the councils of Nicaea (325) and Constantinople (381).
5th–7th centuries	Councils of Ephesus (431) and Chalcedon (451). Christianity is carried northwards by such figures as St Columba (521–597) and St Augustine (died 605), who became the first archbishop of Canterbury.
800	Holy Roman Emperor Charlemagne is crowned by the pope. The Church assists the growth of the feudal system of which it forms the apex.
1054	The Eastern Orthodox Church splits from the Roman Catholic Church.
11th–12th centuries	Secular and ecclesiastical jurisdiction are often in conflict; for example, Emperor Henry IV and Pope Gregory VII, Henry II of England and his archbishop Becket.
1096–1291	The Church supports the Crusades, a series of wars in the Middle East.
1233	The Inquisition is established to suppress heresy.
14th century	Increasing worldliness (against which the foundation of the Dominican and Franciscan monastic orders is a protest) and ecclesiastical abuses lead to dissatisfaction and the appearance of the reformers Wycliffe and Huss.
15th–17th centuries	Thousands of women are accused of witchcraft, tortured, and executed.
early 16th century	The Renaissance brings a re-examination of Christianity in northern Europe by the humanists Erasmus, More, and Colet.
1517	The German priest Martin Luther becomes leader of the Protestant movement and precipitates the Reformation.
1519–64	In Switzerland the Reformation is carried on by Calvin and Zwingli.
1529	Henry VIII renounces papal supremacy and proclaims himself head of the Church of England.
1545–63	The Counter-Reformation is initiated by the Catholic Church at the Council of Trent.
1560	The Church of Scotland is established according to Calvin's Presbyterian system.
17th century	Jesuit missionaries establish themselves in China and Japan. Puritans, Quakers, and other sects seeking religious freedom establish themselves in North America.
18th century	During the Age of Reason, Christian dogmas are questioned, and intellectuals begin to examine society in purely secular terms. In England and America, religious revivals occur among the working classes in the form of Methodism and the Great Awakening. In England the Church of England suffers the loss of large numbers of Nonconformists.
19th century	The evolutionary theories of Darwin and the historical criticism of the Bible challenge the Book of Genesis. Missionaries convert people in Africa and Asia, suppressing indigenous faiths and cultures.
1948	The World Council of Churches is founded as part of the ecumenical movement to reunite various Protestant sects and, to some extent, the Protestant Churches and the Catholic Church.
1950s–80s	Protestant evangelicalism grows rapidly in the USA, spread by television.
1969	A liberation theology of freeing the poor from oppression emerges in South America, and attracts papal disapproval.
1972	The United Reformed Church is formed by the union of the Presbyterian Church in England and the Congregational Church. In the USA, the 1960s–70s sees the growth of cults, some of them nominally Christian, which are a source of social concern.
1980s	The Roman Catholic Church plays a major role in the liberalization of the Polish government; in the USSR the Orthodox Church and other sects are tolerated and even encouraged under Gorbachev.
1988	The Holy Shroud of Turin, claimed by some to be Christ's mortuary cloth, is shown by carbon dating to date from about 1330.
1990s	The Christian Church grapples with the question of its attitude to homosexuality; the policy of most churches is to oppose its public acceptance, declaring that homosexual behaviour conflicts with Christian teachings.
1992	After 359 years, the Roman Catholic Church accepts that Galileo is right: the Earth does go round the Sun.
1993	Legislation to allow the Church of England to ordain women priests gains royal assent in Britain.
1997	The Roman Catholic Church issues a statement called the 'Declaration of Repentance', in which it formally apologizes for its silence when the French government deported Jews to Nazi death camps in German and Poland during World War II.
1998	US archaeologists in Aqaba, Jordan, announce the discovery of the world's oldest Christian church, built by the Christian community of Ayla in the late 3rd century.
1999	British rabbis and Catholic leaders at the Vatican agree to form an amicable partnership and accept the legitimacy of each other's beliefs. Until now, relations were hindered by the Catholic belief that the coming of Jesus Christ superseded the Jewish Covenant between God and Abraham.

Christian X (1870–1947) King of Denmark and Iceland from 1912, when he succeeded his father Frederick VIII. He married Alexandrine, Duchess of Mecklenburg-Schwerin, and was popular for his democratic attitude. During World War II he was held prisoner by the Germans in Copenhagen. He was succeeded by Frederick IX.

Christian Coalition US right-wing political pressure group founded in 1989 by the television evangelist Pat Robertson. The Christian Coalition aims to 'stop the moral decay of government' and to promote the election of 'moral' legislators. By 1995 the group had 1.7 million members in 1,500 branches in all 50 states, making it the group with the most influence over the policies of the Republican Party. Its headquarters are in Chesapeake, Virginia.

Christian Democracy ideology of a number of parties active in Western Europe since World War II, especially in Italy, the Federal Republic of Germany, and France, and (since 1989) in central and Eastern Europe. Christian Democrats are essentially moderate conservatives who believe in a mixed economy and in the provision of social welfare. They are opposed to both communism and fascism but are largely in favour of European integration.

Christianity world religion derived from the teaching of Jesus, as found in the ▷New Testament, during the first third of the 1st century. It has a present-day membership of about 1 billion, and is divided into groups or denominations that differ in some areas of belief and practice. Its main divisions are the ▷Roman Catholic, ▷Eastern Orthodox, and ▷Protestant churches.

Beliefs Christians believe in one God with three aspects: God the Father, God the Son (Jesus), and God the Holy Spirit, who is the power of God working in the world. God created everything that exists and showed his love for the world by coming to Earth as Jesus, and suffering and dying in order to reconcile humanity to himself. Christians believe that three days after his death by crucifixion Jesus was raised to life by God's power, appearing many times in bodily form to his followers, and that he is now alive in the world through the Holy Spirit. Christians speak of the sufferings they may have to endure because of their faith, and the reward of everlasting life in God's presence, which is promised to those who have faith in Jesus and who live according to his teaching. See map on p. 198.

Related Web site: Christian Classics Ethereal Library http://www.ccel.org/

Christian Science (or the Church of Christ, Scientist) sect established in the USA by Mary Baker Eddy in 1879. Christian Scientists believe that since God is good and is a spirit, matter and evil are not ultimately real. Consequently they refuse all medical treatment. The church publishes a daily newspaper, the *Christian Science Monitor*, which reports on international news.

Christie, Agatha (Mary Clarissa) (1890–1976) Born Agatha (Mary Clarissa) Miller. English detective novelist. She is best known for her ingenious plots and for the creation of the characters Hercule Poirot and Miss Jane Marple. She wrote more than 70 novels, including *The Murder of Roger Ackroyd* (1926) and *The Body in the Library* (1942). Her play *The Mousetrap*, which opened in

CHRISTIANITY
See entry on
p. 197.

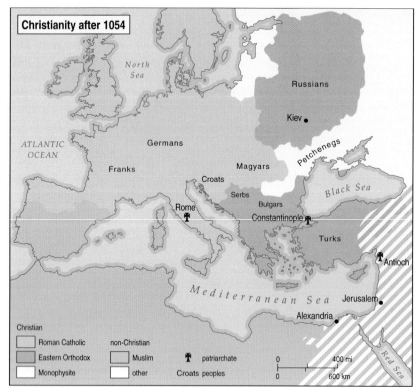

Christianity after 1054

London in 1952, is the longest continuously running show in the world.

Her first crime novel, *The Mysterious Affair at Styles* (1920), introduced the Belgian detective Hercule Poirot. She often broke purist rules, as in *The Murder of Roger Ackroyd* in which the narrator is the murderer. She was at her best writing about domestic murders in the respectable middle-class world. A number of her books have been filmed, for example *Murder on the Orient Express* (1934) (filmed in 1975). She was created a DBE in 1971.

Christie, Linford (1960–) Jamaican-born English sprinter who, with his win in the 1993 world championships, became the first track athlete ever to hold World, Olympic, European, and Commonwealth 100-metre titles simultaneously.

Christina (1626–1689) Queen of Sweden (1632–54). Succeeding her father Gustavus Adolphus at the age of six, she assumed power in 1644, but disagreed with the former regent Oxenstjerna. Refusing to marry, she eventually nominated her cousin Charles Gustavus (Charles X) as her successor. As a secret convert to Roman Catholicism, which was then illegal in Sweden, she had to abdicate in 1654, and went to live in Rome, twice returning to Sweden unsuccessfully to claim the throne.

Christine de Pisan (1364–*c.* 1430) French poet and historian. Her works include love lyrics, philosophical poems, a poem in praise of Joan of Arc, a history of Charles V of France, and various defences of women, including *La Cité des dames/The City of Ladies* (1405), which contains a valuable series of contemporary portraits.

Christmas Christian religious holiday, observed throughout the Western world on December 25 and traditionally marked by feasting and gift-giving. In the Christian church, it is the day on which the birth of Jesus is celebrated, although his actual birth date is unknown. Many of its customs have a non-Christian origin and were adapted from celebrations of the winter ▷solstice.

Christmas Island island in the Indian Ocean, 360 km/224 mi south of Java; area 140 sq km/54 sq mi; population (1994 est) 2,500. Found to be uninhabited when reached by Capt W Mynars on Christmas Day 1643, it was annexed by Britain in 1888, occupied by Japan between 1942 and 1945, and transferred to Australia in 1958. After a referendum in 1984, it was included in Northern Territory. Its phosphate mine was closed in 1987. Tourism and casinos are being developed.

Christophe, Henri (1767–1820) West Indian slave, one of the leaders of the revolt against the French in 1791, who was proclaimed king of Haiti in 1811. His government distributed plantations to military leaders. He shot himself when his troops deserted him because of his alleged cruelty.

Christopher, St Patron saint of travellers. His feast day, 25 July, was dropped from the Roman Catholic liturgical calendar in 1969.

Traditionally he was a martyr in Syria in the 3rd century, and legend describes his carrying the child Jesus over the stream; despite his great strength, he found the burden increasingly heavy, and was told that the child was Jesus Christ bearing the sins of all the world.

chromatic scale musical scale proceeding by semitones. In theory the inclusion of all 12 notes makes it a neutral scale without the focus provided by the seven-tone diatonic major or minor scale; in practice however, owing to small deviations from equal temperament, it is possible for a trained ear to identify the starting point of a randomly chosen chromatic scale.

chromatography (Greek *chromos* 'colour') technique for separating or analysing a mixture of gases, liquids, or dissolved substances. This is brought about by means of two immiscible substances, one of which (**the mobile phase**) transports the sample mixture through the other (**the stationary phase**). The mobile phase may be a gas or a liquid; the stationary phase may be a liquid or a solid, and may be in a column, on paper, or in a thin layer on a glass or plastic support. The components of the mixture are absorbed or impeded by the stationary phase to different extents and therefore become separated. The technique is used for both qualitative and quantitive analyses in biology and chemistry.

In **paper chromatography**, the mixture separates because the components have differing solubilities in the solvent flowing through the paper and in the chemically bound water of the paper.

In **thin-layer chromatography**, a wafer-thin layer of adsorbent medium on a glass plate replaces the filter paper. The mixture separates because of the differing solubilities of the components in the solvent flowing up the solid layer, and their differing tendencies to stick to the solid (adsorption). The same principles apply in **column chromatography**.

In **gas–liquid chromatography**, a gaseous mixture is passed into a long, coiled tube (enclosed in an oven) filled with an inert powder coated in a liquid. A carrier gas flows through the tube. As the mixture proceeds along the tube it separates as the components dissolve in the liquid to differing extents or stay as a gas. A detector locates the different components as they emerge from the tube. The technique is very powerful, allowing tiny quantities of substances (fractions of parts per million) to be separated and analysed.

Preparative chromatography is carried out on a large scale for the purification and collection of one or more of a mixture's constituents; for example, in the recovery of protein from abattoir wastes.

Analytical chromatography is carried out on far smaller quantities, often as little as one microgram (one-millionth of a gram), in order to identify and quantify the component parts of a mixture. It is used to determine the identities and amounts of amino acids in a protein, and the alcohol content of blood and urine samples. The technique was first used in the separation of coloured mixtures into their component pigments.

chromite ($FeCr_2O_4$) iron chromium oxide, the main chromium ore. It is one of the ▷spinel group of minerals, and crystallizes in dark-coloured octahedra of the cubic system. Chromite is usually found in association with ultrabasic and basic rocks; in Cyprus, for example, it occurs with ▷serpentine, and in South Africa it forms continuous layers in a layered ▷intrusion.

chromium (Greek *chromos* 'colour') hard, brittle, grey-white, metallic element, symbol Cr, atomic number 24, relative atomic mass 51.996. It takes a high polish, has a high melting point, and is very resistant to corrosion. It is used in chromium electroplating, in the manufacture of stainless steel and other alloys, and as a catalyst. Its compounds are used for tanning leather and for ▷alums. In human nutrition it is a vital trace element. In nature, it occurs chiefly as chrome iron ore or chromite ($FeCr_2O_4$). Kazakhstan, Zimbabwe, and Brazil are sources.

The element was named in 1797 by the French chemist Louis Vauquelin (1763–1829) after its brightly coloured compounds.

chromium ore essentially the mineral chromite, $FeCr_2O_4$, from which chromium is extracted. South Africa and Zimbabwe are major producers.

chromosome structure in a cell nucleus that carries the ▷genes. Each chromosome consists of one very long strand of DNA, coiled and folded to produce a compact body. The point on a chromosome where a particular gene occurs is known as its locus. Most higher organisms have two copies of each chromosome, together known as a **homologous pair** (they are ▷diploid) but some have only one (they are ▷haploid). There are 46 chromosomes in a normal human cell. See also ▷mitosis and ▷meiosis.

chromosphere (from the Greek words for 'colour' and 'sphere') layer of mostly hydrogen gas about 10,000 km/6,000 mi deep above the visible surface of the Sun (the photosphere). It appears pinkish red during ▷eclipses of the Sun.

chronic in medicine, term used to describe a condition that is of slow onset and then runs a prolonged course, such as rheumatoid arthritis or chronic bronchitis. In contrast, an **acute** condition develops quickly and may be of relatively short duration.

chronic fatigue syndrome a common debilitating condition also known as myalgic encephalomyelitis (ME), postviral fatigue syndrome, or 'yuppie flu'. It is characterized by a diffuse range of symptoms present for at least six months including extreme fatigue, muscular pain, weakness, depression, poor balance and coordination, joint pains, and gastric upset. It is usually diagnosed after exclusion of other diseases and frequently follows a flulike illness.

chronometer instrument for measuring time precisely, originally used at sea. It is designed to remain accurate through all conditions of temperature and pressure. The first accurate marine chronometer, capable of an accuracy of half a minute a year, was made in 1761 by John Harrison in England.

chrysalis pupa of an insect, but especially that of a ▷butterfly or ▷moth. It is essentially a static stage of the creature's life, when the adult insect, benefiting from the large amounts of food laid down by the actively feeding larva, is built up from the disintegrating larval tissues. The chrysalis may be exposed or within a cocoon.

chrysanthemum any of a large group of plants with colourful, showy flowers, containing about 200 species. There are hundreds of cultivated varieties, whose exact wild ancestry is uncertain. In the Far East the common chrysanthemum has been cultivated for more than 2,000 years and is the imperial emblem of Japan. Chrysanthemums can be grown from seed, but new plants are more commonly produced from cuttings or by dividing established plants. (Genus *Chrysanthemum*, family Compositae.)

chrysotile mineral in the ▷serpentine group, $Mg_3Si_2O_5(OH)_4$. A soft, fibrous, silky mineral, the primary source of asbestos.

Chuang the largest minority group in China, numbering about 15 million. They live in southern China, where they cultivate rice fields. Their religion includes elements of ancestor worship. The Chuang language belongs to the Tai family.

chub freshwater fish *Leuciscus cephalus* of the carp family. Thickset and cylindrical, it grows up to 60 cm/2 ft, is dark greenish or grey on the back, silvery yellow below, with metallic flashes on the flanks. It lives generally in clean rivers throughout Europe.

Chubu mountainous coastal region of central Honshu island, Japan, area 66,774 sq km/25,781 sq mi; population (1992) 21,162,000. The chief city is ▷Nagoya. The region, which produces tea, fruits, and fish, contains the Niigata plain, one of the country's largest rice-producing areas. Mount Fuji and several of Japan's longest rivers can also be found in the region.

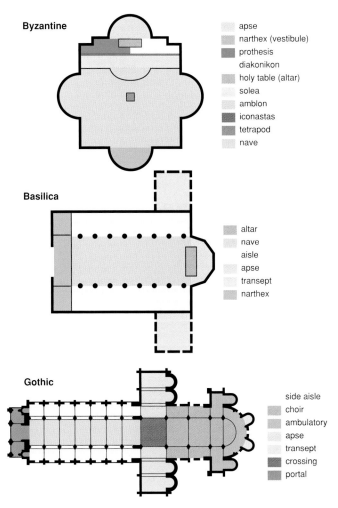

Byzantine

- apse
- narthex (vestibule)
- prothesis
- diakonikon
- holy table (altar)
- solea
- amblon
- iconastas
- tetrapod
- nave

Basilica

- altar
- nave
- aisle
- apse
- transept
- narthex

Gothic

- side aisle
- choir
- ambulatory
- apse
- transept
- crossing
- portal

CHURCH The basic layouts of Byzantine, Basilica, and Gothic churches.

Chugoku southwest region of Honshu island, Japan, area 31,881 sq km/12,309 sq mi; population (1992) 7,754,000. The chief city is ▷Hiroshima. Citrus and grapes are grown in the region. Formerly rich fishing grounds have been damaged by industrial pollution.

Chungking alternative transcription of ▷Chongqing, a city in Sichuan province, China.

church (from Greek *kuriakon*, 'belonging to the lord') in architecture, a building designed as a Christian place of worship; also the Christian community generally, or a subdivision or denomination of it, such as the Protestant Episcopal Church. Churches were first built in the 3rd century, when persecution ceased under the Roman emperor Constantine.

The original church design was based on the Roman ▷basilica, with a central nave, aisles either side, and an apse at one end. Many Western churches are built on an east–west axis with an altar at the east end, facing towards Jerusalem.

The church in the sense of the whole body of Christians is taken to include both those who are alive (the church militant) and those who have died and are in heaven (the church triumphant).

Related Web site: Mission Churches of the Sonoran Desert
http://dizzy.library.arizona.edu/images/swf/mission.html

Church Army religious organization within the Church of England founded in 1882 by Wilson Carlile (1847–1942), an industrialist converted after the failure of his textile firm, who became a cleric in 1880. Originally intended for evangelical and social work in the London slums, it developed along Salvation Army lines, and has done much work among ex-prisoners and for the soldiers of both world wars.

Churchill, Lord Randolph Henry Spencer (1849–1895) British Conservative politician, chancellor of the Exchequer and leader of the House of Commons in 1886; father of Winston Churchill.

Born at Blenheim Palace, Woodstock, Oxfordshire, son of the 7th Duke of Marlborough, he entered Parliament in 1874. In 1880 he formed a Conservative group known as the Fourth Party with Drummond Wolff (1830–1908), J E Gorst, and Arthur Balfour, and in 1885 his policy of Tory democracy was widely accepted by the

party. In 1886 he became chancellor of the Exchequer, but resigned within six months because he did not agree with the demands made on the Treasury by the War Office and the Admiralty. In 1874 he married Jennie Jerome (1854–1921), daughter of a wealthy New Yorker.

Churchill, Winston (Leonard Spencer)

(1874–1965) British Conservative politician, prime minister 1940–45 and 1951–55. In Parliament from 1900, as a Liberal until 1923, he held a number of ministerial offices, including First Lord of the Admiralty 1911–15 and chancellor of the Exchequer 1924–29. Absent from the cabinet in the 1930s, he returned in September 1939 to lead a coalition government from 1940 to 1945, negotiating with Allied leaders in World War II to achieve the unconditional surrender of Germany in 1945. He led a Conservative government between 1951 and 1955. He was awarded the Nobel Prize for Literature in 1953.

Early career Churchill was born at Blenheim Palace, Woodstock, Oxfordshire, the elder son of Lord Randolph Churchill. Educated at Harrow and Sandhurst, he joined the army in 1895. In the dual role of soldier and military correspondent he served in the Spanish–American War in Cuba, and then in India, Egypt, and South Africa, where he made a dramatic escape from imprisonment in Pretoria.

In 1900 he was elected Conservative member of Parliament for Oldham, but he disagreed with Joseph Chamberlain's tariff-reform policy and joined the Liberals. In 1906 he won Northwest Manchester for the Liberals. He had in the meantime been appointed undersecretary of state for the colonies in the Henry Campbell-Bannerman administration. Herbert Asquith made Churchill president of the Board of Trade in 1908, where he introduced legislation for the establishment of labour exchanges. As home secretary in 1910, he lost much of his previously won reputation as a radical by his action in sending the military to aid police against rioting miners in Tonypandy, south Wales.

World War I In 1911 Asquith appointed Churchill First Lord of the Admiralty, a position he still held on the outbreak of World War I. He devised an ill-fated plan to attack the Turkish-held Dardanelles in 1915 in order to relieve pressure on the Russians fighting Turkish troops in the Caucasus. The disaster of the Dardanelles expedition brought political attacks on Churchill that led to his demotion to the Duchy of Lancaster and to his resignation later that year. In 1915–16 he served in the trenches in France, but then resumed his parliamentary duties and was minister of munitions under David Lloyd George in 1917, when he was concerned with the development of the tank. After the armistice he was secretary for war 1918–21 and then as colonial secretary played a leading part in the establishment of the Irish Free State. During the post-war years he was active in support of the Whites (anti-Bolsheviks) in Russia.

Between the wars During the period 1922–24 Churchill was out of Parliament. He left the Liberals in 1923, and was returned for Epping as a Conservative in 1924. Baldwin made him chancellor of the Exchequer, and he brought about Britain's return to the gold standard. During the General Strike of May 1926, Churchill edited the government newspaper, the *British Gazette*, and was prominent in the defeat of the strike. He was out of office 1929–39, and as a back-bench MP he disagreed with the Conservatives on India (he was opposed to any abdication of British power), rearmament (he repeatedly warned of the rate of German rearmament and Britain's unpreparedness), and Neville Chamberlain's policy of appeasement.

WINSTON CHURCHILL Winston Churchill giving his famous 'V for Victory' sign. *Archive Photos*

World War II On the first day of World War II he went back to his old post at the Admiralty. In May 1940 he was called to the premiership as both prime minister and defence minister at the head of an all-party administration, and made a much-quoted 'blood, tears, toil, and sweat' speech to the House of Commons. He had a close relationship with US president Roosevelt, and in August 1941 concluded the Atlantic Charter with him. He travelled to Washington, DC; the Casablanca Conference, Morocco; Cairo, Egypt; Moscow, USSR; and the Tehran Conference, Iran, meeting the other leaders of the Allied war effort. He met Stalin and Roosevelt in the Crimea at the ▷Yalta Conference in February 1945 to draw up plans for the final defeat of Germany and for its occupation and control after its unconditional surrender.

The coalition government was dissolved on 23 May 1945, and Churchill formed a caretaker government drawn mainly from the Conservatives. In June he went to the ▷Potsdam Conference in Germany to discuss the final stages of the war. He was already worried by Soviet intentions in Eastern Europe, but he could have no part in the eventual decisions of the conference, because in July his government was defeated in a general election and he had to return to Britain.

Churchill and the Cold War Although Churchill was voted out of office just as the ▷Cold War started, he still had a significant influence on the course of the Cold War by virtue of his leadership of the UK during World War II, his immense stature as an international statesman, and his subsequent speeches on the subject.

Churchill had been present at all the major meetings held by the UK, USA, and USSR during World War II, Casablanca, Tehran, Yalta, and the Potsdam Conference in Germany. These meetings saw the changing relationships between the great powers played out. By Potsdam the initially friendly alliance against Nazi Germany had crumbled to mistrust and fear between the capitalist allies of Britain and the USA and the communist USSR. Churchill's inability to instill trust between the USA and USSR reflected their incompatible ideologies, rather than lack of effort on his part.

After his electoral defeat, Churchill returned to journalism and public speaking. He went to the USA for a lecture tour, and was invited to make a speech at Westminster College, Fulton, Missouri, USA on 5 March 1946. It was here that Churchill described the existence of an ▷Iron Curtain across Europe between the Soviet-dominated states of Eastern Europe and the democracies of the West. The phrase had previously been used by others, notably the Nazi propaganda minister Joseph Goebbels. Churchill had crystallized the thoughts of many, that the USA and USSR had now become ideological enemies who were playing out a war for power and influence across the world.

Post-war career He became leader of the opposition until the election in October 1951, in which he again became prime minister until his resignation in April 1955.

> ## Winston Churchill
>
> *It was the nation and the race dwelling all around the globe that had the lion's heart. I had the luck to be called upon to give the roar.*
>
> On World War II; 80th birthday address to Parliament, 30 November 1954

His peacetime government saw an apparent abatement of the Cold War, and a revival in the country's economy. There was, however, little progress towards the united Europe of which Churchill had proclaimed himself an advocate. He remained in Parliament as MP for Woodford until the dissolution in 1964. Churchill was made Knight of the Garter in 1953.

Commemoration His home from 1922, Chartwell in Kent, is a museum. His books include a six-volume history of World War II (1948–54) and a four-volume *History of the English-Speaking Peoples* (1956–58).

Related Web site: Speeches of Winston Churchill Sounds Page http://earthstation1.simplenet.com/churchil.html

Church in Wales the Welsh Anglican church; see ▷Wales, Church in.

Church of England established form of Christianity in England, a member of the Anglican Communion. It was dissociated from the Roman Catholic Church in 1534 under Henry VIII; the British monarch is still the supreme head of the Church of England today. The service book until November 2000 was the Book of ▷Common Prayer. It is now *Common Worship.*

The Church of England suffered its largest annual decline in Sunday service attendance for 20 years in 1995, according to the annual Church Statistics report. The average attendance was 1,045,000 – a drop of 36,000 from 1994. In November 1992 the General Synod of the Church of England and the Anglican church in Australia voted in favour of the ordination of women, and the first women priests were ordained in England in 1994. By 1998 there were some 860 stipendiary women clergy.

Organization Two archbishops head the provinces of Canterbury and York, which are subdivided into bishoprics. The Church Assembly (established in 1919) was replaced in 1970 by a **General Synod** with three houses (bishops, other clergy, and laity) to regulate church matters, subject to Parliament and the royal assent. A **Lambeth Conference** (first held in 1867), attended by bishops from all parts of the Anglican Communion, is held every ten years and presided over in London by the archbishop of Canterbury. It is not legislative but its decisions are often put into practice. The **Church Commissioners** for England (dating from 1948) manage the assets of the church (in 1989 valued at £2.64 billion) and endowment of livings.

Main groups The main parties, all products of the 19th century, are: the **Evangelical** or **Low Church**, which maintains the church's Protestant character; the **Anglo-Catholic** or **High Church**, which stresses continuity with the pre-Reformation church and is marked by ritualistic practices, the use of confession, and maintenance of religious communities of both sexes; and the **liberal** or **modernist** movement, concerned with the reconciliation of the church with modern thought. There is also the **Pentecostal Charismatic** movement, emphasizing spontaneity and speaking in tongues.

Related Web site: Church of England http://www.church-of-england.org/

Church of Scotland established form of Christianity in Scotland, first recognized by the state in 1560. It is based on the Protestant doctrines of the reformer ▷Calvin and governed on Presbyterian lines. The church went through several periods of episcopacy (government by bishops) in the 17th century, and those who adhered to episcopacy after 1690 formed the Episcopal Church of Scotland, an autonomous church in communion with the Church of England. In 1843 there was a split in the Church of Scotland (the Disruption), in which almost a third of its ministers and members left and formed the ▷Free Church of Scotland. By an Act of Union of 3 October 1929 the Church of Scotland was united with the United Free Church of Scotland to form the United Church of Scotland. There are over 680,000 members of the Church of Scotland (1998).

Chu Teh Chinese Red Army leader; see ▷Zhu De.

Chuvash (or **Chuvashiya**) autonomous republic in the western Russian Federation; area 18,300 sq km/7,066 sq mi; population (1990) 1,340,000 (68% Chuvash, 25% Russian). The main cities are Cheboksary (capital), Alatyr, and Shumerla. Chuvash lies south of the Volga River, 560 km/350 mi east of Moscow. The main industries are textiles, lumbering, electrical and engineering industries, phosphates, and limestone; there is grain and fruit farming.

chyme general term for the stomach contents. Chyme resembles a thick creamy fluid and is made up of partly digested food, hydrochloric acid, and a range of enzymes.

CIA abbreviation for the US ▷Central Intelligence Agency.

Cibachrome in photography, a process of printing directly from transparencies. It can be home-processed and the rich, saturated colours are highly resistant to fading. It was introduced in 1963.

cicada any of several insects of the family Cicadidae. Most species are tropical, but a few occur in Europe and North America. The adults live on trees, whose juices they suck. The males produce a

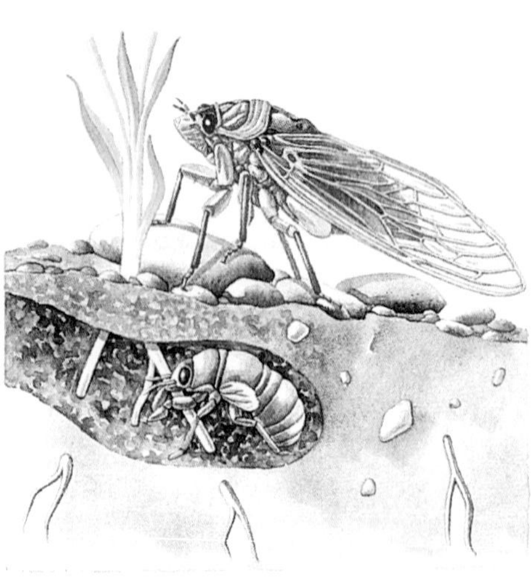

CICADA As in other cicada species, the nymph, or larva, of the Australian double drummer *Thopha saccata* is a strong digger, burrowing down from the surface to feed on the roots of shrubs and trees.

loud, almost continuous, chirping by vibrating membranes in resonating cavities in the abdomen.

Cicadas with a periodic life cycle, such as the 13-year cicada and the 17-year cicada, are found only in the USA. These species spend most of their lives as larvae underground, synchronizing their emergence every 13 or 17 years depending on species.

The rare *Cicadetta montana*, about 2 cm/0.8 in long, lives in the New Forest, England.

Cicero, Marcus Tullius (106–43 BC) Roman orator, writer, and politician. His speeches and philosophical and rhetorical works are models of Latin prose, and his letters provide a picture of contemporary Roman life. As consul in 63 BC he exposed the Roman politician Catiline's conspiracy in four major orations.

Born in Arpinium, Cicero became an advocate in Rome, spent three years in Greece studying oratory, and after the dictator Sulla's death distinguished himself in Rome with the prosecution of the corrupt Roman governor, Verres. When the First Triumvirate was formed 59 BC, Cicero was briefly exiled and devoted himself to literature. He sided with Pompey during the civil war (49–48) but was pardoned by Julius Caesar and returned to Rome. After Caesar's assassination in 44 BC he supported Octavian (the future emperor Augustus) and violently attacked Mark Antony in republican speeches known as the *Philippics*. On the reconciliation of Antony and Octavian, he was executed by Antony's agents.

Related Web site: Cicero Home Page http://www.utexas.edu/depts/classics/documents/Cic.html

MARCUS CICERO The Roman statesman Cicero was a scholar of Ancient Greek, and it was his translation of Greek thought and philosophy that preserved much Greek culture for later generations. He made an enemy of Mark Antony and was put to death. *The Art Archive/Capitoline Museum Rome/Dagli Orti*

cichlid any freshwater fish of the family Cichlidae. Cichlids are somewhat perchlike, but have a single nostril on each side instead of two. They are mostly predatory, and have deep, colourful bodies, flattened from side to side so that some are almost disc-shaped. Many are territorial in the breeding season and may show care of the young. There are more than 1,000 species found in South and Central America, Africa, and India.

Related Web site: Cichlid Home Page http://cichlidresearch.com/index.html#Contents

CID abbreviation for the UK ▷Criminal Investigation Department.

Cid, El, Rodrigo Díaz de Vivar (*c.* 1040–1099) Spanish soldier, nicknamed **El Cid** ('the lord') by the ▷Moors. Born in Castile of a noble family, he fought against the king of Navarre and won his nickname *el Campeador* ('the Champion') by killing the Navarrese champion in single combat. Essentially a mercenary, fighting both with and against the Moors, he died while defending Valencia against them, and in subsequent romances became Spain's national hero.

Much of El Cid's present-day reputation is the result of the exploitation of the legendary character as a model Christian military hero by the Nationalists during the Civil War, with Franco presented as a modern equivalent in his reconquest of Spain.

Related Web site: El Cid http://www.newadvent.org/cathen/03769a.htm

cigarette beetle small beetle that feeds preferentially on tobacco products, such as cigarettes and cigars. It may, however, feed on a wide range of other products for example, raisins, ginger, cocoa, drugs, and even straw.

Classification The cigarette beetle *Lasioderma serricorne* is a member of the family Anobiidae (furniture beetles) in order Coleoptera, class Insecta, phylum Arthropoda.

cilia (singular **cilium**) small hairlike organs on the surface of some cells, particularly the cells lining the upper respiratory tract. Their wavelike movements waft particles of dust and debris towards the exterior. Some single-celled organisms move by means of cilia. In multicellular animals, they keep lubricated surfaces clear of debris. They also move food in the digestive tracts of some invertebrates.

Cilicia ancient region of Asia Minor, now forming part of Turkey, situated between the Taurus Mountains and the Mediterranean. Access from the north across the Taurus range is through the **Cilician Gates**, a strategic pass that has been used for centuries as part of a trade route linking Europe and the Middle East.

Çiller, Tansu (1946–) Turkish politician, prime minister 1993–96 and a forthright exponent of free-market economic policies. She won the leadership of the centre-right True Path Party and the premiership on the election of Suleyman ▷Demirel as president. Her support for a military, as opposed to a diplomatic, approach to ▷Kurdish insurgency provoked international criticism; in 1995 relations with her coalition partners deteriorated, and a general election was called for December. The result was inconclusive and, after prolonged attempts to form a new coalition, she agreed in 1996 to have a rotating premiership with the Motherland Party leader, Mesut Yilmaz. However, this arrangement foundered in June 1996 following allegations of corruption against Çiller. In October 1997 her husband was charged with changing figures on the balance sheet of a US firm owned by the family.

Cimabue, Giovanni (*c.* 1240–1302) Also known as **Cenni di Peppi**. Italian painter. Active in Florence, he is traditionally styled the 'father of Italian painting'. His paintings retain the golden background of Byzantine art but the figures have a new naturalism. Among the works attributed to him are *Maestà* (*c.* 1280; Uffizi, Florence), a huge Gothic image of the Virgin, with a novel softness and solidity that points forwards to Giotto.

cinchona any of a group of tropical American shrubs or trees belonging to the madder family. The drug ▷quinine is produced from the bark of some species, and these are now cultivated in India, Sri Lanka, the Philippines, and Indonesia. (Genus *Chinchona*, family Rubiaceae.)

Cincinnati city and port in southwestern Ohio, USA, on the northern bank of the Ohio River; seat of Hamilton County; population (1994 est) 358,000; metropolitan area (1994 est) 1,894,000. The city is an important inland port on the Ohio–Mississippi system, and a major manufacturing centre; its chief industries include aircraft and car machinery, clothing, furniture making, wine, chemicals, and meatpacking. Founded in 1788, Cincinnati was incorporated as a city in 1819. It attracted large numbers of European immigrants, particularly Germans, during the 19th century.

Cincinnatus, Lucius Quinctius (lived 5th century BC) Roman general. Having served as consul in 460 BC, he retired from political life to work on his farm. However, he was called back and appointed dictator in 458 BC, and he defeated the Aequi (an Italian people) in a brief campaign. Having held office for just 16 days, he returned to his farm and resumed life as a yeoman farmer. He became a legend for republican idealism.

cine camera camera that takes a rapid sequence of still photographs called frames. When the frames are projected one after the other on to a screen, they appear to show movement, because our eyes hold on to the image of one picture until the next one appears.

cinema (Greek *kinema* 'movement') form of art and entertainment consisting of moving pictures, in either black and white or colour, projected on a screen. Cinema draws on other arts, such as literature, drama, and music. Its development, beginning in the 1890s, has been closely linked to technological advances, including action and colour ▷photography, sound reproduction, and film processing and printing. The first sound films were released in 1926 and 1927.

The silent era In the 1890s the French film pioneers Auguste and Louis ▷Lumière developed the cinematograph, a device to project pictures onto a screen to give the illusion of movement. The Lumières' films and those of many other early film-makers were short documentary recordings of everyday events such as workers leaving a factory, the arrival of a train at a station, or the feeding of a baby. The early years of the 20th century saw the emergence of narrative film and the evolution of a more sophisticated film language (editing patterns, camera movements, optical effects).

Hollywood before 1960 By the 1920s the US film industry was centred on a group of studios based near Los Angeles. These Hollywood studios adopted a mass-production system modelled on other American industries. All Hollywood films conformed to a standard pattern and by the mid-1930s their content and idiom were limited by the stringent Production Code (see ▷censorship, film and ▷Hays Code).

The early years of American cinema were dominated by historical epics, melodramas, slapstick comedies, and westerns. Documentaries were pioneered by Robert ▷Flaherty. After the introduction of sound in the late 1920s, popular genres included the musical, the gangster picture, the screwball comedy, the horror film, the period drama, and the crime thriller. The development of animation began at this time. Walt ▷Disney's Mickey Mouse, for example, first appeared in the cartoon *Steamboat Willie* (1928), and the first feature-length animated film, *Snow White and the Seven Dwarfs*, was released in 1937.

The development of a star system dates from 1909, when players such as Mary ▷Pickford and Ben Turpin began to win acclaim. Stars of Hollywood's 'golden era' of the 1930s and 1940s include Humphrey ▷Bogart, James ▷Cagney, Joan Crawford, Bette ▷Davis, Henry ▷Fonda, Clark ▷Gable, Judy ▷Garland, Cary ▷Grant, Katharine ▷Hepburn, Myrna Loy, the ▷Marx Brothers, William Powell, Barbara ▷Stanwyck, James ▷Stewart, and Spencer ▷Tracy.

Despite earlier experiments, colour film-making really began with Technicolor. In the USA, colour was initially reserved for epic productions such as *Gone with the Wind* (1939) and lavish musicals like *The Wizard of Oz* (1939), but by the mid-1950s it had become the industrial norm in Hollywood. At that time various wide-screen processes were introduced, of which ▷CinemaScope was the most successful.

World cinema before 1960 In France in the 1930s, Jean ▷Renoir made his classic films, and a series of poetic realist films, such as Julien Duvivier's *Pépé le Moko* (1936) and Marcel ▷Carné's *Quai des brumes/Port of Shadows* (1938). Jean ▷Cocteau's main work in the cinema dates from the 1940s–50s. Louis ▷Malle began his career in the 1950s.

In Britain the 1930s–50s were a sustained period of creativity, with such film-makers as Alexander ▷Korda, Michael ▷Powell and Emeric ▷Pressburger, and Carol ▷Reed. The Ealing Studios came into their own, and J Arthur Rank established a film empire.

In Italy immediately after World War II, the ▷neo-realist movement, pioneered by Luchino Visconti, produced such classic films as Roberto ▷Rossellini's *Roma, città aperta/Rome, Open City* (1945) and Vittorio ▷De Sica's *Ladri di biciclette/Bicycle Thieves* (1948).

World cinema after 1960 One of the most significant movements of the 1960s was the French New Wave, which began with such films as Jean-Luc ▷Godard's *A bout de souffle/Breathless* (1959) and François ▷Truffaut's *Jules et Jim* (1962). They self-consciously played with film form, subverting the American conventions; they juxtaposed high art and popular culture; and they presented an often left-wing critique of modern life.

The 1960s and 1970s saw the development of significant national film movements in, for example, Britain (Lindsay Anderson, Tony ▷Richardson, John ▷Schlesinger), Czechoslovakia (Miloš Forman, Věra Chytilová, Jiří Menzel), Germany (Rainer Werner ▷Fassbinder, Werner ▷Herzog, Wim Wenders), and Spain (Carlos Saura, José Luis Borau, Victor ▷Erice). In the next two decades in Europe, new directors such as Krzysztof ▷Kieślowski, Pedro Almodóvar, Aki Kaurismaki, Jean-Jacques Beneix, Patrice Leconte, and Derek Jarman rose to prominence. The cinemas of Africa, the Middle East, and Latin America also began to be shown in the West. Antipodean film-makers like Jane ▷Campion, Peter ▷Weir, George Miller, and Lee Tamahori, and Canadian film-makers like Denys Arcand and Atom ▷Egoyan won international acclaim. The national cinemas of China, Hong Kong, Taiwan, and Japan produced some of the most intriguing films of the late 1980s and 1990s, establishing the reputations of Chen Kaige, Zhang Yimou, Hou Hsiao-hsien, Tian Zhuangzhuang, Juzo Itami, Takeshi 'Beat' Takeshi, John Woo, Wong Kar-Wai, and others.

The 1990s also saw a revival in the fortunes of British cinema, with films such as the romantic comedy *Four Weddings and a Funeral* (1994) and the crime film *Lock, Stock and Two Smoking Barrels* (1997) enjoying critical and commercial success on both sides of the Atlantic.

US cinema after 1960 In the USA, film-makers like Robert ▷Altman, Francis ▷Coppola, Arthur Penn, and Martin ▷Scorsese adapted New Wave stylistic techniques for the American mainstream. Woody ▷Allen also developed a more verbose, comic style of film-making that would prove to be hugely influential on the next generation of film-makers.

The late 1960s and early 1970s saw restructuring of the US film industry and innovation among the new generation of film-makers. But there followed a gradual return to the more conservative values traditionally associated with Hollywood cinema.

The success of big-budget commercial films such as *Jaws* (1975), *Star Wars* (1977), and *ET the Extra-Terrestrial* (1982) ushered in an era of US film-making dominated by the blockbuster mentality and special effects, enhanced in the 1990s by the development of computer-generated images. The era was dominated by a conservatism in US film and witnessed a return of sorts to the comfortable film-making practices of yesteryear dominated by genre – the western, romantic comedy, and war film, for example, were all revived in the 1990s, as witness the success of *Unforgiven* (1992), *Sleepless in Seattle* (1993), and *Saving Private Ryan* (1998) – and the Hollywood star, who became the major 'player' in the US film industry, with the likes of Arnold ▷Schwarzenegger, Jim ▷Carrey, Tom ▷Hanks, Demi Moore, and Bruce Willis commanding exorbitant salaries.

On the other hand, in the 1980s and 1990s a number of young independent film-makers and small production companies emerged, operating outside the Hollywood studios. Working with smaller budgets but a greater degree of artistic freedom, many of these film-makers innovatively revived the traditions of both the ▷B film and the New Wave. Landmark films include the Coen brothers' *Blood Simple* (1984), Spike ▷Lee's *She's Gotta Have It* (1986), Steven Soderbergh's *sex, lies and videotape* (1989), and Quentin ▷Tarantino's *Reservoir Dogs* (1992). Soderbergh's film, in particular, triggered a revival of the independent sector that escalated throughout the mid-to-early 1990s. Recent independent US films, written and directed by such twenty- and thirty-something film-makers as Hal ▷Hartley, Richard Linklater, Whit Stillman, and Kevin ▷Smith, have tended to give priority to the spoken word and leave out the visual pyrotechnics associated with mainstream cinema, epitomised by blockbusters like *Jurassic Park* (1993) and *Titanic* (1997).

Robert Bresson
French film director

Make visible what, without you, might perhaps never have been seen.

Notes on the Cinematographer

Technological developments With satellite and cable television dramatically expanding the audience for film, and motion pictures annually setting and breaking new box-office records, the 1990s further blurred the lines between TV and the cinema. The arrival of DVD, a revolution in computer imaging, and the impact of the Internet promise to have a further impact on film consumerism in the 21st century, affecting the way in which films are viewed and received. In 2000 the first large-scale test of digital light processing (DLP) for cinema presentations was carried out by Disney for their film *Dinosaur*. The new technique of digital delivery was used in 15 cinemas across the USA. It involved downloading the film on to a hard drive without using celluloid in the projection room. If DLP expands, cinemas will be able to receive films via satellite, fibre-optic cable, or DVD disk, and will save the industry costs of film development and distribution.

Related Web site: Database http://www.uk.imdb.com/

CinemaScope trade name for a wide-screen process using anamorphic lenses, in which images are compressed during filming and then extended during projection over a wide curved screen. The first film to be made in CinemaScope was *The Robe* (1953) made by Twentieth Century Fox.

cinéma vérité (French 'cinema truth') school of documentary film-making that aims to capture real events and situations as they occur without major directorial, editorial, or technical control. It first came into vogue around 1960 with the advent of lightweight cameras and sound equipment.

CINEMA US actor Marilyn Monroe and English actor Laurence Olivier in 1957 filming *The Prince and the Showgirl*. *Image Bank*

Cinerama wide-screen process devised in 1937 by Fred Waller of Paramount's special-effects department. Originally three 35-mm cameras and three projectors were used to record and project a single image. Three aspects of the image were recorded and then projected on a large curved screen, with the result that the images blended together to produce an illusion of vastness. The first Cinerama film was the travelogue *This Is Cinerama* (1952); the first story feature was *How the West Was Won* (1962).

cinnabar mercuric sulphide mineral, HgS, the only commercially useful ore of mercury. It is deposited in veins and impregnations near recent volcanic rocks and hot springs. The mineral itself is used as a red pigment, commonly known as **vermilion**. Cinnabar is found in the USA (California), Spain (Almadén), Peru, Italy, and Slovenia.

cinnamon dried inner bark of a tree belonging to the laurel family, grown in India and Sri Lanka. The bark is ground to make the spice used in curries and confectionery. Oil of cinnamon is obtained from waste bark and is used as flavouring in food and medicine. (*Cinnamomum zeylanicum*, family Lauraceae.)

Related Web site: Cinnamon http://www.botanical.com/botanical/mgmh/c/cinnam69.html

cinquefoil any of a group of plants that usually have five-lobed leaves and brightly coloured flowers. They are widespread in northern temperate regions. (Genus *Potentilla*, family Rosaceae.)

Related Web site: Five-Leaf Grass http://www.botanical.com/botanical/mgmh/f/fivele20.html

Cinque Ports group of ports in southern England, originally five, Sandwich, Dover, Hythe, Romney, and Hastings, later including Rye, Winchelsea, and others. Probably founded in Roman times, they rose to importance after the Norman conquest and until the end of the 15th century were bound to supply the ships and men necessary against invasion. Their importance declined in the 16th and 17th centuries with the development of a standing navy.

The office of Lord Warden of the Cinque Ports survives as an honorary distinction (Winston Churchill 1941–65, Robert Menzies 1965–78, the Queen Mother from 1979). The official residence is Walmer Castle.

circadian rhythm metabolic rhythm found in most organisms, which generally coincides with the 24-hour day. Its most obvious manifestation is the regular cycle of sleeping and waking, but body temperature and the concentration of ▷hormones that influence mood and behaviour also vary over the day. In humans, alteration of habits (such as rapid air travel round the world) may result in the circadian rhythm being out of phase with actual activity patterns, causing malaise until it has had time to adjust.

Circe in Greek mythology, an enchantress living on the island of Aeaea. In Homer's *Odyssey*, she turned the followers of ▷Odysseus into pigs. Odysseus, protected by the herb moly provided by Hermes, messenger of the gods, forced her to release his men.

circle perfectly round shape, the path of a point that moves so as to keep a constant distance from a fixed point (the centre).

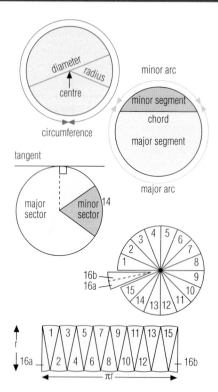

Although most animals have a heart or hearts to pump the blood, in some small invertebrates normal body movements circulate the fluid. In the **open system**, found in snails and other molluscs, the blood (more correctly called ▷haemolymph) passes from the arteries into a body cavity (haemocoel), and from here is gradually returned by other blood vessels to the heart, via the gills. Insects and other arthropods have an open system with a heart. In the **closed system** of earthworms, blood flows directly from the main artery to the main vein, via smaller lateral vessels in each body segment.

The human circulatory system performs a number of functions: it supplies the cells of the body with the food and oxygen they need to survive; it carries carbon dioxide and other wastes away from the cells; it helps to regulate the temperature of the body and conveys substances that protect the body from disease. In addition, the system transports hormones, which help to regulate the activities of various parts of the body.

circumcision surgical removal of all or part of the foreskin (prepuce) of the penis, usually performed on the newborn; it is practised among Jews and Muslims. In some societies in Africa and the Middle East, female circumcision or clitoridectomy (removal of the labia minora and/or clitoris; see ▷female genital mutilation) is practised on adolescents as well as babies; it is illegal in the West.

Male circumcision is usually carried out for cultural reasons and not as a medical necessity, apart from cases where the opening of the prepuce is so small as to obstruct the flow of urine. Some evidence indicates that it protects against the development of cancer of the penis later in life and that women with circumcised partners are at less risk from cancer of the cervix. There is also evidence that circumcision in men provides some protection against HIV infection and that circumcised men with HIV are less likely to infect their partners.

circumference in geometry, the curved line that encloses a curved plane figure, for example a ▷circle or an ellipse. Its length varies according to the nature of the curve, and may be ascertained by the appropriate formula. The circumference of a circle is πd or $2\pi r$, where d is the diameter of the circle, r is its radius, and π is the constant pi, approximately equal to 3.1416.

circus (Latin 'circle') entertainment, often held in a large tent ('big top'), involving performing animals, acrobats, and clowns. In 1871 P T ▷Barnum created the 'Greatest Show on Earth' in the USA. The popularity of animal acts decreased in the 1980s.

cirque French name for a ▷corrie, a steep-sided, armchair-shaped hollow in a mountainside.

cirrhosis any degenerative disease in an organ of the body, especially the liver, characterized by excessive development of connective tissue, causing scarring and painful swelling. Cirrhosis of the liver may be caused by an infection such as viral hepatitis, chronic obstruction of the common bile duct, chronic alcoholism or drug use, blood disorder, heart failure, or malnutrition. However, often no cause is apparent. If cirrhosis is diagnosed early, it can be arrested by treating the cause; otherwise it will progress to coma and death.

CIRCLE Technical terms used in the geometry of the circle; the area of a circle can be seen to equal πr^2 by dividing the circle into segments which form a rectangle.

Each circle has a **radius** (the distance from any point on the circle to the centre), a **circumference** (the boundary of the circle, part of which is called an arc), **diameters** (straight lines crossing the circle through the centre), **chords** (lines joining two points on the circumference), **tangents** (lines that touch the circumference at one point only), **sectors** (regions inside the circle between two radii), and **segments** (regions between a chord and the circumference).

The ratio of the distance all around the circle (the circumference) to the diameter is an ▷irrational number called π (**pi**), roughly equal to 3.1416. A circle of radius r and diameter d has a circumference $C = \pi d$, or $C = 2\pi r$, and an area $A = \pi r^2$. The area of a circle can be shown by dividing it into very thin sectors and reassembling them to make an approximate rectangle. The proof of $A = \pi r^2$ can be done only by using ▷integral calculus.

circuit breaker switching device designed to protect an electric circuit by breaking the circuit if excessive current flows. It has the same action as a ▷fuse, and many houses now have a circuit breaker between the incoming mains supply and the domestic circuits. Circuit breakers usually work by means of ▷solenoids. Those at electricity-generating stations have to be specially designed to prevent dangerous arcing (the release of luminous discharge) when the high-voltage supply is switched off. They may use an air blast or oil immersion to quench the arc.

circulatory system system of vessels in an animal's body that transports essential substances (▷blood or other circulatory fluid) to and from the different parts of the body. It was first discovered and described by English physician, William ▷Harvey. All mammals except for the simplest kinds – such as sponges, jellyfish, sea anemones, and corals – have some type of circulatory system. Some invertebrates (animals without a backbone), such as insects, spiders, and most shellfish, have an 'open' circulatory system which consists of a simple network of tubes and hollow spaces. Other invertebrates have pumplike structures that send blood through a system of blood vessels. All vertebrates (animals with a backbone), including human beings, have a 'closed' circulatory system which principally consists of a pumping organ – the ▷heart – and a network of blood vessels.

Fish have a single circulatory system in which blood passes once around the body before returning to a two-chambered heart. In birds and mammals, there is a double circulation system – the lung or pulmonary circuit and the body or systemic circuit – whereby blood passes to the lungs and back to the heart before circulating around the remainder of the body. In all vertebrates, blood flows in one direction. Valves in the heart, large arteries, and veins prevent backflow, and the muscular walls of the arteries assist in pushing the blood around the body. A network of tiny ▷capillaries carries the blood from arteries to veins.

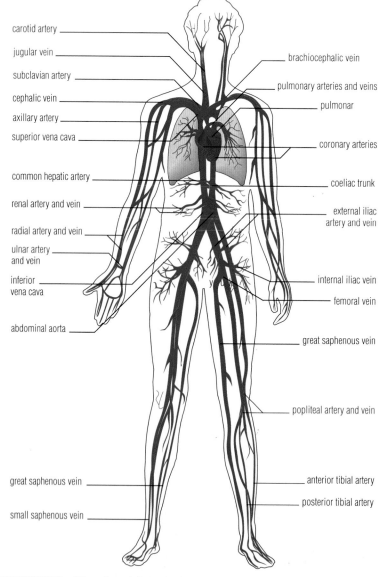

CIRCULATORY SYSTEM Blood flows through 96,500 km/60,000 mi of arteries and veins, supplying oxygen and nutrients to organs and limbs. Oxygen-poor blood (blue) circulates from the heart to the lungs where oxygen is absorbed. Oxygen-rich blood (red) flows back to the heart and is then pumped round the body through the aorta, the largest artery, to smaller arteries and capillaries. Here oxygen and nutrients are exchanged with carbon dioxide and waste products and the blood returns to the heart via the veins. Waste products are filtered by the liver, spleen, and kidneys, and nutrients are absorbed from the stomach and small intestine.

CIS abbreviation for ▷Commonwealth of Independent States, established in 1992 by 11 former Soviet republics.

Cisalpine Gaul region of the Roman province of Gallia (northern Italy) south of the Alps; **Transalpine Gaul**, the region north of the Alps, comprised what is now Belgium, France, the Netherlands, and Switzerland.

CISC (acronym for complex instruction-set computer) in computing, a term referring to the design of the CPU and its instruction set. CISC computers are characterized by having large numbers of instructions, varying a lot in size and complexity. Usually, the various stages of instruction execution are followed, and only when all the stages have been finished can a new instruction start to be executed. RISC CPUs, by comparison, usually have few instructions in the instruction set, and the instructions are smaller and simpler. Complex problems are solved by executing several of the smaller instructions.

Ciskei part of the former independent ▷Black National State within South Africa, independent from 1981 (but not recognized by the United Nations) until 1994 when it was re-integrated into South Africa, in Eastern Cape Province. The region covered an area of 7,700 sq km/2,970 sq mi, and produces wheat, sorghum, sunflower, vegetables, timber, metal products, leather, and textiles. It was one of two homelands of the Xhosa people created by South Africa, the other being Transkei; Xhosa is spoken here.

Cistercian order Roman Catholic monastic order established at Citeaux in 1098 by St Robert de Champagne, abbot of Molesmes, as a stricter form of the Benedictine order. Living mainly by agricultural labour, the Cistercians made many advances in farming methods in the Middle Ages. The ▷Trappists, so called after the original house at La Trappe in Normandy (founded by Dominique de Rancé in 1664), followed a particularly strict version of the rule.

cistron in genetics, the segment of ▷DNA that is required to synthesize a complete polypeptide chain. It is the molecular equivalent of a ▷gene.

CITES (acronym for Convention on International Trade in Endangered Species) international agreement under the auspices of the World Conservation Union with the aim of regulating trade in ▷endangered species of animals and plants. The agreement came into force in 1975 and by 1997 had been signed by 138 states. It prohibits any trade in a category of 8,000 highly endangered species and controls trade in a further 30,000 species.

Animals and plants listed in Appendix 1 of CITES are classified endangered, and all trade in that species is banned; those listed in Appendix 2 are classified vulnerable, and trade in the species is controlled without a complete ban; those listed in Appendix 3 are subject to domestic controls while national governments request help in controlling international trade.

cithara ancient musical instrument resembling a ▷lyre but with a flat back. It was strung with wire and plucked with a plectrum or (after the 16th century) with the fingers. The bandurria and laud, still popular in Spain, are instruments of the same type.

Citizens' Advice Bureau (CAB) UK organization established in 1939 to provide information and advice to the public on any subject, such as personal problems, financial, house purchase, or consumer rights. If required, the bureau will act on behalf of citizens, drawing on its own sources of legal and other experts. There are more than 900 bureaux located all over the UK.

citizens' band (CB) short-range radio communication facility (around 27 MHz) used by members of the public in the USA and many European countries to talk to one another or call for emergency assistance.

Citizen's Charter series of proposals aimed at improving public services in the UK, unveiled by prime minister John Major in 1991. Major's 'programme for a decade' covered the activities of a range of public-sector bodies, including the police, the health service, schools, local authorities, and public and private utility companies.

citizenship status as a member of a state. In most countries citizenship may be acquired either by birth or by naturalization. The status confers rights such as voting and the protection of the law and also imposes responsibilities such as military service, in some countries.

The UK has five different categories of citizenship, with varying rights. Under the British Nationality Act 1981, amended by the British Nationality (Falkland Islands) Act 1983 and the Hong Kong Act 1985, only a person designated as a **British citizen** has a right of abode in the UK; basically, anyone born in the UK to a parent who is a British citizen, or to a parent who is lawfully settled in the UK. Four other categories of citizenship are defined: **British dependent territories citizenship**, **British overseas citizenship**, **British subject**, and **Commonwealth citizen**. Rights of abode in the UK differ widely for each. See also Nationalism and Citizenship Focus Feature on pp. 668–669.

Largest Cities in the World

Source: United Nations Population Division, Department of Economic and Social Affairs
Urban agglomerations with populations of over 7 million.

2000

Rank	City	Population (millions)
1	Tokyo, Japan	28.0
2	Mexico City, Mexico	18.1
3	Mumbai (formerly Bombay), India	18.0
4	São Paulo, Brazil	17.7
5	New York (NY), USA	16.6
6	Shanghai, China	14.2
7	Lagos, Nigeria	13.5
8	Los Angeles (CA), USA	13.1
9	Calcutta, India	12.9
10	Buenos Aires, Argentina	12.4
11	Seoul, South Korea	12.2
12	Beijing, China	12.0
13	Karachi, Pakistan	11.8
14	Delhi, India	11.7
15	Dhaka, Bangladesh	11.0
16=	Cairo, Egypt	10.8
	Metro Manila, Philippines	10.8
18=	Osaka, Japan	10.6
	Rio de Janeiro, Brazil	10.6
20	Tianjin, China	10.2
21	Jakarta, Indonesia	9.8
22	Paris, France	9.6
23	Istanbul, Turkey	9.4
24	Moscow, Russian Federation	9.3
25	London, UK	7.6
26=	Lima, Peru	7.4
	Tehran, Iran	7.4
28	Bangkok, Thailand	7.2

citric acid ($HOOCCH_2C(OH)(COOH)CH_2COOH$) organic acid widely distributed in the plant kingdom; it is found in high concentrations in citrus fruits and has a sharp, sour taste. At one time it was commercially prepared from concentrated lemon juice, but now the main source is the fermentation of sugar with certain moulds.

citronella lemon-scented oil used in cosmetics and insect repellents, obtained from a South Asian grass (*Cymbopogon nardus*).

citrus any of a group of evergreen and aromatic trees or shrubs, found in warm parts of the world. Several species – the orange, lemon, lime, citron, and grapefruit – are cultivated for their fruit. (Genus *Citrus*, family Rutaceae.)

city (French cité from Latin civitas) generally, a large and important town. In the Middle East and ancient Europe, and in the ancient civilizations of Mexico and Peru, cities were states in themselves. In the early Middle Ages, European cities were usually those towns that were episcopal sees (seats of bishops).

city technology college (CTC) in the UK, one of a network of some 20 proposed schools, financed jointly by government and industry, designed to teach the National Curriculum with special emphasis on technological subjects in inner-city areas to students aged 11 to 18. The first school was opened in 1988. By 1994 only 15 schools had opened in England and Wales (still 15 in mid-1998), industry having proved reluctant to fund the scheme, which was abandoned in its original form.

City, the financial centre of ▷London, England. It is situated on the north bank of the River Thames, between Tower Bridge and London Bridge, in the oldest part of the capital. The ▷Bank of England, Lloyd's, the Royal Exchange, and the head offices of the 'big four' banks (Barclays, Lloyds, TSB, HSBC, and National Westminster) are in the City.

civet small to medium-sized carnivorous mammal found in Africa and Asia, belonging to the family Viverridae, which also includes ▷mongooses and ▷genets. Distant relations of cats, they generally have longer jaws and more teeth. All have a scent gland in the inguinal (groin) region. Extracts from this gland are taken from the **African civet** *Civettictis civetta* and used in perfumery.

As well as eating animal matter, many species, for example, the Southeast Asian **palm civet** *Arctogalidia trivirgata*, are fond of fruit.

Civic Forum (Czech Občanske Forum) Czech democratic movement, formed in November 1989, led by Václav ▷Havel. In December 1989 it participated in forming a coalition government after the collapse of communist rule in Czechoslovakia. The party began to splinter during 1991: from it emerged the right-of-centre Civic Democratic Party, led by Václav Klaus, the social-democratic Civic Movement, led by Jiri Dienstbier, and the centre-right Civic Democratic Alliance (CDA).

civil aviation operation of passenger and freight transport by air. With increasing traffic, control of air space is a major problem. In the USA, the Federal Aviation Agency (FAA) is responsible for regulating development of aircraft, air navigation, traffic control, and communications and the Civil Aeronautics Board prescribes safety regulations and investigates accidents. In Europe, Eurocontrol was established in 1963 by Belgium, France, West Germany, Luxembourg, the Netherlands, and the UK to supervise both military and civil movement in the air space over member countries. Close cooperation is maintained with authorities in other countries, and there is also a tendency to coordinate services and other facilities between national airlines; for example, the establishment of Air Union in 1963 by France (Air France), West Germany (Lufthansa), Italy (Alitalia), and Belgium (Sabena).

Related Web site: International Civil Aviation Organization
http://www.icao.int

civil disobedience deliberate breaking of laws considered unjust, a form of nonviolent direct action; the term was coined by the US writer Henry Thoreau in an essay of that name in 1849. It was advocated by Mahatma ▷Gandhi to prompt peaceful withdrawal of British power from India. Civil disobedience has since been employed by, for instance, the US civil-rights movement in the 1960s and the peace movement in the 1980s.

civil engineering branch of engineering that is concerned with the construction of roads, bridges, airports, aqueducts, waterworks, tunnels, canals, irrigation works, and harbours.

civilization (Latin *civis* 'citizen') highly developed human society with structured division of labour. The earliest civilizations evolved in the Old World from advanced ▷Neolithic farming societies in the Middle East (Sumer in 3500 BC; Egypt in 3000 BC), the Indus Valley (in 2500 BC), and China (in 2200 BC). In the New World, similar communities evolved civilizations in Mesoamerica (the Olmec in 1200 BC) and Peru (the Chavin in 800 BC).

civil law legal system based on ▷Roman law. It is one of the two main European legal systems, ▷English (common) law being the other. Civil law may also mean the law relating to matters other than criminal law, such as ▷contract and ▷tort.

civil list in the UK, the annual sum provided from public funds to meet the official expenses of the sovereign and immediate dependents; private expenses are met by the ▷privy purse.

civil rights rights of the individual citizen. In many countries they are specified (as in the Bill of Rights of the US constitution) and guaranteed by law to ensure equal treatment for all citizens. In the USA, the struggle for the civil rights of former slaves and their descendants, both through legislation and in practice, has been a major theme since the American ▷Civil War.

civil-rights movement general term for efforts by African-American people to affirm their constitutional rights and improve their status in society after World War II. Having made a significant contribution to the national effort in wartime, they began a sustained campaign for full ▷civil rights which challenged racial discrimination and segregation; the Civil Rights Commission was created by the Civil Rights Act of 1957. Further favourable legislation followed, such as the Civil Rights Act 1964 and the 1965 Voting Rights Act. Other civil-rights movements have included women (see ▷women's movement) and homosexuals (see ▷homosexuality).

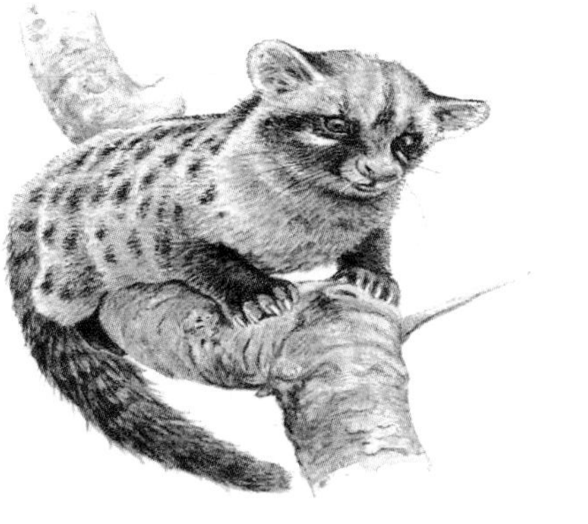

CIVET The African palm civet *Nandinia binotata* spends most of its life in trees, resting among the branches during the day and searching for food at night.

civil service body of administrative staff appointed to carry out the policy of a government. In the USA, federal employees are restricted in the role they may play in political activity, and they retain their posts (except at senior levels) when there is a change in administration. Members of the UK civil service may not take an active part in politics, and do not change with the government.

civil society part of a society or culture outside the government and state-run institutions. For Karl Marx and G W F Hegel, civil society was that part of society where self-interest and materialism were rampant, although Adam ▷Smith believed that enlightened self-interest would promote the general good. Classical writers and earlier political theorists such as John ▷Locke used the term to describe the whole of a civilized society.

Civil War, American

Civil War, American (or the War Between the States) war (1861–65) between the Southern or Confederate States of America (see ▷Confederacy) and the Northern or Union states. The former wished to maintain certain 'states' rights', in particular the right to determine state law on the institution of slavery, and claimed the right to secede from the Union; the latter fought primarily to maintain the Union, with slave emancipation (proclaimed in 1863) a secondary issue.

The issue of slavery had brought to a head long-standing social and economic differences between the two oldest sections of the country. A series of political crises was caused by the task of determining whether newly admitted states, such as California, should permit or prohibit slavery in their state constitutions. The political parties in the late 1850s came to represent only sectional interests – Democrats in the South, Republicans in the North. This breakdown of an underlying national political consensus (which had previously sustained national parties) led to the outbreak of hostilities, only a few weeks after the inauguration of the first Republican president, Abraham Lincoln.

The war, and in particular its aftermath, when the South was occupied by Northern troops in the period known as the ▷Reconstruction, left behind much bitterness. Industry prospered in the North, while the economy of the South, which had been based on slavery, stagnated for some time.

Related Web sites: American Civil War http://www.historyplace.com/civilwar/index.html

Images of the US Civil War http://jefferson.village.virginia.edu/vshadow2/cwimages.html

Letters and Diaries of the US Civil War (Pre-War Years) http://jefferson.village.virginia.edu/vshadow2/letters.html

Maps of the US Civil War http://Jefferson.village.virginia.edu/vshadow2/pics/ormaps.html

Civil War, English

Civil War, English conflict between King Charles I and the Royalists (also called Cavaliers) on one side and the Parliamentarians (also called Roundheads) on the other. Their differences centred initially on the king's unconstitutional acts, but later became a struggle over the relative powers of crown and Parliament. Hostilities began in 1642 and a series of Royalist defeats (at Marston Moor in 1644, and then at Naseby in 1645) culminated in Charles's capture in 1647, and execution in 1649. The war continued until the final defeat of Royalist forces at Worcester in 1651. Oliver ▷Cromwell then became Protector (ruler) from 1653 until his death in 1658.

Civil War, American: Key Dates

1861 February	Having seceded from the Union, seven southern states (South Carolina, Mississippi, Florida, Alabama, Georgia, Louisiana, and Texas) send representatives to Montgomery, Alabama, to form the rebel Confederate States of America under the presidency of Jefferson Davis. Their constitution legalizes slavery.
April	Rebel forces attack a Federal garrison at Fort Sumter, Charleston, South Carolina, capturing it on 14 April. President Lincoln proclaims a blockade of southern ports.
April–May	Four more states secede from the Union: Virginia (part remaining loyal, eventually becoming West Virginia), Arkansas, Tennessee, and North Carolina.
July	Battle of Bull Run is the first major military engagement of the war, near Manassas Junction, Virginia; Confederate army under generals P G T Beauregard and Thomas 'Stonewall' Jackson forces Union army to retreat to Washington DC.
1862 February	Union general Ulysses S Grant captures strategically located forts Henry and Donelson in Tennessee.
April	Battle of Shiloh, the bloodiest Americans had yet fought, when at terrible cost Grant's army forces rebel troops to withdraw. Confederate government introduces conscription of male white citizens aged 18–35.
June–July	Seven Days' battles in Virginia between Union army under George B McClellan and Confederate forces under generals Jackson and Robert E Lee; McClellan withdraws, but continues to threaten the Confederate capital at Richmond, Virginia.
August	At second Battle of Bull Run, Lee's troops force Union army to fall back again to Washington DC.
September	At Battle of Antietam, near Sharpsburg, Maryland, McClellan forces Lee to give up his offensive, but fails to pursue the enemy. Lincoln removes him from his command.
December	Lee inflicts heavy losses on Federal forces attacking his position at Battle of Fredericksburg, Virginia.
1863 January	Lincoln's Emancipation Proclamation comes into effect, freeing slaves in the Confederate states (but not those in border states which have remained loyal to the Union). Some 200,000 blacks eventually serve in Union armies.
March	Federal government introduces conscription.
May	Battle of Chancellorsville, Virginia; Lee and Jackson rout Union forces.
July	Lee fails to break through Union lines at decisive Battle of Gettysburg, Pennsylvania, while Grant captures Vicksburg and the west and takes control of the Mississippi, cutting the Confederacy in two.
November	Grant's victory at Chattanooga, Tennessee, leads to his appointment as general in chief by Lincoln (March 1864). Lincoln's Gettysburg Address.
1864 May	Battle of the Wilderness, Virginia. Lee inflicts heavy casualties on Union forces, but Grant continues to move south through Virginia. They clash again at Battle of Spotsylvania.
June	Battle of Cold Harbor claims 12,000 casualties in a few hours. Grant writes: 'I propose to fight it out along this line if it takes all summer'.
September	Union general William T Sherman occupies Atlanta, Georgia, and marches through the state to the sea, cutting a wide swathe of destruction.
November	Lincoln is re-elected president.
December	Sherman marches into Savannah, Georgia, continuing over the next three months into South and North Carolina.
1865 March	Lee fails to break through Union lines at Battle of Petersburg, Virginia.
April	Lee abandons Confederate capital at Richmond, Virginia, and surrenders to Grant at Appomattox courthouse, Virginia. John Wilkes Booth assassinates President Lincoln at Ford's Theatre, Washington DC.
May	Last Confederate soldiers lay down their arms. The war has taken the lives of 359,528 Union troops and 258,000 Confederates, and cost $20 billion.

Causes ▷Charles I became the king of Great Britain and Ireland in 1625, and quickly became involved in a number of disputes with Parliament. These led to the latter's dissolution in 1629, after which Charles ruled absolutely for 11 years, the Eleven Years' Tyranny. By 1639, people had many reasons to be angry with Charles: his belief in the ▷divine right of kings; his spending – Charles was an art collector, and lavished money on his court and his favourites; his creation of ▷monopolies as a form of patronage; his levies of ▷ship money for the support of the navy; and his use of the ▷Star Chamber court to suppress the Puritans and make judgements in his favour. His officials and associates were also unpopular. ▷Strafford, Charles's advisor and lord deputy in Ireland, was using the army to ruthlessly enforce royal rule in Ireland. The Puritans felt threatened by Charles's deputy, Archbishop William ▷Laud, who had brought Arminianism into the Church of England, new ideas that emphasized links with the pre-Reformation church. Charles's Catholic wife ▷Henrietta Maria was also disliked, as she encouraged him to aid Catholics and make himself an absolute ruler.

In 1639, however, war was declared with Scotland, the first of the Bishops' Wars over Charles's attempts to impose royal control over the church in Scotland. In 1640, Charles called the ▷Short Parliament in order to raise funds. His request for war taxes was refused, and the Parliament was quickly dissolved, but, after defeat in Scotland in the second Bishops' War (1640), Charles called the ▷Long Parliament of 1640. The members of Parliament (MPs) were determined (in the words of the leader John ▷Pym) 'to make their country happy by removing all grievances'. The Long Parliament imprisoned Laud, declared extra-parliamentary taxation illegal, and voted that Parliament could not be dissolved without its own assent. In November 1641 Parliament presented the ▷Grand Remonstrance – a list of complaints. In January 1642 Charles tried to arrest the five parliamentary leaders who, he said, had 'traitorously tried to take away the King's royal power'. When this failed, the king went north to Nottingham, where he declared war against Parliament on 22 August 1642.

For many years, historians believed that the English Civil War grew out of a potent mixture of constitutional, religious, and social forces which had developed over centuries of history. ▷Magna Carta (1215) had claimed that all men should be free, and Parliament's power had been increasing since Tudor times. At the same time, Puritan hostility to the bishops, and long-term social factors such as inflation and enclosure added to the stresses between the king and the people. As the country moved towards democracy and freedom, it seemed inevitable that king and Parliament would clash. This is the traditional view of the causes of the Civil War.

Revisionist historians, however, do not think the Civil War was an inevitable development of history; they believe it grew suddenly out of the events of November 1641. They point out that, by winter 1641, Charles had agreed to everything that most people wanted. In December 1640 he abolished ship money, and during 1641 agreed to call a Parliament every three years, not to collect taxes without Parliament's consent, and to abolish the Star Chamber. Meanwhile Laud was imprisoned (December 1640) and Strafford executed (12 May 1641). By November 1641 the problems of government seemed to have been solved. However, in October 1641 the Catholic Great Rebellion broke out in Ireland. To defeat it the King needed an army but the Parliamentary leaders, worried that he might use it

AMERICAN CIVIL WAR American soldiers pose before their boxing match in front of a barracks during the Civil War era, c. 1865. *Archive Photos*

against them, suggested that Parliament ought to control the army. It was a direct attack on the king's power, and led to the attempt to arrest the five MPs.

Choosing sides Most lords and earls supported Charles, as did most Catholics. Amongst the gentry, also, most young people fought for Charles – fighting for the king seemed exciting and romantic. Many people who disagreed with Charles also fought for him, simply out of loyalty – most famously, Edmund ▷Verney.

Most of the people who fought for Parliament were ▷Puritans. They were people who believed in Parliamentary government and did not trust Charles to keep his promises. Most lawyers, merchants, and trades people (many of whom were Puritans) also fought for Parliament.

Some people tried to remain neutral; the majority of the population did not want to fight at all. Individuals made up their own minds. The war split friends and families. Edmund Verney fought for the king, his son Ralph joined the Parliamentarians.

Events of the war The Royalist and Parliamentarian armies first met at the Battle of ▷Edgehill, South Warwickshire, in October 1642, which had no conclusive outcome. After this initial battle, a series of victories followed for both sides. The king had the initial advantage, for his troops (as Cromwell pointed out after Edgehill) were 'gentleman's sons and persons of quality'. Charles tried to take London in 1642 – when he was halted at Turnham Green (November 1642) – and again in 1643, when he mounted a three-pronged attack from the north, from Cornwall, and from his headquarters at Oxford. Although, the Royalists took control of most of Yorkshire after the Battle of Adwalton Moor in June 1643, the plan failed. As the war went on, the tide turned in Parliament's favour. The navy supported Parliament, which gave Parliament control of the ports. Parliament's strength was in the southeast, the richest part of the country. Also, in November 1643, Parliament formed an alliance with the Scots, the Solemn League and Covenant. Most of all, Cromwell had formed a new army of well-trained, passionately Puritan 'ironsides'. His new army won the Battle of ▷Marston Moor in July 1644. In April 1645 Parliament reorganized all of its forces into the ▷New Model Army. The army was nationally organized and regularly paid. It was commanded by Cromwell and Thomas ▷Fairfax, and won a resounding victory at the Battle of ▷Naseby, near Leicester, which brought the first stage of the war to an end in June 1645.

The second Civil War The Royalist army was disbanded in 1646 and in May 1946 King Charles took refuge with the Scottish army based in the north of England, but was handed over as a prisoner to the Parliamentarians in January 1647. During 1647, however, he was kidnapped by the Roundhead army (which was increasingly at odds with Parliament). He escaped, but was recaptured and held at Carisbroke Castle on the Isle of Wight. From there he concluded a secret pact with the Scots, agreeing to establish Presbyterianism in return for their support. The second Civil War began in March 1648 with a series of uprisings by Royalist supporters in Wales, Kent, and Essex, but these were put down by Cromwell and Fairfax. The Scots invaded the north of England later in the year, but were defeated by Parliamentary forces at the Battle of Preston in August 1648. King Charles was captured, tried, and executed for treason on 30 January 1649.

Civil War, Spanish war (1936–39) precipitated by a military revolt led by General Franco against the Republican government. Inferior military capability led to the gradual defeat of the Republicans by 1939, and the establishment of Franco's dictatorship.

Franco's insurgents (Nationalists, who were supported by fascist Italy and Nazi Germany) seized power in the south and northwest, but were suppressed in areas such as Madrid and Barcelona by the workers' militia. The loyalists (Republicans) were aided by the USSR and the volunteers of the International Brigade, which included several writers, among them George Orwell.

Clackmannanshire unitary authority in central Scotland, bordering the north side of the Firth of Forth. A former county (until 1974), it was a district of Central region (1975–96).

area 161 sq km/62 sq mi **towns** Alloa (administrative headquarters), Tillicoultry **physical** compact geographical area comprising the extensive flat flood plain of the River Devon, which rises dramatically at the Ochil Hills to Ben Cleuch (721 m/2,365 ft) **industries** brewing, distilling, manufacture of bottles and knitwear **agriculture** intensive on flood plain of Forth; less intensive on Ochil Hills **population** (1996) 47,700

cladistics method of biological classification that uses a formal step-by-step procedure for objectively assessing the extent to which organisms share particular characteristics, and for assigning them to taxonomic groups called **clades**. Clades comprise all the species descended from a known or inferred common ancestor plus the ancestor itself, and may be large – consisting of a hierarchy of other clades.

Civil War, English: Key Dates

1625	James I dies, and is succeeded by Charles I, whose first parliament is dissolved after refusing to grant him tonnage and poundage (taxation revenues) for life.
1627	'Five Knights' case in which men who refuse to pay a forced loan are imprisoned.
1628	Coke, Wentworth, and Eliot present the Petition of Right, requesting the king not to tax without parliamentary consent, not to billet soldiers in private homes, and not to impose martial law on civilians. Charles accepts this as the price of parliamentary taxation to pay for war with Spain and France. The Duke of Buckingham is assassinated.
1629	Parliament is dissolved following disagreement over religious policy, tonnage and poundage, beginning Charles' 'Eleven Years' Tyranny'. War with France ends.
1630	War with Spain ends.
1632	Strafford is made lord deputy in Ireland.
1633	Laud becomes archbishop of Canterbury. Savage punishment of puritan William Prynne for his satirical pamphlet 'Histriomastix'.
1634	Ship money is first collected in London.
1634–37	Laud attempts to enforce ecclesiastical discipline by metropolitan visits.
1637	The conviction of John Hampden for refusal to pay ship money infringes the Petition of Right.
1638	Covenanters in Scotland protest at the introduction of the Laudian Prayer Book into the Kirk.
1639	First Bishops' War. Charles sends army to Scotland after its renunciation of episcopacy. Agreement is reached without fighting.
1640	Short Parliament April–May votes for taxes for the suppression of the Scots, but dissolves to forestall petition against Scottish war. Second Bishops' War ends in defeat for English at Newburn-on-Tyne. Scots receive pension and hold Northumberland and Durham in Treaty of Ripon. Long Parliament is called, passing the Triennial Act and abolishing the Star Chamber. High Commission and Councils of the North and of Wales is set up.
1641	Strafford is executed. English and Scots are massacred at Ulster. Grand Remonstrance is passed appealing to mass opinion against episcopacy and the royal prerogative. Irish Catholic nobles are massacred.
1642 January	Charles leaves Westminster after an unsuccessful attempt to arrest five members of the Commons unites both Houses of Parliament and the City against him.
February	Bishop's Exclusion Bill is passed, barring clergy from secular office and the Lords.
May–June	Irish rebels establish supreme council. Militia Ordinance is passed, assuming sovereign powers for parliament. Nineteen Propositions are rejected by Charles.
August	Charles raises his standard at Nottingham. Outbreak of first Civil War.
October	General Assembly of the Confederate Catholics meets at Kilkenny. Battle of Edgehill inconclusive.
1643	Irish truce leaves rebels in control of more of Ireland. Solemn League and Covenant, alliance between English Parliamentarians and Scots, pledges to establish Presbyterianism in England and Ireland, and to provide a Scottish army. Scots intervene in Civil War.
1643–49	Westminster Assembly attempts to draw up Calvinist religious settlement.
1644	Committee of Both Kingdoms to coordinate Scottish and Parliamentarians' military activities is established. Royalists are decisively beaten at Marston Moor.
1645	Laud is executed. The New Model Army is created. Charles pulls out of Uxbridge negotiations on a new constitutional position. Cromwell and the New Model Army destroy Royalist forces at Naseby.
1646	Charles flees to Scotland. Oxford surrenders to Parliament. End of first Civil War.
1647 May	Charles agrees with Parliament to accept Presbyterianism and to surrender control of the militia.
June–August	Army seizes Charles and resolves not to disband without satisfactory terms. Army presents Heads of Proposals to Charles.
October–December	Army debates Levellers' Agreement of the People at Putney. Charles escapes to the Isle of Wight, and reaches agreement with the Scots by Treaty of Newport.
1648 January	Vote of No Addresses passed by Long Parliament declares an end to negotiations with Charles.
August	Cromwell defeats Scots at Preston. Second Civil War begins.
November–December	Army demands trial of Charles I. Pride's Purge of Parliament transfers power to the Rump of independent MPs.
1649 January–February	Charles is tried and executed. Rump elects Council of State as its executive.
May	Rump declares England a Commonwealth. Cromwell lands in Dublin.
September–October	Massacres of garrisons at Drogheda and Wexford by Cromwell. Large numbers of native Irish were transplanted.
1650 September	Cromwell defeated Scots under Leslie at Dunbar.
1651	Scots under Charles II invaded England, but were decisively defeated at Worcester (3 September) by Cromwell. Charles fled to the Continent and lived in exile for nine years.

Claes, Willy (1938–) Belgian politician, secretary general of the ▷North Atlantic Treaty Organization (NATO) 1994–95, with a proven reputation as a consensus-builder. He was a clear favourite for the post, but subsequent allegations about his involvement (while Belgian foreign minister) in illegal dealings with Agusta, the Italian aircraft manufacturer, eventually forced his resignation in November 1995.

Clair, René (1898–1981) Adopted name of René-Lucien Chomette. French film-maker. He was originally a poet, novelist, and journalist. His early comedy *Sous les Toits de Paris/Under the Roofs of Paris* (1930) made great use of the new innovation of sound. His other films include *Un Chapeau de paille d'Italie/The Italian Straw Hat* (1927), *Le Million* (1931), *A nous la Liberté* (1931), and *Porte des Lilas/Gates of Paris* (1957).

clam common name for a ▷bivalve mollusc. The giant clam *Tridacna gigas* of the Indopacific can grow to 1 m/3 ft across in 50 years and weigh, with the shell, 500 kg/1,000 lb.

A giant clam produces a billion eggs in a single spawning.

The term is usually applied to edible species, such as the North American hard clam *Venus mercenaria*, used in clam chowder, and whose shells were formerly used as money by North American Indians. A giant clam may produce a billion eggs in a single spawning.

clan (Gaelic *clann* 'children') social grouping based on ▷kinship. Some traditional societies are organized by clans, which are either matrilineal or patrilineal, and whose members must marry into another clan in order to avoid in-breeding.

Clapton, Eric (1945–) English blues and rock guitarist, singer, and songwriter. Originally a blues purist, then one of the pioneers of heavy rock with Cream (1966–68), he returned to the blues after making the landmark album *Layla and Other Assorted Love Songs* (1970) by Derek and the Dominos. Solo albums include *Journeyman* (1989) and the acoustic *Unplugged* (1992), for which he received six Grammy awards (1993). He won a Grammy award for Record of the Year with 'Change the World' in 1997 and in 2002 for his song 'Reptile'.

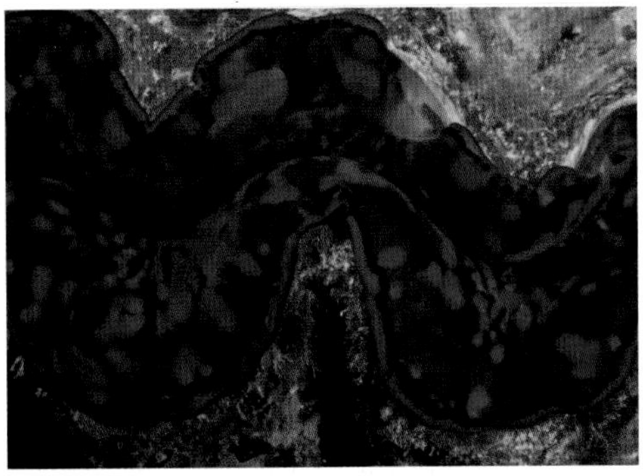

CLAM A close-up of a giant clam, whose natural habitat is the Pacific and Indian Oceans. *Image Bank*

Clare county on the west coast of the Republic of Ireland, in the province of Munster, situated between Galway Bay in the north and the Shannon estuary in the south; county town ▷Ennis; area 3,190 sq km/1,231 sq mi; population (1996) 94,000. Other towns include Kilrush, Kilkee, and Shannon, an important 'new' town noted for its light industry, and electronics and aerospace industries. Dairying and cattle rearing are the principal farming activities; there are also important salmon fisheries and extensive oyster beds. Slate and black marble are quarried and worked; lead is also found.
The Shannon is a source of hydroelectricity: there is a power station at Ardnacrusha, 5 km/3 mi north of Limerick.

Clare, St (*c.* 1194–1253) Christian saint. Born in Assisi, Italy, at 18 she became a follower of St Francis, who founded for her the convent of San Damiano. Here she gathered the first members of the **Order of Poor Clares**. In 1958 she was proclaimed the patron saint of television by Pius XII, since in 1252 she saw from her convent sickbed the Christmas services being held in the Basilica of St Francis in Assisi. Feast day 12 August. Canonized 1255.

> **Arthur C Clarke**
> *Any sufficiently advanced technology is indistinguishable from magic.*
> The Lost Worlds of 2001 (1971)

Clare, John (1793–1864) English poet.
His work includes *Poems Descriptive of Rural Life and Scenery* (1820), *The Village Minstrel* (1821), *The Shepherd's Calendar* (1827), and *The Rural Muse* (1835). The dignified simplicity and truth of his descriptions of both landscape and emotions were rediscovered and appreciated in the 20th century.

Clarendon, Edward Hyde (1609–1674) 1st Earl of Clarendon. English politician and historian, chief adviser to Charles II from 1651 to 1667. A member of Parliament in 1640, he joined the Royalist side in 1641. The **Clarendon Code** (1661–65), a series of acts passed by the government, was directed at Nonconformists (or Dissenters) and was designed to secure the supremacy of the Church of England.

In the ▷Short and ▷Long Parliaments Clarendon attacked Charles I's unconstitutional actions and supported the impeachment of Charles's minister Strafford. In 1641 he broke with the revolutionary party and became one of the royal advisers. When civil war began he followed Charles to Oxford, and was knighted and made chancellor of the Exchequer. On the king's defeat in 1646 he followed Prince Charles to Jersey, where he began his *History of the Rebellion*, published 1702–04, which provides memorable portraits of his contemporaries. In 1651 he became chief adviser to the exiled Charles II. At the Restoration he was created Earl of Clarendon, while his influence was further increased by the marriage of his daughter Anne to James, Duke of York. His moderation earned the hatred of the extremists, however, and he lost Charles's support by openly expressing disapproval of the king's private life. After the disasters of the Dutch war in 1667, he went into exile.

clarinet any of a family of single-reed woodwind instruments of cylindrical bore. The clarinet did not establish itself in the orchestra until after the middle of the 18th century. In their concertos for clarinet, Mozart and Weber exploited the instrument's range of tone from the dark low register rising to brilliance, and its capacity for sustained dynamic control. The ability of the clarinet both to blend and to contrast with other instruments makes it popular for chamber music and as a solo instrument. It is also heard in military and concert bands and as a jazz instrument.

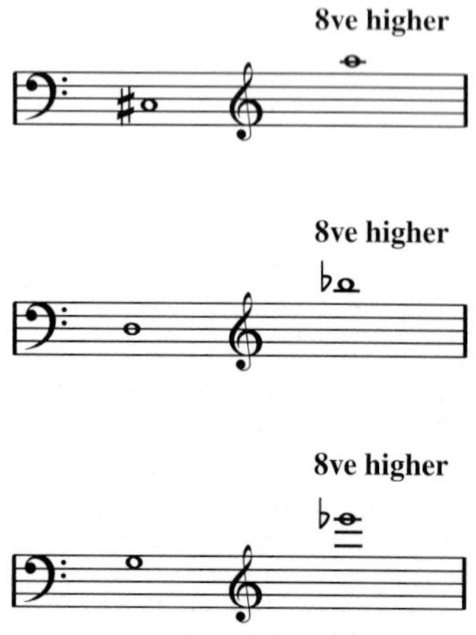

CLARINET The sounding compass of the A clarinet (top); of the B flat (centre); and of the E flat (bottom).

Clark, Kenneth (Mackenzie), Baron Clark (1903–1983) English art historian, director of the National Gallery, London, from 1934 to 1945. His books include *Leonardo da Vinci* (1939), *Landscape into Art* (1949), and *The Nude* (1956).

Clark, Mark Wayne (1896–1984) US general in World War II. In 1942 he became Chief of Staff for ground forces, and deputy to General Eisenhower. He led a successful secret mission by submarine to get information in north Africa to prepare for the Allied invasion, and commanded the 5th Army in the invasion of Italy. He remained in this command until the end of the war when he took charge of the US occupation forces in Austria.

Clarke, Arthur C(harles) (1917–) English science fiction and non-fiction writer. He originated the plan for a system of communications satellites in geostationary orbit in 1945. His works include the short story 'The Sentinel' (1951) (filmed in 1968 by Stanley Kubrick as *2001: A Space Odyssey*), and the novels *Childhood's End* (1953), *2010: Odyssey Two* (1982), *3001: The Final Odyssey* (1997), *Rendezvous with Rama* (1997), and *A Fall of Moondust* (1998).

Clarke was born in Minehead, Somerset, served in the Royal Air Force during World War II as a radar instructor, and then studied physics at King's College, London. He became chair of the British Interplanetary Society in 1946, the year his first story was published. In 1956 he moved to Sri Lanka. His popular-science books generally concern space exploration; his fiction is marked by an optimistic belief in the potential of science and technology.

His non-fiction works include *Interplanetary Flight* (1950) and *The Exploration of Space* (1951); his science fiction includes *Prelude to Space* (1950), *The Sands of Mars* (1951), *Islands in the Sky* (1952), *Childhood's End* (1953), *Earthlight* (1955), *Tales from the White Hart* (1957), and *Of Time and Stars* (1972).

Clarke, Kenneth Harry (1940–) British Conservative politician. A cabinet minister 1985–97, he held the posts of education secretary 1990–92 and home secretary 1992–93.
He succeeded Norman Lamont as chancellor of the Exchequer in May 1993, bringing to the office a more open and combative approach. Along with his colleagues Malcolm Rifkind, Tony Newton, and Patrick Mayhew, in 1996 he became the longest continuously serving minister since Lord Palmerston in the early 19th century.

Clash, the English rock band (1976–85), a driving force in the British ▷punk movement. Reggae and rockabilly were important elements in their sound. Their albums include *The Clash* (1977), *London Calling* (1979), and *Combat Rock* (1982).

class used in biological classification, it is a subdivision of phylum and forms a group of related ▷orders. For example, all mammals belong to the class Mammalia and all birds to the class Aves. Among plants, all class names end in 'idae' (such as Asteridae) and among fungi in 'mycetes'; there are no equivalent conventions among animals. Related classes are grouped together in a ▷phylum.

class in sociology, the main grouping of social stratification in industrial societies, based primarily on economic and occupational factors, but also referring to people's style of living or sense of group identity.

class action in law, a court procedure where one or more claimants represent a larger group of people who are all making the same kind of claim against the same defendant. The court's decision is binding on all the members of the group.

classical economics school of economic thought that dominated 19th-century thinking. It originated with Adam ▷Smith's *The Wealth of Nations* (1776), which embodied many of the basic concepts and principles of the classical school. Smith's theories were further developed in the writings of John Stuart Mill and David Ricardo. Central to the theory were economic freedom, competition, and *laissez-faire* government. The idea that economic growth could best be promoted by free trade, unassisted by government, was in conflict with ▷mercantilism.

The belief that agriculture was the chief determinant of economic health was also rejected in favour of manufacturing development, and the importance of labour productivity was stressed. The theories put forward by the classical economists still influence economists today.

classicism term used in art, music, and literature, to characterize work that emphasizes the qualities traditionally associated with ancient Greek and Roman art, that is, reason, balance, objectivity, and restraint, as opposed to the individuality of expression typical of Romanticism. Classicism and Romanticism are often considered as opposite poles of art, but in fact many artists show elements of both in their work. At certain times, however, classicism has been a dominant trend, notably during the Renaissance and the neoclassical periods. At both these times ancient art exercised a strong direct influence, but this is not an essential component of classicism. The word is often used imprecisely and sometimes conveys no more than an idea of clarity or conservatism.

classification in biology, the arrangement of organisms into a hierarchy of groups on the basis of their similarities. The basic grouping is a ▷species, several of which may constitute a ▷genus, which in turn are grouped into families, and so on up through orders, classes, phyla (in plants, sometimes called divisions), and finally to kingdoms.

The oldest method of classification, called **phenetic classification**, aims to classify organisms on the basis of as many as possible of their observable characteristics: their morphology, anatomy, physiology, and so on. Greek philosopher Theophrastus adopted this method in the 4th century BC, when he classified plants into trees, shrubs, undershrubs, and herbs.

Awareness of evolutionary theory, however, led to the development of **phylogenetic classification**, which aims to classify organisms in a way that mirrors their evolutionary and genetic relationship. Species are grouped according to shared characteristics believed to be derived from common ancestors (care being taken to exclude shared characteristics known to be due to ▷convergent evolution – such as the wings of bats and birds). In practice, most present-day systems of classification compromise between the phenetic and the phylogenetic approaches.

▷Cladistics is a recent phylogenetic method that applies a strict, objective procedure, often assisted by computer analysis, to classify species according to characteristics derived from a common ancestor.

Related Web site: Linnaeus, Carolus http://www.ucmp.berkeley.edu/history/linnaeus.html

clathrate compound formed when the small molecules of one substance fill in the holes in the structural lattice of another, solid, substance – for example, sulphur dioxide molecules in ice crystals. Clathrates are therefore intermediate between mixtures and true compounds (which are held together by ▷ionic or covalent chemical bonds).

Claude Lorrain (1600–1682) Born Claude Gelée. French painter who worked in Rome. One of the leading classical painters of the 17th century, he painted landscapes in a distinctive, luminous style that had a great impact on late 17th- and 18th-century taste. In his paintings insignificant figures (mostly mythological or historical) are typically lost in great expanses of poetic scenery, as in *The Enchanted Castle* (1664; National Gallery, London).

Claudius I (10 BC–AD 54) Born Tiberius Claudius Drusus Nero Germanicus. nephew of ▷Tiberius, and son of Drusus Nero, made Roman emperor by the Praetorian Guard in AD 41, after the murder of his nephew ▷Caligula. Claudius was a scholar and historian. During his reign the Roman empire was considerably extended, and in 43 he took part in the invasion of Britain.

Claudius was believed to have been weak and easily led by his wives and his senior freedmen, who served as his principal secretaries. Lame, and suffering from a speech impediment, Claudius was frequently the object of ridicule. He wrote historical works and an autobiography, none of which survives. His life is imaginatively reconstructed by the novelist Robert Graves in his books *I Claudius* (1934) and *Claudius the God* (1934).

Clause 28 (or Section 28) in British law, section 28 of the Local Government Act 1988 that prohibits local authorities promoting homosexuality by publishing material, or by promoting the teaching in state schools of the acceptability of homosexuality as a 'pretended family relationship'. There was widespread opposition to the introduction of the provision.

Clausewitz, Carl Philipp Gottlieb von (1780–1831) Prussian officer whose book *Vom Kriege/On War* (1832) exerted a powerful influence on military strategists well into the 20th century. Although he advocated the total destruction of an enemy's forces as one of the strategic targets of warfare, his most important idea was to see war as an extension of political policy and not as an end in itself.

clausius in engineering, a unit of ▷entropy (the loss of energy as heat in any physical process). It is defined as the ratio of energy to temperature above absolute zero.

claustrophobia ▷phobia involving fear of enclosed spaces.

Claverhouse, John Graham (*c.* 1649–1689) Viscount Dundee. Scottish soldier. Appointed by ▷Charles II to suppress the ▷Covenanters from 1677, he was routed at Drumclog in 1679, but three weeks later won the battle of Bothwell Bridge, by which the rebellion was crushed. Until 1688 he was engaged in continued persecution and became known as 'Bloody Clavers', regarded by the Scottish people as a figure of evil. His army then joined the first ▷Jacobite rebellion and defeated the loyalist forces at the Battle of Killiecrank ie, where he was mortally wounded.

clavichord small domestic keyboard instrument. Of delicate tone, the clavichord was developed in the 16th century on the principle of the monochord. Notes are sounded by a metal blade striking the string. The sound is clear and precise, and a form of vibrato (bebung) is possible by varying finger pressure on the key. It was superseded in the 18th century by the ▷fortepiano.

clavicle (Latin *clavis* 'key') the collar bone of many vertebrates. In humans it is vulnerable to fracture, since falls involving a sudden force on the arm may result in very high stresses passing into the chest region by way of the clavicle and other bones. It is connected at one end with the sternum (breastbone), and at the other end with the shoulder-blade, together with which it forms the arm socket. The wishbone of a chicken is composed of its two fused clavicles.

claw hard, hooked, pointed outgrowth of the digits of mammals, birds, and most reptiles. Claws are composed of the protein keratin, and grow continuously from a bundle of cells in the lower skin layer. Hooves and nails are modified structures with the same origin as claws.

clay very fine-grained ▷sedimentary deposit that has undergone a greater or lesser degree of consolidation. When moistened it is plastic, and it hardens on heating, which renders it impermeable. It may be white, grey, red, yellow, blue, or black, depending on its composition. Clay minerals consist largely of hydrous silicates of aluminium and magnesium together with iron, potassium, sodium, and organic substances. The crystals of clay minerals have a layered structure, capable of holding water, and are responsible for its plastic properties. According to international classification, in mechanical analysis of soil, clay has a grain size of less than 0.002 mm/0.00008 in.

Clay, Cassius Marcellus, Jr original name of boxer Muhammad ▷Ali.

Clay, Henry (1777–1852) US politician. He stood unsuccessfully three times for the presidency: as a Democratic-Republican in 1824, as a National Republican in 1832, and as a Whig in 1844. He supported the War of 1812 against Britain, and tried to hold the Union together on the slavery issue with the Missouri Compromise of 1820 and again in the compromise of 1850. He was secretary of state from 1825 until 1829 and devised an 'American system' for the national economy.

clay mineral one of a group of hydrous silicate minerals that form most of the fine-grained particles in clays. Clay minerals are normally formed by weathering or alteration of other silicate minerals. Virtually all have sheet silicate structures similar to the ▷micas. They exhibit the following useful properties: loss of water on heating; swelling and shrinking in different conditions;, cation exchange with other media; and plasticity when wet. Examples are kaolinite, illite, and montmorillonite.

cleavage in geology and mineralogy, the tendency of a rock or mineral to split along defined, parallel planes related to its internal structure; the clean splitting of slate is an example. It is a useful distinguishing feature in rock and mineral identification. Cleavage occurs as a result of realignment of component minerals during deformation or metamorphism. It takes place where bonding between atoms is weakest, and cleavages may be perfect, good, or poor, depending on the bond strengths; a given rock or mineral may possess one, two, three, or more orientations along which it will cleave.

clef in music, a symbol prefixed to a five-line stave indicating the pitch range to which the written notes apply. Introduced as a visual aid in plainchant notation, it takes the form of a stylized letter centred on a particular line, indicating the pitch of that line.

cleg another name for ▷horsefly.

Cleisthenes (born *c.* 570) Athenian statesman, later celebrated as the founder of Athenian democracy. Although an early collaborator of the Pisistratids, the Athenian tyrants, he was later exiled with his family, the Alcmaeonidae, and intrigued and campaigned against Hippias and Hipparchus. After their removal in 510 BC, in 508 to 507 BC he won over the people by offering to place the constitution on a more democratic basis. His democracy was established by his reforms over the next few years.

cleistogamy production of flowers that never fully open and that are automatically self-fertilized. Cleistogamous flowers are often formed late in the year, after the production of normal flowers, or during a period of cold weather, as seen in several species of violet *Viola*.

clematis any of a group of temperate woody climbing plants with colourful showy flowers. They belong to the buttercup family. (Genus *Clematis*, family Ranunculaceae.)

Related Web site: Clematis http://www.botanical.com/botanical/mgmh/c/clemat73.html

Clémenceau, Georges Eugène Benjamin (1841–1929) French radical politician, prime minister 1906–09 and 1917–20 when he chaired the Versailles peace conference but failed to secure the Rhine as a frontier for France in the treaty.

> **Georges Clémenceau**
> *Il est plus facile de faire la guerre que la paix.*
> *It is easier to make war than to make peace.*
> Speech at Verdun, 20 July 1919

Clemens, Samuel Langhorne real name of the US writer Mark ▷Twain.

Clement I, St early Christian leader and pope; see ▷Clement of Rome, St.

Clement VII (1478–1534) pope 1523–34. He refused to allow the divorce of Henry VIII of England and Catherine of Aragón. Illegitimate son of a brother of Lorenzo de' Medici, the ruler of Florence, he commissioned monuments for the Medici chapel in Florence from the Renaissance artist Michelangelo.

Clement of Rome, St (lived late 1st century) one of the early Christian leaders and writers known as the fathers of the church. According to tradition he was the third or fourth bishop of Rome, and a disciple of St Peter. He was pope AD 88–97 or 92–101. He wrote a letter addressed to the church at Corinth (First Epistle of Clement), and many other writings have been attributed to him.

Cleon (died 422 BC) Athenian politician and general in the ▷Peloponnesian War. He became 'leader of the people' (demagogue) after the death of ▷Pericles to whom he was opposed. He was an aggressive imperialist and advocated a vigorous war policy against the Spartans. He was killed by the Spartans at Amphipolis in 422 BC.

Cleopatra (*c.* 68–30 BC) Queen of Egypt 51–48 and 47–30 BC. When the Roman general Julius Caesar arrived in Egypt, he restored Cleopatra to the throne from which she had been ousted. Cleopatra and Caesar became lovers and she went with him to Rome. After Caesar's assassination in 44 BC she returned to Alexandria and resumed her position as queen of Egypt. In 41 BC she was joined there by Mark Antony, one of Rome's rulers. In 31 BC Rome declared war on Egypt and scored a decisive victory in the naval Battle of Actium off the west coast of Greece. Cleopatra fled with her 60 ships to Egypt; Antony abandoned the struggle and followed her. Both he and Cleopatra committed suicide.

Cleopatra was Macedonian, and the last ruler of the Macedonian dynasty, which ruled Egypt from 323 until annexation by Rome 31. She succeeded her father Ptolemy XII jointly with her brother Ptolemy XIII, and they ruled together from 51 to 49 BC, when she was expelled by him.

Her reinstatement in 48 BC by Caesar caused a war between Caesar and Ptolemy XIII, who was defeated and killed. The younger brother, Ptolemy XIV, was elevated to the throne and married to her, in the tradition of the pharaohs, although she actually lived with Caesar and they had a son, Ptolemy XV, known as Caesarion (he was later killed by Octavian).

After Caesar's death, Cleopatra and Mark Antony had three sons. In 32 BC he divorced his wife Octavia, the sister of Octavian, who then induced the Roman senate to declare war on Egypt. Shakespeare's play *Antony and Cleopatra* recounts that Cleopatra killed herself with an asp (poisonous snake) after Antony's suicide.

Film versions of her life were made in 1934 and 1963.

Related Web site: Great African Queens http://www.swagga.com/queen.htm

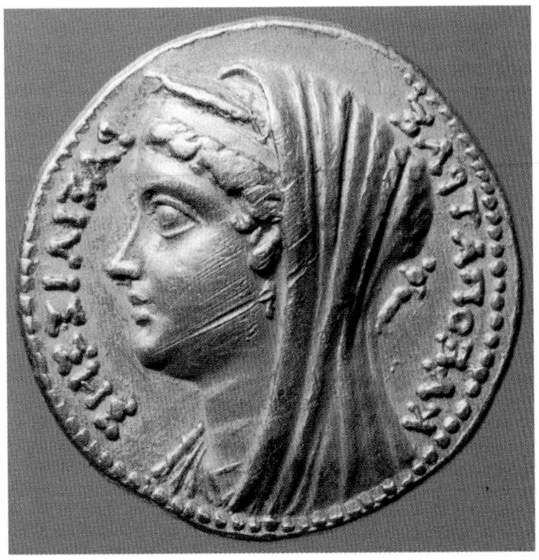

CLEOPATRA The head of Cleopatra I, Queen of Egypt in the first century BC, on a coin. *The Art Archive*

Cleopatra's Needle name given to two ancient Egyptian granite obelisks erected at Heliopolis in the 15th century BC by Thutmose III, and removed to Alexandria by the Roman emperor Augustus in about 14 BC; they have no connection with Cleopatra's reign. One of the pair was taken to England in 1878 and erected on the Victoria Embankment in London. It is 21 m/68.5 ft high.

Clermont-Ferrand city and administrative centre of Puy-de-Dôme *département* in the Auvergne region of France, situated 140 km/87 mi east of Limoges; population (1990) 140,200. It is a centre for agriculture; the rubber industry here, including the manufacture of car tyres, is the largest in France. The town has over 20 mineral springs and supplies a large amount of the country's bottled water. Other products include chemicals, preserves, foodstuffs, and clothing.

Cleveland port and city in northeastern Ohio, USA, on Lake Erie, at the mouth of the Cuyahoga River; seat of Cuyahoga County; population (1990) 505,600. Cleveland is the centre of a seven-county (including Cuyahoga, Portage, Summit, Lake, Medina, and Lorain) metropolitan area (CMSA) with a population (1990) of 2,759,800. An industrial, commercial, and transportation centre, and formerly one of the leading iron and steel producers in the USA, the city has also figured prominently in petroleum, chemicals, automobile manufacturing, and electric power. Cleveland's current industries include chemical and food processing, steel (although not on the scale seen previously), and the manufacture of electrical products and auto parts. Printing and publishing and international and Great Lakes ore shipping also figure prominently. It is also the location of dozens of corporate headquarters.

Cleveland, (Stephen) Grover (1837–1908) 22nd and 24th president of the USA, 1885–89 and 1893–97; the first Democratic president elected after the Civil War. He attempted to check corruption in public life and reduce tariffs. These policies provoked political opposition, and he was defeated by the Republican Benjamin Harrison in 1888. He was returned to office in 1892 and during the economic depression that followed the 'Panic of 1893' pressed Congress to repeal the Sherman Silver Purchase Act to protect the gold standard.

In foreign policy he was a noninterventionist, blocking the annexation of Hawaii and refusing to go to war with Spain over Cuba in 1895. In 1895 he initiated arbitration that settled a boundary dispute between Britain and Venezuela. An unswerving conservative, he refused to involve the government in economic affairs but used federal troops to end the Pullman strike in 1894. Within a year of his taking office for the second time, 4 million were unemployed and the USA was virtually bankrupt.

click beetle ▷beetle that can regain its feet from lying on its back by jumping into the air and turning over, clicking as it does so.

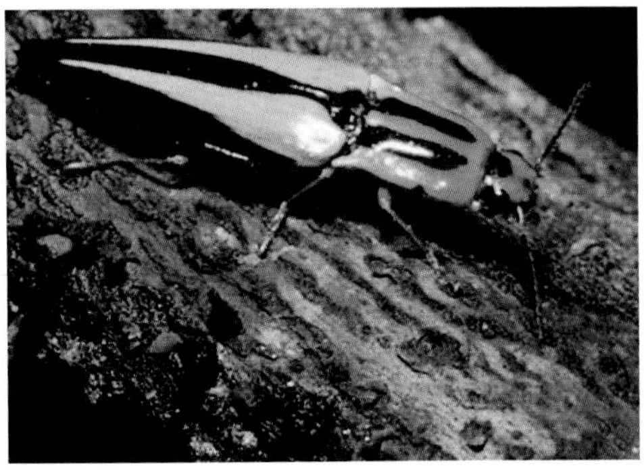

CLICK BEETLE Peruvian click beetle *Semiotus affinis* on a log in the rainforest. *K G Preston-Mafham/Premaphotos Wildlife*

client–server architecture in computing, a system in which the mechanics of looking after data are separated from the programs that use the data. For example, the 'server' might be a central database, typically located on a large computer that is reserved for this purpose. The 'client' would be an ordinary program that requests data from the server as needed.

Most Internet services are examples of client–server applications, including the World Wide Web, FTP, Telnet, and Gopher.

Cliff, Clarice (1899–1972) English pottery designer. Her Bizarre ware, characterized by brightly coloured floral and geometric decoration on often geometrically shaped china, became increasingly popular in the 1930s and increasingly collectable in the 1970s and 1980s. Contemporary artists such as Laura Knight and Vanessa Bell also designed for her Bizarre range.

climate combination of weather conditions at a particular place over a period of time – usually a minimum of 30 years. A classification of climate encompasses the averages, extremes, and frequencies of all meteorological elements such as temperature, atmospheric pressure, precipitation, wind, humidity, and sunshine, together with the factors that influence them. The primary factors involved are: latitude (as a result of the Earth's rotation and orbit); ocean currents; large-scale movements of wind belts and air masses over the Earth's surface; temperature differences between land and sea surfaces; topography; continent positions; and vegetation. In the long term, changes in the Earth's orbit and the angle of its axis inclination also affect climate. Climatology, the scientific study of climate, includes the construction of computer-generated models, and considers not only present-day climates, their effects and their classification, but also long-term climate changes, covering both past climates (paleoclimates) and future predictions. Climatologists are especially concerned with the influences of human activity on climate change, among the most important of which, at both a local and global level, are those currently linked with ▷ozone depleters the ▷greenhouse effect, and ▷global warming.

Climate classification The word climate comes from the Greek *klima*, meaning an inclination or slope (referring to the angle of the Sun's rays, and thus latitude) and the earliest known classification of climate was that of the ancient Greeks, who based their system on latitudes. In recent times, many different systems of classifying climate have been devised, most of which follow that formulated by the German climatologist Wladimir Köppen (1846–1940) in 1900. These systems use vegetation-based classifications such as desert, tundra, and rainforest. Classification by air mass is used in conjunction with this method. This idea was first introduced in 1928 by the Norwegian meteorologist Tor Bergeron, and links the climate of an area with the movement of the air masses it experiences.

In the 18th century, the British scientist George Hadley developed a model of the general circulation of atmosphere based on convection. He proposed a simple pattern of cells of warm air rising at the Equator and descending at the poles. In fact, due to the rotation of the Earth, there are three such cells in each hemisphere. The first two of these consist of air that rises at the Equator and sinks at latitudes north and south of the tropics; the second two exist at the mid-latitudes where the rising air from the sub-tropics flows towards the cold air masses of the third pair of cells circulating from the two polar regions. Thus, in this model, there are six main circulating cells of air above ground producing seven terrestrial zones. There are three rainy regions (at the Equator and the temperate latitudes) resulting from the moisture-laden rising air (see ▷intertropical convergence zone), interspersed and bounded by four dry or desert regions (at the poles and sub-tropics) resulting from the dry descending air. See also The World's Changing Climate Focus Feature on pp. 396–397.

Related Web site: World Environmental Changes Landmarks http://www.bbc.co.uk/education/landmarks/

climate change change in the climate of an area or of the whole world over an appreciable period of time. That is, a single winter that is colder than average does not indicate climate change. It is the change in average weather conditions from one period of time (30–50 years) to the next. See ▷climate.

climatology study of climate, its global variations and causes.

clinical psychology branch of psychology dealing with the understanding and treatment of health problems, particularly mental disorders. The main problems dealt with include anxiety, phobias, depression, obsessions, sexual and marital problems, drug and alcohol dependence, childhood behavioural problems, psychoses (such as schizophrenia), mental disability, and brain disease (such as dementia) and damage. Other areas of work include forensic psychology (concerned with criminal behaviour) and health psychology.

Assessment procedures assess intelligence and cognition (for example, in detecting the effects of brain damage) by using psychometric tests. **Behavioural approaches** are methods of treatment that apply learning theories to clinical problems. **Behaviour therapy** helps clients change unwanted behaviours (such as phobias, obsessions, sexual problems) and to develop new skills (such as improving social interactions). **Behaviour modification** relies on operant conditioning, making selective use of rewards (such as praise) to change behaviour. This is helpful for children, the mentally disabled, and for patients in institutions, such as mental hospitals. **Cognitive therapy** is an approach to treating emotional problems, such as anxiety and depression, by teaching clients how to deal with negative thoughts and attitudes. **Counselling**, developed by Carl Rogers, is widely used to help clients solve their own problems. **Psychoanalysis**, as developed by Sigmund Freud and Carl Jung, is little used by clinical psychologists today. It emphasizes childhood conflicts as a source of adult problems.

Clinton, Bill (1946–) Born William Jefferson Clinton. 42nd president of the USA 1993–2000. A Democrat, he served as governor of Arkansas 1979–81 and 1983–93, establishing a liberal and progressive reputation. As president, he sought to implement a New Democrat programme, combining social reform with economic conservatism as a means of bringing the country out of recession. He introduced legislation to reduce the federal deficit and cut crime. Following accusations of perjury and obstruction of justice Clinton underwent an impeachment trial (the second such trial in US history) in early 1999 but was acquitted. Clinton presided over a period of unchecked expansion for the US economy, which regained global pre-eminence, and sought, with mixed success to promote peace and stability in the Balkans, Middle East, and Northern Ireland. His wife, Hillary, was, in November 2000, elected to the US senate, representing New York state, becoming the first First Lady to hold public office. However, Clinton's centrist New Democrat legacy was placed in danger by the narrow defeat of his loyal vice-president, Al Gore, by the Republican right-winger, George W Bush, in the 2000 presidential election.

Related Web site: William J Clinton Forty-Second President 1993– http://www.whitehouse.gov/WH/glimpse/presidents/html/bc42.html

Clinton, Hillary Diane Rodham (1947–) US lawyer, senator, and former First Lady. In 1993 her husband, President Bill Clinton, appointed her to head his task force on the reform of the national health-care system, but her proposal of health insurance for all US citizens was blocked by Congress in 1994. A formidable figure, Hillary Clinton became the first ever First Lady to be subpoenaed to appear before a Federal Grand Jury. She moved to New York in 1999 in order to stand as a candidate for the vacant Senate seat in New York, which she won in November 2000.

> **Bill Clinton**
> *There is nothing wrong with America that cannot be cured by what is right with America.*
> Inaugural speech as US president 1993

Hillary Rodham was born in the suburbs of Chicago, Illinois. She graduated from Yale law school in 1973 and married Bill Clinton in 1975. She was one of the team of lawyers appointed to work on the impeachment of President Richard Nixon in 1974. The Clintons moved to Arkansas in 1976, where Hillary joined the Rose law firm. As head of the Arkansas Education Standards Committee from 1983, she succeeded in getting the state to pass a law in 1985 allowing the dismissal of teachers for incompetence. From 1994 the Clintons were investigated over alleged irregularities in property deals made by them when in Arkansas (the ▷Whitewater affair). In 2000, the prosectutor concluded there was insufficient evidence to prosecute. A separate investigation also concluded in 2000 that there was insufficient evidence to prosecute Hillary Clinton over claims that she had been involved in misusing FBI files about Republican officials in the Bush and Reagan administrations.

A long time advocate of children's rights, she published the book *It Takes a Village and Other Lessons Children Teach Us* (1996).

Related Web site: Clinton, Hillary Rodham http://www.whitehouse.gov/WH/EOP/First_Lady/html/HILLARY_Bio.html

clitoris (Greek *kleitoris* 'little hill') in anatomy, part of the female reproductive system. The glans of the clitoris is visible externally. It connects to a pyramid-shaped pad of erectile tissue. Attached to this are two 'arms' that extend backwards into the body towards the anus and are approximately 9 cm/3.5 in in length. Between these arms are the clitoral bulbs, lying one on each side of the vaginal cavity.

Clive, Robert (1725–1774) 1st Baron Clive. British soldier and administrator who established British rule in India by victories over French troops at Arcot and over the nawab (prince) of Bengal at Plassey in 1757. This victory secured Bengal for the East India Company, and Clive was appointed governor of the province from 1757. He returned to Britain on account of ill health in 1760, but was governor for a further year in 1765–6. On his return to Britain in 1766, his wealth led to allegations that he had abused his power. Although acquitted by a Parliamentary enquiry, he committed suicide.

Clive became a clerk in the East India Company's service in Madras (now Chennai) in 1743, then joined the army. During a dispute in 1751 over the succession to the Carnatic, an important trading region, Clive marched from Madras with 500 troops, seized Arcot, capital of the Carnatic, and defended it for seven weeks against 10,000 French and Italian troops. He then sallied out and relieved the British forces besieged in Trichinopoli. He returned to Britain a national hero, and was hailed as 'Clive of India'. He returned to India in 1755 as governor of Fort St David, and after the incident of the ▷Black Hole of Calcutta, when the city was besieged by the nawab of Bengal, Clive defeated the nawab's 34,000 strong army, with a force of only 1,900 troops outside Calcutta in February 1757.

cloaca the common posterior chamber of most vertebrates into which the digestive, urinary, and reproductive tracts all enter; a cloaca is found in most reptiles, birds, and amphibians; many fishes; and, to a reduced degree, marsupial mammals. Placental mammals, however, have a separate digestive opening (the anus) and urinogenital opening. The cloaca forms a chamber in which products can be stored before being voided from the body via a muscular opening, the cloacal aperture.

clock rate frequency of a computer's internal electronic clock. Every computer contains an electronic clock, which produces a sequence of regular electrical pulses used by the control unit to synchronize the components of the computer and regulate the ▷fetch–execute cycle by which program instructions are processed.

A fixed number of time pulses is required in order to execute each particular instruction. The speed at which a computer can process instructions therefore depends on the clock rate: increasing the clock rate will decrease the time required to complete each particular instruction.

cloisonné ornamental craft technique in which thin metal strips are soldered in a pattern onto a metal surface, and the resulting compartments (*cloisons*) filled with coloured ▷enamels and fired. The technique was probably developed in the Byzantine Middle East and traded to Asia and Europe. Cloisonné vases and brooches were made in medieval Europe, but the technique was perfected in Japan and China during the 17th, 18th, and 19th centuries.

cloister (from Latin *claustrum* 'an enclosure') in architecture, a quadrangle surrounded by walkways or covered passages for shelter from rain, attached to monastic buildings and cathedrals, and often also to colleges. The church would be linked to other areas of the convent or monastery via the cloisters.

clone an exact replica. In genetics, any one of a group of genetically identical cells or organisms. An identical ▷twin is a clone; so, too, are bacteria living in the same colony. 'Clone' also describes genetically engineered replicas of DNA sequences. The term has also been adopted by computer technology to describe a (nonexistent) device that mimics an actual one to enable certain software programs to run correctly.

British scientists confirmed in February 1997 that they had cloned an adult sheep from a single cell to produce a lamb with the same genes as its mother. A cell was taken from the udder of

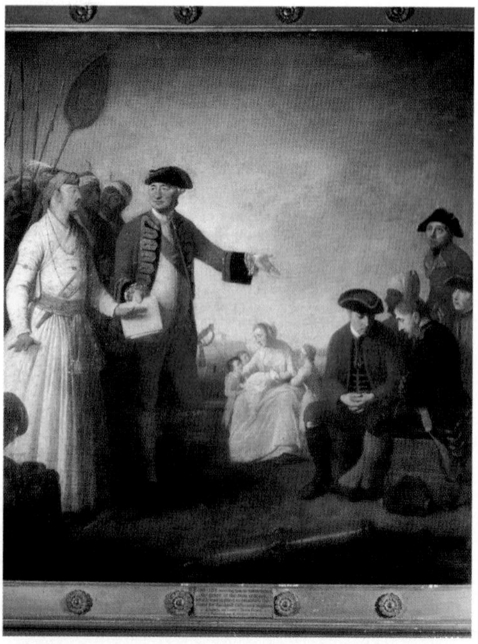

ROBERT CLIVE British soldier and administrator Robert Clive in a painting by E Penny dated 1773, showing Clive receiving a gift from the nawab of Bengal. *The Art Archive/India Office Library*

the mother sheep, and its DNA combined with an unfertilized egg that had had its DNA removed. The fused cells were grown in the laboratory and then implanted into the uterus of a surrogate mother sheep. The resulting lamb, Dolly, came from an animal that was six years old. Dolly was revealed to be not an exact clone, however, in 1999 when research showed her mitochondria to have come mainly from the egg cell rather than the udder cell.

This was the first time cloning had been achieved using cells other than reproductive cells. The cloning breakthrough has ethical implications, as the same principle could be used with human cells and eggs. The news was met with international calls to prevent the cloning of humans. The UK, Spain, Germany, Canada, and Denmark already have laws against cloning humans, as do some individual states in the USA (legislators introduced bills to ban human cloning and associated research nationally in March 1997). France and Portugal also have very restrictive laws on cloning.

The UK government in mid-August 2000 approved the cloning of human embryos for medical purposes.

Related Web site: Dr Frankenstein, I presume? http://www. salonmagazine.com/feb97/news/news2970224.html

Close, Glenn (1947–   ) US film and stage actor. She received Academy Award nominations for her roles as the embittered 'other woman' in *Fatal Attraction* (1987) and as the scheming antiheroine of *Dangerous Liaisons* (1988). She played Gertrude in Franco Zeffirelli's film of *Hamlet* (1990), and appeared as an opera star in *Meeting Venus* (1991). In 1996, she starred as Cruella DeVil in Disney's live-action remake of *101 Dalmatians*. She reprised the role in the sequel, *102 Dalmatians*, in 2000.

closed in mathematics, descriptive of a set of data for which an operation (such as addition or multiplication) done on any members of the set gives a result that is also a member of the set.

closed shop any place of work, such as a factory or an office, where all workers within a section must belong to a single, officially recognized trade union.

udder cell from first sheep

ovum from second sheep stripped of DNA

cells fused

embryo forms with udder cell DNA

implant embryo in surrogate mother

offspring is clone of first sheep

CLONE The cloning of Dolly the sheep by the Roslin Institute in Edinburgh was a genetic milestone. It was the first successful clone produced using genetic material from an adult (udder) cell rather than from a gamete (egg or sperm). The DNA from the udder cell was fused with an ovum stripped of its own DNA. The fused cells divided in vitro to form an embryo that was then implanted into a surrogate mother. The resulting lamb was a clone of the ewe that had provided the udder cell.

clothes moth moth whose larvae feed on clothes, upholstery, and carpets. The adults are small golden or silvery moths. The natural habitat of the larvae is in the nests of animals, feeding on remains of hair and feathers, but they have adapted to human households and can cause considerable damage, for example, the common clothes moth *Tineola bisselliella*.

cloud water vapour condensed into minute water particles that float in masses in the atmosphere. Clouds, like fogs or mists, which occur at lower levels, are formed by the cooling of air containing water vapour, which generally condenses around tiny dust particles.

Clouds are classified according to the height at which they occur and their shape. **Cirrus** and **cirrostratus** clouds occur at around 10 km/33,000 ft. The former, sometimes called mares'-tails, consist of minute specks of ice and appear as feathery white wisps, while cirrostratus clouds stretch across the sky as a thin white sheet. Three types of cloud are found at 3–7 km/10,000–23,000 ft: cirrocumulus, altocumulus, and altostratus. **Cirrocumulus** clouds occur in small or large rounded tufts, sometimes arranged in the pattern called mackerel sky. **Altocumulus** clouds are similar, but larger, white clouds, also arranged in lines. **Altostratus** clouds are like heavy cirrostratus clouds and may stretch across the sky as a grey sheet. **Stratocumulus** clouds are generally lower, occurring at 2–6 km/6,500–20,000 ft. They are dull grey clouds that give rise to a leaden sky that may not yield rain. Two types of clouds, **cumulus** and **cumulonimbus**, are placed in a special category because they are produced by daily ascending air currents, which take moisture into the cooler regions of the atmosphere. Cumulus clouds have a flat base generally at 1.4 km/4,500 ft where condensation begins, while the upper part is dome-shaped and extends to about 1.8 km/6,000ft. Cumulonimbus clouds have their base at much the same level, but extend much higher, often up to over 6 km/20,000 ft. Short heavy showers and sometimes thunder may accompany them. **Stratus** clouds, occurring below 1–2.5 km/3,000–8,000 ft, have the appearance of sheets parallel to the horizon and are like high fogs.

In addition to their essential role in the water cycle, clouds are important in the regulation of radiation in the Earth's atmosphere. They reflect short-wave radiation from the Sun, and absorb and re-emit long-wave radiation from the Earth's surface.

Related Web site: Clouds and Precipitation http://ww2010.atmos.uiuc.edu/(Gh)/guides/mtr/cld/home.rxml

cloud chamber apparatus, now obsolete, for tracking ionized particles. It consists of a vessel fitted with a piston and filled with air or other gas, saturated with water vapour. When the volume of the vessel is suddenly expanded by moving the piston outwards, the vapour cools and a cloud of tiny droplets forms on any nuclei, dust, or ions present. As fast-moving ionizing particles collide with the air or gas molecules, they show as visible tracks.

Clouet French portrait painters and draughtsmen of the 16th century, father and son. The father, **Jean** (or **Janet**) (*c.* 1485–1541), is assumed to have been of Flemish origin. He became painter and *valet de chambre* to Francis I in 1516. His son, **François** (*c.* 1520–1572), succeeded his father in Francis I's service in 1541 and worked also under Henry II, Francis II, and Charles IX.

clove dried, unopened flower bud of the clove tree. A member of the myrtle family, the tree is a native of the Maluku Islands, Indonesia. Cloves are used for flavouring in cookery and confectionery. Oil of cloves, which has tonic qualities and relieves wind, is used in medicine. The aroma of cloves is also shared by the leaves, bark, and fruit of the tree. (*Eugenia caryophyllus*, family Myrtaceae.)

Related Web site: Cloves http://www.botanical.com/botanical/mgmh/c/cloves76.html

clover any of an Old World group of low-growing leguminous plants (see ▷legume), usually with leaves consisting of three leaflets and small flowers in dense heads. Sweet clover refers to various species belonging to the related genus *Melilotus*. (True clover genus *Trifolium*, family Leguminosae.)

Clovis (465–511) Also known as **Chlodovech**. Merovingian king of the Franks (481–511), who extended his realm from a small area around Tournai to encompass most of modern France and parts of modern Germany. He succeeded his father Childeric I as king of the Salian (western) Franks; defeated the Gallo-Romans (Romanized Gauls) near Soissons; and defeated the Alemanni, a confederation of Germanic tribes, near Cologne. He embraced Christianity and subsequently proved a powerful defender of orthodoxy against the Arian Visigoths, whom he defeated at Poitiers. He made Paris his capital.

club moss (or **lycopod**) any of a group of mosslike plants that do not produce seeds but reproduce by ▷spores. They are related to the ferns and horsetails. (Order Lycopodiales, family Pteridophyta.)

Cluj-Napoca (German **Klausenberg**) city in Transylvania, Romania, located on the River Somes; population (1993) 322,000. It is a communications centre for Romania and the Hungarian plain. Industries include machine tools, furniture, and knitwear.

Cluny town in Saône-et-Loire *département* of Burgundy, eastern France, on the River Grosne, 23 km/14 mi northwest of Mâcon; population (1990) 4,700. Its abbey, now in ruins, was from 910 to 1790 the foundation house of the Cluniac order, originally a reformed branch of the Benedictines. Cluny was once a lace-making centre; it has a large cattle market, and attracts many tourists. See picture on p. 210.

cluster in music, the effect of playing simultaneously and without emphasis all the notes within a chosen interval. It was introduced by the US composer Henry Cowell in the piano piece *The Banshee* (1925), for which using a ruler on the keys is recommended. Its use in film and radio incidental music symbolizes a hallucinatory or dreaming state, presumably because it resembles an internalized disturbance of normal hearing.

clutch any device for disconnecting rotating shafts, used especially in a car's transmission system. In a car with a manual gearbox, the driver depresses the clutch when changing gear, thus disconnecting the engine from the gearbox.

CLUB MOSS Club mosses are named after their clublike fertile heads. Here the heads can be seen on a plant of *Lycopodium cernum* from the high mountain forests of Borneo. *Premaphotos Wildlife*

CLUNY Consecration of the abbey of Cluny by Pope Urban II in 1095, from the 12th-century *Book of Offices*. See article on p. 209. *Art Archive*

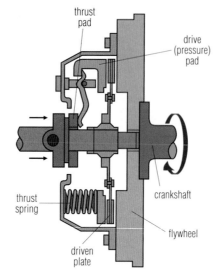

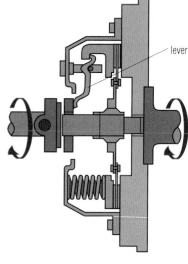

disengaged (pedal pressed down)   engaged (pedal up)

CLUTCH The clutch consists of two main plates: a drive plate connected to the engine crankshaft and a driven plate connected to the wheels. When the clutch is disengaged, the drive plate does not press against the driven plate. When the clutch is engaged, the two plates are pressed into contact and the rotation of the crankshaft is transmitted to the wheels.

Clwyd former county of north Wales, created in 1974 and, in 1996, divided between ▷Conwy, ▷Denbighshire, ▷Flintshire, ▷Powys, and ▷Wrexham unitary authorities.

Clwyd river in northeast Wales, rising in the Denbigh Moors and Clwydian Hills, and flowing past St Asaph and Rhuddlan into the Irish Sea at Rhyl; length 64km/40 mi. The Elwy is the main tributary. The Clwyd valley has fine scenery.

Clyde third longest river and firth in Scotland, and longest in southern Scotland; 171 km/106 mi long. Formerly one of the world's great industrial waterways, and famed for its shipbuilding, its industrial base has declined in recent years and the capacity of the ports on the Clyde has reduced.

Clytemnestra in Greek mythology, the daughter of King Tyndareus of Sparta and ▷Leda, half-sister of ▷Helen, and wife of ▷Agamemnon, king of Mycenae. After killing her first husband in battle, Agamemnon had married her by force, and later sacrificed their daugher Iphegenia to secure fair winds for the Greek expedition to Troy. With the help of her lover Aegisthus, she murdered her husband and the seer ▷Cassandra, whom he brought back from the Trojan War, but was killed in turn by her son ▷Orestes, aided by her daughter Electra.

CND in Britain, abbreviation for ▷Campaign for Nuclear Disarmament.

Cnossus alternative form of ▷Knossos, city of ancient Crete.

Cnut alternative spelling of ▷Canute.

CO abbreviation for **commanding officer**.

CO abbreviation for the state of ▷Colorado, USA.

c/o abbreviation for **care of**.

co. abbreviation for **company**.

coal black or blackish mineral substance formed from the compaction of ancient plant matter in tropical swamp conditions. It is used as a fuel and in the chemical industry. Coal is classified according to the proportion of carbon it contains. The main types are ▷anthracite (shiny, with about 90% carbon), **bituminous coal** (shiny and dull patches, about 75% carbon), and **lignite** (woody,

grading into peat, about 50% carbon). Coal burning is one of the main causes of ▷acid rain. See picture.

coal gas gas produced when coal is destructively distilled or heated out of contact with the air. Its main constituents are methane, hydrogen, and carbon monoxide. Coal gas has been superseded by ▷natural gas for domestic purposes.

coal mining extraction of coal from the Earth's crust. Coal mines may be opencast adit, or deepcast. The least expensive is opencast but this may result in scars on the landscape.

History In Britain, coal was mined on a small scale from Roman times, but production expanded rapidly between 1550 and 1700. Coal was the main source of energy for the Industrial Revolution, and many industries were located near coalfields to cut transport costs. Competition from oil as a fuel, cheaper coal from overseas (USA, Australia), the decline of traditional users (town gas, railways), and the exhaustion of many underground workings resulted in the closure of mines (850 in 1955, 54 in 1992), but rises in the price of oil, greater productivity, and the discovery of new, deep coal seams suitable for mechanized extraction (for example, at Selby in Yorkshire) improved the position of the British coal industry 1973–90. It remains very dependent on the use of coal in electricity generation, however, and is now threatened by a trend towards using natural gas from the North Sea and Irish Sea gas fields for this purpose. The percentage of electricity generated from coal dropped from 74% 1992 to just over 50%in 1995.

More that 100,000 miners have died in mining accidents this century – over 1,000 times more deaths than in the nuclear industry.

Pit closures In October 1992, Trade and Industry Secretary Michael Heseltine announced that 31 of the country's coal mines would be closed, putting some 30,000 miners out of work. After widespread protest from the public and from MPs from all parties, the government announced that 10 pits would close and the remaining 21 would be put under review. In March 1993 a revised closure programme reprieved 12 of the 21 collieries while they were assessed for economic viability. By August 1993, 18 collieries had closed. In 1995, 30 major deep mines and 35 opencast mines formerly owned by British Coal, were still being worked. In 1997 doubts were expressed about the future of even these pits.

coal tar black oily material resulting from the destructive distillation of bituminous coal.

coastal erosion the erosion of the land by the constant battering of the sea's waves, primarily by the processes of hydraulic action, corrasion, attrition, and corrosion. ▷Hydraulic action occurs when the force of the waves compresses air pockets in coastal rocks and cliffs. The air expands explosively, breaking the rocks apart. Rocks and pebbles flung by waves against the cliff face wear it away by the process of ▷corrasion. Chalk and limestone coasts are often broken down by ▷solution (also called corrosion). Attrition is the process by which the eroded rock particles themselves are worn down, becoming smaller and more rounded.

Frost shattering (or freeze-thaw), caused by the expansion of frozen sea water in cavities, and ▷biological weathering, caused by the burrowing of rock-boring molluscs, also result in the breakdown of the coastal rock.

Where resistant rocks form headlands, the sea erodes the coast in successive stages. First it exploits weaknesses, such as faults and cracks in ▷cave openings, and then gradually wears away the interior of the caves until their roofs are pierced through to form blowholes. In time, caves at either side of a headland may unite to form a natural arch. When the roof of the arch collapses, a ▷stack is formed. This may be worn down further to produce a stump and a ▷wave-cut platform.

Beach erosion occurs when more sand is eroded and carried away from the beach than is deposited by ▷longshore drift. Beach erosion can occur due to the construction of artificial barriers, such as ▷groynes, or due to the natural periodicity of the **beach cycle**, whereby high tides and the high waves of winter storms tend to carry sand away from the beach and deposit it offshore in the form of bars. During the calmer summer season some of this sand is redeposited on the beach.

CLWYD A view over the River Clwyd, Conwy, Wales. *Image Bank*

COAL MINING Miners on their way home after a shift down the pit during the 1920s. Mechanization of their work was primitive, conditions underground were unpleasant and often dangerous, and the reward was not overgenerous, but there was such a camaraderie among the men that their leisure hours and interests were frequently also shared. *Image Bank*

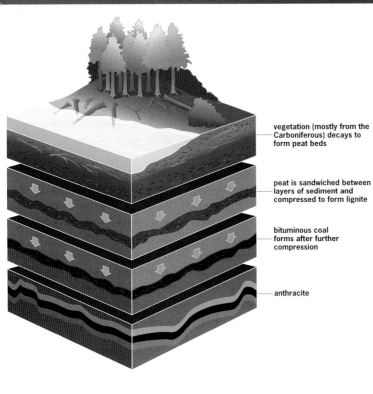

vegetation (mostly from the Carboniferous) decays to form peat beds

peat is sandwiched between layers of sediment and compressed to form lignite

bituminous coal forms after further compression

anthracite

COAL The formation of coal. Coal forms where vegetable matter accumulates but is prevented from complete decay and forms peat beds. Over time it becomes buried and compressed, forming lignite. Increased pressure and temperature produces bituminous coal with a higher carbon content. At great depths, high temperatures reduce methane and anthracite is formed with a very high carbon concentration.

In Britain, the southern half of the coastline is slowly sinking (on the east coast, at the rate of half a centimetre a year) whilst the northern half is rising, as a result of rebounding of the land mass (responding to the removal of ice from the last Ice Age). Some areas may be eroding at a rate of 6 m/20 ft per year. Current opinion is to surrender the land to the sea, rather than build costly sea defences in rural areas. In 1996, it was reported that 29 villages had disappeared from the Yorkshire coast since 1926 as a result of tidal battering.

    Related Web site: Coasts in Crisis http://pubs.usgs.gov/circular/c1075/

coastguard governmental organization whose members patrol a nation's seacoast to prevent smuggling, assist distressed vessels, watch for oil slicks, and so on. In 1994 the Coastguard became an Executive Agency and is responsible for all civil maritime search and rescue operations around the UK coastline and up to 1,000 mi into the North Atlantic.

Coates, Nigel (1949–) English architect. While teaching at the Architectural Association in London in 1983, Coates and a group of students founded NATO (Narrative Architecture Today) and produced an influential series of manifestos and drawings on the theme of the regeneration of derelict areas of London.

coati (or coatimundi) any of several species of carnivores of the genus *Nasua*, in the same family, Procyonidae, as the raccoons. A coati is a good climber and has long claws, a long tail, a good sense of smell, and a long, flexible piglike snout used for digging. Coatis live in packs in the forests of South and Central America.

    The common coati *Nasua nasua* of South America is about 60 cm/2 ft long, with a tail about the same length.

coaxial cable electric cable that consists of a solid or stranded central conductor insulated from and surrounded by a solid or braided conducting tube or sheath. It can transmit the high-frequency signals used in television, telephone, and other telecommunications transmissions.

cobalt (German *Kobalt* 'evil spirit') hard, lustrous, grey, metallic element, symbol Co, atomic number 27, relative atomic mass 58.933. It is found in various ores and occasionally as a free metal, sometimes in metallic meteorite fragments. It is used in the preparation of magnetic, wear-resistant, and high-strength alloys; its compounds are used in inks, paints, and varnishes.

    The isotope Co-60 is radioactive (half-life 5.3 years) and is produced in large amounts for use as a source of gamma rays in industrial radiography, research, and cancer therapy. Cobalt was named in 1730 by Swedish chemist Georg Brandt (1694–1768);

the name derives from the fact that miners considered its ore malevolent because it interfered with copper production.

cobalt-60 radioactive (half-life 5.3 years) isotope produced by neutron radiation of cobalt in heavy-water reactors, used in large amounts for gamma rays in cancer therapy, industrial radiography, and research, substituting for the much more costly radium.

cobalt ore cobalt is extracted from a number of minerals, the main ones being smaltite, $(CoNi)As_3$; linnaeite, Co_3S_4; cobaltite, CoAsS; and glaucodot, $(CoFe)AsS$.

Cobbett, William (1763–1835) English Radical politician and journalist, who published the weekly *Political Register* (1802–35). He spent much of his life in North America. His crusading essays on the conditions of the rural poor were collected as 'Rural Rides' (1830).

Cobden, Richard (1804–1865) British Liberal politician and economist, cofounder with John Bright of the Anti-Corn Law League in 1838. A member of Parliament from 1841, he opposed class and religious privileges and believed in disarmament and free trade.

COBOL (acronym for common business-oriented language) high-level computer-programming language, designed in the late 1950s for commercial data-processing problems; it has become the major language in this field. COBOL features powerful facilities for file handling and business arithmetic. Program instructions written in this language make extensive use of words and look very much like English sentences. This makes COBOL one of the easiest languages to learn and understand.

cobra any of several poisonous snakes, especially the genus *Naja*, of the family Elapidae, found in Africa and southern Asia, species of which can grow from 1 m/3 ft to over 4.3 m/14 ft. The neck stretches into a hood when the snake is alarmed. Cobra venom contains nerve toxins powerful enough to kill humans.

    The Indian cobra *Naja naja* is about 1.5 m/5 ft long, and found over most of southern Asia. Some individuals have 'spectacle' markings on the hood. The hamadryad *N. hannah* of southern and southeast Asia can be 4.3 m/14 ft or more, and eats snakes. The ringhals *Hemachatus hemachatus* of South Africa and the black-necked cobra *N. nigricollis*, of the African savannah are both about 1 m/3 ft long. Both are able to spray venom towards the eyes of an attacker. A species of cobra, *Naja manadalayensis*, was identified in Myanmar in 2000. It is a 'spitting' cobra (able to project its venom). This makes a total of four African species and six Asian.

    Related Web site: King Cobra http://www.nationalgeographic.com/features/97/kingcobra/index-n.html

coca South American shrub belonging to the coca family, whose dried leaves are the source of the drug cocaine. It was used as a holy drug by the Andean Indians. (*Erythroxylon coca*, family Erythroxylaceae.)

    Related Web site: Coca, Bolivian http://www.botanical.com/botanical/mgmh/c/cocobo78.html

cocaine alkaloid ($C_{17}H_{21}NO_4$) extracted from the leaves of the coca tree. It has limited medical application, mainly as a local anaesthetic agent that is readily absorbed by mucous membranes (lining tissues) of the nose and throat. It is both toxic and addictive. Its use as a stimulant is illegal. ▷Crack is a derivative of cocaine.

    Related Web site: Cocaine Anonymous World Services http://www.ca.org/

coccus (plural cocci) member of a group of globular bacteria, some of which are harmful to humans. The cocci contain the subgroups **streptococci**, where the bacteria associate in straight chains, and **staphylococci**, where the bacteria associate in branched chains.

Cochabamba capital of Cochabamba department, central Bolivia, situated on the River Rocha, at an altitude of 2,550 m/8,370 ft on the slopes of the eastern Cordillera, 230 km/144 mi southeast of La Paz; population (1992) 404,100. It is the third-largest city in Bolivia. The Cochabamba valley is a rich agricultural region producing grain, beef, fruit, and timber for the towns of the Altiplano Plateau. The city is a commercial and communications centre with a railway terminus and an international airport, and distributes much of the agricultural produce of eastern Bolivia. It has food-processing and vehicle assembly plants, and there is an oil refinery, linked by pipeline with the Camiri oilfields.

Cochin (or Kochi) former princely state lying west of the Anamalai hills in south India. It was part of Travancore-Cochin from 1949 until merged into Kerala in 1956.

Cochin-China region of Southeast Asia. With Cambodia it formed part of the ancient Khmer empire. In the 17th–18th centuries it was conquered by Annam. Together with Cambodia it became, from 1863 to 1867, the first part of the Indochinese peninsula to be occupied by France. Since 1949 it has been part of Vietnam.

cochineal red dye obtained from the cactus-eating Mexican ▷scale insect *Dactylopius coccus*, used in colouring food and fabrics. There are approximately 70,000 bugs per pound of cochineal.

Cochise (c. 1815–1874) American Indian leader who campaigned relentlessly against white settlement of his territory. Unjustly arrested by US authorities in 1850, he escaped from custody and took American hostages, whom he later executed. A Chiricahua Apache, Cochise joined forces with the Mimbreno Apache and successfully fought off a large force of California settlers in 1862. Finally apprehended by General George Crook in 1871, Cochise made peace with the US government the following year.

cochlea part of the inner ▷ear. It is equipped with approximately 10,000 hair cells, which move in response to sound waves and thus stimulate nerve cells to send messages to the brain. In this way they turn vibrations of the air into electrical signals.

cockatiel Australian parrot *Nymphicus hollandicus*, about 20 cm/8 in long, with greyish or yellow plumage, yellow cheeks, a long tail, and a crest like a cockatoo. Cockatiels are popular as pets and aviary birds.

cockatoo any of several crested parrots, especially of the genus *Cacatua*, family Psittacidae, of the order Psittaciformes. They usually have light-coloured plumage with tinges of red, yellow, or orange on the face, and an erectile crest on the head. They are native to Australia, New Guinea, and nearby islands.

COBRA The Indian cobra often lives in cultivated areas such as rice fields where, if disturbed, it may bite or spit venom. *Image Bank*

There are about 17 species, one of the most familiar being the sulphur-crested cockatoo *C. galerita* of Australia and New Guinea, about 50 cm/20 in long, white with a yellow crest and dark beak.

cockchafer (or **maybug**) European beetle *Melolontha melolontha*, of the scarab family, up to 3 cm/1.2 in long, with clumsy, buzzing flight, seen on early summer evenings. Cockchafers damage trees by feeding on the foliage and flowers.

COCKCHAFER The prominent comblike antennae of this cockchafer *Melolontha melolontha* indicate that it is a male; the antennae of females are much shorter. *Premaphotos Wildlife*

Cockerell, Charles Robert (1788–1863) English architect. He built mainly in a neoclassical style derived from antiquity and from the work of Christopher ▷Wren. His buildings include the Cambridge University Library (now the Cambridge Law Library; 1837–42) and the Ashmolean Museum and Taylorian Institute in Oxford (1841–45).

Cockerell, Christopher Sydney (1910–1999) English engineer who invented the ▷hovercraft in the 1950s.

cockle any of over 200 species of bivalve mollusc with ribbed, heart-shaped shells. Some are edible and are sold in Western European markets.

cockney native of the City of London. According to tradition cockneys must be born within sound of ▷Bow Bells in Cheapside. The term cockney is also applied to the dialect of the Londoner, of which a striking feature is rhyming slang.

cock-of-the-rock South American bird of the genus *Rupicola*. It belongs to the family Cotingidae, which also includes the cotingas and umbrella birds. There are two species: *R. peruviana*, the Andean cock-of-the-rock, and *R. rupicola*, the Guyanan cock-of-the-rock. The male has brilliant orange plumage including the head crest, the female is a duller brown. Males display at a communal breeding area.

COCK-OF-THE-ROCK The Guyanan cock-of-the-rock lives in forested ravines in northern South America.

cockroach any of numerous insects of the family Blattidae, distantly related to mantises and grasshoppers. There are 3,500 species, mainly in the tropics. They have long antennae and biting mouthparts. They can fly, but rarely do so.

The common cockroach, or black-beetle *Blatta orientalis*, is found in human dwellings, is nocturnal, omnivorous, and contaminates food. The German cockroach *Blattella germanica* and American cockroach *Periplaneta americana* are pests in kitchens, bakeries, and warehouses. In Britain only two innocuous species are native, but several have been introduced with imported food and have become severe pests. They are very difficult to eradicate. Cockroaches have a very high resistance to radiation, making them the only creatures likely to survive a nuclear holocaust.

cocktail effect the effect of two toxic, or potentially toxic, chemicals when taken together rather than separately. Such effects are known to occur with some mixtures of drugs, with the active ingredient of one making the body more sensitive to the other.

This sometimes occurs because both drugs require the same ▷enzyme to break them down. Chemicals such as pesticides and food additives are only ever tested singly, not in combination with other chemicals that may be consumed at the same time, so no allowance is made for cocktail effects.

cocoa and chocolate (Aztec *xocolatl*) food products made from the cacao (or cocoa) bean, fruit of a tropical tree *Theobroma cacao*, now cultivated mainly in Africa. Chocolate as a drink was introduced to Europe from the New World by the Spanish in the 16th century; eating-chocolate was first produced in the late 18th century. Cocoa and chocolate are widely used in confectionery and drinks. More than 30 different pesticides are commonly used on cocoa crops, and traces of some have been detected in chocolate.

coconut fruit of the coconut palm, which grows throughout the lowland tropics. The fruit has a large outer husk of fibres, which is removed and used to make coconut matting and ropes. Inside this is the nut which is exported to temperate countries. Its hard shell contains white flesh and clear coconut milk, both of which are tasty and nourishing. (*Cocos nucifera*, family Arecaceae.)

> **Related Web site: Coconut**
> http://www.rbgkew.org.uk/
> ksheets/coconut.html

cocoon pupa-case of many insects, especially of ▷moths and ▷silkworms. This outer web or ball is spun from the mouth by caterpillars before they pass into the ▷chrysalis state.

Cocos Islands (or **Keeling Islands**) group of 27 small coral islands in the Indian Ocean, about 2,700 km/1,678 mi northwest of Perth, Australia; area 14 sq km/5.5 sq mi; population (1996) 655. An Australian external territory since 1955, the islanders voted to become part of Australia in 1984, and in 1992 they became subject to the laws of Western Australia. The main product is copra (dried kernels of coconut, used to make coconut oil), and the islands are a site for ecotourism.

Cocteau, Jean (1889–1963) French poet, dramatist, and film director. A leading figure in European modernism, he worked with the artist ▷Picasso, the choreographer ▷Diaghilev, and the composer ▷Stravinsky. He produced many volumes of poetry, ballets such as *Le Boeuf sur le toit/The Ox on the Roof* (1920), plays like *Orphée/Orpheus* (1926), and a mature novel of bourgeois French life, *Les Enfants Terribles* (1929), which he filmed in 1948.

cod any fish of the family Gadidae, especially the Atlantic cod, *Gadus morhua* found in the North Atlantic and Baltic. It is brown to grey with spots, with a white underbelly, and can grow to 1.5 m/5 ft in length.

The main cod fisheries are in the North Sea, and off the coasts of Iceland and Newfoundland, Canada. Much of the catch is salted and dried. Formerly one of the cheapest fish, decline in numbers from overfishing has made it one of the most expensive.

coda (Italian 'tail') in music, a concluding section of a movement added to emphasize the destination key.

codeine opium derivative that provides ▷analgesia in mild to moderate pain. It also suppresses the cough centre of the brain. It is an alkaloid, derived from morphine but less toxic and addictive.

codex (plural **codices**) book from before the invention of printing: in ancient times wax-coated wooden tablets; later, folded sheets of parchment were attached to the boards, then bound together. The name 'codex' was used for all large works, collections of history, philosophy, poetry, and during the Roman empire designated collections of laws. During the 2nd century AD codices began to replace the earlier rolls in the West. They were widely used by the medieval Christian church to keep records, from about 1200 onwards.

codon (also **coding triplet**) in genetics, a triplet of bases (see ▷base pair) in a molecule of DNA or RNA that directs the placement of a particular amino acid during the process of protein (polypeptide) synthesis. There are 64 codons in the ▷genetic code.

Cody, William Frederick (1846–1917) Called 'Buffalo Bill'. US scout and performer. From 1883 he toured the USA and Europe with a Wild West show which featured the recreation of Indian attacks and, for a time, the cast included Chief ▷Sitting Bull as well as Annie Oakley. His nickname derives from a time when he had a contract to supply buffalo carcasses to railway labourers (over 4,000 in 18 months).

coefficient the number part in front of an algebraic term, signifying multiplication. For example, in the expression $4x^2 + 2xy - x$, the coefficient of x^2 is 4 (because $4x^2$ means $4 \times x^2$), that of xy is 2, and that of x is -1 (because $-1 \times x = -x$).

In general algebraic expressions, coefficients are represented by letters that may stand for numbers; for example, in the equation $ax^2 + bx + c = 0$, a, b, and c are coefficients, which can take any number.

coefficient of relationship the probability that any two individuals share a given gene by virtue of being descended from a common ancestor. In sexual reproduction of diploid species, an individual shares half its genes with each parent, with its offspring, and (on average) with each sibling; but only a quarter (on average) with its grandchildren or its siblings' offspring; an eighth with its great-grandchildren, and so on.

COCONUT A coconut begins to germinate after washing up on a beach.

coelacanth large dark brown to blue-grey fish that lives in the deep waters (200 m/650 ft) of the western Indian Ocean around the Comoros Islands and also off Sulawesi, Indonesia. They can grow to about 2 m/6 ft in length, and weigh up to 73 kg/160 lb. They have bony, overlapping scales, and muscular lobe (limblike) fins sometimes used like oars when swimming and for balance while resting on the sea floor. They feed on other fish, and give birth to live young rather than shedding eggs as most fish do. Coelacanth fossils exist dating back over 400 million years and coelacanth were believed to be extinct until one was caught in 1938 off the coast of South Africa. For this reason they are sometimes referred to as 'living fossils'.

coelenterate any freshwater or marine organism of the phylum Coelenterata, having a body wall composed of two layers of cells. They also possess stinging cells. Examples are jellyfish, hydra, and coral.

coeliac disease disease in which the small intestine fails to digest and absorb food. The disease can appear at any age but has a peak incidence in the 30–50 age group; it is more common in women. It is caused by an intolerance to gluten (a constituent of wheat, rye and barley) and characterized by diarrhoea and malnutrition. Treatment is by a gluten-free diet.

coelom in all but the simplest animals, the fluid-filled cavity that separates the body wall from the gut and associated organs, and

COELACANTH The coelacanth is the sole survivor of an ancient group of fishes.

allows the gut muscles to contract independently of the rest of the body.

Coetzee, J(ohn) M(ichael) (1940–) South African novelist and critic. His novels include *Dusklands* (1974), *In the Heart of the Country* (1975), *Waiting for the Barbarians* (1980), *Foe* (1987), and *The Master of Petersburg* (1994). Uniquely, he has won the Booker Prize twice, in 1983 for *The Life and Times of Michael K*, which is set during a civil war in an unspecified country (obliquely South Africa), and in 1999 for *Disgrace*, an uncompromising story centring on a violent attack by black men on the white protagonist and his daughter, during which she is raped.

A professor at the University of Cape Town since 1971, Coetzee's nonfiction includes *Boyhood: A Memoir* (1998) and the critical work *White Writing* (1988). Coetzee was awarded the Nobel Prize for Literature in 2003.

coevolution evolution of those structures and behaviours within a species that can best be understood in relation to another species. For example, some insects and flowering plants have evolved together: insects have produced mouthparts suitable for collecting pollen or drinking nectar, and plants have developed chemicals and flowers that will attract insects to them. Parasites often evolve and speciate with their hosts.

coffee drink made from the roasted and ground beanlike seeds found inside the red berries of any of several species of shrubs, originally native to Ethiopia and now cultivated throughout the tropics. It contains a stimulant, ▷caffeine. (Genus *Coffea*, family Rubiaceae.)

COFFEE The coffee plant *Coffea arabica* is a small tree, but is pruned into a large bush to make harvesting easier. It produces sweet-smelling white flowers; these are followed by green berries which turn red when ripe. Each berry contains two seeds, which are processed to make coffee for drinking.

coffee house alternative to ale-houses as social meeting place, largely for the professional classes, popular in the 17th and 18th centuries. Christopher Bowman opened the first Coffee House in London (later known as the 'Pasqua Rosee') in St Michael's Alley, Cornhill, in 1652 and others soon followed in both London and

Oxford so that by 1708 London alone boasted 3,000 coffee houses. Their popularity stemmed from their reputations as centres for the dissemination of news and ideas, making them good places to meet others of a like mind and also to conduct business. For this reason, coffee houses were often associated with radical readings and an attempt was made to suppress them by royal proclamation in 1675 but the coffee houses were too popular and the attempt was abandoned within a matter of days. The coffee houses declined in popularity toward the 18th century as coffee itself was largely superseded by the new fashion for tea.

Cognac town in the Charente *département* of western France, on the River ▷Charente 40 km/25 mi west of Angoulême; population (1990) 30,000. Situated in a vine-growing district, Cognac has given its name to a brandy. Under French law the name may be applied only to brandy produced within a strictly limited area around the town. Bottles, corks, barrels, and crates are manufactured here. Francis I of France was born in its castle in 1494.

cognition in psychology, a general term covering the functions involved in synthesizing information – for example, perception (seeing, hearing, and so on), attention, memory, and reasoning.

cognitive therapy (or **cognitive behaviour therapy**) treatment for emotional disorders such as ▷depression and ▷anxiety states. It encourages the patient to challenge the distorted and unhelpful thinking that is characteristic of depression, for example. The treatment may include ▷behaviour therapy.

cohesion in physics, a phenomenon in which interaction between two surfaces of the same material in contact makes them cling together (with two different materials the similar phenomenon is called adhesion). According to kinetic theory, cohesion is caused by attraction between particles at the atomic or molecular level. ▷Surface tension, which causes liquids to form spherical droplets, is caused by cohesion.

coil in medicine, another name for an ▷intrauterine device.

coke clean, light fuel produced, along with town gas, when coal is strongly heated in an airtight oven. Coke contains 90% carbon and makes a useful domestic and industrial fuel (used, for example, in the iron and steel industries).

Coke, Edward (1552–1634) Lord Chief Justice of England 1613–17. He was a defender of common law against royal prerogative; against Charles I he drew up the ▷petition of right in 1628, which defines and protects Parliament's liberties.

cola (or **kola**) any of several tropical trees, especially *Cola acuminata*. In West Africa the nuts are chewed for their high ▷caffeine content, and in the West they are used to flavour soft drinks. (Genus *Cola*, family Sterculiaceae.)

Colbert, Jean-Baptiste (1619–1683) French politician, chief minister to Louis XIV, and controller-general (finance minister) from 1665. He reformed the Treasury, promoted French industry and commerce by protectionist measures, and tried to make France a naval power equal to England or the Netherlands, while favouring a peaceful foreign policy.

Colchester city and river port in Essex, eastern England, on the River Colne, 80 km/50 mi northeast of London; population (1991) 96,100. It is the market centre of an agricultural and shell-fishing area, roses and oysters being notable products. Industries include engineering, printing, and the manufacture of clothing. The oldest recorded town in England, Colchester was the capital of the kingdom of ▷Cymbeline, until his death in about AD 40. As

COFFEE HOUSE A contemporary picture of a coffee house from about 1700. *Philip Sauvain Picture Collection*

Camulodunum, it was the first capital of Roman Britain, and it was burned by ▷Boudicca in AD 60.

cold-blooded of animals, dependent on the surrounding temperature; see ▷poikilothermy.

cold, common minor disease of the upper respiratory tract, caused by a variety of viruses. Symptoms are headache, chill, nasal discharge, sore throat, and occasionally cough. Research indicates that the virulence of a cold depends on psychological factors and either a reduction or an increase of social or work activity, as a result of stress, in the previous six months.

There is little immediate hope of an effective cure since the viruses transform themselves so rapidly.

cold fusion in nuclear physics, the fusion of atomic nuclei at room temperature. If cold fusion were possible it would provide a limitless, cheap, and pollution-free source of energy, and it has therefore been the subject of research around the world. In 1989, Martin Fleischmann and Stanley Pons of the University of Utah, USA, claimed that they had achieved cold fusion in the laboratory, but their results could not be substantiated. The University of Utah announced in 1998 that they would allow the cold fusion patent to elapse, given that the work of Pons and Fleischmann has never been reproduced.

Colditz castle in eastern Germany, near Leipzig, used as a high-security prisoner-of-war camp (Oflag IVC) in World War II. Among daring escapes was that of British Captain Patrick Reid (1910–1990) and others in October 1942, whose story contributed much to its fame. It became a museum in 1989. A highly successful British TV drama series called *Colditz* (1972) was based on prisoners' experiences.

Cold War ideological, political, and economic tensions from 1945 to 1989 between the USSR and Eastern Europe on the one hand and the USA and Western Europe on the other. The Cold War was fuelled by propaganda, undercover activity by intelligence agencies, and economic sanctions; and was intensified by signs of conflict anywhere in the world. Arms-reduction agreements between the USA and USSR in the late 1980s, and a reduction of Soviet influence in Eastern Europe, led to a reassessment of positions, and the 'war' was officially ended in December 1989.

The term 'Cold War' was first used by Bernard Baruch, advisor to US President Truman, in a speech made in April 1947. He spoke about Truman's intent for the USA to 'support free peoples who are resisting attempted subjugation by armed minorities or by outside pressures' (see ▷Truman Doctrine).

Origins Mistrust between the USSR and the West dated from the Russian Revolution of 1917 and contributed to the disagreements which arose during and immediately after World War II over the future structure of Eastern Europe. The Atlantic Charter, signed in 1941 by the USA and the UK, favoured self-determination; whereas the USSR insisted on keeping the territory obtained as a result of the Hitler–Stalin pact of August 1939. After the war the USA was eager to have all of Europe open to Western economic interests, while the USSR, afraid of being encircled and attacked by its former allies, saw Eastern Europe as its own sphere of influence and, in the case of Germany, was looking to extract reparations. As the USSR increased its hold on the countries of Eastern Europe, the USA pursued a policy of 'containment' that involved offering material aid to Western Europe (the ▷Marshall Plan) and to Nazi-victimized countries such as Greece and Turkey; the USSR retaliated by setting up ▷Comecon to offer economic aid to countries within its sphere of influence. Berlin became the focal point of East–West tension (since it was zoned for military occupational governments of the USA, UK, France, and USSR, yet was situated within what was then Soviet-controlled East Germany). This culminated in the Soviet blockade of the US, British, and French zones of the city in 1948, which was relieved by a sustained airlift of supplies (see ▷Berlin blockade). In 1961 the East Berlin government began construction on the ▷Berlin Wall to prevent the flow of East German people to the West.

Increasing tensions The growing divisions between the ▷capitalist and ▷communist worlds were reinforced by the creation of military alliances: the ▷North Atlantic Treaty Organization (NATO) was set up in the West in 1949, and was followed in the East by the ▷Warsaw Pact in 1955. Tensions between the two blocs increased significantly at a number of points during the following two decades, and were prompted on the one hand by the USSR's military suppression of anticommunist revolutions – the East German revolt, 1953, the Hungarian uprising 1956 (see ▷Hungary, **the Hungarian national uprising**), and the

Ron Eccles
Director of the Common Cold Centre in Cardiff

I don't think the public appreciates the magnitude of the problem.

Admitting defeat after ten years attempting to find a cure for the 200-odd viruses that cause the complaint; *Daily Telegraph*, 10 November 1998

revolt known as the ▷Prague Spring in Czechoslovakia 1968); and on the other hand by US participation in the ▷Vietnam War (1964–75) and the ▷Cuban missile crisis of 1962, during which the two superpowers came closer than ever before to nuclear war. The crisis was initiated by the siting of Soviet rockets in ▷Cuba in October 1962, after which US President ▷Kennedy, by means of military threats and negotiation, forced the Soviet leader Nikita ▷Khrushchev to back down and dismantle the missiles. During the 1960s the ▷nonaligned movement appeared – a group of nations who adopted a position of strategic and political neutrality towards the USA, who was accused of pursuing a policy of US imperialism; and towards the USSR, who was seen to be promoting communist ideology through Soviet imperialism.

During the late 1970s and 1980s, tensions between the two blocs were exacerbated still further: first by the USSR's invasion of ▷Afghanistan in 1979 and the resultant war, which continued until 1987; and then by the aggressive foreign policy pursued between 1981 and 1989 by US President Ronald ▷Reagan. In 1980 and 1981, for example, the USA supported the newly formed ▷Solidarity trade-union movement in Poland, and in 1983, Reagan publicly referred to the USSR as an 'evil empire'. The major point of tension, however, arose with the increasing intensification of the arms race (see ▷nuclear warfare), which placed heavy demands upon the economies of both countries, and was given a quite new direction by Reagan's insistence on militarizing space through the ▷Strategic Defense Initiative, popularly known as Star Wars.

COLD WAR A view of the Checkpoint Charlie crossing point, West Berlin, Germany. Checkpoint Charlie was the link between East and West Berlin when the city was divided during the Cold War, and the spot where both sides exchanged captured spies. *Archive Photos*

coleoptile the protective sheath that surrounds the young shoot tip of a grass during its passage through the soil to the surface. Although of relatively simple structure, most coleoptiles are very sensitive to light, ensuring that seedlings grow upwards.

Coleridge, Samuel Taylor (1772–1834) English poet, critic, and philosopher. A friend of the poets Robert ▷Southey and William ▷Wordsworth, he collaborated with the latter on the highly influential collection *Lyrical Ballads* (1798), which expressed their theory of poetic sensation and was the spearhead of the English Romantic Movement. His poems include 'The Rime of the Ancient Mariner', 'Christabel', and 'Kubla Khan' (all written 1797–98); his critical works include *Biographia Literaria* (1817).

Coleridge was educated at Cambridge University where he became friends with Southey. In 1797 he moved to Nether Stowey, Somerset, and worked closely with Wordsworth on *Lyrical Ballads*, producing much of his finest poetry during this period. In 1798 he went to Germany where he studied philosophy and literary criticism. Returning to England, in 1800 he settled in the Lake District with Wordsworth and from 1808 to 1819 gave a series of lectures on prose and drama. Suffering from rheumatic pain, Coleridge became addicted to opium and from 1816 lived in Highgate, London, under medical care. Here he produced his major prose work *Biographia Literaria* (1817), a collection of autobiographical pieces in which he develops his philosophical and critical ideas.

A brilliant talker and lecturer, Coleridge was expected to produce some great work of philosophy or criticism. His *Biographia Literaria*, much of it based on German ideas, is full of insight but its formlessness and the limited extent of his poetic output represents a partial failure of promise.

SAMUEL COLERIDGE The English poet and critic Samuel Coleridge demonstrated that a good poem is complete in itself and cannot be paraphrased. His own writing was at first enhanced, but later ruined, by the opium that he took to relieve rheumatism. His poem 'Kubla Khan' – influenced by laudanum – was unfinished, interrupted, he said, by 'a person from Porlock'. *Archive Photos*

Colette, Sidonie-Gabrielle (1873–1954) French writer. Her best novels reveal an exquisite sensitivity, largely centred on the joys and sorrows of love, and include *Chéri* (1920), *La Fin de Chéri/ The End of Chéri* (1926), and *Gigi* (1944).

She wrote with realism, sharp observation, wit, and style, and had a sensuous awareness of nature, particularly animals, as remembered from her childhood in the countryside.

colic spasmodic attack of pain in the abdomen, usually coming in waves. Colicky pains are caused by the painful muscular contraction and subsequent distension of a hollow organ; for example, the bowels, gall bladder (biliary colic), or ureter (renal colic).

colitis inflammation of the colon (large intestine) with diarrhoea (often bloody). It is usually due to infection or some types of bacterial dysentery.

collage (French 'sticking', 'pasting', or 'paper-hanging') in art, the use of various materials, such as pieces of newspaper, fabric, and wallpaper, to create a picture or design by sticking them on canvas or another suitable surface, often in combination with painted or drawn features. The technique was used in scrapbooks in the 19th century and was first seriously adopted by artists in the early 20th century. Georges Braque and Pablo Picasso became the first major exponents in 1912, and it soon became a distinctive feature of ▷cubism. Subsequently it has featured prominently in several movements, particularly ▷Dada and ▷surrealism, in which the technique was extended to encompass an assortment of three-dimensional objects. Among Dadaists, the best-known exponent of collage was Kurt Schwitters, who made it his life's work, creating a personal variant he called Merz, using refuse such as used bus tickets and pieces of string. Among the surrealists, the most distinctive exponent was probably Max Ernst, who fitted together cuttings from banal 19th-century engravings to form incongruous images that he arranged in 'collage novels'. Among later artists, one of the most original exponents was the Italian Alberto Burri, whose work often features pieces of sacking.

> **Samuel Coleridge**
> 'God save thee, ancient Mariner! / From the fiends that plague thee thus! – / Why look'st thou so?' – With my cross-bow / I shot the Albatross.
> *The Ancient Mariner* pt 1

collagen protein that is the main constituent of ▷connective tissue. Collagen is present in skin, cartilage, tendons, and ligaments. Bones are made up of collagen, with the mineral calcium phosphate providing increased rigidity.

collective bargaining process whereby management, representing an employer, and a trade union, representing employees, agree to negotiate jointly terms and conditions of employment. Agreements can be company-based or industry-wide.

collective responsibility doctrine found in governments modelled on the British system of cabinet government. It is based on convention, or usage, rather than law, and requires that once a decision has been taken by the cabinet, all members of the government are bound by it and must support it or resign their posts.

collective security system for achieving international stability by an agreement among all states to unite against any aggressor. Such a commitment was embodied in the post-World War I ▷League of Nations and also in the ▷United Nations (UN), although the League was not able to live up to the ideals of its founders, nor has the UN been able to do so.

collective unconscious in psychology, a shared pool of memories, ideas, modes of thought, and so on, which, according to the Swiss psychiatrist Carl Jung, comes from the life experience of one's ancestors, indeed from the entire human race. It coexists with the personal ▷unconscious, which contains the material of individual experience, and may be regarded as an immense depository of ancient wisdom.

collectivism in politics, a position in which the collective (such as the state) has priority over its individual members. It is the opposite of ▷individualism, which is itself a variant of anarchy.

College of Arms (or Heralds' College) English heraldic body formed in 1484. There are three kings-of-arms, six heralds, and four pursuivants, who specialize in genealogical and heraldic work. The college establishes the right to a coat of arms, and the kings-of-arms grant arms by letters patent. The office of king-of-arms for Ulster was transferred to the College of Arms in London in 1943.

college of higher education in the UK, a college in which a large proportion of the work undertaken is at degree level or above. Colleges of higher education are centrally funded by the Universities and Colleges Funding Council, and some of the largest became universities in 1992 at the same time as the former polytechnics.

collenchyma plant tissue composed of relatively elongated cells with thickened cell walls, in particular at the corners where adjacent cells meet. It is a supporting and strengthening tissue found in nonwoody plants, mainly in the stems and leaves.

collie any of several breeds of sheepdog originally bred in Britain. They include the border collie, the bearded collie, and the rough collie and its smooth-haired counterpart.

Collier, Lesley Faye (1947–) English ballerina. She became a principal dancer of the Royal Ballet in 1972. She created roles in Kenneth MacMillan's *Anastasia* (1971) and *Four Seasons* (1975), Hans van Manen's *Four Schumann Pieces* (1975), Frederick Ashton's *Rhapsody* (1980), and Glen Tetley's *Dance of Albiar* (1980).

Collins, Joan (Henrietta) (1933–) English film and television actor. Her role as Alexis Carrington in the TV series *Dynasty* (1981–89) brought her international fame.

JOAN COLLINS English actor Joan Collins boards the cruise-liner *Royal Princess* in December 1984 to attend a party held by the producers of the television series *The Love Boat*. *Image Bank*

Collins, Michael (1890–1922) Irish nationalist. He was a ▷Sinn Fein leader, a founder and director of intelligence of the ▷Irish Republican Army (IRA) in 1919, a minister in the provisional government of the Irish Free State in 1922 (see ▷Ireland, Republic of), commander of the Free State forces in the civil war, and for ten days head of state before being killed by Irish republicans.

Born in County Cork, Collins joined the Irish Republican Brotherhood while working in London, and in 1916 returned to Ireland to fight in the ▷Easter Rising. Following his release from prison in December 1916, he became a leading republican organizer and in 1918 was elected Sinn Fein member to the Dáil (Irish parliament). Appointed minister of home affairs and then minister for finance, he continued to maintain a dominant position in the Irish Volunteers (later the IRA) as a director of organization and intelligence. During the Anglo-Irish War (1919–21) he was noted for his skilful infiltration of the British intelligence system in Ireland and ruthless assassination of its operatives. In 1921 Collins helped vice-president Arthur Griffith to negotiate the Anglo-Irish Treaty, and encouraged the support of key IRA figures. He became chairman of the pro-treaty provisional government and, during the ensuing civil war, commander-in-chief of the national army which crushed the opposition in Dublin and the large towns within a few months. When Griffith died on 12 August 1922, Collins became head of state but was ambushed and killed near Cork on 22 August.

Related Web site: Collins, Michael http://www2.cruzio.com/~sbarrett/mcollins.htm

Collins, (William) Wilkie (1824–1889) English author of mystery and suspense novels. He wrote *The Woman in White* (1860) (with its fat villain Count Fosco), often called the first English detective novel, and *The Moonstone* (1868) (with Sergeant Cuff, one of the first detectives in English literature).

Related Web site: Wilkie Collins Appreciation Page http://www.rightword.com.au/writers/wilkie

collision theory theory that explains how chemical reactions take place and why rates of reaction alter. For a reaction to occur the reactant particles must collide. Only a certain fraction of the total collisions cause chemical change; these are called **successful collisions**. The successful collisions have sufficient energy (activation energy) at the moment of impact to break the existing bonds and form new bonds, resulting in the products of the reaction. Increasing the concentration of the reactants and raising the temperature brings about more collisions and therefore more successful collisions, increasing the rate of reaction.

colloid substance composed of extremely small particles of one material (the dispersed phase) evenly and stably distributed in another material (the continuous phase). The size of the dispersed particles (1–1,000 nanometres across) is less than that of particles in suspension but greater than that of molecules in true solution. Colloids involving gases include **aerosols** (dispersions of liquid or solid particles in a gas, as in fog or smoke) and **foams** (dispersions of gases in liquids).

Those involving liquids include **emulsions** (in which both the dispersed and the continuous phases are liquids) and **sols** (solid particles dispersed in a liquid). Sols in which both phases contribute to a molecular three-dimensional network have a jellylike form and are known as **gels**; gelatin, starch 'solution', and silica gel are common examples.

Milk is a natural emulsion of liquid fat in a watery liquid; synthetic emulsions such as some paints and cosmetic lotions have chemical emulsifying agents to stabilize the colloid and stop the two phases from separating out. Colloids were first studied thoroughly by the British chemist Thomas Graham, who defined them as substances that will not diffuse through a semipermeable membrane (as opposed to what he termed crystalloids, solutions of inorganic salts, which will diffuse through).

colobus (or **guereza**) large tree-dwelling African monkey characterized by the almost complete suppression of the thumb. There are five species divided into two groups: the black-and-white colobus and the red colobus. They live in groups and feed on fruit, leaves, flowers, and twigs. A further species, Miss Waldron's red colobus, *Procolobus badius waldroni*, was officially declared extinct in autumn 2000.

Cologne (German **Köln**) industrial and commercial port in North Rhine-Westphalia, Germany, on the left bank of the Rhine, 35 km/22 mi northwest of Düsseldorf; population (1995) 964,200. Cologne is an important transhipment centre, and a major industrial centre for the manufacture of cars (Ford), machinery, electrical goods, chemicals, clothing, and food; other industries include environmental and chemical engineering, and waste management.

Colombia see country box.

Colón chief port and second-largest city of Panama, built on Manzanillo Island at the Caribbean entrance of the Panama Canal, 80 km/50 mi southeast of Panamá, capital city of Colón province; population (1995 est) 158,900. It is a major commercial centre and has an oil refining industry. It is second only to Hong Kong among the major free ports of the world. The free trade zone, created in 1948, has a pivotal role in bolstering the Panamanian economy.

colon in anatomy, the main part of the large intestine, between the caecum and rectum. Water and mineral salts are absorbed from undigested food in the colon, and the residue passes as faeces towards the rectum.

colonialism another name for ▷imperialism.

colonization in ecology, the spread of species into a new habitat, such as a freshly cleared field, a new motorway verge, or a recently flooded valley. The first species to move in are called **pioneers**, and may establish conditions that allow other animals and plants to move in (for example, by improving the condition of the soil or by providing shade). Over time a range of species arrives and the habitat matures; early colonizers will probably be replaced, so that the variety of animal and plant life present changes. This is known as ▷succession.

colophon decorative device on the title page or spine of a book, the trademark of the individual publisher. Originally a colophon was an inscription on the last page of a book giving the writer or printer's name and the place and year of publication.

Colorado river in southwestern USA and northwestern Mexico, rising in the Rocky Mountains and flowing 2,333 km/1,447 mi to the Gulf of California through Colorado, Utah, Arizona (including the Grand Canyon), and extending into northern Mexico. The many dams along its course, including Hoover Dam and Glen Canyon Dam, provide hydroelectric power and irrigation water, but have destroyed wildlife and scenery; they have also created a series of lakes including Lake Powell, Lake Mead, and Lake Havasu.

To the west of the river in southeastern California is the **Colorado Desert**, an arid area of some 5,000 sq km/1,931 sq mi.

Colorado state of the western central USA. It is nicknamed the Centennial State. Colorado was admitted to the Union in 1876 as the 38th US state. Its expansion from World War II onwards has been closely associated with the US's military-industrial surge, with the state serving as the home of numerous military facilities and weapons plants. Colorado is bordered to the east by Kansas and Nebraska, to the north by Nebraska and Wyoming, and to the west by Utah. To the southwest, at the 'Four Corners', it meets Utah, Arizona, and New Mexico. New Mexico extends east along its southern border, which in the southeast also adjoins part of the Oklahoma panhandle.

population (1996 est) 3,823,000   **area** 269,700 sq km/104,104 sq mi   **capital** Denver   **towns and cities** Colorado Springs, Aurora, Lakewood, Fort Collins, Greeley, Pueblo, Boulder, Arvada   **industries and products** cereals, meat and dairy products, oil, coal, molybdenum, uranium, iron, steel, scientific instruments, machinery

COLORADO Beef cattle are the main agricultural product of the state of Colorado, USA, and cowboys still work there, rounding up herds of cattle, and using a lasso as in this picture. *Image Bank*

Colorado beetle (or **potato beetle**) North American black and yellow striped beetle that is a pest on potato crops. Although it was once a serious pest, it can now usually be controlled by using insecticides. It has also colonized many European countries. *Classification* Colarado beetles *Leptinotarsa decemlineata* are in the family Chrysomelidae, order Coleoptera, class Insecta, phylum Arthropoda.

coloratura in music, a rapid ornamental vocal passage with runs and trills. A **coloratura soprano** is a light, high voice suited to such music.

Colosseum amphitheatre in ancient Rome, begun by the emperor Vespasian to replace the one destroyed by fire during the reign of Nero, and completed by his son Titus in AD 80. It was 187 m/615 ft long and 49 m/160 ft high, and seated 50,000 people. Christians were martyred there by lions and gladiators. It could be flooded for mock sea battles. See picture on p. 217.

Colossus of Rhodes bronze statue of Apollo erected at the entrance to the harbour at Rhodes between 292 BC and 280 BC. Said to have been about 30 m/100 ft high, it was counted as one of

a fruitful collision

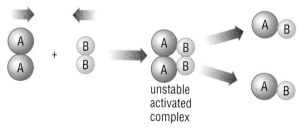

unstable activated complex

an unfruitful collision

COLLISION THEORY Collision theory explains how chemical reactions occur and why rates of reaction differ. For a reaction to occur, particles must collide. If the collision causes a chemical change it is referred to as a fruitful collision.

Colombia

Colombia country in South America, bounded north by the Caribbean Sea, west by the Pacific Ocean, northwestern corner by Panama, east and northeast by Venezuela, southeast by Brazil, and southwest by Peru and Ecuador.

NATIONAL NAME *República de Colombia/Republic of Colombia*
AREA 1,141,748 sq km/440,828 sq mi
CAPITAL Bogotá
MAJOR TOWNS/CITIES Medellín, Cali, Barranquilla, Cartagena, Bucaramanga, Cúcuta, Ibagué
MAJOR PORTS Barranquilla, Cartagena, Buenaventura
PHYSICAL FEATURES the Andes mountains run north–south; flat coastland in west and plains (llanos) in east; Magdalena River runs north to Caribbean Sea; includes islands of Providencia, San Andrés, and Mapelo; almost half the country is forested

Government

HEAD OF STATE AND GOVERNMENT Alvaro Uribe Vélez from 2002
POLITICAL SYSTEM liberal democracy
POLITICAL EXECUTIVE limited presidency
ADMINISTRATIVE DIVISIONS 32 departments and one capital district
ARMED FORCES 158,000; plus paramilitary

COLOMBIA In Colombia few people are of unmixed descent. Indians, such as these Bora, make up a very small part of the population. *Corel*

Economy and resources

CURRENCY Colombian peso
GPD (US$) 82.2 billion (2002 est)
REAL GDP GROWTH (% change on previous year) 1.4 (2001)
GNI (US$) 80.1 billion (2002 est)
GNI PER CAPITA (PPP) (US$) 5,870 (2002 est)
CONSUMER PRICE INFLATION 5.6% (2003 est)
UNEMPLOYMENT 18.2% (2001)
FOREIGN DEBT (US$) 29.7 billion (2001 est)
MAJOR TRADING PARTNERS USA, Venezuela, Germany, Japan, Ecuador, Brazil
RESOURCES petroleum, natural gas, coal, nickel, iron, emeralds (accounts for 95% of world production), gold, manganese, copper, lead, mercury, silver, platinum, limestone, phosphates
INDUSTRIES food processing, chemical products, textiles, steel, petrochemicals, plastics, beverages, transport equipment, cement
EXPORTS petroleum and petroleum products, coal, coffee, gold, bananas, cut flowers, market: USA 42.8% (2001). Illegal trade in cocaine; Colombia is one of the world's main producers of coca, the raw material for cocaine; it is estimated that drug money accounted for about 2% of GDP in 2000; still the main source of illegal cocaine in the USA
IMPORTS machinery and transport equipment, chemicals, minerals, food, metals. Principal source: USA 32.4% (2001)
ARABLE LAND 2% (1998)
AGRICULTURAL PRODUCTS coffee (world's second-largest producer), cocoa, sugar cane, bananas, tobacco, cotton, cut flowers, rice, potatoes, maize; timber; beef production

Population and society

POPULATION 44,222,000 (2003 est)
POPULATION GROWTH RATE 1.3% (2000–15)
POPULATION DENSITY (per sq km) 39 (2003 est)
URBAN POPULATION (% of total) 77 (2003 est)
AGE DISTRIBUTION (% of total population) 0–14 32%, 15–59 61%, 60+ 7% (2002 est)
ETHNIC GROUPS 58% mestizo (mixed Spanish and American Indian descent), 20% European, 14% mulatto, 4% black, 3% black American Indian, 1% American Indian
LANGUAGE Spanish (official) (95%)
RELIGION Roman Catholic
EDUCATION (compulsory years) 5
LITERACY RATE 92% (men); 92% (women) (2003 est)
LABOUR FORCE 1.1% agriculture, 24.1% industry, 74.8% services (1999)
LIFE EXPECTANCY 69 (men); 75 (women) (2000–05)
CHILD MORTALITY RATE (under 5, per 1,000 live births) 23 (2001)
PHYSICIANS (per 1,000 people) 1.2 (1999 est)
HOSPITAL BEDS (per 1,000 people) 1.5 (1999 est)
TV SETS (per 1,000 people) 286 (2001)
RADIOS (per 1,000 people) 549 (2001)
INTERNET USERS (per 10,000 people) 457.8 (2002 est)
PERSONAL COMPUTER USERS (per 100 people) 4.9 (2002 est)

See also ▷Bolívar, Simón; ▷Inca.

See also ▷Bolívar, Simón; ▷Inca.

Chronology

late 15th century: Southern Colombia became part of Inca Empire, whose core lay in Peru.

1522: Spanish conquistador Pascual de Andagoya reached the San Juan River.

1536–38: Spanish conquest by Jimenez de Quesada overcame powerful Chibcha Indian chiefdom, which had its capital in the uplands at Bogotá and was renowned for its gold crafts; became part of Spanish Viceroyalty of Peru, which covered much of South America.

1717: Bogotá became capital of the new Spanish Viceroyalty of Nueva (New) Granada, which also ruled Ecuador and Venezuela.

1809: Struggle for independence from Spain began.

1819: Venezuelan freedom fighter Simón Bolívar, 'the Liberator', who had withdrawn to Colombia in 1814, raised a force of 5,000 British mercenaries and defeated the Spanish at the battle of Boyacá, establishing Colombia's independence; Gran Colombia formed, also comprising Ecuador, Panama, and Venezuela.

1830: Became a separate state, which included Panama, on the dissolution of the Republic of Gran Colombia.

1863: Became major coffee exporter. Federalizing, anti-clerical Liberals came to power, with the country divided into nine largely autonomous 'sovereign' states; the church was disestablished.

1885: Conservatives came to power, beginning 45 years of political dominance; power was recentralized and the church restored to influence.

1899–1903: Civil war between Liberals and Conservatives, ending with Panama's separation as an independent state.

1930: Liberals returned to power at the time of the economic depression; social legislation introduced and a labour movement encouraged.

1946: Conservatives returned to power.

1948: The left-wing mayor of Bogotá was assassinated to a widespread outcry.

1949–57: Civil war, 'La Violencia', during which over 250,000 people died.

1957: Hoping to halt violence, Conservatives and Liberals agreed to form National Front, sharing the presidency.

1970: National Popular Alliance (ANAPO) formed as left-wing opposition to National Front.

1974: National Front accord temporarily ended.

1975: Civil unrest due to disillusionment with government.

1978: Liberals, under Julio Turbay, revived the accord and began an intensive fight against drug dealers.

1982: The Liberals maintained their control of congress but lost the presidency. Conservative president Belisario Betancur granted guerrillas an amnesty and freed political prisoners.

1984: The minister of justice was assassinated by drug dealers; the campaign against them was stepped up.

1989: A drug cartel assassinated the leading presidential candidate and an antidrug war was declared by the president; a bombing campaign by drug traffickers killed hundreds; the police killed José Rodriguez Gacha, one of the most wanted cartel leaders.

1991: A new constitution prohibited the extradition of Colombians wanted for trial in other countries. Several leading drug traffickers were arrested. Many guerrillas abandoned the armed struggle, but the Colombian Revolutionary Armed Forces (FARC) and the National Liberation Army remained active.

1993: Medellín drug-cartel leader Pablo Escobar was shot while attempting to avoid arrest.

1995: President Samper came under pressure to resign over corruption allegations; a state of emergency was declared. Leaders of the Cali drug cartel were imprisoned.

1998: There were clashes between the army and left-wing guerrillas. The conservative Andres Pastrana won presidential elections. Peace talks were held with rebels.

1999: Formal peace talks began between the government and the leading rebel group.

2000: US president Clinton announced $1.3 billion in aid for Colombia, most of which was to go to the armed forces. With his government only receiving 20% public support, President Pastrana appointed a member of the opposition Liberal Party as finance minister.

2001: A deal was signed by Pastrana and Manuel Marulanda, the FARC leader, paving the way for a ceasefire.

2002: An upsurge of violence by the FARC guerrilla group brought to an end three years of peace talks with the Colombian government.

COLOSSEUM An aerial view of the ancient Roman amphitheatre, the Colosseum, in Rome, Italy. *Image Bank*

the ▷Seven Wonders of the World, but in 224 BC fell as a result of an earthquake.

colour in art, the quality or ▷wavelength of light emitted or reflected from an object. Colours may be produced by the use of pigment (paint or dye), by the choice of naturally coloured objects, or (in installation art) by the use of lights or television screens.

colour in physics, quality or wavelength of light emitted or reflected from an object. Visible white light consists of electromagnetic radiation of various wavelengths, and if a beam is refracted through a prism, it can be spread out into a spectrum, in which the various colours correspond to different wavelengths. From long to short wavelengths (from about 700 to 400 nano-metres) the colours are red, orange, yellow, green, blue, indigo, and violet.

The light entering our eyes is either emitted by hot or luminous objects or reflected from the objects we see.

Emitted light Sources of light have a characteristic ▷spectrum or range of wavelengths. Hot solid objects emit light with a broad range of wavelengths, the maximum intensity being at a wavelength which depends on the temperature. The hotter the object, the shorter the wavelengths emitted, as described by ▷Wien's displacement law. Low-pressure gases, such as the vapour of sodium street lights, can emit light at discrete wavelengths. The pattern of wavelengths emitted is unique to each gas and can be used to identify the gas (see ▷spectroscopy).

Reflected light When an object is illuminated by white light, some of the wavelengths are absorbed and some are reflected to the eye of an observer. The object appears coloured because of the mixture of wavelengths in the reflected light. For instance, a red object absorbs all wavelengths falling on it except those in the red end of the spectrum. This process of subtraction also explains why certain mixtures of paints produce different colours. Blue and yellow paints when mixed together produce green because between them the yellow and blue pigments absorb all wavelengths except those around green. A suitable combination of three pigments – cyan (blue-green), magenta (blue-red), and yellow – can produce any colour when mixed. This fact is used in colour printing, although additional black pigment is also added. Cyan, magenta, and yellow are called the subtractive primary colours.

Primary colours In the light-sensitive lining of our eyeball (the ▷retina), cells called cones are responsible for colour vision. There are three kinds of cones. Each type is sensitive to one colour only, either red, green, or blue. The brain combines the signals sent from the set of cones to produce a sensation of colour. When all cones are stimulated equally the sensation is of white light. The three colours to which the cones respond are called the **additive primary colours**. By mixing lights of these three colours, it is possible to produce any colour. This process is called colour mixing by addition, and is used

to produce the colour on a television screen, the inside of which is coated with glowing phosphor dots of red, green, and blue.

Complementary colours Pairs of colours that produce white light, such as yellow and blue, are called complementary colours.

Classifying colours Many schemes have been proposed for classifying colours. The most widely used is the Munsell scheme, which classifies colours according to their hue (dominant wavelength), saturation (the degree of whiteness), and lightness (intensity).

Related Web site: Colour Matters http://www.colormatters.com/entercolormatters.html

colour blindness hereditary defect of vision that reduces the ability to discriminate certain colours, usually red and green. The condition is sex-linked, affecting men more than women.

In the most common types of colour blindness there is confusion among the red–yellow–green range of colours; for example, many colour-blind observers are unable to distinguish red from yellow or yellow from green. The physiological cause of congenital colour blindness is not known, although it probably arises from some defect in the retinal receptors. Lead poisoning and toxic conditions caused by excessive smoking can lead to colour blindness. Between 2% and 6% of men and less than 1% of women are colour-blind.

Coltrane, John William (1926–1967) US jazz saxophonist. He first came to prominence in 1955 with the Miles ▷Davis quintet, later playing with Thelonious Monk in 1957. He was a powerful and individual artist, whose performances featured much experimentation. His 1960s quartet was highly regarded for its innovations in melody and harmony.

Like Charlie Parker, Coltrane marked a watershed in jazz and has been deified by his fans. The free-jazz movement of the 1960s owed much to his extended exploratory solos, for example on 'Giant Steps' (1959), the year he traded tenor saxophone for soprano. A highly original musician, he has been much imitated, but the deeply emotional tone of his playing, for example on 'A Love Supreme' (1964), is impossible to copy.

coltsfoot perennial plant belonging to the daisy family. The single yellow flower heads have many narrow rays (not petals), and the stems have large purplish scales. The large leaf, up to 22 cm/9 in across, is shaped like a horse's foot and gives the plant its name. Coltsfoot grows in Europe, northern Asia, and North Africa, often on bare ground and in waste places, and has been introduced to North America. It was formerly used in medicine. (*Tussilago farfara*, family Compositae.)

colugo (or flying lemur) Southeast Asian climbing mammal of the genus *Cynocephalus*, order Dermoptera, about 60 cm/2 ft long including the tail. It glides between forest trees using a flap of skin that extends from head to forelimb to hindlimb to tail. It may glide 130 m/425 ft or more, losing little height. It feeds largely on buds and leaves, and rests hanging upside down under branches.

Columba, St (521–597) (Latin form of *Colum-cille*, 'Colum of the cell') Irish Christian abbot, missionary to Scotland. He was born in County Donegal of royal descent, and founded monasteries and churches in Ireland. In 563 he sailed with 12 companions to Iona, and built a monastery there that was to play a leading part in the conversion of Britain. Feast day 9 June.

From his base on Iona St Columba made missionary journeys to the mainland. Legend has it that he drove a monster from the River Ness, and he crowned Aidan, an Irish king of Argyll.

COLTSFOOT The coltsfoot, a common roadside plant. *Premaphotos Wildlife*

Columbia river in western North America; length over 2,005 km/1,245 mi. It rises in Columbia Lake on the western slope of the Rocky Mountains in British Columbia, Canada, 130 km/81 mi north of the USA border. It flows through Washington State along the northern border of Oregon, until it reaches the Pacific below Astoria; its estuary is about 55 km/34 mi long and from 5–11 km/3–7 mi wide, and its mouth is the only deep-water harbour between San Francisco and Cape Flattery.

Columbia, District of federal district of the USA, see ▷District of Columbia and ▷Washington, DC.

columbine any of a group of plants belonging to the buttercup family. All are perennial herbs with divided leaves and hanging flower heads with spurred petals. (Genus *Aquilegia*, family Ranunculaceae.)

Related Web site: Columbine http://www.botanical.com/botanical/mgmh/c/columb89.html

COLUMBINE Alpine columbine *Aquilegia alpina*, in flower in the French Alps. *Premaphotos Wildlife*

columbium symbol Cb, former name for the chemical element ▷niobium. The name is still used occasionally in metallurgy.

Columbus city and port in west-central Georgia, USA, 175 km/109 mi south of Atlanta, across the Chattahoochee River from Phenix City, Alabama; seat of Muscogee County; population (1994 est) 186,000. Columbus is one of the largest textile centres in the South, and its industries are powered by hydroelectric plants situated on the Chattahoochee River; other industries include processed food, machinery, iron and steel, and peanuts. It is a distribution centre for surrounding farmlands, and lies just north of Fort Benning, the US Army infantry base.

Columbus capital of ▷Ohio, USA, on the Scioto and Olentangy rivers; seat of Franklin County; population (1994 est) 636,000; metropolitan area (1992) 1,394,000. There are coalfields and natural gas resources nearby, and local industries include the manufacture of cars, aircraft, space equipment, missiles, and electrical goods; it is also a centre for government, banking and insurance. Columbus was founded in 1812, became the state capital in 1816, and was incorporated as a city in 1834.

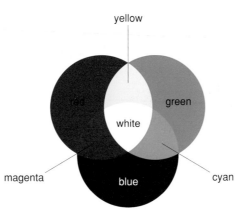

COLOUR The mixing of the primary (red, blue, and green) coloured beams of light. All the colours mixed together produce white.

Features here include the COSI (Center of Science and Industry); Rickenbacker Air Force Base; Batelle Memorial Institute (1929) for research in the metallurgy and mineral industries; Ohio State House (1861); and Columbus Symphony Orchestra.

Columbus, Christopher (1451–1506) Spanish **Cristóbal Colón**. Italian navigator and explorer who made four voyages to the New World: in 1492 to San Salvador Island, Cuba, and Haiti; from 1493 to 1496 to Guadaloupe, Montserrat, Antigua, Puerto Rico, and Jamaica; in 1498 to Trinidad and the mainland of South America; from 1502 to 1504 to Honduras and Nicaragua.

Believing that Asia could be reached by sailing westwards, he eventually won the support of King Ferdinand and Queen Isabella of Spain and set off on his first voyage from Palos on 3 August 1492 with three small ships, the *Niña*, the *Pinta*, and his flagship the *Santa Maria*. Land was sighted on 12 October, probably Watling Island (now San Salvador Island), and within a few weeks he reached Cuba and Haiti, returning to Spain in March 1493.

Born in Genoa, Columbus went to sea at an early age, and settled in Portugal in 1478. After his third voyage in 1498, he became involved in quarrels among the colonists sent to Haiti, and in 1500 the governor sent him back to Spain in chains. Released and compensated by the king, he made his last voyage 1502–04, during which he hoped to find a strait leading to India. He died in poverty in Valladolid and is buried in Seville Cathedral. In 1968 the site of the wreck of the *Santa Maria*, sunk off Hispaniola on 25 December 1492, was located.

> **Related Web site: Columbus Navigation Page** http://www1.minn.net/ ~keithp/index.htm

CHRISTOPHER COLUMBUS In this fresco, Italian explorer Christopher Columbus, centre, is seen preparing for his departure from Palos, Spain, in 1492, on his first voyage to the New World. *The Art Archive/Fondation Thiers Paris/Dagli Orti*

column in architecture, a structure, round or polygonal in plan, erected vertically as a support for some part of a building. Cretan paintings reveal the existence of wooden columns in Aegean architecture in about 1500 BC. The Hittites, Assyrians, and Egyptians also used wooden columns, and they are a feature of the monumental architecture of China and Japan. In classical architecture there are five principal types of column; see ▷order.

combe (or **coombe**) steep-sided valley found on the scarp slope of a chalk ▷escarpment. The inclusion of 'combe' in a placename usually indicates that the underlying rock is chalk.

Combination Acts laws passed in Britain in 1799 and 1800 making trade unionism illegal. They were introduced after the French Revolution for fear that the ▷trade unions would become centres of political agitation. The unions continued to exist, but claimed to be friendly societies or went underground, until the acts were repealed in 1824, largely owing to the radical Francis Place.

combustion burning, defined in chemical terms as the rapid combination of a substance with oxygen, accompanied by the evolution of heat and usually light. A slow-burning candle flame and the explosion of a mixture of petrol vapour and air are extreme examples of combustion. Combustion is an exothermic reaction as heat energy is given out.

Comecon (acronym for Council for Mutual Economic Assistance, or CMEA) economic organization from 1949 to 1991, linking the USSR with Bulgaria, Czechoslovakia, Hungary, Poland, Romania, East Germany (1950–90), Mongolia (from 1962), Cuba (from 1972), and Vietnam (from 1978), with Yugoslavia as an associated member. Albania also belonged between 1949 and 1961. Its establishment was prompted by the ▷Marshall Plan. Comecon was formally disbanded in June 1991.

Comédie Française French national theatre (for both comedy and tragedy) in Paris, founded in 1680 by Louis XIV. Its base is the Salle Richelieu on the right bank of the River Seine, and the Théâtre de l'Odéon, on the left bank, is a testing ground for avant-garde ideas.

comedy drama that aims to make its audience laugh, usually with a happy or amusing ending, as opposed to ▷tragedy. The comic tradition has undergone many changes since its Greek roots; the earliest comedy developed in ancient Greece, in the topical and fantastic satires of Aristophanes. Great comic dramatists include William Shakespeare, Molière, Carlo Goldoni, Pierre de Marivaux, George Bernard Shaw, and Oscar Wilde. Genres of comedy include pantomime, satire, farce, black comedy, and ▷commedia dell'arte.

comet small, icy body orbiting the Sun, usually on a highly elliptical path. A comet consists of a central nucleus a few kilometres across, and has been likened to a dirty snowball because it consists mostly of ice mixed with dust. As a comet approaches the Sun its nucleus heats up, releasing gas and dust which form a tenuous coma, up to 100,000 km/60,000 mi wide, around the nucleus. Gas and dust stream away from the coma to form one or more tails, which may extend for millions of kilometres.

Comets are of many different types, characterized by their orbits, their composition (the ratio of ice to dust, and the amount of frozen volatiles other than water ice, such as methane and carbon monoxide), and their size. Most comets approach the Sun on a hyperbolic orbit and are seen only once; others (the periodic comets) return regularly in elliptical orbits. Famous examples of the periodic comets are ▷Halley's comet, which has a period of 76 years and is one of the largest comets known, with a nucleus about $15 \times 7 \times 7$ km/$9 \times 4 \times 4$ mi across, and comet Encke, which has one of the shortest periods at only 3.3 years. Current thinking is that the nonperiodic comets, and those with very long periods, mostly originate in the ▷Oort cloud, which lies far beyond the orbit of Pluto and which may contain billions of protocomets, only a few of which are gravitationally perturbed into the inner Solar System each decade.

The orbits of the periodic comets suggest a different source, and this is the Kuiper belt, a zone just beyond the orbit of Neptune. This, too, contains a huge number of bodies, most of them too small to be detected by current techniques, although the count is rising steadily. A dozen or more comets are discovered every year, some by amateur astronomers.

Comet Hale-Bopp (C/1995 01) large and exceptionally active ▷comet, which in March 1997 made its closest flyby to Earth since 2000 BC, coming within 190 million km/118 million mi. It has a nucleus of approximately 40 km/25 mi and an extensive gas coma (when close to the Sun Hale-Bopp released 10 tonnes of gas every second). Unusually, Hale-Bopp has three tails: one consisting of dust particles, one of charged particles, and a third of sodium particles.

Comet Hale-Bopp was discovered independently in July 1995 by two amateur US astronomers, Alan Hale and Thomas Bopp.

> **Related Web site: Comet Hale-Bopp Home Page** http://www.jpl. nasa.gov/comet/

comfrey any of a group of plants belonging to the borage family, with rough, hairy leaves and small bell-shaped flowers (blue, purple-pink, or white). They are found in Europe and western Asia. (Genus *Symphytum*, family Boraginaceae.)

> **Related Web site: Comfrey** http://www.botanical.com/botanical/ mgmh/c/comfre92.html

comic book publication in strip-cartoon form. Comic books are usually aimed at children, although in Japan, Latin America, and Europe millions of adults read them. Artistically sophisticated adult comics and **graphic novels** are produced in the USA and several European countries, notably France. Comic books developed from comic strips in newspapers or, like those of Walt ▷Disney, as spin-offs from animated cartoon films.

comic strip (or **strip cartoon**) sequence of several frames of drawings in ▷cartoon style. Strips, which may work independently or form instalments of a serial, are usually humorous or satirical in content. Longer stories in comic-strip form are published separately as ▷comic books. Some have been made into animated films.

COMFREY Common comfrey prefers damp habitats, especially the banks of rivers and streams. Found across Europe, its range extends eastwards as far as Turkey and Siberia. *Premaphotos Wildlife*

Comintern acronym for Communist ▷International.

command economy (or **planned economy**) economy where resources are allocated to factories by the state through central planning. This system is unresponsive to the needs and whims of consumers and to sudden changes in conditions (for example, crop failure or fluctuations in the world price of raw materials).

command language in computing, a set of commands and the rules governing their use, by which users control a program. For example, an ▷operating system may have commands such as SAVE and DELETE, or a payroll program may have commands for adding and amending staff records.

commando member of a specially trained, highly mobile military unit. The term originated in South Africa in the 19th century, where it referred to Boer military reprisal raids against Africans and, in the South African Wars, against the British. Commando units have often carried out operations behind enemy lines.

Comme des Garçons (1942–) Trade name of Rei Kawakubo. Japanese fashion designer. Her asymmetrical, seemingly shapeless designs combine Eastern and Western ideas of clothing. They are often sombre in colour and sometimes torn and crumpled. She became a freelance designer in 1966, after working in a Japanese textile company, and formed Comme des Garçons in 1969. In the early 1980s her avant-garde designs received acclaim in Paris and were widely influential. She continued to question conventions in 1993, producing outfits turned inside out, with unpicked seams and slashed hems, as well as jackets and coats with three sleeves.

commedia dell'arte popular form of Italian improvised comic drama in the 16th and 17th centuries, performed by trained troupes of actors and involving stock characters and situations. It exerted considerable influence on writers such as Molière and Carlo Goldoni, and on the genres of ▷pantomime, harlequinade, and the Punch and Judy show. It laid the foundation for a tradition of mime, strong in France, that has continued with the modern mime of Jean-Louis Barrault and Marcel Marceau.

commensalism in biology, a relationship between two ▷species whereby one (the commensal) benefits from the association, whereas the other neither benefits nor suffers. For example, certain species of millipede and silverfish inhabit the nests of army ants and live by scavenging on the refuse of their hosts, but without affecting the ants.

| Doric | Ionic | Corinthian | Tuscan | Composite |

COLUMN The five orders of column in classical architecture: Doric, Ionic, Corinthian, Tuscan, and Composite.

commissioner for oaths in English law, a person appointed by the Lord Chancellor with power to administer oaths or take affidavits. All practising solicitors have these powers but must not use them in proceedings in which they are acting for any of the parties or in which they have an interest.

committal proceedings in the UK, a preliminary hearing in a magistrate's court to decide whether there is a case to answer before a higher court. The media may only report limited facts about committal proceedings, such as the name of the accused and the charges, unless the defendant asks for reporting restrictions to be lifted.

commodity something produced for sale. Commodities may be consumer goods, such as radios, or producer goods, such as copper bars. **Commodity markets** deal in raw or semi-raw materials that are amenable to grading and that can be stored for considerable periods without deterioration.

Commodus, Lucius Aelius Aurelius (AD 161–192) Roman emperor from 177 (jointly with his father), sole emperor from 180, son of Marcus Aurelius. He was a tyrant, spending lavishly on gladiatorial combats, confiscating the property of the wealthy, persecuting the Senate, and renaming Rome 'Colonia Commodiana'. There were many attempts against his life, and he was finally strangled at the instigation of his mistress, Marcia, and advisers, who had discovered themselves on the emperor's death list.

common denominator denominator that is a common multiple of, and hence exactly divisible by, all the denominators of a set of fractions, and which therefore enables their sums or differences to be found.

For example, $\frac{2}{3}$ and $\frac{3}{4}$ can both be converted to equivalent fractions of denominator 12, $\frac{2}{3}$ being equal to $\frac{8}{12}$ and $\frac{3}{4}$ to $\frac{9}{12}$. Hence their sum is $\frac{17}{12}$ and their difference is $\frac{1}{12}$. The **lowest common denominator** (lcd) is the smallest common multiple of the denominators of a given set of fractions.

common land unenclosed wasteland, forest, and pasture used in common by the community at large. Poor people have throughout history gathered fruit, nuts, wood, reeds, roots, game, and so on from common land; in dry regions of India, for example, the landless derive 20% of their annual income in this way, together with much of their food and fuel. Codes of conduct evolved to ensure that common resources were not depleted. But in the 20th century, in the developing world as elsewhere, much common land has been privatized or appropriated by the state, and what remains is overburdened by those dependent on it.

common law that part of the English law not embodied in legislation. It consists of rules of law based on common custom and usage and on judicial decisions. English common law became the basis of law in the USA and many other English-speaking countries.

Common Market popular name for the **European Economic Community**; see ▷European Union.

common market organization of autonomous countries formed to promote trade; see ▷customs union.

Commons, House of lower chamber of the UK ▷Parliament. It consists of 659 elected members of Parliament, each of whom represents a constituency. Its functions are to debate, legislate, and to scrutinize the activities of government. Constituencies are kept under continuous review by the Parliamentary Boundary Commissions (1944). The House of Commons is presided over by the Speaker. Proceedings in the House of Commons began to be televised from November 1989. After the 1997 election, the Commons included a record 120 women members, including 101 female Labour MPs.

Related Web site: Parliamentary Glossary http://www.ukpol.co.uk/hou.shtml

commonwealth body politic founded on law for the common 'weal' or good. Political philosophers of the 17th century, such as Thomas Hobbes and John Locke, used the term to mean an organized political community. In Britain it is specifically applied to the period between 1649 and 1660 when, after the execution of Charles I in the English ▷Civil War, England was a republic.

History The Commonwealth was proclaimed on 19 May 1649, two months after the execution of Charles I. It was declared that the country would be governed, not by a monarch, but by 'the supreme authority of the nation, the representatives of the people in parliament'. Despite this, control of the press was tightened, and strict laws were made against blasphemy.

The early years of the Commonwealth were spent at war – fighting Royalist uprisings in Scotland and Ireland, and a trade war at sea against the Dutch. Politically, the Commonwealth was a time of ferment. Groups such as the ▷Levellers and ▷Diggers, and religious sects such as the Ranters demanded radical reforms. The Commonwealth saw the publication of Thomas ▷Hobbes's political tract *Leviathan* (1651), which advocated an absolutist government, and James Harrington's *Oceana* (1656), a scheme for an oligarchical political system. The ▷New Model Army also pressed for radical reform. When the ▷Rump – the members of Parliament who still sat in the ▷Long Parliament – failed to make changes, Oliver ▷Cromwell dissolved the Parliament by military force on 20 April 1653. He is said to have shouted, 'In the name of God, go!' and, pointing to the Mace, 'Take away that bauble'.

Cromwell called a 'Parliament of Saints', the ▷Barebones Parliament, but, when that failed to agree, accepted the offer to become Lord Protector, beginning the period known as the ▷Protectorate (1653–59). The Commonwealth came to an end in 1660 with the ▷Restoration of Charles II.

Commonwealth conference any consultation between the prime ministers (or defence, finance, foreign, or other ministers) of the sovereign independent members of the British Commonwealth. These are informal discussion meetings, and the implementation of policies is decided by individual governments.

Commonwealth Games multisport gathering of competitors from British Commonwealth countries, held every four years. The first meeting (known as the British Empire Games) was in Hamilton, Canada, in August 1930. It has been held in Britain on four occasions: London in 1934; Cardiff in 1958; Edinburgh in 1970 and 1986. Manchester will host the 2002 games.

Related Web site: Manchester 2002 XVII Commonwealth Games http://www.commonwealthgames.com.

> **Wentworth Dillon**
> English poet and translator
>
> *But words once spoke can never be recall'd.*
>
> *Art of Poetry*

Commonwealth Immigration Acts successive acts to regulate the entry into the UK of British subjects from the Commonwealth. The Commonwealth Immigration Act, passed by the Conservative government in 1962, ruled that Commonwealth immigrants entering Britain must have employment or be able to offer required skills. Further restrictions have been added since.

Commonwealth of Independent States (CIS) successor body to the ▷Union of Soviet Socialist Republics, initially formed as a new commonwealth of Slav republics on 8 December 1991 by the presidents of the Russian Federation, Belarus, and Ukraine. On 21 December, eight of the nine remaining non-Slav republics – Moldova, Tajikistan, Armenia, Azerbaijan, Turkmenistan, Kazakhstan, Kyrgyzstan, and Uzbekistan – joined the CIS at a meeting held in Kazakhstan's former capital, Alma-Ata (now Almaty). The CIS formally came into existence in January 1992 when President Gorbachev resigned and the Soviet government voted itself out of existence. It has no real, formal political institutions and its role is uncertain. Georgia joined in 1994. There is a 2,000-strong CIS bureaucracy in Moscow.

Related Web site: Commonwealth of Independent States (CIS) http://www.rochester.k12.mn.us/kellogg/rodgers/cis/thecis.htm

Commonwealth, the (British) voluntary association of 54 sovereign countries and their dependencies, the majority of which once formed part of the ▷British Empire and are now independent sovereign states. They are all regarded as 'full members of the Commonwealth'; the newest member being Mozambique, which was admitted in November 1995. Additionally, there are some 20 territories that are not completely sovereign and remain dependencies of the UK or one of the other fully sovereign members, and are regarded as 'Commonwealth countries'. Heads of government meet every two years, apart from those of Nauru and Tuvalu; however, Nauru and Tuvalu have the right to participate in all functional activities. The Commonwealth, which was founded in 1931, has no charter or constitution, and is founded more on tradition and sentiment than on political or economic factors. However, it can make political statements by withdrawing membership; a recent example was Nigeria's suspension between November 1995 and May 1999 because of human-rights abuses. Fiji was readmitted in October 1997, ten years after its membership had been suspended as a result of discrimination against its ethnic Indian community.

On 15 May 1917 Jan Smuts, representing South Africa in the Imperial War Cabinet of World War I, suggested that 'British Commonwealth of Nations' was the right title for the British Empire. The name was recognized in the Statute of Westminster in 1931, but after World War II a growing sense of independent nationhood led to the simplification of the title to the Commonwealth.

In 2000 Queen Elizabeth II was the formal head but not the ruler of 17 member states; 5 member states had their own monarchs; and 33 were republics. The Commonwealth secretariat, headed from April 2000 by London-born Canadian Don McKinnon as secretary general, is based in London. The secretariat's staff come from a number of member countries, which also pay its operating costs.

Common Worship, Book of (until November 2000, known as the *Book of Common Prayer*) the service book of the Church of England and the Episcopal Church, based largely on the Roman breviary.

commune group of people or families living together, sharing resources and responsibilities. There have been various kinds of commune through the ages, including a body of burghers or burgesses in medieval times, a religious community in America, and a communal division in communist China.

Commune, Paris two separate periods in the history of Paris (between 1789 and 1794 and from March to May 1871); see ▷Paris Commune.

communication in biology, the signalling of information by one organism to another, usually with the intention of altering the recipient's behaviour. Signals used in communication may be **visual** (such as the human smile or the display of colourful plumage in birds), **auditory** (for example, the whines or barks of a dog), **olfactory** (such as the odours released by the scent glands of a deer), **electrical** (as in the pulses emitted by electric fish), or **tactile** (for example, the nuzzling of male and female elephants).

communication the sending and receiving of messages. The messages can be verbal or nonverbal; verbal messages can be spoken or written, and transmitted in a variety of ways (see ▷telecommunications). Most nonverbal messages between human beings are in the form of body language. Verbal messages are by no means the clearest and most powerful. The sense of touch, for example, is one of the most forceful methods of communication.

communications satellite relay station in space for sending telephone, television, telex, and other messages around the world. Messages are sent to and from the satellites via ground stations. Most communications satellites are in ▷geostationary orbit, appearing to hang fixed over one point on the Earth's surface.

The first satellite to carry TV signals across the Atlantic Ocean was *Telstar*, which was launched by the United States on 10 July 1962. The world is now linked by a system of communications satellites called Intelsat. Other satellites are used by individual countries for internal communications, or for business or military use. A new generation of satellites, called **direct broadcast satellites**, are powerful enough to transmit direct to small domestic aerials. The power for such satellites is produced by solar cells (see ▷solar energy). The total energy requirement of a satellite is small; a typical communications satellite needs about 2 kW of power, the same as an electric heater.

Related Web site: Advanced Communication Technology Satellite http://acts.grc.nasa.gov/

Communion, Holy in the Christian church, another name for the ▷Eucharist.

communism (French *commun* 'common, general') revolutionary socialism based on the theories of the political philosophers Karl ▷Marx and Friedrich ▷Engels, emphasizing common ownership of the means of production and a planned economy. The principle held is that each should work according to his or her capacity and receive according to his or her needs. Politically, it seeks the overthrow of capitalism through a proletarian revolution. The first communist state was the ▷Union of Soviet Socialist Republics (USSR) after the revolution of 1917. Revolutionary socialist parties and groups united to form communist parties in other countries during the interwar years. After World War II, communism was enforced in those countries that came under Soviet occupation. Communism as the ideology of a nation state survives in only a few countries in the 21st century, notably ▷China, ▷Cuba, ▷North Korea, ▷Laos, and ▷Vietnam, where market forces are being encouraged in the economic sphere.

China emerged after 1961 as a rival to the USSR in world communist leadership, and other countries attempted to adapt communism to their own needs. The late 1980s saw a movement for more individual freedoms in many communist countries, culminating in the abolition or overthrow of communist rule in Eastern European countries and Mongolia, and further state repression in China. The failed hard-line coup in the USSR against President Gorbachev in 1991 resulted in the abandonment of communism there. However, in December 1995 the communists polled strongly in Russian parliamentary elections, with the party's leader, Gennady Zyuganov, running high in the opinion polls.

Reform communist parties have also recovered some strength in other states in central and Eastern Europe, forming governments in Hungary, Lithuania, and Poland from 1993 and remaining the largest parliamentary forces in Moldova and the Ukraine.

Communism Peak alternative form of Pik ▷Kommunizma, the highest mountain in the ▷Pamirs.

community in ecology, an assemblage of plants, animals, and other organisms living within a circumscribed area. Communities are usually named by reference to a dominant feature such as characteristic plant species (for example, a beech-wood community), or a prominent physical feature (for example, a freshwater-pond community).

community in the social sciences, the sense of identity, purpose, and companionship that comes from belonging to a particular place, organization, or social group. The concept dominated sociological thinking in the first half of the 20th century, and inspired the academic discipline of **community studies**.

community council in Wales, name for a ▷parish council.

Community law law of the member states of the ▷European Union, as adopted by the Council of Ministers. The ▷European Court of Justice interprets and applies EU law. Community law forms part of the law of states and prevails over national law. In the UK, community law became effective after enactment of the European Communities Act 1972.

community school/education system based on the philosophy asserting that educational institutions are more effective if they involve all members of the surrounding community.

community service in the penal systems of the UK and the USA, unpaid work in the service of the community (aiding children, the elderly, or the disabled), performed by a convicted person by order of the court as an alternative to prison.

commutative operation in mathematics, an operation that is independent of the order of the numbers or symbols concerned. For example, addition is commutative: the result of adding 4 + 2 is the same as that of adding 2 + 4; subtraction is not as 4 − 2 = 2, but 2 − 4 = −2. Compare ▷associative operation and ▷distributive operation.

commutator device in a DC (direct-current) electric motor that reverses the current flowing in the armature coils as the armature rotates.

A DC generator, or ▷dynamo, uses a commutator to convert the AC (alternating current) generated in the armature coils into DC.

A commutator consists of opposite pairs of conductors insulated from one another, and contact to an external circuit is provided by carbon or metal brushes.

Como (ancient **Comum**) town and resort in Lombardy, Italy, on the southwest shore of Lake Como at the foot of the Alps, 40 km/25 mi north of Milan; population (1990) 88,800. Products include motorcycles, glass, silk, furniture, optical instruments, and metal goods. Tourism is important.

Comoros see country box.

compact disc (or CD) disk for storing digital information, about 12 cm/4.5 in across, mainly used for music, when it can have over an hour's playing time. A laser beam etches the compact disc with microscopic pits that carry a digital code representing the sounds; the pitted surface is then coated with aluminium. During playback, a laser beam reads the code and produces signals that are changed into near-exact replicas of the original sounds.

company in economics, a number of people grouped together as a business enterprise. Types of company include public limited companies, partnerships, joint ventures, sole proprietorships, and branches of foreign companies. Most companies are private and, unlike public companies, cannot offer their shares to the general public.

compass any instrument for finding direction. The most commonly used is a magnetic compass, consisting of a thin piece of magnetic material with the north-seeking pole indicated, free to rotate on a pivot and mounted on a compass card on which the points of the compass are marked. When the compass is properly adjusted and used, the north-seeking pole will point to the magnetic north, from which true north can be found from tables of magnetic corrections.

compensation point in biology, the point at which there is just enough light for a plant to survive. At this point all the food produced by ▷photosynthesis is used up by ▷respiration. For aquatic plants, the compensation point is the depth of water at which there is just enough light to sustain life (deeper water = less light = less photosynthesis).

competition in ecology, the interaction between two or more organisms, or groups of organisms (for example, species), that use a common resource which is in short supply. Competition invariably results in a reduction in the numbers of one or both competitors, and in ▷evolution contributes both to the decline of certain species and to the evolution of ▷adaptations.

competition in economics, rivalry in the marketplace between different business organizations, usually competition for custom between those who have the same commodities to dispose of. Firms can make their products competitive in price, quality, availability, and delivery dates, for example, or compete through advertising.

Michael Foot
British Labour politician and writer

The members of our secret service have apparently spent so much time looking under the beds for communists, they haven't had time to look in the bed.

Attributed remark, referring to the Profumo Affair (1963)

Comoros

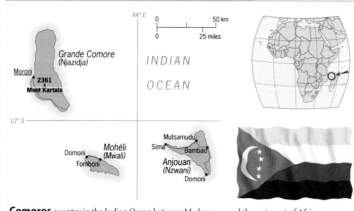

Comoros country in the Indian Ocean between Madagascar and the east coast of Africa, comprising three islands – Njazidja (Grande Comore), Nzwani (Anjouan), and Mwali (Moheli). A fourth island in the group, Mayotte, is a French dependency.

NATIONAL NAME *Jumhuriyyat al-Qumur al-Itthadiyah al-Islamiyah* (Arabic), *République fédérale islamique des Comores* (French)/ *Federal Islamic Republic of the Comoros*
AREA 1,862 sq km/718 sq mi
CAPITAL Moroni
MAJOR TOWNS/CITIES Mutsamudu, Domoni, Fomboni, Mitsamiouli
PHYSICAL FEATURES comprises the volcanic islands of Njazídja, Nzwani, and Mwali (formerly Grande Comore, Anjouan, Moheli)

Government
HEAD OF STATE AND GOVERNMENT Azali Assoumani from 1999
POLITICAL SYSTEM military
POLITICAL EXECUTIVE military
ADMINISTRATIVE DIVISIONS three autonomous island prefectures
ARMED FORCES 800 (2002 est)

Economy and resources
CURRENCY Comorian franc
GPD (US$) 256 million (2002 est)

REAL GDP GROWTH (% change on previous year) 1 (2001)
GNI (US$) 228 million (2002 est)
GNI PER CAPITA (PPP) (US$) 1,640 (2002 est)
CONSUMER PRICE INFLATION 2.5% (2003 est)
UNEMPLOYMENT 20% (2000)
FOREIGN DEBT (US$) 226 million (2001 est)
MAJOR TRADING PARTNERS France, USA, Germany, Kenya, Pakistan, South Africa, Singapore
INDUSTRIES sawmilling, processing of vanilla and copra, printing, soft drinks, plastics, perfume distillation, furniture, jewellery
EXPORTS vanilla, cloves, ylang-ylang, essences, copra, coffee. Principal market: France 38.6% (2000)
IMPORTS rice, petroleum products, transport equipment, meat and dairy products, cement, iron and steel, clothing, footwear. Principal source: France 36.6% (2000)
ARABLE LAND 35% (2000 est)
AGRICULTURAL PRODUCTS vanilla, ylang-ylang, cloves, basil, cassava, sweet potatoes, rice, maize, pulses, coconuts, bananas

Population and society
POPULATION 768,000 (2003 est)
POPULATION GROWTH RATE 2.9% (2000–05)
POPULATION DENSITY (per sq km) 344 (2003 est)
URBAN POPULATION (% of total) 35 (2003 est)
AGE DISTRIBUTION (% of total population) 0–14 43%, 15–59 53%, 60+ 4% (2002 est)
ETHNIC GROUPS population of mixed origin, with Africans, Arabs, and Malaysians predominating; the principal ethnic group is the Antalaotra; others are the Catre, the Makoa, the Oimatsaha, and the Sakalava
LANGUAGE Arabic, French (both official), Comorian (a Swahili and Arabic dialect), Makua
RELIGION Muslim
EDUCATION (compulsory years) 9
LITERACY RATE 64% (men); 49% (women) (2003 est)
LABOUR FORCE 74% agriculture, 10% industry, 16% services (2000)
LIFE EXPECTANCY 59 (men); 62 (women) (2000–05)
TV SETS (per 1,000 people) 5 (1999 est)
INTERNET USERS (per 10,000 people) 42 (2002 est)

COMOROS The Emperor Angelfish *Pomacanthus imperator* is native to the tropical waters of the Indian Ocean. *Stanley Gibbons*

Chronology
5th century AD: First settled by Malay-Polynesian immigrants.
7th century: Converted to Islam by Arab seafarers and fell under the rule of local sultans.
late 16th century: First visited by European navigators.
1886: Moheli island in south became a French protectorate.
1904: Slave trade abolished, ending influx of Africans.
1912: Grande Comore and Anjouan, the main islands, joined Moheli to become a French colony, which was attached to Madagascar from 1914.
1947: Became a French Overseas Territory separate from Madagascar.
1961: Internal self-government achieved.
1975: Independence achieved from France, but island of Mayotte to the southeast voted to remain part of France. Joined the United Nations.
1976: President Ahmed Abdallah was overthrown in a coup by Ali Soilih; relations deteriorated with France as a Maoist-Islamic programme pursued.
1978: Soilih was killed by French mercenaries. A federal Islamic republic was proclaimed, with exiled Abdallah restored as president; diplomatic relations re-established with France.
1979: The Comoros became a one-party state; powers of the federal government increased.
1989: Abdallah killed by French mercenaries who, under French and South African pressure, turned authority over to French administration; Said Muhammad Djohar became president.
1995: Djohar was overthrown in a coup led by Denard, who was persuaded to withdraw by French troops.
1997: Secessionist rebels took control of Anjouan.
1999: The government was overthrown by an army coup, after granting greater autonomy to the islands of Anjouan and Moheli. The new president was Colonel Azali Assoumani.
2000: A coup against the military government was foiled. Hamada Madi appointed prime minister.
2002: The presidential election for the Union of Comoros was marred by violence, and the electoral commission cancelled the results.

In a market where ▷perfect competition is operating, it is assumed that all companies produce identical products and compete only on price. In markets characterized by an ▷oligopoly and other forms of imperfect competition, goods are branded and there is much more emphasis on nonprice competition such as advertising. In a ▷monopoly, where there is only one producer, there is no competition. Governments attempt to increase competition through competition policy.

competition, perfect in commerce, see ▷perfect competition.

compiler computer program that translates programs written in a ▷high-level language into machine code (the form in which they can be run by the computer). The compiler translates each high-level instruction into several machine-code instructions – in a process called **compilation** – and produces a complete independent program that can be run by the computer as often as required, without the original source program being present.

Different compilers are needed for different high-level languages and for different computers. In contrast to using an ▷interpreter, using a compiler adds slightly to the time needed to develop a new program because the machine-code program must be recompiled after each change or correction. Once compiled, however, the machine-code program will run much faster than an interpreted program.

complement in mathematics, the set of the elements within the universal set that are not contained in the designated set. For example, if the universal set is the set of all positive whole numbers and the designated set S is the set of all even numbers, then the complement of S (denoted S') is the set of all odd numbers.

complementary medicine in medicine, systems of care based on methods of treatment or theories of disease that differ from those taught in most western medical schools. See ▷medicine, alternative.

complex in psychology, a group of ideas and feelings that have become repressed because they are distasteful to the person in whose mind they arose, but are still active in the depths of the person's unconscious mind, continuing to affect his or her life and actions, even though he or she is no longer fully aware of their existence. Typical examples include the ▷Oedipus complex and the ▷inferiority complex.

complex number in mathematics, a number written in the form $a + ib$, where a and b are ▷real numbers and i is the square root of -1 (that is, $i^2 = -1$); i used to be known as the 'imaginary' part of the complex number. Some equations in algebra, such as those of the form

$$x^2 + 5 = 0$$

cannot be solved without recourse to complex numbers, because the real numbers do not include square roots of negative numbers.

The sum of two or more complex numbers is obtained by adding separately their real and imaginary parts, for example:

$$(a + bi) + (c + di) = (a + c) + (b + d)i$$

Complex numbers can be represented graphically on an Argand diagram, which uses rectangular ▷Cartesian coordinates in which the x-axis represents the real part of the number and the y-axis the imaginary part. Thus the number $z = a + bi$ is plotted as the point (a, b). Complex numbers have applications in various areas of science, such as the theory of alternating currents in electricity.

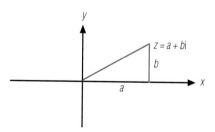

COMPLEX NUMBER A complex number can be represented graphically as a line whose end-point coordinates equal the real and imaginary parts of the complex number. This type of diagram is called an Argand diagram after the French mathematician Jean Argand (1768–1822) who devised it.

Compositae daisy family, comprising dicotyledonous flowering plants characterized by flowers borne in composite heads. It is the largest family of flowering plants, the majority being herbaceous. Birds seem to favour the family for use in nest 'decoration', possibly because many species either repel or kill insects (see ▷pyrethrum). Species include the daisy and dandelion; food plants such as the artichoke, lettuce, and safflower; and the garden varieties of chrysanthemum, dahlia, and zinnia.

Composite in classical architecture, one of the five types of ▷column. See ▷order.

composite in industry, any purpose-designed engineering material created by combining materials with complementary properties into a composite form. Most composites have a structure in which one component consists of discrete elements, such as fibres, dispersed in a continuous matrix. For example, lengths of asbestos, glass, or carbon steel, or 'whiskers' (specially grown crystals a few millimetres long) of substances such as silicon carbide may be dispersed in plastics, concrete, or steel.

compost organic material decomposed by bacteria under controlled conditions to make a nutrient-rich natural fertilizer for use in gardening or farming. A well-made compost heap reaches a high temperature during the composting process, killing most weed seeds that might be present.

compound chemical substance made up of two or more ▷elements bonded together, so that they cannot be separated by physical means. Compounds are held together by ionic or covalent bonds.

The name of a compound may give a clue to its composition.

If the name ends in -ide (with the notable exceptions of hydroxides and ammonium chloride) it usually contain two elements. For example calcium oxide is a compound of calcium and oxygen.

If the name ends in -ate or -ite the compound contains oxygen; compounds ending in -ate have a greater proportion of oxygen than those ending in -ite. For example, sodium sulphate (Na_2SO_4) contains more oxygen than does sodium sulphite (Na_2SO_3).

If the name starts with per- the compound contains extra oxygen. For example, hydrogen peroxide H_2O_2 contains one more oxygen than hydrogen oxide (water) H_2O.

The prefix thio- indicates that the compound contains an atom of sulphur in place of an oxygen. For example, sodium thiosulphate ($Na_2S_2O_3$) contains one more sulphur and one less oxygen than the more common sodium sulphate (Na_2SO_4).

The proportions of the different elements in a compound are shown by the chemical formula of that compound. For example, a molecule of sodium sulphate, represented by the formula Na_2SO_4 contains two atoms of sodium, one of sulphur, and four of oxygen.

compound interest interest calculated by computing the rate against the original capital plus reinvested interest each time the interest becomes due. When simple interest is calculated, only the interest on the original capital is added.

comprehensive school secondary school that admits pupils of all abilities, and therefore without any academic selection procedure. In England 86.8% of all pupils attend a comprehensive school. Other state secondary schools are middle, deemed secondary (5.2%), secondary modern (2.6%), secondary grammar (4.2%), and technical (0.1%). There were 4,462 state secondary schools in 1995 to 1996, with 3,675,600 pupils.

Compton, Denis Charles Scott (1918–1997) English cricketer and football player. He played for Middlesex and England, and was a right-handed batsman of prodigious talent and great style, who in 78 tests between 1937 and 1957 scored 5,807 runs at an average of 50.06. In the 1947 English season he scored 3,816 runs (at an average of 90.85) and 18 hundreds, records which are unlikely ever to be surpassed. As a footballer he won Football League and FA Cup winners' medals with Arsenal and played in 12 wartime internationals for England.

Related Web site: Compton, Denis http://www.usa8.cricket.org/link_to_database/PLAYERS/ENG/C/COMPTON_DCS_01000701/

Compton-Burnett, Ivy (1884–1969) English novelist. She used dialogue to show reactions of small groups of characters dominated by the tyranny of family relationships. Her novels, set at the turn of the century, include *Pastors and Masters* (1925), *More Women than Men* (1933), and *Mother and Son* (1955).

> **Ivy Compton-Burnett**
> *As regards plots I find real life no help at all. Real life seems to have no plots.*
> R Lehmann et al. *Orion I*

compulsory purchase in the UK, the right of the state and authorized bodies to buy land required for public purposes even against the wishes of the owner. Under the Land Compensation Act 1973, fair recompense is payable.

compulsory tendering policy introduced by the UK Conservative government requiring local authorities and other public bodies to put out to tender work which might normally be done 'in house'. This approach stemmed from a political conviction that the private sector was always more efficient and cost-effective than the public.

computer programmable electronic device that processes data and performs calculations and other symbol-manipulation tasks.

There are three types: the ▷digital computer, which manipulates information coded as binary numbers (see ▷binary number system); the ▷analogue computer, which works with continuously varying quantities; and the **hybrid computer**, which has characteristics of both analogue and digital computers.

There are four types of digital computer, corresponding roughly to their size and intended use. **Microcomputers** are the smallest and most common, used in small businesses, at home, and in schools. They are usually single-user machines. **Minicomputers** (or mid-range computers) are found in medium-sized businesses and university departments. They may support from around 10 to 200 users at once. **Mainframes** (or enterprise servers), which can often service several hundred users simultaneously, are found in large organizations, such as national companies and government departments. **Supercomputers** are mostly used for highly complex scientific tasks, such as analysing the results of nuclear physics experiments and weather forecasting.

Under the Computer Misuse Act 1990 three new offences were introduced: unauthorized access to computer material (that is, out of curiosity), unauthorized access with intent to facilitate the commission of a crime (for example fraud or blackmail), and unauthorized modification of computer material (to deter the propagation of malicious codes such as viruses and Trojan horses). See also The Electronic Workplace Focus Feature on pp. 312–313.

computer-aided design use of computers to create and modify design drawings; see ▷CAD.

computer-aided manufacturing use of computers to regulate production processes in industry; see ▷CAM.

computer art art produced with the help of a computer. Since the 1950s the aesthetic use of computers has been increasingly evident in most artistic disciplines, including film animation, architecture, and music. See also Using Computers in Art and Design Focus Feature on pp. 52–53.

computer-assisted learning use of computers in education and training; see ▷CAL.

computer game (or **video game**) any computer-controlled game in which the computer (sometimes) opposes the human player. Computer games typically employ fast, animated graphics on a ▷VDU (visual display unit) and synthesized sound.

Commercial computer games became possible with the advent of the ▷microprocessor in the mid-1970s and rapidly became popular as amusement-arcade games, using dedicated chips. Available games range from chess to fighter-plane simulations.

Some of the most popular computer games in the early 1990s were id Software's *Wolfenstein 3D*, *Doom*, and *Quake*, which were designed to be played across networks including the Internet. A whole subculture built up around those particular games, as users took advantage of id's help to create their own additions to the games.

The computer games industry has been criticized for releasing many violent games with little intellectual content.

computer generation any of the five broad groups into which computers may be classified: **first generation** the earliest computers, developed in the 1940s and 1950s, made from valves and wire circuits; **second generation** from the early 1960s, based on transistors and printed circuits; **third generation** from the late 1960s, using integrated circuits and often sold as families of computers, such as the IBM 360 series; **fourth generation** using ▷microprocessors, large-scale integration (LSI), and sophisticated programming languages, still in use in the 1990s; and **fifth generation** based on parallel processing and very large-scale integration, currently under development.

computer graphics use of computers to display and manipulate information in pictorial form. Input may be achieved by scanning an image, by drawing with a mouse or stylus on a graphics tablet, or by drawing directly on the screen with a light pen.

The output may be as simple as a pie chart, or as complex as an animated sequence in a science fiction film, or a seemingly three-dimensional engineering blueprint. The drawing is stored in the computer as raster graphics or vector graphics.

Vector graphics are stored in the computer memory by using geometric formulas. They can be transformed (enlarged, rotated, stretched, and so on) without loss of picture resolution. It is also possible to select and transform any of the components of a vector-graphics display because each is separately defined in the computer memory. In these respects vector graphics are superior to raster graphics. They are typically used for drawing applications, allowing

Computing: Key Dates

1623	Wilhelm Schickard invents the mechanical calculating machine.
1679	Gottfried Leibniz introduces binary arithmetic, in which only two symbols are used to represent all numbers.
1805	Joseph-Marie Jacquard develops an automatic loom controlled by punch cards.
1820	The first mass-produced calculator, the Arithometer, is developed by Charles Thomas de Colmar.
1823	In the UK, Charles Babbage constructs a Difference Engine for calculating logarithms and trigonometric functions. Later he develops but fails to complete an Analytical Engine, which has the elements of a mechanical computer.
1854	George Boole in the UK publishes his system of symbolic logic, now called Boolean algebra.
1876	Alexander Graham Bell invents the telephone.
1886	William Burroughs develops the first commercially successful mechanical adding machine.
1890	Herman Hollerith develops tabulating machines using punched cards for use in the US Census. Hollerith's company is one of the parts from which IBM (International Business Machines) is formed in 1924, and punched cards – first exploited by Joseph-Marie Jacquard in 1805 – are widely used in data processing until the 1970s.
1936	Alan Turing develops the idea that all solvable problems can be solved using algorithms. He writes a seminal paper, 'On Computable Numbers', that influences John von Neumann and the development of computing.
1937	The first binary adding machine is constructed from telephone relays, strips of tin, bulbs, and other items by George Stibitz, an engineer at the Bell Telephone Laboratories in New Jersey, USA. He calls it the Model K because it is built on his kitchen table.
1938	Konrad Zuse, working in his parents' living room in Berlin, Germany, completes the Z1, the first binary calculating machine.
1942	John Atanasoff and Clifford Berry complete the ABC or Atanasoff–Berry Calculator, one of the first electronic calculating machines. In 1973, a US Judge decides that this is enough of a computer to invalidate patents on the ENIAC, which had been widely considered to be the first electronic computer.
1945	ENIAC (Electronic Numerical Integrator Analyzer And Computer) is completed by J Presper Eckert and John W Mauchly at the Moore School at the University of Pennsylvania. A valve-based machine, it can be reprogrammed using cables and plugboards, that is, essentially by rewiring it. However, Eckert and Mauchly have already proposed building a computer that can store and run programs: EDVAC (Electronic Discrete Variable Computer). John von Neumann's description of the project, 'First Draft of a Report on the EDVAC', is widely circulated and stimulates the building of similar machines following what becomes known as the 'von Neumann architecture'.
1946	Eckert and Mauchly leave the Moore School to found the first commercial computer company, which leads to the UNIVAC (Universal Automatic Computer) and the US mainframe computer industry.
1949	EDSAC (Electronic Delay Storage Automatic Calculator), the first full-scale electronic stored program computer, goes into operation at Cambridge University, England, ahead of Eckert and Mauchly's BINAC (Binary Automatic Computer), which is more than a year behind schedule.
1951	First commercially produced computers are delivered: a Ferranti Mark I going to Manchester University in February, and Eckert and Mauchly's first UNIVAC to the US Census Bureau in March. Whirlwind, the first real-time computer, is designed at MIT by Jay Forrester and Ken Olsen for the US air-defence system. Grace Murray Hopper of Remington Rand invents the first compiler computer program .
1954	The silicon transistor is developed by Gordon Teal of Texas Instruments, USA.
1963	The PDP-8, the first mass-produced minicomputer, is launched by Digital Equipment Corporation (DEC).
1965	The first supercomputer, the CD6600, is developed by Seymour Cray at Control Data Corporation in the USA. Ted Nelson coins the term 'hypertext' and starts to imagine a global network of computers with jump-linked texts, like the World Wide Web.
1968	Doug Engelbart of the Stanford Research Institute, California, demonstrates the first hypertext computer system controlled by a mouse.
1969	Researchers at four US campuses link their computers to form the ARPANET, which is the starting point of the Internet.
1971	The first microprocessor or 'computer on a chip', the Intel 4004, is developed by Marcian 'Ted' Hoff and others at Intel in California, USA. The Poketronic, the first pocket calculator, is launched in the USA.
1972	The first coin-operated video game, Pong, is installed by Nolan Bushnell, who founds Atari in California.
1975	The first commercially successful personal computer, the Altair 8800, is launched in kit form by MITS in New Mexico, USA.
1976	Apple is founded in California by Steve Jobs and Steve Wozniak, who show Wozniak's Apple I computer at the Homebrew Computer Club. *Adventure* or *Colossal Caves*, the first adventure game, is developed by Crowther and Woods.
1978	The first spreadsheet, VisiCalc, is developed by Dan Bricklin and Bob Frankston. *Space Invaders*, a coin-operated video game, is introduced by Taito of Japan.
1980	Clive Sinclair's Sinclair Electronics enters the UK computer market with the Sinclair ZX80, the first computer for less than £100.
1982	TCP/IP – a communications protocol proposed by Vint Cerf and Bob Kahn in 1974 – is made the standard for the ARPANET: this marks the beginning of the Internet as a network of networks.
1983	Apple launches Lisa, its first mouse-operated computer with a graphical user interface inspired by work at Xerox PARC. Microsoft, similarly inspired, announces a graphical 'interface manager' called Windows, and ships a mouse with its first word processor, Microsoft Word.
1984	Apple launches the Macintosh computer, with a built-in black and white screen, using a long television commercial created to be shown only once, during the US Superbowl football final. IBM launches the IBM PC AT (Advanced Technology), which sets the standard for PC-compatibility for the following decade. Novelist William Gibson coins the term 'cyberspace' in an influential work of science fiction, *Neuromancer*. The first commercial publication on CD-ROM is developed by The Library Corporation for IBM PC-compatible computers.
1989	The first pocket-sized PC-compatible computers are announced by Atari (Portfolio) and Poqet (Poqet PC). The first hand-held games console, the GameBoy, is launched in Japan by Nintendo.
1990	Dragon Systems ships Dragon Dictate, the first speech recognition system designed for personal computers. The first remotely operated machine, a toaster, is connected to the Internet.
1990–91	A prototype of the World Wide Web is developed at CERN, Europe's particle physics research centre, by Tim Berners-Lee, who posts his code on the Internet in the alt.hypertext newsgroup.
1992	Philips launches the CD-I (Compact-Disc Interactive) player, based on CD audio technology, to provide interactive multimedia programs for home users.
1993	Apple introduces the Newton MessagePad handheld computer, described as a 'Personal Digital Assistant' (PDA), with built-in handwriting recognition. Mosaic, the first graphical browser for the World Wide Web, is released free of charge by the National Centre for Supercomputing Applications (NCSA) at the University of Illinois, USA.
1994	Cyberia is opened in London, England, providing coffee with Internet access: it claims to be the world's first cybercafé.
1997	IBM's Deep Blue chess machine defeats grandmaster Garry Kasparov in a match by 3.5–2.5.
1998	Microsoft launches Windows 98, an upgrade to its Windows 95 program. It integrates its World Wide Web browser program Internet Explorer into the package, angering rival browser manufacturers, principally Netscape.
2000	Microsoft launches Windows 2000, a new version of its successful Windows program, but containing code that has been completely rewritten to take full advantage of advances in PC development over the past decade. After a long-running dispute between the US government and Microsoft over its unfair marketing of Internet Explorer, a judge recommends that the corporation be broken up into separate companies.

the user to create and modify technical diagrams such as designs for houses or cars.

Raster graphics are stored in the computer memory by using a map to record data (such as colour and intensity) for every ▷pixel that makes up the image. When transformed (enlarged, rotated, stretched, and so on), raster graphics become ragged and suffer loss of picture resolution, unlike vector graphics. They are typically used for painting applications, which allow the user to create artwork on a computer screen much as if they were painting on paper or canvas.

Computer graphics are increasingly used in computer-aided design (▷CAD), and to generate models and simulations in engineering, meteorology, medicine and surgery, and other fields of science.

Related Web site: Gif Wizard http://www.gifwizard.com/

computerized axial tomography medical technique, usually known as ▷CAT scan, for noninvasive investigation of disease or injury.

computer program coded instructions for a computer; see ▷program.

computer simulation representation of a real-life situation in a computer program. For example, the program might simulate the flow of customers arriving at a bank. The user can alter variables, such as the number of cashiers on duty, and see the effect.

More complex simulations can model the behaviour of chemical reactions or even nuclear explosions. The behaviour of solids and liquids at high temperatures can be simulated using quantum simulation. Computers also control the actions of machines – for example, a ▷flight simulator models the behaviour of real aircraft and allows training to take place in safety. Computer simulations are very useful when it is too dangerous, time consuming, or simply impossible to carry out a real experiment or test.

Comte, (Isidore) Auguste (Marie François Xavier) (1798–1857) French philosopher regarded as the founder of sociology, a term he coined in 1830. He sought to establish sociology as an intellectual discipline, using a scientific approach ('positivism') as the basis of a new science of social order and social development.

In his six-volume *Cours de philosophie positive* (1830–42), Comte argued that human thought and social development evolve through three stages: the theological, the metaphysical, and the positive or scientific. Although he originally sought to proclaim society's evolution to a new golden age of science, industry, and rational morality, his radical ideas were increasingly tempered by the political and social upheavals of his time. His influence continued in Europe and the USA until the early 20th century.

Related Web site: Auguste Comte – A General View of Positivism http://www.fordham.edu/halsall/mod/comte-positivism.html

Conakry capital and chief port of the Republic of Guinea; population (1992) 950,000. It is on the island of Tumbo, and is linked with the Kaloum Peninsula by a causeway and (from 1914) by rail with Kankan, 480 km/300 mi to the northeast. One of the major exports is alumina (treated bauxite), which is mined at Fria; iron ore is mined on the nearby Kaloum Peninsula. Other industries include plastics, fisheries, motor vehicle assembly, and tourism. Agricultural products include bananas, oranges, pineapples, palm products, and coffee.

concave of a surface, curving inwards, or away from the eye. For example, a bowl appears concave when viewed from above. In geometry, a concave polygon is one that has an interior angle greater than 180°. Concave is the opposite of ▷convex.

concave lens lens that possesses at least one surface that curves inwards. It is a diverging lens, spreading out those light rays that have been refracted through it. A concave lens is thinner at its centre than at its edges, and is used to correct short-sightedness.

concentration in chemistry, the amount of a substance (▷solute) present in a specified amount of a solution. Either amount may be specified as a mass or a volume (liquids only). Common units used are ▷moles per cubic decimetre, grams per cubic decimetre, grams per 100 cubic centimetres, and grams per 100 grams.

concentration camp prison camp for civilians in wartime or under totalitarian rule. The first concentration camps were devised by the British during the Second Boer War in South Africa in 1899 for the detention of Afrikaner women and children (with the subsequent deaths of more than 20,000 people). A system of hundreds of concentration camps was developed by the Nazis in Germany and occupied Europe (1933–45) to imprison Jews and political and ideological opponents after Adolf ▷Hitler became chancellor in January 1933. The most infamous camps in World War II were the extermination camps of ▷Auschwitz, Belsen,

▷Dachau, Maidanek, Sobibor, and ▷Treblinka. The total number of people who died at the camps exceeded 6 million, and some inmates were subjected to medical experimentation before being killed.

concentric circles two or more circles that share the same centre.

Concepción industrial city in south-central Chile, 350 km/217 mi southwest of Santiago; situated on the north bank of the Bió-Bió River, near its mouth; population (1992) 330,400. It is Chile's third-largest city and capital of Concepción province and of Bió-Bió region. The city is a tourist resort and lies in a rich agricultural district. Industries include coal (from the pits on the Péninsula de Lebú, steel, glass, cement, paper, and textiles. Most of Chile's coal is mined in the vicinity. Its port, Talcahuano, 15 km/9 mi to the north, is Chile's most important naval base.

Auguste Comte
Men are not allowed to think freely about chemistry and biology, why should they be allowed to think freely about political philosophy?
Positive Philosophy

concertina musical instrument, a portable reed organ related to the ▷accordion but smaller in size and hexagonal in shape, with buttons for keys. Metal reeds are blown by wind from pleated bellows which are opened and closed by the player's hands. It was invented in England in the 19th century.

concerto composition, usually in three movements, for solo instrument (or instruments) and orchestra. It developed during the 18th century from the concerto grosso form for orchestra, in which a group of solo instruments (concerto) is contrasted with a full orchestra (ripieno).

conch name applied to various shells, but especially to the fountain shell, a species of gastropod mollusc in the order Mesogastropoda.

Conchobar in Celtic mythology, king of Ulster whose intended bride, ▷Deirdre, eloped with Noísi. She died of sorrow when Conchobar killed her husband and his brothers.

conclave (Latin 'a room locked with a key') secret meeting, in particular the gathering of cardinals in Rome to elect a new pope. They are locked away in the Vatican Palace until they have reached a decision. The result of each ballot is announced by a smoke signal – black for an undecided vote and white when the choice is made.

Concord town in eastern Massachusetts, USA, 29 km/18 mi northwest of Boston; population (1998 est) 17,900. Although electronic equipment, metal products, and leather goods are manufactured here, it is mainly a residential suburb of Boston. Concord was incorporated in 1635, when the early settlers were English.

concordance book containing an alphabetical list of the important words in a major work, with reference to the places in which they occur. The first concordance was one for the Latin Vulgate Bible compiled by a Dominican monk in the 13th century.

concordat agreement regulating relations between the papacy and a secular government, for example, that for France between Pius VII and the emperor Napoleon, which lasted from 1801 to 1905; Mussolini's concordat, which lasted from 1929 to 1978 and safeguarded the position of the church in Italy; and one of 1984 in Italy in which Roman Catholicism ceased to be the Italian state religion.

Concorde the only supersonic airliner, able to cruise at Mach 2, or twice the speed of sound, about 2,170 kph/1,350 mph. Concorde, the result of Anglo-French cooperation, made its first flight in 1969 and entered commercial service seven years later. It was 62 m/202 ft long and had a wing span of nearly 26 m/84 ft. The plane was taken out of commercial service in October 2003.

A Concorde aircraft owned by Air France crashed on 25 July 2000, soon after taking off from Charles de Gaulle airport, Paris. All passengers and crew, totalling 109 people, were killed on board, as well as five people on the ground. It was later discovered that debris on the runway may have pierced a tyre which exploded and tore the fuel tank, which then caused a fire. Air France immediately grounded all Concorde aircraft; British Airways continued to fly until 15 August, when it was announced that the Civil Aviation Authority (CAA) was about to revoke the aircraft's certificate of airworthiness.

Related Web site: Unofficial Concorde Home Page http://www.geocities.com/CapeCanaveral/Lab/8952/e_index.htm

concrete building material composed of cement, stone, sand, and water. It has been used since Egyptian and Roman times. Since the late 19th century, it has been increasingly employed as an economical alternative to materials such as brick and wood, and has been combined with steel to increase its tension capacity.

concrete music see ▷musique concrète.

concussion temporary unconsciousness resulting from a blow to the head. It is often followed by amnesia for events immediately preceding the blow.

Condé, Louis I de Bourbon, Prince of Condé (1530–1569) Prominent French ▷Huguenot leader, founder of the house of Condé and uncle of Henry IV of France. He fought in the wars between Henry II and the Holy Roman Emperor Charles V, including the defence of Metz.

Condé, Louis II (1621–1686) Called 'the Great Condé'. Prince of Condé and French commander who won brilliant victories during the Thirty Years' War at Rocroi (1643) and Lens (1648), but rebelled in 1651 and entered the Spanish service. Pardoned in 1660, he commanded Louis XIV's armies against the Spanish and the Dutch.

condensation conversion of a vapour to a liquid. This is frequently achieved by letting the vapour come into contact with a cold surface. It is the process by which water vapour turns into fine water droplets to form ▷cloud.

Condensation in the atmosphere occurs when the air becomes completely saturated and is unable to hold any more water vapour. As air rises it cools and contracts – the cooler it becomes the less water it can hold. Rain is frequently associated with warm weather fronts because the air rises and cools, allowing the water vapour to condense as rain. The temperature at which the air becomes saturated is known as the ▷dew point. Water vapour will not condense in air if there are not enough condensation nuclei (particles of dust, smoke or salt) for the droplets to form on. It is then said to be supersaturated. Condensation is an important part of the ▷water cycle.

condensation polymerization ▷polymerization reaction in which one or more monomers, with more than one reactive functional group, combine to form a polymer with the elimination of water or another small molecule.

condenser laboratory apparatus used to condense vapours back to liquid so that the liquid can be recovered. It is used in ▷distillation and in reactions where the liquid mixture can be kept boiling without the loss of solvent.

condenser in electronic circuits, a former name for a ▷capacitor.

condenser in optics, a ▷lens or combination of lenses with a short focal length used for concentrating a light source onto a small area, as used in a slide projector or microscope substage lighting unit. A condenser can also be made using a concave mirror.

conditioning in psychology, two major principles of behaviour modification.

In **classical conditioning**, described by Russian psychologist Ivan Pavlov, a new stimulus can evoke an automatic response by being repeatedly associated with a stimulus that naturally provokes that response. For example, the sound of a bell repeatedly associated with food will eventually trigger salivation, even if sounded without food being presented. In **operant conditioning**, described by US psychologists Edward Lee Thorndike (1874–1949) and B F Skinner, the frequency of a voluntary response can be increased by following it with a reinforcer or reward.

condom (or **sheath** or **prophylactic**) barrier contraceptive, made of rubber, which fits over an erect penis and holds in the sperm produced by ejaculation. It is an effective means of preventing pregnancy if used carefully, preferably with a ▷spermicide. A condom with spermicide is 97% effective; one without spermicide is 85% effective as a contraceptive. Condoms can also give some protection against sexually transmitted diseases, including AIDS.

In 1996 the European Union agreed a standard for condoms, which is 17 cm/6.7 in long; although the width can be variable, a regular width was agreed as 5.2 cm/2 in.

In 1992 the female condom became available to buy in the UK. The condom lines the vagina and helps protect against pregnancy and sexually transmitted diseases.

condominium joint rule of a territory by two or more states, for example, Kanton and Enderbury islands in the South Pacific Phoenix group (under the joint control of Britain and the USA for 50 years from 1939).

condor name given to two species of birds in separate genera. The **Andean condor** *Vultur gryphus*, has a wingspan up to 3 m/10 ft, weighs up to 13 kg/28 lb, and can reach up to 1.2 m/3.8 ft in length. It is black, with some white on the wings and a white frill at the base of the neck. It lives in the Andes at heights of up to 4,500 m/14,760 ft, and along the South American coast, and feeds mainly on carrion. The **Californian condor** *Gymnogyps californianus* is a similar bird, with a wingspan of about 3 m/10 ft. It feeds entirely on carrion, and is on the verge of extinction.

CONDOR Condors are an endangered species. They have been the victims of pesticide residues in the environment, which have led to eggshell thinning so severe that parents may crush their eggs while incubating. Poisoning from lead bullets eaten while feeding on the remains of hunters' unrecovered and field-dressed deer, or from poison intended for ground squirrels and coyotes, as well as collisions with power lines, have pushed the condor to the brink of extinction in recent years. *Image Bank*

The Californian condor lays only one egg at a time and may not breed every year. In 1994, only 89 Californian condors remained, of which only four were in the wild. It became the subject of a special conservation effort, and by July 1995 the number had increased to 104.

Condorcet, Marie Jean Antoine Nicolas de Caritat (1743–1794) Marquis de Condorcet. French philosopher, mathematician, and politician, associated with the Encyclopédistes. In *Esquisse d'un tableau des progrès de l'esprit humain/Historical Survey of the Progress of Human Understanding* (1795), he traced human development from barbarity to the brink of perfection. As a mathematician he made important contributions to the theory of probability.

conductance ability of a material to carry an electrical current, usually given the symbol *G*. For a direct current, it is the reciprocal of ▷resistance: a conductor of resistance *R* has a conductance of 1/*R*. For an alternating current, conductance is the resistance *R* divided by the ▷impedance *Z*: $G = R/Z$. Conductance was formerly expressed in reciprocal ohms (or mhos); the SI unit is the ▷siemens (S).

conduction, electrical flow of charged particles through a material giving rise to electric current. Conduction in metals involves the flow of negatively charged free ▷electrons. Conduction in gases and some liquids involves the flow of ▷ions that carry positive charges in one direction and negative charges in the other. Conduction in a ▷semiconductor such as silicon involves the flow of electrons and positive holes.

conduction, heat flow of heat energy through a material without the movement of any part of the material itself (compare ▷conduction, electrical). Heat energy is present in all materials in the form of the kinetic energy of their vibrating molecules, and may be conducted from one molecule to the next in the form of this mechanical vibration. In the case of metals, which are particularly good conductors of heat, the free electrons within the material carry heat around very quickly.

conductor any material that conducts heat or electricity (as opposed to an insulator, or nonconductor). A good conductor has a high electrical or heat conductivity, and is generally a substance rich in free electrons such as a metal. A poor conductor (such as the nonmetals, glass and porcelain) has few free electrons. ▷Carbon is exceptional in being nonmetallic and yet (in some of its forms) a relatively good conductor of heat and electricity. Substances such as ▷silicon and ▷germanium, with intermediate conductivities that are improved by heat, light, or impurities, are known as ▷semiconductors.

cone in botany, the reproductive structure of the conifers and cycads; also known as a strobilus. It consists of a central axis surrounded by numerous, overlapping, scalelike, modified leaves (sporophylls) that bear the reproductive organs. Usually there are

CONE The western yellow or ponderosa pine *Pinus ponderosa* var. *arizonica* exhibits the needlelike leaves and cones typical of gymnosperms. *Premaphotos Wildlife*

separate male and female cones, the former bearing pollen sacs containing pollen grains, and the larger female cones bearing the ovules that contain the ova or egg cells. The pollen is carried from male to female cones by the wind (▷anemophily). The seeds develop within the female cone and are released as the scales open in dry atmospheric conditions, which favour seed dispersal.

cone in geometry, a solid or surface consisting of the set of all straight lines passing through a fixed point (the vertex) and the points of a circle or ellipse whose plane does not contain the vertex.

A circular cone of perpendicular height, with its apex above the centre of the circle, is known as a **right circular cone**; it is generated by rotating an isosceles triangle or framework about its line of symmetry. A right circular cone of perpendicular height h and base of radius r has a volume $V = \frac{1}{3}\pi r^2 h$.

The distance from the edge of the base of a cone to the vertex is called the slant height. In a right circular cone of slant height l, the curved surface area is $\pi r l$, and the area of the base is πr^2. Therefore the total surface area $A = \pi r l + \pi r^2 = \pi r(l + r)$.

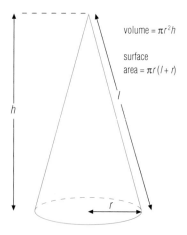

volume = $\pi r^2 h$

surface area = $\pi r (l + r)$

CONE The volume and surface area of a cone are given by formulae involving a few simple dimensions.

Coney Island seaside resort in Brooklyn, in the southwest of Long Island, New York, USA; it is 10 km/6 mi long and about 1 km/0.6 mi at its widest point. Coney Island (now a peninsula) has been popular for its amusement parks and ocean bathing since the 1840s, but this has since declined; it is now mainly a residential area.

Confederacy in US history, popular name for the **Confederate States of America**, the government established by 7 (later 11) Southern states in February 1861 when they seceded from the Union, precipitating the American ▷Civil War. Richmond, Virginia, was the capital, and Jefferson Davis the president. The Confederacy fell after its army was defeated in 1865 and General Robert E ▷Lee surrendered.

The Confederacy suffered from a lack of political leadership as well as a deficit of troops and supplies. Nevertheless, Southern forces won many significant victories. Confederate leaders had hoped to enlist support from Britain and France, but the slavery issue and the Confederacy's uncertain prospects prompted the Europeans to maintain neutrality, although they provided supplies for a time. The Union's blockade and the grinding weight of superior resources made the outcome virtually inevitable. The states of the Confederacy were South Carolina, Georgia, Florida, Alabama, Louisiana, Mississippi, Texas, Virginia, Tennessee, Arkansas, and North Carolina.

Related Web site: Constitution of the Confederate States of America http://odur.let.rug.nl/~usa/D/1851-1875/constitution/css.html

Confederation, Articles of in US history, the initial means by which the 13 former British colonies created a form of national government. Ratified in 1781, the articles established a unicameral legislature, Congress, with limited powers of raising revenue, regulating currency, and conducting foreign affairs. But because the individual states retained significant autonomy, the confederation was unmanageable. The articles were superseded by the US Constitution in 1788.

Related Web site: Constitution of the Confederate States of America http://odur.let.rug.nl/~usa/D/1851-1875/constitution/css.htm

confession in law, a criminal's admission of guilt. Since false confessions may be elicited by intimidation or ill treatment of the accused, the validity of confession in a court of law varies from one legal system to another. For example, in England and Wales a confession, without confirmatory evidence, is sufficient to convict; in Scotland it is not. In the USA a confession that is shown to be coerced does not void a conviction as long as it is supported by independent evidence.

confession in religion, the confession of sins practised in Roman Catholic, Orthodox, and most Far Eastern Christian churches, and since the early 19th century revived in Anglican and Lutheran churches. The Lateran Council of 1215 made auricular confession (self-accusation by the penitent to a priest, who in Catholic doctrine is divinely invested with authority to give absolution) obligatory once a year.

confidence vote in politics, a test of support for the government in the legislature. In political systems modelled on that of the UK, the survival of a government depends on assembly support. The opposition may move a vote of 'no confidence'; if the vote is carried, it requires the government, by convention, to resign.

configuration in computing, the way in which a system, whether it be ▷hardware and/or ▷software, is set up. A minimum configuration is often referred to for a particular application, and this will usually include a specification of processor, disk and memory size, and peripherals required.

CONFIGURATION An engineer configuring a number of PCs (personal computers) so that they will function independently, yet remain linked in a network and (via modems) to a company telephone system. *Image Bank*

confirmation rite practised by a number of Christian denominations, including Roman Catholic, Anglican, and Orthodox, in which a previously baptized person is admitted to full membership of the church. In Reform Judaism there is often a confirmation service several years after the bar or bat mitzvah (initiation into the congregation).

Confucianism body of beliefs and practices based on the Chinese classics and supported by the authority of the philosopher Confucius. The origin of things is seen in the union of **yin** and **yang**, the passive and active principles. Human relationships follow the patriarchal pattern. For more than 2,000 years Chinese political government, social organization, and individual conduct was shaped by Confucian principles. In 1912, Confucian philosophy, as a basis for government, was dropped by the state.

The writings on which Confucianism is based include the ideas of a group of traditional books edited by Confucius, as well as his own works, such as the *Analects*, and those of some of his pupils. The *I Ching* is included among the Confucianist texts.

Doctrine Until 1912 the emperor of China was regarded as the father of his people, appointed by heaven to rule. The Superior Man was the ideal human and filial piety was the chief virtue. Accompanying a high morality was a kind of ancestor worship.

Practices Under the emperor, sacrifices were offered to heaven and earth, the heavenly bodies, the imperial ancestors, various nature gods, and Confucius himself. These were abolished at the Revolution in 1912, but ancestor worship (better expressed as reverence and remembrance) remained a regular practice in the home. Under communism Confucianism continued. The defence minister Lin Biao was associated with the religion, and although

the communist leader Mao Zedong undertook an anti-Confucius campaign from 1974 to 1976, this was not pursued by the succeeding regime.

Related Web site: Confucius http://www.confucius.org/main01.htm

Confucius (551–479 BC) Chinese Kong Fu Zi or K'ung Fu Tzu; born Kong Qiu or K'ung Ch'iu. (Chinese *Kong Fu Zi*, 'Kong the master') Chinese sage whose name is given to the ethical system of Confucianism. He placed emphasis on moral order and observance of the established patriarchal family and social relationships of authority, obedience, and mutual respect. His emphasis on tradition and ethics attracted a growing number of pupils during his lifetime. *The Analects of Confucius*, a compilation of his teachings, was published after his death.

Confucius was born in Lu, in what is now the province of Shangdong, and his early years were spent in poverty. Married at the age of 19, he worked as a minor official, then as a teacher. In 517 there was an uprising in Lu, and Confucius spent the next year or two in the adjoining state of Ch'i. As a teacher he was able to place many of his pupils in government posts but a powerful position eluded him. Only in his fifties was he given an office, but he soon resigned because of the lack of power it conveyed. Then for 14 years he wandered from state to state looking for a ruler who could give him a post where he could put into practice his ideas for relieving suffering among the poor. At the age of 67 he returned to Lu and devoted himself to teaching. At his death five years later he was buried with great pomp, and his grave outside Qufu has remained a centre of pilgrimage. Within 300 years of his death, his teaching was adopted by the Chinese state.

Related Web site: Analects of Confucius, The http://eawc.evansville.edu/anthology/analects.htm

congenital disease in medicine, a disease that is present at birth. It is not necessarily genetic in origin; for example, congenital herpes may be acquired by the baby as it passes through the mother's birth canal.

conger any large marine eel of the family Congridae, especially the genus *Conger*. Conger eels live in shallow water, hiding in crevices during the day and active by night, feeding on fish and crabs. They are valued for food and angling. The European conger *C. conger* is found in the northern Atlantic and in the Mediterranean. It is often 1.8 m/6 ft long, and sometimes as much as 2.7 m/9 ft.

conglomerate in geology, coarse-grained clastic ▷sedimentary rock, composed of rounded fragments (clasts) of pre-existing rocks cemented in a finer matrix, usually sand.

Congo, Democratic Republic of see country box.

Congo, Republic of see country box.

Congo River (or Zaire River) second-longest river in Africa, rising near the Zambia–Democratic Republic of Congo border (and known as the **Lualaba River** in the upper reaches) and flowing 4,500 km/2,800 mi to the Atlantic Ocean, running in a great curve that crosses the equator twice, and discharging a volume of water second only to the River Amazon. The chief tributaries are the Ubangi, Sangha, and Kasai.

Congregationalism form of church government adopted by those Protestant Christians known as Congregationalists, who let each congregation manage its own affairs. The first Congregationalists established themselves in London, England, and were called the Brownists after Robert Browne, who defined the congregational principle in 1580. They opposed King James I and were supporters of Oliver ▷Cromwell. They became one of the most important forces in the founding of New England.

Congress national legislature of the USA, consisting of the House of Representatives (435 members, apportioned to the states of the Union on the basis of population, and elected for two-year terms) and the Senate (100 senators, two for each state, elected for six years, one-third elected every two years). Both representatives

CONGRESS A view of the west side of the Capitol Building, Washington, DC, USA. *Image Bank*

Congo, Democratic Republic of

AGE DISTRIBUTION (% of total population) 0–14 49%, 15–59 46%, 60+ 5% (2002 est)

ETHNIC GROUPS almost entirely of African descent, distributed among over 200 ethnic groups, the most numerous being the Kongo, Luba, Lunda, Mongo, and Zande

LANGUAGE French (official), Swahili, Lingala, Kikongo, Tshiluba (all national languages), over 200 other languages

RELIGION Roman Catholic 41%, Protestant 32%, Kimbanguist 13%, animist 10%, Muslim 1–5%

EDUCATION (compulsory years) 6

LITERACY RATE 76% (men); 55% (women) (2003 est)

LABOUR FORCE 65% agriculture, 15% industry, 20% services (2000)

LIFE EXPECTANCY 41 (men); 43 (women) (2000–05)

CHILD MORTALITY RATE (under 5, per 1,000 live births) 205 (2001)

PHYSICIANS (per 1,000 people) 0.07 (1996 est)

HOSPITAL BEDS (per 1,000 people) 1.5 (1993 est)

TV SETS (per 1,000 people) 135 (1999)

RADIOS (per 1,000 people) 386 (2001 est)

INTERNET USERS (per 10,000 people) 3.8 (2002 est)

See also ▷Hutu; ▷Mobutu, Sese Seko; ▷Rwanda; ▷Tutsi.

Congo, Democratic Republic of or Congo (Kinshasa); formerly Republic of Congo (1960–64), Zaire (1971–97) country in central Africa, bounded west by the Republic of the Congo, north by the Central African Republic and Sudan, east by Uganda, Rwanda, Burundi, and Tanzania, southeast by Zambia, and southwest by Angola. There is a short coastline on the Atlantic Ocean.

NATIONAL NAME *République Démocratique du Congo/Democratic Republic of Congo*

AREA 2,344,900 sq km/905,366 sq mi

CAPITAL Kinshasa

MAJOR TOWNS/CITIES Lubumbashi, Kananga, Mbuji-Mayi, Kisangani, Kolwezi, Likasi, Boma

MAJOR PORTS Matadi, Kalemie

PHYSICAL FEATURES Congo River basin has tropical rainforest (second-largest remaining in world) and savannah; mountains in east and west; lakes Tanganyika, Albert, Edward; Ruwenzori Range

Government

HEAD OF STATE AND GOVERNMENT Joseph Kabila from 2001

POLITICAL SYSTEM military

POLITICAL EXECUTIVE military

ADMINISTRATIVE DIVISIONS 10 provinces and one city (Kinshasa)

ARMED FORCES 81,400 (2002 est)

CONSCRIPTION military service is voluntary

DEATH PENALTY retained and used for ordinary crimes

DEFENCE SPEND (% GDP) 21.7 (2002 est)

HEALTH SPEND (% GDP) 1.5 (2000 est)

DEMOCRATIC REPUBLIC OF CONGO
A stamp featuring the parakeet *Opopsitta diophthalma*.

Economy and resources

CURRENCY congolese franc

GPD (US$) 5.7 billion (2002 est)

REAL GDP GROWTH (% change on previous year) –4.4 (2001)

GNI (US$) 5 billion (2002 est)

GNI PER CAPITA (PPP) (US$) 580 (2002 est)

CONSUMER PRICE INFLATION 13.3% (2003 est)

FOREIGN DEBT (US$) 9.02 billion (2001 est)

MAJOR TRADING PARTNERS Belgium–Luxembourg, South Africa, USA, Nigeria, Finland, Italy, Kenya, Zimbabwe, India

RESOURCES petroleum, copper, cobalt (65% of world's reserves), manganese, zinc, tin, uranium, silver, gold, diamonds (one of the world's largest producers of industrial diamonds)

INDUSTRIES textiles, cement, food processing, tobacco, rubber, engineering, wood products, leather, metallurgy and metal extraction, food production, clothing

EXPORTS mineral products (mainly copper, cobalt, industrial diamonds, and petroleum), agricultural products (chiefly coffee). Principal market: Belgium–Luxembourg 62.2% (2001)

IMPORTS manufactured goods, food and live animals, machinery and transport equipment, chemicals, mineral fuels and lubricants. Principal source: Belgium–Luxembourg 18.3% (2001)

ARABLE LAND 3% (2000 est)

AGRICULTURAL PRODUCTS coffee, palm oil, palm kernels, sugar cane, cassava, plantains, maize, groundnuts, bananas, yams, rice, rubber, seed cotton; forest resources

Population and society

POPULATION 52,771,000 (2003 est)

POPULATION GROWTH RATE 2.6% (2000–15)

POPULATION DENSITY (per sq km) 23 (2003 est)

URBAN POPULATION (% of total) 32 (2003 est)

Chronology

13th century: Rise of Kongo Empire, centred on banks of the Congo River.

1483: First visited by the Portuguese, who named the area Zaire (from Zadi, 'big water') and converted local rulers to Christianity.

16th–17th centuries: Great development of slave trade by Portuguese, Dutch, British, and French merchants, initially supplied by Kongo intermediaries.

18th century: Rise of Luba state, in southern copper belt of north Katanga, and Lunda, in Kasai region in central south.

mid-19th century: Eastern Zaire invaded by Arab slave traders from East Africa.

1874–77: Welsh-born US explorer Henry Morton Stanley navigated Congo River to Atlantic Ocean.

1879–87: Stanley engaged by King Leopold II of Belgium to sign protection treaties with local chiefs and the 'Congo Free State' was awarded to Leopold by 1884–85 Berlin Conference; great expansion in rubber export, using forced labour.

1908: Leopold was forced to relinquish personal control of Congo Free State, after international condemnation of human-rights abuses. Became a colony of the Belgian Congo and important exporter of minerals.

1959: Riots in Kinshasa (Léopoldville) persuaded Belgium to decolonize rapidly.

1960: Independence achieved as Republic of the Congo. Civil war broke out between central government based in Kinshasa (Léopoldville) with Joseph Kasavubu as president, and rich mining province of Katanga.

1961: Former prime minister Patrice Lumumba was murdered in Katanga; fighting between mercenaries engaged by Katanga secessionist leader Moise Tshombe, and United Nations (UN) troops; Kasai and Kivu provinces also sought (briefly) to secede.

1963: Katanga secessionist war ended; Tshombe forced into exile.

1964: Tshombe returned from exile to become prime minister; pro-Marxist groups took control of eastern Zaire. The country was renamed the Democratic Republic of Congo.

1965: Western-backed Col Sese Seko Mobutu seized power in coup, ousting Kasavubu and Tshombe.

1971: Country renamed Republic of Zaire, with Mobutu as president as *authenticité* (Africanization) policy launched.

1972: Mobutu's Popular Movement of the Revolution (MPR) became the only legal political party. Katanga province was renamed Shaba.

1974: Foreign-owned businesses and plantations seized by Mobutu and given to his political allies.

1977: Zairean guerrillas invaded Shaba province from Angola, but were repulsed by Moroccan, French, and Belgian paratroopers.

1980s: The collapse in world copper prices increased foreign debts, and international creditors forced a series of austerity programmes.

1991: After antigovernment riots, Mobutu agreed to end the ban on multiparty politics and share power with the opposition.

1993: Rival pro- and anti-Mobutu governments were created.

1994: There was an influx of Rwandan refugees.

1995: There was secessionist activity in Shaba and Kasai provinces and interethnic warfare in Kivu, adjoining Rwanda in the east.

1996: Thousands of refugees were allowed to return to Rwanda.

1997: Mobutu was ousted by the rebel forces of Laurent Kabila, who declared himself president and changed the name of Zaire back to the Democratic Republic of the Congo. There was fighting between army factions.

1998: There was a rebellion by Tutsi-led forces, backed by Rwanda and Uganda, against President Kabila; government troops aided by Angola and Zimbabwe put down the rebellion. A constituent assembly was appointed prior to a general election. UN-urged peace talks and a ceasefire agreed by rebel forces failed.

1999: A peace deal, signed by both the government and rebel factions, was broken in November with fighting in the north of the country, and a reported bombing by the government of the centre in an attempt to free 700 Zimbabwean troops besieged by rebels.

2000: The war between government and rebel soldiers intensified. President Kabila walked out of a peace conference held in Lusaka, Zambia and called for a summit with Uganda, Rwanda, and Burundi. Ugandan-backed rebels made gains in the northwest of the country. Kabila allowed some United Nations troops into the country, but hindered the operation.

2001: In January President Kabila was assassinated in suspicious circumstances, allegedly by a bodyguard. He was succeeded by his son, Joseph.

2002: Belgium apologized, for the first time, for the 1961 murder of Patrice Lumumba. President Joseph Kabila and Ugandan president Yoweri Museveni signed a peace agreement providing for the withdrawal of Ugandan troops from the country, and Rwanda completed its troop withdrawal. The government signed a peace deal with the country's two main rebel groups, providing for the establishment of a democracy.

and senators are elected by direct popular vote. Congress meets in Washington DC, in the Capitol Building. An ▷act of Congress is a bill passed by both houses.

The Congress of the United States met for the first time on 4 March 1789. It was preceded by the Congress of the Confederation representing the several states under the Articles of Confederation from 1781 to 1789.

In 19th-century history, the term 'congress' refers to a formal meeting or assembly, usually for peace, where delegates assembled to discuss or settle a matter of international concern, such as the Congress of Vienna of 1815, which divided up Napoleon's empire after the Napoleonic Wars; and the Congress of Paris of 1856, which settled some of the problems resulting from the Crimean War.

Related Web sites: US Capitol http://www.aoc.gov/
US Senate http://www.senate.gov/

Congress of Racial Equality (CORE) US nonviolent civil-rights organization, founded in Chicago in 1942 by James Farmer. CORE first concentrated on housing, then sponsored Freedom Rides into the South in 1961 and a lengthy campaign of voter registration. Its work helped achieve such results as the 1965 Voting Rights Act. In recent years, CORE's politically conservative approach has drawn criticism from more militant African-Americans, and its role has been diminished.

Congress Party Indian political party, founded in 1885 as the Indian National Congress. It led the movement to end British rule and was the governing party from independence in 1947 until 1977, when Indira Gandhi lost the leadership she had held since 1966. Congress also held power from 1980 to 1989 and from 1991 to 1996. Heading a splinter group, known as **Congress (I)** ('I' for Indira), she achieved an over-whelming victory in the elections of 1980, and reduced the main Congress Party to a minority.
The 'I' was dropped from the name in 1993 following the assassination of Rajiv ▷Gandhi in 1991, and a small split occurred in the party in 1995.

William Congreve
Musick has charms to sooth a savage breast
The Mourning Bride I. i

---

congress system developed from the Congress of Vienna (1814–15), a series of international meetings in Aachen, Germany, in 1818, Troppau, Austria, in 1820, and Verona, Italy, in 1822.

British opposition to the use of congresses by Klemens ▷Metternich as a weapon against liberal and national movements inside Europe brought them to an end as a system of international arbitration, although congresses continued to meet into the 1830s.

Congreve, William (1670–1729) English dramatist and poet. His first success was the comedy *The Old Bachelor* (1693), followed by *The Double Dealer* (1694), *Love for Love* (1695), the tragedy *The Mourning Bride* (1697), and *The Way of the World* (1700). His plays, which satirize the social affectations of the time, are characterized by elegant wit and wordplay, and complex plots.

congruent in geometry, having the same shape and size, as applied to two-dimensional or solid figures. With plane congruent

---

Congo, Republic of

CONGO, REPUBLIC OF This stamp, bearing the United Nations (UN) logo and the flag of the Republic of Congo, commemorates the admission of the country to the UN in 1960. *Stanley Gibbons*

POPULATION GROWTH RATE 2.8% (2000–15)
POPULATION DENSITY (per sq km) 11 (2003 est)
URBAN POPULATION (% of total) 67 (2003 est)
AGE DISTRIBUTION (% of total population) 0–14 47%, 15–59 48%, 60+ 5% (2002 est)
ETHNIC GROUPS predominantly Bantu; population comprises 15 main ethnic groups and 75 tribes. The Kongo, or Bakongo, account for about 48% of the population, then come the Sanga at about 20%, the Bateke, or Teke, at about 17%, and then the Mboshi, or Boubangui, about 12%
LANGUAGE French (official), Kongo, Monokutuba and Lingala (both patois), and other dialects
RELIGION Christian 50%, animist 48%, Muslim 2%
EDUCATION (compulsory years) 10
LITERACY RATE 90% (men); 78% (women) (2003 est)
LABOUR FORCE 41% agriculture, 19% industry, 40% services (2000)
LIFE EXPECTANCY 47 (men); 50 (women) (2000–05)
CHILD MORTALITY RATE (under 5, per 1,000 live births) 108 (2001)

HOSPITAL BEDS (per 1,000 people) 3.5 (1994 est)
TV SETS (per 1,000 people) 13 (1999)
RADIOS (per 1,000 people) 124 (1997)
INTERNET USERS (per 10,000 people) 15.2 (2002 est)
PERSONAL COMPUTER USERS (per 100 people) 0.4 (2002 est)

Congo, Republic of or Congo (Brazzaville) country in west-central Africa, bounded north by Cameroon and the Central African Republic, east and south by the Democratic Republic of Congo (formerly Zaire), west by the Atlantic Ocean, and northwest by Gabon.

NATIONAL NAME *République du Congo/ Republic of Congo*
AREA 342,000 sq km/132,046 sq mi
CAPITAL Brazzaville
MAJOR TOWNS/CITIES Pointe-Noire, Nkayi, Loubomo, Bouenza, Mossendjo, Ouesso, Owando
MAJOR PORTS Pointe-Noire
PHYSICAL FEATURES narrow coastal plain rises to central plateau, then falls into northern basin; Congo River on the border with the Democratic Republic of Congo; half the country is rainforest

Government

HEAD OF STATE AND GOVERNMENT Denis Sassou-Nguessou from 1997
POLITICAL SYSTEM nationalistic socialist
POLITICAL EXECUTIVE unlimited presidency
ADMINISTRATIVE DIVISIONS nine regions and one capital district
ARMED FORCES 10,000; plus paramilitary forces of 2,000 (2002 est)
CONSCRIPTION national service is voluntary
DEATH PENALTY retains the death penalty for ordinary crimes but can be considered abolitionist in practice; date of last known execution 1982
DEFENCE SPEND (% GDP) 3.1 (2002 est)
EDUCATION SPEND (% GDP) 4.2 (2000 est)
HEALTH SPEND (% GDP) 2.2 (2000 est)

Economy and resources

CURRENCY franc CFA
GPD (US$) 3 billion (2002 est)
REAL GDP GROWTH (% change on previous year) 2.9 (2001)
GNI (US$) 2.2 billion (2002 est)
GNI PER CAPITA (PPP) (US$) 700 (2002 est)
CONSUMER PRICE INFLATION 2% (2003 est)
FOREIGN DEBT (US$) 4.4 billion (2001 est)
MAJOR TRADING PARTNERS France, USA, Italy, South Korea, Germany, China, Belgium, South Africa
RESOURCES petroleum, natural gas, lead, zinc, gold, copper, phosphate, iron ore, potash, bauxite
INDUSTRIES mining, food processing, textiles, cement, metal goods, chemicals, forest products
EXPORTS petroleum and petroleum products, saw logs and veneer logs, veneer sheets, sugar. Principal market: USA 17.2% (2001)
IMPORTS machinery, chemical products, iron and steel, transport equipment, foodstuffs. Principal source: France 20.5% (2001)
ARABLE LAND 0.5% (2000 est)
AGRICULTURAL PRODUCTS cassava, plantains, sugar cane, palm oil, maize, coffee, cocoa; forestry

Population and society

POPULATION 3,724,000 (2003 est)

Chronology

late 15th century: First visited by Portuguese explorers, at which time the Bakongo (a six-state confederation centred south of the Congo River in Angola) and Bateke, both Bantu groups, were the chief kingdoms.

16th century: The Portuguese, in collaboration with coastal peoples, exported slaves from the interior to plantations in Brazil and São Tomé; missionaries spread Roman Catholicism.

1880: French explorer Pierre Savorgnan de Brazza established French claims to coastal region, with the makoko (king) of the Bateke accepting French protection.

1905: There was international outrage at revelations of the brutalities of forced labour as ivory and rubber resources were ruthlessly exploited by private concessionaires.

1910: As Moyen-Congo became part of French Equatorial Africa, which also comprised Gabon and the Central African Republic, with the capital at Brazzaville.

1920s: More than 17,000 were killed as forced labour was used to build the Congo-Ocean railroad; first Bakongo political organization founded.

1940–44: Supported the 'Free French' anti-Nazi resistance cause during World War II, Brazzaville serving as capital for Gen Charles de Gaulle's forces.

1946: Became autonomous, with a territorial assembly and representation in French parliament.

1960: Achieved independence from France, with Abbé Fulbert Youlou, a moderate Catholic Bakongo priest, as the first president.

1963: Alphonse Massamba-Débat became president and a single-party state was established under the socialist National Revolutionary Movement (MNR).

1968: A military coup, led by Capt Marien Ngouabi, ousted Massamba-Débat.

1970: A Marxist People's Republic declared, with Ngouabi's PCT the only legal party.

1977: Ngouabi was assassinated in a plot by Massamba-Débat, who was executed.

early 1980s: Petroleum production increased fivefold.

1990: The PCT abandoned Marxist-Leninism and promised multiparty politics and market-centred reforms in an economy crippled by foreign debt.

1992: Multiparty elections gave the coalition dominated by the Pan-African Union for Social Democracy (UPADS) an assembly majority, with Pascal Lissouba elected president.

1995: A new broad-based government was formed, including opposition groups; market-centred economic reforms were instigated, including privatization.

1997: Violence between factions continued despite the unity government. Sassou-Nguesso took over the presidency.

figures, one figure will fit on top of the other exactly, though this may first require rotation and/or translation of one of the figures.

conical having the shape of a ▷cone.

conic section curve obtained when a conical surface is intersected by a plane. If the intersecting plane cuts both extensions of the cone, it yields a ▷hyperbola; if it is parallel to the side of the cone, it produces a ▷parabola. Other intersecting planes produce ▷circles or ▷ellipses.

The Greek mathematician Apollonius wrote eight books with the title *Conic Sections*, which superseded previous work on the subject by Aristarchus and Euclid.

conifer any of a large number of cone-bearing trees or shrubs. They are often pyramid-shaped, with leaves that are either scaled or needle-shaped; most are evergreen. Conifers include pines, spruces, firs, yews, junipers, monkey puzzles, and larches. (Order Coniferales.)

conjugate in mathematics, a term indicating that two elements are connected in some way; for example, $(a + ib)$ and $(a - ib)$ are conjugate complex numbers.

conjugation a temporary union of two single cells (or hyphae in fungi) with at least one of them receiving genetic material from the other: the bacterial equivalent of sexual reproduction. A fragment of the ▷DNA from one bacterium is passed along a thin tube, the pilus, into another bacterium.

conjunction in astronomy, the alignment of two celestial bodies as seen from Earth. A superior planet (or other object) is in conjunction when it lies behind the Sun. An ▷inferior planet (or other object) comes to **inferior conjunction** when it passes between the Earth and the Sun; it is at **superior conjunction** when it passes behind the Sun.

Planetary conjunction takes place when a planet is closely aligned with another celestial object, such as the Moon, a star, or another planet.

Because the orbital planes of the inferior planets are tilted with respect to that of the Earth, they usually pass either above or below the Sun at inferior conjunction. If they line up exactly, a ▷transit will occur.

Cyril Connolly
Better to write for yourself and have no public, than to write for the public and have no self.
New Statesman, 25 February 1933

conjunctivitis inflammation of the conjunctiva, the delicate membrane that lines the inside of the eyelids and covers the front of the eye. Symptoms include redness, swelling, and a watery or pus-filled discharge. It may be caused by infection, allergy, or other irritant.

Connacht (or Connaught) historic province of the Republic of Ireland, comprising the counties of Galway, Leitrim, Mayo, Roscommon, and Sligo; area 17,130 sq km/6,612 sq mi; population (1996) 433,200. The chief towns are Galway, Roscommon, Castlebar, Sligo, and Carrick-on-Shannon. Mainly lowland, it is agricultural and stock-raising country, with poor land in the west.

Connecticut state in New England, USA. It is nicknamed Constitution State or the Nutmeg State. Connecticut ratified the US Constitution in 1788, becoming the 5th state in the Union. It is bordered to the north by Massachusetts, to the east by Rhode Island, with the Pawcatuck River forming part of the boundary, to the west and southwest by New York, and to the south by the Long Island Sound, across which are New York's Long and Fishers islands.

population (1996 est) 3,274,000 **area** 13,000 sq km/5,018 sq mi **capital** Hartford **towns and cities** Bridgeport, New Haven, Waterbury, Stamford **industries and products** dairy, poultry, and market-garden products; tobacco, watches, clocks, silverware, helicopters, jet engines, nuclear submarines, hardware and l ocks, electrical and electronic equipment, guns and ammunition, optical instruments. Hartford is the centre of the nation's insurance industry

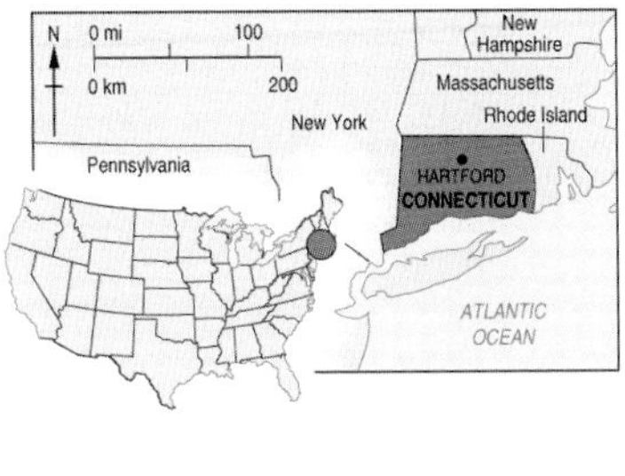

connective tissue in animals, tissue made up of a noncellular substance, the ▷extracellular matrix, in which some cells are embedded. Skin, bones, tendons, cartilage, and adipose tissue (fat) are the main connective tissues. There are also small amounts of connective tissue in organs such as the brain and liver, where they maintain shape and structure.

Connery, Sean (Thomas) (1930–) Scottish film actor. He was the first interpreter of James Bond in several films based on the spy thrillers of Ian Fleming. He has since enjoyed success as a mature actor in such films as *The Name of the Rose* (1986), *Highlander* (1986), and *Indiana Jones and the Last Crusade* (1989). He won an Academy Award for his supporting performance in the crime thriller *The Untouchables* (1987). He was knighted in 1999.

Other films include the Bond movies *Dr No* (1962) and *Goldfinger* (1964), *Marnie* (1964), *The Man Who Would Be King* (1975), *The Hunt for Red October* (1990), *Rising Sun* (1993), *Dragonheart* and *The Rock* (both 1996), *The Avengers* (1998), and *Finding Forrester* (2000).

Connolly, Cyril (Vernon) (1903–1974) English critic and writer. As a founder and editor of the literary magazine *Horizon* (1939–50), he had considerable critical influence. His works include *The Rock Pool* (1936), a novel of artists on the Riviera, and *The Unquiet Grave* (1944), a series of reflections published under the pseudonym of Palinurus.

Connors, Jimmy (James Scott) (1952–) US tennis player who won the Wimbledon title in 1974 and 1982, and subsequently won ten Grand Slam events. He was one of the first players to popularize the two-handed backhand, and won a record 109 tournaments.

conquistador (Spanish 'conqueror') any of the early Spanish conquerors in the Americas. The title is applied in particular to those leaders who overthrew the indigenous empires of Peru and Mexico, and other parts of Central and South America. They include Hernán ▷Cortés, who subjugated Mexico; Francisco ▷Pizarro, conqueror of Peru with Diego de Almagro; and Juan ▷Ponce de León.

Conrad five German kings:

Conrad I (died 918) King of the Germans from 911, when he succeeded Louis the Child, the last of the German Carolingians. During his reign the realm was harassed by ▷Magyar invaders.

Conrad II (*c.* 990–1039) King of the Germans from 1024, Holy Roman Emperor from 1027. He ceded the Sleswick (Schleswig) borderland, south of the Jutland peninsula, to King Canute, but extended his rule into Lombardy and Burgundy.

Conrad III (1093–1152) King of Germany and Holy Roman Emperor from 1138, the first king of the Hohenstaufen dynasty. Throughout his reign there was a fierce struggle between his followers, the ▷Ghibellines, and the ▷Guelphs, the followers of Henry the Proud, duke of Saxony and Bavaria (1108–1139), and later of his son Henry the Lion (1129–1195).

Conrad IV (1228–1254) Elected king of the Germans in 1237. Son of the Holy Roman Emperor Frederick II, he had to defend his right of succession against Henry Raspe of Thuringia (died 1247) and William of Holland (1227–56).

Conrad V (1252–1268) Also known as **Conradin**. Son of Conrad IV, recognized as king of the Germans, Sicily, and Jerusalem by German supporters of the ▷Hohenstaufens in 1254. He led ▷Ghibelline forces against Charles of Anjou at the Battle of Tagliacozzo, northern Italy, in 1266, and was captured and executed.

Conrad, Joseph (1857–1924) Pen-name of Teodor Józef Konrad Nałęcz Korzeniowski. British novelist, born in Ukraine of Polish parents. His greatest works include the novels *Lord Jim* (1900), *Nostromo* (1904), *The Secret Agent* (1907), and *Under Western Eyes* (1911); the short story 'Heart of Darkness' (1902); and the short novel *The Shadow Line* (1917). These combine a vivid and sensuous evocation of various lands and seas with a rigorous, humane scrutiny of moral dilemmas, pitfalls, and desperation.

Conrad went to sea at the age of 17 and first learned English at 21. He is regarded as one of the greatest of modern novelists. His prose style, varying from eloquently sensuous to bare and astringent, keeps the reader in constant touch with a mature, truth-seeking, creative mind.

Joseph Conrad
All ambitions are lawful except those which climb upwards on the miseries or credulities of mankind.
Some Reminiscences

Conran, Terence Orby (1931–) English designer and retailer of furnishings, fashion, and household goods. He was founder of the Storehouse group of companies, including Habitat and Conran Design, with retail outlets in the UK, the USA, and elsewhere. He has been influential in popularizing French country style in the UK.

conscientious objector person refusing compulsory service, usually military, on moral, religious, or political grounds.

conscription legislation for all able-bodied male citizens (and female in some countries, such as Israel) to serve with the armed forces. It originated in France in 1792, and in the 19th and 20th centuries became the established practice in almost all European states. Modern conscription systems often permit alternative national service for conscientious objectors.

consent, age of age at which consent may legally be given to sexual intercourse by a girl or boy.

conservation in the life sciences, action taken to protect and preserve the natural world, usually from pollution, overexploitation, and other harmful features of human activity. The late 1980s saw a great increase in public concern for the environment, with membership of conservation groups, such as ▷Friends of the Earth, ▷Greenpeace, and the US Sierra Club, rising sharply and making the ▷green movement an increasingly powerful political force. Globally the most important issues include the depletion of atmospheric ozone by the action of ▷chlorofluorocarbons (CFCs), the build-up of carbon dioxide in the atmosphere (thought to contribute to an intensification of the ▷greenhouse effect), and ▷deforestation.

Conservation groups in Britain originated in the 1860s; they include the Commons Preservation Society (1865), which fought successfully against the enclosure of Hampstead Heath (1865) and Epping Forest (1866) in London; the National Footpaths Preservation Society (1844); and the ▷National Trust (1895). More recently English Heritage (1983), English Nature (1991, formerly the Nature Conservancy Council), and the Countryside Commission have become heavily involved. In the UK the conservation debate has centred on water quality, road-building schemes, the safety of nuclear power, and the ethical treatment of animals.

Natura 2000 Twelve coastal sites in Great Britain, including five Special Areas of Conservation, have been designated by the European Commission to be part of a network of Natura 2000 sites. The EC will provide funds to help preserve these sites from development, overfishing, and pollution, and to monitor rare plants. They include the north Northumberland coast, with its sea caves, its breeding population of grey seals in the Farne Islands, and Arctic species such as the wolf fish; the Wash and north Norfolk coast, with its population of common seals, waders, and wildfowl, and its extensive salt marshes; and Plymouth Sound and estuaries, with their submerged sandbanks.

'Turning the Tide' A £10 million project, launched in 1997 by the Millennium Commission, to protect and restore Britain's only magnesium limestone cliffs, between Hartlepool and Sunderland. The area is rich in wild flowers, with grassland and denes (steep, wooded valleys). Intensive farming and the use of fertilizers have damaged the flora and fauna of the area. The beaches are polluted as a result of over two centuries of coal mining along the Durham coast. Waste from the mines was dumped into the sea and on to the beaches, leaving heaps of spoil 3.7–4.6 m/12–15 ft high. The restoration project aims to remove spoil from the beaches and return the cliffs to their natural grassland.

Related Web site: Conservation International http://www.conservation.org/

conservation, architectural attempts to maintain the character of buildings and historical areas. In Britain this is subject to a growing body of legislation which has designated around a million listed buildings, the largest number in Western Europe. There are now over 6,000 conservation areas and 500,000 listed buildings throughout England alone.

conservation of energy in chemistry, the principle that states that in a chemical reaction, the total amount of energy in the system remains unchanged.

conservation of mass in chemistry, the principle that states that in a chemical reaction the sum of all the masses of the substances involved in the reaction (reactants) is equal to the sum of all of the masses of the substances produced by the reaction (products) – that is, no matter is gained or lost.

conservatism approach to government favouring the maintenance of existing institutions and identified with a number of Western political parties, such as the British Conservative, US Republican, German Christian Democratic, and Australian Liberal parties. It tends to be explicitly nondoctrinaire and pragmatic but generally emphasizes free-enterprise capitalism, minimal government intervention in the economy, rigid law and order, and the importance of national traditions. In the UK, modern conservatism, under the ideological influence of ▷Thatcherism, has become increasingly radical, attacking entrenched institutions and promoting free-market economies.

Conservative Party
UK political party, one of the two historic British parties; the name replaced **Tory** in general use from 1830 onwards. Traditionally the party of landed interests, it broadened its political base under Benjamin ▷Disraeli's leadership in the 19th century. The present Conservative Party's free-market capitalism is supported by the world of finance and the management of industry. In recent history, the Conservative Party was in power under Margaret ▷Thatcher (1979–90) and John ▷Major (1990–97). After the party's defeat in the 1997 general election, John Major resigned and was succeeded by William ▷Hague. The party's Central Office is located in Smith Square, London, and the current party chairman is Michael Ancram.

In the 1980s the party's economic policies increased the spending power of the majority, but also the gap between rich and poor; nationalized industries were sold off (see ▷privatization); military spending and close alliance with the USA were favoured; and the funding of local government was overhauled with the introduction of the ▷poll tax. The Conservative government of John Major repudiated some of the extreme policies of ▷Thatcherism, notably the poll tax, introduced the new ▷Citizen's Charter, and promoted further privatization or market testing.

Related Web site: Conservative Party http://www.conservatives.com/home.cfm

Constable, John
(1776–1837) English artist; one of the greatest landscape painters of the 19th century. He painted scenes of his native Suffolk, including *The Haywain* (1821; National Gallery, London), as well as castles, cathedrals, landscapes, and coastal scenes in other parts of Britain. Constable inherited the Dutch tradition of sombre realism, in particular the style of Jacob ▷Ruisdael. He aimed to capture the momentary changes of the weather as well as to create monumental images of British scenery, as in *The White Horse* (1819; Frick Collection, New York) and *Salisbury Cathedral from the Bishop's Grounds* (1827; Victoria and Albert Museum, London).

Constable's paintings are remarkable for their atmospheric effects and were admired by many French painters, including Eugène Delacroix. Notable are *The Leaping Horse* (1825; Royal Academy, London); *The Cornfield* (1826; National Gallery, London); and *Dedham Vale* (1828; National Gallery of Scotland, Edinburgh). His many oil sketches are often considered among his best work.

JOHN CONSTABLE *Dedham Lock and Mill*, by English landscape painter John Constable. *The Art Archive/Egyptian Museum Turin/Jacquelin Hyde*

Constance, Lake
(German **Bodensee**) lake bounded by Germany, Austria, and Switzerland, through which the River Rhine flows; area 539 sq km/208 sq mi. It is about 72 km/45 mi long, 13 km/8 mi wide, and lies 396 m/1,300 ft above sea level. At its northwestern end it divides into two, the northern branch being the Überlingen Lake, and the southern the Untersee. The main part of the lake is known as the Obersee.

constant in mathematics, a fixed quantity or one that does not change its value in relation to ▷variables. For example, in the algebraic expression $y^2 = 5x - 3$, the numbers 3 and 5 are

constants. In physics, certain quantities are regarded as universal constants, such as the speed of light in a vacuum.

Constanţa
chief Romanian port on the Black Sea, capital of Constanţa region, and second-largest city of Romania; population (1993) 349,000. It has refineries, shipbuilding yards, and food factories.

constantan (or eureka) high-resistance alloy of approximately 40% nickel and 60% copper with a very low coefficient of thermal expansion (measure of expansion on heating). It is used in electrical resistors.

constant composition, law of
in chemistry, the law that states that the proportions of the amounts of the elements in a pure compound are always the same and are independent of the method by which the compound was produced.

Constantine
city and capital of the department of Constantine in northeast Algeria; population (1998 est) 596,100. It lies 320 km/200 mi south of the capital, Algiers. Products include carpets and leather and woollen goods. The oldest city in Algeria, it was the capital of the Roman province of Numidia, but declined and was ruined, then restored in 313 by Constantine the Great, whose name it bears. It was subsequently ruled by Vandals, Arabs, and Turks and was captured by the French in 1837.

Constantine II
(1940–) King of the Hellenes (Greece). In 1964 he succeeded his father Paul I, went into exile in 1967, and was formally deposed in 1973.

Constantine the Great
(c. AD 285–337) First Christian emperor of Rome and founder of Constantinople. He defeated Maxentius, joint emperor of Rome in AD 312, and in 313 formally recognized Christianity. As sole emperor of the west of the empire, he defeated Licinius, emperor of the east, to become ruler of the Roman world in 324. He presided over the church's first council at Nicaea in 325. Constantine moved his capital to Byzantium on the Bosporus in 330, renaming it Constantinople (now Istanbul).

CONSTANTINE THE GREAT The Pallazio dei Conservatori in the centre of Rome, Italy, houses works such as this colossal marble head which is believed to be part of a huge statue of Constantine dating from 313, following his victory over Maxentius. *Image Bank*

Constantinople
ancient city founded by the Greeks as Byzantium in about 660 BC and refounded by the Roman emperor Constantine (I) the Great in AD 330 as the capital of the Eastern Roman Empire. Constantinople (modern Istanbul, Turkey) was the impregnable bastion of the Eastern Roman Empire and the Byzantine Empire, its successor, until it fell to the Turks on 29 May 1453 after a nearly two-month siege and became the capital of the Ottoman Empire.

constellation
one of the 88 areas into which the sky is divided for the purposes of identifying and naming celestial objects. The first constellations were simple, arbitrary patterns of stars in which early civilizations visualized gods, sacred beasts, and mythical heroes.

The constellations in use today are derived from a list of 48 known to the ancient Greeks, who inherited some from the

Babylonians. The current list of 88 constellations was adopted by the International Astronomical Union, astronomy's governing body, in 1930.

Related Web site: Stars and Constellations http://www.astro.wisc.edu/~dolan/constellations/constellations.html

constipation
in medicine, the infrequent emptying of the bowel. The intestinal contents are propelled by peristaltic contractions of the intestine in the digestive process. The faecal residue collects in the rectum, distending it and promoting defecation. Constipation may be due to illness, alterations in food consumption, stress, or as an adverse effect of certain drugs. An increased intake of dietary fibre (see ▷fibre, dietary) can alleviate constipation. Laxatives may be used to relieve temporary constipation but they should not be used routinely.

constitution
body of fundamental laws of a state, laying down the system of government and defining the relations of the legislature, executive, and judiciary to each other and to the citizens. Since the French Revolution (1789–1799) almost all countries (the UK is an exception) have adopted written constitutions; that of the USA (1787) is the oldest. Of all the world's states, 69 have adopted their current constitutions in the period since 1989.

The proliferation of legislation during the 1970s, often carried on the basis of a small majority in the Commons and by governments elected by an overall minority of votes, led to demands such as those by the organization Charter 88 for the introduction of a written constitution as a safeguard for the liberty of the individual.

The constitution of the UK does not exist as a single document but as an accumulation of customs and precedents, together with laws defining certain of its aspects. Among the latter are ▷Magna Carta 1215, the ▷petition of right 1628, and the Habeas Corpus Act 1679 (see ▷habeas corpus), limiting the royal powers of taxation and of imprisonment; the Bill of Rights 1689 and the Act of Settlement 1701, establishing the supremacy of ▷Parliament and the independence of the judiciary; and the Parliament Acts 1911 and 1949, limiting the powers of the Lords. The Triennial Act 1694, the Septennial Act 1716, and the Parliament Act 1911 limited the duration of Parliament, while the Reform Acts of 1832, 1867, 1884, 1918, and 1928 extended the electorate.

Related Web site: Founding Fathers http://www.nara.gov/exhall/charters/constitution/confath.html

constitutional law
that part of the law relating to the constitution. It sets out the rules defining the powers, limits, and rights of government. In countries without a written constitution, such as the United Kingdom, constitutional law is a mixture of legislation, judicial precedent, and accepted conventional behaviour. Agencies that maintain constitutional law include, in Britain, the law courts and House of Lords; and, in the USA, the Supreme Court.

constructive margin
(or divergent margin) in plate tectonics, a region in which two plates are moving away from each other. Magma, or molten rock, escapes to the surface along this margin to form new crust, usually in the form of a ridge. Over time, as more and more magma reaches the surface, the sea floor spreads – for example, the upwelling of magma at the Mid-Atlantic Ridge causes the floor of the Atlantic Ocean to grow at a rate of about 5 cm/2 in a year.

CONSTANTINOPLE The siege of Constantinople by the Turks in 1453, depicted in a 16th-century fresco. *Art Archive*

constructivism abstract art movement that originated in Russia in about 1914 and subsequently had great influence on Western art. Constructivism usually involves industrial materials such as glass, steel, and plastic in clearly defined arrangements, but the term is difficult to define precisely, as the meaning attached to it has varied according to place and time. Some art historians distinguish between Russian (or Soviet) constructivism and the more diffuse European (or international) constructivism.

consul chief magistrate of the ancient Roman Republic, after the expulsion of the last king in 510 BC. Two consuls were elected annually by the *comitia centuriata* (assembly of the Roman people), and their names were used to date the year. With equal power they shared the full civil authority in Rome and the chief military command in the field. After the establishment of the Roman empire the office became far less important.

consumption in economics, the purchase of goods and services for final use, as opposed to spending by firms on capital goods, known as capital formation.

contact lens lens, made of soft or hard plastic, that is worn in contact with the cornea and conjunctiva of the eye, beneath the eyelid, to correct defective vision. In special circumstances, contact lenses may be used as protective shells or for cosmetic purposes, such as changing eye colour.

CONTACT LENS The manufacture of contact lenses is now a long-established part of the plastics industry. What has changed in recent decades is the use of softer plastics that accommodate their shape to that of the eye. This means that special fitting or measurements are no longer required, and lenses can be made so precisely and in such quantities as to be disposable after use. *Image Bank*

contempt of court behaviour that shows lack of respect for the authority of a court of law, such as disobeying a court order, breach of an injunction, or improper use of legal documents. Behaviour that disrupts, prejudices, or interferes with court proceedings either inside or outside the courtroom may also be

continent any one of the seven large land masses of the Earth, as distinct from the oceans. They are Asia, Africa, North America, South America, Europe, Australia, and Antarctica. Continents are constantly moving and evolving (see ▷plate tectonics). A continent does not end at the coastline; its boundary is the edge of the shallow continental shelf, which may extend several hundred kilometres out to sea.

Continental crust, as opposed to the crust that underlies the deep oceans, is composed of a wide variety of igneous, sedimentary, and metamorphic rocks. The rocks vary in age from recent (currently forming) to almost 4000 million years old. Unlike the ocean crust, the continents are not only high standing, but extend to depths as great at 70 km under high mountain ranges. Continents, as high, dry masses of rock, are present on earth because of the density contrast between them and the rock that underlies the oceans. Continental crust is both thick and light, whereas ocean crust is thin and dense. If the crust were the same thickness and density everywhere, the entire earth would be covered in water.

At the centre of each continental mass lies a shield or ▷craton, a deformed mass of old ▷metamorphic rocks dating from Precambrian times. The shield is thick, compact, and solid (the Canadian Shield is an example), and is usually worn flat. Around the shield is a concentric pattern of fold mountains, with older ranges, such as the Rockies, closest to the shield, and younger ranges, such as the coastal ranges of North America, farther away. This general concentric pattern is modified when two continental masses have drifted together and they become welded with a great mountain range along the join, the way Europe and northern Asia are joined along the Urals. If a continent is torn apart, the new continental edges have no mountains; for instance, South America has mountains (the Andes) along its western flank, but none along the east where it tore away from Africa 200 million years ago.

Continental Congress in US history, the federal legislature of the original 13 states, acting as a provisional government before the ▷American Revolution. It convened in Philadelphia from 1774 to 1789, when the US Constitution was adopted. The Second Continental Congress, convened in May 1775, was responsible for drawing up the ▷Declaration of Independence and, in 1777, the ▷Articles of Confederation.

The Congress authorized an army to resist the British and issued paper money to finance the war effort. It also oversaw the deliberations of the Constitutional Convention.

Related Web sites: Declaration and Resolves of the First Continental Congress, October 1774 http://odur.let.rug.nl/~usa/D/1751-1775/independence/decres.htm
Second Continental Congress: Declaration of the Causes and Necessity of Taking up Arms http://odur.let.rug.nl/~usa/D/1751-1775/war/causes.htm

continental drift in geology, the theory that, about 250–200 million years ago, the Earth consisted of a single large continent (▷Pangaea), which subsequently broke apart to form the continents known today. The theory was proposed in 1912 by German meteorologist Alfred Wegener, but such vast continental movements could not be satisfactorily explained or even accepted by geologists until the 1960s.

The theory of continental drift gave way to the theory of of ▷plate tectonics. Whereas Wegener proposed that continents plowed their way through underlying mantle and ocean floor, plate tectonics states that continents are just part of larger lithospheic

continental rise the portion of the ocean floor rising gently from the abyssal plain toward the steeper continental slope. The continental rise is a depositional feature formed from sediments transported down the slope mainly by turbidity currents. Much of the continental rise consists of coalescing submarine alluvial fans bordering the continental slope.

continental shelf the submerged edge of a continent, a gently sloping plain that extends into the ocean. It typically has a gradient of less than 1°. When the angle of the sea bed increases to 1°–5° (usually several hundred kilometres away from land), it becomes known as the continental slope.

continental slope sloping, submarine portion of a continent. It extends downward from the edge of the continental shelf. In some places, such as south of the Aleutian Islands of Alaska, continental slopes extend directly to the ocean deeps or abyssal plain. In others, such as the east coast of North America, they grade into the gentler continental rises that in turn grade into the abyssal plains.

Continental System system of economic preference and protection within Europe from 1806 to 1813 created by the French emperor Napoleon in order to exclude British trade. Apart from its function as economic warfare, the system also reinforced the French economy at the expense of other European states. It failed owing to British naval superiority.

continuous data data that can take any of an infinite number of values between whole numbers and so may not be measured completely accurately. This type of data contrasts with ▷discrete data, in which the variable can only take one of a finite set of values. For example, the sizes of apples on a tree form continuous data, whereas the numbers of apples form discrete data.

continuum in mathematics, a ▷set that is infinite and everywhere continuous, such as the set of points on a line.

contour on a map, a line drawn to join points of equal height. Contours are drawn at regular height intervals; for example, every 10 m. The closer together the lines are, the steeper the slope. Contour patterns can be used to interpret the relief of an area and to identify land forms.

Contra member of a Central American right-wing guerrilla force attempting to overthrow the democratically elected Nicaraguan Sandinista government between 1979 and 1990. The Contras, many of them mercenaries or former members of the deposed dictator Somoza's guard (see ▷Nicaraguan Revolution), operated mainly from bases outside Nicaragua, mostly in Honduras, with covert US funding, as revealed by the ▷Irangate hearings of 1986–87.

contrabassoon musical instrument, a larger version of the ▷bassoon, sounding an octave lower.

contraceptive any drug, device, or technique that prevents pregnancy. The contraceptive pill (the ▷Pill) contains female hormones that interfere with egg production or the first stage of pregnancy. The 'morning-after' pill can be taken up to 72 hours after unprotected intercourse. Barrier contraceptives include ▷condoms (sheaths) and ▷diaphragms, also called caps or Dutch caps; they prevent the sperm entering the cervix (neck of the womb).

▷Intrauterine devices, also known as IUDs or coils, cause a slight inflammation of the lining of the womb; this prevents the fertilized egg from becoming implanted. See also ▷family planning.

Other contraceptive methods include ▷sterilization (women) and ▷vasectomy (men); these are usually nonreversible. 'Natural' e ejaculation (coitus
ovulation

200 million years ago

140 million years ago

today

CONTINENTAL DRIFT The changing positions of the Earth's continents. Millions of years ago, there was a single large continent, Pangaea. This split 200 million years ago: the continents had started to move apart, to form Gondwanaland in the south and Laurasia in the north. By 50 million years ago the continents were almost in their present positions.

(▷rhythm method). These methods are unreliable and are normally only used on religious grounds. A new development is a sponge impregnated with spermicide that is inserted into the vagina. The use of any contraceptive (birth control) is part of family planning. The effectiveness of a contraceptive method is often given as a percentage. To say that a method has 95% effectiveness means that, on average, out of 100 healthy couples using that method for a year, 95 will not conceive.

In 1998 approximately 55% of women of childbearing age world-wide used contraception, according to the UN Population Fund.
Related Web site: Short Visit to the Museum of Contraception http://www.salon1999.com/07/features/contra.html

contract legal agreement between two or more parties, where each party agrees to do something. For example, a contract of employment is a legal agreement between an employer and an employee and lays out the conditions of employment. Contracts need not necessarily be written; they can be verbal contracts. In consumer law, for example, a contract is established when a good is sold.

contractile root in botany, a thickened root at the base of a corm, bulb, or other organ that helps position it at an appropriate level in the ground. Contractile roots are found, for example, on the corms of plants of the genus *Crocus*. After they have become anchored in the soil, the upper portion contracts, pulling the plant deeper into the ground.

contracting out in industrial relations, an agreement between an employer and employee in Britain whereby the employee does not participate in a financial contributory scheme administered by the employer. This usually applies to pension and health insurance schemes, or payment of trade union or other subscriptions from the gross salary.

contralto low-register female voice, a high (falsetto) male voice, or a low boy's voice; also called an ▷alto.

control experiment essential part of a scientifically valid experiment, designed to show that the factor being tested is actually responsible for the effect observed. In the control experiment all factors, apart from the one under test, are exactly the same as in the test experiments, and all the same measurements are carried out. In drug trials, a placebo (a harmless substance) is given alongside the substance being tested in order to compare effects.

convection heat energy transfer that involves the movement of a fluid (gas or liquid). Fluid in contact with the source of heat expands and tends to rise within the bulk of the fluid. Cooler fluid sinks to take its place, setting up a convection current. This is the principle of natural convection in many domestic hot-water systems and space heaters.

convection current current caused by the expansion of a liquid, solid, or gas as its temperature rises. The expanded material, being less dense, rises, while colder, denser material sinks. Material of neutral buoyancy moves laterally. Convection currents arise in the atmosphere above warm land masses or seas, giving rise to sea breezes and land breezes, respectively. In some heating systems, convection currents are used to carry hot water upwards in pipes.

conventional forces in Europe (CFE) treaty signed by NATO and Warsaw Pact representatives in November 1990, reducing the number of tanks, missiles, aircraft, and other forms of non-nuclear military hardware held by member states.

convergence in mathematics, the property of a series of numbers in which the difference between consecutive terms gradually decreases. The sum of a converging series approaches a limit as the number of terms tends to ▷infinity.

convergent evolution (or convergence) in biology, the independent evolution of similar structures in species (or other taxonomic groups) that are not closely related, as a result of living in a similar way. Thus, birds and bees have wings, not because they are descended from a common winged ancestor, but because their respective ancestors independently evolved flight.

convex of a surface, curving outwards, or towards the eye. For example, the outer surface of a ball appears convex. In geometry, the term is used to describe any polygon possessing no interior angle greater than 180°. Convex is the opposite of ▷concave.

convex lens lens that possesses at least one surface that curves outwards. It is a converging lens, bringing rays of light to a focus. A convex lens is thicker at its centre than at its edges, and is used to correct long-sightedness.

conveyor device used for transporting materials. Widely used throughout industry is the **conveyor belt**, usually a rubber or fabric belt running on rollers. Trough-shaped belts are used, for example in mines, for transporting ores and coal. **Chain conveyors** are also used in coal mines to remove coal from the cutting machines. Overhead endless chain conveyors are used to carry components and bodies in car-assembly works. Other types include **bucket conveyors** and **screw conveyors**, powered versions of the ▷Archimedes screw.

convocation in the Church of England, the synods (councils) of the clergy of the provinces of Canterbury and York. The General Synod, established in 1970, took over the functions and authority of the Convocation of Canterbury and York which continued to exist only in a restricted form. In the Episcopal Church, a convocation is an assembly of clergy as part of a diocese.

convolvulus (or bindweed) any of a group of plants belonging to the morning-glory family. They are characterized by their twining stems and by their petals, which are joined into a funnel-shaped tube. (Genus *Convolvulus*, family Convolvulaceae.)
Related Web site: Convolvulus, Field http://www.botanical.com/botanical/mgmh/c/convol96.html

CONVOLVULUS Despite the beauty of its flowers, convolvulus or field bindweed is a pernicious weed. *Premaphotos Wildlife*

convoy system grouping of ships to sail together under naval escort in wartime. In World War I (1914–18) navy escort vessels were at first used only to accompany troopships, but the convoy system was adopted for merchant shipping when the unrestricted German submarine campaign began in 1917. In World War II (1939–45) the convoy system was widely used by the Allies to keep the Atlantic sea lanes open.

convulsion series of violent contractions of the muscles over which the patient has no control. It may be associated with loss of consciousness. Convulsions may arise from any one of a number of causes, including brain disease (such as ▷epilepsy), injury, high fever, poisoning, and electrocution.

Conwy unitary authority in north Wales, created in 1996 from parts of the former counties of Clwyd and Gwynedd.
area 1,107 sq km/427 sq mi **towns** Conwy (administrative headquarters), Abergele, Llandudno, Llanrwst **physical** rivers Conwy and Elwy **features** ▷Snowdonia National Park; coastline of sandy beaches, including the seaside resort of ▷Colwyn Bay **industries** tourism **population** (1996) 113,000
Related Web site: Betty Crocker http://www.bettycrocker.com/

Cook, James (1728–1779) English naval explorer. After surveying the St Lawrence River in North America in 1759, he made three voyages: 1768–71 to Tahiti, New Zealand, and Australia; 1772–75 to the South Pacific; and 1776–79 to the North and South Pacific, attempting to find the Northwest Passage and charting the Siberian coast. He was largely responsible for Britain's initial interest in acquiring colonies in Australasia. He was killed in Hawaii early in 1779 in a scuffle with islanders.

> **James Cook**
> *At daylight in the morning we discovered a bay, which appeared to be tolerably well sheltered from all winds, into which I resolved to go with the ship.*
> Referring to Botany Bay *Journal*, 28 April 1770

In 1768 Cook was given command of an expedition to the South Pacific to witness the transit of Venus across the Sun. He sailed in the *Endeavour* with Joseph ▷Banks and other scientists, reaching Tahiti in April 1769. He then sailed around New Zealand and made a detailed survey of the east coast of Australia, naming New South Wales and Botany Bay. He returned to England on 12 June 1771.

Now a commander, Cook set out in 1772 with the *Resolution* and *Adventure* to search for the southern continent. The location of Easter Island was determined, and the Marquesas and Tonga Islands plotted. He also went to New Caledonia and Norfolk Island. Cook returned on 25 July 1775, having sailed 100,000 km/60,000 mi in three years.

On 25 June 1776, he began his third and last voyage with the *Resolution* and *Discovery*. On the way to New Zealand, he visited several of the Cook or Hervey Islands and revisited the Hawaiian or Sandwich Islands. The ships sighted the North American coast at latitude 45° N and sailed north hoping to discover the Northwest Passage. He made a continuous survey as far as the Bering Strait, where the way was blocked by ice. Cook then surveyed the opposite coast of the strait (Siberia), and returned to Hawaii early in 1779, where he was killed when his expedition clashed with islanders.

Cook, Robin (Robert Finlayson) (1946–) British Labour politician, foreign secretary 1997–2001, born in Scotland. A member of the moderate-left Tribune Group, he entered Parliament in 1974 and became a leading member of Labour's shadow cabinet, specializing in health matters. When John Smith assumed the party leadership in July 1992, Cook remained in the shadow cabinet as spokesperson for trade and industry. He became shadow foreign secretary under Smith's successor, Tony ▷Blair, in October 1994. As foreign secretary, he placed a new emphasis on human rights as part of an ethical foreign policy. He resigned as Leader of the House of Commons in 2003 in protest over Britain's involvement in the Iraq War.

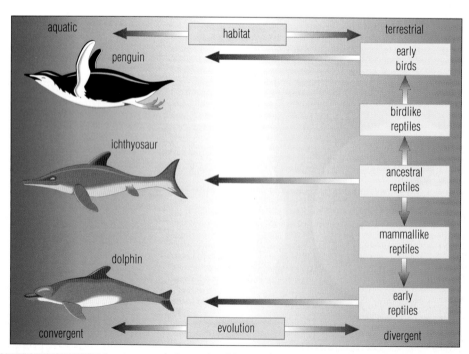
CONVERGENT EVOLUTION Convergent evolution produced the superficially similar streamlined bodies of the dolphin and penguin. Despite their very different evolutionary paths – one as a mammal, the other as a bird – both have evolved and adapted to the aquatic environment they now inhabit.

Cook, Thomas (1808–1892) Pioneer British travel agent and founder of Thomas Cook & Son. He organized his first tour, to Switzerland, in 1863. He introduced traveller's cheques (then called 'circular notes') in the early 1870s.

Cooke, Sam (1931–1964) US soul singer and songwriter. He began his career as a gospel singer and turned to pop music in 1956. His hits include 'You Send Me' (1957) and 'Wonderful World' (1960; re-released 1986). His smooth tenor voice gilded some indifferent material, but his own song 'A Change Is Gonna Come' (1965) is a moving civil-rights anthem.

cooking heat treatment of food to make it more palatable, digestible, and safe. It breaks down connective tissue in meat, making it tender, and softens the cellulose in plant tissue. Some nutrients may be lost in the process, but this does not affect the overall nutritional value of a balanced diet.

Cook Islands group of six large and a number of smaller Polynesian islands 2,600 km/1,600 mi northeast of Auckland, New Zealand; area 290 sq km/112 sq mi; population (1994) 17,400. Their main products include citrus fruit, copra, bananas, pearl-shell, cultivated (black) pearls, and crafts. The islands became a self-governing overseas territory of New Zealand in 1965.

The chief island, Rarotonga, is the site of Avarua, the seat of government. Niue, geographically part of the group, is separately administered. The Cook Islands were visited by Captain James Cook in 1773, annexed by Britain in 1888, and transferred to New Zealand in 1901. They have common citizenship with New Zealand, although they are self-governing, and the prime minister is Terepai Maoate, from 1999.

Related Web site: Welcome to Paradise – the Cook Islands
http://www.ck/index.html

Cook Strait strait dividing North Island and South Island, New Zealand, about 30 km/19 mi in width at its narrowest point. A submarine cable carries electricity from South to North Island.

Coolidge, (John) Calvin (1872–1933) 30th president of the USA 1923–29, a Republican. As governor of Massachusetts in 1919, he was responsible for crushing a Boston police strike. As Warren ▷Harding's vice-president 1921–23, he succeeded to the presidency on Harding's death. He won the 1924 presidential election, and his period of office was marked by economic growth.

As president, Coolidge inherited two scandals from his predecessor: the maladministration of a bureau for war veterans, and an attempt to hand over public oil lands to private companies. Coolidge declined to run for re-election in 1928, supporting the candidacy of his secretary of the interior, Herbert ▷Hoover, who won the presidency. He was known as 'Silent Cal' because of his natural reticence.

Related Web site: Calvin Coolidge – Thirtieth President 1923–1929
http://www.whitehouse.gov/WH/glimpse/presidents/html/cc30.html

Calvin Coolidge
Civilization and profits go hand in hand.
Speech, 27 November 1920

Cooperation Council for the Arab States of the Gulf (CCASG) Arab organization for promoting peace in the Persian Gulf area, established in 1981. Its declared purpose is 'to bring about integration, coordination, and cooperation in economic, social, defence, and political affairs among Arab Gulf states'. Its members include Bahrain, Kuwait, Oman, Qatar, Saudi Arabia, and the United Arab Emirates; its headquarters are in Riyadh, Saudi Arabia.

cooperative business organization with limited liability where each shareholder has only one vote however many shares they own. In a worker cooperative, it is the workers who are the shareholders and own the company. The workers decide on how the company is to be run. In a consumer cooperative, consumers control the company.

Co-op shops and superstores are examples of consumer cooperatives. They are owned by regional cooperative retail groups.

cooperative movement the banding together of groups of people for mutual assistance in trade, manufacture, the supply of credit, housing, or other services. The original principles of the cooperative movement were laid down in 1844 by the Rochdale Pioneers, under the influence of Robert ▷Owen, and by Charles Fourier in France.

Cooperative Party former political party founded in Britain in 1917 by the cooperative movement to maintain its principles in parliamentary and local government. A written constitution was adopted in 1938. The party had strong links with the Labour Party; from 1946 Cooperative Party candidates stood in elections as Cooperative and Labour Candidates and, after the 1959 general election, agreement was reached to limit the party's candidates to 30.

Cooper, Gary (Frank James) (1901–1961) US film actor. One of the great stars of the classical Hollywood era, who created a screen persona of quiet dignity, moral rectititude, and powerful action. He won Academy Awards for his performances in *Sergeant York* (1941) and *High Noon* (1952).

Cooper, James Fenimore (1789–1851) US writer, considered the first great US novelist. He wrote some 50 novels, mostly about the frontier, wilderness life, and the sea, first becoming popular with *The Spy* (1821). He is best remembered for his series of *Leatherstocking Tales*, focusing on the frontier hero Natty Bumppo and the American Indians before and after the American Revolution; they include *The Last of the Mohicans* (1826). Still popular as adventures, his novels have been reappraised for their treatment of social and moral issues in the settling of the American frontier.

coordinate in geometry, a number that defines the position of a point relative to a point or axis (reference line). ▷Cartesian coordinates define a point by its perpendicular distances from two or more axes drawn through a fixed point mutually at right angles to each other. ▷Polar coordinates define a point in a plane by its distance from a fixed point and direction from a fixed line.

coordinate geometry (or **analytical geometry**) system of geometry in which points, lines, shapes, and surfaces are represented by algebraic expressions. In plane (two-dimensional) coordinate geometry, the plane is usually defined by two axes at right angles to each other, the horizontal x-axis and the vertical y-axis, meeting at O, the origin. A point on the plane can be represented by a pair of ▷Cartesian coordinates, which define its position in terms of its distance along the x-axis and along the y-axis from O. These distances are respectively the x and y coordinates of the point.

Lines are represented as equations; for example,

$y = 2x + 1$ gives a straight line, and

$y = 3x^2 + 2x$

gives a ▷parabola (a curve). The graphs of varying equations can be drawn by plotting the coordinates of points that satisfy their equations, and joining up the points. One of the advantages of coordinate geometry is that geometrical solutions can be obtained without drawing but by manipulating algebraic expressions. For example, the coordinates of the point of intersection of two straight lines can be determined by finding the unique values of x and y that satisfy both of the equations for the lines, that is, by solving them as a pair of ▷simultaneous equations. The curves studied in simple coordinate geometry are the ▷conic sections (circle, ellipse, parabola, and hyperbola), each of which has a characteristic equation.

coot freshwater bird of the genus *Fulica* in the rail family, order Gruiformes. Coots are about 38 cm/1.2 ft long, and mainly black. They have a white bill, extending up the forehead in a plate, and big feet with four lobed toes. Coots are omnivores, but feed mainly on water weed, except as chicks, when they feed on insects and other invertebrates.

The Old World coot *F. atra* is found on inland waters in Europe, Asia, North Africa, and Australia. Their nests are built on water-plants and made of dry rushes. The eggs are stone colour with brown specks. In coloration the sexes are alike, but the male is slightly larger.

COOT The giant coot *Fulica gigantea*, 4,300 m/14,100 ft up in the Chilean altiplano. The largest of the coots, it reaches a size of 55 cm/22 in. *K G Preston-Mafham/Premaphotos Wildlife*

Coote, Eyre (1726–1783) Irish general in British India. His victory in 1760 at Wandiwash, followed by the capture of Pondicherry, ended French hopes of supremacy. He returned to India as commander-in-chief in 1779, and several times defeated ▷Hyder Ali, sultan of Mysore.

NICOLAUS COPERNICUS Believing that the theories of Ptolemy regarding the Earth as the centre of the universe were too complicated, Copernicus turned to earlier Greek astronomers such as Aristarchus and Hipparchus. His deduction that the Earth is a moving planet was developed by later astronomers such as Kepler and Galileo. *Archive Photos*

Cope, Wendy (1945–) English poet. Her talent for parody, and for light-hearted demolitions of men, targets male authors such as Ted Hughes or Philip Larkin; the titles *Making Cocoa for Kingsley Amis* (1986) and *Men and their Boring Arguments* (1988) indicate her approach. Her works also include *Serious Concerns* (1993).

copepod ▷crustacean of the subclass Copepoda, mainly microscopic and found in plankton.

Copenhagen (Danish **København**) capital of Denmark, on the islands of Zealand and Amager; population (1995) 1,353,300 (including suburbs).

Features To the east is the royal palace at Amalienborg; the 7th-century Charlottenborg Palace houses the Academy of Arts, and parliament meets in the Christiansborg Palace. The statue of Hans Christian Andersen's *Little Mermaid* (by Edvard Eriksen) is at the harbour entrance. The Tivoli amusement park is in the heart of the city.

History Copenhagen was a fishing village until 1167, when the bishop of Roskilde built the castle on the site of the present Christiansborg palace. A settlement grew up, and it became the Danish capital in 1443. The university was founded in 1479. The city was under German occupation from April 1940 until May 1945.

Related Web site: Excite Travel: Copenhagen, Denmark http://www.city.net/countries/denmark/copenhagen/

Copenhagen, Battle of naval victory on 2 April 1801 by a British fleet under Sir Hyde Parker (1739–1807) and ▷Nelson over the Danish fleet. Nelson put his telescope to his blind eye and refused to see Parker's signal for withdrawal.

Nicolaus Copernicus
Finally we shall place the Sun himself at the centre of the Universe.
De Revolutionibus Orbium Coelestium

Copernicus, Nicolaus (1473–1543) Polish **Mikołaj Kopernik**. Polish astronomer who believed that the Sun, not the Earth, is at the centre of the Solar System, thus defying the Christian church doctrine of the time. For 30 years, he worked on the hypothesis that the rotation and the orbital motion of the Earth are responsible for the apparent movement of the heavenly bodies. His great work *De Revolutionibus Orbium Coelestium/On the Revolutions of the Heavenly Spheres* was the important first step to the more accurate picture of the Solar System built up by Tycho ▷Brahe, ▷Kepler, ▷Galileo, and later astronomers.

Copernicus proposed replacing Ptolemy's ideas with a model in which the planets (including the Earth) orbited a centrally situated Sun. He proposed that the Earth described one full orbit of the Sun in a year, whereas the Moon orbited the Earth. The Earth rotated daily about its axis (which was inclined at 23.5° to the plane of orbit), thus accounting for the apparent daily rotation of the sphere of the fixed stars.

This model was a distinct improvement on the Ptolemaic system for a number of reasons. It explained why the planets Mercury and Venus displayed only 'limited motion'; their orbits were inside that of the Earth's. Similarly, it explained that the planets Mars, Jupiter, and Saturn displayed such curious patterns in their movements ('retrograde motion', loops, and kinks) because they travel in outer orbits at a slower pace than the Earth. The movement of the Earth on its axis accounted for the precession of the equinoxes, previously discovered by ▷Hipparchus.

Copernicus's model represents a complete reformation of astronomy by replacing the **anthropocentric** view of the universe with the **heliocentric** viewpoint. Unable to free himself from the constraints of classical thinking, however, Copernicus was able to imagine only circular planetary orbits. This forced him to retain the system of epicycles, with the Earth revolving around a centre that revolved around another centre, which in turn orbited the Sun. Kepler rescued the model by introducing the concept of elliptical orbits. Copernicus also held to the notion of spheres, in which the planets were supposed to travel. It was Brahe who finally rid astronomy of that concept.

Copland, Aaron (1900–1990) US composer. His early works, such as his piano concerto (1926), were in the jazz idiom but he gradually developed a gentler style with a regional flavour drawn from American folk music. Among his works are the ballet scores *Billy the Kid* (1938), *Rodeo* (1942), and *Appalachian Spring* (1944; based on a poem by Hart Crane). Among his orchestral works is *Inscape* (1967).

Born in New York, Copland studied in France with Nadia Boulanger, and taught from 1940 at the Berkshire Music Center, now the Tanglewood Music Center, near Lenox, Massachusetts. He took avant-garde European styles and gave them a distinctive American pitch. His eight film scores, including *The Heiress* (1949), set new standards for Hollywood.

copper orange-pink, very malleable and ductile, metallic element, symbol Cu (from Latin *cuprum*), atomic number 29, relative atomic mass 63.546. It is used for its durability, pliability, high thermal and electrical conductivity, and resistance to corrosion.

It was the first metal used systematically for tools by humans; when mined and worked into utensils it formed the technological basis for the Copper Age in prehistory. When alloyed with tin it forms bronze, which is stronger than pure copper and may hold a sharp edge; the systematic production and use of this alloy was the basis for the prehistoric Bronze Age. Brass, another hard copper alloy, includes zinc. The element's name comes from the Greek for Cyprus (*Kyprios*), where copper was mined.

copper ore any mineral from which copper is extracted, including native copper, Cu; chalcocite, Cu_2S; chalcopyrite, $CuFeS_2$; bornite, Cu_5FeS_4; azurite, $Cu_3(CO_3)_2(OH)_2$; malachite, $Cu_2CO_3(OH)_2$; and chrysocolla, $CuSiO_3.2H_2O$.

coppicing woodland management practice of severe pruning where trees are cut down to near ground level at regular intervals, typically every 3–20 years, to promote the growth of numerous shoots from the base.

Coppola, Francis (Ford) (1939–) US film director and screenwriter. He directed *The Godfather* (1972), which became one of the biggest moneymaking films of all time, and its sequels *The Godfather Part II* (1974), which won seven Academy Awards, and *The Godfather Part III* (1990). His other films include *Apocalypse Now* (1979), and *Rumblefish* (1983).

FRANCIS COPPOLA US film director Francis Ford Coppola on the set of *The Godfather*. *Archive Photos*

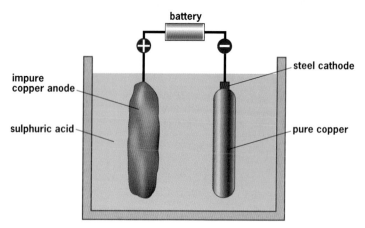

battery

impure copper anode

sulphuric acid

steel cathode

pure copper

COPPER Copper purification by electrolysis. Pure copper dissolves from the impure copper anode, which decreases in size. The copper is deposited at the cathode, which increases in size. When the purification process is complete the cathode is melted down and cast into bars to be sold to manufacturers, such as producers of electrical wiring.

After working on horror 'B-movies', his first successes were *Finian's Rainbow* (1968) and *Patton* (1969), for which his screenplay won an Academy Award. A film-maker of wide-ranging ambition, he has also directed *The Conversation* (1972), *One from the Heart* (1982), *The Outsiders* (1983), *The Cotton Club* (1984), *Tucker: The Man and His Dream* (1988), *Gardens of Stone* (1987), *Bram Stoker's Dracula* (1992), *Jack* (1996), and *The Rainmaker* (1997), based on John Grisham's novel.
Related Web site: Francis Ford Coppola Profile http://www.achievement.org/autodoc/page/cop0pro-1

copra dried meat from the kernel of the ▷coconut, used to make coconut oil.

Copt descendant of those ancient Egyptians who adopted Christianity in the 1st century and refused to convert to Islam after the Arab conquest. They now form a small minority (about 5%) of Egypt's population. **Coptic** is a member of the Hamito-Semitic language family. It is descended from the language of the ancient Egyptians and is the ritual language of the Coptic Christian church. It is written in the Greek alphabet with some additional characters derived from ▷demotic script.

Coptic art the art of the indigenous Christian community of 5th–8th-century Egypt. Flat and colourful in style, with strong outlines and stylized forms, it shows the influence of Byzantine, late Roman, and ancient Egyptian art. Wall paintings, textiles, stone and ivory carvings, and manuscript illuminations remain, the most noted examples of which are in the Coptic Museum, Cairo. The influence of Coptic art was widespread in the Christian world, and Coptic interlacing patterns may have been the source for the designs of Irish and Northumbrian illuminated gospels. For the later period of Fatimid art (10th–11th centuries), see ▷Islamic art.

copulation act of mating in animals with internal ▷fertilization. Male mammals have a ▷penis or other organ that is used to introduce spermatozoa into the reproductive tract of the female. Most birds transfer sperm by pressing their cloacas (the openings of their reproductive tracts) together.

copyright law applying to literary, musical, and artistic works (including plays, recordings, films, photographs, radio and television broadcasts, and, in the USA and the UK, computer programs), which prevents the reproduction of the work, in whole or in part, without the author's consent.
Related Web site: World Intellectual Property Organization http://www.wipo.org/eng/index.htm

coral marine invertebrate of the class Anthozoa in the phylum Cnidaria, which also includes sea anemones and jellyfish. It has a skeleton of lime (calcium carbonate) extracted from the surrounding water. Corals exist in warm seas, at moderate depths with sufficient light. Some coral is valued for decoration or jewellery, for example, Mediterranean red coral *Corallum rubrum*.

Corals live in a symbiotic relationship with microscopic ▷algae (zooxanthellae), which are incorporated into the soft tissue. The algae obtain carbon dioxide from the coral polyps, and the polyps receive nutrients from the algae. Corals also have a relationship to the fish that rest or take refuge within their branches, and which excrete nutrients that make the corals grow faster. The majority of

corals form large colonies although there are species that live singly. Their accumulated skeletons make up large coral reefs and atolls. The Great Barrier Reef, to the northeast of Australia, is about 1,600 km/1,000 mi long, has a total area of 20,000 sq km/7,700 sq mi, and adds 50 million tonnes of calcium to the reef each year. The world's reefs cover an estimated 620,000 sq km/240,000 sq mi.

Coral reefs provide a habitat for a diversity of living organisms. In 1997, some 93,000 species were identified. One third of the world's marine fishes live in reefs. The world's first global survey of coral reefs, carried out in 1997, found around 95% of reefs had experienced some damage from overfishing, pollution, dynamiting, poisoning, and the dragging of ships' anchors. A 1998 research showed that nearly two-thirds of the world's coral reefs were at risk, including 80% of the reefs in the Philippines and Indonesia, 66% of those in the Caribbean, and over 50% of those in the Indian Ocean, the Red Sea, and the Gulf of Arabia.

Fringing reefs are so called because they form close to the shores of continents or islands, with the living animals mainly occupying the outer edges of the reef. **Barrier reefs** are separated from the shore by a saltwater lagoon, which may be as much as 30 km/20 mi wide; there are usually navigable passes through the barrier into the lagoon. **Atolls** resemble a ring surrounding a lagoon, and do not enclose an island. They are usually formed by the gradual subsidence of an extinct volcano, with the coral growing up from where the edge of the island once lay.

A two-year study carried out by the World Conservation Monitoring Centre in Cambridge has shown that nearly two-thirds of the world's coral reefs are at risk, including 80% of the reefs in the Philippines and Indonesia, 66% of those in the Caribbean, and over 50% of those in the Indian Ocean, the Red Sea, and the Gulf of Arabia. The threat comes from the development of coastal towns and cities, with the building of harbours, and dredging of shipping channels, from pollution with sewage, and the production of algae that block out sunlight as a result of agricultural pollution, from destructive fishing practices such as cyanide poisoning and dynamiting, from overfishing, which upsets the ecological balance, and tourism, with trampling of the coral and collection of coral for souvenirs. Careful management, as with the Great Barrier Reef in Australia, keeps coral healthy, and leads to improved fish yields and increased revenues from tourism.

CORAL A picture of the coral off the coast of Costa Rica. Corals are animals, not plants, which exist in tropical seas and frequently form reefs around islands. *Image Bank*

Coral Sea (or Solomon Sea) part of the ▷Pacific Ocean bounded by northeastern Australia, New Guinea, the Solomon Islands, Vanuatu, and New Caledonia; area 4,790,000 sq km/1,849,000 sq mi, with an average depth of 2,400 m/7,870 ft, with three deep trenches on its eastern edge. It contains numerous coral islands and reefs. The Coral Sea Islands are a territory of Australia; they comprise scattered reefs and islands over an area of about 1,000,000 sq km/386,000 sq mi. They are uninhabited except for a meteorological station on Willis Island. The ▷Great Barrier Reef lies along its western edge, just off the east coast of Australia.

coral snake venomous snake. *Elaps corallinus* is a typical specimen; it occurs in the tropical forests of South America, and its small body, less than 1 m/3.3 ft in length, is ringed with coral-red. It is highly poisonous.
Classification Coral snakes are in the family Elapidae, suborder Serpentes, order Squamata, class Reptilia.

coral tree any of several tropical trees with bright red or orange flowers and producing a very lightweight wood. (Genus *Erythrina*, family Fabaceae.)

cor anglais (or **English horn**) musical instrument, an alto ▷oboe, pitched a fifth lower than the oboe in F, with a distinctive tulip-shaped bell and warm nasal tone. It is heard to pastoral effect in Rossini's overture to *William Tell* (1829), and portraying a plaintive Sasha the duck in Prokofiev's *Peter and the Wolf* (1936).

Corbusier, Le French architect; see ▷Le Corbusier.

cordillera group of mountain ranges and their valleys, all running in a specific direction, formed by the continued convergence of two tectonic plates (see ▷plate tectonics) along a line. The term is applied especially to the principal mountain belt of a continent. The Andes of South America are an example.

Cordilleras, The mountainous western section of North America, with the Rocky Mountains and the coastal ranges parallel to the contact between the North American and the Pacific plates.

Córdoba industrial city and capital of Córdoba province, central Argentina, situated on the Primero (or Suquiá)River, 400 m/1,310 ft above sea level at the foot of the Sierra Chica, between the pampas on the east and the Andes on the west; population (1992 est) 1,179,400. Main industries include cement, glass, textiles, and motor vehicles. The city's water and electric power come from the lake created by the San Roque Dam on the River Primero.

Córdoba capital of Córdoba province, southern Spain, on the River Guadalquivir; population (1991) 300,200. Paper, textiles, silverware, and copper products are manufactured, and there is a large trade in agricultural produce, wine, olive oil, and lead. It has many Moorish remains, including the mosque, now a cathedral, founded by 'Abd-ar-Rahman I in 785, which is one of the largest Christian churches in the world. Córdoba was probably founded by the Carthaginians; it was held by the Moors from 711 to 1236.

core in earth science, the innermost part of Earth. It is divided into an outer core, which begins at a depth of 2,900 km/1,800 mi, and an inner core, which begins at a depth of 4,980 km/3,100 mi. Both parts are thought to consist of iron-nickel alloy. The outer core is liquid and the inner core is solid.

Corelli, Arcangelo (1653–1713) Italian composer and violinist. Living at a time when the viol was yielding to the violin, he was one of the first virtuoso exponents of the baroque violin and his music, marked by graceful melody, includes a set of *concerti grossi* and five sets of chamber sonatas.

Corfu (Greek **Kérkyra**) northernmost and second largest of the Ionian islands of Greece, off the coast of Epirus in the Ionian Sea; area 1,072 sq km/414 sq mi; population (1991) 105,000. Its businesses include tourism, fruit, olive oil, and textiles. Its largest town is the port of Corfu (Kérkyra), population (1991) 36,900. Corfu was colonized by the Corinthians about 700 BC. Venice held it 1386–1797, Britain 1815–64.

corgi breed of dog. See ▷Welsh corgi.

Corinth (Greek **Kórinthos**) port in Greece, on the isthmus connecting the Peloponnese with the mainland; population (2001 est) 32,800. The rocky isthmus is bisected by the 6.5 km/4 mi Corinth canal, opened in 1893. The site of the ancient city-state of Corinth lies 7 km/4.5 mi southwest of the port.

Corinthian in classical architecture, one of the five types of column; see ▷order.

Coriolis effect the effect of the Earth's rotation on the atmosphere, oceans, and theoretically all objects moving over the Earth's surface. In the northern hemisphere it causes moving objects and currents to be deflected to the right; in the southern hemisphere it causes deflection to the left. The effect is named after its discoverer, French mathematician Gaspard de Coriolis (1792–1843).

Related Web site: Coriolis Effect http://www.physics.ohio-state.edu/~dvandom/Edu/coriolis.html

Cork largest county of the Republic of Ireland, in the province of Munster; county town ▷Cork; area 7,460 sq km/2,880 sq mi; population (1996) 420,500. Cork is mainly agricultural, but there is some copper and manganese mining, marble quarrying, salmon farming, and river and sea fishing; industries include chemical, and computer hardware and software. There are natural gas and oil fields off the south coast at Kinsale. Angling is a popular sport, and tourism is concentrated in Kinsale, Bantry, Glengarriff, and Youghal; one of the most popular visitor attractions is Charles Fort, Kinsale. Cork is rich in Christian and pre-Christian antiquities.

Cork third-largest city in Ireland; port and county town of County ▷Cork, important industrial and trading centre on the River Lee, at the head of the long inlet of Cork harbour, 21 km/13 mi from the sea; population (1996) 180,000. The lower harbour, at Cobh, can berth liners. The city has breweries, distilleries, container ports, and iron foundries. Other industries include cars, chemicals, food processing, oil refining, pharmaceuticals, pottery, steel, and tanning; manufacturing includes rubber and metal products, and computer hardware and software. St Fin Barre founded a school and an abbey here in the 7th century. The area was subsequently settled by Danes, who were in turn dispossessed by the Normans in 1172.

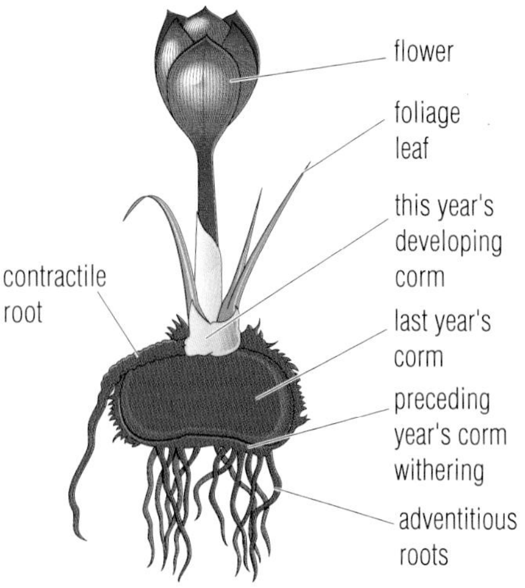

CORM Corms, found in plants such as the gladiolus and crocus, are underground storage organs. They provide the food for growth during adverse conditions such as cold or drought.

cork light, waterproof outer layers of the bark covering the branches and roots of almost all trees and shrubs. The cork oak (*Quercus suber*), a native of southern Europe and North Africa, is cultivated in Spain and Portugal; the exceptionally thick outer layers of its bark provide the cork that is used commercially.

corm short, swollen, underground plant stem, surrounded by protective scale leaves, as seen in the genus *Crocus*. It stores food, provides a means of ▷vegetative reproduction, and acts as a ▷perennating organ.

cormorant any of various diving seabirds, mainly of the genus *Phalacrocorax*, order Pelecaniformes, about 90 cm/3 ft long, with webbed feet, a long neck, hooked beak, and glossy black plumage. Cormorants generally feed on fish and shellfish, which they catch by swimming and diving under water, sometimes to a considerable depth. They collect the food in a pouch formed by the dilatable skin at the front of the throat. Some species breed on inland lakes and rivers.

P. carbo has a bright shiny head and neck, with bluish-black feathers, speckled with white. The general colour above is a greenish black, the throat white, and the bill and feet are dark grey. It is found in all parts of the world in coastal regions.

There are about 30 species of cormorant worldwide, including a flightless form *Nannopterum harrisi* in the Galapagos Islands; the **shag**, or **green cormorant**, *P. aristotelis*; and the **small European cormorant**, *Halietor pygmaeus*, which is a freshwater bird. The **guanay cormorant** *P. bougainvillei*, of the Peruvian coast, is the main producer of the guano of those regions.

There are 8,000 breeding pairs in the UK (fewer than for the grey heron) according to a 1998 RSPB estimate.

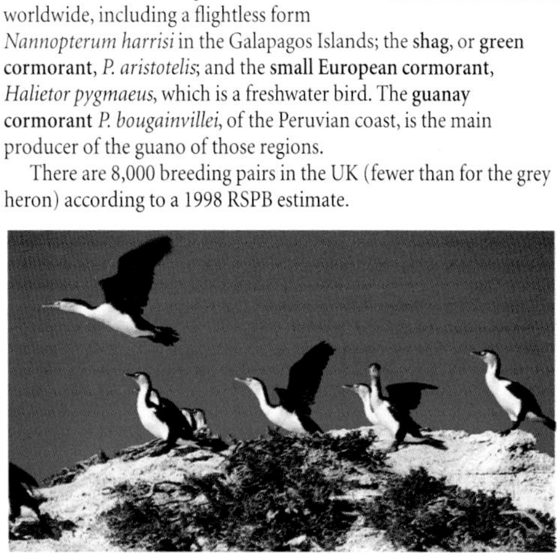

CORMORANT Pied cormorants *Phalacrocorax varius* in Australia. *K G Preston-Mafham/Premaphotos Wildlife*

corn general term for the main ▷cereal crop of a region – for example, wheat in the UK, oats in Scotland and Ireland, ▷maize in the USA.

corncrake (or **landrail**) bird *Crex crex* of the rail family Rallidae, order Gruiformes. About 25 cm/10 in long, the bill and tail are short, the legs long and powerful, and the toes have sharp claws. It is drably coloured, shy, and has a persistent rasping call. The corncrake can swim and run easily, but its flight is heavy. It lives in meadows and crops in temperate regions, but has become rare where mechanical methods of cutting corn are used.

cornea transparent front section of the vertebrate ▷eye. The cornea is curved and behaves as a fixed lens, so that light entering the eye is partly focused before it reaches the lens.

Corneille, Pierre (1606–1684) French dramatist. His tragedies, such as *Horace* (1640), *Cinna* (1641), and *Oedipe* (1659), glorify the strength of will governed by reason, and established the French classical dramatic tradition. His first comedy, *Mélite*, was performed in 1629, followed by others that gained him a brief period of favour with Cardinal Richelieu. His early masterpiece, *Le Cid* (1636), was attacked by the Academicians, although it received public acclaim, and was produced in the same year as *L'Illusion comique/The Comic Illusion.*

Although Corneille enjoyed public popularity, periodic disfavour with Richelieu marred his career, and it was not until 1639 that Corneille (again in favour) produced plays such as *Polyeucte* (1643), *Le Menteur* (1643), and *Rodogune* (1645), leading to his election to the Académie in 1647. His later plays were approved by Louis XIV.

> **Pierre Corneille**
> *When there is no peril in the fight, there is no glory in the triumph.*
> *Le Cid*

cornet three-valved brass-band instrument, soprano member (usually in B flat) of a group of valved horns developed from the coiled post-horn in Austria and Germany between about 1820 and 1850 for military band use. Of cylindrical bore, its compact shape and deeper conical bell allow greater speed and agility of intonation than the trumpet, at the expense of less tonal precision and brilliance. A small E flat cornet is standard in brass bands alongside a B flat cornet section.

cornflower native European and Asian plant belonging to the same genus as the ▷knapweeds but distinguished from them by its deep azure-blue flowers. Formerly a common weed in northern European wheat fields, it is now widely grown in gardens as a ▷herbaceous plant with flower colours ranging from blue through shades of pink and purple to white. (*Centaurea cyanus*, family Compositae.)

Related Web site: Cornflower http://www.botanical.com/botanical/mgmh/c/cornf102.html

> **John Cornforth**
> *For him [the scientist], truth is so seldom the sudden light that shows new order and beauty; more often, truth is the uncharted rock that sinks his ship in the dark.*
> Nobel prize address (1975)

Cornforth, John Warcup (1917–) Australian chemist. Using ▷radioisotopes as markers, he found out how cholesterol is manufactured in the living cell and how enzymes synthesize chemicals that are mirror images of each other (optical ▷isomers). He shared the Nobel Prize for Chemistry in 1975 with Swiss chemist Vladimir Prelog for his work in the stereochemistry of enzyme-catalysed reactions. He was knighted in 1977.

Cornish language extinct member of the ▷Celtic languages, a branch of the Indo-European language family, spoken in Cornwall, England, until 1777. In recent years the language has been revived in a somewhat reconstructed form by people interested in their Cornish heritage.

Corn Laws in Britain until 1846, laws used to regulate the export or import of cereals in order to maintain an adequate supply for consumers and a secure price for producers. For centuries the Corn Laws formed an integral part of the mercantile system in England; they were repealed because they became an unwarranted tax on food and a hindrance to British exports.

The Corn Law of 1815 Although mentioned as early as the 12th century, the Corn Laws only became significant 1815. After the Napoleonic wars, faced with agricultural depression, the landed interests in Parliament used their political power to prevent prices falling. The Corn Law of 1815 prevented the import of wheat unless the price of British grain rose to £4 a quarter (2.91 hl/8 bushels).

To a degree, the law was a success. It did help to protect British farming from foreign competition and to stabilize prices. As they were receiving a high price, farmers were able to continue to introduce improvements. However, the Corn Law pushed the price of bread too high, causing distress to the poor. Business interests argued that, by driving up prices, they also forced up wages and put British industry at a disadvantage in world markets.

William Huskisson, president of the Board of Trade, introduced a sliding scale in 1828 whereby the higher the price of British grain, the lower the duty on imports. The rate of duty was reduced in 1842. However, the principle of protection was still the same.

Repeal The Corn Laws aroused strong opposition and became a hotly contested political issue, as they were regarded by radicals as

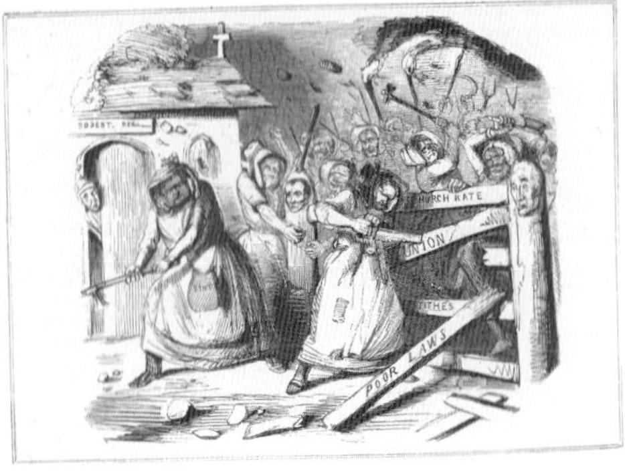

CORN LAWS *Punch* cartoon of 1846 drawing a parallel between the 'Rebecca Riots' which had recently afflicted southwest Wales and the decision of prime minister Robert Peel to abolish the Corn Laws. *Philip Sauvain Picture Collection*

benefiting wealthy landowners at the expense of the ordinary consumer. The industrialists – whose power in Parliament was growing, especially after the Reform Act of 1832 – also opposed the Corn Laws; they argued that ▷protectionism merely caused other countries to close their economies to British goods, and they wanted ▷free trade. It was also argued that the Corn Laws allowed British farming to stay inefficient, and actually held back improvement. In 1838 the ▷Anti-Corn Law League was formed to campaign for the repeal of the laws. Partly as a result of the League, and also partly on account of the Irish potato famine, the laws were repealed by prime minister Robert ▷Peel in 1846, although it destroyed his career.

Related Web site: Corn Laws by T R Malthus http://www.yale.edu/lawweb/avalon/econ/corframe.htm

cornucopia (Latin 'horn of plenty') in Greek mythology, one of the horns of the goat Amalthaea, which Zeus caused to refill perpetually with food and drink. As an artistic symbol it denotes prosperity. In paintings, the cornucopia is depicted as a horn-shaped container spilling over with fruit and flowers.

Cornwall county in southwest England including the Isles of ▷Scilly (Scillies).

area (excluding Scillies) 3,550 sq km/1,370 sq mi **towns and cities** ▷Truro (administrative headquarters), Camborne, Launceston; Bude, Falmouth, Newquay, Penzance, St Ives (resorts) **physical** Bodmin Moor (including Brown Willy 419 m/1,375 ft); Land's End peninsula; rivers Camel, Fal, Fowey, Tamar **features** St Michael's Mount; Poldhu, site of first transatlantic radio signal (1901); the Stannary or Tinners' Parliament; Tate Gallery, St Ives; the Mineral Tramways Project, which aims to preserve the mining landscape, once the centre of the world's hard-rock mining industry; Eden Project, two 'biomes' (tropical rainforest and Mediterranean) built in a disused china-clay pit near St Austell, formed a Millennium Commission Landmark Project, the first part of which opened in 2000; the 'Lost' Gardens of Heligan **agriculture** crops are early in some places: fruit, oats, and vegetables, including swedes, turnips, and mangolds (a root vegetable used as cattle fodder); spring flowers; cattle and sheep rearing; dairy farming; fishing (Mevagissey, Newlyn, and St Ives are the principal fishing ports) **industries** tourism; electronics; kaolin (a white clay used in the manufacture of porcelain; St Austell is the main centre for production) **population** (1996) 483,300 **famous people** John Betjeman, Humphry Davy, Daphne Du Maurier, William Golding

Related Web site: Historical Cornwall http://www.cranstar.co.uk/History.htm

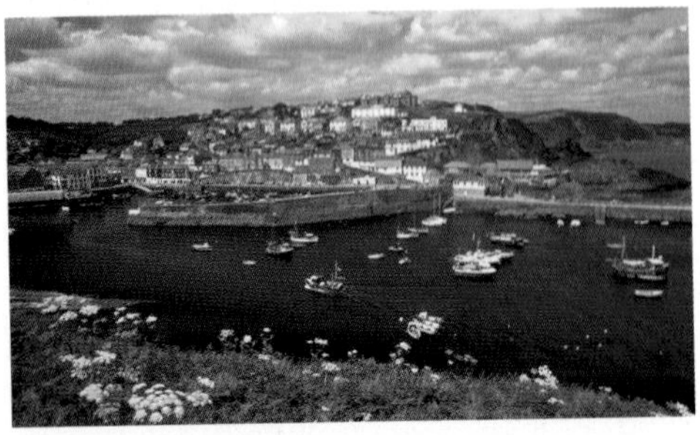

CORNWALL The harbour and village of Mevagissey in Cornwall, England. *Image Bank*

Cornwallis, Charles, 1st Marquis and 2nd Earl (1738–1805) British general in the ▷American Revolution until 1781, when his defeat at Yorktown led to final surrender and ended the war. He then served twice as governor-general of India and once as viceroy of Ireland. He succeeded to the earldom in 1762, and was made a marquis in 1792.

Cornwallis was educated at Eton and Clare College, Cambridge. He joined the army, and in 1761 served on his first campaign, in Germany. He was made constable of the Tower in 1770. During the American Revolution, before his comprehensive defeat at Yorktown, he won victories over General Gates at Camden in 1780 and General Greene at Guilford in 1781. From 1786 onwards, while serving governor-general of India, he instituted many reforms and pacified the country. After capturing Bangalore in 1791 and concluding a treaty with Britain's main adversary Tipu Sahib, he returned to England in 1793. In 1798 he was appointed viceroy of Ireland, where he succeeded in subduing the rebellion led by Wolfe ▷Tone; however, he resigned in 1801 because of the King's refusal to support prime minister William Pitt the Younger's proposal for Catholic emancipation. The following year, he was Britain's chief representative when the Peace of Amiens was concluded with France. In 1805 he was again sent to India, to replace Lord Wellesley as governor-general, but died at Ghazipur.

corolla collective name for the petals of a flower. In some plants the petal margins are partly or completely fused to form a **corolla tube**, for example in bindweed *Convolvulus arvensis*.

corona faint halo of hot (about 2,000,000°C/3,600,000°F) and tenuous gas around the Sun, which boils from the surface. It is visible at solar ▷eclipses or through a **coronagraph**, an instrument that blocks light from the Sun's brilliant disc. Gas flows away from the corona to form the ▷solar wind.

Coronado, Francisco Vásquez de (*c.* 1510–1554) Spanish explorer who sailed to the New World in 1535 in search of gold. In 1540 he set out with several hundred men from the Gulf of California on an exploration of what are today the southernwestern states. Although he failed to discover any gold, his expedition came across the impressive Grand Canyon of the Colorado and introduced the use of the horse to the indigenous Indians.

coronary artery disease (Latin *corona* 'crown', from the arteries encircling the heart) condition in which the fatty deposits of atherosclerosis form in the coronary arteries that supply the heart muscle, narrowing them and restricting the blood flow.

These arteries may already be hardened (arteriosclerosis). If the heart's oxygen requirements are increased, as during exercise, the blood supply through the narrowed arteries may be inadequate, and the pain of ▷angina results. A ▷heart attack occurs if the blood supply to an area of the heart is cut off, for example because a blood clot (thrombus) has blocked one of the coronary arteries. The subsequent lack of oxygen damages the heart muscle (infarct), and if a large area of the heart is affected, the attack may be fatal. Coronary artery disease tends to run in families and is linked to smoking, lack of exercise, and a diet high in saturated (mostly animal) fats, which tends to increase the level of blood ▷cholesterol. It is a common cause of death in many industrialized countries; older men are the most vulnerable group. The condition is treated with drugs or bypass surgery.

Coronary artery disease is the biggest single cause of premature death in the UK.

Related Web site: 'Preventing Recurrent Coronary Heart Disease' http://www.bmj.com/cgi/content/full/316/7142/1400

coronation ceremony of investing a sovereign with the emblems of royalty, as a symbol of inauguration in office. Since the coronation of Harold in 1066, English sovereigns have been crowned in Westminster Abbey, London.

coroner official who investigates the deaths of persons who have died suddenly by acts of violence or under suspicious circumstances, by holding an inquest or ordering a postmortem examination (autopsy).

Corot, Jean-Baptiste Camille (1796–1875) French painter. He created a distinctive landscape style using a soft focus and a low-key palette of browns, ochres, and greens. His early work, including Italian scenes of the 1820s, influenced the ▷Barbizon School of painters. Like them, Corot worked outdoors, but he also continued a conventional academic tradition with his romanticized paintings of women.

According to the wishes of his parents, who had a fashionable dress shop in Paris, after education at the college of Rouen he worked until 1822 in a cloth warehouse, but was then given a small allowance to study painting. He spent a few months with the young and short-lived Michallon, who directed him to the study of nature, afterwards working under another painter, Victor Bertin. It is reasonable to suppose that he was impressed by Constable in the Salon of 1824; going to Rome the following year he showed in his first Italian landscapes a response to effects of sun and cloud that seems, as in the *Claudian Aqueduct* (National Gallery), related to the work of the English master. Their breadth and directness of style marked a new conception of landscape in French art. His first Salon picture, in 1827, was the *Vue prise à Narni* (National Gallery of Canada), and he returned to France in 1828, painting some of his best pictures in the following six years, and working in Paris and Normandy, at Fontainebleu, Ville d'Avray and elsewhere, the light of Italy giving place to harmonies of silvery grey. His stay at Fontainebleau places him in close relation to the Barbizon School. A second visit to Italy in 1834, and another in 1843 produced further masterly works, such as his *Villa d'Este*, though it was long before Corot sold a picture or obtained public recognition, despite the admiration of friends. Late in life, however, he enjoyed great success, generously sharing its rewards with such less fortunate artists as Daumier, though the paintings most popular were not always his best.

Jean-Baptiste Camille Corot

To enter fully into one of my landscapes, one must have the patience to allow the mists to clear . . .

Remark made to T Silvestre (1856)

corporal punishment physical punishment of wrongdoers – for example, by whipping. It is still used as a punishment for criminals in many countries, especially under Islamic law. Corporal punishment of children by parents is illegal in some countries, including Sweden, Finland, Denmark, and Norway.

corporation tax tax levied on a company's profits. It is a form of income tax, and rates vary according to country, but there is usually a flat rate. It is a large source of revenue for governments.

corporatism belief that the state in capitalist democracies should intervene to a large extent in the economy to ensure social harmony. In Austria, for example, corporatism results in political decisions often being taken after discussions between chambers of commerce, trade unions, and the government.

corporative state state in which the members are organized and represented not on a local basis as citizens, but as producers working in a particular trade, industry, or profession. Originating with the syndicalist workers' movement (see ▷syndicalism), the idea was superficially adopted by the fascists during the 1920s and 1930s. Catholic social theory, as expounded in some papal encyclicals, also favours the corporative state as a means of eliminating class conflict.

corpus luteum glandular tissue formed in the mammalian ▷ovary after ovulation from the Graafian follicle, a group of cells associated with bringing the egg to maturity. It secretes the hormone progesterone in anticipation of pregnancy.

Correggio (*c.* 1494–1534) Adopted name of Antonio Allegri. Italian painter of the High Renaissance. His style followed the classical grandeur of ▷Leonardo da Vinci and ▷Titian, but anticipated the ▷baroque in its emphasis on movement, softer forms, and contrasts of light and shade.

correlation the degree of relationship between two sets of information. If one set of data increases at the same time as the other, the relationship is said to be positive or direct. If one set of data increases as the other decreases, the relationship is negative or inverse. Correlation can be shown by plotting a best-fit line on a ▷scatter diagram.

In statistics, such relations are measured by the calculation of ▷coefficients of correlation. These generally measure correlation on a scale with 1 indicating perfect positive correlation, 0 no correlation at all, and −1 perfect inverse correlation. Correlation coefficients for assumed linear relations include the Pearson product moment correlation coefficient (known simply as the correlation coefficient), Kendall's tau correlation coefficient, or Spearman's rho correlation coefficient, which is used in nonparametric statistics (where the data are measured on ordinal rather than interval scales). A high correlation does not always indicate dependence between two variables; it may be that there is a third (unstated) variable upon which both depend.

correspondence in mathematics, the relation between two sets where an operation on the members of one set maps some or all of them onto one or more members of the other. For example, if *A* is the set of members of a family and *B* is the set of months in the year, *A* and *B* are in correspondence if the operation is: '...has a birthday in the month of...'.

corrie (Welsh *cwm*; French, North American *cirque*) Scottish term for a steep-sided hollow in the mountainside of a glaciated area. The weight and movement of the ice has ground out the bottom and worn back the sides. A corrie is open at the front, and its sides and back are formed of ▷arêtes. There may be a lake in the bottom, called a tarn.

corrosion in earth science, an alternative name for ▷solution, the process by which water dissolves rocks such as limestone.

corrosion the eating away and eventual destruction of metals and alloys by chemical attack. The rusting of ordinary iron and steel is the most common form of corrosion. Rusting takes place in moist air, when the iron combines with oxygen and water to form a brown-orange deposit of ▷rust (hydrated iron oxide). The rate of corrosion is increased where the atmosphere is polluted with sulphur dioxide. Salty road and air conditions accelerate the rusting of car bodies.

Corsica (French *Corse*) island region of France, in the Mediterranean off the west coast of Italy, north of Sardinia; it comprises the *départements* of Haute Corse and Corse du Sud; area 8,700 sq km/3,358 sq mi; population (1999 est) 260,200 (including just under 50% native Corsicans). The capital is ▷Ajaccio. The island is largely mountainous and characterized by maquis vegetation (drought-tolerant shrubs such as cork oak and myrtle). The main products are wine and olive oil; tourism is the island's economic mainstay. The languages spoken are French (official) and Corsican, an Italian dialect. Napoleon was born in Ajaccio in 1769, the same year that Corsica became a province of France. The island is the main base of the Foreign Legion.

The Phocaeans of Ionia founded Alalia in about 570 BC, and were succeeded in turn by the Etruscans, the Carthaginians, the Romans, the Vandals, and the Arabs. In the 14th century Corsica fell to the Genoese, and in the second half of the 18th century a Corsican nationalist, Pasquale Paoli (1725–1807), led an independence movement.

Genoa sold Corsica to France in 1768. In World War II Corsica was occupied by Italy from 1942 to 1943. From 1962, French *pieds noirs* (refugees from Algeria), mainly vine growers, were settled in Corsica, and their prosperity helped to fan nationalist feeling, which demands an independent Corsica. This fuelled the National Liberation Front of Corsica (FNLC), banned in 1983, which has engaged in some terrorist bombings (a truce began in June 1988 but ended in January 1991).

French prime minister Lionel Jospin unveiled a plan on 20 July 2000 for limited autonomy for the government of Corsica. In an attempt to end 20 years of violence on the island, he proposed a single political and administrative body with limited independent law-making powers. The proposals marked a great departure from the tradition of heavy-handed government from Paris, but were not met with universal acceptance in Corsica.

Cortés, Hernán Ferdinand (1485–1547) Spanish

conquistador. He conquered the Aztec empire 1519–21, and secured Mexico for Spain.

Cortés went to the West Indies as a young man and in 1518 was given command of an expedition to Mexico. Landing with only

HERNÁN CORTÉS Spanish conquistador Hernán Ferdinand Cortés, on entering Tlaxcala, meets with Aztec resistance, in about 1520. *Archive Photos*

600 men, he was at first received as a god by the Aztec emperor ▷Montezuma II but was expelled from Tenochtitlán (Mexico City) when he was found not to be 'divine'. With the aid of Indian allies he recaptured the city in 1521, and overthrew the Aztec empire. His conquests eventually included most of Mexico and northern Central America.

cortex in biology, the outer part of a structure such as the brain, kidney, or adrenal gland. In botany the cortex includes non-specialized cells lying just beneath the surface cells of the root and stem.

corticosteroid any of several steroid hormones secreted by the cortex of the ▷adrenal glands; also synthetic forms with similar properties. Corticosteroids have anti-inflammatory and ▷immunosuppressive effects and may be used to treat a number of conditions, including rheumatoid arthritis, severe allergies, asthma, some skin diseases, and some cancers. Side effects can be serious, and therapy must be withdrawn very gradually.

cortisone natural corticosteroid produced by the ▷adrenal gland, now synthesized for its anti-inflammatory qualities and used in the treatment of rheumatoid arthritis.

Cortona, Pietro da Italian baroque painter; see ▷Pietro da Cortona.

corundum native aluminium oxide, Al_2O_3, the hardest naturally occurring mineral known apart from diamond (corundum rates 9 on the Mohs scale of hardness); lack of ▷cleavage also increases its durability. Its crystals are barrel-shaped prisms of the trigonal system. Varieties of gem-quality corundum are **ruby** (red) and **sapphire** (any colour other than red, usually blue). Poorer-quality and synthetic corundum is used in industry, for example as an ▷abrasive.

Cosa, Juan de la (c. 1450–1509) Spanish navigator and cartographer who accompanied ▷Columbus on his voyage in 1492, as pilot. He held the same position under Alonzo de Hojeda in 1499, and in 1504 himself led an expedition to North America; in 1509 he was appointed *alguazil* (mayor) over Uraba (Darien in present-day Panama).

Cosgrave, William Thomas

(1880–1965) Irish revolutionary and politician; president of the executive council (prime minister) of the Irish Free State 1922–32, leader of Cumann na nGaedheal 1923–33, and leader of Fine Gael 1935–44. He was born in Dublin and educated by the Christian Brothers. A founding member of ▷Sinn Fein, he fought in the ▷Easter Rising of 1916 but his death sentence was commuted. He supported the Anglo-Irish Treaty (1921) and oversaw the ruthless crushing of Irregular IRA forces during the Irish Civil War (1922–23), executing far more IRA members than his British predecessors.

Cosgrave was elected to Westminster as a Sinn Fein MP in 1917, and was appointed minister for local government in the first Dáil (then the illegal republican parliament) in 1919. Following the deaths of Collins and Griffith in 1922, he succeeded them as chair of the provisional government and president of the Dáil government respectively, and became prime minister of the Irish Free State. After the civil war the Free State settled down under his leadership to a period of dull and conservative stability. Nevertheless this stability was crucial to the new state's democracy, illustrated by the peaceful transference of power to Cosgrave's old enemies in Fianna Fáil in 1932.

cosine in trigonometry, a ▷function of an angle in a right-angled triangle found by dividing the length of the side adjacent to the angle by the length of the hypotenuse (the longest side). It is usually shortened to **cos**.

cosine rule in trigonometry, a rule that relates the sides and angles of triangles. The rule has the formula:

$$a^2 = b^2 + c^2 - 2bc\cos A$$

where *a*, *b*, and *c* are the lengths of the sides of the triangle, and *A* is the angle opposite *a*.

cosmic background radiation (or 3° radiation) electromagnetic radiation left over from the original formation of the universe in the Big Bang between 10 and 20 billion years ago. It corresponds to an overall background temperature of 2.73K (−270.4°C/−454.7°F), or 3°C above absolute zero. In 1992, the US Cosmic Background Explorer satellite, COBE, detected slight 'ripples' in the strength of the background radiation that are believed to mark the first stage in the formation of galaxies.

Cosmic background radiation was first detected in 1965 by US physicists Arno Penzias and Robert Wilson, who in 1978 shared the Nobel Prize for Physics for their discovery.

cosmic radiation streams of high-energy particles and electromagnetic radiation from outer space, consisting of electrons,

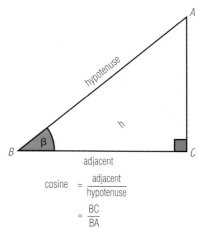

$$\text{cosine} = \frac{\text{adjacent}}{\text{hypotenuse}}$$

$$= \frac{BC}{BA}$$

COSINE The cosine of angle β is equal to the ratio of the length of the adjacent side to the length of the hypotenuse (the longest side, opposite to the right angle).

protons, alpha particles, light nuclei, and gamma rays, which collide with atomic nuclei in the Earth's atmosphere, and produce secondary nuclear particles (chiefly ▷mesons, such as pions and muons) that shower the Earth.

Those of lower energy seem to be galactic in origin, and those of high energy of extragalactic origin. The galactic particles may come from ▷supernova explosions or ▷pulsars. At higher energies, other sources must exist, possibly the giants jets of gas which are emitted from some galaxies.

cosmology branch of astronomy that deals with the structure and evolution of the universe as an ordered whole. Cosmologists construct 'model universes' mathematically and compare their large-scale properties with those of the observed universe.

Modern cosmology began in the 1920s with the discovery that the universe is expanding, which suggested that it began in an explosion, the ▷Big Bang. An alternative – now discarded – view, the ▷steady-state theory, claimed that the universe has no origin, but is expanding because new matter is being continually created.

Related Web site: Brief History of Cosmology http://www-history. mcs.st-and.ac.uk/~history/HistTopics/Cosmology.html

Cossack people of southern and southwestern Russia, Ukraine, and Poland, predominantly of Russian or Ukrainian origin, who took in escaped serfs and lived in independent communal settlements (military brotherhoods) from the 15th to the 19th century. Later they held land in return for military service in the cavalry under Russian and Polish rulers. After 1917, the various Cossack communities were incorporated into the Soviet administrative and collective system.

There are many Cossack settlements in the northern Caucasus. Cossack movements demand the restoration of their traditional military role (granted in part by a 1993 decree) and collective ownership of land.

COSSACK In return for military service, the Cossack peoples of the Ukraine were granted land and self-government. Bands of Cossacks, as shown here, fought against the revolution in 1917, and the communist government subsequently took away many of their privileges. *Image Bank*

Costa Brava (Spanish 'Wild Coast') Mediterranean coastline of northeast Spain, stretching from Port-Bou on the French border southwards to Blanes, northeast of Barcelona. It is noted for its irregular rocky coastline, small fishing villages, and resorts such as Puerto de la Selva, Palafrugell, Playa de Aro, and Lloret del Mar.

Hernán Cortés
I and my companions suffer from a disease of the heart that can be cured only with gold.
Message sent to Montezuma (1519)

Costa del Sol (Spanish 'Coast of the Sun') Mediterranean coastline of Andalusia, southern Spain, stretching for nearly 300 km/190 mi from Gibraltar to Almería. Málaga is the principal port and Marbella, Torremolinos, and Nerja are the chief tourist resorts.

Costa Rica see country box.

cost–benefit analysis process whereby a project is assessed for its social and welfare benefits in addition to considering the financial return on investment. For example, this might take into account the environmental impact of an industrial plant or convenience for users of a new railway. A major difficulty is finding a way to quantify net social costs and benefits.

Costner, Kevin (1955–) US film actor. He emerged as a star in the late 1980s, with roles in *The Untouchables* (1987), *Bull Durham* (1988), and *Field of Dreams* (1989). Increasingly identified with the embodiment of idealism and high principle, Costner went on to direct and star in *Dances with Wolves* (1990), a Western sympathetic to the American Indians, which won several Academy Awards. In 2001 he was acclaimed for his understated performance in *Thirteen Days*.

cost of living cost of goods and services needed for an average standard of living.

In Britain the cost-of-living index was introduced in 1914 and based on the expenditure of a working-class family of a man, woman, and three children; the standard is 100. Known from 1947 as the Retail Price Index (RPI), it is revised to allow for inflation. Supplementary to the RPI are the Consumer's Expenditure Deflator (formerly Consumer Price Index) and the Tax and Price Index (TPI), introduced in 1979. Comprehensive indexation has been advocated as a means of controlling inflation by linking all forms of income (such as wages and investment), contractual debts, and tax scales to the RPI. Index-linked savings schemes were introduced in the UK in 1975. In the USA a consumer price index, based on the expenditure of families in the iron, steel, and related industries, was introduced in 1890. The present index is based on the expenditure of the urban wage-earner and clerical-worker families in 46 large, medium, and small cities, the standard being 100. Increases in social security benefits are linked to it, as are many wage settlements.

cot death (or sudden infant death syndrome (SIDS)) death of an apparently healthy baby, almost always during sleep. It is most common in the winter months, and strikes more boys than girls.

The cause is not known but risk factors that have been identified include prematurity, respiratory infection, overheating, sleeping position, and maternal smoking in pregnancy.

Côte d'Azur Mediterranean coast from Menton to St-Tropez in the *départements* of Alpes-Maritimes and Var, France, renowned for its beaches; it is part of the region ▷Provence-Alpes-Côte d'Azur. The chief resorts are Antibes, Cannes, Nice, Juan-Les-Pins, and Monte Carlo in Monaco.

Côte d'Ivoire see country box.

cotoneaster any of a group of shrubs or trees found in Europe and Asia, belonging to the rose family and closely related to the hawthorn and medlar. The fruits, though small and unpalatable, are usually bright red and conspicuous, often surviving through the winter. Some of the shrubs are cultivated for their attractive appearance. (Genus *Cotoneaster*, family Rosaceae.)

Cotonou chief port and largest city of Benin, on the Bight of Benin; population (1994) 537,000. Palm products and timber are exported, and textiles are manufactured. Although not the official capital, it is the seat of the president, and the main centre of commerce and politics.

Costa Rica

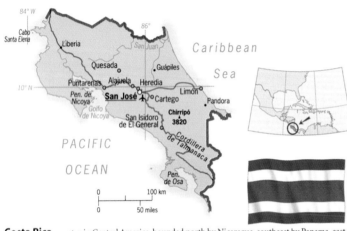

RELIGION Roman Catholic 95% (state religion)
EDUCATION (compulsory years) 9
LITERACY RATE 96% (men); 96% (women) (2003 est)
LABOUR FORCE 19.7% agriculture, 23.2% industry, 57.1% services (1999)
LIFE EXPECTANCY 76 (men); 81 (women) (2000–05)

PHYSICIANS (per 1,000 people) 1.4 (1998 est)
HOSPITAL BEDS (per 1,000 people) 1.7 (1998 est)
TV SETS (per 1,000 people) 231 (2001 est)
RADIOS (per 1,000 people) 816 (2001 est)
INTERNET USERS (per 10,000 people) 933.6 (2002 est)
PERSONAL COMPUTER USERS (per 100 people) 19.7 (2002 est)

Costa Rica country in Central America, bounded north by Nicaragua, southeast by Panama, east by the Caribbean Sea, and west by the Pacific Ocean.

NATIONAL NAME *República de Costa Rica*/Republic of Costa Rica
AREA 51,100 sq km/19,729 sq mi
CAPITAL San José
MAJOR TOWNS/CITIES Alajuela, Cartago, Limón, Puntarenas, San Isidro, Desamparados
MAJOR PORTS Limón, Puntarenas
PHYSICAL FEATURES high central plateau and tropical coasts; Costa Rica was once entirely forested, containing an estimated 5% of the Earth's flora and fauna

Government

HEAD OF STATE AND GOVERNMENT Abel Pacheco de la Espriella from 2002
POLITICAL SYSTEM liberal democracy
POLITICAL EXECUTIVE limited presidency
ADMINISTRATIVE DIVISIONS seven provinces
ARMED FORCES army abolished in 1948; paramilitary forces of 8,400 (2002 est)
DEATH PENALTY abolished in 1877
DEFENCE SPEND (% GDP) 0.6 (2002 est)
EDUCATION SPEND (% GDP) 4.4 (2001 est)
HEALTH SPEND (% GDP) 6.4 (2000 est)

Economy and resources

CURRENCY colón
GPD (US$) 16.9 billion (2002 est)
REAL GDP GROWTH (% change on previous year) 0.9 (2001)
GNI (US$) 16.2 billion (2002 est)
GNI PER CAPITA (PPP) (US$) 8,260 (2002 est)
CONSUMER PRICE INFLATION 10% (2003 est)
UNEMPLOYMENT 6.1% (2001)

FOREIGN DEBT (US$) 7.2 billion (2001 est)
MAJOR TRADING PARTNERS USA, EU, Japan, Venezuela, Mexico, Guatemala
RESOURCES gold, salt, hydro power
INDUSTRIES food processing, chemical products, beverages, paper and paper products, textiles and clothing, plastic goods, electrical equipment
EXPORTS manufactured products, bananas, coffee, sugar, cocoa, textiles, seafood, meat, tropical fruit. Principal market: USA 51.8% (2001)
IMPORTS raw materials for industry and agriculture, consumer goods, machinery and transport equipment, construction materials. Principal source: USA 53.2% (2001)
ARABLE LAND 4.4% (2000 est)
AGRICULTURAL PRODUCTS bananas, coffee, sugar cane, maize, potatoes, tobacco, tropical fruit; livestock rearing (cattle and pigs); fishing

Population and society

POPULATION 4,173,000 (2003 est)
POPULATION GROWTH RATE 1.5% (2000–15)
POPULATION DENSITY (per sq km) 82 (2003 est)
URBAN POPULATION (% of total) 61 (2003 est)
AGE DISTRIBUTION (% of total population) 0–14 31%, 15–59 61%, 60+ 8% (2002 est)
ETHNIC GROUPS about 96% of the population is of European descent, mostly Spanish, and about 2% is of African origin, 1% is Amerindian, 1% Chinese
LANGUAGE Spanish (official)

COSTA RICA A waterfall on the Tabacon River in Costa Rica. This is a volcanic area, and hot springs abound, feeding into the river network. One-third of Costa Rica is given over to national parkland and nature reserves. *Image Bank*

Chronology

1502: Visited by Christopher Columbus, who named the area Costa Rica (the rich coast), observing the gold decorations worn by the Guaymi American Indians.
1506: Colonized by Spain, but there was fierce guerrilla resistance by the indigenous population. Many later died from exposure to European diseases.
18th century: Settlements began to be established in the fertile central highlands, including San José and Alajuela.
1808: Coffee was introduced from Cuba and soon became the staple crop.
1821: Independence achieved from Spain, and was joined initially with Mexico.
1824: Became part of United Provinces (Federation) of Central America, also embracing El Salvador, Guatemala, Honduras, and Nicaragua.
1838: Became fully independent when it seceded from the Federation.
later 19th century: Immigration by Europeans to run and work small coffee farms.
1940–44: Liberal reforms, including recognition of workers' rights and minimum wages, were introduced by President Rafael Angel Calderón

Guradia, founder of the United Christian Socialist Party (PUSC).
1948: Brief civil war following a disputed presidential election.
1949: New constitution adopted. National army abolished and replaced by civil guard. José Figueres Ferrer, cofounder of the PLN, elected president; he embarked on an ambitious socialist programme.
1958–73: Mainly conservative administrations.
1978: Sharp deterioration in the state of the economy.
1982: A harsh austerity programme was introduced.
1985: Following border clashes with Nicaraguan Sandinista forces, a US-trained antiguerrilla guard was formed.
1986: Oscar Arias Sanchez (PLN) won the presidency on a neutralist platform.
1987: Arias won the Nobel Prize for Peace for devising a Central American peace plan signed by the leaders of Nicaragua, El Salvador, Guatemala, and Honduras.
1998: Miguel Angel Rodriguez Echeverria (PUSC) was elected president.
2002: Abel Pacheco de la Espriella elected president.

Cotopaxi active Andean volcano in north-central Ecuador on the border of the Cotopaxi, Napo, and Pichincha provinces. It is located 48 km/30 mi south of ▷Quito at an altitude of 5,897 m/

COTSWOLD HILLS A view of the Cotswold town of Broadway, England. *Image Bank*

19,347 ft above sea level. It one of the highest volcanoes in the world. It is now contained within a 340 sq km/131 sq mi national park, established in 1975.

Cotswold Hills (or **Cotswolds**) range of limestone hills mainly in Gloucestershire, South Gloucestershire, and Bath and North East Somerset, England, 80 km/50 mi long, between Bath and Chipping Camden. They rise to 333 m/1,086 ft at Cleeve Cloud, near Cheltenham, but average about 200 m/600 ft. The area is known for its picturesque villages, built with the local honey-coloured stone.

cotton tropical and subtropical ▷herbaceous plant belonging to the mallow family. Fibres surround the seeds inside the ripened fruits, or bolls, and these are spun into yarn for cloth. (Genus *Gossypium*, family Malvaceae.)

cotton grass (or **bog cotton**) any grasslike plant of a group belonging to the sedge family. White tufts cover the fruiting heads in midsummer; these break off and are carried long distances on the wind. Cotton grass is found in wet places throughout the Arctic and temperate regions of the northern hemisphere, most species growing in acid bogs. (Genus *Eriophorum*, family Cyperaceae.)

cottonwood any of several North American ▷poplar trees with seeds topped by a thick tuft of silky hairs. The eastern cottonwood (*Populus deltoides*), growing to 30 m/100 ft, is native to the eastern

COTTON Harvesters on a cotton plantation in Lost Hills, California, USA. *Image Bank*

Côte d'Ivoire

Côte d'Ivoire country in West Africa, bounded north by Mali and Burkina Faso, east by Ghana, south by the Gulf of Guinea, and west by Liberia and Guinea.

NATIONAL NAME *République de la Côte d'Ivoire/Republic of the Ivory Coast*
AREA 322,463 sq km/124,502 sq mi
CAPITAL Yamoussoukro
MAJOR TOWNS/CITIES Abidjan, Bouaké, Daloa, Man, Korhogo, Gagnoa
MAJOR PORTS Abidjan, San Pedro
PHYSICAL FEATURES tropical rainforest (diminishing as exploited) in south; savannah and low mountains in north; coastal plain; Vridi canal, Kossou dam, Monts du Toura

Government
HEAD OF STATE Laurent Gbagbo from 2000
HEAD OF GOVERNMENT Seydou Diarra from 2003
POLITICAL SYSTEM emergent democracy
POLITICAL EXECUTIVE limited presidency
ADMINISTRATIVE DIVISIONS 18 regions, comprising 57 departments
ARMED FORCES 17,000; plus paramilitary forces of 8,900 (2002 est)
CONSCRIPTION selective conscription for 18 months
DEATH PENALTY abolished in 2000
DEFENCE SPEND (% GDP) 1.4 (2002 est)
EDUCATION SPEND (% GDP) 4.6 (2001 est)
HEALTH SPEND (% GDP) 2.7 (2000 est)

Economy and resources
CURRENCY franc CFA
GPD (US$) 11.7 billion (2002 est)
REAL GDP GROWTH (% change on previous year) –0.9 (2001)
GNI (US$) 10.3 billion (2002 est)
GNI PER CAPITA (PPP) (US$) 1,430 (2002 est)
CONSUMER PRICE INFLATION 4% (2003 est)
FOREIGN DEBT (US$) 10.8 billion (2001 est)
MAJOR TRADING PARTNERS France, Nigeria, the Netherlands, Italy, Belgium–Luxembourg, USA, Mali
RESOURCES petroleum, natural gas, diamonds, gold, nickel, reserves of manganese, iron ore, bauxite
INDUSTRIES agro-processing (dominated by cocoa, coffee, cotton, palm kernels, pineapples, fish), petroleum refining, tobacco
EXPORTS cocoa beans and products, petroleum products, timber, coffee, cotton, tinned tuna. Principal market: France 15.3% (2000)
IMPORTS crude petroleum, machinery and vehicles, pharmaceuticals, fresh fish, plastics, cereals. Principal source: Nigeria 24.8% (2000)
ARABLE LAND 9.3% (2000 est)
AGRICULTURAL PRODUCTS cocoa (world's largest producer), coffee (world's fifth-largest producer), cotton, rubber, palm kernels, bananas, pineapples, yams, cassava, rice, plantains; fishing; forestry

Population and society
POPULATION 16,631,000 (2003 est)
POPULATION GROWTH RATE 1.7% (2000–15)
POPULATION DENSITY (per sq km) 52 (2003 est)
URBAN POPULATION (% of total) 45 (2003 est)
AGE DISTRIBUTION (% of total population) 0–14 41%, 15–59 54%, 60+ 5% (2002 est)
ETHNIC GROUPS five principal ethnic groups: the Akan (41%), in the east and centre, the Voltaic (16%), based in the north, the Malinke (15%) and Southern Mande (11%) in the west, and the Kron (4%), based in the centre and the west
LANGUAGE French (official), over 60 ethnic languages
RELIGION animist 17%, Muslim 39% (mainly in north), Christian 26% (mainly Roman Catholic in south)
EDUCATION (compulsory years) 6
LITERACY RATE 62% (men); 41% (women) (2003 est)
LABOUR FORCE 37% of population: 52.5% agriculture, 11.8% industry, 35.7% services (1997 est)
LIFE EXPECTANCY 41 (men); 41 (women) (2000–05)
CHILD MORTALITY RATE (under 5, per 1,000 live births) 175 (2001)
HOSPITAL BEDS (per 1,000 people) 0.1 (1994 est)
TV SETS (per 1,000 people) 65 (1999 est)
RADIOS (per 1,000 people) 183 (2001 est)
INTERNET USERS (per 10,000 people) 54.6 (2002 est)

See also ▷Houphouet-Boigny, Félix.

CÔTE D'IVOIRE This stamp bears the coat of arms of the Ivory Coast. The elephant was key to the industry that was synonymous with the region.

Chronology

1460s: Portuguese navigators arrived.

16th century: Ivory export trade developed by Europeans and slave trade, though to a lesser extent than neighbouring areas; Krou people migrated from Liberia to the west and Senoufo and Lubi from the north.

late 17th century: French coastal trading posts established at Assini and Grand Bassam.

18th–19th centuries: Akan peoples, including the Baoulé, immigrated from the east and Malinke from the northwest.

1840s: French began to conclude commercial treaties with local rulers.

1893: Colony of Côte d'Ivoire created by French, after war with Mandinkas; Baoulé resistance continued until 1917.

1904: Became part of French West Africa; cocoa production encouraged.

1940–42: Under pro-Nazi French Vichy regime.

1946: Became overseas territory in French Union, with own territorial assembly and representation in French parliament: Felix Houphouet-Boigny, a Western-educated Baoulé chief who had formed the Democratic Party (PDCI) to campaign for autonomy, was elected to the French assembly.

1947: A French-controlled area to the north, which had been added to Côte d'Ivoire in 1932, separated to create new state of Upper Volta (now Burkina Faso).

1950–54: Port of Abidjan constructed.

1958: Achieved internal self-government.

1960: Independence secured, with Houphouët-Boigny as president of a one-party state.

1960s–1980s: Political stability, close links maintained with France and economic expansion of 10% per annum, as the country became one of the world's largest coffee producers.

1986: The country's name was officially changed from Ivory Coast to Côte d'Ivoire.

1987–93: Per capita incomes fell by 25% owing to an austerity programme promoted by the International Monetary Fund.

1990: There were strikes and student unrest. Houphouet-Boigny was re-elected as president as multiparty politics were re-established.

1993: Houphouet-Boigny died and was succeeded by parliamentary speaker and Baoulé Henri Konan Bedie.

1999: After a largely bloodless coup over Christmas 1999 Bedie was replaced by a new military leader, General Robert Guei.

2000: Guei announced suspension of the country's foreign debt repayments in January. A new constitution for the return of civilian rule was approved by referendum. Mutinous soldiers launched three unsuccessful coups against Guei, and a state of emergency was imposed. Guei attempted to sabotage the presidential elections, but was forced to flee. His main opponent, Laurent Gbagbo, declared himself winner amid protest.

2002: A coup was launched by mutinous soldiers against Laurent Gbagbo's government, leading to heavy fighting and hundreds of casualties, including the death of former military ruler, Robert Guei.

USA. The name 'cottonwood' is also given to the downy-leaved Australian tree *Bedfordia salaoina*. (True cottonwood genus *Populus*, family Salicaceae.)

cotyledon structure in the embryo of a seed plant that may form a 'leaf' after germination and is commonly known as a seed leaf. The number of cotyledons present in an embryo is an important character in the classification of flowering plants (▷angiosperms).

couch grass European grass that spreads rapidly by underground stems. It is considered a troublesome weed in North America, where it has been introduced. (*Agropyron repens*, family Gramineae.)
    Related Web site: Grasses http://www.botanical.com/botanical/mgmh/g/grasse34.html

cougar another name for the ▷puma, a large North American cat.

coulomb SI unit (symbol C) of electrical charge. One coulomb is the quantity of electricity conveyed by a current of one ▷ampere in one second.

council in local government in England and Wales, a popularly elected local assembly charged with the government of the area within its boundaries. Under the Local Government Act 1972, they comprise three types: ▷county councils, ▷district councils, and ▷parish councils. Many city councils exist in the USA.

Council of Europe body constituted in 1949 to achieve greater unity between European countries, to facilitate their economic and social progress, and to uphold the principles of parliamentary democracy and respect for human rights. It has a **Committee of foreign ministers**, a **Consultative Assembly**, a **Parliamentary Assembly** (with members from national parliaments), and a **European Commission on Human Rights**, established by the 1950 **European Convention on Human Rights**. If the commission is unable to achieve a friendly settlement after examining alleged violations, the case may be taken to the ▷European Court of Human Rights for adjudication. Its headquarters are in Strasbourg, France.

council tax method of raising revenue for local government in Britain. It replaced the community charge, or ▷poll tax, from April 1993. The tax is based on property values at April 1991, but takes some account of the number of people occupying each property.

counterfeiting fraudulent imitation, usually of banknotes. It is countered by special papers, elaborate watermarks, skilled printing, and sometimes the insertion of a metallic strip. ▷Forgery is also a form of counterfeiting.

counterpoint in music, the art of combining different forms of an original melody with apparent freedom while preserving a harmonious effect. Giovanni Palestrina and Johann Sebastian Bach were masters of counterpoint.

Counter-Reformation movement initiated by the Catholic Church at the Council of Trent (1545–63) to counter the spread of the ▷Reformation. Extending into the 17th century, its dominant forces included the rise of the Jesuits as an educating and missionary group and the deployment of the Spanish ▷Inquisition in Europe and the Americas.
    Related Web site: Counter-Reformation http://www.newadvent.org/cathen/04437a.htm

countertenor the highest natural male voice, as opposed to the ▷falsetto of the male ▷alto. It was favoured by the Elizabethans for its heroic brilliance of tone.

country (or country and western) popular music of the white US South and West; it evolved from the folk music of the English, Irish, and Scottish settlers and has a strong blues influence. Characteristic instruments are slide guitar, mandolin, and fiddle. Lyrics typically extol family values and traditional sex roles, and often have a strong narrative element. Country music encompasses a variety of regional styles, and ranges from mournful ballads to fast and intricate dance music.
    Related Web site: Roughstock's History of Country Music http://www.roughstock.com/history/

county (Latin *comitatus* through French *comté*) administrative unit of a country or state. It was the name given by the Normans to Anglo-Saxon 'shires', and the boundaries of many present-day English counties date back to Saxon times. There are currently 34 English administrative non-metropolitan counties and 6 metropolitan counties, in addition to 34 unitary authorities. Welsh and Scottish counties were abolished in 1996 in a reorganization of local government throughout the UK, and replaced by 22 and 33 unitary authorities respectively. Northern Ireland has 6 geographical

counties, although administration is through 26 district councils. In the USA a county is a subdivision of a state; the power of counties differs widely among states.

county council in England, a unit of local government whose responsibilities include broad planning policy, highways, education, personal social services, and libraries; police, fire, and traffic control; and refuse disposal. The tier below the county council has traditionally been the district council, but with local government reorganization from 1996, there has been a shift towards unitary authorities (based on a unit smaller than the county) replacing both. By 1998 there were 34 two-tier non-metropolitan county councils under which there were 274 district councils. (See also ▷local government.)

county court English court of law created by the County Courts Act 1846 and now governed by the Act of 1984. It exists to try civil cases, such as actions on ▷contract and ▷tort where the claim does not exceed £5,000, and disputes about land, such as between landlord and tenant. County courts are presided over by one or more circuit judges.

county palatine in medieval England, a county whose lord held particular rights, in lieu of the king, such as pardoning treasons and murders. Under William I there were four counties palatine: Chester, Durham, Kent, and Shropshire.

coup d'état (or coup; French 'stroke of state') forcible takeover of the government of a country by elements from within that country, generally carried out by violent or illegal means. It differs from a revolution in typically being carried out by a small group (for example, of army officers or opposition politicians) to install its leader as head of government, rather than being a mass uprising by the people.

Couperin, François le Grand (1668–1733) French composer. He is the best-known member of a musical family which included his uncle Louis Couperin (*c.* 1626–1661), composer for harpsichord and organ. A favoured composer of Louis XIV, Couperin composed numerous chamber concertos and harpsichord suites, and published a standard keyboard tutor *L'Art de toucher le clavecin/The Art of Playing the Harpsichord* (1716) in which he laid down guidelines for fingering, phrasing, and ornamentation.

> **François Couperin**
> *One might venture to say that in many things music . . . has its prose and its poetry.*
> *L'Art de toucher le clavecin (1716)*

Courbet, Gustave (1819–1877) French artist. He was a portrait, genre, and landscape painter. Reacting against academic trends, both classicist and Romantic, he became a major exponent of ▷realism, depicting contemporary life with an unflattering frankness. His *Burial at Ornans* (1850; Musée d'Orsay, Paris), showing ordinary working people gathered around a village grave, shocked the public and the critics with its 'vulgarity'.

His powerful genius found expression in portraiture, figure composition, landscape (the gorges and forests of his native Franche-Comte, and superb paintings of the Normandy coast, *The Wave* being famous in several versions), sensuous paintings of the nude, animal studies, and still life. He went to Paris 1841, his training mainly consisting in the study and imitation of old masters in the Louvre, especially Velázquez and Rembrandt. In defiance of both Romanticism and classicism he evolved the idea of realism, asserting, that is, that painting should consist in 'the representation of real and existing things', his aim therefore being, in his own words, to 'interpret the manners, ideas and aspect of our own time'. In this there were some social and proletarian implications, as might be gathered from his *Stonebreakers* (1849; Dresden, destroyed 1945), and the *Burial at Ornans* (Louvre), with its sombre group of peasants, which caused an uproar when exhibited at the Salon of 1850.

> **Gustave Courbet**
> *I deny that art can be taught.*
> Letter to prospective students (1861)

courgette small variety of ▷marrow, belonging to the gourd family. It is cultivated as a vegetable and harvested before it is fully mature, at 15–20 cm/6–8 in. In the USA and Canada it is known as a zucchini. (*Cucurbita pepo*, family Cucurbitaceae.)

Courrèges, André (1923–) French fashion designer. He is credited with inventing the miniskirt in 1964. His 'space-age' designs – square-shaped short skirts and trousers – were copied worldwide in the 1960s.

court martial court convened for the trial of persons subject to military discipline who are accused of violations of military laws.

Court of Appeal UK law court comprising a Civil Division and a Criminal Division, set up under the Criminal Appeals Act 1968. The Criminal Division of the Court of Appeal has the power to

revise sentences or quash a conviction on the grounds that in all the circumstances of the case the verdict is unsafe or unsatisfactory, or that the judgement of the original trial judge was wrong in law, or that there was a material irregularity during the course of the trial.

Court of Session supreme civil court in Scotland, established in 1532. Cases come in the first place before one of the judges of the Outer House (corresponding to the High Court in England and Wales), and from that decision an appeal lies to the Inner House (corresponding to the Court of Appeal) which sits in two divisions called the First and the Second Division. From the decisions of the Inner House an appeal lies to the House of Lords. The court sits in Edinburgh.

Cousteau, Jacques-Yves (1910–1997) French oceanographer. He pioneered the invention of the aqualung in 1943, as well as techniques in underwater filming. In 1951 he began the first of many research voyages in the ship *Calypso*. His film and television documentaries and books established him as a household name.

Cousteau was born in the Gironde. He joined the navy and worked for naval intelligence during the Nazi occupation. From 1936 he experimented with diving techniques. The compressed air cylinder had been invented in 1933 but restricted the diver to very short periods of time beneath the surface. Testing new breathing equipment, Cousteau was several times nearly killed.

In 1942 Cousteau met Emile Gagnan, an expert on industrial gas equipment. Gagnan had designed an experimental demand valve for feeding gas to car engines. Together, Gagnan and Cousteau developed a self-contained compressed air 'lung', the aqualung. In June 1943 Cousteau made his first dive with it, achieving a depth of 18 m/60 ft.

covalent bond chemical ▷bond produced when two atoms share one or more pairs of electrons (usually each atom contributes an electron). The bond is often represented by a single line drawn between the two atoms. Covalently bonded substances include hydrogen (H_2), water (H_2O), and most organic substances.

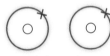

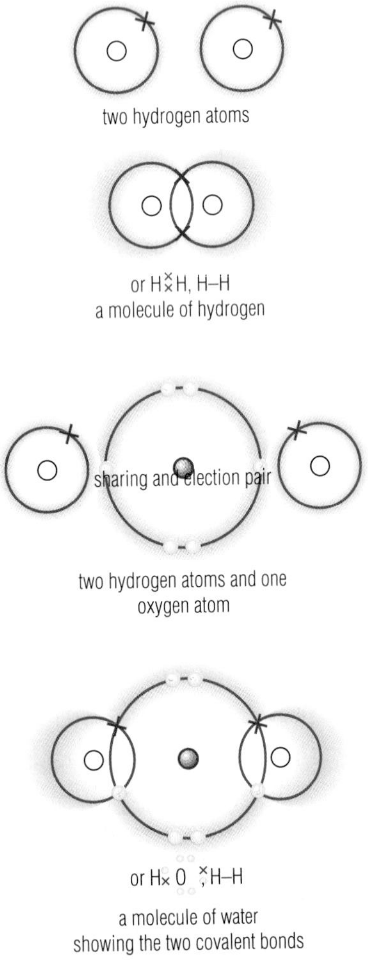

two hydrogen atoms

or H×̈H, H–H
a molecule of hydrogen

sharing and election pair

two hydrogen atoms and one oxygen atom

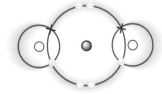

or H× O ×̈H–H

a molecule of water
showing the two covalent bonds

COVALENT BOND The formation of a covalent bond between two hydrogen atoms to form a hydrogen molecule (H_2), and between two hydrogen atoms and an oxygen atom to form a molecule of water (H_2O). The sharing means that each atom has a more stable arrangement of electrons (its outer electron shells are full).

Covenanter in Scottish history, one of the Presbyterian Christians who swore to uphold their forms of worship in a National Covenant, signed on 28 February 1638, when ▷Charles I attempted to introduce a liturgy on the English model into Scotland.

Coventry industrial city in the West Midlands, England, on the River Sherbourne, 29 km/18 mi southeast of Birmingham; population (1994 est) 303,000. Principal industries are engineering and the manufacture of electronic equipment, machine tools, agricultural machinery, manmade fibres, aerospace components, telecommunications equipment, and vehicles, including London taxis and Massey Ferguson tractors.

Features Coventry cathedral, incorporating the ruins of the old cathedral destroyed in an air raid in 1940, was designed by Basil Spence and consecrated in 1962; Belgrade Theatre (1958); the Herbert Art Gallery and Museum; Museum of British Road Transport; the University of Warwick (1965); Coventry University (1992), formerly Coventry or Lanchester Polytechnic. Every three years the city hosts one of the four surviving mystery play cycles performed in England. Under the Phoenix Initiative, a project to mark the millennium, parts of the city centre will be rebuilt to provide public open spaces.

History Leofric, Earl of Mercia and husband of Lady ▷Godiva, founded a Benedictine priory here in 1043. A centre of armaments manufacture during World War II, the city was the target of a massive German air raid on 14 and 15 November 1940 in which 550 people were killed, and over 60,000 buildings were destroyed.

Related Web site: History of Coventry http://www.exponet.co.uk/peter/covpast.htm

Coward, Noël Peirce (1899–1973) English dramatist, actor, revue-writer, director, and composer. He epitomized the witty and sophisticated man of the theatre. From his first success with *The Young Idea* (1923), he wrote and appeared in plays and comedies on both sides of the Atlantic such as *Hay Fever* (1925), *Private Lives* (1930) with Gertrude Lawrence, *Design for Living* (1933), *Blithe Spirit* (1941), and *A Song at Twilight* (1966). His revues and musicals included *On With the Dance* (1925) and *Bitter Sweet* (1929).

cowboy US cattle herder working on horseback; one of the great figures of American history and part of the folklore of the rugged adventurous West portrayed in books, films, and plays. Thousands of cowboys worked across the ▷Great Plains in the heyday of the early US cattle industry 1866–87, initially on the long cattle drives, herding cattle from the ranches to the cow towns, and later on the open range, the vast unfenced grazing grounds belonging to the cattle barons. They represented the spirit of adventure and independence that was seen to epitomize the American spirit during the USA's push to take over the West in the 19th century.

cow parsley (or keck) tall perennial plant belonging to the carrot family, found in Europe, northern Asia, and North Africa. It grows up to 1 m/3 ft tall and has pinnate leaves (leaflets growing either side of a stem), hollow furrowed stems, and heads of delicate white flowers. (*Anthriscus sylvestris*, family Umbelliferae.)

Cowper, William (1731–1800) English poet. His verse anticipates ▷Romanticism and includes the six books of *The Task* (1785). He also wrote hymns (including 'God Moves in a Mysterious Way').

cowrie marine snail of the family Cypreidae, in which the interior spiral form is concealed by a double outer lip. The shells are hard, shiny, and often coloured. Most cowries are shallow-water forms, and are found in many parts of the world, particularly the tropical Indo-Pacific. Cowries have been used as ornaments and fertility charms, and also as currency, for example the Pacific money cowrie *Cypraea moneta*.

cowslip European plant related to the primrose, with several small deep-yellow fragrant flowers growing from a single stem. It is native to temperate regions of the Old World. The oxlip (*Primula elatior*) is also closely related. (*Primula veris*, family Primulaceae.)

coyote wild dog *Canis latrans*, in appearance like a small wolf, living in North and Central America. Its head and body are about 90 cm/3 ft long and brown, flecked with grey or black. Coyotes live in open country and can run at 65 kph/40 mph. Their main foods are rabbits and rodents. Although persecuted by humans for over a century, the species is very successful.

coypu South American water rodent *Myocastor coypus*, about 60 cm/2 ft long and weighing up to 9 kg/20 lb. It has a scaly, ratlike tail, webbed hind feet, a blunt-muzzled head, and large orange incisors. The fur ('nutria') is reddish brown. It feeds on vegetation, and lives in burrows in rivers and lake banks.

WILLIAM COWPER English poet William Cowper. As well as his literacy achievements as a poet, hymn-writer, and translator, Cowper was one of the greatest English letter-writers, writing both of everyday village life and of political and literary events. *Archive Photos*

> **Noël Coward**
> *I believe that since my life began / The most I've had is just / A talent to amuse.*
>
> 'If Love Were All'

Taken to Europe and then to North America to be farmed for their fur, many escaped or were released. In Britain, coypus escaped from fur farms and became established on the Norfolk Broads where their adult numbers reached 5,000. They destroyed crops and local vegetation, and undermined banks and dykes. After a ten-year campaign they were eradicated in 1989 at a cost of over £2 million. In 1993 escaped coypu in Louisiana, USA, were causing serious damage to coastal marshland.

CPU in computing, abbreviation for ▷central processing unit.

CPVE abbreviation for **Certificate of Pre-Vocational Education**, in the UK, an educational qualification introduced in 1986 for students over 16 in schools and colleges who want a one-year course of preparation for work or further vocational study.

CRAB APPLE The wild crab apple *Malus sylvestris*, with its small, tart fruits, is the species from which numerous modern large-fruited dessert, cooking, and cider apples have been derived by careful selection. *Premaphotos Wildlife*

horseshoe crab, which is neither a true crab nor a crustacean.

Types of crab There are many species of true crabs worldwide. The European shore crab *Carcinus maenas*, common on British shores between the tidemarks, is dull green, and grows to 4 cm/1.5 in or more. The edible crab *Cancer paqurus* grows to 14 cm/5.5 in long or more, lives down to 100 m/325 ft, and is extensively fished. Other true crabs include fiddler crabs (*Uca*), the males of which have one enlarged claw to wave at and attract females; the European river crab *Thelphusa fluviatilis*; and spider crabs with small bodies and very long legs, including the Japanese spider crab *Macrocheira kaempferi* with a leg span of 3.4 m/11 ft.

Hermit crabs (division Anomura) have a soft, spirally twisted abdomen and make their homes in empty shells of whelks and winkles for protection. The common hermit crab *Eupagurus bernhardus*, up to 10 cm/4 in long, is found off Atlantic and Mediterranean shores. Some tropical hermit crabs are found a considerable distance from the sea. The robber crab *Birgus latro* grows large enough to climb palm trees and feed on coconuts.

crab apple any of 25 species of wild apple trees, native to temperate regions of the northern hemisphere. Numerous varieties of cultivated apples have been derived from *Malus pumila*, the common native crab apple of southeastern Europe and central Asia.

The fruit of native species is smaller and more bitter than that of cultivated varieties and is used in crab-apple jelly. (Genus *Malus*, family Rosaceae.)

> **William Cowper**
> *God made the country, and man made the town.*
>
> The Task bk 1

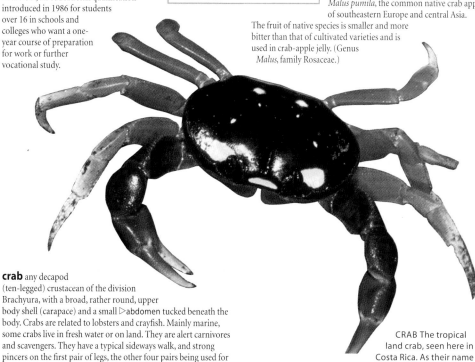

crab any decapod (ten-legged) crustacean of the division Brachyura, with a broad, rather round, upper body shell (carapace) and a small ▷abdomen tucked beneath the body. Crabs are related to lobsters and crayfish. Mainly marine, some crabs live in fresh water or on land. They are alert carnivores and scavengers. They have a typical sideways walk, and strong pincers on the first pair of legs, the other four pairs being used for walking. Periodically, the outer shell is cast to allow for growth. The name 'crab' is sometimes used for similar arthropods, such as the

CRAB The tropical land crab, seen here in Costa Rica. As their name suggests, these crabs live on land. They visit the sea occasionally, principally in order to breed. *Image Bank*

Crabbe, George (1754–1832) English poet. He wrote grimly realistic verse about the poor: *The Village* (1783), *The Parish Register* (1807), *The Borough* (1810) (which includes the story used in Benjamin Britten's opera *Peter Grimes*), and *Tales of the Hall* (1819).

Crab nebula cloud of gas 6,000 light years from Earth, in the constellation ▷Taurus. It is the remains of a star that according to Chinese records, exploded as a ▷supernova observed as a brilliant point of light on 4 July 1054. At its centre is a ▷pulsar that flashes 30 times a second. It was named by Lord Rosse after its crablike shape.

crack street name for a chemical derivative (bicarbonate) of ▷cocaine in hard, crystalline lumps; it is heated and inhaled (smoked) as a stimulant. Crack was first used in San Francisco in the early 1980s, and is highly addictive.

Cracow alternative form of ▷Kraków, a Polish city.

crag in previously glaciated areas, a large lump of rock that a glacier has been unable to wear away. As the glacier passed up and over the crag, weaker rock on the far side was largely protected from erosion and formed a tapering ridge, or **tail**, of debris.

Craig, (Edward Henry) Gordon (1872–1966) English director and stage designer. His innovations and theories on stage design and lighting effects, expounded in *On the Art of the Theatre* (1911), had a profound influence on stage production in Europe and the USA. He was the son of actor Ellen Terry.

Craig, James (1871–1940) 1st Viscount Craigavon. Ulster Unionist politician; first prime minister of Northern Ireland 1921–40. Elected to Westminster as MP for East Down 1906–18 (Mid-Down 1918–21), he was a highly effective organizer of the Ulster Volunteers and unionist resistance to home rule before World War I. In 1921 he succeeded Edward Carson as leader of the Ulster Unionist Party, and was appointed prime minister later that year. As leader of the Northern Ireland government he carried out systematic discrimination against the Catholic minority, abolishing proportional representation in 1929 and redrawing constituency boundaries to ensure Protestant majorities.

Although a stockbroker by trade, Craig took part in the Boer War as captain of the Royal Irish Rifles in South Africa 1900–01. He saw active service in World War I, before serving for a period as a parliamentary secretary 1917–21 in Lloyd George's coalition government. He was knighted in 1918 and made Viscount Craigavon in 1927.

crake any of several small birds of the family Rallidae, order Gruiformes, related to the ▷corncrake.

Cranach, Lucas the Elder (1472–1553) Adopted name of Lucas Müller. German painter, etcher, and woodcut artist. A leading figure in the German Renaissance, he painted religious scenes, allegories (many featuring full-length nudes), and precise and polished portraits, such as *Martin Luther* (1521; Uffizi, Florence).

cranberry any of several trailing evergreen plants belonging to the heath family, related to bilberries and blueberries. They grow in marshy places and bear small, acid, crimson berries, high in vitamin C content, used for making sauce and jelly. (Genus *Vaccinium*, family Ericaceae.)

crane in engineering, a machine for raising, lowering, or placing in position heavy loads. The three main types are the jib crane, the overhead travelling crane, and the tower crane. Most cranes have the machinery mounted on a revolving turntable. This may be mounted on trucks or be self-propelled, often being fitted with caterpillar tracks.

crane in zoology, a large, wading bird of the family Gruidae, order Gruiformes, with long legs and neck, short powerful wings, a naked or tufted head, and unwebbed feet. The hind toe is greatly elevated, and has a sharp claw. Cranes are marsh- and plains-dwelling birds, feeding on plants as well as insects and small animals. They fly well and are usually migratory. Their courtship includes frenzied,

CRANE Japanese cranes on a frozen lake in Hokkaido, Japan. *Image Bank*

leaping dances. They are found in all parts of the world except South America.

The **common crane** *Grus grus* is still numerous in many parts of Europe, and winters in Africa and India. It stands over 1 m/3ft high. The plumage of the adult bird is grey, varied with black and white, with a red patch of bare skin on the head and neck. All cranes have suffered through hunting and loss of wetlands; the population of the North American **whooping crane** *G. americana* fell to 21 wild birds in 1944. Through careful conservation, numbers have now risen to about 200.

crane fly (or **daddy-long-legs**) any fly of the family Tipulidae, with long, slender, fragile legs. They look like giant mosquitoes, but the adults are quite harmless. The larvae live in soil or water. Females have a pointed abdomen; males have a club-shaped one.

cranesbill any of a group of plants containing about 400 species. The plants are named after the long beaklike protrusion attached to the seed vessels. When ripe, this splits into coiling spirals which jerk the seeds out, helping to scatter them. (Genus *Geranium*, family Geraniaceae.)

Related Web site: Cranesbill Root, American http://www.botanical.com/botanical/mgmh/c/crane115.html

Crane, Stephen (1871–1900) US writer and poet who introduced grim realism into the US novel. His book *The Red Badge of Courage* (1895) deals vividly with the US Civil War in a prose of Impressionist, visionary naturalism.

cranium the dome-shaped area of the vertebrate skull that protects the brain. It consists of eight bony plates fused together by sutures (immovable joints). Fossil remains of the human cranium have aided the development of theories concerning human evolution.

crankshaft essential component of piston engines that converts the up-and-down (reciprocating) motion of the pistons into useful rotary motion. The car crankshaft carries a number of cranks. The pistons are connected to the cranks by connecting rods and ▷bearings; when the pistons move up and down, the connecting rods force the offset crank pins to describe a circle, thereby rotating the crankshaft.

Cranmer, Thomas (1489–1556) English cleric, archbishop of Canterbury from 1533. A Protestant convert, he helped to shape the doctrines of the Church of England under ▷Edward VI. He was responsible for the issue of the Prayer Books of 1549 and 1552, and supported the succession of Lady Jane Grey in 1553.

Condemned for heresy under the Catholic Mary I, he at first recanted, but when his life was not spared, resumed his position and was burned at the stake, first holding to the fire the hand which had signed his recantation.

Cranmer suggested in 1529 that the question of Henry VIII's marriage to Catherine of Aragon should be referred to the universities of Europe rather than to the pope, and in 1533 he declared it null and void.

> **Thomas Cranmer**
> *This was the hand that wrote it, therefore it shall suffer punishment.*
> At the stake, 21 March 1556

Crassus the Elder, Marcus Licinius (115–53 BC) Roman general who crushed the Spartacus Revolt in 71 BC and became consul in 70 BC. In 60 BC he joined with Julius Caesar and Pompey the Great in the First Triumvirate and obtained a command in the east in 55 BC. Eager to gain his own reputation for military glory, he invaded Parthia (Mesopotamia and Persia), but was defeated by the Parthians at Carrhae, captured, and put to death.

Crassus the Younger, Marcus Licinius (lived c. 75 BC) Roman general, grandson of the triumvir Marcus Licinius Crassus the Elder. He fought first with Sextus Pompeius and Mark Antony before defecting to Octavian (later the emperor Augustus). In 29 BC he defeated the Bastarnae of modern Romania and Bulgaria, killing their king, Deldo, in single combat.

crater bowl-shaped depression in the ground, usually round and with steep sides. Craters are formed by explosive events such as the eruption of a volcano or the impact of a meteorite.

craton (or **continental shield**) The relatively stable core of a continent that is not currently affected by tectonics along plate

CRANESBILL The meadow cranesbill *Geranium pratense* is widespread in Europe, Asia, and North America. *Premaphotos Wildlife*

boundaries. Cratons generally consist of highly deformed ▷metamorphic rock that formed during ancient orogenic explosions.

Cratons exist in the hearts of all the continents, a typical example being the Canadian Shield.

crayfish freshwater decapod (ten-limbed) crustacean belonging to several families structurally similar to, but smaller than, the lobster. Crayfish are brownish-green scavengers and are found in all parts of the world except Africa. They are edible, and some species are farmed. There are 300–400 species worldwide.

Crazy Horse (1849–1877) Sioux Ta-Sunko-Witko. American Indian Sioux chief, one of the leaders at the massacre of Little Bighorn. He was killed when captured.

creationism theory concerned with the origins of matter and life, claiming, as does the Bible in Genesis, that the world and humanity were created by a supernatural Creator, not more than 6,000 years ago. It was developed in response to Darwin's theory of ▷evolution; it is not recognized by most scientists as having a factual basis.

Crécy, Battle of first major battle of the ▷Hundred Years' War, fought on 26 August 1346. Philip VI of France was defeated by ▷Edward III of England at the village of Crécy-en-Ponthieu, now in Somme *département*, France, 18 km/11 mi northeast of Abbeville. The English archers played a crucial role in Edward's victory, which allowed him to besiege and take Calais.

credit in economics, a means by which goods or services are obtained without immediate payment, usually by agreeing to pay interest. The three main forms are **consumer credit** (usually extended to individuals by retailers), **bank credit** (such as overdrafts or personal loans), and **trade credit** (common in the commercial world both within countries and internationally).

credit in education, a system of evaluating courses so that a partial qualification or unit from one institution is accepted by another on transfer to complete a course. At US universities and colleges, the term also refers to the number of units given upon successful completion of a course.

credit card card issued by a credit company, retail outlet, or bank, which enables the holder to obtain goods or services on credit (usually to a specified limit), payable on specified terms. The first credit card was introduced in 1947 in the USA.

Cree member of an ▷American Indian people numbering about 8,300 (1990) in the USA and 60,000 in Canada (1991). The Cree are distributed over a vast area in Canada from northern Alberta and the NorthWest Territories to Québec. In the USA the majority of Cree live in the Rocky Boys reservation in Montana. Their language belongs to the Algonquian family.

creed in general, any system of belief; in the Christian church the verbal confessions of faith expressing the accepted doctrines of the church. The different forms are the Apostles' Creed, the ▷Nicene Creed, and the ▷Athanasian Creed. The only creed recognized by the Orthodox Church is the Nicene Creed.

creep in civil and mechanical engineering, the property of a solid, typically a metal, under continuous stress that causes it to deform below its ▷yield point (the point at which any elastic solid normally stretches without any increase in load or stress). Lead, tin, and zinc, for example, exhibit creep at ordinary temperatures, as seen in the movement of the lead sheeting on the roofs of old buildings.

creeper any small, short-legged passerine bird of the family Certhidae. They spiral with a mouselike movement up tree trunks, searching for insects and larvae with their thin, down-curved beaks.

The brown creeper *Certhia familiaris* is 12 cm/5 in long, brown above, white below, and is found across North America and Eurasia.

cremation disposal of the dead by burning. The custom was universal among ancient Indo-European peoples, for example, the Greeks, Romans, and Teutons. It was discontinued among Christians until the late 19th century because of their belief in the bodily resurrection of the dead. Overcrowded urban cemeteries gave rise to its revival in the West. It has remained the usual method of disposal in the East.

Creole (Spanish *criar* 'to create') in the West Indies and Spanish America, originally someone of European descent born in the New World; later someone of mixed European and African descent. In Louisiana and other states on the Gulf of Mexico, it applies either to someone of French or Spanish descent or (popularly) to someone of mixed French or Spanish and African descent.

creole language any ▷pidgin language that has ceased to be simply a trade jargon in ports and markets and has become the mother tongue of a particular community, such as the French dialects of the New Orleans area. Many creoles have developed into distinct languages with literatures of their own; for example, Jamaican Creole, Haitian Creole, Krio in Sierra Leone, and Tok Pisin, now the official language of Papua New Guinea.

Related Web site: Journal of Pidgin and Creole Languages http://www.siu.edu/departments/cola/ling/

Crescent City popular nickname for ▷New Orleans, Louisiana, from the location of the Vieux Carré, its oldest section, on a sharp bend of the Mississippi River.

cress any of several plants of the cress family, characterized by a pungent taste. The common European garden cress (*Lepidium sativum*) is cultivated worldwide. (Genera include *Lepidium*, *Cardamine*, and *Arabis*; family Cruciferae.)

Cretaceous period of geological time approximately 143–65 million years ago. It is the last period of the Mesozoic era, during which angiosperm (seed-bearing) plants evolved, and dinosaurs reached a peak. The end of the Cretaceous period is marked by a mass extinction of many lifeforms, most notably the dinosaurs. The north European chalk, which forms the white cliffs of Dover, was deposited during the latter half of the Cretaceous, hence the name Cretaceous, which comes from the Latin *creta*, 'chalk'.

Crete (Greek **Kríti**) largest Greek island in the eastern Mediterranean Sea, 100 km/62 mi southeast of mainland Greece; area 8,378 sq km/3,234 sq mi; population (1991) 536,900. The capital is ▷Iraklion (Heraklion); other major towns are Khaniá (Canea), Rethymnon, and Aghios Nikolaos. The island produces citrus fruit, olives, and wine; tourism is vital to the economy. A Cretan dialect of Greek is spoken.

Crete was home to the ancient ▷Minoan civilization (3000–1400 BC) (see also ▷Knossos), and was successively under Roman, Byzantine, Venetian, and Turkish rule. The island was annexed by Greece in 1913. In 1941 it was captured by German forces from Allied troops who had retreated from the mainland and was retaken by the Allies in 1944.

Crewe town in Cheshire, England; population (1991) 63,400. It grew as a major railway junction, containing the chief construction workshops of British Rail. Crewe is also the centre of the dairy industry, providing cattle breeding, management, and animal health services. Other industries include food-processing and the manufacture of chemicals, clothing, and vehicles.

Crick, Francis Harry Compton (1916–) English molecular biologist who was awarded a Nobel Prize for Physiology or Medicine in 1962, together with Maurice ▷Wilkins and James ▷Watson, for the discovery of the double-helical structure of ▷DNA and of the significance of this structure in the replication and transfer of genetic information.

Using Wilkins's and others' discoveries, Crick and Watson postulated that DNA consists of a double helix consisting of two parallel chains of alternate sugar and phosphate groups linked by pairs of organic bases. They built molecular models which also explained how genetic information could be coded – in the sequence of organic bases. Crick and Watson published their work on the proposed structure of DNA in 1953. Their model is now generally accepted as correct.

See also the Focus Feature on pp. 458–9, on the Human Genome Project.

> **Francis Crick**
> *If you want to understand function, study structure.*
> *What Mad Pursuit* (1988)

cricket in zoology, an insect belonging to any of various families, especially the Gryllidae, of the order Orthoptera. Crickets are related to grasshoppers. They have somewhat flattened bodies and long antennae. The males make a chirping noise by rubbing together special areas on the forewings. The females have a long needlelike egglaying organ (ovipositor). There are around 900 species known worldwide.

cricket bat-and-ball game between two teams of 11 players each. It is played with a small solid ball and long flat-sided wooden bats, on a round or oval field, at the centre of which is a finely mown pitch, 20 m/22 yd long. At each end of the pitch is a wicket made up of three upright wooden sticks (stumps), surmounted by two smaller sticks (bails). The object of the game is to score more runs than the opposing team. A run is normally scored by the batsman striking the ball and exchanging ends with his or her partner until the ball is returned by a fielder, or by hitting the ball to the boundary line for an automatic four or six runs. Cricket became popular in southern England in the late 18th century. Rules were drawn up in 1774 and modified following the formation of the Marylebone Cricket Club (MCC) in 1787. The game's amateur status was abolished in 1963.

Related Web site: CricInfo: The Home of Cricket on the Internet http://www.cricket.org/

> **Lord Mancroft**
> English businessman and writer
> *Cricket – a game which the English, not being a spiritual people, have invented in order to give themselves some conception of eternity.*
> *Bees in Some Bonnets*

crime behaviour or action that is punishable by criminal law. A crime is a public, as opposed to a moral, wrong; it is an offence committed against (and hence punishable by) the state or the community at large. Many crimes are immoral, but not all actions considered immoral are illegal.

What constitutes a crime The laws of each country specify which actions or omissions are criminal. These include serious moral wrongs and offences against the person, such as murder and rape; offences against the state, such as treason or tax evasion (which affect state security and social order); wrongs perpetrated against the community, such as littering; and offences against property, such as theft and the handling of stolen goods. Because crime is socially determined, the definition of what constitutes a crime may vary geographically and over time. Thus, an action may be considered a crime in one society but not in another; for example, drinking alcohol is not generally prohibited in the West, but is a criminal offence in many Islamic countries. Certain categories of crime, however, such as violent crime and theft, are recognized almost universally.

Penalties Crime is dealt with in most societies by the judicial system, comprising the police, the courts, and so on. These may impose penalties ranging from a fine to imprisonment to, in some instances, death, depending upon the severity of the offence and the penalty laid down by the country where the offence was committed. Most European countries have now abolished the death penalty, though it is still retained by a number of African and Asian

CRICKET Most crickets are drably coloured in brown, grey, or black – this Kenyan species *Rhicnogryllus lepidus* is an exception. Its bright livery is probably an example of aposematic (warning) coloration. *Premaphotos Wildlife*

countries as well as some US states. Non-capital and minor offences are also punished in some countries, such as Britain and the USA, by the granting of suspended sentences, where an offender's prison sentence is waived on condition that they do not reoffend during a set period of time. Other common elements in sentencing in Britain and the USA include the provision of probation periods, where offenders are released into the community, but are regularly supervised by probation officers; and community service, where offenders are required, in lieu of a prison sentence, to perform a certain amount of unpaid work for the good of the community.

Theories of punishment There are a number of different theories of punishment, ranging from those which place most emphasis upon the aspect of retribution, where the criminal's punishment is seen as an end in itself (though the punishment's severity may still be linked to that of the crime), to theories which stress the deterrent and reformative aspects of punishment. However, the theory that punishment is intended merely as expiation is not subscribed to by most modern penologists, and in practice the different theories are frequently combined. The most positive theory of penology is aimed at the reform or rehabilitation of the criminal, and stresses the importance of training and educating criminals in preparation for their return to the community as law-abiding citizens.

The most optimistic criminologists are forced to admit, however, that modern methods have so far failed to influence persistent offenders.

English law In English law a crime is defined as an act prohibited by law which is punishable by some sanction applied by the courts of criminal jurisdiction, known as the Crown Court and magistrates' courts. Some criminal acts may also be the subject of civil proceedings; for instance, a motorist found guilty of dangerous driving may subsequently be sued for damages for negligence in a civil court. No act, however antisocial, may be punished as a crime unless it is prohibited by law ('nulla poena sine lege'). Despite the widely differing punishments which they attract, murder, theft, dangerous or careless driving, adulteration of milk, and riding a bicycle without lights are all considered crimes in English law.

Juvenile crime Since the beginning of the 20th century English law has made a number of provisions for the punishment of specifically juvenile crimes (crimes committed by persons between the ages of ten and seventeen). Juvenile courts were first legislated for in England in 1908 and were also used in most US states by the 1920s. In England, juvenile courts cannot deal with cases of murder, but do have the power to commit young adults to special detention centres, formerly known as 'borstals'. The juvenile courts may also enforce care orders, where juvenile offenders are removed from their normal surroundings and relocated in an institution or 'community home' for their own protection; and supervision orders, where the juvenile offender is placed under the supervision of a social worker and may also be required to abide by a curfew or take part in reformative activities.

Crimea (Ukrainian **Krym'**) northern peninsula on the Black Sea, an autonomous republic of ▷Ukraine; formerly an oblast (region) of the Soviet Union (1954–91); area 27,000 sq km/10,425 sq mi; population (1995) 2,632,400. The capital is Simferopol; other main towns are Sevastopol and Yalta. The region produces iron, steel, and oil, and there is fruit- and vine-growing. The land is mainly steppe, but the south coast is a holiday resort.

After successive occupation from the 8th century BC onwards by Scythians, Greeks, Goths, Huns, and Khazars, Crimea became a Tatar khanate in the 13th century. The Genoese trading port of Kaffa (modern Feodosiya) in eastern Crimea was the place from where the ▷Black Death spread from Asia to Western Europe in 1346. Crimea was part of the Ottoman empire between 1475 and 1774. A subsequent brief independence as the Khanate of Crimea was ended by Russian annexation in 1783. It was the scene of conflict between Russia and a coalition of Britain, France, Turkey, and Sardinia in the ▷Crimean War (1853–56). The resort of Yalta was the scene of an important conference of the Allied leaders during World War II.

After the Russian revolution, Crimea became the republic of Taurida from 1917 to 1920 and the Crimean Autonomous Soviet Republic from 1920 until occupied by German forces between 1942 and 1944. It was then reduced to a region, its Tatar people being deported to Uzbekistan for alleged Nazi collaboration. In 1954 Khrushchev made Crimea part of Ukraine. Although the Tatar people were exonerated in 1967 and some were allowed to return, others were forcibly re-exiled in 1979. A drift back to their former homeland began in 1987 and a federal ruling in 1988 confirmed their right to residency. Since 1991 the Crimea has sought to gain independence from the Ukraine; the latter has resisted all secessionist moves. A 1994 referendum in Crimea supported demands for greater autonomy and closer links with Russia.

Related Web site: Crimean Republic http://www.geocities.com/Broadway/Alley/5443/crimopen.htm

Crimean War war (1853–56) between Russia and the allied powers of England, France, Turkey, and Sardinia. The war arose from British and French mistrust of Russia's ambitions in the Balkans. It began with an allied Anglo-French expedition to the Crimea to attack the Russian Black Sea city of Sevastopol. The battles of the River Alma, Balaclava (including the charge of the Light Brigade), and Inkerman in 1854 led to a siege which, owing to military mismanagement, lasted for a year until September 1855. The war was ended by the Treaty of Paris in 1856. The scandal surrounding French and British losses through disease led to the organization of proper military nursing services by Florence Nightingale.

crime fiction variant of ▷detective fiction distinguished by emphasis on character and atmosphere rather than solving a mystery. Examples are the works of US writers Dashiell Hammett and Raymond Chandler during the 1930s and, in the second half of the 20th century, Patricia Highsmith and English author Ruth Rendell.

criminal damage destruction of or damage to property belonging to another without lawful reason. Damaging property by fire is charged as arson.

Criminal Investigation Department (CID) detective branch of the London Metropolitan Police, established in 1878, comprising in 1998 a force of 3,834 (3,458 men and 376 women) recruited entirely from the uniformed police and controlled by an assistant commissioner. Such branches are now also found in the regional police forces.

criminal law body of law that defines the public wrongs (crimes) that are punishable by the state and establishes methods of prosecution and punishment. It is distinct from ▷civil law, which deals with legal relationships between individuals (including organizations), such as contract law.

Related Web site: United Nations Crime and Justice Information Network http://www.ifs.univie.ac.at/~uncjin/uncjin.html

crith unit of mass used for weighing gases. One crith is the mass of one litre of hydrogen gas (H_2) at standard temperature and pressure.

critical mass in nuclear physics, the minimum mass of fissile material that can undergo a continuous ▷chain reaction. Below this mass, too many ▷neutrons escape from the surface for a chain reaction to carry on; above the critical mass, the reaction may accelerate into a nuclear explosion.

Croagh Patrick holy mountain rising to 765 m/2,510 ft in County Mayo, Republic of Ireland, a national place of pilgrimage. An annual pilgrimage on the last Sunday of July commemorates St Patrick, who fasted there for the 40 days of Lent in 441 AD.

Croat the majority ethnic group in ▷Croatia. Their language is generally considered to be identical to that of the Serbs, hence ▷Serbo-Croatian.

Croatia (Serbo-Croatian **Hrvatska**) see country box.

crochet craft technique similar to both knitting and lacemaking, in which one hooked needle is used to produce a loosely looped network of wool or cotton.

Crockett, Davy (David) (1786–1836) US folk hero, born in Tennessee. He served under Andrew ▷Jackson in the war with the Creek American Indians (1813–14), then entered politics, serving on the state legislature from 1821 to 1824. He was a Democratic Congressman 1827–31 and 1833–35. A series of books, of which he may have been part-author, made him into a mythical hero of the frontier, but their Whig associations cost him his office. He clashed with Jackson, who he claimed had betrayed his frontier constituency, and left for Texas in bitterness. He died in the battle of the ▷Alamo during the War of Texan Independence.

crocodile large scaly-skinned ▷reptile with a long, low cigar-shaped body and short legs. Crocodiles can grow up to 7 m/23 ft in length, and have long, powerful tails that propel them when swimming. They are found near swamps, lakes, and rivers in Asia, Africa, Australia, and Central America, where they are often seen floating in the water like logs, with only their nostrils, eyes, and ears above the surface. They are fierce hunters and active mainly at night. Young crocodiles eat worms and insects, but as they mature they add frogs and small fish to their diet. Adult crocodiles will attack animals the size of antelopes and even, occasionally, people. They can live up to 100 years and are related to the ▷alligator and the smaller cayman.

Behaviour In some species, the female lays over 100 hard-shelled eggs in holes or nest mounds of vegetation, which she guards until the eggs hatch, before carrying the hatchlings down to the water in her mouth. When in the sun, crocodiles cool themselves by opening their mouths wide, which also enables scavenging birds to pick their teeth. They can stay underwater for long periods, but must surface to breathe. The nostrils can be closed underwater. They ballast themselves with stones to adjust their buoyancy. Crocodiles have remained virtually unchanged for 200 million years.

Types of crocodile There are 15 species of crocodile, all of them endangered, found in tropical parts of Africa, Asia, Australia, and Central America. The largest is the saltwater (indopacific) crocodile *Crocodylus porosus*, which can grow to 7 m/23 ft or more, and is found in eastern India, Australia, and the western Pacific, in both freshwater and saltwater habitats. The Nile crocodile *C. niloticus* is found in Africa and reaches 6 m/20 ft. The American crocodile *C. acutus*, about 4.6 m/15 ft long, is found from southern Florida to Ecuador. The ▷gavial, or gharial, *Gavialis gangeticus* is sometimes placed in a family of its own. It is an Indian species that grows to 6.5 m/21 ft or more, and has a very long narrow snout specialized for capturing and eating fish. The Cuban crocodile *C. rhombifer* has a short snout, grows up to 3.5 m/11.5 ft, and lives in freshwater swamps in Cuba. Morelet's crocodile *C. moreletti* is found in Central America, where it is overhunted, and grows up to 3.5 m/11.5 ft. Johnston's crocodile *C. johnsoni* is an Australian crocodile that feeds mainly on fish and reaches up to 3 m/9.75 ft in length. The Siamese crocodile *C. siamensis* is probably found only in captivity and grows up to 4 m/13 ft in length. The Philippine crocodile *C. mindorensis* is found in the Philippine Islands and grows to just under 3 m/9.75 ft. The mugger *C. palustris* is an Indian crocodile resembling the Nile crocodile but smaller, reaching up to 4 m/13 ft. The Orinoco crocodile *C. intermedius* grows up to 6 m/19.5 ft. False gharial *Tomistoma schlegelli* is found in rivers in India and Indochina and grows up to 4 m/13 ft. African slender-snouted crocodile *C. cataphractus* grows up to 4 m/13 ft and is found in western and central Africa. Dwarf crocodile *Osteolaemus tetraspis* reaches only 2 m/6.6 ft in length and is found in the tropical forests of west and central Africa. New Guinea crocodile *C. novaguineae* reaches 7 m/23 ft in length.

Differences between crocodiles and alligators Crocodiles differ from alligators in that they have a narrower, more pointed snout and their fourth tooth on the lower jaw can always be seen, even when their mouth is shut. On average, they are larger.

Classification Crocodiles are in the phylum Chordata, subphylum Vertebrata, class Reptilia, subclass Archosauria, order Crocodilia. There are 13 species in the Crocodylidae family, including the Nile crocodile (*Crocodylus niloticus*) and the saltwater crocodile (*C. porosus*).

CROCODILE The female crocodile lays her eggs in nests of mud or vegetation and guards them until hatched, she then carries them to the water in her jaws. *Corel*

crocus any of a group of plants belonging to the iris family, with single yellow, purple, or white flowers and narrow, pointed leaves. They are native to northern parts of the Old World, especially southern Europe and Asia Minor. (Genus *Crocus*, family Iridaceae.)

Croesus (died 547 BC) Last king of Lydia (in western Asia Minor) 560–547 BC. Famed for his wealth, he expanded Lydian power to its greatest extent, conquering all Anatolia west of the river Halys and entering alliances with Media, Egypt, and Sparta. He invaded Persia but was defeated by ▷Cyrus (II) the Great. Lydia was subsequently absorbed into the Persian Empire.

croft small farm in the Highlands of Scotland, traditionally farmed cooperatively with other crofters; the 1886 Crofters Act gave security of tenure to crofters. Today, although grazing land is still shared, arable land is typically enclosed. Crofting is the only form of subsistence farming found in the UK.

Crohn's disease (or **regional ileitis**) chronic inflammatory bowel disease. It tends to flare up for a few days at a time, causing diarrhoea, abdominal cramps, loss of appetite, weight loss, and mild fever. The cause of Crohn's disease is unknown, although stress may be a factor.

Cro-Magnon prehistoric human *Homo sapiens sapiens* believed to be ancestral to Europeans, the first skeletons of which were found in 1868 in the Cro-Magnon cave near Les Eyzies, in the Dordogne region of France. They are thought to have superseded the Neanderthals in the Middle East, Africa, Europe, and Asia about 40,000 years ago. Although modern in skeletal form, they were more robust in build than some present-day humans. They hunted bison, reindeer, and horses, and are associated with Upper Palaeolithic cultures, which produced fine flint and bone tools, jewellery, and naturalistic cave paintings.

Crome, John (1768–1821) English landscape painter. He was a founder of the ▷Norwich School with John Sell Cotman in 1803. His works, which show the influence of Dutch landscape painting, include *The Poringland Oak* (1818; National Gallery, London).

JOHN CROME *The Yarmouth Water Frolic*, by John Crome. *The Art Archive/Kenwood House*

Crompton, Samuel (1753–1827) English inventor at the time of the Industrial Revolution. He developed the 'spinning mule' in 1779, combining the ideas of Richard ▷Arkwright and James ▷Hargreaves. This span a fine, continuous yarn and revolutionized the production of high-quality cotton textiles.

Cromwell, Oliver (1599–1658) English general and politician, Puritan leader of the Parliamentary side in the English ▷Civil War. He raised cavalry forces (later called 'Ironsides') which aided the victories at ▷Edgehill in 1642 and ▷Marston Moor in 1644, and organized the New Model Army, which he led (with General Fairfax) to victory at ▷Naseby in 1645. He declared Britain a republic (the ▷Commonwealth) in 1649, following the execution of Charles I. As Lord Protector (ruler) from 1653, Cromwell established religious toleration and raised Britain's prestige in Europe on the basis of an alliance with France against Spain.

Cromwell was born at Huntingdon, northwest of Cambridge, son of a small landowner. He entered Parliament in 1629 and became active in the events leading to the Civil War. Failing to secure a constitutional settlement with Charles I 1646–48, he defeated the 1648 Scottish invasion at Preston. A special commission, of which Cromwell was a member, tried the king and condemned him to death, and a republic, known as 'the Commonwealth', was set up.

The ▷Levellers demanded radical reforms, but he executed their leaders in 1649. Cromwell's Irish campaign (1649–50) used terror to crush Irish resistance to Parliamentary rule, although its ferocity left a lasting legacy of hatred for British rule among the Catholic Irish. He then defeated the Scots, who had acknowledged Charles II, at Dunbar in 1650 and Worcester in 1651. In 1653, having forcibly expelled the corrupt ▷Rump Parliament he

OLIVER CROMWELL A silver crown of 1658, depicting English statesman and general Oliver Cromwell in Roman style, wearing a laurel wreath. *The Art Archive/British Museum*

Croatia

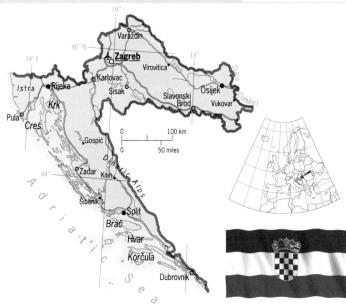

Croatia country in central Europe, bounded north by Slovenia and Hungary, west by the Adriatic Sea, and east by Bosnia-Herzegovina, and Serbia and Montenegro.

NATIONAL NAME *Republika Hrvatska/Republic of Croatia*
AREA 56,538 sq km/21,829 sq mi
CAPITAL Zagreb
MAJOR TOWNS/CITIES Osijek, Split, Dubrovnik, Rijeka, Zadar, Pula
MAJOR PORTS chief port: Rijeka (Fiume); other ports: Zadar, Sibenik, Split, Dubrovnik
PHYSICAL FEATURES Adriatic coastline with large islands; very mountainous, with part of the Karst region and the Julian and Styrian Alps; some marshland

Government

HEAD OF STATE Stjepan Mesic from 2000
HEAD OF GOVERNMENT Ivo Sanader from 2003
POLITICAL SYSTEM emergent democracy
POLITICAL EXECUTIVE limited presidency
ADMINISTRATIVE DIVISIONS 21 counties
ARMED FORCES 51,000; plus paramilitary forces of 10,000 (2002 est)
CONSCRIPTION compulsory for six months
DEATH PENALTY abolished in 1990
DEFENCE SPEND (% GDP) 2.4 (2002 est)
EDUCATION SPEND (% GDP) 4.2 (2000 est)
HEALTH SPEND (% GDP) 8.6 (2000 est)

Economy and resources

CURRENCY kuna
GPD (US$) 22.4 billion (2002 est)
REAL GDP GROWTH (% change on previous year) 3.8 (2001)
GNI (US$) 20.3 billion (2002 est)
GNI PER CAPITA (PPP) (US$) 9,760 (2002 est)
CONSUMER PRICE INFLATION 3% (2003 est)
UNEMPLOYMENT 22.3% (2001)
FOREIGN DEBT (US$) 9.97 billion (2001 est)
MAJOR TRADING PARTNERS Germany, Italy, Slovenia, Austria, Bosnia-Herzegovina, Russia
RESOURCES petroleum, natural gas, coal, lignite, bauxite, iron ore, salt
INDUSTRIES food processing, textiles and footwear, chemicals, ship-building, metal processing, pharmaceuticals, construction materials. Tourism was virtually eliminated during hostilities, but a revival began in 1992

EXPORTS machinery and transport equipment, chemicals, foodstuffs, miscellaneous manufactured items (mainly clothing). Principal market: Italy 23.7% (2001)
IMPORTS machinery and transport equipment, basic manufactures, mineral fuels, miscellaneous manufactured articles. Principal source: Germany 17.1% (2001)
ARABLE LAND 26.1% (2000 est)
AGRICULTURAL PRODUCTS wheat, maize, potatoes, grapes, apples, plums, sugar beet; livestock rearing (cattle and pigs); dairy products

Population and society

POPULATION 4,428,000 (2003 est)
POPULATION GROWTH RATE –0.3% (2000–15)
POPULATION DENSITY (per sq km) 78 (2003 est)
URBAN POPULATION (% of total) 59 (2003 est)
AGE DISTRIBUTION (% of total population) 0–14 18%, 15–59 61%, 60+ 21% (2002 est)
ETHNIC GROUPS in 1991, 77% of the population were ethnic Croats, 12% were ethnic Serbs, and 1% were Slovenes. The civil war that began in 1992 displaced more than 300,000 Croats from Serbian enclaves within the republic, and created some 500,000 refugees from Bosnia in the republic. Serbs are most thickly settled in areas bordering Bosnia-Herzegovina, and in Slavonia, although more than 150,000 fled from Krajina to Bosnia-Herzegovina and Serbia following the region's recapture by the Croatian army in August 1995.
LANGUAGE Croat (official), Serbian
RELIGION Roman Catholic (Croats) 76.5%; Orthodox Christian (Serbs) 11%, Protestant 1.4%, Muslim 1.2%
EDUCATION (compulsory years) 8
LITERACY RATE 99% (men); 98% (women) (2003 est)
LABOUR FORCE 16.6% agriculture, 30.6% industry, 52.8% services (1999)
LIFE EXPECTANCY 70 (men); 78 (women) (2000–05)
CHILD MORTALITY RATE (under 5, per 1,000 live births) 8 (2001)
PHYSICIANS (per 1,000 people) 2.3 (1998 est)

HOSPITAL BEDS (per 1,000 people) 5.9 (1994 est)
TV SETS (per 1,000 people) 293 (2001 est)
RADIOS (per 1,000 people) 340 (2001 est)
INTERNET USERS (per 10,000 people) 1,628.8 (2002 est)
PERSONAL COMPUTER USERS (per 100 people) 15.7 (2002 est)

See also ▷Austro-Hungarian Empire; ▷Tito.

CROATIA The historic town of Zadar was once the capital of Dalmatia (a region of western Croatia). Occupying the end of a low peninsula jutting into the Adriatic Sea, it has in its time been Roman, Byzantine, Venetian, Austrian, Italian, and Yugoslavian. *Image Bank*

Chronology

early centuries AD: Part of Roman region of Pannonia.
AD 395: On division of Roman Empire, stayed in western half, along with Slovenia and Bosnia.
7th century: Settled by Carpathian Croats, from northeast; Christianity adopted.
924: Formed by Tomislav into independent kingdom, which incorporated Bosnia from 10th century.
12th–19th centuries: Autonomy under Hungarian crown, following dynastic union in 1102.
1526–1699: Slavonia, in east, held by Ottoman Turks, while Serbs were invited by Austria to settle along the border with Ottoman-ruled Bosnia, in Vojna Krajina (military frontier).
1797–1815: Dalmatia, in west, ruled by France.
19th century: Part of Austro-Hungarian Habsburg Empire.
1918: On dissolution of Habsburg Empire, joined Serbia, Slovenia, and Montenegro in 'Kingdom of Serbs, Croats, and Slovenes', under Serbian Karageorgevic dynasty.
1929: The Kingdom became Yugoslavia. Croatia continued its campaign for autonomy.
1930s: Ustasa, a Croat terrorist organization, began a campaign against dominance of Yugoslavia by the non-Catholic Serbs.
1941–44: Following German invasion, a 'Greater Croatia' Nazi puppet state, including most of Bosnia and western Serbia, formed under Ustasa leader, Ante Pavelic; more than half a million Serbs, Jews, and members of the Romany community were massacred in extermination camps.
1945: Became constituent republic of Yugoslavia Socialist Federation after communist partisans, led by Croat Marshal Tito, overthrew Pavelic.
1970s: Separatist demands resurfaced, provoking a crackdown.
late 1980s: Spiralling inflation and a deterioration in living standards sparked industrial unrest and a rise in nationalist sentiment, which affected the local communist party.
1989: The formation of opposition parties was permitted.

1990: The communists were defeated by the conservative nationalist CDU led by ex-Partisan Franjo Tudjman in the first free election since 1938. Sovereignty was declared.
1991: The Serb-dominated region of Krajina in the southwest announced its secession from Croatia. Croatia declared independence, leading to military conflict with Serbia, and civil war ensued.
1992: A United Nations (UN) peace accord was accepted; independence was recognized by the European Community (EC) and the USA; Croatia joined the UN. A UN peacekeeping force was stationed in Croatia. Tudjman was elected president.
1993: A government offensive was launched to retake parts of Serb-held Krajina, violating the 1992 UN peace accord.
1994: There was an accord with Muslims and ethnic Croats within Bosnia, to the east, to link the recently formed Muslim–Croat federation with Croatia.
1995: Serb-held western Slavonia and Krajina were captured by government forces; there was an exodus of Croatian Serbs. The offensive extended into Bosnia-Herzegovina to halt a Bosnian Serb assault on Bihac in western Bosnia. Serbia agreed to cede control of eastern Slavonia to Croatia over a two-year period. Zlatko Matesa was appointed prime minister.
1996: Diplomatic relations between Croatia and Yugoslavia were restored. Croatia entered the Council of Europe.
1997: The opposition was successful in local elections. The constitution was amended to prevent the weakening of Croatia's national sovereignty.
1998: Croatia resumed control over East Slavonia.
2000: In parliamentary elections, the ruling Croatian Democratic Union (HDZ) lost heavily to a centre-left coalition. Stipe Mesic, an opponent of Tudjman, was elected to succeed him as president. The Social Democrat leader, Ivica Rajan, became prime minister.
2001: Constitutional changes reduced the powers of the president and turned Croatia into a parliamentary democracy.

summoned a convention ('▷Barebones Parliament'), which was soon dissolved as too radical. Under a constitution (the 'Instrument of Government') drawn up by the army leaders, Cromwell became Protector (king in all but name), beginning the period known as the ▷Protectorate (1653–59). The Parliament of 1654–55 was dissolved as uncooperative, and after a period of military dictatorship, his last Parliament offered him the crown; he refused because he feared the army's republicanism.

Cromwell was seen by Royalists of the time as an ambitious and ruthless tyrant – at best a 'brave, bad man', and at worst 'The English Devil'. However, he was admired by the Whig historians of the 19th century, who saw him as the saviour of Parliament and the father of modern democracy; Cromwell's statue stands outside the House of Commons at Westminster. Although some modern historians have compared Cromwell to Hitler and many – particularly Irish historians – deplore his ruthlessness at the battles of ▷Drogheda and Wexford, others claim that he was merely following the rules of war at the time, and that he was 'a good constable' rather than a dictator.

> **Oliver Cromwell**
> *Take away these baubles.*
>
> Referring to the symbols of Parliamentary power when he dismissed Parliament in 1653

Related Web site: United Nations Crime and Justice Information Network http://www.ifs.univie.ac.at/~uncjin/uncjin.html

Cromwell, Richard (1626–1712) Son of Oliver Cromwell, he succeeded his father as Lord Protector but resigned in May 1659, having been forced to abdicate by the army. He lived in exile after the Restoration until 1680, when he returned.

Cromwell, Thomas (c. 1485–1540) Earl of Essex. English politician who drafted the legislation that made the Church of England independent of Rome. Originally in Lord Chancellor Wolsey's service, he became secretary to ▷Henry VIII in 1534 and the real director of government policy; he was executed for treason. He was created a baron in 1536.

Cromwell had Henry divorced from Catherine of Aragon by a series of acts that proclaimed him head of the church. From 1536 to 1540 Cromwell suppressed the monasteries, ruthlessly crushed all opposition, and favoured Lutheranism. His mistake in arranging Henry's marriage to Anne of Cleves (to cement an alliance with the German Protestant princes against France and the Holy Roman Empire) led to his being accused of treason and beheaded.

> **Henry VIII**
> King of England
>
> *On light pretexts, by false accusations, they made me put to death the most faithful servant I ever had.*
>
> Six months after Cromwell's execution, quoted in Wriothesley *Chronicle* (1875) and Beckingsale *Thomas Cromwell* (1978)

Cronus (or Kronos) in Greek mythology, the youngest of the ▷Titans; ruler of the world under his father ▷Uranus, the sky; and son of ▷Gaia, mother of the Earth. He was eventually overthrown by his son ▷Zeus.

Crookes, William (1832–1919) English scientist whose many chemical and physical discoveries include the metallic element thallium (1861), the radiometer (1875), and the Crookes high-vacuum tube used in X-ray techniques. He was knighted in 1897.

crop in birds, the thin-walled enlargement of the digestive tract between the oesophagus and stomach. It is an effective storage organ especially in seed-eating birds; a pigeon's crop can hold about 500 cereal grains. Digestion begins in the crop, by the moisturizing of food. A crop also occurs in insects and annelid worms.

crop rotation system of regularly changing the crops grown on a piece of land. The crops are grown in a particular order to utilize and add to the nutrients in the soil and to prevent the build-up of insect and fungal pests. Including a legume crop, such as peas or beans, in the rotation helps build up nitrate in the soil, because the roots contain bacteria capable of fixing nitrogen from the air.

A simple seven-year rotation, for example, might include a three-year ley followed by two years of wheat and then two years of barley, before returning the land to temporary grass once more. In this way, the cereal crops can take advantage of the build-up of soil fertility which occurs during the period under grass. In the 18th century a four-field rotation was widely adopted; over four years a field might be planted with autumn-sown cereal, followed by a root crop, then spring cereal, and finally a leguminous crop. Innovative farmers such as Charles 'Turnip' Townshend improved cultivation techniques.

Crosby, Bing (Harry Lillis) (1904–1977) US film actor and singer. He achieved world success with his distinctive style of crooning in such songs as 'Pennies from Heaven' (1936) (featured in a film of the same name) and 'White Christmas' (1942). He won an Academy Award for his acting in *Going My Way* (1944).

Crosby made a series of 'road' film comedies with Bob Hope and Dorothy Lamour (1914–96). His films include *Road to Zanzibar*

(1941), *Holiday Inn* (1942), *Blue Skies* (1946), and *High Society* (1956).

Related Web site: Crosby, Bing http://www.reelclassics.com/Actors/Bing/bing.htm

crossbill species of ▷finch, genus *Loxia*, family Fringillidae, order Passeriformes, in which the hooked tips of the upper and lower beak cross one another, an adaptation for extracting the seeds from conifer cones. The red or common crossbill *Loxia curvirostra* is found in parts of Eurasia and North America, living chiefly in pine forests.

croup inflammation of the larynx in small children, with harsh, difficult breathing and hoarse coughing. Croup is most often associated with viral infection of the respiratory tract.

crow any of 35 species of omnivorous birds in the genus *Corvus*, family Corvidae, order Passeriformes, which also includes choughs, jays, and magpies. Crows are usually about 45 cm/1.5 ft long, black, with a strong bill feathered at the base. The tail is long and graduated, and the wings are long and pointed, except in the jays and magpies, where they are shorter. Crows are considered to be very intelligent. The family is distributed throughout the world, though there are very few species in eastern Australia or South America. The common crows are *C. brachyrhynchos* in North America, and *C. corone* in Europe and Asia.

crowfoot any of several white-flowered aquatic plants belonging to the buttercup family, with a touch of yellow at the base of the petals. The divided leaves are said to resemble the feet of a crow. (Genus *Ranunculus*, family Ranunculaceae.)

Crown colony any British colony that is under the direct legislative control of the Crown and does not possess its own system of representative government. Crown colonies are administered by a crown-appointed governor or by elected or nominated legislative and executive councils with an official majority. Usually the Crown retains rights of veto and of direct legislation by orders in council.

crown court in England and Wales, any of several courts that hear serious criminal cases referred from ▷magistrates' courts after ▷committal proceedings. They replaced quarter sessions and assizes, which were abolished in 1971. Appeals against conviction or sentence at magistrates' courts may be heard in crown courts. Appeal from a crown court is to the Court of Appeal.

Crown jewels (or regalia) symbols of royal authority. The British set (except for the Ampulla and the Anointing Spoon) were broken up at the time of Oliver Cromwell, and the current set dates from the Restoration. In 1671 Colonel ▷Blood attempted to steal them, but was captured, then pardoned and pensioned by Charles II. The Crown Jewels are kept in the Tower of London in the Crown Jewel House.

Crown Prosecution Service body established by the Prosecution of Offences Act 1985, responsible for prosecuting all criminal offences in England and Wales. It is headed by the Director of Public Prosecutions (DPP), and brought England and Wales in line with Scotland (which has a procurator fiscal) in having a prosecution service independent of the police.

crucifixion death by fastening to a cross, a form of capital punishment used by the ancient Romans, Persians, and Carthaginians, and abolished by the Roman emperor Constantine. Specifically, **the Crucifixion** refers to the execution by the Romans of ▷Jesus in this manner.

crude oil the unrefined form of ▷petroleum.

Cruelty, Theatre of theory advanced by Antonin ▷Artaud in his book *Le Théâtre et son double/Theatre and its Double* (1938) and adopted by a number of writers and directors. It aims to substitute gesture and sound for spoken dialogue, and to shock the audience into awareness through the release of feelings usually repressed by conventional behaviour.

Cruikshank, George (1792–1878) English painter and illustrator. He is remembered for his political cartoons and illustrations for Charles Dickens' *Oliver Twist* and Daniel Defoe's *Robinson Crusoe*. From 1835 he published the *Comic Almanack*, a forerunner of *Punch*.

GEORGE CRUIKSHANK *Boney Stark Mad or More Ships Colonies and Commerce*, 1 January 1808, an early cartoon by English illustrator George Cruikshank that shows the influence of English caricaturist James Gillray on his early work. *Art Archive*

Cruise, Tom (1962–) Adopted name of Thomas Cruise Mapother IV. US film actor. One of Hollywood's biggest box-office attractions of the late 1980s and 1990s, he has starred in such films as *Top Gun* (1986), *Rain Man* (1988), *Born on the Fourth of July* (1989), and *Days of Thunder* (1990). Later in his career, he starred with his then wife, Australian actor Nicole Kidman, in director Stanley ▷Kubrick's *Eyes Wide Shut* (1999), and was nominated for an Academy Award for best supporting actor for *Magnolia* (1999). He worked with US director Steven Spielberg on *Minority Report* (2002)

TOM CRUISE Hollywood star Tom Cruise is still a box-office attraction. *Archive Photos*

cruise missile long-range guided missile that has a terrain-seeking radar system and flies at moderate speed and low altitude. It is descended from the German V1 of World War II. Initial trials in the 1950s demonstrated the limitations of cruise missiles, which included high fuel consumption and relatively slow speeds (when compared to intercontinental ballistic missiles – ICBMs) as well as inaccuracy and a small warhead. Improvements to guidance systems by the use of terrain-contour matching (TERCOM) ensured pinpoint accuracy on low-level flights after launch from a mobile ground launcher (ground-launched cruise missile – GLCM), from an aircraft (air-launched cruise missile – ALCM), or from a submarine or ship (sea-launched cruise missile – SLCM).

crusade (French *croisade*) European war against non-Christians and heretics, sanctioned by the pope; in particular, the Crusades, a series of wars undertaken between 1096 and 1291 by European rulers to recover Palestine from the Muslims. Motivated by religious zeal, the desire for land, and the trading ambitions of the major Italian cities, the Crusades were varied in their aims and effects.

The Crusades ostensibly began to ensure the safety of pilgrims visiting the Holy Sepulchre in Jerusalem, and to establish Christian rule in Palestine. They continued for more than 200 years, with hardly a decade passing without one or more expeditions. Later

they were extended to include most of the Middle East, and attacks were directed against Egypt and even against Constantinople (Istanbul). See also The Crusades Focus Feature on pp. 246–247.
Related Web site: Crusade http://www.ukans.edu/kansas/medieval/108/lectures/first_crusade.html

crust the rocky outer layer of Earth, consisting of two distinct parts, the oceanic crust and the continental crust. The **oceanic** crust is on average about 10 km/6 mi thick and consists mostly of basaltic rock overlain by muddy sediments. By contrast, the **continental** crust is largely of granitic composition and is more complex in its structure. Because it is continually recycled back into the mantle by the process of subduction, the oceanic crust is in no place older than about 200 million years. However, parts of the continental crust are over 3.5 billion years old.

crustacean one of the class of arthropods that includes crabs, lobsters, shrimps, woodlice, and barnacles. The external skeleton is made of protein and chitin hardened with lime. Each segment bears a pair of appendages that may be modified as sensory feelers (antennae), as mouthparts, or as swimming, walking, or grasping structures.

cryogenics science of very low temperatures (approaching ▷absolute zero), including the production of very low temperatures and the exploitation of special properties associated with them, such as the disappearance of electrical resistance (▷superconductivity).

cryptogam obsolete name applied to the lower plants. It included the algae, liverworts, mosses, and ferns (plus the fungi and bacteria in very early schemes of classification). In such classifications seed plants were known as phanerogams.

cryptography science of creating and reading codes, for example, those produced by the German Enigma machine used in World War II, those used in the secure transmission of credit card details over the Internet, and those used to ensure the privacy of e-mail messages. Unencoded text (known as **plaintext**) is converted to an unreadable form (known as **cyphertext**) by the process of **encryption**. The recipient must then **decrypt** the message before it can be read. The breaking of such codes is known as **cryptanalysis**. No encryption method is completely unbreakable, but cryptanalysis of a strongly encrypted message can be so time-consuming and complex as to be almost impossible.

cryptosporidium waterborne parasite that causes disease in humans and other animals. It has been found in drinking water in the UK and USA, causing diarrhoea, abdominal cramps, vomiting, and fever, and can be fatal in people with damaged immune systems, such as AIDS sufferers or those with leukaemia. Just 30 cryptosporidia are enough to cause prolonged diarrhoea.

crystal substance with an orderly three-dimensional arrangement of its atoms or molecules, thereby creating an external surface of clearly defined smooth faces having characteristic angles between them. Examples are table salt and quartz.

Each geometrical form, many of which may be combined in one crystal, consists of two or more faces – for example, dome, prism, and pyramid. A mineral can often be identified by the shape of its crystals and the system of crystallization determined. A single crystal can vary in size from a submicroscopic particle to a mass some 30 m/100 ft in length. Crystals fall into seven crystal systems or groups, classified on the basis of the relationship of three or four imaginary axes that intersect at the centre of any perfect, undistorted crystal.

crystallography the scientific study of crystals. In 1912 it was found that the shape and size of the repeating atomic patterns (unit cells) in a crystal could be determined by passing X-rays through a sample. This method, known as ▷X-ray diffraction, opened up an entirely new way of 'seeing' atoms. It has been found that many substances have a unit cell that exhibits all the symmetry of the whole crystal; in table salt (sodium chloride, NaCl), for instance, the unit cell is an exact cube.

Many materials were not even suspected of being crystals until they were examined by X-ray crystallography. It has been shown that purified biomolecules, such as proteins and DNA, can form crystals, and such compounds may now be studied by this method. Other applications include the study of metals and their alloys, and of rocks and soils.
Related Web site: Crystallography and Mineralogy http://www.iumsc.indiana.edu/crystmin.html

CT abbreviation for state of ▷Connecticut, USA.

Ctesiphon (or Ktesiphon) ancient city (now Tak-i-Kesra) in Mesopotamia (now part of Iraq), on the River Tigris, about 32 km/20 mi southeast of Baghdad. Building materials from its ruins were used to build Bahgdad. The facade and arched hall or throne-room of a palace are among the ruins left.

CT scanner medical device used to obtain detailed X-ray pictures of the inside of a patient's body. See ▷CAT scan.

Cuba see country box.

Cuban missile crisis confrontation in international relations in October 1962 when Soviet rockets were installed in Cuba and US president Kennedy compelled Soviet leader Khrushchev, by military threats and negotiation, to remove them. This event prompted an unsuccessful drive by the USSR to match the USA in nuclear weaponry.

cube in geometry, a regular solid figure whose faces are all squares. It has 6 equal-area faces and 12 equal-length edges.

If the length of one edge is *l*, the volume *V* of the cube is given by:

$V = l^3$

and its surface area *A* by:

$A = 6l^2$

cube to multiply a number by itself and then by itself again. For example, 5 cubed = $5^3 = 5 \times 5 \times 5 = 125$. The term also refers to a number formed by cubing; for example, 1, 8, 27, 64 are the first four cubes.

cubism revolutionary style of painting created by Georges Braque and Pablo Picasso in Paris between 1907 and 1914. It was the most radical of the developments that revolutionized art in the years of unprecedented experimentation leading up to World War I, and it changed the course of painting by introducing a new way of seeing and depicting the world. To the cubists, a painting was first and foremost a flat object that existed in its own right, rather than a kind of window through which a representation of the world is seen. Cubism also had a marked, though less fundamental, effect on sculpture, and even influenced architecture and the decorative arts.
Related Web site: Cubism http://www.artlex.com/ArtLex/c/cubism.html

Cuchulain (or Cú Chulainn) (lived 1st century AD) Legendary Celtic hero. A stupendous fighter in Irish hero-tales, he was the chief figure in a cycle associated with his uncle ▷Conchobar mac Nessa, King of Ulster. While still a little boy, he performed his first great feat by slaying a ferocious hound. As a young man, he single-handedly kept a whole army at bay, and won battles in both the real world and the otherworld, but was slain through a combination of magic and treachery. His most famous exploits were recorded in *Taín Bó Cuailnge/The Cattle Raid of Cooley*. Cuchulain became a symbolic figure for the Irish cultural revival in the late 19th century, and a bronze statue of him stands in Dublin General Post Office, commemorating the Easter Rising.

cuckoo species of bird, any of about 200 members of the family Cuculidae, order Cuculiformes, especially the Eurasian cuckoo *Cuculus canorus*, whose name derives from its characteristic call. Somewhat hawklike, it is about 33 cm/1.1 ft long, bluish-grey and barred beneath (females are sometimes reddish), and typically has a long, rounded tail. Cuckoos feed on insects, including hairy caterpillars that are distasteful to most birds. It is a 'brood parasite', laying its eggs singly, at intervals of about 48 hours, in the nests of small insectivorous birds. As soon as the young cuckoo hatches, it ejects all other young birds or eggs from the nest and is tended by its 'foster parents' until fledging. American species of cuckoo hatch and rear their own young.

The North American **roadrunner** *Geococcyx californianus* is a member of the cuckoo family, and the yellow-billed cuckoo, *Coccysus americanus*, incubates its own eggs.

cuckoo flower (or lady's smock) perennial meadow plant of northern temperate regions. From April to June it bears pale lilac flowers, which later turn white. (*Cardamine pratensis*, family Cruciferae.)

cuckoopint (or lords-and-ladies) perennial European plant, a wild arum. It has large arrow-shaped leaves that appear in early spring and flower-bearing stalks enclosed by a bract, or spathe (specialized leaf). The bright red berrylike fruits, which are poisonous, appear in late summer. (*Arum maculatum*, family Araceae.)

cuckoo spit the frothy liquid surrounding and exuded by the larvae of the ▷froghopper.

cuckoo-spit insect another name for ▷froghopper.

cucumber trailing annual plant belonging to the gourd family, producing long, green-skinned fruit with crisp, translucent, edible flesh. Small cucumbers, called gherkins, usually the fruit of *Cucumis anguria*, are often pickled. (*Cucumis sativus*, family Cucurbitaceae.)

Cugnot, Nicolas-Joseph (1725–1804) French engineer who produced the first high-pressure steam engine and, in 1769, the first self-propelled road vehicle. Although it proved the viability of steam-powered traction, the problems of water supply and pressure maintenance severely handicapped the vehicle.

Cukor, George (1899–1983) US film director. He is known for sophisticated dramas and light comedies, such as *The Philadelphia Story* (1940), *Gaslight* (1944), *Born Yesterday* (1950), and *Pat and Mike* (1952).

Culiacán (Spanish **Culiacán Rosales**) capital of Sinaloa state, northwestern Mexico, on the Culiacán River; population (1990) 415,000. It trades in vegetables and textiles. It was founded in 1599.

Culloden, Battle of defeat in 1746 of the ▷Jacobite rebel army of the British prince ▷Charles Edward Stuart (the 'Young Pretender') by the Duke of Cumberland on a stretch of moorland in Inverness-shire, Scotland. This battle effectively ended the military challenge of the Jacobite rebellion.

Although both sides were numerically equal (about 8,000 strong), the English were a drilled and disciplined force, while the Jacobites were a ragbag mixture of French, Irish, and Scots, ill-disciplined and virtually untrained. The English front line opened the battle with a volley of musketry, after which the Jacobites charged and broke through the first English line but were caught by the musket fire of the second line. They retired in confusion, pursued by the English cavalry which broke the Jacobite lines completely and shattered their force. About 1,000 were killed and a further 1,000 captured, together with all their stores and cannon.
Related Web site: Culloden Moor and Story of the Battle http://www.queenofscots.co.uk/culloden/cull.html

cultural anthropology (or social anthropology) subdiscipline of anthropology that analyses human culture and society, the nonbiological and behavioural aspects of humanity. Two principal branches are ethnography (the study at first hand of living cultures) and ethnology (the comparison of cultures using ethnographic evidence).

Cultural Revolution Chinese mass movement from 1966 to 1969 begun by Communist Party leader ▷Mao Zedong, directed against the upper middle class – bureaucrats, artists, and academics – who were killed, imprisoned, humiliated, or 'resettled'. Intended to 'purify' Chinese communism, it was also an attempt by Mao to renew his political and ideological pre-eminence inside China. Half a million people are estimated to have been killed.

The 'revolution' was characterized by the violent activities of the semimilitary Red Guards, most of them students. Many established and learned people were humbled and eventually sent to work on the land, and from 1966 to 1970 universities were closed. Although the revolution was brought to an end in 1969, the resulting bureaucratic and economic chaos had many long-term effects. The ultra-leftist ▷Gang of Four, led by Mao's wife ▷Jiang Qing and defence minister Lin Biao, played prominent roles in the Cultural Revolution. The chief political victims were ▷Liu Shaoqi and ▷Deng Xiaoping, who were depicted as 'bourgeois reactionaries'. After Mao's death, the Cultural Revolution was criticized officially and the verdicts on hundreds of thousands of people who were wrongly arrested and persecuted were reversed. See also ▷China, Cultural Revolution.

culture in biology, the growing of living cells and tissues in laboratory conditions.

culture in sociology and anthropology, the way of life of a particular society or group of people, including patterns of thought, beliefs, behaviour, customs, traditions, rituals, dress, and language, as well as art, music, and literature. Archaeologists use the word to mean the surviving objects or artefacts that provide evidence of a social grouping.
Related Web site: Cultural Exchange http://www.oceanintl.org/newsletter.htm

Cuman member of a powerful alliance of Turkic-speaking peoples of the Middle Ages, which dominated the steppes in the 11th and 12th centuries and built an empire reaching from the River Volga to the Danube.

Cumberland, William Augustus (1721–1765) Duke of Cumberland. British general who ended the ▷Jacobite rising in Scotland with the Battle of ▷Culloden in 1746; his brutal repression of the Highlanders earned him the nickname of 'Butcher'.

Cumbria county of northwest England, created in 1974 from Cumberland, Westmorland, the Furness district of northwest Lancashire, and the Sedbergh district of northwest Yorkshire.
area 6,810 sq km/2,629 sq mi **towns and cities** ▷Carlisle (administrative headquarters), Barrow, Kendal, Penrith, Whitehaven, Workington **physical** Scafell Pike (978 m/3,210 ft), the highest mountain in England, Helvellyn (950 m/3,118 ft); Lake Windermere, the largest lake in England (17 km/10.5 mi long, 1.6 km/1 mi wide), and other lakes (Derwentwater, Grasmere, Haweswater, Ullswater); the rivers Eden and Derwent; the M6 motorway runs north to south through the centre of the county **features** Lake District National Park; Grizedale Forest sculpture project; Furness peninsula; western

THE CRUSADES This early 13th-century crusaders' castle at Sidon, in Lebanon, was built on a small island connected to the mainland by a causeway. It was destroyed in 1291 after the invasion of the Egyptian Mameluke army.
© Image Bank

The Crusades

by Simon Hall

The Crusades were a series of expeditions mounted by European Christians against Muslims in the Middle East. The most significant crusades took place during the 12th and 13th centuries, although they only ended officially in the 18th century. They were part pilgrimage and part military campaign. The term 'crusade' also describes campaigns by European Christians against Muslims in North Africa and Spain, against non-Christians on Europe's northeastern frontiers, and against heretical Christians in Europe itself. They began at the end of the 11th century due to rising self-confidence and prosperity in Europe.

rise of the Seljuk Turks

Christians had lived and worshipped freely in Jerusalem after the Muslim conquest of Palestine in the 7th century, despite regular wars between Muslims and the Christian Byzantine Empire. In 1071, however, the nomadic Seljuk Turks, who had recently become Sunni Muslims, decisively defeated the Byzantines (in the area that is now Turkey) at Manzikert, captured Antioch in 1085, and took Nicaea in 1092. The threat of resurgent Islam in the region led the Byzantine emperor and Christian pilgrims to the Holy Land (modern Israel and Lebanon), and they appealed to Pope Urban II for help in 1095. His solution was a holy war, in which Europeans could travel to Jerusalem as pilgrims and provide military assistance for their fellow Christians

at the same time. The idea received enthusiastic response from both ordinary people and the military nobility, and the same year, several popular crusades, led by charismatic figures like Walter the Penniless and Peter the Hermit, set out for the Middle East. These expeditions were disorderly and undisciplined, and most of the participants died on the way.

First and Second Crusades

A more organized expedition was mounted in 1096–97; a great army under Godfrey de Bouillon, Bohemund of Taranto, and other leaders fought its way through Asia Minor, taking Antioch in 1098 and Jerusalem in 1099. A Christian kingdom of Jerusalem was established, with Godfrey as its first ruler, his brother Baldwin as Count of Edessa (Upper

Mesopotamia), and Bohemund as Prince of Antioch. Godfrey died in 1100 and was succeeded by Baldwin.

For the next half-century, the Christians were hard-pressed by the Turks. Fleets of reinforcements arrived from Genoa, Norway, and Venice. The military-religious orders of the Knights of St John (Hospitallers) and Knights Templar were formed to help defend Jerusalem. Nevertheless, Edessa was lost in 1144 to Imad al-Din Zengi, the Seljuk regent of Mosul (Iraq). In response, the Second Crusade was launched in 1147–48 under Louis VII of France and Conrad III of Germany, but it ended disastrously in a failed attempt to capture Damascus. From the middle of the 12th century the Christian territories were constantly on the defensive, while Zengi and his son Nur al-Din steadily reunited the Muslim territories from Edessa to the Red Sea. In 1169 Nur al-Din, extending beyond the Crusader states, destroyed the Muslim Fatimid power in Egypt, and installed his Kurdish general Saladin as ruler there in 1171.

rise of Saladin and the Third Crusade

Saladin's impact on the region was tremendous. He consolidated his power after the death of Nur al-Din, taking Damascus from his Zengid rivals in 1174 and Aleppo in 1183. He then swept down through the Crusader states with an immense force. He defeated a Christian army under Guy de Lusignan, King of Jerusalem, at the Horns of Hattin (near Lake Tiberias, Israel) and took Jerusalem in 1187. Lusignan moved north to set seige to Acre. Tyre, Tripoli, and Antioch were the only towns that remained in Christian hands.

European Christians reacted to this news with a mixture of anger and fear, and mounted several fresh expeditions. The most important of these was the Third Crusade, which set off in 1189 led by Philip II (Augustus) of France, Frederick I (Barbarossa) of Germany, and Richard I (the Lion-Heart) of England. The Germans went through Asia Minor, and the French and English went by sea to Acre, to assist the seige which had now lasted nearly two years without success. Under Richard's leadership, the Crusaders recovered a narrow strip of the Palestine coast, but were unable to recapture Jerusalem. Richard made a truce with Saladin, and returned to Europe.

Fourth Crusade and beyond

The Fourth Crusade started from Venice in 1202. Instead of reaching Jerusalem, however, the crusaders became involved in Venetian and Byzantine political struggles, helping the deposed Byzantine emperor, Isaac Angelus, to regain his throne. A few months later, in 1204, Angelus's son was assassinated, and the crusaders stormed and sacked Constantinople, setting up the Latin Empire of Constantinople under Baldwin of Flanders.

The failure of the official Crusades expeditions prompted several unofficial ones, including the Children's Crusade of 1212 and the Shepherd's Crusade of 1251. The participants in these came mainly from Normandy, Flanders, and the

Rhineland. They were not trained soldiers and were motivated by religious fervour. Their march through Europe was disorganized. They launched unprovoked attacks on Jews that they encountered and few of them even reached the Mediterranean. Those members of the Children's Crusade who managed to sail for Alexandria, in Egypt, were captured and sold as slaves when they landed.

In 1217–18, King Andrew of Hungary and Duke Leopold IV of Austria led a new crusade to Palestine with only limited success, and an ambitious attack on Egypt, now the centre of Muslim power in the Middle East, led by John of Brienne, King of Jerusalem, in 1218–21, ended in failure. Frederick II of Germany undertook a more successful crusade in 1228. Using diplomacy rather than force, he regained Jerusalem and southern Palestine.

failure and retreat

Jerusalem fell once more to the Turks in 1244, and Louis IX of France (St Louis) launched a disastrous crusade in 1249 against Egypt. He was captured with the greater part of his army, and had to pay 800,000 pieces of gold as a ransom. In 1270 he led a further crusade to Tunis, but died of disease outside the city. Prince Edward of England (later Edward I) led his own followers onwards to Acre a few months later, but achieved little. The remaining crusader states were threatened by the Mongols moving down from the north and the Muslims in surrounding Palestine. After a stunning victory at Ayn Jalut (in modern Syria) in 1260 over the invading Mongols, the Mameluke Sultanate of Egypt reconquered all of Palestine and Syria, taking the last Christian outpost in 1302.

The enthusiasm for crusades died down as European attention turned inwards during the grim 14th century, as the continent was riven by war and the Black Death. Turkish power grew rapidly under the Ottomans, and crusades directed against them were no more than defensive actions against their incursions into the Balkans. Even the final capture of Constantinople by Ottoman Sultan Mehmed II, in 1453, failed to prompt a European crusade for its recovery. The Knights Templar were suppressed in 1307, but the Knights of St John, at Rhodes and later at Malta, continued to fight against the Turkish advance in the Mediterranean.

benefits: trade and knowledge

Despite their military failure, the Crusades brought several benefits to Europe. Relations between European Christian settlers living in the Middle East and their Muslim neighbours were often much more friendly than the supporters of the Crusades might suggest. Trade between Europe and the Middle East increased greatly, particularly in the hands of Venetian and Genoese merchants. Sugar, cotton, and many other things now in everyday use first became known in Europe through the Crusades. There was also a considerable exchange of knowledge; European scholars gained access to learning from classical Greece and Rome that had survived only thanks to Arabic scholars, and these and the works of the Arabic philosophers themselves helped to pave the way for the Renaissance in Europe.

EMBARKING FOR THE CRUSADES European Christians waged a series of wars against the Muslims in Palestine from 1096 to 1291, motivated by the desire to acquire land and goods as well as to deliver the Holy Land. © Philip Sauvain Picture Collection

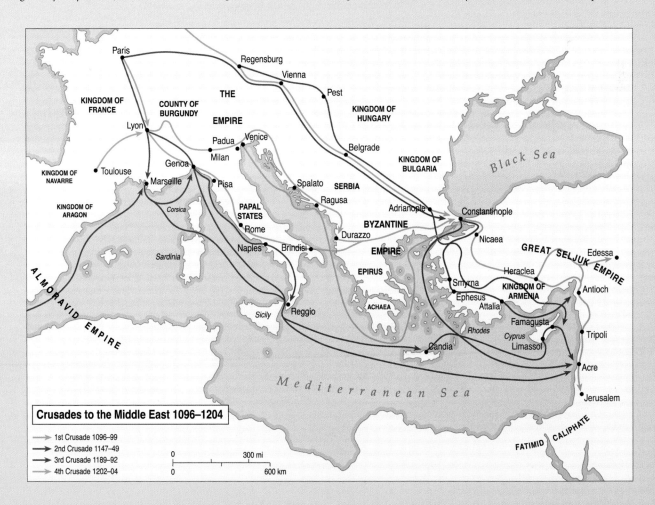

Crusades to the Middle East 1096–1204

- → 1st Crusade 1096–99
- → 2nd Crusade 1147–49
- → 3rd Crusade 1189–92
- → 4th Crusade 1202–04

0   300 mi

0   600 km

Cuba

Cuba island country in the Caribbean Sea, the largest of the West Indies, off the south coast of Florida and to the east of Mexico.

NATIONAL NAME *República de Cuba/Republic of Cuba*
AREA 110,860 sq km/42,803 sq mi
CAPITAL Havana
MAJOR TOWNS/CITIES Santiago de Cuba, Camagüey, Holguín, Guantánamo, Santa Clara, Bayamo, Cienfuegos
PHYSICAL FEATURES comprises Cuba and smaller islands including Isle of Youth; low hills; Sierra Maestra mountains in southeast; Cuba has 3,380 km/2,100 mi of coastline, with deep bays, sandy beaches, coral islands and reefs

Government

HEAD OF STATE AND GOVERNMENT Fidel Castro Ruz from 1959
POLITICAL SYSTEM communist
POLITICAL EXECUTIVE communist
ADMINISTRATIVE DIVISIONS 14 provinces and the special municipality of the Isle of Youth (Isla de la Juventud)
ARMED FORCES 46,000; plus paramilitary forces of 26,500 (2002 est)
CONSCRIPTION compulsory for two years
DEATH PENALTY retained and used for ordinary crimes
DEFENCE SPEND (% GDP) 3.9 (2002 est)
EDUCATION SPEND (% GDP) 8.5 (2001 est)
HEALTH SPEND (% GDP) 6.8 (2000 est)

Economy and resources

CURRENCY Cuban peso
GPD (US$) 26.1 billion (2002 est)

REAL GDP GROWTH (% change on previous year) 3 (2001)
GNI PER CAPITA (PPP) (US$) 2,300 (2002 est)
CONSUMER PRICE INFLATION –0.6% (2003 est)
UNEMPLOYMENT 4.1% (2001)
FOREIGN DEBT (US$) 23.4 billion (2001 est)
MAJOR TRADING PARTNERS Spain, Russia, Canada, China, the Netherlands, France, Venezuela
RESOURCES iron ore, copper, chromite, gold, manganese, nickel, cobalt, silver, salt
INDUSTRIES mining, textiles and footwear, cigarettes, cement, food processing (sugar and its by-products), fertilizers
EXPORTS minerals, sugar, tobacco, citrus fruits, fish products. Principal market: Russia 22.4% (2001)
IMPORTS machinery and transport equipment, mineral fuels, foodstuffs, beverages. Principal source: Spain 21.1% (2001)
ARABLE LAND 33.1% (2000 est)
AGRICULTURAL PRODUCTS sugar cane (world's fourth-largest producer of sugar), potatoes, tobacco, rice, citrus fruits, plantains, bananas; forestry; fishing

Population and society

POPULATION 11,300,000 (2003 est)
POPULATION GROWTH RATE 0.3% (2000–15)
POPULATION DENSITY (per sq km) 102 (2003 est)

URBAN POPULATION (% of total) 76 (2003 est)
AGE DISTRIBUTION (% of total population) 0–14 20%, 15–59 66%, 60+ 14% (2002 est)
ETHNIC GROUPS predominantly of mixed Spanish and African or Spanish and American Indian origin

LANGUAGE Spanish (official)
RELIGION Roman Catholic; also Episcopalians and Methodists
EDUCATION (compulsory years) 6
LITERACY RATE 97% (men); 97% (women) (2003 est)
LABOUR FORCE 15.3% agriculture, 23.0% industry, 61.7% services (1997 est)
LIFE EXPECTANCY 75 (men); 79 (women) (2000–05)
CHILD MORTALITY RATE (under 5, per 1,000 live births) 9 (2001)
PHYSICIANS (per 1,000 people) 5.3 (1998 est)
HOSPITAL BEDS (per 1,000 people) 5.1 (1998 est)
TV SETS (per 1,000 people) 251 (2001 est)
RADIOS (per 1,000 people) 185 (2001 est)
INTERNET USERS (per 10,000 people) 106.8 (2002 est)
PERSONAL COMPUTER USERS (per 100 people) 3.2 (2002 est)

See also ▷Arawak; ▷Castro (Ruz), Fidel; ▷Pigs, Bay of; ▷Spanish-American War.

See also ▷Arawak; ▷Castro (Ruz), Fidel; ▷Pigs, Bay of; ▷Spanish-American War.

Chronology

3rd century AD: The Ciboney, Cuba's earliest known inhabitants, were dislodged by the immigration of Taino, Arawak Indians from Venezuela.

1492: Christopher Columbus landed in Cuba and claimed it for Spain.

1511: Spanish settlement established at Baracoa by Diego Velazquez.

1523: Decline of American Indian population and rise of sugar plantations led to import of slaves from Africa.

mid-19th century: Cuba produced one-third of the world's sugar.

1868–78: Unsuccessful first war for independence from Spain.

1886: Slavery was abolished.

1895–98: Further uprising against Spanish rule, led by José Martí, who died in combat; 200,000 soldiers deployed by Spain.

1898: USA defeated Spain in Spanish-American War; Spain gave up all claims to Cuba, which was ceded to the USA.

1901: Cuba achieved independence; Tomás Estrada Palma became first president of the Republic of Cuba.

1906–09: Brief period of US administration after Estrada resigned in the face of an armed rebellion by political opponents.

1924–33: Gerado Machado established a brutal dictatorship.

1925: Socialist Party founded, from which the Communist Party later developed.

1933: Army sergeant Fulgencio Batista seized power.

1934: USA abandoned its right to intervene in Cuba's internal affairs.

1944: Batista retired and was succeeded by the civilian Ramon Gray San Martin.

1952: Batista seized power again to begin an oppressive and corrupt regime.

1953: Fidel Castro Ruz led an unsuccessful coup against Batista.

1956: Second unsuccessful coup by Castro.

1959: Batista overthrown by Castro and his 9,000-strong guerrilla army. Constitution was replaced by a 'Fundamental Law', making Castro prime minister, his brother Raúl Castro his deputy, and Argentine-born Ernesto 'Che' Guevara third in command.

1960: All US businesses in Cuba appropriated without compensation; USA broke off diplomatic relations.

1961: USA sponsored an unsuccessful invasion by Cuban exiles at the Bay of Pigs. Castro announced that Cuba had become a communist state, with a Marxist-Leninist programme of economic development, and became allied with the USSR.

1962: Cuban missile crisis: Cuba was expelled from the Organization of American States. Castro responded by tightening relations with the USSR, which installed nuclear missiles in Cuba (subsequently removed at US insistence). US trade embargo imposed.

1965: Cuba's sole political party renamed Cuban Communist Party (PCC). With Soviet help, Cuba began to make considerable economic and social progress.

1972: Cuba became a full member of the Moscow-based Council for Mutual Economic Assistance (COMECON).

1976: New socialist constitution approved; Castro elected president.

1976–81: Castro became involved in extensive international commitments, sending troops as Soviet surrogates, particularly to Africa.

1982: Cuba joined other Latin American countries in giving moral support to Argentina in its dispute with Britain over the Falklands.

1984: Castro tried to improve US–Cuban relations by discussing exchange of US prisoners in Cuba for Cuban 'undesirables' in the USA.

1988: A peace accord with South Africa was signed, agreeing to the withdrawal of Cuban troops from Angola, as part of a reduction in Cuba's overseas military activities.

1991: Soviet troops were withdrawn with the collapse of the USSR.

1993: The US trade embargo was tightened; market-oriented reforms were introduced in the face of a deteriorating economy.

1994: There was a refugee exodus; US policy on Cuban asylum seekers was revised.

1998: Castro was confirmed as president for a further five-year term.

1999: In an immigration dispute with the US, which focused on one child, Cuba demanded the return of illegal immigrants, and condemned the use of the US justice system on such matters.

2000: Trade talks were cancelled with European Union (EU) officials after EU countries voted in a UN committee to condemn Cuba's human rights record. The US House of Representatives voted to ease the country's 40-year-old economic embargo of Cuba, allowing exports of food and medicine.

CUBA The town of Morón, east-central Cuba. It is an important transportation and manufacturing centre for the region. *Image Bank*

part of Hadrian's Wall **agriculture** in the north and east there is dairy farming; sheep are also reared; the West Cumberland Farmers is England's largest agricultural cooperative **industries** the traditional coal, iron, and steel industries of the coast towns have been replaced by newer industries including chemicals, plastics, marine engineering, electronics, and shipbuilding (at Barrow-in-Furness, nuclear submarines and warships); tourism; salmon fishing **population** (1996) 490,600 **famous people** Samuel Taylor Coleridge, Stan Laurel, Beatrix Potter, Thomas de Quincey, John Ruskin, Robert Southey, William Wordsworth

Related Web site: Cumbria County Council http://www.cumbria.gov.uk/

cumin seedlike fruit of the herb cumin, which belongs to the carrot family. It has a bitter flavour and is used as a spice in cooking. (*Cuminum cyminum*, family Umbelliferae.)

Related Web site: Cumin http://www.botanical.com/botanical/mgmh/c/cumin127.html

CUMIN The cumin seed comes from a plant of the parsley family.

cummings, e e (1894–1962) Pen-name of Edward Estlin Cummings. US poet and novelist. His work is marked by idiosyncratic punctuation and typography (using only lower case letters, for example), and a subtle, lyric celebration of life. Before his first collection *Tulips and Chimneys* (1923), cummings published an avant-garde novel, *The Enormous Room* (1922), based on his internment in a French concentration camp during World War I.

e e cummings
Listen: there's a hell of a good universe next door: let's go.
Pity this busy monster, manunkind

cuneiform ancient writing system formed of combinations of wedge-shaped strokes, usually impressed on clay. It was probably invented by the Sumerians, and was in use in Mesopotamia as early as the middle of the 4th millennium BC.

Cunningham, Merce (1919–) US choreographer and dancer. He is recognized as the father of postmodernist, or experimental, dance. He liberated dance from its relationship with music, allowing it to obey its own dynamics.

Along with his friend and collaborator, composer John ▷Cage, he introduced chance into the creative process, such as tossing coins to determine options. Influenced by Martha ▷Graham, with whose company he was soloist 1939–45, he formed his own avant-garde dance company and school in New York in 1953. His works include *The Seasons* (1947), *Antic Meet* (1958), *Squaregame* (1976), and *Arcade* (1985).

Cunningham worked closely with composers, such as Cage, and artists, such as Robert Rauschenberg, when staging his works; among them *Septet* (1953), *Suite for Five* (1956), *Crises* (1960), *Winterbranch* (1964), *Scramble* (1967), *Signals* (1970), and *Sounddance* (1974).

Cupid (or Amor; Latin *cupido* 'desire') in Roman mythology, the god of love (Greek Eros); son of the goddess of love, ▷Venus, and either ▷Mars, ▷Jupiter, or ▷Mercury. Joyous and mischievous, he is generally represented as a winged, naked boy with a bow and arrow, sometimes with a blindfold, torch, or quiver. According to the Roman poet Ovid, his golden arrows inspired love, while those of lead put love to flight.

cuprite Cu_2O ore (copper(I) oxide), found in crystalline form or in earthy masses. It is red to black in colour, and is often called ruby copper.

cupronickel copper alloy (75% copper and 25% nickel), used in hardware products and for coinage.

In the UK in 1946, it was substituted for the 'silver' (50% silver, 40% copper, 5% nickel and 5% zinc) previously used in coins. US coins made with cupronickel include the dime, quarter, half-dollar, and dollar.

Curaçao island in the West Indies, one of the ▷Netherlands Antilles; area 444 sq km/171 sq mi; population (1993 est) 146,800. The principal industry, dating from 1918, is the refining of Venezuelan petroleum. Curaçao was colonized by Spain in 1527, annexed by the Dutch West India Company in 1634, and gave its name from 1924 to the group of islands renamed the Netherlands Antilles in 1948. Its capital is the port of Willemstad.

curare black, resinous poison extracted from the bark and juices of various South American trees and plants. Originally used on arrowheads by Amazonian hunters to paralyse prey, it blocks nerve stimulation of the muscles. Alkaloid derivatives (called curarines) are used in medicine as muscle relaxants during surgery.

Curie, Marie (1867–1934) Born Maria Sklodowska. Polish scientist who, with husband Pierre Curie, discovered in 1898 two new radioactive elements in pitchblende ores: polonium and radium. They isolated the pure elements in 1902. Both scientists refused to take out a patent on their discovery and were jointly awarded the Nobel Prize for Physics in 1903, with Henri ▷Becquerel, for their research on radiation phenomena. Marie Curie was also awarded the Nobel Prize for Chemistry in 1911 for the discovery of radium and polonium, and the isolation and study of radium.

From 1896 the Curies worked together on radioactivity, building on the results of Wilhelm ▷Röntgen (who had discovered X-rays) and ▷Becquerel (who had discovered that similar rays are emitted by uranium salts). Marie Curie discovered that thorium emits radiation and found that the mineral pitchblende was even more radioactive than could be accounted for by any uranium and thorium content. In July 1898, the Curies announced the discovery of polonium, followed by the discovery of radium five months later. They eventually prepared 1 g/0.04 oz of pure radium chloride – from 8 tonnes of waste pitchblende from Austria.

They also established that beta rays (now known to consist of electrons) are negatively charged particles. In 1910 with André Debierne (1874–1949), who had discovered actinium in pitchblende in 1899, Marie Curie isolated pure radium metal in 1911.

Related Web site: Essay about Marie and Pierre Curie http://www.nobel.se/physics/articles/curie/

Curitiba capital of Paraná state, on the Curitiba River, southeast Brazil, situated on the Serra do Mar plateau at an altitude of 900 m/2,593 ft; population (1991) 1,248,300 (metropolitan area 2,319,500). It is connected by rail to its seaport Paranaguá, 80 km/50 mi to the east. Curitiba is in the centre of a rich agricultural region which produces timber, coffee, yerba maté, and cereals. Industries include paper, textiles, chemicals, and furniture. Coffee, timber, and maté (a beverage) are exported. It has a cathedral (1893) modelled on the cathedral in Barcelona, Spain, and is the site of the Federal University of Paraná. The city was founded in 1648 as a gold-mining camp and made capital of the state in 1853.

curium synthesized, radioactive, metallic element of the *actinide* series, symbol Cm, atomic number 96, relative atomic mass 247. It is produced by bombarding plutonium or americium with neutrons. Its longest-lived isotope has a half-life of 1.7×10^7 years.

Curium is used to generate heat and power in satellites or in remote places. It was first synthesized in 1944 at the University of California at Berkeley and in 1946 was named after French scientists Pierre and Marie Curie by Glenn Seaborg, its synthesizer.

curlew wading bird of the genus *Numenius* of the sandpiper family, Scolopacidae, order Charadriiformes. The curlew is between 36 cm/14 in and 55 cm/1.8 ft long, and has pale brown plumage with dark bars and mainly white underparts, long legs, and a long, thin, downcurved bill. It feeds on a variety of insects and other invertebrates. Several species live in northern Europe, Asia, and North America. The name derives from its haunting flutelike call.

One species, the Eskimo curlew, is almost extinct, never having recovered from relentless hunting in the late 19th century.

There were only 215 pairs of stone curlews nesting in England in 1998.

currant berry of a small seedless variety of cultivated grape (*Vitis vinifera*). Currants are grown on a large scale in Greece and California and are dried for use in cooking and baking. Because of the similarity of the fruit, the name 'currant' is also given to several species of shrubs (genus *Ribes*, family Grossulariaceae).

Related Web site: Currant, Red http://www.botanical.com/botanical/mgmh/c/currd132.html

current flow of a body of water or air, or of heat, moving in a definite direction. Ocean currents are fast-flowing bodies of seawater moved by the wind or by variations in water density between two areas. They are partly responsible for transferring heat from the Equator to the poles and thereby evening out the global heat imbalance. There are three basic types of ocean current: **drift currents** are broad and slow-moving; **stream currents** are narrow and swift-moving; and **upwelling currents** bring cold, nutrient-rich water from the ocean bottom.

Stream currents include the ▷Gulf Stream and the ▷Japan (or Kuroshio) Current. Upwelling currents, such as the Gulf of Guinea Current and the Peru (Humboldt) current, provide food for plankton, which in turn supports fish and sea birds. At approximate five-to-eight-year intervals, the Peru Current that runs from the Antarctic up the west coast of South America, turns warm, with heavy rain and rough seas, and has disastrous results (as in 1982–83) for Peruvian wildlife and for the anchovy industry. The phenomenon is called **El Niño** (Spanish 'the Child') because it occurs towards Christmas.

current account in economics, that part of the balance of payments concerned with current transactions, as opposed to capital movements. It includes trade (visibles) and service transactions, such as investment, insurance, shipping, and tourism (invisibles). The state of the current account is regarded as a barometer of overall economic health.

current, electric see ▷electric current.

curtain wall in a building, an external, lightweight, non-loadbearing wall (either glazing or cladding) that is hung from a metal frame rather than built up from the ground like a brick wall; the framework it shields is usually of concrete or steel. Curtain walls are typically used in high-rise blocks, one of the earliest examples being the Reliance Building in Chicago (1890–94) by Daniel Burnham and John Wellborn Root. In medieval architecture, the term refers to the outer wall of a castle.

curve in geometry, the ▷locus of a point moving according to specified conditions. The circle is the locus of all points equidistant from a given point (the centre). Other common geometrical curves are the ▷ellipse, ▷parabola, and ▷hyperbola, which are also produced when a cone is cut by a plane at different angles.

Curzon, George Nathaniel (1859–1925) 1st Marquess Curzon of Kedleston. British Conservative politician, viceroy of India 1899–1905. During World War I, he was a member of the cabinet 1916–19. As foreign secretary 1919–24, he negotiated the Treaty of ▷Lausanne with Turkey.

cuscus tree-dwelling marsupial found in Australia, New Guinea, and Sulawesi. There are five species, all about the size of a cat. They have a prehensile tail and an opposable big toe.

Cushing, Harvey Williams (1869–1939) US neurologist who pioneered neurosurgery. He developed a range of techniques for the surgical treatment of brain tumours, and also studied the link between the ▷pituitary gland and conditions such as dwarfism. He first described the chronic wasting disease now known as **Cushing's syndrome**.

custard apple any of several large edible heart-shaped fruits produced by a group of tropical trees and shrubs which are often cultivated. Bullock's heart (*Annona reticulata*) produces a large dark-brown fruit containing a sweet reddish-yellow pulp; it is a native of the West Indies. (Family Annonaceae.)

Custer, George Armstrong (1839–1876) US Civil War general, who became the Union's youngest brigadier general in 1863 as a result of a brilliant war record. He was made a major general in 1865 but, following the end of the American Civil War, his rank was reduced to captain. He later rose to the rank of lieutenant colonel. He took part in an expedition against the Cheyennes in 1868, and several times defeated other American Indian groups in the West during the ▷Plains Wars. Custer campaigned against the Sioux from 1874, and was killed with a detachment of his troops by the forces of Hunkpapa Sioux chief Sitting Bull in the Battle of ▷Little Bighorn, Montana, also known as **Custer's last stand**, on 25 June 1876.

Related Web site: General George A Custer Home Page http://www.garryowen.com/

custody of children the legal control of a minor by an adult. Parents often have joint custody of their children, but this may be altered by a court order, which may be made in various different circumstances. One parent may have 'care and control' over the day-to-day activities of the child while the other or both together have custody. In all cases, the court's role is to give the welfare of the child paramount consideration.

Customs and Excise government department responsible for taxes levied on imports (customs duty). Excise duties are levied on goods produced domestically or on licences to carry on certain trades (such as sale of wines and spirits) or other activities (theatrical entertainments, betting, and so on) within a country.

Related Web site: Her Majesty's Customs and Excise http://www.hmce.gov.uk/

customs union organization of autonomous countries where trade between member states is free of restrictions, but where a ▷tariff or other restriction is placed on products entering the customs union from nonmember states. Examples include the ▷European Union (EU), the Caribbean Community (CARICOM), the Central American Common Market, and the Central African Economic Community.

cuticle the horny noncellular surface layer of many invertebrates such as insects; in botany, the waxy surface layer on those parts of plants that are exposed to the air, continuous except for ▷stomata and lenticels. All types are secreted by the cells of the ▷epidermis. A cuticle reduces water loss and, in arthropods, acts as an ▷exoskeleton.

cuttlefish any of a family, Sepiidae, of squidlike cephalopods with an internal calcareous shell (cuttlebone). The common cuttle *Sepia officinalis* of the Atlantic and Mediterranean is up to 30 cm/1 ft long. It swims actively by means of the fins into which the sides of its oval, flattened body are expanded, and jerks itself backwards by shooting a jet of water from its 'siphon'.

It is capable of rapid changes of colour and pattern. The large head has conspicuous eyes, and the ten arms are provided with suckers. Two arms are very much elongated, and with them the cuttlefish seizes its prey. It has an ink sac from which a dark fluid can be discharged into the water, distracting predators from the cuttle itself. The dark brown pigment sepia is obtained from the ink sacs of cuttlefish.

Cuvier, Georges (Léopold Chrêtien Frédéric Dagobert) (1769–1832) Baron Cuvier. French comparative anatomist, the founder of palaeontology. In 1799 he showed that some species have become extinct by reconstructing extinct giant animals that he believed were destroyed in a series of giant deluges. These ideas are expressed in *Recherches sur les ossiments fossiles de quadrupèdes/Researches on the Fossil Bones of Quadrupeds* (1812) and *Discours sur les révolutions de la surface du globe/Discourse on the Revolutions of the Surface of the Globe* (1825).

Cuyp, Aelbert (1620–1691) Dutch painter. His serene landscapes are bathed in a golden light; for example, *A Herdsman with Cows by a River* (*c.* 1650; National Gallery, London). He also painted seascapes and portraits. Both his father, **Jacob Gerritsz Cuyp** and his uncle **Benjamin Gerritsz** were painters.

Cuzco capital of Cuzco department, south-central Peru, 560 km/350 mi southeast of Lima; situated in a small valley in the Andes at a height of over 3,350 m/11,000 ft above sea level; population (1993) 255,600. The city is a commercial centre, the hub of the South American travel network, and a tourist resort. Manufactures include woollen and leather goods, beer, and fertilizers.

Cuzco was founded *c.* 1200 as the ancient capital of the ▷Inca empire and was captured by the Spanish conquistador Francisco Pizarro in 1533. It is the archaeological capital of the Americas and the oldest continually inhabited city on the continent.

CV abbreviation for curriculum vitae.

cyanide CN^- ion derived from hydrogen cyanide (HCN), and any salt containing this ion (produced when hydrogen cyanide is neutralized by alkalis), such as potassium cyanide (KCN). The principal cyanides are potassium, sodium, calcium, mercury, gold, and copper. Certain cyanides are poisons.

cyanobacteria (singular **cyanobacterium**) alternative name for ▷blue-green algae. These organisms are actually not algae but bacteria. The ancestors of modern cyanobacteria generated the oxygen that caused a transformation some 2 billion years ago of the Earth's atmosphere.

cyanocobalamin chemical name for vitamin B_{12}, which is normally produced by micro-organisms in the gut. The richest sources are liver, fish, and eggs. It is essential to the replacement of cells, the maintenance of the myelin sheath which insulates nerve fibres, and the efficient use of folic acid, another vitamin in the B complex. Deficiency can result in pernicious anaemia (defective production of red blood cells), and possible degeneration of the nervous system.

cybernetics (Greek *kubernan* 'to steer') science concerned with how systems organize, regulate, and reproduce themselves, and also how they evolve and learn. In the laboratory, inanimate objects are created that behave like living systems. Applications range from the creation of electronic artificial limbs to the running of the fully automated factory where decision-making machines operate up to managerial level.

cyberspace imaginary, interactive 'worlds' created by networked computers; often used interchangeably with 'virtual world'. The invention of the word 'cyberspace' is generally credited to US science fiction writer William Gibson in his novel *Neuromancer* (1984).

cycad any of a group of plants belonging to the ▷gymnosperms, whose seeds develop in cones. Some are superficially similar to palms, others to ferns. Their large cones (up to 0.5 m/1.6 ft in length) contain fleshy seeds. There are ten genera and about 80–100 species, native to tropical and subtropical countries. Cycads were widespread during the Mesozoic era (245–65 million years ago). (Order Cycadales.)

Cyclades (Greek **Kikládhes**) group of about 200 Greek islands in the Aegean Sea, lying between mainland Greece and Turkey; area 2,579 sq km/996 sq mi; population (1991) 95,100. They include Andros, Melos, Paros, Naxos, and Siros, on which is the capital Hermoupolis.

cyclamen any of a group of perennial plants belonging to the primrose family, with heart-shaped leaves and petals that are twisted at the base and bent back, away from the centre of the downward-facing flower. The flowers are usually white or pink, and several species are cultivated. (Genus *Cyclamen*, family Primulaceae.)

Related Web site: Ivy-Leaved Cyclamen http://www.botanical.com/botanical/mgmh/c/cycya133.html

CYCLAMEN *Cyclamen persicum*, flowering prolifically in the month of March in Israel. *Premaphotos Wildlife*

cycle in physics, a sequence of changes that moves a system away from, and then back to, its original state. An example is a vibration that moves a particle first in one direction and then in the opposite direction, with the particle returning to its original position at the end of the vibration.

cyclic compound any of a group of organic chemicals that have rings of atoms in their molecules, giving them a closed-chain structure.

cycling riding a ▷bicycle for sport, pleasure, or transport. Cycle racing can take place on oval artificial tracks, on the road, or across country (cyclocross and mountain biking).

cycloid in geometry, a curve resembling a series of arches traced out by a point on the circumference of a circle that rolls along a straight line. Its applications include the study of the motion of wheeled vehicles along roads and tracks.

cyclone alternative name for a ▷depression, an area of low atmospheric pressure with winds blowing in a counter-clockwise direction in the northern hemisphere and a clockwise direction in the southern hemisphere. A severe cyclone that forms in the tropics is called a tropical cyclone or ▷hurricane.

Cyclops (Greek 'circle-eyed') in Greek mythology, one of a race of Sicilian giants with one eye in the middle of their foreheads. According to Homer, they lived as shepherds. ▷Odysseus blinded the Cyclops ▷Polyphemus in Homer's *Odyssey*.

Cygnus large prominent constellation of the northern hemisphere, represented as a swan. Its brightest star is first-magnitude Alpha Cygni or ▷Deneb.

cylinder in geometry, a tubular solid figure with a circular base. In everyday use, the term applies to a **right cylinder**, the curved surface of which is at right angles to the base.

The volume V of a cylinder is given by the formula $V = \pi r^2 h$, where r is the radius of the base and h is the height of the cylinder. Its total surface area A has the formula $A = 2\pi r(h + r)$, where $2\pi rh$ is the curved surface area, and $2\pi r^2$ is the area of both circular ends.

cymbal ancient percussion instrument of indefinite pitch, consisting of a shallow circular brass dish suspended at the centre; either used in pairs clashed together or singly, struck with a beater. Smaller finger cymbals or **crotala**, of ancient origin but used in the 20th century by Debussy and Stockhausen, are precise in pitch. Turkish or 'buzz' cymbals incorporate loose rivets to extend the sound.

Cymbeline (or **Cunobelin**) (lived 1st century AD) King of the Catuvellauni (AD 5–40), who fought unsuccessfully against the Roman invasion of Britain. His capital was at Colchester.

Cymru Welsh name for ▷Wales.

Cynewulf (lived 8th century or 9th century) Anglo-Saxon poet. He is thought to have been a Northumbrian monk and is the undoubted author of 'Juliana' and part of the 'Christ' in the Exeter Book (a collection of poems now in Exeter Cathedral, England), and of the 'Fates of the Apostles' and 'Elene' in the Vercelli Book (a collection of Old English manuscripts housed in Vercelli, northern Italy), in all of which he inserted his name by using runic acrostics.

cynic member of a school of Greek philosophy (cynicism), founded in Athens about 400 BC by Antisthenes, a disciple of Socrates, who advocated a stern and simple morality and a complete disregard of pleasure and comfort.

cypress any of a group of coniferous trees or shrubs containing about 20 species, originating from temperate regions of the northern hemisphere. They have tiny scalelike leaves and cones made up of woody, wedge-shaped scales containing an aromatic ▷resin. (Genera *Cupressus* and *Chamaecyparis*, family Cupressaceae.)

Cyprus see country box. See also map on p. 253.

Cyrano de Bergerac, Savinien (1619–1655) French writer. Joining a corps of guards at the age of 19, he performed heroic feats. He is the hero of a classic play by Edmond ▷Rostand, in which his excessively long nose is used as a counterpoint to his chivalrous character.

Cyrenaic member of a school of Greek ▷hedonistic philosophy founded in about 400 BC by Aristippus of Cyrene. He regarded pleasure as the only absolutely worthwhile thing in life but taught that self-control and intelligence were necessary to choose the best pleasures.

Cyrenaica area of eastern Libya, colonized by the Greeks in the 7th century BC; later held by the Egyptians, Romans, Arabs, Turks, and Italians. Present cities in the region are Benghazi, Derna, and Tobruk. There are archaeological ruins at Cyrene and Apollonia.

Cyril and Methodius, Sts Two brothers, both Christian saints: Cyril (826–869) and Methodius (815–885). Born in Thessalonica, they were sent as missionaries to what is today Moravia. They invented a Slavonic alphabet, and translated the Bible and the liturgy from Greek to Slavonic. The language (known as **Old Church Slavonic**) remained in use in churches and for literature among Bulgars, Serbs, and Russians up to the 17th century. The **cyrillic alphabet** is named after Cyril and may also have been invented by him. Their feast day is 14 February.

Cyrus (II) the Great (died 530 BC) King of Persia 559–530 BC and founder of the Achaemenid Persian Empire. The son of the vassal king of Persia and of a daughter of his Median overlord Astyages, Cyrus rebelled in about 550 BC with the help of mutiny in the Median army and replaced the Median Empire with a Persian one. In 547 BC he defeated ▷Croesus of Lydia at Pteria and Sardis, conquering Asia Minor. In 539 BC he captured Babylon from Nabu-naid (Nabonidus) the Chaldaean, formerly his ally against the

Cyprus

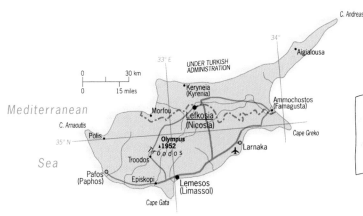

Cyprus island in the Mediterranean Sea, off the south coast of Turkey and west coast of Syria.

NATIONAL NAME *Kipriaki Dimokratia/Greek Republic of Cyprus* (south); *Kibris Cumhuriyeti/Turkish Republic of Northern Cyprus* (north)

AREA 9,251 sq km/3,571 sq mi (3,335 sq km/1,287 sq mi is Turkish-occupied)

CAPITAL Nicosia (divided between Greek and Turkish Cypriots)

MAJOR TOWNS/CITIES Limassol, Larnaca, Paphos, Lefkosia, Gazimagusa

MAJOR PORTS Limassol, Larnaca, and Paphos (Greek); Kyrenia and Famagusta (Turkish)

PHYSICAL FEATURES central plain between two east–west mountain ranges

Government

HEAD OF STATE AND GOVERNMENT Tassos Papadopoulos (Greek) from 2003 and Rauf Denktas (Turkish) from 1976

POLITICAL SYSTEM liberal democracy

POLITICAL EXECUTIVE limited presidency

ADMINISTRATIVE DIVISIONS six districts

ARMED FORCES National Guard of 10,000; Turkish Republic of Northern Cyprus (TRNC) 4,000, plus 60,000 reserves (2002 est)

CONSCRIPTION for 25 months, then reserve to age 50 (officers 65)

DEATH PENALTY abolished in 2002

DEFENCE SPEND (% GDP) 2.4 (2002 est)

EDUCATION SPEND (% GDP) 5.7 (2001 est)

HEALTH SPEND (% GDP) 7.9 (2000 est)

Economy and resources

CURRENCY Cyprus pound and Turkish lira

GPD (US$) 9.1 billion (2002 est)

REAL GDP GROWTH (% change on previous year) 4.1 (2001)

GNI (US$) 9.4 billion (2002 est)

GNI PER CAPITA (PPP) (US$) 18,040 (2002 est)

CONSUMER PRICE INFLATION 4% (2003 est)

UNEMPLOYMENT 3% (2001)

FOREIGN DEBT (US$) 6.3 billion (2001 est)

MAJOR TRADING PARTNERS UK, USA, Russia, Germany, Greece, United Arab Emirates

RESOURCES copper precipitates, beutonite, umber and other ochres

INDUSTRIES food processing, beverages, textiles, clothing and leather, chemicals and chemical petroleum, metal products, wood and wood products, tourism, financial services

EXPORTS pharmaceutical products, clothing, potatoes, manufactured foods, cigarettes, minerals, citrus fruits, industrial products. Principal market: UK 20.5% (2001)

IMPORTS mineral fuels, textiles, vehicles, metals, tobacco, consumer goods, basic manufactures, machinery and transport equipment, food and live animals. Principal source: USA 9.8% (2001)

ARABLE LAND 12% (2000 est)

AGRICULTURAL PRODUCTS government-controlled area: barley, potatoes, grapes, citrus fruit, olives; TRNC area: wheat, barley, potatoes, citrus fruit, olives; livestock rearing (sheep and goats)

Population and society

POPULATION 802,000 (2003 est)

POPULATION GROWTH RATE 0.8% (2000–05)

POPULATION DENSITY (per sq km) 87 (2003 est)

URBAN POPULATION (% of total) 71 (2003 est)

AGE DISTRIBUTION (% of total population) 0–14 22%, 15–59 62%, 60+ 16% (2002 est)

ETHNIC GROUPS about 80% of the population is of Greek origin, while about 18% are of Turkish descent, and live in the northern part of the island within the self-styled Turkish Republic of Northern Cyprus

LANGUAGE Greek, Turkish (both official), English

RELIGION Greek Orthodox 78%, Sunni Muslim 18%, Maronite, Armenian Apostolic

EDUCATION (compulsory years) 9

LITERACY RATE 99% (men); 96% (women) (2003 est)

LABOUR FORCE 9.9% agriculture, 23.5% industry, 66.6% services (1997)

LIFE EXPECTANCY 76 (men); 81 (women) (2000–05)

CHILD MORTALITY RATE (under 5, per 1,000 live births) 6 (2001)

PHYSICIANS (per 1,000 people) 2.6 (2001 est)

HOSPITAL BEDS (per 1,000 people) 4.4 (2001 est)

TV SETS (per 1,000 people) 325 (1997)

RADIOS (per 1,000 people) 406 (1997)

INTERNET USERS (per 10,000 people) 3,000 (2002 est)

PERSONAL COMPUTER USERS (per 100 people) 27.6 (2002 est)

See also ▷Assyria; ▷Greece; ▷Turkey. See map on p. 253.

Chronology

14th–11th centuries BC: Colonized by Myceneans and Achaeans from Greece.

9th century BC: Phoenicans settled in Cyprus.

7th century BC: Several Cypriot kingdoms flourished under Assyrian influence.

414–374 BC: Under Evagoras of Salamis (in eastern Cyprus) the island's ten city kingdoms were united into one state and Greek culture, including the Greek alphabet, was promoted.

333–58 BC: Became part of the Greek Hellenistic and then, from 294 BC, the Egypt-based Ptolemaic empire.

58 BC: Cyprus was annexed by the Roman Empire.

AD 45: Christianity introduced.

AD 395: When the Roman Empire divided, Cyprus was allotted to the Byzantine Empire.

7th–10th centuries: Byzantines and Muslim Arabs fought for control of Cyprus.

1191: Richard the Lionheart of England conquered Cyprus as a base for Crusades; he later sold it to a French noble, Guy de Lusignan, who established a feudal monarchy which ruled for three centuries.

1498: The Venetian Republic took control of Cyprus.

1571: Conquered by Ottoman Turks, who introduced Turkish Muslim settlers, but permitted Christianity to continue in rural areas.

1821–33: Period of unrest, following execution of popular Greek Orthodox Archbishop Kyprianos.

1878: Anglo-Turkish Convention: Turkey ceded Cyprus to British administration in return for defensive alliance.

1914: Formally annexed by Britain after Turkey entered World War I as a Central Power.

1915: Greece rejected an offer of Cyprus in return for entry into World War I on Allied side.

1925: Cyprus became a crown colony.

1931: Greek Cypriots rioted in support of demand for union with Greece (*enosis*); legislative council suspended.

1948: Greek Cypriots rejected new constitution because it did not offer links with Greece.

1955: The National Organization of Cypriot Fighters (EOKA) began a terrorist campaign for *enosis*.

1958: Britain proposed autonomy for Greek and Turkish Cypriot communities under British sovereignty; plan accepted by Turks, rejected by Greeks; violence increased.

1959: Britain, Greece, and Turkey agreed to Cypriot independence, with partition and *enosis* both ruled out.

1960: Cyprus became an independent republic with Archbishop Makarios as president; Britain retained two military bases.

1963: Makarios proposed major constitutional reforms; Turkish Cypriots withdrew from government and formed separate enclaves; communal fighting broke out.

1964: United Nations (UN) peacekeeping force installed.

1968: Intercommunal talks made no progress; Turkish Cypriots demanded federalism; Greek Cypriots insisted on unitary state.

1974: Coup by Greek officers in Cypriot National Guard installed Nikos Sampson as president; Turkey, fearing *enosis*, invaded northern Cyprus; Greek Cypriot military regime collapsed; President Makarios restored.

1975: Northern Cyprus declared itself the Turkish Federated State of Cyprus, with Rauf Denktaş as president.

1977: Makarios died; succeeded by Spyros Kyprianou.

1983: Denktaş proclaimed independent Turkish Republic of Cyprus; recognized only by Turkey.

1985: Summit meeting between Kyprianou and Denktaş failed to reach agreement; further peace talks failed in 1989 and 1992.

1988: Kyprianou was succeeded as Greek Cypriot president by Georgios Vassiliou.

1993: Glafkos Clerides (DISY) replaced Vassiliou.

1994: The European Court of Justice declared trade with northern Cyprus illegal.

1996: Further peace talks were jeopardized by the boundary killing of a Turkish Cypriot soldier; there was mounting tension between north and south.

1997: UN-mediated peace talks between Clerides and Denktaş collapsed.

1998: President Clerides was re-elected. Denktaş refused to meet a British envoy. US mediation failed. Full EU membership negotiations commenced. Greek Cyprus rejected Denktaş's confederation proposals.

2000: Turkish Cypriot President Denktaş was re-elected for a fourth five-year term.

2004: Cyprus was set to join the EU on 1 May.

CYPRUS A satellite photograph of Cyprus. The snows on Mount Olympus, the tallest mountain on the island, can clearly be seen in the dark surroundings of the central mountains. *Image Bank*

Czech Republic

Czech Republic formerly Czechoslovakia (with Slovakia) (1918–93) landlocked country in east-central Europe, bounded north by Poland, northwest and west by Germany, south by Austria, and east by the Slovak Republic.

NATIONAL NAME *Ceská Republika/Czech Republic*
AREA 78,864 sq km/30,449 sq mi
CAPITAL Prague
MAJOR TOWNS/CITIES Brno, Ostrava, Olomouc, Liberec, Plzen, Hradec Králové, Ceské Budejovice
PHYSICAL FEATURES mountainous; rivers: Morava, Labe (Elbe), Vltava (Moldau)

Government

HEAD OF STATE Václav Klaus from 2003
HEAD OF GOVERNMENT Vladimir Spidla from 2001
POLITICAL SYSTEM liberal democracy
POLITICAL EXECUTIVE parliamentary
ADMINISTRATIVE DIVISIONS four municipalities and 72 districts
ARMED FORCES 49,400 (2002 est)
CONSCRIPTION compulsory for 12 months
DEATH PENALTY abolished in 1990
DEFENCE SPEND (% GDP) 2.1 (2002 est)
EDUCATION SPEND (% GDP) 4.4 (2001 est)
HEALTH SPEND (% GDP) 7.2 (2000 est)

Economy and resources

CURRENCY koruna (based on the Czechoslovak koruna)
GPD (US$) 69.6 billion (2002 est)
REAL GDP GROWTH (% change on previous year) 3.3 (2001)
GNI (US$) 56.7 billion (2002 est)

GNI PER CAPITA (PPP) (US$) 14,500 (2002 est)
CONSUMER PRICE INFLATION 1.1% (2003 est)
UNEMPLOYMENT 8.6% (2001)
FOREIGN DEBT (US$) 14.9 billion (2001 est)
MAJOR TRADING PARTNERS Germany, Slovak Republic, Austria, Italy, France, Poland, Russia
RESOURCES coal, lignite
INDUSTRIES steel, cement, motor cars, textiles, bicycles, beer, trucks and tractors; tourism
EXPORTS machinery and transport equipment, basic manufactures, miscellaneous manufactured articles, chemicals, beer. Principal market: Germany 38.1% (2001)
IMPORTS machinery and transport equipment, basic manufactures, chemicals and chemical products, mineral fuels. Principal source: Germany 32.9% (2001)
ARABLE LAND 39.9% (2000 est)
AGRICULTURAL PRODUCTS wheat, barley, sugar beet, potatoes, hops; livestock rearing (cattle, pigs, and poultry); dairy farming

Population and society

POPULATION 10,236,000 (2003 est)
POPULATION GROWTH RATE −0.2% (2000–15)
POPULATION DENSITY (per sq km) 130 (2003 est)

URBAN POPULATION (% of total) 75 (2003 est)
AGE DISTRIBUTION (% of total population) 0–14 16%, 15–69 65%, 60+ 19% (2002 est)
ETHNIC GROUPS predominantly Western Slav Czechs (94%); there is also a sizeable Slovak minority (4%) and small Polish (0.6%), German (0.5%), and Hungarian (0.2%) minorities
LANGUAGE Czech (official), Slovak
RELIGION Roman Catholic 39%, atheist 30%, Protestant 5%, Orthodox 3%

EDUCATION (compulsory years) 9
LITERACY RATE 99% (men); 99% (women) (2003 est)
LABOUR FORCE 5.1% agriculture, 39.5% industry, 55.4% services (2000)
LIFE EXPECTANCY 72 (men); 79 (women) (2000–05)
CHILD MORTALITY RATE (under 5, per 1,000 live births) 5 (2001)
PHYSICIANS (per 1,000 people) 3.4 (1999 est)
HOSPITAL BEDS (per 1,000 people) 4.5 (1999 est)
TV SETS (per 1,000 people) 534 (2001 est)
RADIOS (per 1,000 people) 803 (1997)
INTERNET USERS (per 10,000 people) 2,464.5 (2002 est)
PERSONAL COMPUTER USERS (per 100 people) 17.7 (2002 est)

See also ▷Austro-Hungarian Empire; ▷Bohemia; ▷Czechoslovakia; ▷Prague Spring; ▷Slovak Republic; ▷Thirty Years' War.

Chronology

5th century: Settled by West Slavs.

8th century: Part of Charlemagne's Holy Roman Empire.

9th century: Kingdom of Greater Moravia, centred around the eastern part of what is now the Czech Republic, founded by the Slavic prince Sviatopluk; Christianity adopted.

906: Moravia conquered by the Magyars (Hungarians).

995: Independent state of Bohemia in the northwest, centred around Prague, formed under the Premysl rulers, who had broken away from Moravia; became kingdom in 12th century.

1029: Moravia became a fief of Bohemia.

1355: King Charles IV of Bohemia became Holy Roman Emperor.

early 15th century: Nationalistic Hussite religion, opposed to German and papal influence, founded in Bohemia by John Huss.

1526: Bohemia came under the control of the Austrian Catholic Habsburgs.

1618: Hussite revolt precipitated the Thirty Years' War, which resulted in the Bohemians' defeat, more direct rule by the Habsburgs, and re-Catholicization.

1867: With creation of dual Austro-Hungarian monarchy, Bohemia was reduced to a province of Austria, leading to a growth in national consciousness.

1918: Austro-Hungarian Empire dismembered; Czechs joined Slovaks in forming Czechoslovakia as independent democratic nation, with Tomas Masaryk president.

1938: Under the Munich Agreement, Czechoslovakia was forced to surrender the Sudeten German districts in the north to Germany.

1939: The remainder of Czechoslovakia annexed by Germany, Bohemia-Moravia being administered as a 'protectorate'; President Eduard Benes set up a government-in-exile in London; liquidation campaigns against intelligentsia.

1945: Liberated by Soviet and US troops; communist-dominated government of national unity formed under Benes; 2 million Sudeten Germans expelled.

1948: Benes ousted; communists assumed full control under a Soviet-style single-party constitution.

1950s: Political opponents purged; nationalization of industries.

1968: 'Prague Spring' political liberalization programme, instituted by Communist Party leader Alexander Dubcek, crushed by invasion of Warsaw Pact forces to restore the 'orthodox line'.

1969: New federal constitution, creating a separate Czech Socialist Republic; Gustáv Husák became Communist Party leader.

1977: The formation of the 'Charter '77' human-rights group by intellectuals encouraged a crackdown against dissidents.

1987: Reformist Milos Jakes replaced Husák as communist leader, and introduced a *prestvaba* ('restructuring') reform programme on the Soviet leader Mikhail Gorbachev's *perestroika* model.

1989: Prodemocracy demonstrations in Prague; new political parties formed and legalized, including Czech-based Civic Forum under Havel; Communist Party stripped of powers. New 'grand coalition' government formed; Havel appointed state president. Amnesty granted to 22,000 prisoners.

1991: The Civic Forum split into the centre-right Civic Democratic Party (CDP) and the centre-left Civic Movement (CM), evidence of increasing Czech and Slovak separatism.

1992: Václav Klaus, leader of the Czech-based CDP, became prime minister; Havel resigned as president following nationalist Slovak gains in assembly elections. The creation of separate Czech and Slovak states and a customs union were agreed. A market-centred economic-reform programme was launched, including mass privatization.

1993: The Czech Republic became a sovereign state within the United Nations (UN), with Klaus as prime minister. Havel was elected president.

1994: The Czech Republic joined NATO's 'partnership for peace' programme. Strong economic growth was registered.

1996: The Czech Republic applied for European Union (EU) membership.

1997: The former communist leader Milos Jakes was charged with treason. The ruling coalition survived a currency crisis. The Czech Republic was invited to begin EU membership negotiations. Klaus resigned after allegations of misconduct.

1998: Havel was re-elected president. The centre-left Social Democrats won a general election and a minority government was formed by Milos Zeman, including communist ministers and supported from outside by Václav Klaus. Full EU membership negotiations commenced.

1999: The Czech Republic became a full member of NATO.

2004: The Czech Republic was set to join the EU on 1 May.

CZECH REPUBLIC Prague, capital of the Czech Republic, retains an old-world dignity, the country having survived World War II undamaged by enemy bombing. Staromestske Square is at the centre of the 'Golden City', so-called for the distinctive colour of its many stuccoed walls. *Corel*

CYPRUS See Country Box.

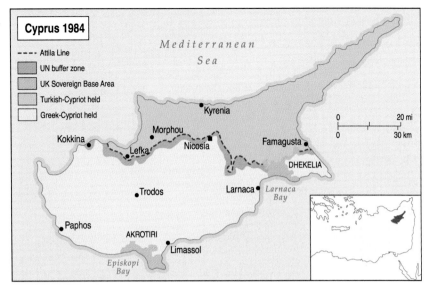

Cyprus 1984

- - - - Attila Line
UN buffer zone
UK Sovereign Base Area
Turkish-Cypriot held
Greek-Cypriot held

Mediterranean Sea

Kyrenia

Morphou

Kokkina

Lefka Nicosia

Famagusta

DHEKELIA

Trodos

Larnaca *Larnaca Bay*

Paphos

AKROTIRI

Limassol

Episkopi Bay

0   20 mi
0   30 km

Medes, and extended his frontiers to the borders of Egypt. He was killed while campaigning in Central Asia, and was succeeded by his son Cambyses II.

cystic fibrosis hereditary disease involving defects of various tissues, including the sweat glands, the mucous glands of the bronchi (air passages), and the pancreas. The sufferer experiences repeated chest infections and digestive disorders and generally fails to thrive. In 1989 a gene for cystic fibrosis was identified by teams of researchers in Michigan, USA, and Toronto, Canada. This discovery enabled the development of a screening test for carriers; the disease can also be detected in the unborn child.

Inheriting the disease One person in 22 is a carrier of the disease. If two carriers have children, each child has a one-in-four chance of having the disease, so that it occurs in about one in 2,000 pregnancies. Around 10% of newborns with cystic fibrosis develop an intestinal blockage (meconium ileus) which requires surgery. It is the commonest fatal hereditary disease amongst white people.

Treatment Cystic fibrosis was once universally fatal at an early age; now, although there is no definitive cure, treatments have raised both the quality and expectancy of life. Results in 1995 from a four-year US study showed that the painkiller ibuprofen, available over the counter, slowed lung deterioration in children by almost 90% when taken in large doses.

Management of cystic fibrosis is by diets and drugs, physiotherapy to keep the chest clear, and use of antibiotics to combat infection and minimize damage to the lungs. Some sufferers have benefited from heart-lung transplants.

Gene therapy In 1993, UK researchers (at the Imperial Cancer Research Fund, Oxford, and the Wellcome Trust, Cambridge)

successfully introduced a corrective version of the gene for cystic fibrosis into the lungs of mice with induced cystic fibrosis, restoring normal function. Trials in human subjects began in 1993, and the cystic fibrosis defect in the nasal cavities of three patients in the USA was successfully corrected, though a later trial was halted after a patient became ill following a dose of the genetically altered virus. Patients treated by gene therapy administered in the form of a nasal spray showed signs of improvement following a preliminary trial in 1996. In 1997, US researchers successful cured mice with cystic fibrosis by administering gene therapy in utero. The fetus breathes in the corrective gene attached to an adenovirus and it becomes incorporated in the developing cells. All the mice were born healthy and survived to old age. Cystic fibrosis is seen as a promising test case for ▷gene therapy. There were approximately 6,500 cystic fibrosis sufferers in Britain in 1997.

cystitis inflammation of the bladder, usually caused by bacterial infection, and resulting in frequent and painful urination. It is more common in women. Treatment is by antibiotics and copious fluids with vitamin C.

Cystitis is more common after sexual intercourse, and it is thought that intercourse encourages bacteria, especially *Escherichia coli*, which are normally present on the skin around the anus and vagina, to enter the urethra and ascend to the bladder. By drinking water before intercourse, and passing urine afterwards, the incidence of cystitis can be reduced, because the bacteria are driven back down the urethra.

cytokine in biology, chemical messenger that carries information from one cell to another, for example the ▷lymphokines.

cytology the study of the structure ▷cells and their functions. Major advances have been made possible in this field by the development of ▷electron microscopes.

cytoplasm the part of the cell outside the ▷nucleus. Strictly speaking, this includes all the ▷organelles (mitochondria, chloroplasts, and so on), but often cytoplasm refers to the jellylike matter in which the organelles are embedded (correctly termed the cytosol). The cytoplasm is the site of protein synthesis.

In many cells, the cytoplasm is made up of two parts: the ectoplasm (or plasmagel), a dense gelatinous outer layer concerned with cell movement, and the endoplasm (or plasmasol), a more fluid inner part where most of the organelles are found.

cytotoxic drug any drug used to kill the cells of a malignant tumour; it may also damage healthy cells. Side effects include nausea, vomiting, hair loss, and bone-marrow damage. Some cytotoxic drugs are also used to treat other diseases and to suppress rejection in transplant patients.

czar alternative spelling of ▷tsar, an emperor of Russia.

Czechoslovakia former country in eastern central Europe, which came into existence as an independent republic in 1918 after the break-up of the ▷Austro-Hungarian empire at the end of World War I. It consisted originally of the Bohemian crownlands (▷Bohemia, ▷Moravia, and part of ▷Silesia) and ▷Slovakia, the area of Hungary inhabited by Slavonic peoples; to this was added as a trust, part of Ruthenia when the Allies and associated powers recognized the new republic under the treaty of St Germain-en-Laye. Besides the Czech and Slovak peoples, the country included substantial minorities of German origin, long settled in the north, and of Hungarian (or Magyar) origin in the south. Despite the problems of welding into a nation such a mixed group of people, Czechoslovakia made considerable political and economic progress until the troubled 1930s. It was the only East European state to retain a parliamentary democracy throughout the interwar period, with five coalition governments (dominated by the Agrarian and National Socialist parties), with Tomas ▷Masaryk serving as president.

Czech Republic see country box.

Czerny, Carl (1791–1857) Austrian pianist, teacher, and composer. He was first taught the piano by his father, played brilliantly at the age of ten, and became a pupil of Beethoven about that time; he also took advice from Johann Hummel and Muzio Clementi. Not liking to appear in public, he took to teaching and soon had an enormous following of pupils, among which he chose only the most gifted. This left him enough leisure for composition, which he cultivated so assiduously as to produce almost 1,000 works. He is chiefly remembered for his books of graded studies and technical exercises used in piano teaching, including the *Complete Theoretical and Practical Pianoforte School* (1839) which is still in widespread use.

Częstochowa city in Poland, on the River Warta, 193 km/ 120 mi southwest of Warsaw; population (1993) 258,700. It produces iron goods, chemicals, paper, and cement. The basilica of Jasna Góra is a centre for Catholic pilgrims (it contains the painting known as the Black Madonna).

D abbreviation for **500**, in the Roman numeral system.

d abbreviation for **day**; **diameter**; **died**; in the UK, d was the symbol for a **penny** (Latin *denarius*) until decimalization of the currency in 1971.

dab small marine flatfish of the flounder family, especially the genus *Limanda*. Dabs live in the North Atlantic and around the coasts of Britain and Scandinavia.

DAC abbreviation for ▷digital-to-analogue converter.

Dacca alternative name for ▷Dhaka, the capital of Bangladesh.

dace freshwater fish *Leuciscus leuciscus* of the carp family. Common in England and mainland Europe, it is silvery and grows up to 30 cm/1 ft.

Dachau site of a Nazi ▷concentration camp during World War II, in Bavaria, Germany. The first such camp to be set up, it opened early in 1933 and functioned as a detention and forced labour camp until liberated in 1945.

DACHAU Liberation of Dachau in 1945. Inmates in striped prison uniforms reach through the fence as US Army corporal Larry Mutinsk distributes cigarettes. *Archive Photos*

dachshund (German 'badger-dog') small dog of German origin, bred originally for digging out badgers. It has a long body and short legs. Several varieties are bred: standard size (up to 10 kg/22 lb), miniature (5 kg/11 lb or less), long-haired, smooth-haired, and wire-haired.

Dacia ancient region covering much of modern Romania. The various Dacian tribes were united around 60 BC, and for many years posed a threat to the Roman empire; they were finally conquered by the Roman emperor Trajan AD 101–07, and the region became a province of the same name. It was abandoned by the emperor Aurelian to the invading Goths about 270.

Dada (or **Dadaism**) artistic and literary movement founded in 1915 in a spirit of rebellion and disillusionment during World War I and lasting until about 1922. Although the movement had a fairly short life and was concentrated in only a few centres (New York being the only non-European one), Dada was highly influential, establishing the tendency for avant-garde art movements to question traditional artistic conventions and values. There are several accounts of how the name Dada (French for hobby horse) originated; the most often quoted is that it was chosen at random by inserting a penknife into a dictionary, symbolizing the antirational nature of the movement.

Dadd, Richard (1817–1886) English painter. In 1843 he murdered his father and was committed to an asylum, but continued to paint minutely detailed pictures of fairy tales, such as *The Fairy Feller's Master Stroke* (1855–64; Tate Gallery, London).

daddy-long-legs popular name for a ▷crane fly.

Dadra and Nagar Haveli since 1961, a Union Territory of west India, between Gujarat and Maharashtra states; area 490 sq km/189 sq mi; population (2001 est) 186,000. The capital is Silvassa. Until 1954 it was part of Portuguese Daman. It produces rice, wheat, and millet. 40% of the total area is forest.

Daedalus in Greek mythology, a talented Athenian artisan. He made a wooden cow to disguise Pasiphae, wife of King Minos of Crete, when she wished to mate with a bull, and then constructed a ▷Labyrinth to house the creature of their union, the ▷Minotaur. Having incurred the displeasure of Minos, Daedalus fled from Crete with his son ▷Icarus, using wings made from feathers fastened with wax.

daffodil any of several Old World species of bulbous plants belonging to the amaryllis family, characterized by their trumpet-shaped yellow flowers which appear in spring. The common daffodil of northern Europe (*Narcissus pseudonarcissus*) has large yellow flowers and grows from a large bulb. There are numerous cultivated forms in which the colours range from white to deep orange. (Genus *Narcissus*, family Amaryllidaceae.)

    Related Web site: Daffodil http://www.botanical.com/botanical/mgmh/d/daffod01.html

Dafydd ap Gwilym (*c.* 1340–*c.* 1400) Welsh poet. His work exhibits a complex but graceful style, concern with nature and love rather than with heroic martial deeds, and has references to classical and Italian poetry.

Dagestan (or **Daghestan**; 'mountain kingdom') autonomous republic in the southwestern Russian Federation, in northern Caucasia; area 50,300 sq km/19,421 sq mi; population (1996) 2,098,000 (42% urban). The main cities are ▷Makhachkala (capital) and Derbent. Situated mainly on the northeastern slopes of the main Caucasus Mountains, Dagestan is bounded on the east by the northwestern shore of the Caspian Sea; the Nogay steppe lowland is in the north, and the principal river is the Terek. There are plentiful oil and natural-gas deposits. Chief industries are oil and gas extraction, metalworking, and traditional crafts (carpet weaving); agricultural activities centre on the raising of livestock, the cultivation of grain and grapevines, and horticulture.

Daguerre, Louis Jacques Mandé (1787–1851) French pioneer of photography. Together with Joseph Niépce, he is credited with the invention of photography (though others were reaching the same point simultaneously). In 1838 he invented the ▷daguerreotype, a single image process superseded ten years later by ▷Fox Talbot's negative/positive process.

daguerreotype in photography, a single-image process using mercury vapour and an iodine-sensitized silvered plate; it was invented by Louis Daguerre in 1838.

LOUIS DAGUERRE The rights to Daguerre's daguerreotype process were assigned to the French Academy of Sciences. *Archive Photos*

Dahl, Roald (1916–1990) British writer, of Norwegian ancestry. He is celebrated for short stories with a twist, such as *Tales of the Unexpected* (1979), and for his children's books, including *James and the Giant Peach* (1961), *Charlie and the Chocolate Factory* (1964), *The BFG* (1982), and *Matilda* (1988). Many of his works have been successfully adapted for television or film. He also wrote the screenplay for the James Bond film *You Only Live Twice* (1967), and the script for *Chitty Chitty Bang Bang* (1968). The enormous popularity of his children's books can be attributed to his weird imagination, the success of his child characters in outwitting their elders, and his repulsive detail. *The Collected Short Stories* was published in 1991. His autobiography *Going Solo* (1986) recounted his experiences as a fighter pilot in the RAF. After surviving a crash landing he was posted to Washington, where he worked with British security.

    Related Web site: Roald Dahl Home Page http://www.roalddahlfans.com/

Dahlhaus, Carl (1928–1989) German musicologist. A prolific writer on music theory and history, his books and articles cover an enormous range of topics and periods; he is best known for his studies in 19th-century music and history. He was extremely influential in German-speaking musicology, and increasingly so in English-speaking circles from the early 1980s when his major works began to be translated. Dahlhaus believed that music cannot be divorced from the society and culture which produces it; therefore, an understanding of musical history can only flow from an understanding of history in a wider sense. He was influenced by the historical theories of Hegel and Marx, and by the philosophical approach to music taken by Theodor Adorno. His theoretical writings include *Esthetics of Music* (1967) and *Foundations of Music History* (1977); historical studies include *Nineteenth-Century Music* (1980), *Ludwig van Beethoven* (1987), and the articles collected as *Schoenberg and the New Music* (1987).

dahlia any of a group of perennial plants belonging to the daisy family, comprising 20 species and many cultivated forms. Dahlias are stocky plants with tuberous roots and showy flowers that come in a wide range of colours. They are native to Mexico and Central America. (Genus *Dahlia*, family Compositae.)

    Related Web site: Dahlias http://www.botanical.com/botanical/mgmh/d/dahlia02.html

Dahomey former name (until 1975) of the People's Republic of ▷Benin.

Dáil Éireann lower house of the legislature of the Republic of Ireland (Oireachtas). It consists of 166 members elected by adult suffrage through the single transferable vote system of proportional representation from 41 constituencies for a five-year term.

Daimler, Gottlieb Wilhelm (1834–1900) German engineer who pioneered the car and the internal-combustion engine together with Wilhelm Maybach. In 1885 he produced a motor

DAGUERREOTYPE A daguerreotype of the Hiller family, made in about 1885. *The Art Archive/Apsley House/Eileen Tweedy*

GOTTLIEB WILHELM DAIMLER German engineer Gottlieb Daimler (in back seat) with his Daimler-Wagen, one of the earliest roadworthy cars produced. *Archive Photos*

bicycle and in 1889 his first four-wheeled motor vehicle. He combined the vaporization of fuel with the high-speed four-stroke petrol engine.

Daimler's work on the internal-combustion engine began in earnest in 1872 when he teamed up with Nikolaus Otto at a gas-engine works; Maybach was the chief designer. Daimler built his first petrol engines in 1883. The Daimler Motoren Gesellschaft was founded in 1890, and Daimler engines were also manufactured under licence; a Daimler-powered car won the first international car race: Paris to Rouen 1894.

daisy any of numerous species of perennial plants belonging to the daisy family, especially the field daisy of Europe and North America (*Chrysanthemum leucanthemum*) and the English common daisy (*Bellis perennis*), with a single white or pink flower rising from a rosette of leaves. (Family Compositae.)
  Related Web site: Daisy, Common http://www.botanical.com/botanical/mgmh/d/daisyc03.html

daisy bush any of several Australian and New Zealand shrubs with flowers like daisies and felted or hollylike leaves. (Genus *Olearia*, family Compositae.)

daisywheel printing head in a computer printer or typewriter that consists of a small plastic or metal disc made up of many spokes (like the petals of a daisy). At the end of each spoke is a character in relief. The daisywheel is rotated until the spoke bearing the required character is facing an inked ribbon, then a hammer strikes the spoke against the ribbon, leaving the impression of the character on the paper beneath.

Dakar capital, chief port (with artificial harbour), and administrative centre of Senegal; population (1992) 1,729,800. It is situated at the tip of the Cape Verde peninsula, the westernmost point of Africa. It is a major industrial centre, with industries including crude-oil refining, engineering, chemicals, brewing, and tobacco and food processing. Dakar contains the Grand Mosque, National Museum, and a university (established in 1949).

Dakota see ▷North Dakota and ▷South Dakota.

Daladier, Edouard (1884–1970) French Radical politician, prime minister in 1933, 1934, and 1938–40, when he signed the Munich Agreement in 1938 (ceding the Sudeten districts of Czechoslovakia to Germany). After declaring war on Germany in September 1939, his government failed to aid Poland and, at home, imprisoned pacifists and communists. After his government resigned in March 1940, Daladier was arrested by the Vichy authorities, tried with Léon Blum at Riom in 1942, then deported to Germany, 1943–45. He was re-elected as a deputy 1946–58.

Dalai Lama (1935–) Title of Tenzin Gyatso. (Tibetan 'oceanic guru') Tibetan Buddhist monk, political ruler of Tibet 1940–59, when he went into exile in protest against Chinese annexation and oppression. He has continued to campaign for self-government, and was awarded the Nobel Prize for Peace in 1989 for his work as spiritual and temporal leader of Tibet. Tibetan Buddhists believe that each Dalai Lama is a reincarnation of his predecessor and also of ▷Avalokiteśvara. His deputy is called the ▷Panchen Lama.

Dalai Lama is the title of the second hierarch of the Gelugpa monastic order. Tenzin Gyatso was chosen to be the 14th Dalai Lama in 1937 and enthroned in Lhasa in 1940. He temporarily fled 1950–51 when the Chinese overran Tibet, and in March 1959 – when a local uprising against Chinese rule was suppressed – made a dramatic escape from Lhasa to India. He then settled at Dharmsala in the Punjab. The Chinese offered to lift the ban on his living in Tibet, providing he would refrain from calling for Tibet's independence. The Dalai Lama has limited himself to pressing for self-government in internal affairs and the cessation of forcible Sinification in Tibet. He concerns himself closely with the welfare

of the many Tibetans who have fled into exile. In May 1998 he announced that he would team up with The Body Shop to support their programme for human rights.

In the 15th century, when the office was founded, Dalai Lama was purely a religious title. The fifth Dalai Lama (1617–1682) united Tibet politically and assumed temporal as well as spiritual powers.
  Related Web site: His Holiness the Dalai Lama http://www.dalailama.com/

Dalap-Uliga-Darrit capital of the Marshall Islands, formed from the three main inhabited areas on the Majuro atoll; population (1998) 19,664.

Dales (or Yorkshire Dales) series of river valleys in northern England, running east from the Pennines in West Yorkshire; a National Park was established in 1954. The principal valleys are Airedale, Nidderdale, Swaledale, Teesdale, Wensleydale, and Wharfedale. The three main peaks are Ingleborough, Whernside, and Pen-y-Ghent.

Dalglish, Kenny (Kenneth Mathieson) (1951–) Scottish footballer and football manager. A prolific goalscorer for Glasgow Celtic and then Liverpool, he was the first player to score 100 goals in both the English and Scottish first divisions. He won nine trophies as a player with Celtic and 12 with Liverpool including three European Cups. Overall, Dalglish made a record 102 international appearances for Scotland and equalled Denis Law's record of 30 goals. As a manager he won the league championship with Liverpool in 1986, 1988, and 1990, and with Blackburn Rovers in 1995.

Dalí, Salvador Felippe Jacinto (1904–1989) Spanish painter and designer. In 1929 he joined the surrealists (see ▷surrealism) and became notorious for his flamboyant eccentricity. Influenced by the psychoanalytic theories of Sigmund ▷Freud, he developed a repertoire of striking, hallucinatory images – distorted human figures, limp pocket watches, and burning giraffes – in superbly executed works, which he termed 'hand-painted dream photographs'. *The Persistence of Memory* (1931; Museum of Modern Art, New York) is typical. By the late 1930s he had developed a more conventional style – this, and his apparent fascist sympathies, led to his expulsion from the surrealist movement in 1938. It was in this more traditional though still highly inventive and idiosyncratic style that he painted such celebrated religious works as *The Crucifixion* (1951; Glasgow Art School). He also painted portraits of his wife Gala.

Dalí, born near Barcelona, initially came under the influence of the Italian Futurists. He is credited as co-creator of Luis Buñuel's surrealist film *Un Chien andalou* (1928), but his role is thought to have been subordinate; he abandoned film-making after collaborating on the script for Buñuel's *L'Age d'or/The Golden Age* (1930). He also designed ballet costumes, scenery, jewellery, and furniture. The books *The Secret Life of Salvador Dalí* (1942) and *Diary of a Genius* (1966) are autobiographical. He was buried beneath a crystal dome in the museum of his work at Figueras on the Costa Brava, Spain.
  Related Web site: Salvador Dalí Art Gallery http://www.salvadordalimuseum.org/

Dalian (or Talien or Dairen) port in Liaoning province, China, on the Liaodong Peninsula, facing the Yellow Sea; population (1994) 2,638,300. Industries include engineering, oil-refining, shipbuilding, food-processing (soybeans), and the manufacture of chemicals, textiles, railway locomotives, and fertilizers. It has ice-free, deep water facilities, and comprises the naval base of Lüshun (known under 19th-century Russian occupation as Port Arthur) and the commercial port of Dalian, together formerly known as Lüda.
  Related Web site: Dalian http://www.chinapages.com/liaoning/dalian/dalian.htm

Dallas commercial city in northeastern Texas, USA, on the Trinity River; seat of Dallas County; population (1994 est) 1,023,000, metropolitan area (with Fort Worth) (1994 est) 4,362,000. The second-largest city in Texas (Houston is the

largest), Dallas is the hub of a rich cotton-farming and oil-producing region, and is one of the leading cultural and manufacturing centres in the Southwest; its industries include banking, insurance, oil, aviation, aerospace, and electronics. Dallas was founded in 1841, and was incorporated as a city in 1871.

Dalmatia region divided between Croatia, Montenegro, and Bosnia-Herzegovina. The capital is Split. It lies along the eastern shore of the Adriatic Sea and includes a number of islands. The interior is mountainous. Important products are wine, olives, and fish. Notable towns in addition to the capital are Zadar, Sibenik, and Dubrovnik.
  History Dalmatia became Austrian in 1815 and by the treaty of Rapallo in 1920 became part of the kingdom of the Serbs, Croats, and Slovenes (Yugoslavia from 1931; Serbia and Montenegro from 2003), except for the town of Zadar (Zara) and the island of Lastovo (Lagosta), which were given to Italy until transferred to Yugoslavia (now Serbia and Montenegro) in 1947.

Dalmatian breed of dog, about 60 cm/24 in tall, with a distinctive smooth white coat with spots that are black or brown. Dalmatians are born white; the spots appear later. They were formerly used as coach dogs, running beside horse-drawn carriages to fend off highwaymen.

Dalton, John (1766–1844) English chemist who proposed the theory of atoms, which he considered to be the smallest parts of matter. He produced the first list of relative atomic masses in 'Absorption of Gases' in 1805 and put forward the law of partial pressures of gases (Dalton's law). From experiments with gases, Dalton noted that the proportions of two components combining to form another gas were always constant. He suggested that if substances combine in simple numerical ratios, then the macroscopic weight proportions represent the relative atomic masses of those substances. He also propounded the law of partial pressures, stating that for a mixture of gases the total pressure is the sum of the pressures that would be developed by each individual gas if it were the only one present.

dam structure built to hold back water in order to prevent flooding, to provide water for irrigation and storage, and to provide hydroelectric power. The biggest dams are of the earth- and rock-fill type, also called embankment dams. Early dams in Britain, built before and about 1800, had a core made from puddled clay (clay which has been mixed with water to make it impermeable). Such dams are generally built on broad valley sites. Deep, narrow gorges dictate a concrete dam, where the strength of reinforced concrete can withstand the water pressures involved. See illustration on p. 256.
  Related Web site: Dams: Panoramic Photographs, 1851–1991 http://lcweb2.loc.gov/cgi-bin/query/r?ammem/pan:(dam)

Dam, Carl Peter Henrik (1895–1976) Danish biochemist who was awarded a Nobel Prize for Physiology or Medicine in 1943 for his discovery of vitamin K. He shared the prize with US biochemist Edward Doisy, who received the award for determining the chemical nature of vitamin K.

damages in law, compensation for a ▷tort (such as personal injuries caused by negligence) or breach of contract. In the case of breach of contract the complainant can claim all the financial loss he or she has suffered. Damages for personal injuries include compensation for loss of earnings, as well as for the injury itself. The court might reduce the damages if the claimant was partly to

DAM Theodore Roosevelt Dam, Arizona, USA. *Image Bank*

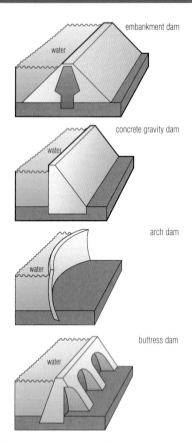

DAM There are two basic types of dam: the gravity dam and the arch dam. The gravity dam relies upon the weight of its material to resist the forces imposed upon it; the arch dam uses an arch shape to take the forces in a horizontal direction into the sides of the river valley. The largest dams are usually embankment dams. Buttress dams are used to hold back very wide rivers or lakes.

blame. In the majority of cases, the parties involved reach an out-of-court settlement (a compromise without going to court).

Daman town and mainland part of the Union Territory of Daman and Diu, western India.

Daman and Diu Union Territory of west India; area 112 sq km/43 sq mi; capital Daman; population (2001 est) 133,000. **Daman** has an area of 72 sq km/28 sq mi. The port and capital, Daman, is on the west coast, 160 km/100 mi north of Mumbai (formerly Bombay), on the estuary of the Daman Ganga River flowing in the Gulf of Khambhat. The economy is based on tourism and fishing. **Diu** is an island off the Kathiawar peninsula with an area of 40 sq km/15 sq mi. The main town is also called Diu. The economy is based on tourism, coconuts, pearl millet, and salt.

History Daman was seized by Portugal in 1531 and ceded to Portugal by the Shah of Gujarat in 1539; Diu was captured by the Portuguese in 1534. Both areas were annexed by India in 1961 and were part of the Union Territory of ▷Goa, Daman, and Diu until Goa became a separate state in 1987.

Damascus (Arabic **Dimashq** or **ash-Sham**) capital of Syria, on the River Barada, 100 km/62 mi southeast of Beirut; population

(1993) 1,497,000. It produces silk, wood products, textiles, brass, and copperware. Said to be the oldest continuously inhabited city in the world, Damascus was an ancient city even in Old Testament times.

History The Assyrians destroyed Damascus in about 733 BC. In 332 BC it fell to one of the generals of Alexander the Great; and in 63 BC it came under Roman rule. In AD 635 it was taken by the Arabs, and has since been captured many times, by Egyptians, Mongolians, and Turks. In 1918, during World War I, it was taken from the Turks by the British with Arab aid and in 1920 became the capital of French-mandated Syria. The 'street which is called straight' (Acts ix. 11) is associated with St Paul, who was converted while on the road to Damascus.

Features Most notable of the old buildings is the Omayyad Mosque (705), built on the site of a 5th-century Christian cathedral. The mausoleum of ▷Saladin is here. The fortress dates from 1219.

Dame in the UK honours system, the title of a woman who has been awarded the Order of the Bath, Order of St Michael and St George, Royal Victorian Order, or Order of the British Empire. It is also the legal title of the wife or widow of a knight or baronet, placed before her name.

Damocles (lived 4th century BC) In classical legend, a courtier of the elder Dionysius, ruler of Syracuse, Sicily. When Damocles made too much of his sovereign's good fortune, Dionysius invited him to a feast where he symbolically hung a sword over Damocles' head by a single horse-hair to demonstrate the precariousness of the happiness of kings.

damper any device that deadens or lessens vibrations or oscillations; for example, one used to check vibrations in the strings of a piano. The term is also used for the movable plate in the flue of a stove or furnace for controlling the draught.

Dampier, William (1651–1715) English explorer and hydrographic surveyor who circumnavigated the world three times.

damselfly long, slender, colourful ▷dragonfly of the suborder Zygoptera, with two pairs of similar wings that are generally held vertically over the body when at rest, unlike those of other dragonflies.

damson cultivated variety of plum tree, distinguished by its small oval edible fruits, which are dark purple or blue-black in colour. (*Prunus domestica* var. *institia*.)
Related Web site: Bullace http://www.botanical.com/botanical/mgmh/b/bullac86.html

Danby, Francis (1793–1861) Irish painter. In Romantic and imaginative landscape and subject pictures, for example *The Deluge* (Tate Gallery, London), he may be compared with John Martin and Washington Allston. He studied in Dublin, worked in Bristol and London, and lived abroad 1830–42.

dance rhythmic movement of the body, usually performed in time to music. Its primary purpose may be religious, magical, martial, social, or artistic – the last two being characteristic of nontraditional societies. The pre-Christian era had a strong tradition of ritual dance, and ancient Greek dance still exerts an influence on dance movement today. Although Western folk and social dances have a long history, the Eastern dance tradition long predates the Western. The European classical tradition dates from the 15th century in Italy, the first printed dance text from 16th-century France, and the first dance school in Paris from the 17th century. The 18th century saw the development of European classical ▷ballet as we know it today, and the 19th century saw the

FRANCIS DANBY A copy of Irish artist Francis Danby's Romantic painting *The Deluge*. The Art Archive/Tate Gallery London

rise of Romantic ballet. In the 20th century ▷modern dance firmly established itself as a separate dance idiom, not based on classical ballet, and many divergent styles and ideas have grown from a willingness to explore a variety of techniques and amalgamate different traditions.

dance of death (German *Totentanz*; French *danse macabre*) popular theme in painting of the late medieval period, depicting an allegorical representation of death (usually a skeleton) leading the famous and the not-so-famous to the grave. One of the best-known representations is a series of woodcuts (1523–26) by Hans Holbein the Younger. It has also been exploited as a theme in music, for example the *Danse macabre* of Saint-Saëns (1874), an orchestral composition in which the xylophone was introduced to represent dancing skeletons.

dandelion common plant throughout Europe and Asia, belonging to the same family as the daisy. The stalk rises from a rosette of leaves that are deeply indented like a lion's teeth, hence the name (from French *dent de lion*). The flower heads are bright yellow, and the fruit is covered with fine hairs, known as the dandelion 'clock'. (*Taraxacum officinale*, family Compositae.)
Related Web site: Dandelion http://www.botanical.com/botanical/mgmh/d/dandel08.html

Dandie Dinmont breed of ▷terrier that originated in the Scottish border country. It is about 25 cm/10 in tall, short-legged and long-bodied, with drooping ears and a long tail. Its hair, about 5 cm/2 in long, can be greyish or yellowish. It is named after the character Dandie Dinmont in Walter Scott's novel *Guy Mannering* (1815).

> ## John Davies
> English poet
>
> *This wondrous miracle did Love devise, / For dancing is love's proper exercise.*
>
> 'Orchestra, or a Poem of Dancing'

DANCE A wall painting of dancers, in an Etruscan tomb from about 475 BC. *Philip Sauvain Picture Collection*

dandy male figure conspicuous for tasteful fastidiousness, particularly in dress. The famous Regency dandy George ('Beau') Brummell (1778–1840) helped to give literary currency to the figure of the dandy, particularly in England and France, providing a model and symbol of the triumph of style for the Francophile Oscar ▷Wilde and for 19th-century French writers such as Charles ▷Baudelaire, J K Huysmans, and the extravagantly romantic novelist and critic Jules-Amédée Barbey d'Aurevilly (1808–1889), biographer of Brummell.

Dane people of Danish culture from Denmark and northern Germany. There are approximately 5 million speakers of Danish (including some in the USA), a Germanic language belonging to the Indo-European family. The Danes are known for their seafaring culture, which dates back to the Viking age of expansion between the 8th and 10th centuries.

danegeld in English history, a tax imposed from 991 onwards by Anglo-Saxon kings to pay tribute to the Vikings. After the Norman Conquest (1066), the tax was revived and was levied until 1162; the Normans used it to finance military operations.

DAMSELFLY The common blue damselfly *Enallagma cyathigerum* male holding his wings closed above his back, as is usual for members of the suborder Zygoptera. *Premaphotos Wildlife*

Danegeld was first exacted in the reign of Ethelred (II) the Unready (978–1016). This payment was distinct from the tax known as *heregeld*, which was levied annually between 1012 and 1051 to pay for a mercenary squadron of Danish ships in English service and to maintain a standing army.

Danelaw 11th-century name for the area of northern and eastern England settled by the Vikings in the 9th century. It occupied about half of England, from the River Tees to the River Thames. Within its bounds, Danish law, customs, and language prevailed, rather than West Saxon or Mercian law. Its linguistic influence is still apparent in place names in this area.

The Danelaw was not uniformly settled. Danish colonists congregated more densely in some areas than in others – in particular in Yorkshire, around Lincoln, Stamford, Leicester, Nottingham, Derby, and in Norfolk.

Daniel (lived 6th century BC) Jewish folk hero and prophet at the court of Nebuchadnezzar; also the name of a book of the Old Testament, probably compiled in the 2nd century BC. It includes stories about Daniel and his companions Shadrach, Meshach, and Abednego, set during the Babylonian captivity of the Jews.

Danish language member of the North Germanic group of the Indo-European language family, spoken in Denmark and Greenland and related to Icelandic, Faroese, Norwegian, and Swedish. It has had a particularly strong influence on Norwegian. As one of the languages of the Vikings, who invaded and settled in parts of Britain during the 9th to 11th centuries, Old Danish had a strong influence on English.

Danish literature Danish writers of international fame emerged in the 19th century: Hans Christian Andersen, the philosopher Søren Kierkegaard, and the critic Georg Brandes (1842–1927), all of whom played a major part in the Scandinavian literary awakening, encouraging Ibsen and others. The novelists Henrik Pontoppidan (1857–1943), Karl Gjellerup (1857–1919), and Johannes Jensen (1873–1950) were all Nobel prizewinners.

D'Annunzio, Gabriele (1863–1938) Italian poet, novelist, and dramatist. Marking a departure from 19th-century Italian literary traditions, his use of language and style of writing earned him much criticism in his own time. His novels, often combining elements of corruption, snobbery, and scandal, include *L'innocente/ The Intruder* (1891) and *Il triomfo della morte/The Triumph of Death* (1894).

Dante Alighieri (1265–1321) Italian poet. His masterpiece *La divina commedia/The Divine Comedy* (1307–21) is an epic account in three parts of his journey through Hell, Purgatory, and Paradise, during which he is guided part of the way by the poet Virgil; on a metaphorical level, the journey is also one of Dante's own spiritual development. Other works include *De vulgari eloquentia/Concerning the Vulgar Tongue* (1304–06), an original Latin work on Italian, its dialects, and kindred languages; the philosophical prose treatise *Convivio/The Banquet* (1306–08), the first major work of its kind to be written in Italian rather than Latin; *De monarchia/On World Government* (1310–13), expounding his political theories; and *Canzoniere/Lyrics*.

Dante was born in Florence, where in 1274 he first met and fell in love with Beatrice Portinari (described in *La vita nuova/New Life* (1283–92)). His love for her survived her

> ### Dante Alighieri
> *Lasciate ogni speranza voi ch'entrate!*
>
> All hope abandon, ye who enter here.
>
> *Divine Comedy*, 'Inferno' III

marriage to another man and her death in 1290 at the age of 24. According to the writer ▷Boccaccio, from 1283 to 1289 Dante was engaged in study, and after the death of Beatrice he seems to have entered into a period of intense philosophical study. In 1289 he fought in the battle of Campaldino, won by Florence against Arezzo, and from 1295 took an active part in Florentine politics. In 1300 he was one of the six priors of the Republic, favouring the moderate Guelph party rather than the extreme papal Ghibelline faction (see ▷Guelph and Ghibelline); when the Ghibellines seized power in 1302, he was convicted in his absence of misapplication of public money and sentenced to death. He escaped from Florence and spent the remainder of his life in exile, in central and northern Italy.

DANTE ALIGHIERI The Italian poet Dante was born in Florence, Italy, but wrote 'The Divine Comedy' while in exile in Ravenna. *Archive Photos*

Danton, Georges Jacques (1759–1794) French revolutionary. Originally a lawyer, during the early years of the Revolution he was one of the most influential people in Paris. He organized the uprising 10 August 1792 that overthrew Louis XVI and the monarchy, roused the country to expel the Prussian invaders, and in April 1793 formed the revolutionary tribunal and the **Committee of Public Safety**, of which he was the leader until July of that year. Thereafter he lost power to the ▷Jacobins, and, when he attempted to recover it, was arrested and guillotined.

Danube (German **Donau**) second longest of European rivers, rising on the eastern slopes of the Black Forest, and flowing 2,858 km/1,776 mi across Europe to enter the Black Sea in Romania by a swampy delta.

The head of river navigation is Ulm, in Baden-Württemberg; Braila, Romania, is the limit for ocean-going ships. Cities on the Danube include Linz, Vienna, Bratislava, Budapest, Belgrade, Ruse, Braila, and Galati. A canal connects the Danube with the River ▷Main, and thus with the Rhine river system. In 1992 the river was diverted in Slovakia to feed the controversial Gabcikovo Dam.

Danzig German name for the Polish port of ▷Gdańsk.

Daphne in Greek mythology, a river ▷nymph who was changed by her mother, the earth goddess ▷Gaia, into a laurel tree to escape ▷Apollo's amorous pursuit. Determined to possess her, Apollo fashioned her branches and leaves into a crown and decorated his lyre and quiver with her foliage.

d'Arblay, Madame married name of English writer Fanny ▷Burney.

Dardanelles (ancient name **Hellespont**, Turkish name **Canakkale Boğazı**) Turkish strait connecting the Sea of Marmara with the Aegean Sea; its shores are formed by the ▷Gallipoli peninsula on the northwest and the mainland of Anatolia on the southeast. It is 75 km/47 mi long and 5–6 km/3–4 mi wide.

Dar es Salaam (Arabic 'haven of peace') chief seaport in Tanzania, on the Indian Ocean, and administrative capital of Tanzania pending the transfer of government functions to ▷Dodoma which was designated the official capital in 1974; population (1996 est) 1,747,000, having grown very rapidly

from 150,000 in 1964. Industries include food processing, textiles, clothing, footwear, petroleum refining, glass, printing, timber, aluminium, steel, polystyrene, machinery, and car components. Exports include copper, coffee, sisal, and cotton. As well as being the chief port and largest city, it is also the main industrial, commercial, and financial centre of Tanzania, and includes the main international airport.

Dar es Salaam is the Indian Ocean terminus of the Tazara Railway (opened in 1975), and also of the railways to the lake ports of Kigoma and Mwanza; a road links it with Ndola in the Zambian copperbelt, and oil is carried to Zambia by pipeline from Dar es Salaam's refineries. University College (1963) became the University of Dar es Salaam in 1970. The National Museum of Tanzania in the city houses the Olduvai Gorge fossils. In 1973 it was decided by a national vote to move the capital from Dar es Salaam to the inland city of Dodoma, a move which had not been fully completed by 2000.

Dariganga a Mongolian people numbering only 30,000. Their language is a dialect of Khalka, the official language of Mongolia. In the past, the Dariganga were nomads, and lived by breeding camels for use in the Chinese imperial army. With the rise of the communist regime in China, they supported the new Mongolian state, and have become sedentary livestock farmers.

Darius I the Great (c. 558–486 BC) King of Persia 521–486 BC. A member of a younger branch of the Achaemenid dynasty, he won the throne from the usurper Gaumata (died 522 BC) and reorganized the government. In 512 BC he marched against the Scythians, a people north of the Black Sea, and subjugated Thrace and Macedonia.

Darjeeling (or **Darjiling**) town and health resort in West Bengal, northeast India; situated 2,150 m/7,000 ft above sea level, on the southern slopes of the Himalayas; population (1991) 73,100. The centre of a tea-producing district, it is connected by rail with Calcutta, 595 km/370 mi to the south. Formerly the summer capital of the British administration in Bengal, it remains a popular hill resort.

Darjiling alternative spelling for ▷Darjeeling.

darkling beetle beetle in the family Tenebrionidae.

dark matter matter that, according to certain modern theories of ▷cosmology, makes up 90–99% of the mass of the universe but so far remains undetected. Dark matter, if shown to exist, would explain many currently unexplained gravitational effects in the movement of galaxies. Theories of the composition of dark matter include unknown atomic particles (cold dark matter) or fast-moving neutrinos (hot dark matter) or a combination of both.

In 1993 astronomers identified part of the dark matter in the form of stray planets and ▷brown dwarfs, and possibly stars that have failed to ignite. These objects are known as MACHOs (massive astrophysical compact halo objects) and may make up approximately half of the dark matter in the Milky Way's halo.

Darling river in southeast Australia, a tributary of the River Murray; length 2,736 km/1,700 mi. The Darling is formed about 40 km/25 mi northeast of Bourke, at the union of the Culgoa and

GEORGES DANTON French revolutionary Georges Danton was an influential figure during the 1790s. *The Art Archive/Musmadee Carnavalet Paris/Dagli Orti*

Bogan rivers (which rise in central Queensland to the west of the Great Dividing range); it flows southwest before joining the Murray at Wentworth. Its waters are conserved in Menindee Lake (155 sq km/60 sq mi) and others nearby. The river is usually navigable as far as Bourke between August and March.

Darling, Grace Horsley (1815–1842) English heroine. She was the daughter of a lighthouse keeper on the Farne Islands, off Northumberland. On 7 September 1838 the *Forfarshire* was wrecked, and Grace Darling and her father rowed through a storm to the wreck, saving nine lives. She was awarded a medal for her bravery.

Darlington unitary authority (borough status) in northeast England, created in 1997.

area 197 sq km/76 sq mi **towns and cities** ▷Darlington (administrative headquarters); villages of Hurworth on Tees, Middleton St George, Heighington, Hurworth Place **features** River Skerne flows through Darlington, River Tees forms southern boundary of authority; Darlington Railway Centre and Museum houses English engineer George Stephenson's locomotion engine **industries** heavy engineering, iron and steel, vehicle components, bridge building, telecommunications, fitted furniture, textiles, knitting wool, agriculture **population** (1996) 100,600 **famous people** Joseph Dent, Ralph Hodgson

Darlington industrial town and administrative headquarters of ▷Darlington unitary authority in northeast England, on the River Skerne near its junction with the Tees, 53 km/33 mi south of Newcastle; population (1996) 100,600. The town was part of the county of Durham until 1997. Industries include heavy engineering, bridge-building, and the production of iron and steel goods, knitting wool, vehicle components, textiles, and fitted kitchens and bathrooms (Magnet). The world's first passenger railway was opened between Darlington and Stockton on 27 September 1825.

Darnley, Henry Stewart (or Stuart, Lord Darnley) (1545–1567) English aristocrat, second husband of Mary Queen of Scots from 1565, and father of James I of England (James VI of Scotland).

On the advice of her secretary, David Rizzio, Mary refused Darnley the crown matrimonial; in revenge, Darnley led a band of nobles who murdered Rizzio in Mary's presence. Darnley was assassinated in 1567. He was knighted and became Earl of Ross and Duke of Albany in 1565.

Darrow, Clarence Seward (1857–1938) US lawyer, born in Ohio, a champion of liberal causes and defender of the underdog. He defended many trade-union leaders, including Eugene ▷Debs 1894. He was counsel for the defence in the Nathan Leopold and Richard Loeb murder trial in Chicago in 1924, and in the ▷Scopes monkey trial. Darrow matched wits in the latter trial with prosecution attorney William Jennings Bryan. He was an opponent of capital punishment.

Dart, Raymond Arthur (1893–1988) Australian-born South African palaeontologist and anthropologist who in 1924 discovered the first fossil remains of the australopithecenes, early hominids, near Taungs in Botswana.

Dartford industrial town in Kent, southeast England, on the River Darent to the south of the Thames estuary, 27 km/17 mi southeast of London; population (1991) 59,400. Industries include milling, engineering, and the manufacture of cement, chemicals, paper, and pharmaceuticals (Glaxo-Wellcome). The **Dartford Tunnel** (1963) runs under the Thames to Purfleet, Essex. The Queen Elizabeth II bridge opened in 1991, relieving congestion in the tunnel.

Dartmoor plateau of southwest Devon, England; mostly a national park, 956 sq km/369 sq mi in area. Over half the region is around 300 m/1,000 ft above sea level, making it the highest and largest of the moorland areas in southwest England. The moor is noted for its wild aspect and the ▷tors, rugged blocks of bare granite, which crown its loftier points. The highest are Yes Tor, rising to 619 m/2,030 ft, and High Willhays, which climbs to 621 m/2,039 ft.

Darwin port and capital of ▷Northern Territory, Australia; population (1996) 70,251. Darwin is situated at the centre of Australia's north coast, in the northwest of Arnhem Land. It is a service centre for the northern part of Northern Territory, and industries include mining (uranium and copper), horticulture, fruit growing, and tourism. Darwin was destroyed in 1974 by Cyclone Tracy, and rebuilt on the same site. It is a base for tourists visiting Kakadu National Park, Bathurst Island, and Melville Island.

Darwin is the most northerly city of Australia, and the northern terminus of the rail line from Birdum. It is linked to the rest of Australia by the Stuart Highway, which runs south from Darwin to Alice Springs. Founded in 1869, under the name of Palmerston, the city was renamed after Charles ▷Darwin in 1911. During World War II it was an Allied base for action against the Japanese in the Pacific, and suffered repeated bombing, the only Australian town to do so. The Northern Territory University (1989) is located here.

Darwin, Charles Robert (1809–1882) English naturalist who developed the modern theory of ▷evolution and proposed, with Alfred Russel ▷Wallace, the principle of ▷natural selection.

After research in South America and the Galapagos Islands as naturalist on HMS *Beagle* 1831–36, Darwin published *On the Origin of Species by Means of Natural Selection or the Preservation of Favoured Races in the Struggle for Life* (1859). This book explained the evolutionary process through the principles of natural selection and aroused bitter controversy because it disagreed with the literal interpretation of the Book of Genesis in the Bible.

On the Origin of Species also refuted earlier evolutionary theories, such as those of French naturalist J B de ▷Lamarck. Darwin himself played little part in the debates, but his *Descent of Man* (1871) added fuel to the theological discussion, in which English scientist T H ▷Huxley and German zoologist Ernst ▷Haeckel took leading parts.

Related Web site: Darwin and Evolution http://landow.stg.brown.edu/victorian/darwin/darwin5.html

CHARLES DARWIN At a time when most people still believed in the biblical account of creation, Darwin's idea that species evolved gradually caused a storm of controversy. *Archive Photos*

Charles Darwin
What can be more curious than that the hand of a man, formed for grasping, that of a mole for digging, [. . .] and the wing of a bat, should all be constructed on the same pattern, and should include the same bones, in the same relative positions?
On the Origin of Species (1859)

Darwinism, social in US history, an influential but contentious social theory, based on the work of Charles Darwin and Herbert Spencer, which claimed to offer a scientific justification for late 19th-century *laissez-faire* capitalism (the principle of unrestricted freedom in commerce).

Dasam Granth collection of the writings of the tenth Sikh guru (teacher), Gobind Singh, and of poems by a number of other writers. It is written in a script called Gurmukhi, the written form of Punjabi popularized by Guru Angad. It contains a retelling of the Krishna legends, devotional verse, and amusing anecdotes.

dasyure any ▷marsupial of the family Dasyuridae, also known as a 'native cat', found in Australia and New Guinea. Various species have body lengths from 25 cm/10 in to 75 cm/2.5 ft. Dasyures have long, bushy tails and dark coats with white spots. They are agile, nocturnal carnivores, able to move fast and climb.

DAT abbreviation for ▷digital audio tape.

data (singular **datum**) facts, figures, and symbols, especially as stored in computers. The term is often used to mean raw, unprocessed facts, as distinct from information, to which a meaning or interpretation has been applied.

Continuous data is data that can take any of an infinite number of values between whole numbers and so may not be measured completely accurately. This type of data contrasts with **discrete data**, in which the variable can only take one of a finite set of values. For example, the sizes of apples on a tree form continuous data, whereas the numbers of apples form discrete data.

database in computing, a structured collection of data, which may be manipulated to select and sort desired items of information. For example, an accounting system might be built around a database containing details of customers and suppliers. In larger computers, the database makes data available to the various programs that need it, without the need for those programs to be aware of how the data are stored. The term is also sometimes used for simple record-keeping systems, such as mailing lists, in which there are facilities for searching, sorting, and producing records. There are four main types (or 'models') of database: relational, object oriented, hierarchical, and network, of which relational is the most widely used. Object oriented databases have become more popular for certain types of application, and hybrids like object-relational are also available. In a **relational database** data are viewed as a collection of linked tables. A **free-text database** is one that holds the unstructured text of articles or books in a form that permits rapid searching. A telephone directory stored as a database might allow all the people whose names start with the letter B to be selected by one program, and all those living in Chicago by another.

A collection of databases is known as a **databank**. A database-management system (DBMS) is software that ensures that the integrity of the data is maintained by controlling the degree of access of the ▷applications programs using the data.

Databases are usually created using a **database tool** that enables a user to define the database structure by selecting the number of fields, naming those fields, and allocating the type and amount of data that is valid for each field. To sort records within a database, one or more **sort fields** may be selected, so that when the data is sorted, it is ordered according to the contents of these fields. A **key field** is used to give a unique identifier to a particular record. Data programs also determine how data can be viewed on screen or extracted into files.

data communications sending and receiving data via any communications medium, such as a telephone line. The term usually implies that the data are digital (such as computer data) rather than analogue (such as voice messages). However, in the ISDN (▷Integrated Services Digital Network) system, all data – including voices and video images – are transmitted digitally. See also ▷telecommunications.

data compression in computing, techniques for reducing the amount of storage needed for a given amount of data. They include word tokenization (in which frequently used words are stored as shorter codes), variable bit lengths (in which common characters are represented by fewer ▷bits than less common ones), and run-length encoding (in which a repeated value is stored once along with a count).

data processing (DP, or **electronic data processing**, **EDP**) use of computers for performing clerical tasks such as stock control, payroll, and dealing with orders. DP systems are typically ▷batch systems, running on mainframe computers.

data protection safeguarding of information about individuals stored in files and on computers, to protect privacy.

data security in computing, precautions taken to prevent the loss or misuse of data, whether accidental or deliberate. These include measures that ensure that only authorized personnel can gain entry to a computer system or file, and regular procedures for storing and 'backing up' data, which enable files to be retrieved or recreated in the event of loss, theft, or damage.

A number of ▷verification and ▷validation techniques may also be used to prevent data from being lost or corrupted by misprocessing.

data terminator (or **rogue value**) in computing, a special value used to mark the end of a list of input data items. The computer must be able to detect that the data terminator is different from the input data in some way – for instance, a negative number might be used to signal the end of a list of positive numbers, or 'XXX' might be used to terminate the entry of a list of names. This is now considered to be very bad programming technique. A lot of old programs used data terminators, and many programmers used 00 as a year data terminator, leading to problems in the year 2000.

date palm tree, also known as the date palm. The female tree produces the brown oblong fruit, dates, in bunches weighing 9–11 kg/20–25 lb. Dates are an important source of food in the Middle East, being rich in sugar; they are dried for export. The tree also supplies timber and materials for baskets, rope, and animal feed. (Genus *Phoenix*.) See picture on p. 257.

dating in geology, the process of determining the age of minerals, rocks, fossils, and geological formations. There are two types of dating: relative and absolute. **Relative dating** involves determining the relative ages of materials, that is determining the chronological order of formation of particular rocks, fossils, or formations, by means of careful field work. **Absolute dating** is the process of determining the absolute age (i.e., the age in years) of a mineral, rock, or fossil. Absolute dating is accomplished using methods such as ▷radiometric dating (measuring the abundances of particular isotopes in a mineral), fission track dating, and even counting annual layers of sediment.

datura any of a group of plants belonging to the nightshade family, such as the ▷thorn apple, with handsome trumpet-shaped blooms. They have narcotic (pain-killing and sleep-inducing) properties. (Genus *Datura*, family Solanaceae.)

DATE Large plantations of date palms are grown along the arid shores of the Dead Sea in Israel. Cultivation is highly advanced, using trickle irrigation and machine harvesting. *Premaphotos Wildlife*

Daumier, Honoré Victorin (1808–1879) French artist. His sharply dramatic and satirical cartoons dissected Parisian society. He produced over 4,000 lithographs and, mainly after 1860, powerful, sardonic oil paintings that were little appreciated in his lifetime.

HONORÉ DAUMIER *The Print Collectors* (a study of two men in a print shop), by French artist Honoré Daumier, a dramatically lit oil painting that deals with the Parisian art world that he observed around him. *The Art Archive/ London Museum/Eileen Tweedy*

dauphin title of the eldest son of the kings of France, derived from the personal name of a count, whose lands, known as the Dauphiné, traditionally passed to the heir to the throne from 1349 to 1830.

David king of the Hebrews 1004–965 BC. He became king of Judah on the death of King Saul at Mount Gilboa in 1004 BC, then king of Israel in 997 BC. He united the tribes against the Philistines, conquering their cities (such as Ekron), and extending his kingdom over Moab and other surrounding lands. He captured Jerusalem to make it the City of David, capital of the united tribes of Israel and Judah. He was succeeded by his son Solomon, and the Davidic line ruled in Jerusalem until 586 BC when the city was destroyed by ▷Nebuchadnezzar.

David two kings of Scotland:

David I (1084–1153) King of Scotland from 1124. The youngest son of Malcolm III Canmore and St ▷Margaret, he was brought up in the English court of ▷Henry I, and in 1113 married ▷Matilda,

widow of the 1st earl of Northampton. He invaded England in 1138 in support of Queen Matilda, but was defeated at Northallerton in the Battle of the Standard, and again in 1141.

David II (1324–1371) King of Scotland from 1329, son of ▷Robert (I) the Bruce. David was married at the age of four to Joanna, daughter of Edward II of England. In 1346 David invaded England, was captured at the battle of Neville's Cross, and imprisoned for 11 years.

After the defeat of the Scots by Edward III at Halidon Hill in 1333, the young David and Joanna were sent to France for safety. They returned in 1341. On Joanna's death in 1362 David married Margaret Logie, but divorced her in 1370.

David, St (or St Dewi) (lived 5th–6th century) Patron saint of Wales, Christian abbot and bishop. According to legend he was the son of a prince of Dyfed and uncle of King Arthur. Tradition has it that David made a pilgrimage to Jerusalem, where he was consecrated bishop. He founded 12 monasteries in Wales, including a monastery at Menevia (now St Davids), which he made his bishop's seat. He presided over a synod at Brefi and condemned the ideas of the British theologian Pelagius. He was responsible for the adoption of the leek as the national emblem of Wales, but his own emblem is a dove. Feast day 1 March.

David, Gerard (c. 1450–c. 1523) Netherlandish painter. He was active chiefly in Bruges from about 1484. His style follows that of Rogier van der ▷Weyden, but he was also influenced by the taste in Antwerp for Italianate ornament. *The Marriage at Cana* (c. 1503; Louvre, Paris) is an example of his work.

> **Peter Maxwell Davies**
> *I could not remain in a country that so scorns its people that it would deny them music.*
> Remark, November 1993

David, Jacques-Louis (1748–1825) French painter. One of the greatest of the neoclassicists, he sought to give his art a direct political significance. He was an active supporter of the republic during the French Revolution, and was imprisoned 1794–95. In his *Death of Marat* (1793; Musées Royaux, Brussels), he turned political murder into classical tragedy. Later he devoted himself to the newly created empire in grandiose paintings such as *The Coronation of Napoleon* (1805–07; Louvre, Paris).

David studied in Paris and then in Rome, drawing the Roman statues and familiarizing himself with the main figures of the Renaissance. Between 1775 and 1785, inspired by his work in Rome, he evolved his strikingly neoclassical idiom. An important picture from this period is *The Oath of the Horatii* (1784; Louvre, Paris), a work in which he set out to rouse Republican patriotic fervour.

After the death of the Jacobin leader Robespierre, David was twice imprisoned and narrowly escaped the guillotine. His *The Rape of Sabine Women* (1799; Louvre, Paris) is dedicated to his wife, whose calls for clemency helped to secure his release.

When Napoleon came to power, David became his official painter, creating such imperial images as *Napoleon Crossing the Alps* (1800; Louvre, Paris) and *Napoleon Distributing the Eagles* (1810; Versailles). David's major works also include portraits, one of the finest being *Mme Récamier* (1800; Louvre, Paris).

His style, which was inherited by several of his pupils, most notably ▷Ingres, dominated French painting in the first half of the 19th century.

Davies, Peter Maxwell (1934–) English composer and conductor. His music combines medieval and serial codes of practice with a heightened expressionism as in his opera *Taverner* (1972), based on the life and works of the 16th-century composer John Taverner. Other works include the chamber opera *The Lighthouse* (1980), the music-theatre piece *Miss Donnithorne's Maggot* (1974), and the orchestral piece *Mavis in Las Vegas*. He is the associate conductor/composer of the Royal Philharmonic Orchestra, and the BBC Philharmonic, and the composer laureate of the Scottish Chamber Orchestra.

da Vinci Italian painter, sculptor, architect, engineer, and scientist; see ▷Leonardo da Vinci.

Davis, Angela Yvonne (1944–) US left-wing activist for African-American rights, prominent in the student movement of the 1960s. In 1970 she went into hiding after being accused of supplying guns used in the murder of a judge, who had been seized as a hostage in an attempt to secure the release of three black convicts. She was captured, tried, and acquitted. At the University of California she studied under Herbert ▷Marcuse, and was assistant professor of philosophy at the Los Angeles campus 1969–70. In 1980 she was the Communist vice-presidential candidate.

Davis, Bette (Ruth Elizabeth) (1908–1989) US actor. She established a reputation as a forceful dramatic actor with

Of Human Bondage (1934). Later films include *Jezebel* (1938), for which she won an Academy Award for Best Actress, *Now, Voyager* (1942), *All About Eve* (1950), and *The Whales of August* (1987), in which she co-starred with Lillian Gish.

Davis, Jefferson (1808–1889) US politician, president of the short-lived Confederate States of America 1861–65. He was a leader of the Southern Democrats in the US Senate from 1857, and a defender of 'humane' slavery; in 1860 he issued a declaration in favour of secession from the USA. During the Civil War he assumed strong political leadership, but often disagreed with military policy. He was imprisoned for two years after the war, one of the few cases of judicial retribution against Confederate leaders.

Davis sat in the US Senate 1847–51, was secretary of war 1853–57, and returned to the Senate in 1857. During the Civil War, his fiery temper and self-righteousness hindered efforts to achieve broad unity among the Southern states. His call for conscription in the South raised protests that he was a military dictator, violating the ideals of freedom for which the Confederacy was supposed to be fighting.

Davis, John (c. 1550–1605) English navigator and explorer. He sailed in search of the Northwest Passage through the Canadian Arctic to the Pacific Ocean in 1585, and in 1587 sailed to Baffin Bay through the straits named after him. He was the first European to see the Falkland Islands, in 1592.

Davis, Miles Dewey, Jr (1926–1991) US jazz trumpeter, composer, and bandleader. He was one of the most influential and innovative figures in jazz. He pioneered bebop with Charlie Parker in 1945, cool jazz in the 1950s, and jazz-rock fusion from the late 1960s. His albums include *Birth of the Cool* (1957; recorded 1949 and 1950), *Sketches of Spain* (1959), *Bitches Brew* (1970), and *Tutu* (1985).

Davis, born in Illinois, joined Charlie Parker's group 1946–48. In 1948 he began an association with composer and arranger Gil Evans (1912–1988) that was to last throughout his career. His quintet in 1955 featured the saxophone player John Coltrane, who recorded with Davis until 1961; for example, *Kind of Blue* (1959). In 1968 Davis introduced electric instruments, later adding electronic devices to his trumpet and more percussion to his band. He went on to use disco backings, and recorded pop songs and collaborated with rock musicians, remaining changeable to the end.

Related Web site: Milestones: A Miles Davis World Wide Web Site
http://miles.rtvf.nwu.edu/miles/milestones.html

MILES DAVIS US jazz musician Miles Davis performing at the Newport Jazz Festival, Rhode Island, USA, in 1969. *Archive Photos*

Davis, Sammy, Jr (1925–1990) US entertainer. His starring role in the Broadway show *Mr Wonderful* (1956), his television work, and his roles in films with Frank Sinatra – among them, *Ocean's Eleven* (1960) and *Robin and the Seven Hoods* (1964) – made him a celebrity. He also appeared in the film version of the opera *Porgy and Bess* (1959).

Davis, Steve (1957–) English snooker player who won every major honour in the game after turning professional in 1978. He was world champion six times.

Davis, Stuart (1894–1964) US abstract painter. Much of his work shows the influence of both jazz tempos and cubism in its use of hard-edged geometric shapes in primary colours and ▷collage. In the 1920s he produced paintings of commercial packaging, such as *Lucky Strike* (1921; Museum of Modern Art, New York), that foreshadowed pop art.

Davison, Emily Wilding (1872–1913) English militant ▷suffragette who died after throwing herself under the king's horse at the Derby at Epsom (she was trampled by the horse). She joined the Women's Social and Political Union in 1906 and served several prison sentences for militant action such as stone throwing, setting fire to pillar boxes, and bombing Lloyd George's country house.

Davy, Humphry (1778–1829) English chemist. He discovered, by electrolysis, the metallic elements sodium and potassium in 1807, and calcium, boron, magnesium, strontium, and barium in 1808. In addition, he established that chlorine is an element and proposed that hydrogen is present in all acids. He invented the safety lamp for use in mines where methane was present, enabling miners to work in previously unsafe conditions. He was knighted in 1812 and made baronet in 1818.

Davy's experiments on electrolysis of aqueous solutions from 1800 led him to suggest its large-scale use in the alkali industry. He theorized that the mechanism of electrolysis could be explained in terms of species that have opposite electric charges, which could be arranged on a scale of relative affinities – the foundation of the modern electrochemical series. His study of the alkali metals provided proof of French chemist Antoine ▷Lavoisier's idea that all alkalis contain oxygen.

Dawes, Charles Gates (1865–1951) US Republican politician. In 1923 the Allied Reparations Commission appointed him president of the committee that produced the Dawes Plan, a loan of US$200 million that enabled Germany to pay enormous war debts after World War I. It reduced tensions temporarily in Europe but was superseded by the Young Plan (which reduced the total reparations bill) in 1929. Dawes was made US vice-president (under Calvin Coolidge) in 1924, and he shared the Nobel Prize for Peace in 1925 with Austen ▷Chamberlain for his reorganization of German reparation payments. He was ambassador to the UK 1929–32.

Dawes General Allotment Act US federal act passed 8 February 1887 providing 65 hectares of allotment land to American Indian families living on reservations, and extending the protection of US laws to them. The aim of the act was to encourage American Indians to take up agriculture and adopt 'the habits of civilized life' and ultimately for them to be fully assimilated into US society. With the grant of land they also received US citizenship.

> **Richard Dawkins**
> *We are survival machines – robot vehicles blindly programmed to preserve the selfish molecules known as genes. This is a truth which still fills me with astonishment.*
> The Selfish Gene Preface

Dawkins, (Clinton) Richard (1941–) English zoologist, born in Kenya, whose book *The Selfish Gene* (1976) popularized the theories of sociobiology (social behaviour in humans and animals in the context of evolution). In *The Blind Watchmaker* (1986) he explained the modern theory of evolution.

dawn raid in business, sudden and unexpected buying of a significant proportion of a company's shares, usually as a prelude to a takeover bid. The aim is to prevent the target company from having time to organize opposition to the takeover.

day time taken for the Earth to rotate once on its axis. The **solar day** is the time that the Earth takes to rotate once relative to the Sun. It is divided into 24 hours, and is the basis of our civil day. The **sidereal day** is the time that the Earth takes to rotate once relative to the stars. It is 3 minutes 56 seconds shorter than the solar day, because the Sun's position against the background of stars as seen from Earth changes as the Earth orbits it.

Day, Doris (1924–) Stage name of Doris von Kappelhoff. US film actor and singing star of the 1950s and early 1960s. She appeared in musicals and, often with Rock Hudson, coy sex comedies such as *Pillow Talk* (1959) and *Lover Come Back* (1961). Her films also include *Tea for Two* (1950), *Calamity Jane* (1953), *Love Me or Leave Me* (1955), and Alfred Hitchcock's *The Man Who Knew Too Much* (1956).

Dayan, Moshe (1915–1981) Israeli general and politician. As minister of defence 1967 and 1969–74, he was largely responsible for the victory over neighbouring Arab states in the 1967 Six-Day War, but he was criticized for Israel's alleged unpreparedness in the 1973 October War and resigned along with Prime Minister Golda ▷Meir.

Day-Lewis, C(ecil) (1904–1972) Irish poet. With W H Auden and Stephen Spender, he was one of the influential left-wing poets of the 1930s. His later poetry moved from political concerns to a more traditional personal lyricism. He also wrote detective novels under the pseudonym **Nicholas Blake**. He was British poet laureate 1968–72.

D-DAY US Army troops on board a landing craft preparing for the D-day invasion of Normandy on 6 June 1944.
Archive Photos

Day-Lewis, Daniel (1958–) English actor. He first came to prominence in *My Beautiful Laundrette* and *A Room With a View* (both 1985). He won an Academy Award for his performance as a painter suffering from cerebral palsy in *My Left Foot* (1989).
Related Web site: Daniel Day-Lewis http://www.danielday.org/

Dayton city in southwestern Ohio, USA; on the junction of the Great Miami and Stillwater rivers, 75 km/47 mi north of Cincinnati; seat of Montgomery County; population (1994 est) 179,000. It is the centre of an agricultural region and the hub of a large metropolitan area; industries include the manufacture of motor vehicle parts, business machines, household appliances, and electrical equipment. It has an aeronautical research centre and was the home of aviators Wilbur and Orville Wright.

> **James Dean**
> *Death is the only thing left to respect. Everything else can be questioned. But death is truth.*
> Photoplay, September 1985

dBASE family of microcomputer programs used for manipulating large quantities of data; also, a related ▷fourth-generation language. The first version, dBASE II, was published by Ashton-Tate in 1981; it has since become the basis for a recognized standard for database applications, known as xBase.

DCC abbreviation for ▷digital compact cassette.

D-day 6 June 1944, the day of the Allied invasion of Normandy under the command of General Eisenhower to commence Operation Overlord, the liberation of Western Europe from German occupation. The Anglo-US invasion fleet landed on the Normandy beaches on the stretch of coast between the Orne River and St Marcouf. Artificial harbours known as 'Mulberries' were constructed and towed across the Channel so that equipment and armaments could be unloaded on to the beaches. After overcoming fierce resistance the allies broke through the German defences; Paris was liberated on 25 August, and Brussels on 2 September. D-day is also military jargon for any day on which a crucial operation is planned. D+1 indicates the day after the start of the operation.
Related Web site: D-Day http://www.pbs.org/wgbh/pages/amex/dday/index.html

> **Gwen Ffrangcon-Davies**
> Actor
> *My dear, I am always nervous about doing something for the first time.*
> Referring to death, aged 101, February 1992

DDT (abbreviation for dichloro-diphenyl-trichloroethane) $(ClC_6H_5)_2CHC(HCl_2)$ insecticide discovered in 1939 by Swiss chemist Paul Müller. It is useful in the control of insects that spread malaria, but resistant strains develop. DDT is highly toxic and persists in the environment and in living tissue. Despite this and its subsequent danger to wildlife, it has evaded a worldwide ban because it remains one of the most effective ways of controlling malaria. China and India were the biggest DDT users in 1999.

DE abbreviation for ▷Delaware, a state of the USA.

deacon in the Roman Catholic and Anglican churches, an ordained minister who ranks immediately below a priest. In the Protestant churches, a deacon is in training to become a minister or is a lay assistant.

deadly nightshade another name for ▷belladonna, a poisonous plant.

Dead Sea large lake, partly in Israel and partly in Jordan, lying 394 m/1,293 ft below sea level; it is the lowest surface point on earth; area 1,020 sq km/394 sq mi. The chief river entering it is the Jordan; it has no outlet and the water is very salty (340 g of salt per litre of water). The sea is not, however, completely dead. *Dunaliella parva*, a single-celled green alga, and a group of halophilic (salt-loving) ▷Archaea are found here. In 1998, three species of fungi were discovered to be living in the Dead Sea. One of the species is new to science and cannot survive without salt.

Dead Sea Scrolls collection of ancient scrolls (rolls of writing) and fragments of scrolls found 1947–56 in caves on the western side of the Jordan, at ▷Qumran. They include copies of Old Testament books a thousand years older than those previously known to be extant. The documents date mainly about 150 BC–AD 68, when the monastic community that owned them, the Essenes, was destroyed by the Romans because of its support for a revolt against their rule.
Related Web site: Dead Sea Scrolls http://sunsite.unc.edu/expo/deadsea.scrolls.exhibit/intro.html

deafness partial or total deficit of hearing in either ear. Of assistance are hearing aids, lip-reading, a cochlear implant in the ear in combination with a special electronic processor, sign language, and 'cued speech' (manual clarification of ambiguous lip movement during speech). Approximately 10% of people worldwide experience some hearing difficulties. This amounts to approximately 28 million people in the USA alone.

Deakin, Alfred (1856–1919) Australian politician, prime minister 1903–04, 1905–08, and 1909–10. In his second administration, he enacted legislation on defence and pensions.

dean in education, in universities and medical schools, the head of administration; in the colleges of Oxford and Cambridge, UK, the member of the teaching staff charged with the maintenance of discipline; in the USA, a leader in several administrative areas, such as the dean of students or dean of admissions; in Roman Catholicism, senior cardinal bishop, head of the college of cardinals; in the Anglican Communion, head of the chapter of a cathedral or collegiate church (a rural dean presides over a division of an archdeaconry).

Dean, James (Byron) (1931–1955) US actor. A stage performer who had appeared in a small number of minor film roles, Dean was killed in a car accident soon after the public showing of the first film in which he starred, Elia Kazan's *East of Eden* (1955). He posthumously became a cult hero with *Rebel Without a Cause* (1955) and *Giant* (1956). Since his death, his image has endured as the classic icon of teenage rebellion.
Related Web site: Dean, James http://www.reelclassics.com/Actors/Dean/dean.htm

death cessation of all life functions, so that the molecules and structures associated with living things become disorganized and indistinguishable from similar molecules found in nonliving things. In medicine, a person is pronounced dead when the brain ceases to control the vital functions, even if breathing and heartbeat are maintained artificially.

Medical definition Death used to be pronounced with the permanent cessation of heartbeat, but the advent of life-support equipment has made this point sometimes difficult to determine. For removal of vital organs in transplant surgery, the World Health Organization in 1968 set out that a potential donor should exhibit no brain–body connection, muscular activity, blood pressure, or ability to breathe spontaneously.

Death Valley

Death Valley was given its name by gold-seekers, many of whom died while trying to cross the valley in the late 1840s during the California gold rush. Death Valley is the greatest depression in the Western hemisphere, the lowest point in North America, and the seventh deepest in the world: about 1,400 sq km/550 sq mi of its area lie below sea level; the valley's lowest point, near Badwater, is 86 m/282 ft below sea level. On 10 July 1913 Death Valley endured the highest-ever recorded temperature in the western hemisphere (57°C/134°F). It has the lowest yearly average rainfall in the USA (4 cm/1.63 in). Although it is one of the world's hottest and driest places, more than 900 kinds of plant live in the valley. It was declared a national monument in 1933 and became a National Park in 1994; the area includes more than 1.2 million ha/3 million acres of wilderness.

Religious belief In religious belief, death may be seen as the prelude to rebirth (as in Hinduism and Buddhism); under Islam and Christianity, there is the concept of a day of judgement and consignment to heaven or hell; Judaism concentrates not on an afterlife but on survival through descendants who honour tradition.

death cap fungus of the ▷amanita group, the most poisonous mushroom known. The fruiting body, or mushroom, has a scaly white cap and a collarlike structure (volva) near the base of the stalk. (*Amanita phalloides*, family Agaricaceae.)

death penalty another name for ▷capital punishment.

death rate the number of deaths per 1,000 of the population of an area over the period of a year. Death rate is a factor in demographic transition.

death's-head moth largest British ▷hawk moth with downy wings measuring 13 cm/5 in from tip to tip, and its thorax is marked as though with a skull.

Death Valley desert depression in southeastern California, USA; 225 km/140 mi long and 6–26 km/4–16 mi wide; area 8,368 sq km/3,231 sq mi. It is one of the world's hottest and driest places, with summer temperatures sometimes exceeding 51.7°C/125°F and an annual rainfall of less than 5 cm/2 in. Borax, iron ore, tungsten, gypsum, and salts are extracted here.

deathwatch beetle any wood-boring beetle of the family Anobiidae, especially *Xestobium rufovillosum*. The larvae live in oaks and willows, and sometimes cause damage by boring in old furniture or structural timbers. To attract the female, the male beetle produces a ticking sound by striking his head on a wooden surface, and this is taken by the superstitious as a warning of approaching death.

Debrecen second-largest city in Hungary, 193 km/120 mi east of Budapest, in the Great Plain (*Alföld*) region; population (1995) 211,000. It produces tobacco, agricultural machinery, and pharmaceuticals. Lajos ▷Kossuth declared Hungary independent of the ▷Habsburgs here 1849. It is a commercial centre and has a university founded 1912.

de Broglie French physicists; see ▷Broglie, Louis, and ▷Broglie, Maurice.

Debs, Eugene V(ictor) (1855–1926) US labour leader and socialist who organized the Social Democratic Party in 1897 (known as the Socialist Party from 1901). He was the founder and first president of the American Railway Union in 1893, and was imprisoned for six months in 1894 for defying a federal injunction to end the 1894 Pullman strike in Chicago. An ardent socialist and union man, he ran for the US presidency five times as the Socialist Party's candidate.

> **Eugene Debs**
> *I said then, I say now, that while there is a lower class, I am in it; while there is a criminal element, I am of it; while there is a soul in prison, I am not free.*
> Speech at his trial, 14 September 1918

debt something that is owed by a person, organization, or country, usually money, goods, or services. Debt usually occurs as a result of borrowing ▷credit. **Debt servicing** is the payment of interest on a debt. The **national debt** of a country is the total money owed by the national government to private individuals, banks, and so on; **international debt**, the money owed by one country to another, began on a large scale with the investment in foreign countries by newly industrialized countries in the late 19th to early 20th centuries. International debt became a global problem as a result of the oil crisis of the 1970s.

Background to debt crisis As a result of the ▷Bretton Woods Conference in 1944, the World Bank (officially called the International Bank for Reconstruction and Development) was established in 1945 as an agency of the United Nations to finance international development, by providing loans where private capital was not forthcoming. Loans were made largely at prevailing market rates ('hard loans') and therefore generally to the industrialized countries, who could afford them.

In 1960 the International Development Association (IDA) was set up as an offshoot of the World Bank to provide interest-free ('soft') loans over a long period to finance the economies of industrializing countries and assist their long-term development. The cash surpluses of Middle Eastern oil-producing countries were channelled by Western banks to Third World countries. However, a slump in the world economy, and increases in interest rates, resulted in the debtor countries paying an ever-increasing share of their national output in debt servicing (paying off the interest on a debt, rather than paying off the debt itself). As a result, many loans had to be rescheduled (renegotiated so that repayments were made over a longer term).

Relief and rescheduling Today, the countries most at risk include Mexico and Brazil, both of which have a **debt-servicing ratio** (proportion of export earnings which is required to pay off the debt) of more than 50%. In 1987 the world's largest bank, Citibank of New York, announced that it was writing off $3 billion of international loans, mainly owing to Brazil's repeated rescheduling of debt repayments. Disagreement over who should bear the cost of debt relief has delayed any real reform. Austerity measures imposed by the International Monetary Fund (IMF) in exchange for loans have provoked riots and an increase in nationalist sentiment, but Brazil began making repayments on its debt in 1988, and the USA and Mexico have negotiated reduction plans. Poland, which ceased making repayments on international debts 1980–81, received substantial loans in 1990 from the USA and Western Europe to assist its transition to a market-based economy.

debt crisis any situation in which an individual, company, or country owes more to others than it can repay or pay interest on; more specifically, the massive indebtedness of many Third World countries that became acute in the 1980s, threatening the stability of the international banking system as many debtor countries became unable to service their debts.

> **Claude Debussy**
> *The colour of my soul is iron-grey and sad bats wheel about the steeple of my dreams.*
> Letter to Chausson, 1894

debt-for-nature swap agreement under which a proportion of a country's debts are written off in exchange for a commitment by the debtor country to undertake projects for environmental protection. Debt-for-nature swaps were set up by environment groups in the 1980s in an attempt to reduce the debt problem of poor countries, while simultaneously promoting conservation.

Debussy, (Achille-) Claude (1862–1918) French composer. He broke with German Romanticism and introduced new qualities of melody and harmony based on the whole-tone scale, evoking oriental music. His work includes *Prélude à l'après-midi d'un faune/Prelude to the Afternoon of a Faun* (1894), illustrating a poem by Stéphane Mallarmé, and the opera *Pelléas et Mélisande* (1902).

Among his other works are numerous piano pieces, songs, orchestral pieces such as *La Mer/The Sea* (1905) and *Trois Nocturnes* (1899), and the ballet *Jeux* (1913). Debussy also published witty and humorous critical writing about the music of his day, featuring the fictional character Monsieur Croche 'antidilettante' (professional debunker), a figure based on Erik ▷Satie.

decagon in geometry, a ten-sided ▷polygon.

decathlon two-day athletic competition for men consisting of ten events: 100 metres, long jump, shot put, high jump, 400 metres (day one); 110-metre hurdles, discus, pole vault, javelin, 1,500 metres (day two). Points are awarded for performances, and the winner is the athlete with the greatest aggregate score. The decathlon is an Olympic event.

decay, radioactive see ▷radioactive decay.

decibel unit (symbol dB) of measure used originally to compare sound intensities and subsequently electrical or electronic power outputs; now also used to compare voltages. An increase of 10 dB is equivalent to a 10-fold increase in intensity or power. The decibel scale is used for audibility measurements, as one decibel, representing an increase of about 25%, is about the smallest change the human ear can detect. A whisper has an intensity of 20 dB; 140 dB (a jet aircraft taking off nearby) is the threshold of pain.

The difference in decibels between two levels of intensity (or power) L_1 and L_2 is $10 \log_{10}(L_1/L_2)$; a difference of 1 dB thus corresponds to a level of $10^{0.1}$, which is about 1.026.

deciduous of trees and shrubs, that shed their leaves at the end of the growing season or during a dry season to reduce ▷transpiration (the loss of water by evaporation).

Most deciduous trees belong to the ▷angiosperms, plants in which the seeds are enclosed within an ovary, and the term 'deciduous tree' is sometimes used to mean 'angiosperm tree', despite the fact that many angiosperms are evergreen, especially in the tropics, and a few ▷gymnosperms, plants in which the seeds are exposed, are deciduous (for example, larches). The term **broad-leaved** is now preferred to 'deciduous' for this reason.

Examples of deciduous trees are oak and beech.

decimal fraction in mathematics, ▷fraction in which the denominator is any higher power of 10. Thus $\frac{3}{10}$, $\frac{51}{100}$, and $\frac{23}{1000}$ are decimal fractions and are normally expressed as 0.3, 0.51, and 0.023. The use of decimals greatly simplifies addition and multiplication of fractions, though not all fractions can be expressed exactly as decimal fractions.

The regular use of the decimal point appears to have been introduced about 1585, but the occasional use of decimal fractions can be traced back as far as the 12th century.

decimal number system (or denary number system) most commonly used number system, to the base ten. Decimal numbers do not necessarily contain a decimal point; 563, 5.63, and −563 are all decimal numbers. Other systems are mainly used in computing and include the ▷binary number system, octal number system, and ▷hexadecimal number system.

Decimal numbers may be thought of as written under column headings based on the number ten. For example, the number 2,567 stands for 2 thousands, 5 hundreds, 6 tens, and 7 ones. Large decimal numbers may also be expressed in floating-point notation.

decision theory system of mathematical techniques for analysing decision-making problems, for example, over unpredictable factors. The system aims to minimize error. It includes game theory, risk analysis, and utility theory.

Declaration of Independence historic US document stating the theory of government on which the USA was founded, based on the right 'to life, liberty, and the pursuit of happiness'. The statement was issued by the ▷Continental Congress 4 July 1776, renouncing all allegiance to the British crown and ending the political connection with Britain.

Following a resolution moved 7 June, by Richard Henry Lee, 'that these United Colonies are, and of right ought to be, free and independent States', a committee including Thomas ▷Jefferson and Benjamin ▷Franklin was set up to draft a declaration; most of the work was done by Jefferson.

The resolution, coming almost a year after the outbreak of hostilities, was adopted by the representatives of 12 colonies (New York abstained initially) on 2 July, and the Declaration on 4 July; the latter date has ever since been celebrated as Independence Day in the USA. The representatives of New York announced their adhesion 15 July, and the Declaration was afterwards signed by the members of Congress on 2 August.

The declaration enumerated the grievances the colonists harboured against the British crown, which included its use of American Indians to attack colonists, taxation without representation, and denial of civil liberties.

Related Web site: Declaration of Independence http://www.nara.gov/exhall/charters/declaration/decmain.html

Declaration of Rights in Britain, the statement issued by the Convention Parliament in February 1689, laying down the conditions under which the crown was to be offered to William III and Mary. Its clauses were later incorporated in the ▷Bill of Rights.

DECLARATION OF INDEPENDENCE A still-life composition of the historic document of the US Declaration of Independence, superimposed over a US flag. This flag is also known as the 'Stars and Stripes'. The stripes represent the original 13 states, and the 50 stars stand for the number of states now in the Union. *Archive Photos*

decoder in computing, an electronic circuit used to select one of several possible data pathways. Decoders are, for example, used to direct data to individual memory locations within a computer's immediate access memory.

decolonization gradual achievement of independence by former colonies of the European imperial powers, which began after World War I. The process of decolonization accelerated after World War II with 43 states achieving independence 1956–60, 51 1961–80 and 23 from 1981. The movement affected every continent: India and Pakistan gained independence from Britain in 1947; Algeria gained independence from France in 1962, the 'Soviet empire' broke up 1989–91.

decomposer in biology, any organism that breaks down dead matter. Decomposers play a vital role in the ▷ecosystem by freeing important chemical substances, such as nitrogen compounds, locked up in dead organisms or excrement. They feed on some of the released organic matter, but leave the rest to filter back into the soil as dissolved nutrients, or pass in gas form into the atmosphere, for example as nitrogen and carbon dioxide. The principal decomposers are bacteria and fungi, but earthworms and many other invertebrates are often included in this group. The ▷nitrogen cycle relies on the actions of decomposers.

decomposition process whereby a chemical compound is reduced to its component substances. In biology, it is the destruction of dead organisms either by chemical reduction or by the action of decomposers, such as bacteria and fungi.

There are three main types of decompositions. Thermal decomposition occurs as a result of heating. For example, copper(II) carbonate decomposes on heating to give copper oxide and carbon dioxide:

$$CuCO_3 \rightarrow CuO + CO_2$$

Electrolytic decomposition may result when an electrical current is passed through a compound in the molten state or in aqueous solution. For example, molten sodium chloride breaks down into sodium and chlorine:

$$2NaCl \rightarrow 2Na + Cl_2$$

Catalysed decomposition describes the process by which decomposition is aided by the presence of a catalyst. For example, hydrogen peroxide decomposes more quickly with the use of manganese(IV) oxide:

$$2H_2O_2 \rightarrow 2H_2O + O_2$$

decompression sickness illness brought about by a sudden and substantial change in atmospheric pressure. It is caused by a too rapid release of nitrogen that has been dissolved into the bloodstream under pressure; when the nitrogen forms bubbles it causes the ▷bends. The condition causes breathing difficulties, joint and muscle pain, and cramps, and is experienced mostly by deep-sea divers who surface too quickly.

decontamination factor in radiological protection, a measure of the effectiveness of a decontamination process. It is the ratio of the original contamination to the remaining radiation after decontamination: 1,000 and above is excellent; 10 and below is poor.

Decorated in architecture, the second period of English Gothic, covering the latter part of the 13th century and the 14th century. Chief characteristics include ornate window tracery, the window being divided into several lights by vertical bars called mullions; sharp spires ornamented with crockets and pinnacles; complex church vaulting; and slender arcade piers.

decretal in medieval Europe, a papal ruling on a disputed point, sent to a bishop or abbot in reply to a request or appeal. The earliest dates from Siricius 385. Later decretals were collected to form a decretum.

decretum collection of papal decrees. The best known is that collected by Gratian (died 1159) about 1140, comprising some 4,000 items. The decretum was used as an authoritative source of canon law (the rules and regulations of the church).

dedicated computer computer built into another device for the purpose of controlling or supplying information to it. Its use has increased dramatically since the advent of the ▷microprocessor: washing machines, digital watches, cars, and video recorders all now have their own processors.

deduction in philosophy, a form of argument in which the conclusion necessarily follows from the premises. It would be inconsistent ▷logic to accept the premises but deny the conclusion.

Dee river which flows through Aberdeenshire, Scotland and the city of Aberdeen; length 137 km/85 mi. From its source in the Cairngorm Mountains, it flows east into the North Sea at Aberdeen (by an artificial channel in this latter stage). Near Braemar the river passes through a rock gorge, the **Linn of Dee**. ▷Balmoral Castle is on its banks. It is noted for salmon fishing and is the fifth longest river in Scotland.

Dee river that flows through Wales and England; length 112 km/ 70 mi. Rising in Bala Lake, Gwynedd, it flows into the Irish Sea west of Chester. There is another River Dee (61 km/38 mi) in Aberdeenshire, Scotland.

deed legal document that passes an interest in property or binds a person to perform or abstain from some action. Deeds are of two kinds: indenture and deed poll. **Indentures** bind two or more parties in mutual obligations. A **deed poll** is made by one party only, such as when a person changes his or her name.

deep-sea trench another term for ▷ocean trench.

deer any of various ruminant, even-toed, hoofed mammals belonging to the family Cervidae. The male typically has a pair of antlers, shed and regrown each year. Most species of deer are forest-dwellers and are distributed throughout Eurasia and North America, but are absent from Australia and Africa south of the Sahara.

Native to Britain are red deer *Cervus elaphus* and roe deer *Capreolus capreolus*. Red deer are found across Europe and can be 1.2 m/4 ft or more at the shoulder, plain dark brown with yellowish rump, and may have many points to the antlers. The roe deer is smaller, only about 75 cm/2.5 ft at the shoulder, with small erect antlers with three points or fewer. The fallow deer *Dama dama* came originally from the Mediterranean region, and was probably introduced to Britain by William the Conqueror. It typically has a spotted coat and flattened 'palmate' antlers, and stands about 1 m/3 ft high. The little ▷muntjac has been introduced in more recent years from East Asia, and is spreading. Other species in the deer family include the ▷elk, ▷wapiti, ▷reindeer, and the ▷musk deer of central and northeastern Asia, the males of which yield musk and have no antlers.

deerhound breed of large, rough-coated dog, formerly used in Scotland for hunting and killing deer. Slim and long-legged, it grows to 75 cm/30 in or more, usually with a bluish-grey coat.

de Falla, Manuel Spanish composer; see ▷Falla, Manuel de.

defamation in law, an attack on a person's reputation by ▷libel or ▷slander.

Defence, Ministry of British government department created in 1964 from a temporary Ministry of Defence established after World War II together with the Admiralty, Air Ministry, and War Office. It is headed by the secretary of state for defence, and is responsible for defence policy and for control and administration of the armed services. This centralization was influenced by the example of the US Department of ▷Defense.

Defender of the Faith one of the titles of the English sovereign, conferred on Henry VIII in 1521 by Pope Leo X in recognition of the king's treatise against the Protestant Martin Luther. It appears on coins in the abbreviated form **F.D.** (Latin *Fidei Defensor*).

Defenestration of Prague an incident in Prague in 1618 that sparked off the ▷Thirty Years' War. When Ferdinand (1578–1637), Archduke of Styria, was elected king of Bohemia in 1617 and chosen to succeed Matthias as emperor, the Bohemian Protestants feared for their religious and civil freedom. On 23 May 1618, invading the Hradschin Palace, they broke up a meeting of the imperial commissioners and threw two Catholic councillors and their secretary out of the window (though all of them survived the fall).

Defense, Department of US government department presided over by the secretary of defense, with headquarters in the ▷Pentagon. The secretary holds a seat in the president's cabinet; each of the three military services has a civilian secretary, not of cabinet rank, at its head. It was established when the army, navy, and air force were unified by the National Security Act 1947. In 2001, Donald Rumsfeld became the secretary of defense.

deferred share on the stock market, a share that typically warrants a dividend only after a specified dividend has been paid on the ordinary shares; it may, however, be entitled to a dividend on all the profits after that point.

defibrillation use of electrical stimulation to restore a chaotic heartbeat to a rhythmical pattern. In fibrillation, which may occur in most kinds of heart disease, the heart muscle contracts irregularly; the heart is no longer working as an efficient pump. Paddles are applied to the chest wall, and one or more electric shocks are delivered to normalize the beat.

deflation in economics, a reduction in the level of economic activity, usually caused by an increase in interest rates and reduction in the money supply, increased taxation, or a decline in government expenditure.

Defoe, Daniel (1660–1731) English writer. His *Robinson Crusoe* (1719), though purporting to be a factual account of shipwreck and solitary survival, was influential in the development of the novel. The fictional *Moll Flanders* (1722) and the partly factual *A Journal of the Plague Year* (1722) are still read for their concrete realism. A prolific journalist and pamphleteer, he was imprisoned in 1703 for the ironic *The Shortest Way with Dissenters* (1702).

> **Daniel Defoe**
> *Nature has left this tincture in the blood, / That all men would be tyrants if they could.*
> *The Kentish Petition*

Early life Defoe was born in London and educated for the Nonconformist ministry, but became a hosier. He took part in ▷Monmouth's rebellion in 1685, and joined William of Orange in 1688. He was bankrupted three times as a result of various business ventures, once for the then enormous amount of £17,000. After his business had failed, he held a civil-service post from 1695 to 1699.

Work He wrote numerous pamphlets and first achieved fame with the satirical poem *The True-Born Englishman* (1701). Serving five months in Newgate prison for *The Shortest Way with Dissenters*, he wrote his *Hymn to the Pillory* in 1703 and made plans for a political periodical, which was published as the *Review* (1704–13). He travelled in Scotland 1706–07, working to promote the Union, and published *A History of the Union of Great Britain* in 1709. During the next ten years he was almost constantly employed as a political controversialist and pamphleteer. His version of the contemporary short story 'True Relation of the Apparition of One Mrs Veal' (1706) revealed a gift for realistic narrative, and *Robinson Crusoe*, based on the adventure of Alexander Selkirk, was followed by, among others, the pirate story *Captain Singleton* (1720) and the picaresque *Colonel Jack* (1722) and *Roxana* (1724). Since Defoe's death, an increasing number of works have been attributed to him, bringing the total to more than 600.

Related Web site: Robinson Crusoe http://www.bibliomania.com/Fiction/defoe/robin/index.html

deforestation destruction of forest for timber, fuel, charcoal burning, and clearing for agriculture and extractive industries, such as mining, without planting new trees to replace those lost (reafforestation) or working on a cycle that allows the natural forest to regenerate. Deforestation causes fertile soil to be blown away or washed into rivers, leading to ▷soil erosion, drought, flooding, and loss of wildlife. It may also increase the carbon dioxide content of the atmosphere and intensify the ▷greenhouse effect, because there are fewer trees absorbing carbon dioxide from the air for photosynthesis.

Degas, (Hilaire Germain) Edgar (1834–1917) French Impressionist (see ▷Impressionism) painter and sculptor. He devoted himself to lively, informal studies (often using pastels) of ballet, horse racing, and young women working. From the 1890s he turned increasingly to sculpture, modelling figures in wax in a fluent, naturalistic style.

Degas studied under a pupil of ▷Ingres and worked in Italy in the 1850s, painting classical themes. In 1861 he met ▷Manet, and exhibited regularly with the Impressionists 1874–86. His characteristic style soon emerged, showing the influence of Japanese prints and photography in inventive compositions and unusual viewpoints, as in *Woman with Chrysanthemums* (1865) (Metropolitan Museum of Art, New York). An example of his sculpture is *The Little Dancer* (1881) (Tate Gallery, London).

> **Edgar Degas**
> *Everybody has talent at twenty-five. The difficult thing is to have it at fifty.*
> Quoted in R H Ives Gammell *The Shop-Talk of Edgar Degas* (1961)

de Gaulle, Charles André Joseph Marie (1890–1970) French general and first president of the Fifth Republic 1958–69. He organized the Free French troops fighting the Nazis 1940–44, was head of the provisional French government 1944–46, and leader of his own Gaullist party. In 1958 the national assembly asked him to form a government during France's economic recovery and to solve the crisis in Algeria. He became president at the end of 1958, having changed the constitution to provide for a presidential system, and served until 1969.

Born in Lille, he graduated from Saint-Cyr in 1911 and was severely wounded and captured by the Germans in 1916. In June 1940 he refused to accept the new prime minister Pétain's truce with the Germans and on 18 June made his historic broadcast calling on the French to continue the war against Germany. He based himself in England as leader of the Free French troops fighting the Germans 1940–44. In 1944 he entered Paris in triumph and was briefly head of the provisional government before resigning over the new constitution of the Fourth Republic in 1946. In 1947 he founded the Rassemblement du Peuple Français, a nonparty constitutional reform movement, then withdrew from politics in 1953. When national bankruptcy and civil war in Algeria loomed in 1958, de Gaulle was called to form a government. As prime minister he promulgated a constitution subordinating the legislature to the presidency and took office as president in December 1958. Economic recovery followed, as well as Algerian independence after a bloody war. A nationalist, he opposed 'Anglo-Saxon' influence in Europe.

Re-elected president in 1965, he pursued a foreign policy that opposed British entry to the European Economic Union (EEC), withdrew French forces from the North Atlantic Treaty Organization (NATO) in 1966, and pursued the development of a French nuclear deterrent. He violently quelled student demonstrations in May 1968 as soon as they were joined by workers. The Gaullist party, reorganized as Union des Democrats pour la Cinquième République, won an overwhelming majority in the elections of the same year. In 1969 he resigned after the defeat of the government in a referendum on constitutional reform. He retired to the village of Colombey-les-Deux-Eglises in northeastern France.

Degenerate Art (German **Entartete Kunst**) art condemned by the Nazi regime in Germany from 1933. The name was taken from a travelling exhibition mounted by the Nazi Party in 1937 to show modern art as 'sick' and 'decadent' – a view that fitted with Nazi racial theories. The exhibition was paralleled by the official Great German Art Exhibition to display officially approved artists. However, five times as many people (more than 3 million) saw the former as the latter. Artists condemned included Max Beckmann, Emil Nolde, Wassily Kandinsky, Henri Matisse, Ernst Barlach, and Pablo Picasso.

degree in mathematics, a unit (symbol °) of measurement of an angle or arc. A circle or complete rotation is divided into 360°. A degree may be subdivided into 60 minutes (symbol ′), and each minute may be subdivided in turn into 60 seconds (symbol ″).

Temperature is also measured in degrees, which are divided on a decimal scale. See also ▷Celsius, and ▷Fahrenheit.

A degree of latitude is the length along a meridian such that the difference between its north and south ends subtend an angle of 1° at the centre of the Earth. A degree of longitude is the length between two meridians making an angle of 1° at the centre of the Earth.

Dehaene, Jean-Luc (1940–) Belgian politician, prime minister 1992–99. He successfully negotiated constitutional changes to make Belgium a federal state. His centre-left coalition was re-elected in 1995.

De Havilland, Geoffrey (1882–1965) English aircraft designer who designed and whose company produced the Moth biplane, the Mosquito fighter-bomber of World War II, and in 1949 the Comet, the world's first jet-driven airliner to enter commercial service. He was knighted in 1944.

Deighton, Len (Leonard Cyril) (1929–) English author of spy fiction. His novels include *The Ipcress File* (1963) and the trilogy *Berlin Game, Mexico Set,* and *London Match* (1983–85),

EDGAR DEGAS *Four Ballerinas*, one of the many paintings of ballet dancers created by the French painter Edgar Degas during the 1870s. *The Art Archive/Sao Paolo Art Museum Brazil/Dagli Orti*

featuring the spy Bernard Samson. Samson was also the main character in Deighton's trilogy *Spy Hook* (1988), *Spy Line* (1989), and *Spy Sinker* (1990). A further spy trilogy is *Faith* (1994), *Hope* (1995), and *Charity* (1996).

Deimos one of the two moons of Mars. It is irregularly shaped, 15 × 12 × 11 km/9 × 7.5 × 7 mi, orbits at a height of 24,000 km/15,000 mi every 1.26 days, and is not as heavily cratered as the other moon, Phobos. Deimos was discovered in 1877 by US astronomer Asaph Hall (1829–1907), and is thought to be an asteroid captured by Mars's gravity.

deindustrialization decline in the share of manufacturing industries in a country's economy. Typically, industrial plants are closed down and not replaced, and service industries increase.

Deirdre in Celtic mythology, the beautiful intended bride of ▷Conchobar, king of Ulster. She eloped with Noísi, and died of sorrow when Conchobar killed him and his two brothers.

deism (Latin *deus* 'god') belief in a supreme being. The term usually refers to a movement in the 17th and 18th centuries characterized by the belief in a rational 'religion of nature' as opposed to the orthodox beliefs of Christianity. Deists believed that God is the source of natural law but does not intervene directly in the affairs of the world, and that the only religious duty of humanity is to be virtuous.

Dekker, Thomas (c. 1572–c. 1632) English dramatist and pamphleteer. He wrote mainly in collaboration with others. His play *The Shoemaker's Holiday* (1600) was followed by collaborations with Thomas ▷Middleton, John ▷Webster, Philip ▷Massinger, and others. His pamphlets include *The Gull's Hornbook* (1609), a lively satire on the fashions of the day.

de Klerk, F(rederik) W(illem) (1936–) South African National Party politician, president 1989–94. Projecting himself as a pragmatic conservative who sought gradual reform of the apartheid system, he won the September 1989 elections for his party, but with a reduced majority. In February 1990 he ended the ban on the ▷African National Congress (ANC) opposition movement and released its effective leader Nelson ▷Mandela. By June 1991 he had repealed all racially discriminating laws. After a landslide victory for Mandela and the ANC in the first universal suffrage elections in April 1994, de Klerk became second executive deputy president. He shared the Nobel Prize for Peace in 1993 with Mandela for their work towards dismantling apartheid and negotiating the transition to a nonracial democracy.

Trained as a lawyer, he entered the South African parliament in 1972. He served in the cabinets of B J Vorster and P W Botha 1978–89, replacing Botha as party leader in February 1989 and as state president in August 1989.

He entered into negotiations with the ANC in December 1991, and in March 1992 a nationwide, whites-only referendum gave him a clear mandate to proceed with plans for major constitutional reform to end white minority rule. In February 1993 he and Mandela agreed to the formation of a government of national unity after multiracial elections in 1994, but in May 1995 he withdrew the National Party from the governing coalition in order to develop a 'strong and vigilant opposition'.

Despite winning the Nobel peace prize, De Klerk's reputation was badly damaged by revelations to the Truth and Reconciliation Commission, the body charged with exposing the truth about the apartheid years. In August 1997 de Klerk resigned as leader of the National Party claiming that he was retiring to rid the Afrikaner-dominated party of the remains of apartheid. He was succeeded by Marthinus van Schalkwyk in September 1997.

Related Web site: de Klerk, Frederik W http://www.nobel.se/peace/laureates/1993/klerk-bio.html

de Kooning, Willem (1904–1997) Dutch-born US painter. He emigrated to the USA in 1926 and worked as a commercial artist. After World War II he became, together with Jackson Pollock, one of the leaders of the abstract expressionist movement, although he retained figural images, painted with quick, violent brushstrokes. His *Women* series, exhibited in 1953, was criticized for its grotesque depictions of women.

EUGÈNE DELACROIX *Constantinople Captured by Crusaders*, painted by the French Romantic painter Eugène Delacroix in 1841. *The Art Archive*

Delacroix, (Ferdinand Victor) Eugène (1798–1863) French Romantic painter. His prolific output included religious and historical subjects and portraits of friends, among them the musicians Paganini and Chopin. Antagonistic to the French academic tradition, he evolved a highly coloured, fluid style, as in *The Death of Sardanapalus* (1829; Louvre, Paris).

de la Mare, Walter John (1873–1956) English poet and writer. His works include verse for children, such as *Peacock Pie* (1913), and the novels *The Three Royal Monkeys* (1910) (for children) and *The Memoirs of a Midget* (1921) (for adults). He excelled at creating a sense of eeriness and supernatural mystery. *The Listeners* (1912) established his reputation as a writer of delicately imaginative verse in the twin domains of childhood and dreamland.

Delaunay, Robert (1885–1941) French painter. He was a pioneer of abstract art. With his wife Sonia Delaunay-Terk, he developed a style known as ▷Orphism, an early variation of cubism, focusing on the effects of pure colour contrasts.

Delaunay-Terk, Sonia (1885–1979) French painter and textile designer. Born in Russia, she was active in Paris from 1905. With her husband Robert ▷Delaunay, she was a pioneer of abstract art.

De Laurentiis, Dino (1919–) Italian film producer. He has enjoyed a prolific but uneven career working in both Europe and the USA. He has produced films for some of the great European film-makers of the 1950s, 1960s, and 1970s, including Federico Fellini, Jean-Luc Godard, François Truffaut, and Ingmar Bergman.

Delaware (native name *Lenni Lenape*; 'original people' or 'truemen') American Indian people numbering about 10,000 (1997) and living primarily in Bartlesville, Oklahoma, with smaller groups in Wisconsin and Ontario. An Algonquian-speaking people, the Delaware originally lived in the Delaware River Valley for thousands of years. Other peoples called them 'grandfather', suggesting they were the ancestors of many ethnic groups in the area. The name Delaware derives from the first governor of Virginia, Sir Thomas West, Third Lord de la Warr. English colonists later used the term Delaware for the bay, the river, and the American Indians that lived there.

Related Web site: Delaware Tribe of Indians http://www.delawaretribeofindians.nsn.us

Delaware state in northeastern USA. It is nicknamed the First State or the Diamond State. Delaware ratified the US Constitution in 1787, becoming the first state in the Union, hence its nickname. It is one of the most industrialized states in the USA. It is bordered to the north by Pennsylvania, to the west and south by Maryland, with which it shares the upper part of the Delmarva Peninsula, and to the east by the Atlantic Ocean.

population (1996 est) 725,000 **area** 5,300 sq km/2,046 sq mi **capital** Dover **towns and cities** Wilmington, Newark **industries and products** dairy, poultry, and market-garden produce; fishing; chemicals, motor vehicles, and textiles

de la Warr, Thomas West (1577–1618) 3rd or 12th Baron de la Warr. English colonial administrator. Sent to North America as governor of Virginia in 1609, he arrived in 1610 just in time to prevent the desertion of the Jamestown colonists, and by 1611 had revitalized the settlement. He fell ill, returned to England, and died during his return voyage to the colony in 1618.

Both the river and state are named after him.

de Lesseps, Ferdinand, Vicomte French engineer; see ▷Lesseps, Ferdinand, Vicomte de Lesseps.

Delft town in South Holland province, the Netherlands, on the Schie Canal, 14 km/9 mi northwest of Rotterdam; population (1997) 94,000. It is known worldwide for its pottery and Delftware porcelain. Other industries include engineering, electronic equipment and cable production, and printing. There is a technical university, founded in 1863. The Dutch nationalist leader William the Silent was murdered here in 1584. It is the birthplace of the artists Jan Vermeer and Michiel van Miereveld.

Delhi (or Old Delhi) city of India, and administrative capital of the Union Territory of ▷Delhi (state); population (2001 est) 13,660,000. It borders on ▷New Delhi, capital of India, to the south. Manufactured goods include electronic goods, chemicals, and precision instruments, as well as traditional handicrafts such as hand-woven textiles and jewellery. An international airport is 13 km/8 mi away at Palam. The University of Delhi (1922) has over 20,000 students.

Delhi Union Territory of India from 1956, capital ▷Delhi; area 1,500 sq km/579 sq mi; population (1994) 9,500,000. It produces grain, sugar cane, fruit, and vegetables.

Delibes, (Clément Philibert) Léo (1836–1891) French composer. His lightweight, perfectly judged works include the ballet scores *Coppélia* (1870) and *Sylvia* (1876), and the opera *Lakmé* (1883).

Delilah In the Old Testament, the Philistine mistress of ▷Samson. Following instructions from the lords of the Philistines she sought to find the source of Samson's great strength. When Samson eventually revealed that his physical power lay in the length of his hair, she shaved his head while he slept and then delivered him into the hands of the Philistines.

deliquescence phenomenon of a substance absorbing so much moisture from the air that it ultimately dissolves in it to form a solution.

delirium in medicine, a state of acute confusion in which the subject is incoherent, frenzied, and out of touch with reality. It is often accompanied by delusions or hallucinations.

Delius, Frederick Theodore Albert (1862–1934) English composer. His haunting, richly harmonious works include the opera *A Village Romeo and Juliet* (1901); the choral pieces *Appalachia* (1903), *Sea Drift* (1904), and *A Mass of Life* (1905); orchestral works such as *In a Summer Garden* (1908) and *A Song of the High Hills* (1911); chamber music; and songs.

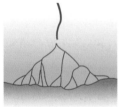

arcuate delta

bird's foot delta

DELTA An arcuate delta and a bird's foot delta. The Mississippi delta is an example of a bird's foot delta and the Ganges delta is an example of an arcuate delta.

de l'Orme, Philibert (c. 1505/10–1570) French architect. He is remembered principally as the author of two important architectural treatises, *Nouvelles Intentions* (1561) and *Architecture* (1567). His building work includes the tomb of Francis I in St Denis, begun in 1547, and extensions to the Château de Chenonceaux in the Loire Valley (1556–59), including the first storey of the picturesque covered bridge.

Delors, Jacques Lucien Jean (1925–) French socialist politician, economy and finance minister 1981–84 under François ▷Mitterrand's presidency, and president of the European Commission, 1985–94, when he oversaw significant budgetary reform, the introduction of the Single European Market, and the negotiation and ratification of the 1992 Maastricht Treaty on European Union.

Delphi city of ancient Greece, situated in a rocky valley north of the gulf of Corinth, on the southern slopes of Mount Parnassus, site of a famous ▷oracle in the temple of Apollo. The site was supposed to be the centre of the Earth and was marked by a conical stone, the *omphalos*. Towards the end of the 6th century BC the Athenian family of the Alcmaeonidae helped to rebuild the temple. The oracle was interpreted by priests from the inspired utterances of the Pythian priestess until it was closed down by the Roman emperor Theodosius I AD 390.

delphinium any of a group of plants containing about 250 species, including the butterfly or Chinese delphinium (*Delphinium grandiflorum*), an Asian form and one of the ancestors of the garden delphinium. Most species have blue, purple, or white flowers on a long spike. (Genus *Delphinium*, family Ranunculaceae.)

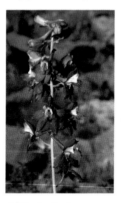

DELPHINIUM A larkspur *Delphinium scaposum* from the deserts of Arizona, USA. *Premaphotos Wildlife*

> **Anonymous**
> *Know thyself*
> Saying written on the wall of the ancient temple of Delphi

del Sarto, Andrea Italian Renaissance painter; see ▷Andrea del Sarto.

delta tract of land at a river's mouth, composed of silt deposited as the water slows on entering the sea. Familiar examples of large deltas are those of the Mississippi, Ganges and Brahmaputra, Rhône, Po, Danube, and Nile; the shape of the Nile delta is like the Greek letter *delta* Δ, and thus gave rise to the name.

The **arcuate delta** of the Nile is only one form. Others are **birdfoot deltas**, like that of the Mississippi which is a seaward extension of the river's ▷levee system; and **tidal deltas**, like that of the Mekong, in which most of the material is swept to one side by sea currents.

Delta Force US antiguerrilla force, based at Fort Bragg, North Carolina, and modelled on the British ▷Special Air Service.

demand in economics, the quantity of a product or service that customers want to buy at any given price. Also, the desire for a commodity, together with ability to pay for it.

demarcation in British industrial relations, the practice of stipulating that particular workers should perform particular tasks. The practice can be the source of industrial disputes.

dementia mental deterioration as a result of physical changes in the brain. It may be due to degenerative change, circulatory disease, infection, injury, or chronic poisoning. **Senile dementia**, a progressive loss of mental faculties such as memory and orientation, is typically a disease process of old age, and can be accompanied by ▷depression.

Dementia is distinguished from amentia, or severe congenital mental insufficiency.

demesne in the Middle Ages in Europe, land kept in the lord's possession, not leased out but, under the ▷feudal system, worked by ▷villeins to supply the lord's household.

Demeter in Greek mythology, the goddess of agriculture, especially corn (Roman ▷Ceres); daughter of the Titans Kronos and Rhea; and mother of ▷Persephone by Zeus. Demeter and her daughter were worshipped in a sanctuary at Eleusis, where the ▷Eleusinian Mysteries, one of the foremost ▷mystery religions of Greece, were celebrated.

DeMille, Agnes George (1909–1993) US dancer and choreographer. She introduced popular dance idioms into ballet with such works as *Rodeo* (1942). One of the most significant contributors to the American Ballet Theater, with dramatic ballets like *Fall River Legend* (1948), based on the Lizzie Borden murder case, she also led the change on Broadway to new-style musicals with her choreography of *Oklahoma!* (1943), *Carousel* (1945), and others.

De Mille, Cecil B(lount) (1881–1959) US film director and producer. He entered films in 1913 with Jesse L Lasky (with whom he later established Paramount Pictures), and was one of the founders of Hollywood. He specialized in lavish biblical epics, such as *The Sign of the Cross* (1932) and *The Ten Commandments* (1923), which he remade in 1956. His other films include *The King of Kings* (1927), *Cleopatra* (1934), *The Plainsman* (1936), *Samson and Delilah* (1949), and the 1952 Academy Award-winning *The Greatest Show on Earth*.

Demirel, Süleyman (1924–) Turkish politician, president from 1993. Leader from 1964 of the Justice Party, he was prime minister 1965–71, 1975–77, and 1979–80. He favoured links with the West, full membership of the European Union, and foreign investment in Turkish industry.

democracy (Greek *demos* 'the community', *kratos* 'sovereign power') government by the people, usually through elected representatives. In the modern world, democracy has developed from the American and French revolutions.

Types of democracy Representative **parliamentary government** existed in Iceland from the 10th century and in England from the 13th century, but the British working classes were excluded almost entirely from the ▷vote until 1867, and women were admitted and property qualifications abolished only in 1918.

In **direct democracy** the whole people meets for the making of laws or the direction of executive officers; for example, in Athens in the 5th century BC. Direct democracy today is represented mainly by the use of the ▷referendum, as in the UK, France, Switzerland, Liechtenstein, and Italy. The populist instrument of citizen's initiatives or propositions is used in certain states of the USA. The citizen's initiative is a bottom-up, grassroots device whereby proposed laws and constitutional changes are put to the public for approval.

The two concepts underlying **liberal democracy** are the right to representative government and the right to individual freedom. In practice the features of a liberal democratic system include representative institutions based on majority rule, through free elections and a choice of political parties; accountability of the government to the electorate; freedom of expression, assembly, and the individual, guaranteed by an independent judiciary; and limitations on the power of government.

> **Florence King**
> US writer
> *Democracy is the fig leaf of elitism.*
> Reflections in a Jaundiced Eye, 'Democracy'

Democratic Party one of the two main political parties of the USA. It tends to be the party of the working person, as opposed to the Republicans, the party of big business, but the divisions between the two are not clear cut. Its stronghold since the Civil War has traditionally been industrial urban centres and the Southern states, but conservative Southern Democrats were largely supportive of Republican positions in the 1980s and helped elect President Reagan. Bill Clinton became the first Democrat president for 13 years in 1993. The party lost control of both chambers of Congress to the Republicans in November 1994, and increasing numbers of Southern Democrat politicians later defected. However, in November 1996 Clinton became the first Democrat president since F D Roosevelt to be elected for a second term, winning 31 states, chiefly in the northeast and west.

Originally called Democratic Republicans, the party was founded by Thomas Jefferson in 1792 to defend the rights of the individual states against the centralizing policy of the Federalists. The party controlled all the Southern states that seceded from the Union in 1860–61. In the 20th century, under the presidencies of Grover Cleveland, Woodrow Wilson, Franklin D Roosevelt, Harry Truman, John F Kennedy, Lyndon B Johnson, Jimmy Carter, and Bill Clinton, the party has adopted more liberal social-reform policies than the Republicans.

From the 1930s, the Democratic Party pursued a number of policies that captured the hearts and minds of the US public, as well as making a significant contribution to their lives. They included Roosevelt's 'New Deal' and Kennedy's 'New Frontier' which was implemented by Lyndon Johnson. The 'New Deal' aimed at pulling the country out of the 1930s depression and putting it back to work, whereas the 'Great Society' programme – encompassing the Economic Opportunity Act, the Civil Rights Act 1964, the Medicare and Voting Rights Act 1965, and the Housing, Higher Education, and Equal Opportunities acts – sought to make the USA a better place for the ordinary, often disadvantaged, citizen.

The Democratic Party has never been a homogenous unit and in the early 1990s it comprised at least five significant factions: the southern conservative rump, the Conservative Democratic Forum (CDF); the northern liberals, moderate on military matters but interventionist on economic and social issues; the radical liberals of the Midwest agricultural states; the Trumanite 'Defense Democrats', liberal on economic and social matters but military hawks; and the non-Congressional fringe, led by Jesse ▷Jackson and seeking a 'rainbow' coalition of African-Americans, Hispanics, feminists, students, peace campaigners, and southern liberals.

Bill Clinton led a reformist 'New Democrat' wing of the party, centred around the Democratic Leadership Council (DLC), which is fiscally conservative, but liberal on social issues.

Related Web site: Democrat Party Online http://www.democrats.org/

Democritus (*c.* 460–*c.* 370 BC) Greek philosopher and speculative scientist who made a significant contribution to metaphysics with his atomic theory of the universe: all things originate from a vortex of tiny, indivisible particles, which he called atoms, and differ according to the shape and arrangement of their atoms.

demography study of the size, structure, dispersement, and development of human ▷populations to establish reliable statistics on such factors as birth and death rates, marriages and divorces, life expectancy, and migration. Demography is used to calculate life tables, which give the life expectancy of members of the population by sex and age.

de Morgan, William (Frend) (1839–1917) English pottery designer and novelist. He set up his own factory in 1888 in London, producing tiles and pottery painted with flora and fauna in a style typical of the ▷Arts and Crafts Movement. When he retired from the pottery industry, he began writing novels in the style of Charles Dickens. *Joseph Vance* (1906) was a great success; it was followed by six other novels.

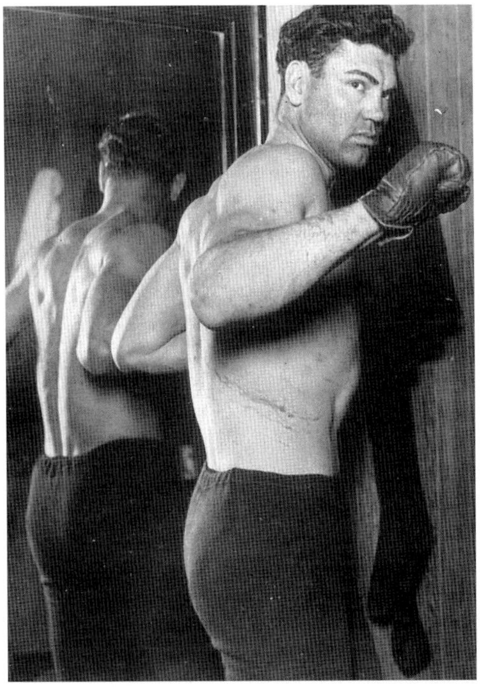

JACK DEMPSEY US heavyweight boxer Jack Dempsey in a fighting stance. *Archive Photos*

Demosthenes (*c.* 384–322 BC) Athenian politician, famed for his oratory. From 351 BC he led the party that advocated resistance to the growing power of ▷Philip of Macedon, and in his *Philippics*, a series of speeches, incited the Athenians to war. This policy resulted in the defeat of Chaeronea in 338 BC, and the establishment of Macedonian supremacy. After the death of Alexander he organized a revolt; when it failed, he took poison to avoid capture by the Macedonians.

Demosthenes
A man is his own easiest dupe, for what he wishes to be true he generally believes to be true.
Third Olynthiac 19

Related Web site: Demosthenes Against Leptines http://www.perseus.tufts.edu/cgi-bin/text?lookup=Dem.+20.init.

Demotic Greek common or vernacular variety of the modern ▷Greek language.

demotic script cursive (joined) writing derived from Egyptian hieratic script, itself a cursive form of ▷hieroglyphic. It was written horizontally, from right to left. Demotic documents are known from the 6th century BC to about AD 470.

Dempsey, Jack (William Harrison) (1895–1983) US heavyweight boxing champion, nicknamed 'the Manassa Mauler'. He beat Jess Willard in 1919 to win the title and held it until 1926, when he lost it to Gene Tunney. He engaged in the 'Battle of the Long Count' with Tunney in 1927.

Denbighshire (Welsh **Sir Ddinbych**) unitary authority in north Wales. A former county, between 1974 and 1996 it was largely merged, together with Flint and part of Merioneth, into Clwyd; a small area along the western border was included in Gwynedd.

area 844 sq km/326 sq mi **towns** Ruthin (administrative headquarters), Denbigh, Llangollen **physical** Clwydian range of mountains rises to a height of 555 m/1,820 ft, with ▷Offa's Dyke along the main ridge; rivers ▷Clwyd, Dee, Elwy **features** Denbigh and Rhuddlan castles; seaside resorts of Rhyl and Prestatyn **industries** agriculture (chiefly dairy), tourism **population** (1996) 91,000

Dench, Judi (Judith Olivia) (1934–) English actor. She made her professional debut as Ophelia in *Hamlet* (1957) with the Old Vic Company. Her Shakespearean roles include Viola in *Twelfth Night* (1969), Lady Macbeth (1976), and Cleopatra (1987). Her films include *Wetherby* (1985), *A Room with a View* (1986), *A Handful of Dust* (1988), *Mrs Brown* (1997), and *Shakespeare in Love* (1998). She was created a DBE in 1988.

dendrite part of a ▷nerve cell or neuron. The dendrites are slender filaments projecting from the cell body. They receive incoming messages from many other nerve cells and pass them on to the cell body.

If the combined effect of these messages is strong enough, the cell body will send an electrical impulse along the axon (the threadlike extension of a nerve cell). The tip of the axon passes its message to the dendrites of other nerve cells.

dendrochronology (or **tree-ring dating**) analysis of the ▷annual rings of trees to date past events by determining the age of timber. Since annual rings are formed by variations in the water-conducting cells produced by the plant during different seasons of the year, they also provide a means of establishing past climatic conditions in a given area.

Deneb (or **Alpha Cygni**) brightest star in the constellation ▷Cygnus, and the 20th-brightest star in the night sky. It is one of the greatest supergiant stars known, with a true luminosity of about 60,000 times that of the Sun. Deneb is 1,800 light years from the Sun.

Deneuve, Catherine (1943–) Born Catherine Dorléac. French actor. Graceful and elegant, she is one of the most famous French stars. Her breakthrough came with Jacques Demy's *Les Parapluies de Cherbourg/Umbrellas of Cherbourg* (1964); since then she has worked with a number of leading film-makers, including Luis Buñuel, Roman Polanski, and François Truffaut.

Deng Xiaoping (or **Teng Hsiao-ping**) (1904–1997) Chinese political leader. A member of the Chinese Communist Party (CCP) from the 1920s, he took part in the ▷Long March (1934–36). He was in the Politburo from 1955 until ousted in the ▷Cultural Revolution (1966–69). Reinstated in the 1970s, he gradually took power and introduced a radical economic modernization programme. He retired from the Politburo in 1987 and from his last official position (as chair of the State Military Commission) in March 1990. He was last seen in public in February 1994. He appointed President Jiang Zemin to succeed him on his death in 1997.

Deng, born in Sichuan province into a middle-class landlord family, joined the CCP as a student in Paris, where he adopted the name Xiaoping ('Little Peace') in 1925, and studied in Moscow in 1926. After the Long March, he served as a political commissar to the People's Liberation Army during the civil war of 1937–49. He entered the CCP Politburo in 1955 and headed the secretariat during the early 1960s, working closely with President Liu Shaoqi. During the Cultural Revolution Deng was dismissed as a 'capitalist roader' and sent to work in a tractor factory in Nanchang for 're-education'.

Deng was rehabilitated by his patron ▷Zhou Enlai in 1973 and served as acting prime minister after Zhou's heart attack in 1974. On Zhou's death in January 1976 he was forced into hiding but returned to office as vice premier in July 1977. By December 1978, although nominally a CCP vice chair, state vice premier, and Chief of Staff to the PLA, Deng was the controlling force in China. His policy of 'socialism with Chinese characteristics', misinterpreted in the West as a drift to capitalism, had success in rural areas. He helped to oust ▷Hua Guofeng in favour of his protégés ▷Hu Yaobang (later in turn ousted) and ▷Zhao Ziyang.

His reputation, both at home and in the West, was tarnished by his sanctioning of the army's massacre of more than 2,000 prodemocracy demonstrators in ▷Tiananmen Square, Beijing, in June 1989. When Deng officially retired from his party and army posts, he claimed to have renounced political involvement, but in 1992 publicly announced his support for market-oriented economic reforms. A subsequent purge of military leaders was later claimed to have been carried out at Deng's instigation.

Deng Xiaoping
Practice is the sole criterion for testing truth.
Pragmatic dictum associated with Deng

denier unit used in measuring the fineness of yarns, equal to the mass in grams of 9,000 metres of yarn. Thus 9,000 metres of 15 denier nylon, used in nylon stockings, weighs 15 g/0.5 oz, and in this case the thickness of thread would be 0.00425 mm/0.0017 in. The term is derived from the French silk industry; the *denier* was an old French silver coin.

denim cotton twill fabric with coloured warp (lengthwise yarns) and undyed weft, originating in France (hence the name 'de Nîmes'). In its most classic form, indigo blue and heavyweight, it is used for jeans and dungarees. It became fashionable in the early 1970s, and many variations followed, including lighter-weight dress fabrics and stone-washed, overdyed, and brushed finishes in many colours.

De Niro, Robert (1943–) US actor. He has frequently appeared in the works of the film-maker Martin ▷Scorsese; for example, *Taxi Driver* (1976). He won Academy Awards for his performances in *The Godfather Part II* (1974) and *Raging Bull* (1980), in which he played a boxer struggling to control his emotional aggression. He is known for his total immersion in his screen roles.

Born in New York, New York, De Niro's first critical success was *Bang the Drum Slowly* (1973), and in the same year he began his long association with Scorsese in *Mean Streets*. It was his role in Francis ▷Coppola's *The Godfather Part II* which cemented his reputation as a powerful method actor.

His magnetism and physical presence can also be seen in, among others, *The Deer Hunter* (1978), *The Untouchables* (1987), *GoodFellas* (1990), *Casino* (1995), and *Heat* (1995). In 2000, he appeared in *Meet the Parents* and *Men of Honor*. He owns a production company based in New York, called the Tribeca Film Center, and De Niro made his directorial debut with *A Bronx Tale* in 1993.

denitrification process occurring naturally in soil, where bacteria break down ▷nitrates to give nitrogen gas, which returns to the atmosphere.

Denktaş, Rauf R (1924–) Turkish-Cypriot nationalist politician. In 1975 the Turkish Federated State of Cyprus (TFSC) was formed in the northern third of the island, with Denktaş as its head, and in 1983 he became president of the breakaway Turkish Republic of Northern Cyprus (TRNC). He was re-elected in 1995, and survived a heart attack in March 1996.

Denmark see country box.

Denpasar capital town of Bali in the Lesser Sunda Islands of Indonesia; population (1995 est) 435,000. Industries include food processing, machinery, papermaking and printing, and handicrafts. There is a university (1962) and, housed in the temple and palace, a museum of Balinese art.

density measure of the compactness of a substance; it is equal to its mass per unit volume and is measured in kg per cubic metre/lb per cubic foot. Density is a ▷scalar quantity. The average density D of a mass m occupying a volume V is given by the formula:

Denmark

Denmark peninsula and islands in northern Europe, bounded to the north by the Skagerrak, east by the Kattegat, south by Germany, and west by the North Sea.

NATIONAL NAME *Kongeriget Danmark/Kingdom of Denmark*
AREA 43,075 sq km/16,631 sq mi
CAPITAL Copenhagen
MAJOR TOWNS/CITIES Århus, Odense, Ålborg, Esbjerg, Randers, Kolding, Horsens
MAJOR PORTS Århus, Odense, Ålborg, Esbjerg
PHYSICAL FEATURES comprises the Jutland peninsula and about 500 islands (100 inhabited) including Bornholm in the Baltic Sea; the land is flat and cultivated; sand dunes and lagoons on the west coast and long inlets on the east; the main island is Sjæland (Zealand), where most of Copenhagen is located (the rest is on the island of Amager)
TERRITORIES the dependencies of Faroe Islands and Greenland

Government

HEAD OF STATE Queen Margrethe II from 1972
HEAD OF GOVERNMENT Anders Fogh Rasmussen from 2001
POLITICAL SYSTEM liberal democracy
POLITICAL EXECUTIVE parliamentary

ADMINISTRATIVE DIVISIONS 14 counties, one city and one borough
ARMED FORCES 22,700; plus 64,900 reservists (2002)
CONSCRIPTION 4–12 months (up to 24 months in certain ranks)
DEATH PENALTY abolished in 1978
DEFENCE SPEND (% GDP) 1.6 (2002 est)
EDUCATION SPEND (% GDP) 8.2 (2001 est)
HEALTH SPEND (% GDP) 8.3 (2000 est)

Economy and resources

CURRENCY Danish krone
GPD (US$) 174.8 billion (2002 est)
REAL GDP GROWTH (% change on previous year) 1 (2001)
GNI (US$) 162.7 billion (2002 est)
GNI PER CAPITA (PPP) (US$) 29,450 (2002 est)
CONSUMER PRICE INFLATION 1.9% (2003 est)
UNEMPLOYMENT 5.2% (2001)
MAJOR TRADING PARTNERS EU (principally Germany, Sweden, UK, and France), Norway, USA, Finland, Japan

RESOURCES crude petroleum, natural gas, salt, limestone
INDUSTRIES mining, food processing, fisheries, machinery, textiles, furniture, electronic goods and transport equipment, chemicals and pharmaceuticals, printing and publishing
EXPORTS machinery and parts, pig meat and pork products, other food products, fish, industrial machinery, chemicals, transport equipment. Principal market: Germany 18.9% (2000)
IMPORTS food and live animals, machinery, transport equipment, iron, steel, electronics, petroleum, cereals, paper. Principal source: Germany 21.3% (2000)
ARABLE LAND 53.8% (2000 est)
AGRICULTURAL PRODUCTS wheat, rye, barley, oats, potatoes, sugar beet, dairy products; livestock production (pigs) and dairy products; fishing

Population and society

POPULATION 5,384,000 (2003 est)
POPULATION GROWTH RATE 0.1% (2000–15)
POPULATION DENSITY (per sq km) 125 (2003 est)
URBAN POPULATION (% of total) 85 (2003 est)
AGE DISTRIBUTION (% of total population) 0–14 18%, 15–59 62%, 60+ 20% (2002 est)
ETHNIC GROUPS all Danes are part of the Scandinavian ethnic group, Eskimo, Faroese, German
LANGUAGE Danish (official), German
RELIGION Evangelical Lutheran 87% (national church), other Protestant and Roman Catholic 3%
EDUCATION (compulsory years) 9
LITERACY RATE 99% (men); 99% (women) (2003 est)
LABOUR FORCE 3.6% agriculture, 26.6% industry, 69.8% services (1998)
LIFE EXPECTANCY 74 (men); 79 (women) (2000–05)
CHILD MORTALITY RATE (under 5, per 1,000 live births) 4 (2001)
PHYSICIANS (per 1,000 people) 3.4 (1999 est)
HOSPITAL BEDS (per 1,000 people) 4.5 (1999 est)
TV SETS (per 1,000 people) 875 (2001 est)
RADIOS (per 1,000 people) 1,400 (2001 est)
INTERNET USERS (per 10,000 people) 4,651.8 (2002 est)
PERSONAL COMPUTER USERS (per 100 people) 57.7 (2002 est)

See also ▷Faroe Islands; ▷Greenland; ▷Norway; ▷Sweden.

Chronology

5th–6th centuries: Danes migrated from Sweden.

8th–10th centuries: Viking raids throughout Europe.

c. 940–85: Harald Bluetooth unified Kingdom of Denmark and established Christianity.

1014–35: King Canute I created an empire embracing Denmark, Norway, and England; the empire collapsed after his death.

12th century: Denmark re-emerged as dominant Baltic power.

1340–75: Valdemar IV restored order after a period of civil war and anarchy.

1397: Union of Kalmar: Denmark, Sweden, and Norway (with Iceland) united under a single monarch.

1449: Sweden broke away from union.

1536: Lutheranism established as official religion of Denmark.

1563–70: Unsuccessful war to recover Sweden. There were two further unsuccessful attempts to reclaim Sweden, 1643–45 and 1657–60.

1625–29: Denmark sided with Protestants in Thirty Years' War.

1665: Frederick III made himself absolute monarch.

1729: Greenland became a Danish province.

1780–81: Denmark, Russia, and Sweden formed 'Armed Neutrality' coalition to protect neutral shipping during the American revolution.

1788: Serfdom abolished.

1800: France persuaded Denmark to revive Armed Neutrality against British blockade.

1801: First Battle of Copenhagen: much of Danish fleet destroyed by British navy.

1807: Second Battle of Copenhagen: British seized rebuilt fleet to pre-empt Danish entry into Napoleonic War on French side.

1814: Treaty of Kiel: Denmark ceded Norway to Sweden as penalty for supporting France in Napoleonic War; Denmark retained Iceland.

1849: Liberal pressure compelled Frederick VII to grant a democratic constitution.

1914–1919: Denmark neutral during World War I.

1918: Iceland achieved full self-government.

1929–40: Welfare state established under left-wing coalition government dominated by Social Democrat Party.

1940–45: German occupation.

1944: Iceland declared independence.

1949: Denmark became a founding member of the North Atlantic Treaty Organization (NATO).

1960: Denmark joined the European Free Trade Association (EFTA).

1973: Denmark withdrew from EFTA and joined the European Economic Community (EEC).

1981: Greenland achieved full self-government.

1992: A referendum rejected the Maastricht Treaty on European union; it was approved in 1993 after the government negotiated a series of 'opt-out' clauses.

1993: Conservative leader Poul Schlüter resigned as prime minister due to a legal scandal.

1994: Schlüter was succeeded as prime minister by Poul Rasmussen, who, leading a Social Democrat-led coalition, won the general election.

1998: The government won a slim majority in assembly elections. A referendum endorsed the Amsterdam European Union (EU) treaty.

2000: A referendum rejected joining Europe's single currency and adopting the euro.

2001: Anders Fogh Rasmussen became prime minister

DENMARK Copenhagen, the capital and main port of Denmark. The commercial and cultural centre of the country, it has shipbuilding, brewing, and chemical industries. *Corel*

$D = m/V$

▷Relative density is the ratio of the density of a substance to that of water at 4°C/39.2°F.

In photography, density refers to the degree of opacity of a negative; in electricity, current density is the amount of current passing through a cross-sectional area of a conductor (usually given in amperes per sq in or per sq cm).

dental caries in medicine, another name for ▷caries.

dental formula way of showing the number of teeth in an animal's mouth. The dental formula consists of eight numbers separated by a line into two rows. The four above the line represent the teeth on one side of the upper jaw, starting at the front. If this reads 2 1 2 3 (as for humans) it means two incisors, one canine, two premolars, and three molars (see ▷tooth). The numbers below the line represent the lower jaw. The total number of teeth can be calculated by adding up all the numbers and multiplying by two.

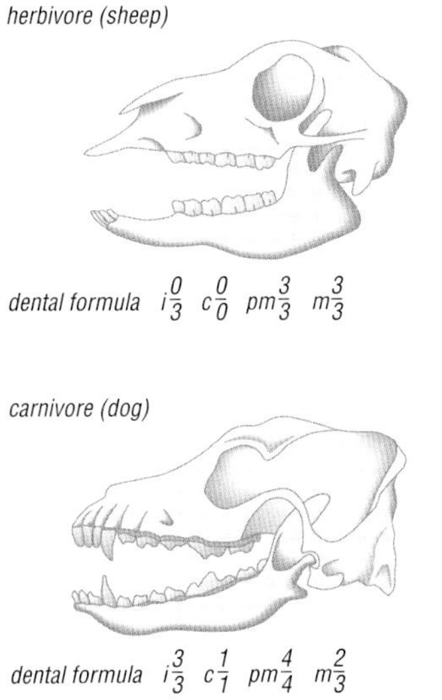
herbivore (sheep)
dental formula $i\frac{0}{3}$ $c\frac{0}{0}$ $pm\frac{3}{3}$ $m\frac{3}{3}$
carnivore (dog)
dental formula $i\frac{3}{3}$ $c\frac{1}{1}$ $pm\frac{4}{4}$ $m\frac{2}{3}$

DENTAL FORMULA The dentition and dental formulae of a typical herbivore (sheep) and carnivore (dog). The dog has long pointed canines for puncturing and gripping its prey and has modified premolars and molars (carnassials) for shearing flesh. In the sheep, by contrast, there is a wide gap, or diastema, between the incisors, developed for cutting through blades of grass, and the grinding premolars and molars; the canines are absent.

dentistry care and treatment of the teeth and gums. **Orthodontics** deals with the straightening of the teeth for aesthetic and clinical reasons, and **periodontics** with care of the supporting tissue (bone and gums).

The bacteria that start the process of dental decay are normal, nonpathogenic members of a large and varied group of micro-organisms present in the mouth. They are strains of oral streptococci, and it is only in the presence of sucrose (from refined sugar) in the mouth that they become damaging to the teeth. ▷Fluoride in the water supply has been one attempted solution to prevent decay, and in 1979 a vaccine was developed from a modified form of the bacterium *Streptococcus mutans*.

The earliest dental school was opened in Baltimore, Maryland, USA, in 1839. In the UK the predecessors of the modern University College Hospital Dental School and Royal Dental Hospital and School, both within the University of London, were established in 1859 and 1860. An International Dental Federation was founded in 1900.

Since 1945 there has been a significant improvement in dental health in the UK. In 1988, 21% of adults had no natural teeth (30% in 1978), and, on average, each adult had 8.4 filled teeth.

Related Web site: Dentistry Now http://www.DentistryNow.com/Mainpage.htm

dentition type and number of teeth in a species. Different kinds of teeth have different functions; a grass-eating animal will have large molars for grinding its food, whereas a meat-eater will need powerful canines for catching and killing its prey. The teeth that are less useful to an animal's lifestyle may be reduced in size or missing altogether. An animal's dentition is represented diagrammatically by a ▷dental formula.

Denver city and capital of ▷Colorado, USA, on the South Platte River, on the western edge of the Great Plains, 24 km/15 mi from the foothills of the Rocky Mountains; population (2000 est) 554,600; Denver–Boulder metropolitan area (1994 est) 2,190,000. At 1,609 m/5,280 ft above sea level, it is known as 'Mile High City'. Denver is the commercial, manufacturing, and transportation centre for the central west region of the USA.

Related Web site: Denver Online http://www.denveronline.com/

deodar Himalayan ▷cedar tree, often planted as a rapid-growing ornamental. Its fragrant, durable wood is valuable as timber. (*Cedrus deodara*, family Pinaceae.)

deontology ethical theory that the rightness of an action consists in its conformity to duty, regardless of the consequences that may result from it. Deontological ethics is thus opposed to any form of utilitarianism or pragmatism.

deoxyribonucleic acid full name of ▷DNA.

De Palma, Brian (Russell) (1940–) US film director. Frequently derided by critics for being derivative of Hitchcock, De Palma is nevertheless a technical master of the cinematic medium, as shown in such films as *Dressed to Kill* (1980) and *Mission: Impossible* (1996).

Depardieu, Gérard (1948–) French actor. His imposing physique and screen presence won him international acclaim as the eponymous hero in *Cyrano de Bergerac* (1990).

His other films include *Les Valseuses/Going Places* (1974), *Novecento/1900* (1977), *Le Camion/The Truck* (1977), *Buffet Froid* (1979), *Le Dernier métro/The Last Metro* (1980), *Le Retour de Martin Guerre/The Return of Martin Guerre* (1981), *Jean de Florette* (1985), *Camille Claudel* (1988), *Hélas pour moi* (1993), *Le Colonel Chabert* (1994) and *Vatel* (2000).

deportation expulsion from a country of an alien who is living there illegally, or whose presence is considered contrary to the public good.

deposit account in banking, an account in which money is left to attract interest, sometimes for a fixed term. Unlike a current account, the deposit account does not give constant access.

deposition in Christian art, a depiction of the body of Christ being taken down from the cross. Notable examples include van der Weyden's *Deposition* (*c.* 1430; Prado, Madrid) and Ruben's *Descent from the Cross* (1612–14; Notre Dame Cathedral, Antwerp).

Depp, Johnny (1963–) US film actor. He became famous as a teen idol in the television series *21 Jump Street* but went on to gain critical acclaim in adult roles, often as lost, brooding eccentrics. He has collaborated on several films with US film director Tim Burton, resulting in starring roles in films such as *Edward Scissorhands* (1990), *Ed Wood* (1994), and *Sleepy Hollow* (1999).

depreciation in economics, the decline of a currency's value in relation to other currencies. Depreciation also describes the fall in value of an asset (such as factory machinery) resulting from age, wear and tear, or other circumstances. It is an important factor in assessing company profits and tax liabilities.

depression in economics, a period of low output and investment, with high unemployment. Specifically, the term describes two periods of crisis in world economy: 1873–96 and 1929 to the mid-1930s.

The term is most often used to refer to the world economic crisis precipitated by the ▷Wall Street crash of 29 October 1929 when millions of dollars were wiped off US share values in a matter of hours. This forced the closure of many US banks involved in stock speculation and led to the recall of US overseas investments. This loss of US credit had serious repercussions on the European economy, especially that of Germany, and led to a steep fall in the levels of international trade as countries attempted to protect their domestic economies. Although most European countries experienced a slow recovery during the mid-1930s, the main impetus for renewed economic growth was provided by rearmament programmes later in the decade.

The Depression of 1873–96 centred on falling growth rates in the British economy but also affected industrial activity in Germany and the USA. The crisis in the British economy is now thought to have lasted longer than these dates suggest.

depression in medicine, an emotional state characterized by sadness, unhappy thoughts, apathy, and dejection. Sadness is a normal response to major losses such as bereavement or unemployment. After childbirth, ▷postnatal depression is common. Clinical depression, which is prolonged or unduly severe, often requires treatment, such as ▷antidepressant medication, ▷cognitive therapy, or, in very rare cases, ▷electroconvulsive therapy (ECT), in which an electrical current is passed through the brain.

Periods of depression may alternate with periods of high optimism, over-enthusiasm, and confidence. This is the manic phase in a disorder known as **manic depression** or **bipolar disorder**. A manic depressive state is one in which a person switches repeatedly from one extreme to the other. Each mood can last for weeks or months. Typically, the depressive state lasts longer than the manic phase.

depression (or **cyclone** or **low**) in meteorology, a region of relatively low atmospheric pressure. In mid latitudes a depression forms as warm, moist air from the tropics mixes with cold, dry polar air, producing warm and cold boundaries (▷fronts) and unstable weather – low cloud and drizzle, showers, or fierce storms. The warm air, being less dense, rises above the cold air to produce the area of low pressure on the ground. Air spirals in towards the centre of the depression in an anticlockwise direction in the northern hemisphere, clockwise in the southern hemisphere, generating winds up to gale force. Depressions tend to travel eastwards and can remain active for several days.

A deep depression is one in which the pressure at the centre is very much lower than that round about; it produces very strong winds, as opposed to a shallow depression, in which the winds are comparatively light. A severe depression in the tropics is called a ▷hurricane, tropical **cyclone**, or typhoon, and is a great danger to shipping; a ▷tornado is a very intense, rapidly swirling depression, with a diameter of only a few hundred metres or so.

De Quincey, Thomas (1785–1859) English writer. His works include *Confessions of an English Opium-Eater* (1821) and the essays 'On the Knocking at the Gate in Macbeth' (1825) and 'On Murder Considered as One of the Fine Arts' (in three parts, 1827, 1839, and 1854). He was a friend of the poets William ▷Wordsworth and Samuel Taylor ▷Coleridge, and his work had a powerful influence on Charles Baudelaire and Edgar Allan Poe, among others.

Derain, André (1880–1954) French painter. He experimented with the strong, almost primary colours associated with ▷fauvism but later developed a more sombre landscape and figurative style. *Pool of London* (1906; Tate Gallery, London) is a typical work. He also produced costumes and scenery for Diaghilev's Ballets Russes.

Derby City industrial city and unitary authority in north central England, on the River Derwent, 200 km/124 mi north of London; the city was part of the county of Derbyshire until 1997.

area 87 sq km/34 sq mi **features** Derby Cathedral, originally a parish church, was rebuilt in the 18th century but retains its 16th-century tower; the University of Derby was established in 1993; the museum collections of Royal Crown Derby porcelain (Royal Doulton) and the Rolls-Royce collection of aero-engines **industries** engineering, chemicals, paper, textiles, plastics; financial services **population** (1996) 218,800 **famous people** Herbert Spencer, Joseph Wright

Related Web site: Derby Tourist Information Web Site http://www.derby.gov.uk/

Derby, Edward (George Geoffrey Smith) Stanley (1799–1869) 14th Earl of Derby. British politician. He was leader of the Conservative Party 1846–68 and prime minister 1852, 1858–59, and 1866–68, each time as head of a minority government. Originally a Whig, he became secretary for the colonies in 1830, and introduced the bill for the abolition of slavery. He joined the Tories in 1834, serving as secretary for war and the colonies in Peel's government. Derby was a protectionist and the split the Tory party over Peel's free-trade policy gave him the leadership for 20 years. During his third adminstration, the second Reform Act (1867) was passed. He inherited the title of Lord Stanley in 1834, became a peer in 1844, and succeeded to the earldom in 1851.

Derbyshire county of north central England (since April 1997 Derby City has been a separate unitary authority).

area 2,550 sq km/984 sq mi **towns and cities** ▷Matlock (administrative headquarters), Buxton, Chesterfield, Glossop, Ilkeston, Long Eaton **physical** Peak District National Park (including Kinder Scout 636 m/2,088 ft); rivers Dane, Derwent, Dove, Goyt, Rother, Trent, Wye; Dove Dale **features** Chatsworth House, Bakewell (seat of the Duke of Devonshire); Haddon Hall; Hardwick Hall; Kedleston Hall

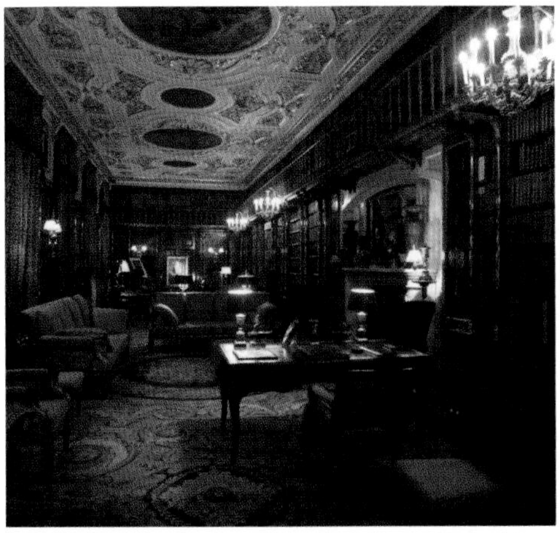

DERBYSHIRE The library at Chatsworth House, Derbyshire, England. *Image Bank*

(designed by Robert Adam); well-dressing at Tissington, Wirksworth, Eyam, and other villages; Castleton Caverns **agriculture** cereals, root crops, and dairy farming (in the south); sheep farming (in the northern hills) **industries** heavy engineering; manufacturing (cotton, hosiery, lace, porcelain, textiles); mineral and metal working (barytes, gypsum, lead, zinc); quarrying (marble, sandstone, pipeclay); motor cars; limestone quarrying **population** (1996) 962,000 **famous people** Thomas Cook, Marquess Curzon of Kedleston, Samuel Richardson

deregulation action to abolish or reduce government controls and supervision of private economic activities, with the aim of improving competitiveness. In Britain, the major changes in the City of London in 1986 (the ▷Big Bang) were in part deregulation. Another UK example was the Building Societies Act 1985 that enabled building societies to compete in many areas with banks.

derivative (or **differential coefficient**) in mathematics, the limit of the gradient of a chord linking two points on a curve as the distance between the points tends to zero; for a function of a single variable, $y = f(x)$, it is denoted by $f'(x)$, $Df(x)$, or dy/dx, and is equal to the gradient of the curve.

dermatitis inflammation of the skin (see ▷eczema), usually related to allergy. **Dermatosis** refers to any skin disorder and may be caused by contact or systemic problems.

dermatology medical speciality concerned with the diagnosis and treatment of skin disorders.

derrick simple lifting machine consisting of a pole carrying a block and tackle. Derricks are commonly used on ships that carry freight. In the oil industry the tower used for hoisting the drill pipes is known as a derrick.

derris climbing leguminous plant (see ▷legume) of southeast Asia. Its roots contain rotenone, a strong insecticide. (*Derris elliptica*, family Fabaceae.)

de Ruyter, Michiel Adriaanszoon Dutch admiral; see Michiel Adriaanszoon de ▷Ruyter.

dervish in Iran and Turkey, a religious mendicant; throughout the rest of Islam a member of an Islamic religious brotherhood, not necessarily mendicant in character. The Arabic equivalent is **fakir**. There are various orders of dervishes, each with its rule and special ritual. The 'whirling dervishes' claim close communion with the deity through ecstatic dancing, reaching spiritual awareness with a trancelike state created by continual whirling. The spinning symbolizes the Earth's orbit of the Sun. 'Howling dervishes' gash themselves with knives to demonstrate the miraculous feats possible to those who trust in Allah.

Derwent river in North Yorkshire, northeast England; length 92 km/57 mi. Rising in the North Yorkshire moors, it flows south through Malton and joins the River Ouse southeast of Selby.

Desai, Anita (1937–) Born Anita Mazumdar. Indian novelist. Her calm, sensitive, and often humorous style is much admired. She won international fame and popularity with *Fire on the Mountain* (1977) and *Clear Light of Day* (1980) and with the imaginative stories of the tension within families in *Games at Twilight* (1978). *Clear Light of Day*, *In Custody* (1984), and *Fasting, Feasting* (1999) were shortlisted for the Booker Prize. She won the Guardian Award for Children's Fiction in 1982 for *The Village by the Sea*.

desalination removal of salt, usually from sea water, to produce fresh water for irrigation or drinking. Distillation has usually been the method adopted, but in the 1970s a cheaper process, using certain polymer materials that filter the molecules of salt from the water by reverse osmosis, was developed.

De Savary, Peter John (1944–) English entrepreneur. He acquired Land's End, Cornwall, England, in 1987 and built a theme park there. He revived Falmouth dock and the port of Hayle in north Cornwall.

Descartes, René (1596–1650) French philosopher and mathematician. He believed that commonly accepted knowledge was doubtful because of the subjective nature of the senses, and attempted to rebuild human knowledge using as his foundation the dictum *cogito ergo sum* ('I think, therefore I am'). He also believed that the entire material universe could be explained in terms of mathematical physics, and founded coordinate geometry as a way of defining and manipulating geometrical shapes by means of algebraic expressions. ▷Cartesian coordinates, the means by which points are represented in this system, are named after him. Descartes also established the science of optics, and helped to shape contemporary theories of astronomy and animal behaviour.

Descartes identified the 'thinking thing' (*res cogitans*), or mind, with the human soul or consciousness; the body, though somehow interacting with the soul, was a physical machine, secondary to, and in principle separable from, the soul. He held that everything has a cause; nothing can result from nothing. He believed that, although all matter is in motion, matter does not move of its own accord; the initial impulse comes from God. He also postulated two quite distinct substances: spatial substance, or matter, and thinking substance, or mind. This is called 'Cartesian dualism', and it preserved him from serious controversy with the church.

Related Web site: Descartes, René http://www.newadvent.org/cathen/04744b.htm

René Descartes

Commonsense is the most widely distributed commodity in the world, for everyone thinks himself so well endowed with it.

Le discours de la méthode

desert arid area with sparse vegetation (or, in rare cases, almost no vegetation). Soils are poor, and many deserts include areas of shifting sands. Deserts can be either hot or cold. Almost 33% of the Earth's land surface is desert, and this proportion is increasing.

The **tropical desert** belts of latitudes from 5° to 30° are caused by the descent of air that is heated over the warm land and therefore has lost its moisture. Other natural desert types are the **continental deserts**, such as the Gobi, that are too far from the sea to receive any moisture; **rain-shadow deserts**, such as California's Death Valley, that lie in the lee of mountain ranges, where the ascending air drops its rain only on the windward slopes; and **coastal deserts**, such as the Namib, where cold ocean currents cause local dry air masses to descend. Desert surfaces are usually rocky or gravelly, with only a small proportion being covered with sand. Deserts can be created by changes in climate, or by the human-aided process of desertification.

Characteristics common to all deserts include irregular rainfall of less than 250 mm/9.75 in per year, very high evaporation rates of often 20 times the annual precipitation, and low relative humidity and cloud cover. Temperatures are more variable; tropical deserts have a big diurnal temperature range and very high daytime temperatures (58°C/136.4°F) has been recorded at Azizia in Libya), whereas mid-latitude deserts have a wide annual range and much lower winter temperatures (in the Mongolian desert the mean temperature is below freezing point for half the year).

Desert soils are infertile, lacking in ▷humus and generally grey or red in colour. The few plants capable of surviving such conditions are widely spaced, scrubby and often thorny. Long-rooted plants (phreatophytes) such as the date palm and musquite commonly grow along dry stream channels. Salt-loving plants (▷halophytes) such as saltbushes grow in areas of highly saline soils and near the edges of ▷playas (dry saline lakes). Others, such as the ▷xerophytes are drought-resistant and survive by remaining leafless during the dry season or by reducing water losses with small waxy leaves. They frequently have shallow and widely branching root systems and store water during the wet season (for example, succulents and cacti with pulpy stems).

desertification spread of deserts by changes in climate, or by human-aided processes. Desertification can sometimes be reversed by special planting (marram grass, trees) and by the use of water-absorbent plastic grains, which, added to the soil, enable crops to be grown. About 30% of land worldwide is affected by desertification (1998), including 1 million hectares in Africa and 1.4 million hectares in Asia.

Desert Storm, Operation code-name of the military action to eject the Iraqi army from Kuwait during 1991. The build-up phase was code-named **Operation Desert Shield** and lasted from August 1990, when Kuwait was first invaded by Iraq, to January 1991 when Operation Desert Storm was unleashed, starting the ▷Gulf War. Desert Storm ended with the defeat of the Iraqi army in the Kuwaiti theatre of operations in late February 1991. The cost of the operation was $53 billion.

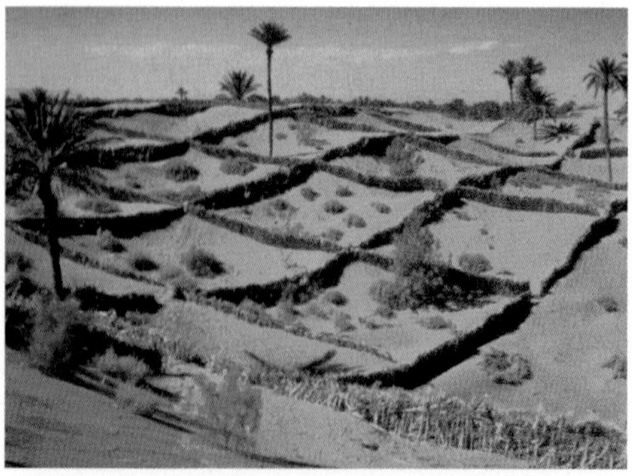

DESERTIFICATION Palm and tamarisk trees are planted inside a barrier in an attempt to stabilize the encroaching sand dunes on a palm plantation in southern Morocco and so show the process of desertification. *Premaphotos Wildlife*

De Sica, Vittorio (1901–1974) Italian film director and actor. His *Ladri di biciclette/Bicycle Thieves* (1949) is a landmark of Italian neo-realism. Later films include *Umberto D* (1955), *Two Women* (1960), and *The Garden of the Finzi-Continis* (1971). His acting credits include *The Earrings of Madame de …* (1953) and *The Millionaires* (1960).

desktop publishing (DTP) use of microcomputers for small-scale typesetting and page makeup. DTP systems are capable of producing camera-ready pages (pages ready for photographing and printing), made up of text and graphics, with text set in different typefaces and sizes. The page can be previewed on the screen before final printing on a laser printer.

A DTP program is able to import text and graphics from other packages; run text as columns, over pages, and around artwork and other insertions; enable a wide range of ▷fonts; and allow accurate positioning of all elements required to make a page.

Related Web site: Ultimate Electronic Publishing Resource http://desktoppublishing.com/

Des Moines capital city of ▷Iowa, USA, on the Des Moines River (a tributary of the Mississippi); seat of Polk County; population (1998 est) 193,200. It is a major road, railway, and air centre for the surrounding Corn Belt region; most of the manufacturing industry is connected with agriculture. Des Moines is the third largest centre in the world for the insurance industry, after London, England, and Hartford, Connecticut.

Desmoulins, (Lucie Simplice) Camille (Benoist) (1760–1794) French revolutionary who summoned the mob to arms on 12 July 1789, so precipitating the revolt that culminated in the storming of the Bastille. A prominent left-wing ▷Jacobin, he was elected to the National Convention in 1792. His *Histoire des Brissotins* was largely responsible for the overthrow of the right-wing ▷Girondins, but shortly after he was sent to the guillotine as too moderate.

de Soto, Hernando (*c.* 1496–1542) Spanish explorer who sailed with Pedro Arias de Avila (*c.* 1440–1531) to Darien, Central America, in 1519, explored the Yucatán Peninsula in 1528, and travelled with Francisco Pizarro in Peru 1530–35. In 1538 he was made governor of Cuba and Florida. In his expedition of 1539 he explored Florida, Georgia, and the Mississippi River.

Desprez, Josquin Franco-Flemish composer; see ▷Josquin Desprez.

Dessalines, Jean Jacques (*c.* 1758–1806) Emperor of Haiti 1804–06. Born in Guinea, he was taken to Haiti as a slave, where in 1802 he succeeded ▷Toussaint L'Ouverture as leader of the black revolt against the French. After defeating the French, he proclaimed Haiti's independence and made himself emperor. He was killed when trying to suppress an uprising provoked by his cruelty.

Dessau, Paul (1894–1979) German composer. His work includes incidental music to Bertolt Brecht's theatre pieces; an opera, *Der Verurteilung des Lukullus/The Trial of Lucullus* (1949), also to a libretto by Brecht; and numerous choral works and songs.

destroyer small, fast warship designed for antisubmarine work. Destroyers played a critical role in the convoy system in World War II.

detective fiction novel or short story in which a mystery is solved mainly by the action of a professional or amateur detective. Where the mystery to be solved concerns a crime, the work may be called **crime fiction**. The traditional formula for the detective story starts with a seemingly intractable mystery, typically a murder, features the astute, often unconventional detective, a wrongly accused suspect to whom the circumstantial evidence points, and concludes with a startling or unexpected denouement, during which the detective explains how he or she arrived at the mystery's solution.

détente (French) reduction of political tension and the easing of strained relations between nations, as seen in the ending of the ▷Cold War 1989–90. The term was first used in the 1970s to describe the new easing of relations between the world's two major superpowers, the USA and the USSR. This resulted in increased contact between East and West in the form of trade agreements and cultural exchanges, and even saw restored relation beween the USA and communist China.

detention in law, depriving a person of liberty following arrest. In England and Wales, the Police and Criminal Evidence Act 1984 established a wide-ranging statutory framework for the regime of detention. Limitations were placed on the length of time that suspects may be held in custody by the police without being charged (to a maximum of 96 hours) and systems of recordkeeping and supervision by designated 'custody officers' were introduced.

DETERGENT Detergent molecules are composed of a salt group which has at one end a long hydrocarbon 'tail'. The hydrocarbon tail is attracted to grease and oil, while the salts remain in the water and become ionized. The oil or grease becomes negatively ionized so its molecules repel one another. By this process the oils and greases are drawn up and become suspended in the water leaving surfaces clean.

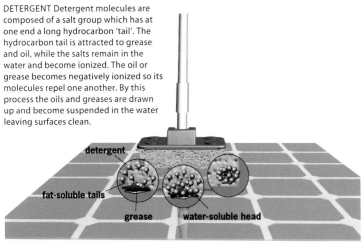

detergent
fat-soluble tails
grease
water-soluble head

detention centre in the UK penal system, an institution where young offenders (aged 14–21) are confined for short periods. Treatment is designed to be disciplinary; for example, the 'short, sharp shock' regime introduced by the Conservative government in 1982.

detergent surface-active cleansing agent. The common detergents are made from ▷fats (hydrocarbons) and sulphuric acid, and their long-chain molecules have a type of structure similar to that of ▷soap molecules: a salt group at one end attached to a long hydrocarbon 'tail'. They have the advantage over soap in that they do not produce scum by forming insoluble salts with the calcium and magnesium ions present in hard water.

To remove dirt, which is generally attached to materials by means of oil or grease, the hydrocarbon 'tails' (soluble in oil or grease) penetrate the oil or grease drops, while the 'heads' (soluble in water but insoluble in grease) remain in the water and, being salts, become ionized. Consequently the oil drops become negatively charged and tend to repel one another; thus they remain in suspension and are washed away with the dirt.

Detergents were first developed from coal tar in Germany during World War I, and synthetic organic detergents were increasingly used after World War II.

Domestic powder detergents for use in hot water have alkyl benzene as their main base, and may also include bleaches and fluorescers as whiteners, perborates to free stain-removing oxygen, and water softeners. Environment-friendly detergents contain no phosphates or bleaches. Liquid detergents for washing dishes are based on epoxyethane (ethylene oxide). Cold-water detergents consist of a mixture of various alcohols, plus an ingredient for breaking down the surface tension of the water, so enabling the liquid to penetrate fibres and remove the dirt. When these surface-active agents (surfactants) escape the normal processing of sewage, they cause troublesome foam in rivers; phosphates in some detergents can also cause the excessive enrichment (▷eutrophication) of rivers and lakes.

determinant in mathematics, an array of elements written as a square, and denoted by two vertical lines enclosing the array. For a 2×2 matrix, the determinant is given by the difference between the products of the diagonal terms. Determinants are used to solve sets of ▷simultaneous equations by matrix methods.

determinism in philosophy, the view that every event is an instance of some scientific law of nature; or that every event has at least one cause; or that nature is uniform. The thesis cannot be proved or disproved. Determinism is also the theory that we do not have free will, because our choices and actions are caused.

deterrence underlying conception of the nuclear arms race: the belief that a potential aggressor will be discouraged from launching a 'first strike' nuclear attack by the knowledge that the adversary is capable of inflicting 'unacceptable damage' in a retaliatory strike. This doctrine is widely known as that of **mutual assured destruction** (MAD). Three essential characteristics of deterrence are: the 'capability to act', 'credibility', and the 'will to act'.

de Tocqueville, Alexis French politician; see ▷Tocqueville, Alexis de.

detonator (or **blasting cap** or **percussion cap**) small explosive charge used to trigger off a main charge of high explosive. The relatively unstable compounds mercury fulminate and lead azide are often used in detonators, being set off by a lighted fuse or, more commonly, an electric current.

detritus in biology, the organic debris produced during the ▷decomposition of animals and plants.

Detroit industrial city and port in southeastern Michigan, USA, 788 km/489 mi west of New York and 395 km/245 mi east of Chicago, situated on the Detroit River opposite the city of Windsor in Ontario, Canada; seat of Wayne County; area 370 sq km/143 sq mi (excluding neighbouring cities), metropolitan area 10,093 sq km/3,897 sq mi; population (1998) 970,196, metropolitan area 5,246,000. Detroit is the headquarters of Ford, Chrysler, and General Motors, hence its nickname, Motown (from 'motor town'). Other manufactured products include steel, machine tools, chemicals, and pharmaceuticals. It is the seventh-largest city in the USA.

Situated 29 km/18 mi above Lake Erie, Detroit is the busiest port in Michigan and is linked to the Atlantic Ocean via the Saint Lawrence Seaway (opened 1959); the Detroit–Windsor tunnel is a major gateway to Canada.

Related Web site: Metropolitan Detroit http://209.238.191.172/

deuterium naturally occurring heavy isotope of hydrogen, mass number 2 (one proton and one neutron), discovered by US chemist Harold Urey in 1932. It is sometimes given the symbol D. In nature, about one in every 6,500 hydrogen atoms is deuterium. Combined with oxygen, it produces 'heavy water' (D_2O), used in the nuclear industry.

deuteron nucleus of an atom of deuterium (heavy hydrogen). It consists of one proton and one neutron, and is used in the bombardment of chemical elements to synthesize other elements.

de Valera, Éamon (1882–1975) Irish nationalist politician, president/Taoiseach (prime minister) of the Irish Free State/Eire/Republic of Ireland 1932–48, 1951–54, and 1957–59, and president 1959–73. Repeatedly imprisoned, de Valera participated in the ▷Easter Rising of 1916 and was leader of the nationalist ▷Sinn Fein party 1917–26, when he formed the republican ▷Fianna Fáil party. He opposed the Anglo-Irish Treaty (1921) but formulated a constitutional relationship with Britain in the 1930s that achieved greater Irish sovereignty.

De Valera was born in New York, the son of a Spanish father and an Irish mother, and sent to Ireland as a child. After studying at Blackrock College and the Royal University at Dublin, he became a teacher of mathematics, French, and Latin in various colleges. He was sentenced to death for his part in the Easter Rising, but the sentence was commuted to penal servitude for life, and he was released under an amnesty in 1917 because he was born in New York. In the same year he was elected to Westminster as MP for East Clare, and president of Sinn Fein. He was rearrested in May 1918, but escaped to the USA in 1919. He returned to Dublin in 1920 from where he directed the struggle against the British government. He authorized the negotiations of 1921, but refused to accept the ensuing treaty arguing that external association with Britain rather than the lesser status of dominion status was attainable.

His opposition to the Anglo-Irish Treaty contributed to the civil war that followed. De Valera was arrested by the Free State government in 1923, and spent a year in prison. In 1926 he formed a new party, Fianna Fáil, which secured a majority in 1932. De Valera became Taoiseach and foreign minister of the Free State, and at once instituted a programme of social and economic protectionism. He played the leading role in framing the 1937 constitution by which southern Ireland became a republic in all but name. In relations with Britain, his government immediately abolished the oath of allegiance and suspended payment of the annuities due under the Land Purchase Acts. Under an agreement concluded in 1938 between the two countries, Britain accepted £10 million in final settlement, and surrendered the right to enter or fortify southern Irish ports. Throughout World War II de Valera maintained a strict neutrality, rejecting an offer by Winston Churchill in 1940 to recognize the principle of a united Ireland in return for Eire's entry into the war. He lost power at the 1948 elections but was again prime minister 1951–54 and 1957–59, and thereafter president of the Republic 1959–66 and 1966–73.

de Valois, Ninette (1898–2001) Stage name of Edris Stannus. Irish choreographer, dancer, and teacher. In setting up the Vic-Wells Ballet in 1931 (later the Royal Ballet and Royal Ballet School) she was, along with choreographer Frederick ▷Ashton, one of the architects of British ballet. Among her works are *Job* (1931), *The Rake's Progress* (1935), *Checkmate* (1937), and *The Prospect Before*

Us (1940), revived by the Birmingham Royal Ballet in honour of her 100th birthday in June 1998. She is reverentially and affectionately known as 'Madam' in the ballet world.

She worked with Sergei Diaghilev in Paris (1923–25) before opening a dance academy in London in 1926. She was created a DBE in 1951.

devaluation in economics, the lowering of the official value of a currency against other currencies, so that exports become cheaper and imports more expensive. Used when a country is badly in deficit in its balance of trade, it results in the goods the country produces being cheaper abroad, so that the economy is stimulated by increased foreign demand.

development in biology, the process whereby a living thing transforms itself from a single cell into a vastly complicated multicellular organism, with structures, such as limbs, and functions, such as respiration, all able to work correctly in relation to each other. Most of the details of this process remain unknown, although some of the central features are becoming understood.

development in the social sciences, the acquisition by a society of industrial techniques and technology; hence the use of the term 'developed' to refer to the nations of the First and Second worlds (the Western capitalist countries and the Eastern communist countries respectively) and the term 'developing' or 'under-developed' to refer to the poorer, non-aligned nations of the Third World. Such references to First, Second, and Third Worlds began to lose their political meaning in the late 1980s with the end of the Cold War, and nowadays many development studies refer to Third World countries as 'the South', and to developed and industrialized nations as 'the North', because most Third World nations are in the southern hemisphere and most industrialized nations are in the northern hemisphere.

development aid see ▷aid, development.

devil in Jewish, Christian, and Muslim theology, the supreme spirit of evil (**Beelzebub, Lucifer, Iblis**), or an evil spirit generally.

devil ray any of several large rays of the genera *Manta* and *Mobula*, in which two 'horns' project forwards from the sides of the huge mouth. These flaps of skin guide the plankton, on which the fish feed, into the mouth. The largest of these rays can be 7 m/23 ft across, and weigh 1,000 kg/2,200 lb. They live in warm seas.

devil's coach horse large, black, long-bodied, omnivorous beetle *Ocypus olens*, about 3 cm/1.2 in long. It has powerful jaws and is capable of giving a painful bite. It emits an unpleasant smell when threatened.

Devil's Island (French **Ile du Diable**) smallest of the Iles du Salut (Salvation isles), off the northeast coast of French Guiana, 43 km/27 mi northwest of Cayenne. The group of islands was collectively and popularly known by the name Devil's Island and formed a penal colony notorious for its terrible conditions.

devolution delegation of authority and duties; in the later 20th century, the movement to decentralize governmental power, for instance, in the UK, the creation of the Scottish Parliament and Welsh Assembly.

Devolution, War of war waged unsuccessfully 1667–68 by Louis XIV of France in an attempt to gain Spanish territory in the Netherlands, of which ownership had allegedly 'devolved' on his wife Maria Theresa.

Devon (or **Devonshire**) county of southwest England; Plymouth and Torbay have been separate unitary authorities since April 1998.
area 6,720 sq km/2,594 sq mi **towns and cities** ▷Exeter (administrative headquarters); resorts: Barnstaple, Bideford, Exmouth, Ilfracombe, Sidmouth, Teignmouth, Tiverton **physical** rivers: Dart, Exe, Plym, Tamar (94 km/58 mi), Taw, Teign, Torridge; National Parks: Dartmoor, Exmoor **features** Lundy bird sanctuary and marine nature reserve in the Bristol Channel **agriculture** sheep and dairy farming, beef cattle; cider and clotted cream; fishing **industries** kaolin in the south; lace (at Honiton); Dartington glass; carpets (Axminster); quarrying (granite, limestone, sandstone); minerals (copper, iron, lead, manganese); tourism **population** (1996) 1,059,300 **famous people** St Boniface, Henry de Bracton, Samuel Taylor Coleridge, John Davis, Francis Drake, Humphrey Gilbert, Richard Grenville, John Hawkins, Charles Kingsley, Thomas Newcomen, Walter Raleigh, Joshua Reynolds, Robert F Scott, Joanna Southcott

Devonian period period of geological time 408–360 million years ago, the fourth period of the Palaeozoic era. Many desert sandstones from North America and Europe date from this time. The first land plants flourished in the Devonian period, corals were abundant in the seas, amphibians evolved from air-breathing fish, and insects developed on land.

The name comes from the county of Devon in southwest England, where Devonian rocks were first studied.

Devonshire, 8th Duke of British politician; see Spencer Compton Cavendish ▷Hartington.

dew precipitation in the form of moisture that collects on the ground. It forms after the temperature of the ground has fallen below the ▷dew point of the air in contact with it. As the temperature falls during the night, the air and its water vapour become chilled, and condensation takes place on the cooled surfaces.

Dewar, James (1842–1923) Scottish chemist and physicist who invented the ▷vacuum flask (Thermos) in 1872 during his research into the properties of matter at extremely low temperatures. He was knighted in 1904.

Dewey, Melvil (1851–1931) US librarian. In 1876, he devised the Dewey decimal system of classification for accessing, storing, and retrieving books, widely used in libraries. The system uses the numbers 000 to 999 to designate the major fields of knowledge, then breaks these down into more specific subjects by the use of decimals. Dewey founded the American Library Association in 1876 and the first school of library science, at Columbia University, in 1887.

dew point temperature at which the air becomes saturated with water vapour. At temperatures below the dew point, the water vapour condenses out of the air as droplets. If the droplets are large they become deposited on the ground as dew; if small they remain in suspension in the air and form mist or fog.

Dhaka (or Dacca) capital of ▷Bangladesh since 1971, in Dhaka region, west of the River Meghna on the ▷Ganges delta; population (1991) 3,397,200. It trades in rice, oilseed, sugar, and tea; industries include jute-processing, tanning, and productions of textiles, chemicals, glass, and metal products.

Features The city has many buildings from different eras: the 17th-century Lal Bagh Fort; several mosques; the early 20th-century supreme court and university; and the more modern Parliament buildings and railway station.

History A former French, Dutch, and English trading post, Dhaka was capital of the Mogul province of East Bengal from 1608 to 1704. It became capital of East Pakistan in 1947, and was handed over to Indian troops in December 1971 to become capital of the new country of Bangladesh.

dharma (Sanskrit 'justice, order') in Hinduism, the consciousness of forming part of an ordered universe, and hence the moral duty of accepting one's station in life. In Buddhism, dharma is the teaching of the Buddha, whose words and principles lead to enlightenment.

Dhofar mountainous southwestern governorate of ▷Oman, on the border with Yemen; population (1993) 189,100. South Yemen supported left-wing guerrilla activity here against the Oman government in the 1970s, while Britain and Iran supported the government's military operations. The guerrillas were defeated in 1975. The capital is Salalah.

dhole wild dog *Cuon alpinus* found in Asia from Siberia to Java. With head and body up to 1 m/39 in long, variable in colour but often reddish above and lighter below, the dhole lives in groups of from 3 to 30 individuals. The species is becoming rare.

diabase alternative name for ▷dolerite (a form of basalt that contains very little silica), especially dolerite that has metamorphosed.

diabetes disease that can be caused by reduced production of the hormone ▷insulin, or a reduced response of the liver, muscle, and fat cells to insulin. This affects the body's ability to use and regulate sugars effectively. *Diabetes mellitus* is a disorder of the islets of Langerhans in the ▷pancreas that prevents the body producing insulin. Treatment is by strict dietary control and oral or injected insulin, depending on the type of diabetes.

Related Web site: 'Recent Advances: Diabetes' http://www.bmj.com/cgi/content/full/316/7139/1221

diagenesis in geology, the physical, chemical, and biological processes by which a sediment becomes a ▷sedimentary rock. The main processes involved include compaction of the grains, and the cementing of the grains together by the growth of new minerals deposited by percolating groundwater. As a whole, diagenesis is actually a poorly understood process.

Diaghilev, Sergei Pavlovich (1872–1929) Russian ballet impresario. In 1909 he founded the Ballets Russes/Russian Ballet (headquarters in Monaco), which he directed for 20 years. Through this company he brought Russian ballet to the West, introducing and encouraging a dazzling array of dancers, choreographers, composers, and artists, such as Anna Pavlova, Vaslav Nijinsky, Bronislava Nijinksa, Mikhail Fokine, Léonide Massine, George Balanchine, Igor Stravinsky, Sergey Prokofiev, Pablo Picasso, and Henri Matisse. Many of the works he commissioned are now firmly established in the concert repertory, including Stravinsky's *Le Sacre du Printemps/The Rite of Spring*.

dialect variation of a spoken language shared by those in a particular area or a particular social or ethnic group. The term is used to indicate a geographical area ('northern dialects' or 'Brooklyn dialect') or social or ethnic group ('African-American dialect').

dialectic Greek term, originally associated with the philosopher Socrates' method of argument through dialogue and conversation. **Hegelian dialectic**, named after the German philosopher ▷Hegel, refers to an interpretive method in which the contradiction between a thesis and its antithesis is resolved through synthesis.

dialectical materialism political, philosophical, and economic theory of the 19th-century German thinkers Karl Marx and Friedrich Engels, also known as ▷Marxism.

dialysis technique for removing waste products from the blood suffering chronic or acute kidney failure. There are two main methods, haemodialysis and peritoneal dialysis.

In **haemodialysis**, the patient's blood is passed through a pump, where it is separated from sterile dialysis fluid by a semipermeable membrane. This allows any toxic substances which have built up in the bloodstream, and which would normally be filtered out by the kidneys, to diffuse out of the blood into the dialysis fluid. Haemodialysis is very expensive and usually requires the patient to attend a specialized unit.

Peritoneal dialysis uses one of the body's natural semipermeable membranes for the same purpose. About two litres of dialysis fluid is slowly instilled into the peritoneal cavity of the abdomen, and drained out again, over about two hours. During that time toxins from the blood diffuse into the peritoneal cavity across the peritoneal membrane. The advantage of peritoneal dialysis is that the patient can remain active while the dialysis is proceeding. This is known as continuous ambulatory peritoneal dialysis (CAPD).

In the long term, dialysis is expensive and debilitating, and ▷transplants are now the treatment of choice for patients in chronic kidney failure.

diameter straight line joining two points on the circumference of a circle that passes through the centre of that circle. It divides a circle into two equal halves.

diamond generally colourless, transparent mineral, an ▷allotrope of carbon. It is regarded as a precious gemstone, and is the hardest substance known (10 on the ▷Mohs scale). Industrial diamonds, which may be natural or synthetic, are used for cutting, grinding, and polishing.

Diana in Roman mythology, the goddess of chastity, hunting, and the Moon; daughter of Jupiter and twin of ▷Apollo. Her Greek equivalent is the goddess ▷Artemis.

Diana, Princess of Wales (1961–1997) Born Diana Frances Spencer. Daughter of the 8th Earl Spencer, Diana married Prince Charles in St Paul's Cathedral, London, in 1981. She had two sons, William and Harry, before her separation from Charles in 1992. In February 1996 she agreed to a divorce, after which she became known as Diana, Princess of Wales. Her worldwide prominence for charity work contributed to a massive outpouring of public grief after her death in a car crash in Paris on 31 August 1997. Her funeral proved to be the biggest British televised event in history.

DIANA A Roman fresco of the Roman goddess Diana with her bow and arrow, from Stabia, near Naples, Italy. *The Art Archive/Archaeological Museum Naples/Dagli Orti*

DIANA, PRINCESS OF WALES Diana, Princess of Wales, on her way to a charity premiere of the film *Apollo 13*, in London. *Archive Photos*

Charles and Diana's decision to separate was announced by Prime Minister John Major in December 1992, when he stated that they had no plans to divorce, and that their constitutional positions were not affected. The Church of England issued a statement saying that the separation would not prevent Charles from leading the church. Diana admitted in a television interview in November 1995 that she had had an affair following her separation from Prince Charles.

Charles and Diana were officially divorced in late August 1996. As part of the settlement, believed to be worth between £15 million and £17 million, the Princess lost the title of Her Royal Highness and was to be known as Diana, Princess of Wales. As Buckingham Palace confirmed, both the queen and the prince continued to regard the princess as a member of the royal family and she continued to live at Kensington Palace. She resigned as the patron of 93 British and Commonwealth charities, and cut her workload to just six charities of her choice: the Centrepoint homeless charity, the National Aids Trust, the Leprosy Mission, which has links with Mother Teresa of Calcutta's mission, the English National Ballet, the Great Ormond Street Hospital for Sick Children, and the Royal Marsden Hospital, which specializes in cancer research and treatment. In the last few years of her life, Diana became deeply involved in the anti-landmine campaign.

Diana died in a car crash in Paris on 31 August 1997, together with her companion, Dodi Fayed, and their chauffeur. The accident happened as their car was being pursued by paparazzi photographers on motorcycles. Her violent and tragic death shocked the British nation and also led to calls for the introduction of tougher privacy laws.

Public response to Diana's death was unprecedented, as hundreds of thousands paid floral tributes and signed books of condolence. The strength of public feeling and criticism directed at the royal family for their apparent indifference to the death of the nationally loved princess led the queen to make an extraordinary live television tribute to the late Princess of Wales, and to arrange Diana's funeral in a way that would allow the public to be involved. The queen normally speaks to the nation on Christmas Day; this was the second exception to this rule in her 45-year reign (the other was on 24 February 1991 at the end of the Gulf War).

A record 31.5 million people – three quarters of British adults – watched the funeral. The BBC's coverage was also broadcast in 185 countries.

diapause period of suspended development that occurs in some species of insects and other invertebrates, characterized by greatly reduced metabolism. Periods of diapause are often timed to coincide with the winter months, and improve the animal's chances of surviving adverse conditions.

diaphragm in mammals, a thin muscular sheet separating the thorax from the abdomen. It is attached by way of the ribs at either side and the breastbone and backbone, and a central tendon. Arching upwards against the heart and lungs, the diaphragm is important in the mechanics of breathing. It contracts at each inhalation, moving downwards to increase the volume of the chest cavity, and relaxes at exhalation.

diaphragm (or cap or Dutch cap) barrier ▷contraceptive that is passed into the vagina to fit over the cervix (neck of the uterus), preventing sperm from entering the uterus. For a cap to be effective, a ▷spermicide must be used and the diaphragm left in place for six to eight hours after intercourse. This method is 97% effective if practised correctly.

diarrhoea frequent or excessive action of the bowels so that the faeces are liquid or semiliquid. It is caused by intestinal irritants (including some drugs and poisons), infection with harmful organisms (as in dysentery, salmonella, or cholera), or allergies.

diary informal record of day-to-day events, observations, or reflections, usually not intended for a general readership. One of the earliest diaries extant is that of a Japanese noblewoman, the *Kagerō Nikki* (954–974), and the earliest known diary in English is that of Edward VI (ruled 1547–53). Notable diaries include those of Samuel ▷Pepys and Anne ▷Frank.

diaspora (Greek 'dispersion') dispersal of the Jews, initially from Palestine after the Babylonian conquest in 586 BC, and then following the Roman sacking of Jerusalem in AD 70 and their crushing of the Jewish revolt of 135. The term has come to refer to all the Jews living outside Israel.

diatom microscopic ▷alga found in all parts of the world in either fresh or marine waters. Diatoms consist of single cells that secrete a hard cell wall made of ▷silica. There are approximately 10,000 species of diatom. (Division Bacillariophyta.)

diatomic molecule molecule composed of two atoms joined together. In the case of an element such as oxygen (O_2), the atoms are identical.

diatonic scale in music, a scale consisting of the seven notes of any major or minor ▷key.

Diaz, Bartholomeu (*c.* 1450–1500) Portuguese explorer, the first European to reach the Cape of Good Hope, in 1488, and to establish a route around Africa. He drowned during an expedition with Pedro Cabral.

Díaz, (José de la Cruz) Porfirio (1830–1915) Mexican soldier and politician, dictator-president (*caudillo*) of Mexico 1877–80 and 1884–1911. He seized power after losing the 1876 presidential election. He dominated the country for the next 34 years, although between 1880 and 1884 his ally, Manuel Gonzáles, was formally president. He centralized the state at the expense of the peasants and Indians, and dismantled all local and regional leadership. Despite significant economic advance, Díaz faced mounting revolutionary opposition in his final years. His retraction of a promise not to seek re-election in 1910 triggered a rebellion, led by Francisco Madero, which led to Díaz's overthrow in May 1911. Díaz fled to France, and died in exile in Paris.

Diaz de Solís, Juan (*c.* 1471–*c.* 1516) Spanish explorer in South America who reached the estuary of the Río de la Plata, and was killed and reputedly eaten by cannibals.

dichloro-diphenyl-trichloroethane full name of the insecticide ▷DDT.

Dickens, Charles (John Huffam) (1812–1870) English novelist. He is enduringly popular for his memorable characters and his portrayal of the social evils of Victorian England. In 1836 he published the first number of the *Pickwick Papers*, followed by *Oliver Twist* (1837), the first of his 'reforming' novels; *Nicholas Nickleby* (1838); *The Old Curiosity Shop* (1840); *Barnaby Rudge* (1841); and ▷*David Copperfield* (1850). Among his later books are *A Tale of Two Cities* (1859) and *Great Expectations* (1861). All his novels were written as serials.

The *Pickwick Papers* were originally intended merely as an accompaniment to a series of sporting illustrations, but the adventures of Pickwick outgrew their setting and established Dickens's reputation. In 1842 he visited the USA, where he was welcomed as a celebrity. On his return home, he satirized US democracy in *Martin Chuzzlewit* (1844). In 1843 he published the first of his Christmas books, *A Christmas Carol. Dombey and Son* (1848) was largely written abroad. *David Copperfield*, his most popular novel and his own favourite, contains many autobiographical incidents and characters; Mr Micawber is usually recognized as a sketch of his father. Dickens inaugurated the weekly magazine *Household Words* in 1850, reorganizing it in 1859 as *All the Year Round*; many of his later stories were published serially in these periodicals. In 1858 he began giving public readings from his

CHARLES DICKENS The English novelist's immense creative energy made him the most popular novelist of his age. Born into a family on the fringes of gentility, he was always conscious of the social and economic abysses of Victorian society. *Archive Photos*

novels, which proved such a success that he was invited to make a second US tour 1867–68.

Among his later novels are *Bleak House* (1853), *Hard Times* (1854), *Little Dorrit* (1857), and *Our Mutual Friend* (1865). *Edwin Drood*, a mystery story influenced by the style of his friend Wilkie ▷Collins, was left incomplete on his death.

Related Web sites: Complete Works of Shakespeare http://the-tech.mit.edu/Shakespeare/works.html
Dickens, Charles http://landow.stg.brown.edu/victorian/dickens/dickensov.html

Dickens, Monica (Enid) (1915–1992) English writer. Her first books were humorous accounts of her experiences in various jobs, beginning as a cook (*One Pair of Hands*, 1939); she went on to become a novelist. She was a great-granddaughter of Charles Dickens.

> **Charles Dickens**
> *Charity begins at home, and justice begins next door.*
> *Martin Chuzzlewit* ch. 27

Dickinson, Emily Elizabeth (1830–1886) US poet. She wrote most of her poetry between 1850 and the late 1860s and was particularly prolific during the Civil War years. She experimented with poetic rhythms, rhymes, and forms, as well as language and syntax. Her work is charact-erized by a wit and boldness that seem to contrast sharply with the reclusive life she led. Very few of her many short, mystical poems were published during her lifetime, and her work became well known only in the 20th century. The first collec-tion of her poetry, *Poems by Emily Dickinson*, was published in 1890.

dicotyledon major subdivision of the ▷angiosperms, containing the great majority of flowering plants. Dicotyledons are characterized by the presence of two seed leaves, or ▷cotyledons, in the embryo, which is usually surrounded by the ▷endosperm. They generally have broad leaves with netlike veins.

DICOTYLEDON The pair of seed leaves typical of this broad group of flowering plants is clearly visible in these tree seedlings, which have germinated in tropical dry forest in Madagascar. *Premaphotos Wildlife*

dictatorship term or office of an absolute ruler, overriding the constitution. (In ancient Rome a dictator was a magistrate invested with emergency powers for six months.) Although dictatorships were common in Latin America during the 19th century, the only European example during this period was the rule of Napoleon III. The crises following World War I produced many dictatorships, including the regimes of Atatürk and Piłsudski (nationalist); Mussolini, Hitler, Primo de Rivera, Franco, and Salazar (all right-wing); and Stalin (communist). The most notable contemporary dictatorship is that of Saddam ▷Hussein in Iraq.

dictionary book that contains a selection of the words of a language, with their pronunciations and meanings, usually arranged in alphabetical order. The term is also applied to any usually alphabetic work of reference containing specialized information about a particular subject, art, or science; for example, a dictionary of music. Bilingual dictionaries provide translations of one language into another.

Diderot, Denis (1713–1784) French philosopher. He is closely associated with the Enlightenment, the European intellectual movement for social and scientific progress, and was editor of the enormously influential *Encyclopédie* (1751–80). An expanded and politicized version of the English encyclopedia (1728) of Ephraim Chambers (*c.* 1680–1740), this work exerted an enormous influence on contemporary social thinking with its materialism and anticlericalism. Its compilers were known as Encyclopédistes.

Diderot's materialism, most articulately expressed in *D'Alembert's Dream*, published after Diderot's death, sees the natural world as nothing more than matter and motion. His account of the origin and development of life is purely mechanical.

didgeridoo (or didjeridu) musical lip-reed wind instrument, made from a hollow eucalyptus branch 1.5 m/4 ft long and blown to produce rhythmic, booming notes of relatively constant pitch. It was first developed and played by Australian Aborigines.

Dido (or **Elissa**) in Greek mythology, a Phoenician princess and legendary founder of ▷Carthage, northern Africa, in 853 BC. She was the sister of ▷Pygmalion, king of Tyre. According to Carthaginian tradition, Dido committed suicide to avoid a marriage, but in the Latin epic *Aeneid*, Virgil places her 300 years earlier, attributing the suicide to her desertion by ▷Aeneas at the fall of Troy (traditionally 1184 BC).

diecasting form of ▷casting in which molten metal is injected into permanent metal moulds or dies.

DIECASTING One of the most useful metal alloys for diecasting comprises 96% zinc and 4% aluminium. Injected molten into a steel die, it solidifies rapidly and does not adhere to the die. Moreover, it can assume the most complex of shapes and has other useful properties. Zinc diecastings are used extensively in the motor industry for car parts and machine tools. *Image Bank*

Diefenbaker, John George (1895–1979) Canadian Progressive Conservative politician, prime minister 1957–63. In 1958, seeking to increase his majority in the House of Commons, Diefenbaker called for new elections; his party won the largest majority in Canadian history. In 1963, however, Diefenbaker refused to accept atomic warheads for missiles supplied by the USA, and the Progressive Conservative Party was ousted after losing a no-confidence vote in parliament.

Diemen, Anthony van (1593–1645) Dutch admiral. In 1636 he was appointed governor general of Dutch settlements in the East Indies, and wrested Ceylon and Malacca from the Portuguese. In 1636 and 1642 he supervised expeditions to Australia, on the second of which the navigator Abel Tasman discovered land not charted by Europeans and named it **Van Diemen's Land**, now Tasmania.

Dien Bien Phu, Battle of decisive battle in the ▷Indochina War at a French fortress in North Vietnam, near the Laotian border. French troops were besieged 13 March–7 May 1954 by the communist Vietminh, and the eventual fall of Dien Bien Phu resulted in the end of French control of Indochina.

Dieppe channel port and holiday resort at the mouth of the River Arques in Seine-Maritime *département*, northern France, 53 km/ 33 mi north of Rouen; population (1999 est) 34,600. There are ferry services from its harbour to Newhaven in England. It is a trading centre for fish and fruit; industries include fishing, shipbuilding, pharmaceuticals, and light manufacturing.

diesel engine ▷internal-combustion engine that burns a lightweight fuel oil. The diesel engine operates by compressing air until it becomes sufficiently hot to ignite the fuel. It is a piston-in-cylinder engine, like the ▷petrol engine, but only air (rather than an air-and-fuel mixture) is taken into the cylinder on the first piston stroke (down). The piston moves up and compresses the air until it is at a very high temperature. The fuel oil is then injected into the hot air, where it burns, driving the piston down on its power stroke. For this reason the engine is called a compression-ignition engine.

Diesel engines have sometimes been marketed as 'cleaner' than petrol engines because they do not need lead additives and produce fewer gaseous pollutants. However, they do produce high levels of the tiny black carbon particles called particulates, which are believed to be carcinogenic and may exacerbate or even cause asthma.

The principle of the diesel engine was first explained in England by Herbert Akroyd (1864–1937) in 1890, and was applied practically by Rudolf Diesel in Germany in 1892.

diesel oil lightweight fuel oil used in diesel engines. Like petrol, it is a petroleum product. When used in vehicle engines, it is also known as **derv** (diesel-engine road vehicle).

European Union ministers agreed in July 1998 to cut sulphur levels in diesel from 500 ppm to 350 ppm by 2005.

diet range of foods eaten by an animal each day; it is also a particular selection of food, or the total amount and choice of food for a specific person or people. Most animals require seven kinds of food in their diet: proteins, carbohydrates, fats, vitamins, minerals, water, and roughage. A diet that contains all of these things in the correct amounts and proportions is termed a balanced diet. The amounts and proportions required varies with different animals, according to their size, age, and lifestyle. The ▷digestive systems of animals have evolved to meet particular needs; they have also adapted to cope with the foods available in the surroundings in which they live. The necessity of finding and processing an appropriate diet is a very basic drive in animal evolution. **Dietetics** is the science of feeding individuals or groups; a dietitian is a specialist in this science.

diet meeting or convention of the princes and other dignitaries of the Holy Roman (German) Empire, for example, the **Diet of Worms** of 1521 which met to consider the question of Luther's doctrines and the governance of the empire under Charles V.

dietetics specialized branch of human nutrition, dealing with the promotion of health through the proper kinds and quantities of food.

Dietrich, Marlene (1901–1992) Born Maria Magdalene Dietrich von Losch. German-born US actor and singer. She became a star in *Der Blaue Engel/The Blue Angel* (1930), directed by Josef

DIFFUSION Diffusion can occur in gases, liquids, and solids. Substances diffuse at different speeds, fastest in gases and slowest in solids. In the gas example, the ring of ammonium chloride forms nearest to the hydrochloric acid end because ammonia diffuses faster than hydrochloric acid.

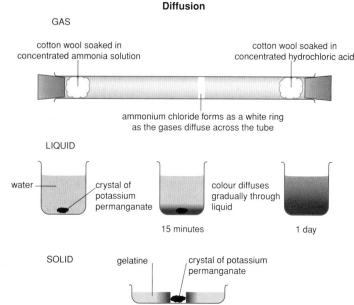

Diffusion

GAS

cotton wool soaked in concentrated ammonia solution

cotton wool soaked in concentrated hydrochloric acid

ammonium chloride forms as a white ring as the gases diffuse across the tube

LIQUID

water   crystal of potassium permanganate   colour diffuses gradually through liquid

15 minutes   1 day

SOLID   gelatine   crystal of potassium permanganate

von ▷Sternberg, with whom she would collaborate throughout the 1930s. Her films include *Morocco* (1930), *Blonde Venus* (1932), *The Devil is a Woman* (1935), *Destry Rides Again* (1939), and *Touch of Evil* (1958). In the 1960s she stopped acting and began a career as a concert singer. Opposed to the Nazi regime, she moved to Hollywood, becoming a US citizen in 1937. Among her later films are *Stagefright* (1950) and *Witness for the Prosecution* (1957).

> **Related Web site: Dietrich, Marlene** http://www.reelclassics.com/ Actresses/Marlene/marlene.htm

difference in mathematics, the result obtained when subtracting one number from another. Also, those elements of one ▷set that are not elements of another.

difference engine mechanical calculating machine designed (and partly built in 1822) by the British mathematician Charles ▷Babbage to produce reliable tables of life expectancy. A precursor of the analytical engine, it was to calculate mathematical functions by solving the differences between values given to ▷variables within equations. Babbage designed the calculator so that once the initial values for the variables were set it would produce the next few thousand values without error.

differential calculus branch of ▷calculus involving applications such as the determination of maximum and minimum points and rates of change.

differentiation in embryology, the process by which cells become increasingly different and specialized, giving rise to more complex structures that have particular functions in the adult organism. For instance, embryonic cells may develop into nerve, muscle, or bone cells.

differentiation in mathematics, a procedure for determining the ▷derivative or gradient of the tangent to a curve $f(x)$ at any point x.

diffraction the spreading out of waves when they pass through a small gap or around a small object, resulting in some change in the direction of the waves. In order for this effect to be observed the size of the object or gap must be comparable to or smaller than the ▷wavelength of the waves. Diffraction occurs with all forms of progressive waves – electromagnetic, sound, and water waves – and explains such phenomena as why long-wave radio waves can bend round hills better than short-wave radio waves.

The wavelength of light ranges from 400 nm to about 700 nm, a few orders of magnitude smaller than radio waves. The gap

through which light travels must be extremely small to observe diffraction. The slight spreading of a light beam through a narrow slit causes the different wavelengths of light to interfere with each other to produce a pattern of light and dark bands. A **diffraction grating** is a plate of glass or metal ruled with close, equidistant parallel lines used for separating a wave train such as a beam of incident light into its component frequencies (white light results in a spectrum). The wavelength of sound is between 0.5 m/1.6 ft and 2.0 m/6.6 ft. When sound waves travel through doorways or between buildings they are diffracted significantly, so that the sound is heard round corners.

diffusion spontaneous and random movement of molecules or particles in a fluid (gas or liquid) from a region in which they are at a high concentration to a region of lower concentration, until a uniform concentration is achieved throughout. The difference in concentration between two such regions is called the **concentration gradient**. No mechanical mixing or stirring is involved. For instance, if a drop of ink is added to water, its molecules will diffuse until their colour becomes evenly distributed throughout. Diffusion occurs more rapidly across a higher concentration gradient and at higher temperature.

In biological systems, diffusion plays an essential role in the transport, over short distances, of molecules such as nutrients, respiratory gases, and neurotransmitters. It provides the means by which small molecules pass into and out of individual cells and micro-organisms, such as amoebae, that possess no circulatory system. Plant and animal organs whose function depends on diffusion – such as the lung – have a large surface area. Diffusion of water across a semi-permeable membrane is termed ▷osmosis.

One application of diffusion is the separation of isotopes, particularly those of uranium. When uranium hexafluoride diffuses through a porous plate, the ratio of the 235 and 238 isotopes is changed slightly. With sufficient number of passages, the separation is nearly complete. There are large plants in the USA and UK for obtaining enriched fuel for fast nuclear reactors and the fissile uranium-235, originally required for the first atom bombs. Another application is the diffusion pump, used extensively in vacuum work, in which the gas to be evacuated diffuses into a chamber from which it is carried away by the vapour of a suitable medium, usually oil or mercury.

Laws of diffusion were formulated by Thomas ▷Graham in 1829 (for gases) and Adolph Fick 1829–1901 (for solutions).

digestion process whereby food eaten by an animal is broken down mechanically, and chemically by ▷enzymes, mostly in the ▷stomach and ▷intestines, to make the nutrients available for absorption and cell metabolism.

> **Related Web site: Human Anatomy** http://library.thinkquest.org/ 28297/body.html

digestive system in the body, all the organs and tissues involved in the digestion of food. In animals, these consist of the mouth, stomach, intestines, and their associated glands. The process of digestion breaks down the food by physical and chemical means into the different elements that are needed by the body for energy and tissue building and repair. Digestion begins in the mouth and is completed in the ▷stomach; from there most nutrients are absorbed into the small intestine from where they pass

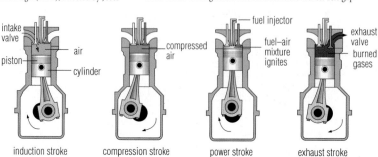

DIESEL ENGINE In a diesel engine, fuel is injected on the power stroke into hot compressed air at the top of the cylinder, where it ignites spontaneously. The four stages are exactly the same as those of the four-stroke or Otto cycle.

intake valve   air   piston   cylinder

induction stroke

compressed air

compression stroke

fuel injector   fuel–air mixture ignites

power stroke

exhaust valve   burned gases

exhaust stroke

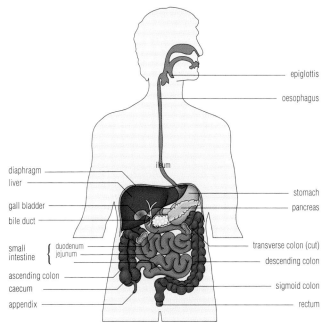

DIGESTIVE SYSTEM The human digestive system. When food is swallowed, it is moved down the oesophagus by the action of muscles (peristalsis) into the stomach. Digestion starts in the stomach as the food is mixed with enzymes and strong acid. After several hours, the food passes to the small intestine. Here more enzymes are added and digestion is completed. After all nutrients have been absorbed, the indigestible parts pass into the large intestine and thence to the rectum. The liver has many functions, such as storing minerals and vitamins and making bile, which is stored in the gall bladder until needed for the digestion of fats. The pancreas supplies enzymes. The appendix appears to have no function in human beings.

through the intestinal wall into the bloodstream; what remains is stored and concentrated into faeces in the large intestine. Birds have two additional digestive organs – the ▷crop and ▷gizzard. In smaller, simpler animals such as jellyfish, the digestive system is simply a cavity (coelenteron or enteric cavity) with a 'mouth' into which food is taken; the digestible portion is dissolved and absorbed in this cavity, and the remains are ejected back through the mouth.

The digestive system of humans consists primarily of the ▷alimentary canal, a tube which starts at the mouth, continues with the pharynx, oesophagus (or gullet), stomach, large and small intestines, and rectum, and ends at the anus. The food moves through this canal by ▷peristalsis whereby waves of involuntary muscular contraction and relaxation produced by the muscles in the wall of the gut cause the food to be ground and mixed with various digestive juices. Most of these juices contain digestive enzymes, chemicals that speed up reactions involved in the breakdown of food. Other digestive juices empty into the alimentary canal from the salivary glands, gall bladder, and pancreas, which are also part of the digestive system.

The fats, proteins, and carbohydrates (starches and sugars) in foods contain very complex molecules that are broken down (see ▷diet; ▷nutrition) for absorption into the bloodstream: starches and complex sugars are converted to simple sugars; fats are converted to fatty acids and glycerol; and proteins are converted to amino acids and peptides. Foods such as vitamins, minerals, and water do not need to undergo digestion prior to absorption into the bloodstream. The small intestine, which is the main site of digestion and absorption, is subdivided into the duodenum, jejunum, and ileum. Covering the surface of its mucous membrane lining are a large number of small prominences called villi which increase the surface for absorption and allow the digested nutrients to diffuse into small blood-vessels lying immediately under the epithelium.

Digger (or **True Leveller**) member of an English 17th-century radical sect that attempted to seize and share out common land. The Diggers became prominent in April 1649 when, headed by Gerrard Winstanley, they set up communal colonies near Cobham, Surrey, and elsewhere. The Diggers wanted to return to what they claimed was a 'golden age' before the Norman Conquest, when they believed that all land was held in common and its fruits were shared fairly between the people, and when men and women were equal. They did not allow private property or possessions; it is sometimes claimed that they were the first communist society. The Diggers' colonies were attacked by mobs and, being pacifists, they made no

resistance. The support they attracted alarmed the government and they were dispersed in 1650. Their ideas influenced the early ▷Quakers.

digit any of the numbers from 0 to 9 in the decimal system. Different bases have different ranges of digits. For example, the ▷hexadecimal system has digits 0 to 9 and A to F, whereas the binary system has two digits (or ▷bits), 0 and 1.

digital in electronics and computing, a term meaning 'coded as numbers'. A digital system uses two-state, either on/off or high/low voltage pulses, to encode, receive, and transmit information. A **digital display** shows discrete values as numbers (as opposed to an analogue signal, such as the continuous sweep of a pointer on a dial).

digital audio tape (DAT) digitally recorded audio tape produced in cassettes that can carry up to two hours of sound on each side and are about half the size of standard cassettes. DAT players/recorders were developed in 1987. Prerecorded cassettes are copy-protected. The first DAT for computer data was introduced in 1988.

digital compact cassette (DCC) digitally recorded audio cassette that is roughly the same size as a standard cassette. It cannot be played on a normal tape recorder, though standard tapes can be played on a DCC machine; this is known as 'backwards compatibility'. The playing time is 90 minutes.

digital computer computing device that operates on a two-state system, using symbols that are internally coded as binary numbers (numbers made up of combinations of the digits 0 and 1); see ▷computer.

digital data transmission in computing, a way of sending data by converting all signals (whether pictures, sounds, or words) into numeric (normally binary) codes before transmission, then reconverting them on receipt. This virtually eliminates any distortion or degradation of the signal during transmission, storage, or processing.

digitalis drug that increases the efficiency of the heart by strengthening its muscle contractions and slowing its rate. It is derived from the leaves of the common European woodland plant *Digitalis purpurea* (foxglove).

digitalis any of a group of plants belonging to the figwort family, which includes the ▷foxgloves. The leaves of the common foxglove (*Digitalis purpurea*) are the source of the drug **digitalis** used in the treatment of heart disease. (Genus *Digitalis*, family Scrophulariaceae.)

digital recording technique whereby the pressure of sound waves is sampled more than 30,000 times a second and the values converted by computer into precise numerical values. These are recorded and, during playback, are reconverted to sound waves.

This technique gives very high-quality reproduction. The numerical values converted by computer represent the original sound-wave form exactly and are recorded on compact disc. When this is played back by ▷laser, the exact values are retrieved. When the signal is fed via an amplifier to a loudspeaker, sound waves exactly like the original ones are reproduced.

digital sampling electronic process used in ▷telecommunications for transforming a constantly varying (analogue) signal into one composed of discrete units, a digital signal. In the creation of recorded music, sampling enables the composer, producer, or remix engineer to borrow discrete vocal or instrumental parts from other recorded work (it is also possible to sample live sound).

digital-to-analogue converter electronic circuit that converts a digital signal into an ▷analogue (continuously varying) signal. Such a circuit is used to convert the digital output from a computer into the analogue voltage required to produce sound from a conventional loudspeaker.

digitizer in computing, a device that converts an analogue video signal into a digital format so that video images can be input, stored, displayed, and manipulated by a computer. The term is sometimes used to refer to a ▷graphics tablet.

Dijon administrative centre of the Côte-d'Or *département*, east-central France, and chief city of the ▷Burgundy region, situated

on the Burgundy canal at the confluence of the rivers Ouche and Suzon; population (1990) 151,600, conurbation 230,000. As well as metallurgical, electrical, electronic, pharmaceutical, and other industries, it has a has a trade in Burgundy wines, is famed for its mustard, spiced bread, and gastronomic specialities, and is an important railway centre.

DIK-DIK Dik-diks are shy, secretive animals. At sunset and during the night they browse on leaves, shoots, and buds. They do not need to drink.

dik-dik any of several species of tiny antelope, genus *Madoqua*, found in Africa south of the Sahara in dry areas with scattered brush. Dik-diks are about 60 cm/2 ft long and 35 cm/1.1 ft tall, and are often seen in pairs. Males have short, pointed horns. The dik-dik is so named because of its alarm call.

dilatation and curettage (D and C) common gynaeco-logical procedure in which the cervix (neck of the womb) is widened, or dilated, giving access so that the lining of the womb can be scraped away (curettage). It may be carried out to terminate a pregnancy, treat an incomplete miscarriage, discover the cause of heavy menstrual bleeding, or for biopsy.

Dili (or Dilli or Dilly) capital, chief port, and main commercial centre of East Timor, situated on the Ombai Strait on the northern coast; population (1990) 60,150. Coffee, cotton, rice, sandalwood, copra, and hides are the chief exports, while industries include soap, perfume, pottery, and textiles, as well as crafts such as basketry and sandalwood carving.

dill herb belonging to the carrot family, whose bitter seeds and aromatic leaves are used in cooking and in medicine. (*Anethum graveolens*, family Umbelliferae.)

DILL Dill grows to a height of 45–90 cm/1.5–3 ft, and resembles fennel with feathery leaves and yellow flowers. A native plant of Asia and Eastern Europe, dill is now common throughout much of Europe.

dilution process of reducing the concentration of a solution by the addition of a solvent. The extent of a dilution normally indicates the final volume of solution required. A fivefold dilution would mean the addition of sufficient solvent to make the final volume five times the original.

dimension in science, any directly measurable physical quantity such as mass (M), length (L), and time (T), and the derived units obtainable by multiplication or division from such quantities. For example, acceleration (the rate of change of velocity) has dimensions (LT^{-2}), and is expressed in such units as km s^{-2}. A quantity that is a ratio, such as relative density or humidity, is dimensionless.

In geometry, the dimensions of a figure are the number of measures needed to specify its size. A point is considered to have zero dimension, a line to have one dimension, a plane figure to have two, and a solid body to have three.

Dimitrov, Georgi Mikhailovich (1882–1949) Bulgarian communist, prime minister from 1946. He was elected a deputy in 1913 and from 1919 was a member of the executive of the Comintern, an international communist organization (see the ▷International). In 1933 he was arrested in Berlin and tried with others in Leipzig for allegedly setting fire to the parliament building (see ▷Reichstag Fire). Acquitted, he went to the USSR, where he became general secretary of the Comintern until its dissolution in 1943.

Dinaric Alps extension of the European ▷Alps that runs parallel to the eastern Adriatic coast, stretching from Slovenia along the frontier between Croatia and Bosnia-Herzegovina into western Serbia and Montenegro and northern Albania. The highest peak is Durmitor at 2,522 m/8,274 ft.

Dine, Jim (1935–) Born James Dine. US pop artist. He experimented with combinations of paintings and objects, such as a bathroom sink attached to a canvas. Dine was a pioneer of happenings in the 1960s and of ▷environment art.

Dinesen, Isak pen-name of Danish writer Karen ▷Blixen.

Dingaan (1795–*c.* 1843) Zulu chief who obtained the throne in 1828 by murdering his predecessor, Shaka, and became notorious for his cruelty. In warfare with the Boer immigrants into Natal he was defeated on 16 December 1838 – 'Dingaan's Day'. He escaped to Swaziland, where he was deposed by his brother Mpande and subsequently assassinated.

dingo wild dog of Australia. Descended from domestic dogs brought from Asia by Aborigines thousands of years ago, it belongs to the same species *Canis familiaris* as other domestic dogs. It is reddish brown with a bushy tail, and often hunts at night. It cannot bark.

Dinka member of a Nilotic minority group in southern Sudan. The Dinka are transhumant pastoralists, moving their cattle from river-area camps in the dry season to savannah forest and permanent settlements in the wet season. They inhabit approximately 388,600 sq km/150,000 sq mi around the river system that flows into the White Nile. Their language belongs to the Chari-Nile branch of the Nilo-Saharan family. The Dinka number around 1–2 million.

dinosaur (Greek *deinos* 'terrible', *sauros* 'lizard') any of a group (sometimes considered as two separate orders) of extinct reptiles living between 205 million and 65 million years ago. Their closest living relations are crocodiles and birds. Many species of dinosaur evolved during the millions of years they were the dominant large land animals. Most were large (up to 27 m/90 ft), but some were as small as chickens. They disappeared 65 million years ago for reasons not fully understood, although many theories exist, perhaps the most widely accepted being that the Earth was struck by a comet.

Classification Dinosaurs are divisible into two unrelated stocks, the orders **Saurischia** ('lizard-hip') and **Ornithischia** ('bird-hip'). Members of the former group possess a reptile-like pelvis and are mostly bipedal and carnivorous, although some are giant amphibious quadrupedal herbivores. Members of the latter group have a bird-like pelvis, are mainly four-legged, and entirely herbivorous.

The Saurischia are divided into: **theropods** ('beast-feet'), including all the bipedal carnivorous forms with long hindlimbs and short forelimbs (▷tyrannosaurus, megalosaurus); and **sauropodomorphs** ('lizard-feet forms'), including sauropods, the large quadrupedal herbivorous and amphibious types with massive limbs, long tails and necks, and tiny skulls (diplodocus, brontosaurus).

The Ornithischia were almost all plant-eaters, and eventually outnumbered the Saurischia. They are divided into four suborders: **ornithopods** ('bird-feet'), Jurassic and Cretaceous bipedal forms (iguanodon) and Cretaceous hadrosaurs with duckbills; **stegosaurs** ('plated' dinosaurs), Jurassic quadrupedal dinosaurs with a double row of triangular plates along the back and spikes on the tail (stegosaurus); **ankylosaurs** ('armoured' dinosaurs), Cretaceous quadrupedal forms, heavily armoured with bony plates

DINOSAUR Dinosaur excavation in the badlands of Alberta, Canada. In this part of the country more than 300 dinosaur skeletons have been found. The Dinosaur Provincial Park in eastern Alberta is now a World Heritage site. *Corel*

(nodosaurus); and **ceratopsians** ('horned' dinosaurs), Upper Cretaceous quadrupedal horned dinosaurs with very large skulls bearing a neck frill and large horns (triceratops).

These two main dinosaur orders form part of the superorder Archosaurus ('ruling reptiles'), comprising a total of five orders. The other three are **Pterosaurs** ('winged lizards'), including ▷pterodactyls, of which no examples exist today, **crocodilians**, and **birds**. All five orders are thought to have evolved from a 'stem-order', the **Thecondontia**.

Species Brachiosaurus, a long-necked plant-eater of the sauropod group, was about 12.6 m/40 ft to the top of its head, and weighed 80 tonnes. Compsognathus, a meat-eater, was only the size of a chicken, and ran on its hind legs. Stegosaurus, an armoured plant-eater 6 m/20 ft long, had a brain only about 3 cm/1.25 in long. Not all dinosaurs had small brains. At the other extreme, the hunting dinosaur stenonychosaurus, 2 m/6 ft long, had a brain size comparable to that of a mammal or bird of today, stereoscopic vision, and grasping hands. Many dinosaurs appear to have been equipped for a high level of activity. ▷Tyrannosaurus was a huge, two-footed, meat-eating theropod dinosaur of the Upper Cretaceous in North America and Asia. The largest carnivorous dinosaur was *Giganotosaurus carolinii*. It lived in Patagonia about 97 million years ago, was 12.5 m/41 ft long, and weighed 6–8 tonnes. Its skeleton was discovered in 1995.

Theories of extinction A popular theory of dinosaur extinction suggests that the Earth was struck by a giant meteorite or a swarm of comets 65 million years ago and this sent up such a cloud of debris and dust that climates were changed and the dinosaurs could not adapt quickly enough. The evidence for this includes a bed of rock rich in ▷iridium – an element rare on Earth but common in extraterrestrial bodies – dating from the time.

An alternative theory suggests that changes in geography brought about by the movements of continents and variations in sea level led to climate changes and the mixing of populations between previously isolated regions. This resulted in increased competition and the spread of disease.

Archaeological findings The term 'dinosaur' was coined in 1842 by the English palaeontologist Richard Owen, although there were findings of dinosaur bones as far back as the 17th century. In 1822 G A Mantell (1790–1852) found teeth of iguanodon in a quarry in Sussex. The first dinosaur to be described in a scientific journal was in 1824, when William Buckland, professor of geology at Oxford University, published his finding of a 'megalosaurus or great fossil lizard' found at Stonesfield, a village northwest of Oxford, England, although a megalosaurus bone had been found in 1677.

One of the largest dinosaur species found in the UK was a sauropod, *Cetiosaurus oxoniensis*, discovered in 1870 near Bletchingdon, north of Oxford. It was around 15 m/49 ft long, although specimens have been discovered in North Africa up to 18 m/60 ft long. In 1992 another large dinosaur, *Iguanodon bernissartensis*, was discovered near Ockley in Surrey, England, by amateur fossil hunters.

An almost complete fossil of a dinosaur skeleton was found in 1969 in the Andean foothills, South America; it had been a two-legged carnivore 2 m/6 ft tall and weighed more than 100 kg/220 lb. More than 230 million years old, it is the oldest known dinosaur. In 1982 a number of nests and eggs were found in 'colonies' in Montana, suggesting that some bred together like modern seabirds. In 1987 finds were made in China that may add much to the traditional knowledge of dinosaurs, chiefly gleaned from North American specimens. In 1989 and 1990 an articulated *Tyrannosaurus rex* was unearthed by a palaeontological team in Montana, with a full skull, one of only six known. Short stretches of dinosaur DNA were extracted in 1994 from unfossilized bone retrieved from coal deposits approximately 80 million years old.

Recent discoveries The discovery of a small dinosaur was announced in China in 1996. Sinosauropteryx lived about 120 million years ago and was 0.5 m/1.6 ft tall. It had short forelegs, a long tail, and short feathers, mainly on its neck and shoulders.

In 1997 US scientists claimed that 65-million-year-old remains discovered in the Atlantic Ocean were proof that a massive asteroid impact on Earth killed the dinosaurs. A sea-drilling expedition discovered three samples that have the signature of an asteroid impact. Previous evidence from sediment suggested that the dinosaurs did not become extinct at exactly the same time as an impact occurred. The new evidence appeared to substantiate the theories of geologists such as Walter Alvarez, who championed the theory that the dinosaurs disappeared from fossil history because of such an impact.

US palaeontologists discovered in 1997 a dinosaur wishbone in place in the skeleton of a velociraptor. This was the first time a wishbone had been found in place and scientists claimed that this constitutes strong evidence for birds having evolved from dinosaurs.

The fossil of a previously unknown dinosaur was discovered in Niger in 1998. The crocodile-like fish-eater has been named *Suchomimus* and lived 100 million years ago. It was about 11m/36 ft in length (with a 1-m/3-ft jaw) and weighed about 4 tonnes.

A new species of carnivorous dinosaur was discovered in Argentina in 2000. Several skeletons were found at the same site, so the species is thought to have been social, and about 1 m/3.3 ft longer than Tyrannosaurus.

Related Web sites: Dinosauria http://www.ucmp.berkeley.edu/diapsids/dinosaur.html
Dinosaur Trace Fossils http://www.emory.edu/COLLEGE/ENVS/research/ichnology/ dinotraces.html
World's First Dinosaur Skeleton: Hadrosaurus Foulkii http://www.levins.com/dinosaur.html

Dio Cassius (*c.* AD 150–*c.* 235) Roman historian. He wrote, in Greek, a Roman history in 80 books (of which 26 survive), covering the period from the founding of the city to AD 229, including the only surviving account of the invasion of Britain by Claudius in 43 BC.

Diocletian (AD 245–313) Born Gaius Aurelius Valerius Diocletianus. Roman emperor 284–305 who initiated severe persecution of Christians in 303. He was commander of the *protectores domestici* (Roman staff officers) under the emperor Numerian, and proclaimed emperor by his troops following Numerian's death. He defeated his rival Carinus in 285. In 293 he appointed Maximian (*c.* 240–*c.* 310) as co-ruler and reorganized and subdivided the empire, with two joint and two subordinate emperors. This was known as the Tetrarchic system. In 305 he abdicated in favour of Galerius, living in retirement until his death.

diode combination of a cold anode and a heated cathode, or the semiconductor equivalent, which incorporates a *p–n* junction. Either device allows the passage of direct current in one direction only, and so is commonly used in a ▷rectifier to convert alternating current (AC) to direct current (DC).

Diogenes (*c.* 412–*c.* 323 BC) Ascetic Greek philosopher of the ▷cynic school. He believed in freedom and self-sufficiency for the individual, and that the virtuous life was the simple life; he did not believe in social mores. His own writings do not survive.

Related Web site: Diogenes of Sinope http://www.utm.edu/research/iep/d/diogsino.htm

DIOGENES The Greek philosopher Diogenes of Sinope. *Archive Photos*

Dionysius Two tyrants of the ancient Greek city of Syracuse in Sicily. **Dionysius the Elder** (*c.* 430–367 BC) seized power in 405 BC. His first two wars with Carthage further extended the power of Syracuse, but in a third (383–378 BC) he was defeated. He was a patron of ▷Plato. He was succeeded by his son, **Dionysius the Younger**, who was driven out of Syracuse by Dion in 356 BC; he was tyrant again in 353 BC, but in 343 BC returned to Corinth.

Dionysus in Greek mythology, the god of wine, mystic ecstasy, and orgiastic excess; son of princess ▷Semele and Zeus. In his original savage form he was attended by ▷satyrs, lustful, drunken creatures; and **maenads**, women considered capable of tearing animals to pieces with their bare hands when under his influence. Later, as a more benign deity, his rites became less extreme; the Roman ▷Bacchus embodied this form.

dioptre optical unit in which the power of a ▷lens is expressed as the reciprocal of its focal length in metres. The usual convention is that convergent lenses are positive and divergent lenses negative. Short-sighted people need lenses of power about −0.7 dioptre; a typical value for long sight is about +1.5 dioptre.

Dior, Christian (1905–1957) French couturier. He established his own Paris salon in 1947 and made an impact with the 'New Look' – long, cinch-waisted, and full-skirted – after wartime austerity.

He worked with Robert Piquet as design assistant in 1938 and for Lucien Lelong 1941–46. His first collection in 1947 was an instant success and he continued to be popular during the 1950s when he created elegant and sophisticated looks with slim skirts and large box-shaped jackets. His last collection in 1957 was based on a waistless shift-style dress with the skirt narrowing towards the hem.

diorite igneous rock intermediate in composition between mafic (consisting primarily of dark-coloured minerals) and felsic (consisting primarily of light-coloured minerals) – the coarse-grained plutonic equivalent of ▷andesite. Constituent minerals include ▷feldspar and amphibole or pyroxene with only minor amounts of ▷quartz.

Diouf, Abdou (1935–) Senegalese left-wing politician, president 1981–2000. He became prime minister in 1970 under President Leopold Senghor and, on his retirement, succeeded him, being re-elected in 1988 and 1993. Despite a controversial law passed in 1998 making him 'president for life', presidential elections were held in March 2000 in which he was defeated. Six months later he withdrew from politics. His presidency was characterized by authoritarianism.

dioxin any of a family of over 200 organic chemicals, all of which are heterocyclic hydrocarbons (see ▷cyclic compounds). The term is commonly applied, however, to only one member of the family, 2,3,7,8-tetrachlorodibenzo-*p*-dioxin (2,3,7,8-TCDD), a highly toxic chemical that occurs, for example, as an impurity in the defoliant Agent Orange, used in the Vietnam War, and sometimes in the weedkiller 2,4,5-T. It has been associated with a disfiguring skin complaint (chloracne), birth defects, miscarriages, and cancer.

diphtheria acute infectious disease in which a membrane forms in the throat (threatening death by ▷asphyxia), along with the production of a powerful toxin that damages the heart and nerves. The organism responsible is a bacterium (*Corynebacterium diphtheriae*). It is treated with antitoxin and antibiotics.

Although its incidence has been reduced greatly by immunization, an epidemic in the former Soviet Union resulted in 47,802 cases and 1,746 deaths in 1994, and 1,500 deaths in 1995. In 1995 the World Health Organization (WHO) declared the epidemic 'an international public health emergency' after 20 linked cases were identified in other parts of Europe. The epidemic showed signs of abating in 1996, with a 59% decrease in the number of cases for the first three months, compared with the same period in 1995.

diplodocus plant-eating sauropod dinosaur that lived about 145 million years ago, the fossils of which have been found in the western USA. Up to 27 m/88 ft long, most of which was neck and tail, it weighed about 11 tonnes. It walked on four elephantine legs, had nostrils on top of the skull, and peglike teeth at the front of the mouth.

diploid having paired ▷chromosomes in each cell. In sexually reproducing species, one set is derived from each parent, the ▷gametes, or sex cells, of each parent being ▷haploid (having only one set of chromosomes) due to ▷meiosis (reduction cell division).

diplomacy process by which states attempt to settle their differences through peaceful means such as negotiation or ▷arbitration. See ▷foreign relations.

dip, magnetic angle at a particular point on the Earth's surface between the direction of the Earth's magnetic field and the horizontal. It is measured using a **dip circle**, which has a magnetized needle suspended so that it can turn freely in the vertical plane of the magnetic field. In the northern hemisphere the needle dips below the horizontal, pointing along the line of the magnetic field towards its north pole. At the magnetic north and south poles, the needle dips vertically and the angle of dip is 90°. See also ▷angle of declination.

dipole the uneven distribution of magnetic or electrical characteristics within a molecule or substance so that it behaves as though it possesses two equal but opposite poles or charges, a finite distance apart.

dipole, magnetic see ▷magnetic dipole.

dipper (or **water ouzel**) any of various birds of the genus *Cinclus*, family Cinclidae, order Passeriformes, found in hilly and mountainous regions across Eurasia and North America, where there are clear, fast-flowing streams. It can swim, dive, or walk along the bottom, using the pressure of water on its wings and tail to keep it down, while it searches for insect larvae and other small animals. Both wings and tail are short, the beak is fairly short and straight, and the general colour of the bird is brown, the throat and part of the breast being white.

Dirac, Paul Adrien Maurice (1902–1984) English physicist who worked out a version of quantum mechanics consistent with special ▷relativity. The existence of antiparticles, such as the positron (positive electron), was one of its predictions. He shared the Nobel Prize for Physics in 1933 (with Austrian physicist Erwin ▷Schrödinger) for his work on the development of quantum mechanics.

> **Paul Dirac**
>
> *A theory with mathematical beauty is more likely to be correct than an ugly one that fits some experimental data. God is a mathematician of a very high order, and He used very advanced mathematics in constructing the universe.*
>
> Scientific American, May 1963

direct access (or **random access**) type of file access. A direct-access file contains records that can be accessed by the computer directly because each record has its own address on the storage disk. Direct access storage mediums include CD-ROMs and magnetic disks (such as floppy disks).

direct cost or **variable cost** cost of production materials, fuel, and so on which varies directly with the volume of output. For example, steel is a direct cost for a car manufacturer because if twice the number of cars are produced, twice the amount of steel will be used in the production process.

direct current (DC) electric current that flows in one direction, and does not reverse its flow as ▷alternating current does. The electricity produced by a battery is direct current.

direct debit in banking, an instruction by a depositor with the bank to pay a certain sum of money at regular intervals.

directed number in mathematics, number with a positive (+) or negative (−) sign attached, for example +5 or −5. On a graph, a positive sign shows a movement to the right or upwards; a negative sign indicates movement downwards or to the left.

Director of Public Prosecutions (DPP) in the UK, the head of the ▷Crown Prosecution Service (established in 1985), responsible for the conduct of all criminal prosecutions in England and Wales. The DPP was formerly responsible only for the prosecution of certain serious crimes, such as murder.

Directory the five-man ruling executive in France 1795–99. Established by the constitution of 1795, it failed to deal with the political and social tensions in the country and became increasingly unpopular after military defeats. It was overthrown by a military coup 9 November 1799 that brought Napoleon Bonaparte to power.

directory in computing, a list of file names, together with information that enables a computer to retrieve those files from backing storage. The computer operating system will usually store and update a directory on the backing storage to which it refers. So, for example, on each ▷disk used by a computer a directory file will be created listing the disk's contents.

The term is also used to refer to the area on a disk where files are stored; the main area, the **root** directory, is at the top-most level, and may contain several separate **sub-directories**.

Dis in Roman mythology, the god of the underworld, also known as Orcus; he is equivalent to the Greek god ▷Pluto, ruler of Hades. Dis is also a synonym for the underworld itself.

disaccharide ▷sugar made up of two monosaccharides or simple sugars. Sucrose, $C_{12}H_{22}O_{11}$, or table sugar, is a disaccharide.

disarmament reduction of a country's weapons of war. Most disarmament talks since World War II have been concerned with nuclear-arms verification and reduction, but biological, chemical, and conventional weapons have also come under discussion at the United Nations and in other forums. Attempts to limit the arms race (initially between the USA and the USSR and since 1992 between the USA and Russia) have included the ▷Strategic Arms Limitation Talks (SALT) of the 1970s and the ▷Strategic Arms Reduction Talks (START) of the 1980s–90s.

In the UK the Campaign for Nuclear Disarmament lobbies on this issue.

Related Web site: Stockholm International Peace Research Institute (SIPRI) http://www.sipri.se

discharge tube device in which a gas conducting an electric current emits visible light. It is usually a glass tube from which virtually all the air has been removed (so that it 'contains' a near vacuum), with electrodes at each end. When a high-voltage current is passed between the electrodes, the few remaining gas atoms in the tube (or some deliberately introduced ones) ionize and emit coloured light as they conduct the current along the tube. The light originates as electrons change energy levels in the ionized atoms.

disciple follower, especially of a religious leader. The word is used in the Bible for the early followers of Jesus. The 12 disciples closest to him are known as the ▷apostles.

disco music international style of dance music of the 1970s with a heavily emphasized beat, derived from ▷funk. It was designed to be played in discotheques rather than performed live; hence the production was often more important than the performer, and drum machines came to dominate.

discrete data data that can take only whole-number or fractional values, that is, distinct values. The opposite is ▷continuous data, which can take all in-between values. Examples of discrete data include frequency and population data. However, measurements of time and other dimensions can give rise to continuous data.

discrimination distinction made (social, economic, political, legal) between individuals or groups such that one has the power to treat the other unfavourably. **Negative discrimination**, often based on ▷stereotype, includes anti-Semitism, apartheid, caste, racism, ▷sexism, and slavery. **Positive discrimination**, or ▷affirmative action, is sometimes practised in an attempt to counteract the effects of previous long-term negative discrimination. Minorities and, in some cases, majorities have been targets for discrimination.

discus circular disc thrown by athletes who rotate the body to gain momentum from within a circle 2.5 m/8 ft in diameter. The men's discus weighs 2 kg/4.4 lb and the women's 1 kg/2.2 lb. Discus throwing was a competition in ancient Greece at gymnastic contests, such as those of the Olympic Games. It is an event in the modern Olympics and athletics meetings.

disease condition that disturbs or impairs the normal state of an organism. Diseases can occur in all living things, and normally affect the functioning of cells, tissues, organs, or systems. Diseases are usually characterized by specific symptoms and signs, and can be mild and short-lasting – such as the common cold – or severe enough to decimate a whole species – such as ▷Dutch elm disease. Diseases can be classified as infectious or noninfectious. Infectious diseases are caused by micro-organisms, such as bacteria and viruses, invading the body; they can be spread across a species, or transmitted between one or more species. All other diseases can be grouped together as noninfectious diseases. These can have many causes: they may be inherited (▷congenital diseases); they may be caused by the ingestion or absorption of harmful substances, such as toxins; they can result from poor nutrition or hygiene; or they may arise from injury or ageing. The causes of some diseases are still unknown.

disinfectant agent that kills, or prevents the growth of, bacteria and other micro-organisms. Chemical disinfectants include carbolic acid (phenol, used by Joseph ▷Lister in surgery in the 1870s), ethanol, methanol, chlorine, and iodine.

disinvestment withdrawal of investments in a country for political reasons. The term is also used in economics to describe non-replacement of stock as it wears out.

disk in computing, a common medium for storing large volumes of data (an alternative is ▷magnetic tape). A **magnetic disk** is rotated at high speed in a disk-drive unit as a read/write (playback or record) head passes over its surfaces to record or read the magnetic variations that encode the data. Recently, **optical disks**, such as ▷CD-ROM (compact-disc read-only memory) and ▷WORM (write once, read many times), have been used to store computer data. Data are recorded on the disk surface as etched microscopic pits and are read by a laser-scanning device.

Optical disks have an enormous capacity – ranging from 650 megabytes for CD-ROM to 2.6 gigabytes for magneto-optical drives.

Magnetic disks come in several forms: **fixed hard disks** are built into the disk-drive unit, occasionally stacked on top of one another. A fixed disk cannot be removed: once it is full, data must be deleted in order to free space or a complete new disk drive must be added to the computer system in order to increase storage capacity. Hard disks can now store up to 22 gigabytes, and the smallest hard disk it is possible to buy is 4 gigabytes. Arrays of such disks were also used to store minicomputer and mainframe data in RAID storage systems, replacing large fixed disks and removable hard disks.

Removable hard disks are still found in minicomputer and mainframe systems. The disks are contained, individually or as stacks (disk packs), in a protective plastic case, and can be taken out of the drive unit and kept for later use. By swapping such disks around, a single hard-disk drive can be made to provide a potentially infinite storage capacity. However, access speeds and capacities tend to be lower that those associated with large fixed hard disks. A **floppy disk** (or diskette) is the most common form of backing store for microcomputers. It is much smaller in size and capacity than a hard disk, normally holding 0.5–2 megabytes of data. The floppy disk is so called because it is manufactured from

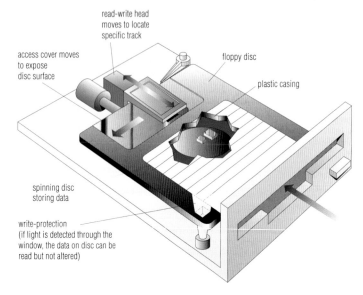

DISK DRIVE A floppy disk drive. As the disk is inserted into the drive, its surface is exposed to the read-write head, which moves over the spinning disk surface to locate a specific track.

read-write head moves to locate specific track

access cover moves to expose disc surface

floppy disc

plastic casing

spinning disc storing data

write-protection (if light is detected through the window, the data on disc can be read but not altered)

thin flexible plastic coated with a magnetic material. The earliest form of floppy disk was packaged in a card case and was easily damaged; more recent versions are contained in a smaller, rigid plastic case and are much more robust. All floppy disks can be removed from the drive unit.

disk drive mechanical device that reads data from, and writes data to, a magnetic ▷disk.

disk formatting in computing, preparing a blank magnetic disk in order that data can be stored on it. Data are recorded on a disk's surface on circular tracks, each of which is divided into a number of sectors. In formatting a disk, the computer's operating system adds control information such as track and sector numbers, which enables the data stored to be accessed correctly by the disk-drive unit.

Disney, Walt(er Elias) (1901–1966) US film producer, animator, and pioneer of family entertainment, whose career spanned the development of the motion picture medium. *Disney* created many world-famous cartoon characters, made phenomenally successful feature-length animated films, including *Snow White and the Seven Dwarfs* (1938), and opened his first theme park in 1955. The creator of Mickey Mouse, the first to add music and effects to cartoons, and founder of the Disneyland theme park, he was the originator of the modern multimedia corporation.

Disney formed the Disney Brothers Studio in 1923. His first cartoon with sound was released in 1928 and featured Mickey Mouse, and in 1929 he began using colour in his cartoons. *Snow White and the Seven Dwarfs* broke all box-office records on its release and was followed by a series of feature-length classics. In the

1950s Disney started making action films and in 1961 he set up the film studio Buena Vista International.

Disney was born in Chicago, Illinois, the youngest of five children. When he left McKinley High School he had a variety of jobs including working for his father's short-lived O Zell company, and at night he attended art classes. As a Red Cross ambulance driver during World War I (he was too young to enlist), he kept drawing and, on his return to Kansas, met US animator Ub Iwerks. Together they set up as commercial artists in a small studio called Laugh-O-Grams, and produced a first series of animated cartoons. When the studio went bankrupt he moved to Los Angeles in California and formed the Disney Brothers Studio in partnership with his brother Roy in 1923. He created the *Alice in Cartoonland* series and then, in 1927, a fully animated series called *Oswald the Rabbit* (although he subsequently lost the rights to the character).

From the late 1920s, Disney was at the forefront of innovation in the film industry. His first sound cartoon featured Mickey Mouse (created earlier in his silent film, *Plane Crazy*) in *Steamboat Willie* in 1928, which premiered in New York. He then introduced Technicolor into his production of the *Silly Symphonies*, a series of animated pieces set to classical music, the first of which was *The Skeleton Dance* (1929). His *Flowers in Trees* won him the first of his Academy Awards in 1932 and Mickey Mouse debuted in colour in 1935. He introduced the multiplane camera technique, a device that added depth to the cartoon, in the *Old Mill* in 1937, and also started merchandising the Disney cartoon characters which by then included Donald Duck, Pluto, and Goofy. The characters also appeared in comic books worldwide.

Disney produced his first animated feature film *Snow White and the Seven Dwarfs* in 1937, which broke all box-office records. It was produced at an unheard-of cost of $2 million during the Great Depression. Other famous full-length classics followed: *Pinocchio* and *Fantasia* (both 1940), *Dumbo* (1941), and *Bambi* (1942).

Disney was the first Hollywood producer to embrace television; he made an historic deal with the ABC network to produce and appear in a weekly programme in 1954 and was the first to present a colour television series called the *Wonderful World of Color* in 1961. In 1955 Disney opened his magic kingdom, Disneyland, a $17 million theme park in Anaheim, California. The second Disneyworld, in Orlando, Florida, opened after his death in 1971. In 1983 a Tokyo Disneyland opened in Japan, and in 1992 Euro Disney opened at Marne-la-Vallé, 32 km/20 mi east of Paris, France. Disney's California Adventure opened in 2001 adjacent to the original Disneyland. A Walt Disney amusement park is being built in Hong Kong and is scheduled to open in 2005.

dispersion in physics, a particular property of ▷refraction in which the angle and velocity of waves passing through a dispersive medium depends upon their frequency. In the case of visible light the frequency corresponds to colour. The splitting of white light into a spectrum (see ▷electromagnetic waves) when it passes through a prism occurs because each component frequency of light moves through at a slightly different angle and speed. A rainbow is formed when sunlight is dispersed by raindrops.

displacement activity in animal behaviour, an action that is performed out of its normal context, while the animal is in a state of stress, frustration, or uncertainty. Birds, for example, often peck

at grass when uncertain whether to attack or flee from an opponent; similarly, humans scratch their heads when nervous.

Disraeli, Benjamin (1804–1881) 1st Earl of Beaconsfield. British Conservative politician and novelist. Elected to Parliament in 1837, he was chancellor of the Exchequer under Lord ▷Derby in 1852, 1858–59, and 1866–68, and prime minister in 1868 and 1874–80. His imperialist policies brought India directly under the crown, and he was personally responsible for purchasing control of the Suez Canal. The central Conservative Party organization is his creation. His popular, political novels reflect an interest in social reform and include *Coningsby* (1844) and *Sybil* (1845).

After a period in a solicitor's office, Disraeli wrote the novels *Vivian Grey* (1826), *Contarini Fleming* (1832), and others, and the pamphlet 'Vindication of the English Constitution' (1835). Entering Parliament in 1837 after four unsuccessful attempts, he was laughed at as a dandy, but when his maiden speech was shouted down, he said: 'The time will come when you will hear me.' Excluded from ▷Peel's government of 1841–46, Disraeli formed his Young England group to keep a critical eye on Peel's Conservatism. Its ideas were expounded in the novel trilogy *Coningsby*, *Sybil*, and *Tancred* (1847).

When Peel decided in 1846 to repeal the Corn Laws, Disraeli opposed the measure in a series of witty and effective speeches; Peel's government fell soon after, and Disraeli gradually came to be recognized as the leader of the Conservative Party in the Commons. During the next 20 years the Conservatives formed short-lived minority governments in 1852, 1858–59, and 1866–68, with Lord Derby as prime minister and Disraeli as chancellor of the Exchequer and leader of the Commons. In 1852 Disraeli first proposed discrimination in income tax between earned and unearned income, but without success. The 1858–59 government legalized the admission of Jews to Parliament, and transferred the government of India from the East India Company to the crown. In 1866 the Conservatives took office after defeating a Liberal Reform Bill, and then attempted to secure the credit of widening the franchise by the Reform Bill of 1867. On Lord Derby's retirement in 1868 Disraeli became prime minister, but a few months later was defeated by Gladstone in a general election. During the six years of opposition that followed he published another novel, *Lothair* (1870), and established Conservative Central Office, the prototype of modern party organizations. In 1874 Disraeli took office for the second time, with a majority of 100. Some useful reform measures were carried, such as the Artisans' Dwelling Act, which empowered local authorities to undertake slum clearance, but the outstanding feature of the government's policy was its imperialism. It was Disraeli's personal initiative that purchased from the Khedive of Egypt a controlling interest in the Suez Canal, conferred on the Queen the title of Empress of India, and sent the Prince of Wales on the first royal tour of that country. Disraeli accepted an earldom in 1876. The Bulgarian revolt of 1876 and the subsequent Russo-Turkish War of 1877–78 provoked one of many political

> **Benjamin Disraeli**
> *Justice is truth in action.*
> Speech in House of Commons, 11 February 1851

GLADSTONE AND DISRAELI Cartoon from *Punch* in 1872 depicting Disraeli (front) and Gladstone as two opposing lions making speeches in Lancashire. *Philip Sauvain Picture Collection*

WALT DISNEY US animator Walt Disney (pictured here with his grandson in 1955). *Image Bank*

duels between Disraeli and Gladstone, the Liberal leader, and was concluded by the Congress of Berlin in 1878, where Disraeli was the principal British delegate and brought home 'peace with honour' and Cyprus. The government was defeated in 1880, and a year later Disraeli died.

dissection cutting apart of bodies to study their organization, or tissues to gain access to a site in surgery. Postmortem dissection was considered a sin in the Middle Ages. In the UK before 1832, hanged murderers were the only legal source of bodies, supplemented by graverobbing (Burke and Hare were the most notorious grave robbers). The Anatomy Act of 1832 authorized the use of deceased institutionalized paupers unclaimed by next of kin, and by the 1940s bequests of bodies had been introduced.

Dissenter in Britain, former name for a Protestant refusing to conform to the established Christian church. For example, Baptists, Presbyterians, and Independents (now known as Congregationalists) were Dissenters.

dissident in one-party states, a person intellectually dissenting from the official line. Dissidents have been sent into exile, prison, labour camps, and mental institutions, or deprived of their jobs. In the former USSR the number of imprisoned dissidents declined from more than 600 in 1986 to fewer than 100 in 1990, of whom the majority were ethnic nationalists. In China the number of prisoners of conscience increased after the 1989 Tiananmen Square massacre. The most prominent pro-democracy activist, Wang Dan, was sentenced to 11 years' imprisonment in 1996 for allegedly plotting to overthrow the government (he was released on medical grounds in April 1998 and allowed to visit the USA).

dissociation in chemistry, the process whereby a single compound splits into two or more smaller products, which may be capable of recombining to form the reactant.

distance learning home-based study by correspondence course or by radio, television, or audio or video tape. The establishment of the ▷Open University in 1969 put the UK in the forefront of distance learning; the ▷Open College and individual institutions also offer distance-learning packages.

distance ratio in a machine, the distance moved by the input force, or effort, divided by the distance moved by the output force, or load. The ratio indicates the movement magnification achieved, and is equivalent to the machine's velocity ratio.

distemper any of several infectious diseases of animals characterized by catarrh, cough, and general weakness. Specifically, it refers to a virus disease in young dogs, also found in wild animals, which can now be prevented by vaccination. In 1988 an allied virus killed over 10,000 common seals in the Baltic and North seas.

distillation technique used to purify liquids or to separate mixtures of liquids possessing different boiling points. **Simple distillation** is used in the purification of liquids (or the separation of substances in solution from their solvents) – for example, in the production of pure water from a salt solution.

The solution is boiled and the vapours of the solvent rise into a separate piece of apparatus (the condenser) where they are cooled and condensed. The liquid produced (the distillate) is the pure solvent; the non-volatile solutes (now in solid form) remain in the distillation vessel to be discarded as impurities or recovered as required. Mixtures of liquids (such as ▷petroleum or aqueous ethanol) are separated by **fractional distillation**, or fractionation. When the mixture is boiled, the vapours of its most volatile component rise into a vertical ▷fractionating column where they condense to liquid form. However, as this liquid runs back down the column it is reheated to boiling point by the hot rising vapours of the next-most-volatile component and so its vapours ascend the column once more. This boiling-condensing process occurs repeatedly inside the column, eventually bringing about a temperature gradient along its length. The vapours of the more volatile components therefore reach the top of the column and enter the condenser for collection before those of the less volatile components. In the fractional distillation of petroleum, groups of compounds (fractions) possessing similar relative molecular masses and boiling points are tapped off at different points on the column.

The earliest-known reference to the process is to the distillation of wine in the 12th century by Adelard of Bath. The chemical retort used for distillation was invented by Muslims, and was first seen in the West about 1570.

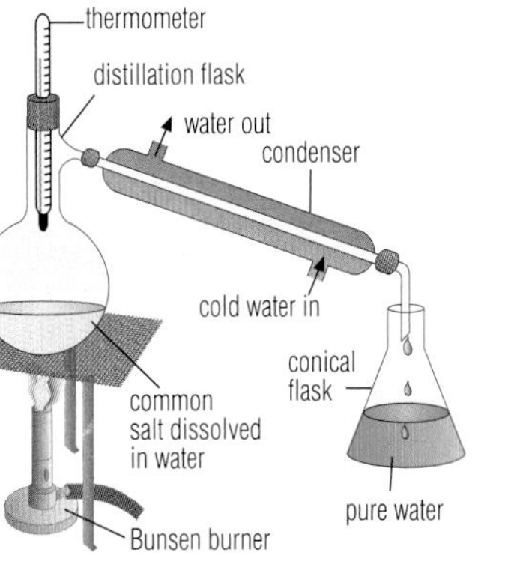

DISTILLATION Laboratory apparatus for simple distillation.

distributive operation in mathematics, an operation, such as multiplication, that bears a relationship to another operation, such as addition, such that $a \times (b + c) = (a \times b) + (a \times c)$. For example, $3 \times (2 + 4) = (3 \times 2) + (3 \times 4) = 18$. Multiplication may be said to be distributive over addition. Addition is not, however, distributive over multiplication because $3 + (2 \times 4) \neq (3 + 2) \times (3 + 4)$.

district council lower unit of local government in England. In 1998 there were 274 district councils under 34 (two-tier) non-metropolitan county councils, and 36 single-tier metropolitan district councils. Their responsibilities cover housing, local planning and development, roads (excluding trunk and classified), bus services, environmental health (refuse collection, clean air, food safety and hygiene, and enforcement of the Offices, Shops and Railway Premises Act 1963), council tax, museums and art galleries, parks and playing fields, swimming baths, cemeteries, and so on.

District of Columbia seat of the federal government of the USA, coextensive with the city of Washington, DC, situated on the Potomac and Anacostia rivers; area 178 sq km/69 sq mi; population (1996 est) 543,000. Government agencies are its main source of employment, but tourism and the manufacture of scientific and technical equipment are also important to the economy. The district was ceded by Maryland as the site of the national capital in 1790.

Diu island off the Kathiawar peninsula, northwest India, part of the Union Territory of ▷Daman and Diu.

diuretic any drug that increases the output of urine by the kidneys. It may be used in the treatment of high blood pressure and to relieve ▷oedema associated with heart, lung, kidney or liver disease, and some endocrine disorders.

diver (or **loon**) any of four species of marine bird of the order Gaviiformes, specialized for swimming and diving, found in northern regions of the northern hemisphere. The legs are set so far back that walking is almost impossible, but they are powerful swimmers and good flyers, and only come ashore to nest. They have straight bills, short tail-feathers, webbed feet, and long bodies; they feed on fish, crustaceans, and some water plants. During the breeding period they live inland and the female lays two eggs which hatch into down-covered chicks. Of the four species, the largest is the white-billed diver *Gavia adamsii*, an Arctic species 75 cm/2.5 ft long.

DIVER The red-throated diver.

diverticulitis inflammation of diverticula (pockets of herniation) in the large intestine. It is usually triggered by infection and causes diarrhoea or constipation, and lower abdominal pain. Usually it can be controlled by diet and antibiotics.

divertissement (French 'entertainment') dance, or suite of dances, within a ballet or opera, where the plot comes to a halt for a display of technical virtuosity, such as the character dances in the last act of *Coppélia* by Delibes, or the last acts of *Sleeping Beauty* and *A Midsummer Night's Dream*.

dividend in business, the amount of money that company directors decide should be taken out of net profits for distribution to shareholders. It is usually declared as a percentage or fixed amount per ▷share.

divination art of ascertaining future events or eliciting other hidden knowledge by supernatural or nonrational means. Divination played a large part in the ancient civilizations of the Egyptians, Greeks (see ▷oracle), Romans, and Chinese (using the ▷*I Ching*), and is still practised throughout the world.

Divine Light Mission religious movement founded in India in 1960, which gained a prominent following in the USA in the 1970s. It proclaims Guru Maharaj Ji as the present age's successor to the gods or religious leaders Krishna, Buddha, Jesus, and Muhammad. He is believed to be able to provide his followers with the knowledge required to attain salvation.

divine right of kings Christian political doctrine that hereditary monarchy is the system approved by God, hereditary right cannot be forfeited, monarchs are accountable to God alone for their actions, and rebellion against the lawful sovereign is therefore blasphemous.

diving sport of entering water either from a springboard 1 m/3 ft or 3 m/10 ft above the water, or from a platform, or highboard, 10 m/33 ft above the water. Various differing starts are adopted, facing forwards or backwards, and somersaults, twists, and combinations thereof are performed in midair before entering the water. A minimum pool depth of 5 m/16.5 ft is needed for high or platform diving. Points are awarded and the level of difficulty of each dive is used as a multiplying factor.

diving apparatus any equipment used to enable a person to spend time underwater. Diving bells were in use in the 18th century, the diver breathing air trapped in a bell-shaped chamber. This was followed by cumbersome diving suits in the early 19th century. Complete freedom of movement came with the ▷aqualung, invented by Jacques ▷Cousteau in the early 1940s. For work at greater depths the technique of saturation diving was developed in the 1970s in which divers live for a week or more breathing a mixture of helium and oxygen at the pressure existing on the seabed where they work (as in work on North Sea platforms and tunnel building).

divorce legal dissolution of a lawful marriage. It is distinct from an annulment, which is a legal declaration that the marriage was invalid. The ease with which a divorce can be obtained in different countries varies considerably and is also affected by different religious practices.

Related Web site: Divorce.co.uk http://www.divorce.co.uk

Diwali ('garland of lamps') Hindu festival in October/November celebrating Lakshmi, goddess of light and wealth, as well as the New Year and the story of the *Rāmāyana*. It is marked by the lighting of lamps and candles (inviting the goddess into the house), feasting, and the exchange of gifts. For Sikhs, Diwali celebrates Guru Hargobind's release from prison.

Dix, Otto (1891–1969) German painter. He was a major exponent of the harsh realism current in Germany in the 1920s and closely associated with the *Neue Sachlichkeit* group. He is known chiefly for his unsettling 1920s paintings of prostitutes and sex murders and for his powerful series of works depicting the hell of trench warfare, for example *Flanders: After Henri Barbusse 'Le Feu'* (1934–36; Nationalgalerie, Berlin).

Dix was a considerable portraitist, as exemplified in *Dr Heinrich Stadelmann* (1920; Art Gallery of Ontario, Toronto), and he also painted allegorical works in a style reminiscent of 16th-century Flemish and Italian masters. He trained at the art academies of Dresden and Dusseldorf, and his early work shows the influence of ▷Kokoschka and Italian ▷Futurism. In 1933 he was dismissed from his teaching post at the Dresden Art Academy by the Nazis, and branded a decadent. His experiences as a serving soldier in World War I and as a prisoner-of-war 1945–46 instilled in him a profound horror of armed conflict.

Dixie southern states of the USA. Dixie encompasses those states that joined the ▷Confederacy during the American Civil War.

Dixieland jazz jazz style that originated in New Orleans, USA, in the early 20th century and worked its way up the Mississippi. It is characterized by improvisation and the playing back and forth of the cornet, trumpet, clarinet, and trombone. The steady background beat is supplied by the piano, bass, and percussion instrument players, who also have their turns to solo. It is usually played by bands of four to eight members.

Noted Dixieland musicians were King Oliver, Jelly Roll ▷Morton, and Louis ▷Armstrong.

dizziness another word for ▷vertigo.

Djakarta variant spelling of ▷Jakarta, the capital of Indonesia.

Djibouti (or **Jibuti**) chief port and capital of the Republic of ▷Djibouti, on a peninsula 240 km/149 mi southwest of Aden and 565 km/351 mi northeast of Addis Ababa; population (1995) 383,000. Industries include petroleum refining, textiles, and rail freighting. The city is an important regional bunkering and supply centre for the export trade in petroleum, and is the main export route for Ethiopian coffee.

Djibouti see country box.

Djilas, Milovan (1911–1995) Yugoslav dissident and political writer. A close wartime colleague of Marshal ▷Tito, he was dismissed from high office in 1954 and twice imprisoned 1956–61 and 1962–66 because of his advocacy of greater political pluralism and condemnation of the communist bureaucracy. He was formally rehabilitated in 1989.

DNA (abbreviation for deoxyribonucleic acid) the molecular basis of heredity. A complex giant molecule that contains, in chemically coded form, the information needed for a cell to make proteins. DNA is a ladderlike double-stranded ▷nucleic acid which forms the basis of genetic inheritance in all organisms, except for a few viruses that have only ▷RNA. DNA is organized into ▷chromosomes and, in organisms other than bacteria, it is found only in the cell nucleus.

Structure DNA is made up of two chains of ▷nucleotide subunits, with each nucleotide containing either a purine (adenine or guanine) or pyrimidine (cytosine or thymine) base. The bases link up with each other (adenine linking with thymine, and cytosine with guanine) to form ▷base pairs that connect the two strands of the DNA molecule like the rungs of a twisted ladder.

Heredity The specific way in which the pairs form means that the base sequence is preserved from generation to generation. Hereditary information is stored as a specific sequence of bases. A set of three bases – known as a **codon** – acts as a blueprint for the manufacture of a particular ▷amino acid, the subunit of a protein molecule.

Codons Geneticists identify the codons by the initial letters of the constituent bases – for example, the base sequence of codon CAG is cytosine–adenine–guanine. The meaning of each of the codons in the ▷genetic code has been worked out by molecular geneticists. There are four different bases, which means that there must be 4 × 4 × 4 = 64 different codons. Proteins are usually made up of only 20 different amino acids, so many amino acids have

more than one codon (for example, GGT, GGC, GGA, and GGG all code for the same amino acid, glycine). The first chromosome to have its DNA sequenced by geneticists was chromosome 22 (one of the smallest human chromosomes, but linked to schizophrenia), which had its estimated 800 genes and 33.5 million bases sequenced in 1999, leaving only a few gaps.

Blueprint for the organism The information encoded by the codons is transcribed (see ▷transcription) by messenger RNA and is then translated into amino acids in the ribosomes and cytoplasm. The sequence of codons determines the precise order in which amino acids are linked up during manufacture and, therefore, the kind of protein that is to be produced. Because proteins are the chief structural molecules of living matter and, as enzymes, regulate all aspects of metabolism, it may be seen that the genetic code is effectively responsible for building and controlling the whole organism.

Laboratory techniques The sequence of bases along the length of DNA can be determined by cutting the molecule into small portions, using restriction enzymes. This technique can also be used for transferring specific sequences of DNA from one organism to another.

Ancient DNA The oldest sequenced DNA to be found is that of a nemonychid weevil trapped in amber from the Cretaceous period, and estimated as being 120–135 million years old. US researchers extracted DNA from human hair 10,000 years old in 1994. Dinosaur DNA was extracted in 1994 from unfossilized dinosaur bones found in a coal mine in Utah.

> Related Web site: Molecular Expressions: The DNA Collection
> http://micro.magnet.fsu.edu/micro/gallery/dna/dna4.html

DNA fingerprinting (or DNA profiling) another name for ▷genetic fingerprinting.

Dnieper (or Dnepr; Greek **Borysthenes**) river rising in the Valdai Hills west of Moscow, in the Smolensk region of the Russian Federation, and flowing south through Belarus and Ukraine to

enter the Black Sea near Kherson; total length 2,250 km/1,400 mi. The Dnieper is the third longest European river (after the Volga and Danube).

Dnipropetrovs'k city in Ukraine, on the right bank of the River Dnieper and capital of an oblast of the same name; population (1990) 1,200,000. It is the centre of a major industrial region, with iron, steel, chemical, and engineering industries. The city draws much of its power from the Dneproges Dam, 60 km/37 mi downstream.

D-notice in the UK, a censorship notice issued by the Department of Defence to the media to prohibit the publication of information on matters alleged to be of national security. The system dates from 1922.

do. abbreviation for ditto.

Dobell, William (1899–1970) Australian portraitist and genre painter, born in New South Wales. He studied art in the UK and the Netherlands 1929–39. His portrait of *Joshua Smith* (1943; Sir Edward Hayward, Adelaide, Australia) provoked a court case (Dobell was accused of caricaturing his subject). He was knighted in 1966.

Dobermann (or Dobermann pinscher) breed of smooth-coated dog with a docked tail, much used as a guard dog. It stands up to 70 cm/27.5 in tall, has a long head with a flat, smooth skull, and is often black with brown markings. It takes its name from the man who bred it in 19th-century Germany.

Döblin, Alfred (1878–1957) German novelist. His *Berlin-Alexanderplatz* (1929) owes much to James Joyce's *Ulysses* in its minutely detailed depiction of the inner lives of a city's inhabitants, scrutinizing the social and psychological pressures exerted by the city; it is considered by many to be the finest 20th-century German novel. Other works include *November 1918: Eine deutsche Revolution/A German Revolution* (1939–50; published in four parts) about the formation of the Weimar Republic.

Djibouti

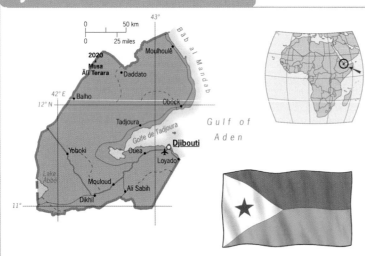

Djibouti formerly French Somaliland (1888–1967), French Territory of the Afars and Issas (1966–77) country on the east coast of Africa, at the south end of the Red Sea, bounded east by the Gulf of Aden, southeast by Somalia, south and west by Ethiopia, and northwest by Eritrea.

NATIONAL NAME *Jumhouriyya Djibouti/Republic of Djibouti*
AREA 23,200 sq km/8,957 sq mi
CAPITAL Djibouti (and chief port)
MAJOR TOWNS/CITIES Tadjoura, Obock, Dikhil, Ali-Sabieh
PHYSICAL FEATURES mountains divide an inland plateau from a coastal plain; hot and arid

Government

HEAD OF STATE Ismail Omar Guelleh from 1999
HEAD OF GOVERNMENT Dileita Mohamed Dileita from 2001
POLITICAL SYSTEM authoritarian nationalist
POLITICAL EXECUTIVE unlimited presidency
ADMINISTRATIVE DIVISIONS five districts
ARMED FORCES 9,800; plus paramilitary forces of 2,500 (2002 est)
DEATH PENALTY abolished in 1995

Economy and resources

CURRENCY Djibouti franc
GPD (US$) 597 million (2002 est)
REAL GDP GROWTH (% change on previous year) 1.9 (2001)
GNI (US$) 590 million (2002 est)
GNI PER CAPITA (PPP) (US$) 2,070 (2002 est)
CONSUMER PRICE INFLATION 2% (2003 est)
UNEMPLOYMENT 58% (1996 est)
FOREIGN DEBT (US$) 338 million (2001 est)
MAJOR TRADING PARTNERS Somalia, France, Ethiopia, Yemen, Saudi Arabia, United Arab Emirates, Italy, UK
INDUSTRIES mineral water bottling, dairy products and other small-scale enterprises; an important port serving the hinterland
EXPORTS hides, cattle, coffee (largely re-exports). Principal market: Somalia 56% (2000)
IMPORTS vegetable products, foodstuffs, beverages, vinegar, tobacco, machinery and

transport equipment, mineral products. Principal source: Saudi Arabia 18% (2000)
ARABLE LAND 10% (1995)
AGRICULTURAL PRODUCTS mainly market gardening; livestock rearing (over 50% of the population are pastoral nomads); fishing

Population and society

POPULATION 703,000 (2003 est)
POPULATION GROWTH RATE 1% (2000–05)
POPULATION DENSITY (per sq km) 30 (2003 est)
URBAN POPULATION (% of total) 85 (2003 est)
AGE DISTRIBUTION (% of total population) 0–14 43%, 15–59 51%, 60+ 6% (2002 est)
ETHNIC GROUPS population divided mainly into two Hamitic groups; the Issas (Somalis) (60%)in the south, and the minority Afars (or Danakil) (35%) in the north and west. There are also minorities of Europeans (mostly French), as well as Arabs, Sudanese, Indians
LANGUAGE French (official), Issa (Somali), Afar, Arabic
RELIGION Sunni Muslim
EDUCATION (compulsory years) 6
LABOUR FORCE 75.2% agriculture, 11% industry, 13.8% services (1999)
LIFE EXPECTANCY 45 (men); 47 (women) (2000–05)
TV SETS (per 1,000 people) 48 (1999 est)
INTERNET USERS (per 10,000 people) 68.6 (2002 est)

DJIBOUTI This stamp depicts a column of travertine or tufa, in Lake Abbe on the western border of Djibouti. *Stanley Gibbons*

Chronology

3rd century BC: The north settled by Able immigrants from Arabia, whose descendants are the Afars (Danakil).

early Christian era: Somali Issas settled in coastal areas and south, ousting Afars.

825: Islam introduced by missionaries.

16th century: Portuguese arrived to challenge trading monopoly of Arabs.

1862: French acquired a port at Obock.

1888: Annexed by France as part of French Somaliland.

1900s: Railroad linked Djibouti port with the Ethiopian hinterland.

1946: Became overseas territory within French Union, with representation in French parliament.

1958: Voted to become overseas territorial member of French Community.

1967: French Somaliland renamed the French Territory of the Afars and the Issas.

early 1970s: Issas (Somali) peoples campaigned for independence, but the minority Afars, of Ethiopian descent, and Europeans sought to remain French.

1977: Independence was achieved as Djibouti, with Hassan Gouled Aptidon, the leader of the independence movement, elected president.

1981: A new constitution made the People's Progress Assembly (RPP) the only legal party.

1984: The policy of neutrality was reaffirmed. The economy was undermined by severe drought.

1992: A new multiparty constitution was adopted; fighting erupted between government forces and Afar Front for Restoration of Unity and Democracy (FRUD) guerrilla movement in the northeast.

1993: Opposition parties were allowed to operate, but Gouled was re-elected president.

1994: A peace agreement was reached with Afar FRUD militants, ending the civil war.

1999: Ismail Omar Guelleh was elected president.

2001: Dileita Mohamed Dileita replaced Hamdaou as prime minister.

2002: Full multiparty democracy implemented instead of only four political parties.

Dobzhansky, Theodosius (1900–1975) Adopted name of Feodosy Grigorevich Dobrzhansky. Ukrainian-born US geneticist who established evolutionary genetics as an independent discipline. He showed that genetic variability between individuals of the same species is very high and that this diversity is vital to the process of evolution.

dock (or **sorrel**) in botany, any of a number of plants belonging to the buckwheat family. They are tall, annual or perennial herbs, often with lance-shaped leaves and small greenish flowers. Native to temperate regions, there are 30 North American and several British species. (Genus *Rumex*, family Polygonaceae.)

> **Related Web site: Docks** http://www.botanical.com/botanical/mgmh/d/docks-15.html

Docklands urban development area east of St Katherine's Dock, London, occupying the site of the former Wapping and Limehouse docks, the Isle of Dogs, and Royal Docks. It comprises 2,226 hectares/5,550 acres of former wharves, warehouses, and wasteland. Plans for its redevelopment were set in motion in 1981 and by 1993 over 13,000 private housing units had been built, including terraced houses at Maconochies Wharf, Isle of Dogs. Distinguished buildings include the Tidal Basin Pumping Station in Royal Docks, designed by Richard Rogers, and the printing plant for the *Financial Times*, designed by Nicholas Grimshaw. The Limehouse Link motorway and tunnel, linking Tower Hill and Canary Wharf, opened in 1993. The tallest building is the ▷Canary Wharf tower. Docklands is served by the London City airport (Stolport) and the Docklands Light Railway (DLR). The London Underground Jubilee Line was extended to Canary Wharf in 1999.

document in computing, data associated with a particular application. For example, a **text document** might be produced by a ▷word processor and a **graphics document** might be produced with a ▷CAD package. An ▷OMR or OCR document is a paper document containing data that can be directly input to the computer using a ▷document reader.

documentation in computing, the written information associated with a computer program or applications package. Documentation is usually divided into two categories: program documentation and user documentation.

document reader in computing, an input device that reads marks or characters, usually on preprepared forms and documents. Such devices are used to capture data by ▷optical mark recognition (OMR), ▷optical character recognition (OCR), and ▷mark sensing.

dodder parasitic plant belonging to the morning-glory family, without leaves or roots. The thin stem twines around the host plant, and penetrating suckers withdraw nourishment. (Genus *Cuscuta*, family Convolvulaceae.)

dodecahedron regular solid with 12 pentagonal faces and 12 vertices. It is one of the five regular ▷polyhedra, or Platonic solids.

Dodecanese (Greek *Dhodhekánisos*; 'twelve islands') group of islands in the Aegean Sea; area 2,663 sq km/1,028 sq mi; population (1991) 162,400. Once Turkish, the islands were Italian 1912–47, when they were ceded to Greece. They include ▷Rhodes and ▷Kos. Chief products include fruit, olives, and sponges.

dodecaphony music composed according to the ▷twelve-tone system of composition.

Dodgson, Charles Lutwidge real name of English author Lewis ▷Carroll.

dodo extinct flightless bird *Raphus cucullatus*, order Columbiformes, formerly found on the island of Mauritius, but exterminated by early settlers around 1681. Although related to the pigeons, it was larger than a turkey, with a bulky body, rudimentary wings, and short curly tail-feathers. The bill was blackish in colour, forming a horny hook at the end.

Dodoma official capital (replacing ▷Dar es Salaam in 1974) of ▷Tanzania; 1,132 m/3,713 ft above sea level; population (1994 est) 215,000. Dar es Salaam remains the administrative capital, pending the transfer of government functions to Dodoma. It is a centre of communications, linked by rail with Dar es Salaam and Kigoma on Lake Tanganyika, and by road with Kenya to the north and Zambia and Malawi to the south. There is an airport. Dodoma is a marketplace for locally-grown coffee and peanuts, but has a limited industrial base, which includes the manufacture of bricks.

Doe, Samuel Kanyon (1950–1990) Liberian politician and soldier, head of state 1980–90. After seizing power in a coup, Doe made himself general and army commander-in-chief. As chair of the People's Redemption Council (PRC) he was the first Liberian ruler to come from an indigenous Liberian group, ending the political dominance of the US-Liberian elite. He lifted the ban on political parties in 1984 and was elected president in 1985, as leader of the newly formed National Democratic Party of Liberia. Despite alleged electoral fraud, he was sworn in during January 1986. Having successfully put down an uprising in April 1990, Doe was deposed and killed by rebel forces in September 1990. His regime was notable for incompetence and a poor human-rights record.

dog any carnivorous mammal of the family Canidae, including wild dogs, wolves, jackals, coyotes, and foxes. Specifically, the domestic dog *Canis familiaris*, the earliest animal descended from the wolf. Dogs were first domesticated around 14,000 years ago, and migrated with humans to all the continents. They have been selectively bred into many different varieties for use as working animals and pets.

Characteristics The dog has slender legs and walks on its toes (**digitigrade**). The forefeet have five toes, the hind feet four, with non-retractile claws. The head is small and the muzzle pointed, but the shape of the head differs greatly in various breeds. The average life of a dog is from 10 to 14 years, though some live to be 20. The dog has a very acute sense of smell and can readily be trained, for it has a good intelligence.

Wild dogs Of the wild dogs, some are solitary, such as the long-legged maned wolf *Chrysocyon brachurus* of South America, but others hunt in groups, such as the African hunting dog *Lycaonpictus* (classified as a vulnerable species) and the ▷wolf. ▷Jackals scavenge for food, and the raccoon dog *Nyctereutes procyonoides* of east Asia includes plant food as well as meat in its diet. The Australian wild dog is the ▷dingo.

Breeds There are over 400 different breeds of dog throughout the world. The UK Kennel Club (1873) groups those eligible for registration (150 breeds) into sporting breeds (hound, gundog, and terrier) and nonsporting (utility, working, and toy). Numerous foreign dogs have been imported into the UK, including the dachshund, German shepherd, and boxer from Germany, the chow-chow from China, and the poodle from France.

There are over 7 million dogs in the UK, of which 0.5 million are strays. About £70 million per year is spent on rounding up and looking after strays, and on hospital treatment for people suffering from dog bites (over 200,000 per year). The RSPCA investigates over 80,000 complaints of dog abuse per year. See also ▷dog, dangerous.

> **Related Web sites: Dog Lovers Page** http://www.petnet.com.au/dogs/dogbreedindex.html

dog, dangerous any of the breeds listed in a 1991 amendment to the UK Dangerous Dogs Act 1989, which have to be muzzled in public. These include pit-bull terriers (which must also be registered with the police) and the Japanese *tosa*. Earlier legislation includes the Dogs Act 1871, with regard to keeping dogs under proper control, and the Dogs (Protection of Livestock) Act 1953.

doge chief magistrate in the ancient constitutions of Venice and Genoa. The first doge of Venice was appointed in 697 with absolute power (modified in 1297), and from his accession dates Venice's prominence in history. The last Venetian doge, Lodovico Manin, retired in 1797 and the last Genoese doge in 1804.

Dōgen (1200–1253) Japanese Buddhist monk, pupil of Eisai; founder of the Sōtō school of Zen. He did not reject study, but stressed the importance of *zazen*, seated meditation, for its own sake.

dogfish any of several small sharks found in the northeast Atlantic, Pacific, and Mediterranean. The sandy dogfish *Scyliorhinus caniculus* is found around the coasts of Britain, Scandinavia, and Europe. Bottom-living, it is sandy brown and covered with spots, and grows to about 75 cm/2.5 ft. It is edible, and is known in restaurants as 'rock eel' or 'rock salmon'. Various other species of small shark may also be called dogfish.

Dogon member of a people of eastern Mali and northwestern Burkina Faso. They number approximately 250,000 and their language belongs to the Voltaic (Gur) branch of the Niger-Congo family. See Dogon culture on p. 278.

Dogs, Isle of district of east London, England, part of the Greater London borough of ▷Tower Hamlets. It is bounded on three sides by the River Thames, and is part of the Docklands urban development area.

dog's mercury plant belonging to the spurge family, common in woods of Europe and southwest Asia. It grows to 30 cm/1 ft, has oval, light-green leaves, and spreads over woodland floors in patches of plants of a single sex. Male flowers are small, greenish yellow, and held on an upright spike above the leaves; female flowers droop below the upper leaves. (*Mercurialis perennis*, family Euphorbiaceae.)

dogwhelk marine mollusc, some of which live on rocky shores whilst others burrow. The shell aperture is grooved to house the inhalant siphon keeping it clear of the mud.

dogwood any of a group of trees and shrubs belonging to the dogwood family, native to temperate regions of North America, Europe, and Asia. The flowering dogwood (*Cornus florida*) of the eastern USA is often cultivated as an ornamental for its beautiful blooms consisting of clusters of small greenish flowers surrounded by four large white or pink petal-like bracts (specialized leaves). (Genus *Cornus*, family Cornaceae.)

Doha (Arabic **Ad Dawhah**) capital and chief port of Qatar; population (2001 est) 299,300. It is the country's only main town and port and is the sultan's residence. Industries include oil refining, refrigeration plants, engineering, and food processing. It has a deep-water port and an international airport. It is the centre of vocational training for all the Gulf states.

Dohnányi, Ernst (Ernö) von (1877–1960) Hungarian pianist, conductor, composer, and teacher. As a pianist his powers were prodigious, while as a composer he drew upon the classical German tradition, especially Brahms. His compositions include *Variations on a Nursery Song* (1913) and *Second Symphony for Orchestra* (1948).

Doi Inthanon highest mountain in Thailand, rising to 2,595 m/8,513 ft southwest of Chiang Mai in northwestern Thailand.

DOGON The masks of the Dogon people of the West African republic of Mali represent their ancestors. The masks are symbolic of their ancestors' place in history in relation to the balance between good and evil, and the lives of their successors, the present Dogon tribespeople. *Image Bank*

Dogon culture

Ancestors of the Dogon are believed to have migrated to the areas in which they now live some time around the 10th century. Today, the population is most heavily concentrated in the Bandiagara district of Mali, the villages set among the rocky mountains and plateaux of the area.

The Dogon are agricultural people, mainly growing such grain crops as millet and sorghum, which are consumed locally, but they also produce other crops (for example onions) which are exported throughout the Sudan region. They keep animals (goats, sheep, cows, and poultry) and undertake fishing annually, as a collective venture.

Dogon villages are organized within a framework of patrilineages and extended families. Family households usually consist of a man, his wives, and their unmarried children. The Dogon lack centralized political authority and are divided into districts, made up of several villages, under a hogan, a spiritual leader.

The elaborately carved wooden masks and figures, which are used in religious ceremonies, are the best-known feature of Dogon culture. Common patterns are spirals and checkerboard motifs and the main colours used are black, white, and red. Figures are carved for the family shrine, to house the spirits of the deceased. Masks are used every year during the four weeks prior to sowing, to drive the spirits away at the end of a mourning period and at a ceremony that takes place every 60 years involving the initiation of selected young men who will take on the life-time responsibility of preserving the mask tradition.

doldrums area of low atmospheric pressure along the Equator, in the ▷intertropical convergence zone where the northeast and southeast trade winds converge. The doldrums are characterized by calm or very light winds, during which there may be sudden squalls and stormy weather. For this reason the areas are avoided as far as possible by sailing ships.

Dole, Bob (Robert Joseph) (1923–) US Republican politician, leader of his party in the Senate 1985–87 and 1995–96. He unsuccessfully stood as a candidate for the Republican presidential nomination in 1980 and 1988; in 1996 he captured the nomination, but lost the presidential election to Democrat Bill Clinton. Regarded initially as a hardline right-of-centre 'mainstreet' Republican, his views later moderated, particularly in the social sphere. He retired from politics in 1996 and became a special counsel to a Washington law firm.

dolerite igneous rock formed below the Earth's surface, a form of basalt, containing relatively little silica (mafic in composition).

Dolin, Anton (1904–1983) Stage name of (Sydney Francis) Patrick (Chippendall Healey) Kay. English dancer and choreographer. He was the first British male dancer to win an international reputation. As a dancer, his reputation rested on his commanding presence, theatricality, and gymnastic ability. His most famous partnership was with Alicia Markova. After studying under Nijinsky, he was a leading member of Diaghilev's company 1924–29. He formed the Markova–Dolin Ballet Company with Markova 1935–38, and was a guest soloist with the American Ballet Theater 1940–46.

Doll, (William) Richard Shaboe (1912–) English physician who, working with Bradford Hill, provided the first statistical proof of the link between smoking and lung cancer in 1950. In a later study of the smoking habits of doctors, they were able to show that stopping smoking immediately reduces the risk of cancer. He was knighted in 1971.

dollar monetary unit of several countries, containing 100 cents. In the USA, the dollar was adopted in 1785 and is represented by the symbol '$'. US dollars originally were issued as gold or silver coins; today both metal and paper dollars circulate, but paper predominates. Australia, Canada, and Hong Kong are among the other countries that use the dollar unit, but none of these dollars is equivalent in value to the US dollar.

Dollfuss, Engelbert (1892–1934) Austrian Christian Socialist politician. He was appointed chancellor in 1932, and in 1933 suppressed parliament and ruled by decree. In February 1934 he crushed a protest by the socialist workers by force, and in May Austria was declared a 'corporative' state. The Nazis attempted a coup on 25 July; the Chancellery was seized and Dollfuss murdered.

dolomite in mineralogy, white mineral with a rhombohedral structure, calcium magnesium carbonate (CaMg (CO$_3$)$_2$). Dolomites are common in geological successions of all ages and are often formed when ▷limestone is changed by the replacement of the mineral calcite with the mineral dolomite.

Dolomites mountain range in the ▷Alps of northern Italy, chiefly composed of dolomitic limestone. Peaks include the Marmolada (the highest at 3,342 m/10,964 ft), the Sorapis, the Sassolungo, the Sella, the Tofane, and the Cima Tosa. The peaks rise in unusual shapes, and are streaked with veins of vivid colours.

dolphin any of various highly intelligent aquatic mammals of the family Delphinidae, which also includes porpoises. There are about 60 species. Most inhabit tropical and temperate oceans, but there are some freshwater forms in rivers in Asia, Africa, and South America. The name 'dolphin' is generally applied to species having a beaklike snout and slender body, whereas the name 'porpoise' is reserved for the smaller species with a blunt snout and stocky body. Dolphins use sound (▷echolocation) to navigate, to find prey, and for communication. The common dolphin *Delphinus delphis* is found in all temperate and tropical seas. It is up to 2.5 m/8 ft long, and is dark above and white below, with bands of grey, white, and yellow on the sides. It has up to 100 teeth in its jaws, which make the 15 cm/6 in 'beak' protrude forward from the rounded head. The corners of its mouth are permanently upturned, giving the appearance of a smile, though dolphins cannot actually smile. Dolphins feed on fish and squid.

River dolphins There are five species of river dolphin, two South American and three Asian, all of which are endangered. The two South American species are the **Amazon river dolphin** or **boto** *Inia geoffrensis*, the largest river dolphin (length 2.7 m/8.9 ft, weight 180 kg/396 lb) and the **La Plata river dolphin** *Pontoporia blainvillei* (length 1.8 m/5.9 ft, weight 50 kg/110 lb). The **tucuxi** *Sotalia fluviatilis* is not a true river dolphin, but lives in the Amazon and Orinoco rivers, as well as in coastal waters.

The Asian species are the **Ganges river dolphin** *Platanista gangetica*, the **Indus river dolphin** *Platanista minor* (length 2 m/

DOLPHIN A bottlenose dolphin, Bay Islands, Honduras. *Image Bank*

6.6 ft, weight 70 kg/154 lb) (fewer than 500 remaining), and the **Yangtze river dolphin** or **baiji** *Lipotes vexillifer* (length 2 m/6.6 ft, weight 70 kg/154 lb). In January 2000, there were believed to be only five Yangtze river dolphins remaining in the wild.

As a result of living in muddy water, river dolphins' eyes have become very small. They rely on echolocation to navigate and find food. Some species of dolphin can swim at up to 56 kph/35 mph, helped by special streamlining modifications of the skin.

All dolphins power themselves by beating the tail up and down, and use the flippers to steer and stabilize. The flippers betray dolphins' land-mammal ancestry with their typical five-toed limb-bone structure. Dolphins have great learning ability and are popular performers in aquariums. The species most frequently seen is the bottle-nosed dolphin *Tursiops truncatus*, found in all warm seas, mainly grey in colour and growing to a maximum 4.2 m/14 ft. The US Navy began training dolphins for military purposes in 1962, and in 1987 six dolphins were sent to detect mines in the Persian Gulf. Marine dolphins are endangered by fishing nets, speedboats, and pollution. In 1990 the North Sea states agreed to introduce legislation to protect them.

Also known as **dolphin** is the totally unrelated true fish *Coryphaena hippurus*, up to 1.5 m/5 ft long.

> **Related Web site: Bottlenose Dolphin** http://www.seaworld.org/animal_bytes/dolphinab.html

Domagk, Gerhard (1895–1964) German pathologist who was awarded a Nobel Prize for Physiology or Medicine in 1939 for his discovery of the first antibacterial ▷sulphonamide drug. In 1932 he found that a coal-tar dye called Prontosil red contains chemicals with powerful antibacterial properties. Sulphanilamide became the first of the sulphonamide drugs, used – before antibiotics were discovered – to treat a wide range of conditions, including pneumonia and septic wounds.

domain small area in a magnetic material that behaves like a tiny magnet. The magnetism of the material is due to the movement of electrons in the atoms of the domain. In an unmagnetized sample of material, the domains point in random directions, or form closed loops, so that there is no overall magnetization of the sample. In a magnetized sample, the domains are aligned so that their magnetic effects combine to produce a strong overall magnetism.

dome in architecture, a roof form which is usually hemispherical and constructed over a circular, square, or octagonal space in a building. A feature of Islamic and Roman architecture, the dome was revived during the Renaissance period.

The dome first appears in Assyrian architecture, later becoming a feature of Islamic mosques (after the notable example in the Byzantine church of Hagia Sophia, Istanbul (532–37) and Roman ceremonial buildings: the Pantheon in Rome (about AD 112), is 43.5 m/143 ft in diameter.

Rediscovered during the Renaissance, the dome features prominently in Brunelleschi's Florence Cathedral (1420–34), Bramante's Tempietto at San Pietro in Montorio, Rome (1502–10), and St Peter's, Rome (1588–90). Other notable examples are St Paul's, London (1675–1710), by Christopher Wren, and the Panthéon, Paris (1757–90), by Jacques Soufflot (1709–1780).

DOLOMITES The jagged peaks of the Dolomites tower over a village in the Tyrol, Italy. The dolomitic limestone of which the mountains are formed has been carved by erosion into saw-edged ridges, deep gorges, and rocky pinnacles. *Image Bank*

DOME View of the geodesic dome at La Villette, Paris, France, invented by US architect Buckminster Fuller. It is a lightweight structure of interlocking units allowing large spaces to be enclosed efficiently. *The Art Archive/Eileen Tweedy*

In the 20th century Buckminster Fuller developed the geodesic dome (a type of space-frame).

Domenichino (1581–1641) Adopted name of Domenico Zampieri. Italian ▷baroque painter and architect, active in Bologna, Naples, and Rome. He began as an assistant to the ▷Carracci family of painters and continued the early baroque style in, for example, frescoes 1624–28 in the choir of the church of S Andrea della Valle, Rome. He is considered one of the pioneers of landscape painting in the baroque period.

Dome of the Rock building in Jerusalem dating from the 7th century AD that enshrines the rock from which, in Muslim tradition, Muhammad ascended to heaven on his ▷Night Journey. It stands on the site of the Jewish national Temple and is visited by pilgrims.

Domesday Book record of the survey of England carried out in 1086 by officials of ▷William the Conqueror in order to assess land tax and other dues, find out the value of the crown lands, and enable the king to estimate the power of his vassal barons. The name is derived from the belief that its judgement was as final as that of Doomsday.

The commissioners' method was to hold formal sessions and to take sworn answers to a set list of questions, including a formalized description of the agriculture of each place, how much land there was, who held it, what it was worth in the time of King Edward the Confessor and in 1086, and the status and numbers of people who lived there. Domesday Book reflects the great changes which the Norman Conquest brought about in England, particularly feudal land tenure following the introduction of the ▷feudal system.

Related Web site: Domesday Book http://www.fordham.edu/halsall/source/domesday1.html

dominance in genetics, the masking of one allele (an alternative form of a gene) by another allele. For example, if a ▷heterozygous person has one allele for blue eyes and one for brown eyes, his or her eye colour will be brown. The allele for blue eyes is described as ▷recessive and the allele for brown eyes as dominant.

dominant in music, the fifth note of the diatonic scale, for example, G in the C major scale. The chord of the dominant is related to the tonic chord by the dominant note, which corresponds to its third harmonic. Classical modulation involves a harmonic progression from the tonic to the dominant and back. The return may be a symmetrical journey, as in the binary form of a sonata by Scarlatti, or an abrupt resolution of dominant to tonic chords in a 'perfect' cadence.

Domingo, Placido (1941–) Spanish lyric tenor. He specializes in Italian and French 19th-century operatic roles to which he brings a finely tuned dramatic temperament. A member of a musical family, he emigrated to Mexico in 1950. As a youth, he sang baritone roles in zarzuela (musical theatre), moving up to tenor as a member of the Israel National Opera 1961–64. Since his New York debut in 1965 he has established a world reputation as a sympathetic leading tenor. In 1986 he starred in the film version of *Otello*. His other films include the 1988 version of Puccini's *Tosca* set in Rome, and the 1990 Zeffirelli production of Leoncavallo's *I pagliacci/The Strolling Players*. He also sang with José ▷Carreras and Luciano ▷Pavarotti in a recording of operatic hits released to coincide with the World Cup soccer series in Rome in 1990, and again in the USA in 1994. He was named artistic director of the Los Angeles Opera in November 1998, assuming the post in 2000.

Related Web site: Domingo, Placido http://www.placidodomingo.com/

Dominic, St (c. 1170–1221) Founder of the Roman Catholic Dominican order of preaching friars. Feast day 7 August. Canonized 1234.

Dominica see country box.

Dominican order Roman Catholic order of friars founded in 1215 by St Dominic. The Dominicans are also known as Friars Preachers, Black Friars, or Jacobins. The order is worldwide and there is also an order of contemplative nuns; the habit is black and white. The first house was established in Toulouse, France, in 1215; in 1216 the order received papal recognition, and the rule was drawn up in 1220–21. They soon spread all over Europe, the first house in England being established in Oxford in 1221. The English Dominicans were suppressed in 1559, but were restored to a corporate existence in 1622. Dominicans have included Thomas Aquinas, Girolamo Savonarola, and Bartolome de las Casas. In 1983 there were 7,200 friars and 4,775 nuns.

Dominican Republic see country box.

Dominions term formerly used to describe those countries of the ▷British Empire and Commonwealth enjoying complete autonomy in internal and external affairs. In this context the term was first applied to Canada, the formal title of which is the Dominion of Canada. It was subsequently applied as a generic term, though not as a formal title (except in the case of New Zealand, which has since ceased to use it), to describe Australia, South Africa, and, in 1922, the Irish Free State.

Domino, 'Fats' (Antoine) (1928–) US rock-and-roll pianist, singer, and songwriter. He was an exponent of the New Orleans style. His hits include 'Ain't That a Shame' (1955) and 'Blueberry Hill' (1956). In 1998 he was awarded the National Medal of Arts.

Domitian, (Titus Flavius Domitianus) (AD 51–96) Roman emperor from AD 81. He finalized the conquest of Britain (see ▷Agricola), strengthened the Rhine–Danube frontier, and suppressed immorality as well as freedom of thought in philosophy and religion. His reign of terror led to his assassination.

Don (ancient Greek **Tanais**) navigable river in the western Russian Federation; length 1,870 km/1,162 mi; basin covers 422,000 sq km/163,000 sq mi. The Don rises in the central Russian uplands near the city of Tula, flows southeast towards the Volga near Volgograd, then turns southwest to empty into the northeast of the Sea of Azov. In its lower reaches the Don is 1.5 km/1 mi wide, and for about four months of the year it is closed by ice. It has long been a major traffic artery linking inland European Russia with the Black Sea. Its chief tributaries are the Donets, Voronezh, Khoper, and Medveditsa, and it is linked to the Volga by the Volga–Don Canal. The main port is Rostov-on-Don, which lies near the river's mouth.

Donatello (c. 1386–1466) Born Donato di Niccolo Bardi. Italian sculptor of the early Renaissance. He was instrumental in reviving the classical style, as in his graceful bronze statue of the youthful *David* (about 1433; Bargello, Florence) and his equestrian statue of the general *Gattamelata* (1447–50; Piazza del Santo, Padua). The course of Florentine art in the 15th century was strongly influenced by his work.

Donatello introduced true perspective in his relief sculptures, such as the panel of *St George Slaying the Dragon* (about 1415–17, Or San Michele, Florence). He absorbed classical influences during a stay in Rome 1430–32, and *David* is said to be the first life-size, free-standing nude since antiquity. In his later work, such as his wood-carving of the aged *Mary Magdalene* (about 1456, Baptistry, Florence), he sought dramatic expression through a distorted, emaciated figural style.

DONATELLO Head of the boy David in bronze by the Florentine sculptor Donatello. *The Art Archive/Bargello Museum Florence/Dagli Orti*

Donau German name for the River ▷Danube.

Doncaster industrial town and administrative headquarters of Doncaster metropolitan borough, South Yorkshire, England, on the River Don, 56 km/35 mi southwest of York; population (1999 est) 292,100. It has been an important centre for railway engineering (locomotives and rolling stock) since the 19th century. Traditional iron, steel, and coal production has declined, although active collieries remain, including the Rossington deep mine. Synthetic textiles, confectionery (butterscotch), agricultural equipment, electrical equipment, fencing, brass fittings, and optical fibres are also produced.

The St Leger (1776), the world's oldest classic horse race, is held annually at Doncaster racecourse in September, and the Lincolnshire Handicap horse race is held in March. The Earth Centre, Europe's largest centre for ecological research and display, was constructed here as a Millennium Commission Landmark Project. It opened in July 2000.

Donegal mountainous county in the northwest of the Republic of Ireland, surrounded on three sides by the Atlantic Ocean, and bordering the counties of Londonderry, Tyrone, and Fermanagh (Northern Ireland), and Leitrim (Republic of Ireland); area 4,830 sq km/1,864 sq mi; county town Lifford; population (1996) 130,000. Ballyshannon is the largest town, and the market town and port of **Donegal** is at the head of **Donegal Bay** in the southwest. The severe climate renders much of the county barren, although the soil is suitable for potatoes, oats, and barley in places. Commercial

DOME The Cupola Brunelleschi in Florence, Italy, designed and built by the architect Brunelleschi in 1436. *Image Bank*

Stephen Rynne
Irish writer

Donegal is strong meat: strong scenery, strong weather, strong bodies, strong spirits.

Stephen Rynne *All Ireland* (1956).

activities include sheep and cattle raising, tweed, linen, and carpet manufacture, and some salmon and deep-sea fishing. Tourism is also very important; the county is noted for dramatic scenery and geology as well as archaeological and historic remains, and the castles of Donegal and Glenveagh as well as Glenveagh National Park are among the top visitor attractions in the county. The River Erne hydroelectric project (1952) involved the building of a large artificial lake (405 ha/1,000 acres) and a power station at Ballyshannon.

Donen, Stanley (1924–) US film director. Formerly a dancer, he co-directed two of Gene Kelly's best musicals, *On the Town* (1949) and *Singin' in the Rain* (1952). His other films include *Seven Brides for Seven Brothers* (1954), *Charade* (1963), *Two for the Road* (1968), and *Blame It on Rio* (1984).

Donets Basin (or Donbas) highly industrialized area in Ukraine, situated in the bend formed by the rivers Don and Donets. The Donets Basin has one of Europe's richest coalfields, together with extensive deposits of salt, mercury, and lead.

Donetsk city in Ukraine; capital of Donetsk region (oblast), situated in the ▷Donets Basin, a major coal-mining area, 600 km/ 372 mi southeast of Kiev; population (1996) 1,121,000. Donetsk has blast furnaces, rolling mills, and other heavy industries.

Dongola town in Northern State, northern Sudan. It has palm groves and produces dates; there is some light engineering and livestock rearing. There are road and river links to Khartoum. The town was founded in about 1811 to replace Old Dongola, 120 km/75 mi upriver, which was destroyed by the ▷Mamelukes.

Old Dongola, a trading centre on a caravan route, was the capital of the Christian kingdom of ▷Nubia between the 6th and 14th centuries.

Dönitz, Karl (1891–1980) German admiral, originator of the wolf-pack submarine technique, which sank Allied shipping in World War II. He succeeded Hitler in 1945, capitulated, and was imprisoned 1946–56.

Donizetti, (Domenico) Gaetano (Maria) (1797–1848) Italian composer. He created more than 60 operas, including *Lucrezia Borgia* (1833), *Lucia di Lammermoor* (1835), *La Fille du régiment* (1840), *La Favorite* (1840), and *Don Pasquale* (1843). They show the influence of Rossini and Bellini, and are characterized by a flow of expressive melodies.

Don Juan (Italian **Don Giovanni**) character of Spanish legend, Don Juan Tenorio, supposed to have lived in the 14th century and notorious for his debauchery. Tirso de Molina, Molière, Mozart, Byron, and George Bernard Shaw featured him in their works.

donkey another name for ▷ass.

Donne, John (1572–1631) English metaphysical poet. His work consists of love poems, religious poems, verse satires, and sermons. His sermons rank him with the century's greatest orators, and his fervent poems of love and hate, violent, tender, or abusive, give him a unique position among English poets. A Roman Catholic in his youth, he converted to the Church of England and finally became dean of St Paul's Cathedral, London.

His earliest poetry consisted of the 'conceited verses' (using elaborate metaphors to link seemingly dissimilar subjects) passed

GAETANO DONIZETTI A contemporary Italian portrait of the Italian operatic composer Gaetano Donizetti aged around 43 years. *The Art Archive/Dagli Orti*

Dominica

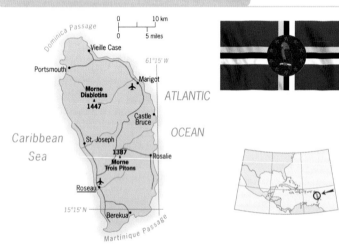

Dominica island in the eastern Caribbean, between Guadeloupe and Martinique, the largest of the Windward Islands, with the Atlantic Ocean to the east and the Caribbean Sea to the west.

NATIONAL NAME *Commonwealth of Dominica*
AREA 751 sq km/290 sq mi
CAPITAL Roseau
MAJOR TOWNS/CITIES Portsmouth, Marigot, Mahaut, Atkinson, Grand Bay
MAJOR PORTS Roseau, Portsmouth, Berekua, Marigot, Rosalie
PHYSICAL FEATURES second-largest of the Windward Islands, mountainous central ridge with tropical rainforest

Government

HEAD OF STATE Nicholas Liverpool from 2003
HEAD OF GOVERNMENT Roosevelt Skerrit from 2004
POLITICAL SYSTEM liberal democracy
POLITICAL EXECUTIVE parliamentary
ADMINISTRATIVE DIVISIONS ten parishes
ARMED FORCES defence force disbanded in 1981; police force of approximately 300

Economy and resources

CURRENCY East Caribbean dollar; pound sterling and Euro are also accepted
GPD (US$) 254 million (2002 est)
REAL GDP GROWTH (% change on previous year) 0.5 (2003 est)
GNI (US$) 228 million (2002 est)
GNI PER CAPITA (PPP) (US$) 4,840 (2002 est)

CONSUMER PRICE INFLATION 0.5% (2003 est)
UNEMPLOYMENT 20% (2000)
FOREIGN DEBT (US$) 253 million (2001 est)
MAJOR TRADING PARTNERS USA, UK, Jamaica, the Netherlands, South Korea, Belgium, Japan, Trinidad and Tobago
RESOURCES pumice, limestone, clay
INDUSTRIES banana packaging, oils, soap, canned juice, cigarettes, rum, beer, furniture, paint, cardboard boxes, candles, tourism
EXPORTS bananas, soap, coconuts, grapefruit, galvanized sheets. Principal market: Jamaica 26.5% (1999)
IMPORTS food and live animals, basic manufactures, machinery and transport equipment, mineral fuels. Principal source: USA 38.3% (1999)
ARABLE LAND 9% (1998)
AGRICULTURAL PRODUCTS bananas, coconuts, mangoes, avocados, papayas, ginger, citrus fruits, vegetables; livestock rearing; fishing

Population and society

POPULATION 79,000 (2003 est)
POPULATION GROWTH RATE –0.1 (2000–05)

POPULATION DENSITY (per sq km) 105 (2003 est)
URBAN POPULATION (% of total) 72 (2003 est)
AGE DISTRIBUTION (% of total population) 0–14 38%, 15–59 47%, 60+ 15% (2001 est)
ETHNIC GROUPS majority descended from African slaves; a small number of the indigenous Arawaks remain
LANGUAGE English (official), a Dominican patois (reflecting former French rule)
RELIGION Roman Catholic 80%
EDUCATION (compulsory years) 10
LITERACY RATE 96% (men); 95% (women) (2001 est)
LABOUR FORCE 23.7% agriculture, 18.2% industry, 58.1% services (1997)
LIFE EXPECTANCY 72 (men); 77 (women) (2000–05)
TV SETS (per 1,000 people) 232 (1999 est)
INTERNET USERS (per 10,000 people) 1,602.6 (2002 est)

DOMINICA Red Rock Beach in Dominica, often referred to as the 'Nature Island' of the Caribbean. *Image Bank*

1493: Visited by the explorer Christopher Columbus, who named the island Dominica ('Sunday Island').

1627: Presented by the English King Charles I to the Earl of Carlisle, but initial European attempts at colonization were fiercely resisted by the indigenous Carib community.

later 18th century: Succession of local British and French conflicts over control of the fertile island.

1763: British given possession of the island by the Treaty of Paris, but France continued to challenge this militarily until 1805, when there was formal cession in return for the sum of £12,000.

1834: Slaves, who had been brought in from Africa, were emancipated.

1870: Became part of the British Leeward Islands federation.

1940: Transferred to British Windward Islands federation.

1951: Universal adult suffrage established.

1958–62: Part of the West Indies Federation.

1960: Granted separate, semi-independent status, with a legislative council and chief minister.

1961: Edward le Blanc, leader of the newly formed DLP, became chief minister.

1978: Independence was achieved as a republic within the Commonwealth, with Patrick John (DLP) as prime minister.

1980: The DFP won a convincing victory in a general election, and Eugenia Charles became the Caribbean's first woman prime minister.

1983: A small force participated in the US-backed invasion of Grenada.

1985: The regrouping of left-of-centre parties resulted in the new Labour Party of Dominica (LPD).

1991: A Windward Islands confederation comprising St Lucia, St Vincent, Grenada, and Dominica was proposed.

1993: Charles resigned the DFP leadership, but continued as prime minister.

1995: DUWP won a general election; Edison James was appointed prime minister and Eugenia Charles retired from politics.

1998: Vernon Shaw elected president.

2000: Rosie Douglas was elected prime minister, leading a DLP-DFP coalition, but died in October. He was replaced by Pierre Charles.

round in manuscript among his friends at the Inns of Court (finally published in the 1633 *Poems*). Most of these were apparently written in the 1590s. They record a series of actual or fictitious love affairs, in which the lover woos, not by praising his mistress's beauty, but by arguing, cajoling, and plunging off into philosophical speculation and flights of fancy. They show a strange blend of the conversational (most of these poems open with a phrase that might come straight from colloquial speech) with the involved, and of the outspokenly erotic with theoretical questions apparently having little to do with the experience of love. His religious poems show the same passion and ingenuity as his love poetry.

Common to all the poems is the imaginative power of their imagery, which ransacks the intellectual world for symbols, curious and sometimes far-fetched, but always compellingly apt. The sermons, in an elegant prose style less rugged and harsh than that of the poems, show the same preoccupation with humanity's place in the universe and its approaching end.

Related Web site: Donne, John http://www.luminarium.org/ sevenlit/donne/index.html

Don Quixote de la Mancha satirical romance by the Spanish novelist Miguel de Cervantes, published in two parts (1605 and 1615). Don Quixote, a self-styled knight, embarks on a series of chivalric adventures accompanied by his servant Sancho Panza. Quixote's imagination leads him to see harmless objects as enemies to be fought, as in his tilting at windmills. English translators include Tobias Smollett (1775). See picture on p. 282.

Doomsday Book variant spelling of ▷Domesday Book, the English survey of 1086.

Doors, the US psychedelic rock group formed in 1965 in Los Angeles by Jim Morrison (1943–1971, vocals), Ray Manzarek (1935– , keyboards), Robby Krieger (1946– , guitar), and John Densmore (1944– , drums). Their first hit was 'Light My Fire' from their debut album *The Doors* 1967. They were noted for Morrison's poetic lyrics and flamboyant performance.

doo-wop US pop-music form of the 1950s, a style of harmony singing without instrumental accompaniment or nearly so, almost exclusively by male groups. The name derives from the practice of having the lead vocalist singing the lyrics against a backing of nonsense syllables from the other members of the group. Many of the doo-wop groups were named after birds; for example, the Ravens and the Orioles.

dopamine neurotransmitter, hydroxytyramine $C_8H_{11}NO_2$, an intermediate in the formation of adrenaline. There are special nerve cells (neurons) in the brain that use dopamine for the transmission of nervous impulses. One such area of dopamine neurons lies in the basal ganglia, a region that controls movement. Patients suffering from the tremors of Parkinson's disease show nerve degeneration in this region. Another dopamine area lies in the limbic system, a region closely involved with emotional responses. It has been found that schizophrenic patients respond well to drugs that limit dopamine excess in this area.

doppelgänger (German 'double-goer') apparition of a living person, a person's double, or a guardian spirit. The German composer and writer E T A Hoffman wrote a short story called 'Die Doppelgänger' in 1821. English novelist Charles Williams (1886–1945) used the idea to great effect in his novel *Descent into Hell* (1937).

Dominican Republic

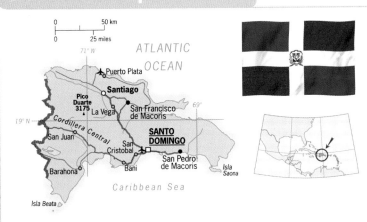

Dominican Republic formerly Hispaniola (with Haiti) (until 1844) country in the West Indies (eastern Caribbean), occupying the eastern two-thirds of the island of Hispaniola, with Haiti covering the western third; the Atlantic Ocean is to the east and the Caribbean Sea to the west.

NATIONAL NAME *República Dominicana/Dominican Republic*
AREA 48,442 sq km/18,703 sq mi
CAPITAL Santo Domingo
MAJOR TOWNS/CITIES Santiago, La Romana, San Pedro de Macoris, San Francisco de Macoris, La Vega, San Juan, San Cristóbal
PHYSICAL FEATURES comprises eastern two-thirds of island of Hispaniola; central mountain range with fertile valleys; Pico Duarte 3,174 m/10,417 ft, highest point in Caribbean islands

Government

HEAD OF STATE AND GOVERNMENT Rafael Mejía Domínguez from 2000
POLITICAL SYSTEM liberal democracy
POLITICAL EXECUTIVE limited presidency
ADMINISTRATIVE DIVISIONS 29 provinces and a national district (Santo Domingo)
ARMED FORCES 24,500; plus paramilitary forces of 15,000 (2002 est)
CONSCRIPTION military service is voluntary
DEATH PENALTY abolished in 1966
DEFENCE SPEND (% GDP) 0.7 (2002 est)
EDUCATION SPEND (% GDP) 6.3 (2000 est)
HEALTH SPEND (% GDP) 1.9 (1998)

Economy and resources

CURRENCY Dominican Republic peso
GPD (US$) 21.3 billion (2002 est)
REAL GDP GROWTH (% change on previous year) 2.7 (2001)
GNI (US$) 20.0 billion (2002 est)
GNI PER CAPITA (PPP) (US$) 5,870 (2002 est)
CONSUMER PRICE INFLATION 14.4% (2003 est)
UNEMPLOYMENT 15.2% (2001)
FOREIGN DEBT (US$) 6.1 billion (2001 est)
MAJOR TRADING PARTNERS USA, the Netherlands, Venezuela, Mexico, Japan, France, Canada, Haiti, Panama
RESOURCES ferro-nickel, gold, silver
INDUSTRIES food processing (including sugar refining), petroleum refining, beverages, chemicals, cement
EXPORTS ferro-nickel, raw sugar and derivatives, molasses, coffee, cocoa, tobacco, gold, silver. Principal market: USA 87.3% (2000)
IMPORTS petroleum and petroleum products, coal, foodstuffs, wheat, raw materials, machinery. Principal source: USA 60.5% (2000)

ARABLE LAND 22.7% (2000 est)
AGRICULTURAL PRODUCTS sugar cane, cocoa, coffee, bananas, tobacco, rice, tomatoes

Population and society

POPULATION 8,745,000 (2003 est)
POPULATION GROWTH RATE 1.3% (2000–15)
POPULATION DENSITY (per sq km) 179 (2003 est)
URBAN POPULATION (% of total) 67 (2003 est)
AGE DISTRIBUTION (% of total population) 0–14 32%, 15–59 61%, 60+ 7% (2002 est)
ETHNIC GROUPS about 73% of the population are mulattos, of mixed European and African descent; about 16% are European; 11% African
LANGUAGE Spanish (official)
RELIGION Roman Catholic
EDUCATION (compulsory years) 8
LITERACY RATE 85% (men); 85% (women) (2003 est)
LABOUR FORCE 17% agriculture, 24.4% industry, 58.6% services (1999)
LIFE EXPECTANCY 69 (men); 70 (women) (2000–05)
CHILD MORTALITY RATE (under 5, per 1,000 live births) 47 (2001)
PHYSICIANS (per 1,000 people) 2.2 (1999 est)
HOSPITAL BEDS (per 1,000 people) 1.5 (1999 est)
TV SETS (per 1,000 people) 96 (1998)
RADIOS (per 1,000 people) 181 (1999 est)
INTERNET USERS (per 10,000 people) 344.5 (2002 est)

See also ▷Arawak; ▷Carib; ▷Haiti.

DOMINICAN REPUBLIC The ruined San Francisco monastery. *Image Bank*

Chronology

14th century: Settled by Carib Indians, who followed an earlier wave of Arawak Indian immigration.

1492: Visited by Christopher Columbus, who named it Hispaniola ('Little Spain').

1496: At Santo Domingo the Spanish established the first European settlement in the western hemisphere, which became capital of all Spanish colonies in America.

first half of 16th century: One-third of a million Arawaks and Caribs died, as a result of enslavement and exposure to European diseases; black African slaves were consequently brought in to work the island's gold and silver mines, which were swiftly exhausted.

1697: Divided between France, which held the western third (Haiti), and Spain, which held the east (Dominican Republic, or Santo Domingo).

1795: Santo Domingo was ceded to France.

1808: Following a revolt by Spanish Creoles, with British support, Santo Domingo was retaken by Spain.

1821: Became briefly independent after uprising against Spanish rule, and then fell under the control of Haiti.

1844: Separated from Haiti to form Dominican Republic.

1861–65: Under Spanish protection.

1904: The USA took over the near-bankrupt republic's debts.

1916–24: Temporarily occupied by US forces.

1930: Military coup established personal dictatorship of Gen Rafael Trujillo Molina.

1937: Army massacred 19,000–20,000 Haitians living in the Dominican provinces adjoining the frontier.

1961: Trujillo assassinated.

1962: First democratic elections resulted in Juan Bosch, founder of the left-wing Dominican Revolutionary Party (PRD), becoming president.

1963: Bosch overthrown in military coup.

1965: 30,000 US marines intervened to restore order and protect foreign nationals after Bosch had attempted to seize power.

1966: New constitution adopted. Joaquín Balaguer, protégé of Trujillo and leader of the centre-right Christian Social Reform Party (PRSC), became president.

1978: PRD returned to power.

1985: PRD president Jorge Blanco was forced by the International Monetary Fund to adopt austerity measures to save the economy.

1986: The PRSC returned to power.

1996: Leonel Fernández of the left-wing PLD was elected president.

2000: Presidential elections were won by Hipólito Mejía, a social democrat.

DON QUIXOTE DE LA MANCHA A statue of Don Quixote, in Madrid, Spain. See entry on p. 283. *Image Bank*

Doppler effect change in the observed frequency (or wavelength) of waves due to relative motion between the wave source and the observer. The Doppler effect is responsible for the perceived change in pitch of a siren as it approaches and then recedes, and for the ▷red shift of light from distant galaxies. It is named after the Austrian physicist Christian Doppler.
Related Web site: Doppler Effect http://www.ncsa.uiuc.edu/Cyberia/Bima/doppler.html

dor beetle oval-shaped, stout beetle measuring on average 20 mm/0.8 in, and with a metallic sheen. In general, dor beetles feed on dung, mostly of herbivorous animals.

Dorchester market town and administrative headquarters of ▷Dorset, southern England, on the River Frome, north of Weymouth, 192 km/119 mi southwest of London; population (1991) 15,000. It is the service centre of an agricultural region and has light engineering industries. Tourism plays an important role in the town's economy. The hill fort Maiden Castle to the southwest was occupied from about 4000 BC, although the first identifiable settlement dates from 2000 BC. The novelist Thomas ▷Hardy was born nearby.

Dordogne river in southwest France, rising on the slopes of the Puy de Sancy in the Massif Central, Puy-de-Dôme *département*, and flowing 490 km/300 mi through Souillac, Bergerac, Castillon, Libourne, and Cubzac, to join the River Garonne at Ambes, 23 km/14 mi north of Bordeaux. The river is a major source of hydroelectric power, and the last 180 km/112 mi of its course sees much river traffic. It gives its name to the Dordogne *département*.

Doré, (Paul) Gustave (1832–1883) French artist. Chiefly known as a prolific illustrator, he was also active as a painter, etcher, and sculptor. He produced closely worked engravings of scenes from, for example, Rabelais, Dante, Cervantes, the Bible, Milton, and Edgar Allan Poe.

Dorian people of ancient Greece. They entered Greece from the north and took most of the Peloponnese from the Achaeans, perhaps destroying the ▷Mycenaean civilization; this invasion appears to have been completed before 1000 BC. Their chief cities were Sparta, Argos, and Corinth.

Doric in classical architecture, one of the five types of column; see ▷order.

dormancy in botany, a phase of reduced physiological activity exhibited by certain buds, seeds, and spores. Dormancy can help a plant to survive unfavourable conditions, as in annual plants that pass the cold winter season as dormant seeds, and plants that form dormant buds.

dormancy in the UK, state of a peerage or baronetcy when it is believed that heirs to the title exist, but their whereabouts are unknown. This sometimes occurs when a senior line dies out and a cadet line has long since gone abroad.

dormitory town rural settlement that has a high proportion of commuters in its population. The original population may have been displaced by these commuters and the settlements enlarged by housing estates. Dormitory towns have increased in the UK since 1960 as a result of counterurbanization.

dormouse small rodent, of the family Gliridae, with a hairy tail. There are about ten species, living in Europe, Asia, and Africa. They are arboreal (live in trees) and nocturnal, hibernating during winter in cold regions. They eat berries, nuts, pollen, and insects.

The dormouse derives its name from French *dormir* 'to sleep' because of its hibernating habit. The common dormouse *Muscardinus avellanarius* lives all over Europe in thickets and forests with undergrowth. It is reddish fawn and 15 cm/6 in long, including the tail. The fat or edible dormouse *Glis glis* lives in continental Europe, and is 30 cm/1 ft long including the tail. It was a delicacy at Roman feasts, and was introduced to southeastern England by the Romans.

Dorpat German name for the Estonian city of ▷Tartu.

dorsal in vertebrates, the surface of the animal closest to the backbone. For most vertebrates and invertebrates this is the upper surface, or the surface furthest from the ground. For bipedal primates such as humans, where the dorsal surface faces backwards, then the word is 'back'.

Dorset county of southwest England (since April 1997 Bournemouth and Poole have been separate unitary authorities).
area 2,541 sq km/981 sq mi **towns and cities** ▷Dorchester (administrative headquarters), Shaftesbury, Sherborne; Lyme Regis, Weymouth, Poole (resorts) **physical** Chesil Beach, a shingle bank along the coast 19 km/11 mi long, connecting Isle of Portland to the mainland; Dorset Downs (chalk); River Stour, and rivers Frome and Piddle (which flow into Poole Harbour); clay beds in the north and west; Canford Heath, the home of some of Britain's rarest breeding birds and reptiles (including the nightjar, Dartford warbler, sand lizard, and smooth snake) **features** Isle of Purbeck, a peninsula where china clay and Purbeck 'marble' are quarried, and which includes Corfe Castle and the holiday resort of Swanage; Cranborne Chase; Maiden Castle (prehistoric earthwork); Tank Museum at Royal Armoured Corps Centre, Bovington, where the cottage of the soldier and writer T E ▷Lawrence is a museum; Wimborne Minster; abbey church of Sherborne **agriculture** dairy farming **industries** Wytch Farm is the largest onshore oilfield in the UK; production at Wareham onshore oilfield started in 1991; quarrying (marble from the Isle of Purbeck, and Portland stone, which has been used for buildings all over the world); manufacturing (rope, twine, and net at Bridport); sand and gravel extraction; tourism **population** (1996) 681,900 **famous people** Anthony Ashley Cooper, Thomas Hardy, Thomas Love Peacock
Related Web site: The English County of Dorset http://www.dorset-cc.gov.uk/dorset2.htm

DORSET A village in the county of Dorset, England. *Image Bank*

Dorset, 1st Earl of Dorset, title of English poet Thomas ▷Sackville.

Dorsey, Tommy (1905–1956) Born Thomas Dorsey. US bandleader, musician, and composer during the swing era. He worked together with his brother Jimmy (James) Dorsey (1904–1957) in the Dorsey Brothers Orchestra 1934–35 and 1953–56, but they led separate bands in the intervening period. The Jimmy Dorsey band was primarily a dance band; the Tommy Dorsey band was more jazz-oriented and featured the singer Frank Sinatra 1940–42. Both Dorsey bands featured in a number of films in the 1940s, and the brothers appeared together in *The Fabulous Dorseys* (1947).

Dortmund city and industrial centre in the ▷Ruhr, in North Rhine-Westphalia, Germany, 58 km/36 mi northeast of Düsseldorf; population (1995) 600,000. It is the largest mining town of the Westphalian coalfield and the southern terminus of the Dortmund–Ems Canal. The enlargement of the Wesel–Datteln Canal (1989), connecting Dortmund to the Rhine River, allows barges to travel between Dortmund and Rotterdam in the Netherlands. Industries include coal, iron, and steel (headquarters of Hoesch), mechanical engineering, and brewing (output exceeds that of Munich), and high-tech industries are developing. There is also a modern university.

dory marine fish *Zeus faber* found in the Mediterranean and Atlantic. It grows up to 60 cm/2 ft, and has nine or ten long spines at the front of the dorsal fin, and four at the front of the anal fin. It is considered to be an excellent food fish and is also known as John Dory.

DOS (acronym for disk operating system) computer ▷operating system specifically designed for use with disk storage; also used as an alternative name for a particular operating system, ▷MS-DOS.
Related Web site: DOS Command Index http://www.easydos.com/dosindex.html

Dos Santos, José Eduardo (1942–) Angolan left-wing politician, president from 1979, a member of the People's Movement for the Liberation of Angola (MPLA). By 1989, he had negotiated the withdrawal of South African and Cuban forces, and in 1991 a peace agreement to end the civil war. In 1992 his victory in multiparty elections was disputed by Jonas Savimbi, leader of the rebel group National Union for the Total Independence of Angola (▷UNITA), and fighting resumed, escalating into full-scale civil war in 1993. Representatives of the two leaders signed a peace agreement in 1994. Dos Santos' proposal to make Savimbi vice-president was declined by the latter in 1996.

Dostoevsky, Fyodor Mihailovich (1821–1881) Russian novelist. Remarkable for their profound psychological insight, Dostoevsky's novels have greatly influenced Russian writers, and since the beginning of the 20th century have been increasingly influential abroad. In 1849 he was sentenced to four years' hard labour in Siberia, followed by army service, for printing socialist propaganda. *The House of the Dead* (1861) recalls his prison experiences, followed by his major works *Crime and Punishment* (1866), *The Idiot* (1868–69), and *The Brothers Karamazov* (1879–80).

Born in Moscow, the son of a physician, Dostoevsky was for a short time an army officer. His first novel, *Poor Folk*, appeared in 1846. In 1849, during a period of intense tsarist censorship, he was arrested as a member of a free-thinking literary circle and sentenced to death. After a last-minute reprieve he was sent to the penal settlement at Omsk for four years, where the terrible conditions increased his epileptic tendency. Finally pardoned in 1859, he published the humorous *Village of Stepanchikovo*, *The House of the Dead*, and *The Insulted and the Injured* (1862). Meanwhile he had launched two unsuccessful liberal periodicals, in the second of which his *Letters from the Underworld* (1864) appeared. Compelled to work by pressure of debt, he quickly produced *Crime and Punishment* (1866) and *The Gambler* (1867), before fleeing the country to escape from his creditors. He then wrote *The Idiot* (in which the hero is an epileptic like himself), *The Eternal Husband* (1870), and *The Possessed* (1871–72). Returning to Russia in 1871, he again entered journalism and issued the personal miscellany *Journal of an Author*, in which he discussed contemporary problems. In 1875 he published *A Raw Youth*, but the great work of his last years is *The Brothers Karamazov*.
Related Web site: Dostoevsky http://www.kiosek.com/dostoevsky/

dot matrix printer computer printer that produces each character individually by printing a pattern, or matrix, of very small dots. The printing head consists of a vertical line or block of either 9 or 24 printing pins. As the printing head is moved from side to side across the paper, the pins are pushed forwards selectively to strike an inked ribbon and build up the dot pattern for each character on the paper beneath. See illustration on p. 285.

dotterel bird *Eudromias morinellus* of the plover family, in order Charadriiformes, nesting on high moors and tundra in Europe and Asia, and migrating south for the winter. About 23 cm/9 in long, its plumage is patterned with black, brown, and white in summer, duller in winter, but always with white eyebrows and breastband. The female is larger than the male, and mates up to five times with different partners, each time laying her eggs and leaving them in the sole care of the male, who incubates and rears the brood. Three pale-green eggs with brown markings are laid in hollows in the ground.

Douala (or Duala) chief port and industrial centre of Cameroon, on the Wouri River estuary by the Gulf of Guinea; population (1991) 884,000. Industries include aluminium, chemicals, textiles, and pulp. Known as Kamerunstadt until 1907, it was capital of German Cameroon, which became a German protectorate in 1884, 1885–1901.

double bass large, bowed four-stringed (sometimes five-stringed) musical instrument, the bass of the ▷violin family. It is descended from the bass viol or violone. Until 1950, after which

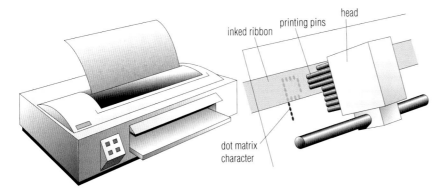

DOT MATRIX PRINTER Dot matrix printers have now largely been superseded by inkjet and laser printers.

it was increasingly superseded by the electric bass, it also provided bass support (plucked) for jazz and dance bands. Performers include Domenico Dragonetti, composer of eight concertos, the Russian-born US conductor Serge Koussevitsky (1874–1951), and the jazz player and composer Charles Mingus. The double bass features in the well loved 'Elephants' solo, No. 5 of Saint-Saëns's *Carnival of the Animals* (1897).

double coconut treelike ▷palm plant, also known as **coco de mer**, of the Seychelles. It produces a two-lobed edible nut, one of the largest known fruits. (*Lodoicea maldivica*.)

double decomposition reaction between two chemical substances (usually ▷salts in solution) that results in the exchange of a constituent from each compound to create two different compounds.

double entendre (French 'double meaning') an ambiguous word or phrase, usually one that is coarse or indelicate.

double star two stars that appear close together. Many stars that appear single to the naked eye appear double when viewed through a telescope. Some double stars attract each other due to gravity, and orbit each other, forming a genuine ▷binary star, but other double stars are at different distances from Earth, and lie in the same line of sight only by chance. Through a telescope both types look the same.

Doughty, Charles Montagu (1843–1926) English travel writer, author of *Travels in Arabia Deserta* (1888), an account of an astonishing and dangerous journey in an unusual literary style, written after two years in the Middle East searching for biblical relics. He was a role model for English soldier T E ▷Lawrence ('Lawrence of Arabia'). Latterly he wrote epic poems of an experimental linguistic and metrical nature.

Douglas capital of the Isle of Man in the Irish Sea; population (1991) 22,200. It is situated in the southeast of the island, and is a holiday resort and terminus of shipping routes to and from Fleetwood and Liverpool. Banking and financial services are important, and the Manx parliament, ▷Tynwald, meets here.

Douglas, Alfred (Bruce), Lord Douglas (1870–1945) English poet. He became closely associated in London with the Irish writer Oscar ▷Wilde. Their relationship led to Wilde's conviction for homosexual activity, imprisonment, and early death, through the enmity of Douglas's father, the 8th Marquess of Queensberry. Douglas wrote the self-justificatory *Oscar Wilde and Myself* (1914) and the somewhat contradictory *Oscar Wilde, A Summing-Up* (1940).

Douglas, Gavin (or **Gawin**) (c. 1475–1522) Scottish poet. He translated into Scots Virgil's *Aeneid* (1513), including the thirteenth book added by Maffeo Vegio. He wrote the allegorical *The Palace of Honour* (c. 1501). His language is more archaic than that of some of his predecessors, but Douglas had fire and a power of vivid description and his allegories are ingenious.

Douglas, Kirk (1916–) Stage name of Issur Danielovitch Demsky. US film actor. Usually cast as a dynamic though ill-fated hero, as in *Spartacus* (1960), he was a major star of the 1950s and 1960s, appearing in such films as *Ace in the Hole* (1951), *The Bad and the Beautiful* (1953), *Lust for Life* (1956), *The Vikings* (1958), *Seven Days in May* (1964), and *The War Wagon* (1967). He received the American Film Institute's life achievement award in 1991 and a lifetime achievement Academy Award in 1995. In March 1999 he received the Screen Actors Guild life achievement award.

> ### Alfred Douglas
> *I am the Love that dare not speak its name.*
> 'Two Loves'

> ### Gavin Douglas
> *And all small fowlys singis on the spray: / Welcum the lord of lycht and lamp of day.*
> *Eneados* bk 12, prologue 1.251

Douglas, Michael (Kirk) (1944–) US film actor and producer. He made his feature-film acting debut in *Hail, Hero!* (1969) and produced the award-winning *One Flew Over the Cuckoo's Nest* (1975). He won an Academy Award for his portrayal of a ruthless entrepreneur in *Wall Street* (1987). He married Welsh actor Catherine Zeta-Jones in an extravagant ceremony in 2000.

Douglas-Hamilton family name of dukes of Hamilton, seated at Lennoxlove, East Lothian, Scotland.

Douglas-Home, Alec (1903–1995) Baron Home of the Hirsel; born Alexander Frederick Douglas-Home. British Conservative politician. He was foreign secretary 1960–63, and succeeded Harold Macmillan as prime minister in 1963. He renounced his peerage (as 14th Earl of Home) and re-entered the Commons after successfully contesting a by-election, but failed to win the 1964 general election, and resigned as party leader in 1965. He was again foreign secretary 1970–74, when he received a life peerage. The playwright William ▷Douglas-Home was his brother. He was knighted in 1962.

Douglas-Home, William (1912–1992) Scottish dramatist. He is noted for his comedies, which include *The Chiltern Hundreds* (1947), *The Secretary Bird* (1968), *Lloyd George Knew My Father* (1972), and *The Kingfisher* (1977). He was the younger brother of the politician Alec Douglas-Home.

Douglas fir any of some six species of coniferous evergreen tree belonging to the pine family. The most common is *Pseudotsuga menziesii*, native to western North America and east Asia. It grows up to 60–90 m/200–300 ft in height, has long, flat, spirally-arranged needles and hanging cones, and produces hard, strong timber. *P. glauca* has shorter, bluish needles and grows to 30 m/100 ft in mountainous areas. (Genus *Pseudotsuga*, family Pinaceae.)

Douglass, Frederick (1817–1895) Born Frederick Augustus Washington Bailey. US antislavery campaigner active during the American Civil War 1861–65. He issued a call to African-Americans to take up arms against the South and helped organize two black regiments. After the Civil War, he held several US government posts, including minister to Haiti 1889–91. He published appeals for full civil rights for blacks and also campaigned for women's suffrage.

Doulton, Henry (1820–1897) English ceramicist. He developed special wares for the chemical, electrical, and building industries, and established the world's first stoneware-drainpipe factory in 1846. From 1870 he created art pottery and domestic tablewares in Lambeth, South London, and Burslem, near Stoke-on-Trent. He was knighted in 1887.

Doumer, Paul (1857–1932) French politician. He was elected president of the Chamber in 1905, president of the Senate in 1927, and president of the republic in 1931. He was assassinated by Gorgulov, a White Russian emigré.

Dounreay site of the world's first fast-breeder nuclear reactor (1962) on the north coast of Scotland, in the Highland unitary authority, 12 km/7 mi west of Thurso. It is now a nuclear reprocessing plant.

Douro (Spanish **Duero**) river in Spain and Portugal, the third largest in the Iberian peninsula; length 775 km/482 mi. It rises in Spain, on the south side of the Peña de Urbión in the province of Soria, and flows west across the plateau of Castile. It follows the Spanish-Portuguese frontier for 105 km/65 mi, and reaches the Atlantic Ocean at São João de Foz, 5 km/3 mi south of ▷Porto. Navigation at the river mouth is hindered by sand bars. There are hydroelectric installations along its course.

dove person who takes a moderate, sometimes pacifist, view on political issues. The term originated in the US during the Vietnam War. Its counterpart is a ▷hawk. In more general usage today, a dove is equated with liberal policies, and a hawk with conservative ones.

dove another name for ▷pigeon.

Dover market town and seaport in Kent, southeast England, on the coast of the English Channel; population (1991) 34,200. It is Britain's nearest point to mainland Europe, 34 km/21 mi from Calais, France. Dover is the world's busiest passenger port and England's principal cross-channel port, with ferry, Seacat (high-speed catamaran), and cross-channel train services. Industries include electronics, paper manufacturing, and light engineering

Dover, Strait of (French **Pas-de-Calais**) stretch of water separating England from France, and connecting the English Channel with the North Sea. It is about 35 km/22 mi long and 34 km/21 mi wide at its narrowest part (from Dover pier to Cap Griz-Nez); its greatest depth is 55 m/180 ft. It is one of the world's busiest sea lanes. The main ports are Dover and Folkestone (England), and Calais and Boulogne (France).

Dowding, Hugh Caswall Tremenheere, 1st Baron Dowding (1882–1970) British air chief marshal. He was chief of Fighter Command at the outbreak of World War II in 1939, a post he held through the Battle of Britain 10 July–12 October 1940.

Dowell, Anthony James (1943–) English classical ballet dancer. He is known for his elegant poise, accurate finish, and exemplary classical style. He was principal dancer with the Royal Ballet 1966–86, and was artistic director 1986–2001.

Dow Jones Index (or Dow Jones Industrial 30 Share Index) scale for measuring the average share price and percentage change of 30 major US industrial companies. It has been calculated and published since 1897 by the financial news publisher Dow Jones and Co.
Related Web site: Dow Jones Indexes http://indexes.dowjones.com/

Dowland, John (c. 1563–c. 1626) English composer of lute songs. He introduced daring expressive refinements of harmony and ornamentation to English Renaissance style in the service of an elevated aesthetic of melancholy, as in the masterly *Lachrymae* (1605).

> ### John Dowland
> *Semper Dowland Semper Dolens. Always Dowland, always sad.*
> Title of pavan

DOVER The white cliffs of Dover epitomize England's historical defences against invasion from the continent of Europe only 34 km/21 mi away. The British politician Stanley Baldwin, in a speech to the House of Commons in July 1934, said 'When you think about the defence of England, you no longer think of the chalk cliffs of Dover. You think of the Rhine.' He was referring to the Maginot Line of fortifications just completed on the Franco-German border. *Image Bank*

Down county of southeastern Northern Ireland.
area 2,470 sq km/953 sq mi **towns and cities** Downpatrick (county town), Bangor, Newtownards, Newry, and Banbridge; the northern part lies within the commuter belt for Belfast, and includes part of the city of Belfast, east of the River Lagan **physical** Mourne Mountains; Strangford sea lough **industries** light manufacturing, plastics, linen, high technology and computer companies, fishing, quarrying **agriculture** County Down has very fertile land in the north. The principal crops are barley, potatoes, and oats; there is livestock rearing and dairying **population** (1981) 339,200 **government** the county returns two members to the UK Parliament
Related Web site: County Down http://www.interknowledge.com/northern-ireland/ukidwn00.htm

Downing Street street in Westminster, London, leading from Whitehall to St James's Park, named after Sir George Downing (died 1684), a diplomat under Cromwell and Charles II. **Number 10** is the official residence of the prime minister and **number 11** is the residence of the chancellor of the Exchequer. **Number 12** is the office of the government whips. After his appointment as prime minister in May 1997, Tony Blair chose to use Number 11 to accommodate his family, using Number 10 as his office and for Cabinet meetings. The chancellor of the Exchequer, Gordon Brown, retained his office in Number 11 but used the flat above Number 10 as his residence.

Down's syndrome condition caused by a chromosomal abnormality (the presence of an extra copy of chromosome 21), which in humans produces mental retardation; a flattened face; coarse, straight hair; and a fold of skin at the inner edge of the eye (hence the former name 'mongolism'). The condition can be detected by prenatal testing.

The incidence for Down's syndrome births in developed countries is one in 700 live births (2000). Mothers aged over 40 are more likely to give birth to a Down's syndrome child, and in 1995 French researchers discovered a link between Down's syndrome incidence and paternal age, with men over 40 having an increased likelihood of fathering a Down's syndrome baby.

The syndrome is named after J L H Down (1828–1896), an English physician who studied it. All people with Down's syndrome who live long enough eventually develop early-onset ▷Alzheimer's disease, a form of dementia. This fact led to the discovery in 1991 that some forms of early-onset Alzheimer's disease are caused by a gene defect on chromosome 21.
Related Web site: Down's Syndrome Web Page http://www.nas.com/downsyn/

dowry property or money given by the bride's family to the groom or his family as part of the marriage agreement; the opposite of ▷bridewealth. In 1961 dowries were made illegal in India; however, in 1992, the Indian government reported more than 15,000 murders or suicides between 1988 and 1991 that were a direct result of insufficient dowries.

Doyle, Arthur Conan (1859–1930) Scottish writer. He created the detective Sherlock ▷Holmes and his assistant Dr Watson, who first appeared in *A Study in Scarlet* (1887) and featured in a number of subsequent stories, including *The Hound of the Baskervilles* (1902). Among Doyle's other works is the fantasy adventure *The Lost World* (1912). In his later years he became a spiritualist and wrote a *History of Spiritualism* (1926).

ARTHUR CONAN DOYLE Scottish writer Arthur Conan Doyle, best known as the creator of the fictional detective Sherlock Holmes, who was so popular that there was a public outcry when Conan Doyle killed him off in 1893. *Archive Photos*

The Sherlock Holmes character featured in several books, including *The Sign of Four* (1890) and *The Valley of Fear* (1915), as well as in volumes of short stories, first published in the *Strand Magazine*. He was knighted in 1902.
Related Web site: Conan Doyle's The Memoirs of Sherlock Holmes: electronic edition http://www.hti.umich.edu/bin/pd-idx?type=header&id=DoyleMemoi

D'Oyly Carte, Richard (1844–1901) English producer of the Gilbert and Sullivan operas. They were performed at the Savoy Theatre, London, which he built. The D'Oyly Carte Opera Company, founded in 1876, was disbanded in 1982 following the ending of its monopoly on the Gilbert and Sullivan operas. The present company, founded in 1988, moved to the Alexandra Theatre, Birmingham, in 1991.

RICHARD D'OYLY CARTE A poster by H M Brock advertising the Gilbert and Sullivan opera *Pirates of Penzance*. *The Art Archive/Victoria and Albert Museum London*

DPP abbreviation for ▷Director of Public Prosecutions.

Drabble, Margaret (1939–) English writer. Her novels include *The Millstone* (1965), *The Middle Ground* (1980), the trilogy *The Radiant Way* (1987), *A Natural Curiosity* (1989), and *The Gates of Ivory* (1991), and *The Witch of Exmoor* (1996). She portrays contemporary life with toughness and sensitivity, often through the eyes of intelligent modern women. She edited the 1985 and 1995 editions of the *Oxford Companion to English Literature*.

> **Margaret Drabble**
> *What fools middle-class girls are to expect other people to respect the same gods and E M Forster.*
> A Summer Bird–cage ch. 11

Draco in astronomy, a large but faint constellation represented as a dragon coiled around the north celestial pole. Due to ▷precession (Earth's axial wobble), the star Alpha Draconis (Thuban) was the pole star 4,700 years ago.

Draco (lived 7th century BC) Athenian politician, the first to codify the laws of the Athenian city-state. These were notorious for their severity; hence **draconian**, meaning particularly harsh.

Dracula in the novel *Dracula* (1897) by Bram Stoker, the caped count who, as a ▷vampire, drinks the blood of beautiful women. The original of Dracula is thought to have been Vlad Tepes, or Vlad the Impaler, ruler of medieval Wallachia, who used to impale his victims and then mock them. Tepes' father took the name *Dracul* from the knightly order of the Dragon. Tepes succeeded to the Wallachian throne in 1456.

draft compulsory military service; also known as ▷conscription.

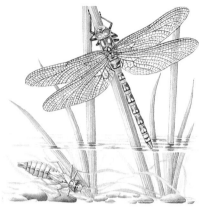

DRAGONFLY Adult dragonflies are long, comparatively slim-bodied insects with two pairs of wings.

dragon name popularly given to various sorts of lizard. These include the ▷flying dragon *Draco volans* of southeast Asia; the komodo dragon *Varanus komodoensis* of Indonesia, at over 3 m/10 ft the largest living lizard; and some Australian lizards with bizarre spines or frills.

dragonfly any of numerous insects of the order Odonata, including the ▷damselfly. They all have long narrow bodies, two pairs of almost equal-sized, glassy wings with a network of veins; short, bristlelike antennae; powerful, 'toothed' mouthparts; and very large compound eyes which may have up to 30,000 facets. They can fly at speeds of up to 64–96 kph/40–60 mph.

dragoon mounted soldier who carried an infantry weapon such as a 'dragon', or short musket, as used by the French army in the 16th century. The name was retained by some later regiments after the original meaning became obsolete.

Drake, Francis (*c.* 1540–1596) English buccaneer and explorer. Having enriched himself as a pirate against Spanish interests in the Caribbean 1567–72, he was sponsored by ▷Elizabeth I for an expedition to the Pacific, sailing round the world 1577–80 in the *Golden Hind*, robbing Spanish ships as he went. This was the second circumnavigation of the globe (the first was by the Portuguese explorer Ferdinand Magellan). Drake also helped to defeat the ▷Spanish Armada in 1588 as a vice admiral in the *Revenge*.

Drake was born in Devon and apprenticed to the master of a coasting vessel, who left him the ship at his death. He accompanied his relative, the navigator John Hawkins, in 1567 and 1572 to plunder the Caribbean, and returned to England in 1573 with considerable booty. After serving in Ireland as a volunteer, he suggested to Queen Elizabeth I an expedition to the Pacific, and in December 1577 he sailed in the *Pelican* with four other ships and 166 men towards South America. In August 1578 the fleet passed through the Straits of Magellan and was then blown south to Cape Horn. The ships became separated and returned to England, all but the *Pelican*, now renamed the *Golden Hind*. Drake sailed north along the coast of Chile and Peru, robbing Spanish ships as far north as California, and then, in 1579, headed southwest across the Pacific. He rounded the South African Cape in June 1580, and reached England in September 1580. Thus the second voyage around the world, and the first made by an English person, was completed in a little under three years. When the Spanish ambassador demanded Drake's punishment, the Queen knighted him on the deck of the *Golden Hind* at Deptford, London. In 1581 Drake was made mayor of Plymouth, in which capacity he brought fresh water into the city by constructing leats from Dartmoor. In 1584–85 he represented the town of Bosinney in Parliament. In a raid on Cádiz in 1587 he burned 10,000 tons of shipping, 'singed the King of Spain's beard', and delayed the invasion of England by the Spanish Armada for a year. He was stationed off the French island of Ushant in 1588 to intercept the Armada, but was driven back to England by unfavourable winds. During the fight in the Channel he served as a vice admiral on the *Revenge*. Drake sailed on his last expedition to the West Indies with Hawkins in 1595, capturing Nombre de Dios on the north coast of Panama but failing to seize Panamá. In January 1596 he died of dysentery off the town of Puerto Bello (now Portobello), Panama.
Related Web site: Drake, Sir Francis http://www.mcn.org/2/oseeler/drake.htm

> **Francis Drake**
> *The advantage of time and place in all practical actions is half the victory; which being lost is irrecoverable.*
> Letter to Queen Elizabeth I, 1588

DRAM (acronym for dynamic random-access memory) computer memory device in the form of a silicon chip commonly used to provide the immediate-access memory of microcomputers. DRAM loses its contents unless they are read and rewritten every 2 milliseconds or so. This process is called **refreshing** the memory. DRAM is slower but cheaper than ▷SRAM, an alternative form of silicon-chip memory.

drama (Greek 'action') in theatre, any play composed to be performed by actors for an audience. The term is also used collectively to group plays into historical or stylistic periods – for example, Greek drama, Restoration drama – as well as referring to the whole body of work written by a dramatist for performance. Drama is distinct from literature in that it is a performing art open to infinite interpretation, the product not merely of the dramatist but also of the collaboration of director, designer, actors, and technical staff. See also ▷theatre, ▷comedy, ▷tragedy, ▷mime, and ▷pantomime.

Dravidian (Sanskrit *Dravida* or *Dramida*) member of a group of non-Indo-European peoples of the Deccan region of India and northern Sri Lanka. The Dravidian language family is large, with about 20 languages spoken in southern India; the main ones are ▷Tamil,which has a literary tradition 2,000 years old; Kanarese; ▷Telugu; ▷Malayalam; and Tulu.

Dreadnought class of battleships built for the British navy after 1905 and far superior in speed and armaments to anything then afloat. The first modern battleship to be built, it was the basis of battleship design for more than 50 years. The first Dreadnought was launched in 1906, with armaments consisting entirely of big guns.

John Drinkwater
Age with the best of all his seasons done, / Youth with his face towards the upland hill.
Olton Pools Dedication

dream series of events or images perceived through the mind during sleep. Their function is unknown, but Sigmund ▷Freud saw them as wish fulfilment (nightmares being failed dreams prompted by fears of 'repressed' impulses). Dreams occur in periods of rapid eye movement (REM) by the sleeper, when the cortex of the brain is approximately as active as in waking hours. Dreams occupy about a fifth of sleeping time.

Dreamtime (or **Dreaming**) mythical past of the Australian Aborigines, the basis of their religious beliefs and creation stories. In the Dreamtime, spiritual beings shaped the land, the first people were brought into being and set in their proper territories, and laws and rituals were established. Belief in a creative spirit in the form of a huge snake, the Rainbow Serpent, occurs over much of Aboriginal Australia, usually associated with waterholes, rain, and thunder. A common feature of religions across the continent is the Aborigines' bond with the land.

Drenthe low-lying northern province of the Netherlands, south of Groningen and Friesland; area 2,660 sq km/1,027 sq mi; population (1997) 460,800. The main cities are Assen (capital), Emmen, and Hoogeveen. The terrain is fenland and moors, with well-drained clay and peat soils. The chief industry is petroleum, and the main agricultural activities are livestock, arable crops, and horticulture.

Dresden capital of the *Land* (state) of ▷Saxony, Germany, lying in a wide basin in the upper Elbe Valley; population (2001 est) 570,700. Products include chemicals, machinery, glassware, and musical instruments; telecommunications and high-tech industries are also important. One of the most beautiful German cities, with a rich architectural and cultural heritage, it was devastated by Allied bombing in 1945; much rebuilding has since taken place, and the city has become an important tourist destination.

Dreyer, Carl Theodor (1889–1968) Danish film director. His wide range of films include the austere silent classic *La Passion de Jeanne d'Arc/The Passion of Joan of Arc* (1928) and the expressionist horror film *Vampyr* (1932), after the failure of which Dreyer made no full-length films until *Vredens Dag/Day of Wrath* (1943). His two late masterpieces are *Ordet/The Word* (1955) and *Gertrud* (1964). His style is restrained and mystical, placing much emphasis on facial detail, subtle camera movement, and elements of decor.

Dreyfus, Alfred (1859–1935) French army officer, victim of miscarriage of justice, anti-Semitism, and cover-up. Employed in the War Ministry, in 1894 he was accused of betraying military secrets to Germany, court-martialled, and sent to the penal colony on ▷Devil's Island, French Guiana. When his innocence was discovered in 1896 the military establishment tried to conceal it, and the implications of the Dreyfus affair were passionately discussed in the press until he was exonerated in 1906.

Dreyfus was born in Mulhouse, eastern France, of a Jewish family. He had been a prisoner in the French Guiana penal colony for two years when it emerged that the real criminal was a Major Esterhazy; the high command nevertheless attempted to suppress the facts and used forged documents to strengthen their case. After a violent controversy, in which the future prime minister Georges ▷Clemenceau and the novelist Emile ▷Zola championed Dreyfus, he was brought back for a retrial in 1899, found guilty with extenuating circumstances, and received a pardon. In 1906 the court of appeal declared him innocent, and he was reinstated in his military rank.

drill in military usage, the repetition of certain fixed movements in response to set commands. Drill is used to get a body of soldiers from one place to another in an orderly fashion, and for parades and ceremonial purposes.

drill large Old World monkey *Mandrillus leucophaeus* similar to a baboon and in the same genus as the ▷mandrill. Drills live in the forests of Cameroon and Nigeria. Brownish-coated, black-faced, and stoutly built, with a very short tail, the male can have a head and body up to 75 cm/2.5 ft long, although females are much smaller.

drilling common woodworking and metal machinery process that involves boring holes with a drill bit. The commonest kind of drill bit is the fluted drill, which has spiral grooves around it to allow the cut material to escape. In the oil industry, rotary drilling is used to bore oil wells. The drill bit usually consists of a number of toothed cutting wheels, which grind their way through the rock as the drill pipe is turned, and mud is pumped through the pipe to lubricate the bit and flush the ground-up rock to the surface.

Drinkwater, John (1882–1937) English poet and dramatist. He was a prolific writer of lyrical and reflective verse, and also wrote many historical plays, including *Abraham Lincoln* (1918) and *Mary Stuart* (1921). His work had an important influence on the revival of serious drama.

driver in computing, a program that controls a peripheral device. Every device connected to the computer needs a driver program.

The driver ensures that communication between the computer and the device is successful.

dromedary variety of Arabian ▷camel. The dromedary or one-humped camel has been domesticated since 400 BC. During a long period without water, it can lose up to one-quarter of its body weight without ill effects.

drone in music, an accompanying constant tone or harmony, usually octave or fifth. It is a feature of many classical and folk traditions, and is produced by many instruments of folk music, including the Indian vina, bagpipes, and hurdy-gurdy. Drone effects in written music include the organ pedal point and the musette dance form.

Drone is also the name given to the three lower pipes of the bagpipes, which produce a fixed chord above which the melody is played on the chanter; also a bowed instrument with a single string stretched on a stick over a bladder; sometimes called a bumbass.

drug any of a range of substances, natural or synthetic, administered to humans and animals as therapeutic agents: to diagnose, prevent, or treat disease, or to assist recovery from injury. Traditionally many drugs were obtained from plants or animals; some minerals also had medicinal value. Today, increasing numbers of drugs are synthesized in the laboratory.

ALFRED DREYFUS French army officer Alfred Dreyfus, who was wrongly convicted of treason in 1895. *Archive Photos*

Drugs are administered in various ways, including: orally, by injection, as a lotion or ointment, as a ▷pessary, by inhalation, or by transdermal patch.

Related Web site: Internet Drug Index http://www.rxlist.com/

drug, generic any drug produced without a brand name that is identical to a branded product. Usually generic drugs are produced when the patent on a branded drug has expired, and are cheaper than their branded equivalents.

drug misuse illegal use of drugs for nontherapeutic purposes. Under the UK Misuse of Drugs regulations drugs used illegally include: narcotics, such as heroin, morphine, and the synthetic opioids; barbiturates; amphetamines and related substances; ▷benzodiazepine tranquillizers; cocaine, LSD, and cannabis. **Designer drugs**, for example ecstasy, are usually modifications of the amphetamine molecule, altered in order to evade the law as well as for different effects, and may be many times more powerful and dangerous. Crack, a highly toxic derivative of cocaine, became available to drug users in the 1980s. Some athletes misuse drugs such as ephedrine and ▷anabolic steroids. Sources of traditional drugs include the 'Golden Triangle' (where Myanmar, Laos, and Thailand meet), Mexico, Colombia, China, Pakistan, and the Middle East

Related Web site: Trashed (NHS promotion site) http://www.trashed.co.uk/index2.html

Druidism religion of the Celtic peoples of the pre-Christian British Isles and Gaul. The word is derived from the Greek *drus* ('oak'), a tree regarded by the Druids as sacred. One of the Druids' chief rites was the cutting of mistletoe from the oak with a golden sickle. They taught the immortality of the soul and a reincarnation doctrine, and were expert in astronomy. The Druids are thought to have offered human sacrifices.

Related Web site: Celtic Druidism http://www.religioustolerance.org/druid.htm

drum any of a class of percussion instruments including **slit drums** made of wood, **steel drums** fabricated from oil containers, and a majority group of **skin drums** consisting of a shell or vessel of wood, metal, or earthenware across one or both ends of which is stretched a membrane of hide or plastic. Drums are struck with the hands or with a stick or pair of sticks; they are among the oldest instruments known.

drupe fleshy ▷fruit containing one or more seeds which are surrounded by a hard, protective layer – for example cherry, almond, and plum. The wall of the fruit (▷pericarp) is differentiated into the outer skin (exocarp), the fleshy layer of tissues (mesocarp), and the hard layer surrounding the seed (endocarp).

DRUPE The succulent flesh around the 'stone' at the centre of a drupe attracts animals to feed on it. In their turn, the animals then distribute the seed. The ivy *Hedera helix*, shown here, produces drupes. *Premaphotos Wildlife*

Druze (or **Druse**) religious sect in the Middle East of some 300,000 people. It began as a branch of Shiite Islam, based on a belief in the divinity of the Fatimid caliph al-Hakim (996–1021) and that he will return at the end of time. Their particular doctrines are kept secret, even from the majority of members. They refer to themselves as the Mowahhidoon, meaning monotheistic. The religion is exclusive, with conversion forbidden, either to or from the sect.

Related Web site: Druse, Druze, Mowahhidoon http://www.religioustolerance.org/druse.htm

dryad (Greek *drys* '(oak) tree') in Greek mythology, a forest ▷nymph or tree spirit, especially of the oak. Each tree had a **hamadryad** who lived and died with it, from the Greek *hama* meaning 'together'.

Dryden, John (1631–1700) English poet and dramatist. He is noted for his satirical verse and for his use of the heroic couplet. His poetry includes the verse satire *Absalom and Achitophel* (1681), *Annus Mirabilis* (1667), and 'A Song for St Cecilia's Day' (1687). Plays include the heroic drama *The Conquest of Granada* (1672), the comedy *Marriage à la Mode* (1673), and *All for Love* (1678), a reworking of Shakespeare's *Antony and Cleopatra.*

On occasion, Dryden trimmed his politics and his religion to the prevailing wind, and, as a Roman Catholic convert under James II, lost the post of poet laureate (to which he had been appointed in 1668) after the Revolution of 1688. Critical works include the essay 'Of Dramatic Poesy' (1668). Later ventures to support himself include a translation of the Roman poet Virgil (1697).

Related Web site: Selected Poetry and Prose by John Dryden
http://www.library.utoronto.ca/utel/rp/authors/dryden.html

John Dryden
Better one suffer, than a nation grieve.
Absalom and Achitophel

dry ice solid carbon dioxide (CO_2), used as a refrigerant. At temperatures above −79°C/−110.2°F, it sublimes (turns into vapour without passing through a liquid stage) to gaseous carbon dioxide.

dry point in printmaking, a technique of engraving on copper, using a hard, sharp tool. The resulting lines tend to be fine and angular, with a strong furry edge created by the metal shavings. Dürer, Rembrandt, and Max Beckmann were outstanding exponents.

dry rot infection of timber in damp conditions by fungi (see ▷fungus), such as *Merulius lacrymans*, that form a threadlike surface. Whitish at first, the fungus later reddens as reproductive spores are formed. Tentacles from the fungus also work their way into the timber, making it dry-looking and brittle. Dry rot spreads rapidly through a building.

Drysdale, (George) Russell (1912–1981) Australian artist. In 1944 he produced a series of wash drawings for the *Sydney Morning Herald* recording the effects of a severe drought in western New South Wales. The bleakness of life in the Australian outback is a recurring theme in his work, which typically depicts the dried-out, scorched landscape with gaunt figures reflecting fortitude in desolation and poverty. Children appear frequently, as in *The Gatekeeper's Wife* (1965; National Library, Canberra).

dry-stone walling the practice of building walls by bonding the stones without mortar. In upland farming areas dry-stone walls often replace hedges and fences as field boundaries. Typically dry-stone walls consist of an outer layer of large stones concealing a core of smaller stones. Dry-stone walling can be seen worldwide and is an ancient skill.

DRY-STONE WALLING Repairs being made to a traditional dry-stone wall in North Yorkshire, England. *R A Preston-Mafham/Premaphotos Wildlife*

DTP abbreviation for ▷desktop publishing.

Dual Entente alliance between France and Russia that lasted from 1893 until the Bolshevik Revolution of 1917.

dualism in philosophy, the belief that reality is essentially dual in nature. The French philosopher René ▷Descartes, for example, referred to thinking and material substance. These entities interact but are fundamentally separate and distinct.

Dualism is contrasted with ▷monism, the theory that reality is made up of only one substance.

Duarte, José Napoleon (1925–1990) El Salvadorean politician, president 1980–82 and 1984–88. He was mayor of San Salvador 1964–70, and was elected president in 1972, but was soon exiled by the army for seven years in Venezuela. He returned in 1980, after the assassination of Archbishop Romero had increased support for the Christian Democratic Party (PDC), and became president, with US backing. He lost the 1982 presidential election, but was successful in May 1984. On becoming president again, he sought a negotiated settlement with the left-wing guerrillas in 1986, but resigned in mid-1988, as he had terminal liver cancer.

Dubai one of the ▷United Arab Emirates; population (1995) 674,100.

Related Web site: Dubai http://www.uaeforever.com/Dubai/

du Barry, comtesse Marie Jeanne (1743–1793) Born Marie Jeanne Bécu. Mistress of ▷Louis XV of France from 1768. At his death in 1774 she was banished to a convent, and during the Revolution fled to London. Returning to Paris in 1793, she was guillotined.

Dubček, Alexander (1921–1992) Czechoslovak politician, chair of the federal assembly 1989–92. He was a member of the Slovak ▷resistance movement during World War II, and became first secretary of the Communist Party 1967–69. He launched a liberalization campaign (called the ▷Prague Spring) that was opposed by the USSR and led to the Soviet invasion of Czechoslovakia in 1968. He was arrested by Soviet troops and expelled from the party in 1970. In 1989 he gave speeches at pro-democracy rallies, and after the fall of the hardline regime, he was elected speaker of the National Assembly in Prague, a position to which he was re-elected in 1990. He was fatally injured in a car crash in September 1992.

Dublin county in the Republic of Ireland, in Leinster province, facing the Irish Sea and bounded by the counties of Meath, Kildare, and Wicklow; county town ▷Dublin; area 920 sq km/355 sq mi; population (1996) 1,058,300. The county is mostly level and low-lying, but rises in the south to 753 m/2,471 ft in Kippure, part of the Wicklow Mountains. The River Liffey enters Dublin Bay. The county is dominated by Ireland's capital city of Dublin and its suburbs, but also contains pastoral and agricultural land. Dún Laoghaire is the other major town and large port.

Alexander Dubček
Socialism with a Human Face.
Motto on the Prague Spring attributed to Dubček

Dublin (official Irish name **Baile Átha Cliath**, 'the town of the ford of the hurdles'; Gaelic *dubh linn* 'dark pool') city and port on the east coast of Ireland, at the mouth of the River Liffey, facing the Irish Sea; capital of the Republic of Ireland, and county town of County ▷Dublin; population (1996) 481,600; Greater Dublin, including Dún Laoghaire (1996) 953,000. Around a quarter of the Republic's population lives in the Dublin conurbation, with a high density of young, professional workers. In the 1990s the city underwent a renaissance, with the restoration of many old city-centre buildings, notably in the Temple Bar area. Dublin is the site of one of the world's largest breweries (Guinness); other industries include textiles, pharmaceuticals, electrical goods, whiskey distilling, glass, food processing, and machine tools. Dublin is a significant centre for culture and tourism, known particularly for its Georgian architecture and plethora of bars.

Features In the Georgian period many fine squares and wide streets were laid out. Important buildings from this period are the City Hall (1769–79; formerly the Royal Exchange); the Bank of Ireland (1729–85; the former parliament building); the Custom House (1791; burned during 1921 but later restored); Leinster House (where the Dáil Éireann (House of Representatives) and the Seanad Éireann (the Senate) sit) with the National Library and the National Museum nearby; the Four Courts (designed in 1786 as the seat of the high court of justice); and the National Gallery.

Other notable buildings are Dublin Castle (the tower of which dates to the early 13th century); the Hugh Lane Municipal Gallery of Modern Art; Collins Barracks (now part of the National Museum of Ireland); and the Abbey and Gate theatres. There is a Roman Catholic pro-cathedral, St Mary's (1816); two Protestant cathedrals, St Patrick's and Christchurch; and three universities – Trinity College, University College (part of the National University of Ireland), and Dublin City University (formerly a technical college). Trinity College library contains the Book of Kells, a splendidly illuminated 8th-century gospel book associated with the monastery of Kells founded by St Columba in County Meath. Kilmainham Jail, where nationalists such as Charles Stewart ▷Parnell were imprisoned, is now a museum.

DUBLIN The O'Connell Bridge over the River Liffey, Dublin, Republic of Ireland, was built in the period 1794–98 by the English-born architect James Gandon and named after the then viceroy, Lord Carlisle. In 1880 it was widened (making it almost square), and in 1882 was renamed after Irish nationalist leader Daniel O'Connell, when the statue in his honour was unveiled. *Image Bank*

History The earliest records of a settlement at Dublin date from AD 140. The city was captured in 840 by Viking invaders; the ruler of Dublin and his Norse and Leinster allies were defeated by Brian Bóruma in 1014 at Clontarf, now a northern suburb of the city. Dublin was the centre of English rule from 1171 (exercised from Dublin Castle; 1220) until 1922. Dublin was the scene of the 1916 ▷Easter Rising against British rule in Ireland.

Related Web site: University of Dublin – Trinity College
http://www.tcd.ie/

dubnium synthesized, radioactive, metallic element of the ▷transactinide series, symbol Db, atomic number 105, relative atomic mass 261. Six isotopes have been synthesized, each with very short (fractions of a second) half-lives. Two institutions claim to have been the first to produce it: the Joint Institute for Nuclear Research in Dubna, Russia, in 1967; and the University of California at Berkeley, USA, who disputed the Soviet claim in 1970. Its temporary name was unnilpentium.

Dubrovnik (Italian **Ragusa**) city and port in Croatia on the Adriatic coast; population (1991) 49,700. It manufactures cheese, liqueurs, silk, and leather.

Dubuffet, Jean Philippe Arthur (1901–1985) French artist. He originated **Art Brut**, 'raw or brutal art', in the 1940s. Inspired by graffiti and children's drawings, he used such varied materials as plaster, steel wool, and straw in his paintings and sculptures to produce highly textured surfaces.

Duccio di Buoninsegna (before 1278–1318/19) Italian painter. As the first major figure in the Sienese school, his influence on the development of painting was profound. His works include his altarpiece for Siena Cathedral, the *Maestà* (1308–11, Cathedral Museum, Siena). In this the figure of the Virgin is essentially Byzantine in style, with much gold detail, but depicted with a new warmth and tenderness.

Duce (Italian 'leader') title bestowed on the fascist dictator Benito ▷Mussolini by his followers and later adopted as his official title.

Duchamp, Marcel (1887–1968) French-born US artist. He achieved notoriety with his *Nude Descending a Staircase No 2* (1912; Philadelphia Museum of Art), influenced by cubism and Futurism. An active exponent of ▷Dada, he invented ▷ready-mades, everyday items (for example, a bicycle wheel mounted on a kitchen stool) which he displayed as works of art.

duck any of about 50 species of short-legged waterbirds with webbed feet and flattened bills, of the family Anatidae, order Anseriformes, which also includes the larger geese and swans. Ducks were domesticated for eggs, meat, and feathers by the ancient Chinese and the ancient Maya (see ▷poultry). Most ducks live in fresh water, feeding on worms and insects as well as vegetable matter. They are generally divided into dabbling ducks and diving ducks.

Anatomy The three front toes of a duck's foot are webbed and the hind toe is free; the legs are scaly. The broad rounded bill is skin-covered with a horny tip provided with little plates (lamellae) through which the duck is able to strain its food from water and mud.

Species of duck The mallard *Anas platyrhynchos*, 58 cm/1.9 ft, found over most of the northern hemisphere, is the species from which all domesticated ducks originated. The male (drake) has a glossy green head, brown breast, grey body, and yellow bill. The female (duck) is speckled brown, with a duller bill. The male moults and resembles the female for a while just after the breeding season.

DUCK The flightless steamer duck, or *Tachyeres brachypterus*, is found in the Falkland Islands. *Image Bank*

There are many other species of duck including ▷teal, ▷eider, mandarin duck, ▷merganser, muscovy duck, pintail duck, ▷shelduck, and ▷shoveler. They have different-shaped bills according to their diet and habitat; for example, the shoveler has a wide spade-shaped bill for scooping insects off the surface of water.

duck-billed platypus another name for the ▷platypus.

duckweed any of a family of tiny plants found floating on the surface of still water throughout most of the world, except the polar regions and tropics. Each plant consists of a flat, circular, leaflike structure 0.4 cm/0.15 in or less across, with a single thin root up to 15 cm/6 in long below. (Genus chiefly *Lemna*, family Lemnaceae.)

DUCKWEED Gibbous duckweed *Lemna gibba*. It is common in the southern British Isles. *Premaphotos Wildlife*

ductless gland alternative name for an ▷endocrine gland.

duel fight between two people armed with weapons. A duel is usually fought according to pre-arranged rules with the aim of settling a private quarrel.

due process of law legal principle, dating from the ▷Magna Carta, the charter of rights granted by King John of England in 1215, and now enshrined in the fifth and fourteenth amendments to the US Constitution, that no person shall be deprived of life, liberty, or property without due process of law (a fair legal procedure). In the USA, the provisions have been given a wide interpretation, to include, for example, the right to representation by an attorney.

Dufay, Guillaume (*c.* 1400–1474) Flemish composer. He wrote secular songs and sacred music, including 84 songs and 8 masses. His work marks a transition from the style of the Middle Ages to the expressive melodies and rich harmonies of the Renaissance.

Dufourspitze second highest of the alpine peaks, 4,634 m/15,203 ft high. It is the highest peak in the Monte Rosa group of the Pennine Alps on the Swiss-Italian frontier.

Dufy, Raoul (1877–1953) French painter and designer. Inspired by ▷fauvism he developed a fluent, brightly coloured style in watercolour and oils, painting scenes of gaiety and leisure, such as horse racing, yachting, and life on the beach. He also designed tapestries, textiles, and ceramics.

dugong marine mammal *Dugong dugong* of the order Sirenia (sea cows), found in the Red Sea, the Indian Ocean, and western Pacific. It can grow to 3.6 m/11 ft long, and has a tapering body with a notched tail and two fore-flippers. All dugongs are listed on Convention on International Trade in Endangered Species (▷CITES) Appendix 1, which bans all trade in the species.

duiker (Afrikaans *diver*) any of several antelopes of the family Bovidae, common in Africa. Duikers are shy and nocturnal, and grow to 30–70 cm/12–28 in tall.

Duiker, Johannes (1890–1935) Dutch architect of the 1920s and 1930s avant-garde period. A member of the De ▷Stijl group, his works demonstrate great structural vigour. They include the Zonnestraal Sanatorium, Hilversum (1926–28) co-designed with Bernard Bijvoet, and the Open Air School (1929–30) and Handelsblad-Cineac News Cinema (1934), both in Amsterdam.

duikerbok small African antelope with crested head, large muzzle, and short, conical horns in the males only.
Classification Duikerboks are in genus *Cephalophus* in the family Bovidae (cattle and antelopes) of order Artiodactyla.

Duisburg (formerly **Duisburg-Hamborn** (until 1934)) river port and industrial city in North Rhine-Westphalia, Germany, at the confluence of the Rhine and Ruhr rivers, 20 km/12 mi northwest of Düsseldorf; population (1995) 535,200. It is the largest inland river port in Europe. Located at the western end of the Ruhrgebiet (Ruhr District), Duisburg possesses the major Rhine docks at Ruhrort through which raw materials, such as iron ore and petroleum are imported. It has the largest concentration of heavy industry (iron and steelmaking, oil refining, heavy engineering, chemicals, and barge building) in the Ruhr.

Dukas, Paul Abraham (1865–1935) French composer and teacher. His scrupulous orchestration and chromatically enriched harmonies were admired by Debussy. He wrote very little, composing slowly and with extreme care. His small output includes the opera *Ariane et Barbe-Bleue/Ariane and Bluebeard* (1907), the ballet *La Péri/The Peri* (1912), and the animated orchestral scherzo *L'Apprenti sorcier/The Sorcerer's Apprentice* (1897).

duke highest title in the English peerage. It originated in England in 1337, when Edward III created his son Edward, Duke of Cornwall.

dulcimer musical instrument, a form of ▷zither, consisting of a shallow open trapezoidal soundbox across which strings are stretched laterally; they are horizontally struck by lightweight hammers or beaters. It produces clearly differentiated pitches of consistent quality and is more agile and wide-ranging in pitch than the harp or lyre. In Hungary the dulcimer is known as a cimbalom, and is a national instrument.

Dulles, Allen Welsh (1893–1969) US lawyer, director of the Central Intelligence Agency (CIA) 1953–61. He helped found the CIA in 1950. He was embroiled in the ▷Bay of Pigs, Cuba, controversial invasion attempt, among others, which forced his resignation. He was the brother of John Foster ▷Dulles.

Dulles, John Foster (1888–1959) US lawyer and politician. Senior US adviser at the founding of the United Nations, he was largely responsible for drafting the Japanese peace treaty of 1951. As secretary of state 1952–59, he was an architect of US ▷Cold War foreign policy and secured US intervention in South Vietnam after the expulsion of the French in 1954. He was highly critical of the UK during the ▷Suez Crisis in 1956.

Dulong, Pierre Louis (1785–1838) French chemist and physicist. In 1819 he discovered, together with physicist Alexis Petit, the law that now bears their names. **Dulong and Petit's law** states that, for many elements solid at room temperature, the product of ▷relative atomic mass and ▷specific heat capacity is approximately constant. He also discovered the explosive nitrogen trichloride in 1811.

dulse any of several edible red seaweeds, especially *Rhodymenia palmata*, found on middle and lower shores of the north Atlantic. They may have a single broad blade up to 30 cm/12 in long rising directly from the holdfast which attaches them to the sea floor, or may be palmate (with five lobes) or fan-shaped. The frond is tough and dark red, sometimes with additional small leaflets at the edge.

Raoul Dufy
*Pictures have broken away
from their frames
to continue on dresses and
on walls.*
Dufy Les Tissus Imprimés Amour de l'Art
No 1 (1920)

Dulwich district of the Greater London borough of Southwark. It includes Dulwich College (1619); the Horniman Museum (1901), with a fine ethnological collection; Dulwich Picture Gallery (1814), the first public art gallery to be opened in London; Dulwich Park; and Dulwich Village.

Dumas, Alexandre (1824–1895) French author, known as Dumas *fils* (the son of Dumas *père*). He is remembered for the play *La Dame aux camélias/The Lady of the Camellias* (1852), based on his own novel, and the source of Verdi's opera *La Traviata*.

Dumas, Alexandre (1802–1870) French writer, known as Dumas *père* (the father). His popular historical romances were the reworked output of a 'fiction-factory' of collaborators. They include *Les Trois Mousquetaires/The Three Musketeers* (1844) and its sequels. He is best known for *Le Comte de Monte Cristo/The Count of Monte Cristo*, which appeared in 12 volumes (1845). His play *Henri III et sa cour/Henry III and His Court* (1829) established French romantic historical drama. Dumas *fils* was his son.
Related Web site: Man in the Iron Mask, The http://www.hoboes.com/html/FireBlade/Dumas/IronMask/

Du Maurier, Daphne (1907–1989) English novelist. Her romantic fiction includes *Jamaica Inn* (1936), *Rebecca* (1938), *Frenchman's Creek* (1942), and *My Cousin Rachel* (1951), and is set in Cornwall. Her work, though lacking in depth and original insights, is made compelling by her storytelling gift.
Jamaica Inn, *Rebecca*, and her short story *The Birds* were made into films by the English director Alfred Hitchcock. She was made a Dame of the British Empire in 1969.

Du Maurier, George (Louis Palmella Busson) (1834–1896) French-born British author and illustrator. He is remembered for the novel *Trilby* (1894), the story of a natural singer able to perform only under the hypnosis of Svengali, her tutor.

Dumbarton Oaks 18th-century mansion in Washington, DC, USA, used for conferences and seminars. It was the scene of a conference held in 1944 that led to the foundation of the United Nations.

Dumfries administrative headquarters of ▷Dumfries and Galloway unitary authority, Scotland; population (1991) 32,100. It is situated on the River Nith, 53 km/33 mi northwest of Carlisle. Industries include plastics, light engineering, and textiles. Robert Burns is buried in the graveyard of St Michael's church.

Dumfries and Galloway unitary authority in southern Scotland, formed in 1996 from the regional council of the same name (1975–96).
area 6,421 sq km/2,479 sq mi *towns* Annan, ▷Dumfries (administrative headquarters), Kirkcudbright, Stranraer, Castle Douglas, Newton Stewart *physical* area characterized by an indented coastline, including Luce Bay and Wigtown Bay, backed by a low-lying coastal strip of varying width; intensively forested in the Galloways. Much of the inland area is upland: east to west this includes Eskdalemuir (Hart Fell 808 m/2,651 ft), the Lowther Hills (Green Lowther 732 m/2,402 ft) and the Galloway Hills (the Merrick 843 m/2,766 ft) *features* Wanlockhead (the highest village in Scotland); the oldest working post office in the world at Sanquhar; Glen Trool National Park; Ruthwell Cross, Whithorn archaeological dig *industries* timber, chemicals, food processing *agriculture* beef and dairy cattle, sheep, forestry *population* (1996) 147,800

dump in computing, the process of rapidly transferring data to external memory or to a printer. It is usually done to help with debugging (see ▷bug) or as part of an error-recovery procedure designed to provide ▷data security. A ▷screen dump makes a printed copy of the current screen display.

dumping in international trade, the selling of goods by one country to another at below marginal cost or at a price below that in its own country. Countries dump in order to get rid of surplus produce or to improve their competitive position in the recipient country. The practice is deplored by ▷free trade advocates because of the artificial, unfair advantage it yields.

Duna Hungarian name for the River ▷Danube.

Dunarea Romanian name for the River ▷Danube.

Dunbar, William (*c.* 1460–*c.* 1520) Scottish poet at the court of James IV. His poems include a political allegory, *The Thrissil and the Rois*, written in 1503, celebrating James IV's marriage with Margaret Tudor, and the lament with the refrain 'Timor mortis conturbat me' ('Fear of death confounds me'), printed in 1508.

William Dunbar
*Fear of death throws me
into confusion.*
Lament for the Makaris

Duncan, Isadora (1878–1927) Born Angela Duncan. US dancer. A pioneer of modern dance, she adopted an emotionally expressive free form, dancing barefoot and wearing a loose tunic, inspired by the ideal of Hellenic beauty. She danced solos accompanied to music by Beethoven and other great composers, believing that the music should fit the grandeur of the dance. She died in an accident when her long scarf caught in the wheel of the sportscar in which she was travelling.

Duncan Smith, Iain (1954–) British Conservative politician, party leader 2001–2003. The candidate of the party's Euro-sceptic and socially-conservative right wing, in September 2001 the party's members chose him in preference to the experienced Euro-phile Kenneth Clarke to replace leader William Hague, who stood down after the party suffered a second successive general election defeat. Duncan Smith had presented himself as the candidate best able to unite policy around a programme of opposition to the UK joining the European single currency, and of reforms in domestic policies, including greater citizen choice in education and health. He was replaced by Michael Howard.

Dundee City city and unitary authority in eastern Scotland, on the north side of the Firth of Tay.

Dundee rests on a gentle slope, rising from the Firth of Tay to a hill known as The Law (174 m/570 ft). The Tay estuary is 3 km/2 mi wide at this point and is easily navigable for large vessels.

There are two universities, University of Dundee (1967), developed from Queen's College (founded in 1881), and University of Abertay (formerly Dundee Institute of Technology). Other notable buildings include the Albert Institute (1867) and Caird Hall. *Discovery*, the ship used by Robert Falcon Scott on his expedition to the Antarctic (1901–04) is moored on the Tay, to the west of the Tay road bridge. At Broughty Ferry, 5 km/3 mi to the east, is a 15th-century castle, with a museum documenting Dundee's 18th-century whaling industry.

area 62 sq km/24 sq mi **towns** Monifieth, Broughty Ferry, Dundee (administrative headquarters) **physical** Firth of Tay **features** Tay Bridges; Scott's ship *Discovery*, which has been restored and is a visitor attraction **agriculture** fishing **industries** biomedical research, oil industry support, high technology manufacturing
population (1996) 155,000

Dundee, John Graham Claverhouse, Viscount Dundee see John Graham ▷Claverhouse.

dune mound or ridge of wind-drifted sand common on coasts and in deserts. Loose sand is blown and bounced along by the wind, up the windward side of a dune. The sand particles then fall to rest on the lee side, while more are blown up from the windward side. In this way a dune moves gradually downwind.

In sandy deserts, the typical crescent-shaped dune is called a **barchan**. **Seif dunes** are longitudinal and lie parallel to the wind direction, and **star-shaped dunes** are formed by irregular winds.

DUNE Sand dunes in Algeria towards the end of the afternoon. The low sun accentuates the ripple effect in the sand caused by the wind's constant pressure at the surface. *Image Bank*

Dunfermline industrial town north of the Firth of Forth in Fife, Scotland; population (1991) 55,100. Industries include engineering, electronics, and textiles. It was the ancient capital of Scotland, with many sites of royal historical significance. Many Scottish kings, including Robert the Bruce and Malcolm Canmore, are buried in **Dunfermline Abbey**.

Dunkirk (French **Dunkerque**) most northerly seaport of France, in Nord *département*, at the entrance to the Strait of Dover; population (1990) 71,100, conurbation 195,000. Its harbour is one of the foremost in France and it stands at the junction of four canals, giving it communication with the rest of France and with Belgium; there is a ferry service to Ramsgate in England. Industries include oil refining, fishing, and the manufacture of textiles, machinery, and soap. Dunkirk was close to the front line during much of World War I, and in World War II, 337,131 Allied troops (including about 110,000 French) were evacuated from the beaches as German forces approached.

Dún Laoghaire (formerly **Kingstown**) major port, residential town, and borough in County Dublin, Republic of Ireland, 10 km/6 mi south of the centre of Dublin; population (1996) 190,000 (Dún Laoghaire – Rathdown). It is a terminal for ferries to Britain, and there are fishing industries. The National Maritime Museum is located here, and it is an important yachting centre and popular tourist resort. The James Joyce museum is located in a Martello tower at Sandycove, 3 km/2 mi south of the town, where the author once stayed.

dunlin small gregarious shore bird *Calidris alpina* of the sandpiper family Scolopacidae, order Charadriformes, about 18 cm/7 in long, nesting on moors and marshes in the far northern regions of Eurasia and North America. Chestnut above and black below in summer, it is greyish in winter; the bill and feet are black.

dunnock (or **hedge sparrow**) European bird *Prunella modularis* family Prunellidae, similar in size and colouring to the sparrow, but with a slate-grey head and breast, and more slender bill. It is characterized in the field by a hopping gait, with continual twitches of the wings whilst feeding. It nests in bushes and hedges.

Duns Scotus, John (*c.* 1265–*c.* 1308) Scottish monk, a leading figure in the theological and philosophical system of medieval ▷scholasticism, which attempted to show that Christian doctrine was compatible with the ideas of the Greek philosophers Aristotle and Plato. The church rejected his ideas, and the word **dunce** is derived from Dunses, a term of ridicule applied to his followers.

In the medieval controversy over universals he advocated nominalism, maintaining that classes of things have no independent reality. He belonged to the Franciscan order, and was known as *Doctor Subtilis* (the Subtle Teacher).

Dunstable (or Dunstaple), **John** (*c.* 1385–1453) English composer of songs and anthems. He is considered one of the founders of Renaissance harmony.

duodecimal system system of arithmetic notation using 12 as a base, at one time considered superior to the decimal number system in that 12 has more factors (2, 3, 4, 6) than 10 (2, 5).

duodenum in vertebrates, a short length of ▷alimentary canal found between the stomach and the small intestine. Its role is in digesting carbohydrates, fats, and proteins. The smaller molecules formed are then absorbed, either by the duodenum or the ileum.

Du Pré, Jacqueline Mary (1945–1987) English cellist. She was celebrated for her proficient technique and powerful interpretations of the classical cello repertory, particularly of Elgar. She had an international concert career while still in her teens and made many recordings.

She married the Israeli pianist and conductor Daniel ▷Barenboim in 1967 and worked with him in concerts, as a duo, and in a conductor-soloist relationship until her playing career was ended by multiple sclerosis. Although confined to a wheelchair for the last 14 years of her life, she continued to work as a teacher and to campaign on behalf of other sufferers of the disease.

duralumin lightweight aluminium ▷alloy widely used in aircraft construction, containing copper, magnesium, and manganese.

Duras, Marguerite (1914–1996) Adopted name of Marguerite Donnadieu. French writer, dramatist, and film-maker. Her work includes short stories ('Des Journées entières dans les arbres' 1954, stage adaptation *Days in the Trees* 1965), plays (*La Musica/The Music* 1967), and film scripts (*Hiroshima, mon amour* 1960, *India Song* 1975). She also directed stage productions and film versions of her work. Her novels include *Le Vice-consul/The Vice-Consul* (1966), evoking an existentialist world from the setting of Calcutta; *L'Amant/The Lover* (1984; Prix Goncourt), which deals with a love affair between a young French woman and a Chinese man; and *Emily L.* (1989). *La Vie matérielle* (1987) appeared in England as *Practicalities* (1990). Her autobiographical novel, *La Douleur* (1986), is set in Paris in 1945.

Durazzo Italian form of ▷Durrës, a port in Albania.

Durban principal port of KwaZulu-Natal, South Africa, and main harbour of the republic; population (urban area, 1996) 1,320,000. Exports include coal, chemicals, steel, granite, wood products, sugar, fruit, grain, rice, and wool; imports include heavy machinery and mining equipment. Durban is also a holiday resort.

Founded in 1824 as Port Natal, it was renamed in 1835 after General Benjamin d'Urban (1777–1849), lieutenant governor of the eastern district of Cape Colony 1834–37. Near the city are the University of Durban-Westville (1961) and the University of Natal (established in 1949 from Natal University College, founded in 1910), which is divided between Durban and Pietermaritzburg.

Dürer, Albrecht (1471–1528) German artist. He was the leading figure of the northern Renaissance. He was born in Nürnberg and travelled widely in Europe. Highly skilled in drawing and a keen student of nature, he perfected the technique of woodcut and engraving, producing woodcut series such as the *Apocalypse* (1498) and copperplate engravings such as *The Knight, Death, and the Devil* (1513) and *Melancholia* (1514). His paintings include altarpieces and meticulously observed portraits, including many self-portraits.

He was apprenticed first to his father, a goldsmith, then in 1486 to Michael Wolgemut (1434–1519), a painter, woodcut artist, and master of a large workshop in Nürnberg. At the age of 13 he drew a portrait of himself from the mirror, the first known self-portrait in the history of European art, and characteristic of his genius. From 1490 he travelled widely, studying Netherlandish and Italian art, then visited Colmar, Basel, and Strasbourg and returned to Nürnberg in 1495. Other notable journeys were to Venice 1505–07, where he met the painter Giovanni Bellini, and to Antwerp in 1520, where he was made court painter to Charles V of Spain and the Netherlands (recorded in detail in his diary).

Related Web site: Albrecht Dürer – An Exhibit of Four of Our Favourite Prints http://glyphs.com/art/durer/

Durga Hindu goddess; one of the many names for the 'great goddess' ▷Mahādevi.

Durham city and administrative headquarters of the county of Durham, northeast England, on the River Wear, 19 km/12 mi south of Newcastle-upon-Tyne; population (1991) 36,900. Formerly a centre for the coalmining industry (the last pit closed in 1993), the city now has light engineering industries and manufactures textiles, carpets, and clothing.

Features Durham has a fine Norman cathedral and the remains of a castle built in 1072 by William I. The cathedral and castle are together a World Heritage Site. Other features include the university's Gulbenkian Museum of Oriental Art and Archaeology (1960), the UK's only museum wholly devoted to the subject, and the annual Miners' Gala. The university was founded in 1832.

Durham county of northeast England (since April 1997 Darlington has been a separate unitary authority).

area 2,232 sq km/862 sq mi **towns and cities** Durham (administrative headquarters), Newton Aycliffe, Peterlee, Chester-le-Street **physical** Pennine Hills; rivers Wear and Tees **features** Beamish open-air industrial museum; site of one of Britain's richest coalfields (pits no longer functioning); Bowes Museum; Barnard Castle; Durham Cathedral; University of Durham (1832), housed in Durham Castle; dales in the west of the county **agriculture** sheep; dairy produce; hill farming **industries** clothing; chemicals; iron and steel processing; light engineering industries; quarrying; cement; pharmaceuticals **population** (1996) 608,100 **famous people** Elizabeth Barrett Browning, Anthony Eden

Related Web site: Durham County Council http://www.durham.gov.uk/

Durham, John George Lambton, 1st Earl of Durham (1792–1840) British politician. Appointed Lord Privy Seal in 1830, he drew up the first Reform Bill in 1832, and as governor general of Canada briefly in 1837 he drafted the Durham Report which resulted in the union of Upper and Lower Canada. He was made a baron in 1828 and an earl in 1833.

Durkheim, Emile (1858–1917) French sociologist, one of the founders of modern sociology, who also influenced social anthropology. He worked to establish sociology as a respectable and scientific discipline, capable of diagnosing social ills and recommending possible cures.

Durkheim was the first lecturer in social science at Bordeaux University 1887–1902, professor of education at the Sorbonne from 1902 and the first professor of sociology there from 1913. He examined the bases of social order and the effects of industrialization on traditional social and moral order.

His four key works are *De la division du travail social/The Division of Labour in Society* (1893), comparing social order in small-scale societies with that in industrial ones; *Les Régles de la méthode/The Rules of Sociological Method* (1895), outlining his own brand of functionalism and proclaiming ▷positivism as the way forward for sociology as a science; *Suicide* (1897), showing social causes of this apparently individual act; and *Les Formes élémentaires de la vie religieuse/The Elementary Forms of Religion* (1912), a study of the beliefs of Australian Aborigines, showing the place of religion in social solidarity.

durra (or **doura**) grass, also known as Indian millet, grown as a cereal in parts of Asia and Africa. *Sorghum vulgare* is the chief cereal in many parts of Africa. See also ▷sorghum. (Genus *Sorghum.*)

Durrell, Gerald (Malcolm) (1925–1995) English naturalist, writer, and zoo curator. He became director of Jersey Zoological Park in 1958, and wrote 37 books, including the humorous memoir *My Family and Other Animals* (1956). He was the brother of the writer Lawrence Durrell.

Durrell, Lawrence (George) (1912–1990) English novelist and poet. He lived mainly in the eastern Mediterranean, the setting of his novels, including the Alexandria Quartet: *Justine, Balthazar, Mountolive*, and *Clea* (1957–60). He also wrote travel books, including *Bitter Lemons* (1957) about Cyprus. His heady prose and bizarre characters reflect his exotic sources of inspiration. He was the brother of the naturalist Gerald Durrell.

Durrës chief port of Albania; population (1991) 86,900. It is a commercial and communications centre, with flour mills, soap and cigarette factories, distilleries, and an electronics plant. It was the capital of Albania 1912–21.

Dushanbe (formerly **Stalinabad** (1929–61)) capital of ▷Tajikistan, situated in the Gissar Valley 160 km/100 mi north of the Afghan frontier; population (1996) 582,000. Dushanbe is a road, rail, and air centre. Its industries include cotton and silk mills, tanneries, meat-packing factories, and printing works. It is the seat of the Tajik state university.

Düsseldorf commercial city and capital of ▷North Rhine-Westphalia, Germany, on the right bank of the River Rhine, 26 km/16 mi northwest of Cologne; population (1995) 571,900. It is a river port and the commercial and financial centre of the Ruhr area, with food processing, brewing, agricultural machinery, textile, and chemical industries.

dust bowl area in the Great Plains region of North America (Texas to Kansas) that suffered extensive wind erosion as the result of drought and poor farming practice in once-fertile soil. Much of the topsoil was blown away in the droughts of the 1930s and the 1980s.

Dutch art painting and sculpture of the Netherlands. The 17th century was the great age of Dutch painting. Among the many masters of this period were Rembrandt; Willem Kalf, who excelled at still lifes; Adriaen van Ostade, who painted Flemish peasant scenes; Gerard Terborch the Younger, the first painter of characteristic Dutch interiors; Albert Cuyp; Jakob van Ruisdael, who specialized in landscapes; Jan Steen; Pieter de Hooch; Jan Vermeer; Willem van de Velde, sea painter to Charles II of England; and Meindert Hobbema. There was a marked decline in Dutch art during the 18th and 19th centuries until the expressionist genius of Vincent van Gogh and, in the 20th century, the abstract painter Piet Mondrian.

Dutch cap common name for a barrier method of contraception; see ▷diaphragm.

Dutch East India Company (VOC, or **Vereenigde Oost-Indische Compagnie**) trading company chartered by the States General (parliament) of the Netherlands, and established in the northern Netherlands in 1602. It was given a monopoly on Dutch trade in the Indonesian archipelago, and certain sovereign rights such as the creation of an army and a fleet.

Dutch East Indies former Dutch colony, which in 1945 became independent as ▷Indonesia.

Dutch elm disease disease of elm trees *Ulmus*, principally Dutch, English, and American elm, caused by the fungus *Certocystis ulmi*. The fungus is usually spread from tree to tree by the elm-bark beetle, which lays its eggs beneath the bark. The disease has no cure, and control methods involve injecting insecticide into the trees annually to prevent infection, or the destruction of all elms in a broad band around an infected area, to keep the beetles out.

Dutch Guiana former Dutch colony, which in 1975 became independent as ▷Suriname.

Dutch language member of the Germanic branch of the Indo-European language family, often referred to by scholars as Netherlandic and taken to include the standard language and dialects of the Netherlands (excluding Frisian) as well as Flemish (in Belgium and northern France) and, more remotely, its offshoot Afrikaans in South Africa.

Duvalier, François (1907–1971) Right-wing president of Haiti 1957–71. Known as **Papa Doc**, he ruled as a dictator, organizing the Tontons Macoutes ('bogeymen') as a private security force to intimidate and assassinate opponents of his regime. He rigged the 1961 elections in order to have his term of office extended until 1967, and in 1964 declared himself president for life. He was excommunicated by the Vatican for harassing the church, and was succeeded on his death by his son Jean-Claude Duvalier.

Duvalier, Jean-Claude (1951–) Right-wing president of Haiti 1971–86. Known as **Baby Doc**, he succeeded his father François Duvalier, becoming, at the age of 19, the youngest president in the world. He continued to receive support from the USA but was pressured into moderating some elements of his father's regime, yet still tolerated no opposition. In 1986, with Haiti's economy stagnating and with increasing civil disorder, Duvalier fled to France, taking much of the Haitian treasury with him.

Dvořák, Antonín Leopold (1841–1904) Czech composer. His Romantic music extends the classical tradition of Beethoven and Brahms and displays the influence of Czech folk music. He wrote nine symphonies; tone poems; operas, including *Rusalka* (1900); large-scale choral works; the *Carnival* (1891–92) and other overtures; violin and cello concertos; chamber music; piano pieces; and songs. International recognition came with two sets of *Slavonic Dances* (1878 and 1886). Works such as his *New World Symphony* (1893) reflect his interest in American folk themes, including black and American Indian music. He was director of the National Conservatory, New York, 1892–95.

Related Web site: Antonín Dvořák http://www.hnh.com/composer/dvorak.htm

ANTONÍN DVOŘÁK Czechoslovakian composer Dvořák is shown conducting in a portrait by Souček. *The Art Archive/Dvořák Museum Prague/Dagli Orti*

Dyak (or **Dayak**) member of any of several peoples of Indonesian Borneo (Kalimantan) and Sarawak, including the Bahau of central and eastern Borneo, the Land Dyak of southwestern Borneo, who are shifting cultivators of dry rice; and the ▷Iban of Sarawak (sometimes called Sea Dyak) who are Malay-speakers living on the coast and along river courses, and grow irrigated (wet) rice and rubber. They are skilled sailors and live in an egalitarian society. They all originated in Sumatra and their languages belong to the Austronesian family. Some anthropologists now call all Dyak peoples Iban.

Dyck, Anthony van (1599–1641) Flemish painter. He was an assistant to Rubens from 1618 to 1620, then worked briefly in England at the court of James I before moving to Italy in 1622. In 1627 he returned to his native Antwerp, where he continued to paint religious works and portraits. From 1632 he lived in England and produced numerous portraits of royalty and aristocrats, such as *Charles I on Horseback* (about 1638; National Gallery, London).

dye substance that, applied in solution to fabrics, imparts a colour resistant to washing. **Direct dyes** combine with the material of the fabric, yielding a coloured compound; **indirect dyes** require the presence of another substance (a mordant), with which the fabric must first be treated; **vat dyes** are colourless soluble substances that on exposure to air yield an insoluble coloured compound.

Naturally occurring dyes include indigo, madder (alizarin), logwood, and cochineal, but industrial dyes (introduced in the 19th century) are usually synthetic: mauve, the first synthetic dye, was developed in 1856. Industrial dyes include ▷azo dyestuffs, ▷acridine, ▷anthracene, and ▷aniline.

Dyfed former county of southwest Wales, created in 1974 and, in 1996, divided between the unitary authorities of ▷Carmarthenshire, ▷Ceredigion, and ▷Pembrokeshire.

dyke in earth science, a sheet of ▷igneous rock created by the intrusion of magma (molten rock) across layers of pre-existing rock. (By contrast, a sill is intruded *between* layers of rock.) It may form a ridge when exposed on the surface if it is more resistant than the rock into which it intruded. A dyke is also a human-made embankment built along a coastline (for example, in the Netherlands) to prevent the flooding of lowland coastal regions.

> **Bob Dylan**
> *Money doesn't talk, it swears.*
> 'It's Alright, Ma (I'm Only Bleeding)'

Dylan, Bob (1941–) Adopted name of Robert Allen Zimmerman. US singer and songwriter. His lyrics provided catchphrases for a generation and influenced innumerable songwriters. He began in the folk-music tradition. His early songs, as on his albums *The Freewheelin' Bob Dylan* (1963) and *The Times They Are A-Changin'* (1964), were associated with the US civil-rights movement and antiwar protest. From 1965 he worked in an individualistic rock style, as on the albums *Highway 61 Revisited* (1965) and *Blonde on Blonde* (1966). His 15th album, *Time Out of Mind*, was released in 1997.

Dylan's early songs range from the simple, preachy 'Blowin' in the Wind' (1962) to brooding indictments of social injustice like 'The Ballad of Hollis Brown' (1963). When he first used an electric rock band in 1965, he was criticized by purists, but the albums that immediately followed are often cited as his best work, with songs of spite ('Like a Rolling Stone') and surrealistic imagery ('Visions of Johanna') delivered in his characteristic nasal whine. The film *Don't Look Back* (1967) documents the 1965 British tour. Of Dylan's 1970s albums, *Blood on the Tracks* (1975) was the strongest.

Slow Train Coming (1979) was his first album as a born-again Christian, a phase that lasted several years and alienated all but the die-hard fans. *Oh, Mercy* (1989) was seen as a partial return to form, but *Under the Red Sky* (1990) did not bear this out. However, *The Bootleg Years* (1991), a collection of 58 previously unreleased items from past years, reasserted his standing. In 1992 he released *Good As I Been to You*, which consisted of traditional tunes and was his first completely solo acoustic album since *Another Side of Bob Dylan* (1964). His song 'Things Have Changed' won the 2001 Academy Award for Best Original Song from the film *Wonder Boys* (2000).

Related Web site: Bob Dylan Music Lounge http://www.geocities.com/SunsetStrip/Alley/8361/index.html

Dynamic HTML in computing, the fourth version of hypertext markup language (HTML), the language used to create Web pages. It is called Dynamic HTML because it enables dynamic effects to be incorporated in pages without the delays involved in downloading Java applets and without referring back to the server.

Related Web site: Dynamic HTML Zone http://www.dhtmlzone.com/alt.html

dynamics in music, symbols indicating relative loudness, changes in loudness such as **crescendo** and **diminuendo**, or loudness in accentuation such as **rinforzando**.

dynamics (or **kinetics**) in mechanics, the mathematical and physical study of the behaviour of bodies under the action of forces that produce changes of motion in them.

dynamite explosive consisting of a mixture of nitroglycerine and diatomaceous earth (diatomite, an absorbent, chalklike material). It was first devised by Alfred Nobel.

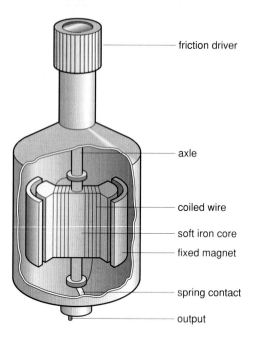

friction driver

axle

coiled wire

soft iron core

fixed magnet

spring contact

output

dynamo in physics, a simple ▷generator or machine for transforming mechanical energy into electrical energy. A dynamo in basic form consists of a powerful field magnet between the poles of which a suitable conductor, usually in the form of a coil (armature), is rotated. The mechanical energy of rotation is thus converted into an electric current in the armature. See diagram on p. 290.

dysentery infection of the large intestine causing abdominal cramps and painful ▷diarrhoea with blood. There are two kinds of dysentery: **amoebic** (caused by a protozoan), common in the tropics, which may lead to liver damage; and **bacterial**, the kind most often seen in the temperate zones.

Both forms are successfully treated with antibacterials and fluids to prevent dehydration.

dyslexia (Greek 'bad', 'pertaining to words') malfunction in the brain's synthesis and interpretation of written information, popularly known as 'word blindness'.

Dyslexia may be described as specific or developmental to distinguish it from reading or writing difficulties which are

DYNAMO Cross-section of a dynamo used to power bicycle lights. The friction driver rotates as the back wheel of the bicycle goes round. This causes the magnet to spin, near the wire coil around the iron core. Electricity is generated in the wires as a result of the change in magnetic field.

acquired. It results in poor ability in reading and writing, though the person may excel in other areas, for example, in mathematics. A similar disability with figures is called **dyscalculia**. **Acquired dyslexia** may occur as a result of brain injury or disease.

Dyslexia affects 5–10% of British schoolchildren.
Related Web site: British Dyslexia Association http://www. bda-dyslexia.org.uk/

dysprosium (Greek *dusprositos* 'difficult to get near') silver-white, metallic element of the ▷lanthanide series, symbol Dy, atomic number 66, relative atomic mass 162.50. It is among the most magnetic of all known substances and has a great capacity to absorb neutrons. It was discovered in 1886 by French chemist Paul Lecoq de Boisbaudran (1838–1912).

dystopia imaginary society whose evil qualities are meant to serve as a moral or political warning. The term was coined in 1868 by the English philosopher John Stuart ▷Mill, and is the opposite of a ▷Utopia. George Orwell's *1984*, published in 1949 and Aldous Huxley's *Brave New World* (1932) are examples of novels about dystopias. Dystopias are common in science fiction.

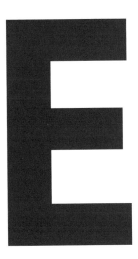

E

eagle any of several genera of large birds of prey of the family Accipitridae, order Falconiformes, including the golden eagle *Aquila chrysaetos* of Eurasia and North America, which has a 2 m/6 ft wingspan. Eagles occur worldwide, usually building eyries or nests in forests or mountains, and all are fierce and powerful birds of prey. The harpy eagle is the largest eagle.

The white-headed bald eagle *Haliaetus leucocephalus* is the symbol of the USA; rendered infertile through the ingestion of agricultural chemicals, it is now rare, except in Alaska.

Another endangered species is the Philippine eagle, sometimes called the Philippine monkey-eating eagle (although its main prey is the flying lemur). Loss of large tracts of forest, coupled with hunting by humans, have greatly reduced its numbers.

In Britain the golden eagle is found in the Highlands of Scotland, with a few recolonizing the Lake District. In the 1980s it was facing extinction due to a reduction in numbers and fertility as a result of the livers of its prey being poisoned by insecticides and seed dressings. In 1996 there were 420 pairs of golden eagles in the UK, mainly in northwestern Scotland and the Hebrides, constituting a fifth of the European population. The sea eagles of the genus *Haliaetus* include the white-tailed sea eagle *H. albicilla*, which was renaturalized in Britain in the 1980s, having died out there in 1916. Mainly a carrion-feeder, it breeds on sea cliffs.

EAGLE The wedge-tailed eagle has been subject to an Australian Nature Conservation Agency-sponsored Recovery Plan since 1992. The plan has aimed to increase public awareness of the eagle's plight, to educate the public about its importance, and to consult with farmers to protect nest sites and reduce disturbances near nests during breeding. *Image Bank*

In August 1999 the Irish government approved a five-year plan to reintroduce the golden eagle to Ireland. Eagle chicks will be imported from Scotland and raised in Donegal before being released into the wild.
Related Web site: Bald Eagle http://www.seaworld.org/animal_bytes/bald_eagleab.html

Eakins, Thomas (1844–1916) US painter, a leading realist. His most memorable subjects are medical and sporting scenes, characterized by strong contrasts between light and shade, as in his controversial *The Gross Clinic* (1875; Jefferson Medical College, Philadelphia), a group portrait of a surgeon, his assistants, and students. In his later years he painted distinguished portraits.

Ealing outer borough of west Greater London; population (1991) 283,600. Local industries are engineering and chemicals. The borough was home to Ealing Studios, founded in 1929, the first British sound-film studios ('Ealing comedies' became a noted genre in British film-making). Historic buildings in Ealing include the 18th-century Pitshanger Manor, Gunnersbury House and Gunnersbury Park (both Regency style), and the art deco Hoover factory, built in 1932.

Eames Charles (1907–1978) and Ray (born Ray Kaiser, 1916–1988). US designers. A husband-and-wife team, they worked together in California 1941–78. They created some of the most highly acclaimed furniture designs of the 20th century: a moulded plywood chair 1945–46; the Lounge Chair, a black leather-upholstered chair, 1956; and a fibreglass armchair 1950–53.

ear organ of hearing in animals. It responds to the vibrations that constitute sound, which are translated into nerve signals and passed to the brain. A mammal's ear consists of three parts: outer ear, middle ear, and inner ear. The **outer ear** is a funnel that collects sound, directing it down a tube to the **ear drum** (tympanic membrane), which separates the outer and **middle ears**. Sounds vibrate this membrane, the mechanical movement of which is transferred to a smaller membrane leading to the **inner ear** by three small bones, the auditory ossicles. Vibrations of the inner ear membrane move fluid contained in the snail-shaped cochlea, which vibrates hair cells that stimulate the auditory nerve connected to the brain. There are approximately 30,000 sensory hair cells (**stereocilia**). Exposure to loud noise and the process of ageing damages the stereocilia, resulting in hearing loss. Three fluid-filled canals of the inner ear detect changes of position; this mechanism, with other sensory inputs, is responsible for the sense of balance.

When a loud noise occurs, muscles behind the eardrum contract automatically, suppressing the noise to enhance perception of sound and prevent injury.
Related Web site: Anatomy and Function of the Ear http://www.voice-center.com/ear_anatomy.html

Earhart, Amelia (1898–1937) US aviation pioneer and author, who in 1928 became the first woman to fly across the Atlantic. With copilot Frederick Noonan, she attempted a round-the-world flight in 1937. Somewhere over the Pacific their plane disappeared.

Born in Atchison, Kansas, Earhart worked as an army nurse and social worker, before discovering that her true calling lay in aviation. In 1928 she became the first woman to fly across the Atlantic as a passenger and in 1932 completed a solo transatlantic flight. During a flight over the Pacific in 1937, her plane disappeared without trace, although clues found in 1989 on Nikumaroro Island, southeast of Kiribati's main island group, suggest that she and her copilot might have survived a crash only to die of thirst.
Related Web site: Earhart, Amelia http://www.ellensplace.net/eae_intr.html

> **Amelia Earhart**
> *Failure must be but a*
> *challenge to others.*
> Last Flight

AMELIA EARHART The first woman to fly solo across the Atlantic Ocean, Amelia Earhart is shown here on a visit to Honolulu, Hawaii, in the mid-1930s. *Archive Photos*

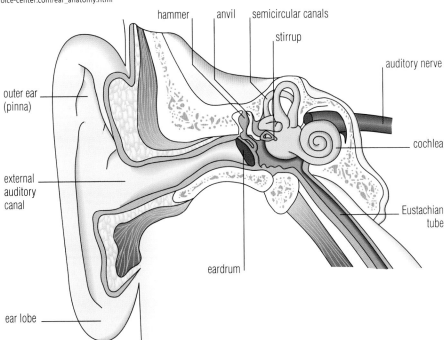

EAR The structure of the ear. The three bones of the middle ear – hammer, anvil, and stirrup – vibrate in unison and magnify sounds about 20 times. The spiral-shaped cochlea is the organ of hearing. As sound waves pass down the spiral tube, they vibrate fine hairs lining the tube, which activate the auditory nerve connected to the brain. The semicircular canals are the organs of balance, detecting movements of the head.

earl in the British peerage, the third title in order of rank, coming between marquess and viscount; it is the oldest of British titles, deriving from the Anglo-Saxon post of ealdorman. For some time earls were called counts, and their wives are still called countesses.

Earl Marshal (Anglo-Saxon mearh 'horse', **sceale** 'groom') in England, one of the great officers of state. The king's marshal early became one of the chief officers of state, and, under the Norman and Plantagenet kings, a judge in the Courts of Chivalry. The Earl Marshal is now head of the ▷College of Arms, through which he regulates all matters connected with armorial bearings and standards, and controls the arrangements for state functions. The office has been hereditary since 1672 in the family of Howard, the dukes of Norfolk. In Scotland a similar dignity was hereditary in the family of Keith from the 14th century until 1716.

Earth third planet from the Sun. It is almost spherical, flattened slightly at the poles, and is composed of five concentric layers: inner ▷core, outer core, ▷mantle, ▷crust, and atmosphere. About 70% of the surface (including the north and south polar icecaps) is covered with water. The Earth is surrounded by a life-supporting atmosphere and is the only planet on which life is known to exist.

> **mean distance from the Sun** 149,500,000 km/92,860,000 mi **equatorial diameter** 12,755 km/7,920 mi **circumference** 40,070 km/24,900 mi **rotation period** 23 hr 56 min 4.1 sec **year** (complete orbit, or sidereal period) 365 days 5 hr 48 min 46 sec. Earth's average speed around the Sun is 30 kps/18.5 mps; the plane of its orbit is inclined to its equatorial plane at an angle of 23.5°, the reason for the changing seasons **atmosphere** nitrogen 78.09%; oxygen 20.95%; argon 0.93%; carbon dioxide 0.03%; and less than 0.0001% neon, helium, krypton, hydrogen, xenon, ozone, radon **surface** land surface 150,000,000 sq km/57,500,000 sq mi (greatest height above sea level 8,872 m/29,118 ft Mount Everest); water surface 361,000,000 sq km/139,400,000 sq mi (greatest depth 11,034 m/36,201 ft ▷Mariana Trench in the Pacific). The interior is thought to be an inner core about 2,600 km/1,600 mi in diameter, of solid iron and nickel; an outer core about 2,250 km/1,400 mi thick, of molten iron and nickel; and a mantle of mostly solid rock about 2,900 km/1,800 mi thick. The crust and the uppermost layer of the mantle form about twelve major moving plates, some of which carry the continents. The plates are in constant, slow motion, called tectonic drift **satellite** the ▷Moon **age** 4.6 billion years. The Earth was formed with the rest of the ▷Solar System by consolidation of interstellar dust. Life began 3.5–4 billion years ago.
> **Related Web site: Earth and Moon Viewer** http://www.fourmilab.ch/earthview/vplanet.html

earthquake abrupt motion that propagates through the Earth and along its surfaces. Earthquakes are caused by the sudden release in rocks of strain accumulated over time as a result of ▷tectonics. The study of earthquakes is called ▷seismology. Most earthquakes occur along ▷faults (fractures or breaks) and ▷Benioff zones. Plate tectonic movements generate the major proportion: as two plates move past each other they can become jammed. When sufficient strain has accumulated, the rock breaks, releasing a series of elastic waves (▷seismic waves) as the plates spring free. The force of earthquakes (magnitude) is measured on the ▷Richter scale, and their effect (intensity) on the ▷Mercalli scale. The point at which an earthquake originates is the **seismic focus** or **hypocentre**; the point on the Earth's surface directly above this is the epicentre.

The Alaskan (USA) earthquake of 27 March 1964 ranks as one of the greatest ever recorded, measuring 8.3 to 8.8 on the Richter scale. The 1906 San Francisco earthquake is among the most famous in history. Its magnitude was 8.3 on the Richter scale. The deadliest, most destructive earthquake in historical times is thought to have been in China in 1556. In 1987, a California earthquake was successfully predicted by measurement of underground pressure waves; prediction attempts have also involved the study of such phenomena as the change in gases issuing from the ▷crust, the level of water in wells, slight deformation of the rock surface, a sequence of minor tremors, and the behaviour of animals. The possibility of earthquake prevention is remote. However, rock slippage might be slowed at movement points, or promoted at stoppage points, by the extraction or injection of large quantities of water underground, since water serves as a lubricant. This would ease overall pressure.

> **Related Web sites: Earthquakes and Plate Tectonics** http://wwwneic.cr.usgs.gov/neis/plate_tectonics/rift_man.html
> **Worldwide Earthquake Locator** http://www.geo.ed.ac.uk/quakes/quakes.html

Earth science scientific study of the planet Earth as a whole. The mining and extraction of minerals and gems, the prediction of weather and earthquakes, the pollution of the atmosphere, and the forces that shape the physical world all fall within its scope of study. The emergence of the discipline reflects scientists' concern that an understanding of the global aspects of the Earth's structure and its past will hold the key to how humans affect its future, ensuring that its resources are used in a sustainable

EARTHQUAKE A man photographing the ruins of a building against a backdrop of devastation after the great San Francisco earthquake of 1906. *Archive Photos*

way. It is a synthesis of several traditional subjects such as ▷geology, ▷meteorology, ▷oceanography, ▷geophysics, ▷geochemistry, and ▷palaeontology.

> **Related Web site: Earth Sciences** http://dir.yahoo.com/science/earth_sciences/

Earth Summit (or United Nations Conference on Environment and Development) international meetings aiming at drawing up measures towards environmental protection of the world. The first summit took place in Rio de Janeiro, Brazil, in June 1992. Treaties were made to combat global warming and protect wildlife ('biodiversity') (the latter was not signed by the USA). The second Earth Summit was held in New York in June 1997 to review progress on the environment. The meeting agreed to work towards a global forest convention in 2000 with the aim of halting the destruction of tropical and old-growth forests.

> **Related Web site: Earth Council** http://www.ecouncil.ac.cr/

earthwork an artwork which involves the manipulation of the natural environment and/or the use of natural materials, such as earth, stones, or wood, largely a phenomenon

EARTH In this photograph of Earth from space, the African continent and southern oceans are clearly visible beneath white swirls of cloud. *Corel*

earth electrical connection between an appliance and the ground. In the event of a fault in an electrical appliance, for example, involving connection between the live part of the circuit and the outer casing, the current flows to earth, causing no harm to the user.

earthenware pottery made of porous clay and fired at relatively low temperatures of up to 1,200°C/2,200°F. It does not vitrify but remains porous, unless glazed. Earthenware may be unglazed (flowerpots, wine-coolers) or glazed (most tableware); the glaze and body characteristics form quite separate layers.

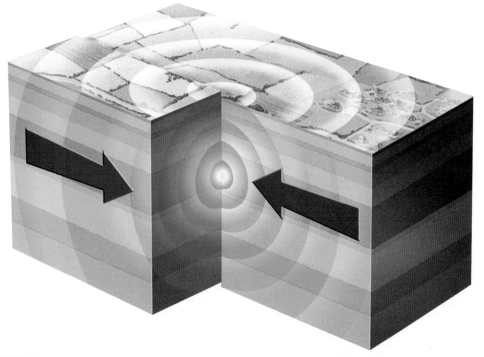

EARTHQUAKE The propagation of seismic waves through the Earth. Waves vibrate outwards from the focus of the earthquake, deep within the Earth. As well as the movement of waves from the epicentre the wave frequency contracts and dilates.

of the late 1960s and 1970s. Although some were exhibited in galleries, most earthworks were vast and usually constructed on remote, deserted sites and hence only known through photographs and plans. Robert Smithson and Michael Heizer (1944–), two leading exponents, engaged in physically overpowering works, for example, Heizer's *Complex One, Central Eastern Nevada* (1972, unfinished), an elongated, pyramidal hill of rammed earth supported by steel and concrete.

earthworm ▷annelid worm of the class Oligochaeta. Earthworms are hermaphroditic and deposit their eggs in cocoons. They live by burrowing in the soil, feeding on the organic matter it contains. They are vital to the formation of humus, aerating the soil and levelling it by transferring earth from the deeper levels to the surface as castings.

The common British earthworms belong to the genera *Lumbricus* and *Allolobophora*. These are comparatively small, but some tropical forms reach over 1 m/3 ft. *Megascolides australis*, of Queensland, can be over 3 m/11 ft long.

EARTHWORM Brandling worm *Eisenia foetida*. Its segments can be clearly seen and although they look smooth each segment has four pairs of bristles.
K G Preston-Mafham/Premaphotos Wildlife

earwig nocturnal insect of the order Dermaptera. The forewings are short and leathery and serve to protect the hindwings, which are large and are folded like a fan when at rest. Earwigs seldom fly. They have a pincerlike appendage in the rear. The male is distinguished by curved pincers; those of the female are straight. Earwigs are regarded as pests because they feed on flowers and fruit, but they also eat other insects, dead or alive. Eggs are laid beneath the soil, and the female cares for the young even after they have hatched. The male dies before the eggs have hatched. When threatened, earwigs spray quinones (irritant chemicals stored as crystals), from their abdominal glands.

A number are found in Britain, such as the common European earwig *Forficula auricularia*.

easement in law, rights that a person may have over the land of another. A common example is a right of way; others are the right to bring water over another's land and the right to a sufficient quantity of light.

east one of the four cardinal points of the compass, indicating that part of the horizon where the Sun rises; when facing north, east is to the right.

East Anglia region of eastern England, formerly a Saxon kingdom, including Norfolk, Suffolk, and parts of Essex and Cambridgeshire. Norwich is the principal city of East Anglia. The Sainsbury Centre for Visual Arts, opened in 1978 at the University of East Anglia, has a collection of ethnographic art and sculpture. East Anglian ports such as Harwich and Felixstowe have greatly developed as trade with the rest of Europe has increased.

East Ayrshire unitary authority in southwest Scotland, created in 1996 from two districts of Strathclyde region.
area 1,269 sq km/490 sq mi **towns** Kilmarnock (administrative headquarters), Cumnock, Stewarton, Galston, Crosshouse **physical** predominantly low lying and undulating in the north, mountainous toward the south; Loch Doon; rivers Ayr, Irvine; Blackcraig Hill (700 m/2,298 ft); Loudoun Hill **features** Burns' House Museum, Mauchline; Loudoun Castle Theme Park; Dunaskin Heritage Museum **industries** textiles, light engineering, food and drink, printing **agriculture** dairy farming, sheep, beef cattle **population** (1996) 124,000 **history** at Loudoun Hill, Robert the Bruce defeated 6,000 of the Earl of Pembroke's men with a force of 600 in 1306

East China Sea see ▷China Sea.

East Dunbartonshire unitary authority in central Scotland, created in 1996 from two districts of Strathclyde region.
area 175 sq km/67 sq mi **towns** Kirkintilloch (administrative headquarters), Bearsden, Milngavie **physical** low-lying lands to the south give way dramatically to the Campsie Fells in the north; Earl's Seat (578 m/1,896 ft); River Kelvin **features** Forth and Clyde Canal; Antonine Wall **population** (1996) 110,000

Easter spring feast of the Christian church, commemorating the Resurrection of Jesus. It is a moveable feast, falling on the first Sunday following the full moon after the vernal equinox (21 March); that is, between 22 March and 25 April.

Easter Island (or Rapa Nui; Spanish Isla de Pascua) Chilean island in the south Pacific Ocean, part of the Polynesian group, about 3,500 km/2,200 mi west of Chile; area about 166 sq km/ 64 sq mi; population (1998) 2,000. It was first reached by Europeans on Easter Sunday 1722. On it stand over 800 huge carved statues (*moai*) and the remains of boat-shaped stone houses, the work of Neolithic peoples from Polynesia. The chief centre is Hanga-Roa.

In 1996, following seven years of work, a New Zealand linguist, Dr Steven Fischer, deciphered a script discovered on the island. This script showed the inhabitants were the first in Oceania to write. According to Dr Fischer, the script, known as 'rongorongo', was made up of chants in Rapanui, the island's Polynesian tongue, and tell the story of creation.

The carved statues are believed to have been religious icons. However, archaeological evidence suggests that, prior to European contact, the island suffered an environmental or cultural crisis resulting in the inhabitants renouncing their earlier religious values, which caused them to damage or overturn many of the statues.
Related Web site: Secrets of Easter Island
http://www.pbs.org/wgbh/nova/easter/

Eastern Cape province of the Republic of South Africa from 1994, formerly part of Cape Province; area 170,616 sq km/65,875 sq mi; population (2000 est) 811,400. The capital is Bisho; the other main towns are East London, Port Elizabeth, and Grahamstown. Industries include motor manufacturing, textiles, and dairy and meat products; agriculture is based on citrus fruits, grain, and sheep-raising. The languages spoken are Xhosa (85%), Afrikaans (9%), and English (3%).

Eastern Orthodox Church see ▷Orthodox Church.

Easter Rising (or Easter Rebellion) in Irish history, a republican insurrection against the British government that began on Easter Monday, April 1916, in Dublin. The rising was organized by the Irish Republican Brotherhood (IRB), led by Patrick ▷Pearse, along with sections of the Irish Volunteers and James Connolly's socialist Irish Citizen Army. Although a military failure, it played a central role in shifting nationalist opinion from allegiance to the constitutional Irish Parliamentary Party (IPP) to separatist republicanism.

Arms from Germany intended for the IRB were intercepted, but the rising proceeded regardless with the seizure of the Post Office and other buildings in Dublin by 1,500 volunteers. The rebellion was crushed by the British Army within five days, both sides suffering major losses: 250 civilians, 64 rebels, and 132 members of the crown forces were killed and around 2,600 injured. Pearse, Connolly, and about a dozen rebel leaders were subsequently executed in Kilmainham Jail. Others, including the future Taoiseach (prime minister) Éamon de Valera, were spared due to US public opinion, and were given amnesty in June 1917.

East Germany see ▷Germany, East.

East India Company, British commercial company (1600–1858) that had a monopoly on trade between England and the Far East; see ▷British East India Company.

East India Company, Dutch trading monopoly of the 17th and 18th centuries; see ▷Dutch East India Company.

East Indies the Malay Archipelago; the Philippines are sometimes included. The term is also used to refer more generally to Southeast Asia.

East Lothian unitary authority in southeast Scotland which was previously a district within Lothian region (1975–96) and a county until 1974.
area 677 sq km/261 sq mi **towns** Haddington (administrative headquarters), North Berwick, Dunbar **physical** area of contrasts, with coastal plains of cliffs, beaches and estuarine marines, broad river valley of the Tyne, volcanic outcrops (Bass Rock, Traprain Law) and gentle slopes of the Lammermuir Hills **features** Tantallon Castle; Muirfield golf course; Traprain Law fort **industries** whisky distilling, agricultural-based **agriculture** arable farming on plains **population** (1996) 85,500

Eastman, George (1854–1932) US entrepreneur and inventor who founded the Eastman Kodak photographic company in 1892. He patented flexible film in 1884, invented the Kodak box camera in 1888, and introduced daylight-loading film in 1892. By 1900 his company was selling a pocket camera for as little as one dollar.

East Pakistan former province of ▷Pakistan, now Bangladesh.

East Renfrewshire unitary authority in central Scotland, created in 1996 from part of Renfrew district in Strathclyde region.
area 174 sq km/67 sq mi **towns** Barrhead, Giffnock (administrative headquarters), Newton Mearns, Clarkston **physical** low-lying plateau rising from the plain of the River Clyde **industries** engineering, cotton textiles **agriculture** sheep, rough grazing, some dairy farming **population** (1996) 86,800

East Riding of Yorkshire unitary authority in northern England created in 1996 from part of the former county of Humberside.
area 2,416 sq km/933 sq mi **towns** Beverley (administrative headquarters), Driffield, Goole, Hornsea, Bridlington **features** Humber Estuary to south of authority; North Sea to east; Flamborough Head chalk cliffs; Spurn Head – dynamic spit at mouth of estuary; River Hull; River Ouse; Holderness Peninsula; The Wolds; Hornsea Mere; Beverley Minster (13th century); All Saints Tower (34 m/110 ft) at Driffield; Sledmere House – 18th century mansion with grounds laid out by Capability Brown; Rudstone has Britain's tallest standing stone (8 m/25 ft); Sewerby Hall (Bridlington) – Georgian mansion including museum dedicated to the aviator Amy Johnson (1903–1941); Hornsea Pottery; Withernsea Lighthouse (39 m/127 ft) including museum **industries** chemicals, pottery, agriculture, agricultural machinery and services, passenger vehicle components, bakery products **population** (1996) 310,000 **famous people** St John of Beverley, William Kent

East River tidal strait running between Manhattan Island and Long Island, in southeastern New York, USA; length 24 km/15 mi, width 0.8 km/0.5 mi to 5.6 km/3.5 mi. The East River separates the boroughs of Manhattan and the Bronx (west and north) from those of Brooklyn and Queens (east and south). It links Long Island Sound with New York Bay and is connected, via the Harlem River and Spuyten Duyvil Creek, with the Hudson River. There are docks and many bridges here, including the Brooklyn Bridge.

East Sussex county of southeast England, created in 1974, formerly part of Sussex (since April 1997 Brighton and Hove has been a separate unitary authority).
area 1,725 sq km/666 sq mi **towns** Lewes (administrative headquarters), Newhaven (cross-channel port), Eastbourne, Rye, Winchelsea; Bexhill-on-Sea, Hastings, St Leonards, Seaford (all coastal resorts) **physical** Beachy Head, highest headland on the south coast (180 m/590 ft), the eastern end of the ▷South Downs; the Weald (including Ashdown Forest); Friston Forest; rivers Cuckmere, Ouse, and East Rother (which flows into the sea near Rye); Romney Marsh **features** the 'Long Man' chalk hill figure at Wilmington, near Eastbourne; prehistoric earthworks; Iron Age hill fort at Mount Caburn, near Lewes; Roman villas; Herstmonceux, with a 15th-century castle (conference and exhibition centre) and adjacent modern buildings, site of the Greenwich Royal Observatory (1958–90); other castles at Hastings, Lewes, Pevensey, and Bodiam; Bayham Abbey; Battle Abbey and the site of the Battle of Hastings; Michelham Priory; Sheffield Park garden; University of Sussex at Falmer, near Brighton, founded in 1961 **agriculture** cereals, hops, fruit and vegetables; fishing (at Hastings) **industries** electronics, gypsum, light engineering, timber **population** (1996) 734,900 **famous people** former homes of Henry James at Rye, Rudyard Kipling at Batemans in Burwash, Thomas Sackville at Buckhurst, Virginia Woolf at Rodmell; Angus Wilson
Related Web site: East Sussex County Council Home Page
http://www.eastsussexcc.gov.uk/

East Timor disputed territory on the island of ▷Timor in the Malay Archipelago, claimed by Indonesia as the province of Timor Timur; prior to 1975, it was a Portuguese colony for almost 460 years; area 14,874 sq km/5,743 sq mi; population (1990) 747,750. The capital is ▷Dili. The main industry is coffee. After 24 years of East Timorese opposition to Indonesian rule, in August 1999 a referendum overwhelming rejected an offer from Indonesia of autonomy within that country. In 2000 United Nations Transitional Administration for East Timor (UNTAET) was put in place to help pave the way to statehood. See country box.

Eastwood, Clint(on) (1930–) US film actor and director. His breakthrough came in the Western *A Fistful of Dollars* (1964), after which he proved himself a box-office attraction in such films as *Dirty Harry* (1973), directed by his regular collaborator Don Siegel, and *In the Line of Fire* (1993). In 1971 he started an accomplished directing career with *Play Misty for Me*, and his latter-day Western *Unforgiven* (1992) won Academy Awards for best film and direction. See picture on p. 297.

A long-serving actor on the television series *Rawhide*, he gained a wider audience when Sergio Leone cast him as the ruthless 'Man with No Name' in the 'spaghetti Western' trilogy *A Fistful of Dollars*, *For a Few Dollars More* (1966), and *The Good, the Bad, and the Ugly* (1966). His directorial credits include *High Plains Drifter* (1973), *The Outlaw Josey Wales* (1976), *Bronco Billy* (1980), *Pale Rider* (1985), *Bird* (1988), *White Hunter, Black Heart* (1990), and *The Bridges of Madison County* (1995). In addition to starring in many of these films, he has also featured in *Coogan's Bluff* (1968), *Hang 'em High* (1968), *Paint Your Wagon* (1969), *Kelly's Heroes* (1970), *Thunderbolt and Lightfoot* (1974), and *Tightrope* (1984), among many others. In 1999 he directed and appeared in *True Crime*. In 2000 he produced, directed, and starred in *Space Cowboys*.

Related Web site: Clint Eastwood – World Wide Web Page
http://www.man-with-no-name.com/

EBCDIC (abbreviation for extended binary-coded decimal interchange code) in computing, a code used for storing and communicating alphabetic and numeric characters. It is an 8-bit code, capable of holding 256 different characters, although only 85 of these are defined in the standard version. It is still used in many mainframe computers, but almost all mini- and microcomputers now use ▷ASCII code.

ebony any of a group of hardwood trees belonging to the ebony family, especially some tropical ▷persimmons native to Africa and Asia. (Genus chiefly *Diospyros*, family Ebenaceae.)

Eboracum Roman name for the English city of ▷York. The archbishop of York signs himself 'Ebor'.

EC (abbreviation for European Community) former name (to 1993) of the ▷European Union.

eccentricity in geometry, a property of a ▷conic section (circle, ellipse, parabola, or hyperbola). It is the distance of any point on the curve from a fixed point (the focus) divided by the distance of that point from a fixed line (the directrix). A circle has an

East Timor

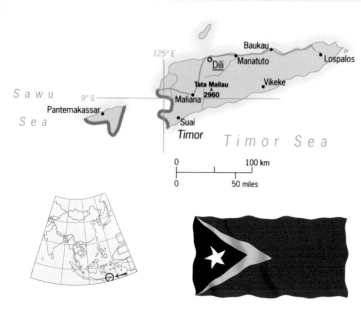

EAST TIMORESE children wait at a food line in Dili

RELIGION Roman Catholic (86%), Islam, Animism
LITERACY RATE 43% (men); 43% (women) (2001 est)
LABOUR FORCE (% of total workers) 73.2% agriculture; 4.8% industry; 22% services (2001 est)
LIFE EXPECTANCY 49 (men); 50 (women) (2000–05)
CHILD MORTALITY RATE (under 5, per 1,000 live births) 124 (2001)

East Timor disputed territory on the island of Timor in the Malay Archipelago, claimed by Indonesia as the province of Timor Timur.

NATIONAL NAME *Repúblika Demokrátika de Timor Leste/Democratic Republic of East Timor*
AREA 14,874 sq km/5,743 sq mi
CAPITAL Dili
MAJOR TOWNS/CITIES Ainaro, Bacau, Maliana, Suai, Viqueque
MAJOR PORTS Dili, Carabela, Com
PHYSICAL FEATURES comprises the largely mountainous eastern half of the island of Timor in the Malay Archipelago, together with two islands, Atauro and Jaco, and an enclave around Ocusse on the northwest coast

Government

HEAD OF STATE Xanana Gusmão from 2002
HEAD OF GOVERNMENT Mari Alkatiri from 2002
POLITICAL SYSTEM emergent democracy
POLITICAL EXECUTIVE parliamentary
ADMINISTRATIVE REGIONS 13 districts divided into 65 sub-districts
ARMED FORCES 650 (2002 est); training began in January 2001 with the aim of deploying 1,500 regulars and 1,500 reservists by January 2004
DEATH PENALTY abolished in 1999

Economy and resources

CURRENCY US dollar
GPD (US$) 388 million (2002 est)
GNI (US$) 402 million (2002 est)
GNI PER CAPITA (US$) 520 (2002 est)

CONSUMER PRICE INFLATION 5% (2002 est)
UNEMPLOYMENT 6% (2001)
MAJOR TRADING PARTNERS Indonesia, Australia
RESOURCES coffee, rice, maize, livestock, fishing, offshore oil and gas fields due to be exploited from 2004
INDUSTRIES textiles, coffee processing, water-bottling, soap, perfumes, processed food; there are also craft industries.
EXPORTS coffee, marble, potential for oil exports IMPORTS rice and other foodstuffs, petroleum products, construction materials
ARABLE LAND 40% (2001 est)
AGRICULTURAL PRODUCTS coffee, maize, cassava, copra, rice, sweet potatoes, cotton, tobacco

Population and society

POPULATION 778,000 (2003 est)
POPULATION GROWTH RATE 3.9% (2000–05)
POPULATION DENSITY (per sq km) 52 (2003 est)
URBAN POPULATION (% of total) 8 (2003 est)
AGE DISTRIBUTION (% of total population) 0–14 39%, 15–59 56%, 60+ 5% (2002 est)
ETHNIC GROUPS 78% Timorese (comprising 12 ethnic groups and including mixed-race), 20% Indonesian, 2% Chinese
LANGUAGE Tetum (national language), Portuguese (official language)

Chronology

1520: Portuguese traders first landed in Timor looking for the sandalwood tree.

1860: The Dutch secured control of West Timor, leaving the Portuguese in control of East Timor.

May 1974: Nicolau Lobato formed the Timorese Social Democratic Association, which became the communist Frente Revolucionária do Timor Leste Independente (Fretilin; in English the Revolutionary Front of an Independent East Timor) in September 1975 to fight for independence.

1975: Fretilin seized control of East Timor and declared independence, pre-empting a planned Portuguese withdrawal. Indonesia reacted by invading in early December. An estimated 100,000–200,000 Timorese, out of a total population of around 650,000, are killed in the military crackdown and the subsequent spread of famine and disease. However, resistance, led by Fretilin, continued.

1976: The Indonesian president, T N J Suharto, signed the Bill of Integration incorporating East Timor as Indonesia's 27th province, Lora Sa'e or Timor Timur. The United Nations (UN) refuses to recognize the annexation and called for Indonesia's withdrawal.

1990: The Indonesian government rejected proposals for unconditional peace negotiations by Xanana Gusmão, commander-in-chief of Fretilin's army, the Falintil.

1991: The Indonesian army killed between 100 and 180 peaceful pro-independence demonstrators during the funeral ceremony for a separatist sympathizer at Santa Cruz cemetery in Dili, and subsequently executed a further 60–100 'subversives'.

1992: Fretilin leader Gusmão was arrested and taken to Jakarta, where he was tried and, in 1993, found guilty of conspiracy and rebellion and sentenced to 20 years' imprisonment.

1994: Under UN auspices, Fretilin Secretary for International Relations, José Ramos-Horta, met Indonesia's foreign minister, Ali Alatas, for the

first time in inaugural official talks on the island's status.

1995: Serious rioting in Dili, involving Timorese Roman Catholics and Muslim immigrants from Indonesia, was defused through the intervention of the Roman Catholic Bishop of Dili, Carlos Belo.

1996: Ramos-Horta and Belo were jointly awarded the Nobel Prize for Peace for their efforts to achieve a peaceful resolution to the East Timor conflict.

1998: The Indonesian president, B J Habibie, who on 21 May had replaced the autocratic and unpopular T N J Suharto, ending his 32 years in power, offered partial autonomy to East Timor, but ruled out independence.

1999: Following UN-brokered talks, Indonesia agreed to hold a referendum in August, offering the East Timorese voters the choice between 'special autonomy' within Indonesia or independence. The East Timorese voted overwhelmingly (79%) for independence. Pro-Indonesian militias, opposed to the vote, embarked on weeks of violence. An Australian-led peacekeeping force, the International Force for East Timor (INTERFET), arrived to liberate East Timor from Indonesia and restore order. The Indonesian government eventually conceded.

2000: INTERFET was replaced by the UN Transitional Administration in East Timor (UNTAET), the handover being completed on 28 February. However, 150,000 East Timorese remained in refugee camps in West Timor. An eight-member power-sharing provisional government, composed half of UNTAET officials and half of East Timorese was formed.

2001: A large voter turnout marked East Timor's first democratic elections. Fretilin won 55 of the 88 seats in East Timor's constituent assembly.

2002: East Timor's assembly approved a draft constitution envisaging a government run along parliamentary lines. East Timor and Indonesia signed two agreements aimed at easing relations. Xanana Gusmão was elected president, and on 20 May, East Timor celebrated its formal independence. The country became the 191st member of the United Nations (UN).

CLINT EASTWOOD Clint Eastwood expresses his delight at having just received two Academy Awards – including the award for Best Director – at the Academy Awards ceremony in Los Angeles, California, USA, in March 1993. See entry on p. 295. *Image Bank*

ECLIPSE The two types of eclipse: lunar and solar. A lunar eclipse occurs when the Moon passes through the shadow of the Earth. A solar eclipse occurs when the Moon passes between the Sun and the Earth, blocking out the Sun's light. During a total solar eclipse, when the Moon completely covers the Sun, the Moon's shadow sweeps across the Earth's surface from west to east at a speed of 3,200 kph/2,000 mph.

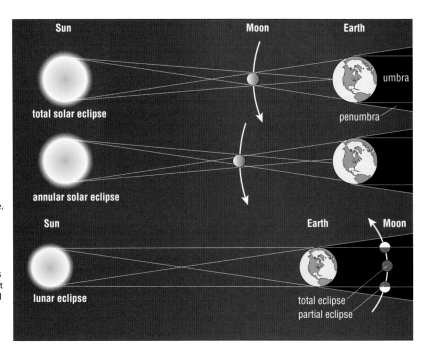

eccentricity of zero; for an ellipse it is less than one; for a parabola it is equal to one; and for a hyperbola it is greater than one.

ecclesiastical law church law. In England, the Church of England has special ecclesiastical courts to administer church law. Each diocese has a consistory court with a right of appeal to the Court of Arches (in the archbishop of Canterbury's jurisdiction) or the Chancery Court of York (in the archbishop of York's jurisdiction). They deal with the constitution of the Church of England, church property, the clergy, services, doctrine, and practice. These courts have no influence on churches of other denominations, which are governed by the usual laws of contract and trust.

ecdysis periodic shedding of the ▷exoskeleton by insects and other arthropods to allow growth. Prior to shedding, a new soft and expandable layer is laid down underneath the existing one. The old layer then splits, the animal moves free of it, and the new layer expands and hardens.

ECG abbreviation for ▷electrocardiogram.

echidna (or spiny anteater) toothless, egg-laying, spiny mammal of the order Monotremata, found in Australia and New Guinea. There are two species: *Tachyglossus aculeatus*, the short-nosed echidna, and the rarer *Zaglossus bruijni*, the long-nosed echidna. They feed entirely upon ants and termites, which they dig out with their powerful claws and lick up with their prehensile tongues. When attacked, an echidna rolls itself into a ball, or tries to hide by burrowing in the earth.

ECHIDNA The short-nosed echidna.

echinoderm marine invertebrate of the phylum Echinodermata ('spiny-skinned'), characterized by a five-radial symmetry.

Echinoderms have a water-vascular system which transports substances around the body. They include starfishes (or sea stars), brittle-stars, sea lilies, sea urchins, and sea cucumbers. The skeleton is external, made of a series of limy plates. Echinoderms generally move by using tube-feet, small water-filled sacs that can be protruded or pulled back to the body.

Echinodermata phylum of invertebrate animals, members of which are called ▷echinoderms.

Echo in Greek mythology, a mountain ▷nymph personifying disembodied sound. According to Ovid's *Metamorphoses*, Hera deprived Echo of her speech, except for the repetition of another's last words, after her chatter had kept the goddess from catching faithless Zeus with the nymphs. After being rejected by ▷Narcissus, she wasted away until only her voice remained.

echo repetition of a sound wave, or of a ▷radar or ▷sonar signal, by reflection from a surface. By accurately measuring the time taken for an echo to return to the transmitter, and by knowing the speed of a radar signal (the speed of light) or a sonar signal (the speed of sound in water), it is possible to calculate the range of the object causing the echo (▷echolocation).

A similar technique is used in echo sounders to estimate the depth of water under a ship's keel or the depth of a shoal of fish.

echolocation (or biosonar) method used by certain animals, notably bats, whales, and dolphins, to detect the positions of objects by using sound. The animal emits a stream of high-pitched sounds, generally at ultrasonic frequencies (beyond the range of human hearing), and listens for the returning echoes reflected off objects to determine their exact location.

The location of an object can be established by the time difference between the emitted sound and its differential return as an echo to the two ears. Echolocation is of particular value under conditions when normal vision is poor (at night in the case of bats, in murky water for dolphins). A few species of bird can also echolocate, including cave-dwelling birds such as some species of swiftlets and the South American oil bird.

The frequency range of bats' echolocation calls is 20–215 kHz. Many species produce a specific and identifiable pattern of sound. Bats vary in the way they use echolocation: some emit pure sounds lasting up to 150 milliseconds, while others use a series of shorter 'chirps'. Sounds may be emitted through the mouth or nostrils depending on species.

Echolocation was first described in the 1930s, though it was postulated by Italian biologist Lazzaro Spallanzani (1729–1799).

eclampsia convulsions occurring during pregnancy following ▷pre-eclampsia.

eclipse passage of an astronomical body through the shadow of another. The term is usually used for solar and lunar eclipses, which may be either partial or total, but may also refer to other bodies, for example, to an eclipse of one of Jupiter's satellites by Jupiter itself. An eclipse of a star by a body in the Solar System is also called an occultation.

A solar eclipse occurs when the Moon passes in front of the Sun as seen from Earth, and can happen only at new Moon. During a

total eclipse the Sun's ▷corona can be seen. A total solar eclipse can last up to 7.5 minutes. Between two and five solar eclipses occur each year but each is visible only from a specific area.

A lunar eclipse occurs when the Moon passes into the shadow of the Earth, becoming dim until emerging from the shadow. Lunar eclipses may be partial or total, and they can happen only at full Moon. Total lunar eclipses last for up to 100 minutes; the maximum number each year is three.

Related Web sites: Lunar Eclipse Computer http://aa.usno.navy.mil/AA/data/docs/LunarEclipse.html

Solar EclipseInformation http://www.eclipse.org.uk/default_hi.htm

eclipsing binary binary (double) star in which the two stars periodically pass in front of each other as seen from Earth.

ecliptic path, against the background of stars, that the Sun appears to follow each year as it is orbited by the Earth. It can be thought of as the plane of the Earth's orbit projected on to the ▷celestial sphere (imaginary sphere around the Earth).

E. coli abbreviation for ▷*Escherichia coli*.

Eco, Umberto (1932–) Italian writer, semiologist, and literary critic. His works include *The Role of the Reader* (1979), the 'philosophical thriller' *The Name of the Rose* (1983), *Foucault's Pendulum* (1988), and *Kant and the Platypus: Essays on Language and Cognition* (1999).

ecology (Greek *oikos* 'house') study of the relationship among organisms and the environments in which they live, including all living and nonliving components. The chief environmental factors governing the distribution of plants and animals are temperature, humidity, soil, light intensity, daylength, food supply, and interaction with other organisms. The term ecology was coined by the biologist Ernst Haeckel in 1866.

Ecology may be concerned with individual organisms (for example, behavioural ecology, feeding strategies), with populations (for example, population dynamics), or with entire communities (for example, competition between species for access to resources in an ecosystem, or predator–prey relationships). Applied ecology is concerned with the management and conservation of habitats and the consequences and control of pollution.

Economic and Monetary Union (EMU) European Union (EU) policy for a single currency and common economic policies. The proposal was announced by what was then a European Community (EC) committee headed by EC Commission president Jacques Delors in April 1989. The December 1991 ▷Maastricht Treaty agreed to the future establishment of a ▷European single currency (ESC), the euro, and set out a timetable and criteria for joining EMU. In June 1994 EU finance ministers agreed to postpone the launch of EMU until 1 January 1999, after it emerged that most countries would be unable to meet the five key economic criteria, which related to the levels of national debt, interest rates, and inflation, and were outlined in the Maastricht Treaty, by the original target date of 1997. In May 1998 EU leaders formalized the creation of the euro monetary zone, to take effect from 1 January 1999.

economic community (or **common market**) organization of autonomous countries formed to promote trade. Examples include the European Union, which was formed as the European Community in 1957, Caribbean Community (CARICOM) 1973, Latin American Economic System 1975, and Central African Economic Community 1985.

Economic Community of Central African States (or **Communauté Economique des Etats de l'Afrique Centrale, CEEAC**) organization formed in 1983 to foster economic cooperation between member states, which include Burundi, Cameroon, Central African Republic, Chad, the Republic of the Congo, Equatorial Guinea, Gabon, Rwanda, São Tomé and Principe, and the Democratic Republic of Congo (formerly Zaire). Angola has observer status.

Economic Community of West African States (ECOWAS; or **Communauté Economique des Etats de l'Afrique de l'Ouest**) organization promoting economic cooperation and development, established in 1975 by the Treaty of Lagos. Its members include Benin, Burkina Faso, Cape Verde, Gambia, Ghana, Guinea, Guinea-Bissau, Côte d'Ivoire, Liberia, Mali, Mauritania, Niger, Nigeria, Senegal, Sierra Leone, and Togo. Its headquarters are in Abuja, Nigeria.

Economic Cooperation Organization (ECO) Islamic regional grouping formed in 1985 by Iran, Pakistan, and Turkey to reduce customs tariffs and promote commerce, with the aim of eventual customs union. In 1992 the newly independent republics of Azerbaijan, Kyrgyzstan, Tajikistan, Turkmenistan, and Uzbekistan were admitted into ECO.

economics (Greek 'household management') social science devoted to studying the production, distribution, and consumption of wealth. It consists of the disciplines of ▷microeconomics, the study of individual producers, consumers, or markets, and ▷macroeconomics, the study of whole economies or systems (in particular, areas such as taxation and public spending).

economy set of interconnected activities concerned with the production, distribution, and consumption of goods and services. The contemporary economy is very complex and includes transactions ranging from the distribution and spending of children's pocket money to global-scale financial deals being conducted by ▷multinational corporations.

economy of scale in economics, the reduction in costs per item (unit costs) that results from large-scale production. The high capital costs of machinery or a factory are spread across a greater number of units as more are produced. This may be a result of automation or ▷mass production. For example, there would sometimes be economies of scale present if a car manufacturer could manufacture cars at £5,000 per car when producing 100,000 cars per year, but at £4,000 per car when producing 200,000 cars per year.

ecosystem in ecology, an integrated unit consisting of a ▷community of living organisms – bacteria, animals, and plants – and the physical environment – air, soil, water, and climate – that they inhabit. Individual organisms interact with each other and with their environment, or habitat, in a series of relationships that depends on the flow of energy and nutrients through the system. These relationships are usually complex and finely balanced, and in theory natural ecosystems are self-sustaining. However, major changes to an ecosystem, such as climate change, overpopulation, or the removal of a species, may threaten the system's sustainability and result in its eventual destruction. For instance, the removal of a major carnivore predator can result in the destruction of an ecosystem through overgrazing by herbivores.

Food chains One of the main features of an ecosystem is its ▷biodiversity. Members are usually classified as producers (those that can synthesize the organic materials they need from inorganic compounds in the environment) or consumers (those that are unable to manufacture their own food directly from these sources and depend upon producers to meet their needs). Thus plants, as producers, capture energy originating from the sun through a process of ▷photosynthesis and absorb nutrients from the soil and water; these stores of energy and nutrients then become available to the consumers – for example, they are passed via the ▷herbivores that eat the plants, to the ▷carnivores that feed on the herbivores. The sequence in which energy and nutrients pass through the system is known as a ▷food chain, and the energy levels within a food chain are termed trophic levels. At each stage of assimilation, energy is lost by consumer functioning, and so there are always far fewer consumers at the end of the chain. This can be represented diagrammatically by a pyramid with the primary producers at the base, and is termed a pyramid of numbers. At each level of the chain, nutrients are returned to the soil through the ▷decomposition of excrement and dead organisms, thus becoming once again available to plants, and completing a cycle crucial to the stability and survival of the ecosystem.

ECSC abbreviation for European Coal and Steel Community.

ecstasy (or **MDMA**) (3,4-methylenedioxymethamphetamine) illegal drug in increasing use since the 1980s. It is a modified ▷amphetamine with mild psychedelic effects, and works by depleting serotonin (a neurotransmitter) in the brain. Its long-term effects are unknown, but Canadian doctors discovered in July 2000 that ecstasy permanently reduces serotonin levels in the brain, as taking ecstasy produces a rush of serotonin that the brain is unable to make up.

ECT abbreviation for ▷electroconvulsive therapy.

ectoparasite ▷parasite that lives on the outer surface of its host.

ectopic in medicine, term applied to an anatomical feature that is displaced or found in an abnormal position. An ectopic pregnancy is one occurring outside the womb, usually in a Fallopian tube.

ectoplasm outer layer of a cell's ▷cytoplasm.

ectotherm 'cold-blooded' animal (see ▷poikilothermy), such as a lizard, that relies on external warmth (ultimately from the Sun) to raise its body temperature so that it can become active. To cool the body, ectotherms seek out a cooler environment.

ECU abbreviation for **European Currency Unit**, the official monetary unit of the European Union. It is based on the value of the different currencies used in the ▷European Monetary System (EMS).

Ecuador see country box.

ecumenical council (Greek *oikoumenikos* 'of the whole world') meeting of church leaders worldwide to determine Christian doctrine; their results are binding on all church members. Seven such councils are accepted as ecumenical by both Eastern and Western churches, while the Roman Catholic Church accepts a further 14 as ecumenical.

ecumenical movement movement for reunification of the various branches of the Christian church. It began in the 19th century with the extension of missionary work to Africa and Asia, where the divisions created in Europe were incomprehensible; the movement gathered momentum from the need for unity in the face of growing secularism in Christian countries and of the challenge posed by such faiths as Islam. The **World Council of Churches** was founded in 1948.

> **Jacob Astley**
> English Royalist general
>
> *O Lord! thou knowest how busy I must be this day: / if I forget thee, do not thou forget me.*
>
> Prayer before the Battle of Edgehill, quoted in Sir Philip Warwick *Memoires*

ecumenical patriarch head of the Eastern Orthodox Church, the patriarch of Istanbul (Constantinople). The bishop of Constantinople was recognized as having equal rights with the bishop of Rome in 451, and first termed 'patriarch' in the 6th century. The office survives today but with only limited authority, mainly confined to the Greek and Turkish Orthodox churches.

eczema inflammatory skin condition, a form of dermatitis, marked by dryness, rashes, itching, the formation of blisters, and the exudation of fluid. It may be allergic in origin and is sometimes complicated by infection.

Edam town in the Netherlands on the ▷IJsselmeer, North Holland province; municipality population (1997), including town of Volendam 26,500. Founded as a customs post in the 13th century, Edam's prosperity in the 16th and 17th centuries was based upon its cheese trade; it still produces round cheeses covered in red wax.

Edda two collections of early Icelandic literature that together constitute our chief source for Old Norse mythology. The term strictly applies to the **Younger** or **Prose Edda**, compiled by Snorri Sturluson, a priest, in about AD 1230.

Eddery, Pat(rick James John) (1952–) Irish-born flat-racing jockey who has ridden 13 English classic winners including the Derby winner on three occasions. He won the jockey's championship in Britain 11 times. By November 1999 he had ridden 100 winners in a British flat racing season for a record 26th time. The previous mark of 25 was held by Lester ▷Piggott.

Eddy, Mary Baker (1821–1910) US founder of the Christian Science movement. Her pamphlet *Science of Man* (1869) was followed by *Science and Health with Key to the Scriptures* (1875), which systematically set forth the basis of Christian Science.

eddy current electric current induced, in accordance with ▷Faraday's laws of electromagnetic induction, in a conductor located in a changing magnetic field. Eddy currents can cause much wasted energy in the cores of transformers and other electrical machines.

edelweiss perennial alpine plant belonging to the daisy family, with a white, woolly, star-shaped flower, found in the high mountains of Europe and Asia. (*Leontopodium alpinum*, family Compositae.)

Eden, (Robert) Anthony (1897–1977) 1st Earl of Avon. British Conservative politician, foreign secretary 1935–38, 1940–45, and 1951–55; prime minister 1955–57, when he resigned after the failure of the Anglo-French military intervention in the ▷Suez Crisis.

Upset by his prime minister's rejection of a peace plan secretly proposed by US president Franklin D Roosevelt in January 1938, Eden resigned as foreign secretary in February 1938 in protest against Chamberlain's decision to open conversations with the fascist dictator Mussolini. He was foreign secretary again in the wartime coalition, formed in December 1940, and in the Conservative government, elected in 1951. With the Soviets, he negotiated an interim peace in Vietnam in 1954. In April 1955 he succeeded Churchill as prime minister. When Egypt nationalized the Suez Canal in 1956, precipitating the ▷Suez Crisis, he authorized the use of force, and a joint Anglo-French force was sent to Egypt. The force was compelled to withdraw after pressure from the USA and the USSR, and this and ill-health led to Eden's resignation in January 1957. He continued to maintain that his action had been justified.

Eden, Garden of in the Old Testament book of Genesis and in the Koran, the 'garden' in which Adam and Eve lived after their creation, and from which they were expelled for disobedience.

Edgar the Peaceful (944–975) King of all England from 959. He was the younger son of Edmund I, and strove successfully to unite English and Danes as fellow subjects.

Edgehill, Battle of first battle of the English Civil War. It took place in 1642, on a ridge in south Warwickshire, between Royalists under ▷Charles I and Parliamentarians under the Earl of Essex. Both sides claimed victory.

Edinburgh capital of Scotland and, as **the City of Edinburgh**, a unitary authority, located near the southern shores of the Firth of Forth.

area 261 sq km/101 sq mi **physical** Water of Leith, Salisbury Crags, Arthur's Seat
industries 85% of the labour force works in the service sector; the largest employers in the city are health, public administration, education, banking, and insurance; manufacturing employment is declining
population (2000 est) 453,400

Key features Edinburgh Castle contains St Margaret's chapel, the oldest building in Edinburgh, dating from the 12th century. The palace of ▷Holyrood House was built in the 15th and 16th centuries on the site of a 12th-century abbey; it is the British sovereign's official Scottish residence. The principal thoroughfares are Princes Street and the Royal Mile.

Edinburgh is the site of the Scottish Parliament, a nation–region tier of government in the UK, with tax-varying powers; a new building to house the Parliament is under construction on the Royal Mile, adjacent to Holyrood House. The new Scottish Parliament's temporary base is the Church of Scotland General Assembly Hall and City of Edinburgh Council buildings, at the Mound and on George IV Bridge, in Edinburgh. The Parliament House, begun in 1632, is now the seat of the supreme courts.

Edinburgh is a cultural centre and hosts the **Edinburgh Festival**, an international arts festival, with the **Edinburgh Fringe Festival** taking place alongside, in August–September each year. The festival was founded in 1947 and has a reputation as one of the world's greatest celebrations of the arts. In 2000, the festival included 182 performances.

History There is evidence of Bronze and Iron Age occupation of Castle Rock, and in Roman times the site was occupied by Celtic

EDINBURGH The centre of Edinburgh, Scotland, with the Castle on the left, the National Gallery of Scotland below, and Princes Street on the far right. *Corel*

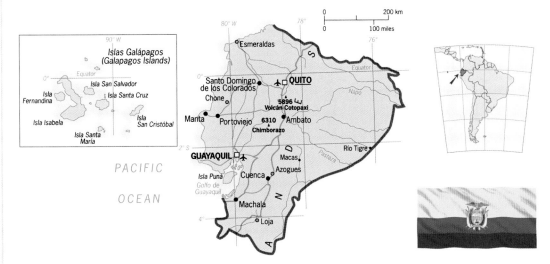

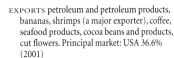

Ecuador country in South America, bounded north by Colombia, east and south by Peru, and west by the Pacific Ocean.

NATIONAL NAME *República del Ecuador/Republic of Ecuador*
AREA 270,670 sq km/104,505 sq mi
CAPITAL Quito
MAJOR TOWNS/CITIES Guayaquil, Cuenca, Machala, Portoviejo, Manta, Ambato, Santo Domingo
MAJOR PORTS Guayaquil
PHYSICAL FEATURES coastal plain rises sharply to Andes Mountains, which are divided into a series of cultivated valleys; flat, low-lying rainforest in the east; Galapagos Islands; Cotopaxi, the world's highest active volcano. Ecuador is crossed by the Equator, from which it derives its name

Government

HEAD OF STATE AND GOVERNMENT Lucio Edwin Gutierrez Borbua from 2003
POLITICAL SYSTEM liberal democracy
POLITICAL EXECUTIVE limited presidency
ADMINISTRATIVE DIVISIONS 21 provinces
ARMED FORCES 59,500 (2002 est)
CONSCRIPTION military service is selective for one year

DEATH PENALTY abolished in 1906
DEFENCE SPEND (% GDP) 3 (2002 est)
EDUCATION SPEND (% GDP) 1.6 (2001 est)
HEALTH SPEND (% GDP) 2.4 (2000 est)

Economy and resources

CURRENCY US dollar from 2000
GPD (US$) 24.3 billion (2002 est)
REAL GDP GROWTH (% change on previous year) 5.6 (2001)
GNI (US$) 19.0 billion (2002 est)
GNI PER CAPITA (PPP) (US$) 3,130 (2002 est)
CONSUMER PRICE INFLATION 7.4% (2003 est)
UNEMPLOYMENT 8.1% (2001)
FOREIGN DEBT (US$) 11.1 billion (2001 est)
MAJOR TRADING PARTNERS USA, Colombia, Germany, Chile, Peru, Japan, Italy, Venezuela
RESOURCES petroleum, natural gas, gold, silver, copper, zinc, antimony, iron, uranium, lead, coal
INDUSTRIES food processing, petroleum refining, cement, chemicals, textiles

EXPORTS petroleum and petroleum products, bananas, shrimps (a major exporter), coffee, seafood products, cocoa beans and products, cut flowers. Principal market: USA 36.6% (2001)
IMPORTS machinery and transport equipment, basic manufactures, chemicals, consumer goods. Principal source: USA 25% (2001)
ARABLE LAND 5.7% (2000 est)
AGRICULTURAL PRODUCTS bananas, coffee, cocoa, rice, potatoes, maize, barley, sugar cane; fishing (especially shrimp industry); forestry

Chronology

1450s: The Caras people, whose kingdom had its capital at Quito, conquered by Incas of Peru.

1531: Spanish conquistador Francisco Pizarro landed on Ecuadorean coast, en route to Peru, where Incas were defeated.

1534: Conquered by Spanish. Quito, which had been destroyed by American Indians, was refounded by Sebastian de Belalcazar; the area became part of the Spanish Viceroyalty of Peru, which covered much of South America, with its capital at Lima (Peru).

later 16th century: Spanish established large agrarian estates, owned by Europeans and worked by American Indian labourers.

1739: Became part of new Spanish Viceroyalty of Nueva Granada, which included Colombia and Venezuela, with its capital in Bogotá (Colombia).

1809: With the Spanish monarchy having been overthrown by Napoleon Bonaparte, the Creole middle class began to press for independence.

1822: Spanish Royalists defeated by Field Marshal Antonio José de Sucre, fighting for Simón Bolívar, 'The Liberator', at battle of Pichincha, near Quito; became part of independent Gran Colombia, which also comprised Colombia, Panama, and Venezuela.

1830: Became fully independent state, after leaving Gran Colombia.

1845–60: Political instability, with five presidents holding power, increasing tension between conservative Quito and liberal Guayaquil on the coast, and minor wars with Peru and Colombia.

1860–75: Power held by Gabriel García Moreno, an autocratic theocrat-Conservative who launched education and public-works programmes.

1895–1912: Dominated by Gen Eloy Alfaro, a radical, anticlerical Liberal from the coastal region, who reduced the power of the church.

Population and society

POPULATION 13,003,000 (2003 est)
POPULATION GROWTH RATE 1.5% (2000–15)
POPULATION DENSITY (per sq km) 48 (2003 est)
URBAN POPULATION (% of total) 64 (2003 est)
AGE DISTRIBUTION (% of total population) 0–14 33%, 15–59 60%, 60+ 7% (2002 est)
ETHNIC GROUPS about 55% mestizo (of Spanish-American and American Indian parentage), 25% American Indian, 10% Spanish, 10% African
LANGUAGE Spanish (official), Quechua, Jivaro, other indigenous languages
RELIGION Roman Catholic
EDUCATION (compulsory years) 6
LITERACY RATE 93% (men); 90% (women) (2003 est)
LABOUR FORCE 7.3% agriculture, 21.4% industry, 71.3% services (1998)
LIFE EXPECTANCY 68 (men); 74 (women) (2000–05)
CHILD MORTALITY RATE (under 5, per 1,000 live births) 30 (2001)
PHYSICIANS (per 1,000 people) 1.7 (1998 est)
HOSPITAL BEDS (per 1,000 people) 1.6 (1998 est)
TV SETS (per 1,000 people) 225 (2001 est)
RADIOS (per 1,000 people) 413 (2001 est)
INTERNET USERS (per 10,000 people) 388.9 (2002 est)
PERSONAL COMPUTER USERS (per 100 people) 3.1 (2002 est)

See also ▷Bolívar, Simón; ▷Inca.

1925–48: Great political instability; no president completed his term of office.

1941: Lost territory in Amazonia after defeat in war with Peru.

1948–55: Liberals in power.

1956: Camilo Ponce became first conservative president in 60 years.

1960: Liberals in power, with José María Velasco Ibarra as president.

1962: Military junta installed.

1968: Velasco returned as president.

1970s: Ecuador emerged as significant oil producer.

1972: Coup put military back in power.

1979: New democratic constitution; Liberals in power but opposed by right- and left-wing parties.

1981: Border dispute with Peru flared up again.

1982: The deteriorating economy and austerity measures provoked strikes, demonstrations, and a state of emergency.

1988: Unpopular austerity measures were introduced.

1992: PUR leader Sixto Duran Ballen was elected president; PSC became the largest party in congress. Ecuador withdrew from OPEC to enable it to increase its oil exports.

1994: There was mounting opposition to Duran's economic liberalization and privatization programme.

1998: A 157-year border dispute was settled with Peru.

2000: After the currency lost 65% of its value in 1999, President Mahuad declared a state of emergency, froze all bank accounts valued at over £100, and said that he would introduce the dollar in favour of the sucre. After a bloodless coup in protest to the measures, Gustavo Noboa was sworn in as president. He nevertheless continued with the introduction of the dollar after positive international response to the plans.

ECUADOR An aerial view of the Andean volcano Cotopaxi, Ecuador, seen breaking through clouds. *Image Bank*

peoples; in about 617 the site was captured by Edwin of the Angles of Northumbria; the city took its name from the fortress of Din Eidin which he built. The early settlement grew up around a castle on Castle Rock, while about a mile to the east another burgh, Canongate, developed around the abbey of Holyrood, founded in 1128 by David I. It remained separate from Edinburgh until 1856. Robert the Bruce, having made Edinburgh the capital in 1325, made Edinburgh a burgh in 1329, and established its port at Leith. In 1544 and 1547 the town was destroyed by the English. After the union with England in 1707, Edinburgh lost its political importance but remained culturally pre-eminent. During the 18th century, Edinburgh was known as the 'Athens of the North' because of its concentration of intellectual talent, for example, Adam Smith, David Hume, and Joseph Black. Development of the area known as New Town started in 1767.

Related Web sites: Edinburgh http://www.city.net/countries/united_kingdom/scotland/edinburgh/
Edinburgh Festival Online http://www.go-edinburgh.co.uk/

Edinburgh, Duke of title of Prince ▷Philip of the UK.

Edison, Thomas Alva (1847–1931) US scientist and inventor, whose work in the fields of communications and electrical power greatly influenced the world in which we live. With more than 1,000 patents, Edison produced his most important inventions in Menlo Park, New Jersey 1876–87, including the phonograph and the electric light bulb in 1879. He also constructed a system of electric power distribution for consumers, the telephone transmitter, and the megaphone.

Telegraphy and telephony Edison's first success came in the area of telegraphy. Perceiving the need for rapid communications after the Civil War, his first invention was an automatic repeater for telegraphic messages. He then invented a tape machine called a 'ticker', which communicated stock exchange prices across the country.

Turning his attention to the transmission of the human voice over long distances in 1876, he patented an electric transmitter system that proved to be less commercially successful than the telephone of Bell and Gray, patented a few months later. Undeterred, Edison set about improving their system, culminating in his invention of the carbon transmitter, which so increased the volume of the telephone signal that it was used as a microphone in the Bell telephone.

> **Thomas Alva Edison**
> *Genius is 1% inspiration and 99% perspiration.*
> Life ch. 24

The light bulb While experimenting with the carbon microphone in the 1870s, Edison had toyed briefly with the idea of using a thin carbon filament as a light source in an incandescent electric lamp. He returned to the idea in 1879. His first major success came on 19 October of that year when, using carbonized sewing cotton mounted on an electrode in a vacuum (one millionth of an atmosphere), he obtained a source that remained aglow for 45 hours without overheating – a major problem with all other materials used. He and his assistants tried 6,000 other organic materials before finding a bamboo fibre that gave a bulb life of 1,000 hours.

Generators and the first power stations To produce a serious rival to gas illumination, a power source was required as well as a cheap and reliable lamp. The alternatives were either generators or heavy and expensive batteries. At that time, the best generators rarely converted more than 40% of the mechanical energy into electrical energy. Edison's first generator consisted of a drum armature of soft iron wire and a simple bi-polar magnet, and was designed to operate one arc lamp and some incandescent lamps in series.

A few months later he built a much more ambitious generator, the largest built to date, weighing 500 kg/1,103 lb and with an efficiency of 82%. Edison's team were at the forefront of development in generator technology over the next decade, during which efficiency was raised above 90%. To complete his electrical system he designed cables to carry power into the home from small (by modern standards) generating stations, and also invented an electricity meter to record its use.

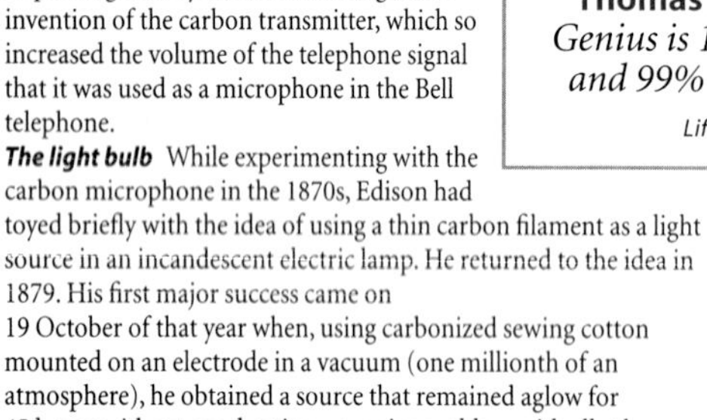

THOMAS EDISON The first motion picture camera, invented by Thomas Edison. *Archive Photos*

The phonograph In 1877 he began the era of recorded sound by inventing the phonograph, a device in which the vibrations of the human voice were engraved by a needle on a revolving cylinder coated with tin foil.

Related Web sites: Inventing Entertainment: The Early Motion Pictures of the Edison Company http://lcweb2.loc.gov/ammem/edhtml/edhome.html

Edmonton capital of ▷Alberta, Canada, on the North Saskatchewan River at an altitude of 665 m/2,182 ft; population (2001 est) 666,100. It is the centre of an oil and mining area to the north and is also an agricultural and dairying region. Manufactured goods include processed foods, petrochemicals, plastic and metal products, lumber, and clothing. Edmonton is known as the 'gateway to the north': it is situated on the Alaska Highway, and petroleum pipelines link the city with Superior in Wisconsin, USA, and Vancouver in British Columbia.

Edmund two kings of England:

Edmund I (921–946) King of England from 939. The son of Edward the Elder, he succeeded his half-brother, Athelstan, as king in 939. He succeeded in regaining control of Mercia, which on his accession had fallen to the Norse inhabitants of Northumbria, and of the Five Boroughs, an independent confederation within the Danelaw. He then moved on to subdue the Norsemen in Cumbria and finally extended his rule as far as southern Scotland. As well as uniting England, he bolstered his authority by allowing St Dunstan to reform the Benedictine order. He was killed in 946 at Pucklechurch, Gloucestershire, by an outlawed robber.

Edmund (II) Ironside (*c.* 981–1016) King of England in 1016, the son of Ethelred II 'the Unready' (*c.* 968–1016). He led the resistance to Canute's invasion in 1015, and on Ethelred's death in 1016 was chosen king by the citizens of London. Meanwhile, the Witan (the king's council) elected Canute. In the struggle for the throne, Canute defeated Edmund at Ashingdon (or Assandun), and they divided the kingdom between them. When Edmund died the same year, Canute ruled the whole kingdom.

Edmund, St (*c.* 840–870) King of East Anglia from 855. In 870 he was defeated and captured by the Danes at Hoxne, Suffolk, and martyred on refusing to renounce Christianity. He was canonized and his shrine at Bury St Edmunds became a place of pilgrimage.

Edo (or Yedo) former name of ▷Tokyo, Japan, until 1868.

education process, beginning at birth, of developing intellectual capacity, manual skill, and social awareness, especially by instruction. In its more restricted sense, the term refers to the process of imparting literacy, numeracy, and a generally accepted body of knowledge.

History of education The earliest known European educational systems were those of ancient Greece. In Sparta the process was devoted mainly to the development of military skills; in Athens, to politics, philosophy, and public speaking, but both were accorded only to the privileged few.

In ancient China, formalized education received impetus from the imperial decree of 165 BC, which established open competitive examinations for the recruitment of members of the civil service, based mainly on a detailed study of literature.

The Romans adopted the Greek system of education and spread it through Western Europe. Following the disintegration of the Roman Empire, widespread education vanished from Europe, although Christian monasteries preserved both learning and Latin. In the Middle Ages, Charlemagne's monastic schools taught the 'seven liberal arts': grammar, logic, rhetoric, arithmetic, geometry, music, and astronomy; elementary schools, generally presided over by a parish priest, instructed children of the poor in reading, writing, and arithmetic. From the monastic schools emerged the theological philosophers of the Scholastic Movement, which in the 11th–13th centuries led to the foundation of the universities of Paris (▷Sorbonne), Bologna, Padua, ▷Oxford, and ▷Cambridge. The capture of Constantinople, capital of the Eastern Roman Empire, by the Turks in 1453 propelled its Christian scholars into exile across Europe, and revived European interest in learning.

The Renaissance humanist movement encouraged the free study of all classical writers, both Latin and Greek, with the aim of assimilating their reasoning and making a philological study of the texts. It owed much to Arabic scholarly activity, which – beginning with the translation and augmentation of Greek scientific texts – had continued unabated during the Dark Ages and had reached Europe via Moorish influences in Sicily and Spain. The curriculum of humanist schools, of which Latin was the foundation, was widely adopted, although by the 17th century it had failed to adapt to society's changing needs and by the early 18th century organized education was at a low level.

> **Horatio Bottomley**
> English newspaper editor
> *I have not had your advantages. What poor education I have received has been gained in the University of Life.*
> Speech at Oxford Union, 2 December 1920

Compulsory attendance at primary schools was first established in the mid-18th century in Prussia, and has since spread almost worldwide. Compulsory schooling in industrialized countries is typically from around age 5 or 6 to around age 15 or 16; public education expenditure is typically around 5% of GNP (Spain 3.2%, Japan 4.4%, Denmark 7.7%).

The role of Church and state In England and Wales, prior to the Reformation, the undivided Church was responsible for education. Thereafter, the question of the control of education became a source of bitter sectarian conflict, and it was not until the 19th century that attempts were made to spread literacy throughout society. In Scotland, as early as 1494, freeholders were required by royal statute to send their heirs to school to acquire 'perfect Latin', and from the late 16th century, under the influence of John ▷Knox, churches in every major town had Latin schools attached.

Education 1750–1870 Before 1800 elementary education was delivered by the ▷public schools and local fee-paying 'grammar' schools, and for the poor by dame schools and, after 1780, Sunday schools. Ragged schools were established after 1820. The government did not fund educational provision, neither did it take any measures such as inspection to ensure the quality of education, though it did intervene to ensure that Leeds Grammar School taught Latin and Greek in preference to more modern subjects such as science. Britain's education system had fallen behind those of countries such as Germany and France.

However, as the Industrial Revolution progressed, it was obvious that skilled engineers, scientists, and mechanics were needed, and that the workforce should be at least literate and numerate. The Factory Act of 1802, which applied throughout the UK, required that during the first four years of their apprenticeship children employed by the owners of the newly arising factories were taught reading, writing, and arithmetic. The requirement was not always observed, but it embodied a new principle. The Factory Act of 1833 required working children to have at least two hours schooling a day – some factories set up factory schools to do this, although the quality of teaching was generally poor.

The British and Foreign Schools Society (1808) and the National Society for Promoting the Education of the Poor in the Principles of the Established Church (1811) set up schools in which basic literacy and numeracy as well as religious knowledge were taught. Schools used the monitorial system of Andrew Bell and Joseph Lancaster, and the primary method of instruction was learning by rote. In 1833 the government made its first grants to education, £20,000 to be divided between the two societies, a sum which was gradually increased year on year. In 1840 a teacher training college was founded at Battersea, London.

Nevertheless, when the Newcastle Commission reported in 1860, it found that less than one half of Britain's children went to school, and that less than half of these could read and write when they left school. It recommended that schools be 'paid by results' as the way to address their inadequacies, and set up a system of inspectors to test the children's learning. In 1862 government grants became available for schools attended by children up to 12.

Education 1870–1902 The Elementary Education Act of 1870 (also known as Forster's Act, after the Liberal reformer William Forster who secured its passage) established district school boards all over the country whose duty was to provide facilities for the elementary education of all children aged 5–11 not otherwise receiving it. The act enabled low school fees to be charged. It allowed the church schools to continue as before and doubled their annual grants, but religious education (RE) was not compulsory in the 'board schools'. Education was made compulsory in 1876 for children aged 5–10. In 1891 elementary education was made free, and in 1899 the school leaving age was raied to 12. Payment by results was dropped in 1900, which encouraged many schools to introduce subjects other than the '3Rs' (reading, writing, and arithematic).

Education 1902 to the present The school boards were abolished by the Education Act of 1902 and their responsibilities transferred to county and borough councils, which became the local education authorities for both higher and elementary education, and for teacher training. This led to the increasing provision of free state secondary ▷grammar schools, and in 1918 the Fisher Act (named

EDUCATION Attic teachers and scholars depicted on an ancient Greek bowl. Ancient Greece was the first known civilization to formalize education, albeit only for those destined for the military or public life. *Philip Sauvain Picture Collection*

after Herbert Fisher, president of the Board of Education) raised the school leaving age to 14. In 1926 the Hadow Commission recommended the provision of free secondary education for all.

Once the principle of elementary education for all was established, the idea of widely available higher education began to be accepted. The Education Act 1944 introduced a system of secondary education for all, and formed the foundation of much education policy today. This has been revised by two further acts in 1980, which repealed 1976 legislation enforcing ▷comprehensive reorganization, and gave new rights to parents; by the 1981 Education Act which made new provisions for the education of children with special needs; and by legislation in 1986 giving further powers to school governors as part of a move towards increased parental involvement in schools, and in 1987 on the remuneration of teachers. In 1988 a major act introduced a compulsory ▷national curriculum in state schools, compulsory testing of children, financial delegation of budgets to schools, and the possibility of direct funding by government for schools that voted to opt out of local council control.

Responsibility for education In the UK, the Department for Education and Employment (DfEE), established in 1944 as the Ministry of Education and headed by a cabinet minister, is responsible for nonmilitary scientific research, for universities throughout Great Britain, and for school education in England. In Wales, primary and secondary education is the responsibility of the Welsh Education Office. There is a Scottish Education Department, under the secretary of state for Scotland. Until direct rule (1972), Northern Ireland had its own Ministry of Education; the responsibility for education is now held by the Education and Library Boards.

Local education authorities (LEAs) are education committees of county and borough councils, responsible for providing educational services locally under the general oversight of the DfEE, but certain of their powers have been curtailed by the 1988 act. The Inner London Education Authority (ILEA) was abolished by the 1988 act and responsibility for education in London passed to the borough councils.

Related Web sites: Home Education Advisory Service http://www.heas.org.uk **Homework High** http://www.homeworkhigh.co.uk/

Edward (1964–) Edward Antony Richard Louis. Prince of the UK, third son of Queen Elizabeth II. He is seventh in line to the throne after Charles, Charles's two sons, Andrew, and Andrew's two daughters. In 1999 he married Miss Sophie Rhys-Jones at Windsor Castle and the couple became the Earl and Countess of Wessex.

Edward (1330–1376) Called 'the Black Prince'. Prince of Wales, eldest son of Edward III of England. The epithet (probably posthumous) may refer to his black armour. During the ▷Hundred Years' War he fought at the Battle of Crécy in 1346 and captured the French king at Poitiers in 1356. He ruled Aquitaine from 1360 to 1371. In 1367 he invaded Castile and restored to the throne the deposed king, Pedro the Cruel (1334–69). During the revolt that eventually ousted him, he caused the massacre of Limoges in 1370.

EDWARD A gilt copper effigy of Edward, 'the Black Prince', on his tomb in Canterbury Cathedral. *The Art Archive/ Canterbury Cathedral/Eileen Tweedy*

Edward eight kings of England or Great Britain:

Edward I (1239–1307) King of England from 1272, son of Henry III (1207–1272). He led the royal forces against Simon de Montfort (the Younger) in the Barons' War of 1264–67, and was on a crusade when he succeeded to the throne. He established English rule over all of Wales in 1282–84, and secured recognition of his overlordship from the Scottish king, although the Scots under Sir William Wallace and Robert (I) the Bruce fiercely resisted actual conquest. His reign saw Parliament move towards its modern form with the ▷Model Parliament of 1295. He married Eleanor of Castile (1254–1290) and in 1299 married Margaret, daughter of Philip III of France. He was succeeded by his son Edward II (1284–1327).

Edward was a noted ▷castle builder, including the northern Welsh Conway castle, Caernarvon castle, Beaumaris castle, and Harlech castle. He was also responsible for building *bastides* to defend the English position in France.

Edward II (1284–1327) King of England from 1307, son of Edward I. Born at Caernarfon Castle, he was created the first Prince of Wales in 1301. Incompetent and frivolous, and unduly influenced by his favourite, Piers Gaveston, Edward struggled throughout his reign with discontented barons, who attempted to restrict his power through the Ordinances of 1311. His invasion of Scotland in 1314 to suppress revolt resulted in defeat at Bannockburn. When he fell under the influence of a new favourite, Hugh le Depenser, he was deposed in 1327 by his wife Isabella (1292–1358), daughter of Philip IV of France, and her lover Roger de ▷Mortimer, and murdered in Berkeley Castle, Gloucestershire. He was succeeded by his son, Edward III.

Edward III (1310–1377) King of England from 1327, son of Edward II. He assumed the government in 1330 from his mother, through whom in 1337 he laid claim to the French throne and thus began the Hundred Years' War. Edward was the victor of Halidon Hill in 1333, Sluys in 1340, Crécy in 1346, and at the siege of Calais 1346–47, and created the Order of the Garter. He was succeeded by his grandson Richard II.

Edward's early experience was against the Scots, including the disastrous Weardale campaign in 1327. Forcing them to battle outside Berwick at Halidon Hill he used a combination of dismounted men-at-arms and archers to crush the Scots. Apart from the naval victory of Sluys his initial campaigns against France were expensive and inconclusive. Resorting to *chevauchée* (raids through enemy territory), he scored a stunning victory at the Battle

> **Edward the Black Prince**
> *He who is steadfast unto death shall be saved and they who suffer in a just cause, theirs is the kingdom of heaven.*
>
> Addressing his soldiers before the Battle of Poitiers 1356, quoted in Jean Froissart *Chronicles*

of Crécy, which delivered the crucial bridgehead of Calais into English hands. Due to the brilliant success of his son Edward of Woodstock (▷Edward the Black Prince) at the Battle of ▷Poitiers in 1356, and later campaigns, Edward achieved the favourable Treaty of Brétigny in 1360. He gave up personal command in the latter part of his reign. An inspiring leader, his Order of the Garter was a chivalric club designed to bind his military nobility to him, and was widely imitated.

Edward improved the status of the monarchy after his father's chaotic reign. He began by attempting to force his rule on Scotland, winning a victory at Halidon Hill in 1333. During the first stage of the Hundred Years' War, English victories included the Battle of Crécy in 1346 and the capture of Calais in 1347. In 1360 Edward surrendered his claim to the French throne, but the war resumed in 1369. During his last years his son John of Gaunt acted as head of government.

Edward IV (1442–1483) King of England 1461–70 and from 1471. He was the son of Richard, Duke of York, and succeeded Henry VI in the Wars of the Roses, temporarily losing his throne to Henry when Edward fell out with his adviser Richard Neville, Earl of ▷Warwick. Edward was a fine warrior and intelligent strategist, with victories at Mortimer's Cross and Towton in 1461, Empingham in 1470, and Barnet and Tewkesbury in 1471. He was succeeded by his son Edward V.

Edward was known as Earl of March until his accession. After his father's death he occupied London in 1461, and was proclaimed king in place of Henry VI by a council of peers. His position was secured by the defeat of the Lancastrians at Towton in 1461 and by the capture of Henry. He quarrelled, however, with Warwick, his strongest supporter, who temporarily restored Henry 1470–71, until Edward recovered the throne by his victories at Barnet and Tewkesbury.

Edward V (1470–1483) King of England in 1483. Son of Edward IV, he was deposed three months after his accession in favour of his uncle (▷Richard III), and is traditionally believed to have been murdered (with his brother) in the Tower of London on Richard's orders.

Edward VI (1537–1553) King of England from 1547, only son of Henry VIII and his third wife, Jane Seymour. The government was entrusted to his uncle, Edward Seymour, 1st Duke of ▷Somerset (who fell from power in 1549), and then to the Earl of Warwick, John Dudley, later created Duke of ▷Northumberland.

> **Edward VI**
> *Methinks I am in prison. Here be no galleries nor gardens to walk in.*
>
> Of Windsor. He was then 12 years old and his uncle, the Duke of Somerset, had just fallen from power.

He was succeeded by his sister Mary I. Edward became a staunch Protestant, and during his reign the ▷Reformation progressed in England under Archbishop Thomas ▷Cranmer (see ▷Reformation, England). Edward died of tuberculosis, and his will, probably prepared by Northumberland, set aside that of his father so as to exclude his half-sisters, Mary and Elizabeth, from the succession. He nominated Lady Jane ▷Grey, a granddaughter of Henry VII, who had recently married Northumberland's son. Technically Jane reigned for nine days, and was deposed by Mary I.

EDWARD VI King Edward VI's coronation medal. *Philip Sauvain Picture Collection*

Edward VII (1841–1910) King of Great Britain and Ireland from 1901. As Prince of Wales he was a prominent social figure, but his mother Queen Victoria considered him too frivolous to take part in political life. In 1860 he made the first tour of Canada and the USA ever undertaken by a British prince.

Edward was born at Buckingham Palace, the eldest son of Queen Victoria and Prince Albert. After his father's death in 1861 he undertook many public duties, took a close interest in politics, and was on friendly terms with the party leaders. In 1863 he married Princess Alexandra of Denmark, and they had six children. He toured India 1875–76. He succeeded to the throne in 1901 and was crowned in 1902.

Although he overrated his political influence, he contributed to the Entente Cordiale of 1904 with France and the Anglo-Russian agreement of 1907.

Edward VIII (1894–1972) King of Great Britain and Northern Ireland January–December 1936, when he renounced the throne to marry Wallis Warfield ▷Simpson (see ▷abdication crisis). He was created Duke of Windsor and was governor of the Bahamas 1940–45.

Eldest son of George V, he received the title of Prince of Wales in 1910 and succeeded to the throne on 20 January 1936. In November 1936 a constitutional crisis arose when Edward wished to marry Mrs Simpson; it was felt that, as a divorcee, she would be unacceptable as queen. On 11 December Edward abdicated and left for France, where the couple were married in 1937. He was succeeded by his brother, George VI.

Edward the Confessor (*c.* 1003–1066) King of England from 1042, the son of Ethelred II. He lived in Normandy until shortly before his accession. During his reign power was held by Earl Godwin and his son ▷Harold, while the king devoted himself to religion, including the rebuilding of Westminster Abbey (consecrated in 1065), where he is buried. His childlessness left four claimants to the English throne on his death and led ultimately to the Norman Conquest in 1066. He was canonized in 1161.

Related Web site: St Edward the Confessor http://www.newadvent.org/cathen/05322a.htm

Edward the Elder (*c.* 870–924) King of the West Saxons. He succeeded his father Alfred the Great in 899. He reconquered southeast England and the Midlands from the Danes, uniting Wessex and Mercia with the help of his sister Aethelflaed. By the time of his death his kingdom was the most powerful in the British Isles. He was succeeded by his son ▷Athelstan.

Edward extended the system of burghal defence begun by Alfred, building new burghs, for example at Hertford and Buckingham, and twin burghs at Bedford and Stamford.

Edward the Martyr (*c.* 963–978) King of England from 975. Son of King Edgar, he was murdered at Corfe Castle, Dorset, probably at his stepmother Aelfthryth's instigation (she wished to secure the crown for her son, Ethelred). He was canonized in 1001.

Edwards, Blake (1922–) Adopted name of William Blake McEdwards. US film director and writer. He was formerly an actor. Specializing in comedies, he directed the series of *Pink Panther* films 1963–78, starring Peter Sellers. His other work includes *Operation Petticoat* (1959), *Breakfast at Tiffany's* (1961), *Victor/Victoria* (1982), *Blind Date* (1987), and *Switch* (1991).

EEC abbreviation for ▷European Economic Community.

EEG abbreviation for ▷electroencephalogram.

eel any fish of the order Anguilliformes. Eels are snakelike, with elongated dorsal and anal fins. They include the freshwater eels of Europe and North America (which breed in the Atlantic), the marine conger eels, and the morays of tropical coral reefs.

A new species of moray eel was discovered in 1995 off the coasts of Oman and Somalia. It is up to 60 cm/2 ft in length with a large black blotch around the gill openings.

eelgrass (or **tape grass** or **glass wrack**) any of several aquatic plants, especially *Zostera marina*. Eelgrass is found in tidal mud flats and is one of the few flowering plants to adapt to marine conditions, being completely submerged at high tide. (Genus *Zostera*, family Zosteraceae.)

EEPROM (acronym for electrically erasable programmable read-only memory) computer memory that can record data and retain it indefinitely. The data can be erased with an electrical charge and new data recorded.

Effelsberg site, near Bonn, Germany, of the world's largest fully steerable radio telescope, the 100-m/328-ft radio dish of the Max Planck Institute for Radio Astronomy, opened in 1971.

efficiency in physics, a general term indicating the degree to which a process or device can convert energy from one form to another without loss. It is normally expressed as a fraction or percentage, where 100% indicates conversion with no loss. The efficiency of a machine, for example, is the ratio of the work done by the machine to the energy put into the machine; in practice it is always less than 100% because of frictional heat losses. Certain electrical machines with no moving parts, such as transformers, can approach 100% efficiency.

EFTA acronym for ▷European Free Trade Association.

EFTPOS acronym for electronic funds transfer at point of sale, a form of electronic funds transfer.

e.g. abbreviation for exempli gratia (Latin 'for the sake of example').

egalitarianism belief that all citizens in a state should have equal rights and privileges. Interpretations of this can vary, from the notion of equality of opportunity to equality in material welfare and political decision-making. Some states reject egalitarianism; most accept the concept of equal opportunities but recognize that people's abilities vary widely. Even those states which claim to be socialist find it necessary to have hierarchical structures in the political, social, and economic spheres. Egalitarianism was one of the principles of the French Revolution.

Egbert (died 839) King of the West Saxons from 802, the son of Ealhmund, an under-king of Kent. By 829 he had united England for the first time under one king.

egg in animals, the ovum, or female ▷gamete (reproductive cell). After fertilization by a sperm cell, it begins to divide to form an embryo. Eggs may be deposited by the female (▷ovipary) or they may develop within her body (▷vivipary and ▷ovovivipary). In the oviparous reptiles and birds, the egg is protected by a shell, and well supplied with nutrients in the form of yolk.

eggar-moth large reddish-brown moth with a highly developed hindwing. The length across the wings is 3.8–11.5 cm/1.5–4.5 in.

eggplant another name for ▷aubergine.

Egmont, Mount (Maori **Taranaki** 'barren mountain') symmetrical dormant volcano in the southwest of the North Island, New Zealand, 29 km/18 mi south of New Plymouth; it is 2,517 m/ 8,260 ft high and lies within Mount Egmont National Park.

ego (Latin 'I') in psychology, the processes concerned with the self and a person's conception of himself or herself, encompassing values and attitudes. In Freudian psychology, the term refers specifically to the element of the human mind that represents the conscious processes concerned with reality, in conflict with the ▷id (the instinctual element) and the ▷superego (the ethically aware element).

egret any of several ▷herons with long tufts of feathers on the head or neck. They belong to the order Ciconiiformes.

Egypt see country box.

Egypt, ancient ancient civilization, based around the River Nile in Egypt, which emerged 5,000 years ago and reached its peak in the 16th century BC. Ancient Egypt was famed for its great power and wealth, due to the highly fertile lands of the Nile delta, which were rich sources of grain for the whole Mediterranean region. Egyptians were advanced in agriculture, engineering, and applied sciences. Many of their monuments, such as the ▷pyramids and the sphinx, survive today.

Related Web site: Exploring Ancient World Cultures: Egypt http://eawc.evansville.edu/egpage.htm

Egyptian art, ancient the art of ancient Egypt falls into three main periods – the Old, Middle, and New Kingdoms – beginning about 3000 BC and spanning 2,000 years overall. During this time, despite some stylistic development, there is remarkable continuity, representing a deeply religious and traditionalist society. Sculpture

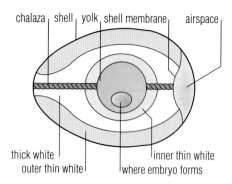

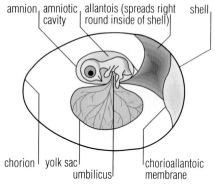

EGG Section through a fertilized bird egg. Inside a bird's egg is a complex structure of liquids and membranes designed to meet the needs of the growing embryo. The yolk, which is rich in fat, is gradually absorbed by the embryo. The white of the egg provides protein and water. The chalaza is a twisted band of protein which holds the yolk in place and acts as a shock absorber. The airspace allows gases to be exchanged through the shell. The allantois contains many blood vessels which carry gases between the embryo and the outside.

and painting are highly stylized, following strict conventions and using symbols of a religion centred on the afterlife and idealization of the dead, their servants, families, and possessions. Depictions of the human form show the face and legs in profile, the upper torso facing forwards, the hips three quarters turned, and the eye enlarged and enhanced.

During Egypt's slow decline in power, the style of art remained conservative and subservient to religion, but the level of technical expertise continued to be high, with an almost constant and prolific production of artefacts. Major collections of Egyptian art are to be found in the National Museum, Cairo, and in the British Museum, London.

The early dynastic period and the Old Kingdom (2920–2134 BC) is exemplified by the monumental statue of the Great Sphinx at

Ancient Egypt: Key Events

5000 BC	Egyptian culture already well established in the Nile Valley, with Neolithic farming villages.
c. 3050	Menes unites Lower Egypt (the delta) with his own kingdom of Upper Egypt.
c. 2630	The architect Imhotep builds the step pyramid at Sakkara.
c. 2550	**Old Kingdom** reaches the height of its power and the kings of the 4th dynasty build the pyramids at El Giza.
c. 2040–1640	**Middle Kingdom**, under which the unity lost towards the end of the Old Kingdom is restored.
c. 1750	Infiltrating Asian Hyksos people establish their kingdom in the Nile Delta.
c. 1550	**New Kingdom** established by the 18th dynasty following the eviction of the Hyksos, with its capital at Thebes. The high point of ancient Egyptian civilization under the pharaohs Thothmes, Hatshepsut, Amenhotep, Akhenaton (who moves the capital to Akhetaton), and Tutankhamen.
c. 1307–1196	19th dynasty: Major building works by Seti I and Ramses II at Thebes, Abydos, and Abu Simbel.
1191	Ramses III defeats the Indo-European Sea Peoples, but after him there is decline, and power within the country passes from the pharaohs to the priests of Amen.
1070–664	**Third Intermediate Period** during this period Egypt is often divided between two or more dynasties; the nobles become virtually independent.
8th–7th centuries	Brief interlude of rule by kings from Nubia.
666	The Assyrians under Ashurbanipal occupy Thebes.
663–609	Psammetichus I restores Egypt's independence and unity.
525	Egypt is conquered by Cambyses and becomes a Persian province.
c. 405–340	Period of independence.
332	Conquest by Alexander the Great. On the division of his empire, Egypt goes to one of his generals, Ptolemy I, and his descendants, the Macedonian dynasty.
30	Death of Cleopatra, last of the Macedonians, and conquest by the Roman emperor Augustus; Egypt becomes a province of the Roman empire.
AD 641	Conquest by the Arabs; the Christianity of later Roman rule is for the most part replaced by Islam.

Egypt

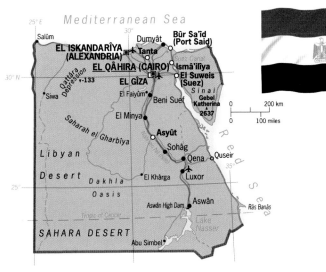

Egypt country in northeast Africa, bounded to the north by the Mediterranean Sea; east by the Palestinian-controlled Gaza Strip, Israel, and the Red Sea; south by Sudan; and west by Libya.

NATIONAL NAME *Jumhuriyyat Misr al-'Arabiyya/Arab Republic of Egypt*
AREA 1,001,450 sq km/386,659 sq mi
CAPITAL Cairo
MAJOR TOWNS/CITIES El Gíza, Shubra Al Khayma, Alexandria, Port Said, El-Mahalla el-Koubra, Tanta, El Mansûra, Suez
MAJOR PORTS Alexandria, Port Said, Suez, Damietta, Shubra Al Khayma
PHYSICAL FEATURES mostly desert; hills in east; fertile land along Nile valley and delta; cultivated and settled area is about 35,500 sq km/13,700 sq mi; Aswan High Dam and Lake Nasser; Sinai

Government

HEAD OF STATE Hosni Mubarak from 1981
HEAD OF GOVERNMENT Atef Obeid from 1999
POLITICAL SYSTEM liberal democracy
POLITICAL EXECUTIVE limited presidency

ADMINISTRATIVE DIVISIONS 26 governorates
ARMED FORCES 443,500 (2002 est)
CONSCRIPTION selective conscription for 12 months–3 years
DEATH PENALTY retained and used for ordinary crimes
DEFENCE SPEND (% GDP) 3.9 (2002 est)
EDUCATION SPEND (% GDP) 4.5 (1999)
HEALTH SPEND (% GDP) 3.8 (2000 est)

Economy and resources

CURRENCY Egyptian pound
GPD (US$) 89.8 billion (2002 est)
REAL GDP GROWTH (% change on previous year) 2.5 (2001)
GNI (US$) 97.6 billion (2002 est)
GNI PER CAPITA (PPP) (US$) 3,710 (2002 est)
CONSUMER PRICE INFLATION 3% (2003 est)
UNEMPLOYMENT 12% (2001)
FOREIGN DEBT (US$) 29.8 billion (2001 est)

MAJOR TRADING PARTNERS EU, USA, Turkey, Japan
RESOURCES petroleum, natural gas, phosphates, manganese, uranium, coal, iron ore, gold
INDUSTRIES petroleum and petroleum products, food processing, petroleum refining, textiles, metals, cement, tobacco, sugar crystal and refined sugar, electrical appliances, fertilizers
EXPORTS petroleum and petroleum products, cotton, textiles, clothing, food, live animals. Principal market: USA 14.4% (2001)
IMPORTS wheat, maize, dairy products, machinery and transport equipment, wood and wood products, consumer goods. Principal source: USA 19.2% (2001)
ARABLE LAND 2.8% (2000 est)
AGRICULTURAL PRODUCTS wheat, cotton, rice, corn, beans, fruit and vegetables; dairy products

Population and society

POPULATION 71,931,000 (2003 est)
POPULATION GROWTH RATE 1.6% (2000–15)

POPULATION DENSITY (per sq km) 72 (2003 est)
URBAN POPULATION (% of total) 43 (2003 est)
AGE DISTRIBUTION (% of total population) 0–14 34%, 15–59 60%, 60+ 6% (2002 est)
ETHNIC GROUPS 99% Eastern Hamitic stock (Egyptians, Bedouins, and Berbers)
LANGUAGE Arabic (official), Coptic (derived from ancient Egyptian), English, French
RELIGION Sunni Muslim 90%, Coptic Christian and other Christian 6%
EDUCATION (compulsory years) 5
LITERACY RATE 68% (men); 47% (women) (2003 est)
LABOUR FORCE 29.8% agriculture, 22.3% industry, 47.9% services (1998)
LIFE EXPECTANCY 67 (men); 71 (women) (2000–05)
CHILD MORTALITY RATE (under 5, per 1,000 live births) 41 (2001)
PHYSICIANS (per 1,000 people) 2 (1996 est)
HOSPITAL BEDS (per 1,000 people) 2.1 (1998 est)
TV SETS (per 1,000 people) 217 (2001 est)
RADIOS (per 1,000 people) 349 (2001 est)
INTERNET USERS (per 10,000 people) 228.5 (2002 est)
PERSONAL COMPUTER USERS (per 100 people) 1.7 (2002 est)

See also ▷Arab–Israeli conflict; ▷Camp David Agreements; ▷Egypt, ancient; ▷Suez Canal.

Chronology

1st century BC–7th century AD: Conquered by Augustus in AD 30, Egypt passed under rule of Roman, and later Byzantine, governors.
AD 639–42: Arabs conquered Egypt, introducing Islam and Arabic; succession of Arab dynasties followed.
1250: Mamelukes seized power.
1517: Became part of Turkish Ottoman Empire.
1798–1801: Invasion by Napoleon followed by period of French occupation.
1801: Control regained by Turks.
1869: Opening of Suez Canal made Egypt strategically important.
1881–82: Nationalist revolt resulted in British occupation.
1914: Egypt became a British protectorate.
1922: Achieved nominal independence under King Fuad I.
1936: Full independence from Britain achieved. King Fuad succeeded by his son Farouk.
1946: Withdrawal of British troops except from Suez Canal zone.
1952: Farouk overthrown by army in bloodless coup.
1953: Egypt declared a republic, with Gen Neguib as president.
1956: Neguib replaced by Col Gamal Nasser. Nasser announced nationalization of Suez Canal; Egypt attacked by Britain, France, and Israel. Ceasefire agreed following US intervention.
1958: Short-lived merger of Egypt and Syria as United Arab Republic (UAR).
1967: Six-Day War with Israel ended in Egypt's defeat and Israeli occupation of Sinai and Gaza Strip.

1970: Nasser died suddenly; succeeded by Anwar Sadat.
1973: An attempt to regain territory lost to Israel led to the Yom Kippur War; ceasefire arranged by US secretary of state Henry Kissinger.
1978–79: Camp David talks in USA resulted in a peace treaty between Egypt and Israel. Egypt expelled from Arab League.
1981: Sadat was assassinated by Muslim fundamentalists and succeeded by Hosni Mubarak.
1983: Relations between Egypt and the Arab world improved; only Libya and Syria maintained a trade boycott.
1987: Egypt was readmitted to the Arab League.
1989: Relations with Libya improved; diplomatic relations with Syria were restored.
1991: Egypt participated in the Gulf War on the US-led side and was a major force in convening a Middle East peace conference in Spain.
1994: The government cracked down on Islamic militants.
1997: Islamic extremists killed and injured tourists at Luxor.
1999: President Mubarak was awarded a fourth term as president, and Atef Obeid was appointed as prime minister.
2000: At least 20 people were killed in clashes in southern Egypt in the worst violence in living memory to occur between Christians and Muslims in Egypt. In parliamentary elections, opposition parties did much better than usual and the banned Muslim Brotherhood won 17 seats, re-establishing their presence in parliament for the first time in a decade.

EGYPT Image of the temple of Kom Ombo, Egypt. Kom Ombo is one of the important Mesolithic sites which have been extensively explored. *Archive Photos*

ANCIENT EGYPTIAN ART A wooden sculpture of Queen Ahmose Merit-Amon, wife of Amenophis I (18th dynasty), from Deir el-Bahari (Cairo Museum, Egypt). *The Art Archives/Museo de Arte Antiga Lisbon*

El Giza, about 2530 BC. A gigantic lion figure with a human head, the sphinx is carved from an outcrop of natural rock, 56.4 m/185 ft long and 19.2 m/63 ft high, and guards the path to the pyramid of Khafre. A rich collection of grave goods survive from the period, including clothes, ornaments, jewellery, and weapons, as well as statues in stone and precious metals. The stylistic conventions of painting – such as showing the human figure with head, legs, and feet in profile, the eyes and shoulders frontally – are established. Vivid wall paintings, such as *Geese of Medum* (National Museum, Cairo) about 2530, show a variety of scenes from the life of the time.

Middle Kingdom (2040–1640 BC), a period when Egypt was reunited under one ruler, is typified by tombs hewn from rock, attempts at realism in frescoes, and deepened perception in portrait sculpture, for example the head of Sesostris III (National Museum, Cairo). Typical of the period are sculptures of figures wrapped in mantles, with only head, hands, and feet showing.

New Kingdom (1550–1070 BC) is represented by a softer and more refined style of painting and a new sophistication in jewellery and furnishings. The golden age of the 18th dynasty, 1550–1070 BC, saw the building of the temples of Karnak and Luxor and the maze of tombs in the Valley of the Kings. The pharaohs of the period, Akhenaton and Tutankhamen, inspired a most extravagant style, as exemplified in the carved images of these godlike creatures, the statues of Akhenaton, the golden coffins of Tutankhamen's mummified body (National Museum, Cairo) about 1361–1352 BC, and the head of Akhenaton's queen, Nefertiti (Museo Archaeologico, Florence) about 1360 BC. The monumental statues of Ramses II in Abu Simbel date from the 13th century BC.

Egyptian religion system of ancient Egyptian beliefs and practices, originating in the worship of totemic animals, representing the ancestors of the clan, and later superimposed with the abstract theology of a priestly caste, who retained suitable totems as the symbols or masks of gods with complex attributes. The main cult was that of ▷Osiris, god of the underworld. Immortality, conferred by the magical rite of mummification, was originally the sole prerogative of the king, but was extended under the New Kingdom to all who could afford it; they were buried with the ▷*Book of the Dead*.

Egyptology the study of ancient Egypt. Interest in the subject was aroused by the Napoleonic expedition's discovery of the ▷Rosetta Stone in 1799. Various excavations continued throughout the 19th century and gradually assumed a more scientific character, largely as a result of the work of the British archaeologist Flinders ▷Petrie from 1880 onwards and the formation of the Egyptian Exploration Fund in 1882. In 1922 another British archaeologist, Howard Carter, discovered the tomb of Tutankhamen, the only royal tomb with all its treasures intact.

Ehrlich, Paul (1854–1915) German bacteriologist and immunologist who was awarded a Nobel Prize for Physiology or Medicine in 1908 with Ilya Mechnikov for their work on immunity. He produced the first cure for ▷syphilis, developing the arsenic compounds, in particular Salvarsan, that were used in the treatment of syphilis before the discovery of antibiotics.

Ehrlich founded ▷chemotherapy – the use of a chemical substance to destroy disease organisms in the body. He was also one of the earliest workers on immunology, and through his studies on blood samples the discipline of haematology was recognized.

Eichmann, (Karl) Adolf (1906–1962) Austrian Nazi. As an ▷SS official during Hitler's regime 1933–45, he was responsible for atrocities against Jews and others, including the implementation of genocide. He managed to escape at the fall of Germany in 1945, but was discovered in Argentina in 1960, abducted by Israeli agents, tried in Israel in 1961 for ▷war crimes, and executed.

eider large marine ▷duck of the genus *Somateria*, family Anatidae, order Anseriformes. They are found on the northern coasts of the Atlantic and Pacific oceans. The **common eider** *S. molissima* is highly valued for its soft down, which is used in quilts and cushions for warmth. The adult male has a black cap and belly and a green nape. The rest of the plumage is white with a pink breast and throat, while the female is a mottled brown. The bill is large and flattened and both bill and feet are olive green.

EIDER Eider ducks are robustly built sea ducks that dive in shallow waters to feed on shellfish and even crabs.

Eid ul-Adha Muslim festival that takes place during the *hajj*, or pilgrimage to Mecca, and commemorates Abraham's willingness to sacrifice his son ▷Ishmael at the command of Allah.

Eid ul-Fitr Muslim festival celebrating the end of Ramadan, the month of fasting.

Eiffel, (Alexandre) Gustave (1832–1923) French engineer who constructed the **Eiffel Tower** for the 1889 Paris Exhibition. The tower, made of iron, is 320 m/1,050 ft high and stands in the Champ de Mars, Paris. Sightseers may ride to the top for a view.

Related Web site: Tour Eiffel http://www.paris.org/Monuments/Eiffel/

Einstein, Albert (1879–1955) German-born US physicist whose theories of ▷relativity revolutionized our understanding of matter, space, and time. Einstein established that light may have a particle nature. He was awarded the Nobel Prize for Physics in 1921 for his work on theoretical physics, especially the **photoelectric law**. He also investigated Brownian motion, confirming the existence of atoms. His last conception of the basic laws governing the universe was outlined in his ▷unified field theory, made public in 1953.

Brownian motion Einstein's first major achievement concerned ▷Brownian movement, the random movement of fine particles that can be seen through a microscope, which was first observed in 1827 by Robert ▷Brown when studying a suspension of pollen grains in water. The motion of the pollen grains increased when the temperature increased but decreased if larger particles were used. Einstein explained this phenomenon as being the effect of large numbers of molecules (in this case, water molecules) bombarding the particles. He was able to make predictions of the movement and sizes of the particles, which were later verified experimentally by the French physicist Jean Perrin. Einstein's explanation of Brownian motion and its subsequent experimental confirmation was one of the most important pieces of evidence for the hypothesis that matter is composed of atoms. Experiments based on this work were used to obtain an accurate value of ▷Avogadro's number (the number of atoms in one mole of a substance) and the first accurate values of atomic size.

The photoelectric effect and the Nobel prize Einstein's work on photoelectricity began with an explanation of the radiation law proposed in 1901 by Max ▷Planck:

$$E = h\nu,$$

where E is the energy of radiation, h is ▷Planck's constant, and ν is the frequency of radiation. Einstein suggested that packets of light energy are capable of behaving as particles called 'light quanta' (later called ▷photons). Einstein used this hypothesis to explain the ▷photoelectric effect, proposing that light particles striking the surface of certain metals cause electrons to be emitted. It had been found experimentally that electrons are not emitted by light of less than a certain frequency ν^0; that when electrons are emitted, their energy increases with an increase in the frequency of the light; and that an increase in light intensity produces more electrons but does not increase their energy. Einstein suggested that the kinetic energy of each electron, $\frac{1}{2}mv^2$, is equal to the difference in the incident light energy, $h\nu$, and the light energy needed to overcome the threshold of emission, $h\nu^0$. This can be written mathematically as:

$$\tfrac{1}{2}mv^2 = h\nu - h\nu^0$$

The speed of light and the special theory of relativity The special theory of relativity started with the premises that (1) the laws of nature are the same for all observers in unaccelerated motion, and (2) the speed of light is independent of the motion of its source. Until then, there had been a steady accumulation of knowledge that suggested that light and other electromagnetic radiation does not behave as predicted by classical physics. For example, various experiments, including the ▷**Michelson**–Morley experiment, failed to measure the expected changes in the speed of light relative to the motion of the Earth. Such experiments are now interpreted as showing that no 'ether' exists in the universe as a medium to carry light waves, as was required by classical physics. Einstein recognized that light has a measured speed that is independent of the speed of the observer. Thus, contrary to everyday experience with phenomena such as sound waves, the velocity of light is the same for an observer travelling at high speed *towards* a light source as it is for an observer travelling rapidly *away* from the light source. To Einstein it followed that, if the speed of light is the same for both these observers, the time and distance framework they use to

GUSTAVE EIFFEL The wrought-iron Eiffel Tower in Paris, France, pictured here during the 1889 World Fair, was designed by Gustave Eiffel. Intended to be dismantled after the fair, the tower has become a landmark and is used for radio and television transmissions. *Archive Photos*

measure the speed of light cannot be the same. Time and distance vary, depending on the velocity of each observer. From the notions of relative motion and the constant velocity of light, Einstein derived the result that, in a system in motion relative to an observer, length would be observed to decrease, time would slow down, and mass would increase. The magnitude of these effects is negligible at ordinary velocities and Newton's laws still hold good. But at velocities approaching that of light, they become substantial. As a system approaches the velocity of light, relative to an observer at rest, its length decreases towards zero, time slows almost to a stop, and its mass increases without limit. Einstein therefore concluded that no system can be accelerated to a velocity equal to or greater than the velocity of light. Einstein's conclusions regarding time dilation and mass increase were verified with observations of fast-moving atomic clocks and cosmic rays. Einstein showed in 1907 that mass is related to energy by the famous equation

$$E = mc^2$$

which indicates the enormous amount of energy that is stored as mass, some of which is released in radioactivity and nuclear reactions, for example in the Sun.

Gravity and the general theory of relativity In the **general theory of relativity** (1916), the properties of space–time were to be conceived as modified locally by the presence of a body with mass; and light rays should bend when they pass by a massive object. A planet's orbit around the Sun arises from its natural trajectory in modified space–time. General relativity theory was inspired by the simple idea that it is impossible in a small region to distinguish between acceleration and gravitation effects (as in a lift one feels heavier when it accelerates upwards). Einstein used the general theory to account for an anomaly in the orbit of the planet Mercury that could not be explained by Newtonian mechanics. Furthermore, the general theory made two predictions concerning light and gravitation. The first was that a red shift is produced if light passes through an intense gravitational field, and this was subsequently detected in astronomical observations in 1925. The second was a prediction that the apparent positions of stars would shift when they are seen near the Sun because the Sun's intense gravity would bend the light rays from the stars as they pass the Sun. Einstein was triumphantly vindicated when observations of a solar eclipse in 1919 showed apparent shifts of exactly the amount he had predicted.

   Related Web site: Life and Theories of Albert Einstein
http://www.pbs.org/wgbh/nova/einstein/index.html

ALBERT EINSTEIN A blackboard with physicist Albert Einstein's theories written in his own handwriting, in the 1920s. *Archive Photos*

einsteinium synthesized, radioactive, metallic element of the actinide series, symbol Es, atomic number 99, relative atomic mass 254.09.

   It was produced by the first thermonuclear explosion, in 1952, and discovered in fallout debris in the form of the isotope Es-253 (half-life 20 days). Its longest-lived isotope, Es-254, with a half-life of 276 days, allowed the element to be studied at length. It is now synthesized by bombarding lower-numbered ▷transuranic elements in particle accelerators. It was first identified by A Ghiorso and his team who named it in 1955 after Albert Einstein, in honour of his theoretical studies of mass and energy.

Eire name of southern Ireland as prescribed in the 1937 Constitution.

Eisenhower, Dwight David ('Ike') (1890–1969) 34th president of the USA 1953–60, a Republican. A general in World War II, he commanded the Allied forces in Italy in 1943, then the Allied invasion of Europe, and from October 1944 all the Allied armies in the West. As president he promoted business interests at

home and conducted the ▷Cold War abroad. His vice-president was Richard Nixon.

   Eisenhower was born at Denison, Texas. A graduate of West Point military academy in 1915, he served in a variety of staff and command posts before World War II. He became commander-in-chief of the US and British forces for the invasion of North Africa in November 1942, commanded the Allied invasion of Sicily in July 1943, and announced the surrender of Italy on 8 September 1943. In December he became commander of the Allied Expeditionary Force for the invasion of Europe and was promoted to General of the Army in December 1944. After the war he served as commander of the US Occupation Forces in Germany, then returned to the USA to become Chief of Staff. He served as president of Columbia University and chair of the joint Chiefs of Staff 1949–50. Eisenhower became supreme commander of the Allied Powers in Europe in 1950, and organized the defence forces in the North Atlantic Treaty Organization (NATO). He resigned from the army in 1952 to campaign for the presidency; he was elected, and re-elected by a wide margin in 1956.

   A popular politician, Eisenhower held office during a period of domestic and international tension, although the USA was experiencing an era of post-war prosperity and growth. Major problems during his administration included the ending of the ▷Korean War, the growing civil-rights movement at home, and the ▷Cold War. His proposals on disarmament and the control of nuclear weapons led to the first International Conference on the Peaceful Uses of Atomic Energy, held under the auspices of the United Nations at Geneva in 1955.

DWIGHT EISENHOWER The future US president Dwight Eisenhower as general and Allied commander during World War II, with paratroopers in England, bound for the first assault on the European continent, June 1944. *Archive Photos*

Eisenman, Peter (1932–) US architect. He came to prominence as a member of the New York Five group, along with Richard Meier and Michael Graves. His work draws on mathematics and philosophy, especially Deconstructionism. Early experiments in complexity, such as House X (1978), led to increasingly scrambled designs, for example, Fin d'Ou T Hou S (1983).

Eisenstein, Sergei Mikhailovich (1898–1948) Latvian-born Soviet film director. One of the giants of the film medium, whose ▷*Battleship Potemkin* (1925) remains a landmark achievement in the history of world cinema. An intellectual, he wrote extensively on the subject of film theory, and helped pioneer the concept of montage (the juxtaposition of shots to create a particular effect) as a means of propaganda. His other films include *Strike* (1925), *October* (1928), and *Alexander Nevsky* (1938).

   Related Web site: Eisenstein, Sergei M http://us.imdb.com/M/person-all?Eisenstein%2C+Sergei+M%2E

eisteddfod (Welsh 'sitting') traditional Welsh gathering lasting up to a week and dedicated to the encouragement of the bardic arts of music, poetry, and literature. The custom dates from pre-Christian times.

Ekman spiral effect in oceanography, theoretical description of a consequence of the ▷Coriolis effect on ocean currents, whereby currents flow at an angle to the winds that drive them. It derives its name from the Swedish oceanographer Vagn Ekman (1874–1954).

El Aaiún Arabic name of ▷Laâyoune.

ELAND A herd of eland, *Tragelaphus Taurotragus oryx*, grazes in a nature reserve on the high veld grasslands of South Africa. *Premaphotos Wildlife*

eland largest species of ▷antelope, *Taurotragus oryx*. Pale fawn in colour, it is about 2 m/6 ft high, and both sexes have spiral horns about 45 cm/18 in long. It is found in central and southern Africa.

Elasmobranchii subclass of class Chondrichthyes (cartilaginous fish), which includes the ▷sharks and rays. They are characterized by having five to seven pairs of gill clefts that open separately to the exterior and are not covered by a protective fold of skin.

elasticity in physics, the ability of a solid to recover its shape once deforming forces (stresses modifying its dimensions or shape) are removed. An elastic material obeys ▷Hooke's law, which states that its deformation is proportional to the applied stress up to a certain point, called the **elastic limit**, beyond which additional stress will deform it permanently. Elastic materials include metals and rubber; however, all materials have some degree of elasticity.

E layer (formerly **Kennelly–Heaviside layer**) the lower regions (90–120 km/56–75 mi) of the ▷ionosphere, which reflect radio waves, allowing their reception around the surface of the Earth. The E layer approaches the Earth by day and recedes from it at night.

Elba (Greek **Aethalia**; Roman **Ilva**) island in the Mediterranean Sea, 10 km/6 mi off the west coast of Italy; area 223 sq km/86 sq mi; population (1981) 35,000. Iron ore is exported from the island's capital, Portoferraio, to the Italian mainland. There is a fishing industry, olives are grown, and tourism is important. Elba was Napoleon's place of exile (1814–15).

Elbe (Czech **Labe**; ancient **Albis**) one of the principal rivers of Germany; length 1,166 km/725 mi. It rises on the southern slopes of the Riesengebirge, Czech Republic, and flows northwest across the German plain to the North Sea. It is navigable for ocean-going vessels as far as Hamburg (101 km/62 mi from the mouth), and for smaller boats as far as its junction with the Vltava (845 km/525 mi). The river basin is approximately 145,039 sq km/56,000 sq mi.

SERGEI EISENSTEIN Latvian-born Soviet film director. *Archive Photos*

Elbrus (or Elbruz; Persian 'two heads') highest peak in Europe; located in the Caucasus Mountains, Caucasia, in the Russian Federation. Its western summit reaches a height of 5,642 m/ 18,510 ft, while the eastern summit stands at 5,595 m/18,356 ft.

elder in botany, any of a group of small trees or shrubs belonging to the honeysuckle family, native to North America, Europe, Asia, and North Africa. Some are grown as ornamentals for their showy yellow or white flower clusters and their colourful black or scarlet berries. (Genus *Sambucus*, family Caprifoliaceae.)

> **Related Web site: Elder** http://www.botanical.com/botanical/mgmh/e/elder-04.html

elder in the Presbyterian church, a lay member who assists the minister (or teaching elder) in running the church.

El Dorado fabled city of gold believed by the 16th-century Spanish and other Europeans to exist somewhere in the area of the Orinoco and Amazon rivers.

Eleanor of Aquitaine (*c.* 1122–1204) Queen of France 1137–51 as wife of Louis VII, and of England from 1154 as wife of ▷Henry II. Henry imprisoned her 1174–89 for supporting their sons, the future Richard I and King John, in revolt against him.

Eleanor of Castile (*c.* 1245–1290) Queen of Edward I of England, the daughter of Ferdinand III of Castile. She married Prince Edward in 1254, and accompanied him on his crusade in 1270. She died at Harby, Nottinghamshire, and Edward erected stone crosses in towns where her body rested on the funeral journey to London. Several **Eleanor Crosses** are still standing, for example, at Northampton.

election process of appointing a person to public office or a political party to government by voting. Elections were occasionally held in ancient Greek democracies; Roman tribunes were regularly elected.

elector (German *Kurfürst*) any of originally seven (later ten) princes of the Holy Roman Empire who had the prerogative of electing the emperor (in effect, the king of Germany). The electors were the archbishops of Mainz, Trier, and Cologne, the court palatine of the Rhine, the Duke of Saxony, the Margrave of Brandenburg, and the king of Bohemia (in force to 1806). Their constitutional status was formalized in 1356 in the document known as the **Golden Bull**, which granted them extensive powers within their own domains, to act as judges, issue coins, and impose tolls.

electoral college in the US government, the indirect system of voting for the president and vice-president. The people of each state officially vote not for the presidential candidate, but for a list of electors nominated by each party. The whole electoral-college vote of the state then goes to the winning party (and candidate). A majority is required for election.

electoral system see ▷vote and ▷proportional representation.

electric arc a continuous electric discharge of high current between two electrodes, giving out a brilliant light and heat. The phenomenon is exploited in the carbon-arc lamp, once widely used in film projectors. In the electric-arc furnace an arc struck between very large carbon electrodes and the metal charge provides the heating. In arc ▷welding an electric arc provides the heat to fuse the metal. The discharges in low-pressure gases, as in neon and sodium lights, can also be broadly considered as electric arcs.

electric charge property of some bodies that causes them to exert forces on each other. Two bodies both with positive or both with negative charges repel each other, whereas bodies with opposite or 'unlike' charges attract each other. ▷Electrons possess a negative charge, and ▷protons an equal positive charge. The ▷SI unit of electric charge is the coulomb (symbol C).

A body can be charged by friction, induction, or chemical change and shows itself as an accumulation of electrons (negative charge) or loss of electrons (positive charge) on an atom or body. Atoms generally have zero net charge but can gain electrons to become negative ions or lose them to become positive ions. So-called ▷static electricity, seen in such phenomena as the charging of nylon shirts when they are pulled on or off, or in brushing hair, is in fact the gain or loss of electrons from the surface atoms. A flow of charge (such as electrons through a copper wire) constitutes an electric current; the flow of current is measured in amperes (symbol A).

> **Related Web site: Static Electricity** http://www.sciencemadesimple.com/static.html

electric current the flow of electrically charged particles through a conducting circuit due to the presence of a ▷potential difference. The current at any point in a circuit is the amount of charge flowing per second; its SI unit is the ampere (coulomb per second).

Current carries electrical energy from a power supply, such as a battery of electrical cells, to the components of the circuit, where it is converted into other forms of energy, such as heat, light, or motion. It may be either ▷direct current or ▷alternating current.

Heating effect When current flows in a component possessing resistance, electrical energy is converted into heat energy. If the resistance of the component is R ohms and the current through it is I amperes, then the heat energy W (in joules) generated in a time t seconds is given by the formula:

$$W = I^2 Rt.$$

Magnetic effect A magnetic field is created around all conductors that carry a current. When a current-bearing conductor is made into a coil it forms an ▷electromagnet with a ▷magnetic field that is similar to that of a bar magnet, but which disappears as soon as the current is switched off. The strength of the magnetic field is directly proportional to the current in the conductor – a property that allows a small electromagnet to be used to produce a pattern of magnetism on recording tape that accurately represents the sound or data stored. The direction of the field created around a conducting wire may be predicted by using ▷Maxwell's screw rule.

Motor effect A conductor carrying current in a magnetic field experiences a force, and is impelled to move in a direction perpendicular to both the direction of the current and the direction of the magnetic field. The direction of motion may be predicted by Fleming's left-hand rule (see ▷Fleming's rules). The magnitude of the force experienced depends on the length of the conductor and on the strengths of the current and the magnetic field, and is greatest when the conductor is at right angles to the field. A conductor wound into a coil that can rotate between the poles of a magnet forms the basis of an ▷electric motor.

electric eel South American freshwater bony fish. It grows to almost 3 m/10 ft and the electric shock produced, normally for immobilizing prey, is enough to stun an adult human. Electric eels are not true eels.

Classification *Electrophorus electricus* is in the order Cypriniformes, class Osteichthyes.

electric field in physics, a region in which a particle possessing electric charge experiences a force owing to the presence of another electric charge. The strength of an electric field, E, is measured in volts per metre (V m⁻¹). It is a type of ▷electromagnetic field.

electric fish any of several unrelated fishes that have electricity-producing powers, including the South American 'electric eel'. These include *Electrophorus electricus*, which is not a true eel, and in which the lateral tail muscles are modified to form electric organs capable of generating 650 volts; the current passing from tail to head is strong enough to stun another animal. Not all electric fishes produce such strong discharges; most use weak electric fields to navigate and to detect nearby objects.

electricity all phenomena caused by ▷electric charge, whether static or in motion. Electric charge is caused by an excess or deficit of electrons in the charged substance, and an electric current is the movement of charge through a material. Substances may be electrical conductors, such as metals, that allow the passage of electricity through them readily, or insulators, such as rubber, that are extremely poor conductors. Substances with relatively poor conductivities that increase with a rise in temperature or when light falls on the material, are known as ▷semiconductors.

Electrical properties of solids The first artificial electrical phenomenon to be observed was that some naturally occurring materials such as amber, when rubbed with a piece of cloth, would then attract small objects such as dust and pieces of paper. Rubbing the object caused it to become electrically charged so that it had an excess or deficit of electrons. When the amber is rubbed with a piece of cloth electrons are transferred from the cloth to the amber so that the amber has an excess of electrons and is negatively charged, and the cloth has a deficit of electrons and is positively charged. This accumulation of charge is called ▷static electricity. This charge on the object exerts an electric field in the space around itself that can attract or repel other objects. It was discovered that there are only two types of charge, positive and negative, and that they neutralize one another. Objects with a like charge always repel one another while objects with an unlike charge attract each other. Neutral objects (such as pieces of paper) can be attracted to charged bodies by electrical induction. For example, the charge on a negatively charged body causes a separation of charge across the neutral body. The positive charges tend to move towards the side near the negatively charged body and the negative charges tend to move towards the opposite side so that the neutral body is weakly attracted to the charged body by ▷induction. The ▷electroscope is a device used to demonstrate the presence of electric charges and

to measure its size and whether it is positive or negative. The electroscope was invented by Michael ▷Faraday.

Current, charge, and energy An ▷electric current in a material is the passage of charge through it. In metals and other conducting materials, the charge is carried by free electrons that are not bound tightly to the atoms and are thus able to move through the material. For charge to flow in a circuit there must be a ▷potential difference (pd) applied across the circuit. This is often supplied in the form of a battery that has a positive terminal and a negative terminal. Under the influence of the potential difference, the electrons are repelled from the negative terminal side of the circuit and attracted to the positive terminal of the battery. A steady flow of electrons around the circuit is produced. Current flowing through a circuit can be measured using an ▷ammeter and is measured in ▷amperes (or amps). A ▷coulomb (C) is the unit of charge, defined as the charge passing a point in a wire each second when the current is exactly 1 amp. The unit of charge is named after Charles Augustin de Coulomb; ▷direct current (DC) flows continuously in one direction; ▷alternating current (AC) flows alternately in each direction. In a circuit the battery provides energy to make charge flow through the circuit. The amount of energy supplied to each unit of charge is called the electromotive force (emf). The unit of emf is the ▷volt (V). A battery has an emf of 1 volt when it supplies 1 joule of energy to each coulomb of charge flowing through it. The energy carried by flowing charges can be used to do work, for example to light a bulb, to cause current to flow through a resistor, to emit radiation, or to produce heat. When the energy carried by a current is made to do work in this way, a potential difference can be measured across the circuit component concerned by a voltmeter or a ▷cathode-ray oscilloscope. The potential difference is also measured in volts. Power, measured in ▷watts, is the product of current and voltage. Potential difference and current measure are related to one another. This relationship was discovered by Georg ▷Ohm, and is expressed by ▷Ohm's law: the current through a wire is proportional to the potential difference across its ends. The potential difference divided by the current is a constant for a given piece of wire. This constant for a given material is called the ▷resistance.

Conduction in liquids and gases In liquids, current can flow by the movement of charged ions through a solution or molten salt (the electrolyte), resulting in the migration of ions to the electrodes: positive ions (cations) to the negative electrode (cathode) and negative ions (anions) to the positive electrode (anode). This process is called ▷electrolysis and represents bi-directional flow of charge as opposite charges move to oppositely charged electrodes. In metals, charges are only carried by free electrons and therefore move in only one direction.

Electromagnetism ▷Magnetic fields are produced either by current-carrying conductors or by permanent magnets. In current-carrying wires, the magnetic field lines are concentric circles around the wire. Their direction depends on the direction of the current and their strength on the size of the current. If a conducting wire is moved within a magnetic field, the magnetic field acts on the free electrons within the conductor, displacing them and causing a current to flow. The force acting on the electrons and causing them to move is greatest when the wire is perpendicular to the magnetic field lines. The direction of the current is given by the left-hand rule. The generation of a current by the relative movement of a conductor in a magnetic field is called ▷electromagnetic induction. This is the basis of how a ▷dynamo works.

Generation of electricity Electricity is the most useful and most convenient form of energy, readily convertible into heat and light and used to power machines. Electricity can be generated in one place and distributed anywhere because it readily flows through wires. It is generated at power stations where a suitable energy source is harnessed to drive ▷turbines that spin electricity generators. Current energy sources are coal, oil, water power (hydroelectricity), natural gas, and ▷nuclear energy. Research is under way to increase the contribution of wind, tidal, solar, and geothermal power. Nuclear fuel has proved a more expensive source of electricity than initially anticipated and worldwide concern over radioactivity may limit its future development. Electricity is generated at power stations at a voltage of about 25,000 volts, which is not a suitable voltage for long-distance transmission. For minimal power loss, transmission must take place at very high voltage (400,000 volts or more). The generated voltage is therefore increased ('stepped up') by a ▷transformer. The resulting high-voltage electricity is then fed into the main arteries of the ▷grid system, an interconnected network of power stations and distribution centres covering a large area. After transmission to a local substation, the line voltage is reduced by a step-down transformer and distributed to consumers. Among specialized power units that convert energy directly to electrical energy without the intervention of any moving mechanisms, the most promising are thermionic converters. These use conventional fuels such as propane gas, as in portable military power packs, or, if refuelling is to be avoided, radioactive fuels, as in uncrewed navigational aids and spacecraft. UK electricity generation was split into four companies in 1990 in preparation for privatization. The nuclear power stations remain in the hands of the state through Nuclear Electric (accounting for 20% of electricity generated); National Power (50%) and PowerGen (30%) generate electricity from fossil-fuel and renewable sources. Transmission lines and substations are owned by the National Grid, which was privatized in 1996. Electricity generated on a commercial scale was available from the early 1880s and used for electric motors driving all kinds of machinery, and for lighting, first by carbon arc, but later by incandescent filaments (first of carbon and then of tungsten), enclosed in glass bulbs partially filled with inert gas under vacuum. Light is also produced by passing electricity through a gas or metal vapour or a fluorescent lamp. Other practical applications include telephone, radio, television, X-ray machines, and many other applications in ▷electronics. An important consideration in the design of electrical equipment is electrical safety. This includes measures to minimize the risk of electric shock or fire caused by electrical faults. Safety measures include the fitting of earth wires, and fuses or circuit breakers, and the insulation of wires.

Related Web site: Electricity and Magnetism http://library. thinkquest.org/12632/magnetism/

electric motor a machine that converts electrical energy into mechanical energy. There are various types, including direct-current and induction motors, most of which produce rotary motion. A linear induction motor produces linear (in a straight line) rather than rotary motion.

A simple **direct-current motor** consists of a horseshoe-shaped permanent ▷magnet with a wire-wound coil (▷armature) mounted so that it can rotate between the poles of the magnet. A ▷commutator reverses the current (from a battery) fed to the coil on each half-turn, which rotates because of the mechanical force exerted on a conductor carrying a current in a magnetic field.

An **induction motor** employs ▷alternating current. It comprises a stationary current-carrying coil (stator) surrounding another coil (rotor), which rotates because of the current induced in it by the magnetic field created by the stator; it thus requires no commutator.

electric ray another name for the ▷torpedo.

electrocardiogram (ECG) graphic recording of the electrical activity of the heart, as detected by electrodes placed on the skin. Electrocardiography is used in the diagnosis of heart disease.

ELECTROCARDIOGRAM One of the first methods for obtaining a read-out of the electrical impulses that cause the heart to 'beat' was electrocardiography. *Image Bank*

electrochemistry the branch of science that studies chemical reactions involving electricity. The use of electricity to produce chemical effects, ▷electrolysis, is employed in many industrial processes, such as the manufacture of chlorine and the extraction of aluminium. The use of chemical reactions to produce electricity is the basis of electrical ▷cells, such as the dry cell and the Leclanché cell.

electroconvulsive therapy (ECT; or **electroshock therapy**) treatment mainly for severe ▷depression, given under anaesthesia and with a muscle relaxant. An electric current is passed through one or both sides of the brain to induce alterations in its electrical activity. The treatment can cause distress and loss of concentration and memory, and so there is much controversy about its use and effectiveness.

electrocution death caused by electric current. It is used as a method of execution in some US states. The condemned person is strapped into a special chair and a shock of 1,800–2,000 volts is administered. See ▷capital punishment.

electrode any terminal by which an electric current passes in or out of a conducting substance; for example, the anode or ▷cathode in a battery or the carbons in an arc lamp. The terminals that emit and collect the flow of electrons in thermionic ▷valves (electron tubes) are also called electrodes: for example, cathodes, plates, and grids.

electrodynamics the branch of physics dealing with electric charges, electric currents and associated forces. ▷Quantum electrodynamics (QED) studies the interaction between charged particles and their emission and absorption of electromagnetic radiation. This subject combines quantum theory and relativity theory, making accurate predictions about subatomic processes involving charged particles such as electrons and protons.

electroencephalogram (EEG) graphic record of the electrical discharges of the brain, as detected by electrodes placed on the scalp. The pattern of electrical activity revealed by electroencephalography is helpful in the diagnosis of some brain disorders, in particular epilepsy.

electrolysis in chemistry, the production of chemical changes by passing an electric current through a solution or molten salt (the electrolyte), resulting in the migration of ions to the electrodes: positive ions (cations) to the negative electrode (cathode) and negative ions (anions) to the positive electrode (anode).

During electrolysis, the ions react with the electrode, either receiving or giving up electrons. The resultant atoms may be liberated as a gas, or deposited as a solid on the electrode, in amounts that are proportional to the amount of current passed, as discovered by English chemist Michael Faraday. For instance, when acidified water is electrolysed, hydrogen ions (H^+) at the cathode receive electrons to form hydrogen gas; hydroxide ions (OH^-) at the anode give up electrons to form oxygen gas and water.

One application of electrolysis is **electroplating**, in which a solution of a salt, such as silver nitrate ($AgNO_3$), is used and the object to be plated acts as the negative electrode, thus attracting silver ions (Ag^+). Electrolysis is used in many industrial processes, such as coating metals for vehicles and ships, and refining bauxite into aluminium; it also forms the basis of a number of electrochemical analytical techniques, such as polarography.

electrolyte solution or molten substance in which an electric current is made to flow by the movement and discharge of ions in accordance with Faraday's laws of ▷electrolysis.

electromagnet coil of wire wound around a soft iron core that acts as a magnet when an electric current flows through the wire. Electromagnets have many uses: in switches, electric bells, ▷solenoids, and metal-lifting cranes.

electromagnetic field in physics, the region in which a particle with an ▷electric charge experiences a force. If it does so only when moving, it is in a pure **magnetic field**; if it does so when stationary, it is in an **electric field**. Both can be present simultaneously.

electromagnetic force one of the four fundamental ▷forces of nature, the other three being the gravitational force or gravity, the weak nuclear force, and the strong nuclear force. The particle that is the carrier for the electromagnetic force is the ▷photon.

electromagnetic induction in electronics, the production of an ▷electromotive force (emf) in a circuit by a change of magnetic flux through the circuit or by relative motion of the circuit and the magnetic flux. In a closed circuit an ▷induced current will be produced. All dynamos and generators make use of this effect. When magnetic tape is driven past the playback head (a small coil) of a tape-recorder, the moving magnetic field induces an emf in the head, which is then amplified to reproduce the recorded sounds.

electromagnetic spectrum the complete range, over all wavelengths and frequencies, of ▷electromagnetic waves. These include radio and television waves, infrared radiation, visible light, ultraviolet light, X-rays, and gamma radiation.

electromagnetic waves oscillating electric and magnetic fields travelling together through space at a speed of nearly 300,000 km/186,000 mi per second. The (limitless) range of possible wavelengths and ▷frequencies of electromagnetic waves, which can be thought of as making up the **electromagnetic spectrum**, includes radio waves, infrared radiation, visible light, ultraviolet radiation, X-rays, and gamma rays.

Radio and television waves lie at the **long wavelength–low frequency** end of the spectrum, with wavelengths longer than 10^{-4} m. Infrared radiation has wavelengths between 10^{-4} m and 7×10^{-7} m. Visible light has yet shorter wavelengths from 7×10^{-7} m to 4×10^{-7} m. Ultraviolet radiation is near the **short wavelength–high frequency** end of the spectrum, with wavelengths between 4×10^{-7} m and 10^{-8} m. X-rays have wavelengths from 10^{-8} m to 10^{-12} m. Gamma radiation has the shortest wavelengths of less than 10^{-10} m. The different wavelengths and frequencies lend specific properties to electromagnetic waves. While visible light is diffracted by a diffraction grating, X-rays can only be diffracted by crystals. Radio waves are refracted by the atmosphere; visible light is refracted by glass or water.

electromotive force (emf) loosely, the voltage produced by an electric battery or generator in an electrical circuit or, more precisely, the energy supplied by a source of electric power in driving a unit charge around the circuit. The unit is the ▷volt.

electron stable, negatively charged ▷elementary particle; it is a constituent of all atoms, and a member of the class of particles known as ▷leptons. The electrons in each atom surround the nucleus in groupings called shells; in a neutral atom the number of electrons is equal to the number of protons in the nucleus. This electron structure is responsible for the chemical properties of the atom (see ▷atomic structure).

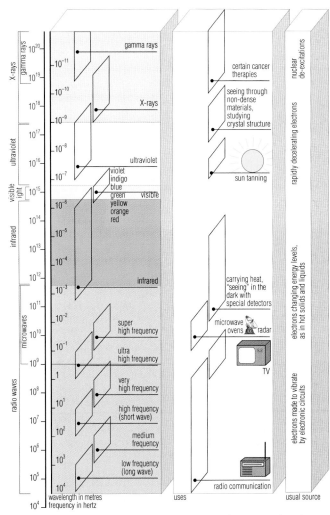

ELECTROMAGNETIC WAVES Radio waves have the lowest frequency. Infrared radiation, visible light, ultraviolet radiation, X-rays, and gamma rays have progressively higher frequencies.

Electrons carry a charge of 1.602177×10^{-19} coulomb and have a mass of 9.109×10^{-31} kg, which is $\frac{1}{1836}$ times the mass of a ▷proton. A beam of electrons will undergo ▷diffraction (scattering) and produce interference patterns in the same way as ▷electromagnetic waves such as light; hence they may be regarded as waves as well as particles.

Related Web site: Look Inside the Atom http://www.aip.org/history/electron/jjhome.htm

electronegativity the ease with which an atom can attract electrons to itself. Electronegative elements attract electrons, so forming negative ions.

electron gun a part in many electronic devices consisting of a series of ▷electrodes, including a cathode for producing an electron beam. It plays an essential role in ▷cathode-ray tubes (television tubes) and ▷electron microscopes.

electronic mail (or e-mail) messages sent electronically from computer to computer via network connections such as Ethernet or the ▷Internet, or via telephone lines to a host system. Messages once sent are stored on the network or by the host system until the recipient picks them up. As well as text, messages may contain enclosed text files, artwork, or multimedia clips.

Subscribers to an electronic mail system type messages in ordinary letter form on a word processor, or microcomputer, and 'drop' the letters into a central computer's memory bank by means of a computer/telephone connector (a ▷modem). The recipient 'collects' the letter by calling up the central computer and feeding a unique password into the system. Due to the high speed of delivery electronic mail is cheaper than an equivalent telephone call or fax.

Related Web site: E-mail: An Introduction http://www.webfoot.com/advice/email.top.html

electronic music music composed mainly of electronically generated and modified sounds. The term was first used in 1954 to describe music made up of synthesized sounds recorded on tape, to distinguish it from ▷musique concrète ('concrete music'), but later included music for electronic sounds with traditional instruments or voices.

Related Web site: Brief History of Electronic Music Instruments http://www.ief.u-psud.fr/~thierry/history/history.html

electronic point of sale (EPOS) system used in retailing in which a bar code on a product is scanned at the cash till and the information relayed to the store computer. The computer will then relay back the price of the item to the cash till. The customer can then be given an itemized receipt while the computer removes the item from stock figures.

electronic publishing distribution of information using computer-based media such as ▷multimedia and ▷hypertext in the creation of electronic 'books'. Critical technologies in the development of electronic publishing were ▷CD-ROM, with its massive yet compact storage capabilities, and the advent of computer networking with its ability to deliver information instantaneously anywhere in the world.

electronics branch of science that deals with the emission of ▷electrons from conductors and ▷semiconductors, with the subsequent manipulation of these electrons, and with the construction of electronic devices. The first electronic device was the thermionic valve, or vacuum tube, in which electrons moved in a vacuum, and led to such inventions as ▷radio, ▷television, ▷radar, and the digital ▷computer. Replacement of valves with the comparatively tiny and reliable ▷transistor from 1948 revolutionized electronic development. Modern electronic devices are based on minute ▷integrated circuits (silicon chips), wafer-thin crystal slices holding tens of thousands of electronic components.

electronic tagging see ▷tagging, electronic.

electron microscope instrument that produces a magnified image by using a beam of ▷electrons instead of light rays, as in an optical ▷microscope. An **electron lens** is an arrangement of electromagnetic coils that control and focus the beam. Electrons are not visible to the eye, so instead of an eyepiece there is a fluorescent screen or a photographic plate on which the electrons form an image. The wavelength of the electron beam is much shorter than that of light, so much greater magnification and resolution (ability to distinguish detail) can be achieved. The development of the electron microscope has made possible the observation of very minute organisms, viruses, and even large molecules.

electrons, delocalized electrons that are not associated with individual atoms or identifiable chemical bonds, but are shared collectively by all the constituent atoms or ions of some chemical substances (such as metals, graphite, and ▷aromatic compounds).

electrons, localized a pair of electrons in a ▷covalent bond that are located in the vicinity of the nuclei of the two contributing atoms. Such electrons cannot move beyond this area.

electron volt unit (symbol eV) for measuring the energy of a charged particle (▷ion or ▷electron) in terms of the energy of motion an electron would gain from a potential difference of one volt. Because it is so small, more usual units are mega-(million) and giga- (billion) electron volts (MeV and GeV).

electrophoresis the ▷diffusion of charged particles through a fluid under the influence of an electric field. It can be used in the biological sciences to separate ▷molecules of different sizes, which diffuse at different rates. In industry, electrophoresis is used in paint-dipping operations to ensure that paint reaches awkward corners.

electroplating deposition of metals upon metallic surfaces by electrolysis for decorative and/or protective purposes. It is used in the preparation of printers' blocks, 'master' audio discs, and in many other processes.

electropositivity in chemistry, a measure of the ability of elements (mainly metals) to donate electrons to form positive ions. The greater the metallic character, the more electropositive the element.

electroscope apparatus for detecting ▷electric charge. The simple gold-leaf electroscope consists of a vertical conducting (metal) rod ending in a pair of rectangular pieces of gold foil, mounted inside and insulated from an earthed metal case or glass jar. An electric charge applied to the end of the metal rod makes the gold leaves diverge, because they each receive a similar charge (positive or negative) and so repel each other.

electrostatics the study of stationary electric charges and their fields (not currents). See ▷static electricity.

electrovalent bond another name for an ▷ionic bond, a chemical bond in which the combining atoms lose or gain electrons to form ions.

electrum naturally occurring alloy of gold and silver used by early civilizations to make the first coins, about the 6th century BC.

element substance that cannot be split chemically into simpler substances. The atoms of a particular element all have the same number of protons in their nuclei (their ▷atomic number).

Electronics: Key Dates

1897	The electron is discovered by English physicist John Joseph Thomson.
1904	English physicist Ambrose Fleming invents the diode valve, which allows flow of electricity in one direction only.
1906	The triode electron valve, the first device to control an electric current, is invented by US physicist Lee De Forest.
1947	John Bardeen, William Shockley, and Walter Brattain invent the junction germanium transistor at the Bell Laboratories, New Jersey, USA.
1952	British physicist G W A Dunner proposes the integrated circuit.
1953	Jay Forrester of the Massachusetts Institute of Technology, USA, builds a magnetic memory smaller than existing vacuum-tube memories.
1954	The silicon transistor is developed by Gordon Teal of Texas Instruments, USA.
1958	The first integrated circuit, containing five components, is built by US electrical physicist Jack Kilby.
1959	The planar transistor, which is built up in layers, or planes, is designed by Robert Noyce of Fairchild Semiconductor Corporation, USA.
1961	Steven Hofstein designs the field-effect transistor used in integrated circuits.
1971	The first microprocessor, the Intel 4004, is designed by Ted Hoff in the USA; it contains 2,250 components and can add two four-bit numbers in 11-millionths of a second.
1974	The Intel 8080 microprocessor is launched; it contains 4,500 components and can add two eight-bit numbers in 2.5-millionths of a second.
1979	The Motorola 68000 microprocessor is introduced; it contains 70,000 components and can multiply two 16-bit numbers in 3.2-millionths of a second.
1981	The Hewlett-Packard Superchip is introduced; it contains 450,000 components and can multiply two 32-bit numbers in 1.8-millionths of a second.
1985	The Inmos T414 transputer, the first microprocessor designed for use in parallel computers, is launched.
1988	The first optical microprocessor, which uses light instead of electricity, is developed.
1989	Wafer-scale silicon memory chips are introduced: the size of a beer mat, they are able to store 200 million characters.
1990	Memory chips capable of holding 4 million bits of information begin to be mass-produced in Japan. The chips can store the equivalent of 520,000 characters, or the contents of a 16-page newspaper. Each chip contains 9 million components packed on a piece of silicon less than 15 mm long by 5 mm wide.
1992	Transistors made from high-temperature superconducting ceramics rather than semiconductors are produced in Japan by Sanyo Electric. The new transistors are ten times faster than semiconductor transistors.
1993	US firm Intel launches the Pentium 64-bit microprocessor. With two separate integer processing units that can run in parallel, it is several times faster than earlier processors.
1996	Japanese researchers complete a computer able to perform 1.08 billion floating-point operations per second.
1997	The US firm Texas Instruments introduces a digital-signal microprocessor chip that can process 1.6 billion instructions a second – about 40 times more powerful than current chips.
1997	The US company Dragon Systems releases the world's first voice recognition software program that is able to recognize and create text from normal continuous speech.
1998	Japanese scientists create an insect robot or 'cybug' by fusing the antennae of a moth onto a wheeled robot containing an electronic brain.

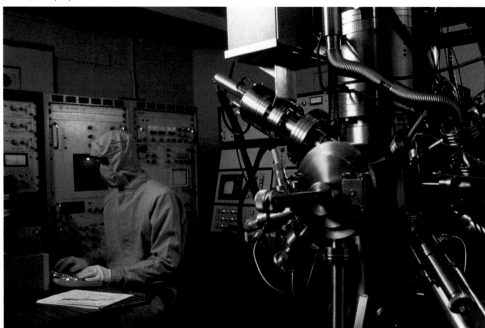

ELECTRON MICROSCOPE A scientist at work with an electron microscope, in a 'clean room' (an area set aside in a laboratory or research establishment where there is need for an absolutely clean, dust-free, and controlled environment).
Image Bank

Elements are classified in the ▷periodic table of the elements. Of the known elements, 92 are known to occur in nature (those with atomic numbers 1–92). Those elements with atomic numbers above 96 do not occur in nature and are synthesized only, produced in particle accelerators. Of the elements, 81 are stable; all the others, which include atomic numbers 43, 61, and from 84 up, are radioactive.

Elements are classified as metals, nonmetals, or metalloids (weakly metallic elements) depending on a combination of their physical and chemical properties; about 75% are metallic. Some elements occur abundantly (oxygen, aluminium); others occur moderately or rarely (chromium, neon); some, in particular the radioactive ones, are found in minute (neptunium, plutonium) or very minute (technetium) amounts. Symbols (devised by Swedish chemist Jöns ▷Berzelius) are used to denote the elements; the symbol is usually the first letter or letters of the English or Latin name (for example, C for carbon, Ca for calcium, Fe for iron, from the Latin *ferrum*). The symbol represents one atom of the element. According to current theories, hydrogen and helium were produced in the ▷Big Bang at the beginning of the universe. Of the other elements, those up to atomic number 26 (iron) are made by nuclear fusion within the stars. The more massive elements, such as lead and uranium, are produced when an old star explodes; as its centre collapses, the gravitational energy squashes nuclei together to make new elements. Two or more elements bonded together form a **compound** so that they cannot be separated by physical means. Compounds are held together by ionic or covalent bonds. The number of atoms of an element that combine to form a molecule is it **atomicity**. A molecule of oxygen (O_2) has atomicity 2; sulphur (S_8) has atomicity 8.

Related Web site: Chemical Elements.com http://www.chemicalelements.com/

elementary particle in physics, a subatomic particle that is not known to be made up of smaller particles, and so can be considered one of the fundamental units of matter. There are three groups of elementary particles: quarks, leptons, and gauge bosons.

Quarks, of which there are 12 types (up, down, charm, strange, top, and bottom, plus the antiparticles of each), combine in groups of three to produce heavy particles called baryons, and in groups of two to produce intermediate-mass particles called mesons. They and their composite particles are influenced by the strong nuclear force. **Leptons** are particles that do not interact via the strong nuclear force. Again, there are 12 types: the electron, muon, tau; their neutrinos, the electron neutrino, muon neutrino, and tau neutrino; and the antiparticles of each. These particles are influenced by the weak nuclear force, as well as by gravitation and electromagnetism. **Gauge bosons** carry forces between other particles. There are four types: gluon, photon, weakon, and graviton. The gluon carries the strong nuclear force, the photon the electromagnetic force, the weakons the weak nuclear force, and the graviton the force of gravity (see ▷forces, fundamental).

Related Web site: Guided Tour of Fermilab Exhibit http://www.fnal.gov/pub/tour.html

elements, the four earth, air, fire, and water. The Greek philosopher ▷Empedocles believed that these four elements made up the fundamental components of all matter and that they were destroyed and renewed through the action of love and discord.

elephant large grazing mammal with thick, grey wrinkled skin, large ears, a long flexible trunk, and huge curving tusks. There are fingerlike projections at the end of the trunk used for grasping food and carrying it to the mouth. The trunk is also used for carrying water to the mouth. The elephant is herbivorous and, because of its huge size, much of its time must be spent feeding on leaves, shoots, bamboo, reeds, grasses, and fruits, and, where possible, cultivated crops such as maize and bananas. Elephants are the largest living land animal.

ELEPHANT Grazing herd of African elephants, Kenya. *Corel*

Elephants

Elephants are highly social animals with strong family ties, and research has shown that they are capable of complex emotions. Females assist each other in the birth of their calves, and families work together in the care of the young and sick members of the herd. If a family member dies they may cover its body with leaves, twigs, and branches, and sometimes stay by the 'grave' for some hours. Elephants communicate using deep growls or rumbles. Some scientists believe that each elephant has its own individual or 'signature' growl by which it can be identified by other members of the herd. Elephants also produce low-frequency calls that are too low for humans to hear, but can be heard by other elephants over distances of up to 9.6 km/6 mi.

ELEPHANTS The Chiang Mai elephant camp in Thailand, now a tourist attraction, houses many elephants rescued from the wild. The young elephants are trained, as shown here, and used in the teak forests to haul logs for transportation by river. *Image Bank*

Elephants usually live in herds containing between 20 and 40 females (cows), led by a mature, experienced cow. Most male (bull) elephants live alone or in small groups; young bulls remain with the herd until they reach sexual maturity. Elephants have the longest gestation period of any animal (18–23 months between conception and birth) and usually produce one calf , which takes 10–15 years to reach maturity. Their tusks, which are initially tipped with enamel but later consist entirely of ivory, continue growing throughout life. They are preceded by milk tusks, which are shed at an early age. Elephants can live up to 60 years in the wild, but those in captivity have been known to reach over 65. There are two species of elephant, the African and the Indian or Asian elephant.

elephantiasis in medicine, a condition of local enlargement and deformity, most often of a leg, though the scrotum, vulva, or breast may also be affected. The commonest form of elephantiasis is the tropical variety (filariasis) caused by infestation by parasitic roundworms (filaria); the enlargement is due to damage of the lymphatic system which impairs immunity. There are approximately 120 million people with elephantiasis worldwide (1998). The World Health Organization (WHO) aims to eradicate the disease by 2020.

Eleusinian Mysteries ceremonies in honour of the Greek deities ▷Demeter, goddess of corn, and her daughter ▷Persephone, queen of the underworld, celebrated in the precincts of the temple of Demeter at Eleusis, in the territory of Athens. They formed the basis of a secret cult, requiring initiation for entrance. The rituals were agrarian in origin and had a strong chthonic (pertaining to the underworld) aspect, dealing with the cycle of growth and decay represented by Persephone's half-yearly absence from her mother.

Elgar, Edward (William) (1857–1934) English composer. Although his celebrated oratorio *The Dream of Gerontius* (1900), based on the written work by the theologian John Henry Newman, was initially unpopular in Britain, its good reception in Düsseldorf, Germany, in 1902 led to a surge of interest in his earlier works,

including the *Pomp and Circumstance Marches* (1901). His *Enigma Variations* (1899) brought him lasting fame.

Among his later works, which tend to be more introspective than the earlier ones, are oratorios, two symphonies, a violin concerto, chamber music, songs, and the symphonic poem *Falstaff* (1902–13), culminating in the poignant *Cello Concerto* of 1919. After this piece, Elgar published no further music of significance. He concentrated on transcriptions and made some early gramophone recordings of his own work.

Related Web site: Elgar Society and Elgar Foundation http://www.elgar.org/

> **Edward Elgar**
> *Music in England was ruined by Hymns Ancient and Modern.*
> Quoted in Redwood
> *An Elgar Companion* (1982)

Elgin marbles collection of ancient Greek sculptures, including the famous frieze and other sculptures from the Parthenon at Athens, are now in the British Museum. Greece has repeatedly asked for them to be returned to Athens.

Elijah (lived *c.* mid-9th century BC) In the Old Testament, a Hebrew prophet during the reigns of the Israelite kings Ahab and Ahaziah. He came from Gilead. He defeated the prophets of ▷Baal, and was said to have been carried up to heaven in a fiery chariot in a whirlwind. In Jewish belief, Elijah will return to Earth to herald the coming of the Messiah.

Related Web site: Elijah http://www.newadvent.org/cathen/05381b.htm

Eliot, George (1819–1880) Pen-name of Mary Ann (later Marian) Evans. English novelist. Her works include the pastoral *Adam Bede* (1859); *The Mill on the Floss* (1860), with its autobiographical elements; *Silas Marner* (1861), containing elements of the folk tale; and *Daniel Deronda* (1876). ▷*Middlemarch*, published serially (1871–72), is considered her greatest novel for its confident handling of numerous characters and central social and moral issues. She developed a subtle psychological presentation of character, and her work is pervaded by a penetrating and compassionate intelligence.

Born in Astley, Warwickshire, George Eliot had a strict evangelical upbringing. In 1841 she was converted to ▷free thought. As assistant editor of the *Westminster Review* under John Chapman from 1851 to 1853, she made the acquaintance of

The Elgin Marbles

The Elgin marbles are a collection of ancient Greek sculptures, dating from the 5th century BC, that were taken from Greece to England between 1803 and 1812. They are also known as The Parthenon Marbles. The pieces were acquired by the British diplomat, Thomas Bruce, the 7th Earl of Elgin, from the Turks, who governed Athens at that time. Elgin was concerned about the potential destruction of the Greek works of art while the Turks and Greeks were in conflict. He obtained permission from the Turks to take the marbles and collected and shipped the sculptures, the majority of which came from the Parthenon on the acropolis of

Athens, including the famous Parthenon frieze. There was widespread criticism of Elgin, who was accused of denying Greece her national treasures. After much debate and discussion about the quality of the sculptures, they were bought from Elgin by the British government in 1816 for £35,000, to be exhibited in the British Museum. Today they are considered masterpieces. Controversy still surrounds the sculptures; Greece has repeatedly asked for the Elgin marbles to be returned but the British Museum has not yet agreed to this. The Greek claims intensified when it was discovered that the marbles had been damaged by cleaning processes.

Thomas Carlyle, Harriet Martineau, Herbert Spencer, and the philosopher and critic George Henry Lewes (1817–1878). Lewes was married but separated from his wife, and from 1854 he and Eliot lived together in a relationship that she regarded as a true marriage and that continued until his death. Lewes strongly believed in her talent and as a result of his encouragement the story 'Amos Barton' was accepted by *Blackwoods Magazine* in 1857. This was followed by a number of other short stories, and their success persuaded Eliot to embark on writing her full-length novels including *Adam Bede* which was highly praised and placed her among the leading contemporary novelists. Lewes died in 1878, bitterly lamented by Eliot. In 1880 she married John Cross (1840–1924).

> **George Eliot**
> *In every parting there is an image of death.*
> *Scenes of Clerical Life*, 'Amos Barton'

Eliot, T(homas) S(tearns) (1888–1965) US-born poet, playwright, and critic, who lived in England from 1915. His first volume of poetry, *Prufrock and Other Observations* (1917), introduced new verse forms and rhythms; subsequent major poems were *The Waste Land* (1922), a long symbolic poem of disillusionment, and 'The Hollow Men' (1925). For children he published *Old Possum's Book of Practical Cats* (1939). Eliot's plays include *Murder in the Cathedral* (1935) and *The Cocktail Party* (1950). His critical works include *The Sacred Wood* (1920), setting out his views on poetic tradition. He was awarded the Nobel Prize for Literature in 1948.

Although he makes considerable demands on his readers, he is regarded as the founder of modernism in poetry: as a critic he profoundly influenced the ways in which literature was appreciated.

Eliot was born in St Louis, Missouri, and was educated at Harvard, the Sorbonne, and Oxford University. He married and settled in London in 1917 and became a British subject in 1927, joining the Anglo-Catholic movement within the Church of England the same year. He was for a time a bank clerk, later lecturing and entering publishing at Faber and Faber, where he became a director. As editor of the highly influential literary magazine *Criterion* from 1922 to 1939, he was responsible for a critical re-evaluation of metaphysical poetry and Jacobean drama, and wrote perceptively about such European poets as ▷Dante Alighieri, Charles ▷Baudelaire, and Jules ▷Laforgue.

Prufrock and Other Observations expressed the disillusionment of the generation affected by World War I. Eliot's reputation was established by the desolate modernity of *The Waste Land*, and 'The Hollow Men' continued on the same note. *Ash Wednesday* (1930) revealed a change in religious attitude and the *Four Quartets* (1944) confirmed his acceptance of the Christian faith. Among his other works are the poetic dramas *Murder in the Cathedral* (about Thomas à ▷Becket), *The Cocktail Party*, *The Confidential Clerk* (1953), and *The Elder Statesman* (1958). His collection *Old Possum's Book of Practical Cats* was used for the popular English composer Andrew Lloyd Webber's musical *Cats* (1981).

> **T S Eliot**
> *April is the cruellest month, breeding / Lilacs out of the dead land, mixing / Memory and desire.*
> *The Waste Land*

Related Web sites: Eliot, T S http://www.bartleby.com/201/index.html
TSEbase: The Online Concordance to T S Eliot's Collected Poems http://web.missouri.edu/~tselist/tse.html

Elisabethville former name of Lubumbashi, a town in the Democratic Republic of Congo.

Elisha (lived mid-9th century BC) In the Old Testament, a Hebrew prophet, successor to Elijah.

elite a small group with power in a society, having privileges and status above others. An elite may be cultural, educational, religious, political (also called 'the establishment' or 'the governing circles'), or social. Sociological interest has centred on how such minorities get, use, and hold on to power, and on what distinguishes elites from the rest of society.

Elizabeth In the New Testament, mother of John the Baptist. She was a cousin of Jesus' mother Mary, who came to see her shortly after the Annunciation; on this visit (called the Visitation), Mary sang the hymn of praise later to be known as the 'Magnificat'.

> **Elizabeth I**
> *My favour is not so lockt up for you, that others shall not partake thereof . . . I will have here but one Mistress, and no Master.*
> To Robert Dudley, Earl of Leicester, quoted in Sir Robert Naunton *Fragmenta Regalia* (1641)

Elizabeth two queens of England or the UK:

Elizabeth I (1533–1603) Called 'the Virgin Queen'. Queen of England from 1558, the daughter of Henry VIII and Anne Boleyn. Through her Religious Settlement of 1559 she enforced the Protestant religion by law. She had ▷Mary Queen of Scots executed in 1587. Her conflict with Roman Catholic Spain led to the defeat of the ▷Spanish Armada in 1588. The Elizabethan age was expansionist in commerce and geographical exploration, and arts and literature flourished. The rulers of many European states made unsuccessful bids to marry Elizabeth, and she manipulated her suitors to strengthen England's position in Europe. She was succeeded by James I.

Elizabeth was born at Greenwich, London on 7 September 1533. She was well educated in several languages. During her Roman Catholic half-sister ▷Mary I's reign, Elizabeth's Protestant sympathies brought her under suspicion, and in 1544 she was imprisoned for eight weeks in the Tower of London. For most of Mary's reign she lived in seclusion at Hatfield, Hertfordshire, until on Mary's death she became queen.

Her reign, 1558–1603 During her reign Elizabeth faced a number of challenges, notably a crisis in religion, the issue of succession ('the marriage problem'), the problem of what to do with Mary Queen of Scots, danger from Spain, and problems with beggars, Ireland, and Parliament.

Religion After the disastrous reign of her sister Mary I, Elizabeth faced opposition from both Catholics and Puritans. The Elizabethan religious settlement tried to provide the Church of England with a *via media* (middle way), a compromise of doctrine that would reconcile Catholic and Protestant. This was generally successful, although compromise proved impossible after Pope Pius V issued the papal bull which excommunicated Elizabeth in 1570, and throughout her reign she faced problems from Catholic recusants (who refused to attend Anglican services) and ▷Jesuit priests such as Edmund Campion. Elizabeth also faced increasing ▷Puritan discontent, and several Puritans were imprisoned or executed.

The marriage problem Many unsuccessful attempts were made by Parliament to persuade Elizabeth to marry or settle the succession. She found courtship a useful political weapon. She used the possibility of marriage as a strategy of foreign policy, and at various times considered marriage proposals from ▷Philip II of Spain, Archduke Charles of Austria, and the French princes Henri, Duke of Anjou, and François, Duke of Alençon. At home she maintained friendships with, among others, the courtiers ▷Leicester, Sir Walter ▷Raleigh, and ▷Essex. However, she announced from the start of her reign that she had no intention of marrying, and declared that she would be satisfied 'if a marble stone should hereafter declare that a Queen, having reigned such a time, lived and died a virgin'. She was known as the Virgin Queen.

Mary Queen of Scots The arrival in England in 1568 of ▷Mary Queen of Scots and her imprisonment by Elizabeth caused a political crisis, and a rebellion of the feudal nobility of the north followed in 1569. Mary became a focus of Catholic plots and in 1587 – with great reluctance – Elizabeth had her executed for treason after the ▷Babington plot.

Danger from Spain Friction between English and Spanish sailors hastened the breach with Spain. A strong Spanish presence in the Low Countries was perceived as a danger to England; in 1563 the Spanish closed Antwerp to English traders. When the Dutch rebelled against Spanish tyranny Elizabeth secretly encouraged them; Philip II retaliated by aiding Catholic conspiracies against her. Spanish support lay behind the Northern rebellion of 1569 and the Irish rebellion of 1579. Philip sent Jesuit priests secretly into England to undermine Elizabeth's position, and both the Ridolfi Plot (1571) and Throckmorton Plot (1584) – intended to place Mary Queen of Scots on the English throne – had Spanish support. In 1585 Philip seized English shipping in a number of Atlantic ports. This undeclared war continued for many years, until the landing of an English army in the Netherlands in 1585 and Mary's execution in 1587, brought it into the open. The ▷Spanish Armada (the fleet sent by Philip to invade England in 1588) met with total disaster. The war with Spain continued with varying fortunes to the end of her reign.

End of the reign Towards the end of her reign, Elizabeth faced economic probelms, which saw an increase in the number of poor people and beggars, and led to the ▷Poor Law of 1601. There were rebellions in Ireland. Parliament showed a new independence, and in 1601 forced Elizabeth to retreat on the question of the crown granting manufacturing and trading monopolies. Yet her prestige remained unabated, as shown by the failure of Essex's rebellion in 1601.

Related Web site: Elizabeth I http://www.luminarium.org/renlit/eliza.htm

ELIZABETH II Queen Elizabeth meeting Canadians on one of her 'walkabouts', in which she greets the public in person. Queen Elizabeth proclaimed the new Canadian constitution in April 1982, severing Canada's last colonial links with Britain. *Corel*

Elizabeth II (1926–) Born Elizabeth Alexandra Mary Windsor. Queen of Great Britain and Northern Ireland from 1952, the elder daughter of George VI. She married her third cousin, Philip, the Duke of Edinburgh, in 1947. They have four children: Charles, Anne, Andrew, and Edward.

Princess Elizabeth Alexandra Mary was born in London on 21 April 1926; she was educated privately, and assumed official duties at 16.

During World War II she served in the Auxiliary Territorial Service, and by an amendment to the Regency Act she became a state counsellor on her 18th birthday. On the death of George VI in 1952 she succeeded to the throne while in Kenya with her husband and was crowned on 2 June 1953.

In June 2002, four days of festivities, including classical and pop concerts, parades and street parties, were staged to celebrate the Golden Jubilee, marking 50 years of her reign.

Elizabeth (1709–1762) Empress of Russia from 1741, daughter of Peter the Great. She carried through a palace revolution and supplanted her cousin, the infant Ivan VI (1730–1764), on the throne. She continued the policy of westernization begun by Peter and allied herself with Austria against Prussia.

Elizabeth, the Queen Mother (1900–2002) Wife of King George VI of Great Britain. She was born Lady Elizabeth Angela Marguerite Bowes-Lyon, and on 26 April 1923 she married Albert, Duke of York, who became King George VI in 1936. Their children are Queen Elizabeth II (1926–) and Princess Margaret (1930–2002). She celebrated her 100th birthday in 2000.

She was the youngest daughter of the 14th Earl of Strathmore and Kinghorne (died 1944), through whom she was descended from Robert Bruce, king of Scotland. When her husband became King George VI she became Queen Consort, and was crowned with him in 1937. She adopted the title Queen Elizabeth, the Queen Mother after his death.

Elizabethan literature literature produced during the reign of Elizabeth I of England (1558–1603). This period saw a remarkable florescence of the arts in England, and the literature of the time is characterized by a new energy, richness, and confidence. Renaissance humanism, Protestant zeal, and geographical discovery all contributed to this upsurge of creative power. Drama was the dominant form of the age, and ▷Shakespeare and ▷Marlowe were popular with all levels of society. Other writers of the period include Edmund Spenser, Sir Philip Sidney, Francis Bacon, Thomas Lodge, Robert Greene, and John Lyly.

Elizabethan drama broke away from religiour domination, which was the major focus of the medieval mystery and morality plays. Elizabethan drama often used poetic metre for its dialogue, especially the five-foot iambic pentameter. Both Shakespeare and Marlowe often used controversial subjects for their drama, including the question of political power (in Marlowe's *Tamberlaine the Great* (two parts; 1587–88) and Shakespeare's *Macbeth* (1606), for example). Other, lesser playwrights wrote in a similar style to Shakespeare and Marlowe; *The Spanish Tragedy* (*c.* 1590) by Thomas Kyd is sometimes said to have been an influence upon Shakespeare's *Hamlet* (1601–02). As the Jacobean period commences, the content of the drama darkens appreciably, and the plays of dramatists such as John Webster are more overtly violent than those of the Elizabethan period, in which (although there are exceptions to this) violent action is often psychological and usually takes place offstage. See also ▷English literature.

elk large deer *Alces alces* inhabiting northern Europe, Asia, Scandinavia, and North America, where it is known as the moose. It is brown in colour, stands about 2 m/6 ft at the shoulders, has very large palmate antlers, a fleshy muzzle, short neck, and long legs. It feeds on leaves and shoots. In North America, the ▷wapiti is called an elk.

ELK The elk *Alces alces*, known as the moose in North America, is the world's largest deer. The flap of skin that hangs from its throat is called the bell.

elkhound Norwegian dog resembling the ▷husky but much smaller. Its coat is thick, with a full undercoat and the tail is bushy. Elkhounds are grey, with a darker shade on the back, and are about 50 cm/20 in high, weighing approximately 22 kg/48 lb.

Ellesmere Island island in the extreme northeast of the Arctic Archipelago, in the Canadian territory of Nunavut; area 196,236 sq km/75,767 sq mi; population is about 100. It is the second-largest island in the Archipelago (Baffin Island is the largest) and is part of the Queen Elizabeth island group, at the northern end of Baffin Bay. Its northern tip, Cape Columbia, is the most northerly point of the North American continent. The island is, for the most part, barren or glacier-covered. It was first sighted in 1616 by William Baffin.

Ellice Islands former name of ▷Tuvalu, a group of islands in the western Pacific Ocean.

Ellington, Duke (Edward Kennedy) (1899–1974) US pianist. He had an outstanding career as a composer and arranger of jazz. He wrote numerous pieces for his own jazz orchestra, accentuating the strengths of individual virtuoso instrumentalists, and became one of the leading figures in jazz over a 55-year period. Some of his most popular compositions include 'Mood Indigo', 'Sophisticated Lady', 'Solitude', and 'Black and Tan Fantasy'. He was one of the founders of big-band jazz.

ellipse curve joining all points (loci) around two fixed points (foci) such that the sum of the distances from those points is always constant. The diameter passing through the foci is the major axis, and the diameter bisecting this at right angles is the minor axis. An ellipse is one of a series of curves known as ▷conic sections. A slice across a cone that is not made parallel to, and does not pass through, the base will produce an ellipse.

Ellis Island island in New York harbour, USA, 1.5 km/1 mi from Manhattan Island; area 0.1 sq km/0.04 sq mi. A former reception centre for immigrants during the immigration waves between 1892 and 1943 (12 million people passed through it from 1892 to 1924), it was later used (until 1954) as a detention centre for nonresidents without documentation, or for those who were being deported. Ellis Island is now a national historic site (1964) and contains the Museum of Immigration (1989).

Ellison, Ralph Waldo (1914–1994) US novelist. His *Invisible Man* (1952) portrays with humour and energy the plight of a black man whom post-war US society cannot acknowledge. It is regarded as one of the most impressive novels published in the USA in the 1950s. He also wrote essays collected in *Shadow and Act* (1964).

Ellora archaeological site in Maharashtra State, India, with 35 sculpted and decorated temple caves – ▷Buddhist, ▷Hindu, and ▷Jainist – dating from the late 6th century to the 10th century.

elm any of a group of trees found in temperate regions of the northern hemisphere and in mountainous parts of the tropics.

ELM The English elm has the typical elm leaf, oval, toothed, and distinctly lopsided. The seed is surrounded by a yellowish petal-like wing.

All have doubly-toothed leaf margins and clusters of small flowers. (Genus *Ulmus*, family Ulmaceae.)
> **Related Web site: Elm, Common** http://www.botanical.com/botanical/mgmh/e/elmcom08.html

El Niño (Spanish 'the child') oceanographic and meteorological condition that occurs when a warm, nutrient-poor current of water moves southward to replace the cold, nutrient-rich surface water of the Peru Current along the west coast of South America. The phenomenon occurs every year around the end of December and lasts for several weeks, but in some years can last for several months. The result is poor fish harvests and global changes in weather patterns.

elongation in astronomy, the angular distance between the Sun and a planet or other solar-system object. This angle is 0° at ▷conjunction, 90° at quadrature, and 180° at ▷opposition.

El Paso city and administrative headquarters of El Paso County, Texas, at the base of the Franklin Mountains, on the Rio Grande, opposite the Mexican city of Ciudad Juárez; population (1994 est) 579,000. It is the centre of an agricultural and cattle-raising area, and there are electronics, food processing, packing, and leather industries, as well as oil refineries and industries based on local iron and copper mines. There are several military installations in the

ELLIS ISLAND Ellis Island in New York Harbor, New York, was the gateway to a new life in the USA for over 12 million immigrants between the years 1892 and 1924. In this photograph a woman and her son are wearing numbered tags as they walk down the pier on their arrival. *Archive Photos*

area. The city is home to the University of Texas at El Paso (formerly Texas Western; founded in 1913).

El Salvador see country box.

Elton, Charles Sutherland (1900–1991) British ecologist, a pioneer of the study of animal and plant forms in their natural environments, and of animal behaviour as part of the complex pattern of life. He defined the concept of food chains and was an early conservationist. Elton was instrumental in establishing the Nature Conservancy Council (1949), and was much concerned with the impact of introduced species on natural systems.

Eluard, Paul (1895–1952) Pen-name of Eugène Grindel. French poet. He expressed the suffering of poverty in his verse, and was a leader of the surrealists (see ▷surrealism). He fought in World War I, which inspired his *Poèmes pour la paix/Poems for Peace* (1918), and was a member of the Resistance in World War II. His books include *Poésie et vérité/Poetry and Truth* (1942) and *Au Rendezvous allemand/To the German Rendezvous* (1944).

Ely city in the Cambridgeshire ▷Fens, eastern England, on the Great Ouse River, 24 km/15 mi northeast of Cambridge; population (1991) 10,300. Economic activities include agriculture (sugar beet), engineering, and the manufacture of agricultural machinery, pottery, chemicals, and plastics. The cathedral, dating from 1083, is one of the largest in England.

Elysée Palace (or **Palais de l'Elysée**) building in Paris erected in 1718 for Louis d'Auvergne, Count of Evreux. It was later the home of Mme de Pompadour, Napoleon I, and Napoleon III, and became the official residence of the presidents of France in 1870, though President Mitterrand chose not to live there.

Elysium (or the **Elysian Fields**) in Greek mythology, an afterworld or paradise, originally identified with the Islands of the Blessed, for those who found favour with the gods. Later poets depicted Elysium as a region in ▷Hades, the underworld. It was ruled over by Rhadamanthys, a judge of the dead.

e-mail abbreviation for ▷electronic mail. See The Electronic Workplace Focus Feature on pp. 312–313.

emancipation being liberated, being set free from servitude or subjection of any kind. The changing role of women in social, economic, and particularly in political terms, in the 19th and 20th centuries is sometimes referred to as the 'emancipation of women' (see ▷women's movement).
> **Related Web site: Spartacus Educational: The Emancipation of Women 1860–1920** http://www.spartacus.schoolnet.co.uk/women.htm

Emancipation Proclamation in US history, President Abraham ▷Lincoln's Civil War announcement, 22 September 1862, stating that from the beginning of 1863 all black slaves in states still engaged in rebellion against the federal government would be emancipated. Slaves in border states still remaining loyal to the Union were excluded.

EMANCIPATION PROCLAMATION US cabinet members hear Lincoln's Emancipation Proclamation of 22 September 1862, freeing all slaves in the Confederacy as of 1 January 1863. *Archive Photos*

embargo the legal prohibition by a government of trade with another country, forbidding foreign ships to leave or enter its ports. Trade embargoes, as economic ▷sanctions, may be imposed on a country seen to be violating international laws.

embezzlement in law, theft by an employee of property entrusted to him or her by an employer.

embolism blockage of a blood vessel by an obstruction called an embolus (usually a blood clot, fat particle, or bubble of air).

AN EARLY OFFICE COMPUTER An example of the large and expensive machines that could only be afforded by a few specialist companies and institutions. The development of small, comparatively cheap, and powerful computers over the last two decades of the 20th century resulted in computers becoming commonplace in business. *Corbis*

The Electronic Workplace

by Paul Bray

Offices and factories have changed out of all recognition during the last generation as workers have learned that technology makes a good servant but a bad master.

the changing workplace

In 1971 the English scientist and novelist C P Snow wrote 'Technology is a queer thing. It brings you great gifts with one hand, and it stabs you in the back with the other.' Snow knew nothing of the personal computer, the mobile phone, the Web site, or the other technological paraphernalia that have become such inescapable elements of working life in the ensuing three decades. Yet he was articulating one of the fundamental truths about new technology: that

its effects are seldom entirely good or bad, and that, for every problem it solves, it has an uncanny knack of creating another.

The photocopier saved many laborious hours in the typing pool; but filing cabinets soon became stuffed with duplicate documents. The personal computer allowed people to create and keep information on disk; but once there, it became inaccessible to anybody else. So the computers were networked, and sharing was encouraged; but the networks proved time consuming to manage and provided a back door for interlopers like viruses and hackers. Even an innovation so humble as direct dialling to office telephone extensions has helped to generate so much demand for numbers that in some parts of the country telephone numbers changed three times in less than a decade.

the communications revolution

The two-edged nature of technology is nowhere more evident than in communications. The personal computer is ceasing to be a storage and processing device and is becoming a communications tool, one among millions of tiny roadside halts on what US Vice-President Al Gore dubbed in 1983 the Information Superhighway – the **Internet**. The upside is that we can communicate with all those other millions of roadside halts. The downside is that they can also communicate with us.

Examine the average business card and you will see why so many working people feel overwhelmed. It will feature several phone numbers – office, mobile, and possibly home – plus a fax number, electronic mail address, Web site, possibly a pager, as well as a bricks-and-mortar address. With so many channels, no wonder we seem to have gone communications-mad. One 2002 report, by analysts IDC, put the number of e-mails sent daily worldwide as 31 billion, a figure that the report-writers estimate will rise to 60 billion by 2006. The impact of this torrent is reported by analysts Gartner, whose 2001 research suggested that a third of employees spend around an hour a day dealing with e-mail, much of which is irrelevant to their work.

Small wonder, then, that beleaguered workers retreat behind yet more technology to shield themselves from the deluge, switching their phones to voice-mail and using filtering software to try to weed out time-wasting e-mails. So, realizing that some of their communications may not get through, senders 'make sure' by sending a fax and an e-mail, and phoning both office and mobile to check that these have arrived.

information overload?

The sheer volume of data available today can easily result in information overload. Study Anglo-Saxon poetry, and you could learn the entire canon by heart, since only about 10,000 lines survive. Study the Internet and you could scarcely read the names of all the new Web sites, since thousands are launched every day. Yet, contrary to popular belief, the Internet contains only only a fraction of the world's computerized information, according to a study by IBM, the largest manufacturer of computers in the world. The rest is stored on private systems.

It would be wrong, however, to suggest that the Internet and associated technologies are necessarily bad for knowledge workers. Used thoughtfully, e-mail can be very efficient. It is cheap, less intrusive than the telephone, and facilitates communication between people in different time-zones. Armed with e-mail, Web-based information, and video-conferencing, teams of workers can be spread across the globe and seldom need to meet in person.

The Web has often become the first port of call when seeking information, from product specifications and government legislation to train times and telephone numbers. Specialized **portal** sites gather together information on particular subjects, and most companies of any size have their own **intranets**. Intranets are mini-Internets for use by staff only, giving access to everything from internal phone lists and job vacancies to stock information and customer databases, with online chat-rooms to help remote workers keep in touch, and sometimes separate areas for trading partners.

Having information at their fingertips can be very enabling for staff, especially those who deal with customer enquiries. Instead of an embarrassed 'I'll call you back' or frantic rifling through filing cabinets, the system can give the answer instantly. If the customer wants to do something the operator is not familiar with, the system can provide on-the-spot training or lead the operator through the necessary steps.

the changing nature of work

New technology is not restricted to white-collar staff; manual workers are being encouraged to use it to cut down on paperwork and to keep abreast of company news. Factory-floor machinery is increasingly controlled by personal computers, with which operators must be familiar, and so-called **process intranets** can collect performance data from the machines and pass it to maintenance engineers and supervisors. Senior managers must also be computer- and Internet-literate, and the days when 'keyboards were only for secretaries' are long gone.

For that matter, may secretaries are long gone, too, replaced by a voice-mail system, an electronic diary, and a word-processing package on their former boss's personal computer. This is just one of the many changes in the workforce that technology has wrought. Automation in office and factory has led to swathes of redundancies. Some industries have suffered more than once, like the banks that shed back-office staff when they computerized in the 1960s and 1970s, and are now closing branches as more customers bank by telephone and Internet.

Telephone call centres have become the new sweatshops. If run badly, they can be like a battery-hen house with a telephone in every cage, where operators are timed when they go to the lavatory and

can answer more calls. But managerial grades are also suffering. The middle-manager, whose job was to summarize information and pass it up the chain, is disappearing because computers can do this automatically. And now that the office junior can e-mail the chairman directly with a bright idea, the traditional hierarchical structure of business is crumbling.

remote working is increasing

The days of the office itself may be numbered. Instead of wasting a couple of hours a day commuting, more people are **teleworking** (that is, working at home or on the road). More than 2 million Britons already work at home at least one day a week, and the number is increasing by about 13% a year.

The reasons are partly commercial – spending more time with customers, recruiting people with specialist skills who live far away, and so on – but technology is a major enabler. Portable computers

THE OFFICES in London of a major multinational company. The offices include built-in technology to allow video conferencing and a presentation room with audio-visual facilities. *Anglo American PLC/Maris_interiors.co.uk/Rob Brown photography*

are made to pre-record their greeting message so they are as powerful as desktop machines, and databases and diaries can be synchronized with the system back at the office so the mobile worker always has up-to-date information. The ubiquitous mobile phone means people are never out of touch, and **unified messaging systems** can forward all phone calls, voice-mails, e-mails, text messages, and faxes

Like all technology-induced changes, teleworking brings its own challenges. No longer restricted to office premises, workers are no longer restricted to office hours, and the dangers of stress and overwork are increased. Greater use of technology means an increased risk of repetitive strain injuries from keyboards and mice, eye-strain from displays, and the putative radiation risks from mobile phones. Loneliness can be a major problem, and work itself may need to be organized and managed differently – parcelled up into self-contained chunks and assessed by results, not by the number of hours the person sits at their desk.

will the office survive?

As more and more staff telework, if only part-time, the nature of the workplace itself will change. Personal desks will be replaced by **hot-desking**, with a smaller pool of desks that can be used by anybody when they are in the office, combined with open-plan 'café' areas where teleworkers can come into the office to socialize and exchange information.

Teleworkers can stay permanently connected to the Internet or their office networks, thanks to 'always-on' technologies such as Broadband for fixed phones and GPRS (general packet radio services) for mobiles. Video-conferencing reduces the need for travel by allowing face-to-face meeting between people in different counties or countries. Mobile phones and handheld computers can access Web pages and corporate databases. making it possible to look up key data in the middle of a meeting ot to check a train timetable from the back of a taxi.

to a single electronic mailbox, accessible from anywhere.

As for the Internet, in evolutionary terms it is still in the Stone Age. In another generation, it will have become as essential and as commonplace as the telephone is today.

embroidery the art of decorating cloth with a needle and thread. It includes ▷broderie anglaise, gros point, and petit point, all of which have been used for the adornment of costumes, gloves, book covers, furnishings, and ecclesiastical vestments. See picture on p. 315.

embryo early developmental stage of an animal or a plant following fertilization of an ovum (egg cell), or activation of an ovum by ▷parthenogenesis. In humans, the term embryo describes the fertilized egg during its first seven weeks of existence; from the eighth week onwards it is referred to as a fetus.

In animals the embryo exists either within an egg (where it is nourished by food contained in the yolk), or in mammals, in the ▷uterus of the mother. In mammals (except marsupials) the embryo is fed through the ▷placenta. The plant embryo is found within the seed in higher plants. It sometimes consists of only a few cells, but usually includes a root, a shoot (or primary bud), and one or two ▷cotyledons, which nourish the growing seedling.

embryology study of the changes undergone by an organism from its conception as a fertilized ovum (egg) to its emergence into the world at hatching or birth. It is mainly concerned with the changes in cell organization in the embryo and the way in which these lead to the structures and organs of the adult (the process of ▷differentiation).

emerald a clear, green gemstone variety of the mineral ▷beryl. It occurs naturally in Colombia, the Ural Mountains in Russia, Zimbabwe, and Australia. The green colour is caused by the presence of the element chromium in the beryl.

emergence (or emergent evolution) a philosophical theory of the early 20th century postulating that life 'emerges' or 'grows naturally' out of matter, mind emerges out of life, and God emerges from mind.

El Salvador

El Salvador country in Central America, bounded north and east by Honduras, south and southwest by the Pacific Ocean, and northwest by Guatemala.

NATIONAL NAME *República de El Salvador/ Republic of El Salvador*
AREA 21,393 sq km/8,259 sq mi
CAPITAL San Salvador
MAJOR TOWNS/CITIES Soyapango, Santa Ana, San Miguel, Nueva San Salvador, Mejicanos, Apopa, Delgado
PHYSICAL FEATURES narrow coastal plain, rising to mountains in north with central plateau

Government

HEAD OF STATE AND GOVERNMENT Francisco Guillermo Flores Pérez from 1999
POLITICAL SYSTEM emergent democracy
POLITICAL EXECUTIVE limited presidency
ADMINISTRATIVE DIVISIONS 14 departments
ARMED FORCES 16,800; plus paramilitary forces of 12,000 (2002 est)
CONSCRIPTION selective conscription for one year
DEATH PENALTY abolished for ordinary crimes in 1983; laws provide for the death penalty for exceptional crimes, such as crimes committed in wartime

DEFENCE SPEND (% GDP) 1.2 (2002 est)
EDUCATION SPEND (% GDP) 2.3 (2000 est)
HEALTH SPEND (% GDP) 8.8 (2000 est)

Economy and resources

CURRENCY US dollar (replaced Salvadorean colón in 2001)
GPD (US$) 14.3 billion (2002 est)
REAL GDP GROWTH (% change on previous year) 1.8 (2001)
GNI (US$) 13.5 billion (2002 est)
GNI PER CAPITA (PPP) (US$) 4,570 (2002 est)
CONSUMER PRICE INFLATION 2.9% (2003 est)
UNEMPLOYMENT 7.5% (2001)
FOREIGN DEBT (US$) 5.1 billion (2001 est)
MAJOR TRADING PARTNERS USA, Guatemala, Costa Rica, Honduras, Mexico, Panama, Japan, Nicaragua
RESOURCES salt, limestone, gypsum
INDUSTRIES food processing, beverages, petroleum products, textiles, chemicals, tobacco, paper products, chemical products

EXPORTS coffee, textiles and garments, sugar, shrimp, footwear, pharmaceuticals. Principal market: USA 65.4% (2001)
IMPORTS petroleum and other minerals, cereals, chemicals, iron and steel, machinery and transport equipment, food and live animals, consumer goods. Principal source: USA 49% (2001)
ARABLE LAND 27% (2000 est)
AGRICULTURAL PRODUCTS coffee, sugar cane, cotton, maize, beans, rice, sorghum; fishing (shrimp)

Population and society

POPULATION 6,515,000 (2003 est)
POPULATION GROWTH RATE 1.6% (2000–15)
POPULATION DENSITY (per sq km) 310 (2003 est)

Chronology

11th century: Pipils, descendants of the Nahuatl-speaking Toltec and Aztec peoples of Mexico, settled in the country and came to dominate El Salvador until the Spanish conquest.

1524: Conquered by the Spanish adventurer Pedro de Alvarado and made a Spanish colony, with resistance being crushed by 1540.

1821: Independence achieved from Spain; briefly joined with Mexico.

1823: Became part of United Provinces (Federation) of Central America, also embracing Costa Rica, Guatemala, Honduras, and Nicaragua.

1833: Unsuccessful rebellion against Spanish control of land led by Anastasio Aquino.

1840: Became fully independent when the Federation was dissolved.

1859–63: Coffee growing introduced by President Gerardo Barrios.

1932: Peasant uprising, led by Augustín Farabundo Martí, suppressed by military at a cost of the lives of 30,000, virtually eliminating American Indian Salvadoreans.

1961: Following a coup, the right-wing National Conciliation Party (PCN) established and in power.

1969: Brief 'Football War' with Honduras, which El Salvador attacked, at the time of a football competition between the two states, following evictions of thousands of Salvadoran illegal immigrants from Honduras.

1977: Allegations of human-rights violations; growth of left-wing Farabundo Martí National Liberation Front (FMLN) guerrilla activities. Gen Carlos Romero elected president.

1979: A coup replaced Romero with a military-civilian junta.

URBAN POPULATION (% of total) 64 (2003 est)
AGE DISTRIBUTION (% of total population) 0–14 35%, 15–59 58%, 60+ 7% (2002 est)
ETHNIC GROUPS about 92% of the population are mestizos, 6% Indians, and 2% of European origin
LANGUAGE Spanish (official), Nahuatl
RELIGION about 75% Roman Catholic, Protestant
EDUCATION (compulsory years) 9
LITERACY RATE 83% (men); 78% (women) (2003 est)
LABOUR FORCE 25.1% agriculture, 24.6% industry, 50.3% services (1998)
LIFE EXPECTANCY 68 (men); 74 (women) (2000–05)
CHILD MORTALITY RATE (under 5, per 1,000 live births) 39 (2001)
PHYSICIANS (per 1,000 people) 1.1 (1998 est)
HOSPITAL BEDS (per 1,000 people) 1.6 (1998 est)
TV SETS (per 1,000 people) 201 (2000 est)
RADIOS (per 1,000 people) 478 (1999)
INTERNET USERS (per 10,000 people) 464.6 (2002 est)
PERSONAL COMPUTER USERS (per 100 people) 2.5 (2002 est)

See also ▷Central America.

1980: The archbishop of San Salvador and human-rights champion, Oscar Romero, was assassinated; the country was on the verge of civil war. José Napoleón Duarte (PDC) became the first civilian president since 1931.

1979–81: 30,000 people were killed by right-wing death squads.

1981: Mexico and France recognized the FMLN guerrillas as a legitimate political force, but the USA actively assisted the government in its battle against them.

1982: Assembly elections were boycotted by left-wing parties. Held amid considerable violence, they were won by far-right National Republican Alliance (ARENA).

1986: Duarte sought a negotiated settlement with the guerrillas.

1989: Alfredo Cristiani (ARENA) became president in rigged elections; rebel attacks intensified.

1991: A peace accord sponsored by the United Nations (UN) was signed by representatives of the government and the socialist guerrilla group, the FMLN, which became a political party.

1993: A UN-sponsored commission published a report on war atrocities; there was a government amnesty for those implicated; top military leaders officially retired.

1999: Francisco Guillermo Flores Pérez was elected president.

2000: The FMLN displaced the ruling ARENA as the largest party in Congress, but did not win an overall majority.

2001: El Salvador adopted the US dollar as its currency, phasing out the colón. A powerful earthquake in January killed over 1,500 people and left 1 million homeless.

EL SALVADOR A group of government soldiers in El Salvador. *Archive Photos*

EMBROIDERY An embroidered picture made in England *c.* 1720 by Elizabeth Haints. See entry on p. 314. *The Art Archive/Victoria and Albert Museum London*

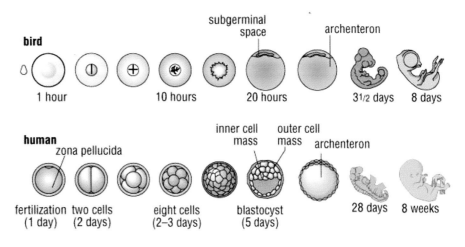

EMBRYO The development of a bird and a human embryo. In the human, division of the fertilized egg, or ovum, begins within hours of conception. Within a week, a hollow, fluid-containing ball – a blastocyte – with a mass of cells at one end has developed. After the third week, the embryo has changed from a mass of cells into a recognizable shape. At four weeks, the embryo is 3 mm/0.1 in long, with a large bulge for the heart and small pits for the ears. At six weeks, the embryo is 1.5 cm/0.6 in long with a pulsating heart and ear flaps. By the eighth week, the embryo (now technically a fetus) is 2.5 cm/1 in long and recognizably human, with eyelids and small fingers and toes.

Emerson, Ralph Waldo (1803–1882) US philosopher, essayist, and poet. He settled in Concord, Massachusetts, which he made a centre of ▷transcendentalism, and wrote *Nature* (1836), which states the movement's main principles emphasizing the value of self-reliance and the godlike nature of human souls. His two volumes of *Essays* (1841, 1844) made his reputation: 'Self-Reliance' and 'Compensation' in the earlier volume are among the best known.

  Related Web site: Emerson, Ralph Waldo http://www2.lucidcafe.com/lucidcafe/library/96May/emerson.html

RALPH WALDO EMERSON US poet and essayist who was highly influential on American thought. *Archive Photos*

Emery, (Walter) Bryan (1903–1971) English archaeologist, who in 1929–34 in ▷Nubia, North Africa, excavated the barrows at Ballana and Qustol, rich royal tombs of the mysterious X-group people (3rd to 6th centuries AD). He also surveyed the whole region 1963–64 before it was flooded as a result of the building of the Aswan High Dam.

emetic any substance administered to induce vomiting. Emetics are used to empty the stomach in many cases of deliberate or accidental drug overdose. The most frequently used is ipecacuanha.

emf in physics, abbreviation for ▷electromotive force.

Emilia-Romagna region of northern central Italy, comprising the provinces of Bologna, Ferrara, Forlì, Modena, Parma, Piacenza, and Reggio nell'Emilia; area 22,100 sq km/8,531 sq mi; population (1992) 3,920,200. The capital is ▷Bologna; other towns include Reggio nell'Emilia, Rimini, Parma, Ferrara, and Ravenna. Agricultural produce includes fruit, wine, sugar beet, beef, dairy products, rice, and wheat. Oil and natural-gas resources have been developed in the Po Valley.

éminence grise (French 'grey eminence') a power behind a throne: that is, a manipulator of power without immediate responsibility. The nickname was originally applied (because of his grey cloak) to the French monk François Leclerc du Tremblay (1577–1638), also known as Père Joseph, who in 1612 became the close friend and behind-the-scenes adviser of Cardinal Richelieu.

Emin Pasha, Mehmed (1840–1892) Adopted name of Eduard Schnitzer. German explorer, physician, and linguist. Appointed by British general Charles Gordon as chief medical officer and then governor of the Equatorial province of southern Sudan, he carried out extensive research in anthropology, botany, zoology, and meteorology.

Emmental district in the valley of the Emme River, Bern canton, Switzerland, where a hard cheese of the same name has been made since the mid-15th century.

emotion in psychology, a powerful feeling; a complex state of body and mind involving, in its bodily aspect, changes in the viscera (main internal organs) and in facial expression and posture, and in its mental aspect, heightened perception, excitement and, sometimes, disturbance of thought and judgement. The urge to action is felt and impulsive behaviour may result.

emotivism a philosophical position in the theory of ethics. Emotivists deny that moral judgements can be true or false, maintaining that they merely express an attitude or an emotional response.

Empedocles (*c.* 493–433 BC) Greek philosopher and scientist who proposed that the universe is composed of four elements – fire, air, earth, and water – which through the action of love and discord are eternally constructed, destroyed, and constructed anew. He lived in Acragas (Agrigentum), Sicily, and according to tradition, he committed suicide by throwing himself into the crater of Mount Etna.

emphysema incurable lung condition characterized by disabling breathlessness. Progressive loss of the thin walls dividing the air spaces (alveoli) in the lungs reduces the area available for the exchange of oxygen and carbon dioxide, causing the lung tissue to expand. The term 'emphysema' can also refer to the presence of air in other body tissues.

empire collective name for a group of countries under the control of a single country or dynasty. Major empires in Europe have included the ▷Roman Empire and the ▷British Empire, and in Asia the ▷Ottoman Empire and Mogul Empire (see ▷Mogul dynasty).

Empire State Building landmark building in New York, USA. It is 443 m/1,454 ft high with 102 floors, and was the highest building in the world until 1972, when it was superseded by the World Trade Center, New York. It was built in 1930 at a cost of over $40,000,000.

empiricism (Greek *empeiria* 'experience' or 'experiment') in philosophy, the belief that all knowledge is ultimately derived from sense experience. It is suspicious of metaphysical schemes based on ▷a priori propositions, which are claimed to be true irrespective of experience. It is frequently contrasted with ▷rationalism.
  Related Web site: Empiricism http://www-philosophy.ucdavis.edu/phi001/emplec.htm

employment law law covering the rights and duties of employers and employees. During the 20th century, statute law rather than common law has increasingly been used to give new rights to employees. Industrial tribunals are statutory bodies that adjudicate in disputes between employers and employees or trade unions and deal with complaints concerning unfair dismissal, sex or race discrimination, and equal pay.

EMS abbreviation for ▷European Monetary System.

EMU abbreviation for ▷Economic and Monetary Union, the proposed ▷European Union (EU) policy for a single currency and common economic policies.

emu flightless bird *Dromaius novaehollandiae*, family Dromaiidae, order Casuariidae, native to Australia. It stands about 1.8 m/6 ft high and has coarse brown plumage, small rudimentary wings, short feathers on the head and neck, and powerful legs, which are well adapted for running and kicking. The female has a curious bag or pouch in the windpipe that enables her to emit a characteristic loud booming note. Emus are monogamous, and the male wholly or partially incubates the eggs.

  In Western Australia emus are farmed for their meat, skins, feathers, and oil.

EMU A flightless bird, the emu weighs 35–40kg/80–90lbs.

emulsion stable dispersion of a liquid in another liquid – for example, oil and water in some cosmetic lotions.

enabling act legislative enactment enabling or empowering a person or corporation to take certain actions. Perhaps the best known example of an enabling law was that passed in Germany in March 1933 by the Reichstag and Reichsrat. It granted Hitler's cabinet dictatorial powers until April 1937, and effectively terminated parliamentary government in Germany until 1950. The law firmly established the Nazi dictatorship by giving dictatorial powers to the government.

enamel vitrified (glasslike) coating of various colours used for decorative purposes on a metallic or porcelain surface. In ▷cloisonné the various sections of the design are separated by thin metal wires or strips. In champlevé the enamel is poured into engraved cavities in the metal surface.

encaustic painting ancient technique of painting, commonly used by the Egyptians, Greeks, and Romans, in which coloured pigments were mixed with molten wax and painted on panels. In the 20th century the technique was used by the US artist Jasper Johns.

encephalitis inflammation of the brain, nearly always due to viral infection but it may also occur in bacterial and other infections. It varies widely in severity, from shortlived, relatively slight effects of headache, drowsiness, and fever to paralysis, coma, and death.

Encke's comet comet with the shortest known orbital period, 3.3 years. It is named after German mathematician and astronomer Johann Franz Encke (1791–1865), who calculated its orbit in 1819 from earlier sightings.

enclosure in Britain, appropriation of ▷common land as private property, or the changing of open-field systems (farming in strips apportioned over two or three large fields) to enclosed fields owned by individual farmers. The enclosed fields were often used for sheep. This process began in the 14th century and became widespread in the 15th and 16th centuries. It caused poverty, homelessness, and rural depopulation, and resulted in revolts in 1536, 1569, and 1607. A further wave of enclosures occurred between about 1760 and 1820 during the ▷agrarian revolution.

Government action Numerous government measures to prevent depopulation were introduced between 1489 and 1640, including the first Enclosure Act (1603), but were sabotaged by landowning magistrates at local level. There was a new wave of enclosures by Acts of Parliament from 1760 to 1820. From 1876 the enclosure of common land in Britain was limited by statutes. Enclosures occurred throughout Europe on a large scale during the 19th century, often at the behest of governments. The last major Enclosure Act was in 1903.

encore (French 'again') in music, an unprogrammed extra item, usually short and well known, played at the end of a concert to please an enthusiastic audience.

encryption encoding a message so that it can only be read by the intended recipient. See ▷cryptography.

encyclical letter addressed by the pope to Roman Catholic bishops for the benefit of the people. The first was issued by Benedict XIV in 1740, but encyclicals became common only in the 19th century. They may be doctrinal (condemning errors), exhortative (recommending devotional activities), or commemorative.

encyclopedia (or encyclopaedia) work of reference covering either all fields of knowledge or one specific subject. Although most encyclopedias are alphabetical, with cross-references, some are organized thematically with indexes, to keep related subjects together.

endangered species plant or animal species whose numbers are so few that it is at risk of becoming extinct. Officially designated endangered species are listed by the World Conservation Union (or IUCN).

Endangered species are not a new phenomenon; extinction is an integral part of evolution. The replacement of one species by another usually involves the eradication of the less successful form, and ensures the continuance and diversification of life in all forms. However, extinctions induced by humans are thought to be destructive, causing evolutionary dead-ends that do not allow for succession by a more fit species. The great majority of recent extinctions have been directly or indirectly induced by humans; most often by the loss, modification, or pollution of the organism's habitat, but also by hunting for 'sport' or for commercial purposes.

According to a 1995 report to Congress by the US Fish and Wildlife Service, although seven of the 893 species listed as endangered under the US Endangered Species Act 1968–93 have become extinct, 40% are no longer declining in number. In February 1996, a private conservation group, Nature Conservancy, reported around 20,000 native US plant and animal species to be rare or imperilled. According to the Red Data List of endangered species, published in 1996 by the World Conservation Union, 25% of all mammal species (including 46% of primates, 36% of insectivores, and 33% of pigs and antelopes), and 11% of all bird species are threatened with extinction.

endive cultivated annual plant, the leaves of which are used in salads and cooking. One variety has narrow, curled leaves; another has wide, smooth leaves. It is related to ▷chicory. (*Cichorium endivia*, family Compositae.)

endocrine gland gland that secretes hormones into the bloodstream to regulate body processes. Endocrine glands are most highly developed in vertebrates, but are also found in other animals, notably insects. In humans the main endocrine glands are the pituitary, thyroid, parathyroid, adrenal, pancreas, ovary, and testis.

endometriosis common gynaecological complaint in which patches of endometrium (the lining of the womb) are found outside the uterus.

endoplasm inner, liquid part of a cell's ▷cytoplasm.

endoplasmic reticulum (ER) a membranous system of tubes, channels, and flattened sacs that form compartments within ▷eukaryotic cells. It stores and transports proteins within cells and

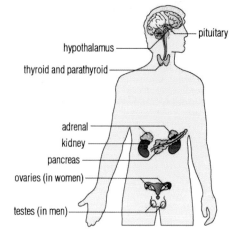

ENDOCRINE GLAND The main human endocrine glands. These glands produce hormones – chemical messengers – which travel in the bloodstream to stimulate certain cells.

also carries various enzymes needed for the synthesis of ▷fats. The ▷ribosomes, or the organelles that carry out protein synthesis, are sometimes attached to parts of the ER.

endorphin natural substance (a polypeptide) that modifies the action of nerve cells. Endorphins are produced by the pituitary gland and hypothalamus of vertebrates. They lower the perception of pain by reducing the transmission of signals between nerve cells.

Endorphins not only regulate pain and hunger, but are also involved in the release of sex hormones from the pituitary gland. Opiates act in a similar way to endorphins, but are not rapidly degraded by the body, as natural endorphins are, and thus have a long-lasting effect on pain perception and mood. Endorphin release is stimulated by exercise.

endoscopy examination of internal organs or tissues by an instrument allowing direct vision. An endoscope is equipped with an eyepiece, lenses, and its own light source to illuminate the field of vision. The endoscope used to examine the digestive tract is a flexible fibreoptic instrument swallowed by the patient.

endoskeleton the internal supporting structure of vertebrates, made up of cartilage or bone. It provides support, and acts as a system of levers to which muscles are attached to provide movement. Certain parts of the skeleton (the skull and ribs) give protection to vital body organs.

endosperm nutritive tissue in the seeds of most flowering plants. It surrounds the embryo and is produced by an unusual process that parallels the ▷fertilization of the ovum by a male gamete. A second male gamete from the pollen grain fuses with two female nuclei within the embryo sac. Thus endosperm cells are triploid (having three sets of chromosomes); they contain food reserves such as starch, fat, and protein that are utilized by the developing seedling.

endotherm 'warm-blooded', or homeothermic, animal. Endotherms have internal mechanisms for regulating their body temperatures to levels different from the environmental temperature. See ▷homeothermy.

endowment insurance a type of life insurance that may produce profits. An endowment policy will run for a fixed number of years during which it accumulates a cash value; it can provide a savings plan for a retirement fund.

end user user of a computer program; in particular, someone who uses a program to perform a task (such as accounting or playing a computer game), rather than someone who writes programs (a programmer).

ENCLOSURE The agrarian revolution saw enclosure of farmland by hedges. Enclosure made crop rotation possible and also allowed room for the use of new farm machinery that was being developed. Enclosure revolutionized the farming system and although a number of farmers profited by the system, many lost their rights to land, particularly with the restrictions to common grazing lands.

Endymion in Greek mythology, a beautiful young shepherd or hunter visited each night by ▷Selene, the Moon goddess. She kissed him as he slept in a cave on Mount Latmos in Caria, sending him into an eternal sleep in which he became ageless.

energy capacity for doing ▷work. Energy can exist in many different forms. For example, potential energy (PE) is energy deriving from position; thus a stretched spring has elastic PE, and an object raised to a height above the Earth's surface, or the water in an elevated reservoir, has gravitational PE. Moving bodies possess kinetic energy (KE). Energy can be converted from one form to another, but the total quantity in a system stays the same (in accordance with the ▷conservation of energy principle). Energy cannot be created or destroyed. For example, as an apple falls it loses gravitational PE but gains KE. Although energy is never lost, after a number of conversions it tends to finish up as the kinetic energy of random motion of molecules (of the air, for example) at relatively low temperatures. This is 'degraded' energy that is difficult to convert back to other forms.

Energy types and transfer A flat battery in a torch will not light the torch. If the battery is fully charged, it contains enough chemical energy to illuminate the torch bulb. When one body A does work on another body B, A transfers energy to B. The energy transferred is equal to the work done by A on B. Energy is therefore measured in ▷joules. The rate of doing work or consuming energy is called power and is measured in ▷watts (joules per second). Energy can be converted from any form into another. A ball resting on a slope possesses ▷potential energy that is gradually changed into ▷kinetic energy of rotation and translation as the ball rolls down. As a pendulum swings, energy is constantly being changed from a potential form at the highest points of the swing to kinetic energy at the lowest point. At positions in between these two extremes, the system possesses both kinetic and potential energy in varying proportions. A weightlifter changes chemical energy from the muscles into potential energy of the weight when the weight is lifted. If the weightlifter releases the weight, the potential energy is converted to kinetic energy as it falls, and this in turn is converted to heat energy and sound energy as it hits the floor. A lump of coal and a tank of petrol, together with the oxygen needed for their combustion, have chemical energy. Other sorts of energy include electrical and nuclear energy, and light and sound.

Resources So-called energy resources are stores of convertible energy. **Nonrenewable resources** include the fossil fuels (coal, oil, and gas) and nuclear-fission 'fuels' – for example, uranium 235. The term 'fuel' is used for any material from which energy can be obtained. We use up fuel reserves such as coal and oil, and convert the energy they contain into other, useful forms. The chemical energy released by burning fuels can be used to do work. **Renewable resources**, such as wind, tidal, and geothermal power, have so far been less exploited. Hydroelectric projects are well established, and wind turbines and tidal systems are being developed.

Energy conservation and efficiency All forms of energy are interconvertible by appropriate processes. Energy is transferred from one form to another, but the sum total of the energy after the conversion is always the same as the initial energy. This is the principle of conservation of energy. This principle can be illustrated by the use of energy flow diagrams, called Sankey diagrams, which show the energy transformations that take place. When a petrol engine is used to power a car, about 75% of the energy from the fuel is wasted. The total energy input equals the total energy output, but a lot of energy is wasted as heat so that the engine is only about 25% efficient. The combustion of the petrol–air mixture produces heat energy as well as kinetic energy. All forms of energy tend to be transformed into heat and cannot then readily be converted into other, useful forms of energy.

Heat transfer A difference in temperature between two objects in thermal contact leads to the transfer of energy as ▷heat. Heat is energy transferred due to a temperature difference. Heat is transferred by the movement of particles (that possess kinetic energy) by conduction, convection, and radiation. ▷Conduction involves the movement of heat through a solid material by the movement of free electrons. For example, thermal energy is lost from a house by conduction through the walls and windows. ▷Convection involves the transfer of energy by the movement of fluid particles. All objects radiate heat in the form of radiation of electromagnetic waves. Hotter objects emit more energy than cooler objects. Methods of reducing energy transfer as heat through the use of insulation are important because the world's fuel reserves are limited and heating homes costs a lot of money in fuel bills. Heat transfer from the home can be reduced by a variety of methods, such as loft insulation, cavity wall insulation, and double glazing. The efficiencies of insulating materials in the building industry are compared by measuring their heat-conducting properties, represented by a U-value. A low U-value indicates a good insulating material.

$E = mc^2$ It is now recognized that mass can be converted into energy under certain conditions, according to Einstein's theory of relativity. This conversion of mass into energy is the basis of atomic power. ▷Einstein's special theory of ▷relativity (1905) correlates any gain, E, in energy with a gain, m, in mass, by the equation $E = mc^2$, in which c is the speed of light. The conversion of mass into energy in accordance with this equation applies universally, although it is only for nuclear reactions that the percentage change in mass is large enough to detect.

energy, alternative energy from sources that are renewable and ecologically safe, as opposed to sources that are non-renewable with toxic by-products, such as coal, oil, or gas (fossil fuels), and uranium (for nuclear power). The most important alternative energy source is flowing water, harnessed as ▷hydroelectric power. Other sources include the oceans' tides and waves (see ▷wave power), ▷wind power (harnessed by windmills and wind turbines), the Sun (▷solar energy), and the heat trapped in the Earth's crust (▷geothermal energy) (see also ▷cold fusion).

energy conservation methods of reducing ▷energy use through insulation, increasing energy efficiency, and changes in patterns of use. Profligate energy use by industrialized countries contributes greatly to air pollution and the ▷greenhouse effect when it draws on nonrenewable energy sources.

energy of reaction energy released or absorbed during a chemical reaction, also called **enthalpy of reaction** or **heat of reaction**. In a chemical reaction, the energy stored in the reacting molecules is rarely the same as that stored in the product molecules. Depending on which is the greater, energy is either released (an exothermic reaction) or absorbed (an endothermic reaction) from the surroundings (see ▷conservation of energy). The amount of energy released or absorbed by the quantities of substances represented by the chemical equation is the energy of reaction.

Enfield outer borough of northeast Greater London. It includes the districts of Edmonton and Southgate.

features the royal hunting ground of Enfield Chase partly survives in the 'green belt'; early 17th-century Forty Hall; Lea Valley Regional Park, opened 1967 **industries** engineering (the Royal Small Arms factory, which closed 1989, produced the Enfield rifle), textiles, furniture, cement, electronics, metal, and plastic products **population** (1991) 257,400.

Engel, (Johann) Carl Ludwig (1778–1840) German architect. From 1815 he worked in Finland. His great neoclassical achievement is the Senate Square in Helsinki, which is defined by his Senate House (1818–22) and University Building (1828–32), and crowned by the domed Lutheran cathedral (1830–40).

Friedrich Engels

English socialism arose with Owen, a manufacturer, and proceeds therefore with great consideration towards the bourgeoisie and great injustice towards the proletariat.

On Robert Owen, in *Condition of the Working Class*

Engels, Friedrich (1820–1895) German social and political philosopher, a friend of, and collaborator with, Karl ▷Marx on *The Communist Manifesto* (1848) and other key works. His later interpretations of Marxism, and his own philosophical and historical studies such as *Origins of the Family, Private Property, and the State* (1884) (which linked patriarchy with the development of private property), developed such concepts as historical materialism. His use of positivism and Darwinian ideas gave Marxism a scientific and deterministic flavour which was to influence Soviet thinking.

In 1842 Engels's father sent him to work in the cotton factory owned by his family in Manchester, England, where he became involved with ▷Chartism. In 1844 his lifelong friendship with Karl Marx began, and together they worked out the materialist interpretation of history and in 1847–48 wrote the *Communist Manifesto*. Returning to Germany during the 1848–49 revolution, Engels worked with Marx on the *Neue Rheinische Zeitung/New Rhineland Newspaper* and fought on the barricades in Baden. After the defeat of the revolution he returned to Manchester, and for the rest of his life largely supported the Marx family.

Engels's first book was *The Condition of the Working Classes in England* (1845). He summed up the lessons of 1848 in *The Peasants' War in Germany* (1850) and *Revolution and Counter-Revolution in Germany* (1851). After Marx's death Engels was largely responsible for the wider dissemination of his ideas; he edited the second and third volumes of Marx's *Das Kapital* (1885 and 1894). Although Engels himself regarded his ideas as identical with those of Marx, discrepancies between their works are the basis of many Marxist debates.

FRIEDRICH ENGELS A portrait of the German political philosopher Friedrich Engels *c.* 1869. *Archive Photos*

engine device for converting stored energy into useful work or movement. Most engines use a fuel as their energy store. The fuel is burnt to produce heat energy – hence the name 'heat engine' – which is then converted into movement. Heat engines can be classified according to the fuel they use (▷petrol engine or ▷diesel engine), or according to whether the fuel is burnt inside (▷internal combustion engine) or outside (▷steam engine) the engine, or according to whether they produce a reciprocating or a rotary motion (▷turbine or Wankel engine).

engineering the application of science to the design, construction, and maintenance of works, machinery, roads, railways, bridges, harbour installations, engines, ships, aircraft and airports, spacecraft and space stations, and the generation, transmission, and use of electrical power. The main divisions of engineering are aerospace, chemical, civil, computer, electrical, electronic, gas, marine, materials, mechanical, mining, production, radio, and structural.

England largest division of the ▷United Kingdom.

area 130,357 sq km/50,331 sq mi **capital** London **towns and cities** Birmingham, Cambridge, Coventry, Leeds, Leicester, Manchester, Newcastle upon Tyne, Nottingham, Oxford, Sheffield, York; ports Bristol, Dover, Felixstowe, Harwich, Liverpool, Portsmouth, Southampton **features** variability of climate and diversity of scenery; among European countries, only the Netherlands is more densely populated **exports** agricultural (cereals, rape, sugar beet, potatoes); meat and meat products; electronic (software) and telecommunications equipment; scientific instruments; textiles

ENGLAND English landscape with a double rainbow by John Constable. *The Art Archive/Victoria and Albert Museum London*

and fashion goods; North Sea oil and gas, petrochemicals, pharmaceuticals, fertilizers; beer; china clay, pottery, porcelain, and glass; film and television programmes, and sound recordings. Tourism is important. There are worldwide banking and insurance interests **currency** pound sterling   **population** (2001 est) 49,181,300. **language** English, with more than 100 minority languages **religion** Christian, with the Church of England as the established church, 31,500,000; and various Protestant groups, of which the largest is the Methodist 1,400,000; Roman Catholic about 5,000,000; Muslim 900,000; Jewish 410,000; Sikh 175,000; Hindu 140,000 **government** returns 529 members to Parliament; a mixture of two-tier and unitary local authorities, with 34 non-metropolitan counties, 46 unitary authorities, 6 metropolitan counties (with 36 metropolitan boroughs), 32 London boroughs, and the Corporation of London

For **government** and history, see ▷Britain, ancient; ▷United Kingdom

Related Web site: Destination England http://www.lonelyplanet.com/destinations/ europe/england

English the natives and inhabitants of England, part of Britain, as well as their descendants, culture, and language. The English have a mixed cultural heritage combining Celtic, Anglo-Saxon, Norman, and Scandinavian elements.

English architecture the main styles in English architecture are Anglo-Saxon, Norman, Early English (of which Westminster Abbey is an example), Decorated, Perpendicular (15th century), Tudor (a name chiefly applied to domestic buildings of about 1485–1558), Jacobean, Stuart (including the Renaissance and Queen Anne styles), Georgian, the Gothic revival of the 19th century, Modern, and postmodern. Notable architects include Christopher Wren, Inigo Jones, John Vanbrugh, Nicholas Hawksmoor, William Chambers, John Soane, Charles Barry, Edwin Landseer Lutyens, Hugh Casson, Basil Spence, Frederick Gibberd, Denys Lasdun, Richard Rogers, Norman Foster, James Stirling, Terry Farrell, Quinlan Terry, and Zahia Hadid.

English art painting and sculpture in England from the 10th century. (For English art before the 10th century, see ▷Celtic art and ▷Anglo-Saxon art.) The strong tradition of manuscript illumination was continued from earlier centuries. Portrait painting flourished from the late 15th century (initially led by artists from Germany and the Low Countries) through the 18th (Thomas ▷Gainsborough, Joshua ▷Reynolds) and into the 20th (David ▷Hockney, Lucian ▷Freud). Landscape painting reached its high point in the 19th century with John ▷Constable and J M W ▷Turner.

The Pre-Raphaelite Brotherhood produced a Victorian version of medievalism. In the early 20th century the Camden Town Group and the Bloomsbury Group responded to modern influences in painting, and in sculpture the work of Jacob ▷Epstein, Henry ▷Moore, and Barbara ▷Hepworth led progressively towards abstraction. In the 1950s pop art began in the UK. Artists in the latter part of the 20th century experimented with mixed and sometimes unusual media such as dead sheep (Damien Hirst) and chocolate (Helen Chadwick, 1953–1996).

English Channel stretch of water between England and France, leading in the west to the Atlantic Ocean, and in the east via the Strait of Dover to the North Sea; it is also known as **La Manche** (French 'the sleeve') from its shape. The ▷Channel Tunnel, opened in 1994, runs between Folkestone, Kent, and Sangatte, west of Calais.

The English Channel is 560 km/348 mi long west–east; 27 km/ 17 mi wide at its narrowest (Cap Gris Nez–Dover) and 177 km/ 110 mi wide at its widest (Ushant–Land's End). The average depth is 40–60 m/131–197 ft, reaching 120 m/394 ft at the entrance to the Strait of Dover and as much as 180 m/590 ft at Hurds Deep, 30 km/ 19 mi northwest of Guernsey.

English horn alternative name for the ▷cor anglais, a musical instrument of the oboe family.

English language member of the Germanic branch of the Indo-European language family. It is traditionally described as having passed through four major stages over about 1,500 years: **Old English** or **Anglo-Saxon** (*c.* 500–1050), rooted in the dialects of invading settlers (Jutes, Saxons, Angles, and Frisians); **Middle English** (*c.* 1050–1550), influenced by Norman French after the Conquest of 1066 and by ecclesiastical Latin; **Early Modern English** (*c.* 1550–1700), including a standardization of the diverse influences of Middle English; and **Late Modern English** (*c.* 1700 onwards), including in particular the development and spread of current Standard English.

Through extensive exploration, colonization, and trade, English spread worldwide from the 17th century onwards and remains the most important international language of trade and technology. It is used in many variations, for example, British, American, Canadian, West Indian, Indian, Singaporean, and Nigerian English, and many pidgins and creoles.

English law one of the major European legal systems, ▷Roman law being the other. English law has spread to many other countries, including former English colonies such as the USA, Canada, Australia, and New Zealand.

Related Web sites: Law Rights http://www.lawrights.co.uk/ **Web Journal of Current Legal Issues** http://webjcli.ncl.ac.uk/

English literature for the earliest surviving English literature see ▷Old English literature.

English toy terrier (or black-and-tan terrier) breed of toy dog closely resembling the ▷Manchester terrier but smaller and with erect ears. It weighs no more than 3.5 kg/8 lb and is 25–30 cm/ 10–12 in high.

Sovereigns of England and the United Kingdom from 899

Edward the Elder made the first major advances towards the unification of England under one sovereign and established the ascendancy of his dynasty.

Reign	Name	Relationship
West Saxon Kings		
899–924	Edward the Elder	son of Alfred the Great
924–39	Athelstan	son of Edward the Elder
939–46	Edmund	half-brother of Athelstan
946–55	Edred	brother of Edmund
955–59	Edwy	son of Edmund
959–75	Edgar	brother of Edwy
975–78	Edward the Martyr	son of Edgar
978–1016	Ethelred (II) the Unready	son of Edgar
1016	Edmund Ironside	son of Ethelred (II) the Unready
Danish Kings		
1016–35	Canute	son of Sweyn I of Denmark who conquered England in 1013
1035–40	Harold I	son of Canute
1040–42	Hardicanute	son of Canute
West Saxon Kings (restored)		
1042–66	Edward the Confessor	son of Ethelred (II) the Unready
1066	Harold II	son of Godwin
Norman Kings		
1066–87	William I	illegitimate son of Duke Robert the Devil
1087–1100	William II	son of William I
1100–35	Henry I	son of William I
1135–54	Stephen	grandson of William II
House of Plantagenet		
1154–89	Henry II	son of Matilda (daughter of Henry I)
1189–99	Richard I	son of Henry II
1199–1216	John	son of Henry II
1216–72	Henry III	son of John
1272–1307	Edward I	son of Henry III
1307–27	Edward II	son of Edward I
1327–77	Edward III	son of Edward II
1377–99	Richard II	son of the Black Prince
House of Lancaster		
1399–1413	Henry IV	son of John of Gaunt
1413–22	Henry V	son of Henry IV
1422–61, 1470–71	Henry VI	son of Henry V
House of York		
1461–70, 1471–83	Edward IV	son of Richard, Duke of York
1483	Edward V	son of Edward IV
1483–85	Richard III	brother of Edward IV
House of Tudor		
1485–1509	Henry VII	son of Edmund Tudor, Earl of Richmond
1509–47	Henry VIII	son of Henry VII
1547–53	Edward VI	son of Henry VIII
1553–58	Mary I	daughter of Henry VIII
1558–1603	Elizabeth I	daughter of Henry VIII
House of Stuart		
1603–25	James I	great-grandson of Margaret (daughter of Henry VII)
1625–49	Charles I	son of James I
1649–60	the Commonwealth	
House of Stuart (restored)		
1660–85	Charles II	son of Charles I
1685–88	James II	son of Charles I
1689–1702	William III and Mary	son of Mary (daughter of Charles I); daughter of James II
1702–14	Anne	daughter of James II
House of Hanover		
1714–27	George I	son of Sophia (granddaughter of James I)
1727–60	George II	son of George I
1760–1820	George III	son of Frederick (son of George II)
1820–30	George IV (regent 1811–20)	son of George III
1830–37	William IV	son of George III
1837–1901	Victoria	daughter of Edward (son of George III)
House of Saxe-Coburg		
1901–10	Edward VII	son of Victoria
House of Windsor		
1910–36	George V	son of Edward VII
1936	Edward VIII	son of George V
1936–52	George VI	son of George V
1952–	Elizabeth II	daughter of George VI

English is the official or primary language of 60 countries. It is estimated that nearly 400 million people speak English as their first language; that 600 million have learned it as a second language, more than any other language, and that one in three of the world's population routinely encounters it.

engraving art of creating a design by means of inscribing blocks of metal, wood, or some other hard material with a point. With **intaglio printing** the design is cut into the surface of a plate, usually metal. It is these cuts, often very fine, which hold the ink. In **relief printing**, by contrast, it is the areas left when the rest has been cut away which are inked for printing. See ▷printmaking.

enharmonic in music, a harmony capable of alternative interpretations, used as a link between passages of normally unrelated keys. For example, an enharmonic modulation from C sharp to F major plays on the equivalence, in keyboard terms, of the notes E sharp and F.

Enlightenment European intellectual movement that reached its high point in the 18th century. Enlightenment thinkers were believers in social progress and in the liberating possibilities of rational and scientific knowledge. They were often critical of existing society and were hostile to religion, which they saw as keeping the human mind chained down by superstition.

enlightenment in Buddhism, the term used to translate the Sanskrit *bodhi*, awakening: perceiving the true nature of the world, the unreality of the self, and becoming liberated from suffering (Sanskrit *duhkha*). By experience of *bodhi*, ▷nirvana is attained.

Ennis county town of County ▷Clare, Republic of Ireland, on the River Fergus, 32 km/20 mi northwest of Limerick; population (1996) 15,300. There are distilleries, flour mills, and furniture manufacturing. In the town are a Roman Catholic cathedral and college, and a Franciscan friary, Ennis Friary, founded about 1241. Shannon international airport is 24 km/15 mi to the south of Ennis.

Enniskillen county town of ▷Fermanagh, Northern Ireland, between Upper and Lower Lough Erne, 184 km/114 mi from Dublin and 141 km/88 mi from Belfast; population (1991) 11,400. It is a market town and shopping centre with some light industry (engineering, food processing); it has been designated for further industrial growth. An IRA bomb exploded here at a Remembrance Day service in November 1987, causing many casualties.

ENNISKILLEN Siege of Enniskillen Castle, Ireland, February 1593. *Art Archive*

Ensor, James Sidney, Baron Ensor (1860–1949) Belgian painter and printmaker. In a bold style employing vivid colours, he created a surreal and macabre world inhabited by masked figures and skeletons. Such works as his famous *Entry of Christ into Brussels* (1888; Musée Royale des Beaux-Arts, Brussels) anticipated expressionism. He was made a baron in 1929.

entablature in classical architecture, the upper part of an ▷order, situated above the column and principally composed of the architrave, frieze, and cornice.

entail in law, the settlement of land or other property on a successive line of people, usually succeeding generations of the original owner's family. An entail can be either **general**, in which case it simply descends to the heirs, or **special**, when it descends according to a specific arrangement – for example, to children by a named wife.

Entebbe city in Uganda, on the northwest shore of Lake Victoria, 20 km/12 mi southwest of Kampala, the capital; 1,136 m/3,728 ft above sea level; population (2002 est) 57,500. Founded 1893, it was the administrative centre of Uganda 1894–1962. The international airport of Uganda is here. Industries include tourism and fishing.

Entente Cordiale (French 'friendly understanding') agreement reached by Britain and France in 1904 recognizing British interests in Egypt and French interests in Morocco. It was expressly designed to check the colonial ambitions of the German Second Empire under ▷William II. Though not a formal alliance, the Entente generated tripartite cooperation between Britain, France, and Russia from 1907 (the Triple Entente), and formed the basis for Anglo-French military collaboration before the outbreak of World War I in 1914.

enterprise zone former special zone introduced in the UK in 1980 and designated by government to encourage industrial and commercial activity, usually in economically depressed areas. Investment was attracted by means of tax reduction and other financial incentives. Enterprise zones no longer exist, but assisted area and intermediate areas survive.

enthalpy in chemistry, alternative term for ▷energy of reaction, the heat energy associated with a chemical change.

entomology study of ▷insects.

entrepreneur in business, a person who successfully manages and develops an enterprise through personal skill and initiative. Examples include John D ▷Rockefeller, Henry ▷Ford, Anita ▷Roddick, and Richard Branson.

entropy in ▷thermo-dynamics, a parameter representing the state of disorder of a system at the atomic, ionic, or molecular level; the greater the disorder, the higher the entropy. Thus the fast-moving disordered molecules of water vapour have higher entropy than those of more ordered liquid water, which in turn have more entropy than the molecules in solid crystalline ice.
In a closed system undergoing change, entropy is a measure of the amount of energy unavailable for useful work. At ▷absolute zero (−273.15°C/−459.67°F/0 K), when all molecular motion ceases and order is assumed to be complete, entropy is zero.

Enver Pasha (1881–1922) Turkish politician and soldier. He led the military revolt of 1908 that resulted in the Young Turks' revolution (see ▷Turkey). He was killed fighting the Bolsheviks in Turkestan.

environmental audit another name for ▷green audit, the inspection of a company to assess its environmental impact.

environmental issues matters relating to the detrimental effects of human activity on the biosphere, their causes, and the search for possible solutions. The political movement that advocates protection of the environment is the ▷green movement. Since the Industrial Revolution, the demands made by both the industrialized and developing nations on the Earth's natural resources are increasingly affecting the balance of the Earth's resources. Over a period of time, some of these resources are renewable – trees can be replanted, soil nutrients can be replenished – but many resources, such as fossil fuels and minerals, are ▷non-renewable and in danger of eventual exhaustion. In addition, humans are creating many other problems that may endanger not only their own survival, but also that of other species. For instance, ▷deforestation and ▷air pollution are not only damaging and radically altering many natural environments, they are also affecting the Earth's climate by adding to the ▷greenhouse effect and ▷global warming, while ▷water pollution is seriously affecting aquatic life, including fish populations, as well as human health.

Environmental pollution is normally taken to mean harm done to the natural environment by human activity. In fact, some environmental pollution can have natural sources, for example volcanic activity, which can cause major air pollution or water pollution and destroy flora and fauna. In terms of environmental issues, however, environmental pollution relates to human actions, especially in connection with energy resources. The demands of the industrialized nations for energy to power machines, provide light, heat, and so on are constantly increasing. The most versatile form of energy is electricity, which can be produced from a wide variety of other energy sources, such as the fossil fuels – coal, oil, and gas – and nuclear power produced from uranium. These are all non-renewable resources and, in addition, their extraction, transportation, utilization, and waste products all give rise to pollutants of one form or another. The effects of these pollutants can have consequences not only for the local environment, but also at a global level.

> **Paul Harrison**
> US dramatist and director
> *The higher our income, the more resources we control and the more havoc we wreak.*
> *Guardian* 1 May 1992

Environmentally Sensitive Area (ESA) scheme introduced by the UK Ministry of Agriculture in 1984, as a result of EC legislation, to protect some of the most beautiful areas of the British countryside from the loss and damage caused by agricultural change. The first areas to be designated ESAs were in the Pennine Dales, the Norfolk Broads, the Breckland, the Suffolk River Valleys, the Test Valley, the South Downs, the Somerset Levels and Moors, West Penwith, Cornwall, the Shropshire Borders, the Cambrian Mountains, and the Lleyn Peninsula.

Environmental Protection Agency (EPA) US agency set up in 1970 to control water and air quality, industrial and commercial wastes, pesticides, noise, and radiation. In its own words, it aims to protect 'the country from being degraded, and its health threatened, by a multitude of human activities initiated without regard to long-ranging effects upon the life-supporting properties, the economic uses, and the recreational value of air, land, and water'.

environment art large sculptural or spatial works that create environments which the spectator may enter and become absorbed in. Environments frequently incorporate sensory stimuli, such as sound or movement, to capture the observer's attention. The US artists Jim ▷Dine and Claes ▷Oldenburg were early exponents in the 1960s.

environment–heredity controversy see ▷nature–nurture controversy.

enzyme biological ▷catalyst produced in cells, and capable of speeding up the chemical reactions necessary for life. They are large, complex ▷proteins, and are highly specific, each chemical reaction requiring its own particular enzyme. The enzyme's specificity arises from its active site, an area with a shape corresponding to part of the molecule with which it reacts (the substrate). The enzyme and the substrate slot together forming an enzyme–substrate complex that allows the reaction to take place, after which the enzyme falls away unaltered.

The activity and efficiency of enzymes are influenced by various factors, including temperature and pH conditions. Temperatures above 60°C/140°F damage (denature) the intricate structure of enzymes, causing reactions to cease. Each enzyme operates best within a specific pH range, and is denatured by excessive acidity or alkalinity.

Digestive enzymes include amylases (which digest starch), lipases (which digest fats), and proteases (which digest protein). Other enzymes play a part in the conversion of food energy into ▷ATP; the manufacture of all the molecular components of the body; the replication of ▷DNA when a cell divides; the production of hormones; and the control of movement of substances into and out of cells.

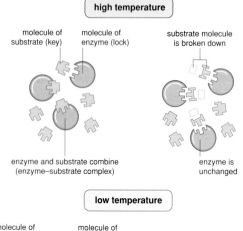

high temperature

molecule of substrate (key) • molecule of enzyme (lock) • substrate molecule is broken down

enzyme and substrate combine (enzyme–substrate complex)

enzyme is unchanged

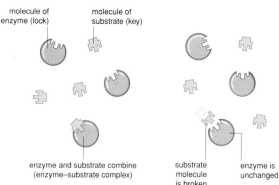

low temperature

molecule of enzyme (lock) • molecule of substrate (key)

enzyme and substrate combine (enzyme–substrate complex)

substrate molecule is broken • enzyme is unchanged

ENZYME Enzymes are catalysts that can help break larger molecules into smaller molecules while remaining unchanged themselves. Like a key for a lock, each enzyme is specific to one molecule. Most also function best within a narrow temperature and pH range. As the temperature rises enzymes catalyse more molecules but beyond a certain temperature most enzymes become denatured.

Enzymes have many medical and industrial uses, from washing powders to drug production, and as research tools in molecular biology. They can be extracted from bacteria and moulds, and ▷genetic engineering now makes it possible to tailor an enzyme for a specific purpose.

Eocene epoch second epoch of the Tertiary period of geological time, roughly 56.5–35.5 million years ago. Originally considered the earliest division of the Tertiary, the name means 'early recent', referring to the early forms of mammals evolving at the time, following the extinction of the dinosaurs.

E & O E abbreviation for **errors and omissions excepted**.

Eos in Greek mythology, the goddess of the dawn (Roman **Aurora**); daughter of the Titans Hyperion and Theia; herald of ▷Helios's chariot bearing the sun. She was cursed to fall in love with many youths by ▷Aphrodite after they quarrelled over Ares, god of war. When distracted by love, Eos would neglect her responsibilities, and the sun could not rise.

ephemeral plant plant with a very short life cycle, sometimes as little as six to eight weeks. It may complete several generations in one growing season.

Ephesus ancient Greek seaport in Asia Minor, a centre of the ▷Ionian Greeks, with a temple of Artemis destroyed by the Goths

EPHESUS The ruins of the Celsus Library at Ephesus, in Turkey. *Image Bank*

---

in AD 262. Now in Turkey, it is one of the world's largest archaeological sites. St Paul visited the city and addressed a letter (▷epistle) to the Christians there.

epic narrative poem or cycle of poems dealing with some great deed – often the founding of a nation or the forging of national unity – and often using religious or cosmological themes. The two main epic poems in the Western tradition are *The Iliad* and *The Odyssey*, attributed to ▷Homer, which were probably intended to be chanted in sections at feasts.

epicentre the point on the Earth's surface immediately above the seismic focus of an ▷earthquake. Most building damage usually takes place at an earthquake's epicentre. The term sometimes refers to a point directly above or below a nuclear explosion ('at ground zero').

Epictetus (*c.* AD 55–135) Greek Stoic philosopher who encouraged people to refrain from self-interest and to promote the common good of humanity. He believed that people were in the hands of an all-wise providence and that they should endeavour to do their duty in the position to which they were called.

Epicureanism system of moral philosophy named after the Greek philosopher Epicurus. He argued that pleasure is the basis of the ethical life, and that the most satisfying form of pleasure is achieved by avoiding pain, mental or physical. This is done by limiting desire as far as possible, and by choosing pleasures of the mind over those of the body.

Epicurus (341–270 BC) Greek philosopher, founder of Epicureanism, who held that all things are made up of atoms. His theory of knowledge stresses the role of sense perception, and in his ethics the most desired condition is a serene detachment based on the avoidance of anxiety and physical pain.

epicycloid in geometry, a curve resembling a series of arches traced out by a point on the circumference of a circle that rolls around another circle of a different diameter. If the two circles have the same diameter, the curve is a ▷cardioid.

Epidaurus (or **Epidavros**) ancient Greek city and port on the east coast of Argolis, in the northeastern Peloponnese. The site contains a well-preserved theatre of the 4th century BC; nearby are the ruins of the temple of Asclepius, the god of healing.

epidemic outbreak of infectious disease affecting large numbers of people at the same time. A widespread epidemic that sweeps across many countries (such as the ▷Black Death in the late Middle Ages) is known as a pandemic.

epidermis outermost layer of ▷cells on an organism's body. In plants and many invertebrates such as insects, it consists of a single layer of cells. In vertebrates, it consists of several layers of cells. The epidermis of plants and invertebrates often has an outer noncellular ▷cuticle that protects the organism from desiccation.

In vertebrates, such as reptiles, birds, and mammals, the outermost layer of cells is dead, forming a tough, waterproof layer, known as ▷skin.

epiglottis small flap located behind the root of the tongue in mammals. It closes off the end of the windpipe during swallowing to prevent food from passing into it and causing choking.

EPICYCLOID A seven-cusped epicycloid, formed by a point on the circumference of a circle (of diameter *d*) that rolls around another circle (of diameter 7*d*/3).

---

epigram short, witty, and pithy saying or short poem. The poem form was common among writers of ancient Rome, including Catullus and Martial. In English, the epigram has been used by Ben Jonson, George Herrick, John Donne, Alexander Pope, Jonathan Swift, W B Yeats, and Ogden Nash. An epigram was originally a religious inscription, such as that on a tomb.

epilepsy medical disorder characterized by a tendency to develop fits, which are convulsions or abnormal feelings caused by abnormal electrical discharges in the cerebral hemispheres of the ▷brain. Epilepsy can be controlled with a number of anticonvulsant drugs.

The term epilepsy covers a range of conditions from mild 'absences', involving momentary loss of awareness, to major convulsions. In some cases the abnormal electrical activity is focal (confined to one area of the brain); in others it is generalized throughout the cerebral cortex. Fits are classified according to their clinical type. They include: the **grand mal** seizure with convulsions and loss of consciousness; the fleeting absence of awareness **petit mal**, almost exclusively a disorder of childhood; **Jacksonian** seizures, originating in the motor cortex; and **temporal-lobe** fits, which may be associated with visual hallucinations and bizarre disturbances of the sense of smell.

Epilepsy affects 1–3% of the world's population. It may arise spontaneously or may be a consequence of brain surgery, organic brain disease, head injury, metabolic disease, alcoholism, or withdrawal from some drugs. Almost a third of patients have a family history of the condition.

Most epileptics have infrequent fits that have little impact on their daily lives. Epilepsy does not imply that the sufferer has any impairment of intellect, behaviour, or personality.

Epiphany festival of the Christian church, held on 6 January, celebrating the coming of the Magi (the three Wise Men) to Bethlehem with gifts for the infant Jesus, and symbolizing the manifestation of Jesus to the world. It is the 12th day after Christmas, and marks the end of the Christmas festivities.
Related Web site: Epiphany http://www.newadvent.org/cathen/05504c.htm

epiphyte any plant that grows on another plant or object above the surface of the ground, and has no roots in the soil. An epiphyte does not parasitize the plant it grows on but merely uses it for support. Its nutrients are obtained from rainwater, organic debris such as leaf litter, or from the air.

Epirus (Greek *Ipiros* 'mainland') region of northwestern Greece; area 9,200 sq km/3,551 sq mi; population (1991) 339,200. Its capital is Yannina, and it consists of the provinces (nomes) of Arta, Thesprotia, Yannina, and Preveza. There is livestock farming. It was part of an ancient Greek region of the same name: the northern part was in Albania, the remainder in northwest Greece.

episcopacy in the Christian church, a system of government in which administrative and spiritual power over a district (diocese) is held by a bishop.

epistemology branch of philosophy that examines the nature of knowledge and attempts to determine the limits of human understanding. Central issues include how knowledge is derived and how it is to be validated and tested.
Related Web site: Epistemology http://www.newadvent.org/cathen/05506a.htm

epistle in the New Testament, any of the 21 letters to individuals or to the members of various churches written by Christian leaders, including the 13 written by St ▷Paul. The term also describes a letter with a suggestion of pomposity and literary affectation, and a letter addressed to someone in the form of a poem, as in the epistles of ▷Horace and Alexander ▷Pope.

epoch subdivision of a geological period in the geological time scale. Epochs are sometimes given their own names (such as the Palaeocene, Eocene, Oligocene, Miocene, and Pliocene epochs comprising the Tertiary period), or they are referred to as the late, early, or middle portions of a given period (as the Late Cretaceous or the Middle Triassic epoch).

Geological time is broken up into **geochronological units** of which epoch is just one level of division. The hierarchy of geochronological divisions is eon, ▷era, period, epoch, age, and chron. Epochs are subdivisions of periods and ages are subdivisions of epochs. Rocks representing an epoch of geological time comprise a **series**.

epoxy resin synthetic ▷resin used as an ▷adhesive and as an ingredient in paints. Household epoxy resin adhesives come in component form as two separate tubes of chemical, one tube containing resin, the other a curing agent (hardener). The two chemicals are mixed just before application, and the mix soon sets hard.

EPROM (acronym for erasable programmable read-only memory) computer memory device in the form of an ▷integrated circuit (chip) that can record data and retain it indefinitely. The data can be erased by exposure to ultraviolet light, and new data recorded. Other kinds of computer memory chips are ▷ROM (read-only memory), ▷PROM (programmable read-only memory), and ▷RAM (random-access memory).

Epsom residential town in Surrey, southeast England, 30 km/19 mi southwest of London; population (1991) 64,400 (with Ewell). In the 17th century it was a spa town producing ▷Epsom salts. The Derby and the Oaks horse races are held annually at **Epsom Downs** racecourse.

Epsom salts $MgSO_4.7H_2O$ hydrated magnesium sulphate, used as a relaxant and laxative and added to baths to soothe the skin. The name is derived from a bitter saline spring at Epsom, Surrey, England, which contains the salt in solution.

Epstein, Jacob (1880–1959) US-born British sculptor. Initially influenced by Rodin, he turned to primitive forms after Brancusi and is chiefly known for his controversial muscular nude figures, such as *Genesis* (1931; Whitworth Art Gallery, Manchester). He was better appreciated as a portraitist; his bust of Albert Einstein (1933) demonstrating a characteristic vigorous modelling in clay. In later years he executed several monumental figures, notably the bronze *St Michael and the Devil* (1959; Coventry Cathedral) and *Social Consciousness* (1953; Fairmount Park, Philadelphia).

In 1904 he moved to England, where most of his major work was done. An early example showing the strong influence of ancient sculptural styles is the angel of the tomb of Oscar Wilde (1912; Père Lachaise cemetery, Paris), condemned as barbaric for its Assyrian idiom. His sculpture from 1912 to 1913 was harsh and mechanistic, having affinities with Vorticism and the work of such contemporary artists as Amedeo Modigliani and Constantin ▷Brancusi. The modernist and semi-abstract *Rock Drill* (1913; Tate Gallery, London) originally incorporated a real drill.

JACOB EPSTEIN Jacob Epstein's *Head of Albert Einstein* (1933), in clay. *The Art Archive/Tate Gallery London/Eileen Tweedy*

equal opportunities the right to be employed or considered for employment without discrimination on the grounds of race, gender, or physical or mental disability.

Equal Opportunities Commission commission established by the UK government in 1975 (1976 in Northern Ireland) to implement the Sex Discrimination Act 1975. Its aim is to prevent discrimination, particularly on sexual or marital grounds.

The US equivalent is the Equal Employment Opportunity Commission (EEOC) established by the Civil Rights Act of 1964. It investigates possible employment discrimination based on race, sex, age, religion, or national origin. The EEOC has the power to initiate suits in the federal district courts.

equation in chemistry, representation of a chemical reaction by symbols and numbers; see ▷chemical equation. For example, the reaction of sodium hydroxide (NaOH) with hydrochloric acid (HCl) to give sodium chloride and water may be represented by:

$$NaOH + HCl \rightarrow NaCl + H_2O$$

equation in mathematics, expression that represents the equality of two expressions involving constants and/or variables, and thus usually includes an equals (=) sign. For example, the equation $A = \pi r^2$ equates the area A of a circle of radius r to the product πr^2.

The algebraic equation $y = mx + c$ is the general one in coordinate geometry for a straight line. See also ▷quadratic equation.

Equator or **terrestrial equator** the ▷great circle whose plane is perpendicular to the Earth's axis (the line joining the poles). Its length is 40,092 km/24,901.8 mi, divided into 360 degrees of longitude. The Equator encircles the broadest part of the Earth, and represents 0° latitude. It divides the Earth into two halves, called the northern and the southern hemispheres.

The **celestial equator** is the circle in which the plane of the Earth's Equator intersects the ▷celestial sphere.

Equatorial Guinea see country box.

equestrianism skill in horse riding, as practised under International Equestrian Federation rules. An Olympic sport, there are three main branches of equestrianism: showjumping, dressage, and three-day eventing. Three other disciplines are under the authority of the International Equestrian Federation (FEI): carriage driving, endurance riding, and vaulting.

Equidae horse family in the order Perissodactyla, which includes the odd-toed hoofed animals. Besides the domestic horse, wild asses, wild horses, onagers, and zebras, there are numerous extinct species known from fossils.

equilateral geometrical figure, having all sides of equal length.

equilibrium in physics, an unchanging condition in which an undisturbed system can remain indefinitely in a state of balance. In a **static equilibrium**, such as an object resting on the floor, there is no motion. In a **dynamic equilibrium**, in contrast, a steady state is maintained by constant, though opposing, changes. For example, in a sealed bottle half-full of water, the constancy of the water level is a result of molecules evaporating from the surface and condensing on to it at the same rate.

equinox time when the Sun is directly overhead at the Earth's ▷Equator and consequently day and night are of equal length at all latitudes. This happens twice a year: on 21 March is the spring, or vernal, equinox, and on 23 September is the autumn equinox.

The variation in day lengths occurs because the Earth is tilted on its axis with respect to the Sun. However, because the Earth not only rotates on its own axis, but also orbits the Sun, at the equinoxes the two planets are positioned so that the circle of light from the Sun passes through both of the Earth's poles.

equity a company's assets, less its liabilities, which are the property of the owner or shareholders. Popularly, equities are stocks and shares which do not pay interest at fixed rates but pay dividends based on the company's performance. The value of equities tends to rise over the long term, but in the short term they are a risk investment because prices can fall as well as rise. Equity is also used to refer to the paid value of mortgaged real property, most commonly a house.

equity system of law supplementing the ordinary rules of law where the application of these would operate harshly in a particular case; sometimes it is regarded as an attempt to achieve 'natural justice'. So understood, equity appears as an element in most legal systems, and in a number of legal codes judges are instructed to apply both the rules of strict law and the principles of equity in reaching their decisions.

era any of the major divisions of geological time that includes several periods but is part of an eon. The eras of the current Phanerozoic in chronological order are the Palaeozoic, Mesozoic, and Cenozoic. We are living in the Recent epoch of the Quaternary period of the Cenozoic era.

Geological time is broken up into **geochronological units** of which era is just one level of division. The hierarchy of geochronological divisions is eon, era, period, ▷epoch, age, and chron. Eras are subdivisions of eons and periods are subdivisions of eras. Rocks representing an era of geological time comprise an **erathem**.

Erasmus, Desiderius (*c.* 1469–1536) Dutch scholar and leading humanist of the Renaissance era, who taught and studied all over Europe and was a prolific writer. His pioneer translation of the Greek New Testament (with parallel Latin text, 1516) exposed the Vulgate as a second-hand document. Although opposed to dogmatism and abuse of church power, he remained impartial during Martin ▷Luther's conflict with the pope.

Erasmus was born in Rotterdam, and as a youth he was a monk in an Augustinian monastery near Gouda. After becoming a priest, he went to study in Paris in 1495. He paid the first of a number of visits to England in 1499, where he met the physician Thomas Linacre, the politician Thomas More, and the Bible interpreter John Colet, and for a time was professor of divinity and Greek at Cambridge University. He also edited the writings of St Jerome and the early Christian authorities, and published *Encomium Moriae/The Praise of Folly* (1511, a satire on church and society that quickly became an international best-seller) and *Colloquia* (1519, dialogues on contemporary subjects). In 1521 he went to Basel, Switzerland, where he edited the writings of the early Christian leaders.

> **Desiderius Erasmus**
> *Let a king recall that to improve his realm is better than to increase his territory.*
> *Querella Pacis*, July 1517

Erastianism belief that the church should be subordinated to the state. The name is derived from Thomas Erastus (1534–1583), a Swiss-German theologian and opponent of Calvinism, who maintained in his writings that the church should not have the power of excluding people as a punishment for sin.

Eratosthenes (*c.* 276–*c.* 194 BC) Greek geographer and mathematician whose map of the ancient world was the first to contain lines of latitude and longitude, and who calculated the Earth's circumference with an error of about 10%. His mathematical achievements include a method for duplicating the cube, and for finding ▷prime numbers (Eratosthenes' sieve).

Eratosthenes' sieve a method for finding ▷prime numbers. It involves writing in sequence all numbers from 2. Then, starting with 2, cross out every second number (but not 2 itself), thus eliminating numbers that can be divided by 2. Next, starting with 3, cross out every third number (but not 3 itself), and continue the process for 5, 7, 11, 13, and so on. The numbers that remain are primes.

erbium soft, lustrous, greyish, metallic element of the ▷lanthanide series, symbol Er, atomic number 68, relative atomic mass 167.26. It occurs with the element yttrium or as a minute part of various minerals. It was discovered in 1843 by Carl Mosander (1797–1858), and named after the town of Ytterby, Sweden, near which the lanthanides (rare-earth elements) were first found.

Erbium has been used since 1987 to amplify data pulses in optical fibre, enabling faster transmission. Erbium ions in the fibreglass, charged with infrared light, emit energy by amplifying the data pulse as it moves along the fibre.

Erebus in Greek mythology, the god of darkness; also the intermediate subterranean region between upper Earth and ▷Hades through which the spirits (shades) passed.

Erebus, Mount the world's southernmost active volcano, located on Ross Island, Antarctica; height 4,072 m/13,359 ft.

ergonomics study of the relationship between people and the furniture, tools, and machinery they use at work. The object is to improve work performance by removing sources of muscular stress and general fatigue: for example, by presenting data and control panels in easy-to-view form, making office furniture comfortable, and creating a generally pleasant environment.

ergot any of a group of parasitic fungi (especially of the genus *Claviceps*), whose brown or black grainlike masses replace the kernels of rye or other cereals. *C. purpurea* attacks the rye plant. Ergot poisoning is caused by eating infected bread, resulting in burning pains, gangrene, and convulsions.

Erhard, Ludwig (1897–1977) German economist and Christian Democrat politician, chancellor of the Federal Republic 1963–66. He became known as the 'father of the German economic miracle'. As economics minister 1949–63 he instituted policies driven by his vision of a 'social market economy', in which a capitalist free market would be tempered by an active role for the state in providing a market-friendly social welfare system. His period as chancellor was less distinguished.

erica any plant of a large group that includes the heathers. There are about 500 species, distributed mainly in South Africa with some in Europe. (Genus *Erica*, family Ericaceae.)

Eric the Red (*c.* 950–1010) Allegedly the first European to find Greenland. According to a 13th-century saga, he was the son of a Norwegian chieftain, and was banished from Iceland in about 982 for murder. He then sailed westward and discovered a land that he called Greenland.

Eridanus in astronomy, the sixth-largest constellation, which meanders from the celestial equator (see ▷celestial sphere) deep into the southern hemisphere of the sky. Eridanus is represented as a river. Its brightest star is ▷Achernar, a corruption of the Arabic for 'the end of the river'.

Eridu ancient city of Mesopotamia of about 5000 BC, according to tradition the cradle of Sumerian civilization. On its site is now the village of Tell Abu Shahrain, Iraq.

Erie city and port on the Pennsylvania bank of Lake Erie, USA; population (1992) 109,300. It has heavy industries and a trade in iron, grain, and freshwater fish. A French fort was built on the site in 1753, and a permanent settlement was laid out in 1795.

Erie, Lake fourth largest of the Great Lakes of North America, connected to Lake Ontario by the Niagara River and bypassed by the Welland Canal; length 388 km/241 mi; width 48–91 km/30–56 mi; area 25,720 sq km/9,930 sq mi. The most southerly of the Great Lakes, it is bounded on the north by Ontario, Canada; on the south and southeast by Ohio, Pennsylvania, and New York; and on the west by Michigan. Lake Erie is an important link in the St Lawrence Seaway.

It is linked to Lake Huron by Lake St Clair and the St Clair and Detroit rivers, and to the Hudson River by the New York State Barge Canal. Lake Erie ports include Cleveland and Toledo in Ohio; Erie in Pennsylvania; and Buffalo in New York. There are several small islands in the western section of the lake, including Pelee, North Bass, Middle Bass, and South Bass islands. The shallowest of the Great Lakes (greatest depth 64 m/210 ft; average depth 19 m/62 ft), Lake Erie lies 170 m/558 ft above mean sea-level. The lake has been severely polluted from industrial and municipal waste.

Eritrea see country box.

Erivan alternative transliteration of ▷Yerevan, the capital of Armenia.

ERM abbreviation for ▷Exchange Rate Mechanism.

ermine the ▷stoat during winter, when its coat becomes white. In northern latitudes the coat becomes completely white, except for a black tip on the tail, but in warmer regions the back may remain brownish. The fur is used commercially.

Ernst, Max (1891–1976) German artist, a major figure in ▷Dada and then ▷surrealism. He worked in France 1922–38 and in the USA from 1941. He experimented with collage, photomontage, and surreal images, creating some of the most haunting and distinctive images of 20th-century art. His works include *The Elephant Celebes* (1921; Tate Gallery, London) and *The Temptation of St Anthony* (1945; Lehmbruck Museum, Duisburg).

Ernst was born in Brühl, near Cologne, and studied philosophy at Bonn. He first exhibited in Berlin in 1916. In 1919 he was a leading figure in Dadaist demonstrations in Cologne, and going to Paris in 1920 he helped André Breton and Paul Eluard in founding the surrealist movement. He became one of its leading visual exponents, creating fantastical images using 19th-century illustrations, and painting bizarre figures, often half animal, and elaborate, dreamlike landscapes. He invented the technique of frottage (rubbing colour or graphite on paper laid over a textured surface), a technique he saw as akin to surrealist automatic writing. In his sculpture, he was influenced by primitive art. He worked in a variety of media, producing a 'collage novel', *La Femme cent têtes* (1929), working on films with Salvador Dalí and Luis Buñuel, and designing sets and costumes for Sergei Diaghilev's Ballets Russes. In 1938 he left the surrealist group after a disagreement with Breton and in 1941 settled in New York, where he became an important figure in the development of American art. He returned to Paris in 1953.

Eros in astronomy, an asteroid, discovered in 1898 by G Witt, that can pass 22 million km/14 million mi from the Earth, as observed in 1975. Eros was the first asteroid to be discovered that has an orbit coming within that of Mars. It is elongated, measures $33 \times 13 \times 13$ km/$21 \times 8 \times 8$ mi (measured in March 2000 by the Near Earth Asteroid Rendezvous (NEAR)), rotates around its shortest axis every 5.3 hours, and orbits the Sun every 1.8 years.

Equatorial Guinea

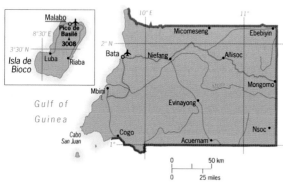

Equatorial Guinea country in west-central Africa, bounded north by Cameroon, east and south by Gabon, and west by the Atlantic Ocean; also five offshore islands including Bioko, off the coast of Cameroon.

NATIONAL NAME *República de Guinea Ecuatorial/Republic of Equatorial Guinea*
AREA 28,051 sq km/10,830 sq mi
CAPITAL Malabo
MAJOR TOWNS/CITIES Bata, Mongomo, Ela Nguema, Mbini, Campo Yaunde, Los Angeles
PHYSICAL FEATURES comprises mainland Río Muni, plus the small islands of Corisco, Elobey Grande and Elobey Chico, and Bioko (formerly Fernando Po) together with Annobón (formerly Pagalú); nearly half the land is forested; volcanic mountains on Bioko

Government

HEAD OF STATE Teodoro Obiang Nguema Mbasogo from 1979
HEAD OF GOVERNMENT Cándido Muatetema Rivas from 2001
POLITICAL SYSTEM authoritarian nationalist
POLITICAL EXECUTIVE unlimited presidency
ADMINISTRATIVE DIVISIONS seven provinces
ARMED FORCES 2,300 (2002 est)
DEATH PENALTY retained and used for ordinary crimes

Economy and resources

CURRENCY franc CFA
GPD (US$) 2.2 billion (2002 est)
REAL GDP GROWTH (% change on previous year) 62.5 (2001)
GNI PER CAPITA (PPP) (US$) 5,590 (2002 est)
CONSUMER PRICE INFLATION 10% (2003 est)
FOREIGN DEBT (US$) 197 million (2003 est)
MAJOR TRADING PARTNERS USA, Spain, China, UK, Japan, Côte d'Ivoire
RESOURCES petroleum, natural gas, gold, uranium, iron ore, tantalum, manganese
INDUSTRIES wood processing, food processing
EXPORTS petroleum, methanol, timber, re-exported ships and boats, textile fibres and waste, cocoa, coffee. Principal market: Spain 53% (2001)
IMPORTS ships and boats, petroleum and related products, food and live animals, machinery and transport equipment, beverages and tobacco, basic manufactures. Principal source: USA 33% (2001)
ARABLE LAND 5% (2000 est)
AGRICULTURAL PRODUCTS cocoa, coffee, cassava, sweet potatoes, bananas, palm oil, palm kernels; exploitation of forest resources (principally of okoumé and akoga timber)

Population and society

POPULATION 494,000 (2003 est)
POPULATION GROWTH RATE 2.8% (2000–05)
POPULATION DENSITY (per sq km) 18 (2003 est)
URBAN POPULATION (% of total) 51 (2003 est)
AGE DISTRIBUTION (% of total population) 0–14 44%, 15–59 50%, 60+ 6% (2002 est)
ETHNIC GROUPS 80–90% of the Fang ethnic group, of Bantu origin; most other groups have been pushed to the coast by Fang expansion; the Bubi are the indigenous ethnic group of Bioko (island)
LANGUAGE Spanish (official), pidgin English, a Portuguese patois (on Annobón, whose people were formerly slaves of the Portuguese), Fang and other African patois (on Río Muni)
RELIGION Roman Catholic, Protestant, animist
EDUCATION (compulsory years) 8
LITERACY RATE 93% (men); 78% (women) (2003 est)
LABOUR FORCE 77% agriculture, 2% industry, 21% services (1990)
LIFE EXPECTANCY 48 (men); 51 (women) (2000–05)
CHILD MORTALITY RATE (under 5, per 1,000 live births) 153 (2001)
PHYSICIANS (per 1,000 people) 0.2 (1996 est)
TV SETS (per 1,000 people) 118 (1999 est)
RADIOS (per 1,000 people) 428 (1997)
INTERNET USERS (per 10,000 people) 34.8 (2002 est)
PERSONAL COMPUTER USERS (per 100 people) 0.7 (2002 est)

See also ▷Fang.

Chronology

1472: First visited by Portuguese explorers.

1778: Bioko (formerly known as Fernando Po) Island ceded to Spain, which established cocoa plantations there in the late 19th century, importing labour from West Africa.

1885: Mainland territory of Mbini (formerly Rio Muni) came under Spanish rule, the whole colony being known as Spanish Guinea, with the capital at Malabu on Bioko Island.

1920s: League of Nations special mission sent to investigate the forced, quasi-slave labour conditions on the Bioko cocoa plantations, then the largest in the world.

1959: Became a Spanish Overseas Province; African population finally granted full citizenship.

early 1960s: On the mainland, the Fang people spearheaded a nationalist movement directed against Spanish favouritism towards Bioko Island and its controlling Bubi tribe.

1963: Achieved internal autonomy.

1968: Independence achieved from Spain. Macias Nguema, a nationalist Fang, became first president, discriminating against the Bubi community.

1970s: The economy collapsed as Spanish settlers and other minorities fled in the face of intimidation by Nguema's brutal, dictatorial regime, which was marked by the murder, torture, and imprisonment of tens of thousands of political opponents and rivals.

1979: Nguema was overthrown, tried, and executed. He was replaced by his nephew, Teodoro Obiang Nguema Mbasogo, who established a military regime, but released political prisoners and imposed restrictions on the Catholic Church.

1992: A new pluralist constitution was approved by referendum.

1993: Obiang's PDGE won the first multiparty elections on low turnout.

1996: Obiang was re-elected amid claims of fraud by opponents. Angel Serafin Seriche Dougan became prime minister, and was reappointed in 1998.

2001: Dougan resigned following allegations of corruption, and was replaced by Cándido Muatetema Rivas.

EQUATORIAL GUINEA The population of gorillas in Equatorial Guinea is under threat, despite their protected status within extensive areas of land. *Stanley Gibbons*

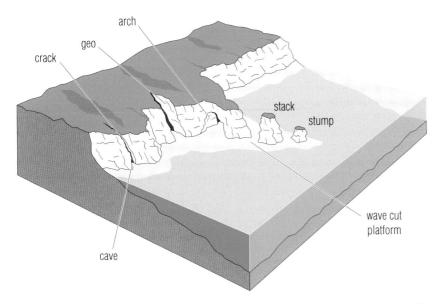

EROSION Typical features of coastal erosion, from the initial cracks in less resistant rocks through to arches, stacks, and stumps that can occur as erosion progresses.

erosion wearing away of the Earth's surface, caused by the breakdown and transportation of particles of rock or soil (by contrast, ▷weathering does not involve transportation). Water, consisting of sea waves and currents, rivers, and rain; ice, in the form of glaciers; and wind, hurling sand fragments against exposed rocks and moving dunes along, are the most potent forces of erosion.

People also contribute to erosion by bad farming practices and the cutting down of forests, which can lead to the formation of dust bowls.

There are several processes of river erosion including ▷hydraulic action, ▷corrasion, ▷attrition, and ▷solution.

Related Web site: Erosion and Deposition http://www.geog.ouc.bc.ca/physgeog/contents/11g.html

EROSION The red scars of soil erosion are now a common feature of the central plateau of Madagascar. *Premaphotos Wildlife*

erratic in geology, a displaced rock that has been transported by a glacier or some other natural force to a site of different geological composition.

error in computing, a fault or mistake, either in the software or on the part of the user, that causes a program to stop running (crash) or produce unexpected results. Program errors, or bugs, are largely eliminated in the course of the programmer's initial testing procedure, but some will remain in most programs. All computer operating systems are designed to produce an **error message** (on the display screen, or in an error file or printout) whenever an error has been detected, reporting that an error has taken place and, wherever possible, diagnosing its cause.

Erse originally a Scottish form of the word *Irish*, a name applied by Lowland Scots to Scottish Gaelic and also sometimes used as a synonym for Irish Gaelic.

Ershad, Hussain Muhammad (1930–) Military ruler of Bangladesh 1982–90. He became chief of staff of the Bangladeshi army in 1979 and assumed power in a military coup in 1982. As president from 1983, Ershad introduced a successful rural-oriented economic programme. He was re-elected in 1986 and lifted martial law, but faced continuing political opposition, which forced him to resign in December 1990.

Erskine, Ralph (1914–) English-born architect. He settled in Sweden in 1939. He specialized in community architecture before it was named as such. A deep social consciousness and a concern to mould building form in response to climate determine his architecture. His Byker Estate in Newcastle-upon-Tyne (1969–80), where a sheltering wall of dwellings embraces the development, involved a lengthy process of consultation with the residents.

> **Ralph Erskine**
> *The job of buildings is to improve human relations; architecture must ease them, not make them worse.*
> The Times, 16 September 1992

Erté (1892–1990) Adopted name of Romain de Tirtoff. Russian designer and illustrator. He was active in France and the USA. An exponent of ▷art deco, he designed sets and costumes for opera, theatre, and ballet, and his drawings were highly stylized and expressive, featuring elegant, curvilinear women.

erythrocyte another name for ▷red blood cell.

ESA abbreviation for ▷European Space Agency.

escalator automatic moving staircase that carries people between floors or levels. It consists of treads linked in an endless belt arranged to form strips (steps), powered by an electric motor that moves both steps and handrails at the same speed. Towards the top and bottom the steps flatten out for ease of passage. The first escalator was exhibited in Paris in 1900.

escape velocity in physics, minimum velocity with which an object must be projected for it to escape from the gravitational pull of a planetary body. In the case of the Earth, the escape velocity is 11.2 kps/6.9 mps; the Moon, 2.4 kps/1.5 mps; Mars, 5 kps/3.1 mps; and Jupiter, 59.6 kps/37 mps.

escarpment (or **cuesta**) large ridge created by the erosion of dipping sedimentary rocks. It has one steep side (scarp) and one gently sloping side (dip). Escarpments are common features of chalk landscapes, such as the Chiltern Hills and the North Downs in England. Certain features are associated with chalk escarpments, including dry valleys (formed on the dip slope), combes (steep-sided valleys on the scarp slope), and springs.

Escherichia coli (or **colon bacillus**) rod-shaped Gram-negative bacterium (see ▷bacteria) that lives, usually harmlessly, in the colon of most warm-blooded animals. It is the commonest cause of urinary tract infections in humans. It is sometimes found in water or meat where faecal contamination has occurred and can cause severe gastric problems.

The mapping of the genome of *E. coli*, consisting of 4,403 genes, was completed in 1997. It is probably the organism about which most molecular genetics is known, and is of pre-eminent importance in recombinant DNA research.

Classification *Escherichia coli* is the only species in the bacterial family Enterobacteriaceae.

Two outbreaks of food poisoning involving a lethal strain of *E. coli* in Scotland in December 1996 and January 1997, resulted in 20 deaths. A resulting report from the Meat and Livestock Commission (MLC) in March 1997 revealed that all stages of food handling in Britain, from the abbatoir to the plate, were suspect to some degree. All stages were identified as needing higher standards. It was revealed that the European Commission had warned the government to clean up Britain's abbatoirs in 1989. Another EC inspection in 1996 still found 'serious weaknesses' in Britain's slaughterhouses, including meat being contaminated by excrement.

Escher, M(aurits) C(ornelis) (1898–1972) Dutch graphic artist. His prints are often based on mathematical concepts and contain paradoxes and illusions. The lithograph *Ascending and Descending* (1960), with interlocking staircases creating a perspective puzzle, is a typical work. His work has continued to fascinate artists, mathematicians, psychologists, and the general public.

Escorial, El monastery and palace standing over 900 m/2,953 ft above sea level on a southeastern slope of the Sierra de Guadarrama, 42 km/26 mi northwest of Madrid, Spain. El Escorial was built (1563–84) for Philip II. It was designed by Juan Bautista de Toledo (assistant to Michelangelo at St Peter's, Rome (1546–48)) and Juan de Herrera (c. 1530–97).

Esenin (or **Yesenin**), **Sergey Aleksandrovich** (1895–1925) Soviet poet, born in Konstantinovo (renamed Esenino in his honour). He went to Petrograd in 1915, attached himself to the Symbolists, welcomed the Russian Revolution, revived peasant traditions and folklore, and initiated the Imaginist group of poets in 1919. A selection of his poetry was translated in *Confessions of a Hooligan* (1973). He was married briefly to US dancer Isadora Duncan 1922–23.

Esfahan (or **Isfahan**; formerly **Ispahan**) city in central Iran and capital of the province of the same name; population (1991) 1,127,000. The town lies on the Zayandeh Rud River at an altitude of 1,600 m/5,250 ft, in the centre of a large fertile oasis. Industries include steel, textiles, carpets, and traditional handicrafts. It was the ancient capital (1598–1722) of ▷Abbas I. Its features include the Great Square, where polo was played, the Sheikh Lutfullah Mosque, the Hall of Forty Pillars known as Chihil Sutun, the Ali Qapu gate, the Khaju and Aliverdi Khan bridges, and the Shah Hussain madrasah, a school for dervishes built in 1710.

Eskimo Algonquian term for Arctic peoples meaning 'eater of raw meat', now considered offensive. See ▷Inuit.

ESP abbreviation for ▷extrasensory perception.

esparto species of grass native to southern Spain, southern Portugal, and the Balearics, but now widely grown in dry, sandy locations throughout the world. The plant is just over 1 m/3 ft high, producing greyish-green leaves, which are used for making paper, ropes, baskets, mats, and cables. (*Stipa tenacissima.*)

Esperanto language devised in 1887 by Polish philologist Ludwig L ▷Zamenhof as an international auxiliary language. For its structure and vocabulary it draws on Latin, the Romance languages, English, and German. At its centenary in 1987, Esperantists claimed 10–15 million users worldwide.

espionage the practice of spying; a way to gather ▷intelligence.

essay short piece of non-fiction, often dealing with a particular subject from a personal point of view. The essay became a recognized genre with the French writer Montaigne's *Essais* (1580) and in English with Francis Bacon's *Essays* (1597). Today the essay is a part of journalism: articles in the broadsheet newspapers are in the essay tradition.

Essen city in North Rhine-Westphalia, Germany, 29 km/18 mi northeast of Düsseldorf; population (1995) 616,400. It is the administrative centre of the ▷Ruhr region, situated between the rivers Emscher and Ruhr. Industries include coalmining, steel, glass-making, chemicals, telecommunications, and electronics. Its 9th–14th-century minster is one of the oldest churches in Germany. Half of the city's buildings were destroyed during World War II.

Essene member of an ancient Jewish religious sect located in the area near the Dead Sea *c.* 200 BC–AD 200, whose members lived a life of denial and asceticism, as they believed that the day of judgement was imminent.

Essequibo longest river in Guyana, South America, draining more than half the total area of the country; length 1,014 km/630 mi; it rises in the Guiana Highlands of southern Guyana and flows north past Bartica to meet the Atlantic at a 32 km/20 mi wide delta. Its course is interrupted by numerous rapids and falls, but its lower course is navigable for large vessels for 80 km/50 mi as far as Bartica. Its major tributaries include the Rupununi, Potaro, Mazaruni, and Cuyuni rivers.

Essex (Old English East-Seaxe) county of southeast England, which has contained the unitary authorities of Southend and Thurrock since April 1998.

area 3,670 sq km/1,417 sq mi **towns and cities** Chelmsford (administrative headquarters), Basildon, Colchester, Harlow, Harwich (port), Clacton-on-Sea (resort) **physical** flat and marshy near the coast; richly wooded in the southwest; rivers: the Blackwater, Crouch, Colne, Lee, Stour, and Thames **features** former royal hunting ground of Epping Forest (2300 ha/5680 acres, controlled from 1882 by the City of London); since 1111 at Little Dunmow (and later at Great Dunmow) the Dunmow flitch (side of cured pork) can be claimed every four years by any couple proving to a jury they have not regretted their marriage within the year (winners are few); Stansted, London's third airport; new Roman Catholic cathedral at Brentwood (designed by Quinlan Terry), dedicated in 1991 **agriculture** cereals (wheat), fruit, sugar beet; livestock rearing, dairy products; oysters **industries** brewing, cars, cement, engineering (at Dagenham, Chelmsford, and Colchester), food processing, oil products (there are large oil refineries at Shellhaven and Canvey) **population** (1996) 1,586,100

Eritrea

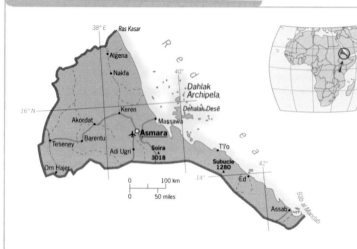

Eritrea country in East Africa, bounded north by Sudan, south by Ethiopia, southeast by Djibouti, and east by the Red Sea.

NATIONAL NAME *Hagere Eretra al-Dawla al-Iritra/State of Eritrea*
AREA 125,000 sq km/48,262 sq mi
CAPITAL Asmara
MAJOR TOWNS/CITIES Assab, Keren, Massawa, Adi Ugri, Ed
MAJOR PORTS Assab, Massawa
PHYSICAL FEATURES coastline along the Red Sea 1,000 km/620 mi; narrow coastal plain that rises to an inland plateau; Dahlak Islands

Government

HEAD OF STATE AND GOVERNMENT Issaias Afwerki from 1993
POLITICAL SYSTEM nationalistic socialist
POLITICAL EXECUTIVE unlimited presidency
ADMINISTRATIVE DIVISIONS six regions
ARMED FORCES 172,200; plus 120,000 reservists (2002 est)

DEATH PENALTY retained and used for ordinary crimes

Economy and resources

CURRENCY nakfa
GPD (US$) 582 million (2002 est)
REAL GDP GROWTH (% change on previous year) 3 (2001)
GNI (US$) 670 million (2002 est)
GNI PER CAPITA (PPP) (US$) 950 (2002 est)
CONSUMER PRICE INFLATION 23.9% (2003 est)
UNEMPLOYMENT 25% (2001)
FOREIGN DEBT (US$) 397 million (2001 est)
MAJOR TRADING PARTNERS Ethiopia, Saudi Arabia, Italy, Sudan, Japan, United Arab Emirates, UK, Korea
RESOURCES gold, silver, copper, zinc, sulphur, nickel, chrome, potash, basalt, limestone, marble, sand, silicates

INDUSTRIES food processing, textiles, leatherwear, building materials, glassware, petroleum products
EXPORTS textiles, leather and leather products, beverages, petroleum products, basic household goods. Principal market: Sudan 27.2% (1998)
IMPORTS machinery and transport equipment, petroleum, food and live animals, basic manufactures. Principal source: Italy 17.4% (1998)
ARABLE LAND 4.9% (2000 est)
AGRICULTURAL PRODUCTS sorghum, teff (an indigenous grain), maize, wheat, millet; livestock rearing (goats and camels); fisheries

Population and society

POPULATION 4,141,000 (2003 est)
POPULATION GROWTH RATE 2.4% (2000–15)
POPULATION DENSITY (per sq km) 35 (2003 est)

URBAN POPULATION (% of total) 20 (2003 est)
AGE DISTRIBUTION (% of total population) 0–14 44%, 15–59 51%, 60+ 5% (2002 est)
ETHNIC GROUPS ethnic Tigrinya 50%, Tigre and Kunama 40%, Afar 4%, Saho 3%
LANGUAGE Tigre, Tigrinya, Arabic, English, Afar, Amharic, Kunama, Italian
RELIGION mainly Sunni Muslim and Coptic Christian, some Roman Catholic, Protestant, and animist
EDUCATION (compulsory years) 7
LITERACY RATE 70% (men); 48% (women) (2003 est)
LABOUR FORCE 80.5% agriculture, 5.0% industry, 14.5% services (1990)
LIFE EXPECTANCY 51 (men); 54 (women) (2000–05)
CHILD MORTALITY RATE (under 5, per 1,000 live births) 111 (2001)
PHYSICIANS (per 1,000 people) 0.03 (1996 est)
TV SETS (per 1,000 people) 39 (2001 est)
RADIOS (per 1,000 people) 464 (2001 est)
INTERNET USERS (per 10,000 people) 22.6 (2002 est)
PERSONAL COMPUTER USERS (per 100 people) 0.3 (2002 est)

See also ▷Ethiopia; ▷Haile Selassie; ▷Mengistu, Haile Mariam.

See also ▷Ethiopia; ▷Haile Selassie; ▷Mengistu, Haile Mariam.

Chronology

4th–7th centuries AD: Part of Ethiopian Aksum kingdom.

8th century: Islam introduced to coastal areas by Arabs.

12th–16th centuries: Under influence of Ethiopian Abyssinian kingdoms.

mid-16th century: Came under control of Turkish Ottoman Empire.

1882: Occupied by Italy.

1889: Italian colony of Eritrea created out of Ottoman areas and coastal districts of Ethiopia.

1920s: Massawa developed into the largest port in East Africa.

1935–36: Used as base for Italy's conquest of Ethiopia and became part of Italian East Africa.

1941: Became British protectorate after Italy removed from North Africa.

1952: Federation formed with Ethiopia by United Nations (UN).

1958: Eritrean People's Liberation Front (EPLF) was formed to fight for independence after a general strike was brutally suppressed by Ethiopian rulers.

1962: Annexed by Ethiopia, sparking a secessionist rebellion which was to last 30 years and claim 150,000 lives.

1974: Ethiopian emperor Haile Selassie was deposed by the military; the EPLF continued the struggle for independence.

1977–78: The EPLF cleared the territory of Ethiopian forces, but the position was soon reversed by the Soviet-backed Marxist Ethiopian government of Col Mengistu Haile Mariam.

mid-1980s: There was severe famine in Eritrea and a refugee crisis as the Ethiopian government sought forcible resettlement.

1990: The strategic port of Massawa was captured by Eritrean rebel forces.

1991: Ethiopian president Mengistu was overthrown. The EPLF secured the whole of Eritrea and a provisional government was formed under Issaias Afwerki.

1993: Independence was approved in a regional referendum and recognized by Ethiopia. A transitional government was established, with Afwerki elected president; 500,000 refugees outside Eritrea began to return.

1998: Border disputes with Ethiopia escalated, with bombing raids from both sides.

1999: The border dispute with Ethiopia erupted into war in February. Peace was agreed the following month, but fighting was renewed.

2000: The Ethiopian military offensive caused Eritrea to pull its forces back to the line it held before the escalation of violence in 1998. A ceasefire was agreed in June and a peace agreement signed in December that provided for UN troops to keep the peace along the border.

ERITREA A road winds through the rugged mountains of Eritrea.

ESSEX Mud flats in the estuary of the River Blackwater, near Maldon in Essex, England. *Aerofilms*

famous people William Gilbert, William Harvey, Joseph Lister, Gerard Manley Hopkins, John Ray

Related Web site: Essex County Council Web Site http://www.essexcc.gov.uk/

Essex, Robert Devereux, 2nd Earl of Essex (1566–1601) English soldier and politician. Having taken part in the Dutch fight against Spain, he became a favourite with Queen ▷Elizabeth I in 1587, but fell from grace because of his policies in Ireland, where he was Lieutenant from 1599, and was executed.

Son of Walter Devereaux, 1st Earl of Essex, and stepson to Robert Dudley, Earl of Leicester, he succeeded to the earldom in 1576. Essex fought in the Netherlands (1585–86), supporting their war of liberation from Spain, and distinguished himself at the Battle of Zutphen. In 1596 he jointly commanded a force that seized and sacked Cádiz. In 1599 he became Lieutenant of Ireland and led an army against Irish rebels under the Earl of Tyrone in Ulster, but was unsuccessful, made an unauthorized truce with Tyrone, and returned without permission to England. He was forbidden to return to court, and when he marched into the City of London at the head of a body of supporters, he was promptly arrested, tried for treason, and beheaded on Tower Green.

Essex, Robert Devereux, 3rd Earl of Essex (1591–1646) English soldier. Eldest son of the 2nd earl, he commanded the Parliamentary army at the inconclusive English Civil War battle of Edgehill in 1642. Following a disastrous campaign in Cornwall, he resigned his command in 1645. He succeeded to the earldom in 1604.

est. abbreviation for estimate(d).

Establishment, the a perceived elite of the professional and governing classes (judges, civil servants, politicians, and so on) who collectively symbolize authority and the status quo.

estate in law, the rights that a person has in relation to any property. **Real estate** is an interest in any land; **personal estate** is an interest in any other kind of property.

estate in European history, an order of society that enjoyed a specified share in government. In medieval theory, there were usually three estates – the **nobility**, the **clergy**, and the **commons** – with the functions of, respectively, defending society from foreign aggression and internal disorder, attending to its spiritual needs, and working to produce the base with which to support the other two orders.

ester organic compound formed by the reaction between an alcohol and an acid, with the elimination of water. Unlike ▷salts, esters are covalent compounds.

Estonia see country box.

Estonian the largest ethnic group in Estonia. There are 1 million speakers of the Estonian language, a member of the Finno-Ugric branch of the Uralic family. Most live in Estonia.

estuary river mouth widening into the sea, where fresh water mixes with salt water and tidal effects are felt.

et al. abbreviation for **et alii** (Latin 'and others'), used in bibliography.

etc. abbreviation for **et cetera** (Latin 'and the rest').

etching printmaking technique in which a metal plate (usually copper or zinc) is covered with a waxy overlayer (ground) and then drawn on with an etching needle. The exposed areas are then 'etched', or bitten into, by a corrosive agent (acid), so that they will hold ink for printing.

ethanal (common name **acetaldehyde**) CH_3CHO one of the chief members of the group of organic compounds known as ▷aldehydes. It is a colourless inflammable liquid boiling at 20.8°C/69.6°F. Ethanal is formed by the oxidation of ethanol or ethene and is used to make many other organic chemical compounds.

ethanoate (common name **acetate**) $CH_3CO_2^-$, negative ion derived from ethanoic (acetic) acid; any salt containing this ion. In textiles, acetate rayon is a synthetic fabric made from modified cellulose (wood pulp) treated with ethanoic acid; in photography, acetate film is a non-flammable film made of cellulose ethanoate.

ethanoic acid (common name **acetic acid**) CH_3CO_2H one of the simplest fatty acids (a series of organic acids). In the pure state it is a colourless liquid with an unpleasant pungent odour; it solidifies to an icelike mass of crystals at 16.7°C/62.4°F, and hence is often called glacial ethanoic acid. Vinegar contains 5% or more ethanoic acid, produced by fermentation.

ethanol (or **ethyl alcohol**) C_2H_5OH alcohol found in beer, wine, cider, spirits, and other alcoholic drinks. When pure, it is a colourless liquid with a pleasant odour, miscible with water or ether; it burns in air with a pale blue flame. The vapour forms an explosive mixture with air and may be used in high-compression internal combustion engines.

It is produced naturally by the fermentation of carbohydrates by yeast cells. Industrially, it can be made by absorption of ethene and subsequent reaction with water, or by the reduction of ethanal in the presence of a catalyst, and is widely used as a solvent.

Ethanol is used as a raw material in the manufacture of ether, chloral, and iodoform. It can also be added to petrol, where it improves the performance of the engine, or be used as a fuel in its own right (as in Brazil). Crops such as sugar cane may be grown to provide ethanol (by fermentation) for this purpose.

> **James Mackintosh**
> Scottish lawyer, philosopher and historian
>
> *Men are never so good or so bad as their opinions.*
>
> *Ethical Philosophy*

Ethelbert (*c.* 552–616) King of Kent 560–616. He was defeated by the West Saxons in 568 but later became ruler of England south of the River Humber. Ethelbert received the Christian missionary Augustine in 597 and later converted to become the first Christian ruler of Anglo-Saxon England. He issued the first written code of laws known in England.

He married a French princess, Bertha.

Ethelred (II) the Unready (968–1016) King of England from 978, following the murder of his half-brother, Edward the Martyr. He was son of King Edgar. Ethelred tried to buy off the Danish raiders by paying Danegeld. In 1002 he ordered the massacre of the Danish settlers, provoking an invasion by Sweyn I of Denmark. War with Sweyn and Sweyn's son, Canute, occupied the rest of Ethelred's reign. His nickname is a corruption of the Old English 'unreed', meaning badly counselled or poorly advised.

ethene (common name **ethylene**) C_2H_4 colourless, flammable gas, the first member of the ▷alkene series of hydrocarbons. It is the most widely used synthetic organic chemical and is used to produce the plastics polyethene (polyethylene), polychloroethene, and polyvinyl chloride (PVC). It is obtained from natural gas or coal gas, or by the dehydration of ethanol.

ether in chemistry, any of a series of organic chemical compounds having an oxygen atom linking the carbon atoms of two hydrocarbon radical groups (general formula R-O-R'); also the common name for ethoxyethane $C_2H_5OC_2H_5$ (also called diethyl ether). This is used as an anaesthetic and as an external cleansing agent before surgical operations. It is also used as a solvent, and in the extraction of oils, fats, waxes, resins, and alkaloids.

Ethoxyethane is a colourless, volatile, inflammable liquid, slightly soluble in water, and miscible with ethanol. It is prepared by treatment of ethanol with excess concentrated sulphuric acid at 140°C/284°F.

ethics (or **moral philosophy**) branch of ▷philosophy concerned with the systematic study of human values. It involves the study of theories of conduct and goodness, and of the meanings of moral terms.

In ancient India and China, sages like Buddha and Lao Zi made recommendations about how people should live, as Jesus and Muhammad did in later centuries. However, ethics as a systematic study first appears with the Greek philosopher Socrates in the 5th century BC. Plato thought that objective standards (forms) of justice and goodness existed beyond the everyday world. In his *Nicomachean Ethics*, Aristotle argued that virtue is natural and so leads to happiness, and that moral virtues are acquired by practice, like skills. The Cyrenaics and Epicureans were hedonists who believed in the wise pursuit of pleasure. The Stoics advocated control of the passions and indifference to pleasure and pain.

The 'Christian ethic' is mainly a combination of New Testament moral teaching with ideas drawn from Plato and Aristotle, combining hedonism and rationalism. Medieval ▷scholasticism saw God's will as the ethical standard but tempered it with Aristotelian ethics.

In the 17th century, the Dutch philosopher Spinoza and the English Thomas Hobbes both believed that morals were deducible from prudence, but Spinoza's moral theory is set in a pantheistic metaphysics. In the 18th century, the English cleric Joseph Butler argued that virtue is natural and that benevolence and self-interest tend to coincide. The Scot David Hume, who influenced Jeremy Bentham, argued that moral judgements are based on feelings about pleasant and unpleasant consequences. For the German Immanuel Kant, morality could not have a purpose outside itself, so the good person acts only from duty, not feeling or self-interest, and in accordance with the categorical imperative (the obligation to obey absolute moral law). Utilitarianism, devised by Bentham and refined by J S Mill in the 19th century, has been immensely influential, especially in social policy.

In the 20th century, the British philosopher G E Moore argued in *Principia Ethica* 1903 that the concept of goodness was simple and indefinable. The French Jean-Paul Sartre's existentialist emphasis on choice and responsibility has been influential, too. The English novelist and philosopher Iris Murdoch has explored the relationship between goodness and beauty, whereas Mary Midgley has tried to update Aristotle's view of human nature by reference to studies of animal behaviour.

Ethics is closely linked to other disciplines, such as anthropology, ethology, political theory, psychology, and sociology. Increasingly, moral philosophers analyse such ethical problems as war, animal rights, abortion, euthanasia, and embryo research; ▷medical ethics has emerged as a specialized branch of ethics.

Ethiopia see country box.

ethnic cleansing the forced expulsion of one ethnic group by another to create a homogenous population, for example, of more than 2 million Muslims by Serbs in Bosnia-Herzegovina 1992–95. The term has also been used to describe the killing of Hutus and Tutsis in Rwanda and Burundi in 1994, and for earlier mass exiles, as far back as the book of Exodus.

ethnicity (from Greek *ethnos* 'a people') people's own sense of cultural identity; a social term that overlaps with such concepts as race, nation, class, and religion.

ethnocentrism viewing other peoples and cultures from the standard of one's own cultural assumptions, customs, and values. In anthropology, ethnocentrism is avoided in preference for a position of ▷relativism.

ethnography study of living cultures, using anthropological techniques like participant observation (where the anthropologist lives in the society being studied) and a reliance on informants. Ethnography has provided much data of use to archaeologists as analogies.

ethnology study of contemporary peoples, concentrating on their geography and culture, as distinct from their social systems. Ethnologists make a comparative analysis of data from different cultures to understand how cultures work and why they change, with a view to deriving general principles about human society.

ethnotourism tourism centred around an indigenous group of people and their culture. Ethnotourists seek the experience of other cultures, a major part of which is participating in another way of life and seeing people carrying out their daily routines. It is important that what is seen and experienced is authentic. Inevitably though, the influx of visitors destroys the very thing they seek. Cultures have come to accommodate and put on shows for tourists. The most popular locations are remote areas of the Amazon, Thailand, and Indonesia. Groups are small, usually 8 to 12 people, and are led by guides familiar with the tribes and their customs, taboos, and codes of conduct.

ethology comparative study of animal behaviour in its natural setting. Ethology is concerned with the causal mechanisms (both the stimuli that elicit behaviour and the physiological mechanisms controlling it), as well as the development of behaviour, its function, and its evolutionary history.

Ethology was pioneered during the 1930s by the Austrians Konrad Lorenz and Karl von Frisch who, with the Dutch zoologist Nikolaas Tinbergen, received the Nobel prize in 1973. Ethologists believe that the significance of an animal's behaviour can be understood only in its natural context, and emphasize the

Estonia

Estonia country in northern Europe, bounded east by Russia, south by Latvia, and north and west by the Baltic Sea.

NATIONAL NAME *Eesti Vabariik/Republic of Estonia*
AREA 45,000 sq km/17,374 sq mi
CAPITAL Tallinn
MAJOR TOWNS/CITIES Tartu, Narva, Kohtla-Järve, Pärnu
PHYSICAL FEATURES lakes and marshes in a partly forested plain; 774 km/481 mi of coastline; mild climate; Lake Peipus and Narva River forming boundary with Russian Federation; Baltic islands, the largest of which is Saaremaa

Government

HEAD OF STATE Arnold Rüütl from 2001
HEAD OF GOVERNMENT Juhan Parts from 2003
POLITICAL SYSTEM emergent democracy
POLITICAL EXECUTIVE dual executive
ADMINISTRATIVE DIVISIONS 15 counties
ARMED FORCES 5,500; plus 24,000 reservists and paramilitary border guard of 2,600 (2002 est)

CONSCRIPTION compulsory for 11 months (men and women)
DEATH PENALTY abolished in 1998
DEFENCE SPEND (% GDP) 1.6 (2002 est)
EDUCATION SPEND (% GDP) 7.5 (2000 est)
HEALTH SPEND (% GDP) 6.1 (2000 est)

Economy and resources

CURRENCY kroon
GPD (US$) 6.4 billion (2002 est)
REAL GDP GROWTH (% change on previous year) 5 (2001)
GNI (US$) 5.6 billion (2002 est)
GNI PER CAPITA (PPP) (US$) 11,120 (2002 est)
CONSUMER PRICE INFLATION 3.6% (2003 est)
UNEMPLOYMENT 12.6% (2001)
FOREIGN DEBT (US$) 1.6 billion (2001 est)
MAJOR TRADING PARTNERS Finland, Russia, Sweden, Germany, Latvia, the Netherlands, Lithuania, UK, Japan, Italy, Denmark

RESOURCES oilshale, peat, phosphorite ore, superphosphates
INDUSTRIES machine building, electronics, electrical engineering, textiles, fish and food processing, consumer goods
EXPORTS foodstuffs, animal products, textiles, timber products, base metals, mineral products, machinery. Principal market: Finland 33.8% (2001)
IMPORTS machinery and transport equipment, food products, textiles, mineral products. Principal source: Finland 18% (2001)
ARABLE LAND 26.5% (2000 est)
AGRICULTURAL PRODUCTS wheat, rye, barley, potatoes, other vegetables; livestock rearing (cattle and pigs); dairy farming

Population and society

POPULATION 1,323,000 (2003 est)
POPULATION GROWTH RATE −0.5% (2000–15)

POPULATION DENSITY (per sq km) 29 (2003 est)
URBAN POPULATION (% of total) 69 (2003 est)
AGE DISTRIBUTION (% of total population) 0–14 16%, 15–59 64%, 60+ 20% (2002 est)
ETHNIC GROUPS 65% Finno-Ugric ethnic Estonians, 28% Russian, 2.5% Ukrainian, 1.5% Belorussian, 1% Finnish
LANGUAGE Estonian (official), Russian
RELIGION Eastern Orthodox, Evangelical Lutheran, Russian Orthodox, Muslim, Judaism
EDUCATION (compulsory years) 9
LITERACY RATE 99% (men); 99% (women) (2003 est)
LABOUR FORCE 8.8% agriculture, 31.8% industry, 59.4% services (1999)
LIFE EXPECTANCY 67 (men); 77 (women) (2000–05)
CHILD MORTALITY RATE (under 5, per 1,000 live births) 12 (2001)
PHYSICIANS (per 1,000 people) 3 (1999 est)
HOSPITAL BEDS (per 1,000 people) 7.4 (1999 est)
TV SETS (per 1,000 people) 629 (2001 est)
RADIOS (per 1,000 people) 1,136 (2001 est)
INTERNET USERS (per 10,000 people) 4,132.8 (2002 est)
PERSONAL COMPUTER USERS (per 100 people) 21.0 (2002 est)

See also ▷Latvia; ▷Lithuania; ▷Russia; ▷Union of Soviet Socialist Republics.

Chronology

1st century AD: First independent state formed.
9th century: Invaded by Vikings.
13th century: Tallinn, in the Danish-controlled north, joined Hanseatic League, a northern European union of commercial towns; Livonia, comprising southern Estonia and Latvia, came under control of German Teutonic Knights and was converted to Christianity.
1561: Sweden took control of northern Estonia.
1629: Sweden took control of southern Estonia from Poland.
1721: Sweden ceded the country to tsarist Russia.
late 19th century: Estonian nationalist movement developed in opposition to Russian political and cultural repression and German economic control.
1914: Occupied by German troops.
1918–19: Estonian nationalists, led by Konstantin Pats, proclaimed and achieved independence, despite efforts by the Russian Red Army to regain control.
1920s: Land reforms and cultural advances under democratic regime.
1934: Pats overthrew parliamentary democracy in a quasi-fascist coup at a time of economic depression; Baltic Entente mutual defence pact signed with Latvia and Lithuania.
1940: Estonia incorporated into Soviet Union (USSR); 100,000 Estonians deported to Siberia or killed.
1941–44: German occupation during World War II.
1944: USSR regained control; 'Sovietization' followed, including agricultural collectivization and immigration of ethnic Russians.
late 1980s: Beginnings of nationalist dissent, encouraged by *glasnost* initiative of reformist Soviet leader Mikhail Gorbachev.

1988: Popular Front (EPF) established to campaign for democracy. Sovereignty declaration issued by state assembly rejected by USSR as unconstitutional.
1989: Estonian replaced Russian as the main language.
1990: The CPE monopoly of power was abolished; pro-independence candidates secured a majority after multiparty elections; a coalition government was formed with EPF leader Edgar Savisaar as prime minister; Arnold Rüütel became president. The prewar constitution was partially restored.
1991: Independence was achieved after an attempted anti-Gorbachev coup in Moscow; the CPE was outlawed. Estonia joined the United Nations (UN).
1992: Savisaar resigned over food and energy shortages; Isamaa leader Lennart Meri became president and free-marketer Mart Laar prime minister.
1993: Estonia joined the Council of Europe and signed a free-trade agreement with Latvia and Lithuania.
1994: The last Russian troops were withdrawn. A radical economic reform programme was introduced; a controversial law on 'aliens' was passed, requiring non-ethnic Estonians to apply for residency. Laar resigned.
1995: Former communists won the largest number of seats in a general election; a left-of-centre coalition was formed under Tiit Vahi.
1996: President Meri was re-elected. The ruling coalition collapsed; Prime Minister Tiit Vahi continued with a minority government.
1997: Vahi, accused of corruption, resigned and was replaced by Mart Siimann. Estonia was invited to begin European Union (EU) membership negotiations.
1998: The legislature voted to ban electoral alliances in future elections.
2002: Siim Kallas became prime minister.
2004: Estonia was set to join the EU on 1 May.

ESTONIA Tallinn, on the shores of the Baltic Sea, is the capital of Estonia. The old city, with its many medieval buildings and churches recalls the days of the Teutonic Knights, and the wealth Tallinn accumulated from Baltic trade. The city is still an important port and industrial centre. *Estonian Tourist Board*

Ethiopia

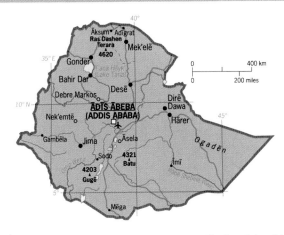

Ethiopia formerly Abyssinia (until the 1920s) country in East Africa, bounded north by Eritrea, northeast by Djibouti, east and southeast by Somalia, south by Kenya, and west and northwest by Sudan.

NATIONAL NAME *Ya'Ityopya Federalawi Dimokrasiyawi Repeblik/Federal Democratic Republic of Ethiopia*
AREA 1,096,900 sq km/423,513 sq mi
CAPITAL Addis Ababa
MAJOR TOWNS/CITIES Jimma, Dire Dawa, Harar, Nazret, Dese, Gonder, Mek'ele, Bahir Dar
PHYSICAL FEATURES a high plateau with central mountain range divided by Rift Valley; plains in east; source of Blue Nile River; Danakil and Ogaden deserts

Government

HEAD OF STATE Girma Woldegiorgis from 2001
HEAD OF GOVERNMENT Meles Zenawi from 1995
POLITICAL SYSTEM emergent democracy
POLITICAL EXECUTIVE limited presidency
ADMINISTRATIVE DIVISIONS nine states and two chartered cities
ARMED FORCES 252,500 (2002 est)
CONSCRIPTION military service is voluntary
DEATH PENALTY retained and used for ordinary crimes
DEFENCE SPEND (% GDP) 8 (2002 est)
EDUCATION SPEND (% GDP) 4.8 (2001 est)
HEALTH SPEND (% GDP) 4.6 (2000 est)

Economy and resources

CURRENCY Ethiopian birr
GPD (US$) 6.0 billion (2002 est)
REAL GDP GROWTH (% change on previous year) 7.7 (2001)
GNI (US$) 6.4 billion (2002 est)
GNI PER CAPITA (PPP) (US$) 720 (2002 est)
CONSUMER PRICE INFLATION 4.5% (2003 est)
FOREIGN DEBT (US$) 5.9 billion (2001 est)
MAJOR TRADING PARTNERS Djibouti, Saudi Arabia, USA, Japan, India, Italy
RESOURCES gold, salt, platinum, copper, potash. Reserves of petroleum have not been exploited
INDUSTRIES food processing, petroleum refining, beverages, textiles
EXPORTS coffee, hides and skins, petroleum products, oilseeds, fruit and vegetables. Principal market: Djibouti 13.2% (2001)
IMPORTS machinery, aircraft and other vehicles, petroleum and petroleum products, basic manufactures, chemicals and related products. Principal source: Saudi Arabia 29.3% (2001)
ARABLE LAND 10% (2000 est)
AGRICULTURAL PRODUCTS coffee, teff (an indigenous grain), barley, maize, sorghum, sugar cane; livestock rearing (cattle and sheep) and livestock products (hides, skins, butter, and ghee)

Population and society

POPULATION 70,678,000 (2003 est)
POPULATION GROWTH RATE 2.1% (2000–15)
POPULATION DENSITY (per sq km) 64 (2003 est)
URBAN POPULATION (% of total) 17 (2003 est)
AGE DISTRIBUTION (% of total population) 0–14 45%, 15–59 50%, 60+ 5% (2002 est)
ETHNIC GROUPS over 80 different ethnic groups, the two main ones are the Amhara and Oromo who comprise about 60% of the population; other groups include Sidamo (9%), Shankella (6%), Somali (16%), and Atar (4%)
LANGUAGE Amharic (official), Arabic, Tigrinya, Orominga, about 100 other local languages
RELIGION Muslim 45%, Ethiopian Orthodox Church (which has had its own patriarch since 1976) 35%, animist 12%, other Christian 8%
EDUCATION (compulsory years) 6
LITERACY RATE 50% (men); 35% (women) (2003 est)
LABOUR FORCE 88.6% agriculture, 2% industry, 9.4% services (1995)
LIFE EXPECTANCY 45 (men); 46 (women) (2000–05)
CHILD MORTALITY RATE (under 5, per 1,000 live births) 172 (2001)
HOSPITAL BEDS (per 1,000 people) 0.3 (1994 est)
TV SETS (per 1,000 people) 6 (1999)
RADIOS (per 1,000 people) 196 (1999)
INTERNET USERS (per 10,000 people) 7.4 (2002 est)
PERSONAL COMPUTER USERS (per 100 people) 0.2 (2002 est)

See also ▷Eritrea; ▷Haile Selassie; ▷Mengistu, Haile Mariam.

See also ▷Eritrea; ▷Haile Selassie; ▷Mengistu, Haile Mariam.

1st–7th centuries AD: Founded by Semitic immigrants from Saudi Arabia, the kingdom of Aksum and its capital, northwest of Ādwa, flourished. It reached its peak in the 4th century when Coptic Christianity was introduced from Egypt.

7th century onwards: Islam was spread by Arab conquerors.

11th century: Emergence of independent Ethiopian kingdom of Abyssinia, which was to remain dominant for nine centuries.

late 15th century: Abyssinia visited by Portuguese explorers.

1889: Abyssinia reunited by Menelik II.

1896: Invasion by Italy defeated by Menelik at Ādwa, who went on to annex Ogaden in the southeast and areas to the west.

1916: Haile Selassie became regent.

1930: Haile Selassie became emperor.

1936: Conquered by Italy and incorporated in Italian East Africa.

1941: Return of Emperor Selassie after liberation by the British.

1952: Ethiopia federated with Eritrea.

1962: Eritrea annexed by Selassie; Eritrean People's Liberation front (EPLF) resistance movement began, a rebellion that was to continue for 30 years.

1963: First conference of Selassie-promoted Organization of African Unity (OAU) held in Addis Ababa.

1973–74: Severe famine in northern Ethiopia; 200,000 died in Wallo province.

1974: Haile Selassie deposed and replaced by a military government.

1977: Col Mengistu Haile Mariam took over the government. Somali forces ejected from the Somali-peopled Ogaden in the southeast.

1977–79: 'Red Terror' period in which Mengistu's single-party Marxist regime killed thousands and promoted collective farming; Tigré People's Liberation Front guerrillas began fighting for regional autonomy in the northern highlands.

1984: The Workers' Party of Ethiopia (WPE) was declared the only legal political party.

1985: The worst famine in more than a decade; Western aid was sent and forcible internal resettlement programmes undertaken in Eritrea and Tigré in the north.

1987: Mengistu Mariam was elected president under a new constitution. There was another famine; food aid was hindered by guerrillas.

1989: Peace talks with Eritrean rebels were mediated by the former US president Jimmy Carter.

1991: Mengistu was overthrown; a transitional government was set up by the opposing Ethiopian People's Revolutionary Democratic Front (EPRDF), headed by Meles Zenawi. The EPLF took control of Eritrea.

1993: Eritrean independence was recognized after a referendum; private farming and market sector were encouraged by the EPRDF government.

1994: A new federal constitution was adopted.

1995: The ruling EPRDF won a majority in the first multiparty elections to an interim parliament. Negasso Ghidada was chosen as president; Zenawi was appointed premier.

1998: There was a border dispute with Eritrea.

1999: The border dispute with Eritrea erupted into war.

2000: A ceasefire with Eritrea was agreed in June and a peace agreement signed that provided for UN troops to keep the peace along the border. Haile Selassie was ceremoniously reburied in Addis Ababa.

2001: Prime Minister Zenawi survived an attempt by his own party, the Tigrayan People's Liberation Front (TPLF), to remove him from office.

ETHIOPIA The dramatic Simen Mountains rise above the northern plateau in Ethiopia.
Image Bank

importance of field studies and an evolutionary perspective.

A development within ethology is ▷sociobiology, the study of the evolutionary function of ▷social behaviour.

ethyl alcohol common name for ▷ethanol.

ethylene common name for ▷ethene.

ethylene glycol alternative name for ▷glycol.

ethyne (common name **acetylene**) CHCH colourless inflammable gas produced by mixing calcium carbide and water. It is the simplest member of the ▷alkyne series of hydrocarbons. It is used in the manufacture of the synthetic rubber neoprene, and in oxyacetylene welding and cutting.

Ethyne was discovered by Edmund Davy in 1836 and was used in early gas lamps, where it was produced by the reaction between water and calcium carbide. Its combustion provides more heat, relatively, than almost any other fuel known (its calorific value is five times that of hydrogen). This means that the gas gives an intensely hot flame; hence its use in oxyacetylene torches.

etiolation in botany, a form of growth seen in plants receiving insufficient light. It is characterized by long, weak stems, small leaves, and a pale yellowish colour (▷chlorosis) owing to a lack of chlorophyll. The rapid increase in height enables a plant that is surrounded by others to quickly reach a source of light, after which a return to normal growth usually occurs.

Etna, Mount volcano on the east coast of Sicily, 3,323 m/ 10,906 ft, the highest in Europe. About 90 eruptions have been recorded since 1800 BC, yet because of the rich soil, the cultivated zone on the lower slopes is densely populated, including the coastal town of Catania.

Eton town in Windsor and Maidenhead unitary authority, southern England, on the north bank of the River Thames, opposite Windsor; population (1991) 2,000. ▷Eton College is one of the UK's oldest, largest, and most prestigious public (private and fee-paying) schools. It was founded in 1440 by Henry VI.

Eton College most prestigious of English ▷public schools (that is, private schools) for boys, in Eton. It has provided the UK with 19 prime ministers and more than 20% of all government ministers between 1900 and 1998.

Etruscan member of an ancient people inhabiting Etruria, Italy (modern-day Tuscany and part of Umbria) from the 8th to 2nd centuries BC. The Etruscan dynasty of the Tarquins ruled Rome 616–509 BC. At the height of their civilization, in the 6th century BC, the Etruscans achieved great wealth and power from their maritime strength. They were driven out of Rome in 509 BC and eventually dominated by the Romans.

étude (French 'study') in music, an exercise designed to develop technique. Although originally intended for practice only, some composers, notably Frédéric Chopin, wrote études of such virtuosity that they are now used as concert showpieces.

etymology study of the origin and history of words within and across languages. It has two major aspects: the study of the phonetic and written forms of words, and of the semantics or meanings of those words.

EU abbreviation for ▷European Union.

eucalyptus any tree of a group belonging to the myrtle family, native to Australia, where they are commonly known as gumtrees.

EUCALYPTUS River red gum trees *Eucalyptus camaldulensis* in Victoria, Australia. *K G Preston-Mafham/Premaphotos Wildlife*

MOUNT ETNA Mount Etna photographed in eruption. *Image Bank*

About 90% of Australian timber belongs to the eucalyptus genus, which contains about 500 species. The trees have dark hardwood timber which is used for heavy construction work such as railway and bridge building. They are mostly tall, aromatic, evergreen trees with pendant leaves and white, pink, or red flowers. (Genus *Eucalyptus*, family Myrtaceae.)

Related Web site: Eucalyptus http://www.botanical.com/botanical/mgmh/e/eucaly14.html

Eucharist chief Christian sacrament, in which bread is eaten and wine drunk in memory of the death of Jesus. Other names for it are the **Lord's Supper**, **Holy Communion**, and (among Roman Catholics, who believe that the bread and wine are transubstantiated, that is, converted to the body and blood of Christ) the **Mass**. The doctrine of transubstantiation was rejected by Protestant churches during the Reformation.

Related Web site: Holy Communion http://www.newadvent.org/cathen/07402a.htm

Euclid (c. 330–c. 260 BC) Greek mathematician who wrote the *Stoicheia/Elements* in 13 books, nine of which deal with plane and solid geometry and four with number theory. His great achievement lay in the systematic arrangement of previous mathematical discoveries and a methodology based on axioms, definitions, and theorems.

Euclid's works, and the style in which they were presented, formed the basis for all mathematical thought and expression for the next 2,000 years. He used two main styles of presentation: the synthetic (in which one proceeds from the known to the unknown via logical steps) and the analytical (in which one posits the unknown and works towards it from the known, again via logical steps). Both methods were based on axioms (statements assumed to be true), and from which mathematical propositions, or theorems, were deduced.

In the *Elements*, Euclid incorporated and developed the work of previous mathematicians as well as including his own many innovations. He was rigorous about the actual detail of the mathematical work, attempting to provide proofs for every one of the theorems. The first six books deal with plane geometry (points, lines, triangles, squares, parallelograms, circles, and so on), and includes hypotheses such as ▷Pythagoras' theorem, which Euclid generalized, and the theorem that only one line can be drawn through a given point parallel to another line.

Books 7 to 9 are concerned with arithmetic and number theory, including Euclid's proof that there are an infinite number of prime numbers. In book 10 Euclid treats irrational numbers, and books 11 to 13 discuss solid geometry, ending with the five Platonic solids (the tetrahedron, octahedron, cube, icosahedron, and dodecahedron).

Related Web site: Introduction to the Works of Euclid http://www.obkb.com/dcljr/euclid.html

Eugène, François, Prince of Savoy (1663–1736) Born François Eugène de Savoie Carignan. French-born Austrian general who had many victories against the Turks, whom he expelled from Hungary in the Battle of Zenta (1697), and against France, including the battles of Blenheim, Oudenaarde, and Malplaquet during the War of the ▷Spanish Succession (1701–14).

eugenics (Greek *eugenes* 'well-born') study of ways in which the physical and mental characteristics of the human race may be improved. The eugenic principle was abused by the Nazi Party in Germany during the 1930s and early 1940s to justify the attempted

---

> ## Euclid
> *There is no royal road to geometry.*
>
> To Ptolemy I, quoted in Proclus *Commentary on Euclid*, Prologue

---

extermination of entire social and ethnic groups and the establishment of selective breeding programmes. Modern eugenics is concerned mainly with the elimination of genetic disease.

Eugénie, Marie Ignace Augustine de Montijo (1826–1920) Empress of France, daughter of the Spanish count of Montijo. In 1853 she married Louis Napoleon, who had become emperor as ▷Napoleon III. She encouraged court extravagance and Napoleon III's intervention in Mexico, and urged him to fight the Prussians. After his surrender to the Germans at Sedan, northeastern France, in 1870, she fled to England.

Euglena genus of single-celled organisms in the ▷protozoan phylum Sarcomastigophora that live in fresh water. They are usually oval or cigar-shaped, less than 0.5 mm/0.2 in long, and have a nucleus, green pigment in chloroplasts, a contractile vacuole, a light-sensitive eyespot, and one or two flagella, with which they swim. A few species are colourless or red.

Classification Euglena are members of the order Euglenida in class Phytomastigophora, subphylum Mastigophora, phylum Sarcomastigophora.

eukaryote in biology, one of the two major groupings (super-kingdoms) into which all organisms are divided. Included are all organisms, except bacteria and cyanobacteria (▷blue-green algae), which belong to the ▷prokaryote grouping.

The cells of eukaryotes possess a clearly defined nucleus, bounded by a membrane, within which DNA is formed into distinct chromosomes. Eukaryotic cells also contain mitochondria, chloroplasts, and other structures (organelles) that, together with a defined nucleus, are lacking in the cells of prokaryotes.

Euler, Leonhard (1707–1783) Swiss mathematician. He developed the theory of differential equations and the calculus of variations, and worked in astronomy and optics. He also enlarged mathematical notation.

Eumenides (or **Semnai**; Greek 'kindly ones') in Greek mythology, an appeasing name for the ▷Furies, used by 458 BC in *Eumenides* by the Greek dramatist ▷Aeschylus. Originally they were worshipped at the foot of the Areopagus in Athens, in Colonus, and outside Attica; their cult was similar to that of ▷Gaia, mother of the Earth.

eunuch (Greek *eunoukhos* 'one in charge of a bed') castrated man. Originally eunuchs were bedchamber attendants in harems in the East, but as they were usually castrated to keep them from taking too great an interest in their charges, the term became applied more generally. In China, eunuchs were employed within the imperial harem from some 4,000 years ago and by medieval times wielded considerable political power. Eunuchs often filled high offices of state in India and Persia.

euphemism ▷figure of speech that substitutes a direct or offensive statement with one that is suitably mild or evasive.

euphonium musical instrument, a tenor four-valved brass band instrument of the bugle type, often mistaken for a tuba, and called a **baryton** in Germany. It is used chiefly in brass and military bands.

Euphrates (Turkish **Firat**; Arabic **Al Furat**) river rising in east Turkey and flowing through Syria and Iraq, joining the River Tigris above Basra to form the River ▷Shatt-al-Arab at the head of the Gulf; length 3,600 km/2,240 mi. The ancient cities of Babylon, Eridu, and Ur were situated along its course.

Eurasia the combined land areas of ▷Europe and ▷Asia.

Eurasian a person of mixed European and Asian parentage; also, native to or an inhabitant of both Europe and Asia.

eureka in chemistry, alternative name for the copper–nickel alloy ▷constantan, which is used in electrical equipment.

Eureka Stockade incident at Ballarat, Australia, when about 150 goldminers, or 'diggers', rebelled against the Victorian state police and military authorities. They took refuge behind a wooden stockade, which was taken in a few minutes by the military on 3 December 1854. Some 30 gold diggers were killed, and a few soldiers killed or wounded, but the majority of the rebels were taken prisoner. Among those who escaped was Peter Lalor, their leader. Of the 13 tried for treason, all were acquitted, thus marking the emergence of Australian democracy.

Related Web site: Eureka Stockade http://users.netconnect.com.au/~ianmac/eureka.html

eurhythmics practice of coordinated bodily movement as an aid to musical development. It was founded about 1900 by the Swiss musician Emile Jaques-Dalcroze, professor of harmony at the Geneva conservatoire. He devised a series of 'gesture' songs, to be sung simultaneously with certain bodily actions.

Euripides (*c*. 485–*c*. 406 BC) Athenian tragic dramatist. He is ranked with Aeschylus and Sophocles as one of the three great tragedians. His plays deal with the emotions and reactions of ordinary people and social issues rather than with deities and the grandiose themes of his contemporaries. He wrote about 90 plays, of which 18 and some long fragments survive. These include *Alcestis* (438 BC), *Medea* (431 BC), *Andromache* (about 430 BC), *Hippolytus* (428 BC), the satyr-drama *Cyclops* (about 424–423 BC), *Electra* (417 BC), *Trojan Women* (415 BC), *Iphigenia in Tauris* (413 BC), *Iphigenia in Aulis* (about 414–412 BC), and *The Bacchae* (about 405 BC) (the last two were produced shortly after his death).

Euripides' questioning of contemporary mores and shrewd psychological analyses made him unpopular, even notorious, during his lifetime, and he was cruelly mocked by the contemporary comic playwright Aristophanes, but he had more influence on the development of later drama than either Aeschylus or Sophocles. He has been called the most modern of the three dramatists, and the 'forerunner of rationalism'. Drawing on the ▷sophists, he transformed tragedy with unheroic themes, sympathetic and disturbing portrayals of women's anger, and plots of incident and reunion.

> **Euripides**
> *Never say that marriage has more of joy than pain.*
> Alcestis (438 BC)

He was essentially a realist whose art reflected the humours and passions of daily life. Plot was almost immaterial to him, and he introduced such innovations as the prologue, which takes the form of a versified programme, and the *deus ex machina*, or god who comes on at the end to wind up the plot.

euro Monetary unit of the European Union (EU). The currency was officially launched on 1 January 1999. The euro, formerly known as the ECU (European Currency Unit), is based on the value of the different currencies used in the ▷European Monetary System.

Countries that achieved financial 'convergence criteria' stipulated in the Maastricht Treaty to join the euro at its launch were: Austria, Belgium, Finland, France, Germany, Republic of Ireland, Italy, Luxembourg, the Netherlands, Portugal, and Spain. Greece joined in January 2001. Euro notes and coins were introduced on 1 January 2002.

Eurodollar in finance, US currency deposited outside the USA and held by individuals and institutions, not necessarily in Europe. Eurodollars originated in the 1960s when East European countries deposited their US dollars in West European banks. Banks holding Eurodollar deposits may lend in dollars, usually to finance trade, and often redeposit with other foreign banks. The practice is a means of avoiding credit controls and exploiting interest rate differentials.

Europa in astronomy, the fourth-largest moon of the planet Jupiter, diameter 3,140 km/1,950 mi, orbiting 671,000 km/417,000 mi from the planet every 3.55 days. It is covered by ice and criss-crossed by thousands of thin cracks, each some 50,000 km/30,000 mi long.

Europa in Greek mythology, a princess carried off by Zeus under the guise of a white bull. She was the daughter of the Phoenician king Agenor of Tyre; sister of Cadmus, founder of Thebes; and the personification of the continent of Europe.

Europe the second-smallest continent, occupying 8% of the Earth's surface.

area 10,400,000 sq km/4,000,000 sq mi **population** (1990 est) 498 million (excluding European Turkey and the former USSR); annual growth rate 0.3%, projected population of 512 million by the year 2000 **language** mostly Indo-European, with a few exceptions, including Finno-Ugric (Finnish and Hungarian), Basque, and Altaic (Turkish); apart from a fringe of Celtic, the northwest is Germanic; Letto-Lithuanian languages separate the Germanic from the Slavonic tongues of Eastern Europe; Romance languages spread east-west from Romania through Italy and France to Spain and Portugal **religion** Christian (Protestant, Roman Catholic, Eastern Orthodox), Muslim (Turkey, Albania, Bosnia-Herzegovina, Serbia and Montenegro, Macedonia, Bulgaria), Jewish **largest cities** (population over 1.5 million) Athens, Barcelona, Berlin, Birmingham, Bucharest, Budapest, Hamburg, Istanbul, Kharkov, Kiev, Lisbon, London, Madrid, Manchester, Milan, Moscow, Paris, Rome, St Petersburg, Vienna, Warsaw **features** Mount Elbrus 5,642 m/18,517 ft in the Caucasus Mountains is the highest peak in Europe; Mont Blanc 4,807 m/15,772 ft is the highest peak in the Alps; lakes (over 5,100 sq km/2,000 sq mi) include Ladoga, Onega, Vänern; rivers (over 800 km/500 mi) include the Volga, Danube, Dnieper Ural, Don, Pechora, Dniester, Rhine, Loire, Tagus, Ebro, Oder, Prut, Rhône **physical** conventionally occupying that part of Eurasia to the west of the Ural Mountains, north of the Caucasus Mountains, and north of the Sea of Marmara, Europe lies entirely in the northern hemisphere between 36° N and the Arctic Ocean. About two-thirds of the continent is a great plain which covers the whole of European Russia and spreads westwards through Poland to the Low Countries and the Bay of Biscay. To the north lie the Scandinavian highlands, rising to 2,472 m/8,110 ft at Glittertind in the Jotenheim range of Norway. To the south, a series of mountain ranges stretch east–west (Caucasus, Balkans, Carpathians, Apennines, Alps, Pyrenees, and Sierra Nevada). The most westerly point of the mainland is Cape Roca in Portugal; the most southerly location is Tarifa Point in Spain; the most northerly point on the mainland is Nordkynn in Norway. A line from the Baltic to the Black Sea divides Europe between an eastern continental region and a western region characterized by a series of **peninsulas** that include Scandinavia (Norway and Sweden), Jutland (mainland Denmark and a small part of Germany), Iberia (Spain and Portugal), and Italy and the Balkans (Greece, Albania, Croatia, Slovenia, Bosnia-Herzegovina, Serbia and Montenegro, Macedonia, Bulgaria, and European Turkey). Because of the large number of bays, inlets, and peninsulas, the coastline is longer in proportion to its size than that of any other continent. The largest **islands** adjacent to continental Europe are the British Isles, Novaya Zemlya, Sicily, Sardinia, Crete, Corsica, Gotland (in the Baltic Sea), and the Balearic Islands; more distant islands associated with Europe include Iceland, Svalbard, Franz Josef Land, Madeira, the Azores, and the Canary Islands. There are three main groups of **lakes**: (1) the Alpine lakes with Geneva, Constance, Lucerne, and Neuchatel in Switzerland; Maggiore, Garda, and Como in Italy; Balaton in Hungary; (2) the Scandinavian group with Vänern, Vättern, and Mälaren in Sweden and Mjøsa and Randsfjord in Norway; and (3) the lakes of the central plain, Ladoga, Onega, Peipus, and Ilmen in Russia; Saimaa and others in Finland. **climate** The greater part of Europe falls within the northern temperate zone, which is modified by the Gulf Stream in the northwest. There are four main climatic zones: the northwest region (stretching from northern Spain through France to Norway), the Mediterranean zone, central Europe, and eastern Europe. The **northwestern region** has mild winters, cool summers, and cloud and rain all the year round with a maximum in the autumn. The **Mediterranean zone** has very mild winters, hot, dry summers, and abundant sunshine; most of the rain falls in the spring and autumn. In **central Europe** winters are cold and the summers warm, with the maximum rainfall in summer. **Eastern Europe** has extremely cold winters. **industries** Nearly 50% of the world's cars are produced in Europe (Germany, France, Italy, Spain, Russia, Georgia, Ukraine, Latvia, Belarus, UK); the rate of fertilizer consumption on agricultural land is four times greater than that in any other continent; Europe produces 43% of the world's barley (Germany, Spain, France, UK), 41% of its rye (Poland, Germany), 31% of its oats (Poland, Germany, Sweden, France), and 24% of its wheat (France, Germany, UK, Romania); Italy, Spain, and Greece produce more than 70% of the world's olive oil.

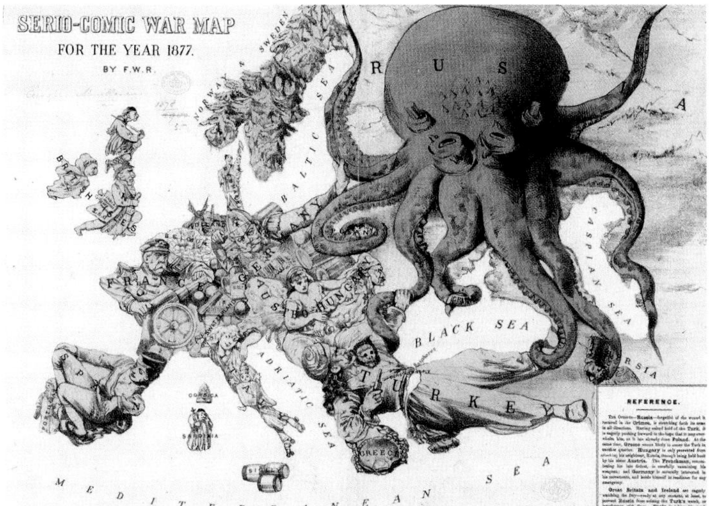

EUROPE Coloured serio-comic war map of 1877, by Frederick Rose. The map shows Russia as an octopus wounded from by its defeat in the Crimea, and Italy as a girl playing with a puppet pope. *Art Archive*

European the natives and inhabitants of the continent of Europe and their descendants. Europe is multicultural and, although most of its languages belong to the Indo-European family, there are also speakers of Uralic (such as Hungarian) and Altaic (such as Turkish) languages, as well as Basque.

European Community (EC) collective term for the European Economic Community, the European Coal and Steel Community, and the European Atomic Energy Community. In 1993 the EC was superceded by the ▷European Union (EU).

European Court of Human Rights court established under the European Convention on Human Rights (1950), whereby cases of alleged human rights violations were referred to the Court by the then *European Commission of Human Rights*, or by a member state of the Council of Europe following a report by the Commission. Under organizational and supervisory reforms, a revised Court came into operation in November 1998.

European Court of Justice the court of the European Union (EU), which is responsible for interpreting ▷Community law and ruling on breaches by member states and others of such law. It sits in Luxembourg with judges from the member states.

Related Web site: Court of Justice of the European Communities
http://europa.eu.int/cj/en/index.htm

European Economic Area agreement in 1991 between the European Community (now the ▷European Union (EU)) and the ▷European Free Trade Association (EFTA) to create a zone of economic cooperation, allowing their 380 million citizens to transfer money, shares, and bonds across national borders and to live, study, or work in one another's countries.

European Economic Community (EEC), organization established in 1957 with the aim of creating a single European market for the products of member states by the abolition of tariffs and other restrictions on trade.

European Free Trade Association (EFTA) organization established in 1960 consisting of Iceland, Norway, Switzerland, and (from 1991) Liechtenstein, previously a nonvoting associate member. There are no import duties between members. Of the original EFTA members, Britain and Denmark left (1972) to join the European Community (EC), as did Portugal (1985); Austria, Finland, and Sweden joined the EC's successor, the European Union (EU), in 1995.

European Monetary Cooperation Fund (EMCF) institution funded by the members of the Exchange Rate Mechanism (ERM) of the ▷European Monetary System to stabilize the exchange rates of member countries if they fluctuate by more than the range permitted by the ERM; if the exchange rate of a currency falls too far, EMCF will buy quantities of the currency on the foreign-exchange market, and if it rises too far, EMCF will sell enough of the currency to bring down the exchange rate.

European Monetary System (EMS) arrangement to promote monetary stability and closer cooperation in the countries of the European Union. It was established in 1979 in the wake of the 1974 oil crisis, which brought growing economic disruption to European economies because of floating exchange rates. Central to the EMS was the ▷Exchange Rate Mechanism (ERM), a voluntary system of semi-fixed exchange rates based on the European Currency Unit (ECU), now the ▷euro.

European Parliament parliament of the ▷European Union, which meets in Strasbourg and Brussels to comment on the legislative proposals of the European Commission. Members are elected for a five-year term. In 2001 the European Parliament had 626 seats, apportioned on the basis of population, of which Germany had 99; the UK, France, and Italy had 87 each; Spain 64; the Netherlands 31; Belgium, Greece, and Portugal 25 each; Sweden 22; Austria 21; Denmark and Finland 16 each; the Republic of Ireland 15; and Luxembourg 6.

Originally merely consultative, the European Parliament became directly elected in 1979, and assumed increased powers. Though still not a true legislative body, it can dismiss the whole Commission and reject the EU budget in its entirety. It also has an important role in monitoring EU spending, questioning EU Commissioners and national ministers, and approving international agreements. It is the only Community institution that meets and deliberates in public. With the spread of the legislative procedure of joint decision-making, the European Parliament has been placed on an equal footing with the EU Council in many areas, and European Parliament amendments are sometimes implemented in Community laws. Full sittings are held one week each month in Strasbourg, France, to amend and vote on draft legislation and policy. Most of the standing and sub-committees, which prepare the work of full sessions, meet in Brussels, Belgium, where additional two-day full parliamentary sessions are also held.

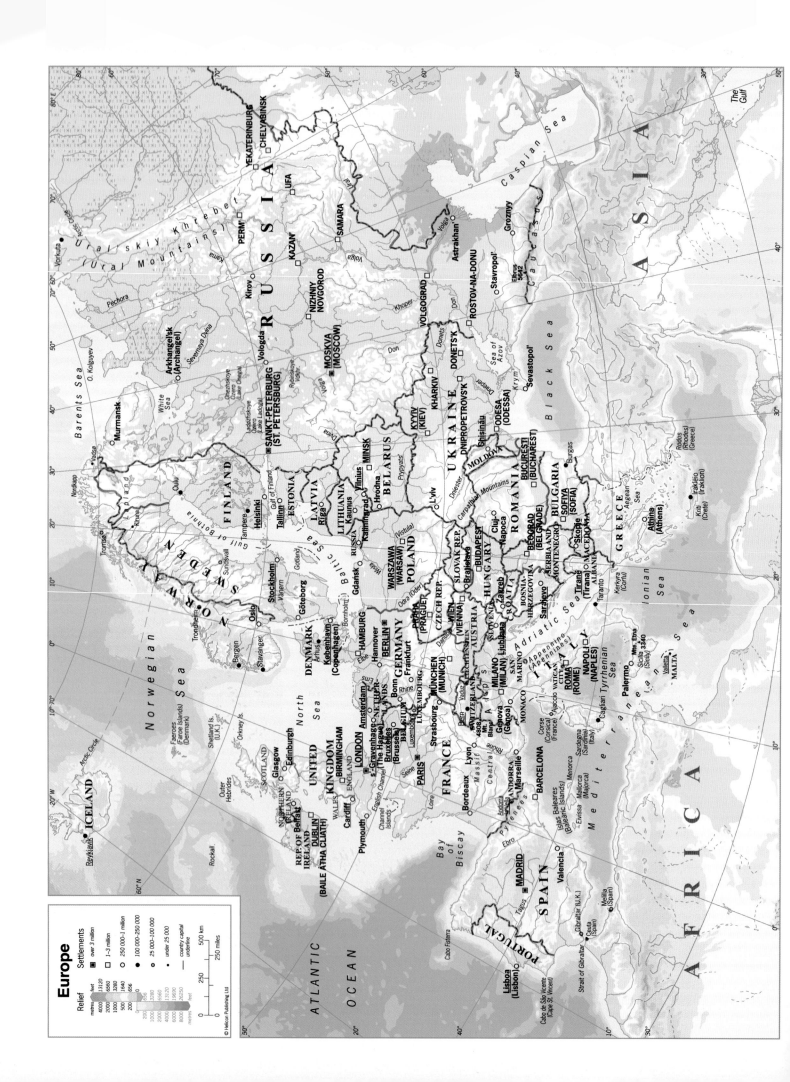

The seat of the Parliament's secretariat, or civil service, is in Luxembourg, though many of its officials are based in Brussels.

Members of the European Parliament (MEPs) do not sit in national delegations in the Parliament, but in multinational political groups. In the June 1999 European Parliament elections, right-wing and centre-right parties made significant gains at the expense of the left-of-centre groups. This transformed a Socialist Group (including UK Labour MEPs) majority of 13 to a centre-right European People's Party and European Democrats' Group (which included the UK Conservative Party MEPs) majority of 53, that is, 233 seats to 180. The third largest bloc is the Liberal Group (in which UK Liberal Democrats are the largest element), with 51 MEPs, followed by the Green/European Free Alliance Group (including UK Green, Welsh Plaid Cymru and Scottish Nationalist MEPs), with 48 MEPs, and the European United Left/Nordic Green Left Group, with 42 MEPs.

European Space Agency (ESA) organization of European countries (Austria, Belgium, Denmark, Finland, France, Germany, Ireland, Italy, the Netherlands, Norway, Portugal, Spain, Sweden, Switzerland, and the UK) that engages in space research and technology. It was founded in 1975, with headquarters in Paris.

ESA has developed various scientific and communications satellites, the ▷*Giotto* space probe, and the ▷*Ariane* rockets. ESA built ▷*Spacelab*, and plans to build its own space station, *Columbus*, for attachment to a US space station. The ESA's earth-sensing satellite ERS-2 was launched successfully in 1995. It will work in tandem with ERS-1, launched in 1991, and should improve measurements of global ozone.

European Union political and economic grouping, comprising 15 countries (in 2001). The six original members - Belgium, France, (West) Germany, Italy, Luxembourg, and the Netherlands - were joined by the United Kingdom, Denmark, and the Republic of Ireland in 1973, Greece in 1981, Spain and Portugal in 1986, and Austria, Finland, and Sweden in 1995. East Germany was incorporated on German reunification in 1990.

Thirteen countries later applied to become new members. Ten of these – Cyprus, Czech Republic, Estonia, Hungary, Latvia, Lithuania, Malta, Poland, Slovak Republic and Slovenia – were set to join in May 2004. Bulgaria and Romania hope to do so by 2007, while Turkey was not in 2003 negotiating its membership.

The European Community (EC) preceded the EU, and comprised the European Coal and Steel Community (set up by the 1951 Treaty of Paris), the European Economic Community, and the European Atomic Energy Community (both set up by the 1957 Treaties of Rome). The EU superseded the EC in 1993, following intergovernmental arrangements for a common foreign and security policy and for increased cooperation on justice and home affairs policy issues set up by the Maastricht Treaty (1992). Other important agreements have been the Single European Act (1986), the Amsterdam Treaty (1997), and the Treaty of Nice (2000). The basic aims of these treaties have been the expansion of trade, the abolition of restrictive economic practices, the encouragement of free movement of capital and labour, and establishment of a closer union among European peoples.

A European Charter of Social Rights (see ▷Social Chapter) was approved at the Maastricht summit in December 1991 by all members except the UK. The UK approved the Charter in 1997. The same meeting secured agreement on a treaty framework for European union, including political and monetary union, and for a new system of police and military cooperation. After initial rejection by Denmark in a national referendum in June 1992, the ▷Maastricht Treaty on European union came into effect on 1 November 1993 and the new designation European Union was adopted, embracing not only the various bodies of its predecessor, the EC, but also two intergovernmental 'pillars', covering common foreign and security policy (CFSP) and cooperation on justice and home affairs. In September 1995, the EU's member nations stated their commitment to the attainment of monetary union by 1999, and in December of the same year they agreed to call the new currency the euro. In May 1998, the leaders of EU governments formalized the creation of the euro monetary zone, or eurozone, and the ▷euro was launched on 1 January 1999.

The aims of the EU include the expansion of trade, reduction of competition, the abolition of restrictive trading practices, the encouragement of free movement of capital and labour within the alliance, and the establishment of a closer union among European people. A single market with free movement of goods and capital was established in January 1993 (see ▷Single European Market). The EU reached agreement on closer economic and political cooperation with 12 Middle Eastern and North African countries in the Barcelona Declaration in November 1995, and an agreement between the USA and the EU to move towards closer economic and political cooperation was signed in December 1995.

The EU has the following institutions: the **European Commission** of 20 members pledged to independence of national interests, who initiate Union action (two members each from France, Germany, Italy, Spain, and the UK; and one each from Austria, Belgium, Denmark, Finland, Greece, Ireland, Luxembourg, Netherlands, Portugal, and Sweden); the **Council of Ministers of the European Union**, which makes decisions on the Commission's proposals; the ▷**European Parliament**, directly elected from 1979; the **Economic and Social Committee**, a consultative body; the **Committee of Permanent Representatives** (COREPER), consisting of civil servants temporarily seconded by member states to work for the Commission; and the ▷**European Court of Justice**, to safeguard interpretation of the Rome Treaties (1957) that established the original alliance.

europium soft, greyish, metallic element of the ▷lanthanide series, symbol Eu, atomic number 63, relative atomic mass 151.96. It is used in lasers and as the red phosphor in colour televisions; its compounds are used to make control rods for nuclear reactors. It was named in 1901 by French chemist Eugène Demarçay (1852–1904) after the continent of Europe, where it was first found.

Euskadi ta Askatasuna (ETA; or Basque Nation and Liberty) illegal organization of militant Basque separatists, founded in 1959, and committed to the independence of the Basque region from Spain. Its main strategy has been based on violence, with more than 800 deaths attributed to the group over the period 1968–2000. It has links with the political party Herri Batasuna (HB), and its French counterpart is Iparretarrak ('ETA fighters from the North Side').

Euskal Herria Basque name for the ▷Basque Country.

eusociality form of social life found in insects such as honey bees and termites, in which the colony is made up of special castes (for example, workers, drones, and reproductives) whose membership is biologically determined. The worker castes do not usually reproduce. Only one mammal, the naked mole rat, has a social organization of this type. A eusocial shrimp was discovered in 1996 living in the coral reefs of Belize. *Synalpheus regalis* lives in colonies of up to 300 individuals, all the offspring of a single reproductive female. See also ▷social behaviour.

Eustachian tube small air-filled canal connecting the middle ▷ear with the back of the throat. It is found in all land vertebrates and equalizes the pressure on both sides of the eardrum.

Euston Road School group of English painters associated with the 'School of Drawing and Painting' founded in 1937 in Euston Road, London, by William Coldstream (b. 1908), Victor Pasmore (1908–1998), Claude Rogers (b. 1907), and Graham Bell (1910–1943). Despite its brief existence, the school influenced many British painters with its emphasis on careful, subdued naturalism.

euthanasia in medicine, mercy killing of someone with a severe and incurable condition or illness. Euthanasia is an issue that creates much controversy on medical and ethical grounds. A patient's right to refuse life-prolonging treatment is recognized in several countries.

eutrophication excessive enrichment of rivers, lakes, and shallow sea areas, primarily by nitrate fertilizers washed from the soil by rain, by phosphates from fertilizers, and from nutrients in municipal sewage, and by sewage itself. These encourage the growth of algae and bacteria which use up the oxygen in the water, thereby making it uninhabitable for fishes and other animal life.

evangelicalism the beliefs of some Protestant Christian movements that stress biblical authority, faith, and the personal commitment of the 'born again' experience.

Evangelical Movement in Britain, a 19th-century group that stressed basic Protestant beliefs and the message of the four Gospels. The movement was associated with the cleric Charles Simeon (1783–1836). It aimed to raise moral enthusiasm and ethical standards among Church of England clergy.

evangelist person travelling to spread the Christian gospel, in particular the authors of the four Gospels in the New Testament: Matthew, Mark, Luke, and John. Proselytizers who appear mainly on television are known as ▷televangelists.

Evans, Arthur John (1851–1941) English archaeologist. His excavations at ▷Knossos on Crete uncovered a vast palace complex, and resulted in the discovery of various Minoan scripts. He proved the existence of a Bronze Age civilization that predated the Mycenean, and named it Minoan after Minos, the legendary king of Knossos.

From 1889, his excavations covered 35 years and also revealed evidence of an earlier Neolithic (New Stone Age) culture. The chief publications detailing his Cretan discoveries are *Scripta Minoa* (two volumes, 1909 and 1952), and four volumes on *The Palace of Minos* (1921–36). An earlier work, *Essay on the Classification of Minoan Civilization*, set out a chronological scheme of Aegean archaeology which, though long accepted, has since come under dispute.

Evans, Edith (Mary) (1888–1976) English character actor. She performed on the London stage and on Broadway. Her many imposing performances include the Nurse in *Romeo and Juliet* (first performed in 1926); her film roles include Lady Bracknell in Oscar Wilde's comedy *The Importance of Being Earnest* (1952). Among her other films are *Tom Jones* (1963) and *Crooks and Coronets* (1969). She was made a DBE in 1946.

evaporation process in which a liquid turns to a vapour without its temperature reaching boiling point. A liquid left to stand in a saucer eventually evaporates because, at any time, a proportion of its molecules will be fast enough (have enough kinetic energy) to escape through the attractive intermolecular forces at the liquid surface into the atmosphere. The temperature of the liquid tends to fall because the evaporating molecules remove energy from the liquid. The rate of evaporation rises with increased temperature because as the mean kinetic energy of the liquid's molecules rises, so will the number possessing enough energy to escape.

A fall in the temperature of the liquid, known as the **cooling effect**, accompanies evaporation because as the faster molecules escape through the surface the mean energy of the remaining molecules falls. The effect may be noticed when wet clothes are worn, and when sweat evaporates from the skin. In the body it plays a part in temperature control.

Eve In the Old Testament, the first woman, wife of ▷Adam. She was tempted by Satan (in the form of a snake) to eat the fruit of the Tree of Knowledge of Good and Evil, and then tempted Adam to eat of the fruit as well, thus bringing about their expulsion from the Garden of Eden.

Related Web site: Eve http://www.newadvent.org/cathen/05646b.htm

Evelyn, John (1620–1706) English diarist and author. He was a friend of the diarist Samuel Pepys, and like him remained in London during the Plague and the Great Fire of London. His fascinating diary, covering the years 1641–1706, and first published in 1818, is an important source of information about 17th-century England. He also wrote some 30 books on a wide variety of subjects, including horticulture and the cultivation of trees, history, religion, and the arts. He was one of the founders of the ▷Royal Society.

evening primrose any of a group of plants that typically have pale yellow flowers which open in the evening. About 50 species are native to North America, several of which now also grow in Europe. Some are cultivated for their oil, which is rich in gamma-linoleic acid (GLA). The body converts GLA into substances which resemble hormones, and **evening primrose oil** is beneficial in relieving the symptoms of ▷premenstrual tension. It is also used in treating such ailments as eczema and chronic fatigue syndrome. (Genus *Oenothera*, family Onagraceae.)

EVENING PRIMROSE The small-flowered evening primrose *Oenothera cambrica* on coastal sand dunes in England.
Ken Preston-Mafham/Premaphotos Wildlife

Everest, Mount (Tibetan *Qomolungma* 'goddess mother of the world'; Nepalese *Sagarmatha* 'head of the earth') world's highest mountain above sea level, in the ▷Himalayas range, on the China–Nepal frontier; height 8,848 m/29,028 ft. It was first climbed by New Zealand mountaineer Edmund ▷Hillary and Sherpa ▷Tenzing Norgay in 1953. More than 360 climbers have reached the summit; over 100 have died during the ascent.

The English name comes from George Everest (1790–1866), surveyor-general of India. In 1987 a US expedition obtained measurements of ▷K2 that disputed Everest's 'highest mountain' status, but satellite measurements have established Mount Everest as the highest.

Related Web site: Alive on Everest
http://www.pbs.org/wgbh/nova/everest/

Did Leigh-Mallory Make the First Ascent of Everest?

On 6 June 1924, two English mountaineers, George Leigh-Mallory and Andrew Irvine, wearing just a few layers of clothing and leather boots, set out to climb Everest. The two men were last sighted on 8 June just 250 m/ 800 ft from the summit and were never seen again. It has been suggested that they may in fact have reached the summit 29 years before the famous ascent of Sir Edmund Hillary and Sherpa Tenzing Norgay. Different theories have been put forward to support this claim and artefacts have been discovered, but it has not been possible to prove whether or not these two climbers did in fact reach the summit.

In April 1999, the **Mallory and Irvine Research Expedition Team** embarked on a search of the mountain to try to solve this great mountaineering mystery. On 1 May they found the body of George Leigh-Mallory. Many interesting items were found on his body, including some of his notes. These notes implied that the climbers were carrying enough oxygen cylinders to see them through to the summit, countering speculation that they were not carrying enough oxygen to complete the ascent.

It is known that Mallory had been lent a camera to take with him to the summit. This has still not been found. If one day it is recovered, it could prove whether or not these two climbers were in fact the first people to reach the summit of Everest.

Everglades subtropical area of swamps, marsh, and lakes in southern Florida, USA; area 7,000 sq km/2,700 sq mi. Formed by the overflow of Lake Okeechobee after heavy rains, it is one of the wildest areas in the USA, with distinctive plant and animal life. The natural vegetation of the swamplands is sawgrass and rushes, with trees such as cypress, palm, and hardwoods where the conditions are slightly drier. Several hundred Seminole, an American Indian people, live here. A national park (established in 1947) covers the southern tip of the Everglades, making up about one-fifth of the Everglades' original area.

evergreen in botany, a plant such as pine, spruce, or holly, that bears its leaves all year round. Most ▷conifers are evergreen. Plants that shed their leaves in autumn or during a dry season are described as ▷deciduous.

evidence in law, the testimony of witnesses and production of documents and other material in court proceedings, in order to prove or disprove facts at issue in the case. Witnesses must swear or affirm that their evidence is true. In English law, giving false evidence is the crime of ▷perjury.

evolution the slow, gradual process of change from one form to another, as in the evolution of the universe from its formation to its present state, or in the evolution of life on Earth. In biology, it is the process by which life has developed by stages from single-celled organisms into the multiplicity of animal and plant life, extinct and existing, that inhabits the Earth. The development of the concept of evolution is usually associated with the English naturalist Charles ▷Darwin who attributed the main role in evolutionary change to ▷natural selection acting on randomly occurring variations. However, these variations in species are now known to be ▷adaptations produced by spontaneous changes or ▷mutations in the genetic material of organisms.

Evolution and creationism Organic evolution traces the development of simple unicellular forms to more complex forms, ultimately to the flowering plants and vertebrate animals, including humans. The Earth contains an immense diversity of living organisms: about a million different species of animals and half a million species of plants have so far been described. Some religions deny the theory of evolution considering it conflicts with their belief that God created all things (see ▷creationism). But most people accept that there is overwhelming evidence that the diversity of life arose by a gradual process of evolutionary divergence and not by individual acts of divine creation. There are several lines of evidence: the fossil record, the existence of similarities or homologies between different groups of organisms, embryology, and geographical distribution.

Natural selection, sexual selection, and chance The idea of continuous evolution can be traced as far back as ▷Lucretius in the 1st century BC, but it did not gain wide acceptance until the 19th century following the work of Scottish geologist Charles ▷Lyell, French naturalist Jean Baptiste ▷Lamarck, Darwin together with Alfred Russel ▷Wallace, and English biologist T H ▷Huxley. Natural selection occurs because those individuals better adapted to their particular environments reproduce more effectively, thus contributing their characteristics (in the form of genes) to future generations. The current theory of evolution, ▷neo-Darwinism, combines Darwin's theory of natural selection with the theories of Austrian biologist Gregor ▷Mendel on genetics.

Currently, neither the general concept of evolution nor the importance of natural selection is doubted by biologists, but there still remains dispute over other possible processes involved in evolutionary change. Besides natural selection, ▷artificial selection, and ▷sexual selection, chance may play a large part in deciding which genes become characteristic of a population – a phenomenon called 'genetic drift'. It is now also clear that evolutionary change does not always occur at a constant rate, but that the process can have long periods of relative stability interspersed with periods of rapid change. This has led to new theories, such as the ▷punctuated equilibrium model. See also ▷adaptive radiation; ▷human species, origins of.

Related Web sites: Coelacanth: the Fish Out of Time http://www. dinofish.com
Evolution Theory and Science http://www.ucmp.berkeley. edu/history/evotheory.html
Virtual Galapagos http://www.terraquest.com/galapagos/

evolutionary stable strategy (ESS) in ▷sociobiology, an assemblage of behavioural or physical characters (collectively termed a 'strategy') of a population that is resistant to replacement by any forms bearing new traits, because the new traits will not be capable of successful reproduction.

Ewe member of a people inhabiting Ghana and Togo, and numbering about 2.5 million. The Ewe live by fishing and farming, and practise an animist religion. Their language belongs to the Kwa branch of the Niger-Congo family. Traditionally independent, the Ewe tribes have been politically unified since the 1950s.

exchange rate price at which one currency is bought or sold in terms of other currencies, gold, or accounting units such as the special drawing right (SDR) of the ▷International Monetary Fund. Exchange rates may be fixed by international agreement or by government policy; or they may be wholly or partly allowed to 'float' (that is, find their own level) in world currency markets.

Exchange Rate Mechanism (ERM) voluntary system for controlling exchange rates within the ▷European Monetary System of the European Union (EU) that was intended to prepare the way for a single currency. The member currencies of the ERM were fixed against each other within a narrow band of fluctuation based on a central European Currency Unit (ECU) rate, but floating against nonmember countries. If a currency deviated significantly from the central ECU rate, the ▷European Monetary Cooperation Fund and the central banks concerned intervened to stabilize the currency.

exchange rate policy policy of government towards the level of the ▷exchange rate of its currency. It may want to influence the exchange rate by using its gold and foreign currency reserves held by its central bank to buy and sell its currency. It can also use interest rates (▷monetary policy) to alter the value of the currency.

excommunication in religion, exclusion of an offender from the rights and privileges of the Roman Catholic Church. The English monarchs King John, Henry VIII, and Elizabeth I were all excommunicated.

excretion in biology, the removal of the waste products of metabolism from living organisms. In plants and simple animals, waste products are removed by ▷diffusion. Plants, for example, excrete O_2, a product of photosynthesis. In mammals, waste products are removed by specialized excretory organs, principally the ▷kidneys, which excrete urea. Water and metabolic wastes are also excreted in the faeces and, in humans, through the sweat glands in the skin; carbon dioxide and water are removed via the lungs. The liver excretes bile pigments.

executor in law, a person appointed in a will to carry out the instructions of the deceased. A person so named has the right to refuse to act. The executor also has a duty to bury the deceased, prove the will, and obtain a grant of probate (that is, establish that the will is genuine and obtain official approval of his or her actions).

Exeter city and administrative headquarters of ▷Devon, England, on the River Exe; population (1994 est) 107,000. Principal industries are brewing, iron and brass founding, light engineering, printing, financial services, and tourism. Other industries include the manufacture of agricultural machinery, textiles, and leather goods. Exeter was founded by the Romans as Isca Dumnoniorum and has medieval, Georgian, and Regency architecture. Exeter Cathedral was built largely between 1280 and 1369. Exeter University was established in 1955.

existentialism branch of philosophy based on the situation of the individual in an absurd or meaningless universe where humans have free will. Existentialists argue that people are responsible for and the sole judge of their actions as they affect others. The origin of existentialism is usually traced back to the Danish philosopher ▷Kierkegaard; among its proponents were Martin Heidegger in Germany and Jean-Paul ▷Sartre in France.

Related Web site: Realm of Existentialism http://members.aol.com/ KatharenaE/private/Philo/philo.html

Exmoor moorland district in north Devon and west Somerset, southwest England, forming (with the coast from Minehead to Combe Martin) a national park since 1954. The park covers an area of around 7,700 ha/19,000 acres, and includes Dunkery Beacon, its highest point at 519 m/1,705 ft; and the Doone Valley.

Exmouth resort town and former port in Devon, southwest England, at the mouth of the River Exe, 14 km/9 mi southeast of Exeter; population (1996 est) 31,920. Small industries include engineering and a pottery specializing in novelty teapots. The port was permanently closed to commercial vessels in 1989, but the town remains a yachting and boating centre.

exocrine gland gland that discharges secretions, usually through a tube or a duct, onto a surface. Examples include sweat glands which release sweat on to the skin, and digestive glands which release digestive juices onto the walls of the intestine. Some animals also have ▷endocrine glands (ductless glands) that release hormones directly into the bloodstream.

exorcism rite used in a number of religions for the expulsion of evil spirits and ghosts. In Christianity it is employed, for example, in the Roman Catholic and Pentecostal churches.

exoskeleton the hardened external skeleton of insects, spiders, crabs, and other arthropods. It provides attachment for muscles and protection for the internal organs, as well as support. To permit growth it is periodically shed in a process called ▷ecdysis.

exosphere the uppermost layer of the ▷atmosphere. It is an ill-defined zone above the thermosphere, beginning at about 700 km/435 mi and fading off into the vacuum of space. The gases are extremely thin, with hydrogen as the main constituent.

expansion in physics, the increase in size of a constant mass of substance caused by, for example, increasing its temperature (thermal expansion) or its internal pressure. The expansivity, or coefficient of thermal expansion, of a material is its expansion (per unit volume, area, or length) per degree rise in temperature.

expectorant any substance, often added to cough mixture, to encourage secretion of mucus in the airways to make it easier to cough up. It is debatable whether expectorants have an effect on lung secretions.

experience curve observed effect of improved performance of individuals and organizations as experience of a repeated task increases.

experiment in science, a practical test designed with the intention that its results will be relevant to a particular theory or set of theories. Although some experiments may be used merely for gathering more information about a topic that is already well understood, others may be of crucial importance in confirming a new theory or in undermining long-held beliefs.

experimental psychology the application of scientific methods to the study of mental processes and behaviour.

explosive any material capable of a sudden release of energy and the rapid formation of a large volume of gas, leading, when compressed, to the development of a high-pressure wave (blast).

exponent (or index) in mathematics, a superscript number that indicates the number of times a term is multiplied by itself; for example $x^2 = x \times x$, $4^3 = 4 \times 4 \times 4$.

exponential in mathematics, descriptive of a ▷function in which the variable quantity is an exponent (a number indicating the power to which another number or expression is raised).

export goods or service produced in one country and sold to another. Exports may be visible (goods such as cars physically exported) or invisible (services such as banking and tourism, that are provided in the exporting country but paid for by residents of another country).

export credit loan, finance, or guarantee provided by a government or a financial institution enabling companies to export goods and services in situations where payment for them may be delayed or subject to risk.

exposition in music, the opening statement of piece in ▷sonata form, in which the principal themes are clearly outlined.

exposure meter instrument used in photography for indicating the correct exposure – the length of time the camera shutter should be open under given light conditions. Meters use substances such as cadmium sulphide and selenium as light sensors. These materials change electrically when light strikes them, the change being proportional to the intensity of the incident light. Many cameras have a built-in exposure meter that sets the camera controls automatically as the light conditions change.

expressionism in music, use of melodic or harmonic distortion for expressive effect, associated with Arnold ▷Schoenberg, Paul ▷Hindemith, Ernst Křenek, and others.

expressionism style of painting, sculpture, and literature that expresses inner emotions; in particular, a movement in early 20th-century art in northern and central Europe. Expressionists tended to distort or exaggerate natural appearance in order to create a reflection of an inner world; the Norwegian painter Edvard Munch's *Skriket/The Scream* (1893; National Gallery, Oslo) is perhaps the most celebrated example. Expressionist writers include August Strindberg and Frank Wedekind.

extinction in biology, the complete disappearance of a species from the planet. Extinctions occur when a species becomes unfit for survival in its natural habitat usually to be replaced by another, better-suited species. An organism becomes ill-suited for survival because its environment is changed or because its relationship to other organisms is altered. For example, a predator's fitness for survival depends upon the availability of its prey.

Past extinctions Mass extinctions are episodes during which large numbers of species have become extinct virtually simultaneously, the best known being that of the dinosaurs, other large reptiles, and various marine invertebrates about 65 million years ago between the end of the ▷Cretaceous period and the beginning of the Tertiary period. The latter, known as the **K–T extinction**, has been attributed to catastrophic environmental changes following a meteor impact or unusually prolonged and voluminous volcanic eruptions.

Another mass extinction occurred about 10,000 years ago when many giant species of mammal died out. This is known as the 'Pleistocene overkill' because their disappearance was probably hastened by the hunting activities of prehistoric humans. The greatest mass extinction occurred about 250 million years ago, marking the Permian–Triassic boundary (see ▷geological time), when up to 96% of all living species became extinct. In 2000, Chinese palaeontologists examined fossils of marine species from the mass extinction at the end of the Permian period, and determined that the extinction took place over 160,000 years. What caused the mass extinction remains undecided, though most earth scientists believe it probably came about through increased volcanic activity or a meteor strike. Mass extinctions apparently occur at periodic intervals of approximately 26 million years.

Current extinctions Humans have the capacity to influence profoundly many habitats and today a large number of extinctions are attributable to human activity. Some species, such as the ▷dodo of Mauritius, the ▷moas of New Zealand, and the passenger ▷pigeon of North America, were exterminated by hunting. Others became extinct when their habitat was destroyed. ▷Endangered species are close to extinction. The rate of extinction is difficult to estimate, but appears to have been accelerated by humans. Conservative estimates put the rate of loss due to deforestation alone at 4,000 to 6,000 species a year. Overall, the rate could be as high as one species an hour, with the loss of one species putting those dependent on it at risk. Australia has the worst record for extinction: 18 mammals have disappeared since Europeans settled there, and 40 more are threatened.

Extinctions in British Isles The last mouse-eared bat *Myotis myotis* in the UK died in 1990. This was the first mammal to have become extinct in the UK for 250 years, since the last wolf was exterminated.

extracellular matrix strong material naturally occurring in animals and plants, made up of protein and long-chain sugars (polysaccharides) in which cells are embedded. It is often called a 'biological glue', and forms part of ▷connective tissues such as bone and skin.

extradition surrender, by one state or country to another, of a person accused of a criminal offence in the state or country to which that person is extradited.

extrasensory perception (ESP) any form of perception beyond and distinct from the known sensory processes. The main forms of ESP are clairvoyance (intuitive perception or vision of events and situations without using the senses); precognition (the ability to foresee events); and telepathy or thought transference (communication between people without using any known visible, tangible, or audible medium). Verification by scientific study has yet to be achieved.

Extremadura autonomous community of western Spain, comprising the provinces of Badajoz and Cáceres; area 41,600 sq km/16,062 sq mi; population (1991) 1,061,900. Irrigated land is used for growing wheat; the remainder is either oak forest or used for pig or sheep grazing. There are food industries. The capital is Mérida.

> **Related Web site: Extremadura** http://www.DocuWeb.ca/SiSpain/english/politics/autonomo/extramad/index.html

extroversion (or **extraversion**) personality dimension described by the psychologists Carl ▷Jung and, later, Hans Eysenck. The typical extrovert is sociable, impulsive, and carefree. The opposite of extroversion is ▷introversion.

extrusive rock (or **volcanic rock**) ▷igneous rock that solidifies on the surface of the Earth (as opposed to intrusive, or plutonic, rocks that solidify below Earth's surface). Most extrusive rocks are finely grained because they crystallize so quickly that the crystals do not have time to grow very large. Extrusive rocks include those that formed from lava flowing out of a volcano (for example basalt), and those made of welded fragments of ash and glass that fell from the sky after being ejected into the air during a volcanic eruption.

Eyck, Aldo van (1918–1999) Dutch architect. He had a strong commitment to social architecture. His works include an orphans' home, the Children's Home (1957–60), and Hubortus House – a refuge for single parents and their children (1978–81; both in Amsterdam).

Eyck, Jan van (c. 1390–1441) Flemish painter, who gained in his lifetime a Europe-wide reputation. One of the first painters to use oil paint effectively, he is noted for his meticulous detail and his brilliance of colour and finish. He painted religious scenes like the altarpiece *The Adoration of the Lamb* (1432; St Bavo Cathedral, Ghent), and portraits, including *The Arnolfini Wedding* (1434; National Gallery, London), which records the betrothal of the Bruges-based Lucchese cloth merchant Giovanni Arnolfini to Giovanna Cenami.

eye the organ of vision. In the human eye, the light is focused by the combined action of the curved **cornea**, the internal fluids, and the **lens**. The insect eye is compound – made up of many separate facets – known as ommatidia, each of which collects light and directs it separately to a receptor to build up an image. Invertebrates have much simpler eyes, with no lenses. Among molluscs, cephalopods have complex eyes similar to those of vertebrates.

The mantis shrimp's eyes contain ten colour pigments with which to perceive colour; some flies and fishes have five, while the human eye has only three.

Human eye This is a roughly spherical structure contained in a bony socket. Light enters it through the cornea, and passes through the circular opening (**pupil**) in the iris (the coloured part of the eye).

The ciliary muscles act on the lens (the rounded transparent structure behind the iris) to change its shape, so that images of objects at different distances can be focused on the ▷retina. This is at the back of the eye, and is packed with light-sensitive cells (rods and cones), connected to the brain by the optic nerve.

> **Related Web site: Eye** http://retina.anatomy.upenn.edu/~lance/eye/eye.html

eyebright any of a group of annual plants belonging to the figwort family. They are 2–30 cm/1–12 in high and have whitish

JAN VAN EYCK Possibly a self-portrait, *The Man in a Turban* (1433), by Flemish painter Jan van Eyck, is thought by some art historians to be a picture of his father-in-law. *The Art Archive/National Gallery London*

flowers streaked with purple. The name indicates their traditional use as an eye-medicine. (Genus *Euphrasia*, family Scrophulariaceae.)

Eyre, Lake lake in northeast South Australia; area up to 9,000 sq km/3,500 sq mi. It is the largest lake in Australia, and includes Lake Eyre North and Lake Eyre South. Much of the lake remains a dry salt crust, while parts form a salt marsh in dry seasons. It is filled only when the rivers which drain into it flood. It is the continent's lowest point, 16 m/52 ft below sea level.

Eyre, Richard (Charles Hastings) (1943–) English stage and film director. He succeeded Peter Hall as artistic director of the National Theatre, London, 1988–97. His stage productions include *Guys and Dolls* (1982), *Bartholomew Fair* (1988), *Richard III* (1990), which he set in 1930s Britain; *Night of the Iguana* (1992), *Macbeth* (1993), *Skylight* (1995), and *Amy's View* and *King Lear* (both 1997). His films include *The Ploughman's Lunch* (1983), *Laughterhouse* (US *Singleton's Pluck*) (1984), *Tumbledown* (1988, for television), *Suddenly Last Summer* (1992), and *The Absence of War* (1995). He also directed the opera *La Traviata* at Covent Garden, London, in 1994.

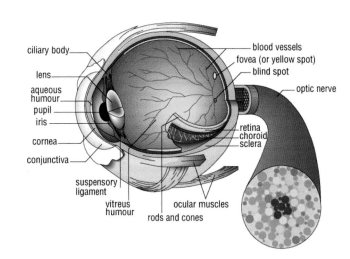

EYE The human eye. The retina of the eye contains about 137 million light-sensitive cells in an area of about 650 sq mm/1 sq in. There are 130 million rod cells for black and white vision and 7 million cone cells for colour vision. The optic nerve contains about 1 million nerve fibres. The focusing muscles of the eye adjust about 100,000 times a day. To exercise the leg muscles to the same extent would need an 80 km/50 mi walk.

F

Fabergé, Peter Carl (1846–1920) Born Karl Gustavovich. Russian goldsmith and jeweller. Among his masterpieces was a series of jewelled Easter eggs, the first of which was commissioned by Alexander III for the tsarina in 1884.

Fabian Society UK socialist organization for research, discussion, and publication, founded in London in 1884. Its name is derived from the Roman commander Fabius Maximus, and refers to the evolutionary methods by which it hopes to attain socialism by a succession of gradual reforms. Early members included the playwright George Bernard Shaw and Beatrice and Sidney Webb. The society helped to found the Labour Representation Committee in 1900, which became the Labour Party in 1906.

Fabius Maximus (*c.* 260–203 BC) Born Quintus Fabius Maximus Verrucosus. Roman general, known as *Cunctator* or 'Delayer' because of his cautious tactics against Hannibal 217–214 BC, when he continually harassed Hannibal's armies but never risked a set battle.

fable story, in either verse or prose, in which animals or inanimate objects are given the mentality and speech of human beings to point out a moral. Fables are common in folklore and children's literature, and range from the short fables of the ancient Greek writer Aesop to the modern novel *Animal Farm* (1945) by George Orwell.

Fabricius, Hieronymus (1537–1619) Italian **Geronimo Fabrizio**; also known as **Girolamo Fabrizio**. Italian anatomist and embryologist. From 1574 he made detailed studies of the veins and blood flow and discovered the existence of one-way valves that direct the blood towards the heart. He also studied the development of chick embryos.

facade in architecture, the front or principal face of a building.

facies body of rock strata possessing unifying characteristics usually indicative of the environment in which the rocks were formed. The term is also used to describe the environment of formation itself or unifying features of the rocks that comprise the facies.

facsimile transmission full name for ▷fax or telefax.

factor a number that divides into another number exactly. For example, the factors of 64 are 1, 2, 4, 8, 16, 32, and 64. In algebra, certain kinds of polynomials (expressions consisting of several or many terms) can be factorized. For example, the factors of $x^2 + 3x + 2$ are $x + 1$ and $x + 2$, since $x^2 + 3x + 2 = (x + 1)(x + 2)$. This is called factorization. See also ▷prime number.

factorial of a positive number, the product of all the whole numbers (integers) inclusive between 1 and the number itself. A factorial is indicated by the symbol '!'. Thus $6! = 1 \times 2 \times 3 \times 4 \times 5 \times 6 = 720$. Factorial zero, 0!, is defined as 1.

factoring lending money to a company on the security of money owed to that company; this is often done on the basis of collecting those debts. The lender is known as the factor. Factoring may also describe acting as a commission agent for the sale of goods.

factory farming intensive rearing of poultry or other animals for food, usually on high-protein foodstuffs in confined quarters. Chickens for eggs and meat, and calves for veal are commonly factory farmed. Some countries restrict the use of antibiotics and growth hormones as aids to factory farming because they can persist in the flesh of the animals after they are slaughtered. The emphasis is on productive yield rather than animal welfare so that conditions for the animals are often very poor. For this reason, many people object to factory farming on moral as well as health grounds.

FA Cup abbreviation for **Football Association Challenge Cup**, the major annual soccer knockout competition in England and Wales, open to all member clubs of the English Football Association. First held in 1871–72, it is the oldest football knockout competition.

faeces remains of food and other waste material eliminated from the digestive tract of animals by way of the anus. Faeces consist of quantities of fibrous material, bacteria and other micro-organisms, rubbed-off lining of the digestive tract, bile fluids, undigested food, minerals, and water.

Faeroe Islands (or **Faeroes**) alternative spelling of the ▷Faroe Islands, in the North Atlantic.

Fagatogo seat of government of American ▷Samoa, situated on Pago Pago Harbour, next to the dependency capital Pago Pago, on Tutuila Island; population (1998 est) 2,300.

Fahd (1923–) In full **Fahd ibn Abdul Aziz al-Saud**. King of Saudi Arabia from 1982. He encouraged the investment of the country's enormous oil wealth in infrastructure and new activities – such as petrochemical industries – in order to diversify the economy, and also built up the country's military forces. When Iraq invaded neighbouring Kuwait in August 1990, King Fahd joined with the USA and other international forces in 'Operation Desert Storm' in the course of the 1990–91 Gulf War, in which Saudi Arabia was used as the base from which Kuwait was liberated in February 1991.

Falling oil prices, since the 1980s, led to a gradual reduction in the country's financial reserves, and to some retrenchment and, in the 1990s, gradual privatization. From the early 1990s King Fahd's absolutist regime faced twin pressures from liberals, campaigning for democratic elections, and from fundamentalist Islamic groups, which opposed the monarchy and sought the full imposition of Islamic *sharia* law. In May 1993 a group of Islamic activists, led by Muhammad al-Masari, formed a Committee for the Defence of Legitimate Rights to monitor the regime's adherence to Islamic principles. In response to pro-democracy pressures, in August 1993 the king established an advisory Shura Council, comprising 60 members of the national elite, drawn from outside the royal family, and also established a system of regional government. In November 1995 King Fahd suffered a stroke, and in January 1996 he temporarily ceded power for one month to Crown Prince Abdullah, his legal successor.

Fahrenheit, Gabriel Daniel (1686–1736) Polish-born Dutch physicist who invented the first accurate thermometer in 1724 and devised the Fahrenheit temperature scale. Using his thermometer, Fahrenheit was able to determine the boiling points of liquids and found that they vary with atmospheric pressure.

Fahrenheit scale temperature scale invented in 1714 by Gabriel Fahrenheit that was commonly used in English-speaking countries until the 1970s, after which the ▷Celsius scale was generally adopted, in line with the rest of the world. In the Fahrenheit scale, intervals are measured in degrees (°F); $°F = (°C \times \frac{9}{5}) + 32$.

Fahrenheit took as the zero point the lowest temperature he could achieve anywhere in the laboratory, and, as the other fixed point, body temperature, which he set at 96°F. On this scale, water freezes at 32°F and boils at 212°F.

fainting sudden, temporary loss of consciousness caused by reduced blood supply to the brain. It may be due to emotional shock or physical factors, such as pooling of blood in the legs from standing still for long periods.

Fairbanks, Douglas Elton Ulman, Sr (1883–1939) US actor. He played acrobatic, swashbuckling heroes in silent films such as *The Mark of Zorro* (1920), *The Three Musketeers* (1921), *Robin Hood* (1922), *The Thief of Bagdad* (1924), and *Don Quixote* (1925). He was married to the film star Mary Pickford 1920–35. In 1919 they founded the film production company United Artists with Charlie Chaplin and D W Griffith.

Fairbanks, Douglas (Elton Ulman), Jr (1909–2000) US actor. He initially appeared in the same type of swashbuckling film roles – *Catherine the Great* (1934), *The Prisoner of Zenda* (1937), and *Sinbad the Sailor* (1947) – as his father, Douglas Fairbanks Sr. Later he produced TV films and acted in a variety of productions.

Fairfax, Thomas (1612–1671) 3rd Baron Fairfax. English general, commander-in-chief of the Parliamentary army in the English ▷Civil War. With Oliver ▷Cromwell he formed the ▷New Model Army and defeated Charles I at the Battle of ▷Naseby. He opposed the king's execution, resigned in protest against the invasion of Scotland in 1650, and participated in the restoration of Charles II after Cromwell's death. Knighted in 1640, he succeeded to the barony in 1648.

Faisal I (1885–1933) King of Iraq from 1921. During his reign, which included the achievement of full independence in 1932, he sought to foster pan-Arabism and astutely maintained a balance between Iraqi nationalists and British interests. He was succeded by his only son, **Ghazi I**, who was killed in an car accident in 1939.

Faisal Ibn Abd al-Aziz (1905–1975) King of Saudi Arabia from 1964. Ruling without a prime minister, he instituted a successful programme of economic modernization, using Saudi Arabia's vast annual oil revenues, which grew from $334 million in 1960 to $22.5 billion in 1974, after the quadrupling of world oil prices in 1973–74. A generous welfare system was established, including free medical care and education to postgraduate level, and subsidized food, water, fuel, electricity, and rents; slavery was outlawed; and financial support was given to other Arab states in their struggle with Israel. In March 1975 Faisal was assassinated by a mentally unstable nephew, Prince Museid, and his half-brother Khalid became king.

Faisalabad city in Punjab province, Pakistan, 120 km/75 mi west of Lahore; population (1998 est) 1,977,000. It lies in an area where cotton and wheat are major crops, and industries in the city include textiles and textile machinery, flour milling, and soap and chemical manufacture. Formerly known as Lyallpur, it was founded in 1892 by the British, and laid out in the shape of a Union Jack.

Falange (Spanish 'phalanx') also known as Falange Española. Former Spanish Fascist Party, founded in 1933 by José Antonio Primo de Rivera (1903–1936), son of military ruler Miguel ▷Primo de Rivera. It was closely modelled in programme and organization on the Italian fascists and on the Nazis. In 1937, when ▷Franco assumed leadership, it was declared the only legal party, and altered its name to Traditionalist Spanish Phalanx.

falcon any bird of prey of the genus *Falco*, family Falconidae, order Falconiformes. Falcons are the smallest of the hawks (15–60 cm/6–24 in). They have short curved beaks with one tooth in the upper mandible; the wings are long and pointed, and the toes elongated. They nest in high places and kill their prey on the wing by 'stooping' (swooping down at high speed). They include the peregrine and kestrel.

The peregrine falcon *F. peregrinus*, up to about 50 cm/1.8 ft long, has become re-established in North America and Britain after near extinction (by pesticides, gamekeepers, and egg collectors). When stooping on its intended prey, it is the fastest creature in the world, timed at 240 kph/150 mph.

Other hawks include the hobby *F. subbuteo*, the merlin *F. columbarius* (called pigeon-hawk in North America), and the kestrel *F. tinnunculus*. The hobby and the merlin are about 30 cm/1 ft in length, steel-blue above and reddish below, and nest on moors. The kestrel is just over 30 cm/1 ft long, with grey head and tail, light chestnut back with black spots, and an unmistakable quivering hover.

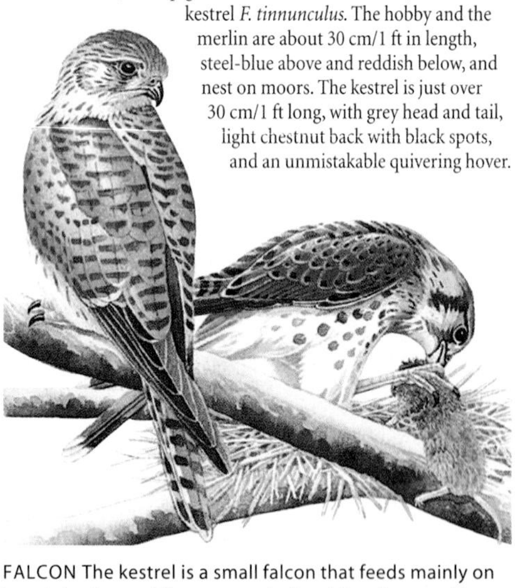

FALCON The kestrel is a small falcon that feeds mainly on invertebrates and tiny mammals. It catches them on the ground and may often be seen hanging in the air beside motorways. The kestrel is often referred to as the 'windhover'.

Faldo, Nick (Nicholas Alexander) (1957–) English golfer who was the first Briton in 54 years to win three British Open titles, and the only person after Jack ▷Nicklaus to win two successive US Masters titles (1989 and 1990). He is one of only seven golfers to win the Masters and British Open in the same year.

Related Web site: Nick Faldo http://www.europeantour.com/players/bio.sps?playerno=53

Falkirk unitary authority in central Scotland, created from the former district of the same name in 1996 from part of the former Central region.

area 297 sq km/115 sq mi **towns** Falkirk (administrative headquarters), Grangemouth **physical** centrally located between Edinburgh and Glasgow, this low-lying area borders the southern side of the Firth of Forth; River Avon flows through **features** Forth and

Clyde and Union canals; Rough Castle; Antonine Wall **industries** chemicals and petrochemicals, bus building, soft drinks, toffees **agriculture** some dairy and arable farming **population** (1996) 142,500

Falkland Islands (Argentine **Islas Malvinas**) British crown colony in the South Atlantic, 480 km/300 mi east of the Straits of Magellan; area 12,173 sq km/4,700 sq mi, made up of two main islands: East Falkland (6,760 sq km/2,610 sq mi) and West Falkland (5,413 sq km/2,090 sq mi); population (1991) 2,120. The capital is ▷Stanley. The main industries are wool, alginates (used as dyes and as a food additive) from seaweed beds, and fishing.

The first European to visit the islands was Englishman John Davis in 1592, and at the end of the 17th century they were named after Lord Falkland, treasurer of the British navy. West Falkland was settled by the French in 1764. The first British settlers arrived in 1765; Spain bought out a French settlement in 1766, and the British were ejected (1770–71), but British sovereignty was never ceded, and from 1833, when a few Argentines were expelled, British settlement was continuous.

Argentina asserts its succession to the Spanish claim to the 'Islas Malvinas', but the inhabitants oppose cession. Occupied by Argentina in April 1982, the islands were recaptured by British military forces in May–June of the same year. In April 1990 Argentina's congress declared the Falkland Islands and other British-held South Atlantic islands part of the new Argentine province of Tierra del Fuego. In September 1995 the UK and Argentina signed an agreement on oil rights in waters surrounding the Falkland Islands. In May 1999 Falkland Islanders agreed to hold their first direct talks with Argentina since the 1982 war. The talks would cover economic cooperation, air links, and visits by Argentine citizens. Under an agreement between the UK and Argentina signed in July 1999, Argentine passport holders could visit Falkland Islands for the first time since the 1982 war. A group of Argentines visited the islands in August.

Related Web site: Chronicle of the Falkland Islands History and War http://www.yendor.com/vanished/falklands-war.html

Falklands War war between Argentina and Britain over disputed sovereignty of the Falkland Islands initiated when Argentina invaded and occupied the islands on 2 April 1982. On the following day, the United Nations Security Council passed a resolution calling for Argentina to withdraw. A British task force was immediately dispatched and, after a fierce conflict in which more than 1,000 Argentine and British lives were lost, 12,000 Argentine troops surrendered and the islands were returned to British rule on 14–15 June 1982.

In April 1990 Argentina's congress declared the Falkland Islands and other British-held South Atlantic islands part of the new Argentine province of Tierra del Fuego.

The cost of the Falklands War was £1.6 billion. It involved 15,000 British military personnel.

Falla, Manuel de (1876–1946) Born Manuel Maria de Falla y Matheu. Spanish composer. The folk idiom of southern Spain is an integral part of his compositions. His opera *La vida breve/Brief Life* (1905; first performed 1913) was followed by the ballets *El amor brujo/Love the Magician* (first performed 1915) and *El sombrero de tres picos/The Three-Cornered Hat* (1919), and his most ambitious concert work, *Noches en los jardines de España/Nights in the Gardens of Spain* (1916). He also wrote songs and pieces for piano and guitar.

Related Web site: Manuel de Falla http://www.hnh.com/composer/falla.htm

Fall of Man, the myth that explains the existence of evil as the result of some primeval wrongdoing by humanity. It occurs independently in many cultures. The biblical version, recorded in the Old Testament (Genesis 3), provided the inspiration for the epic poem *Paradise Lost* (1667) by John ▷Milton.

Fallopian tube (or **oviduct**) in mammals, one of two tubes that carry eggs from the ovary to the uterus. An egg is fertilized by sperm in the Fallopian tubes, which are lined with cells whose ▷cilia move the egg towards the uterus.

Fallopius, Gabriel (1523–1562) Italian **Gabriele Falloppio**. Italian anatomist who discovered the Fallopian tubes, which he described as 'trumpets of the uterus', and named the vagina. As well as the reproductive system, he studied the anatomy of the brain and eyes, and gave the first accurate description of the inner ear.

fallout harmful radioactive material released into the atmosphere in the debris of a nuclear explosion (see ▷nuclear warfare) and descending to the surface of the Earth. Such material can enter the food chain, cause ▷radiation sickness, and last for hundreds of thousands of years (see ▷half-life).

fallow deer one of two species of deer. Fallow deer are characterized by the expansion of the upper part of their antlers in palmate form. Usually they stand about 1 m/3.3 ft high, and have small heads, large ears, and rather long tails. In colour they are fawn, with a number of large white spots, or they may be yellowish-brown or, more rarely, dark brown.

false-colour imagery graphic technique that displays images in false (not true-to-life) colours so as to enhance certain features. It is widely used in displaying electronic images taken by spacecraft; for example, Earth-survey satellites such as *Landsat*. Any colours can be selected by a computer processing the received data.

falsetto in music, the tone-production of male singers resulting in notes above their normal pitch in the female (soprano or alto) register, and sounding like an unbroken voice. Falsetto is the voice normally cultivated by male countertenors.

family in biological classification, a group of related genera (see ▷genus). Family names are not printed in italic (unlike genus and species names), and by convention they all have the ending -idae (animals) or -aceae (plants and fungi). For example, the genera of hummingbirds are grouped in the hummingbird family, Trochilidae. Related families are grouped together in an ▷order.

family planning spacing or preventing the birth of children. Access to family-planning services (see ▷contraceptive) is a significant factor in women's health as well as in limiting population growth. If all those women who wished to avoid further childbirth were able to do so, the number of births would be reduced by 27% in Africa, 33% in Asia, and 35% in Latin America; and the number of women who die during pregnancy or childbirth would be reduced by about 50%.

The average number of pregnancies per woman is two in the industrialized countries, where 71% use family planning, as compared with six or seven pregnancies per woman in the developing world. According to a World Bank estimate, doubling the annual $2 billion spent on family planning would avert the deaths of 5.6 million infants and 250,000 mothers each year.

History English philosopher Jeremy Bentham put forward the idea of birth control in 1797, but it was Francis Place, a Radical, who attempted to popularize it in the 19th century, in a treatise entitled 'Illustrations and Proofs of the Principle of Population' (1822). A US publication by Charles Knowlton, 'The Fruits of Philosophy: or The Private Companion of Young Married People' (1832) was reprinted in England in 1834. When a Bristol publisher was prosecuted for selling it in 1876, two prominent freethinkers and radicals, Annie Besant and Charles ▷Bradlaugh, had the book published in London in order to provoke a test case in court. A successful outcome, and the resulting publicity, helped to spread information on birth control.

In the UK, family planning and birth control became acceptable partly through the efforts of Marie ▷Stopes who opened a clinic in London in 1921. Other clinics subsequently opened in England were amalgamated in 1930 to become the Family Planning Association.

In 1912 two articles by Margaret Sanger, 'What every woman should know' and 'What every girl should know', appeared in the New York socialist newspaper *The Call*, advocating birth control as one means of female emancipation. In 1916 Sanger opened a clinic in Brooklyn, and helped to found the American Birth Control League.

Attitudes changed gradually from opposition to support: for example, in the 1930s the Family Planning Association in the UK ran clinics in hospitals and health centres; Sweden supported municipal clinics; while the USA set up some state public-health programmes incorporating birth control. In 1965, the United Nations Population Commission recommended the provision of technical assistance on birth control to member nations, and the World Health Organization instigated a programme of research.

famine severe shortage of food affecting a large number of people. A report made by the United Nations (UN) Food and Agriculture Organization (FAO), published in October 1999, showed that although the number of people in the developing world without sufficient food declined by 40 million during the first half of the 1990s, there were still, in 1999, 790 million hungry people in poor countries and 34 million in richer ones. The food availability deficit (FAD) theory explains famines as being caused by insufficient food supplies. A more recent theory is that famines arise when one group in a society loses its opportunity to exchange its labour or possessions for food.

Related Web site: Hunger Site http://www.thehungersite.com/index.html

Fang West African people living in the rainforests of Cameroon, Equatorial Guinea, and northwestern Gabon, numbering about 2.5 million. The Fang language belongs to the Bantu branch of the Niger-Congo family.

Fang Lizhi (1936–) Chinese political dissident and astrophysicist. He advocated human rights and political pluralism and encouraged his students to campaign for democracy. After the Red Army massacred the student demonstrators in Tiananmen Square, Beijing, in June 1989, Fang and his wife took refuge in the US embassy in Beijing until June 1990, when they received official permission to leave China.

Fanon, Frantz Omar (1925–1961) French political writer. His experiences in Algeria during the war for liberation in the 1950s led to the writing of *Les Damnés de la terre/The Wretched of the Earth* (1964), which calls for violent revolution by the peasants of the Third World.

fantasia (or **fantasy** or **phantasy** or **fancy**) in music, a free-form instrumental composition for keyboard or chamber ensemble, originating in the late Renaissance, and much favoured by the English composers John Dowland, Orlando Gibbons, and William Byrd. It implies the free manipulation of musical figures without regard to models of form. Later composers include Georg Telemann, Johann Sebastian Bach, and Mozart.

fantasy fiction nonrealistic fiction. The term has been loosely applied to a range of works and attempts to define it more precisely have not been successful. However, a feature shared by most fantasy fiction is its reliance on strangeness of setting (often an imaginary or dream world) and of characters (supernatural or non-human beings).

Fantin-Latour, (Ignace) Henri (Jean Théodore) (1836–1904) French painter. He excelled in delicate still lifes, flower paintings, and portraits. *Homage à Delacroix* (1864; Musée d'Orsay, Paris) is a portrait group featuring several poets, authors, and painters, including Charles Baudelaire and James McNeill Whistler.

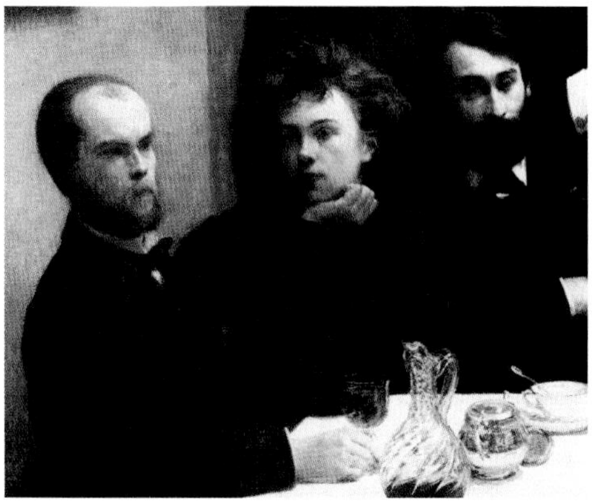

HENRI FANTIN-LATOUR The French artist Henri Fantin-Latour, together with Symbolist poets Paul Verlaine (1844–1896) and Arthur Rimbaud (1854–1891), in a self-portrait. *The Art Archive/Musée d'Orsay Paris/Dagli Orti*

farad SI unit (symbol F) of electrical capacitance (how much electric charge a ▷capacitor can store for a given voltage). One farad is a capacitance of one ▷coulomb per volt. For practical purposes the microfarad (one millionth of a farad, symbol μF) is more commonly used.

The farad is named after English scientist Michael Faraday.

faraday unit of electrical charge equal to the charge on one mole of electrons. Its value is 9.648×10^4 coulombs.

Faraday, Michael (1791–1867) English chemist and physicist. In 1821, he began experimenting with electromagnetism, and discovered the induction of electric currents and made the first dynamo, the first electric motor, and the first transformer. Faraday isolated benzene from gas oils and produced the basic laws of ▷electrolysis in 1834. He also pointed out that the energy of a magnet is in the field around it and not in the magnet itself, extending this basic conception of field theory to electrical and gravitational systems.

Laws of electrolysis Faraday's laws of electrolysis established the link between electricity and chemical affinity, one of the most fundamental concepts in science. Electrolysis is the production of chemical changes by passing an electric current through a solution. It was Faraday who coined the terms ▷anode, ▷cathode, ▷cation, ▷anion, ▷electrode, and ▷electrolyte. He postulated that, during the electrolysis of an aqueous electrolyte, positively charged cations move towards the negatively charged cathode and negatively charged anions migrate to the positively charged anode. Faraday demonstrated that the ions are discharged at each electrode according to the following rules:

(a) the quantity of a substance produced is proportional to the amount of electricity passed;

(b) the relative quantities of different substances produced by the same amount of electricity are proportional to their equivalent weights (that is, the relative atomic mass divided by the oxidation state or ▷valency).

Electromagnetism and the electric motor In 1821, only one year after Hans ▷Oersted had discovered with a compass needle that a

MICHAEL FARADAY A portrait of the English chemist and physicist. *Archive Photos*

current of electricity flowing through a wire produces a magnetic field, Faraday conceived that circular lines of magnetic force are produced around the wire to explain the orientation of Oersted's compass needle.

Faraday's conviction that an electric current gives rise to lines of magnetic force arose from his idea that electricity was a form of vibration and not a moving fluid.

Faraday set about devising an apparatus that would demonstrate the conversion of electrical energy into motive force. His device consisted of two vessels of mercury connected to a battery. Above the vessels and connected to each other were suspended a magnet and a wire, which were free to move and dipped just below the surface of the mercury. In the mercury were fixed a wire and a magnet respectively. When the current was switched on, it flowed through both the fixed and free wires, generating a magnetic field in them. This caused the free magnet to revolve around the fixed wire, and the free wire to revolve around the fixed magnet.

The experiment demonstrated the basic principles governing the electric motor. Although the practical motors that subsequently developed had a very different form to Faraday's apparatus, he is usually credited with the invention of the electric motor.

Faraday is also credited with the simultaneous discovery of electromagnetic induction, although the same discovery had been made in the same way by Joseph ▷Henry in 1830. However, busy teaching, Henry had not been able to publish his findings before Faraday did, although both men are now credited with the independent discovery of induction.

Electrostatic charge In 1832 Faraday showed that an electrostatic charge gives rise to the same effects as current electricity. He demonstrated in 1837 that electrostatic force consists of a field of curved lines of force, and that different substances have specific inductive capacities – that is, they take up different amounts of electric charge when subjected to an electric field.

In 1838, he proposed a theory of electricity elaborating his idea of varying strain in molecules. In a good conductor, a rapid build-up and breakdown of strain took place, transferring energy quickly from one molecule to the next. This also accounted for the decomposition of compounds in electrolysis. At the same time, Faraday wrongly rejected the notion that electricity involved the movement of any kind of electrical fluid (the motion of electrons is involved). However, in that this motion causes a rapid transfer of electrical energy through a conductor, Faraday's ideas are valid.

Polarization of light Finally, Faraday considered the nature of light and in 1846 arrived at a form of the electromagnetic theory of light that was later developed by Scottish physicist James Clerk ▷Maxwell. In 1845, Lord Kelvin suggested that Faraday investigate the action of electricity on polarized light. Faraday had in fact already carried out such experiments with no success, but this could have been because the electrical forces were not strong. Faraday now used an electromagnet to give a strong magnetic field instead and found that it causes the plane of polarization to rotate, the angle of rotation being proportional to the strength of the magnetic field.

Paramagnetism and diamagnetism Several further discoveries resulted from this experiment. Faraday realized that the glass block used to transmit the beam of light must also transmit the magnetic field, and he noticed that the glass tended to set itself at right-angles to the poles of the magnet rather than lining up with it as an iron bar would. He showed that the differing responses of substances to a magnetic field depended on the distribution of the lines of force through them. He called materials that are attracted to a magnetic field paramagnetic, and those that are repulsed diamagnetic. Faraday then went on to point out that the energy of a magnet is in the field around it and not in the magnet itself, and he extended this basic conception of field theory to electrical and gravitational systems.

Faraday's constant constant (symbol *F*) representing the electric charge carried on one mole of electrons. It is found by multiplying Avogadro's constant by the charge carried on a single electron, and is equal to 9.648×10^4 coulombs per mole.

One **faraday** is this constant used as a unit. The constant is used to calculate the electric charge needed to discharge a particular quantity of ions during ▷electrolysis.

Faraday's laws three laws of electromagnetic induction, and two laws of electrolysis, all proposed originally by English scientist Michael Faraday:

induction (1) a changing magnetic field induces an electromagnetic force in a conductor; (2) the electromagnetic force is proportional to the rate of change of the field; (3) the direction of the induced electromagnetic force depends on the orientation of the field.

electrolysis (1) the amount of chemical change during electrolysis is proportional to the charge passing through the liquid; (2) the amount of chemical change produced in a substance by a given amount of electricity is proportional to the electrochemical equivalent of that substance.

farce broad popular comedy involving stereotyped characters in complex, often improbable situations frequently revolving around extramarital relationships (hence the term 'bedroom farce').

Far East geographical term for all Asia east of the Indian subcontinent.

> **Farouk**
> *The whole world is in revolt. Soon there will be only five Kings left – the King of England, the King of Spades, the King of Clubs, the King of Hearts and the King of Diamonds.*
> Remark at a conference in Cairo, 1948

Fargo, William George (1818–1881) US pioneer of long-distance transport. In 1844 he established with Henry Wells (1805–1878) and Daniel Dunning the first express company to carry freight west of Buffalo. Its success led to his appointment in 1850 as secretary of the newly established American Express Company, of which he was president 1868–81. He also established **Wells, Fargo & Company** in 1851, carrying goods express between New York and San Francisco via Panama.

Farnese Italian family, originating in upper Lazio, who held the duchy of Parma 1545–1731. Among the family's most notable members were Alessandro Farnese (1468–1549), who became Pope Paul III in 1534 and granted his duchy to his illegitimate son Pier Luigi (1503–1547); and Elizabeth (1692–1766), niece of the last Farnese duke, who married Philip V of Spain and was a force in European politics of the time.

Faroe Islands (or **Faeroe Islands** or **Faeroes**; Danish *Faerøerne* 'Sheep Islands') island group (18 out of 22 inhabited) in the North Atlantic, between the Shetland Islands and Iceland, forming an outlying part of ▷Denmark; area 1,399 sq km/540 sq mi; population (1992 est) 46,800. The largest islands are Strømø, Østerø, Vagø, Suderø, Sandø, and Bordø. The capital is Thorshavn on Strømø. The main industries are fishing and crafted goods. Faeroese and Danish are spoken.

Related Web site: Faroe Islands Tourist Board http://www.tourist.fo/

Farouk (1920–1965) King of Egypt. He succeeded the throne on the death of his father ▷Fuad I. His early popularity was later overshadowed by his somewhat unsuccessful private life, and more importantly by the humiliating defeat of the Egyptian army in 1948. In 1952 a group called the 'Free Officers', led by Muhammad Neguib and Gamal Abdel Nasser, forced him to abdicate, and he was temporarily replaced by his son Ahmad Fuad II. Exiled for the remainder of his life, he died in Rome in 1965.

Farquhar, George (c. 1677–1707) Irish dramatist. His most notable plays are *The Recruiting Officer* (1706) and *The Beaux Stratagem* (1707). Although typical of the Restoration tradition of comedy of manners, the good-humoured realism of his drama transcends the artificiality and cynicism of the genre.

Farrakhan, Louis (1933–) Born Louis Eugene Walcott. African-American religious and political figure. Leader of the ▷Nation of Islam, Farrakhan preached strict adherence to Muslim values and black separatism. His outspoken views against Jews, homosexuals, and whites caused outrage. In 1995 he organized the 'Million Man March' in Washington, DC; an estimated 400,000 people attended.

Farrell, Terry (1938–) Born Terence Farrell. English architect. He works in a postmodern idiom, largely for corporate clients seeking an alternative to the rigours of modernist or high-tech office blocks. His Embankment Place scheme (1991) sits theatrically on top of Charing Cross station in Westminster, London, and has been likened to a giant jukebox. Alban Gate (1992) in the City of London is a continuation of the language but is more towerlike in form.

Farrow, Mia (Villiers) (1945–) US film and television actor. She starred in Roman Polanski's *Rosemary's Baby* (1968), and in 13 films by Woody ▷Allen, including *Zelig* (1983), *Hannah and Her Sisters* (1986), *Crimes and Misdemeanors* (1989), and *Husbands and Wives* (1992).

Fars (Greek *Persis*) province of southern Iran, comprising fertile valleys among mountain ranges running northwest–southeast; area 133,300 sq km/51,500 sq mi; population (1991) 3,543,800. The capital is ▷Shiraz. The main products are dates, rice, olives, cereals, cotton, tobacco, fruit, and vines. Livestock is also raised. There are imposing ruins of Cyrus the Great's city of Parargardae and of ▷Persepolis.

Farsi (or **Persian**) language belonging to the Indo-Iranian branch of the Indo-European family, and the official language of Iran (formerly Persia). It is also spoken in Afghanistan, Iraq, and Tajikistan.

FARSI A page from a 16th-century Persian copy of Firdausi's epic, the *Shahnama. The Art Archive/British Library*

fascism political ideology that denies all rights to individuals in their relations with the state; specifically, the totalitarian nationalist movement founded in Italy in 1919 by ▷Mussolini and followed by Hitler's Germany in 1933.

Fascism was essentially a product of the economic and political crisis of the years after World War I. Units called *fasci di combattimento* (combat groups), from the Latin *fasces*, were originally established to oppose communism. The fascist party, the *Partitio Nazionale Fascista*, controlled Italy 1922–43. Fascism protected the existing social order by forcible suppression of the working-class movement and by providing scapegoats for popular anger such as minority groups: Jews, foreigners, or blacks; it also prepared the citizenry for the economic and psychological mobilization of war.

> **George Farquhar**
> *Spare all I have, and take my life.*
> *The Beaux Stratagem* V. ii

Fassbinder, Rainer Werner (1946–1982) German film director. He began as a fringe actor and founded his own 'anti-theatre' before moving into films. His works are mainly stylized indictments of contemporary German society. He made more than 40 films, including *Die bitteren Tränen der Petra von Kant/The Bitter Tears of Petra von Kant* (1972), *Angst essen Seele auf/Fear Eats the Soul* (1974), and *Die Ehe von Maria Braun/The Marriage of Maria Braun* (1979).

fast breeder (or **fast breeder reactor**) alternative name for ▷fast reactor, a type of nuclear reactor.

fasting the practice of voluntarily going without food. It can be undertaken as a religious observance, a sign of mourning, a political protest (hunger strike), or for slimming purposes.

fast reactor (or **fast breeder reactor**) ▷nuclear reactor that makes use of fast neutrons to bring about fission. Unlike other reactors used by the nuclear-power industry, it has little or no ▷moderator, to slow down neutrons. The reactor core is surrounded by a 'blanket' of uranium carbide. During operation, some of this uranium is converted into plutonium, which can be extracted and later used as fuel.

Fast breeder reactors can extract about 60 times the amount of energy from uranium that thermal reactors do. In the 1950s, when uranium stocks were thought to be dwindling, the fast breeder was considered to be the reactor of the future. Now, however, when new uranium reserves have been found and because of various technical difficulties in their construction, development of the fast breeder has slowed in most parts of the world.

fat in the broadest sense, a mixture of ▷lipids – chiefly triglycerides (lipids containing three ▷fatty acid molecules linked to a molecule of glycerol). More specifically, the term refers to a lipid mixture that is solid at room temperature (20°C); lipid mixtures that are liquid at room temperature are called **oils**. The higher the proportion of saturated fatty acids in a mixture, the harder the fat.

Boiling fats in strong alkali forms soaps (saponification). Fats are essential constituents of food for many animals, with a calorific value twice that of carbohydrates; however, eating too much fat, especially fat of animal origin, has been linked with heart disease in humans. In many animals and plants, excess carbohydrates and proteins are converted into fats for storage. Mammals and other vertebrates store fats in specialized connective tissues (▷adipose tissues), which not only act as energy reserves but also insulate the body and cushion its organs.

As a nutrient, fat serves five purposes: it is a source of energy (9 kcal/g); makes the diet palatable; provides basic building blocks for cell structure; provides essential fatty acids (linoleic and linolenic); and acts as a carrier for fat-soluble vitamins (A, D, E, and K). Foods rich in fat are butter, lard, margarine, and cooking oils. Products high in monounsaturated or polyunsaturated fats are thought to be less likely to contribute to cardiovascular disease.

William Faulkner
If a writer has to rob his mother, he will not hesitate; the Ode on a Grecian Urn is worth any number of old ladies.
Paris Review, Spring 1956

Fatah, al- Palestinian nationalist organization, founded in 1957 to bring about an independent state of Palestine. It was the first Palestinian resistance group, based 1968–70 in Jordan, then in Lebanon, and from 1982 in Tunisia. Also called the Palestine National Liberation Movement, it is the main component of the ▷Palestine Liberation Organization. Its leader (from 1968) is Yassir ▷Arafat.

fata morgana (Italian 'Morgan the Fairy') mirage, often seen in the Strait of Messina and traditionally attributed to the sorcery of ▷Morgan le Fay. She was believed to reside in Calabria, a region of southern Italy.

Fates (or **Moirai**) in Greek mythology, three female figures who determined the destiny of human lives; later, the duration of human life. They were envisaged as spinners: Clotho spun the thread of life, Lachesis apportioned the thread, and Atropos cut it off. They are analogous to the Roman Parcae or Fata and Norse Norns.

fat hen plant belonging to the goosefoot family, widespread in temperate regions. It grows up to 1 m/3 ft tall and has lance- or diamond-shaped leaves and compact heads of small inconspicuous flowers. Now considered a weed, fat hen was once valued for its fatty seeds and edible leaves. (*Chenopodium album*, family Chenopodiaceae.)

Father Christmas (or **Santa Claus**) popular personification of the spirit of Christmas, derived from the Christian legend of St ▷Nicholas and elements of Scandinavian mythology. He is depicted as a fat, jolly old man with a long white beard, dressed in boots and a red hat and suit trimmed with white fur. He lives with his toy-making elves at the North Pole, and on Christmas Eve he travels in an airborne sleigh, drawn by eight reindeer, to deliver presents to good children, who are fast asleep when he arrives. The most popular legends claim that Father Christmas lands his sleigh on rooftops, secretly entering homes through the chimney.

Father of the Church any of certain teachers and writers of the early Christian church, eminent for their learning and orthodoxy, experience, and sanctity of life. They lived between the end of the 1st and the end of the 7th century, a period divided by the Council of Nicaea in 325 into the ante-Nicene and post-Nicene Fathers.

fathom (Anglo-Saxon *faethm* 'to embrace') in mining, seafaring, and handling timber, a unit of depth measurement (1.83 m/6 ft) used prior to metrication; it approximates to the distance between an adult man's hands when the arms are outstretched.

Fathy, Hassan (1900–1989) Egyptian architect. In his work at the village of New Gournia in Upper Egypt 1945–48, he demonstrated the value of indigenous building technology and natural materials in solving contemporary housing problems. This, together with his book *The Architecture of the Poor* (1973), influenced the growth of community architecture enabling people to work directly with architects in building their homes.

Gabriel Fauré
The artist should love life and show us that it is beautiful; without him, we might doubt it.
Quoted in Mellers *Studies in Contemporary Music* (1947)

Fatimid dynasty of Muslim Shiite caliphs founded in 909 by Obaidallah, who claimed to be a descendant of Fatima (the prophet Muhammad's daughter) and her husband Ali, in North Africa. In 969 the Fatimids conquered Egypt, and the dynasty continued until overthrown by Saladin in 1171.
Related Web site: Fatimids http://www.islam.org/Mosque/ihame/Sec8.htm

fatty acid (or **carboxylic acid**) organic compound consisting of a hydrocarbon chain of an even number of carbon atoms, with a carboxyl group (–COOH) at one end. The covalent bonds between the carbon atoms may be single or double; where a double bond occurs the carbon atoms concerned carry one instead of two hydrogen atoms. Chains with only single bonds have all the hydrogen they can carry, so they are said to be saturated with hydrogen. Chains with one or more double bonds are said to be unsaturated. Fatty acids are produced in the small intestine when fat is digested.

Saturated fatty acids include palmitic and stearic acids; unsaturated fatty acids include oleic (one double bond), linoleic (two double bonds), and linolenic (three double bonds). Linoleic acid accounts for more than one third of some margarines. Supermarket brands that say they are high in polyunsaturates may contain as much as 39%. Fatty acids are generally found combined with glycerol in ▷lipids such as triglycerides.

fatwa in Islamic law, an authoritative legal opinion on a point of doctrine. In 1989 a fatwa calling for the death of British novelist Salman ▷Rushdie was made by the Ayatollah ▷Khomeini of Iran, following publication of Rushdie's controversial and allegedly blasphemous book *The Satanic Verses* (1988).

Faulkner, William (Cuthbert) (1897–1962) US novelist. His works employ difficult narrative styles in their epic mapping of a quasi-imaginary region of the American South. His third novel, *The Sound and the Fury* (1929), deals with the decline of a Southern family, told in four voices, beginning with an especially complex stream-of-consciousness narrative. He was awarded the Nobel Prize for Literature in 1949.

Later works using highly complex structures include *As I Lay Dying* (1930), *Light in August* (1932), and *Absalom, Absalom!* (1936). These were followed by a less experimental trilogy – *The Hamlet* (1940), *The Town* (1957), and *The Mansion* (1959) – covering the rise of the materialistic Snopes family. Oxford, Mississippi, was his model for the town of Jefferson in Yoknapatawpha County, the setting of his major novels. He was recognized as one of America's greatest writers only after World War II.
Related Web site: William Faulkner on the Web http://www.mcsr.olemiss.edu/~egjbp/faulkner/faulkner.html

Guy Fawkes
A desperate disease requires a desperate remedy.
Attributed remark

fault a planar break in rocks, along which the rock formations on either side have moved relative to one another. Faults involve displacements, or offsets, ranging from the microscopic scale to hundreds of kilometres. Large offsets along a fault are the result of the accumulation of smaller movements (metres or less) over long periods of time. Large motions cause detectable ▷earthquakes.

Faults are planar features. Fault orientation is described by the inclination of the fault plane with respect to horizontal and its direction in the horizontal plane (see ▷strike). Faults at high angle with respect to horizontal (in which the fault plane is steep) are classified as either **normal faults**, where the hanging wall (the body of rock above the fault) has moved down relative to the footwall (the body of rock below the fault), or **reverse faults**, where the hanging wall has moved up relative to the footwall. Normal faults occur where rocks on either side have moved apart. Reverse faults occur where rocks on either side have been forced together. A reverse fault that forms a low angle with the horizontal plane is called a **thrust fault**.

A **lateral fault**, or **strike–slip fault**, occurs where the relative movement along the fault plane is sideways. A **transform fault** is a major strike–slip fault along a plate boundary, that joins two other plate boundaries – two spreading centres, two subduction zones, or one spreading centre and one subduction zone. The San Adreas fault is a transform fault.

Faults produce lines of weakness on the Earth's surface (along their strike) that are often exploited by processes of ▷weathering and ▷erosion. Coastal caves and geos (narrow inlets) often form along faults and, on a larger scale, rivers may follow the line of a fault.

Faunus in Roman mythology, one of the oldest Italian deities; god of fertility and prophecy; protector of agriculturists and shepherds. He was later identified with the Greek ▷Pan and represented with goat's ears, horns, tail, and hind legs.

Fauré, Gabriel (Urbain) (1845–1924) French composer. He wrote songs, chamber music, and a choral *Requiem* (1887–89). He was a pupil of Saint-Saëns, became professor of composition at the Paris Conservatoire in 1896, and was its director 1905–20.

Faust legendary magician who sold his soul to the devil. The historical Georg (or Johann) Faust appears to have been a wandering scholar and conjurer in Germany at the start of the 16th century. Christopher Marlowe, J W Goethe, Heinrich Heine, and Thomas Mann all used the legend, and it inspired musical works by Franz Liszt, Hector Berlioz, Charles Gounod, and Richard Wagner.

fauvism (French *fauve* 'wild beast') movement in modern French painting characterized by the use of very bold, vivid colours. The name is a reference to the fact that the works seemed to many people at the time to be crude and untamed. Although short-lived, lasting only about two years (1905–07), the movement was highly influential. It was the first of the artistic movements that transformed European art between the turn of the century and World War I.

Fawcett, Millicent (1847–1929) Born Millicent Garrett. English suffragist and social reformer, younger sister of Elizabeth Garrett ▷Anderson. A non-militant, she rejected the violent acts of some of her contemporaries in the suffrage movement. She joined the first Women's Suffrage Committee in 1867 and became president of the Women's Unionist Association in 1889. She was president of the National Union of Women's Suffrage Societies (NUWWS) 1897–1919.

Fawkes, Guy (1570–1606) English conspirator in the ▷Gunpowder Plot to blow up King James I and the members of both Houses of Parliament. Fawkes, a Roman Catholic convert, was arrested in the cellar underneath the House of Lords on 4 November 1605, tortured, and executed. The event is still commemorated in Britain and elsewhere every 5 November with bonfires, fireworks, and the burning of the 'guy', an effigy.

Fawkes was born in York of Protestant parents. He became a Roman Catholic, and served in the Spanish army in the Netherlands from 1593 to 1604. The leader of the conspiracy, Robert Catesby, asked him to return to England to take part in the plot. Probably because of his experience as a soldier and his reputation for courage and coolness, he was entrusted with actually carrying out the plan. The plot was betrayed to the government, and, under torture, Fawkes revealed the names of his fellow conspirators, but, by then, they had already been captured at Holbeach.
Related Web site: Fawkes, Guy http://www.gunpowder-plot.org/people/g_fawkes.htm

fax (or **facsimile transmission** or **telefax**) transmission of images over a ▷telecommunications link, usually the telephone network. When placed on a fax machine, the original image is scanned by a transmitting device and converted into coded signals, which travel via the telephone lines to the receiving fax machine, where an image is created that is a copy of the original. Photographs as well as printed text and drawings can be sent. The standard transmission takes place at 4,800 or 9,600 bits of information per second.

FBI abbreviation for ▷Federal Bureau of Investigation, agency of the US Department of Justice.

FCO abbreviation for ▷Foreign and Commonwealth Office.

fealty in feudalism, the loyalty and duties owed by a vassal to a lord. In the 9th century fealty obliged the vassal not to take part in any action that would endanger the lord or his property, but by the 11th century the specific duties of fealty were established and included financial obligations and military service. Following an oath of fealty, an act of allegiance and respect (homage) was made by the vassal; when a fief was granted by the lord, it was formalized in the process of investiture.

> **Sally Kempton**
> US writer
>
> *I became a feminist as an alternative to becoming a masochist.*
>
> *Esquire*, July 1970

feather rigid outgrowth of the outer layer of the skin of birds, made of the protein keratin. Feathers provide insulation and facilitate flight. There are several types, including long quill feathers on the wings and tail, fluffy down feathers for retaining body heat, and contour feathers covering the body. The colouring of feathers is often important in camouflage or in courtship and other displays. Feathers are normally replaced at least once a year.

feather star any of an unattached, free-swimming group of sea lilies, order Comatulida. The arms are branched into numerous projections (hence 'feather' star), and grow from a small cup-shaped body. Below the body are appendages that can hold on to a surface, but the feather star is not permanently attached.

fecundity potential rate at which an organism reproduces, as distinct from its ability to reproduce (▷fertility). In vertebrates, it is usually measured as the number of offspring produced by a female each year. Specifically, it refers to the quantity of gametes (usually eggs) produced per female over a given time.

Federal Bureau of Investigation (FBI) agency of the US Department of Justice that investigates violations of federal law not specifically assigned to other agencies, being particularly concerned with internal security. The FBI was established in 1908 and built up a position of powerful autonomy during the autocratic directorship of J Edgar Hoover 1924–72. Robert Mueller was appointed director in 2001; he was previously a federal prosecutor.

Related Web site: Federal Bureau of Investigation Home Page http://www.fbi.gov/homepage.htm

federalism system of government in which two or more separate states unite into a ▷federation under a common central government. A federation should be distinguished from a **confederation**, a looser union of states for mutual assistance. The USA is an example of federal government.

federalist in US history, one who advocated the ratification of the US Constitution 1787–88 in place of the Articles of ▷Confederation. The Federalists became in effect the ruling political party under the first two presidents, George Washington and John Adams, 1789–1801, legislating to strengthen the authority of the newly created federal government.

Federal Reserve System (called the 'Fed') US central banking system and note-issuing authority, established in 1913 to regulate the country's credit and ▷monetary policy. The Fed consists of the 12 federal reserve banks, their 25 branches and other facilities throughout the country; it is headed by a board of governors in Washington, DC, appointed by the president with Senate approval.

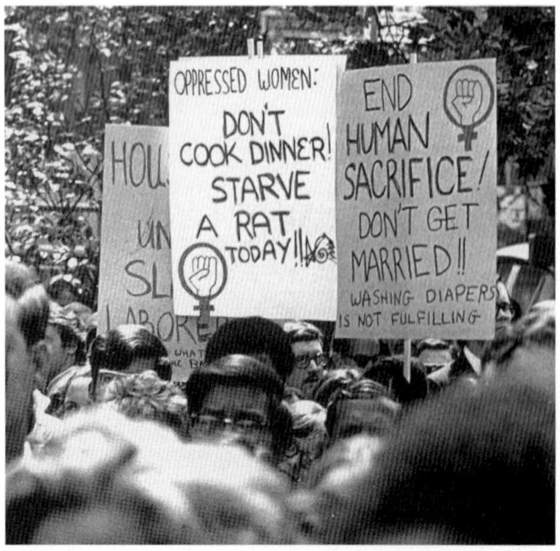

FEMINISM Women's liberation rally. Signs read: 'Oppressed women: don't cook dinner! Starve a rat today!' and 'End human sacrifice! Don't get married!'. *Archive Photos*

federation political entity made up from a number of smaller units or states where the central government has powers over national issues such as foreign policy and defence, while the individual states retain a high degree of regional and local autonomy. A federation should be distinguished from a **confederation**, a looser union of states for mutual assistance. Contemporary examples of federated states established since 1750 include the USA, Canada, Australia, India, the Federal Republic of Germany, Malaysia, and Micronesia.

feedback general principle whereby the results produced in an ongoing reaction become factors in modifying or changing the reaction; it is the principle used in self-regulating control systems, from a simple ▷thermostat and steam-engine ▷governor to automatic computer-controlled machine tools. A fully computerized control system, in which there is no operator intervention, is called a **closed-loop feedback** system. A system that also responds to control signals from an operator is called an **open-loop feedback** system.

feedback in music, a continuous tone, usually a high-pitched squeal, caused by the overloading of circuits between electric guitar and amplifier as the sound of the speakers is fed back through the guitar pickup. Deliberate feedback is much used in rock music.

Feininger, Lyonel Charles Adrian (1871–1956) US abstract artist, an early cubist. He worked at the ▷Bauhaus school of design and architecture in Germany 1919–33, and later helped to found the Bauhaus in Chicago. Inspired by cubism and *der* ▷*Blaue Reiter*, he developed a style based on translucent geometric planes arranged in subtle harmonic patterns.

feldspar group of ▷silicate minerals. Feldspars are the most abundant mineral type in the Earth's crust. They are the chief constituents of ▷igneous rock and are present in most metamorphic and sedimentary rocks. All feldspars contain silicon, aluminium, and oxygen, linked together to form a framework. Spaces within this framework structure are occupied by sodium, potassium, calcium, or occasionally barium, in various proportions. Feldspars form white, grey, or pink crystals and rank 6 on the ▷Mohs scale of hardness.

feldspathoid any of a group of silicate minerals resembling feldspars but containing less silica. Examples are nepheline ($NaAlSiO_4$ with a little potassium) and leucite ($KAlSi_2O_6$). Feldspathoids occur in igneous rocks that have relatively high proportions of sodium and potassium. Such rocks may also contain alkali feldspar, but they do not generally contain quartz because any free silica would have combined with the feldspathoid to produce more feldspar instead.

felicific calculus (or **hedonic calculus**) in ethics, a technique for establishing the rightness and wrongness of an action. Using the calculus, one can attempt to work out the likely consequences of an action in terms of the pain or pleasure of those affected by the action. The calculus is attributed to English utilitarian philosopher Jeremy Bentham.

Fellini, Federico (1920–1993) Italian film director and screenwriter. His work has been a major influence on modern cinema. Many of his films combine dream and fantasy sequences with satire and autobiographical detail. They include *I vitelloni/The Young and the Passionate* (1953), *La strada/The Street* (1954), *Le notti di Cabiria/Nights of Cabiria* (1956), *La dolce vita* (1960), *8½* (1963), *Giulietta degli spiriti/Juliet of the Spirits* (1965), *Amarcord* (1974), and *Ginger e Fred/Ginger and Fred* (1986).

His work is intensely personal and vividly original. Peopled with circus, carnival, and music-hall characters and the high society of Rome, his films created iconic images such as that of the Swedish actor Anita Ekberg in the Trevi Fountain, Rome, in *La dolce vita*.

felsic rock a ▷plutonic rock composed chiefly of light-coloured minerals, such as quartz, feldspar, and mica. It is derived from feldspar, lenad (meaning feldspathoid), and silica. The term felsic also applies to light-coloured minerals as a group, especially quartz, feldspar, and feldspathoids.

female circumcision see ▷female genital mutilation.

female genital mutilation (FGM) the partial or total removal of female external genitalia for cultural, religious, or other non-medical reasons. There are three types: **Sunna**, which involves cutting off the hood, and sometimes the tip, of the clitoris; **clitoridectomy**, the excision of the clitoris and removal of parts of the inner and outer labia; **infibulation** (most widely practised in Sudan and Somalia), the removal of the clitoris, the inner and outer labia, and the stitching of the scraped sides of the vulva across the vagina leaving a small hole to allow passage of urine and menstrual blood.

feminism active belief in equal rights and opportunities for women; feminism includes the many diverse ideas and philosophies that developed from the ▷women's movement in the West.

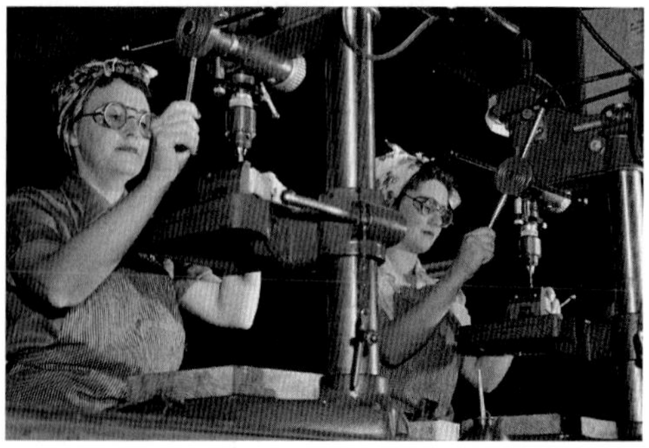

FEMINISM Women working in a factory during World War II. The war exploded the myth that women were only suited to domestic work. When the men went away to fight, women proved themselves to be adept and competent at jobs previously only done by men. *Archive Photos*

femur (or **thigh-bone**) also the upper bone in the hind limb of a four-limbed vertebrate.

fencing sport of fighting with swords including the **foil**, derived from the light weapon used for practising duels; the **épée**, a heavier weapon derived from the duelling sword proper; and the **sabre**, with a curved handle and narrow V-shaped blade. In sabre fighting, cuts count as well as thrusts. Masks and protective jackets are worn, and hits are registered electronically in competitions. Men's fencing has been part of every Olympic programme since 1896; women's fencing was included from 1924 but only using the foil.

Related Web site: Fencing FAQ http://www.ii.uib.no/~arild/fencing/faq/Top-view.html

Fender, (Clarence) Leo (1909–1991) US guitarmaker. He created the solid-body electric guitar, the Fender Broadcaster in 1948 (renamed the Telecaster in 1950), and the first electric bass guitar, the Fender Precision, in 1951. The Fender Stratocaster guitar dates from 1954. In 1965 he sold the Fender name to CBS, which continues to make the instruments.

Fenian movement Irish-American republican secret society, founded in the USA in 1858 to campaign for Irish-American support for armed rebellion following the death of the Irish nationalist leader Daniel O'Connell and the breakup of ▷Young Ireland. Its name, a reference to the ancient Irish legendary warrior band of the **Fianna**, became synonymous with underground Irish republicanism in the 19th century. The collapse of the movement began when an attempt to establish an independent Irish republic by an uprising in Ireland in 1867 failed, as did raids into Canada in 1866 and 1870, and England in 1867. In the 1880s the US-based Fenian society Clan-Na-Gael conducted assassinations and bombings through its agents in England and Ireland in an attempt to force Irish home rule.

The Fenian movement was initiated by James O'Mahony, Michael Doheny (1805–1863), and James Stephens. O'Mahony ran operations in the USA and Stephens was in charge of Ireland, where the movement emerged as the Irish Republican Brotherhood after 1867. Fenian ideology revolved around the notion of

Fencing

Modern fencing involves combat with three types of weapon: the foil, the épée, and the sabre.

Weapon	Description	Point scoring	Target
Foil	introduced in the 17th century; a thin, flexible blade with a rectangular cross section and small guard to protect the hand	thrust (landing with the point) only	torso
Epée	introduced in the 19th century; a stiff blade with a triangular cross section and large guard	thrust only	entire body
Sabre	introduced in the late 19th century; a light flat blade with a knuckle guard which completely covers the hand	cut (touch delivered with the edge of the weapon) and thrust	whole body above the waist

Feminism: Key Dates

431 BC	The Greek dramatist Euripides writes *Medea*, in which the central character raises issues of women's rights. The women of Athens are said to have found the play shocking.
c. 410 BC	The comedies *Lysistrata* and *Ecclesiazusae* by Greek dramatist Aristophanes make fun of the idea of women ruling Athens.
400 BC	The widow of a Persian provincial governor persuades the authorities to allow her to take over her late husband's governorship.
1405	Italian-born French writer Christine de Pisan writes her prose work *Le Livre de la cité des dames/The Book of the City of Women*, in which she defends women against attacks on their intelligence and virtue. She also writes *Le Livre de trois vertus/The Book of Three Virtues*, which asserts women's rights.
1622	French author Marie le Jars de Gournay writes *Egalité des hommes et des femmes/Equality of Men and Women*.
1648	Mexican feminist playwright Sor Juana Inés de la Cruz is born.
1791	Women in Paris begin to organize and demand that French revolutionaries take into account the rights of women. Olympe de Gouge publishes *The Declaration of the Rights of Women* in France.
1792	Mary Wollstonecraft writes *A Vindication of the Rights of Woman*.
1843	Flora Tristan's socialist feminist tract *The Workers' Union* is published in Paris.
1848	The world's first women's rights convention is held in Seneca Falls, New York.
1850	Bessie Rayner Parkes and Barbara Leigh Smith set up a Ladies' Institute at 19 Langham Place, London.
1851	Sojourner Truth asks 'Ain't I a Woman?', raising the issue of slavery at the woman's rights convention in Akron, Ohio.
1855	The American activist Lucy Stone is the first woman to keep her own name after marriage.
1869	John Stuart Mill argues that men and women are equal in *The Subjection of Women*.
1893	New Zealand becomes the first country to give women the vote.
1903	Emmeline Pankhurst forms the Women's Social and Political Union in 1903 at Nelson Street, London. Marie Curie is the first woman to win a Nobel Prize for physics, for her joint research on radiation. She wins the chemistry prize 7 years later.
1906	Suffragettes in England demonstrate at the House of Commons and ten are sent to prison, in one of many years of protest, arrest, and imprisonment. Utako Shimodo, writer and reformer of the education of women in Japan, earns the equivalent of £60,000.
1911	Tan Junying founds the Chinese Suffragette Society in Beijing.
1914	During the First World War, women in developed nations take over jobs previously held by men on a large scale for the first time.
1917	Lenin appoints Alexandra Kollontai as Commissar for Social Welfare in the Russian government. The Soviet Union also institutes maternity leave, government-funded child care, equal pay for equal work, equal education, and the right to hold any political office.
1918	An Act of Parliament in Britain gives women over 30 the right to vote. Women are not granted equal suffrage rights with men until ten years later.
1923	Huda Shaarawi removes her veil in public and co-founds the Egyptian Feminist Union.
1949	Simone de Beauvoir's *The Second Sex* is published.
1955	Rosa Parks is arrested for sitting on a whites-only bus in Montgomery, Alabama.
1956	20,000 women in South Africa protest against apartheid's pass laws, singing 'You strike the women, you strike rock'.
1959	The pharmaceutical company Searle files its application with the Food and Drug Administration in the US to licence the contraceptive pill. The pill becomes available in the US two years later.
1960	Sirimavo Bandaranaike of Ceylon (now Sri Lanka) becomes the first woman premier of a modern parliamentary government.
1963	Betty Friedan's *The Feminine Mystique* is a best seller. The Soviet Tatiana Kuznetsova becomes the first woman to fly in space.
1968	Radical feminists protest outside the Miss America Beauty Contest by throwing hair curlers, bras, and false eyelashes into the 'freedom trashcan'.
1970s	A number of books are published that give modern feminism its philosophic base, among them Germaine Greer's *The Female Eunuch*, Kate Millet's *Sexual Politics*, Shulamith Firestone's *The Dialectic of Sex* and Susan Brownmiller's *Against our Will*.
1970	The Equal Pay Act establishes the principle of equal pay for equal work (effective from 1975).
1972	The Self-Employed Women's Association (SEWA) is founded in India – today it has over 2 million members. The first edition of *Ms Magazine* is co-founded and edited by Gloria Steinem.
1973	The US Supreme Court rules in Roe v. Wade that women have the right to choose an abortion. Billie Jean King beats Bobby Riggs in a televised tennis match watched by nearly 50 million viewers.
1975	As the Decade for Women begins, the United Nations holds conferences examining conditions for women all over the world.
1977	The Mothers of Plaza de Mayo in Argentina begin their protest, holding up photographs of 'the disappeared'.
1978	A national conference of black feminists in London attracts women from all over the world. The Organization of Women of Asian and African Descent is set up.
1981	Women set up camp at Greenham Common in southern England to protest against the deployment of US missiles. bel hooks publishes *'Ain't I a Woman?'*, challenging the white ethnocentricity of western feminism.
1982	Nawal El Saadawi, among others, founds the Women's Rights Association in Cairo. Alice Walker's *The Colour Purple* is published; Walker goes on to develop the concept of womanism. The Chinese writer Zhang Jie publishes her novella *Ark*, widely seen as the first genuinely feminist work to come from modern China.
1990	Some 50 Saudi women protest against customary restrictions by driving for half an hour before being arrested by police.
1991	50 organizations are registered at the Independent Women's Forum in Dubna, Russia, indicating the healthy growth of a new feminism. The following year over 200 groups are represented.
1995	The United Nations Fourth World Conference on Women is held in Beijing, China.

England as an evil power, a mystic commitment to Ireland, and a belief that an independent Irish republic was morally superior to Britain.

A Fenian was more likely to be an artisan than a farmer, and the movement found its greatest support in towns. Although a secret organization, James Stephens published a newspaper, *Irish People* (1863), which compromised Fenian secrecy. Charles Kickham, its leader writer from 1863, was chairman of the Supreme Council of the Irish Republican Brotherhood 1873–82.

fennec small nocturnal desert ▷fox *Fennecus zerda* found in North Africa and Arabia. It has a head and body only 40 cm/1.3 ft long, and its enormous ears act as radiators to lose excess heat. It eats insects and small animals.

fennel any of several varieties of a perennial plant with feathery green leaves, belonging to the carrot family. Fennels have an aniseed (liquorice) flavour, and the leaves and seeds are used in seasoning. The thickened leafstalks of sweet fennel (*F. vulgare dulce*) are eaten as a vegetable. (*Foeniculum vulgare*, family Umbelliferae.)

Fens, the level, low-lying tracts of reclaimed marsh in eastern England, west and south of the Wash, covering an area of around 40,000 sq km/15,500 sq mi, about 115 km/70 mi north–south and 55 km/34 mi east–west. They fall within the counties of Lincolnshire, Cambridgeshire, and Norfolk. Formerly a bay of the North Sea, they are now crossed by numerous drainage canals and form some of the most fertile and productive agricultural land in Britain. The southern peat portion of the Fens is known as the Bedford Level.

Ferdinand five kings of Castile, including:

Ferdinand (I) the Great (c. 1016–1065) King of Castile from 1035. He began the reconquest of Spain from the Moors and united all northwestern Spain under his and his brothers' rule.

Ferdinand II (1452–1516) King-consort of Castile from 1474 (as Ferdinand V), King of Aragon from 1479, and Ferdinand III of Naples from 1504. In 1469 he married his cousin ▷Isabella I, who succeeded to the throne of Castile in 1474; they were known as **the Catholic Monarchs** because they completed the *reconquista*

(reconquest) of the Spanish peninsula from the Muslims by taking the last Moorish kingdom, Granada, in 1492. To celebrate this success they expelled the Jews and financed Christopher ▷Columbus's expedition to the Americas in 1492.

Ferdinand conquered Naples 1500–03 and Navarre in 1512. On his wife's death, the crown of Castile passed to his daughter Joanna and her husband, Philip the Handsome of Burgundy, in 1506. However, on Philip's death and Joanna's subsequent decline into madness, Ferdinand was recognized as ruler of Castile, establishing the rule of one man for all the kingdoms which became permanent under his grandson, Charles I of Spain (later Emperor Charles V).

Ferdinand three Holy Roman emperors:

Ferdinand I (1503–1564) Holy Roman Emperor who succeeded his brother Charles V in 1556; King of Bohemia and Hungary from 1526, King of the Germans from 1531. He reformed the German monetary system and reorganized the judicial Aulic council (*Reichshofrat*). He was the son of Philip the Handsome and grandson of Maximilian I.

Ferdinand II (1578–1637) Holy Roman Emperor from 1619, when he succeeded his uncle Matthias; king of Bohemia from 1617 and of Hungary from 1618. A zealous Catholic, he provoked the Bohemian revolt that led to the Thirty Years' War. He was a grandson of Ferdinand I.

Ferdinand III (1608–1657) Holy Roman Emperor from 1637 when he succeeded his father Ferdinand II; king of Hungary from 1625. Although anxious to conclude the Thirty Years' War, he did not give religious liberty to Protestants.

Ferdinand III King of Naples from 1504, also known as ▷Ferdinand II.

Ferdinand (1865–1927) King of Romania from 1914, when he succeeded his uncle Charles I. In 1916 he declared war on Austria. After the Allied victory in World War I, Ferdinand acquired Transylvania and Bukovina from Austria-Hungary, and Bessarabia from Russia. In 1922 he became king of this Greater Romania. His reign saw agrarian reform and the introduction of universal suffrage.

Ferdinand, Franz (or Francis) (1863–1914) Archduke of Austria. He became heir to Emperor Franz Joseph, his uncle, in 1884 but while visiting Sarajevo on 28 June 1914, he and his wife were assassinated by a Serbian nationalist. Austria used the episode to make unreasonable demands on Serbia that ultimately precipitated World War I.

Fergana (formerly **Novy Margelan** (1877–1910); **Skobolev** (1910–24)) city in eastern Uzbekistan, and capital, cultural, and administrative centre of Fergana wiloyat (region), situated 250 km/155 mi southeast of Tashkent and 65 km/40 mi east of Kokand; population (1995) 190,000. It is an important centre of petroleum and oil extraction and refining, and is the capital of the major cotton- and fruit-growing region of the Fergana Valley.

Fergus mac Roigh in Celtic mythology, a king of Ulster, a great warrior. He was the tutor of ▷Cuchulain.

Ferguson, Alex(ander) (1941–) Scottish football manager. One of British football's most successful managers, since 1986 he has won 15 trophies with Manchester United including six league championship titles and four FA Cups. In 1999, under his charge, Manchester United became the first club to achieve the league

FENNEL A native of the Mediterranean shores, fennel is one of the largest herbs, growing to a height of 1.5 m/5 ft.

championship and FA Cup double three times, having previously performed the feat in 1994 and 1996. Also in 1999 he led Manchester United to the European Cup, thus achieving a unique treble in English football. Earlier, as manager of Aberdeen from 1978 to 1986, he won ten trophies including three Scottish championships and the European Cup Winners' Cup. He was manager of the Scottish national side 1985-86. Knighted 1999.

Fermanagh county of Northern Ireland.
area 1,680 sq km/648 sq mi **towns** ▷Enniskillen (county town), Lisnaskea, Irvinestown **physical** in the centre is a broad trough of low-lying land, in which lie Upper and Lower Lough Erne **industries** clothing, tweeds, cotton thread, food processing, light engineering, china, tourism, electronics **agriculture** small farms, livestock, potatoes **population** (1991) 50,000
Related Web site: Fermanagh District Council http://www.fermanagh.gov.uk/

Fermat, Pierre de (1601–1665) French mathematician who, with Blaise ▷Pascal, founded the theory of ▷probability and the modern theory of numbers. Fermat also made contributions to analytical geometry. In 1657, Fermat published a series of problems as challenges to other mathematicians, in the form of theorems to be proved.

Fermat's last theorem states that equations of the form $x^n + y^n = z^n$ where x, y, z, and n are all ▷integers have no solutions if $n > 2$. Fermat scribbled the theorem in the margin of a mathematics textbook and noted that he could have shown it to be true had he enough space in which to write the proof. The theorem remained unproven for 300 years (and therefore, strictly speaking, constituted a conjecture rather than a theorem). In 1993, Andrew Wiles, the English mathematician of Princeton University, USA, announced a proof; this turned out to be premature, but he put forward a revised proof in 1994. Fermat's last theorem was finally laid to rest in June 1997 when Wiles collected the Wolfskehl prize (the legacy bequeathed in the 19th century for the problem's solution).
Related Web site: Fermat's Last Theorem http://www-groups.dcs.st-and.ac.uk/history/HistTopics/Fermat's_last_theorem.html

Fermat's principle in physics, the principle that a ray of light, or other radiation, moves between two points along the path that takes the minimum time. The principle is named after French mathematician Pierre de Fermat, who used it to deduce the laws of ▷reflection and ▷refraction.

fermentation breakdown of sugars by bacteria and yeasts using a method of respiration without oxygen (▷anaerobic). Fermentation processes have long been utilized in baking bread, making beer and wine, and producing cheese, yogurt, soy sauce, and many other foodstuffs.

In baking and brewing, yeasts ferment sugars to produce ▷ethanol and carbon dioxide; the latter makes bread rise and puts bubbles into beers and champagne.

In the brewing process, complex sugars, such as sucrose, are first broken down by yeast into simple sugars, such as glucose. Glucose is then further decomposed into ethanol and carbon dioxide:

$$C_6H_{12}O_6 \rightarrow 2C_2H_5OH + 2CO_2$$

Many antibiotics are produced by fermentation; it is one of the processes that can cause food spoilage.

Fermi, Enrico (1901–1954) Italian-born US physicist who was awarded the Nobel Prize for Physics in 1938 for his proof of the existence of new radioactive elements produced by bombardment with neutrons, and his discovery of nuclear reactions produced by low-energy neutrons. This research was the basis for studies leading to the atomic bomb and nuclear energy. Fermi built the first nuclear reactor in 1942 at Chicago University and later took part in the Manhattan Project to construct an atom bomb. His theoretical work included the study of the weak nuclear force, one of the fundamental forces of nature, and beta decay.

Neutron bombardment and the Nobel Prize Following the work of the ▷Joliot-Curies, who discovered artificial radioactivity in 1934 using ▷alpha particle bombardment, Fermi began producing new radioactive isotopes by neutron bombardment. Unlike the alpha particle, which is positively charged, the neutron is uncharged. Fermi realized that less energy would be wasted when a bombarding neutron encounters a positively charged target nucleus. He also found that a block of paraffin wax or a jacket of water around the neutron source produced slow, or 'thermal', neutrons. Slow neutrons are more effective at producing artificial radioactive elements because they remain longer near the target nucleus and have a greater chance of being absorbed. He did, however, misinterpret the results of experiments involving neutron bombardment of uranium, failing to recognize that nuclear ▷fission had occurred. Instead, he maintained that the bombardment produced two new ▷transuranic elements. It was left to Lise ▷Meitner and Otto Frisch to explain nuclear fission in 1938.

Nuclear reactors and the atomic bomb In the USA, Fermi continued the work on the fission of uranium (initiated by neutrons) by building the first nuclear reactor, then called an **atomic pile**, because it had a moderator consisting of a pile of purified graphite blocks (to slow the neutrons) with holes drilled in them to take rods of enriched uranium. Other neutron-absorbing rods of cadmium, called control rods, could be lowered into or withdrawn from the pile to limit the number of slow neutrons available to initiate the fission of uranium. The reactor was built on the squash court of Chicago University. On the afternoon of 2 December 1942, the control rods were withdrawn for the first time and a self-sustaining nuclear chain reaction began. Two years later, the USA, through a team led by Arthur Compton and Fermi, had constructed an atomic bomb, in which the same reaction occurred but was uncontrolled, resulting in a nuclear explosion.

Beta decay and the neutrino Fermi's experimental work on beta decay in radioactive materials provided further evidence for the existence of the ▷neutrino, predicted by Austrian physicist Wolfgang Pauli.

Enrico Fermi
Whatever Nature has in store for mankind, unpleasant as it may be, man must accept, for ignorance is never better than knowledge.
In Laura Fermi *Atoms in the Family* (1954)

fermion in physics, a subatomic particle whose spin can only take values that are half-odd-integers, such as $\frac{1}{2}$ or $\frac{3}{2}$. Fermions may be classified as leptons, such as the electron, and hadrons, such as the proton, neutron, mesons, and so on. All elementary particles are either fermions or ▷bosons.

The exclusion principle, formulated by Austrian–US physicist Wolfgang Pauli in 1925, asserts that no two fermions in the same system (such as an atom) can possess the same position, energy state, spin, or other quantized property.

fermium synthesized, radioactive, metallic element of the ▷actinide series, symbol Fm, atomic number 100, relative atomic mass 257.10. Ten isotopes are known, the longest-lived of which, Fm-257, has a half-life of 80 days. Fermium has been produced only in minute quantities in particle accelerators.

It was discovered in 1952 in the debris of the first thermonuclear explosion. The element was named in 1955 in honour of US physicist Enrico ▷Fermi.

fern any of a group of plants related to horsetails and clubmosses. Ferns are spore-bearing, not flowering, plants and most are perennial, spreading by slow-growing roots. The leaves, known as fronds, vary widely in size and shape. Some taller types, such as tree ferns, grow in the tropics. There are over 7,000 species. (Order Filicales.)

Ferns found in Britain include the polypody (*Polypodium vulgare*), shield fern (*Polystichum*), male fern (*Dryopteris filix-mas*), hart's-tongue (*Phyllitis scolopendrium*), maidenhair (*Adiantum capillus-veneris*), and bracken (*Pteridium aquilinum*), an agricultural weed.

Ferrara industrial town and archbishopric in Emilia-Romagna region, northern Italy, on a branch of the Po delta, 52 km/32 mi west of the Adriatic Sea; population (1992) 137,100. It is the principal distribution and market centre of a major fruit-growing area. Industries include sugar-refining, and the manufacture of chemicals and textiles. Ferrara became a powerful city state in the 13th century.

Ferrari, Enzo (1898–1988) Italian founder of the Ferrari car-manufacturing company, which specializes in Grand Prix racing cars and high-quality sports cars. He was a racing driver for Alfa Romeo in the 1920s, went on to become one of their designers, and took over their racing division in 1929. In 1947 the first 'true' Ferrari was seen. To the end of the 1999 season Ferrari had won more world championship Grand Prix than any other team. In 2000 Michael Schumacher brought Ferrari their first Drivers' Championship since 1979.
Related Web site: Ferrari http://www.ferrari.it

ferret domesticated variety of the Old World ▷polecat.

About 35 cm/1.2 ft long, it usually has yellowish-white fur and pink eyes, but may be the dark brown colour of a wild polecat. Ferrets may breed with wild polecats. They have been used since ancient times to hunt rabbits and rats.
Related Web site: Ferret Central http://www.ferretcentral.org/

Ferrier, Kathleen Mary (1912–1953) English contralto. She brought warmth and depth of conviction to English oratorio roles during wartime and subsequently to opera and lieder (songs), including Gluck's *Orfeo ed Euridice*, Mahler's *Das Lied von der Erde/The Song of the Earth*, and the role of Lucretia in Benjamin Britten's *The Rape of Lucretia* (1946).

Ferrier, Susan (Edmonstone) (1782–1854) Scottish novelist. Her anonymously published books are *Marriage* (1818), *The Inheritance* (1824), and *Destiny* (1831), all of which give a lively picture of Scottish manners and society.

ferro-alloy alloy of iron with a high proportion of elements such as manganese, silicon, chromium, and molybdenum. Ferro-alloys are used in the manufacture of alloy steels. Each alloy is generally named after the added metal – for example, ferrochromium.

ferromagnetism form of ▷magnetism that can be acquired in an external magnetic field and usually retained in its absence, so that ferromagnetic materials are used to make permanent magnets. A ferromagnetic material may therefore be said to have a high magnetic permeability and susceptibility (which depends upon temperature). Examples are iron, cobalt, nickel, and their alloys.

fertility an organism's ability to reproduce, as distinct from the rate at which it reproduces (▷fecundity). Individuals become infertile (unable to reproduce) when they cannot generate gametes (eggs or sperm) or when their gametes cannot yield a viable ▷embryo after fertilization.

fertility drug any of a range of drugs taken to increase a female's fertility, developed in Sweden in the mid-1950s. They increase the chances of a multiple birth.

fertilization in ▷sexual reproduction, the union of two ▷gametes (sex cells, often called egg and sperm) to produce a ▷zygote, which combines the genetic material contributed by each parent. In self-fertilization the male and female gametes come from the same plant; in cross-fertilization they come from different plants. Self-fertilization rarely occurs in animals; usually even ▷hermaphrodite animals cross-fertilize each other.

In terrestrial insects, mammals, reptiles, and birds, fertilization occurs within the female's body. In humans it usually takes place in the ▷Fallopian tube. In the majority of fishes and amphibians, and most aquatic invertebrates, fertilization occurs externally, when both sexes release their gametes into the water. In most fungi, gametes are not released, but the hyphae of the two parents grow towards each other and fuse to achieve fertilization. In higher plants, ▷pollination precedes fertilization.

fertilizer substance containing some or all of a range of about 20 chemical elements necessary for healthy plant growth, used to compensate for the deficiencies of poor or depleted soil. Fertilizers may be organic, for example farmyard manure, composts, bonemeal, blood, and fishmeal; or inorganic, in the form of compounds, mainly of nitrogen, phosphate, and potash, which have been used on a very much increased scale since 1945. Compounds of nitrogen and phosphorus are of particular importance.

Fès (or **Fez**; Arabic **Fas**) former capital of Morocco 808–1062, 1296–1548, and 1662–1912, in the Fès valley north of the Great Atlas Mountains, 160 km/100 mi east of Rabat; population (1993) 564,000. Textiles, carpets, and leather are manufactured, and the *fez*, a brimless hat worn in southern and eastern Mediterranean countries, is traditionally said to have originated here. Qarawiyin Islamic University dates from 859; a second university was founded in 1961.

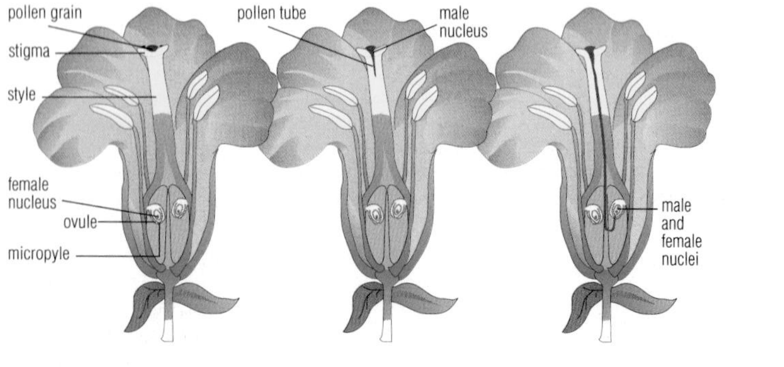

FERTILIZATION In a flowering plant pollen grains land on the surface of the stigma, and if conditions are acceptable the pollen grain germinates, forming a pollen tube, through which the male gametes pass, entering the ovule via the micropyle in order to reach the female egg.

fescue any grass of a widely distributed group. Many are used in temperate regions for lawns and pasture. Many upland species are viviparous, producing young plantlets instead of flowers. (Genus *Festuca*, family Gramineae.)

fetal therapy diagnosis and treatment of conditions arising in the unborn child. While some anomalies can be diagnosed antenatally, fetal treatments are only appropriate in a few cases – mostly where the development of an organ is affected.

fetch-execute cycle (or **processing cycle**) in computing, the two-phase cycle used by the computer's central processing unit to process the instructions in a program. During the fetch phase, the next program instruction is transferred from the computer's immediate-access memory to the instruction register (memory location used to hold the instruction while it is being executed). During the execute phase, the instruction is decoded and obeyed. The process is repeated in a continuous loop.

fetishism in anthropology, belief in the supernormal power of some inanimate object that is known as a fetish. Fetishism in some form is common to most cultures, and often has religious or magical significance.

fetishism in psychology, the transfer of erotic interest to an object, such as an item of clothing, whose real or fantasized presence is necessary for sexual gratification. The fetish may also be a part of the body not normally considered erogenous, such as the feet.

fetus (or **foetus**) stage in mammalian ▷embryo development. The human embryo is usually termed a fetus after the eighth week of development, when the limbs and external features of the head are recognizable.

In the UK, from 1989, the use of aborted fetuses for research and transplant purposes was approved provided that the mother's decision to seek an abortion is not influenced by consideration of this possible use. Each case has to be considered by an ethics committee, which may set conditions for the use of the fetal material.

Related Web site: Visible Embryo http://www.visembryo.com/

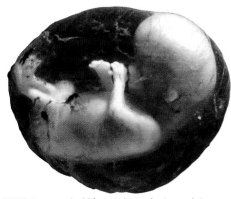

FETUS A ten-week-old fetus in its mother's womb (or uterus). *Image Bank*

feudalism (or the **feudal system**; Latin *feudem* 'fief', coined 1839) the main form of social organization in medieval Europe. A system based primarily on land, it involved a hierarchy of authority, rights, and power that extended from the monarchy downwards. At the head of the system the crown owned all the land. Beneath the crown, an intricate network of duties and obligations linked royalty, tenants-in-chief (such as the barons), under-tenants (knights), and villeins (serfs). Feudalism was reinforced by personal oaths of allegiance and a complex legal system and supported by the Christian medieval church.

In return for military service the monarch allowed powerful vassals to hold land, and often also to administer justice and levy taxes. They in turn 'sublet' such rights, usually keeping part of the land (the ▷demesne) for themselves. At the bottom of the system were the villeins, who worked without pay on their lord's manor lands in return for being allowed to cultivate some for themselves. They could not be sold as if they were slaves, but they could not leave the estate to live or work elsewhere without permission. In medieval England, their work was supervised by a village official called the reeve. Their life was undoubtedly hard, as shown in documents such as 'Pierce the Plowman's Crede' (*c.* 1394) and picture sources such as the Luttrell Psalter (1340). The feudal system declined from the 13th century, gradually giving way to the class system as the dominant form of social ranking, partly because of the growth of a money economy, with medieval trade, commerce, and industry, and partly because of the many peasants' revolts 1350–1550, such as the ▷Peasant's Revolt of 1381. Villeinage, or serfdom, ended in England in the 16th century, but

lasted in France until 1789 and in the rest of Western Europe until the early 19th century. In Russia it continued until 1861.

Related Web site: 'Feudalism to Socialism' http://eserver.org/history/feudalism-to-socialism.txt

fever condition of raised body temperature, usually due to infection.

Feydeau, Georges Léon Jules Marie (1862–1921) French comic dramatist. He is the author of over 60 farces and light comedies, which have been repeatedly revived in France at the Comédie Française and abroad. These include *La Dame de chez Maxim/The Girl from Maxim's* (1899), *Une Puce à l'oreille/A Flea in her Ear* (1907), *Feu la mère de Madame/My Late Mother-in-Law*, and *Occupe-toi d'Amélie/Look after Lulu*, (both 1908).

Feynman, Richard P(hillips)
(1918–1988) US physicist whose work laid the foundations of quantum electrodynamics. He was awarded the Nobel Prize for Physics in 1965 for his work on the theory of radiation. He shared the award with Julian Schwinger and Sin-Itiro Tomonaga. He also contributed to many aspects of particle physics, including quark theory and the nature of the weak nuclear force.

For his work on quantum electrodynamics, he developed a simple and elegant system of Feynman diagrams to represent interactions between particles and how they moved from one space-time point to another. He derived rules for calculating the probability of the interaction represented by each diagram. His other major discoveries are the theory of superfluidity (frictionless flow) in liquid helium, developed in the early 1950s; his work on the weak interaction (with US physicist Murray Gell-Mann) and the strong force; and his prediction that the proton and neutron are not elementary particles. Both particles are now known to be composed of quarks.

Related Web site: Feynman, Richard Phillips http://www-groups.dcs.st-and.ac.uk/history/Mathematicians/Feynman.html

Fez alternative spelling of ▷Fès, a city in Morocco.

ff abbreviation for folios; and the following, used in reference citation and bibliography.

Fianna Fáil (Gaelic 'Soldiers of Destiny') Republic of Ireland political party, founded by the Irish nationalist Éamon ▷de Valera in 1926, and led since 1994 by Bertie ▷Ahern. A broad-based party, it is conservative socially and economically, and generally right of centre. It was the governing party in the Republic of Ireland 1932–48, 1951–54, 1957–73, 1977–81, 1982, 1987–94 (from 1993 in coalition with Labour), and from 1997. Its official aims include the establishment of a united and completely independent all-Ireland republic.

Fibonacci, Leonardo (*c.* 1170–*c.* 1250) Also known as **Leonardo of Pisa**. Italian mathematician. He published *Liber abaci/The Book of the Calculator* in Pisa in 1202, which was instrumental in the introduction of Arabic notation into Europe. From 1960, interest increased in **Fibonacci numbers**, in their simplest form a sequence in which each number is the sum of its two predecessors (1, 1, 2, 3, 5, 8, 13, ...). They have unusual characteristics with possible applications in botany, psychology, and astronomy (for example, a more exact correspondence than is given by ▷Bode's law to the distances between the planets and the Sun).

In 1220, Fibonacci published *Practica geometriae*, in which he used algebraic methods to solve many arithmetical and geometrical problems.

fibre, dietary (or **roughage**) plant material that cannot be digested by human digestive enzymes; it consists largely of cellulose, a carbohydrate found in plant cell walls. Fibre adds bulk to the gut contents, assisting the muscular contractions that force food along the intestine. A diet low in fibre causes constipation and is believed to increase the risk of developing diverticulitis, diabetes, gall-bladder disease, and cancer of the large bowel – conditions that are rare in nonindustrialized countries, where the diet contains a high proportion of unrefined cereals.

fibreglass glass that has been formed into fine fibres, either as long continuous filaments or as a fluffy, short-fibred glass wool. Fibreglass is heat- and fire-resistant and a good electrical insulator. It has applications in the field of fibre optics and as a strengthener for plastics in GRP (glass-reinforced plastics).

fibre optics branch of physics dealing with the transmission of light and images through glass or plastic fibres known as ▷optical fibres.

Related Web site: Fibre Optic Chronology http://www.sff.net/people/Jeff.Hecht/Chron.html

fibrin insoluble protein involved in blood clotting. When an injury occurs fibrin is deposited around the wound in the form of a mesh, which dries and hardens, so that bleeding stops. Fibrin is developed in the blood from a soluble protein, fibrinogen.

fibula the rear lower bone in the hind leg of a vertebrate. It is paired and often fused with a smaller front bone, the tibia.

fiction in literature, any work in which the content is completely or largely invented. The term describes imaginative works of narrative prose (such as the novel or the short story), and is distinguished from non-fiction (such as history, biography, or works on practical subjects) and poetry.

Related Web site: InterText http://www.etext.org/Zines/InterText/

> ### Richard Feynman
> *One does not, by knowing all the physical laws as we know them today, immediately obtain an understanding of anything much.*
>
> *The Character of Physical Law*

field in physics, a region of space in which an object exerts a force on another separate object because of certain properties they both possess. For example, there is a force of attraction between any two objects that have mass when one is in the gravitational field of the other.

Other fields of force include ▷electric fields (caused by electric charges) and ▷magnetic fields (caused by circulating electric currents), either of which can involve attractive or repulsive forces.

Field, Sally (1946–) US film and television actor and director. She won an Academy Award for *Norma Rae* (1979) and again for *Places in the Heart* (1984). Her directorial debut was made in 2000 with *Beautiful*.

fieldfare gregarious thrush *Turdus pilaris* of the family Muscicapidae, order Passeriformes; it has chestnut upperparts with a pale-grey lower back and neck, and a dark tail. The bird's underparts are a rich ochre colour, spotted with black. Its nest is of long fine grass with an intervening layer of mud; it may be built in birch or fir trees at a height of 5 m/16 ft or less. It feeds on berries, insects, and other invertebrates.

Fielding, Henry (1707–1754) English novelist. His greatest work, *The History of Tom Jones, a Foundling* (1749), which he described as 'a comic epic poem in prose', was an early landmark in the development of the English novel, realizing for the first time in English the form's potential for memorable characterization, coherent plotting, and perceptive analysis. The vigour of its comic impetus, descriptions of high and low life in town and country, and its variety of characters made it immediately popular.

In youth a prolific dramatist, Fielding began writing novels with *An Apology for the Life of Mrs Shamela Andrews* (1741), a merciless parody of Samuel ▷Richardson's *Pamela*.

Fielding gave a new prominence to dialogue in his work, which was to have a marked influence on the development of the English novel. He tried to portray life realistically, with humour, though his penetrating analysis of human weakness is also compassionate.

> ### Henry Fielding
> *His designs were strictly honourable, as the phrase is; that is, to rob a lady of her fortune by way of marriage.*
>
> *Tom Jones* bk 11 ch. 4

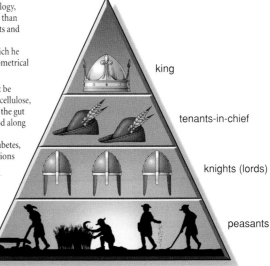

king

tenants-in-chief

knights (lords)

peasants

feudal system

FEUDALISM Feudalism is often depicted diagrammatically as a pyramid, with the monarch at the apex and the peasants (serfs) at the base. Peasants were the largest group in society but they held the least power.

Fields, W C (1880–1946) Stage name of William Claude Dukenfield. US actor and screenwriter. His distinctive speech and professed attitudes such as hatred of children and dogs gained him enormous popularity in such films as *David Copperfield* (1935), *My Little Chickadee* (1940; co-written with Mae West), *The Bank Dick* (1940), and *Never Give a Sucker an Even Break* (1941).

Fife unitary authority in eastern Scotland, which was formerly a region of three districts (1975–96) and a county until 1974.

area 1,321 sq km/510 sq mi **towns** Cupar, Dunfermline, Glenrothes (administrative headquarters), Kirkcaldy, St Andrews **physical** coastal area, predominantly low lying, undulating interior with dramatic escarpment at Lomond Hills; rivers Eden and Leven flow through **features** Rosyth naval base; Old Course, St Andrews **industries** electronics, petrochemicals, light engineering, oil servicing, paper **agriculture** potatoes, cereals, sugar beet, fishing (Pittenweem) **population** (1996) 351,200 **history** Tentsmuir, a coastal sand-dune area in the north, is possibly the earliest settled site in Scotland; the ancient palace of the Stuarts (16th century) was at Falkland; eight Scottish kings buried at Dunfermline

fife (German *pfeife*) small transverse ▷flute, originally with finger holes, without keys, and of similar range to the ▷piccolo. Of Swiss origin, the fife is a popular military band instrument, played on the side drums and associated with historic parades. The name is now used for a military flute in B flat, with six finger holes and several keys.

Fifteen, the ▷Jacobite rebellion of 1715, led by the 'Old Pretender' ▷James Edward Stuart and the Earl of Mar, in order to place the former on the English throne. Mar was checked at Sheriffmuir, Scotland, and the revolt collapsed.

Events Mar raised the standard in Scotland on 6 September 1715, and eight days later he captured Perth. The rebellion was also supported by risings in the Lowlands of Scotland and the north of England, and by a naval attack on Plymouth. In England, 'German George' was not liked, and the revolt hoped to gain from the hatred in Scotland of the Act of Union.

However, the rebellion was badly organized. Mar waited in Perth for nearly two months, allowing the government forces, led by the Duke of Argyll, to seize Stirling. He then failed to co-ordinate his moves with the rebellions in the Lowlands and the north of England. In November, the attack on Plymouth failed, the rebellion in the north of England was defeated at Preston, and Muir's army of 12,000 failed to defeat Argyll's 3,000 soldiers at the battle of Sheriffmuir. Also, by that time it was clear that the hoped-for French troops were not going to arrive. When James Edward Stuart arrived on 22 December 1715, he found that he was too late – the rebellion collapsed.

fifth column group within a country secretly aiding an enemy attacking from without. The term originated in 1936 during the Spanish Civil War, when General Mola boasted that Franco supporters were attacking Madrid with four columns and that they had a 'fifth column' inside the city.

fifth-generation computer anticipated new type of computer based on emerging microelectronic technologies with high computing speeds and ▷parallel processing. The development of very large-scale integration (VLSI) technology, which can put many more circuits onto an integrated circuit (chip) than is currently possible, and developments in computer hardware and software design may produce computers far more powerful than those in current use.

It has been predicted that such a computer will be able to communicate in natural spoken language with its user; store vast knowledge databases; search rapidly through these databases, making intelligent inferences and drawing logical conclusions; and process images and 'see' objects in the way that humans do.

In 1981 Japan's Ministry of International Trade and Industry launched a ten-year project to build the first fifth-generation computer, the 'parallel inference machine', consisting of over a thousand microprocessors operating in parallel with each other. By 1992, however, the project was behind schedule and had only produced 256-processor modules. It has since been suggested that research into other technologies, such as ▷neural networks, may present more promising approaches to artificial intelligence. Compare earlier ▷computer generations.

fig. abbreviation for ▷figure.

fig any of a group of trees belonging to the mulberry family, including the many cultivated varieties of *F. carica*, originally from western Asia. They produce two or three crops of fruit a year. Eaten fresh or dried, figs have a high sugar content and laxative properties. (Genus *Ficus*, family Moraceae.)

Related Web site: Fig, Common http://www.botanical.com/botanical/mgmh/f/figcom12.html

fighting fish any of a southeast Asian genus *Betta* of fishes of the gourami family, especially *B. splendens*, about 6 cm/2 in long and a popular aquarium fish. It can breathe air, using an accessory breathing organ above the gill, and can live in poorly oxygenated

FIGHTING FISH Siamese fighting fish live in brackish water in ponds and drainage channels in Thailand. The males are extremely aggressive and are bred for their large and brightly coloured fins, which they flare during combat.

water. The male has large fins and various colours, including shining greens, reds, and blues. The female is yellowish brown with short fins.

The male builds a nest of bubbles at the water's surface and displays to a female to induce her to lay. Rival males are attacked, and in a confined space fights may occur. In Thailand, public contests are held.

figure of speech poetic, imaginative, or ornamental expression used for comparison, emphasis, or stylistic effect; usually one of a list of such forms dating from discussions of literary and rhetorical style in Greece in the 5th century BC. These figures include euphemism, hyperbole, metaphor, metonymy, onomatopoeia, oxymoron, personification, pun, simile, synecdoche, and zeugma.

figwort any of a group of Old World plants belonging to the figwort family, which also includes foxgloves and snapdragons. Members of the genus have square stems, opposite leaves, and open two-lipped flowers in a cluster at the top of the stem. (Genus *Scrophularia*, family Scrophulariaceae.)

Related Web site: Figwort, Knotted http://www.botanical.com/botanical/mgmh/f/figkno13.html

Fiji Islands see country box.

file in computing, a collection of data or a program stored in a computer's external memory (for example, on ▷disk). It might include anything from information on a company's employees to a program for an adventure game. Serial (or sequential) access files hold information as a sequence of characters, so that, to read any particular item of data, the program must read all those that precede it. Random-access (or direct access) files allow the required data to be reached directly. Files are usually located via a ▷directory.

Fillmore, Millard (1800–1874) 13th president of the USA 1850–53, a Whig. He was Zachary Taylor's vice-president from 1849, and succeeded him on Taylor's death. Fillmore supported the Compromise of 1850 on slavery to reconcile North and South.

FIG The edible fig originated in western Asia and has been cultivated for at least 6,000 years.

film, art of see ▷cinema.

film, photographic strip of transparent material (usually cellulose acetate) coated with a light-sensitive emulsion, used in cameras to take pictures. The emulsion contains a mixture of light-sensitive silver halide salts (for example, bromide or iodide) in gelatin. When the emulsion is exposed to light, the silver salts are invisibly altered, giving a latent image, which is then made visible by the process of developing. Films differ in their sensitivities to light, this being indicated by their speeds. Colour film consists of several layers of emulsion, each of which records a different colour in the light falling on it.

filter in chemistry, a porous substance, such as blotting paper, through which a mixture can be passed to separate out its solid constituents.

filter in electronics, a circuit that transmits a signal of some frequencies better than others. A low-pass filter transmits signals of low frequency and also direct current; a high-pass filter transmits high-frequency signals; a band-pass filter transmits signals in a band of frequencies.

filter in optics, a device that absorbs some parts of the visible ▷spectrum and transmits others. For example, a green filter will absorb or block all colours of the spectrum except green, which it allows to pass through. A yellow filter absorbs only light at the blue and violet end of the spectrum, transmitting red, orange, green, and yellow light.

filtration technique by which suspended solid particles in a fluid are removed by passing the mixture through a filter, usually porous paper, plastic, or cloth. The particles are retained by the filter to form a residue and the fluid passes through to make up the filtrate. For example, soot may be filtered from air, and suspended solids from water. See diagram on p. 344.

fin in aquatic animals, flattened extension from the body that aids balance and propulsion through the water. In fish they may be paired, such as the pectoral and ventral fins, or singular, such as the caudal and dorsal fins, all being supported by a series of cartilaginous or bony rays.

The fins in cetaceans (whales and dolphins) are simple extensions of the soft tissue and have no bony rays. The flippers of seals are modified five-fingered limbs and contain the same bones as the limbs of other vertebrates.

final solution (to the Jewish question; German *Endlosung der Judenfrage*) euphemism used by the Nazis to describe the extermination of Jews (and other racial groups and opponents of the regime) before and during World War II in the ▷Holocaust.

financial gearing relationship between fixed-interest debt and shareholders' ▷equity used to finance a company. The additional profit made by borrowing at fixed interest and earning a greater return on those funds than the interest payable accrues to the shareholders. A high proportion of fixed-interest funding, known as 'high gearing', can leave the firm more vulnerable in poorer trading conditions.

Financial Times Index (FT Index) indicator measuring the daily movement of 30 major industrial share prices on the London Stock Exchange, issued by the UK *Financial Times* newspaper. Other FT indices cover government securities, fixed-interest securities, gold mine shares, and Stock Exchange activity.

finch any of various songbirds of the family Fringillidae, in the order Passeriformes (perching birds). They are seed-eaters with stout conical beaks. The name may also be applied to members of the Emberizidae (buntings), and Estrildidae (weaver-finches).

Related Web site: FinchWorld http://www.finchworld.com/

Fine Gael (Gaelic 'family of the gael') Republic of Ireland political party founded in 1933 by William ▷Cosgrave and led by John ▷Bruton from 1990. It has been socially liberal in recent years but fiscally conservative. Though it formed a coalition government with the Labour and Democratic Left parties 1994–97, it has typically been the main opposition party.

Fine Gael formed in 1933 as a merger of political party Cumann na nGaedheal, which governed the Irish Free State 1923–32, and two minor parties. Cumann na nGaedheal, which supported the 1921 Anglo-Irish Treaty that established the Irish Free State, was founded as the pro-Treaty side of Sinn Fein. It was traditionally associated with larger farmers and the middle class, but tended to draw support from anyone traditionally on the pro-Treaty side. Fine Gael first gained power in that guise as the main party in the coalition governments of 1948–51 and 1954–57. These coalitions also contained small leftist parties. It regained power with the Labour Party 1973–77. In 1977 Fine Gael's new leader Garret ▷FitzGerald moved the party towards social democracy making the 1981–82 and 1982–87 coalitions with Labour more natural, yet these still ended in rancour. The party seemed to flounder after FitzGerald's departure, but regained power in 1994 as part of a rainbow coalition which included Labour and Democratic Left elements.

Fingal's Cave cave on the island of Staffa, Inner Hebrides, Argyll and Bute, Scotland. It is lined with volcanic basalt columns, and is 70 m/230 ft long and 20 m/65 ft high. Visited by the German Romantic composer Felix Mendelssohn in 1829, the cave was the inspiration of his *Hebridean* overture, otherwise known as *Fingal's Cave*.

fingerprint ridge pattern of the skin on a person's fingertips; this is constant through life and no two are exactly alike. Fingerprinting was first used as a means of identifying crime suspects in India, and was adopted by the English police in 1901; it is now widely employed in police and security work.

Finland see country box.

Finland, Gulf of eastern arm of the ▷Baltic Sea, separating Finland from Estonia. It is 420 km/260 mi long and 40–150 km/25–90 mi wide. Helsinki and St Petersburg are the main ports.

Finney, Albert (1936–   ) English stage and film actor. He created the title roles in Keith Waterhouse's stage play *Billy Liar* (1960) and John Osborne's *Luther* (1961), and was associate artistic director of the Royal Court Theatre 1972–75. Later roles for the National Theatre include Tamburlaine in Marlowe's tragedy (1976) and Macbeth (1978). His films include *Saturday Night and Sunday Morning* (1960), *Tom Jones* (1963), *Murder on the Orient Express* (1974), *The Dresser* (1984), *Miller's Crossing* (1990), *The Browning Version* (1994), and *Erin Brockovich* (2000).

Finnish language member of the Finno-Ugric language family, the national language of Finland and closely related to neighbouring Estonian, Livonian, Karelian, and Ingrian languages. At the beginning of the 19th century Finnish had no official status, since Swedish was the language of education, government, and literature in Finland. The publication of the *Kalevala*, a national epic poem, in 1835, contributed greatly to the arousal of Finnish national and linguistic feeling.

Finn Mac Cumhaill (or **Fionn** or **Finn McCool**) ('the fair-haired son of Cumhall') Legendary Irish hero, the best-known character in the hero-tales of Ireland, identified with a general who organized an Irish regular army in the 3rd century. The word 'Fionn' (from Celtic *Vindos*) also has connotations of illumination and wisdom, and his most typical act was the gaining of knowledge

Fiji Islands

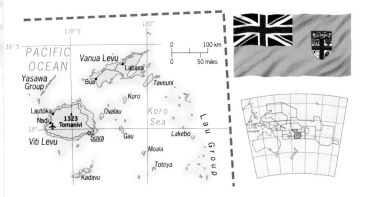

Fiji Islands country comprising 844 islands and islets in the southwest Pacific Ocean, about 100 of which are inhabited.

NATIONAL NAME *Matanitu Ko Viti/Republic of the Fiji Islands*
AREA 18,333 sq km/7,078 sq mi
CAPITAL Suva
MAJOR TOWNS/CITIES Lautoka, Nadi, Ba, Labasa, Nausori, Lami
MAJOR PORTS Lautoka, Levuka
PHYSICAL FEATURES comprises about 844 Melanesian and Polynesian islands and islets (about 100 inhabited), the largest being Viti Levu (10,429 sq km/4,028 sq mi) and Vanua Levu (5,556 sq km/2,146 sq mi); mountainous, volcanic, with tropical rainforest and grasslands; coral reefs; high volcanic peaks

Government

HEAD OF STATE Ratu Josefa Iloilo from 2000
HEAD OF GOVERNMENT Laisenia Qarase from 2000
POLITICAL SYSTEM military
POLITICAL EXECUTIVE military
ADMINISTRATIVE DIVISIONS 14 provinces
ARMED FORCES 3,500 (2002 est)
DEATH PENALTY abolished for ordinary crimes in 1979

Economy and resources

CURRENCY Fiji dollar
GPD (US$) 1.9 billion (2002 est)
REAL GDP GROWTH (% change on previous year) 3.8 (2001)
GNI (US$) 1.8 billion (2002 est)
GNI PER CAPITA (PPP) (US$) 5,310 (2002 est)
CONSUMER PRICE INFLATION 2% (2003 est)
UNEMPLOYMENT 7.6% (1999)
FOREIGN DEBT (US$) 213 million (2001 est)
MAJOR TRADING PARTNERS Australia, New Zealand, Japan, UK, USA, Singapore
RESOURCES gold, silver, copper
INDUSTRIES food processing (sugar, molasses, and copra), ready-made garments, animal feed, cigarettes, cement, tourism
EXPORTS clothing, sugar, gold, fish and fish products, re-exported petroleum products, timber, ginger, molasses. Principal market: Australia 25.6% (2001)
IMPORTS basic manufactured goods, machinery and transport equipment, food, mineral fuels. Principal source: Australia 39.8% (1998)
ARABLE LAND 10% (2000 est)
AGRICULTURAL PRODUCTS sugar cane, coconuts, ginger, rice, tobacco, cocoa; forestry (for timber)

Population and society

POPULATION 839,000 (2003 est)
POPULATION GROWTH RATE 1.1% (2000–05)
POPULATION DENSITY (per sq km) 46 (2003 est)
URBAN POPULATION (% of total) 52 (2003 est)
AGE DISTRIBUTION (% of total population) 0–14 33%, 15–59 61%, 60+ 6% (2002 est)
ETHNIC GROUPS 51% Fijians (of Melanesian and Polynesian descent), 44% Indian
LANGUAGE English (official), Fijian, Hindi
RELIGION Methodist 37%, Hindu 38%, Muslim 8%, Roman Catholic 8%, Sikh
EDUCATION not compulsory
LITERACY RATE 95% (men); 92% (women) (2003 est)
LABOUR FORCE 2.0% agriculture, 33.8% industry, 64.2% services (1998)
LIFE EXPECTANCY 68 (men); 72 (women) (2000–05)
TV SETS (per 1,000 people) 110 (1999 est)
INTERNET USERS (per 10,000 people) 599.4 (2002 est)

Chronology

c. **1500 BC**: Peopled by Polynesian and, later, by Melanesian settlers.

1643: The islands were visited for the first time by a European, the Dutch navigator Abel Tasman.

1830s: Arrival of Western Christian missionaries.

1840s–50s: Western Fiji came under dominance of a Christian convert prince, Cakobau, ruler of Bau islet, who proclaimed himself Tui Viti (King of Fiji), while the east was controlled by Ma'afu, a Christian prince from Tonga.

1857: British consul appointed, encouraging settlers from Australia and New Zealand to set up cotton farms in Fiji.

1874: Fiji became a British crown colony after a deed of cession was signed by King Cakobau.

1875–76: A third of the Fijian population were wiped out by a measles epidemic; a rebellion against the British was suppressed with the assistance of Fijian chiefs.

1877: Fiji became the headquarters of the British Western Pacific High Commission (WPHC), which controlled other British protectorates in the Pacific.

1879–1916: Indian labourers brought in, on ten-year indentured contracts, to work sugar plantations.

1904: Legislative Council formed, with elected Europeans and nominated Fijians, to advise the British governor.

1963: Legislative Council enlarged; women and Fijians were enfranchised. The predominantly Fijian Alliance Party (AP) formed.

1970: Independence was achieved from Britain; Ratu Sir Kamisese Mara of the AP was elected as the first prime minister.

1973: Ratu Sir George Cakobau, the great-grandson of the chief who had sworn allegiance to British in 1874, became governor general.

1985: The FLP was formed by Timoci Bavadra, with trade-union backing.

1987: After a general election had brought to power an Indian-dominated coalition led by Bavadra, Lt-Col Sitiveni Rabuka seized power in a military coup, and proclaimed a Fijian-dominated republic outside the Commonwealth.

1990: A new constitution, favouring indigenous (Melanese) Fijians, was introduced. Civilian rule was re-established, with resignations from the cabinet of military officers, but Rabuka remained home affairs minister, with Mara as prime minister.

1992: A general election produced a coalition government with Rabuka of the FPP as prime minister.

1994: Ratu Sir Kamisese Mara became president.

1997: A nondiscriminatory constitution was introduced. Fiji was re-admitted to the Commonwealth.

1999: President Mara's term was renewed for a further five years. Mahendra Chaudhry became Fiji's first prime minister of Indian descent.

2000: A coup led by George Speight took cabinet members hostage and ended Mara's presidency. The head of Fiji's armed forces, Commodore Frank Bainimarama, announced that he was taking power, proclaimed martial law, and revoked the 1997 non-discriminatory constitution (the aim of Speight's coup). When the hostages were released in July, the military handed over executive power to the new president, Ratu Josefa Iloilo, and installed Laisenia Qarase as prime minister. Speight was arrested and charged with treason.

2001: President Iloilo appointed an interim government with Ratu Tevita Momoedonu as prime minister, and announced elections.

2002: Coup leader George Speight was sentenced to death. However the sentence was commuted by President Iloilo to life imprisonment.

FIJI ISLANDS A view of the South Pacific. Most of the islands have coral reefs which encircle lagoons and calm the coastal waters. *Photodisk*

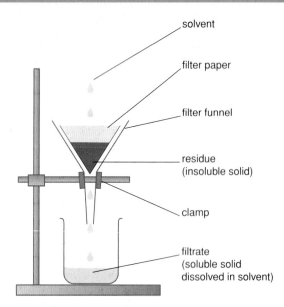

solvent

filter paper

filter funnel

residue
(insoluble solid)

clamp

filtrate
(soluble solid
dissolved in solvent)

FILTRATION The separation of a solid from a liquid by passing through a filter. The suspension is poured into the filter funnel where the filter paper traps all solid particles but allows the liquid to pass through to be collected below. See entry on p. 342.

through chewing his thumb. The Scottish writer James ▷Macpherson featured him (as Fingal) and his followers in the verse of his popular epics 1762–63, which were supposedly written by a 3rd-century bard called ▷Ossian.

Finno-Ugric group or family of more than 20 languages spoken by some 22 million people in scattered communities from Norway in the west to Siberia in the east and to the Carpathian mountains in the south. Members of the family include Finnish, Lapp, and Hungarian.
> Related Web site: Finno-Ugrian Languages http://www.helsinki.fi/hum/sugl/fgrlang.html

finsen unit unit (symbol FU) for measuring the intensity of ultraviolet (UV) light; for instance, UV light of 2 FUs causes sunburn in 15 minutes.

fiord alternative spelling of ▷fjord.

fir any of a group of ▷conifer trees belonging to the pine family. The true firs include the balsam fir (*A. balsamea*) of northern North America and the silver fir (*A. alba*) of Europe and Asia. Douglas firs of the genus *Pseudotsuga* are native to western North America and the Far East. (True fir genus *Abies*, family Pinaceae.)

Firbank, (Arthur Annesley) Ronald (1886–1926) English novelist. His work, set in the Edwardian decadent period, has a malicious humour and witty sophistication. It includes *Caprice* (1917), *Valmouth* (1919), and the bizarre fantasy *Concerning the Eccentricities of Cardinal Pirelli* (1926).

firearm weapon from which projectiles are discharged by the combustion of an explosive. Firearms are generally divided into two

main sections: ▷artillery (ordnance or cannon), with a bore greater than 2.54 cm/1 in, and ▷small arms, with a bore of less than 2.54 cm/1 in. Although gunpowder was known in Europe 60 years previously, the invention of guns dates from 1300 to 1325, and is attributed to Berthold Schwartz, a German monk.

firebrat any insect of the order Thysanura (▷bristletail).

fire clay a ▷clay with refractory characteristics (resistant to high temperatures), and hence suitable for lining furnaces (firebrick). Its chemical composition consists of a high percentage of silicon and aluminium oxides, and a low percentage of the oxides of sodium, potassium, iron, and calcium.

firedamp gas that occurs in coal mines and is explosive when mixed with air in certain proportions. It consists chiefly of methane (CH_4, natural gas or marsh gas) but always contains small quantities of other gases, such as nitrogen, carbon dioxide, and hydrogen, and sometimes ethane and carbon monoxide.

firefly any winged nocturnal beetle of the family Lampyridae. They all emit light through the process of ▷bioluminescence.

Firenze Italian form of ▷Florence, a city in Italy.

Fire of London fire 2–5 September 1666 that destroyed four-fifths of the City of London.

firewood the principal fuel for some 2 billion people, mainly in the Third World. In principle a renewable energy source, firewood is being cut far faster than the trees can regenerate in many areas of Africa and Asia, leading to ▷deforestation.

firework device that produces a display of colour, smoke, noise, or a combination of these three; examples include bangers, Catherine wheels, and Roman candles. They always generate heat. Fireworks were invented in China, and are today common in most countries. Pyrotechnics is the science and art of designing and using fireworks. Fireworks are used for displays and military purposes (including illumination and signalling).

firmware computer program held permanently in a computer's ▷ROM (read-only memory) chips, as opposed to a program that is read in from external memory as it is needed.

First World War another name for ▷World War I, 1914–18.

fiscal policy that part of government policy concerning ▷taxation and other revenues, ▷public spending, and government borrowing (the ▷public sector borrowing requirement).

fiscal year a year as defined by a company or government for financial accounting purposes. A company can choose any 12-month period for its accounting year and in exceptional circumstances may determine a longer or shorter period as its fiscal year. It does not necessarily coincide with the calendar year.

Fischer, Bobby (Robert James) (1943–) US World Chess Champion 1972–5, 1992. In 1958, after proving himself in international competition, he became the youngest grand master in history. He was the author of *Games of Chess* (1959), and was also celebrated for his unorthodox psychological tactics.
> Related Web site: Bobby Fischer Home Page http://www.rio.com/~johnnymc/

Fischer, Emil Hermann (1852–1919) German chemist who produced synthetic sugars and, from these, various enzymes. His descriptions of the chemistry of the carbohydrates and peptides laid the foundations for the science of biochemistry. He was awarded the Nobel Prize for Chemistry in 1902 for his work on the synthesis of sugars and purine compounds.

Fischer, Hans (1881–1945) German chemist awarded the Nobel Prize for Chemistry in 1930 for his work on haemoglobin, the oxygen-carrying, red colouring matter in blood. He determined the molecular structures of three important biological pigments: haemoglobin, chlorophyll, and bilirubin.

Fischer-Dieskau, Dietrich (1925–) German baritone singer. His intelligently focused and subtly understated interpretations of opera and lieder introduced a new depth and intimacy to a wide-ranging repertoire extending in opera from Christoph Willibald von Gluck to Alban Berg's Wozzeck, Hans Werner Henze, and from Bach arias to lieder of Schubert, Hugo Wolf, and Arnold Schoenberg. Since 1973 he has also conducted.

Fischl, Eric (1948–) US realist painter. The most prominent artist of his generation, he is known for his narrative, frequently disturbing paintings of suburban Americans at play. His figures are shown on the beach or indoors, often engaged in such intimate activities as dressing or making love. His straightforward handling of sexual themes has been considered shocking, as in *Bad Boy* (1981; Saatchi Collection, London).

fish aquatic vertebrate that uses gills to obtain oxygen from fresh or sea water. There are three main groups: the bony fishes or Osteichthyes (goldfish, cod, tuna); the cartilaginous fishes or Chondrichthyes (sharks, rays); and the jawless fishes or Agnatha (hagfishes, lampreys). Fishes of some form are found in virtually every body of water in the world except for the very salty water of the Dead Sea and some of the hot larval springs. Of the 30,000 fish species, approximately 2,500 are freshwater.

Bony fishes These constitute the majority of living fishes (about 20,000 species). The skeleton is bone, movement is controlled by mobile fins, and the body is usually covered with scales. The gills are covered by a single flap. Many have a ▷swim bladder with which the fish adjusts its buoyancy. Most lay eggs, sometimes in vast numbers; some ▷cod can produce as many as 28 million. These are laid in the open sea, and probably no more than 28 of them will survive to become adults. Those species that produce small numbers of eggs very often protect them in nests, or brood them in their mouths. Some fishes are internally fertilized and retain eggs until hatched inside the body, then giving birth to live young. Most bony fishes are ray-finned fishes, but a few, including lungfishes and coelacanths, are fleshy-finned.

Cartilaginous fishes These are efficient hunters. There are fewer than 600 known species of sharks and rays. The skeleton is cartilage, the mouth is generally beneath the head, the nose is large and sensitive, and there is a series of open gill slits along the neck region. They have no swimbladder and, in order to remain buoyant, must keep swimming. They may lay eggs ('mermaid's purses') or bear live young. Some types of cartilaginous fishes, such as sharks, retain the shape they had millions of years ago.

Jawless fishes Jawless fish have a body plan like that of some of the earliest vertebrates that existed before true fishes with jaws evolved. There is no true backbone but a notochord. The lamprey attaches itself to the fishes on which it feeds by a suckerlike rasping mouth. Hagfishes are entirely marine, very slimy, and feed on carrion and injured fishes.

The world's largest fish is the whale shark *Rhineodon typus*, more than 20 m/66 ft long; the smallest is the dwarf pygmy goby *Pandaka pygmaea*), 7.5–9.9 mm long. The study of fishes is called ichthyology.

John Evelyn
English diarist and author

This fatal night about ten, began that deplorable fire near Fish Street in London . . . all the sky were of a fiery aspect, like the top of a burning oven, and the light seen above 40 miles round about for many nights.

Diary, 23 September 1666

Fir Trees

The term fir tree is sometimes loosely used to refer to any conifer, but the true firs belong to the genus *Abies* which consists of some 40–50 species. Although the fir tree is similar in appearance to the spruce, it may be identified by the circular scars left on its bark when its needles fall. The scars are not raised above the bark's surface so the bark is left almost smooth. When a needle falls from a spruce part of the bark comes away too, leaving it rough with a peg-like scar. Fir tree cones stand upright on the branches and they break up when the seeds are scattered, leaving their central spikes on the tree. Spruce cones hang downwards and fall off when the seeds are scattered, leaving nothing on the tree.

Common name	Latin name	Max height m	ft	Natural home
Giant fir	*Abies grandis*	91	300	western USA
Red silver fir	*Abies amabilis*	76	250	northwest USA
Red fir	*Abies magnifica*	61	200	western USA
Noble fir	*Abies nobilis*	61	200	north-central USA
Caucasian fir	*Abies nordmanniana*	61	200	Caucasus, Greece, Asia Minor
European silver fir	*Abies alba*	52	170	Europe
Japanese fir	*Abies firma*	46	150	Japan
Colorado white fir	*Abies concolor*	37	120	Colorado and New Mexico, USA
Grecian fir	*Abies cephalonica*	30	100	Greece
Algerian fir	*Abies numidica*	21	70	Algeria
Forrest's fir	*Abies forrestii*	18	60	western China
Balsam fir	*Abies balsamea*	12–23	40–75	Canada and northeast USA
Douglas fir[1]	*Pseudotsuga douglasii*	76	250	North America

[1] The Douglas firs belong to the genus *Pseudotsuga* which consists of about seven species. They have narrower and softer leaves than the *Abies* firs and their mature cones are pendulous and have seed-scales beneath.

Fire of London

Also known as the **Great Fire of London**, this massive fire, the worst London had experienced, broke out accidentally in a bakery in Pudding Lane on 2 September 1666. Encouraged by a strong wind, it quickly spread through the City of London, raging for four days and destroying most of the buildings in the City, reaching as far west as the Temple. In an attempt to stop the fire reaching the Tower of London, gunpowder was used to blow up a house. The fire subsided on 5 September. It destroyed 87 churches, including St Paul's Cathedral, and 13,200 houses, although fewer than 20 people lost their lives.

Christopher Wren played a significant part in rebuilding the devastated city. His major contribution was the design of the magnificent St Paul's Cathedral, built from 1675 to 1711, to replace the

FIRE OF LONDON The Fire of London of 1666, illustrated here in a contemporary painting of the 'Dutch School', swept away much of the medieval city. *The Art Archive/ London Museum*

medieval church burnt down in the fire. With Robert Hooke, he also designed The Monument, which was built from 1671 to 1677. This stone column, 67 m/220 ft high, was erected near the site where the conflagration began, in Pudding Lane, to commemorate the fire.

Perhaps the most famous first-hand account of the fire is found in the *Diary* (1660–69) of Samuel Pepys, which provides an interesting insight into daily life at the time, including a detailed description of the fire. Another account of the fire was given by the diarist John Evelyn.

Classification of Fish

Order	Number of species	Examples
Class: Agnatha (jawless fishes)		
Subclass: Cyclostomota (scaleless fish with round mouths)		
Petromyzoniformes	30	lamprey
Myxiniformes	30	hagfish
Superclass: Pisces (jawed fishes)		
Class: Chondrichthyes (cartilaginous fishes)		
Subclass: Elasmobranchii (sharks and rays)		
Selachii	>200	shark
Batoidei	>300	skate, ray
Subclass: Holocephali (rabbitfishes)		
Chimaeriformes	20	chimaera, rabbitfish
Class: Osteichthyes (bony fishes)		
Subclass: Sarcopterygii (lobe-finned fishes)		
Coelacanthiformes	1	coelacanth
Ceratodiformes	1	Australian lungfish
Lepidosireniformes	4	South American and African lungfish
Subclass: Actinopterygii (ray-finned fishes)		
Polypteriformes	11	bichir, reedfish
Acipensiformes	25	paddlefish, sturgeon
Superorder: Teleostei		
Elopiformes	12	bonefish, tarpon, ladyfish
Anguilliformes	>500	eel
Clupeiformes	390	herring, anchovy
Osteoglossiformes	7	arapaima, African butterfly fish
Mormyriformes	150	elephant-trunk fish, featherback
Salmoniformes	160	salmon, trout, smelt, pike
Gonorhynchiformes	15	milkfish
Ostariophsi	6,000	carp, barb, characin, loach, catfish
Myctophiformes	300	deep-sea lantern fish, Bombay duck
Paracathopteryggi	853	toadfish, trout-perch, codfish
Atheriniformes	575	flying fish, toothcarp, halfbeak
Gasterosteiformes	150	stickleback, pipefish, seahorse
Pleuronectiformes	402	flatfish, flounder
Tetraodontiformes	250	puffer fish, triggerfish, sunfish
Perciformes	6,500	perch, cichlid, damsel fish, gobie, wrass, parrotfish, gourami, marlin,mackerel, tuna, swordfish, spiny eel, mullet, barracuda, sea bream, croaker, ice fish, butterfish

Fish as food The nutrient composition of fish is similar to that of meat, except that there are no obvious deposits of fat. Examples of fish comparatively high in fat are salmon, mackerel, and herring. White fish such as cod, haddock, and whiting contain only 0.4–4% fat. Fish are good sources of B vitamins and iodine, and the fatty fish livers are good sources of A and D vitamins. Calcium can be obtained from fish with soft skeletons, such as sardines. Roe and caviar have a high protein content (20–25%).

Fisher, John, St

(1459–1535) English cleric, created bishop of Rochester in 1504. He was an enthusiastic supporter of the revival in the study of Greek, and a friend of the humanists Thomas More and Desiderius Erasmus. In 1535 he was tried on a charge of denying the royal supremacy of Henry VIII and beheaded. He was canonized in 1935.

fish farming (or **aquaculture**) raising fish (including molluscs and crustaceans) under controlled conditions in tanks and ponds, sometimes in offshore pens. It has been practised for centuries in the Far East, where Japan today produces some 100,000 tonnes of fish a year; the USA, Norway, and Canada are also big producers. In the 1980s 10% of the world's consumption of fish was farmed, notably carp, catfish, trout, Atlantic salmon, turbot, eel, mussels, clams, oysters, and shrimp. See picture on p. 347.

fission in physics, the splitting of a heavy atomic nucleus into two or more major fragments. It is accompanied by the emission of two or three neutrons and the release of large amounts of ▷nuclear energy.

Fission occurs spontaneously in nuclei of uranium-235, the main fuel used in nuclear reactors. However, the process can also be induced by bombarding nuclei with neutrons because a nucleus that has absorbed a neutron becomes unstable and soon splits.

$$^{235}_{92}U + ^{1}_{0}n \rightarrow ^{236}_{92}U \rightarrow 2 \text{ nuclei} + 2\text{–}3 \text{ neutrons} + \text{energy}.$$

The neutrons released spontaneously by the fission of uranium nuclei may therefore be used in turn to induce further fissions, setting up a ▷chain reaction that must be controlled if it is not to result in a nuclear explosion. The minimum amount of fissile material that can undergo a continuous chain reaction is referred to as the ▷critical mass.

fistula in medicine, an abnormal pathway developing between adjoining organs or tissues, or leading to the exterior of the body. A fistula developing between the bowel and the bladder, for instance, may give rise to urinary-tract infection by intestinal organisms.

fit in medicine, popular term for ▷convulsion.

fitness in genetic theory, a measure of the success with which a genetically determined character can spread in future generations. By convention, the normal character is assigned a fitness of one, and variants (determined by other ▷alleles) are then assigned fitness values relative to this. Those with fitness greater than one will spread more rapidly and will ultimately replace the normal allele; those with fitness less than one will gradually die out.

Fitzgerald, Edward (1809–1883) English poet and translator. His poetic version of the *Rubaiyat of Omar Khayyám* (1859) (and often revised), with its resonant and melancholy tone, is generally considered more an original creation than a true translation. It is known throughout all the English-speaking countries and has passed through innumerable editions.

Fitzgerald, Ella (1917–1996) US jazz singer. She is recognized as one of the finest, most lyrical voices in jazz, both in solo work and with big bands. She is celebrated for her smooth interpretations of George and Ira Gershwin and Cole Porter songs.

Fitzgerald excelled at scat singing and was widely imitated in the 1950s and 1960s. She is among the best-selling recording artists in the history of jazz. Her albums include *Ella Fitzgerald Sings the Rodgers and Hart Songbook*, *Duke Ellington Songbook*, and other single-composer sets in the 1950s, and *Ella and Louis* (1956) with trumpeter Louis Armstrong. She also recorded with Count Basie and Duke Ellington.

FISH The anatomy of a fish. All fish move through water using their fins for propulsion. The bony fishes, like the specimen shown here, constitute the largest group of fishes with about 20,000 species.

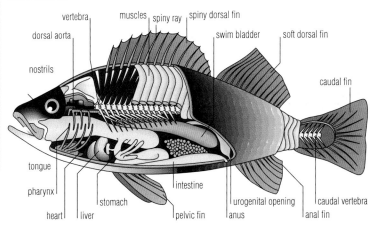

Fitzgerald, F(rancis) Scott (Key) (1896–1940) US novelist and short-story writer. His early autobiographical novel *This Side of Paradise* (1920) made him known in the post-war society of the East Coast, and *The Great Gatsby* (1925) epitomizes the Jazz Age.
Related Web site: F Scott Fitzgerald Home Page http://www.sc.edu/fitzgerald/

FitzGerald, Garret Michael (1926–   ) Irish politician, leader of the Fine Gael party 1977–87. As Taoiseach (prime minister) 1981–82 and 1982–87, he attempted to solve the Northern Ireland dispute, ultimately by participating in the ▷Anglo-Irish Agreement in 1985. He tried to remove some of the overtly Catholic features of the constitution to make the Republic more attractive to Northern Protestants.

Five Civilized Tribes term used to describe the Choctaw, Creek, Chickasaw, ▷Cherokee, and Seminole peoples of the southeast USA. They

> **F Scott Fitzgerald**
> *You can stroke people with words.*
>
> The Crack-up

were considered 'civilized' because they were farmers who lived in settled towns, had a democratic form of government, and had assimilated many European customs, including European dress. The Cherokee also built roads, schools, and churches, and even published a newspaper using their own alphabet. They were forcibly relocated to ▷Indian Territory, beginning in 1838.

Finland

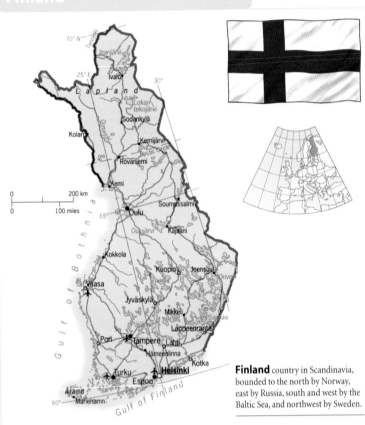

Finland country in Scandinavia, bounded to the north by Norway, east by Russia, south and west by the Baltic Sea, and northwest by Sweden.

NATIONAL NAME *Suomen Tasavalta* (Finnish)/*Republiken Finland* (Swedish)/*Republic of Finland*
AREA 338,145 sq km/130,557 sq mi
CAPITAL Helsinki (Swedish Helsingfors)
MAJOR TOWNS/CITIES Tampere, Turku, Espoo, Vantaa, Oulu
MAJOR PORTS Turku, Oulu
PHYSICAL FEATURES most of the country is forest, with low hills and about 60,000 lakes; one-third is within the Arctic Circle; archipelago in south includes Åland Islands; Helsinki is the most northerly national capital on the European continent. At the 70th parallel there is constant daylight for 73 days in summer and 51 days of uninterrupted night in winter.

Government

HEAD OF STATE Tarja Halonen from 2000
HEAD OF GOVERNMENT Matti Taneli Vanhanen from 2003
POLITICAL SYSTEM liberal democracy
POLITICAL EXECUTIVE dual executive
ADMINISTRATIVE DIVISIONS six provinces, subdivided into 452 municipalities
ARMED FORCES 31,800 (2002 est)
DEATH PENALTY abolished in 1972

Economy and resources

CURRENCY euro (markka until 2002)
GPD (US$) 130.8 billion (2002 est)
REAL GDP GROWTH (% change on previous year) 0.7 (2001)
GNI (US$) 122.2 billion (2002 est)
GNI PER CAPITA (PPP) (US$) 25,440 (2002 est)
CONSUMER PRICE INFLATION 0.8% (2003 est)
UNEMPLOYMENT 9.1% (2001)
MAJOR TRADING PARTNERS Germany, Sweden, UK, USA, Russia, Norway, the Netherlands, France, Italy
RESOURCES copper ore, lead ore, gold, zinc ore, silver, peat, hydro power, forests
INDUSTRIES food processing, paper and paper products, machinery, printing and publishing, wood products, metal products, shipbuilding, chemicals, clothing and footwear
EXPORTS metal and engineering products, gold, paper and paper products, machinery, ships, wood and pulp, clothing and footwear, chemicals. Principal market: Germany 12.5% (2000)
IMPORTS mineral fuels, machinery and transport equipment, food and live animals, chemical and related products, textiles, iron and steel. Principal source: Germany 14.3% (2000)
ARABLE LAND 7.2% (2000 est)
AGRICULTURAL PRODUCTS oats, sugar beet, potatoes, barley, hay; forestry and animal husbandry

Population and society

POPULATION 5,207,000 (2003 est)
POPULATION GROWTH RATE 0.1% (2000–15)
POPULATION DENSITY (per sq km) 15 (2003 est)
URBAN POPULATION (% of total) 59 (2003 est)
AGE DISTRIBUTION (% of total population) 0–14 18%, 15–59 62%, 60+ 20% (2002 est)
ETHNIC GROUPS predominantly Finnish; significant Swedish minority (6% of population); small minorities of native Saami (Lapp) and Russians
LANGUAGE Finnish (93%), Swedish (6%) (both official), Saami (Lapp), Russian
RELIGION Evangelical Lutheran 87%, Greek Orthodox 1%
EDUCATION (compulsory years) 9
LITERACY RATE 99% (men); 99% (women) (2003 est)
LABOUR FORCE 6.1% agriculture, 27.6% industry, 66.3% services (2000)
LIFE EXPECTANCY 74 (men); 82 (women) (2000–05)
CHILD MORTALITY RATE (under 5, per 1,000 live births) 5 (2001)
PHYSICIANS (per 1,000 people) 3.1 (1999 est)
HOSPITAL BEDS (per 1,000 people) 7.5 (1999 est)
TV SETS (per 1,000 people) 678 (2001 est)
RADIOS (per 1,000 people) 1,624 (2001 est)
INTERNET USERS (per 10,000 people) 5,089.3 (2002 est)
PERSONAL COMPUTER USERS (per 100 people) 44.2 (2002 est)

See also ▷Åland Islands.

Chronology

1st century: Occupied by Finnic nomads from Asia who drove out native Saami (Lapps) to the far north.
12th–13th centuries: A series of Swedish crusades conquered Finns and converted them to Christianity.
16th–17th centuries: Finland was a semi-autonomous Swedish duchy with Swedish landowners ruling Finnish peasants; Finland was allowed relative autonomy, becoming a grand duchy in 1581.
1634: Finland fully incorporated into Swedish kingdom.
1700–21: Great Northern War between Sweden and Russia; half of Finnish population died in famine and epidemics.
1741–43 and 1788–90: Further Russo-Swedish wars; much of the fighting took place in Finland.
1808: Russia invaded Sweden (with support of Napoleon).
1809: Finland ceded to Russia as grand duchy with Russian tsar as grand duke; Finns retained their own legal system and Lutheran religion and were exempt from Russian military service.
1812: Helsinki became capital of grand duchy.
19th century: Growing prosperity was followed by rise of national feeling among new Finnish middle class.
1904–05: Policies promoting Russification of Finland provoked a national uprising; Russians imposed military rule.
1917: Finland declared independence.
1918: Bitter civil war between Reds (supported by Russian Bolsheviks) and Whites (supported by Germany); Baron Carl Gustaf Mannerheim led the Whites to victory.
1919: Republican constitution adopted with Kaarlo Juho Ståhlberg as first president.
1927: Land reform broke up big estates and created many small peasant farms.
1939–40: Winter War: USSR invaded Finland after a demand for military bases was refused.
1940: Treaty of Moscow: Finland ceded territory to USSR.
1941: Finland joined the German attack on USSR in the hope of regaining lost territory.
1944: Finland agreed separate armistice with USSR; German troops withdrawn.
1947: Finno-Soviet peace treaty: Finland forced to cede 12% of its total area and to pay $300 million in reparations.
1948: Finno-Soviet Pact of Friendship, Cooperation, and Mutual Assistance (YYA treaty): Finland pledged to repel any attack on USSR through its territories.
1950s: Unstable centre-left coalitions excluded communists from government and adopted strict neutrality in foreign affairs.
1955: Finland joined the United Nations (UN) and the Nordic Council.
1956: There was a general strike as a result of unemployment and inflation.
1973: Trade agreements were signed with the European Economic Community (EEC) and Comecon.
1991: There was a swing towards the Centre Party in a general election.
1995: Finland joined the European Union (EU); the Social Democrats won a general election, with Paavo Lipponen becoming prime minister.
2000: Tarja Halonen was elected president. A former foreign minister, she became the first woman president of Finland.

FINLAND The Lutheran Cathedral in Helsinki, Finland. *Corel*

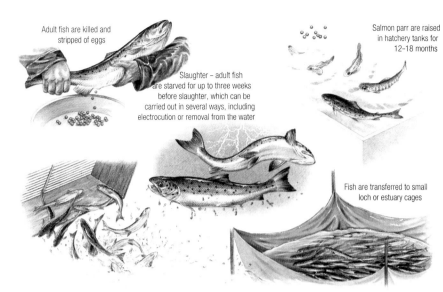

Adult fish are killed and stripped of eggs

Slaughter – adult fish are starved for up to three weeks before slaughter, which can be carried out in several ways, including electrocution or removal from the water

Salmon parr are raised in hatchery tanks for 12–18 months

Fish are transferred to small loch or estuary cages

Grading – fish are sorted by size up to five times in their lives. They are starved for 12 hours before sorting

Transfer from fresh to saltwater results in 15–50% of the fish dying. Additional stresses arise through overcrowding and the prevention of the salmon following their instincts to migrate

FISH FARMING The cycle of events on a fish farm. Fish farming is an intensive form of farming. Fish are crowded together and rely heavily on antibiotics. The resulting organic waste and chemical residues become pollution. See entry on p. 345.

Five Dynasties and Ten Kingdoms chaotic period in Chinese history 907–960 between the ▷Han and ▷Song dynasties, during which regionally based military dictatorships contested for power. The five dynasties, none of which lasted longer than 16 years, were based mainly in northern China and the ten kingdoms in the south.

five pillars of Islam the five duties required of every Muslim: repeating the **creed**, which affirms that Allah is the one God and Muhammad is his prophet; daily **prayer** or ▷salat; giving **alms**; **fasting** during the month of Ramadan; and, if not prevented by ill health or poverty, the hajj, or **pilgrimage** to Mecca, once in a lifetime.

fixed point temperature that can be accurately reproduced and used as the basis of a temperature scale. In the Celsius scale, the fixed points are the temperature of melting ice, defined to be 0°C (32°F), and the temperature of boiling water (at standard atmospheric pressure), defined to be 100°C (212°F).

fjord (or **fiord**) narrow sea inlet enclosed by high cliffs. Fjords are found in Norway, New Zealand, and western parts of Scotland. They are formed when an overdeepened U-shaped glacial valley is drowned by a rise in sea-level. At the mouth of the fjord there is a characteristic lip causing a shallowing of the water. This is due to reduced glacial erosion and the deposition of moraine at this point.

  Fiordland is the deeply indented southwest coast of the South Island, New Zealand; one of the most beautiful inlets is Milford Sound.

FL abbreviation for ▷Florida, a state of the USA.

fl. abbreviation for **floruit** (Latin 'he/she flourished').

flag in botany, another name for ▷iris, especially yellow flag (*Iris pseudacorus*), which grows wild in damp places throughout Europe; it is a true water plant but adapts to garden borders. It has a thick rhizome (underground stem), stiff bladelike leaves, and stems up to 150 cm/5 ft high. The flowers are large and yellow.

Flaherty, Robert (Joseph) (1884–1951) US film director. He was one of the pioneers of documentary film-making. He exerted great influence through his pioneer documentary of Inuit life, *Nanook of the North* (1922), a critical and commercial success.

flame test in chemistry, the use of a flame to identify metal ▷cations present in a solid.

flame tree any of various trees with brilliant red flowers, including the smooth-stemmed semi-deciduous *Brachychiton acerifolium* with scarlet bell-shaped flowers, native to Australia, but spread throughout the tropics.

flamingo long-legged and long-necked wading bird, family Phoenicopteridae, of the stork order Ciconiiformes. Largest of the family is the greater or roseate flamingo *Phoenicopterus ruber*, found in Africa, the Caribbean, and South America, with delicate pink plumage and 1.25 m/4 ft tall. They sift the mud for food with their downbent bills, and build colonies of high, conelike mud nests, with a little hollow for the eggs at the top.

Flamsteed, John (1646–1719) English astronomer. He began systematic observations of the positions of the stars, Moon, and planets at the Royal Observatory he founded at Greenwich, London, in 1676. His observations were published in *Historia Coelestis Britannica* (1725).

Flanders region of the Low Countries that in the 8th and 9th centuries extended from Calais to the Schelde and is now covered by the Belgian provinces of Oost Vlaanderen and West Vlaanderen (East and West Flanders), the French *département* of Nord, and part of the Dutch province of Zeeland. The language is Flemish. East Flanders, capital Ghent, has an area of 3,000 sq km/1,158 sq mi and a population (1995) of 1,349,400. West Flanders, capital Bruges, has an area of 3,100 sq km/1,197 sq mi and a population (1995) of 1,121,100.

> **Gustave Flaubert**
> *Of all the icy blasts that blow on love, a request for money is the most chilling and havoc-wreaking.*
> Madame Bovary ch. 8

flash flood flood of water in a normally arid area brought on by a sudden downpour of rain. Flash floods are rare and usually occur in mountainous areas. They may travel many kilometres from the site of the rainfall.

flat in music, a note or a key that is played lower in pitch than the written value, indicated by the ♭ sign or key signature. It can also refer to inaccurate intonation by a player.

flatfish bony fishes of the order Pleuronectiformes, having a characteristically flat, asymmetrical body with both eyes (in adults) on the upper side. Species include flounders, turbots, halibuts, plaice, and the European soles.

flatworm invertebrate of the phylum Platyhelminthes. Some are free-living, but many are parasitic (for example, tapeworms and flukes). The body is simple and bilaterally symmetrical, with one opening to the intestine. Many are hermaphroditic (with both male and female sex organs) and practise self-fertilization.

Flaubert, Gustave (1821–1880) French writer. One of the major novelists of the 19th century, he was the author of *Madame Bovary* (1857), *Salammbô* (1862), *L'Education sentimentale/Sentimental Education* (1869), and *La Tentation de Saint Antoine/The Temptation of St Anthony* (1874). Flaubert also wrote the short stories *Trois Contes/Three Tales* (1877). His dedication to art resulted in a meticulous prose style, realistic detail, and psychological depth, often revealed through interior monologue.

  Flaubert was born in Rouen. For a while he studied law, but preferred literature. In 1847 he travelled in Brittany and, from 1849 to 1851, in Greece and the Middle East, but for the greater part of his life he lived quietly with his mother and niece at his estate near Rouen. From 1846 until 1854 he was the lover of Louise Colet, but his unrequited love, at the age of 15, for Mme Elisa Schlesinger had more influence on his character.

  Madame Bovary, which took many years to prepare, caused a great scandal, and the author and publisher were prosecuted on a charge of violating morals, but were acquitted. In 1858 Flaubert travelled to Carthage and began a serious archaeological and historical study of its surroundings, which he made use of in his second work, *Salammbô*, a romance of the struggle between Rome and Carthage. With the publication of his next two works, he became a distinguished member of a small literary set, which included Turgenev, Zola, Daudet, and the Goncourts, and was a personal friend of George Sand. His last work, *Bouvard et Pécuchet*, was unfinished, and was published posthumously 1881.

flax any of a group of plants including the cultivated *L. usitatissimum*; **linen** is produced from the fibre in its stems. The seeds yield **linseed oil**, used in paints and varnishes. The plant,

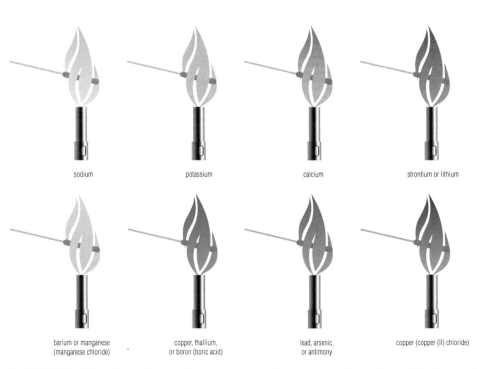

sodium

potassium

calcium

strontium or lithium

barium or manganese (manganese chloride)

copper, thallium, or boron (boric acid)

lead, arsenic, or antimony

copper (copper (II) chloride)

FLAME TEST Metals heated in the flame of a Bunsen burner burn with characteristic coloured flames. This is because when heated the electrons in the metal move around and give off light. Flame tests are useful for identifying unknown metals.

of almost worldwide distribution, has a stem up to 60 cm/24 in high, small leaves, and bright blue flowers. (Genus *Linum*, family Linaceae.)

Related Web site: Flax http://www.botanical.com/botanical/mgmh/f/flax—23.html

Flaxman, John (1755–1826) English neoclassical sculptor and illustrator. From 1775 he worked for the ▷Wedgwood pottery as a designer, and later became one of Europe's leading exponents of the neoclassical style. His public works include the monuments to Nelson and Joshua Reynolds in St Paul's Cathedral, London; and to Robert Burns in Westminster Abbey. In 1810 he became the first professor of sculpture at the Royal Academy.

flea wingless insect of the order Siphonaptera, with blood-sucking mouthparts. Fleas are parasitic on warm-blooded animals. Some fleas can jump 130 times their own height.

Species include the human flea *Pulex irritans*; the rat flea *Xenopsylla cheopis*, the transmitter of plague and typhus; and (fostered by central heating) the cat and dog fleas *Ctenocephalides felis* and *C. canis*.

Britain's largest flea *Histricopsylla talpae* lives on the mole and is about 8 mm/0.25 in long.

fleabane any of several plants of two related groups, belonging to the daisy family. Common fleabane (*P. dysenterica*) has golden-yellow flower heads and grows in wet and marshy places throughout Europe. (Genera *Pulicaria* and *Erigeron*, family Compositae.)

Fleming, Alexander (1881–1955) Scottish bacteriologist who was awarded a Nobel Prize for Physiology or Medicine in 1945 for his discovery of the bactericidal effect of ▷penicillin in 1928. In 1922 he had discovered lysozyme, an antibacterial enzyme present in saliva, nasal secretions, and tears. While studying this, he found an unusual mould growing on a culture dish, which he isolated and grew into a pure culture. This led to his discovery of penicillin, which came into use in 1941. He shared the award with Howard W ▷Florey and Ernst B ▷Chain, whose research had brought widespread realization of the value of penicillin with its isolation and its development as an antibiotic drug.

Related Web site: Fleming, Alexander http://www.pbs.org/wgbh/aso/databank/entries/bmflem.html

Fleming, Ian Lancaster (1908–1964) English author. His suspense novels feature the ruthless, laconic James Bond, British Secret Service agent 007. The first novel in the series was *Casino Royale* (1953); others include *From Russia with Love* (1957), *Goldfinger* (1959), and *The Man with the Golden Gun* (1965). Most of the novels were made into a successful series of Bond films.

IAN FLEMING A photograph of the English author Ian Fleming, taken in New York in February 1962. *Archive Photos*

Fleming's rules memory aids used to recall the relative directions of the magnetic field, current, and motion in an electric generator or motor, using one's fingers. The three directions are represented by the thu*m*b (for *m*otion), forefinger (for *f*ield), and se*c*ond finger (for conventional *c*urrent), all held at right angles to

each other. The right hand is used for generators and the left for motors. The rules were devised by the English physicist John Fleming.

Flemish member of the West Germanic branch of the Indo-European language family, spoken in north Belgium and the Nord *département* of France. It is closely related to Dutch.

Flemish art painting and sculpture of Flanders (now divided between Belgium, the Netherlands, and France). A distinctive Flemish style emerged in the early 15th century based on manuscript illumination and the art of the Burgundian court. It is distinguished by keen observation, minute attention to detail, bright colours, and superb technique – oil painting was a Flemish invention. Apart from portraits, Flemish art is chiefly religious and often set in contemporary landscapes, townscapes, and interiors.

flesh fly medium-sized fly varying from golden-brown to dark grey. The larvae feed on carrion and animal waste, though the larvae of *Wohlfahrtia* often invade the skin of children and young animals and other larvae will cause myiasis (invasion of the tissues) when the skin is already broken by a cut or abrasion. Flesh flies are members of the genera *Sarcophaga* and *Wohlfahrtia* in the family Sarcophagidae of the insect order Diptera, class Insecta, phylum Arthropoda.

Fletcher, John (1579–1625) English dramatist. He is remarkable for his range, which included tragicomedy and pastoral dramas, in addition to comedy and tragedy. He collaborated with Francis ▷Beaumont in some 12 plays, producing, most notably, the tragicomedy *Philaster* (1610) and *The Maid's Tragedy* (c. 1611). He is alleged to have collaborated with ▷Shakespeare on *The Two Noble Kinsmen* and *Henry VIII* (1613).

fleur-de-lis (French 'flower of the lily') heraldic device in the form of a stylized iris flower, borne on coats of arms since the 12th century and adopted by the French royal house of Bourbon.

flight (or **aviation**) method of transport in which aircraft carry people and goods through the air. People first took to the air in ▷balloons in 1783 and began powered flight in 1852 in ▷airships, but the history of flying, both for civilian and military use, is dominated by the ▷aeroplane. The earliest planes were designed for ▷gliding; the advent of the petrol engine saw the first powered flight by the ▷Wright brothers in 1903 in the USA. This inspired the development of aircraft throughout Europe. Biplanes were succeeded by monoplanes in the 1930s. The first jet plane (see ▷jet propulsion) was produced in 1939, and after the end of World War II the development of jetliners brought about a continuous expansion in passenger air travel. In 1969 came the supersonic aircraft ▷Concorde.

Related Web sites: Allstar Network – History of Flight http://www.allstar.fiu.edu/aero/history1.htm
Vertebrate Flight Exhibit http://www.ucmp.berkeley.edu/vertebrates/flight/enter.html

flight simulator computer-controlled pilot-training device, consisting of an artificial cockpit mounted on hydraulic legs, that simulates the experience of flying a real aircraft. Inside the cockpit, the trainee pilot views a screen showing a computer-controlled projection of the view from a real aircraft, and makes appropriate adjustments to the controls. The computer monitors these adjustments, changes both the alignment of the cockpit on its hydraulic legs, and the projected view seen by the pilot. In this way a trainee pilot can progress to quite an advanced stage of training without leaving the ground.

Flinders, Matthew (1774–1814) English navigator who explored the Australian coasts 1795–99 and 1801–03.

flint compact, hard, brittle mineral (a variety of chert), brown, black, or grey in colour, found as nodules in limestone or shale deposits. It consists of cryptocrystalline (grains too small to be visible even under a light microscope) ▷silica, SiO_2, principally in the crystalline form of ▷quartz. Implements fashioned from flint were widely used in prehistory.

Flintshire (Welsh **Sir y Fflint**) unitary authority in north Wales. A former county, it was part of Clwyd between 1974 and 1996.
area 437 sq km/169 sq mi **towns** ▷Mold (administrative headquarters), Flint, Holywell, Buckley, Connah's Quay **physical** bounded by the Irish Sea in the north, the Dee estuary in the east, and the Clwydian Range, which rises to 555 m/1,820 ft, in the southwest; rivers Dee, Alyn **industries** artificial silk, chemicals, optical glass **agriculture** dairy farming, stock-raising **population** (1996) 144,000

flocculation in soils, the artificially induced coupling together of particles to improve aeration and drainage. Clay soils, which have very tiny particles and are difficult to work, are often treated in this way. The method involves adding more lime to the soil.

Flodden, Battle of defeat of the Scots by the English under the Earl of Surrey on 9 September 1513, on a site 5 km/3 mi southeast of Coldstream, in Northumberland, England. ▷James IV of Scotland, declaring himself the active ally of France, crossed the border to England with an invading army of 30,000. The Scots were defeated, suffering heavy losses, and James himself was killed.

Flood, the in the Old Testament, the Koran, and *The Epic of Gilgamesh* (an ancient Sumerian legend), a deluge lasting 40 days and nights, a disaster alleged to have obliterated all humanity except a chosen few (in the Old Testament, the survivors were the family of ▷Noah and the pairs of animals sheltered on his ark).

flooding the inundation of land that is not normally covered with water. Flooding from rivers commonly takes place after heavy rainfall or in the spring after winter snows have melted. The river's discharge (volume of water carried in a given period) becomes too great, and water spills over the banks onto the surrounding flood plain. Small floods may happen once a year – these are called **annual floods** and are said to have a one-year return period. Much larger floods may occur on average only once every 50 years.

FLOODING Erected in 1982 across the River Thames at Woolwich, London, England, the Thames Barrier controls the flow of tide in the river. As a result of global warming, sea levels are expected to rise, and London is likely to be at risk of severe flooding. London was flooded in 1953 and again in 1965. *Image Bank*

flood plain area of periodic flooding along the course of river valleys. When river discharge exceeds the capacity of the channel, water rises over the channel banks and floods the adjacent low-lying lands. As water spills out of the channel some alluvium (silty material) will be deposited on the banks to form ▷levees (raised river banks). This water will slowly seep into the flood plain, depositing a new layer of rich fertile alluvium as it does so. Many important flood plains, such as the inner Nile delta in Egypt, occur in arid areas where their exceptional productivity has great importance for the local economy.

floppy disk in computing, a storage device consisting of a light, flexible disk enclosed in a cardboard or plastic jacket. The disk is placed in a disk drive, where it rotates at high speed. Data are recorded magnetically on one or both surfaces.

Floppy disks were invented by IBM in 1971 as a means of loading programs into the computer. They were originally 20 cm/8 in in diameter and typically held about 240 ▷kilobytes of data. Present-day floppy disks, widely used on ▷microcomputers, are 8.8 cm/3.5 in in diameter, and generally hold up to 2 ▷megabytes, depending on the disk formatting.

Floppy disks are inexpensive, and light enough to send through the post, but have slower access speeds and are more fragile than hard disks. (See also ▷disk.)

Flora in Roman mythology, the goddess of flowers, youth, and spring. Her festival, the **Floralia**, instituted in 238 BC, was initially celebrated at irregular intervals but became annual from 173 BC. It lasted from 28 April to 3 May and included licentious staged exhibitions.

Florence (Italian **Firenze**; Roman **Florentia**) capital of ▷Tuscany, northern Italy, on the River Arno, 88 km/55 mi from the river's mouth; population (1992) 397,400. It has printing, engineering, and optical industries; many crafts, including leather, gold and silver work, and embroidery; and its art and architecture attract large numbers of tourists. Notable medieval and Renaissance citizens included the writers Dante and Boccaccio, and the artists Giotto, Leonardo da Vinci, and Michelangelo.

Flight: Key Events

1783	First human flight, by Jean F Pilâtre de Rozier and the Marquis d'Arlandes, in Paris, using a hot-air balloon made by Joseph and Etienne Montgolfier; first ascent in a hydrogen-filled balloon by Jacques Charles and M N Robert in Paris.
1785	Jean-Pierre Blanchard and John J Jeffries make the first balloon crossing of the English Channel.
1852	Henri Giffard flies the first steam-powered airship over Paris.
1853	George Cayley flies the first true aeroplane, a model glider 1.5 m/5 ft long.
1891–96	Otto Lilienthal pilots a glider in flight.
1903	First powered and controlled flight of a heavier-than-air craft (aeroplane) by Orville Wright, at Kitty Hawk, North Carolina, USA.
1908	First powered flight in the UK by Samuel Cody.
1909	Louis Blériot flies across the English Channel in 36 minutes.
1914–18	World War I stimulates improvements in speed and power.
1919	First east–west flight across the Atlantic by Albert C Read, using a flying boat; first nonstop flight across the Atlantic east–west by John William Alcock and Arthur Whitten Brown in 16 hours 27 minutes; first complete flight from Britain to Australia by Ross Smith and Keith Smith.
1923	Juan de la Cieva flies the first autogiro with a rotating wing.
1927	Charles Lindbergh makes the first west–east solo nonstop flight across the Atlantic.
1928	The first transpacific flight, from San Francisco, USA, to Brisbane, Australia, is made by Charles Kingsford Smith and C T P Ulm.
1930	Frank Whittle patents the jet engine; Amy Johnson becomes the first woman to fly solo from England to Australia.
1937	The first fully pressurized aircraft, the Lockheed XC-35, comes into service.
1939	Erich Warsitz flies the first Heinkel jet plane, in Germany; Igor Sikorsky designs the first helicopter, with a large main rotor and a smaller tail rotor.
1939–45	World War II – developments include the Hawker Hurricane and Supermarine Spitfire fighters, and Avro Lancaster and Boeing Flying Fortress bombers.
1947	A rocket-powered plane, the Bell X-1, is the first aircraft to fly faster than the speed of sound.
1949	The de Havilland Comet, the first jet airliner, enters service; James Gallagher makes the first nonstop round-the-world flight, in a Boeing Superfortress.
1953	The first vertical takeoff aircraft, the Rolls-Royce 'Flying Bedstead', is tested.
1968	The world's first supersonic airliner, the Russian TU-144, flies for the first time.
1970	The Boeing 747 jumbo jet enters service, carrying 500 passengers.
1976	Anglo-French Concorde, making a transatlantic crossing in under three hours, comes into commercial service. A Lockheed SR-17A, piloted by Eldon W Joersz and George T Morgan, sets the world air-speed record of 3,529.56 kph/2,193.167 mph over Beale Air Force Base, California, USA.
1978	A US team makes the first transatlantic crossing by balloon, in the helium-filled *Double Eagle II*.
1979	First crossing of the English Channel by a human-powered aircraft, *Gossamer Albatross*, piloted by Bryan Allen.
1981	The solar-powered *Solar Challenger* flies across the English Channel, from Paris, France, to Kent, England, taking 5 hours for the 262 km/162.8 mi journey.
1986	Dick Rutan and Jeana Yeager make the first nonstop flight around the world without refuelling, in *Voyager*, which completes the flight in 9 days 3 minutes 44 seconds.
1987	Richard Branson and Per Lindstrand make the first transatlantic crossing by hot-air balloon, in *Virgin Atlantic Challenger*.
1988	*Daedalus*, a human-powered craft piloted by Kanellos Kanellopoulos, flies 118 km/74 mi across the Aegean Sea.
1991	Richard Branson and Per Lindstrand cross the Pacific Ocean in the hot-air balloon *Virgin Otsouka Pacific Flyer* from the southern tip of Japan to northwest Canada in 46 hours 15 minutes.
1992	US engineers demonstrate a model radio-controlled ornithopter, the first aircraft to be successfully propelled and manoeuvred by flapping wings.
1993	The US Federal Aviation Authority makes the use of an automatic on-board collision avoidance system (TCAS-2) mandatory in US airspace.
1994	The US Boeing 777 airliner makes its first flight. A scale model scramjet (supersonic combustion ramjet) is tested and produces speeds of 9,000 kph/5,590 mph (Mach 8.2). The scramjet uses oxygen from the atmosphere to burn its fuel.
1996	Japan tests the first fire-fighting helicopter. It is designed to reach skyscrapers beyond the range of fire-engine ladders.
1998	Swiss balloonist Bertrand Piccard, in the balloon *Breitling Orbiter*, sets a record for the longest nonstop, nonrefuelled flight by an aircraft: 9 days 17 hours 55 minutes.
1998	(August) An unpiloted aircraft crosses the Atlantic. The 14-kg/31-lb robot aircraft is designed by Australian and US researchers and it completes the crossing in 26 hours.
1999	Brian Jones and co-pilot Bertrand Piccard, aboard *Breitling Orbiter 3*, complete the first nonstop balloon flight around the world, a distance of 42,803 km/26,602 mi.
2000	David Hempelman-Adams becomes the first man to attempt to fly to the North Pole in a balloon. High winds and tiredness force him to turn back less than 21 km/13 mi short of the pole itself.

Features Florence's architectural treasures include the Ponte Vecchio (1345); the Pitti and Vecchio palaces; the churches of Sta Croce and Sta Maria Novella; the cathedral of Sta Maria del Fiore (1314); and the Uffizi Gallery, which has one of Europe's finest art collections, based on that of the Medicis.

History Florentia was founded by Julius Caesar in the 1st century BC on the site of the Etruscan town of **Faesulae**. It was besieged by the Goths in AD 405 and visited by Charlemagne in 786.

In 1052, Florence passed to Countess Matilda of Tuscany (1046–1115), and from the 11th century onwards gained increasing autonomy. In 1198 it became an independent republic governed by a body of 12 citizens, and had new city walls. In the 13th–14th centuries, the city was the centre of the struggle between the Guelphs (papal supporters) and Ghibellines (supporters of the Holy Roman Emperor). Despite this, Florence became immensely prosperous and went on to reach its cultural peak during the 14th–16th centuries.

From the 15th to the 18th century, the ▷Medici family, originally bankers, were the predominant power, in spite of being twice expelled by revolutions. In the first of these in 1493, a year after Lorenzo de' Medici's death, a republic was proclaimed (with ▷Machiavelli as secretary) which lasted until 1512. From 1494 to 1498, the city was under the control of religious reformer ▷Savonarola. In 1527, the Medicis again proclaimed a republic, which lasted through many years of gradual decline until 1737, when the city passed to Maria Theresa of Austria. The city was ruled by the Habsburg-Lorraine imperial dynasty 1737–1861, and was then the capital of Italy 1865–70. The city was badly damaged in World War II and by floods in 1966.

Florence was the birthplace of the writers Dante and Machiavelli, the sculptors Donatello and Ghiberti, and the founder of nursing, Florence Nightingale.

Related Web sites: Florence and Tuscany http://es.rice.edu/ES/humsoc/Galileo/Student_Work/Florence96/
Gardens, Villas, and Social Life in Renaissance Florence http://www.arts.monash.edu.au/visual_culture/projects/diva/kent.html

floret small flower, usually making up part of a larger, composite flower head. There are often two different types present on one flower head: disc florets in the central area, and ray florets around the edge which usually have a single petal known as the ligule. In the common daisy, for example, the disc florets are yellow, while the ligules are white.

Florey, Howard Walter (1898–1968) Baron Florey.

Australian pathologist who was awarded the Nobel Prize for Physiology or Medicine in 1945 with Ernst ▷Chain for the isolation of penicillin and its development as an antibiotic drug. His research into lysozyme, an antibacterial enzyme discovered by Alexander ▷Fleming (who shared the prize), led him to study penicillin (another of Fleming's discoveries), which he and Chain isolated and prepared for widespread use.

Florida southeasternmost state of the USA. It is nicknamed the Sunshine State. Florida was admitted to the Union in 1845 as the 27th US state. Much of the state is subtropical and is a popular tourist and retirement destination; the Miami region in particular has a thriving cosmopolitan community, serving as a gateway to both the Caribbean and Latin America. Florida is bordered to the north by Georgia and by Alabama. The state consists of a 640 km/400 mi-long peninsula jutting into the Atlantic, which it separates from the Gulf of Mexico, with a 390 km/240 mi-long panhandle to the northwest on the mainland. At the peninsula's southern end, the 220 km/135 mi-long chain of Florida Keys extends to the southwest.

population (2000) 15,982,400, one of the fastest-growing of the states; including 12% Hispanic (especially Cuban) and 13.6% African-American **area** 152,000 sq km/58,672 sq mi **capital** Tallahassee **towns and cities** Miami, Tampa, Jacksonville, Hialeah, Orlando, Fort Lauderdale **industries and products** tourism, leisure industry, citrus fruits, melons, vegetables, sugar cane, fish, shellfish, phosphates, chemicals, electrical and electronic equipment, aircraft, fabricated metals, finance sector

FLORIDA An elderly trader at the fish market in Sarasota, Florida, USA, inspects the size and quality of red snappers fresh in from the western Atlantic Ocean. *Image Bank*

Florida Keys series of small coral islands that curve over 240 km/150 mi southwest from the southern tip of Florida, USA, between the Straits of Florida and Florida Bay. The most important are Key Largo (the largest settlement) and Key West (which has a US naval and air station); economically they depend on fishing and tourism. A causeway links the keys to each other and to the mainland.

flotation, law of law stating that a floating object displaces its own weight of the fluid in which it floats. See ▷Archimedes principle.

flounder small flatfish *Platychthys flesus* of the northeastern Atlantic and Mediterranean, although it sometimes lives in estuaries. It is dull in colour and grows to 50 cm/1.6 ft.

flour beetle beetle that is a major pest of stored agricultural products, such as flour. They are found worldwide in granaries and stores where both the adult beetles and the larvae feed on damaged grain or flour. Neither adults nor larvae can eat intact grains.

Flour beetles are in the genus *Tribolium*, family Tenebrionidae, class Insecta, phylum Arthropoda.

flow chart diagram, often used in computing, to show the possible paths that data can take through a system or program.

A **system flow chart**, or **data flow chart**, is used to describe the flow of data through a complete data-processing system. Different graphic symbols represent the clerical operations involved and the different input, storage, and output equipment required. Although the flow chart may indicate the specific programs used, no details are given of how the programs process the data.

A **program flow chart** is used to describe the flow of data through a particular computer program, showing the exact sequence of operations performed by that program in order to process the data. Different graphic symbols are used to represent data input and output, decisions, branches, and subroutines.

flower the reproductive unit of an angiosperm or flowering plant, typically consisting of four whorls of modified leaves: ▷sepals, ▷petals, ▷stamens, and ▷carpels. These are borne on a central axis or ▷receptacle. The many variations in size, colour, number, and arrangement of parts are closely related to the method of pollination. Flowers adapted for wind pollination typically have reduced or absent petals and sepals and long, feathery ▷stigmas that hang outside the flower to trap airborne pollen. In contrast, the petals of insect-pollinated flowers are usually conspicuous and brightly coloured.

Structure The sepals and petals form the **calyx** and **corolla** respectively and together comprise the **perianth** with the function of protecting the reproductive organs and attracting pollinators.

The stamens lie within the corolla, each having a slender stalk, or filament, bearing the pollen-containing anther at the top. Collectively they are known as the **androecium** (male organs). The inner whorl of the flower comprises the carpels, each usually consisting of an ovary in which are borne the ▷ovules, and a stigma borne at the top of a slender stalk, or style. Collectively the carpels are known as the **gynoecium** (female organs).

Types of flower In size, flowers range from the tiny blooms of duckweeds scarcely visible to the naked eye to the gigantic flowers of the Malaysian *Rafflesia*, which can reach over 1 m/3 ft across. Flowers may either be borne singly or grouped together in ▷inflorescences. The stalk of the whole inflorescence is termed a **peduncle**, and the stalk of an individual flower is termed a **pedicel**. A flower is termed hermaphrodite when it contains both male and female reproductive organs. When male and female organs are carried in separate flowers, they are termed **monoecious**; when male and female flowers are on separate plants, the term **dioecious** is used.

flowering plant term generally used for ▷angiosperms, which bear flowers with various parts, including sepals, petals, stamens, and carpels.

Sometimes the term is used more broadly, to include both angiosperms and ▷gymnosperms, in which case the ▷cones of conifers and cycads are referred to as 'flowers'. Usually, however, the angiosperms and gymnosperms are referred to collectively as ▷seed plants, or spermatophytes.

The earliest flowering plant identified so far has been dated as being between 125 and 142 million years old, by Chinese palaeontologists, in 1998. The fossil *Archefructus* was found in northeast China. In 1996 UK palaeontologists found fossils in southern England of *Bevhalstia pebja*, a wetland herb about 25 cm/10 in high, which has been dated as early Cretaceous, about 130 million years old.

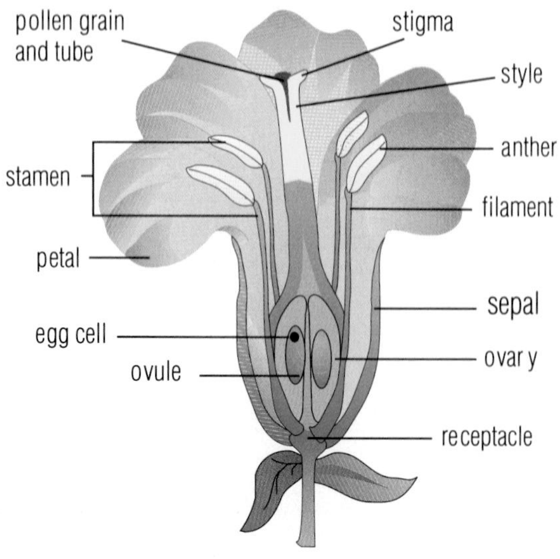

flue-gas desulphurization process of removing harmful sulphur pollution from gases emerging from a boiler. Sulphur compounds such as sulphur dioxide are commonly produced by burning ▷fossil fuels, especially coal in power stations, and are the main cause of ▷acid rain.

flugelhorn valved brass instrument of the ▷bugle type. It is made in three sizes: soprano, alto, and tenor, and is used in military and brass bands. In Britain only the alto instrument, in B flat, is used, normally only in brass bands. The alto flugelhorn has a similar range to the ▷cornet but is of mellower tone.

fluid mechanics the study of the behaviour of fluids (liquids and gases) at rest and in motion. Fluid mechanics is important in the study of the weather, the design of aircraft and road vehicles, and in industries, such as the chemical industry, which deal with flowing liquids or gases.

fluke any of various parasitic flatworms of the classes Monogenea and Digenea, that as adults live in and destroy the livers of sheep, cattle, horses, dogs, and humans. Monogenetic flukes can complete their life cycle in one host; digenetic flukes require two or more hosts, for example a snail and a human being, to complete their life cycle.

fluorescence short-lived ▷luminescence (a glow not caused by high temperature). ▷Phosphorescence lasts a little longer.

Fluorescence is used in strip and other lighting, and was developed rapidly during World War II because it was a more efficient means of illumination than the incandescent lamp. Recently, small bulb-size fluorescence lamps have reached the market. It is claimed that, if widely used, their greater efficiency could reduce demand for electricity. Other important applications are in fluorescent screens for television and cathode-ray tubes.

fluorescence microscopy technique for examining samples under a ▷microscope without slicing them into thin sections. Instead, fluorescent dyes are introduced into the tissue and used as a light source for imaging purposes. Fluorescent dyes can also be bonded to monoclonal antibodies and used to highlight areas where particular cell proteins occur.

fluoridation addition of small amounts of fluoride salts to drinking water by certain water authorities to help prevent tooth decay. Experiments in Britain, the USA, and elsewhere have indicated that a concentration of fluoride of 1 part per million in tap water retards the decay of children's teeth by more than 50%.

Much concern has been expressed about the risks of medicating the population at large by the addition of fluoride to the water supply, but the medical evidence demonstrates conclusively that there is no risk to the general health from additions of 1 part per million of fluoride to drinking water.

The recommended policy in Britain is to add sodium fluoride to the water to bring it up to the required amount, but implementation is up to each local authority.

fluoride negative ion (F^-) formed when hydrogen fluoride dissolves in water; compound formed between fluorine and another element in which the fluorine is the more electronegative element (see ▷electronegativity, ▷halide).

In parts of India, the natural level of fluoride in water is 10 parts per million. This causes fluorosis, or chronic fluoride poisoning, mottling teeth and deforming bones.

fluorine pale yellow, gaseous, nonmetallic element, symbol F, atomic number 9, relative atomic mass 19. It is the first member of the halogen group of elements, and is pungent, poisonous, and highly reactive, uniting directly with nearly all the elements. It occurs naturally as the minerals fluorite (CaF_2) and cryolite (Na_3AlF_6). Hydrogen fluoride is used in etching glass, and the freons, which all contain fluorine, are widely used as refrigerants.

Fluorine was discovered by the Swedish chemist Karl Scheele in 1771 and isolated by the French chemist Henri Moissan in 1886. Combined with uranium as UF_6, it is used in the separation of uranium isotopes.

The Infrared Space Observatory detected hydrogen fluoride molecules in an interstellar gas cloud in the constellation Sagittarius in 1997. It was the first time fluorine had been detected in space.

fluorite (or **fluorspar**) glassy, brittle halide mineral, calcium fluoride CaF_2, forming cubes and octahedra; colourless when pure, otherwise violet, blue, yellow, brown, or green.

fluorocarbon compound formed by replacing the hydrogen atoms of a hydrocarbon with fluorine. Fluorocarbons are used as inert coatings, refrigerants, synthetic resins, and as propellants in aerosols.

flute (or **transverse flute**) side-blown woodwind instrument of considerable antiquity. The flute is difficult to master but capable of intricate melodies and expressive tonal shading. The player blows across an end hole, the air current being split by the opposite edge, which causes pressure waves to form within the tube. The fingers are placed over holes in the tube to create different notes. The standard soprano flute has a range of three octaves or more.

fluvioglacial of a process or landform, associated with glacial meltwater. Meltwater, flowing beneath or ahead of a glacier, is capable of transporting rocky material and creating a variety of landscape features, including eskers, kames, and outwash plains.

fly any insect of the order Diptera. A fly has a single pair of wings, antennae, and compound eyes; the hind wings have become modified into knoblike projections (halteres) used to maintain equilibrium in flight. There are over 90,000 species.

The mouthparts project from the head as a proboscis used for sucking fluids, modified in some species, such as mosquitoes, to pierce a victim's skin and suck blood. Discs at the ends of hairs on their feet secrete a fluid enabling them to walk up walls and across ceilings. Flies undergo complete metamorphosis; their larvae (maggots) are without true legs, and the pupae are rarely enclosed in a cocoon. The sexes are similar and coloration is rarely vivid, though some are metallic green or blue. The fruitfly, genus *Drosophila*, is much used in genetic experiments as it is easy to keep, fast-breeding, and has easily visible chromosomes.

A new species of fly was discovered in Scotland in 1997. The 3-mm yellow fly is in genus *Palloptera*.

FLY A tachinid fly *Blepharella snyderi* in Kakamega Forest, Kenya. The females of the family Tachinidae lay their eggs on or near the bodies of other arthropods (future hosts), or on food which is likely to be eaten by a host at some point. The fly's larvae eventually live as internal parasites in other insects. *Premaphotos Wildlife*

flying dragon lizard *Draco volans* of the family Agamidae. It lives in southeast Asia, and can glide on flaps of skin spread and supported by its ribs. This small (7.5 cm/3 in head and body) arboreal lizard can glide between trees for 6 m/20 ft or more.

FLYING DRAGON A male flying dragon *Draco volans* with wings and throat flap extended in a territorial display in the rainforest of Sulawesi, Indonesia. *Ken Preston-Mafham/ Premaphotos Wildlife*

flying fish any marine bony fishes of the family Exocoetidae, order Beloniformes, best represented in tropical waters. They have winglike pectoral fins that can be spread to glide over the water.

Labels on flower diagram:
pollen grain and tube
stigma
style
anther
stamen
filament
petal
sepal
egg cell
ovary
ovule
receptacle

FLOWER Cross section of a typical flower showing its basic components: sepals, petals, stamens (anthers and filaments), and carpel (ovary and stigma). Flowers vary greatly in the size, shape, colour, and arrangement of these components.

flying fox another name for the fruit bat, a fruit-eating ▷bat of the suborder Megachiroptera.

flying lizard another name for ▷flying dragon.

flying squirrel any of 43 known species of squirrel, not closely related to the true squirrels. They are characterized by a membrane along the side of the body from forelimb to hindlimb (in some species running to neck and tail) which allows them to glide through the air. Several genera of flying squirrel are found in the Old World; the New World has the genus *Glaucomys*. Most species are eastern Asian.

The giant flying squirrel *Petaurista* grows up to 1.1 m/ 3.5 ft including tail.

FLYING SQUIRREL Giant flying squirrels can glide over 400 m/440 yd between trees by stretching the broad, fur-covered membranes that extend from the sides of the body to the toes.

Flynn, Errol (1909–1959) Stage name of Leslie Thomson Flynn. Australian-born US film actor. He portrayed swashbuckling heroes in such films as *Captain Blood* (1935), *Robin Hood* (1938), *The Charge of the Light Brigade* (1938), *The Private Lives of Elizabeth and Essex* (1939), *The Sea Hawk* (1940), and *The Master of Ballantrae* (1953).

flywheel heavy wheel in an engine that helps keep it running and smooths its motion. The ▷crankshaft in a petrol engine has a flywheel at one end, which keeps the crankshaft turning in between the intermittent power strokes of the pistons. It also comes into contact with the ▷clutch, serving as the connection between the engine and the car's transmission system.

FM in physics, abbreviation for ▷frequency modulation.

f-number (or f-stop) measure of the relative aperture of a telescope or camera lens; it indicates the light-gathering power of the lens. In photography, each successive f-number represents a halving of exposure speed.

Fo, Dario (1926–   ) Italian dramatist. His plays are predominantly political satires combining black humour with slapstick. They include *Morte accidentale di un anarchico/Accidental Death of an Anarchist* (1970), and *Non si paga non si paga/Can't Pay? Won't Pay!* (1974). Fo was awarded the Nobel Prize for Literature in 1997.

focal length (or focal distance) the distance from the centre of a lens or curved mirror to the focal point. For a concave mirror or convex lens, it is the distance at which rays of light parallel to the principal axis of the mirror or lens are brought to a focus (for a mirror, this is half the radius of curvature). For a convex mirror or concave lens, it is the distance from the centre to the point from which rays of light originally parallel to the principal axis of the mirror or lens diverge after being reflected or refracted.

Foch, Ferdinand (1851–1929) Marshal of France during World War I. He was largely responsible for the Allied victory at the first battle of the ▷Marne in September 1914, and commanded on the northwestern front October 1914–September 1916. He was appointed commander-in-chief of the Allied armies in the spring of 1918, and launched the Allied counter-offensive in July that brought about the negotiation of an armistice to end the war.

foetus stage in mammalian embryo development; see ▷fetus.

fog cloud that collects at the surface of the Earth, composed of water vapour that has condensed on particles of dust in the atmosphere. Cloud and fog are both caused by the air temperature falling below ▷dew point. The thickness of fog depends on the number of water particles it contains. Officially, fog refers to a condition when visibility is reduced to 1 km/0.6 mi or less, and mist or haze to that giving a visibility of 1–2 km or about 1 mi.

There are two types of fog. An **advection fog** is formed by the meeting of two currents of air, one cooler than the other, or by warm air flowing over a cold surface. Sea fogs commonly occur where warm and cold currents meet and the air above them mixes. A **radiation fog** forms on clear, calm nights when the land surface loses heat rapidly (by radiation); the air above is cooled to below its dew point and condensation takes place. A **mist** is produced by condensed water particles, and a haze by smoke or dust.

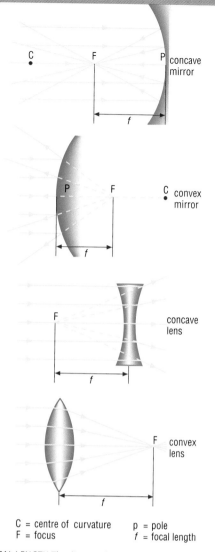

C = centre of curvature   p = pole
F = focus   f = focal length

FOCAL LENGTH The distance from the pole (P), or optical centre, of a lens or spherical mirror to its principal focus (F). The focal length of a spherical mirror is equal to half the radius of curvature ($f = \frac{CP}{2}$). The focal length of a lens is inversely proportional to the power of that lens (the greater the power the shorter the focal length).

In drought areas, for example Baja California, Canary Islands, Cape Verde Islands, Namib Desert, Peru, and Chile, coastal fogs enable plant and animal life to survive without rain and are a potential source of water for human use (by means of water collectors exploiting the effect of condensation).

Industrial areas uncontrolled by pollution laws have a continual haze of smoke over them, and if the temperature falls suddenly, a dense yellow smog forms. At some airports since 1975 it has been possible for certain aircraft to land and take off blind in fog, using radar navigation.

föhn (or foehn) warm dry wind that blows down the leeward slopes of mountains.

The air heats up as it descends because of the increase in pressure, and it is dry because all the moisture was dropped on the windward side of the mountain. In the valleys of Switzerland it is regarded as a health hazard, producing migraine and high blood pressure. A similar wind, chinook, is found on the eastern slopes of the Rocky Mountains in North America.

Fokine, Mikhail (1880–1942) Russian choreographer and dancer. He was chief choreographer to the Ballets Russes 1909–14, and with ▷Diaghilev revitalized and reformed the art of ballet,

MIKHAIL FOKINE Dancers performing in the ballet *Les Sylphides* which was created by Mikhail Fokine in 1909, when he was chief choreographer to Sergei Diaghilev's Ballets Russes. *Image Bank*

promoting the idea of artistic unity among dramatic, musical, and stylistic elements.

fold in geology, a bend in ▷beds or layers of rock. If the bend is arched up in the middle it is called an **anticline**; if it sags downwards in the middle it is called a **syncline**. The line along which a bed of rock folds is called its axis. The axial plane is the plane joining the axes of successive beds. See diagram on p. 352.

folic acid a ▷vitamin of the B complex. It is found in liver, legumes and green leafy vegetables, and whole grain foods, and is also synthesized by the intestinal bacteria. It is essential for growth, and plays many other roles in the body. Lack of folic acid causes anaemia because it is necessary for the synthesis of nucleic acids and the formation of red blood cells.

folk dance dance characteristic of a particular people, nation, or region. Many European folk dances are derived from the dances accompanying the customs and ceremonies of pre-Christian times. Some later became ballroom dances (for example, the minuet and waltz). Once an important part of many rituals, folk dance has tended to die out in industrialized countries. Examples of folk dance are Morris dance, farandole, and jota.

The preservation of folk dance in England was promoted by the work of Cecil Sharp.

Folkestone port and resort on the southeast coast of Kent, England, 10 km/6 mi southwest of Dover; population (1991) 46,200. There are passenger ferry and hovercraft connections with Boulogne, and to the northwest of the town is the British terminal of Eurotunnel, which offers a high-speed train link through the ▷Channel Tunnel to Paris and Brussels for private and haulage traffic.

folklore oral traditions and culture of a people, expressed in legends, riddles, songs, tales, and proverbs. The term was coined in 1846 by W J Thoms (1803–1885), but the founder of the systematic study of the subject was Jacob ▷Grimm; see also ▷oral literature.

Related Web site: Folklore: An Introduction http://virtual.park.uga.edu/~clandrum/folklore.html

advection fog
warm moist air cools either as it passes over a cool sea or comes into contact with cold land surface

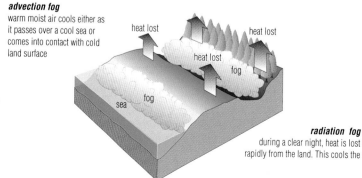

radiation fog
during a clear night, heat is lost rapidly from the land. This cools the

FOG The diagram shows the two types of fog, advection and radiation.

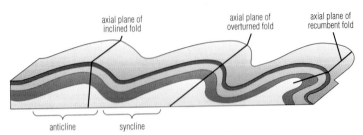

axial plane of inclined fold | axial plane of overturned fold | axial plane of recumbent fold

anticline | syncline

FOLD The folding of rock strata occurs where compression causes them to buckle. Over time, folding can assume highly complicated forms, as can sometimes be seen in the rock layers of cliff faces or deep cuttings in the rock. Folding contributed to the formation of great mountain chains such as the Himalayas. See entry on p. 351.

folk music traditional music, especially from rural areas, which is passed on by listening and repeating, and is usually performed by amateurs. The term is used to distinguish it from the classical music of a country, and from urban popular or commercial music. Most folk music exists in the form of songs, or instrumental music to accompany ▷folk dancing, and is usually melodic and rhythmic rather than harmonic in style.

Each country has its own styles of folk music, based on distinctive ▷scales and modes, and often played on instruments associated with that culture alone, such as the Scottish ▷bagpipes, the Russian ▷balalaika, or the Australian ▷didjeridu. A number of composers of classical music have used folk music in their own pieces to give them a particular national character, and in the late 19th century the use of folk tunes was a prominent feature of ▷nationalism in music.

In the 20th century a number of people, such as the composers Zoltán ▷Kodály and Béla ▷Bartók, and the musicologists Cecil Sharp and Alan Lomax, transcribed and recorded folk music to preserve it for the future. Since World War II, a renewed interest – especially among young people – led to a 'folk revival'. Traditional folk music was performed to a much wider audience, and songwriters such as Pete Seeger, Joan ▷Baez, and Bob ▷Dylan composed popular songs in a folk style.

Elements of folk music have also been combined with rock and pop music, and form an important part of ▷world music.

follicle in botany, a dry, usually many-seeded fruit that splits along one side only to release the seeds within. It is derived from a single ▷carpel. Examples include the fruits of the larkspurs *Delphinium* and columbine *Aquilegia*. It differs from a pod, which always splits open (dehisces) along both sides.

follicle in zoology, a small group of cells that surround and nourish a structure such as a hair (hair follicle) or a cell such as an egg (Graafian follicle; see ▷menstrual cycle).

follicle-stimulating hormone (FSH) a ▷hormone produced by the pituitary gland. It affects the ovaries in women, stimulating the production of an egg cell. Luteinizing hormone is needed to complete the process. In men, FSH stimulates the testes to produce sperm. It is used to treat some forms of infertility.

Fomalhaut (or **Alpha Piscis Austrini**) brightest star in the southern constellation Piscis Austrinus and the 18th-brightest star in the night sky. It is 25 light years from the Sun, with a true luminosity 13 times that of the Sun.

Fomalhaut is one of a number of stars around which IRAS (the Infra-Red Astronomy Satellite) detected excess infrared radiation, presumed to come from a region of solid particles around the star. This material may be a planetary system in the process of formation.

Fon a people living mainly in Benin, and also in Nigeria, numbering about 2.5 million. The Fon language belongs to the Kwa branch of the Niger–Congo family. The Fon founded a kingdom which became powerful in the 18th and 19th centuries through the slave trade, and the region became known as the Slave Coast.

Fonda, Henry (Jaynes) (1905–1982) US actor. His engaging style made him ideal in the role of the American pioneer and honourable man. His many films include *Young Mr Lincoln* (1939), *The Grapes of Wrath* (1940), *My Darling Clementine* (1946), *12 Angry Men* (1957), and *On Golden Pond* (1981), for which he won an Academy Award.

Related Web site: Fonda, Henry http://www.reelclassics.com/Actors/Fonda/fonda.htm

Fonda, Jane (Seymour) (1937–) US actor and producer. She won Academy Awards for her roles in *Klute* (1971) and *Coming Home* (1978). Other films include *Barbarella* (1968) and *They Shoot Horses, Don't They?* (1969).

A member of the Fonda acting dynasty, she became a star in her own right in the 1960s. Her varied films roles include the Western *Cat Ballou* (1965), *The Chase* (1966), *Barefoot in the Park* (1967), *Julia* (1977), *The China Syndrome* (1979), *9 to 5* (1980), *On Golden Pond* (1981), *The Morning After* (1986), and *Old Gringo* (1989).

Related Web site: Fonda, Jane http://mrshowbiz.go.com/people/janefonda/

Fongafale capital of Tuvalu, on Funafuti atoll.

font (or **fount**) complete set of printed or display characters of the same typeface, size, and style (bold, italic, underlined, and so on).

Fontainebleau (Latin **Fons Bellaqueus**) town in Seine-et-Marne *département*, France, situated 60 km/37 mi southeast of Paris near the River Seine; population (1990) 35,500. Its royal palace was founded by Philip the Good, but, as it exists today, was built by Francis I in the 16th century. Louis XIV's mistress, Mme de Montespan, lived here, as did Louis XV's mistress, Mme du Barry. Napoleon signed his abdication here in 1814. Nearby is the village of Barbizon, the haunt of several 19th-century painters (known as the ▷Barbizon School).

Fontainebleau School French school of Mannerist painting and sculpture. It was established at the court of François I, who brought Italian artists to Fontainebleau, near Paris, to decorate his hunting lodge: Rosso Fiorentino arrived in 1530, Francesco Primaticcio came in 1532. They evolved a distinctive decorative style using a combination of stucco relief and painting. Their work, with its exuberant ornamental and figurative style, had a lasting impact on French art in the 16th century.

Fontana, Domenico (1543–1607) Italian architect, born in Melide, Canton Tizino. In 1563 he went to Rome where Cardinal Felice Peretti became his patron. Under his auspices Fontana built a chapel in the Church of Santa Maria Maggiore in 1581 and the Villa Montalto in 1578. When Peretti was elected pope as Sixtus V, Fontana was appointed papal architect and undertook various important commissions in Rome, notably the Lateran Palace (1586–88), the Quirinal, and the Vatican library (1587–90). He also assisted in the completion of the dome of St Peter's (1587–90).

Fonteyn, Margot (1919–1991) Stage name of Peggy (Margaret) Hookham. English ballet dancer. She made her debut with the Vic-Wells Ballet in *Nutcracker* (1934) and first appeared as Giselle in 1937, eventually becoming prima ballerina of the Royal Ballet, London. Renowned for her perfect physique, clear line, musicality, and interpretive powers, she created many roles in Frederick ▷Ashton's ballets and formed a legendary partnership with Rudolf ▷Nureyev. She retired from dancing in 1979.

Foochow alternative transcription of ▷Fuzhou, a port and capital of Fujian province, southeast China.

food anything eaten by human beings and other animals and absorbed by plants to sustain life and health. The building blocks of food are nutrients, and humans can utilize the following nutrients: **carbohydrates** as starches found in bread, potatoes, and pasta; as simple sugars in sucrose and honey; and as fibres in cereals, fruit, and vegetables; **proteins** as from nuts, fish, meat, eggs, milk, and some vegetables; **fats** as found in most animal products (meat, lard, dairy products, fish), also in margarine, nuts and seeds, olives, and edible oils; **vitamins**, found in a wide variety of foods, except for vitamin B_{12}, which is found mainly in foods of animal origin; and **minerals**, found in a wide variety of foods (for example, calcium from milk and broccoli, iodine from seafood, and iron from liver and green vegetables).

Liquids consumed are principally **water**, ubiquitous in nature, and **alcohol**, found in fermented distilled beverages, from 40% in spirits to 0.01% in low-alcohol lagers and beers.

Food is needed both for energy, measured in ▷calories or kilojoules, and nutrients, which are converted to body tissues. Some nutrients, such as fat, carbohydrate, and alcohol, provide mainly energy; other nutrients are important in other ways; for example, fibre is an aid to metabolism. Proteins provide energy and are necessary for building cell and tissue structure.

Related Web site: Restaurants.co.uk http://www.restaurants.co.uk/

food chain in ecology, a sequence showing the feeding relationships between organisms in a particular ▷ecosystem. Each organism depends on the next lowest member of the chain for its food. A pyramid of numbers can be used to show the reduction in food energy at each step up the food chain.

Energy in the form of food is shown to be transferred from ▷autotrophs, or producers, which are principally plants and photosynthetic micro-organisms, to a series of ▷heterotrophs, or consumers. The heterotrophs comprise the ▷herbivores, which feed on the producers; ▷carnivores, which feed on the herbivores; and ▷decomposers, which break down the dead bodies and waste products of all four groups (including their own), ready for recycling.

In reality, however, organisms have varied diets, relying on different kinds of foods, so that the food chain is an oversimplification. The more complex **food web** shows a greater variety of relationships, but again emphasizes that energy passes from plants to herbivores to carnivores.

Environmentalists have used the concept of the food chain to show how poisons and other forms of pollution can pass from one animal to another, threatening rare species. For example, the pesticide DDT has been found in lethal concentrations in the bodies of animals at the top of the food chain, such as the golden eagle *Aquila chrysaetos*.

food poisoning any acute illness characterized by vomiting and diarrhoea and caused by eating food contaminated with harmful bacteria (for example, ▷listeriosis), poisonous food (for example, certain mushrooms, puffer fish), or poisoned food

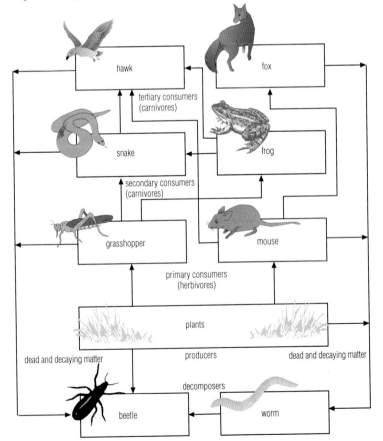

hawk | fox

tertiary consumers (carnivores)

snake | frog

secondary consumers (carnivores)

grasshopper | mouse

primary consumers (herbivores)

plants

dead and decaying matter | producers | dead and decaying matter

decomposers

beetle | worm

FOOD CHAIN The complex interrelationships between animals and plants in a food web. A food web shows how different food chains are linked in an ecosystem. Note that the arrows indicate movement of energy through the web. For example, an arrow shows that energy moves from plants to the grasshopper, which eats the plants.

(such as lead or arsenic introduced accidentally during processing). A frequent cause of food poisoning is ▷Salmonella bacteria. Salmonella comes in many forms, and strains are found in cattle, pigs, poultry, and eggs.

Deep freezing of poultry before the birds are properly cooked is a common cause of food poisoning. Attacks of salmonella also come from contaminated eggs that have been eaten raw or cooked only lightly. Pork may carry the roundworm *Trichinella*, and rye the parasitic fungus ergot. The most dangerous food poison is the bacillus that causes ▷botulism. This is rare but leads to muscle paralysis and, often, death. Food irradiation is intended to prevent food poisoning.

The number of notified cases of food poisoning in Britain for 1997 was 99,976. The actual incidence is as much as ten times higher, as most cases do not get reported.

Two outbreaks of food poisoning involving a lethal strain of *Escherichia coli* in Scotland in December 1996 and January 1997, resulted in 20 deaths.

food supply the availability of food, usually for human consumption. Food supply can be studied at scales ranging from individual households to global patterns. Since the 1940s the industrial and agricultural aspects of food supply have become increasingly globalized. New farming, packaging, and distribution techniques mean that the seasonal aspect of food supply has been reduced in wealthier nations such as the USA and the UK. In some less developed countries there are often problems of food scarcity and distribution caused by climate-related crop failure.

foot imperial unit of length (symbol ft), equivalent to 0.3048 m, in use in Britain since Anglo-Saxon times. It originally represented the length of a human foot. One foot contains 12 inches and is one-third of a yard.

foot unit of metrical pattern in poetry.

The five most common types of foot in English poetry are iamb (v –), trochee (– v), dactyl (– vv), spondee (– –), and anapaest (vv –); the symbol v stands for an unstressed syllable and – for a stressed one.

Foot, Michael Mackintosh (1913–) British Labour politician and writer. A leader of the left-wing Tribune Group, he was secretary of state for employment 1974–76, Lord President of the Council and leader of the House 1976–79, and succeeded James Callaghan as Labour Party leader 1980–83.

foot-and-mouth disease contagious eruptive viral disease of cloven-hoofed mammals, characterized by blisters in the mouth and around the hooves. In cattle it causes deterioration of milk yield and abortions. It is an airborne virus, which makes its eradication extremely difficult.

In the UK, an epidemic of foot-and-mouth broke out in February 2001, devastating the farming industry. By the end of June, over 5 million animals in the UK had been slaughtered. Despite health scares, a 2001 report stated that there had only been 40 confirmed cases of foot-and-mouth disease in humans worldwide.

football, American contact sport similar to the English game of rugby, played between two teams of 11 players, with an inflated oval ball. Players are well padded for protection and wear protective helmets. The **Super Bowl**, first held in 1967, is now an annual meeting between the winners of the National and American Football Conferences.

Related Web site: Pro Football Hall of Fame http://www.profootballhof.com/

football, association (or **soccer**) form of football originating in the UK, popular throughout the world. The modern game is played in the UK according to the rules laid down by the home countries' football associations. Slight amendments to the rules take effect in certain competitions and international matches as laid down by the sport's world governing body, Fédération Internationale de Football Association (FIFA, 1904). FIFA organizes the competitions for the World Cup, held every four years since 1930. The field has a halfway line marked with a centre circle, two penalty areas, and two goal areas. The game is played with an inflated spherical ball. There are two teams each of 11 players, broadly divided into defence (the goalkeeper and defenders), midfield (whose players collect the ball from the defence and distribute it to the attackers), and attack (forwards or strikers). The object of the game is to kick or head the ball into the opponents' goal.

Related Web sites: Football 365 http://www.football365.co.uk/
From the Terrace http://www.fromtheterrace.co.uk/

football, Australian rules game that combines aspects of Gaelic football, rugby, and association football; it is played between two teams of 18 players each, with an inflated oval ball. It is unique to Australia.

football, Gaelic kicking and catching game played mainly in Ireland. The two teams have 15 players each. The game is played on a field with an inflated spherical ball. The goalposts have a crossbar and a net across the lower half. Goals are scored by kicking the ball into the net (three points) or over the crossbar (one point).

Related Web site: Gaelic and Gaelic Culture http://sunsite.unc.edu/gaelic/gaelic.html

Football War popular name for a five-day war between El Salvador and Honduras which began on 14 July 1969, when Salvadorean planes bombed Tegucigelpa. Its army entered Honduras, but the ▷Organization of American States arranged a ceasefire, by which time about 2,000 lives had been lost.

The war is so called because of the mistaken belief that it followed a dispute after a World Cup qualifying match between the two countries. In fact, it arose because of densely populated El Salvador's desire for Honduran territory.

foraminifera any marine protozoan of the order Foraminiferida, with shells of calcium carbonate. Their shells have pores through which filaments project. Some form part of the ▷plankton, others live on the sea bottom.

force any influence that tends to change the state of rest or the uniform motion in a straight line of a body. The action of an unbalanced or resultant force results in the acceleration of a body in the direction of action of the force, or it may, if the body is unable to move freely, result in its deformation (see ▷Hooke's law). Force is a vector quantity, possessing both magnitude and direction; its SI unit is the newton.

Speed and distance In order to understand movement and what causes it, we need to be able to describe it. ▷Speed is a measure of how fast something is moving. Speed is measured by dividing the distance travelled by the time taken to travel that distance. Hence speed is distance moved in unit time. Speed is a ▷scalar quantity in which the direction of travel is not important, only the rate of travel. It is often useful to represent motion using a graph. Plotting distance against time in a distance–time graph enables one to calculate the total distance travelled. The gradient of the graph represents the speed at a particular point, the instantaneous speed. A straight line on the distance–time graph corresponds to a constant speed. A form of this graph that shows the stages on the journey is called a travel graph. A speed–time graph plots speed against time. It shows the instantaneous speed at each point. When the graph is horizontal, the object is stationary because speed is zero.

Velocity and acceleration ▷Velocity is the speed of an object in a given direction. Velocity is therefore a ▷vector quantity, in which both magnitude and direction of movement must be taken into account. ▷Acceleration is the rate of change of velocity with time. This is also a vector quantity. Acceleration happens when there is a change in speed, or a change in direction, or a change in speed and direction.

Forces and motion ▷Galileo discovered that a body moving on a perfectly smooth horizontal surface would neither speed up nor slow down. All moving bodies continue moving with the same

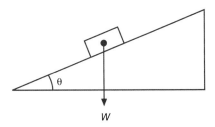

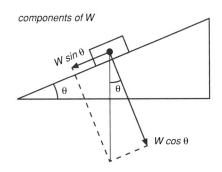

components of W

FORCE In mechanics, the resolution of forces is the division of a single force into two parts that act at right angles to each other. In the diagram, the weight W of an object on a slope, tilted at an angle θ, can be resolved into two parts or components: one acting at a right angle to the slope, equal to $W\cos\theta$, and one acting parallel to and down the slope, equal to $W\sin\theta$.

velocity unless a force is applied to cause an acceleration. The reason we appear to have to push something to keep it moving with constant velocity is because of frictional forces acting on all moving objects on Earth. ▷Friction occurs when two solid surfaces rub on each other; for example, a car tyre in contact with the ground. Friction opposes the relative motion of the two objects in contact and acts to slow the velocity of the moving object. A force is required to push the moving object and to cancel out the frictional force. If the forces combine to give a net force of zero, the object will not accelerate but will continue moving at constant velocity. A resultant force is a single force acting on a particle or body whose effect is equivalent to the combined effects of two or more separate forces. Galileo's work was developed by Isaac ▷Newton. According to Newton's second law of motion, the magnitude of a resultant force is equal to the rate of change of ▷momentum of the body on which it acts; the force F producing an acceleration a ms^{-2} on a body of mass m kilograms is therefore given by:

$$F = ma$$

Thus Newton's second law states that change of momentum is proportional to the size of the external force and takes place in the direction in which the force acts. Momentum is a function both of the mass of a body and of its velocity. This agrees with our experience, because the idea of force is derived from muscular effort, and we know that we have to exert more strength to stop the motion of a heavy body than a light one, just as we have to exert more strength to stop a rapidly moving body than a slowly moving one. Force, then, is measured by change of momentum, momentum being equal to mass multiplied by velocity. (See also ▷Newton's laws of motion.) Newton's third law of motion states that if a body A exerts a force on a body B, then body B exerts an equal force on body A but in the opposite direction. This equal and opposite force is called a ▷reaction force.

Free fall and terminal velocity Galileo also established that freely falling bodies, heavy or light, have the same, constant acceleration and that this acceleration is due to ▷gravity. This acceleration, due to the gravitational force exerted by the Earth, is also known as the acceleration of free fall. It has a value of 10 ms^{-2}. However, air resistance acts when a body falls through the air. This increases greatly as an object's velocity increases, so the object tends to reach a ▷terminal velocity. It then continues to fall with this same velocity (it has stopped accelerating because its ▷weight is cancelled out by air resistance) until it reaches the ground. The acceleration due to gravity can be measured using a pendulum.

Statics Statics is the branch of mechanics concerned with the behaviour of bodies at rest or moving with constant velocity. The forces acting on the body under these circumstances cancel each other out; that is, the forces are in equilibrium.

force majeure (French 'superior force') in politics, the use of force rather than the seeking of a political or diplomatic solution to a problem. By this principle, a government could end a strike by sending in troops, instead of attempting to conciliate the strikers.

force ratio the magnification of a force by a machine; see ▷mechanical advantage.

forces, fundamental in physics, the four fundamental interactions currently known to be at work in the physical universe. There are two long-range forces: the **gravitational force**, or **gravity**, which keeps the planets in orbit around the Sun, and acts between all particles that have mass; and the **electromagnetic force**, which stops solids from falling apart, and acts between all particles with ▷electric charge. There are two very short-range forces which operate over distances comparable with the size of the atomic nucleus: the **weak nuclear force**, responsible for the reactions that fuel the Sun and for the emission of ▷beta particles by some particles; and the **strong nuclear force**, which binds together the protons and neutrons in the nuclei of atoms. The relative strengths of the four forces are: strong, 1; electromagnetic, 10^{-2}; weak, 10^{-6}; gravitational, 10^{-40}.

By 1971, the US physicists Steven Weinberg and Sheldon Glashow, the Pakistani physicist Abdus Salam, and others had developed a theory that suggested that the weak and electromagnetic forces were aspects of a single force called the **electroweak force**; experimental support came from observation at ▷CERN in the 1980s. Physicists are now working on theories to unify all four forces. See ▷supersymmetry.

Ford, Ford Madox (1873–1939) Adopted name of Ford Hermann Hueffer. English author. He wrote more than 80 books, the best known of which are the novels *The Good Soldier* (1915) and *Tietjen's Saga* (1924–28). As the first editor of the *English Review* from 1908 to 1910, he published works by established writers such as Thomas Hardy and Joseph Conrad, as well as the works of D H Lawrence, Wyndham Lewis, and Ezra Pound.

Ford, Gerald R(udolph) (1913–) 38th president of the USA 1974–77, a Republican. He was elected to the House of

Representatives in 1948, was nominated to the vice-presidency by Richard Nixon in 1973 on the resignation of Spiro Agnew, and became president in 1974, when Nixon was forced to resign following the ▷Watergate scandal. He granted Nixon a full pardon in September 1974.

Ford, Henry (1863–1947) US automobile manufacturer. He built his first car in 1896 and founded the Ford Motor Company in 1903. His Model T (1908–27) was the first car to be constructed solely by assembly-line methods and to be mass-marketed; 15 million of these cars were sold.

Ford's innovative policies, such as a $5 daily minimum wage (at the time nearly double the average figure in Detroit) and a five-day working week, revolutionized employment practices, but he opposed the introduction of trade unions. In 1928 he launched the Model A, a stepped-up version of the Model T.

Henry Ford
People can have the Model T in any colour – so long as it's black.
A Nevins *Ford*

Related Web site: Life of Henry Ford http://www.hfmgv.org/histories/hf/henry.html

HENRY FORD In this 1910 photograph, a man demonstrates the ease with which the wheel of a Model T Ford motor car could be changed. Ford's early cars had to be able to cope with rough road conditions and the tyres would often need to be mended. *Archive Photos*

Ford, John (1895–1973) Adopted name of Sean Aloysius O'Feeney. US film director. Active from the silent film era, he became one of the most acclaimed figures of classical Hollywood cinema, winning four Academy Awards for best director. Responsible for a number of impressive westerns such as *The Iron Horse* (1924), *Stagecoach* (1939), *My Darling Clementine* (1946), *She Wore a Yellow Ribbon* (1949), *The Searchers* (1956), and *The Man Who Shot Liberty Valance* (1962), he also directed a range of comedies and dramas, including *The Grapes of Wrath* (1940).

He frequently collaborated with the actors John Wayne, Henry Fonda, James Stewart, and others, and filmed many of his westerns in the stunning landscape of Monument Valley, Arizona. Among his other films are *The Informer* (1935), *The Prisoner of Shark Island* (1936), *Young Mr Lincoln* (1939), *How Green Was My Valley* (1941), *They Were Expendable* (1945), *Rio Grande* (1950), *Wagon Master* (1950), *The Quiet Man* (1952), *Mogambo* (1953), *Mister Roberts* (1955), *Sergeant Rutledge* (1960), *Donovan's Reef* (1963), and *Cheyenne Autumn* (1964).

Related Web site: Ford, John http://www.reelclassics.com/Directors/Ford/ford.htm

Ford, John (*c.* 1586–*c.* 1640) English poet and dramatist. His play *'Tis Pity She's a Whore* (performed in about 1626, printed in 1633) is a study of incestuous passion between brother and sister. His other plays include *The Lover's Melancholy* (1629), *The Broken Heart* (1633), *Love's Sacrifice* (1633), in which Bianca is one of Ford's finest psychological studies of women, and *The Chronicle History of Perkin Warbeck* (1634). Dwelling on themes of pathos and frustration, they reflect the transition from a general to an aristocratic audience for drama.

foreclosure in law, the transfer of title of a mortgaged property from the mortgagor (borrower, usually a home owner) to the mortgagee (loaner, for example a bank) if the mortgagor is in breach of the mortgage agreement, usually by failing to make a number of payments on the mortgage (loan).

Foreign and Commonwealth Office (FCO) UK government department established in 1782 as the Foreign Office. It is responsible for the conduct of foreign policy, representation of British interests abroad, relations with other members of the ▷Commonwealth, and overseas aid policy and administration. Jack Straw was appointed foreign secretary in 2001.

Foreign Legion volunteer corps of foreigners within a country's army. The French **Légion Etrangère**, founded in 1831, is one of a number of such forces. Enlisted volunteers are of any nationality (about half are now French), but the officers are usually French. Headquarters until 1962 was in Sidi Bel Abbés, Algeria; the main base is now Corsica, with reception headquarters at Aubagne, near Marseille, France.

foreign relations a country's dealings with other countries. Specialized diplomatic bodies first appeared in Europe during the 18th century. After 1818 diplomatic agents were divided into: **ambassadors**, papal legates, and nuncios; **envoys** extraordinary, **ministers** plenipotentiary, and other ministers accredited to the head of state; ministers resident; and **chargés d'affaires**, who may deputize for an ambassador or minister, or be themselves the representative accredited to a minor country. Other diplomatic staff may include counsellors and attachés (military, labour, cultural, press). **Consuls** are state agents with commercial and political responsibilities in foreign towns.

forensic medicine in medicine, branch of medicine concerned with the resolution of crimes. Examples of forensic medicine include the determination of the cause of death in suspicious circumstances or the identification of a criminal by examining tissue found at the scene of a crime. Forensic psychology involves the establishment of a psychological profile of a criminal that can assist in identification.

forensic science the use of scientific techniques to solve criminal cases. A multidisciplinary field embracing chemistry, physics, botany, zoology, and medicine, forensic science includes the identification of human bodies or traces. Ballistics (the study of projectiles, such as bullets), another traditional forensic field, makes use of such tools as the comparison microscope and the electron microscope.

Traditional methods such as ▷fingerprinting are still used, assisted by computers; in addition, blood analysis, forensic dentistry, voice and speech spectrograms, and ▷genetic fingerprinting are increasingly applied. Chemicals, such as poisons and drugs, are analysed by ▷chromatography. ESDA (electrostatic document analysis) is a technique used for revealing indentations on paper, which helps determine if documents have been tampered with. Forensic entomology is also a branch of forensic science.

forest area where trees have grown naturally for centuries, instead of being logged at maturity (about 150–200 years). A natural, or old-growth, forest has a multistorey canopy and includes young and very old trees (this gives the canopy its range of heights). There are also fallen trees contributing to the very complex ecosystem, which may support more than 150 species of mammals and many thousands of species of insects. Globally forest is estimated to have covered around 68 million sq km/26.25 million sq mi during prehistoric times. By the late 1990s this is believed to have been reduced by half to 34.1 million sq km/13.2 million sq mi.

The Pacific forest of the west coast of North America is one of the few remaining old-growth forests in the temperate zone. It consists mainly of conifers and is threatened by logging – less than 10% of the original forest remains.

FOREST This image shows the marked changes to the landscape after an area of forest has been completely cut down. *Image Bank*

forestry the science of forest management. Recommended forestry practice aims at multipurpose crops, allowing the preservation of varied plant and animal species as well as human uses (lumbering, recreation). Forestry has often been confined to the planting of a single species, such as a rapid-growing conifer providing softwood for paper pulp and construction timber, for which world demand is greatest. In tropical countries, logging contributes to the destruction of ▷rainforests, causing global environmental problems. Small unplanned forests are ▷woodland.

The earliest planned forest dates from 1368 at Nuremberg, Germany; in Britain, planning of forests began in the 16th century. In the UK, Japan, and other countries, forestry practices have been criticized for concentration on softwood conifers to the neglect of native hardwoods.

FORESTRY In Scandinavia, where atmospheric humidity is generally low, logs are stacked for seasoning in the open air during the summer. Even during the winter, stacks of logs may simply be covered over with a plastic sheet to keep off the snow, leaving the ends open to the weather. *Image Bank*

Forfarshire former name (to 1928) of the former Scottish county of ▷Angus.

forgery the making of a false document, painting, or object with deliberate intention to deceive or defraud. The most common forgeries involve financial instruments such as cheques or credit-card transactions or money (counterfeiting). There are also literary forgeries, forged coins, and forged antiques.

forget-me-not any of a group of plants belonging to the borage family, including *M. sylvatica* and *M. scorpioides*, with small bright blue flowers. (Genus *Myosotis*, family Boraginaceae.)

forging one of the main methods of shaping metals, which involves hammering or a more gradual application of pressure. A blacksmith hammers red-hot metal into shape on an anvil, and the traditional place of work is called a forge. The blacksmith's mechanical equivalent is the drop forge. The metal is shaped by the blows from a falling hammer or ram, which is usually accelerated by steam or air pressure. Hydraulic presses forge by applying pressure gradually in a squeezing action.

formaldehyde common name for ▷methanal.

formalin aqueous solution of formaldehyde (methanal) used to preserve animal specimens.

formatting in computing, short for ▷disk formatting.

Formentera smallest inhabited island in the Spanish Balearic Islands, lying south of Ibiza; area 93 sq km/36 sq mi. The chief town is San Francisco Javier and the main port is La Sabina. The main industry is tourism.

Formica trademark of the Formica Corporation for a heat-proof plastic laminate, widely used as a veneer on wipe-down kitchen surfaces and children's furniture. It is made from formaldehyde resins similar to ▷Bakelite. It was first put on the market in 1913.

formic acid common name for ▷methanoic acid.

Formosa former name for ▷Taiwan.

formula in chemistry, a representation of a molecule, radical, or ion, in which the component chemical elements are represented by their symbols. An **empirical formula** indicates the simplest ratio of the elements in a compound, without indicating how many of them there are or how they are combined. A **molecular formula** gives the number of each type of element present in one molecule. A **structural formula** shows the relative positions of the atoms and the bonds between them. For example, for ethanoic acid, the empirical formula is CH_2O, the molecular formula is $C_2H_4O_2$, and the structural formula is CH_3COOH.

formula in mathematics, a set of symbols and numbers that expresses a fact or rule. $A = \pi r^2$ is the formula for calculating the area of a circle. Einstein's famous formula relating energy and mass is $E = mc^2$.

Forster, E(dward) M(organ) (1879–1970) English novelist, short-story writer, and critic. He was concerned with the interplay of personality and the conflict between convention and instinct. His novels include *A Room with a View* (1908), *Howards End* (1910), and *A Passage to India* (1924). Collections of stories include *The Celestial Omnibus* (1911) and *Collected Short Stories* (1948), and of essays and reviews 'Abinger Harvest' (1936). His most lasting critical work is *Aspects of the Novel* (1927).

Forster published his first novel, *Where Angels Fear to Tread*, in 1905. He enhances the superficial situations of his plots with unexpected insights in *The Longest Journey* (1907), *A Room with a View*, and *Howards End*. These three novels explore Forster's preoccupation with the need to find intellectual and spiritual harmony in a world dominated by narrow social conventions. His many years spent in India and as secretary to the Maharajah of Dewas provided him with the material for his best-known work *A Passage to India*, which explores the relationship between the English and the Indians with insight and wisdom. It is considered to be one of the most influential of modern English novels. *Maurice*, written in 1914 and published in 1971, has a homosexual theme. Many of his works have been successfully adapted for film.

forsythia any of a group of temperate eastern Asian shrubs, which bear yellow bell-shaped flowers in early spring before the leaves appear. (Genus *Forsythia*, family Oleaceae.)

Fort-de-France capital, chief commercial centre, and port of Martinique, West Indies, at the mouth of the Madame River; population (1995 est) 109,000. It trades in sugar, rum, and cacao. There is an airport and the tourist industry is a source of much local revenue.

fortepiano early 18th-century piano invented by Italian instrument maker Bartolommeo Cristofori in 1709. It has small, leather-bound hammers and harpsichord strings. Unlike the harpsichord, it can produce a varying intensity of tone, depending on the pressure of the player's touch, hence the name, which means 'loud-soft' in Italian.

Forth river in central Scotland, with its headstreams, Duchray Water and Avondhu, rising on the northeast slopes of Ben Lomond. It flows east approximately 105 km/65 mi to Kincardine where the **Firth of Forth** begins. The Firth is approximately 80 km/50 mi long, and is 26 km/16 mi wide where it joins the North Sea.

FORTRAN (or fortran; contraction of formula translation) high-level computer-programming language suited to mathematical and scientific computations. Developed by John Backus at IBM in 1956, it is one of the earliest computer languages still in use. A recent version, Fortran 90, is now being used on advanced parallel computers. ▷BASIC was strongly influenced by FORTRAN and is similar in many ways. Fortran 2000 is being developed and is expected to become an ▷ISO standard in 2002.

Fort Sumter fort in Charleston Harbor, South Carolina, USA, 6.5 km/4 mi southeast of Charleston. The first shots of the US Civil War were fired here on 12 April 1861, after its commander had refused the call to surrender made by the Confederate General Beauregard.

Fort Ticonderoga fort in New York State, USA, near Lake Champlain. It was the site of battles between the British and the French 1758–59, and was captured from the British on 10 May 1775 by Benedict ▷Arnold and Ethan Allen (leading the ▷Green Mountain Boys).

Fortune 500 the 500 largest publicly owned US industrial corporations, a list compiled by the US business magazine *Fortune*. An industrial corporation is defined as one that derives at least 50% of its revenue from manufacturing or mining.

Fort Worth city in northeastern Texas, USA, on the Trinity River, 48 km/30 mi west of ▷Dallas; seat of Tarrant County; population (1994 est) 452,000. It is a grain and railway centre serving the southern USA; manufactured products include aerospace equipment, motor vehicles, computers, and refined petroleum.

Forty-Five, the ▷Jacobite rebellion of 1745, led by Prince ▷Charles Edward Stuart. With his army of Highlanders 'Bonnie Prince Charlie' occupied Edinburgh and advanced into England as far as Derby, but then turned back. The rising was crushed by the Duke of Cumberland at Culloden in 1746.

forum (Latin 'market') in an ancient Roman town, the meeting place and market, like the Greek *agora*. In Rome the Forum Romanum contained the Senate House, the public speaking platform, covered halls for trading, temples of Saturn, Concord, and the Divine Augustus, and memorial arches. Later constructions included the Forum of Caesar (temple of Venus), the Forum of ▷Augustus (temple of Mars), and the colonnaded Forum of ▷Trajan, containing Trajan's Column.

fossil (Latin *fossilis* 'dug up') cast, impression, or the actual remains of an animal or plant preserved in rock. Fossils were created during periods of rock formation, caused by the gradual accumulation of sediment over millions of years at the bottom of the sea bed or an inland lake. Fossils may include footprints, an internal cast, or external impression. A few fossils are preserved

FORTH A distant view of the Forth Rail Bridge, which was for several years the world's longest-spanning bridge. It was designed by English engineer Benjamin Baker in the late 1880s, and was one of the first cantilever bridges. *Image Bank*

intact, as with ▷mammoths fossilized in Siberian ice, or insects trapped in tree resin that is today amber. The study of fossils is called ▷palaeontology. Palaeontologists are able to deduce much of the geological history of a region from fossil remains.

Related Web site: Fossil Collections of the World http://www.geocities.com/CapeCanaveral/Lab/8147/index.html

fossil fuel fuel, such as coal, oil, and natural gas, formed from the fossilized remains of plants that lived hundreds of millions of years ago. Fossil fuels are a ▷nonrenewable resource and will eventually run out. Extraction of coal and oil causes considerable environmental pollution, and burning coal contributes to problems of ▷acid rain and the ▷greenhouse effect.

> ### E M Forster
> *I hate the idea of causes, and if I had to choose between betraying my country and betraying my friend, I hope I should have the guts to betray my country.*
> Two Cheers for Democracy, 'What I Believe'

Foster, Jodie (1962–) Stage name of Alicia Christian Foster. US film actor and director. She began acting as a child in a great variety of roles. In 1976 she starred in *Taxi Driver* (by Martin Scorsese) and *Bugsy Malone* when only 14. She won Academy Awards for her performances in *The Accused* (1988) and *The Silence of the Lambs* (1991).

Foster, Norman Robert (1935–) English architect of the high-tech school. His buildings include the Willis Faber & Dumas insurance offices, Ipswich (1975); the Sainsbury Centre for the Visual Arts, Norwich (1977); the headquarters of the Hong Kong and Shanghai Bank, Hong Kong (1986); and Stansted Airport, Essex (1991). In 1999 he won the Pritzker Architecture Prize.

He designed the Millennium Bridge in London, which opened in June 2000, and spans the River Thames between St Paul's Cathedral and the Tate Modern at Southwark.

Foster has won numerous international awards for his industrial architecture and design, including RIBA awards for the Stansted project and the Sackler Galleries extension at the Royal Academy of Art, London (1992), which is a sensitive, yet overtly modern, addition to an existing historic building. He was knighted in 1990. In 1998 Foster and Partners were awarded the Stirling Prize – the RIBA/Sunday Times Building of the Year award for the American Air Museum in Britain, Imperial War Museum, Duxford Airfield.

Foster, Stephen Collins (1826–1864) US songwriter. He wrote about 175 sentimental popular songs including 'The Old Folks at Home' (1851), 'My Old Kentucky Home' (1853), and 'Beautiful Dreamer' (1864), and rhythmic minstrel songs such as

FORUM Roman forum at sunrise, with St Peter's Basilica in the background. *Image Bank*

'Oh! Susanna' (1848) and 'Camptown Races' (1850). Almost wholly self-taught in music, he published his first song as early as 1842.

Foucault, (Jean Bernard) Léon (1819–1868) French physicist who used a pendulum to demonstrate the rotation of the Earth on its axis, and invented the ▷gyroscope in 1852. In 1862 he made the first accurate determination of the velocity of light.

Foucault investigated heat and light, discovered eddy currents induced in a copper disc moving in a magnetic field, invented a polarizer, and made improvements in the electric arc. In 1860, he invented high-quality regulators for driving machinery at a constant speed; these were used in telescope motors and factory engines.

Foucault, Michel Paul (1926–1984) French philosopher who argued that human knowledge and subjectivity are dependent upon specific institutions and practices, and that they change through history. In particular, he was concerned to subvert conventional assumptions about 'social deviants' – the mentally ill, the sick, and the criminal – who, he believed, are oppressed by the approved knowledge of the period in which they live.

Foucault rejected phenomenology and existentialism, and his historicization of the self challenges the ideas of ▷Marxism. He was deeply influenced by the German philosopher Friedrich ▷Nietzsche, and developed an analysis of the operation of power in society using Nietzschean concepts.

His publications include *Histoire de la folie/Madness and Civilization* (1961) and *Les Mots et les choses/The Order of Things* (1966).

> ### Michel Foucault
> *Freedom of conscience entails more dangers than authority and despotism.*
> Madness and Civilization ch. 7

Related Web site: Foucault, Michel http://www.connect.net/ron/foucault.html

Fountains Abbey Cistercian abbey in North Yorkshire, England, situated 13 km/8 mi north of Harrogate. Celebrated as the greatest monument to English monasticism and its architecture, it was founded about 1132, and closed in 1539 at the Dissolution of the Monasteries. The ruins were incorporated into a Romantic landscaped garden (1720–40) with a lake, formal water garden, temples, and a deer park.

four-colour process colour ▷printing using four printing plates, based on the principle that any colour is made up of differing proportions of the primary colours blue, red, and yellow. Ink colours complementary to those represented on the plates are used for printing – cyan for the blue plate, magenta for the red, and yellow for the yellow. The first stage in preparing a colour picture for printing is to produce separate films, one each for the cyan, magenta, and yellow respectively in the picture (colour separations). From these separations three printing plates are made, with a fourth plate for black. The black is used for shading or outlines and type, and also to darken colour without making the ink too dense.

Fourdrinier machine papermaking machine patented by the Fourdrinier brothers Henry and Sealy in England in 1803. On the machine, liquid pulp flows onto a moving wire-mesh belt, and water drains and is sucked away, leaving a damp paper web. This is passed first through a series of steam-heated rollers, which dry it, and then between heavy calendar rollers, which give it a smooth finish.

Such machines can measure up to 90 m/300 ft in length, and are still in use.

Fourier, (François Marie) Charles (1772–1837) French socialist. In *Le Nouveau monde industriel/The New Industrial World* (1829–30), he advocated that society should be organized in self-sufficient cooperative units of about 1,500 people, and marriage should be abandoned.

Fourier, (Jean Baptiste) Joseph (1768–1830) French applied mathematician whose formulation of heat flow in 1807 contains the proposal that, with certain constraints, any mathematical function can be represented by trigonometrical series. This principle forms the basis of **Fourier analysis**, used today in many different fields of physics. His idea, not immediately well received, gained currency and is embodied in his *Théorie analytique de la chaleur/The Analytical Theory of Heat* (1822).

Four Noble Truths in Buddhism, a summary of the basic concepts: there is suffering (Sanskrit *duhkha*); suffering has its roots in desire (*tanha*, clinging or grasping); the cessation of desire is the end of suffering, *nirvana*; and this can be reached by the Noble Eightfold Path of taught by the Buddha.

four-stroke cycle the engine-operating cycle of most petrol and ▷diesel engines. The 'stroke' is an upward or downward movement of a piston in a cylinder. In a petrol engine the cycle begins with the induction of a fuel mixture as the piston goes down on its first stroke. On the second stroke (up) the piston compresses the mixture in the top of the cylinder. An electric spark then ignites the mixture, and the gases produced force the piston down on its third, power, stroke. On the fourth stroke (up) the piston expels the burned gases from the cylinder into the exhaust.

fourth estate another name for the press. The term was coined by the British politician Edmund Burke in analogy with the traditional three ▷estates.

fourth-generation language in computing, a type of programming language designed for the rapid programming of ▷applications but often lacking the ability to control the individual parts of the computer. Such a language typically provides easy ways of designing screens and reports, and of using databases. Other 'generations' (the term implies a class of language rather than a chronological sequence) are ▷machine code (first generation); ▷assembly languages, or low-level languages (second); and conventional high-level languages such as ▷BASIC and ▷Pascal (third).

Fourth of July in the USA, the anniversary of the day in 1776 when the ▷Declaration of Independence was adopted by the Continental Congress. It is a public holiday, officially called **Independence Day**, commemorating independence from Britain.

Fourth Republic the French constitutional regime that was established between 1944 and 1946 and lasted until 4 October 1958: from liberation after Nazi occupation during World War II to the introduction of a new constitution by General de Gaulle.

fowl chicken or chickenlike bird. Sometimes the term is also used for ducks and geese. The red jungle fowl *Gallus gallus* is the ancestor of all domestic chickens. It is a forest bird of Asia, without the size or egg-laying ability of many domestic strains. ▷Guinea fowl are of African origin.

Fowler, Henry Watson (1858–1933) and **Francis George** (1870–1918) English brothers who were scholars and authors of a number of English dictionaries. *Modern English Usage* (1926), the work of Henry Fowler, has become a classic reference work for matters of style and disputed usage.

Fowles, John Robert (1926–   ) English writer. His novels, often concerned with illusion and reality and with the creative process, include *The Collector* (1963), *The Magus* (1965), *The French Lieutenant's Woman* (1969) (filmed in 1981), *Daniel Martin* (1977), *Mantissa* (1982), and *A Maggot* (1985).

fox one of the smaller species of wild dog of the family Canidae, which live in Africa, Asia, Europe, North America, and South America. Foxes feed on a wide range of animals from worms to rabbits, scavenge for food, and also eat berries. They are very adaptable, maintaining high populations close to urban areas.

Most foxes are nocturnal, and make an underground den, or 'earth'. The common or red fox *Vulpes vulpes* is about 60 cm/2 ft long plus a tail ('brush') 40 cm/1.3 ft long. The fur is reddish with black patches behind the ears and a light tip to the tail. Other foxes include the Arctic fox *Alopex lagopus*, the ▷fennec, the grey foxes genus *Urocyon* of North and Central America, and the South American genus *Dusicyon*, to which the extinct Falkland Islands dog belonged.

There are between 240,000 (end of winter) and 500,000 (end of summer) foxes in Britain, with 86% living in rural areas.

Fox, Charles James (1749–1806) English Whig politician, son of the 1st Baron Holland. He entered Parliament in 1769 as a supporter of the court, but went over to the opposition in 1774. As secretary of state in 1782, leader of the opposition to William Pitt the Younger, and foreign secretary in 1806, he welcomed the French Revolution and brought about the abolition of the slave trade.

Fox, George (1624–1691) English founder of the Society of ▷Friends. After developing his belief in a mystical 'inner light', he became a travelling preacher in 1647, and in 1650 was imprisoned for blasphemy at Derby, where the name Quakers was first applied derogatorily to him and his followers, supposedly because he enjoined Judge Bennet to 'quake at the word of the Lord'.

foxglove any of a group of flowering plants found in Europe and the Mediterranean region. They have showy spikes of bell-like flowers, and grow up to 1.5 m/5 ft high. (Genus *Digitalis*, family Scrophulariaceae.)

Related Web site: Digitalis Purpurea http://www.nnlm.nlm.nih.gov/pnr/uwmhg/species.html?COMNAME=Foxglove

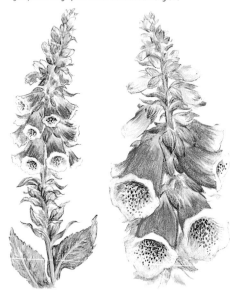

FOXGLOVE Foxgloves have purple, golden or white flowers and prefer semi-shaded positions.

foxhound small, keen-nosed hound, up to 60 cm/2 ft tall and black, tan, and white in colour. There are two recognized breeds: the English foxhound, bred for some 300 years to hunt foxes, and the American foxhound, not quite as stocky, used for foxes and other game.

fox-hunting the pursuit of a fox across country on horseback, aided by a pack of foxhounds specially trained to track the fox's scent. The aim is to catch and kill the fox. In **drag-hunting**, hounds pursue a prepared trail rather than a fox.

foxtrot ballroom dance originating in the USA about 1914. It is believed to be named after Harry Fox, a US vaudeville comedian who did a distinctive trotting dance to ragtime music.

f.p.s. system system of units based on the foot, pound, and second as units of length, mass, and time, respectively. It has now been replaced for scientific work by the ▷SI system.

fractal (from Latin *fractus* 'broken') irregular shape or surface produced by a procedure of repeated subdivision. Generated on a computer screen, fractals are used in creating models of geographical or biological processes (for example, the creation of a coastline by erosion or accretion, or the growth of plants).

Sets of curves with such discordant properties were developed in the 19th century in Germany by Georg Cantor and Karl Weierstrass. The name was coined by the French mathematician Benoit Mandelbrot. Fractals are also used for computer art.

fraction in chemistry, a group of similar compounds, the boiling points of which fall within a particular range and which are separated during fractional ▷distillation (fractionation).

fraction (from Latin *fractus* 'broken') in mathematics, a number that indicates one or more equal parts of a whole. Usually, the number of equal parts into which the unit is divided (denominator) is written below a horizontal or diagonal line, and the number of parts comprising the fraction (numerator) is written above; thus $\frac{2}{3}$ or $\frac{3}{4}$. Such fractions are called **vulgar** or **simple** fractions. The denominator can never be zero.

A **proper fraction** is one in which the numerator is less than the denominator. An **improper fraction** has a numerator that is larger than the denominator, for example $\frac{3}{2}$. It can therefore be expressed as a mixed number, for example, $1\frac{1}{2}$. A combination such as $\frac{5}{0}$ is not regarded as a fraction (an object cannot be divided into zero equal parts), and mathematically any number divided by 0 is equal to infinity.

A **decimal fraction** has as its denominator a power of 10, and these are omitted by use of the decimal point and notation, for example 0.04, which is $\frac{4}{100}$. The digits to the right of the decimal point indicate the numerators of vulgar fractions whose denominators are 10, 100, 1,000, and so on. Most fractions can be expressed exactly as decimal fractions ($\frac{1}{3} = 0.333...$). Fractions are also known as **rational numbers**; that is, numbers formed by a ratio. **Integers** may be expressed as fractions with a denominator of 1, so 6 is $\frac{6}{1}$, for example.

Addition and subtraction To add or subtract with fractions a **common denominator** (a number divisible by both the bottom numbers) needs to be identified. For example, for

$$\tfrac{3}{4} + \tfrac{5}{6}$$

the smallest common denominator is 12. Both the numerators and denominators of the fractions to be added (or subtracted) are then multiplied by the number of times the denominator goes into the common denominator, so $\frac{3}{4}$ is multiplied by 3 and $\frac{5}{6}$ by 2. The numerators can then be simply added or subtracted.

$$\tfrac{9}{12} + \tfrac{10}{12} = \tfrac{19}{12} = 1\tfrac{7}{12}$$

If whole numbers appear in the calculation they can be added/subtracted separately first.

Multiplication and division All whole numbers in a division or multiplication calculation must first be converted into improper fractions. For multiplication, the numerators are then multiplied together and the denominators are then multiplied to provide the solution. For example:

$$7\tfrac{2}{3} \times 4\tfrac{1}{2} = \tfrac{23}{3} \times \tfrac{9}{2} = \tfrac{207}{6} = 34\tfrac{1}{2}$$

In division, the procedure is similar, but the second fraction must be inverted before multiplication occurs. For example:

$$5\tfrac{5}{12} \div 1\tfrac{1}{8} = \tfrac{65}{12} \div \tfrac{9}{8} = \tfrac{65}{12} \times \tfrac{8}{9} = \tfrac{520}{108} = 4\tfrac{22}{27}$$

fractionation (or **fractional distillation**) process used to split complex mixtures (such as ▷petroleum) into their components, usually by repeated heating, boiling, and condensation; see ▷distillation. In the laboratory it is carried out using a ▷fractionating column.

Fragonard, Jean-Honoré (1732–1806) French painter. He was the leading exponent of the rococo style (along with his teacher François Boucher). His light-hearted subjects, often erotic, include *Les heureux Hazards de l'escarpolette/The Swing* (c. 1766; Wallace Collection, London). Madame de Pompadour was one of his patrons.

JEAN-HONORÉ FRAGONARD *The Lock*, a dramatic narrative painting by French painter Jean-Honoré Fragonard. *The Art Archive/Archaeological Museum Naples/Dagli Orti*

FOX The common or red fox is versatile and intelligent. It is a skilful hunter, preying on rodents, hares, birds, and insects.

France

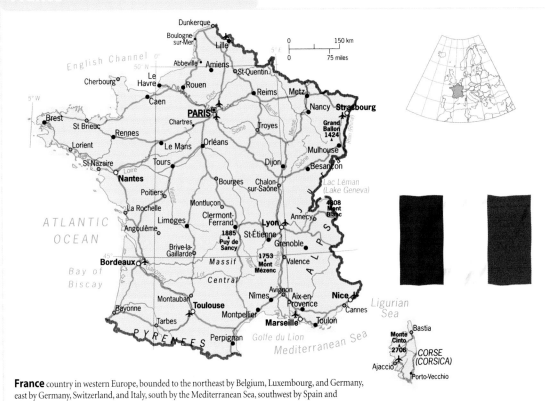

France country in western Europe, bounded to the northeast by Belgium, Luxembourg, and Germany, east by Germany, Switzerland, and Italy, south by the Mediterranean Sea, southwest by Spain and Andorra, and west by the Atlantic Ocean.

NATIONAL NAME *République Française/French Republic*

AREA (including Corsica) 543,965 sq km/210,024 sq mi

CAPITAL Paris

MAJOR TOWNS/CITIES Lyon, Lille, Bordeaux, Toulouse, Nantes, Marseille, Nice, Strasbourg, Montpellier, Rennes, Le Havre

MAJOR PORTS Marseille, Nice, Le Havre

PHYSICAL FEATURES rivers Seine, Loire, Garonne, Rhône; mountain ranges Alps, Massif Central, Pyrenees, Jura, Vosges, Cévennes; Auvergne mountain region; Mont Blanc (4,810 m/15,781 ft); Ardennes forest; Riviera; caves of Dordogne with relics of early humans; the island of Corsica

TERRITORIES Guadeloupe, French Guiana, Martinique, Réunion, St Pierre and Miquelon, Southern and Antarctic Territories, New Caledonia, French Polynesia, Wallis and Futuna, Mayotte, Bassas da India, Clipperton Island, Europa Island, Glorioso Islands, Juan de Nova Island, Tromelin Island

Government

HEAD OF STATE Jacques Chirac from 1995

HEAD OF GOVERNMENT Jean-Pierre Raffarin from 2002

POLITICAL SYSTEM liberal democracy

POLITICAL EXECUTIVE dual executive

FRANCE Château de Fontainebleau, Seine-et-Marne, France, built by Francis I in the 16th century. *Corel*

ADMINISTRATIVE DIVISIONS 21 regional councils containing 96 departments, four overseas departments, and two territorial collectivities

ARMED FORCES 260,400; plus paramilitary gendarmerie of 101,400 (2002 est)

Economy and resources

CURRENCY euro (franc until 2002)

GPD (US$) 1,409.6 billion (2002 est)

REAL GDP GROWTH (% change on previous year) 2 (2001)

GNI (US$) 1,342.7 billion (2002 est)

GNI PER CAPITA (PPP) (US$) 26,180 (2002 est)

CONSUMER PRICE INFLATION 2% (2003 est)

UNEMPLOYMENT 8.8% (2001)

MAJOR TRADING PARTNERS EU (principally Germany, UK, Italy, Belgium, Luxembourg), USA

RESOURCES coal, petroleum, natural gas, iron ore, copper, zinc, bauxite

INDUSTRIES mining, quarrying, food products, transport equipment, non-electrical machinery, electrical machinery, weapons, metals and metal products, yarn and fabrics, wine, tourism, aircraft

EXPORTS machinery and transport equipment, food and live animals, chemicals, beverages, tobacco, textile yarn, fabrics and other basic manufactures, clothing, accessories, perfumery, cosmetics. Principal market: Germany 14.4% (2001)

IMPORTS food and live animals, mineral fuels, machinery and transport equipment, chemicals and chemical products, basic manufactures. Principal source: Germany 16.7% (2001)

ARABLE LAND 33.5% (2000 est)

AGRICULTURAL PRODUCTS wheat, sugar beet, maize, barley, vine fruits, potatoes, fruit, vegetables; livestock and dairy products

Population and society

POPULATION 60,144,000 (2003 est)

POPULATION GROWTH RATE 0.3% (2000–15)

POPULATION DENSITY (per sq km) 109 (2003 est)

URBAN POPULATION (% of total) 76 (2003 est)

AGE DISTRIBUTION (% of total population) 0–14 18%, 15–59 61%, 60+ 21% (2002 est)

ETHNIC GROUPS predominantly French ethnic, of Celtic and Latin descent; Basque minority in southwest; 7% of population are immigrants – a third from Algeria and Morocco, living mainly in the Marseille Midi region and in northern cities; 20% from Portugal; 10% each from Italy and Spain

LANGUAGE French (official; also Basque, Breton, Catalan, Corsican, and Provençal)

RELIGION Roman Catholic, about 90%; also Muslim, Protestant, and Jewish minorities

EDUCATION (compulsory years) 10

LITERACY RATE 99% (men); 99% (women) (2003 est)

LABOUR FORCE 1.3% agriculture, 24.7% industry, 74.0% services (2000)

LIFE EXPECTANCY 75 (men); 83 (women) (2000–05)

CHILD MORTALITY RATE (under 5, per 1,000 live births) 6 (2001)

HOSPITAL BEDS (per 1,000 people) 8.2 (1999 est)

TV SETS (per 1,000 people) 632 (2001 est)

INTERNET USERS (per 10,000 people) 3,138.3 (2002 est)

PERSONAL COMPUTER USERS (per 100 people) 34.7 (2002 est)

Chronology

5th century BC: Celtic peoples invaded the region.

58–51 BC: Romans conquered Celts and formed province of Gaul.

5th century AD: Gaul overrun by Franks and other Germanic tribes.

481–511: Frankish chief Clovis accepted Christianity and formed a kingdom based at Paris; under his successors, the Merovingian dynasty, the kingdom disintegrated.

751–68: Pepin the Short usurped the Frankish throne, reunified the kingdom, and founded the Carolingian dynasty.

768–814: Charlemagne conquered much of Western Europe and created the Holy Roman Empire.

843: Treaty of Verdun divided the Holy Roman Empire into three, with the western portion corresponding to modern France.

9th–10th centuries: Weak central government allowed the great nobles to become virtually independent.

987: Frankish crown passed to House of Capet.

1180–1223: Philip II doubled the royal domain and tightened control over the nobles.

1337: Start of the Hundred Years' War. English won victories at Crécy in 1346 and Agincourt in 1415.

1429: Joan of Arc raised the siege of Orléans; Hundred Years' War ended with Charles VII expelling the English in 1453.

1483: France annexed Burgundy and Brittany after Louis XI had restored royal power.

1562–98: Civil wars between nobles were fought under religious slogans, Catholic versus Protestant (or Huguenot).

1589–1610: Henry IV, first king of Bourbon dynasty, established peace, religious tolerance, and absolute monarchy.

1701–14: War of the Spanish Succession: England, Austria, and allies checked expansionism of France under Louis XIV.

1756–63: Seven Years' War: France lost most of its colonies in India and Canada to Britain.

1789: French Revolution abolished absolute monarchy and feudalism; First Republic proclaimed and revolutionary wars began in 1792.

1799: Napoleon Bonaparte seized power in coup; crowned himself emperor in 1804.

1814: Defeat of France; restoration of Bourbon monarchy; comeback by Napoleon defeated at Waterloo in 1815.

1830: Liberal revolution deposed Charles X in favour of his cousin Louis Philippe, the 'Citizen King'.

1848: Revolution established Second Republic; conflict between liberals and socialists; Louis Napoleon, nephew of Napoleon I, elected president.

1852: Louis Napoleon proclaimed Second Empire, taking title Napoleon III.

1870–71: Franco-Prussian War: France lost Alsace-Lorraine; Second Empire abolished; Paris Commune crushed; Third Republic founded.

1914–18: France resisted German invasion in World War I; Alsace-Lorraine recovered in 1919.

1939: France entered World War II.

1940: Germany invaded and occupied northern France, and all France in 1942.

1944: Allies liberated France; provisional government formed by Gen Charles de Gaulle, leader of Free French.

1946: Fourth Republic proclaimed.

1949: Became a member of NATO; withdrew from military command structure in 1966.

1954: French withdrew from Indo-China after eight years of war; start of war against French rule in Algeria.

1957: France was a founder member of the European Economic Community.

1958: Algerian crisis caused collapse of Fourth Republic; de Gaulle becomes president of the Fifth Republic.

1962: Algeria achieved independence.

1968: Revolutionary students rioted in Paris.

1981: François Mitterrand was elected the Fifth Republic's first socialist president.

1995: Jacques Chirac (RPR) was elected president. There was widespread condemnation of the government's decision to resume nuclear tests in the South Pacific, and this was stopped in 1996 .

1997: A general election was called by President Chirac, with victory for Socialists.

2002: In the first round of the presidential election, Jean-Marie Le Pen, the leader of the far-right Front National (FN), came second. This unexpected success sparked anti-fascist demonstrations. However, in the second round, centre-right incumbent Jacques Chirac won with 82% of the vote (the highest ever margin of victory in the Fifth Republic).

FRANCE A ball at the court of King Charles IX of France (attributed to Dutch painter Frans Pourbus, 1571). *The Art Archive/Museum of Mankind London/Eileen Tweedy*

France: Regions

Region	Capital	Area sq km	Area sq mi	Population (1996 est)
Alsace	Strasbourg	8,280	3,197	1,701,000
Aquitaine	Bordeaux	41,308	15,949	2,880,000
Auvergne	Clermont-Ferrand	26,013	10,044	1,315,000
Basse-Normandie	Caen	17,589	6,791	1,416,000
Brittany (Bretagne)	Rennes	27,208	10,505	2,861,000
Burgundy (Bourgogne)	Dijon	31,582	12,194	1,625,000
Centre	Orléans	39,151	15,116	2,443,000
Champagne-Ardenne	Châlons-sur-Marne	25,606	9,886	1,353,000
Corsica (Corse)	Ajaccio	8,680	3,351	260,000
Franche-Comté	Besançon	16,202	6,256	1,116,000
Haute-Normandie	Rouen	12,317	4,756	1,782,000
Ile de France	Paris	12,012	4,638	11,027,000
Languedoc-Roussillon	Montpellier	27,376	10,570	2,243,000
Limousin	Limoges	16,942	6,541	718,000
Lorraine	Metz	23,547	9,091	2,312,000
Midi-Pyrénées	Toulouse	45,348	17,509	2,506,000
Nord-Pas-de-Calais	Lille	12,414	4,793	4,001,000
Pays de la Loire	Nantes	32,082	12,387	3,154,000
Picardie	Amiens	19,399	7,490	1,864,000
Poitou-Charentes	Poitiers	25,809	9,965	1,622,000
Provence-Alpes-Côte d'Azur	Marseille	31,400	12,123	4,448,000
Rhône-Alpes	Lyon	43,698	16,872	5,608,000

France see country box.

France, Anatole (1844–1924) Pen-name of Jacques Anatole François Thibault. French writer. His works are marked by wit, urbanity, and style. His earliest novel was *Le Crime de Sylvestre Bonnard/The Crime of Sylvester Bonnard* (1881); later books include the satiric *L'Ile des pingouins/Penguin Island* (1908). He was awarded the Nobel Prize for Literature in 1921. His other books include the autobiographical series beginning with *Le Livre de mon ami/My Friend's Book* (1885), *Thaïs* (1890), *Crainquebille* (1905), and *Les Dieux ont soif/The Gods Are Athirst* (1912). He was a socialist and a supporter of the wrongfully accused officer Alfred ▷Dreyfus.

Francesca, Piero della Italian painter; see ▷Piero della Francesca.

Franche-Comté region of eastern France; area 16,200 sq km/ 6,250 sq mi; population (1999) 1,117,000. Its administrative centre is ▷Besançon, and it includes the *départements* of Doubs, Jura, Haute-Saône, and Territoire de Belfort. In the mountainous Jura, there is farming and forestry, and elsewhere there are engineering and plastics industries.

franchise in business, the right given by one company to another to manufacture, distribute, or provide its branded products. It is usual for the franchisor to impose minimum quality conditions on its franchisees to make sure that customers receive a fair deal from the franchisee and ensure that the brand image is maintained.

franchise in politics, the eligibility, right, or privilege to vote at public elections, especially for the members of a legislative body, or parliament. In the UK adult citizens are eligible to vote from the age of 18, with the exclusion of peers, the insane, and criminals. The voting age for adults in the USA was lowered from 21 to 18 by the 26th Amendment in 1971, and the Voting Rights Act of 1965 eliminated local laws that restricted full participation by minorities.

It was 1918 before all men in the UK had the right to vote, and 1928 before women were enfranchised; in New Zealand women were granted the right as early as 1893.

Francia, José Gaspar Rodríguez de (1766–1840) Paraguayan dictator 1814–40, known as **El Supremo**. A lawyer, he emerged as a strongman after independence was achieved in 1811, and was designated dictator by congress in 1814. Hostile to the Argentine regime, he sealed off the country and followed an isolationist policy.

Francis I Emperor of Austria from 1804, also known as ▷Francis II, Holy Roman Emperor.

Francis II (1768–1835) Holy Roman Emperor 1792–1806. He became Francis I, Emperor of Austria in 1804, and abandoned the title of Holy Roman Emperor in 1806. During his reign Austria was five times involved in war with France, 1792–97, 1798–1801, 1805, 1809, and 1813–14. He succeeded his father, Leopold II.

French Rulers 751–1958

In 751 Pépin the Short deposed Childeric III, the last Merovingian ruler, to become king of the Franks. In 1958 the Algerian crisis caused the collapse of the Fourth Republic, and the establishment of a new constitution for the Fifth Republic.

Date of accession	Ruler	Date of accession	Ruler
751	Pépin the Short	1560	Charles IX
768	Charlemagne/Carloman	1574	Henri III
814	Louis I	1574	Henri IV
840	Lothair I	1610	Louis XIII
843	Charles (II) the Bald	1643	Louis XIV
877	Louis II	1715	Louis XV
879	Louis III	1774	Louis XVI
884	Charles (III) the Fat	1792	National Convention
888	Odo	1795	Directory (five members)
893	Charles (III) the Simple	1799	Napoléon Bonaparte (First Consul)
922	Robert I	1804	Napoléon I (Emperor)
923	Rudolf	1814	Louis XVIII (King)
936	Louis IV	1815	Napoléon I (Emperor)
954	Lothair II	1815	Louis XVIII (King)
986	Louis V	1824	Charles X (King)
987	Hugues Capet	1830	Louis XIX (King)
996	Robert II	1830	Henri V (King)
1031	Henri I	1830	Louis-Philippe (King)
1060	Philippe I	1848	Philippe Buchez (President of the National Assembly)
1108	Louis VI	1848	Louis Cavaignac (Minister of War)
1137	Louis VII	1848	Louis Napoléon Bonaparte (President)
1180	Philippe II	1852	Napoléon III (Emperor)
1223	Louis VIII	1871	Adolphe Thiers (President)
1226	Louis IX	1873	Patrice MacMahon (President)
1270	Philippe III	1879	Jules Grevy (President)
1285	Philippe IV	1887	François Sadui-Carnot (President)
1314	Louis X	1894	Jean Casimir-Périer (President)
1316	Jean I	1895	François Faure (President)
1328	Philippe V	1899	Emile Loubet (President)
1322	Charles IV	1913	Armand Fallières (President)
1328	Philippe VI	1913	Raymond Poincaré (President)
1350	Jean II	1920	Paul Deschanel (President)
1356	Charles V	1920	Alexandre Millerand (President)
1380	Charles VI	1924	Gaston Doumergue (President)
1422	Charles VII	1931	Paul Doumer (President)
1461	Louis XI	1932	Albert Le Brun (President)
1483	Charles VIII	1940	Philippe Pétain (Vichy government)
1498	Louis XII	1944	provisional government
1515	François I	1947	Vincent Auriol (President)
1547	Henri II	1954	René Coty (President)
1559	François II		

FRANCIS I A portrait of Francis I, king of France, an early work by contemporary French artist François Clouet. *The Art Archive/Uffizi Gallery Florence/Album/Joseph Martin*

Francis (or **François**) two kings of France:

Francis I (1494–1547) King of France from 1515. He succeeded his cousin Louis XII, and from 1519 European politics turned on the rivalry between him and the Holy Roman emperor Charles V, which led to war in 1521–29, 1536–38, and 1542–44. In 1525 Francis was defeated and captured at Pavia and released only after signing a humiliating treaty. At home, he developed absolute monarchy.

Francis II (1544–1560) King of France from 1559 when he succeeded his father, Henri II. He married Mary Queen of Scots in 1558. He was completely under the influence of his mother, ▷Catherine de' Medici.

Franciscan order Catholic order of friars, **Friars Minor** or **Grey Friars**, founded in 1209 by Francis of Assisi. Subdivisions were the strict Observants; the Conventuals, who were allowed to own property corporately; and the ▷Capuchins, founded in 1529.

Francis Ferdinand archduke of Austria, also known as ▷Franz Ferdinand.

Francis Joseph emperor of Austria-Hungary, also known as ▷Franz Joseph.

Francis of Assisi, St (1182–1226) Born Giovanni Bernadone. Italian founder of the Roman Catholic Franciscan order of friars in 1209 and, with St Clare, of the Poor Clares in 1212. In 1224 he is said to have undergone a mystical experience during which he received the stigmata (five wounds of Jesus). Many stories are told of his ability to charm wild animals, and he is the patron saint of ecologists. His feast day is 4 October. He was canonized in 1228.

> **Related Web site: Francis of Assisi, St** http://www.newadvent.org/cathen/06221a.htm

ST FRANCIS OF ASSISI A 14th-century portrait of St Francis of Assisi and St Clare. *The Art Archive/Civic Museum San Gimignano/Dagli Orti*

francium radioactive metallic element, symbol Fr, atomic number 87, relative atomic mass 223. It is one of the alkali metals and occurs in nature in small amounts as a decay product of actinium. Its longest-lived isotope has a half-life of only 21 minutes. Francium was discovered and named in 1939 by Marguérite Perey to honour her country.

Franco, Francisco (Paulino Hermenegildo Teódulo Bahamonde) (1892–1975) Spanish dictator from 1939. As a general, he led the insurgent Nationalists to victory in the Spanish ▷Civil War 1936–39, supported by Fascist Italy and Nazi Germany, and established a dictatorship. In 1942 Franco reinstated a Cortes (Spanish parliament), which in 1947 passed an act by which he became head of state for life.

Franco was born in Galicia, northwestern Spain. He entered the army in 1910, served in Morocco 1920–26, and was appointed chief of staff in 1935, but demoted to governor of the Canary Islands in 1936. Dismissed from this post by the Popular Front (Republican) government, he plotted an uprising with German and Italian assistance, and on the outbreak of the Civil War organized the invasion of Spain by North African troops and foreign legionaries. After the death of General Sanjurjo, he took command of the Nationalists, proclaiming himself caudillo (leader) of Spain. The defeat of the Republic with the surrender of Madrid in 1939 brought all Spain under his government. The war and first years of power were marked by the execution of tens of thousands of his opponents.

On the outbreak of World War II, in spite of Spain's official attitude of 'strictest neutrality', his pro-Axis sympathies led him to send aid, later withdrawn, to the German side. His government was at first ostracized as fascist by the United Nations, but with the development of the Cold War, Franco came to be viewed more as an anti-communist, which improved relations with other Western countries.

At home, he curbed the growing power of the ▷Falange Española (the fascist party), and in later years slightly liberalized his regime. In 1969 he nominated ▷Juan Carlos as his successor and future king of Spain. He relinquished the premiership in 1973, but remained head of state until his death.

> **Related Web site: Spanish Government and the Axis** http://www.yale.edu/lawweb/avalon/wwii/spain/spmenu.htm

Franco, Itamar (1931–) Brazilian politician and president 1992–94, governor of Minas Gerais state from 1998. During his first months in office he attracted widespread criticism, both from friends (for his working methods and lack of clear policies) and opponents. Franco's greatest achievement was the introduction in 1994 of the Plano Real programme to stabilize the economy. He was defeated by Fernando Henrique Cardoso in the October 1994 presidential election but Cardoso saw the programme implemented. He also introduced a rapid privatization programme and was bold enough to acknowledge the poverty that afflicted the nation, requesting the middle classes to organize themselves into groups to help the disadvantaged.

François French form of ▷Francis, two kings of France.

Franco-Prussian War 1870–71. The Prussian chancellor Otto von Bismarck put forward a German candidate for the vacant Spanish throne with the deliberate, and successful, intention of provoking the French emperor Napoleon III into declaring war. The Prussians defeated the French at Sedan, then besieged Paris. The Treaty of Frankfurt of May 1871 gave Alsace, Lorraine, and a large French indemnity to Prussia. The war established Prussia, at the head of a newly established German empire, as Europe's leading power.

FRANCO-PRUSSIAN WAR A French cartoon entitled *Entrée du Charlemagne moderne à Paris*, depicting the German chancellor Bismarck, with Kaiser Wilhelm of Germany riding a pig (Napoleon) down the Champs Elysées in Paris, France. *The Art Archive/Eileen Tweedy*

frangipani any of a group of tropical American trees, especially the species *P. rubra*, belonging to the dogbane family. Perfume is made from the strongly scented waxy flowers. (Genus *Plumeria*, family Apocynaceae.)

Frank, Anne (Anneliese Marie) (1929–1945) German diarist. She fled to the Netherlands with her family in 1933 to escape Nazi anti-Semitism (the ▷Holocaust). During the German occupation of Amsterdam, they and two other families remained in a sealed-off room, protected by Dutch sympathizers 1942–44, when betrayal resulted in their deportation and Anne's death in Belsen concentration camp. Her diary of her time in hiding was published in 1947.

Previously suppressed portions of her diary were published in 1989. The house in which the family took refuge is preserved as a museum. Her diary has sold 20 million copies in more than 50 languages and has been made into a play and a film publicizing the fate of millions. See picture on p. 360.

> **Related Web site: Anne Frank Online** http://www.annefrank.com/

Frank, Robert (1924–) US photographer. He is best known for his informal and unromanticized pictures of American life. These were published, with a foreword by the US novelist Jack Kerouac, as *The Americans* (1959). Since then he has concentrated mainly on film-making.

Frankenthaler, Helen (1928–) US abstract expressionist painter. She invented the colour-staining technique whereby the unprimed, absorbent canvas is stained or soaked with thinned-out paint, creating deep, soft veils of translucent colour.

Frankfurt am Main (German 'ford of the Franks') city in Hessen, Germany, 72 km/45 mi northeast of Mannheim; population (1995) 651,200. It is a commercial and banking centre, with electrical and machine industries, and an inland port on the River Main. The International Book Fair is held here annually in the autumn. It is the site of the Bundesbank (German Central Bank), and the European Central Bank (from 1999).

> **Related Web site: Frankfurt am Main** http://expedia.msn.com/wg/Europe/Germany/P14119.asp

frankincense resin of various African and Asian trees, burned as incense. Costly in ancient times, it is traditionally believed to be one of the three gifts brought by the Magi to the infant Jesus. (Genus *Boswellia*, family Burseraceae.)

FRANKINCENSE Frankincense trees near Salalah, Oman. *Image Bank*

Franklin, Aretha (1942–) US soul singer. Her gospel background infuses her four-octave voice with a passionate conviction and authority. Her hit singles include 'Respect' (1967), 'Chain of Fools' (1968), and her albums *Lady Soul* (1968), *Amazing Grace* (1972), *Who's Zoomin' Who?* (1985), and *A Rose is a Rose* (1998).

Franklin, Benjamin (1706–1790) US scientist, statesman, writer, printer, and publisher. He proved that lightning is a form of electricity, distinguished between positive and negative electricity, and invented the lightning conductor. He was the first US ambassador to France 1776–85, and negotiated peace with Britain in 1783. As a delegate to the ▷Continental Congress from Pennsylvania 1785–88, he helped to draft the ▷Declaration of Independence and the US Constitution.

BENJAMIN FRANKLIN American statesman and scientist, Benjamin Franklin was a prominent negotiator in the American Declaration of Independence of 1773. *Philip Sauvain Picture Collection*

Francis I

In times of necessity all privileges cease, and not only privileges, but common laws as well, for necessity has no law.

R J Knecht *French Renaissance Monarchy: Francis I & Henry II* (1984)

ANNE FRANK Anne Frank (right) with her sister Margot. The picture is from Margot's photo album of 1932, when Anne would have been about three years old, and the family was still living in Germany. See entry on p. 359. *Archive Photos*

Franklin was born in Boston and self-educated. He was the 15th of 17 children and after two years at school he was apprenticed to a printer at the age of 12. In 1723, he left Boston for Philadelphia and in 1724 sailed for England, where he worked for 18 months in a printer's office. He returned to Philadelphia, set up his own printing business, and bought the *Pennsylvania Gazette*. In 1737, he became deputy postmaster of Philadelphia, and was a member of the colony's legislative body 1751–64. As early as 1754, Franklin was advocating an inter-colonial union to improve the presentation of colonial claims to the British government.

Related Web site: Benjamin Franklin: His Autobiography
http://odur.let.rug.nl/~usa/B/bfranklin/frankxx.htm

Franz Josef Land (Russian **Zemlya Frantsa Iosifa**) archipelago of over 85 islands in the Arctic Ocean, east of Svalbord and northwest of Novaya Zemlya, Russia; area 20,720 sq km/ 8,000 sq mi. There are scientific stations on the islands.

Franz Joseph (or **Francis Joseph**) (1830–1916) Emperor of Austria-Hungary from 1848, when his uncle Ferdinand I abdicated. After the suppression of the 1848 revolution, Franz Joseph tried to establish an absolute monarchy but had to grant Austria a parliamentary constitution in 1861 and Hungary equality with Austria in 1867. He was defeated in the Italian War in 1859 and the Prussian War in 1866. In 1914 he made the assassination of his heir and nephew Franz Ferdinand the excuse for attacking Serbia, thus precipitating World War I.

Frasch process process used to extract underground deposits of sulphur. Superheated steam is piped into the sulphur deposit and melts it. Compressed air is then pumped down to force the molten sulphur to the surface. The process was developed in the USA in 1891 by German-born Herman Frasch (1851–1914).

Fraser river in southern British Columbia, Canada; length 1,370 km/850 mi. It rises in the Yellowhead Pass of the Rocky Mountains and flows northwest into the interior plateau of British Columbia. It then flows south through its lower valley at Hope, then west where it enters the Strait of Georgia, near Vancouver. The Fraser River has acted as the focus of economic life in the southern part of the province: as a salmon fishery, as a means of transportation for the rich lumber reserves of its upper valley, and as a source of irrigation and hydroelectric power.

Fraser, Antonia (1932–) English author. She has published authoritative biographies, including *Mary Queen of Scots* (1969) and *The Six Wives of Henry VIII* (1992), and an investigation of *The Gunpowder Plot* (1996). She has also written historical works, such as *The Weaker Vessel* (1984); and a series of detective novels featuring investigator Jemima Shore.

Fraser, (John) Malcolm (1930–) Australian Liberal politician, prime minister 1975–83; nicknamed 'the Prefect' because of a supposed disregard of subordinates.

fraud in law, an act of deception resulting in injury to another. To establish fraud it has to be demonstrated that (1) a false representation (for example, a factually untrue statement) has been made, with the intention that it should be acted upon; (2) the person making the representation knows it is false or does not attempt to find out whether it is true or not; and (3) the person to whom the representation is made acts upon it to his or her detriment.

Frazer, James (George) (1854–1941) Scottish anthropologist. Frazer's book *The Golden Bough* (12 volumes, 1890–1915), a pioneer study of the origins of religion and sociology on a comparative basis, exerted considerable influence on subsequent anthropologists and writers such as T S Eliot and D H Lawrence. By the standards of modern anthropology, many of its methods and findings are unsound.

Frederick V (1596–1632) Called 'the Winter King'. Elector palatine of the Rhine 1610–23 and king of Bohemia 1619–20 (for one winter, hence the name), having been chosen by the Protestant Bohemians as ruler after the deposition of Catholic emperor ▷Ferdinand II. His selection was the cause of the Thirty Years' War. Frederick was defeated at the Battle of the White Mountain, near Prague, in November 1620, by the army of the Catholic League and fled to Holland.

Frederick two Holy Roman emperors:

Frederick (I) Barbarossa (c. 1123–1190) Called 'red-beard'. Holy Roman Emperor from 1152. Originally duke of Swabia, he was elected emperor in 1152, and was engaged in a struggle with Pope Alexander III 1159–77, which ended in his submission; the Lombard cities, headed by Milan, took advantage of this to establish their independence of imperial control. Frederick joined the Third Crusade, and was drowned while crossing a river in Anatolia.

Frederick II (1194–1250) Holy Roman Emperor from 1212, called 'the Wonder of the World'. He was the son of Holy Roman Emperor ▷Henry VI. He led a crusade in 1228–29 that recovered Jerusalem by treaty without fighting. Frederick quarrelled with the pope, who excommunicated him three times, and a feud began that lasted with intervals until the end of his reign. Frederick, who was a religious sceptic, is often considered the most cultured person of his age. His later years were marred by the rebellions of his chief minister and his son.

Frederick fought for his inheritance, taking the imperial crown from Otto IV in 1212 but not being formally crowned as emperor until 1220, after an early life as king of Sicily.

Frederick three kings of Prussia:

Frederick (II) the Great (1712–1786) King of Prussia from 1740, when he succeeded his father Frederick William I. In that year he started the War of the ▷Austrian Succession by his attack on Austria. In the peace of 1745 he secured Silesia. The struggle was renewed in the ▷Seven Years' War 1756–63. He acquired West Prussia in the first partition of Poland in 1772 and left Prussia as Germany's foremost state. He was an efficient and just ruler in the spirit of the Enlightenment and a patron of the arts.

In his domestic policy he encouraged industry and agriculture, reformed the judicial system, fostered education, and established religious toleration. He corresponded with the French writer Voltaire, and was a talented musician.

He received a harsh military education from his father, and in 1730 was threatened with death for attempting to run away. In the Seven Years' War, in spite of assistance from Britain, Frederick had a hard task holding his own against the Austrians and their Russian allies; the skill with which he did so proved him to be one of the great soldiers of history.

In August 1991, fulfilling his expressed wish to be buried in a simple grave at his beloved Sans Souci Palace at Potsdam, his embalmed remains, along with those of his father, Frederick William I, were taken from the Hohenzollern family castle near Stuttgart and reburied at Sans Souci. (During World War II, Hitler had removed the two bodies from Potsdam's garrison church, where they were first buried in 1786, to a salt mine in Thuringia as Soviet troops approached Berlin in 1945.) Chancellor Kohl attended the reburial as a 'private citizen', but the occasion was criticized for sending the wrong, militaristic, signals for a united Germany to its European neighbours.

Frederick III (1831–1888) King of Prussia and emperor of Germany in 1888. The son of Wilhelm I, he married the eldest daughter (Victoria) of Queen Victoria of the UK in 1858 and, as a liberal, frequently opposed Chancellor Bismarck. He died three months after his accession.

Frederick William (1620–1688) Elector of Brandenburg from 1640, 'the Great Elector'. By successful wars against Sweden and Poland, he prepared the way for Prussian power in the 18th century.

Frederick William four kings of Prussia:

Frederick William I (1688–1740) King of Prussia from 1713, who developed Prussia's military might and commerce.

Frederick William II (1744–1797) King of Prussia from 1786. He was a nephew of Frederick II but had little of his relative's military skill. He was unsuccessful in waging war on the French 1792–95 and lost all Prussia west of the Rhine.

Frederick William III (1770–1840) King of Prussia from 1797. He was defeated by Napoleon in 1806, but contributed to his final overthrow 1813–15 and profited by being allotted territory at the Congress of Vienna.

Frederick William IV (1795–1861) King of Prussia from 1840. He upheld the principle of the ▷divine right of kings, but was forced to grant a constitution in 1850 after the Prussian revolution of 1848. He suffered two strokes in 1857 and became mentally debilitated. His brother William (later emperor) took over his duties.

Free Church the Protestant denominations in England and Wales that are not part of the Church of England; for example, the Methodist Church, Baptist Union, and United Reformed Church (Congregational and Presbyterian). These churches joined for common action in the Free Church Federal Council in 1940.

Free Church of Scotland body of Scottish Presbyterians who seceded from the Established Church of Scotland in the Disruption of 1843. In 1900 all but a small section that retains the old name (known as the **Wee Frees**) combined with the United Presbyterian Church to form the United Free Church of Scotland. Most of this reunited with the Church of Scotland in 1929, although there remains a continuing United Free Church of Scotland. It has 6,000 members, 110 ministers, and 140 churches.

freedom of the press absence of censorship in the press or other media; see ▷press, freedom of.

free enterprise (or **free market**) economic system where private capital is used in business with profits going to private companies and individuals. The term has much the same meaning as ▷capitalism.

freehold in England and Wales, ownership of land for an indefinite period. It is contrasted with a **leasehold**, which is always for a fixed period. In practical effect, a freehold is absolute ownership.

> ### Benjamin Franklin
> *But in this world nothing can be said to be certain, except death and taxes.*
> Letter to Jean Baptiste Le Roy, 13 November 1789

FREDERICK (II) THE GREAT Brought up in the harsh militarism of Prussia, Frederick II became a well-loved and enlightened monarch when he took the throne in 1740. He was a friend of Voltaire and a patron of the arts, and at his palace of Sans Souci he gathered a circle of literary friends. *Archive Photos*

freemasonry beliefs and practices of a group of linked national organizations open to men over the age of 21, united by a common code of morals and certain traditional 'secrets'. Modern freemasonry began in 18th-century Europe. Freemasons do much charitable work, but have been criticized in recent years for their secrecy, their male exclusivity, and their alleged use of influence within and between organizations (for example, the police or local government) to further each other's interests.

Beliefs Freemasons believe in God, whom they call the 'Great Architect of the Universe'.

History Freemasonry is descended from a medieval guild of itinerant masons, which existed in the 14th century and by the 16th was admitting men unconnected with the building trade. The term 'freemason' may have meant a full member of the guild or one working in freestone, that is, a mason of the highest class. There were some 25 lodges in 17th-century Scotland, of which 16 were in centres of masonic skills such as stonemasonry.

The present order of **Free and Accepted Masons** originated with the formation in London of the first Grand Lodge, or governing body, in 1717, and during the 18th century spread from Britain to the USA, continental Europe, and elsewhere. In France and other European countries, freemasonry assumed a political and anticlerical character; it has been condemned by the papacy, and in some countries was suppressed by the state. In Italy the freemasonic lodge P2 was involved in a number of political scandals from the 1980s.

In 1994 there were 359,000 masons registered in England and Wales; there were also an estimated 100,000 in Scotland and 60,000 in Ireland. There are approximately 6 million members worldwide.

Related Web site: Freemasonry Pages http://www.geocities.com/Athens/Delphi/4439/freemasonry.html

free port port or sometimes a zone within a port, where cargo may be accepted for handling, processing, and reshipment without the imposition of tariffs or taxes. Duties and tax become payable only if the products are for consumption in the country to which the free port belongs.

Free Presbyterian Church of Scotland body seceded from the ▷Free Church of Scotland in 1893. In 1990 a further split created the Associated Presbyterian Churches of Scotland and Canada.

free radical in chemistry, an atom or molecule that has an unpaired electron and is therefore highly reactive. Most free radicals are very short-lived. They are by-products of normal cell chemistry and rapidly oxidize other molecules they encounter. Free radicals are thought to do considerable damage. They are neutralized by protective enzymes. Free radicals are often produced by high temperatures and are found in flames and explosions.

The action of ultraviolet radiation from the Sun splits chlorofluorocarbon (CFC) molecules in the upper atmosphere into free radicals, which then break down the ▷ozone layer.

freesia any of a South African group of plants belonging to the iris family, commercially grown for their scented, funnel-shaped flowers. (Genus *Freesia*, family Iridaceae.)

Free State (formerly **Orange Free State** (until 1995)) province of the Republic of South Africa; area 127,993 sq km/49,418 sq mi; population (2000 est) 2,762,700. Lesotho forms an enclave on the KwaZulu-Natal and Eastern Cape Province border. The capital is ▷Bloemfontein; other main towns are Springfontein, Kroonstad, Bethlehem, Harrismith, and Koffiefontein. The main industries are gold, oil from coal, cement, and pharmaceuticals; agricultural production is centred on grain, wool, and cattle.

free thought post-Reformation movement opposed to Christian dogma. It was represented in Britain in the 17th and 18th century by ▷deism; in the 19th century by the radical thinker Richard Carlile (1790–1843), a pioneer of the free press, and the Liberal politicians Charles Bradlaugh and Lord Morley (1838–1923); and in the 20th century by the philosopher Bertrand Russell.

Freetown capital of Sierra Leone; population (1992) 505,000. It has a naval station and a harbour. Industries include cement, plastics, footwear, oil refining, food production, and tobacco processing. Platinum, chromite, rutile, diamonds, and gold are traded. Freetown was founded as a settlement for freed slaves in 1787. It was made capital of the independent Sierre Leone in 1961.

free trade economic system where governments do not interfere in the movement of goods between countries; there are thus no taxes on imports. In the modern economy, free trade tends to hold within economic groups such as the European Union (EU), but not generally, despite such treaties as the ▷General Agreement on Tariffs and Trade (GATT) of 1948 and subsequent agreements to reduce tariffs. The opposite of free trade is ▷protectionism.

The case for free trade, first put forward in the 17th century, received its classic statement in Adam Smith's *Wealth of Nations* (1776). The movement towards free trade began with the younger Pitt's commercial treaty with France in 1786, and triumphed with the repeal of the ▷Corn Laws in 1846. According to traditional economic theory, free trade allows nations to specialize in those commodities that can be produced most efficiently. In Britain, superiority to all rivals as a manufacturing country in the Victorian age made free trade an advantage, but when that superiority was lost the demand for protection was raised, notably by Joseph Chamberlain.

The Ottawa Agreements of 1932 marked the end of free trade until in 1948 GATT came into operation. A series of resultant international tariff reductions was agreed in the Kennedy Round Conference 1964–67, and the Tokyo Round 1974–79 gave substantial incentives to developing countries. In the 1980s recession prompted by increased world oil prices and unemployment swung the pendulum back towards protectionism, which discourages foreign imports by heavy duties, thus protecting home products. Within the EU, all protectionist tariffs were abolished in 1993.

free verse poetry without metrical form. At the beginning of the 20th century, many poets believed that the 19th century had accomplished most of what could be done with regular metre, and rejected it, in much the same spirit as John Milton in the 17th century had rejected rhyme, preferring irregular metres that made it possible to express thought clearly and without distortion.

free will the doctrine that human beings are free to control their own actions, and that these actions are not fixed in advance by God or fate. Some Jewish and Christian theologians assert that God gave humanity free will to choose between good and evil; others that God has decided in advance the outcome of all human choices (▷predestination), as in Calvinism.

freeze-thaw form of physical ▷weathering, common in mountains and glacial environments, caused by the expansion of water as it freezes. Water in a crack freezes and expands in volume by 9% as it turns to ice. This expansion exerts great pressure on the rock causing the crack to enlarge. After many cycles of freeze-thaw, rock fragments may break off to form ▷scree slopes.

freezing change from liquid to solid state, as when water becomes ice. For a given substance, freezing occurs at a definite temperature, known as the **freezing point**, that is invariable under similar conditions of pressure, and the temperature remains at this point until all the liquid is frozen. The amount of heat per unit mass that has to be removed to freeze a substance is a constant for any given substance, and is known as the latent heat of fusion.

freezing point, depression of lowering of a solution's freezing point below that of the pure solvent; it depends on the number of molecules of solute dissolved in it. For a single solvent, such as pure water, all solute substances in the same molar concentration produce the same lowering of freezing point. The depression d produced by the presence of a solute of molar concentration C is given by the equation $d = KC$, where K is a constant (called the cryoscopic constant) for the solvent concerned.

Frege, (Friedrich Ludwig) Gottlob (1848–1925) German philosopher, the founder of modern mathematical logic. He created symbols for concepts like 'or' and 'if ... then', which are now in standard use in mathematics. His *Die Grundlagen der Arithmetik/The Foundations of Arithmetic* (1884) influenced Bertrand ▷Russell and Ludwig ▷Wittgenstein. Frege's chief work is *Begriffsschrift/Conceptual Notation* (1879).

French, John Denton Pinkstone (1852–1925) 1st Earl of Ypres. British field marshal. In the second ▷South African War 1899–1902, he relieved Kimberley and took Bloemfontein; in World War I he was commander-in-chief of the British Expeditionary Force in France 1914–15; he resigned after being criticized as indecisive and became commander-in-chief home forces. He was made KCB in 1900, Viscount in 1916, and Earl 1922.

> **John French**
> *It is a solemn thought that at my signal all these fine young fellows go to their death.*
> Quoted in Brett *Journals and letters of Reginald, Viscount Esher*

French Antarctic Territories (or **French Southern and Antarctic Territories**) territory created in 1955; population approximately 200 research scientists. It includes Adélie Land (area 432,000 sq km/165,500 sq mi) on the Antarctic continent, the Kerguelen and Crozet archipelagos (7,515 sq km/2,901 sq mi), and St Paul and Nouvelle Amsterdam islands (67 sq km/26 sq mi) in the southern seas. It is administered from Paris.

French architecture the architecture of France.

Early Christian The influence of France's rich collection of Roman buildings (ranging from amphitheatres to temples and aqueducts) can be seen in early Christian church building, which began even before the Romans retreated. The baptistery of St Jean at Poitiers and the crypt of Jouarre near Meaux, both 5th century, use Roman architectural effects to their own ends.

Romanesque Such early Roman-influenced buildings gave way to the first distinctive Romanesque architecture, which reached its zenith in the abbey at Cluny (begun 1088). The style developed and took on regional characteristics, such as tunnel and other types of vaulting, for example, St Philibert at Tournus (11th century).

Gothic The abbey church of St Denis, near Paris, 1132–44, marks the beginning of the Gothic style, characterized by the use of pointed arches and rib vaulting. The cathedral of Notre Dame, Paris, begun 1160, is an example of **early Gothic** (1130–90). The cathedrals at Chartres, begun 1194, Reims, begun 1211, and Bourges, begun 1209, are examples of **lancet Gothic** (1190–1240). French **Late Gothic**, or the **Flamboyant style** as it was known in France (1350–1520), characterized by flowing tracery, is best represented at Caudebec-en-Caux in Normandy, about 1426, and Moulins in Burgundy.

Renaissance Arriving in France from Italy late in the 15th century, at first it replaced Gothic very gradually, as in England. Francis I introduced a number of Italian architects at Fontainebleau, Amboise, Blois, and other places. French architects soon acquired the new Italian fashions in design, and during the 16th century built the first part of the New Louvre in Paris (1546), the chateau of St Germain, and many of the picturesque châteaux in the Loire valley, where the Renaissance made its greatest impact, for example Azay-le-Rideau, Chenonceaux, and Chambord 1519–47.

Baroque After a long period of religious warfare, architecture was again given priority. Henry IV's interest in town planning manifested itself in such works as the Place des Vosges, Paris (begun 1605), the Pont Neuf, and the Place Dauphine. The Baroque style found expression in Le Vau's work on the château of Vaux-le-Vicomte 1657–61, the gardens of which were designed by Le Notre; the two later worked extensively at Versailles. Jacques Lemercier designed the older part of the palace at Versailles; the Palais Royal (1633), and the churches of the Sorbonne (begun 1626) and St Roch; and laid out the town and château of Richelieu for the cardinal of that name (begun 1631). Francois Mansart enlarged Lescot's Hôtel Carnavalet and built the church of Val-de-Grace, both in Paris; the beautiful château at Maisons-Lafitte, near Paris, 1642–51; and the Orléans wing at Blois. Under Louis XIV, Hardouin-Mansart enlarged Versailles in 1678, designed the cathedral there, and Les Invalides in Paris, 1680–91; and planned the Place des Victoires and the Place Vendôme both in Paris. See also ▷Baroque.

Neo-Classicism In the 18th century there was a definite move towards Classicism, culminating in the severe works of Boullée and Ledoux. The classical influence continued in the 19th century, perpetuated to some extent by the revolution of 1789, with works such as the Madeleine, Paris, 1804–49, by P A Vignon (1762–1828). By the middle of the century, the grandiose Beaux Arts style was established, most spectacularly in the Opéra, Paris, 1861–74, by Charles Garnier (1825–1898). It was challenged by both the rationalist approach of Labrouste who was responsible for the Library of Sainte Geneviève, Paris, 1843–50, and by the Gothic Revival as detailed in the writings of Viollet-le-Duc. See also ▷Neo-Classicism.

Art nouveau Art nouveau developed towards the end of the 19th century, with centres in Nancy and Paris. Hector Guimard's Paris Metro station entrances, with their flamboyant metal arches, are famous examples of the style. Garnier experimented with pure form, paralleled by the later work of Auguste Perret. See also ▷art nouveau.

The Modern Movement In the 1920s the Swiss-born Le Corbusier emerged as the leading exponent of the Modern Movement in France. His masterpieces range from the cubist Villa Savoye at Poissy (1929–31) to the vast, grid-like Unité d'Habitation at Marseille (1947–52). Since the 1950s technological preoccupations have been evident in much modern architecture in France, beginning with the work of Jean Prouvé, for instance his Refreshment Room at Evian (1957), and continuing in more recent projects, such as the Pompidou Centre, Paris, by Renzo Piano and Richard Rogers (1971–77), and the Institut du Monde Arabe, Paris, 1981–87, by Jean Nouvel. In the 1980s, Paris became the site for a number of *Grands Projets* initiated by President Mitterrand, including the cultural complex at Parc de la Villette by Bernard Tschumi (partially opened 1985), the conversion by Gui Aulenti of the Gare d'Orsay into the Musée d'Orsay in 1986, I M Pei's glass pyramid for the Louvre in 1989, and the Grande Arche at La Défense by Johan Otto von Spreckelsen in 1989. See also ▷Modern Movement.

French art painting, sculpture, and decorative arts of France. As the birthplace of the Gothic style, France was a centre for sculpture and manuscript illumination in the Middle Ages, and of tapestry from the 15th century. 17th-century French painting is particularly rich, dominated by the Italianate Classicism of ▷Claude Lorrain and Nicolas ▷Poussin. Subsequent light-hearted rococo scenes of upper-class leisure gave way with the French Revolution to the Neo-Classicism of Jacques-Louis ▷David and Jean ▷Ingres. In the 19th century, Romanticism was superseded first by ▷realism and then by ▷Impressionism, led by such painters as Claude ▷Monet and Auguste ▷Renoir, which in turn fragmented, via the work of Georges ▷Seurat, Paul ▷Cézanne, and others, into the modern art of the 20th century. Georges ▷Braque (cubism) and Henri ▷Matisse (fauvism) were among the pioneers. In sculpture the towering figure was that of Auguste ▷Rodin. From the mid-19th to the mid-20th century, Paris was the hotbed of Western art.

Among the very earliest artistic remains are the cave paintings of Lascaux in southern France (18,000 BC). The Celtic period (5th century BC to 1st century AD) left many artefacts and from the Roman occupation (1st century to 5th) there are artefacts and fine buildings. During the Ottonian and Carolingian dynasties, the growing power and wealth of the Christian church helped to sow the seeds of a national culture.

Romanesque: 10th–12th centuries The first distinctively French art was Romanesque. The building of ever larger churches, cathedrals, and monasteries gave new impetus to the 'minor arts' that religious buildings and communities require – metalwork, textiles, and manuscript illumination. Sculpture was also one of the outstanding achievements of the period, the expressive, highly stylized forms deriving in part from manuscript illumination, as at the cathedral of Autun and the abbeys of Cluny, Moissac, and Souillac. Enamels achieved a new sophistication, with *champlevé* enamelling being produced in Limoges.

Gothic: 12th–14th centuries In both architecture and the other arts, France played a major role in the development of Gothic. New, soaring cathedrals required large areas of stained glass, some of the finest of which was made for Chartres cathedral. Mural paintings (mostly destroyed) often imitated the colouring of the stained glass. Sculpture acquired a greater elegance and realism, with complex programmes being carved at Chartres, in Paris at Notre Dame, and elsewhere. Portrait sculpture (in the form of sepulchral effigies) began in France in the late 14th century. The carvings produced at the Burgundian court by Claus Sluter during this period are the outstanding examples of late Gothic sculpture. Paris became an international centre for illumination and miniature painting.

15th century As Gothic styles were adapted to the changing needs of society at the end of the Middle Ages, regional schools in painting developed and the first major artists appeared: in Provence, Nicolas Froment; in Burgundy and the north, Simon Marmion (*c.* 1422–1489); and in the Loire country, Jean Fouquet, Jean Bourdichon (*c.* 1457–1521), the Maître de Moulins (worked 1480–1500), Jean Perréal (*c.* 1457–1530). The most important of these is the court portrait painter Jean Fouquet, whose precise realism owes much to Netherlandish painting. His miniatures and those of the Limbourg brothers, creators of the *Très Riches Heures* illuminated prayer books, show remarkable naturalism and flair for ornamentation. Exquisite tapestries were woven, one of the finest being *The Lady with the Unicorn* about 1480 (Musée de Cluny, Paris). With the decline of church commissions, there were few opportunities for sculptors.

Renaissance: 16th century The desire of Francis I to create a centralized art to rival Italy led to his introducing Italian painters (such as Francesco Primaticcio and Niccolò dell'Abbate) into France, and from this followed the development of the School of Fontainebleau. The art of the court portrait and portrait miniature flourished with Corneille de Lyon (*c.* 1503–1574) and the two leading artists of the period, Jean and François Clouet. Although increasingly influenced by Italian styles, these artists were still indebted to Netherlandish painting. Sculptors, on the other hand – such as Jean Goujon, Jean Cousin (*c.* 1522–*c.* 1594), and Germain Pilon (1535–1590) – were more successful in adopting Italian styles. The Renaissance in France also saw brilliant enamelling work, especially by Léonard (*c.* 1505–*c.* 1577) and Jean Limousin (*c.* 1528–*c.* 1610); the extraordinary ceramics of Bernard Palissy; and fine work by goldsmiths.

Baroque: 17th century Under Louis XIV, Poussin's style became 'official', being promulgated by the Royal Academy (founded 1648). The minister Jean-Baptiste Colbert and the painter Charles Le Brun, painter to the king and director of the academy, controlled all aspects of art production, from state portraits to the furniture and tapestry produced at the Gobelins factory. The painters Georges de La Tour and Louis Le Nain are unusual in that they adopted a realistic style, though they too have a classical sense of order and poise. A ceremonial form of portraiture was practised by Nicola de Largillière (1656–1746) and Hyacinthe Rigaud. The etcher Jacques Callot provided forceful records of the harsher realities of the period, his works frequently anticipating those of the Spanish artist Francisco Goya.

In the earlier part of the 17th century, French sculpture was mainly sepulchral. Notable sculptors in this line were François Anguier (*c.* 1604–1669), who modelled the duc de Montmorency's tomb in Moulins, northern Auvergne, and Jacques Sarrazin (1588–1660), sculptor of Prince de Condé, Henry II's tomb in Chantilly, north of Paris. A fresh expansion came with the encouragement of a grandiose secular art by Louis XIV. Girardon, whose masterpiece is Cardinal Richelieu's tomb in the Sorbonne church, Paris, was extensively employed on the sculptural decoration of Versailles. Antoine Coysevox carved portraits remarkable for their vitality.

18th century The grandiose decoration of the Louis XIV style gave way to the lightness and charm of rococo. Jean-Antoine Watteau marks the change of mood, also evident in his followers Jean-Baptiste Pater (1695–1736) and Nicolas Lancret. In Watteau's informal *fêtes galantes*, graceful figures engage in musical and amatory pursuits in theatrical landscape settings which are tinged with melancholy and a sense of the transitory nature of pleasure. A graceful and highly decorative development of this style is found in the work of François Boucher and Jean-Honoré Fragonard, both of whom epitomized the gaiety and frivolity of the court immediately before the Revolution. The style declined sharply in the work of Jean Baptiste Greuze, whose moralizing genre subjects extolling simple virtues became mawkishly sentimental. In contrast with the art of court circles, Jean-Baptiste Chardin painted quiet scenes of domestic bourgeois life. In still life he took up and gave new values to the genre practised by Jean-Baptiste Oudry (1686–1755) and Alexandre-François Desportes (1661–1743) and inspired by Netherlandish models. 18th-century portraiture is represented by the pastellist Maurice Quentin de La Tour and by the elegance of Jean-Marc Nattier (1685–1766), Jean-Baptiste Perroneau (1715–1783), Hubert Drouais (1699–1767) and François-Hubert Drouais (1727–1775), father and son, and Elisabeth Vigée Lebrun. The sculptor Jean Antoine Houdon stands out in the 18th century particularly for his animated and expressive portrait busts.

The end of the 18th century saw a reaction against rococo and a return to 'the antique' advocated by Joseph Marie Vien (1716–1809). The major exponent of this neoclassicism was one of Vien's pupils, David, whose works give dramatic expression to both the Revolution and Napoleon's empire building.

19th century As a return to the past, however, neoclassicism had a Romantic element, which appears in the work of Girodet-Trioson (1767–1824), Pierre Prud'hon, and Baron Antoine-Jean Gros (1771–1835). Full-blown Romanticism is strikingly demonstrated in the works of Théodore Géricault and Eugène Delacroix, though Ingres remained a determined upholder of classicism (the approved style of the Royal Academy throughout the 19th century).

In landscape the beginnings of a new era came with Camille Corot's low-keyed, poetic landscapes, luminous and misty. Although he worked at Barbizon, he is distinct from the Barbizon School, who were 'pure' landscape painters, partly inspired by the Dutch painters Meindert Hobbema and Jacob van Ruisdael. French painters of this group are Jean François Millet, Daubigny (1817–1878), and Theodore Rousseau. By midcentury, realism had become a challenge to both neoclassicism and Romanticism. Gustave ▷Courbet, whose unheroic depictions of everyday life caused a storm of protest, was the main figure of realism, his art closely linked to his political radicalism. More an attitude than a style, realism was advanced by Honoré ▷Daumier, a painter and cartoonist noted for his satirical depictions of French life, and the landscape painter Jean François Millet. Edouard ▷Manet may also be regarded as a realist, his brilliant modern treatment of old-master themes, as in his *Olympia* 1865 (Musée d'Orsay, Paris), causing a scandal.

By focusing on everyday life, realism prepared the way for the best-known movement of the 19th century, Impressionism. ▷Monet, who began as a member of the group inspired by Manet, is one of Impressionism's central figures. His concentration on the sheer appearance of things, with colours and forms subtly altered by variations of atmosphere and light, was the essence of the movement. Other major Impressionists are Renoir, Camille ▷Pissarro, and Berthe ▷Morisot. Edgar Degas brought to Impressionism a classical sense of structure and form. Although aware of Impressionism, Henri de ▷Toulouse-Lautrec developed his own highly independent style derived from posters, Japanese prints, and Degas.

The Impressionist use of colour suggested various new departures: the Neo-Impressionism (or pointillism) of Seurat and Paul Signac; and the forms of post-Impressionism represented by Cézanne and Paul Gauguin, who both had a profound effect on the development of modern art. Their art is the matrix of a succession of brilliant phases of art from the 1890s, beginning with Symbolism (Odilon Redon, Gustave Moreau, and others) and the group les Nabis.

Rodin infused a Romantic intensity of feeling into the cold formulas of 19th-century sculpture. Notable sculptors include François Rude, who executed the sculptural work on the Arc de Triomphe; Antoine-Louis Barye (1795–1875), known for animal sculptures; Albert Bartholomé (1848–1928), known especially for funerary masks; Henri Laurens (1885–1954), and important sculptor and engraver; Antoine Bourdelle (1861–1929), who combined classic Greek manner with a style of exaggeration conveying heroic energies; and Jean-Baptiste Carpeaux. Degas also produced some innovative sculptures.

20th century Among the most important 20th-century innovators were Georges ▷Braque – who, with the Spanish artist Pablo ▷Picasso, developed and perfected the cubist style – and Henri ▷Matisse. Matisse, the central figure in fauvism, produced brilliantly coloured works of a highly decorative, rhythmic nature. The new ideas of painting successively launched in Paris made that city the centre of an international school, 'l'Ecole de Paris'. Some of its representatives, like Picasso, came originally from outside France, but among the notable French painters are Edouard ▷Vuillard, Pierre ▷Bonnard, Pierre Albert Marquet, Robert Delaunay, Fernand Léger, Georges Rouault, and Raoul ▷Dufy. Aristide Maillol revitalized traditional sculptural forms.

After World War II Paris ceased to be the centre of the artistic world and was succeeded by the USA as the most universal influence on contemporary art. Leading artists of the post-war period include Yves Klein and Jean Dubuffet.

French Community former association consisting of France and those overseas territories joined with it by the constitution of the Fifth Republic, following the 1958 referendum. Many of the constituent states withdrew during the 1960s, and it no longer formally exists, but in practice all former French colonies have close economic and cultural as well as linguistic links with France.

French Equatorial Africa federation of French territories in West Africa. Founded in 1910, it consisted of Gabon, Middle Congo, Chad, and Ubangi-Shari (now the Central African Republic), and was ruled from Brazzaville. The federation supported the Free French in World War II and was given representation in the French Fourth Republic 1944–58. In 1958, the states voted for autonomy and the federation was dissolved.

French Guiana (French **Guyane Française**) French overseas *département* from 1946, and administrative region from 1974, on the north coast of South America, bounded west by Suriname and east and south by Brazil; area 83,500 sq km/32,230 sq mi; population (1997 est) 156,900. The main towns are ▷Cayenne and St Laurent. The main economic activity is fishing; other resources include bauxite, tropical hardwood timber, gold, cinnabar, and kaolin. Agricultural products include rice, maize, cocoa, bananas, and sugar, though the country depends largely on imported food.

French horn musical brass instrument, a descendant of the natural hunting horn, valved and curved into a circular loop, with a funnel-shaped mouthpiece and wide bell.

French India former French possessions in India: Pondicherry, Chandernagore, Karaikal, Mahé, and Yanam (Yanaon). They were all transferred to India by 1954.

French language member of the Romance branch of the Indo-European language family, spoken in France, Belgium, Luxembourg, Monaco, and Switzerland in Europe; also in Canada (principally in the province of Québec), various Caribbean and Pacific Islands (including overseas territories such as Martinique and French Guiana), and certain North and West African countries (for example, Mali and Senegal).

French literature the literature of France.

The Middle Ages The *Chanson de Roland* (*c.* 1080) is one of the early *chansons de geste* (epic poems about deeds of chivalry), which were superseded by the Arthurian romances (seen at their finest in the work of Chrétien de Troyes in the 12th century), and by the classical themes of Alexander, Troy, and Thebes. Other aspects of French medieval literature are represented by the anonymous *Aucassin et Nicolette* of the early 13th century; the allegorical *Roman de la Rose/Romance of the Rose*, the first part of which was written by Guillaume de Lorris (*c.* 1230) and the second by Jean de Meung (*c.* 1275); and the satiric *Roman de Renart/Story of Renard* of the late 12th century. The period also produced the historians Villehardouin, Joinville, Froissart, and Comines, and the first great French poet, François Villon.

16th century: the Renaissance One of the most celebrated poets of the Renaissance was Ronsard, leader of *La Pléiade* (a group of seven writers); others included Marot at the beginning of the 16th century and Mathurin Régnier (1573–1613) at its close. In prose

French Revolution: Key Dates 1789–99

1789	(May) Meeting of States General called by Louis XVI to discuss reform of state finances. Nobility opposes reforms.
	(June) Third (commoners) estate demands end to system where first (noble) estate and second (church) estate can outvote them; rejected by Louis. Third estate declares itself a national assembly and 'tennis-court oath' pledges them to draw up new constitution.
	(July) Rumours of royal plans to break up the assembly lead to riots in Paris and the storming of the Bastille. Revolutionaries adopt the tricolour as their flag. Peasant uprisings occur throughout the country.
1789–91	National-assembly reforms include abolition of noble privileges, dissolution of religious orders, appropriation of church lands, centralization of governments, and limits on the king's power.
1791	(June) King Louis attempts to escape from Paris in order to unite opposition to the assembly, but is recaptured.
	(September) The king agrees to a new constitution.
	(October) New legislative assembly meets, divided between moderate Girondists and radical Jacobins.
1792	(January) Girondists form a new government but their power in Paris is undermined by the Jacobins. Foreign invasion leads to the breakdown of law and order. Hatred of the monarchy increases.
	(August) The king is suspended from office and the government dismissed.
	(September) National Convention elected on the basis of universal suffrage; dominated by Jacobins. A republic is proclaimed.
	(December) The king is tried and condemned to death.
1793	(January) The king is guillotined.
	(April) The National Convention delegates power to the Committee of Public Safety, dominated by Robespierre. The Reign of Terror begins.
1794	(July) Robespierre becomes increasingly unpopular, is deposed and executed.
1795	Moderate Thermidoreans take control of the convention and create a new executive Directory of five members.
1795–99	Directory fails to solve France's internal or external problems and becomes increasingly unpopular.
1799	Coup d'état overthrows the Directory and a consulate of three is established, including Napoleon as First Consul with special powers.

the period produced the broad genius of Rabelais and the essayist Montaigne.

17th century The triumph of form came with the great classical dramatists Corneille, Racine, and Molière, the graceful brilliance of La Fontaine, and the poet and critic Boileau. Masters of prose in the same period include the philosophers Pascal and Descartes; the preacher Bossuet; the critics La Bruyère, Fénelon, and Malebranche; and La Rochefoucauld, Cardinal de Retz, Mme de Sévigné, and Le Sage.

18th century The age of the ▷Enlightenment and an era of prose, with Montesquieu, Voltaire, and Rousseau; the scientist Buffon; the encyclopedist Diderot; the ethical writer Vauvenargues; the novelists Prévost and Marivaux; and the memoir writer Saint-Simon.

19th century Poetry came to the fore again with the Romantics Lamartine, Hugo, Vigny, Musset, Leconte de Lisle, and Gautier; novelists of the same school were George Sand, Stendhal, and Dumas *père*, while criticism is represented by Sainte-Beuve, and history by Thiers, Michelet, and Taine. The realist novelist Balzac was followed by the school of naturalism, whose representatives were Flaubert, Zola, the Goncourt brothers, Alphonse Daudet, Maupassant, and Huysmans. Dramatists include Hugo, Musset, and Dumas *fils*. Symbolism, a movement of experimentation and revolt against classical verse and materialist attitudes, with the philosopher Bergson as one of its main exponents, found its first expression in the work of Gérard de Nerval, followed by Baudelaire, Verlaine, Mallarmé, Rimbaud, Corbière, and the prose writer Villiers de l'Isle Adam; later writers in the same tradition were Henri de Régnier and Laforgue.

20th century Drama and poetry revived with Valéry, Claudel, and Paul Fort, who advocated 'pure poetry'; other writers were the novelists Gide and Proust, and the critics Thibaudet (1874–1936) and later St John Perse, also a poet. The surrealist movement, which developed from 'pure poetry' through the work of Eluard and Apollinaire, influenced writers as diverse as Giraudoux, Louis Aragon, and Cocteau. The literary reaction against the symbolists was seen in the work of Charles Péguy, Rostand, de Noailles, and Romain Rolland. Novelists in the naturalist tradition were Henri Barbusse, Jules Romains, Julian Green, François Mauriac, Francis Carco, and Georges Duhamel. Other prose writers were Maurois, Malraux, Montherlant, Anatole France, Saint-Exupéry, Alain-Fournier, Pierre Hamp, and J R Bloch, while the theatre flourished with plays by J J Bernard, Anouilh, Beckett, and Ionesco. World War II had a profound effect on French writing, and distinguished post-war writers include the existentialists Sartre and Camus, Simone de Beauvoir, Alain Robbe-Grillet, Romain Gary, Nathalie Sarraute, and Marguerite Duras.

French Polynesia
French Overseas Territory in the South Pacific, consisting of five archipelagos: Windward Islands, Leeward Islands (the two island groups comprising the ▷Society Islands), ▷Tuamotu Archipelago (including ▷Gambier Islands), ▷Tubuai Islands, and ▷Marquesas Islands; total area 3,940 sq km/1,521 sq mi; population (1994) 216,600. The capital is ▷Papeete on Tahiti. Tourism is the mainstay of the economy; other industries are cultivated pearls, coconut oil, and vanilla. The languages spoken are Tahitian (official) and French.

French Revolution
the period 1789–1799 that saw the end of the monarchy in France. The revolution began as an attempt to create a constitutional monarchy, but by late 1792 demands for

long-overdue reforms resulted in the proclamation of the First Republic. The violence of the revolution; attacks by other nations; and bitter factional struggles, riots, and counter-revolutionary uprisings consumed the republic. This helped bring the extremists to power, and the bloody Reign of Terror followed. French armies then succeeded in holding off their foreign enemies and one of the generals, ▷Napoleon, seized power in 1799.

The States General In the period leading up to the French Revolution, France was involved in the Seven Years' War (1756–1763) and the American Revolutionary Wars (1775–1783). The cost of these wars brought about a financial crisis, and in 1788 King ▷Louis XVI called a meeting of the ▷States General (three 'estates' of nobles, clergy, and commons) in order to raise taxes. During the meeting, the third estate insisted that the three estates should be merged into a single national assembly. Its demands were initially refused by Louis XVI and the first two estates, but the king later changed his position: he allowed the national assembly to be formed and then gathered his armed forces around Paris with the intent of breaking up the assembly by force.

The national assembly These repressive measures led to the storming of the ▷Bastille prison by the Paris mob on 14 July 1789. This was followed by the formation of a revolutionary city government in Paris and a number of peasant uprisings outside Paris. In August, the assembly introduced the 'Declaration of the Rights of Man and of the Citizen', which proclaimed the principles of liberty and equality; the right to own property; and the right of all citizens to resist oppression. The king refused to sanction the Declaration, however, and in October there were more uprisings in Paris. The royal family attempted to flee the country in 1791, but Louis XVI was captured and was later forced to accept a new constitution. This reorganized France into 83 *départements*; reformed the court system and the Catholic Church by requiring both judges and priests to be elected to office; and extended religious tolerance to Protestants and Jews. It also nationalized much of the Catholic Church's property, which was sold off in order to pay off the nation's debts.

War with Austria and Prussia During this period some of the aristocracy moved abroad, and began to agitate for action against the revolution. The revolution's supporters outside France were also increasingly persecuted, and France eventually went to war with Austria and Prussia (who supported Louis XVI) on 20 April 1792. The Austrian and Prussian armies invaded France, and for a time the war threatened to undermine the revolution, but on 10 August the mob stormed the royal palace; imprisoned Louis XVI and his family; and brought the constitutional monarchy to an end. A National Convention was formed by election and, on 21 September, the same body abolished the monarchy and declared France a republic. Louis XVI was subsequently tried, found guilty of treason, and executed at the guillotine on 21 January 1793.

The Reign of Terror In the period after Louis XVI's death, tensions within the National Convention resulted in a power struggle between the moderate ▷Girondins and the more radical ▷Jacobins, led by Maximilien ▷Robespierre, Georges Jaques ▷Danton, and Jean Paul ▷Marat. The Jacobins arrested the Girondin leaders in June 1793, and control of the country was passed to the infamous Committee of Public Safety, which was headed by Robespierre, Lazare Carnot, and Bertrand Barère. The committee announced a policy of terror against all rebels, supporters of the king, and Girondin sympathizers (see ▷Terror, Reign of), during which approximately 18,000 citizens were sent

to the guillotine and many more died in prison without being formally brought to trial. One of the more famous victims of the Terror was Marie Antoinette, the widow of Louis XVI.

Related Web sites: French Revolution Home Page
http://members.aol.com/agentmess/frenchrev/index.html
Glossary of the French Revolution http://www.warwick.ac.uk/fac/arts/History/teaching/french-rev/glossary.html

French West Africa
group of French colonies administered from Dakar 1895–1958. They are now Senegal, Mauritania, Sudan, Burkina Faso, Guinea, Niger, Côte d'Ivoire, and Benin.

frequency
in physics, the number of periodic oscillations, vibrations, or waves occurring per unit of time. The SI unit of frequency is the hertz (Hz), one hertz being equivalent to one cycle per second. Frequency is related to wavelength and velocity by the relationship

$$f = \frac{v}{\lambda}$$

where f is frequency, v is velocity, and λ is wavelength. Frequency is the reciprocal of the period T:

$$f = \frac{1}{T}$$

Human beings can hear sounds from objects vibrating in the range 20–15,000 Hz. Ultrasonic frequencies well above 15,000 Hz can be detected by such mammals as bats. Infrasound (low-frequency sound) can be detected by some animals and birds. Pigeons can detect sounds as low as 0.1 Hz; elephants communicate using sounds as low as 1 Hz. **Frequency modulation** (FM) is a method of transmitting radio signals in which the frequency of the **carrier wave** is changed and then decoded.

One kilohertz (kHz) equals 1,000 hertz; one megahertz (MHz) equals 1,000,000 hertz.

frequency
in statistics, the number of times an event occurs. For example, when two dice are thrown repeatedly and the two scores added together, each of the numbers 2 to 12 may have a frequency of occurrence. The set of data including the frequencies is called a **frequency distribution**, usually presented in a frequency table or shown diagrammatically, by a frequency polygon.

frequency modulation
(FM) method by which radio waves are altered for the transmission of broadcasting signals. FM varies the frequency of the carrier wave in accordance with the signal being transmitted. Its advantage over AM (▷amplitude modulation) is its better signal-to-noise ratio. It was invented by the US engineer Edwin Armstrong.

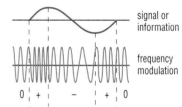

signal or information

frequency modulation

FREQUENCY MODULATION In FM radio transmission, the frequency of the carrier wave is modulated, rather than its amplitude (as in AM broadcasts). The FM system is not affected by the many types of interference which change the amplitude of the carrier wave, and so provides better quality reception than AM broadcasts.

fresco
mural painting technique using water-based paint on wet plaster that has been freshly applied to the wall (*fresco* is Italian for fresh). The technique is ancient and widespread; some of the earliest examples (*c.* 1750–1400 BC) were found in Knossos, Crete (now preserved in the Archeological Museum in Heraklion). However, fresco reached its finest expression in Italy from the 13th to the 17th centuries. See picture on p. 364.

Frescobaldi, Girolamo
(1583–1643) Italian composer and virtuoso keyboard player. He was organist at St Peter's, Rome, 1608–28. His compositions included various forms of both instrumental and vocal music, and his fame rests on numerous keyboard toccatas, fugues, ricercari, and capriccios in which he advanced keyboard technique and exploited ingenious and daring modulations of key.

Fresnel, Augustin Jean
(1788–1827) French physicist who refined the theory of ▷polarized light. Fresnel realized in 1821 that light waves do not vibrate like sound waves longitudinally, in the direction of their motion, but transversely, at right angles to the direction of the propagated wave.

Freud, Anna
(1895–1982) Austrian-born founder of child psychoanalysis in the UK. Her work was influenced by the theories of her father, Sigmund Freud. She held that understanding of the stages of psychological development was essential to the treatment of children, and that this knowledge could only be obtained through observation of the child.

FRESCO A fresco from the *Cycle of Months* by the Bohemian artist Torre Aquila Trento. In high summer, courtiers disport themselves outside a manor house, fishing, hawking, and playing at courtly love, while in the background peasants scythe and rake the fields. See entry on p. 363. *The Art Archive/Torre Aquila Trento/Dagli Orti*

Freud, Lucian (1922–) German-born British painter. One of the greatest contemporary figurative artists, he combines meticulous accuracy with a disquieting intensity, painting from unusual angles and emphasizing the physicality of his subjects, whether nudes, still lifes, or interiors. His *Portrait of Francis Bacon* (1952; Tate Gallery, London) is one of his best-known works. He is a grandson of Sigmund Freud.

Freud, Sigmund (1856–1939) Austrian physician who pioneered the study of the ▷unconscious mind. He developed the methods of free association and interpretation of dreams that are basic techniques of ▷psychoanalysis. The influence of unconscious forces on people's thoughts and actions was Freud's discovery, as was his controversial theory of the repression of infantile sexuality as the root of neuroses in the adult. His books include *Die Traumdeutung/The Interpretation of Dreams* (1900), *Jenseits des Lustprinzips/Beyond the Pleasure Principle* (1920), *Das Ich und das Es/The Ego and the Id* (1923), and *Das Unbehagen in der Kultur/Civilization and its Discontents* (1930). His influence has permeated the world to such an extent that it may be discerned today in almost every branch of thought.

SIGMUND FREUD Sigmund Freud was diagnosed with cancer of the mouth in 1923 and was operated on more than 30 times. Nevertheless, he continued to smoke. *Image Bank*

From 1886 to 1938 Freud had a private practice in Vienna, and his theories and writings drew largely on case studies of his own patients, who were mainly upper-middle-class, middle-aged women. Much of the terminology of psychoanalysis was coined by Freud, and many terms have passed into popular usage, not without distortion. His theories have changed the way people think about human nature and brought about a more open approach to sexual matters. Antisocial behaviour is now understood to result in many cases from unconscious forces, and these new concepts have led to wider expression of the human condition in art and literature. Nevertheless, Freud's theories have caused disagreement among psychologists and psychiatrists, and his methods of psychoanalysis cannot be applied in every case.

Related Web site: **Freud Web** http://landow.stg.brown.edu/victorian/science/freud/Freud_OV.html

Freya (or **Freyja**) in Norse mythology, goddess of married love and the hearth. She was also the goddess of death, Odin's punishment after her dalliance with four dwarfs to gain the necklace Brisingamen. In this capacity, she caused war between mortals and flew over their battlefields in a chariot drawn by two cats. Half the heroes slain were banqueted in her hall Sessrumnir in Asgard, the others being feasted by Odin. Friday is named after her.

friction in physics, the force that opposes the relative motion of two bodies in contact. The **coefficient of friction** is the ratio of the force required to achieve this relative motion to the force pressing the two bodies together.

Friction is greatly reduced by the use of lubricants such as oil, grease, and graphite. Air bearings are now used to minimize friction in high-speed rotational machinery. In other instances friction is deliberately increased by making the surfaces rough – for example, brake linings, driving belts, soles of shoes, and tyres.

Friedan, Betty (Elizabeth) (1921–) Born Elizabeth Goldstein. US liberal feminist. Her book *The Feminine Mystique* (1963) started the contemporary women's movement in the USA and the UK. She was a founder of the National Organization for Women (NOW) in 1966 (and its president 1966–70), the National Women's Political Caucus in 1971, and the First Women's Bank in 1973.

Friedman, Milton (1912–) US economist, a pioneer of ▷monetarism. He argued that a country's economy, and hence inflation, can be controlled through its money supply, although most governments lack the 'political will' to cut government spending and thereby increase unemployment. He was awarded the Nobel Prize for Economics in 1976 for his work on consumption analysis, monetary theory, and economic stabilization.

Friedman believed that inflation is 'always and everywhere a monetary phenomenon'. If the rate of growth of the money supply is limited to the rate of growth of output in the economy (through monetary policy such as changes in interest rates), it should be impossible for increases in costs, such as wages or imports, to be translated into a rise in prices in the economy as a whole.

His advocacy of the use of monetary policy, and his rejection of Keynesian economics, stemmed from his belief in the self-regulating nature of market forces, and the idea that there is a 'natural rate of unemployment'. He argued that this was determined by 'structural and institutional forces in the labour market', such as unemployment benefits and trade unions, and could not be reduced in the long term by increases in government spending.

Friedrich, Caspar David (1774–1840) German Romantic landscape painter. He was active mainly in Dresden. He imbued his subjects – mountain scenes and moonlit seas – with poetic melancholy and was later admired by Symbolist painters. *The Cross in the Mountains* (1808; Gemäldegalerie, Dresden) and *Moonrise over the Sea* (1822; Nationalgalerie, Berlin) are among his best-known works.

Friel, Brian (1929–) Northern Irish dramatist and short-story writer. Friel's work often addresses social and historical pressures that contribute to the Irish political situation. Born in Omagh, County Tyrone, and educated in Northern Ireland, Friel has lived in the Republic since 1967. His first success was with *Philadelphia, Here I Come!* (1964), which examines the issue of emigration in the 1960s. Later plays include the critically acclaimed *Dancing at Lughnasa* (1990).

Friendly Islands another name for ▷Tonga, a country in the Pacific.

friendly society association that makes provisions for the needs of sickness and old age by money payments. In 1995 there were 1,013 orders and branches (17 orders, 996 branches), 18 collecting societies, 294 other centralized societies, 72 benevolent societies, 2,271 working men's clubs, and 131 specially authorized societies in the UK. Among the largest are the National Deposit, Odd Fellows, Foresters, and Hearts of Oak. In the USA similar 'fraternal insurance' bodies are known as **benefit societies**; they include the Modern Woodmen of America (1883) and the Fraternal Order of Eagles (1898).

Friends of the Earth (FoE or FOE) largest international network of environmental pressure groups, established in the UK in 1971, that aims to protect the environment and to promote rational and sustainable use of the Earth's resources. It campaigns on such issues as acid rain; air, sea, river, and land pollution; recycling; disposal of toxic wastes; nuclear power and renewable energy; the destruction of rainforests; pesticides; and agriculture. FoE is represented in 52 countries.

Related Web site: **Friends of the Earth Home Page** http://www.foe.co.uk/

Friends, Society of (or **Quakers**) Christian Protestant sect founded by George ▷Fox in England in the 17th century. They were persecuted for their nonviolent activism, and many emigrated to form communities elsewhere; for example, in Pennsylvania and New England. The worldwide movement had about 219,800 members in 1997. Their worship stresses meditation and the freedom of all to take an active part in the service (called a meeting, held in a meeting house). They have no priests or ministers.

Related Web site: **Religious Society of Friends** http://www.quaker.org/

Friesland maritime province on the northeast side of the IJsselmeer, north Netherlands, which includes the Frisian Islands and land reclaimed from the former Zuider Zee; area 3,400 sq km/1,313 sq mi; population (1997) 615,000 (the inhabitants of the province are called ▷Frisians). The capital is Leeuwarden; other main towns are Drachten, Harlingen, Sneek, and Heerenveen. Small boats are made; agriculture centres on livestock (Friesian cattle, which originated here, and black Friesian horses), dairy products, and arable farming.

frigate bird (or **man-of-war bird**) five species of marine birds belonging to the family Fregatidae, order Pelecaniformes, natives of the tropics. They are black, strongly tinged with brown, with a scarlet pouch. Frigate birds are large, with long tails and wings, and a long hooked beak. They are essentially seabirds, and only come to land during the breeding season. Their chief food is fish.

FRIGATE BIRD A great frigate bird. *Image Bank*

Frigga (or **Frigg**) in Norse mythology, queen of the gods; wife of Odin. Her sons were ▷Balder, the beloved god; Bragi, god of poetry and wisdom; and ▷Thor, god of thunder. She was one of the Aesir, the principal warrior gods who lived in Asgard.

frilled lizard yellowish-brown Australian lizard with a large frill of skin to the sides of the neck and throat. The lizard is about 90 cm/35 in long.

fringe benefit in employment, payment in kind over and above wages and salaries. These may include a pension, subsidized lunches, company car, favourable loan facilities, and health insurance. Fringe benefits may, in part, be subject to income tax.

fringe theatre productions that are anti-establishment or experimental, and performed in converted or informal venues (warehouses, pubs), in contrast to subsidized or mainstream commercial theatre. In the UK, the term originated in the 1960s from the activities held on the 'fringe' of the Edinburgh Festival. The US equivalent is off-off-Broadway (off-Broadway is mainstream theatre that is not on Broadway).

Frink, Elisabeth (1930–1993) English sculptor. She created rugged, naturalistic bronzes, mainly based on human and animal forms; for example, the *Alcock Brown Memorial* (1962) for Manchester airport, *In Memoriam* (heads), and *Running Man* (1980).

Frisch, Ragnar Anton Kittil (1895–1973) Norwegian economist. He shared the first Nobel Prize for Economics in 1969 with Jan ▷Tinbergen for his pioneering work in ▷econometrics (the application of mathematical and statistical methods in economics).

Frisian (or Friesian) member of a Germanic people of northwestern Europe (Friesland and the Frisian Islands). In Roman times they occupied the coast of Holland and may have taken part in the Anglo-Saxon invasions of Britain. Their language is closely akin to Anglo-Saxon, with which it forms the Anglo-Frisian branch of the West Germanic languages, part of the Indo-European family.

Frisian Islands (Dutch *Friesche Eilanden*) chain of low-lying islands 5–32 km/3–20 mi off the northwest coasts of the Netherlands and Germany, with a northerly extension off the west coast of Denmark. They are divided between these three states. They were formed by the natural sinking of the intervening land and are separated from the mainland only by shallow flats (*wadden*). **Texel** is the largest and westernmost island, at the southern end of the chain. Sheep and cattle are raised, and there are a number of small seaside resorts.

fritillary in botany, any of a group of plants belonging to the lily family. The snake's head fritillary (*F. meleagris*) has bell-shaped flowers with purple-chequered markings. (Genus *Fritillaria*, family Liliaceae.)

> **Related Web site: Common Fritillary** http://www.botanical.com/ botanical/mgmh/f/fritil33.html

fritillary in zoology, any of a large grouping of butterflies of the family Nymphalidae. Mostly medium-sized, fritillaries are usually orange and reddish with a black criss-cross pattern or spots above and with silvery spots on the underside of the hindwings.

Friuli-Venezia Giulia
autonomous agricultural and wine-producing region of northeast Italy, bordered to the east by Slovenia, comprising the provinces of Pordenone, Gorizia, Trieste, and Udine; area 7,800 sq km/3,011 sq mi; population (1998) 1,183,900. The most important industrial centres are Udine, which is the region's capital, Gorizia, the ports of ▷Trieste and Monfalcone (dockyards and chemical industries), and Pordenone.

FRITILLARY A Queen of Spain fritillary butterfly *Issoria lathonia. Premaphotos Wildlife*

Frobisher, Martin (*c.* 1535–1594)
English navigator. He made his first voyage to Guinea, West Africa, in 1554. In 1576 he set out in search of the Northwest Passage, and visited Labrador and Frobisher Bay, Baffin Island. Second and third expeditions sailed in 1577 and 1578. Knighted in 1588.

Froebel, Friedrich Wilhelm August (1782–1852)
German educationist. He evolved a new system of education using instructive play, described in *Education of Man* (1826) and other works. In 1836 he founded the first kindergarten (German 'garden for children') in Blankenburg, Germany. He was influenced by the Swiss Johann Pestalozzi.

frog any amphibian of the order Anura (Greek 'tailless'). There are about 24 different families of frog, containing more than 3,800 species. There are no clear rules for distinguishing between frogs and ▷toads.

Frogs usually have squat bodies, with hind legs specialized for jumping, and webbed feet for swimming. Most live in or near water, though as adults they are air-breathing. A few live on land or even in trees. Their colour is usually greenish in the genus *Rana*, but other Ranidae are brightly coloured, for instance black and orange or yellow and white. Many use their long, extensible tongues to capture insects. The eyes are large and bulging. Frogs vary in size from the North American little grass frog *Limnaoedus ocularis*, 12 mm/0.5 in long, to the giant aquatic frog *Telmatobius culeus*, 50 cm/20 in long, of Lake Titicaca, South America. Frogs are widespread, inhabiting all continents except Antarctica, and they have adapted to a range of environments including deserts, forests, grasslands, and even high altitudes, with some species in the Andes and Himalayas existing above 5,000 m/19,600 ft.

Courtship and reproduction In many species the males attract the females in great gatherings, usually by croaking. In some tropical species, the male's inflated vocal sac may exceed the rest of his body in size. Other courtship 'lures' include thumping on the ground and 'dances'.

Some lay eggs in large masses (spawn) in water. The jelly surrounding the eggs provides support and protection and retains warmth. Some South American frogs build mud-pool 'nests', and African tree frogs make foam nests from secreted mucus. In other species, the eggs may be carried in pockets on the mother's back, brooded

FROG Tree frogs have adhesive toe pads that allow them to adhere to the undersides of leaves and crawl up vertical surfaces. Although most tree frogs live and feed in trees, the majority descend to water to breed. *Image Bank*

by the male in his vocal sac or, as with the Eurasian midwife toad *Alytes obstetricans*, wrapped round the male's hind legs until hatching.

Life cycle The tadpoles hatch from the eggs in about a fortnight. At first they are fishlike animals with external gills and a long swimming tail, but no limbs. The first change to take place is the disappearance of the external gills and the development of internal gills, which are still later supplanted by lungs. The hind legs appear before the front legs, and the last change to occur is the diminution and final disappearance of the tail. The tadpole stage lasts about three months. At the end of this time the animal leaves the water. Some species, such as the edible frog, are always aquatic. By autumn the frog grows big and sluggish. It stores fat in a special gland in the abdomen; it is this fat that it lives on during hibernation.

Species Certain species of frog have powerful skin poisons (alkaloids) to deter predators. 'True frogs' are placed in the worldwide family Ranidae, with 800 species, of which the genus *Rana* is the best known. The North American bullfrog *Rana catesbeiana*, with a croak that carries for miles, is able to jump nine times its own length. The flying frogs, genus *Rhacophorus*, of Malaysia, using webbed fore and hind feet, can achieve a 12 m/40 ft glide. The hairy frog *Astylosternus robustus* is found in West Africa; it has long outgrowths on its flanks, which seem to aid respiration. A four-year rainforest study in eastern Madagascar revealed 106 new frog species in 1995. Indian zoologists discovered the first

FRITILLARY The snake's head fritillary *Fritillaria meleagris* (also called the leopard lily and the toad lily) is a plant of damp lowland meadows and pastures, native to Europe. *Premaphotos Wildlife*

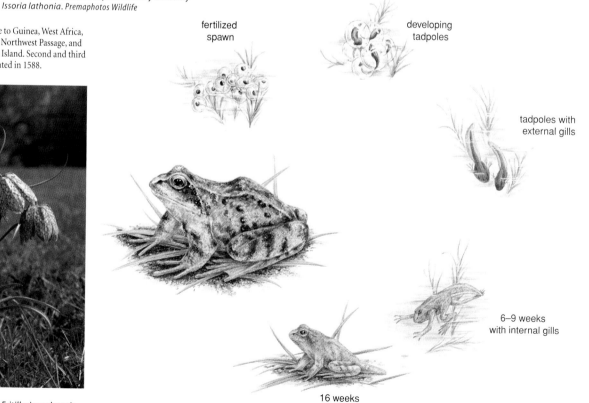

fertilized spawn

developing tadpoles

tadpoles with external gills

6–9 weeks with internal gills

16 weeks

FROG The life cycle of a frog. Frogs lay their eggs (spawn) in fresh, still water. The tadpoles hatch within about two weeks and then over the course of the next three months they grow larger and slowly develop legs and internal gills. By the time they lose their tails they resemble tiny adult frogs and can leave the water.

known leaf-eating frog in 1996, in Tamil Nadu, southern India. *R. hexadactyla* feeds mainly on leaves, flowers, and algae. New species are constantly being discovered. In 1997 a species *Eleutherodactylus pluvicanorus* was discovered in Bolivia; it is 4 cm long and ground-dwelling.

The **common frog** *Rana temporaria* is becoming rare in Britain as small ponds disappear. It hibernates in holes in the ground, and in the early spring it comes above ground to mate. At this season a horny cushion appears on the first finger of the male frog, which may help it to grasp the female during courtship. The eggs are laid in water, and are fertilized as they are laid.

The **marsh frog** *Rana ridibunda* is said to have been first introduced to England in 1935. Its ground colour is like weathered cement with a pattern of square dark brown spots on the legs that remains through all colour changes. When basking in the sun on a grassy bank it assumes a striking green hue. The marsh frog is the largest of all British frogs or toads.

    Related Web site: Whole Frog Project http://george.lbl.gov/ ITG.hm.pg.docs/Whole.Frog/Whole.Frog.html

froghopper (or spittlebug) leaping plant-bug, of the family Cercopidae, in the same order (Homoptera) as leafhoppers and aphids. Froghoppers live by sucking the juice from plants. The pale green larvae protect themselves (from drying out and from predators) by secreting froth ('cuckoo spit') from their anuses.

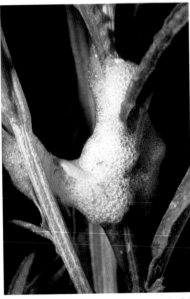

FROGHOPPER Cuckoo spit surrounding a nymph of the froghopper *Philaenus spumarius*. The froth, formed by blowing air through liquid expelled from the insect's anus, hides it from possible predators. Despite this, at least one *Gorytes* species of hunting wasp specializes in extracting these nymphs from their protective froth. *Premaphotos Wildlife*

frogmouth nocturnal bird, related to the nightjar, of which the commonest species, the tawny frogmouth *Podargus strigoides*, is found throughout Australia, including Tasmania. Well camouflaged, it sits and awaits its prey.

Fromm, Erich (1900–1980) German psychoanalyst who moved to the USA in 1933 to escape the Nazis. He believed that human beings experience a separation from nature and from other people which gives them the freedom to decide on the course their lives should take. This gives their lives meaning but also causes anxiety.

> **Erich Fromm**
> *Man always dies before he is fully born.*
> Man for Himself (1947)

frond large leaf or leaflike structure; in ferns it is often pinnately divided. The term is also applied to the leaves of palms and less commonly to the plant bodies of certain seaweeds, liverworts, and lichens.

Fronde French revolts 1648–53 against the administration of the chief minister ▷Mazarin during Louis XIV's minority. In 1648–49 the Paris parlement attempted to limit the royal power, its leaders were arrested, Paris revolted, and the rising was suppressed by the royal army under Louis II Condé. In 1650 Condé led a new revolt of the nobility, but this was suppressed by 1653. The defeat of the Fronde enabled Louis to establish an absolutist monarchy in the later 17th century.

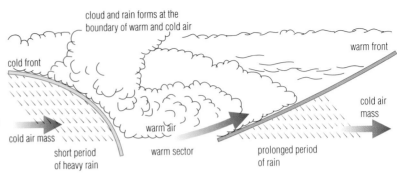

FRONT The boundaries between two air masses of different temperature and humidity. A warm front is when warm air displaces cold air; if cold air replaces warm air, it is a cold front.

cloud and rain forms at the boundary of warm and cold air

cold front / warm front / warm air / cold air mass / cold air mass / short period of heavy rain / warm sector / prolonged period of rain

front in meteorology, the boundary between two air masses of different temperature or humidity. A **cold front** marks the line of advance of a cold air mass from below, as it displaces a warm air mass; a **warm front** marks the advance of a warm air mass as it rises up over a cold one. Frontal systems define the weather of the mid-latitudes, where warm tropical air is continually meeting cold air from the poles.

Warm air, being lighter, tends to rise above the cold; its moisture is carried upwards and usually falls as rain or snow, hence the changeable weather conditions at fronts. Fronts are rarely stable and move with the air mass. An **occluded front** is a composite form, where a cold front catches up with a warm front and merges with it.

frost condition of the weather that occurs when the air temperature is below freezing, 0°C/32°F. Water in the atmosphere is deposited as ice crystals on the ground or exposed objects. As cold air is heavier than warm, ground frost is more common than hoar frost, which is formed by the condensation of water particles in the same way that ▷dew collects.

Frost, Robert Lee (1874–1963) US poet. His accessible, colloquial blank verse, often flavoured with New England speech patterns, is written with an individual voice and penetrating vision. His poems include 'Mending Wall' ('Something there is that does not love a wall'), 'The Road Not Taken', and 'Stopping by Woods on a Snowy Evening' and are collected in *Complete Poems* (1951).

> **Robert Frost**
> *We dance round in a ring and suppose, / But the Secret sits in the middle and knows.*
> 'The Secret Sits'

    Related Web site: Complete Works of Robert Frost http://www.bartleby.com/155/index.html

frostbite the freezing of skin or flesh, with formation of ice crystals leading to tissue damage. The treatment is slow warming of the affected area; for example, by skin-to-skin contact or with lukewarm water. Frostbitten parts are extremely vulnerable to infection, with the risk of gangrene.

frost hollow depression or steep-sided valley in which cold air collects on calm, clear nights. Under clear skies, heat is lost rapidly from ground surfaces, causing the air above to cool and flow downhill (as katabatic wind) to collect in valley bottoms. Fog may form under these conditions and, in winter, temperatures may be low enough to cause frost.

frost shattering alternative name for ▷freeze-thaw.

FRS abbreviation for Fellow of the ▷Royal Society.

fructose $C_6H_{12}O_6$ a sugar that occurs naturally in honey, the nectar of flowers, and many sweet fruits; it is commercially prepared from glucose.

    It is a monosaccharide, whereas the more familiar cane or beet sugar is a disaccharide, made up of two monosaccharide units: fructose and glucose. It is sweeter than cane sugar and can be used to sweeten foods for people with diabetes.

fruit (from Latin *frui* 'to enjoy') in botany, the ripened ovary in flowering plants that develops from one or more seeds or carpels and encloses one or more seeds. Its function is to protect the seeds during their development and to aid in their dispersal. Fruits are often edible, sweet, juicy, and colourful. When eaten they provide vitamins, minerals, and enzymes, but little protein. Most fruits are borne by perennial plants.

Fruits are divided into three agricultural categories on the basis of the climate in which they grow. **Temperate fruits** require a cold season for satisfactory growth; the principal temperate fruits are apples, pears, plums, peaches, apricots, cherries, and soft fruits, such as strawberries. **Subtropical fruits** require warm conditions but can survive light frosts; they include oranges and other citrus fruits, dates, pomegranates, and avocados. **Tropical fruits** cannot tolerate temperatures that drop close to freezing point; they include bananas, mangoes, pineapples, papayas, and litchis. Fruits can also be divided botanically into **dry** (such as the ▷capsule, ▷follicle, ▷schizocarp, ▷nut, ▷caryopsis, pod or legume, lomentum, and ▷achene) and those that become **fleshy** (such as the ▷drupe and the ▷berry). The fruit structure consists of the ▷pericarp or fruit wall, which is usually divided into a number of distinct layers. Sometimes parts other than the ovary are incorporated into the fruit structure, resulting in a false fruit or ▷pseudocarp, such as the apple and strawberry. True fruits include the tomato, orange, melon, and banana. Fruits may be dehiscent, which open to shed their seeds, or indehiscent, which remain unopened and are dispersed as a single unit. Simple fruits (for example, peaches) are derived from a single ovary, whereas compositae or multiple fruits (for example, blackberries) are formed from the ovaries of a number of flowers. In ordinary usage, 'fruit' includes only sweet, fleshy items; it excludes many botanical fruits such as acorns, bean pods, thistledown, and cucumbers.

Methods of seed dispersal Efficient seed dispersal is essential to avoid overcrowding and enable plants to colonize new areas; the natural function of a fruit is to aid in the dissemination of the seeds which it contains. A great variety of dispersal mechanisms exist: winged fruits are commonly formed by trees, such as ash and elm, where they are in an ideal position to be carried away by the wind; some wind-dispersed fruits, such as clematis and cotton, have plumes of hairs; others are extremely light, like the poppy, in which the capsule acts like a pepperpot and shakes out the seeds as it is blown about by the wind. Some fruits float on water; the coconut can be dispersed across oceans by means of its buoyant fruit. Geraniums, gorse, and squirting cucumbers have explosive mechanisms, by which seeds are forcibly shot out at dehiscence. Animals often act as dispersal agents either by carrying hooked or sticky fruits (burs) attached to their bodies, or by eating succulent fruits, the seeds passing through the alimentary canal unharmed.

Recorded world fruit production in the mid-1980s was approximately 300 million tonnes per year. Technical advances in

ROBERT FROST US poet Robert Frost. At a time when other US poets were turning to European culture for inspiration, Frost turned to New England everyday life to develop a home-grown American poetic idiom. *Archive Photos*

FRUIT Fresh fruit and vegetables contain many of the essential dietary minerals and vitamins that we require to stay healthy. *Corel*

storage and transport have made tropical fruits available to consumers in temperate areas, and fresh temperate fruits available all year in major markets.

frustum (from Latin 'a piece cut off') in geometry, a 'slice' taken out of a solid figure by a pair of parallel planes. A conical frustum, for example, resembles a cone with the top cut off. The volume and area of a frustum are calculated by subtracting the volume and area of the 'missing' piece from those of the whole figure.

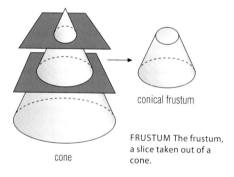

conical frustum

FRUSTUM The frustum, a slice taken out of a cone.

cone

Fry, Elizabeth (1780–1845) Born Elizabeth Gurney. English Quaker philanthropist. From 1813 she began to visit and teach the women in Newgate Prison who lived with their children in terrible conditions. She formed an association for the improvement of conditions for female prisoners in 1817, and worked with her brother, **Joseph Gurney** (1788–1847), on an 1819 report on prison reform. She was a pioneer for higher nursing standards and the education of working women.

Fry, (Edwin) Maxwell (1899–1987) English architect and town-planner. He was a pioneer of the ▷Modern Movement in Britain. Sun House, Hampstead, London (1935), with its horizontally banded windows and white stucco finish is typical of his work. Fry worked in partnership with Walter ▷Gropius 1934–36, and with Denys ▷Lasdun (among others) 1951–58. He was ▷Le Corbusier's senior architect at Chandigarh, India, 1951–54.

Fry, Roger (Eliot) (1866–1934) English artist and art critic. An admirer of the French painter Paul Cézanne, he coined the term and championed ▷post-Impressionism in Britain, expounding the theory of 'significant form' and colour as the criteria for true art. He was a member of the Bloomsbury Group and founded the ▷Omega Workshops to improve design and to encourage young artists. His critical essays, which were very influential in the 1920s and 1930s, are contained in *Vision and Design* (1920).

f-stop in photography, another name for ▷f-number.

ft symbol for ▷foot, a measure of distance.

FT Index abbreviation for ▷Financial Times Index, a list of leading share prices.

Fuad two kings of Egypt, including:

Fuad I (1868–1936) King of Egypt from 1923. Son of the Khedive Ismail, he succeeded his elder brother Hussein Kamel as sultan of Egypt in 1917. Egypt was declared independent in 1922 and the promulgation of the 1923 constitution enabled him to assume the title of king. His pretension to be king of Sudan as well was not realized. Opposed to the constitution, he favoured the restoration of the autocracy of the ruling family and was almost constantly in conflict with the nationalists, represented by the Wafd.

fuchsia any shrub or ▷herbaceous plant of a group belonging to the evening-primrose family. Species are native to South and Central America and New Zealand, and bear red, purple, or pink bell-shaped flowers that hang downwards. (Genus *Fuchsia*, family Onagraceae.)

fuel any source of heat or energy, embracing the entire range of materials that burn in air (combustibles). A **nuclear fuel** is any material that produces energy by nuclear fission in a nuclear reactor. ▷Fossil fuels are formed from the fossilized remains of plants and animals. See also Fuels of the Future Focus Feature on pp. 368–369.

fuel-air explosive warhead containing a highly flammable petroleum and oxygen mixture; when released over a target, this mixes with the oxygen in the atmosphere and produces a vapour which, when ignited, causes a blast approximately five times more powerful than conventional high explosives.

fuel cell cell converting chemical energy directly to electrical energy. It works on the same principle as a battery but is continually fed with fuel, usually hydrogen. Fuel cells are silent and reliable (no moving parts) but expensive to produce.

Hydrogen is passed over an ▷electrode (usually nickel or platinum) containing a ▷catalyst, which strips electrons off the atoms. These pass through an external circuit while hydrogen ions (charged atoms) pass through an ▷electrolyte to another electrode, over which oxygen is passed. Water is formed at this electrode (as a by-product) in a chemical reaction involving electrons, hydrogen ions, and oxygen atoms. If the spare heat also produced is used for hot water and space heating, 80% efficiency in fuel is achieved.

Related Web site: Batteries Not Included http://whyfiles.news.wisc. edu/shorties/fuel_cell.html

fuel injection injecting fuel directly into the cylinders of an internal combustion engine, instead of by way of a carburettor. It is the standard method used in ▷diesel engines, and is now becoming standard for petrol engines. In the diesel engine, oil is injected into the hot compressed air at the top of the second piston stroke and explodes to drive the piston down on its power stroke. In the petrol engine, fuel is injected into the cylinder at the start of the first induction stroke of the ▷four-stroke cycle.

Fuentes, Carlos (1928–) Mexican novelist, lawyer, and diplomat. His first novel *La región más transparente/Where the Air Is Clear* (1958) encompasses the history of the country from the Aztecs to the present day.

Fugard, Athol Harold Lanigan (1932–) South African dramatist, director, and actor. His plays often deal with the effects of apartheid. His first successful play was *The Blood Knot* (1961), which was produced in London and New York. This was followed by *Hello and Goodbye* (1965) and *Boesman and Lena* (1969). Other plays include *Statements After an Arrest under the Immorality Act* (1973), *A Lesson from Aloes* (1980), *Master Harold and the Boys* (1982), *A Place with the Pigs* (1987), *My Children! My Africa!* (1989), and *The Township Plays* (1993).

fugue (Latin 'flight') in music, a contrapuntal form with two or more subjects (principal melodies) for a number of parts, which enter in succession in direct imitation of each other or transposed to a higher or lower key, and may be combined in augmented form (larger note values). It represents the highest form of contrapuntal ingenuity in works such as Johann Sebastian Bach's *Das musikalische Opfer/The Musical Offering* (1747), on a theme of Frederick II of Prussia, and *Die Kunst der Fuge/The Art of the Fugue* published in 1751, and Beethoven's *Grosse Fuge/Great Fugue* for string quartet (1825–26).

Führer (or Fuehrer) (German 'leader') title adopted by Adolf ▷Hitler as leader of the Nazi Party.

Fujian (or Fukien) maritime province of southeast China, lying opposite Taiwan, bounded to the southwest by Guangdong, to the west and northwest by Jiangxi, to the northeast by Zhejiang, and to the southeast by the Taiwan Strait on the China Sea; area 123,100 sq km/47,500 sq mi; population (1994) 32,610,000. The main cities are ▷Fuzhou (capital), Xiamen, Zhangzhou, and Nanping. The main industries are steel-rolling, electrical goods, tourism, handicrafts, and leather goods. Agricultural products are rice, sweet potatoes, sugar, special aromatic teas, tobacco, timber, and citrus fruit.

Fujimori, Alberto (1938–) Peruvian politician, president 1990-2000. As leader of the newly formed Cambio 90 (Change 90), he campaigned on a pro-market reformist ticket and defeated his more experienced Democratic Front opponent. Lacking an assembly majority and faced with increasing opposition to his policies, he closed congress and imposed military rule in early 1992, to fight the ▷Sendero Luminoso (Shining Path) guerrillas and the left-wing Movimento Revolucionario Túpac Amarú (MRTA; in English the Túpac Amarú Revolutionary Movement). In 1993 a plebiscite narrowly approved his constitutional reform proposals, allowing him to achieve re-election in 1995. In May 2000, he was re-elected for a constitutionally unsound third term. Within months his regime collapsed, however, after the head of intelligence, Vladimiro Montesinos, was involved in a bribery scandal, and he resigned in November.

Fuji, Mount Japanese volcano and highest peak, on Honshu Island, near Tokyo; height 3,778 m/12,400 ft. Extinct since 1707, it has a ▷Shinto shrine and a weather station on its summit. Fuji has long been revered for its picturesque cone-shaped crater peak, and figures prominently in Japanese art, literature, and religion.

Related Web site: Introduction to Mt Fuji Climbing http://www. sunplus.com/fuji/scott/scott2-1.html

Fujiwara in Japanese history, the ruling clan 858–1185. During that period (the latter part of the ▷Heian), the office of emperor became merely ceremonial, with power exercised by chancellors and regents, who were all Fujiwara and whose daughters in every generation married into the imperial family. There was a Fujiwara in Japanese government as recently as during World War II.

Fujiyama another name for Mount Fuji (see ▷Fuji, Mount).

Fukien alternative transcription of ▷Fujian, a province of southeast China.

Fula West African empire founded by people of predominantly Fulani extraction. The Fula conquered the Hausa states in the 19th century.

Fulani member of a West African people from the southern Sahara and Sahel. The Fulani language is divided into four dialects and belongs to the West Atlantic branch of the Niger-Congo family; it has more than 10 million speakers. Traditionally they are nomadic pastoralists and traders; many are now settled agriculturalists or live in cites. Fulani groups are found in Senegal, Guinea, Mali, Burkina Faso, Niger, Nigeria, Chad, and Cameroon.

Fulbright, (James) William (1905–1995) US Democratic politician. A US senator 1945–75, he was responsible for the Fulbright Act 1946, which provided grants for thousands of Americans to study abroad and for overseas students to study in the USA. Fulbright chaired the Senate Foreign Relations Committee 1959–74, and was a strong internationalist and supporter of the United Nations.

A moderate dove Fulbright was a member of the US House of Representatives 1942–45 before becoming senator for Arkansas. After World War II he anticipated the creation of the UN, calling for US membership in an international peacekeeping body. He was an advocate of military and economic aid to Western nations but a powerful critic of US involvement in the Vietnam War and other military ventures against small countries.

Fuller, (Richard) Buckminster (1895–1983) US architect, engineer, and social philosopher. He embarked on an unorthodox career in an attempt to maximize energy resources through improved technology. In 1947 he invented the lightweight geodesic dome, a hemispherical ▷space-frame of triangular components linked by rods, independent of buttress or vault and capable of covering large-span areas. Within 30 years over 50,000 had been built. See picture on p. 370.

Related Web site: Buckminster Fuller Virtual Institute http://gate.cruzio.com/~joemoore/ index.html

> **Buckminster Fuller**
> *Now there is one outstandingly important fact regarding Spaceship Earth, and that is that no instruction book came with it.*
> Operating Manual for Spaceship Earth

Fuller, Roy (Broadbent) (1912–1991) English poet and novelist. His early verse, including the collections *Poems* (1940) and *The Middle of a War* (1944), was concerned with social problems. With *Counterparts*

(continued on p. 370)

A SOLAR-POWERED VEHICLE in Palm Springs, California, USA. Solar energy is a renewable energy source that is increasingly being harnessed for a variety of applications, including domestic heating systems, the powering of space shuttles and satellites, and even, as here, in some cars. *Anthony Cooper, Ecoscene*

Fuels of the Future

by Sarah Chester

Since the Industrial Revolution in the 18th century, people in the Western world have needed fossil fuels (coal, oil, and gas) to run the many machines used in industry and everyday life. However, preparing for the demise of 'the age of oil' is becoming increasingly important, as concerns about limited resources of fossil fuels and the environmental consequences of burning them become pressing. Ways to increase efficiency in the use of energy and alternative energy sources are being developed.

why is there a need for alternative energy?

Although technologies for finding and extracting fossil fuels are advancing all the time, there is still only a finite supply.

Burning any type of fossil fuel leads to environmental pollution, such as increased levels of carbon dioxide in the atmosphere, which most scientists believe is a major cause of **global warming**. Fossil-fuel combustion has increased atmospheric concentrations of carbon dioxide by more than 25% since pre-industrial times. In addition, burning fossil fuels at high temperatures, such as in boilers, jets, or car engines, allows reaction of oxygen with nitrogen in the atmosphere, leading to the formation of nitrogen oxides. Nitrogen oxides, along with sulphur dioxide, another by-product of burning fossil fuels, dissolve in rainwater, producing nitric acids and sulphuric acids, which are components of **acid rain**. Both nitrogen oxides and sulphur dioxide are poisonous to humans, and **acid rain** destroys buildings, forests, and lakes.

Nuclear power is initially less polluting, as it does not produce any greenhouse gases, sulphur, or nitrogen oxides. However, the radioactivity from its waste products lives on for hundreds of years, and many people feel that the potential health risks resulting from radiation escaping from nuclear power stations by accident are unacceptable.

energy efficiency

To improve fuel economy and to lower emissions, advances are being made in energy efficiency. The car industry has been investigating ways to reduce the emissions of the internal combustion engine. One of the products of their research is the exhaust gas recirculation valve. This valve sends some of the exhaust gas back into the engine cylinders, thereby reducing combustion temperature and consequently the emission of nitrogen oxides.

Other new technologies include **gasoline direct injection**. It has been found that fuel is burned more completely if it is injected directly into the engine cylinder. More complete combustion leads to lower emissions and little or no nitrogen oxides due to the lower combustion temperatures.

However, because these developments still involve the use of fossil fuels, they can only reduce pollution rather than eliminate it. Alternative methods of automotive power are being researched. An exciting development is the possibility of installing **fuel cells** in electric vehicles. Fuel cells are extremely energy efficient and clean. They have been in existence for over 150 years and have provided electricity on spacecraft since the 1960s. Fuel cells are similar to batteries in that they convert chemical energy into an electric current, but, unlike batteries, they are endlessly rechargeable. They work by means of the reaction of hydrogen with oxygen from the air in a chemical medium known as an electrolyte, which generates electricity. The only by-product from this reaction is water. As hydrogen in air is highly explosive, it is potentially very dangerous to have a tank of hydrogen gas in a car, so research is underway into methods of extracting hydrogen from other chemicals, including methanol (a type of alcohol), for use in fuel cells.

Energy efficiency is also being increased in other industries, notably **electricity generation**. Most electricity power plants require steam under pressure to rotate a turbine. This activates a generator, producing electricity. Much of the steam is still produced by boiling water, heated by burning fossil fuels. More energy-efficient ways of rotating turbines are now in use, including gas turbines. Gas turbines work by burning a fuel in air, producing a high-temperature, high-pressure gas. The gas is forced out of the combustor and pushes against the turbine blades, causing them to rotate and produce electricity. Turbines are now being developed that use natural gas as the fuel.

WIND GENERATORS in Andalusia, Spain. Turbines such as these have the potential to generate huge amounts of electricity by harnessing the power of the wind. However, wind farms are thought by some people to spoil the landscape and create an unpleasant noise. *Genevieve Leaper, Ecoscene*

renewable energy

The need to reduce emissions of **greenhouse gases** has been recognized globally, and it is hoped that renewable energy sources will replace fossil fuels in the future. Renewable energy is dependent on sources of natural energy in our environment, such as sunshine, wind, movement of water, and the internal heat of the Earth. As these sources are constantly replenished, they will last for millions of years. However, generators for renewable sources are expensive to build and can themselves have a negative effect on the environment. In the UK, approximately 2% of electricity is currently derived from renewable energy.

geothermal energy

Although this type of energy is not strictly renewable, as the supply from geothermal wells will eventually run out, electricity generation can be made more efficient and cleaner by using **steam** produced from reservoirs of hot water found several miles underneath the Earth's surface.

hydroelectric power

The conversion of energy from flowing water into electricity is known as hydroelectric power (or hydropower). The most common type of hydropower plant uses a dam on a river to store water in a reservoir. Water is released from the reservoir to the turbine, thus rotating it and activating the generator. However, there are concerns about the damage that hydropower can cause to river habitats and freshwater fish populations, and vegetation building up behind dams may actually release large amounts of carbon dioxide into the atmosphere.

wind power

Wind turbines, grouped together in windy areas, could theoretically produce as much as 20% of the UK's electricity requirements. Wind power is clean and economically competitive, but there are concerns about its environmental impact. Some people consider wind turbines to be an eyesore on the local landscape – they are inevitably sited on prominent ridges and hills, which are usually in attractive countryside. There have also been concerns about the noise generated by the turbines, and the blades are thought to kill thousands of birds every year.

solar energy

In recent years, large-scale 'solar thermal' plants have been set up in places that receive plenty of sunshine. These focus the Sun's rays so as to heat water and produce steam for electricity generation. Even in the UK, not famed for its sunny climate, solar energy is slowly becoming more popular, and passive solar designs, which use large south-facing glazed areas to trap the solar heat, are commonplace in modern offices and houses. **Photovoltaic cells** use solar energy to generate electricity through chemical reactions. Mainly used only for powering space satellites, these cells are becoming less expensive and are increasingly being used worldwide in rural areas where there is no grid electricity.

biomass energy

By using biomass energy (the animal and plant resources in the environment), we have the potential to reduce greenhouse gas emissions by replacing fossil fuel use, to recycle more water and nutrients, and to limit pollution. There are several sources of biomass energy, including fumes from domestic and industrial wastes at landfill sites; the combustion of biomass, such as the use of bagasse (residue from the extraction of sugar) by the sugar industry to produce heat and electricity; the planting of **biomass feedstocks** (fast-growing, carbon-dioxide absorbing trees and grasses) to replace those used for combustion, thus counteracting carbon dioxide emissions; the production of carbon-rich efficient fuel by heating biomass feedstocks in the absence of oxygen; the use of **bio-diesel** (an alternative fuel made directly from crops such as rapeseed, sunflower, and soya, or by recycling cooking oil). Bio-diesel is not without emissions but has far less of an impact upon the environment than petroleum-based diesel.

However, the global biomass industry is currently underdeveloped due to the high costs involved in setting up a biomass business, along with the lack of public and political awareness of the potential of biofuels as a cleaner energy source.

alternatives for the future

The use of fossil fuels continues to shape our social, economic, and political outlook on the world, and also, importantly, attitudes to our environment. The effects of pollution from fossil fuel combustion are in evidence everywhere – from global warming to acid rain. Many energy-efficient systems and alternative energy sources are now being embraced, although these are not without their own issues. It is clear that the global advantages of alternative energy sources far outweigh any local disadvantages, and there is a growing need for mankind to satisfy its energy needs in the future by balanced use of renewable sources.

OIL Waste gases are flared off into the twilight sky above an oil refinery in Michigan, USA. Oil was first produced in the state as early as 1886, although production was at its height between 1925 and 1955. Since then, the quantity of oil obtained from the wells has drastically declined. © *Image Bank*

BUCKMINSTER FULLER Buckminster Fuller pictured in front of a geodesic dome, c. 1960. See entry on p. 367. *Image Bank*

(*continued from p. 367*)

(1954), his work became more personal and allusive. His novels are particularly concerned with mental turmoil and difficult relationships: they include *Image of a Society* (1956), *My Child, My Sister* (1965), and *The Carnal Island* (1970). *The Strange and the Good: Collected Memoirs* was published in 1989.

fullerene form of carbon, discovered in 1985, based on closed cages of carbon atoms. The molecules of the most symmetrical of the fullerenes are called ▷buckminsterfullerenes (or buckyballs). They are perfect spheres made up of 60 carbon atoms linked together in 12 pentagons and 20 hexagons fitted together like those of a spherical football. Other fullerenes, with 28, 32, 50, 70, and 76 carbon atoms, have also been identified.

Fullerenes can be made by arcing electricity between carbon rods. They may also occur in candle flames and in clouds of interstellar gas. Fullerene chemistry may turn out to be as important as organic chemistry based on the benzene ring. Already, new molecules based on the buckyball enclosing a metal atom, and 'buckytubes' (cylinders of carbon atoms arranged in hexagons), have been made. They were proved to be 200 times tougher than any other known fibre by Israeli and US materials scientists in 1998. Applications envisaged include using the new molecules as lubricants, semiconductors, and superconductors, and as the starting point for making new drugs.
Related Web site: Nobel Prize in Chemistry 1999 http://www.nobel.se/chemistry/laureates/1999/illpres/index.html

fuller's earth soft, greenish-grey rock resembling clay, but without clay's plasticity. It is formed largely of clay minerals, rich in montmorillonite, but a great deal of silica is also present. Its absorbent properties make it suitable for removing oil and grease, and it was formerly used for cleaning fleeces ('fulling'). It is still used in the textile industry, but its chief application is in the purification of oils. Beds of fuller's earth are found in the southern USA, Germany, Japan, and the UK.

FULLER'S EARTH The Bentonite Hills in Capitol Reef National Park, Utah, USA, have a landscape quite unlike any other within the park. The well-drained fuller's earth soils are capable of supporting only a few hardy examples of the resident fauna and flora in an area where aridity is already extreme. *Premaphotos Wildlife*

fulmar any of several species of petrels of the family Procellariidae, which are similar in size and colour to herring gulls. The northern fulmar *Fulmarus glacialis* is found in the North Atlantic and visits land only to nest, laying a single egg.

fulminate any salt of fulminic (cyanic) acid (HOCN), the chief ones being silver and mercury. The fulminates detonate (are exploded by a blow); see ▷detonator.

fumitory any of a group of plants native to Europe and Asia. The common fumitory (*F. officinalis*) grows to 50 cm/20 in and produces pink flowers tipped with blackish red; it has been used in medicine for stomach and liver complaints. (Genus *Fumeria*, family Fumariaceae.)
Related Web site: Fumitory http://www.botanical.com/botanical/mgmh/f/fumito36.html

Funchal capital and chief port of the Portuguese island of Madeira, on the south coast; population (1991) 109,900. Tourism and Madeira wine are the main industries.

function in computing, a small part of a program that supplies a specific value – for example, the square root of a specified number, or the current date. Most programming languages incorporate a number of built-in functions; some allow programmers to write their own. A function may have one or more arguments (the values on which the function operates). A **function key** on a keyboard is one that, when pressed, performs a designated task, such as ending a program.

function in mathematics, a function f is a non-empty set of ordered pairs $(x, f(x))$ of which no two can have the same first element. Hence, if $f(x) = x^2$ two ordered pairs are $(-2,4)$ and $(2,4)$. The set of all first elements in a function's ordered pairs is called the **domain**; the set of all second elements is the **range**. In the algebraic expression

$$y = 4x^3 + 2$$

the dependent variable y is a function of the independent variable x, generally written as $f(x)$.

functional group in chemistry, a small number of atoms in an arrangement that determines the chemical properties of the group and of the molecule to which it is attached (for example, the carboxyl group COOH, or the amine group NH_2). Organic compounds can be considered as structural skeletons, with a high carbon content, with functional groups attached.

Functionalism in architecture and design, the principle of excluding everything that serves no practical purpose. Central to 20th-century ▷modernism, the Functionalist ethic developed as a reaction against the 19th-century practice of imitating and combining earlier styles. Its finest achievements are in the realms of industrial architecture and office furnishings.

fundamental in musical acoustics, the lowest ▷harmonic of a musical tone, corresponding to the audible pitch.

fundamental constant physical quantity that is constant in all circumstances throughout the whole universe. Examples are the electric charge of an electron, the speed of light, Planck's constant, and the gravitational constant.

fundamental forces see ▷forces, fundamental.

fundamentalism in religion, an emphasis on basic principles or articles of faith. **Christian fundamentalism** emerged in the USA just after World War I (as a reaction to theological modernism and the historical criticism of the Bible) and insisted on belief in the literal truth of everything in the Bible. **Islamic fundamentalism** insists on strict observance of Muslim Shari'a law.

fundamental particle another term for ▷elementary particle.

fungicide any chemical ▷pesticide used to prevent fungus diseases in plants and animals. Inorganic and organic compounds containing sulphur are widely used.

fungus (plural **fungi**) any of a unique group of organisms that includes moulds, yeasts, rusts, smuts, mildews, mushrooms, and

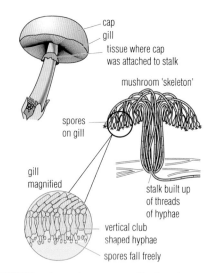

FUNGUS Fungi grow from spores as fine threads, or hyphae. Mushrooms and toadstools are the fruiting bodies formed by the hyphae. Gills beneath the caps of these aerial structures produce masses of spores.

toadstools. There are around 70,000 species of fungi known to science (1998), though there may be as many as 1.5 million actually in existence. They are not considered to be plants for three main reasons: they have no leaves or roots; they contain no chlorophyll (green colouring) and are therefore unable to make their own food by ▷photosynthesis; and they reproduce by ▷spores. Some fungi are edible but many are highly poisonous; they often cause damage and sometimes disease to the organic matter they live and feed on, but some fungi are exploited in the production of food and drink (for example, yeasts in baking and brewing) and in medicine (for example, penicillin).
Related Web site: Fungi http://www.herb.lsa.umich.edu/kidpage/factindx.htm

funk dance music of black US origin, relying on heavy percussion in polyrhythmic patterns. Leading exponents include James Brown and George Clinton.

fur the ▷hair of certain animals. Fur is an excellent insulating material and so has been used as clothing. This is, however, vociferously criticized by many groups on humane grounds, as the methods of breeding or trapping animals are often cruel. Mink, chinchilla, and sable are among the most valuable, the wild furs being finer than the farmed. Fur such as mink is made up of a soft, thick, insulating layer called underfur and a top layer of longer, lustrous guard hairs.

Furs have been worn since prehistoric times and have long been associated with status and luxury (ermine traditionally worn by royalty, for example), except by certain ethnic groups like the Inuit. The fur trade had its origin in North America, where in the late 17th century the Hudson's Bay Company was established. The chief centres of the fur trade are New York, London, St Petersburg, and Kastoria in Greece. It is illegal to import furs or skins of endangered species listed by ▷CITES (such as the leopard). Many synthetic fibres are widely used as substitutes.

In the UK, the number of mink farms decreased to fewer than 20 in 1997.

Furies (or Erinyes) in Greek mythology, spirits of vengeance, principally of murder within the family but also of other breaches of natural order such as filial disobedience, inhospitality, and oath-breaking; they may have been considered the personifications of curses. The Furies were also associated with fertility, and were appeasingly called the ▷Eumenides 'kindly ones'. Represented as winged maidens with serpents twisted in their hair, they inhabited Hades, the underworld.

Fundamental Constants

Physical constants, or fundamental constants, are physical quantities that are constant in all circumstances throughout the whole universe.

Constant	Symbol	Value in SI units
acceleration of free fall	g	9.80665 m s^{-2}
Avogadro's constant	N_A	6.0221367×10^{23} mol^{-1}
Boltzmann's constant	k	1.380658×10^{-23} J K^{-1}
elementary charge	e	$1.60217733 \times 10^{-19}$ C
electronic rest mass	m_e	$9.1093897 \times 10^{-31}$ kg
Faraday's constant	F	9.6485309×10^4 C mol^{-1}
gas constant	R	8.314510 J K^{-1} mol^{-1}
gravitational constant	G	6.672×10^{-11} N m^2 kg^{-2}
Loschmidt's number	N_L	2.686763×10^{25} m^{-3}
neutron rest mass	m_n	$1.6749286 \times 10^{-27}$ kg
Planck's constant	h	$6.6260755 \times 10^{-34}$ J s
proton rest mass	m_p	$1.6726231 \times 10^{-27}$ kg
speed of light in a vacuum	c	2.99792458×10^8 m s^{-1}
standard atmosphere	atm	1.01325×10^5 Pa
Stefan–Boltzmann constant	σ	5.67051×10^{-8} W m^{-2} K^{-4}

furlong unit of measurement, originating in Anglo-Saxon England, equivalent to 220 yd (201.168 m).

furnace structure in which fuel such as coal, coke, gas, or oil is burned to produce heat for various purposes. Furnaces are used in conjunction with ▷boilers for heating, to produce hot water, or steam for driving turbines – in ships for propulsion and in power stations for generating electricity. The largest furnaces are those used for smelting and refining metals, such as the ▷blast furnace, electric furnace, and ▷open-hearth furnace.

FURNACE Copper ore is being separated in a furnace at Hidalgo, New Mexico. This reverberatory furnace has a firebox at one end, where flames engulf the copper ore and melt it. The heat removes the impurities in the ore, either as gas or as slag, which rises to the top of the molten metal and is skimmed off. *Image Bank*

furniture movable functional items such as tables, chairs, and beds needed to make a room or a home more comfortable and easier to live and work in. Furniture may be made from a wide variety of materials, including wood, stone, metal, plastic, papier-mâché, glass, cane, and textiles. Styles vary from plain utilitarian to richly ornate, and decoration may be added in the form of carving, inlay, veneer, paint, gilding, or upholstery.

furniture beetle wood-boring beetle. See ▷woodworm.

further education college centre of education for students over school-leaving age that provides courses for skills towards an occupation or trade, and general education at a level below that of a degree course. Further education colleges were removed from local authority control in 1993.

Furtwängler, (Gustav Heinrich Ernst Martin) Wilhelm (1886–1954) German conductor. He was leader of the Berlin Philharmonic Orchestra 1924–54. His interpretations of Wagner, Bruckner, and Beethoven were valued expressions of monumental national grandeur, but he also gave first performances of Bartók, Schoenberg's *Variations for Orchestra* (1928), and Hindemith's opera *Mathis der Maler/Mathis the Painter* (1934), a work implicitly critical of the Nazi regime. He ascended rapidly from theatre to opera orchestras in Mannheim 1915–20 and Vienna, Austria, 1919–24, then to major appointments in Leipzig and Vienna.

furze another name for ▷gorse, a shrub.

fuse in electricity, a wire or strip of metal designed to melt when excessive current passes through. It is a safety device that halts surges of current which would otherwise damage equipment and cause fires. In explosives, a fuse is a cord impregnated with chemicals so that it burns slowly at a predetermined rate. It is used to set off a main explosive charge, sufficient length of fuse being left to allow the person lighting it to get away to safety.

Fuseli, (John) Henry (1741–1825) Born Johann Heinrich Füssli. Swiss-born British Romantic artist. He painted macabre and dreamlike images, such as *The Nightmare* (1781; Institute of Arts, Detroit), which come close in feelings of horror and the unnatural to the English gothic novels of his day. His subjects include scenes from Milton and Shakespeare.

fusel oil liquid with a characteristic unpleasant smell, obtained as a by-product of the distillation of the product of any alcoholic fermentation, and used in paints, varnishes, essential oils, and plastics. It is a mixture of fatty acids, alcohols, and esters.

fusion in music, a combination of styles; the term usually refers to jazz-rock fusion. Jazz trumpeter Miles Davis began to draw on rock music in the late 1960s, and jazz-rock fusion flourished in the 1970s with bands like Weather Report (formed in 1970 in the USA) and musicians like English guitarist John McLaughlin.

fusion in physics, the fusing of the nuclei of light elements, such as hydrogen, into those of a heavier element, such as helium. The resultant loss in their combined mass is converted into energy. Stars and thermonuclear weapons are powered by nuclear fusion.

Very high temperatures and pressures are thought to be required in order for fusion to take place. Under these conditions the atomic nuclei can approach each other at high speeds and overcome the mutual repulsion of their positive charges. At very close range another force, the strong nuclear force, comes into play, fusing the particles together to form a larger nucleus. As fusion is accompanied by the release of large amounts of energy, the process might one day be harnessed to form the basis of commercial energy production. So far no successful fusion reactor – one able to produce the required conditions and contain the reaction – has been built. However, an important step

along the road to fusion power was taken in 1991. In an experiment that lasted 2 seconds, a 1.7 megawatt pulse of power was produced by the Joint European Torus (JET) at Culham, Oxfordshire, UK. This was the first time that a substantial amount of fusion power had been produced in a controlled experiment, as opposed to a bomb. In 1997 JET produced a record 21 megajoule of fusion power, and tested the first large-scale plant of the type needed to supply and process tritium in a future fusion power station.
Related Web site: Fusion http://www.pppl.gov/~rfheeter/

future in business, a contract to buy or sell a specific quantity of a particular commodity or currency (or even a purely notional sum, such as the value of a particular stock index) at a particular date in the future. There is usually no physical exchange between buyer and seller. It is only the difference between the ground value and the market value that changes. Such transactions are a function of the **futures market**.

futures trading buying and selling commodities (usually cereals and metals) at an agreed price for delivery several months ahead. The notional value of the futures contracts traded annually worldwide is $140,000 billion (1994). The volume of crude oil futures and options traded on the New York Mercantile Exchange amounts to 200 million barrels a day, almost four times the amount actually produced.

Futurism avant-garde art movement founded in 1909 that celebrated the dynamism of the modern world. It was chiefly an Italian movement and was mainly expressed in painting, but it also embraced other arts, including literature and music, and it had extensive influence outside Italy, particularly in Russia. In Italy the movement virtually died out during World War I, but in Russia it continued to flourish into the 1920s.
Related Web site: Futurism Menu http://www.milanoweb.com/mazzotta/futurismo/ingindex.html#future

Fuzhou (or **Foochow**; formerly **Minhow**) industrial port and capital of Fujian province, on the Min River in southeast China; population (1994) 1,354,800. It is a centre for shipbuilding and steel production; rice, sugar, tea, and fruit pass through the port. Traditionally renowned for its handicrafts, particularly carving and lacquerware, Fuzhou's industries now include electronics, food-processing, and the manufacture of textiles and building materials. There are joint foreign and Chinese factories.

fuzzy logic in mathematics and computing, a form of knowledge representation suitable for notions (such as 'hot' or 'loud') that cannot be defined precisely but depend on their context. For example, a jug of water may be described as too hot or too cold, depending on whether it is to be used to wash one's face or to make tea.

The central idea of fuzzy logic is **probability of set membership**. For instance, referring to someone 175 cm/5 ft 9 in tall, the statement 'this person is tall' (or 'this person is a member of the set of tall people') might be about 70% true if that person is a man, and about 85% true if that person is a woman.

Fyn (German **Fünen**) island forming part of Denmark and lying between the mainland and Zealand; capital Odense; area 2,976 sq km/1,149 sq mi; population (1995) 467,700.

G

g symbol for ▷**gram**.

GA abbreviation for the state of ▷Georgia, USA.

gabbro mafic (consisting primarily of dark-coloured crystals) igneous rock formed deep in the Earth's crust. It contains pyroxene and calcium-rich feldspar, and may contain small amounts of olivine and amphibole. Its coarse crystals of dull minerals give it a speckled appearance.

Gable, (William) Clark (1901–1960) US actor. A star for more than 30 years, he played a range of hard-boiled, comic, and romantic roles. He won an Academy Award for his performance in Frank Capra's *It Happened One Night* (1934), and starred as Rhett Butler in *Gone With the Wind* (1939).

He started his career as a call boy, toured with the Jewell Players, and appeared on Broadway. His first major film role was in *The Painted Desert* (1931). His other films include *Red Dust* (1932), *Manhattan Melodrama* (1934), *China Seas* (1935), *Mutiny on the Bounty* (1935), *San Francisco* (1936), *Idiot's Delight* (1939), *Mogambo* (1953), *Teacher's Pet* (1958), and *The Misfits* (1961). He was nicknamed the 'King of Hollywood'.

Related Web site: Gable, Clark http://www.reelclassics.com/ Actors/Gable/gable.htm

Gabo, Naum (1890–1977) Adopted name of Naum Neemia Pevsner. Russian-born US abstract sculptor. One of the leading exponents of constructivism, he was one of the first artists to make ▷kinetic sculpture. In later works he often used transparent plastics in works that attempt to define space rather than occupy it, as in *Linear Construction* (1942; Tate Gallery, London).

Gabon see country box.

Gaborone capital of ▷Botswana, mainly an administrative and government-service centre; population (1995 est) 158,000. The city lies at altitude 1000 m/3300 ft and has an airport. Light industries include motor vehicle assembly, textiles, brewing, printing and publishing, and construction. The city developed after 1962 when it replaced Mafikeng as capital in preparation for the country's independence in 1966.

Gabriel In the New Testament, the archangel who foretold the birth of John the Baptist to Zacharias and of Jesus to the Virgin Mary. He is also mentioned in the Old Testament in the book of Daniel. In Muslim belief, Gabriel revealed the Koran to Muhammad and escorted him on his ▷Night Journey.

Gaddafi alternative form of ▷Khaddhafi, Libyan leader.

Gaddi Italian family of artists. **Gaddo** (*c.* 1260–1332) was a painter and mosaic worker, a friend of Cimabue, whose influence has been perceived in the *Coronation of the Virgin with Saints and Angels*, a mosaic in the cathedral at Florence attributed to Gaddo. Other works attributed to him are the mosaics in Santa Maria Maggiore and those of the choir of the old St Peter's, Rome. His son, **Taddeo** (*c.* 1300–1366) was a pupil of Giotto and is considered one of his most important followers. His paintings include the frescoes *Virgin and Child between Four Prophets* and other scenes from the life of the Virgin in the Baroncelli Chapel in Santa Croce at Florence (1332), as well as works at Pisa, Pistoia and in various

galleries. The son of Taddeo, **Agnolo** (died 1396), perhaps trained by his father, was placed on the latter's death in the care of Jacopo del Casentino and Giovanni da Milano. He worked in the Vatican in 1369, probably with his brother Giovanni. Frescoes in Santa Croce depicting the legend of the Cross, and in the cathedral of Prato (1392–95), representing the legends of the Virgin and the Sacred Girdle, are attributed to him. He died while working on an altarpiece for San Miniato. He employed a number of assistants, and Cennino Cennini was among his pupils, embodying the methods of the followers of Giotto in his treatise on art.

gadfly fly that bites cattle, such as a ▷botfly or ▷horsefly.

gadolinium silvery-white metallic element of the lanthanide series, symbol Gd, atomic number 64, relative atomic mass 157.25. It is found in the products of nuclear fission and used in electronic components, alloys, and products needing to withstand high temperatures.

Gadsden Purchase in US history, the purchase of approximately 77,700 sq km/30,000 sq mi in what is now New Mexico and Arizona by the USA in 1853. The land was bought from Mexico for $10 million in a treaty, negotiated by James Gadsden (1788–1858) of South Carolina, to construct a transcontinental railroad route, the Southern Pacific, completed in the 1880s.

Gaelic football see ▷football, Gaelic.

Gaelic language member of the Celtic branch of the Indo-European language family, spoken in Ireland, Scotland, and (until 1974) the Isle of Man. Gaelic has been in decline for several centuries, though efforts are being made to keep it alive, for example by means of the government's Gaelic Broadcasting Fund, established in 1993, which subsidises television and radio programmes in Gaelic for transmission in Scotland.

Related Web site: Gaelic and Gaelic Culture http://sunsite.unc.edu/ gaelic/gaelic.html

Gagarin, Yuri (Alexeyevich) (1934–1968) Soviet cosmonaut who in 1961 became the first human in space aboard the spacecraft *Vostok 1*. Gagarin was born in the Smolensk region. He became a pilot in 1957, and on 12 April 1961 completed one orbit of the Earth, taking 108 minutes from launch to landing. He died in a plane crash while training for the *Soyuz 3* mission.

Related Web site: Gagarin, Yuri http://www.allstar.fiu.edu/ aerojava/gagarin.htm

Gagauz (or **Gagauze**) member of a people of whom 153,000 (90%) live in southern Moldova. Orthodox Christians, they have always been distinct from the Turks, although their language is related. Their origin is unclear, although many migrated to Russia in the late 18th and early 19th centuries as a result of the Russo-Turkish wars and the Turkish oppression of Christians. In 1990, Gagauz separatists unilaterally declared a breakaway republic.

Gaia (or **Ge**) in Greek mythology, the goddess of the Earth. She sprang from primordial Chaos and herself produced Uranus, by whom she was the mother of the Cyclopes and ▷Titans.

Gaia hypothesis theory that the Earth's living and nonliving systems form an inseparable whole that is regulated and kept adapted for life by living organisms themselves. The planet therefore functions as a single organism, or a giant cell. The hypothesis was elaborated by British scientist James Lovelock and first published in 1968.

Related Web site: Earthdance: Living Systems in Evolution http://www.ratical.com/LifeWeb/ Erthdnce/erthdnce.html

Gaidar, Yegor Timurovich (1956–) Russian politician and economist. He served as first deputy prime minister in charge of the economy, then early in 1992 was made acting prime minister – a title that was never confirmed because of the opposition of an increasingly hostile Russian parliament. That opposition grew too strong for his continued tenure of office; President Boris ▷Yeltsin accepted his resignation in December 1992, and he was replaced by Viktor ▷Chernomyrdin. He later returned to the government, again as first deputy prime minister in charge of economic reform 1993–94.

gain in electronics, the ratio of the amplitude of the output signal produced by an amplifier to that of the input signal. In a ▷voltage amplifier the voltage gain is the ratio of the output voltage to the input voltage; in an inverting ▷operational amplifier (op-amp) it is equal to the ratio of the resistance of the feedback resistor to that of the input resistor.

> ### James Ephraim Lovelock
> British scientist
>
> *When I first introduced Gaia, I had vague hopes that it might be denounced from the pulpit and thus made acceptable to my scientific colleagues. As it was, Gaia was embraced by theologians and by a wide range of New Age writers and thinkers but denounced by biologists.*
>
> *Earthwatch* (1992)

YURI GAGARIN Soviet cosmonaut Yuri Gagarin standing in a crowd of people in 1962. *Archive Photos*

Gainsborough, Thomas (1727–1788) English landscape and portrait painter. In 1760 he settled in Bath, where his elegant and subtly characterized society portraits brought great success. In 1774 he went to London, becoming one of the original members of the Royal Academy and the principal rival of Joshua Reynolds. He was one of the first British artists to follow the Dutch example in painting realistic landscapes rather than imaginative Italianate scenery, as in *Mr and Mrs Andrews* (about 1750; National Gallery, London).

Although he learned painting and etching in London, Gainsborough was largely self-taught. His method of painting – what Reynolds called 'those odd scratches and marks ... this chaos which by a kind of magic at a certain distance assumes form' – is full of temperament and life. The portrait of his wife (Courtauld Institute, London) and *The Morning Walk* (National Gallery) show his sense of character and the elegance of his mature work.

A constant tendency to experiment produced the remarkable 'fancy pictures' or imaginative compositions of his late years, *Diana and Actaeon* (Royal Collection), unfinished when he died, being an example. Hundreds of drawings, often in a mixture of media, show his continued pursuit of landscape for its own sake.

THOMAS GAINSBOROUGH His portrait of his two daughters, *Margaret and Mary Chasing a Butterfly*, is one of his most natural and lyrical pictures. *The Art Archive/National Gallery London*

Gaitskell, Hugh (Todd Naylor) (1906–1963) British Labour Party leader from 1955. In 1950 he became minister of economic affairs, and then chancellor of the Exchequer until October 1951. As party leader, he tried to reconcile internal differences on nationalization and disarmament.

gal symbol for ▷gallon, ▷galileo.

Galahad in Arthurian legend, one of the knights of the Round Table. His virtue allowed him to succeed in the quest for the ▷Holy Grail, and he died in ecstasy, having seen its mystery.

He was the son of ▷Lancelot of the Lake and Elaine, daughter of the Fisher King, whom Lancelot believed to be his beloved ▷Guinevere.

Galapagos Islands (official name **Archipiélago de Colón**) group of 12 large and several hundred smaller islands in the Pacific about 800 km/500 mi off the coast of Ecuador, to which they belong; area 7,800 sq km/3,000 sq mi; population (1999 est) 16,900. This island group, of volcanic origin, includes the six main islands of San Cristóbal (where the capital of the same name is situated), Santa Cruz, Isabela, Floreana, Santiago, and Fernandina, as well as 12 smaller islands, with other islets. Volcán Wolf, at 1707 m/5600 ft, on Isabela I is the highest peak. The Galapagos National Park was established in 1934 and, because of the unique fauna, the islands have been established as a UNESCO World Heritage Site.

Galaţi (German **Galatz**) port on the River Danube in Romania; population (1993) 324,000. Industries include shipbuilding, iron, steel, textiles, food processing, and cosmetics.

galaxy congregation of millions or billions of stars, held together by gravity. **Spiral galaxies**, such as the ▷Milky Way, are flattened in shape, with a central bulge of old stars surrounded by a disc of younger stars, arranged in spiral arms like a Catherine wheel.

Barred spirals are spiral galaxies that have a straight bar of stars across their centre, from the ends of which the spiral arms emerge. The arms of spiral galaxies contain gas and dust from which new stars are still forming.

Elliptical galaxies contain old stars and very little gas. They include the most massive galaxies known, containing a trillion stars. At least some elliptical galaxies are thought to be formed by mergers between spiral galaxies. There are also irregular galaxies. Most galaxies occur in clusters, containing anything from a few to thousands of members.

Our own Galaxy, the Milky Way, is about 100,000 light years in diameter, and contains at least 100 billion stars. It is a member of a small cluster, the Local Group. The Sun lies in one of its spiral arms, about 25,000 light years from the centre.

GALAXY An image of a spiral galaxy, one of the main classes of galaxy, of which Andromeda and our own Milky Way are examples. There may be billions of stars in such a system, held together by gravity. With the advanced technology now available to astronomers, especially the Hubble Space Telescope, the mysteries of galactic structure are being uncovered. *Image Bank*

Gabon

Gabon country in central Africa, bounded north by Cameroon, east and south by the Congo, west by the Atlantic Ocean, and northwest by Equatorial Guinea.

NATIONAL NAME *République Gabonaise/Gabonese Republic*
AREA 267,667 sq km/103,346 sq mi
CAPITAL Libreville
MAJOR TOWNS/CITIES Port-Gentil, Franceville (or Masuku), Lambaréné, Mouanda, Oyem, Mouila
MAJOR PORTS Port-Gentil and Owendo
PHYSICAL FEATURES virtually the whole country is tropical rainforest; narrow coastal plain rising to hilly interior with savannah in east and south; Ogooué River flows north–west

Government

HEAD OF STATE Omar Bongo from 1967
HEAD OF GOVERNMENT Jean-François Ntoutoume-Emane from 1999
POLITICAL SYSTEM emergent democracy
POLITICAL EXECUTIVE limited presidency
ADMINISTRATIVE DIVISIONS nine provinces
ARMED FORCES 4,700; plus paramilitary forces of 2,000 (2002 est)
DEATH PENALTY retained and used for ordinary crimes

Economy and resources

CURRENCY franc CFA
GPD (US$) 5.0 billion (2002 est)
REAL GDP GROWTH (% change on previous year) 1.9 (2001)
GNI (US$) 4.0 billion (2002 est)
GNI PER CAPITA (PPP) (US$) 5,320 (2002 est)
CONSUMER PRICE INFLATION 2% (2003 est)
UNEMPLOYMENT 21% (2000)
FOREIGN DEBT (US$) 2.9 billion (2001 est)
MAJOR TRADING PARTNERS France, USA, Japan, the Netherlands, China, South Korea, Spain, Belgium
RESOURCES petroleum, natural gas, manganese (one of world's foremost producers and exporters), iron ore, uranium, gold, niobium, talc, phosphates
INDUSTRIES mining, food processing (particularly sugar), petroleum refining, processing of other minerals, timber preparation, chemicals
EXPORTS petroleum and petroleum products, manganese, timber and wood products, uranium. Principal market: USA 50% (2000)
IMPORTS machinery and apparatus, transport equipment, food products, metals and metal products. Principal source: France 65% (2000)
ARABLE LAND 1.3% (2000 est)
AGRICULTURAL PRODUCTS cassava, sugar cane, cocoa, coffee, plantains, maize, groundnuts, bananas, palm oil; forestry (forests cover approximately 75% of the land)

Population and society

POPULATION 1,329,000 (2003 est)
POPULATION GROWTH RATE 2.2% (2000–15)
POPULATION DENSITY (per sq km) 5 (2003 est)
URBAN POPULATION (% of total) 84 (2003 est)
AGE DISTRIBUTION (% of total population) 0–14 41%, 15–59 50%, 60+ 9% (2002 est)
ETHNIC GROUPS 40 Bantu peoples in four main groupings: the Fang, Eshira, Mbede, and Okande; there are also Pygmies and about 10% Europeans (mainly French)
LANGUAGE French (official), Fang (in the north), Bantu languages, and other local dialects
RELIGION Christian 60% (mostly Roman Catholic), animist about 4%, Muslim 1%
EDUCATION (compulsory years) 10
LITERACY RATE 80% (men); 62% (women) (2000 est)
LABOUR FORCE 64.2% agriculture, 10.8% industry, 25% services (1994)
LIFE EXPECTANCY 56 (men); 58 (women) (2000–05)
CHILD MORTALITY RATE (under 5, per 1,000 live births) 90 (2001)
PHYSICIANS (per 1,000 people) 0.5 (1994 est)
HOSPITAL BEDS (per 1,000 people) 3.3 (1994 est)
TV SETS (per 1,000 people) 326 (2001 est)
RADIOS (per 1,000 people) 501 (2000 est)
INTERNET USERS (per 10,000 people) 192.5 (2002 est)
PERSONAL COMPUTER USERS (per 100 people) 2.0 (2002 est)

GABON A 15 franc stamp from Gabon. It depicts a manganese mine in Moanda, where there is a large deposit of this metallic element. *Stanley Gibbons*

See also ▷Fang; ▷Pygmy.

Chronology

12th century: Immigration of Bantu speakers into an area previously peopled by Pygmies.

1472: Gabon Estuary first visited by Portuguese navigators, who named it Gabao ('hooded cloak'), after the shape of the coastal area.

17th–18th centuries: Fang, from Cameroon in the north, and Omiene peoples colonized the area, attracted by the presence in coastal areas of European traders, who developed the ivory and slave trades, which lasted until the mid-19th century.

1839–42: Mpongwe coastal chiefs agreed to transfer sovereignty to France; Catholic and Protestant missionaries attracted to the area.

1849: Libreville ('Free Town') formed by slaves from a slave ship liberated by the French.

1889: Became part of French Congo, with Congo.

1910: Became part of French Equatorial Africa, which also comprised Congo, Chad, and Central African Republic.

1890s–1920s: Human and natural resources exploited by private concessionary companies.

1940–44: Supported the 'Free French' anti-Nazi cause during World War II.

1946: Became overseas territory within the French Community, with its own assembly.

1960: Independence achieved; Léon M'ba, a Fang of the pro-French Gabonese Democratic Block (BDG), became the first president.

1967: M'ba died and was succeeded by his protégé Albert Bernard Bongo, drawn from the Teke community.

1968: A One-party state established, with the BDG dissolved and replaced by Gabonese Democratic Party (PDG).

1973: Bongo converted to Islam and changed his first name to Omar, but continued to follow a pro-Western policy course and exploit rich mineral resources to increase prosperity.

1989: A coup attempt against Bongo was defeated; the economy deteriorated.

1990: The PDG won the first multiparty elections since 1964. French troops were sent in to maintain order following antigovernment riots.

1993: A national unity government was formed, including some opposition members.

1998: A new party, Rassemblement des Gaullois, was recognized. President Bongo was re-elected.

1999: Jean-François Ntoutoume-Emane was appointed prime minister.

By the end of a five-year study in 1995, US astronomers had identified 600 previously uncatalogued galaxies, mostly 200–400 million light years away, leading to the conclusion that there may be 30–100% more galaxies than previously estimated. Two galaxies were discovered obscured by galactic dust at the edge of the Milky Way. One, named MB1, is a spiral galaxy 17,000 light years across; the other, MB2, is an irregular-shaped dwarf galaxy about 4,000 light years across. In 1996 US astronomers discovered a further new galaxy 17 million light years away. The galaxy, NGC2915, is a blue compact dwarf galaxy and 95% of its mass is in the form of dark matter. In 1997 an international team of astronomers detected the furthest known object in the universe, which is a galaxy lying 13 billion light years away. In 1998 Dutch researchers discovered a large galaxy close to our own. The galaxy is 20 million light years away in the Local Void, an area of space that is generally considered to be fairly empty.

Galbraith, John Kenneth (1908–)
Canadian-born US economist who criticized the neoclassical view that in the economy market forces were in a state approximating ▷perfect competition. He suggested that the 'affluent society' develops an economic imbalance, devoting too many resources to the production of consumer goods and not enough to public services and infrastructure.

Galbraith was critical of the view put forward by the advocates of monetarism that state spending was unable to reduce unemployment. His commitment to the development of the public sector was in sympathy with ▷Keynesian economics. In his book *The Affluent Society* (1958), he documents the tendency of free-market capitalism to create private splendour and public squalor.

JOHN GALBRAITH The US economist J K Galbraith, photographed in about 1964. *Image Bank*

Galen (c. 129–c. 200) Greek physician and anatomist whose ideas dominated Western medicine for almost 1,500 years. Central to his thinking were the threefold circulation of the blood and the theory of ▷humours (blood, phlegm, choler/yellow bile, and melancholy/black bile) that contributed to mental and physical state. His *On Anatomical Procedures*, a detailed description of animal dissections when work on human corpses was forbidden, became a standard text on anatomy when rediscovered in Western Europe in the 16th century. He remained the highest medical authority until Andreas ▷Vesalius and William ▷Harvey exposed the fundamental errors of his system.

> **Related Web site: On the Natural Faculties**
> http://classics.mit.edu/Galen/natfac.html

galena mineral consisting of lead sulphide, PbS, the chief ore of lead. It is lead-grey in colour, has a high metallic lustre and breaks into cubes because of its perfect cubic cleavage. It may contain up to 1% silver, and so the ore is sometimes mined for both metals. Galena occurs mainly among limestone deposits in Australia, Mexico, Russia, Kazakhstan, the UK, and the USA.

Galicia region of central Europe, extending from the northern slopes of the Carpathian Mountains to the Romanian border.

Once part of the Austrian Empire, it was included in Poland after World War I and divided in 1945 between Poland and the USSR.

Galicia mountainous but fertile autonomous community of northwest Spain, comprising the provinces of La Coruña, Lugo, Orense, and Pontevedra; area 29,400 sq km/11,350 sq mi; population (1996 est) 2,742,600. Industries include fishing, and tungsten and tin mining; Galicia has the largest fishing fleet in the European Union. The climate is very wet, and the region is traversed northeast to southwest by the River Miño. The chief harbours are La Coruña, Vigo, and El Ferrol. The Galician language (Gallego) is similar to Portuguese. The capital is ▷Santiago de Compostela.

Galilee region of northern Israel (once a Roman province in Palestine) which includes Nazareth and Tiberias, frequently mentioned in the Gospels of the New Testament.

Galilee, Sea of alternative name for Lake ▷Tiberias in northern Israel.

Galileo (1564–1642) born Galileo Galilei. Italian mathematician, astronomer, and physicist. He developed the astronomical telescope and was the first to see sunspots, the four main satellites of Jupiter, and the appearance of Venus going through phases, thus proving it was orbiting the Sun. Galileo discovered that freely falling bodies, heavy or light, have the same, constant acceleration and that this acceleration is due to gravity. He also determined that a body moving on a perfectly smooth horizontal surface would neither speed up nor slow down. He invented a thermometer, a hydrostatic balance, and a compass, and discovered that the path of a projectile is a parabola.

Galileo's work founded the modern scientific method of deducing laws to explain the results of observation and experiment, although the story of his dropping cannonballs from the Leaning Tower of Pisa is questionable. His observations were an unwelcome refutation of the Aristotelian ideas taught at universities, largely because they made plausible for the first time the Sun-centred theory of Polish astronomer Nicolaus ▷Copernicus. Galileo's persuasive *Dialogo sopra i due massimi sistemi del mondo/Dialogues on the Two Chief Systems of the World* (1632) was banned by the church authorities in Rome and he was made to recant by the Inquisition.

Astronomy and the invention of the telescope In July 1609, hearing that a Dutch scientist had made a telescope, Galileo worked out the principles involved and made a number of telescopes. He compiled fairly accurate tables of the orbits of four of Jupiter's satellites and proposed that their frequent eclipses could serve as a means of determining longitude on land and at sea. His observations on sunspots and Venus going through phases supported Copernicus's theory that the Earth rotated and orbited the Sun. Galileo's results published in *Sidereus Nuncius/The Starry Messenger* (1610) were revolutionary.

He believed, however – following both Greek and medieval tradition – that orbits must be circular, not elliptical, in order to maintain the fabric of the cosmos in a state of perfection. This preconception prevented him from deriving a full formulation of the law of inertia, which was later to be attributed to the contemporary French mathematician René ▷Descartes.

The pendulum Galileo made several fundamental contributions to mechanics. He rejected the impetus theory that a force or push is required to sustain motion. While watching swinging lamps in Pisa Cathedral, Galileo determined that each oscillation of a pendulum takes the same amount of time despite the difference in amplitude, and recognized the potential importance of this observation to timekeeping. In a later publication, he presented his derivation that the square of the period of a pendulum varies with its length (and is independent of the mass of the pendulum bob).

Mechanics and the law of falling bodies Galileo discovered before Newton that two objects of different weights – an apple and a melon, for instance – falling from the same height would hit the ground at the same time. He realized that gravity not only causes a body to fall, but also determines the motion of rising bodies and, furthermore, that gravity extends to the centre of the Earth. Galileo then showed that the motion of a projectile is made up of two components: one component consists of uniform motion in a horizontal direction, and the other component is vertical motion under acceleration or deceleration due to gravity.

Galileo used this explanation to refute objections to Copernicus. It had been argued, against Copernicus, that a turning Earth would not carry along birds and clouds. Galileo explained that the motion of a bird, like a projectile, has a horizontal component that is provided by the motion of the Earth and that this horizontal component of motion always exists to keep such objects in position even though they are not attached to the ground.

Galileo came to an understanding of uniform velocity and uniform acceleration by measuring the time it takes for bodies to move various distances. He had the brilliant idea of slowing vertical motion by measuring the movement of balls rolling down inclined planes, realizing that the vertical component of this motion is a uniform acceleration due to gravity. It took Galileo many years to arrive at the correct expression of the law of falling bodies, which he presented in *Discorsi e dimostrazioni matematiche intorno a due nove scienze/Discourses and Mathematical Discoveries Concerning Two New Sciences* (1638) as:

$$s = \tfrac{1}{2}at^2$$

where *s* is speed, *a* is the acceleration due to gravity, and *t* is time. He found that the distance travelled by a falling body is proportional to the square of the time of descent.

A summation of his life's work, *Discourses* also included the facts that the trajectory of a projectile is a parabola, and that the law of falling bodies is perfectly obeyed only in a vacuum, and that air resistance always causes a uniform terminal velocity to be reached.

> **Related Web site: IMSS – History of Science Multimedia Catalogue Galileo Galilei**
> http://galileo.imss.firenze.it/museo/4/index.html

GALILEO A fresco dating from 1841 in the Observatory Academy, Florence, Italy, which shows the 17-year-old Italian mathematician and astronomer Galileo contemplating a swinging lamp in Pisa Cathedral, and coming to the realization that each swing, long or short, takes the same time. *The Art Archive/Observatory Academy Florence Italy/Dagli Orti*

gall abnormal outgrowth on a plant that develops as a result of attack by insects or, less commonly, by bacteria, fungi, mites, or nematodes. The attack causes an increase in the number of cells or an enlargement of existing cells in the plant. Gall-forming insects generally pass the early stages of their life inside the gall.

Gall wasps are responsible for the conspicuous bud galls forming on oak trees, 2.5–4 cm/1–1.5 in across, known as 'oak apples'. The organisms that cause galls are host-specific. Thus, for example, gall wasps tend to parasitize oaks, and ▷sawflies willows.

Galla (or **Oromo**) member of a Cushitic people inhabiting southern Ethiopia and northwestern Kenya. Galla is a Hamito-Semitic (Afro-Asiatic) language, and is spoken by about 12 million people. Most are sedentary agriculturalists, except for some in the south who are nomadic pastoralists. They originally spread south from the Ethiopian plateau and Ethiopian empire. The southern

---

John Kenneth Galbraith
Politics is not the art of the possible. It consists in choosing between the disastrous and the unpalatable.
Letter to President Kennedy, 2 March 1962

Galileo
In questions of science the authority of a thousand is not worth the humble reasoning of a single individual.
Arago's Eulogy of Laplace, Smithsonian Report 1874

Galen
That physician will hardly be thought very careful of the health of others who neglects his own.
Of Protecting the Health bk V

Galla adhere to traditional beliefs, whereas those in the north are Muslims or Christians.

gall bladder small muscular sac, part of the digestive system of most, but not all, vertebrates. In humans, it is situated on the underside of the liver and connected to the small intestine by the bile duct. It stores bile from the liver.

Gallic Wars series of military campaigns 58–51 BC in which Julius Caesar, as proconsul of Gaul, annexed Transalpine Gaul (the territory that formed the geographical basis of modern-day France). His final victory over the Gauls led by Vercingetorix 52 BC left him in control of the land area from the Rhine to the Pyrenees and from the Alps to the Atlantic. The final organization of the provinces followed under Augustus.

Gallipoli port in European Turkey, giving its name to the peninsula (ancient name **Chersonesus**) on which it stands. In World War I, at the instigation of Winston Churchill, an unsuccessful attempt was made between February 1915 and January 1916 by Allied troops to force their way through the Dardanelles and link up with Russia. The campaign was fought mainly by Australian and New Zealand (▷Anzac) forces, who suffered heavy losses. An estimated 36,000 Commonwealth troops died during the nine-month campaign.

> Related Web site: Gallipoli 1915 http://www.focusmin.com.au/~focus/anzac-01.htm/

gall midge minute and fragile long-legged flies, with longish hairy antennae. The larvae are small maggots, ranging in colour from white or yellow, to orange and bright red, that feed on developing fruits which become deformed and decay, and frequently produce ▷galls on plants.

Gallo, Robert Charles (1937–) US scientist credited with identifying the virus responsible for ▷AIDS. Gallo discovered the virus, now known as human immunodeficiency virus (HIV), in 1984; the French scientist Luc Montagnier of the Pasteur Institute, Paris, discovered the virus, independently, in 1983.

gallon imperial liquid or dry measure, equal to 4.546 litres, and subdivided into four quarts or eight pints. The US gallon is equivalent to 3.785 litres.

gallstone pebblelike, insoluble accretion formed in the human gall bladder or bile ducts from cholesterol or calcium salts present in bile. Gallstones may be symptomless or they may cause pain, indigestion, or jaundice. They can be dissolved with medication or removed, either by means of an endoscope or, along with the gall bladder, in an operation known as cholecystectomy.

Gallup, George Horace (1901–1984) US journalist and statistician, who founded in 1935 the American Institute of Public Opinion and devised the Gallup Poll, in which public opinion is sampled by questioning a number of representative individuals (see ▷opinion poll).

gall wasp small (only a few millimetres long), dark-coloured insect with a compressed abdomen. Most gall wasps form ▷galls, though a few live within the galls formed by other species; these are called **inquilines**. Others feed on gall-formers and inquilines. Gall wasps are in the family Cynipidae, order Hymenoptera, class Insecta, phylum Arthropoda.

Galsworthy, John (1867–1933) English novelist and dramatist. His work examines the social issues of the Victorian period. He wrote *The Forsyte Saga* (1906–22) and its sequel, the novels collectively entitled *A Modern Comedy* (1929). His plays include *The Silver Box* (1906). He was awarded the Nobel Prize for Literature in 1932.

Galsworthy first achieved recognition with *The Silver Box* and *The Man of Property* (1906), the first instalment of the *Forsyte Saga* series, which also includes *In Chancery* (1920) and *To Let* (1921). Soames Forsyte, the central character, is the embodiment of Victorian values and feeling for property, and the wife whom he also 'owns' – Irene – was based on Galsworthy's wife. *A Modern Comedy* contains *The White Monkey* (1924), *The Silver Spoon* (1926), and *Swan Song* (1928), and (included in later editions) the short stories *On Forsyte Change* (1930).

Galton, Francis (1822–1911) English scientist, inventor, and explorer who studied the inheritance of physical and mental attributes with the aim of improving the human species. He was the first to use twins to try to assess the influence of environment on development, and is considered the founder of ▷eugenics (a term he coined).

Galvani, Luigi (1737–1798) Italian physiologist who discovered galvanic, or voltaic, electricity in 1762, when investigating the contractions produced in the muscles of dead frogs by contact with pairs of different metals. His work led quickly to Alessandro ▷Volta's invention of the electrical ▷cell, and later to an understanding of how nerves control muscles.

galvanizing process for rendering iron rust-proof, by plunging it into molten zinc (the dipping method), or by electroplating it with zinc.

Galway county on the west coast of the Republic of Ireland, in the province of Connacht; county town ▷Galway; area 5,940 sq km/2,293 sq mi; population (1996) 188,900. Lead is found at Tynagh, and copper, lead, and zinc near Loughrea; marble is quarried and processed at Recess and Inverin. The main farming activity is cattle and sheep grazing. The Connemara National Park is in Galway. Towns include Salthill, a suburb of **Galway** city and seaside resort, Ballinasloe, Clifden, and Tuam.

Galway fishing port and county town of County ▷Galway, Republic of Ireland; 200 km/124 mi west of Dublin; principal city of ▷Connacht province; population (1996) 57,200. It produces textiles and chemicals, and there is salmon and eel fishing; Galway has recently become important for its computer industry. Queen's College (founded in about 1845) was renamed University College in 1908, and is part of the National University of Ireland; teaching has been bilingual, conducted in both English and Irish, since 1929. Galway is an important centre of the Irish language; **Galway Theatre**, An Taibhdhearc, only stages plays in Irish.

Gama, Vasco da (c. 1469–1524) Portuguese navigator. He commanded an expedition in 1497 to discover the route to India around the Cape of Good Hope (in modern South Africa). On Christmas Day 1497 he reached land, which he named Natal. He then crossed the Indian Ocean, arriving at Calicut (now Kozhikode in Kerala) in May 1498, and returned to Portugal in September 1499.

Da Gama was born in Sines, southwest Portugal, and was chosen by King Manoel I for his 1497 expedition. In 1502 he founded a Portuguese colony in Mozambique. In the same year he attacked and plundered Calicut in revenge for the murder of some Portuguese sailors. After 20 years of retirement, he was dispatched to India again as Portuguese viceroy in 1524, but died two months after his arrival in Goa.

Gambetta, Léon Michel (1838–1882) French politician, organizer of resistance during the Franco-Prussian War, and founder in 1871 of the Third Republic. In 1881–82 he was prime minister for a few weeks.

Gambia river in western Africa, 1,000 km/620 mi long, which gives its name to The Gambia. It rises in Guinea and flows west through Senegal and The Gambia to the Atlantic Ocean.

Gambia, The see country box.

gamelan percussion ensemble consisting largely of tuned knobbed gongs and keyed metallophones found in Indonesia (especially Java and Bali) and Malaysia. Most modern gamelan are tuned to a five-note or seven-note system. Gamelan music is performed as an accompaniment for dance and theatre.

gamete cell that functions in sexual reproduction by merging with another gamete to form a ▷zygote. Examples of gametes include sperm and egg cells. In most organisms, the gametes are haploid (they contain half the number of chromosomes of the parent), owing to reduction division or ▷meiosis.

In higher organisms, gametes are of two distinct types: large immobile ones known as eggs or egg cells (see ▷ovum) and small ones known as ▷sperm. They come together at ▷fertilization. In some lower organisms the gametes are all the same, or they may belong to different mating strains but have no obvious differences in size or appearance.

game theory group of mathematical theories, developed in 1944 by German-born US mathematician Oscar Morgenstern (1902–1977) and Hungarian-born US mathematician John ▷Von Neumann, that seeks to abstract from invented game-playing scenarios and their outcome the essence of situations of conflict and/or cooperation in the real political, business, and social world.

gametophyte the ▷haploid generation in the life cycle of a plant that produces gametes; see ▷alternation of generations.

gamma radiation very high-frequency electromagnetic radiation, similar in nature to X-rays but of shorter wavelength, emitted by the nuclei of radioactive substances during decay or by the interactions of high-energy electrons with matter. Cosmic gamma rays have been identified as coming from pulsars, radio galaxies, and quasars, although they cannot penetrate the Earth's atmosphere.

Gamma rays are stopped only by direct collision with an atom and are therefore very penetrating; they can, however, be stopped by about 4 cm/1.5 in of lead or by a very thick concrete shield.

They are less ionizing in their effect than alpha and beta particles, but are dangerous nevertheless because they can penetrate deeply into body tissues such as bone marrow. They are not deflected by either magnetic or electric fields. Gamma radiation is used to kill bacteria and other micro-organisms, sterilize medical devices, and change the molecular structure of plastics to modify their properties (for example, to improve their resistance to heat and abrasion).

gamma-ray astronomy in astronomy, study of celestial objects that emit gamma rays (energetic photons with very short wavelengths). Much of the radiation detected comes from collisions between hydrogen gas and cosmic rays in our Galaxy. Some sources have been identified, including the Crab nebula and the Vela pulsar (the most powerful gamma-ray source detected).

Gamsakhurdia, Zviad (1939–1993) Georgian politician, president 1990–92. He was a fervent nationalist and an active anticommunist. After nationalist success in parliamentary elections when Georgia achieved independence in 1991, he was elected head of state by a huge margin. His increasingly dictatorial style of government and his hostile attitude to non-ethnic Georgians led to his forced removal and flight to neighbouring Armenia in 1992. He returned to western Georgia in 1993 to lead a rebellion against Edvard ▷Shevardnadze's presidency, but Shevardnadze, with Russian help, destroyed his ill-equipped supporters, and the deposed president was later reported dead, although uncertainty remained as to whether he had committed suicide or been killed by Russian troops.

Gance, Abel (1889–1981) French film director. His films were grandiose melodramas. *Napoléon* 1927 was one of the most ambitious silent epic films. It features colour tinting and triple-screen sequences, as well as multiple-exposure shots, and helped further the technological and aesthetic development of the film medium.

Ganda (or **Baganda**) member of the majority ethnic group in Uganda; the Baganda also live in Kenya. Traditionally farmers, the Ganda are a Bantu people, many of whom now work in cities. Most are Christians. Their language, Luganda, belongs to the Niger-Congo language family and has about 3 million speakers.

Gandhi, Indira Priyadarshani (1917–1984) Born Indira Priyadarshani Nehru. Indian politician, prime minister of India 1966–77 and 1980–84, and leader of the ▷Congress Party 1966–77 and subsequently of the Congress (I) party. She was assassinated in 1984 by members of her Sikh bodyguard, resentful of her use of troops to clear malcontents from the Sikh temple at ▷Amritsar.

Her father, Jawaharlal Nehru, was India's first prime minister. She married Feroze Gandhi in 1942 (died 1960, not related to Mahatma Gandhi) and had two sons, Sanjay Gandhi (1946–1980), who died in an aeroplane crash, and Rajiv ▷Gandhi, who was assassinated in 1991. In 1975 the validity of her re-election to parliament was questioned, and she declared a state of emergency. During this time Sanjay Gandhi implemented a social and economic programme (including an unpopular family-planning policy) that led to his mother's defeat in 1977.

> Related Web site: Gandhi, Indira Priyadarshini http://www.indiasurvey.com/biodata/indiragandhi.htm

Gandhi, Mahatma (1869–1948) Honorific name of Mohandas Karamchand Gandhi. (Sanskrit *Mahatma* 'Great Soul') Indian nationalist leader. A pacifist, he led the struggle for Indian independence from the UK by advocating nonviolent noncooperation (*satyagraha* 'truth and firmness') from 1915. He was imprisoned several times by the British authorities. He was influential in the nationalist Congress Party and in the independence negotiations in 1947. He was assassinated by a Hindu nationalist in the violence that followed the partition of British India into India and Pakistan. Religious violence in India and Pakistan soon waned, and his teachings came to inspire nonviolent movements in other parts of the world, notably in the USA under civil rights leader Martin Luther King, Jr, and in South Africa under Nelson Mandela.

> **Mahatma Gandhi**
> *Rights that do not flow from duty well performed are not worth having.*
> *Non-Violence in Peace and War,* vol. 2, ch. 269 (1949)

Gandhi began to develop the principles of *satyagraha*, the practice of nonviolent resistance, while practising as a lawyer in South Africa, where he lived from 1893. He led the Indian community there in opposition to racial discrimination until 1914, when the South African government made important concessions to his demands. He returned to India in January 1915 and became the leader in the country's complex struggle for independence from British rule. He organized hunger strikes, boycotts of British goods, and events of civil disobedience, and campaigned for social reform. In 1920, when the British failed to make amends, Gandhi proclaimed an organized campaign of noncooperation. Indians in public office resigned, government agencies were boycotted,

MAHATMA GANDHI Indian politician Mahatma Gandhi. Leader of the nationalist movement 1915–47, Gandhi is regarded as the founder of the Indian state. *Archive Photos*

and Indian children were withdrawn from government schools. Gandhi was arrested by the British, but they were soon forced to release him.

India's economic independence was an important issue for Gandhi's *swaraj* (self-ruling) movement. As a remedy for the extreme poverty affecting Indian villagers as a result of exploitation by British industrialists, Gandhi advocated the revival of cottage industries. He began to use a spinning wheel as a token of the renewal of native Indian industries and the return to the simple village life he expounded.

In 1921 the Indian National Congress, the group that spearheaded the movement for independence, gave Gandhi complete executive authority. However, a series of armed revolts against Britain broke out and Gandhi withdrew from active politics 1924–30. In 1930, he led a 265 km/165 mi long march from Ahmadabad, Gujarat, to the Arabian Sea, and produced salt by evaporating sea water as a gesture of defiance against the British monopoly in salt production. In 1932 he began to fast as a method of protest. The fasts were effective measures against the British, because revolution could well have broken out had he died. He formally resigned from politics in 1934, but continued to travel through India teaching *ahimsa* (nonviolence) and demanding the eradication of 'untouchability', the policy of shunning members of India's lowest caste. In real terms, his political power remained immense and, in 1939, he returned to active political life because of the pending federation of Indian principalities with the rest of India. Gandhi stood steadfastly against the partition of India,

but ultimately had to concede to it, hoping that internal peace would be achieved after the Muslim demand for separation had been met.

Related Web site: Mahatma Gandhi Ashram http://www.nuvs. com/ashram/

Gandhi, Rajiv (1944–1991) Indian politician, prime minister from 1984 (following his mother Indira Gandhi's assassination) to November 1989. As prime minister, he faced growing discontent with his party's elitism and lack of concern for social issues. He was assassinated at an election rally.

Elder son of Indira Gandhi and grandson of Nehru, Rajiv Gandhi was born into the Kashmiri Brahmin family that had governed India for all but four years since 1947. He initially displayed little interest in politics and became a pilot with Indian Airlines. But after the death in a plane crash of his brother **Sanjay** (1946–1980), he was elected to his brother's Amethi parliamentary seat in 1981. In the December 1984 parliamentary elections he won a record majority. His reputation was tarnished by a scandal concerning alleged kickbacks to senior officials from an arms deal with the Swedish munitions firm Bofors and, following his party's defeat in the general election of November 1989, Gandhi was forced to resign as premier. He was killed by a bomb on 21 May in the middle of the 1991 election campaign at a rally near Madras (now Chennai), while attempting to regain office.

Ganesh Hindu god, son of Siva and Parvati; he is represented as elephant-headed and is worshipped as a remover of obstacles.

Gambia, The

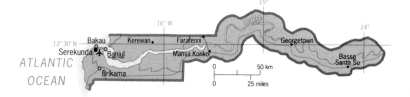

Gambia, The country in west Africa, bounded north, east, and south by Senegal and west by the Atlantic Ocean.

NATIONAL NAME *Republic of the Gambia*
AREA 10,402 sq km/4,016 sq mi
CAPITAL Banjul
MAJOR TOWNS/CITIES Serekunda, Brikama, Bakau, Farafenni, Sukuta, Gunjur, Basse
PHYSICAL FEATURES consists of narrow strip of land along the River Gambia; river flanked by low hills

Government

HEAD OF STATE AND GOVERNMENT Yahya Jammeh from 1994
POLITICAL SYSTEM transitional
POLITICAL EXECUTIVE transitional
ADMINISTRATIVE DIVISIONS five divisions and one city (Banjul)
ARMED FORCES 800 (2002 est)
CONSCRIPTION military service is voluntary
DEATH PENALTY retains the death penalty for ordinary crimes but can be considered abolitionist in practice; date of last known execution 1981
DEFENCE SPEND (% GDP) 1 (2002 est)
EDUCATION SPEND (% GDP) 2.7 (2001 est)
HEALTH SPEND (% GDP) 4.1 (2000 est)

Economy and resources

CURRENCY dalasi
GPD (US$) 388 million (2002 est)
REAL GDP GROWTH (% change on previous year) 4.6% (2001)
GNI (US$) 392 million (2002 est)
GNI PER CAPITA (PPP) (US$) 1,680 (2002 est)
CONSUMER PRICE INFLATION 6% (2003 est)
UNEMPLOYMENT 25% (2000)
FOREIGN DEBT (US$) 526 million (2001 est)
MAJOR TRADING PARTNERS UK, Belgium, Luxembourg, China, Italy, Hong Kong, Japan

RESOURCES ilmenite, zircon, rutile, petroleum (well discovered, but not exploited)
INDUSTRIES food processing (fish, fish products, and vegetable oils), beverages, construction materials
EXPORTS groundnuts and related products, cotton lint, fish and fish preparations, hides and skins. Principal market: UK 53% (2001)
IMPORTS food and live animals, basic manufactures, machinery and transport equipment, mineral fuels and lubrications, miscellaneous manufactured articles, chemicals. Principal source: China (including Hong Kong) 59.2% (2001)
ARABLE LAND 23% (2000 est)
AGRICULTURAL PRODUCTS groundnuts, cotton, rice, citrus fruits, avocados, sesame seed, millet, sorghum, maize; livestock rearing (cattle); fishing

Population and society

POPULATION 1,425,000 (2003 est)
POPULATION GROWTH RATE 2.1% (2000–15)
POPULATION DENSITY (per sq km) 126 (2003 est)
URBAN POPULATION (% of total) 33 (2003 est)
AGE DISTRIBUTION (% of total population) 0–14 40%, 15–59 55%, 60+ 5% (2002 est)
ETHNIC GROUPS wide mix of ethnic groups, the largest is the Madinka (about 40%); other main groups are the Fula (13.5%), Wolof (13%), Jola (7%), and Serahuli (7%)
LANGUAGE English (official), Mandinka, Fula, Wolof, other indigenous dialects
RELIGION Muslim 85%, with animist and Christian minorities

EDUCATION free, but not compulsory
LITERACY RATE 47% (men); 33% (women) (2003 est)
LABOUR FORCE 50% of population: 79.6% agriculture, 4.2% industry, 16.2% services (1994)
LIFE EXPECTANCY 53 (men); 56 (women) (2000–05)
CHILD MORTALITY RATE (under 5, per 1,000 live births) 126 (2001)
PHYSICIANS (per 1,000 people) 0.14 (2001 est)
HOSPITAL BEDS (per 1,000 people) 1 (2000 est)
TV SETS (per 1,000 people) 3 (1999)
RADIOS (per 1,000 people) 394 (1999)
INTERNET USERS (per 10,000 people) 134.6 (2002 est)
PERSONAL COMPUTER USERS (per 100 people) 1.4 (2002 est)

See also ▷Fulani; ▷Mali Empire.

THE GAMBIA Red-eyed doves *Streptopelia semitorquata* in a forest in The Gambia. *K G Preston-Mafham/Premaphotos Wildlife*

Chronology

13th century: Wolof, Malinke (Mandingo), and Fulani tribes settled in the region from east and north.

14th century: Became part of the great Muslim Mali Empire, which, centred to northeast, also extended across Senegal, Mali, and southern Mauritania.

1455: The Gambia River was first sighted by the Portuguese.

1663 and 1681: The British and French established small settlements at Fort James and Albreda.

1843: The Gambia became a British crown colony, administered with Sierra Leone until 1888.

1965: Independence was achieved as a constitutional monarchy within the Commonwealth, with Dawda K Jawara of the People's Progressive Party (PPP) as prime minister at the head of a multiparty democracy.

1970: The Gambia became a republic, with Jawara as president.

1982: The Gambia formed the Confederation of Senegambia with Senegal.

1994: Jawara was ousted in a military coup, and fled to Senegal; Yahya Jammeh was named acting head of state.

1996: A civilian constitution was adopted.

2002: The ruling Alliance for Patriotic Reorientation and Construction (APRC) retained power overwhelmingly in parliamentary elections.

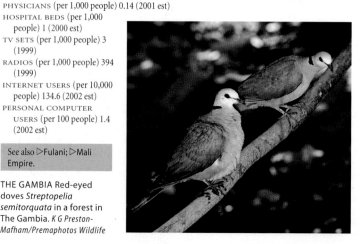

Ganges (Hindi **Ganga**) major river of India and Bangladesh; length 2,510 km/1,560 mi. It is the most sacred river for Hindus.

ganglion (plural **ganglia**) solid cluster of nervous tissue containing many cell bodies and ▷synapses, usually enclosed in a tissue sheath; found in invertebrates and vertebrates.

gangrene death and decay of body tissue (often of a limb) due to bacterial action; the affected part gradually turns black and causes blood poisoning.

Gangrene sets in as a result of loss of blood supply to the area. This may be due to disease (diabetes, atherosclerosis), an obstruction of a major blood vessel (as in ▷thrombosis), injury, or frostbite. Bacteria colonize the site unopposed, and a strong risk of blood poisoning often leads to surgical removal of the tissue or the affected part (amputation).

gannet any of three species of North Atlantic seabirds (Family Sulidae, order Pelecaniformaes.); the largest is *Sula bassana*. When fully grown, it is white with buff colouring on the head and neck; the beak is long and thick and compressed at the point; the wings are black-tipped with a span of 1.7 m/5.6 ft. It breeds on cliffs in nests made of grass and seaweed, laying a single white egg. Gannets feed on fish that swim near the surface, such as herrings and pilchards. Diving swiftly and sometimes from a considerable height upon their prey, they enter the water with closed wings and neck outstretched. They belong to the same family as the ▷booby.

The gannets are the largest seabirds of the North Atlantic; they are found also in the southeast Pacific and in temperate waters off Africa.

Gannets can be found nesting on several rocky stations on the coast of the British Isles, including Ailsa Craig, St Kilda, Suliskerry, and Grassholme. In the late autumn they migrate to the west coast of Africa.

GANNET The Cape gannet *Morus capensis*. It forms dense breeding colonies around the coasts of South Africa, incubating its single egg with its feet. *Premaphotos Wildlife*

Gansu (or **Kansu**) province of northwest China, bounded to the north by Mongolia and Inner Mongolia, to the east by Ningxia Hui Autonomous Region and Shaanxi, to the south by Sichuan, and to the west by Qinghai and Xinjiang Uygur Autonomous Region; area 530,000 sq km/205,000 sq mi; population (1996) 24,670,000. The main cities are ▷Lanzhou (capital), Yumen, Tianshui, Dunhuang, and Jiayuguan. Chief industries are coal, oil, hydroelectric power from the Huang He River, mining, metal-processing, and tourism. Agriculture is based on the cultivation of spring wheat, millet, sorghum, flax, and fruit, and animal rearing.

Ganymede in astronomy, the largest moon of the planet Jupiter, and the largest moon in the Solar System, 5,260 km/3,270 mi in diameter (larger than the planet Mercury). It orbits Jupiter every 7.2 days at a distance of 1.1 million km/700,000 mi. Its surface is a mixture of cratered and grooved terrain. Molecular oxygen was identified on Ganymede's surface in 1994.

Ganymede in Greek mythology according to Homer, a youth so beautiful he was taken as cupbearer to Zeus, king of the gods.

The Ganges: Purification and Pollution

It is estimated that the Ganges supports over 500 million people – those who live along its course depend on it for irrigation, fishing, industry, transportation, energy, and drinking water. It is also worshipped by millions of Hindus as the goddess Ganga 'the mother of India'. Hindus believe that they will be purified by bathing in its waters and will ensure favourable reincarnation if their ashes are scattered over its waters. For this reason millions of Hindu pilgrims bathe in its waters – estimates suggest that sometimes as many as 10 million people bathe in the Ganges in one day – and thousands of bodies are cremated each day on the burning ghats or pyres by the river, especially at the city of Varanasi in the north. Many half-cremated bodies are thrown into the river. The river is polluted by the untreated sewage and chemical waste from over 100 cities.

He was deemed responsible for the annual flooding of the Nile, and was later identified with the constellation ▷Aquarius.

Garbo, Greta (1905–1990) Stage name of Greta Lovisa Gustafsson. Swedish-born US film actor. She went to the USA in 1925, and her captivating beauty and leading role in *Flesh and the Devil* (1927) made her one of Hollywood's greatest stars. Her later films include *Mata Hari* (1931), *Grand Hotel* (1932), *Queen Christina* (1933), *Anna Karenina* (1935), *Camille* (1936), and *Ninotchka* (1939). Her ethereal qualities and romantic mystery on the screen intermingled with her seclusion in private life. She retired in 1941.

García Lorca, Federico Spanish poet. See ▷Lorca, Federico García.

García Márquez, Gabriel (Gabo) (1928–) Colombian novelist. His sweeping novel *Cien años de soledad/One Hundred Years of Solitude* (1967) (which tells the story of a family over a period of six generations) is an example of magic realism, a technique used to heighten the intensity of realistic portrayal of social and political issues by introducing grotesque or fanciful material. He was awarded the Nobel Prize for Literature in 1982.

His other books include *El amor en los tiempos del cólera/ Love in the Time of Cholera* (1985) and *The General in His Labyrinth* (1991), which describes the last four months of Simón Bolívar's life.

García Perez, Alan (1949–) Peruvian politician and president 1985–90; leader of the moderate, reformist left-wing American Popular Revolutionary Alliance party (APRA; Aprista Party). He inherited an ailing economy and was forced to trim his socialist programme. His government was marked by scandals, economic crisis, and the failure to confront growing political violence caused by guerrillas and drugs traffickers. He lost to political novice Alberto Fujimori in the 1990 presidential elections.

Garda, Lake (Italian **Lago di Garda**; ancient **Lacus Benacus**) largest lake in Italy; situated on the border between the regions of Lombardy and Veneto; area 370 sq km/143 sq mi.

garden city in the UK, a town built in a rural area and designed to combine town and country advantages, with its own industries, controlled developments, private and public gardens, and cultural centre. The idea was proposed by Ebenezer ▷Howard, who in 1899 founded the Garden City Association, which established the first garden city: Letchworth in Hertfordshire.

gardenia any of a group of subtropical and tropical trees and shrubs found in Africa and Asia, belonging to the madder family, with evergreen foliage and flattened rosettes of fragrant waxen-looking flowers, often white in colour. (Genus *Gardenia*, family Rubiaceae.)

Garfield, James A(bram) (1831–1881) 20th president of the USA 1881, a Republican. A compromise candidate for the presidency, he held office for only four months before being assassinated in a Washington, DC, railway station by a disappointed office-seeker. His short tenure was marked primarily by struggles within the Republican Party over influence and cabinet posts.

garfish European marine fish with a long spearlike snout. The common garfish (*Belone belone*) has an elongated body measuring 75 cm/2.5 ft in length. (Family Belonidae, order Beloniformes.)

gargoyle (French *gargouille* 'throat') in architecture, a lead or stone spout projecting from the roof gutter

> ### Gabriel García Márquez
> *She discovered with great delight that one does not love one's children just because they are one's children, but because of the friendship formed while raising them.*
>
> Love in the Time of Cholera, 207 (1985)

JAMES A GARFIELD James A Garfield, 20th president of the USA, who was shot by an assassin on 2 July 1881, finally dying on 19 September. *Archive Photos*

of a building with the purpose of directing water away from the wall. The term is usually applied to the ornamental forms found in Gothic architecture; these were carved in stone in the form of fantastic animals, angels, or human heads.

Garibaldi, Giuseppe (1807–1882) Italian soldier who played a central role in the unification of Italy by conquering Sicily and Naples in 1860. From 1834 a member of the nationalist Mazzini's ▷Young Italy society, he was forced into exile until 1848 and again 1849–54. He fought against Austria 1848–49, in 1859, and in 1866, and led two unsuccessful expeditions to liberate Rome from papal rule in 1862 and 1867.

Born in Nice, he became a sailor and then joined the nationalist movement ▷Risorgimento. Condemned to death for treason, he escaped to South America where he became a mercenary. He returned to Italy during the 1848 revolution, served with the Sardinian army against the Austrians, and commanded the army of the Roman republic in its defence of the city against the French. He subsequently lived in exile until 1854, when he settled on the island of Caprera.

In 1860, at the head of his 1,000 redshirts, he won Sicily and Naples for the new kingdom of Italy. He served in the Austrian War of 1866 and fought for France in the Franco-Prussian War 1870–71.

Garland, Judy (1922–1969) Stage name of Frances Gumm. US singer and actor. Her performances are marked by a compelling intensity. Her films include *The Wizard of Oz* (1939) (which featured the tune that was to become her theme song, 'Over the Rainbow'), *Babes in Arms* (1939), *Strike Up the Band* (1940), *Meet Me in St Louis* (1944), *Easter Parade* (1948), *A Star is Born* (1954), and *Judgment at Nuremberg* (1961).

garlic perennial Asian plant belonging to the lily family, whose strong-smelling and sharp-tasting bulb, made up of several small segments, or cloves, is used in cooking. The plant has white flowers. It is widely cultivated and has been used successfully as a fungicide in the cereal grass

> ### Judy Garland
> *If I'm such a legend, then why am I so lonely? If I'm a legend, then why do I sit at home for hours staring at the damned phone . . .?*
>
> Quoted in J Gruen, Close-Up

GARLIC Garlic is a perennial bulb of the onion family. It grows about 30 cm/12 in high, and has pale spherical flowers. It has been used since ancient Egyptian times as a herb. In the Middle Ages, it was thought to keep away vampires, perhaps because of the strong smell imparted to the breath of regular users.

▷sorghum. It also has antibacterial properties. (*Allium sativum*, family Liliaceae.)

garnet group of ▷silicate minerals with the formula $X_3Y_3(SiO_4)_3$, where *X* is calcium, magnesium, iron, or manganese, and *Y* is usually aluminium or sometimes iron or chromium. Garnets are used as semiprecious gems (usually pink to deep red) and as abrasives. They occur in metamorphic rocks such as gneiss and schist.

Garrick, David (1717–1779) English actor and theatre manager. From 1747 he became joint licensee of the Drury Lane Theatre, London, with his own company, and instituted a number of significant theatrical conventions including concealed stage lighting and banishing spectators from the stage. He played Shakespearean characters such as Richard III, King Lear, Hamlet, and Benedick, and collaborated with George Colman (1732–1794) in writing the play *The Clandestine Marriage* (1766). He retired from the stage in 1766, but continued as a manager.

He was a pupil of the lexicographer Samuel ▷Johnson.

Garter, Order of the senior British order of knighthood (see ▷knighthood, order of), founded by Edward III in about 1347. Its distinctive badge is a garter of dark-blue velvet, with the motto of the order – *Honi soit qui mal y pense* ('Shame be to him who thinks evil of it') – in gold letters. Knights of the Garter write KG after their names.

Garvey, Marcus (Moziah) (1887–1940) Jamaican political thinker and activist, an early advocate of black nationalism. He led a Back to Africa movement for black Americans to establish a black-governed country in Africa. The Jamaican cult of ▷Rastafarianism is based largely on his ideas.

Garvey founded the UNIA (Universal Negro Improvement Association) in 1914, and moved to the USA in 1916, where he established branches in New York and other northern cities. Aiming to achieve human rights and dignity for black people through pride and economic self-sufficiency, he was considered one of the first militant black nationalists.

gas in physics, a form of matter, such as air, in which the molecules move randomly in otherwise empty space, filling any size or shape of container into which the gas is put.

A sugar-lump sized cube of air at room temperature contains 30 trillion molecules moving at an average speed of 500 metres per second (1,800 kph/1,200 mph). Gases can be liquefied by cooling, which lowers the speed of the molecules and enables attractive forces between them to bind them together.

Gascoigne, Paul (1967–) Called 'Gazza'. English footballer who played for Newcastle United 1985–87, Tottenham Hotspur 1988–91, Lazio, Italy 1992–95, Glasgow Rangers 1995–97 and then joined Middlesbrough until July 2000, when he joined Everton. An attacking midfield player with superb passing and dribbling skills, he was the best player of his generation in England but his talent was dissipated by a wayward lifestyle and a fragile temperament. He made his full England debut in September 1988 and by August 1998 had won 57 caps.

Gascony ancient province of southwest France. With Guienne it formed the duchy of Aquitaine in the 12th century. Henry II of England gained possession of it through his marriage to Eleanor of Aquitaine in 1152, and it was often in English hands until 1451. Thereafter it was ruled by the king of France until it was united with the French royal domain in 1607 under Henry IV.

gas engine internal-combustion engine in which a gas (coal gas, producer gas, natural gas, or gas from a blast furnace) is used as the fuel.

The first practical gas engine was built in 1860 by Jean Etienne Lenoir, and the type was subsequently developed by Nikolaus August Otto, who introduced the ▷four-stroke cycle.

Gaskell, Elizabeth Cleghorn (1810–1865) Born Elizabeth Cleghorn Stevenson. English novelist. Her most popular book, *Cranford* (1853), is the study of a small, close-knit circle in a small town, modelled on Knutsford, Cheshire, where she was brought up. Her other books, which often deal with social concerns, include *Mary Barton* (1848), *North and South* (1855), *Sylvia's Lovers* (1863–64), and the unfinished *Wives and Daughters* (1866). She wrote a frank and sympathetic biography of her friend Charlotte ▷Brontë (1857).

Related Web site: Gaskell Web http://lang.nagoya-u.ac.jp/~matsuoka/Gaskell.html

gas laws physical laws concerning the behaviour of gases. They include ▷Boyle's law and ▷Charles's law, which are concerned with the relationships between the pressure, temperature, and volume of an ideal (hypothetical) gas. These two laws can be combined to give the **general** or **universal gas law**, which may be expressed as:

$$\frac{(\text{pressure} \times \text{volume})}{\text{temperature}} = \text{constant}$$

Van der Waals' law includes corrections for the nonideal behaviour of real gases.

gasohol motor fuel that is 90% petrol and 10% ethanol (alcohol). The ethanol is usually obtained by fermentation, followed by distillation, using maize, wheat, potatoes, or sugar cane. It was used in early cars before petrol became economical, and its use was revived during the 1940s war shortage and the energy shortage of the 1970s, for example in Brazil.

gastroenteritis inflammation of the stomach and intestines, giving rise to abdominal pain, vomiting, and diarrhoea. It may be caused by food or other poisoning, allergy, or infection. Dehydration may be severe and it is a particular risk in infants.

gastrolith stone that was once part of the digestive system of a dinosaur or other extinct animal. Rock fragments were swallowed to assist in the grinding process in the dinosaur digestive tract, much as some birds now swallow grit and pebbles to grind food in their crop. Once the animal has decayed, smooth round stones remain – often the only clue to their past use is the fact that they are geologically different from their surrounding strata.

gastropod any member of a very large group of ▷molluscs (soft-bodied invertebrate animals). Gastropods have a single shell (in a spiral or modified spiral form) and eyes on stalks, and they move on a flattened, muscular foot. They have well-developed heads and rough, scraping tongues called radulae. Some are marine, some freshwater, and others land creatures, but they all tend to live in damp places. (Class Gastropoda.)

gas turbine engine in which burning fuel supplies hot gas to spin a ▷turbine. The most widespread application of gas turbines has been in aviation. All jet engines (see under ▷jet propulsion) are modified gas turbines, and some locomotives and ships also use gas turbines as a power source.

They are also used in industry for generating and pumping purposes.

Gates, Bill (1955–) Born William Henry Gates, III. US businessman and computer programmer. He co-founded Microsoft Corporation in 1975 with school friend Paul Allen. Together they adapted the computer language ▷BASIC, traditionally used on large computers, for use on personal computers. They licensed the BASIC language and the operating system ▷MS-DOS to IBM for use in the IBM personal computer (PC), which was first marketed in 1981. Microsoft began to develop computer ▷software, and in 1990 introduced the ▷graphical user interface ▷Windows, which made computers more user-friendly by operating with on-screen symbols ('icons') and pull-down menus which are activated by a ▷mouse.

MS-DOS was accepted as standard for the software industry, and consequently Windows has been widely accepted as the standard software for PCs, including the word-processing program Word and the spreadsheet Excel. Within two months of the release of Windows 95, around seven million copies were sold. However, this domination of the software market has been attacked. In the early 1990s Microsoft was under the investigation of the US Federal Trade Commission, and accused of creating a monopoly. In 1997 the accusations were renewed and Microsoft was ordered to cease its policy of requiring computer companies to install its Internet Explorer Web browser as part of the Windows package. This court order was lifted in 1998.

In 1999 Gates's personal wealth and assets were estimated at $90 billion and, despite a reduction in his wealth due to a slump in technology shares, Bill Gates remains one of the world's richest people. In 2002, Gate's net worth was put at $52.8 billion. However, Microsoft was accused of violation of anti-monopoly legislation and in 2000 a US judge ordered Microsoft to be broken up into two separate concerns. Although the ruling to break up the company was overturned on appeal in June 2001, the verdict that Microsoft had abused its monopoly with its Windows software was upheld in October 2001, forcing the company to accept penalties for breaking US competition laws. Gates stepped down as chief executive in January 2000, in order to devote his time to building new, Internet-based software for the future, as well as concentrating on the Bill and Melinda Gates Foundation for charitable causes and programmes.

Related Web site: Gates, Bill http://www.pathfinder.com/time/time100/builder/profile/gates.html

Gateshead port in Tyne and Wear, northeast England; population (1994 est) 127,000. It is situated on the south bank of the River Tyne, opposite Newcastle upon Tyne. Formerly a port for the Tyne coalfields and a railway workshop centre, it now manufactures chemicals, plastics, and glass; other industries include engineering, printing, and tourism.

Gatling, Richard Jordan (1818–1903) US inventor of a rapid-fire gun. Patented in 1862, the Gatling gun had ten barrels arranged as a cylinder rotated by a hand crank. Cartridges from an overhead hopper or drum dropped into the breech mechanism, which loaded, fired, and extracted them at a rate of 320 rounds per minute.

GATT acronym for ▷General Agreement on Tariffs and Trade.

Gatwick site of Gatwick Airport, West Sussex, England, situated 42 km/26 mi south of central London. Designated as London's second airport in 1954, it is now one of the city's three international airport facilities. Nearly 30 million passengers a year pass through its two terminals. A rail connection links Gatwick to Victoria Station, London.

gaucho part American Indian, part Spanish cattle herder of the Argentine and Uruguayan pampas. The gauchos supported the Argentine ruler, Ortiz de Rosas, 1835–52.

Gaudí, Antonio (1852–1926) Spanish architect. He is distinguished for his flamboyant ▷art nouveau style. Gaudí worked mainly in Barcelona, designing both domestic and industrial buildings. He introduced colour, unusual materials, and audacious technical innovations. His spectacular Church of the Holy Family, Barcelona, begun 1883, is still under construction.

His design for Casa Milá, a blocks of flats in Barcelona (begun 1905), is wildly imaginative, with an undulating facade, vertically thrusting wrought-iron balconies, and a series of sculpted shapes that protrude from the roof. The central feature of his Parque Güell in Barcelona is a snakelike seat faced with a mosaic of broken tiles and cutlery.

ANTONIO GAUDÍ The Church of the Holy Family in Barcelona, Spain, the unfinished work of Antonio Gaudí.
The Art Archive/Red-Head

Gaudier-Brzeska, Henri (1891–1915) Born Henri Gaudier. French sculptor, active in London from 1911. He is regarded as one of the outstanding sculptors of his generation. He studied art in Bristol, Nuremberg, and Munich, and became a member of the English Vorticist movement, which sought to reflect the energy of the industrial age through an angular, semi-abstract style. His works include the portrait *Horace Brodsky* (1913; Tate Gallery, London); and *Birds Erect* (1914; Museum of Modern Art, New York).

gauge any scientific measuring instrument – for example, a wire gauge or a pressure gauge. The term is also applied to the width of a railway or tramway track.

gauge boson (or **field particle**) any of the particles that carry the four fundamental forces of nature (see ▷forces, fundamental). Gauge bosons are ▷elementary particles that cannot be subdivided, and include the photon, the graviton, the gluons, and the weakons.

Gauguin, (Eugène Henri) Paul (1848–1903) French post-Impressionist painter. Going beyond the Impressionists' concern with ever-changing appearances, he developed a heavily symbolic and decorative style characterized by his sensuous use of pure colours. In his search for a more direct and intense experience of life, he moved to islands in the South Pacific, where he created many of his finest works. Among his paintings is *The Yellow Christ* (1889; Albright-Knox Art Gallery, Buffalo, New York State).

Born in Paris, Gauguin spent his childhood in Peru. After a few years as a stockbroker, he took up full-time painting in 1883 and became a regular contributor to the Impressionists' last four group exhibitions 1880–86. In the period 1886–91 he spent much of his time in the village of Pont Aven in Brittany, where he concentrated on his new style, Synthetism, based on the use of powerful, expressive colours and boldly outlined areas of flat tone. Influenced by Symbolism, he chose subjects reflecting his interest in the beliefs of other cultures. He made brief visits to Martinique and Panama 1887–88, and in 1888 spent two troubled months with Vincent van Gogh in Arles, Provence. He lived in Tahiti 1891–93 and 1895–1901, and from 1901 in the Marquesas Islands, where he died. It was in Tahiti that he painted one of his best-known works, *Where Do We Come From? What Are We? Where Are We Going?* (1897; Museum of Fine Art, Boston). Gauguin has touched the modern imagination as an escapist from a sophisticated civilization, but the new life he gave to colour was his great legacy to modern painting. His life is vividly recorded in his letters, journals, and the poetical fragment of autobiography *Noa-Noa.*

Paul Gauguin
Art is either plagiarism or revolution.
Quoted in Huneker *Pathos of Distance*, 128

PAUL GAUGUIN Painted in Tahiti, *The White Horse* is an example of what Paul Gauguin called his 'Synthetist-Symbolic' style. He meant that the painting combines images and ideas, and is not intended to represent real life. *The Art Archive/Musée d'Orsay Paris/Dagli Orti*

Gaul the Celtic-speaking peoples who inhabited France and Belgium in Roman times; also their territory. Certain Gauls invaded Italy around 400 BC, sacked Rome 387 BC, and settled between the Alps and the Apennines; this district, known as Cisalpine Gaul, was conquered by Rome in about 225 BC.

Gaulle, Charles de French politician, see Charles ▷de Gaulle.

gaullism political philosophy deriving from the views of Charles ▷de Gaulle but not necessarily confined to Gaullist parties, or even to France. Its basic tenets are the creation and preservation of a strongly centralized state and an unwillingness to enter into international obligations at the expense of national interests. President Chirac's Rally for the Republic is an influential neo-Gaullist party in contemporary France, and was the first main political party in France to appoint a woman as head, when Michèle Alliot-Marie was elected its leader in November 1999.

Gaultier, Jean-Paul (1952–) French fashion designer. After working for Pierre Cardin, he launched his first collection in 1978, designing clothes that went against fashion trends, inspired by London's street style. Humorous and showy, his clothes are among the most influential in the French ready-to-wear market. He designed the costumes for Peter Greenaway's film *The Cook, the Thief, His Wife and Her Lover* (1989) and the singer Madonna's outfits for her world tour in 1990.

gauss centimetre-gram-second (c.g.s.) unit (symbol Gs) of magnetic induction or magnetic flux density, replaced by the SI unit, the ▷tesla, but still commonly used. It is equal to one line of magnetic flux per square centimetre. The Earth's magnetic field is about 0.5 Gs, and changes to it over time are measured in gammas (one gamma equals 10^{-5} gauss).

Gauss, Carl Friedrich (1777–1855) German mathematician who worked on the theory of numbers, non-Euclidean geometry, and the mathematical development of electric and magnetic theory. A method of neutralizing a magnetic field, used to protect ships from magnetic mines, is called 'degaussing'.

Gautama family name of the historical ▷Buddha.

Gauteng (Sotho 'Place of Gold') province of the Republic of South Africa from 1994, known as Pretoria-Witwatersrand-Vereeniging before 1995, and historically part of the Transvaal; area 18,760 sq km/7,243 sq mi; population (1995 est) 7,048,300. The Vaal River and Magaliesberg Mountains pass through the province. The main cities are ▷Johannesburg (capital), Pretoria, Vereeniging, Krugersdorp, Benoni, and Germiston. The most important industries are gold mining, coal, iron and steel, uranium, and chemicals; tobacco and maize are cultivated.

Gautier, Théophile (1811–1872) French Romantic poet. His later works emphasized the perfection of form and the polished beauty of language and imagery, for example *Emaux et camées/ Enamels and Cameos* (1852). He was also a novelist (*Mademoiselle de Maupin* (1835)) and later turned to journalism. His belief in the supreme importance of form in art, at the cost both of sentiment and ideas, inspired the poets who were later known as *Les Parnassiens.*

gavial large reptile related to the crocodile. It grows to about 7 m/ 23 ft long, and has a very long snout with about 100 teeth in its jaws. Gavials live in rivers in northern India, where they feed on fish and frogs. They have been extensively hunted for their skins, and are now extremely rare. (Species *Gavialis gangeticus.*)

Gawain in Arthurian legend, one of the knights of the Round Table who participated in the quest for the ▷Holy Grail. He is the hero of the 14th-century epic poem *Sir Gawayne and the Greene Knight.*

Related Web site: Sir Gawain and the Green Knight http://etext.lib.virginia.edu/cgibin/browse-mixed?id=AnoGawa&tag=public&images=images/mideng&data=/lv1/Archive/mideng-parsed

Gay, John (1685–1732) English poet and dramatist. He wrote *Trivia* (1716), a verse picture of 18th-century London. His *The Beggar's Opera* (1728), a 'Newgate pastoral' using traditional songs and telling of the love of Polly for highwayman Captain Macheath, was an extraordinarily popular success. Its satiric political touches led to the banning of *Polly*, a sequel. Bertolt Brecht (1898–1956) based his *Threepenny Opera* (1928) on the story of *The Beggar's Opera.*

Related Web site: Selected Poetry of John Gay (1685–1732) http://www.library.utoronto.ca/utel/rp/authors/gay.html

John Gay
Do you think your mother and I should have liv'd comfortably so long together, if ever we had been married?
The Beggar's Opera, I. viii (1728)

Gaye, Marvin (1939–1984) Born Marvin Pentz Gay, Jr. US pop singer and songwriter. His early hits, including 'Stubborn Kinda Fellow' (1962), 'I Heard It Through the Grapevine' (1968), and 'What's Goin' On' (1971), exemplified the Detroit ▷Motown sound. He enjoyed a comeback in the early 1980s, with the hit single 'Sexual Healing' (1982). Among his albums are the seminal *What's Going On* (1971) and *Let's Get It On* (1973).

gay politics political activity by homosexuals in pursuit of equal rights and an end to discrimination. A gay political movement first emerged in the late 1960s in New York with the founding of the Gay Liberation Front. It aimed to counter negative and critical attitudes to homosexuality and encouraged pride and solidarity among homosexuals.

Gaza Strip strip of land on the Mediterranean sea, 10 km/6 mi wide and 40 km/25 mi long, extending northeast from the Egyptian border; area 363 sq km/140 sq mi; population (2000 est) 1,022,200, mainly Palestinians, plus about 6,000 Israeli settlers, most of whom arrived during the 1990s and who occupy a fifth of the territory. The Gaza Strip was occupied by Israel from 1967 until 1994, when responsibility for its administration was transferred to the Palestine National Authority. The capital is Gaza; other main centres of population are Khan Yunis and Rafah. The area is dependent on Israel for the supply of electricity. Agriculture is the main activity, producing citrus fruit, wheat, and olives. Prior to the great influx of Palestinian refugees in 1948 the area was rural, and it is geographically part of the ▷Negev. Industry is on a small scale.

Part of the British mandate of Palestine until 1948, it was then occupied by Egypt. It was first invaded by Israel in 1956, before being reoccupied in 1967 and retained in 1973. Clashes between the Israeli authorities and the Arab Palestinian inhabitants escalated to the ▷Intifada (uprising) in 1987. In April 1992 the UN Security Council issued a statement condemning Israel for allowing 'the continued deterioration of the situation in the Gaza Strip', after clashes between Israeli troops and Palestinian demonstrators left five Palestinians dead and more than 60 wounded. Under the terms of an historic Israeli–PLO accord, signed in September 1993, the area was transferred to Palestinian control in May 1994, although Israel remained responsible for its foreign policy and defence until a final overall agreement for all the formerly-occupied territories was implemented. There were further clashes in 2000–01, in the second intifada.

Related Web site: Gaza Strip http://www.umsl.edu/services/govdocs/wofact96/97.htm

gazelle any of a number of lightly built, fast-running antelopes found on the open plains of Africa and southern Asia. (Especially species of the genus *Gazella.*)

GCHQ abbreviation for **Government Communications Headquarters**, the centre of the British government's electronic surveillance operations, in Cheltenham, Gloucestershire. It monitors broadcasts of various kinds from all over the world. It was established in World War I, and was successful in breaking the German Enigma code in 1940.

GCSE abbreviation for **General Certificate of Secondary Education**, in the UK, from 1988, the examination for 16-year-old pupils, superseding both GCE O level and CSE, and offering qualifications for up to 60% of school leavers in any particular subject.

Related Web site: GCSE Bitesize http://www.bbc.co.uk/education/gcsebitesize/

Gdańsk (German Danzig) Polish port; population (1993) 466,500. Oil is refined, and textiles, televisions, and fertilizers are produced. In the 1980s there were repeated antigovernment strikes at the Lenin shipyards; many were closed 1996.

GDP abbreviation for ▷gross domestic product.

gear toothed wheel that transmits the turning movement of one shaft to another shaft. Gear wheels may be used in pairs, or in threes if both shafts are to turn in the same direction. The gear ratio – the ratio of the number of teeth on the two wheels – determines the torque ratio, the turning force on the output shaft compared with the turning force on the input shaft. The ratio of the angular velocities of the shafts is the inverse of the gear ratio.

The common type of gear for parallel shafts is the **spur gear**, with straight teeth parallel to the shaft axis. The **helical gear** has teeth cut along sections of a helix or corkscrew shape; the double form of the helix gear is the most efficient for energy transfer. **Bevel gears**, with tapering teeth set on the base of a cone, are used to connect intersecting shafts. See picture on p. 380.

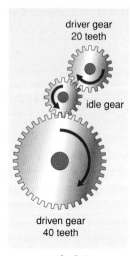
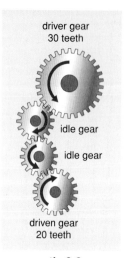

driver gear
40 teeth

driven gear
20 teeth

ratio 1:2
(one turn of the driver to
every two of the driven)

driver gear
20 teeth

idle gear

driven gear
40 teeth

ratio 2:1
(two turns of the driver to
every one of the driven)

driver gear
30 teeth

idle gear

idle gear

driven gear
20 teeth

ratio 2:3
(two turns of the driver to
every three of the driven)

GEAR Gear ratio is calculated by dividing the number of teeth on the driver gear by the number of teeth on the driven gear (gear ratio = $\frac{driver}{driven}$). A high driven to driver ratio (middle) is a speed-reducing ratio. See entry on p. 379.

gearing, financial see ▷financial gearing.

Geber Latin name of Arabic alchemist ▷Jabir ibn Hayyan.

Gebrselassie, Haile (1973–) Ethiopian long-distance runner who won the men's 10,000-metre gold medal at both the 1996 and 2000 Olympics and has also won three consecutive 10,000-metre world titles, 1993–97. Between 1994 and 1997 he broke the 5,000-metre world record three times, the 10,000-metre record twice, and in 1996 set world indoor records at 3,000 and 5,000 metres. On 25 January 1998 in Karlsruhe, Germany, he reduced his own 3,000-metre world record of 7 minutes 30.72 seconds by over four and a half seconds. In June 1998 he regained the 5,000 and 10,000 metres world records he lost to the Kenyan runners Daniel Komen and Paul Tergat in 1997. He made his debut at the marathon distance in London, England, in April 2002: his time of 2 hours 6 minutes 35 seconds shattered the record for a debut, though he finished in third place.

gecko any lizard of the family Gekkonidae. Geckos are common worldwide in warm climates, and have large heads and short, stout bodies. Many have no eyelids. They are able to climb vertically and walk upside down on smooth surfaces in their search for flies, spiders, and other prey.

There are about 850 known species of gecko. There are 102 Australian species, 17 new species having been discovered there 1986–96. A new species of gecko *Tarentola mindiae* was identified in Egypt's Western Desert in 1997. In June 2000 US researchers explained the mechanism whereby geckos are able to walk across ceilings and up walls. Each foot is covered with nearly 5,000 tiny hairs less than a tenth of the diameter of human hair, called setae. Each seta is tipped with hundreds of spatula-shaped structures. The setae generate a force of over 10 kg/22 lb when clinging on, by force of attraction between molecules (explained by ▷van der Waals' law).

The name comes from the clicking sound made by the lizard.

Geddes, Patrick (1854–1932) Scottish town planner. He established the importance of surveys, research work, and properly planned 'diagnoses before treatment'. His major work is *City Development* (1904). His protégé was Lewis ▷Mumford.

Gehry, Frank Owen (1929–) US architect, based in Los Angeles. His architecture approaches abstract art in its use of collage and montage techniques. He was awarded the 1998 National Medal of Arts.

Geiger, Hans (Wilhelm) (1882–1945) German physicist who produced the ▷Geiger counter. He spent the period 1906–12 in Manchester, England, working with Ernest ▷Rutherford on ▷radioactivity. In 1908 they designed an instrument to detect and count alpha particles, positively charged ionizing particles produced by radioactive decay.

Geiger counter any of a number of devices used for detecting nuclear radiation and/or measuring its intensity by counting the number of ionizing particles produced (see ▷radioactivity). It detects the momentary current that passes between ▷electrodes in a suitable gas when a nuclear particle or a radiation pulse causes the ionization of that gas. The electrodes are connected to electronic devices that enable the number of particles passing to be

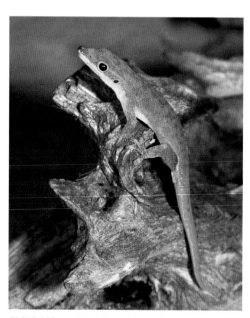

GECKO A blue-tailed day gecko from the Indian Ocean island of Madagascar. *Image Bank*

measured. The increased frequency of measured particles indicates the intensity of radiation. The device is named after the German physicist Hans ▷Geiger.

The Geiger–Müller, Geiger–Klemperer, and Rutherford–Geiger counters are all devices often referred to loosely as Geiger counters.

Geingob, Hage Gottfried (1941–) Namibian politician, from 1990 the first prime minister of an independent Namibia. He played a major role in the South West Africa's People's Organization (SWAPO), as its representative in Botswana 1963–34, and as a petitioner to the United Nations 1964–71 to obtain international recognition for SWAPO. In 1975 he was the founding director of the UN Institute for Namibia in Lusaka, educating future administrators for an independent Namibia. In 1989 he returned to Namibia as the head of SWAPO's election campaign and played a leading role in drawing up the post-independence constitution.

Geingob qualified as a schoolteacher before gaining a Masters degree in political science in the USA.

gel solid produced by the formation of a three-dimensional cage structure, commonly of linked large-molecular-mass polymers,

> **Bob Geldof**
> *I don't think that the possible death of 120 million people is a matter for charity. It is a matter of moral imperative.*
>
> To UK prime minister Margaret Thatcher on the threatened famine in Africa, 1985

in which a liquid is trapped. It is a form of ▷colloid. A gel may be a jellylike mass (pectin, gelatin) or have a more rigid structure (silica gel).

Gelderland (English **Guelders**) province of the east Netherlands, bounded on the southeast by Germany, on the southwest by the River Maas, and on the northwest by the Ijsselmeer; area 5,020 sq km/1,938 sq mi; population (1997) 1,886,100. The capital is Arnhem; other main cities are Apeldoorn, Nijmegen, and Ede. Textiles, electrical goods, and paper are produced; agriculture is based on livestock, wheat, fruit, and vegetables.

Geldof, Bob (1954–) Born Robert Frederick Xenon. Irish rock singer, born in Dun Laoghaire. He was the leader of the group the Boomtown Rats 1975–86. In the mid-1980s he instigated the charity Band Aid, which raised some £60 million for famine relief, primarily for Ethiopia.

gelignite type of ▷dynamite.

Gelon (c. 540–478 BC) Tyrant of Syracuse. Gelon took power in Gela, then capital of Sicily, in 491, and then transferred the capital to Syracuse. He refused to help the mainland Greeks against Xerxes in 480 BC, but later the same year defeated the Carthaginians under Hamilcar Barca at Himera, on the north coast of Sicily, leaving Syracuse as the leading city in the western Greek world.

gem mineral valuable by virtue of its durability (hardness), rarity, and beauty, cut and polished for ornamental use, or engraved. Of 120 minerals known to have been used as gemstones, only about 25 are in common use in jewellery today; of these, the diamond, emerald, ruby, and sapphire are classified as precious, and all the others semiprecious; for example, the topaz, amethyst, opal, and aquamarine.

Birthstones		
Month	**Stone**	**Quality**
January	garnet	constancy
February	amethyst	sincerity
March	aquamarine, bloodstone	courage
April	diamond	innocence
May	emerald	love
June	alexandrite, pearl	health and purity
July	ruby	contentment
August	peridot, sardonyx	married happiness
September	sapphire	clear thinking
October	opal, tourmaline	hope
November	topaz	fidelity
December	turquoise, zircon	wealth

Gemayel, Amin (1942–) Lebanese politician, a Maronite Christian; president 1982–88. He succeeded his brother, president-elect **Bechir Gemayel** (1947–1982), on his assassination on 14 September 1982. The Lebanese parliament was unable to agree on a successor when his term expired, so separate governments were formed under rival Christian and Muslim leaders. Following the end of his term of office as president, Gemayel was largely instrumental in ending Lebanon's civil war in 1989.

Gemeinschaft and Gesellschaft German terms (roughly, 'community' and 'association') coined by Ferdinand Tönnies in 1887 to contrast social relationships in traditional rural societies with those in modern industrial societies. He saw *Gemeinschaft* (traditional) as intimate and positive, and *Gesellschaft* (modern) as impersonal and negative.

Gemini prominent zodiacal constellation in the northern hemisphere represented as the twins Castor and Pollux. Its brightest star is Pollux; Castor is a system of six stars. The Sun passes through Gemini from late June to late July. Each December, the Geminid meteors radiate from Gemini. In astrology, the dates for Gemini are between about 21 May and 21 June (see ▷precession).

Gemini project US space programme (1965–66) in which astronauts practised rendezvous and docking of spacecraft, and working outside their spacecraft, in preparation for the ▷Apollo Moon landings.

gemsbok species of antelope that inhabits the desert regions of southern Africa. It stands about 1.2 m/4 ft in height, and its general colour is greyish. Its horns are just over 1 m/3.3 ft long.

Classification The gemsbok *Oryx gazella* is in family Bovidae, order Artiodactyla.

gen. in grammar, abbreviation for genitive.

gender in grammar, one of the categories into which nouns are divided in many languages, such as masculine, feminine, and neuter (as in Latin, German, and Russian), masculine and feminine (as in French, Italian, and Spanish), or animate and inanimate (as in some American Indian languages).

gene unit of inherited material, encoded by a strand of ▷DNA and transcribed by ▷RNA. In higher organisms, genes are located on the ▷chromosomes. A gene consistently affects a particular character in an individual – for example, the gene for eye colour. Also termed a Mendelian gene, after Austrian biologist Gregor ▷Mendel, it occurs at a particular point, or locus, on a particular chromosome and may have several variants, or ▷alleles, each specifying a particular form of that character – for example, the alleles for blue or brown eyes. Some alleles show ▷dominance. These mask the effect of other alleles, known as ▷recessive.

In the 1940s, it was established that a gene could be identified with a particular length of DNA, which coded for a complete protein molecule, leading to the 'one gene, one enzyme' principle. Later it was realized that proteins can be made up of several polypeptide chains, each with a separate gene, so this principle was modified to 'one gene, one polypeptide'. However, the fundamental idea remains the same, that genes produce their visible effects simply by coding for proteins; they control the structure of those proteins via the genetic code, as well as the amounts produced and the timing of production.

In modern genetics, the gene is identified either with the ▷cistron (a set of ▷codons that determines a complete polypeptide) or with the unit of selection (a Mendelian gene that determines a particular character in the organism on which ▷natural selection can act). Genes undergo ▷mutation and ▷recombination to produce the variation on which natural selection operates.

Related Web sites: Genetic Technology http://whyfiles.news.wisc.edu/075genome/

Your Genes, Your Choices: Exploring the Issues Raised by Genetic Research http://ehrweb.aaas.org/ehr/books/index.html

gene amplification technique by which selected DNA from a single cell can be duplicated indefinitely until there is a sufficient amount to analyse by conventional genetic techniques.

gene bank collection of seeds or other forms of genetic material, such as tubers, spores, bacterial or yeast cultures, live animals and plants, frozen sperm and eggs, or frozen embryos. These are stored for possible future use in agriculture, plant and animal breeding, or in medicine, genetic engineering, or the restocking of wild habitats where species have become extinct. Gene banks may be increasingly used as the rate of extinction increases, depleting the Earth's genetic variety (biodiversity).

gene pool total sum of ▷alleles (variants of ▷genes) possessed by all the members of a given population or species alive at a particular time.

General Agreement on Tariffs and Trade (GATT) organization within the United Nations founded in 1948 with the aim of encouraging ▷free trade between nations by reducing tariffs, subsidies, quotas, and regulations that discriminate against imported products. GATT was effectively replaced by the ▷World Trade Organization in January 1995.

General Motors the USA's largest company, a vehicle manufacturer founded in 1908 in Flint, Michigan, from a number of small carmakers; it went on to acquire many more companies, including those that produced the Oldsmobile, Pontiac, Cadillac, and Chevrolet. It has headquarters in Detroit, Michigan, and New York.

> **Bradford Snell**
> Historian
>
> *The Nazis could not have invaded Poland without General Motors.*
>
> On the supply of General Motors – and Ford – vehicles to Nazi Germany prior to the USA's declaration of war in 1941; *Independent on Sunday*, 6 December 1998

general strike refusal to work by employees in several key industries, with the intention of paralysing the economic life of a country. In British history, the General Strike was a nationwide strike called by the Trade Union Congress (TUC) on 3 May 1926 in support of striking miners. Elsewhere, the general strike was used as a political weapon by anarchists and others (see ▷syndicalism), especially in Spain and Italy. See also ▷strike.

The immediate cause of the 1926 general strike was the report of a royal commission on the coal-mining industry (*Samuel Report* (1926)) which, among other things, recommended a cut in wages. The mine-owners wanted longer hours as well as lower wages. The miners' union, under the leadership of A J Cook, resisted with the slogan 'Not a penny off the pay, not a minute on the day'. A coal strike started in early May 1926 and the miners asked the TUC to bring all major industries out on strike in support of the action; eventually it included more than 2 million workers. The Conservative government under Stanley Baldwin used troops, volunteers, and special constables to maintain food supplies and essential services, and had a monopoly on the information services, including BBC radio. After nine days the TUC ended the general strike, leaving the miners – who felt betrayed by the TUC – to remain on strike, unsuccessfully, until November 1926. The Trades Disputes Act of 1927 made general strikes illegal.

generator machine that produces electrical energy from mechanical energy, as opposed to an electric motor, which does the opposite. A simple generator (known as a dynamo in the UK) consists of a wire-wound coil (▷armature) that is rotated between the poles of a permanent magnet. The movement of the wire in the magnetic field induces a current in the coil by ▷electromagnetic induction, which can be fed by means of a ▷commutator as a continuous direct current into an external circuit. Slip rings instead of a commutator produce an alternating current, when the generator is called an alternator.

Genet, Jean (1910–1986) French dramatist, novelist, and poet. His turbulent life and early years spent in prison are reflected in his drama, characterized by ritual, role-play, and illusion, in which his characters come to act out their bizarre and violent fantasies. His plays include *Les Bonnes/The Maids* (1947), *Le Balcon/The Balcony* (1957), and two plays dealing with the Algerian situation: *Les Nègres/The Blacks* (1959) and *Les Paravents/The Screens* (1961). His novels include *Notre Dame des fleurs/Our Lady of the Flowers* (1944) and *Miracle de la rose/Miracle of the Rose* (1946), which depict a world of criminality and homosexual eroticism.

genet any of several small, nocturnal, carnivorous mammals belonging to the mongoose and civet family. Most species live in Africa, but the common genet *G. genetta* is also found in Europe and the Middle East. It is about 50 cm/1.6 ft long with a 45 cm/1.5 ft tail, weighs up to 2 kg/4.4 lb, with the male slightly larger than the female, and is greyish yellow in colour with rows of black spots. It is a good climber. Females have up to four young that begin to fend for themselves after about the age of four months. (Genus *Genetta*, family Viverridae.)

GENET The small spotted genet *Genetta genetta* at night. Genets feed on rodents, reptiles, insects, and birds.
K G Preston-Mafham/Premaphotos Wildlife

gene therapy medical technique for curing or alleviating inherited diseases or defects that are due to a gene malfunction; certain infections, and several kinds of cancer in which affected cells from a sufferer would be removed from the body, the ▷DNA repaired in the laboratory (▷genetic engineering), and the normal functioning cells reintroduced. In 1990 a genetically engineered gene was used for the first time to treat a patient.

The first human being to undergo gene therapy, in 1990, was one of the so-called 'bubble babies' – a four-year-old American girl suffering from a rare enzyme (ADA) deficiency that cripples the immune system. Unable to fight off infection, such children are nursed in a germ-free bubble; they usually die in early childhood.

Cystic fibrosis is the most common inherited disorder and the one most keenly targeted by genetic engineers; the treatment has been pioneered in patients in the USA and UK. Gene therapy is not the final answer to inherited disease; it may cure the patient but it cannot prevent him or her from passing on the genetic defect to any children. However, it does hold out the promise of a cure for various other conditions, including heart disease and some cancers; US researchers have successfully used a gene gun to target specific tumour cells. In 1995 tumour growth was halted in mice when DNA-coated gold bullets were fired into tumour cells.

By the end of 1995, although 600 people had been treated with gene therapy, nobody had actually been cured. Even in the ADA trials, the most successful to date, the children were still receiving injections of synthetic ADA, possibly the major factor in their improvement.

genetically modified foods (or **GM foods**) foods produced using genetic engineering technology. Individual genes can be copied or transferred from one living organism to another, to incorporate specific characteristics into the organism or remove undesirable characteristics. The technology, developed in the 1980s, may be used, for example, to produce crops with higher yields, enhanced taste, resistance to pests, or a longer growing season. The first genetically modified (GM) food, the 'Flavr Savr' tomato, went on sale in the USA in 1994. GM ingredients appearing in foods on the market today include tomatoes, soya, and maize, however there remain some reservations about GM products, and some companies and countries, including Britain, have taken steps to delay the growing of GM crops until risks have been assessed, and to introduce legislation forcing GM products to be declared as such.

genetic code the way in which instructions for building proteins, the basic structural molecules of living matter, are 'written' in the genetic material ▷DNA. This relationship between the sequence of bases (the subunits in a DNA molecule) and the sequence of ▷amino acids (the subunits of a protein molecule) is the basis of heredity. The code employs ▷codons of three bases each; it is the same in almost all organisms, except for a few minor differences recently discovered in some protozoa.

Only 2% of DNA is made up of base sequences, called **exons**, that code for proteins. The remaining DNA is known as 'junk' DNA or **introns**.

genetic disease any disorder caused at least partly by defective genes or chromosomes. In humans there are some 3,000 genetic diseases, including cystic fibrosis, Down's syndrome, haemophilia, Huntington's chorea, some forms of anaemia, spina bifida, and Tay-Sachs disease.

genetic engineering an all-inclusive term that describes the deliberate manipulation of genetic material by biochemical techniques. It is often achieved by the introduction of new ▷DNA, usually by means of a virus or ▷plasmid. This can be for pure research, ▷gene therapy, or to breed functionally specific plants, animals, or bacteria. These organisms with a foreign gene added are said to be transgenic. At the beginning of 1995 more than 60 plant species had been genetically engineered, and nearly 3,000 transgenic crops had been field-tested.

Practical uses In genetic engineering, the splicing and reconciliation of genes is used to increase knowledge of cell function and reproduction, but it can also achieve practical ends. For example, plants grown for food could be given the ability to fix nitrogen, found in some bacteria, and so reduce the need for expensive fertilizers, or simple bacteria may be modified to produce rare drugs. A foreign gene can be inserted into laboratory cultures of bacteria to generate commercial biological products, such as synthetic insulin, hepatitis-B vaccine, and interferon. Gene splicing was invented in 1973 by the US scientists Stanley Cohen and Herbert Boyer, and patented in the USA in 1984.

US figures for the 1997 and 1998 performance of genetically modified crops of maize, cotton, and soya released by the US Department of Agriculture in July 1999, revealed that in two-thirds of the crops studied there was no real improvement in yield and in over half of those modified to be insect resistant farmers had still needed to use similar quantities of pesticide as required for unmodified crops.

New developments Developments in genetic engineering have led to the production of growth hormone, and a number of other bone-marrow stimulating hormones. New strains of animals have also been produced; a new strain of mouse was patented in the USA in 1989 (the application was rejected in the European Patent Office). A ▷vaccine against a sheep parasite (a larval tapeworm) has been developed by genetic engineering; most existing vaccines protect against bacteria and viruses.

The first genetically engineered food went on sale in 1994; the 'Flavr Savr' tomato, produced by the US biotechnology company Calgene, was available in California and Chicago.

Safety measures There is a risk that when transplanting genes between different types of bacteria (*Escherichia coli*, which lives in the human intestine, is often used) new and harmful strains might be produced. For this reason strict safety precautions are observed, and the altered bacteria are disabled in some way so they are unable to exist outside the laboratory.

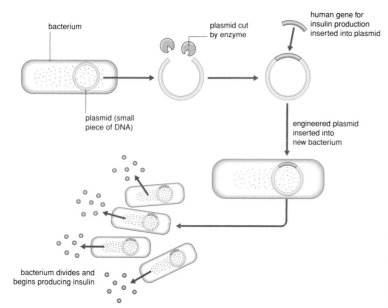

bacterium

plasmid cut by enzyme

human gene for insulin production inserted into plasmid

plasmid (small piece of DNA)

engineered plasmid inserted into new bacterium

bacterium divides and begins producing insulin

GENETIC ENGINEERING The genetic modification of a bacterium to produce insulin. The human gene for the production of insulin is collected from a donor chromosome and spliced into a vector plasmid (DNA found in bacteria but separate from the bacterial chromosomes). The plasmids and recipient bacteria are mixed together, during which process the bacteria absorb the plasmids. The plasmids replicate as the bacteria divide asexually (producing clones) and begin to produce insulin.

There are also concerns for the environmental consequences of genetically modified crops and in 1999 US ecologists found evidence that maize modified to contain the insecticidal *Bt* genes from the soil bacterium *Bacillus thuringiensis* maybe harmful to the monarch butterfly caterpillar. Monarchs feed on milkweed, which often grows near maize fields and some of the transgenic maize pollen is contaminating the milkweed.

In 1998 there were approximately 300 experimental crops of genetically engineered plants but resistance to transgenic plants increased in Britain and led to activists destroying crops from 19 separate sites. There are an estimated 150 local groups throughout Britain formed in the late 1990s to protest against genetic engineering within food and agriculture.

In spring 1999 the UK Department of Environment, Transport and the Regions began a £3.3-million four-year trial to assess the risk to nature posed by genetically modified crops of maize and oilseed rape.

genetic fingerprinting (or genetic profiling) technique developed in the UK by Professor Alec Jeffreys (1950–   ), and now allowed as a means of legal identification. It determines the pattern of certain parts of the genetic material ▷DNA that is unique to each individual. Like conventional fingerprinting, it can accurately distinguish humans from one another, with the exception of identical siblings from multiple births. It can be applied to as little material as a single cell.

genetics branch of biology concerned with the study of ▷heredity and variation; it attempts to explain how characteristics of living organisms are passed on from one generation to the next. The science of genetics is based on the work of Austrian biologist Gregor ▷Mendel whose experiments with the cross-breeding (hybridization) of peas showed that the inheritance of characteristics and traits takes place by means of discrete 'particles' (▷genes). These are present in the cells of all organisms, and are now recognized as being the basic units of heredity. All organisms possess ▷genotypes (sets of variable genes) and ▷phenotypes (characteristics produced by certain genes). Modern geneticists investigate the structure, function, and transmission of genes.

Before the publication of Mendel's work in 1865, it had been assumed that the characteristics of both parents were blended during inheritance, but Mendel showed that the genes remain intact, although their combinations change. As a result of his experiments with the cultivation of the common garden pea, Mendel introduced the concept of hybridization (see ▷monohybrid inheritance). Since Mendel, the study of genetics has advanced greatly, first through ▷breeding experiments and light-microscope observations (classical genetics), later by means of biochemical and electron microscope studies (molecular genetics).

In 1944, Canadian-born bacteriologist Oswald Avery, together with his colleagues at the Rockefeller Institute, Colin McLeod and Maclyn McCarty, showed that the genetic material was deoxyribonucleic acid (▷DNA), and not protein as was previously thought. A further breakthrough was made in 1953 when James ▷Watson and Francis ▷Crick published their molecular model for the structure of DNA, the double helix, based on X-ray diffraction photographs. The following decade saw the cracking of the ▷genetic code. The genetic code is said to be universal since the same code applies to all organisms from bacteria and viruses to higher plants and animals, including humans. Today the deliberate manipulation of genes by biochemical techniques, or ▷genetic engineering, is commonplace.

Related Web site: **Natural History of Genetics** http://gslc.genetics. utah.edu/

genetic screening in medicine, the determination of the genetic make-up of an individual to determine if he or she is at risk of developing a hereditary disease later in life. Genetic screening can also be used to determine if an individual is a carrier for a particular genetic disease and, hence, can pass the disease on to any children. Genetic counselling should be undertaken at the same time as genetic screening of affected individuals. Diseases that can be screened for include cystic fibrosis, Huntington's chorea, and certain forms of cancer.

Geneva (French **Genève**; German **Genf**) city in Switzerland, capital of Geneva canton, on the southwestern shore of ▷Lake Geneva; population (1994 est) 174,400. It is a point of convergence of natural routes and is a cultural and commercial centre. Industries include the manufacture of watches, scientific and optical instruments, foodstuffs, jewellery, and musical boxes. CERN, the particle physics research organization, is here, as are the headquarters of the International Red Cross and the World Health Organization. The United Nations has its second-largest office (after New York) in Geneva.

Related Web site: **Geneva** http://www.geneva-guide.ch/

Geneva Convention international agreement of 1864 regulating the treatment of those wounded in war, and later extended to cover the types of weapons allowed, the treatment of prisoners and the sick, and the protection of civilians in wartime. The rules were revised at conventions held in 1906, 1929, and 1949, and by the 1977 Additional Protocols.

Geneva, Lake (French **Lac Léman**; German **Genfersee**) largest of the central European lakes, between Switzerland and France; area 580 sq km/225 sq mi. The main part of the lake lies in western Switzerland. It is in the shape of a crescent 72 km/45 mi long and 13 km/8 mi wide.

Geneva Protocol international agreement of 1925 designed to prohibit the use of poisonous gases, chemical weapons, and bacteriological methods of warfare. It came into force in 1928 but was not ratified by the USA until 1974.

Genghis Khan (or **Chingiz Khan**) (c. 1155–1227) (Greek 'World Conqueror') Mongol conqueror, ruler of all Mongol peoples from 1206. He conquered the empires of northern China 1211–15 and Khwarazm 1219–21, and invaded northern India in 1221, while his lieutenants advanced as far as the Crimea. When he died, his empire ranged from the Yellow Sea to the Black Sea; it continued to expand after his death to extend from Hungary to Korea. Genghis Khan controlled probably a larger area than any other individual in history. He was not only a great military leader, but the creator of a stable political system.

The ruins of his capital Karakorum are southwest of Ulaanbaatar in Mongolia; his alleged remains are preserved at Ejin Horo, Inner Mongolia.

Genoa (Italian **Genova**; ancient **Genua**) historic city in northwest Italy, capital of Liguria, on the Gulf of Genoa, 400 km/249 mi northwest of Rome; population (1992) 667,600. It is Italy's largest port, with a major container port facility at Voltri, 10 km/6 mi to the west. Industries include oil-refining, chemicals, engineering, and the manufacture of textiles.

genocide deliberate and systematic destruction of a national, racial, religious, or ethnic group defined by the exterminators as undesirable. The term is commonly applied to the policies of the Nazis during World War II (what they called the 'final solution' – the extermination of all 'undesirables' in occupied Europe, particularly the Jews). See ▷Holocaust.

genome the full complement of ▷genes carried by a single (haploid) set of ▷chromosomes. The term may be applied to the genetic information carried by an individual or to the range of genes found in a given species. The human genome is made up of between 27,000 and 40,000 genes, according to a rough draft of the sequenced genome completed by the ▷Human Genome Project in June 2000.

genotype particular set of ▷alleles (variants of genes) possessed by a given organism. The term is usually used in conjunction with ▷phenotype, which is the product of the genotype and all environmental effects. See also ▷nature–nurture controversy.

Genova Italian form of ▷Genoa, a city in Italy.

genre a particular kind of work within an art form, differentiated by its structure, content, or style. For instance, the novel is a literary genre and the historical novel is a genre of the novel. The Western is a genre of film, and the symphonic poem is a musical genre.

Gentile da Fabriano (c. 1370–c. 1427) Born Niccolò di Giovanni di Massio. Italian painter of frescoes and altarpieces who worked in a Gothic style uninfluenced by the fashions of contemporary Florence. Gentile was active in Venice, Florence, Siena, Orvieto, and Rome and collaborated with the artists ▷Pisanello and Jacopo Bellini. His *Adoration of the Magi* (1423; Uffizi, Florence), painted for the church of Santa Trinità in Florence, is typically rich in detail and colour.

Gentileschi, Artemisia (c. 1593–c. 1652) Italian painter. She trained under Agostino Tassi (c. 1580–1644) and her father Orazio Gentileschi, though her work is more melodramatic than his. Active in England 1638–39, Florence, and Rome, she settled in Naples from about 1630, working in a heavily Caravaggesque style. She focused on macabre and grisly subjects popular during her day, most notably *Judith Decapitating Holofernes* (c. 1620).

Gentili, Alberico (1552–1608) Italian jurist. He practised law in Italy but having adopted Protestantism was compelled to flee to England, where he lectured on Roman law in Oxford. His publications, such as *De Jure Belli/On the Law of War* (1598), made him the first true international law writer and scholar.

gentry the lesser nobility, particularly in England and Wales, not entitled to sit in the House of Lords. By the later Middle Ages, it included knights, esquires, and gentlemen, and after the 17th century, baronets.

genus (plural **genera**) group of one or more ▷species with many characteristics in common. Thus all doglike species (including dogs, wolves, and jackals) belong to the genus *Canis* (Latin 'dog').

Species of the same genus are thought to be descended from a common ancestor species. Related genera are grouped into ▷families.

GENGHIS KHAN This 1891 illustration shows subjects offering tribute to Genghis Khan, whose name meant 'Universal Ruler'. *Archive Photos*

geochemistry science of chemistry as it applies to geology. It deals with the relative and absolute abundances of the chemical elements and their ▷isotopes in the Earth, and also with the chemical changes that accompany geologic processes.

geochronology the branch of geology that deals with the dating of rocks, mineral and fossils in order to create an accurate and precise geological history of the Earth. The ▷geological time scale is a result of these studies. It puts stratigraphic units in chronological order and assigns actual dates, in millions of years, to those units.

geode in geology, a subspherical cavity into which crystals have grown from the outer wall into the centre. Geodes often contain very well-formed crystals of quartz (including amethyst), calcite, or other minerals.

geodesy the science of measuring and mapping Earth's surface for making maps and correlating geological, gravitational, and magnetic measurements. Geodetic surveys, formerly carried out by means of various measuring techniques on the surface, are now commonly made by using radio signals and laser beams from orbiting satellites.

Geoffrey of Monmouth (*c.* 1100–1154) Welsh writer and chronicler. While a canon at Oxford, he wrote *Historia Regum Britanniae/History of the Kings of Britain* (*c.* 1139), which included accounts of the semi-legendary kings Lear, Cymbeline, and Arthur. He is also thought by some to be the author of *Vita Merlini*, a life of the legendary wizard. He was bishop-elect of St Asaph, North Wales, in 1151 and ordained a priest in 1152.

geography the study of the Earth's surface; its topography, climate, and physical conditions, and how these factors affect people and society. It is usually divided into **physical geography**, dealing with landforms and climates, and **human geography**, dealing with the distribution and activities of peoples on Earth.

History Early preclassical geographers concentrated on map-making, surveying, and exploring. In classical Greece theoretical ideas first became a characteristic of geography. ▷Aristotle and ▷Pythagoras believed the Earth to be a sphere, ▷Eratosthenes was the first to calculate the circumference of the world, and Herodotus investigated the origin of the Nile floods and the relationship between climate and human behaviour.

During the medieval period the study of geography progressed little in Europe, but the Muslim world retained much of the Greek tradition, embellishing the 2nd-century maps of ▷Ptolemy. During the early Renaissance the role of the geographer as an explorer and surveyor became important once again.

The foundation of modern geography as an academic subject stems from the writings of Friedrich ▷Humboldt and Johann Ritter, in the late 18th and early 19th centuries, who for the first time defined geography as a major branch of scientific inquiry.

Related Web site: The Geography Portal http://www.m8i.net/

geological time time scale embracing the history of the Earth from its physical origin to the present day. Geological time is traditionally divided into eons (Archaean or Archaeozoic, Proterozoic, and Phanerozoic in ascending chronological order), which in turn are subdivided into eras, periods, epochs, ages, and finally chrons.

The terms eon, era, period, epoch, age and chron are **geochronological units** representing intervals of geological time. Rocks representing an interval of geological time comprise a **chronostratigraphic** (or **time-stratigraphic**) **unit**. Each of the hierarchical geochronological terms has a chronostratigraphic equivalent. Thus, rocks formed during an eon (a geochronological unit) are members of an eonothem (the chronostratigraphic unit equivalent of eon). Rocks of an era belong to an erathem. The chronostratigraphic equivalents of period, epoch, age, and chron are system, series, stage, and chronozone, respectively.

geology science of the Earth, its origin, composition, structure, and history. It is divided into several branches, inlcuding **mineralogy** (the minerals of Earth), **petrology** (rocks), **stratigraphy** (the deposition of successive beds of sedimentary rocks), **palaeontology** (fossils), and **tectonics** (the deformation and movement of the Earth's crust), **geophysics** (using physics to study the Earth's surface, interior, and atmosphere), and **geochemistry** (the science of chemistry as it applies to biology).

Related Web site: Essential Guide To Rocks http://www.bbc.co.uk/education/rocks/

geometric mean in mathematics, the *n*th root of the product of *n* positive numbers. The geometric mean *m* of two numbers *p* and *q* is such that $m = \sqrt{(p \times q)}$. For example, the geometric mean of 2 and 8 is $\sqrt{(2 \times 8)} = \sqrt{16} = 4$.

geometric progression (or geometric sequence) in mathematics, a sequence of terms (progression) in which each term is a constant multiple (called the **common ratio**) of the one preceding it. For example, 3, 12, 48, 192, 768, ... is a geometric progression with a common ratio 4, since each term is equal to the previous term multiplied by 4. Compare ▷arithmetic progression.

geometry branch of mathematics concerned with the properties of space, usually in terms of plane (two-dimensional) and solid (three-dimensional) figures. The subject is usually divided into **pure geometry**, which embraces roughly the plane and solid geometry dealt with in Greek mathematician ▷Euclid's *Stoicheia/Elements*, and **analytical** or ▷coordinate geometry, in which problems are solved using algebraic methods. A third, quite distinct, type includes the non-Euclidean geometries.

Pure geometry This is chiefly concerned with properties of figures that can be measured, such as lengths, areas, and angles and is therefore of great practical use. An important idea in Euclidean geometry is the idea of **congruence**. Two figures are said to be congruent if they have the same shape and size (and area). If one figure is imagined as a rigid object that can be picked up, moved and placed on top of the other so that they exactly coincide, then the two figures are congruent. Some simple rules about congruence may be stated: two line segments are congruent if they are of equal length; two triangles are congruent if their corresponding sides are equal in length or if two sides and an angle in one is equal to those in the other; two circles are congruent if they have the same radius; two polygons are congruent if they can be divided into congruent triangles assembled in the same order.

The idea of picking up a rigid object to test congruence can be expressed more precisely in terms of elementary 'movements' of figures: a translation (or glide) in which all points move the same distance in the same direction (that is, along parallel lines); a rotation through a defined angle about a fixed point; a reflection (equivalent to turning the figure over).

Two figures are congruent to each other if one can be transformed into the other by a sequence of these elementary movements. In Euclidean geometry a fourth kind of movement is also studied; this is the enlargement in which a figure grows or shrinks in all directions by a uniform scale factor. If one figure can be transformed into another by a combination of translation, rotation, reflection, and enlargement then the two are said to be similar. All circles are similar. All squares are similar. Triangles are similar if corresponding angles are equal.

Coordinate geometry A system of geometry in which points, lines, shapes, and surfaces are represented by algebraic expressions. In plane (two-dimensional) coordinate geometry, the plane is usually defined by two axes at right angles to each other, the horizontal *x*-axis and the vertical *y*-axis, meeting at O, the origin. A point on the plane can be represented by a pair of ▷Cartesian coordinates, which define its position in terms of its distance along the *x*-axis and along the *y*-axis from O. These distances are respectively the *x* and *y* coordinates of the point.

Lines are represented as equations; for example,

$y = 2x + 1$ gives a straight line, and

$y = 3x^2 + 2x$

gives a ▷parabola (a curve). The graphs of varying equations can be drawn by plotting the coordinates of points that satisfy their equations, and joining up the points. One of the advantages of coordinate geometry is that geometrical solutions can be obtained without drawing but by manipulating algebraic expressions. For example, the coordinates of the point of intersection of two straight lines can be determined by finding the unique values of *x* and *y* that satisfy both of the equations for the lines, that is, by solving them as a pair of ▷simultaneous equations. The curves studied in simple coordinate geometry are the ▷conic sections (circle, ellipse, parabola, and hyperbola), each of which has a characteristic equation.

Geometry probably originated in ancient Egypt, in land measurements necessitated by the periodic inundations of the River Nile, and was soon extended into surveying and navigation. Early geometers were the Greek mathematicians Thales, Pythagoras, and Euclid. Analytical methods were introduced and developed by the French philosopher René ▷Descartes in the 17th century. From the 19th century, various non-Euclidean geometries were devised by Carl Friedrich Gauss, János Bolyai, and Nikolai Lobachevsky. These were later generalized by Bernhard Riemann and found to have applications in the theory of relativity.

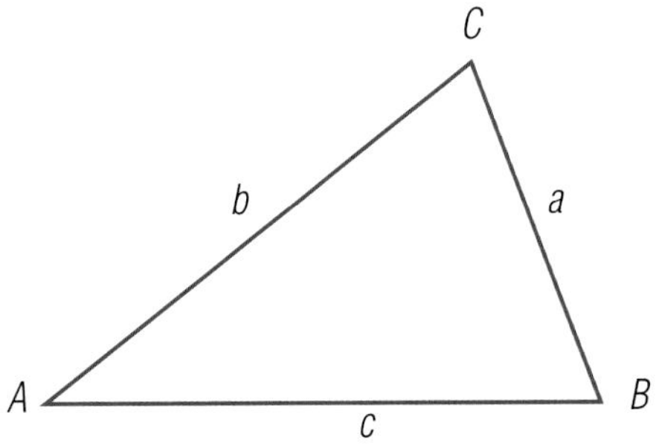

the sine rule states that

$$\frac{a}{\sin A} = \frac{b}{\sin B} = \frac{c}{\sin C}$$

or

$$\frac{\sin A}{a} = \frac{\sin B}{b} = \frac{\sin C}{c}$$

GEOMETRY The sine rule relates the sides and angles of a triangle, stating that the ratio of the length of each side and the sine of the angle opposite is constant.

geomorphology branch of geology, developed in the late 19th century, dealing with the morphology, or form, of the Earth's surface; nowadays it is also considered to be an integral part of physical geography. Geomorphological studies involve investigating the nature and origin of surface landforms, such as mountains, valleys, plains, and plateaux, and the processes that influence them. These processes include the effects of tectonic forces, ▷weathering, running water, waves, glacial ice, and wind, which result in the ▷erosion, transportation, and deposition of ▷rocks and ▷soils. The underlying dynamics of these forces are the energy derived from the Earth's gravitational field, the flow of solar energy through the hydrological cycle, and the flow of heat from the Earth's molten interior. The mechanisms of these processes are both destructive and constructive; out of the destruction or modification of one landform another will be created. In addition to the natural processes that mould landforms, human activity can produce changes, either directly or indirectly, and cause the erosion, transportation, and deposition of rocks and soils: for example, by poor land management practices and techniques in farming and forestry, and in the mining and construction industries.

geophysics branch of earth science using physics (for instance gravity, seismicity, and magnetism) to study the Earth's surface, interior, and atmosphere. Geophysics includes several sub-fields such as seismology, paleomagnetism, and remote sensing.

George six kings of Great Britain:

George I (1660–1727) King of Great Britain and Ireland from 1714. He was the son of the first elector of Hannover, Ernest Augustus (1629–1698), and his wife ▷Sophia, and a great-grandson of James I. He succeeded to the electorate in 1698, and became king on the death of Queen Anne. He attached himself to the Whigs, and spent most of his reign in Hannover, never having learned English.

He was heir through his father to the hereditary lay bishopric of Osnabrück and the duchy of Calenberg, which was one part of the Hanoverian possessions of the house of Brunswick. He acquired the other part by his marriage to **Sophia Dorothea of Zell** (1666–1726) in 1682. They were divorced in 1694, and she remained in seclusion until her death. George's children were George II and **Sophia Dorothea** (1687–1757), who married Frederick William (later king of Prussia) in 1706 and was the mother of Frederick the Great.

George II (1683–1760) King of Great Britain and Ireland from 1727, when he succeeded his father, George I. He was accused, with his minister John Carteret, of favouring Hannover at the expense of Britain's interest in the War of the Austrian Succession; his victory at Dettingen in 1743 was the last battle to be commanded by a British king. He married Caroline of Anspach in 1705, and was succeeded by his grandson, George III.

Under Queen Caroline's influence, Robert ▷Walpole retained his ministry, begun during the reign of George I, and until his resignation in 1742, managed to keep Britain at peace. The Jacobite rebellion of 1745 was successfully put down by George's favourite son, William Augustus, Duke of Cumberland.

George III (1738–1820) King of Great Britain and Ireland from 1760, when he succeeded his grandfather George II. His rule was marked by intransigence resulting in the loss of the American colonies, for which he shared the blame with his chief minister Lord North, and the emancipation of Catholics in England. Possibly suffering from ▷porphyria, he was believed to be insane. His condition deteriorated dramatically after 1811. He was succeeded by his son George IV. He married Princess ▷Charlotte Sophia of Mecklenburg-Strelitz in 1761. See picture on p. 384.

GEORGE III A portrait of 'Mad King George', by Nathaniel Dance. The king suffered from an illness now thought to be porphyria, a rare genetic abnormality that causes various disorders, including mental disturbances. See entry on p. 383. *The Art Archive/Gripsholm Castle Sweden/Dagli Orti*

George IV (1762–1830) King of Great Britain and Ireland from 1820, when he succeeded his father George III, for whom he had been regent during the king's period of insanity 1811–20. In 1785 he secretly married a Catholic widow, Maria Fitzherbert, but in 1795 also married Princess ▷Caroline of Brunswick, in return for payment of his debts. He was a patron of the arts. His prestige was undermined by his treatment of Caroline (they separated in 1796), his dissipation, and his extravagance. He was succeeded by his brother, the duke of Clarence, who became William IV.

George V (1865–1936) King of Great Britain and Northern Ireland from 1910, when he succeeded his father Edward VII. He was the second son, and became heir in 1892 on the death of his elder brother Albert, Duke of Clarence. In 1893, he married Princess Victoria Mary of Teck (Queen Mary), formerly engaged to his brother. During World War I he made several visits to the front. In 1917, he abandoned all German titles for himself and his family. The name of the royal house was changed from Saxe-Coburg-Gotha to Windsor.

His mother was Princess Alexandra of Denmark, sister of Empress Marie of Russia.

George VI (1895–1952) King of Great Britain and Northern Ireland from 1936, when he succeeded after the abdication of his brother Edward VIII, who had succeeded their father George V. Created Duke of York in 1920, he married in 1923 Lady Elizabeth Bowes-Lyon (1900–   ), and their children are Elizabeth II and Princess Margaret. During World War II, he visited the Normandy and Italian battlefields.

GEORGE VI Souvenir programme for coronation of King George VI. *The Art Archive/Imperial War Museum*

George two kings of Greece:

George I (1845–1913) King of Greece 1863–1913. The son of Christian IX of Denmark, he was nominated to the Greek throne and, in spite of early unpopularity, became a highly successful constitutional monarch. He was assassinated by a Greek, Schinas, at Salonika.

George II (1890–1947) King of Greece 1922–23 and 1935–47. He became king on the expulsion of his father Constantine I in 1922 but was himself overthrown in 1923. Restored by the military in 1935, he set up a dictatorship under Joannis Metaxas, and went into exile during the German occupation 1941–45.

George, St (died *c.* 303) Patron saint of England. The story of St George rescuing a woman by slaying a dragon, evidently derived from the Greek ▷Perseus legend, first appears in the 6th century. The cult of St George was introduced into Western Europe by the Crusaders. His feast day is 23 April.

He is said to have been martyred at Lydda in Palestine in 303, probably under the Roman emperor Diocletian. His association with England probably began when his story became popular among medieval Crusaders.

Georgetown capital and main port of Guyana, situated on the east bank of the Demerara River at its mouth on the Atlantic coast; population (1992) 200,000. There are food processing and shrimp fishing industries. Principal exports include sugar, bauxite, and rice.

George Town (or **Penang**) chief port of the Federation of Malaysia, and capital of Penang, on the island of Penang; population (2000 est) 180,600. Its sheltered harbour has made it a port of call between India and China. The port handles most of the exports of the Malay Peninsula, including tin, rubber, and copra. Local industries include smelting, milling of rice and coconuts, soap manufacture, and the assembly of electronic goods.

Georgia see country box.

Georgia state in southeastern USA. It is nicknamed the Empire State of the South or the Peach State. Georgia ratified the US Constitution in 1788, becoming the 4th state to join the Union. Historically it was a cotton-producing state associated with slavery; as the birthplace of Martin Luther King Jr, it also has strong links with the history of the civil-rights movement. Georgia is bordered to the northeast by South Carolina, to the north by North Carolina and Tennessee, to the west by Alabama, and to the south by Florida. In the southeast, Georgia has a coastline some 145 km/90 mi long on the Atlantic, off which are many of the Sea Islands.

population (1996 est) 7,353,000   **area** 152,600 sq km/58,900 sq mi **capital** Atlanta   **towns and cities** Columbus, Savannah, Macon, Albany   **industries and products** poultry, livestock, tobacco, maize, peanuts, cotton, soybeans, china clay, crushed granite, marble, clothing and textiles, carpets, aircraft, paper products, lumber, turpentine, finance sector, tourism

Related Web site: Colonials Collide at Bloody March http://www.thehistorynet.com/MilitaryHistory/articles/1096_text.htm

Georgian or **Grazinian** the people of a number of related groups which make up the largest ethnic group in Georgia and the surrounding area. There are 3–4 million speakers of Georgian, a member of the Caucasian language family.

Georgian period of English architecture, furniture making, and decorative art between 1714 and 1830. The architecture is mainly classical in style, although external details and interiors were often rich in ▷rococo carving. Furniture was frequently made of mahogany and satinwood, and mass production became increasingly common; designers included Thomas Chippendale, George Hepplewhite, and Thomas Sheraton. The silver of this period is particularly fine, and ranges from the earlier, simple forms to the ornate, and from the neoclassical style of Robert Adam to the later, more decorated pre-Victorian taste.

geostationary orbit circular path 35,900 km/22,300 mi above the Earth's Equator on which a ▷satellite takes 24 hours, moving from west to east, to complete an orbit, thus appearing to hang stationary over one place on the Earth's surface. Geostationary orbits are used particularly for communications satellites and weather satellites.

geothermal energy energy extracted for heating and electricity generation from natural steam, hot water, or hot dry rocks in the Earth's crust. Water is pumped down through an injection well where it passes through joints in the hot rocks. It rises to the surface through a recovery well and may be converted to steam or run through a heat exchanger. Dry steam may be directed through turbines to produce electricity. It is an important source of energy in volcanically active areas such as Iceland and New Zealand.

Related Web site: Geothermal Information Office http://www.alliantgeo.com/

GEOTHERMAL ENERGY Wairakei geothermal power station, New Zealand. *Image Bank*

Gerald of Wales English name of ▷Giraldus Cambrensis, medieval Welsh bishop and historian.

geranium any of a group of plants either having divided leaves and white, pink, or purple flowers (geraniums), or having a hairy stem, and white, pink, red, or black-purple flowers (▷pelargoniums). Some geraniums are also called ▷cranesbill. (Genera *Geranium* and *Pelargonium*, family Geraniaceae.)

Gérard, François Pascal (1770–1837) French painter. He was a successful portrait painter both in the Napoleonic period and during the Restoration, painting about 300 portraits of celebrities, including those of Napoleon, the politician Talleyrand, the sculptor Antonio Canova, the writer Madame de Staël, and the socialite Madame Récamier.

FRANÇOIS GÉRARD *Cupid and Psyche* (1798), by the French neoclassical painter François Gérard (1770–1837). *Archive Photos*

Georgia

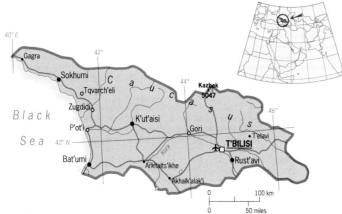

Georgia country in the Caucasus of southeastern Europe, bounded north by Russia, east by Azerbaijan, south by Armenia, and west by the Black Sea.

NATIONAL NAME *Sak'art'velo/Georgia*
AREA 69,700 sq km/26,911 sq mi
CAPITAL Tbilisi
MAJOR TOWNS/CITIES Kutaisi, Rustavi, Batumi, Zugdidi, Gori
PHYSICAL FEATURES largely mountainous with a variety of landscape from the subtropical Black Sea shores to the ice and snow of the crest line of the Caucasus; chief rivers are Kura and Rioni

Government

HEAD OF STATE Mikhail Saakashvili from 2004
HEAD OF GOVERNMENT Zurab Zhvania from 2004
POLITICAL SYSTEM emergent democracy
POLITICAL EXECUTIVE limited presidency
ADMINISTRATIVE DIVISIONS 53 regions, nine cities and two autonomous republics
ARMED FORCES 10,500 (2002 est)
CONSCRIPTION compulsory for 18 months
DEATH PENALTY abolished in 1997
DEFENCE SPEND (% GDP) 0.6 (2002 est)
EDUCATION SPEND (% GDP) 5.2 (2000 est)
HEALTH SPEND (% GDP) 7.1 (1998)

Economy and resources

CURRENCY lari
GPD (US$) 3.3 billion (2002 est)
REAL GDP GROWTH (% change on previous year) 4.5 (2001)
GNI (US$) 3.3 billion (2002 est)
GNI PER CAPITA (PPP) (US$) 2,210 (2002 est)
CONSUMER PRICE INFLATION 5% (2003 est)
UNEMPLOYMENT 15.8% (2001)
FOREIGN DEBT (US$) 2.07 billion (2001 est)
MAJOR TRADING PARTNERS Russia, Turkey, Azerbaijan, USA, Germany, EU
RESOURCES coal, manganese, barytes, clay, petroleum and natural gas deposits, iron and other ores, gold, agate, marble, alabaster, arsenic, tungsten, mercury
INDUSTRIES metalworking, light industrial goods, motor cars, food processing, textiles (including silk), chemicals, construction materials
EXPORTS aluminium and metal products, machinery, wine, tea, food and tobacco products. Principal market: Russia 23% (2001)
IMPORTS mineral fuels, chemical and petroleum products, machinery, medicines, food products (mainly wheat and flour),

light industrial products, beverages. Principal source: Turkey 15.3% (2001)
ARABLE LAND 11.4% (2000 est)
AGRICULTURAL PRODUCTS grain, tea, citrus fruits, wine grapes, flowers, tobacco, almonds, sugar beet; sheep and goat farming; forest resources

Population and society

POPULATION 5,126,000 (2003 est)
POPULATION GROWTH RATE –0.3% (2000–15)
POPULATION DENSITY (per sq km) 74 (2003 est)
URBAN POPULATION (% of total) 57 (2003 est)
AGE DISTRIBUTION (% of total population) 0–14 19%, 15–59 62%, 60+ 19% (2002 est)
ETHNIC GROUPS 70% ethnic Georgian, 8% Armenian, 7% ethnic Russian, 6% Azeri, 3% Ossetian, 2% Abkhazian, and 2% Greek
LANGUAGE Georgian (official), Russian, Abkazian, Armenian, Azeri
RELIGION Georgian Orthodox, also Muslim
EDUCATION (compulsory years) 9
LITERACY RATE 99% (men); 99% (women) (2003 est)
LABOUR FORCE 48.5% agriculture, 8.5% industry, 43.0% services (1998)
LIFE EXPECTANCY 70 (men); 78 (women) (2000–05)
CHILD MORTALITY RATE (under 5, per 1,000 live births) 29 (2001)
PHYSICIANS (per 1,000 people) 4.8 (1999 est)
HOSPITAL BEDS (per 1,000 people) 4.8 (1999 est)
TV SETS (per 1,000 people) 502 (1999)
RADIOS (per 1,000 people) 559 (1999 est)
INTERNET USERS (per 10,000 people) 149.0 (2002 est)
PERSONAL COMPUTER USERS (per 100 people) 3.2 (2002 est)

See also ▷Abkhazia; ▷Ossetia; ▷Russia; ▷Union of Soviet Socialist Republics.

Chronology

4th century BC: Georgian kingdom founded.

1st century BC: Part of Roman Empire.

AD 337: Christianity adopted.

458: Tbilisi founded by King Vakhtang Gorgasal.

mid-7th century: Tbilisi brought under Arab rule and renamed Tiflis.

1121: Tbilisi liberated by King David II the Builder, of the Gagrationi dynasty. An empire was established across the Caucasus region, remaining powerful until Mongol onslaughts in the 13th and 14th centuries.

1555: Western Georgia fell to Turkey and Eastern Georgia to Persia (Iran).

1783: Treaty of Georgievsk established Russian dominance over Georgia.

1804–13: First Russo-Iranian war fought largely over Georgia.

late 19th century: Abolition of serfdom and beginnings of industrialization, but Georgian church suppressed.

1918: Independence established after Russian Revolution.

1921: Invaded by Red Army; Soviet republic established.

1922–36: Linked with Armenia and Azerbaijan as the Transcaucasian Federation.

1930s: Rapid industrial development, but resistance to agricultural collectivization and violent political purges instituted by the Georgian Soviet dictator Joseph Stalin.

1936: Became separate republic within the USSR.

early 1940s: 200,000 Meskhetians deported from southern Georgia to Central Asia on Stalin's orders.

1972: Drive against endemic corruption launched by new Georgian Communist Party (GCP) leader Eduard Shevardnadze.

1978: Violent demonstrations by nationalists in Tbilisi.

1981–88: Increasing demands for autonomy were encouraged from 1986 by the *glasnost* initiative of the reformist Soviet leader Mikhail Gorbachev.

1989: The formation of the nationalist Georgian Popular Front led the minority Abkhazian and Ossetian communities in northwest and central-north Georgia to demand secession, provoking interethnic clashes. A state of emergency was imposed in Abkhazia; 20 pro-independence demonstrators were killed in Tbilisi by Soviet troops; Georgian sovereignty was declared by parliament.

1990: A nationalist coalition triumphed in elections and Gamsakhurdia became president. The GCP seceded from the Communist Party of the USSR.

1991: Independence was declared. The GCP was outlawed and all relations with the USSR severed. Demonstrations were held against the increasingly dictatorial Gamsakhurdia; a state of emergency was declared.

1992: Gamsakhurdia fled to Armenia; Shevardnadze, with military backing, was appointed interim president. Georgia was admitted into the United Nations (UN). Clashes continued in South Ossetia and Abkhazia, where independence had been declared.

1993: The conflict with Abkhazi separatists intensified, forcing Shevardnadze to seek Russian military help. Otar Patsatsia was appointed prime minister.

1994: Georgia joined the Commonwealth of Independent States (CIS). A military cooperation pact was signed with Russia. A ceasefire was agreed with the Abkhazi separatists; 2,500 Russian peacekeeping troops were deployed in the region and paramilitary groups disarmed. Inflation exceeded 5,000% per annum.

1996: A cooperation pact with the European Union (EU) was signed as economic growth resumed. Elections to the secessionist Abkhazi parliament were declared illegal by the Georgian government.

1997: A new opposition party, Front for the Reinstatement of Legitimate Power in Georgia, was formed. There were talks between the government and the breakaway Abkhazi government.

1998: There was another outbreak of fighting in Abkhazia.

2000: President Shevardnadze won a second term as president in elections. In May, Giorgi Arsenishvili became secretary of state (prime minister). The government signed a pact with the Abkhazian prime minister, Vyacheslav Tsugba, both sides repudiating the use of force to settle the conflict.

GEORGIA These apartment buildings stand above the Kura River, which flows through the Georgian capital, Tbilisi. *Corel*

Germany

Germany country in central Europe, bounded north by the North and Baltic Seas and Denmark, east by Poland and the Czech Republic, south by Austria and Switzerland, and west by France, Luxembourg, Belgium, and the Netherlands.

NATIONAL NAME *Bundesrepublik Deutschland/Federal Republic of Germany*
AREA 357,041 sq km/137,853 sq mi
CAPITAL Berlin
MAJOR TOWNS/CITIES Cologne, Hamburg, Munich, Essen, Frankfurt am Main, Dortmund, Stuttgart, Düsseldorf, Leipzig, Dresden, Hannover
MAJOR PORTS Hamburg, Kiel, Bremerhaven, Rostock
PHYSICAL FEATURES flat in north, mountainous in south with Alps; rivers Rhine, Weser, Elbe flow north, Danube flows southeast, Oder and Neisse flow north along Polish frontier; many lakes, including Müritz; Black Forest, Harz Mountains, Erzgebirge (Ore Mountains), Bavarian Alps, Fichtelgebirge, Thüringer Forest

Government

HEAD OF STATE Johannes Rau from 1999
HEAD OF GOVERNMENT Gerhard Schroeder from 1998
POLITICAL SYSTEM liberal democracy
POLITICAL EXECUTIVE parliamentary
ADMINISTRATIVE DIVISIONS 16 states
ARMED FORCES 296,100 (2002 est)

CONSCRIPTION 10–23 months (mainly voluntary)
DEATH PENALTY abolished in the Federal Republic of Germany in 1949 and in the German Democratic Republic in 1987
DEFENCE SPEND (% GDP) 1.5 (2002 est)
EDUCATION SPEND (% GDP) 4.5 (2001 est)
HEALTH SPEND (% GDP) 10.6 (2000 est)

Economy and resources

CURRENCY euro (Deutschmark until 2002)
GPD (US$) 1,976.2 billion (2002 est)
REAL GDP GROWTH (% change on previous year) 0.6 (2001)
GNI (US$) 1,870.4 billion (2002 est)
GNI PER CAPITA (PPP) (US$) 26,220 (2002 est)
CONSUMER PRICE INFLATION 1% (2003 est)
UNEMPLOYMENT 7.8% (2001)
MAJOR TRADING PARTNERS EU (particularly France, the Netherlands, UK, and Ireland), USA, Japan, Switzerland
RESOURCES lignite, hard coal, potash salts, crude oil, natural gas, iron ore, copper, timber, nickel, uranium

GERMANY The Reichstag Building in Berlin. *Corel*

INDUSTRIES mining, road vehicles, chemical products, transport equipment, nonelectrical machinery, metals and metal products, electrical machinery, electronic goods, cement, food and beverages

EXPORTS road vehicles, electrical machinery, metals and metal products, textiles, chemicals. Principal market: France 11.1% (2001)

IMPORTS road vehicles, electrical machinery, food and live animals, clothing and accessories, crude petroleum and petroleum products. Principal source: France 9.4% (2001)

ARABLE LAND 33.1% (2000 est)

AGRICULTURAL PRODUCTS potatoes, sugar beet, barley, wheat, maize, rapeseed, vine fruits; livestock (cattle, pigs, and poultry) and fishing

Population and society

POPULATION 82,476,000 (2003 est)

POPULATION GROWTH RATE –0.2% (2000–15)

POPULATION DENSITY (per sq km) 231 (2003 est)

URBAN POPULATION (% of total) 88 (2003 est)

AGE DISTRIBUTION (% of total population) 0–14 15%, 15–59 61%, 60+ 24% (2002 est)

ETHNIC GROUPS predominantly Germanic (92%; notable Danish and Slavonic ethnic minorities in the north; significant population of foreigners (92%), numbering about 7.4 million (1998). The largest community is Turkish (2 million), followed by nationals of the former Yugoslavia (Serbia and Montenegro from 2003) (1.4 million)

LANGUAGE German (official)

RELIGION Protestant (mainly Lutheran) 38%, Roman Catholic 34%

EDUCATION (compulsory years) 12

LITERACY RATE 99% (men); 99% (women) (2003 est)

LABOUR FORCE 2.8% agriculture, 34.5% industry, 62.6% services (2000)

LIFE EXPECTANCY 75 (men); 81 (women) (2000–05)

CHILD MORTALITY RATE (under 5, per 1,000 live births) 5 (2001)

PHYSICIANS (per 1,000 people) 3.6 (1999 est)

HOSPITAL BEDS (per 1,000 people) 9.1 (1999 est)

TV SETS (per 1,000 people) 586 (2001 est)

RADIOS (per 1,000 people) 570 (2001 est)

INTERNET USERS (per 10,000 people) 4,240.5 (2002 est)

PERSONAL COMPUTER USERS (per 100 people) 43.1 (2002 est)

See also ▷Prussia; ▷Reformation.

c. 1000 BC: Germanic tribes from Scandinavia began to settle the region between the rivers Rhine, Elbe, and Danube.

AD 9: Romans tried and failed to conquer Germanic tribes.

5th century: Germanic tribes plundered Rome, overran Western Europe, and divided it into tribal kingdoms.

496: Clovis, King of the Franks, conquered the Alemanni tribe of western Germany.

772–804: After series of fierce wars, Charlemagne extended Frankish authority over Germany, subjugated Saxons, imposed Christianity, and took title of Holy Roman Emperor.

843: Treaty of Verdun divided the Holy Roman Empire into three, with eastern portion corresponding to modern Germany; local princes became virtually independent.

919: Henry the Fowler restored central authority and founded Saxon dynasty.

962: Otto the Great enlarged the kingdom and revived title of Holy Roman Emperor.

1024–1254: Emperors of Salian and Hohenstaufen dynasties came into conflict with popes; frequent civil wars allowed German princes to regain independence.

12th century: German expansion eastwards into lands between rivers Elbe and Oder.

13th–14th centuries: Hanseatic League of Allied German cities became a great commercial and naval power.

1438: Title of Holy Roman Emperor became virtually hereditary in the Habsburg family of Austria.

1517: Martin Luther began the Reformation; Emperor Charles V tried to suppress Protestantism; civil war ensued.

1555: Peace of Augsburg: Charles V forced to accept that each German prince could choose the religion of his own lands.

1618–48: Thirty Years' War: bitter conflict, partly religious, between certain German princes and emperor, with foreign intervention; the war wrecked the German economy and reduced the Holy Roman Empire to a name.

1701: Frederick I, Elector of Brandenburg, promoted to King of Prussia.

1740: Frederick the Great of Prussia seized Silesia from Austria and retained it through war of Austrian Succession (1740–48) and Seven Years' War (1756–63).

1772–95: Prussia joined Russia and Austria in the partition of Poland.

1792: Start of French Revolutionary Wars, involving many German states, with much fighting on German soil.

1806: Holy Roman Empire abolished; France formed puppet Confederation of the Rhine in western Germany and defeated Prussia at Battle of Jena.

1813–15: National revival enabled Prussia to take part in the defeat of Napoleon at Battles of Leipzig and Waterloo.

1814–15: Congress of Vienna rewarded Prussia with Rhineland, Westphalia, and much of Saxony; loose German Confederation formed by 39 independent states.

1848–49: Liberal revolutions in many German states; Frankfurt Assembly sought German unity; revolutions suppressed.

1862: Otto von Bismarck became prime minister of Prussia.

1866: Seven Weeks' War: Prussia defeated Austria, dissolved German Confederation, and established North German Confederation under Prussian leadership.

1870–71: Franco-Prussian War; southern German states agreed to German unification; German Empire proclaimed, with King of Prussia as emperor and Bismarck as chancellor.

1890: Wilhelm II dismissed Bismarck and sought to make Germany a leading power in world politics.

1914: Germany encouraged the Austrian attack on Serbia that started World War I; Germany invaded Belgium and France.

1918: Germany defeated; a revolution overthrew the monarchy.

1919: Treaty of Versailles: Germany lost land to France, Denmark, and Poland; demilitarization and reparations imposed; Weimar Republic proclaimed.

1922–23: Hyperinflation: in 1922, one dollar was worth 50 marks; in 1923, one dollar was worth 2.5 trillion marks.

1929: Start of economic slump caused mass unemployment and brought Germany close to revolution.

1933: Adolf Hitler, leader of Nazi Party, became chancellor.

1934: Hitler took title of Führer (leader), murdered rivals, and created one-party state with militaristic and racist ideology; rearmament reduced unemployment.

1938: Germany annexed Austria and Sudeten; occupied remainder of Czechoslovakia in 1939.

1939: German invasion of Poland started World War II; Germany defeated France in 1940, attacked USSR in 1941, and pursued extermination of Jews.

1945: Germany defeated and deprived of its conquests; eastern lands transferred to Poland; USA, USSR, UK, and France established zones of occupation.

1948–49: Disputes between Western allies and USSR led to Soviet blockade of West Berlin.

1949: Partition of Germany: US, French, and British zones in West Germany became Federal Republic of Germany with Konrad Adenauer as chancellor; Soviet zone in East Germany became communist German Democratic Republic led by Walter Ulbricht.

1953: Uprising in East Berlin suppressed by Soviet troops.

1955: West Germany became a member of NATO; East Germany joined the Warsaw Pact.

1957: West Germany was a founder member of the European Economic Community.

1961: East Germany constructed the Berlin Wall to prevent emigration to West Berlin (part of West Germany).

1969: Willy Brandt, Social Democratic Party chancellor of West Germany, sought better relations with USSR and East Germany.

1971: Erich Honecker succeeded Ulbricht as Communist Party leader, and became head of state in 1976.

1982: Helmut Kohl (Christian Democratic Union) became the West German chancellor.

1989: There was a mass exodus of East Germans to West Germany via Hungary; East Germany opened its frontiers, including the Berlin Wall.

1990: The communist regime in East Germany collapsed; Germany was reunified with Kohl as chancellor.

1991: Germany took the lead in pressing for closer European integration in the Maastricht Treaty.

1998: Unemployment reached a post-war high of 12.6%. The CDU–CSU–FDP coalition was defeated in a general election and a 'Red–Green' coalition government was formed by the SPD and the Greens, with Gerhard Schroeder as chancellor.

1999: Social Democrat Johannes Rau was elected president.

2000: Former chancellor Helmut Kohl admitted financial irregularities within his party, and a criminal investigation was launched as he resigned his honorary leadership of the CDU.

2001: Kohl was heavily fined for accepting illegal donations to his party, but spared a criminal trial.

2002: Chancellor Gerhard Schroeder was re-elected in general elections, but by a close margin. Germany became the first EU country to enshrine animal rights in the constitution.

Germany: States

State	Capital	Area		Population (1997 est)
		sq km	sq mi	
Baden-Württemberg	Stuttgart	35,752	13,804	10,393,000
Bavaria	Munich	70,551	27,240	12,057,000
Berlin	Berlin	889	343	3,447,000
Brandenburg	Potsdam	29,479	11,382	2,562,000
Bremen	Bremen	404	156	676,000
Hamburg	Hamburg	755	292	1,707,000
Hessen	Wiesbaden	21,114	8,152	6,031,000
Lower Saxony	Hannover	47,606	18,381	7,832,000
Mecklenburg-West Pomerania	Schwerin	23,170	8,946	1,816,000
North Rhine-Westphalia	Düsseldorf	34,077	13,157	17,962,000
Rhineland-Palatinate	Mainz	19,852	7,665	4,010,000
Saarland	Saarbrücken	2,570	992	1,083,000
Saxony	Dresden	18,412	7,109	4,538,000
Saxony-Anhalt	Magdeburg	20,446	7,894	2,715,000
Schleswig-Holstein	Kiel	15,770	6,089	2,750,000
Thuringia	Erfurt	16,171	6,244	2,485,000

GERMANY Linderhof Palace and its fountain in Bavaria, Germany. *Image Bank*

gerbil any of numerous rodents with elongated back legs, good at hopping or jumping. Gerbils range from mouse- to rat-size, and have hairy tails. Many of the 13 genera live in dry, sandy, or sparsely vegetated areas of Africa and Asia. (Family Cricetidae.)

The Mongolian jird or gerbil (*Meriones unguiculatus*) is a popular pet.

GERBIL A hairy-footed gerbil *Gerbillurus paeba* photographed in the Kalahari Desert in southern Africa. Gerbils live in burrows and feed at night, mostly on seeds and roots. *Premaphotos Wildlife*

Gerhardie, William Alexander (1895–1977) Born William Alexander Gerhardi. English novelist, born in Russia. His novels include *Futility: A Novel on Russian Themes* (1922) and *The Polyglots* (1925), both of which draw on his Russian upbringing.

geriatrics medical speciality concerned with diseases and problems of the elderly.

Géricault, (Jean Louis André) Théodore (1791–1824) French painter and graphic artist. One of the main figures of the Romantic movement, he brought a new energy and emotional intensity to painting. His subjects included spirited horses, Napoleonic cavalry officers, and portraits, including remarkable studies of the insane, such as *A Kleptomaniac* (1822–23; Musée des Beaux Arts, Ghent). His *The Raft of the Medusa* (1819; Louvre, Paris), a vast history piece, was notorious in its day for its grim depiction of a recent scandal in which shipwrecked sailors had turned to murder and cannibalism in order to survive.

germ colloquial term for a micro-organism that causes disease, such as certain ▷bacteria and ▷viruses. Formerly, it was also used to mean something capable of developing into a complete organism (such as a fertilized egg, or the ▷embryo of a seed).

German the native people or inhabitants of Germany, or a person of German descent, as well as their culture and language. In eastern Germany the Sorbs (or Wends) comprise a minority population who speak a Slavic language. The Austrians and Swiss Germans speak German, although they are ethnically distinct. German-speaking minorities are found in France (Alsace-Lorraine), Romania (Transylvania), the Czech Republic, Siberian Russia, Central Asia, Poland, and Italy (Tyrol).

German art painting and sculpture in the Germanic north of Europe from the 8th century AD to the present. This includes Germany, Austria, and Switzerland. The Gothic style is represented by a wealth of woodcarvings and paintings for churches. Influences came from first the Low Countries and then Renaissance Italy, shown in the work of such painters as Albrecht ▷Dürer and Hans Holbein. The baroque and neoclassical periods, though important in Germany, had no individual artists of that stature; the Romantic movement produced the nature mysticism of Caspar David Friedrich. In the 20th century, expressionism began as an almost entirely German movement; ▷Dada was founded in Switzerland; and the ▷Bauhaus school of art and design was influential worldwide. Recent German art includes the multimedia work of Joseph Beuys, dealing with wartime experiences.

Germanic languages branch of the Indo-European language family, divided into **East Germanic** (Gothic, now extinct), **North Germanic** (Danish, Faroese, Icelandic, Norwegian, Swedish), and **West Germanic** (Afrikaans, Dutch, English, Flemish, Frisian, German, Yiddish).

Germanicus Caesar (15 BC–AD 19) Roman general. He was the adopted son of the emperor ▷Tiberius and married the emperor ▷Augustus' granddaughter Agrippina. Although he refused the suggestion of his troops that he claim the throne on the death of Augustus, his military victories in Germany made Tiberius jealous. Sent to the Middle East, he died near Antioch, possibly murdered at the instigation of Tiberius. He was the father of ▷Caligula and Agrippina, mother of ▷Nero.

germanium brittle, grey-white, weakly metallic (▷metalloid) element, symbol Ge, atomic number 32, relative atomic mass 72.6. It belongs to the silicon group, and has chemical and physical properties between those of silicon and tin. Germanium is a semiconductor material and is used in the manufacture of transistors and integrated circuits. The oxide is transparent to infrared radiation, and is used in military applications. It was discovered in 1886 by German chemist Clemens Winkler (1838–1904).

In parts of Asia, germanium and plants containing it are used to treat a variety of diseases, and it is sold in the West as a food supplement despite fears that it may cause kidney damage.

German language member of the Germanic group of the Indo-European language family, the national language of Germany and Austria, and an official language of Switzerland. There are many spoken varieties of German, including High German (*Hochdeutsch*) and Low German (*Plattdeutsch*).

German literature the literature of Germany. The earliest written records date from the late 8th century and consist of glosses and translations from Latin of religious and philosophical works. However, there existed a tradition of oral literature, *Heldenlieder*, or songs describing the deeds of heroes, battle songs, pagan hymns, and laments, which provided a rich source for the developing vernacular literature.

German measles (or rubella) mild, communicable virus disease, usually caught by children. It is marked by a sore throat, pinkish rash, and slight fever, and has an incubation period of two to three weeks. If a woman contracts it in the first three months of pregnancy, it may cause serious damage to the unborn child.

Immunization is recommended for girls who have not contracted the disease, at about 12–14 months or at puberty.

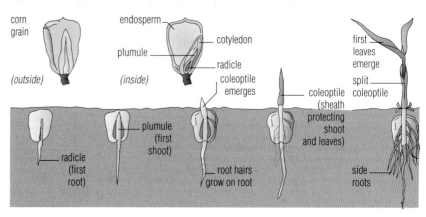

GERMINATION The germination of a corn grain. The plumule and radicle emerge from the seed coat and begin to grow into a new plant. The coleoptile protects the emerging bud and the first leaves.

German shepherd (or Alsatian) breed of dog. It is about 63 cm/25 in tall and has a wolflike appearance, a thick coat with many varieties of colouring, and a distinctive way of moving. German shepherds are used as police dogs because of their courage and intelligence.

German silver (or nickel silver) silvery alloy of nickel, copper, and zinc. It is widely used for cheap jewellery and the base metal for silver plating. The letters EPNS on silverware stand for electroplated nickel silver.

German Spring Offensive Germany's final offensive on the Western Front during World War I. By early 1918, German forces outnumbered the Allies on the Western Front. Germany staged three separate offensives, which culminated in the Second ▷Battle of the Marne, fought between 15 July and 6 August. It marked the turning point of World War I. After winning the battle the Allies advanced steadily, and by September, Germany had lost all the territory it had gained during the spring.

Germany (Federal Republic of) see country box.

Germany, East (German Democratic Republic, GDR) country 1949–90, formed from the Soviet zone of occupation in the partition of Germany following World War II. East Germany became a sovereign state in 1954, and was reunified with West Germany in October 1990. For history after 1949, see ▷Germany.

Germany, West (formerly Federal Republic of Germany, FRG) country 1949–90, formed from the British, US, and French occupation zones in the partition of Germany following World War II; reunified with East Germany in October 1990. For history after 1949, see ▷Germany.

germination in botany, the initial stages of growth in a seed, spore, or pollen grain. Seeds germinate when they are exposed to favourable external conditions of moisture, light, and temperature, and when any factors causing dormancy have been removed.

Geronimo (1829–1909) Apache **Goyahkla**. Chief of the Chiricahua Apache Indians and war leader. From 1875 to 1885, he fought US federal troops, as well as settlers encroaching on tribal reservations in the Southwest, especially in southeastern Arizona and New Mexico.

Gershwin, George (1898–1937) Born Jacob Gershvin. US composer. His musical comedies, mostly to lyrics by his brother Ira Gershwin (1896–1983), were among Broadway's most successful in the 1920s and 1930s, including *Strike up the Band* (1927), *Funny Face* (1927), and *Girl Crazy* (1930). He also wrote concert works including the tone poems *Rhapsody in Blue* (1924) and *An American in Paris* (1928). His opera *Porgy and Bess* (1935) incorporated jazz rhythms and popular song styles in an operatic format.

Successful songs from the Gershwin brothers' musicals include 'I Got Rhythm', ''S Wonderful', and 'Embraceable You'.

Gestalt (German 'form') concept of a unified whole that is greater than, or different from, the sum of its parts; that is, a complete structure whose nature is not explained simply by analysing its constituent elements. A chair, for example, will generally be recognized as a chair despite great variations between individual chairs in such attributes as size, shape, and colour.

> **Ira Gershwin**
> *From Gershwin emanated a new American music . . . based on a new native gusto and wit and awareness. His was a modernity that reflected the civilization we live in as excitingly as the headline in today's newspaper.*
>
> On George Gershwin. Quoted in
> E Jablonski and L D Stewart,
> *The Gershwin Years*

GERMANICUS CAESAR A marble bust of the Roman general Germanicus Caesar. *The Art Archive/ Capitoline Museum Rome/Dagli Orti*

Gestapo (contraction of **Geheime Staatspolizei**) Nazi Germany's secret police, formed in 1933, and under the direction of Heinrich ▷Himmler from 1934.

gestation in all mammals except the ▷monotremes (platypus and spiny anteaters), the period from the time of implantation of the embryo in the uterus to birth. This period varies among species; in humans it is about 266 days, in elephants 18–22 months, in cats about 60 days, and in some species of marsupial (such as opossum) as short as 12 days.

Gethsemane site of the garden where Judas Iscariot, according to the New Testament, betrayed Jesus. It is on the Mount of Olives, in east Jerusalem. When Jerusalem was divided between Israel and Jordan in 1948, Gethsemane fell within Jordanian territory.

Getty, J(ean) Paul (1892–1976) US oil billionaire, president of the Getty Oil Company from 1947, and founder of the Getty Museum (housing the world's highest-funded art collections) in Malibu, California.

Gettysburg site of one of the decisive battles of the American ▷Civil War: a Confederate defeat by Union forces 1–3 July 1863, at Gettysburg, Pennsylvania, 80 km/50 mi northwest of Baltimore. The site is now a national cemetery, at the dedication of which President Lincoln delivered the **Gettysburg Address** on 19 November 1863, a speech in which he reiterated the principles of freedom, equality, and democracy embodied in the US Constitution.

The South's heavy losses at Gettysburg came in the same week as their defeat at Vicksburg, and the Confederacy remained on the defensive for the rest of the war. The battle ended Robert E ▷Lee's invasion of the North.

The address begins with 'Fourscore and seven years ago', and ends with an assertion of 'government of the people, by the people, and for the people'.

Confederate advance After his victory at Chancellorsville, Lee decided to advance north into Union territory. He marched up the western side of the Blue Ridge mountains and sent General J E B (Jeb) Stuart's cavalry to the east to act as scouts. Unfortunately, Stuart instead set off to find a Union force to defeat, and failed to carry out any scouting. When the Confederates reached Chambersburg, they found that two Union corps were a few kilometres away and that General Joseph Hooker had been replaced as commander of the Union Army of the Potomac by the more dangerous General George Meade.

First clash at Gettysburg Lee sent General Ambrose P Hill's corps over the mountains to report on the Union forces' strength, but a Union cavalry patrol discovered them and Meade began moving his army toward Gettysburg. The two forces met close to the town and fighting broke out more or less immediately. The Union forces eventually passed through the town and took up a strong position on Cemetery Hill; Lee moved his troops on to a ridge across the valley, and ordered an attack the following morning.

Confederate attacks This attack was a shambles, owing to the Confederate general James Longstreet's failure to support General Richard Ewell during the morning attack. By the time Lee got him moving, the Union lines had outflanked his corps. The following day Lee planned another concerted attack. Longstreet again failed to move, allowing Ewell to make his attack and be beaten back.

Confederate defeat Ammunition began to run low, and General George A Pickett, waiting to make a frontal attack when Ewell and Longstreet had done their part, was warned that unless he made his assault now, there would be no covering fire available. Longstreet ordered him to advance. Pickett's division poured from a ravine and was blown to shreds by concentrated Union artillery fire. At the same time Hill made an attack on the Union lines, which was driven off by the appearance of a strong Union reserve. Lee saw that there was no hope of victory, and set off back to Virginia.

Related Web sites: Battle of Gettysburg Home Page http://www.militaryhistoryonline.com/gettysburg/
Gettysburg Address http://lcweb.loc.gov/exhibits/gadd/

Getz, Stan (1927–1991) Born Stanley Gayetzby. US saxophonist. He was one of the foremost tenor-sax players of his generation. In the 1950s he was a leading exponent of the cool jazz school, as on the album *West Coast Jazz* (1955). In the 1960s he turned to the Latin American bossa nova sound, which gave him a hit single, 'The Girl from Ipanema' (1964). Later he experimented with jazz-rock fusion.

geyser natural spring that intermittently discharges an explosive column of steam and hot water into the air due to the build-up of steam in underground chambers. One of the most remarkable geysers is Old Faithful, in Yellowstone National Park, Wyoming, USA. Geysers also occur in New Zealand and Iceland.

g-force force that pilots and astronauts experience when their craft accelerate or decelerate rapidly. One *g* is the ordinary pull of gravity.

Early astronauts were subjected to launch and reentry forces of up to six *g* or more; in the space shuttle, more than three *g* is experienced on liftoff. Pilots and astronauts wear *g*-suits that prevent their blood pooling too much under severe *g*-forces, which can lead to unconsciousness.

Ghana see country box.

Ghana, ancient trading empire that flourished in northwestern Africa between the 5th and 13th centuries. Founded by the Soninke people, the Ghana Empire was based, like the Mali Empire that superseded it, on the Saharan gold trade. Trade consisted mainly of the exchange of gold from inland deposits for salt from the coast. At its peak in the 11th century, it occupied an area that includes parts of present-day Mali, Senegal, and Mauritania. Wars with the Berber tribes of the Sahara led to its fragmentation and collapse in the 13th century, when much of its territory was absorbed into Mali.

From its capital at Kumbi Saleh, most trade routes ran north across the Sahara and west to the coast.

Ghats, Eastern and Western twin mountain ranges in south India, east and west of the central plateau; a few peaks reach about 3,000 m/9,800 ft. The name is a European misnomer, the Indian word *ghat* meaning 'pass', not 'mountain'.

Ghent (Flemish **Gent**; French **Gand**) port city and capital of East Flanders province, northwest Belgium, situated at the junction of the rivers Lys and Schelde, 55 km/34 mi northwest of Brussels; population (1997) 225,500. Industries include textiles, chemicals, electronics, metallurgy, and motor-vehicle manufacturing. The cathedral of St Bavon (12th–14th centuries) has paintings by van Eyck and Rubens.

ghetto (Old Venetian *gèto* 'foundry') any deprived area occupied by a minority group, whether voluntarily or not. Originally a ghetto was the area of a town where Jews were compelled to live, decreed by a law enforced by papal bull 1555. The term came into use 1516 when the Jews of Venice were expelled to an island within the city which contained an iron foundry. Ghettos were abolished, except in Eastern Europe, in the 19th century, but the concept and practice were revived by the Germans and Italians 1940–45.

Ghibelline in medieval Germany and Italy, a supporter of the emperor and member of a rival party to the Guelphs (see ▷Guelph and Ghibelline).

Ghiberti, Lorenzo (1378–1455) Italian sculptor and goldsmith. In 1402 he won the commission for a pair of gilded bronze doors for the baptistry of Florence's cathedral. He produced a second pair 1425–52, the *Gates of Paradise*, one of the masterpieces of the early Italian Renaissance. They show a sophisticated use of composition and perspective, and the influence of classical models. Around 1450 he wrote *Commentarii/Commentaries*, the earliest surviving autobiography of an artist and an important source of information on the art of his time.

Ghirlandaio, Domenico (*c.* 1449–1494) Adopted name of Domenico di Tommaso Bigordi. Italian fresco painter. He was the head of a large and prosperous workshop in Florence. His fresco cycle (1486–90) in Sta Maria Novella, Florence, includes portraits of many Florentines and much contemporary domestic detail. He also worked in Pisa, Rome, and San Gimignano, and painted many portraits.

Ghost Dance American Indian religious revivalist movement that spread through the ▷Plains Indians and other ethnic groups in the 1890s. In January 1889, a Paiute American Indian named Wovoka had a vision that the old ways would be restored, the buffalo herds would return, white people would disappear, and the American Indians would be reunited with friends and relatives in the ghost world. This vision became the nucleus for the Ghost Dance, in which American Indian peoples engaged in frenzied trance-inducing dancing, believing it would eliminate the whites and leave only the American Indians and their ancestors. The movement spread rapidly, creating a fervour and unity among the various ethnic groups that caused fear among white settlers, and which ultimately contributed to the massacre at ▷Wounded Knee after government agents called on the US Army to quell the movement.

GI abbreviation for **government issue**, hence (in the USA) a common soldier.

Giacometti, Alberto (1901–1966) Swiss sculptor and painter. In the 1940s, he developed a highly original style, creating thin, rough-textured single figures in bronze. These emaciated figures have often been seen as an expression of the acute sense of alienation of people in the modern world. *Man Pointing* (1947) is one of many examples in the Tate collection, London.

Giambologna (1529–1608) Also known as **Giovanni da Bologna** or **Jean de Boulogne**. Flemish-born sculptor. He was active mainly in Florence and Bologna. In 1583 he completed his public commission for the Loggia dei Lanzi in Florence, *The Rape of the Sabine Women*, a dynamic group of muscular, contorted figures and a prime example of Mannerist sculpture.

Giant's Causeway stretch of basalt columns forming a headland on the north coast of Antrim, Northern Ireland. It was formed by an outflow of lava in Tertiary times which has solidified in polygonal columns. The Giant's Causeway and Causeway Coast became a World Heritage Site in 1986.

Gibberd, Frederick Ernest (1908–1984) English architect and town planner. He was a pioneer of the ▷Modern Movement in England. His works include the new towns of Harlow, England, and Santa Teresa, Venezuela; the Catholic Cathedral, Liverpool (1962–67); and the Central London Mosque, Regent's Park (1970–77).

gibberellin plant growth substance (see also ▷auxin) that promotes stem growth and may also affect the breaking of dormancy in certain buds and seeds, and the induction of flowering. Application of gibberellin can stimulate the stems of dwarf plants to additional growth, delay the ageing process in leaves, and promote the production of seedless fruit (▷parthenocarpy).

gibbon any of a group of several small southern Asian apes. The **common** or **lar gibbon** (*H. lar*) is about 60 cm/2 ft tall, with a body that is hairy except for the buttocks, which distinguishes it from other types of apes. Gibbons have long arms and no tail. They spend most of their time in trees and are very agile when swinging from branch to branch. On the ground they walk upright, and are more easily caught by predators. (Genus *Hylobates*, including the subgenus *Symphalangus*.)

The **siamang** (*S. syndactylus*) is the largest of the gibbons, growing to 90 cm/36 in tall; it is entirely black. Gibbons are found from Assam through the Malay peninsula to Borneo, but are becoming rare, with certain species classified as endangered.

Gibbon, Edward (1737–1794) English historian. He wrote one major work, arranged in three parts, *The History of the Decline and Fall of the Roman Empire* (1776–88), a continuous narrative from the 2nd century AD to the fall of Constantinople in 1453.

He began work on it while in Rome in 1764. Although immediately successful, he was compelled to reply to attacks on his account of the early development of Christianity by a 'Vindication' in 1779. His *Autobiography*, pieced together from fragments, appeared in 1796.

From 1783 Gibbon lived in Lausanne, Switzerland, but he returned to England and died in London.

Gibbon, Lewis Grassic (1901–1935) Pen-name of James Leslie Mitchell. Scottish novelist. He was the author of the trilogy *A Scots Quair*, comprising *Sunset Song*, *Cloud Howe*, and *Grey Granite* (1932–34), set in the Mearns, south of Aberdeen, where he was born and brought up. Under his real name he wrote anthropological works and novels, which included *Stained Radiance* (1930) and *Spartacus* (1933).

Gibbons, Grinling (1648–1720) Dutch woodcarver who settled in England around 1667. He produced delicately carved wooden panels (largely of birds, flowers, and fruit) for St Paul's Cathedral, London, and for many large English country houses including Petworth House, Sussex, and Hampton Court, Surrey. He was carpenter to English monarchs from Charles II to George I.

Gibbs, James (1682–1754) Scottish neoclassical architect. He studied under the late-baroque architect Carlo Fontana (1638–1714) in Rome and was a close friend and follower of Christopher ▷Wren. His buildings include St Mary-le-Strand, London (1714–17), St Martin-in-the-Fields, London (1722–26), and the circular Radcliffe Camera, Oxford (1737–49), which shows the influence of Italian Mannerism.

Gibraltar (Arabic Jebel Tariq, 'Mountain of Tariq') British dependency, situated on a narrow rocky promontory at the southern tip of Spain; the **Rock of Gibraltar** formed one of the Pillars of ▷Hercules with Mount Acho, near Ceuta, across the Strait

GIBRALTAR The Rock of Gibraltar is a lump of limestone, geologically very different from the surrounding landscape. It marks the position of the Strait of Gibraltar, the narrow neck that separates Europe from Africa and provides the only link between the Atlantic Ocean and the Mediterranean Sea. *Image Bank*

Ghana

Ghana formerly the Gold Coast (until 1957), country in West Africa, bounded north by Burkina Faso, east by Togo, south by the Gulf of Guinea, and west by Côte d'Ivoire.

NATIONAL NAME *Republic of Ghana*
AREA 238,540 sq km/92,100 sq mi
CAPITAL Accra
MAJOR TOWNS/CITIES Kumasi, Tamale, Tema, Sekondi-Takoradi, Cape Coast, Koforidua, Bolgatanga, Obuasi
MAJOR PORTS Sekondi, Tema
PHYSICAL FEATURES mostly tropical lowland plains; bisected by River Volta

Government

HEAD OF STATE AND GOVERNMENT John Agyekum Kufuor from 2001
POLITICAL SYSTEM emergent democracy
POLITICAL EXECUTIVE limited presidency
ADMINISTRATIVE DIVISIONS ten regions
ARMED FORCES 7,000 (2002 est)
CONSCRIPTION military service is voluntary
DEATH PENALTY retained and used for ordinary crimes
DEFENCE SPEND (% GDP) 0.5 (2002 est)
EDUCATION SPEND (% GDP) 4.1 (2000 est)
HEALTH SPEND (% GDP) 4.2 (2000 est)

Economy and resources

CURRENCY cedi
GPD (US$) 6.0 billion (2002 est)
REAL GDP GROWTH (% change on previous year) 4.3 (2001)
GNI (US$) 5.4 billion (2002 est)
GNI PER CAPITA (PPP) (US$) 2,000 (2002 est)
CONSUMER PRICE INFLATION 11.8% (2003 est)
UNEMPLOYMENT 20% (1997 est)

FOREIGN DEBT (US$) 6.7 billion (2001 est)
MAJOR TRADING PARTNERS the Netherlands, Nigeria, UK, USA, Germany, Côte d'Ivoire, France
RESOURCES diamonds, gold, manganese, bauxite
INDUSTRIES food processing, textiles, clothes and leather goods, vehicles, aluminium, cement, paper, chemicals, petroleum products, tourism
EXPORTS gold, cocoa and related products, timber, manganese (one of the world's largest exporters). Principal market: the Netherlands 14% (2001)
IMPORTS raw materials, machinery and transport equipment, petroleum, food, basic manufactures. Principal source: Nigeria 22% (2001)
ARABLE LAND 15.9% (2000 est)
AGRICULTURAL PRODUCTS cocoa (world's third-largest producer), coffee, bananas, oil palm, maize, rice, cassava, plantain, yams, coconuts, kola nuts, limes, shea nuts; forestry (timber production)

Population and society

POPULATION 20,922,000 (2003 est)
POPULATION GROWTH RATE 1.6% (2000–15)
POPULATION DENSITY (per sq km) 88 (2003 est)
URBAN POPULATION (% of total) 37 (2003 est)
AGE DISTRIBUTION (% of total population) 0–14 40%, 15–59 55%, 60+ 5% (2002 est)
ETHNIC GROUPS over 75 ethnic groups; most significant are the Akan in the south and west (44%), the Mole-Dagbani in the north (16%), the Ewe in the south (13%), the Ga in the region of the capital city (8%), and the Fanti in the coastal area
LANGUAGE English (official), Ga, other African languages
RELIGION Christian 40%, animist 32%, Muslim 16%
EDUCATION (compulsory years) 9
LITERACY RATE 83% (men); 67% (women) (2003 est)
LABOUR FORCE 60% agriculture, 15% industry, 25% services (2000)
LIFE EXPECTANCY 57 (men); 59 (women) (2000–05)
CHILD MORTALITY RATE (under 5, per 1,000 live births) 100 (2001)
PHYSICIANS (per 1,000 people) 0.04 (1997 est)
HOSPITAL BEDS (per 1,000 people) 1.5 (1997 est)
TV SETS (per 1,000 people) 118 (2001 est)
RADIOS (per 1,000 people) 710 (2001 est)
INTERNET USERS (per 10,000 people) 23.1 (2002 est)
PERSONAL COMPUTER USERS (per 100 people) 0.4 (2002 est)

See also ▷Ashanti; ▷Ghana, ancient; ▷Gold Coast.

Chronology

5th–12th century: Ghana Empire (from which present-day country's name derives) flourished, with its centre 500 mi/800 km to the northwest, in Mali.

13th century: In coastal and forest areas Akan peoples founded the first states.

15th century: Gold-seeking Mande traders entered northern Ghana from the northeast, founding Dagomba and Mamprussi states; Portuguese navigators visited coastal region, naming it the 'Gold Coast', building a fort at Elmina, and slave trading began.

17th century: Gonja kingdom founded in north by Mande speakers; Ga and Ewe states founded in southeast by immigrants from Nigeria; in central Ghana, controlling gold reserves around Kumasi, the Ashanti, a branch of the Akans, founded what became the most powerful state in precolonial Ghana.

1618: British trading settlement established on Gold Coast.

18th–19th centuries: Centralized Ashanti kingdom at its height, dominating between Komoe River in the west and Togo Mountains in the east and active in slave trade; Fante state powerful along coast in the south.

1874: Britain, after ousting the Danes and Dutch and defeating the Ashanti, made the Gold Coast (the southern provinces) a crown colony.

1898–1901: After three further military campaigns, Britain finally subdued and established protectorates over Ashanti and the northern territories.

early 20th century: The colony developed into a major cocoa-exporting region.

1917: West Togoland, formerly German-ruled, was administered with the Gold Coast as British Togoland.

1949: Campaign for independence launched by Kwame Nkrumah, who formed the Convention People's Party (CPP) and became prime minister in 1952.

1957: Independence achieved, within the Commonwealth, as Ghana, which included British Togoland; Nkrumah became prime minister. Policy of 'African socialism' and nonalignment pursued.

1960: Became a republic, with Nkrumah as president.

1964: Ghana became a one-party state, dominated by the CCP, and developed links with communist bloc.

1972: A coup placed Col Ignatius Acheampong at the head of a military government as the economy deteriorated.

1978: Acheampong was deposed in a bloodless coup. Flight-Lt Jerry Rawlings, a populist soldier who launched a drive against corruption, came to power.

1979: There was a return to civilian rule.

1981: Rawlings seized power again. All political parties were banned.

1992: A pluralist constitution was approved in a referendum, lifting the ban on political parties. Rawlings won presidential elections.

1996: The New Democratic Congress (NDC) won an assembly majority.

2001: John Kufuor, leader of the liberal New Patriotic Party, was elected president.

GHANA Groundnuts, or peanuts, being spread out to dry in Fihini, in the north of the country. They are a staple food in Ghana. *Corel*

of Gibraltar on the north African coast; area 6.5 sq km/2.5 sq mi; population (1993) 29,000. Gibraltar is mainly a trading centre for the import and re-export of goods.

The fortress was taken by the Moors in 711 who finally ceded it to Spain in 1462. Captured from Spain in 1704 by English admiral George Rooke (1650–1709), it was ceded to Britain under the Treaty of Utrecht (1713). A referendum in 1967 confirmed the wish of the people to remain in association with the UK, but Spain continues to claim sovereignty and closed the border from 1969 to 1985. In 1989, the UK government announced it would reduce the military garrison by half. Ground troops were withdrawn in 1991, but navy and airforce units remained.

Gibraltar, Strait of strait between north Africa and Spain, forming the entrance from the Atlantic Ocean to the Mediterranean Sea, with the Rock of Gibraltar to the north side and Mount Acho to the south, the so-called Pillars of ▷Hercules.

Gibson, Guy Penrose (1918–1944) English bomber pilot of World War II. He became famous as leader of the 'dambuster raids' 16–17 May 1943; he formed 617 squadron specifically to bomb the ▷Ruhr Dams, and as wing commander led the raid personally, dropping the first bomb on the Mohne Dam. He was awarded the Victoria Cross for his leadership in this action.

Gibson Desert desert in central Western Australia, between the Great Sandy Desert to the north and the Great Victoria Desert in the south; area 220,000 sq km/85,000 sq mi.

Gide, André (Paul Guillaume) (1869–1951) French novelist. His work is largely autobiographical and concerned with the conflict between desire and conventional morality. It includes *Les Nourritures terrestres/Fruits of the Earth* (1897), *L'Immoraliste/The Immoralist* (1902), *La Porte étroite/Strait is the Gate* (1909), *Les Caves du Vatican/The Vatican Cellars* (1914), and *Les Faux-monnayeurs/The Counterfeiters* (1926). He was a cofounder of the influential literary periodical *Nouvelle Revue française* (1908), and kept an almost lifelong *Journal*. He was awarded the Nobel Prize for Literature in 1947.

Gielgud, (Arthur) John (1904–2000) English actor and director. One of the greatest Shakespearean actors of his time, he made his debut at the Old Vic in 1921 and played Hamlet in 1929. His stage appearances ranged from roles in works by Anton Chekhov and Richard Sheridan to those of Alan Bennett, Harold Pinter, and David Storey. He won an Academy Award for his role as a butler in the film *Arthur* (1981).

Gielgud's other films include *Secret Agent* (1936), *Richard III* (1955), *Becket* (1964), *Oh! What a Lovely War* (1969), *Murder on the Orient Express* (1974), *Providence* (1977), *Chariots of Fire* (1980), *Prospero's Books* (1991), *Shining Through* and *The Power of One* (both 1992), *First Knight* (1995), and *Portrait of a Lady* (1996). Television appearances included *The Best of Friends* (1992) and *Scarlett* (1994).

Giffard, Henri (1825–1882) French inventor of the first passenger-carrying powered and steerable airship, called a dirigible, built in 1852. The hydrogen-filled airship was 43 m/144 ft long, had a 2,200-W/3-hp steam engine that drove a three-bladed propeller, and was steered using a saillike rudder. It flew at an average speed of 5 kph/3 mph.

giga- prefix signifying multiplication by 10^9 (1,000,000,000 or 1 billion), as in **gigahertz**, a unit of frequency equivalent to 1 billion hertz.

gigabyte in computing, a measure of ▷memory capacity, equal to 1,024 ▷megabytes. It is also used, less precisely, to mean 1,000 billion ▷bytes.

gila monster lizard native to the southwestern USA and Mexico. It is one of the only two existing venomous lizards, the other being the Mexican beaded lizard of the same genus. It has poison glands in its lower jaw, but its bite is not usually fatal to humans. (Species *Heloderma suspectum*.)

Gilbert, Cass (1859–1934) US architect, born at Zanesville, Ohio. He began practice in 1883, and was a major developer of the ▷skyscraper. He designed the Woolworth Building, New York (1908–1913), the highest building in America (265 m/868 ft) when built and famous for its use of Gothic decorative detail.

Gilbert, Humphrey (c. 1539–1583) English soldier and navigator who claimed Newfoundland (landing at St John's) for Elizabeth I in 1583. He died when his ship sank on the return voyage. He was knighted in 1570.

Gilbert, Walter (1932–) US molecular biologist who studied genetic control, seeking the mechanisms that switch genes on and off. By 1966 he had established the existence of the lac repressor, a molecule that suppresses lactose production. He was awarded the Nobel Prize for Chemistry in 1980 for his work on the sequencing of ▷DNA nucleotides. He shared the award with Frederick ▷Sanger and Paul ▷Berg.

Gilbert, William (1540–1603) English scientist who studied magnetism and static electricity, deducing that the Earth's magnetic field behaves as if a bar magnet joined the North and South poles. His book on magnets, published in 1600, is the first printed scientific book based wholly on experimentation and observation.

Gilbert, W(illiam) S(chwenck) (1836–1911) English humorist and dramatist. He collaborated with composer Arthur ▷Sullivan, providing the libretti for their series of light comic operas from 1871 performed by the ▷D'Oyly Carte Opera Company; they include *HMS Pinafore* (1878), *The Pirates of Penzance* (1879), and *The Mikado* (1885).

W S GILBERT A costume design for the Duke of Plaza Toro, in the Richard D'Oyly Carte company's production of *The Gondoliers*, by W S Gilbert and Arthur Sullivan, at the Savoy Theatre, London, England. The design is by Charles Ricketts (1866–1931). *The Art Archive/Theatre Museum London*

Gilbert and Ellice Islands former British colony in the Pacific, known since independence (1978) as the countries of ▷Tuvalu and ▷Kiribati.

Gilbert and George Gilbert Proesch (1943–) and George Passmore (1942–). English painters and performance artists. They became known in the 1960s for their presentations of themselves as works of art, or 'living sculptures', holding poses for many hours. They also produce large emblematic photoworks. Their use of both erotic and ambiguous political material has made them controversial. They received the Turner Award in 1986. Their work has been very widely exhibited, notably in China in 1993.

gilding application of gilt (gold or a substance that looks like it) to a surface. From the 19th century, gilt was often applied to ceramics and to the relief surfaces of woodwork or plasterwork to highlight a design.

Gilgit mountainous region on the northwest frontier of Kashmir, under the rule of Pakistan; formerly a British Agency established in 1889; area 38,021 sq km/14,680 sq mi. It is drained by the Gilgit and Indus rivers. The region's town, Gilgit, was formerly a Buddhist centre. It lies at nearly 1,500 m/5,000 ft above sea level; during the winter the town can be approached only by plane.

gill in biology, the main respiratory organ of most fishes and immature amphibians, and of many aquatic invertebrates. In all types, water passes over the gills, and oxygen diffuses across the gill membranes into the circulatory system, while carbon dioxide passes from the system out into the water.

In aquatic insects, these gases diffuse into and out of air-filled canals called tracheae.

gill imperial unit of volume for liquid measure, equal to one-quarter of a pint or five fluid ounces (0.142 litre), traditionally used in selling alcoholic drinks.

Gill, (Arthur) Eric (Rowton) (1882–1940) English sculptor, graphic designer, engraver, and writer. He designed the typefaces Perpetua in 1925 and Gill Sans (without serifs) in 1927, and created monumental stone sculptures with clean, simplified outlines, such as *Prospero and Ariel* (1929–31) on Broadcasting House, London.

Gillespie, Dizzy (John Birks) (1917–1993) US jazz trumpeter. With Charlie ▷Parker, he was the chief creator and exponent of the ▷bebop style (*Groovin' High* is a CD re-issue of their seminal 78-rpm recordings). Gillespie influenced many modern jazz trumpeters, including Miles Davis.

Although associated mainly with small combos, Gillespie formed his first big band in 1945 and toured with a big band in the late 1980s, as well as in the intervening decades; a big band can be heard on *Dizzy Gillespie at Newport* (1957).

Gillespie was born in South Carolina. He moved to Philadelphia and then, in 1937, to New York, where he made his first recordings as a soloist. He was a member of popular bandleader Cab Calloway's orchestra 1939–41, with shorter spells in other bands, and formed his own quartet 1942. The following year he made his first recording with Parker.

The hipster image that Gillespie invented, with goatee, black beret, and sunglasses, was adoped by beboppers everywhere. Though his candidacy for US president in 1964 was tongue in cheek (he promised to rename the White House the Blues House), Gillespie was a serious musician and internationalist. He toured widely on a cultural mission for the State Department 1956, the first jazz musician to be so honoured. In 1968 he joined the Baha'i faith, which expects members to work for world peace. His formation of the United Nations Orchestra in the late 1980s, incorporating a strong Latin element, amounted almost to a summary of his life and work.

Gillray, James (1757–1815) English caricaturist. Creator of over 1,500 cartoons, his fierce, sometimes gross caricatures satirized George III, the Prince of Wales, politicians, and the social follies of his day, and later targeted the French and Napoleon.

Initially a letter engraver and actor, he was encouraged to become a caricaturist by the works of William Hogarth, and he was celebrated for his coloured etchings, directed against the French and the English court. Gillray's works form a brilliant if unconventional history of the late Georgian and Napoleonic period. He spared no one, and one of his most brutal caricatures, *Dido in Despair*, was directed against Admiral Nelson's mistress Lady Hamilton.

JAMES GILLRAY A cartoon by the English caricaturist James Gillray, 24 October 1798. John Bull (the personification of England) is taking a luncheon served by Admiral Nelson, whose victory at the Battle of the Nile (or Aboukir Bay) is being celebrated by this satire. *The Art Archive/British Museum/Eileen Tweedy*

gilt-edged securities stocks and shares issued and guaranteed by the British government to raise funds and traded on the Stock Exchange. A relatively risk-free investment, gilts bear fixed interest and are usually redeemable on a specified date. The term is now used generally to describe securities of the highest value.

ginger southeast Asian reedlike perennial plant; the hot-tasting spicy underground root is used as a food flavouring and in preserves. (*Zingiber officinale*, family Zingiberaceae.)

Related Web site: Ginger http://www.botanical.com/botanical/mgmh/g/ginger13.html

Gingrich, Newt(on Leroy) (1943–) US Republican politician, speaker of the ▷House of Representatives from 1995. A radical-right admirer of Reagan, he was the driving force behind his party's victory in the 1994 congressional elections, when it gained a House majority for the first time since 1954. On taking office, he sought to implement a conservative, populist manifesto – 'Contract with America' – designed to reduce federal powers, balance the budget, tackle crime, and limit congressional terms.

Gingrich was a professor of military history before entering Congress as House representative for Georgia in 1979. He established himself as a powerful and partisan speaker, and became House minority whip for the Republican Party in 1989. He set about attacking the leadership of the incumbent Democratic Party with charges of sleaze and corruption and, after their defeat in the 1994 mid-term elections, was elected speaker. He fulfilled his party's pledge to put all measures in its manifesto to a House floor vote within the first 100 days of the new Congress. However, many were subsequently watered down by the Republican-controlled Senate, and Gingrich's personal popularity fell during 1995–96.

In December 1995 Gingrich faced investigation by special committee following allegations that he had violated tax laws. He was reprimanded and fined $300,000 by the House's ethics committee in January 1997, but was nevertheless re-elected speaker. In 1998, after Republican losses in the House, he resigned his position as speaker.

ginkgo (or **maidenhair tree**) tree belonging to the ▷gymnosperm (or naked-seed-bearing) division of plants. It may reach a height of 30 m/100 ft by the time it is 200 years old. (*Ginkgo biloba*.)

Ginsberg, (Irwin) Allen (1926–1997) US poet and political activist. His reputation as a visionary, overtly political poet was established by *Howl* (1956), which expressed and shaped the spirit of the ▷Beat Generation and criticized the materialism of contemporary US society. Ginsberg, like many of his generation of poets, found his authorial voice via experimentation with drugs, alternative religion, and the hippie culture; his poetry drew, for example, on Oriental philosophies and utilized mantric breath meditations.

> **Allen Ginsberg**
> *What if someone gave a war & Nobody came?*
> 'Graffiti'

Ginsberg travelled widely – to Cuba, India, and Czechoslovakia in the 1960s, and China and Nicaragua in the 1980s – spreading his Zen-socialist politics of radical but passive dissent. His other major poem, *Kaddish* (1961), dealt with the breakdown and death of his schizophrenic mother. His *Collected Poems 1947–1980* was published in 1985.

ALLEN GINSBERG Photographed in an anti-Vietnam War protest in the early 1970s, poet Allen Ginsberg carries a prayer bell in one hand. *Archive Photos*

ginseng plant with a thick forked aromatic root used in alternative medicine as a tonic. (*Panax ginseng*, family Araliaceae.)
  Related Web site: Ginseng http://www.botanical.com/botanical/mgmh/g/ginsen15.html

Giorgione, da Castelfranco (1475–1510) Born Giorgio Barbarelli. Italian Renaissance painter. Active in Venice, he created the Renaissance poetic landscape, with its rich colours, soft forms, and gentle sense of intimacy. An example is his *Sleeping Venus* (about 1510; Gemäldegalerie, Dresden), a work that was probably completed by ▷Titian.

Giotto (*c.* 1267/77–1337) Born Giotto di Bondone. Italian painter and architect. Widely considered the founder of modern painting, he had a profound influence on the development of European art. He broke away from the conventions of the Byzantine style and introduced a new naturalism, painting saints as real people, solid, lifelike, and expressive. His style gave a greater narrative coherence, dramatic power, and dignity to the depiction of biblical incidents. His main works are cycles of frescoes in churches in Florence and Padua.

Giotto was born in Vespignano, north of Florence, and was probably taught by Giovanni Cimabue. Becoming famous in his lifetime, he was given important commissions in Tuscany, Rome, and Naples. Most of this work is lost, but the series of frescoes that decorates the walls of the Arena chapel, Padua, is enough to establish him as one of the major figures of Western art. Painted 1303–06, these frescoes illustrate the life of Christ and the life of the Virgin Mary in 38 scenes. Giotto seems to have been influenced by the contemporary Roman painter Pietro Cavallini (*c.* 1250–*c.* 1330), the sculptors Nicola and Giovanni Pisano, and antique sculpture, but his figures display an unprecedented majesty and sense of form, and convey great dramatic power.

The sole surviving work of Giotto as an architect is the bell tower (campanile) of Florence cathedral, begun in 1334, when he was made director of public works in Florence. It was unfinished at his death, and the design was later altered.

GIORGIONE The painting by Giorgione known as *The Tempest* is one of the most critically discussed pictures of all time. No one knows what it represents. The contrast between the darkness of the mood, the tension of the coming storm, and the calm passivity of the two figures, 'the soldier' and 'the gypsy', give the painting a great sense of foreboding. *The Art Archive/Accademia Venice/Dagli Orti*

GIOTTO This painting by the Italian painter Giotto di Bondone depicts the three magi, or 'wise men', visiting the baby Jesus. It also shows Halley's Comet, which may have given rise to the story of the star in the east that came to rest over Bethlehem. *The Art Archive/Scrovegni Chapel Padua/Dagli Orti*

giraffe world's tallest mammal. It stands over 5.5 m/18 ft tall, the neck accounting for nearly half this amount. The giraffe has two to four small, skin-covered, hornlike structures on its head and a long, tufted tail. The fur has a mottled appearance and is reddish brown and cream. Giraffes are found only in Africa, south of the Sahara Desert. They eat leaves and vegetation that is out of reach of smaller mammals, and are ruminants; that is, they chew the cud. (Species *Giraffa camelopardalis*, family Giraffidae.)
  Related Web site: Giraffe http://www.seaworld.org/animal_bytes/giraffeab.html

Giraldus Cambrensis (*c.* 1146–*c.* 1220) Welsh **Gerallt Gymro**. Welsh historian, born in Pembrokeshire. He studied in Paris, took holy orders in about 1172, and soon afterwards became archdeacon of Brecknock. In 1184 he accompanied Prince John to Ireland. He was elected bishop of St Davids in 1198, but failed to gain possession of his see. He wrote a history of the conquest of Ireland by Henry II. His books include *Expugnatio Hibernica* (*The Conquest of Ireland*); *Topographia Hibernica* (*The Topography of Ireland*), a descriptive account of the island; *Itinerarium Cambriae* (*Journey through Wales*) (1191); and *De Rebus a se Gestis: Gemma Ecclesiastica* (*Concerning Things Done by Himself: the Jewel of the Church*), an autobiography.

Girl Guides female equivalent of the ▷Scout organization, founded in 1910 in the UK by Robert Baden-Powell and his sister Agnes. There are three branches: Brownie Guides (age 7–11); Guides (10–16); Ranger Guides (14–20); they are led by Guiders (adult leaders). The World Association of Girl Guides and Girl Scouts (as they are known in the USA) has some 9 million members (1998).

Gironde navigable estuary 75 km/46 mi long on the southwest coast of France between Bordeaux and the sea, formed by the mouths of the Garonne and ▷Dordogne rivers. It flows into the Bay of Biscay between the Médoc and Côtes vineyards. The estuary has sand banks and strong tides, but is used by ocean-going vessels. The passenger port is Le Verdon-sur-Mer. There are oil refineries at Pauillac and Bec d'Ambès.

Girondin (or **Girondist, Brissotin**) member of the moderate republican party in the French Revolution, so called because a number of its leaders came from the Gironde region of

GIRAFFE A Rothchild's giraffe and baby in Nakuru National Park, Kenya. *Image Bank*

GIRONDIN French Girondin Charlotte Corday (d'Armont), who is most famed for stabbing the Jacobin leader, Jean Paul Marat. *Archive Photos*

southwestern France. The Girondins controlled the Legislative Assembly from late 1791 to late 1792, but were ousted by the radical Montagnards under Jean Paul ▷Marat in 1793. Many Girondin leaders were executed during the ▷Reign of Terror.

Giscard d'Estaing, Valéry (1926–) French centre-right politician and head of state, president of France 1974–81. At home he secured divorce and abortion law reforms early on, reduced the voting age to 18, and amended the constitution to enable the parliamentary opposition to refer legislation to the Constitutional Council. In Europe, he helped initiate the new Exchange Rate Mechanism in 1978 and direct elections to the European Parliament from 1979. Faced with increasingly difficult economic circumstances, he brought in Raymond ▷Barre as prime minister to manage a deflationary programme from 1976. Defeated by Mitterrand in 1981, he was re-elected to the National Assembly in 1984, resigning in 1989 in order to sit in the European Parliament.

Giscard had served as finance minister under the presidencies of Charles ▷de Gaulle 1962–66, and Georges ▷Pompidou 1969–74, but remained outside the Gaullist movement, projecting himself as leader of a 'new centre': European, Atlanticist, and committed to enhancing parliament's role. In 1978 he founded a broad-based confederation, the Union pour la Démocratie Française (UDF), and led it until 1996.

Gissing, George Robert (1857–1903) English writer. His work deals with social issues and has a tone of gloomy pessimism. Among his books are *New Grub Street* (1891), about a writer whose marriage breaks up, and the semi-autobiographical *Private Papers of Henry Ryecroft* (1903).

Givenchy, Hubert James Marcel Taffin de (1927–) French fashion designer. His simple, reasonably priced mix-and-match blouses, skirts, and slacks earned him instant acclaim when he opened his couture house in Paris 1952. He was noted for his embroidered and printed fabrics and his imaginative use of accessories.

Giza, El (or al-Jizah) city and governorate of Egypt, situated on the west bank of the Nile to the southwest of ▷Cairo, of which it forms a suburb of the greater metropolitan area; population of city (1998 est) 4,479,000, and governorate (1995 est) 4,525,000. It has textile, footwear, brewing, and film industries. It is noted for its archaeological sites; 8 km/5 mi to the southwest are the pyramids of Khufu, Khafre, and Menkure, and the Great Sphinx.

gizzard muscular grinding organ of the digestive tract, below the ▷crop of birds, earthworms, and some insects, and forming part of the ▷stomach. The gizzard of birds is lined with a hardened horny layer of the protein keratin, preventing damage to the muscle layer during the grinding process. Most birds swallow sharp grit which aids maceration of food in the gizzard.

glacial deposition the laying-down of rocky material once carried by a glacier and the product of ▷glacial erosion. When ice melts, it deposits the material that it has been carrying. The material deposited by a glacier is called ▷till, or in Britain **boulder clay**. It comprises angular particles of all sizes from boulders to clay that are unsorted and lacking in stratification.

glacial erosion the wearing-down and removal of rocks and soil by a ▷glacier. Glacial erosion forms impressive landscape features, including ▷glacial troughs (U-shaped valleys), ▷arêtes (steep ridges), ▷corries (enlarged hollows), and ▷pyramidal peaks (high mountain peaks with concave faces).

glacial trough (or U-shaped valley) steep-sided, flat-bottomed valley formed by a glacier. The erosive action of the glacier and of the debris carried by it results in the formation not only of the trough itself but also of a number of associated features, such as truncated spurs (projections of rock that have been sheared off by the ice) and hanging valleys (smaller glacial valleys that enter the trough at a higher level than the trough floor). Features characteristic of glacial deposition, such as drumlins and eskers, are commonly found on the floor of the trough, together with linear lakes called ribbon lakes.

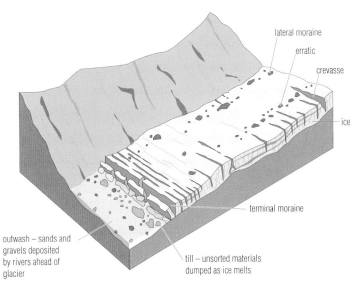

GLACIAL DEPOSITION A glacier picks up large boulders and rock debris from the valley and deposits them at the snout of the glacier when the ice melts. Some deposited material is carried great distances by the ice to form erratics.

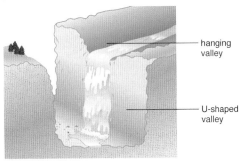

GLACIAL TROUGH Cross section of a glacial trough with a hanging valley (a smaller glacial trough). Glacial troughs are U-shaped and carved out by glaciers.

glacier tongue of ice, originating in mountains in snowfields above the snowline, which moves slowly downhill and is constantly replenished from its source. The geographic features produced by the erosive action of glaciers (▷glacial erosion) are characteristic and include ▷glacial troughs (U-shaped valleys), ▷corries, and ▷arêtes. In lowlands, the laying down of rocky debris carried by glaciers (▷glacial deposition) produces a variety of landscape features, such as ▷moraines, ▷eskers, and drumlins.

Glaciers form where annual snowfall exceeds annual melting and drainage. The area at the top of the glacier is called the zone of **accumulation**. The lower area of the glacier is called the ablation zone. In the zone of accumulation, the snow compacts to ice under the weight of the layers above and moves downhill under the force of gravity. The ice moves plastically under pressure, changing its shape and crystalline structure permanently. Partial melting of ice at the sole of the glacier also produces a sliding component of glacial movement, as the ice travels over the bedrock. In the ablation zone, melting occurs and glacial ▷till is deposited.

When a glacier moves over an uneven surface, deep **crevasses** are formed in rigid upper layers of the ice mass; if it reaches the sea or a lake, it breaks up to form **icebergs**. A glacier that is formed by one or several valley glaciers at the base of a mountain is called a **piedmont** glacier. A body of ice that covers a large land surface or continent, for example Greenland or Antarctica, and flows outward in all directions is called an **ice sheet**.

Related Web site: Glaciers http://www.nsidc.colorado.edu/glaciers/

gladiator in ancient Rome, a trained fighter, recruited mainly from slaves, criminals, and prisoners of war, who fought to the death in arenas for the entertainment of spectators. The custom was introduced into Rome from Etruria in 264 BC and continued until the 5th century AD.

Gladio code name for the Italian branch of a secret paramilitary network backed by the Central Intelligence Agency and the North Atlantic Treaty Organization (NATO), the ▷Allied Coordination Committee, made public and disbanded in 1990. The name Gladio has also been used for the entire network.

gladiolus any plant of a group of southern European and African cultivated perennials belonging to the iris family, with brightly coloured funnel-shaped flowers borne on a spike; the swordlike leaves spring from a corm (swollen underground stem). (Genus *Gladiolus*, family Iridaceae.)

GLACIER A view of the Muldrow Glacier in Mount McKinley National Park, Alaska, USA. *Archive Photos*

GLADIOLUS The mountains of South Africa are rich in species of gladioli. This is a *Gladiolus ecklonii* from the grasslands of the Natal Drakensberg region. *Premaphotos Wildlife*

Gladstone, William Ewart (1809–1898) British Liberal politician, four times prime minister. He entered Parliament as a Tory in 1833 and held ministerial office, but left the party in 1846 and after 1859 identified himself with the Liberals. He was chancellor of the Exchequer 1852–55 and 1859–66, and prime minister 1868–74, 1880–85, 1886, and 1892–94. He introduced elementary education in 1870 and vote by secret ballot in 1872 and many reforms in Ireland, although he failed in his efforts to get a Home Rule Bill passed.

Gladstone was born in Liverpool. In Robert Peel's government he was president of the Board of Trade 1843–45 and colonial secretary 1845–46. He left the Tory Party with the Peelite group in 1846. He was chancellor of the Exchequer in Aberdeen's government 1852–55 and in the Liberal governments of Palmerston and John Russell 1859–66. In his first term as prime minister he carried through a series of reforms, including the disestablishment of the Church of Ireland, the Irish Land Act, and the abolition of the purchase of army commissions and of religious tests in the universities.

> **William Gladstone**
> *All the world over,*
> *I will back the masses*
> *against the classes.*
> Speech in Liverpool, 28 June 1886

Gladstone strongly resisted Benjamin Disraeli's imperialist and pro-Turkish policy during the latter's government of 1874–80, not least because of Turkish pogroms against subject Christians, and by his Midlothian campaign of 1879 helped to overthrow Disraeli. Gladstone's second government carried the second Irish Land Act and the Reform Act of 1884 but was confronted with problems in Ireland, Egypt, and South Africa, and lost prestige through its failure to relieve General ▷Gordon in Sudan. Returning to office in 1886, Gladstone introduced his first Home Rule Bill, which was defeated by the secession of the Liberal Unionists, and he thereupon resigned. After six years' opposition he formed his last government; his second Home Rule Bill was rejected by the Lords, and in 1894 he resigned. He led a final crusade against the massacre of Armenian Christians in 1896.

Related Web site: Gladstone, William Ewart http://www.spartacus.schoolnet.co.uk/PRgladstone.htm

LONDON SKETCH BOOK.

RT. HON. W. E. GLADSTONE, M.P.,
First Lord of the Treasury and Chancellor of the Exchequer.
Double, double toil and trouble.

WILLIAM GLADSTONE English statesman William Ewart Gladstone, depicted here in a 1850s caricature as a member of Parliament and first lord of the treasury. *Archive Photos*

Glamorgan (Welsh **Morgannwg**) three counties of south Wales – ▷Mid Glamorgan, ▷South Glamorgan, and ▷West Glamorgan – created in 1974 from the former county of Glamorganshire. All are on the Bristol Channel. In 1996 Mid Glamorgan was divided amongst Rhondda Cynon Taff, Merthyr Tydfil, Bridgend, and Vale of Glamorgan; South Glamorgan was divided amongst Cardiff and Vale of Glamorgan; and West Glamorgan was divided into Neath Port Talbot and Swansea.

gland specialized organ of the body that manufactures and secretes enzymes, hormones, or other chemicals. In animals, glands vary in size from small (for example, tear glands) to large (for example, the pancreas), but in plants they are always small, and may consist of a single cell. Some glands discharge their products internally, ▷endocrine glands, and others, externally ▷exocrine glands. Lymph nodes are sometimes wrongly called glands.

glandular fever (or infectious mononucleosis) viral disease characterized at onset by fever and painfully swollen lymph nodes (in the neck); there may also be digestive upset, sore throat, and skin rashes. Lassitude persists for months and even years, and recovery can be slow. It is caused by the Epstein–Barr virus.

Glasgow city and, as **Glasgow City**, unitary authority in west-central Scotland; the unitary authority was formed in 1995 from the majority of land from Glasgow District Council of Strathclyde Region. Glasgow is the largest of Scotland's four cities. It is the third most visited city in Britain, and the UK's fourth largest manufacturing centre.

area 176 sq km/68 sq mi **industries** primarily a service economy, with 83% of employment in the service sector; industries also include engineering, chemicals, printing, whisky blending, brewing, electronics, textiles, light manufacturing **population** (2000 est) 609,300 **features** Buildings include the Cathedral of St Mungo, which dates mainly from the 13th century; Provand's Lordship (1475; the oldest dwelling-house in the city); the Cross Steeple (part of the historic Tolbooth); the University of Glasgow, established in 1451 (present buildings constructed in 1868–70 to designs by George Gilbert ▷Scott). Other buildings of note include the Kelvingrove Art Gallery; the Glasgow School of Art, designed by C R ▷Mackintosh; the Burrell Collection at Pollock Park, bequeathed by shipping magnate William Burrell (1861–1958); the Gallery of Modern Art; the Mitchell Library; and 19th-century Greek Revival buildings designed by Alexander Thomson. Glasgow's Hampden Park Stadium is a Millennium Commission Landmark Project. **history** There was a settlement on the Clyde when St Mungo arrived in the 6th century to convert the Strathclyde Britons. William the Lion made Glasgow a burgh of barony in about 1178, and it became a royal burgh under James VI in 1636. The Union of Scotland and England in 1707, though at first resented, brought increasing prosperity; in the 18th century trade with the Americas for tobacco, sugar, and cotton was very important. By 1775, the city's prosperity was at its height as a result of overseas trade. In the 19th century the Industrial Revolution had a great influence on the city, and its shipbuilding industry developed. By 1811, Glasgow was larger than any other city in Britain, apart from London. During the 19th century, there was a major influx of immigrants from Ireland and the Scottish highlands, contributing to overcrowding and insanitary conditions. This was a period of intense building of tenement housing.

GLASGOW The Kelvingrove Art Gallery and Museum in Glasgow, Scotland, is noted for its collection of European painting from the 15th century onwards. *Image Bank*

glasnost (Russian 'openness') Soviet leader Mikhail ▷Gorbachev's policy of liberalizing various aspects of Soviet life, such as introducing greater freedom of expression and information and opening up relations with Western countries. *Glasnost* was introduced and adopted by the Soviet government in 1986.

glass transparent or translucent substance that is physically neither a solid nor a liquid. Although glass is easily shattered, it is one of the strongest substances known. It is made by fusing certain types of sand (silica); this fusion occurs naturally in volcanic glass (see ▷obsidian).

In the industrial production of common types of glass, the type of sand used, the particular chemicals added to it (for example, lead, potassium, barium), and refinements of technique determine the type of glass produced. Types of glass include: soda glass; flint glass, used in cut-crystal ware; optical glass; stained glass; heat-resistant glass; and glasses that exclude certain ranges of the light spectrum. Blown glass is either blown individually from molten glass (using a tube up to 1.5 m/4.5 ft long), as in the making of expensive crafted glass, or blown automatically into a mould – for example, in the manufacture of light bulbs and bottles; pressed glass is simply pressed into moulds, for jam jars, cheap vases, and light fittings; while sheet glass, for windows, is made by putting the molten glass through rollers to form a 'ribbon', or by floating molten glass on molten tin in the 'float glass' process; ▷fibreglass is made from fine glass fibres. Metallic glass is produced by treating alloys so that they take on the properties of glass while retaining the malleability and conductivity characteristic of metals.

Glass, Philip (1937–) US composer. As a student of Nadia Boulanger, he was strongly influenced by Indian music; his work is characterized by repeated rhythmic figures that are continually expanded and modified. His compositions include the operas *Einstein on the Beach* (1976), *Akhnaten* (1984), *The Making of the Representative for Planet 8* (1988), and the '*Low' Symphony* (1992) on themes from David Bowie's *Low* album.

glasses pair of lenses fitted in a frame and worn in front of the ▷eyes to correct or assist defective vision. Common defects of the eye corrected by lenses are short sight (myopia) by using concave (spherical) lenses, long sight (hypermetropia) by using convex (spherical) lenses, and astigmatism by using cylindrical lenses.

glass-reinforced plastic (GRP) a plastic material strengthened by glass fibres, sometimes erroneously called ▷fibreglass. Glass-reinforced plastic is a favoured material for boat hulls and for the bodies and some structural components of high-performance cars and aircraft; it is also used in the manufacture of passenger cars.

glass snake (or **glass lizard**) any of a worldwide group of legless lizards. Their tails are up to three times the head–body length and are easily broken off. (Genus *Ophisaurus*, family Anguidae.)

Glastonbury market town in Somerset, southwest England, on the River Brue, 8 km/5 mi southwest of Wells; population (1996 est) 8,100. Light industries include injection moulding, and the production of footwear and leather goods. Tourism and warehousing are also important. **Glastonbury Tor**, a hill crowned by a ruined 14th-century church tower, rises to 159 m/522 ft. Glastonbury lake village, occupied from around 150 BC to AD 50, lies 5 km/3 mi to the northwest.

glaucoma condition in which pressure inside the eye (intraocular pressure) is raised abnormally as excess fluid accumulates. It occurs when the normal outflow of fluid within the chamber of the eye (aqueous humour) is interrupted. As pressure rises, the optic nerve suffers irreversible damage, leading to a reduction in the field of vision and, ultimately, loss of eyesight.

Related Web site: Glaucoma Research Foundation http://www.glaucoma.org/

Glencoe valley in the Highland unitary authority, Scotland, extending 16 km/10 mi east from Rannoch Moor to Loch Leven. The mountains rise steeply on either side to over 1,000 m/3,300 ft, and the River Coe flows through the valley. Thirty-eight members of the Macdonald clan were massacred in Glencoe on 13 February 1692 by government troops led by Robert Campbell of Glenlyon; 300 escaped.

Glendower, Owen (c. 1350–1416) Also known as **Owain Glyndwr**. Welsh nationalist leader. He led a rebellion against Henry IV of England, taking the title 'Prince of Wales' in 1400, and successfully led the Welsh defence against English invasions in 1400–02, although Wales was reconquered 1405–13. He gained control of most of the country and established an independent Welsh parliament, but from 1405 onwards suffered repeated defeats at the hands of Prince Hal, later ▷Henry V.

Glendower allied himself with English rebels, including the Percies, and also the French, but his allies were defeated. He went into hiding and disappeared from history.

gliding the art of using air currents to fly unpowered aircraft. Technically, gliding involves the gradual loss of altitude; gliders designed for soaring flight (utilizing air rising up a cliff face or hill, warm air rising as a thermal above sun-heated ground, and so on) are known as sailplanes.

globalization the process by which different parts of the globe become interconnected by economic, social, cultural, and political means, or through natural phenomena. Globalization has become increasingly rapid over the last 30 years. ▷Global warming and the international operation of financial markets are examples of processes operating on a global scale.

global warming an increase in average global temperature of approximately 0.5°C/1°F over the past century. Global temperature has been highly variable in Earth history and many fluctuations in global temperature have occurred in historical times, but this most recent episode of warming coincides with the spread of industrialization, prompting the hypothesis that it is the result of an accelerated ▷greenhouse effect caused by atmospheric pollutants, especially carbon dioxide gas. See The World's Changing Climate Focus Feature on pp. 396–397.

    Related Web site: Global Warming http://pooh.chem.wm.edu/ chemWWW/courses/chem105/projects/group1/page1.html

globefish another name for the ▷puffer fish.

globular cluster spherical or near-spherical ▷star cluster containing from approximately 10,000 to millions of stars. About 120 globular clusters are distributed in a spherical halo around our Galaxy. They consist of old stars, formed early in the Galaxy's history. Globular clusters are also found around other galaxies.

glockenspiel tuned percussion instrument of light metal bars mounted on a carrying frame for use in military bands or on a standing frame for use in an orchestra (in which form it resembles a small xylophone or celesta). It is played with hammers or via a piano keyboard attachment.

Glorious Revolution in British history, the events surrounding the removal of ▷James II from the throne and his replacement in 1689 by his daughter Mary and William of Orange as joint sovereigns (▷Mary II and ▷William III), bound by the ▷Bill of Rights.

Events James had become increasingly unpopular on account of his unconstitutional behaviour and Catholicism. In June 1688 seven prominent politicians invited the Protestant William to invade. In September 1688 William issued a Declaration of Reasons, supporting the 'warming pan' theory that James's son was an impostor, and promising to defend the Protestant faith. In November his fleet set sail for England, landing at Torbay on 5 November. James's army and navy deserted him, and he lost his nerve and fled to France.

    The Glorious Revolution was bloodless in England, but involved fierce wars in both Scotland and Ireland. William and Mary ascended the throne, but the Bill of Rights limited the power of the crown, established the power of Parliament, and established a constitutional monarchy in England. The Act of ▷Settlement of 1701 ensured future Protestant succession to the throne, and William was succeeded by Anne, second daughter of James II.

    Related Web site: Glorious Revolution of 1688 http://www. lawsch.uga.edu/~glorious/

glottis in medicine, narrow opening at the upper end of the larynx that contains the vocal cords.

Gloucester (Roman Glevum) city, port, and administrative headquarters of ▷Gloucestershire, southwest England, on the River Severn, 67 km/42 mi northeast of Bristol; population (1996 est) 106,800. It is a finance and insurance centre, and manufactures aerospace equipment, ice cream and frozen foods, machinery (lifting, fuel vending, compressors), optical equipment, information technology, and camping goods. Salmon fisheries in the Severn are a valuable resource.

Gloucestershire county of southwest England.

    area 2,640 sq km/1,019 sq mi **towns and cities** ▷Gloucester (administrative headquarters), Cheltenham, Cirencester, Stroud, Tewkesbury **physical** Cotswold Hills; River Severn and tributaries **features** Berkeley Castle, where Edward II was murdered; Prinknash Abbey, where pottery is made; Cotswold Farm Park, near Stow-on-the-Wold, which has rare and ancient breeds of farm animals; pre-Norman churches at Cheltenham and Cleeve; Gloucester Cathedral; Tewkesbury Abbey, with early 12th-century nave

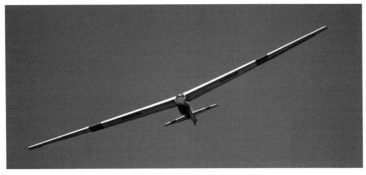

GLIDING As well as being a popular sport in its own right, gliding is one of the cheapest ways of learning to fly. *Image Bank*

agriculture cereals (in the Cotswolds), fruit (apples and pears), cider, dairy products ('double Gloucester' cheese was formerly made here), sheep farming **industries** aerospace industry, light engineering, manufacturing (bricks, carpets, furniture, glass, pins, pottery, tiles, watches), plastics, timber **population** (1996) 556,300 **famous people** Gustav Holst, Edward Jenner, John Keble

    Related Web site: Glosnet http://www.gloscc.gov.uk/

glow-worm wingless female of any of a large number of luminous beetles (fireflies). The luminous organs, situated under the abdomen, at the end of the body, give off a greenish glow at night and attract winged males for mating. There are about 2,000 species of glow-worms, distributed worldwide. (Family Lampyridae.)

Gluck, Christoph Willibald von

(1714–1787) Bohemian-German composer. His series of 'reform' operas moved music away from the formal conventions of the day, in which the interests of singers predominated; in particular, endless recitative was replaced by orchestral accompaniments, which improved dramatic flow. In 1762 his *Orfeo ed Euridice/Orpheus and Eurydice* revolutionized the 18th-century conception of opera by giving free scope to dramatic effect. It was followed by *Alceste/Alcestis* (1767) and *Paride ed Elena/Paris and Helen* (1770).

> ### Christoph Willibald von Gluck
> *There is no musical rule that I have not willingly sacrificed to dramatic effect.*
> Preface to *Alceste* (1767)

CHRISTOPH GLUCK A portrait of German composer Christoph Gluck, by an unknown artist. None of his many operas was in German: the lighter operas were in French while the more serious compositions were in Italian. *The Art Archive/Society Friends Music Vienna/Dagli Orti*

glucose (or **dextrose** or **grape sugar**) $C_6H_{12}O_6$ sugar present in the blood and manufactured by green plants during ▷photosynthesis. The ▷respiration reactions inside cells involves the oxidation of glucose to produce ▷ATP, the 'energy molecule' used to drive many of the body's biochemical reactions.

    In humans and other vertebrates optimum blood glucose levels are maintained by the hormone ▷insulin.

Glucose is prepared in syrup form by the hydrolysis of cane sugar or starch, and may be purified to a white crystalline powder. Glucose is a monosaccharide sugar (made up of a single sugar unit), unlike the more familiar sucrose (cane or beet sugar), which is a disaccharide (made up of two sugar units: glucose and fructose).

glue ear (or **secretory otitis media**) condition commonly affecting small children, in which the Eustachian tube, which normally drains and ventilates the middle ▷ear, becomes blocked with mucus. The resulting accumulation of mucus in the middle ear muffles hearing. It is the leading cause of deafness (usually transient) in children.

glue-sniffing (or **solvent misuse**) inhalation of the fumes from organic solvents of the type found in paints, lighter fuel, and glue, for their hallucinatory effects. As well as being addictive, solvents are dangerous for their effects on the user's liver, heart, and lungs. It is believed that solvents produce hallucinations by dissolving the cell membrane of brain cells, thus altering the way the cells conduct electrical impulses.

gluon in physics, a ▷gauge boson that carries the ▷strong nuclear force, responsible for binding quarks together to form the strongly interacting subatomic particles known as ▷hadrons. There are eight kinds of gluon.

    Gluons cannot exist in isolation; they are believed to exist in balls ('glueballs') that behave as single particles. Glueballs may have been detected at CERN in 1995 but further research is required to confirm their existence.

glyceride ▷ester formed between one or more acids and glycerol (propan-1,2,3-triol). A glyceride is termed a mono-, di-, or triglyceride, depending on the number of hydroxyl groups from the glycerol that have reacted with the acids.

glycerine another name for ▷glycerol.

glycerol (or **glycerine** or **propan-1,2,3-triol**) HOCH₂CH(OH)CH₂OH thick, colourless, odourless, sweetish liquid. It is obtained from vegetable and animal oils and fats (by treatment with acid, alkali, superheated steam, or an enzyme), or by fermentation of glucose, and is used in the manufacture of high explosives, in antifreeze solutions, to maintain moist conditions in fruits and tobacco, and in cosmetics.

glycine CH₂(NH₂)COOH the simplest amino acid, and one of the main components of proteins. When purified, it is a sweet, colourless crystalline compound.

glycol (or **ethylene glycol** or **ethane-1,2-diol**) HOCH₂CH₂OH thick, colourless, odourless, sweetish liquid. It is used in antifreeze solutions, in the preparation of ethers and esters (used for explosives), as a solvent, and as a substitute for glycerol.

GMT abbreviation for ▷**Greenwich Mean Time**.

gnat any of a group of small two-winged biting insects belonging to the mosquito family. The eggs are laid in water, where they hatch into wormlike larvae, which pass through a pupal stage (see ▷pupa) to emerge as adults. (Family Culicidae) Only the female is capable of drawing blood; the male does not have piercing jaws.

    Species include *Culex pipiens*, abundant in England; the carrier of malaria *Anopheles maculipennis*; and the banded mosquito *Aedes aegypti*, which transmits yellow fever.

gneiss coarse-grained ▷metamorphic rock, formed under conditions of high temperature and pressure, and often occurring in association with schists and granites. It has a foliated, or layered, structure consisting of thin bands of micas and/or amphiboles dark in colour alternating with bands of granular quartz and feldspar that are light in colour. Gneisses are formed during regional ▷metamorphism; **paragneisses** are derived from metamorphism of sedimentary rocks and **orthogneisses** from metamorphism of granite or similar igneous rocks.

Gnosticism esoteric cult of divine knowledge (a synthesis of Christianity, Greek philosophy, Hinduism, Buddhism, and the mystery cults of the Mediterranean), which flourished during the 2nd and 3rd centuries and was a rival to, and influence on, early Christianity. The medieval French Cathar heresy and the modern Mandean sect (in southern Iraq) descend from Gnosticism.

    Related Web site: Gnosticism http://www.newadvent.org/ cathen/06592a.htm

GNP abbreviation for ▷gross national product.

gnu another name for ▷wildebeest.

Goa state on the west coast of India, lying 400 km/250 mi south of Mumbai (formerly Bombay); area 3,700 sq km/1,428 sq mi; population (est 2001) 1,364,000. The capital is Panaji. Tourism is

(continued on p. 398)

The World's Changing Climate

by Simon Torok

The surface of the Earth is warmed by energy from the Sun. The Earth then radiates energy through the atmosphere into space. Gases in the lower atmosphere such as carbon dioxide, methane, and water vapour are warmed by the radiation released by the Earth's surface. The atmosphere then radiates heat back towards the ground, adding to the heat the ground receives from the Sun. This process is called 'the greenhouse effect'. Without the natural greenhouse effect, the surface of the planet would be about 34°C/61°F colder than it is now, and life as we know it would not be possible.

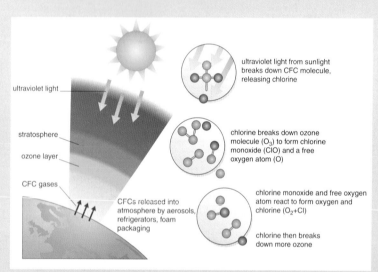

THE OZONE LAYER'S destruction by chlorofluorocarbons (CFCs). CFCs discharged into the atmosphere break down in sunlight releasing chlorine, which breaks down the ozone to form chlorine monoxide and a free oxygen atom. These products react together to form oxygen and chlorine, leaving the chlorine to break down another ozone molecule, and so on.

global warming

The rising concentration of **greenhouse gases** in the atmosphere is increasing the amount of radiation trapped near the Earth's surface. It is this enhanced greenhouse effect, also called **global warming**, that most scientists believe is changing the planet's climate. Everyone agrees that the world is getting warmer, but there is debate about whether the activity of human beings is responsible. Most scientists now believe it is; the enhanced greenhouse effect is due to the world's growing population burning more fossil fuels (such as coal, oil, and natural gas) for energy, as well as expanding agriculture and increasing deforestation.

after the Industrial Revolution

About 200 years ago, the Industrial Revolution ushered in an era in which humans rely on fossil fuels to run the many machines used in industry and everyday life. The burning of fossil fuels releases carbon dioxide into the atmosphere. Since the Industrial Revolution, there has been a steady increase in the production of carbon dioxide, and an increase in global population. Some of the carbon dioxide is absorbed by trees and plants or dissolved into the oceans; these are known as **carbon sinks**. But human activities have been producing carbon dioxide faster than it can be absorbed naturally, while widespread forest clearance has reduced the carbon sinks.

Scientists have been measuring the amount of carbon dioxide in the atmosphere for about 40 years, over which time the concentration has risen by about 15%. Older records of carbon dioxide levels, obtained from bubbles of air trapped in Antarctic ice, extend back 300,000 years. Carbon dioxide levels are now 32% higher than before the Industrial Revolution, higher than they have been for 160,000 years. Other greenhouse gases have also increased: methane levels have more than doubled and nitrous oxide levels have increased by 15%. Humans have also introduced greenhouse gases to the atmosphere that did not exist until this century, such as **chlorofluorocarbons** (CFCs). We are changing the atmosphere faster than ever before.

rising temperatures

Additional greenhouse gases add to the natural greenhouse effect and are likely to make the planet warmer than it would otherwise be. Temperature changes vary from region to region, but records show that the Earth is about 0.6°C/1°F warmer than it was a century ago, with most of the warming occurring in the past 40 years. The 1990s were the Earth's warmest decade since measurements began in 1860, with eight of the ten warmest years occurring since 1990. The warmest year ever recorded was 1998.

Changes in **natural phenomena** can also indicate changes in temperature, and over a longer period of time. Evidence of warming includes melting glaciers, the temperature of the upper layers of the Earth's crust, coral growth, sea-floor sediments, and the width of tree rings. These records show the 1900s to have been the warmest century in the past 1,000 years.

changes in the weather

As well as rises in temperature, many other aspects of the world's climate have changed. Some countries have experienced heavier rainfall, while other areas have suffered drought. There has been a reduction in the number of frosts and an increase in the number of heatwaves in many parts of the world. Mountain glaciers have shrunk, Arctic sea-ice has thinned by 40%, and sea levels have risen by 10–25 cm/4–10 in. (Sea levels rise because water expands as it warms, and because the melting of glaciers adds to the amount of water.) Scientists expect to see more such changes in the future.

But it is not possible to say for certain that all these changes have been due to the enhanced greenhouse effect. The temperature of the Earth may change naturally due to variations in the amount of energy emitted by the Sun, wobbles in the Earth's orbit around the Sun, and fluctuations in greenhouse gases, and, in the shorter term, because of variations in ocean currents and the cooling effect of dust emitted by volcanoes. Any warming due to human activities is superimposed on, and hidden by, these natural variations.

Over a longer time scale, there have been ice ages and warm periods fluctuating every 100,000 years or so over the past million years. The past 11,500 years have been relatively warm with short cool periods, such as the Little Ice Age that occurred in the Middle Ages. But although temperatures vary naturally between ice ages and warm periods, there is no record of the average global temperature ever having increased as rapidly as it did in the 20th century.

predicted changes

If greenhouse gases continue to be emitted as a result of human activities the way they do today, carbon dioxide levels will rise to at least double their pre-industrial levels by the end of the 21st century, even if we reduce global greenhouse gas emissions to the levels that they were in 1990. To guarantee no further increases in carbon dioxide in the

A CYCLONIC STORM, or hurricane, off Hawaii, USA. Satellites provide invaluable information about the cloud and wind patterns of entire weather systems. Tropical cyclones begin in the hot, moist air over tropical oceans. As an area of very low pressure develops, air is sucked in, creating a violent storm of spiralling winds. © *NASA*

atmosphere, we will need rapidly to reduce the levels of emissions by about 60 to 70% of current levels. Such major reductions are unlikely, so further changes in the climate will probably be felt over the next 100 years.

Scientists use sophisticated computer programs running on powerful supercomputers to predict how the climate will change in the future. The programs create a global, three-dimensional model based on the physical laws that govern how the atmosphere, land, and oceans behave. Scientists first simulate the current climate, then increase the amount of greenhouse gases in the simulated atmosphere to see what effect this has. A doubling of carbon dioxide concentrations will increase the average global temperature by between 1.5 and 4.5°C/2.5 and 7.5°F.

The warming over the next 100 years is predicted to be greater than any temperature change over the past 10,000 years.

It is not clear how global warming will change other aspects of the weather around the world. Some areas may receive more rain while others receive less. In general, global rainfall is likely to increase but evaporation will also increase, leaving soils drier. Scientists expect a greater number of extreme weather events, such as storms, floods, heatwaves, and droughts. By the end of the 21st century, the sea level is expected to rise by 15–100 cm/6–38 in above current levels.

These predictions are based on the assumption that changes will occur gradually. However, there are concerns that abrupt and massive changes in climate may take place, as have occurred in the distant past, due to unexpected changes in ocean currents.

impacts on our world

A few degrees of warming does not sound much, but the effects of such warming are serious. Increased temperature will cause a rise in the number of deaths related to heat stress. Infectious diseases such as malaria are expected to spread as disease-carrying insects are able to move to areas that are currently too cold. Drier soils will make food more difficult to grow and change the distribution of crops, with some areas facing increased risk of famine. Pests and weeds will flourish. Changing river flow patterns could reduce the amount of available fresh water. Small rises in sea levels increase the risk of storm surges that could flood low-lying coastal areas, and small islands and salt marsh habitats could be lost.

Tropical forests and grasslands could die, and many plants and animals unable to adapt to such rapid changes in climate could become extinct.

Societies will need to adapt to these negative impacts, but there may also be positive changes in various regions. For example, forest production will increase due to the higher concentrations of carbon dioxide, and some areas may experience tourism and agricultural benefits from the warmer temperatures.

If the climate changes we have experienced at the end of the 20th century are a result of human activities, it is likely that changes in climate will continue to occur during the 21st century due to the long life of greenhouse gases.

political response

Advice from the Intergovernmental Panel on Climate Change (IPCC), an international group of more than 2,000 experts, has led to governments agreeing to stabilize greenhouse-gas concentrations to prevent dangerous interference with the world's climate. The first such legal agreement, the United Nations Framework Convention on Climate Change, took place in Rio de Janeiro, Brazil, in 1992, and in Kyoto, Japan, in 1997. A protocol was proposed that would require countries to cut their emissions. However, there is still disagreement about how this should be achieved, and a summit in The Hague, the Netherlands, in 2000 was inconclusive.

A DRY RIVER BED showing the effects of drought in Queensland, Australia. As the world's climate changes and average temperatures rise, many areas are experiencing severe droughts, while others are falling victim to flooding. *Alan Towse, Ecoscene*

(*continued from p. 395*) very important to the economy; local industries include clothing, footwear, pesticides, iron ore, manganese, and fishing nets. Agriculture is based on the cultivation of rice, pulses, cashew nuts, coconuts, and ragi (a cereal).

Related Web site: Goa http://travel.indiamart.com/goa/

GOA Boys mending nets in a fishing village in Goa, India. *Image Bank*

goat ruminant mammal (it chews the cud), closely related to sheep. Both male and female goats have horns and beards. They are sure-footed animals, and feed on shoots and leaves more than on grass. (Genus *Capra*, family Bovidae.)

Domestic varieties are descended from the **scimitar-horned wild goat** (*C. aegagrus*) and have been kept for over 9,000 years in southern Europe and Asia. They are kept for milk or for mohair (angora and cashmere goats). Wild species include the **ibex** (*C. ibex*) of the Alps and **markhor** (*C. falconeri*) of the Himalayas, 1 m/3 ft high and with long twisted horns. The **Rocky Mountain goat** (*Oreamnos americanus*) is a 'goat antelope' and is not closely related to true goats.

Gobi vast desert region of Central Asia in the independent state of Mongolia, and Inner Mongolia, China. It covers an area of 1,280,000 sq km/490,000 sq mi (800 km/500 mi north–south and 1,600 km/1,000 mi east–west), and lies on a high plateau 900–1,500 m/2,950–4,920 ft above sea level. It is mainly rocky, with shifting sands and salt marshes at lower levels. The desert is sparsely populated, mainly by nomadic herders. It is rich in the fossil remains of extinct species, and Stone Age implements.

Gobind Singh (1666–1708) Indian religious leader, the tenth and last guru (teacher) of Sikhism, 1675–1708, and founder of the Sikh brotherhood known as the ▷Khalsa. On his death, the Sikh holy book, the *Guru Granth Sahib*, replaced the line of human gurus as the teacher and guide of the Sikh community.

During a period of Sikh persecution, Gobind Singh asked those who were willing to die for their faith to join him. The first five willing to risk their lives were named the *panj pyares* 'faithful ones' by him and proclaimed the first members of the Khalsa. He also introduced the names Singh (lion) for male Sikhs, and Kaur (princess) for female Sikhs.

goby small marine bony fish. Nearly all gobies are found in the shallow coastal waters of the temperate and tropical oceans.

God the concept of a supreme being, a unique creative entity, basic to several monotheistic religions (for example Judaism, Christianity, Islam); in many polytheistic cultures (for example Norse, Roman, Greek), the term 'god' refers to a supernatural being who personifies the force behind an aspect of life (for example Neptune, Roman god of the sea).

Godard, Jean-Luc (1930–) French film director. A politically motivated, neo-modernist film-maker, he was one of the leaders of New Wave cinema. He made his name with *A bout de souffle/Breathless* (1959), in which his challenging, subversive approach to conventional narrative cinema was clear in his handling of a story based on US gangster movies.

Godard was a critic for the film journal *Cahiers du Cinéma* in the 1950s. His work has continued to explore cinematic conventions, and his anthropological eye has trenchantly examined the iconography of his time. His frequently experimental works constantly allude to and quote from the other arts, whether painting, music, literature, or the cinema itself. They include *Vivre sa Vie/It's My Life* (1962), *Le Mépris/Contempt* (1963), *Pierrot le fou* (1965), *2 ou 3 choses que je sais d'elle/Two or Three Things I Know About Her* (1967), *Weekend* (1968), *Tout va bien* (1972), *Sauve qui peut (la vie)/Slow Motion* (1980), *Je vous salue, Marie/Hail Mary* (1985), *Histoire(s) du cinéma* (1989), and *Nouvelle Vague* (1990).

Goddard, Robert Hutchings (1882–1945) US rocket pioneer. He launched the first liquid-fuelled rocket at Auburn, Massachusetts, in 1926. By 1935 his rockets had gyroscopic control and could carry cameras to record instrument readings. Two years later a Goddard rocket gained the world altitude record with an ascent of 3 km/1.9 mi.

ROBERT GODDARD Robert H Goddard, the 'father of US rocketry', in the 1930s. *Archive Photos*

Goddard Space Flight Center NASA installation at Greenbelt, Maryland, USA, responsible for the operation of NASA's unmanned scientific satellites, including the ▷Hubble Space Telescope. It is also home of the National Space Science Data centre, a repository of data collected by satellites.

Godiva, or Godgifu, Lady (*c.* 1040–1080) Wife of Leofric, Earl of Mercia (died 1057). Legend has it that her husband promised to reduce the heavy taxes on the people of Coventry if she rode naked through the streets at noon. The grateful citizens remained indoors as she did so, but 'Peeping Tom' bored a hole in his shutters and was struck blind.

Godthåb (Greenlandic **Nuuk**) capital and largest town of Greenland; population (1993) 12,200. It is a storage centre for oil and gas, and the chief industry is fish processing.

Godunov, Boris Fyodorovich (1552–1605) Tsar of Russia from 1598, elected after the death of Fyodor I, son of Ivan the Terrible. He was assassinated by a pretender to the throne who professed to be Dmitri, a brother of Fyodor and the rightful heir. The legend that has grown up around this forms the basis of Pushkin's play *Boris Godunov* (1831) and Mussorgsky's opera of the same name (1874).

An apocryphal story of Boris killing the true Dmitri in order to gain the throne was fostered by Russian historians anxious to discredit Boris because he was not descended from the main ruling families.

Godunov's rule was marked by a strengthening of the Russian church. It was also the beginning of the Time of Troubles, a period of instability.

Godwin, William (1756–1836) English philosopher, novelist, and father of the writer Mary Shelley. His *Enquiry Concerning Political Justice* (1793) advocated an anarchic society based on a faith in people's essential rationality. At first a Nonconformist minister, he later became an atheist. His first wife was Mary ▷Wollstonecraft.

JOSEPH GOEBBELS The skull at the microphone adds a dimension of fear to this quotation from Joseph Goebbels, the German minister of propaganda, at the time of the invasion of Russia during World War II. *The Art Archive/ Eileen Tweedy*

Goebbels, (Paul) Joseph (1897–1945) German Nazi leader. As minister of propaganda from 1933, he brought all cultural and educational activities under Nazi control and built up sympathetic movements abroad to carry on the 'war of nerves' against Hitler's intended victims.

He was born in the Rhineland, became a journalist, joined the Nazi party in 1924 when it was still in its early days, and was given control of its propaganda in 1929. He was totally committed to Nazism and as minister of propaganda his organizational abilities and oratory were major factors in disseminating the party line throughout Germany and abroad. He was appointed special plenipotentiary for total war in August 1944 and was granted powers to draft any able-bodied person in the Reich into war work. In the final days of Berlin he moved into the Führerbunker, poisoned his six children, and then ordered an SS officer to shoot him and his wife.

Goering, Hermann Wilhelm (1893–1946) Nazi leader, German field marshal from 1938. He was part of Hitler's inner circle, and with Hitler's rise to power was appointed commissioner for aviation from 1933 and built up the Luftwaffe (airforce). He built a vast economic empire in occupied Europe, but later lost favour and was expelled from the party in 1945. Tried at Nürnberg for war crimes, he poisoned himself before he could be executed.

HERMANN GOERING Creator of the Luftwaffe, Goering was tried for war crimes. *Philip Sauvain Picture Collection*

Goering was born in Bavaria. He was a renowned fighter pilot in World War I, and joined the Nazi party in 1922. He was elected to the Reichstag in 1928 and became its president in 1932. He was appointed minister of the interior for Prussia in 1933. This position gave him full control of the police and security forces; he organized the Gestapo and had the first concentration camps built, then handed control to the SS to enable him to concentrate on developing the Luftwaffe. He supervised the four-year economic plan to ready the country for war 1935–39. The Luftwaffe's failure to break the British air defences was a serious blow to his reputation from which he never really recovered, and he retired to his country estate in 1942.

Goes, Hugo van der

(c. 1440–1482) Flemish painter. Chiefly active in Ghent. His works were highly praised by Italian artists, particularly his *Portinari Altarpiece* (c. 1475; Uffizi, Florence), typically rich both in symbolism and naturalistic detail.

Goethe, Johann Wolfgang von

(1749–1832) German poet, novelist, dramatist, and scholar. He is generally considered the founder of modern German literature, and was the leader of the Romantic ▷Sturm und Drang movement. His masterpiece is the poetic play *Faust* (1808 and 1832). His other works include the partly autobiographical *Die Leiden des Jungen Werthers/The Sorrows of the Young Werther* (1774); the classical dramas *Iphigenie auf Tauris/Iphigenia in Tauris* (1787), *Egmont* (1788), and *Torquato Tasso* (1790); the *Wilhelm Meister* novels (1795–1829); the short novel *Die Wahlverwandschaften/Elective Affinities* (1809); and scientific treatises including *Farbenlehre/Treatise on Colour* (1810).

Goethe was born in Frankfurt-am-Main, and studied law. Inspired by Shakespeare, to whose work he was introduced by the critic J G von Herder, he wrote the play *Götz von Berlichingen* (1773), heralding the *Sturm und Drang* movement. The inspiration for *Die Leiden des Jungen Werthers* came from an unhappy love affair. He took part in public life at the court of Duke Charles Augustus in Weimar 1775–86, and pursued his interests in scientific research. A year and a half spent in Italy 1786–88 was a period of great development for Goethe, when he outgrew the *Sturm und Drang* movement and worked towards the Greek ideal of calm and harmony.

The publication of *Wilhelm Meisters Lehrjahre/Wilhelm Meister's Apprenticeship* (1795–96) established Goethe's enduring fame throughout Europe. *Faust*, written in the intervals between other work, over a period of more than 50 years, reflects the evolution of Goethe's own thinking and character, from youth to age. The two parts of the work are as dissimilar as the influences under which

> **Johann Wolfgang von Goethe**
> *He who seizes the right moment, /
> Is the right man.*
> Faust

JOHANN GOETHE The German poet initially contributed to the *Sturm und Drang* movement popular in Germany in the 1770s. *Archive Photos*

VINCENT VAN GOGH *The Church at Auvers-sur-Oise*, painted in 1890 by Dutch painter Vincent van Gogh. *The Art Archive/Musée d'Orsay Paris/ Dagli Orti*

they were written, the first being romantic, the second classical in form and spirit.

Gogh, Vincent (Willem) van

(1853–1890) Dutch post-Impressionist painter. He began painting in the 1880s, his early works often being sombre depictions of peasant life, such as *The Potato Eaters* (1885; Van Gogh Museum, Amsterdam). Influenced by the Impressionists and by Japanese prints, he developed a freer style characterized by intense colour and expressive brushwork, as seen in his *Sunflowers* series (1888). His influence on modern art, particularly on expressionism, has been immense. His numerous works (over 800 paintings and 700 drawings) include still lifes, portraits (many self-portraits), and landscapes, such as *The Starry Night* (1889; Museum of Modern Art, New York) and *Crows over Wheatfield* (1890; Van Gogh Museum, Amsterdam). His most creative time was 1888 in Arles, Provence, in the company of the painter Paul Gauguin, when he produced views of the town and such pictures as *Orchard in Blossom* and *The Chair and Pipe*.

> **Vincent van Gogh**
> *I am not an adventurer by choice, but by fate.*
> Letter, 1886

His painting *Irises* (1889) was sold for the record price of $53.9 million at Sotheby's, New York, in 1987.

Related Web site: Vincent Van Gogh Exhibition Gallery http://www. vangoghgallery.com/

Gogol, Nicolai Vasilyevich

(1809–1852) Russian writer. His first success was a collection of stories, *Evenings on a Farm near Dikanka* (1831–32), followed by *Mirgorod* (1835). Later works include *Arabesques* (1835), the comedy play *The Inspector General* (1836), and the picaresque novel *Dead Souls* (1842), which satirizes Russian provincial society.

Goh Chok Tong

(1941–) Singaporean politician, prime minister from 1990. A trained economist, Goh became a member of parliament for the ruling People's Action Party in 1976. Rising steadily through the party ranks, he was appointed deputy prime minister in 1985, and subsequently chosen by the cabinet as Lee Kuan Yew's successor, first as prime minister and from 1992 also as party leader.

goitre enlargement of the thyroid gland seen as a swelling on the neck. It is most pronounced in simple goitre, which is caused by iodine deficiency. More common is toxic goitre or ▷hyperthyroidism, caused by overactivity of the thyroid gland.

Golan Heights

(Arabic **Jawlan**) plateau on the Syrian border with Israel, bitterly contested in the ▷Arab–Israeli Wars and

annexed by Israel on 14 December 1981. In the 1996 peace talks Syria insisted that Israel withdraw from the Golan Heights, following its capture in 1967. Demands for the return of the Golan to Syrian control have stalled negotiations towards normalization of Israeli–Syrian relations.

Related Web site: Peace with the Golan – Tourism on the Golan Heights http://www.golan.org.il/tourism3.html

gold heavy, precious, yellow, metallic element; symbol Au (from Latin *aurum*, 'gold'), atomic number 79, relative atomic mass 197.0. It occurs in nature frequently as a free metal (see ▷native metal) and is highly resistant to acids, tarnishing, and corrosion. Pure gold is the most malleable of all metals and is used as gold leaf or powder, where small amounts cover vast surfaces, such as gilded domes and statues.

The elemental form is so soft that it is alloyed for strength with a number of other metals, such as silver, copper, and platinum. Its purity is then measured in ▷carats on a scale of 24 (24 carats is pure gold). It is used mainly for decorative purposes (jewellery, gilding) but also for coinage, dentistry, and conductivity in electronic devices.

Gold has been known and worked from ancient times, and currency systems were based on it in Western civilization, where mining it became an economic and imperialistic goal. In 1990 the three leading gold-producing countries were South Africa, 605.4 tonnes; USA, 295 tonnes; and Russia, 260 tonnes. In 1989 gold deposits were found in Greenland with an estimated yield of 12 tonnes per year.

Related Web site: Gold Prospecting http://www.klws.com/gold/gold.html

GOLD Gold and cornelian earrings from a tomb in the Bruznoe necropolis at Simferopol on the Black Sea. These finely-wrought earrings belong to the Alani culture of the 3rd to 4th centuries. *Art Archive*

Gold Coast former name for ▷Ghana, but historically the west coast of Africa from Cape Three Points to the Volta River, where alluvial gold is washed down. Portuguese and French navigators visited this coast in the 14th century, and a British trading settlement developed into the colony of the Gold Coast in 1618. With its dependencies of Ashanti and Northern Territories plus the trusteeship territory of Togoland, it became Ghana in 1957. The name is also used for many coastal resort areas – for example, in Florida, USA.

goldcrest smallest European bird, about 9 cm/3.5 in long and weighing 5 g/0.011 lb; a ▷warbler. It is olive green, with a bright orange-yellow streak running from the beak to the back of the head and a black border above the eye. The tail is brown, marked with black and white, and the cheeks, throat, and breast are a greyish white. (Species *Regulus regulus*, family Muscicapidae, order Passeriformes.)

GOLDCREST The smallest European bird, the goldcrest, is widespread in Europe and Asia and builds its nest high up in trees.

Golden Fleece in Greek legend, the fleece of the winged ram Chrysomallus, which hung on an oak tree at Colchis and was guarded by a dragon. It was stolen by ▷Jason and the Argonauts.

Golden Horde the invading Mongol-Tatar army that first terrorized Europe from 1237 under the leadership of Batu Khan, a grandson of Genghis Khan. ▷Tamerlane broke their power in 1395, and ▷Ivan III ended Russia's payment of tribute to them in 1480.

goldenrod one of several tall and leafy North American perennial plants, belonging to the daisy family. Flower heads are mostly composed of many small yellow flowers, or florets. (Genus *Solidago*, family Compositae.)

golden section visually satisfying ratio, first constructed by the Greek mathematician ▷Euclid and used in art and architecture. It is found by dividing a line AB at a point O such that the rectangle produced by the whole line and one of the segments is equal to the square drawn on the other segment. The ratio of the two segments is about 8:13 or 1:1.618, and a rectangle whose sides are in this ratio is called a **golden rectangle**. The ratio of consecutive ▷Fibonacci numbers tends to the golden ratio.

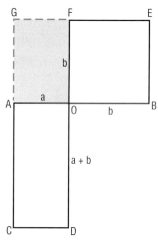

GOLDEN SECTION The golden section is the ratio a:b, equal to 8:13. A golden rectangle is one, like that shaded in the picture, that has its length and breadth in this ratio. These rectangles are said to be pleasant to look at and have been used instinctively by artists in their pictures.

goldfinch songbird found in Eurasia, North Africa, and North America. (Species *Carduelis carduelis*, family Fringillidae, order Passeriformes.)

goldfish fish belonging to the ▷carp family, found in East Asia. It is greenish-brown in its natural state, but has been bred by the Chinese for centuries, taking on highly coloured and sometimes freakishly shaped forms. Goldfish can occur in a greater range of colours than any other animal tested. (Species *Carassius auratus*, family Cyprinidae.)

Golding, William (Gerald) (1911–1993) English novelist. His work is often principally concerned with the fundamental corruption and evil inherent in human nature. His first book, *Lord of the Flies* (1954; filmed in 1962), concerns the degeneration into savagery of a group of English schoolboys marooned on a Pacific island after their plane crashes; it is a chilling allegory about the savagery lurking beneath the thin veneer of modern 'civilized' life. *Pincher Martin* (1956) is a study of greed and self-delusion. Later novels include *The Spire* (1964). He was awarded the Nobel Prize for Literature in 1983 and knighted in 1988.

Golding's novels deal with universal themes and anxieties: evil, greed, guilt, primal instincts, and unknown forces. *Darkness Visible* (1979) is a disturbing book full of symbolism. The Sea Trilogy – *Rites of Passage* (1980; Booker Prize), *Close Quarters* (1987), and *Fire Down Below* (1989) – tells the story of a voyage to Australia in Napoleonic times through the eyes of a callow young aristocrat.

Related Web site: Golding, William http://members.aol.com/Kiwi11020/goldingmain1.html

Goldman, Emma (1869–1940) US political organizer, feminist and co-editor of the anarchist monthly magazine *Mother Earth* 1906–17. In 1908 her citizenship was revoked and in 1919 she was deported to Russia. Breaking with the Bolsheviks in 1921, she spent the rest of her life in exile. Her writings include *My Disillusionment in Russia* (1923) and *Living My Life* (1931).

GOLD RUSH Early prospectors in the US gold rush, about 1867. After gold was discovered in California in 1848, men streamed west in their thousands – they were dubbed the 'forty-niners' because they left home in 1849. *Archive Photos*

gold rush large influx of gold prospectors to an area where gold deposits have recently been discovered. The result is a dramatic increase in population. Cities such as Johannesburg, Melbourne, and San Francisco either originated or were considerably enlarged by gold rushes. Melbourne's population trebled from 77,000 to some 200,000 between 1851 and 1853, while San Francisco boomed from a small coastal village of a few hundred people to the largest city in the western USA during the California gold rush of 1848–56.

Goldsmith, James Michael (1933–1997) Franco-British industrialist, publisher, and politician. He was one of the UK's wealthiest people. Early in his career he built up a grocery empire, Cavenham Foods, then went on to become the owner of several industrial, commercial (he was cofounder of Mothercare), and financial enterprises. His political activities resulted in his securing a seat in the European Parliament in 1991, representing a French constituency, and the formation in Britain of the Referendum Party in 1995.

Goldsmith, Oliver (1728–1774) Irish playwright, novelist, poet, and essayist. His works include the novel *The Vicar of Wakefield* (1766), an outwardly artless and gentle story which is also social and political satire, and in which rural honesty, kindness, and patience triumph over urban values; it became one of the most popular works of fiction in English. Other works include the poem 'The Deserted Village' (1770) and the play *She Stoops to Conquer* (1773). In 1761 Goldsmith met Samuel ▷Johnson and became a member of his circle.

> **Samuel Goldwyn**
> *Any man who goes to a psychiatrist should have his head examined.*
> Quoted in Norman Zierold, *The Moguls*

Related Web site: Selected Poetry of Oliver Goldsmith (1730?–1774) http://www.library.utoronto.ca/utel/rp/authors/goldsmit.html

OLIVER GOLDSMITH The Irish poet and playwright Oliver Goldsmith was a member of the Literary Club in London, England. His comedy *She Stoops to Conquer* was a break from the formal comedies of the time, as he had written it with the express purpose of making people laugh. *Archive Photos*

gold standard system under which a country's currency is exchangeable for a fixed weight of gold on demand at the central bank. It was almost universally applied 1870–1914, but by 1937 no single country was on the full gold standard. Britain abandoned the gold standard in 1931; the USA abandoned it in 1971. Holdings of gold are still retained because it is an internationally recognized commodity, which cannot be legislated upon or manipulated by interested countries.

Goldwyn, Samuel (1882–1974) Adopted name of Schmuel Gelbfisz (Samuel Goldfish). US film producer. Born in Poland, he emigrated to the USA in 1896. He founded the Goldwyn Pictures Corporation in 1917, which merged into Metro-Goldwyn-Mayer (MGM) in 1924, although he was not part of the deal. He remained an independent producer for many years, making classics such as *Wuthering Heights* (1939), *The Little Foxes* (1941), *The Best Years of Our Lives* (1946), and *Guys and Dolls* (1955).

SAMUEL GOLDWYN US film producer Samuel Goldwyn and Adolph Zuko sitting together at the Milestone award presentation in the Hilton Hotel, Hollywood, USA, on 6 May 1966. *Archive Photos*

golf outdoor game in which a small rubber-cored ball is hit with a wooden- or iron-faced club into a series of holes using the least number of shots. On the first shot for each hole, the ball is hit from a tee, which elevates the ball slightly off the ground; subsequent strokes are played off the ground. Most courses have 18 holes and are approximately 5,500 m/6,000 yd in length. Golf developed in Scotland in the 15th century. The major golfing events are the British Open (first held in 1860), US Open (first held 1895), US Masters (first held in 1934), and US Professional Golfers Association (PGA) (first held in 1916).

Related Web site: GolfWeb http://www.golfweb.com/

Golgi, Camillo (1843–1926) Italian cell biologist who was awarded a Nobel Prize for Physiology or Medicine in 1906 with Santiago Ramón y Cajal for their discovery of the fine structure of the nervous system.

Golgi apparatus (or **Golgi body**) stack of flattened membranous sacs found in the cells of ▷eukaryotes. Many molecules travel through the Golgi apparatus on their way to other organelles or to the endoplasmic reticulum. Some are modified or assembled inside the sacs. The Golgi apparatus is named after the Italian physician Camillo Golgi.

Goliath In the Old Testament, a champion of the ▷Philistines, who was said to have been slain by a stone from a sling by the young ▷David in single combat in front of their opposing armies.

Goliath beetle large beetle found only in tropical countries. The biggest Goliath beetle *Goliathus giganteus*, found in equatorial Africa, may be more than 150 mm/6 in long and is one of the largest insects.

Gomułka, Władysaw (1905–1982) Polish communist politician, party leader 1943–48 and 1956–70. He introduced moderate reforms, including private farming and tolerance for Roman Catholicism.

gonad the part of an animal's body that produces the sperm or egg cells (ova) required for sexual reproduction. The sperm-producing gonad is called a ▷testis, and the egg-producing gonad is called an ▷ovary.

gonadotrophin any hormone that supports and stimulates the function of the gonads (sex glands); some gonadotrophins are used as ▷fertility drugs.

Goncharov, Ivan Alexandrovitch (1812–1891) Russian novelist. His first novel, *A Common Story* (1847), was followed in 1858 by his humorous masterpiece *Oblomov*, which satirized the indolent Russian landed gentry.

Goncourt, de Edmond (1822–1896) and Jules (1830–1870) French writers. The brothers collaborated in producing a compendium, *L'Art du XVIIIème siècle/18th-Century Art* 1859–75, historical studies, and a *Journal* published 1887–96 that depicts French literary life of their day. Edmond de Goncourt founded the Académie Goncourt, opened in 1903, which awards an annual prize, the Prix Goncourt, to the author of the best French novel of the year.

Gond member of a heterogenous people of central India, about half of whom speak unwritten languages belonging to the Dravidian family. The rest speak Indo-European languages such as Hindi. There are over 4 million Gonds, most of whom live in Madhya Pradesh, eastern Maharashtra, and northern Andra Pradesh, although some live in Orissa. Traditionally, the Gonds practised shifting cultivation; cereal farming and cattle remain the basis of the economy.

Gondwanaland (or **Gondwana**) southern landmass formed 200 million years ago by the splitting of the single world continent ▷Pangaea. (The northern landmass was ▷Laurasia.) It later fragmented into the continents of South America, Africa, Australia, and Antarctica, which then drifted slowly to their present positions. The baobab tree found in both Africa and Australia is a relic of this ancient land mass.

gonorrhoea common sexually transmitted disease arising from infection with the bacterium *Neisseria gonorrhoeae*, which causes inflammation of the genito-urinary tract. After an incubation period of two to ten days, infected men experience pain while urinating and a discharge from the penis; infected women often have no external symptoms.

Untreated gonorrhoea carries the threat of sterility to both sexes; there is also the risk of blindness in a baby born to an infected mother. The condition is treated with antibiotics, though ever-increasing doses are becoming necessary to combat resistant strains.

González, Julio (1876–1942) Spanish sculptor and painter. He established the use of wrought and welded iron as an expressive sculptural medium. Influenced by the cubism of his close friend Pablo Picasso, and also by Russian constructivism and surrealism, his early sculptures are open, linear designs using rods and bands of iron, as in *Woman with a Mirror* about 1936–37 (IVAM, Centre Julio González, Valencia).

González Márquez, Felipe (1942–) Spanish socialist politician, leader of the Socialist Workers' Party (PSOE), and prime minister 1982–96. His party was re-elected in 1989 and 1993, but his popularity suffered as a result of economic upheaval and revelations of corruption within his administration. During 1995 he was himself briefly under investigation for alleged involvement with anti-terrorist death squads in the 1980s, and in March 1996, he and his party were narrowly defeated in the general elections.

good in economics, a term often used to denote any product, including services. Equally, a good is often distinguished from a service, as in 'goods and services'. The opposite of a **normal good**, a product for which demand increases as a person's income increases, is an **inferior good**, a product for which demand decreases as income increases. A **free good** is one which an individual or organization can consume in infinite quantities at no cost, like the air we breathe. However, most goods are **economic goods**, which are scarce in supply and therefore have an opportunity cost. In a free market, economic goods are allocated through prices.

Good Friday in the Christian church, the Friday before Easter, which is observed in memory of the Crucifixion (the death of Jesus on the cross).

Good Friday Agreement Multi-party settlement proposed on 10 April 1998 in the Northern Ireland peace process.

Good Hope, Cape of South African headland forming a peninsula between Table Bay and False Bay, Cape Town. The first European to sail around it was Bartolomeu ▷Diaz in 1488. Formerly named Cape of Storms, it was given its present name by King John II of Portugal.

CAPE OF GOOD HOPE Vegetation on the Cape of Good Hope is characterized by low shrubs and grass. *Image Bank*

Good King Henry perennial plant belonging to the goosefoot family, growing to 50 cm/1.6 ft, with triangular leaves which are mealy when young. Spikes of tiny greenish-yellow flowers appear above the leaves in midsummer. (*Chenopodium bonus-henricus*, family Chenopodiaceae.)

Goodman, Benny (1909–1986) US clarinettist, composer, and band-leader, nicknamed the 'King of Swing'. He played in various jazz and dance bands from 1921. In 1934 he founded a 12-piece band, which combined the expressive improvisatory style of black jazz with disciplined precision ensemble playing. He is associated with such numbers as 'Blue Skies' and 'Let's Dance'.

Goodyear, Charles (1800–1860) US inventor who developed rubber coating in 1837 and vulcanized rubber in 1839, a method of curing raw rubber to make it strong and elastic.

goose any of several large aquatic birds belonging to the same family as ducks and swans. There are about 12 species, found in North America, Greenland, Europe, North Africa, and Asia north of the Himalayas. Both sexes are similar in appearance: they have short, webbed feet, placed nearer the front of the body than in other members of the family, and a slightly hooked beak. Geese feed entirely on grass and plants, build nests of grass and twigs on the ground, and lay 5–9 eggs, white or cream-coloured, according to the species. (Genera mainly *Anser* and *Branta*, family Anatidae, order Anseriformes.)

> **Mikhail Gorbachev**
> *No party has a monopoly over what is right.*
> *The Observer*, March 2 1986

The **barnacle goose** (*B. leucopsis*) is about 60 cm/2 ft long and weighs about 2 kg/4.5 lb. It is black and white, marbled with blue and grey, and the beak is black. The **bean goose** (*A. fabalis*) is a grey species of European wild goose with an orange or yellow and black beak. It breeds in northern Europe and Siberia. The **Brent goose** (*B. bernicla*) is a small goose, black or brown, white, and grey in colour. It is almost completely herbivorous, feeding on eel grass and algae. The world population of Brent geese was 25,000 in 1996. The **greylag goose** (*A. anser*) is the ancestor of domesticated geese.

Other species include the **Canada goose** (*B. canadensis*) (common to North America and introduced into Europe in the 18th century), the **pink-footed goose** (*A. brachyrhynchus*), the **white-fronted goose** (*A. albifrons*), and the **ne-ne** or **Hawaiian goose** (*B. sandvicensis*).

The greylag goose is the only species that nests in Great Britain. It is found in the west of Scotland and in west central Ireland.

GOOSE A gaggle of geese in Dordogne, France. This *département* is well-known for pâté de foie gras, the rich delicacy prepared from fatted goose liver. Force-feeding of the birds happens for about three weeks before they are killed; the liver becomes so enlarged that the bird can hardly walk. *Image Bank*

gooseberry edible fruit of a low-growing bush (*Ribes uva-crispa*) found in Europe and Asia, related to the ▷currant. It is straggling in its growth, and has straight sharp spines in groups of three and rounded, lobed leaves. The flowers are green and hang on short stalks. The sharp-tasting fruits are round, hairy, and generally green, but there are reddish and white varieties.

goosefoot any of a group of plants belonging to the goosefoot family, closely related to spinach and beets. The seeds of white goosefoot (*C. album*) were used as food in Europe from Neolithic times, and also from early times in the Americas. White goosefoot grows to 1 m/3 ft tall and has lance- or diamond-shaped leaves and packed heads of small inconspicuous flowers. The green part is eaten as a spinach substitute. (Genus *Chenopodium*, family Chenopodiaceae.)

gopher any of a group of burrowing rodents. Gophers are a kind of ground squirrel represented by some 20 species distributed across western North America, Europe, and Asia. Length ranges from 15 cm/6 in to 90 cm/16 in, excluding the furry tail; colouring ranges from plain yellowish to striped and spotted species. (Genus *Citellus*, family Sciuridae.) The name **pocket gopher** is applied to the eight genera of the North American family Geomyidae.

gopher tortoise land tortoise occurring in the southern USA. It has a domed shell and scaly legs. Its forelegs are flattened for digging the burrow where it lives. Gopher tortoises reach lengths of up to 37 cm/14.5 in.

Classification The gopher tortoise *Gopherus polyphemus* is in family Cheloniidae, order Testudinae, class Reptilia.

Gorbachev, Mikhail Sergeyevich (1931–) Soviet president, in power 1985–91. He was a member of the Politburo from 1980. As general secretary of the Communist Party (CPSU) 1985–91 and president of the Supreme Soviet 1988–91, he introduced liberal reforms at home (▷*perestroika* and ▷*glasnost*), proposed the introduction of multiparty democracy, and attempted to halt the arms race abroad. He became head of state in 1989. He was awarded the Nobel Prize for Peace in 1990 for promoting greater openness in the USSR and helping to end the Cold War.

Gorbachev radically changed the style of Soviet leadership, encountering opposition to the pace of change from both conservatives and radicals, but failed both to realize the depth of hostility this aroused against him in the CPSU and to distance himself from the party. His international reputation suffered in the light of harsh state repression of nationalist demonstrations in the Baltic states. Following an abortive coup attempt by hardliners in August 1991, international acceptance of independence for the Baltic states, and accelerated moves towards independence in other republics, Gorbachev's power base as Soviet president was greatly weakened and in December 1991 he resigned. He contested the Russian presidential elections in June 1996, but attracted a humiliating 0.5% of the vote.

Related Web site: Gorbachev, Mikhail http://www.pathfinder.com/time/time100/leaders/profile/gorbachev.html

Gordian knot in Greek mythology, the knot tied by King Gordius of Phrygia that – so an oracle revealed – could be unravelled only by the future conqueror of Asia. According to tradition, Alexander the Great, unable to untie it, cut it with his sword in 334 BC.

Gordimer, Nadine (1923–) South African novelist and short story writer. Internationally acclaimed for her fiction and regarded by many as South Africa's conscience, Gordimer was for many years one of the most prominent opponents of apartheid and censorship. Much of Gordimer's fiction is set in Johannesburg and is generated by a complex of public and private concerns, chief among which are the family, sexuality, interracial social interaction and the imperatives of political commitment in the context of apartheid. She was awarded the Nobel Prize for Literature in 1991.

Gordimer's own political ideology evolved from the liberal humanism that dominates her novels from her autobiographical debut *The Lying Days* (1953) through *The Late Bourgeois World* (1966), to the radicalism that increasingly informs such subsequent novels as the Booker Prize-winning *The Conservationist* (1974), *July's People* (1981), and *My Son's Story* (1990). *None to Accompany Me* (1994) is set during South Africa's transition from apartheid to democracy, while *The House Gun* (1998) focuses on issues raised by a murder in the post-apartheid context. Also a consummate practitioner of the short story, Gordimer's many collections include *Jump and Other Stories* (1991), which appeared the year she was awarded the Nobel Prize for Literature. Her nonfiction includes the essay collections *The Essential Gesture* (1988) and *Living in Hope and History: Notes from Our Century* (1999).

Gordon, Charles George (1833–1885) British general sent to Khartoum in the Sudan in 1884 to rescue English garrisons that were under attack by the ▷Mahdi, Muhammad Ahmed; he was himself besieged for ten months by the Mahdi's army. A relief expedition arrived on 28 January 1885 to find that Khartoum had been captured and Gordon killed two days before. See picture on p. 402.

Gordon setter breed of dog. See ▷setter.

Gore, Al(bert Arnold, Jr) (1948–) US politician, vice-president from 1993. A Democrat, he was a member of the House of Representatives 1977–79, and was senator for Tennessee 1985–92. He was on the conservative wing of the party, but held liberal views on such matters as women's rights, environmental

CHARLES GORDON *General Gordon's Last Stand* by
W G Joy. *The Art Archive*

issues, and abortion. As vice-president he was unusually active in
foreign affairs, and put forward proposals for 'reinventing
government' by cutting red tape and improving efficiency. Gore
narrowly failed to become president when, in November 2000, he
won a plurality of the popular vote (48.3%) but won four fewer
electoral college seats than the Republican, George W ▷Bush, who
won 48.1% of the vote. His lack of warmth as a campaigner and
failure to attach to himself credit for the Clinton administration's
economic success was suggested to explain this failure.

gorge narrow steep-sided valley (or canyon) that may or may not
have a river at the bottom. A gorge may be formed as a ▷waterfall
retreats upstream, eroding away the rock at the base of a river
valley; or it may be caused by rejuvenation, when a river begins to
cut downwards into its channel once again (for example, in
response to a fall in sea level). Gorges are common in limestone
country, where they may be formed by the collapse of the roofs of
underground caverns.

Gorgon in Greek mythology according to the Greek poet Hesiod,
any of three monsters; the sisters **Stheno** and **Euryale**, daughters of
the sea god Phorcys and Ceto, and the mortal ▷Medusa. They had
wings, claws, enormous teeth, and snakes for hair; direct sight of
them turned living creatures to stone. Medusa was slain by
▷Perseus who watched her reflection in his shield, although her
head retained its power to transform.

gorilla largest of the apes, found in the dense forests of West
Africa and mountains of central Africa. The male stands about
1.8 m/6 ft high and weighs about 200 kg/450 lb. Females are about
half this size. The body is covered with blackish hair, silvered on
the back in older males. Gorillas live in family groups; they are
vegetarian, highly intelligent, and will attack only in self-defence.
They are dwindling in numbers, being shot for food by some local
people, or by poachers taking young for zoos, but protective
measures are having some effect. (Species *Gorilla gorilla*.)

GORILLA Juvenile female mountain gorilla in the Parc
National des Volcans/Volcano National Park, Rwanda.
Ken Preston-Mafham/Premaphotos Wildlife

Gorillas construct stoutly built nests in trees for overnight use.
The breast-beating movement, once thought to indicate rage,
actually signifies only nervous excitement. There are three races –
western lowland, eastern lowland, and mountain gorillas – and US
scientists suggested in 1994 that there may be two separate species
of gorilla. In 1998 the Worldwide Fund for Nature estimated that
there were 111,000 western lowland gorillas remaining, 10,000
eastern lowland, and 620 mountain gorillas.

    Related Web site: Gorilla http://www.seaworld.org/
animal_bytes/gorillaab.html

Göring, Hermann German spelling of ▷Goering, Nazi leader.

Gorky (Russian Gor'kiy) name 1932–91 of ▷Nizhniy-Novgorod,
a city in central Russia. The city was named after the writer Maxim
Gorky in 1932, but reverted to its original name after the collapse
of the Soviet Union.

Gorky, Arshile (1904–1948) Adopted name of Vosdanig
Manoüg Adoian. Armenian-born US painter. He painted in several
modernist styles before developing a semi-abstract surreal style,
using organic shapes and vigorous brushwork. His works, such as
The Liver Is the Cock's Comb (1944; Albright-Knox Art Gallery,
Buffalo), are noted for their sense of fantasy.

Gorky, Maxim (1868–1936) Pen-name of Alexei Maximovich
Peshkov. Russian writer. Born in Nizhniy-Novgorod (named
Gorky 1932–90 in his honour), he was exiled 1906–13 for his
revolutionary principles. His works, which include the play *The
Lower Depths* (1902) and the memoir *My Childhood* (1913–14),
combine realism with optimistic faith in the potential of the
industrial proletariat.

gorse (or **furze** or **whin**) any of a group of plants native to
Europe and Asia, consisting of thorny shrubs with spine-shaped
leaves growing thickly along the stems and bright-yellow coconut-
scented flowers. (Genus *Ulex*, family Leguminosae.)

GORSE Western gorse *Ulex gallii*. It is found in Europe
in western Spain, Portugal, France and the British Isles.
Premaphotos Wildlife

goshawk (or **northern goshawk**) woodland hawk similar in
appearance to the peregrine falcon, but with shorter wings and legs.
It is native to most of Europe, Asia, and North America, and is used
in falconry. The male is much smaller than the female. It is ash grey
on the upper part of the body and whitish underneath with brown
horizontal stripes; it has a dark head and cheeks with a white stripe
above the eye. The tail has dark bands across it. (Species *Accipiter
gentilis*, order Falconiformes.)

Gospel (Middle English 'good news') in the New Testament
generally, the message of Christian salvation; in particular the four
written accounts of the life of Jesus in the books of Matthew, Mark,
Luke, and John. Although the first three give approximately the
same account or synopsis (thus giving rise to the name 'Synoptic
Gospels'), their differences from John have raised problems for
theologians.

gospel music vocal music developed in the 1920s in the black
Baptist churches of the US South from spirituals. Outstanding
among the early gospel singers was Mahalia Jackson, but from the
1930s to the mid-1950s male harmony groups predominated,
among them the Dixie Hummingbirds, the Swan Silvertones, and
the Five Blind Boys of Mississippi.

Gossaert, Jan Flemish painter, known as ▷Mabuse.

Göteborg (English **Gothenburg**) port and industrial city (ships,
vehicles, chemicals) on the west coast of Sweden, at the mouth of
the Göta River; population (1994 est) 444,600. It is Sweden's
second-largest city and is linked with Stockholm by the Göta Canal
(built 1832).

GOTH Silver buckle
with precious stones
and the head of an
eagle from the
Tarnovka necropolis in
Mangup, Crimea, 7th
century AD. In the late
4th century AD, the
Ostrogoths, who had
developed an empire
north of the Black Sea
in the 3rd century AD,
were defeated by the
Huns, and most of them
migrated eastwards to
central Europe;
however, a pocket of
them remained behind
in the Crimea and this
branch of Ostrogoths
preserved their identity
into the Middle Ages.
The Art Archive

Goth East Germanic people who settled near the Black Sea around
AD 2nd century. There are two branches, the eastern Ostrogoths
and the western Visigoths. The **Ostrogoths** were conquered by the
Huns in 372. They regained their independence in 454 and under
Theodoric the Great conquered Italy 488–93; they disappeared as a
nation after the Byzantine emperor Justinian I reconquered Italy
535–55.

    The **Visigoths** migrated to Thrace. Under ▷Alaric they raided
Greece and Italy 395–410, sacked Rome, and established a kingdom
in southern France. Expelled from there by the Franks, they
established a Spanish kingdom which lasted until the Moorish
conquest of 711.

Gothenburg English form of ▷Göteborg, a city in Sweden.

Gothic architecture style of architecture that flourished in
Europe from the mid-12th century to the end of the 15th century.
It is characterized by the vertical lines of tall pillars and spires,
greater height in interior spaces, the pointed arch, rib vaulting, and
the flying buttress.

    Gothic architecture originated in Normandy and Burgundy in
the 12th century. Essentially the style of the Catholic countries of
Europe, including Hungary and Poland, it attained its highest
excellence in France and England. It developed forms on a regional
basis, often of great complexity and beauty, and was used for all
secular buildings as well as for cathedrals, churches, and
monasteries. The style prevailed in Western Europe until the 16th
century when Classic architecture was revived.

France In France, Gothic architecture may be divided into four
periods. **Early Gothic** (1130–90) saw the introduction of ogival
(pointed) vaults, for example Notre Dame, Paris (begun 1160). In
lancet Gothic (1190–1240) pointed arches were tall and narrow, as
in Chartres Cathedral (begun 1194), and Bourges Cathedral (begun
1209). **Rayonnant Gothic** (1240–1350) takes its name from the
series of chapels that radiate from the cathedral apse, as in Sainte
Chapelle, Paris, 1226–30. **Late Gothic** or the **Flamboyant style**
(1350–1520) is exemplified in St Gervais, Paris.

Italy In Italy Gothic had a classical basis, characterized by vast
spans with simple arches on a basilican plan. A notable example of
Italian Gothic is Milan Cathedral.

Germany In Germany, the Gothic style until the end of the 13th
century was at first heavily influenced by that of France; for
example Cologne Cathedral, the largest in northern Europe, was
built after the model of Amiens. Many churches were built of brick,
not stone.

England In England the Gothic style is divided into Early English
(1200–75), for example, Salisbury Cathedral; Decorated (1300–75),
for example, York Minster; and Perpendicular (1400–1575), for
example, Winchester Cathedral.

The pointed arch and window designs The real basis of Gothic
architecture, and that which differentiates it from the heavier
Romanesque style, is its elaborate and highly scientific system of
vaulting and buttressing, made possible by the presence of the
pointed arch. One result of the improved system was an increase of
window area in the walls between buttresses – the walls no longer
had to carry the main weight of the roof and could therefore be
thinner and pierced with impunity. Lancet windows (windows
topped by pointed arches) were grouped in twos or threes under an
enclosing arch, the remaining contained space being pierced with

small circular openings. Later the stonework between the various windows and openings ('lights') was reduced to slender stone bars ('mullions'), and the whole enclosed group of 'lights' became a single window. The upper portion of the window within the arch was filled with tracery, consisting at first of geometrical patterns, then later of flowing patterns, and finally of quasi-rectangular openings in the form of a grid (an effect achieved largely by the introduction of horizontal transoms in the larger windows).

These phases of window design, rather than any vital principle of construction, led to the formal division of English Gothic architecture into its three main stages.

Related Web site: Late Gothic Architecture http://www.tulane.edu/lester/text/Gothic/Late.Gothic/Late.Gothic.html

Gothic art style that succeeded Romanesque as the most popular force in European art and prevailed in most countries, particularly in northern Europe, from the late 12th century to the beginning of the 16th century, when it gave way to ▷Renaissance influence. The term 'Gothic' was coined with reference to architecture, and it is only in architecture that it has a clear meaning, with pointed arches being the most obvious characteristic. The term is used as a convenient label for other visual arts of the period, but its meaning in these contexts is rarely precise.

gothic novel literary genre established by Horace Walpole's *The Castle of Otranto* (1765) and marked by mystery, violence, and horror; other exponents were the English writers Anne Radcliffe, Matthew 'Monk' Lewis, Mary Shelley, the Irish writer Bram Stoker, and Edgar Allan Poe in the USA.

gouache (or **body colour**) painting medium in which watercolour is mixed with white pigment. Applied in the same way as watercolour, gouache gives a chalky finish similar to that of ▷tempera painting. It has long been popular in continental Europe, where Dürer and Boucher were both masters of the technique. Poster paints are usually a form of gouache.

Gould, Stephen Jay (1941–2002) US palaeontologist and writer. In 1972 he proposed that the evolution of species did not occur at a steady rate but could suddenly accelerate, with rapid change occurring over a few hundred thousand years. His books include *Ever Since Darwin* (1977), *The Panda's Thumb* (1980), *The Flamingo's Smile* (1985), *Wonderful Life* (1990), and *The Structure of Evolutionary Theory* (2002).

Gounod, Charles François (1818–1893) French composer and organist. His operas, notably *Faust* (1859) and *Roméo et Juliette* (1867), and church music, including *Messe solennelle/Solemn Mass* (1849), combine graceful melody and elegant harmonization. His *Méditation sur le prélude de Bach/Meditation on Bach's 'Prélude'* (1889) for soprano and instruments, based on Prelude No. 1 of Bach's *Well-Tempered Clavier*, achieved popularity as 'Gounod's *Ave Maria*'.

gourd any of a group of plants that includes melons and pumpkins. In a narrower sense, the name applies only to the genus *Lagenaria*, of which the bottle gourd or ▷calabash (*L. siceraria*) is best known. (Family Cucurbitaceae.)

gout hereditary form of ▷arthritis, marked by an excess of uric acid crystals in the tissues, causing pain and inflammation in one or more joints (usually of the feet or hands). Acute attacks are treated with anti-inflammatories.

government any system whereby political authority is exercised. Modern systems of government distinguish between liberal democracies, totalitarian (one-party) states, and autocracies (authoritarian, relying on force rather than ideology). The Greek philosopher Aristotle was the first to attempt a systematic classification of governments. His main distinctions were between government by one person, by few, and by many (monarchy, oligarchy, and democracy), although the characteristics of each may vary between states and each may degenerate into tyranny (rule by an oppressive elite in the case of oligarchy or by the mob in the case of democracy).

Types of government The French philosopher Montesquieu distinguished between **constitutional governments** – whether monarchies or republics – which operated under various legal and other constraints, and **despotism**, which was not constrained in this way. Many of the words used (dictatorship, tyranny, totalitarian, democratic) have acquired negative or positive connotations that make it difficult to use them objectively.

The term **liberal democracy** was coined to distinguish Western types of democracy from the many other political systems that claimed to be democratic. Its principal characteristics are the existence of more than one political party, relatively open processes of government and political debate, and a separation of powers.

Totalitarian has been applied to both fascist and communist states and denotes a system where all power is centralized in the state, which in turn is controlled by a single party that derives its legitimacy from an exclusive ideology.

Autocracy describes a form of government that has emerged in a number of Third World countries, where state power is in the hands either of an individual or of the army; normally ideology is not a central factor, individual freedoms tend to be suppressed where they may constitute a challenge to the authority of the ruling group, and there is a reliance upon force.

Other useful distinctions are between **federal** governments (where powers are dispersed among various regions which in certain respects are self-governing) and **unitary** governments (where powers are concentrated in a central authority); and between **presidential** (where the head of state is also the directly elected head of government, not part of the legislature) and **parliamentary** systems (where the government is drawn from an elected legislature that can dismiss it).

Distribution In 1995, 73 of the world's 192 sovereign states were liberal democracies and 72 were emergent democracies, 13 had authoritarian nationalist regimes, 12 absolutist, 8 nationalistic-socialist, 7 military, 5 communist, and 2 Islamic-nationalist.

> **Stephen Jay Gould**
> *If we are still here to witness the destruction of our planet [by the Sun] some five billion years or more hence, then we will have achieved something so unprecedented in the history of life that we should be willing to sing our swan song with joy.*
> The Panda's Thumb (1980)

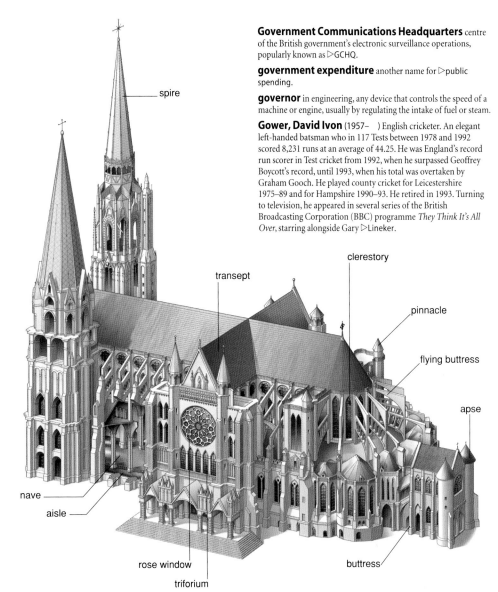

spire

transept

clerestory

pinnacle

flying buttress

apse

nave

aisle

rose window

triforium

buttress

GOTHIC ARCHITECTURE
A Gothic cathedral showing a cutaway section.

Government Communications Headquarters centre of the British government's electronic surveillance operations, popularly known as ▷GCHQ.

government expenditure another name for ▷public spending.

governor in engineering, any device that controls the speed of a machine or engine, usually by regulating the intake of fuel or steam.

Gower, David Ivon (1957–) English cricketer. An elegant left-handed batsman who in 117 Tests between 1978 and 1992 scored 8,231 runs at an average of 44.25. He was England's record run scorer in Test cricket from 1992, when he surpassed Geoffrey Boycott's record, until 1993, when his total was overtaken by Graham Gooch. He played county cricket for Leicestershire 1975–89 and for Hampshire 1990–93. He retired in 1993. Turning to television, he appeared in several series of the British Broadcasting Corporation (BBC) programme *They Think It's All Over*, starring alongside Gary ▷Lineker.

Gowon, Yakubu (1934–) Nigerian politician, head of state 1966–75. He became army chief of staff following a coup in January 1966, and five months later seized power in a further coup. Unsuccessful in his efforts to prevent the secession of the eastern region of ▷Biafra, Nigeria was plunged into civil war 1967–70. After leading the federal army to victory, he reunited the country with his policy of 'no victor, no vanquished'. His later administration was plagued by allegations of corruption and Gowon's failure to timetable a return to civilian rule. Deposed by a bloodless coup in 1975, he went into exile in the UK, returning to Nigeria in 1983.

Goya, Francisco José de Goya y Lucientes (1746–1828) Spanish painter and engraver. One of the major figures of European art, Goya depicted all aspects of Spanish life – portraits, including those of the royal family, religious works, scenes of war and of everyday life. Towards the end of his life, he created strange, nightmarish works, the 'Black Paintings', with such horrific images as *Saturn Devouring One of His Sons* (c. 1822; Prado, Madrid). His series of etchings include *The Disasters of War* (1810–14), depicting the horrors of the French invasion of Spain.

Goya was born in Aragón. After studying in Italy, he returned to Spain and was employed on a number of paintings for the royal tapestry factory as well as numerous portraits. In 1789 he was appointed court painter to Charles IV. The eroticism of his *Naked Maja* and *Clothed Maja* (c. 1800–05; Prado, Madrid) caused such outrage that he was questioned by the Inquisition. *The Shootings of May 3rd 1808* (1814; Prado, Madrid), painted for Ferdinand VII, is passionate in its condemnation of the inhumanity of war. Technically, Goya attained brilliant effects by thin painting over a red earth ground. Much influenced by Rembrandt ('Rembrandt, Velázquez, and Nature' were, he said, his guides), he turned in later years to a dusky near-monochrome. His skill, however, seemed to increase with age, and the *Milkmaid of Bordeaux*, one of his last paintings, shows him using colour with great freedom.

Gozo (or Gozzo; ancient **Gaulus**; Maltese **Ghawdex**) island in the Mediterranean Sea, 6 km/4 mi northwest of ▷Malta; it is one of three main islands (with Malta and Comino) that form the state of Malta; area 67 sq m/26 sq mi; population (1994 est) 27,600 (with Comino). The chief town is Victoria. The island is very fertile, and products include fruit and vegetables. On Gozo are the megalithic ruins of Ggantija (the Giant's Temple, a citadel begun during the rule of the Arabs 870–1127), a baroque cathedral, and a modern Romanesque church.

Gozzoli, Benozzo (*c.* 1421–1497) Florentine painter. He is known for his fresco *The Procession of the Magi* (1459–61) in the Chapel of the Palazzo Medici-Riccardi, Florence, where the walls are crowded with figures, many of them portraits of the Medici family.

Graafian follicle fluid-filled capsule that surrounds and protects the developing egg cell inside the ovary during the ▷menstrual cycle. After the egg cell has been released, the follicle remains and is known as a corpus luteum.

Graaf, Regnier de (1641–1673) Dutch physician and anatomist who discovered the ovarian follicles, which were later named **Graafian follicles**. He named the ovaries and gave exact descriptions of the testicles. He was also the first to isolate and collect the secretions of the pancreas and gall bladder.

Gracchus Tiberius Sempronius (*c.* 163–133 BC) and Gaius Sempronius (*c.* 153–121 BC). In ancient Rome, two brothers who worked for agrarian reform. As ▷tribune (magistrate) 133 BC, Tiberius tried to redistribute land away from the large slave-labour farms in order to benefit the poor as well as increase the number of those eligible for military service by providing them with the miniumum property requirement. He was murdered by a mob of senators. Gaius, tribune 123–122 BC, revived his brother's legislation, and introduced other reforms, but was outlawed by the Senate and killed in a riot.

Graces in Greek mythology, three goddesses (Aglaia, Euphrosyne, Thalia), daughters of Zeus and Hera, personifications of pleasure, charm, and beauty; the inspirers of the arts and the sciences.

Grace, W(illiam) G(ilbert) (1848–1915) English cricketer. By profession a doctor, he became the most famous sportsman in Victorian England. A right-handed batsman, he began playing first-class cricket at the age of 16, scored 152 runs in his first Test match, and scored the first triple century in 1876. Throughout his career, which lasted nearly 45 years, he scored 54,896 runs and took 2,876 wickets.

Graf, Steffi (1969–) German lawn-tennis player who brought Martina ▷Navratilova's long reign as the world's number-one female player to an end. Graf reached the semi-final of the US Open in 1985 at the age of 16, and won five consecutive Grand Slam singles titles 1988–89. In 1994 she became the first defending Wimbledon ladies' singles champion to lose her title in the first round. In June 1999 she won her sixth French Open singles title, and her 22nd Grand Slam singles in total. Only Chris Evert, with seven victories, has won the women's French Open more times, and only Margaret Court has won more Grand Slam singles titles.
In August 1999 Graf announced her retirement from competitive tennis. She married fellow tennis player Andre Agassi in 2001.
Related Web site: Steffi Graf International Supporters' Club http://www.sgisc.com/

graffiti art art inspired by urban graffiti. Critical and financial interest in graffiti art emerged in the 1970s in New York, with artists and critics seeing graffiti as a direct and genuine expression of urban culture, free of the manipulation of the art market. Leading graffiti artists were Jean-Michel Basquiat (1960–1988) and Keith Haring (1958–1990).

GRAFFITI ART The US artist Jean-Michel Basquiat (1960–1988) first gained recognition with his graffiti on the streets and subways of New York City, New York, in 1981. Within a year, his paintings and drawings had taken the New York art scene by storm and were soon selling in galleries throughout the world. *Archive Photos*

grafting in medicine, the operation by which an organ or other living tissue is removed from one organism and transplanted into the same or a different organism.

In horticulture, it is a technique widely used for propagating plants, especially woody species. A bud or shoot on one plant, termed the **scion**, is inserted into another, the **stock**, so that they continue growing together, the tissues combining at the point of union. In this way some of the advantages of both plants are obtained. Grafting is usually only successful between species that are closely related and is most commonly practised on roses and fruit trees. The grafting of nonwoody species is more difficult but it is sometimes used to propagate tomatoes and cacti. See also ▷transplant.

Graham, Billy (William Franklin) (1918–) US Protestant evangelist, known for the dramatic staging and charismatic eloquence of his preaching. Graham has preached to millions during worldwide crusades and on television, bringing many thousands to conversion to, or renewal of, Christian faith.

Graham, Martha (1894–1991) US dancer, choreographer, teacher, and director. The greatest exponent of modern dance in the USA, she developed a distinctive vocabulary of movement, the **Graham Technique**, now taught worldwide. Her pioneering technique, designed to express inner emotion and intention through dance forms, represented the first real alternative to classical ballet.

Graham founded her own dance school in 1927 and started a company with students from the school 1929. She created over 170 works, including *Appalachian Spring* (1944; score by Aaron Copland), *Clytemnestra* (1958; the first full-length modern dance work), and *Lucifer* (1975).
She danced in most of the pieces she choreographed until her retirement from performance in the 1960s. Graham had a major influence on such choreographers in the contemporary dance movement as Robert Cohan, Glen Tetley, Merce Cunningham, Norman Morrice, Paul Taylor, and Robert North.

Graham, Thomas (1805–1869) Scottish chemist who laid the foundations of physical chemistry (the branch of chemistry concerned with changes in energy during a chemical transformation) by his work on the diffusion of gases and liquids. **Graham's law** (1829) states that the diffusion rate of a gas is inversely proportional to the square root of its density.

Grahame, Kenneth (1859–1932) Scottish-born writer. The early volumes of sketches of childhood, *The Golden Age* (1895) and *Dream Days* (1898), were followed by his masterpiece *The Wind in the Willows* (1908) which became a children's classic. Begun as a bedtime story for his son, it is a charming tale of life on the river bank, with its blend of naturalistic style and fantasy, and its memorable animal characters, the practical Rat, Mole, Badger, and conceited, bombastic Toad. It was dramatized by A A Milne as *Toad of Toad Hall* (1929) and by Alan Bennett (1990).

Kenneth Grahame
Believe me, my young friend, there is nothing – absolutely nothing – half so much worth doing as simply messing about in boats.
Wind in the Willows ch. 2

grain the smallest unit of mass in the three English systems (avoirdupois, troy, and apothecaries' weights) used in the UK and USA, equal to 0.0648 g. It was reputedly the weight of a grain of wheat. One pound avoirdupois equals 7,000 grains; one pound troy or apothecaries' weight equals 5,760 grains.

gram metric unit of mass; one-thousandth of a kilogram.

grammar (Greek *grammatike tekhne* 'art of letters') the rules for combining words into phrases, clauses, sentences, and paragraphs. The standardizing impact of print has meant that spoken or colloquial language is often perceived as less grammatical than written language, but all forms of a language, standard or otherwise, have their own grammatical systems. People often acquire several overlapping grammatical systems within one language; for example, a formal system for writing and standard communication and a less formal system for everyday and peer-group communication.

grammar school in the UK, secondary school catering for children of high academic ability, about 20% of the total, usually measured by the Eleven Plus examination. Most grammar schools have now been replaced by ▷comprehensive schools.

In the USA the term is sometimes used for a primary school (also called elementary school).

Grampian Mountains range that includes **Ben Nevis**, the highest mountain in the British Isles at 1,343 m/4,406 ft, and the Cairngorm Mountains, which include the second highest mountain, **Ben Macdhui** 1,309 m/4,295 ft. The region includes Aviemore, a winter holiday and sports centre.

Gramsci, Antonio (1891–1937) Italian Marxist who attempted to unify social theory and political practice. He helped to found the Italian Communist Party in 1921 and was elected to parliament in 1924, but was imprisoned by the Fascist leader Mussolini from 1926; his *Quaderni di carcere/Prison Notebooks* were published posthumously in 1947.

Gramsci believed that politics and ideology were independent of the economic base, that no ruling class could dominate by economic factors alone, and that the working class could achieve liberation by political and intellectual struggle. His concept of **hegemony** argued that real class control in capitalist societies is ideological and cultural rather than physical, and that only the working class 'educated' by radical intellectuals could see through and overthrow such bourgeois propaganda.

His humane and gradualist approach to Marxism, specifically his emphasis on the need to overthrow bourgeois ideology, influenced European Marxists in their attempt to distance themselves from orthodox determinist Soviet communism.

Granada capital of Granada province in Andalusia, southern Spain, situated to the north of the Sierra Nevada on the River Genil; population (1991) 254,000. Products include textiles, soap, and paper; there are also food industries and tourism. Granada has many palaces and monuments, including the Alhambra, a fortified hilltop palace built in the 13th and 14th centuries by the Moorish kings; a Gothic and Renaissance archiepiscopal cathedral (1523–1703); and a university, founded in 1533.

Grand Canal (or **Imperial Canal**; Chinese **Da Yunhe**) the world's longest canal, running north from Hangzhou to Tianjin, China; 1,600 km/1,000 mi long and 30–61 m/100–200 ft wide. The earliest section was completed in 486 BC; the central section linking the Chang Jiang and Huang He rivers was built from AD 605 to 610; and the northern section was built between 1282 and 1292 during the reign of Kublai Khan.

Grand Canyon gorge in northwestern Arizona, USA, containing the ▷Colorado River. It is 350 km/217 mi long, 6–29 km/4–18 mi wide, and reaches depths of over 1.7 km/1.1 mi. The gorge cuts through a multicoloured series of rocks – mainly limestones, sandstones, and shales, and ranging in age from the Precambrian to the Cretaceous – and various harder strata stand out as steps on its slopes. It is one of the country's most popular national parks and millions of tourists visit it each year.
Protected since 1893, and accessible by rail since 1901, the Grand Canyon was made a national park in 1919, and is a World Heritage Site. Most visitors approach the canyon via the more accessible South Rim; the North Rim is around 300–500 m/1,000–1,500 ft higher, and is closed during the winter. The national park has an area of 4,931 sq km/1,904 sq mi, and is bounded by Glen Canyon to the east and Lake Mead to the west. On its way through the canyon the Colorado River drops 670 m/2,200 ft through dozens of rapids.
Related Web site: Grand Canyon http://www.kaibab.org/

Grand Guignol genre of short horror play originally produced at the Grand Guignol theatre in Montmartre, Paris (named after the bloodthirsty character Guignol in late 18th-century marionette plays).

grand opera type of opera without any spoken dialogue (unlike the *opéra-comique*), as performed at the Paris Opéra, France, in the 1820s to 1880s. Grand operas were extremely long (five acts), and included incidental music and a ballet.

Grand Remonstrance petition passed by the English Parliament in November 1641 that listed all the alleged misdeeds of ▷Charles I – 'the evils under which we have now many years suffered'. It then went on to blame those it thought responsible – the 'Jesuited papists', the bishops and Charles's councillors and courtiers. It demanded parliamentary approval for the king's ministers and the reform of the church. Charles refused to accept the Grand Remonstrance and countered by trying to arrest five leading members of the House of Commons. The worsening of relations between king and Parliament led to the outbreak of the English Civil War in 1642.

grand slam in tennis, the winning of four major tournaments in one season: the Australian Open, the French Open, Wimbledon, and the US Open. In golf, it is also winning the four major tournaments in one season: the US Open, the British Open, the Masters, and the US PGA (Professional Golfers Association)

National Tournament. In baseball, a grand slam is a home run with runners on all the bases. A grand slam in bridge is when all 13 tricks are won by one team.

Related Web site: Sky Sports Online Tennis http://www.sky.com/sports/tennis/

grand unified theory in physics, a sought-for theory that would combine the theory of the strong nuclear force (called ▷quantum chromodynamics) with the theory of the weak nuclear and electromagnetic forces. The search for the grand unified theory is part of a larger programme seeking a ▷unified field theory, which would combine all the forces of nature (including gravity) within one framework.

Grange Movement in US history, a farmers' protest in the South and Midwest states against economic hardship and exploitation. The National Grange of the Patrons of Husbandry, formed in 1867, was a network of local organizations, employing cooperative practices and advocating 'granger' laws. The movement petered out in the late 1870s, to be superseded by the ▷Greenbackers.

granite coarse-grained intrusive ▷igneous rock, typically consisting of the minerals quartz, feldspar, and biotite mica. It may be pink or grey, depending on the composition of the feldspar. Granites are chiefly used as building materials.

GRANITE The smooth granite domes near Ambalavo, Madagascar, that are typical of this area. *K G Preston-Mafham/Premaphotos Wildlife*

Grant, Cary (1904–1986) Stage name of Archibald Alexander Leach. English-born actor, a US citizen from 1942. His witty, debonair personality made him a screen favourite for more than three decades. Among his many films are *She Done Him Wrong* (1933), *Bringing Up Baby* (1938), *The Philadelphia Story* (1940), *Notorious* (1946), *To Catch a Thief* (1955), *North by Northwest* (1959), and *Charade* (1963).

Grant was a frequent collaborator with the directors Alfred Hitchcock, Howard Hawks, and George Cukor. Further films include *The Awful Truth* (1937), *Topper* (1937), *His Girl Friday* (1940), *Arsenic and Old Lace* (1944), *Monkey Business* (1952), and *An Affair to Remember* (1957). He received an honorary Academy Award in 1969.

Grant, Duncan (James Corrowr) (1885–1978) Scottish painter and designer. A pioneer of post-Impressionism in the UK, he was influenced by Paul Cezanne and the Fauves, and became a member of the ▷Bloomsbury Group. He lived with the painter Vanessa Bell from about 1914 and worked with her on decorative projects, such as those at the ▷Omega Workshops. Later works, such as *Snow Scene* (1921), show great fluency and a subtle use of colour.

Grant, Ulysses S(impson) (1822–1885) Born Hiram Ulysses Grant. US Civil War general in chief for the Union and 18th president of the USA 1869–77. As a Republican president, he carried through a liberal ▷Reconstruction policy in the South. He failed to suppress extensive political corruption within his own party and cabinet, which tarnished the reputation of his second term.

Grant was the son of an Ohio farmer. He had an unsuccessful career in the army 1839–54 and in business. On the outbreak of the Civil War he received a commission on the Mississippi front. He took command there in 1862, and by his capture of Vicksburg in 1863 brought the whole Mississippi front under Northern control. In 1864 he was made commander in chief. He slowly wore down the Confederate general Lee's resistance, and in 1865 received his surrender at Appomattox.

Grant was elected president in 1868 and re-elected in 1872. As president, he reformed the civil service and ratified the Treaty of Washington with the UK in 1871.

Related Web site: Ulysses S Grant – Eighteenth President 1869–1877 http://www.whitehouse.gov/WH/glimpse/presidents/html/ug18.html

grant-maintained school in the UK, a state school that has voluntarily withdrawn itself from local authority support (an action called **opting out**), and instead is maintained directly by central government. The schools are managed by their own boards of governors. In 1996 there were 1,090 grant-maintained schools, of which 60% were secondary schools.

grape fruit of any grape ▷vine, especially *V. vinifera*. (Genus *Vitis*, family Vitaceae.)

GRAPE Grapes grown in the valley of the River Douro in Portugal. *Image Bank*

grapefruit round, yellow, juicy, sharp-tasting fruit of the evergreen grapefruit tree. The tree grows up to 10 m/more than 30 ft and has dark shiny leaves and large white flowers. The large fruits grow in grapelike clusters (hence the name). Grapefruits were first established in the West Indies and subsequently cultivated in Florida by the 1880s; they are now also grown in Israel and South Africa. Some varieties have pink flesh. (*Citrus paradisi*, family Rutaceae.)

graph pictorial representation of numerical data, such as statistical data, or a method of showing the mathematical relationship between two or more variables by drawing a diagram.

graphical user interface (GUI or WIMP) in computing, a type of ▷user interface in which programs and files appear as icons (small pictures), user options are selected from pull-down menus, and data are displayed in windows (rectangular areas), which the operator can manipulate in various ways. The operator uses a pointing device, typically a ▷mouse, to make selections and initiate actions.

The concept of the graphical user interface was developed by the Xerox Corporation in the 1970s, was popularized with the Apple Macintosh computers in the 1980s, and is now available on many types of computer – most notably as Windows, an operating system for IBM PC-compatible microcomputers developed by the software company Microsoft.

graphic equalizer control used in hi-fi systems that allows the distortions introduced into the sound output by unequal amplification of different frequencies to be corrected.

graphics tablet (or **bit pad**) in computing, an input device in which a stylus or cursor is moved, by hand, over a flat surface. The computer can keep track of the position of the stylus, so enabling the operator to input drawings or diagrams into the computer.

graphite blackish-grey, laminar, crystalline form of ▷carbon. It is used as a lubricant and as the active component of pencil lead.

Graphite, like ▷diamond and ▷fullerene, is an allotrope of carbon. The carbon atoms are strongly bonded together in sheets, but the bonds between the sheets are weak, allowing other atoms to enter regions between the layers causing them to slide over one another. Graphite has a very high melting point (3,500°C/6,332°F), and is a good conductor of heat and electricity. It absorbs neutrons and is therefore used to moderate the chain reaction in nuclear reactors.

graph notation in music, an invented sign language representing unorthodox sounds objectively in pitch and time, or alternatively representing sounds of orthodox music in a visually unorthodox manner. A form of graph notation for speech patterns used in phonetics was adopted by Karlheinz Stockhausen in *Carré/Squared* (1959–60).

graphology the study of the writing systems of a language, including the number and formation of letters, spelling patterns, accents, and punctuation. In the 19th century it was believed that analysis of a person's handwriting could give an indication of his or her personality, a belief still held in a more limited fashion today.

graph plotter alternative name for a ▷plotter.

Grappelli, Stéphane (1908–1997) French jazz violinist. He played in the Quintette du Hot Club de France (1934–39), in partnership with the guitarist Django ▷Reinhardt. Romantic improvisation was a hallmark of his style. Grappelli spent World War II in the UK and returned several times to record there, including a number of jazz albums with the classical violinist Yehudi Menuhin in the 1970s. Of his other collaborations, an LP with the mandolinist David Grisman (1945–) reached the US pop chart in 1981. He died in Paris, France, on 1 December 1997.

grass any of a very large family of plants, many of which are economically important because they provide grazing for animals and food for humans in the form of cereals. There are about 9,000 species distributed worldwide except in the Arctic regions. Most are perennial, with long, narrow leaves and jointed, hollow stems; flowers with both male and female reproductive organs are borne on spikelets; the fruits are grainlike. Included in the family are bluegrass, wheat, rye, maize, sugarcane, and bamboo. (Family Gramineae.)

Grass, Günter (Wilhelm) (1927–) German writer. The grotesque humour and socialist feeling of his novels *Die Blechtrommel/The Tin Drum* (1959) and *Der Butt/The Flounder* (1977) are also characteristic of many of his poems. Deeply committed politically, Grass's works contain a mixture of scurrility, humour, tragedy, satire, and marvellously inventive imagery. In 2000 he published *My Century*, a collection of a hundred short stories, one for each year of the 20th century, as well as a novel, *Too Far Afield*. He was awarded the Nobel Prize for Literature in 1999.

> **Günter Grass**
> *Art is so wonderfully irrational, exuberantly pointless, but necessary all the same. Pointless and yet necessary, that's hard for a puritan to understand.*
> Interview in *New Statesman and Society*, 22 June 1990

Die Blechtrommel One of the most successful post-war German novels, *Die Blechtrommel* is narrated by an impossible midget, Oskar, who willed himself to stop growing at the age of three, a device that enables the author to hover between fantasy and realism and achieve a detachment to make the scenes and characters of German life before and during the Nazi regime stand out with extraordinary clarity and humour.

grasshopper any of several insects with strongly developed hind legs, enabling them to leap into the air. The hind leg in the male usually has a row of protruding joints that produce the characteristic chirping sound when rubbed against the hard wing veins. ▷Locusts, ▷crickets, and katydids are related to grasshoppers. (Families Acrididae and Tettigoniidae, order Orthoptera.)

The **short-horned grasshoppers** constitute the family Acrididae, and include locusts. All members of the family feed voraciously on vegetation. Eggs are laid in a small hole in the ground, and the unwinged larvae become adult after about six moults.

There are several sober-coloured, small, and harmless species of grasshoppers in Britain. The **long-horned grasshoppers** or **bush crickets**, of the family Tettigoniidae, have a similar life history but differ from the Acrididae in having long antennae and in producing their chirping by the friction of the wing covers over one another (stridulation). The great green bush cricket (*Tettigonia viridissima*), 5 cm/2 in long, is a British species of this family, which also comprises the North American katydids, notable stridulators.

grass of Parnassus plant, unrelated to grasses, found growing in marshes and on wet moors in Europe and Asia. It is low-growing, with a rosette of heart-shaped stalked leaves, and has five-petalled white flowers with conspicuous veins growing singly on stem tips in late summer. (*Parnassia palustris*, family Parnassiaceae.)

GRASS SNAKE Grass snake *Natrix natrix* basking in the sun.
Mark Preston-Mafham/Premaphotos Wildlife

grass snake olive-green, grey or brownish non-venomous snake *Natrix natrix* found near water in lowland areas with woodland. They are about 80 cm/32 in long and feed mainly on frogs, toads, and newts, which they hunt in the water. They are the largest British reptiles. There is also a grass snake in the USA.

grass tree Australian plant belonging to the lily family. The tall, thick stems have a grasslike tuft at the top above which rises a flower spike resembling a spear; this often appears after bushfires and in some species can grow to a height of 3 m/10 ft. (Genus *Xanthorrhoea*, family Liliaceae.)

Graubünden (French **Grisons**) Swiss canton, the largest in Switzerland; area 7,106 sq km/2,743 sq mi; population (1999) 186,000. The capital is Chur. The inner valleys are the highest in Europe, and the main sources of the River Rhine rise here. It also includes the resort of Davos and, in the Upper Engadine, St Moritz. Ladin (a form of Romansch) is still widely spoken. Graubünden entered the Swiss Confederation in 1803.

gravel coarse ▷sediment consisting of pebbles or small fragments of rock, originating in the beds of lakes and streams or on beaches. Gravel is quarried for use in road building, railway ballast, and for an aggregate in concrete. It is obtained from quarries known as gravel pits, where it is often found mixed with sand or clay.

Graves, Robert (Ranke) (1895–1985) English poet and writer. He was severely wounded on the Somme in World War I, and his frank autobiography *Goodbye to All That* (1929) contains outstanding descriptions of the war. *Collected Poems* (1975) contained those verses he wanted preserved, some of which were influenced by the American poet Laura Riding, with whom he lived for some years. His fiction includes two historical novels of imperial Rome, *I Claudius* and *Claudius the God* (both 1934). His most significant critical work is *The White Goddess: A Historical Grammar of Poetic Myth* (1948, revised edition 1966).

Poetry Graves first achieved notice for his war poetry, but he largely rejected his early poetry and developed much further in his later verse. The poems of his maturity (1926–39), are technically confident, rhetorically simple, and are among the finest of modern love poems. After World War II, he became increasingly interested in Sufist and Eastern religious philosophy and mythology, the subject of many of his later poems. His works include *Collected Poems* (1965), *Poems 1965–68* (1968), *Poems 1968–1970* (1970), and *Poems 1970–72* (1972).

gravimetry measurement of the Earth's gravitational field. Small variations in the gravitational field (gravimetric anomalies) can be caused by varying densities of rocks and structure beneath the surface. Such variations are measured by a device called a gravimeter (or gravity-meter), which consists of a weighted spring that is pulled further downwards where the gravity is stronger. Gravimetry is used by geologists to map the subsurface features of the Earth's crust, such as underground masses of dense rock such as iron ore, or light rock such as salt.

gravitational field the region around a body in which other bodies experience a force due to its gravitational attraction. The gravitational field of a massive object such as the Earth is very strong and easily recognized as the force of gravity, whereas that of an object of much smaller mass is very weak and difficult to detect. Gravitational fields produce only attractive forces.

gravitational force (or gravity) one of the four fundamental ▷forces of nature, the other three being the electromagnetic force, the weak nuclear force, and the strong nuclear force. The gravitational force is the weakest of the four forces, but it acts over great distances. The particle that is postulated as the carrier of the gravitational force is the ▷graviton.

gravitational lensing bending of light by a gravitational field, predicted by German-born US physicist Albert Einstein's general theory of relativity. The effect was first detected in 1917 when the light from stars was found to be bent as it passed the totally eclipsed Sun. More remarkable is the splitting of light from distant quasars into two or more images by intervening galaxies. In 1979 the first double image of a quasar produced by gravitational lensing was discovered and a quadruple image of another quasar was later found.

graviton in physics, the ▷gauge boson that is the postulated carrier of the gravitational force.

gravity force of attraction that arises between objects by virtue of their masses. On Earth, gravity is the force of attraction between any object in the Earth's gravitational field and the Earth itself. It is regarded as one of the four fundamental ▷forces of nature, the other three being the ▷electromagnetic force, the ▷strong nuclear force, and the ▷weak nuclear force. The gravitational force is the weakest of the four forces, but it acts over great distances. The particle that is postulated as the carrier of the gravitational force is the ▷graviton.

One of the earliest gravitational experiments was undertaken by Nevil ▷Maskelyne in 1774 and involved the measurement of the attraction of Mount Schiehallion (Scotland) on a plumb bob.

Measuring forces of attraction An experiment for determining the force of attraction between two masses was first planned in the mid-18th century by the Reverend J Mitchell, who did not live to work on the apparatus he had designed and completed. After Mitchell's death the apparatus came into the hands of Henry ▷Cavendish, who largely reconstructed it but kept to Mitchell's original plan. The attracted masses consisted of two small balls, connected by a stiff wooden beam suspended at its middle point by a long, fine wire. The whole of this part of the apparatus was enclosed in a case, carefully coated with tinfoil to secure, as far as possible, a uniform temperature within the case. Irregular distribution of temperature would have resulted in convection currents of air which would have had a serious disturbing effect on the suspended system. To the beam was attached a small mirror with its plane vertical. A small glazed window in the case allowed any motion of the mirror to be observed by the consequent deviations of a ray of light reflected from it. The attracting masses consisted of two equal, massive lead spheres. Using this apparatus, Cavendish, in 1797, obtained for the gravitational constant *G* the value 6.6×10^{-11} N m^2 kg^{-2}. The apparatus was refined by Charles Vernon Boys and he obtained the improved value 6.6576×10^{-11} N m^2 kg^{-2}. The value generally used today is 6.6720×10^{-11} N m^2 kg^{-2}.

Related Web site: Exploring Gravity http://www.curtin.edu.au/curtin/dept/phys-sci/gravity/index2.htm

gravure one of the three main ▷printing methods, in which printing is done from a plate etched with a pattern of recessed cells in which the ink is held. The greater the depth of a cell, the greater the strength of the printed ink. Gravure plates are expensive to make, but the process is economical for high-volume printing and reproduces illustrations well.

Gray, Thomas (1716–1771) English poet. His *Elegy Written in a Country Churchyard* (1751), a dignified contemplation of death, was instantly acclaimed and is one of the most quoted poems in the English language. Other poems include *Ode on a Distant Prospect of Eton College* (1747), *The Progress of Poesy*, and *The Bard* (both 1757). He is now seen as a forerunner of ▷Romanticism.

A close friend of Horace ▷Walpole at Eton, Gray made a continental tour with him from 1739 to 1741, an account of which is given in his vivid letters. His first poem, *Ode on a Distant Prospect of Eton College*, was published anonymously in 1747 and again in 1748 with *Ode on the Spring* and *Ode on the Death of a Favourite Cat* in *A Collection of Poems By Several Hands*, edited by Robert Dodsley (1703–1764). *Poems by Mr Gray* was published in 1768.

Related Web site: Selected Poetry of Thomas Gray (1716–1771) http://www.library.utoronto.ca/utel/rp/authors/gray.html

gray SI unit (symbol Gy) of absorbed radiation dose. It replaces the rad (1 Gy equals 100 rad), and is defined as the dose absorbed when one kilogram of matter absorbs one joule of ionizing radiation. Different types of radiation cause different amounts of damage for the same absorbed dose; the SI unit of **dose equivalent** is the ▷sievert.

grayling freshwater fish with a long multirayed dorsal (back) fin and silver to purple body colouring. It is found in northern parts of Europe, Asia, and North America, where it was once common in the Great Lakes. (Species *Thymallus thymallus*, family Salmonidae.)

Graz capital of Styria province, and second-largest city in Austria, situated on the River Mur, 150 km/93 mi southwest of Vienna; population (1995) 243,700. Industries include engineering and the manufacture of chemicals, iron, steel, automobiles, precision and optical instruments, paper, textiles, and leather. Tourism is also important. It has a 15th-century cathedral and a university founded in 1586. Lippizaner horses are bred near here.

Great Artesian Basin the largest area of artesian water in the world. It underlies much of Queensland, New South Wales, and South Australia, and in prehistoric times formed a sea. It has an area of 1,750,000 sq km/675,750 sq mi.

Great Australian Bight broad bay of the Indian Ocean in southern Australia, notorious for storms. It was discovered by a Dutch navigator, Captain Thyssen, in 1627.

Great Barrier Reef chain of ▷coral reefs and islands about 2,000 km/1,250 mi long, in the Coral Sea, off the east coast of Queensland, Australia, about 16–241 km/10–150 mi offshore. The Great Barrier Reef is made up of 3,000 individual reefs, and is believed to be the world's largest living organism. Only ten navigable channels break through the reef. The most valuable products of the reef are pearls, pearl shells, trepangs (edible sea slugs), and sponges. The reef is popular with tourists. In 1976 it became a Marine Park and was declared a World Heritage Site by UNESCO in 1981.

Annually, a few nights after the full moon in November, 135 species of hard coral release their eggs and sperm for fertilization and the sea turns pink. The phenomenon, one of the wonders of the natural world, was discovered in 1983, and is triggered by a mechanism dependent on the moon, the tides, and water temperatures.

Related Web site: Great Barrier Reef Marine Park Authority http://www.gbrmpa.gov.au/

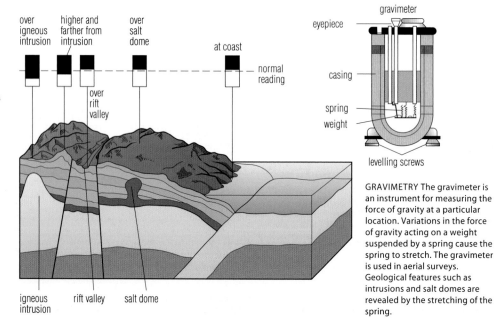

GRAVIMETRY The gravimeter is an instrument for measuring the force of gravity at a particular location. Variations in the force of gravity acting on a weight suspended by a spring cause the spring to stretch. The gravimeter is used in aerial surveys. Geological features such as intrusions and salt domes are revealed by the stretching of the spring.

Great Bear popular name for the constellation ▷Ursa Major.

Great Bear Lake freshwater lake in the western Northwest Territories, Canada, on the Arctic Circle; area 31,153 sq km/12,028 sq mi; depth 410 m/1,345 ft.

Great Britain official name for ▷England, ▷Scotland, and ▷Wales, and the adjacent islands (except the Channel Islands and the Isle of Man) from 1603, when the English and Scottish crowns were united under James I of England (James VI of Scotland). With ▷Northern Ireland it forms the ▷United Kingdom.

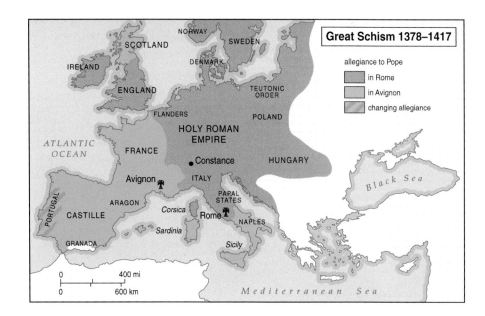

Great Schism 1378–1417

allegiance to Pope
- in Rome
- in Avignon
- changing allegiance

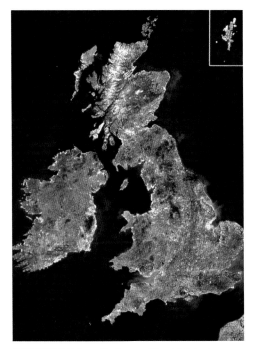

GREAT BRITAIN A satellite image of Great Britain. *Image Bank*

great circle circle drawn on a sphere such that the diameter of the circle is a diameter of the sphere. On the Earth, all meridians of longitude are half great circles; among the parallels of latitude, only the Equator is a great circle.

Great Dane breed of large, short-haired dog, often fawn or brindle in colour, standing up to 76 cm/30 in tall, and weighing up to 70 kg/154 lb. It has a large head and muzzle, and small, erect ears. It was formerly used in Europe for hunting boar and stags.

Great Dividing Range eastern Australian mountain range, extending 3,700 km/2,300 mi N–S from Cape York Peninsula, Queensland, to Victoria. It includes the Carnarvon Range, Queensland, which has many Aboriginal cave paintings, the Blue Mountains in New South Wales, and the Australian Alps.

Great Exhibition world fair held in Hyde Park, London, UK, in 1851, proclaimed by its originator Prince Albert as 'the Great Exhibition of the Industries of All Nations'. In practice, it glorified British manufacture: over half the 100,000 exhibits were from Britain or the British Empire. Over 6 million people attended the exhibition. The exhibition hall, popularly known as the **Crystal Palace**, was constructed of glass with a cast-iron frame, and designed by Joseph ▷Paxton.

Great Lake Australia's largest freshwater lake, 1,030 m/3,380 ft above sea level, in Tasmania; area 114 sq km/44 sq mi. It is used for hydroelectric power and is a tourist attraction.

Great Lakes series of five

GREAT EXHIBITION Dickinson's picture of the 'India' section at the Great Exhibition, in London, England, in 1851. *The Art Archive/Victoria and Albert Museum London/Eileen Tweedy*

freshwater lakes along the USA–Canadian border: Superior, ▷Michigan, Huron, ▷Erie, and ▷Ontario; total area 245,000 sq km/94,600 sq mi. Interconnected by a network of canals and rivers, the lakes are navigable by large ships, and they are connected with the Atlantic Ocean via the ▷St Lawrence River and by the St Lawrence Seaway (completed in 1959), which is navigable by medium-sized ocean-going ships. In March 1998 a bill was passed through Congress designating Lake ▷Champlain the sixth Great Lake, although controversy over this continues.

Physical The Great Lakes are said to contain 20% of the world's surface fresh water, and drain a basin of approximately 751,100 sq km/290,000 sq mi.

Industries Nickel, copper, gold, silver, cobalt, arsenic, bismuth, and pitchblende are found to the north of Lakes Huron and Superior, and rich forest lands on their Canadian shores have given rise to a large wood-pulp industry. The ▷Niagara Falls are a valuable source of electric power both to the USA and to Canada. The lakes are ice-bound for some five months of the year, but are used for the rest of the year by bulk carriers known as 'lakers'. The principal cargoes are iron ore and grain, both of which originate at Lake Superior ports. Iron ore is carried to other lake ports for transport to steel mills. Grain may be shipped to processing centres such as Buffalo, New York, or sent directly overseas.

Ports The chief ports of the Great Lakes are Fort William, Port Arthur, Hamilton, Toronto, and Kingston in Canada; and Duluth, Chicago, Milwaukee, Detroit, Cleveland, Erie, Toledo, and Buffalo in the USA.

Great Leap Forward change in the economic policy of the People's Republic of China introduced by ▷Mao Zedong under the second five-year plan of 1958 to 1962. The aim was to achieve rapid and simultaneous agricultural and industrial growth through the creation of large new agro-industrial communes. The inefficient and poorly planned allocation of state resources led to the collapse of the strategy by 1960 and the launch of a 'reactionary programme', involving the use of rural markets and private subsidiary plots. More than 20 million people died in the Great Leap famines of 1959 to 1961. See also ▷China, the Great Leap Forward.

Great Patriotic War (1941–45) war between the USSR and Germany during ▷World War II.

Great Plains (formerly the **Great American Desert**) semi-arid region to the east of the Rocky Mountains, stretching as far as the 100th meridian of longitude through Oklahoma, Kansas, Nebraska, and the Dakotas. The plains, which cover one-fifth of the USA, extend from Texas in the south over 2,400 km/1,500 mi north to Canada. The Great Plains have extensive oil and coal reserves, many of which are actively worked. Ranching and wheat farming have resulted in overuse of water resources to such an extent that available farmland has been reduced by erosion.

Great Power any of the major European powers of the 19th century: Russia, Austria (Austria-Hungary), France, Britain, and Prussia.

Great Red Spot prominent oval feature, 14,000 km/8,500 mi wide and some 30,000 km/20,000 mi long, in the atmosphere of the planet ▷Jupiter, south of the Equator. It was first observed in 1664. Space probes show it to be an anticlockwise vortex of cold clouds, coloured possibly by phosphorus.

Great Rift Valley volcanic valley formed 10–20 million years ago owing to rifting of the Earth's crust and running about 8,000 km/5,000 mi from the Jordan Valley through the Red Sea to central Mozambique in southeast Africa. It is marked by a series of lakes, including Lake Turkana (formerly Lake Rudolf), and volcanoes, such as Mount Kilimanjaro. The rift system associated with the Rift Valley extends into northern Botswana, with geological faults controlling the location of the Okavango Delta.

Great Sandy Desert desert in northern Western Australia; 415,000 sq km/160,000 sq mi. It is also the name of an arid region in southern Oregon, USA.

Great Schism in European history, the period 1378–1417 in which rival popes had seats in Rome and in Avignon; it was ended by the election of Martin V during the Council of Constance 1414–17.

Great Slave Lake freshwater lake in the Northwest Territories, Canada; area 28,450 sq km/10,980 sq mi. It is about 480 km/298 mi long and 100 km/62 mi wide, and is the deepest lake (615 m/2,020 ft) in North America. The lake forms two large bays, McLeod's Bay in the north and Christie's Bay in the south. It is connected with Artillery Lake, Clinton-Golden Lake, and Aylmer Lake, and the Mackenzie River flows out from it on the west. The Great Slave Lake contains many fish, including salmon and trout, and has major commercial fisheries.

Great Trek in South African history, the movement of 12,000–14,000 Boer (Dutch) settlers from Cape Colony in 1835 and 1845 to escape British rule. They established republics in Natal and the Transvaal. It is seen by many white South Africans as the main event in the founding of the present republic and was cited as a justification for whites-only rule.

Great Wall of China continuous defensive wall stretching from western Gansu to the Gulf of Liaodong (2,250 km/1,450 mi). It was once even longer. It was built under the Qin dynasty from 214 BC to prevent incursions by the Turkish and Mongol peoples and extended westwards by the Han dynasty. Some 8 m/25 ft high, it consists of a brick-faced wall of earth and stone, has a series of square watchtowers, and has been carefully restored. It is so large that it can be seen from space.

GREAT WALL OF CHINA The Great Wall of China, photographed here near Beijing (Peking), China, is built of stone for much of its length, where it lies in rocky, hilly terrain. However, in desert areas where stone was not easily available, the builders constructed an earth fortification. *Image Bank*

Great War another name for ▷World War I.

Great Yarmouth holiday resort and port in Norfolk, eastern England, at the mouth of the River Yare, 32 km/20 mi east of Norwich; population (1991) 56,200. It is Norfolk's largest port. Formerly a herring-fishing port, it is now a container port and a base for North Sea oil and gas. Other industries include shipbuilding, tourism and leisure, food processing, engineering, the manufacture of electronic components, shipwreck salvage, and some fishing.

grebe any of a group of 19 species of water birds. The **great crested grebe** (*Podiceps cristatus*) is the largest of the Old World grebes. It feeds on fish, and lives on ponds and marshes in Europe, Asia, Africa, and Australia. It grows to 50 cm/20 in long and has a white breast, with chestnut and black feathers on its back and head. Dark ear tufts and a prominent collar or crest of feathers around the base of the head appear during the breeding season; these are lost in winter. (Family Podicipedidae, order Podicipediformes.)

Grebes have broad, flat feet, and the toes are partially webbed, the legs being set extremely far back on the body. The wings are short and rounded, there is practically no tail, and flight is low. Both sexes are similar in appearance.

GREBE The great crested grebe is easily recognized by its long slender neck and daggerlike bill.

Greco, El (1541–1614) Born Doménikos Theotokopoulos. Spanish painter called 'the Greek' because he was born in Crete. He studied in Italy, worked in Rome from about 1570, and by 1577 had settled in Toledo. He painted elegant portraits and intensely emotional religious scenes with increasingly distorted figures and unearthly light, such as *The Burial of Count Orgaz* (1586; Church of S Tomé, Toledo).

His passionate insistence on rhythm and movement and vehement desire for intensity of expression were conveyed by the

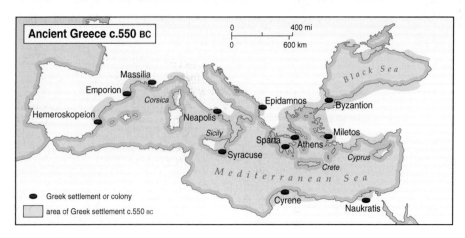

Ancient Greece c.550 BC

elongation and distortion of figures, and unusual and disturbing colour schemes with calculated clashes of crimson, lemon yellow, green, and blue, and livid flesh tones. Perspective and normal effects of lighting were disregarded, and the young El Greco is recorded as having said that the daylight blinded him to the inner light. The characteristic El Greco can be seen in the *Martyrdom of St Maurice* (1581–84; Madrid, Escorial). The huge *Burial of Count Orgaz* combines austere dignity with rapturous sublimity. Later compositions include *The Agony in the Garden* (National Gallery, London, and other versions) and the soaring vertical ascent of *Pentecost*, *Resurrection*, and *Adoration of the Shepherds* (Prado, Madrid).

Greece see country box.

Greece, ancient ancient civilization that flourished 2,500 years ago on the shores of the Ionian and Aegean Seas (modern Greece and the west coast of Turkey). Although its population never exceeded 2 million, ancient Greece made great innovations in philosophy, politics, science, architecture, and the arts, and Greek culture forms the basis of western civilization to this day.

Related Web site: Perseus Project Home Page http://www.perseus.tufts.edu/

Greek architecture the architecture of ancient Greece is the base for virtually all architectural developments in Europe. The Greeks invented the ▷entablature, which allowed roofs to be hipped (inverted V-shape), and perfected the design of arcades with support columns. There were three styles, or orders, of columns: Doric (with no base), Ionic (with scrolled capitals), and Corinthian (with acanthus-leafed capitals).

Of the Greek orders, the **Doric** is the oldest; it is said to have evolved from a former timber prototype. The finest example of a Doric temple is the Parthenon in Athens (447–438 BC). The origin of the **Ionic** is uncertain. The earliest building in which the Ionic capital appears is the temple of Artemis (Diana) at Ephesus (530 BC). The gateway to the Acropolis in Athens (known as the Propylaea) has internal columns of the Ionic order. The most perfect example is the Erechtheum (421–406 BC) in Athens.

The **Corinthian** order belongs to a later period of Greek art. A leading example is the temple of Zeus (Jupiter) Olympius in Athens (174 BC), completed under Roman influence AD 129. The monumental and sumptuously ornamental Mausoleum in Halicarnassus (353 BC) was one of the ▷Seven Wonders of the World.

GREEK ART A detail of an Attic red-figure vase depicting an Amazon fighting cavalry, dating to the 4th century BC (Archaeological Museum, Naples, Italy). *The Art Archive/ Musée Baron Gerard Bayeux*

Greek art the sculpture, painting (almost entirely vase decoration), mosaic, and crafts of ancient Greece. It is usually divided into three periods: **archaic** (late 8th century–480 BC), showing Egyptian influence; **classical** (480–323 BC), characterized by dignified and eloquent realism; and **hellenistic** (323–27 BC), more exuberant or dramatic. Sculptures of human figures dominate all periods, and vase painting was a focus for artistic development for many centuries.

Greek language member of the Indo-European language family, which has passed through at least five distinct phases since the 2nd millennium BC: **ancient Greek** 14th–12th centuries BC; **Archaic Greek**, including Homeric epic language, until 800 BC; **classical Greek** until 400 BC; **hellenistic Greek**, the common language of Greece, Asia Minor, West Asia, and Egypt to the 4th century AD, and **Byzantine Greek**, used until the 15th century and still the ecclesiastical language of the Greek Orthodox Church. **modern Greek** is principally divided into the general vernacular (demotic Greek) and the language of education and literature (Katharevousa).

Greek literature literature of Greece, ancient and modern.
Ancient The Archaic period of ancient Greek literature (8th century–*c*. 480 BC) begins with ▷Homer, reputed author of the epic narrative poems the *Iliad* and *Odyssey*, but there is evidence that parts of the Homeric epics embody an oral literary tradition going much further back into the past. Other heroic legends were handled a little later by the so-called cyclic poets, for example, Arctinus, but these are lost. Towards the end of the 8th century other literary forms began to appear: the didactic poetry of ▷Hesiod, whose *Works and Days* deals with morals as they pertain to agricultural life, and the various kinds of lyric which flourished for two centuries, particularly in Ionia and the Aegean islands. Besides choral lyric (Alcman, Stesichorus), there were elegiac and iambic (Archilochus, Mimnermus, Semonides of Amorgos, ▷Solon, Theognis, Tyrtaeus); epigram (Simonides of Ceos); table-songs (Terpander); and political lyrics (Alcaeus). This kind of poetry served also as a vehicle of moral ideas for Solon, Theognis, and Tyrtaeus, of invective for Archilochus, of ardent passion for Sappho, or of the merely elegant and affected as in Anacreon. At the very end of the Archaic period stands the first Greek historian, Hecataeus of Miletus, who wrote in prose.

During the **classical period** (*c*. 480–323 BC) lyric poetry reached its perfection with Pindar and Bacchylides. New literary genres appeared, especially in Athens, which for 150 years after the Persian Wars was the intellectual and artistic capital of the Greek world. Drama reached unsurpassed heights: tragedy with ▷Aeschylus, ▷Sophocles, and ▷Euripides, and comedy with Eupolis, Cratinus, and ▷Aristophanes. In the second half of the 5th and most of the 4th centuries BC prose flowered in several forms, including history, philosophy, and speeches (Herodotus, Thucydides, ▷Xenophon, ▷Plato, ▷Aristotle, Isocrates, and ▷Demosthenes).

During the **Hellenistic period** (323–27 BC), after the death of Alexander the Great, Athens lost its preponderance, but its philosophical schools continued to flourish with such teachers as ▷Epicurus, ▷Zeno of Citium, and ▷Theophrastus, as also did comedy (▷Menander). The principal centres of Greek culture now were Antioch, Pergamum, Pella and, above all, the Ptolemaic court at Alexandria with its library which attracted poets and scientists alike. Alexandrian poetry revived some forms that had fallen into disuse: epic (▷Apollonius of Rhodes), didactic (Aratus), epigram and hymn (Callimachus). Herodas reintroduced mime, which had been first given literary form in the 5th century by Sophron. In this period also bucolic (pastoral) poetry begins with Theocritus. It was, moreover, an age of erudition, notably in the field of philology and textual criticism, exemplified in the work of Aristophanes of Byzantium and Callimachus, and in that of mathematics and

See also ▷Athens; ▷Byzantine Empire; ▷Mycenaean civilization; ▷Roman Empire.

GREECE The Temple of Hephaistos and Athena, Athens, Greece, dates from 449 BC, and is a fine example of a Doric temple. *Corel*

Greece country in southeast Europe, comprising the southern part of the Balkan peninsula, bounded to the north by Serbia and Montenegro, Macedonia and Bulgaria, to the northwest by Albania, to the northeast by Turkey, to the east by the Aegean Sea, to the south by the Mediterranean Sea, and to the west by the Ionian Sea.

NATIONAL NAME *Elliniki Dimokratia/Hellenic Republic*
AREA 131,957 sq km/50,948 sq mi
CAPITAL Athens
MAJOR TOWNS/CITIES Thessaloniki, Peiraias, Patras, Iraklion, Larisa, Peristerio, Kallithéa
MAJOR PORTS Peiraias, Thessaloniki, Patras, Iraklion
PHYSICAL FEATURES mountainous (Mount Olympus); a large number of islands, notably Crete, Corfu, and Rhodes, and Cyclades and Ionian Islands

Government

HEAD OF STATE Konstantinos Stephanopoulos from 1995
HEAD OF GOVERNMENT Kostantinos Karamanlis from 2004
POLITICAL SYSTEM liberal democracy
POLITICAL EXECUTIVE parliamentary
ADMINISTRATIVE DIVISIONS 13 regions, divided into 54 administrative divisions, and one autonomous region (Mount Athos)
ARMED FORCES 177,600 (2002)
DEATH PENALTY abolished for ordinary crimes in 1993; laws provide for the death penalty for exceptional crimes, such as crimes committed in wartime

Economy and resources

CURRENCY euro (drachma until 2002)
GPD (US$) 132.8 billion (2002 est)
REAL GDP GROWTH (% change on previous year) 4.1 (2001)
GNI (US$) 123.9 billion (2002 est)
GNI PER CAPITA (PPP) (US$) 18,240 (2002 est)
CONSUMER PRICE INFLATION 3.3% (2003 est)
UNEMPLOYMENT 10.5% (2001)
MAJOR TRADING PARTNERS Germany, Italy, France, the Netherlands, USA, UK, Turkey, Iran, Cyprus
RESOURCES bauxite, nickel, iron pyrites, magnetite, asbestos, marble, salt, chromite, lignite
INDUSTRIES food products, metals and metal products, textiles; radio, television, and communications equipment; petroleum refining, machinery and transport equipment, tourism, wine
EXPORTS fruit and vegetables, chemicals, clothing, mineral fuels and lubricants, textiles, iron and steel, aluminium and aluminium alloys. Principal market: Germany 12.3% (1999)
IMPORTS petroleum and petroleum products, machinery and transport equipment, food, live animals, chemicals and chemical products. Principal source: Italy 13.5% (1999)
ARABLE LAND 21.3% (2000 est)
AGRICULTURAL PRODUCTS fruit and vegetables, cereals, sugar beet, tobacco, olives; livestock and dairy products

Population and society

POPULATION 10,976,000 (2003 est)
POPULATION GROWTH RATE −0.2% (2000–15)
POPULATION DENSITY (per sq km) 83 (2003 est)
URBAN POPULATION (% of total) 61 (2003 est)
AGE DISTRIBUTION (% of total population) 0–14 15%, 15–59 61%, 60+ 24% (2002 est)
ETHNIC GROUPS predominantly Greek (98%); also Turks, Slavs, and Albanians
LANGUAGE Greek (official)
RELIGION Greek Orthodox, over 96%; about 1% Muslim
EDUCATION (compulsory years) 9
LITERACY RATE 99% (men); 96% (women) (2003 est)
LABOUR FORCE 17.8% agriculture, 23.0% industry, 59.2% services (1998)
LIFE EXPECTANCY 76 (men); 81 (women) (2000–05)
HOSPITAL BEDS (per 1,000 people) 4.9 (1998 est)
TV SETS (per 1,000 people) 519 (2001 est)
INTERNET USERS (per 10,000 people) 1,547.4 (2002 est)
PERSONAL COMPUTER USERS (per 100 people) 8.2 (2002 est)

c. **2000–1200 BC**: Mycenaean civilization flourished.

c. **1500–1100 BC**: Central Greece and Peloponnese invaded by tribes of Achaeans, Aeolians, Ionians, and Dorians.

c. **1000–500 BC**: Rise of the Greek city states; Greek colonies established around the shores of the Mediterranean.

c. **490–404 BC**: Ancient Greek culture reached its zenith in the democratic city state of Athens.

357–338 BC: Philip II of Macedon won supremacy over Greece; cities fought to regain and preserve independence.

146 BC: Roman Empire defeated Macedon and annexed Greece.

476 AD: Western Roman Empire ended; Eastern Empire continued as Byzantine Empire, based at Constantinople, with essentially Greek culture.

1204: Crusaders partitioned Byzantine Empire; Athens, Achaea, and Thessaloniki came under Frankish rulers.

late 14th century–1461: Ottoman Turks conquered mainland Greece and captured Constantinople in 1453; Greek language and culture preserved by Orthodox Church.

1685: Venetians captured Peloponnese; regained by Turks in 1715.

late 18th century: Beginnings of Greek nationalism among émigrés and merchant class.

1814: *Philike Hetairia* ('Friendly Society') formed by revolutionary Greek nationalists in Odessa.

1821: *Philike Hetairia* raised Peloponnese brigands in revolt against Turks; War of Independence ensued.

1827: Battle of Navarino: Britain, France, and Russia intervened to destroy Turkish fleet; Count Ioannis Kapodistrias elected president of Greece.

1829: Treaty of Adrianople: under Russian pressure, Turkey recognized independence of small Greek state.

1832: Great Powers elected Otto of Bavaria as king of Greece.

1843: Coup forced King Otto to grant a constitution.

1862: Mutiny and rebellion led King Otto to abdicate.

1863: George of Denmark became king of the Hellenes.

1864: Britain transferred Ionian islands to Greece.

1881: Following Treaty of Berlin in 1878, Greece was allowed to annex Thessaly and part of Epirus.

late 19th century: Politics dominated by Kharilaos Trikoupis, who emphasized economic development, and Theodoros Deliyiannis, who emphasized territorial expansion.

1897: Greco-Turkish War ended in Greek defeat.

1908: Cretan Assembly led by Eleutherios Venizelos proclaimed union with Greece.

1910: Venizelos became prime minister and introduced financial, military, and constitutional reforms.

1912–13: Balkan Wars: Greece annexed a large area of Epirus and Macedonia.

1916: 'National Schism': Venizelos formed rebel pro-Allied government while royalists remained neutral.

1917–18: Greek forces fought on Allied side in World War I.

1919–22: Greek invasion of Asia Minor; after Turkish victory, a million refugees came to Greece.

1924: Republic declared amid great political instability.

1935: Greek monarchy restored with George II.

1936: Gen Ioannia Metaxas established right-wing dictatorship.

1940: Greece successfully repelled Italian invasion.

1941–44: German occupation of Greece; rival monarchist and communist resistance groups operated from 1942.

1946–49: Civil war: communists defeated by monarchists with military aid from Britain and USA.

1952: Became a member of NATO.

1967: 'Greek Colonels' seized power under George Papadopoulos; political activity banned; King Constantine II exiled.

1973: Republic proclaimed with Papadopoulos as president.

1974: Cyprus crisis caused downfall of military regime; Constantinos Karamanlis returned from exile to form Government of National Salvation and restore democracy.

1981: Andreas Papandreou was elected Greece's first socialist prime minister; Greece entered the European Community.

1989–93: The election defeat of Panhellenic Socialist Movement (PASOK) was followed by unstable coalition governments.

1993: PASOK returned to power.

1996: Costas Simitis succeeded Papandreou as prime minister.

1997: Direct talks with Turkey resulted in an agreement to settle all future disputes peacefully.

2000: Costas Simitis was re-elected as prime minister, and Kostis Stephanopoulos was re-elected as president. Greece and Turkey signed a series of agreements aimed at improving relations between the two countries.

2001: Greece adopted the euro.

geography (▷Eratosthenes, ▷Euclid). Most of the great names of the Hellenistic period belong to the 3rd century. From 150 BC the influence of Rome became progressively stronger, and the Greek narrative of its ascendancy is that of ▷Polybius. The 1st century BC also saw the first Greek anthology of epigrams, compiled by Meleager, and the work of the Jewish writers Philo Judaeus and Josephus, and the New Testament writers.

In the **Roman period** (*c.* 27 BC–*c.* AD 330) the city of Rome became the capital of the civilized world, and Latin the literary language *par excellence*. However, Greek continued to be spoken throughout the Mediterranean basin, and the following writers were outstanding: Flavius Arrianus, Dion Cassius, and Dionysius of Halicarnassus on history; ▷Epictetus, ▷Plutarch, and Marcus Aurelius on ethics and related subjects; Strabo and Pausanias on geography; ▷Ptolemy on astronomy; ▷Galen on medicine; Dionysius of Halicarnassus, Apollonius Dyscolus, Demetrius (author of *On Style*), and Longinus on grammar and literary criticism; Plotinus on neo-Platonism; and the theologians Clement and Origen on Christianity. The Roman period was also an age of compilers (Aelianus, Athenaeus, Diodorus Siculus). Rhetoric was represented by Aelius Aristides and moral satire by ▷Lucian, while the novel appeared with Heliodorus (*Theagenes and Charicleia*).

For the Byzantine period (AD 330–1453) see ▷Byzantine literature.

Modern After the fall of Constantinople, the Byzantine tradition was perpetuated in the classical Greek writing of, for example, the 15th-century chronicles of Cyprus, various historical works in the 16th and 17th centuries, and educational and theological works in the 18th century. The 17th and 18th centuries saw much controversy over whether to write in the Greek vernacular (Demotic), the classical language (*Katharevousa*), or the language of the Eastern Orthodox Church. Adamantios Korais (1748–1833), the first great modern writer, produced a compromise language; he was followed by the prose and drama writer and poet Aleksandros Rhangavis ('Rangabe') (1810–1892), and many others.

The 10th-century epic of *Digenis Akritas* is usually considered to mark the beginnings of modern Greek vernacular literature, and the Demotic was kept alive in the flourishing Cretan literature of the 16th and 17th centuries, in numerous popular songs, and in the Klephtic ballads of the 18th century. With independence in the 19th century the popular movement became prominent with the Ionian poet Dionysios Solomos (1798–1857), Andreas Kalvos (1796–1869), and others, and later with Iannis Psichari (1854–1929), short-story writer and dramatist, and the prose writer Alexandros Papadiamandis (1851–1911), who influenced many younger writers, for example Konstantinos Hatzopoulos (1868–1921), poet and essayist. After the 1920s, the novel began to emerge with Stratis Myrivilis (1892–1969) and Nikos Kazantzakis (1885–1957), author of *Zorba the Greek* (1946) and also a poet. There were also the Nobel-prize-winning poets George Seferis and Odysseus Elytis.

Greek Orthodox Church see ▷Orthodox Church.

Greeley, Horace (1811–1872) US editor, publisher, and politician. He founded the *New York Tribune* in 1841 and, as a strong supporter of the Whig party, advocated many reform causes in his newspaper – among them, feminism and abolitionism. He was an advocate of American westward expansion, and is remembered for his advice 'Go west, young man, go west'. One of the founders of the Republican party in 1854, Greeley was the unsuccessful presidential candidate of the breakaway Liberal Republicans in 1872.

Green, Henry (1905–1973) Pen-name of Henry Vincent Yorke. English novelist. His works (for example *Loving* (1945), *Nothing* (1950), and *Doting* (1952) are characterized by an experimental colloquial prose style and extensive use of dialogue; he was greatly influenced by James ▷Joyce.

green audit inspection of a company to assess the total environmental impact of its activities or of a particular product or process.

Greenaway, Peter (1942–) Welsh film director. His films are highly stylized and cerebral, richly visual, and often controversial. His feeling for perspective and lighting reveal his early training as a painter. *The Draughtsman's Contract* (1983), a tale of 18th-century country-house intrigue, is dazzling in its visual and narrative complexity.

Greenbacker in US history, a supporter of an alliance of agrarian and industrial organizations 1874–88, known as the **Greenback Labor Party**, which campaigned for currency inflation by increasing the paper dollars ('greenbacks') in circulation. In 1880 the party's presidential nominee polled only 300,000 votes; the movement was later superseded by ▷Populism.

green belt area surrounding a large city, officially designated not to be built on but preserved where possible as open space for agricultural and recreational use. In the UK the first green belts were established from 1938 around conurbations such as London in order to prevent urban sprawl. New towns were set up to take the overspill population.

greenbottle type of ▷blowfly.

Greene, (Henry) Graham (1904–1991) English writer. His novels of guilt, despair, and penitence are set in a world of urban seediness or political corruption in many parts of the world. They include *Brighton Rock* (1938), *The Power and the Glory* (1940), *The Heart of the Matter* (1948), *The Third Man* (1949), *The Honorary Consul* (1973), and *Monsignor Quixote* (1982). In 1999 his novel *The End of the Affair* (1951) was made into a film, directed by Neil Jordan.

> **Graham Greene**
> *He felt the loyalty we all feel to unhappiness – the sense that that is where we really belong.*
> *The Heart of the Matter* bk 3, pt 2, ch. 2

Stamboul Train (1932) proved the success of a format used by Greene with equal skill in other works, which he preferred to describe as 'entertainments'. They include *A Gun for Sale* (1936), *The Confidential Agent* (1939), *The Ministry of Fear* (1943), and *The Third Man* (written as a film script). *Brighton Rock*, about the criminal underworld, is in fact a religious novel, while *The Power and the Glory* explores the inner struggles of a weak, alcoholic priest in Mexico. A World War II period of service for the Foreign Office in Sierra Leone is reflected in the setting of *The Heart of the Matter*. Greene also wrote lighter, comic novels, including *Our Man in Havana* (1958) and *Travels with My Aunt* (1969).

Related Web site: May We Borrow Your Husband? http://www.wh1.tu-dresden.de/~andy/englisch/literature/greene/HusbandIndex.html

greenfinch olive-green songbird common in Europe and North Africa. It has bright-yellow markings on the outer tail feathers and wings; males are much brighter in colour than females. (Species *Carduelis chloris*, family Fringillidae, order Passeriformes.)

greenfly plant-sucking insect, a type of ▷aphid.

Greenham Common site of a continuous peace demonstration on public land near Newbury, Berkshire, UK, outside a US airbase. The women-only camp was established in September 1981 in protest against the siting of US cruise missiles in the UK. The demonstrations ended with the closure of the base. The last US cruise missiles were withdrawn in March 1991.

greenhouse effect phenomenon of the Earth's atmosphere by which solar radiation, trapped by the Earth and re-emitted from the surface as infrared radiation, is prevented from escaping by various gases in the atmosphere. Greenhouse gases trap heat because they readily absorb infrared radiation. The result of the greenhouse effect is a rise in the Earth's temperature (▷global warming). The main greenhouse gases are carbon dioxide, methane, and ▷chlorofluorocarbons (CFCs) as well as water vapour. Fossil-fuel consumption and forest fires are the principal causes of carbon dioxide build-up; methane is a by product of agriculture (rice, cattle, sheep).

The United Nations Environment Programme estimates that by 2025, average world temperatures will have risen by 1.5°C/2.7°F with a consequent rise of 20 cm/7.9 in in sea level. Low-lying areas and entire countries would be threatened by flooding and crops would be affected by the change in climate. However, predictions about global warming and its possible climatic effects are tentative and often conflict with each other.

At the 1992 Earth Summit it was agreed that by 2000 countries would stabilize carbon dioxide emissions at 1990 levels, but to halt the acceleration of global warming, emissions would probably need to be cut by 60%. Any increases in carbon dioxide emissions are expected to come from transport. The Berlin Mandate, agreed unanimously at the climate conference in Berlin in 1995, committed industrial nations to the continuing reduction of greenhouse gas emissions after 2000. Australia is in favour of different targets for different nations, and refused to sign a communiqué at the South Pacific Forum meeting in the Cook Islands in 1997 which insisted on legally binding reductions in greenhouse gas emissions. The United Nations Framework Convention on Climate Change (UNFCCC) adopted the Kyoto Protocol in 1997, committing the world's industrialized countries to cutting their annual emissions of harmful gases. By July 2001 the Protocol had been signed by 84 parties and ratified by 37; the USA announced its refusal to ratify the Protocol in June 2001.

Dubbed the 'greenhouse effect' by Swedish scientist Svante Arrhenius, it was first predicted in 1827 by French mathematician Joseph Fourier.

Related Web site: The Greenhouse Effect: How the Earth Stays Warm http://www.enviroweb.org/edf/ishappening/greeneffect/index.html

Greenland (Greenlandic **Kalaallit Nunaat**) world's largest island, a dependency of Denmark, lying between the North Atlantic and Arctic Oceans east of North America; area 2,175,600 sq km/840,000 sq mi; population (1993) 55,100, comprising Inuit (Ammassalik Eskimoan), Danish, and other Europeans. The capital is Godthåb (Greenlandic *Nuuk*) on the west coast. The main economic activities are fishing and fish-processing.

Greenland was discovered in about 982 by Eric the Red, who founded colonies on the west coast soon after Inuit from the North American Arctic had made their way to Greenland. Christianity was introduced to the Vikings in about 1000. In 1261 the Viking colonies accepted Norwegian sovereignty, but early in the 15th century all communication with Europe ceased, and by the 16th century the colonies had died out, but the Inuit had moved on to the east coast. It became a Danish colony in the 18th century, and following a referendum in 1979 was granted full internal self-government in 1981.

Related Web site: Greenland Guide http://www.greenland-guide.dk/

Greenland Sea area of the ▷Arctic Ocean between Spitsbergen and Greenland, to the north of the Norwegian Sea; area 1,200,000 sq km/460,000 sq mi, mainly ice-bound in winter. It consists of two large basins, reaching depths of 4,850 m/15,900 ft, separated by the West Jan Mayen Rise.

greenmail payment made by a target company to avoid a takeover; for example, buying back a portion of its own shares from a potential predator (a person or a company) at an inflated price.

Green Man (or **Jack-in-the-Green**) in English folklore, a figure dressed and covered in foliage, associated with festivities celebrating the arrival of spring.

Green Mountain Boys in US history, irregular troops who fought to protect the Vermont part of what was then New Hampshire colony from land claims made by neighbouring New York. In the American Revolution they captured ▷Fort Ticonderoga from the British. Their leader was Ethan Allen (1738–1789), who was later captured by the British. Vermont declared itself an independent republic, refusing to join the Union until 1791. It is popularly known as the Green Mountain State.

green movement collective term for the individuals and organizations involved in efforts to protect the environment. The movement encompasses political parties such as the ▷Green Party and organizations like ▷Friends of the Earth and ▷Greenpeace. See also ▷environmental issues. See Green Movement: Key Dates on p. 411.

Green Paper publication issued by a British government department setting out various aspects of a matter on which legislation is contemplated, and inviting public discussion and suggestions. In due course it may be followed by a ▷White Paper, giving details of proposed legislation. The first Green Paper was published in 1967.

Green Party political party aiming to 'preserve the planet and its people', based on the premise that incessant economic growth is unsustainable. The leaderless party structure reflects a general commitment to decentralization. Green parties sprang up in Western Europe in the 1970s and in Eastern Europe from 1988. Parties in different countries are linked to one another but unaffiliated with any pressure group.

Related Web site: Green Party of England and Wales http://www.greenparty.org.uk/

Greenpeace international environmental pressure group, founded in 1971, with a policy of nonviolent direct action backed by scientific research. During a protest against French atmospheric nuclear testing in the South Pacific in 1985, its ship *Rainbow Warrior* was sunk by French intelligence agents, killing a crew member. In 1995 it played a prominent role in opposing the disposal of waste from an oil rig in the North Sea, and again attempted to disrupt French nuclear tests in the Pacific. In 1997 Greenpeace had a membership in 43 'chapters' worldwide.

Related Web site: Greenpeace http://www.greenpeace.org/

green pound exchange rate used by the European Union (EU) for the conversion of EU agricultural prices to sterling. The prices for all EU members are set in European Currency Units (ECUs) and are then converted into green currencies for each national currency.

green revolution in agriculture, the change in methods of arable farming instigated in the 1940s and 1950s in countries of the developing world. The intent was to provide more and better food for their populations, albeit with a heavy reliance on chemicals and machinery. It was abandoned by some countries in the 1980s. Much of the food produced was exported as ▷cash crops, so that local diet did not always improve.

Green Movement: Key Dates

1798	Thomas Malthus's *Essay on the Principle of Population* published, setting out the idea that humans are also bound by ecological constraints.
1824	Society for the Prevention of Cruelty to Animals founded.
1835–39	Droughts and famine in India result in the first connections being made between environmental damage (deforestation) and climate change.
1864	George Marsh's 'Man and Nature' is the first comprehensive study of humans' impact on the environment.
1865	The Commons Preservation Society is founded, raising the issue of public access to the countryside, and is taken further by the mass trespasses of the 1930s.
1872	Yellowstone National Park is created in the USA; a full system of national parks is established 40 years later.
1893	The National Trust is founded in the UK to buy land in order to preserve places of natural beauty and cultural landmarks.
1930	Chlorofluorocarbons (CFCs) are invented; they are hailed as a boon for humanity as they are not only cheap and nonflammable but are also thought not to be harmful to the environment.
1934	Drought exacerbates soil erosion, causing the 'Dust Bowl Storm' in the USA, during which some 350 million tons of topsoil are blown away.
1948	The United Nations creates a special environmental agency, the International Union for the Conservation of Nature (IUCN).
1952	Air pollution causes massive smog in London, England, killing some 4,000 people and leading to clean-air legislation.
1960s	Public awareness of the damage to the environment caused by pollution increases, encouraged by such books as Rachel Carson's *Silent Spring* and Garret Hardin's essay 'The Tragedy of the Commons', which challenges individuals to recognize their personal responsibility for environmental degradation as a result of lifestyle choices.
1969	Friends of the Earth is launched in the USA as a breakaway group from the increasingly conservative Sierra Club; there is an upsurge of more radical active groups within the environmental movement over the following years.
1972	*Blueprint for Survival*, a detailed analysis of the human race's ecological predicament and proposed solutions, is published in the UK by Teddy Goldsmith and others from the *Ecologist* magazine.
1974	The first scientific warning of serious depletion of the protective ozone layer in upper atmosphere by CFCs is announced.
1980	US president Jimmy Carter commissions the report *Global 2000*, reflecting the entry of environmental concerns into mainstream politics.
1983	The German political party The Greens (Die Grünen) win 27 seats in the Bundestag (government).
1985	The Greenpeace ship *Rainbow Warrior* is sunk by French intelligence agents in a New Zealand harbour during a protest against French nuclear testing in the South Pacific. One crew member is killed.
1988	NASA scientist James Hansen warns the US Congress about global warming, announcing 'The greenhouse effect is here.'
1989	European elections put green issues firmly on political agenda as Green parties across Europe attract unprecedented support; especially in the UK, where the Greens receive some 15% of votes cast (though not of seats).
1989	*The Green Consumer Guide* is published in the UK, one of many such books worldwide advocating 'green consumerism.'
1991	The Gulf War has massive environmental consequences, primarily as a result of the huge quantity of oil discharged into the Persian Gulf from Kuwait's oilfields.
1992	United Nations Earth Summit in Rio de Janeiro arouses great media interest but achieves little progress in tackling difficult global environmental issues because many nations fear possible effects on trade.
1994	Protests against roadbuilding in many parts of the UK; for example, in 'Battle of Wanstonia', green activists occupy buildings and trees in East London in attempt to halt construction of M11 motorway.
1995	Animal-rights activists campaign against the export of live animals; activist Jill Phipps is killed on 1 February during a protest at Coventry airport. In May Greenpeace's London headquarters are raided by the Ministry of Defence and files and computer disks are confiscated.
1996	A new political force, Real World, is formed from a coalition of 32 campaigning charities and pressure groups.
1997	The second Earth Summit takes place in New York. Delegates report on progress since the 1992 Rio Summit, but fail to agree on a deal to address the world's escalating environmental crisis. Delegates at the Kyoto, Japan, conference on global warming agree to cut emission of greenhouse gases by 5.2% from 1990 levels during the years 2008–2012.
1999	Genetically modified (GM) crops are identified as a potential threat to the environment. In the UK legislation is introduced requiring all foodstuffs containing any GM ingredients to be clearly labelled. The number of demonstrations at GM crop test sites escalates. In the USA, GM crops are grown and eaten extensively, with little public protest.
2000	Despite being caught red-handed, a group of UK anti-GM protesters who vandalized a government-run experimental GM maize crop on private land are found not guilty by a sympathetic jury.

greenshank greyish shorebird of the sandpiper group. It has long olive-green legs and a long, slightly upturned bill, with white underparts and rump and dark grey wings. It breeds in northern Europe and regularly migrates through the Aleutian Islands, southwest of Alaska. (Species *Tringa nebularia*, family Scolopacidae, order Charadriiformes.)

Greenwich Mean Time (GMT) local time on the zero line of longitude (the **Greenwich meridian**), which passes through the Old Royal Observatory at Greenwich, London. It was replaced in 1986 by coordinated universal time (UTC), but continued to be used to measure longitudes and the world's standard time zones.

Greer, Germaine (1939–   ) Australian academic and feminist, author of *The Female Eunuch* (1970). The book is a polemical study of how patriarchy – through the nuclear family and capitalism – subordinates women by forcing them to conform to feminine stereotypes that effectively 'castrate' them. With its publication, Greer became identified as a leading figure in the women's movement.

However, the book has been criticized by other feminists for placing too much emphasis on sexual liberation as the way forward. In *Sex and Destiny: The Politics of Human Fertility* (1984), a critique of the politics of fertility and contraception, Greer seemed to reverse this position. Her other works include *The Obstacle Race* (1979), a study of women and painting; *The Change* (1991), a positive view of the menopause; and *The Whole Woman* (1999), a review of the feminist movement over the past 30 years.

> ### Germaine Greer
> *I love men like some people like good food or wine.*
>
> The Observer, 18 February 1979

Gregorian chant any of a body of plainsong choral chants associated with Pope Gregory the Great (540–604), which became standard in the Roman Catholic Church.
> Related Web site: Gregorian Chants http://www.music.princeton.edu/chant_html/

Gregory name of 16 popes, including:

Gregory (I) the Great (*c*. 540–604) Also known as **St Gregory**. Pope from 590 who asserted Rome's supremacy and exercised almost imperial powers. In 596 he sent St ▷Augustine to England. He introduced the choral **Gregorian chant** into the liturgy. His feast day is 12 March.
> Related Web site: Pope St Gregory I http://www.newadvent.org/cathen/06780a.htm

Gregory VII (*c*. 1020–1085) Born Hildebrand. Pope from 1073 and Catholic saint. He was chief minister to several popes before his election to the papacy, and was one of the great ecclesiastical reformers. He aroused the imperial wrath by prohibiting the abuse of investiture, and was declared deposed by the Holy Roman Emperor Henry IV in 1076. His feast day is 25 May. He was canonized in 1606.

He claimed power to depose kings, denied lay rights to make clerical appointments, and attempted to suppress simony (the buying and selling of church preferments) and to enforce clerical celibacy, making enemies of both rulers and the church.
> Related Web site: Pope St Gregory VII http://www.newadvent.org/cathen/06791c.htm

Gregory XIII (1502–1585) Pope from 1572 who introduced the reformed Gregorian calendar, still in use, in which a century year is not a leap year unless it is divisible by 400.

Gregory of Tours, St (*c*. 538–594) French Christian bishop of Tours from 573, author of a *History of the Franks*. His feast day is 17 November.

Grenada see country box.

Grenadines chain of about 600 small islands in the Caribbean Sea, part of the group known as the Windward Islands. They are divided between ▷St Vincent and ▷Grenada.

GRENADINES The Tobago Cays in the Grenadines (a chain of islets in the West Indies). The Cays are a group of five islets that lie off the coast of Mayreau and Union islands of the Grenadines. They lie within a small lagoon surrounded by a horseshoe reef, and have some of the most beautiful beaches in the Caribbean Sea. Overfishing, anchor damage, and the removal of black coral have led to the death of some of the reef, and the Cays have recently been declared a wildlife reserve. *Image Bank*

Grenoble alpine city and administrative centre of the Isère *département*, Rhône-Alpes region, southeast France, situated on the rivers Isère and Drac; population (1990) 154,000, conurbation 400,000. Industries include electrometallurgy, engineering, nuclear research, hydroelectric power, computers, technology, chemicals, plastics, cement, textiles, foodstuffs, paper, and gloves. Grenoble was the birthplace of the novelist ▷Stendhal (1783), commemorated by a museum, and the Beaux-Arts gallery has a modern collection. There is a 12th–13th-century cathedral, a major university (1339), and the Institut Laue-Langevin for nuclear research. It is the site of the ESRF (European Synchrotron Radiation Facility), the brightest X-ray machine in the world, inaugurated in 1994. The 1968 Winter Olympics were held here.

Grenville, George (1712–1770) English Whig politician, prime minister, and chancellor of the Exchequer, whose introduction of the ▷Stamp Act of 1765 to raise revenue from the colonies was one of the causes of the American Revolution. His government was also responsible for prosecuting the radical John ▷Wilkes.

Grenville, Richard (*c*. 1541–1591) English naval commander and adventurer who died heroically aboard his ship *The Revenge* when attacked by Spanish warships. Grenville fought in Hungary and Ireland (1566–69), and was knighted about 1577. In 1585 he commanded the expedition that founded Virginia, USA, for his cousin Walter ▷Raleigh. From 1586 to 1588 he organized the defence of England against the Spanish Armada.

Grenville, William Wyndham (1759–1834) 1st Baron Grenville. British Whig politician, home secretary from 1791, foreign secretary from 1794; he resigned along with Prime Minister Pitt the Younger in 1801 over George III's refusal to assent to Catholic emancipation. He headed the 'All the Talents' coalition of 1806–07 that abolished the slave trade.

Gresham, Thomas (c. 1519–1579) English merchant financier who founded and paid for the Royal Exchange and propounded Gresham's law: 'bad money tends to drive out good money from circulation'. He also founded Gresham College in London. The college was provided for by his will, and among the professorships was one for music, which has continued to the present day. Knighted in 1559.

Gretna Green village in Dumfries and Galloway region, Scotland, where runaway marriages were legal after they were banned in England in 1754; all that was necessary was the couple's declaration, before witnesses, of their willingness to marry. From 1856 Scottish law required at least one of the parties to be resident in Scotland for a minimum of 21 days before the marriage, and marriage by declaration was abolished in 1940.

Grey, Charles (1764–1845) 2nd Earl Grey. British Whig politician. He entered Parliament in 1786, and in 1806 became First Lord of the Admiralty, and foreign secretary soon afterwards. As prime minister 1830–34, he carried the Great Reform Bill of 1832 that reshaped the parliamentary representative system and the act abolishing slavery throughout the British Empire in 1833. He succeeded to the earldom in 1807.

Grey, Edward (1862–1933) 1st Viscount Grey of Fallodon. British Liberal politician, MP for Berwick on Tweed 1885–1916, nephew of Charles Grey. As foreign secretary 1905–16 he negotiated an entente with Russia in 1907, and backed France against Germany in the Agadir Incident of 1911. He published his memoirs, *Twenty-Five Years* in 1925. Baronet 1882, Viscount 1916.

Grey, Lady Jane (1537–1554) Queen of England for nine days, 10–19 July 1553, the great-granddaughter of Henry VII. She was married in 1553 to Lord Guildford Dudley (died 1554), son of the Duke of ▷Northumberland. Edward VI was persuaded by Northumberland to set aside the claims to the throne of his sisters Mary and Elizabeth. When Edward died on 6 July 1553, Jane reluctantly accepted the crown and was proclaimed queen four days later. Mary, although a Roman Catholic, had the support of the populace, and the Lord Mayor of London announced that she was queen on 19 July. Grey was executed on Tower Green.

Grey, (Pearl) Zane (1872–1939) US author of Westerns. He wrote more than 80 books, including *Riders of the Purple Sage* (1912), and was primarily responsible for the creation of the Western as a literary genre.

greyhound ancient breed of dog, with a long narrow head, slight build, and long legs. It stands up to 75 cm/30 in tall. It is renowned for its swiftness, and can exceed 60 kph/40 mph. Greyhounds were bred to hunt by sight, their main quarry being hares. Hunting hares with greyhounds is the basis of the ancient sport of coursing. Track-based greyhound racing is a popular spectator sport.

grey market dealing in shares using methods that are legal but perhaps officially frowned upon – for example, before issue and flotation.

grid network by which electricity is generated and distributed over a region or country. It contains many power stations and switching centres and allows, for example, high demand in one area to be met by surplus power generated in another.

grid reference a cadastral numbering system to specify location on a map. The numbers representing grid lines at the bottom of the map (eastings) are given before those at the side (northings). Successive decimal digits refine the location within the grid system.

Grenada

Grenada island country in the Caribbean, the southernmost of the Windward Islands.

AREA (including the southern Grenadine Islands, notably Carriacou and Petit Martinique) 344 sq km/133 sq mi
CAPITAL St George's
MAJOR TOWNS/CITIES Grenville, Sauteurs, Victoria, Gouyave
PHYSICAL FEATURES southernmost of the Windward Islands; mountainous; Grand-Anse beach; Annandale Falls; the Great Pool volcanic crater

Government

HEAD OF STATE Queen Elizabeth II from 1974, represented by Governor General Daniel Williams from 1996
HEAD OF GOVERNMENT Keith Mitchell from 1995
POLITICAL SYSTEM liberal democracy
POLITICAL EXECUTIVE parliamentary
ADMINISTRATIVE DIVISIONS 15 constituencies
ARMED FORCES no standing army; 730-strong regional security unit
DEATH PENALTY retains the death penalty for ordinary crimes but can be considered abolitionist in practice; date of last known execution 1978

Economy and resources

CURRENCY East Caribbean dollar
GPD (US$) 414 million (2002 est)
REAL GDP GROWTH (% change on previous year) –3.2 (2001)
GNI (US$) 356 million (2002 est)
GNI PER CAPITA (PPP) (US$) 6,330 (2002 est)
CONSUMER PRICE INFLATION 1.5% (2003 est)
UNEMPLOYMENT 15.2% (1998)
FOREIGN DEBT (US$) 285 million (2001 est)
MAJOR TRADING PARTNERS USA, UK, Trinidad and Tobago, the Netherlands, Germany, St Lucia
INDUSTRIES agricultural products (nutmeg oil distillation), rum, beer, soft drinks, cigarettes, clothing, tourism
EXPORTS nutmeg, cocoa, bananas, cocoa, mace, fresh fruit. Principal market: USA 35.8% each (2000)
IMPORTS foodstuffs, mineral fuels, machinery and transport equipment, basic manufactures, beverages, tobacco. Principal source: USA 37.9% (2000)
ARABLE LAND 3% (2000 est)
AGRICULTURAL PRODUCTS cocoa, bananas, nutmeg (world's second-largest producer), mace, sugar cane, fresh fruit and vegetables; livestock (for domestic use); fishing

Population and society

POPULATION 80,000 (2003 est)
POPULATION GROWTH RATE 0.3% (2000–05)
POPULATION DENSITY (per sq km) 233 (2003 est)
URBAN POPULATION (% of total) 39 (2003 est)
AGE DISTRIBUTION (% of total population) 0–14 38%, 15–59 55%, 60+ 7% (2001 est)
ETHNIC GROUPS majority is of black African descent
LANGUAGE English (official), some French-African patois
RELIGION Roman Catholic 53%, Anglican about 14%, Seventh Day Adventist, Pentecostal, Methodist
EDUCATION (compulsory years) 11
LITERACY RATE 95% (2001 est)
LABOUR FORCE 24% agriculture, 14% industry, 62% services (1998)
LIFE EXPECTANCY 68 (men); 67 (women) (2000–05)
CHILD MORTALITY RATE (under 5, per 1,000 live births) 25 (2001)
HOSPITAL BEDS (per 1,000 people) 5.3 (1996 est)
TV SETS (per 1,000 people) 376 (1999 est)
INTERNET USERS (per 10,000 people) 613.2 (2002 est)
PERSONAL COMPUTER USERS (per 100 people) 13.2 (2002 est)

Chronology

1498: Sighted by the explorer Christopher Columbus; Spanish named it Grenada since its hills were reminiscent of the Andalusian city.

1650: Colonized by French settlers from Martinique, who faced resistance from the local Carib Indian community armed with poison arrows, before the defeated Caribs performed a mass suicide.

1783: Ceded to Britain as a colony by the Treaty of Versailles; black African slaves imported to work cotton, sugar, and tobacco plantations.

1795: Abortive rebellion against British rule led by Julien Fedon, a black planter.

1834: Slavery abolished.

1950: Left-wing Grenada United Labour Party (GULP) founded by trade union leader Eric Gairy.

1951: Universal adult suffrage granted and GULP elected to power in a nonautonomous local assembly.

1958–62: Part of the Federation of the West Indies.

1967: Internal self-government achieved.

1974: Independence achieved within the Commonwealth, with Gairy as prime minister.

1979: Autocratic Gairy was removed in a bloodless coup led by left-wing Maurice Bishop of the New Jewel Movement. The constitution was suspended and a People's Revolutionary Government established.

1982: Relations with the USA and Britain waned as ties with Cuba and the USSR strengthened.

1983: After attempts to improve relations with the USA, Bishop was overthrown by left-wing opponents, precipitating a military coup by Gen Hudson Austin. The USA invaded; there were 250 fatalities. Austin was arrested and the 1974 constitution was reinstated.

1984: Newly formed centre-left New National Party (NNP) won a general election and its leader became prime minister.

1991: Integration of Windward Islands proposed.

1995: A general election was won by the NNP, led by Keith Mitchell. A plague of pink mealy bugs caused damage to crops estimated at $60 million.

1999: The ruling NNP gained a sweeping general election victory.

GRENADA The town of St George's, from the vantage point at Fort George. The capital of Grenada, St George's has a deep, landlocked harbour, called Carenage, which, like Grand Etang in the centre of the island, occupies a volcanic caldera (a large crater formed after the collapse of the original peak). *Grenada Board of Tourism*

Grieg, Edvard (Hagerup) (1843–1907) Norwegian nationalist composer. Much of his music is small-scale, particularly his songs, dances, sonatas, and piano works, strongly identifying with Norwegian folk music. Among his orchestral works are the piano concerto in A minor (1869) and the incidental music for Henrik Ibsen's drama *Peer Gynt* (1876), commissioned by Ibsen and the Norwegian government.

Grieve, Christopher Murray real name of Scottish poet Hugh ▷McDiarmid.

grievous bodily harm (GBH) in English law, very serious physical damage suffered by the victim of a crime. The courts have said that judges should not try to define grievous bodily harm but leave it to the jury to decide.

griffin mythical monster, the supposed guardian of hidden treasure, with the body, tail, and hind legs of a lion, and the head, forelegs, and wings of an eagle, though in classical times all four legs were those of a lion.

Griffith, D(avid) W(ark) (1875–1948) US film director. He was an influential figure in the development of cinema as an art. He made hundreds of one-reelers 1908–13, in which he pioneered the techniques of masking, fade-out, flashback, crosscut, close-up, and long shot. After much experimentation with photography and new techniques, he directed *The Birth of a Nation* (1915), about the aftermath of the Civil War, later criticized as degrading to African-Americans.

> **Walter Adolf Gropius**
> *The human mind is like an umbrella – it functions best when open.*
> The Observer 1965

griffon small breed of dog originating in Belgium. Red, black, or black and tan in colour and weighing up to 5 kg/11 lb, griffons are square-bodied and round-headed. There are rough- and smooth-coated varieties.

griffon Bruxelloise breed of terrierlike toy dog originally bred in Belgium. It weighs up to 4.5 kg/10 lb and has a harsh and wiry coat that is red or black in colour. The smooth-haired form of the breed is called the **petit Brabançon**.

Grimaldi, Joseph (1779–1837) English clown. Born in London, he was the son of an Italian actor. He appeared on the stage at two years old. He gave his name 'Joey' to all later clowns, and excelled as 'Mother Goose', performed at Covent Garden in 1806.

Grimm brothers Jakob (Ludwig Karl) (1785–1863) and Wilhelm (1786–1859), philologists and collectors of German fairy tales such as 'Hansel and Gretel' and 'Rumpelstiltskin'. Joint compilers of an exhaustive dictionary of German, they saw the study of language and the collecting of folk tales as strands in a single enterprise.

Related Web site: Grimm's Fairy Tales http://www.cs.cmu.edu/~spok/grimmtmp/

Grimm's law in linguistics, the rule (formulated 1822 by Jakob Grimm) by which certain prehistoric sound changes have occurred in the consonants of Indo-European languages: for example Latin *p* became English and German *f* sound, as in *pater – father, Vater.*

Grimsby fishing port and administrative headquarters of ▷North East Lincolnshire, England, on the River Humber, 24 km/15 mi southeast of Hull; population (1995) 89,400. It declined in the 1970s when Icelandic waters were closed to British fishing fleets. Chemicals and processed foods are manufactured, and marine-related industries and tourism are important. The ports of Grimsby and Immingham, 10 km/6 mi up river, are managed jointly from Grimsby, and together deal with 46 million tonnes of freight a year.

Grimshaw, Nicholas Thomas (1939–) English architect. His work has developed along distinctly High Tech lines, diverging sharply from that of his former partner, Terry ▷Farrell. His *Financial Times* printing works, London (1988), is an uncompromising industrial building, exposing machinery to view through a glass outer wall. The British Pavilion for Expo '92 in Seville, created in similar vein, addressed problems of climatic control, incorporating a huge wall of water in its facade and sail-like mechanisms on the roof.

Gris, Juan (1887–1927) Adopted name of José Victoriano Gonzalez. Spanish painter, one of the earliest cubists. He developed a distinctive geometrical style, often strongly coloured. He experimented with paper collage and made designs for Serge Diaghilev's Ballets Russes (1922–23).

Grisons French name for the Swiss canton of ▷Graubünden.

Gromyko, Andrei Andreyevich (1909–1989) President of the USSR 1985–88. As ambassador to the USA from 1943, he took part in the Tehran, Yalta, and Potsdam conferences; as United Nations representative 1946–49, he exercised the Soviet veto 26 times. He was foreign minister 1957–85. It was Gromyko who formally nominated Mikhail Gorbachev as Communist Party leader in 1985.

Groningen most northerly province of the Netherlands, located on the Ems estuary and also including the innermost West Friesian Islands, bounded to the north by the North Sea, to the south by the province of Drenthe, to the east by Germany, and to the west by Friesland; area 2,350 sq km/907 sq mi; population (1997) 558,100. The capital is Groningen; other major towns are Hoogezand-Sappemeer, Stadskanaal, Veendam, Delfzijl, and Winschoten. The chief industries are natural gas, textiles, sugar refining, shipbuilding, and papermaking. Agriculture centres on arable and livestock farming, dairy produce, tobacco, and fishing.

grooming in biology, the use by an animal of teeth, tongue, feet, or beak to clean fur or feathers. Grooming also helps to spread essential oils for waterproofing. In many social species, notably monkeys and apes, grooming of other individuals is used to reinforce social relationships.

Gropius, Walter Adolf (1883–1969) German architect, in the USA from 1937. He was an early exponent of the ▷international style, defined by glass curtain walls, cubic blocks, and unsupported corners. A founder director of the ▷Bauhaus school in Weimar 1919–28, he advocated teamwork in design and artistic standards in industrial production. He was responsible for the new Bauhaus premises in Dessau 1925–26.

grosbeak any of various thick-billed ▷finches. The **pine grosbeak** (*Pinicola enucleator*) breeds in Arctic forests. Its plumage is similar to that of the pine ▷crossbill. (Family Fringillidae, order Passeriformes.)

gross a particular figure or price, calculated before the deduction of specific items such as commission, discounts, interest, and taxes. The opposite is ▷net.

gross domestic product (GDP) value of the output of all goods and services produced within a nation's borders, normally given as a total for the year. It thus includes the production of foreign-owned firms within the country, but excludes the income from domestically owned firms located abroad. See also ▷gross national product.

Grossglockner highest mountain in Austria, rising to 3,797 m/12,457 ft in the Hohe Tauern range of the Tirol Alps, on the borders of Carinthia, Salzburg, and the Tirol. It was first climbed in 1800.

gross national product (GNP) the most commonly used measurement of the wealth of a country. GNP is defined as the total value of all goods and services produced by firms owned by the country concerned. It is measured as the ▷gross domestic product plus income from abroad, minus income earned during the same period by foreign investors within the country; see also ▷national income.

Grosz, George (1893–1959) German-born US expressionist painter and graphic artist. He was a founder of the Berlin Dada group in 1918, and excelled in savage satirical drawings criticizing the government and the military establishment. After numerous prosecutions, he fled his native Berlin in 1932 and went to the USA.

Grotius, Hugo (1583–1645) Dutch **Huig de Groot**. Dutch jurist and politician. His book *De Jure Belli et Pacis/On the Law of War and Peace* (1625) is the foundation of international law.

> **Hugo Grotius**
> *Not to know something is a great part of wisdom.*
> Docta Ignorantia

groundnut another name for ▷peanut.

groundwater water present underground in porous rock strata and soils; it emerges at the surface as springs and streams. The groundwater's upper level is called the **water table**. Rock strata that are filled with groundwater that can be extracted are called **aquifers**. Aquifers must be both porous (filled with holes) and permeable – full of holes that are interconnected so that the water is able to flow.

Most groundwater near the surface moves slowly through the ground while the water table stays in the same place. The depth of the water table reflects the balance between the rate of infiltration, called recharge, and the rate of discharge at springs or rivers or pumped water wells. The force of gravity makes underground water run 'downhill' underground just as it does above the surface. The greater the slope and the permeability, the greater the speed. Velocities vary from 100 cm/40 in per day to 0.5 cm/0.2 in.

The water table dropped in the UK during the drought of the early 1990s; however, under cities such as London and Liverpool the water table rose because the closure of industries meant that less water was being removed.

Related Web site: Groundwater Quality and the Use of Lawn and Garden Chemicals by Homeowners http://www.ext.vt.edu/pubs/envirohort/426-059/426-059.html

group in chemistry, a vertical column of elements in the ▷periodic table. Elements in a group have similar physical and chemical properties; for example, the group I elements (the ▷alkali metals: lithium, sodium, potassium, rubidium, caesium, and francium) are all highly reactive metals that form univalent ions. There is a gradation of properties down any group: in group I, melting and boiling points decrease, and density and reactivity increase.

grouper any of several species of large sea perch (spiny-finned fish), found in warm waters. Some species grow to 2 m/6.5 ft long, and can weigh 300 kg/660 lbs. (Family Serranidae.)

The spotted **giant grouper** (*Promicrops itaiara*) is 2–2.5 m/6–8 ft long, may weigh over 300 kg/700 lb and is sluggish in movement. Formerly game fish, groupers are now commercially exploited as food.

GROUPER A grouper fish off the Tuamotu Islands, French Polynesia. *Image Bank*

Group of Eight (G8); formerly Group of Seven (G7) 1975–98, the eight leading industrial nations of the world: the USA, Japan, Germany, France, the UK, Italy, Canada, and Russia, which account for more than three-fifths of global GDP. Founded as the Group of Seven (G7) in 1975, without Russia, the heads of government have met once a year to discuss economic and, increasingly, political matters. Russia attended the annual summits from 1991, and became a full member in 1998, when the name of the organization was changed. Summits are also attended by the president of the European Commission.

The group formed during the 1970s with the aim of coordinating international management of exchange rates following the collapse of the Bretton Woods system of fixed rates. However, its intervention in the mid-1980s was later blamed for the 1987 stock-market crash.

Related Web site: G8 Information Center http://www.g7.utoronto.ca/

grouse plump fowl-like game bird belonging to a subfamily of the pheasant family, which also includes the ptarmigan, capercaillie, and prairie chicken. Grouse are native to North America and northern Europe. They spend most of their time on the ground. During the mating season the males undertake elaborate courtship displays in small individual territories (▷leks). (Subfamily Tetraonidae, family Phasianidae, order Galliformes.)

Among the most familiar are the **red grouse** (*Lagopus scoticus*), a native of Britain; the ▷ptarmigan; the **ruffed grouse** (*Bonasa umbellus*), common in North American woods; and the **capercaillie** (*Tetrao urogallus*) and **blackcock** (*Tetrao tetrix*), both known in Britain. The grouse-shooting season is 12 August to 10 December.

groyne wooden or concrete barrier built at right angles to a beach in order to block the movement of material along the beach by ▷longshore drift. Groynes are usually successful in protecting individual beaches, but because they prevent beach material from passing along the coast they can mean that other beaches, starved of sand and shingle, are in danger of being eroded away by the waves. This happened, for example, at Barton-on-Sea in Hampshire, England, in the 1970s, following the construction of a large groyne at Bournemouth.

Groznyy (or Grozny; Russian 'terrible', 'awesome') capital of ▷Chechnya and of the former Soviet republic of Checheno-Ingush; population (1996) 388,000. Situated on the Sunzha River, a tributary of the Terek, it is the biggest city of the Caucasian foothills. From the late 19th century, it became a major oil centre with pipelines to the Caspian Sea at Makhachkala, the Black Sea at Tuapse, and Trudovaya (near Gorlovka in the Donets Basin). Chemical and engineering industries are also located here.

Half its residential areas were damaged beyond repair and its infrastructure destroyed by bombing, shelling, and street fighting during the struggle for Chechen independence from the Russian Federation in 1994–95.

Grünewald, Matthias (c. 1475–1528) Also known as Mathis Gothardt-Neithardt. German painter, architect, and engineer. His altarpiece at Isenheim, southern Alsace, (1515, Unterlinden Museum, Colmar, France), with its grotesquely tortured figure of Jesus and its radiant *Resurrection*, is his most important work.

MATTHIAS GRÜNEWALD Panels showing the Nativity and the Concert of Angels, from the Isenheim Altarpiece, by German painter Matthias Grünewald, *c.* 1515 (Unterlinden Museum, Colmar, France). *The Art Archive/Eileen Tweedy*

grunge rock-music style of the early 1990s, characterized by a thick, abrasive, distorted sound. Grunge evolved from ▷punk in the Seattle, Washington, area of the USA and came to prominence with the chart success of the band ▷Nirvana in 1991.

g-scale scale for measuring force by comparing it with the force due to ▷gravity (*g*), often called ▷g-force.

Guadalajara industrial city (textiles, glass, soap, pottery), capital of Jalisco state, western Mexico; population (2000 est) 1,646,200; metropolitan area (2000 est) 3,677,500. The second largest city in Mexico, 535 km/332 mi northwest of Mexico City, Guadalajara is a key communications centre. There are two universities and an airport.

Guadalcanal Island largest of the ▷Solomon Islands; area 6,500 sq km/2,510 sq mi; population (1991) 60,700. The principal population centres are ▷Honiara, capital of the Solomon Islands, Aola, and Lunga, all on the north coast. Gold, copra, and rubber are produced. The population are Melanesians (or Papuasians). In 1942, during World War II, it was the scene of a battle for control of the area that was won by US forces after six months of fighting.

Guadeloupe group of islands in the Leeward Islands, West Indies (nine of which are inhabited), an overseas *département* of France; area 1,705 sq km/658 sq mi; population (1999 est) 422,500. The main islands are Basse-Terre and Grande-Terre. The chief town and seat of government is Basse-Terre; the largest town is Pointe-à-Pitre. Agriculture is the basis of the economy, though tourism (mostly from the USA) is also important. Sugar cane is a major crop, and bananas account for about half of export earnings. Industries include cement, rum distilling, and sugar refining.

Guam largest and southernmost of the ▷Mariana Islands in the West Pacific, an unincorporated territory of the USA; 540 sq km/ 208 sq mi; population (1992) 140,200. The main towns are Hagatna (capital), Apra (port), and Tamuning. Tourism is important to the island's economy, as are fishing and the cultivation of sweet potatoes. The land is largely limestone plateau in the north and volcanic in the south, with much jungle. Guam is the site of a major US air and naval base.

guanaco hoofed ruminant (cud-chewing) mammal belonging to the camel family, found in South America on the pampas and mountain plateaux. It grows up to 1.2 m/4 ft at the shoulder, with the head and body measuring about 1.5 m/5 ft in length. It is sandy brown in colour, with a blackish face, and has fine wool. It lives in small herds and is the ancestor of the domestic ▷llama and ▷alpaca. It is also related to the other wild member of the camel family, the ▷vicuna. (Species *Lama guanacoe*, family Camelidae.)

Guanajuato town in Mexico and administrative capital of the state of Guanajuato, situated on the banks of the Rio Guanajuato; population (1995) 128,200. Gold and silver are mined, and the town has some small-scale industry, primarily ceramics and bakeries. Guanajuato has many fine Spanish colonial churches and buildings and has developed a considerable tourist industry. The town is a UNESCO World Heritage Zone, because of its historical interest.

Guangdong (or **Kwangtung**) province of south China, bounded to the north by Hunan and Jiangxi; to the northeast by Fujian; to the south by the South China Sea, Hong Kong, Macau, and the island province of Hainan; and to the west by Guangxi Zhuang Autonomous Region; area 197,000 sq km/76,062 sq mi; population (1996) 69,610,000. The capital is ▷Guangzhou; other major cities are Maoming, Shantou, Shenzhen, and Zhanjiang. The main industries are minerals, electronics, household appliances, and textiles; agriculture is based on rice, sugar, fruit, tobacco, and fish.

Guangxi Zhuang Autonomous Region (or **Guangxi** or **Kwangsi Chuang Autonomous Region**) autonomous region in south China, bounded to the north by Guizhou, to the northeast by Hunan, to the east by Guangdong, to the south by the Gulf of Tongking, to the southwest by Vietnam, and to the west by Yunnan; area 236,700 sq km/91,400 sq mi; population (1996) 45,890,000 (including the Zhuang people, related to the Thai, who form China's largest ethnic minority). The capital is ▷Nanning; other main cities are Guilin, Liuzhou, and Wuzhou. Tourism is an important part of the economy, and the main industries are sugar-refining, metallurgy, fishing, food-processing, and timber. Agriculture is based on the cultivation of rice, maize, barley, millet, sugar, tropical fruits, and tea.

Guangzhou (or **Kwangchow** or **Canton**) capital of ▷Guangdong province, south China; population (1993) 3,560,000. Industries include shipbuilding, engineering, and the manufacture of automobiles, electronics, chemicals, and textiles.

Guanyin in Chinese Buddhism, the goddess of mercy. In Japan she is **Kannon** or **Kwannon**, an attendant of the Amida Buddha (Amitābha). Her origins were in India as the male bodhisattva Avalokiteśvara.

guarana Brazilian woody climbing plant. A drink with a high caffeine content is made from its roasted seeds, and it is the source of the drug known as zoom in the USA. Starch, gum, and several oils are extracted from it for commercial use. (*Paullinia cupana*, family Sapindaceae.)

Guaraní member of an American Indian people who formerly inhabited the area that is now Paraguay, southern Brazil, and Bolivia. The Guaraní live mainly in reserves; few retain the traditional ways of hunting in the tropical forest, cultivation, and ritual warfare. About 1 million speak Guaraní, a member of the Tupian language group.

GUANAJUATO San Miguel Allende, Guanajuato, Mexico. Once a major silver-mining centre, Guanajuato is today a government seat and college town, as well as a UNESCO (United Nations Educational, Scientific, and Cultural Organization) World Heritage Site. The great wealth it enjoyed in the 16th and 17th centuries can be seen in the town's many richly appointed churches. *Image Bank*

GUANGXI ZHUANG AUTONOMOUS REGION The Detian Waterfall in the Guangxi Zhuang Autonomous Region, China. *Image Bank*

guard cell in plants, a specialized cell on the undersurface of leaves for controlling gas exchange and water loss. Guard cells occur in pairs and are shaped so that a pore, or ▷stomata, exists between them. They can change shape with the result that the pore disappears. During warm weather, when a plant is in danger of losing excessive water, the guard cells close, cutting down evaporation from the interior of the leaf.

Guardi, Francesco (1712–1793) Italian painter. He produced souvenir views of his native Venice that were commercially less successful than Canaletto's but are now considered more atmospheric, with subtler use of reflected light.

Guatemala see country box.

Guatemala City capital of ▷Guatemala, situated in the Guatemalan Highlands at an altitude of 1,500 m/4,920 ft on a plateau in the Sierra Madre mountains of the Gutemalan Highlands; population (1994 est) 823,300. A group of volcanoes overlooks the city: Acatenango (3,976 m/13,044 ft); Fuego (3,763 m/12,346 ft); Agua (3,760 m/12,336 ft). Industries include textiles, tyres, silverware, footwear, and cement. Half of the industrial output of Guatemala emanates from Guatemala City. It was founded in 1776 as Guatemala's third capital after earthquakes destroyed the earlier capitals of Antigua and Ciudad Vieja in 1773 and 1542 respectively. It was itself severely damaged by subsequent earthquakes in 1917–18, and 1976.
Related Web site: About Guatemala http://www.tradepoint.org.gt/travelguate.html

guava tropical American tree belonging to the myrtle family; the astringent yellow pear-shaped fruit is used to make guava jelly, or it can be stewed or canned. It has a high vitamin C content. (*Psidium guajava*, family Myrtaceae.)

Guayaquil largest city and chief port of Ecuador near the mouth of the Guayas River; population (1997 est) 1,973,900. The economic centre of Ecuador and the capital of Guayas province, the port is the world's leading exporter of bananas and industries include textiles, iron and steel, engineering, pharmaceuticals, and petroleum refining. The city was founded in 1537 by the Spanish explorer Francisco de Orellana.

Gucci Italian-US company manufacturing and retailing leather luggage and accessories from the 1960s, and designing clothes for men and women from 1969. The Gucci family firm was founded in Italy in the 15th century.

gudgeon any of an Old World group of freshwater fishes of the carp family, especially the species *G. gobio* found in Europe and northern Asia on the gravel bottoms of streams. It is olive-brown, spotted with black, and up to 20 cm/8 in long, with a distinctive barbel (sensory bristle, or 'whisker') at each side of the mouth. (Genus *Gobio*, family Cyprinidae.)

guelder rose (or **snowball tree**) cultivated shrub or small tree, native to Europe and North Africa, with round clusters of white flowers which are followed by shiny red berries. (*Viburnum opulus*, family Caprifoliaceae.)

Guelders another name for ▷Gelderland, a province of the Netherlands.

Guelph and Ghibelline rival parties in medieval Germany and Italy, which supported the papal party and the Holy Roman emperors respectively.

Guérin, Camille (1872–1961) French bacteriologist who, with Albert Calmette, developed the ▷BCG vaccine for tuberculosis in 1921.

Guernica large oil painting (3.5 m × 7.8 m/11 ft 5 in × 25 ft 6 in) by Pablo Picasso as a mural for the Spanish pavilion at the Paris Exposition Universelle in 1937 (now in the Museo Nacional Centro de Arte Reina Sofía, Madrid), inspired by the bombing of Guernica, the seat of the Basque parliament during the Spanish Civil War. The painting, executed entirely in black, white, and grey, was the culmination of years of experimentation. It has since become a symbol of the senseless destruction of war.

Guernsey second largest of the ▷Channel Islands; area 63 sq km/24.3 sq mi; population (1991) 58,900. The capital is St Peter Port. Products include electronics, tomatoes, flowers, and butterflies; and since 1975 it has been a major financial centre. Guernsey cattle, which are a distinctive pale fawn colour and give rich, creamy milk, originated here.

guerrilla (Spanish 'little war') irregular soldier fighting in a small, unofficial unit, typically against an established or occupying power, and engaging in sabotage, ambush, and the like, rather than pitched battles against an opposing army. Guerrilla tactics have been used both by resistance armies in wartime (for example, the Vietnam War) and in peacetime by national liberation groups and militant political extremists (for example, the Tamil Tigers).

Guevara, Che (Ernesto) (1928–1967) Latin American revolutionary. He was born in Resario, Argentina, and trained there as a doctor, but left his homeland in 1953 because of his opposition to the right-wing president Juan Perón. In effecting the Cuban revolution of 1959 against the Cuban dictator Fulgencio Batista, he was second only to Castro and Castro's brother Raúl. Between 1961 and 1965, he served as Cuba's minister of industry. In 1965 he went to the Congo to fight against white mercenaries, and then to Bolivia, where he was killed in an unsuccessful attempt to lead a peasant rising near Vallegrande. He was an orthodox Marxist and renowned for his guerrilla techniques.

In November 1995 the location of the mass grave in which Guevara's body was buried was revealed by a witness to the burial to be in the village of Valle Grande in Bolivia. The remains of Guevara were unearthed in 1997 and returned to Cuba for a hero's burial.

Guggenheim Museum (in full Solomon R Guggenheim Museum) museum of modern art. Founded by Solomon R Guggenheim, it opened 1939 in New York and in 1959 moved to a highly original building on 5th Avenue, designed by Frank Lloyd Wright. Its collection, constantly updated, is particularly strong on early 20th-century European artists, such as Marc Chagall, Vasily Kandinsky, Paul Klee, Alexander Calder, and Lyonel Feininger. A new $45 million/£285 million Guggenheim Museum is planned to be built on Wall Street, New York, with which the 5th Avenue collection will be shared. There are also Guggenheim Museums in Bilbao, Spain, and in Berlin, Germany.

Guiana northeastern part of South America that includes ▷French Guiana, ▷Guyana, and ▷Suriname.

Guienne ancient province of southwestern France which formed the duchy of Aquitaine with Gascony in the 12th century. Its capital was Bordeaux. It became English 1154 and passed to France 1453.

guild (or gild) medieval association, particularly of artisans or merchants, formed for mutual aid and protection and the pursuit of a common purpose, religious or economic. Guilds became politically powerful in Europe but after the 16th century their position was undermined by the growth of capitalism.

Guildford cathedral city and county town (since 1257) of Surrey, southeast England, on the River Wey, 48 km/30 mi southwest of

Guatemala

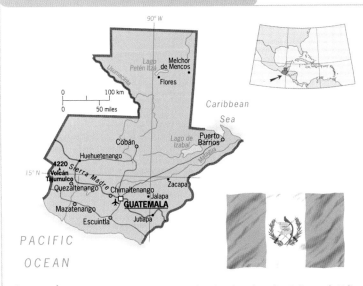

Guatemala country in Central America, bounded north and northwest by Mexico, east by Belize and the Caribbean Sea, southeast by Honduras and El Salvador, and southwest by the Pacific Ocean.

c. AD 250–900: Part of culturally advanced Maya civilization.

1524: Conquered by the Spanish adventurer Pedro de Alvarado and became a Spanish colony.

1821: Independence achieved from Spain, joining Mexico initially.

1823: Became part of United Provinces (Federation) of Central America, also embracing Costa Rica, El Salvador, Honduras, and Nicaragua.

1839: Achieved full independence.

1844–65: Rafael Carrera held power as president.

1873–85: The country was modernized on liberal lines by President Justo Rufino Barrios, the army was built up, and coffee growing introduced.

1944: Juan José Arevalo became president, ending a period of rule by dictators. Socialist programme of reform instituted by Arevalo, including establishing a social security system and redistributing land expropriated from large estates to landless peasants.

1954: Col Carlos Castillo Armas became president in a US-backed coup, after United Fruit Company plantations had been nationalized. Land reform halted.

1966: Civilian rule was restored.

1970s: More than 50,000 died in a spate of political violence as the military regime sought to liquidate left-wing dissidents.

1970: The military were back in power.

1976: An earthquake killed 27,000 and left more than 1 million homeless.

1981: Growth of an antigovernment guerrilla movement. Death squads and soldiers killed an estimated 11,000 civilians during the year.

1985: A new constitution was adopted; PDCG won the congressional elections.

1989: Over 100,000 people were killed, and 40,000 reported missing, since 1980.

1991: Diplomatic relations established with Belize, which Guatemala had long claimed.

1994: Peace talks were held with Guatemalan Revolutionary National Unity (URNG) rebels. Right-wing parties secured a majority in congress after elections.

1995: The government was criticized by USA and United Nations for widespread human-rights abuses. There was a ceasefire by rebels.

1996: A peace agreement was signed which ended the 36-year war.

2000: Alfonso Portillo, a right-wing candidate, became president. The US dollar was accepted as a second currency.

NATIONAL NAME *República de Guatemala/Republic of Guatemala*
AREA 108,889 sq km/42,042 sq mi
CAPITAL Guatemala City
MAJOR TOWNS/CITIES Quezaltenango, Escuintla, Puerto Barrios (naval base), Mixco, Villa Nueva, Chinautla
PHYSICAL FEATURES mountainous; narrow coastal plains; limestone tropical plateau in north; frequent earthquakes

Government

HEAD OF STATE AND GOVERNMENT Oscar Berger Perdomo from 2004
POLITICAL SYSTEM liberal democracy
POLITICAL EXECUTIVE limited presidency
ADMINISTRATIVE DIVISIONS 22 departments
ARMED FORCES 31,400; plus paramilitary forces of 19,000 (2002 est)
DEATH PENALTY retained and used for ordinary crimes

Economy and resources

CURRENCY quetzal and US dollar
GPD (US$) 23.3 billion (2002 est)
REAL GDP GROWTH (% change on previous year) 2.1 (2001)
GNI (US$) 20.9 billion (2002 est)
GNI PER CAPITA (PPP) (US$) 3,880 (2002 est)
CONSUMER PRICE INFLATION 5% (2003 est)
UNEMPLOYMENT 7.5% (1999)

FOREIGN DEBT (US$) 5.7 billion (2001 est)
MAJOR TRADING PARTNERS USA, El Salvador, Mexico, Costa Rica, Venezuela, Germany, Japan, Honduras
RESOURCES petroleum, antimony, gold, silver, nickel, lead, iron, tungsten
INDUSTRIES food processing, textiles, pharmaceuticals, chemicals, tobacco, non-metallic minerals, sugar, electrical goods, tourism
EXPORTS coffee, bananas, sugar, oil, cardamoms, shellfish, tobacco. Principal market: USA 55.3% (2001)
IMPORTS raw materials and intermediate goods for industry, consumer goods, mineral fuels and lubricants. Principal source: USA 32.8% (2001)
ARABLE LAND 12.5% (2000 est)
AGRICULTURAL PRODUCTS coffee, sugar cane, bananas, cardamoms, cotton; one of the largest sources of essential oils (citronella and lemon grass); livestock rearing; fishing (chiefly shrimp); forestry (mahogany and cedar)

Population and society

POPULATION 12,347,000 (2003 est)
POPULATION GROWTH RATE 2.4% (2000–15)
POPULATION DENSITY (per sq km) 113 (2003 est)
URBAN POPULATION (% of total) 41 (2003 est)

AGE DISTRIBUTION (% of total population) 0–14 43%, 15–59 52%, 60+ 5% (2002 est)
ETHNIC GROUPS two main ethnic groups: American Indians and ladinos (others, including Europeans, black Africans, and mestizos). American Indians are descended from the highland Mayas
LANGUAGE Spanish (official), 22 Mayan languages (45%)
RELIGION Roman Catholic 70%, Protestant 10%, traditional Mayan
EDUCATION (compulsory years) 6
LITERACY RATE 78% (men); 63% (women) (2003 est)
LABOUR FORCE 58.1% agriculture, 18.1% industry, 23.8% services (1995)
LIFE EXPECTANCY 63 (men); 69 (women) (2000–05)
CHILD MORTALITY RATE (under 5, per 1,000 live births) 58 (2001)
PHYSICIANS (per 1,000 people) 0.9 (1998 est)
HOSPITAL BEDS (per 1,000 people) 1 (1998 est)
TV SETS (per 1,000 people) 61 (1999 est)
RADIOS (per 1,000 people) 79 (1997)
INTERNET USERS (per 10,000 people) 333.4 (2002 est)
PERSONAL COMPUTER USERS (per 100 people) 1.4 (2002 est)

See also ▷Maya.

GUATEMALA Guatemalans in Easter masks. Fairs and religious festivals are an important part of life in all areas of Guatemala and are heavily attended throughout the year. *Image Bank*

London; urban population (1991) 60,000; borough population (1996 est) 124,600. Industries include telecommunications, engineering, and the manufacture of plastics and pharmaceuticals. Features include a ruined Norman castle, a cathedral (founded in 1936 and consecrated in 1961), the main campus of the University of Surrey (1966), and the Yvonne Arnaud Theatre (opened in 1965).

Guilin (or Kweilin) resort city in northeast Guangxi Zhuang Autonomous Region, south China, on the Li River; population (1994) 550,500. Its spectacular limestone mountains, rock formations, and underground caves are one of China's major tourist attractions. Machinery, electronics, textiles, and cement are manufactured, and rice, vegetable oil, and cinnamon produced. Tin and tungsten are mined nearby.

guillemot any of several diving seabirds belonging to the auk family that breed on rocky North Atlantic and Pacific coasts. The common guillemot (*U. aalge*) has a long straight beak and short tail and wings; the feet are three-toed and webbed, the feathers are sooty brown and white. It breeds in large colonies on sea cliffs. The black guillemot (*C. grylle*) of northern coasts is much smaller and mostly black in summer, with orange legs when breeding. Guillemots build no nest, but lay one large, almost conical egg. (Genera *Uria* and *Cepphus*, family Alcidae, order Charadriiformes.)

guillotine beheading device consisting of a metal blade that descends between two posts. It was common in the Middle Ages and was introduced to France in 1791 by physician Joseph Ignace Guillotin (1738–1814), who recommended the use of the guillotine for all sentences of death. It was subsequently used for executions during the French Revolution. It is still in use in some countries.

guillotine in politics, a device used by UK governments in which the time allowed for debating a bill in the House of Commons is restricted so as to ensure its speedy passage to receiving the royal assent (that is, to becoming law). The tactic of guillotining was introduced during the 1880s to overcome attempts by Irish members of Parliament to obstruct the passing of legislation. The guillotine is also used as a parliamentary process in France.

Guimard, Hector Germain (1867–1942) French architect. He was a leading exponent of the ▷art nouveau style in France. His flamboyant designs of glazed canopies for a number of Paris Métro station exteriors are one of art nouveau's most enduring images.

Guinea see country box.

Guinea-Bissau see country box.

guinea fowl any of a group of chickenlike African birds, including the helmet guinea fowl (*Numida meleagris*), which has a horny growth on the head, white-spotted feathers, and fleshy cheek wattles (loose folds of skin). It is the ancestor of the domestic guinea fowl. Guinea fowl are mostly gregarious ground-feeders, eating insects, leaves, and snails; at night they roost in trees. (Family Numididae, order Galliformes.)

GUINEA FOWL Vulturine guinea fowl *Acryllium vulturinum* on the savannah in Kenya. They grow to about 60 cm/ 24 in. *K G Preston-Mafham/Premaphotos Wildlife*

Guinea

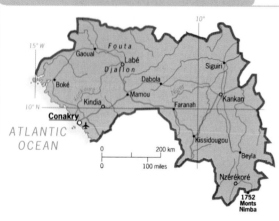
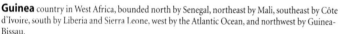

Guinea country in West Africa, bounded north by Senegal, northeast by Mali, southeast by Côte d'Ivoire, south by Liberia and Sierra Leone, west by the Atlantic Ocean, and northwest by Guinea-Bissau.

NATIONAL NAME *République de Guinée/Republic of Guinea*
AREA 245,857 sq km/94,925 sq mi
CAPITAL Conakry
MAJOR TOWNS/CITIES Labé, Nzérékoré, Kankan, Kindia, Mamou, Siguiri
PHYSICAL FEATURES flat coastal plain with mountainous interior; sources of rivers Niger, Gambia, and Senegal; forest in southeast; Fouta Djallon, area of sandstone plateaux, cut by deep valleys

Government

HEAD OF STATE Lansana Conté from 1984
HEAD OF GOVERNMENT François Fall from 2004
POLITICAL SYSTEM emergent democracy
POLITICAL EXECUTIVE limited presidency
ADMINISTRATIVE DIVISIONS eight administrative regions, including Conakry; the country is subdivided into 34 regions, including Conekry (which is divided into three communities)
ARMED FORCES 9,700; plus paramilitary forces of 9,600 (2002 est)
CONSCRIPTION military service is compulsory for two years
DEATH PENALTY retained and used for ordinary crimes
DEFENCE SPEND (% GDP) 1.8 (2002 est)
EDUCATION SPEND (% GDP) 1.9 (2001 est)
HEALTH SPEND (% GDP) 3.4 (2000 est)

Economy and resources

CURRENCY Guinean franc
GPD (US$) 3.4 billion (2002 est)

REAL GDP GROWTH (% change on previous year) 3.3 (2001)
GNI (US$) 3.1 billion (2002 est)
GNI PER CAPITA (PPP) (US$) 1,980 (2002 est)
CONSUMER PRICE INFLATION 3.5% (2003 est)
FOREIGN DEBT (US$) 2.9 billion (2001 est)
MAJOR TRADING PARTNERS France, USA, Belgium, Spain, Côte d'Ivoire
RESOURCES bauxite (world's top exporter of bauxite and second-largest producer of bauxite ore), alumina, diamonds, gold, granite, iron ore, uranium, nickel, cobalt, platinum
INDUSTRIES processing of agricultural products, cement, beer, soft drinks, cigarettes
EXPORTS bauxite, aluminium, gold, diamonds, coffee. Principal market: Belgium 16.4% (2001)
IMPORTS foodstuffs, mineral fuels, semi-manufactured goods, consumer goods, textiles and clothing, machinery and transport equipment. Principal source: France 15.9% (2000)
ARABLE LAND 3.6% (2000 est)
AGRICULTURAL PRODUCTS cassava, millet, rice, fruits, oil palm, groundnuts, coffee, vegetables, sweet potatoes, yams, maize; livestock rearing (cattle); fishing; forestry

Population and society

POPULATION 8,480,000 (2003 est)
POPULATION GROWTH RATE 1.9% (2000–15)

Chronology

c. AD 900: The Susi people, a community related to the Malinke, immigrated from the northeast, pushing the indigenous Baga towards the Atlantic coast.

13th century: Susi kingdoms established, extending their influence to the coast; northeast Guinea was part of Muslim Mali Empire, centred to northeast.

mid-15th century: Portuguese traders visited the coast and later developed trade in slaves and ivory.

1849: French protectorate established over coastal region around Nunez River, which was administered with Senegal.

1890: Separate Rivières du Sud colony formed.

1895: Renamed French Guinea, the colony became part of French West Africa.

1946: French Guinea became an overseas territory of France.

1958: Full independence from France achieved as Guinea, after referendum, rejected remaining within French Community; Sékou Touré of the Democratic Party of Guinea (PDG) elected president.

POPULATION DENSITY (per sq km) 34 (2003 est)
URBAN POPULATION (% of total) 29 (2003 est)
AGE DISTRIBUTION (% of total population) 0–14 44%, 15–59 52%, 60+ 4% (2002 est)
ETHNIC GROUPS 24 ethnic groups, including the Malinke (30%), Peuhl (30%), and Soussou (16%)
LANGUAGE French (official), Susu, Pular (Fulfude), Malinke, and other African languages
RELIGION Muslim 85%, Christian 6%, animist
EDUCATION (compulsory years) 6
LITERACY RATE 55% (men); 27% (women) (2000 est)
LABOUR FORCE 87.2% agriculture, 1.9% industry, 10.9% services (1990)
LIFE EXPECTANCY 49 (men); 50 (women) (2000–05)
CHILD MORTALITY RATE (under 5, per 1,000 live births) 169 (2001)
PHYSICIANS (per 1,000 people) 0.1 (1996 est)
HOSPITAL BEDS (per 1,000 people) 0.6 (1995 est)
TV SETS (per 1,000 people) 44 (2001 est)
RADIOS (per 1,000 people) 52 (2001 est)
INTERNET USERS (per 10,000 people) 23.1 (2002 est)
PERSONAL COMPUTER USERS (per 100 people) 0.4 (2002 est)

See also ▷French Community; ▷Mali Empire.

1960s and 1970s: Touré established socialist one-party state, leading to deterioration in economy as 200,000 fled abroad.

1979: Strong opposition to Touré's rigid Marxist policies forced him to accept a return to mixed economy and legalize private enterprise.

1984: Touré died. A bloodless military coup brought Col Lansana Conté to power; the PDG was outlawed and political prisoners released; and there were market-centred economic reforms.

1991: Antigovernment general strike and mass protests.

1992: The constitution was amended to allow for multiparty politics.

1993: Conté was narrowly re-elected in the first direct presidential election.

1998–99: President Conté was re-elected, and named his prime minister as Lamine Sidime.

2000–01: From October 2000, civil wars in Liberia and Sierra Leone began to spill over into Guinea, creating hundreds of thousands of refugees.

GUINEA A stamp from the Republic of Guinea, depicting a sea shell of the order *crenatus achatinus*. *Stanley Gibbons*

guinea pig species of ▷cavy, a type of rodent.
Related Web site: Guinea Pig Care http://www.aracnet.com/~seagull/Guineas/#Care

Guinea worm parasitic, microscopic ▷nematode worm found in India and Africa, affecting some 650,000 people in Nigeria alone. It enters the body via drinking water and migrates to break out through the skin. (Species *Dracunculus medinensis*.)

Guinevere (Welsh *Gwenhwyfar*) in British legend, the wife of King Arthur. Her adulterous love affair with the knight ▷Lancelot of the Lake led ultimately to Arthur's death.

Guinness, Alec (1914–2000) English actor of stage and screen. A versatile performer, he made early appearances in Ealing comedies, notably playing eight parts in *Kind Hearts and Coronets* (1949). In 1957 he played Colonel Nicholson in *The Bridge on the River Kwai*, for which he won awards including an Academy Award, a New York Critics' award, and a Golden Globe. Other films include *The Lavender Hill Mob* (1952), *The Ladykillers* (1955), and *Star Wars* (1977). He was made a CBE in 1955, knighted in 1959, and made a CH (Companion of Honour) in 1994.

Guise, Francis (1519–1563) 2nd Duke of Guise. French soldier and politician. He led the French victory over Germany at Metz in 1552 and captured Calais from the English in 1558. Along with his brother **Charles** (1527–1574), he was powerful in the government of France during the reign of Francis II. He was assassinated attempting to crush the ▷Huguenots.

Guise, Henri (1550–1588) 3rd Duke of Guise. French noble who persecuted the Huguenots and was partly responsible for the Massacre of ▷St Bartholomew in 1572. He was assassinated.

guitar flat-bodied musical instrument with six or twelve strings which are plucked or strummed with the fingers. The fingerboard is usually fretted, although some modern electric guitars are fretless. The Hawaiian guitar is laid across the player's lap, and uses a metal bar to produce a distinctive gliding tone. The solid-bodied electric guitar, developed in the 1950s by Les Paul and Leo Fender, mixes and amplifies vibrations from electromagnetic pickups at different points to produce a range of tone qualities.

guitarfish sharklike ray that lives in the shallow waters of tropical seas. Unlike rays, which swim by flapping their pectoral fins, it swims like a shark by lashing its long, thick muscular tail. Guitarfish tend to be small, though one species can reach 2 m/6.6 ft in length.

Guiyang (or *Kweiyang*) capital of Guizhou province, south China; population (1994) 1,602,400. It is an important transport and industrial centre, producing aluminium, iron, steel, machinery, chemicals, pharmaceuticals, textiles, and construction materials. There are coal and bauxite mines nearby.

Guizhou (or *Kweichow*) province of south China, bounded to the north by Sichuan, to the east by Hunan, to the south by Guangxi Zhuang Autonomous Region, and to the west by Yunnan; area 174,000 sq km/67,000 sq mi; population (1996) 35,550,000 (ethnic minorities comprise about 25% of the population). The capital is ▷Guiyang; other main cities are Zunyi, Anshun, and Duyun. Chief industries include non-ferrous minerals, machinery, food-processing, and timber; agriculture is based on the cultivation of rice, maize, tobacco, tea, and rapeseed.

Guizot, François Pierre Guillaume (1787–1874) French politician and historian, professor of modern history at the Sorbonne, Paris 1812–30. He wrote histories of French and European culture and became prime minister 1847. His resistance to all reforms led to the revolution of 1848.

Gujarat (or *Gujerat*) state of west India, formed from north and west Mumbai state in 1960; bordered to the north by Pakistan and the Rajasthan state, with Madhya Pradesh and Maharashtra states to the east and southeast; area 196,000 sq km/75,500 sq mi; population (2001 est) 50,612,000 (90% Hindu). The capital is Gandhinagar (founded in 1961); other major towns are ▷Ahmadabad and ▷Vadodara; the main port is Kandla. The state is heavily industrialized, with the main industries being petrochemicals, oil (from Kalol, refined at Koyali near Baroda), gas, textiles, coal, limestone, pharmaceuticals, soda ash, electrical engineering, machine tools, cement, fertilizers, and dairy products. Agriculture is based on wheat, millet, cotton, rice, maize, tobacco, groundnuts, and fishing.

Guinea-Bissau

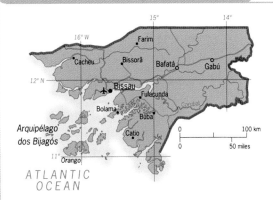

Guinea-Bissau formerly Portuguese Guinea (until 1974) country in West Africa, bounded north by Senegal, east and southeast by Guinea, and southwest by the Atlantic Ocean.

NATIONAL NAME *República da Guiné-Bissau/Republic of Guinea-Bissau*
AREA 36,125 sq km/13,947 sq mi
CAPITAL Bissau (and chief port)
MAJOR TOWNS/CITIES Barfatá, Bissorã, Bolama, Gabú, Bubaque, Cacheu, Catio, Farim
PHYSICAL FEATURES flat coastal plain rising to savannah in east

Government

HEAD OF STATE AND GOVERNMENT Veríssimo Correia Seabra from 2003
POLITICAL SYSTEM military
POLITICAL EXECUTIVE military
ADMINISTRATIVE DIVISIONS nine regions
ARMED FORCES 9,300; plus paramilitary gendarmerie of 2,000 (2002 est)
CONSCRIPTION selective conscription
DEATH PENALTY abolished in 1993
DEFENCE SPEND (% GDP) 1.6 (2002 est)
EDUCATION SPEND (% GDP) 2.1 (2000 est)
HEALTH SPEND (% GDP) 3.9 (2000 est)

Economy and resources

CURRENCY Guinean peso
GPD (US$) 216 million (2002 est)
REAL GDP GROWTH (% change on previous year) 4.5 (2001)
GNI (US$) 193 million (2002 est)
GNI PER CAPITA (PPP) (US$) 750 (2002 est)
CONSUMER PRICE INFLATION 3% (2003 est)

FOREIGN DEBT (US$) 822 million (2001 est)
MAJOR TRADING PARTNERS Uruguay, Senegal, Thailand, India, Portugal, China, Taiwan
RESOURCES bauxite, phosphate, petroleum (largely unexploited)
INDUSTRIES food processing, brewing, cotton processing, fish and timber processing
EXPORTS cashew nuts, palm kernels, groundnuts, fish and shrimp, timber. Principal market: Uruguay 40.7% (2001)
IMPORTS foodstuffs, machinery and transport equipment, fuels, construction materials. Principal source: Portugal 22.9% (2001)
ARABLE LAND 10.7% (2000 est)
AGRICULTURAL PRODUCTS groundnuts, sugar cane, plantains, palm kernels, rice, coconuts, millet, sorghum, maize, cashew nuts; fishing; forest resources

Population and society

POPULATION 1,493,000 (2003 est)
POPULATION GROWTH RATE 2.4% (2000–05)
POPULATION DENSITY (per sq km) 41 (2003 est)
URBAN POPULATION (% of total) 34 (2003 est)
AGE DISTRIBUTION (% of total population) 0–14 44%, 15–59 50%, 60+ 6% (2002 est)
ETHNIC GROUPS majority originated in Africa, and comprises five main ethnic groups: the Balanta in the central region, the Fulani in the north, the Malinke in the northern central area, and the Mandyako and Pepel near the coast
LANGUAGE Portuguese (official), Crioulo (a Cape Verdean dialect of Portuguese), African languages
RELIGION animist 58%, Muslim 40%, Christian 5% (mainly Roman Catholic)
EDUCATION (compulsory years) 6
LITERACY RATE 58% (men); 23% (women) (2003 est)
LABOUR FORCE 82% agriculture, 3.8% industry, 14.2% services (2000)
LIFE EXPECTANCY 44 (men); 47 (women) (2000–05)

CHILD MORTALITY RATE (under 5, per 1,000 live births) 211 (2001)
PHYSICIANS (per 1,000 people) 0.2 (1996 est)
HOSPITAL BEDS (per 1,000 people) 1.5 (1994 est)
TV SETS (per 1,000 people) 36 (2001 est)
RADIOS (per 1,000 people) 204 (2001 est)
INTERNET USERS (per 10,000 people) 39.9 (2002 est)

Chronology

10th century: Known as Gabu, became a tributary kingdom of the Mali Empire to northeast.

1446: Portuguese arrived, establishing nominal control over coastal areas and capturing slaves to send to Cape Verde.

1546: Gabu kingdom became independent of Mali and survived until 1867.

1879: Portugal, which had formerly administered the area with Cape Verde islands, created the separate colony of Portuguese Guinea.

by 1915: The interior had been subjugated by the Portuguese.

1956: African Party for the Independence of Portuguese Guinea and Cape Verde (PAIGC) formed to campaign for independence from Portugal.

1961: The PAIGC began to wage a guerrilla campaign against Portuguese rule.

1973: Independence was declared in the two-thirds of the country that had fallen under the control of the PAIGC; heavy losses were sustained by Portuguese troops who tried to put them down.

1974: Independence separately from Cape Verde accepted by Portugal, with Luíz Cabral (PAIGC) president.

1981: PAIGC was confirmed as the only legal party, with João Vieira as its secretary general; Cape Verde decided not to form a union.

1984: A new constitution made Vieira head of both government and state.

1991: Other parties were legalized in response to public pressure.

1994: PAIGC secured a clear assembly majority and Vieira narrowly won the first multiparty presidential elections.

1999: President Vieira ousted by the army.

2000: Kumba Ialá became president, and Caetano N'Tchama became prime minister.

2001: Former foreign minister Faustino Imbali became prime minister

2002: Mario Pires replaced Imbali as prime minister.

GUINEA-BISSAU This stamp portrays a dancer in traditional costume. *Stanley Gibbons*

Gujarati inhabitants of Gujarat on the northwest coast of India. The Gujaratis number approximately 30 million and speak their own Indo-European language, Gujarati, which has a long literary tradition. They are predominantly Hindu (90%), with Muslim (8%) and Jain (2%) minorities.

Gujarati language member of the Indo-Iranian branch of the Indo-European language family, spoken in and around the state of Gujarat in western India. It is written in its own script, a variant of the Devanagari script used for Sanskrit and Hindi.

gulag Russian term for the system of prisons and labour camps used to silence dissidents and opponents of the Soviet regime.

Gulf States oil-rich countries sharing the coastline of the ▷Gulf (Bahrain, Iran, Iraq, Kuwait, Oman, Qatar, Saudi Arabia, and the United Arab Emirates). In the USA, the term refers to those states bordering the Gulf of Mexico (Alabama, Florida, Louisiana, Mississippi, and Texas).

Gulf Stream warm ocean ▷current that flows north from the warm waters of the Gulf of Mexico along the east coast of America, from which it is separated by a channel of cold water originating in the southerly Labrador current. Off Newfoundland, part of the current is diverted east across the Atlantic, where it is known as the **North Atlantic Drift**, dividing to flow north and south, and warming what would otherwise be a colder climate in the British Isles and northwest Europe.

At its beginning the Gulf Stream is 80–150 km/50–93 mi wide and up to 850 m/2,788 ft deep, and moves with an average velocity of 130 km/80 mi a day. Its temperature is about 26°C. As it flows northwards, the current cools and becomes broader and less rapid.

Gulf War war 16 January–28 February 1991 between Iraq and a coalition of 28 nations led by the USA. The invasion and annexation of Kuwait by Iraq on 2 August 1990 provoked a build-up of US troops in Saudi Arabia, eventually totalling over 500,000. The UK subsequently deployed 42,000 troops, France 15,000, Egypt 20,000, and other nations smaller contingents.

An air offensive lasting six weeks, in which 'smart' weapons came of age, destroyed about one-third of Iraqi equipment and inflicted massive casualties. A 100-hour ground war followed, which effectively destroyed the remnants of the 500,000-strong Iraqi army in or near Kuwait.

A dispute over a shared oilfield and the price of oil was one of the main reasons for Iraq's invasion of Kuwait. Resolutions made in August 1990 by the United Nations (UN) Security Council for immediate withdrawal of Iraqi troops went unheeded, and a trade embargo and blockade were instituted. In November the USA doubled its troop strength in Saudi Arabia to 400,000, and in December 1990 the UN Security Council authorized the use of force if Iraq did not withdraw before 15 January 1991. Talks between the USA and Iraq failed, as did peace initiatives by the UN and France. By January 1991 coalition forces totalled some 725,000. Within 24 hours of the deadline, US and allied forces launched massive air bombardments against Baghdad, hitting strategic targets such as military air bases and communications systems. Saddam Hussein replied by firing missiles at the Israeli cities of Tel Aviv and Haifa (by which tactic he hoped to bring Israel into the war and thus break up the Arab alliance against him), as well as cities in Saudi Arabia; most of these missiles were intercepted.

The ground war started on 24 February and the superior range of the US artillery soon devastated the retreating Iraqi forces; by the end of February the war was over, Iraq defeated, and Kuwait once more independent, though under a pall of smoke from burning oil wells and facing extensive rebuilding. Political considerations prevented the military from following up their comprehensive victory with the complete annihilation of Iraqi forces and it was widely considered that the Iraqi leader Saddam Hussein had been allowed to stay in place, albeit much chastened, in order to avoid destabilizing the strategically crucial Middle East region.

About 90,000 tonnes of ordnance was dropped by US planes on Iraq and occupied Kuwait, of which precision-guided weapons amounted to 7%; of these, 90% hit their targets whereas only 25% of the conventional bombs did so. British forces dropped 3,000 tonnes of ordnance, including 6,000 bombs, of which 1,000 were laser-guided. Napalm and fuel-air explosives were also used by coalition forces, but cluster bombs and multiple-launch rockets were predominant. The cost to the USA of the war was $61.1 billion (£36.3 billion), including $43.1 billion contributed by the allies. Estimates of Iraqi casualties are in the range of 80,000–150,000 troops and 100,000–200,000 civilians. In May 1991 some 15,000 Iraqi prisoners of war were still in allied custody, and the war created 2–3 million refugees. Severe environmental damage, including ▷oil spills, affected a large area.

Related Web site: Gulf War Frontline http://www2.pbs.org/wgbh/pages/frontline/gulf/index.html

gull any of a group of seabirds that are usually 25–75 cm/10–30 in long, white with grey or black on the back and wings, and have large beaks. Immature birds are normally a mottled brown colour. Gulls are sociable, noisy birds and they breed in colonies. (Genus principally *Larus*, subfamily Larinae, family Laridae, order Charadriiformes.)

The **common black-headed gull** (*L. ridibundus*), common on both sides of the Atlantic Ocean, is grey and white with (in summer) a dark-brown head and a red beak; it breeds in large colonies on wetlands, making a nest of dead rushes and laying, on average, three eggs. The **great black-headed gull** (*L. ichthyaetus*) is native to Asia. The **herring gull** (*L. argentatus*), common in the northern hemisphere, has white and pearl-grey plumage and a yellow beak. The **oceanic great black-backed gull** (*L. marinus*), found in the Atlantic, is over 75 cm/2.5 ft long.

The **kelp gull** or **Southern black-backed gull** (*L. dominicanus*) is common throughout the southern hemisphere. It feeds mainly on limpets, which are swallowed whole, with the shell later spat out and left in a heap around the nest area.

gum in botany, complex polysaccharides (carbohydrates) formed by many plants and trees, particularly by those from dry regions. They form four main groups: plant exudates (gum arabic); marine plant extracts (agar); seed extracts; and fruit and vegetable extracts. Some are made synthetically.

gum arabic substance obtained from certain species of ▷acacia trees, especially *A. senegal*, with uses in medicine, confectionery, and adhesive manufacture.

gumtree common name for the ▷eucalyptus tree.

gun any kind of firearm or any instrument consisting of a metal tube from which a projectile is discharged; see also ▷artillery, ▷machine gun, ▷pistol, and ▷small arms.

gun metal type of ▷bronze, an alloy high in copper (88%), also containing tin and zinc, so-called because it was once used to cast cannons. It is tough, hard-wearing, and resists corrosion.

Gunnell, Sally (1966–) British hurdler. She won the 1986 Commonwealth 100-metre hurdles gold medal before moving on to 400-metre hurdles, at which she won Olympic, World, Commonwealth, and European titles. In winning gold at the 1993 World Championships she set a new world record with a time of 52.74 seconds.

gunpowder (or **black powder**) the oldest known ▷explosive, a mixture of 75% potassium nitrate (saltpetre), 15% charcoal, and 10% sulphur. Sulphur ignites at a low temperature, charcoal burns readily, and the potassium nitrate provides oxygen for the explosion. As gunpowder produces lots of smoke and burns quite slowly, it has progressively been replaced since the late 19th century by high explosives, although it is still widely used for quarry blasting, fuses, and fireworks. Gunpowder has high ▷activation energy; a gun based on gunpowder alone requires igniting by a flint or a match.

It was probably first invented in China, where it was chiefly used for fireworks. It is possible that knowledge of it was transmitted from the Middle East to Europe. The writings of the English monk Roger Bacon show that he was experimenting with gunpowder in 1249. His mixture contained saltpetre, charcoal, and sulphur. The development of effective gunpowder was essential for the growing significance of cannons and handguns in the late medieval period. The Arabs produced the first known working gun, in 1304. Gunpowder was used in warfare from the 14th century but it was not generally adapted to civil purposes until the 17th century, when it began to be used in mining.

GULL The great black-backed gull (seen nesting here) is found in Atlantic regions and is the largest of the gulls. *Image Bank*

GUNPOWDER PLOT The main conspirators of the Gunpowder Plot of 1605. Robert Catesby was the leader of the plot, while Guy Fawkes was the explosives expert. Their disaffection with James I arose from his failure to implement tolerance measures for Catholics as had been widely anticipated. *Philip Sauvain Picture Collection*

Gunpowder Plot in British history, the Catholic conspiracy to blow up James I and his parliament on 5 November 1605. It was discovered through an anonymous letter. Guy ▷Fawkes was found in the cellar beneath the Palace of Westminster, ready to fire a store of explosives. Several of the conspirators were killed as they fled, and Fawkes and seven others were captured and executed.

In 1604 the conspirators, led by Robert Catesby, took possession of a vault below the House of Lords where they stored barrels of gunpowder. Lord Monteagle, a Catholic peer, received the anonymous letter warning him not to attend Parliament on 5 November. A search was made, and Guy Fawkes was discovered in the vault and arrested.

The event is commemorated annually in England on 5 November by fireworks and burning 'guys' (effigies) on bonfires. The searching of the vaults of Parliament before the opening of each new session, however, was not instituted until the ▷Popish Plot of 1678.

Related Web site: Gunpowder Plot http://www.bcpl.lib.md.us/~cbladey/guy/html/main.html

Guomindang (or **Kuomintang**) Chinese National People's Party, founded in 1894 by ▷Sun Zhong Shan (Sun Yat-sen), which overthrew the Manchu Empire in 1912. During the ▷Chinese revolution (1927–49) the right wing, led by ▷Jiang Jie Shi (Chiang Kai-shek), was in conflict with the left, led by ▷Mao Zedong until the communist victory of 1949 (except for the period of the Japanese invasion from 1937 to 1945). It survives as the dominant political party of Taiwan, where it is still spelled **Kuomintang**. However, in recent years there have been splits between mainland-born hardliners and moderates, led by the president of Taiwan and Kuomintang leader ▷Lee Teng-hui.

Gupta dynasty Indian hereditary rulers that reunified and ruled over much of northern and central India 320–550. The dynasty's stronghold lay in the Magadha region of the middle Ganges valley, with the capital ▷Pataliputra. Gupta influence was extended through military conquest east, west, and south by Chandragupta I, Chandragupta II, and Samudragupta. Hun raids in the northwest from the 6th century undermined the Guptas' decentralized administrative structure.

The dynasty grew out of the array of states left from the disintegration of the Kushan empire (about 200). Its conquest brought about varying degrees of independence and created a prosperous society in which Sanskrit grew out of its religious sphere to become the official language, at least in northern India.

At the empire's height, the Hindu and Buddhist religions, commerce, and the arts flourished in what is seen as a golden or classical age of Indian civilization.

gurdwara Sikh place of worship and meeting. As well as a room housing the *Guru Granth Sahib*, the holy book, the gurdwara contains a kitchen and eating area for the *langar*, or communal meal.

Gurkha member of any of several peoples living in the mountains of Nepal: the Gurung, Limbu, Magar, Rai, and Tamang, whose young men have been recruited since 1815 for the British and Indian armies. They are predominantly Tibeto-Mongolians, but their language is Khas, a dialect of a northern Indic language.

gurnard any of a group of coastal fish that creep along the sea bottom with the help of three fingerlike appendages detached from the pectoral fins. Gurnards are both tropical and temperate zone fish. (Genus *Trigla*, family Trigilidae.)

guru (Hindi *gurū*) Hindu or Sikh leader, or religious teacher.

The Ten Gurus

Guru Nanak, the founder of the Sikh faith, was succeeded by nine further gurus, or teachers, each of whom was chosen by his predecessor. In 1708 the collection of Sikh writings was instituted as the Guru for all time to come, and Sikhs revere their scripture, the Guru Granth Sahib, as they would a living teacher.

- Guru Nanak Dev (1469–1539)
- Guru Angad Dev (born 1504, guru 1539–52)
- Guru Amar Das (born 1479, guru 1552–1574)
- Guru Ram Das (born 1534, guru 1574–81)
- Guru Arjan Dev (born 1563, guru 1581–1606)
- Guru Hargobind (born 1595, guru 1606–1644)
- Guru Har Rai (born 1630, guru 1644–61)
- Guru Harkrishan (born 1656, guru 1661–64)
- Guru Tegh Bahadur (born 1621, guru 1664–75)
- Guru Gobind Singh (born 1666, guru 1675–1708)

Gush Emunim (Hebrew 'bloc of the faithful') Israeli fundamentalist group, founded 1973, which claims divine right to settlement of the West Bank, Gaza Strip, and Golan Heights as part of Israel. The claim is sometimes extended to the Euphrates.

gust a temporary increase in ▷wind speed, lasting less than two minutes. Gusts are caused by rapidly moving air in higher layers of the atmosphere, mixing with slower air nearer the ground. Gusts are common in urban areas, where winds are funnelled between closely-spaced high buildings. Gusting winds do far more damage to buildings and crops than steady winds. The strongest gusts can exceed speeds of 100 m/328 ft per second.

Gustavus (or Gustaf) six kings of Sweden, including:

Gustavus I (or Gustaf I) king of Sweden, better known as ▷Gustavus Vasa.

Gustavus II (or Gustaf II) king of Sweden, better known as ▷Gustavus Adolphus.

Gustavus Adolphus (1594–1632) Also known as **Gustavus II** or **Gustaf II**. King of Sweden from 1611, when he succeeded his father Charles IX. He waged successful wars with Denmark, Russia, and Poland, and in the ▷Thirty Years' War became a champion of the Protestant cause. Landing in Germany 1630, he defeated the German general Wallenstein at Lützen, southwest of Leipzig 6 November 1632, but was killed in the battle. He was known as the 'Lion of the North'.

GUSTAVUS ADOLPHUS A great Swedish military commander and one of the best battle tacticians of the 17th century, Gustavus Adolphus, when not engaged in warfare, used his time to completely reform the Swedish educational system. Most notably, he instituted grammar schools and upgraded the university at Uppsala, Sweden. He also founded many towns, one of which is now the city of Göteborg, Sweden. *The Art Archive/Gripsholm Castle Sweden/Dagli Orti*

Gustavus Vasa (1496–1560) Also known as **Gustavus I** or **Gustaf I**. King of Sweden from 1523, when he was elected after leading the Swedish revolt against Danish rule. He united and pacified the country and established Lutheranism as the state religion.

GUSTAVUS VASA Gustavus I (called Gustavus Vasa), king of Sweden, aged 62 years, in a painting from 1558 by W Boy. *The Art Archive/Gripsholm Castle Sweden/Dagli Orti*

gut (or **alimentary canal**) in the ▷digestive system, the part of an animal responsible for processing food and preparing it for entry into the blood.

Gutenberg, Johannes (*c.* 1398–1468) Born Johann Gensfleisch zur Laden zum Gutenberg. German printer, the inventor of European printing from movable metal type (although Laurens Janszoon Coster has a rival claim). Gutenberg began work on the process in the 1440s and in 1450 set up a printing business in Mainz. By 1456 he had produced the first printed Bible (known as the Gutenberg Bible). It is not known what other books he printed.

He punched and engraved a steel character (letter shape) into a piece of copper to form a mould which he filled with molten metal. The letters were in Gothic script and of equal height.

Related Web site: Gutenberg, Johann http://www.newadvent. org/cathen/07090a.htm

Guthrie, Woody (1912–1967) Born Woodrow Wilson Guthrie. US folk singer and songwriter. His left-wing protest songs, 'dustbowl ballads', and 'talking blues' influenced, among others, Bob Dylan; they include 'Deportees', 'Hard Travelin', and 'This Land Is Your Land'.

Related Web site: Guthrie, Woody http://xroads.virginia.edu/~1930s/ RADIO/c_w/guthrie.html

gutta-percha juice of various tropical trees of the sapodilla family (such as the Malaysian *Palaquium gutta*), which can be hardened to form a flexible, rubbery substance used for electrical insulation, dentistry, and golf balls; it has now been largely replaced by synthetic materials.

guttation secretion of water on to the surface of leaves through specialized pores, or hydathodes. The process occurs most frequently during conditions of high humidity when the rate of transpiration is low. Drops of water found on grass in early morning are often the result of guttation, rather than dew. Sometimes the water contains minerals in solution, such as calcium, which leaves a white crust on the leaf surface as it dries.

Guyana see country box.

Guzmán Blanco, Antonio (1829–1899) Venezuelan dictator and military leader (*caudillo*), who seized power 1870 and remained absolute ruler until 1889. He modernized Caracas to become the political capital; committed resources to education, communications, and agriculture; and encouraged foreign trade.

Gwent former county of south Wales, 1974–1996, now divided between ▷Blaenau Gwent, ▷Caerphilly, ▷Monmouthshire, ▷Newport, and ▷Torfaen unitary authorities.

Gwyn (or Gwynn), **Nell (Eleanor)** (1650–1687) English comedy actor from 1665. She was formerly an orange-seller at Drury Lane Theatre, London. The poet Dryden wrote parts for her, and from 1669 she was the mistress of Charles II. See picture on p. 421.

Gwynedd unitary authority in northwest Wales, created 1996 from part of the former county of Gwynedd.

area 2,546 sq km/983 sq mi   towns ▷Caernarfon (administrative headquarters)   physical area includes the highest mountain in Wales, ▷Snowdon (1,085 m/3,560 ft), and the largest Welsh lake, Llyn Tegid (▷Bala Lake)   features ▷Snowdonia National Park, seaside resorts, Bardsey Island   industries gold mining at ▷Dolgellau, textiles, electronics, slate, tourism   agriculture cattle and sheep-farming   population (1996) 116,000   Most of Gwynedd lies within ▷Snowdonia National Park. The Lleyn Peninsula, which juts out into the Irish Sea and forms the northern limit of Cardigan Bay, is a rural area with many seaside resorts. Off the tip of the peninsula is the former pilgrimage centre of Bardsey Island, with its 6th-century ruined abbey. In Tremadog Bay is the fantasy resort of Portmeirion, built by Clough Williams-Ellis.

Related Web site: Croeso I Gyngor Gwynedd http://www. gwynedd.gov.uk/

Gwynedd, kingdom of medieval Welsh kingdom comprising north Wales and Anglesey. It was the most powerful kingdom in Wales during the 10th and 11th centuries: its king Gruffydd ap Llewellyn dominated Wales in the mid-11th century and nearly succeeded in uniting the Welsh. When the Normans invaded England, Gwynedd led Welsh resistance against Norman efforts to extend their writ over the border, with mixed success. Llewellyn ap Gruffydd styled himself Prince of Wales in 1258, and the English king Henry III was forced to acknowledge him as such in 1267. Edward I rightly recognized Gwynedd as the key to subduing the Welsh and he launched a major offensive against Llewellyn in 1277,

Guttenberg.

JOHANNES GUTENBERG An engraving intended to show the appearance of German printer and inventor Johannes Gutenberg, although there is no authenticated contemporary portrait of the man. *Image Bank*

ultimately destroying the kingdom. Gwynedd was broken up and the lands of the ruling dynasty passed to the English Prince of Wales.

gymnastics physical exercises, originally for health and training (so called from the way in which men of ancient Greece trained: *gymnos* 'naked'). The *gymnasia* were schools for training competitors for public games.

Men's gymnastics includes high bar, parallel bars, horse vault, rings, pommel horse, and floor exercises. Women's gymnastics includes asymmetrical bars, side horse vault, balance beam, and floor exercises. Also popular are sports acrobatics, performed by gymnasts in pairs, trios, or fours to music, where the emphasis is on dance, balance, and timing, and rhythmic gymnastics, choreographed to music and performed by individuals or six-girl teams, with small hand apparatus such as a ribbon, ball, or hoop.

Related Web site: Sport of Gymnastics http://www.usa-gymnastics. org/gymnastics/

gymnosperm (Greek 'naked seed') in botany, any plant whose seeds are exposed, as opposed to the structurally more advanced ▷angiosperms, where they are inside an ovary. The group includes conifers and related plants such as cycads and ginkgos, whose seeds develop in ▷cones. Fossil gymnosperms have been found in rocks about 350 million years old.

gynaecology medical speciality concerned with disorders of the female reproductive system.

gynoecium (or gynaecium) collective term for the female reproductive organs of a flower, consisting of one or more ▷carpels, either free or fused together.

Guyana

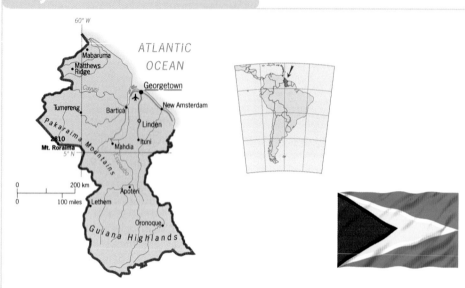

Guyana country in South America, bounded north by the Atlantic Ocean, east by Suriname, south and southwest by Brazil, and northwest by Venezuela.

NATIONAL NAME *Cooperative Republic of Guyana*
AREA 214,969 sq km/82,999 sq mi
CAPITAL Georgetown (and chief port)
MAJOR TOWNS/CITIES Linden, New Amsterdam, Bartica, Corriverton
MAJOR PORTS New Amsterdam
PHYSICAL FEATURES coastal plain rises into rolling highlands with savannah in south; mostly tropical rainforest; Mount Roraima; Kaietur National Park, including Kaietur Falls on the Potaro (tributary of Essequibo) 250 m/821 ft

Government

HEAD OF STATE Bharrat Jagdeo from 1999
HEAD OF GOVERNMENT Samuel Hinds from 1999
POLITICAL SYSTEM liberal democracy
POLITICAL EXECUTIVE limited presidency
ADMINISTRATIVE DIVISIONS ten regions
ARMED FORCES 1,600; plus paramilitary forces of 1,500 (2002 est)
CONSCRIPTION military service is voluntary
DEATH PENALTY retained and used for ordinary crimes
DEFENCE SPEND (% GDP) 0.7 (2002 est)
EDUCATION SPEND (% GDP) 4.1 (2000 est)
HEALTH SPEND (% GDP) 5.1 (2000 est)

Economy and resources

CURRENCY Guyanese dollar
GPD (US$) 710 million (2002 est)
REAL GDP GROWTH (% change on previous year) 1.9 (2001)
GNI (US$) 651 million (2002 est)
GNI PER CAPITA (PPP) (US$) 3,780 (2002 est)
CONSUMER PRICE INFLATION 4.5% (2003 est)
UNEMPLOYMENT 9% (2001)
FOREIGN DEBT (US$) 1.1 billion (2001 est)

MAJOR TRADING PARTNERS USA, Canada, UK, Trinidad and Tobago, Italy, Netherlands Antilles
RESOURCES gold, diamonds, bauxite, copper, tungsten, iron, nickel, quartz, molybdenum
INDUSTRIES agro-processing (sugar, rice, coconuts, and timber), mining, rum, pharmaceuticals, textiles
EXPORTS sugar, gold, bauxite, alumina, rice, rum, timber, molasses, shrimp. Principal market: USA 22.5% (2000)
IMPORTS mineral fuels and lubricants, machinery, capital goods, consumer goods. Principal source: USA 32.7% (2000)
ARABLE LAND 2.4% (2000 est)
AGRICULTURAL PRODUCTS sugar cane, rice, coffee, cocoa, coconuts, copra, tobacco, fruit and vegetables; forestry (timber production; approximately 77% of total land area was forested in 1995)

Population and society

POPULATION 765,000 (2003 est)
POPULATION GROWTH RATE 0.2% (2000–05)
POPULATION DENSITY (per sq km) 4 (2003 est)
URBAN POPULATION (% of total) 38 (2003 est)
AGE DISTRIBUTION (% of total population) 0–14 30%, 15–59 63%, 60+ 7% (2002 est)
ETHNIC GROUPS about 51% descended from settlers from the subcontinent of India; about 43% Afro-Indian; small minorities of American Indians, Chinese, Europeans, and people of mixed race
LANGUAGE English (official), Hindi, American Indian languages
RELIGION Christian 57%, Hindu 34%, Sunni Muslim 9%
EDUCATION (compulsory years) 10

LITERACY RATE 99% (men); 98% (women) (2003 est)
LABOUR FORCE 33% agriculture, 20% industry, 47% services (2000)
LIFE EXPECTANCY 60 (men); 66 (women) (2000–05)
CHILD MORTALITY RATE (under 5, per 1,000 live births) 72 (2001)
PHYSICIANS (per 1,000 people) 0.2 (1997 est)
TV SETS (per 1,000 people) 70 (1999 est)

GUYANA Aerial photograph of a river running through the equatorial rainforest of Guyana. *Photodisk*

RADIOS (per 1,000 people) 468 (1999 est)
INTERNET USERS (per 10,000 people) 1,422.1 (2002 est)
PERSONAL COMPUTER USERS (per 100 people) 2.7 (2003 est)

Chronology

1498: The explorer Christopher Columbus sighted Guyana, whose name, 'land of many waters', was derived from a local American Indian word.

***c*. 1620**: Settled by Dutch West India Company, who established armed bases and brought in slaves from Africa.

1814: After a period of French rule, Britain occupied Guyana during the Napoleonic Wars and purchased Demerara, Berbice, and Essequibo.

1831: Became British colony under name of British Guiana.

1834: Slavery was abolished, resulting in an influx of indentured labourers from India and China to work on sugar plantations.

1860: Settlement of the Rupununi Savannah commenced.

1860s: Gold was discovered.

1899: International arbitration tribunal found in favour of British Guiana in a long-running dispute with Venezuela over lands west of Essequibo River.

1953: Assembly elections won by left-wing People's Progressive Party (PPP), drawing most support from the Indian community; Britain suspended constitution and installed interim administration, fearing communist takeover.

1961: Internal self-government granted; Cheddi Jagan (PPP) became prime minister.

1964: Racial violence between the Asian- and African-descended communities.

1966: Independence achieved from Britain as Guyana, with PNC leader Forbes Burnham as prime minister.

1970: Guyana became a republic within the Commonwealth, with Raymond Arthur Chung as president; Burnham remained as prime minister.

1980: Burnham became the first executive president under the new constitution, which ended the three-year boycott of parliament by the PPP.

1992: PPP had a decisive victory in the first completely free assembly elections for 20 years; a privatization programme was launched.

1997: Cheddi Jagan died. His wife, Janet Jagan, was elected president.

1998: Violent antigovernment protests. Government and opposition agreed to an independent audit of elections.

1999: A constitutional reform commission was appointed. Bharrat Jagdeo replaced Janet Jagan as president.

2001: The 1997 elections were declared void, new elections were called, and President Jagdeo was re-elected.

Gypsy English name for a member of the ▷Romany people.

gyre circular surface rotation of ocean water in each major sea (a type of ▷current). Gyres are large and permanent, and occupy the northern and southern halves of the three major oceans. Their movements are dictated by the prevailing winds and the ▷Coriolis effect. Gyres move clockwise in the northern hemisphere and anticlockwise in the southern hemisphere.

gyroscope mechanical instrument, used as a stabilizing device and consisting, in its simplest form, of a heavy wheel which is mounted on an axis fixed in a ring that can be rotated about another axis, which is also fixed in a ring capable of rotation about a third axis. Applications of the gyroscope principle include the gyrocompass, the gyropilot for automatic steering, and gyro-directed torpedoes.

NELL GWYN A portrait of Nell Gwyn, who started her acting career at the age of 15. In 1669 she became the mistress of Charles II, to whom she bore two sons. See entry on p. 419. *Archive Photos*

H

Haakon seven kings of Norway, including:

Haakon IV (1204–1263) King of Norway from 1217, the son of Haakon III. Under his rule, Norway flourished both militarily and culturally; he took control of the Faroe Islands, Greenland in 1261, and Iceland 1262–64. His court was famed throughout northern Europe.

Haakon VII (1872–1957) King of Norway from 1905. Born Prince Charles, the second son of Frederick VIII of Denmark, he was elected king of Norway on the country's separation from Sweden, and in 1906 he took the name Haakon. On the German invasion in 1940 he refused to accept Vidkun ▷Quisling's collaborationist government, and instead escaped to London and acted as constitutional head of the government-in-exile. He served as a powerful personification of Norwegian nationhood.

Haarlem industrial city and capital of the province of North Holland, the Netherlands, 20 km/12 mi west of Amsterdam; population (1997) 147,400. At Velsea, to the north, a road and rail tunnel runs under the North Sea Canal, linking North and South Holland. Industries include chemicals, pharmaceuticals, textiles, and printing. Haarlem is in an area of flowering bulbs and has a 15th–16th-century cathedral and a Frans Hals museum.

habeas corpus (Latin 'you may have the body') in law, a writ directed to someone who has custody of a person, ordering him or her to bring the person before the court issuing the writ and to justify why the person is detained in custody.

Haber, Fritz (1868–1934) German chemist whose conversion of atmospheric nitrogen to ammonia opened the way for the synthetic fertilizer industry. His study of the combustion of hydrocarbons led to the commercial 'cracking' or fractional distillation of natural oil (petroleum) into its components (for example, diesel fuel, petrol, and paraffin). In electrochemistry, he was the first to demonstrate that oxidation and reduction take place at the electrodes; from this he developed a general electrochemical theory. He was awarded the Nobel Prize for Chemistry in 1918 for his work on the synthesis of ammonia from its elements.

At the outbreak of World War I in 1914, Haber was asked to devise a method of producing nitric acid for making high explosives. Later he became one of the principals in the German chemical-warfare effort, devising weapons and gas masks, which led to protests against his Nobel prize in 1918.

Haber process (or **Haber–Bosch process**) industrial process by which ammonia is manufactured by direct combination of its elements, nitrogen and hydrogen. The reaction is carried out at 400–500°C/752–932°F and at 200 atmospheres pressure. The two gases, in the proportions of 1:3 by volume, are passed over a ▷catalyst of finely divided iron.

Around 10% of the reactants combine, and the unused gases are recycled. The ammonia is separated either by being dissolved in water or by being cooled to liquid form.

habitat in ecology, the localized environment in which an organism lives, and which provides for all (or almost all) of its needs. The diversity of habitats found within the Earth's ecosystem is enormous, and they are changing all the time. Many can be considered inorganic or physical; for example, the Arctic ice cap, a cave, or a cliff face. Others are more complex; for instance, a woodland, or a forest floor. Some habitats are so precise that they are called **microhabitats**, such as the area under a stone where a particular type of insect lives. Most habitats provide a home for many species.

Habsburg (or **Hapsburg**) European royal family, former imperial house of Austria-Hungary. A Habsburg, Rudolf I, became king of Germany in 1273 and began the family's control of Austria and Styria. They acquired a series of lands and titles, including that of Holy Roman Emperor which they held during 1273–91, 1298–1308, 1438–1740, and 1745–1806. The Habsburgs reached the zenith of their power under the emperor Charles V (1519–1556) who divided his lands, creating an Austrian Habsburg line (which ruled until 1918) and a Spanish line (which ruled to 1700).

The name comes from the family castle in Aargau, Switzerland.

hacienda large estate typical of most of Spanish colonial and post-colonial Latin America. Typically inherited, haciendas were often built up by the purchase of crown or private lands, or lands traditionally worked by the Indian community. They used cheap, seasonal labour to farm produce, fairly inefficiently, for domestic and export markets. Socially, the hacienda served as a means of control by the ruling oligarchy.

hacking unauthorized access to a computer, either for fun or for malicious or fraudulent purposes. Hackers generally use microcomputers and telephone lines to obtain access. In computing, the term is used in a wider sense to mean using software for enjoyment or self-education, not necessarily involving unauthorized access. The most destructive form of hacking is the introduction of a computer ▷virus.

Hacking can be divided into four main areas: ▷viruses, phreaking, software piracy (stripping away the protective coding that should prevent the software being copied), and accessing operating systems.

A 1996 US survey co-sponsored by the FBI showed 41% of academic, corporate, and government organizations interviewed had had their computer systems hacked into during 1995. White hat hackers are computer experts hired by companies to hack into their networks to expose weaknesses in security.

In the UK, hacking is illegal under the Computer Misuse Act 1990. A survey 1993–96 of 10,000 organizations in the UK showed that only 3% had been troubled by hackers.

Hackman, Gene (Eugene Allen) (1931–) US actor. He won an Academy Award as 'Popeye' Doyle in *The French Connection* (1971), and has continued to play mainly combative roles in such films as *Night Moves* (1975), *Mississippi Burning* (1988), *Unforgiven* (1992; Academy Award), *Get Shorty* (1995), *Enemy of the State* (1998), *Heartbreakers* (2001), and *Heist* (2001).

hadal zone the deepest level of the ocean, below the abyssal zone, at depths of greater than 6,000 m/19,500 ft. The ocean trenches are in the hadal zone. There is no light in this zone and pressure is over 600 times greater than atmospheric pressure.

Hadar (or **Beta Centauri**) second-brightest star in the constellation of ▷Centaurus, and the 11th-brightest in the night sky. It is a blue-white giant star of magnitude 0.61, some 320 light years from the Sun. It is a ▷binary star, comprising two stars of magnitudes 0.7 and 3.9.

haddock marine fish belonging to the cod family and found off the North Atlantic coastline. It is brown with silvery underparts and black markings above the pectoral fins. It can grow up to 1 m/3 ft in length. Haddock are important food fish; about 45 million kg/100 million lb are taken annually off the New England fishing banks alone. (Species *Melanogrammus aeglefinus*, family Gadidae.)

Hades in Greek mythology, the underworld where spirits (shades) went after death, usually depicted as a cavern or pit underneath the Earth, the entrance of which was guarded by the three-headed dog ▷Cerberus. It was presided over by the god ▷Pluto, originally also known as Hades (Roman **Dis**). Pluto was the brother of Zeus and married ▷Persephone, daughter of Demeter and Zeus.

Hadith collection of the teachings of ▷Muhammad and stories about his life, regarded by Muslims as a guide to living second only to the ▷Koran.

Hadlee, Richard John (1951–) New Zealand cricketer who broke Ian Botham's world record of 373 test wickets and improved the total to 431, a figure which has since been beaten by Kapil Dev in 1994. He played for Canterbury (NZ) and Nottinghamshire (England). In 1990 he retired from test cricket.

Hadrian, Publius Aelius Hadrianus (AD 76–138) Roman emperor 117–138. He was adopted by the emperor Trajan, whom he succeeded. He pursued a policy of non-expansion and consolidation after the vast conquests of Trajan's reign. His defensive policy aimed at fixing the boundaries of the empire, which included the building of Hadrian's Wall in Britain. He travelled more widely than any other emperor, and consolidated both the army and Roman administration.

Hadrian's Wall line of fortifications built by the Roman emperor Hadrian across northern Britain from the Cumbrian coast on the west to the North Sea on the east. The wall itself ran from Bowness on the Solway Firth to Wallsend on the River Tyne, a distance of 110 km/68 mi. It was defended by 16 forts and smaller intermediate fortifications. It was breached by the Picts on several occasions and finally abandoned in about 383. Referred to colloquially as the **Picts' Wall**, it was covered in some parts with a glistening, white coat of mortar. Numerous modifications were made to the original plan, usually owing to the need to conserve labour and resources for such an enormous project.

In 1985 Roman letters (on paper-thin sheets of wood), the earliest and largest collection of Latin writing, were discovered at Vindolanda Fort. Hadrian's Wall was declared a World Heritage Site in 1987.

hadron in physics, a subatomic particle that experiences the strong nuclear force. Each is made up of two or three indivisible particles called ▷quarks. The hadrons are grouped into the ▷baryons (protons, neutrons, and hyperons), consisting of three quarks, and the ▷mesons, consisting of two quarks.

haematite principal ore of iron, consisting mainly of iron(III) oxide, Fe_2O_3. It occurs as **specular haematite** (dark, metallic lustre), **kidney ore** (reddish radiating fibres terminating in smooth, rounded surfaces), and a red earthy deposit.

haematology medical speciality concerned with disorders of the blood.

haemoglobin protein used by all vertebrates and some invertebrates for oxygen transport because the two substances combine reversibly. In vertebrates it occurs in red blood cells (erythrocytes), giving them their colour.

In the lungs or gills where the concentration of oxygen is high, oxygen attaches to haemoglobin to form **oxyhaemoglobin**. This process effectively increases the amount of oxygen that can be carried in the bloodstream. The oxygen is later released in the body tissues where it is at a low concentration, and the deoxygenated blood returned to the lungs or gills. Haemoglobin will combine also with carbon monoxide to form carboxyhaemoglobin, which reduces the amount of oxygen that can be carried in the blood

haemolymph circulatory fluid of those molluscs and insects that have an 'open' circulatory system. Haemolymph contains water, amino acids, sugars, salts, and white cells like those of blood. Circulated by a pulsating heart, its main functions are to transport digestive and excretory products around the body. In molluscs, it also transports oxygen and carbon dioxide.

haemophilia any of several inherited diseases in which normal blood clotting is impaired. The sufferer experiences prolonged bleeding from the slightest wound, as well as painful internal bleeding without apparent cause.

Haemophilias are nearly always sex-linked, transmitted through the female line only to male infants; they have afflicted a number of European royal households. Males affected by the most common form are unable to synthesize Factor VIII, a protein involved in the clotting of blood. Treatment is primarily with Factor VIII (now mass-produced by recombinant techniques), but the haemophiliac remains at risk from the slightest incident of bleeding. The disease is a painful one that causes deformities of joints.

Ireland became the first country in Europe to introduce genetically engineered Factor VIII for the treatment of haemophiliacs, in 1998. Shortly after, the UK government brought it in for patients under 16, to remove the risk of contracting Creutzfeldt-Jakob disease (CJD).

haemorrhage loss of blood from the circulatory system. It is 'manifest' when the blood can be seen, as when it flows from a wound, and 'occult' when the bleeding is internal, as from an ulcer or internal injury.

Rapid, profuse haemorrhage causes ▷shock and may prove fatal if the circulating volume cannot be replaced in time. Slow, sustained bleeding may lead to ▷anaemia. Arterial bleeding is potentially more serious than blood lost from a vein. It may be stemmed by applying pressure directly to the wound.

haemorrhoids distended blood vessels (▷varicose veins) in the area of the anus, popularly called **piles**.

haemostasis natural or surgical stoppage of bleeding. In the natural mechanism, the damaged vessel contracts, restricting the flow, and blood ▷platelets plug the opening, releasing chemicals essential to clotting.

Hâfiz, Shams al-Din Muhammad (*c.* 1326–*c.* 1390) Persian lyric poet. He was born in Shiraz and taught in a Dervish college there. His *Diwan*, a collection of short odes, extols the pleasures of life and satirizes his fellow Dervishes.

hafnium (Latin *Hafnia* 'Copenhagen') silvery, metallic element, symbol Hf, atomic number 72, relative atomic mass 178.49. It occurs in nature in ores of zirconium, the properties of which it resembles. Hafnium absorbs neutrons better than most metals, so it is used in the control rods of nuclear reactors; it is also used for light-bulb filaments.

It was named in 1923 by Dutch physicist Dirk Coster (1889–1950) and Hungarian chemist Georg von Hevesy after the city of Copenhagen, where the element was discovered.

hagfish eel-like marine fish. Hagfish are virtually blind and jawless, with slit mouths surrounded by four pairs of tentacles. They attack other fish, usually those which are dead or dying, and rasp away all the flesh with their powerful, tooth-studded tongues, leaving only the skeleton of their prey. When not seeking food they burrow in mud at the bottom of the sea.

Haggard, H(enry) Rider (1856–1925) English novelist. He used his experience in the South African colonial service in his romantic adventure tales, including *King Solomon's Mines* (1885) and *She* (1887), the best of which also illuminate African traditions and mythology. He also published *Rural England* (1902).

His first book, *Cetewayo and his White Neighbours*, appeared in 1882. In 1884 he published *Dawn*, the first of his novels, and followed it with others, most of which were very successful. The most popular was *King Solomon's Mines*; others include *Jess* (1887), *Allan Quatermain* (1887), and *The World's Desire* (1890), written with Andrew ▷Lang. He was knighted in 1912.

Hagia Sophia (Greek 'holy wisdom') Byzantine building in Istanbul, Turkey, built 532–37 as a Christian cathedral, replacing earlier churches. From 1453 to 1934 it was an Islamic mosque; in 1922 it became a museum.

Hague, The (Dutch **'s-Gravenhage** or **Den Haag**) legislative and judicial capital of the Netherlands, seat of the Netherlands government and capital of South Holland province, linked by canal to Rotterdam and Amsterdam, 3 km/2 mi from the North Sea; population (1997) 442,200.

Hague, William Jefferson (1961–) British Conservative politician, leader of the Conservative Party 1997–2001. He entered the House of Commons in 1989, representing the constituency of Richmond, Yorkshire, and was private secretary to the chancellor of the Exchequer 1990–93, parliamentary under-secretary of state for social security 1993–94, minister for social security and disabled people 1994–95, and secretary of state for Wales 1995–97. After the Conservative Party's defeat in the May 1997 general election, he succeeded John ▷Major as party leader. In 1998 he committed the party to oppose joining the European single currency for at least a decade and launched major reforms of the party's organization. However, he resigned as party leader in 2001 following a second Conservative general election defeat.

> ### Stella Hague
> William Hague's mother
>
> *The first girl spoke on My Little Pony, the second boy on 'what I did in the holidays'. William spoke on reform of the House of Lords.*
>
> On William Hague's childhood;
> *Independent*, 26 July 1997

Haifa (or **Hefa**) chief seaport and industrial centre of Israel, situated in the northwest of the country at the foot of Mount Carmel, about 85 km/53 mi north of Tel Aviv-Yafo; population (1997 est) 264,300. The deepwater port dates from 1933, and has been considerably expanded since the foundation of the state of Israel in 1948 as a result of the rise of industry in the hinterland. Industries include textiles, steel, oil refining, chemicals, glass, cement, soap, building materials, metal goods, shipbuilding, and vehicle assembly. Israel's main naval base is here. It is the capital of a district of the same name.

Haig, Alexander Meigs (1924–) US general and Republican politician. He became President Nixon's White House chief of staff at the height of the ▷Watergate scandal, was NATO commander 1974–79, and secretary of state to President Reagan 1981–82.

Haig, Douglas (1861–1928) 1st Earl Haig. Scottish army officer, commander-in-chief in World War I, born in Edinburgh, Scotland. His Somme offensive in France in the summer of 1916 made considerable advances only at enormous cost to human life, and his Passchendaele offensive in Belgium from July to November 1917 achieved little at a similar loss. He was created field marshal in 1917 and, after retiring, became first president of the ▷British Legion in 1921.

A national hero at the time of his funeral, Haig's reputation began to fall after Lloyd George's memoirs depicted him as treating soldiers' lives with disdain, while remaining far from battle himself.

> ### Douglas Haig
> *Every position must be held to the last man: there must be no retirement. With our backs to the wall, and believing in the justice of our cause, each one must fight on to the end.*
>
> Order given, 12 April 1918

haiku seventeen-syllable Japanese verse form, usually divided into three lines of five, seven, and five syllables. ▷Bashō popularized the form in the 17th century. It evolved from the 31-syllable *tanka* form dominant from the 8th century.

HAILE SELASSIE Haile Selassie on the cover of *Weekly Illustrated* 15 June 1935. *Philip Sauvain Picture Collection*

hail precipitation in the form of pellets of ice (hailstones). It is caused by the circulation of moisture in strong convection currents, usually within cumulonimbus ▷clouds.

Water droplets freeze as they are carried upwards. As the circulation continues, layers of ice are deposited around the droplets until they become too heavy to be supported by the currents and they fall as a hailstorm.

Haile Selassie, Ras (Prince) Tafari (1892–1975) Called 'the Lion of Judah'. Emperor of Ethiopia 1930–74. He pleaded unsuccessfully to the League of Nations against the Italian conquest of his country 1935–36, and was then deposed and fled to the UK. He went to Egypt in 1940 and raised an army, which he led into Ethiopia in January 1941 alongside British forces, and was restored to the throne on 5 May. He was deposed by a military coup in 1974 and died in captivity the following year. Followers of the Rastafarian religion (see ▷Rastafarianism) believe that he was the Messiah, the incarnation of God (Jah).

Hainan island province of south China, in the South China Sea, off the southwest coast of Guangdong province; area 34,000 sq km/13,000 sq mi; population (1996) 7,340,000. The capital is Haikou; major towns are Wenchang, Xincun, Tongzha, and Sanya. Hainan is China's second-largest island. Tourism and food-processing are the main industries, while the most important agricultural activities are rice, sugar, rubber, pineapples, sugar, betel nuts, and animal husbandry.

Hainaut (Flemish **Henegouwen**) industrial province of southwest Belgium, bounded on the south by France; area 3,800 sq km/1,467 sq mi; population (1997) 1,284,300. The capital is ▷Mons; the other major towns are Charleroi, Tournai, and Soignies. Chief industries are iron, steel, glass, and textiles; fertile arable land in the north produces wheat, sugar beet, barley, and oil-seed rape. The rivers Schelde and Sambre pass through the province.

hair fine filament growing from mammalian skin. Each hair grows from a pit-shaped follicle embedded in the second layer of the skin, the dermis. It consists of dead cells impregnated with the protein ▷keratin.

The average number of hairs on a human head varies from 98,000 (red-heads) to 120,000 (blondes). Each grows at the rate of 5–10 mm/0.2–0.4 in per month, lengthening for about three years before being replaced by a new one. A coat of hair helps to insulate land mammals by trapping air next to the body. The thickness of this layer can be varied at will by raising or flattening the coat. In some mammals a really heavy coat may be so effective that it must be shed in summer and a thinner one grown. Hair also aids camouflage, as in the zebra and the white winter coats of Arctic animals; and protection, as in the porcupine and hedgehog; bluffing enemies by apparently increasing the size, as in the cat; sexual display, as in humans and the male lion; and its colouring or erection may be used for communication. In 1990 scientists succeeded for the first time in growing human hair in vitro.

hairstreak any of a group of small butterflies, related to blues and coppers. Hairstreaks live in both temperate and tropical regions. Most of them are brownish or greyish-blue with hairlike tips streaked with white at the end of their hind wings. (Genera *Callophrys* and other related genera, family Lycaenidae.)

HAIRSTREAK The purple hairstreak butterfly *Quercusia quercus* is typical of lowland oakwoods in the British Isles. It spends most of its time perched up on the canopy of woods and forests and seldom comes down to ground level. *Premaphotos Wildlife*

Haiti see country box.

Haitink, Bernard (1929–) Dutch conductor. He was associated with the Concertgebouw Orchestra, Amsterdam, from 1958, and the London Philharmonic Orchestra from 1967; he was musical director at Glyndebourne 1977–87 and at the Royal Opera House, Covent Garden, London, 1987–98. He is a noted interpreter of Mahler and Shostakovitch.

hajj pilgrimage to Mecca that should be undertaken by every Muslim at least once in a lifetime, unless he or she is prevented by financial or health difficulties. A Muslim who has been on hajj may take the additional name Hajji. Many of the pilgrims on hajj also visit Medina, where the prophet Muhammad is buried.
Related Web site: Reflections From the Hajj http://www.erols.com/ameen/hajjexp.htm#kabah

hake any of various marine fishes belonging to the cod family, found in northern European, African, and American waters. They have silvery elongated bodies and grow up to 1 m/3 ft in length. They have two dorsal fins and one long anal fin. The silver hake (*M. bilinearis*) is an important food fish. (Genera *Merluccius* and *Urophycis*, family Gadidae.)

Hakkinen, Mika Pauli (1968–) Finnish motor racing driver who won the 1998 and 1999 Formula 1 World Drivers' Championship. He made his Formula 1 debut in 1991 (for Lotus-Judd), a year after winning the British Formula 3 title. Switching to McLaren, he finished fourth in the championship in 1993 and 1994, and fifth in 1996, but it was not until the final race of the 1997 season that he won his first Formula 1 Grand Prix. In 1998, however, he won a further eight Grand Prix to take the drivers' crown and help McLaren-Mercedes to the Constructors' title.

Hakluyt, Richard (c. 1552–1616) English geographer whose chief work is *The Principal Navigations, Voyages and Discoveries of the English Nation* (1598–1600). He was assisted by Sir Walter Raleigh.

Halab Arabic name of ▷Aleppo, a city in Syria.

halal (Arabic 'lawful') conforming to the rules laid down by Islam. The term can be applied to all aspects of life, but usually refers to food permissible under Muslim dietary laws, including meat from animals that have been slaughtered in the correct ritual fashion.

Hale-Bopp, Comet commonly referred to as ▷Comet Hale-Bopp.

Hale, George Ellery (1868–1938) US astronomer. He made pioneer studies of the Sun and founded three major observatories. In 1889 he invented the spectroheliograph, a device for photographing the Sun at particular wavelengths. In 1917 he established on Mount Wilson, California, a 2.5-m/100-in reflector, the world's largest telescope until superseded in 1948 by the 5-m/200-in reflector on Mount Palomar, which Hale had planned just before he died.

He, more than any other, was responsible for the development of observational astrophysics in the USA. He also founded the Yerkes Observatory in Williams Bay, Wisconsin, in 1897, with the largest refractor, 102 cm/40 in, ever built at that time.

Haley, Bill (1925–1981) Born William John Haley. US musician. A pioneering rock 'n' roll singer, he led country-and-western bands around Philadelphia, Pennsylvania, between 1942–52, when he formed the rhythm and blues-styled Bill Haley and His Comets. In 1954 his recordings of 'Rock Around the Clock' and 'Shake, Rattle and Roll' were among the earliest rock 'n' roll hits. He had his last hit record in 1956, but continued to record and tour in rock 'n' roll revival shows until 1980.

half-life during ▷radioactive decay, the time in which the strength of a radioactive source decays to half its original value. In theory, the decay process is never complete and there is always some residual radioactivity. For this reason, the half-life of a radioactive isotope is measured, rather than the total decay time. It may vary from millionths of a second to billions of years.

Radioactive substances decay exponentially; thus the time taken for the first 50% of the isotope to decay will be the same as the time taken by the next 25%, and by the 12.5% after that, and so on. For example, carbon-14 takes about 5,730 years for half the material to

Haiti

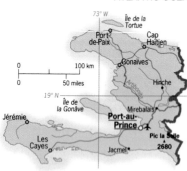

ATLANTIC OCEAN

Caribbean Sea

Haiti formerly Hispaniola (with Dominican Republic) (until 1844) country in the Caribbean, occupying the western part of the island of Hispaniola; to the east is the Dominican Republic.

NATIONAL NAME *République d'Haïti/Republic of Haiti*
AREA 27,750 sq km/10,714 sq mi
CAPITAL Port-au-Prince
MAJOR TOWNS/CITIES Cap-Haïtien, Gonaïves, Les Cayes, St Marc, Carrefour, Delmas, Pétionville
PHYSICAL FEATURES mainly mountainous and tropical; occupies western third of Hispaniola Island in Caribbean Sea

Government

HEAD OF STATE Boniface Alexandre from 2004
HEAD OF GOVERNMENT Gérard Latortue from 2004
POLITICAL SYSTEM transitional
POLITICAL EXECUTIVE transitional
ADMINISTRATIVE DIVISIONS nine departments, subdivided into *arrondissements* and communes
ARMED FORCES armed forces effectively dissolved in 1995 following restoration of civilian rule in 1994; 5,300 in paramilitary forces (2002 est)
CONSCRIPTION military service is voluntary
DEATH PENALTY abolished in 1987
DEFENCE SPEND (% GDP) 1 (2002 est)
EDUCATION SPEND (% GDP) 1.1 (2001 est)
HEALTH SPEND (% GDP) 4.9 (2000 est)

Economy and resources

CURRENCY gourde
GPD (US$) 3.6 billion (2002 est)
REAL GDP GROWTH (% change on previous year) –1.1 (2001)
GNI (US$) 3.7 billion (2002 est)

GNI PER CAPITA (PPP) (US$) 1,580 (2002 est)
CONSUMER PRICE INFLATION 9.5% (2003 est)
UNEMPLOYMENT 60% (2001)
FOREIGN DEBT (US$) 1.33 billion (2001 est)
MAJOR TRADING PARTNERS USA, Netherlands Antilles, France, Italy, Germany, Japan, UK
RESOURCES marble, limestone, calcareous clay, unexploited copper and gold deposits
INDUSTRIES food processing, metal products, machinery, textiles, chemicals, clothing, toys, electronic and electrical equipment, tourism; much of industry closed down during the international embargo imposed by the UN after Aristide was deposed in 1991
EXPORTS manufactured articles, coffee, essential oils, sisal. Principal market: USA 90% (1999)
IMPORTS food and live animals, mineral fuels and lubricants, textiles, machinery, chemicals, pharmaceuticals, raw materials, vehicles. Principal source: USA 59.6% (1999)
ARABLE LAND 20.3% (2000 est)
AGRICULTURAL PRODUCTS coffee, sugar cane, rice, maize, sorghum, cocoa, sisal, sweet potatoes, bananas, cotton

Population and society

POPULATION 8,326,000 (2003 est)
POPULATION GROWTH RATE 1.7% (2000–15)
POPULATION DENSITY (per sq km) 300 (2003 est)
URBAN POPULATION (% of total) 38 (2003 est)

AGE DISTRIBUTION (% of total population) 0–14 39%, 15–59 55%, 60+ 6% (2002 est)
ETHNIC GROUPS about 95% black African descent, the remainder are mulattos or Europeans
LANGUAGE French (20%), Creole (both official)
RELIGION Christian 95% (of which 70% are Roman Catholic), voodoo 4%
EDUCATION (compulsory years) 6
LITERACY RATE 55% (men); 51% (women) (2003 est)
LABOUR FORCE 66% agriculture, 10% industry, 24% services (2000)

LIFE EXPECTANCY 49 (men); 50 (women) (2000–05)
CHILD MORTALITY RATE (under 5, per 1,000 live births) 123 (2001)
PHYSICIANS (per 1,000 people) 0.2 (1998 est)
HOSPITAL BEDS (per 1,000 people) 0.7 (1998 est)
TV SETS (per 1,000 people) 6 (2001 est)
RADIOS (per 1,000 people) 18 (2001 est)
INTERNET USERS (per 10,000 people) 96.4 (2002 est)

See also ▷Arawak; ▷Aristide, Jean-Bertrand; ▷Dominican Republic; ▷Duvalier, François.

Chronology

14th century: Settled by Carib Indians, who followed an earlier wave of Arawak Indian immigration.

1492: The first landing place of the explorer Christopher Columbus in the New World, who named the island Hispaniola ('Little Spain').

1496: At Santo Domingo, now in the Dominican Republic to the east, the Spanish established the first European settlement in the western hemisphere, which became capital of all Spanish colonies in America.

first half of 16th century: A third of a million Arawaks and Caribs died, as a result of enslavement and exposure to European diseases; black African slaves were consequently brought in to work the island's gold and silver mines, which were swiftly exhausted.

1697: Spain ceded western third of Hispaniola to France, which became known as Haiti, but kept the east, which was known as Santo Domingo (the Dominican Republic).

1785: John James Audubon, US ornithologist, naturalist, and artist, born in Saint-Dominique, now in Haiti.

1804: Independence achieved after uprising against French colonial rule led by the former slave Toussaint l'Ouverture, who had died in prison in 1803, and Jean-Jacques Dessalines.

1818–43: Ruled by Jean-Pierre Boyer, who excluded the blacks from power.

1821: Santo Domingo fell under the control of Haiti until 1844.

1847–59: Blacks reasserted themselves under President Faustin Soulouque.

1844: Hispaniola was split into Haiti and the Dominican Republic

1915: Haiti invaded by USA as a result of political instability caused by black-mulatto friction; remained under US control until 1934.

1956: Dr François Duvalier (Papa Doc), a voodoo physician, seized power in military coup and was elected president one year later.

1964: Duvalier pronounced himself president for life, establishing a dictatorship based around a personal militia, the Tonton Macoutes.

1971: Duvalier died, succeeded by his son Jean-Claude (Baby Doc); thousands murdered during Duvalier era.

1988: A military coup installed Brig-Gen Prosper Avril as president, with a civilian government under military control.

1990: Left-wing Catholic priest Jean-Bertrand Aristide was elected president.

1991: Aristide was overthrown in a military coup led by Brig-Gen Raoul Cedras. Sanctions were imposed by the Organization of American States (OAS) and the USA.

1993: United Nations (UN) embargo was imposed. Aristide's return was blocked by the military.

1994: The threat of a US invasion led to the regime recognizing Aristide as president.

1995: UN peacekeepers were drafted in to replace US troops. Assembly elections were won by Aristide's supporters. René Préval was elected to replace Aristide as president.

1998: Jacques-Edouard Alexis was nominated prime minister and endorsed by the assembly.

1999: President Préval dissolved parliament. Elections were repeatedly delayed.

2000: Aristide's Fanmi Lavalas Party won parliamentary elections, which were boycotted by the opposition.

2001: Aristide became president for the third time.

HAITI A stamp commemorating the 25th General Assembly of the Organization of American States, which was held in 1995 in Montrouis, Haiti. *Stanley Gibbons*

decay; another 5,730 for half of the remaining half to decay; then 5,730 years for half of that remaining half to decay, and so on. Plutonium-239, one of the most toxic of all radioactive substances, has a half-life of about 24,000 years.

halftone process technique used in printing to reproduce the full range of tones in a photograph or other illustration. The intensity of the printed colour is varied from full strength to the lightest shades, even if one colour of ink is used. The picture to be reproduced is photographed through a screen ruled with a rectangular mesh of fine lines, which breaks up the tones of the original into areas of dots that vary in frequency according to the intensity of the tone. In the darker areas the dots run together; in the lighter areas they have more space between them.

halibut any of a group of large flatfishes found in the Atlantic and Pacific oceans. The largest of the flatfishes, they may grow up to 2 m/6 ft in length and weigh 90–135 kg/200–300 lb. They are a very dark mottled brown or green above and pure white on the underside. The Atlantic halibut (*H. hippoglossus*) is caught offshore at depths from 180 m/600 ft to 730 m/2,400 ft. (Genus *Hippoglossus*, family Pleuronectidae.)

Halicarnassus ancient city in Asia Minor (now Bodrum in Turkey), where the tomb of Mausolus, built about 350 BC by widowed Queen Artemisia, was one of the Seven Wonders of the World. The Greek historian Herodotus was born there.

halide any compound produced by the combination of a ▷halogen, such as chlorine or iodine, with a less electronegative element (see ▷electronegativity). Halides may be formed by ▷ionic bonds or by ▷covalent bonds.

Halifax capital of ▷Nova Scotia, Canada, on the eastern shore of the province; population (2001 est) 359,100. It is the largest and most important city of the Canadian Maritime Provinces (consisting of Nova Scotia, Prince Edward Island, and New Brunswick), and is the main port in eastern Canada; industries include oil refining, food processing, and aerospace. Halifax Harbour is ice-free all year round, due to the warm Gulf Stream current. There are six military bases located here, and the city is a centre for oceanography.

Halifax town in West Yorkshire, northern England, on the River Calder, 13 km/8 mi northwest of Huddersfield; population (1991) 91,100. Important in the woollen cloth trade since medieval times, the town produces textiles, carpets, and clothing; other industries include engineering and the manufacture of confectionery (Nestlé). It is the headquarters of the Halifax plc (formerly Halifax Building Society).

halite mineral form of sodium chloride, NaCl. Common ▷salt is the mineral halite. When pure it is colourless and transparent, but it is often pink, red, or yellow. It is soft and has a low density.

Hall, Peter (Reginald Frederick) (1930–) English theatre, opera, and film director. He was director of the Royal Shakespeare Theatre in Stratford-upon-Avon 1960–68 and developed the Royal Shakespeare Company 1968–73 until appointed director of the National Theatre 1973–88, succeeding Laurence Olivier. He founded the Peter Hall Company in 1988. He was knighted in 1977.

Hall's stage productions include Samuel Beckett's *Waiting for Godot* (1955), *The Wars of the Roses* (1963), Harold Pinter's *The Homecoming* (stage 1967 and film 1973), *The Oresteia* (1981), and Tennessee Williams's *Orpheus Descending* (1988). He has directed operas at Covent Garden, London; Bayreuth, Germany; and New York, and in 1984 was appointed artistic director of opera at Glyndebourne, East Sussex, with productions of *Carmen* (1985) and *Albert Herring* (1985–86).

He established a new repertory company based at the Old Vic Theatre, London, in 1996. In the same year, he directed *Carmen* in New York and *The Oedipus Plays* in London.

Hall, Radclyffe (1880–1943) Pen-name of Marguerite Radclyffe-Hall. English novelist. *The Well of Loneliness* (1928) brought her notoriety because of its lesbian theme. It was successfully prosecuted for obscenity and banned in the UK, but republished in 1949. Her other works include the novel *Adam's Breed* (1926; Femina Vie Heureuse and Tait Black Memorial prizes) and five early volumes of poetry.

Haller, Albrecht von (1708–1777) Swiss physician and scientist, founder of neurology. He studied the muscles and nerves, and concluded that nerves provide the stimulus that triggers muscle contraction. He also showed that it is the nerves, not muscle or skin, that receive sensation.

Halley, Edmond (1656–1742) English astronomer. He not only identified the comet that was later to be known by his name, but also compiled a star catalogue, detected the ▷proper motion of stars using historical records, and began a line of research that, after his death, resulted in a reasonably accurate calculation of the astronomical unit.

Halley calculated that the comet sightings reported in 1456, 1531, 1607, and 1682 all represented reappearances of the same comet. He reasoned that the comet would follow a parabolic path and announced in 1705 in his *Synopsis Astronomia Cometicae* that it would reappear in 1758. When it did, public acclaim for the astronomer was such that his name was irrevocably attached to it.

He made many other notable contributions to astronomy, including the discovery of the proper motions of ▷Aldebaran, ▷Arcturus, and ▷Sirius, and working out a method of obtaining the solar parallax by observations made during a transit of Venus. He was Astronomer Royal from 1720.

Related Web site: Halley, Edmond http://es.rice.edu/ES/humsoc/Galileo/Catalog/Files/halley.html

Halley's comet comet that orbits the Sun roughly every 75 years, named after English mathematician, physicist, and astronomer Edmond Halley, who calculated its orbit. It is the brightest and most conspicuous of the periodic comets. Recorded sightings go back over 2,000 years. It travels around the Sun in the opposite direction to the planets. Its orbit is inclined at almost 20° to the main plane of the Solar System and ranges between the orbits of Venus and Neptune. It will next reappear in 2061.

The comet was studied by space probes at its last appearance in 1986. The European probe *Giotto* showed that the nucleus of Halley's comet is a tiny and irregularly shaped chunk of ice, measuring some 15 km/10 m long by 8 km/5 m wide, coated by a layer of very dark material, thought to be composed of carbon-rich compounds. This surface coating has a very low ▷albedo, reflecting just 4% of the light it receives from the Sun. Although the comet is one of the darkest objects known, it has a glowing head and tail produced by jets of gas from fissures in the outer dust layer. These vents cover 10% of the total surface area and become active only when exposed to the Sun. The force of these jets affects the speed of the comet's travel in its orbit.

hallmark official mark stamped on British gold, silver, and (from 1913) platinum, instituted in 1327 (royal charter of London Goldsmiths) in order to prevent fraud. After 1363 personal marks of identification were added. Now tests of metal content are carried out at authorized assay offices in London, Birmingham, Sheffield, and Edinburgh; each assay office has its distinguishing mark, to which is added a maker's mark, date letter, and mark guaranteeing standard.

Halloween evening of 31 October, immediately preceding the Christian feast of All Hallows or All Saints' Day. Customs associated with Halloween in the USA and the UK include children wearing masks or costumes, and 'trick or treating' – going from house to house collecting sweets, fruit, or money.

Hallstatt archaeological site in Upper Austria, southwest of Salzburg. The salt workings date from prehistoric times. In 1846 over 3,000 graves were discovered belonging to a 9th–5th century BC Celtic civilization transitional between the Bronze and Iron ages.

hallucinogen any substance that acts on the ▷central nervous system to produce changes in perception and mood and often hallucinations. Hallucinogens include ▷LSD, ▷peyote, and ▷mescaline. Their effects are unpredictable and they are illegal in most countries.

halogen any of a group of five nonmetallic elements with similar chemical bonding properties: fluorine, chlorine, bromine, iodine, and astatine. They form a linked group in the ▷periodic table of the elements, descending from fluorine, the most reactive, to astatine, the least reactive. They combine directly with most metals to form salts, such as common salt (NaCl). Each halogen has seven electrons in its valence shell, which accounts for the chemical similarities displayed by the group.

halon organic chemical compound containing one or two carbon atoms, together with ▷bromine and other ▷halogens. The most commonly used are halon 1211 (bromochlorodifluoromethane) and halon 1301 (bromotrifluoromethane). The halons are gases and are widely used in fire extinguishers. As destroyers of the ▷ozone layer, they are up to ten times more effective than ▷chlorofluorocarbons (CFCs), to which they are chemically related.

halophyte plant adapted to live where there is a high concentration of salt in the soil, for example, in salt marshes and mud flats.

Hals, Frans (*c.* 1581–1666) Flemish-born painter. The pioneer in the Dutch school of free, broad brushwork, he painted directly on to the canvas to create portraits that are spontaneous and full of life. His work includes the famous *Laughing Cavalier* (1624; Wallace Collection, London), and group portraits of military companies, governors of charities, and others.

Halton unitary authority in northwest England, created in 1998 from part of Cheshire.

area 74 sq km/29 sq mi **towns and cities** Runcorn, Widnes (administrative headquarters), Ditton **features** River Mersey divides Runcorn from Widnes and Ditton; Manchester Ship Canal and Bridgewater Canal reach Mersey at Runcorn; St Helen's Canal reaches Mersey via a series of locks at Widnes; Catalyst: the Museum of the Chemical Industry is at Widnes; Norton Priory Museum (Runcorn) is on the site of a 12th-century priory **industries** industrial chemicals, pharmaceuticals, plastics manufacturing and coatings, light engineering, scientific instruments **population** (1996) 122,300 **famous people** Charles Barkla, Thomas Caine, Robert Mond

hamadryad (or **king cobra** or **giant cobra**) large and poisonous cobra found from India to China and the Philippines, sometimes reaching a length of 5 m/16 ft. It is one of the longest and most venomous of snakes, and is yellow with black crossbands.

Classification The hamadryad *Ophiophagus hannah* is in family Elapidae, suborder Serpentes, order Squamata, class Reptilia.

Hamburg largest inland port of Europe, in Germany, on the Elbe and Alster rivers, 103 km/64 mi from the mouth of the Elbe; population (1999 est) 1,704,700. Industries include marine engineering, ship-repairing, oil-refining, printing, publishing, and the production of chemicals, electronics, processed foods, and cosmetics. It is the capital of the *Land* (state) of Hamburg, and has been an archbishopric since 834. In alliance with Lübeck, it founded the ▷Hanseatic League. The city suffered extensive bomb damage during World War II.

HAMBURG Container vessels line the docksides at Europe's largest inland port, Hamburg, in Germany. *Image Bank*

Hamburg administrative region (German *Land*) of Germany, situated between Schleswig-Holstein and Lower Saxony; area 760 sq km/293 sq mi; population (1999 est) 1,704,700. The capital is ▷Hamburg. The main industries are oil refining, chemicals, electrical goods, marine engineering, ship-repairing, food-processing, printing, and publishing. The area is mostly urban, but small parts of fenland are used for dairying and apple orchards.

Hamed, 'Prince' Naseem (1974–) English boxer. Born in Sheffield of Yemeni extraction and known as 'Prince' Naseem for his showmanship qualities. An exceptionally strong puncher for a featherweight, he is widely regarded as one of British boxing's greatest talents. He made his professional debut in 1992 and was unbeaten until April 2001, when he lost on a unanimous points decision to Mexico's Marco Antonio Barrera. He won the European bantamweight title and the World Boxing Council (WBC) International super-bantamweight championship in 1994, before capturing the World Boxing Organization (WBO) world featherweight title in September 1995. He won the IBF version of the world featherweight title in February 1997, but relinquished it after a few months. In January 1999 he was awarded an MBE.

Related Web site: Prince Naseem Official Web Site http://www.princenaseem.com/

Hamilcar Barca (died 229 BC) Carthaginian general, the father of ▷Hannibal the Great. Hamilcar rose to prominence in 249 BC at the first Battle of Eryx, during the later stages of the First Punic War. He negotiated the peace treaty with the Carthaginians at the end of the war in 241 BC, and suppressed the revolt of Carthage's foreign troops, the Mercenary War (241–237 BC). He then campaigned in Spain until his death, substantially enlarging and enriching the Carthaginian Empire.

Hamilton capital (since 1815) of Bermuda, on Bermuda Island; population about (2000 est) 1,010. It has a deep-sea harbour.

Related Web site: Hamilton – Heart of the Mighty Waikato http://www.chemistry.co.nz/waikato.htm

Hamilton city and port in southwestern Ontario, Canada, at the head of Lake Ontario, 65 km/40 mi southwest of Toronto and

90 km/56 mi northwest of the Niagara Falls; population (1991) 318,500; metropolitan area 599,800. Hamilton Harbour, one of the largest landlocked harbours on the Great Lakes, is linked with Lake Ontario via the Burlington Canal (completed in 1830). The city lies at the centre of a fruit-growing district, and is Canada's leading producer of steel; other industries include the manufacture of heavy machinery, electrical equipment, farm and machine tools, chemicals, and textiles.

Hamilton, Alexander (1757–1804) US politician who influenced the adoption of a constitution with a strong central government and was the first secretary of the Treasury 1789–95. He led the Federalist Party, and incurred the bitter hatred of Aaron ▷Burr when he voted against Burr and in favour of Thomas Jefferson for the presidency in 1801. Challenged to a duel by Burr, Hamilton was wounded and died the next day.

Hamilton was a member of the Constitutional Convention of 1787. He was a strong advocate of the wealthy urban sector of American life and encouraged renewed ties with Britain, remaining distrustful of revolutionary France. In the cabinet, he soon came into conflict with Thomas Jefferson, who was secretary of state. Hamilton was for centralization of power, Jefferson was opposed to it. Hamilton looked to the leadership of money and property; Jefferson was a thorough-going democrat.

Hamilton, Emma, Lady (*c.* 1761–1815) Born Amy Lyon. English courtesan. In 1782 she became the mistress of Charles Greville and in 1786 of his uncle Sir William Hamilton (1730–1803), the British envoy to the court of Naples, who married her in 1791. After Admiral ▷Nelson's return from the Nile in 1798 during the Napoleonic Wars, she became his mistress and their daughter, Horatia, was born in 1801.

After Nelson's death in battle in 1805, Lady Hamilton spent her inheritance and died in poverty in Calais, France. She had been a great beauty and had posed for several artists, especially George ▷Romney.

Hamilton, James (1606–1649) 3rd Marquis and 1st Duke of Hamilton. Scottish adviser to Charles I. He led an army against the ▷Covenanters (supporters of the National Covenant of 1638 to establish Presbyterianism) in 1639 and subsequently took part in the negotiations between Charles and the Scots. In the second English Civil War he led the Scottish invasion of England, but was captured at Preston and executed. He succeeded as marquis in 1625, and was made a duke in 1643.

Hamilton, Richard (1922–) English artist, a pioneer of pop art. His collage *Just What Is It That Makes Today's Homes So Different, So Appealing?* (1956; Kunsthalle, Tübingen, Germany) is often cited as the first pop art work: its 1950s interior, inhabited by the bodybuilder Charles Atlas and a pin-up, is typically humorous, concerned with popular culture and contemporary kitsch.

Hammarskjöld, Dag (Hjalmar Agne Carl) (1905–1961) Swedish secretary general of the United Nations (UN) 1953–61. His role as a mediator and negotiator, particularly in areas of political conflict, helped to increase the prestige and influence of the UN significantly, and his name is synonymous with the peacekeeping work of the UN today. He was killed in a plane crash while involved in a controversial peacekeeping mission in Congo (now the Democratic Republic of Congo). He was posthumously awarded the Nobel Prize for Peace in 1961 for his peacekeeping work as secretary general of the UN.

Hammarskjöld was born in Jönköping, Sweden, the son of the Swedish prime minister 1914–17, and attended university in Uppsala and Stockholm, where he read economics. After serving as chairman of the bank of Sweden, he entered government, and in 1951 joined the Swedish delegation to the UN. In 1953 he was elected to replace the first secretary general of the UN, Trygve Lie, and was reelected in 1957.

Related Web site: Hammarskjöld, Dag http://www.nobel.se/peace/laureates/1961/hammarskjold-bio.html

hammer throwing event in track and field athletics. The hammer is a spherical weight attached to a wire with a handle. The competitors spin the hammer over their heads to gain momentum, within the confines of a circle, and throw it as far as they can. The senior men's hammer weighs 7.26 kg/16 lb and may originally have been a blacksmith's hammer. Women and junior men throw lighter implements.

Related Web site: Hammer Throw http://www.geocities.com/Colosseum/8682/ham.htm

Hammer, Armand (1898–1990) US entrepreneur, one of the most remarkable business figures of the 20th century. A pioneer in trading with the USSR from 1921, he later acted as a political mediator. He was chair of the US oil company Occidental Petroleum until his death, and was also an expert on art.

Dag Hammarskjöld
The only kind of dignity which is genuine is that which is not diminished by the indifference of others.
Markings

hammerhead any of several species of shark found in tropical seas, characterized by having eyes at the ends of flattened hammerlike extensions of the skull. Hammerheads can grow to 4 m/13 ft in length. (Genus *Sphyrna*, family Sphyrnidae.)

Hammerstein, Oscar, II (1895–1960) US lyricist and librettist. He collaborated with Richard ▷Rodgers over a period of 16 years on some of the best-known US musicals, including *Oklahoma!* (1943, Pulitzer prize), *Carousel* (1945), *South Pacific* (1949, Pulitzer prize), *The King and I* (1951), and *The Sound of Music* (1959).

He was a grandson of the opera impresario Oscar Hammerstein (I) (1846–1919). He earned his first successes with *Rose Marie* (1924), with music by Rudolf Friml (1879–1972); *Desert Song* (1926), music by Sigmund Romberg (1887–1951); and *Show Boat* (1927), music by Jerome Kern. *Show Boat* represented a major step forward in integration of plot and character. After a period of moderate success in film music, he joined Rodgers and began their 16-year collaboration. His adaptation of *Carmen* as a musical (*Carmen Jones*) was premiered in 1943.

HAMPTON COURT PALACE Hampton Court Palace, near Richmond, England. Henry VIII's third wife, Jane Seymour, gave birth to the future Edward VI there in 1540, and Henry married Catherine Howard and later Katherine Parr in the palace. The last monarch to live at the palace was George II. *Image Bank*

Hammett, (Samuel) Dashiell (1894–1961) US crime novelist. He introduced the 'hard-boiled' detective character into fiction and attracted a host of imitators, with works including *The Maltese Falcon* (1930, filmed 1941), *The Glass Key* (1931, filmed 1942), and his most successful novel, the light-hearted *The Thin Man* (1932, filmed 1934). His Marxist politics were best expressed in *Red Harvest* (1929), which depicts the corruption of capitalism in 'Poisonville'.

Hammett was a former Pinkerton detective agent. In 1951 he was imprisoned for contempt of court for refusing to testify during the McCarthy era of anticommunist witch hunts. He lived with the dramatist Lillian ▷Hellman for the latter half of his life.

Hammond organ electric ▷organ invented in the USA by Laurens Hammond in 1934. It is widely used in gospel music. Hammond applied valve technology to miniaturize Thaddeus Cahill's original 'tone-wheel' concept, introduced draw-slide registration to vary timbre, and incorporated a distinctive tremulant using rotating speakers. The Hammond organ was a precursor of the ▷synthesizer.

Hammurabi (died *c.* 1750 BC) Sixth ruler of the first dynasty of Babylon, reigned 1792–1750 or 1728–1686 BC. He united his country and took it to the height of its power. He authorized a legal code, of which a copy was found in 1902.

Hampden, John (1594–1643) English politician. His refusal in 1636 to pay ship money, a compulsory tax levied to support the navy, made him a national figure. In the Short and Long Parliaments he proved himself a skilful debater and parliamentary strategist.

King Charles I's attempt to arrest him and four other leading MPs made the Civil War inevitable. He raised his own regiment on the outbreak of hostilities, and on 18 June 1643 was mortally wounded at the skirmish of Chalgrove Field in Oxfordshire.

HAMMURABI The Code of Hammurabi on a Babylonian plaque, dating from around the 18th century BC (Louvre Museum, Paris, France). *The Art Archive/Eileen Tweedy*

Hampshire county of south England (since April 1997 Portsmouth and Southampton have been separate unitary authorities).

area 3,679 sq km/1,420 sq mi **towns and cities** ▷Winchester (administrative headquarters), Aldershot, Andover, Basingstoke, Eastleigh, Gosport, Romsey, and Lymington **physical** New Forest (area 373 sq km/144 sq mi), in the southeast of the county, a Saxon royal hunting ground; rivers Avon, Ichen, and Test (which has trout fishing) **features** Hampshire Basin, where Britain has onshore and offshore oil; Danebury, 2,500-year-old Celtic hill fort; Beaulieu (including National Motor Museum); Broadlands (home of Lord Mountbatten); Highclere castle (home of the Earl of Carnarvon, with gardens by Capability Brown); Hambledon, where the first cricket club was founded in 1750; site of the Roman town of Silchester; Jane Austen's cottage at Chawton (1809–17), now a museum; Twyford Down section of the M3 motorway was completed in 1994 despite protests **agriculture** market gardening (watercress) **industries** aeronautics, brewing, chemicals, electronics, light engineering (at Basingstoke), oil from refineries at Fawley, perfume, pharmaceuticals **population** (1996) 1,627,400 **famous people** Jane Austen, Charles Dickens, Gilbert White

Related Web site: Hampshire County Council http://www.hants.gov.uk/hcc/index.html

Hampton, Lionel (1909–2002) US jazz musician. He was a top bandleader of the 1940s and 1950s. Originally a drummer, Hampton introduced the vibraphone, an electronically vibrated percussion instrument, to jazz music. With the Benny Goodman band from 1936, he fronted his own big band 1941–65 and subsequently led small groups.

Hampton Court Palace former royal residence near Richmond, England, 24 km/15 mi west of central London. Hampton Court is one of the greatest historical monuments in the UK, and contains some of the finest examples of Tudor architecture and of Christopher ▷Wren's work. It was built in 1515 by Cardinal ▷Wolsey and presented by him to Henry VIII who subsequently enlarged and improved it. In the 17th century William (III) and Mary (II) made it their main residence outside London, and the palace was further enlarged by Wren. Part of the building was extensively damaged by fire in 1986.

hamster any of a group of burrowing rodents with a thickset body, short tail, and cheek pouches to carry food. Several genera are found across Asia and in southeastern Europe. Hamsters are often kept as pets. (Genera include *Cricetus* and *Mesocricetus*, family Cricetidae.)

Species include the European and Asian **black-bellied** or **common hamster** (*C. cricetus*), about 25 cm/10 in long, which can be a crop pest and stores up to 90 kg/200 lb of seeds in its burrow. The **golden hamster** (*M. auratus*) lives in western Asia and southeastern Europe. All golden hamsters now kept as pets originated from one female and 12 young captured in Syria in 1930.

Hamsun, Knut (1859–1952) Pseudonym of Knut Pedersen. Norwegian novelist. His first novel *Sult/Hunger* (1890) was largely autobiographical. Other works include *Pan* (1894) and *Markens grøde/The Growth of the Soil* (1917). He was the first of many European and American writers to attempt to capture 'the unconscious life of the soul'. He was awarded the Nobel Prize for Literature in 1920. His hatred of capitalism made him sympathize with Nazism and he was fined in 1946 for collaboration.

Han the majority ethnic group in China, numbering about 990 million. The Hans speak a wide variety of dialects of the same monosyllabic language, a member of the Sino-Tibetan family. Their religion combines Buddhism, Taoism, Confucianism, and ancestor worship.

Hancock, John (1737–1793) US politician and a leader of the American Revolution. As president of the Continental Congress 1775–77, he was the first to sign the Declaration of Independence of 1776. Because he signed it in a large, bold hand, his name became a colloquial term for a signature in the USA. He was governor of Massachusetts 1780–85 and 1787–93.

Hancock, Tony (Anthony John) (1924–1968) English lugubrious radio and television comedian. His radio show *Hancock's Half Hour* (1951–53) showed him famously at odds with everyday life; it was followed by a television show of the same name in 1956. He also appeared in films, including *The Rebel* (1961) and *The Wrong Box* (1966).

hand unit used in measuring the height of a horse from front hoof to shoulder (withers). One hand equals 10.2 cm/4 in.

Handel, George Frideric (1685–1759) Born Georg Friedrich Händel. German composer, a British subject from 1726. His first opera, *Almira*, was performed in Hamburg in 1705. In 1710 he was appointed Kapellmeister to the elector of Hanover (the future George I of England). In 1712 he settled in England, where he established his popularity with such works as the *Water Music* (1717), written for George I. His great choral works include the *Messiah* (1742) and the later oratorios *Samson* (1743), *Belshazzar* (1745), *Judas Maccabaeus* (1747), and *Jephtha* (1752).

Visits to Italy 1706–10 inspired a number of operas and oratorios, and in 1711 his opera *Rinaldo* was performed in London. *Saul* and *Israel in Egypt* (both 1739) were unsuccessful, but his masterpiece, the oratorio *Messiah*, was acclaimed on its first performance in Dublin, Ireland, in 1742. Other works include the pastoral *Acis and Galatea* (1718) and a set of variations for harpsichord that were later nicknamed 'The Harmonious Blacksmith'.

> **George Frideric Handel**
> *[Telemann] could write a motet for eight voices more quickly than one could write a letter.*
> Quoted in Young *Handel* (1946)

GEORGE HANDEL Born a German (in Saxony), and by inclination a maestro of Italian opera, it is nonetheless as one of the most English of composers that Handel has long been remembered. *The Art Archive Museo Musicale Bologna/ Dagli Orti*

Han dynasty Chinese ruling family from 206 BC to AD 220 established by Liu Bang (256–195 BC) after he overthrew the ▷Qin dynasty, and named after the Han River. There was territorial expansion to the west, southwest, and north, including the conquest of Korea by Emperor Wudi or Wu-ti (ruling 141–87 BC) and the suppression of the Xiongnu invaders. Under the Han, a Confucianist-educated civil service was established and Buddhism introduced.

Divided into the eras of the Western Han (206 BC–AD 8) and the Eastern Han (AD 25–220), it was a time of internal peace, except for the period AD 8 to 25. The building of new canals allowed long-distance trading, while the arts and technologies (including the invention of paper) flourished. The dynasty collapsed under the weight of court intrigues, rebellions, and renewed threat from the Xiongnu, and was replaced by the ▷Three Kingdoms.

Hangchow alternative transcription of ▷Hangzhou, port and capital of Zhejiang province, China.

hang-gliding technique of unpowered flying using air currents, perfected by US engineer Francis Rogallo in the 1970s. The aeronaut is strapped into a carrier, attached to a sail wing of nylon stretched on an aluminium frame like a paper dart, and jumps into the air from a high place, where updraughts of warm air allow soaring on the thermals. See ▷gliding.

Related Web site: Hang-Para Gliding FAQ http://www.sky-adventures.com/hang/HGfaq.html

hanging execution by suspension, usually with a drop of 0.6–2 m/2–6 ft, so that the powerful jerk of the tightened rope breaks the neck. This was once a common form of ▷capital punishment in Europe and is still practised in some states in the USA.

Hanging Gardens of Babylon in antiquity, gardens at Babylon, the capital of Mesopotamia, considered one of the ▷Seven Wonders of the World. According to legend, King Nebuchadnezzar constructed the gardens in the 6th century BC for one of his wives, who was homesick for her birthplace in the Iranian mountains. Archaeological excavations at the site of Babylon, 88 km/55 mi south of Baghdad in modern Iraq, have uncovered a huge substructure that may have supported irrigated gardens on terraces.

hanging valley valley that joins a larger glacial trough at a higher level than the trough floor. During glaciation the ice in the smaller valley was unable to erode as deeply as the ice in the trough, and so the valley was left perched high on the side of the trough when the ice retreated. A river or stream flowing along the hanging valley often forms a waterfall as it enters the trough.

Hangzhou (or **Hangchow**) port and capital of ▷Zhejiang province, China, on the mouth of the Qiantang River, at the southern terminus of the ▷Grand Canal, 175 km/109 mi southwest of Shanghai; population (1994) 1,412,700. Products include jute, steel, machine tools, chemicals, electronics, processed foods, tea, silk and cotton textiles, fans, and gold-embroidered goods. Hangzhou has fine landscaped gardens, and was the capital of China from 1127 to 1278 under the Song dynasty.

Hanks, Tom (1956–) US actor. His mainstream appeal, often seen in romantic comedies such as *Sleepless in Seattle* (1993), made his casting as an AIDS-afflicted lawyer in *Philadelphia* (1993) (Academy Award) surprising. His other roles include a drunken baseball coach in *A League of their Own* (1992), the title role in *Forrest Gump* (1994) (Academy Award), a leading part in *Saving Private Ryan* (1998), and as a death row prison guard in *The Green Mile* (1999).

Hannibal (247–182 BC) Called 'the Great'. Carthaginian general from 221 BC, son of Hamilcar Barca. His siege of Saguntum (now Sagunto, near Valencia) precipitated the Second ▷Punic War with Rome. Following a campaign in Italy (after crossing the Alps in 218), Hannibal was the victor at Trasimene in 217 and Cannae in 216, but he failed to take Rome. In 203 he returned to Carthage to meet a Roman invasion but was defeated at Zama in 202 and exiled in 196 at Rome's insistence.

Hannibal's invasion of Italy, his seemingly endless string of devastating victories over the Romans, and his inspiring personality earned him immortality as a military genius and iconic hero. Fulfilling an oath sworn at the age of 9 to always hate the Romans, Hannibal ravaged Italy for 16 years. Though defeating the Roman army in almost a dozen battles, relentless Roman resistance and the problems of supplying his invasion army prevented him from achieving a decisive victory. When the Romans finally fielded a general willing to experiment and innovate in battle as much as he had done, Publius Cornelius ▷Scipio, Hannibal had to come to the defence of his own homeland. He was defeated at Zama in 202. He tried a political career, but was forced out of Carthage by opponents in 195 BC and spent the remainder of his life as a curiosity and mercenary among foreign courts, finally committing suicide.

Hannover (or **Hanover**) industrial city and capital of Lower Saxony, Germany, on the rivers Leine and Ihme; population (1995) 524,600. Industries include mechanical engineering, telecommunications, and the manufacture of electrical goods, rubber, and textiles. From 1386 it was a member of the ▷Hanseatic League, and from 1692 capital of the electorate of Hannover (created a kingdom in 1815). ▷George I of Great Britain and Ireland was also Elector of Hannover.

Related Web site: Hannover – City of Fairs http://www.expo.hannover.de/english/start/tourist.htm

Hanoi capital of Vietnam, on the Red River; population (1997 est) 3,500,800. Central Hanoi has one of the highest population densities in the world: 1,300 people per hectare/3,250 per acre. Industries include tanning and food processing, especially rice milling.

Hanover, House of German royal dynasty that ruled Great Britain and Ireland from 1714 to 1901. Under the Act of ▷Settlement of 1701, the succession passed to the ruling family of Hannover, Germany, on the death of Queen Anne. On the death of Queen Victoria, the crown passed to Edward VII of the house of Saxe-Coburg.

Hanseatic League (German *Hanse* 'group, society') confederation of northern European trading cities from the 12th century to 1669. At its height in the late 14th century the Hanseatic League included over 160 cities and towns, among them Lübeck, Hamburg, Cologne, Breslau, and Kraków. The basis of the league's power was its monopoly of the Baltic trade and its relations with Flanders and England. The decline of the Hanseatic League from the 15th century was caused by the closing and moving of trade routes and the development of nation states.

Hansom, Joseph Aloysius (1803–1882) English architect and inventor. His works include the Birmingham town hall (1831), but he is remembered as the designer of the **hansom cab** (1834), a two-wheel carriage with a seat for the driver on the outside.

Hanukkah (or **Hanukah** or **Chanukkah**) in Judaism, an eight-day festival of lights that takes place at the beginning of December. It celebrates the recapture and rededication of the Temple in Jerusalem by Judas Maccabaeus in 164 BC.

Related Web site: Hanukkah – Festival of Lights http://www.ahavat-israel.com/torat/chanukah.html

Haora (or **Howrah**) city of West Bengal, northeast India, on the right bank of the River Hooghly opposite ▷Calcutta; population (1991) 947,000. The capital of Haora district, it has jute and cotton factories; rice, flour, and saw mills; iron and steel works and chemical factories; and railway engineering works. Haora suspension bridge, opened in 1943, spans the river. It is on a railway junction.

haploid having a single set of ▷chromosomes in each cell. Most higher organisms are ▷diploid – that is, they have two sets – but their gametes (sex cells) are haploid. Some plants, such as mosses, liverworts, and many seaweeds, are haploid, and male honey bees are haploid because they develop from eggs that have not been fertilized. See also ▷meiosis.

Hapsburg alternative form of ▷Habsburg, former imperial house of Austria-Hungary.

Harare (formerly **Salisbury**) capital of Zimbabwe, in Mashonaland East Province, about 1,525 m/5,000 ft above sea level; population (1992) 1,184,200. It is the centre of a rich farming area producing tobacco and maize. The city's industries include milling, textiles, electrical and mechanical engineering, motor assembly, railway rolling stock, chemicals, furniture, consumer goods, and metallurgical and food processing.

Harbin (or **Haerhpin** or **Pinkiang**) port and capital of ▷Heilongjiang province, northeast China, on the Songhua River; population (1994) 2,887,800. It is a major rail junction. Industries include metallurgy, food processing, and sugar-refining; the manufacture of machinery and paper; and tourism. Harbin was developed by Russian settlers after Russia was granted trading rights here in 1896, and more Russians arrived as refugees after the October Revolution (1917). In World War II, it was the key objective of the Soviet invasion of Manchuria in August 1945.

Related Web site: Welcome to the City of Harbin http://china.muzi.net/travel/city/harbin.htm

hard disk in computing, a storage device usually consisting of a rigid metal ▷disk coated with a magnetic material. Data are read from and written to the disk by means of a disk drive. The hard disk may be permanently fixed into the drive or in the form of a disk pack that can be removed and exchanged with a different pack. Hard disks vary from large units with capacities of more than 3,000 megabytes, intended for use with mainframe computers, to small units with capacities as low as 20 megabytes, intended for use with microcomputers.

A hard disk drive that is only thumbnail-sized was released by IBM in 1999, holding 340 megabytes. A one gigabyte version was released in 2000.

Hardenberg, Friedrich von real name of German Romantic poet ▷Novalis.

Hardicanute (*c.* 1019–1042) King of Denmark from 1028, and of England from 1040; son of Canute. In England he was considered a harsh ruler.

Hardie, (James) Keir (1856–1915) Scottish socialist, the first British Labour politician, member of Parliament 1892–95 and 1900–15. He worked in the mines as a boy and in 1886 became secretary of the Scottish Miners' Federation. In 1888 he was the first Labour candidate to stand for Parliament; he entered Parliament independently as a Labour member in 1892, he became chair of the Labour party 1906–08 and 1909–10, and in 1893 was a chief founder of the Independent Labour Party.

Hardie was born in Lanarkshire but represented the parliamentary constituencies of West Ham, London 1892–95 and Merthyr Tydfil, Wales, from 1900. A pacifist, he strongly opposed the Boer War and World War I, and his idealism in his work for socialism and the unemployed made him a popular hero.

Harding, Warren G(amaliel) (1865–1923) 29th president of the USA 1921–23, a Republican. As president he concluded the peace treaties of 1921 with Germany, Austria, and Hungary, and in the same year called the Washington Naval Conference to resolve conflicting British, Japanese, and US ambitions in the Pacific. He opposed US membership of the ▷League of Nations. There were charges of corruption among members of his cabinet (the ▷Teapot Dome Scandal), with the secretary of the interior later convicted for taking bribes.

Harding was born in Ohio. Before entering politics, he was a newspaper editor and publisher. He was an Ohio state senator 1898–1904 and lieutenant governor 1904–05, entering the US Senate in 1915. The various treaties stemming from the Washington Conference, providing for naval disarmament, and ostensibly stabilizing international relations between the great power signatories, were considered at the time a diplomatic coup for the USA and Harding, which reinforced the traditional US position of neutrality. He died in office, shortly after undeniable evidence of corruption in his administration began to surface. He was succeeded by Calvin ▷Coolidge.

Related Web site: Warren G Harding – Twenty-ninth President 1921–1923 http://www.whitehouse.gov/WH/glimpse/presidents/html/wh29.html

hardness physical property of materials that governs their use. Methods of heat treatment can increase the hardness of metals. A scale of hardness was devised by German–Austrian mineralogist Friedrich Mohs in the 1800s, based upon the hardness of certain minerals from soft talc (Mohs hardness 1) to diamond (10), the hardest of all materials.

Hardouin-Mansart, Jules (1646–1708) French architect born in Paris. He superintended the construction of all the principal buildings of Louis XIV, including the lavish baroque extensions to the palace of Versailles (1678–1708), its colonnade, the cathedral, and the Grand Trianon.

hardware mechanical, electrical, and electronic components of a computer system, as opposed to the various programs, which constitute ▷software.

Hardware associated with a microcomputer might include the power supply and housing of its processor unit, its circuit boards, VDU (screen), disk drive, keyboard, and printer.

hard water water that does not lather easily with soap, and produces a deposit or 'scale' in kettles. It is caused by the presence of certain salts of calcium and magnesium.

Hardy, Oliver Born Oliver Norvell Hardy, Jr. US film comedian, member of the duo ▷Laurel and Hardy.

Hardy, Thomas (1840–1928) English novelist and poet. His novels, set in rural 'Wessex' (his native West Country), portray intense human relationships played out in a harshly indifferent natural world. They include *Far From the Madding Crowd* (1874), *The Return of the Native* (1878), *The Mayor of Casterbridge* (1886), *The Woodlanders* (1887), *Tess of the d'Urbervilles* (1891), and *Jude the Obscure* (1895). His poetry includes the *Wessex Poems* (1898), the blank-verse epic of the Napoleonic Wars *The Dynasts* (1903–08), and several volumes of lyrics. Many of his books have been successfully dramatized for film and television.

> **Thomas Hardy**
> *We two kept house, the Past and I.*
> *The Ghost of the Past*

Hardy was born in Dorset and trained as an architect. His first success was *Far From the Madding Crowd* and *Tess of the d'Urbervilles*, subtitled 'A Pure Woman', outraged public opinion by portraying as its heroine a woman who had been seduced. *Jude the Obscure* received an even more hostile reception, which reinforced Hardy's decision to confine himself to verse in his later years.

In his novels Hardy dramatizes with uncompromising directness a belief in the futility of fighting against the cruelties of circumstance, the inevitability of each individual's destiny, and the passing of all beauty. His poems, many of which are now rated as highly as the best of his prose fiction, often contain a compressed version of the same theme, either by seeing ahead from a happy present to a grim future or else looking back from the bitterness of the present to a past that was full of promise.

Related Web sites: Far from the Madding Crowd http://www.bibliomania.com/Fiction/hardy/crowd/index.html

hare mammal closely related to the rabbit, similar in appearance but larger. Hares have very long black-tipped ears, long hind legs, and short upturned tails. (Genus *Lepus*, family Leporidae, order Lagomorpha.) Throughout the long breeding season (June–August) there are chases and 'boxing matches' among males and females; the expression 'mad as a March hare' arises from this behaviour. The young ('leverets') are left by the mother immediately after birth. She stays about 200 m away where she is unlikely to draw attention to her litter and feeds them for just 10 minutes every 24 hours. Hares are largely nocturnal and avoid predators during the day by their stillness.

Unlike rabbits, hares do not burrow. Their furry, open-eyed young are cared for in a grassy hollow in the ground called a form. According to a 1997–99 survey, there are 752,608 hares in Britain. Killing of hares is unregulated in Britain, the only EC country where this is the case.

Hare, David (1947–) English dramatist and screenwriter. He co-founded the theatre company Joint Stock in 1974. His plays satirize the decadence of post-war Britain, and include *Slag* (1970), *Teeth 'n' Smiles* (1975), *Fanshen* (1975) on revolutionary Chinese communism, *Plenty* (1978), and *Pravda* (1985) (with Howard ▷Brenton) on Fleet Street journalism. More recent plays include *My Zinc Bed* (2000) and *The Breath of Life* (2002).

harebell perennial plant of the ▷bellflower family, with bell-shaped blue flowers, found on dry grassland and heaths. It is known in Scotland as the bluebell. (*Campanula rotundifolia*, family Campanulaceae.)

HAREBELL The harebell, also known as the witches' thimble, is a plant of northern temperate regions. *Premaphotos Wildlife*

Hare Krishna popular name for a member of the ▷International Society for Krishna Consciousness, derived from their chant.

Hargobind (1595–1644) Indian religious leader, sixth guru (teacher) of Sikhism 1606–44. He encouraged Sikhs to develop military skills in response to growing persecution. At the festival of ▷Diwali, Sikhs celebrate his release from prison.

Hargreaves, James (*c.* 1720–1778) English inventor who co-invented a carding machine for combing wool in 1760. In *c.* 1764 he invented his 'spinning jenny' (patented in 1770), which enabled a number of threads to be spun simultaneously by one person.

Haridwar (or **Hardwar**) city in Uttar Pradesh, India, 170 km/106 mi northeast of Delhi, on the right bank of the River Ganges at the foot of the Shiwalik Hills; population (1991) 147,300. The name means 'door of Hari' (or Vishnu). In Hindu legend Vishnu's footprint was found on the river bank; it is one of the seven holy cities of the Hindu religion and a pilgrimage centre.

Harijan (Hindi 'children of god') member of the Indian ▷caste of untouchables. The term was introduced by Mahatma Gandhi during the independence movement.

Harlow, Jean (1911–1937) Stage name of Harlean Carpentier. US film actor. She was the original 'platinum blonde' and the wisecracking sex symbol of the 1930s. Her films include *Hell's Angels* (1930), *Red Dust* (1932), *Platinum Blonde* (1932), *Dinner at Eight* (1933), *China Seas* (1935), and *Saratoga* (1937), during the filming of which she died (her part was completed by a double).

harmattan in meteorology, a dry and dusty northeast wind that blows over West Africa.

harmonica musical instrument, a pocket-sized reed organ blown directly from the mouth, invented by Charles Wheatstone in 1829; see ▷mouth organ.

Related Web site: Harmonica World http://www.bekkoame.ne.jp/~mshige/

harmonics in music, a series of partial vibrations that combine to form a musical tone. The number and relative prominence of harmonics produced determines an instrument's tone colour (timbre). An oboe is rich in harmonics, the flute has few. Harmonics conform to successive divisions of the sounding air column or string; their pitches are harmonious.

harmonium keyboard reed organ of the 19th century, powered by foot-operated bellows and incorporating lever-action knee swells to influence dynamics. It was invented by Alexandre Debain in Paris, France, about 1842.

harmony in music, any simultaneous combination of sounds, as opposed to melody, which is a succession of sounds. Although the term suggests a pleasant or agreeable sound, it is applied to any combination of notes, whether consonant or dissonant. The theory of harmony deals with the formation of chords and their interrelation and logical progression.

harness racing form of horse racing, also known as trotting or pacing, in which the horses are harnessed, pull a light vehicle (sulky) and compete at either a trotting or pacing gait. If a horse breaks the pace and gallops, the driver must start it again.

Harold two kings of England:

Harold I (1016–1040) King of England from 1035. The illegitimate son of Canute, known as **Harefoot**, he claimed the crown on the death of his father, when the rightful heir, his half-brother Hardicanute, was in Denmark and unable to ascend the throne. He was elected king in 1037, but died three years later, as Hardicanute was preparing to invade England.

Harold (II) Godwinson (*c.* 1020–1066) last Anglo-Saxon king of England, January to October 1066. He was defeated and killed by William of Normandy (▷William (I) the Conqueror) at the Battle of Hastings.

He succeeded his father Earl Godwin in 1053 as Earl of Wessex. Harold was Edward the Confessor's military commander, and became so powerful that one chronicler described him as the 'sub-king'. In about 1063 William of Normandy tricked or forced him into swearing to support his claim to the English throne, and when the Witan (a council of high-ranking religious and secular men) elected Harold to succeed Edward the Confessor, William prepared to invade. Meanwhile, Harold's treacherous brother Tostig (died 1066) joined the King of Norway Harald (III) Hardrada in invading Northumbria. Harold routed and killed them at Stamford Bridge on 25 September. Three days later William landed at Pevensey, Sussex, and Harold was killed at the Battle of Hastings on 14 October.

HAROLD GODWINSON An illustration from a 13th-century manuscript shows King Harold of England wounded in the eye at the Battle of Hastings in 1066. *The Art Archive*

harp plucked musical string instrument, with the strings stretched vertically and parallel to one member of a triangular framework. A second member of the triangle is a wood and brass soundbox of triangular shape; the third member locates pegs by means of which the strings are tensioned. The orchestral harp is the largest instrument of its type. It has up to 47 diatonically tuned strings, in the range B0–C7 (seven octaves), and seven double-action pedals to alter pitch. Before the pedals are depressed, the strings sound the diatonic scale of C flat major, but each note can be raised a semitone or a whole tone by one of the pedals. Thus all the notes of the chromatic scale can be sounded.

Harper's Ferry town in Jefferson County, West Virginia, in the Blue Ridge Mountains, where the Potomac and Shenandoah rivers meet; population (1990) 300. It was first settled in 1732 and incorporated as a town in 1763. In 1859 the antislavery leader John ▷Brown seized the federal government's arsenal here, an action that helped precipitate the American Civil War.

harpsichord the largest and grandest of 18th-century keyboard string instruments, used in orchestras and as a solo instrument. The strings are plucked by 'jacks' made of leather or quill, and multiple keyboards offering variation in tone are common. However, unlike the piano, the tone cannot be varied by the player's touch. The revival of the harpsichord repertoire in the 20th century owed much to Wanda Landowska and Ralph Kirkpatrick (1911–1984).

Harpy (Greek 'snatcher') in early Greek mythology, a wind spirit; in later legend, such as the story of the ▷Argonauts, a female monster with a horrific face, pale with hunger, and the body of a vulture. Often associated with the underworld, harpies were believed to abduct those people who disappeared without trace, and were perceived as an instrument of torment used by the gods.

harrier any of a group of birds of prey. Harriers have long wings and legs, a small head with a short beak, an owl-like frill of thickset feathers around the face, and soft plumage. They eat frogs, birds, snakes, and small mammals, and are found mainly in marshy areas throughout the world. (Genus *Circus*, family Accipitridae, order Falconiformes.)

Three species occur in Britain: the hen harrier (*C. cyaneus*), Montagu's harrier (*C. pygargus*), and marsh harrier (*C. aeruginosus*). Hen harriers are one of the UK's rarest birds of prey, with only about 630 breeding females counted during the 1988–89 survey. 1997 figures gathered from selected roosting sites indicated that there had been a 40% decline in the 1990s, and by 2000 the numbers of breeding females had dropped to 570 in Britain.

harrier breed of hound, similar to a ▷foxhound but smaller, used in packs for hare-hunting.

Harris part of the Outer ▷Hebrides, Western Isles, Scotland; area 500 sq km/193 sq mi; population (1971) 2,900. It is joined to Lewis by a narrow isthmus. Harris tweed cloths are produced here.

Harris, Joel Chandler (1848–1908) US author. He wrote tales narrated by the former slave 'Uncle Remus', based on black folklore and involving the characters Brer Rabbit, Brer Fox, Brer Wolf, and Brer Bear.

En set by de fier, en smoke his pipe, en read de newspapers same like enny man w'at got a fambly.
(See page 107.)

JOEL HARRIS Brer Rabbit is shown, in an illustration by J A Shepherd from 1901, relaxing in front of his fireplace. *The Art Archive*

Harrison, Benjamin (1833–1901) 23rd president of the USA 1889–93, a Republican. He called the first Pan-American Conference, which led to the establishment of the Pan-American Union, to improve inter-American cooperation and develop commercial ties. In 1948 this became the ▷Organization of American States.

Events of his presidency included the settlement with Britain of the Bering Sea fur-seal question, an attempt to negotiate the annexation of Hawaii, and the passing of the ▷McKinley Tariff Act, the Sherman Silver Purchase Act, and the Sherman Anti-Trust Act.

Harrison, George (1943–2001) English rock and pop guitarist, singer, and songwriter. He played lead guitar and sang in the legendary English rock group the Beatles, and wrote occasional songs for the group, including 'Something' (1969). After the group split up in 1970, Harrison began a solo career with hit singles including 'My Sweet Lord' (1970).

Harrison, Rex (Reginald Carey) (1908–1990) English film and theatre actor. He appeared in over 40 films and numerous plays, often portraying sophisticated and somewhat eccentric characters, such as the waspish Professor Higgins in *My Fair Lady* (1964; Academy Award), the musical version of *Pygmalion*. His other films include *Blithe Spirit* (1945), *The Ghost and Mrs Muir* (1947), and *Dr Doolittle* (1967).

Harrison, Tony (1937–) English poet, translator, and dramatist. He caused controversy with his poem *V* (1987), dealing with the desecration of his parents' grave by Liverpool football supporters, and the play *The Blasphemers' Banquet* (1989), which attacked (in the name of Molière, Voltaire, Byron, and Omar Khayyam) the death sentence on Salman ▷Rushdie. He has also translated and adapted Molière.

Harrison, William Henry (1773–1841) 9th president of the USA in 1841. Elected in 1840 as a Whig, he died one month after taking office. His political career was based largely on his reputation as an Indian fighter, and his campaign was constructed to give the impression that he was a man of the people with simple tastes and that the New Yorker, Martin ▷Van Buren, his opponent, was a 'foppish' sophisticate.

Harrogate resort and spa town in North Yorkshire, northern England, about 24 km/15 mi north of Leeds; population (1996 est) 69,800. Employment is mainly in the service sector, particularly related to conference business, tourism, and finance. A US communications station is located at Menwith Hill.

Harry (1984–) Born Henry Charles Albert David. Prince of the UK; second child of the Prince and Princess of Wales.

Harry attended Ludgrove School, Wokingham (1992–97) and Eton College, Windsor. He is third in line to the throne after his father, Prince ▷Charles, and his older brother, Prince ▷William.

hartebeest large African antelope with lyre-shaped horns set close on top of the head in both sexes. It can grow to 1.5 m/5 ft tall at the rather humped shoulders and up to 2 m/6 ft long. Although they are clumsy-looking runners, hartebeest can reach speeds of 65 kph/40 mph. (Species *Alcelaphus buselaphus*, family Bovidae.)

Hartington, Spencer Compton Cavendish, Marquess of Hartington and 8th Duke of Devonshire (1833–1908) British politician, first leader of the Liberal Unionists 1886–1903. As war minister he opposed devolution for Ireland in cabinet and later led the revolt of the Liberal Unionists that defeated Gladstone's Irish Home Rule Bill of 1886. Hartington refused the premiership three times, in 1880, 1886, and 1887, and led the opposition to the Irish Home Rule Bill in the House of Lords in 1893.

Hartlepool town, port, and, since 1996, unitary authority in northeast England, formed from part of the county of Cleveland.
area 94 sq km/36 sq mi **features** redeveloped dock area including the Museum of Hartlepool (opened in 1995); the Gray Art Gallery and Museum; remains of the medieval town walls; Early English church of St Hilda with a Norman doorway **industries** the local economy depends on metal industries, engineering, support services for the oil industry, fishing, and brewing. A nuclear power station is located 5 km/3 mi southeast of the town at Seaton Carew **population** (1996) 90,400 **famous people** Christopher Furness, Compton Mackenzie, Edward Mellanby, Kenneth Mellanby

Hartley, L(eslie) P(oles) (1895–1972) English novelist and short-story writer. His early works explored the sinister. His chief works are the trilogy *The Shrimp and the Anemone* (1944), *The Sixth Heaven* (1946), and *Eustace and Hilda* (1947; Tait Black Memorial Prize), on the intertwined lives of a brother and sister. Later works include *The Go-Between* (1953; filmed 1971) and *The Hireling* (1957), which explore sexual relationships between the classes.

hart's-tongue fern with straplike undivided fronds, up to 60 cm/24 in long, which have clearly visible brown spore-bearing organs on the undersides. The plant is native to Europe, Asia, and eastern North America, and is found on walls, in shady rocky places, and in woods. (*Phyllitis scolopendrium*, family Polypodiaceae.)

Hartz Mountains range running N–S in Tasmania, Australia, with two remarkable peaks: Hartz Mountain (1,254 m/4,113 ft) and Adamsons Peak (1,224 m/4,017 ft).

Harvard University the oldest educational institution in the USA, founded in 1636 at New Towne (later Cambridge), Massachusetts, and named after John Harvard (1607–1638), who bequeathed half his estate and his library to it. Women were first admitted in 1969; the women's college of the university is **Radcliffe College**.

"A PROSPECT OF THE COLLEDGES AT CAMBRIDGE IN NEW ENGLAND." *American print. c. 1739.*

HARVARD UNIVERSITY The oldest college in the USA, Harvard University was founded in 1636. *Philip Sauvain Picture Collection*

harvestman small animal (an ▷arachnid) related to spiders with very long, thin legs and a small body. Harvestmen are different from true spiders in that they do not have a waist or narrow part to the oval body. They feed on small insects and spiders, and lay their eggs in autumn, to hatch the following spring or early summer. They are found from the Arctic to the tropics. (Order Opiliones.)

harvest mite another name for the ▷chigger, a parasitic mite.

Harvey, William (1578–1657) English physician who discovered the circulation of blood. In 1628 he published his book *De motu cordis/On the Motion of the Heart and the Blood in Animals*. He also explored the development of chick and deer embryos.

Harvey's discovery marked the beginning of the end of medicine as taught by ▷Galen, which had been accepted for 1,400 years.

Haryana (Hindi 'God's home') state of northwest India; area 44,200 sq km/17,061 sq mi; population (2001 est) 20,821,000. The capital is ▷Chandigarh (also capital of ▷Punjab state). The state lies on the Gangetic plain, drained by the Yamuna River. Chief industries are textiles, cement, iron ore, and processing of agricultural products; agriculture is based on wheat (with Punjab accounting for one-third of India's total production), sugar, cotton, oilseed, rice, and pulses.

Hasdrubal Barca Carthaginian general, son of Hamilcar Barca and younger brother of Hannibal. He remained in command in Spain when Hannibal invaded Italy during the Second Punic War and, after fighting there against Scipio until 208, marched to Hannibal's relief. He was defeated and killed in the Metaurus valley, northeastern Italy.

hashish drug made from the resin contained in the female flowering tops of hemp (▷cannabis).

Hasidism (or **Hassidism**, or **Chasidism**, or **Chassidism**) sect of Orthodox Judaism, originating in 18th-century Poland under the leadership of Israel Ba'al Shem Tov (*c.* 1700–1760). Hasidic teachings encourage prayer, piety, and 'serving the Lord with joy'. Many of the Hasidic ideas are based on the ▷kabbala.

Hassan II (1929–1999) King of Morocco 1961–99. He succeeded the throne upon the death of his father Mohamed V. Following riots in Casablanca in 1965, he established a royal dictatorship and survived two coup attempts. The occupation of the former Spanish Western Sahara in 1976 enabled him to rally strong popular support and consolidate his power. He returned to constitutional government in 1984, with a civilian prime minister leading a government of national unity. He was succeeded by his 35-year-old son Muhammad.

It was not until February 1998 that the opposition accepted and participated in the formation of an elected government that was still controlled by the monarchy. In the late 1990s the king's poor health led to a debate about the succession and the likely survival of the monarchical system in Morocco.

hassium synthesized, radioactive element of the ▷transactinide series, symbol Hs, atomic number 108, relative atomic mass 265. It was first synthesized in 1984 by the Laboratory for Heavy Ion Research in Darmstadt, Germany. Its temporary name was unniloctium.

Hastert, Denny (1942–) Born J Dennis Hastert. US Republican politician, speaker of the House of Representatives from 1999. Known as 'the Coach' for his work as a high-school teacher and wrestling coach 1964–80, Hastert served in the Illinois General Assembly from 1980 until 1986, when he was first elected a representative to Congress for the 14th District of Illinois. He was appointed in 1993 as the House Republican representative on the White House Healthcare Reform Task Force, chaired by Hillary ▷Clinton, and chaired the Speaker's Steering Committee on Health and the Resource Group on Health. He was appointed Chief Deputy Whip for the Republicans in 1995, and was a member of the Commerce Committee and the Committee of Government Reform and Oversight.

Hastings resort in East Sussex, southeast England, on the English Channel; population (1996) 85,000. Fishing is an important activity; the town has Britain's largest fleet of beach-launched fishing boats and a new wholesale fish market. Other industries include engineering and the manufacture of scientific and aerospace-related instruments, plastics, electronics, and domestic appliances. William the Conqueror landed at Pevensey to the west and defeated Harold at the Battle of ▷Hastings in 1066.

Hastings, Warren (1732–1818) English colonial administrator. A protégé of Lord Clive, who established British rule in India, Hastings carried out major reforms, and became governor general of Bengal in 1774. Impeached for corruption on his return to England in 1785, he was acquitted in 1795.

Hastings, Battle of battle on 14 October 1066 at which William, Duke of Normandy (▷William (I) the Conqueror) defeated King ▷Harold II of England. Harold was killed leaving the throne open for William to complete the ▷Norman Conquest. The site is 10 km/6 mi inland from Hastings, at Senlac, Sussex; it is marked by Battle Abbey. The story of the battle is told in a sequence of scenes in the ▷Bayeux Tapestry.

Related Web site: Battle of Hastings http://battle1066.com/index.html

Hathor ('temenos (dwelling) of Horus') in ancient Egyptian mythology, a sky goddess; wife or mother of the sky god ▷Horus; goddess of dance, music, and love, (equivalent to Greek **Aphrodite**); also, goddess of desert cemeteries. She may appear as the great celestial cow, creator of the world; or as a human with cow's horns

HATHOR The statue of the Egyptian goddess of creation, Hathor (pronounced *Hat-hor*), found in the Temple of Hatshepsut at Dayr al-Bahri, Thebes, Egypt. *Image Bank*

and ears. Other variations include a hornlike hairstyle, or a headdress in the shape of a sun-disc with cow's horns. She was popular with women as their protector, and was later associated with the principal goddess ▷Isis whose headdress was indistinguishable.

Hatshepsut (c. 1473–c. 1458 BC) Queen (pharaoh) of ancient Egypt during the 18th dynasty. She was the daughter of Thutmose I, and the wife and half-sister of Thutmose II. Throughout his reign real power lay with Hatshepsut, and she continued to rule after his death, as regent for her nephew Thutmose III.

Hattersley, Roy Sydney George (1932–) British Labour politician and author. On the right wing of the Labour Party, he was prices secretary 1976–79, and deputy leader of the party 1983–1992. In 1994 he announced his retirement from active politics, and later expressed disagreement with some of the policies of the new party leadership, which he considered had swung too far to the right in its views on promoting income distribution through the taxation and welfare system.

Hausa member of a people living along the southern edge of the Sahara Desert, especially in northwestern Nigeria, southern Niger, and Dahomey, and numbering 9 million. The Hausa are Muslim farmers and skilled artisans, weavers, leatherworkers, potters, and metalworkers. Their language belongs to the Chadic subfamily of the Hamito-Semitic (Afro-Asiatic) language group.

Haussmann, Georges Eugène (1809–1891) Baron Haussmann. French administrator, financier, and civil servant. In 1853 he was made prefect of the Seine by Louis Napoleon who had vast schemes for the embellishment of Paris. Haussmann replanned medieval Paris 1853–70 to achieve the current city plan, with long wide boulevards and parks. The improvements transformed Paris, but their cost (which amounted to £34,000,000) and his authoritarianism led to considerable opposition, and in 1870 he was forced to resign.

Haute-Normandie (English **Upper Normandy**) coastal region of northwest France lying between Basse-Normandie and Picardy and bisected by the River Seine; area 12,300 sq km/ 4,750 sq mi; population (1999) 1,780,200. It comprises the *départements* of Eure and Seine-Maritime; its administrative centre is ▷Rouen. Ports include Le Havre, Dieppe and Fécamp. The area is fertile and has many beech forests. Industries include dairy-farming and fishing, cars are manufactured, and the region is a petrochemical centre.

Havana capital and port of Cuba, on the northwest coast of the island; population (1995 est) 2,219,000. Products include cigars and tobacco, sugar, coffee, and fruit. The old city centre is a world heritage site, and the oldest building in the city and in Cuba is La Fuerza, a fortress built in 1538.

History Founded on the south coast as **San Cristóbal de la Habana** by Spanish explorer Diego Velásquez in 1515, it was moved to its present site on a natural harbour in 1519. It became the capital of Cuba in the late 16th century. Taken by Anglo-American forces in 1762, it was returned to Spain in 1763 until independence in 1898. The blowing up of the US battleship *Maine* in the harbour that year began the ▷Spanish-American War. There is a university dating from 1721.

Havel, Václav (1936–) Czech dramatist and politician, president of Czechoslovakia 1989–92 and of the Czech Republic from 1993. His plays include *The Garden Party* (1963) and *Largo Desolato* (1985), about a dissident intellectual. Havel became widely known as a human-rights activist. He was imprisoned 1979–83 and again in 1989 for support of Charter 77, a human-rights manifesto. As president of Czechoslovakia he sought to preserve a united republic, but resigned in recognition of the breakup of the federation in 1992. In 1993 he became president of the newly independent Czech Republic. In December 1996 he underwent surgery for lung cancer but was re-elected president, by the Czech parliament, in January 1998.

Hawaii Pacific state of the USA. It is nicknamed the Aloha State. Hawaii was admitted to the Union in 1959 as the 50th US state. The only state not part of North America, Hawaii, variously described as part of Oceania or Polynesia, comprises a west-northwest–east-southeast oriented island chain 2,700km/1,700 mi in length, the east end of which lies some 3,400km/2,100 mi southwest of California. The chief islands are Hawaii (the largest), Maui, Kahoolawe, Oahu (the most densely populated), Lanai, Molokai, and Kauai. From the 6th century, the islands were a Polynesian kingdom. Captain James Cook, who called Hawaii 'the Sandwich Islands', arrived as the first known European in 1778. The Tropic of Cancer passes through the islands.

population (1995) 1,186,800 (34% of European descent, 25% Japanese, 14% Filipino, 12% Hawaiian, 6% Chinese)
area 16,800 sq km/6,485 sq mi **capital** ▷Honolulu on Oahu
towns and cities Hilo, Kailua, Kaneohe **industries and products** tourism is the chief source of income; other industries include sugar,

coffee, pineapples, macadamia nuts, orchids and other flowers, livestock, poultry, dairy goods, clothing
Related Web site: Best of Hawaii http://www.bestofhawaii.com/

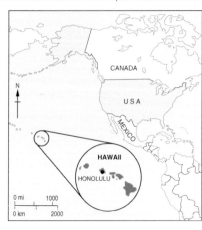

hawfinch European ▷finch, about 18 cm/7 in long. It feeds on berries and seeds, and can crack cherry stones with its large, powerful beak. The male bird has brown plumage, a black throat and black wings with a bold white shoulder stripe, a short white-tipped tail, and a broad band of grey at the back of the neck. (Species *Coccothraustes coccothraustes*, family Fringillidae, order Passeriformes.)

hawk any of a group of small to medium-sized birds of prey, belonging to the same family as eagles, kites, ospreys, and vultures. Hawks have short, rounded wings, a long tail, and keen eyesight; the ▷sparrow hawk and ▷goshawk are examples.

hawk person who believes in the use of military action rather than mediation as a means of solving a political dispute. The term first entered the political language of the USA during the 1960s, when it was applied metaphorically to those advocating continuation and escalation of the Vietnam War. Those with moderate, or even pacifist, views were known as ▷doves.

Hawke, Bob (Robert James Lee) (1929–) Australian Labor politician, prime minister 1983–91, on the right wing of the party. He was president of the Australian Council of Trade Unions 1970–80. He announced his retirement from politics in 1992.

Hawking, Stephen (William) (1942–) English physicist whose work in general ▷relativity – particularly gravitational field theory – led to a search for a quantum theory of gravity to explain ▷black holes and the ▷Big Bang, singularities that classical relativity theory does not adequately explain. His book *A Brief History of Time* (1988) gives a popular account of cosmology and became an international best-seller. He later co-wrote (with Roger Penrose) *The Nature of Space and Time* (1996).

Hawking's objective of producing an overall synthesis of quantum mechanics and relativity theory began around the time of the publication in 1973 of his seminal book *The Large Scale Structure of Space-Time*, written with G F R Ellis. His most remarkable result, published in 1974, was that black holes could in fact emit particles in the form of thermal radiation – the so-called **Hawking radiation**.

Hawkins, Coleman (Randolph) (1904–1969) US virtuoso tenor saxophonist. He was, until 1934, a soloist in the swing band led by Fletcher Henderson (1898–1952), and helped bring the jazz saxophone to prominence as a solo instrument.

hawk moth any member of a family of ▷moths with more than 1,000 species distributed throughout the world, but found mainly in tropical regions. (Family Sphingidae.)

HAWK MOTH A hawk moth *Batocnema coquereli* resting during daytime, in the rainforest.
K G Preston-Mafham/Premaphotos Wildlife

Hawks, Howard (Winchester) (1896–1977) US director, screenwriter, and producer. He made a wide range of classic films in virtually every American genre. Swift-moving and immensely accomplished, his films include the gangster movie *Scarface* (1932), the screwball comedy *Bringing Up Baby* (1938), the *film noir The Big Sleep* (1946), the musical comedy *Gentlemen Prefer Blondes* (1953), and the Western *Rio Bravo* (1959).

Despite the generic diversity of his work, his films are united by their common themes, their prioritization of story over all else, their celebration of community and friendship, and their restrained visual style (with the camera invariably placed at eye level). He regularly worked with the actors Cary Grant, Humphrey Bogart, and John Wayne. His films include *Twentieth Century* (1934), *Only Angels Have Wings* (1939), *His Girl Friday* (1940), *Sergeant York* (1941), *Ball of Fire* (1942), *To Have and Have Not* (1945), *Red River* (1948), and *Monkey Business* (1952).

Related Web site: Hawks, Howard http://www.reelclassics.com/ Directors/Hawks/hawks.htm

Hawksmoor, Nicholas (1661–1736) English architect. He was assistant to Christopher ▷Wren in designing various London churches and St Paul's Cathedral, and joint architect of Castle Howard and Blenheim Palace with John ▷Vanbrugh. His genius is displayed in a quirky and uncompromising style incorporating elements from both Gothic and classical sources.

After 1712 Hawksmoor completed six of the 50 new churches planned for London under the provisions made by the Fifty New Churches Act of 1711: St Alphege, Greenwich (1712–14); St Anne, Limehouse (1712–24); St George-in-the-East (1714–34); St Mary Woolnoth (1716–27); St George, Bloomsbury (1720–30); and Christ Church, Spitalfields (1714–29).

He worked for Wren in various capacities at Chelsea and Greenwich Hospitals, Winchester, Whitehall, Kensington and St James's Palaces. He also designed the quadrangle and hall of All Souls' College, Oxford (1729). The original west towers of Westminster Abbey, long attributed to Wren, were designed by Hawksmoor in 1734, and completed in 1745 after his death.

Haworth Parsonage home of the English novelists Charlotte, Emily, and Anne ▷Brontë. Their father, Patrick Brontë, was vicar of Haworth, a hillside village on the edge of the Yorkshire moors, from 1820 until his death in 1861. *Wuthering Heights*, *Jane Eyre*, and *Agnes Grey* were written here in 1847. The house was given to the Brontë Society in 1928 and is now a Brontë museum. Haworth is now part of the town of ▷Keighley.

hawthorn any of a group of shrubs or trees belonging to the rose family, growing abundantly in eastern North America, and also in Europe and Asia. All have alternate, toothed leaves and bear clusters of showy white, pink, or red flowers. Their small applelike fruits can be red, orange, blue, or black. Hawthorns are popular as ornamentals. (Genus *Crataegus*, family Rosaceae.)

Hawthorne, Nathaniel (1804–1864) US writer. He was the author of American literature's first great classic novel, *The Scarlet*

JOSEPH HAYDN Austrian composer Franz Joseph Haydn at the clavichord, as painted by Guttenbrunn. Haydn's studiously consistent arrangement of four movements within all his symphonies standardized the symphonic form. *The Art Archive/Private Collection/Eileen Tweedy*

Letter (1850). Set in 17th-century Puritan Boston, it tells the powerful allegorical story of a 'fallen woman' and her daughter who are judged guilty according to men's, not nature's, laws. He wrote three other novels, including *The House of the Seven Gables* (1851), and many short stories, a form he was instrumental in developing, including *Tanglewood Tales* (1853), classic Greek legends retold for children.

Hawthorne's fiction is marked by its haunting symbolism and its exploration of guilt, sin, and other complex moral and psychological issues. It had a profound effect on writers of his own time, notably his friend Herman Melville, and continues to influence writers.

Haydn, (Franz) Joseph (1732–1809) Austrian composer. He was a major exponent of the classical sonata form in his numerous chamber and orchestral works (he wrote more than 100 symphonies). He also composed choral music, including the oratorios *The Creation* (1798) and *The Seasons* (1801). He was the first great master of the string quartet, and was a teacher of Mozart and Beethoven. Haydn was employed by the Hungarian Esterházy family from 1761, and was responsible for all the musical entertainment at their palace. His work also includes operas, church music, and songs, and the 'Emperor's Hymn', adopted as the Austrian, and later the German, national anthem.

Hayek, Friedrich August von (1899–1992) Austrian economist who taught at the London School of Economics 1931–50. His *The Road to Serfdom* (1944) was a critical study of socialist trends in Britain. He was awarded the Nobel Prize for Economics in 1974 with Gunnar Myrdal for his analysis of the interdependence of economic, social, and institutional phenomena.

Hayes, Rutherford (Birchard) (1822–1893) 19th president of the USA 1877–81, a Republican. He was a major general on the Union side in the Civil War. During his presidency federal troops were withdrawn from the Southern states (after ▷Reconstruction) and the civil service was reformed.

Related Web site: Rutherford B Hayes – Nineteenth President 1877–1881 http://www.whitehouse.gov/WH/glimpse/presidents/ html/rh19.html

hay fever allergic reaction to pollen, causing sneezing, with inflammation of the nasal membranes and conjunctiva of the eyes. Symptoms are due to the release of ▷histamine. Treatment is by antihistamine drugs. An estimated 25% of Britons, 33% of Americans, and 40% of Australians suffer from hayfever.

Scientists prefer to call it **seasonal rhinitis** since it is not caused only by grass pollen but by that of flowers and trees as well; some people also react to airborne spores and moulds which are prevalent in autumn.

Hays Office film regulation body in the USA 1922–45. Officially known as the Motion Picture Producers and Distributors of America, it was created by the major film companies to improve the industry's image and provide internal regulation, including a strict moral code.

Hayworth, Rita (1918–1987) Stage name of Margarita Carmen Cansino. US dancer and film actor. She gave vivacious performances in 1940s musicals and played erotic roles in *Gilda* (1946) and *Affair in Trinidad* (1952). She was married to Orson Welles 1943–48 and appeared in his film *The Lady from Shanghai* (1948). She gave assured performances in *Pal Joey* (1957) and *Separate Tables* (1958).

hazardous waste waste substance, usually generated by industry, that represents a hazard to the environment or to people living or working nearby. Examples include radioactive wastes, acidic resins, arsenic residues, residual hardening salts, lead from car exhausts, mercury, nonferrous sludges, organic solvents, asbestos, chlorinated solvents, and pesticides. The cumulative effects of toxic waste can take some time to become apparent (anything from a few hours to many years), and pose a serious threat to the ecological stability of the planet; its economic disposal or recycling is the subject of research.

hazel any of a group of shrubs or trees that includes the European common hazel or cob (*C. avellana*), of which the filbert is the cultivated variety. North American species include the American hazel (*C. americana*). (Genus *Corylus*, family Corylaceae.)

Hazlitt, William (1778–1830) English essayist and critic. His work is characterized by invective, scathing irony, an intuitive critical sense, and a gift for epigram. His essays include 'Characters

HAZEL The hazel is a common plant in hedgerows and the shrub layer of lowland oakwoods. *Premaphotos Wildlife*

of Shakespeare's Plays' (1817), 'Lectures on the English Poets' (1818–19), 'English Comic Writers' (1819), and 'Dramatic Literature of the Age of Elizabeth' (1820).

Other works are *Table Talk* (1821–22); *The Spirit of the Age* (1825), literary studies in which he argues that the personality of the writer is germane to a criticism of what they write; and *Liber Amoris* (1823), in which he revealed aspects of his love life.

> **William Hazlitt**
> *When I am in the country I wish to vegetate like the country.*
> *Table Talk*, 'On Going a Journey'

H-bomb abbreviation for ▷hydrogen bomb.

HDTV abbreviation for ▷high-definition television.

headache pain felt within the skull. Most headaches are caused by stress or tension, but some may be symptoms of brain or ▷systemic disease, including ▷fever.

headland an area of land running out into the sea. Headlands are often high points on the coastline and may be made of more resistant rock than that in adjacent bays.

head louse parasitic insect that lives in human hair (see ▷louse).

headward erosion the backwards erosion of material at the source of a river or stream. Broken rock and soil at the source are carried away by the river, causing erosion to take place in the opposite direction to the river's flow. The resulting lowering of the land behind the source may, over time, cause the river to cut backwards into a neighbouring valley to 'capture' another river.

harmful/irritant   toxic

radioactive   explosive

flammable   corrosive

oxidizing/supports fire   biohazardous/infectious

environmentally dangerous

HAZARDOUS WASTE The internationally recognized symbols, warning of the potential dangers of handling certain substances.

Healey, Denis Winston (1917–) Baron Healey. British Labour politician. While secretary of state for defence 1964–70 he was in charge of the reduction of British forces east of Suez. He was chancellor of the Exchequer 1974–79. In 1976 he contested the party leadership, losing to James Callaghan, and again in 1980, losing to Michael Foot, to whom he was deputy leader 1980–83. In 1987 he resigned from the shadow cabinet.

health service government provision of medical care on a national scale.

Health service, UK In the UK, the National Health Service Act (1946) was largely the work of Aneurin ▷Bevan, Labour minister of health. It instituted a health service from July 1948 that sought to provide free medical, dental, and optical treatment as rights; see ▷United Kingdom, **nationalization and the welfare state**.

Successive governments, both Labour and Conservative, introduced charges for some services. The **National Health Service** (NHS) now includes hospital care, but limited fees are made for ordinary doctors' prescriptions, eye tests and spectacles, and dental treatment, except for children and people on very low incomes. A White Paper published 1989 by the Conservative government proposed legislation for decentralizing the control of hospitals and changes in general practice giving greater responsibilities to doctors to manage in general practice. Private health schemes such as BUPA are increasingly used in the UK.

The NHS employs about 1.25 million people, including part-timers, and in the financial year 2000–01 had a £54,200,000 million (2000–01) budget. It offers free health care to the population at a cost of 6% of the ▷GDP, compared with an average cost among developed countries of 7.6% of GDP. However, the number of available hospital beds in public hospitals decreased by 25% between 1971 and 1987, while the number of private hospital beds increased by 157%. The NHS managed to increase the number of patients treated during the same period by the use of new technology and faster recovery times from operations, so the fall in numbers of beds was not matched by a fall in the number of patients treated. On average, 317,000 beds are occupied in NHS hospitals. The number of frontline NHS staff (nurses and midwives) on hospital wards fell by 13%, or about 50,000, between 1989 and 1994, while the number of managers increased by 400%, or more than 18,300. The number of nurses in training fell by more than 19,000, almost a third, in the same period. The fall in numbers of nurses and midwives continued under the Labour government (from 1997), although schemes have been implemented to recruit and train more staff. Nurses have been recruited from countries such as the Philippines to fill the gaps in British hospitals during the 1990s. The rise in management posts reflects the increasing managerial style of the NHS introduced under the internal market system that followed the 1989 Conservative reforms. This was designed to ensure the maximum possible efficiency of patient care and use of resources in the NHS by introducing market economics to the system. Following their election in 1997, Labour set about dismantling these reforms and introducing their own ideas to improve the NHS.

According to a report released in June 2000 by the World Health Organization (WHO), the UK was ranked 18th in the world for overall health care among 191 countries. France was ranked first, Italy second, and the USA 37th. The rankings were based on the population's overall health, inequalities of health, how well the system performs, and how satisfied patients were with it, how people at different income levels are served, and how costs are distributed.

Related Web site: **NHS** http://www.nhs.uk

health, world the health of people worldwide is monitored by the ▷World Health Organization (WHO). Outside the industrialized world in particular, poverty and degraded environmental conditions mean that easily preventable diseases are widespread: WHO estimated in 1990 that 1 billion people, or 20% of the world's population, were diseased, in poor health, or malnourished. In North Africa and the Middle East, 25% of the population were ill.

Heaney, Seamus (Justin) (1939–) Irish poet and critic. Born near Castledawson, County Londonderry, he has written powerful verse about the political situation in Northern Ireland and reflections on Ireland's cultural heritage. Collections include *Death of a Naturalist* (1966), *Field Work* (1979), *The Haw Lantern* (1987), *The Spirit Level* (1996; Whitbread Book of the Year), and *Opened Ground: Poems 1966–1996* (1998). Critical works include *The Redress of Poetry* (1995). His *Beowulf: A New Translation* (1999), a modern version of the Anglo-Saxon epic, won the Whitbread Book of the Year award. He was professor of poetry at Oxford University 1989–94 and was awarded the Nobel Prize for Literature in 1995.

Heaney was educated at Queen's University, Belfast. His *Death of a Naturalist* was the first collection from a group of Ulster poets, including James Simmons, Derek Mahon, and Michael Longley, with whom he was associated. Heaney's early work, in this collection and in *Door into the Dark* (1969), was marked by a densely descriptive evocation of rural life. The poems of *Wintering Out* (1972) and *North* (1975) explore history and prehistory as a vehicle for oblique comment on the contemporary 'Troubles' of Northern Ireland. Later collections, including *Field Work* (1979), *Station Island* (1984), *The Haw Lantern* (1987), and *The Spirit Level* (1996), mix increasingly self-conscious political language with more private love-poetry and elegy, and display a continuing concern with the natural world, and with the wider responsibilities of poetry.

The technical mastery and linguistic and thematic richness of Heaney's work have gained an international audience, and exercised a powerful influence on contemporary poetry.

Related Web site: **Seamus Heaney** http://sunsite.unc.edu/dykki/poetry/heaney/heaney-cov.html

hearing aid any device to improve the hearing of partially deaf people. Hearing aids usually consist of a battery-powered transistorized microphone/amplifier unit and earpiece. Some miniaturized aids are compact enough to fit in the ear or be concealed in the frame of eyeglasses.

Hearst, William Randolph (1863–1951) US newspaper publisher, celebrated for his introduction of banner headlines, lavish illustration, and the sensationalist approach known as 'yellow journalism'. A campaigner in numerous controversies, and a strong isolationist, he was said to be the model for Citizen Kane in the 1941 film of that name by Orson Welles.

He was also a Hollywood film-maker (promoting the career of his long-time mistress Marian Davies), as well as an unsuccessful presidential candidate. He collected art treasures, antiques, zoo animals, and castles – one of which, San Simeon (Hearst Castle) in California, is a state museum and zoo.

heart muscular organ that rhythmically contracts to force blood around the body of an animal with a circulatory system. Annelid worms and some other invertebrates have simple hearts consisting of thickened sections of main blood vessels that pulse regularly. An earthworm has ten such hearts. Vertebrates have one heart. A fish heart has two chambers – the thin-walled atrium (once called the auricle) that expands to receive blood, and the thick-walled ventricle that pumps it out. Amphibians and most reptiles have two atria and one ventricle; birds and mammals have two atria and two ventricles. The beating of the heart is controlled by the autonomic nervous system and an internal control centre or pacemaker, the sinoatrial node.

The cardiac cycle The cardiac cycle is the sequence of events during one complete cycle of a heart beat. This consists of the simultaneous contraction of the two atria, a short pause, then the simultaneous contraction of the two ventricles, followed by a longer pause while the entire heart relaxes. The contraction phase is called

'systole' and the relaxation phase which follows is called 'diastole'. The whole cycle is repeated 70–80 times a minute under resting conditions.

When the atria contract, the blood in them enters the two relaxing ventricles, completely filling them. The mitral and tricuspid valves, which were open, now begin to shut and as they do so, they create vibrations in the heart walls and tendons, causing the first heart sound. The ventricles on contraction push open the pulmonary and aortic valves and eject blood into the respective vessels. The closed mitral and tricuspid valves prevent return of blood into the atria during this phase. As the ventricles start to relax, the aortic and pulmonary valves close to prevent backward flow of blood, and their closure causes the second heart sound. By now, the atria have filled once again and are ready to start contracting to begin the next cardiac cycle.

Related Web sites: **Circulatory System: Online Learning** http://library.thinkquest.org/25896/

heart attack (or myocardial infarction) sudden onset of gripping central chest pain, often accompanied by sweating and vomiting, caused by death of a portion of the heart muscle following obstruction of a coronary artery by thrombosis (formation of a blood clot). Half of all heart attacks result in death within the first two hours, but in the remainder survival has improved following the widespread use of thrombolytic (clot-buster) drugs.

heartburn burning sensation behind the breastbone (sternum). It results from irritation of the lower oesophagus (gullet) by excessively acid stomach contents, as sometimes happens during pregnancy and in cases of duodenal ulcer or obesity. It is often due to a weak valve at the entrance to the stomach that allows its contents to well up into the oesophagus.

heart–lung machine apparatus used during heart surgery to take over the functions of the heart and the lungs temporarily. It has a pump to circulate the blood around the body and is able to add oxygen to the blood and remove carbon dioxide from it. A heart–lung machine was first used for open-heart surgery in the USA in 1953.

heat form of energy possessed by a substance by virtue of the vibrational movement (kinetic energy) of its molecules or atoms. Heat energy is transferred by conduction, convection, and radiation. It always flows from a region of higher ▷temperature (heat intensity) to one of lower temperature. Its effect on a substance may be simply to raise its temperature, or to cause it to expand, melt (if a solid), vaporize (if a liquid), or increase its pressure (if a confined gas).

Measurement Quantities of heat are usually measured in units of energy, such as joules (J) or calories (cal). The specific heat of a substance is the ratio of the quantity of heat required to raise the temperature of a given mass of the substance through a given range of temperature to the heat required to raise the temperature of an equal mass of water through the same range. It is measured by a ▷calorimeter.

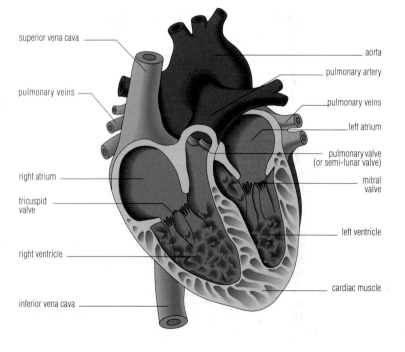

superior vena cava
aorta
pulmonary artery
pulmonary veins
pulmonary veins
left atrium
pulmonary valve (or semi-lunar valve)
right atrium
mitral valve
tricuspid valve
left ventricle
right ventricle
cardiac muscle
inferior vena cava

HEART The structure of the human heart. During an average lifetime, the human heart beats more than 2,000 million times and pumps 500 million l/ 110 million gal of blood. The average pulse rate is 70–72 beats per minute at rest for adult males, and 78–82 beats per minute for adult females.

Conduction, convection, and radiation Conduction is the passing of heat along a medium to neighbouring parts with no visible motion accompanying the transfer of heat; for example, when the whole length of a metal rod is heated when one end is held in a fire. Convection is the transmission of heat through a fluid (liquid or gas) in currents; for example, when the air in a room is warmed by a fire or radiator. Radiation is heat transfer by infrared rays. It can pass through a vacuum, travels at the same speed as light, and can be reflected and refracted; for example, heat reaches the Earth from the Sun by radiation. For the transformation of heat, see ▷thermodynamics.

heat capacity in physics, the quantity of heat required to raise the temperature of an object by one degree. The **specific heat capacity** of a substance is the heat capacity per unit of mass, measured in joules per kilogram per kelvin ($J\,kg^{-1}\,K^{-1}$).

heath in botany, any of a group of woody, mostly evergreen shrubs, including ▷heather, many of which have bell-shaped pendant flowers. They are native to Europe, Africa, and North America. (Common Old World genera *Erica* and *Calluna*, family Ericaceae.)

Heath, Edward (Richard George)

(1916–) British Conservative politician, party leader 1965–75. He was born at Broadstairs, Kent, and was educated at Chatham House Grammar School, Ramsgate, and Balliol College, Oxford. Heath was president of the Oxford Union in 1939. During World War II he was commissioned in the Royal Artillery 1940–46. In 1950 he entered politics and was elected Conservative MP for Bexley. As prime minister 1970–74 he took the UK into the European Community (EC) but was brought down by economic and industrial-relations crises at home. He was replaced as party leader by Margaret Thatcher in 1975, and became increasingly critical of her policies and her opposition to the UK's full participation in the EC. During John Major's administration, he continued his attacks on 'Eurosceptics' within the party. He retired from politics in 2001.

In 1990 he undertook a mission to Iraq in an attempt to secure the release of British hostages. He returned in 1993 to negotiate the release of three Britons held prisoner by Iraq.

heather low-growing evergreen shrub of the ▷heath family, common on sandy or acid soil. The common heather (*Calluna vulgaris*) is a carpet-forming shrub, growing up to 60 cm/24 in high and bearing pale pink-purple flowers. It is found over much of Europe and has been introduced to North America.

HEATHER In its heath and moorland habitats, the common heather, also called ling, provides an important source of both food and shelter for moorland birds such as the grouse and insects such as the fox moth. *Premaphotos Wildlife*

Heathrow major international airport to the west of London in the Greater London borough of Hounslow, approximately 24 km/14 mi from the city centre. Opened in 1946, it is one of the world's busiest airports, with four terminals. In 2001 the government gave the go-ahead for a fifth terminal. Heathrow was the target of three mortar attacks by the Irish Republican Army (IRA) in March 1994, all of which failed to detonate.

heat of reaction alternative term for ▷energy of reaction.

heat shield any heat-protecting coating or system, especially the coating (for example, tiles) used in spacecraft to protect the astronauts and equipment inside from the heat of re-entry when returning to Earth. Air friction can generate temperatures of up to 1,500°C/2,700°F on re-entry into the atmosphere.

heat storage any means of storing heat for release later. It is usually achieved by using materials that undergo phase changes, for example, Glauber's salt and sodium pyrophosphate, which melts at 70°C/158°F. The latter is used to store off-peak heat in the home: the salt is liquefied by cheap heat during the night and then freezes to give off heat during the day.

heatstroke (or **sunstroke**) rise in body temperature caused by excessive exposure to heat. Mild heatstroke is experienced as feverish lassitude, sometimes with simple fainting; recovery is prompt following rest and replenishment of salt lost in sweat. Severe heatstroke causes collapse akin to that seen in acute ▷shock, and is potentially lethal without prompt treatment, including cooling the body carefully and giving fluids to relieve dehydration. Death rates increase by half during heatwaves; heat stress is responsible for more deaths than any meteorological cause, including cyclones and floods.

heat treatment in industry, the subjection of metals and alloys to controlled heating and cooling after fabrication to relieve internal stresses and improve their physical properties. Methods include ▷annealing, ▷quenching, and ▷tempering.

heaven in Christianity and some other religions, the abode of God and the destination of the virtuous after death. In Islam, heaven is seen as a paradise of material delights, though such delights are generally accepted as being allegorical.

heavy metal in music, a style of rock characterized by histrionic guitar solos and a macho swagger. Heavy metal developed out of the hard rock of the late 1960s and early 1970s, was performed by such groups as ▷Led Zeppelin and Deep Purple (formed in 1968), and enjoyed a resurgence in the late 1980s. Bands include Van Halen (formed 1974), Def Leppard (formed 1977), and Guns n' Roses (formed 1987).

heavy water (or **deuterium oxide**) D_2O water containing the isotope deuterium instead of hydrogen (relative molecular mass 20 as opposed to 18 for ordinary water).

Its chemical properties are identical with those of ordinary water, but its physical properties differ slightly. It occurs in ordinary water in the ratio of about one part by mass of deuterium to 5,000 parts by mass of hydrogen, and can be concentrated by electrolysis, the ordinary water being more readily decomposed by this means than the heavy water. It has been used in the nuclear industry because it can slow down fast neutrons, thereby controlling the chain reaction.

Hebei (or **Hopei**, **Hopeh**, or **Chihli**) province of north China, bounded to the north by Inner Mongolia, to the northeast by Liaoning, to the east by the Bohai Gulf, to the south by Shandong and Henan, and to the west by Shanxi; area 185,900 sq km/71,800 sq mi; population (1996) 64,840,000. The capital is ▷Shijiazhuang; other major cities are Baoding, Tangshan, Handan, and Zhangjiakou. The province includes the special municipalities of Beijing and Tianjin. The main industries are textiles, coal, iron, steel, and oil; agricultural production is based on winter wheat, barley, maize, and cotton.

Hebrew member of the Semitic people who lived in Palestine at the time of the Old Testament and who traced their ancestry to ▷Abraham of Ur, a city of Sumer.

Hebrew Bible the sacred writings of Judaism (some dating from as early as 1200 BC), called by Christians the ▷Old Testament. It includes the Torah (the first five books, ascribed to Moses), historical and prophetic books, and psalms, originally written in Hebrew and later translated into Greek (Septuagint) and other languages.

Hebrew language member of the ▷Afro-Asiatic language family spoken in Southwest Asia by the ancient Hebrews, sustained for many centuries in the ▷Diaspora as the liturgical language of Judaism, and revived by the late-19th-century Haskalah intellectual movement, which spread modern European culture among Jews. The language developed in the 20th century as Israeli Hebrew, the national language of the state of Israel. It is the original language of the Old Testament of the Bible.

Hebrides group of more than 500 islands (fewer than 100 inhabited) off the west coast of mainland Scotland; total area 2,900 sq km/1,120 sq mi. The Hebrides were settled by Scandinavians during the 6th–9th centuries and passed under Norwegian rule from about 890 to 1266.

Related Web site: Virtual Hebrides – Trusadh nan Eilean http://www.hebrides.com/

Hebron (Arabic **El Khalil**) city on the west bank of the Jordan, occupied by Israel in 1967; population (1996) 120,500. The population is mainly Arab Muslim, but just outside the city is a large Israeli settlement called Qiryat Arba. Industries include leather, stone cutting, and ceramics. Hebron experienced frequent front-line confrontation between Israelis and Arabs in the ▷Intifada and throughout the Israel–Palestine peace process.

Hecate (Greek 'worker from afar') in Greek mythology, the goddess of the underworld and magic arts. Her association with night led to her identification with the goddesses ▷Selene and ▷Artemis. She is first mentioned by Hesiod as having universal power to confer wealth and all the blessings of daily life. Ovid depicted her in *Fasti* with three bodies and heads, standing back-to-back to see in three directions.

hectare metric unit of area equal to 100 ares or 10,000 square metres (2.47 acres), symbol ha.

Trafalgar Square, London's only metric square, was laid out as one hectare.

Hector in Greek mythology, a Trojan prince; son of King Priam and Hecuba, husband of ▷Andromache, and father of Astyanax. He was the foremost warrior in the siege of ▷Troy until killed by the Greek hero ▷Achilles.

hedge (or **hedgerow**) row of closely planted shrubs or low trees, generally acting as a land division and windbreak. Hedges also serve as a source of food and as a refuge for wildlife, and provide a ▷habitat not unlike the understorey of a natural forest.

HEDGE A traditionally laid hedge, in Alcester, Warwickshire, England. Many ancient hedgerows have been destroyed as a result of increasing mechanization and changes in farming practices. *K G Preston-Mafham/ Premaphotos Wildlife*

hedgehog insectivorous mammal native to Europe, Asia, and Africa. The body, including the tail, is 30 cm/1 ft long. It is greyish brown in colour, has a piglike snout, and its back and sides are covered with sharp spines. When threatened it rolls itself into a ball bristling with spines. Hedgehogs feed on insects, slugs, mice, frogs, young birds, and carrion. Long-eared hedgehogs and desert hedgehogs are placed in different genera. (Genus *Erinaceus*, family Erinaceidae, order Insectivora.)

Hedgehogs normally shelter by day and go out at night. They find food more by smell and sound than by sight. The young are born in the late spring or early summer, and are blind, helpless, and covered with soft spines. For about a month they feed on their mother's milk, after which she teaches them to find their own food. In the autumn, hedgehogs make a nest of leaves and moss in the roots of a tree or in a hole in the ground and hibernate until spring.

There is concern for the survival of hedgehogs in the wild in Europe.

hedge sparrow another name for the ▷dunnock, a small European bird.

hedonism ethical theory that pleasure or happiness is, or should be, the main goal in life. Hedonist sects in ancient Greece were the ▷Cyrenaics, who held that the pleasure of the moment is the only human good, and the ▷Epicureans, who advocated the pursuit of pleasure under the direction of reason. Modern hedonistic philosophies, such as those of the British philosophers Jeremy

Bentham and J S Mill, regard the happiness of society, rather than that of the individual, as the aim.

Hefei (or **Hofei** or **Luzhou**) capital of ▷Anhui province, eastern China; population (1994) 1,126,600. Once just a trading hub for agricultural products, especially rice, it is now a centre of heavy industry. Products include textiles, chemicals, steel, electronics, and domestic appliances.

Hegel, Georg Wilhelm Friedrich (1770–1831) German philosopher who conceived of mind and nature as two abstractions of one indivisible whole, Spirit. His system, which is a type of ▷idealism, traces the emergence of Spirit in the logical study of concepts and the process of world history.

For Hegel, concepts unfold, and in unfolding they generate the reality that is described by them. To understand reality is to understand our concepts, and vice versa. The development of a concept involves three stages, which he calls **dialectic**. The dialectic moves from the thesis, or indeterminate concept (for example, a thing in space), to the antithesis, or determinate concept (for example, an animal), and then to the synthesis (for example, a cat), which is the resolution of what Hegel thinks is the contradiction between the indeterminate and determinate concepts. As logic, Hegel's dialectic is worthless. As an account of how intellectual and social development occurs, it is shrewd.

Georg Hegel

The English have undertaken the weighty responsibility of being the missionaries of civilization to the world . . .

The Philosophy of History

Hegel's works include *The Phenomenology of Spirit* (1807), *Encyclopaedia of the Philosophical Sciences* (1817), and *Philosophy of Right* (1821).

Related Web site: Hegel, Georg Wilhelm Friedrich http://plato.stanford.edu/entries/hegel/

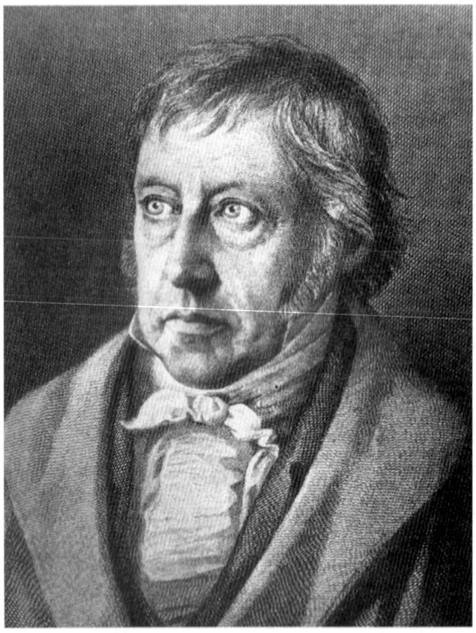

GEORG HEGEL The German philosopher Georg Hegel in middle age. *Image Bank*

hegemony (Greek *hegemonia* 'authority') political dominance of one power over others in a group in which all are supposedly equal. The term was first used for the dominance of Athens over the other Greek city states, later applied to Prussia within Germany, and, in more recent times, to the USA and the USSR with regard to the rest of the world.

Hegira flight of the prophet Muhammad (▷Hijrah).

Heian in Japanese history, the period 794–1185, from the foundation of Kyoto as the new capital to the seizure of power by the Minamoto clan. The cut-off date may also be given as 1186, 1192, or 1200. The Heian period was the golden age of Japanese literature and of a highly refined culture at court; see also ▷Japanese art.

Heidegger, Martin (1889–1976) German philosopher. He believed that Western philosophy had 'forgotten' the fundamental question of the 'meaning of being' and, in *Sein und Zeit/Being and Time* (1927), analysed the different types of being appropriate to people and to things in general. He lectured and wrote extensively on German and Greek philosophy, and in the later part of his career focussed his attention on the nature of language and technology. His work was an important influence upon the existentialist philosophy of Jean-Paul Sartre.

Heidegger was born in Messkirsch, Baden, Germany, and was educated at the University of Freiburg, where he studied theology and then philosophy, with the phenomenologist Edmund ▷Husserl. He taught mainly at the University of Freiburg and, in 1933, when he was made University Rector, gave an inaugural address in which he praised the 'inner truth and greatness' of Hitler's National Socialist Party. In the same year he became a party member, and, though he resigned from the party and the rectorate ten months later, was subsequently banned from university teaching from the end of World War II until 1951.

Related Web site: Heidegger, Martin http://www.regent.edu/acad/schcom/rojc/mdic/martin1.html

Heidelberg city in Baden-Württemberg, Germany, on the River Neckar, 19 km/12 mi southeast of Mannheim; population (1995) 138,400. Industries include publishing, brewing and the manufacture of tobacco products and optics. It is a major tourist centre. Heidelberg University, the oldest in Germany, was established in 1386. The city is overlooked by the ruins of its 13th–17th-century castle, standing 100 m/330 ft above the river.

Heidelberg School group of Australian Impressionist artists (including Tom Roberts, Arthur Streeton, and Charles Conder) working near the village of Heidelberg in Melbourne in the 1880s–90s. The school had its most famous exhibition 1889, called the '9 by 5', from the size of the cigar-box lids used.

Heifetz, Jascha (1901–1987) Russian-born US violinist. He was one of the great virtuosos of the 20th century. He first performed at the age of five, and before he was 17 had played in most European capitals, and in the USA, where he settled in 1917. He popularized a clear, unemotional delivery suited to radio and recordings.

Heike alternative name for ▷Taira, an ancient Japanese clan.

Heilongjiang (or **Heilungkiang**) province of northeast China, bordered to the north and east by Russia, to the south by Jilin, and to the northwest by Inner Mongolia; area 463,600 sq km/178,950 sq mi; population (1996) 37,280,000. The capital is ▷Harbin; other main cities are Qiqihar, Hegang, and Jiamusi. China's largest oilfield is located in the province, at Daqing; other industries are engineering, food processing, timber and wood products, building materials, and ice-skates. Agriculture is based on maize, sugar beet, dairy farming, and sheep rearing.

Heine, Heinrich (Christian Johann) (1797–1856) German Romantic poet and journalist. He wrote *Reisebilder* (1826–31), blending travel writing and satire, and *Das Buch der Lieder/The Book of Songs* (1827). Disillusioned by undercurrents of anti-Semitism and antiliberal censorship, he severed his ties with Germany and from 1831 lived mainly in Paris. His *Neue Gedichte/New Poems* appeared in 1844. He excelled in both the Romantic lyric and satire. Franz Schubert and Robert Schumann set many of his lyrics to music.

His first volume of verse, *Gedichte/Poems*, appeared 1821, followed by *Lyrisches Intermezzo* (1823). In Paris he wrote penetrating political essays and turned towards satire; for example, *Deutschland* (1844), a political satire in verse. His *Atta Troll* (1847) has been described as 'the swansong of Romanticism'.

Heisenberg, Werner (Karl) (1901–1976) German physicist who developed ▷quantum theory and formulated the ▷uncertainty principle, which places absolute limits on the achievable accuracy of measurement. He was awarded the Nobel Prize for Physics in 1932 for his creation of quantum mechanics, work he carried out when only 24.

Heisenberg was concerned not to try to picture what happens inside the atom but to find a mathematical system that explained it. His starting point was the spectral lines given by hydrogen, the simplest atom. Assisted by Max ▷Born, Heisenberg presented his ideas in 1925 as a system called **matrix mechanics**. He obtained the frequencies of the lines in the hydrogen spectrum by mathematical treatment of values within matrices or arrays. His work was the first precise mathematical description of the workings of the atom and with it Heisenberg is regarded as founding quantum mechanics, which seeks to explain atomic structure in mathematical terms. Heisenberg also was able to predict from studies of the hydrogen spectrum that hydrogen exists in two allotropes – ortho-hydrogen and para-hydrogen – in which the two nuclei of the atoms in a hydrogen molecule spin in the same or opposite directions respectively. The ▷allotropes were discovered in 1929. In 1927 Heisenberg made the discovery of the

Werner Karl Heisenberg

Science clears the fields on which technology can build.

Attributed remark

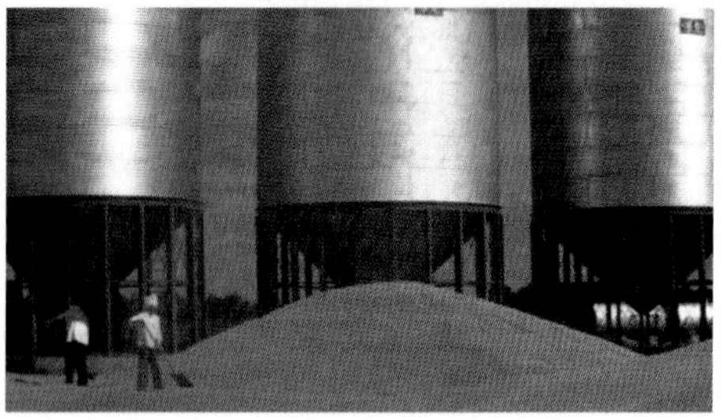

HEILONGJIANG Grain stores in Heilongjiang, in the wheat-growing area of the north of China. *Image Bank*

uncertainty principle, for which he is best known. The uncertainty principle states that there is a theoretical limit to the precision with which a particle's position and momentum can be measured. In other words, it is impossible to specify precisely both the position and the simultaneous momentum (mass multiplied by velocity) of a particle. There is always a degree of uncertainty in either, and as one is determined with greater precision, the other can only be found less exactly. Multiplying together the uncertainties of the position and momentum yields a value approximately equal to ▷Planck's constant. The idea that the result of an action can be expressed only in terms of the probability of a certain effect was revolutionary, and it discomforted even Albert Einstein, but is generally accepted today. In 1927 Heisenberg used the Pauli exclusion principle, which states that no two electrons can have identical sets of quantum numbers the same, to show that ferromagnetism (the ability of some materials to acquire magnetism in the presence of an external magnetic field) is caused by electrostatic interaction between the electrons.

Related Web site: Heisenberg, Werner Karl http://www-groups.dcs.st-and.ac.uk/history/Mathematicians/Heisenberg.html

Hejaz (or **Hedjaz** or **Al Hedjaz**, or **Hijāz** or **Al Hijāz**) historic region of Saudi Arabia, on the Red Sea; area about 290,000 sq km/111,970 sq mi. A former independent kingdom, it merged in 1932 with Nejd to form ▷Saudi Arabia. Historically its principal city has been ▷Mecca. The other main cities are ▷Jiddah, on the coast, Taif, a mountain resort at an altitude of 1,800 m/5,905 ft, and ▷Medina.

Hekmatyar, Gulbuddin (1949–) Afghani leader of the Mujahedin (Islamic fundamentalist guerrillas), prime minister 1993–94 and 1996. Strongly anticommunist and leading the Hezb-i-Islami (Islamic Party) faction, he resisted the takeover of Kabul by moderate Mujahedin forces in April 1992 and refused to join the interim administration, continuing to bombard the city until being driven out. In June 1993, under a peace agreement with President Burhanuddin Rabbani, Hekmatyar was re-admitted to the city as prime minister, but his forces renewed their attacks on Kabul during 1994. He was subsequently dismissed from the premiership, but returned to Kabul in June 1996, when he became combined prime minister, defence minister, and finance minister. However, in September he was driven out of Kabul by the Talibaan (fundamentalist student army) who had seized control of much of Afghanistan.

Helen in Greek mythology, the most beautiful of women; daughter of ▷Leda and Zeus (transformed as a swan). She was abducted as a young girl by Theseus, but rescued by her brothers ▷Castor and Pollux (Greek Polydeuces). Helen married ▷Menelaus, king of Sparta, and bore him Hermione, but during his absence was seduced by ▷Paris, prince of Troy; their flight precipitated the Trojan wars.

Helicon mountain in central Greece, on which was situated a spring and a sanctuary sacred to the ▷Muses.

helicopter powered aircraft that achieves both lift and propulsion by means of a rotary wing, or rotor, on top of the fuselage. It can take off and land vertically, move in any direction, or remain stationary in the air. It can be powered by piston or jet engine. The autogiro was a precursor.

The rotor of a helicopter has two or more blades of aerofoil cross-section like an aeroplane's wings. Lift and propulsion are achieved by angling the blades as they rotate. Experiments using the concept of helicopter flight date from the early 1900s, with the first successful liftoff and short flight in 1907. Ukrainian–US engineer Igor ▷Sikorsky built the first practical single-rotor craft in the USA in 1939.

A single-rotor helicopter must also have a small tail rotor to counter the torque, or tendency of the body to spin in the opposite

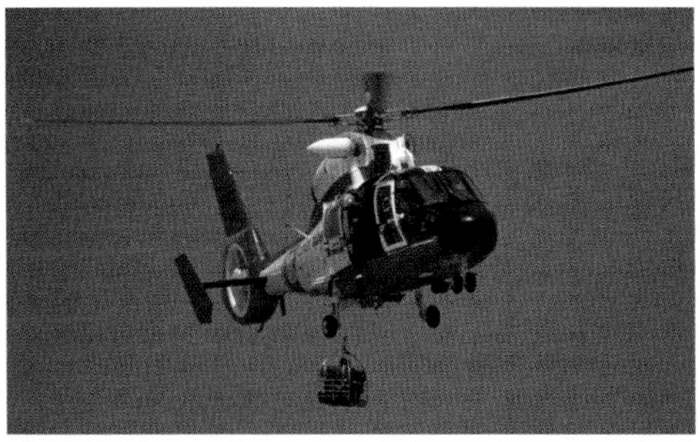

HELICOPTER The US Coastguard HH-65 Dauphin rescue helicopter. *Image Bank*

direction to the main rotor. Twin-rotor helicopters, like the Boeing Chinook, have their rotors turning in opposite directions to prevent the body from spinning. Helicopters are now widely used in passenger service, rescue missions on land and sea, police pursuits and traffic control, fire-fighting, and agriculture. In war they carry troops and equipment into difficult terrain, make aerial reconnaissance and attacks, and carry the wounded to aid stations. A fire-fighting helicopter was tested in Japan in 1996, designed to reach skyscrapers beyond the reach of fire-engine ladders.

Naval carriers are increasingly being built, with helicopters with depth charges and homing torpedoes being guided to submarine or surface targets beyond the carrier's attack range. The helicopter may also use dunking ▷sonar to find targets beyond the carrier's radar horizon. As many as 30 helicopters may be used on large carriers, in combination with V/STOL aircraft, such as the Harrier.

Related Web site: Helicopter Aviation http://www.ai.mit.edu/projects/cbcl/heli/

Heliopolis ancient Egyptian centre (the biblical **On**) of the worship of the sun god Ra, northeast of Cairo and near the village of Matariah. Heliopolis was also the Greek name for ▷Baalbek.

Helios (Roman **Sol**) in Greek mythology, the god of the Sun; a ▷Titan who drove the Sun's chariot across the sky. He was the father of ▷Phaethon, who almost set the Earth alight. From the 5th century BC, Helios was identified with the god ▷Apollo.

heliotrope decorative plant belonging to the borage family, with distinctive spikes of blue, lilac, or white flowers, including the Peruvian or cherry pie heliotrope (*H. peruvianum*). (Genus *Heliotropium*, family Boraginaceae.)

helium (Greek *helios* 'Sun') colourless, odourless, gaseous, non-metallic element, symbol He, atomic number 2, relative atomic mass 4.0026. It is grouped with the ▷inert gases, is nonreactive, and forms no compounds. It is the second most abundant element (after hydrogen) in the universe, and has the lowest boiling (−268.9°C/−452°F) and melting points (−272.2°C/−458°F) of all the elements. It is present in small quantities in the Earth's atmosphere from gases issuing from radioactive elements (from ▷alpha decay) in the Earth's crust; after hydrogen it is the second lightest element.

Helium is a component of most stars, including the Sun, where the nuclear-fusion process converts hydrogen into helium with the production of heat and light. It is obtained by compression and fractionation of naturally occurring gases. It is used for inflating balloons and as a dilutant for oxygen in deep-sea breathing systems. Liquid helium is used extensively in low-temperature physics (cryogenics).

helix in mathematics, a three-dimensional curve resembling a spring, corkscrew, or screw thread. It is generated by a line that encircles a cylinder or cone at a constant angle.

hell in various religions, a place of posthumous punishment. In Hinduism, Buddhism, and Jainism, hell is a transitory stage in the progress of the soul, but in Christianity and Islam it is eternal (▷purgatory is transitory). Judaism does not postulate such punishment.

hellebore poisonous European ▷herbaceous plant belonging to the buttercup family. The stinking hellebore (*H. foetidus*) has greenish flowers early in the spring. (Genus *Helleborus*, family Ranunculaceae.)

helleborine one of several temperate Old World orchids, including the marsh helleborine (*E. palustris*) and the hellebore orchid (*E. helleborine*) introduced to North America. (Genera *Epipactis* and *Cephalanthera*, family Orchidaceae.)

Hellene (Greek *Hellas* 'Greece') alternative name for a Greek.

Hellenic period (from *Hellas*, Greek name for Greece) classical period of ancient Greek civilization, from the first Olympic Games in 776 BC until the death of Alexander the Great in 323 BC.

Hellenistic period period in Greek civilization from the death of Alexander in 323 BC until the accession of the Roman emperor Augustus in 27 BC. Alexandria in Egypt was the centre of culture and commerce during this period, and Greek culture spread throughout the Mediterranean region and the near East.

Heller, Joseph (1923–1999) US novelist. He drew on his experiences in the US air force in World War II to write his best-selling *Catch-22* (1961), satirizing war, the conspiracy of bureaucratic control, and the absurdism of history. A film based on the book appeared in 1970.

Hellespont former name of the ▷Dardanelles, the strait that separates Europe from Asia.

Hellman, Lillian Florence (1907–1984) US dramatist. Her work is concerned with contemporary political and social issues. *The Children's Hour* (1934) on accusations of lesbianism, *The Little Foxes* (1939) on industrialists, and *Toys in the Attic* (1960) are all examples of a social critique cast in the form of the 'well-made play'. In the 1950s she was summoned to appear before the House Committee on Un-American Activities.

> **Lillian Hellman**
> *Cynicism is an unpleasant way of saying the truth.*
> *The Little Foxes*

Helmand longest river in Afghanistan. Rising in the Hindu Kush, west of Kabul, it flows southwest for 1,125 km/703 mi before entering the marshland surrounding Lake Saberi on the Iranian frontier.

Helmont, Jan Baptist van (1579–1644) Flemish chemist and physician. Helmont was the first to realize that there are gases other than air, and established the present scientific sense of the word 'gas' (from Greek *cháos*). He also investigated the chemical properties of the fluids of the human body. His chief work, *Ortus medicinae*, was published by his son in 1648.

Héloïse (1101–1164) Abbess of Paraclete in Champagne, France, correspondent and lover of ▷Abelard. She became deeply interested in intellectual study in her youth and was impressed by the brilliance of Abelard, her teacher, whom she secretly married.

After her affair with Abelard, and the birth of a son, Astrolabe, she became a nun in 1129, and with Abelard's assistance, founded a nunnery at Paraclete. Her letters show her strong and pious character and her devotion to Abelard.

Helpmann, Robert Murray (1909–1986) Australian dancer, choreographer, and actor. The leading male dancer with the Sadler's Wells Ballet, London 1933–50, he partnered Margot ▷Fonteyn in the 1940s. He was knighted in 1968.

Helsingfors Swedish name for ▷Helsinki, the capital of Finland.

Helsinki (Swedish **Helsingfors**) capital and port of Finland; population (1994) 516,000. Industries include shipbuilding, engineering, and textiles. The port is kept open by icebreakers in winter.

Helsinki was founded in 1550 by King Gustavus Vasa of Sweden, north of its present location. After Finland was ceded to Russia in 1809, Helsinki became capital of the grand duchy in 1812 and remained the capital after independence in 1917. The city contains the parliament house, an 18th-century cathedral, many buildings by the German-born architect Carl Ludwig Engel of the early 19th century, and many in national Romantic style from around 1900, including the railway station by Eliel Saarinen.

Helsinki Conference international meeting in 1975 at which 35 countries, including the USSR and the USA, attempted to reach agreement on cooperation in security, economics, science, technology, and human rights. This established the Conference on Security and Cooperation in Europe, which is now known as the Organization for Security and Cooperation in Europe.

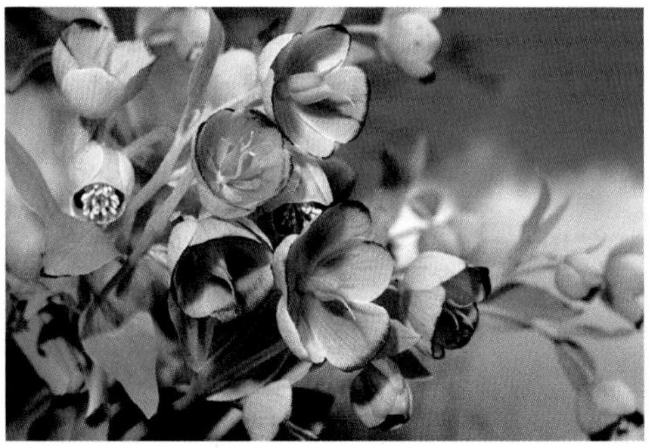

HELLEBORE The stinking hellebore *Helleborus foetidus* is one of around 20 known species, all of which thrive in rich, chalk soils and are native to Europe and W Asia. The petalloid sepals assume the function of petals, which are absent in the hellebore. *Premaphotos Wildlife*

Helvetia region, corresponding to western Switzerland, occupied by the Celtic Helvetii 1st century BC–5th century AD. In 58 BC Caesar repulsed their invasion of southern Gaul at Bibracte (near Autun) and Helvetia became subject to Rome. Helvetian is another word for Swiss.

Hemingway, Ernest (Miller) (1899–1961) US writer. War, bullfighting, and fishing are used symbolically in his work to represent honour, dignity, and primitivism – prominent themes in his short stories and novels, which include *A Farewell to Arms* (1929), *For Whom the Bell Tolls* (1941), and *The Old Man and the Sea* (1952; Pulitzer prize). His deceptively simple writing style attracted many imitators. He was awarded the Nobel Prize for Literature in 1954.

He became a journalist and was wounded while serving on a volunteer ambulance crew in Italy in World War I. In 1921 he settled in Paris, where he met the writers Gertrude ▷Stein and Ezra ▷Pound. His style was influenced by Stein, who also introduced him to bullfighting, a theme in his first novel, *Fiesta (The Sun Also Rises)* (1927), and the memoir *Death in the Afternoon* (1932). *A Farewell to Arms* deals with wartime experiences on the Italian front, and *For Whom the Bell Tolls* has a Spanish Civil War setting. He served as war correspondent both in that conflict and in Europe during World War II. His last years were spent mainly in Cuba. He committed suicide.

Related Web site: Hemingway, Ernest http://www.lostgeneration.com/hrc.htm

hemlock plant belonging to the carrot family, native to Europe, western Asia, and North Africa. It grows up to 2 m/6 ft high and produces delicate clusters of small white flowers. The whole plant, especially the root and fruit, is poisonous, causing paralysis of the nervous system. The name 'hemlock' is also given to some North American and Asiatic conifers (genus *Tsuga*) belonging to the pine family. (*Conium maculatum*, family Umbelliferae.)

hemp annual plant originally from Asia, now cultivated in most temperate countries for the fibres produced in the outer layer of the stem, which are used in ropes, twines, and, occasionally, in a type of linen or lace. The drug ▷cannabis is obtained from certain varieties of hemp. (*Cannabis sativa*, family Cannabaceae.)

Henan (or **Honan**) province of east central China, bounded to the north by Hebei, to the east by Shandong and Anhui, to the south by Hubei, and to the west by Shaanxi and Shanxi provinces; area 167,000 sq km/64,500 sq mi; population (1996) 91,720,000. The capital is ▷Zhengzhou; other major cities are Luoyang, Kaifeng, and Anyang. The main industries are coal, oil, textiles, cement, glass, and fertilizers. Agricultural products are cereals, cotton, fruit, tobacco, and peanuts.

henbane poisonous plant belonging to the nightshade family, found on waste ground throughout most of Europe and western Asia. It is a branching plant, up to 80 cm/31 in high, with hairy leaves and a sickening smell. The yellow flowers are bell-shaped. Henbane is used in medicine as a source of the drugs hyoscyamine and scopolamine. (*Hyoscyamus niger*, family Solanaceae.)

Hendrix, Jimi (James Marshall) (1942–1970) US rock guitarist, songwriter, and singer. He was legendary for his virtuoso experimental technique and flamboyance. *Are You Experienced?* (1967) was his first album. His performance at the 1969 Woodstock festival included a memorable version of *The Star-Spangled Banner* and is recorded in the film *Woodstock* (1970). He greatly expanded the vocabulary of the electric guitar and influenced both rock and jazz musicians.

Hendry, Stephen (1969–) Scottish snooker player who in 1990 became the youngest ever world champion at the age of 21 years 106 days. He won the title five years in succession, an unprecedented achievement in modern snooker. The world number one from 1990 to 1998, he has won more ranking event tournaments than any other player. He has also made a record seven maximum breaks of 147 in competition. He was awarded the MBE in 1994.

Hengist (died *c.* 488) Legendary leader, with his brother Horsa, of the Jutes, who originated in Jutland and settled in Kent about 450, the first Anglo-Saxon settlers in Britain.

henna small shrub belonging to the loosestrife family, found in Iran, India, Egypt, and North Africa. The leaves and young twigs are ground to a powder, mixed to a paste with hot water, and applied to the fingernails and hair to give an orange-red hue. The colour may then be changed to black by applying a preparation of indigo. (*Lawsonia inermis*, family Lythraceae.)

Henrietta Maria (1609–1669) Queen of England 1625–49. The daughter of Henry IV of France, she married ▷Charles I of England in 1625. By encouraging him to aid Roman Catholics and make himself an absolute ruler, she became highly unpopular and was exiled 1644–60 during the English Civil War. She returned to England at the Restoration but retired to France in 1665.

Henry Born Henry Charles Albert David. Prince of the UK (see ▷Harry).

Henry eight kings of England:

Henry I (1068–1135) King of England from 1100. Youngest son of William the Conqueror, he succeeded his brother William II. He won the support of the Saxons by marrying a Saxon princess, Matilda, daughter of Malcolm III of Scotland. An able administrator, he established a system of travelling judges and a professional bureaucracy, notably the setting up of the Exchequer as a formal government department to deal with the crown's financial matters (the chancellor of the Exchequer is still the government minister in charge of the Treasury in Britain). Henry quarrelled with St ▷Anselm, the archbishop of Canterbury, who claimed that the king had no right to invest bishops to vacant sees. For a while, Anselm was forced into exile, but in the end Henry had to concede defeat.

Henry's only legitimate son, William, was drowned in 1120, and Henry tried to settle the succession on his daughter ▷Matilda. However, Matilda was unpopular and the throne was taken by Henry's nephew Stephen who, towards the end of his reign, agreed to adopt Matilda's son Henry (later Henry II) as his heir.

Henry II (1133–1189) King of England from 1154. The son of ▷Matilda and Geoffrey V, Count of Anjou, he succeeded King ▷Stephen (*c.* 1097–1154). He brought order to England after the chaos of Stephen's reign, curbing the power of the barons and reforming the legal system. His attempt to bring the church courts under control had to be abandoned after the murder of Thomas à ▷Becket, archbishop of Canterbury, in 1170. The English conquest of Ireland began during Henry's reign. On several occasions his sons rebelled, notably 1173–74. Henry was succeeded by his son Richard (I) the Lionheart.

Henry was lord of Scotland, Ireland, and Wales, and Count of Anjou, Brittany, Poitou, Normandy, Maine, and Gascony. He claimed Aquitaine through marriage to the heiress ▷Eleanor of Aquitaine in 1152. Henry's many French possessions caused him to live for more than half his reign outside England. This made it essential for him to establish a judicial and administrative system which would work during his absence. Before the reign of Henry II, execution of the law was the job of a number of different courts – the shire courts for major offences, the hundred courts for petty crimes, the manor courts for village issues, and the church courts for the clergy. Trials still might involve trial by battle or by ordeal. In 1166 Henry published the Assize of Clarendon, which established regular visits to towns by royal justices 'on eyre' and trial by a 'jury' of 12 men who – unlike in modern courts, where the jury is required to judge the evidence – were called upon to give evidence.

Henry's parallel attempt to bring the medieval church courts under royal control, in a collection of decrees known as the Constitutions of ▷Clarendon (1164), had to be dropped after the murder of Becket. Initially his chancellor and friend, Becket was persuaded to become archbishop of Canterbury in 1162 in the hope that he would help the king curb the power of the ecclesiastical courts. However, once consecrated, Becket felt bound to defend church privileges, and he was murdered in Canterbury Cathedral in 1170 by four knights of the king's household.

Henry III (1207–1272) King of England from 1216, when he succeeded John, but the royal powers were exercised by a regency until 1232, and by two French nobles, Peter des Roches and Peter des Rivaux, until the barons forced their expulsion in 1234, marking the start of Henry's personal rule. His financial commitments to the papacy and his foreign favourites antagonized the barons who issued the Provisions of Oxford in 1258, limiting the king's power. Henry's refusal to accept the provisions led to the second Barons' War in 1264, a revolt of nobles led by his brother-in-law Simon de ▷Montfort. Henry was defeated at Lewes, Sussex, and imprisoned, but restored to the throne after the royalist victory at Evesham in 1265. He was succeeded by his son Edward I.

On his release Henry was weak and senile and his eldest son, Edward, took charge of the government.

Henry IV (1367–1413) Born Henry Bolingbroke. King of England from 1399, the son of ▷John of Gaunt. In 1398 he was banished by ▷Richard II but returned in 1399 to head a revolt and be accepted as king by Parliament. He was succeeded by his son Henry V.

He had difficulty in keeping the support of Parliament and the clergy, and had to deal with baronial unrest and Owen ▷Glendower's rising in Wales. In order to win support he had to conciliate the Church by a law for the burning of heretics, and to

HENRY III Just over a week after the death of his father, John, in October 1216, the nine-year-old Henry III was crowned king of England by Peter des Roches, bishop of Winchester. The regency council that ruled in his name effectively clung to power until 1234, when Henry was 27 years old. *The Art Archive*

make many concessions to Parliament. The Percy family was defeated at Shrewsbury in 1403, and the Earl of Northumberland was beaten at Bramham Moor in 1408.

Henry V (1387–1422) King of England from 1413, son of Henry IV. Invading Normandy in 1415 (during the ▷Hundred Years' War), he captured Harfleur and defeated the French at ▷Agincourt. He invaded again in 1417–19, capturing Rouen. His military victory forced the French into the Treaty of Troyes in 1420, which gave Henry control of the French government. He married ▷Catherine of Valois in 1420 and gained recognition as heir to the French throne by his father-in-law Charles VI, but died before him. He was succeeded by his son Henry VI.

Henry was knighted at the age of 12 by Richard II on his Irish expedition of 1399, and experienced war early. He was wounded in the face by an arrow fighting against his military tutor Harry 'Hotspur' at Shrewsbury. Campaigns in Wales against Owen Glendower taught him the realities of siege warfare. He was succeeded by his son Henry VI.

Henry VI (1421–1471) King of England from 1422, son of Henry V. He assumed royal power in 1442 and sided with the party opposed to the continuation of the Hundred Years' War with France. After his marriage in 1445, he was dominated by his wife, ▷Margaret of Anjou. He was deposed in 1461 during the Wars of the ▷Roses, was captured in 1465, temporarily restored in 1470, but again imprisoned in 1471 and then murdered.

Henry was eight months old when he succeeded to the English throne, and shortly afterwards, by the death in 1422 of his maternal grandfather, Charles VI, he became titular king of France. Unlike his father, Henry was disinclined to warfare, and when Joan of Arc revived French patriotism the English gradually began to lose their French possessions. By 1453 only Calais remained of his father's conquests.

The unpopularity of the government, especially after the loss of the English conquests in France, encouraged Richard, Duke of York, to claim the throne, and though York was killed in 1460, his son Edward IV proclaimed himself king in 1461.

Henry VII (1457–1509) King of England from 1485, when he overthrew Richard III at the Battle of ▷Bosworth. A descendant of ▷John of Gaunt, Henry, by his marriage to Elizabeth of York in 1486, united the houses of York and Lancaster. Yorkist revolts continued until 1497, but Henry restored order after the Wars of the Roses by the ▷Star Chamber and achieved independence from Parliament by amassing a private fortune through confiscations. He was succeeded by his son Henry VIII.

Born in Pembroke, Wales, the son of Edmund Tudor, Earl of Richmond (*c.* 1430–1456), Henry lived in Brittany, France, from 1471 to 1485, when he landed in Britain to lead the rebellion against Richard III. Henry succeeded in crushing the independence of the nobility by means of a policy of forced loans and fines. His chancellor, Cardinal Morton, was made responsible for the collection of these fines, and they were enforced by the privy councillors Empson and Dudley. This form of taxation became known as Morton's Fork, the dilemma being that, if a subject liable for taxation lived an extravagant lifestyle, obviously they could afford to pay the fine; if they lived austerely they should have sufficient funds saved with which to pay. To further curb the pretensions of the nobility, there were no unions of his children with the baronage. He married his son Henry to Catherine of Aragón, daughter of the joint sovereigns of Spain, his daughter Margaret to James IV of Scotland, and his youngest daughter Mary to Louis XII of France.

Henry VIII (1491–1547) King of England from 1509, when he succeeded his father Henry VII and married Catherine of Aragón, the widow of his brother.

During the period 1513–29 Henry pursued an active foreign policy, largely under the guidance of his Lord Chancellor, Cardinal Wolsey, who shared Henry's desire to make England stronger. Wolsey was replaced by Thomas More in 1529 for failing to persuade the pope to grant Henry a divorce. After 1532 Henry broke with papal authority, proclaimed himself head of the church in England, dissolved the monasteries, and divorced Catherine. His subsequent wives were Anne Boleyn, Jane Seymour, Anne of Cleves, Catherine Howard, and Catherine Parr. He was succeeded by his son Edward VI.

Henry divorced Catherine of Aragón in 1533 because she was too old to give him an heir, and married Anne Boleyn, who was beheaded in 1536, ostensibly for adultery. Henry's third wife, Jane Seymour, died in 1537. He married Anne of Cleves in 1540 in pursuance of Thomas ▷Cromwell's policy of allying with the German Protestants, but rapidly abandoned this policy, divorced Anne, and beheaded Cromwell. His fifth wife, Catherine Howard, was beheaded in 1542, and the following year he married Catherine Parr, who survived him. Henry never completely lost his popularity, but wars with France and Scotland towards the end of his reign sapped the economy, and in religion he not only executed Roman Catholics, including Thomas More, for refusing to acknowledge his supremacy in the church, but also Protestants who maintained his changes had not gone far enough.

Related Web site: Henry VIII http://www.tudorhistory.org/henry8/

HENRY VIII A contemporary portrait of King Henry VIII of England with his jester Will Summers. *The Art Archive/British Museum*

HENRY II This picture, by an artist from the 16th-century Sienese school of painting, shows King Henry II of France and King Philip II of Spain. They have just agreed a peace treaty at Câteau Cambrésis, France, on 3 April 1559. *The Art Archive/Sienese State Archives/Dagli Orti*

Henry four kings of France, including:

Henry II (1519–1559) King of France from 1547. He captured the fortresses of Metz and Verdun from the Holy Roman Emperor Charles V and Calais from the English. He was killed in a tournament.

Henry III (1551–1589) King of France from 1574. He fought both the ▷Huguenots (headed by his successor, Henry of Navarre) and the Catholic League (headed by the third Duke of Guise). Guise expelled Henry from Paris in 1588 but was assassinated. Henry allied with the Huguenots under Henry of Navarre to besiege the city, but was assassinated by a monk.

Henry IV (1553–1610) King of France from 1589. Son of Antoine de Bourbon and Jeanne, Queen of Navarre, he was brought up as a Protestant and from 1576 led the ▷Huguenots. On his accession he settled the religious question by adopting Catholicism while tolerating Protestantism. He restored peace and strong government to France and brought back prosperity by measures for the promotion of industry and agriculture and the improvement of communications. He was assassinated by a Catholic extremist.

Henry seven Holy Roman emperors, including:

Henry (I) the Fowler (c. 876–936) King of Germany from 919, and duke of Saxony from 912. He secured the frontiers of Saxony, ruled in harmony with its nobles, and extended German influence over the Danes, the Hungarians, and the Slavonic tribes. He was about to claim the imperial crown when he died.

Henry (III) the Black (1017–1056) King of Germany from 1028, Holy Roman Emperor from 1039 (crowned In 1046). He raised the empire to the height of its power, and extended its authority over Poland, Bohemia, and Hungary.

Henry IV (1050–1106) Holy Roman Emperor from 1056. He was involved from 1075 in a struggle with the papacy. Excommunicated twice (1076 and 1080), Henry deposed ▷Gregory VII and set up the antipope Clement III (died 1191) by whom he was crowned Holy Roman Emperor 1084.

Henry VI (1165–1197) Holy Roman Emperor 1191–97. He conquered the Norman Kingdom of Sicily in the name of his wife, Constance, aunt and heiress of William II of Sicily, and was crowned at Palermo, Sicily, on Christmas Day, 1194. As part of his plan for making the empire universal, he captured and imprisoned Richard I of England and compelled him to do homage.

King Richard (I) the Lionheart of England was handed into Henry's power after falling into the hands of Duke Leopold of Austria when returning from crusade. Richard was released for a large ransom only after agreeing that England should become a fief of the Holy Roman Empire.

henry SI unit (symbol H) of ▷inductance (the reaction of an electric current against the magnetic field that surrounds it). One henry is the inductance of a circuit that produces an opposing voltage of one volt when the current changes at one ampere per second.

Henry, Joseph (1797–1878) US physicist, inventor of the electromagnetic motor in 1829 and of a telegraphic apparatus. He also discovered the principle of electromagnetic induction, roughly at the same time as Michael ▷Faraday, and the phenomenon of self-induction. The unit of inductance, the henry, is named after him.

Henry, O (1862–1910) Pen-name of William Sydney Porter. US short-story writer. His stories are written in a colloquial style and employ skilled construction with surprise endings. Among his collections are *Cabbages and Kings* (1904), *The Four Million* (including 'The Gift of the Magi', 1906), *The Voice of the City* (1908), and *Rolling Stones* (1913).

Henry the Lion
(1129–1195) Duke of Bavaria 1156–80, Duke of Saxony 1142–80, and Duke of Lüneburg 1180–85. He was granted the Duchy of Bavaria by the Emperor Frederick Barbarossa. He founded Lübeck and Munich. In 1162 he married Matilda, daughter of Henry II of England. His refusal in 1176 to accompany Frederick Barbarossa to Italy led in 1180 to his being deprived of the Duchies of Bavaria and Saxony. Henry led several military expeditions to conquer territory in the East.

Henry the Navigator (1394–1460) Portuguese prince, the fourth son of John I. He is credited with setting up a school for navigators in 1419 and under his patronage Portuguese sailors explored and colonized Madeira, the Cape Verde Islands, and the Azores; they sailed down the African coast almost to Sierra Leone.

Related Web site: Henry the Navigator http://www.thornr.demon.co.uk/kchrist/phenry.html

Henry, William (1774–1836) English chemist and physician. In 1803 he formulated Henry's law, which states that when a gas is dissolved in a liquid at a given temperature, the mass that dissolves is in direct proportion to the pressure of the gas.

HENRY THE NAVIGATOR Henry the Navigator (right, with hat), Prince of Portugal, with St Vincent and the Portuguese royal family, from an altarpiece by Nuno Goncalves (c. 1460–70; Museo de Arte Antiga, Lisbon, Portugal). *The Art Archive*

Henson, Jim (1936–1990) Born James Maury Henson. US puppeteer who created the television Muppet characters, including Kermit the Frog, Miss Piggy, and Fozzie Bear. The Muppets became popular on the children's educational TV series *Sesame Street*, which first appeared in 1969 and soon became regular viewing in over 80 countries. In 1976 Henson created *The Muppet Show*, which ran for five years and became one of the world's most widely seen TV programmes, reaching 235 million viewers in 100 countries. Several Muppet movies followed.

Henze, Hans Werner (1926–) German composer. His immense and stylistically restless output is marked by a keen literary sensibility and seductive use of orchestral coloration, as in the opera *Elegy for Young Lovers* (1961) and the cantata *Being Beauteous* (1963). Among recent works are the opera *Das Verratene Meer/The Sea Betrayed* (1992).

hepatitis any inflammatory disease of the liver, usually caused by a virus. Other causes include alcohol, drugs, gallstones, ▷lupus erythematous, and amoebic ▷dysentery. Symptoms include weakness, nausea, and jaundice.

Five different hepatitis viruses have been identified; A, B, C, D, and E. The hepatitis A virus (HAV) is the commonest cause of viral hepatitis, responsible for up to 40% of cases worldwide. It is spread by contaminated food. Hepatitis B, or serum hepatitis, is a highly contagious disease spread by blood products or in body fluids. It often culminates in liver failure, and is also associated with liver cancer, although only 5% of those infected suffer chronic liver damage. During 1995, 1.1 million people died of hepatitis B. Around 300 million people are ▷carriers. Vaccines are available against hepatitis A and B.

Hepatitis C is mostly seen in people needing frequent transfusions. In 1999 there were an estimated 150 million people worldwide infected with hepatitis C and 75% of these will go on to develop chronic liver infections. Hepatitis D, which only occurs in association with hepatitis B, is common in the Mediterranean region. Hepatitis E is endemic in India and South America.

In 1998, the World Health Organization estimated that some 350 million people were infected with hepatitis B.

Hepburn, Audrey (1929–1993) Born Audrey Hepburn-Ruston. English actor. She often played innocent, childlike characters. Slender and doe-eyed, she set a different style from the more ample women stars of the 1950s. After playing minor parts in British films in the early 1950s, she became a Hollywood star in *Roman Holiday* (1951), for which she won an Academy Award, and later starred in such films as *Funny Face* (1957) and *My Fair Lady* (1964).

Hepburn, Katharine (1909–2003) US actor. An acclaimed actor of the classical Hollywood era, Hepburn won four Academy Awards and was nominated on 12 separate occasions. Feisty self-assurance was her trademark in both comic and dramatic roles. She was a frequent collaborator with the director George ▷Cukor, and appeared in several films with her off-screen partner Spencer Tracy, including *Woman of the Year* (1942) and *Pat and Mike* (1952).

Hephaestus in Greek mythology, the god of fire and metalcraft (Roman **Vulcan**); the lame son of Zeus and Hera; and in Homer's *Odyssey*, husband of Aphrodite, goddess of love. He created armour for the Greek hero ▷Achilles, Harmonia's magic necklace, and other objects famed in legend.

Hepplewhite, George (died 1786) English furnituremaker associated with Neo-Classicism. His reputation rests upon his book of designs *The Cabinetmaker and Upholsterer's Guide*, published posthumously in 1788, which contains over 300 designs, characterized by simple elegance and utility. No piece of furniture has been identified as being made by him.

Hepworth, (Jocelyn) Barbara (1903–1975) English sculptor. She developed a distinctive abstract style, creating slender upright forms reminiscent of standing stones or totems; and round, hollowed forms with spaces bridged by wires or strings, as in *Pelagos* (1946; Tate Gallery, London). Her preferred medium was stone, but she also worked in concrete, wood, and aluminium, and many of her later works were in bronze.

Hepworth was an admirer of Henry ▷Moore, Constantin Brancusi, and Hans Arp. She married first the sculptor John Skeaping and in 1933 the painter Ben ▷Nicholson, whose influence encouraged her interest in abstract forms. In 1939 she moved to St Ives, Cornwall (where her studio is now a museum). She was made DBE in 1965.

Hera (Greek 'lady') in Greek mythology, the goddess of women and marriage (Roman **Juno**); sister and consort of Zeus; and mother of ▷Hephaestus, god of fire and metalcraft, the war god Ares, and Hebe, the original cupbearer to the gods. The peacock was sacred to her; the eyes in its tail were transplanted from her servant, the 100-eyed Argus, who had watched over Zeus' lover Io.

Heracles (or **Alcides**) in Greek mythology, an immortalized hero (Roman **Hercules**); son of Zeus and Alcmene; and famed for his strength. While serving Eurystheus, king of Argos, he performed 12 labours, including the cleansing of the ▷Augean stables. Driven mad by the goddess ▷Hera, he murdered his children by Megara, his first wife, and was mistakenly poisoned by his second wife Deianira.

Heraclitus (c. 544–c. 483 BC) Greek philosopher who believed that the cosmos is in a ceaseless state of flux and motion, fire being the fundamental material that accounts for all change and motion in the world.

Nothing in the world ever stays the same, hence the dictum, 'one cannot step in the same river twice'.

Heraclius (c. 575–641) Byzantine emperor from 610. His reign marked a turning point in the empire's fortunes. Of Armenian descent, he recaptured Armenia in 622, and other provinces 622–28 from the Persians, but lost them to the Muslims 629–41.

Heraklion alternative name for ▷Iraklion, a port in Crete, Greece.

heraldry insignia and symbols representing a person, family, or dynasty; the science of armorial bearings. Heraldry originated with simple symbols used on shields and banners for recognition in battle. By the 14th century, it had become a complex pictorial language with its own regulatory bodies (courts of chivalry), used by noble families, corporate bodies, cities, and realms. The world's oldest heraldic court is the English ▷College of Arms founded in 1484.

In a coat of arms, the charges (heraldic symbols) are placed on the shield, or escutcheon. The surface of the shield is called the field, and coats of arms are distinguished not only by their charges, but also by the colouring of this field, which represents a combination of metals, tinctures (colours), or furs. There are two heraldic metals: or (gold) and argent (silver); five colours, azure (blue), gules (red), sable (black), vert (green), and purpure (purple). The most common furs are ermine and vair. It is a general rule in English heraldry that metal should not rest on metal nor colour on colour. A coat of arms may be differenced (modified) to represent a family, or any individual member of that family, by the addition of any of a variety of symbols; for example, an eldest son has a label (a horizontal bar with three shorter bars descending from it) across the top of his coat of arms; a second son has a crescent on his.

The royal arms of each sovereign state indicate the public authority of its ruler. In Britain, the quartered royal standard (properly a banner) is the insignia of the ruling authority – the crown.

Herat capital of Herat province, and the largest city in western Afghanistan, on the north banks of the Hari Rud River; population (2001 est) 161,700. A principal road junction, the city is

NON SANZ DROICT

The Armorial Bearings of
WILLIAM SHAKESPEARE
of Stratford-upon-Avon.

College of Arms,
London.

Chester Herald
and Registrar.

HERALDRY An armorial bearing made for the English playwright William Shakespeare of Stratford-upon-Avon, England. The shield carries a pen but no other insignia, and no metals nor furs are used. The Shakespeare family were not of noble birth, so their right to a shield would have been doubtful. *The Art Archive/College of Arms/Eileen Tweedy*

922 m/3,026 ft above sea level and lies in an area which has been the site of cities since the time of Alexander the Great and contains many ancient ruins and buildings, including a 15th-century mosque and the tomb of the poet and saint Abdollah Ansari. Herat is now the marketing centre for an irrigated, fertile, and densely-peopled agricultural area in western Afghanistan, and its industries include handicrafts, textiles, and the milling of oilseeds, flour, and rice, while Karakul furs are also an important item of local commerce.

herb any plant (usually a flowering plant) tasting sweet, bitter, aromatic, or pungent, used in cooking, medicine, or perfumery; technically, a herb is any plant in which the aerial parts do not remain above ground at the end of the growing season.

herbaceous plant plant with very little or no wood, dying back at the end of every summer. The herbaceous perennials survive winters as underground storage organs such as bulbs and tubers.

herbalism in alternative medicine, the prescription and use of plants and their derivatives for medication. Herbal products are favoured by alternative practitioners as 'natural medicine', as opposed to modern synthesized medicines and drugs, which are regarded with suspicion because of the dangers of side effects and dependence.

> **Related Web site: Herbal** http://www.geocities.com/Athens/4177/herbal.htm

Herbert, George (1593–1633) English poet. His volume of religious poems, *The Temple*, appeared in 1633, shortly before his death. His intense though quiet poems embody his religious struggles ('The Temper', 'The Collar') or poignantly contrast mortality and eternal truth ('Vertue', 'Life') in a deceptively simple language.

The high regard in which he was held in the 17th century waned early in the 18th, and for a century or more his poetry was considered uncouth. The Romantic poet Coleridge did much to restore it to favour. It is noted for its colloquial phraseology, pliable verse forms, and quiet music; its apparent simplicity is its greatest strength.

> **Related Web site: Herbert, George** http://www.luminarium.org/sevenlit/herbert/index.html

herbivore animal that feeds on green plants (or photosynthetic single-celled organisms) or their products, including seeds, fruit, and nectar. The most numerous type of herbivore is thought to be the zooplankton, tiny invertebrates in the surface waters of the oceans that feed on small photosynthetic algae. Herbivores are more numerous than other animals because their food is the most abundant. They form a vital link in the food chain between plants and carnivores.

Mammalian herbivores that rely on cellulose as a major part of their diet, for instance cows and sheep, generally possess millions of specialized bacteria in their gut. These are capable of producing the enzyme cellulase, necessary for digesting cellulose; no mammal is able to manufacture cellulase on its own.

herb Robert wild ▷geranium found throughout Europe and central Asia and naturalized in North America. About 30 cm/12 in high, it has hairy leaves and small pinkish to purplish flowers. (*Geranium robertianum*, family Geraniaceae.)

Herculaneum ancient city of Italy between Naples and Pompeii. Along with Pompeii, it was buried when Vesuvius erupted in AD 79. It was excavated from the 18th century onwards.

Hercules in astronomy, the fifth-largest constellation, lying in the northern hemisphere. Despite its size it contains no prominent stars. Its most important feature is the best example in the northern hemisphere of a ▷globular cluster of stars 22,500 light years from the Sun, which lies between Eta and Zeta Herculis.

Hercules in Roman mythology, Roman form of the deified Greek hero ▷Heracles. Possibly the first foreign cult accepted in Rome, he was popular with merchants due to his legendary travel and ability to ward off evil, and was seen as the personification of strength.

Hercules beetle largest beetle in the world: males measure up to 17 cm/6.6 in in length; females are smaller. Hercules beetles are found mainly in the tropical and subtropical regions.

heredity in biology, the transmission of traits from parent to offspring. See also ▷genetics.

Hereford city in the county of Herefordshire, west-central England, on the River Wye, 34 km/21 mi southwest of Worcester; population (1996 est) 48,900. It is an agricultural centre, with a livestock market noted for its white-faced Hereford cattle. The city has the UK's largest cider industry. Other activities include brewing, food processing (chicken), tourism, and the manufacture of non-ferrous alloys and components. The cathedral, dating from 1079, has the largest chained library in the world and a medieval *Mappa Mundi* (map of the world).

Herefordshire unitary authority in west England, created in 1998 from part of the former county of Hereford and Worcester. **area** 2,288 sq km/884 sq mi **towns and cities** ▷Hereford (administrative headquarters), Leominster, Ross-on-Wye, Ledbury **features** River Wye; Herefordshire Beacon (340 m/1,115 ft) Iron Age fort; Hereford Cathedral (11th century) houses the late 13th/early 14th-century Mappa Mundi, and the Chained Library, with over 1,400 chained books and 200 manuscripts dating from the 8th to 12th centuries; Waterworks Museum (Hereford) in restored Victorian pump house; Croft Castle (Leominster); St Mary's Church (Kempley) with medieval wall paintings; The Prospect, a walled clifftop garden in Ross-on-Wye designed by John Kyrle in the 17th century; Norman Church (Kilpeck) with notable carvings **industries** agriculture, orchards and cider industry, agricultural services and machinery, precision engineering, light engineering, plastics manufacture **population** (1996) 166,100 **famous people** Thomas Knight, John Kyrle, Walter Map, John Masefield

heresy (Greek *hairesis* 'parties' of believers) any doctrine opposed to orthodox belief, especially in religion. Those holding ideas considered heretical by the Christian church have included Gnostics, Arians, Pelagians, Montanists, Albigenses, Waldenses, Lollards, and Anabaptists.

HERESY This image shows the pope defending the church against the heretics of the Reformation. Any religious doctrine opposed to the orthodox belief of the time may be defined as heresy. *Philip Sauvain Picture Collection*

HERCULANEUM When Vesuvius erupted in AD 79, the Italian city of Herculaneum was buried with lava and hot ash in a manner completely different from Pompeii, which was twice the distance away from the volcano. Herculaneum was probably better preserved because of this, and also because of the unusual humidity of the area, but excavation of the city is more difficult. *The Art Archive*

Hereward the Wake (lived 11th century) legendary Saxon hero of the English resistance to the Normans in 1070. Helped by a Danish army, the rebels attacked and sacked Peterborough Abbey. William bribed the Danes to return home, but Hereward continued the revolt. His stronghold in the Isle of Ely was captured in 1071 by William (I) the Conqueror during the Siege of Ely. Although his actual fate is unkown, legends grew up about him, and he has remained a hero of fiction.

Herman, Woody (Woodrow Charles) (1913–1987) US jazz bandleader and clarinetist. A child prodigy, he was leader of his own orchestra at 23, and after 1945 formed his Thundering Herd band. Soloists in this or later versions of the band included Lester ▷Young and Stan ▷Getz.

hermaphrodite organism that has both male and female sex organs. Hermaphroditism is the norm in such species as earthworms and snails, and is common in flowering plants. Cross-fertilization is common among hermaphrodites, with the parents functioning as male and female simultaneously, or as one or the other sex at different stages in their development. Human hermaphrodites are extremely rare.

hermeneutics philosophical tradition concerned with the nature of understanding and interpretation of human behaviour and social traditions. From its origins in problems of biblical interpretation, hermeneutics has expanded to cover many fields of enquiry, including aesthetics, literary theory, and science. The German philosophers Wilhelm Dilthey, Martin ▷Heidegger, and Hans-Georg Gadamer were influential contributors to this tradition.

Hermes in Greek mythology, the messenger of the gods; son of Zeus and ▷Maia, one of the Pleiades. Homer's *Odyssey* presented the god as the conductor of the dead (shades) to ▷Hades, in which capacity he became associated with the underworld and dreams. Identified with the Roman ▷Mercury and ancient Egyptian ▷Thoth, he protected thieves, travellers, and merchants. As a god of good fortune, he presided over some forms of popular divination, public competitions, and games of dice.

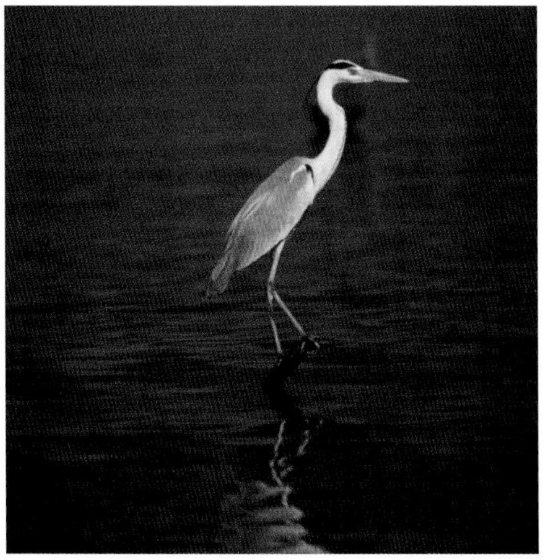

HERON The grey heron *Ardea cinerea* can be seen in this typical fishing pose from western Europe through Asia to Japan and into Africa and Madagascar. It builds an untidy stick nest, usually high up in trees, forming colonies known as heronries. *Premaphotos Wildlife*

hermit (Greek *eremites* from *eremia* 'desert') person living in seclusion, generally practising asceticism for religious reasons.

Hermitage Museum one of the world's largest and finest museums of art, in St Petersburg, Russia. Founded by Russian empress ▷Catherine the Great in 1764 and housed in some of St Petersburg's grandest buildings, the Hermitage collection now numbers over 3,000,000 items, presenting the development of world culture and art from the Stone Age to the present day.

hermit crab type of ▷crab.

hernia (or **rupture**) protrusion of part of an internal organ through a weakness in the surrounding muscular wall, usually in the groin. The appearance is that of a rounded soft lump or swelling.

Hero and Leander in Greek mythology, a pair of lovers. Hero, virgin priestess of Aphrodite, at Sestos on the Hellespont, fell in love at a festival with Leander on the opposite shore at Abydos. He used to swim to her at night, guided by the light, but during a storm the flame blew out and he was drowned. Seeing his body, Hero threw herself into the sea.

Herod Agrippa I (10 BC–AD 44) Ruler of Palestine from AD 41. His real name was Marcus Julius Agrippa, erroneously called 'Herod' in the Bible. Grandson of Herod the Great, he was made tetrarch (governor) of Palestine by the Roman emperor Caligula and king by Emperor Claudius AD 41. He put the apostle James to death and imprisoned the apostle Peter. His son was Herod Agrippa II.

Herod Agrippa II (*c.* 40–*c.* 93 AD) King of Chalcis (now southern Lebanon), son of Herod Agrippa I. He was appointed by the Roman emperor Claudius about AD 50, and in AD 60 tried the apostle Paul. He helped the Roman commander Titus (subsequently emperor) take and sack Jerusalem in AD 70, then went to Rome, where he died.

Herod Antipas (21 BC–AD 39) Tetrarch (governor) of the Roman province of Galilee, northern Palestine, 4 BC–AD 39, son of Herod the Great. He divorced his wife to marry his niece Herodias, and was responsible for the death of John the Baptist. Jesus was brought before him on Pontius Pilate's discovery that he was a Galilean and hence of Herod's jurisdiction, but Herod returned him without giving any verdict. In AD 38 Herod Antipas went to Rome to try to persuade Emperor Caligula to give him the title of king, but was instead banished.

Herodotus (lived 5th century BC) Greek historian, described as the 'Father of History'. He wrote a nine-book account of the Greek-Persian struggle that culminated in the defeat of the Persian invasion attempts in 490 and 480 BC. The work contains lengthy digressions on peoples, places, and earlier history. Herodotus was the first historian to apply critical evaluation to his material while also recording divergent opinions.

> **Herod the Great**
> *You can find out from my past actions how I behave towards my benefactors.*
> Quoted in Josephus *Jewish Antiquities* bk 15.193

Herod the Great (74–4 BC) King of the Roman province of Judaea, southern Palestine, from 40 BC. With the aid of Mark Antony, he established his government in Jerusalem in 37 BC. He rebuilt the Temple in Jerusalem, but his Hellenizing tendencies made him suspect to orthodox Jewry. His last years were a reign of terror, and in the New Testament Matthew alleges that he ordered the slaughter of all the infants in Bethlehem to ensure the death of Jesus, whom he foresaw as a rival. He was the father of Herod Antipas.

heroin (or **diamorphine**) powerful ▷opiate analgesic, an acetyl derivative of ▷morphine. It is more addictive than morphine but causes less nausea. It has an important place in the control of severe pain in terminal illness, severe injuries, and heart attacks, but is widely used illegally.

In 1971 there were 3,000 registered heroin addicts in the UK; in 1989 there were over 100,000.

heron large to medium-sized wading bird belonging to the same family as bitterns, egrets, night herons, and boatbills. Herons have sharp bills, broad wings, long legs, slender bodies, and soft plumage. They are found mostly in tropical and subtropical regions, but also in temperate zones, on lakes, fens, and mudflats, where they wade searching for prey. (Genera include *Ardea*, *Butorides*, and *Nycticorax*; family Ardeidae, order Ciconiiformes.)

They capture small animals, such as fish, molluscs, and worms, by spearing them with their long bills. Herons nest in trees or bushes, on ivy-covered rocks, or in reedbeds, making a loose fabric of sticks lined with grass or leaves; they lay greenish or drab-coloured eggs, varying in number from two to seven according to the different species.

The common heron (*A. cinerea*) nests in Europe, Asia, and parts of Africa in large tree-top colonies. The bird is about 1 m/3 ft long, and has a long neck and legs. The plumage is chiefly grey, but there are black patches on the sides and a black crest. The legs are olive green and the bill yellow, except during the breeding season, when it is pink. Although it is a wading bird, it is rarely seen to swim or walk. It feeds on fish, frogs, and rats. In 1996 there were an estimated 6,600 heron pairs in Britain.

> **James Herriot**
> *I have long held the notion that if a vet can't catch his patient there's not much to worry about.*
> *Vet in Harness*

herpes any of several infectious diseases caused by viruses of the herpes group. **Herpes simplex I** is the causative agent of a common inflammation, the cold sore. **Herpes simplex II** is responsible for genital herpes, a highly contagious, sexually transmitted disease characterized by painful blisters in the genital area. It can be transmitted in the birth canal from mother to newborn. Herpes zoster causes ▷shingles; another herpes virus causes chickenpox.

A number of antivirals treat these infections, which are particularly troublesome in patients whose immune systems have been suppressed medically; for example, after a transplant operation. The drug acyclovir, originally introduced for the treatment of genital herpes, has now been shown to modify the course of chickenpox and the related condition shingles, by reducing the duration of the illness.

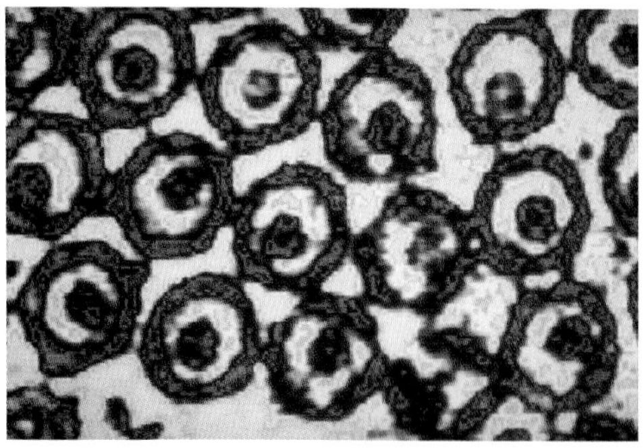

HERPES A false-colour micrograph of the *Herpes simplex* or cold sore virus. Herpes is the name given to any of several infectious diseases – including cold sores, genital herpes, shingles, chickenpox, and glandular fever – caused by the viruses in the herpes group. *SmithKline Beecham Plc*

A vaccine for shingles was tested by US researchers in 1999.

The Epstein–Barr virus of ▷glandular fever also belongs to this group.

Related Web site: Childhood Infections – Herpes
http://KidsHealth.org/parent/infections/herpes.html

Herrick, Robert (1591–1674) English poet and cleric. He published *Hesperides: or the Works both Humane and Divine of Robert Herrick* (1648), a collection of verse admired for its lyric quality, including the well-known poems 'Gather ye rosebuds' and 'Cherry ripe'.

The 'divine' poems are, on the whole, unremarkable, but the 'humane' works are rich and varied, owing much to Roman models such as ▷Catullus and ▷Martial and to native influences such as Ben ▷Jonson and popular ballads. They range in scale from couplets to Horatian odes and verse epistles, and cover such subjects as religion, politics, love, erotic fantasy, the value of poetry, and the changing cycles of life in the countryside.

Related Web site: Selected Poetry of Robert Herrick (1591–1674)
http://www.library.utoronto.ca/utel/rp/authors/herrick.html

herring any of various marine fishes belonging to the herring family, but especially the important food fish *Clupea harengus*. A silvered greenish blue, it swims close to the surface, and may be 25–40 cm/10–16 in long. Herring travel in schools several kilometres long and wide. They are found in large quantities off the east coast of North America, and the shores of northeastern Europe. Overfishing and pollution have reduced their numbers. (Family Clupeidae.)

Herriot, Edouard (1872–1957) French radical politician. A leading parliamentarian of the inter-war period, Herriot was president of his party (1919–26, 1931–35, and 1945–56) and prime minister (1924–25, 1926, and 1932). As president of the chamber of deputies 1936–40 and a staunch republican, he challenged the legality of the 1940 parliamentary vote establishing the Vichy regime.

Herriot, James (1916–1995) Pen-name of James Alfred Wight. English writer. A practising veterinary surgeon in Yorkshire from 1939, he wrote of his experiences in a series of humorous books which described the life of a young vet working in a Yorkshire village in the late 1930s. His first three books were published as a compilation under the title *All Creatures Great and Small* (1972).

Herron, Ron(ald James) (1930–1994) English architect and founder member of Archigram, a radical architectural group of the 1960s. He designed Walking City, a proposed city on wheels with full environmental controls, inspired by space exploration. Walking City became a seminal icon of technology and mobility. The Pompidou Centre in Paris was inspired by Herron's drawing *Oasis* (1968).

Herschel, John Frederick William (1792–1871) English scientist, astronomer, and photographer who discovered thousands of close double stars, clusters, and nebulae. He coined the terms 'photography', 'negative', and 'positive', discovered sodium thiosulphite as a fixer of silver halides, and invented the cyanotype process; his inventions also include astronomical instruments.

Herschel, (Frederick) William (1738–1822) German-born English astronomer. He was a skilled telescopemaker, and pioneered the study of binary stars and nebulae. He discovered the planet Uranus in 1781 and infrared solar rays in 1801. He catalogued over 800 double stars, and found over 2,500 nebulae, catalogued by his sister Caroline Herschel; this work was continued by his son John Herschel. By studying the distribution of stars, William established the basic form of our Galaxy, the Milky Way. He was knighted in 1816.

Herschel discovered the motion of binary stars around one another, and recorded it in his *Motion of the Solar System in Space* (1783). In 1789 he built, in Slough, a 1.2-m/4-ft telescope of 12 m/40 ft focal length (the largest in the world at the time), but he made most use of a more satisfactory 46-cm/18-in instrument. He discovered two satellites of Uranus and two of Saturn.

Hertfordshire county of southeast England, to the north of London.

area 1,630 sq km/629 sq mi **towns and cities** Hertford (administrative headquarters), Bishop's Stortford, Hatfield, Hemel Hempstead, Letchworth (the first ▷garden city; followed by Welwyn in 1919), Stevenage (the first ▷new town, designated in 1946), St Albans, Watford, Hitchin **physical** rivers Lea, Stort, Colne; part of the Chiltern Hills **features** Hatfield House; Knebworth House (home of Lord Lytton); Brocket Hall (home of Palmerston and Melbourne); home of George Bernard ▷Shaw at Ayot St Lawrence; Berkhamsted Castle (Norman); Rothamsted agricultural experimental station **agriculture** barley for brewing industry, dairy farming, market gardening, horticulture **industries** aircraft, computer electronics, electrical goods, engineering, paper and printing, plastics, pharmaceuticals, tanning, sand and gravel worked in the south **population** (1996) 1,015,800 **famous people** Henry Bessemer, Graham Greene, Cecil Rhodes

hertz SI unit (symbol Hz) of frequency (the number of repetitions of a regular occurrence in one second). Radio waves are often measured in megahertz (MHz), millions of hertz, and the ▷clock rate of a computer is usually measured in megahertz. The unit is named after German physicist Heinrich Hertz.

Hertz, Heinrich Rudolf (1857–1894) German physicist who studied electromagnetic waves, showing that their behaviour resembles that of light and heat waves.

Hertzsprung–Russell diagram in astronomy, a graph on which the surface temperatures of stars are plotted against their luminosities. Most stars, including the Sun, fall into a narrow band called the main sequence. When a star grows old it moves from the main sequence to the upper right part of the graph, into the area of the giants and supergiants. At the end of its life, as the star shrinks to become a white dwarf, it moves again, to the bottom left area. It is named after the Danish astronomer Ejnar Hertzsprung and the US astronomer Henry Russell, who independently devised it in the years 1911–13.

THEODOR HERZL Founder of Zionism, Herzl organized the Zionist World Congress in Basel in 1897, at which the Zionist Organization was formed. He died more than 40 years before the State of Israel was formed, but did much to make Zionism a significant international political movement. *Image Bank*

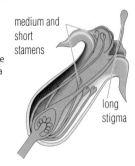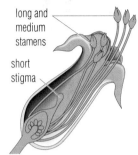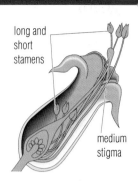

HETEROSTYLY The diagram shows which lengths of the stamens and stigma differ in flowers of different plants of the same species. This is a device to ensure cross-pollination by visiting insects.

Herzegovina (or **Hercegovina**) part of ▷Bosnia-Herzegovina (which was formerly, until 1991, a republic of Yugoslavia).

Herzl, Theodor (1860–1904) Austrian founder of the Zionist movement. The ▷Dreyfus case convinced him that the only solution to the problem of anti-Semitism was the resettlement of the Jews in a state of their own. His book *Der Judenstaad/Jewish State* (1896) launched political ▷Zionism, and he became the first president of the World Zionist Organization in 1897.

Herzog, Werner (1942–) Adopted name of Werner Stipetic. German film director. He often takes his camera to exotic and impractical locations. His original and visually splendid films include *Aguirre der Zorn Gottes/Aguirre Wrath of God* (1972), *Nosferatu Phantom der Nacht/Nosferatu Phantom of the Night* (1979), and *Fitzcarraldo* (1982).

Heseltine, Michael (Ray Dibdin) (1933–) British Conservative politician, deputy prime minister 1995–97. A member of Parliament from 1966 (for Tavistock 1966–74 and for Henley from 1974), he was secretary of state for the environment 1990–92 and for trade and industry 1992–95.

Hesiod (lived 8th century BC) Greek poet. The earliest of the Greek didactic poets, he is often contrasted with ▷Homer as the other main representative of the early epic. He is the author of *Works and Days*, a moralizing and didactic poem of rural life, and *Theogony*, an account of the origin of the world and of the gods. Both poems include the myth of ▷Pandora.

> ### Hesiod
> *Between us and virtue the immortal gods placed sweat: long and steep is the path that leads to her.*
> *Works and Days* (289–90)

Hesse (German **Hessen**) administrative region (German *Land*) in central Germany, bordered on the west by the state of Rhineland-Palatinate, on the south by Bavaria and Baden-Württemberg, on the east by Thuringia, and on the north by North Rhine-Westphalia and Lower Saxony; area 21,100 sq km/8,150 sq mi; population (1999 est) 6,951,400. The capital is Wiesbaden; other major cities are Frankfurt-am-Main, Kassel, Darmstadt, Fulda, Giessen, and Offenbach-am-Main. The chief industries are timber, chemicals, textiles, automobiles, electrical engineering, optical instruments, computers, telecommunications, printing, and publishing. Agriculture is based on the cultivation of oats, wheat, potatoes, barley, flax, and sugar beet; wine is produced in the west of the state, in the Rheingau area bordering the Rhine.

Hesse, Hermann (1877–1962) German writer, a Swiss citizen from 1923. A conscientious objector in World War I and a pacifist opponent of Hitler, he published short stories, poetry, and novels, including *Peter Camenzind* (1904), *Siddhartha* (1922), and *Steppenwolf* (1927). Later works, such as *Das Glasperlenspiel/The Glass Bead Game* (1943), show the influence of Indian mysticism and Jungian psychoanalysis. Above all, Hesse was the prophet of individualism. He was awarded the Nobel Prize for Literature in 1946.

Hess, (Walter Richard) Rudolf (1894–1987) German Nazi leader. Imprisoned with Adolf Hitler 1924–25, he became his private secretary, taking down *Mein Kampf* from his dictation. In 1933 he was appointed deputy *Führer* to Hitler, a post he held until replaced by Goering in September 1939. On 10 May 1941 he landed by air in the UK with his own compromise peace proposals and was held a prisoner of war until 1945, when he was tried at Nürnberg as a war criminal and sentenced to life imprisonment. He died in Spandau prison, Berlin.

He was effectively in charge of the Nazi party organization until his flight in 1941. For the last years of his life he was the only prisoner left in Spandau.

Heston, Charlton (1924–) Stage name of John Charles Carter. US film actor. He often starred in biblical and historical epics; for example, as Moses in *The Ten Commandments* (1956), and in the title role in *Ben Hur* (1959, Academy Award). His other film appearances include *Touch of Evil* (1958), *Major Dundee* (1965), *Earthquake* (1974), and *True Lies* (1994).

heterosexuality sexual preference for, or attraction mainly to, persons of the opposite sex.

heterostyly in botany, having ▷styles of different lengths. Certain flowers, such as primroses (*Primula vulgaris*), have different-sized ▷anthers and styles to ensure cross-fertilization (through ▷pollination) by visiting insects.

heterotroph any living organism that obtains its energy from organic substances produced by other organisms. All animals and fungi are heterotrophs, and they include herbivores, carnivores, and saprotrophs (those that feed on dead animal and plant material).

heterozygous in a living organism, having two different ▷alleles for a given trait. In ▷homozygous organisms, by contrast, both chromosomes carry the same allele. In an outbreeding population an individual organism will generally be heterozygous for some genes but homozygous for others.

heuristics in computing, a process by which a program attempts to improve its performance by learning from its own experience.

Hewish, Antony (1924–) English radio astronomer who, with Martin ▷Ryle, was awarded the Nobel Prize for Physics in 1974 for his work on the development of radioastronomy, particularly the aperture-synthesis technique, and the discovery of ▷pulsars, rapidly rotating neutron stars that emit pulses of energy.

hexadecimal number system (or **hex**) number system to the base 16, used in computing. In hex the decimal numbers 0–15 are represented by the characters 0, 1, 2, 3, 4, 5, 6, 7, 8, 9, A, B, C, D, E, F. Hexadecimal numbers are easy to convert to the computer's internal ▷binary code and are more compact than binary numbers.

Each place in a number increases in value by a power of 16 going from right to left; for instance, 8F is equal to $15 + (8 \times 16) = 143$ in decimal. Hexadecimal numbers are often preferred by programmers writing in low-level languages because they are more easily converted to the computer's internal ▷binary (base-two) code than are decimal numbers, and because they are more compact than binary numbers and therefore more easily keyed, checked, and memorized. (See also ▷ASCII.)

Heydrich, Reinhard Tristan Eugen (1904–1942) German Nazi, head of the *Sicherheitsdienst* (SD), the party's security service, and Heinrich ▷Himmler's deputy. He was instrumental in organizing the ▷final solution, the policy of genocide used against Jews and others. 'Protector' of Bohemia and Moravia from 1941, he was ambushed and killed the following year by three members of the Czechoslovak forces in Britain, who had landed by parachute. Reprisals followed, including several hundred executions and the massacre in Lidice.

Heyerdahl, Thor (1914–) Norwegian ethnologist. He sailed on the ancient-Peruvian-style raft ▷*Kon-Tiki* from Peru to the Tuamotu Archipelago along the Humboldt Current in 1947, and in 1969–70 used ancient-Egyptian-style papyrus-reed boats to cross the Atlantic. His experimental approach to historical reconstruction is not regarded as having made any important scientific contribution.

Heywood, Thomas (c. 1570–c. 1650) English actor and dramatist. He wrote or adapted over 220 plays, including the domestic tragedy *A Woman Kilde with Kindnesse* (1602–03). He also wrote an *Apology for Actors* (1612), in answer to attacks on the morality of the theatre.

Hezbollah (or **Hizbollah**; 'Party of God') extremist Muslim organization founded by the Iranian Revolutionary Guards who were sent to Lebanon after the 1979 Iranian revolution. Its aim is to spread the Islamic revolution of Iran among the Shiite population of Lebanon. Hezbollah is believed to be the umbrella movement of the groups that held many of the Western hostages taken from 1984.

HI abbreviation for ▷Hawaii, a state of the USA.

Hiawatha 16th-century American Indian teacher and Onondaga chieftain. He is said to have welded the Five Nations (later joined by a sixth) of the ▷Iroquois into the league of the Long House, as the confederacy was known in what is now upper New York State. The hero of H W Longfellow's epic poem *The Song of Hiawatha* (1855) is an unrelated fictitious character.

hibernation state of dormancy in which certain animals spend the winter. It is associated with a dramatic reduction in all metabolic processes, including body temperature, breathing, and heart rate.

The body temperature of the Arctic ground squirrel falls to below 0°C/32°F during hibernation. Hibernating bats may breathe only once every 45 minutes, and can go for up to 2 hours without taking a breath.

HIBERNATION Ladybirds hibernating on a pine tree.
K G Preston-Mafham/Premaphotos Wildlife

hibiscus any of a group of plants belonging to the mallow family. Hibiscuses range from large ▷herbaceous plants to trees. Popular as ornamental plants because of their brilliantly coloured, red to white, bell-shaped flowers, they include *H. syriacus* and *H. rosa-sinensis* of Asia and the rose mallow (*H. palustris*) of North America. (Genus *Hibiscus*, family Malvaceae.)

Hickok, Wild Bill (1837–1876) Born James Butler Hickok. US pioneer and law enforcer, a legendary figure in the West. In the Civil War he was a sharpshooter and scout for the Union army. He then served as marshal in Kansas, killing as many as 27 people. He was a prodigious gambler and was fatally shot from behind while playing poker in Deadwood, South Dakota.

hickory tree belonging to the walnut family, native to North America and Asia. It provides a valuable timber, and all species produce nuts, though some are inedible. The pecan (*C. illinoensis*) is widely cultivated in the southern USA, and the shagbark (*C. ovata*) in the northern USA. (Genus *Carya*, family Juglandaceae.)

hieroglyphic (Greek 'sacred carved writing') Egyptian writing system of the mid-4th millennium BC–3rd century AD, which combines picture signs with those indicating letters. The direction of writing is normally from right to left, the signs facing the beginning of the line. It was deciphered in 1822 by the French Egyptologist J F Champollion (1790–1832) with the aid of the ▷Rosetta Stone, which has the same inscription carved in hieroglyphic, demotic, and Greek. The earliest hieroglyphics were discovered by German archaeologist Gunter Dreyer on clay tablets in southern Egypt in 1998, and record linen and oil deliveries and also taxes paid. From the tomb of King Scorpion I, they are dated to between 3300 BC and 3200 BC and challenge the widely held belief that Sumerians were the first people to write. Hieroglyphics were replaced by cursive writing from about 700 BC onwards.

hi-fi (abbreviation for high-fidelity) faithful reproduction of sound from a machine that plays recorded music or speech. A typical hi-fi system includes a turntable for playing vinyl records, a cassette tape deck to play magnetic tape-recordings, a tuner to pick up radio broadcasts, an amplifier to serve all the equipment, possibly a compact-disc player, and two or more loudspeakers.

Higgs boson (or **Higgs particle**) postulated ▷elementary particle whose existence would explain why particles have mass. The current theory of elementary particles, called the ▷standard model, cannot explain how mass arises. To overcome this difficulty, Peter Higgs of the University of Edinburgh and Thomas Kibble of Imperial College, London proposed in 1964 a new particle that binds to other particles and gives them their mass. Physicists in Geneva announced in September 2000 that they believed that they had successfully created a Higgs boson. However in July 2001 this was revealed to be an error in the data; in December 2001 nuclear physicists at the research organization CERN concluded that the Higgs boson did not exist.

High Church group in the ▷Church of England that emphasizes aspects of Christianity usually associated with Catholics, such as ceremony and hierarchy. The term was first used in 1703 to describe those who opposed Dissenters, and later for groups such as the 19th-century ▷Oxford Movement.

high commissioner representative of one independent Commonwealth country in the capital of another, ranking with ambassador. Also a high administrative officer in a dependency or protectorate.

high-definition television (HDTV) ▷television system offering a significantly greater number of scanning lines, and therefore a clearer picture, than that provided by conventional systems. Typically, HDTV has about twice the horizontal and vertical resolution of current 525-line (such as the American standard, NTSC) or 625-line standards (such as the British standard, PAL); a frame rate of at least 24 Hz; and a picture aspect ratio of 9:16 instead of the current 3:4. HDTV systems have been in development since the mid-1970s.

Higher in Scottish education, a public examination taken at the age of 17, one year after the Scottish O grade. Highers are usually taken in four or five subjects and qualify students for entry to ▷higher education.

higher education in most countries, education beyond the age of 18 leading to a university or college degree or similar qualification.

Related Web site: Higher Education Statistics Agency
http://www.hesa.ac.uk/

high jump field event in athletics in which competitors leap over a horizontal crossbar held between rigid uprights at least 3.66 m/12 ft apart. The bar is placed at increasingly higher levels. Elimination occurs after three consecutive failures to clear the bar.

Highland unitary authority in northern Scotland, created from the region bearing the same name in 1996.

> **area** 26,157 sq km/10,100 sq mi (one-third of Scotland) **towns** ▷Inverness (administrative headquarters), Thurso, Wick, Fort William, Aviemore **physical** mainland Highland consists of a series of glaciated ancient plateau masses dissected by narrow glens and straths (valleys); in the northeast (Caithness), old red sandstone rocks give a softer, lower topography; Ben Nevis (1,343 m/4,406 ft), Cairngorm Mountains; Loch Ness; Cuillin Hills, Skye; includes many of the Inner Hebridean islands **features** Caledonian Canal; John O'Groats; Skye Road Bridge **industries** winter sports, timber, aluminium smelting, pulp and paper production, whisky distilling, cottage and croft industries **agriculture** salmon fishing, sheep farming, grouse and deer hunting **population** (1996) 207,500 **history** location of many key historical moments in Scottish history, including the 'massacre' of Glencoe, the Battle of Culloden and the Highland Clearances

Highland Clearances forced removal of tenants from large estates in Scotland during the early 19th century, as landowners 'improved' their estates by switching from arable to sheep farming. It led ultimately to widespread emigration to North America.

Highlands one of the three geographical divisions of Scotland, lying to the north of a geological fault line that stretches from Stonehaven in the North Sea to Dumbarton on the Clyde. It is a mountainous region of hard rocks, shallow infertile soils, and high rainfall.

high-level language in computing, a programming language designed to suit the requirements of the programmer; it is independent of the internal machine code of any particular computer. High-level languages are used to solve problems and are often described as **problem-oriented languages**; for example, ▷BASIC was designed to be easily learnt by first-time programmers; ▷COBOL is used to write programs solving business problems; and ▷FORTRAN is used for programs solving scientific and mathematical problems. In contrast, **low-level languages**, such as ▷assembly languages, closely reflect the machine codes of specific computers, and are therefore described as **machine-oriented languages**.

high-tech (or **high technology**) in architecture, an approach to design, originating in the UK in the 1970s, which concentrates on technical innovation, often using exposed structure and services as a means of creating exciting forms and spaces. The Hong Kong and Shanghai Bank, Hong Kong (1986), designed by Norman ▷Foster, is a masterpiece of high-tech architecture.

highwayman in English history, a thief on horseback who robbed travellers on the highway (those who did so on foot were known as **footpads**).

With the development of regular coach services in the 17th and 18th centuries, the highwaymen's activities became notorious, and the Bow Street Runners were organized to suppress them. Highwaymen continued to flourish well into the 19th century.

Among the best-known highwaymen were Jonathan Wild, Claude Duval, John Nevison (1639–1684), the original hero of the 'ride to York', Dick ▷Turpin and his partner Tom King, and Jerry Abershaw (c. 1773–1795). Favourite haunts were Hounslow and Bagshot heaths and Epping Forest, around London.

hijacking illegal seizure or taking control of a vehicle and/or its passengers or goods. The term dates from 1923 and originally referred to the robbing of freight lorries. Subsequently it (and its derivative 'skyjacking') has been applied to the seizure of aircraft, usually in flight, by an individual or group, often with some political aim. International treaties (Tokyo 1963, The Hague 1970, and Montréal 1971) encourage cooperation against hijackers and make severe penalties compulsory.

Hijrah (or **Hegira**; Arabic 'flight') the flight from Mecca to Medina of the prophet Muhammad, which took place in AD 622 as a result of the persecution of the prophet and his followers. The Muslim calendar dates from this event, and the day of the Hijrah is celebrated as the Muslim New Year.

Hilbert, David (1862–1943) German mathematician, philosopher, and physicist whose work was fundamental to 20th-century mathematics. He founded the formalist school with *Grundlagen der Geometrie/Foundations of Geometry* (1899), which was based on his idea of postulates.

Hildebrand Benedictine monk who became Pope ▷Gregory VII.

Hildebrandt, Johann Lucas von (1668–1745) Italian-born Austrian architect. He trained under Carlo Fontana (1638–1714), the leading baroque architect in late 17th-century

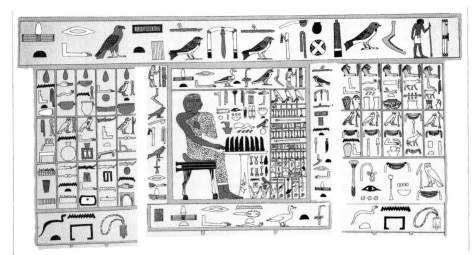

HIEROGLYPHIC Hieroglyphics from the tomb of Prince Rahotep at Medun, from about 2800 BC. The prince is shown together with inscriptions representing the articles with which he was buried. *Philip Sauvain Picture Collection*

Rome, and was successor to Viennese court architect Johann Fischer von Erlach (1656–1723). His baroque masterpiece is the Belvedere, Vienna (1693–1724), which comprises the Upper and Lower Palaces, divided by magnificent gardens.

Hill, David Octavius Scottish landscape painter and photographer. He collaborated with fellow Scottish photographer Robert Adamson. See ▷Hill and Adamson.

Hill, (Norman) Graham (1929–1975) English motor-racing driver. He won the Dutch Grand Prix in 1962, progressing to the world driver's title in 1962 and 1968. In 1972 he became the first Formula 1 World Champion to win the Le Mans Grand Prix d'Endurance (Le Mans 24-Hour Race). He was also the only driver to win the Formula 1 world championship, Le Mans 24-Hour Race, and the Indianapolis 500 Race in his career as a driver. Hill started his Formula 1 career with Lotus in 1958, went to BRM 1960–66, returned to Lotus 1967–69, moved to Brabham 1970–72, and formed his own team, Embassy Shadow, 1973–75. He was killed in an air crash. His son Damon won his first Grand Prix in 1993, making them the first father and son both to win a Grand Prix.

Hill, Rowland (1795–1879) English Post Office official who reformed the postage system with the introduction of adhesive stamps. His pamphlet *Post Office Reform* (1837) prompted the introduction of the penny prepaid post in 1840 (previously the addressee paid, according to distance, on receipt).

Hill and Adamson David Octavius Hill (1802–1870) and Robert R Adamson (1821–1848). Scottish photographers who worked together 1843–48. They made extensive use of the ▷calotype process in their portraits of leading members of the Free Church of Scotland and their views of Edinburgh and the Scottish fishing village of Newhaven. They produced some 2,500 calotypes. Their work was rediscovered around 1900.

hill figure in Britain, any of a number of figures, usually of animals, cut from the turf to reveal the underlying chalk. Their origins are variously attributed to Celts, Romans, Saxons, Druids, or Benedictine monks, although most are of modern rather than ancient construction. Examples include 17 White Horses, and giants such as the Cerne Abbas Giant, near Dorchester, Dorset, associated with a prehistoric fertility cult.

Nearly 50 hill figures are known in Britain, of which all but four are on the southern chalk downs of England. Some are landmarks or memorials; others have a religious or ritual purpose. It is possible that the current figures are on the site of, or reinforce, previous ones. There may have been large numbers of figures dotted on the landscape in the Iron Age, which were not maintained. The White Horse at Uffington, on the Berkshire Downs, used to be annually 'scoured' in a folk ceremony.

Other hill-figure designs include the Long Man of Wilmington on Windover Hill, East Sussex; crosses, such as the Bledlow and Whiteleaf crosses on the Chiltern Hills; a collection of military badges made at Fovant Down, Wiltshire (1916); an aeroplane, and a crown. A stag at Mormond Hill, Aberdeenshire, Scotland, is cut into white quartz.

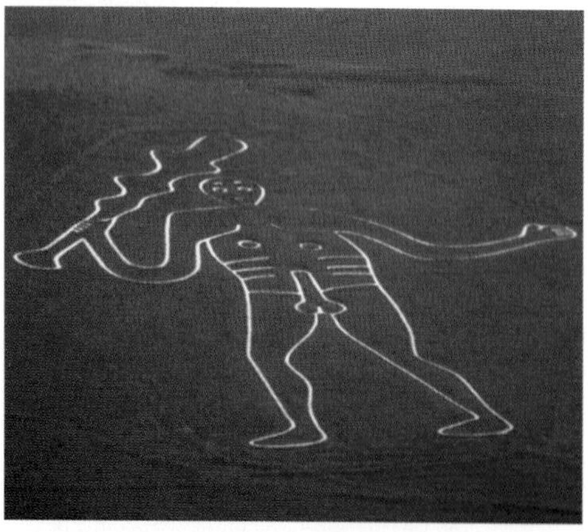

HILL FIGURE The Cerne Abbas Giant, measuring 55 m/180 ft long, on a hillside near the village of Cerne Abbas, Dorset, England. *Image Bank*

Hillary, Edmund (Percival) (1919–) New Zealand mountaineer. In 1953, with Nepalese Sherpa mountaineer Tenzing Norgay, he reached the summit of Mount Everest, the first to climb the world's highest peak. As a member of the Commonwealth Transantarctic Expedition 1957–58, he was the first person since R F Scott to reach the South Pole overland, on 3 January 1958. He was knighted in 1953.

On the way to the South Pole he laid depots for Vivian Fuchs's completion of the crossing of the continent.

Related Web site: Edmund Hillary Profile http://www.achievement.org/autodoc/page/hil0pro-1

Hilliard, Nicholas (*c.* 1547–1619) English miniaturist and goldsmith. Court artist to Elizabeth I and James I, he painted many leading figures of Tudor and Stuart society, including Francis Drake, Walter Raleigh, and Mary Queen of Scots, as well as several portraits of Elizabeth I herself. Some of his minatures, in particular *An Unknown Young Man Amid Roses* (*c.* 1590; Victoria and Albert Museum, London), place the sitter in a closely observed natural setting.

NICHOLAS HILLIARD *Portrait of an Unknown Young Man against a Background of Flames*, by English miniaturist Nicholas Hilliard, was painted for a locket. The fashion for miniatures, with their rather mannered subjects, was at its height in the late 16th century, and they were usually commissioned as gifts. *The Art Archive/Modovita Monastery Rumania/Dagli Orti*

Hillsborough Agreement another name for the ▷Anglo-Irish Agreement (1985).

Hilton, James (1900–1954) English-born US novelist. His books include *Lost Horizon* (1933), envisaging Shangri-la, a remote district of Tibet where time stands still; and *Goodbye, Mr Chips* (1934), a portrait of an old schoolteacher, written in four days for serialization in the *British Weekly* in 1933.

Himachal Pradesh state of northwest India, to the south of Kashmir and west of Tibet; area 55,700 sq km/21,500 sq mi; population (2001 est) 6,235,000 (mainly Hindu; some Buddhists). The capital is Shimla, which lies at an altitude of 2,213 m/7,200 ft. Himachal Pradesh is a mainly agricultural state, partly forested, producing fruit, grain, rice, and seed potatoes. The chief industry is timber; other industries are the small-scale mining of slate, gypsum, and limestone; iron foundry; the production of resin, fertilizer, and turpentine; and electronics. The mountain scenery attracts increasing numbers of tourists.

Himalayas vast mountain system of central Asia, extending from the Indian states of Kashmir in the west to Assam in the east, covering the southern part of Tibet, Nepal, Sikkim, and Bhutan. It is the highest mountain range in the world. The two highest peaks are Mount ▷Everest and ▷K2. Other peaks include ▷Kanchenjunga, Makalu, Annapurna, and Nanga Parbat, all over 8,000 m/26,000 ft.

Related Web site: Himalayas: Where Earth Meets Sky http://library.advanced.org/10131/javascriptmenu_final.html

Himmler, Heinrich (1900–1945) German Nazi leader, head of the ▷SS elite corps from 1929, the police and the ▷Gestapo secret police from 1936, and supervisor of the extermination of the Jews in Eastern Europe. During World War II he replaced Hermann Goering as Hitler's second-in-command. He was captured in May 1945 and committed suicide.

Born in Munich, he joined the Nazi Party in 1925 and became chief of the Bavarian police in 1933. His accumulation of offices meant he had command of all German police forces by 1936, which made him one of the most powerful people in Germany. He was appointed minister of the interior in 1943 in an attempt to stamp out defeatism and following the July Plot in 1944 became commander-in-chief of the home forces. In April 1945 he made a proposal to the Allies that Germany should surrender to the USA and Britain but not to the USSR, which was rejected.

Hīnayāna (Sanskrit 'lesser vehicle') Mahāyāna Buddhist name for ▷Theravāda Buddhism.

Hindemith, Paul (1895–1963) German composer and teacher. His operas *Cardillac* (1926, revised 1952) and *Mathis der Maler/Mathis the Painter* (1933–35) are theatrically astute and politically aware; as a teacher in Berlin 1927–33 he encouraged the development of a functional modern repertoire ('Gebrauchsmusik'/'utility music') for home and school.

> **Paul Hindemith**
> *Tonality is a natural force, like gravity.*
> *The Craft of Musical Composition* 1937

Hindenburg, Paul Ludwig Hans Anton von Beneckendorf und Hindenburg (1847–1934) German field marshal and right-wing politician. During World War I he was supreme commander and, with Erich von Ludendorff, practically directed Germany's policy until the end of the war. He was president of Germany 1925–33.

Born in Poznań of a Prussian Junker (aristocratic landowner) family, he was commissioned in 1866, served in the Austro-Prussian and Franco-German wars, and retired in 1911. Given the command in East Prussia in August 1914, he received the credit for the defeat of the Russians at Tannenberg and was promoted to supreme commander and field marshal. Re-elected president in 1932, he was compelled to invite Adolf Hitler to assume the chancellorship in January 1933.

Hindenburg Line German western line of World War I fortifications running from Arras to Laon, built 1916–17. Part of the line was taken by the British in the third battle of Arras, but it generally resisted attack until the British offensive of summer 1918.

Hindi language member of the Indo-Iranian branch of the Indo-European language family, the official language of the Republic of India, although resisted as such by the Dravidian-speaking states of the south. Hindi proper is used by some 30% of Indians, in such northern states as Uttar Pradesh and Madhya Pradesh.

Related Web site: Hindi Language and Literature http://www.cs.colostate.edu/~malaiya/hindiint.html

Hinduism (Hindu *sanatana dharma* 'eternal tradition') religion originating in northern India about 4,000 years ago, which is superficially and in some of its forms polytheistic, but has a concept of the supreme spirit, ▷Brahman, above the many divine manifestations. These include the triad of chief gods (the Trimurti): ▷Brahma, ▷Vishnu, and ▷Siva (creator, preserver, and destroyer). Central to Hinduism are the beliefs in reincarnation and ▷*karma*; the oldest scriptures are the ▷*Vedas*. Temple worship is almost universally observed and there are many festivals. There are over 805 million Hindus worldwide. Women are not regarded as the equals of men but should be treated with kindness and respect. Muslim influence in northern India led to the veiling of women and the restriction of their movements from about the end of the 12th century.

Roots Hindu beliefs originated in the ▷Indus Valley civilization about 4,500 years ago, which passed on a rich assortment of myths and legends to the ▷Dravidians. Following the invasion of northern India by the Aryans, about 3,000 years ago, these myths were absorbed into Aryan ritual and religion, which now forms much of the tradition of Hindu religion. Ancient Babylonian and Egyptian influences are also discernible.

Scriptures The *Veda* collection of hymns, compiled by the Aryans, was followed by the philosophical ▷*Upanishads*, centring on the doctrine of Brahman; and the epics, containing both Aryan and pre-Aryan material, ▷*Rāmāyana* and ▷*Mahābhārata* (which includes the ▷*Bhagavad-Gītā*). All were in existence before the Christian era. The ▷*Puranas*, sacred historical texts dating from the 4th century AD, reflect the many cultural streams of India.

Beliefs Hindu belief and ritual can vary greatly even between villages. Some deities achieve widespread popularity such as ▷Krishna, Hanuman, ▷Lakshmi, and ▷Mahādevī; others, more localized and specialized, are referred to particularly in times of sickness or need. Some deities manifest themselves in different incarnations or avatars such as ▷Rama or Krishna, both avatars of the god Vishnu.

Underlying this multifaceted worship is the creative strength of Brahman, the supreme being. Hindus believe that all living things are part of Brahman: they are sparks of *atman* or divine life that transmute from one body to another, sometimes descending into the form of a plant or an insect, sometimes the body of a human. This is all according to its *karma* or past actions which are the cause of its sufferings or joy as it rises and falls in *samsara* (the endless cycle of birth and death). Humans have the opportunity, through knowledge and devotion, to break the karmic chain and achieve final liberation, or *moksha*. The *atman* is then free to return to Brahman.

The creative force of the universe is recognized in the god Brahma. Once he has brought the cosmos into being, it is sustained by Vishnu and then annihilated by the god Siva, only to be created once more by Brahma. Vishnu and Siva are, respectively, the forces of light and darkness, preservation and destruction, with Brahma as the balancing force that enables the existence and interaction of life. The cosmos is seen as both real and an illusion ▷*maya*, since its reality is not lasting; the cosmos is itself personified as the goddess Maya.

HINDUISM A Hindu priest making offerings in Varanasi, Uttar Pradesh, India. *Corel*

Practice Hinduism has a complex of rites and ceremonies performed within the framework of the *jati*, or caste system, under the supervision of the Brahman priests and teachers. In India, caste is traditionally derived from the four classes of early Hindu society: brahmans (priests), kshatriyas (nobles and warriors), vaisyas (traders and cultivators), and sudras (servants). A fifth class, the untouchables, regarded as polluting in its origins, remained (and still largely remains) on the edge of Hindu society. The Indian Constituent Assembly (1947) made discrimination against the Scheduled Castes or Depressed Classes illegal, but strong prejudice continues.

Western influence ▷The International Society for Krishna Consciousness (ISKON), the Western organization of the Hare Krishna movement, was introduced to the West by Swami Prabhupada (1896–1977). Members are expected to lead ascetic lives. It is based on devotion to Krishna which includes study of the *Bhagavad-Gītā*, temple and home ritual, and the chanting of the name Hare (saviour) Krishna. Members are expected to avoid meat, eggs, alcohol, tea, coffee, drugs, and gambling. Sexual relationships should be only for procreation within the bonds of marriage.

Hindu Kush mountain range in central Asia, length 800 km/500 mi, greatest height Tirich Mir, 7,690 m/25,239 ft, in Pakistan. The narrow Khyber Pass (53 km/33 mi long) connects Pakistan with Afghanistan and was used by ▷Babur and other invaders of India. The present road was built by the British in the Afghan Wars.

Hindustan ('land of the Hindus') the whole of India, but more specifically the plain of the ▷Ganges and ▷Yamuna rivers, or that part of India north of the ▷Deccan.

Hindustani member of the Indo-Iranian branch of the Indo-European language family, closely related to Hindi and Urdu and originating in the bazaars of Delhi. It is a ▷lingua franca in many parts of the Republic of India.

Hingis, Martina (1980–) Czech-born Swiss tennis player. In 1996 she became the youngest-ever winner of a Grand Slam title when she won the Wimbledon women's doubles title at the age of 15 years 282 days. In January 1997, at 16 years 92 days, she won the women's singles at the Australian Open. Three months later she became the youngest player to be ranked as number one in the world since the women's official rankings began. In 1997, at 16 years 279 days she became the youngest winner of a singles title at Wimbledon since Lottie Dod won the women's singles in 1887 at the age of 15 years 285 days. In the same year she became the US Open singles champion. In early 1998 she retained her Australian Open singles title, defeating the 1994 Wimbledon champion Conchita Martinez of Spain in the final. She won the women's singles at the Australian Open for the third year in a row in January 1999, also achieving her third successive doubles title at the same championships. She won the 2000 French Open doubles title (with Mary Pierce of France).

Hingis, Martina http://www.hingis.org/

Hipparchus (*c.* 190–*c.* 120 BC) Greek astronomer and mathematician. He invented trigonometry and calculated the lengths of the solar year and the lunar month, discovered the precession of the equinoxes, made a catalogue of 850 fixed stars, and advanced Eratosthenes' method of determining the situation of places on the Earth's surface by lines of latitude and longitude.

Hipparcos (acronym for **high precision parallax collecting satellite**) satellite launched by the European Space Agency in 1989. Named after the Greek astronomer Hipparchus, it is the world's first ▷astrometry satellite and is providing precise positions, distances, colours, brightnesses, and apparent motions for over 100,000 stars.

hippie member of a youth movement of the late 1960s, also known as **flower power**, which originated in San Francisco, California, and was characterized by nonviolent anarchy, concern for the environment, and rejection of Western materialism. The hippies formed a politically outspoken, anti-war, artistically prolific counterculture in North America and Europe. Their colourful psychedelic style, inspired by drugs such as ▷LSD, emerged in fashion, graphic art, and music by bands such as Love (1965–71), the Grateful Dead, Jefferson Airplane (1965–74), and ▷Pink Floyd.

Hippocrates (*c.* 460–*c.* 377 BC) Greek physician, often called the founder of medicine. Important Hippocratic ideas include cleanliness (for patients and physicians), moderation in eating and drinking, letting nature take its course, and living where the air is good. He believed that health was the result of the 'humours' of the body being in balance; imbalance caused disease. These ideas were later adopted by ▷Galen.

He was born and practised on the island of Kos, where he founded a medical school. He travelled throughout Greece and Asia Minor, and died in Larisa, Thessaly. He is known to have discovered aspirin in willow bark. The *Corpus Hippocraticum/Hippocratic Collection*, a group of some 70 works, is attributed to him but was probably not written by him, although the works outline his approach to medicine. They include *Aphorisms* and the Hippocratic Oath, which embodies the essence of medical ethics.

Related Web site: Works by Hippocrates http://classics.mit.edu/Browse/browse-Hippocrates.html

Hippocrates

Life is short, the Art long, opportunity fleeting, experience treacherous, judgment difficult.

Aphorisms I, 1

Hippolytus in Greek mythology, the charioteer son of ▷Theseus, loved by his stepmother Phaedra. Enraged by his rejection, she falsely accused him of dishonouring her and committed suicide, turning Theseus against his son. The sea god ▷Poseidon, who owed Theseus a wish, sent a monster as Hippolytus drove on the shore near Troezen; the frightened chariot horses dragged him to death. His story was dramatized in *Hippolytus* by ▷Euripides .

hippopotamus (Greek 'river horse') large herbivorous, short-legged, even-toed hoofed mammal. The **common hippopotamus** (*Hippopotamus amphibius*) is found in Africa. It weighs up to 3,200 kg/7,040 lb, stands about 1.6 m/5.25 ft tall, and has a brown or slate-grey skin. It is an endangered species. (Family Hippopotamidae.)

Hippos are social animals and live in groups. Because they dehydrate rapidly (at least twice as quickly as humans), they must stay close to water. When underwater, adults need to breath every 2–5 minutes and calves every 30 seconds. When out of water, their skin exudes an oily red fluid that protects them against the Sun's ultraviolet rays. The hippopotamus spends the day wallowing in rivers or waterholes, only emerging at night to graze. It can eat up to 25–40 kg/55–88 lb of grass each night. The **pygmy hippopotamus** (*Choeropsis liberiensis*) lives in West Africa.

HIPPOPOTAMUS The *Hippopotamus amphibius* in a river in Tanzania. *Ken Preston-Mafham/Premaphotos Wildlife*

There are about 157,000 hippos in Africa (1993 estimate), but they are under threat from hunters because of the value of their meat, hides, and large canine teeth (up to 0.5 m/1.6 ft long), which are used as a substitute for ivory.

Related Web site: Hippopotamus http://www.seaworld.org/animal_bytes/hippopotamusab.html

hire purchase (**HP**) form of credit under which the buyer pays a deposit and makes instalment payments at fixed intervals over a certain period for a particular item. The buyer has immediate possession, but does not own the item until the final instalment has been paid.

Hirohito (1901–1989) Regnal name **Shōwa**. Emperor of Japan from 1926, when he succeeded his father Taishō (Yoshihito). After the defeat of Japan in World War II in 1945, he was made a figurehead monarch by the US-backed constitution of 1946. He is believed to have played a reluctant role in General ▷Tōjō's prewar expansion plans. He was succeeded by his son ▷Akihito.

As the war turned against Japan from June 1942, Tōjō involved him more in national life, calling upon the people to make sacrifices in his name. He belatedly began to exert more influence over his government as defeat became imminent in 1945, but was too late to act before the atomic bombs were dropped on Hiroshima and Nagasaki. His speech on Japanese radio on 15 August 1945 announcing the previous day's surrender was the first time a Japanese emperor had directly addressed his people. The Shōwa emperor ruled Japan with dignity during and after the US occupation following World War II. He was a scholar of botany and zoology and the author of books on marine biology.

Hiroshige, Andō (1797–1858) Japanese artist. He was one of the leading exponents of ▷ukiyo-e prints, an art form whose flat, decorative style and choice of everyday subjects influenced such artists as James Whistler and Vincent van Gogh. His landscape prints, often employing snow or rain to create atmosphere, include *Tōkaidō gojūsan tsugi/53 Stations on the Tōkaidō Highway* (1833).

Hiroshige was born in Edo (now Tokyo), and most of his subjects were taken from the vicinity of Edo or were scenes on the old Tokaido highway between Edo and Kyoto. His last series, *Meishō Edo hyakkei/100 Famous Views of Edo* (1856–58), was incomplete at his death. He is thought to have made over 5,000 different prints.

Hiroshima industrial city and port on the south coast of Honshu island, Japan; population (1994) 1,077,000. On 6 August 1945 it was destroyed by the first wartime use of an atomic bomb. The city has largely been rebuilt since then. The main industries include food processing and the manufacture of cars and machinery.

Related Web site: Atomic Bombings of Hiroshima and Nagasaki http://www.yale.edu/lawweb/avalon/abomb/mpmenu.htm

Hispania Roman provinces of Spain and Portugal. The republican provinces were Hispania Citerior ('Nearer', the Ebro region), and Ulterior ('Farther', the Guadalquivir region). Under the empire the peninsula was divided into three administrative areas: Lusitania in the west, Baetica in the south, and Tarraconensis. The Roman emperors Trajan and Hadrian came from Baetica.

Hispanic Spanish-speaking person in the USA, especially of Latin American descent, either native-born or immigrant from Mexico, Cuba, Puerto Rico, or any other Spanish-speaking country.

Hispaniola (Spanish 'little Spain') West Indian island, first landing place of Columbus in the New World, 6 December 1492; it is now divided into ▷Haiti and the ▷Dominican Republic.

Hiss, Alger (1904–1996) US diplomat and liberal Democrat, a former State Department official, imprisoned in 1950 for perjury when he denied having been a Soviet spy. There are doubts about the justice of Hiss's conviction.

histamine inflammatory substance normally released in damaged tissues, which also accounts for many of the symptoms of ▷allergy. It is an amine, $C_5H_9N_3$. Substances that neutralize its activity are known as ▷antihistamines. Histamine was first described in 1911 by British physiologist Henry Dale (1875–1968).

histogram in statistics, a graph showing frequency of data, in which the horizontal axis details discrete units or class boundaries, and the vertical axis represents the frequency. Blocks are drawn such that their areas (rather than their height as in a bar chart) are proportional to the frequencies within a class or across several class boundaries. There are no spaces between blocks.

historical materialism the application of the principles of ▷dialectical materialism to history and sociology. This decrees that the social, political, and cultural superstructure of a society is determined by its economic base and that developments are therefore governed by laws with no room for the influence of individuals. In this theory, change occurs through the meeting of opposing forces (thesis and antithesis) which leads to the production of a higher force (synthesis).

historical novel fictional prose narrative set in the past. Literature set in the historic rather than the immediate past has always abounded, but in the West, Walter Scott began the modern tradition by setting imaginative romances of love, impersonation, and betrayal in a past based on known fact; his use of historical detail, and subsequent imitations of this technique by European writers, gave rise to the genre.

history record of the events of human societies. The earliest surviving historical records are inscriptions concerning the achievements of Egyptian and Babylonian kings. As a literary form in the Western world, historical writing, or **historiography**, began in the 5th century BC with the Greek Herodotus, who was first to pass beyond the limits of a purely national outlook. Contemporary historians make extensive use of statistics, population figures, and primary records to justify historical arguments.

Greek and Roman history A generation after Herodotus, Thucydides brought to history a strong sense of the political and military ambitions of his native Athens. His close account of the ▷Peloponnesian War was continued by ▷Xenophon. Later Greek history and Roman history tended towards rhetoric; Sallust tried to recreate the style of Thucydides, but Livy wrote an Augustan history of his city and its conquests, and Tacitus expressed his cynicism about the imperial dynasty.

Medieval and Renaissance European history Medieval history was dominated by a religious philosophy sustained by the Christian church. English chroniclers of this period are Bede, William of Malmesbury, and Matthew Paris. France produced great chroniclers of contemporary events in Jean Froissart and Philippe Comines. The Renaissance revived historical writing and the study of history both by restoring classical models and by creating the science of textual criticism. A product of the new secular spirit was Machiavelli's *History of Florence* (1520–23).

18th- and 19th-century Western history This critical approach continued into the 17th century, but the 18th century ▷Enlightenment disposed of the attempt to explain history in theological terms, and an interpretive masterpiece was produced by Edward Gibbon, *The Decline and Fall of the Roman Empire* (1776–88). An attempt to formulate a historical method and a philosophy of history, that of the Italian Giovanni Vico, remained almost unknown until the 19th century. Romanticism left its mark on 19th-century historical writing in the tendency to exalt the contribution of the individual 'hero', and in the introduction of a more colourful and dramatic style and treatment, variously illustrated in the works of the French historian Jules Michelet and the British writers Thomas Carlyle and Thomas Macaulay.

20th-century history During the 20th century the study of history has been revolutionized, partly through the contributions of other disciplines, such as the sciences and anthropology. The deciphering of the Egyptian and Babylonian inscriptions was of great importance. Researchers and archaeologists have traced developments in prehistory, and have revealed forgotten civilizations such as that of Crete. Anthropological studies of primitive society and religion, which began with James Frazer's *Golden Bough* (1890), have attempted to analyse the bases of later forms of social organization and belief. The changes brought about by the Industrial Revolution and the accompanying perception of economics as a science forced historians to turn their attention to economic questions. Karl Marx's attempt to find in economic development the most significant, although not the only, determining factor in social change, has influenced many historians. History from the point of view of ordinary people is now recognized as an important element in historical study. Associated with this is the collection of spoken records known as **oral history**.

A comparative study of civilizations is offered in A J Toynbee's *Study of History* (1934–54) and on a smaller scale by J M Roberts's *History of the World* (1992). Contemporary historians make a distinction between historical evidence or records, historical writing, and historical method or approaches to the study of history. The study of historical method is also known as **historiography**.

Related Web site: Hyper History http://www.hyperhistory.com/online_n2/History_N2/a.html

Hitachi Japanese electrical and electronic company, one of the world's largest and most diversified manufacturers of industrial machinery. It has offices in 39 countries and over 100 factories, which manufacture 40,000 different products, ranging from electrical home appliances and stereo and high-tech telecommunications equipment (for which it is best known) to

---

Hitchcock, The Master of Suspense

Selected Cameo Appearances

Film	Date	Role
The Thirty-Nine Steps	1935	seven minutes after the beginning of the film, walking in the street throwing litter
The Lady Vanishes	1938	in a train station, wearing a black coat and smoking a cigarette, near the end of the film
Suspicion	1941	in a village scene, about 45 minutes after the beginning of the film, posting a letter
Spellbound	1945	about 40 minutes after the beginning of the film, coming out of a hotel elevator smoking a cigarette and carrying a violin case
Rear Window	1954	about 30 minutes after the beginning of the film, winding a clock in the songwriter's apartment
Vertigo	1958	11 minutes after the beginning of the film, in a street scene, carrying a black case
North by Northwest	1959	at the end of the opening credits, missing a bus
Psycho	1960	seen through an office window, standing on the street wearing a cowboy hat
The Birds	1963	at the beginning of the film, walking two dogs out of the pet shop
Torn Curtain	1966	soon after the beginning of the film, sitting in a hotel lobby holding a baby
Frenzy	1972	in the crowd scene by a river, listening to a politician's speech at the beginning of the film

ALFRED HITCHCOCK A promotional still for the Hitchcock film *The Birds*, an adaptation of a story by Daphne du Maurier made in 1963, shows the film director posing with a seagull and a raven. *Archive Photos*

---

heavy industrial machinery, such as hydroelectric turbines and nuclear generators. As one of Japan's largest private employers, it had net sales in 1990–91 of over £31 billion.

Hitchcock, Alfred (Joseph) (1899–1980) English film director, a US citizen from 1955. A master of the suspense thriller, he was noted for his meticulously drawn storyboards that determined his camera angles and for cameo walk-ons in his own films. His *Blackmail* (1929) was the first successful British talking film. *The Thirty-Nine Steps* (1935) and *The Lady Vanishes* (1938) are British suspense classics. He went to Hollywood in 1940, and his work there included *Rebecca* (1940), *Notorious* (1946), *Strangers on a Train* (1951), *Rear Window* (1954), *Vertigo* (1958), *North by Northwest* (1959), *Psycho* (1960), and *The Birds* (1963).

Hitler, Adolf (1889–1945) German Nazi dictator, born in Austria. He was *Führer* (leader) of the ▷Nazi Party from 1921 and wrote *Mein Kampf/My Struggle* (1925–27). As chancellor of Germany from 1933 and head of state from 1934, he created a dictatorship by playing party and state institutions against each other and continually creating new offices and appointments. His position was not seriously challenged until the July Plot of 1944, which failed to assassinate him. In foreign affairs, he reoccupied the Rhineland and formed an alliance with the Italian Fascist Benito ▷Mussolini in 1936, annexed Austria in 1938, and occupied Sudeten under the ▷Munich Agreement. The rest of Czechoslovakia was annexed in March 1939. The ▷Ribbentrop–Molotov pact was followed in September by the invasion of Poland and the declaration of war by Britain and France (see ▷World War II). He committed suicide as Berlin fell.

Hitler was born in Braunau-am-Inn, and spent his early years in poverty in Vienna and Munich. After serving as a volunteer in the German army during World War I, he was employed as a spy by the military authorities in Munich and in 1919 joined, in this capacity, the German Workers' Party. By 1921 he had assumed its leadership, renamed it the National Socialist German Workers' Party (Nazi Party for short), and provided it with a programme that mixed nationalism with ▷anti-Semitism. Having led an unsuccessful uprising in Munich in 1923, he served nine months in prison, during which he wrote his political testament, *Mein Kampf.*

The party did not achieve national importance until the elections of 1930; by 1932, although Field Marshal ▷Hindenburg defeated Hitler in the presidential elections, it formed the largest group in the Reichstag (parliament). As the result of an intrigue directed by Chancellor Franz von Papen, Hitler became chancellor in a Nazi–Nationalist coalition on 30 January 1933. The opposition

was rapidly suppressed, the Nationalists removed from the government, and the Nazis declared the only legal party. In 1934 Hitler succeeded Hindenburg as head of state. Meanwhile, the drive to war began; Germany left the ▷League of Nations, conscription was reintroduced, and in 1936 the Rhineland was reoccupied.

Hitler and Mussolini, who were already both involved in the Spanish Civil War, formed an alliance (the ▷Axis) in 1936, joined by Japan in 1940. Hitler conducted the war in a ruthless but idiosyncratic way, took and ruled most of the neighbouring countries with repressive occupation forces, and had millions of Slavs, Jews, Romanies, homosexuals, and political enemies killed in ▷concentration camps and massacres. He narrowly escaped death on 20 July 1944 from a bomb explosion at a staff meeting, prepared by high-ranking officers. On 29 April 1945, when Berlin was largely in Soviet hands, he married his mistress Eva Braun in his bunker under the chancellery building and on the following day committed suicide with her.

Related Web site: Rise of Hitler http://www.historyplace.com/worldwar2/riseofhitler/index.htm

ADOLF HITLER Adolf Hitler in a poster from the 1930s, bearing the slogan 'One People, one Reich, one Führer'. *Archive Photos*

Philip Guedalla
English writer and historian

History repeats itself. Historians repeat each other.

Supers and Supermen,
'Some Historians'

Ein Volk, ein Reich, ein Führer!

Hitler–Stalin pact another name for the
▷Ribbentrop–Molotov pact.

Hittite member of any of a succession of peoples who inhabited Anatolia and northern Syria from the 3rd millennium to the 1st millennium BC. The city of Hattusas (now Boğazköy in central Turkey) became the capital of a strong kingdom which overthrew the Babylonian Empire. After a period of eclipse the Hittite New Empire became a great power (about 1400–1200 BC), which successfully waged war with Egypt. The Hittite language is an Indo-European language.

HIV (abbreviation for human immunodeficiency virus) the infectious agent that is believed to cause ▷AIDS. It was first discovered in 1983 by Luc Montagnier of the Pasteur Institute in Paris, who called it lymphocyte-associated virus (LAV). Independently, US scientist Robert Gallo of the National Cancer Institute in Bethesda, Maryland, claimed its discovery in 1984 and named it human T-lymphocytotrophic virus 3 (HTLV-III).
The development of HIV Many people who have HIV in their blood are not ill; in fact, it was initially thought that during the delay between infection with HIV and the development of AIDS the virus lay dormant. However, US researchers estimated in 1995 that HIV reproduces at a rate of a billion viruses a day, even in individuals with no symptoms, but is held at bay by the immune system producing enough white blood cells (CD4 cells) to destroy them. Gradually, the virus mutates so much that the immune system is unable to continue to counteract; people with advanced AIDS have virtually no CD4 cells remaining. These results indicate the importance of treating HIV-positive individuals before symptoms develop, rather than delaying treatment until the onset of AIDS.
HIV statistics In January 2000 the United Nations (UN) AIDS programme (UNAIDS) estimated there were 34 million HIV-positive people in the world, 95% of whom lived in the developing world. In sub-Saharan Africa, HIV infections numbered 24.5 million (equivalent to 9% of the adult population), in South and Southeast Asia, 5.6 million (0.5%), in South America 1.3 million (0.5%), in North America 900,000 (0.6%), in East Asia 530,000 (0.06%), in the Caribbean 360,000 (2.1%), in Western Europe 520,000 (0.2%), in Eastern Europe and Central Asia 420,000 (0.2%), in North Africa and the Middle East 220,000 (0.1%), and in Australia and New Zealand 150,000 (0.1%). In sub-Saharan Africa, 55% of adult infections were among women and in the Caribbean the rate was 37%. Elsewhere, typically over 70% of infections are among men. In 2001 there were 5 million new cases of HIV infections worldwide – around 14,000 new cases a day.

Hmong member of a Southeast Asian highland people. They are predominantly hill farmers, rearing pigs and cultivating rice and grain, and many are involved in growing the opium poppy. Estimates of the size of the Hmong population vary between 1.5 million and 5 million, the greatest number being in China. Although traditional beliefs, which have many Taoist elements, remain important, many have adopted Christianity. Their language belongs to the Sino-Tibetan family. The names **Meo** or **Miao**, sometimes used to refer to the Hmong, are considered derogatory.

hoatzin tropical bird found only in tropical rainforests, usually over rivers, especially in the Amazon and Orinoco basins of South America. A hoatzin resembles a small pheasant in size and appearance. The beak is thick and the facial skin blue. Adults are olive-coloured with white markings above and red-brown below. The hoatzin is the only bird in its family. (Species *Opisthocomus hoatzin*, family Opisthocomidae, order Galliformes.)

Hoban, James (1762–1831) Irish-born architect. He emigrated to the USA where he designed the White House, Washington, DC; he also worked on the Capitol and other public buildings.

Hobart capital and principal port of ▷Tasmania, Australia; population (1996) 126,118. Hobart is situated on the southeast coast of the island, at the mouth of the River Derwent. Industries include zinc processing, brewing, electronics, engineering, fruit and vegetable processing, chocolate making, shipbuilding, and the production of textiles, paper, furniture, and newsprint. Hobart is a centre for yachting, fishing, and trading; exports include fruit, textiles, and processed food. The University of Tasmania (founded in 1890) is located here.
   Australia's second-oldest city after Sydney, Hobart was founded in 1804 and named after Lord Hobart (1760–1816), then secretary of state for the colonies.

Hobbema, Meindert Lubbertzsoon (1638–1709) Dutch landscape painter. A pupil of Ruisdael, his early work is derivative, but later works are characteristically realistic and unsentimental. His best-known work is *The Avenue, Middelharnis* (1689; National Gallery, London).

THOMAS HOBBES Title page of Hobbes's *Leviathan or the matter, form, and power of a Commonwealth, Ecclesiastical and Civil*. English philosopher Thomas Hobbes wrote this treatise in 1651, believing that without the fear inherent in absolute rule, the natural state of the human race is selfish and moved only by a need for power. *The Art Archive/British Library*

Hobbes, Thomas (1588–1679) English political philosopher and the first thinker since Aristotle to attempt to develop a comprehensive theory of nature, including human behaviour. In *Leviathan* (1651), he advocates absolutist government as the only means of ensuring order and security; he saw this as deriving from the ▷social contract.
   He was tutor to the exiled Prince Charles (later Charles II).

hobby small ▷falcon found across Europe and northern Asia. It is about 30 cm/1 ft long, with a grey-blue back, streaked front, and chestnut thighs. It is found in open woods and heaths, and feeds on insects and small birds. (Species *Falco subbuteo*.)

> ### Jimmy Hoffa
> *An ego is just imagination. And if a man doesn't have imagination he'll be working for someone else for the rest of his life.*
> Esquire

Ho Chi Minh (1890–1969) Adopted name of Nguyen Tat Thanh. North Vietnamese communist politician, prime minister 1954–55, and president 1954–69. Having trained in Moscow shortly after the Russian Revolution, he headed the communist Vietminh from 1941 and fought against the French during the ▷Indochina War 1946–54, becoming president and prime minister of the republic at the armistice. Aided by the communist bloc, he did much to develop industrial potential. He relinquished the premiership in 1955, but continued as president. In the years before his death, Ho successfully led his country's fight against US-aided South Vietnam in the ▷Vietnam War 1954–75.
   Related Web site: Ho Chi Minh http://www.pathfinder.com/time/time100/leaders/profile/hochiminh.html

Ho Chi Minh City (formerly **Saigon** (until 1976)) chief port and industrial city of South Vietnam; population (1997 est) 3,571,000 (the largest city in Vietnam). It lies on the Saigon River, 54 km/ 34 mi from the South China Sea. Industries include shipbuilding, textiles, rubber, and food products. Saigon was the capital of the Republic of Vietnam (South Vietnam) from 1954 to 1976, when it was renamed, and the city was also the former capital of French Indochina.

Hockney, David (1937–   ) English painter, printmaker, and designer, resident in California. One of the best-known figures in British pop art, he developed a distinctive figurative style, as in his portrait *Mr and Mrs Clark and Percy* (1971; Tate Gallery, London). He has experimented prolifically with technique, and produced drawings; etchings, including *Six Fairy Tales from the Brothers Grimm* (1970); photo collages; and opera sets for Glyndebourne, East Sussex; La Scala, Milan; and the Metropolitan, New York.

Born in Yorkshire, he studied at Bradford School of Art and then at the Royal College of Art, London, from 1959 to 1962. He exhibited at the Young Contemporaries Show in 1961 and held his first solo exhibition in 1963, showing paintings that exploited pictorial ambiguities in a witty, self-consciously naive manner.
   In 1964 he went to California and many of his later paintings are concerned with Los Angeles life, his views of swimming pools reflecting a preoccupation with surface pattern and effects of light. His drawings in pencil or pen and ink, many of them portraits of friends, are carried out with seemingly effortless ability.
   As well as illustrations to Grimm, in 1963 he produced a series of etchings updating Hogarth's *The Rake's Progress*. In 1975 he designed the sets and costumes for the Glyndebourne Festival Theatre production of Igor Stravinsky's opera *The Rake's Progress*. During the 1980s his work included some experiments with unconventional media, including prints created on a photocopier, but he still regards painting as his main activity. In 1992 he began a series called *Very New Paintings*, depicting Californian scenery. In 1999 he was awarded the Royal Academy Summer Exhibition Award.
   He was the subject of Jack Hazan's semidocumentary film *A Bigger Splash* (1974).

Hodgkin, Dorothy Mary Crowfoot (1910–1994) English biochemist who analysed the structure of penicillin, insulin, and vitamin B_{12}. Hodgkin was the first to use a computer to analyse the molecular structure of complex chemicals, and this enabled her to produce three-dimensional models. She was awarded the Nobel Prize for Chemistry in 1964 for her work in the crystallographic determination of the structures of biochemical compounds, notably penicillin and cyanocobalamin (vitamin B_{12}).

Hodgkin's disease (or **lymphadenoma**) rare form of cancer mainly affecting the lymph nodes and spleen. It undermines the immune system, leaving the sufferer susceptible to infection.
   However, it responds well to radiotherapy and ▷cytotoxic drugs, and long-term survival is usual.

Hoffa, Jimmy (James Riddle) (1913–1975) US labour leader, president of the International Brotherhood of Teamsters (lorry drivers' union) from 1957. He was jailed 1967–71 for attempted bribery of a federal court jury after he was charged with corruption. He was released by President Richard Nixon with the stipulation that he did not engage in union activities, but was evidently attempting to reassert influence when he disappeared in 1975. He is generally believed to have been murdered.

Hoffman, Dustin (1937–   ) US actor. He became popular in the 1960s with his unconventional looks, short stature, and versatility. He won Academy Awards for his performances in *Kramer vs Kramer* (1979) and *Rain Man* (1988). His other films

HO CHI MINH CITY City Hall in Ho Chi Minh City, Vietnam, which still has many buildings dating from the period of French colonial rule. *Image Bank*

include *The Graduate* (1967), *Midnight Cowboy* (1969), *Little Big Man* (1970), *All the President's Men* (1976), *Runaway Jury* (2003), and *Neverland* (2004).

Hoffmann, Amadeus (Ernst Theodor Wilhelm)
(1776–1822) German composer and writer. He composed the opera *Undine* (1816), but is chiefly remembered as an author and librettist of fairy stories, including 'Nussknacker/Nutcracker' (1816). His stories inspired Jacques ▷Offenbach's *Tales of Hoffmann*.

Hoffmann, Josef
(1870–1956) Austrian architect. Influenced by art nouveau, he was one of the founders of the Wiener Werkstätte/Vienna Workshops (a modern design cooperative of early 20th-century Vienna), and a pupil of Otto ▷Wagner. One of his best-known works is the Purkersdorf Sanatorium (1903–05).

hog any member of the ▷pig family. The **river hog** (*Potamochoerus porcus*) lives in Africa, south of the Sahara. Reddish or black, up to 1.3 m/4.2 ft long plus tail, and 90 cm/3 ft at the shoulder, this gregarious animal roots for food in many types of habitat. The **giant forest hog** (*Hylochoerus meinerzthageni*) lives in thick forests of central Africa and grows up to 1.9 m/6 ft long. The ▷wart hog is another African wild pig. The **pygmy hog** (*Sus salvanus*), the smallest of the pig family, is about 65 cm long (25 cm at the shoulder) and weighs 8–9 kg.

Hogarth, William
(1697–1764) English painter and engraver. He produced portraits and moralizing genre scenes, such as the story series of prints *A Rake's Progress* (1735; Soane Museum, London). His portraits are remarkably direct and full of character, for example *Heads of Six of Hogarth's Servants* (*c.* 1750–55; Tate Gallery, London) and his oil sketch masterpiece *The Shrimp Girl* (National Gallery, London).

hogback geological formation consisting of a ridge with a sharp crest and abruptly sloping sides, the outline of which resembles the back of a hog. Hogbacks are the result of differential erosion on steeply dipping rock strata composed of alternating resistant and soft beds. Exposed, almost vertical resistant beds provide the sharp crests.

Hogmanay
Scottish name for New Year's Eve. A traditional feature is first-footing, visiting the homes of friends and neighbours after midnight to welcome in the new year with salt, bread, whisky, and other gifts. Children may also go from house to house singing carols and receiving oatmeal cakes.

hognose North American colubrine, nonvenomous snake with a flattened head and a projecting snout for burrowing. (Genus *Heterodon*, family Elapidae, suborder Serpentes, order Squamata, class Reptilia.)

hogweed any of a group of plants belonging to the carrot family. The giant hogweed (*H. mantegazzianum*) grows over 3 m/9 ft high. (Genus *Heracleum*, family Umbelliferae.)

Hohenstaufen
German family of princes, several members of which were Holy Roman Emperors 1138–1208 and 1214–54. They were the first German emperors to make use of associations with Roman law and tradition to aggrandize their office, and included Conrad III; Frederick I (Barbarossa), the first to use the title Holy Roman Emperor (previously the title Roman emperor was used); Henry VI; and Frederick II.

The last of the line, Conradin, was executed in 1268 with the approval of Pope Clement IV while attempting to gain his Sicilian inheritance. They were supported by the Ghibellines (see ▷Guelph and Ghibelline), who took their name from the family's castle of Waiblingen.

Hohenzollern
German family, originating in Württemberg, the main branch of which held the titles of ▷elector of Brandenburg from 1415, king of Prussia from 1701, and German emperor from 1871. The last emperor, Wilhelm II, was dethroned in 1918 after the disastrous course of World War I. Another branch of the family were kings of Romania 1881–1947.

Hohhot
(or **Huhehot**; formerly **Kweisui**) city and capital of ▷Inner Mongolia Autonomous Region, China; population (1993) 730,000. It is an important industrial centre and trading hub between north and west China and Mongolia. Cotton textiles, wool, fur, steel, building materials, machinery, electronics, chemicals, flour, dairy goods, and diesel engines are produced. Hohot contains Lamaist monasteries and temples.

Hokkaido
(formerly **Yezo** or **Ezo** until 1868); Japanese *hoku* 'north'; *kai* 'sea'; *do* 'road') northernmost and second-largest of the four main islands of Japan, separated from Honshu to the south by Tsugaru Strait (20 km/12 mi wide), and from Sakhalin (Russia) to the north by Soya Strait; area 83,500 sq km/32,239 sq mi; population (1995) 5,692,000 (including 16,000 ▷Ainu). The capital is ▷Sapporo; other major cities are Hakodate, Asahikawa, Otaru, and Muroran. The main industries are coal, mercury, manganese, oil, natural gas, and tourism; agriculture centres on rice cultivation, dairying, forestry, and fishing.

Hokusai, Katsushika
(1760–1849) Japanese artist. He was the leading printmaker of his time and a major exponent of ▷ukiyo-e. He published *Fugaku sanjū-rokkei/36 Views of Mount Fuji* (*c.* 1823–29), and produced outstanding pictures of almost every kind of subject – birds, flowers, courtesans, and scenes from legend and everyday life. *Under the Wave at Kanagawa* (British Museum, London) is typical.

Holbein, Hans, the Elder
(*c.* 1464–1524) German painter. Painting mainly religious works, he belonged to the school of Rogier van der ▷Weyden and Hans Memling in his early paintings but showed Italianate influence in such a work as the *Basilica of St Paul* (1502; Staatsgalerie, Augsburg). His principal work is the altarpiece *St Sebastian* (1515–17; Alte Pinakothek, Munich). He was the father of Hans ▷Holbein the Younger.

Holbein, Hans, the Younger
(1497–1543) German painter and woodcut artist who spent much of his career as a portrait artist at the court of Henry VIII of England. One of the finest graphic artists of his age, he executed a woodcut series *Dance of Death* (*c.* 1525), and designed title pages for Luther's New Testament and Thomas More's *Utopia*.

He was born in Augsburg. In 1515 he went to Basel, where he became friendly with the scholar and humanist Erasmus and illustrated his *Praise of Folly*. He painted three portraits of Erasmus in 1523.

He travelled widely in Europe and while in England as painter to Henry VIII he created a remarkable evocation of the English court in a series of graphic, perceptive portraits. Among his sitters were Henry VIII and Thomas More. During his time at the English court, he also painted miniature portraits, inspiring Nicholas Hilliard. One of his pictures of this period is *The (French) Ambassadors* (1533; National Gallery, London). Pronounced Renaissance influence emerged in the *Meyer Madonna* (1526), a fine altarpiece in Darmstadt.

HOLLY With its bright red berries and its glossy, sharply spined leaves, holly is easily recognized. Male and female flowers grow on separate trees, and it is the female flowers that produce berries. Holly has long been used for hedging. *Premaphotos Wildlife*

HANS HOLBEIN, THE YOUNGER Portrait of King Henry VIII of England, by German painter and engraver Hans Holbein. The portrait is a piece of Tudor propaganda designed to emphasize Henry's strength, power, and prestige. *The Art Archive/Windsor Castle*

Holden, William
(1918–1981) Stage name of William Franklin Beedle. US film actor. He was a star in the late 1940s and 1950s. He played a wide variety of leading roles in such films as *Sunset Boulevard* (1950), *Stalag 17* (1953), *Bridge on the River Kwai* (1957), *The Wild Bunch* (1969), and *Network* (1976).

Holford, William Graham,
Baron Holford (1907–1975) British architect, born in South Africa. A leading architect/planner of his generation, he was responsible for much post-war redevelopment, including the plan for the City of London (with Charles Holden) and the precinct for St Paul's Cathedral, London (1955–56). He was knighted in 1953 and made a baron in 1965.

Holiday, Billie
(1915–1959) Stage name of Eleanora Gough McKay. US jazz singer, also known as 'Lady Day'. She made her debut in clubs in Harlem, New York, and became known for her emotionally charged delivery and idiosyncratic phrasing. Holiday brought a blues feel to her performances with swing bands. Songs she made her own include 'Stormy Weather', 'Strange Fruit', 'I Cover the Waterfront', 'That Ole Devil Called Love', and 'Lover Man (Oh, Where can You Be?)'.

Holinshed (or Hollingshead), Raphael
(*c.* 1520–*c.* 1580) English historian. He published two volumes of the *Chronicles of England, Scotland, and Ireland* (1578), which are a mixture of fact and legend. The *Chronicles* were used as a principal source by Elizabethan dramatists for their plots. Nearly all Shakespeare's English history plays, as well as *Macbeth*, *King Lear*, and *Cymbeline*, are based on Holinshed's work.

holistic medicine umbrella term for an approach that virtually all alternative therapies profess, which considers the overall health and lifestyle profile of a patient, and treats specific ailments not primarily as conditions to be alleviated but rather as symptoms of more fundamental disease.

Holland popular name for the ▷Netherlands; also two provinces of the Netherlands, see ▷North Holland and ▷South Holland.

Holland, John Philip
(1840–1914) Irish engineer who developed some of the first military submarines used by the US navy. He began work in Ireland in the late 1860s and emigrated to the USA in 1873. Holland's first successful submarine was launched in 1881 and, after several failures, he built the *Holland* in 1893, which was bought by the US navy in 1895. He introduced many of the innovations that would be incorporated in later attack submarines.

Hollerith, Herman
(1860–1929) US inventor of a mechanical tabulating machine, the first device for high-volume data processing. Hollerith's tabulator was widely publicized after being successfully used in the 1890 census. The firm he established, the Tabulating Machine Company, was later one of the founding companies of IBM.

holly any of a group of trees or shrubs that includes the English Christmas holly (*I. aquifolium*), an evergreen with spiny, glossy leaves, small white flowers, and poisonous scarlet berries on the female tree. Leaves of the Brazilian holly (*I. paraguayensis*) are used to make the tea *yerba maté*. (Genus *Ilex*, family Aquifoliaceae.)

Holly, Buddy
(1936–1959) Stage name of Charles Hardin Holley. US rock-and-roll singer, guitarist, and songwriter. He had a distinctive, hiccuping vocal style and was an early experimenter with recording techniques. Many of his hits with his band, the Crickets, such as 'That'll Be the Day' (1957), 'Peggy Sue' (1957), and 'Maybe Baby' (1958), have become classics. His albums include *The Chirping Crickets* (1958) and *Buddy Holly* (1958). He died in a plane crash.

Related Web site: Rave On http://www.visuallink.net/kdwilt/index.html

hollyhock tall flowering plant belonging to the mallow family. *A. rosea*, originally a native of Asia, produces spikes of large white, yellow, pink, or red flowers, 3 m/10 ft high when cultivated as a biennial; it is a popular cottage garden plant. (Genus *Althaea*, family Malvaceae.)

SHERLOCK HOLMES Photograph of a man dressed as the Arthur Conan Doyle character Sherlock Holmes, with his trademark pipe and deerstalker hat. *Archive Photos*

HOLOGRAPHY The image shows how to record a transmission hologram. Light from a laser is divided into two beams. One beam goes directly to the photographic plate. The other beam reflects off the object before hitting the photographic plate. The two beams combine to produce a pattern on the plate which contains information about the 3-D shape of the object. If the exposed and developed plate is illuminated by laser light, the pattern can be seen as a 3-D picture of the object.

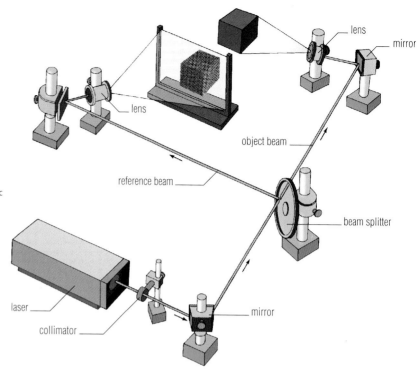

Hollywood district in the city of Los Angeles, California; the centre of the US film industry from 1911. It is the home of film studios such as Twentieth Century Fox, MGM, Paramount, Columbia Pictures, United Artists, Disney, and Warner Bros. Many film stars' homes are situated nearby in Beverly Hills and other communities adjacent to Hollywood.

Holmes, Sherlock fictitious private detective, created by the Scottish writer Arthur Conan ▷Doyle in *A Study in Scarlet* (1887) and recurring in novels and stories until 1927. Holmes' ability to make inferences from slight clues always astonishes the narrator, Dr Watson.

holmium (Latin *Holmia* 'Stockholm') silvery, metallic element of the ▷lanthanide series, symbol Ho, atomic number 67, relative atomic mass 164.93. It occurs in combination with other rare-earth metals and in various minerals such as gadolinite. Its compounds are highly magnetic.

   The element was discovered in 1878, spectroscopically, by the Swiss chemists J L Soret and Delafontaine, and independently in 1879 by Swedish chemist Per Cleve (1840–1905), who named it after Stockholm, near which it was found.

Holocaust, the the annihilation of an estimated 16 million people by the Nazi regime between 1933 and 1945, principally in the numerous extermination and ▷concentration camps, most notably ▷Auschwitz (Oświęcim), Sobibor, ▷Treblinka, and Maidanek in Poland, and Belsen, ▷Buchenwald, and ▷Dachau in Germany. Camps were built on railway lines to facilitate transport. Of the victims around 6 million were Jews (over 67% of European Jews); around 10 million Ukrainian, Polish, and Russian civilians and prisoners of war, Romanies, socialists, homosexuals, and others (labelled 'defectives') were also imprisoned and/or exterminated. Victims were variously starved, tortured, experimented on, and worked to death. Millions were executed in gas chambers, shot, or hanged. It was euphemistically termed the ▷final solution (of the Jewish question). The precise death toll will never be known. Holocaust museums and memorial sites have been established in Israel and in other countries.

   In Germany it is illegal to deny the fact of the Holocaust, and many Germans and foreign nationals have faced court charges for doing so. Controversy also arises in Israel, the Jewish state established after the Holocaust and World War II. In 2000 an ultra-orthodox rabbi caused outrage when he suggested that the victims of the Holocaust were being punished for their sins. The Holocaust was such a traumatic event, that it continues to fuel debate and high emotions amongst both the survivors and post-war generations.

   Related Web site: Holocaust Timeline http://www.historyplace. com/worldwar2/holocaust/timeline.html

Holocene epoch epoch of geological time that began 10,000 years ago, and continues into the present; the second and current epoch of the Quaternary period. During this epoch the glaciers

retreated, the climate became warmer, and human civilizations developed significantly.

holography method of producing three-dimensional (3-D) images, called holograms, by means of ▷laser light. Holography uses a photographic technique (involving the splitting of a laser beam into two beams) to produce a picture, or hologram, that contains 3-D information about the object photographed. Some holograms show meaningless patterns in ordinary light and produce a 3-D image only when laser light is projected through them, but reflection holograms produce images when ordinary light is reflected from them (as found on credit cards).

   Related Web site: Amateur Holography http://members.aol.com/ gakall/holopg.html

Holst, Gustav(us Theodore von) (1874–1934) English composer of distant Swedish descent. He wrote operas, including *Sávitri* (1908) and *At the Boar's Head* (1924); ballets; choral works, including *Choral Hymns from the Rig Veda* (1908–12) and *The*

THE HOLOCAUST A Nazi soldier stands outside a Jewish shop in the late 1930s. There is a Star of David pasted on the window, and a sign that says 'Germans! Wake up! Don't buy from Jews!' *Archive Photos*

Hymn of Jesus (1917); orchestral suites, including *The Planets* (1914–16); and songs. He was a lifelong friend of Ralph ▷Vaughan Williams, with whom he shared an enthusiasm for English folk music. His musical style, although tonal and drawing on folk song, tends to be severe. He was the father of Imogen Holst (1907–1984), musicologist and his biographer.

   Related Web site: Gustav Holst http://wso.williams.edu/~ktaylor/ gholst

Holy Alliance 'Christian Union of Charity, Peace, and Love' initiated by Alexander I of Russia in 1815 and signed by every crowned head in Europe. The alliance became associated with Russian attempts to preserve autocratic monarchies at any price, and served as an excuse to meddle in the internal affairs of other states. Ideas of an international army acting in the name of the alliance were rejected by Britain and Austria in 1818 and 1820.

Holy Communion another name for the ▷Eucharist, a Christian sacrament.

Holy Grail in medieval Christian legend, the dish or cup used by Jesus at the Last Supper; credited with supernatural powers and a symbol of Christian grace. In certain stories incorporated in Arthurian legend, it was an object of quest by King Arthur's knights, together with the spear with which Jesus was wounded at the Crucifixion. ▷Galahad was the only knight to achieve the mission.

   According to one story, the blood of Jesus was collected in the Holy Grail by ▷Joseph of Arimathaea at the Crucifixion, and brought to Britain where he allegedly built the first church, at Glastonbury. At least three churches in Europe possess vessels claimed to be the Holy Grail.

   Related Web site: Holy Grail http://www.newadvent.org/ cathen/06719a.htm

Holy Office tribunal of the Roman Catholic Church that deals with ecclesiastical discipline; see ▷Inquisition.

holy orders Christian priesthood, as conferred by the laying on of hands by a bishop. It is held by the Roman Catholic, Eastern Orthodox, and Anglican churches to have originated in Jesus' choosing of the apostles.

Holy Roman Empire empire of Charlemagne and his successors, and the German Empire 962–1806, both being regarded as the Christian (hence 'holy') revival of the Roman Empire. At its height it comprised much of Western and Central Europe. See ▷Habsburg.

Holyrood House royal residence in Edinburgh, Scotland. The palace was built from 1498 to 1503, on the site of a 12th-century abbey, by James IV. It has associations with Mary Queen of Scots, and Charles Edward, the Young Pretender. Holyrood was the royal palace of the Scottish kings until the Union, and is now a palace of the British monarchy, used during state visits but otherwise open to the public.

Holy See the diocese of the ▷pope.

Holy Spirit third person of the Christian ▷Trinity, also known as the Holy Ghost or the Paraclete, usually depicted as a white dove.

Holy Week in the Christian church, the last week of ▷Lent, when Christians commemorate the events that led up to the crucifixion of Jesus. Holy Week begins on Palm Sunday and includes Maundy Thursday, which commemorates the Last Supper.

Home, Alec Douglas- British Conservative politician. See ▷Douglas-Home.

Home Counties those counties in close proximity to London, England: Hertfordshire, Essex, Kent, Surrey, Buckinghamshire, and formerly Berkshire and Middlesex.

home front organized sectors of domestic activity in wartime, mainly associated with World Wars I and II. Features of the UK home front in World War I included greater government control over industry, the introduction of British summer time, and the introduction of women into jobs previously undertaken only by men as many were on active military service. In World War II measures on the UK home front included the organization of the black-out, evacuation, air-raid shelters, the Home Guard, rationing, and the distribution of gas masks.

Home Guard unpaid force formed in Britain in May 1940 to repel the expected German invasion, and known until July 1940 as the Local Defence Volunteers. It consisted of men aged 17–65 who had not been called up, formed part of the armed forces of the Crown, and was subject to military law. Over 2 million strong in 1944, it was disbanded on 31 December 1945, but revived in 1951, then placed on a reserve basis in 1955. It ceased activity in 1957.

homeland (or **Bantustan**) before 1980, name for the ▷Black National States in the Republic of South Africa.

Homelands Policy South Africa's apartheid policy which set aside ▷Black National States for black Africans.

homeopathy (or **homoeopathy**) system of alternative medicine based on the principle that symptoms of disease are part of the body's self-healing processes, and on the practice of administering extremely diluted doses of natural substances found to produce in a healthy person the symptoms manifest in the illness being treated. Developed by the German physician Samuel Hahnemann (1755–1843), the system is widely practised today as an alternative to allopathic (orthodox) medicine, and many controlled tests and achieved cures testify its efficacy.

Related Web site: Homeopathy http://www.homeopathyhome.com/

homeostasis maintenance of a constant environment around living cells, particularly with regard to pH, salt concentration, temperature, and blood sugar levels. Stable conditions are important for the efficient functioning of the ▷enzyme reactions within the cells. In humans, homeostasis in the blood (which provides fluid for all tissues) is ensured by several organs. The ▷kidneys regulate pH, urea, and water concentration. The lungs regulate oxygen and carbon dioxide (see ▷breathing). Temperature is regulated by the liver and the skin. Glucose levels in the blood are regulated by the ▷liver and the pancreas.

homeothermy maintenance of a constant body temperature in endothermic (warm-blooded) animals, by the use of chemical processes to compensate for heat loss or gain when external temperatures change. Such processes include generation of heat by the breakdown of food and the contraction of muscles, and loss of heat by sweating, panting, and other means.

Homer according to ancient tradition, the author of the Greek narrative epics, the *Iliad* and the *Odyssey* (both derived from oral tradition). Little is known about the man, but modern research suggests that both poems should be assigned to the 8th century BC, with the *Odyssey* the later of the two.

The epics, dealing with military values, social hierarchy, and the emotions and objectives of a heroic class of warriors, supported or opposed by the gods, had an immediate and profound effect on Greek society and culture and were a strong influence on the Roman poet ▷Virgil in the composition of his *Aeneid*.

Related Web site: Works by Homer
http://classics.mit.edu/Browse/browse-Homer.html

Homer, Winslow (1836–1910) US painter and lithographer. A leading realist, he is known for his vivid seascapes, in both oil and watercolour, most of which date from the 1880s and 1890s. *The Gulf Stream* (1899; Metropolitan Museum of Art, New York) is an example.

home rule, Irish movement to repeal the Act of ▷Union of 1801 that joined Ireland to Britain, and to establish an Irish parliament responsible for internal affairs. In 1870 Isaac Butt formed the Home Rule Association and the movement was led in Parliament from 1880 by Charles Stewart ▷Parnell. After 1918 the demand for an independent Irish republic replaced that for home rule.

The British prime minister William Gladstone's home rule bills of 1886 and 1893 were both defeated. A third bill was introduced by the Liberals in 1912, which aroused opposition in Ireland where the Protestant minority in Ulster feared domination by the Catholic majority. Ireland appeared on the brink of civil war but the outbreak of World War I rendered further consideration of home rule inopportune.

In 1920 the Government of Ireland Act introduced separate parliaments in the North and South and led to the treaty of 1921 that established the Irish Free State.

> **George Bernard Shaw**
> Irish dramatist
>
> *A healthy nation is as unconscious of its nationality as a healthy man of his bones. But if you break a nation's nationality it will think of nothing else but getting it set again. It will listen to no reformer, to no philosopher, to no preacher, until the demand of the nationalist is granted.*
>
> 'Preface for Politicians' in *Prefaces* (1934, revised 1938).

home service force (HSF) military unit established in the UK in 1982, linked to the ▷Territorial Army (TA) and recruited from volunteers aged 18–60 with previous army (TA or regular) experience. It was introduced to guard key points and installations likely to be the target of enemy 'special forces' and saboteurs, so releasing other units for mobile defence roles. It was stood down in 1992.

Homestead Act in US history, an act of Congress in 1862 to encourage settlement of land in the west by offering 65-hectare/160-acre plots cheaply or even free to those willing to cultivate and improve the land for a stipulated amount of time. By 1900 about 32 million hectares/80 million acres had been distributed. Homestead lands are available to this day.

homicide in law, the killing of a human being. This may be unlawful, lawful, or excusable, depending on the circumstances. Unlawful homicides include murder, ▷manslaughter, ▷infanticide, and causing death by dangerous driving. Lawful homicide occurs where, for example, a police officer is justified in killing a criminal in the course of apprehension or when a person is killed in self-defence or defence of others.

homoeopathy variant spelling of ▷homeopathy.

Homo erectus species of hominid (of the human family) that walked upright and lived more than 1.5 million years ago. Fossil remains have been found in Java, China, Africa, and Europe. See ▷human species, origins of.

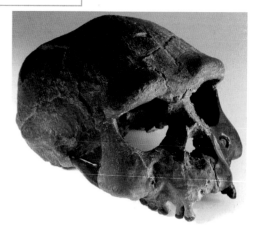

HOMO ERECTUS The skull of a *Homo erectus* from Sangiran Java (Anthropological Institute, Turin, Italy). *The Art Archive/Palazzo Ducale Mantua/Dagli Orti*

homologous in biology, a term describing an organ or structure possessed by members of different taxonomic groups (for example, species, genera, families, orders) that originally derived from the same structure in a common ancestor. The wing of a bat, the arm of a monkey, and the flipper of a seal are homologous because they all derive from the forelimb of an ancestral mammal.

homologous series any of a number of series of organic chemicals with similar chemical properties in which members differ by a constant relative molecular mass.

homophony music comprising a melody lead and accompanying harmony, in contrast to heterophony and ▷polyphony in which different melody lines of equal importance are combined.

homosexuality sexual preference for, or attraction to, persons of one's own sex; in women it is referred to as ▷lesbianism.

Both sexes use the term 'gay'. Men and women who are attracted to both sexes are referred to as bisexual. The extent to which homosexual behaviour is caused by biological or psychological factors is an area of disagreement among experts.

Although some ancient civilizations (notably ancient Greece and Confucian China) accepted homosexuality, other societies have punished homosexual acts. In 12th-century Europe sodomy was punishable by burning and since then homosexuals have suffered varying degrees of prejudice and prosecution. In the latter half of the 20th century discrimination against homosexuals has decreased as a result of pressure from campaigners (see ▷gay politics).

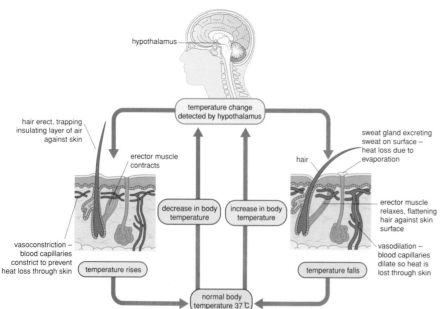

HOMEOSTASIS The ability of warm-blooded animals to control their body temperature by physiological means is an example of homeostasis (maintenance of a constant environment around living cells). As temperature increases, the change is detected by the hypothalamus and the skin responds by sweating and dilating capillaries near the skin surface so heat is lost by evaporation and convection. If the temperature falls, blood capillaries constrict and sweating ceases. Shivering causes heat generation within the muscles.

Laws relating to homosexuality and the age of consent differ from country to country. In some countries homosexual acts are illegal. In European Union (EU) countries homosexuality between consenting adults is legal. Male homosexuals fear further discrimination as a result of the discovery of the ▷AIDS virus.

In 1992 the Isle of Man's parliament, Tynwald, decriminalized homosexuality, becoming one of the last territories in the EU to do so. In Denmark from 1989, gay men in a registered partnership have all the legal rights of married couples except for adoption. In Britain homosexuality ceased to be illegal over the age of 21 in 1967, and the age of consent was lowered to 18 in 1994.

In 1997 the General Synod of the Church of England approved a motion stating that practicing homosexuals could be lay members of the Church, but not priests.

Related Web site: Advocate Magazine http://www.advocate.com/

homozygous in a living organism, having two identical ▷alleles for a given trait. Individuals homozygous for a trait always breed true; that is, they produce offspring that resemble them in appearance when bred with a genetically similar individual; inbred varieties or species are homozygous for almost all traits. ▷Recessive alleles are only expressed in the homozygous condition. ▷Heterozygous organisms have two different alleles for a given trait.

Homs (or **Hims**) city and administrative centre of Homs governorate, west Syria, near the Orontes River; population (1993) 537,000. Silk, cereals, and fruit are produced in the area, and industries include silk textiles, oil refining, and jewellery. Known in ancient times as Emesa, it was once famous for its Temple of the Sun. ▷Zenobia, Queen of Palmyra, was defeated here by the Roman emperor ▷Aurelian in 272.

Honan alternative name of ▷Henan, a province of China.

Honduras see country box.

Honecker, Erich (1912–1994) German communist politician, in power in East Germany 1973–89, elected chair of the council of state (head of state) in 1976. He governed in an outwardly austere and efficient manner and, while favouring East–West détente, was a loyal ally of the USSR. In 1989, following a wave of pro-democracy demonstrations, he was replaced as leader of the Socialist Unity Party (SED) and head of state by Egon ▷Krenz, and expelled from the Communist Party. He died in exile in Chile.

Honegger, Arthur (1892–1955) Swiss composer. He was one of the group of composers known as ▷*Les Six*. His work was varied in form, for example, the opera *Antigone* (1927), the ballet *Skating Rink* (1922), the dramatic oratorio *Le Roi David/King David* (1921), programme music (*Pacific 231*, 1923), and the *Symphonie liturgique/Liturgical Symphony* (1946). He also composed incidental music for Abel Gance's silent movie classics *La Roue/The Wheel* (1923) and *Napoléon* (1927).

Hōnen (1133–1212) Japanese Buddhist monk who founded the ▷Pure Land school of Buddhism.

honey sweet syrup produced by honey ▷bees from the nectar of flowers. It is stored in honeycombs and made in excess of their needs as food for the winter. Honey comprises various sugars, mainly laevulose and dextrose, with enzymes, colouring matter, acids, and pollen grains. It has antibacterial properties and was widely used in ancient Egypt, Greece, and Rome as a wound salve. It is still popular for sore throats, in hot drinks or in lozenges.

honeyeater (or **honey-sucker**) any of a group of small, brightly coloured birds with long, curved beaks and long tails, native to Australia. They have a long tongue divided into four at the end to form a brush for collecting nectar from flowers. (Family Meliphagidae.)

HONEYEATER The Kauaioo was thought to be extinct, like the other three species of Hawaiian honeyeaters, but was rediscovered in 1960. It was saved by its relatively plain feathers; the other, more colourful, Hawaiian honeyeaters were hunted to extinction.

honeysuckle vine or shrub found in temperate regions of the world. The common honeysuckle or woodbine (*L. periclymenum*) of Europe is a climbing plant with sweet-scented flowers, reddish and yellow-tinted outside and creamy white inside; it now grows in the northeastern USA. (Genus *Lonicera*, family Caprifoliaceae.)

HONEYSUCKLE In Shakespeare's time, honeysuckle was called woodbine.

Hong Kong special administrative region in the southeast of China, comprising Hong Kong Island, the mainland Kowloon Peninsula and New Territories, and many small islands, of which the largest is Lantau; area 1,070 sq km/413 sq mi; population (1995 est) 6,189,800 (57% Hong Kong Chinese, most of the remainder refugees from the mainland). The capital buildings are located in Victoria (Hong Kong City), and other towns and cities include Kowloon and Tsuen Wan (in the New Territories). A former British crown colony, it reverted to Chinese control in July 1997.

An enclave of Guangdong province, China, it has one of the world's finest natural harbours. Hong Kong Island is connected with Kowloon by undersea railway and ferries. A world financial centre, its stock market has four exchanges. Main exports are textiles, clothing, electronic goods, clocks, watches, cameras, and plastic products, and tourism is important.

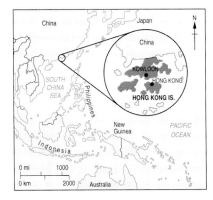

HONG KONG Hong Kong lies in China near the mouth of the Pearl River (Zhu Jiang) southeast of Guangzhou. Hong Kong means 'fragrant harbour', but its waters are now badly polluted. *Image Bank*

A large proportion of the exports and imports of southern China are transshipped here. The currency used is the Hong Kong dollar; the languages spoken are English and Chinese; religions include Confucianism, Buddhism, and Taoism, with Muslim and Christian minorities.

Honiara port and capital of the Solomon Islands, on the northwest coast of Guadalcanal Island in the southwest Pacific Ocean; population (1996 est) 43,700. The city, which is on the River Mataniko, grew around a World War II US military base, and replaced Tulagi as the capital of the Solomon Islands in 1952 and is now served by the international airport, Henderson Airfield, which lies 16 km/10 mi to the east. Exports include coconuts, copra, fish, and a little gold from the island's central Gold Ridge.

Honolulu (or **Honolulu on Oaha**; Hawaiian 'sheltered bay') state capital and port of ▷Hawaii, USA, on the south coast of ▷Oahu; seat of Honolulu County; population (2000 est) 371,700. The city is the economic centre of Hawaii. It has a natural harbour (formed by a lagoon within the coral reef) with extensive shipping facilities. Honolulu is a trading centre for European and Indian goods, and is the principal point of entry to the islands. It is often called the 'Crossroads of the Pacific'. With its warm climate and tropical vegetation, Honolulu has become a holiday resort. In addition to tourism, other industries include food processing, machinery, clothing, and building materials. It was incorporated as a city in 1907.

Honolulu's port handles 3 million tonnes of general cargo and 2.5 million tonnes of petroleum a year. William Brown, a British sea captain, was the first European to see Honolulu, in 1794. It became the Hawaiian royal capital in the 19th century, and was annexed by the USA in 1848. ▷Pearl Harbor Naval Base and Hickam Air Force Base are situated 11 km/7 mi to the northwest.

honours list military and civil awards approved by the sovereign of the UK and published on New Year's Day and on her official birthday in June. Many Commonwealth countries, for example, Australia and Canada, also have their own honours list.

Honshu principal island of Japan, lying between Hokkaido to the northeast and Kyushu to the southwest. Its land mass comprises approximately four-fifths of the country total area; area 231,100 sq km/89,228 sq mi, including 382 smaller islands; population (1995) 100,995,000. The capital is ▷Tokyo; other major cities are Yokohama, Osaka, Kobe, Nagoya, and Hiroshima. Honshu is linked by bridges and tunnels with the islands of Hokkaido, Kyushu, and Shikoku. A chain of volcanic mountains runs along the island and there are frequent earthquakes.

HONSHU Pole Rising Festival, Honshu, Japan. *Image Bank*

Hooch, Pieter de (1629–1684) Dutch painter. He painted harmonious domestic interiors and courtyards, his style influenced by Jan Vermeer. *The Courtyard of a House in Delft* (1658; National Gallery, London) is a typical work.

Hood, Raymond Mathewson (1881–1934) US architect. He designed several New York skyscrapers of the 1920s and 1930s, and was a member of the team responsible for the Rockefeller Center, New York (1929). Two of his skyscrapers, the *Daily News* building (1930) and the McGraw-Hill building (1931), with its distinctive green-tile cladding, are seminal works of the ▷art deco style.

Hood, Samuel (1724–1816) 1st Viscount Hood. English admiral. A masterly tactician, he defeated the French at Dominica in the West Indies in 1783, and in the ▷Revolutionary Wars captured Toulon and Corsica. He was made a baronet in 1779 and a viscount in 1796.

Hood, Thomas (1799–1845) English poet and humorist. He entered journalism and edited periodicals, including his own *Hood's Monthly Magazine* in 1844. Although remembered for his light comic verse, for example, 'Miss Kilmansegg' (1841), he also wrote serious poems such as 'The Dream of Eugene Aram' (1839), about a notorious murderer; 'Song of the Shirt' (1843), a protest against poorly paid labour; and 'Bridge of Sighs' (1843), about the suicide of a prostitute.

hoof horny covering that protects the sensitive parts of the foot of an animal. The possession of hooves is characteristic of the orders Artiodactyla (even-toed ungulates such as deer and cattle), and Perissodactyla (horses, tapirs, and rhinoceroses).

Hooghly (or **Hugli**) river and city in West Bengal, India; population (1991) 151,800. The river is the western and most commercially important stream of the ▷Ganges delta, providing access to ▷Calcutta; length 320 km/198 mi. The city is on the site of a factory set up by the East India Company in 1640, which was moved to Calcutta, 40 km/25 mi downstream, 1686–90. Alongside the River Hooghly there is a concentration of factories which process cotton, rice, and jute, and manufacture rubber goods and chemicals.

THOMAS HOOD The English poet and humorist.
Archive Photos

Hooke, Robert (1635–1703) English scientist and inventor, originator of ▷Hooke's law, and considered the foremost mechanic of his time. His inventions included a telegraph system, the spirit level, marine barometer, and sea gauge. He coined the term 'cell' in biology.

He studied elasticity, furthered the sciences of mechanics and microscopy, invented the hairspring regulator in timepieces, perfected the air pump, and helped improve such scientific instruments as microscopes, telescopes, and barometers. His work on gravitation and in optics contributed to the achievements of his contemporary Isaac ▷Newton.

Hooker, John Lee (1917–2001) US blues guitarist, singer, and songwriter. One of the foremost blues musicians, his first record, 'Boogie Chillen' (1948), was a blues hit and his percussive guitar style made him popular with a rock audience from the 1950s. His albums include *Urban Blues* (1968) and *Boom Boom* (1992) (also the title of his 1962 song).

Honduras

Honduras country in Central America, bounded north by the Caribbean Sea, southeast by Nicaragua, south by the Pacific Ocean, southwest by El Salvador, and west and northwest by Guatemala.

NATIONAL NAME *República de Honduras/Republic of Honduras*
AREA 112,100 sq km/43,281 sq mi
CAPITAL Tegucigalpa
MAJOR TOWNS/CITIES San Pedro Sula, La Ceiba, El Progreso, Choluteca, Juticalpa, Danlí
MAJOR PORTS La Ceiba, Puerto Cortés
PHYSICAL FEATURES narrow tropical coastal plain with mountainous interior, Bay Islands, Caribbean reefs

Government

HEAD OF STATE AND GOVERNMENT Ricardo Maduro from 2001
POLITICAL SYSTEM liberal democracy
POLITICAL EXECUTIVE limited presidency
ADMINISTRATIVE DIVISIONS 18 departments
ARMED FORCES 8,300; plus paramilitary forces of 6,000 (2002 est)
CONSCRIPTION military service is voluntary
DEATH PENALTY abolished in 1956
DEFENCE SPEND (% GDP) 1.7 (2002 est)
EDUCATION SPEND (% GDP) 3.4 (1999)
HEALTH SPEND (% GDP) 6.8 (2000 est)

Economy and resources

CURRENCY lempira
GPD (US$) 6.6 billion (2002 est)
REAL GDP GROWTH (% change on previous year) 2.6 (2001)
GNI (US$) 6.2 billion (2002 est)
GNI PER CAPITA (PPP) (US$) 2,450 (2002 est)
CONSUMER PRICE INFLATION 8.4% (2003 est)
UNEMPLOYMENT 28.5% (2001)
FOREIGN DEBT (US$) 4.7 billion (2001 est)
MAJOR TRADING PARTNERS USA, Guatemala, Japan, El Salvador, Germany,

Nicaragua, Mexico
RESOURCES lead, zinc, silver, gold, tin, iron, copper, antimony
INDUSTRIES food processing, petroleum refining, cement, beverages, wood products, chemical products, textiles, beer, rum
EXPORTS bananas, lobsters and prawns, coffee, zinc, meat. Principal market: USA 45.7% (2001)
IMPORTS machinery, industrial raw materials, appliances and electrical equipment, mineral fuels and lubricants, chemical products, consumer goods. Principal source: USA 46.2% (2001)
ARABLE LAND 9.5% (2000 est)
AGRICULTURAL PRODUCTS coffee, bananas, maize, sorghum, plantains, beans, rice, sugar cane, citrus fruits; fishing (notably shellfish); livestock rearing (cattle); timber production

Population and society

POPULATION 6,941,000 (2003 est)
POPULATION GROWTH RATE 1.9% (2000–15)
POPULATION DENSITY (per sq km) 62 (2003 est)
URBAN POPULATION (% of total) 56 (2003 est)
AGE DISTRIBUTION (% of total population) 0–14 41%, 15–59 54%, 60+ 5% (2002 est)
ETHNIC GROUPS about 90% of mixed American Indian and Spanish descent (known as ladinos or mestizos); there are also Salvadorean, Guatemalan, American, and European minorities
LANGUAGE Spanish (official), English, American Indian languages
RELIGION Roman Catholic 97%
EDUCATION (compulsory years) 6

LITERACY RATE 76% (men); 77% (women) (2003 est)
LABOUR FORCE 35.1% agriculture, 22.0% industry, 42.9% services (1999)
LIFE EXPECTANCY 67 (men); 71 (women) (2000–05)
CHILD MORTALITY RATE (under 5, per 1,000 live births) 38 (2001)
PHYSICIANS (per 1,000 people) 0.8 (1998 est)
HOSPITAL BEDS (per 1,000 people) 1.1 (1998 est)
TV SETS (per 1,000 people) 96 (2001 est)
RADIOS (per 1,000 people) 413 (2001 est)
INTERNET USERS (per 10,000 people) 298.1 (2002 est)
PERSONAL COMPUTER USERS (per 100 people) 1.4 (2002 est)

See also ▷Contra; ▷Maya; ▷Mosquito Coast.

HONDURAS A colonial building in Yuscarán, a southeastern town in Honduras. Spanish conquest in the 16th century was initially stimulated by the pursuit of gold, and the Honduran gold-mining town of Gracias became the capital of Spanish Central America. When the gold had been exhausted, the Spanish moved their administrative centre to Guatemala, but prospectors returned in the 1570s when silver was struck. *PhotoDisk*

Hooker was born in Mississippi and learned from the delta folk-blues players before moving north and taking up the urban, electric style on early recordings like 'Hobo Blues' and 'Crawlin' King Snake' (both 1949); however, he never entirely abandoned the acoustic guitar. His career benefited from both the vogue for folk music in the 1950s and the blues boom of the 1960s. Despite many collaborations with rock musicians, he retained a traditional blues sound.

Related Web site: Hooker, John Lee http://www.virginrecords.com/hooker/

Hooker, Joseph Dalton (1817–1911) English botanist who travelled to the Antarctic and India, and made many botanical discoveries. His works include *Flora Antarctica* (1844–47), *Genera plantarum* (1862–83), and *Flora of British India* (1875–97).

Hooke's law law stating that the deformation of a body is proportional to the magnitude of the deforming force, provided that the body's elastic limit (see ▷elasticity) is not exceeded. If the elastic limit is not reached, the body will return to its original size once the force is removed. The law was discovered by English physicist Robert Hooke in 1676.

For example, if a spring is stretched by 2 cm by a weight of 1 N, it will be stretched by 4 cm by a weight of 2 N, and so on; however, once the load exceeds the elastic limit for the spring, Hooke's law will no longer be obeyed and each successive increase in weight will result in a greater extension until finally the spring breaks.

hookworm parasitic roundworm (see ▷worm) with hooks around its mouth. It lives mainly in tropical and subtropical regions, but also in humid areas in temperate climates. The eggs are hatched in damp soil, and the larvae bore into the host's skin, usually through the soles of the feet. They make their way to the small intestine, where they live by sucking blood. The eggs are expelled with faeces, and the cycle starts again. The human hookworm causes anaemia, weakness, and abdominal pain. It is common in areas where defecation occurs outdoors. (Genus *Necator.*)

hoopoe bird slightly larger than a thrush, with a long, thin, slightly downward-curving bill and a bright pinkish-buff crest tipped with black that expands into a fan shape on top of the head. The wings and tail are banded with black and white, and the rest of the plumage is buff-coloured. The hoopoe is found throughout southern Europe and Asia down to southern Africa, India, Malaya. (Species *Upupa epops*, family Upupidae, order Coraciiformes.)

Hoopoes visit Britain during the spring and autumn migration, but seldom breed during that time.

HOOPOE
The hoopoe is the sole member of its family, the Upupidae. With its orange-pink body plumage, boldly striped wings and tail, and huge, erectile crest, it is an unmistakable bird.

Hoover, Herbert (Clark) (1874–1964) 31st president of the USA 1929–33, a Republican. He was secretary of commerce 1921–28. Hoover lost public confidence after the stock-market crash of 1929, when he opposed direct government aid for the unemployed in the Depression that followed.

Hoover was born in West Branch, Iowa. He became a mining engineer, and travelled widely before World War I. After the war he organized relief work in occupied Europe. A talented administrator, he was subsequently associated with numerous international relief organizations, and became food administrator for the USA 1917–19. President Wilson later made him a member of the War Trade Council, and as such he took part at Paris in the negotiation of the Versailles Treaty. In 1928 he defeated the Democratic

candidate for the presidency, Al Smith (1873–1944), winning by a wide margin.

The shantytowns, or Hoovervilles, of the homeless that sprang up around large cities after the stock-market crash were evidence of his failure to cope with the effects of the Depression and prevent the decline of the economy. He was severely criticized for his adamant opposition to federal relief for the unemployed, even after the funds of states, cities, and charities were exhausted. In 1933 he was succeeded by F D Roosevelt.

Hoover, J(ohn) Edgar (1895–1972) US lawyer and director of the Federal Bureau of Investigation (FBI) from 1924 until his death. He built up a powerful network for the detection of organized crime, including a national fingerprint collection. His drive against alleged communist activities after World War II and his opposition to the Kennedy administration brought much criticism for abuse of power.

Hoover was born in Washington, DC. He entered the Department of Justice in 1917, and in 1921 became assistant director of the Bureau of Investigation. He served under eight presidents, none of whom would dismiss him since he kept files on them and their associates. During his tenure, the FBI grew from a corrupt Bureau of Investigation to a respected and highly professional national police agency, with responsibility for counterespionage within the USA as well as counterterrorism. Hoover waged a personal campaign of harassment against leaders of the civil-rights movement, notably Martin Luther ▷King, Jr.

Hoover Dam highest concrete dam in the USA, 221 m/726 ft, on the Colorado River at the Arizona–Nevada border. It was begun during the administration of President Herbert Hoover and built 1931–36. Known as **Boulder Dam** 1933–47, under the administration of Franklin D Roosevelt, its name was restored by President Harry Truman as the reputation of Herbert Hoover was revived. It impounds Lake Mead, and has a hydroelectric power capacity of 1,300 megawatts.

Hope, Bob (1903–2003) Stage name of Leslie Townes Hope. British-born US comedian. His earliest success was on Broadway and as a radio star in the 1930s. Employing a wise-cracking, cowardly persona, his film appearances include seven 'Road' films (1940–62) with Bing ▷Crosby and Dorothy Lamour (1914–96). These include *The Road to Singapore* (1940), *The Road to Zanzibar* (1941), *The Road to*

> **Herbert Hoover**
> *When there is a lack of honour in government, the morals of the whole people are poisoned.*
> The New York Times, 9 August 1964

Morocco (1942), *The Road to Utopia* (1946), *The Road to Rio* (1946), *The Road to Bali* (1952), and *The Road to Hong Kong* (1953). He made other films, including two *Paleface* comic westerns (1948–52) with Jane ▷Russell. Hope received an honorary British knighthood on 17 May 1998 at the British Embassy in Washington, DC.

Hopei alternative transcription of ▷Hebei, a province of China.

Hopewell ▷American Indian agricultural culture of the central USA that flourished between 200 BC and AD 400. The Hopewell people grew maize, beans, and squash supplemented by fish and game. They were skilled metalworkers especially of copper and silver, had a distinctive pottery style which used incised lines to create naturalistic motifs, and made exquisite stone ceremonial pipes carved into animal shapes. The Hopewell built burial mounds up to 12 m/40 ft high and structures such as Serpent Mound in Ohio; see also ▷Moundbuilder.

Hopi (Hopi *Hopitue* 'Peaceful People') member of an ▷American Indian people who live in the southwest USA, especially northeast Arizona and number about 11,000 (1995). They have lived in Arizona since prehistoric times and are direct descendants of the ancient Anasazi. A ▷Pueblo people, they farm and herd sheep and live in houses of stone or adobe (mud brick), forming about a dozen autonomous villages on rocky plateaus, or mesas. The Hopi speak a Shoshonean dialect of the Uto-Aztecan language family.

Hopkins, Anthony (Philip) (1937–) Welsh actor. A successful stage actor both in London and on Broadway, Hopkins won acclaim for his performance as Richard the Lion-Heart in his second film, *The Lion in Winter* (1968). His performance as a cannibalistic serial killer in *The Silence of the Lambs* (1991) gained him an Academy Award.

> **Gerard Manley Hopkins**
> *The world is charged with the grandeur of God.*
> 'God's Grandeur'

Hopkins, Frederick Gowland (1861–1947) English biochemist who was awarded a Nobel Prize for Physiology or Medicine in 1929 for his discovery of trace substances, now known as vitamins, that stimulate growth. His research into diets revealed the necessity of these vitamins for the maintenance of health. Hopkins shared the prize with Christiaan Eijkman, who had arrived at similar conclusions. He was knighted in 1925.

Hopkins, Gerard Manley (1844–1889) English poet and Jesuit priest. His works are marked by originality of diction and rhythm and include 'The Wreck of the Deutschland' (1876), and 'The Windhover' and 'Pied Beauty' (both 1877). His collected works were published posthumously in 1918 by his friend, the poet Robert ▷Bridges. His employment of 'sprung rhythm' (the combination of traditional regularity of stresses with varying numbers of syllables in each line) greatly influenced later 20th-century poetry.

His poetry is profoundly religious and records his struggle to gain faith and peace, but also shows freshness of feeling and delight in nature.

Related Web site: Poems of Gerard Manley Hopkins http://www.bartleby.com/122/index.html

Hopper, Dennis (1936–) US film actor and director. He caused a sensation with the anti-establishment *Easy Rider* (1969). His work as an actor includes *Rebel Without a Cause* (1955), *The American Friend/Der amerikanische Freund* (1977), *Apocalypse Now* (1979), *Blue Velvet* (1986), and *Speed* (1994).

Hopper, Edward (1882–1967) US painter and etcher, one of the foremost American realists. His views of life in New England and New York in the 1930s and 1940s, painted in rich, dark colours, convey a brooding sense of emptiness and solitude, as in *Nighthawks* (1942; Art Institute, Chicago).

Born in Nyack, New York, he studied at the Commercial Art School, New York, and then at the New York School of Art, where his teacher Robert Henri, associated with the ▷Ashcan School, was an important influence.

He visited Europe several times between 1906 and 1910, though he remained uninfluenced by avant-garde development, preferring to devote himself to painting the urban background of American life in a style which, though highly individual, drew on the strong tradition of American realism. An example is his street scene *Early Sunday Morning* (1930; Whitney Museum of American Art, New York).

hops female fruit heads of the hop plant *Humulus lupulus*, family Cannabiaceae; these are dried and used as a tonic and in flavouring beer. In designated areas in Europe, no male hops may be grown,

HOOVER DAM The power-generating station at the base of Hoover Dam in Boulder Canyon, Nevada, USA. *Archive Photos*

HOPS A female hop plant showing the fruits which, in cultivated varieties, are used in brewing. The genus *Humulus* is a small one, with *H. lupulus* coming from Europe and W Asia and one species each from North America and E Asia. *Premaphotos Wildlife*

since seedless hops produced by the unpollinated female plant contain a greater proportion of the alpha acid that gives beer its bitter taste.

Horace (65–8 BC) Born Quintus Horatius Flaccus. Roman lyric poet and satirist. He became a leading poet under the patronage of Emperor Augustus. His works include *Satires* (35–30 BC); the four books of *Odes* (*c.* 25–24 BC); *Epistles*, a series of verse letters; and an influential critical work, *Ars poetica*. They are distinguished by their style, wit, discretion, and patriotism.

horehound any of a group of plants belonging to the mint family. The white horehound (*M. vulgare*), found in Europe, North Africa, and western Asia and naturalized in North America, has a thick hairy stem and clusters of dull white flowers; it has medicinal uses. (Genus *Marrubium*, family Labiatae.)

> **Related Web site: Directory of Herbs – Horehound** http://hortweb. cas.psu.edu/vegcrops/herbs/Marrubiumvulgare.html

hormone in biology, chemical secretion of the ductless ▷endocrine glands and specialized nerve cells concerned with control of body functions. The major glands are the thyroid, parathyroid, pituitary, adrenal, pancreas, ovary, and testis. There are also hormone-secreting cells in the kidney, liver, gastrointestinal tract, thymus (in the neck), pineal (in the brain), and placenta. Hormones bring about changes in the functions of various organs according to the body's requirements. The ▷hypothalamus, which adjoins the pituitary gland at the base of the brain, is a control centre for overall coordination of hormone secretion; the thyroid hormones determine the rate of general body chemistry; the adrenal hormones prepare the organism during stress for 'fight or flight'; and the sexual hormones such as oestrogen and testosterone govern reproductive functions.

The endocrine system, together with the ▷nervous system, forms the neuroendocrine system. Thus, chemical messages can be relayed to the appropriate part, or parts, of the body in response to stimulants either through nervous impulses via the nerves or through hormones secreted in the blood, or by both together. Hormones regulate ▷homeostasis (a constant state within the body) and the body's responses to external and internal stimuli, and also control tissue development, morphogenesis (the development of an organism's form and structure), and reproduction. Many human diseases that are caused by hormone deficiency can be treated with hormone preparations.

In plants, hormones are organic chemicals, and are usually referred to as 'growth substances'. These are synthesized by plants, and the five major types are abscisic acid, auxin, cytokinin, ethylene (ethene), and gibberellin. These substances regulate growth and development, and are usually produced in a particular part of the plant, such as the shoot tip, and transported to other parts where they take effect.

hormone-replacement therapy (HRT) use of ▷oestrogen and progesterone to help limit the unpleasant effects of the menopause in women. The treatment was first used in the 1970s.

At the menopause, the ovaries cease to secrete natural oestrogen. This results in a number of symptoms, including hot flushes, anxiety, and a change in the pattern of menstrual bleeding. It is also associated with osteoporosis, or a thinning of bones, leading to an increased incidence of fractures, frequently of the hip, in older women. Oestrogen preparations, taken to replace the decline in natural hormone levels, combined with regular exercise can help to maintain bone strength in women. In order to improve bone density, however, HRT must be taken for five years, during which time the woman will continue to menstruate. Many women do not find this acceptable. In 1997 about 33% of British women and 40% of US women opted for post-menopausal HRT. A 1999 US survey revealed that white women are more likely to use hormone replacement than African-Americans or Mexican-Americans.

Hormuz (or Ormuz) small island in the Strait of Hormuz belonging to Iran; area 41 sq km/16 sq mi. It is strategically important because oil tankers leaving the Gulf for Japan and the West have to pass through the strait to reach the Arabian Sea.

horn member of a family of lip-reed wind instruments used for signalling and ritual, and sharing features of a generally conical bore (although the orchestral horn is of part conical and part straight bore) and curved shape, producing a pitch of rising or variable inflection.

horn broad term for hardened processes on the heads of some members of order Artiodactyla: deer, antelopes, cattle, goats, and sheep; and the rhinoceroses in order Perissodactyla. They are used usually for sparring rather than serious fighting, often between members of the same species rather than against predators.

Horn, Gyula (1932–   ) Hungarian economist and politician, president of the Hungarian Socialist Party (HSP) from 1990 and prime minister 1994–98. Under his leadership the ex-communist HSP enjoyed a resurgence, capturing an absolute majority in the July 1994 assembly elections. Despite opposition to the ongoing economic restructuring programme, Horn, as a trained economist, recognized the need to press on with reforms and formed a coalition with the centrist Free Democrats. He pursued a free-market economic programme, which, by attracting foreign inward investment, brought economic recovery. However, Horn lost power after the May 1998 general elections, following a collapse in support for his coalition partners, the Free Democrats, and was replaced by László Kovásc.

hornbeam any of a group of trees belonging to the birch family. They have oval leaves with toothed edges and hanging clusters of flowers, each with a nutlike seed attached to the base. The trunk is usually twisted, with smooth grey bark. (Genus *Carpinus*, family Betulaceae.)

hornbill any of a group of omnivorous birds found in Africa, India, and Malaysia. They are about 1 m/3 ft long, and have powerful down-curved beaks, usually surmounted by a bony growth or casque. During the breeding season, the female walls herself into a hole in a tree and does not emerge until the young are hatched. There are about 45 species. (Family Bucerotidae, order Coraciiformes.)

> ### Horace
> *Sapere aude.*
> *Dare to be wise.*
> Epistles I. 2

HORNBILL The beak of the yellow-billed hornbill *Tockus flavirostris*, common in dry bush country from Ethiopia to South Africa, illustrates one of the extremes to which beaks have evolved. There is, however, no satisfactory explanation for this bizarre adaptation. This species lacks the prominent casque found in some of the larger members of the family. *Premaphotos Wildlife*

Hornbills feed chiefly on the ground, their food consisting of insects, small mammals, and reptiles. The great hornbill (*Buceros bicornis*) of Southeast Asia can reach up to 1.3 m/4.3 ft in length.

The southern ground hornbill lives in groups of about three to five birds (though sometimes as many as ten) with only one breeding pair, and the rest acting as helpers. On average, only one chick is reared successfully every nine years. Lifespan can be 40 years or more.

hornblende green or black rock-forming mineral, one of the amphiboles. It is a hydrous ▷silicate composed mainly of calcium, iron, magnesium, and aluminium in addition to the silicon and oxygen that are common to all silicates. Hornblende is found in both igneous and metamorphic rocks and can be recognized by its colour and prismatic shape.

Horn, Cape (Spanish *Cabo de Hornos*) southernmost point of South America, in Magallanes region, Chile; situated on Horn Island to the south of ▷Tierra del Fuego archipelago. The cape is notorious for gales and heavy seas, and was the sea route between the Atlantic and the Pacific Oceans until the opening of the Panama Canal in 1914. Cape Horn was discovered in 1616 by Dutch explorer Willem Schouten (1580–1625), and named after his birthplace (Hoorn).

hornet type of ▷wasp.

hornfels ▷metamorphic rock formed by rocks heated by contact with a hot igneous body. It is fine-grained, brittle, and lacks foliation (a planar structure).

hornwort nonvascular plant (with no 'veins' to carry water and food), related to the ▷liverworts and ▷mosses. Hornworts are found in warm climates, growing on moist shaded soil. (Class Anthocerotae, order Bryophyta.)

The name is also given to a group of aquatic flowering plants which are found in slow-moving water. They have whorls of finely divided leaves and may grow up to 2 m/7 ft long. (Genus *Ceratophyllum*, family Ceratophyllaceae.)

horoscope in Western astrology, a chart of the position of the Sun, Moon, and planets relative to the ▷zodiac at the moment of birth, used to assess a person's character and forecast future influences.

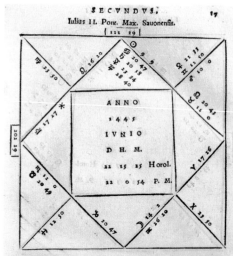

HOROSCOPE For a number of reasons, this horoscope chart is exceptional. Firstly, it is the chart of Pope Julius II (born June 1445), but it is also notable for the fact that it is squared off instead of being displayed as overlapping circles. It was first published as part of a *Tractatus Astrologicus* in 1546 – 33 years after the pope's death. The astrologer, in the text beneath, lists the pope's many outstanding achievements and cites them as inspiration for his work. *The Art Archive/Dagli Orti*

Horowitz, Vladimir (1904–1989) Russian-born US pianist. He made his US debut in 1928 with the New York Philharmonic Orchestra. A leading interpreter of Liszt, Schumann, and Rachmaninov, he toured worldwide until the early 1950s, when he retired to devote more time to recording. His rare concert appearances 1965–86 displayed undiminished brilliance.

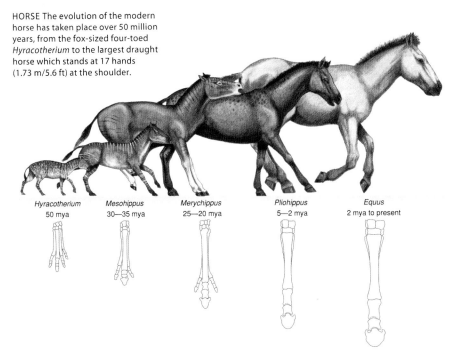

HORSE The evolution of the modern horse has taken place over 50 million years, from the fox-sized four-toed *Hyracotherium* to the largest draught horse which stands at 17 hands (1.73 m/5.6 ft) at the shoulder.

| *Hyracotherium* 50 mya | *Mesohippus* 30—35 mya | *Merychippus* 25—20 mya | *Pliohippus* 5—2 mya | *Equus* 2 mya to present |

horse hoofed, odd-toed, grazing mammal belonging to the same family as zebras and asses. The many breeds of domestic horse of Euro-Asian origin range in colour from white to grey, brown, and black. The yellow-brown **Mongolian wild horse**, or **Przewalski's horse** (*Equus przewalskii*), named after its Polish 'discoverer' in *c*. 1880, is the only surviving species of wild horse. (Species *Equus caballus*, family Equidae.)

Przewalski's horse became extinct in the wild because of hunting and competition with domestic animals for food; about 800 survive in captivity. However, in the late 1990s 55 Przewalski's horses were successfully reintroduced to the wild in Mongolia.

There are basically three types of domestic horse: the light riding horse, the heavy horse or draught horse, and the pony.

Light horse Breeds of light horse include the **Arab**, small, agile, highly spirited, and intelligent; the **Thoroughbred**, derived from the Arab via English mares, used in horse racing for its speed (the present stock is descended from three Arab horses introduced to Britain in the 18th century, especially the Darley Arabian; they are therefore closely related and so have only a limited range of genetic characteristics to improve with breeding); the **Anglo-Arab**, a French breed derived from crosses between English Thoroughbreds and Arabs; the North American **standard-bred**, developed from Thoroughbreds for pacing and trotting races; the **Tennessee Walking Horse**, developed for overseeing southern US plantations, with a special gait (smooth and comfortable for hours but as fast as a trot); the **quarter horse**, used by cowboys for herding; the **hackney**, a high-stepping harness horse; and the **Lippizaner**, a pure white horse, named after its place of origin in Slovenia (bred in Austria and Italy since the 16th century, these horses are used for advanced dressage, as practised at the Spanish Riding School in Vienna).

Heavy horse Among breeds of heavy horse in Britain are the **shire**, the largest draught horse in the world at 17 hands (1 hand = 10.2 cm/4 in), descended from the medieval war horses which carried knights in armour, and marked by long hair or 'feathering' round the fetlocks (ankles); the **Clydesdale**, smaller than the shire but possessing great strength and endurance; and the **Suffolk punch**, a sturdy all-round chestnut-coloured working horse.

Pony The pony, with a smaller build (under 14.2 hands, or 1.47 m/58 in), combines the qualities of various of the larger breeds of horse. Pony breeds include the **Highland**, the largest and strongest of native British breeds, unequalled for hardiness and staying power; the **Welsh cob**, similar to the Highland but faster; the smaller **New Forest**; and, smaller again, the **Exmoor** and **Dartmoor**. The smallest breed of pony is the hardy **Shetland**, about 70 cm/27 in high. The **Dales** and **Fell** ponies of Cumbria were formerly used by farmers as working horses. The **Connemara** is a large Irish breed, frequently used as a polo pony.

The **mule** is the usually sterile offspring of a female horse and a male ass, and a hardy pack animal; the **hinny** is a similarly sterile offspring of a male horse and a female ass, but less useful as a beast of burden.

Related Web site: Breeds of Livestock – Horse Breeds http://www.ansi.okstate.edu/breeds/horses/

horse chestnut any of a group of trees, especially *A. hippocastanum*, originally from southeastern Europe but widely planted elsewhere. Horse chestnuts have large palmate (five-lobed) leaves, showy upright spikes of white, pink, or red flowers, and large, shiny, inedible seeds (conkers) in prickly green capsules. The horse chestnut is not related to the true chestnut. In North America it is called buckeye. (Genus *Aesculus*, family Hippocastanaceae.)

Related Web site: Chestnut, Horse http://www.botanical.com/botanical/mgmh/c/chehor58.html

horsefly any of over 2,500 species of fly. The females suck blood from horses, cattle, and humans; the males live on plants and suck nectar. The larvae are carnivorous. (Family Tabanidae.)

HORSEFLY A female horsefly, or cleg, *Haematopota pluvialis* feeding on human blood. *Premaphotos Wildlife*

horsepower imperial unit (abbreviation hp) of power, now replaced by the ▷watt. It was first used by the engineer James ▷Watt, who employed it to compare the power of steam engines with that of horses.

horse racing sport of racing mounted or driven horses. Two forms in Britain are **flat racing**, for thoroughbred horses over a flat course, and **National Hunt racing**, in which the horses have to clear obstacles.

In Britain, racing took place in Stuart times and with its royal connections became known as the 'sport of kings'. Early racecourses included Chester, Ascot, and Newmarket. The English classics were introduced in 1776 with the St Leger (run at Doncaster), followed by the Oaks in 1779 and the Derby in 1780 (both run at Epsom), and the 2,000 Guineas in 1809 and the 1,000 Guineas in 1814 (both run at Newmarket). The first governing body for the sport was the Jockey Club, founded about 1750; it still has a regulatory role, but the British Horseracing Board became the governing body in 1993. The National Hunt Committee was established in 1866.

Related Web site: Mining Co. Guide to Horse Racing http://horseracing.miningco.com/

horseradish hardy perennial plant, native to southeastern Europe but naturalized elsewhere. The thick cream-coloured root is strong-tasting and is often made into a savoury sauce to accompany food. (*Armoracia rusticana*, family Cruciferae.)

horsetail plant related to ferns and club mosses; some species are also called **scouring rush**. There are about 35 living species, bearing their spores on cones at the stem tip. The upright stems are ribbed and often have spaced whorls of branches. Today they are of modest size, but hundreds of millions of years ago giant treelike forms existed. (Genus *Equisetum*, order Equisetales.)

Horta, Victor, Baron Horta (1861–1947) Belgian ▷art nouveau architect. He was responsible for a series of apartment buildings in Brussels, the first of which, the Hôtel Tassel (1892), is striking in its use of sinuous forms and decorative ironwork in the interior, particularly the staircase. His sumptuous Hôtel Solvay (1895–1900) and Maison du Peuple (1896–99) are more complete, interior and exterior being unified in a stylistic whole.

Horthy, Miklós Horthy de Nagybánya (1868–1957) Hungarian politician and admiral. Leader of the counter-revolutionary White government, he became regent in 1920 on the overthrow of the communist Bela ▷Kun regime by Romanian and Czechoslovak intervention. He represented the conservative and military class, and retained power until World War II, trying (although allied to Hitler) to retain independence of action. In 1944 he tried to negotiate a surrender to the USSR but Hungary was taken over by the Nazis and he was deported to Germany. He was released from German captivity the same year by the Western Allies. He was not tried at Nuremberg, however, but instead allowed to go to Portugal, where he died.

Horthy's relations with Germany were somewhat ambivalent. He ordered Hungarian forces to invade Yugoslavia in August 1941 in support of Hitler's aims in the region and the following month formally declared an anti-Soviet alliance with Germany. In November 1940 he joined the Tripartite Pact. In April 1941 Hungarian forces took part in the German attack on Yugoslavia. Horthy declared war with the USSR in June 1941, and with the USA in December 1941. However, he refused to send more troops to the Eastern Front in May 1943 and went further in 1944, demanding the return of Hungarian troops from Germany and an end to the use of Hungary as a supply base, and attempting to halt the deportation of Hungarian Jews. He backed down on all these points when Hitler threatened to occupy Hungary and from then on began trying to remove Hungary from the war.

horticulture art and science of growing flowers, fruit, and vegetables. Horticulture is practised in gardens and orchards, along with millions of acres of land devoted to vegetable farming. Some areas, like California, have specialized in horticulture because they have the mild climate and light fertile soil most suited to these crops.

The growth of industrial towns in the 19th century led to the development of commercial horticulture in the form of nurseries and market gardens, pioneering methods such as glasshouses, artificial heat, herbicides and pesticides, synthetic fertilizers, and machinery. In Britain, over 500,000 acres/200,000 hectares are devoted to commercial horticulture; vegetables account for almost three-quarters of the produce.

Horus (the Elder; or **Haroeris**) in ancient Egyptian mythology, the falcon-headed sky god whose eyes were the Sun and the Moon; adult son of the principal goddess ▷Isis or ▷Hathor (otherwise his wife), whom she magically conceived by the dead ▷Osiris, ruler of the Underworld. He injured his eye while avenging his father's

HORSERADISH The horseradish has wavy, indented leaves and small white flowers. It grows to a height of 60–90 cm/2–3 ft and has a thick taproot.

HORUS The falcon-headed Egyptian god, Horus, is on the left in this picture, receiving gifts from a newly dead Egyptian. *The Art Archive/Cairo Museum/Dagli Orti*

murder by ▷Set, the good eye being the Sun and the bad representing the Moon. Every pharaoh was believed to be his incarnation, becoming Osiris on death and ruling the Underworld. The next pharaoh was then thought to be a new incarnation of Horus.

Hoskins, Bob (Robert William) (1942–) English character actor. He progressed to fame from a series of supporting roles, and has played a range of both comic and dramatic parts, effortlessly shifting from humorous sidekick or love-interest to menacing sociopath. Films include *The Long Good Friday* (1980), *The Cotton Club* (1984), *Mona Lisa* (1986), *A Prayer for the Dying* (1987), *Who Framed Roger Rabbit?* (1988), *Mermaids* (1990), *Shattered* (1991), and *Nixon* (1995), in which he played the FBI chief J Edgar Hoover.

host in biology, an organism that is parasitized by another. In ▷commensalism, the partner that does not benefit may also be called the host.

HOST An orb web spider *Nephila clavipes* in Argentina acting as host to the larva of a parasitic wasp. *Premaphotos Wildlife*

hot spot a relatively large region of persistent volcanism that is not associated with an island arc, and not necessarily associated with an ocean-spreading centre (although it can be coincident with one). Hot spots occur in the oceans and on the continents, commonly within, rather than on the edges of, lithospheric plates. Examples include Hawaii, Iceland, and Yellowstone. Hot spots are thought to be the surface manifestations of stationary 'plumes' of hot mantle material that is continuously rising to the surface from some unknown depth in the mantle, possible the core-mantle boundary. The detailed chemistry of hot spot volcanic rocks is distinctly different from ridge or arc volcanics.

Hottentot (Dutch 'stammerer') South African term for a variety of different African peoples; it is non-scientific and considered derogatory by many. The name ▷Khoikhoi is preferred.

Houdini, Harry (1874–1926) Stage name of Erich Weiss. US escapologist and conjuror. He was renowned for his escapes from

ropes and handcuffs, from trunks under water, from straitjackets, and from prison cells.

Houphouët-Boigny, Félix (1905–1993) Côte d'Ivoire right-wing politician, president 1960–93. He held posts in French ministries, and became president of the Republic of Côte d'Ivoire on independence in 1960, maintaining close links with France, which helped to boost an already thriving economy and encourage political stability. Pro-Western and opposed to communist intervention in Africa, Houphouët-Boigny was strongly criticized for maintaining diplomatic relations with South Africa. He was re-elected for a seventh term in 1990 in multi-party elections, amid allegations of ballot rigging and political pressure.

hour period of time comprising 60 minutes; 24 hours make one calendar day.

Hours, Book of in medieval Europe, a collection of liturgical prayers for the use of the faithful. Some Books of Hours were also used as calendars.

BOOK OF HOURS 'Agenda for the Month of May', an excerpt from the Playfair *Book of Hours* (French, late 15th century). *The Art Archive/Victoria and Albert Museum London/Graham Brandon*

housefly fly found in and around human dwellings, especially *M. domestica*, a common worldwide species. Houseflies are grey and have mouthparts adapted for drinking liquids and sucking moisture from food and manure. (Genus *Musca*.)

house music dance music of the 1980s originating in the inner-city clubs of Chicago, USA, combining funk with European high-tech pop, and using dub, digital sampling, and cross-fading. **Acid house** has minimal vocals and melody, instead surrounding the mechanically emphasized 4/4 beat with stripped-down synthesizer riffs and a wandering bass line. Other variants include **hip house**, with rap elements, and **handbag** (mainstream).

House of Commons see ▷Commons, House of.

House of Lords see ▷Lords, House of.

House of Representatives lower chamber of the US ▷Congress, with 435 members elected at regular two-year intervals, every even year, in November. States are represented in proportion to their population. The Speaker of the House is the majority party's leader.

Related Web site: House of Representatives http://www.house.gov/

House Un-American Activities Committee (HUAC) Congressional committee, established in 1938 as the Special Committee to Investigate Un-American Activities under the chairmanship of Martin Dies. Noted for its public investigation of alleged subversion, particularly of communists, it was renamed the House Internal Security Committee in 1969. It achieved its greatest notoriety during the 1950s through its hearings on communism in the movie industry. It was abolished in 1975.

housing provision of residential accommodation. All countries have found some degree of state housing provision or subsidy essential, even in free-enterprise economies such as the USA. In the UK, flats and houses to rent (intended for people with low incomes) are built by local authorities under the direction of the secretary of state for environment, but houses in England and Wales would have to last 2,500 years at the rate of replacement being achieved by local authorities in 1991.

Housman, A(lfred) E(dward) (1859–1936) English poet and classical scholar. His *A Shropshire Lad* (1896), a series of deceptively simple, nostalgic, ballad-like poems, has been popular since World War I. This was followed by *Last Poems* (1922), *More Poems* (1936), and *Collected Poems* (1939).

Houston city and port in southeastern Texas, USA; linked by the Houston Ship Canal to the Gulf of Mexico, in the Gulf Coastal Plain; population (2000 est) 1,953,600; population of metropolitan

area (1994 est) 4,099,000. A major centre of finance and commerce, Houston is also one of the busiest US ports. Industrial products include refined petroleum, oilfield equipment, and petrochemicals, chief of which are synthetic rubber, plastics, insecticides, and fertilizers. Other products include iron and steel, electrical and electronic machinery, paper products, and milled rice. The Lyndon B Johnson Space Center (1961), the command post for flights by US astronauts, is located here. Houston was first settled in 1826 and incorporated as a city in 1839.

Related Web site: Houston http://www.houston-guide.com/

Houston, Sam (Samuel) (1793–1863) US general who won independence for Texas from Mexico in 1836 and was president of the Republic of Texas 1836–45. The city of Houston, Texas, is named after him.

Houston, Whitney (1963–) US soul ballad singer. She has had a string of consecutive number-one hits in the USA and Britain. They include 'Saving All My Love for You' (1985), 'I Wanna Dance With Somebody (Who Loves Me)' (1987), 'Where Do Broken Hearts Go' (1988), 'I Will Always Love You' (1992), and 'When You Believe' (with Mariah ▷Carey, featured in the 1998 film *Prince of Egypt*). Her album *My Love Is Your Love* (1999) sold five million copies worldwide by mid-1999, three million of those outside the USA.

hovercraft vehicle that rides on a cushion of high-pressure air, free from all contact with the surface beneath, invented by English engineer Christopher ▷Cockerell in 1959. Hovercraft need a smooth terrain when operating overland and are best adapted to use on waterways. They are useful in places where harbours have not been established. See diagram on p. 455.

Related Web site: Build a Real Working Hovercraft http://www.flash.net/~spartech/ReekoScience/ExpHoverCraft.htm

HOVERCRAFT Hovercrafts, also known as 'air-cushion vehicles', can travel efficiently across land or water. The weight of the craft is supported by air pressure, causing it to hover just above the surface. *Image Bank*

hoverfly brightly coloured winged insect. Hoverflies usually have spots, stripes, or bands of yellow or brown against a dark-coloured background, sometimes with dense hair covering the body surface. Many resemble bees, bumble bees, and wasps (displaying Batesian ▷mimicry) and most adults feed on nectar and pollen. (Family Syrphidae (numbering over 2,500 species), suborder Cyclorrhapha, order Diptera, class Insecta, phylum Arthropoda.)

Howard, Catherine (*c.* 1520–1542) Queen consort of ▷Henry VIII of England from 1540. In 1541 the archbishop of Canterbury, Thomas Cranmer, accused her of being unchaste before marriage to Henry and she was beheaded in 1542 after Cranmer made further charges of adultery.

Howard, Ebenezer (1850–1928) English town planner. Aiming to halt the unregulated growth of industrial cities, he pioneered the ideal of the ▷garden city through his book *Tomorrow* (1898; republished as *Garden Cities of Tomorrow* in 1902). He also inspired and took an active part in building the garden cities of Letchworth and Welwyn.

Howard, Michael (1941–) British Conservative politician, leader of the Conservative party from 2003. As home secretary (1993–97) he championed the restoration of law and order as a key electoral issue.

After a successful legal career, he entered the House of Commons in 1983 and, under Margaret Thatcher, made rapid ministerial progress through the departments of trade and industry, environment, and employment, until being appointed home secretary by John Major in 1993. His populist approach to law and order won him the plaudits of grass-roots party members, but he was forced to retreat on a number of key points, including that of police restructuring.

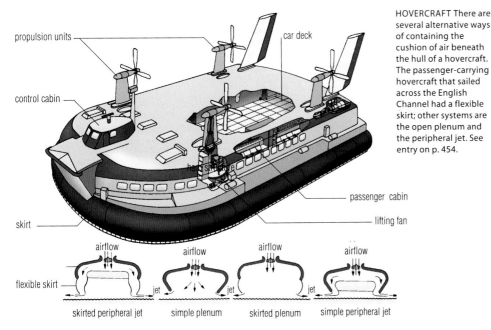

HOVERCRAFT There are several alternative ways of containing the cushion of air beneath the hull of a hovercraft. The passenger-carrying hovercraft that sailed across the English Channel had a flexible skirt; other systems are the open plenum and the peripheral jet. See entry on p. 454.

skirted peripheral jet   simple plenum   skirted plenum   simple peripheral jet

Howe, (Richard Edward) Geoffrey (1926–) Baron Howe of Aberavon. British Conservative politician, member of Parliament for Surrey East. As chancellor of the Exchequer 1979–83 under Margaret Thatcher, he put into practice the monetarist policy that reduced inflation at the cost of a rise in unemployment. In 1983 he became foreign secretary, and in 1989 deputy prime minister and leader of the House of Commons. On 1 November 1990 he resigned in protest at Thatcher's continued opposition to the UK's greater integration in Europe.

Howe, William (1729–1814) 5th Viscount Howe. British general. During the American Revolution he won the Battle of Bunker Hill in 1775, and as commander-in-chief in America 1776–78 captured New York and defeated Washington at Brandywine and Germantown. He resigned in protest at lack of home government support.

howitzer cannon, in use since the 16th century, with a particularly steep angle of fire. It was much developed in World War I for demolishing the fortresses of the trench system. The multinational NATO FH70 field howitzer is mobile and fires, under computer control, three 43 kg/95 lb shells at 32 km/20 mi range in 15 seconds.

Hoxha, Enver (1908–1985) Albanian communist politician, the country's leader from 1954. He founded the Albanian Communist Party in 1941, and headed the liberation movement 1939–44. He was prime minister 1944–54, also handling foreign affairs 1946–53, and from 1954 was first secretary of the Albanian Party of Labour. In policy he was a Stalinist and independent of both Chinese and Soviet communism.

Hoyle, Fred(erick) (1915–2001) English astronomer, cosmologist, and writer. His astronomical research dealt mainly with the internal structure and evolution of the stars. In 1948 he developed with Hermann Bondi and Thomas Gold the ▷steady-state theory of the universe. In 1957, with William Fowler, he showed that chemical elements heavier than hydrogen and helium may be built up by nuclear reactions inside stars. He was knighted in 1972.

HP abbreviation for ▷hire purchase.

hp abbreviation for ▷horsepower.

Hrabal, Bohumil (1914–1997) Czech writer, born in Moravia. He began writing after 1962. His novels depict ordinary people caught up in events they do not control or comprehend, including *Ostre sledované vlaky/Closely Observed Trains* (1965; filmed 1967), *I Served the King of England* (1975; published 1986), *The Millions of Arlequin* (1981), *Snowdrop Festivities* (1981; filmed 1984), and *Too Loud a Solitude* (filmed 1994).

Hsuan Tung name adopted by Henry ▷P'u-i on becoming emperor of China in 1908.

Hua Guofeng (or **Hua Kuofeng**) (1920–) Chinese politician, leader of the Chinese Communist Party (CCP) 1976–81, premier 1976–80. He dominated Chinese politics 1976–77, seeking economic modernization without major structural reform. From 1978 he was gradually eclipsed by Deng Xiaoping. Hua was ousted from the Politburo in September 1982 but remained a member of the CCP Central Committee.

Born near Tiayuan, in Shanxi province in northern China, Hua was the illegitimate son of a rich landlord's daughter who, after being disowned by her family, later married a communist underground labour organizer. Brought up in Shaanxi province, Hua joined the Chinese Communist Party (CCP) in 1938 and fought under ▷Zhu De, the Red Army leader, during the liberation struggle and civil war of 1937–49, serving as a political commissar and propagandist. After the establishment of the People's Republic in 1949, Hua began a steady climb up the CCP administrative ladder, working in Hunan, Mao Zedong's home province, where he specialized in agriculture and education. He entered the CCP Central Committee in 1969, was made party leader in Hunan in 1970, and joined the CCP Politburo in 1973.

Huai-Hai, Battle of decisive campaign 1948–49 in the Chinese Civil War (1946–49). The name is derived from the two main defensive positions held by the nationalist ▷Guomindang force: the Huang (Huai) River in Shandong and Jiangsu provinces, and the Lung Hai railway. Communist forces from the east and west captured Suzhou (Soochow), a key railway junction, on 1 December 1948. On 6 January 1949 they secured a crushing victory at Yungchung to the southwest, facilitating an advance on Shanghai, which fell in the spring of 1949.

Huang He (or **Hwang Ho**; English **Yellow River**) river in China, named after its muddy waters; length 5,464 km/3,395 mi. Rising in Qinghai province in the west of the country, it winds eastwards to the Bohai Gulf. Sometimes known as 'China's sorrow' because of disastrous floods, it is now largely controlled through hydroelectric works, dykes, and embankments. The barriers, however, are ceasing to work because silt is continually raising the river bed.

> **Fred Hoyle**
> *Space isn't remote at all.*
> *It's only an hour's drive*
> *away if your car could go*
> *straight upwards.*
> The Observer, September 1979

Hubble, Edwin (Powell) (1889–1953) US astronomer. He discovered the existence of ▷galaxies outside our own, and classified them according to their shape. His theory that the universe is expanding is now generally accepted.

His data on the speed at which galaxies were receding (based on their ▷red shifts) were used to determine the portion of the universe that we can never come to know, the radius of which is called the **Hubble radius**. Beyond this limit, any matter will be travelling at the speed of light, so communication with it will never be possible. The ratio of the velocity of galactic recession to distance has been named the **Hubble constant**.

Hubble discovered ▷Cepheid variable stars in the Andromeda galaxy in 1924, proving it to lie far beyond our own Galaxy. In 1925 he introduced the classification of galaxies as spirals, barred spirals, and ellipticals. In 1929 he announced **Hubble's law**, stating that the galaxies are moving apart at a rate that increases with their distance from each other.

Hubble's law law that relates a galaxy's distance from us to its speed of recession as the universe expands, announced in 1929 by US astronomer Edwin Hubble. He found that galaxies are moving apart at speeds that increase in direct proportion to their distance apart. The rate of expansion is known as Hubble's constant.

Hubble Space Telescope (HST) space-based astronomical observing facility, orbiting the Earth at an altitude of 610 km/380 mi. It consists of a 2.4 m/94 in telescope and four complimentary scientific instruments, is roughly cylindrical, 13 m/43 ft long, and 4 m/13 ft in diameter, with two large solar panels. HST produces a wealth of scientific data, and allows astronomers to observe the birth of stars, find planets around neighbouring stars, follow the expanding remnants of exploding stars, and search for black holes in the centre of galaxies. HST is a cooperative programme between the European Space Agency (ESA) and the US agency NASA, and is the first spacecraft specifically designed to be serviced in orbit as a permanent space-based observatory. It was launched in 1990.

By having a large telescope above Earth's atmosphere, astronomers are able to look at the universe with unprecedented clarity. Celestial observations by HST are unhampered by clouds and other atmospheric phenomena that distort and attenuate starlight. In particular, the apparent twinkling of starlight caused by density fluctuations in the atmosphere limits the clarity of ground-based telescopes. HST performs at least ten times better than such telescopes and can see almost back to the edge of the universe and to the beginning of time (see ▷Big Bang).

Before HST could reach its full potential, a flaw in the shape of its main mirror, discovered two months after the launch, had to be corrected. In 1993, as part of a planned servicing and instrument upgrade mission, NASA astronauts aboard the space shuttle *Endeavor* installed a set of corrective lenses to compensate for the error in the mirror figure. COSTAR (corrective optics space telescope axial replacement), a device containing ten coin-sized mirrors, now feeds a corrected image from the main mirror to three of the HST's four scientific instruments. HST is also being used to detail the distribution of dust and stars in nearby galaxies, watch the collisions of galaxies in detail, infer the evolution of galaxies, and measure the age of the universe.

In December 1995 HST was trained on an 'empty' area of sky near the Plough, now termed the **Hubble Deep Field**. Around 1,500 galaxies, mostly new discoveries, were photographed.

Two new instruments were added in February 1997. The Near Infrared Camera and Multi-Object Spectrometer (NICMOS) will enable Hubble to see things even further away (and therefore older) than ever before. The Space Telescope Imaging Spectograph will work 30 times faster than its predecessor as it can gather information about different stars at the same time.

In May 1997, three months after astronauts installed new equipment, US scientists reported that Hubble had made an extraordinary finding. Within 20 minutes of searching, it discovered evidence of a black hole 300 million times the mass of the Sun. It is located in the middle of galaxy M84 about 50 million light-years from Earth. Further findings in December 1997 concerned different shapes of dying stars. Previously, astronomers had thought that most stars die with a round shell of burning gas expanding into space. The photographs taken by the HST show shapes such as pinwheels and jet exhaust. This may be indicative of how the Sun will die.

Galaxies photographed by the HST in 1998 were born at least 12 billion years ago. These were the deepest images ever obtained. In April 2000, 10 years after its launch, the telescope had taken 271,000 separate observations of 13,670 objects, and had been serviced by astronauts 13 times. In March 2002 a pair a powerful solar wings and an advanced camera were installed. The next plan from NASA is to launch a Next Generation Space Telescope (NGST) in about 2008, which will use an infrared camera which, it is hoped, will be able to display what the universe was like before the stars were formed.

Hubei (or **Hupei** or **Hupeh**) province of central China, bounded to the north by Henan, to the east by Anhui, to the south by Jiangxi and Hunan, and to the west by Sichuan and Shaanxi provinces; area 187,500 sq km/72,375 sq mi; population (1996) 58,250,000. The capital is ▷Wuhan; other major cities and towns are Huangshi, Shashi, Yichang, and Xiangfan. The main industries are the mining of copper, gypsum, iron ore, phosphorus, and salt; and the production of steel, machinery, domestic appliances, textiles, food processing, and fibre-optic cables. Agriculture is based on the cultivation of rice, cotton, rapeseed, wheat, beans, and vegetables.

hubris in Greek thought, an act of transgression or overweening pride. In ancient Greek tragedy, hubris was believed to offend the gods, and to lead to retribution.

huckleberry berry-bearing bush closely related to the ▷blueberry in the USA and bilberry in Britain. Huckleberry bushes have edible dark-blue berries. (Genus *Gaylussacia*, family Ericaceae.)

Huddersfield (Anglo-Saxon **Oderesfelt**) industrial town in West Yorkshire, on the River Colne, between Leeds and Manchester; population (1991) 119,000. A thriving centre of woollen manufacture by the end of the 18th century, it now produces textiles and related products, and has electrical and mechanical engineering, food processing (biscuits), publishing, and building industries. The service sector is the principal employer.

Hudson river in northeastern USA; length 485 km/300 mi. It rises in the Adirondack Mountains and flows south, emptying into a bay of the Atlantic Ocean at New York City. The Hudson forms the boundary between New Jersey and New York, and the states are linked by bridges and tunnels. The New York Barge Canal system links the Hudson to Lake Champlain, Lake Erie, and the St Lawrence River. It is navigable by small ocean-going vessels as far upstream as Albany and Troy, about 150 mi/240 km from its mouth, and for eight months of the year barge traffic can reach the Great Lakes.

Related Web site: Explore the Hudson Valley's Rich History
http://www.hudsonriver.com/history.htm

Hudson, Henry (c. 1565–1611) English explorer. Under the auspices of the Muscovy Company (1607–08), he made two unsuccessful attempts to find the Northeast Passage to China. In September 1609, commissioned by the Dutch East India Company, he reached New York Bay and sailed 240 km/150 mi up the river that now bears his name, establishing Dutch claims to the area. In 1610 he sailed from London in the *Discovery* and entered what is now the Hudson Strait. After an icebound winter, he was turned adrift by a mutinous crew in what is now Hudson Bay.

Hudson, Rock (1925–1985) Stage name of Roy Harold Scherer, Jr. US film actor. He was a star from the mid-1950s to the mid-1960s, and entered the film industry with no previous acting experience. He specialized in melodrama, often working with director Douglas Sirk, and in romantic comedy, co-starring on three occasions with Doris Day. He enjoyed a successful TV career in the 1970s. His films include *Magnificent Obsession* (1954), *Giant* (1956), *Written on the Wind* (1956), and *Pillow Talk* (1959).

Hudson Bay inland sea of northeastern Canada, linked with the Atlantic Ocean by **Hudson Strait** and with the Arctic Ocean by Foxe Channel and the Gulf of Boothia; area 1,233,000 sq km/ 476,000 sq mi. It is bordered by (clockwise) the provinces of Québec, Ontario, Manitoba, and the Northwest Territories. It is named after Henry Hudson, who reached it in 1610.

Hudson Bay occupies a basin in the Canadian Shield, and is mostly shallow, with low shorelines, especially in the south and west. Southampton Island lies in the northwest of the bay, and James Bay is the major inlet at its southern end. The eastern shores are rocky, with some steep bluffs and a small chain of islands. Several rivers empty into the bay, including the Churchill, Nelson, Albany, Moose, and Rupert and Severn. It is ice-free and navigable during the summer, when grain is shipped from Churchill, Manitoba, but the bay is obstructed by drifting ice for nine months of the year. Hudson Bay abounds in fish, and whales, dolphins, seals, and walruses also inhabit its waters and coastline. The Hudson Bay area is sparsely settled, chiefly by trappers, American Indians, and Inuit.

Hudson River School group of US landscape painters of the early 19th century. They painted the dramatic scenery of the Hudson River Valley and the Catskill Mountains in New York State, their style influenced by the Romantic landscapes of J M W ▷Turner and John Martin. The best-known members of the school were Thomas Cole, who set up his studio at Catskill in 1826, and Albery Bierstadt.

Hudson's Bay Company chartered company founded by Prince ▷Rupert in 1670 to trade in furs with North American Indians. In 1783 the rival North West Company was formed, but in 1851 this became amalgamated with the Hudson's Bay Company. It is still Canada's biggest fur company, but today also sells general merchandise through department stores and has oil and natural gas interests.

Huelva port and capital of Huelva province in Andalusia, southwest Spain, situated on the Atlantic coast, on a small peninsula formed by the junction of the Tinto and the Odiel rivers; population (1991) 141,000. Industries include shipbuilding and oil refining; there is a large petrochemical complex here which produces fertilizers, sulphuric acid, and explosives, as well as petrol and oil products. There are also fisheries, and a trade in ores from the Rio Tinto mines.

Huesca capital of Huesca province in Aragón, northeast Spain, situated on the River Isuela; population (1991) 44,100. Industries include engineering and food processing. Among its buildings are a 13th-century cathedral and the former palace of the kings of Aragón.

HOWARD HUGHES A photograph of Howard Hughes as a test pilot, preparing to fly the XF-11 for the US Air Force in 1947. In later life, he became a recluse, and few photographs exist of him after middle age. *Archive Photos*

Hughes, Howard (Robard) (1905–1976) US tycoon. Inheriting wealth from his father, who had patented a successful oil-drilling bit, he created a legendary financial empire. A skilled pilot, he manufactured and designed aircraft. He formed a film company in Hollywood and made the classic film *Hell's Angels* (1930) about aviators of World War I; later successes included *Scarface* (1932) and *The Outlaw* (1944). From his middle years he was a recluse.

Hughes, Richard (Arthur Warren) (1900–1976) English writer. His study of childhood, *A High Wind in Jamaica*, was published in 1929; his story of a ship's adventures in a hurricane, *In Hazard* in 1938; and the historical novel *The Fox in the Attic* in 1961. He also wrote some poetry and plays (his *Collected Plays* appeared in 1928), and short stories.

Hughes, Ted (Edward James) (1930–1998) English poet. He was the poet laureate from 1984 until his death. His work is characterized by its harsh portrayal of the crueller aspects of nature, by its reflection of the agonies of personal experience, and by the employment of myths of creation and being, as in *Crow* (1970) and *Gaudete* (1977). His free-verse renderings, *Tales from Ovid* won the 1997 Whitbread Book of the Year Award, and his collection *Birthday Letters* was awarded the 1998 Forward Prize and the 1998 Whitbread Book of the Year Award.

His collections include *The Hawk in the Rain* (1957), *Lupercal* (1960), *Wodwo* (1967), *Wolfwatching* (1989), and *Winter Pollen: Occasional Prose* (1994). His novels for children include *The Iron Man* (1968).

Hughes, Thomas (1822–1896) English writer. He is best known as the author of *Tom Brown's School Days* (1857), a story of Rugby School under Thomas ▷Arnold, with an underlying religious sense, which was the forerunner of the modern school story. It had a sequel, *Tom Brown at Oxford* (1861).

Hugo, Victor (Marie) (1802–1885) French novelist, poet, and dramatist. The verse play *Hernani* (1830) firmly established Hugo as the leader of French Romanticism. This was the first of a series of dramas produced in the 1830s and early 1840s, including *Le Roi s'amuse* (1832) and *Ruy Blas* (1838). His melodramatic novels include *Notre-Dame de Paris* (1831), and *Les Misérables* (1862).

Hugo's position in French literature is important: he gave French Romanticism a peculiarly decorative character and kept the Romantic spirit alive in France for some 30 years after its apparent demise. His writing is notable for its vitality, wide scope, graceful lyrical power, rhetorical magnificence, the ability to express pathos, awe, and indignation; and the variety of style and skill displayed in his handling of metre and language. Despite a lack of humour and proportion, and an all-pervading egoism, Hugo remains a literary giant.

Related Web site: Hugo's Les Miserables (Fantine, Cosette, Marius)
http://www.hti.umich.edu/bin/pd-idx?type=header&id=HugoVMiser

Huguenot French Protestant in the 16th century; the term referred mainly to Calvinists. Persecuted under Francis I and Henry II, the Huguenots survived both an attempt to exterminate them (the Massacre of ▷St Bartholomew on 24 August 1572) and the religious wars of the next 30 years. In 1598 ▷Henry IV (himself formerly a Huguenot) granted them toleration under the Edict of ▷Nantes. Louis XIV revoked the edict in 1685, attempting their forcible conversion, and 400,000 emigrated.

Hui one of the largest minority ethnic groups in China, numbering about eight and a half million. Members of the Hui live all over China, but are concentrated in the northern central region. They have been Muslims since the 10th century, for which they have suffered persecution both before and since the communist revolution.

Hull shortened name of ▷Kingston upon Hull, a city and unitary authority on the north bank of the Humber estuary, northeast England.

Hull, Cordell (1871–1955) US Democratic politician. As F D Roosevelt's secretary of state 1933–44, he was a vigorous champion of free trade, and opposed German and Japanese aggression. He was identified with the Good Neighbor policy of nonintervention in Latin America. An advocate of collective security after World War II, he was called by Roosevelt 'the father of the United Nations'. He was awarded the Nobel Prize for Peace in 1945 for his work in organizing the United Nations (UN).

He was a member of Congress 1907–33. After December 1941 foreign policy was handled more directly by Roosevelt, but Hull was active in reaching agreements with ▷Vichy France, though these were largely cancelled by the rising influence of General Charles ▷de Gaulle.

human body the physical structure of the human being. It develops from the single cell of the fertilized ovum, is born at 40 weeks, and usually reaches sexual maturity between 11 and 18 years of age. The bony framework (skeleton) consists of more than 200 bones, over half of which are in the hands and feet. Bones are held together by joints, some of which allow movement. The circulatory system supplies muscles and organs with blood, which provides oxygen and food and removes carbon dioxide and other waste products. Body functions are controlled by the nervous system and hormones.

In the upper part of the trunk is the thorax, which contains the lungs and heart. Below this is the abdomen, containing the digestive system (stomach and intestines); the liver, spleen, and pancreas; the urinary system (kidneys, ureters, and bladder); and, in women, the reproductive organs (ovaries, uterus, and vagina). In men, the prostate gland and seminal vesicles only of the reproductive system are situated in the abdomen, the testes being in the scrotum, which, with the penis, is suspended in front of and below the abdomen.

The bladder empties through a small channel (urethra); in the female this opens in the upper end of the vulval cleft, which also contains the opening of the vagina, or birth canal; in the male, the urethra is continued into the penis. In both sexes, the lower bowel terminates in the anus, a ring of strong muscle situated between the buttocks.

Human Body: Composition

Chemical element or substance	Body weight (%)
Pure elements	
Oxygen	65
Carbon	18
Hydrogen	10
Nitrogen	3
Calcium	2
Phosphorus	1.1
Potassium	0.35
Sulphur	0.25
Sodium	0.15
Chlorine	0.15
Magnesium, iron, manganese, copper, iodine, cobalt, zinc	traces
Water and solid matter	
Water	60–80
Total solid material	20–40
Organic molecules	
Protein	15–20
Lipid	3–20
Carbohydrate	1–15
Other	0–1

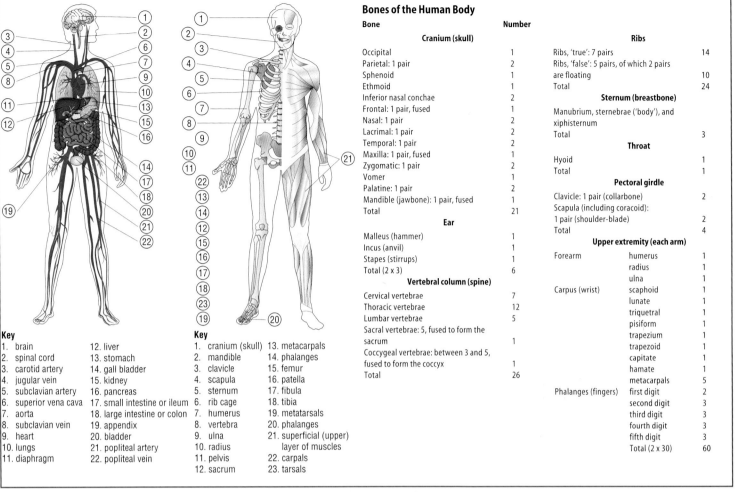

Bones of the Human Body

Bone	Number		Ribs	
Cranium (skull)				
Occipital	1		Ribs, 'true': 7 pairs	14
Parietal: 1 pair	2		Ribs, 'false': 5 pairs, of which 2 pairs	
Sphenoid	1		are floating	10
Ethmoid	1		Total	24
Inferior nasal conchae	2		**Sternum (breastbone)**	
Frontal: 1 pair, fused	1		Manubrium, sternebrae ('body'), and	
Nasal: 1 pair	2		xiphisternum	
Lacrimal: 1 pair	2		Total	3
Temporal: 1 pair	2		**Throat**	
Maxilla: 1 pair, fused	1		Hyoid	1
Zygomatic: 1 pair	2		Total	1
Vomer	1		**Pectoral girdle**	
Palatine: 1 pair	2		Clavicle: 1 pair (collarbone)	2
Mandible (jawbone): 1 pair, fused	1		Scapula (including coracoid):	
Total	21		1 pair (shoulder-blade)	2
Ear			Total	4
Malleus (hammer)	1		**Upper extremity (each arm)**	
Incus (anvil)	1		Forearm	humerus	1
Stapes (stirrups)	1			radius	1
Total (2 x 3)	6			ulna	1
Vertebral column (spine)			Carpus (wrist)	scaphoid	1
Cervical vertebrae	7			lunate	1
Thoracic vertebrae	12			triquetral	1
Lumbar vertebrae	5			pisiform	1
Sacral vertebrae: 5, fused to form the				trapezium	1
sacrum	1			trapezoid	1
Coccygeal vertebrae: between 3 and 5,				capitate	1
fused to form the coccyx	1			hamate	1
Total	26			metacarpals	5
			Phalanges (fingers)	first digit	2
				second digit	3
				third digit	3
				fourth digit	3
				fifth digit	3
				Total (2 x 30)	60

Key
1. brain
2. spinal cord
3. carotid artery
4. jugular vein
5. subclavian artery
6. superior vena cava
7. aorta
8. subclavian vein
9. heart
10. lungs
11. diaphragm
12. liver
13. stomach
14. gall bladder
15. kidney
16. pancreas
17. small intestine or ileum
18. large intestine or colon
19. appendix
20. bladder
21. popliteal artery
22. popliteal vein

Key
1. cranium (skull)
2. mandible
3. clavicle
4. scapula
5. sternum
6. rib cage
7. humerus
8. vertebra
9. ulna
10. radius
11. pelvis
12. sacrum
13. metacarpals
14. phalanges
15. femur
16. patella
17. fibula
18. tibia
19. metatarsals
20. phalanges
21. superficial (upper) layer of muscles
22. carpals
23. tarsals

HUMAN BODY The adult human body has approximately 650 muscles, 100 joints, 100,000 km/60,000 mi of blood vessels and 13,000 nerve cells. There are 206 bones in the adult body, nearly half of them in the hands and feet.

Human Genome Project (HGP) research scheme to map the complete nucleotide (see ▷nucleic acid) sequence of human ▷DNA. It was begun in 1990 and a working draft of the genome (a mapping of 97% of the genome, sequencing of 85%, and completion of 24% of the human genome) was achieved in June 2000, with the results published in February 2001. The publicly-funded Human Genome Organization (HUGO) is coordinating the $300 million project (the largest research project ever undertaken in the life sciences), which took place in over 20 centres around the world. Sequencing was also carried out commercially by US biotechnology company Celera Genomics. The detailed mapping of the genome was completed in for 2003.

Research found the human genome to consist of between 27,000 and 40,000 different ▷genes, far fewer than expected, and one gene may contain more than 2 million nucleotides. The knowledge gained from mapping all these genes is expected to help prevent or treat many crippling and lethal diseases, but there are potential ethical problems associated with knowledge of an individual's genetic make-up.

Sequencing Each strand of DNA carries a sequence of chemical building blocks, the nucleotides. The different combinations of nucleotides code for the production of different proteins in the cell, and thus determine the structure of the body and its individual variations. To establish the nucleotide sequence, DNA strands are broken into fragments, which are duplicated (by being introduced into cells of yeast or the bacterium *Escherichia coli*) and distributed to the research centres.

Genes account for only a small amount of the DNA sequence. Over 90% of DNA appears not to have any function, although it is perfectly replicated each time the cell divides, and handed on to the next generation. Many higher organisms have large amounts of redundant DNA and it may be that this is an advantage, in that a pool of DNA is available to form new genes if one is lost by mutation.

Whose genome? The genome sequenced is not that of any one person. The HGP collected blood and sperm samples from a large number of donors and then processed the DNA of a small number (10–20) of these, ensuring that neither their scientists nor the donors would know whose DNA was finally used. As all humans share the same basic set of genes the information gained will be applicable to everyone. See also The Human Genome Project Focus Feature on pp. 458–459.
Related Web site: Human Genome Project Information http://www.ornl.gov/TechResources/Human_Genome/home.html

humanism belief in the high potential of human nature rather than in religious or transcendental values. Humanism culminated as a cultural and literary force in 16th-century Renaissance Europe in line with the period's enthusiasm for classical literature and art, growing individualism, and the ideal of the all-round male who should be statesman and poet, scholar and warrior. ▷Erasmus is a great exemplar of Renaissance humanism.
Related Web site: British Humanist Association http://www.humanism.org.uk/

human reproduction an example of ▷sexual reproduction, where the male produces sperm and the female eggs. These gametes contain only half the normal number of chromosomes, 23 instead of 46, so that on fertilization the resulting cell has the correct genetic complement. Fertilization is internal, which increases the chances of conception; unusually for mammals, copulation and pregnancy can occur at any time of the year. Human beings are also remarkable for the length of childhood and for the highly complex systems of parental care found in society. The use of contraception and the development of laboratory methods of insemination and fertilization are issues that make human reproduction more than a merely biological phenomenon.

human rights civil and political ▷rights of the individual in relation to the state; see also ▷civil rights. Under the terms of the ▷United Nations Charter human rights violations by countries have become its proper concern, although the implementation of this obligation is hampered by Article 2 (7) of the charter prohibiting interference in domestic affairs. The Universal Declaration of ▷Human Rights, passed by the General Assembly on 10 December 1948, is based on a belief in the inherent rights, equality, and freedom of human beings and sets out in 28 articles the fundamental freedoms – civil, political, economic – to be promoted. The declaration has considerable moral force but is not legally binding on states.
Related Web site: Amnesty International Online http://www.amnesty.org/

Human Rights, Universal Declaration of charter of civil and political rights drawn up by the United Nations in 1948. They include the right to life, liberty, education, and equality before the law; to freedom of movement, religion, association, and information; and to a nationality.

Under the **European Convention on Human Rights** of 1950, the Council of Europe established the **European Commission of Human Rights**, which investigates complaints by states or individuals. Its findings are examined by the **European Court of Human Rights** (established 1959), whose compulsory jurisdiction has been recognized by a number of states, including the UK.
Related Web site: Human Rights Caravan http://rights.amnesty.org/

Human Rights Watch US non-partisan pressure group that monitors and publicizes human-rights abuses by governments, especially attacks on those who defend human rights in their own countries. It comprises **Africa Watch, Americas Watch, Asia Watch, Middle East Watch**, and **Helsinki Watch**; the last-named monitors compliance with the 1975 Helsinki accords by the 35 signatory countries.

human species, origins of evolution of humans from ancestral ▷primates. The African apes (gorilla and chimpanzee) are shown by anatomical and molecular comparisons to be the closest living relatives of humans. The oldest known hominids (of the human group) had been the australopithecines, found in Africa, dating from 3.5–4.4 million years ago. But in December 2000, scientists unearthed the fossilized remains of a hominid dating back 6 million years. The first to use tools came 2 million years ago, and the first hominids to use fire and move out of Africa appeared 1.7 million years ago. ▷Neanderthals were not direct ancestors of the human species. Modern humans are all believed to descend from one African female of 200,000 years ago, although there is a rival theory that humans evolved in different parts of the world simultaneously.

(continued on p. 460)

The Human Genome Project

by Paul Wymer

June 2001 witnessed the completion of the first draft of the entire human genome, a DNA sequence of some 3.2 billion chemical units called nucleotides. A high-quality reference sequence was completed in April 2003, marking the end of the Human Genome Project (HGP), two years ahead of schedule. Coincidentally this was also the 50th anniversary of Watson and Crick's publication of DNA structure that launched the era of molecular biology.

drafting the human genome

DNA is the chemical repository of inherited instructions for the development and functioning of all living things. As well as determining the entire nucleotide sequence within human DNA, work derived from the HGP aims to identify the relatively small parts of the sequence representing the 30–40,000 human genes. Available to researchers worldwide, the human genome reference sequence provides an unprecedented resource. It will serve throughout the 21st century as a basis for research and discovery.

Many other genome projects – on microbes, plants, and animals – have been completed since the inception of the HGP, and many more are underway. The data produced enable detailed comparisons between different organisms, including humans.

sequence and consequence

DNA is made up of four different **nucleotides** characterized by the bases adenine, guanine, thymine, and cytosine. The genetic code that gives us our unique characteristics is defined by the sequence of these bases along the DNA molecule. This base sequence determines the order of building blocks (amino acids) in the proteins coded for by different genes.

The development of advanced robotics and computer software for large-scale DNA sequencing has proceeded at a remarkable pace. The '**shotgun**' strategy, coupled with automated DNA sequencing machines, has proved an extremely successful combination. The 'shotgun' strategy for serquencing the entire DNA in an organism was

CHROMOSOME The 23 pairs of chromosomes of a normal human male.

developed by US scientist Dr Craig Venter. It involves the preparation of a 'library' of random DNA fragments by the breaking up of entire genomic DNA to make it more amenable to analysis. These fragments are then reproduced many times and a large number are sequenced from both ends until

THE SANGER CENTRE is a publicly funded research centre founded by the Wellcome Trust and the British Medical Research Council. Research at the centre concentrates on the large-scale sequencing and analysis of genomes, with the centre providing the focus for the UK's involvement in the international Human Genome Project. Although rival organization Celera Genomics published a draft of the human genome first, scientists at the Sanger Centre have claimed that their results are more precise. *The Sanger Centre*

every part of the genome has been sequenced several times on average (this is determined by statistical means). Finally, the order in which the fragments fit together is established to provide the complete genome sequence.

Nonetheless, it is a huge step from elucidating the DNA sequence of the genome to knowing where within that sequence genes are located and what they do. Mere acquisition of DNA sequences conveys little more about the biology of the organisms from which they are derived than a company telephone directory can reveal about the complexities of the company's business. It is conceivable, however, that many of the major genes involved in, for example, susceptibility to heart disease and various cancers, will be identified in the near future. This will make it possible to 'type' people according to the variants of these genes that they carry and hence determine the likelihood that they will develop these diseases.

making sense of sequence

The vast amount of DNA sequence information generated by research groups around the world is stored in computer databases, connected to each other via the Internet. In extracting meaning from sequence information, scientists are faced with a task analogous to decoding an unknown language. By themselves the letters make no sense, but their particular combination into words and sentences is crucial. As in a real language, the subtlest changes, just like changing a single letter in a word, can thoroughly alter the message. DNA sequences for microbes, plants, animals, and humans from laboratories around the world can be compared and duplications can be detected. Also, similarities that point to evolutionary relationships, new classifications, and, ultimately, better understanding of life form and function can be recognized.

genetics and disease

While we all share a common genome, humans as a population are not clones. The genome is what defines us as *Homo sapiens* and alterations in DNA make us individuals. Despite our common genome, we are predisposed to different diseases, we respond to the environment in different ways, and we differ in the way we react to drugs – just as we are inherently different in our ability to perform particular tasks. Genetic explanations of the mechanism of diseases will enable the development of drugs with a more precise action, producing higher response rates and lowering the risk of adverse effects. Recent research, for example, has identified some schizophrenic patients who have a mutation in a particular neuroreceptor gene. This group of patients is not likely to benefit from the drug Clozapine, often used to treat schizophrenia. This knowledge is very valuable, as the drug is costly and can have severe side effects. However, a potential drawback for pharmaceutical companies would be the costs involved in tailoring drugs, which would then be sold to fewer customers.

genetic screening

Many genes have already been mapped to their approximate positions on the **chromosomes**. These positions are determined in relation to known 'markers', DNA fragments that provide landmarks throughout the genome. Once the location of a disease gene is known, it is relatively straightforward to test for its presence in different people. This is known as genetic screening. For disorders caused by a single gene, such as cystic fibrosis and Duchenne muscular dystrophy, tests can now be applied to indicate the presence or absence of the faulty gene. Such tests may be carried out antenatally on the unborn fetus, on test-tube embryos, or on adults. If the genetic conditions contributing to multi-factorial diseases are identified, it may be possible to test for increased susceptibility to common illnesses, such as coronary heart disease.

CRAIG VENTER (right), US geneticist and businessman, discussing the mapping of the human genome at a meeting in Brisbane, Australia, in 1999. Venter was head of Celera Genomics, a private company, and was responsible for the development of the shotgun strategy for sequencing DNA. This strategy has produced results faster than expected. *Applied Biosystems*

Although genetic testing at the chromosome level has been in existence for some time, for example in prenatal testing for Down's syndrome, recent progress has focused attention on the sensitive issues that this type of testing entails. For example, some genetic tests permit diagnosis of disorders in patients before they have developed any symptoms. Others can identify carriers of recessive genetic diseases. Such tests can raise very difficult choices for individuals, as illustrated by the discovery of the gene for Huntingdon's disease.

Huntingdon's disease is a degenerative condition of the central nervous system that generally develops in middle age. No cure is currently available. Sufferers gradually deteriorate to a point where they require total care before death occurs. The disease affects about one in 5,000 people in the UK. The gene responsible for Huntington's disease was identified in 1993 and mapped to the tip of chromosome 4, making direct testing possible. Since testing began, it is thought that only a small minority of those who have a 50% chance of carrying the faulty gene –that is, those with a parent who has the condition – have chosen to undergo testing; probably around 5% of such people. Those who do seek testing usually undergo extensive counselling and discussion before proceeding.

Diagnosis of a single gene disorder for which no cure is currently available is one dilemma, but as the Human Genome Project progresses, new issues with consequences for the individual and for society are regularly created. For example, how do we deal with the discovery of genes that apparently predispose people towards certain kinds of behaviour, such as violence? Should the population be screened for certain genetic conditions and, if so, how do we use the information? A worst-case scenario could see the development of a genetic underclass, with people denied insurance and employment and discriminated against in society because of what is written in their genes.

gene therapy

Gene therapy involves the introduction of a healthy gene into a cell to replace a diseased gene. Unlike conventional treatments, which attempt to deal with the consequences of a defect, gene therapy aims to correct the defect itself. In order to function, the therapeutic gene must reach the nucleus of the target cell, which contains the cell's genetic material. Various **vectors** have been used to transfer the material into the cell. Viruses were the first to be investigated. These have a natural ability to enter a cell and can be manipulated to make them harmless. Another method involves the use of liposomes, hollow membranous spheres which encapsulate the gene. Liposomes fuse with the cell membrane, releasing their gene into the cell. Whatever the vector, gene therapy is carried out in one of two ways.

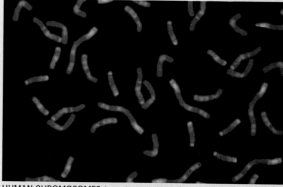

HUMAN CHROMOSOMES, hugely magnified. A chromosome is a threadlike structure of nucleic acids and protein, carrying a set of linked genes, and (in the case of humans and most other higher organisms) paired with an identical copy. © *Image Bank*

In *in vivo* gene therapy, the vector is injected into the body and has to find its way to the target tissue. The other way is *ex vivo*, in which a sample of tissue, tumour cells for example, is taken from the patient, treated with the vector, and then replaced. While hundreds of trials are currently in progress, the success of gene therapy remains largely unproven.

ownership and control

The decoding of the human genome is an immense achievement and its impact on health care will be far-reaching. The major challenge that lies ahead is in ensuring appropriate management of the ownership of the new knowledge and of its potential effects on the individual.

(continued from p. 457)

Miocene apes Genetic studies indicate that the last common ancestor between chimpanzees and humans lived 5 to 10 million years ago. There are only fragmentary remains of ape and hominid fossils from this period. Dispute continues over the hominid status of *Ramapithecus*, the jaws and teeth of which have been found in India and Kenya in late Miocene deposits, dating from between 14 and 10 million years ago. The lower jaw of a fossil ape found in the Otavi Mountains, Namibia, comes from deposits dated between 10 and 15 million years ago, and is similar to finds from East Africa and Turkey. It is thought to be close to the initial divergence of the great apes and humans.

Australopithecines Bones of the earliest human ancestor then known were found in Ethiopia in 1998 and are dated as 5 million years old. *A. afarensis*, found in Ethiopia and Kenya, date from 3.9 to 4.4 million years ago. The most complete australopithecine skeleton to date was found in South Africa in April 2000. It is about 1.8 million years old and from a female *Australopithecus robustus*. These hominids walked upright and they were either direct ancestors or an offshoot of the line that led to modern humans. They may have been the ancestors of *Homo habilis* (considered by some to be a species of *Australopithecus*), who appeared about 2 million years later, had slightly larger bodies and brains, and were probably the first to use stone tools. Also living in Africa at the same time was *A. africanus*, a gracile hominid thought to be a meat-eater, and *A. robustus*, a hominid with robust bones, large teeth, heavy jaws, and thought to be a vegetarian. They are not generally considered to be our ancestors.

A new species of *Australopithecus* was discovered in Ethiopia in 1999. Named *A. garhi*, the fossils date from 2.5 million years ago and also share anatomical features with *Homo* species.

Homo erectus Over 1.7 million years ago, *Homo erectus*, believed by some to be descended from *H. habilis*, appeared in Africa. *H. erectus* had prominent brow ridges, a flattened cranium, with the widest part of the skull low down, and jaws with a rounded tooth row, but the chin, characteristic of modern humans, is lacking. They also had much larger brains (900–1,200 cu cm), and were probably the first to use fire and the first to move out of Africa. Their remains are found as far afield as China, West Asia, Spain, and southern Britain. Modern human *H. sapiens sapiens* and the Neanderthals *H. sapiens neanderthalensis* are probably descended from *H. erectus*.

Australian palaeontologists announced the discovery of stone tools dated at about 800,000 to 900,000 years old and belonging to *H. erectus* on Flores, an island near Bali, in 1998. The discovery provides strong evidence that *H. erectus* were seafarers and had the language abilities and social structure to organize the movements of large groups to colonize new islands. In 2000 Japanese archaeologists discovered that *H. erectus* were probably building hut-like shelters around 500,000 years ago, the oldest known artificial structures.

Neanderthals Neanderthals were large-brained and heavily built, probably adapted to the cold conditions of the ice ages. They lived in Europe and the Middle East, and disappeared about 40,000 years ago, leaving *H. sapiens sapiens* as the only remaining species of the hominid group. Possible intermediate forms between Neanderthals and *H.sapiens sapiens* have been found at Mount Carmel in Israel and at Broken Hill in Zambia, but it seems that *H.sapiens sapiens* appeared in Europe quite rapidly and either wiped out the Neanderthals or interbred with them.

Modern humans There are currently two major views of human evolution: the 'out of Africa' model, according to which *H. sapiens* emerged from *H.erectus*, or a descendant species, in Africa and then spread throughout the world; and the multiregional model, according to which selection pressures led to the emergence of similar advanced types of *H. sapiens* from *H. erectus* in different parts of the world at around the same time. Analysis of DNA in recent human populations suggests that *H. sapiens* originated about 200,000 years ago in Africa from a single female ancestor, 'Eve'. The oldest known fossils of *H.sapiens* also come from Africa, dating from 150,000–100,000 years ago. Separation of human populations would have occurred later, with separation of Asian, European, and Australian populations taking place between 100,000 and 50,000 years ago.

In September 1998 researchers at the University of California, USA, announced the discovery of the first major biochemical and genetic difference between humans and great apes—the first gene for 'humanness'. Comparison of samples from 60 humans from diverse ethnic groups with samples from great apes showed that the outer surfaces of human cells have different form of one common sugar molecule termed sialic acid. Sialic acid plays a role in health and may be involved in differences in disease between humans and primates.

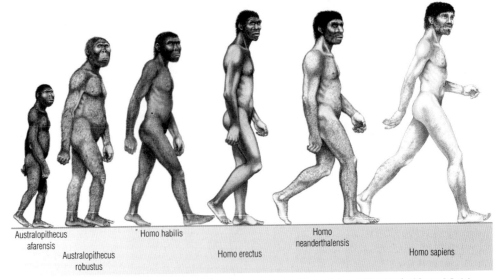

Australopithecus afarensis

Australopithecus robustus

Homo habilis

Homo erectus

Homo neanderthalensis

Homo sapiens

HUMAN SPECIES In evolutionary terms, the period from the appearance of the early hominid *Australopithecus* 3.5–4.4 million years ago, to the development of modern humans approximately 200,000 years ago, has been fairly short.

The human genome consists of between 60,000 to 100,000 genes. Of these only about 1.5% or about 900 to 1,500 differ between humans and the great apes.

Humayun (or Nasir ud-Din Muhammad) (1508–1556) Second Mogul emperor of North India (1530–40 and 1554–56). The son of ▷Babur, he inherited an unsettled empire and faced constant challenges from his three brothers. Following defeat by the Afghan Sher Shad Suri (died 1545), he fled into exile in Persia in 1540. Returning to India, he reoccupied Delhi and Agra in 1555 but died within a year. He was succeeded by his son ▷Akbar.

Humber estuary in northeast England formed by the Ouse and Trent rivers, which meet east of Goole and flow east for 60 km/38 mi to enter the North Sea below Spurn Head. It is an important commercial waterway, and the main ports are ▷Kingston upon Hull on the north side, and ▷Grimsby on the south side. The Humber Bridge (1981) joins the two banks.

Humberside former county of northeast England, created in 1974 out of north Lincolnshire and parts of the East and West Ridings of Yorkshire. It was abolished in 1996 when the unitary authorities of East Riding of Yorkshire, Kingston upon Hull, North East Lincolnshire, and North Lincolnshire were created.

Humbert anglicized form of ▷Umberto, two kings of Italy.

Humboldt, (Friedrich Wilhelm Heinrich) Alexander (1769–1859) Baron von Humboldt. German geophysicist, botanist, geologist, and writer who, with French botanist Aimé Bonpland (1773–1858), explored the regions of the Orinoco and Amazon rivers in South America 1800–04, and gathered 60,000 plant specimens. He was a founder of ecology.

Humboldt, (Karl) Wilhelm, Baron von Humboldt (1767–1835) German philologist whose stress on the identity of thought and language influenced Noam ▷Chomsky. He was the brother of Friedrich Humboldt.

Humboldt Current former name of the ▷Peru Current.

Hume, David (1711–1776) Scottish philosopher whose *Treatise of Human Nature* (1739–40) is a central text of British ▷empiricism (the theory that experience is the only source of knowledge). Examining meticulously our modes of thinking, he concluded that they are more habitual than rational. Consequently, he not only rejected the possibility of knowlege that goes beyond the bounds of experience (speculative metaphysics), but also arrived at generally sceptical positions about reason, causation, necessity, identity, and the self.

Hume's law in moral philosophy states that it is never possible to deduce evaluative conclusions from factual premises; this has come to be known as the 'is/ought problem'.

Hume, John (1937–) Northern Ireland politician, leader of the Social Democratic and Labour Party (SDLP) from 1979. Hume was a founder member of the Credit Union Party, which later became the SDLP. An MP since 1969, and a member of the European Parliament, he has been one of the chief architects of the peace process in Northern Ireland. He shared the Nobel Prize for Peace in 1998 with David ▷Trimble for their efforts to further the peace process.

humidity the quantity of water vapour in a given volume of the atmosphere (absolute humidity), or the ratio of the amount of water vapour in the atmosphere to the saturation value at the same temperature (relative humidity). At ▷dew point the relative humidity is 100% and the air is said to be saturated. Condensation (the conversion of vapour to liquid) may then occur. Relative humidity is measured by various types of ▷hygrometer.

hummingbird any of various small, brilliantly coloured birds found in the Americas. The name comes from the sound produced by the rapid vibration of their wings when hovering near flowers to feed.

Hummingbirds have long, needlelike bills and tongues to obtain nectar from flowers and capture insects. They are the only birds able to fly backwards. The **Cuban bee hummingbird** (*Mellisuga helenae*), the world's smallest bird, is 5.5 cm/2 in long and weighs less than 2.5 g/0.1 oz. There are over 300 species. (Family Trochilidae, order Apodiformes.)

The long cleft tongue of a hummingbird is in the form of a double tube, which can be extended a considerable distance beyond the bill and withdrawn again very rapidly; the sternum (breastbone) is greatly developed, forming a suitable base for the wing muscles; the plumage has a metallic lustre.

Related Web site: Hummingbirds! http://www.hummingbirds.net/

hummingbird moth type of ▷hawk moth.

humours, theory of theory prevalent in the West in classical and medieval times that the human body was composed of four kinds of fluid: phlegm, blood, choler or yellow bile, and melancholy or black bile. Physical and mental characteristics were explained by different proportions of humours in individuals.

Humphries, (John) Barry (1934–) Australian actor and author. He is best known for his satirical one-person shows and especially for the creation of the character of Mrs (later Dame) Edna Everage. His comic strip 'The Adventures of Barry Mackenzie', published in the British weekly *Private Eye* 1963–74, was the basis for two films, *The Adventures of Barry Mackenzie* (1972) and *Barry Mackenzie Holds His Own* (1974), in which Humphries also acted.

humus component of ▷soil consisting of decomposed or partly decomposed organic matter, dark in colour and usually richer towards the surface. It has a higher carbon content than the original material and a lower nitrogen content, and is an important source of minerals in soil fertility.

Hun member of any of a number of nomad Mongol peoples who were first recorded historically in the 2nd century BC, raiding across the Great Wall into China. They entered Europe about AD 372, settled in the area that is now Hungary, and imposed their supremacy on the Ostrogoths and other Germanic peoples. Under the leadership of Attila they attacked the Byzantine Empire, invaded Gaul, and threatened Rome. After Attila's death in 453 their power was broken by a revolt of their subject peoples. The **White Huns**, or Ephthalites, a kindred people, raided Persia and northern India in the 5th and 6th centuries.

> ### Cornelia Otis Skinner
> US writer and actor
>
> *If it is true that we have sprung from the ape, there are occasions when my own spring appears not to have been very far.*
>
> The Ape in Me, title essay

HUNDRED YEARS' WAR An illustration in a 15th-century manuscript shows the siege of Brest, France. The Duke of Lancaster, with cannon, ladders, and arrows, laid siege to Brest Castle in 1373. The scene is typical of the sporadic fighting of the Hundred Years' War. *The Art Archive/JFB*

Hundred Years' War: Key Events	
1340	The English are victorious at the naval Battle of Sluis.
1346	Battle of Crécy, a victory for the English.
1347	The English take Calais.
1356	Battle of Poitiers, where Edward the Black Prince defeats the French. King John of France is captured.
late 1350s– early 1360s	France undergoes civil wars, brigandage, and the popular uprising of the Jacquerie.
1360	Treaty of Brétigny. France accepts English possession of Calais and of a greatly enlarged Duchy of Gascony. John is ransomed for £500,000.
1369–1414	The tide turns in favour of the French, and when there is another truce in 1388, only Calais, Bordeaux, and Bayonne are in English hands. A state of half-war continues for many years.
1415	Henry V invades France and wins a victory at Agincourt, followed by conquest of Normandy.
1420	In the Treaty of Troyes, Charles VI of France is forced to disinherit his son, the Dauphin, in favour of Henry V, who is to marry Catherine, Charles's daughter. Most of northern France is in English hands.
1422–28	After the death of Henry V his brother, the Duke of Bedford, is generally successful.
1429	Joan of Arc raises the siege of Orléans, and the Dauphin is crowned Charles VII at Rheims.
1430–53	Even after Joan's capture and death the French continue their successful counter-offensive, and in 1453 only Calais is left in English hands.

HUNDRED YEARS' WAR An illustration in the chronicles of French poet and chronicler Jean Froissart (around 1400) featuring Edward the Black Prince, son of Edward III of England. *The Art Archive/British Library/British Library*

Hunan province of south central China, bounded to the north by Hubei, to the east by Jiangxi, to the south by Guangdong and Guangxi Zhuang Autonomous Region, and to the west by Guizhou and Sichuan; area 210,500 sq km/81,300 sq mi; population (1996) 64,280,000. The capital is Changsha; other main cities and towns are Hengyang, Shaoyang, Xiangtan, and Zhuzhou. The main industries are minerals, engineering, chemicals, and electrical goods. Agriculture is based on rice, tea, tobacco, and rapeseed.

hundred days in European history, the period 20 March– 28 June 1815, marking the French emperor Napoleon's escape from imprisonment on Elba to his departure from Paris after losing the battle of Waterloo on 18 June.

hundredweight imperial unit (abbreviation cwt) of mass, equal to 112 lb (50.8 kg). It is sometimes called the long hundredweight, to distinguish it from the short hundredweight or **cental**, equal to 100 lb (45.4 kg).

Hundred Years' War series of conflicts between England and France 1337–1453. Its causes were the French claim (as their fief) to Gascony in southwest France, held by the English kings, and medieval trade rivalries in Flanders.

Medieval England and France had a long history of war before 1337, and the Hundred Years' War has sometimes been interpreted as merely an intensification of these struggles. It was caused by fears of French intervention in Scotland, which the English were trying to subdue, and by the claim of England's Edward III (through his mother Isabella, daughter of Philip IV of France) to the crown of France. See table of key events in the war, above.

Hungarian (or **Magyar**) the majority population of Hungary or a people of Hungarian descent; also, their culture and language. Hungarian minorities are found in the Slovak Republic, Serbia and Montenegro and Romania, where the Székely of Transylvania regard themselves as ethnically distinct but speak Hungarian, as do the Csángó of Moldova.

Hungarian language member of the Finno-Ugric language group, spoken principally in Hungary but also in parts of the Slovak Republic, Romania, and Serbia and Montenegro. Hungarian is known as **Magyar** among its speakers. It is written in a form of the Roman alphabet in which *s* corresponds to English *sh*, and *sz* to *s*.

Hungarian literature written literature has been traced back to 1200 but it was a rich surviving oral literature that influenced Bálint Balassi (1554–1594) and the development of a secular poetic tradition in the 16th century. Hapsburg Hungary welcomed the baroque, reflected in major poets such as Miklós Zrínyi (1620–1664). The Enlightenment stimulated writers such as the lyric poet Mihály Csokonai Vitéz (1773–1805) but the national

epics of János Arany and the revolutionary fervour of his friend Sándor Petöfi reached a much wider public. The Hungarian novel, influenced by European realism, was developed by the arch-romantic Mór Jókai (1825–1904) and his biographer Kálmán Mikszáth (1847–1910). In the early 20th century the leftist literary magazine *Nyugat* involved distinguished writers including the Symbolist poet Endre Ady (1877–1919). Socialist writing, such as the work of Tibor Déry (1894–1977), flourished between the wars. Although the suppression of the 1956 uprising discouraged writers who had benefited from a post-Stalinist thaw, influentially courageous and troubled poets such as Ferenc Juhász (1928–) and László Nagy (1925–1978) have continued to confront the intractable problems of life, death, and Hungary.

Hungary see country box.

Hun Sen (1950–) Cambodian political leader, prime minister 1985–93, deputy prime minister from 1993, and single effective leader from July 1997. His leadership was characterized by the promotion of economic liberalization and a thawing in relations with exiled non-Khmer opposition forces as a prelude to a compromise political settlement. After the defeat of his Cambodian People's Party (CCP) in the 1993 elections, Hun Sen agreed to participate in a power-sharing arrangement as second premier. In July 1997 he launched a successful coup to oust the first deputy prime minister, Prince Norodom Ranariddh, and secure full effective control over Cambodia. In February 1998 he accepted a Japanese-brokered peace plan to allow for Ranariddh's return, after he was found guilty in a March 1998 show trial and then pardoned by his father, King Norodom Sihanouk. Following the November 1998 elections in which Hun Sen's CCP won 41% of the vote, Hun Sen formed a coalition between the two main rival political parties, FUNCINPEC and the CCP.

Hunt, (William) Holman (1827–1910) English painter, one of the founders of the ▷Pre-Raphaelite Brotherhood in 1848. His paintings, characterized both by a meticulous attention to detail and a clear moral and religious symbolism, include *The Awakening Conscience* (1853; Tate Gallery, London) and *The Light of the World* (1854; Keble College, Oxford).

Hunt, (James Henry) Leigh (1784–1859) English essayist and poet. He influenced and encouraged the Romantics. His verse, though easy and agreeable, is little appreciated today, and he is best remembered as an essayist. He recycled parts of his *Lord Byron and some of his Friends* (1828), in which he criticized Byron's character, as *Autobiography* (1850). The character of Harold Skimpole in Charles Dickens's *Bleak House* was allegedly based on him.

Hunter, John (1728–1793) Scottish surgeon, pathologist, and comparative anatomist who insisted on rigorous scientific method. He was the first to understand the nature of digestion.

St Joan of Arc
French military leader

King of England, and you Duke of Bedford . . . give up to the Maid sent here by the King of Heaven the key of all the noble cities of France you have taken and ravaged . . . . I have come here . . . to drive you man for man from France.

Letter to the English forces besieging Orleans, March 1429

hunting dog (or **painted dog**) wild dog (weight 23–35 kg/ 51–77 lb) that once roamed over virtually the whole of sub-Saharan Africa. A pack might have a range of almost 4,000 km/2,500 mi, hunting zebra, antelope, and other game. Individuals can run at 50 kph/30 mph for up to 5 km/3 mi, with short bursts of even higher speeds. The number of hunting dogs that survive has been reduced to a fraction of the original population. According to a 1997 World Conservation Union report, there were fewer than 3,000 hunting dogs remaining in the wild, with many existing populations too small to be viable. (Species *Lycaon pictus*, family Canidae.)

The maximum pack size found today is usually eight to ten, whereas in the past several hundred might have hunted together. Habitat destruction and the decline of large game herds have played a part in its decline, but the hunting dog has also suffered badly from the effects of distemper, a disease which was introduced into East Africa early in the 20th century.

HUNTING DOG The hunting dog *Lycaon pictus* is gradually becoming extinct over large areas of its former range in Africa. It usually lives in close, hierarchical packs and, by taking turns in leading the chase, is able to run down swift prey such as antelopes. *Premaphotos Wildlife*

Hungary

Hungary country in central Europe, bounded north by the Slovak Republic, northeast by Ukraine, east by Romania, south by Serbia and Montenegro, and Croatia, and west by Austria and Slovenia.

NATIONAL NAME *Magyar Köztársaság/Republic of Hungary*
AREA 93,032 sq km/35,919 sq mi
CAPITAL Budapest
MAJOR TOWNS/CITIES Miskolc, Debrecen, Szeged, Pécs, Györ, Nyíregyháza, Székesfehérvár, Kecskemét
PHYSICAL FEATURES Great Hungarian Plain covers eastern half of country; Bakony Forest, Lake Balaton, and Transdanubian Highlands in the west; rivers Danube, Tisza, and Raba; more than 500 thermal springs

Government

HEAD OF STATE Ferenc Mádl from 2000
HEAD OF GOVERNMENT Péter Medgyessy from 2002
POLITICAL SYSTEM liberal democracy
POLITICAL EXECUTIVE parliamentary
ADMINISTRATIVE DIVISIONS 19 counties and the capital city (with 22 districts)
ARMED FORCES 33,400 (2002 est)
CONSCRIPTION 16 months (men aged 18–23)
DEATH PENALTY abolished in 1990
DEFENCE SPEND (% GDP) 1.8 (2002 est)
EDUCATION SPEND (% GDP) 5 (2001 est)
HEALTH SPEND (% GDP) 6.8 (2000 est)

Economy and resources

CURRENCY forint
GPD (US$) 65.8 billion (2002 est)
REAL GDP GROWTH (% change on previous year) 3.8 (2001)
GNI (US$) 53.7 billion (2002 est)
GNI PER CAPITA (PPP) (US$) 12,810 (2002 est)
CONSUMER PRICE INFLATION 5.3% (2003 est)

UNEMPLOYMENT 5.7% (2001)
FOREIGN DEBT (US$) 19.5 billion (2001 est)
MAJOR TRADING PARTNERS Germany, Italy, Austria, USA, Russia, France, UK, Japan, the Netherlands
RESOURCES lignite, brown coal, natural gas, petroleum, bauxite, hard coal
INDUSTRIES food and beverages, tobacco, steel and iron production,, chemicals, petroleum and plastics, engineering, transport equipment, pharmaceuticals, textiles, cement
EXPORTS raw materials, semi-finished products, industrial consumer goods, food and agricultural products, transport equipment. Principal market: Germany 35.6% (2001)
IMPORTS mineral fuels, raw materials, semi-finished products, transport equipment, food products, consumer goods. Principal source: Germany 24.9% (2001)
ARABLE LAND 49.8% (2000 est)
AGRICULTURAL PRODUCTS wheat, maize, sugar beet, barley, potatoes, sunflowers, grapes; livestock and dairy products

Population and society

POPULATION 9,877,000 (2003 est)
POPULATION GROWTH RATE –0.4% (2000–15)
POPULATION DENSITY (per sq km) 106 (2003 est)
URBAN POPULATION (% of total) 65 (2003 est)
AGE DISTRIBUTION (% of total population) 0–14 16%, 15–59 64%, 60+ 20% (2002 est)
ETHNIC GROUPS 90% indigenous, or Magyar; there is a large Romany community

of around 600,000; other ethnic minorities include Germans, Croats, Romanians, Slovaks, Serbs, and Slovenes
LANGUAGE Hungarian (official)
RELIGION Roman Catholic 65%, Calvinist 20%, other Christian denominations, Jewish, atheist
EDUCATION (compulsory years) 10
LITERACY RATE 99% (men); 99% (women) (2003 est)
LABOUR FORCE 6.7% agriculture, 34.5% industry, 58.8% services (2000)
LIFE EXPECTANCY 68 (men); 76 (women) (2000–05)
CHILD MORTALITY RATE (under 5, per 1,000 live births) 9 (2001)
PHYSICIANS (per 1,000 people) 3.6 (1998 est)
HOSPITAL BEDS (per 1,000 people) 8.2 (1999 est)
TV SETS (per 1,000 people) 448 (1999)
RADIOS (per 1,000 people) 690 (1999 est)
INTERNET USERS (per 10,000 people) 1,576.0 (2002 est)
PERSONAL COMPUTER USERS (per 100 people) 10.8 (2002 est)

See also ▷Austro-Hungarian Empire; ▷Warsaw Pact.

HUNGARY The Lanchid Bridge in Budapest, Hungary, illuminated at dusk, casts reflections in the River Danube. The two halves of the city, Buda on the right bank of the Danube and Pest on the left, are also joined by many other bridges. *Image Bank*

Chronology

1st century AD: Region formed part of Roman Empire.

4th century: Germanic tribes overran central Europe.

c. 445: Attila the Hun established a short-lived empire, including Hungarian nomads living far to the east.

c. 680: Hungarians settled between the Don and Dniepr rivers under Khazar rule.

9th century: Hungarians invaded central Europe; ten tribes united under árpád, chief of the Magyar tribe, who conquered the area corresponding to modern Hungary in 896.

10th century: Hungarians colonized Transylvania and raided their neighbours for plunder and slaves.

955: Battle of Lech: Germans led by Otto the Great defeated the Hungarians.

1001: St Stephen founded the Hungarian kingdom to replace tribal organization and converted the Hungarians to Christianity.

12th century: Hungary became a major power when King Béla III won temporary supremacy over the Balkans.

1308–86: Angevin dynasty ruled after the Arpádian line died out.

1456: Battle of Belgrade: János Hunyadi defeated Ottoman Turks and saved Hungary from invasion.

1458–90: Under Mátyás I Corvinus, Hungary enjoyed military success and cultural renaissance.

1526: Battle of Mohács: Turks under Suleiman the Magnificent decisively defeated the Hungarians.

16th century: Partition of Hungary between Turkey, Austria, and the semi-autonomous Transylvania.

1699: Treaty of Karlowitz: Austrians expelled the Turks from Hungary, which was reunified under Habsburg rule.

1707: Prince Ferenc Rákóczi II led an uprising against the Austrians.

1780–90: Joseph II's attempts to impose uniform administration throughout the Austrian Empire provoked nationalist reaction among the Hungarian nobility.

early 19th century: 'National Revival' movement led by Count Stephen Széchenyi and Lajos Kossuth.

1848: Hungarian Revolution: nationalists proclaimed self-government; Croat minority resisted Hungarian rule.

1849: Austrians crushed revolution with Russian support.

1867: Austria conceded equality to Hungary within the dual monarchy of Austria-Hungary.

1918: Austria-Hungary collapsed in military defeat; Count Mihály Károlyi proclaimed Hungarian Republic.

1920: Treaty of Trianon: Hungary lost 72% of its territory to Czechoslovakia, Romania, and Yugoslavia; Admiral Miklós Horthy restored the Kingdom of Hungary with himself as regent.

1938–41: Diplomatic collaboration with Germany allowed Hungary to regain territories lost in 1920; Hungary declared war on USSR in alliance with Germany in 1941.

1944: Germany occupied Hungary and installed a Nazi regime.

1945: USSR 'liberated' Hungary.

1947: Peace treaty restored 1920 frontiers.

1949: Hungary became a Soviet-style dictatorship; communist leader Mátyás Rákosi pursued Stalinist policies.

1956: Hungarian uprising: anti-Soviet demonstrations led the USSR to invade, crush dissent, and install János Kádár as communist leader.

1961: Kádár began to introduce limited reforms.

1988: The Hungarian Democratic Forum was formed by opposition groups.

1989: The communist dictatorship was dismantled, and a transitional constitution restored multi-party democracy. The opening of the border with Austria destroyed the 'Iron Curtain'.

1990: Elections won by a centre–right coalition.

1991: The withdrawal of Soviet forces was completed.

1996: A friendship treaty with the Slovak Republic was signed, as was a cooperation treaty with Romania.

1997: Hungary was invited to join NATO and to begin negotiations for membership of the European Union. A referendum showed clear support in favour of joining NATO.

1998: Viktor Orban, leader of right-of-centre Fidesz, became prime minister after the general election.

1999: Hungary became a full member of NATO.

2000: Ferenc Mádl was elected president.

2004: Hungary was set to join the EU on 1 May.

Huntingdonshire former English county, merged in 1974 into a much-enlarged Cambridgeshire.

Huntington's chorea rare hereditary disease of the nervous system that mostly begins in middle age. It is characterized by involuntary movements (▷chorea), emotional disturbances, and rapid mental degeneration progressing to ▷dementia. There is no known cure but the genetic mutation giving rise to the disease was located in 1993, making it easier to test individuals for the disease and increasing the chances of developing a cure.

Hupei alternative transcription of ▷Hebei, a province of China.

Hurd, Douglas (Richard) (1930–) British Conservative politician, home secretary 1985–89 and foreign secretary 1989–95. In November 1990 he was an unsuccessful candidate in the Tory leadership contest following Margaret Thatcher's unexpected resignation.

Huron (or **Wyandot**; French *hure* 'rough hair of the head') member of an ▷American Indian people living in Ontario near lakes Huron, Erie, and Ontario in the 16th and 17th centuries. The Hurons formed a trading alliance with the French, until they were almost wiped out by the Iroquois 1648–50 over control of the fur trade. Descendants of surviving Hurons now live in Québec and Oklahoma. Their language belongs to the Iroquoian family.

hurricane (or **tropical cyclone** or **typhoon**) a severe ▷depression (region of very low atmospheric pressure) in tropical regions, called **typhoon** in the North Pacific. It is a revolving storm originating at latitudes between 5° and 20° N or S of the Equator, when the surface temperature of the ocean is above 27°C/80°F. A central calm area, called the eye, is surrounded by inwardly spiralling winds (anticlockwise in the northern hemisphere and clockwise in the southern hemisphere) of up to 320 kph/200 mph. A hurricane is accompanied by lightning and torrential rain, and can cause extensive damage. In meteorology, a hurricane is a wind of force 12 or more on the ▷Beaufort scale.

During 1995 the Atlantic Ocean region suffered 19 tropical storms, 11 of them hurricanes. This was the third-worst season since 1871, causing 137 deaths. The most intense hurricane recorded in the Caribbean/Atlantic sector was Hurricane Gilbert in 1988, with sustained winds of 280 kph/175 mph and gusts of over 320 kph/200 mph.

In October 1987 and January 1990, winds of near-hurricane strength were experienced in southern England. Although not technically hurricanes, they were the strongest winds there for three centuries.

Related Web sites: Disasters: Panoramic Photographs, 1851–1991 http://lcweb2.loc.gov/cgi-bin/query/r?ammem/pan: and (+fires+earthquake+storms+railroad+accidents+floods+ cyclones+hurricane+))
Hurricane & Tropical Storm Tracking http://hurricane.terrapin.com/

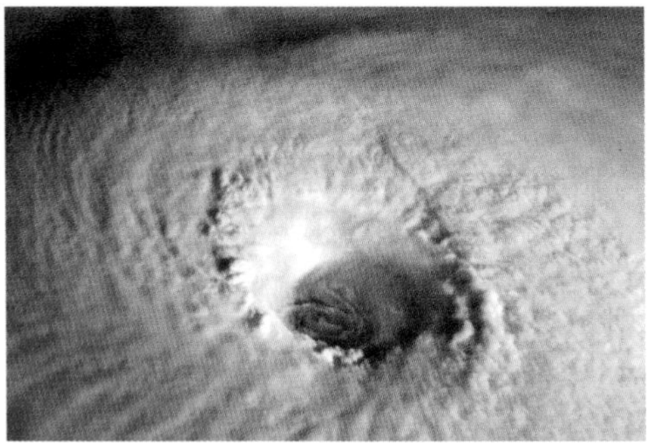

HURRICANE The eye of typhoon Odessa, seen from the NASA space shuttle. Odessa had one of the strongest circular storm patterns ever seen by shuttle crews, and a very tightly formed eye. The tighter the eye in a circular storm, the stronger the winds underneath. *Image Bank*

Husák, Gustáv (1913–1991) Czechoslovak politician, leader of the Communist Party of Czechoslovakia (CCP) 1969–87 and president 1975–89. After the 1968 Prague Spring of liberalization, his task was to restore control, purge the CCP, and oversee the implementation of a new, federalist constitution. He was deposed in the popular uprising of November–December 1989 and expelled from the CCP in February 1990.

husky any of several breeds of sledge dog used in Arctic regions, growing up to about 60 cm/23 in high, and weighing up to about 27 kg/60 lbs, with pricked ears, thick fur, and a bushy tail. The Siberian husky is the best known.

Huss, John (*c.* 1373–1415) Czech **Jan Hus**. Bohemian Christian church reformer, rector of Prague University from 1402, who was excommunicated for attacks on ecclesiastical abuses. He was summoned before the Council of Constance in 1414, defended the English reformer John Wyclif, rejected the pope's authority, and was burned at the stake. His followers were called Hussites.

Hussein, Saddam (1937–) Iraqi politician, in power from 1968, president 1979–2003. He presided over the Iran–Iraq war 1980–88, and harshly repressed Kurdish rebels seeking independence in northern Iraq. He annexed Kuwait in 1990 but was driven out by a US-dominated coalition army in February 1991. Defeat in the ▷Gulf War led to unrest, and both the Kurds in the north and Shiites in the south rebelled. His savage repression of both revolts led to charges of genocide. He was removed from power in the ▷Iraq War (2003) by a US- and UK-led international coalition concerned at his apparent contravention of United Nations resolutions passed after the Gulf War that required Iraqi disarmament. After several months in hiding he was arrested in December 2003 by US troops.

Saddam joined the Arab Ba'ath Socialist Party as a young man and soon became involved in revolutionary activities. In 1959 he was sentenced to death and took refuge in Egypt, but a coup in 1963 made his return possible, although in the following year he was imprisoned for plotting to overthrow the regime he had helped to install. After his release he took a leading part in the 1968 revolution, removing the civilian government and establishing a Revolutionary Command Council (RCC). He progressively eliminated real or imagined opposition to become president in 1979.

The 1990 Kuwait annexation followed a long-running border dispute and was prompted by the need for more oil resources after the expensive war against Iran. Saddam, who had received US economic aid during the war with Iran and had used poison gas against civilian populations in his war with Kurdish rebels without any falling-off in trade with the West, suddenly found himself almost universally condemned.

> **Aldous Huxley**
> *Consistency is contrary to nature, contrary to life. The only completely consistent people are the dead.*
> *Do What You Will*, 'Wordsworth in the Tropics'

When the Kurds rebelled again after the end of the war, he sent the remainder of his army to crush them, bringing international charges of genocide against him and causing hundreds of thousands of Kurds to flee their homes in northern Iraq. His continued indiscriminate bombardment of Shiites in southern Iraq led the UN to impose a 'no-fly zone' in the area August 1992. In September 1996, the US retaliated against Saddam's encroachment into UN protected territories in northern Iraq, carrying out missile attacks on Iraqi military bases in the area. In March 1998, a major confrontation with the UN over the inspection of weapons of mass destruction held by Iraq was narrowly averted.

> **Thomas Henry Huxley**
> *All truth, in the long run, is only common sense clarified.*
> Quoted in J Huxley *Essays in Popular Science* (1926)

Hussein ibn Ali (1856–1931) Born Sharif Husayan Hussein ibn Ali. King of the Hejaz 1916–24 and founder of the modern Hashemite dynasty. Emir (grand sherif) of the Muslim holy city of Mecca 1908–16, at the start of World War I he sided with the Turks and Germany. However, T E ▷Lawrence persuaded him, in 1916, to join an Arab Revolt against Turkish rule, when he was proclaimed the independent King of the Hejaz region of Arabia. In 1919 he proclaimed himself king of all the Arab countries. This led to conflict with ▷Ibn Saud of the neighbouring emirate of Nejd. Hussein accepted the caliphate in 1924, but was forced to abdicate in 1924 by Ibn Saud. He took refuge in Cyprus and died in Amman, Jordan.

Hussein ibn Talal (1935–1999) King of Jordan 1952–99. By 1967 he had lost all his kingdom west of the River Jordan in the Arab-Israeli Wars, and in 1970 suppressed the Palestine Liberation Organization acting as a guerrilla force against his rule on the remaining East Bank territories. Subsequently, he became a moderating force in Middle Eastern politics, and in 1994 signed a peace agreement with Israel, ending a 46-year-old state of war between the two countries.

A great-grandson of ▷Hussein ibn Ali, he became king following the mental incapacitation of his father, Talal. After Iraq's annexation of Kuwait in 1990 he attempted to mediate between the opposing sides, at the risk of damaging his relations with both sides. In 1993 he publicly distanced himself from Iraqi leader Saddam ▷Hussein.

King Hussein died on 7 February 1999 at the age of 63. His funeral was attended by hundreds of foreign dignitaries. He was succeeded by his son, ▷Abdullah ibn Hussein.

Husserl, Edmund Gustav Albrecht (1859–1938) German philosopher, regarded as the founder of ▷phenomenology, the study of mental states as consciously experienced. His early phenomenology resembles linguistic philosophy because he examined the meaning and our understanding of words.

Hussite follower of John ▷Huss. Opposed to both German and papal influence in Bohemia, the Hussites waged successful war against the Holy Roman Empire from 1419, but Roman Catholicism was finally re-established in 1620.

Huston, John (Marcellus) (1906–1987) US film director, screenwriter, and actor. An impulsive and individualistic film-maker, he often dealt with the themes of greed, treachery in human relationships, and the loner. His works as a director include *The Maltese Falcon* (1941), *The Treasure of the Sierra Madre* (1948), *The Asphalt Jungle* (1950), *The African Queen* (1951), and *The Dead* (1987).

Hutton, James (1726–1797) Scottish geologist, known as the 'founder of geology', who formulated the concept of ▷uniformitarianism. In 1785 he developed a theory of the igneous origin of many rocks.

Hutu member of the majority ethnic group of Burundi and Rwanda, numbering around 9.5 million. The Hutu tend to live as peasant farmers. They have been dominated by the ▷Tutsi minority since the 14th century and there is a long history of violent conflict between the two groups. The Hutu language belongs to the Bantu branch of the Niger-Congo family.

Huxley, Aldous (Leonard) (1894–1963) English writer of novels, essays, and verse. From the disillusionment and satirical eloquence of *Crome Yellow* (1921), *Antic Hay* (1923), and *Point Counter Point* (1928), Huxley developed towards the Utopianism exemplified by *Island* (1962). His most popular work, the science fiction novel *Brave New World* (1932) shows human beings mass-produced in laboratories and rendered incapable of freedom by indoctrination and drugs.

Huxley's later devotion to mysticism led to his experiments with the hallucinogenic drug mescalin, recorded in *The Doors of Perception* (1954). His other works include the philosophical novel *Eyeless in Gaza* (1936), *After Many a Summer* (1939; Tait Black Memorial Prize), the biography of Père Joseph *Grey Eminence* (1941), and *The Devils of Loudun* (1952). He was the grandson of the scientist and humanist Thomas Henry Huxley and brother of the biologist and writer of popular science books Julian Huxley.

Huxley, T(homas) H(enry) (1825–1895) English scientist and humanist. Following the publication of Charles Darwin's *On the Origin of Species* (1859), he became known as 'Darwin's bulldog', and for many years was a prominent champion of evolution. In 1869 he coined the word 'agnostic' to express his own religious attitude, and is considered the founder of scientific humanism.

From 1846 to 1850 Huxley was the assistant ship's surgeon on HMS *Rattlesnake* on its voyage around the South Seas. The observations he made on the voyage, especially of invertebrates, were published and made his name in the UK.

Hu Yaobang (1915–1989) Chinese politician, Communist Party (CCP) chair 1981–87. A protégé of the communist leader Deng Xiaoping, Hu presided over a radical overhaul of the party structure and personnel 1982–86. His death ignited the pro-democracy movement, which was eventually crushed in ▷Tiananmen Square in June 1989.

Huygens (or Huyghens)**, Christiaan** (1629–1695) Dutch mathematical physicist and astronomer. He proposed the wave theory of light, developed the pendulum clock in 1657, discovered polarization, and observed Saturn's rings. He made important advances in pure mathematics, applied mathematics, and mechanics, which he virtually founded. His work in astronomy was an impressive defence of the Copernican view of the Solar System.

Mechanics Huygens used the idea of relative frames of reference, considering the motion of one body relative to the other. He anticipated the law of conservation of momentum stating that in a system of bodies under impact the centre of gravity is conserved. In *De Motu Corporum* 1656, he was also able to show that the quantity

$$\tfrac{1}{2}mv^2$$

is conserved in an elastic collision.

Huygens also studied centrifugal force and showed, in 1659, its similarity to gravitational force, although he lacked the Newtonian concept of acceleration. He considered projectiles and gravity, developing the mathematically primitive ideas of ▷Galileo.

The pendulum clock In 1657, Huygens developed a clock regulated by a pendulum, an idea that he published and patented. By 1658, major towns in Holland had pendulum tower clocks. Huygens worked at the theory first of the simple pendulum and then of harmonically oscillating systems throughout the rest of his life, publishing the *Horologium Oscillatorium* in 1673. He derived the relationship between the period of a simple pendulum and its length.

The theory of light The *Traité de la Lumière/Treatise on Light* (1690) contained Huygens' famous wave or pulse theory of light. Two years earlier, Huygens had been able to use his principle of secondary wave fronts to explain ▷reflection and ▷refraction, showing that refraction is related to differing velocities of light in media. He theorized that light is transmitted as a pulse moving through a medium, or ether, by setting up a whole train of vibrations in the ether in a serial displacement.

Astronomy and the telescope Huygens' comprehensive study of geometric optics led to the invention of a telescope eyepiece that reduced chromatic aberration. It consisted of two thin plano-convex lenses, rather than one fat lens, with the field lens having a focal length three times greater than that of the eyepiece lens. Its main disadvantage was that cross-wires could not be fitted to measure the size of an image. Huygens then developed a micrometer to measure the angular diameter of celestial objects.

With a home-made telescope, he discovered Titan, one of Saturn's moons, in 1655. Later that year he observed that Titan's period of revolution was about 16 days and that it moved in the same plane as the so-called 'arms' of Saturn. The theory behind Huygens' hypothesis followed later in *Systema Saturnium* (1659), which included observations on the planets, their satellites, the ▷Orion nebula and the determination of the period of Mars, and provided further evidence for the Copernican view of the Solar System.

Related Web site: Huygens, Christiaan http://www-history.mcs.st-and.ac.uk/history/Mathematicians/Huygens.html

Hwang Ho alternative transcription of ▷Huang He, a river in China.

hyacinth any of a group of bulb-producing plants belonging to the lily family, native to the eastern Mediterranean and Africa. The cultivated hyacinth (*H. orientalis*) has large, scented, cylindrical heads of pink, white, or blue flowers. (Genus *Hyacinthus*, family Liliaceae.)

The ▷water hyacinth, a floating plant from South America, is unrelated.

hybrid offspring from a cross between individuals of two different species, or two inbred lines within a species. In most cases, hybrids between species are infertile and unable to reproduce sexually. In plants, however, doubling of the chromosomes (see ▷polyploid) can restore the fertility of such hybrids.

Hybrids between different genera were believed to be extremely rare (an example is the *Cupressocyparis leylandii* cypress which, like some hybrids, shows exceptional vigour, or heterosis) but research in the late 1990s shows that hybridization is much more common than traditionally represented. One British evolutionary biologist estimated in 1999 that approximately 10% of animal species and 20% of plant species produced fertile offspring through interspecies mating. Blue whales, for example, hybridize with fin whales and different species of birds of paradise also hybridize. In the wild, a 'hybrid zone' may occur where the ranges of two related species meet.

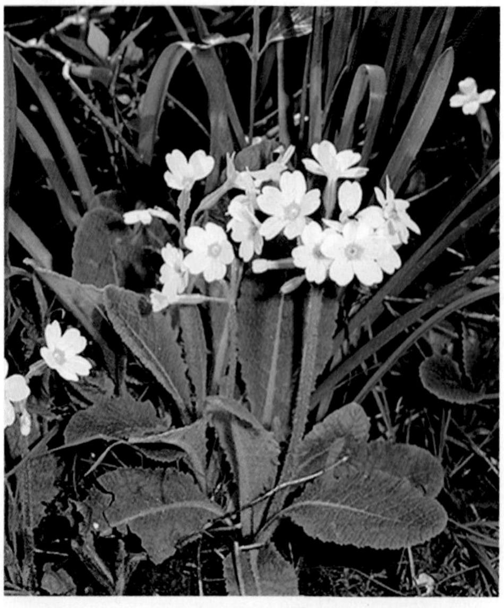

HYBRID The false oxlip, a hybrid produced by crossing the true oxlip *Primula elatior* with the primrose *Primula vulgaris*. *K G Preston-Mafham/Premaphotos Wildlife*

Hyderabad capital city of the southern central Indian state of ▷Andhra Pradesh, on the River Musi; population (1991) 4,280,000. Products include carpets, silks, and metal inlay work. More recently industries such as textiles, pharmaceuticals, electrical machinery, and chemicals have become important. It was formerly the capital of the state of Hyderabad. Buildings include the Jama Masjid mosque and Golconda fort. It is an important educational and research centre, with Osmania University founded by the Nizam in 1939.

Hyderabad city in Sind province, southeast Pakistan, lying 10 km/6 mi east of the ▷Indus River, 150 km/95 mi northeast of Karachi; population (1998 est) 1,151,300. It produces gold, pottery, glass, embroidered leather saddles for camels, and furniture. Industries include textiles, cement, glass and soap, and there is a thermal power station nearby.

Hyder Ali (or **Haidar Ali**) (*c.* 1722–1782) Indian general, sultan of Mysore in southwestern India from 1759. In command of the army in Mysore from 1749, he became the ruler of the state in 1761, and rivalled British power in the area until his triple defeat by Sir Eyre ▷Coote in 1781 during the Anglo-French wars. He was the father of Tipu Sultan.

Hydra in astronomy, the largest constellation, winding across more than a quarter of the sky between ▷Cancer and ▷Libra in the southern hemisphere. Hydra is named after the multi-headed sea serpent slain by Hercules. Despite its size, it is not prominent; its brightest star is second-magnitude Alphard.

Hydra in Greek mythology, a huge monster with nine heads. If one were cut off, two would grow in its place. One of the 12 labours of ▷Heracles was to kill it.

hydra in zoology, any of a group of freshwater polyps, belonging among the ▷coelenterates. The body is a double-layered tube (with six to ten hollow tentacles around the mouth), 1.25 cm/0.5 in long when extended, but capable of contracting to a small knob. Usually fixed to waterweed, hydras feed on minute animals that are caught and paralysed by stinging cells on the tentacles. (Genus *Hydra*, family Hydridae, phylum Coelenterata, subphylum Cnidaria.)

hydrangea any of a group of flowering shrubs belonging to the saxifrage family, native to Japan. Cultivated varieties of *H. macrophylla* normally produce round heads of pink flowers, but these may be blue if there are certain chemicals in the soil, such as alum or iron. The name comes from the Greek for 'water vessel', after the cuplike seed capsules. (Genus *Hydrangea*, family Hydrangeaceae.)

hydration in earth science, a form of ▷chemical weathering caused by the expansion of certain minerals as they absorb water. The expansion weakens the parent rock and may cause it to break up.

hydraulic action in earth science, the erosive force exerted by water (as distinct from the forces exerted by rocky particles carried by water). It can wear away the banks of a river, particularly at the outer curve of a meander (bend in the river), where the current flows most strongly.

hydraulic radius measure of a river's channel efficiency (its ability to discharge water), used by water engineers to assess the likelihood of flooding. The hydraulic radius of a channel is defined as the ratio of its cross-sectional area to its wetted perimeter (the part of the cross-section that is in contact with the water).

hydraulics field of study concerned with utilizing the properties of water and other liquids, in particular the way they flow and transmit pressure, and with the application of these properties in engineering. It applies the principles of ▷hydrostatics and hydrodynamics. The oldest type of hydraulic machine is the **hydraulic press**, invented by Joseph ▷Bramah in England in 1795. The hydraulic principle of pressurized liquid increasing a force is commonly used on vehicle braking systems, the forging press, and the hydraulic systems of aircraft and excavators.

hydrocarbon any of a class of chemical compounds containing only hydrogen and carbon (for example, the alkanes and alkenes). Hydrocarbons are obtained industrially principally from petroleum and coal tar.

Unsaturated hydrocarbons contain at least one double or triple carbon–carbon ▷bond, whereas saturated hydrocarbons contain only single bonds.

hydrocephalus potentially serious increase in the volume of cerebrospinal fluid (CSF) within the ventricles of the brain. In infants, since their skull plates have not fused, it causes enlargement of the head, and there is a risk of brain damage from CSF pressure on the developing brain.

hydrochloric acid (HCl) highly corrosive solution of hydrogen chloride (a colourless, acidic gas) in water. The concentrated acid is about 35% hydrogen chloride and is corrosive. The acid is a typical

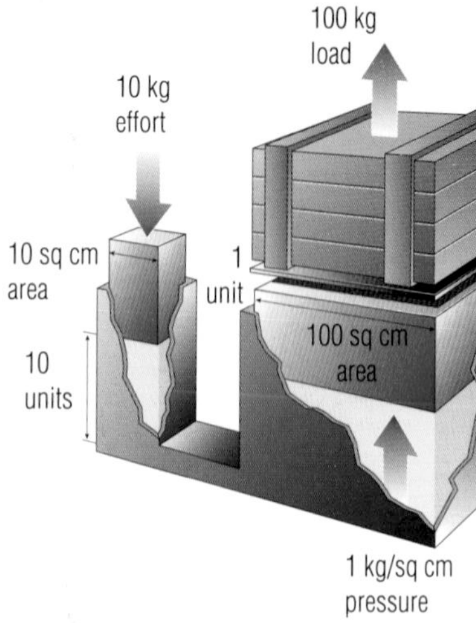

HYDRAULICS The hydraulic jack transmits the pressure on a small piston to a larger one. A larger total force is developed by the larger piston but it moves a smaller distance than the small piston.

strong, monobasic acid forming only one series of salts, the chlorides. It has many industrial uses, including recovery of zinc from galvanized scrap iron and the production of chlorine. It is also produced in the stomachs of animals for the purposes of digestion.

hydrocyanic acid (or **prussic acid**) solution of hydrogen cyanide gas (HCN) in water. It is a colourless, highly poisonous, volatile liquid, smelling of bitter almonds.

hydrodynamics branch of physics dealing with fluids (liquids and gases) in motion.

hydroelectric power electricity generated by moving water. In a typical scheme, water stored in a reservoir, often created by damming a river, is piped into water ▷turbines, coupled to electricity generators. In ▷pumped storage plants, water flowing through the turbines is recycled. A tidal power station exploits the rise and fall of the tides. About one-fifth of the world's electricity comes from hydroelectric power.

hydrofoil wing that develops lift in the water in much the same way that an aeroplane wing develops lift in the air. A hydrofoil boat is one whose hull rises out of the water owing to the lift, and the boat skims along on the hydrofoils. The first hydrofoil was fitted to a boat in 1906. The first commercial hydrofoil went into operation in 1956. One of the most advanced hydrofoil boats is the Boeing jetfoil. Hydrofoils are now widely used for fast island ferries in calm seas.

hydrogen (Greek *hydro* + *gen* 'water generator') colourless, odourless, gaseous, nonmetallic element, symbol H, atomic number 1, relative atomic mass 1.00797. It is the lightest of all the elements and occurs on Earth, chiefly in combination with oxygen, as water. Hydrogen is the most abundant element in the universe, where it accounts for 93% of the total number of atoms and 76% of the total mass. It is a component of most stars, including the Sun, whose heat and light are produced through the nuclear-fusion process that converts hydrogen into helium. When subjected to a pressure 500,000 times greater than that of the Earth's atmosphere, hydrogen becomes a solid with metallic properties, as in one of the inner zones of Jupiter.

Hydrogen's common and industrial uses include the hardening of oils and fats by hydrogenation, the creation of high-temperature flames for welding, and as rocket fuel. It has been proposed as a fuel for road vehicles.

Its isotopes ▷deuterium and ▷tritium (half-life 12.5 years) are used in nuclear weapons, and deuterons (deuterium nuclei) are used in synthesizing elements. The element's name refers to the generation of water by the combustion of hydrogen, and was coined in 1787 by French chemist Louis Guyton de Morveau (1737–1816).

hydrogenation addition of hydrogen to an unsaturated organic molecule (one that contains double bonds or triple bonds). It is widely used in the manufacture of margarine and low-fat spreads by the addition of hydrogen to vegetable oils.

hydrogen bomb bomb that works on the principle of nuclear ▷fusion. Large-scale explosion results from the thermonuclear release of energy when hydrogen nuclei are fused to form helium nuclei. The first hydrogen bomb was exploded at Enewetak Atoll in the Pacific Ocean by the USA in 1952.

hydrogen carbonate (or **bicarbonate**) compound containing the ion HCO_3^-, an acid salt of carbonic acid (solution of carbon dioxide in water). When heated or treated with dilute acids, it gives off carbon dioxide. The most important compounds are sodium hydrogen carbonate (bicarbonate of soda), and calcium hydrogen carbonate.

hydrograph graph showing how the discharge of a river varies with time. By studying hydrographs, water engineers can predict when flooding is likely and take action to prevent its taking place.

hydrological cycle also known as the ▷water cycle, by which water is circulated between the Earth's surface and its atmosphere.

hydrology study of the location and movement of inland water, both frozen and liquid, above and below ground. It is applied to major civil engineering projects such as irrigation schemes, dams, and hydroelectric power, and in planning water supply. Hydrologic studies are also undertaken to assess drinking water supplies, to track water underground, and to understand the role of water in geological processes such as fault movement and mineral deposition.

hydrolysis chemical reaction in which the action of water or its ions breaks down a substance into smaller molecules. Hydrolysis occurs in certain inorganic salts in solution, in nearly all non-metallic chlorides, in esters, and in other organic substances. It is one of the mechanisms for the breakdown of food by the body, as in the conversion of starch to glucose.

hydrolysis in earth science, a form of ▷chemical weathering caused by the chemical alteration of certain minerals as they react with water. For example, the mineral feldspar in granite reacts with water to form a white clay called ▷china clay.

hydrometer in physics, an instrument used to measure the relative density of liquids (the density compared with that of water). A hydrometer consists of a thin glass tube ending in a sphere that leads into a smaller sphere, the latter being weighted so that the hydrometer floats upright, sinking deeper into less dense liquids than into denser liquids. Hydrometers are used in brewing and to test the strength of acid in car batteries.

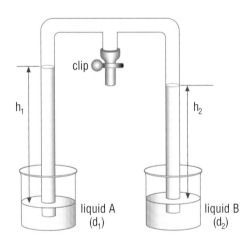

HYDROMETER Hare's apparatus is used to compare the density of two liquids. When air is removed from the top of the apparatus, the liquids rise in the tubes to heights which are inversely proportional to their densities.

hydrophily type of ▷pollination where the pollen is transported by water. Water-pollinated plants occur in 31 genera in 11 different families. They are found in habitats as diverse as rainforests and seasonal desert pools. Pollen is either dispersed underwater or on the water's surface.

hydrophobia another name for the disease ▷rabies.

hydrophone underwater ▷microphone and ancillary equipment capable of picking up waterborne sounds. It was originally developed to detect enemy submarines but is now also used, for example, for listening to the sounds made by whales.

hydrophyte plant adapted to live in water, or in waterlogged soil.

hydroponics cultivation of plants without soil, using specially prepared solutions of mineral salts. Beginning in the 1930s, large crops were grown by hydroponic methods, at first in California but since then in many other parts of the world.

hydrosphere the portion of the Earth made of water, ice, and water vapour, including the oceans, seas, rivers, streams, swamps, lakes, groundwater, and atmospheric water vapour. In some cases

HYDROPONICS Soya beans being grown hydroponically. Hydroponics allows for the commercial cultivation of crops through the use of nutrient-enriched solutions instead of soil. *Image Bank*

its definition is extended to include the water locked up in Earth's crust and mantle.

hydrostatics in physics, the branch of ▷statics dealing with fluids in equilibrium – that is, in a static condition. Practical applications include shipbuilding and dam design.

hydrothermal vein crack in rock filled with minerals precipitated through the action of circulating high-temperature fluids. Igneous activity often gives rise to the circulation of heated fluids that migrate outwards and move through the surrounding rock. When such solutions carry metallic ions, ore-mineral deposition occurs in the new surroundings on cooling.

hydrothermal vent (or **smoker**) crack in the ocean floor, commonly associated with an ▷ocean ridge, through which hot, mineral-rich water flows into the cold ocean water, forming thick clouds of suspended material. The clouds may be dark or light, depending on the mineral content, thus producing 'white smokers' or 'black smokers'. In some cases the water is clear.

hydroxide any inorganic chemical compound containing one or more hydroxyl (OH) groups and generally combined with a metal. Hydroxides include sodium hydroxide (caustic soda, $NaOH$), potassium hydroxide (caustic potash, KOH), and calcium hydroxide (slaked lime, $Ca(OH)_2$).

hydroxyl group an atom of hydrogen and an atom of oxygen bonded together and covalently bonded to an organic molecule. Common compounds containing hydroxyl groups are alcohols and phenols.

hydroxypropanoic acid technical name for ▷lactic acid.

hyena any of three species of carnivorous doglike mammals living in Africa and Asia. Hyenas have extremely powerful jaws.

HYENA The spotted (or laughing) hyena feeds mainly on carrion, although it is also a major predator of herbivores. It is named after the wailing, 'laughing' call it produces. *Image Bank*

They are scavengers, feeding on the remains of animals killed by predators such as lions, although they will also attack and kill live prey. (Genera *Hyaena* and *Crocuta*, family Hyaenidae, order Carnivora.)

The species are the **striped hyena** (*H. hyaena*) found from Asia Minor to India; the **brown hyena** (*H. brunnea*), found in South Africa; and the **spotted** or **laughing hyena** (*C. crocuta*), common south of the Sahara. The ▷aardwolf also belongs to the hyena family.

hygrometer in physics, any instrument for measuring the humidity, or water vapour content, of a gas (usually air). A wet and dry bulb hygrometer consists of two vertical thermometers, with one of the bulbs covered in absorbent cloth dipped into water. As the water evaporates, the bulb cools, producing a temperature difference between the two thermometers. The amount of evaporation, and hence cooling of the wet bulb, depends on the relative humidity of the air.

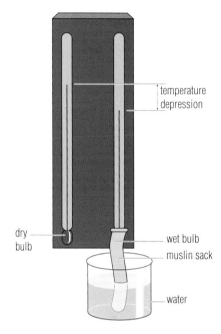

HYGROMETER The most common hygrometer, or instrument for measuring the humidity of a gas, is the wet and dry bulb hygrometer. The wet bulb records a lower temperature because water evaporates from the muslin, taking heat from the wet bulb. The degree of evaporation and hence cooling depends upon the humidity of the surrounding air or other gas.

Hymen in Greek mythology, the god of the marriage ceremony; personification of the refrain of a wedding song. In art, he is represented as a boy crowned with flowers, carrying a burning bridal torch.

hymn song in praise of a deity. Examples include Akhenaton's hymn to the Aton in ancient Egypt, the ancient Greek Orphic hymns, Old Testament psalms, extracts from the New Testament (such as the 'Ave Maria'), and hymns by the British writers John Bunyan ('Who Would True Valour See') and Charles Wesley ('Hark! The Herald Angels Sing'). The earliest sources of modern hymn melodies can be traced to the 11th and 12th centuries, and the earliest polyphonic settings date from the late 14th century. ▷Gospel music and carols are forms of Christian hymn singing.

hyoscine (or **scopolamine**) drug that acts on the autonomic nervous system and prevents muscle spasm. It is frequently included in premedication to dry up lung secretions and as a postoperative sedative. It is also used to treat ulcers, to relax the womb in labour, for travel sickness, and to dilate the pupils before an eye examination. It is an alkaloid, $C_{17}H_{21}NO_2$, obtained from various plants of the nightshade family (such as ▷belladonna).

hyperactivity condition of excessive activity in young children, combined with restlessness, inability to concentrate, and difficulty in learning. There are various causes, ranging from temperamental predisposition to brain disease. In some cases food additives have come under suspicion; in such instances modification of the diet may help. Mostly there is improvement at puberty, but symptoms may persist in the small proportion diagnosed as having ▷attention-deficit hyperactivity disorder.

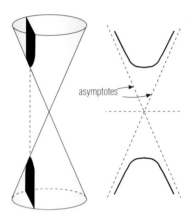

HYPERBOLA The hyperbola is produced when a cone is cut by a plane. It is one of a family of curves called conic sections: the circle, ellipse, and parabola. These curves are produced when the plane cuts the cone at different angles and positions.

hyperbola in geometry, a curve formed by cutting a right circular cone with a plane so that the angle between the plane and the base is greater than the angle between the base and the side of the cone. All hyperbolae are bounded by two asymptotes (straight lines which the hyperbola moves closer and closer to but never reaches).

A hyperbola is a member of the family of curves known as ▷conic sections.

hyperbole ▷figure of speech that is an intentional exaggeration or overstatement, used for emphasis or comic effect. Many everyday idioms are hyperbolic: 'waiting for ages' and 'a flood of tears'.

hypercharge in physics, a property of certain ▷elementary particles, analogous to electric charge, that accounts for the absence of some expected behaviour (such as certain decays).

hypermetropia (or **long-sightedness**) defect of vision in which a person is able to focus on objects in the distance, but not on close objects. It is caused by the failure of the lens to return to its normal rounded shape, or by the eyeball being too short, with the result that the image is focused on a point behind the retina. Hyperme-tropia is corrected by wearing glasses fitted with converging lenses, each of which acts like a magnifying glass.

hypertension abnormally high ▷blood pressure due to a variety of causes, leading to excessive contraction of the smooth muscle cells of the walls of the arteries. It increases the risk of kidney disease, stroke, and heart attack.

Hypertension is one of the major public health problems of the developed world, affecting 15–20% of adults in industrialized countries (1996). It may be of unknown cause (**essential hypertension**), or it may occur in association with some other condition, such as kidney disease (**secondary or symptomatic hypertension**). It is controlled with a low-salt diet and drugs.

hypertext system for viewing information (both text and pictures) on a computer screen in such a way that related items of information can easily be reached. For example, the program might display a map of a country; if the user clicks (with a ▷mouse) on a particular city, the program will display information about that city.

hyperthyroidism (or **thyrotoxicosis**) overactivity of the thyroid gland due to enlargement or tumour. Symptoms include accelerated heart rate, sweating, anxiety, tremor, and weight loss. Treatment is by drugs or surgery.

hypnosis artificially induced state of relaxation or altered attention characterized by heightened suggestibility. There is evidence that, with susceptible persons, the sense of pain may be diminished, memory of past events enhanced, and illusions or hallucinations experienced. Posthypnotic amnesia (forgetting what happened during hypnosis) and posthypnotic suggestion (performing an action after hypnosis that had been suggested during it) have also been demonstrated.

hypnotic any substance (such as ▷barbiturate, ▷benzodiazepine, alcohol) that depresses brain function, inducing sleep. Prolonged use may lead to physical or psychological addiction.

hypo in photography, a term for sodium thiosulphate, discovered in 1819 by John ▷Herschel, and used as a fixative for photographic images since 1837.

hypocaust floor raised on tile piers, heated by hot air circulating beneath it. It was first used by the Romans for baths about 100 BC, and was later introduced to private houses.

hypodermic syringe instrument used for injecting fluids beneath the skin into either muscles or blood vessels. It consists of a small graduated tube with a close-fitting piston and a nozzle onto which a hollow needle can be fitted.

hypogeal term used to describe seed germination in which the ▷cotyledons remain below ground. It can refer to fruits that develop underground, such as peanuts *Arachis hypogea*.

hypoglycaemia condition of abnormally low level of sugar (glucose) in the blood (below 60 g/100 ml), which starves the brain. It causes weakness, sweating, and mental confusion, sometimes fainting.

hypotenuse the longest side of a right-angled triangle, opposite the right angle. It is of particular application in Pythagoras' theorem (the square of the hypotenuse equals the sum of the squares of the other two sides), and in trigonometry where the ratios ▷sine and ▷cosine are defined as the ratios opposite/hypotenuse and adjacent/hypotenuse respectively.

hypothalamus region of the brain below the ▷cerebrum which regulates rhythmic activity and physiological stability within the body, including water balance and temperature. It regulates the production of the pituitary gland's hormones and controls that part of the ▷nervous system governing the involuntary muscles.

hypothermia condition in which the deep (core) temperature of the body falls below 35°C. If it is not discovered, coma and death ensue. Most at risk are the aged and babies (particularly if premature).

hypothesis in science, an idea concerning an event and its possible explanation. The term is one favoured by the followers of the philosopher Karl ▷Popper, who argue that the merit of a scientific hypothesis lies in its ability to make testable predictions.

hypothyroidism (or **myxoedema**) deficient functioning of the thyroid gland, causing slowed mental and physical performance, weight gain, sensitivity to cold, and susceptibility to infection.

hyrax any of a group of small, rodentlike, herbivorous mammals that live among rocks in desert areas, and in forests in Africa, Arabia, and Syria. They are about the size of a rabbit, with a plump body, short legs, short ears, brownish fur, and long, curved front teeth. (Family Procaviidae, order Hyracoidea.)

HYSSOP The hyssop is a bushy herb formerly used in medicine. It is also used, like its relation mint, in cooking.

hyssop aromatic herb belonging to the mint family, found in Asia, southern Europe, and around the Mediterranean. It has blue flowers, oblong leaves, and stems that are woody near the ground but herbaceous (fleshy) above. (*Hyssopus officinalis*, family Labiatae.)

hysterectomy surgical removal of all or part of the uterus (womb). The operation is performed to treat fibroids (benign tumours growing in the uterus) or cancer; also to relieve heavy menstrual bleeding. A woman who has had a hysterectomy will no longer menstruate and cannot bear children.

Instead of a full hysterectomy it is sometimes possible to remove the lining of the womb, the endometrium, by a 'keyhole' procedure known as endometrial resection, using either diathermy or a laser. This procedure avoids the complications, such as infections, that have occurred in as many as 45% of women after hysterectomy.

HYRAX A rock hyrax *Heterohyrax brucei* eating leaves in Tanzania. *Ken Preston-Mafham/Premaphotos Wildlife*

IA abbreviation for ▷Iowa, a state of the USA.

Iapetus Ocean (or **Proto-Atlantic**) sea that existed in early ▷Palaeozoic times between the continent that was to become Europe and that which was to become North America. The continents moved together in the late Palaeozoic, obliterating the ocean. When they moved apart once more, they formed the Atlantic.

Iaşi (German **Jassy**) city in northeastern Romania; population (1993) 328,000. It has chemical, machinery, electronic, and textile industries. It was the capital of the principality of Moldavia 1568–1889.

Ibadan city in southwest Nigeria, capital of Oyo State, 145 km/90 mi northeast of Lagos; population (1992 est) 1,295,000. Ibadan is the second-largest city in the country, and is a major commercial, industrial, and administrative centre. It is a marketplace for cocoa and other local agricultural produce. Industries include chemicals, electronics, plastics, and motor vehicle assembly.

Iban (or **Sea Dyak**) the ▷Dyak people of central Borneo. Approximately 250,000 Iban live in the interior uplands of Sarawak, while another 10,000 live in the border area of western Kalimantan. Traditionally the Iban live in long houses divided into separate family units, and practise shifting cultivation. Their languages belong to the Austronesian family.

Ibáñez, Vicente Blasco (1867–1928) Spanish novelist and politician. His novels include *La barraca/The Cabin* (1898), the most successful of his regional works; *Sangre y arena/Blood and Sand* (1908), the story of a famous bullfighter; and *Los cuatro jinetes del Apocalipsis/The Four Horsemen of the Apocalypse* (1916), a product of the effects of World War I. He was actively involved in revolutionary politics.

Ibarruri, Dolores (1895–1989) Called 'La Pasionaria' (the passion flower). Spanish Basque politician, journalist, and orator; she was first elected to the Cortes (Spanish parliament) in 1936. She helped to establish the Popular Front government and was a Loyalist leader in the Civil War. When Franco came to power in 1939 she left Spain for the USSR, where she was active in the Communist Party. She returned to Spain in 1977 after Franco's death and was re-elected to the Cortes (at the age of 81) in the first parliamentary elections for 40 years.

> **Dolores Ibarruri**
> *Il vaut mieux mourir debout que de vivre à genoux!*
>
> *It is better to die on your feet than to live on your knees!*
> Speech in Paris, 3 September 1936

Iberian Peninsula name given by ancient Greek navigators to the Spanish peninsula, derived from the River Iberus (Ebro). Anthropologists have given the name 'Iberian' to a Neolithic people, traces of whom are found in the Spanish peninsula, southern France, the Canary Isles, Corsica, and part of North Africa.

ibex any of various wild goats found in mountainous areas of Europe, northeastern Africa, and Central Asia. They grow to 100 cm/3.5 ft, and have brown or grey coats and heavy horns. They are herbivorous and live in small groups.

ibid. abbreviation for **ibidem** (Latin 'in the same place'), reference to a book, chapter, or page previously cited.

ibis any of various wading birds, about 60 cm/2 ft tall, belonging to the same family as spoonbills. Ibises have long legs and necks, and long, downward-curved beaks, rather blunt at the end; the upper part is grooved. Their plumage is generally black and white. Various species occur in the warmer regions of the world. (Family Threskiornidae, order Ciconiiformes.)

The **scarlet ibis** (*Guara ruber*), a South American species, is brilliant scarlet with a few black patches. The scarlet colour is caused by an accumulation of pigment from the aquatic invertebrates that it feeds on.

The **glossy ibis** (*Plegadis falcinellus*) is found in all continents except South America. The **Japanese ibis** is in danger of extinction because of the loss of its habitat; fewer than 25 birds remain. The **sacred ibis** (*Threskiornis aethiopica*) of ancient Egypt is still found in the Nile basin. The northern bald ibis *Geronticus eremita* is one of the world's rarest birds, with only 60 pairs remaining in the wild in 1998; they are concentrated at two sites in Morocco.

> **Henrik Ibsen**
> *The minority is always right.*
> An Enemy of the People, IV

Ibiza one of the ▷Balearic Islands, a popular tourist resort; area 596 sq km/230 sq mi; population (1990 est) 71,000. The capital and port, also called Ibiza, has a cathedral, built sometime between the 14th and 16th centuries.

Since the late 1980s, the island of Ibiza has become synonymous with dance music, and is one of the most popular resorts for young people, with holiday-makers flooding to the island every summer, especially from the UK. The island contains many huge dance clubs, including Pacha, Amnesia, and Es Paradise, and some of the largest clubs in the UK run events on the island every summer – Radio 1 has also had a strong presence on the island since the mid-1990s, with DJs broadcasting live from the famous Café del Mar.

Ibn Battuta (1304–1368) Arab traveller born in Tangier. In 1325, he went on an extraordinary 120,675-km/75,000-mi journey via Mecca to Egypt, East Africa, India, and China, returning some 30 years later. During this journey he also visited Spain and crossed the Sahara to Timbuktu. The narrative of his travels, *The Adventures of Ibn Battuta*, was written with an assistant, Ibn Juzayy.

Ibn Saud (1880–1953) Born Abdul Aziz al-Saud. First king of Saudi Arabia from 1932. His personal hostility to ▷Hussein ibn Ali, the British-supported political and religious leader of the Al Hijaz (Hejaz) region of western Arabia, meant that he stood back from the Arab Revolt of World War I, organized by T E ▷Lawrence and in which ▷Abdullah ibn Hussein and ▷Faisal I, of Iraq, participated. However, after the war, supported by the Wahabi-inspired Ikhwan (Brethren), Ibn Saud extended his dominions to the Red Sea coast, capturing Jedda and the Muslim holy cities of Mecca and Medina (with their lucrative pilgrimage revenue). By 1921, all central Arabia had been brought under his rule, and in 1924 he successfully invaded the Hejaz, defeating Hussein ibn Ali, who, in 1919, had proclaimed himself king of all the Arab countries. In January 1926, at Mecca, he was proclaimed King of Hejaz and Nejd and in 1932 the territories were unified, under the title 'Kingdom of Saudi Arabia'. In 1934 Saudi forces attacked Yemen and captured further territories in the south, including the towns of Najran and Jizan.

Oil was discovered in 1938, with oil concessions being leased to US and British companies, and exports began in 1946. During the 'first oil boom' (1947–52), the country was transformed from a poor pastoral kingdom into an affluent modernizing state, as annual oil revenues increased from $10 million to $212 million. During World War II, Ibn Saud remained neutral, but sympathetic towards the UK and the USA. In 1945 he founded the Arab League to encourage Arab unity.

Ibn Sina Arabic name of ▷Avicenna, scholar, and translator.

Ibo (or **Igbo**) member of a West African people occupying southeastern Nigeria and numbering about 18 million. Primarily subsistence farmers, they also trade and export palm oil and kernels, and make pottery, woodcarvings, and music. They are divided into five main groups, and their languages belong to the Kwa branch of the Niger-Congo family.

Ibsen, Henrik (Johan) (1828–1906) Norwegian dramatist and poet. His realistic and often controversial plays revolutionized European theatre. Driven into voluntary exile (1864–91) by opposition to the satirical *Kjærlighedens komedie/Love's Comedy* (1862), he wrote the symbolic verse dramas *Brand* (1866) and *Peer Gynt* (1867), followed by realistic plays dealing with social issues, including *Samfundets støtter/Pillars of Society* (1877), *Et dukkehjem/A Doll's House* (1879), *Gengangere/Ghosts* (1881), *En folkefiende/An Enemy of the People* (1882), and *Hedda Gabler* (1890). By the time he returned to Norway, he was recognized as the country's greatest living writer.

In his 'social problem' plays, Ibsen went beyond simply dealing with contemporary social issues and attitudes. He returned persistently to themes that had preoccupied him in *Brand* and *Peer Gynt*: the gulf between the ideal and the actual; the struggle to achieve personal integrity and fulfil one's vocation; the influence of the past and its 'inheritance of sin' on individuals and society generally. Nor did he reject symbolism, though he used it with great subtlety in the works written abroad, so that it did not jar with his naturalistic portrayal of contemporary life. After his return to Norway in 1891, he made a more overt use of symbolism to dramatize the confrontation of tortured and aspiring souls with their ultimate destinies, in the plays *Bygmester Solness/The Master Builder* (1892), *Lille Eyolf/Little Eyolf* (1894), *John Gabriel Borkman* (1896), and *Naar vi døde vaagner/When We Dead Awaken* (1899). His influence on European and American theatre in the 20th century has been profound.

IC abbreviation for ▷integrated circuit.

Icarus in astronomy, an ▷Apollo asteroid 1.5 km/1 mi in diameter, discovered in 1949 by German-born astronomer Walter Baade. It orbits the Sun every 409 days at a distance of 28–300 million km/18–186 million mi (0.19–2.0 astronomical units). It was the first asteroid known to approach the Sun closer than does the planet Mercury. In 1968 it passed 6 million km/ 3.7 million mi from Earth.

Icarus in Greek mythology, the son of ▷Daedalus, who with his father escaped from the labyrinth in Crete by making wings of feathers fastened with wax. Icarus plunged to his death when he flew too near the Sun and the wax melted.

ICBM abbreviation for **intercontinental ballistic missile**; see ▷nuclear warfare.

ice solid formed by water when it freezes. It is colourless and its crystals are hexagonal. The water molecules are held together by hydrogen bonds.

The freezing point of ice, used as a standard for measuring temperature, is 0° for the Celsius and Réaumur scales and 32° for the Fahrenheit. Ice expands in the act of freezing (hence burst pipes), becoming less dense than water (0.9175 at 5°C/41°F). In 1998 US geologists succeeded in creating ice made up of irregular crystals. The new type of ice was created by exerting an enormous pressure (6,500 atmospheres) on water molecules, till their hydrogen atoms were squeezed into a disorderly state.

ice age any period of extensive glaciation occurring in the Earth's history, but particularly that in the Pleistocene epoch, immediately preceding historic times. On the North American continent, ▷glaciers reached as far south as the Great Lakes, and an ice sheet spread over northern Europe, leaving its remains as far south as Switzerland. There were several glacial advances separated by interglacial stages, during which the ice melted and temperatures were higher than today.

Other ice ages have occurred throughout geological time: there were four in the Precambrian era, one in the Ordovician, and one at the end of the Carboniferous and beginning of the Permian. The occurrence of an ice age is governed by a combination of factors (the **Milankovitch hypothesis**): (1) the Earth's change of attitude in relation to the Sun, that is, the way it tilts in a 41,000-year cycle and at the same time wobbles on its axis in a 22,000-year cycle, making the time of its closest approach to the Sun come at different seasons; and (2) the 92,000-year cycle of eccentricity in its orbit round the Sun, changing it from an elliptical to a near circular orbit, the severest period of an ice age coinciding with the approach to circularity. There is a possibility that the Pleistocene ice age is not yet over. It may reach another maximum in another 60,000 years.

Related Web site: Cracking the Ice Age http://www.pbs.org/wgbh/nova/ice/

Ice Age, Little period of particularly severe winters that gripped northern Europe between the 13th and 17th centuries. Contemporary writings and paintings show that Alpine glaciers were much more extensive than at present, and rivers such as the Thames, which do not ice over today, were so frozen that festivals could be held on them.

iceberg floating mass of ice, about 80% of which is submerged, rising sometimes to 100 m/300 ft above sea level. Glaciers that reach the coast become extended into a broad foot; as this enters the sea, masses break off and drift towards temperate latitudes, becoming a danger to shipping.

ice hockey game played on ice between two teams of six, developed in Canada from field hockey or bandy. Players, who wear skates and protective clothing, use a curved stick to advance the puck (a rubber disc) and shoot it at the opponents' goal, a netted cage, guarded by the goalminder, or goalie. The other positions are the left and right defencemen and the left wing, centre, and right wing. The latter three are offensive players. The team with the most goals scored at the end of the three 20-minute periods wins; an overtime period may be played if a game ends in a tie.

Related Web site: National Hockey League http://www.nhl.com/

Iceland see country box.

Icelandic language member of the northern Germanic branch of the Indo-European language family, spoken only in Iceland and the most conservative in form of the Scandinavian languages. Despite seven centuries of Danish rule, lasting until 1918, Icelandic has remained virtually unchanged since the 12th century.

Iceni ancient people of eastern England, who revolted against Roman occupation under the chieftainship of ▷Boudicca.

ice-skating see ▷skating.

ichneumon fly any of a large group of parasitic wasps. There are several thousand species in Europe, North America, and other regions. They have slender bodies, and the females have unusually long, curved ovipositors (egg-laying instruments) that can pierce several inches of wood. The eggs are laid in the eggs, larvae, or pupae of other insects, usually butterflies or moths. (Family Ichneumonidae.) See picture on p. 469.

icon in computing, a small picture on the computer screen, or ▷VDU, representing an object or function that the user may manipulate or otherwise use. It is a feature of ▷graphical user interface (GUI) systems. Icons make computers easier to use by allowing the user to point to and click with a ▷mouse on pictures, rather than type commands.

icon in the Greek or Eastern Orthodox Church, a representation of Jesus, Mary, an angel, or a saint, in painting, low relief, or mosaic. The painted icons were traditionally done on wood. After the 17th century, and mainly in Russia, a *riza*, or gold and silver covering that leaves only the face and hands visible (and may be adorned with jewels presented by the faithful in thanksgiving), was often added as protection.

Related Web site: Icon Gallery http://www.christusrex.org/www1/lviv/Gallery/Gallery.Entrance.html

Iceland

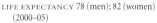

Iceland island country in the North Atlantic Ocean, situated south of the Arctic Circle, between Greenland and Norway.

NATIONAL NAME *Lýðveldið Island/Republic of Iceland*
AREA 103,000 sq km/39,768 sq mi
CAPITAL Reykjavik
MAJOR TOWNS/CITIES Akureyri, Kópavogur, Hafnarjördur, Gardhabaer, Keflavik, Reykjanesbaer, Vestmannaeyjar
PHYSICAL FEATURES warmed by the Gulf Stream; glaciers and lava fields cover 75% of the country; active volcanoes (Hekla was once thought the gateway to Hell); geysers, hot springs, and new islands created offshore (Surtsey in 1963); subterranean hot water heats 85% of Iceland's homes; Sidujokull glacier moving at 100 metres a day

Government

HEAD OF STATE Ólafur Ragnar Grímsson from 1996
HEAD OF GOVERNMENT Davíd Oddsson from 1991
POLITICAL SYSTEM liberal democracy
POLITICAL EXECUTIVE parliamentary
ADMINISTRATIVE DIVISIONS 23 counties and 14 independent towns
ARMED FORCES no defence forces of its own; US forces under NATO are stationed there: 2,500 military personnel and a 130-strong coastguard (2002 est)
DEATH PENALTY abolished in 1928
EDUCATION SPEND (% GDP) 5.9 (2001 est)
HEALTH SPEND (% GDP) 8.9 (2000 est)

Economy and resources

CURRENCY krona
GPD (US$) 8.6 billion (2002 est)
REAL GDP GROWTH (% change on previous year) 3.6 (2001)
GNI (US$) 7.9 billion (2002 est)
GNI PER CAPITA (PPP) (US$) 28,590 (2002 est)
CONSUMER PRICE INFLATION 2.1% (2003 est)

UNEMPLOYMENT 1.4% (2001)
MAJOR TRADING PARTNERS EU (principally Germany, UK, the Netherlands, Portugal, and Denmark), Norway, USA, Japan, Sweden
RESOURCES aluminium, diatomite, hydroelectric and thermal power, fish
INDUSTRIES mining, fish processing, processed aluminium, fertilizer, construction, cement
EXPORTS fish and fish products, aluminium, ferrosilicon, diatomite, fertilizer, animal products. Principal market: UK 19.4% (2000)
IMPORTS machinery and transport equipment, industrial supplies, motor vehicles, petroleum and petroleum products, foodstuffs, textiles. Principal source: Germany 11.8% (2000)

ARABLE LAND 0.1% (2000 est)
AGRICULTURAL PRODUCTS hay, potatoes, turnips; fishing industry, dairy products and livestock (lamb)

Population and society

POPULATION 290,000 (2003 est)
POPULATION GROWTH RATE 0.7% (2000–05)
POPULATION DENSITY (per sq km) 3 (2003 est)
URBAN POPULATION (% of total) 93 (2003 est)
AGE DISTRIBUTION (% of total population) 0–14 23%, 15–59 62%, 60+ 15% (2002 est)
ETHNIC GROUPS most of the population is descended from Norwegians and Celts
LANGUAGE Icelandic (official)
RELIGION Evangelical Lutheran about 90%, other Protestant and Roman Catholic about 4%
EDUCATION (compulsory years) 9
LITERACY RATE 99% (men); 99% (women) (2003 est)
LABOUR FORCE 8.3% agriculture, 23% industry, 68.7% services (2000)

LIFE EXPECTANCY 78 (men); 82 (women) (2000–05)
CHILD MORTALITY RATE (under 5, per 1,000 live births) 4 (2001)
TV SETS (per 1,000 people) 505 (1999 est)
RADIOS (per 1,000 people) 1075 (1999 est)
INTERNET USERS (per 10,000 people) 6,076.4 (2002 est)
PERSONAL COMPUTER USERS (per 100 people) 45.1 (2002 est)

Chronology

7th century: Iceland discovered by Irish seafarers.

874: First Norse settler, Ingólfr Arnarson, founded a small colony at Reykjavik.

c. 900: Norse settlers came in larger numbers, mainly from Norway.

930: Settlers established an annual parliament, the Althing, to make laws and resolve disputes.

985: Eric the Red left Iceland to found a settlement in Greenland.

1000: Icelanders adopted Christianity.

1263: Icelanders recognized the authority of the king of Norway after a brief civil war.

1397: Norway and Iceland were united with Denmark and Sweden under a single monarch.

15th century: Norway and Iceland were increasingly treated as appendages of Denmark, especially after Sweden seceded in 1449.

1783: Poisonous volcanic eruption caused great loss of life.

1814: Norway passed to the Swedish crown; Iceland remained under Danish rule.

1845: Althing was re-established in modernized form.

1874: New constitution gave Iceland limited autonomy.

1918: Iceland achieved full self-government under the Danish crown.

1940: British forces occupied Iceland after Germany invaded Denmark; US troops took over in 1941.

1944: Iceland became an independent republic under President Sveinn Björnsson.

1949: Iceland became a member of NATO.

1958: The introduction of an exclusive fishing limit led to the first 'Cod War', when Icelandic patrol boats clashed with British fishing boats.

1972–73: Iceland extended its fishing limit, renewing confrontations with Britain.

1975–76: The further extension of the fishing limit caused the third 'Cod War' with the UK.

1985: Iceland declared itself a nuclear-free zone.

1991: Davíd Oddsson was appointed prime minister.

1992: Iceland defied a world ban to resume its whaling industry.

2003: Prime Minister Oddsson's conservative Sjálfstædisflokkurinn (SSF; Independence Party) and its liberal coalition partner, the Framsóknarflokkurinn (FSF; Progressive Party), retained a slim majority in legislative elections.

ICELAND A time-lapse photograph showing sunrise in Heimey, Iceland. *Image Bank*

ICHNEUMON FLY The female of the ichneumon fly (or wasp) *Rhyssa persuasoria*. She is using her long ovipositor to insert an egg into a larva of the wood wasp *Sirex gigas*, which lives in a tunnel burrowed into a pine trunk. See entry on p. 468. *Premaphotos Wildlife*

Iconium city of ancient Turkey; see ▷Konya.

iconoclast (Greek 'image-breaker') literally, a person who attacks religious images, originally in obedience to the injunction of the Second Commandment not to worship 'graven images'. Under the influence of Islam and Judaism, an iconoclastic movement calling for the destruction of religious images developed in the Byzantine Empire, and was endorsed by the Emperor Leo III in 726. Fierce persecution of those who made and venerated icons followed, until iconoclasm was declared a heresy in the 9th century. The same name was applied to those opposing the use of images at the Reformation, when there was much destruction in churches. Figuratively, the term is used for a person who attacks established ideals or principles.

iconography in art history, significance attached to symbols that can help to identify subject matter (for example, a saint holding keys usually represents St Peter) and place a work of art in its historical context. The pioneer of this approach was the German art historian Erwin Panofsky.

ID abbreviation for ▷Idaho, a state of the USA.

id. abbreviation for **idem** (Latin 'the same'), used in reference citation.

id in Freudian psychology, the mass of motivational and instinctual elements of the human mind, whose activity is largely governed by the arousal of specific needs. It is regarded as the ▷unconscious element of the human psyche, and is said to be in conflict with the ▷ego and the ▷superego.

Idaho state of northwestern USA. It is nicknamed Gem State. Idaho, one of the Mountain States, was admitted to the Union in 1890 as the 43rd US state. It is bordered to the east by Montana and Wyoming, to the south by Utah and Nevada, to the west by Oregon and Washington, and to the north by British Columbia, Canada.

> **population** (1995) 1,163,300 **area** 216,500 sq km/83,569 sq mi **capital** Boise **towns and cities** Pocatello, Idaho Falls, Nampa, Lewiston **industries and products** potatoes, wheat, livestock, timber, silver, lead, zinc, antimony, tourism, leisure industry

idealism in philosophy, the theory that states that the external world is fundamentally immaterial and a dimension of the mind. Objects in the world exist but, according to this theory, they lack substance.

identikit a set of drawings of different parts of the face used to compose a likeness of a person for identification. It was evolved by Hugh C McDonald in the USA. It has largely been replaced by photofit, based on photographs, which produces a more realistic likeness.

Ides in the Roman calendar, the 15th day of March, May, July, and October, and the 13th day of all other months (the word originally indicated the full moon); Julius Caesar was assassinated on the Ides of March 44 BC.

i.e. abbreviation for **id est** (Latin 'that is').

Ife town in western Nigeria, traditionally the oldest of the Yoruba kingdoms in the region. Ife was established in the 6th century and became an important Iron-Age town. It was the cultural and religious, though not political, centre of the region, and reached its peak about 1300. Many sculptures in bronze, brass, clay, and ivory have been excavated in and around the town.

Ifugao an indigenous people of northern Luzon in the Philippines, numbering approximately 70,000. In addition to practising shifting cultivation on highland slopes, they build elaborate terraced rice fields. Their language belongs to the Austronesian family.

igloo temporary ▷Inuit dwelling constructed of blocks of ice piled high in a dome. The entranceway is long and narrow.

IGLOO The traditional temporary dwelling of the Inuit, constructed from blocks of frozen snow and ice. Nowadays, most igloos are for show rather than for actually living in. *Image Bank*

Ignatius of Antioch, St (died *c.* 110) Christian martyr. Traditionally a disciple of St John, he was bishop of Antioch, and was thrown to the wild beasts in Rome. He wrote seven epistles, important documents of the early Christian church. Feast day 1 February.

igneous rock rock formed from the solidification of molten rock called magma. The acidic nature of this rock type means that areas with underlying igneous rock are particularly susceptible to the effects of acid rain. Igneous rocks that crystallize slowly from magma below the Earth's surface have large crystals. Examples include dolerite and granite.

Igneous rocks that crystallize from magma below the Earth's surface are called **plutonic** or **intrusive**, depending on the depth of formation. They have large crystals produced by slow cooling; examples include dolerite and ▷granite. Those extruded at the surface from ▷lava are called **extrusive** or **volcanic**. Rapid cooling results in small crystals; ▷basalt is an example.

> **Related Web site: Types of Rocks: Igneous, Metamorphic and Sedimentary** http://www.zephyrus.demon.co.uk/virtualschool/lessons/Lesson008.htm

ignis fatuus another name for ▷will-o'-the-wisp.

ignition temperature (or **fire point**) minimum temperature to which a substance must be heated before it will spontaneously burn independently of the source of heat; for example, ethanol has an ignition temperature of 425°C/798°F and a flash point of 12°C/54°F.

Iguaçu Falls (or **Iguassú Falls**) waterfall in South America, on the border between Brazil and Argentina. The falls lie 19 km/12 mi above the junction of the River Iguaçu with the Paraná. The falls are divided by forested rocky islands and form a spectacular tourist attraction. The water plunges in 275 falls, many of which have separate names. They have a height of 82 m/269 ft and a width of about 4 km/2.5 mi.

> **Related Web site: Iguaçu Falls – Great Water** http://darkwing.uoregon.edu/~sergiok/brasil/iguacu.html

iguana any of about 700 species of lizard, chiefly found in the Americas. The **common iguana** (*I. iguana*) of Central and South America is a vegetarian and may reach 2 m/6 ft in length. (Especially genus *Iguana*, family Iguanidae.)

iguanodon plant-eating ▷dinosaur whose remains are found in deposits of the Lower ▷Cretaceous age, together with the remains of other dinosaurs of the same order (ornithiscians) such as stegosaurus and ▷triceratops. It was 5–10 m/16–32 ft long and, when standing upright, 4 m/13 ft tall. It walked on its hind legs, using its long tail to balance its body. (Order *Ornithiscia*.)

IJsselmeer lake in the Netherlands, area 1,217 sq km/470 sq mi. It was formed in 1932 after the ▷Zuider Zee was cut off from the North Sea by a dyke 32 km/20 mi long (the *Afsluitdijk*); it has been freshwater since 1944. The rivers Vecht, IJssel, and Zwatewater flow into the lake.

Ikhnaton another name for ▷Akhenaton, pharaoh of Egypt.

IL abbreviation for ▷Illinois, a state of the USA.

Ile-de-France region of northern France; area 12,000 sq km/4,600 sq mi; population (1999 est) 10,952,000. It includes the French capital, ▷Paris, and the towns of Versailles, Sèvres, and St-Cloud, and comprises the *départements* of Essonne, Val-de-Marne, Val-d'Oise, Ville de Paris, Seine-et-Marne, Hauts-de-Seine, Seine-St-Denis, and Yvelines. From here the early French kings extended their authority over the whole country.

Ile de la Tortue (French **La Tortue** 'turtle') island off the north coast of ▷Haiti; area 180 sq km/69 sq mi. It was a pirate lair during the 17th century.

ileum part of the small intestine of the ▷digestive system, between the duodenum and the colon, that absorbs digested food.

Iliescu, Ion (1930–) Romanian president 1990–96, and from 2000. A former member of the Romanian Communist Party (PCR) and of Nicolae Ceauşescu's government, Iliescu swept into power on Ceauşescu's fall as head of the National Salvation Front.

Ilium in classical mythology, an alternative name for the city of ▷Troy, taken from its founder Ilus.

illegitimacy in law, the status of a child born to a mother who is not legally married; a child may be legitimized by subsequent marriage of the parents. The nationality of the child is usually that of the mother.

Illimani highest peak in the Bolivian Andes, rising to 6,402 m/21,004 ft east of the city of La Paz.

Illinois midwestern state of the USA. It is nicknamed Prairie State. Illinois was admitted to the Union in 1818 as the 21st US state. A major agricultural state, Illinois is bordered to the east by Indiana, to the southeast by Kentucky, with the Ohio River serving as a boundary, to the west by Missouri and Iowa, with the Mississippi River as a boundary, and to the north by Wisconsin. In the northeast, it has a shore of *c.* 100 km/60 mi on Lake Michigan, occupied by Chicago and its northern suburbs.

> **population** (1995) 11,829,900 **area** 146,100 sq km/56,395 sq mi **capital** Springfield **towns and cities** Chicago, Rockford, Peoria, Decatur, Aurora **industries and products** soybeans, cereals, meat and dairy products, livestock, machinery, electrical and electronic equipment

Illyria ancient name for the eastern coastal region of the Adriatic, north of the Gulf of Corinth. Its three constituent districts were Dalmatia, Iapydia, and Liburnia. It later formed the Roman province of Illyricum. The Albanians are the survivors of its ancient peoples.

image picture or appearance of a real object, formed by light that passes through a lens or is reflected from a mirror. If rays of light actually pass through an image, it is called a **real image**. Real images, such as those produced by a camera or projector lens, can be projected onto a screen. An image that cannot be projected onto a screen, such as that seen in a flat mirror, is known as a **virtual image**.

imaginary number term often used to describe the non-real element of a ▷complex number. For the complex number ($a + ib$), ib is the imaginary number where $i = \sqrt{(-1)}$, and b any real number.

Imagism movement in Anglo-American poetry that flourished from 1912 to 1914 and affected much US and British poetry and critical thinking thereafter. A central figure was Ezra ▷Pound, who asserted the principles of free verse, complex imagery, and poetic impersonality.

imago sexually mature stage of an ▷insect.

imam (Arabic 'leader') in a mosque, the leader of congregational prayer, but generally any notable Islamic leader.

IMF abbreviation for ▷International Monetary Fund.

Imhotep (born c. 2630 BC) Egyptian physician, architect, and vizier (chief adviser) of King Zoser (3rd dynasty). He is thought to have designed the step pyramid at ▷Sakkara, the first pyramid ever constructed. Reputedly King Zoser's doctor, Imhotep was raised to the status of god of healing after his death and his tomb (believed to be in the north Sakkara cemetery) became a centre of healing. He was said to be the son of ▷Ptah, the Egyptian god of the creative force, and was later identified with ▷Asclepius, the Greek god of medicine.

Imhotep was important to ancient Egyptian medicine for the next 2,500 years, as Egyptian medical belief required that doctors treat their patients with both spiritual and rational methods. Doctors gave prayers to Imhotep as they treated their patients in the belief that he would intervene to help the healing process. Imhotep continued to be worshipped after the end of the ancient Egyptian period c. 400 BC. The ancient Greeks considered Imhotep and their god of healing Asclepius to be the same person, while the Romans continued to revere him over 3,000 years after his death. The Roman emperors Claudius I and Tiberius had inscriptions placed on their temples in Egypt praising Imhotep.

Immaculate Conception in the Roman Catholic Church, the belief that the Virgin Mary was, by a special act of grace, preserved free from ▷original sin from the moment she was conceived. This article of the Catholic faith was for centuries the subject of heated controversy, opposed by St Thomas Aquinas and other theologians, but generally accepted from about the 16th century. It became a dogma in 1854 under Pope Pius IX.

Related Web site: Immaculate Conception http://www.newadvent. org/cathen/07674d.htm

immigration and emigration movement of people from one country to another. Immigration is movement to a country; emigration is movement from a country. Immigration or emigration on a large scale is often for economic reasons or because of religious, political, or social persecution (which may create ▷refugees), and often prompts restrictive legislation by individual countries. The USA has received immigrants on a larger scale than any other country, more than 50 million during its history.

immiscible describing liquids that will not mix with each other, such as oil and water. When two immiscible liquids are shaken together, a turbid mixture is produced. This normally forms separate layers on being left to stand.

immunity the protection that organisms have against foreign micro-organisms, such as bacteria and viruses, and against cancerous cells (see ▷cancer). The cells that provide this protection are called white blood cells, or leucocytes, and make up the immune system. They include neutrophils and ▷macrophages, which can engulf invading organisms and other unwanted material, and natural killer cells that destroy cells infected by viruses and cancerous cells. Some of the most important immune cells are the B cells and ▷T cells. Immune cells coordinate their activities by means of chemical messengers or ▷lymphokines, including the antiviral messenger ▷interferon. The lymph nodes play a major role in organizing the immune response.

Immunity is also provided by a range of physical barriers such as the skin, tear fluid, acid in the stomach, and mucus in the airways. ▷AIDS is one of many viral diseases in which the immune system is affected.

immunization conferring immunity to infectious disease by artificial methods. The most widely used technique is ▷vaccination. Immunization is an important public health measure. If most of the population has been immunized against a particular disease, it is impossible for an epidemic to take hold.

Related Web site: Immunology http://www.nutramed.com/ immunology/index.htm

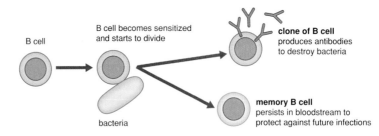

IMMUNITY B cells, a type of lymphocyte (white blood cell), have an important role in the body's immune system. When a B cell encounters an invading bacterium it starts to divide, forming two different types of cell. One type is a clone of itself that begins to produce antibodies to fight the infection; the other is a memory cell that will persist in the bloodstream, ready to produce antibodies should re-infection occur.

immunocompromised lacking a fully effective immune system. The term is most often used in connection with infections such as ▷AIDS where the virus interferes with the immune response (see ▷immunity).

immunodeficient lacking one or more elements of a working immune system. Immune deficiency is the term generally used for patients who are born with such a defect, while those who acquire such a deficiency later in life are referred to as ▷immuno-compromised or immunosuppressed.

immunoglobulin human globulin ▷protein that can be separated from blood and administered to confer immediate immunity on the recipient. It participates in the immune reaction as the antibody for a specific ▷antigen (disease-causing agent).

immunosuppressive any drug that suppresses the body's normal immune responses to infection or foreign tissue. It is used in the treatment of autoimmune disease (see ▷autoimmunity); as part of chemotherapy for leukaemias, lymphomas, and other cancers; and to help prevent rejection following organ transplantation. Immunosuppressed patients are at greatly increased risk of infection.

impact printer computer printer that creates characters by striking an inked ribbon against the paper beneath. Examples of impact printers are dot-matrix printers, daisywheel printers, and most types of line printer.

impala African ▷antelope found from Kenya to South Africa in savannahs and open woodland. The body is sandy brown. Males have lyre-shaped horns up to 75 cm/2.5 ft long. Impala grow up to 1.5 m/5 ft long and 90 cm/3 ft tall. They live in herds and spring high in the air when alarmed. (Species *Aepyceros melampus*, family Bovidae.)

impeachment judicial procedure by which government officials are accused of wrongdoing and brought to trial before a legislative body. In the USA the House of Representatives may impeach offenders to be tried before the Senate, as in the case of President Andrew Johnson in 1868. Richard ▷Nixon resigned the US presidency in 1974 when threatened by impeachment. President Bill ▷Clinton's impeachment trial took place in 1999.

impedance the total opposition of a circuit to the passage of alternating electric current. It has the symbol Z. It includes the resistance R and the reactance X (caused by ▷capacitance or ▷inductance); the impedance can then be found using the equation $Z^2 = R^2 + X^2$.

imperialism policy of extending the power and rule of a government beyond its own boundaries. A country may attempt to dominate others by direct rule and settlement – the establishment of a colony – or by less obvious means such as control of markets for goods or raw materials. These less obvious means are often called ▷neocolonialism.

imperial system traditional system of units developed in the UK, based largely on the foot, pound, and second (f.p.s.) system.

imperium (Latin 'command' or 'rule') in ancient Rome, the legal and military power granted to certain magistrates, for example, consul, praetor, or dictator. The term also extends to command over a province (proconsul). Repeated grants of imperium, with the additional powers of a tribune, became the basis of the principate of Augustus and subsequent emperors. The term was also used for the rule of Rome over the Roman empire.

IMPALA This male impala in the Kruger National Park, South Africa, is part of a bachelor herd. A pursued impala can reach speeds of 60 kph/ 37 mph and clear obstacles 3 m/10 ft high in a single leap. *Premaphotos Wildlife*

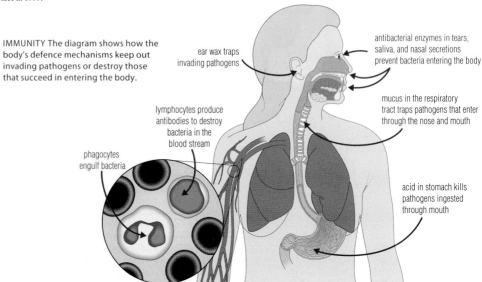

IMMUNITY The diagram shows how the body's defence mechanisms keep out invading pathogens or destroy those that succeed in entering the body.

ear wax traps invading pathogens

antibacterial enzymes in tears, saliva, and nasal secretions prevent bacteria entering the body

lymphocytes produce antibodies to destroy bacteria in the blood stream

mucus in the respiratory tract traps pathogens that enter through the nose and mouth

phagocytes engulf bacteria

acid in stomach kills pathogens ingested through mouth

Imphal capital of ▷Manipur state on the Manipur River, India; population (1991) 201,000. It is a communications and trade centre (tobacco, sugar, fruit). Imphal was besieged between March and June 1944, when Japan invaded Assam, but held out with the help of supplies dropped by air.

implantation in mammals, the process by which the developing ▷embryo attaches itself to the wall of the mother's uterus and stimulates the development of the ▷placenta. In humans it occurs 6–8 days after ovulation.

import product or service that one country purchases from another for domestic consumption, or for processing and re-exporting (Hong Kong, for example, is heavily dependent on imports for its export business). Imports may be visible (goods) or invisible (services). If an importing country does not have a counterbalancing value of exports, it may experience balance-of-payments difficulties and accordingly consider restricting imports by some form of protectionism (such as an import tariff or import quotas).

Impressionism movement in painting that originated in France in the 1860s and had enormous influence in European and North American painting in the late 19th century. The Impressionists wanted to depict real life, to paint straight from nature, and to capture the changing effects of light. The term was first used abusively to describe Claude Monet's painting *Impression: Sunrise* (1872). The other leading Impressionists included Paul Cézanne, Edgar Degas, Edouard Manet, Camille Pissarro, Pierre-Auguste Renoir, and Alfred Sisley, but only Monet remained devoted to Impressionist ideas throughout his career.

Related Web sites: First Impressionist Exhibition, 1874 http://www.artchive.com/74nadar.htm
WebMuseum: Impressionism http://www.southern.net/wm/paint/theme/impressionnisme.html

imprinting in ▷ethology, the process whereby a young animal learns to recognize both specific individuals (for example, its mother) and its own species. Imprinting is characteristically an automatic response to specific stimuli at a time when the animal is especially sensitive to those stimuli (the **sensitive period**). Thus, goslings learn to recognize their mother by following the first moving object they see after hatching; as a result, they can easily become imprinted on other species, or even inanimate objects, if these happen to move near them at this time. In chicks, imprinting occurs only between 10 and 20 hours after hatching. In mammals, the mother's attachment to her infant may be a form of imprinting made possible by a sensitive period; this period may be as short as the first hour after giving birth.

impromptu in music, a 19th-century character piece in the style of an improvisation. Composers of piano impromptus include Schubert and Chopin.

improvisation creating a play, a poem, or any other imaginative work, without preparation. The term is used in GCSE English for the unprepared piece of drama most students undertake as part of their assessment in the Speaking and Listening section of their examination. The word has already been twisted from its original meaning in this context, and the term 'prepared improvisation' is being used to show that some preparation time has been allowed.

IN abbreviation for ▷Indiana, a state of the USA.

in abbreviation for ▷inch, a measure of distance.

inbreeding in ▷genetics, the mating of closely related individuals. It is considered undesirable because it increases the risk that offspring will inherit copies of rare deleterious ▷recessive alleles (genes) from both parents and so suffer from disabilities.

Inca member of an ancient Peruvian civilization of Quechua-speaking American Indians that began in the Andean highlands about AD 1200. By the time the Spanish conquered the region in the

INCA Inca stonework at the ruined city of Machu Picchu, Peru. Walls constructed by the Incas have a perfect line of inclination towards the centre from bottom to top, and the edges and corners of each stone are rounded. *Corel*

1530s, the Inca people ruled an area that stretched from Ecuador in the north to Chile in the south. Inca means 'king', and was the title of the ruler as well as the name of the people.

Incan art see ▷pre-Columbian art.

incandescence emission of light from a substance in consequence of its high temperature. The colour of the emitted light from liquids or solids depends on their temperature, and for solids generally the higher the temperature the whiter the light. Gases may become incandescent through ionizing radiation, as in the glowing vacuum ▷discharge tube.

incarnation assumption of living form (plant, animal, human) by a deity; for example, the gods of Greece and Rome, Hinduism, and Christianity (Jesus as the second person of the Trinity).

incendiary bomb bomb containing inflammable matter. Usually dropped by aircraft, incendiary bombs were used in World War I and incendiary shells were used against Zeppelin aircraft. Incendiary bombs were a major weapon in attacks on cities in World War II, causing widespread destruction. To hinder firefighters, delayed-action high-explosive bombs were usually dropped with them. In the Vietnam War, US forces used ▷napalm in incendiary bombs.

incest sexual intercourse between persons thought to be too closely related to marry; the exact relationships that fall under the incest taboo vary widely from society to society. A biological explanation for the incest taboo is based on the necessity to avoid ▷inbreeding.

Within groups in which ritual homosexuality is practised, for example in New Guinea, an incest taboo applies also to these relations, suggesting that the taboo is as much social as biological in origin.

inch imperial unit of linear measure, a twelfth of a foot, equal to 2.54 centimetres.

It was defined in statute by Edward II of England as the length of three barley grains laid end to end.

Inchon (formerly **Chemulpo**) chief port of Seoul, South Korea; population (1995 est) 2,307,600. The city lies where the Han River enters the Yellow Sea. The building of a rail link with Seoul in 1900 boosted the port's trade. Exports include rice, wheat, paper, and electronic goods.

inclination angle between the ▷ecliptic and the plane of the orbit of a planet, asteroid, or comet. In the case of satellites orbiting a planet, it is the angle between the plane of orbit of the satellite and the equator of the planet.

inclusive fitness in ▷genetics, the success with which a given variant (or allele) of a ▷gene is passed on to future generations by a particular individual, after additional copies of the allele in the individual's relatives and their offspring have been taken into account.

income support in the UK, ▷social security benefit payable to people who are unemployed or who work for less than 24 hours per week and whose financial resources fall below a certain level. It replaced supplementary benefit in 1988. Originally payable to anyone over 18 not in full-time employment and without adequate resources, as of October 1996 it was restricted to groups such as pensioners or long-term disabled who were not required to be available for work. Payments were reduced if savings exceeded a set amount.

income tax direct tax levied on personal income, mainly wages and salaries, but which may include the value of receipts other than in cash. It is one of the main instruments for achieving a government's income redistribution objectives. In contrast, **indirect taxes** are duties payable whenever a specific product is purchased; examples include VAT and customs duties.

Most countries impose income taxes on company (corporation) profits and on individuals (personal), although the rates and systems differ widely from country to country. In the case of companies in particular, income tax returns are prepared by an accountant, who will take advantage of the various exemptions, deductions, and allowances available. Personal income taxes are usually progressive so that the poorest members of society pay little or no tax, while the rich make much larger contributions. In the 1980s many countries underwent tax reforms that led to simplification and reductions in income tax rates. This had the effect of stimulating economic activity by increasing consumer spending and in some cases discouraged tax evasion. In the UK the rates of tax and allowances are set out yearly in the annual Finance Act, which implements the recommendations agreed to by the House of Commons in the budget presented by the chancellor of the Exchequer. William Pitt introduced an income tax between 1799 and 1801 to finance the wars with revolutionary France; it was re-imposed between 1803 and 1816 for the same purpose, and was so unpopular that all records of it were destroyed when it was abolished. Peel reintroduced the tax in 1842 and it has been levied ever since, forming an important part of government finance. At its lowest, from 1874 to 1876, it was 0.83%; at its highest, between 1941 and 1946, the standard rate was 50%.

In the UK, not all earnings are taxed. Individuals are permitted to a certain amount tax free – this is known as their tax allowance; employees' tax is deducted under the PAYE system. In 1993, there were three rates of income tax: 20%, 25%, and 40%. A major change in the UK system of taxation was introduced on 6 April 1996. The self-assessment system, in force since the tax year 1996–97, does not affect the amount of tax payable, but requires the taxpayer to deliver a completed tax return and optionally also calculate the amount of income tax due. Prior to 1996–97, the Inland Revenue would raise the appropriate assessment, or assessments, showing the amount of tax due based on tax returns which showed profits, income, and so on. The impact of self-assessment is largely limited to those who are self-employed, those with investment income liable to a higher income tax rate, and those receiving income from the exploitation of land. For the most part, employees whose tax is deducted under the PAYE system are not affected by the new system.

incontinence failure or inability to control evacuation of the bladder or bowel (or both in the case of double incontinence). It may arise as a result of injury, childbirth, disease, or senility.

incorporation in law, the formation of an association that has corporate personality and is therefore distinct from its individual members, who have no liability for its debts. Corporations (such as companies) can own property and have their own rights and liabilities in legal proceedings.

incubus in the popular belief of the Middle Ages in Europe, a male demon who had sexual intercourse with women in their sleep. Supposedly the women then gave birth to witches and demons. **Succubus** is the female equivalent.

indemnity in law, an undertaking to compensate another for damage, loss, trouble, or expenses, or the money paid by way of such compensation – for example, under fire-insurance agreements.

indentured labour work under a restrictive contract of employment for a fixed period in a foreign country in exchange for payment of passage, accommodation, and food. Indentured labour was the means by which many British people emigrated to North America during the colonial era, and in the 19th–early 20th centuries it was used to recruit Asian workers for employment elsewhere in European colonial empires.

Independence city in western Missouri, USA, a suburb of ▷Kansas City, on the Missouri River; seat of Jackson County; population (1994 est) 112,000. It is the centre of an agricultural region; industries include steel, agricultural machinery, Portland cement, petroleum refining, and flour milling.

Independence Day public holiday in the USA commemorating the adoption of the ▷Declaration of Independence, 4 July 1776.

INDEPENDENCE DAY American July 4 celebrations, in an illustration by Charles G Bush, about 1860. *Archive Photos*

independent school in the UK, a school run privately without direct assistance from the state. Just over 7% of children (1998) attend private fee-paying schools. There are some 2,420 independent schools in Britain, with about 600,000 pupils. A group of old-established and prestigious independent schools are known as ▷public schools. Pupil numbers fell back for the first time in a decade in 1993.

The independent sector includes most boarding education in the UK. Although most independent secondary schools operate a highly selective admissions policy for entrants at the age of 11 or 13, some specialize in the teaching of slow learners or difficult children and a few follow particular philosophies of progressive education.

Related Web site: Independent Schools Information Service
http://www.isis.org.uk/

indeterminacy principle alternative name for ▷uncertainty principle.

index in economics, an indicator of a general movement in wages and prices over a specified period.

index (plural **indices**; Latin 'sign, indicator') in mathematics, another term for ▷exponent, the number that indicates the power to which a term should be raised.

India see country box.

India Acts legislation passed in 1858, 1919, and 1935 which formed the basis of British rule in India until independence in 1947. The 1858 Act abolished the administrative functions of the British ▷East India Company, replacing them with direct rule from London. The 1919 Act increased Indian participation at local and provincial levels but did not meet nationalist demands for complete internal self-government (▷Montagu-Chelmsford reforms). The 1935 Act outlined a federal structure but was never implemented.

Indiana state of the midwest USA. It is nicknamed the Hoosier State. Indiana was admitted to the Union in 1816 as the 19th US state. It is bordered to the northeast by Michigan, to the east by Ohio, to the south and southeast by Kentucky, and to the west by Illinois. In the northwest, Indiana has a shoreline of *c.* 72 km/45 mi on Lake Michigan.

population (1995) 5,803,500 **area** 93,700 sq km/36,168 sq mi
capital ▷Indianapolis **towns and cities** Fort Wayne, Gary, Evansville, South Bend **industries and products** maize, pigs, cattle, soybeans, limestone, machinery, electrical goods, coal, steel, iron, chemicals, glass, oil

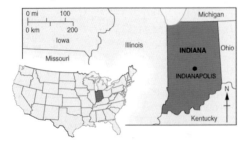

Indianapolis state capital and largest city of ▷Indiana, on the White River, 300 km/186 mi southeast of Chicago; seat of Marion County; population (1994 est) 752,000; population of metropolitan area (1992) 1,424,000. Situated in the rich Corn Belt agricultural region, the city is an industrial centre; products include electronic components, pharmaceuticals, processed foods, machinery, plastics, and rubber. It is the venue for the Indianapolis 500 car race.

Indian art the arts of the Indian subcontinent (present-day India, Pakistan, and Bangladesh). Indian art dates back to the ancient Indus Valley civilization, about 3000–1500 BC, centred on the cities of Harappa and ▷Mohenjo Daro. Surviving artefacts reflect the influence of ▷Mesopotamian art. Beginning about 1800 BC, the Aryan invasions gave rise to the Hindu religion and arts celebrating its gods, heroes, and scenes from the two great epics, the *Mahābhārata* and the *Rāmāyana*. From the 6th century BC, Buddhist art developed, following the life and enlightenment of the Buddha Sakyamuni. A third strand was added in the 16th–17th centuries when the Mogul Empire introduced ▷Islamic art to the subcontinent.

Buddhist art Early Buddhist art developed in relation to the architecture of the stupa (temple shrines to the Buddha and his disciples), typically using symbols to represent the Buddha. The first appearance of the Buddha in human form was in the sculptures of the Mathura tradition (2nd century BC) and those of Gandhara (2nd–6th centuries BC) – possibly the greatest school of Buddhist sculpture. The Gandhara sculptures show Greek influence and, along with the Buddhist religion, were exported to China, Korea, and Japan. The profound depth of relief of the Mathura work was followed by the gentler sculptures of Gupta (about 5th century AD). The Ajanta caves near Mumbai (formerly Bombay), first begun about 200 BC, contain the finest example of Gupta art – mural paintings from the 5th–7th centuries which, though religious in intent, reflect a sophisticated, courtly society.

Hindu art From the 4th century AD, influenced by Buddhist art, Hindu artists created huge temple complexes; for example, at Orissa, Konarak, and ▷Khajurāho. They also built cave sanctuaries, the most famous being at Elephanta, near Mumbai, with a monumental depiction of the three forces of creation, preservation, and destruction, portrayed as Shiva with three heads. The caves at Ellora feature an ensemble of religious art (Buddhist, Hindu, and Jain) dating from the 6th and 7th centuries. At Khajurāho, celestial dancing girls, the Asparas, adorn the temple facades. Later Hindu art includes the jewel-like depictions from the lives of Krishna and Rama in palm-leaf manuscripts, known as Rajput paintings.

Mogul art From the 11th century, Muslim invaders destroyed Buddhist and Hindu temple art and introduced the mosque and, with it, Islamic art styles. By the 16th century, the Moguls had established an extensive empire. Persian painters were imported and Hindu artists trained in their workshops, a fusion that formed part of the liberal emperor ▷Akbar's cultural plan and resulted in the exquisite miniature paintings of the courts of ▷Jahangir and ▷Shah Jahan. The subjects of miniature painting ranged from portraiture and histories to birds, animals, and flowers.

INDIAN ART A painting from the Ajanta caves, India. These Buddhist cave temples, which date from 200 BC to the 7th century AD, were cut from solid granite, and are decorated with many such paintings. *Philip Sauvain Picture Collection*

Indian corn another name for ▷maize.

Indian languages traditionally, the languages of the subcontinent of India; since 1947, the languages of the Republic of India. These number some 200, depending on whether a variety is classified as a language or a dialect. They fall into five main groups, the two most widespread of which are the Indo-European languages (mainly in the north) and the Dravidian languages (mainly in the south).

Indian literature literature of the Indian subcontinent, written in Sanskrit, in the Dravidian languages such as Tamil, in the vernacular languages derived from Sanskrit, such as Urdu and Hindi, and, largely in the 20th century, English.

Sanskrit The oldest surviving examples of Indian literature are the sacred Hindu texts from the Vedic period of about 1500–200 BC. These include the ▷Vedas and the later *Upanishads* 800–200 BC, which are philosophical reflections upon the *Vedas*. Of the same period are the *Sutras* 500–200 BC, collections of aphorisms and doctrinal summaries, including the *Kamasutra* on erotic love. During the epic period (400 BC–AD 400) two major epics were written down: the ▷*Mahābhārata* (which contains the ▷*Bhagavad-Gītā*) and the shorter ▷*Rāmāyana*, both about 300 BC. By the classical period (from AD 400), lyric poetry, romances, and drama had developed, the leading poet and dramatist of the period being ▷Kālidāsa. The *Panchatantra*, a collection of Hindu myths, were written down in the 4th century AD.

Dravidian The Dravidian languages of the south, which are unrelated to Sanskrit, had their own strong and ancient literary traditions, though gradually they were influenced by the literatures of the north. The two major works of Tamil are the verse anthologies the *Pattuppattu* and the *Ettutogaiad*, both 1st century AD.

Vernacular By AD 1000 extensive vernacular literatures had developed – largely through popularizations of Sanskrit classics – in those languages derived from Sanskrit, such as Urdu, Hindi, and Gujarati. From the 17th century, Urdu poetry flourished at the Mogul court, where it was strongly influenced by classical Persian literature. The poets Asadullah Ghalib (1797–1869) and Muhammad Iqbāl wrote in Urdu and Persian. Bengali literature in particular was encouraged by the wide use of printing presses in the 19th century. Bengali writers include Bankim Chandra Chatterji, Romesh Chunder Dutt (1848–1909), and Rabindranath Tagore who was awarded the Nobel Prize for Literature 1913. The spiritual and political leader Mahatma Gandhi wrote in Gujarati.

Indian Mutiny (or **Sepoy Rebellion** or **Mutiny**) revolt of Indian soldiers (sepoys) against the British in India from 1857 to 1858. The uprising was confined to the north, from Bengal to the Punjab, and central India. It led to the end of rule by the ▷British East India Company and its replacement by direct British crown administration.

Indian National Congress (INC) official name for the ▷Congress Party of India.

Indian Ocean ocean between Africa and Australia, with India to the north, and the southern boundary being an arbitrary line from Cape Agulhas to south Tasmania; area 73,500,000 sq km/28,370,000 sq mi; average depth 3,872 m/12,708 ft. The greatest depth is the Java Trench 7,725 m/25,353 ft. It includes two great bays on either side of the Indian peninsula, the Bay of Bengal to the east, and the Arabian Sea with the gulfs of Aden and Oman to the west.

INDIA The landscape of Kashmir is mostly mountainous, but there are several large river valleys such as this one, the Liddar Valley. *Image Bank*

Indian Removal Act US federal act signed by President Andrew ▷Jackson on 28 May 1830 empowering him to offer land in ▷Indian Territory to all American Indians situated east of the Mississippi River, in exchange for their lands there. Most northern American Indian peoples, except the Iroquois, were peacefully relocated, but the ▷Five Civilized Tribes in the southeast refused. The ▷Cherokees successfully challenged the removal laws in the US Supreme Court in 1832, but the ruling was ignored by President Andrew Jackson. The Florida Seminoles fought relocation for seven years in the second Seminole Wars 1835–42. Nearly 100,000 American Indians were forcibly relocated and between a quarter and a third died during the journey and resettlement. Tennessee Senator Davy ▷Crockett was among those who spoke out against the Act.

Indian Reorganization Act US federal act passed in 18 June 1934, aimed at re-establishing government by American Indian peoples and preserving American Indian culture. A survey of reservation life under the ▷Dawes General Allotment Act discovered appalling living conditions and recommended drastic reforms. The Indian Reorganization Act returned thousands of acres of land to reservations, provided federal financial and technical aid to ethnic groups, supplied health and education services, and encouraged the adoption of written constitutions. The Act forms the basis of current federal legislation on American Indians.

Indian Territory initially most of the land west of the Mississippi River; after 1834 the term was restricted to the present state of Oklahoma. After the Indian Relocation Act of 1830, most of the American Indians east of the Mississippi were relocated to Indian Territory, some forcibly, including the ▷Five Civilized Tribes 1835–43. Indian Territory became the Territory of Oklahoma in 1890; 'Oklahoma' means 'red people' in the Choctaw language.

India of the Princes the 562 Indian states ruled by princes during the period of British control. They occupied an area of 1,854,347 sq km/715,967 sq mi (45% of the total area of pre-partition India) and had a population of over 93 million. At the partition of British India in 1947 the princes were given independence by the British government but were advised to adhere to either India or Pakistan. Between 1947 and 1950 all except Kashmir were incorporated in either country.

indicator in chemistry, a compound that changes its structure and colour in response to its environment. The commonest chemical indicators detect changes in ▷pH (for example, ▷litmus and ▷universal indicator), or in the oxidation state of a system (redox indicators).

indicator species plant or animal whose presence or absence in an area indicates certain environmental conditions, such as soil type, high levels of pollution, or, in rivers, low levels of dissolved oxygen. Many plants show a preference for either alkaline or acid soil conditions, while certain trees require aluminium, and are found only in soils where it is present. Some lichens are sensitive to sulphur dioxide in the air, and absence of these species indicates atmospheric pollution.

indie (short for independent) in music, a record label that is neither owned nor distributed by one of the large conglomerates ('majors') that dominate the industry. Without a corporate bureaucratic structure, the independent labels are often quicker to respond to new trends and more idealistic in their aims. What has become loosely known as **indie music** therefore tends to be experimental, amateurish, or at the cutting edge of street fashion.

indigenous the people, animals, or plants that are native to a country, but especially a people whose territory has been colonized by others (particularly Europeans). In 1995 it was estimated that there were approximately 220 million indigenous people in the world. Examples of indigenous peoples include Australian Aborigines and American Indians. A World Council of Indigenous Peoples is based in Canada. The United Nations declared 1993 the International Year of Indigenous Peoples.

indigo violet-blue vegetable dye obtained from various tropical plants such as the anil, but now replaced by a synthetic product. It was once a major export crop of India. (Plant genus *Indigofera*, family Leguminosae.)

indium (Latin *indicum* 'indigo') soft, ductile, silver-white, metallic element, symbol In, atomic number 49, relative atomic mass 114.82. It occurs in nature in some zinc ores, is resistant to abrasion, and is used as a coating on metal parts. It was discovered in 1863 by German metallurgists Ferdinand Reich (1799–1882) and Hieronymus Richter (1824–1898), who named it after the two indigo lines of its spectrum.

individualism in politics, a view in which the individual takes precedence over the collective: the opposite of ▷collectivism. The term **possessive individualism** has been applied to the writings of John ▷Locke and Jeremy ▷Bentham, describing society as comprising individuals interacting through market relations.

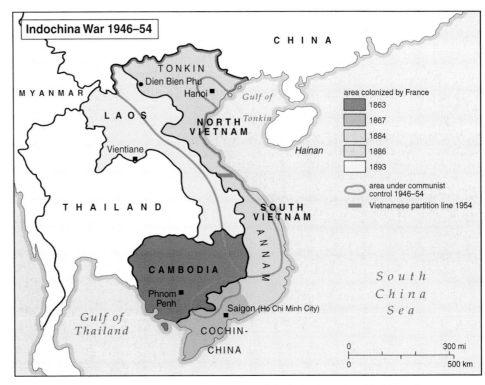

Indochina War 1946–54

area colonized by France
1863
1867
1884
1886
1893

area under communist control 1946–54

Vietnamese partition line 1954

Indo-Aryan languages another name for the ▷Indo-European languages.

Indochina, French name given by the French to their colonies in Southeast Asia: ▷Cambodia, ▷Laos, and ▷Vietnam, which became independent after World War II.

Indochina War war of independence 1946–54 between the nationalist forces of what was to become Vietnam and France, the occupying colonial power.

In 1945 Vietnamese nationalist communist leader ▷Ho Chi Minh proclaimed an independent Vietnamese republic, which soon began an armed struggle against French forces. France in turn set up a noncommunist state four years later. In 1954, after the siege of ▷Dien Bien Phu, a ceasefire was agreed between France and China that resulted in the establishment of two separate states, North and South Vietnam, divided by the 17th parallel. Attempts at reunification of the country led subsequently to the ▷Vietnam War.

Indo-European languages family of languages that includes some of the world's major classical languages (Sanskrit and Pali in India, Zend Avestan in Iran, Greek and Latin in Europe), as well as several of the most widely spoken languages (English worldwide; Spanish in Iberia, Latin America, and elsewhere; and the Hindi group of languages in northern India). Indo-European languages were once located only along a geographical band from India through Iran into northwestern Asia, Eastern Europe, the northern Mediterranean lands, northern and Western Europe and the British Isles.

Indo-Germanic languages former name for the ▷Indo-European languages.

Indonesia see country box.

Indra Hindu god of the sky, shown as a four-armed man on a white elephant, carrying a thunderbolt. The intoxicating drink ▷soma is associated with him.

induced current electric current that appears in a closed circuit when there is relative movement of its conductor in a magnetic field. The effect is known as the **dynamo effect**, and is used in all ▷dynamos and generators to produce electricity. See ▷electromagnetic induction.

inductance in physics, phenomenon in which a changing current in a circuit builds up a magnetic field which induces an ▷electromotive force either in the same circuit and opposing the current (self-inductance) or in another circuit (mutual inductance). The SI unit of inductance is the henry (symbol H).

A component designed to introduce inductance into a circuit is called an ▷inductor (sometimes inductance) and is usually in the form of a coil of wire. The energy stored in the magnetic field of the coil is proportional to its inductance and the current flowing through it. See ▷electromagnetic induction.

induction in obstetrics, deliberate intervention to initiate labour before it starts naturally; then it usually proceeds normally.

Induction involves rupture of the fetal membranes (amniotomy) and the use of the hormone oxytocin to stimulate contractions of the womb. In biology, induction is a term used for various processes, including the production of an ▷enzyme in response to a particular chemical in the cell, and the ▷differentiation of cells in an ▷embryo in response to the presence of neighbouring tissues.

induction coil type of electrical transformer, similar to an ignition coil, that produces an intermittent high-voltage alternating current from a low-voltage direct current supply.

inductor device included in an electrical circuit because of its inductance.

indulgence in the Roman Catholic Church, the total or partial remission of temporal punishment for sins that remain to be expiated after penitence and confession have secured exemption from eternal punishment. The doctrine of indulgence began as the commutation of church penances in exchange for suitable works of charity or money gifts to the church, and became a great source of church revenue. This trade in indulgences roused Martin Luther to post his 95 theses on the church door in Wittenberg, and so initiated the Reformation in 1517. The Council of Trent (1563) recommended moderate retention of indulgences, and they continue, notably in 'Holy Years'.

Related Web site: Indulgences http://www.newadvent.org/cathen/07783a.htm

Der Ablaßhandel im Anfang des 16. Jahrhunderts.
Holzschnitt von Jörg Breu d. Ä.

INDULGENCE A woodcarving showing Johann Tetzel selling indulgences in Wittenberg (1517). *Philip Sauvain Picture Collection*

Indus river in Asia, rising in Tibet and flowing 3,180 km/1,975 mi to the Arabian Sea. In 1960 the use of its waters, including those of its five tributaries (rivers Ravi, Beas,

(continued on p. 477)

India

INDIA The palace in Jaipur, the capital of Rajasthan, India. The intricate latticed windows allowed the courtiers to look out on the city below unobserved from the street. They also allowed cooling breezes to enter. *Corel*

India country in southern Asia, bounded to the north by China, Nepal, and Bhutan; east by Myanmar and Bangladesh; northwest by Pakistan and Afghanistan; and southeast, south, and southwest by the Indian Ocean.

NATIONAL NAME *Bharat* (Hindi)/*India*; *Bharatiya Janarajya* (unofficial)/*Republic of India*
AREA 3,166,829 sq km/1,222,713 sq mi
CAPITAL New Delhi
MAJOR TOWNS/CITIES Mumbai (formerly Bombay), Kolkata (formerly Calcutta), Chennai (formerly Madras), Bangalore, Hyderabad, Ahmadabad, Kanpur, Pune, Nagpur, Bhopal, Jaipur, Lucknow, Surat
MAJOR PORTS Kolkata, Mumbai, Chennai
PHYSICAL FEATURES Himalayas on northern border; plains around rivers Ganges, Indus, Brahmaputra; Deccan peninsula south of the Narmada River forms plateau between Western and Eastern Ghats mountain ranges; desert in west; Andaman and Nicobar Islands, Lakshadweep (Laccadive Islands)

Government

HEAD OF STATE Abdul Kalam from 2002
HEAD OF GOVERNMENT Atal Behari Vajpayee from 1998
POLITICAL SYSTEM liberal democracy
POLITICAL EXECUTIVE parliamentary
ADMINISTRATIVE DIVISIONS 28 states and seven centrally administered union territories
ARMED FORCES 1,298,000 (2002 est)
CONSCRIPTION none, although all citizens are constitutionally obliged to perform national service when called upon
DEATH PENALTY retained and used for ordinary crimes
DEFENCE SPEND (% GDP) 2.7 (2002 est)

EDUCATION SPEND (% GDP) 4.1 (2000 est)
HEALTH SPEND (% GDP) 4.9 (2000 est)

Economy and resources

CURRENCY rupee
GPD (US$) 515.0 billion (2002 est)
REAL GDP GROWTH (% change on previous year) 5.4 (2001)
GNI (US$) 501.53 billion (2002 est)
GNI PER CAPITA (PPP) (US$) 2,570 (2002 est)
CONSUMER PRICE INFLATION 4.1% (2003 est)
UNEMPLOYMENT 9.2% (2001)
FOREIGN DEBT (US$) 87.7 billion (2001 est)
MAJOR TRADING PARTNERS USA, UK, Germany, Japan, Belgium, China, Switzerland, United Arab Emirates
RESOURCES coal, iron ore, copper ore, bauxite, chromite, gold, manganese ore, zinc, lead, limestone, crude oil, natural gas, diamonds
INDUSTRIES mining (including coal, iron and manganese ores, diamonds, and gold), manufacturing (iron and steel, mineral oils, shipbuilding, chemical products, road transport, cotton cloth, sugar, petroleum refining products)
EXPORTS tea (world's largest producer), coffee, fish, iron and steel, leather, textiles, clothing, polished diamonds, handmade carpets, engineering goods, chemicals. Principal market: USA 20.9% (2000)
IMPORTS nonelectrical machinery, mineral fuels and lubricants, pearls, precious and semiprecious stones, chemicals, transport equipment. Principal source: UK 6.3% (2001)

ARABLE LAND 54.4% (2000 est)
AGRICULTURAL PRODUCTS cotton, tea, wheat, rice, coffee, cashew nuts, jute, spices, sugar cane, oil seeds

Population and society

POPULATION 1,065,462,000 (2003 est)
POPULATION GROWTH RATE 1.3% (2000–15)
POPULATION DENSITY (per sq km) 324 (2003 est)
URBAN POPULATION (% of total) 28 (2003 est)
AGE DISTRIBUTION (% of total population) 0–14 33%, 15–59 59%, 60+ 8% (2002 est)
ETHNIC GROUPS 72% of Indo-Aryan descent; 25% (predominantly in south) Dravidian; 3% Mongoloid
LANGUAGE Hindi, English, Assamese, Bengali, Gujarati, Kannada, Kashmiri, Konkani, Malayalam, Manipuri, Marathi, Nepali, Oriya, Punjabi, Sanskrit, Sindhi, Tamil, Telugu, Urdu (all official), more than 1,650 dialects

RELIGION Hindu 80%, Sunni Muslim 10%, Christian 2.5%, Sikh 2%, Buddhist, Jewish
EDUCATION (compulsory years) 8
LITERACY RATE 70% (men); 48% (women) (2003 est)
LABOUR FORCE 61% agriculture, 17% industry, 22% services (1997 est)
LIFE EXPECTANCY 63 (men); 65 (women) (2000–05)
CHILD MORTALITY RATE (under 5, per 1,000 live births) 93 (2001)
PHYSICIANS (per 1,000 people) 0.5 (1999 est)
HOSPITAL BEDS (per 1,000 people) 0.9 (1999 est)
TV SETS (per 1,000 people) 83 (2001 est)
RADIOS (per 1,000 people) 121 (1997)
INTERNET USERS (per 10,000 people) 159.1 (2002 est)
PERSONAL COMPUTER USERS (per 100 people) 0.7 (2002 est)

See also ▷Buddhism; ▷Congress Party; ▷East India Company; ▷Gandhi; ▷Hinduism; ▷Kashmir.

India (cont.)

Chronology

c. 2500–1500 BC: The earliest Indian civilization evolved in the Indus Valley with the city states of Harappa and Mohenjo Daro.

c. 1500–1200 BC: Aryan peoples from the northwest overran northern India and the Deccan; Brahmanism (a form of Hinduism) developed.

321 BC: Chandragupta, founder of the Mauryan dynasty, began to unite northern India in a Hindu Empire.

268–232 BC: Mauryan Empire reached its height under Asoka, who ruled two-thirds of India from his capital Pataliputra.

c. 180 BC: Shunga dynasty replaced the Mauryans; Hindu Empire began to break up into smaller kingdoms.

AD 320–480: Gupta dynasty reunified northern India.

c. 500: Raiding Huns from central Asia destroyed the Gupta dynasty; India reverted to many warring kingdoms.

11th–12th centuries: Rajput princes of northern India faced repeated Muslim invasions by Arabs, Turks, and Afghans, and in 1206 the first Muslim dynasty was established at Delhi.

14th–16th centuries: Muslim rule extended over northern India and the Deccan; south remained independent under the Hindu Vijayanagar dynasty.

1498: Explorer Vasco da Gama reached India, followed by Portuguese, Dutch, French, and English traders.

1526: Last Muslim invasion: Zahir ud-din Muhammad (Babur) defeated the Sultan of Delhi at Battle of Panipat and established the Mogul Empire, which was consolidated by Akbar the Great (1556–1605).

1600: East India Company founded by English merchants, who settled in Madras, Bombay, and Calcutta.

17th century: Mogul Empire reached its zenith under Jahangir (1605–27), Shah Jehan (1628–58), and Aurangzeb (1658–1707).

1739: Persian king Nadir Shah invaded India and destroyed Mogul prestige; the British and French supported rival Indian princes in subsequent internal wars.

1757: Battle of Plassey: Robert Clive defeated Siraj al-Daulah, nawab of Bengal; Bengal came under control of the British East India Company.

1772–85: Warren Hastings, British governor general of Bengal, raised the Indian army and pursued expansionist policies.

early 19th century: British took control throughout India by defeating powerful Indian states in a series of regional wars.

1858: 'Indian Mutiny': mutiny in Bengal army erupted into widespread anti-British revolt; rebels sought to restore Mogul emperor.

1858: British defeated the rebels; East India Company dissolved; India came under the British crown.

1885: Indian National Congress founded in Bombay as a focus for nationalism.

1909: Morley–Minto Reforms: Indians received the right to elect members of Legislative Councils; Hindus and Muslims formed separate electorates.

1919: British forces killed 379 Indian demonstrators at Amritsar; India Act (Montagu–Chelmsford Reforms) conceded a measure of provincial self-government.

1920–22: Mohandas Gandhi won control of the Indian National Congress, which launched a campaign of civil disobedience in support of the demand for complete self-rule.

1935: India Act provided for Indian control of federal legislature, with defence and external affairs remaining the viceroy's responsibility.

1940: Muslim League called for India to be partitioned along religious lines.

1947: British India partitioned into two independent dominions of India (mainly Hindu) and Pakistan (mainly Muslim) amid bloody riots; Jawaharlal Nehru of Congress Party became prime minister.

1950: India became a republic within the Commonwealth.

1962: India lost a brief border war with China; retained Kashmir in war with Pakistan in 1965.

1966: Indira Gandhi, daughter of Nehru, became prime minister.

1971: India defeated Pakistan in a war and helped East Pakistan become independent as Bangladesh.

1975: Found guilty of electoral corruption, Mrs Gandhi declared a state of emergency and arrested opponents.

1977–79: The Janata Party formed a government under Morarji Desai.

1980: Mrs Gandhi, heading a Congress Party splinter group, Congress (I), was returned to power.

1984: Troops cleared Sikh separatists from the Golden Temple, Amritsar; Mrs Gandhi was assassinated by Sikh bodyguards; her son Rajiv Gandhi became prime minister.

1989: After financial scandals, Congress lost elections; V P Singh formed a Janata Dal minority government.

1990: Direct rule was imposed on Jammu and Kashmir after an upsurge in Muslim separatist violence; rising interethnic and religious conflict was seen in the Punjab and elsewhere.

1992: The destruction of a mosque at Ayodhya, northern India, by Hindu extremists resulted in widespread violence.

1995: Bombay was renamed Mumbai.

1997: Kocheril Raman Narayanan became the first 'untouchable' to be elected president.

1998: Atal Behari Vajpayee, leader of the Bharatiya Janata party, was elected prime minister. The creation of three new states was proposed. India carried out five underground nuclear explosions, meeting with international condemnation.

1999: The Indian government renounced further nuclear weapons testing and promised to sign the Comprehensive Test Ban Treaty. India used air power to attack 'infiltrators' in Kashmir. Kashmir peace talks were offered to Pakistan.

2000: Relations with Pakistan worsened after India accused Pakistan of involvement (which it denied) of the hijacking of an Indian airliner by Kashmiri militants. Three new states are created: Uttaranchal is carved out of Uttar Pradesh, Jharkhand out of Bihar, and Chattisgarh out of Madhya Pradesh. India declared a unilateral ceasefire in Kashmir in November, renewing it twice over the following months.

2001: Over 30,000 people were killed in an earthquake in Gujarat. A census showed the population exceeded one billion.

2002: Hindu–Muslim clashes in Gujarat led to around 800 deaths, and the Indian supreme court barred all religious activity at a disputed site in Ayodhya that is sacred to both faiths.

2003: International tensions between India and Pakistan were re-ignited as a massacre of 24 Hindus by Islamic militants in Indian-administered Kashmir was followed by the test-firing by both countries of missiles capable of delivering nuclear weapons. However India and Pakistan went on to begin their first formal ceasefire in the disputed territory in 20 years.

India: States and Union Territories

State	Capital	Area sq km	Area sq mi	Population (2001 est)
Andhra Pradesh	Hyderabad	275,045	106,195	81,293,000
Arunachal Pradesh	Itanagar	83,743	32,333	1,163,000
Assam	Dispur	78,438	30,285	27,428,000
Bihar	Patna	173,877	67,134	77,633,000
Goa	Panaji	3,702	1,429	1,364,000
Gujarat	Gandhinagar	196,024	75,685	50,612,000
Haryana	Chandigarh	44,212	17,070	20,821,000
Himachal Pradesh	Shimla	55,673	21,495	6,235,000
Jammu and Kashmir[1]	Srinagar	222,236	85,805	9,763,000
Karnataka	Bangalore	191,791	74,051	54,907,000
Kerala	Trivandrum	38,863	15,005	33,462,000
Madhya Pradesh	Bhopal	443,446	171,215	64,920,000
Maharashtra	Mumbai[2]	307,713	118,808	97,663,000
Manipur	Imphal	22,327	8,620	2,373,000
Meghalaya	Shillong	22,429	8,660	2,324,000
Mizoram	Aizawl	21,081	8,139	976,000
Nagaland	Kohima	16,579	6,401	1,817,000
Orissa	Bhubaneshwar	155,707	60,118	37,557,000
Punjab	Chandigarh	50,400	19,454	24,475,000
Rajasthan	Jaipur	342,239	132,138	56,728,000
Sikkim	Gangtok	7,096	2,740	516,000
Tamil Nadu	Chennai[3]	130,058	50,215	64,158,000
Tripura	Agartala	10,486	4,049	3,631,000
Uttar Pradesh	Lucknow	294,411	113,672	164,346,000
West Bengal	Calcutta	88,752	34,267	83,438,000
Union Territory				
Andaman and Nicobar Islands	Port Blair	8,249	3,185	381,000
Chandigarh	Chandigarh	114	44	976,000
Dadra and Nagar Haveli	Silvassa	491	190	186,000
Daman and Diu	Daman	112	43	133,000
Delhi	Delhi	1,483	573	13,660,000
Lakshadweep	Kavaratti	32	12	65,000
Pondicherry	Pondicherry	492	190	1,052,000

[1] Includes area occupied by Pakistan and China.
[2] Prior to 1995 called Bombay.
[3] Prior to 1996 called Madras.

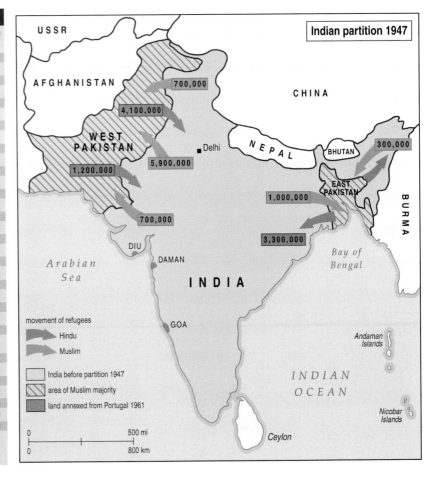

Indian partition 1947

Indonesia

INDONESIA A Sasak potter in Masbagik village, Indonesia. *Image Bank*

Indonesia formerly Dutch East Indies (until 1949) country in southeast Asia, made up of 13,677 islands situated on or near the Equator, between the Indian and Pacific oceans. It is the world's fourth most populous country, surpassed only by China, India, and the USA.

NATIONAL NAME *Republik Indonesia/Republic of Indonesia*
AREA 1,904,569 sq km/735,354 sq mi
CAPITAL Jakarta
MAJOR TOWNS/CITIES Surabaya, Bandung, Medan, Semarang, Palembang, Tangerang, Bandar Lampung, Ujung Pandang, Malang
MAJOR PORTS Tanjung Priok, Surabaya, Semarang (Java), Ujung Pandang (Sulawesi)
PHYSICAL FEATURES comprises 13,677 tropical islands (over 6,000 of them are inhabited): the Greater Sundas (including Java, Madura, Sumatra, Sulawesi, and Kalimantan (part of Borneo)), the Lesser Sunda Islands/Nusa Tenggara (including Bali, Lombok, Sumbawa, Flores, Sumba, Alor, Lomblen, Timor, Roti, and Savu), Maluku/Moluccas (over 1,000 islands including Ambon, Ternate, Tidore, Tanimbar, and Halmahera), and Irian Jaya (part of New Guinea); over half the country is tropical rainforest; it has the largest expanse of peatlands in the tropics

Government

HEAD OF STATE AND GOVERNMENT Megawati Sukarnoputri from 2001
POLITICAL SYSTEM emergent democracy
POLITICAL EXECUTIVE limited presidency
ADMINISTRATIVE DIVISIONS 27 provinces, subdivided into 55 municipalities
ARMED FORCES 297,000; plus paramilitary forces of 195,000 (2002 est)
DEATH PENALTY retained and used for ordinary crimes

Economy and resources

CURRENCY rupiah
GPD (US$) 172.9 billion (2002 est)
REAL GDP GROWTH (% change on previous year) 3.3 (2001)
GNI (US$) 149.9 billion (2002 est)
GNI PER CAPITA (PPP) (US$) 2,990 (2002 est)
CONSUMER PRICE INFLATION 9% (2003 est)
UNEMPLOYMENT 9.4% (2001)
FOREIGN DEBT (US$) 97.3 billion (2001 est)
MAJOR TRADING PARTNERS Japan, Singapore, USA, Australia, South Korea, Germany, the Netherlands
RESOURCES petroleum (principal producer of petroleum in the Far East), natural gas, bauxite, nickel (world's third-largest producer), copper, tin (world's second-largest producer), gold, coal, forests
INDUSTRIES petroleum refining, food processing, textiles, wood products, tobacco, chemicals, fertilizers, rubber, cement
EXPORTS textiles and garments, petroleum and petroleum products, natural and manufactured gas, rubber, palm oil, wood and wood products, electrical and electronic products, coffee, fishery products, coal, copper, tin, pepper, tea. Principal market: Japan 25.6% (2001)
IMPORTS machinery, transport and electrical equipment, manufactured goods, chemical and mineral products. Principal source: Japan 22.5% (2001)
ARABLE LAND 11.3% (2000 est)
AGRICULTURAL PRODUCTS rice, cassava, maize, coffee, spices, tea, cocoa, tobacco, sugar cane, sweet potatoes, palm, rubber, coconuts, nutmeg; fishing

Population and society

POPULATION 219,883,000 (2003 est)
POPULATION GROWTH RATE 1.2% (2000–15)
POPULATION DENSITY (per sq km) 115 (2003 est)
URBAN POPULATION (% of total) 44 (2003 est)
AGE DISTRIBUTION (% of total population) 0–14 30%, 15–59 62%, 60+ 8% (2002 est)
ETHNIC GROUPS comprises more than 300 ethnic groups, the majority of which are of Malay descent; important Malay communities include Javanese (about 45% of the population), Sundanese (14%), and Madurese (7%); the largest non-Malay community is the Chinese (2%); substantial numbers of Indians, Melanesians, Micronesians, and Arabs
LANGUAGE Bahasa Indonesia (closely related to Malay; official), Javanese, Dutch, over 550 regional languages and dialects
RELIGION Muslim 87%, Protestant 6%, Roman Catholic 3%, Hindu 2% and Buddhist 1% (the continued spread of Christianity, together with an Islamic revival, have led to greater religious tensions)
EDUCATION (compulsory years) 6
LITERACY RATE 93% (men); 84% (women) (2003 est)
LABOUR FORCE 45.0% agriculture, 16.3% industry, 38.8% services (1998)
LIFE EXPECTANCY 65 (men); 67 (women) (2000–05)
CHILD MORTALITY RATE (under 5, per 1,000 live births) 45 (2001)
PHYSICIANS (per 1,000 people) 0.2 (1996 est)
HOSPITAL BEDS (per 1,000 people) 0.7 (1996 est)
TV SETS (per 1,000 people) 153 (2001 est)
RADIOS (per 1,000 people) 159 (2001 est)
INTERNET USERS (per 10,000 people) 377.2 (2002 est)
PERSONAL COMPUTER USERS (per 100 people) 1.2 (2002 est)

See also ▷Dutch East India Company; ▷Java; ▷Sumatra.

Chronology

3000–500 BC: Immigrants from southern China displaced original Melanesian population.

6th century AD: Start of Indian cultural influence; small Hindu and Buddhist kingdoms developed.

8th century: Buddhist maritime empire of Srivijaya expanded to include all Sumatra and Malay peninsula.

13th century: Islam introduced to Sumatra by Arab merchants; spread throughout the islands over next 300 years.

14th century: Eastern Javanese kingdom of Majapahit destroyed Srivijaya and dominated the region.

c. 1520: Empire of Majapahit disintegrated; Javanese nobles fled to Bali.

16th century: Portuguese merchants broke the Muslim monopoly on the spice trade.

1602: Dutch East India Company founded.

1619: Dutch East India Company captured the port of Jakarta in Java and renamed it Batavia.

17th century: Dutch introduced coffee plants and established informal control over central Java through divide-and-rule policy among local rulers.

1749: After frequent military intervention, the Dutch East India Company obtained formal sovereignty over Mataram.

1799: The Netherlands took over interests of bankrupt Dutch East India Company.

1808: French forces occupied Java; British expelled them in 1811 and returned Java to the Netherlands in 1816.

1824: Anglo-Dutch Treaty: Britain recognized entire Indonesian archipelago as Dutch sphere of influence.

1825–30: Java War: Prince Dipo Negoro led unsuccessful revolt against Dutch rule; further revolt 1894–96.

1908: Dutch completed conquest of Bali.

1927: Communist revolts suppressed; Achmed Sukarno founded Indonesian Nationalist Party (PNI) to unite diverse anti-Dutch elements.

1929: Dutch imprisoned Sukarno and tried to suppress PNI.

1942–45: Japanese occupation; PNI installed as anti-Western puppet government.

1945: When Japan surrendered, President Sukarno declared an independent republic, but the Dutch set about restoring colonial rule by force.

1947: Dutch 'police action': an all-out attack on Java and Sumatra conquered two-thirds of the republic.

1949: Under US pressure, the Dutch agreed to transfer sovereignty of the Netherlands Indies (except Dutch New Guinea or Irian Jaya) to the Republic of the United States of Indonesia.

1950: Sukarno abolished federalism and proclaimed unitary Republic of Indonesia dominated by Java; revolts in Sumatra and South Moluccas.

1959: To combat severe political instability, Sukarno imposed authoritarian 'guided democracy'.

1963: The Netherlands ceded Irian Jaya to Indonesia.

1968: Suharto formally replaced Sukarno as president and proclaimed 'New Order' under strict military rule.

1970s: Rising oil exports brought significant agricultural and industrial growth.

1975: Indonesia invaded East Timor when Portuguese rule collapsed; 200,000 died in ensuing war.

1986: After suppressing a revolt on Irian Jaya, Suharto introduced a programme to settle 65,000 Javanese there and on outer islands.

1996: The government initiated a crackdown on its opponents.

1997: Hundreds killed in ethnic riots in west Kalimantan province. Drought and famine in Irian Jaya. Forest fires in Borneo and Sumatra caused catastrophic environmental damage.

1998: Following mass riots, Suharto stepped down as president. There was some withdrawal of troops from East Timor and partial autonomy was offered. Irian Jaya's status as a military occupation zone ended, following a ceasefire agreement with separatist rebels. Troops killed 16 student demonstrators in Jakarta. Political parties were legalized.

1999: Ethnic violence continued in Borneo, with over 500 people killed. The government held its promised referendum on independence for East Timor on 30 August, but after an overwhelming vote in favour, pro-Indonesian militias rampaged through the country, killing hundreds and displacing thousands of citizens. Intervention by UN troops ended the violence. Abdurrahman Wahid became president in October 1999. He refused to rule out repression to solve the unrest in Aceh.

2000: Following violence between Muslims and Christians in Maluku, Indonesian Muslims called for a holy war in Maluku against the Christians. Jaya unilaterally declared independence. Corruption charges against ex-president Suharto were dropped on grounds of ill-health, but the high court overruled this and restarted the trial.

2001: Financial scandals involving President Wahid provoked riots. A temporary ceasefire was declared in Aceh, but collapsed when Wahid sent in troops.

2002: A massive car bomb exploded at a nightclub in the tourist centre of Kuta on the island of Bali, killing around 200 people and injuring 300. The Indonesian authorities blamed Islamic extremists. Christian and Muslim leaders from the eastern Molucca islands signed a peace accord to end three years of sectarian fighting which had claimed 5,000 lives since 1999 and created 750,000 refugees. The government and separatist rebels in Aceh province signed a peace deal aimed at ending three decades of fighting.

2003: Following the collapse of a ceasefire agreement with Aceh separatists, President Megawati declared martial law and launched a major military operation, involving up to 45,000 troops and paramilitary police, against the Free Aceh Movement.

(continued from p. 473)
Sutlej) and Pakistan (rivers Indus, Jhelum, Chenab). In the 3rd and 2nd millennia BC ▷Indus Valley civilization flourished at centres like Harappa and Mojenjo Daro.

industrial design branch of artistic activity that came into being as a result of the need to design machine-made products, introduced by the Industrial Revolution in the 18th century. The purpose of industrial design is to ensure that goods satisfy the demands of fashion, style, function, materials, and cost.

industrial dispute disagreement between an employer and its employees, usually represented by a trade union, over some aspect of the terms or conditions of employment. A dispute is often followed by industrial action, in the form of a ▷strike or a ▷work to rule.

industrial estate area planned for industry, where space is available for large buildings and further expansion. Industrial estates often have good internal road layouts and occupy accessible sites near main road junctions but away from the central business district.

industrialization process by which an increasing proportion of a country's economic activity is involved in industry. It is essential for economic development and largely responsible for the growth of cities (▷urbanization).

It is usually associated with the modernization of developing countries, beginning with the manufacture of simple goods that can replace imports.

industrial law (or **labour law**) the body of law relating to relationships between employers (and their representatives), employees (and their representatives), and government.

industrial relations relationship between employers and employees, and their dealings with each other. In most industries, wages and conditions are determined by **free collective bargaining** between employers and ▷trade unions. Some European and American countries have **worker participation** through profit-sharing and industrial democracy. Another solution is **co-ownership**, in which a company is entirely owned by its employees. The aim of good industrial relations is to achieve a motivated, capable workforce that sees its work as creative and fulfilling. A breakdown in industrial relations can lead to an industrial dispute where one party takes industrial action.

Industrial Revolution acceleration of technical and economic development that became evident in Britain in the second half of the 18th century. The traditional agricultural economy was replaced by one dominated by machinery and manufacturing, made possible through technical advances such as the steam engine. This transferred the balance of political power from the landowner to the industrial capitalist and created an urban working class. As the first country to have an industrial revolution, Britain for a while was the 'workshop of the world'. The Industrial Revolution, therefore, became the basis of 19th-century British world power and the British Empire. From 1830 to the early 20th century, the Industrial Revolution spread throughout Europe and the USA, and to Japan and the various colonial empires.

The term 'Industrial Revolution' has been criticized on the grounds that it implies a sudden and dramatic change, whereas the process of industrialization was long-drawn-out, erratic, and varied from industry to industry and from region to region.

    Related Web site: Industrial Revolution: A Trip to the Past
http://members.aol.com/mhirotsu/kevin/trip2.html

industrial sector any of the different groups into which industries may be divided: primary, secondary, tertiary, and quaternary. **Primary** industries extract or use raw materials; for example, mining and agriculture. **Secondary** industries are manufacturing industries, where raw materials are processed or components are assembled. **Tertiary** industries supply services such as retailing. The **quaternary** sector of industry is concerned with the professions and those services that require a high level of skill, expertise, and specialization. It includes education, research and development, administration, and financial services such as accountancy.

industrial tribunal independent panel that rules on disputes between employers and employees or trade unions relating to statutory terms and conditions of employment. Employment issues brought before it include unfair dismissal, redundancy, equal opportunities, and discrimination at work.

Industrial Workers of the World (**IWW**) labour movement founded in Chicago, USA in 1905, and in Australia in 1907, the members of which were popularly known as the **Wobblies**. The IWW was

> ## David Hume
> *Avarice, the spur of industry.*
> *Essays: Moral and Political,*
> *'Of Civil Liberty'*

dedicated to the overthrow of capitalism and the creation of a single union for workers, but divided on tactics.

industry the extraction and conversion of raw materials, the manufacture of goods, and the provision of services. Industry can be either low technology, unspecialized, and

Industrial Revolution: Key Events	
1701	The seed drill is invented by Jethro Tull. This is a critical point of the agrarian revolution which frees labour from the fields and lowers crop prices.
1709	Abraham Darby introduces coke smelting to his ironworks at Coalbrookdale in Shropshire.
1712	The first workable steam-powered engine is developed by Thomas Newcomen.
1740	Crucible steelmaking is discovered by Benjamin Huntsman, a clockmaker of Doncaster.
1759	The first Canal Act is passed by the British Parliament; this leads to the construction of a national network of inland waterways for transport and industrial supplies. By 1830 there are 6,500 km/4,000 mi of canals in Britain.
c. 1764	The spinning jenny, which greatly accelerates cotton spinning, is invented by James Hargreaves in Blackburn.
1764	Pierre Trosanquet, a French engineer, develops a new method of road building. Similar techniques are used by Thomas Telford in Britain to build modern roads from 1803.
1769	James Watt patented a more reliable and efficient version of the Newcomen engine.
1779	The spinning mule, which makes the production of fine yarns by machine possible, is developed in Bolton by Samuel Crompton.
1785	The power loom marks the start of the mechanized textile industry.
1794	The problem of supplying cotton fast enough for the textile industry is solved by Eli Whitney's cotton gin.
1797	The first true industrial lathe is invented, virtually simultaneously, by Henry Maudslay in England and David Wilkinson in the USA.
1798	Techniques of mass production of interchangeable parts are developed by the arms industry in the USA, led by Eli Whitney.
1802	The first electric battery capable of mass production is designed by William Cruickshank in England.
1811–16	Textile workers known as Luddites stage widespread protests against low pay and unemployment in Nottinghamshire, which involve destroying new machines.
c. 1812	The population of Manchester passes 100,000.
c. 1813	Industrial employment overtakes agricultural employment in England for the first time.
1825	The first regular railway services start between Stockton and Darlington in northeast England.
1826	The Journeymen Steam Engine Fitters, the first substantial industrial trade union, is established in Manchester.
1829	With his steam locomotive *Rocket*, English engineer George Stephenson wins a contest to design locomotives for the new Manchester–Liverpool railway.
1831–52	British industrial production doubles.
1832	Hippolyte Pixii of France produces a prototype electricity generator using magnets.
1832	The Reform Act concerning elections to the British Parliament gives representation to the industrial cities.
1833	The first effective Factory Act is passed in Britain regulating child labour in cotton mills.
c. 1840	The USA becomes the world leader for railroads, with over 5,000 km/3,000 mi laid. By 1860 this will rise to 50,000 km/30,000 mi.
1840s	Cornelius Vanderbilt and John Jacob Astor become the most prominent millionaires of the industrial age.
1842	Cotton-industry workers in England stage a widespread strike.
1846	Repeal of the Corn Law in Britain reduces agricultural prices, thereby helping industry.
1851	Britain celebrates its industrial achievements in the Great Exhibition.
1852–80	British industrial production doubles again.
1858	The 'great stink' of London dramatizes the increasing pollution in the cities.
c. 1860	New York City becomes the first US city with over 1 million inhabitants.

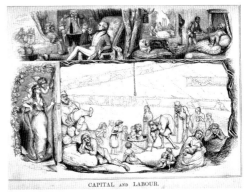

INDUSTRIAL REVOLUTION A *Punch* cartoon of 1844 entitled *Capital and Labour* contrasts the luxurious life of a mineowner with the harsh working conditions in the pits. *Philip Sauvain Picture Collection*

labour-intensive, as in countries with a large unskilled labour force, or highly automated, mechanized, and specialized, using advanced technology, as in the industrialized countries. Major recent trends in industrial activity have been the growth of electronic, robotic, and microelectronic technologies, the expansion of the offshore oil industry, and the prominence of Japan and other Pacific-region countries in manufacturing and distributing electronics, computers, and motor vehicles.

Indus Valley civilization one of the four earliest ancient civilizations of the Old World (the other three being the ▷Sumerian civilization of 3500 BC; ▷Egypt 3000 BC; and ▷China 2200 BC), developing in the northwest of the Indian subcontinent c. 2500 BC.

▷Mohenjo Daro and Harappa were the two main city complexes, but many more existed along the Indus Valley, now in Pakistan. Remains include grid-planned streets with municipal drainage, public and private buildings, baths, temples, and a standardized system of weights and measures – all of which testify to centralized political control. Evidence exists for trade with Sumer and Akkad. The ▷Aryan invasion of c. 1500 BC probably led to its downfall.

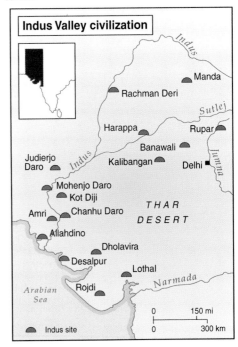

Indus Valley civilization

(Map shows sites: Manda, Rachman Deri, Harappa, Rupar, Judierjo Daro, Banawali, Kalibangan, Delhi, Mohenjo Daro, Kot Diji, Amri, Chanhu Daro, Allahdino, Dholavira, Desalpur, Lothal, Rojdi, Indus site; rivers Indus, Sutlej, Jumna, Narmada; THAR DESERT; Arabian Sea; scale 0 150 mi, 0 300 km)

inert gas (or **noble gas**) any of a group of six elements (helium, neon, argon, krypton, xenon, and radon), so named because they were originally thought not to enter into any chemical reactions. This is now known to be incorrect: in 1962, xenon was made to combine with fluorine, and since then, compounds of argon, krypton, and radon with fluorine and/or oxygen have been described.

The extreme unreactivity of the inert gases is due to the stability of their electronic structure. All the electron shells (energy levels) of inert gas atoms are full and, except for helium, they all have eight electrons in their outermost (▷valency) shell. The apparent stability of this electronic arrangement led to the formulation of the ▷octet rule to explain the different types of chemical bond found in simple compounds.

inertia in physics, the tendency of an object to remain in a state of rest or uniform motion until an external force is applied, as described by Isaac Newton's first law of motion (see ▷Newton's laws of motion).

INF abbreviation for **intermediate nuclear forces**, as in the ▷Intermediate Nuclear Forces Treaty.

infante (and infanta) title given in Spain and Portugal to the sons (other than the heir apparent) and daughters, respectively, of the sovereign. The heir apparent in Spain bears the title of prince of Asturias.

infanticide in law, the killing of a child under 12 months old, and more generally, any killing of a newborn child. It is often seen as a method of population control, especially among hunter-gatherers and nomadic societies where it may be impossible for a mother to carry around more than one small child and still perform the tasks necessary for survival. In some societies, especially in India and China, more girls are killed than boys because of the higher value placed on male offspring. It is estimated that more than one million children worldwide are killed each year because they are born female. Infanticide may also be practised on deformed or sick infants or for religious or ritual purposes; in some African societies twin births are thought to be supernatural and the twins are left to die.

infant mortality rate measure of the number of infants dying under one year of age, usually expressed as the number of deaths per 1,000 live births. Improved sanitation, nutrition, and medical care have considerably lowered figures throughout much of the world; for example in the 18th century in the USA and UK infant mortality was about 500 per thousand, compared with under 10 per thousand in 1989. The lowest infant mortality rate is in Japan, at 4.5 per 1,000 live births. In much of the developing world, however, the infant mortality rate remains high.

infection invasion of the body by disease-causing organisms (pathogens, or germs) that become established, multiply, and produce symptoms. Bacteria and viruses cause most diseases, but diseases are also caused by other micro-organisms, protozoans, and other parasites.

inferiority complex in psychology, a ▷complex or cluster of repressed fears, described by Alfred ▷Adler, based on physical inferiority. The term is popularly used to describe general feelings of inferiority and the overcompensation that often ensues.

inferior planet planet (Mercury or Venus) whose orbit lies within that of the Earth, best observed when at its greatest elongation from the Sun, either at eastern elongation in the evening (setting after the Sun) or at western elongation in the morning (rising before the Sun).

infertility in medicine, inability to reproduce. In women, this may be due to blockage in the Fallopian tubes, failure of ovulation, a deficiency in sex hormones, or general ill health. In men, impotence, an insufficient number of sperm or abnormal sperm may be the cause of infertility. Clinical investigation will reveal the cause of the infertility in about 75% of couples and assisted conception may then be appropriate.

infinity mathematical quantity that is larger than any fixed assignable quantity; symbol ∞. By convention, the result of dividing any number by zero is regarded as infinity.

inflammation defensive reaction of the body tissues to disease or damage, including redness, swelling, and heat. Denoted by the suffix *-itis* (as in appendicitis), it may be acute or chronic, and may be accompanied by the formation of pus. This is an essential part of the healing process.

inflation in economics, a rise in the general level of prices. The many causes include cost-push inflation, which results from rising production costs. **Demand-pull inflation** occurs when overall demand exceeds supply. **Suppressed inflation** occurs in controlled economies and is reflected in rationing, shortages, and black-market prices. **Hyperinflation** is inflation of more than 50% in one month. **Deflation**, a fall in the general level of prices, is the reverse of inflation.

inflation tax tax imposed on companies that increase wages by more than an amount fixed by law (except to take account of increased profits or because of a profit-sharing scheme).

inflorescence in plants, a branch, or system of branches, bearing two or more individual flowers. Inflorescences can be divided into two main types: cymose (or definite) and racemose (or indefinite). In a **cymose inflorescence**, the tip of the main axis produces a single flower and subsequent flowers arise on lower side

INFLORESCENCE Inflorescence (arrangement of flowers on a stalk) of the dragonmouth *Horminium pyrenaicum*. Here a flower spike consists of whorls of flowers (verticillasters) with gaps between them. *Premaphotos Wildlife*

branches, as in forget-me-not *Myosotis* and chickweed *Stellaria*; the oldest flowers are, therefore, found at the tip. A **racemose inflorescence** has an active growing region at the tip of its main axis, and bears flowers along its length, as in hyacinth *Hyacinthus*; the oldest flowers are found near the base or, in cases where the inflorescence is flattened, towards the outside.

The stalk of the inflorescence is called a peduncle; the stalk of each individual flower is called a pedicel.

Types of racemose inflorescence include the **raceme**, a spike of similar, stalked flowers, as seen in lupin *Lupinus*. A **corymb**, seen in candytuft *Iberis amara*, is rounded or flat-topped because the pedicels of the flowers vary in length, the outer pedicels being longer than the inner ones. A **panicle** is a branched inflorescence made up of a number of racemes; such inflorescences are seen in many grasses, for example, the oat *Avena*. The pedicels of an **umbel**, seen in members of the carrot family (Umbelliferae), all arise from the same point on the main axis, like the spokes of an umbrella. Other types of racemose inflorescence include the ▷catkin, a pendulous inflorescence, made up of many small stalkless flowers; the **spadix**, in which tiny flowers are borne on a fleshy axis; and the capitulum, in which the axis is flattened or rounded, bears many small flowers, and is surrounded by large petal-like bracts.

influenza any of various viral infections primarily affecting the air passages, accompanied by ▷systemic effects such as fever, chills, headache, joint and muscle pains, and lassitude. Treatment is with bed rest and analgesic drugs such as aspirin or paracetamol.

Depending on the virus strain, influenza varies in virulence and duration, and there is always the risk of secondary (bacterial) infection of the lungs (pneumonia). Vaccines are effective against known strains but will not give protection against newly evolving viruses. The 1918–19 influenza pandemic (see ▷epidemic) killed about 20 million people worldwide.

information technology (**IT**) collective term for the various technologies involved in processing and transmitting information. They include computing, telecommunications, and microelectronics. The term became popular in the UK after the Government's 'Information Technology Year' in 1972.

Word processing, databases, and spreadsheets are just some of the computing ▷software packages that have revolutionized work in the office environment. Not only can work be done more quickly than before, but IT has given decisionmakers the opportunity to consider far more data when making decisions.

infrared astronomy study of infrared radiation produced by relatively cool gas and dust in space, as in the areas around forming stars. In 1983, the US-Dutch-British Infra-Red Astronomy Satellite (IRAS) surveyed almost the entire sky at infrared wavelengths. It found five new comets, thousands of galaxies undergoing bursts of star formation, and the possibility of planetary systems forming around several dozen stars.

Planets and gas clouds emit their light in the far and mid-infrared regions of the spectrum. The Infrared Space Observatory (ISO), launched in 1995, observed a broad wavelength (3–200 micrometres) in these regions. It is 10,000 times more sensitive than IRAS, and searches for ▷brown dwarfs (cool masses of gas smaller than the Sun).

infrared radiation invisible electromagnetic ▷radiation of wavelength between about 0.75 micrometres and 1 millimetre – that is, between the limit of the red end of the visible spectrum and the shortest microwaves. All bodies above the ▷absolute zero of temperature absorb and radiate infrared radiation. Infrared radiation is used in medical photography and treatment, and in industry, astronomy, and criminology.

Infrared absorption spectra are used in chemical analysis, particularly for organic compounds. Objects that radiate infrared radiation can be photographed or made visible in the dark on specially sensitized emulsions. This is important for military purposes and in detecting people buried under rubble. The strong absorption by many substances of infrared radiation is a useful method of applying heat.

infrastructure relatively permanent facilities that serve an industrial economy. Infrastructure usually includes roads, railways, other communication networks, energy and water supply, and education and training facilities. Some definitions also include sociocultural installations such as health-care and leisure facilities.

ingestion process of taking food into the mouth. The method of food capture varies but may involve biting, sucking, or filtering. Many single-celled organisms have a region of their cell wall that acts as a mouth. In these cases surrounding tiny hairs (cilia) sweep food particles together, ready for ingestion.

Ingres, Jean-Auguste-Dominique (1780–1867) French painter. A leading Neo-Classicist, he was a student of Jacques Louis ▷David. He studied and worked in Rome *c.* 1807–20, where he began the *Odalisque* series of sensuous female nudes, then went to Florence, and returned to France in 1824. His portraits painted in the 1840s–50s are meticulously detailed and highly polished.

A master draughtsman, he considered drawing 'the probity of art', and developed his style – based on the study of ▷Raphael and marked by clarity of line and a cool formality – in fierce opposition to the Romanticism of Eugène ▷Delacroix. His major works, which exercised a profound influence on 19th-century French Academic art, include *Roger and Angelica* (1819; Louvre, Paris), *La Grande Baigneuse* (1808; Louvre, Paris), and *La Grande Odalisque* (1814; Louvre, Paris), and the portraits *Madame Moitessier* (1856; National Gallery, London) and *François Marius* (1807; Musée Granet, Aix-en-Provence).

Ingushetia (or **Ingushetiya**) autonomous republic of the Russian Federation, on the northern slopes of the Caucasus mountains; area 2,000 sq km/770 sq mi; population (1994 est) 250,000 (Ingush 85%). The capital is Nazran. The chief industries are farming and cattle-raising; there is also petroleum drilling. The predominant religion is Islam.

inheritance tax in the UK, a tax charged on the value of an individual's estate on his or her death, including gifts made within the previous seven years. It replaced capital transfer tax in 1986 (which in turn replaced estate duty in 1974).

inhibition, neural in biology, the process in which activity in one ▷nerve cell suppresses activity in another. Neural inhibition in networks of nerve cells leading from sensory organs, or to muscles, plays an important role in allowing an animal to make fine sensory discriminations and to exercise fine control over movements.

initiative in politics, a device whereby constitutional voters may play a direct part in making laws. A proposed law may be drawn up and signed by petitioners, and submitted to the legislature. A ▷referendum may be taken on a law that has been passed by the legislature but that will not become operative unless the voters assent to it. Switzerland was the first country to make use of the device.

injunction court order that forbids a person from doing something, or orders him or her to take certain action. Breach of an injunction is ▷contempt of court.

ink coloured liquid used for writing, drawing, and printing. Traditional ink (blue, but later a permanent black) was produced from gallic acid and tannic acid, but inks are now based on synthetic dyes.

Inkatha Freedom Party (**IFP**; from the grass coil worn by Zulu women for carrying head loads; its many strands give it strength) South African political party, representing the nationalist aspirations of the country's largest ethnic group, the ▷Zulus. It was founded as a paramilitary organization in 1975 by its present leader,

Chief Gatsha ▷Buthelezi, with the avowed aim of creating a nonracial democratic political situation. The party entered South Africa's first multiracial elections in April 1994, after an initial violent boycott, and emerged with 10% of the popular vote.

Related Web site: History and Profile of the Inkatha Freedom Party
http://www.ifp.org.za/

ink-jet printer computer printer that creates characters and graphics by spraying very fine jets of quick-drying ink onto paper. Ink-jet printers range in size from small machines designed to work with microcomputers to very large machines designed for high-volume commercial printing.

INLA abbreviation for ▷Irish National Liberation Army.

Innocent thirteen popes including:

Innocent III (*c.* 1161–1216) Pope from 1198. He asserted papal power over secular princes, in particular over the succession of Holy Roman emperors. He also made King ▷John of England his vassal, compelling him to accept Stephen ▷Langton as archbishop of Canterbury. He promoted the fourth Crusade and crusades against the non-Christian Livonians and Letts, and the Albigensian heretics of southern France.

Innocents' Day (or **Childermas**) festival of the Roman Catholic Church, celebrated 28 December in memory of the Massacre of the Innocents, the children of Bethlehem who were allegedly slaughtered by King ▷Herod after the birth of Jesus.

Innsbruck capital of Tirol state, west Austria; population (1995) 119,600. It is a tourist and winter sports centre, and a route junction for the Brenner Pass. Local industries include mechanical engineering, bellmaking, and bookbinding. The 1964 and 1976 Winter Olympics were held here.

Inns of Court four private legal societies in London, England: Lincoln's Inn, Gray's Inn, Inner Temple, and Middle Temple. All barristers (advocates in the English legal system) must belong to one of the Inns of Court. The main function of each Inn is the education, government, and protection of its members. Each is under the administration of a body of Benchers (judges and senior barristers).

inoculation injection into the body of dead or weakened disease-carrying organisms or their toxins (▷vaccine) to produce immunity by inducing a mild form of a disease.

inorganic chemistry branch of chemistry dealing with the chemical properties of the elements and their compounds, excluding the more complex covalent compounds of carbon, which are considered in ▷organic chemistry.

The origins of inorganic chemistry lay in observing the characteristics and experimenting with the uses of the substances (compounds and elements) that could be extracted from mineral ores. These could be classified according to their chemical properties: elements could be classified as metals or nonmetals; compounds as acids or bases, oxidizing or reducing agents, ionic compounds (such as salts), or covalent compounds (such as gases). The arrangement of elements into groups possessing similar properties led to Mendeleyev's ▷periodic table of the elements, which prompted chemists to predict the properties of undiscovered elements that might occupy gaps in the table. This, in turn, led to the discovery of new elements, including a number of highly radioactive elements that do not occur naturally.

input device device for entering information into a computer. Input devices include keyboards, joysticks, mice, light pens, touch-sensitive screens, scanners, graphics tablets, speech-recognition devices, and vision systems. Compare ▷output device.

Keyboards, the most frequently used input devices, are used to enter instructions and data via keys. There are many variations on the layout and labelling of keys. Extra numeric keys may be added, as may special-purpose function keys, whose effects can be defined by programs in the computer.

The **graphics tablet** is an input device in which a stylus or cursor is moved, by hand, over a flat surface. The computer can keep track of the position of the stylus, enabling the operator to input drawings or diagrams into the computer. The **joystick** signals to a computer the direction and extent of displacement of a hand-held lever.

Light pens resemble ordinary pens and are used to indicate locations on a computer screen. With certain computer-aided design (▷CAD) programs, the light pen can be used to instruct the computer to change the shape, size, position, and colours of sections of a screen image.

Scanners produce a digital image of a document for input and storage in a computer, using technology similar to that of a photocopier. Small scanners can be passed over the document surface by hand; larger versions have a flat bed, like that of a photocopier, on which the input document is placed and scanned.

Input devices that are used commercially – for example, by banks, postal services, and supermarkets – must be able to read and capture large volumes of data very rapidly. Such devices include **document readers** for ▷magnetic-ink character recognition (MICR), ▷optical character recognition (OCR), and ▷optical mark recognition (OMR); mark-sense readers; bar-code scanners; magnetic-strip readers; and point-of-sale (POS) terminals. Punched-card and paper-tape readers were used in earlier commercial applications but are now obsolete.

inquest inquiry held by a ▷coroner into an unexplained death. At an inquest, a coroner is assisted by a jury of between 7 and 11 people. Evidence is on oath, and medical and other witnesses may be summoned.

Inquisition tribunal of the Roman Catholic Church established in 1233 to suppress heresy, originally by excommunication. The Inquisition operated in France, Italy, Spain, and the Holy Roman Empire, and was especially active after the ▷Reformation; it was later extended to the Americas. Its trials were conducted in secret, without torture, and penalties ranged from fines, through flogging and imprisonment, to death by burning.

insanity in medicine and law, any mental disorder in which the patient cannot be held responsible for their actions. The term is no longer used to refer to psychosis.

insect any of a vast group of small invertebrate animals with hard, segmented bodies, three pairs of jointed legs, and, usually, two pairs of wings; they belong among the ▷arthropods and are distributed throughout the world. An insect's body is divided into three segments: head, thorax, and abdomen. On the head is a pair of feelers, or antennae. The legs and wings are attached to the thorax, or middle segment of the body. The abdomen, or end segment of the body, is where food is digested and excreted and where the reproductive organs are located.

Insects vary in size from 0.02 cm/0.007 in to 35 cm/13.5 in in length. The world's smallest insect is believed to be a 'fairy fly' wasp in the family Mymaridae, with a wingspan of 0.2 mm/0.008 in. (Class Insecta.)

Many insects hatch out of their eggs as ▷larvae (an immature stage, usually in the form of a caterpillar, grub, or maggot) and have to pass through further major physical changes (▷metamorphosis) before reaching adulthood. An insect about to go through metamorphosis hides itself or makes a cocoon in which to hide, then rests while the changes take place; at this stage the insect is called a ▷pupa, or a chrysalis if it is a butterfly or moth. When the changes are complete, the adult insect emerges.

The **classification** of insects is largely based upon characteristics of the mouthparts, wings, and metamorphosis. Insects are divided into two subclasses (one with two divisions) and 29 orders. More than 1 million species are known, and several thousand new ones are discovered each year.

The study of insects is called **entomology**.

Classification of Insects

Order	Number of species	Examples
Class: Insecta		
Subclass: Apterygota (wingless insects)		
Collembola[1]	2,000	springtails
Diplura	660	two-pronged bristletails, campodeids, japygids
Protura	120	minute insects living in soil
Thysanura	600	three-pronged bristletails, silverfish
Subclass: Pterygota (winged insects or forms secondary wingless), incorporating two superorders:		
Superorder: Exopterygota (young resemble adults but have externally-developing wings)		
Ephemeroptera	2,000	mayflies
Odonata	5,000	dragonflies, damselflies
Grylloblattodea	12	wingless soil-living insects of North America
Plecoptera	3,000	stoneflies
Zoraptera	20	tiny insects living in decaying plants
Isoptera	2,000	termites
Dermaptera	1,500	earwigs
Embioptera	200	web-spinners
Dictyoptera	3,700	cockroaches, praying mantises
Orthoptera	24,000	crickets, grasshoppers, locusts, mantids, roaches
Phasmida	2,500	stick insects, leaf insects
Psocoptera	1,600	booklice, barklice, psocids
Mallophaga	2,500	biting lice, mainly parasitic on birds
Anoplura	250	sucking lice, mainly parasitic on mammals
Hemiptera	39,500	true bugs, including shield- and bedbugs, froghoppers, pond skaters, water boatmen
Homoptera	45,000	aphids, cicadas, hoppers, whiteflies
Thysanoptera	5,000	thrips
Superorder: Endopterygota (young are unlike adults and undergo sudden metamorphosis)		
Neuroptera	4,500	lacewings, alderflies, snakeflies
Mecoptera	450	scorpion flies
Lepidoptera	138,000	butterflies, moths
Trichoptera	7,000	caddisflies
Diptera	150,000	true flies, including bluebottles, mosquitoes, leatherjackets, midges
Siphonaptera	1,750	fleas
Hymenoptera	130,000	bees, wasps, ants, sawflies, chalcids
Coleoptera	250,000	beetles, including weevils, ladybirds, glow-worms, woodworms, chafers

[1] Some zoologists recognize the Collembola taxon as a class rather than an order.

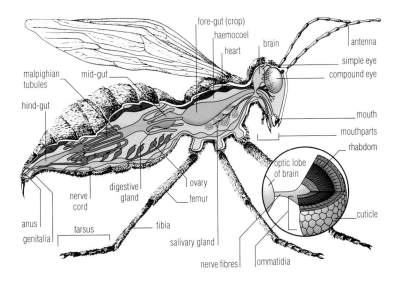

INSECT The general features of the insect body include a segmented body divided into head, thorax, and abdomen, jointed legs, feelers or antennae, and usually two pairs of wings. Insects often have compound eyes with a large field of vision.

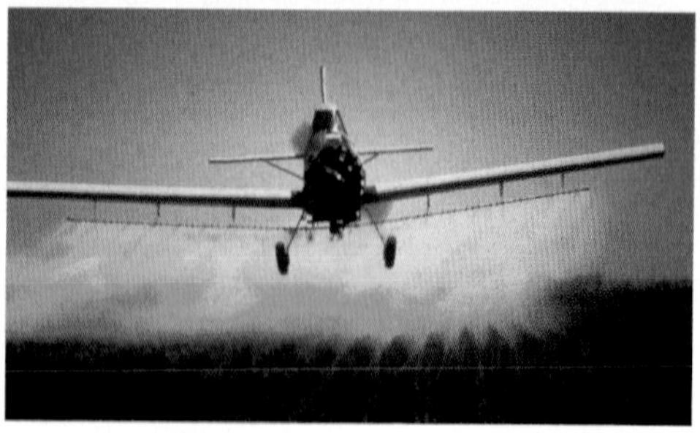

INSECTICIDE Spraying crops with insecticide and pesticide from an aeroplane allows a large area to be sprayed quickly and also avoids having to drive vehicles through fields, thus potentially damaging the crops. *Image Bank*

insecticide any chemical pesticide used to kill insects. Among the most effective insecticides are synthetic organic chemicals such as ▷DDT and dieldrin, which are chlorinated hydrocarbons. These chemicals, however, have proved persistent in the environment and are also poisonous to all animal life, including humans, and are consequently banned in many countries. Other synthetic insecticides include organic phosphorus compounds such as malathion. Insecticides prepared from plants, such as derris and pyrethrum, are safer to use but need to be applied frequently and carefully.

insectivore any animal whose diet is made up largely or exclusively of ▷insects. In particular, the name is applied to mammals of the order Insectivora, which includes the shrews, hedgehogs, moles, and tenrecs.

According to the Red List of endangered species published by the ▷World Conservation Union for 1996, 36% of insectivore species are threatened with extinction.

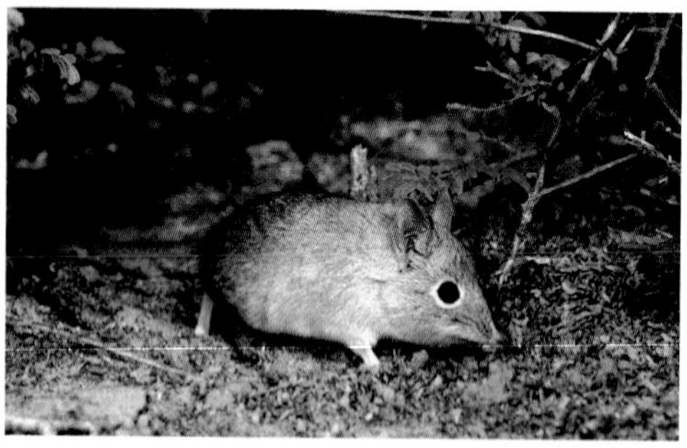

INSECTIVORE The elephant shrew *Elephantulus intufi* foraging for termites, which form an important part of its diet. *K G Preston-Mafham/Premaphotos Wildlife*

insectivorous plant plant that can capture and digest live prey (normally insects), to obtain nitrogen compounds that are lacking in its usual marshy habitat. Some are passive traps, for example, the pitcher plants *Nepenthes* and *Sarracenia*. One pitcher-plant species has container-traps holding 1.6 l/3.5 pt of the liquid that 'digests' its food, mostly insects but occasionally even rodents. Others, for example, sundews *Drosera*, butterworts *Pinguicula*, and Venus flytraps *Dionaea muscipula*, have an active trapping mechanism. Insectivorous plants have adapted to grow in poor soil conditions where the number of micro-organisms recycling nitrogen compounds is very much reduced. In these circumstances other plants cannot gain enough nitrates to grow. See also ▷leaf.

inselberg (or **kopje**; German 'island mountain') prominent steep-sided hill of resistant solid rock, such as granite, rising out of a plain, usually in a tropical area. Its rounded appearance is caused by so-called onion-skin ▷weathering, in which the surface is eroded in successive layers.

insemination, artificial see ▷artificial insemination.

insider trading (or **insider dealing**) illegal use of privileged information in dealing on a stock exchange, for example, when a company takeover bid is imminent. Insider trading is in theory detected by the Securities and Exchange Commission (SEC) in the USA, and by the Securities and Investment Board (SIB) in the UK. Neither agency, however, has any legal powers other than public disclosure and they do not bring prosecutions themselves.

instinct in ▷ethology, behaviour found in all equivalent members of a given species (for example, all the males, or all the females with young) that is presumed to be genetically determined.

Examples include a male robin's tendency to attack other male robins intruding on its territory and the tendency of many female mammals to care for their offspring. Instincts differ from ▷reflexes in that they involve very much more complex actions, and learning often plays an important part in their development.

insulator any poor ▷conductor of heat, sound, or electricity. Most substances lacking free (mobile) ▷electrons, such as non-metals, are electrical or thermal insulators. Usually, devices of glass or porcelain, called insulators, are used for insulating and supporting overhead wires.

insulin protein ▷hormone, produced by specialized cells in the islets of Langerhans in the pancreas, that regulates the metabolism (rate of activity) of glucose, fats, and proteins. Insulin was discovered by Canadian physician Frederick ▷Banting and Canadian physiologist Charles ▷Best, who pioneered its use in treating ▷diabetes.

insurance contract guaranteeing compensation to the payer of a premium against loss by fire, death, accident, and so on, which is known as **assurance** in the case of a fixed sum and **insurance** where the payment is proportionate to the loss.

intaglio design cut into the surface of gems or seals by etching or engraving; an ▷engraving technique.

integer any whole number. Integers may be positive or negative; 0 is an integer, and is often considered positive. Formally, integers are members of the set

$$Z = \{\dots -3, -2, -1, 0, 1, 2, 3, \dots\}$$

Fractions, such as $\frac{1}{2}$ and 0.35, are known as non-integral numbers ('not integers').

integral calculus branch of mathematics using the process of ▷integration. It is concerned with finding volumes and areas and summing infinitesimally small quantities.

integrated circuit (**IC** or **silicon chip**) miniaturized electronic circuit produced on a single crystal, or chip, of a semiconducting material – usually silicon. It may contain many millions of components and yet measure only 5 mm/0.2 in square and 1 mm/0.04 in thick. The IC is encapsulated within a plastic or ceramic case, and linked via gold wires to metal pins with which it is connected to a ▷printed circuit board and the other components that make up such electronic devices as computers and calculators.

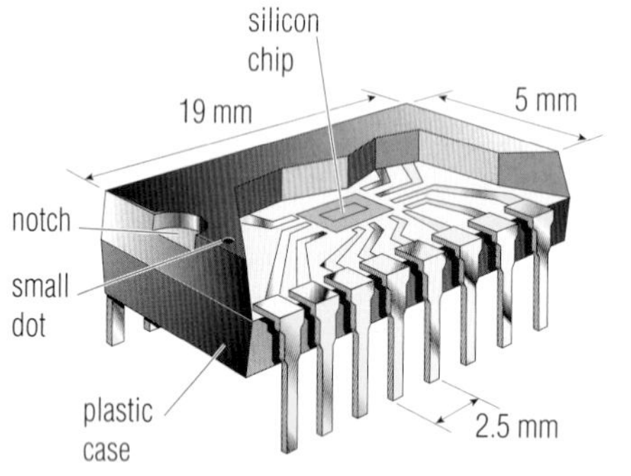

INTEGRATED CIRCUIT An integrated circuit (IC), or silicon chip.

Integrated Services Digital Network (**ISDN**) internationally developed telecommunications system for sending signals in ▷digital format. It involves converting the 'local loop' – the link between the user's telephone (or private automatic branch exchange) and the digital telephone exchange – from an ▷analogue system into a digital system, thereby greatly increasing the amount of information that can be carried. The first large-scale use of ISDN began in Japan in 1988.

Related Web site: ISDN Tutorial http://www.ralphb.net/ISDN/

integration in mathematics, a method in ▷calculus of determining the solutions of definite or indefinite integrals.
An example of a definite integral can be thought of as finding the area under a curve (as represented by an algebraic expression or function) between particular values of the function's variable.
In practice, integral calculus provides scientists with a powerful tool for doing calculations that involve a continually varying quantity (such as determining the position at any given instant of a space rocket that is accelerating away from Earth). Its basic principles were discovered in the late 1660s independently by the German philosopher ▷Leibniz and the British scientist ▷Newton.

intelligence in military and political affairs, information, often secretly or illegally obtained, about other countries. **Counter-intelligence** is information on the activities of hostile agents. Much intelligence is gained by technical means, such as satellites and the electronic interception of data.

The British intelligence services consist of M(ilitary) I(ntelligence) 6, the nickname of the Secret Intelligence Service, which operates mainly under Foreign Office control; the counter-intelligence service, the Security Service, who are also called M(ilitary) I(ntelligence) 5, which is responsible directly to the prime minister for internal security and has Scotland Yard's ▷Special Branch as its executive arm; and Government Communications Headquarters (▷GCHQ), which carries out electronic surveillance for the other two branches. The chief of MI6 from 1994 is David Spedding; the director-general of MI5 was Stella Rimington from 1992–96 and from 1996 is Stephen Lander. The overall head of intelligence in the UK is the chair of the Joint Intelligence Committee (Pauline Neville-Jones from 1994). The British intelligence services budget for 1994 was £975 million, about half of which was spent on GCHQ and £150 million by M15. Staff numbered almost 11,000, including 6,500 working at GCHQ and 2,000 at MI5. US equivalents of MI6 include the Central Intelligence Agency (CIA) and the National Security Agency; the Federal Bureau of Investigation (FBI) is responsible for US counter-intelligence. **Double agents** increase their income, but may decrease their lifespan, by working for both sides (for example, Mata Hari); **moles** are those within the service who betray their own side, usually defecting (fleeing to the other side) when in danger of discovery (for example, Kim Philby); a **sleeper** is a spy who is inactive, sometimes for many years, until needed. The motive for work in intelligence may be service to country (T E Lawrence, John Buchan, Graham Greene, Ian Fleming, and John Le Carré afterwards used their experiences in their books), money, or idealism (for example, the German scientist Klaus Fuchs or the art historian Anthony Blunt).

From 1991, in a government move to reduce secrecy and increase the accountability of the British intelligence services, information was gradually released into the public domain. The names of those in charge, and the whereabouts, of MI5 and MI6 were made public (until 1992, MI6 did not officially exist in peacetime). (GCHQ's base in Cheltenham, Gloucestershire, was already public knowledge.) It was also announced that, in future, the accounts of all three branches of the service would be audited by the National Audit Office. In addition, legislation was expected to be passed giving powers to a House of Commons select committee to scrutinize the work of the services. Following the end of the Cold War 1990, and the IRA ceasefire 1994–96, MI5 faced the threat of substantial job losses, and began to participate in some criminal investigations formerly conducted solely by the police. In 1995 the service had an annual budget of £150 million and a staff of 2,000. In recent years it has taken over responsibility for intelligence-gathering about the IRA from Special Branch, and now also helps the police in efforts to combat organized crime. MI5 was found in breach of the European Convention on Human Rights 1990 in having carried out secret surveillance of civil-liberties campaigners and covert vetting of applicants for jobs with military contractors.

intelligence in psychology, a general concept that summarizes the abilities of an individual in reasoning and problem solving, particularly in novel situations. These consist of a wide range of verbal and nonverbal skills and therefore some psychologists dispute a unitary concept of intelligence.

intensity in physics, the power (or energy per second) per unit area carried by a form of radiation or wave motion. It is an indication of the concentration of energy present and, if measured at varying distances from the source, of the effect of distance on this. For example, the intensity of light is a measure of its brightness, and may be shown to diminish with distance from its source in accordance with the ▷inverse square law (its intensity is inversely proportional to the square of the distance).

interactive computing in computing, a system for processing data in which the operator is in direct communication with the computer, receiving immediate responses to input data. In ▷batch processing, by contrast, the necessary data and instructions are prepared in advance and processed by the computer with little or no intervention from the operator.

interactive video (**IV**) computer-mediated system that enables the user to interact with and control information (including text, recorded speech, or moving images) stored on video disk. IV is most commonly used for training purposes, using analogue video disks, but has wider applications with digital video systems such as CD-I (Compact Disc Interactive, from Philips and Sony) which are based on the CD-ROM format derived from audio compact discs.

Inter-American Development Bank (IADB) bank founded in 1959, at the instigation of the Organization of American States (OAS), to finance economic and social development, particularly in the less wealthy regions of the Americas. Its membership includes the states of Central and Southern America, the Caribbean, and the USA, as well as Austria, Belgium, Canada, Denmark, Finland, France, Germany, Israel, Italy, Japan, the Netherlands, Norway, Portugal, Spain, Sweden, Switzerland, and the UK. Its headquarters are in Washington DC.

interdict in the Christian church, a punishment that excludes an individual, community, or realm from participation in spiritual activities except for communion. It was usually employed against heretics or realms whose ruler was an excommunicant.

interest in finance, a sum of money paid by a borrower to a lender in return for the loan, usually expressed as a percentage per annum. **Simple interest** is interest calculated as a straight percentage of the amount loaned or invested. In **compound interest**, the interest earned over a period of time (for example, per annum) is added to the investment, so that at the end of the next period interest is paid on that total.

interface in computing, the point of contact between two programs or pieces of equipment. The term is most often used for the physical connection between the computer and a peripheral device, which is used to compensate for differences in such operating characteristics as speed, data coding, voltage, and power consumption. For example, a **printer interface** is the cabling and circuitry used to transfer data from a computer to a printer, and to compensate for differences in speed and coding.

interference in physics, the phenomenon of two or more wave motions interacting and combining to produce a resultant wave of larger or smaller amplitude (depending on whether the combining waves are in or out of ▷phase with each other).

Interference of white light (multiwavelength) results in spectral coloured fringes; for example, the iridescent colours of oil films seen on water or soap bubbles (demonstrated by ▷Newton's rings). Interference of sound waves of similar frequency produces the phenomenon of beats, often used by musicians when tuning an instrument. With monochromatic light (of a single wavelength), interference produces patterns of light and dark bands. This is the basis of ▷holography, for example. Interferometry can also be applied to radio waves, and is a powerful tool in modern astronomy.

interferometer in physics, a device that splits a beam of light into two parts, the parts being recombined after travelling different paths to form an interference pattern of light and dark bands. Interferometers are used in many branches of science and industry where accurate measurements of distances and angles are needed.

interferon (or **IFN**) naturally occurring cellular protein that makes up part of mammalian defences against viral disease. Three types (alpha, beta, and gamma) are produced by infected cells and enter the bloodstream and uninfected cells, making them immune to virus attack.

Related Web site: Antiviral Agents Bulletin http://www.bioinfo.com/antiviral.html

Intermediate Nuclear Forces Treaty agreement signed 8 December 1987 between the USA and the USSR to eliminate all ground-based nuclear missiles in Europe that were capable of hitting only European targets (including European Russia). It reduced the countries' nuclear arsenals by some 2,000 (4% of the total). The treaty included provisions for each country to inspect the other's bases.

intermediate technology application of mechanics, electrical engineering, and other technologies, based on inventions and designs developed in scientifically sophisticated cultures, but utilizing materials, assembly, and maintenance methods found in technologically less developed regions.

intermediate vector boson alternative name for ▷weakon, the elementary particle responsible for carrying the ▷weak nuclear force.

intermezzo in music, initially a one-act comic opera, such as Giovanni Pergolesi's *La serva padrona/The Maid as Mistress* (1732); also a short orchestral interlude played between the acts of an opera to denote the passage of time. By extension, an intermezzo has come to mean a short piece to be played between other more substantial works, such as Brahms's *Three Intermezzos for Piano* (1892).

intermolecular force (or **van der Waals' force**) force of attraction between molecules. Intermolecular forces are relatively weak; hence simple molecular compounds are gases, liquids, or low-melting-point solids.

internal-combustion engine heat engine in which fuel is burned inside the engine, contrasting with an external-combustion engine (such as the steam engine) in which fuel is burned in a separate unit. The ▷diesel engine and ▷petrol engine are both internal-combustion engines. Gas ▷turbines and ▷jet and ▷rocket engines are also considered to be internal-combustion engines because they burn their fuel inside their combustion chambers.

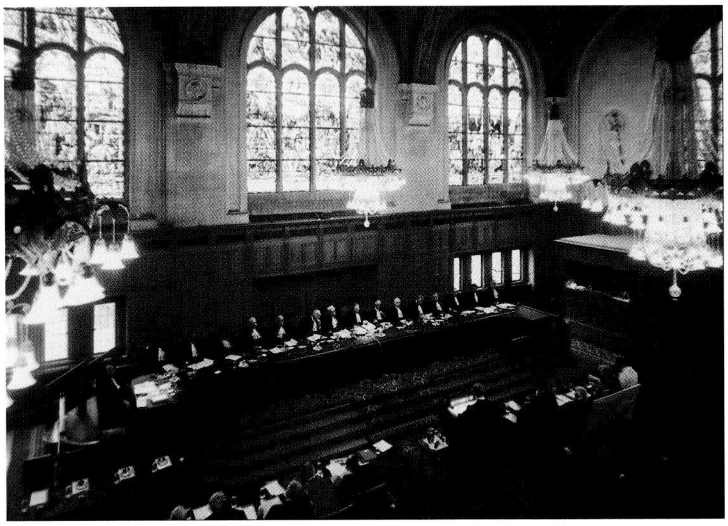

INTERNATIONAL COURT OF JUSTICE Interior of the United Nations International Court of Justice in The Hague, the Netherlands. *Corel*

International Bank for Reconstruction and Development specialized agency of the United Nations. Its popular name is the ▷World Bank.

International Brigade international volunteer force on the Republican side in the Spanish ▷Civil War (1936–39).

International Court of Justice main judicial organ of the ▷United Nations, in The Hague, the Netherlands. It hears international law disputes as well as playing an advisory role to UN organs. It was set up by the UN charter in 1945 and superseded the World Court. There are 15 judges, each from a different member state.

International Date Line (IDL) imaginary line that approximately follows the 180° line of longitude. The date is put forward a day when crossing the line going west, and back a day when going east. The IDL was chosen at the International Meridian Conference 1884.

International Gothic late Gothic style of painting and sculpture flourishing in Europe in the late 14th and 15th centuries. It is characterized by bright colours, a courtly elegance, and a naturalistic rendering of detail. Originally evolving in the court art of France and Burgundy, it spread to many parts of Europe, its leading exponents including the Italian ▷Simone Martini and the Franco-Flemish ▷Limbourg brothers.

International Labour Organization (ILO) specialized agency of the United Nations, originally established in 1919, which formulates standards for labour and social conditions. Its headquarters are in Geneva, Switzerland. It was awarded the Nobel Peace Prize in 1969. By 1997, the agency was responsible for over 70 international labour conventions.

international law body of rules generally accepted as governing the relations between countries, pioneered by Hugo ▷Grotius, especially in matters of human rights, territory, and war.

Neither the League of Nations nor the United Nations proved able to enforce international law, successes being achieved only when the law coincided with the aims of a predominant major power – for example, in the ▷Korean War. The scope of the law is now extended to space – for example, the 1967 treaty that (among other things) banned nuclear weapons from space.

Related Web site: International Law Association (ILA) http://www.ila-hq.org/

> **Helmut Kohl**
> Chancellor of Germany
>
> *The way the world public with hypocritical lust follows the most private events on the Internet, that – and I use this expression deliberately – makes me puke.*
>
> On the Clinton tapes, and allied affairs; *Daily Telegraph*, 22 September 1998

International Monetary Fund (IMF) specialized agency of the United Nations, headquarters Washington, DC, established under the 1944 ▷Bretton Woods agreement and operational since 1947. It seeks to promote international monetary cooperation and the growth of world trade, and to smooth multilateral payment arrangements among member states. IMF standby loans are available to members in balance-of-payments difficulties (the amount being governed by the member's quota), usually on the basis that the country must agree to take certain corrective measures.

International Society for Krishna Consciousness (**ISKCON** or **Gaudiya Vaisnavism**) Hindu sect based on the demonstration of intense love for Krishna (an incarnation of the god Vishnu), especially by chanting the mantra 'Hare Krishna'. Members wear distinctive yellow robes, and men often have their heads partly shaven. Their holy books are the Hindu scriptures and particularly the *Bhagavad-Gītā*, which they study daily.

Related Web site: Hare Krishna http://www.iskcon.org/

international style (or **International Modern**) architectural style, an early and influential phase of the ▷Modern Movement, originating in Western Europe in the 1920s but finding its fullest expression in the 1930s, notably in the USA. It is characterized by a dominance of geometric, especially rectilinear, forms; emphasis on asymmetrical composition; large expanses of glazing; and white rendered walls. Examples are Walter ▷Gropius's Bauhaus building, Dessau, Germany, (1925–26); ▷Le Corbusier's Villa Savoye, Poissy, France, (1927–31); Alvar ▷Aalto's Viipuri Library, Finland (now in Russia), (1927–35); and ▷Mies van der Rohe's Barcelona Pavilion (1929).

International, the coordinating body established by labour and socialist organizations, including: **First International** or **International Working Men's Association** (1864–72), formed in London under Karl ▷Marx; **Second International** (1889–1940), founded in Paris; **Third (Socialist) International** or **Comintern** (1919–43), formed in Moscow by the Soviet leader Lenin, advocating from 1933 a popular front (communist, socialist, liberal) against the German dictator Hitler; **Fourth International** or **Trotskyist International** (1938), somewhat indeterminate, anti-Stalinist; **Revived Socialist International** (1951), formed in Frankfurt, Germany, a largely anticommunist association of social democrats.

Internet Global public computer network that provides the communication infrastructure for applications such as ▷e-mail, the World Wide Web, and FTP. The Internet is not one individual network, but an interconnected system of smaller networks using common protocols to pass packets of information from one computer to another.

Early work on the Internet began in the 1960s at the Advanced Research Projects Agency (ARPA), in the USA. It was based on theories of ▷packet switching, particularly those of Leonard Kleinrock. In 1967 work by Lawrence Roberts, Vinton Cerf, and Bob Kahn led to the publishing of plans for the ARPANET network. They were put into practice in 1969, when the ARPANET was used to connect four university computers. In 1972 the ARPANET had its first public demonstration at the International Computer Communication Conference. In the same year, Ray Tomlinson designed the first application for this new network: e-mail. The ARPANET had used a protocol called NCP, but it had compatibility problems. Engineers needed to design protocols that could meet the needs of an open-architecture network. Roberts and Cerf then led the team that created the Transmission Control Protocol/Internet Protocol (TCP/IP), which swiftly became the standard Internet protocol. In 1983 the ARPANET switched from using NCP to TCP/IP, and the network was separated into military (MILNET) and non-military systems. By 1985 the Internet was well-established among scientific researchers and developers, and was beginning to be used for daily computer communications. By the early 1990s access had become cheap enough for domestic users to have their own links on home personal computers.

The impact of the Internet on the economy has been huge. In 1999 Internet-related activities accounted for nearly 2.5 million jobs, of which 650,000 were newly created, and had generated almost US$524 billion in revenue. By 2000, it was estimated that there were between 580 and 655 million Internet users worldwide. The number of users was expected to rise to between 709 and 945 million users in 2004.

Related Web site: Brief History of the Internet http://www.isoc.org/internet-history/brief.html

internment detention of suspected criminals without trial. Foreign citizens are often interned during times of war or civil unrest.

interplanetary matter gas, dust, and charged particles from a variety of sources, which occupies the space between the planets. Dust left over from the formation of the Solar System, or from disintegrating comets, orbits the Sun in or near the ecliptic plane and is responsible for scattering sunlight to cause the ▷zodiacal light (mainly the smaller particles) and for ▷meteor showers in the Earth's atmosphere (larger particles). The charged particles mostly originate in the ▷solar wind, but some are cosmic rays from deep space.

Interpol (acronym for International Criminal Police Organization) agency founded following the Second International Judicial Police Conference (1923) with its headquarters in Vienna, and reconstituted after World War II with its headquarters in Paris. It has an international criminal register, fingerprint file, and methods index.

interpreter computer program that translates and executes a program written in a high-level language. Unlike a ▷compiler, which produces a complete machine-code translation of the high-level program in one operation, an interpreter translates the source program, instruction by instruction, each time that program is run.

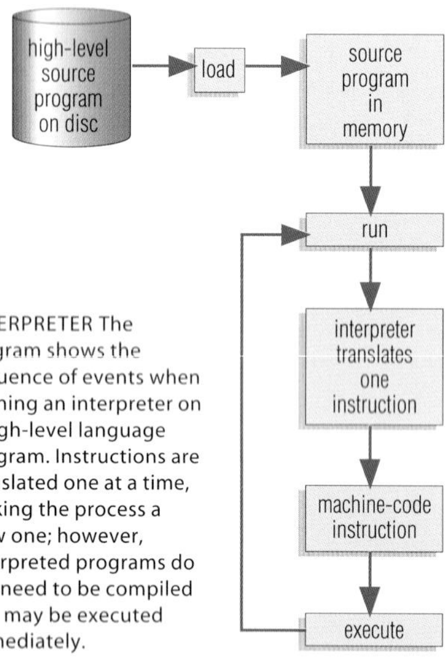

INTERPRETER The diagram shows the sequence of events when running an interpreter on a high-level language program. Instructions are translated one at a time, making the process a slow one; however, interpreted programs do not need to be compiled and may be executed immediately.

intersex individual that is intermediate between a normal male and a normal female in its appearance (for example, a genetic male that lacks external genitalia and so resembles a female).

intertropical convergence zone (ITCZ) area of heavy rainfall found in the tropics and formed as the trade winds converge and rise to form cloud and rain. It moves a few degrees northwards during the northern summer and a few degrees southwards during the southern summer, following the apparent movement of the Sun. The ITCZ is responsible for most of the rain that falls in Africa. The ▷doldrums are also associated with this zone.

interval in music, the pitch difference between two notes, expressed in terms of the diatonic scale, for example a fifth, or as a harmonic ratio, 3:2.

intestacy absence of a will at a person's death. Special legal rules apply on intestacy for appointing administrators to deal with the deceased person's affairs, and for disposing of the deceased person's property in accordance with statutory provisions.

intestine in vertebrates, the digestive tract from the stomach outlet to the anus. The human **small intestine** is 6 m/20 ft long, 4 cm/1.5 in in diameter, and consists of the duodenum, jejunum, and ileum; the **large intestine** is 1.5 m/5 ft long, 6 cm/2.5 in in diameter, and includes the caecum, colon, and rectum. Both are muscular tubes comprising an inner lining that secretes alkaline digestive juice, a submucous coat containing fine blood vessels and nerves, a muscular coat, and a serous coat covering all, supported by a strong peritoneum, which carries the blood and lymph vessels, and the nerves. The contents are passed along slowly by ▷peristalsis (waves of involuntary muscular action). The term intestine is also applied to the lower digestive tract of invertebrates.

Intifada (Arabic 'resurgence' or 'throwing off') Palestinian uprising, specifically between December 1987 and September 1993, during which time a loosely organized group of Palestinians (the **Liberation Army of Palestine**, also called Intifada) rebelled against armed Israeli troops in the occupied territories of the Gaza Strip and the West Bank. Their campaign for self-determination included stone-throwing and petrol bombing. The 1993 peace accord between Israel and the Palestine Liberation Organization provided limited autonomy for Gaza and Jericho and initiated the Israel–Palestine peace process. However, extremist groups that had participated in the Intifada, notably the militant wing of the Hamas fundamentalist group, opposed the accord and continued a campaign of violence within Israel. A second Intifada began in September 2000, after a visit by right-wing Israeli politician Ariel Sharon to the holy site of Haram al-Sharif (Temple Mount) in Jerusalem. This continued into 2001.

The uprising began in December 1987 in the Gaza Strip. Rumours that a fatal traffic collision had been caused by Israeli security service agents in retaliation for the stabbing of an Israeli the previous week led to demonstrations by teenagers armed with slingshots. It subsequently spread, despite attempts at repression. Some 1,300 Palestinians and 80 Israelis were killed in the uprising up to the end of 1991. Many Palestinian private homes were dynamited by military order, under a still-valid British emergency regulation promulgated in 1946 to put down Jewish guerrillas. The number of soldiers on duty on the West Bank at the beginning of 1989 was said to be more than three times the number needed to conquer it during the Six-Day War.

Related Web site: Intifada Diary – Ten Years After http://www.birzeit.edu/diary/intifada/

intrauterine device (**IUD**; or **coil**) a contraceptive device that is inserted into the womb (uterus). It is a tiny plastic object, sometimes containing copper. By causing a mild inflammation of the lining of the uterus it prevents fertilized eggs from becoming implanted.

IUDs are not usually given to women who have not had children. They are generally very reliable, as long as they stay in place, with a success rate of about 98%. Some women experience heavier and more painful periods, and there is a very slight risk of a pelvic infection leading to infertility.

introversion in psychology, preoccupation with the self, generally coupled with a lack of sociability. The opposite of introversion is ▷extroversion.

intrusion mass of ▷igneous rock that has formed by 'injection' of molten rock, or magma, into existing cracks beneath the surface of the Earth, as distinct from a volcanic rock mass which has erupted from the surface. Intrusion features include vertical cylindrical structures such as stocks, pipes, and necks; sheet structures such as dykes that cut across the strata and sills that push between them; laccoliths, which are blisters that push up the overlying rock; and batholiths, which represent chambers of solidified magma and contain vast volumes of rock.

intrusive rock (or **plutonic rock**) ▷igneous rock formed beneath the Earth's surface. Magma, or molten rock, cools slowly at these depths to form coarse-grained rocks, such as granite, with large crystals. (▷Extrusive rocks, which are formed on the surface, are generally fine-grained.) A mass of intrusive rock is called an intrusion.

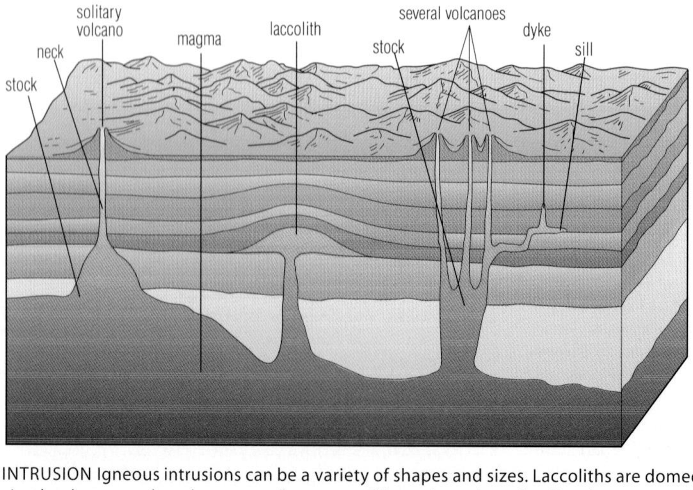

INTRUSION Igneous intrusions can be a variety of shapes and sizes. Laccoliths are domed circular shapes, and can be many miles across. Sills are intrusions that flow between rock layers. Pipes or necks connect the underlying magma chamber to surface volcanoes.

intuition rapid, unconscious thought process. In philosophy, intuition is that knowledge of a concept which does not derive directly from the senses. Thus, we may be said to have an intuitive idea of God, beauty, or justice. The concept of intuition is similar to Bertrand ▷Russell's theory of knowledge by acquaintance. In both cases, it is contrasted with empirical knowledge.

Inuit (*inuk* 'a man') member of a people inhabiting the Arctic coasts of Alaska, the eastern islands of the Canadian Arctic, Labrador, and the ice-free coasts of Greenland. Until recent times there was a remarkable homogeneity in culture throughout this area, which traditionally relied on fish, sea mammals, and land animals for food, heat, light, clothing, tools, and shelter. The total number of Inuit (1993 est) is 125,000.

Inverclyde unitary authority in western Scotland, created in 1996 from Inverclyde district in Strathclyde region.

area 161 sq km/62 sq mi **towns** Greenock (administrative headquarters), Port Glasgow, Gourock **physical** coastal lowland on the Firth of Clyde estuary, rising sharply to an inland plateau of 305 m/1,000 ft **features** Inverkip Marina **industries** electronics **population** (1996) 90,000 **history** key part in the industrial history of Scotland as a port and a heavy engineering centre

Invergordon Mutiny incident in the British Atlantic Fleet, Cromarty Firth, Scotland, on 15 September 1931. Ratings refused to prepare the ships for sea following the government's cuts in their pay; the cuts were consequently modified.

Inverness main town in, and the administrative centre of, ▷Highland unitary authority, Scotland, at the head of the Moray Firth, lying in a sheltered site at the mouth of the River Ness; population (1991) 41,200. It is a tourist centre with tanning, oil-related engineering, distilling, and electronics industries. Culloden Moor, scene of the massacre of clansmen loyal to Charles Edward Stuart by the English Army in April 1746, is situated to the east of Inverness.

Inverness-shire largest of the former Scottish counties, it was part of Highland Region 1975–96, and is now part of the Highland unitary authority.

inverse square law in physics, the statement that the magnitude of an effect (usually a force) at a point is inversely proportional to the square of the distance between that point and the object exerting the force.

inversion in music, the mirror image of a melody used in counterpoint; alternatively a chord in which the natural order of notes is rearranged.

invertebrate animal without a backbone. The invertebrates form all of the major divisions of the animal kingdom called phyla, with the exception of vertebrates. Invertebrates include the sponges, coelenterates, flatworms, nematodes, annelids, arthropods, molluscs, and echinoderms. Primitive aquatic chordates such as sea squirts and lancelets, which only have notochords and do not possess a vertebral column of cartilage or bone, are sometimes called invertebrate chordates, but this is misleading, since the notochord is the precursor of the backbone in advanced chordates.

Oxford zoologists estimated in 1996 that two or more British invertebrate species become extinct each year, a rate of 1% per century.

investment in economics, the purchase of any asset with the potential to yield future financial benefit to the purchaser (such as a house, a work of art, stocks and shares, or even a private education).

investment trust public company that makes investments in other companies on behalf of its shareholders. It may issue shares to raise capital and issue fixed interest securities.

in vitro fertilization (**IVF**; 'fertilization in glass') allowing eggs and sperm to unite in a laboratory to form embryos. The embryos (properly called pre-embryos in their two- to eight-celled state) are stored by cooling to the temperature of liquid air (cryopreservation) until they are implanted into the womb of the otherwise infertile mother (an extension of ▷artificial insemination). The first baby to be produced by this method was born in 1978 in the UK. In cases where the Fallopian tubes are blocked, fertilization may be carried out by **intra-vaginal culture**, in which egg and sperm are incubated (in a plastic tube) in the mother's vagina, then transferred surgically into the uterus.

Recent extensions of the in vitro technique have included the birth of a baby from a frozen embryo (Australia, 1984) and from a frozen egg (Australia, 1986). Pioneers in the field have been the British doctors Robert Edwards and Patrick Steptoe. As yet the success rate is relatively low; only 15–20% of in vitro fertilizations result in live births.

Io in astronomy, the third-largest moon of the planet Jupiter, 3,630 km/2,260 mi in diameter, orbiting in 1.77 days at a distance of 422,000 km/262,000 mi. It is the most volcanically active body in the Solar System, covered by hundreds of vents that erupt not lava but sulphur, giving Io an orange-coloured surface.

iodide compound formed between iodine and another element in which the iodine is the more electronegative element (see ▷electronegativity, ▷halide).

iodine (Greek *iodes* 'violet') greyish-black nonmetallic element, symbol I, atomic number 53, relative atomic mass 126.9044. It is a member of the ▷halogen group. Its crystals give off, when heated, a violet vapour with an irritating odour resembling that of chlorine. It only occurs in combination with other elements. Its salts are known as iodides, which are found in sea water. As a mineral nutrient it is vital to the proper functioning of the thyroid gland, where it occurs in trace amounts as part of the hormone thyroxine. Absence of iodine from the diet leads to ▷goitre. Iodine is used in photography, in medicine as an antiseptic, and in making dyes.

Its radioactive isotope ^{131}I (half-life of eight days) is a dangerous fission product from nuclear explosions and from the nuclear reactors in power plants, since, if ingested, it can be taken up by the thyroid and damage it. It was discovered in 1811 by French chemist B Courtois (1777–1838).

iodoform (chemical name **triiodomethane**) CHI_3, an antiseptic that crystallizes into yellow hexagonal plates. It is soluble in ether, alcohol, and chloroform, but not in water.

IOM abbreviation for Isle of ▷Man, an island in the Irish Sea.

ion atom, or group of atoms, that is either positively charged (▷cation) or negatively charged (▷anion), as a result of the loss or gain of electrons during chemical reactions or exposure to certain forms of radiation. In solution or in the molten state, ionic compounds such as salts, acids, alkalis, and metal oxides conduct electricity. These compounds are known as ▷electrolytes.

Ions are produced during ▷electrolysis, for example the salt zinc chloride ($ZnCl_2$) dissociates into the positively charged Zn^{2+} and negatively charged Cl^- when electrolysed.

Iona island in the Inner Hebrides; area 850 hectares/2,100 acres. A centre of early Christianity, it is the site of a monastery founded in 563 by St ▷Columba. It later became a burial ground for Irish, Scottish, and Norwegian kings. It has a 13th-century abbey.

ion engine rocket engine that uses ▷ions (charged particles) rather than hot gas for propulsion. Ion engines have been successfully tested in space, where they will eventually be used for gradual rather than sudden velocity changes. In an ion engine, atoms of mercury, for example, are ionized (given an electric charge by an electric field) and then accelerated at high speed by a more powerful electric field.

Ionesco, Eugène (1912–1994) Romanian-born French dramatist. He was a leading exponent of the Theatre of the ▷Absurd. Most of his plays are in one act and concern the futility of language as a means of communication. These include *La Cantatrice chauve/The Bald Prima Donna* (1950) and *La Leçon/The Lesson* (1951). Later full-length plays include *Le Rhinocéros* (1958) and *Le Roi se meurt/Exit the King* (1961).

The comic wordplay of *La Cantatrice chauve* was inspired by the artificial sentences of a teach-yourself English book, and parodies both everyday conversation and the theatre.
It has played in Paris virtually without a break since its first performance in 1950.

Ionia in classical times the east coast of the Aegean Sea and the offshore islands, settled about 1000 BC by the Ionians; it included the cities of Ephesus, Miletus, and later Smyrna, and the islands of Chios and Samos.

Ionian member of a Hellenic people from beyond the Black Sea who crossed the Balkans *c.* 1980 BC and invaded Asia Minor. Driven back by the ▷Hittites, they settled all over mainland Greece, later being supplanted by the Achaeans.

Ionian Islands (Greek **Ionioi Nisoi**) island group off the west coast of Greece; area 860 sq km/332 sq mi; population (1991) 191,000. A British protectorate from 1815 until their cession to Greece in 1864, they include Cephalonia (Greek *Kefallínia*); Corfu (*Kérkyra*), a Venetian possession (1386–1797); Cythera (*Kíthira*); Ithaca (*Itháki*), the traditional home of ▷Odysseus; Leukas (*Levkás*); Paxos (*Paxoí*); and Zanté (*Zakynthos*).

Ionian Sea part of the Mediterranean Sea that lies between Italy and Greece, to the south of the Adriatic Sea, and containing the Ionian Islands.

Ionic in classical architecture, one of the five types of column; see ▷order.

ionic bond (or **electrovalent bond**) bond produced when atoms of one element donate electrons to atoms of another element, forming positively and negatively charged ▷ions respectively. The attraction between the oppositely charged ions constitutes the bond. Sodium chloride (Na^+Cl^-) is a typical ionic compound.

Each ion has the electronic structure of an inert gas (see ▷noble gas structure). The maximum number of electrons that can be gained is usually two.

ionic compound substance composed of oppositely charged ions. All salts, most bases, and some acids are examples of ionic compounds. They possess the following general properties: they are crystalline solids with a high melting point; are soluble in water and insoluble in organic solvents; and always conduct electricity when molten or in aqueous solution. A typical ionic compound is sodium chloride (Na^+Cl^-).

Mohammad Khatami
President of Iran

In the past five decades, we have never been successful in our experience with freedom . . . We Iranians are all dictators, in a sense.

Time, 19 January 1998

ionization potential measure of the energy required to remove an ▷electron from an ▷atom. Elements with a low ionization potential readily lose electrons to form ▷cations.

ionization therapy enhancement of the atmosphere of an environment by instrumentally boosting the negative ion content of the air.

Fumes, dust, cigarette smoke, and central heating cause negative ion deficiency, which particularly affects sufferers from respiratory disorders such as bronchitis, asthma, and sinusitis. Symptoms are alleviated by the use of ionizers in the home or workplace. In severe cases, ionization therapy is used as an adjunct to conventional treatment.

ionosphere ionized layer of Earth's outer ▷atmosphere (60–1,000 km/38–620 mi) that contains sufficient free electrons to modify the way in which radio waves are propagated, for instance by reflecting them back to Earth. The ionosphere is thought to be produced by absorption of the Sun's ultraviolet radiation. The British Antarctic Survey estimates that the ionosphere is decreasing at a rate of 1 km/0.6 mi every five years, based on an analysis of data from 1960 to 1998. Global warming is the probable cause.

ion plating method of applying corrosion-resistant metal coatings. The article is placed in argon gas, together with some coating metal, which vaporizes on heating and becomes ionized (acquires charged atoms) as it diffuses through the gas to form the coating. It has important applications in the aerospace industry.

IOW abbreviation for Isle of ▷Wight, an island and unitary authority off the coast of southern England.

Iowa state of the midwest USA. It is nicknamed Hawkeye State. Iowa was admitted to the Union in 1846 as the 29th US state. It is a major constituent of the US Corn Belt, with grain and cereal crops and livestock-rearing historically comprising a significant proportion of the state's income. Iowa is bordered to the south by Missouri, to the west Nebraska and South Dakota, to the north by Minnesota, and to the east by Wisconsin and Illinois, with the Mississippi River forming the state boundary.

population (1995) 2,841,800 **area** 145,754 sq km/56,276 sq mi **capital** ▷Des Moines **towns and cities** Cedar Rapids, Davenport, Sioux City, Waterloo **industries and products** cereals, soybeans, grasses and grains, pigs and cattle, poultry, dairy farming, chemicals, farm machinery, electrical goods, hardwood lumber, minerals, finance and insurance sectors

Related Web site: Iowa Office of the State Archaeologist
http://www.uiowa.edu/~osa/

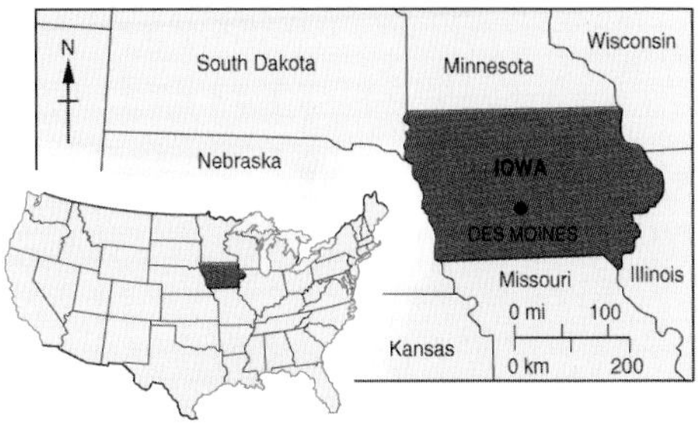

ipecacuanha (or **ipecac**) South American plant belonging to the madder family, the dried roots of which are used in medicine as an emetic (to cause vomiting) and to treat amoebic dysentery (infection of the intestine with amoebae). (*Psychotria ipecacuanha*, family Rubiaceae.)

Ipoh capital of Perak state, Peninsular Malaysia; population (2000 est) 566,200. The economy is based on tin mining.

Ipswich (Saxon **Gyppeswyk**) river port and administrative headquarters of ▷Suffolk, eastern England, on the Orwell estuary, 111 km/69 mi northeast of London; population (1996 est) 113,000. An important wool port in the 16th century, it now provides financial and distribution services, and is the location of British Telecom's laboratories. Other industries include engineering, and the manufacture of computer software, machinery, beer, flour, fibre optics, videotape and multi-media products, building materials, plastics, and electrical goods.

IQ (abbreviation for intelligence quotient) the ratio between a subject's 'mental' and chronological ages, multiplied by 100. A score of 100 ± 10 in an intelligence test is considered average.

Iqbāl, Muhammad (1876–1938) Islamic poet and thinker. His literary works, in Urdu and Persian, were mostly verse in the classical style, suitable for public recitation. He sought through his writings to arouse Muslims to take their place in the modern world. He was knighted in 1922.

IRA abbreviation for ▷Irish Republican Army.

Irákleio (or **Heraklion**) chief commercial port and capital city of Crete, Greece; population (1991) 117,200. There is a ferry link to Piraeus on the mainland. The archaeological museum contains a fine collection of antiquities from the island.

Iran see country box.

Irangate US political scandal in 1987 involving senior members of the Reagan administration (the name echoes the Nixon administration's ▷Watergate). Congressional hearings 1986–87 revealed that the US government had secretly sold weapons to Iran in 1985 and traded them for hostages held in Lebanon by pro-Iranian militias, and used the profits to supply right-wing Contra guerrillas in Nicaragua with arms. The attempt to get around the law (Boland amendment) specifically prohibiting military assistance to the Contras also broke other laws in the process.

Arms, including Hawk missiles, were sold to Iran via Israel (at a time when the USA was publicly calling for a worldwide ban on sending arms to Iran), violating the law prohibiting the sale of US weapons for resale to a third country listed as a 'terrorist nation', as well as the law requiring sales above $14 million to be reported to Congress. The negotiator in the field was Lt Col Oliver North, a military aide to the National Security Council, reporting in the White House to the national-security adviser (first Robert McFarlane, then John Poindexter). North and his associates were also channelling donations to the Contras from individuals and from other countries, including $2 million from Taiwan, $10 million from the sultan of Brunei, and $32 million from Saudi Arabia. The Congressional Joint Investigative Committee reported in November 1987 that the president bore 'ultimate responsibility' for allowing a 'cabal of zealots' to seize control of the administration's policy, but found no firm evidence that President Reagan had actually been aware of the Contra diversion. Reagan persistently claimed to have no recall of events, and some evidence was withheld on grounds of 'national security'. The hearings were criticized for finding that the president was not responsible for the actions of his subordinates. North was tried and convicted in May 1989 on charges of obstructing Congress and unlawfully destroying government documents. Poindexter was found guilty on all counts in 1990. Former defence secretary Caspar Weinberger was pardoned in 1992 by President George Bush to prevent further disclosures. In December 1993 the independent prosecutor Lawrence Walsh published his final report. It asserted that Reagan and Bush were fully aware of attempts to free US hostages in Lebanon in 1985–86 by means of unsanctioned arms sales to Iran. The total cost of the Irangate enquiries came to $35 million.

Iranian language the main language of Iran, more commonly known as Persian or ▷Farsi.

Iran

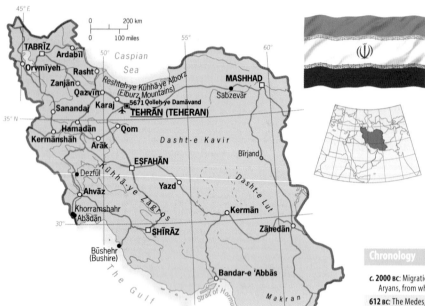

IRAN Iran is a country of contrasts. While influenced by Western culture, it is governed by religious law, and there are extremes of both rich and poor in spite of a wealthy oil economy. *Corel*

Iran (formerly Persia, until 1935) country in southwest Asia, bounded north by Armenia, Azerbaijan, the Caspian Sea, and Turkmenistan; east by Afghanistan and Pakistan; south and southwest by the Gulf of Oman and the Persian Gulf; west by Iraq; and northwest by Turkey.

NATIONAL NAME *Jomhûrî-ye Eslâmi-ye Îrân/Islamic Republic of Iran*
AREA 1,648,000 sq km/636,292 sq mi
CAPITAL Tehran
MAJOR TOWNS/CITIES Esfahan, Mashhad, Tabriz, Shiraz, Ahvaz, Kermanshah, Qom, Karaj
MAJOR PORTS Abadan
PHYSICAL FEATURES plateau surrounded by mountains, including Elburz and Zagros; Lake Rezayeh; Dasht-e-Kavir desert; occupies islands of Abu Musa, Greater Tunb and Lesser Tunb in the Gulf

Government

HEAD OF STATE AND GOVERNMENT Mohammad Khatami from 1997
LEADER OF THE ISLAMIC REVOLUTION Seyed Ali Khamenei from 1989
POLITICAL SYSTEM Islamic nationalist
POLITICAL EXECUTIVE unlimited presidency
ADMINISTRATIVE DIVISIONS 28 provinces
ARMED FORCES 520,000; plus 350,000 army reserves and paramilitary forces of 40,000 (2002 est)
DEATH PENALTY retained and used for ordinary crimes

Economy and resources

CURRENCY rial
GPD (US$) 107.5 billion (2002 est)
REAL GDP GROWTH (% change on previous year) 5.1 (2001)
GNI (US$) 112.1 billion (2002 est)
GNI PER CAPITA (PPP) (US$) 6,340 (2002 est)
CONSUMER PRICE INFLATION 17% (2003 est)
UNEMPLOYMENT 15% (2001)
FOREIGN DEBT (US$) 10.6 billion (2001 est)
MAJOR TRADING PARTNERS Germany, Japan, Italy, United Arab Emirates, China, France, South Korea
RESOURCES petroleum, natural gas, coal, magnetite, gypsum, iron ore, copper, chromite, salt, bauxite, decorative stone
INDUSTRIES mining, petroleum refining, textiles, food processing, transport equipment

EXPORTS crude petroleum and petroleum products, gas, agricultural goods, carpets, metal ores. Principal market: Japan 19.2% (2001)
IMPORTS machinery and motor vehicles, paper, textiles, iron and steel and mineral products, chemicals and pharmaceuticals. Principal source: Germany 10.1% (2001)
ARABLE LAND 8.8% (2000 est)
AGRICULTURAL PRODUCTS wheat, barley, sugar beet, sugar cane, rice, fruit, tobacco, livestock (cattle, sheep, and chickens) for meat and wool production

Population and society

POPULATION 68,920,000 (2003 est)
POPULATION GROWTH RATE 1.6% (2000–15)
POPULATION DENSITY (per sq km) 42 (2003 est)
URBAN POPULATION (% of total) 66 (2003 est)
AGE DISTRIBUTION (% of total population) 0–14 35%, 15–59 60%, 60+ 5% (2002 est)
ETHNIC GROUPS about 66% of Persian origin, 25% Turkic, 5% Kurdish, and 4% Arabic
LANGUAGE Farsi (official), Kurdish, Turkish, Arabic, English, French
RELIGION Shiite Muslim (official) 91%, Sunni Muslim 8%; Zoroastrian, Christian, Jewish, and Baha'i comprise about 1%
EDUCATION (compulsory years) 5
LABOUR FORCE 23.0% agriculture, 30.7% industry, 46.3% services (1996)
LIFE EXPECTANCY 69 (men); 72 (women) (2000–05)
CHILD MORTALITY RATE (under 5, per 1,000 live births) 42 (2001)

See also ▷Iran–Iraq War; ▷Islam; ▷Khomeini, Ayatollah; ▷Kurd; ▷Persia, ancient.

Chronology

c. 2000 BC: Migration from southern Russia of Aryans, from whom Persians claim descent.

612 BC: The Medes, from northwest Iran, destroyed Iraq-based Assyrian Empire to the west and established their own empire which extended into central Anatolia (Turkey-in-Asia).

550 BC: Cyrus the Great overthrew Medes' empire and founded the First Persian Empire, the Achaemenid, conquering much of Asia Minor, including Babylonia (Palestine and Syria) in 539 BC. Expansion continued into Afghanistan under Darius I, who ruled 521–486 BC.

499–449 BC: The Persian Wars with Greece ended Persian domination of the ancient world.

330 BC: Collapse of Achaemenid Empire following defeat by Alexander the Great.

AD 224: Sassanian Persian Empire founded by Ardashir, with its capital at Ctesiphon, in the northeast.

637: Sassanian Empire destroyed by Muslim Arabs at battle of Qadisiya; Islam replaced Zoroastrianism.

750–1258: Dominated by the Persianized Abbasid dynasty, who reigned as caliphs (Islamic civil and religious leaders), with a capital in Baghdad (Iraq).

1380s: Conquered by the Mongol leader, Tamerlane.

1501: Emergence of Safavids; the arts and architecture flourished, particularly under Abbas I, 'the Great', who ruled 1588–1629.

1736: The Safavids were deposed by the warrior Nadir Shah Afshar, who ruled until 1747.

1790: Rise of the Qajars, who transferred the capital from Esfahan in central Iran to Tehran, further north.

19th century: Increasing influence in the north of tsarist Russia, which took Georgia and much of Armenia 1801–28. Britain exercised influence in the south and east, and fought Iran 1856–57 over claims to Herat (western Afghanistan).

1906: Parliamentary constitution adopted after a brief revolution.

1925: Qajar dynasty overthrown, with some British official help, in a coup by Col Reza Khan, a nationalist Iranian Cossack military officer, who was crowned shah ('king of kings'), with the title Reza Shah Pahlavi.

1920s onwards: Economic modernization, Westernization, and secularization programme launched, which proved unpopular with traditionalists.

1935: Name changed from Persia to Iran.

1941: Pahlavi Shah was forced to abdicate during World War II by Allied occupation forces and was succeeded by his son Muhammad Reza Pahlavi, who continued the modernization programme.

1946: British, US, and Soviet occupation forces left Iran.

1951: Oilfields nationalized by radical prime minister Muhammad Mossadeq as anti-British and US sentiment increased.

1953: Mossadeq deposed, the nationalization plan changed, and the US-backed shah, Muhammad Reza Shah Pahlavi, took full control of the government.

1963: Hundreds of protesters, who demanded the release of the arrested fundamentalist Shiite Muslim leader Ayatollah Ruhollah Khomeini, were killed by troops.

1970s: Spiralling world oil prices brought rapid economic expansion.

1975: The shah introduced a single-party system.

1978: Opposition to the shah was organized from France by Ayatollah Ruhollah Khomeini, who demanded a return to the principles of Islam. Hundreds of demonstrators were killed by troops in Jaleh Square, Tehran.

1979: Amid mounting demonstrations by students and clerics, the shah left the country; Khomeini returned to create a nonparty theocratic Islamic state. Revolutionaries seized 66 US hostages at the embassy in Tehran; US economic boycott.

1980: Iraq invaded Iran, provoking a bitter war. The exiled shah died.

1981: US hostages were released.

1985–87: Fighting intensified in the Iran–Iraq War, with heavy loss of life.

1989: Khomeini issued a fatwa (public order) for the death of British writer Salman Rushdie for blasphemy against Islam.

1990: Generous peace terms with Iraq were accepted to close the Iran–Iraq war.

1991: Nearly 1 million Kurds arrived from northwest Iraq, fleeing persecution by Saddam Hussein after the Gulf War between Iraq and UN forces.

1993: Free-market economic reforms were introduced.

1997: Moderate politician Seyyed Muhammad Khatami was elected president.

1998: There were signs of rapprochement with the West. There was increased tension with Afghanistan, after the murder of Iranian civilians by the Taliban.

1999: Diplomatic relations with the UK were to be restored.

2000: Ali Akbar Mohtashami, a former radical, was elected in August to lead the reforming majority in Iran's parliament.

2001: Eight of Khatami's prominent supporters were convicted of crimes relating to expression and thought.

2002: The government passed the first foreign investment law since the 1950s as part of reforms to open the economy and lessen dependence on oil revenues.

2003: Pressure on the government from the United Nations International Atomic Energy Agency to address Western concerns over suspected nuclear weapon ambitions ended in an agreement to suspend uranium enrichment, allow spot checks of nuclear installations, and submit a list of present and past nuclear activities. An earthquake measuring 6.7 on the Richter scale devastated the southeastern town of Bam, with a death toll of around 41,000.

Iraq

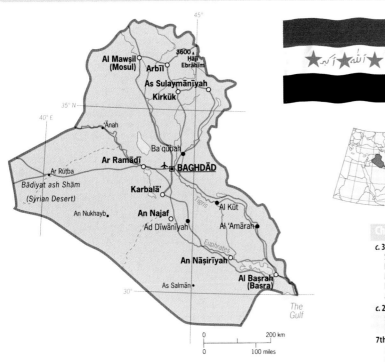

IRAQ An oil pumping station in Iraq. *Corel*

Iraq country in southwest Asia, bounded north by Turkey, east by Iran, southeast by the Persian Gulf and Kuwait, south by Saudi Arabia, and west by Jordan and Syria.

NATIONAL NAME *al-Jumhuriyya al'Iraqiyya/Republic of Iraq*
AREA 434,924 sq km/167,924 sq mi
CAPITAL Baghdad
MAJOR TOWNS/CITIES Mosul, Basra, Kirkuk, Hillah, An Najaf, An Nasiriya, As Sulamaniya, Irbil
MAJOR PORTS Basra
PHYSICAL FEATURES mountains in north, desert in west; wide valley of rivers Tigris and Euphrates running northwest–southeast; canal linking Baghdad and the Gulf opened in 1992

Government

HEAD OF STATE AND GOVERNMENT Iraqi governing council from 2004
POLITICAL SYSTEM pending (2003)
POLITICAL EXECUTIVE pending (2003)
ADMINISTRATIVE DIVISIONS 18 provinces
ARMED FORCES 389,000; plus 650,000 army reserves (2002 est)
CONSCRIPTION military service is compulsory for 18–24 months
DEATH PENALTY retained and used for ordinary crimes
DEFENCE SPEND (% GDP) 5 (2001 est)
HEALTH SPEND (% GDP) 3.7 (2000 est)

Economy and resources

CURRENCY Iraqi dinar
GPD (US$) 25.9 billion (2002 est)
REAL GDP GROWTH (% change on previous year) –6.0 (2001)
GNI PER CAPITA (PPP) (US$) 1,250 (2002 est)
CONSUMER PRICE INFLATION 70% (2002 est)
FOREIGN DEBT (US$) 18.4 billion (2001 est)
MAJOR TRADING PARTNERS USA, Italy, France, Spain, China, Jordan, Australia
RESOURCES petroleum, natural gas, sulphur, phosphates
INDUSTRIES chemical, petroleum, coal, rubber and plastic products, food processing, nonmetallic minerals, textiles, mining

EXPORTS crude petroleum (accounting for more than 95% of total foreign-currency earnings in 2000), dates and other dried fruits. Principal market: USA 61.1% (2001)
IMPORTS machinery and transport equipment, basic manufactured articles, cereals and other foodstuffs, iron and steel, military goods. Principal source: France 20.7% (2001)
ARABLE LAND 11.9% (2000 est)
AGRICULTURAL PRODUCTS dates, wheat, barley, maize, sugar beet, sugar cane, tobacco, melons, rice; livestock rearing (notably production of eggs and poultry meat)

Population and society

POPULATION 25,175,000 (2003 est)
POPULATION GROWTH RATE 2.0% (2000–15)
POPULATION DENSITY (per sq km) 57 (2003 est)
URBAN POPULATION (% of total) 67 (2003 est)
AGE DISTRIBUTION (% of total population) 0–14 41%, 15–59 54%, 60+ 5% (2002 est)
ETHNIC GROUPS about 79% Arab, 16% Kurdish (mainly in northeast), 3% Persian, 2% Turkish
LANGUAGE Arabic (80%) (official), Kurdish (15%), Assyrian, Armenian
RELIGION Shiite Muslim 60%, Sunni Muslim 37%, Christian 3%
EDUCATION (compulsory years) 6
LITERACY RATE 56% (men); 24% (women) (2003 est)
LABOUR FORCE 12% agriculture, 20% industry, 68% services (1997 est)
LIFE EXPECTANCY 60 (men); 62 (women) (2000–05)
CHILD MORTALITY RATE (under 5, per 1,000 live births) 133 (2001)
PHYSICIANS (per 1,000 people) 0.6 (1998 est)
HOSPITAL BEDS (per 1,000 people) 1.5 (1998 est)
TV SETS (per 1,000 people) 82 (1999 est)
RADIOS (per 1,000 people) 229 (1999)

See also ▷Gulf War; ▷Hussein, Saddam; ▷Iran–Iraq War; ▷Ottoman Empire; ▷Sumerian civilization.

Chronology

c. 3400 BC: The world's oldest civilization, the Sumerian, arose in the land between the rivers Euphrates and Tigris, known as lower Mesopotamia, which lies in the heart of modern Iraq. Its cities included Lagash, Eridu, Uruk, Kish, and Ur.
c. 2350 BC: The confederation of Sumerian city-states was forged into an empire by the Akkadian leader Sargon.
7th century BC: In northern Mesopotamia, the Assyrian Empire, based around the River Tigris and formerly dominated by Sumeria and Euphrates-centred Babylonia, created a vast empire covering much of the Middle East.
612 BC: The Assyrian capital of Nineveh was destroyed by Babylon and Mede (in northwest Iran).
c. 550 BC: Mesopotamia came under Persian control.
AD 114: Conquered by the Romans.
266: Came under the rule of the Persian-based Sassanians.
637: Sassanian Empire destroyed by Muslim Arabs at battle of Qadisiya, in southern Iraq; Islam spread.
750–1258: Dominated by Abbasid dynasty, who reigned as caliphs (Islamic civil and religious leaders) in Baghdad.
1258: Baghdad invaded and burned by Tatars.
1401: Baghdad destroyed by Mongol ruler Tamerlane.
1533: Annexed by Suleiman the Magnificent, becoming part of the Ottoman Empire until the 20th century, despite recurrent anti-Ottoman insurrections.
1916: Occupied by Britain during World War I.
1920: Iraq became a British League of Nations protectorate.
1921: Hashemite dynasty established, with Faisal I installed by Britain as king.
1932: Independence achieved from British protectorate status, with Gen Nuri-el Said as prime minister.
1941–45: Occupied by Britain during World War II.
1955: Signed the Baghdad Pact collective security treaty with the UK, Iran, Pakistan, and Turkey.
1958: Monarchy overthrown in military-led revolution, in which King Faisal was assassinated; Iraq became a republic; joined Jordan in an Arab Federation; withdrew from Baghdad Pact as left-wing military regime assumed power.
1963: Joint socialist-nationalist Ba'athist-military coup headed by Col Salem Aref and backed by US Central Intelligence Agency; reign of terror launched against the left.
1968: Ba'athist military coup put Maj-Gen Ahmed Hassan al-Bakr in power.
1979: Al-Bakr was replaced by Saddam Hussein of the Arab Ba'ath Socialist Party.
1980: The war between Iraq and Iran broke out.
1985–87: Fighting in the Iran–Iraq war intensified, with heavy loss of life.
1988: There was a ceasefire and talks began with Iran. Iraq used chemical weapons against Kurdish rebels in the northwest.
1989: There was an unsuccessful coup against President Hussein.
1990: A peace treaty favouring Iran was agreed. Iraq invaded and annexed Kuwait. US forces massed in Saudi Arabia at the request of King Fahd. The United Nations (UN) ordered Iraqi withdrawal and imposed a total trade ban and sanctioned the use of force. All foreign hostages were released.
1991: US-led Allied forces launched an aerial assault on Iraq and destroyed its infrastructure; a land–sea–air offensive to free Kuwait was successful. Uprisings of Kurds and Shiites were brutally suppressed by surviving Iraqi troops. Allied troops established 'safe havens' for Kurds in the north.
1992: The UN imposed a 'no-fly zone' over southern Iraq to protect Shiites.
1993: Iraqi incursions into the 'no-fly zone' prompted US-led alliance aircraft to bomb strategic targets in Iraq.
1994: Iraq renounced its claim to Kuwait, but failed to fulfil the other conditions required for the lifting of UN sanctions.
1996: Iraqi-backed attacks on Kurds prompted US retaliation; these air strikes destroyed Iraqi military bases in the south.
1997: Iraq continued to resist the US and Allied pressure to allow UN weapons inspections.
1998: Iraq expelled UN weapons inspectors, whose report showed that Iraq had failed to meet UN requirements on the destruction of chemical and biological weapons. US and UK forces launched Operation Desert Fox which lasted four days; there were further clashes between US–UK forces and Baghdad over the no-fly zone.
1999: US–UK air strikes resumed for a short time.
2000: The UN head of humanitarian aid efforts in Iraq resigned in protest at continuing sanctions. The Iraq–Syria border was re-opened, and Iraq began pumping oil to Syria in contravention of the UN-approved oil-for-food programme.
2001: Iraq signed free-trade agreements with Egypt and Syria. UK and US aircraft bombed radar sites near Baghdad, aiming to enforce the no-fly zones, despite a lack of unilateral support.
2002: Under increasing threat of military intervention by the USA, the Iraqi government agreed to re-admit United Nations (UN) weapons inspectors. The UN Security Council agreed unanimously on Resolution 1441, giving Saddam Hussein a final chance to comply with commitments to disarm weapons of mass distruction (WMD) or face 'serious consequences'.
2003: The USA and UK started controversial military action in March, nominally to rid Iraq of weapons of mass destruction (WMD). Following a rapid military advance through Iraq, US ground forces took control of the capital, Baghdad. Saddam Hussein's regime collapsed, his sons Uday and Qusay were killed, and widespread looting by Iraqi civilians followed. A new 25-member Iraqi governing council, appointed by US and UK officials and broadly representing the country's religious and ethnic balance, held its inaugural meeting in July. Iraqi insurgents and suicide bombers maintained almost daily attacks on US and other targets, including the International Red Cross, killing and wounding dozens of people. Saddam Hussein was captured alive and without resistance by US troops near Tikrit in December.

Iran–Iraq War war between Iran and Iraq (1980–88), claimed by the former to have begun with the Iraqi offensive on 21 September 1980, and by the latter with the Iranian shelling of border posts on 4 September 1980. Occasioned by a boundary dispute over the ▷Shatt-al-Arab waterway, it fundamentally arose because of Saddam Hussein's fear of a weakening of his absolute power base in Iraq by Iran's encouragement of the Shiite majority in Iraq to rise against the Sunni government. An estimated 1 million people died in the war.

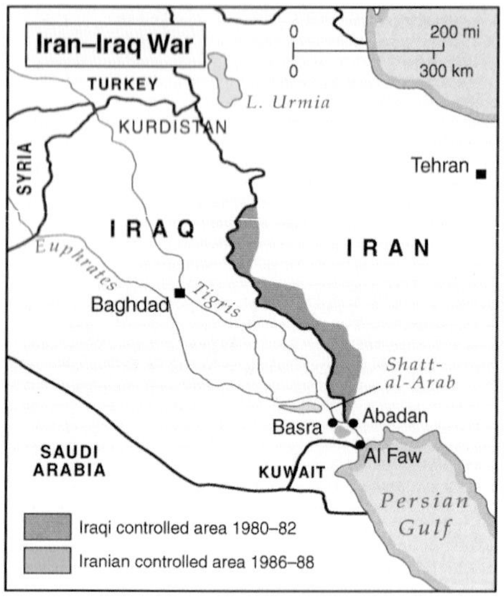

Iraq see country box.

Iraq War War (2003) between Iraq and an international coalition led by the USA and the UK. The conflict arose over issues surrounding the disarmament process accepted by Iraq as part of peace terms concluding the Gulf War (1991). Required to destroy and cease all development of weapons of mass destruction (including chemical, biological, and nuclear weapons), Iraq had expelled all United Nations (UN) weapons inspectors in 1998. Increasingly concerned that Iraq was continuing to develop such weapons in the inspectors' absence, the UN security council passed Resolution 1441 in November 2002 requiring both the return of the inspectors under Swedish diplomat Hans Blix and a full declaration of all Iraqi weapons programmes. Inspectors were admitted in November, and an Iraqi declaration issued the following month, but Iraqi actions were not deemed by the USA and the UK to conform to the full compliance required by Resolution 1441. US and UK efforts to secure a further UN resolution authorizing military action to forcefully disarm the Iraqi regime of Saddam Hussein were unsuccessful, and many countries expressed concern that the weapons inspectors had not been given enough time to assess the situation. In February 2003 France, Germany, and Russia all announced that they would veto any further resolutions brought to the security council, forcing the USA and the UK to forgo attempts to gain UN backing for war. On 20–21 March the USA and UK launched air strikes on Iraqi strategic targets, beginning the first phase of military action.

By the end of March, the Iraqi government remained defiant and reports of increasing civilian casualties provoked worldwide concern. US ground forces based in the Gulf advanced on Baghdad to confront the elite troops of the Iraqi Republican Guard. Meanwhile, British forces surrounded Iraq's second city of Basra in the south of the country. US forces took control of Baghdad on 9 April. It marked the collapse of Saddam Hussein's regime, although many senior government figures remained at large, and widespread looting by Iraqi civilians ensued. British troops meanwhile secured Basra. On 21 April retired US general Jay Garner arrived in Baghdad to become the US civil administrator for Iraq. However, France, Russia and Germany called for a central UN role in overseeing Iraq's post-war reconstruction and opposed the lifting of UN sanctions.

Irbil (or **Arbil** or **Erbil**) Kurdish capital city, in a governorate of the same name in northern Iraq; population (1998 est) 659,300. The city lies near Mosul and is one of the oldest settlements in the world, having been founded before 2300 BC by the Sumerians. Its position on the caravan route between Baghdad and Mosul helped it to become, as it still is, an important centre of commerce. In 1974 Irbil became the capital of a Kurdish autonomous region set up by the Iraqi government. It was captured by the Kurdish Democratic Party in 1996 with the help of Saddam Hussein.

Ireland an island lying to the west of Great Britain between the Atlantic Ocean and the Irish Sea. It comprises the provinces of Ulster, Leinster, Munster, and Connacht, and is divided into the Republic of ▷Ireland (which occupies the south, centre, and northwest of the island) and ▷Northern Ireland (which occupies the northeastern corner and forms part of the United Kingdom).

Ireland, John Nicholson (1879–1962) English composer. His works include the mystic orchestral prelude *The Forgotten Rite* (1913), a piano concerto (1930), and several song cycles. His pupils included Benjamin Britten and E J Moeran.

Ireland, Northern see ▷Northern Ireland.

Ireland, Republic of see country box.

Ireton, Henry (1611–1651) English general. During the Civil War he joined the parliamentary forces and fought at ▷Edgehill in 1642, Gainsborough in 1643, and ▷Naseby in 1645. After the Battle of Naseby, Ireton, who was opposed to both the extreme republicans and ▷Levellers, strove for a compromise with Charles I, but then played a leading role in his trial and execution.

Irian Jaya western portion of the island of New Guinea, disputed province of Indonesia; area 420,000 sq km/162,000 sq mi; population (1995 est) 1,794,000. The capital is Jayapura. The main industries include copper, palm oil, copra, maize, groundnuts, pepper, tuna, gold, oil, coal, and phosphates. It is mostly a mountainous and forested region, with the Pegunungan Maoke range rising to 5,029 m/16,499 ft at Jaya Peak. The province declared independence from Indonesia, as West Papua, in June 2000. However, the president of Indonesia stated that the declaration was unrepresentative of true feeling in the province.

iridium (Latin *iridis* 'rainbow') hard, brittle, silver-white, metallic element, symbol Ir, atomic number 77, relative atomic mass 192.2. It is resistant to tarnish and corrosion. Iridium is one of the so-called platinum group of metals; it occurs in platinum ores and as a free metal (▷native metal) with osmium in osmiridium, a natural alloy that includes platinum, ruthenium, and rhodium. It is alloyed with platinum for jewellery and used for watch bearings and in scientific instruments. It was named in 1804 by English chemist Smithson Tennant (1761–1815) for its iridescence in solution.

iridium anomaly unusually high concentrations of the element iridium found world-wide in sediments that were deposited at the Cretaceous-Tertiary boundary (▷K-T boundary) 65 million years ago. Since iridium is more abundant in extraterrestrial material, its presence is thought to be evidence for a large meteorite impact that may have caused the extinction of the dinosaurs and other life at the end of the Cretaceous.

iris in anatomy, the coloured muscular diaphragm that controls the size of the pupil in the vertebrate eye. It contains radial muscle that increases the pupil diameter and circular muscle that constricts the pupil diameter. Both types of muscle respond involuntarily to light intensity.

iris in botany, any of a group of perennial northern temperate flowering plants belonging to the iris family. The leaves are usually sword-shaped; the purple, white, or yellow flowers have three upright inner petals and three outward- and downward-curving ▷sepals. The wild yellow iris is called a flag. (Genus *Iris*, family Iridaceae.)

Irish people of Irish culture from Ireland or those of Irish descent. The Irish mainly speak English, though there are approximately 30,000–100,000 speakers of Irish Gaelic (see ▷Gaelic language), a Celtic language belonging to the Indo-European family.

Irish Gaelic first official language of the Irish Republic, but much less widely used than the second official language, English. See ▷Gaelic language.

Seán Ó Faoláin
Irish writer and critic

If we turn to early Irish literature, we find ourselves wandering in delighted bewilderment through a darkness shot with lightning and purple flame.

The Irish (1948)

Irish literature early Irish literature, in Gaelic, consists of the sagas, which are mainly in prose, and a considerable body of verse. The chief cycles are that of Ulster, which deals with the mythological ▷Conchobar and his followers, and the Ossianic, which has influenced European literature through ▷Macpherson's version.

Irish National Liberation Army (**INLA**) guerrilla organization committed to the end of British rule in Northern Ireland and Irish reunification. The INLA, founded in 1974, is a left-wing offshoot of the ▷Irish Republican Army (IRA). Among its activities was the killing of British politician Airey Neave in 1979. The INLA initially rejected the IRA's call for a ceasefire in 1994; its assassination in 1997 of loyalist leader Billy Wright threatened to destabilize the peace process and bomb attacks occurred in London in 1998. However, after the Omagh bomb atrocity in 1998 the INLA became the first republican subversive group to state explicitly that the war was over and voice strong support for the peace process.

The INLA has repeatedly been devastated by internecine feuds. In 1987 alone, 13 members were killed in a vendetta between rival factions. Its leader, Gino Gallagher, was shot and killed in Belfast in January 1996 by feuding INLA members.

Irish Republican Army (**IRA**) militant Irish nationalist organization formed in 1919, the paramilitary wing of ▷Sinn Fein. Its aim is to create a united Irish socialist republic including Ulster. To this end, the IRA has frequently carried out bombings and shootings. Despite its close association with Sinn Fein, it is not certain that the politicians have direct control of the military, the IRA usually speaking as a separate, independent organization. The chief common factor shared by Sinn Fein and the IRA is the aim of a united Ireland.

IRA splinter groups In 1969 the IRA split into two wings, one 'official' and the other 'provisional'. The official wing sought reunification by political means, while the Provisional IRA, or Provos as they became known, carried on with terrorist activities, their objective being the expulsion of the British from Northern Ireland. It is this wing, of younger, strongly sectarian, Ulster Catholics, who are now generally regarded and spoken of as the IRA. The left-wing Irish Republican Socialist Party, with its paramilitary wing, the ▷Irish National Liberation Army, split from the IRA in 1974.

Irkutsk city in southern Siberian Russia, capital of Irkutsk oblast (region); population (1990) 635,000. Irkutsk is situated near Lake Baikal on the River Angara; there is a large hydroelectric station near the city. Coal is mined here, while manufactured goods include iron, steel, motor vehicles, and machine tools. Its industrial development dates from the arrival of the Trans-Siberian railway in 1898.

Related Web site: WWW Irkutsk http://www.icc.ru/fed/title_eng.html

iron (Germanic *eis* 'strong') hard, malleable and ductile, silver-grey, metallic element, symbol Fe (from Latin *ferrum*), atomic number 26, relative atomic mass 55.847. It is the fourth most abundant element (the second most abundant metal, after aluminium) in the Earth's crust. Iron occurs in concentrated deposits as the ores hematite (Fe_2O_3), spathic ore ($FeCO_3$), and magnetite (Fe_3O_4). It sometimes occurs as a free metal, occasionally as fragments of iron or iron–nickel meteorites.

Iron is the most common and most useful of all metals; it is strongly magnetic and is the basis for ▷steel, an alloy with carbon and other elements (see also ▷cast iron).

In electrical equipment it is used in all permanent magnets and electromagnets, and forms the cores of transformers and magnetic amplifiers. It is noted for becoming oxidized (rusted) in moist air. In the human body, iron is an essential component of haemoglobin, the molecule in red blood cells that transports oxygen to all parts of the body. A deficiency in the diet causes a form of anaemia.

Iron, Ralph pseudonym of the South African writer Olive Schreiner when she published her novel *The Story of an African Farm* (1883).

Iron Age developmental stage of human technology when weapons and tools were made from iron. Preceded by the Stone and Bronze ages, it is the last technological stage in the Three Age System framework for prehistory. Iron was

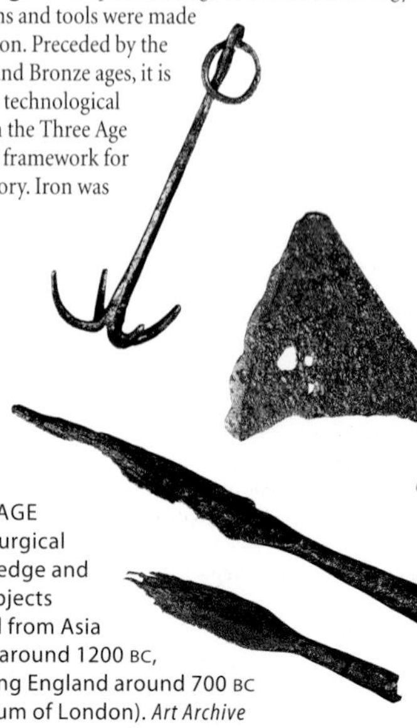

IRON AGE Metallurgical knowledge and iron objects spread from Asia Minor around 1200 BC, reaching England around 700 BC (Museum of London). *Art Archive*

Ireland, Republic of

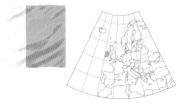

Ireland (or *Éire*) country occupying the main part of the island of Ireland, in northwest Europe. It is bounded to the east by the Irish Sea, south and west by the Atlantic Ocean, and northeast by Northern Ireland.

NATIONAL NAME *Poblacht Na hÉireann/Republic of Ireland*
AREA 70,282 sq km/27,135 sq mi
CAPITAL Dublin
MAJOR TOWNS/CITIES Cork, Limerick, Galway, Waterford, Dundalk, Bray
MAJOR PORTS Cork, Dun Laoghaire, Limerick, Waterford, Galway
PHYSICAL FEATURES central plateau surrounded by hills; rivers Shannon, Liffey, Boyne; Bog of Allen; Macgillicuddy's Reeks, Wicklow Mountains; Lough Corrib, lakes of Killarney; Galway Bay and Aran Islands

Government

HEAD OF STATE Mary McAleese from 1997
HEAD OF GOVERNMENT Bertie Ahern from 1997
POLITICAL SYSTEM liberal democracy
POLITICAL EXECUTIVE parliamentary
ADMINISTRATIVE DIVISIONS 26 counties within four provinces
ARMED FORCES 10,500 (2002 est)
CONSCRIPTION military service is voluntary
DEATH PENALTY abolished in 1990
DEFENCE SPEND (% GDP) 0.6 (2002 est)
EDUCATION SPEND (% GDP) 4.4 (2001 est)
HEALTH SPEND (% GDP) 6.7 (2002 est)

Economy and resources

CURRENCY euro (Irish pound, or punt Eireannach, until 2002)
GPD (US$) 119.9 billion (2002 est)
REAL GDP GROWTH (% change on previous year) 5.7 (2001)
GNI (US$) 92.6 billion (2002 est)
GNI PER CAPITA (PPP) (US$) 28,040 (2002 est)
CONSUMER PRICE INFLATION 2.9% (2003 est)
UNEMPLOYMENT 3.9% (2001)
MAJOR TRADING PARTNERS UK, USA, Germany, France, Japan, the Netherlands, Italy, Spain, Sweden, Singapore

RESOURCES lead, zinc, peat, limestone, gypsum, petroleum, natural gas, copper, silver
INDUSTRIES textiles, machinery, chemicals, electronics, motor vehicle manufacturing and assembly, food processing, beer, tourism
EXPORTS beef and dairy products, live animals, machinery and transport equipment, electronic goods, chemicals. Principal market: UK 21.8% (2000)
IMPORTS petroleum products, machinery and transport equipment, chemicals, foodstuffs, animal feed, textiles and clothing. Principal source: UK 31.3% (2000)
ARABLE LAND 15.2% (2000 est)
AGRICULTURAL PRODUCTS barley, potatoes, sugar beet, wheat, oats; livestock (cattle) and dairy products

Population and society

POPULATION 3,956,000 (2003 est)
POPULATION GROWTH RATE 0.8% (2000–15)
POPULATION DENSITY (per sq km) 56 (2003 est)
URBAN POPULATION (% of total) 60 (2003 est)
AGE DISTRIBUTION (% of total population) 0–14 21%, 15–59 64%, 60+ 15% (2002 est)
ETHNIC GROUPS most of the population has Celtic origins
LANGUAGE Irish Gaelic, English (both official)
RELIGION Roman Catholic 92%, Church of Ireland, other Protestant denominations 3%
EDUCATION (compulsory years) 9
LITERACY RATE 99% (men); 99% (women) (2003 est)
LABOUR FORCE 7.9% agriculture, 28.6% industry, 63.5% services (2000)
LIFE EXPECTANCY 74 (men); 80 (women) (2000–05)
CHILD MORTALITY RATE (under 5, per 1,000 live births) 6 (2001)
PHYSICIANS (per 1,000 people) 2.3 (1999 est)

HOSPITAL BEDS (per 1,000 people) 9.7 (1999 est)
TV SETS (per 1,000 people) 406 (1999)
RADIOS (per 1,000 people) 699 (1997)
INTERNET USERS (per 10,000 people) 2,709.2 (2002 est)
PERSONAL COMPUTER USERS (per 100 people) 42.1 (2002 est)

See also ▷Anglo-Irish Agreement; ▷Easter Rising; ▷Fianna Fáil; ▷home rule, Irish; ▷Irish Republican Army.

Chronology

3rd century BC: The Gaels, a Celtic people, invaded Ireland and formed about 150 small kingdoms.

AD c. 432: St Patrick introduced Christianity.

5th–9th centuries: Irish Church was a centre of culture and scholarship.

9th–11th centuries: The Vikings raided Ireland until defeated by High King Brian Bóruma at Clontarf in 1014.

12th–13th centuries: Anglo-Norman adventurers conquered much of Ireland, but no central government was formed and many became assimilated.

14th–15th centuries: Irish chieftains recovered their lands, restricting English rule to the Pale around Dublin.

1536: Henry VIII of England made ineffectual efforts to impose the Protestant Reformation on Ireland.

1541: Irish parliament recognized Henry VIII as king of Ireland; Henry gave peerages to Irish chieftains.

1579: English suppressed Desmond rebellion, confiscated rebel lands, and tried to 'plant' them with English settlers.

1610: James I established plantation of Ulster with Protestant settlers from England and Scotland.

1641: Catholic Irish rebelled against English rule; Oliver Cromwell brutally reasserted English control (1649–50); Irish landowners evicted and replaced with English settlers.

1689–91: Williamite War: following the 'Glorious Revolution', the Catholic Irish unsuccessfully supported James II against Protestant William III in civil war. Penal laws barred Catholics from obtaining wealth and power.

1720: Act passed declaring British Parliament's right to legislate for Ireland.

1739–41: Famine killed one-third of population of 1.5 million.

1782: Protestant landlords led by Henry Grattan secured end of restrictions on Irish trade and parliament.

1798: British suppressed revolt by Society of United Irishmen (with French support) led by Wolfe Tone.

1800: Act of Union abolished Irish parliament and created United Kingdom of Great Britain and Ireland, effective 1801.

1829: Daniel O'Connell secured Catholic Emancipation Act, which permitted Catholics to enter parliament.

1846–52: Potato famine reduced population by 20% through starvation and emigration.

1870: Land Act increased security for tenants but failed to halt agrarian disorder; Isaac Butt formed political party to campaign for Irish home rule (devolution).

IRELAND St Patrick, patron saint of Ireland. He converted much of Ireland from paganism to Christianity. *Archive Photos*

1885: Home-rulers, led by Charles Stewart Parnell, held balance of power in Parliament; first Home Rule Bill rejected in 1886; second Home Rule Bill defeated in 1893.

1905: Arthur Griffith founded the nationalist movement Sinn Fein ('Ourselves Alone').

1914: Ireland came close to civil war as Ulster prepared to resist implementation of Home Rule Act (postponed because of World War I).

1916: Easter Rising: nationalists proclaimed a republic in Dublin; British crushed revolt and executed 15 leaders.

1919: Sinn Fein MPs formed Irish parliament in Dublin in defiance of British government.

1919–21: Irish Republican Army (IRA) waged guerrilla war against British forces.

1921: Anglo-Irish Treaty partitioned Ireland; northern Ireland (Ulster) remained part of the United Kingdom; southern Ireland won full internal self-government with dominion status.

1922: Irish Free State proclaimed; IRA split over Anglo-Irish Treaty led to civil war (1922–23).

1932: Anti-Treaty party, Fianna Fáil, came to power under Éamon de Valera.

1937: New constitution established Eire (Gaelic name for Ireland) as a sovereign state and refused to acknowledge partition.

1949: After remaining neutral in World War II, Eire left the Commonwealth and became the Republic of Ireland.

1973: Ireland joined European Economic Community.

1985: The Anglo-Irish Agreement gave the Republic of Ireland a consultative role, but no powers, in the government of Northern Ireland.

1990: Mary Robinson was elected as the first female president.

1993: The Downing Street Declaration, a joint Anglo-Irish peace proposal for Northern Ireland, was issued.

1997: Mary McAleese was elected president; she appointed Bertie Ahern as her prime minister.

1998: A multiparty agreement (the Good Friday Agreement) was reached on the future of Northern Ireland. The subsequent referendum showed a large majority in favour of dropping Ireland's claim to Northern Ireland. Strict legislation was passed against terrorism.

1999: The IRA agreed to begin decommissioning discussions and a coalition government was established, with David Trimble as first minister. Powers were devolved to the province by the British government in December.

2000: After it was revealed that there had been no arms handover, the British Secretary of State for Northern Ireland suspended the Northern Ireland Assembly and reintroduced direct rule. Within hours of the suspension of the Assembly, the British government announced a new IRA initiative on arms decommissioning.

produced in Thailand *c.* 1600 BC, but was considered inferior in strength to bronze until *c.* 1000 BC, when metallurgical techniques improved, and the alloy steel was produced by adding carbon during the smelting process.

Ironworking was introduced into different regions over a wide time span, appearing in Thailand *c.* 1600 BC, Asia Minor *c.* 1200 BC, central Europe *c.* 900 BC, China *c.* 600 BC, and in remoter areas during exploration and colonization by the Old World. It reached the Fiji Islands with an expedition in the late 19th century. Iron Age cultures include ▷Hallstatt (named after a site in Austria) and ▷La Tène (named after a site in Switzerland).

Economy and society The economic working of iron, particularly for use in agricultural tools and weapons, was a great step forward in material culture. Unlike copper and tin used in bronze, iron ores are widely available and this enabled the spread of cheap, durable metal tools. The Iron Age saw the development of hierarchical systems, with tribes and chiefs, and the strengthening of defences, such as hill forts and enclosures. Complex trade routes were established between the Mediterranean and northern Europe, especially using rivers. Conspicuous consumption increased among chiefs, particularly of alcohol, and intense competition increased the output of prestige goods. Ritual behaviour is evidenced by depositions in pits and water, or bogland; and skeletal remains suggest the practice of disarticulation (separation of joints), possibly as part of ritual process. Celtic beliefs and practices became significant, and were written about by classical authors, such as Tacitus and Julius Caesar.

End of the Iron Age In areas that became part of the Roman Empire, the Iron Age is succeeded in archaeological terminology by a Roman period, but elsewhere the Iron Age continues until some other literate culture, often Christianity, becomes dominant. In Scandinavia, the Roman Iron Age and the periods of migrations and Vikings are considered to be Iron Age by Scandinavian scholars, since they are essentially prehistoric (or protohistoric) rather than historic periods. In Britain, the Iron Age dates from about 700 BC until the Roman invasion of AD 43, although Iron Age culture lingered beyond this date, particularly in Cornwall.

ironclad wooden warship covered with armour plate. The first to be constructed was the French *Gloire* in 1858, but the first to be launched was the British HMS *Warrior* in 1859. The first battle between ironclads took place during the American Civil War, when the Union *Monitor* fought the Confederate *Virginia* (formerly the *Merrimack*) on 9 March 1862. The design was replaced by battleships of all-metal construction in the 1890s.

Iron Curtain in Europe after World War II, the symbolic boundary between capitalist West and communist East during the ▷Cold War. The term was popularized by the UK prime minister Winston Churchill from 1946.

An English traveller to Bolshevik Russia, Ethel Snowden (1881–1951), used the term with reference to the Soviet border in 1920. The Nazi minister Goebbels used it a few months before Churchill in 1945 to describe the divide between Soviet-dominated and other nations that would follow German capitulation.

Iron Gate (Romanian **Porţile de Fier**) narrow gorge, interrupted by rapids, in Romania. A hydroelectric scheme undertaken between 1964 and 1970 by Romania and Yugoslavia transformed this section of the River Danube into a lake 145 km/90 mi long and eliminated the rapids as a navigation hazard. Before flooding, in 1965, an archaeological survey revealed Europe's oldest urban settlement, Lepenski Vir.

Iron Guard profascist group controlling Romania in the 1930s. To counter its influence, King Carol II established a dictatorship in 1938 but the Iron Guard forced him to abdicate in 1940.

iron ore any mineral from which iron is extracted. The chief iron ores are ▷magnetite, a black oxide; ▷haematite, or kidney ore, a reddish oxide; limonite, brown, impure oxyhydroxides of iron; and siderite, a brownish carbonate. Iron ores are found in a number of different forms, including distinct layers in igneous intrusions, as components of contact metamorphic rocks, and as sedimentary beds. Much of the world's iron is extracted in Russia, Kazakhstan, and the Ukraine. Other important producers are the USA, Australia, France, Brazil, and Canada; over 40 countries produce significant quantities of ore.

iron pyrites (or **pyrite**) (FeS_2) common iron ore. Brassy yellow, and occurring in cubic crystals, it is often called 'fool's gold', since only those who have never seen gold would mistake it.

Iroquois member of a confederation of ▷American Indian peoples of northeastern North America formed about 1570. Known originally as the Five Nations, it was composed of the Cayuga, ▷Mohawk, Oneida, Onondaga, and Seneca. The Tuscarora joined after 1722, and it became known as the **Six Nations**. The organization was analyzed by Benjamin Franklin and provided one of the sources used by the colonists to form their own confederacy and write their own constitution. Their descendants now live in Ontario, Québec, New York, and Oklahoma and number about 50,000 (1990). Iroquois also refers to the American Indian groups which speak a language belonging to the Iroquoian language family and also includes ▷Cherokee and ▷Huron.

irrationalism feature of many philosophies rather than a philosophical movement. Irrationalists deny that the world can be comprehended by conceptual thought, and often see the human mind as determined by unconscious forces.

irrational number in mathematics, number that cannot be expressed as an exact ▷fraction. Irrational numbers include some square roots (for example, $\sqrt{2}$, $\sqrt{3}$, and $\sqrt{5}$ are irrational) and numbers such as π (the ratio of the circumference of a circle to its diameter, which is approximately equal to 3.14159) and e (the base of ▷natural logarithms, approximately 2.71828). If an irrational number is expressed as a decimal it would extend infinitely without repeating.

Irrawaddy (Myanmar **Ayeryarwady**) chief river of Myanmar (Burma), flowing roughly north–south for 2,090 km/1,300 mi across the centre of the country into the Bay of Bengal. Its sources are the Mali and N'mai rivers; its chief tributaries are the Chindwin and Shweli.

irredentist (Latin *redemptus*, bought back) person who wishes to reclaim the lost territories of a state. The term derives from an Italian political party founded in about 1878 intending to incorporate Italian-speaking areas into the newly formed state.

irrigation artificial water supply for dry agricultural areas by means of dams and channels. Drawbacks are that it tends to concentrate salts at the surface, ultimately causing soil infertility, and that rich river silt is retained at dams, to the impoverishment of the land and fisheries below them. Irrigation has been practised for thousands of years, in Eurasia as well as the Americas. An example is the channelling of the annual Nile flood in Egypt, which has been done from earliest times to its present control by the Aswan High Dam.

IRRIGATION Modern methods of irrigation, such as this pivot irrigation system operating in Burkina Faso, west Africa, improve crop yields and reduce the dependency on seasonal rains. However, such schemes are capital-intensive and often lead to the cultivation of high-value crops at the expense of less profitable cereal staples. *Premaphotos Wildlife*

Irving, Henry (1838–1905) Stage name of John Henry Brodribb. English actor. He established his reputation from 1871, chiefly at the Lyceum Theatre in London, where he became manager in 1878. He staged a series of successful Shakespearean productions, including *Romeo and Juliet* (1882), with himself and Ellen ▷Terry playing the leading roles. He was the first actor to be knighted, in 1895.

Irving, Washington (1783–1859) US essayist and short-story writer. He published a mock-heroic *History of New York* (1809), supposedly written by the Dutchman 'Diedrich Knickerbocker'. In 1815 he went to England where he published *The Sketch Book of Geoffrey Crayon, Gent* (1820), which contained such stories as 'Rip Van Winkle' and 'The Legend of Sleepy Hollow'. His other works include *The Alhambra* (1832), sketches about Spanish subjects, and *Tour of the Prairies* (1835), about the American West. His essays and tales remain popular.

Isaac In the Old Testament, a Hebrew patriarch, son of ▷Abraham and Sarah, and father of Esau and Jacob.

Isabella two Spanish queens:

Isabella (I) the Catholic (1451–1504) Queen of Castile from 1474, after the death of her brother Henry IV. By her marriage with ▷Ferdinand of Aragon in 1469, the crowns of two of the Christian states in the Spanish peninsula cemented their dynastic link. Her youngest daughter was Catherine of Aragon, first wife of Henry VIII of England. Under Isabella and her husband (the Catholic king), the reconquista was finally fulfilled with the taking of the Moorish city Granada in 1492. She introduced the Inquisition into Castile, expelled the Jews, and gave financial encouragement to Columbus.

Isabella II (1830–1904) Queen of Spain from 1833, when she succeeded her father Ferdinand VII (1784–1833). The Salic Law banning a female sovereign had been repealed by the Cortes (parliament), but her succession was disputed by her uncle Don Carlos de Bourbon (1788–1855). After seven years of civil war, the ▷Carlists were defeated. She abdicated in favour of her son Alfonso XII in 1868.

Isaiah (lived 8th century BC) In the Old Testament, the first major Hebrew prophet. The Book of Isaiah in the Old Testament was traditionally believed to be written by him, but it is now thought that large parts of it are the work of at least two other writers.

ischaemic heart disease (IHD) disorder caused by reduced perfusion of the coronary arteries due to atherosclerosis. It is the commonest cause of death in the Western world, leading to more than a million deaths each year in the USA and about 160,000 in the UK. See also ▷coronary artery disease.

Early symptoms of IHD include ▷angina or palpitations, but sometimes a heart attack is the first indication that a person is affected.

ISDN abbreviation for ▷Integrated Services Digital Network, a telecommunications system.

Isherwood, Christopher (William Bradshaw) (1904–1986) English-born US novelist. He lived in Germany from 1929–33 just before Hitler's rise to power, a period that inspired *Mr Norris Changes Trains* (1935) and *Goodbye to Berlin* (1939), creating the character of Sally Bowles, the basis of the musical *Cabaret* (1968). Returning to England, he collaborated with W H ▷Auden in three verse plays.

Ishiguro, Kazuo (1954–) Japanese-born British novelist. His novel *An Artist of the Floating World* won the 1986 Whitbread Prize, and *The Remains of the Day*, about an English butler coming to realize the extent of his self-sacrifice and self-deception, won the 1989 Booker Prize and was made into a successful film in 1993. His works, which are characterized by a sensitive style and subtle structure, include *The Unconsoled* (1995), and *When We Were Orphans* (2000), which was shortlisted for the 2000 Booker Prize.

Ishmael In the Old Testament, the son of ▷Abraham and his wife Sarah's Egyptian maid Hagar; traditional ancestor of Muhammad and the Arab people. He and his mother were driven away by Sarah's jealousy. Muslims believe that it was Ishmael, not Isaac, whom God commanded Abraham to sacrifice, and that Ishmael helped Abraham build the ▷Kaaba in Mecca.

Ishtar (or **Istar**) Mesopotamian goddess of fertility, sexual love, wedlock, maternity, and war, worshipped by the Babylonians and Assyrians, and personified as the legendary queen ▷Semiramis. She was the equivalent of the Canaanite and Syrian ▷Astarte.

Isidore of Seville (*c.* 560–636) Spanish philosopher, theologian, writer, and missionary. His *Etymologiae* was the model for later medieval encyclopedias and helped to preserve classical thought during the Middle Ages. As archbishop of Seville from 600, he strengthened the church in Spain and converted many Jews and Aryan Visigoths. His *Chronica Maiora* remains an important source for the history of Visigothic Spain.

Isis (Ancient Egyptian 'seat') principal goddess of ancient Egypt; the daughter of Geb and Nut (Earth and Sky); and the personification of the throne of her brother-husband ▷Osiris. She searched for the body of Osiris after he was murdered by his brother, Set. Her son, the sky god ▷Horus, defeated and captured Set, but beheaded his mother because she would not allow Set to be killed. She was later identified with ▷Hathor, and by the Greeks with ▷Demeter, goddess of agriculture, and Zeus' lover Io.

Iskandariya Arabic name for the Egyptian port of ▷Alexandria.

Islam (Arabic 'submission', that is, to the will of Allah) religion founded in the Arabian peninsula in the early AD 600s. It emphasizes the oneness of God, his omnipotence, beneficence, and inscrutability. Its sacred book is the **Koran**, which Muslims believe was divinely revealed to ▷Muhammad, the prophet or messenger of Allah. There are two main Muslim sects: ▷Sunni and ▷Shiite. Others include **Sufism**, a mystical movement which originated in the AD 700s. The word Muslim means 'one who makes his peace with God and Man'.

Beliefs The fundamental beliefs of Islam are contained in the *shahada* (testimony) – 'I bear witness that there is no God but Allah and Muhammad is the Prophet of Allah' – which is a constituent part of the *adhan* (call to worship). Other beliefs central to Islam are the Creation, the Fall of Adam, angels and ▷jinn, heaven and hell, the Day of Judgement, God's predestination of good and evil, and the succession of scriptures revealed to the prophets, who include Moses and Jesus. The perfect, final form of the scriptures is the Koran or Quran (literally 'reading'). It contains Muhammad's teachings, and was written down about 20 years after his death. It is divided into 114 **suras** (chapters), each of which is divided into a number of *ayat* (verses).

Muslim populations Roughly speaking all lands where Arabic is spoken, together with Turkey, Iran, Afghanistan, Pakistan, and North Africa as far as the Tropic of Cancer, are solidly Muslim. In the Central Asian republics there are about 20 million in Uzbekistan, probably 8 million in Kazakhstan, and around 5 million altogether in Kyrgyzstan, Tajikistan, and Turkmenistan. Other Muslim populations include China (29 million); the Balkan states (4.5 million); Malaysia (10 million); Indonesia (172 million), the Philippines (3.3 million), and sub-Saharan Africa (about 75 million). Islam is the second-largest religion in the UK, with about 1 million followers.

    Related Web site: Islamic Calendar http://www.cob. ohio-state.edu/~wmuhanna/hijri-intro.html

Islamabad capital of Pakistan from 1967 (replacing Karachi), in the Potwar district, at the foot of the Margala Hills and immediately northwest of Rawalpindi; population (1998 est) 524,500. The city was designed by Constantinos Doxiadis in the 1960s. Landmarks include the Shahrazad Hotel and national Assembly Building. The Federal Capital Territory of Islamabad has an area of 907 sq km/350 sq mi and a population (1998 est) of 799,000. Islamabad is the centre of an agricultural region in the Vale of Kashmir.

Islamic architecture the architecture of the Muslim world, highly diverse but unified by climate, culture, and a love of geometric and arabesque ornament, as well as by the mobility of ideas, artisans, and architects throughout the region. The central public buildings are ▷mosques, often with a dome and minaret; domestic houses face an inner courtyard and are grouped together, with vaulted streets linking the blocks.

    The **mosque** is the centre of religious life throughout the Islamic world, the *masjid* or 'place of prostration'. The major mosque in a city is the *masjid al-jum'a*, the Friday mosque. The mosque form originated in Muhammad's house in Medina (where he fled from Mecca in 622). It was a mud-walled courtyard enclosure with a shaded perimeter. The elements of the mosque are essentially functional rather than symbolic. There is no division between the sacred and secular. A *mihrab* niche indicates the orientation to Mecca. To the right of the *mihrab* stands the *minbar*, the pulpit. A minaret signifies the presence of the mosque and provides a platform from which the muezzin calls the faithful to prayer. A courtyard *sahn* is a place of gathering for the community. The Arab-type mosque plan of columned halls surrounding a courtyard is found throughout North Africa, Arabia, Syria, and Mesopotamia; an example is the mosque of Ahmad ibn Tulun, Cairo, Egypt (876–79). The other great mosque type is the four-*eyvan* mosque originating in Iran. Here the courtyard has a high *eyvan*, or arched recess, in the centre of each side. This plan comes from the Persian house and is seen at its noblest in the Masjid-i-Jum'a in Esfahan, Iran, 8th–18th centuries. A very flexible plan form, it is found from Cairo to central Asia in mosques, theological colleges, caravanserais, and hospitals.

    In the Ottoman Empire, the stimulus of the ▷Hagia Sophia (532–37), Istanbul, the great church of Justinian, inspired the development of the imperial Turkish mosque in which the open courtyard of the Arab and Iranian mosques is translated into a great space enclosed by a large central dome; an example is the Suleymaniye, Istanbul (1550–57) by Sinan. The **minaret** was originally square, following the towers of Christian churches. Spiral minarets are found but most commonly they take the form of a tapering cylindrical tower. The **Islamic city** is a highly organic entity. The basic cellular unit is the courtyard house, representing the desire for privacy and familial obligations of Muslim life.

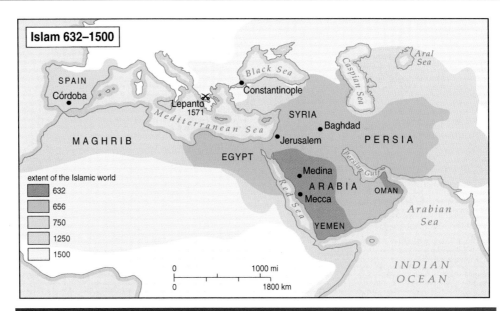

Islam: Key Dates

3rd–6th centuries
The eastern Roman Empire and the Persian Sassanians are in continuous conflict for the domination of Syria, Egypt, and Asia Minor.

571
Birth of Muhammad, the prophet of Islam, in Mecca.

6th–7th centuries
Islam begins in Arabia, calling for a new way of life based on submission to God. An Islamic state is established that develops further during the formative period of the four Orthodox caliphs or successors to the prophet, Abu Bakr, Umar, Uthman, and Ali. During this period the Persians are defeated (637) and their capital Cteisphon is captured.

8th century
Islam expands under the Umayyad and Abbasid dynasties to Spain and Sind; southern France is invaded; Southern Italy is occupied. The early schools of Islamic law continue to develop during this period and legal doctrine becomes integrated into the legal practices of the courts.

9th century
Turkish slave Mamelukes rise to power in Baghdad and a dictatorship is established in Egypt that occupies Syria, in a move towards the fragmentation of the main Islamic state.

10th century
The Fatimid Shiite Isma'ili sect conquers Cairo in 969. Al-Azhar University is founded in 972. With the insanity of the Fatimid caliph (who believes himself God) and his death in 1018, a new religion appears in the form of the Druze Shia subsect, comprised of those adherents who believe in the caliph's divinity.

11th century
The Abbasid and Fatimid dynasties and the Byzantine empire decline. The central Asian Turkish nomads known as the Seljuks emerges. Islamic law becomes stagnant. The first Christian Crusade captures Muslim-held Jerusalem in 1099.

12th century
Muslims are reunited in a jihad or holy war, and recapture Jerusalem under the leadership of Saladin. The Mongols emerge as a new force in the Middle East, seizing Persia and part of Syria.

13th century
The Mongols continue their march, sacking Baghdad. With the fall of the city 1258 and the death of the caliph Mustasim, the Abbasid caliphate ends. Only two years later the Mongols are defeated by Qutuz at the decisive Battle of Ayn Jalut on the way to Damascus, ending their expansion towards the heartland of the Muslim world. Thirty years later the Mongol khan converts to Islam. This is followed by the emergence of the first Ottomans in Turkey.

14th century
Ottoman Turks invade Bulgarian territory up to the Balkans.

15th century
In the Second Battle of Kossova in 1446 Serbia is annexed to Turkey, with Bosnia as its vassal. Muhammad al-Fath conquers Constantinople in 1453. Albania is annexed to the Ottoman Turkish empire. In 1492, Granada, the last Muslim state in Spain, falls to the monarchs of Spain, Ferdinand and Isabella. The Safavid dynasty is founded in Persia.

16th–17th centuries
Ottoman power reaches its height during the reign of the Ottoman Suleiman the Magnificent 1520–65. The first unsuccessful Ottoman siege of Vienna is in 1529, and the second in 1683. With the defeat of the Ottomans in the naval battle of Lepanto, their dominance of the Mediterranean ends. The forcible conversion of Muslims to Catholicism begins in Spain.

18th century
In Arabia, Muhammad ibn-Abd-al-Wahab (1703–1792) preaches a return to fundamental Muslim values.

19th century
Muhammad Ali is appointed pasha of Egypt by the Turks in 1805, after subduing the Mamelukes. He occupies Mecca and Taif in 1813 and continues across Arabia, expelling the Saudis from their capital Dariyya in 1818. European powers take control of many territories that previously came under Muslim rule. In 1876 Britain purchases shares in the Suez Canal and becomes involved in Egypt, with military occupation following in 1882. In 1878 Turkey hands Cyprus to Britain and a year later, after the Treaty of Berlin, Turkey loses 80 percent of its European territory.

20th century
European expansion continues in the Middle East. During World War I, the Arabs revolt against Ottoman Turkish rule. In 1921, the British make kings of two sons of the Sharif of Mecca, Abdullah ibn Hussein of Transjordan and Faisal of Iraq. Mustafa Kemal abolishes the Turkish sultanate in 1922 and becomes the first president of Turkey. Reza Shah seizes the government in Persia in 1925. Abdul Aziz Ibn Saud captures Riyadh and Mecca, assuming the title of king in 1926. Hasan al-Banna founds the Muslim Brotherhood in Egypt in 1928. Egyptian president Gamal Abdel Nasser nationalizes the Suez Canal in 1956 and executes Sayyid Qutb, the leader of the Muslim Brotherhood. The secular Pahlavi dynasty in Iran ends in 1979 with the return from exile of Ayatollah Khomeini, who declares Iran an Islamic Republic. The Iraq–Iran War is followed by Saddam Hussein's invasion of Kuwait (1990) and the Gulf War. Revivalist movements arise, calling for a return to fundamental Islamic values; in Algeria this leads to violent unrest. Islamic regimes are established in Iran, Afghanistan, Sudan, and Pakistan.

The houses are grouped into quarters, often of a tribal or ethnic character. Each quarter has its own mosques and facilities. At the centre of the city stands the focus of the community, the congregational mosque, the *masjid al-jum'a*. The arteries of this intricate organism are the vaulted streets of the souk, or bazaar, which thread outwards from the *masjid al-jum'a* towards the great gates of the enclosing fortified walls. The key monuments and facilities of the city are found along the souk – the religious colleges, baths, hospitals, and fountains. Examples of these are found in Fez, Morocco; Aleppo, Syria; and Esfahan, Iran. **Islamic private houses** are invariably inward-looking courtyard houses. A bent corridor (for privacy) leads from the gated entry from the public lane into a courtyard paved with tiles, often planted with shade trees and with a pool at the centre. Surrounding the courtyard are the principal rooms of the house. Different sides of the courtyard may provide separate accommodation for sections of the extended family.

Decoration and colour In Islam there is a general dislike of figurative representation. As a consequence, architectural decoration relies on calligraphic script and abstract ornament, often combined with a passion for colour, intensified by the desert environment. The domes and courts of such buildings as the 17th-century Masjid-i-Sháh, Esfahan, Iran, are entirely clothed in faience tiles. Arabic script is used extensively in the earliest surviving Islamic building, the Dome of the Rock, Jerusalem, (AD 691), and thereafter the word of God plays a significant role in architectural decoration.

Islamic gardens In a largely arid region, the Islamic garden represents an image of paradise. The basic plan is a rectangular enclosure walled against the dust of the desert and divided into at least four sections by water channels. Pavilions are placed at focal points within the gardens. An example is Chehel Sutun, Esfahan, 17th century.

Islamic art art and design of the Muslim world, dating from the foundation of the Islamic faith in the 7th century AD. The traditions laid down by Islam created devout, painstaking craftsmen whose creative purpose was the glory of God. Elements and motifs were borrowed from ▷Byzantine, ▷Coptic, and ▷Persian Sassanian (AD 224–642) traditions and fused into a distinctive decorative style, based on arabic calligraphy. Sculpture was prohibited and carvers turned instead to exquisite inlay and fretwork, notably on doors and screens, in Islamic monuments such as the Alhambra Palace, Granada, Spain, and the Taj Mahal, India. Today, Islamic art is to be found predominately in Egypt, Iran, Iraq, Turkey, the Indian subcontinent, and the Central Asian Republics.

island area of land surrounded entirely by water. Australia is classed as a continent rather than an island, because of its size.

Islands can be formed in many ways. **Continental islands** were once part of the mainland, but became isolated (by tectonic movement, erosion, or a rise in sea level, for example). **Volcanic islands**, such as Japan, were formed by the explosion of underwater volcanoes. **Coral islands** consist mainly of ▷coral, built up over many years. An **atoll** is a circular coral reef surrounding a lagoon; atolls were formed when a coral reef grew up around a volcanic island that subsequently sank or was submerged by a rise in sea level. **Barrier islands** are found by the shore in shallow water, and are formed by the deposition of sediment eroded from the shoreline.

island arc curved chain of volcanic islands. Island arcs are common in the Pacific where they ring the ocean on both sides; the Aleutian Islands off Alaska are an example. The volcanism that forms island arcs is a result of subduction of an oceanic plate beneath another plate, as evidenced by the presence of ocean trenches on the convex side of the arc, and the Benioff zone of high seismic activity beneath.

Largest Islands in the World

Island	Location	Area sq km	Area sq mi
Greenland	northern Atlantic	2,175,600	840,000
New Guinea	southwestern Pacific	800,000	309,000
Borneo	southwestern Pacific	744,100	287,300
Madagascar	Indian Ocean	587,041	226,657
Baffin	Canadian Arctic	507,450	195,875
Sumatra	Indian Ocean	424,760	164,000
Honshu	northwestern Pacific	230,966	89,176
Great Britain	northern Atlantic	218,078	84,200
Victoria	Canadian Arctic	217,206	83,896
Ellesmere	Canadian Arctic	196,160	75,767
Sulawesi	Indian Ocean	189,216	73,057
South Island, New Zealand	southwestern Pacific	149,883	57,870
Java	Indian Ocean	126,602	48,900
North Island, New Zealand	southwestern Pacific	114,669	44,274
Cuba	Caribbean Sea	110,860	42,803
Newfoundland	northwestern Atlantic	108,860	42,030
Luzon	western Pacific	104,688	40,420
Iceland	northern Atlantic	103,000	39,768
Mindanao	western Pacific	94,630	36,537
Ireland (Northern Ireland and the Republic of Ireland)	northern Atlantic	84,406	32,590
Hokkaido	northwestern Pacific	83,515	32,245
Sakhalin	northwestern Pacific	76,400	29,500
Hispaniola (Dominican Republic and Haiti)	Caribbean Sea	76,192	29,418
Banks	Canadian Arctic	70,028	27,038
Tasmania	southwestern Pacific	67,800	26,171
Sri Lanka	Indian Ocean	65,610	25,332
Devon	Canadian Arctic	55,247	21,331

Isle of Man see ▷Man, Isle of.

Isle of Wight see ▷Wight, Isle of.

islets of Langerhans groups of cells within the pancreas responsible for the secretion of the hormone insulin. They are sensitive to the blood sugar, producing more hormone when glucose levels rise.

Islington inner borough of north Greater London, including the suburbs of Finsbury, Barnsbury, and Holloway; population (1991) 164,700. Features include the Sadler's Wells music hall, built in 1638 when Clerkenwell springs were exploited and Islington Spa became famous, and the present Sadler's Wells theatre (1927–31), where opera and ballet companies were established under the direction of Lilian Baylis.

Ismail (1830–1895) Khedive (governor) of Egypt 1866–79. A grandson of Mehmet Ali, he became viceroy of Egypt in 1863, and in 1866 received the title of khedive from the Ottoman sultan. He amassed huge foreign debts and in 1875 Britain, at Prime Minister Disraeli's suggestion, bought the khedive's Suez Canal shares for nearly £4 million, establishing Anglo-French control of Egypt's finances. In 1879 the UK and France persuaded the sultan to appoint Tewfik, his son, khedive in his place.

Ismail I (1486–1524) Shah of Persia from 1501. He was the founder of the **Safavi dynasty**, and established the first national government since the Arab conquest and Shiite Islam as the national religion.

Isma'ili member of an Islamic group, the second-largest ▷Shiite community in Islam (after the ▷Twelver Shi'is). Isma'ilis comprise several smaller groups, the most important of which are the Nizari Isma'ilis, from 1094; the Da'udi Isma'ilis; the Musta'li Isma'ilis; and the Sulaymani Isma'ilis.

ISO in photography, a numbering system for rating the speed of films, devised by the International Standards Organization.

isobar line drawn on maps and weather charts linking all places with the same atmospheric pressure (usually measured in millibars). When used in weather forecasting, the distance between the isobars is an indication of the barometric gradient (the rate of change in pressure).

Where the isobars are close together, cyclonic weather is indicated, bringing strong winds and a depression, and where far apart anticyclonic, bringing calmer, settled conditions.

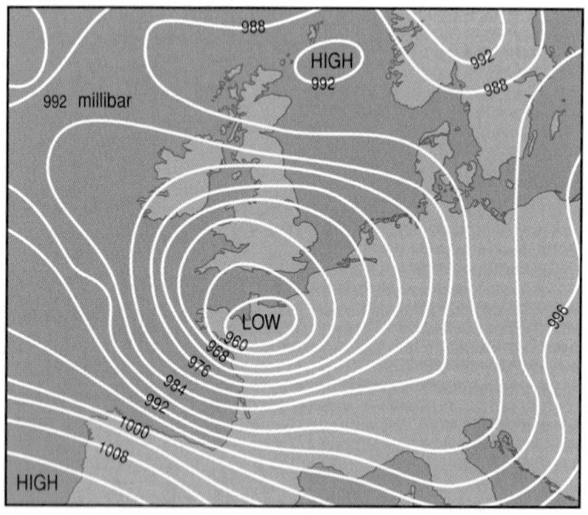

ISOBAR This image shows the isobars around a low-pressure area or depression. In the northern hemisphere, winds blow anticlockwise around lows, approximately parallel to the isobars, and clockwise around highs. In the southern hemisphere, the winds blow in the opposite directions.

isolationism in politics, concentration on internal rather than foreign affairs; a foreign policy having no interest in international affairs that do not affect the country's own interests.

Isolde (or **Iseult**) in Celtic and medieval legend, the wife of King Mark of Cornwall who was brought from Ireland by King Mark's nephew ▷Tristan. She and Tristan accidentally drank the aphrodisiac given to her by her mother for her marriage, were separated as lovers, and finally died together.

isomer chemical compound having the same molecular composition and mass as another, but with different physical or chemical properties owing to the different structural arrangement of its constituent atoms. For example, the organic compounds butane ($CH_3(CH_2)_2CH_3$) and methyl propane ($CH_3CH(CH_3)CH_3$) are isomers, each possessing four carbon atoms and ten hydrogen atoms but differing in the way that these are arranged with respect to each other.

Structural isomers have obviously different constructions, but **geometrical** and **optical isomers** must be drawn or modelled in order to appreciate the difference in their three-dimensional arrangement. Geometrical isomers have a plane of symmetry and arise because of the restricted rotation of atoms around a bond; optical isomers are mirror images of each other. For instance, 1,1-dichloroethene ($CH_2{=}CCl_2$) and 1,2-dichloroethene ($CHCl{=}CHCl$) are structural isomers, but there are two possible geometric isomers of the latter (depending on whether the chlorine atoms are on the same side or on opposite sides of the plane of the carbon–carbon double bond).

isorhythm in music, a form in which a given rhythm cyclically repeats, although the corresponding melody notes may change. It was used in European medieval music, and is still practised in classical Indian music. The composers Alban Berg, John Cage, and Olivier Messiaen used isorhythmic procedures.

isostasy the condition of gravitational equilibrium of all parts of the Earth's ▷crust. The crust is in isostatic equilibrium if, below a certain depth, the weight and thus pressure of rocks above is the same everywhere. The idea is that the lithosphere floats on the asthenosphere as a piece of wood floats on water. A thick piece of wood floats lower than a thin piece, and a denser piece of wood floats lower than a less dense piece. There are two theories of the mechanism of isostasy, the Airy hypothesis and the Pratt hypothesis, both of which have validity. In the **Airy hypothesis** crustal blocks have the same density but different thicknesses: like ice cubes floating in water, higher mountains have deeper roots. In the **Pratt hypothesis**, crustal blocks have different densities allowing the depth of crustal material to be the same. In practice, both mechanisms are at work.

isotope one of two or more atoms that have the same atomic number (same number of protons), but which contain a different number of neutrons, thus differing in their atomic mass (see ▷relative atomic mass). They may be stable or radioactive (see ▷radioisotope), naturally occurring, or synthesized. For example, hydrogen has the isotopes ^{2}H (▷deuterium) and ^{3}H (▷tritium). The term was coined by English chemist Frederick Soddy, pioneer researcher in atomic disintegration.

Elements at the lower end of the periodic table have atoms with roughly the same number of protons as neutrons. These elements are called **stable isotopes**. The stable isotopes of oxygen include ^{16}O, ^{17}O, and ^{18}O. Elements with high atomic mass numbers have many more neutrons than protons and are therefore less stable. It is these isotopes that are more prone to ▷radioactive decay. Examples are ^{238}U (uranium-238), and ^{60}Co (cobalt-60).

Isozaki, Arata (1931–) Japanese architect. One of Kenzo ▷Tange's team 1954–63, he has tried to blend Western postmodernist with elements of traditional Japanese architecture. His works include Ochanomizu Square, Tokyo (retaining the existing facades), the Museum of Contemporary Art, Los Angeles (begun 1984), and buildings for the 1992 Barcelona Olympics.

Israel see country box.

Israel, ancient kingdom of north ▷Palestine, formed after the death of Solomon by Jewish peoples seceding from the rule of his son Rehoboam and electing Jeroboam as their leader.

Israëls, Jozef (1824–1911) Dutch painter. In 1870 he settled in The Hague and became a leader of the **Hague School** of landscape painters, who shared some of the ideals of the ▷Barbizon School in France. His low-keyed and sentimental scenes of peasant life recall the work of ▷Millet.

Istanbul city and chief seaport of Turkey; population (1990) urban area 6,407,200; city 6,293,400. It produces textiles, tobacco, cement, glass, and leather. Founded as **Byzantium** about 660 BC, it was renamed **Constantinople** (AD 330) and was the capital of the ▷Byzantine Empire until captured by the Turks in 1453. As **Istamboul** it was capital of the Ottoman Empire until 1922.

Features the harbour of the Golden Horn; Hagia Sophia (Emperor Justinian's church of the Holy Wisdom (537), later a mosque and since 1922 a museum); Sultan Ahmet Mosque, known as the Blue Mosque, from its tiles; Topkapi Palace of the Sultans, with a harem of 400 rooms (now a museum). The Selimye Barracks in the suburb of **Usküdar** (Scutari) was used as a hospital in the Crimean War; the rooms used by Florence Nightingale, with her personal possessions, are preserved as a museum. The Istanbul Biennial, one of the world's biggest art shows, began in 1987.

ISTANBUL The Blue Mosque (or Sultan Ahmet Mosque) in Istanbul was built between 1609 and 1616 by Mehmet Aga for Sultan Ahmet I. Modelled on two other great religious buildings of Istanbul – Hagia Sophia and the Suleimaniye Mosque – it is known as the Blue Mosque because of the predominantly blue and green tilework and painting of its interior. *Image Bank*

IT abbreviation for ▷information technology.

Itagaki, Taisuke (1837–1919) Japanese military and political leader. Involved in the overthrow of the ▷Tokugawa shogunate and the ▷Meiji restoration of 1868, Itagaki became leader of the people's rights movement. He was the founder of Japan's first political party, the Jiyūtō (Liberal Party), in 1881.

Itaipu Dam world's largest hydroelectric plant, situated on the Paraná River, southwestern Brazil. A joint Brazilian-Paraguayan venture, it came into operation in 1984 and has a capacity of 12,600 mega-watts; it supplies hydroelectricity to a wide area.

Italian people who are native to inhabitants of Italy and their descendants, culture, and language. The language belongs to the Romance group of Indo-European languages.

Italian art painting and sculpture of Italy from the early Middle Ages to the present. In the 4th century AD Christian art emerged from Roman art, which was adapted to give expression to religious beliefs and sentiments. Throughout the next 14 centuries Roman art was to be the source of constant reappraisals and renewals in the evolution of the visual arts in Italy, and was fundamental to the major development of the Renaissance. It is from antique art, blended with Byzantine and then Gothic influences, that Italian art emerged.

Italian language member of the Romance branch of the Indo-European language family, the most direct descendant of Latin. Broadcasting and films have standardized the Italian national tongue, but most Italians speak a regional dialect as well as standard Italian.

Italian literature the literature of Italy originated in the 13th century with the Sicilian school, which imitated Provençal poetry. *Medieval* The works of St Francis of Assisi and Jacopone da Todi reflect the religious faith of that time. Guido Guinicelli (1230–*c.* 1275) and Guido Cavalcanti developed the spiritual conception of love and influenced Dante Alighieri, whose *Divina commedia/Divine Comedy* (1307–21) is generally recognized as the greatest work of Italian literature. Petrarch was a humanist and a poet, celebrated for his sonnets, while Boccaccio is principally known for his tales.
Renaissance The *Divina commedia* marked the beginning of the Renaissance. Boiardo dealt with the Carolingian epics in his *Orlando innamorato/Roland in Love* (1487), which was completed and transformed by Lodovico Ariosto as *Orlando furioso/ The Frenzy of Roland* (1516). Their contemporaries Niccolò Machiavelli and Francesco Guicciardini (1483–1540) are historians of note. Torquato Tasso wrote his epic *Gerusalemme liberata/Jerusalem Delivered* (1574) in the spirit of the Counter-Reformation.

17th century This period was characterized by the exaggeration of the poets Giovanni Battista Marini (1569–1625) and Gabriello Chiabrera (1552–1638). In 1690 the 'Academy of Arcadia' was formed, including among its members Innocenzo Frugoni (1692–1768) and Metastasio. Other writers include Salvator Rosa, the satirist. *18th century* Giuseppe Parini (1729–1799) ridiculed the abuses of his day, while Vittorio Alfieri attacked tyranny in his dramas. Carlo Goldoni wrote comedies.
19th century Ugo Foscolo is chiefly remembered for his patriotic verse. Giacomo Leopardi is not only the greatest lyrical poet since Dante but also a master of Italian prose. The Romantic Alessandro Manzoni is best known as a novelist, and influenced among others the novelist Antonio Fogazzaro. A later outstanding literary figure, Giosuè Carducci, was followed by the verbose Gabriele d'Annunzio, writing of sensuality and violence, and Benedetto Croce, historian and philosopher, who between them dominated Italian literature at the turn of the century.
20th century Writers include the realist novelists Giovanni Verga and Grazia Deledda, winner of the Nobel prize 1926, the dramatist Luigi Pirandello, and the novelists Ignazio Silone and Italo Svevo. Poets of the period include Dino Campana and Giuseppe Ungaretti; and among the modern school are Nobel prizewinners Eugenio Montale and Salvatore Quasimodo. Novelists of the post-Fascist period include Alberto Moravia, Carlo Levi, Cesare Pavese, Vasco Pratolini, Elsa Morante, Natalia Ginsburg, Giuseppe Tomasi, Prince of Lampedusa, and the writers Italo Calvino, Leonardo Sciascia, and Primo Levi.

Italian Somaliland former Italian trust territory on the Somali coast of Africa extending to 502,300 sq km/193,900 sq mi. Established in 1892, it was extended in 1925 with the acquisition of Jubaland from Kenya; administered from Mogadishu; and under British rule 1941–50. Thereafter it reverted to Italian authority before uniting with British Somaliland in 1960 to form the independent state of Somalia.

italic style of printing in which the letters slope to the right *like this*, introduced by the printer Aldus Manutius of Venice in 1501. It is usually used side by side with the erect Roman type to distinguish titles of books, films, and so on, and for purposes of emphasis and (mainly in the USA) citation. The term 'italic' is also

Italy: Regions				
Region	Capital	Area		Population (1997)
		sq km	sq mi	
Abruzzo	L'Aquila	10,794	4,168	1,276,000
Basilicata	Potenza	9,992	3,858	610,300
Calabria	Catanzaro	15,080	5,822	2,071,100
Campania	Naples	13,595	5,249	5,796,900
Emilia-Romagna	Bologna	22,123	8,542	3,947,100
Friuli-Venezia Giulia[1]	Trieste	7,846	3,029	1,184,700
Lazio	Rome	17,203	6,642	5,242,700
Liguria	Genoa	5,416	2,091	1,641,800
Lombardy	Milan	23,856	9,211	8,989,000
Marche	Ancona	9,694	3,743	1,450,900
Molise	Campobasso	4,438	1,714	329,900
Piedmont	Turin	25,399	9,807	4,291,400
Puglia	Bari	19,347	7,470	4,090,100
Sardinia[1]	Cagliari	24,090	9,301	1,661,400
Sicily[1]	Palermo	25,708	9,926	5,108,100
Trentino-Alto Adige[1]	Trento	13,613	5,256	924,300
Tuscany	Florence	22,992	8,877	3,527,300
Umbria	Perugia	8,456	3,265	831,700
Valle d'Aosta[1]	Aosta	3,262	1,259	119,600
Veneto	Venice	18,364	7,090	4,469,200

[1] Special autonomous region.

used for the handwriting style developed for popular use in 1522 by Vatican chancery scribe Ludovico degli Arrighi.

Italy see country box.

iteroparity in biology, the repeated production of offspring at intervals throughout the life cycle. It is usually contrasted with ▷semelparity, where each individual reproduces only once during its life.

Ithaca (Greek *Itháki*) Greek island in the Ionian Sea, area 93 sq km/36 sq mi. Important in pre-classical Greece, Ithaca was (in Homer's poem) the birthplace of ▷Odysseus, though this is sometimes identified with the island of Leukas (some archaeologists have equated ancient Ithaca with Leukas rather than modern Ithaca).

Ivan six rulers of Russia, including:

Ivan (III) the Great (1440–1505) Grand Duke of Muscovy from 1462. He revolted against Tatar overlordship by refusing tribute to Grand Khan Ahmed in 1480. He claimed the title of tsar (Caesar), and used the double-headed eagle as the Russian state emblem. See map on p. 493.

Ivan (IV) the Terrible (1530–1584) Grand Duke of Muscovy from 1533. He assumed power in 1544 and was crowned as first tsar of Russia in 1547. He conquered Kazan in 1552, Astrakhan in 1556, and Siberia in 1581. He reformed the legal code and local administration in 1555 and established trade relations with England. In his last years he alternated between debauchery and religious austerities, executing thousands and, in rage, his own son.
His regime was marked by brutality, evidenced by the destruction (sacking) of Novgorod. See map on p. 493.

Ivanisevic, Goran (1971–) Croatian tennis player. A tall left-handed player, he is known for his fast serve and sometimes fiery temperament. He turned professional in 1988, aged 17, and had broken into the world's top ten by 1990, a year in which he reached five singles finals and three doubles finals. He reached No. 2 in the world in 1992, a position he again held in 1997. His serve-and-volley style is most suited to the grass courts of Wimbledon where he lost three finals, in 1992, 1994, and 1998, before finally claiming the title in 2001 as an unseeded player, defeating Australian Pat Rafter over five sets in what was widely regarded as one of the greatest matches of the modern era.

Ives, Charles Edward (1874–1954) US composer. He experimented with ▷atonality, quarter tones, clashing time signatures, and quotations from popular music of the time. He wrote four symphonies, including the *Dvorakian Symphony No. 1* (1895–98); chamber music, including the *Concord Sonata* (piano sonata no. 2, 1909–15); and the orchestral works *Three Places in New England* (1903–14), *New England Holidays* (1904–13), and *The Unanswered Question* (1908).

IVF abbreviation for ▷in vitro fertilization.

Iviza alternative spelling of ▷Ibiza, one of the ▷Balearic Islands.

ivory hard white substance of which the teeth and tusks of certain mammals are made. Among the most valuable are elephants' tusks, which are of unusual hardness and density. Ivory is used in carving

ITALIAN ART A glazed terracotta altarpiece of the Virgin and Child with angels, a chalice, and a dove overhead, by the Italian sculptor Giovanni della Robbia (1469–1529). *The Art Archive/Pulci-Beraldi Chapel Sta Croce Florence/Dagli Orti*

Israel

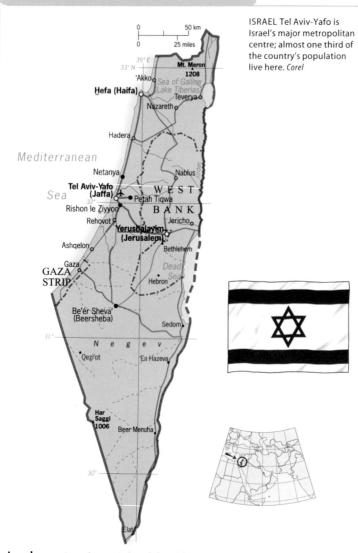

0   50 km
0   25 miles

ISRAEL Tel Aviv-Yafo is Israel's major metropolitan centre; almost one third of the country's population live here. *Corel*

Israel country in southwest Asia, bounded north by Lebanon, east by Syria and Jordan, south by the Gulf of Aqaba, and west by Egypt and the Mediterranean Sea.

NATIONAL NAME *Medinat Israel/State of Israel*
AREA 20,800 sq km/8,030 sq mi (as at 1949 armistice)
CAPITAL Jerusalem (not recognized by the United Nations)
MAJOR TOWNS/CITIES Tel Aviv-Yafo, Haifa, Bat-Yam, Holon, Ramat Gan, Petach Tikva, Rishon Le Ziyyon, Beersheba
MAJOR PORTS Tel Aviv-Yafo, Haifa, 'Akko (formerly Acre), Eilat
PHYSICAL FEATURES coastal plain of Sharon between Haifa and Tel Aviv noted since ancient times for its fertility; central mountains of Galilee, Samaria, and Judea; Dead Sea, Lake Tiberias, and River Jordan Rift Valley along the east are below sea level; Negev Desert in the south; Israel occupies Golan Heights, West Bank, East Jerusalem, and Gaza Strip (the last was awarded limited autonomy, with West Bank town of Jericho, in 1993)

Government

HEAD OF STATE Moshe Katsav from 2000
HEAD OF GOVERNMENT Ariel Sharon from 2001
POLITICAL SYSTEM liberal democracy
POLITICAL EXECUTIVE parliamentary
ADMINISTRATIVE DIVISIONS six districts, 61 municipalities, 150 local councils, and 53 regional councils

ARMED FORCES 161,500; plus 425,000 reservists (2002 est)
CONSCRIPTION voluntary for Christians, Circassians, and Muslims; compulsory for Jews and Druzes (men 36 months, women 21 months)
DEATH PENALTY abolished for ordinary crimes; laws provide for the death penalty for exceptional crimes, such as crimes committed in wartime
DEFENCE SPEND (% GDP) 9.7 (2002 est)
EDUCATION SPEND (% GDP) 7.3 (2001 est)
HEALTH SPEND (% GDP) 10.9 (2000 est)

Economy and resources

CURRENCY shekel
GPD (US$) 101 billion (2002 est)
REAL GDP GROWTH (% change on previous year) –0.9 (2001)
GNI (US$) 103 billion (2002 est)
GNI PER CAPITA (PPP) (US$) 19,920 (2002 est)
CONSUMER PRICE INFLATION 3.2% (2003 est)
UNEMPLOYMENT 9.3% (2001)
FOREIGN DEBT (US$) 48.3 billion (2001 est)
MAJOR TRADING PARTNERS USA, UK, Germany, Belgium–Luxembourg, UK, Italy, Japan, Switzerland, the Netherlands
RESOURCES potash, bromides, magnesium, sulphur, copper ore, gold, salt, petroleum, natural gas

INDUSTRIES food processing, beverages, tobacco, electrical machinery, chemicals, petroleum and coal products, metal products, diamond polishing, transport equipment, tourism
EXPORTS machinery and parts, citrus fruits, worked diamonds, software, food products, chemical products, textiles and clothing. Principal market: USA 38.2% (2001)
IMPORTS machinery and parts, rough diamonds, chemicals and related products, crude petroleum and petroleum products, military equipment, motor vehicles. Principal source: USA 20.1% (2001)
ARABLE LAND 16.1% (2000 est)
AGRICULTURAL PRODUCTS citrus fruits, vegetables, potatoes, wheat, melons, pumpkins, avocados; poultry and fish production

Population and society

POPULATION 6,433,000 (2003 est)
POPULATION GROWTH RATE 1.6% (2000–15)
POPULATION DENSITY (per sq km) 291 (2003 est)
URBAN POPULATION (% of total) 92 (2003 est)

AGE DISTRIBUTION (% of total population) 0–14 28%, 15–59 59%, 60+ 13% (2002 est)
ETHNIC GROUPS around 81% of the population is Jewish, the majority of the remainder Arab. Under the Law of Return 1950, 'every Jew shall be entitled to come to Israel as an immigrant'; those from the East and Eastern Europe are Ashkenazim, and those from Mediterranean Europe (Spain, Portugal, Italy, France, Greece) and Arab Africa are Sephardim (over 50% of the population is now of Sephardic descent); an Israeli-born Jew is a Sabra
LANGUAGE Hebrew, Arabic (both official), English, Yiddish, other European and west Asian languages
RELIGION Israel is a secular state, but the predominant faith is Judaism 80%; also Sunni Muslim (about 15%), Christian, and Druze
LABOUR FORCE 2.3% agriculture, 24.8% industry, 72.9% services (1999)
LIFE EXPECTANCY 77 (men); 81 (women) (2000–05)

See also ▷Arab–Israeli conflict; ▷Camp David Agreements; ▷Jerusalem; ▷Palestine; ▷Zionism.

Chronology

c. **2000 BC**: Abraham, father of the Jewish people, is believed to have come to Palestine from Mesopotamia.

c. **1225 BC**: Moses led the Jews out of slavery in Egypt towards the promised land of Palestine.

11th century BC: Saul established a Jewish kingdom in Palestine; developed by kings David and Solomon.

586 BC: Jews defeated by Babylon and deported; many returned to Palestine in 539 BC.

333 BC: Alexander the Great of Macedonia conquered the entire region.

3rd century BC: Control of Palestine contested by Ptolemies of Egypt and Seleucids of Syria.

142 BC: Jewish independence restored after Maccabean revolt.

63 BC: Palestine fell to Roman Empire.

70 AD: Romans crushed Zealot rebellion and destroyed Jerusalem; start of dispersion of Jews (diaspora).

614: Persians took Jerusalem from Byzantine Empire.

637: Muslim Arabs conquered Palestine.

1099: First Crusade captured Jerusalem; Christian kingdom lasted a century before falling to sultans of Egypt.

1517: Palestine conquered by the Ottoman Turks.

1897: Theodor Herzl organized the First Zionist Congress at Basel to publicize Jewish claims to Palestine.

1917: The Balfour Declaration: Britain expressed support for the creation of a Jewish National Home in Palestine.

1918: British forces expelled the Turks from Palestine, which became a British League of Nations mandate in 1920.

1929: Severe violence around Jerusalem caused by Arab alarm at doubling of Jewish population in ten years.

1933: Jewish riots in protest at British attempts to restrict Jewish immigration.

1937: The Peel Report, recommending partition, accepted by most Jews but rejected by Arabs; open warfare ensued between 1937 and 1938.

1939: Britain postponed independence plans on account of World War II, and increased military presence.

1946: Resumption of terrorist violence; Jewish extremists blew up British headquarters in Jerusalem.

1947: United Nations (UN) voted for partition of Palestine.

1948: Britain withdrew; Independent State of Israel proclaimed with David Ben-Gurion as prime minister; Israel repulsed invasion by Arab nations; many Palestinian Arabs settled in refugee camps in the Gaza Strip and West Bank.

1952: Col Gamal Nasser of Egypt stepped up blockade of Israeli ports and support of Arab guerrillas in Gaza.

1956: War between Israel and Egypt; Israeli invasion of Gaza and Sinai followed by withdrawal in 1957.

Israel (cont.)

1964: Palestine Liberation Organization (PLO) founded to unite Palestinian Arabs with the aim of overthrowing the state of Israel.

1967: Israel defeated Egypt, Syria, and Jordan in the Six-Day War; Gaza, West Bank, east Jerusalem, Sinai, and Golan Heights captured.

1969: Yassir Arafat became chair of the PLO; escalation of terrorism and border raids.

1973: Yom Kippur War: Israel repulsed surprise attack by Egypt and Syria.

1977: President Anwar Sadat of Egypt began peace initiative.

1979: Camp David talks ended with signing of peace treaty between Israel and Egypt; Israel withdrew from Sinai.

1980: United Jerusalem was declared the capital of Israel.

1982: Israeli forces invaded southern Lebanon to drive out PLO guerrillas; occupation continued until 1985.

1988: The Israeli handling of Palestinian uprising (Intifada) in the occupied territories provoked international criticism.

1990: The PLO formally recognized the state of Israel.

1991: Iraq launched missile attacks on Israel during the Gulf War; Middle East peace talks began in Madrid.

1992: A Labour government was elected under Yitzhak Rabin.

1993: Rabin and Arafat signed a peace accord; Israel granted limited autonomy to Gaza Strip and Jericho. Ezer Weizman was elected president.

1994: Arafat became the head of an autonomous Palestinian authority in Gaza and Jericho; a peace agreement was reached between Israel and Jordan.

1995: Rabin was assassinated by a Jewish opponent of the peace accord.

1996: A Likud government was elected under Binjamin Netanyahu, a critic of the peace accord. A revival of communal violence was seen and the peace process was threatened.

1997: A Jewish settlement in east Jerusalem was widely condemned. There were suicide bombs by Hamas in Jerusalem.

1998: Violence flared on the West Bank between Palestinians and Israeli troops. The Wye Peace Agreement was signed with the PLO. A land-for-security deal was approved by the Knesset, and the promised Israeli withdrawal from the Lebanon was subsequently placed in doubt. President Clinton attempted to restart the peace process.

1999: The South Lebanon 'security zone' was expanded. Yasser Arafat delayed the declaration of an independent state until after the Israeli elections. Ehud Barak (Labour) was elected prime minister and restarted peace negotiations.

2000: Israel withdrew from the Golan Heights. Moshe Katsav, who opposed Barak's peace initiative, became president. In September, renewed violence between Palestinians and Israeli security forces broke out and quickly escalated, following a visit by right-wing Israeli politician Ariel Sharon to Muslim holy sites in Jerusalem. Repeated efforts to end the violence failed, and Barak announced his resignation in December.

2001: Ariel Sharon was elected prime minister.

2002: After months of violence and military reprisals against the Palestinians, the army besieged Yasser Arafat's Ramallah headquarters for 11 days before withdrawing under US pressure and United Nations (UN) Security Council demands.

2003: An international blueprint (the so-called 'road map', designed by the USA, European Union, United Nations, and Russia) for a phased settlement of the Palestinian-Israeli conflict by 2005–06 was released and endorsed by the government under US diplomatic pressure. However, the government authorized the building of a controversial security wall. The Palestine National Authority's new government under Mahmoud Abbas was sworn in, but Abbas was later forced to resign and was replaced by Ahmed Qureia. A peace initiative drafted by unofficial Israeli and Palestinian negotiators, and known as the Geneva Accord, gained significant international support but was rejected by the government. Palestinian suicide bombings and Israeli retaliation, including the first direct air attack on Syrian territory since 1973, continued throughout the year.

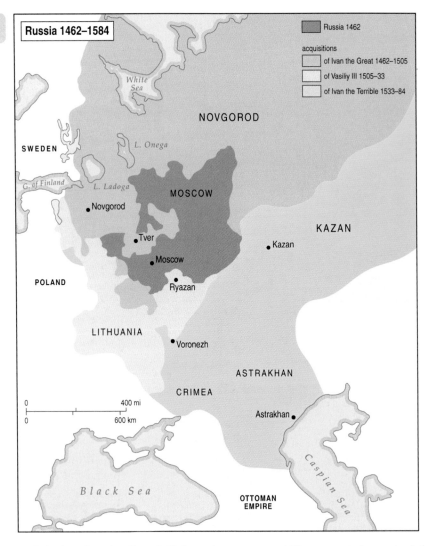

```
Russia 1462–1584
```

Russia 1462

acquisitions
☐ of Ivan the Great 1462–1505
☐ of Vasiliy III 1505–33
☐ of Ivan the Terrible 1533–84

White Sea

NOVGOROD

SWEDEN
L. Onega
G. of Finland
L. Ladoga
MOSCOW
• Novgorod
KAZAN
• Tver
• Kazan
• Moscow
POLAND
• Ryazan
LITHUANIA
• Voronezh
ASTRAKHAN
CRIMEA
• Astrakhan

0 — 400 mi
0 — 600 km

Black Sea
Caspian Sea
OTTOMAN EMPIRE

IVAN THE GREAT AND IVAN THE TERRIBLE Map showing the acquisitions within Russia in the 15th and 16th centuries. See entries on p. 491.

and other decorative work, and is so valuable that poachers continue to illegally destroy the remaining wild elephant herds in Africa to obtain it.

Ivory, James (Francis) (1928–) US film director. He established his reputation with the Indian-made *Shakespeare Wallah* (1965), which began collaborations with Ishmail ▷Merchant and the writer Ruth Prawer ▷Jhabvala. Ivory subsequently directed films in various genres in India, the USA, and Europe, but became associated with adaptations of classic literature, including *The Bostonians* (1984) and *Howards End* (1992).

ivy any of an Old World group of woody climbing, trailing, or creeping evergreen plants. English or European ivy (*H. helix*) has shiny five-lobed leaves and clusters of small, yellowish-green flowers followed by black berries. It climbs by means of rootlike suckers put out from its stem, and causes damage to trees. (Genus *Hedera*, family Araliaceae.)

Ivy League eight long-established colleges and universities in the USA with prestigious academic and social reputations: Brown, Columbia, Cornell, Dartmouth, Harvard, Pennsylvania, Princeton, and Yale.

Iwo Jima, Battle of intense fighting between Japanese and US forces 19 February–17 March 1945 during World War II. In February 1945, US marines landed on the island of Iwo Jima, a Japanese air base, intending to use it to prepare for a planned final assault on mainland Japan. The 22,000 Japanese troops put up a fanatical resistance but the island was finally secured on 16 March. US casualties came to 6,891 killed and 18,700 wounded, while only 212 of the Japanese garrison survived.

IWW abbreviation for ▷Industrial Workers of the World.

Izetbegović, Alija (1925–) Bosnia-Herzegovinan politician, president 1990–96.

A lifelong opponent of communism, he founded the Stranka Demokratski Akcije (SDA; Party of Democratic Action) in 1990, ousting the communists in the multiparty elections that year. Adopting a moderate stance during the civil war in Bosnia-Herzegovina, he sought an honourable peace for his country in the face of ambitious demands from Serb and Croat political leaders, and signed the Dayton peace accord in November 1995. He served the Bosnian Muslims on the rotating three-person collective presidency 1996–2000, when he retired.

Izmir (formerly **Smyrna**) port and naval base in Turkey; population (1990) 1,757,400. Products include steel, electronics, and plastics. The largest annual trade fair in the Middle East is held here. It is the headquarters of ▷North Atlantic Treaty Organization SE Command.

IVORY Ivory was used as ornamentation for numerous objects, such as the handle of this late 18th-century fan, possibly of Dutch origin, in Chinoiserie style. *The Art Archive/Private Collection*

Italy

ITALY The town of Sorrento, on the Gulf of Naples, Campania region, Italy. *Corel*

Italy country in southern Europe, bounded north by Switzerland and Austria, east by Slovenia, Croatia, and the Adriatic Sea, south by the Ionian and Mediterranean seas, and west by the Tyrrhenian and Ligurian seas and France. It includes the Mediterranean islands of Sardinia and Sicily.

NATIONAL NAME *Repubblica Italiana/Italian Republic*
AREA 301,300 sq km/116,331 sq mi
CAPITAL Rome
MAJOR TOWNS/CITIES Milan, Naples, Turin, Palermo, Genoa, Bologna, Florence
MAJOR PORTS Naples, Genoa, Palermo, Bari, Catania, Trieste
PHYSICAL FEATURES mountainous (Maritime Alps, Dolomites, Apennines) with narrow coastal lowlands; continental Europe's only active volcanoes: Vesuvius, Etna, Stromboli; rivers Po, Adige, Arno, Tiber, Rubicon; islands of Sicily, Sardinia, Elba, Capri, Ischia, Lipari, Pantelleria; lakes Como, Maggiore, Garda

Government

HEAD OF STATE Carlo Azeglio Ciampi from 1999
HEAD OF GOVERNMENT Silvio Berlusconi from 2001
POLITICAL SYSTEM liberal democracy
POLITICAL EXECUTIVE parliamentary
ADMINISTRATIVE DIVISIONS 103 provinces within 20 regions (of which five have a greater degree of autonomy)
ARMED FORCES 216,800 (2002 est)
CONSCRIPTION up to ten months
DEATH PENALTY abolished in 1994
DEFENCE SPEND (% GDP) 1.9 (2002 est)
EDUCATION SPEND (% GDP) 4.6 (2001 est)
HEALTH SPEND (% GDP) 8.1 (2000 est)

Economy and resources

CURRENCY euro (lira until 2002)
GPD (US$) 1,180.9 billion (2002 est)
REAL GDP GROWTH (% change on previous year) 1.8 (2001)
GNI (US$) 1,097.9 billion (2002 est)

GNI PER CAPITA (PPP) (US$) 25,320 (2002 est)
CONSUMER PRICE INFLATION 2.4% (2003 est)
UNEMPLOYMENT 9.4% (2001)
MAJOR TRADING PARTNERS EU (principally Germany, France, the Netherlands, Spain, and UK), USA
RESOURCES lignite, lead, zinc, mercury, potash, sulphur, fluorspar, bauxite, marble, petroleum, natural gas, fish
INDUSTRIES machinery and machine tools, textiles, leather, footwear, food and beverages, steel, motor vehicles, chemical products, wine, tourism
EXPORTS machinery and transport equipment, textiles, clothing and leather goods, wine (leading producer and exporter), metals and metal products, chemicals, wood, paper and rubber goods. Principal market: Germany 14.5% (2001)
IMPORTS mineral fuels and lubricants, machinery and transport equipment, chemical products, foodstuffs, metal products. Principal source: Germany 17.7% (2001)
ARABLE LAND 27.1% (2000 est)
AGRICULTURAL PRODUCTS sugar beet, grapes, wheat, maize, tomatoes, olives, citrus fruits, vegetables; fishing

Population and society

POPULATION 57,423,000 (2003 est)
POPULATION GROWTH RATE –0.3% (2000–15)
POPULATION DENSITY (per sq km) 191 (2003 est)
URBAN POPULATION (% of total) 67 (2003 est)
AGE DISTRIBUTION (% of total population) 0–14 14%, 15–59 61%, 60+ 25% (2002 est)

ETHNIC GROUPS mainly Italian; some minorities of German origin
LANGUAGE Italian (official), German and Ladin (in the north), French (in the Valle d'Aosta region), Greek and Albanian (in the south)
RELIGION Roman Catholic 98%
EDUCATION (compulsory years) 8
LITERACY RATE 99% (men); 98% (women) (2003 est)
LABOUR FORCE 5.4% agriculture, 32.4% industry, 62.2% services (2000)
LIFE EXPECTANCY 76 (men); 82 (women) (2000–05)

Chronology

4th and 3rd centuries BC: Italian peninsula united under Roman rule.
AD 476: End of Western Roman Empire.
568: Invaded by Lombards.
756: Papal States created in central Italy.
800: Charlemagne united Italy and Germany in Holy Roman Empire.
12th and 13th centuries: Papacy and Holy Roman Empire contended for political supremacy; papal power reached its peak under Innocent III (1198–1216).
1183: Cities of Lombard League (founded in 1164) became independent.
14th century: Beginnings of Renaissance in northern Italy.
15th century: Most of Italy ruled by five rival states: the city-states of Milan, Florence, and Venice; the Papal States; and the Kingdom of Naples.
1494: Charles VIII of France invaded Italy.
1529–59: Spanish Habsburgs secured dominance in Italy.
17th century: Italy effectively part of Spanish Empire; economic and cultural decline.
1713: Treaty of Utrecht gave political control of most of Italy to Austrian Habsburgs.
1796–1814: France conquered Italy, setting up satellite states and introducing principles of French Revolution.
1815: Old regimes largely restored; Italy divided between Austria, Papal States, Naples, Sardinia, and four duchies.
1831: Giuseppe Mazzini founded the 'Young Italy' movement with the aim of creating a unified republic.
1848–49: Liberal revolutions occurred throughout Italy; reversed everywhere except Sardinia, which became a centre of nationalism under the leadership of Count Camillo di Cavour.
1859: France and Sardinia forcibly expelled Austrians from Lombardy.
1860: Sardinia annexed duchies and Papal States (except Rome); Giuseppe Garibaldi overthrew Neapolitan monarchy.
1861: Victor Emmanuel II of Sardinia proclaimed King of Italy in Turin.
1866: Italy gained Venetia after defeat of Austria by Prussia.
1870: Italian forces occupied Rome in defiance of Pope, completing unification of Italy.
1882: Italy joined Germany and Austria-Hungary in Triple Alliance.

See also ▷Renaissance; ▷Rome, ancient; ▷Vatican City State.

1896: Attempt to conquer Ethiopia defeated at Battle of Adowa.
1900: King Umberto I assassinated by an anarchist.
1912: Annexation of Libya and Dodecanese after Italo-Turkish War.
1915: Italy entered World War I on side of Allies.
1919: Peace treaties awarded Trentino, South Tyrol, and Trieste to Italy.
1922: Mussolini established fascist dictatorship following period of strikes and agrarian revolts.
1935–36: Conquest of Ethiopia.
1939: Invasion of Albania.
1940: Italy entered World War II as ally of Germany.
1943: Allies invaded southern Italy; Mussolini removed from power; Germans occupied northern and central Italy.
1945: Allies completed liberation.
1946: Monarchy replaced by a republic.
1947: Peace treaty stripped Italy of its colonies.
1948: New constitution adopted; Christian Democrats emerged as main party of government in political system marked by ministerial instability.
1957: Italy became a founder member of European Economic Community (EEC).
1963: Creation of first of long series of fragile centre-left coalition governments.
1976: Communists attempt to join the coalition, the 'historic compromise', rejected by the Christian Democrats.
1978: Christian Democrat Aldo Moro, the architect of historic compromise, was murdered by Red Brigade guerrillas infiltrated by Western intelligence agents.
1983–87: Bettino Craxi, Italy's first Socialist prime minister, led the coalition. The economy improved.
1993: A major political crisis was triggered by the exposure of government corruption and Mafia links, and governing parties were discredited. A new electoral system replaced proportional representation, with 75% majority voting.
1999: Carlo Azeglio Ciampi was elected president. Former prime minister Prodi became president of the new European Commission.
2000: After his centre-left coalition was beaten in regional elections, Massimo d'Alema resigned his position as prime minister, which he had held since 1998, and Giuliano Amato was sworn in as head of Italy's 58th government since 1945. Amato later conceded leadership of the coalition in the next general election to Francesco Rutelli, the mayor of Rome.

J in physics, the symbol for **joule**, the SI unit of energy.

Jabir ibn Hayyan (*c.* 721–*c.* 776) Latin **Geber**. Arabian alchemist, regarded by some as the founder of molecular chemistry. His influence lasted for more than 600 years, and in the late 1300s his Latin name, Geber, was adopted by a Spanish alchemist whose writings spread the knowledge and practice of alchemy throughout Europe.

jaborandi plant belonging to the rue family, native to South America. It is the source of **pilocarpine**, used in medicine to contract the pupil of the eye. (*Pilocarpus microphyllus*, family Rutaceae.)

jacamar insect-eating bird related to the woodpeckers, found in dense tropical forest in Central and South America. It has a long, straight, sharply-pointed bill, a long tail, and paired toes. The plumage is golden bronze with a steely lustre. Jacamars are usually seen sitting motionless on trees from which they fly out to catch insects on the wing, then return to crack them on a branch before eating them. The largest species is *Jacamerops aurea*, which is nearly 30 cm/12 in long. (Family Galbulidae, order Piciformes.)

jacana (or **lily-trotter**) wading bird with very long toes and claws enabling it to walk on the floating leaves of water plants. There are seven species. Jacanas are found in Mexico, Central America, South America, Africa, South Asia, and Australia, usually in marshy areas. (Family Jacanidae, order Charadriiformes.)

JACANA The American jacana, or lily trotter, is a common waterbird of lagoons and marshes in Mexico and Central America. Jacanas have extremely long toes and claws for walking on floating vegetation.

jacaranda any of a group of tropical American trees belonging to the bignonia family, with fragrant wood and showy blue or violet flowers, commonly cultivated in the southern USA. (Genus *Jacaranda*, family Bignoniaceae.)

jack tool or machine for lifting, hoisting, or moving heavy weights, such as motor vehicles. A **screw jack** uses the principle of the screw to magnify an applied effort; in a car jack, for example, turning the handle many times causes the lifting screw to rise slightly, and the effort is magnified to lift heavy weights. A **hydraulic jack** uses a succession of piston strokes to increase pressure in a liquid and force up a lifting ram.

jackal any of several wild dogs found in South Asia, southern Europe, and North Africa. Jackals can grow to 80 cm/2.7 ft long, and have greyish-brown fur and a bushy tail. (Genus *Canis.*)

The **golden jackal** (*C. aureus*) of South Asia, southern Europe, and North Africa is 45 cm/1.5 ft high and 60 cm/2 ft long. It is greyish-yellow, and darker on the back. A nocturnal animal, it preys on smaller mammals and poultry, although packs will attack larger animals; it will also scavenge. The **side-striped jackal** (*C. adustus*) is found over much of Africa; the **black-backed jackal** (*C. mesomelas*) occurs only in the south of Africa.

jackdaw bird belonging to the crow family, native to Europe and Asia. It is mainly black, but greyish on the sides and back of the head, and about 33 cm/1.1 ft long. It nests in tree holes or on buildings. Usually it lays five bluish-white eggs, mottled with tiny dark brown spots. Jackdaws feed on a wide range of insects, molluscs, spiders, worms, birds' eggs, fruit, and berries. (Species *Corvus monedula*, family Corvidae, order Passeriformes.)

Jackson largest city and state capital of ▷Mississippi, on the Pearl River, in the central part of the state, 70 km/43 mi east of Vicksburg; seat of Hinds County; population (2001 est) 185,800. It produces electrical machinery, furniture, cottonseed oil, and iron and steel castings, and owes its prosperity to the discovery of gas fields to the south in the 1930s.

Jackson, Andrew (1767–1845) 7th president of the USA 1829–37, a Democrat. A major general in the War of 1812, he defeated a British force at New Orleans in 1815 (after the official end of the war in 1814) and was involved in the war that led to the purchase of Florida in 1819. The political organization he built as president, with Martin Van Buren (1782–1862), was the basis for the modern ▷Democratic Party.

After an unsuccessful attempt in 1824, he was elected president in 1828. This was the first election in which electors were chosen directly by voters rather than state legislators. He demanded and received absolute loyalty from his cabinet members and made wide use of his executive powers. In 1832 he vetoed the renewal of the US bank charter and was re-elected, whereupon he continued his struggle against the power of finance. His administration is particularly associated with the spoils system.

Related Web site: Andrew Jackson – Seventh President 1829–1837 http://www.whitehouse.gov/WH/glimpse/presidents/html/aj7.html

Jackson, Colin Ray (1967–) Welsh athlete who won the 110-metre hurdles gold medal at the 1993 World Championships at Stuttgart in a world record time of 12.91 seconds. He gained a silver medal at the 1988 Olympic Games, and won three consecutive European titles (1990–98) and two consecutive Commonwealth titles, (1990–94). In August 2000 he became the first athlete to win ten AAA titles. At the world championships in Seville, Spain, in 1999, he regained his 110-metre hurdles title, which he had previously won in 1993. After a disappointing fifth place in the 2000 Olympic Games, he confirmed his retirement from major championships.

Jackson, Glenda (1936–) English actor and politician, Labour member of Parliament from 1992, and parliamentary undersecretary for transport from 1997. Her many stage appearances for the Royal Shakespeare Company include *Marat/Sade* (1966), Hedda in *Hedda Gabler* (1975), and Cleopatra in *Antony and Cleopatra* (1978). Among her films are the Academy Award-winning *Women in Love* (1969), *Sunday Bloody Sunday* (1971), and *A Touch of Class* (1973). On television she played Queen Elizabeth I in *Elizabeth R* (1971).

Jackson, Jesse Louis (1941–) US Democratic politician, cleric and campaigner for minority rights. He contested his party's 1984 and 1988 presidential nominations in an effort to increase voter registration and to put black issues on the national agenda.

He is an eloquent public speaker, and in 1998 emerged as a spiritual adviser to President Bill Clinton. He withdrew from politics indefinitely after it emerged in January 2001 that he had fathered a child during an affair in 1998.

'STONEWALL' JACKSON US General Thomas 'Stonewall' Jackson at the First Battle of Bull Run, near Manassas, Virginia, 21 July 1861. Under Jackson, Confederate troops stopped some 30,000 Union troops from marching to Richmond, Virginia (the Confederate capital), and drove them back to Washington, DC. The Second Battle of Bull Run, which took place the following summer, also went in favour of the Confederacy. *Archive Photos*

Born in North Carolina and educated in Chicago, Jackson emerged as a powerful Baptist preacher and black activist politician, working first with the civil-rights leader Martin Luther King, Jr, then on building the political machine that gave Chicago a black mayor in 1983. Jackson sought to construct what he called a **rainbow coalition** of ethnic-minority and socially deprived groups. He took the lead in successfully campaigning for US disinvestment in South Africa in 1986.

Jackson, Michael (Joseph) (1958–) US rock singer and songwriter. His videos and live performances are meticulously choreographed. His first solo hit was 'Got to Be There' (1971); his worldwide popularity peaked with the albums *Thriller* (1982), *Bad* (1987), and *Dangerous* (1991). Jackson's career faltered after allegations of child abuse, but he returned with the albums *History* (1995) and *Blood on the Dance Floor* (1997). He was inducted into the Rock and Roll Hall of Fame in the USA in 2001.

Jackson, 'Stonewall' (Thomas Jonathan) (1824–1863) US Confederate general in the American Civil War. He acquired his nickname and his reputation at the Battle of Bull Run, from the firmness with which his brigade resisted the Northern attack. In 1862 he organized the Shenandoah Valley campaign and assisted Robert E ▷Lee's invasion of Maryland. He helped to defeat General Joseph E ▷Hooker's Union army at the battle of Chancellorsville, Virginia, but was fatally wounded by one of his own soldiers in the confusion of battle.

Jacksonville city and port in northeastern Florida, USA; population (1994 est) 665,000. It is one of the chief southern commercial centres on the Atlantic coast, with extensive rail, air, and highway connections; it is also a port of entry and a tourist resort. Manufactured goods include wood and paper products, ships, chemicals, cigars, and processed food. The port, situated on St John's River, has naval installations and ship-repair yards. To the north the Cross-Florida Barge Canal links the Atlantic with the Gulf of Mexico. Jacksonville dates from 1816, and was incorporated as a city in 1832.

> **Jesse Jackson**
> *We've removed the ceiling above our dreams. There are no more impossible dreams.*
> The Independent, 9 June 1988

Jack the Ripper Popular name for the unidentified mutilator and murderer of at least five women prostitutes in the Whitechapel area of London in 1888.

Jacob In the Old Testament, Hebrew patriarch, son of Isaac and Rebecca, who obtained the rights of seniority from his twin brother Esau by trickery. He married his cousins Leah and Rachel, serving their father Laban seven years for each, and at the time of famine in Canaan joined his son Joseph in Egypt. His 12 sons were the traditional ancestors of the 12 tribes of Israel.

Related Web site: Jacob http://www.newadvent.org/cathen/08261a.htm

Jacob, François (1920–) French biochemist who was awarded a Nobel Prize in Physiology or Medicine in 1965, with Jacques ▷Monod and André Lwoff, for their work on the genetic control of enzyme and virus synthesis. They pioneered research into molecular genetics and showed how the production of proteins from ▷DNA is controlled.

Jacobean style in the arts, particularly in architecture and furniture, during the reign of James I (1603–25) in England. Following the general lines of Elizabethan design, but using classical features with greater complexity and with more profuse ornamentation, it adopted many motifs from contemporary Italian design.

Jacobin member of an extremist republican club of the French Revolution founded in Versailles 1789. Helped by ▷Danton's speeches, they proclaimed the French republic, had the king executed, and overthrew the moderate ▷Girondins 1792–93. Through the Committee of Public Safety, they began the Reign of Terror, led by ▷Robespierre. After his execution in 1794, the club was abandoned and the name 'Jacobin' passed into general use for any left-wing extremist.

Jacobite in Britain, a supporter of the royal house of Stuart after the deposition of James II in 1688. They include the Scottish Highlanders, who rose unsuccessfully under ▷Claverhouse in 1689, despite initial victory at the Battle of ▷Killiecrankie; and those who rose in Scotland and northern England in 1715 (the ▷Fifteen) under the leadership of ▷James Edward Stuart, the Old Pretender, and followed his son ▷Charles Edward Stuart in an invasion of England from 1745 to 1746 (the ▷Forty-Five) that reached Derby. After the defeat at ▷Culloden, Jacobitism disappeared as a political force.

Jacquard, Joseph Marie (1752–1834) French textile manufacturer. He invented a punched-card system for programming designs on a carpetmaking loom (the **Jacquard loom**). In 1801 he constructed looms that used a series of punched cards to control the pattern of longitudinal warp threads depressed before each sideways passage of the shuttle. On later machines the punched cards were joined to form an endless loop that represented the 'program' for the repeating pattern of a carpet.

Jacquard-style punched cards were used in the early computers of the 1940s–1960s.

Jacquerie French peasant uprising of 1358, caused by the ravages of the English army and French nobility during the Hundred Years' War, which reduced the rural population to destitution. The word derives from the nickname for French peasants, Jacques Bonhomme.

Jacuzzi, Candido (1903–1986) Italian-born US engineer who invented the Jacuzzi, a pump that produces a whirlpool effect in a bathtub. The Jacuzzi was commercially launched as a health and recreational product in the mid-1950s.

jade semiprecious stone consisting of either jadeite, $NaAlSi_2O_6$ (a pyroxene), or nephrite, $Ca_2(Mg,Fe)_5Si_8O_{22}(OH,F)_2$ (an amphibole), ranging from colourless through shades of green to black according to the iron content. Jade ranks 5.5–6.5 on the Mohs scale of hardness.

JADE A Mayan jade mask pectoral or belt ornament (probably from the ancient Mayan city at Palenque in Mexico) (Museum of Mankind, London, England).
The Art Archive/Gordon Boys' School, Woking/Eileen Tweedy

Jade Emperor (or **Yu Huang**) in Chinese religion, the supreme god of pantheistic Taoism, also known as the **August Personage of Jade** and **Father Heaven**, who watches over human actions and is the ruler of life and death. His court inspects the earth annually, making a detailed account from which he apportions praise or blame; the gods could be promoted or lose their rank accordingly.

Jaffa (Arabic **Yafa**; Hebrew **Yafo**; biblical **Joppa**) city and former port in west Israel, part of ▷Tel Aviv-Yafo from 1950. It is also a tourist centre.

Jaffna capital of Jaffna district, Northern Province, Sri Lanka; population (1990) 129,000. It was the focal point of Hindu Tamil nationalism and the scene of recurring riots during the 1980s.

Jagan, Cheddi Berret (1918–1997) Guyanese left-wing politician, president 1992–97. With his wife, Janet Jagan, he co-founded the People's Progressive Party (PPA) in 1950, of which he was the leader, and was the first prime minister of British Guyana 1961–64. As presidential candidate in August 1992, he opposed privatization as leading to 'recolonization'. The PPA won a decisive victory, and Jagan became president (succeeding Desmond Hoyte). Vice president Samuel Hinds succeeded to the presidency on Jagan's death, but in elections in December 1997, Jagan's wife, Janet, was elected as president.

Jagger, Mick (Michael Philip) (1943–) English singer and songwriter. He is the lead singer of the rock band the ▷Rolling Stones, with whom he has enjoyed enormous success dating back to the 1960s. In the 1980s, Jagger also launched a solo career. His albums include *She's the Boss* (1985), *Primitive Cool* (1987), and *Wandering Spirit* (1993). In 1985, Jagger also recorded a version of 'Dancing in the Streets' with David ▷Bowie as part of the Live Aid charity campaign.

jaguar largest species of cat in the Americas, formerly ranging from the southwestern USA to southern South America, but now extinct in most of North America. It can grow up to 2.5 m/8 ft long including the tail. Male jaguars weigh up to 150 kg/330 lb; females up to 90 kg/198 lb. The background colour of the fur varies from creamy white to brown or black, and is covered with black spots. The jaguar is usually solitary and lives approximately 11 years in the wild. (Species *Panthera onca*, family Felidae.)

The gestation period is 100 days and between one and four cubs are born. Jaguars are good swimmers and favour territory that is near water or flooded seasonally.

In 1999 there were 10,000–15,000 jaguars in the wild.
Related Web site: Jaguar http://dialspace.dial.pipex.com/town/plaza/abf90/jaguar.htm

jaguarundi wild cat found in forests in Central and South America. Up to 1.1 m/3.5 ft long, it is very slim with rather short legs and short rounded ears. It is uniformly coloured dark brown or chestnut. A good climber, it feeds on birds and small mammals and, unusually for a cat, has been reported to eat fruit. (Species *Felis yaguaroundi*, family Felidae.)

Jahangir (1569–1627) Adopted name of Salim. ('Holder of the World') Third Mogul emperor of India (1605–27), succeeding his father ▷Akbar the Great. The first part of his reign was marked by peace, prosperity, and a flowering of the arts, but the latter half by rebellion and succession conflicts.

Jahweh another spelling of ▷Jehovah, the Lord (meaning God) in the Hebrew Bible.

Jainism (Hindi *jaina* 'person who overcomes') ancient Indian religion, sometimes regarded as an offshoot of Hinduism. Jains emphasize the importance of not injuring living beings, and their code of ethics is based on sympathy and compassion for all forms of life. They also believe in ▷karma but not in any deity. It is a monastic, ascetic religion. There are two main sects: the Digambaras and the Swetambaras. Jainism practises the most extreme form of nonviolence (*ahimsā*) of all Indian sects, and influenced the philosophy of Mahatma Gandhi. Jains number approximately 6 million; there are Jain communities throughout the world but the majority live in India.
Related Web site: Outline of Jain History
http://www.cs.colostate.edu/~malaiya/jainhout1.html

Jaipur capital of Rajasthan, India, 240 km/150 mi southeast of Delhi; population (1991) 1,458,000. Products include textiles and metal products. Founded by Jai Singh II in 1728, it was formerly the capital of the state of Jaipur, which was merged with Rajasthan in 1949.

Jakarta (or **Djakarta**) (1619–1949 **Batavia**) capital of Indonesia on the northwest coast of Java, at the estuary of the River Liwung on Jakarta Bay; population (2000 est) 8,389,400. It is a leading commercial and industrial zone. Industries include textiles, chemicals, and plastics; a canal links it with its port of Tanjung Priok where rubber, oil, tin, coffee, tea, and palm oil are among its exports; also a tourist centre.

Jakeš, Miloš (1922–) Czech communist politician, a member of the Politburo from 1981 and party leader 1987–89. A conservative, he supported the Soviet invasion of Czechoslovakia in 1968. He was forced to resign in November 1989 following a series of prodemocracy mass rallies.

Der indische Großmogul Jehangir mit seinen Wesiren bei einer Beratung. Miniatur, um 1614. London, Victoria und Albert Museum.

JAHANGIR Third of the emperors of the Mogul dynasty, Jahangir, the son of Akbar, was considered to be the greatest of the Moguls. His reign was marred by an addiction to alcohol and opium. *Philip Sauvain Picture Collection*

Jalalabad capital of Nangarhar province, east Afghanistan, on the road from Kabul to Peshawar in Pakistan; population (1998 est) 142,000. The town stands on the Kabul River, at a height of 590 m/1,940 ft, and lies on the route connecting Kabul and Peshawar via the Khyber Pass. Jalalabad is well-placed to handle much of the trade between Afghanistan to the west and Pakistan and India to the east, and is the commercial centre for the irrigated plain around it. It trades in almonds, rice, grain, and fruit, while industries include sugar refining and handicrafts.

Jamaica see country box.

James two kings of Britain:

James I (1566–1625) King of England from 1603 and Scotland (as **James VI**) from 1567. The son of Mary Queen of Scots and her second husband, Lord Darnley, he succeeded to the Scottish throne on the enforced abdication of his mother and assumed power in 1583. He established a strong centralized authority, and in 1589 married Anne of Denmark (1574–1619).

As successor to Elizabeth I in England, he alienated the ▷Puritans by his High Church views and Parliament by his assertion of ▷divine right, and was generally unpopular because of his favourites, such as ▷Buckingham, and his schemes for an alliance with Spain. He was succeeded by his son Charles I.

As king of Scotland, he curbed the power of the nobility, although his attempts to limit the authority of the Kirk (Church of Scotland) were less successful.

Upon his accession to the English throne on the death of Elizabeth I, James acted mainly upon the advice of Robert Cecil, Earl of Salisbury, but on the latter's death all restraint vanished.

His religious policy consisted of asserting the supreme authority of the crown and suppressing both Puritans and Catholics who

JAMES I of England was a physically weak man, but he was extremely learned and wrote two books advocating the 'divine right of kings'. *Philip Sauvain Picture Collection*

objected. The preparation of the ▷Authorized Version of the ▷Bible in English, published in 1611, was ordered by James.

He thwarted Guy Fawkes's plot to blow up Parliament during its opening in 1605. The ▷gunpowder plot, with its anti-Catholic reaction, gave James a temporary popularity which soon dissipated. It was during his reign that the Puritan ▷Pilgrims (or 'Pilgrim Fathers') sailed to the New World to escape persecution in England. His foreign policy, aimed primarily at achieving closer relations with Spain, was also disliked.

James II (1633–1701) King of England and Scotland (as **James VII**) from 1685. The second son of Charles I, he succeeded his brother, Charles II. In 1660 James married Anne Hyde ((1637–1671), mother of Mary II and Anne) and in 1673 ▷Mary of Modena (mother of James Edward Stuart). He became a Catholic in 1671, which led first to attempts to exclude him from the succession, then to the rebellions of ▷Monmouth and Argyll, and finally to the Whig and Tory leaders' invitation to William of Orange to take the throne in 1688. James fled to France, then led an uprising in Ireland in 1689, but after defeat at the Battle of the ▷Boyne (1690) remained in exile in France.

At the Restoration in 1660 he had been appointed lord high admiral and warden of the Cinque Ports, but after the passing of the

▷Test Act in 1673 (which excluded Catholics from public office) he was forced to give up his offices.

James seven kings of Scotland:

James I (1394–1437) King of Scotland (1406–37), who assumed power in 1424. He was a cultured and strong monarch whose improvements in the administration of justice brought him popularity among the common people. He was assassinated by a group of conspirators led by the Earl of Atholl.

Related Web site: Selected Poetry of James I, Of Scotland (1394–1437) http://www.library.utoronto.ca/utel/rp/authors/james1sc.html

James II (1430–1460) King of Scotland from 1437, who assumed power in 1449. The only surviving son of James I, he was supported by most of the nobles and parliament. He sympathized with the Lancastrians during the Wars of the ▷Roses, and attacked English possessions in southern Scotland. He was killed while besieging Roxburgh Castle.

Almost continual civil war raged during the period of his minority; the prize of the victors was the custody of the king. In 1449 he married Mary, daughter of the Duke of Gueldres. He was succeeded by his son James III.

James III (1451–1488) King of Scotland from 1460, who assumed power in 1469. His reign was marked by rebellions by the

nobles, including his brother Alexander, Duke of Albany. He was murdered during a rebellion supported by his son, who then ascended the throne as James IV.

Eldest son of James II, he became king at the age of nine. In 1469 he married Margaret, daughter of King Christian I of Denmark.

James IV (1473–1513) King of Scotland from 1488. He came to the throne after his followers murdered his father, James III, at Sauchieburn. His reign was internally peaceful, but he allied himself with France against England, invaded in 1513, and was defeated and killed at the Battle of ▷Flodden. James IV was a patron of poets and architects as well as a military leader.

In 1503 he married Margaret Tudor ((1489–1541), daughter of Henry VII), which eventually led to his descendants succeeding to the English crown. He was succeeded by his son James V.

James V (1512–1542) King of Scotland from 1513, who assumed power in 1528. During the long period of his minority, he was caught in a struggle between pro-French and pro-English factions. When he assumed power, he allied himself with France and upheld Catholicism against the Protestants. Following an attack on Scottish territory by Henry VIII's forces, he was defeated near the border at Solway Moss in 1542.

Son of James IV and Margaret Tudor, he succeeded his father at the age of one year. His first wife, Madeline, daughter of King Francis I of France, died in 1537; the following year he married Mary of Guise. Their daughter, Mary Queen of Scots, succeeded him.

Jamaica

Jamaica island in the Caribbean Sea, south of Cuba and west of Haiti.

AREA 10,957 sq km/4,230 sq mi
CAPITAL Kingston
MAJOR TOWNS/CITIES Montego Bay, Spanish Town, St Andrew, Portmore, May Pen
PHYSICAL FEATURES mountainous tropical island; Blue Mountains (so called because of the haze over them)

Government

HEAD OF STATE Queen Elizabeth II from 1962, represented by Governor General Howard Cooke from 1991
HEAD OF GOVERNMENT Percival Patterson from 1992
POLITICAL SYSTEM liberal democracy
POLITICAL EXECUTIVE parliamentary
ADMINISTRATIVE DIVISIONS 14 parishes within three counties
ARMED FORCES 2,800 (2002 est)
CONSCRIPTION military service is voluntary
DEATH PENALTY retained and used for ordinary crimes
DEFENCE SPEND (% GDP) 0.5 (2002 est)
EDUCATION SPEND (% GDP) 6.3 (2001 est)
HEALTH SPEND (% GDP) 5.5 (2000 est)

Economy and resources

CURRENCY Jamaican dollar
GPD (US$) 8.0 billion (2002 est)

REAL GDP GROWTH (% change on previous year) 1.7 (2001)
GNI (US$) 7.4 billion (2002 est)
GNI PER CAPITA (PPP) (US$) 3,550 (2002 est)
CONSUMER PRICE INFLATION 7% (2003 est)
UNEMPLOYMENT 15% (2001)
FOREIGN DEBT (US$) 4.9 billion (2001 est)
MAJOR TRADING PARTNERS USA, UK, Mexico, Venezuela, EU, Canada, Norway
RESOURCES bauxite (one of world's major producers), marble, gypsum, silica, clay
INDUSTRIES mining and quarrying, bauxite processing, food processing, petroleum refining, clothing, cement, glass, tourism
EXPORTS alumina, bauxite, gypsum, sugar, bananas, garments, rum. Principal market: USA 39.3% (2000)
IMPORTS mineral fuels, machinery and transport equipment, basic manufactures and consumer goods, chemicals, food and live animals, miscellaneous manufactured articles. Principal source: USA 44.7% (2000)
ARABLE LAND 16.1% (2000 est)
AGRICULTURAL PRODUCTS sugar cane, bananas, citrus fruit, coffee, cocoa, coconuts; livestock rearing (goats, cattle, and pigs)

Population and society

POPULATION 2,651,000 (2003 est)

JAMAICA Coffee beans ripening in the Blue Mountains, Jamaica. *Corel*

POPULATION GROWTH RATE 1.0% (2000–15)
POPULATION DENSITY (per sq km) 241 (2003 est)
URBAN POPULATION (% of total) 58 (2003 est)
AGE DISTRIBUTION (% of total population) 0–14 31%, 15–59 59%, 60+ 10% (2002 est)
ETHNIC GROUPS 76% of African descent; about 15% of mixed African-European origin. There are also about 3% Indian, 3% European, and 1% Chinese minorities
LANGUAGE English (official), Jamaican Creole
RELIGION Protestant 70%, Rastafarian
EDUCATION (compulsory years) 6
LITERACY RATE 84% (men); 92% (women) (2003 est)
LABOUR FORCE 21.4% agriculture, 18.5% industry, 60.1% services (1998)
LIFE EXPECTANCY 74 (men); 78 (women) (2000–05)
CHILD MORTALITY RATE (under 5, per 1,000 live births) 20 (2001)
PHYSICIANS (per 1,000 people) 1.4 (1998 est)
HOSPITAL BEDS (per 1,000 people) 2,1 (1998 est)
TV SETS (per 1,000 people) 194 (2001 est)
RADIOS (per 1,000 people) 796 (2001 est)
INTERNET USERS (per 10,000 people) 2,291.8 (2002 est)
PERSONAL COMPUTER USERS (per 100 people) 5.4 (2002 est)

See also ▷Arawak; ▷West Indies, Federation of the.

Chronology

c. AD 900: Settled by Arawak Indians, who gave the island the name Jamaica ('well watered').

1494: The explorer Christopher Columbus reached Jamaica.

1509: Occupied by Spanish; much of Arawak community died from exposure to European diseases; black African slaves brought in to work sugar plantations.

1655: Captured by Britain and became its most valuable Caribbean colony.

1838: Slavery abolished.

1870: Banana plantations established as sugar cane industry declined in face of competition from European beet sugar.

1938: Serious riots during the economic depression and, as a sign of growing political awareness, the People's National Party (PNP) was formed by Norman Manley.

1944: First constitution adopted.

1958–62: Part of West Indies Federation.

1959: Internal self-government granted.

1962: Independence achieved within the Commonwealth, with Alexander Bustamante of the centre-right Jamaica Labour Party (JLP) as prime minister.

1981: Diplomatic links with Cuba were severed, and a free-market economic programme was pursued.

1988: The island was badly damaged by Hurricane Gilbert.

1992: Percival Patterson of the PNP became prime minister.

1998: Violent crime increased as the economy declined.

James VI of Scotland. See ▷James I of England.

James VII of Scotland. See ▷James II of England.

James, St several Christian saints, including:

James, St (lived 1st century AD) Called 'the Great'. New Testament apostle, originally a Galilean fisher. He was the son of Zebedee and brother of the apostle John. He was put to death by ▷Herod Agrippa. James is the patron saint of Spain. Feast day 25 July.

James, St (lived 1st century AD) Called 'the Just'. The New Testament brother of Jesus, to whom Jesus appeared after the Resurrection. Leader of the Christian church in Jerusalem, he was the author of the biblical Epistle of James.

James, St (lived 1st century AD) Called 'the Little'. In the New Testament, a disciple of Christ, son of Alphaeus. Feast day 3 May.

James Francis Edward Stuart (1688–1766) British prince, known as the **Old Pretender** (for the ▷Jacobites, he was James III). Son of James II, he was born at St James's Palace and after the ▷Glorious Revolution of 1688 was taken to France. He landed in Scotland in 1715 to head a Jacobite rebellion (the ▷Fifteen) but withdrew through lack of support. In his later years he settled in Rome.

James, Henry (1843–1916) US novelist, who lived in Europe from 1875 and became a naturalized British subject in 1915. His novels deal with the social, moral, and aesthetic issues arising from the complex relationship of European to American culture. His major novels include *The Portrait of a Lady* (1881), *The Bostonians* (1886), *What Maisie Knew* (1887), *The Ambassadors* (1903), and *The Golden Bowl* (1904). He also wrote more than a hundred shorter works of fiction, notably the novella *The Aspern Papers* (1888) and the supernatural/psychological riddle *The Turn of the Screw* (1898).

Initially a master of psychological realism, noted for the complex subtlety of his prose style, James became increasingly experimental, writing some of the essential works of early modernism. Other major novels include *Roderick Hudson* (1876), *The American* (1877), *Washington Square* (1881), *The Tragic Muse* (1890), *The Spoils of Poynton* (1897), *The Awkward Age* (1899), and *The Wings of the Dove* (1902). He also wrote travel sketches, including *The American Scene* (1906), which records his impressions on returning to the USA after 20 years' absence, and literary criticism, including *Notes on Novelists* (1914).

James, Jesse Woodson (1847–1882) US bank and train robber. He was a leader, with his brother Frank (1843–1915), of the Quantrill raiders, a Confederate guerrilla band in the Civil War. Jesse was killed by Bob Ford, an accomplice; Frank remained unconvicted and became a farmer.

In 1995 a US circuit court judge approved a scientist's proposal to exhume the body buried in James's grave and, using genetic testing, resolve whether or not the outlaw had faked his own death. The test determined that the remains really were those of James.

James, P(hyllis) D(orothy), Baroness James of Holland Park (1920–) English detective novelist. She created the characters Superintendent Adam Dalgliesh and private investigator Cordelia Gray. She was a tax official, hospital administrator, and civil servant in the Home Office, involved with police matters, before turning to writing. Her books include *Death of an Expert Witness* (1977), *The Skull Beneath the Skin* (1982), *A Taste for Death* (1986), *Original Sin* (1994), *Certain Justice* (1997), *Death in Holy Orders* (2001), and her memoirs, *Time to be in Earnest: A Fragment of Autobiography* (1999). She was created a baronesss in 1991.

James, William (1842–1910) US psychologist and philosopher. He was among the first to take an approach emphasizing the ends or purposes of behaviour and to advocate a scientific, experimental psychology. His *Varieties of Religious Experience* (1902) is one of the most important works on the psychology of religion.

James (I) the Conqueror (1208–1276) King of Aragón from 1213, when he succeeded his father. He conquered the Balearic Islands and took Valencia from the ▷Moors, dividing it with Alfonso X of Castile by a treaty of 1244. Both these exploits are recorded in his autobiography *Libre dels feyts/Chronicle*. He largely established Aragón as the dominant power in the Mediterranean.

Jameson, Leander Starr (1853–1917) Scottish colonial administrator, born in Edinburgh, Scotland. In South Africa, early in 1896, he led the **Jameson Raid** from Mafeking into the Transvaal to support the non-Boer colonists there, in an attempt to overthrow the government (for which he served some months in prison). Returning to South Africa, he succeeded Cecil ▷Rhodes as leader of the Progressive Party of Cape Colony, where he was prime minister 1904–08. He was made 1st baronet in 1911.

Jammu winter capital of the state of ▷Jammu and Kashmir, India, 130 km/80 mi north of Amritsar; population (1991) 206,000. It stands on the River Tavi, a tributary of the Chenab, and was linked to India's rail system in 1972.

Jammu and Kashmir state of north India; area 222,200 sq km/85,791 sq mi; population (2001 est) 10,069,900 (Indian-occupied territory). The main cities are ▷Jammu (winter capital), ▷Srinagar (summer capital and the seat of state government), and Leh.

The state has semi-arid alluvial plains in the south and is mountainous towards the north, with the ▷Karakoram range reaching heights of 4,000 m/13,000 ft, divided by river valleys (the ▷Jhelum), and the Vale of Kashmir (1,600 m/5,250 ft), the most densely populated area. Agricultural products include grain and rice, and fruit round Dal Lake near Srinagar, in the Vale of Kashmir. Sheep and goats are reared in the far north.

JAMMU AND KASHMIR Shikara boats, Srinagar, Jammu and Kashmir, India. *Image Bank*

Janáček, Leoš (1854–1928) Czech composer. He became director of the Conservatory at Brno in 1919 and professor at the Prague Conservatory in 1920. His music, highly original and influenced by Moravian folk music, includes arrangements of folk songs, operas (*Jenůfa*, (1904), *The Cunning Little Vixen* (1924)), and the choral *Glagolitic Mass* (1926).

Janata alliance of political parties in India formed in 1971 to oppose Indira Gandhi's ▷Congress Party. Victory in the election brought Morarji Desai to power as prime minister but he was unable to control the various groups within the alliance and resigned in 1979. His successors fared little better, and the elections of 1980 overwhelmingly returned Indira Gandhi to office.

Janata Dal (or **People's Party**) Indian centre-left coalition, formed in October 1988 under the leadership of V P ▷Singh and comprising the Janata, Lok Dal (B), Congress (S), and Jan Morcha parties. In a loose alliance with the Hindu fundamentalist Bharatiya Janata Party and the Communist Party of India, the Janata Dal was victorious in the November 1989 general election, taking power out of the hands of the Congress (I) Party. Following internal splits, its minority government fell in November 1990. Since 1992, several breakaway Janata Dal factions have been formed. The party has drawn particularly strong support from Hindu lower castes and, with its secular outlook, recently from Muslims. It formed the core of the new government of H D Deve Gowda in June 1996 and that of Inder Kumar Gujral in April 1997. In the 1998 general election the party formed part of the United Front, an alliance with regional parties, which lost much support and finished third in the hung parliament.

Jancsó, Miklós (1921–) Hungarian film director and screenwriter. He developed a powerfully individualist style which complimented his political narratives. His films include *Szegénylegények/The Round-up* (1965), *Csillagosok, katonák/The Red and the White* (1967), *Fényes szelek/The Confrontation* (1968), and *Még kér a nép/Red Psalm* (1971), for which he received the Best Director award at the Cannes Film Festival.

Janequin, Clément (c. 1472–c. 1560) French composer of chansons and psalms. He was choirmaster of Angers Cathedral 1534–37 and was based in Paris from 1549.

His songs of the 1520s–30s are witty and richly textured in imitative effects, for example 'Le Chant des oiseaux/Birdsong', 'La Chasse/The Hunt', and 'Les Cris de Paris/Street Cries of Paris'.

janissary (Turkish *yeniçeri* 'new force') bodyguard of the Ottoman sultan, the Turkish standing army from the late 14th century until 1826. Until the 16th century janissaries were Christian boys forcibly converted to Islam; after this time they were allowed to marry and recruit their own children. The bodyguard ceased to exist when it revolted against the decision of the sultan in 1826 to raise a regular force. The remaining janissaries were killed in battle or executed after being taken prisoner.

Jansen, Cornelius Otto (1585–1638) Dutch Roman Catholic theologian, founder of ▷Jansenism with his book *Augustinus* (1640).

Jansenism Christian teaching of Cornelius Jansen, which divided the Roman Catholic Church in France in the mid-17th century. Emphasizing the more predestinatory approach of St Augustine of Hippo's teaching, Jansenism was supported by the philosopher Pascal and Antoine Arnauld (a theologian linked with the abbey of Port Royal). Jansenists were excommunicated in 1719.

jansky unit of radiation received from outer space, used in radio astronomy. It is equal to 10^{-26} watts per square metre per hertz, and is named after US engineer Karl Jansky.

Janus in Roman mythology, the god of all openings, including doorways and passageways, and the beginning of the day, month, and year. January was dedicated to him. He is represented as having two faces, one looking forwards and one back, (in sculpture, a **herm**), and was associated with wisdom because he knew the past and could foresee the future. In Roman ritual he was invoked first in a list of gods, and at the beginning of any enterprise.

Japan see country box.

Japan Current (or **Kuroshio**) warm ocean ▷current flowing from Japan to North America.

Japanese inhabitants of Japan; people of Japanese culture or descent. Japan is an unusually homogeneous society, which has always been adept at assimilating influences from other cultures but has not readily received immigrants; discrimination against foreigners is legal in Japan. The ▷Japanese language is the only one spoken, though English is considered fashionable and is much used in advertising. Religion is syncretic and it is common for Japanese to take part in both Buddhist and Shinto rituals while professing belief in neither.

Japanese art the painting, sculpture, printmaking, and design of Japan. Early Japanese art was influenced by China. Painting later

JAPANESE ART An example of Japanese art in the 19th century. The landscape background is signed by Hiroshige II while the travellers in the foreground are the work of Kunisada. *Philip Sauvain Picture Collection*

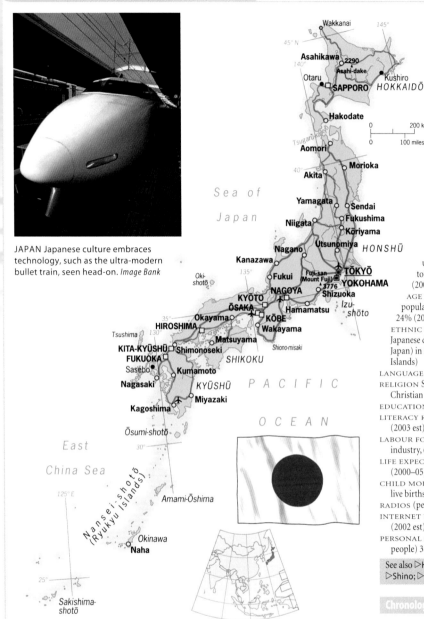

JAPAN Japanese culture embraces technology, such as the ultra-modern bullet train, seen head-on. *Image Bank*

Japan country in northeast Asia, occupying a group of islands of which the four main ones are Hokkaido, Honshu, Kyushu, and Shikoku. Japan is situated between the Sea of Japan (to the west) and the north Pacific (to the east), east of North and South Korea.

NATIONAL NAME *Nihon-koku/State of Japan*
AREA 377,535 sq km/145,766 sq mi
CAPITAL Tokyo
MAJOR TOWNS/CITIES Yokohama, Osaka, Nagoya, Fukuoka, Kitakyushu, Kyoto, Sapporo, Kobe, Kawasaki, Hiroshima
MAJOR PORTS Osaka, Nagoya, Yokohama, Kobe
PHYSICAL FEATURES mountainous, volcanic (Mount Fuji, volcanic Mount Aso, Japan Alps); comprises over 1,000 islands, the largest of which are Hokkaido, Honshu, Kyushu, and Shikoku

Government

HEAD OF STATE Emperor Akihito from 1989
HEAD OF GOVERNMENT Junichiro Koizumi from 2001
POLITICAL SYSTEM liberal democracy
POLITICAL EXECUTIVE parliamentary
ADMINISTRATIVE DIVISIONS 47 prefectures
ARMED FORCES self-defence forces of 239,900 (2002 est)
DEATH PENALTY retained and used for ordinary crimes

Economy and resources

CURRENCY yen
GPD (US$) 3,978.8 billion (2002 est)
REAL GDP GROWTH (% change on previous year) 0.7 (2001)
GNI (US$) 4,265.6 billion (2002 est)
GNI PER CAPITA (PPP) (US$) 26,070 (2002 est)
CONSUMER PRICE INFLATION –0.7% (2003 est)
UNEMPLOYMENT 5% (2001)
MAJOR TRADING PARTNERS USA, China, Australia, South Korea, Indonesia, UK, Germany, Taiwan, Singapore, Thailand, Malaysia
RESOURCES coal, iron, zinc, copper, natural gas, fish
INDUSTRIES motor vehicles, steel, machinery, electrical and electronic equipment, chemicals, textiles
EXPORTS electrical machinery, motor vehicles, electronic goods and components, chemicals, iron and steel products, scientific and optical equipment. Principal market:

USA 30.1% (2001)
IMPORTS machinery and equipment, mineral fuels, foodstuffs, live animals, bauxite, iron ore, copper ore, coking coal, chemicals, textiles, wood. Principal source: USA 18.1% (2001)
ARABLE LAND 12.3% (2000 est)
AGRICULTURAL PRODUCTS rice, potatoes, cabbages, sugar cane, sugar beet, citrus fruit; one of the world's leading fishing nations

Population and society

POPULATION 127,654,000 (2003 est)
POPULATION GROWTH RATE 0.1% (2000–15)
POPULATION DENSITY (per sq km) 338 (2003 est)
URBAN POPULATION (% of total) 79 (2003 est)
AGE DISTRIBUTION (% of total population) 0–14 14%, 15–59 62%, 60+ 24% (2002 est)
ETHNIC GROUPS more than 99% of Japanese descent; Ainu (aboriginal people of Japan) in north Japan (Hokkaido, Kuril Islands)
LANGUAGE Japanese (official), Ainu
RELIGION Shinto, Buddhist (often combined), Christian (less than 1%)
EDUCATION (compulsory years) 9
LITERACY RATE 99% (men); 99% (women) (2003 est)
LABOUR FORCE 5.1% agriculture, 31.2% industry, 63.7% services (2000)
LIFE EXPECTANCY 78 (men); 85 (women) (2000–05)
CHILD MORTALITY RATE (under 5, per 1,000 live births) 5 (2001)
RADIOS (per 1,000 people) 960 (1998)
INTERNET USERS (per 10,000 people) 4,488.6 (2002 est)
PERSONAL COMPUTER USERS (per 100 people) 38.2 (2002 est)

See also ▷Hiroshima; ▷Russo-Japanese War; ▷Shino; ▷shogun; ▷Sino-Japanese Wars.

Chronology

660 BC: According to legend, Jimmu Tenno, descendent of the Sun goddess, became the first emperor of Japan.

c. 400 AD: The Yamato, one of many warring clans, unified central Japan; Yamato chiefs are the likely ancestors of the imperial family.

5th–6th centuries: Writing, Confucianism, and Buddhism spread to Japan from China and Korea.

646: Start of Taika Reform: Emperor Kotoku organized central government on Chinese model.

794: Heian became imperial capital; later called Kyoto.

858: Imperial court fell under control of Fujiwara clan, who reduced the emperor to a figurehead.

11th century: Central government grew ineffectual; real power exercised by great landowners (daimyo) with private armies of samurai.

1185: Minamoto clan seized power under Yoritomo, who established military rule.

1192: Emperor gave Yoritomo the title of shogun (general); the shogun ruled in the name of the emperor.

1274: Mongol conqueror Kublai Khan attempted to invade Japan, making a second attempt in 1281; on both occasions Japan was saved by a typhoon.

1336: Warlord Takauji Ashikaga overthrew Minamoto shogunate; emperor recognized Ashikaga shogunate in 1338.

16th century: Power of Ashikagas declined; constant civil war.

1543: Portuguese sailors were the first Europeans to reach Japan; followed by Spanish, Dutch, and English traders.

1549: Spanish missionary St Francis Xavier began to preach Roman Catholic faith in Japan.

1585–98: Warlord Hideyoshi took power and attempted to conquer Korea in 1592 and 1597.

1603: Ieyasu Tokugawa founded new shogunate at Edo, reformed administration, and suppressed Christianity.

1630s: Japan adopted policy of isolation: all travel forbidden and all foreigners expelled except a small colony of Dutch traders in Nagasaki harbour.

1853: USA sent warships to Edo with demand that Japan open diplomatic and trade relations; Japan conceded in 1854.

1867: Revolt by isolationist nobles overthrew the Tokugawa shogunate.

1868: Emperor Mutsuhito assumed full powers, moved the imperial capital from Kyoto to Edo (renamed Tokyo), and launched policy of swift Westernization.

1894–95: Sino-Japanese War: Japan expelled Chinese from Korea.

1902–21: Japan entered a defensive alliance with Britain.

1904–05: Russo-Japanese War: Japan drove Russians from Manchuria and Korea; Korea annexed in 1910.

1914: Japan entered World War I and occupied German possessions in Far East.

1923: Earthquake destroyed much of Tokyo and Yokohama.

1931: Japan invaded Chinese province of Manchuria and created puppet state of Manchukuo; Japanese government came under control of military and extreme nationalists.

1937: Japan resumed invasion of China.

1940: After Germany defeated France, Japan occupied French Indo-China.

1941: Japan attacked US fleet at Pearl Harbor; USA and Britain declared war on Japan.

1942: Japanese conquered Thailand, Burma, Malaya, Dutch East Indies, Philippines, and northern New Guinea.

1945: USA dropped atomic bombs on Hiroshima and Nagasaki; Japan surrendered.

1947: MacArthur supervised introduction of democratic 'Peace Constitution', accompanied by demilitarization and land reform.

1952: Occupation ended.

1955: Liberal Democratic Party (LDP) founded with support of leading business people.

1956: Japan admitted to United Nations.

1950s–70s: Rapid economic development; growth of manufacturing exports led to great prosperity.

1993: An economic recession and financial scandals brought the downfall of the LDP government. A coalition government was formed.

1995: An earthquake devastated Kobe.

1997: A financial crash occurred after bank failures.

1998: Keizo Obuchi, leader of the LDP, became prime minister. The government introduced a new $200 billion economic stimulus package after the worst recession since World War II.

2000: After Prime Minister Obuchi suffered a stroke, Yoshiro Mori was appointed in his place.

2001: Junichiro Koizumi was appointed prime minister after a vote of no-confidence in Yoshiro Mori.

2002: Koizumi made an historic visit to communist North Korea, prompting an unprecedented apology from North Korean leader Kim Jong Il for the abduction of about 12 Japanese nationals by Korean special forces in the 1970s and 1980s. Koizumi apologized for Japan's occupation of Korea before and during World War II.

2003: The island of Hokkaido was struck by powerful earthquakes measuring up to 8.0 on the Richter scale, some of the strongest tremors in the world during 2003.

developed a distinct Japanese character, bolder and more angular, with the spread of Zen Buddhism in the 12th century. Ink painting and calligraphy flourished, followed by book illustration and decorative screens. Japanese prints developed in the 17th century, with multicolour prints invented around 1765. Buddhist sculpture proliferated from 580, and Japanese sculptors excelled at portraits. Japanese pottery stresses simplicity.

Japanese language language of East Asia, spoken almost exclusively in the islands of Japan. Traditionally isolated, but possibly related to Korean, Japanese was influenced by Mandarin Chinese especially in the 6th–9th centuries and is written in Chinese-derived ideograms supplemented by two syllabic systems.

Japanese literature prose, poetry, and drama of Japan. Characteristic of the classical literature is the intermingling of prose and poetry, the forms of the latter being determined by the number of syllables. *The Tale of Genji* (*c.* 1005) by ▷Murasaki Shikibu has been called the world's first novel. Modern novelists include Yukio Mishima and Jun-ichirō Tanizaki.

jargon language that is complex and hard to understand, usually because it is highly technical or occupational, used in the wrong contexts, or designed to impress or confuse ('technical jargon'; 'writing in pseudoscientific jargon'; 'using a meaningless jargon').

jarrah type of ▷eucalyptus tree of western Australia, with durable timber.

Jarry, Alfred (1873–1907) French satiric dramatist. His grossly farcical *Ubu Roi* (1896) foreshadowed the Theatre of the ▷Absurd and the French Surrealist movement in its freedom of staging and subversive humour.

Jaruzelski, Wojciech Witold (1923–) Polish army general, appointed first secretary of the Polish United Workers Party (PUWP) in 1981. He was responsible for the imposition of martial law in Poland in December 1981. He was prime minister 1981–85 and president 1985–90. During martial law he attempted to suppress the ▷Solidarity trade union, interning its leaders and political dissidents. In 1989 he approved the 'Round Table' talks with the opposition that led to partially free parliamentary elections and to the appointment of a coalition government under a noncommunist prime minister, Tadeusz ▷Mazowiecki.

Jarvik 7 the first successful artificial heart intended for permanent implantation in a human being. Made from polyurethane plastic and aluminium, it is powered by compressed air. Barney Clark became the first person to receive a Jarvik 7, in Salt Lake City, Utah, USA, in 1982; it kept him alive for 112 days.

jasmine any of a group of subtropical plants with white or yellow flowers. The common jasmine (*J. officinale*) has fragrant pure white flowers that yield jasmine oil, used in perfumes; the Chinese winter jasmine (*J. nudiflorum*) has bright yellow flowers that appear before the leaves. (Genus *Jasminum*, family Oleaceae.)

Jason in Greek mythology, the leader of the Argonauts who sailed in the *Argo* to Colchis in search of the ▷Golden Fleece. He eloped with ▷Medea, daughter of the king of Colchis, who had helped him achieve his goal, but later deserted her.

Jassy German name for the Romanian city of ▷Iaşi.

Jat an ethnic group living in Pakistan and northern India, and numbering about 11 million; they are the largest group in northern India. The Jat are predominantly farmers. They speak Punjabi, a language belonging to the Iranian branch of the Indo-European family. They are thought to be related to the Romany people.

jaundice yellow discoloration of the skin and whites of the eyes caused by an excess of bile pigment in the bloodstream. Approximately 60% of newborn babies exhibit some degree of jaundice, which is treated by bathing in white, blue, or green light that converts the bile pigment bilirubin into a water-soluble compound that can be excreted in urine. A serious form of jaundice occurs in rhesus disease (see ▷rhesus factor).

Bile pigment is normally produced by the liver from the breakdown of red blood cells, then excreted into the intestines. A build-up in the blood is due to abnormal destruction of red cells (as in some cases of ▷anaemia), impaired liver function (as in ▷hepatitis), or blockage in the excretory channels (as in gallstones or ▷cirrhosis). The jaundice gradually recedes following treatment of the underlying cause.

Jaurès, (Auguste Marie Joseph) Jean (Léon) (1859–1914) French socialist politician. He was considered a commanding intellectual presence within the socialist movement in France, through his writings (which included a magisterial social history of the French revolution), his oratory, and his journalism. In the decade leading up to the outbreak of World War I, Jaurès' impassioned opposition to the rising tide of militarism in Europe brought him centre stage within the Second International.

Java (or **Jawa**) most populated island of Indonesia, situated between Sumatra and Bali; area (with the island of Madura) 132,000 sq km/51,000 sq mi; population (with Madura; 2000 est) 118,230,300. The capital is ▷Jakarta (which is also the capital of Indonesia). About half the island is under cultivation, the rest being thickly forested. Mountains and sea breezes keep the temperature down, but humidity is high, with heavy rainfall from December to March. Ports include Surabaya and Semarang.

Javanese the largest ethnic group in the Republic of Indonesia. There are more than 50 million speakers of Javanese, which belongs to the western branch of the Austronesian family. Although the Javanese have a Hindu-Buddhist heritage, they are today predominantly Muslim, practising a branch of Islam known as *Islam Jawa*, which contains many Sufi features.

javelin spear used in athletics events. The men's javelin is about 260 cm/8.5 ft long, weighing 800 g/28 oz; the women's 230 cm/ 7.5 ft long, weighing 600 g/21 oz. It is thrown from a scratch line at the end of a run-up. The centre of gravity on the men's javelin was altered in 1986 to reduce the vast distances (90 m/100 yd) that were being thrown.

jaw one of two bony structures that form the framework of the mouth in all vertebrates except lampreys and hagfishes (the agnathous or jawless vertebrates). They consist of the upper jawbone (maxilla), which is fused to the skull, and the lower jawbone (mandible), which is hinged at each side to the bones of the temple by ▷ligaments.

jay any of several birds belonging to the crow family, generally brightly coloured and native to Europe, Asia, and the Americas. In the Eurasian **common jay** (*Garrulus glandarius*), the body is fawn with patches of white, blue, and black on the wings and tail. (Family Corvidae, order Passeriformes.)

> **Thomas Jefferson**
> *A little rebellion now and then is a good thing.*
> Letter to James Madison, 30 January 1787

Jayawardene, Junius Richard (1906–1996) Sri Lankan politician. Leader of the United Nationalist Party from 1973, he became prime minister in 1977 and the country's first president 1978–88. Jayawardene embarked on a free-market economic strategy, but was confronted with increasing Tamil–Sinhalese ethnic unrest, forcing the imposition of a state of emergency in 1983.

jazz polyphonic syncopated music, characterized by solo virtuosic improvisation, which developed in the USA at the turn of the 20th century. Initially music for dancing, often with a vocalist, it had its roots in black American and other popular music. Developing from ▷blues and spirituals (religious folk songs) in the southern states, it first came to prominence in the early 20th century in New Orleans, St Louis, and Chicago, with a distinctive flavour in each city.

Traits common to all types of jazz are the modified rhythms of West Africa; the emphasis on improvisation; western European harmony emphasizing the dominant seventh and the clash of major and minor thirds; characteristic textures and ▷timbres, first exemplified by a singer and rhythm section (consisting of a piano, bass, drums, and guitar or a combination of these instruments), and later by the addition of the saxophone and various brass instruments, and later still by the adoption of electrically amplified instruments.

JAZZ US pianist Duke Ellington, in a photograph from the 1920s. *Archive Photos*

Jazz Age the hectic and exciting 1920s in the USA, when 'hot jazz' became fashionable as part of the general rage for spontaneity and social freedom. The phrase is attributed to the novelist F Scott Fitzgerald.

jazz dance dance based on African techniques and rhythms, developed by black Americans around 1917. It entered mainstream dance in the 1920s, mainly in show business, and from the 1960s the teachers and choreographers Matt Mattox and Luigi expanded its vocabulary. Contemporary choreographers as diverse as Jerome ▷Robbins and Alvin Ailey used it in their work.

Jedda alternative spelling for the Saudi Arabian port ▷Jiddah.

Jefferson, Thomas (1743–1826) 3rd president of the USA 1801–09, founder of the Democratic Republican Party. He published *A Summary View of the Rights of America* (1774) and as a member of the Continental Congresses of 1775–76 was largely responsible for the drafting of the ▷Declaration of Independence. He was governor of Virginia 1779–81, ambassador to Paris 1785–89, secretary of state 1789–93, and vice-president 1797–1801.

Jefferson was born in Virginia into a wealthy family, educated at William and Mary College, and became a lawyer. His interests included music, painting, architecture, and the natural sciences; he was very much a product of the 18th-century Enlightenment. He designed the Capitol at Richmond, Virginia, (1785–1809), and the University of Virginia, Charlottesville (opened 1825). His political philosophy of 'agrarian democracy' placed responsibility for upholding a virtuous American republic mainly upon a citizenry of independent yeoman farmers. Ironically, his two terms as president saw the adoption of some of the ideas of his political opponents, the ▷Federalists. In January 2000 the Thomas Jefferson Memorial Foundation announced that after DNA tests had been carried out on the descendants of Jefferson's slave Sally Hemings, it had found that there was a strong likelihood that Jefferson had fathered at least one, and probably all six, of her children. Such a relationship with his slave adds a controversial element to the acceptance of Jefferson's opposition to slavery.

Related Web site: Autobiography by Thomas Jefferson
http://www.bibliomania.com/NonFiction/Jefferson/Autobiography/chap00.html

Jeffreys, Alec John (1950–) English geneticist who discovered the DNA probes necessary for accurate ▷genetic fingerprinting so that a murderer or rapist could be identified by, for example, traces of blood, tissue, or semen.

Jeffreys of Wem, George, 1st Baron Jeffreys of Wem (1644–1689) Welsh judge, popularly known as 'the hanging judge'. He became Chief Justice of the King's Bench in 1683, and presided over many political trials, notably those of Philip Sidney, Titus Oates, and Richard Baxter, becoming notorious for his brutality.

JEFFREYS OF WEM was appointed Lord Chancellor by James II as a reward for his support for the crown, such as his brutal punishment of those who had supported Monmouth's rebellion in the 'bloody assizes' in 1685. *Philip Sauvain Picture Collection*

Jehovah (or **Jahweh**) in the Old Testament, the name of God, revealed to Moses; in Hebrew texts of the Old Testament the name was represented by the letters YHVH (without the vowels 'a o a') because it was regarded as too sacred to be pronounced.

Jehovah's Witness member of a religious organization originating in the USA in 1872 under Charles Taze Russell (1852–1916). Jehovah's Witnesses attach great importance to Christ's second coming, which Russell predicted would occur in 1914, and which Witnesses still believe is imminent. All Witnesses are expected to take part in house-to-house preaching; there are no clergy.

Jekyll, Gertrude (1843–1932) English landscape gardener and writer. She created over 300 gardens, many in collaboration with the architect Edwin ▷Lutyens. In her books, she advocated colour design in garden planning and natural gardens of the cottage type, with plentiful herbaceous borders.

Originally a painter and embroiderer, she took up landscape design at the age of 48 when her eyesight deteriorated. Her home at Munstead Wood, Surrey, was designed for her by Lutyens.

Jellicoe, Geoffrey Alan (1900–1996) English architect, landscape architect, and historian. His contribution to 20th-century thinking on landscapes and gardens has been mainly through his writings, notably *The Landscape of Man* (1975). However, he also made an impact as a designer, working in a contemplative and poetic vein and frequently incorporating water and sculptures. Representative of his work are the Kennedy Memorial (1965) at Runnymede, where a granite path winds uphill to a memorial stone by an American Scarlet oak; and the Sutton Place gardens, Sussex (1980–84). He was knighted in 1979.

jellyfish marine invertebrate, belonging among the ▷coelenterates (subphylum Cnidaria), with an umbrella-shaped body made of a semi-transparent jellylike substance, often tinted with blue, red, or orange colours, and having stinging tentacles that trail in the water. Most adult jellyfish move freely, but during parts of their life cycle many are polyp-like and attached to rocks, the seabed, or another underwater surface. They feed on small animals that are paralysed by stinging cells in the jellyfish tentacles.

Most jellyfish cause no more discomfort to humans than a nettle sting, but contact with the tentacles of the subtropical Portuguese man-of-war (*Physalia physalis*) or the Australian box jellyfish (*Chironex fleckeri*) can be life-threatening.

A new species of giant jellyfish was discovered in the eastern Pacific in 1998. *Chrysaora achlyos* has 6-m/20-ft tentacles and a bell that is 1 m/3.3 ft in diameter. The largest jellyfish is the lion's mane sea jelly *Cyanea capillata arctica*. One individual had a bell of 2.3 m/7.5 ft diameter and 36.5 m/120 ft tentacles.

Jencks, Charles (1939–) US architectural theorist, living in Britain. He coined the term 'postmodern architecture' and wrote *The Language of Post-Modern Architecture* (1984).

Jenkins, Roy Harris (1920–2003) Baron Jenkins of Hillhead. British politician, born in Monmouthshire, Wales. He became a Labour minister in 1964, was home secretary 1965–67 and 1974–76, and chancellor of the Exchequer 1967–70. He was president of the European Commission 1977–81. In 1981 he became one of the founders of the Social Democratic Party and was elected as an SDP MP in 1982, but lost his seat in 1987. In the same year, he was elected chancellor of Oxford University and made a life peer. In 1997 he was appointed head of a commission, set up by the Labour government, to recommend, in 1998, a new voting system for elections to Parliament.

Jenner, Edward (1749–1823) English physician who pioneered vaccination. In Jenner's day, smallpox was a major killer. His discovery in 1796 that inoculation with cowpox gives immunity to smallpox was a great medical breakthrough.

Jenner observed that people who worked with cattle and contracted cowpox from them never subsequently caught smallpox. In 1798 he published his findings that a child inoculated with cowpox, then two months later with smallpox, did not get smallpox. He coined the word 'vaccination' from the Latin word for cowpox, *vaccinia*.

Jerablus ancient Syrian city, adjacent to Carchemish on the River Euphrates.

jerboa any of a group of small nocturnal rodents with long and powerful hind legs developed for leaping. There are about 25 species of jerboa, native to desert areas of North Africa and Southwest Asia. (Family Dipodidae.)

The common North African jerboa (*Jaculus orientalis*) is a typical species. Its body is about 15 cm/6 in long and the tail is 25 cm/10 in long with a tuft at the tip. At speed it moves in a series of long jumps with its forefeet held close to its body.

Jeremiah (lived 7th–6th century BC) Old Testament Hebrew prophet, whose ministry continued from 626 to 586 BC. He was imprisoned during ▷Nebuchadnezzar's siege of Jerusalem on suspicion of intending to desert to the enemy. On the city's fall, he retired to Egypt.

> **Edward Jenner**
> *The deviation of man from the state in which he was originally placed by nature seems to have proved him to be a prolific source of diseases.*
> *An Inquiry into the Causes and Effects of the Variolae Vaccinae, or Cow-pox*

> **Jerome K Jerome**
> *It is impossible to enjoy idling thoroughly unless one has plenty of work to do.*
> *Idle Thoughts of an Idle Fellow, 'On Being Idle'*

Jericho town in the Jordan valley, west of the River Jordan and north of the Dead Sea, 24 km/15 mi northeast of Jerusalem; population (1995 est) 25,000. The site of the old city is the centre of a fertile district where palms, rose trees, grapes, and balsams are grown. It was occupied by Israel from 1967–94 when responsibility for its administration was transferred to the Palestine National Authority, after the Israeli–Palestine Liberation Organization peace agreement in 1993. Jericho was settled by 8000 BC, and by 6000 BC had become a walled city with 2,000 inhabitants. It is claimed to be the site of the world's earliest known town, dating from around 9000 BC. Successive archaeological excavations since 1907 have shown 20 layers of settlement, and that the walls of the city were destroyed many times. In the Old Testament it was the first Canaanite stronghold captured by the Israelites, and its walls, according to the Book of ▷Joshua, fell to the blast of Joshua's trumpets.

Jerome, St (c. 340–420) One of the early Christian leaders and scholars known as the Fathers of the Church. His Latin versions of the Old and New Testaments form the basis of the Roman Catholic Vulgate. He is usually depicted with a lion. His feast day is 30 September.
Related Web site: Jerome, St http://www.newadvent.org/cathen/08341a.htm

Jerome, Jerome K(lapka) (1859–1927) English journalist and writer. His works include the novel *Three Men in a Boat* (1889), a humorous account of a trip on the Thames from Kingston to Oxford; the humorous essays 'Idle Thoughts of an Idle Fellow' (1889); and the play *The Passing of the Third Floor Back* (story 1908, dramatized version 1910).

Jersey largest of the ▷Channel Islands; capital St Helier; area 117 sq km/45 sq mi; population (1991) 85,200. It is governed by a lieutenant governor representing the English crown and an assembly. Jersey cattle were originally bred here. Jersey gave its name to a woollen garment.
Related Web site: States of Jersey http://www.jersey.gov.uk/

Jersey City city in northeastern New Jersey, USA, on a peninsula bordered by the Hudson and Hackensack rivers to the north, and by New York and Newark bays to the south; seat of Hudson County; population (1994 est) 226,000. Jersey City is separated from New York by 2 km/1.2 mi of river, and connected with Manhattan Island via the Hudson River tunnels. A former port, it is now an industrial centre; products include pharmaceuticals, steel and metal products, electrical equipment, and chemicals.

EDWARD JENNER Distress at the idea of inoculation is shown in this 19th-century caricature. The child is about to be infected with cowpox matter in order to protect him from smallpox. Smallpox epidemics killed thousands of people until English physician Edward Jenner established this successful source of immunity. *The Art Archive/Bibliotheque des Arts Decoratifs Paris/Dagli Orti*

Jerusalem (Arabic **al-Quds**; Hebrew **Yerushalayim**) ancient city of Palestine, 762 m/2,500 ft above sea level, situated in hills 55 km/34 mi from the Mediterranean, divided in 1948 between Jordan and the new republic of Israel; area (pre-1967) 37.5 sq km/ 14.5 sq mi, (post-1967) 108 sq km/42 sq mi, including areas of the West Bank; population of the city (1997 est) 621,100; district (1997 est) 701,700. In 1950 the western New City was proclaimed as the Israeli capital, and, having captured from Jordan the eastern Old City in 1967, Israel affirmed in 1980 that the united city was the country's capital; the United Nations does not recognize East Jerusalem as part of Israel, and regards Tel Aviv as the capital.

Features These include the seven gates into the Old City through the walls built by Selim I (1467–1520); the Church of the Holy Sepulchre (built by Emperor Constantine in 335) and the mosque of the Dome of the Rock. The latter stands on the site of the ▷Temple built by King Solomon in the 10th century BC, and the Western ('Wailing') Wall, held sacred by Jews, is part of the walled platform on which the Temple once stood. The Hebrew University of Jerusalem opened in 1925.

Religions Christianity, Judaism, and Islam, with Roman Catholic, Anglican, Eastern Orthodox, and Coptic bishoprics. In 1967 Israel guaranteed freedom of access of all faiths to their holy places.

Related Web sites: Jerusalem in Old Maps and Views
http://www.israel-mfa.gov.il/mfa/go.asp?MFAH00jb0
Virtual Tour of Jerusalem http://www.md.huji.ac.il/vjt/

Jerusalem artichoke a variety of ▷artichoke.

Jesuit (or **the Society of Jesus**) member of the largest and most influential Roman Catholic religious order founded by Ignatius ▷Loyola in 1534, with the aims of protecting Catholicism against the Reformation and carrying out missionary work. During the 16th and 17th centuries Jesuits took a leading role in the ▷Counter-Reformation, the defence of Catholicism against Protestantism – many, for instance, came to England to work to undermine the Elizabethan religious settlement. Others worked as missionaries in Japan, China, Paraguay, and among the North American Indians. The order had (1991) about 29,000 members (15,000 priests plus students and lay members). There are Jesuit schools and universities.

Related Web site: Jesuits and the Sciences 1540–1995 http://www.luc.edu/libraries/science/jesuits/index.html

Jesus (*c*. 4 BC–AD 29 or 30) Hebrew preacher on whose teachings ▷Christianity was founded. According to the accounts of his life in the four Gospels, he was born in Bethlehem, Palestine, son of God and the Virgin Mary, and brought up by Mary and her husband Joseph as a carpenter in Nazareth. After adult baptism, he gathered 12 disciples, but his preaching antagonized the Roman authorities and he was executed by crucifixion. Three days later there came reports of his ▷resurrection and, later, his ascension to heaven.

Through his legal father Joseph, Jesus belonged to the tribe of Judah and the family of David, the second king of Israel, a heritage needed by the Messiah for whom the Hebrew people were waiting. In AD 26 or 27 his cousin John the Baptist proclaimed the coming of the promised Messiah and baptized Jesus, who then made two missionary journeys through the district of Galilee. His teaching, summarized in the Sermon on the Mount, aroused both religious opposition from the ▷Pharisees and secular opposition from the party supporting the Roman governor ▷Herod Antipas. When Jesus returned to Jerusalem (probably AD 29), a week before the Passover festival, he was greeted by the people as the Messiah, and the Hebrew authorities (aided by the apostle Judas) had him arrested and condemned to death, after a hurried trial by the Sanhedrin (supreme Jewish court). The Roman procurator, Pontius Pilate, confirmed the sentence, stressing the threat posed to imperial authority by Jesus' teaching.

Related Web sites: From Jesus to Christ: The First Christians
http://www.pbs.org/wgbh/pages/frontline/shows/religion/
Jesus Christ http://www.newadvent.org/cathen/08374c.htm

JET (abbreviation for Joint European Torus) research facility at Culham, near Abingdon, Oxfordshire, UK, that conducts experiments on nuclear fusion. It is the focus of the European effort to produce a safe and environmentally sound fusion-power reactor. On 9 November 1991 the JET tokamak, operating with a mixture of deuterium and iritium, produced a 1.7 megawatt pulse of power in an experiment that lasted two seconds. In 1997 isotopes of deuterium and tritium were fused to produce a record 21 mega-joule of nuclear fusion power. JET has tested the first large-scale plant of the type needed to process and supply tritium in a future fusion power station.

jet lag the effect of a sudden switch of time zones in air travel, resulting in tiredness and feeling 'out of step' with day and night. In 1989 it was suggested that use of the hormone melatonin helped to lessen the effect of jet lag by resetting the body clock. See also ▷circadian rhythm.

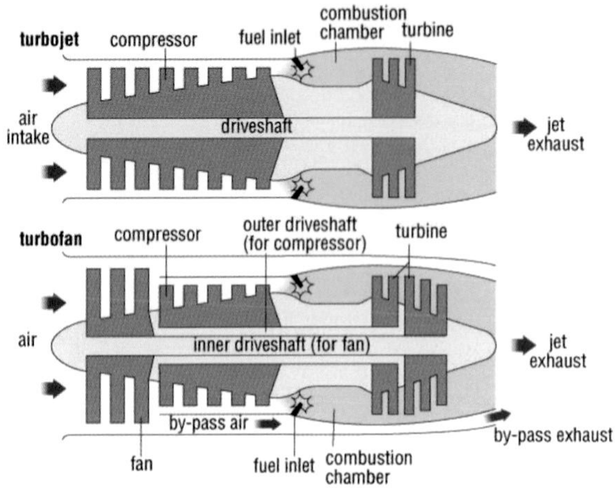

JET PROPULSION The diagram shows two forms of jet engine. In the turbojet, air passing into the air intake is compressed by the compressor and fed into the combustion chamber where fuel burns. The hot gases formed are expelled at high speed from the rear of the engine, driving the engine forwards and turning a turbine which drives the compressor. In the turbofan, air flows around the combustion chamber and mixes with the exhaust gases. This arrangement is more efficient and quieter than the turbojet.

jet propulsion method of propulsion in which an object is propelled in one direction by a jet, or stream of gases, moving in the other. This follows from Isaac ▷Newton's third law of motion: 'To every action, there is an equal and opposite reaction.' The most widespread application of the jet principle is in the jet engine, the most common kind of aircraft engine.

Jet Propulsion Laboratory NASA installation at Pasadena, California, operated by the California Institute of Technology. It is the command centre for NASA's deep-space probes such as the Voyager, Magellan, and Galileo missions, with which it communicates via the Deep Space Network of radio telescopes at Goldstone, California; Madrid, Spain; and Canberra, Australia.

jet stream narrow band of very fast wind (velocities of over 150 kph/95 mph) found at altitudes of 10–16 km/6–10 mi in the upper troposphere or lower stratosphere. Jet streams usually occur about the latitudes of the Westerlies (35°–60°).

Jew follower of ▷Judaism, the Jewish religion. The term is also used to refer to those who claim descent from the ancient Hebrews, a Semitic people of the Middle East. Today, some may recognize their ethnic heritage but not practise the religious or cultural traditions. The term came into use in medieval Europe, based on the Latin name for Judeans, the people of Judah. Prejudice against Jews is termed ▷anti-Semitism.

jewellery objects worn for ornament, such as rings, brooches, necklaces, pendants, earrings, and bracelets. Jewellery has been made from a wide variety of materials, including precious metals, gemstones, amber, teeth, bone, glass, and plastics.

Jew's harp musical instrument consisting of a two-pronged metal frame inserted between the teeth, and a springlike tongue plucked with the finger. The resulting drone excites resonances in the mouth. Changes in the shape of the mouth cavity will vary the pitch of these resonances to produce a melody.

Jezebel In the Old Testament, daughter of the king of Sidon. She married King Ahab of Israel, and was brought into conflict with the prophet Elijah by her introduction of the worship of Baal.

Jhabvala, Ruth Prawer (1927–) German-born novelist, short-story writer, and screenplay writer. She was educated in England and has spent much of her adult life in India, the setting of some of her most widely acclaimed novels, including *Heat and Dust* (1975), which won the Booker Prize. Among her best-known screenplays are the films *A Room with a View* (1985), an adaptation of a novel by E M ▷Forster, and *Jefferson in Paris* (1995).

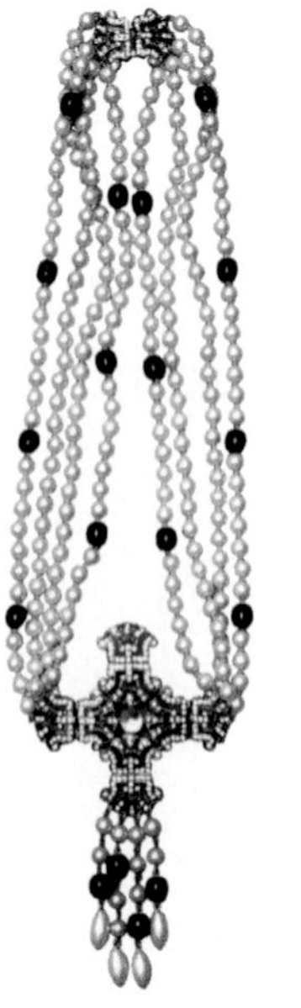

JEWELLERY A necklace featuring various kinds of pearls together with glass crystal, designed in the 1940s by the Italian jeweller Marangoni. *The Art Archive/ Private Collection/Dagli Orti*

Jharkhand state of northeast India bordered by Bihar, West Bengal, Orissa, Chhattisgarh, and Uttar Pradesh; area 74,677 sq km/28,833 sq mi; population (2001 est) 27,894,000. It was carved from Bihar and was incorporated in November 2000. The capital is Ranchi. Jharkhand accounts for nearly half of India's mineral wealth. Minerals extracted include bauxite, limestone, mica, coal, iron, and copper ore. Industries include the Tata Iron and Steel Company and the Bokaro Steel Plant. The area is home to 30 tribal groups who are estimated to form one-third of the population. The principal languages spoken are Santali, Kurukh, Mundari, and Nagpuria.

Jharkhand was recognized as a separate state following years of protest by the indigenous population. It has 22 districts. Major cities include Dhandbad, Bokaro, Jamshedpur, and Sindi. Only 30% of the state's land is cultivable and, in 2000, 57% of the state's population lived below the poverty line.

Jharkhand is also home to Palamau Forest, and contains several well-known tourist spots, including Hudru Falls, Lodha, and a wildlife sanctuary for tigers at Betla National Park.

Jiang Jie Shi (or **Chiang Kai-shek**) (1887–1975) Chinese nationalist Kuomintang (▷Guomindang) general and politician, president of China 1928–31 and 1943–49, and of ▷Taiwan from 1949, where he set up a US-supported right-wing government on his expulsion from the mainland by the communist forces.

Jiang took part in the revolution of 1911 that overthrew the Qing dynasty of the Manchus, and on the death of the Kuomintang leader Sun Zhong Shan (Sun Yat-sen) was made commander-in-chief of the nationalist armies in southern China in 1925. Collaboration with the communists, broken in 1927, was resumed after the Xi'an Incident in 1936 when China needed to pool military strength in the struggle against the Japanese invaders of World War II. After the Japanese surrender in 1945, civil war between the nationalists and communists erupted, and in December 1949 Jiang and his followers took refuge on the island of Taiwan, maintaining a large army in the hope of reclaiming the mainland. His authoritarian regime enjoyed US support until his death. His son Jiang Qing-guo then became president.

Jiang Qing (or **Chiang Ching**) (1914–1991) Chinese communist politician, third wife of the party leader ▷Mao Zedong. In 1960 she became minister for culture, and played a key role in the 1966–69 ▷Cultural Revolution as the leading member of the Shanghai-based ▷Gang of Four, who attempted to seize power in 1976. She was imprisoned in 1981.

Jiang was a Shanghai actor when in 1937 she met Mao Zedong at the communist headquarters in Yan'an; she became his wife in 1939. She emerged as a radical, egalitarian Maoist. Her influence waned during the early 1970s and her relationship with Mao became embittered. On Mao's death in September 1976, the Gang of Four, with Jiang as a leading figure, sought to seize power by organizing military coups in Shanghai and Beijing. They were arrested for treason by Mao's successor Hua Guofeng and tried 1980–81. The Gang were blamed for the excesses of the Cultural Revolution, but Jiang asserted during her trial that she had only followed Mao's orders as an obedient wife. This was rejected, and Jiang received a death sentence in January 1981, which was subsequently commuted to life imprisonment.

Jiang Qing-guo (or **Chiang Ching-kuo**) (1910–1988) Taiwanese politician, eldest son of Jiang Jie Shi (Chiang Kai-shek), prime minister 1972–78, president 1978–88. After Jiang Jie Shi's Kuomintang (▷Guomindang, nationalist) forces fled to Taiwan in 1949, in the wake of the communist takeover of the Chinese mainland, Jiang Qing-guo worked to strengthen the security and intelligence forces and established a youth wing for the ruling Kuomintang. He became Taiwan's prime minister in 1972 and, after the death of his father in April 1975, Kuomintang leader and, from 1978, head of state.

Jiangsu (or **Kiangsu**) province on the coast of east China, bounded to the north by Shandong, to the east by the Yellow Sea, to the southeast by Shanghai, to the south by Zhejiang, and to the west by Anhui; area 102,200 sq km/39,450 sq mi; population (1996) 71,100,000, the most densely populated province in China. The capital is ▷Nanjing.

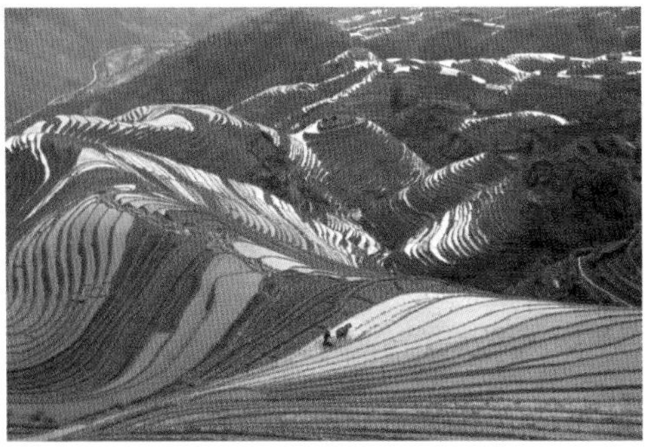

JIANGXI Terraced field in Jiangxi province, China. In this hilly region, where agriculture remains concentrated in the river valleys and limestone plains, intensive terracing is used to maximize the area of land under cultivation. *Image Bank*

Jiangxi (or **Kiangsi**) province of southeast China, bounded to the north by Hubei and Anhui, to the east by Zhejiang and Fujian, to the south by Guangdong, and to the west by Hunan; area 164,800 sq km/63,600 sq mi; population (1996) 41,050,000. The capital is ▷Nanchang; other cities and towns include Ganzhou, Ji'an, Jingdezhen, Jiujiang, and Pingxiang. The Chang Jiang River and Lake Poyang are found in the province. The main industries are porcelain, coal, tungsten, copper, and uranium; agricultural products include rice, tea, cotton, tobacco, and timber.

Jiang Zemin (1926–) Chinese communist politician, leader of the Chinese Communist Party from 1989 and state president from 1993. He succeeded ▷Zhao Ziyang as Communist Party leader after the Tiananmen Square massacre of 1989. He was re-elected state president in March 1998 by China's parliament, the National People's Congress and has continued to press on with a combination of market-centred economic reform, coupled with unswerving adherence to the CCP's 'political line'. He has also launched a campaign against official corruption.

The son-in-law of ▷Li Xiannian and a graduate in engineering, Jiang joined the Chinese Communist Party's politburo in 1967 after serving in the Moscow embassy and as mayor of Shanghai. During the 1989 student protests, he secured a peaceful end to the demonstrations in Shanghai and was rewarded by being appointed Communist Party leader. He subsequently succeeded his patron ▷Deng Xiaoping as head of the influential central military commission and replaced ▷Yang Shangkun as state president in March 1993.

> **Jiang Zemin**
> *You should not imagine that there is no ideological education in capitalist countries.*
> On the film *Titanic*

Jibuti variant spelling of ▷Djibouti, a republic of northeast Africa.

Jiddah (or **Jedda**) port in Hejaz, Saudi Arabia, on the eastern shore of the Red Sea, about 80 km/50 mi west of Mecca; population (1992 est) 2,046,300. The country's leading industrial centre, its industries include cement, steel, and oil refining. It exports hides, mother-of-pearl, coffee, and carpets. Pilgrims pass through here on their way to Mecca.

jigger (or **sandflea**) flea found in tropical and subtropical countries. The males of the species are free-living and measure about 1 mm/0.03 in in length. The females, which are slightly bigger, are parasites of humans and other animals.

jihad (Arabic 'conflict') holy war undertaken by Muslims against nonbelievers. In the Mecca Declaration (1981), the Islamic powers pledged a jihad against Israel, though not necessarily military attack.

Jilin (or **Kirin**) province of northeast China, bounded to the northeast by Heilongjiang, to the southeast by Russia, to the south by North Korea, to the southwest by Liaoning, and to the northwest by Inner Mongolia; area 187,000 sq km/72,000 sq mi; population (1996) 26,100,000. The capital is ▷Changchun, and other cities and towns include Jilin, Tonghua, Baicheng, and Liaoyuan. Major industries include coal, iron ore, engineering, food-processing, and chemicals; agricultural products include maize, sorghum, soybeans, and millet.

Related Web site: Outline of Jilin Province of China http://www.chinarainbow.com/english/intro.htm

Jim Crow the systematic practice of segregating black Americans, which was common in the southern USA until the 1960s. **Jim Crow laws** are laws designed to deny civil rights to blacks or to enforce the policy of segregation, which existed until Supreme Court decisions and civil-rights legislation of the 1950s and 1960s (Civil Rights Act 1964, Voting Rights Act 1965) denied their legality.

Ji'nan (**Tsinan** or **Chinan**) city and capital of ▷Shandong province, China; population (1999) 1,713,000. Industries include engineering, food-processing, flour-milling, and the manufacture of textiles, iron, steel, heavy goods vehicles, tools, and chemicals.

Jin dynasty (or **Chin dynasty**) hereditary rulers of northern China, including Manchuria and part of Mongolia, from 1122 to 1234, during the closing part of the ▷Song era (960–1279). The dynasty was founded by Juchen (Jurchen) nomad hunters, who sacked the northern Song capital Kaifeng in 1126, forcing the Song to retreat south to Hangzhou. The Jin eventually ruled northern China as far south as the Huai River. Over time, the Juchen became Sinicized, but from 1214 they lost much of their territory to the ▷Mongols led by Genghis Khan.

jingoism blinkered, war-mongering patriotism. The term originated in 1878, when the British prime minister Disraeli developed a pro-Turkish policy, which nearly involved the UK in war with Russia. His supporters' war song included the line 'We don't want to fight, but by jingo if we do . . .'.

Jinnah, Muhammad Ali (1876–1948) Indian politician, Pakistan's first governor general from 1947. He was president of the ▷Muslim League in 1916 and 1934–48, and by 1940 was advocating the need for a separate state of Pakistan. At the 1946 conferences in London he insisted on the partition of British India into Hindu and Muslim states.

jinni (plural **jinn**) in Muslim mythology, a member of a class of spirits able to assume human or animal shape.

Jinsha Jiang river rising in southwest China and forming the ▷Chang Jiang (Yangtze Kiang) at Yibin.

Jivaro an American Indian people of the tropical forests of southeastern Ecuador and northeastern Peru. They live by farming, hunting, fishing, and weaving; the Jivaro language belongs to the Andean-Equatorial family. They were formerly notorious for preserving the hair and shrunken skin of the heads of their enemies as battle trophies.

Joan of Arc, St (*c.* 1412–1431) French **Jeanne d'Arc**. French military leader who inspired the French at the Siege of Orléans 1428–29 and at the Battle of Patay, north of Orléans, in 1429. As a young peasant girl, she was the wrong age, class, and gender to engage in warfare, yet her 'heavenly voices' instructed her to expel the English, who had occupied northern France during the Hundred Years' War, and secure the coronation of ▷Charles VII of France. Because of her strength of character, she achieved both aims. Her subsequent attempt to take Paris was overambitious, however, and she was captured in May 1430 at Compiègne by the Burgundians, who sold her to the English. She was found guilty of witchcraft and heresy by a tribunal of French ecclesiastics who supported the English, and burned to death at the stake in Rouen on 30 May 1431.

Charles made no attempt to save her, but after the recapture of Normandy he instituted a retrial, held between 1450 and 1456, that exonerated her. After the French defeat in the Franco-Prussian War in 1870–71, Joan experienced a revival as a military figurehead. She was canonized in 1920.

Related Web site: Joan of Arc, St http://www.newadvent.org/cathen/08409c.htm

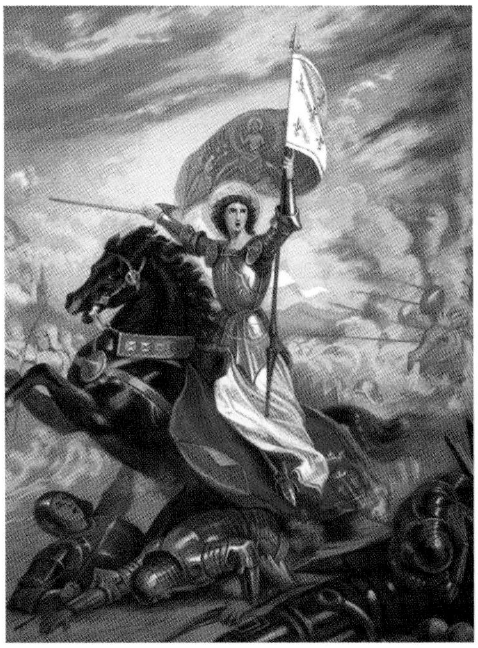

ST JOAN OF ARC Illustration of Joan of Arc from *La Prophetie de Merlin*. *Archive Photos*

Job (lived *c.* 5th century BC) In the Old Testament, Hebrew leader who in the **Book of Job** questioned God's infliction of suffering on the righteous while enduring great sufferings himself.

jobseekers allowance social security benefit included by the UK Conservative government in the Jobseekers Act 1995. The allowance became effective from October 1996. It replaced unemployment benefit and ▷income support, combining them into one payment for the unemployed. The Labour government inherited the jobseekers allowance after winning the May 1997 general election.

Jodhpur city in Rajasthan, India, 490 km/310 mi southwest of Delhi; population (1991) 668,000. Handicraft industries such as ivory carving and lacquerware are important, and railway parts, textiles, and bicycles are manufactured here. It is a market centre. It was formerly the capital of Jodhpur princely state, founded by Rao Jodha on the edge of the Thar Desert. A style of riding breeches is named after the town.

Jodrell Bank site in Cheshire, England, of the Nuffield Radio Astronomy Laboratories of the University of Manchester. Its largest instrument is the 76 m/250 ft radio dish (the Lovell Telescope), completed in 1957 and modified in 1970. A 38 × 25 m/125 × 82 ft elliptical radio dish was introduced in 1964, capable of working at shorter wave lengths.

These radio telescopes are used in conjunction with five smaller dishes up to 230 km/143 mi apart in an array called MERLIN (**m**ulti-**e**lement **r**adio-**l**inked **in**terferometer **n**etwork) to produce detailed maps of radio sources.

Related Web site: Jodrell Bank http://www.jb.man.ac.uk/index.html

Joffre, Joseph Jacques Césaire (1852–1931) Marshal of France during World War I. He was chief of general staff in 1911. The German invasion of Belgium in 1914 took him by surprise, but his stand at the Battle of the ▷Marne resulted in his appointment as supreme commander of all the French armies in 1915. His failure to make adequate preparations at Verdun in 1916 and the military disasters on the ▷Somme led to his replacement by Nivelle in December 1916.

Johannesburg largest city of South Africa, situated on the ▷Witwatersrand in Gauteng Province; population (city area, 1998) 849,600 (urban area, 1996) 2,200,000. It is the centre of a large gold-mining industry; other industries include engineering works, meat-chilling plants, and clothing factories.

Features Notable buildings include the law courts, Escom House (Electricity Supply Commission), the South African Railways Administration Building, the City Hall, Chamber of Mines and Stock Exchange, the Witwatersrand (1921) and Rand Afrikaans (1966) universities, and the Union Observatory.

History Johannesburg was founded after the discovery of gold by the Australian prospector George Harrison in 1886, and was probably named after Jan (Johannes) Meyer, the first mining commissioner.

John two kings of France, including:

John II (1319–1364) King of France from 1350. He was defeated and captured by the Black Prince at Poitiers (1356) and imprisoned in England. Released in 1360, he failed to raise the money for his ransom and returned to England in 1364, where he died.

John name of 23 popes, including:

John XXII (1249–1334) Born Jacques Dues. Pope 1316–34. He spent his papacy in Avignon, France, engaged in a long conflict with the Holy Roman Emperor, Louis of Bavaria, and the Spiritual Franciscans, a monastic order who preached the absolute poverty of the clergy.

John XXIII (1881–1963) Born Angelo Giuseppe Roncalli. Pope from 1958. He improved relations with the USSR in line with his encyclical *Pacem in Terris/Peace on Earth* (1963), established Roman Catholic hierarchies in newly emergent states, and summoned the Second Vatican Council, which reformed church liturgy and backed the ecumenical movement.

John three kings of Poland, including:

John III, Sobieski (1624–1696) King of Poland from 1674. He became commander-in-chief of the army in 1668 after victories over the Cossacks and Tatars. A victory over the Turks in 1673 helped to get him elected to the Polish throne, and he saved Vienna from the besieging Turks in 1683.

John six kings of Portugal, including:

John I (1357–1433) King of Portugal from 1385. An illegitimate son of Pedro I, he was elected by the Cortes (parliament). His claim was supported by an English army against the rival king of Castile, thus establishing the Anglo-Portuguese Alliance in 1386.

He married Philippa of Lancaster, daughter of ▷John of Gaunt.

John IV (1604–1656) King of Portugal from 1640. Originally duke of Braganza, he was elected king when the Portuguese rebelled against Spanish rule. His reign was marked by a long war against Spain, which did not end until 1668.

John VI (1769–1826) King of Portugal and regent for his insane mother **Maria I** from 1799 until her death in 1816. He fled to Brazil when the French invaded Portugal in 1807 and did not return until 1822. On his return Brazil declared its independence, with John's elder son Pedro as emperor.

John, St (lived 1st century AD) New Testament apostle. Traditionally, he wrote the fourth Gospel and the Johannine Epistles (when he was bishop of Ephesus), and the Book of Revelation (while exiled to the Greek island of Patmos). His emblem is an eagle; his feast day is 27 December.

John, Augustus Edwin (1878–1961) Welsh painter. He is known for his vivacious portraits, including *The Smiling Woman* (1910; Tate Gallery, London), portraying his second wife, Dorelia McNeill. His sitters included such literary figures as Thomas Hardy, Dylan Thomas, W B Yeats, T E Lawrence, and James Joyce.

John's portraits are outstanding in their combined certainty of drawing and temperamental handling of paint. His sense of colour and a modified post-Impressionism appear in their most assured in his landscapes of the south of France and his flower pieces. He produced beautiful drawings of the figure at every stage of his career, and also some etchings.

His sister was the artist Gwen ▷John.

Born in Tenby, South Wales, he studied at the Slade School of Art, and taught at the University College, Liverpool, from 1901 to 1902. He began to exhibit at the New English Art Club in 1903. From 1910 to 1919 John led a nomadic existence in Ireland, Dorset, and Wales, producing many poetic small oil paintings of figures in landscape. His cartoon for a mural decoration, *Galway* (1916; Tate Gallery), shows an inclination for large-scale work which was never fully realized. During World War I he was an official artist to the Canadian Corps. Elected to the Royal Academy in 1928, he resigned in 1938 because of the Academy's rejection of a sculpture by Epstein, but accepted re-election in 1940. He received the Order of Merit in 1942.

His autobiography appeared in two parts: *Chiaroscuro* (1952) and *Finishing Touches* (1964).

John, Elton (1947–) Stage name of Reginald Kenneth Dwight. English pop singer, pianist, and composer whose long and flamboyant career reached unparalleled heights in 1997 when he rewrote his 'Candle in the Wind' hit for the funeral of Diana, Princess of Wales, a personal friend. In the 1970s he had seven consecutive hit albums. *Goodbye Yellow Brick Road* (1973) includes the hit 'Bennie and the Jets'; among his many other highly successful songs are 'Rocket Man', 'Crocodile Rock', and 'Daniel' (all 1972), 'Candle in the Wind' (1973), 'Pinball Wizard' (1975), 'Blue Eyes' (1982), 'Nikita' (1985), and 'Sacrifice' (1989), the last from his album *Sleeping with the Past*. He wrote the Academy Award-winning music (with lyrics by Tim Rice) for the animated film and stage production *The Lion King* (1995) and in 2000 wrote and recorded the soundtrack to *The Road to Eldorado*.

Related Web site: Illustrated Elton John Discography
http://ej.kylz.com/

John, Gwen(dolen Mary) (1876–1939) Welsh painter. She lived in France for most of her life. Many of her paintings depict young women or nuns (she converted to Catholicism in 1913), but she also painted calm, muted interiors. Her style was characterized by a sensitive use of colour and of tone.

John (I) Lackland (1167–1216) King of England from 1199 and acting king from 1189 during his brother Richard (I) the Lion-Heart's absence on the Third Crusade.

Although branded by contemporaries as cruel and power-hungry, he is now recognized as a hardworking, able, reforming monarch, who travelled the country tirelessly. He improved the legal system, was the first king to keep records of government writs, and built a large navy that defeated the French fleet before it could invade. He tried vigorously to extend his kingdom, conducting campaigns in Wales, Ireland, and Normandy, and cowing Scotland into a peace treaty. However, he lost Normandy and nearly all other English possessions in France by 1205. The taxes needed to finance his campaigns brought conflict with his barons, and he was forced to sign the ▷Magna Carta in 1215. Later repudiation of it led to the first ▷Barons' War 1215–17, during which he died. He was succeeded by his son Henry III.

John was nicknamed 'Lackland', probably because, as the youngest of Henry II's five sons, it was difficult to find a portion of his father's French possessions for him to inherit. In 1205 he disputed the pope's choice of Stephen ▷Langton as archbishop of Canterbury, and Pope Innocent III placed England under an interdict, suspending all religious services, including baptisms, marriages, and burials. John retaliated by seizing church revenues, and was excommunicated. Eventually, John submitted, accepting the papal nominee, and agreed to hold the kingdom as a fief of the papacy. After the Battle of ▷Bouvines in 1214, when John's attempt to regain Normandy was defeated by Philip II of France, royal authority collapsed. The barons rebelled and forced him to sign Magna Carta, and the Scots, Welsh, and French attacked England.

John's subsequent bad reputation was only partially deserved. Contemporaries accused him of plotting to depose his brother Richard while acting king; of killing his nephew Arthur, Duke of Brittany (1187–1203), a rival for the English throne; and of numerous acts of cruelty to the English barons and their families. His conflict with the pope was resented by the monastic chroniclers of the time, and these provided much of the evidence upon which his reign was later judged.

John Bull imaginary figure who is a personification of England, similar to the American Uncle Sam. He is represented in cartoons and caricatures as a prosperous farmer of the 18th century.

The name was popularized by Dr John ▷Arbuthnot's political satire *History of John Bull* (1712), advocating the Tory policy of peace with France.

John Dory marine bony fish also called a ▷dory.

John of Gaunt (1340–1399) English noble and politician, fourth (and third surviving) son of Edward III, Duke of Lancaster from 1362. He distinguished himself during the Hundred Years' War. During Edward's last years, and the years before Richard II attained the age of majority, he acted as head of government, and Parliament protested against his corrupt rule.

He was called John of Gaunt because he was born in Ghent, Flanders. In 1359 he married Blanche, daughter of Henry, Duke of Lancaster (died 1361), whose title passed to John of Gaunt in 1362; their son became Henry IV of England. Blanche died in 1369 and three years later he married Constance, daughter of Pedro III of Castile. Their daughter Philippa (1359–1415) married King John I of Portugal (1357–1433). John of Gaunt assumed the title of King of Castile in 1372, but his efforts to establish his claim against his rival, Henry of Trastamare, proved unsuccessful; in 1387 he renounced all claims in favour of his daughter Catherine, who married Henry III of Castile (1379–1406) in 1393.

Constance died in 1394, and John of Gaunt married his mistress of long standing, Katharine Swynford (*c.* 1350–1403), with whom he already had four children; they were legitimized in 1397 by charter of Richard II, and founded the house of Beaufort, from whom Henry VII was descended.

John of Salisbury (*c.* 1115–1180) English philosopher and historian. His *Policraticus* portrayed the church as the guarantee of liberty against the unjust claims of secular authority.

John of the Cross, St (1542–1591) Spanish Carmelite friar from 1564, who was imprisoned several times for attempting to impose the reforms laid down by St Teresa of Avila. His verse describes spiritual ecstasy.

John o' Groats village in the northeast of the Highland unitary authority, Scotland, about 3 km/2 mi west of Duncansby Head, Britain's northernmost point. It is the furthest point from Land's End on the British mainland.

John Paul two popes:

John Paul I (1912–1978) Born Albino Luciani. Pope 26 August–28 September 1978. His name was chosen as the combination of his two immediate predecessors.

John Paul II (1920–) Born Karol Jozef Wojtyla. Pope from 1978, the first non-Italian to be elected pope since 1522. He was born near Kraków, Poland. He has upheld the tradition of papal infallibility and has condemned artificial contraception, women priests, married priests, and modern dress for monks and nuns – views that have aroused criticism from liberalizing elements in the church.

In a March 1995 encyclical, the Pope stated in unequivocal terms his opposition to abortion, birth control, in vitro fertilization, genetic manipulation, and euthanasia, and employed the church's strongest language to date against capital punishment. In March 2000, he undertook a pilgrimage to the Holy Land, visiting Jordan, Israel, and the Palestinian Territories.

Related Web site: John Paul II http://www.vatican.va/holy_father/john_paul_ii/

Philip Johnson
Architecture is the art of how to waste space.
The New York Times 27 December 1964

Johns, Jasper (1930–) US painter, sculptor, and printmaker. He was one of the foremost exponents of ▷pop art. He rejected abstract art, favouring such mundane subjects as flags, maps, and numbers as a means of exploring the relationship between image and reality. His work employs pigments mixed with wax (encaustic) to create a rich surface with unexpected delicacies of colour.

Johns, W(illiam) E(arl) (1893–1968) Called 'Captain'. English author. From 1932 he wrote popular novels about World War I flying ace 'Biggles', now sometimes criticized for chauvinism, racism, and sexism. Johns was a flying officer in the RAF (there is no rank of captain) until his retirement in 1930.

Johnson, Amy (1903–1941) English aviator. She made a solo flight from England to Australia in 1930, in 9½ days, and in 1932 made the fastest ever solo flight from England to Cape Town, South Africa. Her plane disappeared over the English Channel in World War II while she was serving with the Air Transport Auxiliary.

Johnson, Andrew (1808–1875) 17th president of the USA 1865–69, a Democrat. He was a congressman from Tennessee 1843–53, governor of Tennessee 1853–57, senator 1857–62, and vice-president in 1865. He succeeded to the presidency on Abraham Lincoln's assassination (15 April 1865). His conciliatory policy to the defeated South after the Civil War involved him in a feud with the Radical Republicans, culminating in his impeachment in 1868 before the Senate, which failed to convict him by one vote.

Among Johnson's achievements was the purchase of Alaska from Russia in 1867. When he tried to dismiss Edwin Stanton, a cabinet secretary, his political opponents seized on the opportunity to charge him with 'high crimes and misdemeanours' and attempted to remove him from office; it was this battle that ended in his impeachment. Johnson's tenure as president was characterized by frustration and political stalemate. He presided over the re-entry of the Southern states into the Union. He returned to the Senate in 1875, but died shortly afterwards.

Related Web site: Andrew Johnson – Seventeenth President 1865–1869 http://www.whitehouse.gov/WH/glimpse/presidents/html/aj17.html

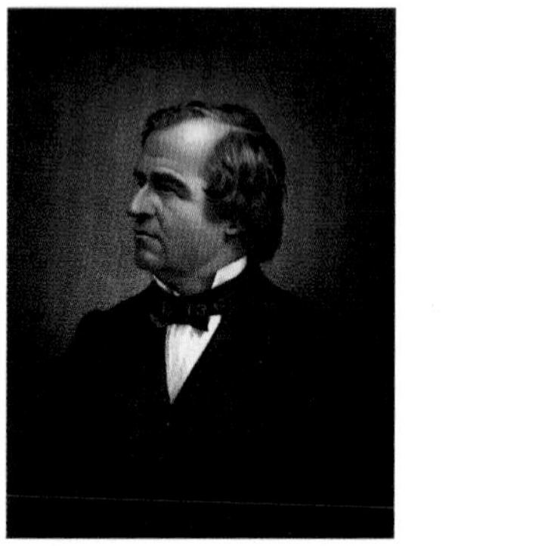

ANDREW JOHNSON The 17th US president, who took office after the assassination of Abraham Lincoln.
© Bettmann/CORBIS

Johnson, Jack (1878–1946) Born John Arthur Johnson. US heavyweight boxer. He overcame severe racial prejudice to become the first black to win the world heavyweight title in 1908 and was one of boxing's greatest and most controversial champions. After winning the title in Australia in 1908 with a knockout of Tommy Burns, he defended the championship successfully against a succession of 'great white hopes', including former champion James J Jeffries. He lost the championship in 1915 to Jess Willard by a knockout in the 26th round.

Johnson, Lyndon Baines (1908–1973) 36th president of the USA 1963–69, a Democrat. He was a member of Congress 1937–49 and the Senate 1949–60. Born in Texas, he brought critical Southern support as J F Kennedy's vice-presidential running mate in 1960, and became president on Kennedy's assassination.

After Kennedy's assassination, Johnson successfully won congressional support for many of Kennedy's New Frontier proposals, most conspicuously in the area of civil rights. He moved beyond the New Frontier to declare 'war on poverty' supported by Great Society legislation (civil rights, education, alleviation of poverty). His foreign policy met with considerably less success. After the ▷Tonkin Gulf Incident, which escalated US involvement in the Vietnam War, support won by Johnson's domestic reforms dissipated, and he declined to run for re-election in 1968.

Related Web site: Lyndon B Johnson Library and Museum
http://www.lbjlib.utexas.edu/

Johnson, Philip Cortelyou (1906–) US architect and architectural historian. Originally designing in the style of ▷Mies van der Rohe, he later became an exponent of ▷postmodernism. He designed the giant AT&T building in New York 1978, a pink skyscraper with a Chippendale-style cabinet top.

SAMUEL JOHNSON The *Portrait of Samuel Johnson* by the English portrait painter Joshua Reynolds.
The Art Archive/Musee du Louvre Paris/Dagli Orti

Johnson, Samuel (1709–1784) Also known as **Dr Johnson**. English lexicographer, author, and critic. He was also a brilliant conversationalist and the dominant figure in 18th-century London literary society. His *Dictionary* (1755), provided in its method the pedigree for subsequent lexicography and remained authoritative for over a century. In 1764 he founded, at the suggestion of the painter Joshua Reynolds, a club, known from 1779 as the Literary Club, whose members at various times included also the political philosopher Edmund Burke, the dramatist Oliver Goldsmith, the actor David Garrick, and James ▷Boswell, Johnson's biographer.

Johnson's first meeting with Boswell was in 1763. A visit with Boswell to Scotland and the Hebrides in 1773 was recorded in *A Journey to the Western Isles of Scotland* (1775). Other works include a satire imitating Juvenal, *The Vanity of Human Wishes* (1749), the philosophical romance *Rasselas* (1759), an edition of Shakespeare (1765), and the classic *Lives of the English Poets* (1779–81).

Johnson's prose style is balanced, judicious, and sometimes ponderous, and as a critic he displayed great creative insight. His edition of Shakespeare is the forerunner of modern scholarly editions and his 'Preface to Shakespeare' remains a classic critical essay of permanent value. He viewed art as an important vehicle for the expression of truth and this serious attitude sometimes lead to heavy-handed moral instruction, but his well-known wit and humanity are documented in Boswell's classic *The Life of Samuel Johnson LL.D* (1791).

> **Related Web site: Selected Poetry and Prose Of Samuel Johnson (1709–1784)** http://www.library.utoronto.ca/utel/rp/authors/johnson.html

John the Baptist, St (*c.* 12 BC–*c.* AD 27) In the New Testament, an itinerant preacher. After preparation in the wilderness, he proclaimed the coming of the Messiah and baptized Jesus in the River Jordan. He was later executed by ▷Herod Antipas at the request of Salome, who demanded that his head be brought to her on a platter.

John was the son of Zacharias and Elizabeth (a cousin of Jesus' mother), and born in Nazareth, Galilee. He and Jesus are often shown together as children.

As an adult, he is depicted with a shaggy beard and robes, usually green.

> **Related Web site: John the Baptist, St** http://www.newadvent.org/cathen/08486b.htm

joint in any animal with a skeleton, a point of movement or articulation. In vertebrates, it is the point where two bones meet. Some joints allow no motion (the sutures of the skull), others allow a very small motion (the sacroiliac joints in the lower back), but most allow a relatively free motion. Of these, some allow a gliding motion (one vertebra of the spine on another), some have a hinge action (elbow and knee), and others allow motion in all directions (hip and shoulder joints) by means of a ball-and-socket arrangement. The ends of the bones at a moving joint are covered with cartilage for greater elasticity and smoothness, and enclosed in an envelope (capsule) of tough white fibrous tissue lined with a membrane which secretes a lubricating and cushioning ▷synovial fluid. The joint is further strengthened by ligaments. In invertebrates with an ▷exoskeleton, the joints are places where

the exoskeleton is replaced by a more flexible outer covering, the arthrodial membrane, which allows the limb (or other body part) to bend at that point.

Joint European Torus experimental nuclear-fusion machine, known as ▷JET.

Joliot-Curie, Frédéric (1900–1958) Born Frédéric Jean Joliot. French physicist. With his wife, Irène ▷Joliot-Curie, he was awarded the Nobel Prize for Chemistry in 1935 for their discovery of artificial ▷radioactivity.

Joliot was born in Paris, France, and graduated from the Ecole Supérieure de Physique et de Chimie Industrielle. He joined the Radium Institute in 1925. In 1937 he became professor of nuclear physics at the Collège de France. He succeeded his wife as director of the Radium Institute in 1956.

Joliot-Curie, Irène (1897–1956) French physicist, daughter of Pierre and Marie ▷Curie. She and her husband Frédéric ▷Joliot were jointly awarded the Nobel Prize for Chemistry in 1935 for their discovery of artificial radioactivity. She was professor of physics at the Sorbonne from 1937, and director of the Radium Institute 1946–56.

Jolson, Al (1886–1950) Stage name of Asa Yoelson. Russian-born US singer and entertainer. Popular in Broadway theatre and vaudeville, he was chosen to star in the first talking picture, *The Jazz Singer* (1927).

Jonah (lived 7th century BC) Hebrew prophet whose name is given to a book in the Old Testament. According to this, he fled by ship to evade his mission to prophesy the destruction of Nineveh, the ancient capital of Assyria. The crew threw him overboard in a storm, as a bringer of ill fortune, and he spent three days and nights in the belly of a whale before coming to land.

Jonathan, Chief (Joseph) Leabua (1914–1987) Lesotho politician. A leader in the drive for independence, Jonathan became prime minister of Lesotho in 1965. His rule was ended by a coup in 1986.

As prime minister, Jonathan played a pragmatic role, allying himself in turn with the South African government and the Organization of African Unity.

> **Samuel Johnson**
> *Language is the dress of thought.*
> *Lives of the English Poets,* 'Cowley'

Jones, Allen (1937–) English painter, sculptor, and printmaker. He was a leading figure in the ▷pop art movement of the 1960s. His colourful paintings are executed in the style of commercial advertising, and unabashedly celebrate the female form, for example, *Perfect Match* (1966–67; Wallraf-Richartz Museum, Cologne). One of the most committed exponents of pop art, he has continued to work in this vein into the 1990s.

Jones, Inigo (1573–1652) English classical architect. He introduced the ▷Palladian style to England. He was employed by James I to design scenery for Ben Jonson's masques and was appointed Surveyor of the King's Works 1615–42. He designed the Queen's House, Greenwich (1616–35), and the Banqueting House in Whitehall, London (1619–22).

Jones, Marion (1975–) US track and field athlete. A former college basketball star, she came to international prominence in 1997 when she won the world 100-metre title in Athens. In 1998 she won 36 consecutive sprint and long jump events, and became the first woman to be ranked world number one in three events in the

JONAH This 4th-century mosaic from the Basilica Aquileia, Italy, shows the Hebrew prophet Jonah sitting under a gourd plant outside the city of Nineveh, waiting for the judgement of God. *The Art Archive/Victoria and Albert Museum London*

same year. At the Sydney Olympic Games in 2000, she competed in five events, winning gold medals in the 100 metres, 200 metres, and 4 × 400-metre relay, and bronze medals in the long jump and 4 × 100-metre relay.

> **Ben Jonson**
> *Suns, that set, may rise again; / But if once we lose this light, / 'Tis with us perpetual night.*
> *Volpone* III. vi

Jones, Thomas Gwynn (1871–1949) Welsh poet. He won the National Eisteddfod chair at Bangor in 1902 with 'Ymadawiad Arthur' ('The Passing of Arthur'), a poem which, for its application of a modern creative mind to traditional strict metre, heralded a new era in Welsh literature, and won again in 1909 with 'Gwlad y Bryniau' ('The Land of the Hills'); from then his place in Welsh literature was assured. He also wrote some volumes of essays, several plays, and a book in English on Welsh folklore.

Jonestown commune of the **People's Temple Sect**, northwest of Georgetown, Guyana, established in 1974 by the American Jim Jones (1933–1978), who originally founded the sect among San Francisco's black community. After a visiting US congressman was shot dead, Jones enforced mass suicide on his followers by instructing them to drink cyanide; 914 died, including over 240 children.

jonquil species of small ▷daffodil, with yellow flowers. It is native to Spain and Portugal, and is cultivated in other countries. (*Narcissus jonquilla*, family Amaryllidaceae.)

Jonson, Ben(jamin) (1572–1637) English dramatist, poet, and critic. *Every Man in his Humour* (1598) established the English 'comedy of humours', in which each character embodies a 'humour', or vice, such as greed, lust, or avarice. This was followed by *Cynthia's Revels* (1600) and *The Poetaster* (1601). His first extant tragedy is *Sejanus* (1603), with Burbage and Shakespeare as members of the original cast. His great comedies are *Volpone, or The Fox* (1606), *The Alchemist* (1610), and *Bartholomew Fair* (1614). He wrote extensively for court entertainment in the form of ▷masques produced with scenic designer Inigo ▷Jones.

> **Related Web site: Jonson, Ben** http://www.luminarium.org/sevenlit/jonson/index.html

Joplin, Janis (Lyn) (1943–1970) US blues and rock singer. She sang with the San Francisco group Big Brother and the Holding Company 1966–68. Together they appeared at the Monterey International Pop Festival in 1967, and recorded the album *Cheap Thrills* in 1968, which included the legendary 'Ball and Chain'. Joplin then embarked on a solo career, releasing *I've Got Dem Ol' Kozmic Blues Again Mama!* in 1969 and touring extensively. Her biggest hit, 'Me and Bobby McGee', written by Kris Kristofferson, was released on the posthumous *Pearl* album (1971). Among her other solo tracks are 'Down on Me' and 'Cry Baby', which are collected in the 1993 anthology *Janis*.

Joplin, Scott (1868–1917) US ▷ragtime pianist and composer. He first came to attention as a pianist at brothels in St Louis and Chicago, and was considered the leading exponent of 'classic rag', in which the standard syncopated rhythm was treated with some sophistication. His 'Maple Leaf Rag' (1899) was the first instrumental sheet music to sell a million copies, and 'The Entertainer', as the theme tune of the film *The Sting* (1973), revived his popularity. He was an influence on Jelly Roll Morton and other early jazz musicians.

> **Related Web site: Scott Joplin** http://www.geocities.com/BourbonStreet/2783/

Jordaens, Jacob (1593–1678) Flemish painter. His style follows Rubens, whom he assisted in various commissions. Much of his work is exuberant and on a large scale, including scenes of peasant life and mythological subjects, as well as altarpieces and portraits.

Jordan see country box.

Jordan (Arabic **Nahr al-Urdunn**; Hebrew **Ha-Yarden**) river rising on Mount Hermon, Syria, at 550 m/1,800 ft above sea level and flowing south for about 320 km/200 mi via the Lake of Tiberias (the Sea of Galilee) to the Dead Sea, 390 m/1,290 ft below sea level. It is the lowest river in the world. It occupies the northern part of the Great Rift Valley; its upper course forms the boundary of Israel with Syria and the kingdom of Jordan; its lower course runs through Jordan. The West Bank has been occupied by Israel since 1967.

Joseph In the New Testament, the husband of the Virgin Mary, a descendant of King David of the Tribe of Judah, and a carpenter by trade.

Although Jesus was not the son of Joseph, Joseph was his legal father. According to Roman Catholic tradition, he had a family by a previous wife, and was an elderly man when he married Mary.

Joseph In the Old Testament, the 11th and favourite son of ▷Jacob, sold into Egypt by his jealous half-brothers. After he had

Jordan

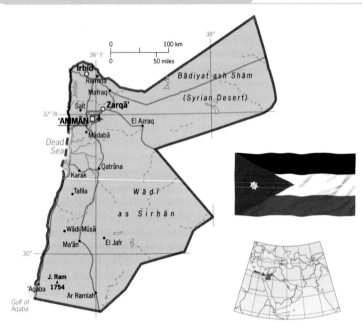

JORDAN Jarash was one of the cities of the Decapolis, a confederation of ten Roman cities dating from the 1st century BC. This vast and spectacular city, which lay on the southeastern frontier of the Roman Empire, is famous for both its well-preserved town plan and individual monuments. This is the Nymphaeum, which served as a public fountain and Temple of the Nymphs. *Corel*

Jordan country in southwest Asia, bounded north by Syria, northeast by Iraq, east, southeast, and south by Saudi Arabia, south by the Gulf of Aqaba, and west by Israel.

NATIONAL NAME *Al-Mamlaka al-Urduniyya al-Hashemiyyah/Hashemite Kingdom of Jordan*
AREA 89,206 sq km/34,442 sq mi (excluding the West Bank 5,879 sq km/2,269 sq mi)
CAPITAL Amman
MAJOR TOWNS/CITIES Zarqa, Irbid, Saet, Ma'an
MAJOR PORTS Aqaba
PHYSICAL FEATURES desert plateau in east; Rift Valley separates east and west banks of River Jordan

Government

HEAD OF STATE King Abdullah ibn Hussein from 1999
HEAD OF GOVERNMENT Ali Abu al-Ragheb from 2000
POLITICAL SYSTEM emergent democracy
POLITICAL EXECUTIVE parliamentary
ADMINISTRATIVE DIVISIONS 12 governorates
ARMED FORCES 100,200; plus paramilitary forces of 10,000 (2002 est)
CONSCRIPTION military service is voluntary
DEATH PENALTY retained and used for ordinary crimes
DEFENCE SPEND (% GDP) 9.3 (2002 est)
EDUCATION SPEND (% GDP) 5 (2000 est)
HEALTH SPEND (% GDP) 8.1 (2000 est)

Economy and resources

CURRENCY Jordanian dinar
GPD (US$) 9.3 billion (2002 est)
REAL GDP GROWTH (% change on previous year) 4.6 (2001)
GNI (US$) 9.1 billion (2002 est)
GNI PER CAPITA (PPP) (US$) 4,070 (2002 est)
CONSUMER PRICE INFLATION 2.5% (2003 est)
UNEMPLOYMENT 13.7% (2000)
FOREIGN DEBT (US$) 11.2 billion (2001 est)
MAJOR TRADING PARTNERS Germany, India, Saudi Arabia, Iraq, Italy, UK, USA, Israel, France, Japan
RESOURCES phosphates, potash, shale

INDUSTRIES mining and quarrying, petroleum refining, chemical products, alcoholic drinks, food products, phosphate, cement, potash, tourism
EXPORTS phosphate, potash, fertilizers, foodstuffs, pharmaceuticals, fruit and vegetables, cement. Principal market: India 11.7% (2001)
IMPORTS machinery and transport equipment, food and live animals, basic manufactures, mineral fuels. Principal source: Germany 8.8% (2001)
ARABLE LAND 2.7% (2000 est)
AGRICULTURAL PRODUCTS wheat, barley, maize, tobacco, vegetables, fruits, nuts; livestock rearing (sheep and goats)

Population and society

POPULATION 5,473,000 (2003 est)
POPULATION GROWTH RATE 2.2% (2000–15)
POPULATION DENSITY (per sq km) 61 (2003 est)
URBAN POPULATION (% of total) 79 (2003 est)
AGE DISTRIBUTION (% of total population) 0–14 40%, 15–59 55%, 60+ 5% (2002 est)
ETHNIC GROUPS majority of Arab descent (98%); small Circassian, Armenian, and Kurdish minorities
LANGUAGE Arabic (official), English
RELIGION over 90% Sunni Muslim (official religion), small communities of Christians and Shiite Muslims
EDUCATION (compulsory years) 10
LITERACY RATE 96% (men); 87% (women) (2003 est)
LABOUR FORCE 5.5% agriculture, 22.8% industry, 71.7% services (2000)
LIFE EXPECTANCY 70 (men); 73 (women) (2000–05)
CHILD MORTALITY RATE (under 5, per 1,000 live births) 33 (2001)
PHYSICIANS (per 1,000 people) 1.7 (1998 est)
HOSPITAL BEDS (per 1,000 people) 1.8 (1998 est)
TV SETS (per 1,000 people) 111 (2001 est)

RADIOS (per 1,000 people) 372 (2001 est)
INTERNET USERS (per 10,000 people) 577.0 (2002 est)
PERSONAL COMPUTER USERS (per 100 people) 3.8 (2002 est)

Chronology

13th century BC: Oldest known 'states' of Jordan, including Gideon, Ammon, Moab, and Edom, established.

c. 1000 BC: East Jordan was part of kingdom of Israel, under David and Solomon.

4th century BC: Southeast Jordan occupied by the independent Arabic-speaking Nabataeans.

64 BC: Conquered by the Romans and became part of the province of Arabia.

AD 636: Became largely Muslim after the Byzantine forces of Emperor Heraclius were defeated by Arab armies at battle of Yarmuk, in northern Jordan.

1099–1187: Part of Latin Kingdom established by Crusaders in Jerusalem.

from early 16th century: Part of Turkish Ottoman Empire, administered from Damascus.

1920: Trans-Jordan (the area east of the River Jordan) and Palestine (which includes the West Bank) placed under British administration by League of Nations mandate.

1923: Trans-Jordan separated from Palestine and recognized by Britain as a substantially independent state under the rule of Emir Abdullah ibn Hussein, a member of the Hashemite dynasty of Arabia.

1946: Trans-Jordan achieved independence from Britain, with Abd Allah as king; name changed to Jordan.

1948: British mandate for Palestine expired, leading to fighting between Arabs and Jews, who each claimed the area.

1950: Jordan annexed West Bank; 400,000 Palestinian refugees flooded into Jordan, putting pressure on the economy.

1952: Partially democratic constitution introduced.

1958: Jordan and Iraq formed Arab Federation that ended when Iraqi monarchy was deposed.

1967: Israel defeated Egypt, Syria, and Jordan in Arab–Israeli Six-Day War, and captured and occupied the West Bank, including Arab Jerusalem. Martial law imposed.

1970–71: Jordanians moved against increasingly radicalized Palestine Liberation Organization (PLO), which had launched guerrilla raids on Israel from Jordanian territory, resulting in bloody civil war, before the PLO leadership fled abroad.

1976: Political parties were banned and elections postponed until further notice.

1980: Jordan emerged as an important ally of Iraq in its war against Iran, an ally of Syria, with whom Jordan's relations were tense.

1984: Women voted for the first time; the parliament was recalled.

1985: King Hussein ibn Tal Abdulla el Hashim and PLO leader Yassir Arafat put forward a framework for a Middle East peace settlement. There was a secret meeting between Hussein and the Israeli prime minister.

1988: Hussein announced his willingness to cease administering the West Bank as part of Jordan, passing responsibility to the PLO; parliament was suspended.

1989: There were riots over price increases of up to 50% following a fall in oil revenues. In the first parliamentary elections for 23 years the Muslim Brotherhood won 25 of 80 seats but were exiled from government.

1990: Hussein unsuccessfully tried to mediate after Iraq's invasion of Kuwait. There were huge refugee problems as thousands fled to Jordan from Kuwait and Iraq.

1991: 24 years of martial law ended, the ban on political parties was lifted, and Jordan remained neutral during the Gulf War involving Iraq.

1993: Candidates loyal to Hussein won a majority in the parliamentary elections; several leading Islamic fundamentalists lost their seats.

1994: An economic cooperation pact was signed with the PLO. A peace treaty was signed with Israel, ending the 46-year-old state of war.

1999: King Hussein died and his eldest son, Abdullah, succeeded him. Ali Abu al-Ragheb was appointed prime minister. In May, Abdullah held talks with Yassir Arafat prior to Israeli peace negotiations.

See also ▷Hussein, ibn Talal; ▷Israel; ▷Ottoman Empire; ▷Palestine.

risen to power there, they and his father joined him to escape from famine in Canaan.

Joseph two Holy Roman emperors:

Joseph I (1678–1711) Holy Roman Emperor from 1705 and king of Austria, of the house of Habsburg. He spent most of his reign involved in fighting the War of the ▷Spanish Succession.

Joseph II (1741–1790) Holy Roman Emperor from 1765, son of Francis I (1708–1765). The reforms he carried out after the death of his mother, ▷Maria Theresa in 1780 provoked revolts from those who lost privileges.

Josephine, Marie Josèphe Rose Tascher de la Pagerie (1763–1814) As wife of ▷Napoleon Bonaparte, she was empress of France 1804–09. Born on the island of Martinique, she married in 1779 Alexandre de Beauharnais, who played a part in the French Revolution, and in 1796 Napoleon, who divorced her in 1809 because she had not produced children.

Joseph of Arimathaea, St (lived 1st century AD) In the New Testament, a wealthy Hebrew, member of the Sanhedrin (supreme court), and secret supporter of Jesus. On the evening of the Crucifixion he asked the Roman procurator Pilate for Jesus' body and buried it in his own tomb. Feast day 17 March.

Josephson, Brian David (1940–) Welsh physicist, a leading authority on ▷superconductivity. He shared the Nobel Prize for Physics in 1973 for his theoretical predictions of the properties of a supercurrent through a tunnel barrier (the **Josephson effect**), which led to the development of the Josephson junction.

Josephson junction device used in 'superchips' (large and complex integrated circuits) to speed the passage of signals by a phenomenon called 'electron tunnelling'. Although these superchips respond a thousand times faster than the ▷silicon chip, they have the disadvantage that the components of the Josephson junctions operate only at temperatures close to ▷absolute zero. They are named after English theoretical physicist Brian Josephson.

Josephus, Flavius (AD 37–c. 100) Jewish historian and general, born in Jerusalem. He became a Pharisee and commanded the Jewish forces in Galilee in their revolt against Rome from AD 66 (which ended with the mass suicide at Masada). When captured, he gained the favour of the Roman emperor Vespasian and settled in Rome as a citizen. He wrote *Antiquities of the Jews*, an early history to AD 66; *The Jewish War*; and an autobiography.

Joshua (lived 13th century BC) In the Old Testament, successor of Moses, who led the Jews in their return to, and conquest of, the land of Canaan. The city of Jericho was the first to fall – according to the Book of Joshua, the walls crumbled to the blast of his trumpets.

Jospin, Lionel (1937–) French socialist politician, first secretary of the Socialist Party (PS) 1981–88 and 1995–97, then prime minister, under President Jacques ▷Chirac, 1997–2002 heading a 'pluralist left' coalition with communist, green, and left radical parties.

Josquin Des Prez (or Josquin des Prés) (1440–1521) Franco-Flemish composer. His synthesis of Flemish structural counterpoint and Italian harmonic expression, acquired in the service of the Rome papal chapel 1484–1503, marks a peak in Renaissance vocal music. In addition to Masses on secular as well as sacred themes, including the *Missa 'L'Homme armé'/Mass on 'The Armed Man'* (1504), he also wrote secular chansons such as 'El grillo'/'The Cricket' employing imitative vocal effects.

Joubert, Piet (Petrus Jacobus) (1831–1900) Boer general in South Africa. He opposed British annexation of the Transvaal 1877, proclaimed its independence in 1880, led the Boer forces in the First ▷South African War against the British 1880–81, defeated ▷Jameson in 1896, and fought in the Second South African War.

joule SI unit (symbol J) of work and energy, replacing the ▷calorie (one calorie equals 4.2 joules).

It is defined as the work done (energy transferred) by a force of one newton acting over one metre. It can also be expressed as the work done in one second by a current of one ampere at a potential difference of one volt. One watt is equal to one joule per second.

Joule, James Prescott (1818–1889) English physicist. His work on the relations between electrical, mechanical, and chemical effects led to the discovery of the first law of ▷thermodynamics.

He determined the mechanical equivalent of heat (**Joule's equivalent**) in 1843, and the SI unit of energy, the ▷joule, is named after him. He also discovered **Joule's law**, which defines the relation between heat and electricity; and, with Irish physicist Lord ▷Kelvin in 1852, the **Joule–Kelvin** (or **Joule–Thomson**) effect.

journalism profession of reporting, photographing, or editing news events for the mass media – ▷newspapers, magazines, radio, television, documentary films, and newsreels – and for news agencies.

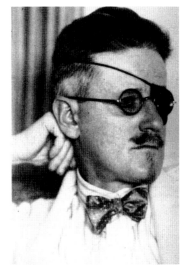

JAMES JOYCE The controversial Irish writer James Joyce was troubled by failing eyesight for most of his life. *Archive Photos*

journeyman a man who served his apprenticeship in a trade and worked as a fully qualified employee. The term originated in the regulations of the medieval trade ▷guilds; it derives from the French *journée* ('a day') because journeymen were paid daily.

Joyce, James (Augustine Aloysius) (1882–1941) Irish writer. Joyce was born in Dublin, one of a large and poor family, and educated at University College, Dublin. His originality lies in evolving a literary form to express the complexity of the human mind, and he revolutionized the form of the English novel with his 'stream of consciousness' technique. His works include the short story collection *Dubliners* (1914), *A Portrait of the Artist as a Young Man* (1916), *Ulysses* (1922), and *Finnegans Wake* (1939).

Ulysses, which records the events of a single Dublin day, experiments with language and combines direct narrative with the unspoken and unconscious reactions of the characters. Banned at first for obscenity in the USA and the UK, it made a great impact and is generally regarded as Joyce's masterpiece. It was first published in Paris, where Joyce settled after World War I. *Finnegans Wake*, a story about a Dublin publican and his family, continued Joyce's experiments with language. In this work the word-coining which had been a feature of *Ulysses* was pushed to its limits and punning language and allegory are used to explore various levels of meaning, while attempting a synthesis of all existence.

Related Web site: James Joyce Web Site http://www.2street.com/joyce

joystick in computing, an input device that signals to a computer the direction and extent of displacement of a hand-held lever. It is similar to the joystick used to control the flight of an aircraft.

Joysticks are sometimes used to control the movement of a cursor (marker) across a display screen, but are much more

Joystick

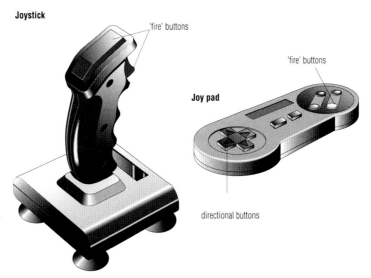

JOYSTICK The directional and other controls on a conventional joystick may be translated to a joy pad, which enables all controls to be activated by buttons.

frequently used to provide fast and direct input for moving the characters and symbols that feature in computer games. Unlike a ▷mouse, which can move a pointer in any direction, simple games joysticks are often capable only of moving an object in one of eight different directions. Today, many joysticks and control pads feature some form of force feedback.

JP abbreviation for ▷justice of the peace.

Juan Carlos (1938–) King of Spain. The son of Don Juan, pretender to the Spanish throne, he married Princess Sofia, eldest daughter of King Paul of Greece, in 1962. In 1969 he was nominated by ▷Franco to succeed on the restoration of the monarchy intended to follow Franco's death; his father was excluded because of his known liberal views. Juan Carlos became king in 1975, and played a vital role in the smooth transition to democratic stability. He was instrumental in the defeat of an attempted military coup in 1981.

Related Web site: Royal Household http://www.DocuWeb.ca/SiSpain/english/politics/royal/king.html

Juárez, Benito Pablo (1806–1872) Mexican politician, president 1861–65 and 1867–72. In 1861 he suspended repayments of Mexico's foreign debts, which prompted a joint French, British, and Spanish expedition to exert pressure. French forces invaded and created an empire for ▷Maximilian, brother of the Austrian emperor. After their withdrawal in 1867, Maximilian was executed, and Juárez returned to the presidency.

Judaea see ▷Judah.

Judah (or **Judaea**) name used in Graeco-Roman times for the southernmost district of Palestine, now divided between Israel and Jordan. After the death of King Solomon in 922 BC, Judah adhered to his son Rehoboam and the Davidic line, whereas the rest of Israel elected Jeroboam as ruler of the northern kingdom. In New Testament times, Judah was the Roman province of Judaea, and in current Israeli usage it refers to the southern area of the West Bank.

Judaism the religion of the ancient Hebrews and their descendants the Jews, based, according to the Old Testament, on a covenant between God and Abraham about 2000 BC, and the renewal of the covenant with Moses about 1200 BC. Judaism is the oldest monotheistic faith, the forebear of Christianity and Islam. It rests on the concept of one eternal invisible God, whose will is revealed in the Torah and who has a special relationship with the Jewish people. The Torah comprises the first five books of the Bible (the Pentateuch), which contains the history, laws, and guide to life for correct behaviour. Besides those living in Israel, there are large Jewish populations in the USA, the former USSR (mostly Russia, Ukraine, Belarus, and Moldova), the UK and Commonwealth nations, and in Jewish communities throughout the world. There are approximately 18 million Jews, with about 9 million in the Americas, 5 million in Europe, and 4 million in Asia, Africa, and the Pacific.

Scriptures As well as the Torah, the Hebrew Bible contains histories, writings of the prophets, and writings such as the Psalms and Proverbs. A further source of authority on Jewish ritual, worship, and practice is the *Talmud*, combining the *Mishnah*, rabbinical commentary on the law handed down orally from AD 70 and put in writing about 200; the *Gemara*, legal discussions in the schools of Palestine and Babylon from the 3rd and 4th centuries; and the *Midrash*, a collection of commentaries on the scriptures written 400–1200, mainly in Palestine. Material in the *Talmud* can be generally divided into *halakah*, consisting of legal and ritual matters, and *aggadah* (or *haggadah*), mainly concerned with ethical and theological matters expounded in narrative form.

Observances The synagogue (in US non-Orthodox usage, temple) is the local building for congregational worship (originally simply the place where the Torah was read and expounded); its characteristic feature is the Ark, the enclosure where the Torah scrolls are kept. Rabbis are ordained teachers schooled in the Jewish law and ritual who act as spiritual leaders and pastors of their communities; some devote themselves to study. Religious practices include: circumcision, daily services in Hebrew, observance of the Sabbath (sunset on Friday to sunset Saturday) as a day of rest, and, among Orthodox

Jews, strict dietary laws (see ▷kosher). High holy days include **Rosh Hashanah** marking the Jewish New Year (first new moon after the autumn equinox) and, a week later, the religious fast **Yom Kippur** (Day of Atonement). Other holidays are celebrated throughout the year to commemorate various events of biblical history.

Divisions In the late Middle Ages, when Europe and W Asia were divided into Christian and Islamic countries, the Jewish people also found itself divided into two main groups. Jews in central and eastern Europe, namely in Germany and Poland, were called **Ashkenazi**. **Sephardic** Jews can trace their tradition back to the Mediterranean countries, particularly Spain and Portugal under Muslim rule. When they were expelled in 1492 they settled in N Africa, the E Mediterranean, the Far East, and N Europe. The two traditions differ in a number of ritual and cultural ways but their theology and basic Jewish practice is the same. The Hasidic sects of eastern Europe and some N African and Oriental countries also differ from other groups in their rites but they, too, maintain the concept of divine authority. In the 19th and early 20th centuries there was a move by some Jewish groups away from traditional or orthodox observances. This trend gave rise to a number of groups within Judaism. **Orthodox Jews**, who form the majority, assert the supreme authority of the Torah and adhere to all the traditions of Judaism, including the strict dietary laws (see ▷kosher) and the segregation of women in the synagogue. **Reform Judaism** rejects the idea that Jews are the chosen people, has a liberal interpretation of the dietary laws, and takes a critical attitude towards the Torah. **Conservative Judaism** is a compromise between Orthodox and Reform in its acceptance of the traditional law, making some allowances for modern conditions, although its services and ceremonies are closer to Orthodox than to Reform. **Liberal Judaism**, or **Reconstructionism**, goes further than Reform in attempting to adapt Judaism to the needs of the modern world and to interpret the Torah in the light of current scholarship. In all the groups except Orthodox, women are not segregated in the synagogue, and there are female rabbis in both Reform and Liberal Judaism.

Many people who call themselves Jews prefer to identify Judaism with a historical and cultural tradition rather than with strict religious observance, and a contemporary debate (complicated by the history of non-Jewish attitudes towards Jews) centres on the question of how to define a Jew. As in other religions, fundamentalist movements have emerged; for example, Gush Emunim.

In England, the majority of the country's Jewish community are Orthodox, under the leadership of the Chief Rabbi (from 1991 Dr Jonathan Sacks). The progressive Jewish community is divided into Liberal and Reform Judaism, both groups receiving rabbinic leadership from Leo Baeck College (London).

Related Web site: Jewish Culture and History http://www.igc.apc.org/ddickerson/judaica.html

Judaism: Key Events

c. 2000 BCE
Led by Abraham, the ancient Hebrews emigrate from Mesopotamia to Canaan.

18th century BCE–1580 BCE
Some settle on the borders of Egypt and are put to forced labour.

13th century BCE
They are rescued by Moses, who leads them out of Egypt to Canaan, the 'Promised Land'. Moses receives the Ten Commandments from God and brings them to the people. The main invasion of Canaan is led by Joshua in about 1274 BCE.

12th–11th centuries BCE
During the period of Judges, ascendancy is established over the Canaanites.

c. 1000 BCE
Complete conquest of Palestine and the union of all Judea is achieved under David, and Jerusalem becomes the capital.

10th century BCE
Solomon succeeds David and enjoys a reputation for great wealth and wisdom, but his lack of a constructive policy leads, after his death, to the secession of the north of Judea (Israel) under Jeroboam, with only the tribe of Judah remaining under the house of David as the southern kingdom of Judah.

9th–8th centuries BCE
Assyria becomes the dominant power in the Middle East. Israel purchases safety by tribute, but the basis of the society is corrupt, and prophets such as Amos, Isaiah, and Micah predict destruction. At the hands of Tiglathpileser and his successor Shalmaneser IV, the northern kingdom (Israel) is made into Assyrian provinces after the fall of Samaria in 721 BCE, although the southern kingdom of Judah is spared as an ally.

586–458 BCE
Nebuchadnezzar takes Jerusalem and carries off the major part of the population to Babylon. Judaism is retained during exile, and is reconstituted by Ezra on the return to Jerusalem.

520 BCE
The Temple, originally built by Solomon, is restored.

c. 444 BCE
Ezra promulgates the legal code that is to govern the future of the Jewish people.

4th–3rd centuries BCE
After the conquest of the Persian Empire by Alexander the Great, the Syrian Seleucid rulers and the Egyptian Ptolemaic dynasty struggle for control of Palestine, which comes under the government of Egypt, although with a large measure of freedom.

2nd century BCE
With the advance of Syrian power, Antiochus IV attempts to intervene in the internal quarrels of the Hebrews, even desecrating the Temple, and a revolt breaks out in 165 BCE led by the Maccabee family.

63 BCE
Judea's near-independence ends when internal dissension causes the Roman general Pompey to intervene, and Roman suzerainty is established.

1st century CE
A revolt leads to the destruction of the Temple (66–70) by the Roman emperor Titus. Judean national sentiment is encouraged by the work of Rabbi Johanan ben Zakkai (*c.* 20–90), and, following him, the president of the Sanhedrin (supreme court) is recognized as the patriarch of Palestinian Jewry.

2nd–3rd centuries
Greatest of the Sanhedrin presidents is Rabbi Judah Ha-Nasi, who codifies the traditional law in the *Mishnah*. The Palestinian *Talmud* (*c.* 375) adds the *Gemara* to the *Mishnah*.

4th–5th centuries
The intellectual leadership of Judaism passes to the descendants of the 6th century BCE exiles in Babylonia, who compile the Babylonian *Talmud*.

8th–13th centuries
Judaism enjoys a golden era, producing the philosopher Saadiah, the poet Jehudah Ha-levi (*c.* 1075–1141), the codifier Moses Maimonides, and others.

14th–17th centuries
Where Christianity becomes the dominant or state religion, the Jews are increasingly segregated from mainstream life and trade by the Inquisition, anti-Semitic legislation, or by expulsion. The Protestant and Islamic states and their colonies allow for refuge. Persecution leads to messianic hopes, strengthened by the 16th-century revival of Kabbalism, culminating in the messianic movement of Shabbatai Sevi in the 17th century.

18th–19th centuries
Outbreaks of persecution increase with the rise of European nationalism. In the UK, the first synagogue is founded in 1701. Reform Judaism, a rejection of religious orthodoxy and an attempt to interpret it for modern times, begins in Germany in 1810 and is soon established in England and the USA. In the late 19th century, large numbers of Jews fleeing persecution (pogroms) in Russia and Eastern Europe emigrate to the USA, leading to the development of large Orthodox, Conservative, and Reform communities there. Many become Americanized and lose interest in religion.

20th century
Zionism, a nationalist movement dedicated to achieving a secure homeland where the Jewish people would be free from persecution, is founded in 1896; this leads to the establishment of the state of Israel in 1948. Liberal Judaism (more radical than Reform) develops in the USA. The Nazi German regime (1933–45) exterminates 6 million European Jews. Hundreds of thousands of survivors take refuge in pre-existing Jewish settlements in what eventually becomes the new state of Israel. Although most Israeli and American Jews are not affiliated with synagogues after the 1950s, they continue to affirm their Jewish heritage. Both Orthodox and Hasidic Judaism, however, flourish in their new homes and grow rapidly in the 1970s and 1980s. Conflict with Palestinian separatists and the subsequent peace process increase tensions between secular and Orthodox Jews in Israel. The Catholic Church apologizes (1997) for its silence during the Holocaust. The German government establishes (1998) a fund to compensate Holocaust survivors.

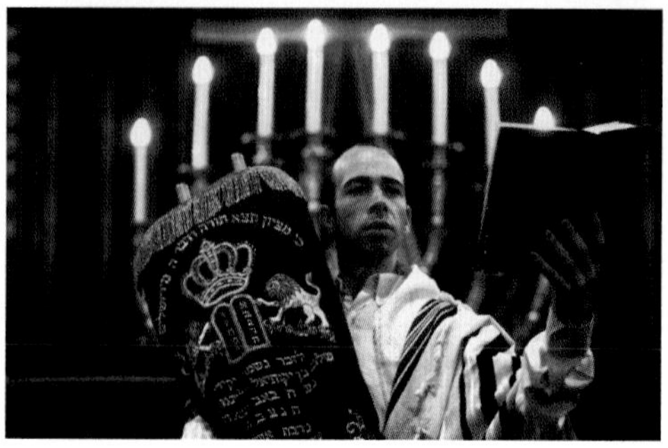

JUDAISM In this photograph, there are various items of Judaic religious significance. The man is wearing a prayer shawl, and is holding the rolled-up scrolls on which the Torah (first five books of the Hebrew Bible) is inscribed. In his left hand is a prayer book, and the nine-branched *menorah* (candlestick) is behind him. *Image Bank*

Judas Iscariot (lived 1st century AD) In the New Testament, the disciple who betrayed Jesus Christ. Judas was the treasurer of the group. At the last Passover supper, he arranged, for 30 pieces of silver, to point out Jesus to the chief priests so that they could arrest him. Afterward Judas was overcome with remorse and committed suicide.

Related Web site: Judas Iscariot http://www.newadvent.org/cathen/08539a.htm

Jude, St (lived 1st century AD) Supposed half-brother of Jesus and writer of the Epistle of Jude in the New Testament; patron saint of lost causes. Feast day 28 October.

judicial review in English law, action in the High Court to review the decisions of lower courts, tribunals, and administrative bodies. Various court orders can be made: ▷certiorari (which quashes the decision); **mandamus** (which commands a duty to be performed); **prohibition** (which commands that an action should not be performed because it is unauthorized); a **declaration** (which sets out the legal rights or obligations); or an ▷injunction.

judiciary in constitutional terms, the system of courts and body of judges in a country. The independence of the judiciary from other branches of the central authority is generally considered to be an essential feature of a democratic political system. This independence is often written into a nation's constitution and protected from abuse by politicians.

Judith In the Old Testament, a Jewish widow who saved her community from a Babylonian siege by pretending to seduce, and then beheading, the enemy general Holofernes. Her story is much represented in Western art.

judo (Japanese *jū do*, 'gentle way') form of wrestling of Japanese origin. The two combatants wear loose-fitting, belted jackets and trousers to facilitate holds, and falls are broken by a square mat; when one has established a painful hold that the other cannot break, the latter signifies surrender by slapping the ground with a free hand. Degrees of proficiency are indicated by the colour of the belt: for novices, white, then yellow, orange (2 degrees), green (2 degrees), blue (2 degrees), brown (2 degrees), then black (Dan grades; 10 degrees, of which 1st to 5th Dan wear black belts, 6th to 9th wear red and white, and 10th wears solid red).

Related Web site: Judo Information Site http://JudoInfo.com

Juggernaut (or **Jagannath**) a name for Vishnu, the Hindu god, meaning 'Lord of the World'. His temple is in Puri, Orissa, India. A statue of the god, dating from about 318, is annually carried in procession on a large vehicle (hence the word 'juggernaut'). Devotees formerly threw themselves beneath its wheels.

Jugoslavia alternative spelling of ▷Yugoslavia.

jugular vein one of two veins in the necks of vertebrates; they return blood from the head to the superior (or anterior) ▷vena cava and thence to the heart.

jujube any of a group of trees belonging to the buckthorn family, with berrylike fruits. The common jujube (*Z. jujuba*) of Asia, Africa, and Australia, cultivated in southern Europe and California, has fruit the size of small plums, known as Chinese dates when preserved in syrup. See also ▷lotus. (Genus *Zizyphus*, family Thamnaceae.)

Juliana (1909–) Queen of the Netherlands 1948–80. The daughter of Queen Wilhelmina (1880–1962), she married Prince Bernhard of Lippe-Biesterfeld in 1937. She abdicated in 1980 and was succeeded by her daughter ▷Beatrix.

Julian the Apostate (332–363) Roman emperor. Born in Constantinople, the nephew of Constantine the Great, he was brought up as a Christian but early in life became a convert to paganism. Sent by Constantius to govern Gaul in 355, he was proclaimed emperor by his troops in 360, and in 361 was marching on Constantinople when Constantius' death allowed a peaceful succession. He revived pagan worship and refused to persecute heretics. He was killed in battle against the Persians of the ▷Sassanian Empire.

Julius II (1443–1513) Born Giuliano della Rovere. Pope (1503–13). A politician who wanted to make the Papal States the leading power in Italy, he formed international alliances first against Venice and then against France. He began the building of St Peter's Church in Rome in 1506 and was a patron of the artists Michelangelo and Raphael.

Juneau ice-free port and state capital of ▷Alaska, USA, opposite Douglas Island on Gastineau Channel, in the south Alaskan panhandle (narrow strip of land that projects from one state into another); population (1992) 28,400. The city is the commercial and distribution centre for the fur-trading and mining industries of the panhandle region; also important are salmon fishing, fish processing, lumbering and tourism. Gold-mining remained important here until the closure of the mine in 1944, but in the 1990s there has been some resumption of it.

Related Web site: Juneau, Alaska – The Capital City http://www.juneau.lib.ak.us/juneau.htm

Jung, Carl Gustav (1875–1961) Swiss psychiatrist. He collaborated with Sigmund ▷Freud from 1907 until their disagreement in 1914 over the importance of sexuality in causing psychological problems. Jung studied myth, religion, and dream symbolism, saw the unconscious as a source of spiritual insight, and distinguished between introversion and extroversion.

Jung devised the word-association test in the early 1900s as a technique for penetrating a subject's unconscious mind. He also developed his theory concerning emotional, partly repressed ideas which he termed 'complexes'. In place of Freud's emphasis on infantile sexuality, Jung introduced the idea of a 'collective unconscious' which is made up of many archetypes or 'congenital conditions of intuition'.

jungle popular name for ▷rainforest.

juniper any of a group of aromatic evergreen trees or shrubs of the cypress family, found throughout temperate regions. Junipers produce a valuable wood and their berries are used to flavour gin and in cooking. Some junipers are mistakenly called ▷cedars. (Genus *Juniperus*, family Cupressaceae.)

Junkers, Hugo (1859–1935) German aeroplane designer. In 1919 he founded in Dessau the aircraft works named after him. Junkers planes, including dive bombers, night fighters, and troop carriers, were used by the Germans in World War II.

Juno in Roman mythology, the principal goddess, identified with the Greek ▷Hera. The wife of Jupiter and queen of heaven, she was concerned with all aspects of women's lives and also regarded as a patroness of commerce.

junta (Spanish 'council') the military rulers of a country, especially after an army takeover, as in Turkey in 1980. Other examples include Argentina, under Juan Perón and his successors; Chile, under Augusto Pinochet; Paraguay, under Alfredo Stroessner; Peru, under Manuel Odría; Uruguay, under Juan Bordaberry, and Myanmar since 1988. Juntas rarely remain collective bodies, eventually becoming dominated by one member.

Jupiter fifth planet from the Sun, and the largest in the Solar System, with a mass equal to 70% of all the other planets combined, 318 times that of Earth's. Its main feature is the Great Red Spot, a cloud of rising gases, 14,000 km/8,500 mi wide and 30,000 km/20,000 mi long, revolving anticlockwise.

mean distance from the Sun 778 million km/484 million mi **equatorial diameter** 142,800 km/88,700 mi **rotation period** 9 hr 51 min **year** (complete orbit) 11.86 Earth years **atmosphere** consists of clouds of white ammonia crystals, drawn out into belts by the planet's high speed of rotation (the fastest of any planet). Darker orange and brown clouds at lower levels may contain sulphur, as well as simple organic compounds. Temperatures range from −140°C/−220°F in the upper atmosphere to as much as 24,000 °C/43,000°F near the core. This is the result of heat left over from Jupiter's formation, and it is this that drives the turbulent weather patterns of the planet. The Great Red Spot was first observed in 1664. Its top is higher than the surrounding clouds; its colour is thought to be due to red phosphorus. The Southern Equatorial Belt in which the Great Red Spot occurs is subject to large fluctuation. In 1989 it sustained a dramatic and sudden fading. Jupiter's strong magnetic field gives rise to a large surrounding magnetic 'shell', or magnetosphere, from which bursts of radio waves are detected. Jupiter's faint rings are made up of dust from its moons, particularly the four inner moons **surface** largely composed of hydrogen and helium, liquefied by pressure in its interior, it probably has a rocky core larger than Earth. In 1995, the *Galileo* probe revealed Jupiter's atmosphere to consist of 0.2% water, less than previously estimated **satellites** Jupiter has 28 known moons. The four largest moons, Io, Europa (which is the size of our Moon), Ganymede, and Callisto, are the **Galilean satellites**, discovered in 1610 by ▷Galileo Galilei (Ganymede, which is larger than Mercury, is the largest moon in the Solar System). Three small moons were discovered in 1979 by the US *Voyager* space probes, as was a faint ring of dust around Jupiter's equator 55,000 km/34,000 mi above the cloud tops. One of Jupiter's small inner moons, Almathea (diameter 250 km/155 mi), was shown by pictures from *Galileo* in April 2000, to have a long narrow bright region, as yet unidentified. A new moon was first observed in October 1999 orbiting Jupiter by US researchers at the Kitt Peak Observatory, Arizona. It was thought to be an asteroid and named S/1999J1, but was confirmed to be a moon in July 2000. The moon is only 5 km/3 mi in diameter and orbits Jupiter once every two years at a distance of 24 million km/15 million mi. Ten previously unobserved moons were discovered orbiting Jupiter in November and December 2000. These moons are all believed to be less than 5 km/3.1 mi in diameter, and were observed by astronomers at the Mauna Kea observatory, Hawaii. Comet Shoemaker-Levy 9 crashed into Jupiter in July 1994. Impact zones were visible for several months.

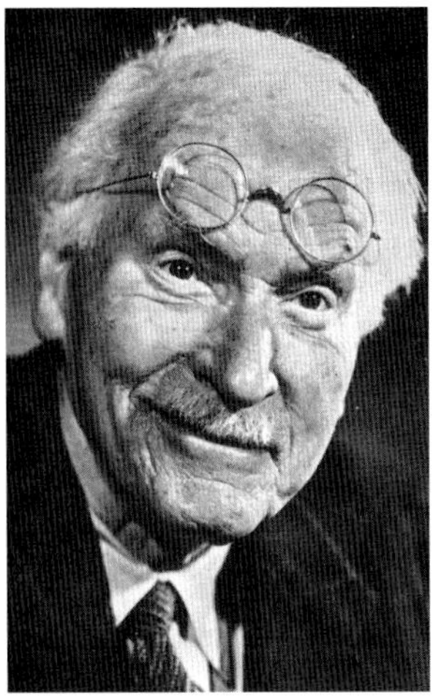

CARL JUNG For many years a colleague of Sigmund Freud, Carl Jung had a disagreement with the founder of modern psychology and set up his own practice in Zürich, Switzerland. Jung believed that all races share a collective unconsciousness which holds thought patterns which have developed over centuries. *Archive Photos*

> **Carl Jung**
> *Show me a sane man and I will cure him for you.*
> *The Observer* 19 July 1975

Jupiter (or **Jove**; Latin *Diovis pater* 'father of heaven') in Roman mythology, the supreme god reigning on Mount Olympus, identified with the Greek ▷Zeus; son of Saturn and Ops; and husband of Juno, his sister. His titles included Fulgur (thrower of lightning), Tonans (maker of thunder), Invictus (protector in battle), and Triumphator (bestower of victory). His main temple was on the Capitoline Hill in Rome; destination of the solemn triumphal processions of victorious generals. As the particular protector of Rome, he was honoured by consuls taking office.

Juppé, Alain Marie (1945–) French neo-Gaullist politician, foreign minister 1993–95 and prime minister 1995–97. In 1976, as a close lieutenant of Jacques Chirac, he helped to found the right-of-centre Rally for the Republic (RPR) party, of which he later became secretary general, then president. He was appointed premier by newly-elected president Chirac in May 1995 but, within months, found his position under threat as a result of a housing scandal. Opposition to his government's economic programme, particularly welfare cuts, provoked a general strike in November 1995.

Jura island of the Inner ▷Hebrides, Argyll and Bute; area 380 sq km/147 sq mi; population (1991) 196. It is separated from the Scottish mainland by the **Sound of Jura**. The whirlpool Corryvreckan (Gaelic 'Brecan's cauldron') is off the north coast. It has a range of mountains known as the 'Paps of Jura', the highest of which is Beinn an Oir at 784 m/2,572 ft.

Jura Mountains series of parallel mountain ranges running along the French–Swiss frontier between the Rivers Rhône and Rhine, a distance of 250 km/156 mi. The highest peak is Crête de la Neige (1,723 m/5,650 ft). The mountains give their name to the Jura *département* of France, and in 1979 a Jura canton was established in Switzerland, formed from the French-speaking areas of Berne.

Jurassic period period of geological time 208–146 million years ago; the middle period of the Mesozoic era. Climates worldwide were equable, creating forests of conifers and ferns; dinosaurs were abundant, birds evolved, and limestones and iron ores were deposited.

The name comes from the Jura Mountains in France and Switzerland, where the rocks formed during this period were first studied.

jurisprudence the science of law in the abstract – that is, not the study of any particular laws or legal system, but of the principles upon which legal systems are founded.

jury body of lay people (usually 12) sworn to decide the facts of a case and reach a verdict in a court of law. Juries, used mainly in English-speaking countries, are implemented primarily in criminal cases, but also sometimes in civil cases; for example, inquests and libel trials.

justice of the peace (**JP**) in England, an unpaid ▷magistrate. In the USA, where JPs receive fees and are usually elected, their courts are the lowest in the states, and deal only with minor offences, such as traffic violations; they may also conduct marriages.

justiciar the chief justice minister of Norman and early Angevin kings, second in power only to the king. By 1265, the government had been divided into various departments, such as the Exchequer and Chancery, which meant that it was no longer desirable to have one official in charge of all.

Justin, St (*c.* 100–*c.* 163) One of the early Christian leaders and writers known as the Fathers of the Church. Born in Palestine of a Greek family, he was converted to Christianity and wrote two *Apologies* in its defence. He spent the rest of his life as an itinerant missionary, and was martyred in Rome. Feast day 1 June.

Justinian (*c.* 483–565) Born Flavius Anicianus Justinianus. East Roman emperor 527–565, renowned for overseeing the reconquest of Africa, Italy, and parts of Spain. He ordered the codification of Roman law, which has influenced European jurisprudence; he built the church of Hagia Sophia in Constantinople, and closed the university in Athens in 529. His achievements, however, were short-lived. His reconquests and ambitious building projects overstretched the empire's resources and within a few years of his death much of his newly conquered territory had been lost.

Jute member of a Germanic people who originated in Jutland but later settled in Frankish territory. They occupied Kent, southeast England, in about 450, according to tradition under Hengist and Horsa, and conquered the Isle of Wight and the opposite coast of Hampshire in the early 6th century.

jute fibre obtained from two plants of the linden family: *C. capsularis* and *C. olitorius*. Jute is used for sacks and sacking, upholstery, webbing (woven strips used to support upholstery), string, and stage canvas. (Genus *Corchorus*, family Tiliaceae.)

Jutland (Danish **Jylland**) peninsula of northern Europe; area 29,500 sq km/11,400 sq mi. It is separated from Norway by the Skagerrak and from Sweden by the Kattegat, with the North Sea to the west. The larger northern part belongs to Denmark, the southern part to Germany.

Jutland, Battle of World War I naval battle between British and German forces on 31 May 1916, off the west coast of Jutland. Its outcome was indecisive, but the German fleet remained in port for the rest of the war.

Juvenal (*c.* AD 60–140) Born Decimus Junius Juvenalis. Roman satirical poet. His 16 surviving *Satires* give an explicit and sometimes brutal picture of the corrupt Roman society of his time. Very little is known of his life, but his native place, if not his birthplace, was Aquinum (now Aquino, southern Italy). Juvenal is twice mentioned by ▷Martial, and he may be the author of a well-known dedication (probably to an altar to Ceres) by one Juvenal who held military rank and some civil offices at Aquinum. This reference to military service agrees with the story of Sidonius Apollinaris (5th century) that Juvenal quarrelled with Paris, a famous ballet dancer in the reign of Domitian, and was sent to the Egyptian frontier as an officer of a local garrison.

> **Juvenal**
> *Sed quis custodiet ipsos custodes?*
> *But who will guard the guards themselves?*
> *Satires* VI. 347

juvenile delinquency offences against the law that are committed by young people.

juvenile offender young person who commits a criminal offence. In UK law, young people under the age of 17 are commonly referred to as juveniles, although for some purposes a distinction is made between 'children' (under the age of 14) and 'young persons' (14–16). A juvenile under the age of ten may not be found guilty of an offence.

K

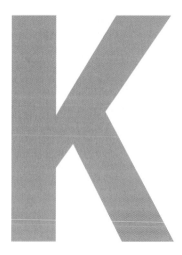

K abbreviation for thousand, as in a salary of £30K.

K symbol for **kelvin**, a scale of temperature.

k symbol for **kilo-**, as in kg (kilogram) and km (kilometre).

K2 (or **Chogori**) second highest mountain above sea level, 8,611 m/28,251 ft, in the Karakoram range, in a disputed region of Pakistan. It was first climbed in 1954 by an Italian expedition.

Kaaba (Arabic 'chamber') in Mecca, Saudi Arabia, an oblong building in the quadrangle of the Great Mosque, into the northeastern corner of which is built the Black Stone declared by the prophet Muhammad to have been given to Abraham by the archangel Gabriel, and revered by Muslims.

Kabardino-Balkaria (or **Kabardino-Balkariya**) republic in the far southwestern Russian Federation, on the border with Georgia; area 12,500 sq km/4,826 sq mi; population (1996) 790,000 (58% urban) (48% Kabarda, 32% Russians, 9% Balkars).
The capital is Nalchik, and other cities include Tyrnyauz and Prokhladnyy. The republic is on the northern slopes and foothills of the main Caucasus mountain range and contains the highest Caucasian peaks (Elbrus and Dykh Tau). It is crossed by the Rivers Terek, the Chegem, the Cherek, and the Baksan. Mineral deposits include wolfram, molybdenum, lead, zinc, and coal.

kabbala (or **cabbala**; Hebrew 'tradition') ancient esoteric Jewish mystical tradition of philosophy containing strong elements of pantheism, yet akin to neo-Platonism. Kabbalistic writing reached its peak between the 13th and 16th centuries. It is largely rejected by current Judaic thought as medieval superstition, but is basic to the Hasid sect.
Related Web site: Kabbalah FAQ http://www.digital-brilliance.com/kab/faq.htm

Kabinda part of Angola; see ▷Cabinda.

Kabul capital of Afghanistan, 1,800 m/5,900 ft above sea level, on the **River Kabul**; population (1997 est) 500,000. Products include textiles, plastics, leather, and glass. It commands the strategic routes to Pakistan via the ▷Khyber Pass. The city was captured by the ▷Talibaan on 27 September 1996.
Features Kabul's university (1932), closed since September 1996, when the Talibaan took control of the city; the tomb of ▷Babur, founder of the Mogul empire; the Dar ol-Aman Palace, which houses the parliament and government departments.
History Kabul has been in existence for over 3,000 years. In 1504 it became capital of the Mogul Empire under Babur, but in 1526 was replaced by Delhi as the imperial capital. In 1747 it became part of an independent Afghan state, and in 1776 replaced ▷Kandahar as the capital of Afghanistan. It was captured by the British in 1839 and 1879, and was under Soviet control 1979–89. In 1992 the city saw fierce fighting during the ▷Mujahedin takeover and ousting of the Soviet-backed ▷Najibullah regime, and by the end of 1993 it had been reduced almost to rubble in the course of the civil war.

Kádár, János (1912–1989) Hungarian communist leader, in power 1956–88, after suppressing the national uprising. As leader of the Hungarian Socialist Workers' Party (HSWP) and prime minister 1956–58 and 1961–65, Kádár introduced a series of market-socialist economic reforms, while retaining cordial political relations with the USSR.

Kafka, Franz (1883–1924) Austrian novelist. He wrote in German. His three unfinished allegorical novels *Der Prozess/The Trial* (1925), *Das Schloss/The Castle* (1926), and *Amerika/America* (1927) were posthumously published despite his instructions that they should be destroyed. His short stories include 'Die Verwandlung/The Metamorphosis' (1915), in which a man turns into a huge insect. His vision of lonely individuals trapped in bureaucratic or legal labyrinths can be seen as a powerful metaphor for modern experience.
Kafka's work has considerably influenced other modern writers, including Samuel ▷Beckett and Albert ▷Camus.

Kafue river in central Zambia, a tributary of the Zambezi, 965 km/600 mi long. The upper reaches of the river form part of the Kafue National Park (1951). Kafue town, 44 km/27 mi south of Lusaka, population (1998 est) 40,800, is the centre of Zambia's heavy industry, which includes engineering and textiles.
A hydroelectric power station opened in 1972 on the lower Kafue River at Kafue Gorge; its 600,000-kilowatt generating facility was expanded to 900,000 in the late 1970s by the construction of a storage dam upstream.

Kagoshima industrial city and port on Kyushu island, southwest Japan, 150 km/93 mi southeast of Nagasaki; population (1994) 534,000. It is the seat of the prefecture of the same name. Satsumayaki porcelain, starch, caramel, vegetable oil, tobacco, wood crafts, and a silk fabric called *tsumugi* are produced here. Kagoshima is often compared to Naples, its twin city.

Kahlo, Frida (1907–1954) Mexican painter. Combining the folk arts of South America with classical and modern styles, she concentrated on surreal self-portraits in which she explored both her own physical disabilities (she was crippled in an accident when 15) and broader political and social issues. Her work became popular during the 1980s. She was the wife of the painter Diego Rivera.

Kaieteur Falls waterfall on the River Potaro, a tributary of the Essequibo, Guyana. At 250 m/822 ft, it is five times as high as Niagara Falls.

Kaifeng (or **Pien-ching**) city in Henan province; population (1994) 788,500. Formerly the provincial capital and once a capital of China (907–1127), it lost its importance because of the silting-up of the nearby Huang He River. Industries include zinc-smelting, and the manufacture of fertilizers, textiles, beverages, and agricultural machinery.

Kairouan (or **Kairwan**, Arabic **al-Qayrawan**) Muslim holy city in Tunisia, south of Tunis; population (1994) 102,600. Chief products are carpets, leather goods, and copperware. The city, said to have been founded in AD 617, ranks after Mecca and Medina as a place of pilgrimage.

Kaiser title formerly used by the Holy Roman emperors, Austrian emperors 1806–1918, and German emperors 1871–1918. The word, like the Russian 'tsar', is derived from the Latin *Caesar*.

kakapo nocturnal flightless parrot that lives in burrows in New Zealand. It is green, yellow, and brown with a disc of brown feathers round its eyes, like an owl. It weighs up to 3.5 kg/7.5 lb. When in danger, its main defence is to remain perfectly still. Because of the introduction of predators such as dogs, cats, rats, and ferrets, it is in danger of extinction. In 1998 there were only 56 birds left in the wild. (Species *Strigops habroptilus*, order Psittaciformes.)

Kalaallit Nunaat Greenlandic name for ▷Greenland.

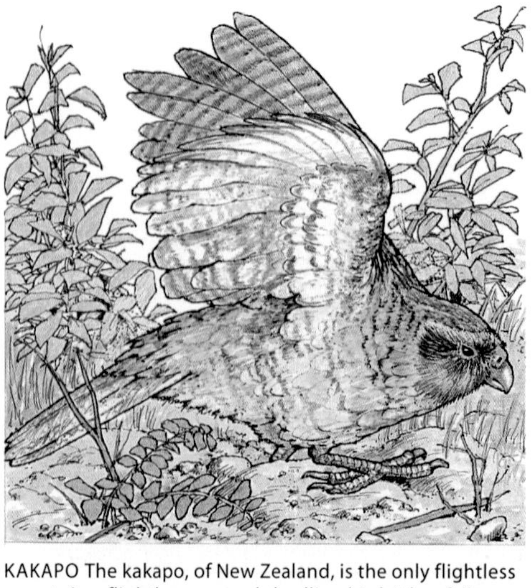

KAKAPO The kakapo, of New Zealand, is the only flightless parrot. As a flightless, ground-dwelling bird, it has fallen easy prey to introduced ground predators such as stoats and rats. Only two breeding populations on small, offshore islands survive in the wild.

Kalahari Desert arid to semi-arid desert area forming most of Botswana and extending into Namibia, Zimbabwe, and South Africa; area about 900,000 sq km/347,400 sq mi. The only permanent river, the Okavango, flows into a delta in the northwest forming marshes rich in wildlife.
Related Web site: Night Creatures of Kalahari http://www.pbs.org/wgbh/nova/kalahari/

Kali in Hindu mythology, the goddess of destruction and death. She is the wife of ▷Siva.

Kālidāsa (lived 5th century AD) Indian epic poet and dramatist. His works, in Sanskrit, include the classic drama *Sakuntalā*, the love story of King Dushyanta and the nymph Sakuntala.

Kalimantan name given to the Indonesian part of the island of Borneo; area 543,900 sq km/210,000 sq mi. It is divided into four provincees: Kalimantan Barat, population (2000 est) 4,034,200, capital Pontianak; Kalimantan Selatan, population (2000 est) 2,985,200, capital Banjarmasin; Kalimantan Tengah, population (2000 est) 1,857,000, capital Palangkaraya; and Kalimantan Timur, population (2000 est) 2,449,400, capital Samarinda. Other towns include Balikpapan. The land is mostly low-lying, with mountains in the north rising to 2,274 m/7,462 ft at Mount Raya. Industries include petroleum, rubber, coffee, copra, pepper, and timber.

Kaliningrad (formerly **Königsberg**) city and port in western Russia; population (1995 est) 926,400. Industries include shipbuilding, fisheries, engineering, and paper manufacture. The port of Kaliningrad remains ice-free throughout the year; as well as being an important commercial centre, it is also the principal base of the Russian Baltic fleet. The city was the capital of East Prussia until this territory was divided between the USSR and Poland in 1945 under the Potsdam Agreement, when it was renamed in honour of Soviet President Mikhail Kalinin (1875–1946). As Königsberg, the city was the birthplace and residence of the German philosopher Immanuel Kant (1724–1804).
Related Web site: Kalingrad in Your Pocket http://www.inyourpocket.com/Kaliningrad/index.htm

Kali-Yuga in Hinduism, the last of the four **yugas** (ages) that make up one cycle of creation. The Kali-Yuga, in which Hindus believe we are now living, is characterized by wickedness and disaster, and leads up to the destruction of this world in preparation for a new creation and a new cycle of yugas.

Kalki in Hinduism, the last avatar (manifestation) of Vishnu, who will appear at the end of the Kali-Yuga, or final age of the world, to destroy it in readiness for a new creation.

Kalmyk (or **Kalmykiya** or **Kalmuck**; Kalmyk **Khal'mg Tangch**) republic in the southwest of the Russian Federation; area 75,900 sq km/29,305 sq mi; population (1996) 319,000 (39% urban) (45% Kalmyks, 38% Russians). The capital is Elista, and Yashkul is another city. The republic is west of the lower Volga and has a short coastline on the northwestern shore of the Caspian Sea. Physical features include dry steppe and semi-desert lowland, and there is a continental climate. Industries include machine building, metalworking, food processing, fish canning.

Kaltenbrunner, Ernst (1903–1946) Austrian Nazi leader. After the annexation of Austria in 1938 he joined police chief Himmler's staff, and as head of the Security Police (SD) from 1943 was responsible for the murder of millions of Jews (see the ▷Holocaust) and Allied soldiers in World War II. After the war, he was tried at Nürnberg for war crimes and hanged in October 1946.

Kamakura city of Kanagawa prefecture, Honshu island, Japan, 15 km/9 mi southwest of Yokohama, on Sagami Bay; population (1993 est) 174,300. It is an exclusive commuter area for Tokyo. The mild climate and historic buildings, especially the Buddhist temples, attract tourists. Lacquer ware has been an important craft since the 13th century. Kamakura was the seat of the first shogunate (1192–1333), which established the rule of the samurai class.

Kamchatka Peninsula mountainous region in the Russian Far East, separating the Sea of ▷Okhotsk from the Pacific Ocean and the Bering Sea. The Kamchatka Peninsula is over 1,200 km/746 mi long, covers an area of 370,000 sq km/142,857 sq mi, and contains a total of over 160 volcanoes (22 of them active), together with many hot springs and geysers. The region has an extremely severe climate and predominantly tundra vegetation, with forests in sheltered valleys. The Kamchatka Peninsula is home to a huge number of animal and bird species, including the brown bear, sea eagle, and sable. There are coal, sulphur, gold, mica, and other mineral deposits.

kame geological feature, usually in the form of a mound or ridge, formed by the deposition of rocky material carried by a stream of glacial meltwater. Kames are commonly laid down in front of or at the edge of a glacier (kame terrace), and are associated with the disintegration of glaciers at the end of an ice age.

Kamenev, Lev Borisovich (1883–1936) Born Lev Borisovich Rosenfeld. Russian leader of the Bolshevik movement after 1917 who, with Stalin and Zinoviev, formed a ruling triumvirate in the USSR after Lenin's death in 1924. His alignment with the Trotskyists led to his dismissal from office and from the Communist Party by Stalin in 1926. Arrested in 1934 after Kirov's assassination, Kamenev was secretly tried and sentenced, then retried, condemned, and shot in 1936 for allegedly plotting to murder Stalin.

kamikaze (Japanese 'wind of the gods') pilots of the Japanese air force in World War II who deliberately crash-dived their planes, loaded with bombs, usually on to ships of the US Navy.

Kampala capital of Uganda, on Lake Victoria; population (1991) 773,500. It is linked by rail with Mombasa. Products include tea, coffee, fruit, and vegetables. Industries include engineering, chemicals, paint manufacture, textiles, footwear, brewing, distilling, and food processing.

Kampuchea former name (1975–89) of ▷Cambodia.

Kanchenjunga Himalayan mountain on the Nepal–Sikkim border, 8,586 m/28,170 ft high, 120 km/75 mi southeast of Mount Everest. The name means 'five treasure houses of the great snows'. Kanchenjunga was first climbed by a British expedition in 1955.

Kandahar city in Afghanistan, 450 km/280 mi southwest of Kabul, capital of Kandahar; population (1995 est) 341,000. A province and a trading centre, with wool and cotton factories, and other industries which include silk and felt. The city is a market for other agricultural products, including wool, tobacco, grains, fresh and dried fruit, and livestock, especially sheep. When Afghanistan became independent in 1747, Kandahar was its first capital.

Kandinsky, Vasily (1866–1944) Russian-born painter. He was a pioneer of abstract art. Between 1910 and 1914 he produced the series *Improvisations* and *Compositions*, the first known examples of purely abstract work in 20th-century art. He was an originator of the expressionist ▷*Blaue Reiter* movement 1911–12, and taught at the ▷Bauhaus school of design in Germany 1921–33.

Born in Moscow, he studied in Munich and in 1902 joined the Berlin ▷Sezession. He travelled widely 1903–08, finally settling in Murnau with the painter Gabriele Münter. By this stage his original experiments with post-Impressionist styles had given way to a fauvist freedom of colour and form. These early paintings used glowing mosaic-like colours to evoke a fairy-tale world inspired by Russian folklore. The elements of his paintings – such as a horse and rider – gradually became more and more abstract as he concentrated exclusively on the expressive qualities of colour and line.

He spent World War I in Russia and his work after his return to Germany shows the influence of Malevich and Lissitzky in its more disciplined structure. His abstract works had few imitators, but his theories on composition, published in *Concerning the Spiritual in Art* (1912), were taken up by the abstractionists. Further theories were published in *Reminiscences* (1913) and *Point and Line to Plane* (1926).

A teacher at the Bauhaus in 1922, he left Nazi Germany for Paris in 1933, becoming a French citizen in 1939.

Kandy city in central Sri Lanka, on the Mahaweli River; capital of a district of the same name; population (2001 est) 110,000. It lies 116 km/72 mi northeast of Colombo. It is the focus both of a major tea-growing area and of the Sinhalese Buddhist culture. One of the most sacred Buddhist shrines is situated in Kandy. Called the Dalada Maligawa (Temple of the Tooth), it contains an alleged tooth of the Buddha.

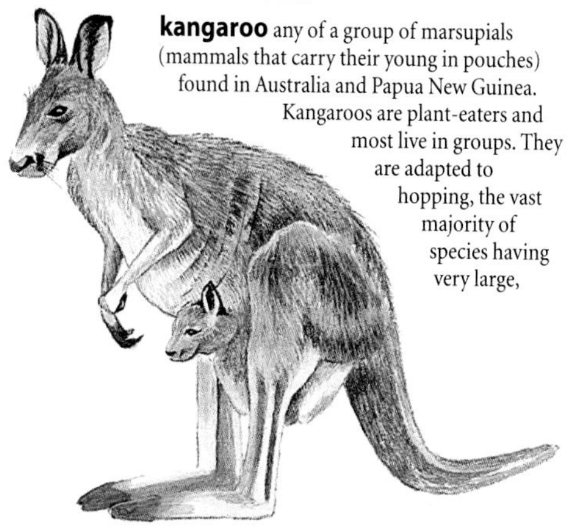

KANGAROO The giant grey kangaroo may reach a weight of 90 kg/200 lb and a height of over 1.5 m/5 ft. Like the red kangaroo, the grey kangaroo lives in small herds, sheltering by rocky outcrops during the heat of the day and emerging during the night to feed and drink.

kangaroo any of a group of marsupials (mammals that carry their young in pouches) found in Australia and Papua New Guinea. Kangaroos are plant-eaters and most live in groups. They are adapted to hopping, the vast majority of species having very large, powerful back legs and feet compared with the small forelimbs. The larger types can jump 9 m/30 ft in a single bound. Most are nocturnal. Species vary from small rat kangaroos, only 30 cm/1 ft long, through the medium-sized wallabies, to the large red and great grey kangaroos, which are the largest living marsupials. These may be 1.8 m/5.9 ft long with 1.1 m/3.5 ft tails. (Family Macropodidae.)

In Papua New Guinea and northern Queensland, tree kangaroos (genus *Dendrolagus*) occur. These have comparatively short hind limbs. The great grey kangaroo (*Macropus giganteus*) produces a single young ('joey') about 2 cm/1 in long after a very short gestation, usually in early summer. At birth the young kangaroo is too young even to suckle. It remains in its mother's pouch, attached to a nipple which squirts milk into its mouth at intervals. It stays in the pouch, with excursions as it matures, for about 280 days.

A new species of kangaroo was discovered 1994 in New Guinea. Local people know it as 'bondegezou'. It weighs 15 kg/33 lb and is 1.2 m/3.9 ft in height. As it shows traits of both arboreal and ground-dwelling species, it may be a 'missing link'.

Kannada (or **Kanarese**) language spoken in southern India, the official state language of Karnataka; also spoken in Tamil Nadu and Maharashtra. There are over 20 million speakers of Kannada, which belongs to the Dravidian family. Written records in Kannada date from the 5th century AD.

Kano capital of Kano state in northern Nigeria, trade centre of an irrigated area; population (1992 est) 699,900. Kano is a major centre for the groundnut and cattle trade. Products include bicycles, glass, furniture, textiles, chemicals, flour, vegetable oil, and cereals. Kano is a tourist centre with trade in leather, brass, cloth, silverware, and beads. Founded about 1000 BC, Kano is a walled city, with New Kano extending beyond the walls.

Kanpur (formerly **Cawnpore**) commercial and industrial city and capital of Kanpur district, Uttar Pradesh, India, 65 km/40 mi southwest of Lucknow, on the River Ganges; population (2001 est) 2,532,100. Industries include cotton, wool, jute, chemicals, plastics, iron, and steel. It has benefited from its rail links with Calcutta, particularly during the growth of its cotton industry in the last century.

Kansas state in central USA. It is nicknamed the Sunflower State. Kansas was admitted to the Union in 1861 as the 34th US state. It is considered both a part of the US Midwest and as one of the Great Plains states. It is bordered to the south by Oklahoma, to the west by Colorado, to the north by Nebraska, and to the east by Missouri.

population (1995) 2,565,300 **area** 213,200 sq km/82,296 sq mi **capital** ▷Topeka **towns and cities** Kansas City, Wichita, Overland Park **industries and products** wheat, corn, sorghum, sunflowers, beef and dairy cattle, coal, petroleum, natural gas, lead, zinc, aircraft, minerals

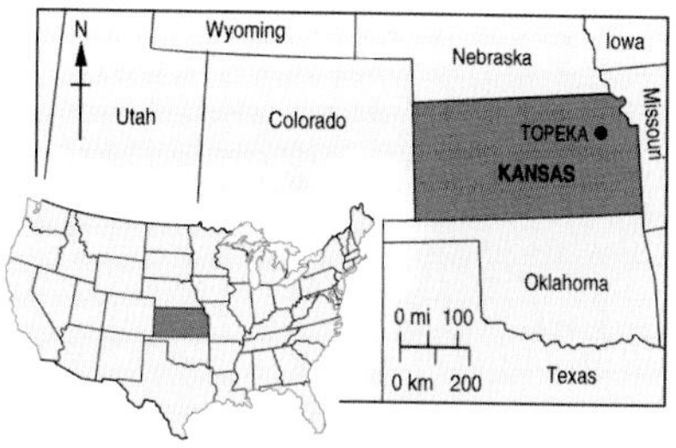

Kansas City city and administrative headquarters of Wyandotte County, northeast Kansas, at the confluence of the Kansas and Missouri rivers; population (1994 est) 143,000. It is adjacent to Kansas City, Missouri. The city is an agricultural market with stockyards, meatpacking plants, grain elevators, and flour mills. Other industries include oil refining, auto assembly, and the manufacture of aircraft engines, furniture, clothing, steel and aluminium products, chemicals, soap, and farm machinery. Among its educational institutions are the University of Kansas Medical Center, Kansas City Kansas Community College (1923), and Donnelly College (1949).

Kansu alternative spelling for the Chinese province ▷Gansu.

Kant, Immanuel (1724–1804) German philosopher. He believed that knowledge is not merely an aggregate of sense impressions but is dependent on the conceptual apparatus of the human understanding, which is itself not derived from experience. In ethics, Kant argued that right action cannot be based on feelings or inclinations but conforms to a law given by reason, the **categorical imperative**.

It was in his *Kritik der reinen Vernunft/Critique of Pure Reason* (1781) that Kant inaugurated a revolution in philosophy by turning attention to the mind's role in constructing our knowledge of the objective world. He also argued that God's existence could not be proved theoretically.

His other main works are *Kritik der praktischen Vernunft/Critique of Practical Reason* (1788) and *Kritik der Urteilskraft/Critique of Judgement* (1790).

Related Web site: Kant, Immanuel
http://www.island-of-freedom.com/KANT.HTM

> **Immanuel Kant**
> *Two things fill the mind with ever-increasing wonder and awe . . . the starry heavens above me and the moral law within me.*
> *Critique of Practical Reason*, conclusion

Kanto flat, densely populated region of east Honshu island, Japan; area 32,377 sq km/12,501 sq mi; population (1995) 1,423,800. It is the largest plain and most heavily populated area in Japan. The chief city is Tokyo.

KANU (acronym for Kenya African National Union) political party founded in 1944 and led by Jomo ▷Kenyatta from 1947, when it was the Kenya African Union (KAU); it became KANU on independence in 1964. The party formed Kenyatta's political power base in 1963 when he became prime minister; in 1964 he became the first president of Kenya. KANU was the sole political party 1982–91. It secured an overwhelming majority in multiparty elections in 1993, but opposition parties disputed the results and their claims of malpractices were partly supported by independent Commonwealth observers.

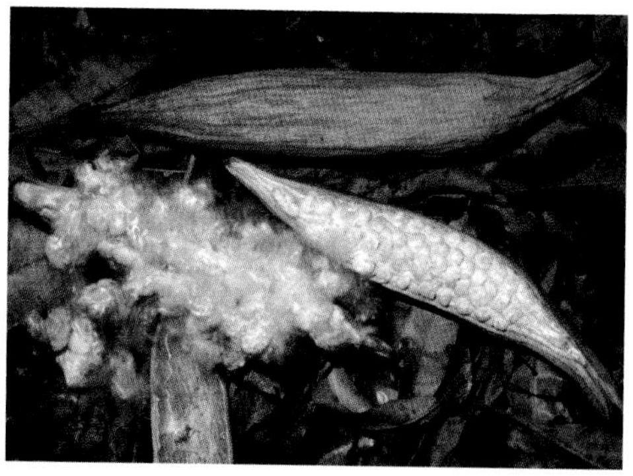

KAPOK When the seed pods of the kapok tree *Bombax ceiba* or the closely related silk-cotton tree *Ceiba pentandra* split open, they release the dense masses of kapok that surround the seeds. Despite the development of synthetic materials, kapok is still in demand, as is the oil extracted from the seeds which is used in making soap and cooking. *Premaphotos Wildlife*

Kaohsiung city and port on the west coast of Taiwan; population (1998) 1,462,302. Industries include aluminium ware, fertilizers, cement, oil refineries, iron and steel works, shipyards, and food processing. Kaohsiung began to develop as a commercial port after 1858; its industrial development came about while it was occupied by Japan 1895–1945.

kaolin group of clay minerals, such as ▷kaolinite, $Al_2Si_2O_5(OH)_4$, derived from the alteration of aluminium silicate minerals, such as ▷feldspars and ▷mica. It is used in medicine to treat digestive upsets, and in poultices.

kaolinite white or greyish ▷clay mineral, hydrated aluminium silicate, $Al_2Si_2O_5(OH)_4$, formed mainly by the decomposition of feldspar in granite. It is made up of platelike crystals, the atoms of which are bonded together in two-dimensional sheets, between which the bonds are weak, so that they are able to slip over one another, a process made more easy by a layer of water. China clay (kaolin) is derived from it. It is mined in France, the UK, Germany, China, and the USA.

kapok silky hairs that surround the seeds of certain trees, particularly the **kapok tree** (*Bombax ceiba*) of India and Malaysia and the **silk-cotton tree** (*Ceiba pentandra*) of tropical America. Kapok is used for stuffing cushions and mattresses and for sound insulation; oil obtained from the seeds is used in food and soap.

Karachay-Cherkessia (or **Karachay-Cherkess Republic** or **Karachayevo-Cherkesiya**) republic in the southwestern Russian Federation, part of Stavropol territory; area 14,100 sq km/5,444 sq mi; population (1996) 436,000 (46% urban) (42% Russian, 31% Karachay). Cherkessk is the capital, and Karachayevsk is another city. The republic is located on the northern slopes of the Caucasus

Mountains, with lowland steppe in the north and forested foothills in the south. There are rich coal and mineral deposits (lead, zinc, and copper). Industries include mining, production of chemicals, foodstuffs, light industries, and grain and vegetable cultivation. Tourism is increasingly important in the republic.

Karachi largest city and chief port of Pakistan, northwest of the Indus delta; population (1996 est) 10 million; 4 million live in makeshift settlements. It is the capital of ▷Sind province. Industries include shipbuilding, engineering, chemicals, plastics, and textiles. A nuclear power plant has been developed at Paradise Point, 25 km/15 mi to the west of the city. It was the capital of Pakistan 1947–59, when it was replaced by ▷Islamabad.

Karadžić, Radovan (1945–) Montenegrin-born leader of the Bosnian Serbs, leader of the community's unofficial government 1992–96. He co-founded the Serbian Democratic Party of Bosnia-Herzegovina (SDS-BH) in 1990 and launched the siege of Sarajevo in 1992, plunging the country into a prolonged and bloody civil war. A succession of peace initiatives for the region failed due to his ambitious demands for Serbian territory, and he was subsequently implicated in war crimes allegedly committed in Bosnia-Herzegovina. In the autumn of 1995, in the wake of a sustained NATO bombardment of Bosnian Serb positions around Sarajevo, Karadžić agreed to enter peace negotiations; in November he signed the US-sponsored Dayton peace accord, under the terms of which he was forced to step down as the Bosnian Serb prime minister. The accord divided Bosnia into separate Moslem, Croat, and Serb areas, and although this seemingly excluded him from further power, he remained a dominant backstage force. He was charged with genocide and crimes against humanity at the Yugoslav War Crimes Tribunal in The Hague, Netherlands, in November 1995 but subsequently defied NATO orders to arrest him on sight by continuing to travel openly about the region. He stepped down as party leader in July 1996. His position was further weakened when, in January 1998, the moderate Milorad Dodik became prime minister of the Bosnian Serb Republic.

Distrusted in the West and viewed as an intransigent figure, he is nevertheless viewed as moderate by many Bosnian Serbs.

Karajan, Herbert von (1908–1989) Austrian conductor. He dominated European classical music performance after 1947. He was principal conductor of the Berlin Philharmonic Orchestra 1955–89, and artistic director of the Vienna State Opera 1957–64 and of the Salzburg Festival 1956–60. A perfectionist, he cultivated an orchestral sound of notable smoothness and transparency; he also staged operas and directed his own video recordings. He recorded the complete Beethoven symphonies four times, and had a special affinity with Mozart and Bruckner, although his repertoire extended from Bach to Schoenberg.

Kara-Kalpak (or **Karakalpakstan**) large autonomous region in northwest ▷Uzbekistan; area 158,000 sq km/61,000 sq mi; population 1,343,000. The capital is Nukus and Munyak is another city in the region. The north of the region consists mainly of lowland around the delta of the ▷Amu Darya, which formerly flowed into the Aral Sea, the southern half of which is within the region. There are plentiful salt deposits. Industries include heavily irrigated cultivation of cotton, rice, and wheat; there is also some viticulture and manufacture of leather goods.

Karakoram mountain range in central Asia, divided among China, Pakistan, and India. Peaks include K2, Masharbrum, Gasharbrum, and Mustagh Tower. **Ladakh** subsidiary range is in northeastern Kashmir on the Tibetan border.

Kara-Kum (Turkmen **Garagum** 'black sand') sandy desert occupying some 90% of the republic of Turkmenistan; area about 310,800 sq km/120,000 sq mi. The Kara-Kum lies to the east of the Caspian Sea, between the Aral Sea to the north and the Iranian border to the south. It is separated from the Kyzyl-Kum desert by the ▷Amu Darya River. The desert is crossed by the Trans-Caspian railway and the **Kara-Kum Canal**, the largest irrigation canal in the world. The area has rich oil, gas, and sulphur deposits, all of which are being increasingly exploited. Air temperatures of over 50°C have been recorded here.

Karamanlis, Constantinos (1907–1998) Greek politician of the New Democracy Party. A lawyer and an anticommunist, he was prime minister 1955–58, 1958–61, and 1961–63 (when he went into self-imposed exile because of a military coup). He was recalled as prime minister on the fall of the regime of the 'colonels' in July 1974, and was president 1980–85.

Kara Sea (Russian **Kavaskoye More**) part of the Arctic Ocean off the north coast of the Russian Federation, bounded to the northwest by the island of Novaya Zemlya and to the northeast by Severnaya Zemlya; area 880,000 sq km/339,768 sq mi; average depths 30–100 m/98–328 ft, with a maximum of 620 m/2,034 ft. Novy Port on the Gulf of Ob is the chief port. Dikson is also a main port and is located on the mouth of the Yenisey River, which flows into the Kara Sea.

karate (Japanese 'empty hand') one of the ▷martial arts. Karate is a type of unarmed combat derived from *kempo*, a form of the Chinese Shaolin boxing. It became popular in the West in the 1930s.

Karbala (or **Kerbala**) holy city of the Shiite Muslims and administrative centre of the governorate of the same name, in Iraq, 96 km/60 mi southwest of Baghdad; population (1998 est) 402,500. The city lies on the edge of the Syrian desert and is linked by canal to the Hindiyah branch of the River Euphrates. The chief modern industries are the manufacture of textiles, shoes, and cement.

Karelia (or **Kareliya**) autonomous republic in the northwest of the Russian Federation, bordering on Finland to the west; area 172,400 sq km/66,550 sq mi; population (1997) 780,000. The capital is Petrozavodsk. The republic is extensively forested with numerous lakes, of which Ladoga and Onega are the largest in Europe. Industries include fishing, timber, chemicals, coal, and mineral and stone quarrying.

Karen member of any of a group of Southeast Asian peoples. Numbering 1.9 million, they live in eastern Myanmar (Burma), Thailand, and the Irrawaddy delta. Traditionally they practised shifting cultivation. Buddhism and Christianity are their main religions, and their language belongs to the Thai division of the Sino-Tibetan family. In 1984 the Burmese government began a military campaign against the Karen National Liberation Army, the armed wing of the Karen National Union. The Myanmar State Law and Order Council (SLORC) increased the use of Karen civilians as forced labourers 1995–96, especially to build the Ye-Tavoy railway and road. Karen villages were also relocated, crops destroyed and property confiscated, forcing thousands to flee to Thailand.

Boris Karloff
The Monster was the best friend I ever had.
Of Frankenstein's monster character

Kariba Dam concrete dam on the Zambezi River, on the Zambia–Zimbabwe border, about 386 km/240 mi downstream from the Victoria Falls, constructed 1955–60 to supply power to both countries.

Karl-Marx-Stadt former name (1953–90) of ▷Chemnitz, a city in Germany.

Karloff, Boris (1887–1969) Stage name of William Henry Pratt. English-born US actor. He achieved Hollywood stardom with his role as the monster in the film *Frankenstein* (1931). Several sequels followed, as well as appearances in such films as *The Mummy* (1932), *Scarface* (1932), *The Lost Patrol* (1934), *The Body Snatcher* (1945), and *The Raven* (1963).

karma (Sanskrit 'action') in Hinduism, the sum of a human being's actions, carried forward from one life to the next, resulting in an improved or worsened fate. Buddhism has a similar belief, except that no permanent personality is envisaged, the karma relating only to volitional tendencies carried on from birth to birth, unless the power holding them together is dispersed in the attainment of nirvana.

Karnak village of modern Egypt on the east bank of the River Nile. It gives its name to the temple of Ammon (constructed by Seti I and Rameses I) around which the major part of the ancient city of ▷Thebes was built. An avenue of rams leads to ▷Luxor.

Karnataka (formerly **Mysore** (until 1973)) state in southwest India; area 191,800 sq km/74,035 sq mi; population (2001 est) 54,907,000, of which the majority is Hindu. The capital is ▷Bangalore, and Mangalore is a port. The state has a western coastal plain; inland the forested Western Ghats rise to heights of 1,250 m/4,000 ft. Industries include manganese, chromite, iron ore, bauxite, mica, copper, and India's only sources of gold (from the Kolar fields) and silver; teak and sandalwood processing. The Tungabhadra dam provides hydroelectricity, and irrigates up to 500,000 ha/1.23 million acres in Karnataka and Andrha Pradesh. Agricultural products include rice on the coastal western plain; inland millet, groundnuts, rice with irrigation; cotton in the north; and coffee and tea on the slopes of the Western Ghats. The language is Kannada.

Related Web site: Destination Karnataka http://www.lonelyplanet.com/dest/ind/kar.htm

Kärnten German name for ▷Carinthia, a province of Austria.

Karoo (Khoikhoi *karusa* 'hard') two areas of semi-desert in Eastern Cape Province, South Africa, divided into the **Great Karoo** and **Little Karoo** by the Swartberg Mountains. The two Karoos together have an area of about 260,000 sq km/100,000 sq mi.

Karpov, Anatoly Yevgenyevich (1951–) Russian chess player. He succeeded Bobby Fischer of the USA as world champion in 1975, and held the title until losing to Gary Kasparov in 1985. He lost to Kasparov again in 1990. In January 1998 Karpov won the FIDE World Chess Championship defeating Viswanathan Anand of India in the final. He lost the FIDE World Chess title in 1999 to Russian Alexander Khalifman.

karst landscape characterized by remarkable surface and underground forms, created as a result of the action of water on permeable limestone. The feature takes its name from the Karst region on the Adriatic coast in Slovenia and Croatia, but the name is applied to landscapes throughout the world, the most dramatic of which is found near the city of Guilin in the Guangxi province of China.

karyotype in biology, the set of ▷chromosomes characteristic of a given species. It is described as the number, shape, and size of the chromosomes in a single cell of an organism. In humans, for example, the karyotype consists of 46 chromosomes, in mice 40, crayfish 200, and in fruit flies 8.

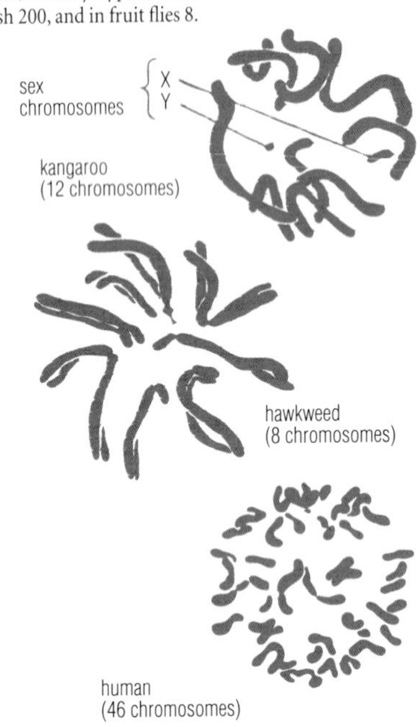

KARYOTYPE The characteristics, or karyotype, of the chromosomes vary according to species. The kangaroo has 12 chromosomes, the hawkweed 8, and a human being 46.

Kashmir disputed area on the border of India and Pakistan in the northwest of the former state of Kashmir, now ▷Jammu and Kashmir; area 78,900 sq km/30,445 sq mi. Physical features include the west Himalayan peak Nanga Parbat (8,126 m/26,660 ft), Karakoram Pass, Indus River, and Baltoro Glacier. Azad ('free') Kashmir in the west has its own legislative assembly based in Muzaffarabad while Gilgit and Baltistan regions to the north and east are governed directly by Pakistan. The ▷Northern Areas are claimed by India and Pakistan. Cities in the region include Gilgit and Skardu.

Fighting took place between the pro-India Hindu ruling class and the pro-Pakistan Muslim majority involving Indian and Pakistani troops, until a UN ceasefire was agreed on 1 January 1949. There was open war between the two countries 1965 and 1971. The area is today officially divided under the terms of the 1972 Simla Agreement between the Pakistani area of Kashmir and the Indian state of Jammu and Kashmir. However, since 1990 it has been riven by Muslim separatist violence, claiming an estimated 60,000 lives (to 2004). Hopes for peace were raised in November 2003 when India and Pakistan both agreed to a ceasefire in a run-up to further summit talks in January 2004.

Kashmiri inhabitants of or natives to the state of Jammu and Kashmir, a disputed territory divided between India and Pakistan. There are approximately 6 million Kashmiris, 4 million of whom live on the Indian side of the ceasefire line.

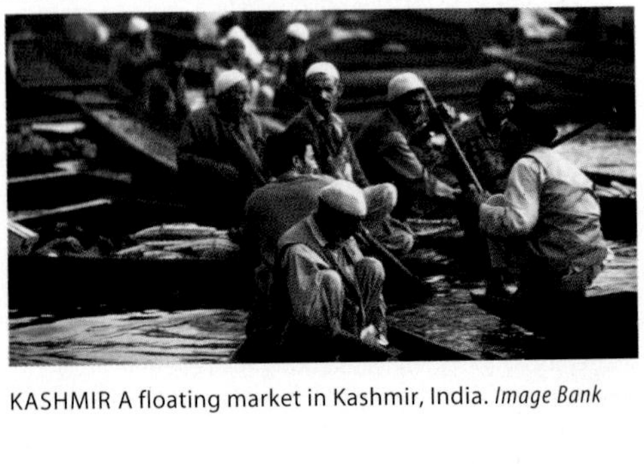

KASHMIR A floating market in Kashmir, India. *Image Bank*

Kasparov, Garry Kimovich (1963–) Born Garri Weinstein. Russian chess player. When he beat his compatriot Anatoly Karpov to win the world title in 1985, he was the youngest-ever champion at 22 years 210 days. He held this crown for 15 years until November 2000 when he was beaten by a former Russian pupil, Vladimir Kramnik. During that time Kasparov lost only once – to IBM computer Deep Blue in 1997.

Related Web site: Garry Kasparov's International Chess Master Academy http://www.chess.ibm.com/meet/html/d.1.html

Kathmandu (or **Katmandu**) capital of Nepal, situated at 1,370 m/4,500 ft in the southern Himalayas, in the Valley of Nepal, at the junction of the Baghmati and Vishnumati rivers; population (2001 est) 696,900. Tourism is an important economic activity.

GARRY KASPAROV From 1993 Kasparov led the Professional Chess Association, a breakaway from FIDE, who ran the existing world championships. *Image Bank*

Kattegat sea passage between Denmark and Sweden. It is about 240 km/150 mi long and 135 km/85 mi wide at its broadest point, and joins the Skagerrak on the north to the Baltic Sea on the south. Its sandbanks are a navigational hazard.

katydid (or **bush cricket** or **longhorn grasshopper**) one of over 4,000 insect species, most of which are tropical, related to grasshoppers.

Katyn Forest forest near Smolensk, southwest of Moscow, Russia, where 4,500 Polish officer prisoners of war (captured in the German-Soviet partition of Poland 1940) were shot; 10,000 others were killed elsewhere. In 1989 the USSR accepted responsibility for the massacre.

KATYDID A Costa Rican katydid. This insect has long antennae and most members of the species are wingless. *Image Bank*

Kaunas (formerly **Kovno** (until 1917)) industrial city in Lithuania, at the confluence of the Neris and Niemen (Neman) rivers, 80 km/50 mi northwest of Vilnius; population (1991) 430,000. Kaunas has engineering, textile, and food industries and is an important river port and railway junction. It was the capital of independent Lithuania from 1920 until 1940.

Kaunda, Kenneth David (1924–) Zambian politician, president 1964–91. Imprisoned 1958–60 as founder of the Zambia African National Congress, in 1964 he became the first prime minister of Northern Rhodesia, then the first president of independent Zambia. In 1973 he introduced one-party rule. He supported the nationalist movement in Southern Rhodesia, now Zimbabwe, and survived a coup attempt in 1980 thought to have been promoted by South Africa. He was elected chair of the Organization of African Unity in 1970 and 1987. In November 1991 he lost the first multiparty elections to Frederick Chiluba.

In July 1995 he was elected president of the United National Independence Party (UNIP) and announced his return to active politics, though his decision was not widely applauded. In May 1996 the Zambian constitution was controversially amended, making it impossible for non-second-generation Zambians to stand for the presidency, thereby effectively debarring Kaunda from future contests. The move was criticized by Commonwealth observers. In 1998, while under house arrest, he was charged with concealing knowledge of an abortive coup in October 1997. In June 1998 he was freed, after a five-months' detention.

kauri pine New Zealand coniferous tree (see ▷conifer). Its fossilized gum deposits are valued in varnishes; the wood is used for carving and handicrafts. (*Agathis australis*, family Araucariaceae.)

Kavanagh, Dan pseudonym of the English writer Julian ▷Barnes, under which he has written detective novels.

Kawabata, Yasunari (1899–1972) Japanese novelist. He translated Lady ▷Murasaki, and was the author of *Snow Country* (1947) and *A Thousand Cranes* (1952). His novels are characterized by melancholy and loneliness. He was the first Japanese to be awarded the Nobel Prize for Literature, in 1968.

Kawasaki industrial city of Kanagawa prefecture, Honshu island, Japan; population (2000) 1,250,000. It is situated between Tokyo and Yokohama in the important Keihin industrial zone, the largest industrial zone in Japan, and is a major port for the import of raw materials. The main industries are iron, steel, shipbuilding, chemicals, and textiles. It is noted for its cherry blossoms at Inadazutsumi on the banks of the Tamagawa.

Kaye, Danny (1913–1987) Stage name of David Daniel Kaminski. US actor, comedian, and singer. He appeared in many films, including *Wonder Man* (1944), *The Secret Life of Walter Mitty* (1946), and *Hans Christian Andersen* (1952). He had his own television show 1963–67.

Kayseri (ancient **Caesarea Mazaca**) capital of Kayseri province, central Turkey; population (1990) 421,400. It produces textiles, carpets, and tiles. In Roman times it was capital of the province of Cappadocia.

Kazakh (or **Kazak**) a pastoral Kyrgyz people of Kazakhstan. Kazakhs also live in China (Xinjiang, Gansu, and Qinghai), Mongolia, and Afghanistan. There are 5–7 million speakers of Kazakh, a Turkic language belonging to the Altaic family. They are predominantly Sunni Muslim, although pre-Islamic customs have survived.

Kazakhstan see country box.

Kazan city and port on the ▷Volga, capital and economic centre of ▷Tatarstan, in the western Russian Federation; population (1996) 1,085,000. Kazan is the centre of Tatarstan culture. It has large engineering plants (manufacturing ships, machine tools, compressors, and dental equipment), chemical works (producing explosives, synthetic rubber, soap, and photographic materials), and a large leather and fur industry. It is also a major transportation centre, with its river port, airport, and location at a major railway junction.

Kazan, Elia (1909–2003) Born Elia Kazanjoglous. Turkish-born US stage and film director. In the theatre he directed, among others, *The Skin of Our Teeth* (1942), *A Streetcar Named Desire* (1947), *Death of a Salesman* (1949), and *Cat on a Hot Tin Roof* (1955). He became a film director in 1944, and won Academy Awards for *Gentleman's Agreement* (1947) and *On the Waterfront* (1954).

Kazantzakis, Nikos (1885–1957) Greek writer. His works include the poem *I Odysseia/The Odyssey* (1938), which continues Homer's *Odyssey*, and the novels *Zorba the Greek* (1946), *Christ Recrucified* (1948), *The Greek Passion*, and *The Last Temptation of Christ* (both 1951). *Zorba the Greek* was filmed in 1964 and *The Last Temptation of Christ* (controversially) in 1988.

kea hawklike greenish parrot found in New Zealand. It eats insects, fruits, and discarded sheep offal. The Maori name imitates its cry. (Species *Nestor notabilis*, family Psittacidae, order Psittaciformes.) In 2000 there were only about 2,000 keas remaining.

Kean, Edmund (1787–1833) English tragic actor. He was noted for his portrayal of villainy in the Shakespearean roles of Shylock, Richard III, and Iago. He died on stage, playing Othello opposite his son as Iago.

Keating, Paul John (1944–) Australian politician, Labor Party (ALP) leader and prime minister 1991–96. He was treasurer and deputy leader of the ALP 1983–91. In 1993 he announced plans for Australia to become a federal republic by the year 2001, which incited a mixed reaction among Australians. He and his party lost the February 1996 general election to John Howard, leader of the Liberal Party.

> **Kenneth Kaunda**
> *The moment you have protected an individual you have protected society.*
> The Observer 6 May 1962

Keaton, Buster (Joseph Francis) (1896–1966) US comedian, actor, and film director. After being a star in vaudeville, he became one of the great comedians of the silent film era, with an inimitable deadpan expression masking a sophisticated acting ability. His films include *One Week* (1920), *The Navigator* (1924), *Sherlock, Jr* (1924), *The General* (1927), *The Cameraman* (1928), and *Steamboat Bill, Jr* (1928).

Keaton, the 'Great Stone Face', rivalled Charlie Chaplin in popularity until studio problems ended his creative career. He then made only shorts and guest appearances, as in Chaplin's *Limelight* (1952) and *A Funny Thing Happened on the Way to the Forum* (1966).

Keats, John (1795–1821) English Romantic poet. He produced work of the highest quality and promise before dying at the age of 25. *Poems* (1817), *Endymion* (1818), the great odes (particularly 'Ode to a Nightingale' and 'Ode on a Grecian Urn' written in 1819, published in 1820), and the narratives 'Isabella; or the Pot of Basil' (1818), 'Lamia' (1819), and 'The Eve of St Agnes' (1820), show his lyrical richness and talent for drawing on both classical mythology and medieval lore.

Born in London, Keats studied at Guy's Hospital from 1815–17, but then abandoned medicine for poetry. *Endymion* was harshly reviewed by the Tory *Blackwood's Magazine* and *Quarterly Review*, largely because of Keats's friendship with the radical writer Leigh Hunt (1784–1859). In 1819 he fell in love with Fanny Brawne (1802–1865). Suffering from tuberculosis, he sailed to Italy in 1820 in an attempt to regain his health, but died in Rome. Valuable insight into Keats's poetic development is provided by his *Letters*, published in 1848.

Keats's poetry often deals with the relationship between love and death, beauty and decay. The odes reflect his feelings about the death of his brother and human mortality. 'Ode to a Nightingale' is a symbol of beauty's power to surmount death, a theme which reappears in 'Ode on a Grecian Urn', where the figures on the vase are seen to epitomize an enduring truth, while 'Ode to Autumn' asserts the fulfilment of complete fruition and ripeness.

Related Web site: Keats, John http://www.bartleby.com/126/index.html

JOHN KEATS The poetry of English Romantic poet John Keats aims to find a balance between the beauty of the world and the inevitability of its passing. His work was much influenced by the early death of his brother, and by his own ill health and poverty. He died in 1821 of tuberculosis. *Archive Photos*

Keble, John (1792–1866) Anglican priest and religious poet. His sermon on the decline of religious faith in Britain, preached in 1833, heralded the start of the ▷Oxford Movement, a Catholic revival in the Church of England. He wrote four of the *Tracts for the Times* (theological treatises in support of the movement), and was professor of poetry at Oxford 1831–41. His book of poems, *The Christian Year* (1827), was very popular in the 19th century. Keble College, Oxford, was founded in 1870 in his memory.

Kedah state in northwest Peninsular Malaysia; capital Alor Setar; area 9,400 sq km/3,628 sq mi; population (1993) 1,412,000. Products include rice, rubber, tapioca, tin, and tungsten. Kedah was transferred by Siam (Thailand) to Britain in 1909, and was one of the Unfederated Malay States until 1948.

Keeling Islands another name for the ▷Cocos Islands, an Australian territory.

keeshond (or **Dutch barge dog**) sturdily built dog with erect ears and curled tail. It has a long grey top-coat, forming a mane around the neck, and a short, very thick undercoat, with darker 'spectacles' around the eyes. The ideal height is 46 cm/18 in for dogs; 43 cm/17 in for bitches, and the ideal weight is 25–30 kg/55–66 lb.

Keïta, Salif (1949–) Malian singer and songwriter. His combination of traditional rhythms and vocals with electronic instruments made him popular in the West in the 1980s; in Mali he worked 1973–83 with the band Les Ambassadeurs and became a star throughout West Africa, moving to France in 1984. His albums include *Soro* (1987) and *Amen* (1991).

Keitel, Wilhelm (1882–1946) German field marshal in World War II, chief of the supreme command from 1938 and Hitler's chief military adviser. He dictated the terms of the French armistice in 1940 and was a member of the court that sentenced many officers to death for their part in the July Plot 1944. He signed Germany's unconditional surrender in Berlin on 8 May 1945. Tried at Nürnberg for war crimes, he was hanged.

Kazakhstan

KAZAKHSTAN Women gutting fresh fish in the open air at Atyrau, Kazakhstan, on the coast of the Caspian Sea. *Image Bank*

Kazakhstan country in central Asia, bounded north by Russia, west by the Caspian Sea, east by China, and south by Turkmenistan, Uzbekistan, and Kyrgyzstan.

NATIONAL NAME *Kazak Respublikasy/Republic of Kazakhstan*
AREA 2,717,300 sq km/1,049,150 sq mi
CAPITAL Astana (formerly Akmola)
MAJOR TOWNS/CITIES Qaraghandy, Pavlodar, Semey, Petropavlosk, Shymkent
PHYSICAL FEATURES Caspian and Aral seas, Lake Balkhash; Steppe region; natural gas and oil deposits in the Caspian Sea

Government
HEAD OF STATE Nursultan Nazarbayev from 1990
HEAD OF GOVERNMENT Daniyel Akhmetov from 2003
POLITICAL SYSTEM authoritarian nationalist
POLITICAL EXECUTIVE unlimited presidency
ADMINISTRATIVE DIVISIONS 14 regions and one city (Astana)
ARMED FORCES 60,000; plus paramilitary forces of 34,500 (2002 est)
DEATH PENALTY retained and used for ordinary crimes

Economy and resources
CURRENCY tenge
GPD (US$) 24.2 billion (2002 est)
REAL GDP GROWTH (% change on previous year) 13.2 (2001)
GNI (US$) 22.3 billion (2002 est)
GNI PER CAPITA (PPP) (US$) 5,480 (2002 est)
CONSUMER PRICE INFLATION 6.4% (2003 est)
UNEMPLOYMENT 8.9% (2001)
FOREIGN DEBT (US$) 4.1 billion (2001 est)
MAJOR TRADING PARTNERS Russia, Germany, EU, Bermuda, CIS (Commonwealth of Independent States), USA
RESOURCES petroleum, natural gas, coal, bauxite, chromium, copper, iron ore, lead, zinc, titanium, magnesium, tungsten, molybdenum, gold (second largest reserves in the world), silver, manganese
INDUSTRIES metal processing, heavy engineering, mining and quarrying, chemicals, fuel, power, machine-building, textiles, food processing, household appliances

EXPORTS ferrous and non-ferrous metals, mineral products (including petroleum and petroleum products), chemicals. Principal market: Russia 20.2% (2001)
IMPORTS energy products and electricity, machinery and transport equipment, chemicals, food products. Principal source: Russia 45.4% (2001)
ARABLE LAND 8% (2000 est)
AGRICULTURAL PRODUCTS fruits, sugar beet, vegetables, potatoes, cotton, cereals; livestock rearing (particularly sheep); karakul and astrakhan wool

Population and society
POPULATION 15,433,000 (2003 est)
POPULATION GROWTH RATE –0.2% (2000–15)
POPULATION DENSITY (per sq km) 6 (2003 est)
URBAN POPULATION (% of total) 56 (2003 est)
AGE DISTRIBUTION (% of total population) 0–14 26%, 15–59 63%, 60+ 11% (2002 est)
ETHNIC GROUPS 50% of Kazakh descent, 32% ethnic Russian, 4.5% Ukrainian, 2% German, 2% Uzbek, and 2% Tatar
LANGUAGE Kazakh (related to Turkish; official), Russian
RELIGION Sunni Muslim 50–60%, Russian Orthodox 30–35%
EDUCATION (compulsory years) 11
LITERACY RATE 99% (men); 99% (women) (2003 est)
LABOUR FORCE 22.0% agriculture, 18.3% industry, 59.7% services (1999)
LIFE EXPECTANCY 61 (men); 72 (women) (2000–05)
CHILD MORTALITY RATE (under 5, per 1,000 live births) 76 (2001)
PHYSICIANS (per 1,000 people) 3.5 (1999 est)
HOSPITAL BEDS (per 1,000 people) 8.5 (1999 est)
TV SETS (per 1,000 people) 241 (2001 est)
RADIOS (per 1,000 people) 411 (2001 est)
INTERNET USERS (per 10,000 people) 93.2 (2002 est)

See also ▷Kazakh; ▷Russian Federation; ▷Union of Soviet Socialist Republics.

Chronology

early Christian era: Settled by Mongol and Turkic tribes.

8th century: Spread of Islam.

10th century: Southward migration into east Kazakhstan of Kazakh tribes, displaced from Mongolia by the Mongols.

13th–14th centuries: Part of Mongol Empire.

late 15th century: Kazakhs emerged as distinct ethnic group from Kazakh Orda tribal confederation.

early 17th century: The nomadic, cattle-breeding Kazakhs split into smaller groups, united in the three Large, Middle, and Lesser Hordes (federations), led by khans (chiefs).

1731–42: Faced by attacks from the east by Oirot Mongols, protection was sought from the Russian tsars, and Russian control was gradually established.

1822–48: Conquest by tsarist Russia completed; khans deposed. Large-scale Russian and Ukrainian peasant settlement of the steppes after the abolition of serfdom in Russia in 1861.

1887: Alma-Alta (now Almaty), established in 1854 as a fortified trading centre and captured by the Russians in 1865, destroyed by an earthquake.

1916: 150,000 killed as anti-Russian rebellion brutally repressed.

1917: Bolshevik coup in Russia followed by outbreak of civil war in Kazakhstan.

1920: Autonomous republic in USSR.

early 1930s: More than 1 million died of starvation during the campaign to collectivize agriculture.

1936: Joined USSR and became a full union republic.

early 1940s: Volga Germans deported to the republic by Soviet dictator Joseph Stalin.

1954–56: Part of Soviet leader Nikita Khrushchev's ambitious 'Virgin Lands' agricultural extension programme; large influx of Russian settlers made Kazakhs a minority in their own republic.

1986: There were nationalist riots in Alma-Alta (now Almaty) after the reformist Soviet leader Mikhail Gorbachev ousted the local communist leader and installed an ethnic Russian.

1989: Nursultan Nazarbayev, a reformist and mild nationalist, became leader of the Kazakh Communist Party (KCP) and instituted economic and cultural reform programmes, encouraging foreign inward investment.

1990: ; economic sovereignty was declared.

1991: Nazarbayev became head of state and condemned the attempted anti-Gorbachev coup in Moscow; the KCP was abolished. The country joined the new Commonwealth of Independent States (CIS); and independence was recognized by the USA.

1992: Kazakhstan was admitted into the United Nations (UN) and the Conference on Security and Cooperation in Europe (CSCE; now the Organization on Security and Cooperation in Europe, OSCE).

1993: Presidential power was increased by a new constitution. A privatization programme was launched. START-1 (disarmament treaty) and Nuclear Non-Proliferation Treaty were both ratified by Kazakhstan.

1994: There was economic, social, and military union with Kyrgyzstan and Uzbekistan.

1995: An economic and military cooperation pact was signed with Russia. Kazakhstan achieved nuclear-free status.

1997: Astana (formerly known as Akmola) was designated as the new capital.

1998: A treaty of 'eternal friendship' and a treaty of deepening economic cooperation was signed with Uzbekistan.

1999: Kasymzhomart Tokaev was appointed prime minister.

2002: A final border agreement was signed with Uzbekistan and an agreement on eternal friendship. Otan and the People's Co-operative Party of Kazakhstan (PCPK), the country's two main political parties, merged.

Kekulé von Stradonitz, Friedrich August (1829–1896) German chemist whose theory in 1858 of molecular structure revolutionized organic chemistry. He proposed two resonant forms of the ▷benzene ring.

Kelantan state in northeast Peninsular Malaysia; capital Kota Bharu; area 14,900 sq km/5,751 sq mi; population (1993) 1,221,700. It produces rice, rubber, copra, tin, manganese, and gold. Kelantan was transferred by Siam (Thailand) to Britain 1909 and until 1948 was one of the Unfederated Malay States.

kelim oriental carpet or rug that is flat, pileless, and reversible. Kelims are made by a tapestry-weave technique. Weft thread of one colour is worked to and fro in one area of the pattern; the next colour continues the pattern from the adjacent warp thread, so that no weft thread runs across the full width of the carpet.

Kellogg–Briand Pact agreement negotiated in 1927 between the USA and France to renounce war and seek settlement of disputes by peaceful means. It took its name from the US secretary of state Frank B Kellogg (1856–1937) and the French foreign minister Aristide Briand. Most other nations subsequently signed. Some successes were achieved in settling South American disputes, but the pact made no provision for measures against aggressors and became ineffective in the 1930s, with Japan in Manchuria, Italy in Ethiopia, and Hitler in central Europe.

Kells, Book of 8th-century illuminated manuscript of the Gospels produced at the monastery of Kells in County Meath, Ireland. It is now in Trinity College Library, Dublin.

Kelly, Gene (Eugene Curran) (1912–1996) US film actor, dancer, choreographer, and director. He was a major star of the 1940s and 1950s in a series of MGM musicals, including *On the Town* (1949), *Singin' in the Rain* (1952) (both of which he codirected), and *An American in Paris* (1951). He also directed *Hello Dolly* (1969).

Kelly, Grace (Patricia) (1929–1982) US film actor. She starred in *High Noon* (1952), *The Country Girl* (1954), for which she received an Academy Award, and *High Society* (1955). She also starred in three Hitchcock films – *Dial M for Murder* (1954), *Rear Window* (1954), and *To Catch a Thief* (1955). She retired from acting after marrying Prince Rainier III of Monaco in 1956.

Kelly, Petra (1947–1992) German politician and activist. She was a vigorous campaigner against nuclear power and other environmental issues and founded the German Green Party in 1972. She was a member of the Bundestag (parliament) 1983–90, but then fell out with her party.

Kelman, James (1946–) Scottish novelist and short-story writer. His works are angry, compassionate, and ironic, and make effective use of the trenchant speech patterns of his native Glasgow. These include the novels *The Busconductor Hines* (1984), *A Disaffection* (1989), and *How Late It Was, How Late* (1994; Booker Prize); *The Good times* (1998) comprises 21 'narratives' in which men try to come to terms with their redundancy in life.

keloid in medicine, overgrowth of fibrous tissue, usually produced at the site of a scar. Surgical removal is often unsuccessful, because the keloid returns.

kelp collective name for a group of large brown seaweeds. Kelp is also a term for the powdery ash of burned seaweeds, a source of iodine. (Typical families Fucaceae and Laminariaceae.)

Kelvin scale temperature scale used by scientists. It begins at ▷absolute zero (−273.15°C) and increases in kelvins, the same degree intervals as the Celsius scale; that is, 0°C is the same as 273.15 K and 100°C is 373.15 K. It is named after the Scottish physicist William Thomson, 1st Baron ▷Kelvin.

Kelvin, William Thomson (1824–1907) 1st Baron Kelvin. Irish physicist who introduced the **kelvin scale**, the absolute scale of temperature. His work on the conservation of energy in 1851 led to the second law of ▷thermodynamics. He was knighted in 1866, and made baron in 1892.

Kelvin's knowledge of electrical theory was largely responsible for the first successful transatlantic telegraph cable. In 1847 he concluded that electrical and magnetic fields are distributed in a manner analogous to the transfer of energy through an elastic solid. From 1849 to 1859 Kelvin also developed the work of English scientist Michael ▷Faraday into a full theory of magnetism, arriving at an expression for the total energy of a system of magnets.

Kemal Atatürk, Mustafa Turkish politician; see ▷Atatürk.

Kemble, (John) Philip (1757–1823) English actor and theatre manager. He excelled in tragedy, including the Shakespearean roles of Hamlet and Coriolanus. As manager of Drury Lane 1788–1803 and Covent Garden 1803–17 in London, he introduced many innovations in theatrical management, costume, and scenery.

Kempe, Margerie (*c.* 1373–*c.* 1439) Born Margerie Brunham. English Christian mystic. She converted to religious life after a period of mental derangement, and travelled widely as a pilgrim. Her *Boke of Margery Kempe* (about 1420) describes her life and experiences, both religious and worldly. It has been called the first autobiography in English.

Kempis, Thomas à medieval German monk and religious writer; see ▷Thomas à Kempis.

Keneally, Thomas Michael (1935–) Australian novelist and playwright. He won the Booker Prize with *Schindler's Ark* (1982), a novel based on the true account of Polish Jews saved from the gas chambers in World War II by a German industrialist. Other works include *Woman of the Inner Sea* (1992) and *Bettany's Book* (2000).

Kennedy, Charles (1959–) British politician, leader of the Liberal Democrat party from 1999– . Kennedy was Britain's youngest Member of Parliament when he was elected in 1983, at the age of 23, and became Liberal Democrat president 1990–94. He won a comfortable victory in the leadership contest to choose a successor to Paddy Ashdown, who had stepped down after 11 years as leader of the UK's third political party. He inhertited a party which had at long last made a crucial leap into government through its coalition with Labour in the Scottish Parliament. To the anger of many in his party Kennedy refused to rule out greater cross-party cooperation. He told his party colleagues he would continue to work with Labour in some areas, but only where his own party backed such cooperation.

Kennedy, Edward Moore ('Ted') (1932–) US Democratic politician. He aided his brothers John and Robert Kennedy in their presidential campaigns of 1960 and 1968, respectively, and entered politics as a senator for Massachusetts in 1962. He failed to gain the presidential nomination in 1980, largely because of questions about his delay in reporting a car crash at Chappaquiddick Island, near Cape Cod, Massachusetts, in 1969, in which his passenger, Mary Jo Kopechne, was drowned.

Kennedy, John F(itzgerald) ('Jack') (1917–1963) 35th president of the USA 1961–63, a Democrat; the first Roman Catholic and the youngest person to be elected president. In foreign policy he carried through the unsuccessful ▷Bay of Pigs invasion of Cuba, and secured the withdrawal of Soviet missiles from the island in 1962. His programme for reforms at home, called the **New Frontier**, was posthumously executed by Lyndon Johnson. Kennedy was assassinated while on a visit to Dallas, Texas, on 22 November 1963. Lee Harvey Oswald (1939–1963), who was within a few days shot dead by Jack Ruby (1911–1967), was named as the assassin.

> **Joseph P Kennedy**
> *When the going gets tough, the tough get going.*
> J H Cutler *Honey Fitz*

> **John F Kennedy**
> *Conformity is the jailer of freedom and the enemy of growth.*
> Address to UN General Assembly, 25 September 1961

Background The son of financier Joseph Kennedy, he was born in Brookline, Massachusetts, educated at Harvard and briefly at the London School of Economics, and served in the navy in the Pacific during World War II, winning the Purple Heart and the Navy and Marine Corps medal.

Early political career After a brief career in journalism he was elected to the House of Representatives in 1946. At this point he was mainly concerned with domestic politics and showed few signs of the internationalism for which he later became famous. In 1952 he was elected to the Senate from Massachusetts, defeating Republican Henry Cabot Lodge, Jr, one of Eisenhower's leading supporters. In 1953 he married socialite Jacqueline Lee Bouvier (1929–1995).

Presidential candidate Kennedy made his name as a supporter of civil-rights legislation and as a prominent internationalist, but his youth and his Roman Catholicism were considered serious barriers to the White House. His victory in all seven primaries that he entered, however, assured his place as Democratic candidate for the presidency in 1960. His programme was a radical one, covering promises to deal with both civil rights and social reform. On television Kennedy debated well against the Republican candidate Richard ▷Nixon, yet went on to win the presidency by one of the narrowest margins ever recorded.

Presidency Critics suggest style was more important than substance in the Kennedy White House, but he inspired a generation of idealists and created an aura of positive activism. He brought academics and intellectuals to Washington as advisers, and his wit and charisma combined with political shrewdness disarmed many critics. His inaugural address, with its emphasis on the 'new frontier', was reminiscent of Franklin D Roosevelt. In fact Kennedy did not succeed in carrying through any major domestic legislation, though, with the aid of his brother Robert ▷Kennedy, who was attorney general, desegregation continued and the Civil Rights Bill was introduced. He created the ▷Peace Corps – volunteers who

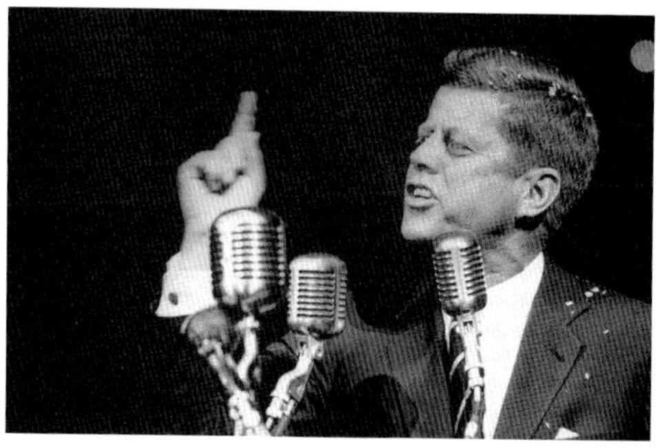

JOHN F KENNEDY John F Kennedy, speaking just after winning the US presidential election, at Hyannis Port, Massachusetts, 9 November 1960. *Archive Photos*

give various types of health, agricultural, and educational aid overseas – and he proposed the Alliance for Progress for aid to Latin America.

Foreign affairs It was in foreign affairs that Kennedy's presidency was most notable. Early in 1961 came the fiasco of the Bay of Pigs, which, though partially carried over from the previous administration, was undoubtedly Kennedy's responsibility. This was redeemed by his masterly handling of the ▷Cuban missile crisis in 1962, where his calm and firm approach had a prolonged effect on US–Soviet relations. The Nuclear ▷Test Ban Treaty of 1963 achieved a further lessening of tension. Kennedy's internationalism won him a popular European reputation not attained by any of his predecessors. He visited Western Europe in 1961 and 1963, and was tumultuously received on each occasion. The US involvement in the Vietnam War began during Kennedy's administration.

Assassination On 22 November, while on a tour of Texas, Kennedy was shot while being driven through Dallas and died shortly afterwards. His presumed assassin, Lee Harvey Oswald, was himself shot on 24 November while under arrest. Kennedy's death caused worldwide grief and his funeral was attended by heads of state and their representatives from all over the world. He was buried in Arlington National Cemetery.

Related Web sites: Kennedy Assassination http://mcadams.posc.mu.edu/home.htm
Kennedy, John F http://www.geocities.com/~newgeneration/

Kennedy, Joseph (Patrick) (1888–1969) US industrialist and diplomat. As ambassador to the UK 1937–40, he was a strong advocate of appeasement of Nazi Germany. He groomed each of his sons – Joseph Patrick Kennedy, Jr (1915–1944), John F ▷Kennedy, Robert ▷Kennedy, and Edward ▷Kennedy – for a career in politics.

Kennedy, Nigel Paul (1956–) English violinist. He is credited with expanding the audience for classical music. His 1986 recording of Vivaldi's *Four Seasons* sold more than 1 million copies. He announced a temporary retirement from the concert platform in 1992. On his return he made recordings of his own compositions, and in early 1999 abandoned his classical roots altogether, announcing major new projects based on his interpretation of the music of US musicians The Doors and Jimi Hendrix. However, 2000 saw Kennedy return to the classical arena, with new recordings of works by J S Bach and an international performance tour.

Kennedy, Robert Francis (1925–1968) US Democratic politician and lawyer. He was presidential campaign manager for his brother John F ▷Kennedy in 1960, and as attorney general 1961–64 pursued a racket-busting policy and worked to enforce federal law in support of civil rights. He was assassinated during his campaign for the 1968 Democratic presidential nomination.

Kennedy Space Center ▷NASA launch site on Merritt Island, near Cape Canaveral, Florida, used for *Apollo* and space-shuttle launches. The first flight to land on the Moon (1969) and *Skylab*, the first orbiting laboratory (1973), were launched here.

The Center is dominated by the Vehicle Assembly Building, 160 m/525 ft tall, used for assembly of ▷*Saturn* rockets and space shuttles.

Related Web site: Kennedy Space Centre
http://www.ksc.nasa.gov/

Kennelly–Heaviside layer former term for the ▷E layer of the ionosphere.

Kenneth two kings of Scotland:

Kenneth I (died 860) Called 'MacAlpin'. King of Scotland from about 844. Traditionally, he is regarded as the founder of the Scottish kingdom (Alba) by virtue of his final defeat of the Picts about 844. He invaded Northumbria six times, and drove the Angles and the Britons over the River Tweed.

Kenneth II (died 995) King of Scotland from 971, son of Malcolm I. He invaded Northumbria several times, and his chiefs were in constant conflict with Sigurd the Norwegian over the area of Scotland north of the River Spey. He is believed to have been murdered by his subjects.

Kent county of southeast England, known as the 'garden of England' (since April 1998 Medway Towns has been a separate unitary authority).

area 3,730 sq km/1,440 sq mi **towns and cities** ▷Maidstone (administrative headquarters), Ashford, Canterbury, Deal, Dover (ferry terminus), Gravesend, Hythe, New Ash Green (a new town), Sevenoaks, Royal Tunbridge Wells; resorts: Folkestone, Margate, Ramsgate **physical** the North Downs; White Cliffs of Dover; rivers: Thames, Darent, Medway (traditionally, a 'man of Kent' comes from east of the Medway and a 'Kentish man' from west Kent), Stour; marshes (especially Romney Marsh); the Isles of Grain, Thanet and Sheppey (on which is the resort of Sheerness, formerly a royal dockyard); the Weald (an agricultural area); Dungeness (peninsula and headland) **features** Leeds Castle (converted to a palace by Henry VIII); Ightham Mote; Hever Castle (where Henry VIII courted Anne Boleyn); Chartwell (Churchill's country home), Knole, Sissinghurst Castle and gardens; the Brogdale Experimental Horticulture Station at Faversham has the world's finest collection of apple and other fruit trees; the former RAF Manston became Kent International Airport in 1989; Dungeness nuclear power station **agriculture** cereals, hops, apples, soft fruit, vegetables; in Kent are found about half the orchards, half the hops, and one fifth of the soft fruit grown in England and Wales; livestock production **industries** cement (Gravesend), paper, oil refining, shipbuilding, tourism. The East Kent coalfield ceased production in 1989 **population** (2001 est) 1,331,100 **famous people** Edward Heath, Christopher Marlowe

KENT The drawbridge at Hever Castle, Kent, England. *Image Bank*

Kent, William (1685–1748) English architect, landscape gardener, and interior designer. Working closely with Richard ▷Burlington, he was foremost in introducing the ▷Palladian style to Britain from Italy, excelling in richly carved, sumptuous interiors and furnishings, as at Holkham Hall, Norfolk, begun in 1734.

Immensely versatile, he also worked in a neo-Gothic style, and was a pioneer of Romantic landscape gardening, for example, the grounds of Stowe House, Buckinghamshire, and Rousham Park, Oxfordshire (1738–40). Horace Walpole called him 'the father of modern gardening'.

Kentigern, St (c. 518–603) Called 'Mungo'. First bishop of Glasgow, born at Culross, Scotland. Anti-Christian factions forced him to flee to Wales, where he founded the monastery of St Asaph. In 573 he returned to Glasgow and founded the cathedral there. Feast day 14 January.

Kenton, Stan(ley Newcomb) (1912–1979) US exponent of progressive jazz. Kenton broke into West Coast jazz in 1941 with his 'wall of brass' sound, noted for its mild experimentations in a self-described 'progressive jazz' style. He helped introduce Afro-Cuban rhythms to US jazz, and combined jazz and classical music in compositions like 'Artistry in Rhythm' (1943), his orchestra's theme song.

Kentucky state in south-central USA. It is nicknamed the Bluegrass State. Kentucky was admitted to the Union in 1792 as the 15th US state. Extending over 640 km/400 mi from east–west, Kentucky has the Ohio River along its entire northern boundary; across which are the states of Ohio, Indiana, and Illinois. To the east, the Tug Fork and Big Sandy rivers separate it from West Virginia. To the southeast, it is bordered by Virginia, with the Cumberland Gap at the extreme south; from this point along its southern boundary, as far as the Mississippi River, it is bordered by Tennessee. Across a small stretch of the Mississippi, on the west, it faces the New Madrid region of Missouri.

population (1995) 3,860,200 **area** 104,700 sq km/40,414 sq mi **capital** Frankfort **towns and cities** Louisville, Lexington, Owensboro, Covington, Bowling Green **industries and products** tobacco, cereals, textiles, coal, whisky, horses, transport vehicles

Kenya see country box.

Kenya, Mount (or **Kirinyaga**) extinct volcano from which Kenya takes its name, height 5,199 m/17,057 ft. It is situated almost exactly on the Equator. The first European to climb it was Halford Mackinder in 1899.

Kenyatta, Jomo (c. 1894–1978) Adopted name of Kamau Ngengi. Kenyan nationalist politician, prime minister from 1963, as well as the first president of Kenya from 1964 until his death. He led the Kenya African Union from 1947 (KANU from 1963) and was active in liberating Kenya from British rule.

A member of the Kikuyu ethnic group, Kenyatta was born near Fort Hall, son of a farmer. Brought up at a Church of Scotland mission, he joined the Kikuyu Central Association (KCA), devoted to recovery of Kikuyu lands from white settlers, and became its president. He spent some years in the UK, returning to Kenya in 1946. He became president of the Kenya African Union (successor to the banned KCA in 1947). In 1953 he was sentenced to seven years' imprisonment for his management of the guerrilla organization ▷Mau Mau, though some doubt has been cast on his complicity. Released to exile in northern Kenya in 1958, he was allowed to return to Kikuyuland in 1961 and became prime minister in 1963 (also president from 1964) of independent Kenya. His slogans were *'Uhuru na moja'* (Freedom and unity) and *'Harambee'* (Let's get going).

Kenzo (1940–) Trade name of Kenzo Takada. Japanese fashion designer. He has been active in France from 1964. He opened his shop Jungle JAP in 1970, and by 1972 he was well established, known initially for unconventional designs based on traditional Japanese clothing. His fabrics are characterized by rich pattern and colour combinations.

Kepler, Johannes (1571–1630) German mathematician and astronomer. He formulated what are now called **Kepler's laws** of planetary motion. Kepler's laws are the basis of our understanding of the Solar System, and such scientists as Isaac ▷Newton built on his ideas.

Kepler was one of the first advocates of Sun-centred cosmology, as put forward by ▷Copernicus. Unlike Copernicus and ▷Galileo, Kepler rejected the Greek and medieval belief that orbits must be circular in order to maintain the fabric of the cosmos in a state of perfection.

Early work Kepler also produced a calendar of predictions for the year 1595. In 1596, he published his *Prodromus dissertationum cosmographicarum seu mysterium cosmographicum* in which he demonstrated that the five Platonic solids (the only five regular polyhedrons) could be fitted alternately inside a series of spheres to form a 'nest'. The nest described quite accurately (within 5%) the distances of the planets from the Sun. Kepler regarded this discovery as a divine inspiration that revealed the secret of the Universe.

In 1601 Kepler was bequeathed all of Tycho ▷Brahe's data on planetary motion. He had already made a bet that, given Tycho's

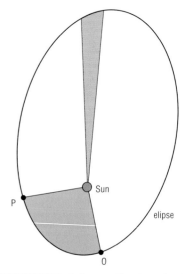

JOHANNES KEPLER Kepler's second law states that the pink-shaded area equals the blue-shaded area if a planet moves from P to O in the same time that it moves from X to Y. The law says, in effect, that a planet moves fastest when it is closest to the Sun.

unfinished tables, he could find an accurate planetary orbit within a week. It was five years before Kepler obtained his first planetary orbit, that of Mars. His analysis of these data led to the discovery of his three laws. In 1604 his attention was diverted from the planets by his observation of the appearance of a new star, 'Kepler's nova'. Kepler had observed the first supernova visible since the one discovered by Brahe in 1572.

Kepler's laws Kepler's first two laws of planetary motion were published in *Astronomia Nova* (1609). The first law stated that planets travel in elliptical rather than circular, or epicyclic, orbits and that the Sun occupies one of the two foci of the ellipses. The second law established the Sun as the main force governing the orbits of the planets. It stated that the line joining the Sun and a planet traverses equal areas of space in equal periods of time, so that the planets move more quickly when they are nearer the Sun. He also suggested that the Sun itself rotates, a theory that was confirmed using Galileo's observations of sunspots, and he postulated that this established some sort of 'magnetic' interaction between the planets and the Sun, driving them in orbit. This idea, although incorrect, was an important precursor of Newton's gravitational theory.

Kepler's third law was published in *De Harmonices Mundi*. It described in precise mathematical language the link between the distances of the planets from the Sun and their velocities – specifically, that the orbital velocity of a planet is inversely proportional to its distance from the Sun.

Rudolphine Tables and other work Kepler finally completed and published the *Rudolphine Tables* (1627) based on Brahe's observations. These were the first modern astronomical tables, enabling astronomers to calculate the positions of the planets at any time in the past, present, or future. The publication also included other vital information, such as a map of the world, a catalogue of stars, and the latest aid to computation, ▷logarithms.

Related Web site: Kepler, Johannes http://es.rice.edu/ES/humsoc/Galileo/People/kepler.html

Kerala state of southwest India; area 38,900 sq km/15,015 sq mi; population (2001 est) 33,462,000. The capital is ▷Trivandrum and Kozhikode and Cochin are other towns. The state extends along the southwest coast from Karnataka almost to the southern tip of India and is bounded on the east by the highlands of the Western Ghats. Industries include textiles, chemicals, electrical goods, and fish. Agricultural products include tea, coffee, rice, coconuts, fruit, and oilseed.

keratin fibrous protein found in the ▷skin of vertebrates and also in hair, nails, claws, hooves, feathers, and the outer coating of horns.

Kerbala (or ▷Karbala) holy city of the Shiite Muslims in Iraq.

kerb crawling accosting women in the street from a motor vehicle for the purposes of ▷prostitution. In the UK, this is an offence under the Sexual Offences Act 1985.

Kerekou, Mathieu Ahmed (1933–) Benin socialist politician and soldier, president 1980–91 and from 1996. In 1972, while deputy head of the Dahomey army, he led a coup to oust the ruling president and establish his own military government.

Kenya

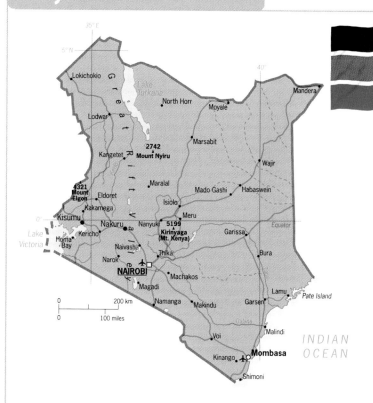

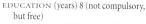

EDUCATION (years) 8 (not compulsory, but free)

LITERACY RATE 91% (men); 80% (women) (2003 est)

LABOUR FORCE 18.6% agriculture, 19.5% industry, 61.9% services (1999)

LIFE EXPECTANCY 44 (men); 46 (women) (2000–05)

CHILD MORTALITY RATE (under 5, per 1,000 live births) 122 (2001)

PHYSICIANS (per 1,000 people) 0.1 (1998 est)

HOSPITAL BEDS (per 1,000 people) 1.8 (1996 est)

TV SETS (per 1,000 people) 26 (2001 est)

RADIOS (per 1,000 people) 221 (2001 est)

INTERNET USERS (per 10,000 people) 125.3 (2002 est)

PERSONAL COMPUTER USERS (per 100 people) 0.6 (2002 est)

See also ▷Kenyatta, Jomo; ▷Mau Mau.

KENYA A market in Kenya. *Image Bank*

Kenya country in east Africa, bounded to the north by Sudan and Ethiopia, to the east by Somalia, to the southeast by the Indian Ocean, to the southwest by Tanzania, and to the west by Uganda.

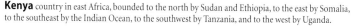

NATIONAL NAME *Jamhuri ya Kenya/Republic of Kenya*

AREA 582,600 sq km/224,941 sq mi

CAPITAL Nairobi

MAJOR TOWNS/CITIES Mombasa, Kisumu, Nakuru, Eldoret, Nyeri

MAJOR PORTS Mombasa

PHYSICAL FEATURES mountains and highlands in west and centre; coastal plain in south; arid interior and tropical coast; semi-desert in north; Great Rift Valley, Mount Kenya, Lake Nakuru (salt lake with world's largest colony of flamingos), Lake Turkana (Rudolf)

Government

HEAD OF STATE AND GOVERNMENT Mwai Kibaki from 2002

POLITICAL SYSTEM authoritarian nationalist

POLITICAL EXECUTIVE unlimited presidency

ADMINISTRATIVE DIVISIONS seven provinces and the Nairobi municipality

ARMED FORCES 24,400; plus paramilitary forces of 5,000 (2002 est)

CONSCRIPTION military service is voluntary

DEATH PENALTY retained and used for ordinary crimes

DEFENCE SPEND (% GDP) 3.2 (2002 est)

EDUCATION SPEND (% GDP) 6.4 (2001 est)

HEALTH SPEND (% GDP) 8.3 (2000 est)

Economy and resources

CURRENCY Kenyan shilling

GPD (US$) 12.1 billion (2002 est)

REAL GDP GROWTH (% change on previous year) 1.2 (2001)

GNI (US$) 11.3 billion (2002 est)

GNI PER CAPITA (PPP) (US$) 990 (2002 est)

CONSUMER PRICE INFLATION 4.8% (2003 est)

UNEMPLOYMENT 30% (urban, 1995 est)

FOREIGN DEBT (US$) 5.6 billion (2001 est)

MAJOR TRADING PARTNERS Uganda, United Arab Emirates, UK, Tanzania, Germany, Japan, Pakistan

RESOURCES soda ash, fluorspar, salt, limestone, rubies, gold, vermiculite, diatonite, garnets

INDUSTRIES food processing, petroleum refining and petroleum products, textiles and clothing, leather products, chemicals, cement, paper and paper products, beverages, tobacco, ceramics, rubber and metal products, vehicle assembly, tourism

EXPORTS coffee, tea, horticultural products, petroleum products, soda ash, cement. Principal market: Uganda 20.4% (2001)

IMPORTS crude petroleum, motor vehicles, industrial machinery, iron and steel, chemicals, basic manufactures. Principal source: United Arab Emirates 14.5% (2001)

ARABLE LAND 7% (2000 est)

AGRICULTURAL PRODUCTS coffee, tea, maize, wheat, sisal, sugar cane, pineapples, cotton, horticulture; dairy products

Population and society

POPULATION 31,987,000 (2003 est)

POPULATION GROWTH RATE 1.5% (2000–15)

POPULATION DENSITY (per sq km) 55 (2003 est)

URBAN POPULATION (% of total) 36 (2003 est)

AGE DISTRIBUTION (% of total population) 0–14 42%, 15–59 54%, 60+ 4% (2002 est)

ETHNIC GROUPS main ethnic groups are the Kikuyu (about 21%), the Luhya (14%), the Luo (13%), the Kalenjin (11%), the Kamba (11%), the Kisii (6%), and the Meru (5%); there are also Asian, Arab, and European minorities

LANGUAGE English, Kiswahili (both official), many local dialects

RELIGION Roman Catholic 28%, Protestant 8%, Muslim 6%, traditional tribal religions

8th century: Arab traders began to settle along coast of East Africa.

16th century: Portuguese defeated coastal states and exerted spasmodic control over them.

18th century: Sultan of Oman reasserted Arab overlordship of East African coast, making it subordinate to Zanzibar.

19th century: Europeans, closely followed by Christian missionaries, began to explore inland.

1887: British East African Company leased area of coastal territory from sultan of Zanzibar.

1895: Britain claimed large inland region as East African Protectorate.

1903: Railway from Mombasa to Uganda built using Indian labourers, many of whom settled in the area; British and South African settlers began to farm highlands.

1920: East African Protectorate became crown colony of Kenya, with legislative council elected by white settlers (and by Indians and Arabs soon afterwards).

1923: Britain rejected demand for internal self-government by white settlers.

1944: First African appointment to legislative council; Kenyan African Union (KAU) founded to campaign for African rights.

1947: Jomo Kenyatta became leader of KAU, which was dominated by Kikuyu tribe.

1952: Mau Mau (Kikuyu secret society) began terrorist campaign to drive white settlers from tribal lands; Mau Mau largely suppressed by 1954 but state of emergency lasted for eight years.

1953: Kenyatta charged with management of Mau Mau activities and imprisoned by the British. He

was released in 1959, but exiled to northern Kenya.

1956: Africans allowed to elect members of legislative council on a restricted franchise.

1960: Britain announced plans to prepare Kenya for majority African rule.

1961: Kenyatta allowed to return to help negotiate Kenya's independence.

1963: Kenya achieved independence with Kenyatta as prime minister.

1964: Kenya became a republic with Kenyatta as president.

1969: Kenya became one-party state under Kenyan African National Union (KANU).

1978: President Kenyatta died and was succeeded by Daniel arap Moi.

1984: There were violent clashes between government troops and the ethnic Somali population at Wajir.

1989: Moi announced the release of political prisoners.

1991: A multiparty system was conceded after an opposition group was launched.

1997: There were demonstrations calling for democratic reform. Constitutional reforms were adopted.

1998: A bomb exploded at the US embassy in Nairobi, killing over 230 people and injuring 5,000; an anti-American Islamic group claimed responsibility.

1999: A framework agreement was signed with the leaders of Uganda and Tanzania, intending to reestablish the East African Community (EAC) which had collapsed in 1977, hoping to lead to a common market and political federation similar to that of the European Union (EU).

He embarked on a programme of 'scientific socialism', changing his country's name to Benin to mark this change of direction. In 1987 he resigned from the army and confirmed a civilian administration. He was re-elected president in 1989, but lost to Nicéphore Soglo in the 1991 presidential elections. He surprisingly won the March 1996 presidential elections despite claims of fraud.

Kerensky, Alexandr Feodorovich (1881–1970) Russian revolutionary politician, prime minister of the second provisional government before its collapse in November 1917, during the ▷Russian Revolution. He was overthrown by the Bolshevik revolution and fled to France in 1918 and to the USA in 1940.

Kerguelen Islands (or **Desolation Islands**) volcanic archipelago in the Indian Ocean, part of the French Southern and Antarctic Territories; area 7,215 km/2,787 sq mi. They were discovered in 1772 by the Breton navigator Yves de Kerguelen and annexed by France in 1949. Uninhabited except for scientists (centre for joint study of geomagnetism with Russia), the islands support a unique wild cabbage containing a pungent oil.

Kérkyra Greek form of ▷Corfu, an island in the Ionian Sea.

Kermanshah (now **Bakhtaran**; Farsi 'city of the kings') capital of Kermanshahan province, northwest Iran, a major city of Iranian Kurdistan; population (1991) 624,100. The province (area 23,700 sq km/9,148 sq mi; population (1991) 1,622,200) is on the Iraqi border. Industries include oil refining, carpets, and textiles. Founded in the 4th century, its prosperity derived from its fertile agricultural hinterland and its site on caravan routes to Baghdad. In the years following the Islamic revolution in 1979 the city and province were known as Bakhtaran.

kernel the inner, softer part of a ▷nut, or of a seed within a hard shell.

kerosene thin oil obtained from the distillation of petroleum; a highly refined form is used in jet aircraft fuel. Kerosene is a mixture of hydrocarbons of the ▷paraffin series.

Kerouac, Jack (Jean Louis) (1922–1969) US novelist. He named and epitomized the ▷Beat Generation of the 1950s. The first of his autobiographical, myth-making books, *The Town and the City* (1950), was followed by the rhapsodic ▷*On the Road* (1957). Other works written with similar free-wheeling energy and inspired by his interests in jazz and Buddhism include *The Dharma Bums* (1958), *Doctor Sax* (1959), and *Desolation Angels* (1965). His major contribution to poetry was *Mexico City Blues* (1959).

Kerouac became a legendary symbol of youthful rebellion from the late 1950s, but before his early death from alcoholism, he had become a semi-recluse, unable to cope with his fame.

Related Web site: Kerouac, Jack http://www.charm.net/~brooklyn/People/JackKerouac.html

JACK KEROUAC After a year at Columbia University, New York, the US poet and writer Jack Kerouac dropped out and travelled around the USA, often working as a labourer while gathering material for his novel. In the late 1950s he was recognized as the voice of the rebellious young and it was he who named them the Beat Generation. *Archive Photos*

Kerry county of the Republic of Ireland, west of Cork, in the province of Munster; county town Tralee; area 4,700 sq km/1,814 sq mi; population (1996) 126,100. Industries include engineering, woollens, shoes, cutlery, fishing, and farming (dairy farming in the north, cattle grazing in the south). Tourism is important; Muckross House and Abbey are among the top visitor attractions. Other towns include Caherciveen, Castleisland, Dingle, Killarney, and Listowel. Kerry is low-lying in the north and mountainous in the south, with the Slieve Mish and Caha Mountains, and ▷Macgillycuddy's Reeks, where Carrauntoohill (Ireland's highest peak at 1,041m/3,415 ft) is situated; other peaks include Brandon (953 m/3,127 ft) and Mangerton (840 m/2,756 ft).

Related Web site: Kerry Insight http://www.kerry-insight.com/

KERRY A beehive stone structure at Skellig, County Kerry, Republic of Ireland. These distinctive structures, known as *clochans*, were used as monks' cells, and can be found on a number of offshore islands, including Bishop's Island (County Clare), High Island (County Galway), and Innishmurray (County Sligo). *Image Bank*

Kerry blue terrier compact and sturdy dog, with a soft, full coat of bluish tone. It is 46 cm/18 in high and weighs 15–17 kg/33–37.4 lb. Its ears lie close to the head and it has a thin tail that is held erect.

Kerry, John Forbes (1943–) US Democratic Party politician, Senator for Massachusetts from 1984 and Democrat candidate for the presidency in 2004. A decorated Vietnam War veteran, he came back as an outspoken opponent of the war and gained national fame in 1971 when he testified on Vietnam to the Senate Foreign Relations Committee. He supported the 2003 US-led war against Iraq, but later came to believe that President George W Bush had misled the American people.

> **Jack Kerouac**
> *I had nothing to offer anybody except my own confusion.*
> On the Road

Kesselring, Albert (1885–1960) German field marshal in World War II, commander of the Luftwaffe (air force) 1939–40, during the invasions of Poland and the Low Countries and the early stages of the Battle of Britain. He later served under Field Marshal Rommel in North Africa, took command in Italy in 1943, and was commander-in-chief on the western front March in 1945. His death sentence for war crimes at the Nürnberg trials in 1947 was commuted to life imprisonment, but he was released in 1952.

kestrel (or **windhover**) small hawk that breeds in Europe, Asia, and Africa. About 30 cm/1 ft long, the male has a bluish-grey head and tail and is light chestnut brown back with black spots on the back and pale with black spots underneath. The female is slightly larger and reddish brown above, with bars; she does not have the bluish-grey head. The kestrel hunts mainly by hovering in midair while searching for prey. It feeds on small mammals, insects, frogs, and worms. (Species *Falco tinnunculus*, family Falconidae, order Falconiformes.)

The kestrel rarely builds its own nest, but uses those of other birds, such as crows and magpies, or scrapes a hole on a cliff-ledge. It is found all over Europe and Asia and most parts of Africa, and most birds migrate southwards in winter.

The **lesser kestrel** (*Falco naumanni*) is an inhabitant of southern Europe. The **American kestrel** or **sparrowhawk** (*F. sparverius*) is somewhat smaller, and occurs in most of North America. It is russet, grey, and tan in colour, with the male having more grey on its wings.

In the British Isles, the population of *F. tinnunculus* has increased greatly in recent years.

ketone member of the group of organic compounds containing the carbonyl group (C=O) bonded to two atoms of carbon (instead of one carbon and one hydrogen as in ▷aldehydes). Ketones are liquids or low-melting-point solids, slightly soluble in water. An example is propanone (acetone, CH_3COCH_3, used as a solvent.

kettle hole pit or depression formed when a block of ice from a receding glacier becomes isolated and buried in glacial debris (till). As the block melts the till collapses to form a hollow, which may become filled with water to form a kettle lake or pond. Kettle holes range from 5 m/15 ft to 13 km/8 mi in diameter, and may exceed 33 m/100 ft in depth.

Kew Gardens popular name for the Royal Botanic Gardens, Kew, Surrey, England. They were founded in 1759 by Augusta of Saxe-Coburg (1719–1772), the mother of King George III, as a small garden and were passed to the nation by Queen Victoria in 1840. By then they had expanded to almost their present size of 149 hectares/368 acres and since 1841 have been open daily to the public. They contain a collection of over 25,000 living plant species and many fine buildings. The gardens are also a centre for botanical research.

key in music, the ▷diatonic scale around which a piece of music is written. For example, a passage in the key of C major uses mainly the notes of the C major scale, and harmonies made up of the notes of that scale. The first note of the scale is known as the ▷tonic; it gives the name of the key and is the note on which the music usually starts and finishes.

keyboard in computing, an input device resembling a typewriter keyboard, used to enter instructions and data. There are many variations on the layout and labelling of keys. Extra numeric keys may be added, as may special-purpose function keys, whose effects can be defined by programs in the computer.

Keynes, John Maynard (1883–1946) 1st Baron Keynes. English economist. His *General Theory of Employment, Interest, and Money* (1936) proposed the prevention of financial crises and unemployment by adjusting demand through government control of credit and currency. He is responsible for that part of economics that studies whole economies, now known as ▷macroeconomics.

Keynes led the British delegation at the Bretton Woods Conference in 1944, which set up the International Monetary Fund.

His theories were widely accepted in the aftermath of World War II, and he was one of the most influential economists of the 20th century. His ideas are today often contrasted with ▷monetarism, the theory that economic policy should be based on control of the money supply. He was made a baron in 1942.

Keynes was a fellow of King's College, Cambridge. He worked at the Treasury during World War I, and took part in the peace conference as chief Treasury representative, but resigned in protest against the financial terms of the treaty. He justified his action in *The Economic Consequences of the Peace* (1919).

> **John Maynard Keynes**
> *But this long run is a misleading guide to current affairs. In the long run we are all dead.*
> A Tract on Monetary Reform

Keynesian economics the economic theory of English economist John Maynard Keynes, which argues that a fall in national income, lack of demand for goods, and rising unemployment should be countered by increased government expenditure to stimulate the economy. It is opposed by monetarists (see ▷monetarism).

key stage in Britain, the National Curriculum term for the stages of a pupil's progress through school. There are four key stages, each ending with a national standard attainment test (SAT). The key stages are the years 5–7, 7–11, 11–14, and 14–17. Key Stage 1 covers the years 5–7. GCSE is the test for pupils at the end of Key Stage 4.

kg symbol for ▷kilogram.

KESTREL The dainty Madagascar kestrel *Falco newtoni*, whose main prey is often lizards. It is superficially similar to the common European kestrel, with which it also shares the habit of nesting on buildings and living successfully alongside humans. *Premaphotos Wildlife*

KGB secret police of the USSR, the **Komitet Gosudarstvennoy Bezopasnosti** (Committee of State Security), which was in control of frontier and general security and the forced-labour system. KGB officers held key appointments in all fields of daily life, reporting to administration offices in every major town. On the demise of the USSR in 1991, the KGB was superseded by the Federal Counterintelligence Service, which was renamed the Federal Security Service (FSB) in April 1995, when its powers were expanded to enable it to combat corruption and organized crime, and to undertake foreign-intelligence gathering. Its main successor is the Russian Federal Security Service (FSB), which focuses on 'economic security' and combating foreign espionage.

Khabarovsk large krai (territory) in the Russian Far East; area 824,600 sq km/318,378 sq mi; population (1996) 1,571,000 (81% urban). The capital is Khabarovsk, and other towns include Birobidzhan, Okhotsk, Komsomolsk-na-Amure, and Sovetskaya Gavan. The territory extends for over 2,000 km/1,243 mi along the eastern Siberian coast north of the Manchuria and the Amur River, almost entirely enclosing the Sea of Okhotsk. It encompasses the ▷Jewish Autonomous Region (Oblast). It is mountainous and extensively forested, with a cold monsoonal climate. Mineral resources include gold, coal, tin, iron ore, manganese, and molybdenum. Industries include engineering, mining, metallurgy, pulp and paper production; lumbering and fishing.

Khachaturian, Aram Il'yich (1903–1978) Armenian composer. His use of folk themes is shown in the ballets *Gayaneh* (1942), which includes the 'Sabre Dance', and *Spartacus* (1956).

Khaddhafi (or **Gaddafi** or **Qaddafi**), **Moamer al** (1942–) Libyan revolutionary leader. Overthrowing King Idris in 1969, he became virtual president of a republic, although he nominally gave up all except an ideological role in 1974. He favours territorial expansion in North Africa reaching as far as the Democratic Republic of Congo (formerly Zaire), has supported rebels in Chad, and has proposed mergers with a number of countries. During the ▷Gulf War, however, he advocated diplomacy rather than war. Imbued with Nasserism, he was to develop afterwards his own theories (*Green Book*), based on what he called 'natural socialism' of an egalitarian nature.

Khaddhafi's alleged complicity in international terrorism led to his country's diplomatic isolation during the 1980s and in 1992 United Nations sanctions were imposed against Libya after his refusal to allow extradiction of two suspects in the Lockerbie and Union de Transports Aériens bombings.

In 1995 Khaddhafi faced an escalating campaign of violence by militant Islamicists, the strongest challenge to his regime to date. In 2000 a hostage crisis in the Philippines, in which the Abu Sayyaf muslim guerrilla kidnapped people of various nationalities who were holidaying in the area, was mediated by Libya. The country agreed to pay $24 million/£16 million in ransom money for the hostages remaining in September 2000. The money was taken from the Khaddhafi International Association for Charitable Organizations, with Khaddhafi appearing to hope that by ending the Jolo island crisis his image on the international stage would be further enhanced and his country might win a more respectable role.

Khakass (or **Khakasiya**) republic of the Russian Federation, in southern Siberia, adjacent to ▷Krasnoyarsk krai (territory); area 61,900 sq km/23,900 sq mi; population (1996) 586,000 (72% urban) (80% Russians, 11% Khakass). The capital is ▷Abakan and Chernogorsk is another town. The republic is situated between the Kuznetsky Alatau Mountains in the west and the Sayan Mountains in the southeast. It is located in the Minusinsk Basin west of the upper River Yenisey. Coal, iron-ore, and gold deposits are found here. Industries include mining and lumbering; hydroelectric power generation (at Sayanogorsk on the Yenisey); and breeding of sheep, goats, and cattle.

al-Khalil Arabic name for ▷Hebron in the Israeli-occupied West Bank.

Khalistan projected independent Sikh state. See ▷Sikhism.

Khalsa the brotherhood of the Sikhs, created by Guru Gobind Singh at the festival of Baisakhi in 1699. The Khalsa was originally founded as a militant group to defend the Sikh community from persecution.

Khama, Seretse (1921–1980) Botswanan politician, prime minister of Bechuanaland in 1965, and first president of Botswana 1966–80. He founded the Bechuanaland Democratic Party in 1962 and led his country to independence in 1966. Botswana prospered under his leadership, both economically and politically, and he won every post-independence election until his death in July 1980. He was knighted in 1966.

khamsin hot southeasterly wind that blows from the Sahara desert over Egypt and parts of the Middle East from late March to May or June. It is called *sharav* in Israel.

Khan, Imran Niazi (1952–) Pakistani cricketer and politician. In cricket he was an all-rounder, and played in England for both Worcestershire and Sussex, making his test debut in 1971. He played 88 test matches for Pakistan, of which 48 were as captain. In 1992 he captained his country to victory in the World Cup. He scored 17,771 first-class runs at an average of 36.87, and took 1,287 wickets at an average of 22.32. He retired from cricket in 1992, and moved into Pakistani politics in 1996, launching the Pakistan Tehreek-e-Insaaf (PTI; in English the Pakistani Justice Movement). However, the party failed to win a single seat in the 1997 election. Despite an apparent lack of public support, Khan has remained the chair of the party.

Khan, Jahangir (1963–) Pakistani squash player. He won the World Open championship a record six times 1981–85 and 1988, and was World Amateur champion in 1979, 1983, and 1985. He announced his retirement in 1993.

Khardung Pass road linking the Indian town of Leh with the high-altitude military outpost on the Siachen Glacier at an altitude of 5,401 m/17,730 ft in the Karakoram range, Kashmir. It is thought to be the highest road in the world.

Kharkov (Ukrainian **Kharkiv**) major city in eastern Ukraine, capital of the Kharkov oblast, 400 km/250 mi east of Kiev and 40km/25 mi south of the border with the Russian Federation; population (1990) 1,618,000. An important railway junction and industrial city, Kharkov is situated at the confluence of the Kharkov, Lopan, and Udy rivers, and lies close to the ▷Donets Basin coalfield and ▷Krivoy Rog iron mines. Its industrial enterprises include engineering and railway rolling-stock works, agricultural and mining machinery factories, and chemical plants.

Khartoum capital and trading centre of Sudan, in Khartoum State, at the junction of the Blue and White Nile rivers; population (1998 est) 1,038,600, and of Khartoum North, across the Blue Nile, 890,000. ▷Omdurman is also a suburb of Khartoum, giving the urban area a population of over 3 million. It has long served as a major communications centre between the Arab countries of North Africa and central African countries. The city lies in a rich cotton-growing area and an oil pipeline reached it from Port Sudan on the Red Sea. Industries include tanning, textiles, light engineering, food processing, glassware, and printing.

> **Nikita Khrushchev**
> *We are in favour of a détente, but if anybody thinks that for this reason we shall forget about Marx, Engels, and Lenin, he is mistaken. This will happen when shrimps learn to whistle.*
> At Geneva conference July 1955

Khashoggi, Adnan (1935–) Saudi entrepreneur and arms dealer who built up a large property company, Triad, based in Switzerland, and through ownership of banks, hotels, and real estate became a millionaire. In 1975 he was accused by the USA of receiving bribes to secure military contracts in Arab countries, and in 1986 he was financially disadvantaged by the slump in oil prices and political problems in Sudan. In April 1989 he was arrested in connection with illegal property deals. He successfully weathered all three setbacks.

khedive title granted by the Turkish sultan to his Egyptian viceroy in 1867, retained by succeeding rulers until 1914.

Khmer (or **Kmer**) the largest ethnic group in Cambodia, numbering about 7 million. Khmer minorities also live in eastern Thailand and South Vietnam. The Khmer language belongs to the Mon-Khmer family of Austro-Asiatic languages.

Khmer Republic former name (1970–76) of ▷Cambodia.

Khmer Rouge communist movement in Cambodia (Kampuchea) formed in the 1960s. Controlling the country 1974–78, it was responsible for mass deportations and executions under the leadership of ▷Pol Pot. Since then it has conducted guerrilla warfare, and in 1991 gained representation in the governing body.

The Khmer Rouge formed the largest opposition group to the US-backed regime led by Lon Nol 1970–75. By 1974 they controlled the countryside, and in 1975 captured the capital, Phnom Penh. Initially former prime minister Prince ▷Sihanouk was installed as head of state, but internal disagreements led to the creation of the Pol Pot government 1976. From 1978, when Vietnam invaded the country, the Khmer Rouge conducted a guerrilla campaign against the Vietnamese forces. Pol Pot retired as military leader in 1985 and was succeeded by the more moderate Khieu Samphan. After the withdrawal of Vietnamese forces in 1989, the Khmer Rouge continued its warfare against the Vietnamese-backed government. A UN-brokered peace treaty in October 1991 between Cambodia's four warring factions gave the Khmer Rouge its share of representation in the ruling Supreme National Council, but failed to win a renunciation of the guerrillas' goal of regaining domination of Cambodia. Fighting between Khmer Rouge and government forces continued into 1994.

Khoikhoi (formerly **Hottentot**; *Khoi-khoin* 'men of men') member of any of several peoples living in Namibia and Cape Province of South Africa. They number about 30,000. Their language is related to San (spoken by the Kung) and uses clicks for certain consonants; it belongs to the Khoisan family. The Khoikhoi once inhabited a wider area, but were driven into the Kalahari Desert by invading Bantu peoples and Dutch colonists in the 18th century. They live as nomadic hunter-gatherers, in family groups, and have animist beliefs.

Khoisan the smallest group of languages in Africa. It includes fewer than 50 languages, spoken mainly by the people of the Kalahari Desert (including the Khoikhoi and Kung). Two languages from this group are spoken in Tanzania. The Khoisan languages are known for their click consonants (clicking sounds made with the tongue, which function as consonants).

Khomeini, Ayatollah Ruhollah (1900–1989) Iranian Shiite Muslim leader. Exiled from 1964 for his opposition to Shah Pahlavi, he returned when the shah left the country in 1979, and established a fundamentalist Islamic republic. His rule was marked by a protracted war with Iraq, and suppression of opposition within Iran, executing thousands of opponents.

Related Web site: Khomeini, Ayatollah Ruhollah http://www.pathfinder.com/time/time100/leaders/profile/khomeini.html

Khorana, Har Gobind (1922–) Indian-born US biochemist who was awarded a Nobel Prize for Physiology or Medicine in 1968 for his part in the interpretation of genetic code and its function in protein synthesis. In 1976 he led the team that first synthesized a biologically active ▷gene. His work provides much of the basis for gene therapy and biotechnology.

Khrushchev, Nikita Sergeyevich (1894–1971) Soviet politician, secretary general of the Communist Party 1953–64, premier 1958–64. He emerged as leader from the power struggle following Stalin's death and was the first official to denounce Stalin, in 1956. His de-Stalinization programme gave rise to revolts in Poland and Hungary in 1956. Because of problems with the economy and foreign affairs (a breach with China in 1960; conflict with the USA in the ▷Cuban missile crisis of 1962), he was ousted by Leonid Brezhnev and Alexei Kosygin.

Born near Kursk, the son of a miner, Khrushchev fought in the post-Revolutionary civil war 1917–20, and in World War II organized the guerrilla defence of his native Ukraine. He denounced Stalinism in a secret session of the party in February 1956.

Many victims of the purges of the 1930s were either released or posthumously rehabilitated, but when Hungary revolted in October 1956 against Soviet domination, there was immediate Soviet intervention. In 1958 Khrushchev succeeded Bulganin as chair of the council of ministers (prime minister). His policy of competition with capitalism was successful in the space programme, which launched the world's first satellite (▷*Sputnik*). Because of the Cuban crisis and the personal feud with Mao Zedong that led to the Sino-Soviet split, he was compelled to resign in 1964, although by 1965 his reputation was to some extent officially restored. In April 1989 his 'secret speech' against Stalin in February 1956 was officially published for the first time.

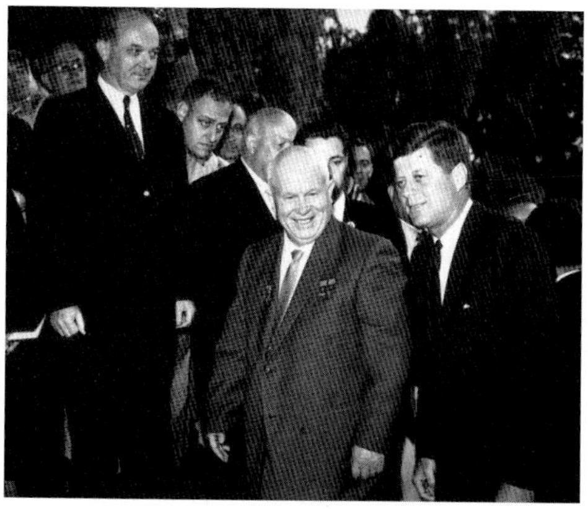

NIKITA KHRUSHCHEV The Soviet leader, photographed in 1961 with US president John F Kennedy in Vienna, Austria, was a strong supporter of the Russian space programme and of competition with the USA. *Archive Photos*

Khulna capital of Khulna region, southwestern Bangladesh, situated close to the Ganges delta; population (1991) 545,800. Industry includes shipbuilding and textiles; it trades in jute, rice, salt, sugar, and oilseed.

Khuzestan province of southwest Iran, on the northern shores of the Gulf; area 66,560 sq km/25,700 sq mi; population (1991) 3,175,900. It has Iran's chief oil resources. Cities include the administrative centre of ▷Ahvaz and the ports of ▷Abadan and Khorramshahr. A large proportion of the population is Arab. The province is often referred to by Arabs as Arabistan.

Khwārizmī, al-, Muhammad ibn-Mūsā (*c.* 780–*c.* 850) Persian mathematician. He wrote a book on algebra, from part of whose title (*al-jabr*) comes the word 'algebra', and a book in which he introduced to the West the Hindu–Arabic decimal number system. The word 'algorithm' is a corruption of his name. He was born in Khwarizm (now Khiva, Uzbekistan), but lived and worked in Baghdad. He compiled astronomical tables and was responsible for introducing the concept of zero into Arab mathematics.

Khyber Pass pass through the mountain range that separates Pakistan from Afghanistan; length 53 km/33 mi; width varies from 140 m/460 ft at its widest to about 15 m/50 ft at its narrowest. On either side are rock faces rising to a height of 915 m/3,000 ft in some places, the highest point at Landi Kotal, 520 m/1,700 ft higher than Jamrud at the entrance to the pass. The Khyber Pass was used by invaders of India. The present road was constructed by the British during the Afghan Wars (1839–42 and 1878–80).

Kiangsi alternative spelling of ▷Jiangxi, a province of China.

Kiangsu alternative spelling of ▷Jiangsu, a province of China.

kibbutz Israeli communal collective settlement with collective ownership of all property and earnings, collective organization of work and decision-making, and communal housing for children. A modified version, the *Moshav Shitufi*, is similar to the collective farms that were typical of the USSR. Other Israeli cooperative rural settlements include the *Moshav Ovdim*, which has equal opportunity, and the similar but less strict *Moshav* settlement.

Kickapoo (Algonquian 'he moves about') ▷American Indian people numbering about 3,200 (1996) and living in Oklahoma (2,000), Kansas (500), and Texas (700). An Algonquian-speaking people, the Kickapoo originated in the Great Lakes region and were once part of the Shawnee ethnic group.

Kidd, 'Captain' William (*c.* 1645–1701) Scottish pirate who privateered for the British against the French off the North American coast, and in 1695 was given a royal commission to suppress piracy in the Indian Ocean. Instead, he joined a group of pirates in Madagascar. In 1699, on his way to Boston, Massachusetts, he was arrested, taken to England, and hanged.

kidnapping the abduction of a person against his or her will. It often involves holding persons for ransom. It may also take place in child-custody disputes or involve psychosexual motives.

kidney in vertebrates, one of a pair of organs responsible for fluid regulation, excretion of waste products, and maintaining the ionic composition of the blood. The kidneys are situated on the rear wall of the abdomen. Each one consists of a number of long tubules (see ▷nephron); the outer parts filter the aqueous components of blood, and the inner parts selectively reabsorb vital salts, leaving waste products in the remaining fluid (urine), which is passed through the ureter to the bladder.

The action of the kidneys is vital, although if one is removed, the other enlarges to take over its function. A patient with two defective kidneys may continue near-normal life with the aid of a kidney machine or continuous ambulatory peritoneal ▷dialysis (CAPD); or a kidney transplant may be recommended. Other diseases of the kidney can include the formation of kidney stones. These hard stones can build up as a result of high levels of blood calcium or high levels of uric acid, and can cause intense pain as they travel down the ureter, as well as causing bleeding in the tissues of the urinary tract.

kidney machine medical equipment used in ▷dialysis.

Kiefer, Anselm (1945–) German neo-expressionist painter. He studied under Joseph ▷Beuys and his works include monumental landscapes on varied surfaces, often with the paint built up into heavily textured impasto with other substances. Much of his neo-expressionist work deals with recent German history.

Kiel Baltic port and capital of Schleswig-Holstein, Germany; population (1995) 247,300. It is a naval and commercial facility. Chief industries include fishing, marine engineering, ship-repairing, electronics, engineering, food-processing, and tourism. It is at the terminus of the ▷Kiel Canal. **Kiel Week** in June is a major yachting venue. In World War I it was the headquarters of the German Imperial Fleet.

Kiel Canal (German **Nord-Ostsee Kanal**; formerly **Kaiser Wilhelm Canal**) waterway connecting the Baltic with the North Sea; 96 km/60 mi long. It provides passage for ocean-going vessels. Built by Germany in the years before World War I, the canal allowed the German navy to move from its Baltic bases to the open sea without travelling through international waters. It was declared an international waterway by the Treaty of Versailles in 1919.

Kierkegaard, Søren Aabye (1813–1855) Danish philosopher and theologian, often considered to be the founder of ▷existentialism. He argued that no system of thought could explain the unique experience of the individual. He defended Christianity, suggesting that God cannot be known through reason, but only through a 'leap of faith'. His chief works are *Enten-Eller/Either-Or* (1843) and *Begrebet Angest/Concept of Dread* (1844).

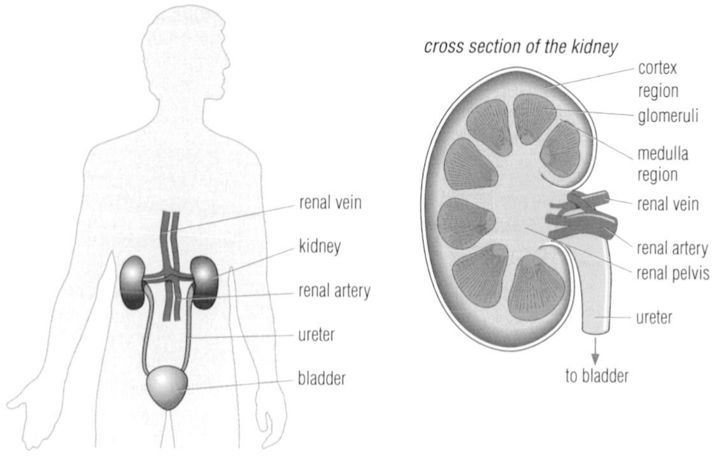
renal vein
kidney
renal artery
ureter
bladder
cross section of the kidney
cortex region
glomeruli
medulla region
renal vein
renal artery
renal pelvis
ureter
to bladder

KIDNEY The diagrams above show how the kidney functions. Blood enters the kidney through the renal artery. The blood is filtered through the glomeruli to extract the nitrogenous waste products and excess water that make up urine. The urine flows through the ureter to the bladder; the cleaned blood then leaves the kidney via the renal vein.

Kieślowski, Krzysztof (1941–1996) Polish film director and screenwriter. One of the great European auteurs of the 1980s and 1990s, his films are often personal narratives with broader moral and political implications. His 'Three Colours' trilogy – *Trois couleurs: Bleu/Blue* (1993), *Trois couleurs: Blanc/White* (1993), and *Trois couleurs: Rouge/Red* (1994) – is based on the French flag and the concepts of liberty, equality, and fraternity.

Kieślowski began his film career making documentaries during the 1970s, before directing such feature films as *Amator/Camera Buff* (1979), *Przypadek/Blind Chance* (1981), and *Bez Końca/No End* (1984). He won international recognition for his series of ten short television films *Dekalog/Decalogue* (1988), which offered contemporary readings of the Ten Commandments. Two of these were made into feature-length films, *Krotki film o milosci/A Short Film About Killing* and *Krotki film o zabijaniu/A Short Film About Love* (both 1988). These were followed by the Franco-Polish coproduction *La Double Vie de Véronique/The Double Life of Veronique* (1991).

Related Web site: Krzysztof Kieslowski Home Page http://www-personal.engin.umich.edu/~zbigniew/Kieslowski/kieslowski.html

Kiev (Ukrainian **Kyiv**) capital and largest city of Ukraine, situated at the confluence of the Desna and Dnieper rivers; population (1990) 2,616,000. Kiev was the capital of Russia in the Middle Ages. It is a major industrial centre, producing chemicals, clothing, leather goods, machine tools, and electrical goods, and is also a market city for the abundant agricultural produce of the western Ukraine. Kiev University was founded in 1834.

Features St Sophia cathedral, the oldest cathedral in Ukraine (11th century) and Kiev-Pechersky Monastery (both now museums) survive, together with the remains of the Golden Gate, an arched entrance to the old walled city, built in 1037. The gate is surmounted by the small Church of the Annunciation. The Kiev ballet and opera companies are renowned worldwide.

History Kiev was founded in the 5th century by ▷Vikings. The Slav domination of Russia began with the rise of Kiev, the 'mother of Russian cities'; Kiev replaced ▷Novgorod as the capital of the state of Kievan Rus in 882 and was the original centre of the Orthodox Christian faith from 988. It was for a long time an important trading centre on the route from the Baltic to the Black Sea, but declined in importance in the 12th century. The Russian capital was moved to Vladimir in 1169, and Kiev was sacked by Mongols under Batu Khan in 1240. From the 14th–late 17th centuries, the city was successively under Tatar, Lithuanian and Polish control. It was annexed by Russia in 1686. In World War II, Kiev, then the third-largest city of the USSR, was occupied and largely destroyed by German forces 1941–43. During this period, around 200,000 of the city's inhabitants, including its entire Jewish population, were murdered.

Kigali capital of ▷Rwanda, central Africa, 80 km/50 mi east of Lake Kivu; population (2001 est) 327,700. Products include coffee, tea, hides, textiles, cigarettes, shoes, paints, and varnishes.

Kikuyu member of the dominant ethnic group in Kenya, numbering about 3 million. The Kikuyu are primarily cultivators of millet, although many have entered the professions. Their language belongs to the Bantu branch of the Niger-Congo family.

Kildare county of the Republic of Ireland, in the province of Leinster; county town Naas; area 1,690 sq km/ 652 sq mi; population (1996) 135,000. The principal rivers are the Barrow, the Boyne, the Lesser Barrow, and the Liffey. Kildare is wet and boggy in the north with extensive grassy plains and rolling hills, and includes part of the Bog of Allen. The town of Maynooth houses a constituent part of the National University of Ireland; originally the college was a seminary for Roman Catholic priests. The Curragh, at Tully, is a plain that is the site of the national stud and headquarters of Irish horse racing; steeplechase racing also takes place at Punchestown. Cattle are grazed in the north, and in the south products include oats, barley, potatoes, and cattle. Other main towns include Athy, Droichead Nua, and Kildare.

Kilimanjaro volcano in ▷Tanzania, the highest mountain in Africa, 5,895 m/19,340 ft. It is situated between Lake Victoria and the coast. It culminates in two peaks, Kibo (5,895 m/19,340 ft) and Mawenzi (5,149 m/16,893 ft), both craters of extinct volcanoes. The first recorded ascent was by the German geographer Hans Meyer and the Austrian mountaineer Ludwig Purtscheller in 1889.

Kilkenny county of the Republic of Ireland, in the province of Leinster; county town Kilkenny; area 2,060 sq km/795 sq mi; population (1996) 75,300. It has the rivers Nore, Suir, and Barrow. Industries include coalmining, clothing, footwear, brewing, and agricultural activities include cattle rearing and dairy farming. Principal towns include Castlecomer, Callan, Graiguenamanagh, and Thomastown.

Related Web site: Welcome to Country Kilkenny, Ireland http://www.countykilkenny.com/

killer whale (or **orca**) toothed whale belonging to the dolphin family, found in all seas of the world. It is black on top, white below, and grows up to 9 m/30 ft long. It is the only whale that has been observed to prey on other whales, as well as on seals and seabirds. (Species *Orcinus orca*, family Delphinidae.)

It has been tamed and trained to perform for audiences and has proved to be gentle, friendly, intelligent, and hard working.

Related Web site: Killer Whales http://www.seaworld.org/killer_whale/killerwhales.html

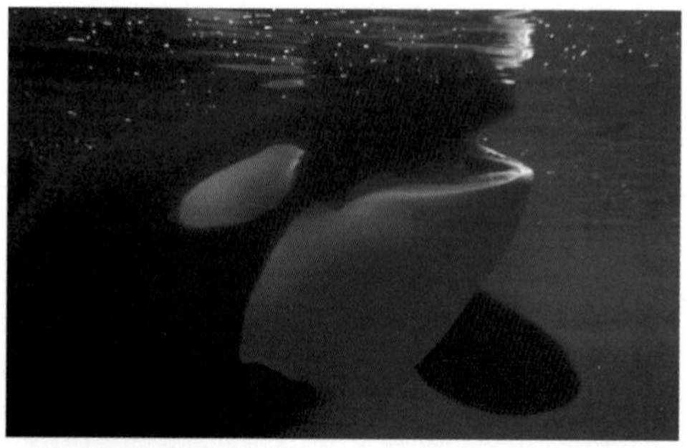

KILLER WHALE There have been no known instances of killer whales attacking and killing humans. They live in groups of up to 50 individuals and often swim in formation. *Image Bank*

Killiecrankie, Battle of in British history, during the first ▷Jacobite uprising, defeat on 27 July 1689 of General Mackay (for William of Orange) by John Graham of ▷Claverhouse, Viscount Dundee, a supporter of James II, at Killiecrankie, Scotland. Despite the victory, Claverhouse was killed by a chance shot and the revolt soon petered out; the remaining forces were routed at Dunkeld on 21 August.

The battle was for control of the strategically important Blair Castle in Perthshire. Claverhouse's Highlanders spent several weeks plundering the Lowlands before Mackay moved north from Dunkeld with a force of about 3,000 solders. Claverhouse's army, which was inferior in numbers, was stationed along the Pass of Killiecrankie. Barefoot and armed with claymores, they suddenly rushed upon the marching troops down the steep sides of the gorge. Mackay's men were untrained, and they broke and fled.

kiln high-temperature furnace used commercially for drying timber, roasting metal ores, or for making cement, bricks, and pottery. Oil- or gas-fired kilns are used to bake ceramics at up to 1,760°C/3,200°F; electric kilns do not generally reach such high temperatures.

kilo- prefix denoting multiplication by 1,000, as in kilohertz, a unit of frequency equal to 1,000 hertz.

kilobyte (**K** or **KB**) in computing, a unit of memory equal to 1,024 ▷bytes. It is sometimes used, less precisely, to mean 1,000 bytes. In the metric system, the prefix 'kilo-' denotes multiplication by 1,000 (as in kilometre, a unit equal to 1,000 metres). However, computer memory size is based on the ▷binary number system, and the most convenient binary equivalent of 1,000 is 2^{10}, or 1,024.

kilogram SI unit (symbol kg) of mass equal to 1,000 grams (2.24 lb). It is defined as a mass equal to that of the international prototype, a platinum-iridium cylinder held at the International Bureau of Weights and Measures in Sèvres, France.

kilometre unit of length (symbol km) equal to 1,000 metres, equivalent to 3,280.89 ft or 0.6214 (about $\frac{5}{8}$) of a mile.

kilowatt unit (symbol kW) of power equal to 1,000 watts or about 1.34 horsepower.

kilowatt-hour commercial unit of electrical energy (symbol kWh), defined as the work done by a power of 1,000 watts in one hour and equal to 3.6 megajoules. It is used to calculate the cost of electrical energy taken from the domestic supply.

Kim Il Sung (1912–1994) North Korean communist politician and marshal. He became prime minister in 1948 and led North Korea in the ▷Korean War 1950–53. He became president in 1972, retaining the presidency of the Communist Workers' party. He liked to be known as the 'Great Leader' and campaigned constantly for the reunification of Korea. His son **Kim Jong Il**, known as the 'Dear Leader', succeeded him.

Kim Jong Il (1942–) North Korean communist politician, national leader from 1994, when he succeeded his father, ▷Kim Il Sung in what was the first dynastic succession in the communist world. Despite his official designation 'Dear Leader', he lacked his father's charisma and did not automatically inherit the public adulation accorded to him. In October 1997 he formally became general secretary of the ruling communist party amid famine in North Korea.

Kim Young Sam (1927–) South Korean democratic politician, president 1993–98. In 1990 he merged the National Democratic Party (NNP) with the ruling party to form the Democratic Liberal Party (DLP), now known as the New Korean Party. In the December 1992 presidential election he captured 42% of the national vote, assuming office in February 1993. As president, he encouraged greater political openness, some deregulation of the economy, and a globalization (segyehwa) initiative.

Kimberley diamond-mining capital city of Northern Cape Province, South Africa, 153 km/95 mi northwest of Bloemfontein, and 1,223 m/4,012 ft above sea level; population (1991) 167,100. Its mines have been controlled by De Beers Consolidated Mines since 1887. It is an important railway junction.

kimberlite an igneous rock that is ultramafic (containing very little silica); a type of alkaline ▷peridotite with a porphyritic texture (larger crystals in a fine-grained matrix), containing mica in addition to olivine and other minerals. Kimberlite represents the world's principal source of diamonds.

kimono traditional Japanese costume. Worn in the Heian period (more than 1,000 years ago), it is still used by women for formal wear and informally by men.

kindergarten (German 'children's garden') another term for ▷nursery school.

kinesis (plural **kineses**) in biology, a nondirectional movement in response to a stimulus; for example, woodlice move faster in drier surroundings. **Taxis** is a similar pattern of behaviour, but there the response is directional.

kinetic art in the visual arts, a work of art (usually sculpture) that incorporates real or apparent movement (from the Greek word for movement, *kinesis*). The term was coined by Naum Gabo and Antoine Pevsner in a manifesto of constructivist art (see ▷constructivism) issued in Moscow in 1920 and known as the 'Realist Manifesto'. ▷Op art is sometimes counted as a type of kinetic art, as Op paintings give an illusion of movement because they appear to flicker. Kinetic art also sometimes merges with other types of avant-garde art, including ▷performance art.

kinetic energy the energy of a body resulting from motion. It is contrasted with ▷potential energy.

The kinetic energy of a moving body is equal to the work that would have to be done in bringing that body to rest, and is dependent upon both the body's mass and speed. The kinetic energy in joules of a mass m kg travelling with speed v m s^{-1} is given by the formula:

$$KE = \frac{mv^2}{2}$$

All atoms and molecules possess some amount of kinetic energy because they are all in some state of motion (see ▷kinetic theory). Adding heat energy to a substance increases the mean kinetic energy and hence the mean speed of its constituent molecules – a change that is reflected as a rise in the temperature of that substance.

kinetics the branch of chemistry that investigates the rates of chemical reactions.

kinetics branch of ▷dynamics dealing with the action of forces producing or changing the motion of a body; **kinematics** deals with motion without reference to force or mass.

kinetic theory theory describing the physical properties of matter in terms of the behaviour – principally movement – of its component atoms or molecules. The temperature of a substance is dependent on the velocity of movement of its constituent particles, increased temperature being accompanied by increased movement. A gas consists of rapidly moving atoms or molecules and, according to kinetic theory, it is their continual impact on the walls of the containing vessel that accounts for the pressure of the gas. The slowing of molecular motion as temperature falls, according to kinetic theory, accounts for the physical properties of liquids and solids, culminating in the concept of no molecular motion at ▷absolute zero (0 K/−273.15°C).

By making various assumptions about the nature of gas molecules, it is possible to derive from the kinetic theory the gas laws (such as ▷Avogadro's hypothesis, ▷Boyle's law, and ▷Charles's law).

King, B B (Riley) (1925–) US blues guitarist, singer, and songwriter. One of the most influential electric-guitar players, he became an international star in the 1960s. His albums include *Blues Is King* (1967), *Lucille Talks Back* (1975), *Blues 'n' Jazz* (1983), and *Deuces Wild* (1997).

King, Billie Jean (1943–) Born Billie Jean Moffitt. US tennis player. She won a record 20 Wimbledon titles 1961–79 and 39 Grand Slam titles, and fought for equal treatment and equal pay for women tennis players. In 1973 she formed the Women's Tennis Association and the Players' Union. In 1974, with Olympic swimmer Donna de Varona and others, she created the Women's Sports Foundation to support and promote women in sport. That same year, in front of a worldwide audience, she beat Bobby Riggs, a self-confessed chauvinist and critic of women in sport.

King, Martin Luther, Jr (1929–1968) US civil-rights campaigner, black leader, and Baptist minister. He first came to national attention as leader of the ▷Montgomery, Alabama, bus boycott in 1955, and was one of the organizers of the march of 200,000 people on Washington, DC, in 1963 to demand racial equality. He was awarded the Nobel Prize for Peace in 1964 for his work as a civil-rights leader and an advocate of nonviolence. On 4 April 1968 he was assassinated in Memphis, Tennessee. Although the assassination has commonly been considered to be the work of an individual, James Earl Ray, in December 1999 a civil lawsuit brought by King's family to a circuit court in Memphis, Tennessee, found that the assassination was the work of mobsters and 'several government agencies'.

> **Martin Luther King, Jr**
> *Injustice anywhere is a threat to justice everywhere.*
> Letter from Birmingham jail, Alabama 16 April 1963

King was a founder of the Southern Christian Leadership Conference in 1957. A brilliant and moving speaker, he was the symbol of, and a leading figure in, the campaign for integration and equal rights in the late 1950s and early 1960s. In the mid-1960s his moderate approach was criticized by black militants. He was the target of intensive investigation by the federal authorities, chiefly the FBI under J Edgar ▷Hoover. His personal life was scrutinized and criticized by those opposed to his policies.

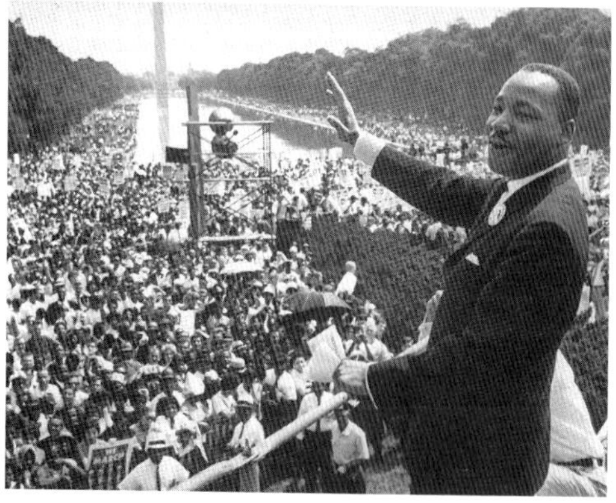

MARTIN LUTHER KING At the march on Washington, DC, USA, 28 August 1963, over 200,000 people gathered peacefully to demand equal rights and justice for all citizens. King made his famous 'I have a dream' speech here, in which he voiced his faith and hope in a fully equal society. *Archive Photos*

King's birthday (15 January) is observed on the third Monday in January as a public holiday in the USA.

Related Web site: Martin Luther King Jr Papers Project
http://www.stanford.edu/group/King/

King, Stephen Edwin (1947–) US writer of best-selling horror novels with small-town or rural settings. Many of his works have been filmed, including *Carrie* (1974), *The Shining* (1978), and *Christine* (1983).

King, W(illiam) L(yon) Mackenzie (1874–1950) Canadian Liberal prime minister 1921–26, 1926–30, and 1935–48. He maintained the unity of the English- and French-speaking populations, and was instrumental in establishing equal status for Canada with the UK.

king crab (or **horseshoe crab**) marine ▷arthropod found on the Atlantic coast of North America, and the coasts of Asia. The upper side of the body is entirely covered with a dark, rounded shell, and it has a long spinelike tail. It is up to 60 cm/2 ft long. It is unable to swim, and lays its eggs in the sand at the high-water mark. (Class Arachnida, subclass Xiphosura.)

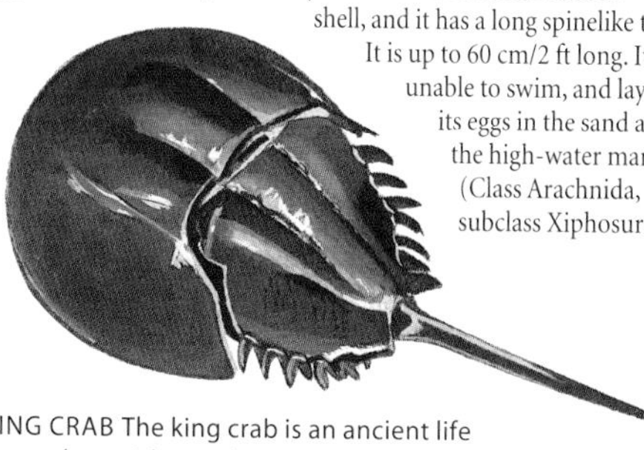

KING CRAB The king crab is an ancient life form, almost identical to fossils from the Triassic period about 225 million years ago.

kingdom the primary division in biological ▷classification. At one time, only two kingdoms were recognized: animals and plants. Today most biologists prefer a five-kingdom system, even though it still involves grouping together organisms that are probably unrelated. One widely accepted scheme is as follows: **Kingdom Animalia** (all multicellular animals); **Kingdom Plantae** (all plants, including seaweeds and other algae, except blue-green); **Kingdom Fungi** (all fungi, including the unicellular yeasts, but not slime moulds); **Kingdom Protista** or **Protoctista** (protozoa, diatoms, dinoflagellates, slime moulds, and various other lower organisms with eukaryotic cells); and **Kingdom Monera** (all prokaryotes – the bacteria and cyanobacteria, or ▷blue-green algae). The first four of these kingdoms make up the eukaryotes.

When only two kingdoms were recognized, any organism with a rigid cell wall was a plant, and so bacteria and fungi were considered plants, despite their many differences. Other organisms, such as the photosynthetic flagellates (euglenoids), were claimed by both kingdoms. The unsatisfactory nature of the two-kingdom system became evident during the 19th century, and the biologist Ernst ▷Haeckel was among the first to try to reform it. High-power microscopes have revealed more about the structure of cells; it has become clear that there is a fundamental difference between cells without a nucleus (▷prokaryotes) and those with a nucleus (▷eukaryotes). However, these differences are larger than those between animals and higher plants, and are unsuitable for use as kingdoms. At present there is no agreement on how many kingdoms there are in the natural world.

Although the five-kingdom system is widely favoured, some schemes have as many as 20.

kingfisher any of a group of heavy-billed birds found near streams, ponds, and coastal areas around the world. The head is exceptionally large, and the long, angular bill is keeled; the tail and wings are relatively short, and the legs very short, with short toes. Kingfishers plunge-dive for fish and aquatic insects. The nest is usually a burrow in a riverbank. (Family Alcedinidae, order Coraciiformes.)

There are 88 species of kingfisher, the largest being the Australian ▷kookaburra. The Alcedinidae are sometimes divided into the subfamilies Daceloninae, Alcedininae, and Cerylinae.

The common **European kingfisher** (*Alcedo atthis*) has greenish-blue plumage, with a bright blue head and tail, and white patches at the side of the neck; the bill is black with an orange-tinted base, and it is a bright chestnut colour below with red legs. It is generally found by rivers, canals, and streams, sitting on a branch overhanging the water, waiting to dive onto fish, which form its principal diet; having sighted the prey it dives perpendicularly, with folded wings, and returning with its catch, dashes it against a stone or tree-branch before swallowing it. Kingfishers also feed on insects, and on small crustaceans. Their eggs are usually laid in a chamber at the end of a tunnel that the breeding pair have excavated in a suitable bank by a stream.

Kingsley, Charles (1819–1875) English author. A rector, he was known as the 'Chartist clergyman' because of such social novels as *Yeast* (1848) and *Alton Locke* (1850). His historical novels include *Westward Ho!* (1855) and *Hereward the Wake* (1866). He also wrote, for children, *The Water Babies* (1863). He was deeply interested in social questions, and threw himself wholeheartedly into the schemes of social relief which were supported under the name of Christian Socialism, writing many tracts and articles as 'Parson Lot'.

Related Web site: Selected Poetry of Charles Kingsley (1819–1875) http://www.library.utoronto.ca/utel/rp/authors/kingsley.html

Kingston capital and principal port of Jamaica, West Indies, the cultural and commercial centre of the island; population (1991) 587,800 (metropolitan area). Founded in 1693, Kingston became the capital of Jamaica in 1872.

Kingston upon Hull (or **Hull**) city, port, and unitary authority, created in 1996 from part of the former county of Humberside, situated where the River Hull flows into the north side of the Humber estuary, northeast England.

area 71 sq km/27 sq mi **features** 13th-century Holy Trinity Church; restored docklands area; Town Docks Museum; Ferens Art Gallery (1927); University of Hull (1954) and University of Humberside (1992), formerly Humberside Polytechnic; linked with the south bank of the estuary by the Humber Bridge, the world's longest single-span suspension bridge **industries** fish processing, flour milling, sawmilling, marine engineering, food processing, and the manufacture of electrical goods, vegetable oils, paint, pharmaceuticals, chemicals, caravans, aircraft, and paper; 11 km/7 mi of modern docks located on the Humber estuary; the largest timber port in the UK, it also handles grain, oilseeds, wool, and the export/import of manufactured goods; ferries to Rotterdam and Zeebrugge – following the building of the Queen Elizabeth Dock in 1971, the port's roll-on/roll-off freight traffic expanded rapidly **population** (1996) 265,000 **famous people** Amy Johnson, Stevie Smith, William Wilberforce; Philip Larkin was librarian at the University of Hull

Related Web site: Kingston upon Hull City Council http://www.hullcc.gov.uk/index.html

Kingstown capital and principal port of St Vincent and the Grenadines, West Indies, in the southwest of the island of St Vincent; population (1991) 26,200.

kinkajou Central and South American carnivorous mammal belonging to the raccoon family. Yellowish-brown, with a rounded face and slim body, the kinkajou grows to 55 cm/1.8 ft with a 50 cm/1.6 ft tail, and has short legs with sharp claws. It spends its time in trees and has a prehensile tail, which it uses as an extra limb when moving from branch to branch. It feeds largely on fruit. (Species *Potos flavus*, family Procyonidae.)

Kinnock, Neil Gordon (1942–) British Labour politician, party leader 1983–92. Born and educated in Wales, he was elected to represent a Welsh constituency in Parliament in 1970 (Islwyn from 1983). He was further left than prime ministers Wilson and Callaghan, but as party leader (in succession to Michael Foot) adopted a moderate position, initiating a major policy review 1988–89. He resigned as party leader after Labour's defeat in the 1992 general election. In 1994 he left parliament to become a European commissioner and was given the transport portfolio. In July 1999 it was announced that Kinnock would become vice-president of the European Commission with responsibility for internal reform, which happened in October.

Kinshasa (formerly **Léopoldville** (until 1966)) capital of the Democratic Republic of Congo on the Congo River, 400 km/250 mi inland from the port of Matadi; population (1994 est) 4,655,300. Industries include ship building and repairing, chemicals, textiles, engineering, food processing, and furniture. It was founded by the explorer Henry Morton Stanley in 1881. The National University of Kinshasa is here.

kinship in anthropology, human relationship based on blood or marriage, and sanctified by law and custom. Kinship forms the basis for most human societies and for such social groupings as the family, clan, or tribe.

Kipling, (Joseph) Rudyard (1865–1936) English writer, born in India. *Plain Tales from the Hills* (1888), about Anglo-Indian society, contains the earliest of his masterly short stories. His books for children, including *The Jungle Book* (1894–95), *Just So Stories* (1902), *Puck of Pook's Hill* (1906), and the picaresque novel *Kim* (1901), reveal his imaginative identification with the exotic. Poems such as 'If–', 'Danny Deever', and 'Gunga Din', express an empathy with common experience, which contributed to his great popularity, together with a vivid sense of 'Englishness' (sometimes denigrated as a kind of jingoist imperialism). He was awarded the Nobel Prize for Literature in 1907.

Born in Bombay (now Mumbai), Kipling was educated at the United Services College at Westward Ho!, Devon, England, which provided the background for *Stalky and Co* (1899). He worked as a journalist in India from 1882–89 and during these years wrote the stories which appeared in *Plain Tales from the Hills*, *Soldiers Three* (1890), and *Wee Willie Winkie* (1890). Returning to London in 1889 he published the novel *The Light that Failed* (1890) and *Barrack-Room Ballads* (1892). He lived largely in the USA from 1892–99, where he produced the two *Jungle Books* and *Captains Courageous* (1897). Settling in Sussex, southeast England, he published *Kim* (his last work set in India), usually regarded as his greatest work of fiction; the *Just So Stories*; *Puck of Pook's Hill*; and *Rewards and Fairies* (1910).

> **Rudyard Kipling**
> *If you can dream – and not make dreams your master; / If you can think – and not make thoughts your aim; / If you can meet with Triumph and Disaster / And treat those two impostors just the same.*
> 'If'

Kipling's work is increasingly valued for its complex characterization and subtle moral viewpoints.

Related Web site: Complete Collection of Poems by Rudyard Kipling http://www.geocities.com/Athens/Aegean/1457/

Kirchner, Ernst Ludwig (1880–1938) German artist. He was a leading member of the expressionist *die* ▷*Brücke* group in Dresden from 1905 and in Berlin from 1911. In Berlin he painted city scenes and portraits, using lurid colours and bold diagonal paint strokes recalling woodcut technique.

Kirghiz (or **Kirgiz**) member of a pastoral people numbering approximately 1.5 million. The Kirghiz live in Tajikistan, Uzbekistan, Kyrgyzstan, China (Xinjiang), and Afghanistan (Wakhan corridor). They are Sunni Muslims, and their Turkic language belongs to the Altaic family.

Kirghizia alternative form of ▷Kyrgyzstan, a country in central Asia.

Kiribati see country box.

Kirin alternative name for ▷Jilin, a Chinese province.

Kirkland, Gelsey (1953–) US ballerina. She danced with effortless technique and innate musicality. She joined the New York City Ballet in 1968, where George ▷Balanchine staged a new *Firebird* for her (1970) and Jerome ▷Robbins chose her for his *Goldberg Variations* (1971) and other ballets. In 1974 Mikhail ▷Baryshnikov sought her out and she joined the American Ballet Theater in 1975, where they danced in partnership, for example in *Giselle*.

Kirkwall administrative headquarters and port of the ▷Orkney Islands, Scotland, on the north coast of the largest island, Mainland; population (1991) 6,700. The main industry is distilling. The Norse cathedral of St Magnus dates from 1137. The Bishop's Palace is also 12th-century, and the Earl's Palace was completed in 1606.

Kirov, Sergei Mironovich (1886–1934) Russian Bolshevik leader who joined the party in 1904 and played a prominent part in the 1918–20 civil war. As one of ▷Stalin's closest associates, he became first secretary of the Leningrad Communist Party. His assassination, possibly engineered by Stalin, led to the political trials held during the next four years as part of the ▷purge.

Kishinev Russian name for ▷Chişinău, the capital of Moldova.

Kissinger, Henry (Alfred) (1923–) German-born US diplomat. After a brilliant academic career at Harvard University, he was appointed national security adviser in 1969 by President Nixon, and was secretary of state 1973–77. His missions to the USSR and China improved US relations with both countries, and he took part in negotiating US withdrawal from Vietnam in 1973 and in Arab-Israeli peace negotiations 1973–75. He shared the Nobel Prize for Peace in 1973 with North Vietnamese diplomat Le Duc Tho for their efforts in securing the peace settlement of the Vietnam War.

His secret trips to Beijing and Moscow led to Nixon's visits to both countries and a general détente. In 1976 he was involved in the negotiations in Africa arising from the Angola and Rhodesia crises. In 1983, President Reagan appointed him to head a bipartisan commission on Central America. He was widely regarded as the most powerful member of Nixon's administration.

kiss of life (or **artificial ventilation**) in first aid, another name for ▷artificial respiration.

Kiswahili another name for the ▷Swahili language.

Kitaj, R(onald) B(rooks) (1932–) US painter and graphic artist, active in Britain. His work is mainly figurative, and employs a wide range of allusions to art, history, and literature. *The Autumn of Central Paris (After Walter Benjamin)* (1972–74) is a typical work. His distinctive use of colour and economy of line was in part inspired by studies of the Impressionist painter Degas, and has similarities with oriental art.

Kitakyushu industrial port city in Fukuoka prefecture, on the Hibiki Sea, north Kyushu island, Japan; population (1994) 1,015,000. Kitakyushu, which means 'north Kyushu city', was formed in 1963 by the amalgamation of Moji, Kokura, Tobata, Yawata, and Wakamatsu. Industries include food-processing and the manufacture of appliances, ceramics, and semiconductors. A tunnel, built in 1942, and a bridge link the port with Honshu.

Kitasato, Shibasaburō (1852–1931) Japanese bacteriologist who discovered the plague bacillus while investigating an outbreak of plague in Hong Kong. He was the first to grow the tetanus bacillus in pure culture. He and German bacteriologist Emil von ▷Behring discovered that increasing nonlethal doses of tetanus toxin give immunity to the disease.

Kitchener city in southwestern Ontario, Canada, 96 km/60 mi west of Toronto and 145 km/90 mi northwest of the Niagara Falls; population (2001 est) 190,400; population of metropolitan area (with Waterloo) 414,300. It lies at an altitude of 335 m/1,099 ft in the fertile valley of the Grand River, and is twinned with the neighbouring city of Waterloo. Kitchener is the centre of a rich agricultural district; industries include the manufacturing of agricultural machinery, tyres, processed food, textiles, and electrical equipment.

> **Henry Kissinger**
> *Power is the ultimate aphrodisiac.*
> *Guardian* 28 November 1976

Kitchener, Horatio (Herbert) (1850–1916) 1st Earl Kitchener of Khartoum. Irish soldier and administrator. He defeated the Sudanese at the Battle of ▷Omdurman in 1898 and reoccupied Khartoum. In South Africa, he was commander-in-chief 1900–02 during the Boer War, and he commanded the forces in India 1902–09. Appointed war minister on the outbreak of World War I, he was successful in his campaign calling for voluntary recruitment.

Kitchener was born in County Kerry, Ireland. He was commissioned in 1871, and transferred to the Egyptian army in 1882. Promoted to commander-in-chief in 1892, he forced a French expedition to withdraw from the Sudan in the Fashoda Incident. During the Boer War he acted first as Lord Roberts's chief of staff and then as commander-in-chief. He conducted war by a scorched-earth policy and created the earliest concentration camps for civilians. Subsequently he commanded the forces in India and acted as British agent in Egypt, and in 1914 received an earldom. As British secretary of state for war from 1914, he modernized the British forces. He was one of the first to realize that the war would not be 'over by Christmas', and planned for an entrenched three-year war, for which he began raising new armies. He bears some responsibility for the failure of the ▷Gallipoli campaign, having initially refused any troops for the venture, and from then on his influence declined. He drowned when his ship struck a German mine on the way to Russia.

kitchen-sink painters loose-knit group of British painters, active in the late 1940s and early 1950s. They depicted drab, everyday scenes with an aggressive technique and often brilliant, 'crude' colour. The best known were John Bratby, Derrick Greaves (1927–), Edward Middleditch (1923–1987), and Jack Smith (1928–).

kite quadrilateral with two pairs of adjacent equal sides. The geometry of this figure follows from the fact that it has one axis of symmetry.

kite any of a group of birds of prey found in all parts of the world. Kites have long, pointed wings and, usually, a forked tail. There are about 20 species. (Family Accipitridae, order Falconiformes.)

The **red kite** (*Milvus milvus*), found in Europe, has the characteristic forked tail and narrow wings, and is about 60 cm/2 ft long. Its general colour is reddish-brown, with tail feathers of a light red, barred with brown; the beak is black and strongly curved downwards. The kite feeds on small birds, fishes, small mammals, carrion, and sometimes insects. Its nest, which is formed largely of rags and twigs, is generally placed in the cleft of a tree.

Wales used to be the only place in the UK where the kite was found; it was formerly common in urban areas as a carrion eater. A reintroduction programme released 120 kites from Sweden and Spain into southern England and northern Scotland 1988–1992. In 1993, 21 chicks were raised. As a result of the reintroduction programme there were populations of 120 red kites in England and 70 in Scotland in 1995. In 1998, 195 kites were fledged from a 100 nests in the reintroduced kite populations in England and Scotland, with a further 165 fledged in Wales by the 160 breeding pairs there. In 1999, due to extensive conservation efforts, there were 295 breeding pairs of kites in Wales.

The darker and slightly smaller **black kite** (*M. migrans*) is found over most of the Old World. It is a scavenger as well as a hunter.

North America has five species, including the American **swallow-tailed kite** (*Elanoides forficatus*) of the southeastern USA, which catches insects in flight as well as dropping down on snakes and lizards.

kittiwake bird of the genus *Rissa*, in the ▷gull family Laridae, order Charadriiformes. The chief characteristic which distinguishes the kittiwakes from the rest of the gulls is the rudimentary condition or absence of the hind toe. There are two species, *R. tridactyla*, with dark brown feet and white under the wing-coverts, and *R. brevirostris*, with vermilion-coloured feet and grey under the wing-coverts. The kittiwake feeds mainly on fish, which it dives for. It is found around northern and arctic coasts.

Kitwe commercial centre for the Zambian copperbelt; population (1998 est) 424,100. It is the headquarters of the Zambia Chamber of Mines. Nkana township and copper mine is adjacent; to the south are Zambia's emerald mines. The local supplies of copper have helped the growth of an electrical equipment industry. Other industries include engineering, brewing, iron goods, fibreglass, paint, furniture, and plastics.

kiwi flightless bird found only in New Zealand. It has long hairlike brown plumage, minute wings and tail, and a very long beak with nostrils at the tip. It is nocturnal and insectivorous. It lays one or two white eggs per year, each weighing up to 450 g/15.75 oz. (Species *Apteryx australis*, family Apterygidae, order Apterygiformes.)

KITTIWAKE A kittiwake *Rissa tridactyla* nesting on the Farne Islands. *R A Preston-Mafham/Premaphotos Wildlife*

Kiwis live in burrows and a pair will share a territory of up to 40 hectares. The female is about a third bigger than the male and the egg she lays is up to a quarter of her own bodyweight. Incubation takes up to 80 days and the male may carry incubate the egg alone. By 2 weeks the chick is fully independent.

There are three main types of kiwi: brown, great spotted, and little spotted. All kiwi species have declined since European settlement of New Zealand, and the little spotted kiwi is most at risk. It survives only on one small island reservation, which was stocked with birds from the mainland. In 1999 there were fewer than 80,000 kiwis remaining in total. See picture on p. 524.

Kiribati

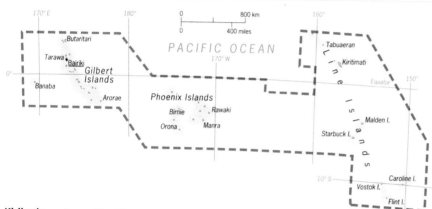

KIRIBATI This stamp commemorates the International Year of the Child in 1979. This was also the year in which Kiribati became an independent republic. *Stanley Gibbons*

Kiribati formerly part of the Gilbert and Ellice Islands (until 1979) republic in the west central Pacific Ocean, comprising three groups of coral atolls: the 16 Gilbert Islands, 8 uninhabited Phoenix Islands, 8 of the 11 Line Islands, and the volcanic island of Banaba; population (1997 est) 82,400.

NATIONAL NAME *Ribaberikan Kiribati/Republic of Kiribati*
AREA 717 sq km/277 sq mi
CAPITAL Bairiki (on Tarawa atoll)
MAJOR TOWNS/CITIES principal islands are the Gilbert Islands, the Phoenix Islands, the Line Islands, Banaba
MAJOR PORTS Bairiki, Betio (on Tarawa)
PHYSICAL FEATURES comprises 33 Pacific coral islands: the Kiribati (Gilbert), Rawaki (Phoenix), Banaba (Ocean Island), and three of the Line Islands including Kiritimati (Christmas Island); island groups crossed by Equator and International Date Line

Government

HEAD OF STATE AND GOVERNMENT Anote Tong from 2003
POLITICAL SYSTEM liberal democracy
POLITICAL EXECUTIVE limited presidency
ADMINISTRATIVE DIVISIONS three units (island groups) and six districts
ARMED FORCES no standing army

Economy and resources

CURRENCY Australian dollar
GPD (US$) 44 million (2002 est)
REAL GDP GROWTH (% change on previous year) –0.2 (2001)
GNI (US$) 77 million (2002 est)

GNI PER CAPITA (PPP) (US$) 2,070 (2002 est)
CONSUMER PRICE INFLATION 5.6% (2001 est)
FOREIGN DEBT (US$) 8.6 million (2001 est)
MAJOR TRADING PARTNERS Australia, Bangladesh, Japan, Fiji Islands, USA, Marshall Islands, Denmark
RESOURCES phosphate, salt
INDUSTRIES handicrafts, coconut-based products, soap, foods, furniture, leather goods, garments, tourism
EXPORTS copra, fish, seaweed, bananas, breadfruit, taro. Principal market: Bangladesh 51.4% (1999)
IMPORTS foodstuffs, machinery and transport equipment, mineral fuels, basic manufactures. Principal source: Australia 44.5% (1999)
ARABLE LAND 50.7% (2000 est)
AGRICULTURAL PRODUCTS copra, coconuts, bananas, vegetables, melons, screw-pine, papaya, breadfruit; livestock rearing (pigs and chickens); fishing

Population and society

POPULATION 88,000 (2003 est)
POPULATION GROWTH RATE 1.3% (2000–05)
POPULATION DENSITY (per sq km) 121 (2003 est)

URBAN POPULATION (% of total) 39 (2003 est)
AGE DISTRIBUTION (% of total population) 0–14 41%, 15–59 53%, 60+ 6% (2001 est)
ETHNIC GROUPS predominantly Micronesian, with a Polynesian minority; also European and Chinese minorities
LANGUAGE English (official), Gilbertese
RELIGION Roman Catholic, Protestant (Congregationalist)
EDUCATION (compulsory years) 9
LITERACY RATE 93% (men); 92% (women) (2001 est)
LABOUR FORCE 6.2% agriculture, 6.4% industry, 87.4% services (1995)
LIFE EXPECTANCY 58 (men); 63 (women) (2001 est)

Chronology

1st millennium BC: Settled by Austronesian-speaking peoples.
1606: Visited by Spanish explorers.
late 18th century: Visited by British naval officers.
1857: Christian mission established.
1892: Gilbert (Kiribati) and Ellice (Tuvalu) Islands proclaimed a British protectorate.
1916–39: Uninhabited Phoenix Islands, Christmas Island, Ocean Island, and Line Island (Banaba) added to colony.
1942–43: While occupied by Japanese it was the scene of fierce fighting with US troops.
late 1950s: UK tested nuclear weapons on Christmas Island (Kiritimati).

PHYSICIANS (per 1,000 people) 0.3 (1998 est)
HOSPITAL BEDS (per 1,000 people) 4.4 (1994 est)
TV SETS (per 1,000 people) 23 (1999 est)

See also ▷Australasia and Oceania; ▷Tuvalu.

1963: Legislative council established.
1974: Legislative council replaced by an elected House of Assembly.
1975: The mainly Melanesian-populated Ellice Islands separated to become Tuvalu.
1977: The predominantly Micronesian-populated Gilbert Islands was granted internal self-government.
1979: The Gilbert Islands achieved independence within the Commonwealth, as the Republic of Kiribati, with Ieremia Tabai as president.
1985: Kiribati's first political party, the opposition Christian Democrats, was formed.
1994: The government resigned after losing a vote of confidence. Teburoro Tito of the MTM was elected president.

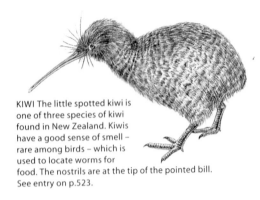

KIWI The little spotted kiwi is one of three species of kiwi found in New Zealand. Kiwis have a good sense of smell – rare among birds – which is used to locate worms for food. The nostrils are at the tip of the pointed bill. See entry on p.523.

kiwi fruit (or **Chinese gooseberry**) fruit of a vinelike plant grown commercially on a large scale in New Zealand. Kiwi fruits are egg-sized, oval, and similar in flavour to gooseberries, though much sweeter, with a fuzzy brown skin. (*Actinidithia chinensis*, family Actinidiaceae.)

Klaipeda (formerly German **Memel**) main port of Lithuania, on the Baltic coast at the mouth of the River Dane; population (1991) 206,000. Klaipeda lies 290 km/180 mi northwest of Vilnius. Industries include shipbuilding, fisheries, and iron foundries; the city also trades in timber and grain. Klaipeda was founded in 1252 on the site of a local fortress as the castle of Memelburg by the ▷Teutonic Knights, joined the ▷Hanseatic League soon after, and has changed hands between Sweden, Russia, and Prussia/Germany. The city was part of independent Lithuania from 1923, and after a period of German occupation (1939–45), it became part of the Soviet Republic of Lithuania (1945–91).

Klammer, Franz (1953–) Austrian skier. He won a record 25 World Cup downhill races 1974–1985, plus one win in the combined event. He was an Olympic gold medallist in 1976. He was the combined world champion in 1974, and the World Cup downhill champion 1975–78 and 1983. He was the most successful Austrian skier in World Cup competition until February 2000 when Hermann Maier achieved his 27th victory.

Klaproth, Martin Heinrich (1743–1817) German chemist who first identified the elements uranium and zirconium, in 1789, and was the second person to isolate titanium, chromium, and cerium. He was a pioneer of analytical chemistry.

Klaus, Václav (1941–) Czech politician and economist, prime minister of the Czech Republic 1993–97. Before the break-up of Czechoslovakia, he served in the government of Václav Havel and was chair of Civic Forum from 1990, breaking away to form the right-of-centre Civic Democratic Party (CDP) in 1991. The architect of Eastern Europe's initially most successful economic reform programme, he was a keen promoter of membership of the European Union.

Klee, Paul (1879–1940) Swiss painter and graphic artist. He was one of the most original and prolific artists of the 20th century. Endlessly inventive and playful, and suggesting a childlike innocence, his works are an exploration of the potential of line, plane, and colour. *Twittering Machine* (1922; Museum of Modern Art, New York) is typical.

Klee studied in Munich and absorbed a variety of influences from painters old and modern (Blake, Goya, Hans von Marées, and Cézanne among them) before setting out – in his own words – to work 'as one new-born'. With Kandinsky, Marc, and Macke, he took part in founding the ▷*Blaue Reiter* group in 1912, and taught at the Bauhaus 1921–31, though the style he developed – influenced as much by the art of children and the insane as it was by any school or movement – was unique and makes him difficult to classify neatly.

He moved to the Düsseldorf Academy in 1931 and to Bern in 1933 when the Nazis came into power.

His influential views on art, which reflect his time at the Bauhaus, were presented in *Pedagogical Sketchbook* (1925).

Klein, Calvin (Richard) (1942–) US fashion designer. His collections are characterized by the smooth and understated, often in natural fabrics such as mohair, wool, and suede, in subtle colours. He set up his own business in 1968, specializing in designing coats and suits, and expanded into sportswear in the mid-1970s. His designer jeans became a status symbol during the same period.

Klein, Melanie (1882–1960) Born Melanie Reizes. Austrian child psychoanalyst. She pioneered child psychoanalysis and play

---

studies, and was influenced by Sigmund ▷Freud's theories. She published *The Psychoanalysis of Children* (1960).

Klemperer, Otto (1885–1973) German conductor. He was celebrated for his interpretation of contemporary and classical music (especially Beethoven and Brahms). He conducted the Los Angeles Orchestra 1933–39 and the Philharmonia Orchestra, London, from 1959.

kleptomania (Greek *kleptēs* 'thief') behavioural disorder characterized by an overpowering desire to possess articles for which one has no need. In kleptomania, as opposed to ordinary theft, there is no obvious need or use for what is stolen and sometimes the sufferer has no memory of the theft.

Klimt, Gustav (1862–1918) Austrian painter. He was influenced by *Jugendstil* (art nouveau) and was a founding member of the Vienna ▷Sezession group in 1897. His paintings, often sensual and erotic, have a jewelled effect similar to mosaics, for example *The Kiss* (1909; Musée des Beaux-Arts, Strasbourg). His many portraits include *Judith I* (1901; österreichische Galerie, Vienna).

Klimt's paintings and other decorative works (for example, the mosaics for the Palais Stoclet, Brussels) are characterized by academic forms that are obscured by massed repetitive decorative elements. His use of decorative fragments and gold backgrounds is derived from Byzantine mosaics, but his depiction of women – as seductive and dangerous – is typical of *fin-de-siècle* decadence. Examples are the *Jurisprudence* panel (1903–07; destroyed 1945) and his ideal woman as *Pallas Athene*.

klipspringer small African antelope. It reaches about 60 cm at the shoulder and males weigh about 10 kg; females are heavier, weighing 13 kg. Klipspringers are browsers, feeding on leaves, berries, flowers, and seed pods and can survive for long periods without water. They are common in rocky or mountainous areas in the Ethiopian highlands, Namibia, and Angola.

Klondike former gold-mining area in northwest ▷Yukon Territory, Canada, near Dawson, where the Klondike and Yukon rivers meet. It is named after the river valley (length 193 km/120 mi) near where gold was found in August 1896. By 1898, at the height of the 'Klondike Gold Rush', over 30,000 people had moved into the area.

Klopstock, Friedrich Gottlieb (1724–1803) German poet. His religious epic *Der Messias/The Messiah* (1748–73) and *Oden/Odes* (1771) anticipated Romanticism. Written in hexameters, *Der Messias* is a very uneven poem, some parts of it being imbued with deep feeling and fervour, while others are flat and trivial.

km symbol for ▷kilometre.

knapweed any of several weedy plants belonging to the daisy family. In the common knapweed (*C. nigra*), also known as **hardhead**, the hard, dark buds break open at the top into pale purple composite flowers. It is native to Europe and has been introduced to North America. (Genus *Centaurea*, family Compositae.)

Kneller, Godfrey (1646–1723) Born Gottfried Kniller. German-born portrait painter who lived in England from 1674. A successful and prolific painter of nearly 6,000 portraits, he dominated English portraiture of the late 17th and early 18th centuries. He was court painter to Charles II, James II, William III, and George I. Kneller was knighted in 1692 and made a baronet in 1715.

Knesset the Israeli parliament, consisting of a single chamber of 120 deputies elected for a period of four years.

knifefish any of a group of fishes in which the body is deep at the front and drawn to a narrow or pointed tail at the rear, the main fin being the well-developed long ventral (stomach) fin that completes the knifelike shape. The ventral fin is rippled for forward or backward movement. Knifefishes produce electrical fields, which they use for navigation. (Genus *Gymnotus* and other allied genera, family Gymnotidae.)

Knight, Charles (1874–1953) US palaeontological artist who was influential in bringing dinosaurs to life in the public

---

KNAPWEED Knapweed *Centaurea nemoralis* is found in Asia, Europe, and N Africa. *Premaphotos Wildlife*

imagination. His extensive knowledge of anatomy and his collaborations with palaeontologists, such as Edward Drinker Cope and Henry Fairfield Osborn, mean his paintings accurately reflect scientific thinking of the time.

knighthood, orders of fraternity carrying with it the rank of knight, admission to which is granted as a mark of royal favour or as a reward for public services. During the Middle Ages in Europe such fraternities fell into two classes: religious and secular. The first class, including the ▷Templars and the Knights of ▷St John, consisted of knights who had taken religious vows and devoted themselves to military service against the Saracens (Arabs) or other non-Christians. The secular orders probably arose from bands of knights engaged in the service of a prince or great noble.

knitting method of making fabric by looping and knotting yarn with two needles. Knitting may have developed from ▷crochet, which uses a single hooked needle, or from **netting**, using a shuttle.

Knock village and parish in County Mayo, Republic of Ireland, 11 km/7 mi northeast of Claremorris. A national place of pilgrimage, Knock is known as the site of alleged apparitions of the Virgin Mary (the first on 21 August 1879), and for its church shrine, the Basilica of Our Lady, 'Queen of Ireland', which seats 12,000 and was opened in 1976. Horan International Airport, opened in 1986,

ORDERS OF KNIGHTHOOD Taken from the mid-15th-century French *Livre des Belles Dames*, this picture shows French *chevalier* (or knight) Jean de Saintre kneeling before a noble lady. His pointed shoes indicate his importance – as a man gained in rank or social standing, he was entitled to wear longer footwear. *The Art Archive/British Library/British Library*

receives transatlantic flights; it was named after Monsignor James Horan, a parish priest who launched the project to attract pilgrims.

knocking in a spark-ignition petrol engine, a phenomenon that occurs when unburned fuel-air mixture explodes in the combustion chamber before being ignited by the spark. The resulting shock waves produce a metallic knocking sound. Loss of power occurs, which can be prevented by reducing the compression ratio, re-designing the geometry of the combustion chamber, or increasing the octane number of the petrol (usually by the use of tetraethyl lead anti-knock additives, or increasingly by MTBE – methyl tertiary butyl ether in unleaded petrol).

Knossos Middle and Late Bronze Age settlement, 8 km/5 mi south of present-day Iraklion, Crete. Knossos is one of the main cities of what is known as the ▷Minoan civilization (a modern name derived from the legend of King Minos). The archaeological site, excavated by Arthur Evans in 1899–1935, includes the palace throne room, the remains of frescoes, and construction on more than one level. The Greek myth of Theseus's encounter with the Minotaur in a labyrinth was possibly derived from the ritual 'bull-leaping' by young people depicted in the palace frescoes and from the mazelike layout of the palace.

knot wading bird belonging to the sandpiper family. It is about 25 cm/10 in long, with a short bill, neck, and legs. In the winter, it is grey above and white below, but in the breeding season, it is brick-red on the head and chest and black on the wings and back. It feeds on insects and molluscs. (Species *Calidris canutus*, family Scolopacidae, order Charadriiformes.)

knot in navigation, unit by which a ship's speed is measured, equivalent to one ▷nautical mile per hour (one knot equals about 1.15 miles per hour). It is also sometimes used in aviation.

knotgrass annual plant belonging to the dock family. The bases of the small lance-shaped leaves enclose the slender stems, giving a superficial resemblance to grass. Small pinkish flowers are followed by seeds that are eaten by birds. Knotgrass grows worldwide except in the polar regions. (*Polygonum aviculare*, family Polygonaceae.)

knowledge-based system (KBS) computer program that uses an encoding of human knowledge to help solve problems. It was discovered during research into ▷artificial intelligence that adding heuristics (rules of thumb) enabled programs to tackle problems that were otherwise difficult to solve by the usual techniques of computer science.

Chess-playing programs have been strengthened by including knowledge of what makes a good position, or of overall strategies, rather than relying solely on the computer's ability to calculate variations.

Knox, John (*c.* 1505–1572) Scottish Protestant reformer, founder of the Church of Scotland. He spent several years in exile for his beliefs, including a period in Geneva where he met John ▷Calvin. He returned to Scotland in 1559 to promote Presbyterianism. His books include *First Blast of the Trumpet Against the Monstrous Regiment of Women* (1558).

Originally a Roman Catholic priest, Knox is thought to have been converted by the reformer George Wishart. When Wishart was burned for heresy, Knox went into hiding, but later preached the reformed doctrines.

Captured by French troops in Scotland in 1547, he was imprisoned in France, sentenced to the galleys, and released only by the intercession of the British government in 1549. In England he assisted in compiling the Prayer Book, as a royal chaplain from 1551. On Mary's accession in 1553 he fled the country and in 1557 was, in his absence, condemned to be burned. In 1559 he returned to Scotland. He was tried for treason but acquitted in 1563. He wrote a *History of the Reformation in Scotland* (1586).

koala marsupial (mammal that carries its young in a pouch) found only in eastern Australia. It feeds almost entirely on eucalyptus shoots. It is about 60 cm/2 ft long, and resembles a bear (it is often incorrectly described as a 'koala bear'). The popularity of its greyish fur led to its almost complete extermination by hunters. Under protection since 1936, it rapidly increased in numbers, but recently numbers have fallen from 400,000 in 1985 to 40,000–80,000 in 1995. (Species *Phascolarctos cinereus*, family Phalangeridae.)

A three-year trial began in November 1996 in southern Australia, overpopulated by koalas, to bring their numbers under control by giving males vasectomies and females hormone implants preventing ovulation. In 1997, the programme of sterilization continued, and a relocation plan, following earlier trials, began.

kōan in Zen Buddhism, a superficially nonsensical question or riddle used by a Zen master to help a pupil achieve satori (▷enlightenment). It is used in the Rinzai school of Zen.

Kobe deep-water port on Osaka Bay in Hyogo prefecture, southern Honshu island, Japan; population (2000) 1,494,000. It was a ▷treaty port between 1868 and 1899, for foreigners exempt from Japanese law. **Port Island**, an artificial island of 5 sq km/3 sq mi in Kobe harbour, was created in 1960–68 from the rock of nearby mountains. It was one of the world's largest construction projects, and is now a residential and recreation area with a luxury hotel, amusement park, and conference centres. It is linked to the city by a driverless, computerized monorail.

København Danish name for ▷Copenhagen, the capital of Denmark.

Koch, (Heinrich Hermann) Robert (1843–1910) German bacteriologist who was awarded a Nobel Prize for Physiology or Medicine in 1905 for his investigations and discoveries in relation to tuberculosis. Koch and his assistants devised the techniques for culturing bacteria outside the body, and formulated the rules for showing whether or not a bacterium is the cause of a disease.

His techniques enabled him to identify the bacteria responsible for tuberculosis (1882), cholera (1883), and other diseases. He investigated anthrax bacteria in the 1870s and showed that they form spores which spread the infection.

Koch was a great teacher, and many of his pupils, such as Shibasaburō ▷Kitasato, Paul ▷Ehrlich, and Emil von ▷Behring, became outstanding scientists.

Kodály, Zoltán (1882–1967) Hungarian composer and educationalist. With Béla Bartók, he recorded and transcribed Magyar folk music, the scales and rhythm of which he incorporated in a deliberately nationalist style. His works include the cantata *Psalmus Hungaricus* (1923), a comic opera *Háry János* (1925–27), and orchestral dances and variations. His 'Kodály method' of school music education is widely practised.

Koestler, Arthur (1905–1983) Hungarian-born British writer. Imprisoned by the Nazis in France 1940, he escaped to England. His novel *Darkness at Noon* (1940), regarded as his masterpiece, is a fictional account of the Stalinist purges, and draws on his experiences as a prisoner under sentence of death during the Spanish Civil War. He also wrote extensively about creativity, science, parapsychology, politics, and culture.

Koestler's other novels include *Thieves in the Night* (1946), *The Lotus and the Robot* (1960), and *The Call Girls* (1972). His non-fiction includes *The Yogi and the Commissar* (1945), *The Sleepwalkers* (1959), *The Act of Creation* (1964), *The Ghost in the Machine* (1967), *The Roots of Coincidence* (1972), *The Heel of Achilles* (1974), and *The Thirteenth Tribe* (1976).

Autobiographical works include *Arrow in the Blue* (1952) and *The Invisible Writing* (1954). He was a member of the Voluntary Euthanasia Society and committed suicide with his wife after suffering for a long time from Parkinson's disease.

Koh-i-noor (Persian 'mountain of light') diamond, originally part of the Aurangzeb treasure, seized in 1739 by the shah of Iran from the Moguls in India, taken back by Sikhs, and acquired by Britain in 1849 when the Punjab was annexed.

Kohl, Helmut (1930–) German conservative politician, leader of the Christian Democratic Union (CDU) 1976–98, West German chancellor (prime minister) 1982–90, and German chancellor 1990–98. He oversaw the reunification of East and West Germany 1989–90 and in 1990 won a resounding victory to become the first chancellor of a reunited Germany. His miscalculation of the true costs of reunification and their subsequent effects on the German economy led to a dramatic fall in his popularity, but as the economy recovered, so did his public esteem, enabling him to achieve a historic fourth electoral victory in 1994. In November 1996 Kohl entered his 15th year as chancellor, overtaking the record previously held by Konrad Adenauer, Kohl's political mentor. His close working relationship with President Mitterrand of France was the foundation for accelerating progress towards closer European integration, and Kohl was a strong backer of the project of a single European currency. His popularity slipped as a result of record levels of unemployment, which reached 12.6% in January 1998, and he lost office following his defeat by Gerhard Schroeder of the Social Democratic Party (SDP) in the elections of September 1998. In January 2000 Kohl resigned his position as honorary leader of the Christian Democrats after he admitted to receiving secret and therefore illegal payments on behalf of his party when he was chancellor.

Kohl studied law and history before entering the chemical industry. Elected to the Rhineland-Palatinate *Land* (state) parliament in 1959, he became state premier in 1969. After the 1976 Bundestag (federal parliament) elections Kohl led the CDU in opposition. He became federal chancellor in 1982, when the Free Democratic Party (FDP) withdrew support from the socialist Schmidt government, and was elected at the head of a new coalition that included the FDP. From 1984 Kohl was implicated in the Flick bribes scandal over the illegal business funding of political parties, but he was cleared of all charges in 1986, and was re-elected chancellor in January 1987, December 1990, and October 1994. However, in December 1999 he admitted to keeping secret party bank accounts when he was chancellor. A subsequent inquiry into his accounts centred on a covert payment of 1 million marks/£330,000 by an arms dealer to the treasurer of the Christian Democrats while Kohl was chancellor and party chairman in 1991. The inquiry would try to establish whether the payment was linked to a sale of arms to Saudi Arabia. It also spread the scandal on to other members of the Christian Democrats, including the Kohl's replacement leader, Wolfgang Schäuble, and Manfred Kanther, former regional chief of the party, and an ex-aide to Kohl. Both resigned from their positions.

kohlrabi variety of kale, which is itself a variety of ▷cabbage; it is used for food and resembles a turnip. The leaves of kohlrabi shoot from a round swelling on the main stem. (*Brassica oleracea caulorapa* or *B. oleracea gongylodes*, family Cruciferae.)

Koivisto, Mauno Henrik (1923–) Finnish politician, prime minister 1968–70 and 1979–82, and president 1982–94. He was finance minister 1966–67 and led a Social Democratic Party coalition as prime minister 1968–70. He became interim president in 1981 after the resignation of Urho Kekkonen, and was elected president the following year. As president he shared power with Centre Party prime minister Esko Aho in Finland's unusual 'dual executive'.

Kok, Wim (1938–) Dutch trade unionist and politician, leader of the Labour Party (PvdA) and prime minister 1994–99. After an inconclusive general election in May 1994, Kok eventually succeeded in forming a broad-based three-party coalition of the PvdA with the People's Party of Freedom and Democracy (VVD) and Democrats 66 (D-66), both centrist parties. After D-66 withdrew in May 1999, the coalition government was forced to resign.

Kokoschka, Oskar (1886–1980) Austrian expressionist painter. Initially influenced by the Vienna ▷Sezession painters, he painted vivid landscapes, and highly charged allegories and portraits, for example *The Bride of the Wind (The Tempest)* (1914; Kunstmuseum, Basel). His writings include expressionist plays and poetry.

kola alternative spelling of ▷cola, any of a group of tropical trees.

Kola Peninsula (Russian **Kol'skiy Poluostrov**) peninsula in the far northwestern Russian Federation, between the Barents Sea and the White Sea. Administratively, it forms part of Murmansk oblast (region). Its total area is 129,500 sq km/50,000 sq mi, and it has a population of 1.3 million (of whom 2,000 are Saami). To the northwest the low-lying granite plateau adjoins Norway's thinly populated county of Finnmark.

Kolchak, Alexander Vasilievich (1874–1920) Russian admiral, commander of the White forces in Siberia after the Russian Revolution. He proclaimed himself Supreme Ruler of Russia in 1918, but was later handed over to the Bolsheviks by his own men and shot.

Kolkata alternative form of ▷Calcutta, a city in India.

Kollontai, Alexandra Mikhailovna (1872–1952) Born Alexandra Mikhailovna Domontovich. Russian revolutionary, politician, and writer. In 1905 she published *On the Question of the Class Struggle*, and, as commissar for public welfare, was the only female member of the first Bolshevik government. She campaigned for domestic reforms such as acceptance of free love, simplification of divorce laws, and collective child care.

Kollwitz, Käthe (1867–1945) Born Käthe Schmidt. German graphic artist and sculptor. One of the leading expressionists, she is noted for the harrowing drawings, woodcuts, etchings, and lithographs on the themes of social injustice and human suffering, as in the woodcut cycle *Never Again War!* (1924).

Köln German form of ▷Cologne, a city in Germany.

Komi member of a Finnish people living mainly in the tundra and coniferous forests of the autonomous republic of Komi in the northwestern Urals, Russia. They raise livestock, grow timber, and mine coal and oil. They have been Christians (Russian Orthodox) since the 14th century, and their language, Zyryan, belongs to the Finno-Ugric branch of the Uralic family.

Komi republic in the northwestern Russian Federation; area 415,900 sq km/160,579 sq mi; population (1996) 1,185,000 (74% urban) (58% Russian, 23% Komi). The capital is ▷Syktyvkar and Vorkuta is another city. The republic is partly in the Arctic Circle and is largely lowland (*taiga*) with coniferous forests. There are large coal seams (Pechora Basin) and oil deposits, and rich mineral resources (natural gas, oil shale, and bauxite). Industries include coal mining, oil and natural-gas extraction, and lumbering; and grain and dairy farming.

Kommunizma, Pik (or **Communism Peak**; formerly **Garmo Peak** (to 1933), **Stalin Peak** (1933–61)) highest mountain in the ▷Pamirs, a mountain range in Tajikistan in Central Asia; height 7,495 m/24,590 ft. It was first climbed by a Soviet expedition in 1933.

Kongo African kingdom flourishing in the lower Congo region in the 14th–18th centuries. Although it possessed a sophisticated system of government, its power began to decline early in the 17th century under the impact of intensified slave trading and the interventions of Portuguese merchants and missionaries. In the late 19th century the kingdom was incorporated in the Portuguese colony of Angola. The Kongo people rebelled against colonial rule 1913–17.

Kongur Shan mountain peak in China, 7,719 m/25,325 ft high, part of the ▷Pamir Plateau. The 1981 expedition that first reached the summit was led by British climber Chris Bonington.

Kong Zi Pinyin form of ▷Confucius, Chinese philosopher.

Koniev, Ivan Stepanovich (1898–1973) Soviet marshal who in World War II liberated Ukraine from the invading German forces 1943–44 and then in 1945 advanced from the south on Berlin to link up with the British-US forces. He commanded all Warsaw Pact forces 1955–60.

Königsberg former name of ▷Kaliningrad, a Baltic port in Russia.

Königsberg bridge problem long-standing puzzle that was solved by topology (the geometry of those properties of a figure which remain the same under distortion). In the city of Königsberg (now Kaliningrad in Russia), seven bridges connect the banks of the River Pregol'a and the islands in the river. For many years, people were challenged to cross each of the bridges in a single tour and return to their starting point. In 1736 Swiss mathematician Leonhard Euler converted the puzzle into a topological network, in which the islands and river banks were represented as nodes (junctions), and the connecting bridges as lines. By analysing this network he was able to show that it is not traversable – that is, it is impossible to cross each of the bridges once only and return to the point at which one started.

Konoe, Fumimaro, Prince (1891–1945) Japanese politician and prime minister 1937–39 and 1940–41. He helped to engineer the fall of the ▷Tōjō government in 1944 but committed suicide after being suspected of war crimes.

Kon-Tiki legendary creator god of Peru and sun king who ruled the country later occupied by the ▷Incas and was supposed to have migrated out into the Pacific. The name was used by explorer Thor ▷Heyerdahl in 1947 for his raft.

Konya (Roman **Iconium**) city in southwestern central Turkey; population (1990) 513,300. Carpets and silks are made here, and the city contains the monastery of the dancing ▷dervishes.

kookaburra (or **laughing jackass**) largest of the world's ▷kingfishers, found in Australia, with an extraordinary laughing call. It feeds on insects and other small creatures. The body and tail

KOOKABURRA The kookaburra is common in Australian forest and woodland. *G Preston-Mafham/Premaphotos Wildlife*

measure 45 cm/18 in, the head is greyish with a dark eye stripe, and the back and wings are flecked brown with grey underparts. It nests in shady forest regions, but will also frequent the vicinity of houses, and its cry is one of the most familiar sounds of the bush in eastern Australia. (Species *Dacelo novaeguineae*, family Alcedinidae, order Coraciiformes.)

kora instrument of West African origin, with 21 strings, made from gourds, with a harplike sound. Traditionally played by griots (hereditary troubadours) of the old Mali empire to accompany praise songs and historical ballads, it was first incorporated into an electronically amplified band by Guinean musician Mory Kante.

Koran (or **Quran**) the sacred book of ▷Islam, written in Arabic. It is said to have been divinely revealed through the angel Gabriel, or Jibra'el, to the prophet Muhammad between about AD 610 and 632. The Koran is the prime source of all Islamic ethical and legal doctrines.

Related Web site: Koran http://etext.virginia.edu/koran.html

KORAN A copy of the *Koran* (the sacred book of Islam) from the Sultanahmet Mosque in Istanbul, Turkey. *Image Bank*

Korda, Alexander (Laszlo) (1893–1956) Hungarian-born British film producer and director. He was a dominant figure in the British film industry during the 1930s and 1940s. His films as director include *Marius* (1931), in France, and *The Private Life of Henry VIII* (1933), in England. He was the producer of *The Scarlet Pimpernel* (1935), *The Thief of Bagdad* (1940), *The Third Man* (1949), and *Richard III* (1956), among many others.

Kordofan (or **Kurdufan**) former province of central Sudan, known as the 'White Land'; area 146,932 sq km/56,730 sq mi; population (1983) 3,093,300. In 1994 it was divided into three new federal states: North, South, and West Kordofan. Although it has never been an independent state, it has a character of its own. It is mainly undulating plain, with acacia scrub producing gum arabic, marketed in the chief towns of El Obeid in the north and Kaduqli in the south. Formerly a rich agricultural region, it is threatened by desertification.

Korea peninsula in East Asia, divided into north and south; see ▷North Korea, and ▷South Korea.

Korean person who is native to or an inhabitant of Korea; also the language and culture. There are approximately 33 million Koreans in South Korea, 15 million in North Korea, and 3 million elsewhere, principally in Japan, China (Manchuria), Russia, Kazakhstan, Uzbekistan, and the USA.

Korean language language of Korea, written from the 5th century AD in Chinese characters until the invention of an alphabet by King Sejong 1443. The linguistic affiliations of Korean are unclear, but it may be distantly related to Japanese.

Korea, North see ▷North Korea.

Korean War war from 1950 to 1953 between ▷North Korea (supported by China) and ▷South Korea, aided by the United Nations (the troops were mainly US). North Korean forces invaded South Korea on 25 June 1950, and the Security Council of the United Nations, owing to a walk-out by the USSR, voted to oppose them. The North Koreans held most of the South when US reinforcements arrived in September 1950 and forced their way through to the North Korean border with China. The Chinese retaliated, pushing them back to the original boundary by October 1950; truce negotiations began in 1951, although the war did not end until 1953.

By September 1950 the North Koreans had overrun most of the South, with the UN forces holding a small area, the Pusan perimeter, in the southeast. The course of the war changed after the surprise landing of US troops later the same month at Inchon on

> **Koran**
> *On that day shall men come forth in bands to behold their works. And whosoever shall have wrought an atom's weight of good shall behold it. And whosoever shall have wrought an atom's weight of evil shall behold it.*
> xcix, 1–6

KOREAN WAR US troops are shown landing from helicopters during the Korean War in the 1950s. *Archive Photos*

South Korea's northwest coast. The troops, led by General Douglas ▷MacArthur, fought their way through North Korea to the Chinese border in little over a month. On 25 October 1950 Chinese troops attacked across the Yalu River, driving the UN forces below the ▷38th parallel. Truce talks began in July 1951, and the war ended two years later, with the restoration of the original boundary on the 38th parallel.

Related Web site: Korean War Veterans National Museum and Library http://www.theforgottenvictory.org/

Korea, South see ▷South Korea.

Korolev, Sergei Pavlovich (1906–1966) Russian designer of the first Soviet intercontinental missile, used to launch the first ▷Sputnik satellite 1957 and the ▷Vostok spacecraft, also designed by Korolev, in which Yuri ▷Gagarin made the world's first space flight in 1961.

Kos (or **Cos**) fertile Greek island, one of the Dodecanese, in the Aegean Sea; area 287 sq km/111 sq mi. It gives its name to the Cos lettuce.

Kościuszko, Tadeusz Andrzej (1746–1817) Polish general and nationalist. He served with George Washington in the American Revolution (1776–83). He returned to Poland in 1784, fought against the Russian invasion that ended in the partition of Poland, and withdrew to Saxony. He returned again in 1794 to lead the revolt against the occupation, but was defeated by combined Russian and Prussian forces and imprisoned until 1796.

Kosciusko, Mount highest mountain in Australia (2,228 m/7,310 ft), in the Snowy Mountains of the Australian Alps in southeast New South Wales, close to the border with Victoria.

kosher (Hebrew 'appropriate') conforming to religious law with regard to the preparation and consumption of food; in Judaism, conforming to the Mosaic law of the Book of Deuteronomy. For example, only animals that chew the cud and have cloven hooves (cows and sheep, but not pigs) may be eaten. There are rules governing their humane slaughter and their preparation (such as complete draining of blood) which also apply to fowl. Only fish with scales and fins may be eaten; not shellfish. Milk products may not be cooked or eaten with meat or poultry, or until four hours after eating them. Utensils for meat must be kept separate from those for milk.

Kosovo (or **Kossovo**) autonomous region 1945–1990 of southern Serbia; capital ▷Priština; area 10,900 sq km/4,207 sq mi; population (1991) 2,012,500, consisting of about 210,000 Serbs and about 1.8 million Albanians. Products include wine, nickel, lead, and zinc. In 1990 fighting broke out between police, ethnic Albanians, who were agitating for unification of Kosovo with Albania, and Kosovo Serbs, who wished Kosovo to be merged with the rest of Serbia. The Serbian parliament formally annexed Kosovo in September, and Serbian troops were sent to the region in 1998. In 1999, after an 11-week bombing campaign against Serbia, NATO forces moved in to Kosovo to keep the peace, and the United Nations (UN) took over the civil administration of the province.

Related Web site: Kosova http://albanian.com/main/countries/kosova/index.html

Kosovo Liberation Army (KLA; Albanian **Ushtria çlirimtare e Kosovës (UCK)**) paramilitary force operating in the predominantly ethnic Albanian region of Kosovo in southern Serbia, which fought for the independence of Kosovo. The KLA emerged as an organized movement in 1996, and by 1998 found itself in command of an uprising, which quickly spread across parts of the province. Labelled a terrorist organization by the Serb authorities (and Russia), the KLA took large tracts of land 1997–98, but the Serbs began to fight back in the summer of 1998 and by April 1999 – a month into a NATO offensive against Yugoslavia – the organization had been decimated. Thousands of new Kosovar recruits from European countries began to arrive. The KLA participated in the February 1999 Rambouillet peace talks and signed the agreement. It cooperated and coordinated its operations with NATO's air forces in its bombing campaign against Yugoslav military targets.

Kossuth, Lajos (1802–1894) Hungarian nationalist and leader of the revolution of 1848. He proclaimed Hungary's independence of Habsburg rule, became governor of a Hungarian republic in 1849, and, when it was defeated by Austria and Russia, fled first to Turkey and then to exile in Britain and Italy.

Koštunica, Vojislav (1944–) Serbian nationalist politician and Yugoslavian president from October 2000 after a disputed poll victory. A wave of demonstrations was required before the election result was recognized by outgoing president Slobodan ▷Milošević. An economic liberal who was an advocate of Serbia establishing peace with its neighbours and joining Europe and European institutions, Koštunica also has strong anti-NATO views and initially pledged not to hand Milošević over to the International War Crimes Tribunal before finally doing so in Summer 2001.

Kosygin, Alexei Nikolaievich (1904–1980) Soviet politician, prime minister 1964–80. He was elected to the Supreme Soviet in 1938, became a member of the Politburo in 1946, deputy prime minister in 1960, and succeeded Khrushchev as premier (while Brezhnev succeeded him as party secretary). In the late 1960s Kosygin's influence declined.

koto Japanese musical instrument; a long ▷zither of ancient Chinese origin, having 13 silk strings supported by movable bridges. It rests on the floor and the strings are plucked with ivory plectra, producing a brittle sound.

Kourou second-largest town of French Guiana, northwest of Cayenne, site of the Guiana Space Centre of the European Space Agency; population (1996) 20,000 (20% of the total population of French Guiana).

Kovac, Michal (1930–) Slovak politician, president 1993–98, when Czechoslovakia split in two to become the Czech and Slovak republics. He was known to favour some confederal arrangement with the Czech Republic and, in consequence, his election was welcomed by the Czech government.

Kovalevskaia, Sofya Vasilevna (1850–1891) Born Sofya Vasilevna Krukovskya. Russian mathematician and novelist who worked on partial differential equations and Abelian integrals. In 1886 she won the Prix Bordin of the French Academy of Sciences for a paper on the rotation of a rigid body about a point, a problem the 18th-century mathematicians ▷Euler and ▷Lagrange had both failed to solve.

Kowloon peninsular area on the Chinese coast, until July 1997 part of the British crown colony of Hong Kong; population (2001 est) 2,024,000; the city of Kowloon is a residential area.

Krafft-Ebing, Richard, Baron von (1840–1902) German pioneer psychiatrist and neurologist. He published *Psychopathia Sexualis* (1886).

Krajina region on the frontier between Croatia and Bosnia-Herzegovina; the chief town is Knin. Dominated by Serbs, the region proclaimed itself an autonomous Serbian province after Croatia declared its independence from Yugoslavia in 1991. Krajina was the scene of intense inter-ethnic fighting during the civil war in Croatia 1991–92 and, following the ceasefire in January 1992, 10,000 UN troops were deployed here and in eastern and western Slavonia.

Krakatoa (Indonesian **Krakatau**) volcanic island in Sunda Strait, Indonesia, that erupted in 1883, causing 36,000 deaths on Java and Sumatra from the tidal waves that followed. The island is now uninhabited.

Kraków (or **Cracow**) city in Poland, on the River Vistula; population (2001 est) 735,800. It is an industrial centre producing railway wagons, paper, chemicals, and tobacco. It was capital of Poland from 1320 to 1611.

Founded in 1364, its university, at which the astronomer ▷Copernicus was a student, is one of the oldest in central Europe. There is a 14th-century Gothic cathedral.

Krasnodar (formerly **Ekaterinodar** (before 1920)) capital city, economic and cultural centre of ▷Krasnodar krai (territory), Russian Federation; population (1996 est) 648,000. The city stands on the River Kuban, 250 km/155 mi south of Rostov-on-Don, in the centre of a highly fertile agricultural region. Its industries include food processing, engineering, and oil refining. It is also

an important railway junction. There has been considerable development of financial, business, and other services since the collapse of communism in 1991. It is linked by pipeline with the Caspian oilfields.

Krasnodar krai (territory) in the southwestern Russian Federation; area 83,600 sq km/32,278 sq mi; population (1996) 5,044,000 (54% urban). The capital is ▷Krasnodar, and Armavir, Novorossiysk, Maikop, and Sochi are other cities. The territory is in northwestern ▷Caucasia, adjacent to the Black Sea and the Sea of Azov, and crossed by the River Kuban. It is lowland with black earth soil (*chernozem*) in the north, with the heavily forested northwestern part of the main Caucasian range in the south. There are oil, natural gas, and cement-marl deposits. Industries include food processing, engineering, oil extraction and refining, cement production, and manufacture of farm machinery. It is one of the main agricultural regions of the Russian Federation, growing wheat, sunflowers, rice, tobacco, fruit, and wine, and there is extensive livestock rearing.

Krasnoyarsk capital, economic and cultural centre of ▷Krasnoyarsk krai (territory), in central Siberia, Russian Federation; population (1996 est) 871,000. Situated on the Yenisey River and the ▷Trans-Siberian Railway, Krasnoyarsk played a key role in the opening up and industrial development of Siberia. Heavy-engineering works, chemical plants, and a number of light industries (including food processing) are sited within the city. Upstream from Krasnoyarsk lies a large hydroelectric power facility.

Krasnoyarsk krai (territory) in the Russian Federation, in central Siberia; area 2,401,600 sq km/927,258 sq mi (including Arctic Ocean Islands); population (1996) 3,106,000 (74% urban). The capital is ▷Krasnoyarsk and Kansk and Norilsk are other cities. The territory stretches some 3,000 km/1,870 mi north–south along the River Yenisey valley from the Arctic Ocean to the Sayan Mountains. There is lowland to the west of the Yenisey, and plateau to the east. The climate is severe, with permafrost in the north, within the Arctic Circle. The area is largely covered with coniferous forests, but with tundra in the north and fertile steppe in the south. There are huge coal, graphite, iron-ore, gold, non-ferrous metals, and uranium deposits.

Kravchuk, Leonid (1934–) Ukrainian politician, president 1990–94. Formerly a member of the Ukrainian Communist Party (UCP), he became its ideology chief in the 1980s. After the suspension of the UCP in August 1991, Kravchuk became an advocate of independence and market-centred economic reform. Faced with a rapidly deteriorating economic situation in 1993, he assumed direct control of government, eliminating the post of prime minister. He was, however, defeated by former prime minister Leonid Kuchma in the July 1994 presidential elections.

Krebs, Hans Adolf (1900–1981) German-born British biochemist who was awarded a Nobel Prize for Physiology or Medicine in 1953 for his discovery of the citric acid cycle, also known as the ▷Krebs cycle, the final pathway by which food molecules are converted into energy in living tissues. He was knighted in 1958.

Krebs first became interested in the process by which the body degrades amino acids. He discovered that nitrogen atoms are the first to be removed (deamination) and are then excreted as urea in the urine. He then investigated the processes involved in the production of urea from the removed nitrogen atoms, and by 1932 he had worked out the basic steps in the urea cycle.

Krebs cycle (or **citric acid cycle** or **tricarboxylic acid cycle**) final part of the chain of biochemical reactions by which organisms break down food using oxygen to release energy (respiration). It takes place within structures called ▷mitochondria in the body's cells, and breaks down food molecules in a series of small steps, producing energy-rich molecules of ▷ATP.

Kreisler, Fritz (1875–1962) Austrian violinist and composer. He was a US citizen from 1943. His prolific output of recordings in the early 20th century introduced a wider public to classical music from old masters such as Johann Sebastian Bach and François Couperin to moderns such as Manuel de Falla and Sergei Rachmaninov. He also composed and recorded romantic pieces in the style of the classics, often under a pseudonym. He gave the first performance of Edward Elgar's *Violin Concerto* in 1910, dedicated to him by the composer.

Kremer, Gerhard Flemish mapmaker and mathematician, see ▷Mercator, Gerardus.

Krenz, Egon (1937–) East German communist politician. A member of the East German Socialist Unity Party (SED) from 1955, he joined its politburo in 1983 and was a hardline protégé of Erich ▷Honecker, succeeding him as party leader and head of state in 1989 after widespread prodemocracy demonstrations. Pledging a 'new course', Krenz opened the country's western border and promised more open elections, but his conversion to pluralism

proved weak in the face of popular protest and he resigned in December 1989 after only a few weeks as party general secretary and head of state. In 1997 a Berlin court found Krenz guilty of manslaughter in connection with the deaths of East Germans who had attempted to flee to the West during the period of communist rule, and sentenced him to six and a half years' imprisonment. In 1999 an appeal against his conviction was unsuccessful and his conviction was upheld.

krill any of several Antarctic ▷crustaceans, the most common species being *Euphausia superba*. Similar to a shrimp, it is up to 5 cm/2 in long, with two antennae, five pairs of legs, seven pairs of light organs along the body, and is coloured orange above and green beneath. It is the most abundant animal, numbering perhaps 600 trillion (million million). (Order Euphausiacea.)

Krishna incarnation of the Hindu god ▷Vishnu. The devotion of the ▷bhakti movement is usually directed towards Krishna; an example of this is the ▷International Society for Krishna Consciousness. Many stories are told of Krishna's mischievous youth, and he is the charioteer of Arjuna in the *Bhagavad-Gītā*.

Krishna Menon, Vengalil Krishnan (1897–1974) Indian politician who was a leading light in the Indian nationalist movement. He represented India at the United Nations 1952–62, and was defence minister 1957–62, when he was dismissed by Nehru following China's invasion of northern India.

He was a barrister of the Middle Temple in London, and a Labour member of St Pancras Borough Council 1934–47. He was secretary of the India League in the UK from 1929, and in 1947 was appointed Indian high commissioner in London. He became a member of the Indian parliament in 1953, and minister without portfolio in 1956. He was dismissed by Nehru in 1962 when China invaded India after Menon's assurances to the contrary.

Kristallnacht ('night of (broken) glass') night of 9–10 November 1938 when the Nazi Sturmabteilung (SA) militia in Germany and Austria mounted a concerted attack on Jews, their synagogues, homes, and shops. It followed the assassination of a German embassy official in Paris by a Polish-Jewish youth. Subsequent measures included German legislation against Jews owning businesses or property, and restrictions on their going to school or leaving Germany. It was part of the ▷Holocaust.

Kristiansen, Ingrid (1956–) Norwegian athlete, an outstanding long-distance runner of 5,000-metre, 10,000-metre, marathon, and cross-country races. She has won all the world's leading marathons. In 1986 she knocked 45.68 seconds off the world 10,000-metre record. She was the world cross-country champion in 1988 and won the London marathon 1984–85 and 1987–88.

Krivoy Rog (Ukrainian **Kryvyy Rih**; Russian 'crooked horn') city in south-central Ukraine on the Ingulets River, 130 km/81 mi southwest of Dnipropetrovs'k; population (1990) 717,000. The district surrounding Krivoy Rog is rich in iron ore, and the city's industries centre on metallurgical products. Mining machinery, cement, and foodstuffs are also produced. Exploitation of the iron-ore deposits began on a large scale in the 1880s. Krivoy Rog was occupied by German forces 1941–44.

Kroc, Ray(mond A) (1902–1984) US restaurateur. By 1960 he had 228 McDonald's restaurants with profits of US$37 million/£23 million. He controlled all facets of franchising, even establishing Hamburger University in Elk Grove, Illinois, and requiring that all franchise owners attend to learn how to prepare the food. He was chairman of the board of McDonald's Corporation (1968–77) and senior chairman (1977–84). He bought the San Diego Padres in 1974 and established the Kroc Foundation for charitable giving.

Kronstadt uprising revolt in March 1921 by sailors of the Russian Baltic Fleet at their headquarters in Kronstadt, outside Petrograd (now St Petersburg). On the orders of the leading Bolshevik, Leon Trotsky, Red Army troops, dressed in white camouflage, crossed the ice to the naval base and captured it on 18 March. The leaders were subsequently shot.

Kropotkin, Peter Alexeivich, Prince Kropotkin (1842–1921) Russian anarchist. Imprisoned for revolutionary activities in 1874, he escaped to the UK in 1876 and later moved to Switzerland. Expelled from Switzerland in 1881, he went to France, where he was imprisoned 1883–86. He lived in Britain until 1917, when he returned to Moscow. Among his works are *Memoirs of a Revolutionist* (1899), *Mutual Aid* (1902), and *Modern Science and Anarchism* (1903).

Kruger National Park game reserve in Mpumalanga Province, South Africa, bordering Mozambique and Zimbabwe, between the Limpopo and Crocodile rivers; area about 20,720 sq km/8,000 sq mi. The Sabie Game Reserve was established in 1898 by President Kruger, and the park declared in 1926.

Kruger, (Stephanus Johannes) Paul(us) (1825–1904)
President of the Transvaal 1883–1900. He refused to remedy the
grievances of the uitlanders (English and other non-Boer white
residents) and so precipitated the Second ▷South African War.

Krupp German steelmaking armaments firm, founded in 1811
by Friedrich Krupp (1787–1826) and developed by his son **Alfred
Krupp** by pioneering the Bessemer steelmaking process. The
company developed the long-distance artillery used in World War I,
and supported Hitler's regime in preparation for World War II, after
which the head of the firm, Alfred Krupp (1907–1967), was
imprisoned.

Krym' Ukrainian name for ▷Crimea.

krypton (Greek *kryptos* 'hidden') colourless, odourless, gaseous,
nonmetallic element, symbol Kr, atomic number 36, relative atomic
mass 83.80. It is grouped with the inert gases and was long believed
not to enter into reactions, but it is now known to combine with
fluorine under certain conditions; it remains inert to all other
reagents. It is present in very small quantities in the air (about 114
parts per million). It is used chiefly in fluorescent lamps, lasers,
and gas-filled electronic valves.

Krypton was discovered in 1898 in the residue from liquid air
by British chemists William Ramsay and Morris Travers; the name
refers to their difficulty in isolating it.

KS abbreviation for ▷Kansas, a state of the USA.

K-T boundary geologists' shorthand for the boundary between
the rocks of the ▷Cretaceous and the ▷Tertiary periods 65 million
years ago. It coincides with the end of the extinction of the
dinosaurs and in many places is marked by a layer of clay or rock
enriched in the element iridium. Extinction of the dinosaurs at the
K-T boundary and deposition of the iridium layer are thought to
be the result of either impact of an asteroid or comet that crashed
into the Yucatán Peninsula (forming the **Chicxulub crater**), perhaps
combined with a period of intense volcanism on the continent of
India.

Kuala Lumpur capital of the Federation of Malaysia; area 240
sq km/93 sq mi; population (1997 est) 1,374,000. The city
developed after 1873 with the expansion of tin and rubber trading;
these are now its main industries. Formerly within the state of
Selangor, of which it was also the capital, it was created a federal
territory in 1974.

Kublai Khan (or Khubilai Khan or Kubla Khan) (*c.* 1216–1294)
Mongol emperor of China from 1259. He completed his
grandfather ▷Genghis Khan's conquest of northern China from
1240, and on his brother Mangu's death in 1259 established himself
as emperor of China. He moved the capital to Khanbalik or
Cambuluc (now the site of Beijing) and founded the Yuan dynasty,
successfully expanding his empire into southern China, Tartary, and
Tibet. He also conquered Indochina and Burma, and conducted
campaigns in other neighbouring countries to secure tribute
claims, but was defeated in an attempt to take Japan in 1281.

Kubrick, Stanley (1928–1999) US film director, producer,
and screenwriter. His work was eclectic in subject matter and
ambitious in scale and technique. It includes *Paths of Glory* (1957),
Dr Strangelove (1964), *2001: A Space Odyssey* (1968), *A Clockwork
Orange* (1971), and *Full Metal Jacket* (1987). His last film,
Eyes Wide Shut, was completed just before his death and was
released in 1999.

A former photographer in the USA, Kubrick was based in
England for much of his film-making career. Critically acclaimed
and much admired among his film-making peers, he was
responsible for *Killer's Kiss* (1955), *The Killing* (1956), *Lolita* (1962),
and *The Shining* (1980). More than any of his US contemporaries,
he achieved complete artistic control over his films.
    Related Web site: Kubrick Multimedia Film Guide http://www.
indelibleinc.com/kubrick

Kuchma, Leonid (1938–   ) Ukrainian politician, prime
minister 1992–93 and president from 1994. A traditional Soviet
technocrat, he worked his way up the hierarchy of the Communist
Party (CPSU) and, when the USSR was dissolved and Ukraine
gained independence in 1991, was well placed to assume a senior
position within the Ukrainian administration. As prime minister,
he established himself as a moderate reformer and in July 1994
defeated the incumbent Leonid Kravchuk to become president.
Once in power, his programme for reform followed a considerably
more pro-Western course than originally pledged. The economy
declined and Kuchma repeatedly replaced ministers in an attempt
to reverse the trend. He was, nevertheless, re-elected in 1999.

kudu either of two species of African antelope. The **greater kudu**
(*T. strepsiceros*) is fawn-coloured with thin white vertical stripes,
and stands 1.3 m/4.2 ft at the shoulder, with head and body 2.4 m/8
ft long. Males have long spiral horns. The greater kudu is found in
bush country from Angola to Ethiopia. The similar **lesser kudu** (*T.
imberbis*) lives in East Africa and is 1 m/3 ft at the shoulder. (Genus
Tragelaphus, family Bovidae.)

KUDU One of the largest African antelopes, the greater
kudu *Tragelaphus strepsiceros* lives in small herds on the
savannah. Normally only the males have the spirally
twisted horns. *Premaphotos Wildlife*

kudzu Japanese creeper belonging to the ▷legume family, which
helps fix nitrogen (see ▷nitrogen cycle) and can be used as a feed
crop for animals, but became a pest in the southern USA when
introduced to check soil erosion. (*Pueraria lobata*, family
Leguminosae.)

Kuhn, Thomas Samuel (1922–1996) US historian and
philosopher of science, who showed that social and cultural
conditions affect the directions of science. *The Structure of Scientific
Revolutions* (1962) argued that even scientific knowledge is relative,
dependent on the ▷paradigm (theoretical framework) that
dominates a scientific field at the time.

Ku Klux Klan US secret society dedicated to white supremacy.
It was founded in 1866 to oppose ▷Reconstruction in the Southern
states after the American ▷Civil War and to deny political rights to
the black population. Members wore hooded white robes to hide
their identity, and burned crosses at their night-time meetings. In
the late 20th
century the Klan
evolved into a
paramilitary
extremist group
and forged loose
ties with other
white supremacist
groups.
It was originally
headed by former
Confederate
general Nathan
Bedford Forrest
and was
disbanded 1869
under pressure
from members

who opposed violence. Scattered groups continued a campaign of
lynching and flogging, prompting the government to pass the
restrictive Ku Klux Klan Acts of 1871. The society re-emerged 1915
in Atlanta, Georgia, and increased in strength during the 1920s as a
racist, anti-Semitic, anti-Catholic, and anticommunist
organization, with membership reaching more than 4 million. It
was publicized in the 1960s for terrorizing civil-rights activists and
organizing racist demonstrations. In the 1990s it began actively
recruiting and organizing in the UK, with membership coming
primarily from existing extreme-right groupings.

kulak Russian term for a peasant who could afford to hire labour
and often acted as village usurer. The kulaks resisted the Soviet
government's policy of collectivization, and in 1930 they were
'liquidated as a class', with up to 5 million being either killed or
deported to Siberia.

Kulturkampf German word for a policy introduced by
Chancellor Bismarck in Germany in 1873 that isolated the Catholic
interest and attempted to reduce its power in order to create a
political coalition of liberals and agrarian conservatives. The
alienation of such a large section of the German population as the
Catholics could not be sustained, and the policy was abandoned
after 1876 to be replaced by an anti-socialist policy.

Kumasi (formerly **Coomassie**) second-largest city in Ghana,
capital of Ashanti region, situated 160 km/100 mi from the
coast within the forest zones and 180 km/112 mi northwest of
the capital and port of Accra; population (1998 est) 607,900.
Kumasi is a major centre of Ghana's transport system, with an
airport, as well as road and rail communications. It trades in cocoa,
rubber, and cattle and its market is one of the largest in Africa.
Food processing, brewing, logging, lumber, and tourism are the
main industries.

kumquat small orange-yellow fruit of any of several evergreen
trees native to East Asia and cultivated throughout the tropics. The
trees grow 2.4–3.6 m/8–12 ft high and have dark green shiny leaves
and white scented flowers. The fruit is eaten fresh (the skin is
edible), preserved, or candied. The oval or Nagami kumquat is the
most common variety. (Genus *Fortunella*, family Rutaceae.)

Kun, Béla (1886–1937) Hungarian politician. He created a
Soviet republic in Hungary in March 1919, which was overthrown
in August 1919 by a Western blockade and Romanian military
actions. The succeeding regime under Admiral ▷Horthy effectively
liquidated both socialism and liberalism in Hungary.

Kundera, Milan (1929–   ) Czech writer. His first novel,
The Joke (1967), brought him into official disfavour in Prague, and,
unable to publish further works, he moved to France. Other novels
include *The Book of Laughter and Forgetting* (1979) and *The
Unbearable Lightness of Being* (1984; filmed 1988).
    **Related Web site: Milan Kundera, The Unbearable Lightness of
Being, and Prague** http://www.georgetown.edu/irvinemj/
english016/kundera/kundera.html

Kung (formerly **Bushman**) member of a small group of hunter-
gatherer peoples of the northeastern Kalahari, southern Africa, still
living to some extent nomadically. Their language belongs to the
▷Khoisan family.

kung fu (Mandarin **ch'üan fa**) Chinese art of unarmed combat,
one of the ▷martial arts. It is practised in many forms, the most
popular being *wing chun*, 'beautiful springtime'. The basic principle
is to use attack as a form of defence.
    Related Web site: Planet Wing Chun http://www.wingchun.com/

Kunming (formerly **Yünnan**) capital of ▷Yunnan province,
China, on Lake Dianchi, about 2,000 m/6,500 ft above sea level;
population (1994) 1,625,000. It is an important trading centre
between the far west and central and south China. Industries
include engineering and the manufacture of chemicals,
textiles, iron, steel, machinery, cigarettes, heavy goods
vehicles, plastics, and cement. Copper is smelted with nearby
hydroelectric power.

Kuomintang original spelling of the Chinese nationalist party,
now known (outside Taiwan) as ▷Guomindang.

Kurd member of a people living mostly in the Taurus and Sagros
mountains of eastern Turkey, western Iran, and northern Iraq in the
region called ▷Kurdistan. The Kurds have suffered repression in
several countries, most brutally in Iraq, where in 1991 more than
1 million were forced to flee their homes. They speak an Indo-
Iranian language and are predominantly Sunni Muslims, although
there are some Shiites in Iran.

Kurdish language language belonging to the Indo-Iranian
branch of the Indo-European family, closely related to Farsi
(Persian). It is spoken by the Kurds, a geographically divided ethnic
group. Its numerous dialects fall into two main groups: northern

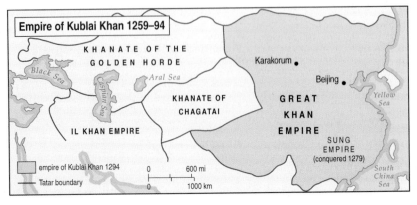

Empire of Kublai Khan 1259–94

KHANATE OF THE
GOLDEN HORDE

Black Sea

Aral Sea

Caspian Sea

Karakorum •

Beijing •

KHANATE OF
CHAGATAI

IL KHAN EMPIRE

GREAT
KHAN
EMPIRE

Yellow
Sea

SUNG
EMPIRE
(conquered 1279)

South
China
Sea

☐ empire of Kublai Khan 1294
— Tatar boundary

0   600 mi
0   1000 km

Kurmanji and southern Kurmanji (also known as Sorani). Around 60% of Kurds speak one of the northern Kurmanji dialects. Related languages include Zaza and Gurani. Three different alphabets are used – Arabic, Latin, and Cyrillic.

Kurdistan (or **Kordestan**) mountain and plateau region in southwest Asia near Mount Ararat, where the borders of Iran, Iraq, Syria, Turkey, Armenia, and Azerbaijan meet; area 193,000 sq km/74,600 sq mi; total population 25–30 million. It is the home of the ▷Kurds and is the area over which Kurdish nationalists have traditionally fought to win sovereignty. It is also

the name of a northwest Iranian province in the Zagros Mountains, covering 25,000 sq km/9,650 sq mi, population (1991) 1,233,500. The chief towns of the region are ▷Kermanshah (Iran); Irbil, Sulaymaniyah, and ▷Kirkuk (Iraq); Divarbakir, Erzurum, and ▷Van (Turkey); and Qamishle (Syria). See map on p. 531.

Kuril Islands (or **Kuriles**) chain of about 50 small islands belonging to Russia, stretching from the northeast of Hokkaido, Japan, to the south of Kamchatka, Russia, area 14,765 sq km/5,700 sq mi; population (1990) 25,000. Some of the islands are of volcanic origin with active volcanoes and hot springs. Two of the Kurils

(Etorofu and Kunashiri) are claimed by Japan for historical reasons; they are of strategic importance and have mineral deposits. The surrounding waters are rich in salmon and cod.

Kurosawa, Akira (1910–1998) Japanese director. His film *Rashōmon* (1950) introduced Western audiences to Japanese cinema. Epics such as *Shichinin no samurai/Seven Samurai* (1954) combine spectacle with intimate human drama. Kurosawa's films with a contemporary setting include *Yoidore tenshi/Drunken Angel* (1948) and *Ikiru/Living* (1952), both using illness as metaphor.

Kuwait

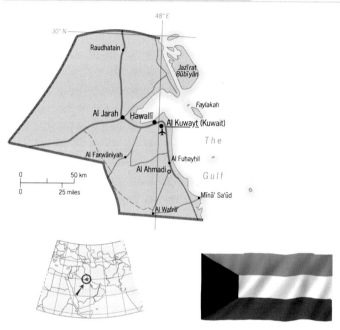

KUWAIT Water towers outside Kuwait city. Water, always scarce in this desert country, is provided from both underground freshwater supplies and the distillation of seawater. *Corel*

LANGUAGE Arabic (78%) (official), English, Kurdish (10%), Farsi (4%)
RELIGION Sunni Muslim 45%, Shiite Muslim 40%; Christian, Hindu, and Parsi about 5%
EDUCATION (compulsory years) 8
LITERACY RATE 85% (men); 82% (women) (2003 est)
LABOUR FORCE 1.6% agriculture, 7.0% industry, 91.4% services (2000)
LIFE EXPECTANCY 75 (men); 79 (women) (2000–05)
CHILD MORTALITY RATE (under 5, per 1,000 live births) 10 (2001)
PHYSICIANS (per 1,000 people) 1.3 (1999 est)
HOSPITAL BEDS (per 1,000 people) 6.1 (1999 est)
TV SETS (per 1,000 people) 482 (2001 est)
RADIOS (per 1,000 people) 632 (1999)
INTERNET USERS (per 10,000 people) 1,057.5 (2002 est)
PERSONAL COMPUTER USERS (per 100 people) 12.1 (2002 est)

See also ▷Iran–Iraq War; ▷Gulf War.

Kuwait country in southwest Asia, bounded north and northwest by Iraq, east by the Persian Gulf, and south and southwest by Saudi Arabia.

NATIONAL NAME *Dowlat al-Kuwayt/State of Kuwait*
AREA 17,819 sq km/6,879 sq mi
CAPITAL Kuwait (and chief port)
MAJOR TOWNS/CITIES as-Salimiya, Hawalli, Al Farwaaniyah, Abraq Kheetan, Al Jahrah, Al Ahmadi, Al Fuhayhil
PHYSICAL FEATURES hot desert; islands of Faylakah, Bubiyan, and Warbah at northeast corner of Arabian Peninsula

Government

HEAD OF STATE Sheikh Jabir al-Ahmad al-Jabir al-Sabah from 1977
HEAD OF GOVERNMENT Sabah al-Ahmad al-Jabir al-Sabah from 2003
POLITICAL SYSTEM absolutist
POLITICAL EXECUTIVE absolute
ADMINISTRATIVE DIVISIONS six governorates
ARMED FORCES 15,500 (2002 est)
CONSCRIPTION compulsory for two years (one year for university students)
DEATH PENALTY retained and used for ordinary crimes
DEFENCE SPEND (% GDP) 10.7 (2002 est)
EDUCATION SPEND (% GDP) 3.3 (2001 est)
HEALTH SPEND (% GDP) 3 (2000 est)

Economy and resources

CURRENCY Kuwaiti dinar
GPD (US$) 32.8 billion (2002 est)
REAL GDP GROWTH (% change on previous year) –1.0 (2001)
GNI (US$) 37.4 billion (2002 est)
GNI PER CAPITA (PPP) (US$) 18,800 (2002 est)
CONSUMER PRICE INFLATION 2% (2003 est)

UNEMPLOYMENT 1.1% (2001)
FOREIGN DEBT (US$) 10.5 billion (2001 est)
MAJOR TRADING PARTNERS USA, Japan, Germany, France, South Korea, UK, Italy, Singapore, the Netherlands, Pakistan
RESOURCES petroleum, natural gas, mineral water
INDUSTRIES petroleum refining, petrochemicals, food processing, gases, construction
EXPORTS petroleum and petroleum products (accounted for more than 93% of export revenue in 1994), chemical fertilizer, gas (natural and manufactured), basic manufactures. Principal market: Japan 21.2% (2000)
IMPORTS consumer goods, machinery and transport equipment, basic manufactures (especially iron, steel, and textiles) and other manufactured goods, live animals and food. Principal source: USA 12.9% (2000)
ARABLE LAND 0.4% (2000 est)
AGRICULTURAL PRODUCTS melons, tomatoes, cucumbers, onions; livestock rearing (poultry); fishing

Population and society

POPULATION 2,521,000 (2003 est)
POPULATION GROWTH RATE 2.1% (2000–15)
POPULATION DENSITY (per sq km) 142 (2003 est)
URBAN POPULATION (% of total) 96 (2003 est)
AGE DISTRIBUTION (% of total population) 0–14 28%, 15–59 67%, 60+ 5% (2002 est)
ETHNIC GROUPS about 45% Kuwaiti, 35% non-Kuwaiti Arab, 9% Indian and Pakistani, 4% Iranian

Chronology

c. **3000 BC**: Archaeological evidence suggests that coastal parts of Kuwait may have been part of a commercial civilization contemporary with the Sumerian, based in Mesopotamia (the Tigris and Euphrates valley area of Iraq).

c. **323 BC**: Visited by Greek colonists at the time of Alexander the Great.

7th century AD: Islam introduced.

late 16th century: Fell under nominal control of Turkish Ottoman Empire.

1710: Control was assumed by the Utab, a member of the Anaza tribal confederation in northern Arabia, and Kuwait city was founded, soon developing from a fishing village into an important port.

1756: Autonomous Sheikhdom of Kuwait founded by Abd Rahman of the al-Sabah family, a branch of the Utab.

1776: British East India Company set up a base in the Gulf.

1899: Concerned at the potential threat of growing Ottoman and German influence, Britain signed a treaty with Kuwait, establishing a self-governing protectorate in which the Emir received an annual subsidy from Britain in return for agreeing not to alienate any territory to a foreign power.

1914: Britain recognized Kuwait as an 'independent government under British protection'.

1922–33: Agreement on frontiers with Iraq, to the north, and Nejd (later Saudi Arabia) to the southwest.

1938: Oil discovered; large-scale exploitation after World War II transformed the economy.

1961: Full independence achieved from Britain, with Sheikh Abdullah al-Salem al-Sabah as emir. Attempted Iraqi invasion discouraged by dispatch of British troops to the Gulf.

1962: Constitution introduced, with franchise restricted to 10% of the population.

1977: Crown Prince Jabir Al Ahmad Al Jabir Al Sabah became Emir. The National Assembly was dissolved.

1978: Sheikh Saad al-Abdullah al-Salem al-Sabah was appointed prime minister by the emir.

1981: The National Assembly was reconstituted.

1983: Shiite guerrillas bombed targets in Kuwait; 17 were arrested.

1986: The National Assembly was dissolved.

1987: Kuwaiti oil tankers were reflagged and received US Navy protection; there were missile attacks by Iran.

1988: Aircraft hijacked by pro-Iranian Shiites demanding the release of convicted guerrillas; Kuwait refused.

1989: Two of the convicted guerrillas were released.

1990: Prodemocracy demonstrations were suppressed. Kuwait was annexed by Iraq in August, causing extensive damage to property and environment. The emir set up a government in exile in Saudi Arabia.

1991: US-led coalition forces defeated Iraqi forces in Kuwait in the Gulf War. The new government omitted any opposition representatives.

1992: The reconstituted national assembly was elected, with opposition nominees, including Islamic candidates, winning the majority of seats.

1993: Incursions by Iraq into Kuwait were repelled by US-led air strikes on Iraqi military sites.

1994: The massing of Iraqi troops on the Kuwaiti border prompted a US-led response. Iraqi president Saddam Hussein publicly renounced any claim to Kuwait.

1999: A decree to secure a political voice for women in Kuwait was defeated in parliament, in the belief that female participation in politics would violate the principles of Islam and Kuwaiti traditions.

2000: The high court upheld parliament's refusal to allow women the vote.

Yōjimbō (1961), *Kagemusha* (1981), and *Ran* (1985), loosely based on Shakespeare's *King Lear*, are historical films with an increasingly bleak outlook.

Kuroshio (or **Japan Current**) warm ocean ▷current flowing from Japan to North America.

Kursk capital city, economic and cultural centre of Kursk oblast (region), western Russian Federation, on the banks of the River Seim, and bordered on the west by Ukraine; population (1996 est) 442,000. It has engineering, chemical, textile, and light industries, and is an important railway junction. Kursk and the surrounding region was the site of a decisive tank battle in July–August 1943, which signalled the ultimate defeat of German forces on the Eastern Front.

Kuti, Fela Anikulapo (1938–1997) Nigerian singer, songwriter, and musician. He was a strong proponent of African nationalism and ethnic identity. His albums of big-band African funk include *Coffin for Head of State* (1978), *Teacher Don't Teach Me Nonsense* (1987), and *Underground System* (1993).

Kutuzov, Mikhail Illarionovich (1745–1813) Prince of Smolensk. Commander of the Russian forces in the Napoleonic Wars. He commanded an army corps at ▷Austerlitz and the army in its retreat in 1812. After the burning of Moscow that year, he harried the French throughout their retreat and later took command of the united Prussian armies.

Kuwait see country box.

Kuwait (Arabic Al Kuwayt); formerly Qurein) chief port and capital of the state of Kuwait, on the southern shore of Kuwait Bay; population (1995 est) 28,700. Kuwait is a banking and investment centre. It was heavily damaged during the Gulf War.

Kwangchow alternative transliteration of ▷Guangzhou, capital of Guangdong province, China.

Kwangju (or **Kwangchu**) capital of South Cholla province, southwestern South Korea; population (1995 est) 1,257,500. It is at the centre of a rice-growing region. Beverages, textiles, and motor vehicles are also important industries. The city dates from the first century BC, but grew rapidly in modern times after being linked by rail to Seoul in 1914.

Kyrgyzstan

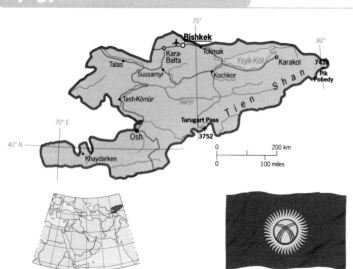

Kyrgyzstan country in central Asia, bounded north by Kazakhstan, east by China, west by Uzbekistan, and south by Tajikistan.

NATIONAL NAME *Kyrgyz Respublikasy/Kyrgyz Republic*
AREA 198,500 sq km/76,640 sq mi
CAPITAL Bishkek (formerly Frunze)
MAJOR TOWNS/CITIES Osh, Karakol, Kyzyl-Kiya, Tokmak, Djalal-Abad
PHYSICAL FEATURES mountainous, an extension of the Tien Shan range

Government

HEAD OF STATE Askar Akayev from 1991
HEAD OF GOVERNMENT Nikolai Tanaev from 2002
POLITICAL SYSTEM emergent democracy
POLITICAL EXECUTIVE limited presidency
ADMINISTRATIVE DIVISIONS seven regions and the municipality of Bishkek, the capital
ARMED FORCES 10,900 (2002 est)
CONSCRIPTION compulsory for 18 months
DEATH PENALTY retained and used for ordinary crimes
DEFENCE SPEND (% GDP) 1.9 (2002 est)
EDUCATION SPEND (% GDP) 3.7 (2001 est)
HEALTH SPEND (% GDP) 6 (2000 est)

Economy and resources

CURRENCY som
GPD (US$) 1.6 billion (2002 est)
REAL GDP GROWTH (% change on previous year) 5.3 (2001)
GNI (US$) 1.5 billion (2002 est)
GNI PER CAPITA (PPP) (US$) 1,520 (2002 est)
CONSUMER PRICE INFLATION 3.9% (2003 est)
UNEMPLOYMENT 9% (2001)
FOREIGN DEBT (US$) 1.6 billion (2001 est)
MAJOR TRADING PARTNERS Germany, Russia, Uzbekistan, Kazakhstan, Turkey, China, USA

RESOURCES petroleum, natural gas, coal, gold, tin, mercury, antimony, zinc, tungsten, uranium
INDUSTRIES metallurgy, machinery, electronics and instruments, textiles, food processing (particularly sugar refining), mining
EXPORTS non-ferrous metallurgy, wool, cotton yarn, tobacco, electric power, electronic and engineering products, food and beverages. Principal market: Germany 28.7% (2001)
IMPORTS petroleum, natural gas, engineering products, food products, chemicals. Principal source: Russia 23.9% (2001)
ARABLE LAND 7.1% (2000 est)
AGRICULTURAL PRODUCTS grain, potatoes, cotton, tobacco, sugar beet, hemp, kenat, kendyr, medicinal plants; livestock rearing (sheep, cattle, goats, yaks, and horses) is the mainstay of agricultural activity

Population and society

POPULATION 5,138,000 (2003 est)
POPULATION GROWTH RATE 1.1% (2000–15)
POPULATION DENSITY (per sq km) 26 (2003 est)
URBAN POPULATION (% of total) 34 (2003 est)
AGE DISTRIBUTION (% of total population) 0–14 32%, 15–59 598%, 60+ 9% (2002 est)
ETHNIC GROUPS 60% ethnic Kyrgyz, 15% Russian, 14% Uzbek, 2% Ukrainian; Dungan, German, Kazakh, Korean, Tajik, Tartar and Uighar minorities
LANGUAGE Kyrgyz (a Turkic language; official), Russian
RELIGION Sunni Muslim 70%, Russian Orthodox 20%

KYRGYZSTAN The yurt, a circular tent made of felt bound onto a wicker frame, is a typical dwelling for the nomads of Kyrgyzstan. Travelling widely in search of water and pasture for their livestock, the 40,000 or so Kyrgyz nomads find this form of accommodation ideal, as it is cheap, lightweight, and collapsible. *Simon Harris-Ward*

EDUCATION (compulsory years) 9
LITERACY RATE 99% (men); 98% (women) (2003 est)
LABOUR FORCE 52.4% agriculture, 11.6% industry, 36.0% services (1999)
LIFE EXPECTANCY 65 (men); 72 (women) (2000–05)
CHILD MORTALITY RATE (under 5, per 1,000 live births) 61 (2001)
PHYSICIANS (per 1,000 people) 3 (1999 est)
HOSPITAL BEDS (per 1,000 people) 9.5 (1999 est)

TV SETS (per 1,000 people) 49 (2001 est)
RADIOS (per 1,000 people) 112 (1997)
INTERNET USERS (per 10,000 people) 298.3 (2002 est)
PERSONAL COMPUTER USERS (per 100 people) 1.3 (2002 est)

See also ▷Manchu; ▷Russian Federation; ▷Turkestan; ▷Union of Soviet Socialist Republics.

Chronology

8th century: Spread of Islam.

10th century onwards: Southward migration of Kyrgyz people from upper Yenisey River region to Tien Shan region; accelerated following rise of Mongol Empire in 13th century.

13th–14th centuries: Part of Mongol Empire.

1685: Came under control of Mongol Oirots following centuries of Turkic rule.

1758: Kyrgyz people became nominal subjects of Chinese Empire, following Oirots' defeat by Chinese rulers, the Manchus.

early 19th century: Came under suzerainty of Khanate (chieftaincy) of Kokand, to the west.

1864–76: Incorporated into tsarist Russian Empire.

1916–17: Many Kyrgyz migrated to China after Russian suppression of rebellion in Central Asia and outbreak of civil war following 1917 October Revolution in Russia, with local armed guerrillas (*basmachi*) resisting Bolshevik Red Army.

1917–1924: Part of independent Turkestan republic.

1920s: Land reforms resulted in settlement of many formerly nomadic Kyrgyz; literacy and education improved.

1924: Became autonomous republic within USSR.

1930s: Agricultural collectivization programme provoked *basmachi* resistance and local 'nationalist communists' were purged from Kyrgyz Communist Party (KCP).

1936: Became full union republic within USSR.

1990: A state of emergency was imposed in Bishkek after ethnic clashes.

1991: Askar Akayev, a reform communist, was chosen as president, and condemned the attempted coup in Moscow against the reformist Mikhail Gorbachev; Kyrgyzstan joined the new Commonwealth of Independent States (CIS).

1992: Kyrgyzstan joined the United Nations and Conference on Security and Cooperation in Europe (CSCE; now the Organization on Security and Cooperation in Europe, OSCE). Economic reform was instituted.

1994: The country joined the Central Asian Union, with Kazakhstan and Uzbekistan.

1996: A constitutional amendment increased the powers of the president.

1997: Private ownership of land was legalized but the privatization programme was suspended.

1998: A referendum approved the private ownership of land.

1999: Amengeldy Muraliyev was appointed prime minister.

2000: Islamist rebels crossed into the country from Afghanistan via Tajikistan, reportedly seeking to create an Islamic state in east Uzbekistan. Akayer was re-elected president and Kurmanbek Bakiyev was appointed prime minister.

2002: Prime Minister Bakiyev resigned after 13 days of anti-government protests and hunger strikes. The civil unrest followed the killing by police of five protesters after the arrest of opposition politician Azimbek Beknazarov.

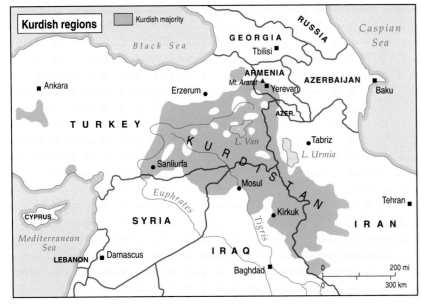

KURDISH REGIONS Kurdish lands stretch from Turkey to Iran. See entry on p. 529.

Kwangsi Chuang Autonomous Region alternative transliteration of ▷Guangxi Zhuang Autonomous Region, China.

Kwangtung alternative transliteration of ▷Guangdong, a province of China.

Kwannon (or **Kannon**) in Buddhism, a form, often regarded as female (and known to the West as 'goddess of mercy'), of the bodhisattva ▷Avalokiteśvara. Kwannon is the most important bodhisattva in all main schools of Buddhism, and is an attendant of Amida Buddha. Kwannon is sometimes depicted with many arms extending compassion.

kwashiorkor severe protein deficiency in children under five years, resulting in retarded growth, lethargy, ▷oedema, diarrhoea, and a swollen abdomen. It is common in Third World countries with a high incidence of malnutrition.

KwaZulu former Black National State in former Natal Province, South Africa. In 1994 it became part of ▷KwaZulu-Natal Province. It achieved self-governing status in 1971. In 1994 it was placed under a state of emergency in the run-up to the first multiracial elections, after mounting violence by the Zulu-based ▷Inkatha party threatened to destabilize the election process. Homelands were to progressively disappear under the 1993 nonracial constitution, but Inkatha's leader (and the homeland's chief minister), Mangosuthu Buthelezi, won substantial concessions for KwaZulu prior to agreeing to participate in the elections.

KwaZulu-Natal province of the Republic of South Africa, formed from the former province of Natal and the former Black National State of KwaZulu; area 91,481 sq km/35,321 sq mi; population (1995 est) 8,713,100 (75% Zulu). The capital is Pietermaritzburg, and Durban and Richards Bay are other towns. The province is a narrow plain bounded by the Drakensberg Mountains to the west and the Indian Ocean to the east. Industries include oil refining, coal, iron and steel, engineering, and food processing. Agricultural products include sugar, maize, fruit, black wattle, maize, tobacco, and vegetables. Languages spoken are Zulu (80%), English (15%), and Afrikaans (2%).

Features Ndumu Game Reserve, Kosi Bay Nature Reserve, Sodwana Bay National Park, and Maple Lane Nature Reserve are features of the province. St Lucia National Park extends from the coral reefs of the Indian Ocean north of Umfolozi River (where whales, dolphins, turtles, and crayfish are found), over forested sandhills to inland grasslands and swamps of Lake St Lucia, 324 sq km/125 sq mi (where reedbuck, buffalo, crocodiles, hippopotami, black rhinos, cheetahs, pelicans, flamingos, and storks are found). It is under threat from titanium mining.

History The British colony of Natal annexed Zululand in 1897 and it became part of the Union of South Africa in 1910. KwaZulu-Natal was created in May 1994.

Kweichow alternative transliteration of ▷Guizhou, a province of China.

Kweilin alternative transliteration of ▷Guilin, a city in Guangxi Zhuang Autonomous Region, China.

KY abbreviation for ▷Kentucky, a state of the USA.

kyanite aluminium silicate, Al_2SiO_5, a pale-blue mineral occurring as blade-shaped crystals. It is an indicator of high-pressure conditions in metamorphic rocks formed from clay sediments. Andalusite, kyanite, and sillimanite are all polymorphs (see ▷polymorphism).

Kyd, Thomas (c. 1557–1595) English dramatist. He was the author of a bloody revenge tragedy, *The Spanish Tragedy* (printed about 1590), which anticipated elements present in Shakespeare's *Hamlet*. His *Pompey the Great* (1594) was translated from the French of Robert Garnier. He probably wrote *Solyman and Perseda* (1592), and perhaps had a part in *Arden of Feversham* (1592), the first of many domestic tragedies.

Kyoto (or **Kioto**) former capital of Japan 794–1868 (when the capital was changed to Tokyo) on Honshu island, linked by canal with Lake Biwa, 510 km/317 mi west of Tokyo and 40 km/25 mi northeast of Osaka; population (2000 est) 1,468,000. Industries include electrical, chemical, and machinery plants; silk weaving; and the manufacture of porcelain, bronze, lacquerware, dolls, and fans.

Kyprianou, Spyros (1932–) Cypriot politician, president 1977–88. Foreign minister 1961–72, he founded the federalist, centre-left Democratic Front in 1976.

Kyrgyzstan (or **Kirghizia**) see country box.

Kyushu (or **Kiushu**) southernmost of the main islands of Japan, separated from Shikoku island by the Bungo Strait, from Honshu island by the Kammon Strait, and from Korea by the Korea Strait; connected to Honshu by bridge and rail tunnel; area 42,150 sq km/16,270 sq mi, including about 370 small islands; population (2000 est) 13,446,000. The capital is ▷Nagasaki, and Fukuoka, Kumamoto, Kagoshima, and Kitakyushu are other cities. The island is mountainous, with a subtropical climate. It is volcanic and the active volcano Aso-take (1,592 m/5,225 ft) has the world's largest crater. Industries include semiconductors, coal, gold, silver, iron, tin, timber, tourism, cattle, and hogs. Agricultural products include rice, tea, oranges, tobacco, and sweet potatoes.

KYOTO The Tofuku-ji Zen garden in Kyoto, Japan. Zen gardens are designed to suggest an infinite yet enclosed space, and are closer to landscape painting than to nature. The most austere type of Zen garden is the dry landscape. These were first created in the late 15th century and are intended purely for meditation. *Image Bank*

L

L Roman numeral for 50.

l symbol for ▷litre, a measure of liquid volume.

LA abbreviation for ▷Louisiana, a state of the USA; **Los Angeles**, a city in California, USA.

Laâyoune (Arabic **El Aaiún**) capital of ▷Western Sahara; population (1998 est) 139,000. It has expanded from a population of 25,000 in 1970 as a result of Moroccan investment (Morocco lays claim to Western Sahara). Laâyoune is the main urban centre of the country, which was formerly the Spanish Sahara, and lies in an artificial oasis where, through irrigation, cereals and vegetables are grown. To the southwest, especially at Bu Craa, there are large deposits of phosphates, which are linked to the coast by a conveyor belt 29 km/18 mi long, though exploitation has been handicapped by a shortage of water in the area. Since 1976 it has been capital of the (not internationally recognized) Laâyoune province.

Lab abbreviation for ▷Labour, a political party in the UK; or ▷Labrador, an area in northeastern Canada.

Labanotation comprehensive system of accurate dance notation (*Kinetographie Laban*) devised in 1928 by Rudolf von Laban. It uses a set of graphic symbols arranged on a vertical staff that represents the human body. The varying length of the symbols indicates the timing of the movements. It is commonly used as a means of copyright protection for choreographers.

labelled compound (or **tagged compound**) chemical compound in which a radioactive isotope is substituted for a stable one. The path taken by such a compound through a system can be followed, for example by measuring the radiation emitted.

labelling in sociology, defining or describing a person in terms of his or her behaviour; for example, describing someone who has broken a law as a criminal. Labelling theory deals with human interaction, behaviour, and control, particularly in the field of deviance.

labellum lower petal of an orchid flower; it is a different shape from the two lateral petals and gives the orchid its characteristic appearance. The labellum is more elaborate and usually larger than the other petals. It often has distinctive patterning to encourage ▷pollination by insects; sometimes it is extended backwards to form a hollow spur containing nectar.

Labor, Knights of in US history, a national labour organization founded by Philadelphia tailor Uriah Stephens in 1869 and committed to cooperative enterprise, equal pay for both sexes, and an eight-hour day. The Knights grew rapidly in the mid-1880s under Terence V Powderly (1849–1924) but gave way to the ▷American Federation of Labor after 1886.

Labor Party in Australia, a political party based on socialist principles. It was founded in 1891 and first held office in 1904. It formed governments 1929–31 and 1939–49, but in the intervening periods internal discord provoked splits, and reduced its effectiveness. It returned to power under Gough Whitlam 1972–75, and again under Bob Hawke in 1983, he was succeeded as party leader and prime minister by Paul Keating in 1991, who subsequently lost the 1996 general election.

Labour Day legal national holiday in honour of workers. In Canada and the USA, **Labor Day** is celebrated on the first Monday in September. In many countries it coincides with ▷May Day, the first day of May.

Labour Party UK political party based on socialist principles, originally formed to represent workers. It was founded in 1900 and first held office in 1924. The first majority Labour government 1945–51 introduced ▷nationalization and the National Health Service, and expanded ▷social security. Labour was again in power 1964–70, 1974–79 and from 1997. The party leader (Tony ▷Blair from 1994) is elected by an electoral college, with a weighted representation of the Parliamentary Labour Party (30%), constituency parties (30%), and trade unions (40%).

The Labour Party, the Trades Union Congress, and the cooperative movement together form the National Council of Labour, whose aims are to coordinate political activities and take joint action on specific issues.

Although the Scottish socialist Keir Hardie and John Burns, a workers' leader, entered Parliament independently as Labour members in 1892, it was not until 1900 that a conference representing the trade unions, the Independent Labour Party (ILP), and the ▷Fabian Society, founded the Labour Party, known until 1906, when 29 seats were gained, as the Labour Representation Committee. All but a pacifist minority of the Labour Party supported World War I, and in 1918 a socialist programme was first adopted, with local branches of the party set up to which individual members were admitted. By 1922 the Labour Party was recognized as the official opposition, and in 1924 formed a minority government (with Liberal support) for a few months under the party's first secretary Ramsay MacDonald.

A second minority government in 1929 followed a conservative policy, and in 1931 MacDonald and other leaders, faced with a financial crisis, left the party to support the national government. The ILP seceded in 1932.

In 1936–39 there was internal dissension on foreign policy; the leadership's support of nonintervention in Spain was strongly criticized and Stafford Cripps, Aneurin Bevan, and others were expelled for advocating an alliance of all left-wing parties against the government of Neville Chamberlain. The Labour Party supported Winston Churchill's wartime coalition, but then withdrew and took office for the first time as a majority government under Clement ▷Attlee, party leader from 1935, after the 1945 elections. The ▷welfare state was developed by nationalization of essential services and industries, a system of national insurance was established in 1946, and the National ▷Health Service was founded 1948. Defeated in 1951, Labour was split by disagreements on further nationalization, and unilateral or multilateral disarmament, but achieved unity under Hugh Gaitskell's leadership 1955–63.

Under Harold ▷Wilson the party returned to power 1964–70 and, with a very slender majority, 1974–79. James ▷Callaghan, who had succeeded Wilson in 1976, was forced to a general election in 1979 and lost. Michael ▷Foot was elected to the leadership in 1980; Neil ▷Kinnock succeeded him in 1983 after Labour had lost another general election. The party adopted a policy of unilateral nuclear disarmament in 1986 and expelled the left-wing faction Militant Tendency, but rifts remained. Labour lost the 1987 general election, a major reason being its non-nuclear policy. In spite of the Conservative government's declining popularity, Labour was defeated in the 1992 general election, following which Neil Kinnock stepped down as party leader. Party membership fell to a low of 260,000 in 1990 and John Smith succeeded Kinnock in July 1992 but died suddenly in May 1994. Tony Blair was elected to succeed him July in 1994, in the first fully democratic elections to the post, and launched a campaign to revise the party's constitution by scrapping Clause 4, concerning common ownership of the means of production, and ending trade union direct sponsorship of MPs; a new charter was approved in April 1995.

Under the title **New Labour**, Blair sought to move the party nearer to the 'middle ground' of politics to secure the 'middle England' vote. By 1996 Labour Party membership was 365,000 and rising and it led the Conservatives in the opinion polls by more than 20 points. The Labour Party returned to power after a landslide victory in the May 1997 general election. Membership peaked in Janurary 1998, at 405,000, and began to gradually decline for the first time since Blair became leader, amid concerns among traditional members that control over the party had become too centralized. The opinion-poll rating of Blair slumped to its lowest since he took office in September 2000, following popular protests over fuel prices and general discontent with Labour policies. For the first time since Labour won power in 1997, opinion polls put the popularity of the Conservative Party ahead of Labour by four percentage points.

Labour Representation Committee in British politics, a forerunner (1900–06) of the Labour Party. The committee was founded in February 1900 after a resolution drafted by Ramsay ▷MacDonald, and moved by the Amalgamated Society of Railway Workers (now the National Union of Railwaymen), was carried at the 1899 Trades Union Congress (TUC). The resolution called for a special congress of the TUC parliamentary committee to campaign for more Labour members of Parliament. Ramsay MacDonald became its secretary. Following his efforts, 29 Labour members of Parliament were elected in the 1906 general election, and the Labour Representation Committee was renamed the Labour Party.

labour theory of value in classical economics, the theory that the price (value) of a product directly reflects the amount of labour it involves. According to the theory, if the price of a product falls, either the share of labour in that product has declined or that expended in the production of other goods has risen.

Labrador area in northeastern Canada, part of the province of ▷Newfoundland, lying between Ungava Bay on the northwest, the Atlantic Ocean on the east, and the Strait of Belle Isle on the southeast; area 266,060 sq km/102,730 sq mi; population (1991) 30,000. The most easterly part of the North American mainland, Labrador consists primarily of a gently sloping plateau with an irregular coastline of numerous bays, fjords, inlets, and cliffs (60–120 m/200–400 ft high). Its industries include fisheries, timber and pulp, and the mining of various minerals, especially iron ore. Hydroelectric resources include Churchill Falls, where one of the world's largest underground power houses is situated (opened in 1971). There is a Canadian Air Force base at Goose Bay on Lake Melville.

La Bruyère, Jean de (1645–1696) French writer and moralist. He was born in Paris, studied law, took a post in the revenue office, and in 1684 entered the service of the French commander the Prince of ▷Condé as tutor to his grandson. His 'Caractères/The Characters' (1688), a penetrating study of human behaviour in the form of satirical pen-portraits of his contemporaries, made him many enemies. The work is remarkable also for its highly critical account of French society in the last years of the 17th century. La Bruyère's style is notable for its rich vocabulary and infinite variety of phrase.

laburnum any of a group of flowering trees or shrubs belonging to the pea family; the seeds develop in pealike pods but are poisonous. *L. anagyroides*, native to the mountainous parts of central Europe, is often grown as an ornamental tree. The flowers, in long drooping clusters, are bright yellow and appear in early spring; some varieties have purple or reddish flowers. (Genus *Laburnum*, family Leguminosae.)

Labyrinth in Greek legend, the maze designed by the Athenian artisan Daedalus at Knossos in Crete for King Minos, as a home for the Minotaur – a monster, half man and half bull. After killing the Minotaur, Theseus, the prince of Athens, was guided out of the Labyrinth by a thread given to him by the king's daughter Ariadne.

labyrinthitis inflammation of the part of the inner ear responsible for the sense of balance (the labyrinth). It results in dizziness, which may then cause nausea and vomiting. It is usually caused by a viral infection of the ear (▷otitis), which resolves in a few weeks. The nausea and vomiting may respond to anti-emetic drugs.

lac resinous incrustation produced by the female of the lac insect (*Laccifer lacca*), which eventually covers the twigs of trees in India and the Far East. The gathered twigs are known as **stick lac**, and yield a useful crimson dye; **shellac**, which is used in varnishes, polishes, and leather dressings, is manufactured commercially by melting the separated resin and spreading it into thin layers or flakes.

Laccadive, Minicoy, and Amindivi Islands former name of the Indian island group ▷Lakshadweep.

laccolith intruded mass of igneous rock that forces apart two strata and forms a round lens-shaped mass many times wider than thick. The overlying layers are often pushed upward to form a dome. A classic development of laccoliths is illustrated in the Henry, La Sal, and Abajo mountains of southeastern Utah, USA, found on the Colorado plateau.

lace delicate, decorative, openwork textile fabric. Lace is a European craft with centres in Belgium, Italy, France, Germany, and England.

lacewing any of a group of insects found throughout the world. Lacewings take their name from the intricate veining of their two pairs of semitransparent wings. They have narrow bodies and long thin antennae. The larvae (called aphid lions) are predators, especially on aphids. (Families Hemerobiidae (brown lacewings) and Chrysopidae (green lacewings), order Neuroptera.)

laches in law, neglect and unreasonable delay in enforcing an equitable right. If the court is satisfied that a plaintiff has taken an unnecessarily long time in pursuing a case, the action may be struck out.

lac insect small plant-sucking insect related to ▷scale insects and mealy bugs. The females of most species lack legs and have reduced antennae; their bodies are globular and enclosed within a dense resinous secretion called ▷lac. Lac insects are members of the family Lacciferidae, order Hemiptera (suborder Homoptera), class Insecta, phylum Arthropoda.

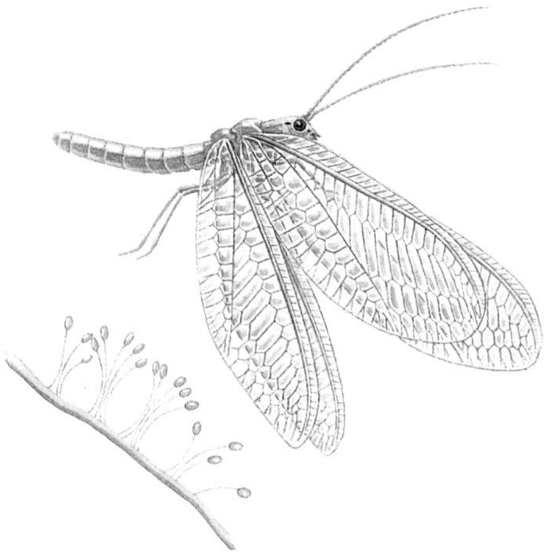

LACEWING Lacewing adults are slender-bodied flies with two pairs of wings covered with a network of veins – hence the name.

Laclos, Pierre-Ambroise-François Choderlos de (1741–1803) French author. An army officer, he wrote a single novel in letter form, *Les Liaisons dangereuses/Dangerous Liaisons* (1782), an analysis of moral corruption. A cynical and unscrupulous libertine, the Vicomte de Valmont, encouraged by the Marquise de Merteuil, seduces and destroys two innocent women. A moral twist is given at the end of the book when Valmont is killed in a duel and the Marquise de Merteuil is hideously disfigured by smallpox.

lacquer waterproof resinous varnish obtained from Oriental trees *Toxicodendron verniciflua*, and used for decorating furniture and art objects. It can be applied to wood, fabric, leather, or other materials, with or without added colours. The technique of making and carving small lacquerwork objects was developed in China, probably as early as the 4th century BC, and was later adopted in Japan.

Lacroix, Christian Marie Marc (1951–) French fashion designer. He opened his couture and ready-to-wear business in 1987, after working with Jean ▷Patou. He made headlines with his fantasy creations, including the short puffball skirt, rose prints, and low décolleté necklines. Lacroix uses experimental fabrics, sometimes handwoven by traditional rural and community workshops.

lacrosse Canadian ball game, adopted from the North American Indians, and named after a fancied resemblance of the lacrosse stick (crosse) to a bishop's crosier. Thongs across the curved end of the crosse form a pocket to carry the small rubber ball. The field is approximately 100 m/110 yd long and a minimum of 55 m/60 yd wide in the men's game, which is played with 10 players per side; the women's field is larger, and there are 12 players per side. The goals are just under 2 m/6 ft square, with loose nets. The world championship was first held in 1967 for men, and in 1969 for women.

lactation secretion of milk in mammals, from the mammary glands. In late pregnancy, the cells lining the lobules inside the mammary glands begin extracting substances from the blood to produce milk. The supply of milk starts shortly after birth with the production of colostrum, a clear fluid consisting largely of water, protein, antibodies, and vitamins. The production of milk continues practically as long as the baby continues to suckle.

lacteal Small vessel responsible for absorbing fat in the small intestine. Occurring in the fingerlike villi of the ▷ileum, lacteals have a milky appearance and drain into the lymphatic system.

Before fat can pass into the lacteal, bile from the liver causes its emulsification into droplets small enough for attack by the enzyme lipase. The products of this digestion form into even smaller droplets, which diffuse into the villi. Large droplets re-form before entering the lacteal and this causes the milky appearance.

lactic acid (or 2-hydroxypropanoic acid) $CH_3CHOHCOOH$ organic acid, a colourless, almost odourless liquid, produced by certain bacteria during fermentation and by active muscle cells when they are exercised hard and are experiencing ▷oxygen debt. An accumulation of lactic acid in the muscles may cause cramp. It occurs in yogurt, buttermilk, sour cream, poor wine, and certain plant extracts, and is used in food preservation and in the preparation of pharmaceuticals.

lactose white sugar, found in solution in milk; it forms 5% of cow's milk. It is commercially prepared from the whey obtained in cheese-making. Like table sugar (sucrose), it is a disaccharide, consisting of two basic sugar units (monosaccharides), in this case, glucose and galactose. Unlike sucrose, it is tasteless.

Ladakh subsidiary range of the ▷Karakoram Mountains and district of northeast Kashmir, India, on the border of Tibet in the upper ▷Indus valley, lying about 3,900 m/12,800 ft above sea level; chief town Leh. After China occupied Tibet in 1951, it made claims on the area, and since 1962 has occupied most of northeast Ladakh.

Ladoga, Lake (Russian Ladozhskoye Ozero) largest lake in Europe, and the second largest in the Russian Federation after the Caspian Sea, situated in the far northwest of the Russian Federation, in the Republic of Karelia and Leningrad oblast (region), northeast of the city of St Petersburg. Lake Ladoga covers an area of 17,700 sq km/6,834 sq mi (with its islands, 18,135 sq km/7,002 sq mi). The main feeder rivers are the Volkhov, Svir, and Vuoksa, and the lake's outlet is by way of the Neva River into the Gulf of Finland. Its average depth is 51 m/167 ft, and its maximum depth 230 m/755 ft. A valuable commercial fishing industry is based here.

Lady in the UK, the formal title of the daughter of an earl, marquess, or duke, and of any woman whose husband's rank is above that of baronet or knight; the title 'Lady' is prefixed to her first name. The wife of a baronet or a knight is also called 'Lady', but uses the title by courtesy only, and has it prefixed to her surname.

ladybird (or ladybug) any of various small beetles, generally red or yellow in colour, with black spots. There are more than 5,200 species worldwide. As larvae and adults, they feed on aphids and scale-insect pests. (Family Coccinellidae, order Coleoptera.)

Ladybirds have been used as a form of ▷biological control since the 19th century and the US ladybird harvest was worth an annual $3–5 million by 1991.

There are 42 species in Britain. In 1987 the 5-spot ladybird (*Coccinella 5-punctata*) was observed for the first time in Britain since the early 1950s. The 13-spot ladybird (*Hippodamia 13-punctata*) was declared extinct in Britain by the Nature Conservancy Council 1991. The **orange ladybird** *Halyzia sedecimguttata* is a large pale orange beetle with 16 spots. It is an unusual ladybird in that it feeds on mildew instead of aphids.

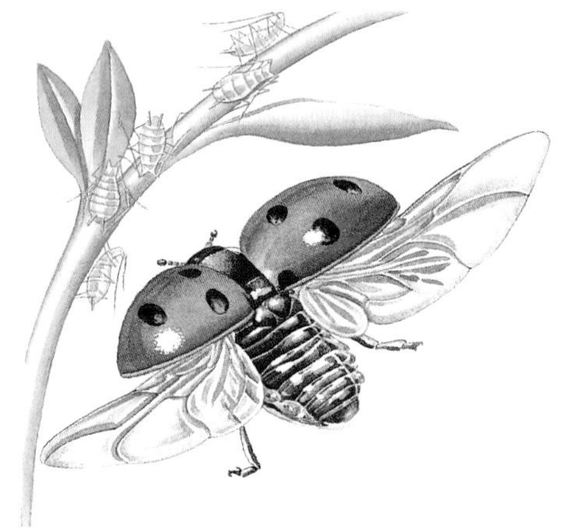

LADYBIRD Ladybirds' red colouration with black spots is a warning to potential predators, such as birds, that they are unpleasant to eat.

Lady Day British name for the Christian festival (25 March) of the Annunciation of the Virgin Mary; until 1752 it was the beginning of the legal year in England, and it is still a quarter day (date for the payment of quarterly rates or dues).

lady's smock another name for the ▷cuckoo flower.

Laënnec, René Théophile Hyacinthe (1781–1826) French physician, inventor of the ▷stethoscope in 1816. He advanced the diagnostic technique of ▷auscultation (listening to the internal organs) with his book *Traité de l'auscultation médiaté* in 1819, which quickly became a medical classic.

Lafayette, Marie Joseph Paul Yves Roch Gilbert de Motier (1757–1834) Marquis de Lafayette. French soldier and politician. He fought against Britain in the American Revolution 1777–79 and 1780–82. During the French Revolution he sat in the National Assembly as a constitutional royalist and in 1789 presented the Declaration of the Rights of Man. After the storming of the ▷Bastille, he was given command of the National Guard. In 1792 he fled the country after attempting to restore the monarchy and was imprisoned by the Austrians until 1797. He supported Napoleon Bonaparte in 1815, sat in the chamber of deputies as a Liberal from 1818, and played a leading part in the revolution of 1830.

He was a popular hero in the USA, and the cities of Lafayette in Louisiana and Indiana are named after him, as was the Lafayette Escadrille – American aviators flying for France during World War I, before the USA entered the war in 1917.

La Fontaine, Jean de (1621–1695) French poet. He was born at Château-Thierry, Champagne, and from 1656 lived largely in Paris, the friend of the playwrights Molière and Racine, and the poet Boileau. His works include *Contes et nouvelles en vers* (1665–74), a series of witty and bawdy tales in verse, and *Fables choisies mises en vers* (1668–94), his universally known verse fables.

The subjects of the *Contes* are taken from various writers including Boccaccio, Ariosto, and Machiavelli, while the *Fables* are derived from numerous sources including Aesop, Phaedrus, Babrius, and other ancient writers, or from 16th-century authors such as Rabelais and Marot. He also wrote *Les Amours de Psyché et de Cupidon/The Loves of Cupid and Psyche* (1669).

Laforgue, Jules (1860–1887) French poet. He experimented with new kinds of verse forms, rhythms, and vocabulary, and pioneered ▷free verse. His work, which was also influenced by the Symbolists, is often marked by a lyrical irony. It made a considerable impact on 20th-century poets, including Ezra Pound and T S Eliot. His books of verse include *Les Complaintes* (1885) and *Imitation de Notre-Dame la lune* (1886), while his best-known prose work is the collection of short stories *Moralités légendaires* (1887).

Lagash Sumerian city north of Shatra, Iraq, under independent and semi-independent rulers from about 3000–2700 BC. Besides objects of high artistic value, it has provided about 30,000 clay tablets giving detailed information on temple administration. Lagash was discovered in 1877 and excavated by Ernest de Sarzec, then French consul in Basra.

Lagerlöf, Selma Ottiliana Lovisa (1858–1940) Swedish novelist. Her first work was the romantic historical novel *Gösta Berling's saga/The Story of Göst Berling* (1891). The children's fantasy *Nils Holgerssons underbara resa/The Wonderful Voyage of Nils Holgersson* (1906–07) grew from her background as a schoolteacher. She was the first woman to be awarded the Nobel Prize for Literature, in 1909.

lagoon coastal body of shallow salt water, usually with limited access to the sea. The term is normally used to describe the shallow sea area cut off by a ▷coral reef or barrier islands.

Lagos chief port and former capital of Nigeria, located at the western end of an island in a lagoon and linked by bridges with the mainland via Iddo Island; population (1992 est) 1,347,000. Industries include chemicals, metal products, fish, food processing, light engineering, chemicals, and brewing. Its surrounding waters are heavily polluted.

One of the most important slaving ports, Lagos was bombarded and occupied by the British in 1851, becoming the colony of Lagos in 1862. Abuja was designated the new capital in 1982 (officially recognized as such in 1992). The University of Lagos was founded in 1962. Onikan National Museum has one of the world's richest collections of African art.

Lagrange, Joseph Louis (1736–1813) Born Giuseppe Lodovico Lagrange. Italian-born French mathematician. His *Mécanique analytique* (1788) applied mathematical analysis, using principles established by Isaac ▷Newton, to such problems as the movements of planets when affected by each other's gravitational force. He presided over the commission that introduced the metric system in 1793.

Lagrangian points five locations in space where the centrifugal and gravitational forces of two bodies neutralize each other; a third, less massive body located at any one of these points will be held in equilibrium with respect to the other two. Three of the points, L1–L3, lie on a line joining the two large bodies. The other two points, L4 and L5, which are the most stable, lie on either side of this line. Their existence was predicted in 1772 by French mathematician Joseph Louis Lagrange.

La Guardia, Fiorello (Henry) (1882–1947) US Republican politician. He was mayor of New York 1933–45. Elected against the opposition of the powerful Tammany Hall Democratic Party organization, he improved the administration of the city, suppressed racketeering, and organized unemployment relief, slum-clearance schemes, and social services. Although nominally a Republican, he supported the Democratic president Franklin D Roosevelt's ▷New Deal.

lahar mudflow formed of a fluid mixture of water and volcanic ash. During a volcanic eruption, melting ice may combine with ash to form a powerful flow capable of causing great destruction. The lahars created by the eruption of Nevado del Ruiz in Colombia, South America, in 1985 buried 22,000 people in 8 m/26 ft of mud.

Lahnda language spoken by 15–20 million people in Pakistan and northern India. It is closely related to Punjabi and Romany, and belongs to the Indo-Iranian branch of the Indo-European language family.

Lahore capital of the province of ▷Punjab, Pakistan, situated on a tributary of the River Ravi, 50 km/30 mi west of Amritsar in India; population (1991) 3,200,000. Lahore is a commercial and banking centre, and industries include engineering, textiles, carpets, and chemicals. It is associated with the Mogul rulers ▷Akbar, ▷Jahangir, and ▷Aurangzeb, whose capital it was in the 16th and 17th centuries.

Laibach German name of ▷Ljubljana, a city in Slovenia.

Lailat ul-Barah (the **Night of Forgiveness**) Muslim festival which takes place two weeks before the beginning of the fast of Ramadan (the ninth month of the Islamic year) and is a time for asking and granting forgiveness.

Lailat ul-Isra Wal Mi'raj Muslim festival that celebrates the prophet Muhammad's ▷Night Journey.

Lailat ul-Qadr (the **Night of Power**) Muslim festival which celebrates the giving of the Koran to Muhammad. It usually falls at the end of Ramadan.

Laing, R(onald) D(avid) (1927–1989) Scottish psychoanalyst. He was the originator of the social theory of mental illness; for example, that schizophrenia is promoted by family pressure for its members to conform to standards alien to themselves. His books include *The Divided Self* (1960) and *The Politics of the Family* (1971).

Influenced by existentialist philosophy, Laing inspired the antipsychiatry movement. He observed interactions between people in an attempt to understand and describe their experience and thinking. In *The Divided Self* he criticized the psychiatrist's role as one that, with its objective scientific outlook, depersonalized the patient. By investigating the personal interactions within the families of diagnosed schizophrenics, he found that the seemingly bizarre behaviour normally regarded as indicating the illness began to make sense.

> **R D Laing**
> *We are bemused and crazed creatures, strangers to our true selves, to one another, and to the spiritual and material world – mad, even, from an ideal standpoint we can glimpse but not adopt.*
> *The Politics of Experience* Introduction

laissez faire (French 'let alone') theory that the state should not intervene in economic affairs, except to break up a monopoly. The phrase originated with the Physiocrats, 18th-century French economists whose maxim was *laissez faire et laissez passer* (literally, 'let go and let pass' – that is, leave the individual alone and let commodities circulate freely). The degree to which intervention should take place is still one of the chief problems of economics. The Scottish economist Adam ▷Smith justified the theory in *The Wealth of Nations* (1776).

lake body of still water lying in depressed ground without direct communication with the sea. Lakes are common in formerly glaciated regions, along the courses of slow rivers, and in low land near the sea. The main classifications are by origin: **glacial lakes**, formed by glacial scouring; **barrier lakes**, formed by landslides and glacial moraines; **crater lakes**, found in volcanoes; and **tectonic lakes**, occurring in natural fissures.

Crater lakes form in the ▷calderas of extinct volcanoes, for example Crater Lake, Oregon. Subsidence of the roofs of limestone caves in ▷karst landscape exposes the subterranean stream network and provides a cavity in which a lake can develop. Tectonic lakes form during tectonic movement, as when a rift valley is formed. Lake Tanganyika was created in conjunction with the East African Great Rift Valley. Glaciers produce several distinct types of lake, such as the lochs of Scotland and the Great Lakes of North America.

Lakes are mainly freshwater, but salt and bitter lakes are found in areas of low annual rainfall and little surface runoff, so that the rate of evaporation exceeds the rate of inflow, allowing mineral salts to accumulate. The Dead Sea has a salinity of about 250 parts per 1,000 and the Great Salt Lake, Utah, about 220 parts per 1,000. Salinity can also be caused by volcanic gases or fluids, for example Lake Natron, Tanzania.

In the 20th century large artificial lakes have been created in connection with hydroelectric and other works. Some lakes have become polluted as a result of human activity. Sometimes ▷eutrophication (a state of overnourishment) occurs, when agricultural fertilizers leaching into lakes cause an explosion of aquatic life, which then depletes the lake's oxygen supply until it is no longer able to support life.

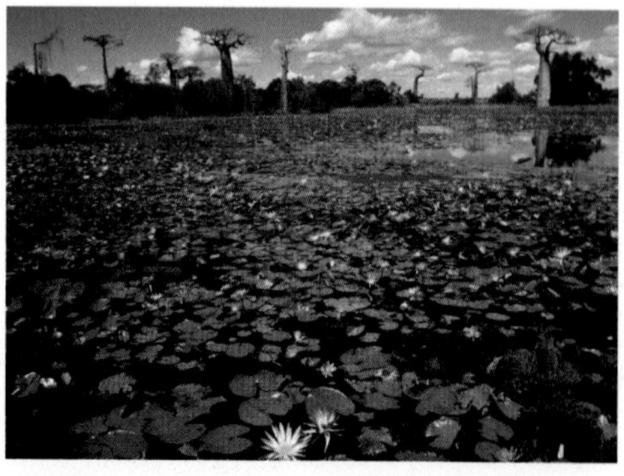

LAKE A lake near Morondava in Madagascar. The water lilies are *Nymphaea stellata* and the trees in the distance, growing on dry land, are baobabs *Adansonia grandidieri*. Most lakes are the focal point of an ecosystem, drawing together a broad range of animal and plant life.
Premaphotos Wildlife

Lake District region in Cumbria, northwest England. It contains the principal English lakes, separated by wild uplands rising to many peaks, including ▷Scafell Pike (978 m/3,210 ft), the highest peak in England. The area was made a national park in 1951, covering 2,292 sq km/885 sq mi, and is a popular tourist destination.

Related Web site: Lake District National Park Authority http://www.lake-district.gov.uk/index.htm

Lakeland terrier medium-sized wire-haired terrier weighing about 7–8 kg/15.5–17.5 lb with an ideal height of no more than 37 cm/14.5 in. Its skull is moderately broad, with small, V-shaped ears and dark eyes; the body is short and the tail traditionally docked.

Lakshadweep group of 36 coral islands, 10 inhabited, in the Indian Ocean, 320 km/200 mi off the Malabar coast, forming a Union Territory of India; area 32 sq km/12 sq mi; population (2001 est) 65,000. The administrative headquarters are on Kavaratti Island. Products include coir, copra, and fish. There is a tourist resort on Bangarem, an uninhabited island with a large lagoon. The religion is Islam.

Lakshmi Hindu goddess of wealth and beauty, consort of Vishnu; her festival is ▷Diwali.

Lalique, René (1860–1945) French designer and manufacturer of ▷Art Nouveau glass, jewellery, and house interiors. The Lalique factory continues in production at Wingen-sur-Moder, Alsace, under his son Marc and granddaughter Marie-Claude.

Lallans variant of 'lowlands' and a name for Lowland Scots, whether conceived as a language in its own right or as a northern dialect of English. Because of its rustic associations, Lallans has been known since the 18th century as 'the Doric', in contrast with the 'Attic' usage of Edinburgh ('the Athens of the North'). See ▷Scots language.

Lamaism Buddhism of Tibet and Mongolia, a form of Mahāyāna Buddhism. Buddhism was introduced into Tibet in AD 640, but the real founder of Tibetan Buddhism was the Indian missionary Padma Sambhava, who was active in about 750. Tibetan Buddhism developed several orders, based on lineages of teachings transmitted by reincarnated lamas (teachers). In the 14th–15th centuries Tsong-kha-pa founded the sect of Geluk-Pa ('virtuous'), which became the most powerful order in the country. Its head is the ▷Dalai Lama, who is considered an incarnation of the Bodhisattva Avalokiteśvara.

Lamarck, Jean Baptiste Pierre Antoine de Monet (1744–1829) Chevalier de Lamarck. French naturalist. His theory of evolution, known as **Lamarckism**, was based on the idea that acquired characteristics (changes acquired in an individual's lifetime) are inherited by the offspring, and that organisms have an intrinsic urge to evolve into better-adapted forms. *Philosophie zoologique/Zoological Philosophy* (1809) outlined his 'transformist' (evolutionary) ideas.

Zoological Philosophy tried to show that various parts of the body developed because they were necessary, or disappeared because of disuse when variations in the environment caused a change in habit. If these body changes were inherited over many generations, new species would eventually be produced.

Lamarck was the first to distinguish vertebrate from invertebrate animals by the presence of a bony spinal column. He was also the first to establish the crustaceans, arachnids, and annelids among the invertebrates. It was Lamarck who coined the word 'biology'.

Lamartine, Alphonse Marie Louis de (1790–1869) French poet. He wrote romantic poems, including *Méditations poétiques/Poetical Meditations* (1820), followed by *Nouvelles méditations/New Meditations* (1823), and *Harmonies poétiques et religieuses/Poetical and Religious Harmonies* (1830). His *Histoire des Girondins/History of the Girondins* (1847) helped to inspire the revolution of 1848. Lamartine was the first to sound a more personal note in his poetry and to establish a direct bond between himself and his public.

A distinguished orator, he entered the Chamber of Deputies 1833 and served as a deputy for several years. He was a leader in the revolution and became minister of foreign affairs in the provisional government in 1848. He was defeated in the presidential election by Louis-Napoleon (▷Napoleon III).

Lamb, Charles (1775–1834) English essayist and critic. He collaborated with his sister **Mary Lamb** (1764–1847) on *Tales from Shakespeare* (1807), and his *Specimens of English Dramatic Poets Contemporary with Shakespeare, with Notes* (1808) revealed him as a penetrating critic and helped to revive interest in Elizabethan plays. As 'Elia' he contributed essays to the *London Magazine* from 1820 (collected 1823 and 1833). Lamb's essays are still widely read and admired; they include 'A Dissertation on Roast Pig', 'Mrs Battle's Opinions on Whist', 'Dream Children', and 'The Supernatural Man'.

He was born in the Temple, London, and was educated at Christ's Hospital. As a friend of Coleridge, some of his poems were included in the second edition of *Poems on Various Subjects* (1797). He was a clerk with the East India Company at India House 1792–1825, when he retired to Enfield. His sister Mary stabbed their mother to death in a fit of insanity in 1796, and Charles cared for her between her periodic returns to an asylum.

lambada Brazilian dance music that became internationally popular in 1989. It combines elements of calypso, zouk, and reggae. The record 'Lambada' by Kaoma was the best-selling single of 1989 in Europe.

Lambeth Conference meeting of bishops of the Anglican Communion every ten years, presided over by the archbishop of Canterbury; its decisions on doctrinal matters are not binding.

lamina in flowering plants (▷angiosperms), the blade of the ▷leaf on either side of the midrib. The lamina is generally thin and flattened, and is usually the primary organ of ▷photosynthesis. It has a network of veins through which water and nutrients are conducted. More generally, a lamina is any thin, flat plant structure, such as the ▷thallus of many seaweeds.

Lammas ('loaf-mass') medieval festival of harvest, celebrated 1 August. At one time it was an English quarter day (date for payment of quarterly rates or dues), and is still a quarter day in Scotland.

lammergeier (or **bearded vulture**) Old World vulture with a wingspan of 2.7 m/9 ft. It ranges over southern Europe, North Africa, and Asia, in wild mountainous areas. It feeds on offal and carrion and drops bones onto rocks to break them and so get at the marrow. (Species *Gypaetus barbatus*, family Accipitridae.)

Lamont, Norman Stewart Hughson (1942–) British Conservative politician, chief secretary of the Treasury 1989–90, chancellor of the Exchequer 1990–93, born in the Shetland Islands. In September 1992, despite earlier assurances to the contrary, he was forced to suspend the UK's membership of the European Community (now the European Union) ▷Exchange Rate Mechanism (ERM). He was replaced as chancellor by Kenneth Clarke in May 1993, after which he became a fierce right-wing critic of the Major administration. He lost his House of Commons seat in the May 1997 general election.

Lampedusa, Giuseppe Tomasi di (1896–1957) Italian aristocrat. He was the author of *Il gattopardo/The Leopard* (1958; translated into English 1960), a novel set in his native Sicily during the period following its annexation by Garibaldi in 1860. It chronicles the reactions of an aristocratic family to social and political upheavals.

lamprey any of various eel-shaped jawless fishes. A lamprey feeds on other fish by fixing itself by its round mouth to its host and boring into the flesh with its toothed tongue. Lampreys breed in fresh water, and the young live as larvae for about five years before migrating to the sea. (Family Petromyzontidae.)

Henry I of England is said to have died from eating too many, hence the phrase 'a surfeit of lampreys'. The sea lamprey was once a food fish in Europe.

Lancashire county of northwest England (since April 1998 Blackpool and Blackburn have been separate unitary authorities).

area 3,040 sq km/1,173 sq mi **towns and cities** Preston (administrative headquarters), which forms part of Central Lancashire New Town from 1970 (together with Fulwood, Bamber Bridge, Leyland, and Chorley); Lancaster, Accrington, Burnley; ports Fleetwood and Heysham; seaside resorts Morecambe and Southport
features the River Ribble; the Pennines; the Forest of Bowland

(moors and farming valleys); Pendle Hill **industries** formerly a world centre of cotton manufacture, now replaced with high-technology aerospace, nuclear fuels, and electronics industries. There is dairy farming and market gardening **population** (1996) 1,424,700 **famous people** Kathleen Ferrier, Gracie Fields, George Formby, Rex Harrison

Related Web site: Lancashire
http://www.lancashire.com/regionf.htm

Lancaster city in Lancashire, northwest England, on the River Lune; population (1991) 44,500. Until 1974 it was the county town of Lancashire (now Preston is the county town). Industries include the manufacture of paper, furniture, plastics, chemicals, textiles, and wall and floor coverings (linoleum). Manufacturing accounts for 12% of employment, while tourism accounts for 10%. The service sector is the largest employer, and there is an important livestock market. Education facilities include the University of Lancaster (1964) and St Martin's College. The city's castle was originally established in the 11th century on the site of a Roman fort.

Lancaster, Burt (Burton Stephen) (1913–1994) US film actor. A star from his first film, *The Killers* (1946), he proved adept both at action roles and more complex character parts as in *From Here to Eternity* (1953), *Elmer Gantry* (1960; Academy Award), *The Leopard/Il Gattopardo* (1963), *The Swimmer* (1968), and *Atlantic City* (1980).

Lancaster, Chancellor of the Duchy of public office created in 1351 and attached to the crown since 1399. The office of Chancellor of the Duchy is a sinecure without any responsibilities, usually held by a member of the cabinet with a special role outside that of the regular ministries; for example, Harold Lever as financial adviser to the Wilson–Callaghan governments from 1974.

Lancaster, House of English royal house, a branch of the Plantagenets. It originated in 1267 when Edmund (died 1296), the younger son of Henry III, was granted the earldom of Lancaster. Converted to a duchy for Henry of Grosmont (died 1361), it passed to John of Gaunt in 1362 by his marriage to Blanche, Henry's daughter. John's son, Henry IV, established the royal dynasty of Lancaster in 1399, and he was followed by two more Lancastrian kings, Henry V and Henry VI.

lancelet any of a variety of marine animals about 2.5 cm/1 in long. They have no skull, brain, eyes, heart, vertebral column, centralized brain, or paired limbs, but there is a notochord (a supportive rod) which runs from end to end of the body, a tail, and a number of gill slits. Found in all seas, lancelets burrow in the sand but when disturbed swim freely. (Genus *Amphioxus*, phylum Chordata, subphylum Cephalocordata.)

Lancelot of the Lake in British legend, one of King Arthur's knights of the Round Table. Originally a Celtic folk hero, he was first introduced into the Arthurian cycle of tales in the 12th century. He was designated Queen ▷Guinevere's lover in the early 13th century by French poet ▷Chrétien de Troyes, who made him a symbol of fidelity and chivalrous love.

Lanchow alternative transcription of ▷Lanzhou, capital of Gansu province, China.

Land (plural ***Länder***) federal state of Germany or Austria.

Land, Edwin Herbert (1909–1991) US inventor of the ▷Polaroid Land camera in 1947. The camera developed the film in one minute inside the camera and produced an 'instant' photograph.

Land League Irish peasant-rights organization, formed in 1879 by Michael Davitt and Charles Stewart ▷Parnell to fight against tenant evictions. Through its skilful use of the boycott against anyone who took a farm from which another had been evicted, it forced Gladstone's government to introduce a law in 1881 restricting rents and granting tenants security of tenure.

The Land League was supported by the use of intimidation from the Irish Republican Brotherhood (IRB) an offshoot of the Irish-American ▷Fenian movement. The IRB ensured that landlords were unable to collect rents and that no other Irish farmers took the unoccupied farms. Support also came from Irish parliamentary nationalists, led by Charles Stewart Parnell, in the House of Commons at Westminster. The combination of intimidation and parliamentary action gave the Land League success. By attacking the economic wealth generated by Ireland for Britain and the large Protestant landowners of Ireland, the Land League achieved victory where previous campaigns for rights in Ireland had failed.

landlord and tenant in law, the relationship that exists between an owner of land or buildings (the landlord) and a person granted the right to occupy them (the tenant). The landlord grants a lease or tenancy, which may be for a year, a term of years, a week, or any other definite, limited period.

Landor, Walter Savage (1775–1864) English poet and essayist. He lived much of his life abroad, dying in Florence, where he had fled to avoid a libel suit in 1858. His works include the epic poem *Gebir* (1798), the tragedy *Count Julian* (1812), and *Imaginary Conversations of Literary Men and Statesmen* (1824–29). Landor has a high place among prose writers for his restrained and finished style; his shorter poems have the same classic simplicity.

> **Walter Savage Landor**
> *States, like men, have their growth, their manhood, their decrepitude, their decay.*
> *Imaginary Conversations*, 'Leonora di Este and Panigarola'

land reclamation the conversion of derelict or otherwise unusable areas into productive land. For example, where industrial or agricultural activities, such as sand and gravel extraction, or open-cast mining have created large areas of derelict or waste ground, the companies involved are usually required to improve the land so that it can be used.

Land Registry, HM official body set up in 1925 to register legal rights to land in England and Wales. There has been a gradual introduction, since 1925, of compulsory registration of land in different areas of the country. This requires the purchaser of land to register details of his or her title and all other rights (such as mortgages and ▷easements) relating to the land. Once registered, the title to the land is guaranteed by the Land Registry, subject to those interests that cannot be registered; this makes the buying and selling of land easier and cheaper. The records are open to public inspection (since December 1990).

Landsbergis, Vytautas (1932–) Lithuanian politician, president 1990–93. He became active in nationalist politics in the 1980s, founding and eventually chairing the anticommunist Sajudis independence movement in 1988. When Sajudis swept to victory in the republic's elections in March 1990, Landsbergis chaired the Supreme Council of Lithuania, becoming, in effect, president. He immediately drafted the republic's declaration of independence from the USSR, which, after initial Soviet resistance, was recognized in September 1991. In October 1996, after a general election, he took the chair of the new parliament.

landscape painting comparatively late product of art in the West, though the contemplation of mountain and water and their rendering in pictures were cultivated in China in the early centuries AD. In Western art it first appears as a background and as such became an element in the illuminated manuscripts and paintings of the Middle Ages. The Flemish painter Patenier is usually credited with having first made landscape a primary feature of interest. ▷Impressionism was the last great phase of landscape objectively treated, though it was not the end of its development. ▷Cézanne made landscape into a study of essential structure underlying all natural forms; Vincent van ▷Gogh made it a vehicle for expressing personal emotion.

Landseer, Edwin Henry (1802–1873) English painter, sculptor, and engraver of animal studies. Much of his work reflects the Victorian taste for sentimental and moralistic pictures, for example *Dignity and Impudence* (1839; Tate Gallery, London). His sculptures include the lions at the base of Nelson's Column in Trafalgar Square, London (1857–67). He was knighted in 1850.

Born in London, at the age of 14 he entered the Royal Academy schools, where he took lessons from Benjamin Haydon. His works show close knowledge of animal forms and he established a vogue for Highland animal and sporting scenes, much encouraged by Queen Victoria's patronage. Among his best-known works are *The Old Shepherd's Chief Mourner* (1837); *Monarch of the Glen* (1851), painted for the House of Lords; and *The Stag at Bay* (1846). His works were popularized by enormous numbers of engravings, and in the 19th century he was considered the foremost European animal painter. He was buried in St Paul's Cathedral.

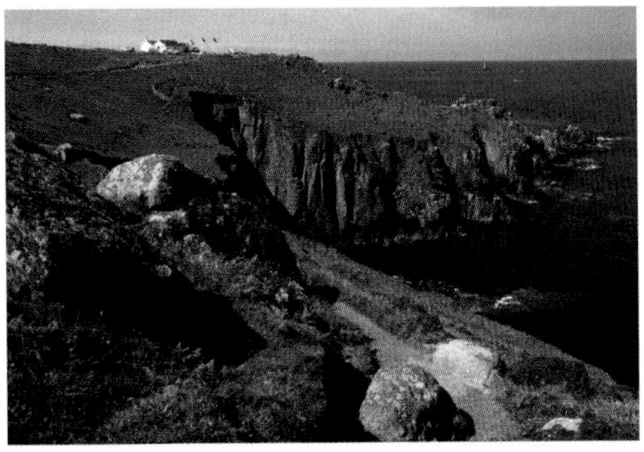

LAND'S END Land's End, in Cornwall, is a distinctive headland of granite cliffs that rise about 18m/59ft from the Atlantic Ocean. *Image Bank*

Land's End promontory of southwest Cornwall, 15 km/9 mi southwest of Penzance, the westernmost point of England.

landslide sudden downward movement of a mass of soil or rocks from a cliff or steep slope. Landslides happen when a slope becomes unstable, usually because the base has been undercut or because materials within the mass have become wet and slippery.

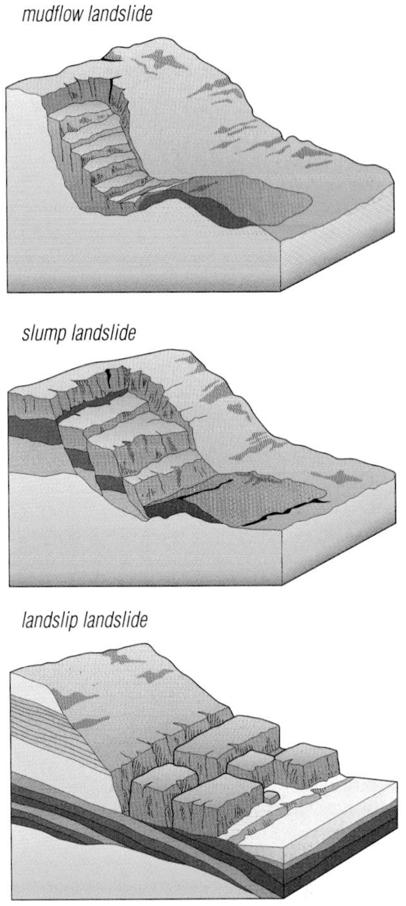

LANDSLIDE Types of landslide. A mudflow is a tongue of mud that slides downhill. A slump is a fall of a large mass that stays together after the fall. A landslip occurs when beds of rock move along a lower bed.

Landsteiner, Karl (1868–1943) Austrian-born US immunologist who was awarded a Nobel Prize for Physiology or Medicine in 1930 for his discovery of the ABO ▷blood group system in the period 1900–02. He also aided in the discovery of the Rhesus blood factors in 1940, and discovered the polio virus.

Lanfranc (*c.* 1010–1089) Italian archbishop of Canterbury from 1070. Following the ▷Norman Conquest, he was the adviser of ▷William (I) the Conqueror. As archbishop he rebuilt ▷Canterbury Cathedral, replaced English clergy with Normans, enforced clerical celibacy, and separated the ecclesiastical from the secular courts.

Lang, Andrew (1844–1912) Scottish historian and folklore scholar. His writings include historical works; anthropological studies, such as *Myth, Ritual and Religion* (1887) and *The Making of Religion* (1898), which involved him in controversy with the anthropologist James G ▷Frazer; novels; and the series of children's books which he inspired and edited, beginning with *The Blue Fairy Book* (1889).

Lang, Fritz (1890–1976) Austrian film director. His films are characterized by a strong sense of fatalism and alienation. His German films include *Metropolis* (1927) and *M* (1931), in which Peter Lorre starred as a child-killer. His US films include *Rancho Notorious* (1952) and *The Big Heat* (1953).

His expressionist German films betrayed the influence of the French serials in his predilection for international crime subjects. He was also very successful in mythological and science fiction subjects. He left Nazi Germany in 1933 and settled in the USA where he made a number of noteworthy social problem pictures and *films noirs*, such as *Fury* (1936) and *Scarlet Street* (1945). He returned to work in Germany in the late 1950s and featured in Jean-Luc Godard's *Le Mépris/Contempt* (1963).

lang, k(athryn) d(awn) (1961–) Canadian singer. Her mellifluous voice and androgynous image have gained her a wide following beyond the country-music field where she first established herself. Her albums include *Angel With a Lariat* (1987), *Shadowland* (1988), *Absolute Torch and Twang* (1989), the mainstream *Ingénue* (1992), *Even Cowgirls get the Blues* (1993), and *All You Can Eat* (1995).

Lange, David Russell (1942–) New Zealand Labour centre-left politician, prime minister 1983–89. A skilled parliamentary debater, he became Labour's deputy leader in 1979, and in 1983 replaced Wallace Rowling as party leader. Taking advantage of economic difficulties and a changing public mood, Lange led Labour to a decisive win in the 1984 general election, replacing Robert ▷Muldoon of the National Party as prime minister. The centre-piece of his policy programme was non-nuclear military policy. This was put into effect, despite criticism from the USA, becoming law in 1987. It prevented US nuclear-armed or nuclear-powered ships visiting New Zealand's ports and resulted in the USA suspending its defence obligations to New Zealand under the ANZUS treaty. Lange's government also introduced a free-market economic policy, which was a significant and controversial departure for Labour, and improved Maori rights and the position of women. His government was re-elected in 1987, but in August 1989 Lange unexpectedly resigned, as a result of health problems but also pressure being exerted by supporters of the right-wing former finance minister, Roger Douglas. Lange, who had become a critic of Douglas' liberalizing policies, had dismissed Douglas in 1988. Lange was replaced as prime minister by Geoffrey Palmer and served under him as attorney general until 1990.

Langland, William (*c.* 1332–*c.* 1400) English poet. His alliterative *The Vision of William Concerning Piers the Plowman* (see *Piers Plowman*) was written in three (or possibly four) versions between about 1367 and 1386. The poem forms a series of allegorical visions, in which Piers develops from the typical poor peasant to a symbol of Jesus, and condemns the social and moral evils of 14th-century England. It is a masterpiece in combining the depiction of a spiritual pilgrimage with scenes of contemporary social life for a satirical purpose.

Langobard another name for ▷Lombard, member of a Germanic people.

Langton, Stephen (*c.* 1150–1228) English priest who was mainly responsible for drafting the charter of rights, the ▷Magna Carta.

He studied in Paris, where he became chancellor of the university, and in 1206 was created a cardinal. When in 1207 Pope Innocent III secured Langton's election as archbishop of Canterbury, King ▷John I refused to recognize him, and he was not allowed to enter England until 1213. He supported the barons in their struggle against John and worked for revisions to both church and state policies.

Langtry, Lillie (1853–1929) Stage name of Emilie Charlotte le Breton. English actor. She was the mistress of the future Edward VII. She was known as the 'Jersey Lily' from her birthplace in the Channel Islands and considered to be one of the most beautiful women of her time.

language human communication through speech, writing, or both. Different nationalities or ethnic groups typically have different languages or variations on particular languages; for example, Armenians speaking the Armenian language and British and Americans speaking distinctive varieties of the English language. One language may have various ▷dialects, which may be seen by those who use them as languages in their own right. There are about 6,000 languages spoken worldwide, but 90% of these are in some danger of falling into disuse. More than half the world's population speaks one of just five languages – Chinese, English, Hindi, Russian, and Spanish.

The term language is also used for systems of communication with languagelike qualities, such as **animal language** (the way animals communicate), **body language** (gestures and expressions used to communicate ideas), **sign language** (gestures for the deaf or for use as a ▷lingua franca, as among American Indians), and **computer languages** (such as BASIC and COBOL).

> **Related Web site: Foundation for Endangered Languages**
> http://www.bris.ac.uk/Depts/Philosophy/CTLL/FEL/

Languedoc former province of southern France, bounded by the River Rhône, the Mediterranean Sea, and the regions of Guienne and Gascony. In 1791 Languedoc was replaced by the eight *départements* of Haute-Loire, Lozère, Ardèche, Aude, Tarn, Hérault, Gard, and Haute-Garonne. Lower Languedoc was united with the former province of Roussillon to form the modern region of ▷Languedoc-Roussillon.

LILLIE LANGTRY An undated portrait of the English actor Lillie Langtry, who was also painted by English artists Millais and Berne-Jones. Daughter of the dean of Jersey, she married Edward Langtry at the age of 21 years, three years before becoming the mistress of Edward, Prince of Wales (who called her 'My Fair Lily'). *Archive Photos*

Languedoc-Roussillon region of southern France, comprising the *départements* of Aude, Gard, Hérault, Lozère, and Pyrénées-Orientales; area 27,400 sq km/10,600 sq mi; population (1999 est) 2,295,600. The administrative centre is ▷Montpellier. Products include fruit, vegetables, and wine.

langur any of various leaf-eating Old World monkeys that live in trees in South Asia. There are about 20 species. Langurs are related to the colobus monkey of Africa. (Genus *Presbytis* and other related genera.)

lanolin sticky, purified wax obtained from sheep's wool and used in cosmetics, soap, and leather preparation.

Lansdowne, William Petty Fitzmaurice, 1st Marquis of Lansdowne, British Whig politician; see Lord ▷Shelburne.

lanternfish any of about 300 species of small deep-sea bony fish. They are less than 15 cm/6 in long, with a large mouth, large eyes, and many luminous organs along the underside of the body, the function of which is not understood. They feed on plankton. Lanternfish are in the order Myctophiformes, class Osteichthyes.

lanthanide any of a series of 15 metallic elements (also known as rare earths) with atomic numbers 57 (lanthanum) to 71 (lutetium). One of its members, promethium, is radioactive. All occur in nature. Lanthanides are grouped because of their chemical similarities (most are trivalent, but some can be divalent or tetravalent), their properties differing only slightly with atomic number. Lanthanides were called rare earths originally because they were not widespread and were difficult to identify and separate from their ores by their discoverers. The series is set out in a band in the periodic table of the elements, as are the ▷actinides.

lanthanum (Greek *lanthanein* 'to be hidden') soft, silvery, ductile and malleable, metallic element, symbol La, atomic number 57, relative atomic mass 138.91, the first of the lanthanide series. It is used in making alloys. It was named in 1839 by Swedish chemist Carl Mosander (1797–1858).

Lanzarote most easterly of the Spanish Canary Islands; area 795 sq km/307 sq mi; capital Arrecife. The desertlike volcanic landscape is dominated by the Montañas de Fuego ('Mountains of Fire') with over 300 volcanic cones.

Lanzhou (or Lanchow) capital of ▷Gansu province, China, on the Huang He River, 190 km/120 mi south of the Great Wall; population (1994) 1,612,600. Industries include oil-refining and the manufacture of chemicals, fertilizers, machinery, and synthetic rubber.

Lao people who live along the Mekong river system in Laos (2 million) and northern Thailand (9 million). The Lao language is a member of the Sino-Tibetan family. The majority of Lao live in rural villages. During the wet season, May–October, they grow rice in irrigated fields, though some shifting or swidden cultivation is practised on hillsides. Vegetables and other crops are grown during drier weather. The Lao are predominantly Buddhist though a belief in spirits, **phi**, is included in Lao devotions. There are some Christians among the minority groups.

Laocoön in classical mythology, a Trojan priest of Apollo and a visionary, brother of Anchises. He and his sons were killed by serpents when he foresaw disaster for Troy in the ▷Trojan horse left by the Greeks. The scene of their death is the subject of a classical marble group, rediscovered in the Renaissance, and forms an episode in Virgil's *Aeneid*.

Laois (or Laoighis, previously spelt Leix; also formerly **Queen's County**) county of the Republic of Ireland, in the province of Leinster; county town Portlaoise; area 1,720 sq km/664 sq mi; population (1996) 52,900. Other towns are Abbeyleix, Mountmellick, Mountrath, and Portarlington. Laois is flat, except for the Slieve Bloom Mountains in the northwest, the highest point of which is Mount Arderin (529 m/1,734 ft), and there are many bogs. The Barrow and the Nore are the chief rivers. Agriculture includes dairying, and mixed cattle and arable farming (sugar beet), and industries include peat, woollens, and agricultural machinery. Part of the Leinster coalfield lies within the county. There is a large peat-fired power station near Portarlington, and at the Clonsast Bog (1,619 ha/4,000 acres) is an important peat industry.

Laos see country box.

Laotian an Indochinese people who live along the Mekong river system. There are approximately 9 million Laotians in Thailand and 2 million in Laos. The Laotian language is a Thai member of the Sino-Tibetan family.

Lao Zi (or Lao Tzu) (*c.* 604–531 BC) Chinese philosopher. He is commonly regarded as the founder of ▷Taoism, with its emphasis on the Tao, the inevitable and harmonious way of the universe. Nothing certain is known of his life. The *Tao Te Ching*, the Taoist scripture, is attributed to him but apparently dates from the 3rd century BC. He is often depicted on a water-buffalo or an ox, with a book in his hand.

La Pampa department of central Argentina, bounded by the Río Colorado to the south, and characterized by the plains of the eastern pampas and salt marshes; population (1991) 260,000; area 143,400 sq km/55,367 sq mi; capital Santa Rosa. Cereal crops are grown and there is stock raising.

laparotomy exploratory surgical procedure involving incision into the abdomen. The use of laparotomy, as of other exploratory surgery, has decreased sharply with advances in medical imaging and the direct-viewing technique known as ▷endoscopy.

La Paz capital city of Bolivia, in Murillo province, 3,800 m/12,400 ft above sea level; population (1992) 711,000 (metropolitan

LANZAROTE The Canary Island of Lanzarote seen from the air. The beaches are of black sand created by the erosion of volcanic material. *Image Bank*

Laos

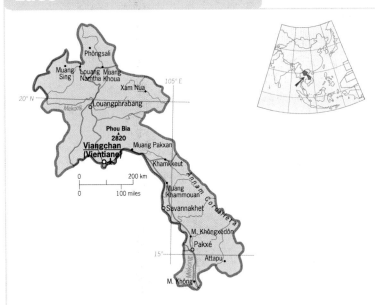

Laos landlocked country in southeast Asia, bounded north by China, east by Vietnam, south by Cambodia, west by Thailand, and northwest by Myanmar.

NATIONAL NAME *Sathalanalat Praxathipatai Paxaxôn Lao/Democratic People's Republic of Laos*
AREA 236,790 sq km/91,424 sq mi
CAPITAL Vientiane
MAJOR TOWNS/CITIES Louangphrabang (the former royal capital), Pakse, Savannakhet
PHYSICAL FEATURES landlocked state with high mountains in east; Mekong River in west; rainforest covers nearly 60% of land

Government

HEAD OF STATE Khamtay Siphandon from 1998
HEAD OF GOVERNMENT Boungnang Volachit from 2001
POLITICAL SYSTEM communist
POLITICAL EXECUTIVE communist
ADMINISTRATIVE DIVISIONS 16 provinces, one municipality (Vientiane), and one special region
ARMED FORCES 29,100 (2002 est)
CONSCRIPTION military service is compulsory for a minimum of 18 months
DEATH PENALTY retained and used for ordinary crimes
DEFENCE SPEND (% GDP) 0.8 (2002 est)
EDUCATION SPEND (% GDP) 2.3 (2001 est)
HEALTH SPEND (% GDP) 3.4 (2000 est)

Economy and resources

CURRENCY new kip
GPD (US$) 1.7 billion (2002 est)
REAL GDP GROWTH (% change on previous year) 5.7 (2001)
GNI (US$) 1.7 billion (2002 est)
GNI PER CAPITA (PPP) (US$) 1,610 (2002 est)
CONSUMER PRICE INFLATION 7% (2003 est)
UNEMPLOYMENT 4.3% (2000)
FOREIGN DEBT (US$) 2.6 billion (2001 est)
MAJOR TRADING PARTNERS Thailand, Vietnam, Japan, Germany, France, China, Italy, USA, UK, Singapore
RESOURCES coal, tin, gypsum, baryte, lead, zinc, nickel, potash, iron ore; small quantities of gold, silver, precious stones
INDUSTRIES processing of agricultural produce, sawmilling, textiles and garments, handicrafts, basic consumer goods
EXPORTS electricity, timber and wood products, textiles and garments, motorcycles, coffee, tin, gypsum. Principal market: Vietnam 41.7% (2001)
IMPORTS food (particularly rice and sugar), consumer goods, mineral fuels, machinery and transport equipment, cement, cotton yarn, gold, silver. Principal source: Thailand 52.5% (2001)
ARABLE LAND 3.8% (2000 est)
AGRICULTURAL PRODUCTS rice, maize, tobacco, cotton, coffee, sugar cane, cassava, potatoes, sweet potatoes; livestock rearing (pigs, poultry, and cattle); fishing; forest resources including valuable wood such as Teruk (forest covered about 47% of the country in 1995); opium is produced but its manufacture is controlled by the state

Population and society

POPULATION 5,657,000 (2003 est)
POPULATION GROWTH RATE 2.2% (2000–15)
POPULATION DENSITY (per sq km) 24 (2003 est)
URBAN POPULATION (% of total) 21 (2003 est)
AGE DISTRIBUTION (% of total population) 0–14 42%, 15–59 53%, 60+ 5% (2002 est)
ETHNIC GROUPS Laotian, predominantly the lowland Lao Lum (over 60%); the upland and mountain-dwelling Lao Theung (22%), and the tribal Laotai and the Lao Soung (9%); Vietnamese Chinese (1%)
LANGUAGE Lao (official), French, English, ethnic languages
RELIGION Theravada Buddhist 85%, animist beliefs among mountain dwellers
EDUCATION (compulsory years) 5
LITERACY RATE 78% (men); 57% (women) (2003 est)
LABOUR FORCE 77% agriculture, 6% industry, 17% services (1997 est)
LIFE EXPECTANCY 53 (men); 56 (women) (2000–05)
CHILD MORTALITY RATE (under 5, per 1,000 live births) 100 (2001)

Chronology

***c.* 2000–500 BC**: Early Bronze Age civilizations in central Mekong River and Plain of Jars regions.
5th–8th centuries: Occupied by immigrants from southern China.
8th century onwards: Theravāda Buddhism spread by Mon monks.
9th–13th centuries: Part of the sophisticated Khmer Empire, centred on Angkor in Cambodia.
12th century: Small independent principalities, notably Louangphrabang, established by Lao invaders from Thailand and Yunnan, southern China; they adopted Buddhism.
14th century: United by King Fa Ngum; the first independent Laotian state, Lan Xang, formed. It was to dominate for four centuries, broken only by a period of Burmese rule 1574–1637.
17th century: First visited by Europeans.
1713: The Lan Xang kingdom split into three separate kingdoms, Louangphrabang, Vientiane, and Champassac, which became tributaries of Siam (Thailand) from the late 18th century.
1893–1945: Laos was a French protectorate, comprising the three principalities of Louangphrabang, Vientiane, and Champassac.
1945: Temporarily occupied by Japan.
1946: Retaken by France, despite opposition by the Chinese-backed Lao Issara (Free Laos) nationalist movement.
1950: Granted semi-autonomy in French Union, as an associated state under the constitutional monarchy of the king of Louangphrabang.
1954: Independence achieved from France under the Geneva Agreements, but civil war broke out between a moderate royalist faction of the Lao Issara, led by Prince Souvanna Phouma, and the communist Chinese-backed Pathet Lao (Land of the Lao) led by Prince Souphanouvong.
1957: A coalition government, headed by Souvanna Phouma, was established by the Vientiane Agreement.

PHYSICIANS (per 1,000 people) 0.2 (1998 est)
HOSPITAL BEDS (per 1,000 people) 2.8 (1996 est)
TV SETS (per 1,000 people) 52 (2001 est)
RADIOS (per 1,000 people) 148 (2001 est)
INTERNET USERS (per 10,000 people) 27.1 (2002 est)
PERSONAL COMPUTER USERS (per 100 people) 0.3 (2002 est)

1959: Savang Vatthana became king.
1960: Right-wing pro-Western government seized power, headed by Prince Boun Gum.
1962: Geneva Agreement established a new coalition government, led by Souvanna Phouma, but civil war continued, the Pathet Lao receiving backing from the North Vietnamese, and Souvanna Phouma from the USA.
1973: Vientiane ceasefire divided the country between the communists and the Souvanna Phouma regime and brought the withdrawal of US, Thai, and North Vietnamese forces.
1975: Communists seized power; a republic was proclaimed, with Prince Souphanouvong as head of state and the Communist Party leader Kaysone Phomvihane as prime minister.
1979: Food shortages and the flight of 250,000 refugees to Thailand led to an easing of the drive towards nationalization and agricultural collectivization.
1985: Greater economic liberalization received encouragement from the Soviet Union's reformist leader Mikhail Gorbachev.
1989: The first assembly elections since communist takeover were held; Vietnamese troops were withdrawn from the country.
1991: A security and cooperation pact was signed with Thailand, and an agreement reached on the phased repatriation of Laotian refugees.
1995: The US lifted its 20-year aid embargo.
1996: The military tightened its grip on political affairs, but inward investment and private enterprise continued to be encouraged, fuelling economic expansion.
1997: Membership of the Association of South East Asian Nations (ASEAN) was announced.
1998: Khamtay Siphandon became president and was replaced as prime minister by Sisavath Keobounphanh.
2001: Boungnang Volachit became prime minister.

LAOS Agriculture is the chief component of the economy in Laos, but farming methods are old-fashioned. Buffalo, such as the ones shown here, are essential on farms that have no machinery. Rice is the main crop along the river valleys, while coffee and tobacco are also cultivated. In isolated mountain regions illegal crops of opium are grown for export. *Corel*

area 1,126,000). It is in a canyon formed by the La Paz River, and is the world's highest capital city. Products include textiles and copper. It has been the seat of government since 1898, but Sucre is the legal capital and seat of the judiciary.

lapis lazuli rock containing the blue mineral lazurite in a matrix of white calcite with small amounts of other minerals. It occurs in silica-poor igneous rocks and metamorphic limestones found in Afghanistan, Siberia, Iran, and Chile. Lapis lazuli was a valuable pigment of the Middle Ages, also used as a gemstone and in inlaying and ornamental work.

LAPIS LAZULI A flask in lapis lazuli with a chain in gilded copper, from the late 16th century. (Museo degli Argenti, Pitti Palace, Florence). *Art Archive*

Laplace, Pierre Simon (1749–1827) Marquis de Laplace. French astronomer and mathematician. In 1796 he theorized that the Solar System originated from a cloud of gas (the nebular hypothesis). He studied the motion of the Moon and planets, and published a five-volume survey of ▷celestial mechanics, *Traité de méchanique céleste* (1799–1825). Among his mathematical achievements was the development of probability theory.

Traité de mécanique céleste contained the law of universal attraction – the law of gravity as applied to the Earth – and explanations of such phenomena as the ebb and flow of tides and the precession of the equinoxes. He became Marquis in 1817.

Related Web site: Laplace, Pierre Simon http://www-history.mcs. st-and.ac.uk/history/Mathematicians/Laplace.html

Lapland region of Europe within the Arctic Circle in Norway, Sweden, Finland, and the Kola Peninsula of northwest Russia, without political definition. Its chief resources are chromium, copper, iron, timber, hydroelectric power, and tourism. The indigenous population are the ▷Saami (formerly known as Lapps), 10% of whom are nomadic, the remainder living mostly in coastal settlements. Lapland has low temperatures, with two months of continuous daylight in summer and two months of continuous darkness in winter. There is summer agriculture.

La Plata capital of Buenos Aires province, Argentina, on the Río de la Plata 48 km/30 mi southeast of the city of Buenos Aires; population (1991) 542,600; metropolitan area (1992 est) 676,100. It is 9 km/6 mi from its port, Ensenada, the main outlet for produce from the Pampas. Industries include meat packing and petroleum refining. It has one of the country's best universities. The city was founded in 1882 by Governor Daroo Rocha.

laptop computer portable microcomputer, small enough to be used on the operator's lap. It consists of a single unit, incorporating a keyboard, ▷floppy disk and ▷hard disk drives, and a screen. The screen often forms a lid that folds back in use. It uses a liquid-crystal or gas-plasma display, rather than the bulkier and heavier cathode-ray tubes found in most display terminals. A typical laptop computer measures about 210 × 297 mm/ 8.3 × 11.7 in (A4), is 5 cm/2 in in depth, and weighs less than 3 kg/6 lb 9 oz. In the 1980s there were several types of laptop computer, but in the 1990s designs converged on systems known as ▷notebook computers.

lapwing bird belonging to the plover family, also known as the **green plover** and, from its call, as the **peewit**. Bottle-green above and white below, with a long thin crest and rounded wings, it is about 30 cm/1 ft long. It inhabits moorland in Europe and Asia, making a nest scratched out of the ground, and is also often seen on farmland. (Species *Vanellus vanellus*, family Charadriidae.)

Lapwings have declined in Britain by 62% since the late 1960s.

Lara, Brian (1969–) Trinidadian cricket player. A left-handed batsman, he plays first-class cricket for Trinidad and Tobago and for Warwickshire. In April 1994, he broke the world individual Test batting record with an innings of 375 against England, and 50 days later, he broke the world record for an individual innings in first-class cricket with an unbeaten 501 for Warwickshire against Durham. In February 2000, after two years in the position, Lara stepped down as West Indies captain. Under his captaincy the West Indies had a record of five wins, one draw, and nine defeats.

larch any of a group of trees belonging to the pine family. The common larch (*L. decidua*) grows to 40 m/130 ft. It is one of the few ▷conifers to shed its leaves annually. The small needlelike leaves are replaced every year by new bright-green foliage, which later darkens. (Genus *Larix*, family Pinaceae.)

LARCH A native of the mountains of central Europe, the larch is now widely cultivated for timber and is often used to shelter hardwood saplings. *Premaphotos Wildlife*

Large Electron Positron Collider (LEP) the world's largest particle ▷accelerator, in operation 1989–2000 at the CERN laboratories near Geneva in Switzerland. It occupies a tunnel 3.8 m/12.5 ft wide and 27 km/16.7 mi long, which is buried 180 m/590 ft underground and forms a ring consisting of eight curved and eight straight sections. In June 1996, LEP resumed operation after a £210 million upgrade. The upgraded machine, known as LEP2, can generate collision energy of 161 gigaelectron volts.

La Rioja autonomous community of northern Spain; area 5,000 sq km/1,930 sq mi; population (2001 est) 270,400. The River Ebro passes through the region, but it is a tributary of the Río

Oja, which gives its name to the region. La Rioja produces red and white wines with a characteristic flavour that derives from their storage in oak barrels. The capital is Logroño.

Related Web site: La Rioja http://www. DocuWeb.ca/SiSpain/english/politics/ autonomo/rioja/index.html

lark any of a group of songbirds found mainly in the Old World, but also in North America. Larks are brownish-tan in colour and usually about 18 cm/7 in long; they nest on the ground in the open. The **skylark** (*Alauda arvensis*) sings as it rises almost vertically in the air. It is light brown and 18 cm/7 in long. (Family Alaudidae, order Passeriformes.) Skylarks have declined in Britain by 58% since the late 1960s.

The **woodlark** (*Lullula arborea*), the **crested lark** (*Galerida cristata*), and the **shore lark** (*Eremophila alpestris*) belong to the same family. The **Australian lark** belongs to the genus *Mirafra*.

Larkin, Philip Arthur (1922–1985) English poet. His perfectionist, pessimistic verse appeared in *The Less Deceived* (1955), and in the later volumes *The Whitsun Weddings* (1964), and *High Windows* (1974) which confirmed him as one of the most powerful and influential of 20th-century English poets. After his death, his letters and other writings, which he had instructed should be destroyed, revealed an intolerance and misanthropy not found in his published material. From 1955 until his death he was librarian at the University of Hull. He edited *The Oxford Book of 20th-Century English Verse* (1973). *Collected Poems* was published in 1988.

larkspur any of several plants included with the ▷delphiniums. (Genus *Delphinium*, family Ranunculaceae.)

La Rochefoucauld, François, Duc de (1613–1680) French writer. His 'Réflexions, ou sentences et maximes morales/Reflections, or Moral Maxims', published anonymously in 1665, is a collection of brief, epigrammatic, and cynical observations on life and society, with the epigraph 'Our virtues are mostly our vices in disguise'. The work is remarkable for its literary excellence and its bitter realism in the dissection of basic human motives, making La Rochefoucauld a forerunner of modern 'psychological' writers.

La Rochelle fishing port on the Bay of Biscay in western France; population (1990) 73,700, conurbation 100,000. It is the administrative centre of Charente-Maritime *département*. Industries include shipbuilding, chemicals, motor vehicles, fish-canning, and saw-milling. A Huguenot stronghold, it was taken by Cardinal Richelieu in the siege of 1627–28.

Larousse, Pierre Athenase (1817–1875) French grammarian and lexicographer. His encyclopedic dictionary, the *Grand dictionnaire universel du XIXème siècle/Great Universal 19th-Century Dictionary* (1865–76), continues to be published in revised form.

Lartigue, Jacques-Henri Charles Auguste (1894–1986) French photographer. He began taking photographs of his family at the age of seven, and went on to make ▷autochrome colour prints of women. During his lifetime he took over 40,000 photographs, documenting everyday people and situations.

larva stage between hatching and adulthood in those species in which the young have a different appearance and way of life from the adults. Examples include tadpoles (frogs) and caterpillars (butterflies and moths). Larvae are typical of the invertebrates, some of which (for example, shrimps) have two or more distinct larval stages. Among vertebrates, it is only the amphibians and some fishes that have a larval stage.

The process whereby the larva changes into another stage, such as a pupa (chrysalis) or adult, is known as ▷metamorphosis.

laryngitis inflammation of the larynx, causing soreness of the throat, a dry cough, and hoarseness. The acute form is due to a virus or other infection, excessive use of the voice,

LARVA The larva of the monarch butterfly *Danaus plexippus*. *Premaphotos Wildlife*

or inhalation of irritating smoke, and may cause the voice to be completely lost. With rest, the inflammation usually subsides in a few days.

larynx in mammals, a cavity at the upper end of the trachea (windpipe) containing the vocal cords. It is stiffened with cartilage and lined with mucous membrane. Amphibians and reptiles have much simpler larynxes, with no vocal cords. Birds have a similar cavity, called the **syrinx**, found lower down the trachea, where it branches to form the bronchi. It is very complex, with well-developed vocal cords.

la Salle, René Robert Cavelier, Sieur de (1643–1687) French explorer. He made an epic voyage through North America, exploring the Mississippi River down to its mouth, and in 1682 founded Louisiana. When he returned with colonists, he failed to find the river mouth again, and was eventually murdered by his mutinous men.

Las Casas, Bartolomé de (1474–1566) Spanish missionary, historian, and colonial reformer, known as **the Apostle of the Indies**. He was one of the first Europeans to call for the abolition of Indian slavery in Latin America. He took part in the conquest of Cuba in 1513, but subsequently worked for American Indian freedom in the Spanish colonies. *Apologetica historia de las Indias* (first published 1875–76) is his account of Indian traditions and his witnessing of Spanish oppression of the Indians.

BARTOLEMÉ DE LAS CASAS Bartolomé de Las Casas, Spanish missionary and historian. *Archive Photos*

Lascaux cave system near Montignac-sur-Vezère in the Dordogne, southwestern France, with prehistoric wall art, discovered in 1940. It is richly decorated with realistic and symbolic paintings of aurochs (wild cattle), horses, and red deer of the Upper Palaeolithic period (Old Stone Age, about 15,000 BC), preserved under a glaze of calcite formation.

Lasdun, Denys Louis (1914–2001) English modernist architect. Many of his designs emphasize the horizontal layering of a building, creating the effect of geological strata extending into the surrounding city or landscape. This effect can be seen in his designs for the University of East Anglia, Norwich (1962–68); and the National Theatre (1967–76) on London's South Bank.

laser (acronym for light amplification by stimulated emission of radiation) device for producing a narrow beam of light, capable of travelling over vast distances without dispersion, and of being focused to give enormous power densities (10^8 watts per cm^2 for high-energy lasers). The laser operates on a principle similar to that of the ▷maser (a high-frequency microwave amplifier or oscillator). The uses of lasers include communications (a laser beam can carry much more information than can radio waves), cutting, drilling, welding, satellite tracking, medical and biological research, and surgery. Sound wave

vibrations from the window glass of a room can be picked up by a reflected laser beam. Lasers are also used as entertainment in theatres, concerts, and light shows.

Laser material Any substance in which the majority of atoms or molecules can be put into an excited energy state can be used as laser material. Many solid, liquid, and gaseous substances have been used, including synthetic ruby crystal (used for the first extraction of laser light in 1960, and giving a high-power pulsed output) and a helium–neon gas mixture, capable of continuous operation, but at a lower power.

Applications Carbon dioxide gas lasers (CO$_2$ lasers) can produce a beam of 100 watts or more power in the infrared (wavelength 10.6 µm) and this has led to an important commercial application, the cutting of material for suits and dresses in hundreds of thicknesses at a time. Dye lasers, in which complex organic dyes in solution are the lasing material, can be tuned to produce light of any chosen wavelength over a range of a sizeable fraction of the visible spectrum.

laser printer computer printer in which the image to be printed is formed by the action of a laser on a light-sensitive drum, then transferred to paper by means of an electrostatic charge. Laser printers are page printers, printing a complete page at a time. The printed image, which can take the form of text or pictures, is made up of tiny dots, or ink particles. The quality of the image generated depends on the fineness of these dots – most laser printers can print up to 120 dots per cm/300 dots per in across the page.

laser surgery use of intense light sources to cut, coagulate, or vaporize tissue. Less invasive than normal surgery, it destroys diseased tissue gently and allows quicker, more natural healing. It can be used by way of a flexible endoscope to enable the surgeon to view the diseased area at which the laser needs to be aimed.

Las Palmas (or **Las Palmas de Gran Canaria**) tourist resort on Gran Canaria, Canary Islands; population (1995) 373,800. Products include sugar and bananas. It lies in the northeast of the island on a narrow coastal strip, with the Atlantic Ocean on one side and cliffs containing rock houses on the other. There is a cathedral here, partly 15th century.

La Spezia port in northwest Italy and chief Italian naval base, 80 km/50 mi southeast of Genoa, on the Riviera di Levante; population (1992) 100,500. Industries include shipbuilding, engineering, oil-refining, and the manufacture of electrical goods and textiles. The English poet Percy Bysshe Shelley drowned in the Gulf of La Spezia in 1822.

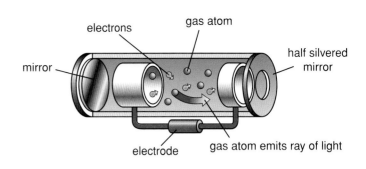

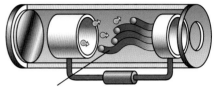

light ray hits another energized atom causing more light to be emitted

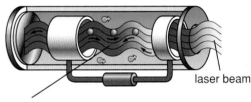

light rays bounce between the mirrors causing a build up of light

LASER In a gas laser, electrons moving between the electrodes pass energy to gas atoms. An energized atom emits a ray of light. The ray hits another energized atom causing it to emit a further light ray. The rays bounce between mirrors at each end causing a build-up of light. Eventually it becomes strong enough to pass through the half-silvered mirror at one end, producing a laser beam.

Lassa fever acute disease caused by an arenavirus, first detected in 1969, and spread by a species of rat found only in West Africa. It is classified as a haemorrhagic fever and characterized by high fever, headache, muscle pain, and internal bleeding. There is no known cure, the survival rate being less than 50%.

Las Vegas city in southeastern Nevada, USA; seat of Clark County; population (2000 est) 478,000. With its many nightclubs and gambling casinos, Las Vegas attracts millions of visitors each year. It is also a major convention centre. Founded in 1855 in a ranching area, the modern community developed with the coming of the railroad in 1905 and was incorporated as a city in 1911. The first casino hotel opened here in 1947. Las Vegas is the easiest place to get married in the USA, with numerous chapels along the Strip (main street) and hotel chapels.

    Related Web site: Las Vegas http://www.klas-tv.com/

lat. abbreviation for ▷latitude.

La Tène prehistoric settlement at the east end of Lake Neuchâtel, Switzerland, which has given its name to a culture of the Iron Age dating from the 5th century BC to the Roman conquest.

latent heat in physics, the heat absorbed or released by a substance as it changes state (for example, from solid to liquid) at constant temperature and pressure.

lateral line system system of sense organs in fishes and larval amphibians (tadpoles) that detects water movement. It usually consists of a row of interconnected pores on either side of the body that divide into a system of canals across the head. See picture on p. 540.

lateral moraine linear ridge of rocky debris deposited near the edge of a ▷glacier. Much of the debris is material that has fallen from the valley side onto the glacier's edge, having been weathered by ▷freeze-thaw (the alternate freezing and thawing of ice in cracks). Where two glaciers merge, two lateral moraines may join together to form a **medial moraine** running along the centre of the merged glacier.

Lateran Treaties series of agreements that marked the reconciliation of the Italian state with the papacy in 1929. They

---

Lascaux Cave Art

The cave system at Lascaux, in the Dordogne, southwestern France, contains fine examples of prehistoric art – paintings, drawings, and engravings of animals (some greater than life size) such as wild cattle, horses, and deer. The artwork, which probably dates from about 15,000–13,000 BC (Old Stone Age) demonstrates advanced artistic quality and technical skill. The paintings have a light background and the colours, yellow, red, brown, and black, were rubbed onto the surface or blown by a tube. The portrayals of animals are stylized, often in a twisted perspective, with the horns or antlers seen from the front but the body appearing in profile. Traps and arrows

depicted near the animals have led to the suggestion that the caves were used as a centre for performing hunting and magical rites.

When the caves were discovered by schoolboys in 1940, the artwork was extremely well preserved. However, following the opening of the caves to the public in 1948 it rapidly deteriorated. The caves were closed in 1963 and a replica was opened in 1983. Since 1979 the caves have been listed by UNESCO as a World Heritage Site. Reconstruction of the cave art has been useful in suggesting how long the original pieces of work would have taken to complete.

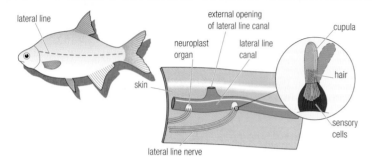

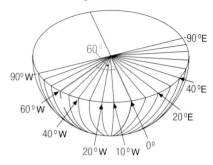

LATERAL LINE SYSTEM In fishes, the lateral line system detects water movement. Arranged along a line down the length of the body are two water-filled canals, just under the skin. The canals are open to the outside, and water movements cause water to move in the canals. Nerve endings detect the movements. See entry on p. 539.

were hailed as a propaganda victory for the fascist regime. The treaties involved recognition of the sovereignty of the ▷Vatican City State, the payment of an indemnity for papal possessions lost during unification in 1870, and agreement on the role of the Catholic Church within the Italian state in the form of a concordat between Pope Pius XI and the dictator Mussolini.

latex (Latin 'liquid') fluid of some plants (such as the rubber tree and poppy), an emulsion of resins, proteins, and other organic substances. It is used as the basis for making rubber. The name is also applied to a suspension in water of natural or synthetic rubber (or plastic) particles used in rubber goods, paints, and adhesives.

lathe machine tool, used for turning. The workpiece to be machined, usually wood or metal, is held and rotated while cutting tools are moved against it. Modern lathes are driven by electric motors, which can drive the spindle carrying the workpiece at various speeds.

Latimer, Hugh (c. 1485–1555) English bishop. After his conversion to Protestantism in 1524 during the ▷Reformation he was imprisoned several times but was protected by cardinal Thomas ▷Wolsey and Henry VIII. After the accession of the Catholic ▷Mary I, he was burned for heresy.

Latin Indo-European language of ancient Italy. Latin has passed through four influential phases: as the language of (1) republican Rome, (2) the Roman Empire, (3) the Roman Catholic Church, and (4) Western European culture, science, philosophy, and law during the Middle Ages and the Renaissance. During the third and fourth phases, much Latin vocabulary entered the English language. It is the parent form of the ▷Romance languages, noted for its highly inflected grammar and conciseness of expression.

Latin America large territory in the Western hemisphere south of the USA, consisting of Mexico, Central America, South America, and the West Indies. The main languages spoken are Spanish, Portuguese, and French.

Latin American Economic System (LAES or Sistema Económico Latino-Americana (**SELA**)) international coordinating body for economic, technological, and scientific cooperation in Latin America and the Caribbean, aiming to create and promote multinational enterprises in the region and provide markets. Founded in 1975 as the successor to the Latin American Economic Coordination Commission, its members include Argentina, Barbados, Bolivia, Brazil, Chile, Colombia, Costa Rica, Cuba, Dominican Republic, Ecuador, El Salvador, Grenada, Guatemala, Guyana, Haiti, Honduras, Mexico, Jamaica, Nicaragua, Panama, Paraguay, Peru, Spain (from 1979), Suriname, Trinidad and Tobago, Uruguay, and Venezuela. Its headquarters are in Caracas, Venezuela.

Latin American Integration Association (or *Asociación Latino-Americana de Integración* (ALADI)) organization aiming to create a common market in Latin America; to promote trade it applies tariff reductions preferentially on the basis of the different stages of economic development that individual member countries have reached. Formed in 1980 to replace the Latin American Free Trade Association (formed in 1961), it has 11 members: Argentina, Bolivia, Brazil, Chile, Colombia, Ecuador, Mexico, Paraguay, Peru, Uruguay, and Venezuela. Its headquarters are in Bogotá, Colombia.

Latin literature literature written in the Latin language.

Early literature Only a few hymns and inscriptions survive from the earliest period of Latin literature before the 3rd century BC.

Greek influence began with the work of Livius Andronicus (*c.* 284–204 BC), who translated the *Odyssey* and Greek plays into Latin. Naevius and Ennius both attempted epics on patriotic themes; the former used the native 'Saturnian' metre, but the latter introduced the Greek hexameter. Plautus and Terence successfully adapted Greek comedy to the Latin stage. Accius and Pacuvius produced tragic verse. Lucilius (190–103 BC) founded Latin verse satire, while the writings of Cato the Elder were the first important works in Latin prose.

Golden Age (70 BC–AD 18) In the *De Rerum natura* of Lucretius, and the passionate lyrics of Catullus, Latin verse reached maturity. Cicero set a standard for Latin prose, in his orations, philosophical essays, and letters. To the same period of the Roman republic belong the commentaries of Caesar on his own campaigns. Other prose writers of this period include Cornelius Nepos, Sallust, and Marcus Terentius Varro.

Augustan Age (43 BC–AD 18) Within the Golden Age, this is usually regarded as the finest period of Latin literature. There is strong patriotic feeling in the work of the poets Virgil and Horace and the historian Livy, who belonged to the emperor Augustus' court circle. Virgil produced the one great Latin epic, the *Aeneid*, while Horace brought charm and polish to both lyric and satire. Younger poets of the period were Ovid, who wrote ironically about love and mythology, and the elegiac and erotic poets Tibullus and Propertius. Tragedy was again in vogue, and was attempted by Asinius Pollio (76 BC–AD 5), Varius Rufus (74–14 BC), and Augustus himself.

Silver Age (AD 18–*c.* 130) The second major period of imperial literature begins with the writers of Nero's reign: the Stoic philosopher Seneca; Lucan, author of the epic *Pharsalia*; the satirist Persius; and the novelist Petronius. Around the end of the 1st century and the beginning of the 2nd came the historian and annalist Tacitus and the satirical poet Juvenal; other writers of this period were the epigrammatist Martial, the scientific encyclopedist Pliny the Elder, the letter-writer Pliny the Younger, the critic Quintilian, the historian Suetonius, and the epic poet Statius.

2nd–5th centuries There was only one pagan writer of importance, the romancer Apuleius, but there were some able Christian writers, such as Tertullian and Cyprian, who were followed by Arnobius (died 327) and Lactantius (died 325). In the 4th century there was a poetic revival, with Ausonius, Claudian, and the Christian poets Prudentius and St Ambrose.

The classical period ends, and the Middle Ages begin, with St Augustine's *City of God* and St Jerome's translation of the Bible.

Middle Ages Throughout the Middle Ages, Latin remained the language of the church and was normally employed for theology, philosophy, histories, and other learned works. Latin verse, adapted to rhyme and non-classical metres, was used both for hymns and for the secular songs of scholars, as in the *Carmina Burana*. Medieval Latin vernacular gradually evolved into the regional and national ▷Romance languages, including French, Italian, and Spanish. Even after the Reformation, Latin retained its prestige as the international language of scholars and was used as such by the English writers Thomas More, Francis Bacon, John Milton, and many others.

latitude and longitude imaginary lines used to locate position on the globe. Lines of latitude are drawn parallel to the Equator, with 0° at the Equator and 90° at the north and south poles. Lines of longitude are drawn at right angles to these, with 0° (the Prime Meridian) passing through Greenwich, England.

The 0-degree line of latitude is defined by Earth's equator, a characteristic definable by astronomical observation. It was determined as early as AD 150 by Egyptian astronomer ▷Ptolemy in his world atlas. The prime meridian, or 0-degree line of longitude, is a matter of convention rather than physics. Prior to the latter half of the 18th century, sailors navigated by referring to their position east or west of any arbitrary meridian. When Nevil Maskelyne (1732–1811), English astronomer and fifth Astronomer Royal, published the *Nautical Almanac* he referred all of his

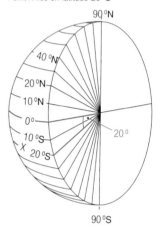

LATITUDE AND LONGITUDE The diagram above shows how to locate a point on a globe using latitude and longitude. Longitude is the angle between the terrestrial meridian through a place and the standard meridian 0° passing through Greenwich, England. Latitude is the angular distance of a place from the equator.

lunar–stellar distance tables to the Greenwich meridian. These tables were relied upon for computing longitudinal position and so the Greenwich meridian became widely accepted.

Chronometers, time keeping devices with sufficient accuracy for longitude determination, invented by English instrument-maker John Harrison (1693–1776) and perfected in 1759, would gradually replace the lunar distance method for navigation, but reliance on the Greenwich meridian persisted because the *Nautical Almanac* was used by sailors to verify their position. The Greenwich meridian was officially adopted as the prime meridian by the International Meridian Conference held in Washington, DC, in 1884.

La Tour, Georges de (1593–1652) French painter. Many of his pictures – which range from religious paintings to domestic genre scenes – are illuminated by a single source of light, with deep contrasts of light and shade, as in *Joseph the Carpenter* about (1645; Louvre, Paris).

Latter-day Saint member of the Christian sect known as the ▷Mormons.

Latvia see country box.

Latvian language (or **Lettish**) language of Latvia; with Lithuanian it is one of the two surviving members of the Balto-Slavic branch of the Indo-European language family.

Latynina, Larissa Semyonovna (1935–) Soviet gymnast. She has won more Olympic medals than any person in any sport. She won 18 between 1956 and 1964, including nine gold medals. She won a total of 12 individual Olympic and world championship gold medals.

Laud, William (1573–1645) English priest; archbishop of Canterbury from 1633. Laud's High Church policy, support for Charles I's unparliamentary rule, censorship of the press, and persecution of the Puritans all aroused bitter opposition, while his strict enforcement of the statutes against enclosures and of laws regulating wages and prices alienated the propertied classes. His attempt to impose the use of the Prayer Book on the Scots precipitated the English ▷Civil War. Impeached by Parliament in 1640, he was imprisoned in the Tower of London. In 1645 he was beheaded.

Latvia

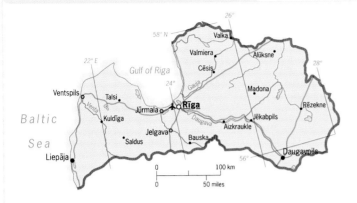

Latvia country in northern Europe, bounded east by Russia, north by Estonia, north and northwest by the Baltic Sea, south by Lithuania, and southeast by Belarus.

NATIONAL NAME *Latvijas Republika/Republic of Latvia*
AREA 63,700 sq km/24,594 sq mi
CAPITAL Riga
MAJOR TOWNS/CITIES Daugavpils, Leipaja, Jurmala, Jelgava, Ventspils
MAJOR PORTS Ventspils, Leipaja
PHYSICAL FEATURES wooded lowland (highest point 312 m/1,024 ft), marshes, lakes; 472 km/293 mi of coastline; mild climate

Government

HEAD OF STATE Vaira Vike-Freiberga from 1999
HEAD OF GOVERNMENT Indulis Emsis from 2004
POLITICAL SYSTEM emergent democracy
POLITICAL EXECUTIVE parliamentary
ADMINISTRATIVE DIVISIONS 26 districts and seven municipalities
ARMED FORCES 5,500 (2002 est)
CONSCRIPTION compulsory for 12 months
DEATH PENALTY abolished for ordinary crimes in 1999; laws provide for the death penalty for exceptional crimes, such as crimes committed in wartime
DEFENCE SPEND (% GDP) 1.8 (2002 est)
EDUCATION SPEND (% GDP) 5.9 (2001 est)
HEALTH SPEND (% GDP) 5.9 (2000 est)

Economy and resources

CURRENCY lat
GPD (US$) 8.4 billion (2002 est)

REAL GDP GROWTH (% change on previous year) 7.7 (2001)
GNI (US$) 8.1 billion (2002 est)
GNI PER CAPITA (PPP) (US$) 8,940 (2002 est)
CONSUMER PRICE INFLATION 3% (2003 est)
UNEMPLOYMENT 7.7% (2001)
FOREIGN DEBT (US$) 3.5 billion (2001 est)
MAJOR TRADING PARTNERS Germany, Russia, Lithuania, Finland, Sweden, Estonia, EU
RESOURCES peat, gypsum, dolomite, limestone, amber, gravel, sand
INDUSTRIES food processing, machinery and equipment (major producer of electric railway passenger cars and long-distance telephone exchanges), chemicals and chemical products, sawn timber, paper and woollen goods
EXPORTS timber and timber products, textiles, food and agricultural products, machinery and electrical equipment, metal industry products. Principal market: Germany 16.7% (2001)
IMPORTS mineral fuels and products, machinery and electrical equipment, chemical industry products. Principal source: Germany 17% (2001)
ARABLE LAND 29.7% (2000 est)
AGRICULTURAL PRODUCTS oats, barley, rye, potatoes, flax; cattle and dairy farming and pig breeding are the chief agricultural occupations

Population and society

POPULATION 2,307,000 (2003 est)
POPULATION GROWTH RATE –0.7% (2000–15)
POPULATION DENSITY (per sq km) 36 (2003 est)
URBAN POPULATION (% of total) 60 (2003 est)
AGE DISTRIBUTION (% of total population) 0–14 16%, 15–59 63%, 60+ 21% (2002 est)
ETHNIC GROUPS 56% of Latvian ethnic descent, 32% ethnic Russian, 4% Belorussian, 3% Ukrainian, 2% Polish, 1% Lithuanian
LANGUAGE Latvian (official)
RELIGION Lutheran, Roman Catholic, Russian Orthodox
EDUCATION (compulsory years) 9
LITERACY RATE 99% (men); 99% (women) (2003 est)

LABOUR FORCE 15.3% agriculture, 26.1% industry, 58.6% services (1999)
LIFE EXPECTANCY 66 (men); 76 (women) (2000–05)
CHILD MORTALITY RATE (under 5, per 1,000 live births) 21 (2001)
PHYSICIANS (per 1,000 people) 2.8 (1999 est)
HOSPITAL BEDS (per 1,000 people) 10.3 (1999 est)
TV SETS (per 1,000 people) 840 (2001 est)
RADIOS (per 1,000 people) 700 (2001 est)
INTERNET USERS (per 10,000 people) 1,331.0 (2002 est)
PERSONAL COMPUTER USERS (per 100 people) 17.2 (2002 est)

See also ▷Russian Federation; ▷Union of Soviet Socialist Republics.

Chronology

9th–10th centuries: Invaded by Vikings and Russians.

13th century: Conquered by crusading German Teutonic Knights, who named the area Livonia and converted population to Christianity; Riga joined the Hanseatic League, a northern European union of commercial towns.

1520s: Lutheranism established as a result of the Reformation.

16th–17th centuries: Successively under Polish, Lithuanian, and Swedish rule.

1721: Tsarist Russia took control.

1819: Serfdom abolished.

1900s: Emergence of an independence movement.

1914–18: Under partial German occupation during World War I.

1918–19: Independence proclaimed and achieved after Russian Red Army troops expelled by German, Polish, and Latvian forces.

1920s: Land reforms introduced by Farmers' Union government.

1934: Democracy overthrown and, at time of economic depression, an autocratic regime was established; Baltic Entente mutual defence pact made with Estonia and Lithuania.

1940: Incorporated into Soviet Union (USSR) as constituent republic, following secret German–Soviet agreement.

1941–44: Occupied by Germany.

1944: USSR regained control; mass deportations of Latvians to Central Asia, followed by immigration of ethnic Russians; agricultural collectivization.

1960s and 1970s: Extreme repression of Latvian cultural and literary life.

1980s: Nationalist dissent began to grow, influenced by the Polish Solidarity movement and Mikhail Gorbachev's *glasnost* ('openness') initiative in the USSR.

1988: The Latvian Popular Front was established to campaign for independence. The prewar flag was readopted and official status was given to the Latvian language.

1989: The Latvian parliament passed a sovereignty declaration.

1990: The Popular Front secured a majority in local elections and its leader, Ivan Godmanir, became the prime minister. The Latvian Communist Party split into pro-independence and pro-Moscow wings. The country entered a 'transitional period of independence' and the Baltic Council was reformed.

1991: Soviet troops briefly seized key installations in Riga. There was an overwhelming vote for independence in a referendum. Full independence was achieved following the failure of the anti-Gorbachev coup attempt in Moscow; the Communist Party was outlawed. Joined United Nations (UN); a market-centred economic reform programme was instituted.

1992: The curbing of rights of non-citizens prompted Russia to request minority protection by the UN.

1993: The right-of-centre Latvian Way won the general election; a free-trade agreement was reached with Estonia and Lithuania.

1994: The last Russian troops departed.

1995: A trade and cooperation agreement was signed with the European Union (EU). A general election produced a hung parliament in which extremist parties received most support. Applied for EU membership.

1996: Guntis Ulmanis was re-elected president. The finance minister and deputy prime minister resigned from the eight-party coalition.

1997: A new political party was formed, the Latvian National Party of Reforms. Former Communist leader Alfreds Rubiks was released from prison.

1998: The DPS withdrew from the government, leaving the coalition as a minority. Citizenship laws were relaxed to make it easier for ethnic Russians to acquire citizenship.

1999: Andris Skele became prime minister. Vaira Vike-Freiberga was sworn in as president.

2000: Andris Skele resigned as prime minister after a disagreement within his coalition. He was replaced by Andris Berzins, who headed a coalition of the same parties as before as well as the additional New Party.

2004: Latvia was set to join the EU 1 May.

LATVIA A street in the old part of the city of Riga, Latvia. *Image Bank*

laudanum alcoholic solution (tincture) of the drug ▷opium. Used formerly as a narcotic and painkiller, it was available in the 19th century from pharmacists on demand in most of Europe and the USA.

Lauderdale, John Maitland, 1st Duke of Lauderdale (1616–1682) Scottish politician. Formerly a zealous ▷Covenanter, he joined the Royalists in 1647, and as high commissioner for Scotland 1667–79 persecuted the Covenanters. He was created Duke of Lauderdale in 1672, and was a member of the ▷Cabal ministry 1667–73.

Laughton, Charles (1899–1962) English actor who became a US citizen in 1950. Initially a classical stage actor, he joined the Old Vic in 1933. His films include such roles as the king in *The Private Life of Henry VIII* (1933; Academy Award), Captain Bligh in *Mutiny on the Bounty* (1935), and Quasimodo in *The Hunchback of Notre Dame* (1939). In 1955 he directed *Night of the Hunter* and in 1962 appeared in *Advise and Consent.*

Laurasia northern landmass formed 200 million years ago by the splitting of the single world continent ▷Pangaea. (The southern landmass was ▷Gondwanaland.) It consisted of what was to become North America, Greenland, Europe, and Asia, and is believed to have broken up about 100 million years ago with the separation of North America from Europe.

laurel any of a group of European evergreen trees with glossy aromatic leaves, yellowish flowers, and black berries. The leaves of sweet bay or poet's laurel (*L. nobilis*) are used in cooking. Several species are cultivated worldwide. (Genus *Laurus*, family Lauraceae.)

Laurel and Hardy Stan Laurel (stage name of Arthur Stanley Jefferson) (1890–1965) and Oliver Hardy (1892–1957). US film comedians. They were one of the most successful comedy teams in film history (Laurel was slim, Hardy rotund). Their partnership began in 1927, survived the transition from silent films to sound, and resulted in more than 200 short and feature-length films. Among these are *Pack Up Your Troubles* (1932), *Our Relations* (1936), and *A Chump at Oxford* (1940). *The Music Box* (1932) won an Academy Award as Best Short Film. Laurel received a special Academy Award in 1960.

laurustinus evergreen shrub belonging to the honeysuckle family, of Mediterranean origin. It has clusters of white flowers in winter. (*Viburnum tinus*, family Caprifoliaceae.)

Lausanne resort and capital of Vaud canton, west Switzerland, above the north shore of Lake Geneva; population (1995) 143,200. It is a major railway junction on the Paris–Milan route through the Simplon Pass. Industries include publishing and the manufacture of chocolate and scientific instruments. It hosts international fairs and conferences, and is the headquarters of the International Olympic Committee. An Olympic Museum opened in 1993. The canton is mainly French-speaking and Protestant.

lava magma that erupts from a ▷volcano and cools to form extrusive ▷igneous rock. Lava types differ in composition, temperature, gas content, and viscosity (resistance to flow).

The three major lava types are basalt (dark, fluid, and relativey low silica content), rhyolite (light, viscous, high silica content), and andesite (an intermediate lava).

Laval, Pierre (1883–1945) French extreme-rightwing politician, he gravitated between the wars from socialism through the centre ground (serving as prime minister and foreign secretary 1931–32 and again 1935–36) to the extreme right. As head of the Vichy government and foreign minister 1942–44, he was responsible for the deportation of Jews and for requisitioning French labour to Germany.

Born near Vichy and elected as a socialist deputy in 1914, Laval had trained as a lawyer and acquired considerable wealth from his legal practice. In his second term as premier he negotiated the Hoare–Laval Pact in 1935, providing concessions to Italy in Abyssinia (now Ethiopia). In July 1940 he was instrumental in securing the voting of full powers to Marshal ▷Pétain and served as his vice premier until December 1940. At Hitler's insistence Laval was reinstated as head of government from April 1942, reducing Pétain to the role of figurehead. He fled the country in 1944 but was captured in Austria, tried for treason in France in October 1945, and was executed by firing squad, after trying to poison himself.

lavender sweet-smelling purple-flowering herb belonging to the mint family, native to western Mediterranean countries. The bushy low-growing species *L. angustifolia* has long, narrow, upright leaves of a silver-green colour. The small flowers, borne on spikes, vary in colour from lilac to deep purple and are covered with small fragrant oil glands. Lavender oil is widely used in pharmacy and perfumes. (Genus *Lavandula*, family Labiatae.)

laver any of several edible purplish-red seaweeds, including purple laver (*P. umbilicalis*). Growing on the shore and in the sea, attached to rocks and stones, laver forms thin, roundish sheets of tissue up to 20 cm/8 in across. It becomes almost black when dry. (Genus *Porphyra*, family Rhodophyceae.)

Lavoisier, Antoine Laurent (1743–1794) French chemist. He proved that combustion needs only a part of the air, which he called oxygen, thereby destroying the theory of phlogiston (an imaginary 'fire element' released during combustion). With astronomer and mathematician Pierre de ▷Laplace, he showed in 1783 that water is a compound of oxygen and hydrogen. In this way he established the basic rules of chemical combination.

Lavoisier established that organic compounds contain carbon, hydrogen, and oxygen. From quantitative measurements of the changes during breathing, he showed that carbon dioxide and water are normal products of respiration.

Related Web site: Lavoisier, Antoine Laurent http://www.newadvent.org/cathen/09052a.htm

law body of rules and principles under which justice is administered or order enforced in a state or nation. In Western Europe there are two main systems: Roman law and English law. US law is a modified form of English law.

Law, Andrew Bonar (1858–1923) British Conservative politician, born in New Brunswick, Canada, of Scottish descent. He succeeded Balfour as leader of the opposition in 1911, became colonial secretary in Asquith's coalition government 1915–16, chancellor of the Exchequer 1916–19, and Lord Privy Seal 1919–21 in Lloyd George's coalition. He formed a Conservative cabinet in 1922, but resigned on health grounds.

Law made a fortune in Scotland as a banker and iron-merchant before entering Parliament in 1900.

Law Commission in the UK, either of two statutory bodies established in 1965 (one for England and Wales and one for Scotland) which consider proposals for law reform and publish their findings. They also keep British law under constant review, systematically developing and reforming it by, for example, the repeal of obsolete and unnecessary enactments.

D H Lawrence

An author should be in among the crowd, kicking their shins or cheering on some mischief or merriment . . . Whoever reads me will be in the thick of the scrimmage . . .

Letter, 1925

law courts bodies that adjudicate in legal disputes. Civil and criminal cases are usually dealt with by separate courts. In many countries there is a hierarchy of courts that provide an appeal system.

In England and Wales the court system was reorganized under the Courts Act 1971. The higher courts are: the **House of Lords** (the highest court for the whole of Britain), which deals with both civil and criminal appeals; the **Court of Appeal**, which is divided between criminal and civil appeal courts; the **High Court of Justice** dealing with important civil cases; **crown courts**, which handle criminal cases; and **county courts**, which deal with civil matters. **Magistrates' courts** deal with minor criminal cases and are served by ▷justices of the peace or stipendiary (paid) magistrates; and **juvenile courts** are presided over by specially qualified justices. There are also special courts, such as the Restrictive Practices Court and the Employment Appeal Tribunal.

The courts are organized in six circuits. The towns of each circuit are first-tier (High Court and circuit judges dealing with both criminal and civil cases), second-tier (High Court and circuit judges dealing with criminal cases only), or third-tier (circuit judges dealing with criminal cases only). Cases are allotted according to gravity among High Court and circuit judges and recorders (part-time judges with the same jurisdiction as circuit judges). In 1971 solicitors were allowed for the first time to appear in and conduct cases at the level of the crown courts, and solicitors as well as barristers of ten years' standing became eligible for appointment as recorders, who after five years become eligible as circuit judges. In the UK in 1989 there were 5,500 barristers and 47,000 solicitors. In Scotland, the supreme civil court is the **Court of Session**, with appeal to the House of Lords; the highest criminal court is the **High Court of Justiciary**, with no appeal to the House of Lords.

LAW COURTS Law courts on Fleet Street in London, England. *The Art Archive/Eileen Tweedy*

law lords in England, the ten Lords of Appeal in Ordinary who, together with the Lord Chancellor and other peers, make up the House of Lords in its judicial capacity. The House of Lords is the final court of appeal in both criminal and civil cases. Law lords rank as life peers.

Lawrence, D(avid) H(erbert) (1885–1930) English writer. His work expresses his belief in emotion and the sexual impulse as creative and true to human nature, but his ideal of the complete, passionate life is seen to be threatened by the encroachment of the modern and technological world. His writing first received attention after the publication of the semi-autobiographical *The White Peacock* (1911) and *Sons and Lovers* (1913). Other novels include *The Rainbow* (1915), *Women in Love* (1921), and *Lady Chatterley's Lover*, printed privately in Italy in 1928. Lawrence also wrote short stories (for example, 'The Woman Who Rode Away', written in Mexico from 1922–25) and poetry (*Collected Poems*, 1928).

Lawrence tried to forge a new kind of novel, with a structure and content so intense that it would reflect emotion and passion more genuinely than ever before. This often led to conflict with official and unofficial prudery, and his interest in sex as a life force and bond was often censured. *The Rainbow* was suppressed for obscenity, and *Lady Chatterley's Lover* could only be published in an expurgated form in the UK in 1932. Not until 1960, when the obscenity law was successfully challenged, was it published in the original text.

Related Web site: Poems of D H Lawrence http://www.bartleby.com/128/index.html

Lawrence, T(homas) E(dward) (1888–1935) Called 'Lawrence of Arabia'. British soldier, scholar, and translator. Appointed to the military intelligence department in Cairo, Egypt, during World War I, he took part in negotiations for an Arab revolt against the Ottoman Turks, and in 1916 attached himself to the emir Faisal. He became a guerrilla leader of genius, combining raids on Turkish communications with the organization of a joint Arab revolt, described in his book *The Seven Pillars of Wisdom* (1926).

Lawrence, Thomas (1769–1830) English painter. He was the leading portraitist of his day, becoming painter to George III in 1792 and president of the Royal Academy from 1820 to 1830. One of his finest portraits is *Queen Charlotte* (1789; National Gallery, London).

lawrencium synthesized, radioactive, metallic element, the last of the actinide series, symbol Lr, atomic number 103, relative atomic mass 262. Its only known isotope, Lr-257, has a half-life of 4.3 seconds and was originally synthesized at the University of California at Berkeley in 1961 by bombarding californium with boron nuclei. The original symbol, Lw, was officially changed in 1963. The element was named after Ernest Lawrence (1901–1958), the US inventor of the cyclotron.

Lawson, Nigel, Baron Lawson of Blaby (1932–) British Conservative politician. A former financial journalist, he was financial secretary to the Treasury 1979–81, secretary of state for energy 1981–83, and chancellor of the Exchequer 1983–89. He resigned as chancellor after criticusm by government adviser Alan Walters, supported by prime minister Margaret Thatcher, over his policy of British membership of the ▷European Monetary System.

laxative substance used to relieve constipation (infrequent bowel movement). Current medical opinion discourages regular or prolonged use. Regular exercise and a diet high in vegetable fibre are believed to be the best means of preventing and treating constipation.

Layamon English poet. His name means 'law man' or 'judge', and according to his own account he was a priest of Areley (now Areley Kings), Worcestershire. He was the author of the *Brut*, a chronicle of about 16,000 alliterative lines on the history of Britain from the arrival of ▷Brutus, the legendary Roman senator and general, to ▷Cadwalader, which gives the earliest version of the Arthurian legend in English.

The *Brut* is based on the French rendering by Robert Wace of the Latin *Historia Regum Britanniae* by ▷Geoffrey of Monmouth, with

additions from Celtic legend. The first important poem written in Middle English, the *Brut* is written mainly in alliterative lines but occasionally uses rhyme and assonance; it therefore shows English verse in transition. Two composite manuscript copies survive (housed in the British Museum).

Lazarus in the New Testament, the brother of Martha, a friend of Jesus, raised by him from the dead. Lazarus is also the name of a beggar in a parable told by Jesus (Luke 16).

Lazio (Roman **Latium**) region of west central Italy, comprising the provinces of Viterbo, Rieti, Rome, Frosinone, and Latina; area 17,200 sq km/6,600 sq mi; capital Rome; population (1992 est) 5,162,100. It is the third-largest region of Italy, over half its population living in the city of ▷Rome. Products include olives, wine, chemicals, pharmaceuticals, and textiles. Home of the Latins from the 10th century BC, it was dominated by the Romans from the 4th century BC.

lb (Latin 'libra') symbol for ▷pound (weight).

lbw abbreviation for **leg before wicket** (cricket).

lc in typography, abbreviation for **lower case**, or 'small' letters, as opposed to capitals.

LCD abbreviation for ▷liquid-crystal display.

L-dopa chemical, normally produced by the body, which is converted by an enzyme to dopamine in the brain. It is essential for integrated movement of individual muscle groups.

LEA in the UK, abbreviation for **local education authority**, the body of local government responsible for the state schools and further education establishments in a district.

Leach, Bernard Howell (1887–1979) English potter. His simple designs of stoneware and *raku* ware, inspired by a period of study in Japan from 1909 to 1920, pioneered a revival of studio pottery in Britain. In 1920 he established the Leach Pottery, a communally-run workshop at St Ives, Cornwall, with the Japanese potter Shoji Hamada (1894–1978).

leaching process by which substances are washed through or out of the soil. Fertilizers leached out of the soil drain into rivers, lakes, and ponds and cause water pollution. In tropical areas, leaching of the soil after the destruction of forests removes scarce nutrients and can lead to a dramatic loss of soil fertility. The leaching of soluble minerals in soils can lead to the formation of distinct soil horizons as different minerals are deposited at successively lower levels.

lead heavy, soft, malleable, grey, metallic element, symbol Pb (from Latin *plumbum*), atomic number 82, relative atomic mass 207.19. Usually found as an ore (most often in galena), it occasionally occurs as a free metal (▷native metal), and is the final stable product of the decay of uranium. Lead is the softest and weakest of the commonly used metals, with a low melting point; it is a poor conductor of electricity and resists acid corrosion. As a cumulative poison, lead enters the body from lead water pipes, lead-based paints, and leaded petrol. (In humans, exposure to lead shortly after birth is associated with impaired mental health between the ages of two and four.) The metal is an effective shield against radiation and is used in batteries, glass, ceramics, and alloys such as pewter and solder.

leaded petrol petrol that contains antiknock, a mixture of the chemicals tetraethyl lead and dibromoethane. The lead from the exhaust fumes enters the atmosphere, mostly as simple lead compounds, which are poisonous to the developing nervous systems of children.

lead ore any of several minerals from which lead is extracted. The primary ore is galena or lead sulphite PbS. This is unstable, and on prolonged exposure to the atmosphere it oxidizes into the minerals cerussite $PbCO_3$ and anglesite $PbSO_4$. Lead ores are usually associated with other metals, particularly silver – which can be mined at the same time – and zinc, which can cause problems during smelting.

leaf lateral outgrowth on the stem of a plant, and in most species the primary organ of ▷photosynthesis. The chief leaf types are cotyledons (seed leaves), scale leaves (on underground stems), foliage leaves, and bracts (in the axil of which a flower is produced).

Typically leaves are composed of three parts: the sheath or leaf base, the petiole or stalk, and the lamina or blade. The lamina has a network of veins through which water and nutrients are conducted. Structurally the leaf is made up of ▷mesophyll cells surrounded by the epidermis and usually, in addition, a waxy layer, termed the cuticle, which prevents excessive evaporation of water from the leaf tissues by transpiration. The epidermis is interrupted by small pores, or stomata, through which gas exchange between the plant and the atmosphere occurs.

A **simple leaf** is undivided, as in the beech or oak. A **compound leaf** is composed of several leaflets, as in the blackberry, horse-chestnut, or ash tree (the latter being a ▷pinnate leaf). Leaves that are shed in the autumn are termed **deciduous**, while evergreen leaves are termed **persistent**.

leaf-hopper any of numerous species of plant-sucking insects. They feed on the sap of leaves. Each species feeds on a limited range of plants. (Family Cicadellidae, order Homoptera.)

leaf insect any of various insects about 10 cm/4 in long, with a green or brown, flattened body, remarkable for closely resembling the foliage on which they live. They are most common in Southeast Asia. (Genus *Phyllium*, order Phasmida.)

LEAF INSECT This adult female *Phyllium* leaf insect, a newly discovered species when it was photographed in New Guinea, is mimicking a dead brown leaf. Other species are green and mimic living leaves. *Premaphotos Wildlife*

League of Nations international organization formed after World War I to solve international disputes by arbitration. Established in Geneva, Switzerland, in 1920, the League included representatives from states throughout the world, but was severely weakened by the US decision not to become a member, and had no power to enforce its decisions. It was dissolved in 1946. Its subsidiaries included the **International Labour Organization** and the **Permanent Court of International Justice** in The Hague, the Netherlands, both now under the auspices of the ▷United Nations (UN).

Related Web site: League of Nations
http://www.library.miami.edu/gov/League.html

Leakey, Louis Seymour Bazett (1903–1972) Kenyan archaeologist, anthropologist, and palaeontologist. With his wife Mary Leakey, he discovered fossils of extinct animals in the ▷Olduvai Gorge in Tanzania, as well as many remains of an early human type. Leakey's conviction that human origins lie in Africa was opposed to contemporary opinion.

Leakey, Mary Douglas (1913–1996) Born Mary Douglas Nicol. English archaeologist and anthropologist. In 1948 she discovered, on Rusinga Island, Lake Victoria, East Africa, the prehistoric ape skull known as *Proconsul*, about 20 million years old; and human footprints at Laetoli, to the south, about 3.75 million years old.

Leakey, Richard Erskine Frere (1944–) Kenyan palaeoanthropologist. In 1972 he discovered at Lake Turkana, Kenya, an apelike skull estimated to be about 2.9 million years old; it had some human characteristics and a brain capacity of 800 cu cm/49 cu in. In 1984 his team found an almost complete skeleton of *Homo erectus* some 1.6 million years old. He is the son of Louis and Mary Leakey.

He was appointed director of the Kenyan Wildlife Service in 1988, waging a successful war against poachers and the ivory trade, but was forced to resign in 1994 in the face of political interference. He was reappointed to the post in 1998. In 1995 he co-founded the Kenyan political party Safina (Swahili for Noah's Ark), which aimed to clean up Kenya. The party was accused of racism and colonialism by President Daniel arap Moi. Nevertheless, in July 1999 the president appointed Leakey head of the civil service in the country. He resigned in March 2001, having completed the task but having made many enemies in the government.

Leamington (officially **Royal Leamington Spa**) town and former health resort in Warwickshire, England, adjoining Warwick, on the River Leam, southeast of Birmingham; population (1991) 42,300. Public administration and services, distribution, tourism, and leisure industries provide the main employment. Manufacturing is more significant than the national average and includes engineering and automotive industries, producing brakes, steering, transmission, and other components. The Royal Pump Room offers spa treatment.

Lean, David (1908–1991) English film director. His films, painstakingly crafted, include early work codirected with the playwright Noël Coward, such as *Brief Encounter* (1946). Among his later films are such accomplished epics as *The Bridge on the River Kwai* (1957; Academy Award), *Lawrence of Arabia* (1962; Academy Award), and *Dr Zhivago* (1965).

The unfavourable reaction to *Ryan's Daughter* (1970) caused him to withdraw from film-making for over a decade, but *A Passage to India* (1984) represented a return to form. He was knighted in 1984.

Lear, Edward (1812–1888) English artist and humorist. His *Book of Nonsense* (1846) popularized the ▷limerick (a five-line humorous verse). His *Nonsense Songs, Botany and Alphabets* (1871), includes two of his best-known poems, 'The Owl and the Pussycat' and 'The Jumblies'. He first attracted attention with his paintings of birds, and later turned to landscapes. He travelled to Italy, Greece, Egypt, and India, publishing books on his travels with his own illustrations, and spent most of his later life in Italy.

learning theory in psychology, any theory or body of theories about how behaviour in animals and human beings is acquired or modified by experience. Two main theories are classical and operant ▷conditioning.

leasehold in law, land or property held by a tenant (lessee) for a specified period (unlike ▷freehold, outright ownership), usually at a rent from the landlord (lessor).

leather material prepared from the hides and skins of animals, by tanning with vegetable tannins and chromium salts. Leather is a durable and water-resistant material, and is used for bags, shoes, clothing, and upholstery. There are three main stages in the process of converting animal skin into leather: cleaning, tanning, and dressing. Tanning is often a highly polluting process.

leatherjacket larva of the ▷crane fly.

leaven element inducing fermentation. The term is applied to the yeast added to dough in bread making; it is used figuratively to describe any pervasive influence, usually in a good sense, although in the Old Testament it symbolized corruption, and unleavened bread was used in sacrifice.

> **Edward Lear**
> *Far and few, far and few, /
> Are the lands where the
> Jumblies live; / Their heads
> are green, and their hands
> are blue, / And they went
> to sea in a Sieve.*
>
> *Nonsense Songs*, 'The Jumblies'

Leavis, F(rank) R(aymond) (1895–1978) English literary critic. With his wife Q(ueenie) D(orothy) Leavis (1906–1981), he

EDWARD LEAR English humorist Edward Lear began to earn his living, at the age of 15 years, as an illustrator. *Archive Photos*

cofounded and edited the influential literary review *Scrutiny* (1932–53). He championed the work of D H Lawrence and James Joyce and in 1962 attacked C P Snow's theory of 'the two cultures' (the natural alienation of the arts and sciences in intellectual life). His critical works, introducing a new seriousness to the study of literature, include *New Bearings in English Poetry* (1932), which placed T S ▷Eliot centrally in the modern poetic tradition, *The Great Tradition* (1948), and *The Common Pursuit* (1952).

Lebanon see country box.

Lebanon conflict

Mediterranean Sea

Tripoli

Baalbek

Beirut

LEBANON

Sidon

Damascus

Tyre

SYRIA

Golan Heights

ISRAEL

L. Tiberias

● mixed Christian, Shi'ite and Sunni

Muslim occupied
● Sunni militia
Druse militia
Shi'ite militia
Syrian army

Christian occupied
Israeli and South Lebanese armies
Phalangist militia

0   40 mi
0   60 km

Lebensraum (German 'living space') theory developed by Adolf Hitler for the expansion of Germany into Eastern Europe, and in the 1930s used by the Nazis to justify their annexation of neighbouring states on the grounds that Germany was overpopulated.

Leblanc, Nicolas (1742–1806) French chemist who in the 1780s developed a process for making soda ash (sodium carbonate, Na_2CO_3) from common salt (sodium chloride, NaCl). Soda ash was widely used industrially in making glass, paper, soap, and various chemicals.

Lebowa former black homeland assigned to the North Sotho people in former northern Transvaal Province, South Africa, now in Northern Transvaal. It consisted of five separate areas of territory. It achieved self-governing status in 1972.

Le Brun, Charles (1619–1690) French baroque artist. Court painter to Louis XIV from 1662, he became director of the French Academy and of the Gobelins factory, which produced art, tapestries, and furnishings for the new palace of Versailles.

Le Carré, John (1931–) Pen-name of David John Moore Cornwell. English writer of thrillers. His low-key realistic accounts of complex espionage include *The Spy Who Came in from the Cold* (1963), *Tinker Tailor Soldier Spy* (1974), *Smiley's People* (1980), *The Russia House* (1989), *The Night Manager* (1993), *Our Game* (1995), *The Tailor of Panama* (1996), and *The Constant Gardener* (2000). He was a member of the Foreign Service 1960–64.

Le Chatelier's principle (or Le Chatelier-Braun principle) in science, the principle that if a change in conditions is imposed on a system in equilibrium, the system will react to counteract that change and restore the equilibrium.

lecithin lipid (fat), containing nitrogen and phosphorus, that forms a vital part of the cell membranes of plant and animal cells. The name is from the Greek *lekithos* 'egg yolk', eggs being a major source of lecithin.

Leconte de Lisle, Charles Marie René (1818–1894) French poet. He was born on the Indian Ocean Island of Réunion and settled in Paris in 1846. He played an important part in

formulating the aims of the anti-Romantic group *Les Parnassiens* and became their acknowledged leader. His work, characterized by classic regularity and faultlessness of form, drew inspiration from the ancient world; it includes *Poèmes antiques/Antique Poems* (1852), *Poèmes barbares/Barbaric Poems* (1862), and *Poèmes tragiques/Tragic Poems* (1884). Although he advocated impassivity, his poems express a pessimistic awareness of the transitoriness of things.

Le Corbusier (1887–1965) Adopted name of Charles-Edouard Jeanneret. Swiss-born French architect. He was an early and influential exponent of the ▷Modern Movement and one of the most innovative of 20th-century architects. His distinct brand of Functionalism first appears in his town-planning proposals of the early 1920s, which advocate 'vertical garden cities' with zoning of living and working areas and traffic separation as solutions to urban growth and chaos. From the 1940s several of his designs for multistorey villas were realized, notably his Unité d'Habitation, Marseille, (1947–52), using his Modulor system of standard-sized units mathematically calculated according to the proportions of the human figure (see ▷Fibonacci, ▷golden section).

His white-stuccoed, cubist-style villas of the 1920s were designed as 'machines for living in', making the most of space and light through open-plan interiors, use of *pilotis* (stilts carrying the building), and roof gardens. He moved on to a more expressive mode (anticipating Brutalism) with rough, unfinished exteriors, as in the Ministry of Education, Rio de Janeiro, 1936–45, designed with Lucio Costa (1902–98) and Oscar ▷Niemeyer. In the reconstruction period after World War II, Le Corbusier's urbanization theories were highly influential, disseminated through the work of the urban planning body CIAM, although only in the gridlike layout of the new city of Chandigarh, India, 1951–56, was he able to see his visions of urban zoning fully realized. His sculptural design for the church of Notre-Dame du Haut du Ronchamp 1950–54, worked out in the minutest detail, is a supreme example of aesthetic Functionalism.

Le Corbusier was originally a painter and engraver, but turned his attention to the problems of contemporary industrial society. His books *Vers une Architecture/Towards a New Architecture* 1923 and *Le Modulor* 1948 have had worldwide significance for town planning and building design.

Related Web site: Le Corbusier http://studwww.rug.ac.be/~jvervoor/architects/corbusier/corbusier.html

LED abbreviation for ▷light-emitting diode.

Leda in Greek mythology, wife of Tyndareus of Sparta and mother of ▷Clytemnestra. Zeus, transformed as a swan, was the father of her daughter ▷Helen of Troy and, in some traditions, the brothers ▷Castor and Pollux (Greek Polydeuces). In other variants, Castor was fathered by Tyndareus or, according to Homer, both brothers were his sons.

Le Duc Anh (1920–) Vietnamese soldier and communist politician, president 1992–97. A member of the politburo's military faction, he is regarded as a conservative, anxious to maintain tight party control over domestic policies.

Led Zeppelin UK rock group 1969–80, founders of the ▷heavy metal genre. Their overblown style, with long instrumental solos, was based on rhythm and blues. Many of their songs, such as 'Stairway to Heaven', 'Rock and Roll', 'Black Dog' and 'Kashmir', have become classics, most of them collected on the 1992 *Remasters* compilation. Among their most celebrated records were the group's untitled fourth album, popularly known as *Led Zeppelin IV* (1971) and their 1975 *Physical Graffiti*.

Related Web site: Electric Magic http://www.led-zeppelin.com/

Lee, Bruce (1941–1973) Stage name of Lee Yuen Kam. US 'Chinese Western' film actor. He was an expert in ▷kung fu, who popularized the oriental martial arts in the West with pictures such as *Jing wu men/Fists of Fury* (1972) (made in Hong Kong) and *Enter the Dragon* (1973), his last film.

Lee, Laurie (1914–1997) English writer. His autobiographical *Cider with Rosie* (1959) is a classic evocation of childhood; subsequent volumes are *As I Walked Out One Summer Morning* (1969), and *A Moment of War* (1991), in which he describes the horrors of the Spanish Civil War in 1936. His travel writing includes *A Rose for Winter* (1955). *Selected Poems* was published in 1983.

Lee, Robert E(dward) (1807–1870) US military strategist and Confederate general in the ▷American Civil War. As military adviser to Jefferson ▷Davis, president of the Confederacy, and as

commander of the Army of Northern Virginia, he made several raids into Northern territory, but was defeated at ▷Gettysburg and surrendered in 1865 at ▷Appomattox.

Lee was born in Virginia. He graduated from West Point, was commissioned in 1829, and served in the Mexican War 1846–48. In 1859 he suppressed John ▷Brown's raid on Harper's Ferry. On the outbreak of the Civil War in 1861 he joined the army of the Confederacy of the Southern States, and in 1862 received the command of the Army of Northern Virginia and won the Seven Days' Battle defending Richmond, Virginia, the Confederate capital, against General George McClellan's Union forces.

In 1863 Lee won victories at Fredericksburg and Chancellorsville, and in 1864 at Cold Harbor, but was besieged in Petersburg from June 1864 to April 1865. He surrendered to General Ulysses ▷Grant on 9 April 1865 at Appomattox Court House.

ROBERT E LEE US Confederate general Robert E Lee. During the American Civil War he was commander of the army of North Virginia, and military adviser to Jefferson Davis, president of the Confederacy. At the onset of the Civil War he resigned from the US army to accept command of the Confederate forces. *Archive Photos*

Lee, Spike (Shelton Jackson) (1957–) US film director, actor, and writer. Much of his work presents the harsh realities of contemporary working-class African-American life in a direct, often controversial manner. His films, in which he sometimes appears, include *She's Gotta Have It* (1986), *Do The Right Thing* (1989), *Jungle Fever* (1991), *Malcolm X* (1992), *Clockers* (1995), *He Got Game* (1998), *Summer of Sam* (1999), and *Bamboozled* (2000). See picture on p. 546.

Lee Kuan Yew (1923–) Singaporean politician, prime minister 1959–90. Lee founded the anticommunist Socialist People's Action Party in 1954 and entered the Singapore legislative assembly in 1955. He was elected the country's first prime minister in 1959, and took Singapore out of the Malaysian federation in 1965. He remained in power until his resignation in 1990, and was succeeded by Goh Chok Tong. Until 1992 he held on to the party leadership.

leech any of a group of ▷annelid worms. Leeches live in fresh water, and in tropical countries infest damp forests. As bloodsucking animals they are injurious to people and animals, to whom they attach themselves by means of a strong mouth adapted to sucking. (Class Hirudinea.)

Formerly, the **medicinal leech** (*Hirudo medicinalis*) was used extensively for 'bleeding' for a variety of ills. It is still cultivated as the source of the anticoagulant hirudin.

Leech, John (1817–1864) English caricaturist. He illustrated many books, including Dickens's novel *A Christmas Carol*, and during 1841–64 contributed about 3,000 humorous drawings and political cartoons to *Punch* magazine. His work provides a valuable record of Victorian social life.

Lebanon

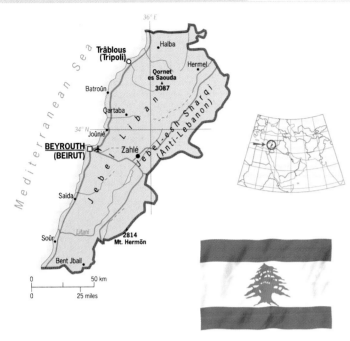

Lebanon country in western Asia, bounded north and east by Syria, south by Israel, and west by the Mediterranean Sea.

NATIONAL NAME *Jumhouria al-Lubnaniya/Republic of Lebanon*
AREA 10,452 sq km/4,035 sq mi
CAPITAL Beirut (and chief port)
MAJOR TOWNS/CITIES Tripoli, Zahlé, Baabda, Baalbek, Jezzine
MAJOR PORTS Tripoli, Tyre, Sidon, Jounie
PHYSICAL FEATURES narrow coastal plain; fertile Bekka valley running north–south between Lebanon and Anti-Lebanon mountain ranges

Government

HEAD OF STATE Emile Lahoud from 1998
HEAD OF GOVERNMENT Rafik Hariri from 2000
POLITICAL SYSTEM emergent democracy
POLITICAL EXECUTIVE dual executive
ADMINISTRATIVE DIVISIONS five governorates
ARMED FORCES 71,800; plus 18,000 Syrian troops (2002 est)
CONSCRIPTION compulsory for 12 months
DEATH PENALTY retained and used for ordinary crimes
DEFENCE SPEND (% GDP) 3.2 (2002 est)
EDUCATION SPEND (% GDP) 3 (2001 est)
HEALTH SPEND (% GDP) 11.8 (2000 est)

Economy and resources

CURRENCY Lebanese pound
GPD (US$) 17.3 billion (2002 est)
REAL GDP GROWTH (% change on previous year) 0.8 (2001)
GNI (US$) 17.7 billion (2002 est)
GNI PER CAPITA (PPP) (US$) 4,470 (2002 est)
CONSUMER PRICE INFLATION 2% (2003 est)
UNEMPLOYMENT 18% (1997 est)
FOREIGN DEBT (US$) 10.8 billion (2001 est)
MAJOR TRADING PARTNERS Italy, Saudi Arabia, United Arab Emirates, Syria, Germany, USA, France, Kuwait, Switzerland, China
RESOURCES there are no commercially viable mineral deposits; small reserves of lignite and iron ore

INDUSTRIES food processing and mineral water, petroleum refining, textiles, furniture and woodworking, paper and paper products, cement, paints
EXPORTS paper products, textiles, fruit and vegetables, jewellery. Principal market: Saudi Arabia 9.6% (2001)
IMPORTS electrical equipment, vehicles, petroleum, metals, machinery, consumer goods. Principal source: Italy 10.9% (2001)
ARABLE LAND 18.6% (2000 est)
AGRICULTURAL PRODUCTS citrus fruits, potatoes, melons, apples, grapes (viticulture is significant), wheat, sugar beet, olives, bananas; livestock rearing (goats and sheep); although illegal, hashish is an important export crop

Population and society

POPULATION 3,653,000 (2003 est)
POPULATION GROWTH RATE 1.2% (2000–15)
POPULATION DENSITY (per sq km) 351 (2003 est)
URBAN POPULATION (% of total) 91 (2003 est)
AGE DISTRIBUTION (% of total population) 0–14 30%, 15–59 61%, 60+ 9% (2002 est)
ETHNIC GROUPS about 95% Arab, with Armenian, Assyrian, Jewish, Turkish, and Greek minorities

LANGUAGE Arabic (official), French, Armenian, English
RELIGION Muslim 70% (Shiite 35%, Sunni 23%, Druze 7%, other 5%); Christian 30% (mainly Maronite 19%), Druze 3%; other Christian denominations including Greek Orthodox, Armenian, and Roman Catholic
EDUCATION not compulsory
LITERACY RATE 93% (men); 82% (women) (2003 est)
LABOUR FORCE 3.7% agriculture, 30.3% industry, 66% services (1997 est)
LIFE EXPECTANCY 72 (men); 75 (women) (2000–05)
CHILD MORTALITY RATE (under 5, per 1,000 live births) 32 (2001)
PHYSICIANS (per 1,000 people) 2.1 (1998 est)
HOSPITAL BEDS (per 1,000 people) 2.7 (1998 est)
TV SETS (per 1,000 people) 336 (2001 est)
RADIOS (per 1,000 people) 182 (2001 est)
INTERNET USERS (per 10,000 people) 1,171.3 (2002 est)
PERSONAL COMPUTER USERS (per 100 people) 8.1 (2002 est)

See also ▷Druze; ▷Hezbollah; ▷Palestine Liberation Organization; ▷Shiite.

Chronology

5th century BC–1st century AD: Part of the eastern Mediterranean Phoenician Empire.

1st century: Came under Roman rule; Christianity introduced.

635: Islam introduced by Arab tribes, who settled in southern Lebanon.

11th century: Druze faith developed by local Muslims.

1516: Became part of the Turkish Ottoman Empire.

1860: Massacre of thousands of Christian Maronites by the Muslim Druze led to French intervention.

1920–41: Administered by French under League of Nations mandate.

1943: Independence achieved as a republic, with a constitution that enshrined Christian and Muslim power-sharing.

1945: Joined the Arab League.

1948–49: Lebanon joined the first Arab war against Israel; Palestinian refugees settled in the south.

1958: Revolt by radical Muslims opposed to pro-Western policies of the Christian president, Camille Chamoun.

1964: Palestine Liberation Organization (PLO) founded in Beirut.

1967: More Palestinian refugees settled in Lebanon following the Arab–Israeli war.

1971: PLO expelled from Jordan; established headquarters in Lebanon.

1975: Outbreak of civil war between conservative Christians and leftist Muslims backed by PLO.

1976: Ceasefire agreed; Syrian-dominated Arab deterrent force formed to keep the peace, but considered by Christians as an occupying force.

1978: Israel launched a limited invasion of southern Lebanon in search of PLO guerrillas. An international United Nations peacekeeping force was unable to prevent further fighting.

1979: Part of southern Lebanon declared an 'independent free Lebanon' by a right-wing army officer.

1982: Israel again invaded Lebanon. Palestinians withdrew from Beirut under the supervision of an international peacekeeping force; the PLO moved its headquarters to Tunis.

1983: An agreement was reached for withdrawal of Syrian and Israeli troops but abrogated under Syrian pressure; intense fighting was seen between Christian Phalangists and Muslim Druze militias.

1984: Most of the international peacekeeping force were withdrawn. Radical Muslim militia took control of west Beirut.

1985: Lebanon was in chaos; many foreigners were taken hostage and Israeli troops withdrawn.

1987: Syrian troops were sent into Beirut.

1988: Gen Michel Aoun was appointed to head the caretaker military government; Premier Selim el-Hoss set up a rival government; the threat of partition hung over country.

1989: Gen Aoun declared a 'war of liberation' against Syrian occupation; Arab League-sponsored talks resulted in a ceasefire and a revised constitution recognizing Muslim majority; René Mouhawad was assassinated after 17 days as president; Maronite Christian Elias Hrawi was named as his successor; Aoun occupied the presidential palace, rejecting the constitution.

1990: The release of Western hostages began. Gen Aoun, crushed by Syrians, surrendered and legitimate government was restored.

1991: The government extended its control to the whole country. A treaty of cooperation with Syria was signed.

1992: The remaining Western hostages were released. A pro-Syrian administration was re-elected after many Christians boycotted general election.

1993: Israel launched attacks against Shia fundamentalist Hezbollah strongholds in southern Lebanon before the USA and Syria brokered an agreement to avoid the use of force.

1996: Israel launched a rocket attack on southern Lebanon in response to Hezbollah activity. USA, Israel, Syria, and Lebanon attempted to broker a new ceasefire.

1998: Army chief General Emile Lahoud was elected president.

2000: Israeli withdrawal from southern Lebanon. Lebanese troops assumed control in the region from Hezbollah guerillas. Rafik Hariri, a businessman and former prime minister of Lebanon, won a landslide victory in September to become prime minister for a second time.

LEBANON St Paul's Church in Beirut, Lebanon. *Image Bank*

SPIKE LEE US film director Spike Lee. Known primarily for his films, including *She's Gotta Have It* (1986) and *Malcolm X* (1992), Spike Lee has also produced music videos (for artists including Michael Jackson, Prince, and Stevie Wonder) and has written a number of books, including *By Any Means Necessary: The Trials and Tribulations of Making Malcolm X* (1996), *Mo' Better Blues* (1991) and *Spike Lee's Gotta Have It: Inside Guerrilla Film Making* (1988). See entry on p. 544. *Archive Photos*

Leeds industrial city and metropolitan borough in West Yorkshire, England, 40 km/25 mi southwest of York, on the River Aire; population (1991) 424,200 (city), 680,700 (district). Industries include engineering, printing, chemicals, glass, woollens, clothing, plastics, paper, metal goods, and leather goods. Notable buildings include the Town Hall (1858) designed by Cuthbert Brodrick, the University of Leeds (1904), the Leeds City Art Gallery (1888), Temple Newsam House (early 16th century, altered in about 1630), and the Cistercian Abbey of Kirkstall (1147). It is a centre of communications where road, rail, and canals (to Liverpool and Goole) meet.

Opera North is based here. The Leeds Music Festival and the Leeds International Pianoforte Competition are held here every three years. The City of Leeds Open Brass Band Championships take place each May. The Royal Armouries Museum opened in 1996, housing a national collection of arms and armour formerly in the White Tower at the Tower of London. There is a famous cricket ground at Headingley.

> **Related Web site: City of Leeds** http://www.leeds.gov.uk/

Scrooge's third Visitor.

JOHN LEECH An illustration from *A Christmas Carol*, by English novelist Charles Dickens, in a hand-coloured engraving by English engraver John Leech. *The Art Archive*

leek onionlike plant belonging to the lily family. The cultivated leek is a variety of the wild species *A. ampeloprasum* of the Mediterranean area and Atlantic islands. The lower leaf parts and white bulb are eaten as a vegetable. (Genus *Allium*, family Liliaceae.)

Lee Teng-hui (1923–) Taiwanese right-wing politician, vice-president 1984–88, president and Kuomintang (see ▷Guomindang) party leader from 1988. The country's first island-born leader, he was viewed as a reforming technocrat. He was directly elected president in March 1996, defying Chinese opposition to the democratic contest.

Leeuwenhoek, Anton van (1632–1723) Dutch pioneer of microscopic research. He ground his own lenses, some of which magnified up to 300 times. With these he was able to see individual red blood cells, sperm, and bacteria, achievements not repeated for more than a century.
> **Related Web site: Leeuwenhoek, Antony van** http://www.ucmp.berkeley.edu/history/leeuwenhoek.html

Leeward Islands (1) group of islands, part of the ▷Society Islands, in ▷French Polynesia, South Pacific; (2) general term for the northern half of the Lesser ▷Antilles in the West Indies; (3) former British colony in the West Indies (1871–1956) comprising Antigua, Montserrat, St Kitts and Nevis, Anguilla, and the Virgin Islands.

left-handedness using the left hand more skilfully and in preference to the right hand for most actions. It occurs in about 9% of the population, predominantly males. It is caused by dominance of the right side of the brain.

left wing in politics, the socialist parties. The term originated in the French national assembly of 1789, where the nobles sat in the place of honour to the right of the president, and the commons sat to the left. This arrangement has become customary in European parliaments, where the progressives sit on the left and the conservatives on the right. It is also usual to speak of the right, left, and centre, when referring to the different elements composing a single party.

legacy in law, a gift of personal property made by a testator in a will and transferred on the testator's death to the legatee. **Specific legacies** are definite named objects; a **general legacy** is a sum of money or item not specially identified; a **residuary legacy** is all the remainder of the deceased's personal estate after debts have been paid and the other legacies have been distributed.

legal aid public assistance with legal costs. In Britain it is given only to those below certain thresholds of income and unable to meet the costs. There are separate provisions for civil and criminal cases. Since 1989 legal aid is administered by the Legal Aid Board.

legal tender currency that must be accepted in payment of debt. Cheques and postal orders are not included. In most countries, limits are set on the amount of coinage, particularly of small denominations, that must legally be accepted.

legend (Latin *legere* 'to read', *legenda* 'to be read') traditional or undocumented story about famous people, commonly religious in character and frequently posing problems of authenticity. Legends are typically narrative, in the form of verse or prose novella, although more complex forms such as drama or ballad are possible. It is typical for legends to avoid a strict documentary account in favour of a more poetic and religious interpretation of reality. The term was originally applied to the books of readings designed for use in Christian religious service, and was extended to the stories of saints' lives read in monasteries.

Léger, Fernand (1881–1955) French painter and designer. He was associated with ▷cubism. From around 1909 he evolved a characteristic style of simplified forms, clear block outlines, and bold colours. Mechanical forms are constant themes in his work, which includes designs for the Swedish Ballet 1921–22, murals, and the abstract film *Ballet mécanique/Mechanical Ballet* (1924).

legionnaires' disease pneumonia-like disease, so called because it was first identified when it broke out at a convention of the American Legion in Philadelphia in 1976. Legionnaires' disease is caused by the bacterium *Legionella pneumophila*, which breeds in warm water (for example, in the cooling towers of air-conditioning systems). It is spread in minute water droplets, which may be inhaled. The disease can be treated successfully with antibiotics, though mortality can be high in elderly patients.

legislature lawmaking body or bodies in a political system. Some legislatures are unicameral (having one chamber), and some bicameral (with two).

legitimacy the justification of a ruling group's right to exercise power. Principles of legitimacy have included divine right, popular

approval, and, in the case of communist parties, an insight into the true meaning of history.

Legnano, Battle of defeat of Holy Roman Emperor Frederick Barbarossa by members of the Lombard League in 1176 at Legnano, northwest of Milan. It was a major setback to the emperor's plans for imperial domination over Italy and showed for the first time the power of infantry against feudal cavalry.

Le Guin, Ursula K(roeber) (1929–) US writer of science fiction and fantasy. Her novels include *The Left Hand of Darkness* (1969), which questions sex roles; the *Earthsea* series (1968–91); *The Dispossessed* (1974), which compares an anarchist and a capitalist society; and *Always Coming Home* (1985).

legume plant of the family Leguminosae, which has a pod containing dry seeds. The family includes peas, beans, lentils, clover, and alfalfa (lucerne). Legumes are important in agriculture because of their specialized roots, which have nodules containing bacteria capable of fixing nitrogen from the air and increasing the fertility of the soil. The edible seeds of legumes are called **pulses**.

LEGUME Leguminous fruits on the eastern redbud *Cercis canadensis* growing in the Smokey Mountains of Tennessee, USA. *Premaphotos Wildlife*

Lehár, Franz (1870–1948) Hungarian composer. He wrote many operettas, among them *The Merry Widow* (1905), *The Count of Luxembourg* (1909), *Gypsy Love* (1910), and *The Land of Smiles* (1929). He also composed songs, marches, and a violin concerto.

Le Havre industrial port in the *département* of Seine-Maritime in Normandy, northwest France, on the north side of the estuary of the River Seine, 90 km/56 mi from Rouen; population (1999 est) 190,600, conurbation 250,000. It serves 500 harbours worldwide. It is the second-largest port in France, and has cross-channel passenger links. The major industries include engineering, chemicals, car manufacturing, and oil refining.

Lehmann, Rosamond Nina (1901–1990) English novelist. Her books include *Dusty Answer* (1927), *The Weather in the Streets* (1936), *The Echoing Grove* (1953), and, following a long silence, *A Sea-Grape Tree* (1976), a sequel to *The Ballad and the Source* (1944). Once neglected as too romantic, her novels regained popularity in the 1980s because of their sensitive portrayal of female emotions. She was the sister of the poet and essayist John Lehmann.

Leibniz, Gottfried Wilhelm (1646–1716) German mathematician, philosopher, and diplomat. Independently of, but concurrently with, English scientist Isaac ▷Newton, he developed the branch of mathematics known as ▷calculus and was one of the founders of symbolic logic. Free from all concepts of space and number, his logic was the prototype of future abstract mathematics. *Calculus and controversy* It was in London in 1673 that Leibniz became acquainted with the work of Newton and Isaac Barrow and began to work on problems that led him to his independent discovery of differential and integral calculus. Leibniz is due the credit for first using the **infinitesimals** (very small quantities that were precursors of the modern idea of limits) as differences. He devised a notation for integration and differentiation that was so much more convenient than Newton's **fluxions** that it remains in standard use today.

In 1699 the Swiss mathematician and Fellow of the Royal Society, Fatio de Duillier, accused Leibniz of stealing the idea from Newton, a charge which the Royal Society formally upheld in 1711. Leibniz himself never sought to conceal that it was after his 1673 visit to London, by which time Newton had worked out his calculus of fluxions, that he began his investigations into tangents and quadratures, the research that eventually led to his discovery of calculus. Newton's discovery, probably made in 1665, was not published for many years and there is no doubt that Leibniz arrived at his calculus independently. As he put it, he, Newton and Barrow were 'contemporaries in these discoveries'. Leibniz always communicated his findings to fellow mathematicians; most mathematicians of the time were working on the same problems and they all knew the work that had been done on infinitesimal quantities.

Monads In his metaphysical works, such as *The Monadology* (1714), he argued that everything consisted of innumerable units, **monads**, the individual properties of which determined each thing's past, present, and future. Monads, although independent of each other, interacted predictably; this meant that Christian faith and scientific reason need not be in conflict and that 'this is the best of all possible worlds'. Leibniz's optimism is satirized in French philosopher Voltaire's novel *Candide*.

Related Web site: Leibniz, Gottfried Wilhelm http://mally.stanford.edu/leibniz.html

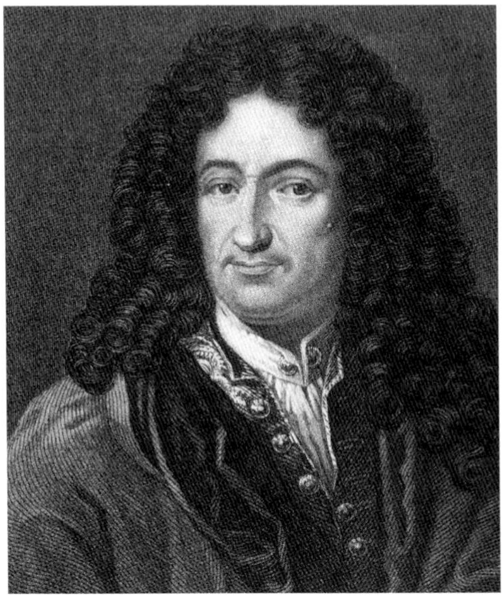

GOTTFRIED LEIBNIZ A portrait of the German mathematician and philosopher Gottfried Leibniz. Leibniz discovered calculus at the same time as Isaac Newton, and made other progress in the field of abstract mathematics. As well as this, he sought the reunion of Catholics and Protestants and wrote metaphysical studies, laying the foundation for 18th century philosophy. *Archive Photos*

Leibovitz, Annie (1950–) US photographer. Her elaborately staged portraits of US celebrities appeared first in *Rolling Stone* magazine and later in *Vanity Fair*. The odd poses in which her sitters allow themselves to be placed suggest an element of self-mockery.

Leicester City industrial city and unitary authority in central England, on the River Soar. It was part of the county of Leicestershire to 1997.

area 73 sq km/28 sq mi **features** 14th-century Guildhall, St Martin's Cathedral, and two universities (University of Leicester, established in 1957, and De Montfort University, formerly Leicester Polytechnic, established in 1992); Bradgate House, the home of Lady Jane Grey, located in Bradgate Park, 10 km/6 mi northwest of Leicester; there is an Eco House in the city, an environment-friendly show home, demonstrating ways in which people can reduce the ecological impact of their homes **industries** engineering, food processing, electronics, chemicals, and the manufacture of hosiery, footwear, knitwear, plastics, scientific and medical instruments, electrical products, and construction and woodworking machinery **population** (1996) 270,500 **famous people** Joe Orton, C P Snow

Leicester, Robert Dudley, Earl of Leicester (*c.* 1532–1588) English courtier. Son of the Duke of Northumberland, he was created Earl of Leicester in 1564. He led the disastrous military expedition (1585–87) sent to help the Netherlands against Spain. Despite this failure, he retained the favour of Queen ▷Elizabeth I, who gave him command of the army prepared to resist the threat of Spanish invasion in 1588.

His father was executed in 1553 for supporting Lady Jane Grey's claim to the throne, and Leicester was himself briefly imprisoned in the Tower of London. His good looks attracted Queen Elizabeth, who made him Master of the Horse in 1558 and a privy councillor in 1559. He was a supporter of the Protestant cause.

Elizabeth might have married him if he had not been already married to Amy Robsart. When his wife died in 1560 after a fall downstairs, Leicester was suspected of murdering her. In 1578 he secretly married the widow of the Earl of Essex.

Leicestershire county of central England (since April 1997 Leicester City and Rutland have been separate unitary authorities).

area 2,084 sq km/804 sq mi **towns and cities** Loughborough, Melton Mowbray, Market Harborough (administrative headquarters at Glenfield, Leicester) **physical** rivers Soar and Wreake; Charnwood Forest (in the northwest); Vale of Belvoir (under which are large coal deposits) **features** Belvoir Castle, seat of the dukes of Rutland since the time of Henry VIII, rebuilt by James Wyatt in 1816; Donington Park motor-racing circuit, Castle Donington; Leicestershire has traditionally had several fox-hunts, including the Quorn hunt **agriculture** good pasture with horses, cattle, and sheep (especially the New Leicester breed, first bred by Robert Bakewell in the 18th century at Dishley); dairy products (including Stilton cheese at Melton Mowbray); cereals **industries** engineering (Loughborough); hosiery (at Earl Shilton, Hinckley, and Loughborough); footwear; bell founding; coal (Asfordby); quarrying of limestone (Barrow-on-Soar, Breedon-on-the-Hill), ironstone (in the northwest), and granite (Enderby, Stoney, and Mountsorrel, known for its paving stones) **population** (2001 est) 610,300 **famous people** Thomas Babington Macaulay, Titus Oates, C P Snow

Related Web site: Leicestershire at the Heart of the Shires http://www.leics.gov.uk/

Leics abbreviation for ▷Leicestershire, an English county.

Leiden (or **Leyden**) city in South Holland province, the Netherlands, on the Oude Rijn River, 10 km/6 mi from the North Sea, and 27 km/17 mi north of Rotterdam; population (1997) 117,000. Industries include textiles and cigars. It has been a printing centre since 1580, with a university established in 1575. It is linked by canal to Haarlem, Amsterdam, and Rotterdam. The painters Rembrandt and Jan Steen were born here.

Leif Ericsson (lived *c.* 970) Norse explorer, son of Eric the Red, who sailed west from Greenland to find a country first sighted by Norsemen 986. He visited Baffin Island then sailed along the Labrador coast to Newfoundland, which was named 'Vinland' (Wine Land), because he discovered grape vines growing there.

The story was confirmed in 1961 when a Norwegian expedition, led by Helge Ingstad, discovered the remains of a Viking settlement (dated *c.* 1000) near the fishing village of L'Anse-aux-Meadows at the northern tip of Newfoundland.

Leigh, Mike (1943–) English dramatist and film-maker. He directs his own plays, which evolve through improvisation before they are scripted. His films, sharp social satires, include *Life Is Sweet* (1991) and *Secrets and Lies* (1995).

Leigh, Vivien (1913–1967) Stage name of Vivien Mary Hartley. Indian-born English actor. She won Academy Awards for her performances as Scarlett O'Hara in *Gone With the Wind* (1939) and as Blanche du Bois in *A Streetcar Named Desire* (1951). She was married to Laurence ▷Olivier 1940–60, and starred with him in the play *Antony and Cleopatra* (1951).

Leigh-Mallory, Trafford Leigh (1892–1944) British air chief marshal in World War II. He took part in the Battle of Britain and was commander-in-chief of Allied air forces during the invasion of France.

Leinster southeastern historic province of the Republic of Ireland, comprising the counties of Carlow, Dublin, Kildare, Kilkenny, Laois, Longford, Louth, Meath, Offaly, Westmeath, Wexford, and Wicklow; area 19,630 sq km/7,580 sq mi; population (1996) 1,924,700.

Leipzig major commercial and industrial city in west Saxony, Germany, on the Weisse Elster (a tributary of the River Elbe), 145 km/90 mi southwest of Berlin; population (1995) 478,200. Industries include printing, publishing, and the production of furs, leather goods, paper, and musical instruments. It hosts numerous trade shows, including important industrial and book fairs. The city is also a centre for the arts, culture, and education, and has a university founded in 1409.

leishmaniasis any of several parasitic diseases caused by microscopic protozoans of the genus *Leishmania*, identified by William Leishman (1865–1926), and transmitted by sandflies. It occurs in two main forms: **visceral** (also called kala-azar), in which various internal organs are affected, and **cutaneous**, where the disease is apparent mainly in the skin. Leishmaniasis occurs in the Mediterranean region, Africa, Asia, and Central and South America.

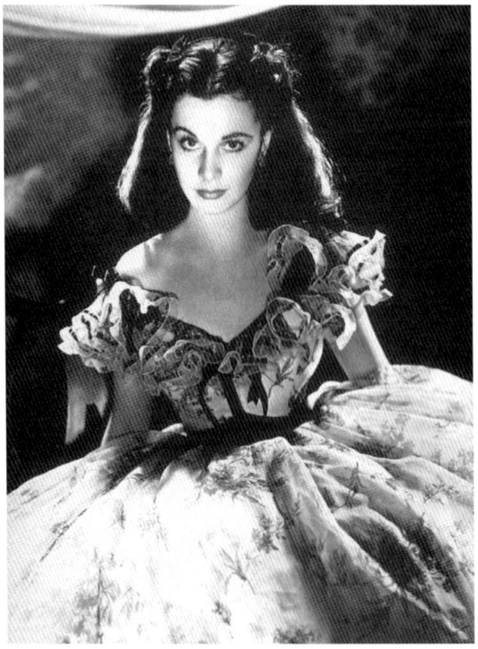

VIVIEN LEIGH Indian-born British actor Vivien Leigh as she appeared in the classic film *Gone With the Wind* (1939) in the role of Scarlett O'Hara. This promotional studio picture makes Vivien Leigh look much younger than her actual 26 years. Her lead man, Clark Gable (who played Rhett Butler), was 38 years old at the time. *Image Bank*

There are 12 million cases of leishmaniasis annually. The disease kills 8,000 people a year in South America and results in hundreds of thousands more suffering permanent disfigurement and disability through skin lesions, joint pain, and swelling of the liver and spleen.

leitmotif (German **Leitmotiv**; German 'leading motive') in music, a recurring theme or motive used to illustrate a character or idea. The term is strongly associated with Richard ▷Wagner, who frequently employed this technique with great sophistication in his music dramas; it is also strongly prevalent in music for film.

Leitrim county of the Republic of Ireland, in the province of Connacht, bounded on the northwest by Donegal Bay; county town Carrick-on-Shannon; area 1,530 sq km/591 sq mi; population (1996) 25,100. Carrick-on-Shannon, Mohill, and Manorhamilton are the most important towns. The rivers Shannon, Bonet, Drowes, and Duff run through Leitrim. There is some coal, and iron and lead in the mountainous areas, but the county is generally not very productive – even the soil is heavy – and is the poorest county in the Republic of Ireland. Potatoes and oats are grown, and some cattle and sheep are reared. Industries include linen, woollens, and potteries. Parke's Castle is one of the most popular tourist attractions in the county.

lek in biology, a closely spaced set of very small ▷territories each occupied by a single male during the mating season. Leks are found in the mating systems of several ground-dwelling birds (such as grouse) and a few antelopes, and in some insects.

Lely, Peter (1618–1680) Adopted name of Pieter van der Faes. Dutch painter. He was active in England from 1641, painting fashionable portraits in the style of van Dyck. His subjects included Charles I, Cromwell, and Charles II. He painted a series of admirals, *Flagmen* (National Maritime Museum, London), and one of *The Windsor Beauties* (Hampton Court, Richmond), fashionable women of Charles II's court.

Lemaître, Georges Edouard (1894–1966) Belgian cosmologist. He proposed the ▷Big Bang theory of the origin of the universe in 1933. US astronomer Edwin ▷Hubble had shown that the universe was expanding, but it was Lemaître who suggested that the expansion had been started by an initial explosion, the Big Bang, a theory that is now generally accepted.

Le Mans industrial city and administrative centre of the Sarthe *département* in western France; population (1990) 148,500, conurbation 191,000. It has a motor-racing circuit where the annual endurance 24-hour race (established 1923) for sports cars and their prototypes is held at the Sarthe circuit. It is linked to Paris by a high-speed rail system.

Le Marche (English **the Marches**) region of east central Italy, comprising the provinces of Ancona, Ascoli Piceno, Macerata, and

Pesaro e Urbino; capital Ancona; area 9,700 sq km/3,750 sq mi; population (1992 est) 1,434,000. Agriculture produces wheat, maize, vines, potatoes, tomatoes, and root crops; and fishing is important.

lemming any of a group of small rodents distributed worldwide in northern latitudes. They are about 12 cm/5 in long, with thick brownish fur, a small head, and a short tail. Periodically, when their population exceeds the available food supply, lemmings undertake mass migrations. (Genus *Lemmus* and other related genera, family Cricetidae.)

Lemmon, Jack (1925–2001) Born John Uhler Lemmon III. US actor. He collaborated with Billy ▷Wilder on the comedies *Some Like It Hot* (1959) and *The Apartment* (1960), and teamed up with Walter ▷Matthau on the popular *The Odd Couple* (1968). His performance in *Save the Tiger* (1973) won him an Academy Award.

Lemnos (Greek Limnos) Greek island in the north of the Aegean Sea; area 476 sq km/184 sq mi; population (1991) 17,600. Towns include Kastron and Mudros. The island is of volcanic origin, rising to 430 m/1,411 ft. Industries include mulberries and other fruit, tobacco, and sheep.

lemon sharp-tasting yellow citrus fruit of the small, evergreen, semitropical lemon

LEMON The lemon tree and its fruit.

tree. It may have originated in northwestern India, and was introduced into Europe by the Spanish Moors in the 12th or 13th century. It is now grown in Italy, Spain, California, Florida, South Africa, and Australia, and is widely used for flavouring and as a garnish. (*Citrus limon*, family Rutaceae.)

lemon balm perennial herb belonging to the mint family, with lemon-scented leaves. It is widely used in teas, liqueurs, and medicines. (*Melissa officinalis*, family Labiatae.)

lemur any of various prosimian ▷primates of the Family Lemuridae, found in Madagascar and the Comoros Islands. There are about 16 species, ranging from mouse-sized to dog-sized animals; the pygmy mouse lemur (*Microcebus myoxinus*), weighing 30 g/1 oz, is the smallest primate. The diademed sifaka, weighing 7 kg/15 lb, is the largest species of lemur. Lemurs are arboreal, and some species are nocturnal. They have long, bushy tails, and feed on fruit, insects, and small animals. Many are threatened with extinction owing to loss of their forest habitat and, in some cases, from hunting.

In 2000 researchers identified three new species of mouse lemur in Madagascar.

Related Web site: Lemur http://www.seaworld.org/animal_bytes/lemurab.html

Lena one of the largest rivers of the Russian Federation, in eastern Siberia; length 4,400 km/2,734 mi; total drainage area 490,000 sq km/189,189 sq mi. The Lena rises in the Baikal Mountains, west of Lake Baikal, and flows northeast to Yakutsk, then north into the Laptev Sea (an inlet of the Arctic Ocean), where it forms a large delta 400 km/240 mi wide and covering some 30,000 sq km/11,583 sq mi. The river is navigable almost throughout its course, but is frozen for eight months of the year. Its main tributaries are the Vitim, Olekma, Aldan, and the Vilyui. The main ports on the Lena's course are Osetrovo (since 1954 part of Ust-Kut) and Yakutsk.

lend-lease in US history, an act of Congress passed in March 1941 that gave the president power to order 'any defense article for the government of any country whose defense the president deemed vital to the defense of the USA'. During World War II, the USA negotiated many lend-lease agreements, notably with Britain and the USSR.

Lendl, Ivan (1960–) Czech-born US lawn-tennis player. He won eight Grand Slam singles titles, including the US and French titles three times each, taking more than $15 million in prize money. He retired from the game in December 1994, citing a degenerative spinal condition.

L'Enfant, Pierre Charles (1754–1825) French-born US architect and engineer. He is remembered for his survey and plan for the city of Washington 1791–92. Although he was dismissed from the project before he was able to design any major buildings, the constructed layout is much as he conceived it, clearly reflecting the plan of his native Versailles.

Lenin, Vladimir Ilyich (1870–1924) Adopted name of Vladimir Ilyich Ulyanov. Russian revolutionary, first leader of the USSR, and communist theoretician. Active in the 1905 Revolution, Lenin had to leave Russia when it failed, settling in Switzerland in 1914. He returned to Russia after the February revolution of 1917 (see ▷Russian Revolution). He led the Bolshevik revolution of November 1917 and became leader of a Soviet government, concluded peace with Germany, and organized a successful resistance to ▷White Russian (pro-tsarist) uprisings and foreign intervention during the ▷Russian civil war 1918–21. His modification of traditional Marxist doctrine to fit conditions prevailing in Russia became known as **Marxism-Leninism**, the basis of ▷communist ideology.

Lenin was born on 22 April 1870 in Simbirsk (now renamed Ulyanovsk), on the River Volga, and became a lawyer in St Petersburg. His brother was executed in 1887 for attempting to assassinate Tsar Alexander III. A Marxist from 1889, Lenin was sent to Siberia for spreading revolutionary propaganda 1895–1900. He then edited the political paper *Iskra* ('The Spark') from abroad, and visited London several times. In *What is to be Done?* (1902), he advocated that a professional core of Social Democratic Party activists should spearhead the revolution in Russia, a suggestion accepted by the majority (*bolsheviki*) at the London party congress 1903. From Switzerland he attacked socialist support for World War I as aiding an 'imperialist' struggle, and wrote *Imperialism* (1917).

After the renewed outbreak of revolution February–March 1917, he was smuggled back into Russia in April by the Germans so that he could take up his revolutionary activities and remove Russia from the war, allowing Germany to concentrate the war effort on the Western Front. On arriving in Russia, Lenin established himself at the head of the Bolsheviks, against the provisional government of Kerensky. A complicated power struggle ensued, but eventually Lenin triumphed on 8 November 1917; a Bolshevik government

> ### Vladimir Lenin
> *It is true that liberty is precious – so precious that it must be rationed.*
> Quoted in S and B Webb
> *Soviet Communism*

> ### John Lennon
> *Will the people in the cheaper seats clap your hands? All the rest of you, if you'll just rattle your jewellery.*
> Royal Variety Performance,
> 4 November 1963

VLADIMIR LENIN Russian revolutionary leader Vladimir Ilyich Lenin feared that the Russian peasants and workers would be unable to sustain a Marxist revolution in 1917. Lenin believed that the people needed the leadership of a small party of professional revolutionaries, who would then control the new, classless society. *Archive Photos*

was formed, and peace negotiations with Germany were begun, leading to the signing of the ▷Treaty of Brest Litovsk on 3 March 1918.

From the overthrow of the provisional government in November 1917 until his death, Lenin effectively controlled the USSR, although an assassination attempt in 1918 injured his health. He founded the Third (Communist) ▷International in 1919. With communism proving inadequate to put the country on its feet, he introduced the private-enterprise ▷New Economic Policy in 1921.

Related Web site: Vladimir Ilyich Lenin Internet Archive http://csf.colorado.edu/psn/marx/Other/Lenin/

Leningrad former name (1924–91) of the Russian city ▷St Petersburg.

Leninism modification of ▷Marxism by ▷Lenin which argues that in a revolutionary situation the industrial proletariat is unable to develop a truly revolutionary consciousness without strong leadership.

Lennon, John Winston (1940–1980) UK rock singer, songwriter, and guitarist; a founder member of the ▷Beatles. He lived in the USA from 1971. Both before the band's break-up in 1970 and in his solo career, he collaborated intermittently with his wife **Yoko Ono** (1933–). 'Give Peace a Chance', a hit in 1969, became an anthem of the peace movement. His solo work alternated between the confessional and the political, as on the album *Imagine* (1971). He was shot dead by a fan.

An anthology of Lennon's solo work and an album of previously unrecorded material, *Wonsaponatime*, were both released in 1998.

Related Web site: Bagism: site for Lennon fans http://www.bagism.com/

lens in optics, a piece of a transparent material, such as glass, with two polished surfaces – one concave or convex, and the other plane, concave, or convex – that modifies rays of light. A convex lens brings rays of light together; a concave lens makes the rays diverge. Lenses are essential to spectacles, microscopes, telescopes, cameras, and almost all optical instruments.

The image formed by a single lens suffers from several defects or ▷aberrations, notably **spherical aberration** in which an image becomes blurred, and **chromatic aberration** in which an image in white light tends to have coloured edges. Aberrations are corrected by the use of compound lenses, which are built up from two or more lenses of different refractive index.

LEMUR The rufous mouse lemur *Microcebus rufus* is a small nocturnal primate from rainforests on the island of Madagascar. The long muzzle terminating in a moist naked snout and large external ears are typical of a prosimian. *Premaphotos Wildlife*

LENT A traditional 'pancake race' in London, 1962. These races are held on the day before Lent in the Christian calendar, Shrove Tuesday. *Archive Photos*

lens, gravitational see ▷gravitational lensing.

Lent in the Christian church, the 40-day period of fasting that precedes Easter, beginning on Ash Wednesday, but omitting Sundays.

Related Web site: Lent http://www.newadvent.org/cathen/09152a.htm

lentil annual Old World plant belonging to the pea family. The plant, which resembles vetch, grows 15–45 cm/6–18 in high and has white, blue, or purplish flowers. The seeds, contained in pods about 1.6 cm/0.6 in long, are widely used as food. (*Lens culinaris*, family Leguminosae.)

Lenya, Lotte (1898–1981) Adopted name of Karoline Wilhelmine Blamauer. Austrian actor and singer. She was married five times, twice to the composer Kurt Weill, first in 1926, with whom she emigrated to the USA in 1935. She appeared in several of the Brecht–Weill operas, notably *Die Dreigroschenoper/The Threepenny Opera* (1928). Her plain looks and untrained singing voice brought added realism to her stage roles.

Lenz's law in physics, a law stating that the direction of an electromagnetically induced current (generated by moving a magnet near a wire or a wire in a magnetic field) will be such as to oppose the motion producing it. It is named after the German physicist Heinrich Friedrich Lenz (1804–1865), who announced it in 1833.

Leo zodiacal constellation in the northern hemisphere, represented as a lion. The Sun passes through Leo from mid-August to mid-September. Its brightest star is first-magnitude Regulus at the base of a pattern of stars called the Sickle. In astrology, the dates for Leo are between about 23 July and 22 August (see ▷precession).

Leo thirteen popes, including:

Leo (I) the Great, (St Leo) (*c.* 390–461) Pope from 440. He helped to establish the Christian liturgy. Leo summoned the Chalcedon Council where his Dogmatical Letter was accepted as the voice of St Peter. Acting as ambassador for the emperor Valentinian III (425–455), Leo saved Rome from devastation by the Huns by buying off their king, Attila.

Leo III (*c.* 750–816) Pope from 795. After the withdrawal of the Byzantine emperors, the popes had become the real rulers of Rome. Leo III was forced to flee because of a conspiracy in Rome and took refuge at the court of the Frankish king Charlemagne. He returned to Rome in 799 and crowned Charlemagne emperor on Christmas Day 800, establishing the secular sovereignty of the pope over Rome under the suzerainty of the emperor (who became the Holy Roman Emperor).

Leo X, Giovanni de' Medici (1475–1521) Pope from 1513. The son of Lorenzo the Magnificent of Florence, he was created a cardinal at 13. He bestowed on Henry VIII of England the title of Defender of the Faith. A patron of the arts, he sponsored the rebuilding of St Peter's Church, Rome. He raised funds for this by selling indulgences (remissions of punishment for sin), a sale that led the religious reformer Martin Luther to rebel against papal authority. Leo X condemned Luther in the bull *Exsurge domine* (1520) and excommunicated him in 1521.

Leo (III) the Isaurian (*c.* 680–741) Byzantine emperor and soldier. He seized the throne in 717, successfully defended Constantinople against the Saracens 717–18, and attempted to suppress the use of images in church worship (see ▷iconoclast).

León capital of León province in Castilla–León, northwest Spain, situated on a plateau 821 m/2,694 ft high at the confluence of the Torio and Bernesga rivers; population (2001) 137,400. Linen, chemicals, pottery, and leather are manufactured. León was built on the site of a Roman camp. In the 10th century, after its recapture from the Moors, it became the capital of the kingdom of León until 1230, when it was merged with Castile. It has an 11th-century church, a Gothic cathedral, and parts of the old walls remain.

Leonard, Elmore John, Jr (1925–) US novelist and screenwriter. A prolific writer, Leonard is the author of numerous Westerns and crime novels. His writing, given more to character and mood than plot, is marked by vivid dialogue. His crime novels, in particular, are reflections of the peculiarities and violence of contemporary US society.

Leonardo da Vinci (1452–1519) Italian painter, sculptor, architect, engineer, and scientist. One of the greatest figures of the Italian Renaissance, he was active in Florence, Milan, and, from 1516, France. As state engineer and court painter to the Duke of Milan, he painted the *Last Supper* mural (*c.* 1495; Sta Maria delle Grazie, Milan), and on his return to Florence painted the *Mona Lisa* (*c.* 1503–05; Louvre, Paris). His notebooks and drawings show an immensely inventive and enquiring mind, studying aspects of the natural and scientific world from anatomy and botany to aerodynamics and hydraulics.

Milan Leonardo left Florence for Milan in *c.* 1482, offering his services to Ludovico Sforza, the Duke of Milan, primarily as a military and naval engineer, as a sculptor next, and as a painter incidentally. As a military engineer he was responsible for the construction of assault machines, pontoons, a steam cannon, and a tortoise-shaped assault tank. For a castle in Milan he created a forced-air central heating system and also a water-pumping mechanism. Leonardo's inventions ranged from complex cranes to pulley systems, lathes, drilling machines, a paddlewheel boat, flying machines, and an underwater breathing apparatus.

Soon after his arrival, however, he painted Ludovico's mistress, Cecilia Gallerani (the *Lady with an Ermine*, Kraków, Czartoryski Collection), and, in partnership with Ambrogio da Predis in 1483, an altarpiece to which Leonardo contributed the central panel, *The Virgin of the Rocks*. (The existence of two versions, one in the Louvre, Paris, and one in the National Gallery, London, may be explained by the revision of the altarpiece in 1506 after a long period of haggling, when presumably a first version of the panel was sent to France and the other was finally accepted by the confraternity of the Immaculate Conception.)

Other undertakings were the bronze equestrian monument to Francesco Sforza, of which only the model was completed, and the world-famous fresco of the *Last Supper* in the refectory of Sta Maria delle Grazie. This painting, in which he used an experimental oil medium, suffered from the damp wall on which it was painted.

Venice, Rome, and Florence Having left Milan to return to Florence in 1499, the following year Leonardo travelled to Venice, where he may have met Italian painter ▷Giorgione, who was greatly impressed by his treatment of light and shade. Leonardo developed the use of both *chiaroscuro* (the contrast of light and shadow) and also *sfumato* (the subtle graduation of colours and tones), both techniques helping to extend the emotional depth and complexity of painting.

After mapping the country and planning canals and harbours for Caesar Borgia in Rome, in 1503 Leonardo was commissioned by the Signory of Florence to produce a battle scene on the walls of the Council Hall. Michelangelo was commissioned the same time for a similar work. After working on the *Battle of Anghiari* for two years, Leonardo left the work unfinished, and an experimental technique again destroyed what he had done. Over the same time, Leonardo also worked on the portrait of *Mona Lisa* (*La Gioconda*; Louvre), the wife of wealthy merchant Francesco Zanobi del Giocondo. The mysterious smiling picture depicted all the subtle elusiveness of expression that Leonardo loved.

Later years In 1506 Leonardo returned to Milan (now under French domination) as the city's engineer and architect, moved on to Rome in 1513 for three years, and then accepted Francis I's invitation to France. He spent his last years in the small castle of Cloux near the royal residence of Amboise on the Loire. His last painting was the *St John the Baptist* (*c.* 1514–15), now in the Louvre.

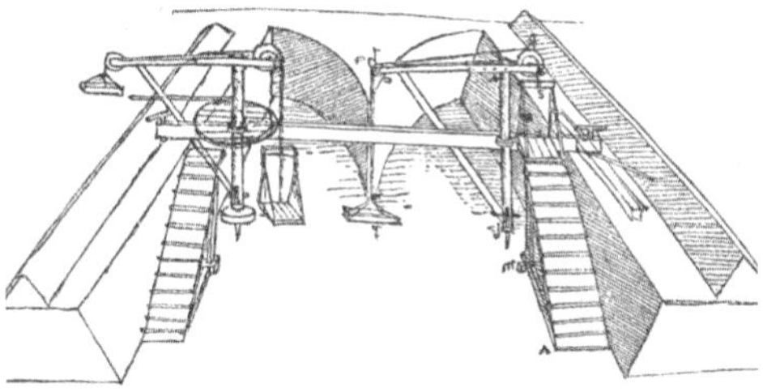

LEONARDO DA VINCI A sketch by Italian artist and scientist Leonardo da Vinci of a device for excavating a canal, which piles the earth it removes onto the bank. Da Vinci worked from 1482 to 1499 for the Duke of Milan as court artist and civil engineer. *Archive Photos*

Leoncavallo, Ruggero (1858–1919) Italian operatic composer. He played in restaurants, composing in his spare time, until the success of *I pagliacci/The Strolling Players* (1892). His other operas include *La Bohème/Bohemian Life* (1897) (contemporary with Puccini's version) and *Zaza* (1900).

Leone, Sergio (1921–1989) Italian film director and screenwriter. One of the pioneers of the 'spaghetti Western', he was largely responsible for making a star of the actor Clint ▷Eastwood, starting with *Per un pugno di dollari/A Fistful of Dollars* (1964).

Leonidas King of Sparta. He was killed in 480 BC while defending the pass of Thermopylae with 300 Spartans, 700 Thespians, and 400 Thebans against a huge Persian army.

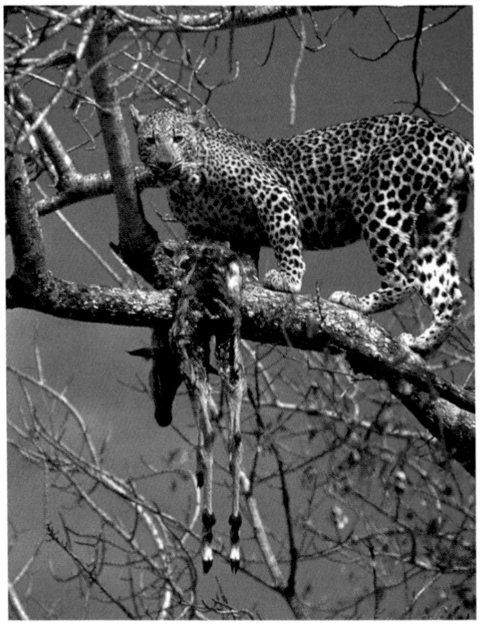

LEOPARD A leopard with an impala kill in South Africa. Leopards are good climbers and often drag their prey high into trees for safety. *Image Bank*

leopard (or panther) large wild cat found in Africa and Asia. The background colour of the coat is golden, and the black spots form rosettes that differ according to the variety; **black panthers** are simply a colour variation and retain the patterning as a 'watered-silk' effect. The leopard is 1.5–2.5 m/5–8 ft long, including the tail, which may measure 1 m/3 ft. (Species *Panthera pardus*, family Felidae.)

The **snow leopard** or **ounce** (*Panthera uncia*), which has irregular rosettes of much larger black spots on a light cream or grey background, is a native of mountains in central Asia. The **clouded leopard** (*Neofelis nebulosa*) is rather smaller, about 1.75 m/5.8 ft overall, with large blotchy markings rather than rosettes, and is found in Southeast Asia. There are seven subspecies, of which six are in danger of extinction, including the **Amur leopard** and the **South Arabian leopard**. One subspecies, the **Zanzibar leopard**, may already be extinct. The last **Judean desert leopard** died May 1995, although a small population survives in the Negev Desert.

Leopold III (1901–1983) King of the Belgians 1934–51. Against the prime minister's advice he surrendered to the German army in World War II in 1940. Post-war charges against his conduct led to a regency by his brother Charles and his eventual abdication in 1951 in favour of his son Baudouin.

Lepanto, Battle of sea battle on 7 October 1571 between the Ottoman Empire and 'Holy League' forces from Spain, Venice, Genoa, and the Papal States jointly commanded by the Spanish soldier Don John of Austria. The battle took place in the Mediterranean Gulf of Corinth off Lepanto (the Greek port of **Naupaktos**), then in Turkish possession. It was not decisive, but the combined western fleets halted Turkish expansion and broke Muslim sea power.

Le Pen, Jean-Marie (1928–) French extreme-rightwing politician. He was the founder of the National Front (FN) in 1972. His talents as a public speaker, his demagogic mixing of nationalism with law-and-order populism – calling for immigrant repatriation, stricter nationality laws, and the restoration of capital punishment – and his hostility to the European Union attracted a wide swathe of electoral support in the 1980s and 1990s.

leprosy (or Hansen's disease) chronic, progressive disease caused by the bacterium *Mycobacterium leprae*, closely related to that of tuberculosis. The infection attacks the skin and nerves. Once common in many countries, leprosy is still endemic in 28 countries and confined almost entirely to the tropics. It is controlled with drugs. In 1998 there were an estimated 1.5 million cases of leprosy, with 60% of these being in India. Worldwide there are 700,000 new cases of leprosy a year (2001).

There are two principal manifestations. **Lepromatous leprosy** is a contagious, progressive form distinguished by the appearance of raised blotches and lumps on the skin and thickening of the skin and nerves, with numbness, weakness, paralysis, and ultimately deformity of the affected parts. In **tuberculoid leprosy**, sensation is lost in some areas of the skin; sometimes there is loss of pigmentation and hair. The visible effects of long-standing leprosy (joint damage, paralysis, loss of fingers or toes) are due to nerve damage and injuries of which the sufferer may be unaware. Damage to the nerves remains, and the technique of using the patient's muscle material to encourage nerve regrowth is being explored.

In January 1998 the Indian government authorized the sale of the world's first leprosy vaccine.

lepton any of a class of ▷elementary particles that are not affected by the strong nuclear force. The leptons comprise the ▷electron, ▷muon, and ▷tau, and their ▷neutrinos (the electron neutrino, muon neutrino, and tau neutrino), as well as their six ▷antiparticles.

In July 2000, researchers at Fermilab, in the USA, amassed the first direct evidence for the existence of the tau lepton.

Lermontov, Mikhail Yurevich (1814–1841) Russian Romantic poet and novelist. In 1837 he was sent into active military service in the Caucasus for writing a revolutionary poem on the death of Pushkin, which criticized court values, and for participating in a duel. Among his works are the psychological novel *A Hero of Our Time* (1840) and a volume of poems *October* (1840).

Lerner, Alan Jay (1918–1986) US lyricist. He collaborated with Frederick Loewe on musicals including *Brigadoon* (1947), *Paint Your Wagon* (1951), *My Fair Lady* (1956), *Gigi* (1958), and *Camelot* (1960).

lesbianism homosexuality (sexual attraction to one's own sex) between women, so called from the Greek island of Lesbos (now Lesvos), the home of ▷Sappho the poet and her followers to whom the behaviour was attributed.

Lesbos alternative spelling of ▷Lesvos, an island in the Aegean Sea.

Lesotho see country box.

less developed country (LDC) any country late in developing an industrial base, and dependent on cash crops and unprocessed minerals. The terms 'less developed' and 'developing' imply that industrial development is desirable or inevitable; many people prefer to use ▷'Third World'.

Lesseps, Ferdinand Marie (1805–1894) Vicomte de Lesseps. French engineer. He designed and built the ▷Suez Canal 1859–69. He began work on the Panama Canal in 1881, but withdrew after failing to construct it without locks.

Lessing, Doris May (1919–) Born Doris May Tayler. English novelist and short-story writer, brought up in Rhodesia. Concerned with social and political themes, particularly the place of women in society, her work includes *The Grass is Singing* (1950), the five-novel series *Children of Violence* (1952–69), *The Golden Notebook* (1962), *The Good Terrorist* (1985), *The Fifth Child* (1988), *London Observed* (1992), and *Love Again* (1996), and *Ben, in the World* (2000). *Under My Skin* (1994) and *Walking in the Shade* (1997) are volumes of autobiography. She has also written an 'inner space fiction' series *Canopus in Argus: Archives* (1979–83), and under the pen-name 'Jane Somers', *The Diary of a Good Neighbour* (1981).

FERDINAND LESSEPS French engineer responsible for the Suez Canal. *Archive Photos*

Les Six (French 'The Six') group of French composers: Georges ▷Auric, Louis Durey, Arthur ▷Honegger, Darius Milhaud, Francis ▷Poulenc, and Germaine Tailleferre. Formed in 1917, the group had Jean ▷Cocteau as its spokesperson and adopted Erik ▷Satie as its guru; it was dedicated to producing works free from foreign influences and reflecting contemporary attitudes. The group split up in the early 1920s.

Lesvos Greek island in the Aegean Sea, near the coast of Turkey; area 2,154 sq km/ 831 sq mi; population (1991) 103,700. The capital is Mytilene. Industries include olives, wine, and grain. The island was called Lesbos in ancient times and was an Aeolian settlement, home of the poets Alcaeus and Sappho. It was conquered by the Turks from Genoa in 1462 and was annexed to Greece in 1913.

> **Related Web site: Lesvos – More Than Just Another Greek Island** http://www.lesvos.com/

Lethe (Greek 'oblivion') in Greek mythology, a river of the underworld whose waters when drunk, usually by the shades (dead), brought forgetfulness of the past.

letterpress method of printing from raised type, pioneered by Johann ▷Gutenberg in Europe in the 1450s.

lettuce annual plant whose large edible leaves are commonly used in salads. There are many varieties, including the cabbage lettuce, with round or loose heads, the Cos lettuce, with long, upright heads, and the Iceberg lettuce, with tight heads of crisp leaves. They are all believed to have been derived from the wild species *L. serriola*. (Genus *Lactuca*, especially *L. sativa*, family Compositae.)

leucocyte another name for a ▷white blood cell.

leucotomy (or **lobotomy**) a brain operation to sever the connections between the frontal lobe and underlying structures. It was widely used in the 1940s and 1950s to treat severe psychotic or depressive illness. Though it achieved some success, it left patients dull and apathetic; there was also a considerable risk of epilepsy. It was largely replaced by the use of psychotropic drugs from the late 1950s.

leukaemia any one of a group of cancers of the blood cells, with widespread involvement of the bone marrow and other blood-forming tissue. The central feature of leukaemia is runaway production of white blood cells that are immature or in some way abnormal. These rogue cells, which lack the defensive capacity of healthy white cells, overwhelm the normal ones, leaving the victim vulnerable to infection. Treatment is with radiotherapy and ▷cytotoxic drugs to suppress replication of abnormal cells, or by bone-marrow transplantation.

Abnormal functioning of the bone marrow also suppresses production of red blood cells and blood ▷platelets, resulting in ▷anaemia and a failure of the blood to clot.

Leukaemias are classified into acute or chronic, depending on their known rates of progression. They are also grouped according to the type of white cell involved.

Levant (Italian *il levante*, 'the East') former name for the eastern Mediterranean region or, more specifically, the Mediterranean coastal regions of Turkey, Syria, Lebanon, Israel, and Palestine.

levee naturally formed raised bank along the side of a river channel. When a river overflows its banks, the rate of flow is less than that in the channel, and silt is deposited on the banks. With each successive flood the levee increases in size so that eventually the river may be above the surface of the surrounding flood plain. Notable levees are found on the lower reaches of the Mississippi in the USA and the Po in Italy.

level (or **spirit level**) instrument for finding horizontal level, or adjusting a surface to an even level, used in surveying, building construction, and archaeology. It has a glass tube of coloured liquid, in which a bubble is trapped, mounted in an elongated frame. When the tube is horizontal, the bubble moves to the centre.

Levellers democratic party in the English ▷Civil War. The Levellers found wide support among ▷Cromwell's New Model Army and the yeoman farmers, artisans, and small traders, and proved a powerful political force from 1647 to 1649. Their

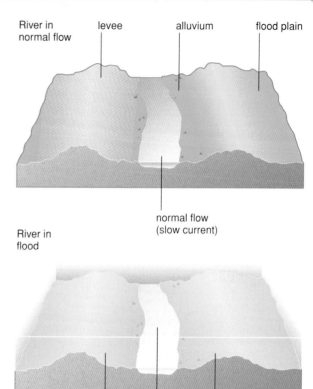

LEVEE Levees are formed on the banks of meandering rivers when the river floods over its flood plain. The flow of the flood water is slower over the levees than it is in the river bed and so silt is deposited there.

programme included the establishment of a republic, government by a parliament of one house elected by all men over 21, elections every year, freedom of speech, religious toleration, and sweeping social reforms, including education for everyone. They were led by John ▷Lilburne, whose wife Elizabeth campaigned for a 'proportional share in the freedom of this commonwealth' for women. Cromwell's refusal to implement this programme led to mutinies by Levellers in the army, which, when suppressed by Cromwell at Burford in 1649, ended the movement.

True Levellers (also known as ▷Diggers) were denounced by the Levellers because of their more radical methods.

Leven, Loch lake in Perth and Kinross, Scotland; area 16 sq km/ 6 sq mi. The River Leven flows from Loch Leven. It has six islands; Mary Queen of Scots was imprisoned on Castle Island until she escaped in 1568. The whole loch has been a National Nature Reserve since 1964. The loch is known for its trout fisheries.

lever simple machine consisting of a rigid rod pivoted at a fixed point called the fulcrum, used for shifting or raising a heavy load or applying force. Levers are classified into orders according to where the effort is applied, and the load-moving force developed, in relation to the position of the fulcrum.

A **first-order** lever has the load and the effort on opposite sides of the fulcrum – for example, a see-saw or pair of scissors. A **second-order** lever has the load and the effort on the same side of the fulcrum, with the load nearer the fulcrum – for example, nutcrackers or a wheelbarrow. A **third-order** lever has the effort nearer the fulcrum than the load, with both on the same side of it – for example, a pair of tweezers or tongs. The mechanical advantage of a lever is the ratio of load to effort, equal to the perpendicular distance of the effort's line of action from the fulcrum divided by the distance to the load's line of action. Thus tweezers, for instance, have a mechanical advantage of less than one.

leveraged buyout in business, the purchase of a controlling proportion of the shares of a company by its own management, financed almost exclusively by borrowing. It is so called because the ratio of a company's long-term debt to its equity (capital assets) is known as its 'leverage'.

Levi, Primo (1919–1987) Italian novelist. He joined the antifascist resistance during World War II, was captured, and sent to the concentration camp at Auschwitz. He wrote of these experiences in *Se questo è un uomo/If This Is a Man* (1947). His other books, all based on his experience of the war, include *Period Tables* (1975) and *Moments of Reprieve* (1981).

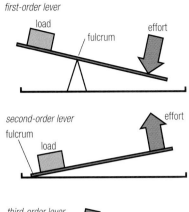

first-order lever

load | fulcrum | effort

second-order lever

fulcrum | load | effort

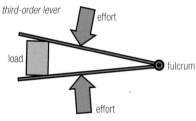

third-order lever

effort | load | fulcrum | effort

LEVER Types of lever. Practical applications of the first-order lever include the crowbar, seesaw, and scissors. The wheelbarrow is a second-order lever; tweezers or tongs are third-order levers.

Levi-Montalcini, Rita (1909–) Italian neurologist who was awarded a Nobel Prize for Physiology or Medicine in 1986 with her co-worker, US biochemist Stanley Cohen, for their discovery of factors that promote the growth of nerve and epidermal cells. This nerve-growth factor controls how many cells make up the adult nervous system.

Levinson, Barry (1932–) US film director and screenwriter. Working in Hollywood's mainstream, he has been responsible for some of the best adult comedy films of the 1980s and 1990s. The offbeat realism of *Diner* (1982) gave way to such large-budget movies as *Good Morning Vietnam* (1987), *Tin Men* 1987, *Rain Man* (1988; Academy Awards for best picture and best director), and *Bugsy* (1991).

Lévi-Strauss, Claude (1908–) French anthropologist. He helped to formulate the principles of ▷structuralism by stressing the interdependence of cultural systems and the way they relate to each other, maintaining that social and cultural life can be explained by a postulated unconscious reality concealed behind the reality by which people believe their lives to be ordered.

levitation counteraction of gravitational forces on a body. As claimed by medieval mystics, spiritualist mediums, and practitioners of transcendental meditation, it is unproven. In the laboratory it can be produced scientifically; for example, electrostatic force and acoustical waves have been used to suspend water drops for microscopic study. It is also used in technology; for example, in magnetic levitation as in ▷maglev trains.

Lewes, Battle of battle in 1264 caused by the baronial opposition to the English King Henry III, led by Simon de Montfort, Earl of Leicester (1208–65). The king was defeated and captured at the battle.

Lewis (or **Lewis-with-Harris**) largest and most northerly island in the Outer ▷Hebrides, Western Isles; area 2,220 sq km/857 sq mi; population (1991) 21,700. Its main town is Stornoway. It is separated from northwest Scotland by the Minch. The island is 80 km/50 mi long from north to south, and its greatest breadth is 45 km/28 mi. There are many lochs and peat moors. The Callanish standing stones on the west coast are thought to be up to 5,000 years old, second only to Stonehenge in archaeological significance in the UK.

Lewis, (William) Arthur (1915–1991) British economist born on St Lucia, West Indies. He specialized in the economic problems of developing countries and created a model relating the terms of trade between less developed and more developed nations to their respective levels of labour productivity in agriculture. He shared the Nobel Prize for Economics in 1979 with an American, Theodore Schultz, for his analysis of economic processes in developing nations. He wrote many books, including the *Theory of Economic Growth* (1955). He was knighted in 1963.

Lewis, Carl (1961–) Born Frederick Carlton Lewis. US track and field athlete. He won nine gold medals and one silver in four successive Olympic Games. At the 1984 Olympic Games he equalled the performance of Jesse ▷Owens, winning gold medals in the 100 and 200 metres, 400-metre relay, and long jump. He officially ended his career in 1997 at the age of 36. In November 1999 he was voted 'Sportsman of the Century' by the International Olympic Committee (IOC), and in December 1999 the US magazine *Sports Illustrated* named him the 'Best Olympian of the 20th Century'.

Lewis, C Day Irish poet; see Cecil ▷Day-Lewis.

Lewis, C(live) S(taples) (1898–1963) English academic and writer, born in Belfast. He became a committed Christian in 1931 and wrote the Chronicles of Narnia, a series of seven novels of Christian allegory for children set in the magic land of Narnia, beginning with *The Lion, the Witch, and the Wardrobe* (1950). His other works include the medieval study *The Allegory of Love* (1936) and the space fiction *Out of the Silent Planet* (1938). He wrote essays in popular theology such as *The Screwtape Letters* (1942) and *Mere Christianity* (1952), and the autobiographical *Surprised by Joy* (1955).

Lewis, Jerry (1926–) Stage name of Joseph Levitch. US comic actor and director. He worked in partnership with Dean Martin 1946–56; their film debut was in *My Friend Irma* (1949). He was revered as a solo performer by French critics ('*Le Roi du Crazy*'), but films that he directed, such as *The Nutty Professor* (1963), were less well received in the USA. He appeared in a straight role opposite Robert De Niro in *The King of Comedy* (1982).

Lewis, Jerry Lee (1935–) US rock-and-roll and country singer and pianist. His trademark was the boogie-woogie-derived 'pumping piano' style in hits such as 'Whole Lotta Shakin' Going On' and 'Great Balls of Fire' (1957); later recordings include 'What Made Milwaukee Famous' (1968).

Lewis, John Frederick (1805–1876) English painter. His pictures of Egyptian subjects – for example, *The Hareem* (1850; Victoria and Albert Museum, London) – combine minuteness of detail with brilliance of colour. They were admired by the critic John Ruskin as an anticipation of Pre-Raphaelitism.

Lewis, Lennox Claudius (1966–) English boxer who won the World Boxing Council (WBC) world heavyweight title in 1992, becoming the first British boxer to do so in the 20th century. He was awarded the title when the reigning champion, Riddick Bowe, refused to fight him. After defending the title successfully for nearly two years, he lost to Oliver McCall in September 1994, but he regained the title in February 1997. He became the undisputed heavyweight world champion in November 1999 after winning a rematch with the joint World Boxing Association (WBA) and International Boxing Federation (IBF) world champion Evander Holyfield. He lost his WBC, IBF, and IBO titles in April 2001 when he was surprisingly knocked out in the fifth round by the US challenger Hasim Rahman. He regained his titles later that year, before winning a much anticipated fight with Mike Tyson in June 2002.

Related Web site: Lennox Lewis Official Web Site http://www.lennox-lewis.com/

Lewis, (Percy) Wyndham (1882–1957) English writer and artist. He pioneered Vorticism, which, with its feeling of movement, sought to reflect the age of industry. He had a hard and aggressive style in both his writing and his painting. His literary works include the novel *The Apes of God* (1930); the essay collection *Time and Western Man* (1927); and an autobiography, *Blasting and Bombardiering* (1937). In addition to paintings of a semi-abstract kind, he made a number of portraits; among his sitters were the poets Edith Sitwell, Ezra Pound, and T S Eliot.

Through Vorticism, a variant of cubist and Futurist ideas, Lewis opposed the 'everyday visual real' and favoured machinelike forms. He edited *Blast* from 1914 to 1915, a literary and artistic magazine which proclaimed the principles of the movement. Both in his paintings and in his numerous written works – including the novels *Tarr* (1918) and *The Childermass* (1928) – he was an intellectual independent, and one of his later literary products, *The Demon of Progress in the Arts* (1954), was an attack on formalized extremism. His painting *The Surrender of Barcelona* (1936; Tate Gallery, London) applies mechanistic treatment to an imagined scene of the past.

Lexington and Concord, Battle of first battle of the ▷American Revolution, 19 April 1775, at Lexington, Massachusetts, USA. The first shots were fired when British troops, sent to seize illegal military stores and arrest rebel leaders John Hancock and Samuel Adams, were attacked by the local militia (minutemen). Although a somewhat inconclusive action in itself, it sparked wider rebellion and so precipitated the revolution.

Leyden alternative form of ▷Leiden, a city in the Netherlands.

Leyden, Lucas van Dutch painter; see ▷Lucas van Leyden.

Lhasa (called 'the Forbidden City') capital of the autonomous region of ▷Tibet, China, at 5,000 m/16,400 ft; population (1992) 124,000. Products include handicrafts and light industry. The holy city of ▷Lamaism, Lhasa was closed to Westerners until 1904, when members of a British expedition led by Col Francis E Younghusband visited the city. It was annexed with the rest of Tibet 1950–51 by China, and the spiritual and temporal head of state, the Dalai Lama, fled in 1959 after a popular uprising against Chinese rule. Monasteries have been destroyed and monks killed, and an influx of Chinese settlers has generated resentment. In 1988 and 1989 nationalist demonstrators were shot by Chinese soldiers.

Related Web site: Lhasa Archive Project http://www.asianart.com/lhasa_restoration/index.html

liability in accounting, a financial obligation. Liabilities are placed alongside assets on a balance sheet to show the wealth of the individual or company concerned at a given date. Business organizations often distinguish between **current liabilities** such as overdrafts, trade credit, and provisions, and **long-term liabilities** such as debentures, mortgages, and unsecured loans.

liana woody, perennial climbing plant with very long stems, which grows around trees right up to the top, where there is more sunlight. Lianas are common in tropical rainforests, where individual stems may grow up to 78 m/255 ft long. They have an unusual stem structure that makes them flexible, despite being woody.

LHASA A young Tibetan monk in Lhasa. The monastic practice of lamaism is one of meditation, chanting, and recitation. The monks wear traditional simple robes and have very few material possessions. *Corel*

Lesotho

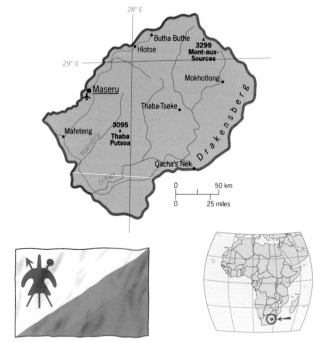

Lesotho landlocked country in southern Africa, an enclave within South Africa.

NATIONAL NAME *Mmuso oa Lesotho/Kingdom of Lesotho*
AREA 30,355 sq km/11,720 sq mi
CAPITAL Maseru
MAJOR TOWNS/CITIES Qacha's Nek, Teyateyaneng, Mafeteng, Hlotse, Roma, Quthing
PHYSICAL FEATURES mountainous with plateaux, forming part of South Africa's chief watershed

Government

HEAD OF STATE King Letsie III from 1996
HEAD OF GOVERNMENT Bethuel Pakalitha Mosisili from 1998
POLITICAL SYSTEM emergent democracy
POLITICAL EXECUTIVE parliamentary
ADMINISTRATIVE DIVISIONS ten districts
ARMED FORCES 2,000 (2002 est)
CONSCRIPTION military service is voluntary
DEATH PENALTY retained and used for ordinary crimes
DEFENCE SPEND (% GDP) 2.9 (2002 est)
EDUCATION SPEND (% GDP) 10.1 (2000 est)
HEALTH SPEND (% GDP) 6.3 (2000 est)

Economy and resources

CURRENCY loti
GPD (US$) 730 million (2002 est)
REAL GDP GROWTH (% change on previous year) 4 (2001)
GNI (US$) 981 million (2002 est)
GNI PER CAPITA (PPP) (US$) 2,710 (2002 est)
CONSUMER PRICE INFLATION 8.5% (2003 est)
UNEMPLOYMENT 35% (2000)
FOREIGN DEBT (US$) 848 million (2001 est)
MAJOR TRADING PARTNERS SACU (South African Customs Union) members: Lesotho, Botswana, Swaziland, Namibia, and South Africa; USA, Canada, Taiwan, Hong Kong, Italy and other EU countries

RESOURCES diamonds, uranium, lead, iron ore; believed to have petroleum deposits
INDUSTRIES food products and beverages, textiles and clothing, mining, baskets, furniture
EXPORTS clothing, footwear, furniture, food and live animals (cattle), hides, wool and mohair, baskets. Principal market: USA and Canada 62.8% (2001)
IMPORTS food and live animals, machinery and transport equipment, electricity, petroleum products. Principal source: SACU 82.8% (2001)
ARABLE LAND 10.7% (2000 est)

AGRICULTURAL PRODUCTS maize, wheat, sorghum, asparagus, peas, and other vegetables; livestock rearing (sheep, goats, and cattle)

Population and society

POPULATION 1,802,000 (2003 est)
POPULATION GROWTH RATE 0.8% (2000–15)
POPULATION DENSITY (per sq km) 59 (2003 est)
URBAN POPULATION (% of total) 30 (2003 est)
AGE DISTRIBUTION (% of total population) 0–14 39%, 15–59 54%, 60+ 7% (2002 est)
ETHNIC GROUPS almost entirely Bantus (of Southern Sotho) or Basotho

LANGUAGE English (official), Sesotho, Zulu, Xhosa
RELIGION Protestant 42%, Roman Catholic 38%, indigenous beliefs
EDUCATION (compulsory years) 7
LITERACY RATE 75% (men); 94% (women) (2003 est)
LABOUR FORCE 76.3% agriculture, 11.1% industry, 12.6% services (1994 est)
LIFE EXPECTANCY 32 (men); 38 (women) (2000–05)
CHILD MORTALITY RATE (under 5, per 1,000 live births) 132 (2001)
PHYSICIANS (per 1,000 people) 0.05 (1998 est)
TV SETS (per 1,000 people) 16 (1999)
RADIOS (per 1,000 people) 53 (1999)
INTERNET USERS (per 10,000 people) 96.9 (2000)

Chronology

18th century: Formerly inhabited by nomadic hunter-gatherer San, Zulu-speaking Ngunis, and Sotho-speaking peoples settled in the region.

1820s: Under the name of Basutoland, Sotho nation founded by Moshoeshoe I, who united the people to repulse Zulu attacks from south.

1843: Moshoeshoe I negotiated British protection as tension with South African Boers increased.

1868: Became British territory, administered by Cape Colony (in South Africa) from 1871.

1884: Became British crown colony, after revolt against Cape Colony control; Basuto chiefs allowed to govern according to custom and tradition, but rich agricultural land west of the Caledon River was lost to South Africa.

1900s: Served as a migrant labour reserve for South Africa's mines and farms.

1952: Left-of-centre Basutoland African Congress, later Congress Party (BCP), founded by Ntsu Mokhehle to campaign for self rule.

1966: Independence achieved within Commonwealth, as Kingdom of Lesotho, with Moshoeshoe II as king and Chief Leabua Jonathan of the conservative Basotho National Party (BNP) as prime minister.

1970: State of emergency declared; king briefly forced into exile after attempting to increase his authority.

1973: State of emergency lifted; BNP won majority of seats in general election.

1975: Members of ruling party attacked by South African-backed guerrillas, who opposed African National Congress (ANC) guerrillas using Lesotho as a base.

1986: South Africa imposed a border blockade, forcing the deportation of 60 ANC members.

1990: Moshoeshoe II was dethroned and replaced by his son, as King Letsie III.

1993: Free multiparty elections ended the military rule.

1994: Fighting between rival army factions was ended by a peace deal, brokered by the Organization of African Unity.

1995: King Letsie III abdicated to restore King Moshoeshoe II to the throne.

1996: King Moshoeshoe II was killed in car accident; King Letsie III was restored to the throne.

1998: The LCD attained general election victory amidst claims of rigged polls; public demonstrations followed. South Africa sent troops to support the government. An interim political authority was appointed prior to new elections. Bethuel Mosisili became the new prime minister.

LESOTHO A field of maize interspersed with cosmos flowers near the village of Malalea. The cosmos plant was brought into South Africa along with alfalfa, which was imported from South America to provide fodder for horses during the Boer War. Cosmos grows more widely during droughts, when the fields are left uncultivated. Across the plateau are the Maluti Mountains. *www.malealea.co.ls*

Liao river in northeast China; length 1,450 km/900 mi. The main headstream rises in the mountains of Inner Mongolia and flows east, then south to the Gulf of Liaodong. It is frozen from December to March.

Liao dynasty family that ruled part of northeastern China and Manchuria 945–1125 during the ▷Song era. It was founded by cavalry-based Qidan (Khidan) people, Mongolian-speakers who gradually became Sinicized. They were later defeated by the nomadic Juchen (Jurchen) who founded the ▷Jin dynasty.

Liaoning province of northeast China, bounded to the east by Jilin, to the southeast by North Korea, to the south by Korea Bay and the Gulf of Liaodong, to the southwest by Hebei, and to the northwest by Inner Mongolia; area 151,000 sq km/58,300 sq mi; population (1996) 41,160,000. The capital is ▷Shenyang, and other cities and towns include Anshan, Fushun, Liaoyang, and Dalian (port). The province includes the Dongbei (Manchurian) Plain and the grasslands of the Mongolian Plateau. It is one of China's most heavily industrialized areas, and industries include coal, iron, salt, and oil. Agricultural products include cereals. Liaoning was developed by Japan between 1905 and 1945, including the Liaodong Peninsula, whose ports had been conquered from the Russians.

Liaquat Ali Khan, Nawabzada (1895–1951) Indian politician, deputy leader of the ▷Muslim League 1940–47, first prime minister of Pakistan from 1947. He was assassinated by objectors to his peace policy with India.

libel in law, defamation published in a permanent form, such as in a newspaper, book, or broadcast.

Liberal Democrats UK political party of the centre, led from 1999 by Charles Kennedy. Britain's third main party, the Liberal Democrats are successors to the Liberal Party and the Social Democratic Party, which merged in 1998 to form the Social and Liberal Democrats (SLD). The name Liberal Democrats was adopted in 1989. It is a progressive party, which supports closer integration within the European Union, constitutional reform (including proportional representation and regional government), and greater investment in state education and the National Health Service, financed by higher direct taxes. The party has strong libertarian and environmentalist wings. It has been in coalition, with Labour, in the Scottish Parliament since 1999, and in the Welsh Assembly since 2000. It won 52 seats at the June 2001 general election – the best result for the Liberals and their successors for more than 70 years.

Under the leadership of Paddy Ashdown (1988–99) the Liberal Democrats became close allies of 'New Labour', which won power in 1997. Liberal Democrats were given seats by Prime Minister Tony Blair on a joint cabinet committee, which discussed constitutional issues, Europe, health, and education. Since 1999, with Kennedy as leader, relations with Labour have remained cordial, but less close. On certain issues, such as government investment in education and the health service, the Liberal Democrats have moved, in many voters' minds, to the left of New Labour.

> **Herbert Samuel**
> British Liberal politician
>
> *A library is thought in cold storage.*
>
> *Book of Quotations*

liberalism political and social theory that favours representative government, freedom of the press, speech, and worship, the abolition of class privileges, the use of state resources to protect the welfare of the individual, and international ▷free trade. It is historically associated with the Liberal Party in the UK and the Democratic Party in the USA.

Liberalism developed during the 17th–19th centuries as the distinctive theory of the industrial and commercial classes in their struggle against the power of the monarchy, the church, and the feudal landowners. Economically it was associated with ▷*laissez faire*, or nonintervention. In the late 19th and early 20th centuries its ideas were modified by the acceptance of universal suffrage and a certain amount of state intervention in economic affairs, in order to ensure a minimum standard of living and to remove extremes of poverty and wealth. The classical statement of liberal principles is found in *On Liberty* and other works of the British philosopher J S Mill.

Related Web site: Liberalism http://plato.stanford.edu/entries/liberalism/

Liberal Party British political party, the successor to the ▷Whig Party, with an ideology of liberalism. In the 19th century it represented the interests of commerce and industry. Its outstanding leaders were Palmerston, Gladstone, and Lloyd George. From 1914 it declined, and the rise of the Labour Party pushed the Liberals into the middle ground. The Liberals joined forces with the Social Democratic Party (SDP) as the Alliance for the 1983 and 1987 elections. In 1988 a majority of the SDP voted to merge with the Liberals to form the ▷Social and Liberal Democrats.

The Liberal Party was officially formed on 6 June 1857, marking a shift of support for the party from aristocrats to include also progressive industrialists, backed by supporters of the utilitarian reformer Jeremy ▷Bentham, Nonconformists (especially in Welsh and Scottish constituencies), and the middle classes. During the Liberals' first period of power, from 1830 to 1841, they promoted parliamentary and municipal government reform and the abolition of slavery, but their *laissez-faire* theories led to the harsh Poor Law of 1834. Except for two short periods, the Liberals were in power from 1846 to 1866, but the only major change was the general adoption of free trade. Liberal pressure forced Prime Minister Robert Peel to repeal the Corn Laws of 1846, thereby splitting the ruling Conservative (or Tory) party.

Extended franchise (1867) and Gladstone's emergence as leader began a new phase, dominated by the Manchester school with a programme of 'peace, retrenchment, and reform'. Gladstone's 1868–74 government introduced many important reforms, including elementary education and vote by ballot. The party's left, composed mainly of working-class Radicals and led by Charles ▷Bradlaugh (a lawyer's clerk) and Joseph ▷Chamberlain (a wealthy manufacturer), repudiated *laissez faire* and inclined towards republicanism, but in 1886 the Liberals were split over the policy of home rule for Ireland, and many became Liberal Unionists or joined the Conservatives.Except for the period 1892 to 1895, the Liberals remained out of power until 1906, when, reinforced by Labour and Irish support, they returned with a huge majority. Old-age pensions, National Insurance, limitation of the powers of the Lords, and the Irish Home Rule Bill followed. Lloyd George's alliance with the Conservatives from 1916 to 1922 divided the Liberal Party between him and his predecessor Asquith, and although reunited in 1923 the Liberals continued to lose votes. They briefly joined the National Government (1931–32). After World War II they were reduced to a handful of members of Parliament.

A revival began under the leadership (1956–67) of Jo Grimond and continued under Jeremy Thorpe, who resigned after a period of controversy within the party in 1976. After a caretaker return by Grimond, David Steel became the first party leader in British politics to be elected by party members who were not MPs. Between 1977 and 1978 Steel entered into an agreement to support Labour in any vote of confidence in return for consultation on measures undertaken. After the 1987 general election, Steel suggested a merger of the Liberal Party and the SDP, and the Liberal Democrat Party was formed on 3 March 1988, with Paddy Ashdown elected leader in July of that year.

Liberal Party, Australian political party established 1944 by Robert Menzies, after a Labor landslide, and derived from the former United Australia Party.

After the voters rejected Labor's extensive nationalization plans, the Liberals were in power 1949–72 and 1975–83 and were led in succession by Harold Holt, John Gorton, William McMahon, Billy Snedden, Malcolm Fraser, John Hewson, Alexander Downer, and John Howard. It returned to power in 1996 in a coalition with the National Party.

liberation theology Christian theory of Jesus' primary importance as the 'Liberator', personifying the poor and devoted to freeing them from oppression. Enthusiastically (and sometimes violently) adopted in Latin America, it embodies a Marxist interpretation of the class struggle, especially by Third World nations. It has been criticized by some Roman Catholic authorities, including Pope John Paul II.

Liberia see country box.

libido in Freudian psychology, the energy of the sex instinct, which is to be found even in a newborn child. The libido develops through a number of phases, described by Sigmund Freud in his theory of infantile sexuality. The source of the libido is the ▷id.

LIBOR (acronym for London Interbank Offered Rates) loan rates for a specified period that are offered to first-class banks in the London interbank market. Banks link their lending to LIBOR as an alternative to the base lending rate when setting the rate for a fixed term, after which the rate may be adjusted. The LIBOR rate is the main benchmark for much of the Eurodollar loan market.

Libra faint zodiacal constellation on the celestial equator (see ▷celestial sphere) adjoining Scorpius, and represented as the scales of justice. The Sun passes through Libra during November. The constellation was once considered to be a part of Scorpius, seen as the scorpion's claws. In astrology, the dates for Libra are between about 23 September and 23 October (see ▷precession).

library collection of information (usually in the form of books) held for common use. The earliest was in Nineveh in Babylonian times. The first public library was opened in Athens in 330 BC. All ancient libraries were reference libraries: books could be consulted but not borrowed. Lending or circulating libraries did not become popular until the 18th century; they became widespread in the 19th century with the rapid development of public libraries. Free public libraries probably began in the 15th century. In the UK, the first documented free public library was established in Manchester in 1852, after the 1850 Public Library Act. The first free, public, tax-supported library in the USA was opened in Boston in 1854.

libretto (Italian 'little book') the text of an opera or other dramatic vocal work, or the scenario of a ballet.

Libreville (French 'free town') capital of Gabon, on the northern shore of the Gabon River estuary; population (1993) 419,600. Products include timber, oil, cement, and minerals (including uranium and manganese). It is the main port and transport centre of the country, together with Owendo on the southern edge of the town. Libreville was founded in 1849 as a refuge for slaves freed by the French. Since the 1970s the city has developed rapidly due to the oil trade. It was capital of French Equatorial Guinea 1888–1904. There is a cathedral, the Sainte-Exupéry French Cultural Centre, and a university (1976).

Libya see country box.

lichen any organism of a unique group that consists of associations of a specific ▷fungus and a specific ▷alga living together in a mutually beneficial relationship. Found as coloured patches or spongelike masses on trees, rocks, and other surfaces, lichens flourish in harsh conditions. (Group Lichenes.)

Related Web site: Fun With Lichens http://mgd.nacse.org/hyperSQL/lichenland/

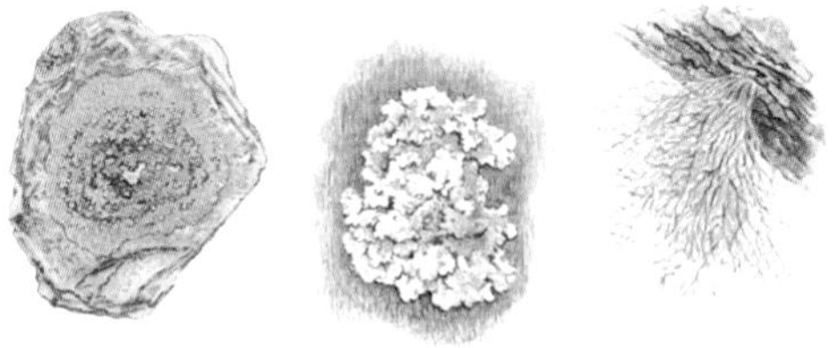

LICHEN A lichen is a symbiotic association between an alga and a fungus – in other words, each lichen is not one organism but two. Lichen grow very slowly, usually as encrustations on rocks, walls or wood. They are found throughout the world but are unable to survive where the atmosphere is polluted, so they are good indicators of clean air.

Lichtenstein, Roy (1923–1997) US pop artist. He is best known for using advertising imagery and comic-strip techniques, often focusing on popular ideals of romance and heroism, as in *Whaam!* (1963; Tate Gallery, London). He has also produced sculptures in brass, plastic, and enamelled metal.

Related Web site: Roy Lichtenstein Foundation http://www.lichtensteinfoundation.org/

Liddell Hart, Basil Henry (1895–1970) British military strategist. He was an exponent of mechanized warfare, and his ideas were adopted in Germany in 1935 in creating the 1st Panzer Division, combining motorized infantry and tanks. From 1937 he advised the UK War Office on army reorganization. Knighted in 1966.

Liebig, Justus (1803–1873) Baron von Liebig. German organic chemist who extended chemical research into other scientific fields, such as agricultural chemistry and biochemistry. He introduced the theory of compound ▷radicals and discovered chloroform and chloral, and demonstrated the use of fertilizers.

Liebknecht, Karl (1871–1919) German socialist, son of Wilhelm Liebknecht. A founder of the German Communist Party, originally known as the Spartacus League (see ▷Spartacist), in 1918, he was one of the few socialists who refused to support World War I. He led an unsuccessful revolt with Rosa Luxemburg in Berlin in 1919 and both were murdered by army officers.

Liebknecht, Wilhelm (1826–1900) German socialist. A friend of the communist theoretician Karl Marx, with whom he took part in the ▷revolutions of 1848, he was imprisoned for opposition to the Franco-Prussian War 1870–71. He was one of the founders of the Social Democratic Party 1875. He was the father of Karl Liebknecht.

Liechtenstein see country box.

lied (German 'song', plural **lieder**) musical dramatization of a poem, usually for solo voice and piano; referring especially to the Romantic songs of Franz Schubert, Robert Schumann, Johannes Brahms, and Hugo Wolf.

lie detector instrument that records graphically certain body activities, such as thoracic and abdominal respiration, blood pressure, pulse rate, and galvanic skin response (changes in electrical resistance of the skin). Marked changes in these activities when a person answers a question may indicate that the person is lying.

Liège (Flemish **Luik**) industrial city, capital of Liège province in eastern Belgium, southeast of Brussels, almost bisected by the River Meuse, and bounded on the east side by Germany; population

(1997) 189,500. It is one of the largest river ports in Europe. Weapons, textiles, paper, and chemicals are manufactured here. The city has a university, founded in 1817, and several ancient churches; the oldest, St Martin's, dates from 692.

liege in the feudal system, the allegiance owed by a vassal to his or her lord (the liege lord).

Lifar, Serge (1905–1986) Ukrainian dancer and choreographer. Born in Kiev, he studied under ▷Nijinsky, joined the Diaghilev company in 1923, and was artistic director and principal dancer of the Paris Opéra 1929–44 and 1947–59. He completely revitalized the company and in so doing, reversed the diminished fortunes of French ballet.

life the ability to grow, reproduce, and respond to such stimuli as light, heat, and sound. Life on Earth may have begun about 4 billion years ago when a chemical reaction produced the first organic substance. Over time, life has evolved from primitive single-celled organisms to complex multicellular ones. There are now some 10 million different species of plants and animals living on the Earth. The earliest fossil evidence of life is threadlike chains of cells discovered in 1980 in deposits in northwestern Australia; these 'stromatolites' have been dated as being 3.5 billion years old.

▷Biology is the study of living organisms – their evolution, structure, functioning, classification, and distribution – while ▷biochemistry is the study of the chemistry of living organisms. Biochemistry is especially concerned with the function of the chemical components of organisms such as proteins, carbohydrates, lipids, and nucleic acids.

Life probably originated in the primitive oceans. The original atmosphere, 4 billion years ago, consisted of carbon dioxide, nitrogen, and water. Laboratory experiments have shown that more complex organic molecules, such as ▷amino acids and ▷nucleotides, can be produced from these ingredients by passing electric sparks through a mixture. The climate of the early atmosphere was probably very violent, with lightning a common feature, and these conditions could have resulted in the oceans becoming rich in organic molecules, producing the so-called 'primeval soup'. These molecules may have organized themselves into clusters capable of reproducing and eventually developing into simple cells. Soon after life developed, ▷photosynthesis would have become the primary source of energy for life. By this process, life would have substantially affected the chemistry of the atmosphere and, in turn, that of its own environment. Once the atmosphere had changed to its present composition, life could only be created by the replication of living organisms (a process called ▷biogenesis).

Related Web site: GCSE Biology http://www.purchon.co.uk/science/biology.html

life cycle in biology, the sequence of developmental stages through which members of a given species pass. Most vertebrates have a simple life cycle consisting of ▷fertilization of sex cells or ▷gametes, a period of development as an ▷embryo, a period of juvenile growth after hatching or birth, an adulthood including ▷sexual reproduction, and finally death. Invertebrate life cycles are generally more complex and may involve major reconstitution of the individual's appearance (▷metamorphosis) and completely different styles of life. Plants have a special type of life cycle with two distinct phases, known as ▷alternation of generations. Many insects such as cicadas, dragonflies, and mayflies have a long larvae or pupae phase and a short adult phase. Dragonflies live an aquatic life as larvae and an aerial life during the adult phase. In many invertebrates and protozoa there is a sequence of stages in the life cycle, and in parasites different stages often occur in different host organisms. See picture on p. 556.

Liberia

Liberia country in West Africa, bounded north by Guinea, east by Côte d'Ivoire, south and southwest by the Atlantic Ocean, and northwest by Sierra Leone.

NATIONAL NAME *Republic of Liberia*
AREA 111,370 sq km/42,999 sq mi
CAPITAL Monrovia (and chief port)
MAJOR TOWNS/CITIES Bensonville, Saniquillie, Gbarnga, Voinjama, Buchanan
MAJOR PORTS Buchanan, Greenville
PHYSICAL FEATURES forested highlands; swampy tropical coast where six rivers enter the sea

Government

HEAD OF STATE AND GOVERNMENT Gynde Bryant from 2003
POLITICAL SYSTEM emergent democracy
POLITICAL EXECUTIVE limited presidency
ADMINISTRATIVE DIVISIONS 13 counties
ARMED FORCES 15,000 (2002 est)
CONSCRIPTION military service is voluntary
DEATH PENALTY retained and used for ordinary crimes
DEFENCE SPEND (% GDP) 4.5 (2002 est)
HEALTH SPEND (% GDP) 4 (2000 est)

Economy and resources

CURRENCY Liberian dollar
GPD (US$) 564 million (2002 est)
REAL GDP GROWTH (% change on previous year) 5.3 (2001)

GNI (US$) 489 million (2002 est)
CONSUMER PRICE INFLATION 15% (2003 est)
UNEMPLOYMENT 65% (2000)
FOREIGN DEBT (US$) 16.9 billion (2001 est)
MAJOR TRADING PARTNERS Germany, France, South Korea, Japan, USA, Italy, China, Singapore
RESOURCES iron ore, diamonds, gold, barytes, kyanite
INDUSTRIES beverages (soft drinks and beer), mineral products, chemicals, tobacco and other agricultural products, cement, mining, rubber, furniture, bricks, plastics
EXPORTS rubber, timber, coffee, cocoa, iron ore, palm-kernel oil, diamonds, gold. Principal market: Germany 50% (2001)
IMPORTS food and live animals, machinery and transport equipment, mineral fuels, rice, basic manufactures. Principal source: France 26.9% (2001)
ARABLE LAND 3.9% (2000 est)
AGRICULTURAL PRODUCTS rice, cassava, coffee, citrus fruits, cocoa, palm kernels, sugar cane; timber production; rubber plantation

Chronology

1821: Purchased by the philanthropic American Colonization Society and turned into settlement for liberated black slaves from southern USA.

1847: Recognized as an independent republic.

1869: The True Whig Party founded, which was to dominate politics for more than a century, providing all presidents.

1926: Large concession sold to Firestone Rubber Company as foreign indebtedness increased.

1980: President Tolbert was assassinated in military coup led by Sgt Samuel Doe, who banned political parties and launched an anticorruption drive.

1984: A new constitution was approved in a referendum. The National Democratic Party (NDPL) was founded by Doe as political parties were relegalized.

1985: Doe and the NDPL won decisive victories in the allegedly rigged elections.

1990: Doe was killed as bloody civil war broke out, involving Charles Taylor and Gen Hezekiah Bowen, who led rival rebel armies, the National Patriotic Front (NPFL) and the Armed Forces of Liberia (AFL). The war left 150,000 dead and 2 million homeless. A West African peacekeeping force was drafted in.

Population and society

POPULATION 3,367,000 (2003 est)
POPULATION GROWTH RATE 2.5% (2000–15)
POPULATION DENSITY (per sq km) 30 (2003 est)
URBAN POPULATION (% of total) 47 (2003 est)
AGE DISTRIBUTION (% of total population) 0–14 43%, 15–59 53%, 60+ 4% (2002 est)
ETHNIC GROUPS 95% indigenous peoples, including the Kpelle, Bassa, Gio, Kru, Grebo, Mano, Krahn, Gola, Ghandi, Loma, Kissi, Vai, and Bella; 5% descended from repatriated US slaves
LANGUAGE English (official), over 20 Niger-Congo languages
RELIGION animist 70%, Sunni Muslim 20%, Christian 10%
EDUCATION (compulsory years) 9
LITERACY RATE 73% (men); 40% (women) (2003 est)
LABOUR FORCE 69% agriculture, 8% industry, 23% services (1997 est)
LIFE EXPECTANCY 41 (men); 42 (women) (2000–05)

See also ▷Doe, Samuel.

1992: Monrovia was under siege by Taylor's rebel forces.

1995: Ghanaian-backed peace proposals were accepted by rebel factions; an interim Council of State was established, comprising leaders of three main rebel factions.

1996: There was renewed fighting in the capital. A peace plan was reached in talks convened by the Economic Community of West African States (ECOWAS); Ruth Perry became Liberia's first female head of state.

1997: The National Patriotic Party (NPP) won a majority in assembly elections and its leader, Charles Taylor, became head of state.

1998: There was fighting in Monrovia between President Taylor's forces and opposition militias.

2000: A massive offensive against rebels in northern Liberia was launched in September.

2001: Fighting worsened, and the UN renewed its arms embargo and the ban on diamond trading.

2003: Despite a ceasefire agreement, hundreds of people were killed in the ongoing civil war as rebel forces seeking the overthrow of President Taylor launched assaults on Monrovia and Buchanan. West African peacekeeping forces supported by 200 US marines took control of the situation and President Taylor resigned and went into exile. Rebel factions and government representatives signed a power-sharing agreement appointing Gyude Bryant, an industrialist and cleric, to lead a new transitional administration.

LIBERIA The red cross marked on the ten-cent stamp from Liberia signifies a surcharge raising funds for the humanitarian organization the International Red Cross.
Stanley Gibbons

Libya

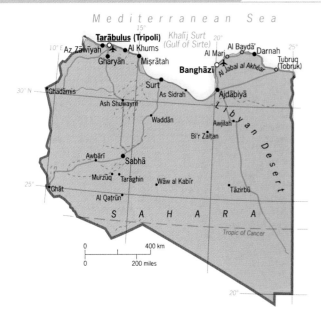

Libya country in North Africa, bounded north by the Mediterranean Sea, east by Egypt, southeast by Sudan, south by Chad and Niger, and west by Algeria and Tunisia.

POPULATION DENSITY (per sq km) 3 (2003 est)
URBAN POPULATION (% of total) 89 (2003 est)
AGE DISTRIBUTION (% of total population) 0–14 33%, 15–59 61%, 60+ 6% (2002 est)
ETHNIC GROUPS majority are of Berber and Arab origin (97%), with a small number of Tebou and Touareg nomads and semi-nomads, mainly in south
LANGUAGE Arabic (official), Italian, English
RELIGION Sunni Muslim 97%
EDUCATION (compulsory years) 9
LITERACY RATE 92% (men); 72% (women) (2003 est)
LABOUR FORCE 17.9% agriculture, 29.9% industry, 52.2% services (1996)

LIFE EXPECTANCY 71 (men); 75 (women) (2000–05)
CHILD MORTALITY RATE (under 5, per 1,000 live births) 19 (2001)
PHYSICIANS (per 1,000 people) 1.3 (1998 est)
HOSPITAL BEDS (per 1,000 people) 4.3 (1998 est)
TV SETS (per 1,000 people) 139 (1999 est)
RADIOS (per 1,000 people) 259 (1997)
INTERNET USERS (per 10,000 people) 225.0 (2002 est)
PERSONAL COMPUTER USERS (per 100 people) 2.3 (2002 est)

See also ▷Khaddhafi, Moamer al.

NATIONAL NAME *Al-Jamahiriyya al-'Arabiyya al-Libiyya ash-Sha'biyya al-Ishtirakiyya al-'Uzma/Great Libyan Arab Socialist People's State of the Masses*
AREA 1,759,540 sq km/679,358 sq mi
CAPITAL Tripoli
MAJOR TOWNS/CITIES Benghazi, Misurata, Az Zawiyah, Tobruk, Ajdabiya, Darnah
MAJOR PORTS Benghazi, Misratah, Az Zawiyah, Tobruk, Ajdabiya, Darnah
PHYSICAL FEATURES flat to undulating plains with plateaux and depressions stretch southwards from the Mediterranean coast to an extremely dry desert interior

Government

HEAD OF STATE Moamer al-Khaddhafi from 1969
HEAD OF GOVERNMENT Mubarak al-Shamikh from 2000
POLITICAL SYSTEM nationalistic socialist

POLITICAL EXECUTIVE unlimited presidency
ADMINISTRATIVE DIVISIONS three provinces and ten governorates
ARMED FORCES 76,000 (2002 est)
CONSCRIPTION conscription is selective for two years
DEATH PENALTY retained and used for ordinary crimes
DEFENCE SPEND (% GDP) 3.8 (2002 est)
HEALTH SPEND (% GDP) 3.3 (2000 est)

Economy and resources

CURRENCY Libyan dinar
GPD (US$) 13.3 billion (2002 est)
REAL GDP GROWTH (% change on previous year) 3.1 (2001)
CONSUMER PRICE INFLATION 2.4% (2003 est)
UNEMPLOYMENT 30% (2000)
FOREIGN DEBT (US$) 5.1 billion (2001 est)
MAJOR TRADING PARTNERS Italy, Germany, Spain, UK, France, Turkey, Tunisia, South Korea
RESOURCES petroleum, natural gas, iron ore, potassium, magnesium, sulphur, gypsum
INDUSTRIES petroleum refining, processing of agricultural products, cement and other building materials, fish processing and canning, textiles, clothing and footwear
EXPORTS crude petroleum and natural gas (accounted for 95% of 2000 export earnings), chemicals and related products. Principal market: Italy 42% (2000)
IMPORTS machinery and transport equipment, basic manufactures, food and live animals, miscellaneous manufactured articles. Principal source: Italy 25.4% (2000)
ARABLE LAND 1% (2000 est)
AGRICULTURAL PRODUCTS barley, wheat, grapes, olives, dates; livestock rearing (sheep, goats, and camels); fishing

Population and society

POPULATION 5,551,000 (2003 est)
POPULATION GROWTH RATE 1.9% (2000–15)

LIBYA This stamp shows US troops departing from their Libyan base in 1970. Each June there is a national holiday celebrating Evacuation Day.
Stanley Gibbons

Chronology

7th century BC: Tripolitania, in western Libya, was settled by Phoenicians, who founded Tripoli; it became an eastern province of Carthaginian kingdom, which was centred on Tunis to the west.

4th century BC: Cyrenaica, in eastern Libya, colonized by Greeks, who called it Libya.

74 BC: Became a Roman province, with Tripolitania part of Africa Nova province and Cyrenaica combined with Crete as a province.

19 BC: The desert region of Fezzan (Phazzania), inhabited by Garmante people, was conquered by Rome.

6th century AD: Came under control of Byzantine Empire.

7th century: Conquered by Arabs, who spread Islam: Egypt ruled Cyrenaica and Morrocan Berber Almohads controlled Tripolitania.

mid-16th century: Became part of Turkish Ottoman Empire, who combined the three ancient regions into one regency in Tripoli.

1711: Karamanli (Qaramanli) dynasty established virtual independence from Ottomans.

1835: Ottoman control reasserted.

1911–12: Conquered by Italy.

1920s: Resistance to Italian rule by Sanusi order and Umar al-Mukhtar.

1934: Colony named Libya.

1942: Italians ousted, and area divided into three provinces: Fezzan (under French control), Cyrenaica, and Tripolitania (under British control).

1951: Achieved independence as United Kingdom of Libya, under King Idris, former Amir of Cyrenaica and leader of Sanusi order.

1959: Discovery of oil transformed economy, but also led to unsettling social changes.

1969: King deposed in military coup led by Col Moamer al Khaddhafi. Revolution Command Council set up and Arab Socialist Union (ASU) proclaimed the only legal party in a new puritanical Islamic-socialist republic which sought Pan-Arab unity.

1970s: Economic activity collectivized, oil industry nationalized, opposition suppressed by Khaddhafi's revolutionary regime.

1972: Proposed federation of Libya, Syria, and Egypt abandoned.

1980: A proposed merger with Syria was abandoned. Libyan troops began fighting in northern Chad.

1986: The US bombed Khaddhafi's headquarters, following allegations of his complicity in terrorist activities.

1988: Diplomatic relations with Chad were restored, political prisoners were freed, and the economy was liberalized.

1989: The US navy shot down two Libyan planes. There was a reconciliation with Egypt.

1992: Khaddhafi came under international pressure to extradite the alleged terrorists suspected of planting a bomb on a plane that crashed in Lockerbie in Scotland for trial outside Libya. UN sanctions were imposed; several countries severed diplomatic and air links with Libya.

1995: There was an antigovernment campaign of violence by Islamicists. Hundreds of Palestinians and thousands of foreign workers were expelled.

1999: Lockerbie suspects were handed over for trial in the Netherlands, to be tried by Scottish judges. Having handed over the suspects, and after Libya paid compensation to the family of PC Yvonne Fletcher, who was murdered outside the Libyan Embassy in London in 1984, full diplomatic relations with the UK were restored and UN sanctions were suspended.

2000: Khaddhafi installed a new head of government, Prime Minister Mubarak al-Shamikh.

2001: Libyan national Abdelbaset Ali Mohmed al-Megrahi was found guilty of the Lockerbie bombing.

2002: Libya withdrew from the Arab League.

2003: Colonel Khaddhafi confirmed that his regime had sought to develop weapons of mass destruction (WMD) but, following negotiations with the USA and UK, planned to dismantle all covert programmes and open the country's sites to international inspection.

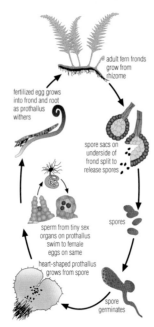

LIFE CYCLE The life cycle of a fern. Ferns have two distinct forms that alternate during their life cycle. For the main part of its life, a fern consists of a short stem (or rhizome) from which roots and leaves grow. The other part of its life is spent as a small heart-shaped plant called a prothallus. See entry on p. 554.

Diagram labels:
- adult fern fronds grow from rhizome
- fertilized egg grows into frond and root as prothallus withers
- spore sacs on underside of frond split to release spores
- spores
- sperm from tiny sex organs on prothallus swim to female eggs on same
- heart-shaped prothallus grows from spore
- spore germinates

life expectancy average lifespan that can be presumed of a person at birth. It depends on nutrition, disease control, environmental contaminants, war, stress, and living standards in general.

life sciences scientific study of the living world as a whole, a new synthesis of several traditional scientific disciplines including ▷biology, ▷zoology, and ▷botany, and newer, more specialized areas of study such as ▷biophysics and ▷sociobiology.

LIFFE (acronym for London International Financial Futures and Options Exchange) one of the exchanges in London where ▷futures contracts are traded. It opened in September 1982. By 1998 it was the largest futures and options exchange in Europe.

Liffey river in the east of the Republic of Ireland; length 129 km/80 mi. The Liffey is formed by two streams that rise in the Wicklow Mountains near Enniskerry. It flows through County Kildare, past Kilcullen and Newbridge, and into Dublin Bay. The **Liffey Plain** is excellent land for pasture, and has the lowest rainfall in the Republic of Ireland.

ligament strong, flexible connective tissue, made of the protein ▷collagen, which joins bone to bone at moveable joints and sometimes encloses the joints. Ligaments prevent bone dislocation (under normal circumstances) but allow joint flexion. The ligaments around the joints are composed of white fibrous tissue. Other ligaments are composed of yellow elastic tissue, which is adapted to support a continuous but varying stress, as in the ligament connecting the various cartilages of the ▷larynx (voice box).

Ligeti, György Sándor (1923–) Hungarian-born Austrian composer. He developed a dense, highly

LIGHT BULB The first electric light bulb, invented by Thomas Edison, had carbonized thread as its filament, and burned for 45 hours. Edison experimented with many other filaments, including red hair and a mixture of lamp black and tar. *Archive Photos*

chromatic, polyphonic style in which melody and rhythm are sometimes lost in shifting blocks of sound. He achieved international prominence with *Atmosphères* (1961) and *Requiem* (1965), which achieved widespread fame as background music for Stanley Kubrick's film epic *2001: A Space Odyssey* (1968). Other works include an opera *Le Grand Macabre* (1978) and *Poème symphonique* (1962), for 100 metronomes.

light ▷electromagnetic waves in the visible range, having a wavelength from about 400 nanometres in the extreme violet to about 770 nanometres in the extreme red. Light is considered to exhibit particle and wave properties, and the fundamental particle, or quantum, of light is called the photon. The speed of light (and of all electromagnetic radiation) in a vacuum is approximately 300,000 km/186,000 mi per second, and is a universal constant denoted by *c*.

Isaac ▷Newton was the first to discover, in 1666, that sunlight is composed of a mixture of light of different colours in certain proportions and that it could be separated into its components by dispersion. Before his time it was supposed that dispersion of light produced colour instead of separating already existing colours. The ancients believed that light travelled at infinite speed; its finite speed was first discovered by Danish astronomer Ole Römer in 1676.

Related Web site: Light! http://library.thinkquest.org/28160/

light bulb incandescent filament lamp, first demonstrated by Joseph Swan in the UK in 1878 and Thomas Edison in the USA in 1879. The present-day light bulb is a thin glass bulb filled with an inert mixture of nitrogen and argon gas. It contains a filament made of fine tungsten wire. When electricity is passed through the wire, it glows white hot, producing light.

light-emitting diode (LED) electronic component that converts electrical energy into light or infrared radiation in the range of 550 nm (green light) to 1300 nm (infrared). They are used for displaying symbols in electronic instruments and devices. An LED is a ▷diode made of ▷semiconductor material, such as gallium arsenide phosphide, that glows when electricity is passed through it. The first digital watches and calculators had LED displays, but many later models use ▷liquid-crystal displays.

lighthouse structure carrying a powerful light to warn ships or aeroplanes that they are approaching a place (usually land) dangerous or important to navigation. The light is magnified and directed out to the horizon or up to the zenith by a series of mirrors or prisms. Increasingly lighthouses are powered by electricity and automated rather than staffed; the more recent models also emit radio signals.

Related Web site: Lighthouse Society of Great Britain http://www.lsgb.co.uk/

LIGHTHOUSE This lighthouse is at Tranoy, Norway. Lighthouses are built either on the seabed, or onshore, and provide shipping traffic with a guide for coastal navigation. *Image Bank*

lightning high-voltage electrical discharge between two charged rainclouds or between a cloud and the Earth, caused by the build-up of electrical charges. Air in the path of lightning ionizes (becomes conducting), and expands; the accompanying noise is heard as thunder. Currents of 20,000 amperes and temperatures of 30,000°C/54,000°F are common. Lightning causes nitrogen oxides to form in the atmosphere and approximately 25% of the atmospheric nitrogen oxides are formed in this way.

According to a 1997 US survey on lightning strength and frequency, using information gathered from satellite images and data from the US Lightning Detection Network, there are 70–100 lightning flashes per second worldwide, with an average peak current of 36 kiloamps. See diagram on p. 558.

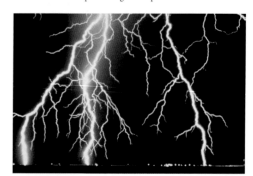

LIGHTNING Lightning at a power plant in Red Rock, Arizona, USA. *Image Bank*

Lightning conductor device that protects a tall building from lightning strike by providing an easier path for current to flow to earth than through the building. It consists of a thick copper strip of very low resistance connected to the ground below. A good connection to the ground is essential and is made by burying a large metal plate deep in the damp earth. In the event of a direct lightning strike, the current in the conductor may be so great as to melt or even vaporize the metal, but the damage to the building will nevertheless be limited.

light watt unit of radiant power (brightness of light). One light watt is the power required to produce a perceived brightness equal to that of light at a wavelength of 550 nanometres and 680 lumens.

light year in astronomy, the distance travelled by a beam of light in a vacuum in one year, approximately 9.4605×10^{12} km/5.9128×10^{12} mi.

lignin naturally occurring substance produced by plants to strengthen their tissues. It is difficult for ▷enzymes to attack lignin, so living organisms cannot digest wood, with the exception of a few specialized fungi and bacteria. Lignin is the essential ingredient of all wood and is, therefore, of great commercial importance.

lignite type of ▷coal that is brown and fibrous, with a relatively low carbon content. As a fuel it is less efficient because more of it must be burned to produce the same amount of energy generated by bituminous coal. Lignite also has a high sulphur content and is more polluting. It is burned to generate power in Scandinavia and some former eastern block countries because it is the only fuel resource available without importing.

Liguria coastal region of northwest Italy, which lies between the western Alps and the Gulf of Genoa in the Mediterranean, comprising the provinces of Genova, La Spezia, Imperia, and Savona; area 5,418 sq km/2,093 sq mi; population (2001 est) 1,560,800. ▷Genoa is the chief city and port. The region includes the resorts of the Italian Riviera and tourism is very important. Industries include shipbuilding, heavy engineering, horticulture, and the production of chemicals, metals, and textiles.

Likud alliance of right-wing Israeli political parties that defeated the Labour Party coalition in the May 1977 election and brought Menachem Begin to power. In 1987 Likud became part of an uneasy national coalition with Labour, formed to solve Israel's economic crisis. In 1989 another coalition was formed under Yitzhak Shamir. Likud was defeated by the Labour Party in the 1992 general election. Under the leadership of Binjamin Netanyahu 1993–1999 and Ariel Sharon since 1999, it adopted a much harder line than Labour in the Middle East peace process. In May 1996 Netanyahu became Israel's first directly-elected prime minister, forming a Likud-led government. He was defeated in May 1999 by Ehud Barak of the Labour party, who in turn was defeated by Sharon in 2001.

lilac any of a group of flowering Old World shrubs, with clusters (panicles) of small, sweetly scented, white or purple flowers on the main stems. The common lilac (*S. vulgaris*) is a popular garden ornamental. (Genus *Syringa*, family Oleaceae.)

Lilienthal, Otto (1848–1896) German aviation pioneer who inspired US aviators Orville and Wilbur ▷Wright. From 1891 he made and successfully flew many gliders, including two biplanes, before he was killed in a glider crash.

Lille (Flemish **Ryssel** or **Russel**; Latin **Insula**; *l'ile* 'island') industrial city and administrative centre of the Nord *département* in the Nord-Pas-de-Calais region of France, on the River Deûle; population (1999 est) 182,200, metropolitan area 936,000. The world's first entirely automatic underground train system was opened here in 1982. The Eurostar train stops here, at the new Eurolille station. Industries include textiles, chemicals, engineering, and distilling.

Lillee, Dennis Keith (1949–) Australian cricketer. He is regarded as the best fast bowler of his generation. He made his Test debut in the 1970–71 season and subsequently played for his country 70 times. Lillee took 355 wickets in Test cricket. He played Sheffield Shield cricket for Western Australia and at the end of his career made a comeback with Tasmania.

Lilongwe capital of ▷Malawi since 1975, on the Lilongwe River; population (2001 est) 473,000. Products include tobacco, groundnuts, and textiles. Capital Hill, 5 km/3 mi from the old city, is the site of government buildings and offices.

lily any of a group of plants belonging to the lily family, of which there are about 80 species, most with showy, trumpet-shaped flowers growing from bulbs. The lily family includes hyacinths, tulips, asparagus, and plants of the onion genus. The name 'lily' is also applied to many lilylike plants of related genera and families. (Genus *Lilium*, family Liliaceae.)

lily of the valley plant belonging to the lily family, growing in woods in Europe, northern Asia, and North America. The small bell-shaped white flowers hang downwards from short stalks attached to a central stem; they are strongly scented. The plant is often cultivated. (*Convallaria majalis*, family Liliaceae.) See picture on p. 558.

Lima capital and largest city of Peru, on the River Rimac, 13 km/8 mi from its Pacific port of Callao; population (1993) 5,706,100. It comprises about one-third of the country's total population. Industries include textiles, chemicals, glass, and cement.

Features Surviving structures of the Spanish colonial period include the National University of San Marcos, founded in 1551, and the oldest in the Western Hemisphere; the government palace (the rebuilt palace of the viceroys); the Senate House, originally the headquarters of the Inquisition; the church of Santo Domingo built on land granted to a Dominican friar in 1535 (built 1540–99); La Merced church, built on the site of the first mass in Lima in 1534. The cathedral, begun in 1555 and built on the southeastern side of the Plaza de Armas, was destroyed by earthquakes and was reconstructed several times, most recently in 1746. A third of the population live in overcrowded shanty towns (Pueblo Jóvenes) on the outskirts of the city.

History It was founded as Ciudad de los Reyes (City of the Kings) by the Spaniard Francisco Pizarro in January 1535, and became the seat of the Spanish viceroys of Peru; it was rebuilt after its destruction by an earthquake in 1746.

limbo in Christian theology, a region for the souls of those who were not admitted to the divine vision. *Limbus infantum* was a place where unbaptized infants enjoyed inferior blessedness, and *limbus patrum* was where the prophets of the Old Testament dwelt. The word was first used in this sense in the 13th century by Thomas Aquinas.

Liechtenstein

Liechtenstein landlocked country in west-central Europe, bounded east by Austria and west by Switzerland.

NATIONAL NAME *Fürstentum Liechtenstein*/Principality of Liechtenstein
AREA 160 sq km/62 sq mi
CAPITAL Vaduz
MAJOR TOWNS/CITIES Balzers, Schaan, Ruggell, Triesen, Eschen
PHYSICAL FEATURES landlocked Alpine; includes part of Rhine Valley in west

Government

HEAD OF STATE Prince Hans Adam II from 1989
HEAD OF GOVERNMENT Otmar Hasler from 2001
POLITICAL SYSTEM liberal democracy
POLITICAL EXECUTIVE parliamentary
ADMINISTRATIVE DIVISIONS 11 communes
ARMED FORCES no standing army since 1868; there is a police force of 59 men and 19 auxiliaries
DEATH PENALTY abolished in 1987

Economy and resources

CURRENCY Swiss franc
GPD (US$) 1.14 billion (1999)
REAL GDP GROWTH (% change on previous year) 1.5 (1999)
GNI PER CAPITA (PPP) (US$) 24,000 (1998 est)
CONSUMER PRICE INFLATION 0.7% (2003 est)
UNEMPLOYMENT 1.1% (2000)

MAJOR TRADING PARTNERS Switzerland and other EFTA countries, EU countries
RESOURCES hydro power
INDUSTRIES small machinery, textiles, ceramics, chemicals, furniture, precision instruments, pharmaceutical products, heating appliances, financial services, tourism
EXPORTS small machinery, artificial teeth and other material for dentistry, stamps, precision instruments, ceramics. Principal market: Switzerland 14.5% (1996)
IMPORTS machinery and transport equipment, foodstuffs, textiles, metal goods. Principal source: European Economic Area (EEA) 45.4% (1996)
ARABLE LAND 25% (2000 est)
AGRICULTURAL PRODUCTS maize, potatoes; cattle rearing and dairy farming

Population and society

POPULATION 34,000 (2003 est)
POPULATION GROWTH RATE 1.1% (2000–05)
POPULATION DENSITY (per sq km) 216 (2003 est)
URBAN POPULATION (% of total) 22 (2003 est)
AGE DISTRIBUTION (% of total population) 0–14 18%, 15–59 69%, 60+ 13% (2001 est)
ETHNIC GROUPS indigenous population of Alemannic origin; one-third of the population are foreign-born resident

workers (mainly Italian and Turkish)
LANGUAGE German (official), an Alemannic dialect
RELIGION Roman Catholic 80%, Protestant 7%
EDUCATION (compulsory years) 8
LITERACY RATE 99% (men); 99% (women) (2003 est)

Chronology

c. AD 500: Settled by Germanic-speaking Alemanni tribe.
1342: Became a sovereign state.
1434: Present boundaries established.
1719: Former independent lordships of Schellenberg and Vaduz were united by Princes of Liechtenstein to form the present state.
1815–66: A member of the German Confederation.
1868: Abolished standing armed forces.
1871: Liechtenstein was the only German principality to stay outside the newly formed German Empire.
1918: Patriotic Union (VU) party founded, drawing most support from the mountainous south.
1919: Switzerland replaced Austria as the foreign representative of Liechtenstein.

LABOUR FORCE 1.5% agriculture, 46% industry, 52.5% services (1996)
LIFE EXPECTANCY 79 (men); 84 (women) (2000–05)
CHILD MORTALITY RATE (under 5, per 1,000 live births) 11 (2001)
TV SETS (per 1,000 people) 483 (2000)
RADIOS (per 1,000 people) 686 (1997)

1921: Adopted Swiss currency; constitution created a parliament.
1923: United with Switzerland in customs and monetary union.
1938: Prince Franz Josef II came to power.
1970: After 42 years as the main governing party, the northern-based Progressive Citizens' Party (FBP) was defeated by VU which, except for 1974–78, became a dominant force in politics.
1978: Joined the Council of Europe.
1984: The franchise was extended to women in the national elections.
1989: Prince Franz Josef II died; he was succeeded by Hans Adam II.
1990: Joined the United Nations.
1991: Became the seventh member of the European Free Trade Association.
1993: Mario Frick of VU became Europe's youngest head of government, aged 28, after two general elections.
2001: Otmar Hasler was elected prime minister.

LIECHTENSTEIN The church and church hall in Planken. Liechtenstein is divided into 11 administrative regions, called communes or *gemeinden*, which have considerable autonomy and are governed by mayors and city councils. Planken is the smallest commune in terms of population, with just over 300 inhabitants. *Liechtenstein Government Press and Information Office*

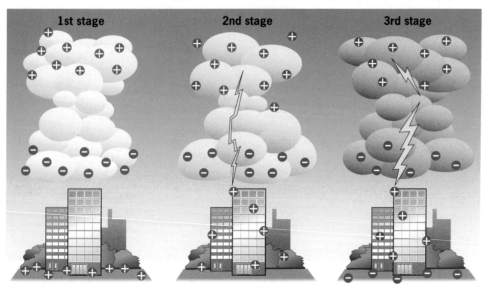

1st stage **2nd stage** **3rd stage**

LIGHTNING The build-up of electrical charge during a thunderstorm that causes lightning. Negative charge builds up at the bottom of a cloud; positive charges rise from the ground and also within the cloud, moving to the top of it. A conducting channel forms through the cloud and a giant spark jumps between opposite charges causing lightning to strike within the cloud and from cloud to ground. See entry on p. 556.

Limbourg (Flemish **Limburg**) province of northeast Belgium, bounded north and east by the Netherlands; the River Meuse marks the frontier; area 2,422 sq km/935 sq mi; population (1997) 780,000. The capital is Hasselt, and Genk and Tongeren are other towns. The province includes the River Demer, Kempen heathland in the north, rich coalfields, and agriculture in the south. Industries include coal, sugar refining, food processing, chemicals, electronics, engineering, glass, and metallurgy. Agriculture includes dairy farming and market gardening. The province was formerly part of the feudal duchy of Limburg (which was divided in 1839 into today's Belgian and Dutch provinces).

Limbourg brothers Franco-Flemish painters, **Paul** (Pol), **Herman**, and **Jan** (Hennequin, Janneken), active in the late 14th and early 15th centuries, first in Paris, then at the ducal court of Burgundy. They produced richly detailed manuscript illuminations, including two Books of ▷Hours. Patronized by Jean de France, duc de Berry, from about 1404, they illustrated two Books of Hours that are masterpieces of the International Gothic style, the Belles Heures about 1408 (Metropolitan Museum of Art, New York), and Les Tres Riches Heures du Duc de Berry about 1413–15 (Musée Conde Chaantilly). Their miniture paintings include a series of scenes representing the months, presenting an almost fairytale world of pinnacled castles with lords and ladies, full of detail and brilliant decorative effects. All three brothers were dead by 1416.

LILY OF THE VALLEY Widely cultivated for its beautiful, fragrant, white, nodding flowers, the lily of the valley is native to woods in the northern hemisphere. Small, detachable buds ('pips') can be force-grown for indoor blooms in winter. See entry on p.557. *Image Bank*

Limburg southernmost province of the Netherlands, bounded by Germany to the east, Belgium to the west and south, and North Brabant to the north; area 2,170 sq km/838 sq mi; population (1997) 1,136,200. The capital is ▷Maastricht, and Kerkrade, Heerlen, and Roermond are other towns. The province includes the Maas (Meuse) and Roer rivers, and features sandy soils in river plain, marl soils in the south, and is hilly towards the south. Industries include chemicals, cement, and fertilizers, and agriculture includes mixed arable farming, and horticulture.

lime (or **quicklime**) CaO (technical name **calcium oxide**) white powdery substance used in making mortar and cement. It is made commercially by heating calcium carbonate ($CaCO_3$), obtained from limestone or chalk, in a lime kiln. Quicklime readily absorbs water to become calcium hydroxide $Ca(OH)_2$, known as slaked lime, which is used to reduce soil acidity.

lime sharp-tasting green or greenish-yellow citrus fruit of the small thorny lime bush, native to India. The white flowers are followed by the fruits, which resemble lemons but are more round in shape; they are rich in vitamin C. (*Citrus aurantifolia*, family Rutaceae.)

lime (or **linden**) any of a group of ▷deciduous trees native to the northern hemisphere. The leaves are heart-shaped and coarsely toothed, and the flowers are cream-coloured and fragrant. (Genus *Tilia*, family Tiliaceae.)

Limerick county of the Republic of Ireland, in the province of Munster; county town ▷Limerick; area 2,690 sq km/1,038 sq mi; population (1996) 165,000. The principal river is the ▷Shannon, and towns include Abbeyfeale, Kilmallock, Newcastle West, and Rathkeale. Limerick is hilly in the southwest (Mullaghreirk Mountains) and in the northeast (Galtee Mountains). The low-lying region in the west is very fertile, and is known as the 'Golden Vale'. Dairy cattle, sheep, pigs, and poultry are reared extensively, and corn, sugar-beet, and potatoes are grown. Lace is also produced.

Limerick county town of County ▷Limerick and fourth-largest city in the Republic of Ireland, on the Shannon estuary; population (1996) 79,000. The city is divided into three parts: English Town, which is the old city on King's Island (an island in the Shannon estuary); Irish Town; and Newtown Pery, which now forms the centre of the modern city. Industries include flour milling, tanning, meat products, and brewing. The **University of Limerick**, 5 km/3 mi north of the city, is a modern campus.

limerick five-line humorous verse, often nonsensical, which first appeared in England about 1820 and was popularized by Edward ▷Lear. An example is: 'There was a young lady of Riga, Who rode with a smile on a tiger; They returned from the ride With the lady inside, And the smile on the face of the tiger.'

limestone sedimentary rock composed chiefly of calcium carbonate $CaCO_3$, either derived from the shells of marine organisms or precipitated from solution, mostly in the ocean. Various types of limestone are used as building stone.

limestone pavement bare rock surface resembling a block of chocolate, found on limestone plateaus. It is formed by the weathering of limestone into individual upstanding blocks, called clints, separated from each other by joints, called grykes. The weathering process is thought to entail a combination of freeze-thaw (the alternate freezing and thawing of ice in cracks) and carbonation (the dissolving of minerals in the limestone by weakly acidic rainwater). Malham Tarn in North Yorkshire is an example of a limestone pavement.

Limitation, Statutes of in English law, acts of Parliament limiting the time within which legal action must be inaugurated. Actions for breach of contract and most other civil wrongs must be started within six years. Personal injury claims must usually be brought within three years. In actions in respect of land and of contracts under seal, the period is 12 years.

limited company company for whose debts the members are liable only to a limited extent. The capital of a limited company is divided into small units, and profits are distributed according to shareholding.

limited liability legal safeguard that allows shareholders to be liable for their company's debts only up to and including the value of their shareholding. For example, if a limited liability company goes bankrupt with debts of £1 million, the shareholders are not liable for any of that debt, although the value of their shares in the company would be worthless.

limiting factor in biology, any factor affecting the rate of a metabolic reaction. Levels of light or of carbon dioxide are limiting factors in ▷photosynthesis because both are necessary for the production of carbohydrates. In experiments, photosynthesis is observed to slow down and eventually stop as the levels of light decrease.

limits, territorial and fishing the limits of sea area to which an adjoining coastal state can claim territorial or fishing rights under ▷maritime law.

LIMESTONE The edge of a limestone quarry in the UK. The cliff face reveals the various 'beach levels', where the shells of tiny marine organisms were laid down over vast periods of time. Towards the camera (now largely worked out) would have been stratum upon stratum of compressed shells forming a consistent mass of limestone that was once the sea bed. *Image Bank*

limnology study of lakes and other bodies of open fresh water, in terms of their plant and animal biology, chemistry, and physical properties.

Limnos Greek name for ▷Lemnos.

Limoges administrative centre of the *département* of Haute-Vienne and of the ▷Limousin region, central France, situated on the River Vienne, 175 km/109 mi northeast of Bordeaux; population (1990) 136,400. It is the centre of the modern French porcelain industry; other industries include shoes, textiles, electrical equipment, and metal goods. Fine enamels were made here as early as Merovingian times, and their production flourished in the 12th century. The city was sacked by the Black Prince, the eldest son of Edward III of England, in 1370. It has a university.

Limousin modern planning region and former province of central France; area 16,900 sq km/6,544 sq mi; population (1990) 722,900. The modern region consists of the *départements* of Corrèze, Creuse, and Haute-Vienne. The administrative centre is ▷Limoges; Brive-la-Gaillarde, Tulle, and Gueret are the other towns of note. A thinly populated and largely infertile region, it is crossed by the mountains of the Massif Central. Fruit and vegetables are produced in the more fertile lowlands. Kaolin is mined here.

limpet any of various marine ▷snails belonging to several families and genera, found in the Atlantic and Pacific oceans. A limpet has a conical shell and adheres firmly to rocks by its disclike foot. Limpets leave their fixed positions only to graze on seaweeds, always returning to the same spot. The **common limpet** (*P. vulgata*) can be seen on rocks at low tide (especially genera *Acmaea* and *Patella*).

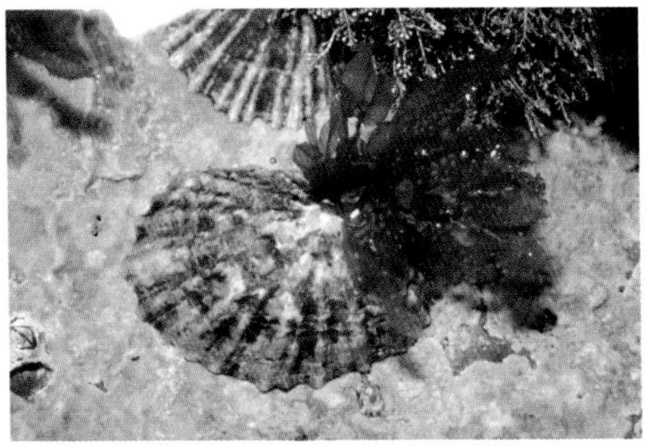

LIMPET The common limpet *Patella vulgata*, found on rocky shores in the cooler regions of the Atlantic and the Pacific, is a true limpet. It does not have a small hole in its shell through which to expel waste matter. *Premaphotos Wildlife*

Limpopo river in southeast Africa, rising in the Magaliesberg to the west of Pretoria in Gauteng Province, South Africa, and flowing through Mozambique to the Indian Ocean at Delagoa Bay; length 1,600 km/1,000 mi. It is also known as Crocodile River.

Lin Biao (or Lin Piao) (1908–1971) Chinese communist soldier and politician, deputy leader of the Chinese Communist Party 1969–71. He joined the communists in 1927, became a commander of ▷Mao Zedong's Red Army, and led the Northeast People's Liberation Army after 1945 during the ▷Chinese revolution (1927–49). He became defence minister in 1959, and as vice chair of the party from 1969 he was expected to be Mao's successor. In 1972 the government announced that Lin had been killed in an aeroplane crash in Mongolia on 17 September 1971 while fleeing to the USSR following an abortive coup attempt.

Lincoln industrial and cathedral city, administrative headquarters of ▷Lincolnshire, England, situated on the River Witham, 210 km/130 mi north of London; population (1991) 80,300. Products include bricks, excavators, cranes, gas turbines, radios, vehicle components, cattle feed, matting, pharmaceuticals, power units for oil platforms, and cosmetics. Other industries include heavy engineering, iron foundries, seed milling, and food processing.

During the Roman period, Lincoln was the flourishing colony of **Lindum**, and in the Middle Ages it was a centre for the wool trade. Paulinus built a church here in the 7th century, and the 11th–15th-century cathedral has the earliest Gothic work in Britain. The 12th-century High Bridge is the oldest in Britain still to have buildings on it.

Lincoln industrial city and capital of ▷Nebraska, USA, 80 km/50 mi southwest of Omaha in the southeastern part of the state; seat of Lancaster County; population (1994 est) 203,000. It is the centre of a rich agricultural area; industries include processed food, railway rolling stock, engineering, pharmaceuticals, electronic and electrical equipment, and small motor vehicles and motor cycles.

Lincoln, Abraham (1809–1865) 16th president of the USA 1861–65, a Republican. In the American ▷Civil War, his chief concern was the preservation of the Union from which the Confederate (Southern) slave states had seceded on his election. In 1863 he announced the freedom of the slaves with the Emancipation Proclamation. He was re-elected in 1864 with victory for the North in sight, but was assassinated at the end of the war.

Early career Lincoln was born in a log cabin in Kentucky. Self-educated, he practised law from 1837 in Springfield, Illinois. He was a member of the state legislature 1832–42, during which period he was known as Honest Abe, and in 1846 sat in Congress, although his law practice remained his priority. The repeal of the Missouri Compromise in 1854 and the reopening of the debate on the extension of slavery in the new territories of the USA drew him back into politics. He joined the new Republican Party in 1856 and two years later was chosen as their candidate for senator in Illinois, opposing the incumbent Stephen Douglas, who had been largely responsible for repeal of the Compromise. In the ensuing debate, Lincoln revealed his power as an orator, but failed to wrest the post from Douglas. However, he had established a national reputation and in 1860 was chosen by the Republicans, now pledged to oppose the extension of slavery, as their presidential candidate. He was elected on a minority vote, defeating Douglas and another Democratic Party candidate.

Presidency Prior to Lincoln's inauguration, seven Southern states proclaimed their formal secession from the Union. Lincoln's inaugural address in March 1861 was conciliatory: he declared he had no intention of interfering with slavery where it already existed, but pronounced the Union indissoluble, declaring that no state had the right to secede from it. His refusal to concede to Confederate demands for the evacuation of the federal garrison at Fort Sumter, Charleston, South Carolina the following month precipitated the first hostilities of the Civil War.

In 1862, following an important Union victory at Antietam, Lincoln proclaimed the emancipation of all slaves in states engaged in rebellion, thereby surpassing the limits of the constitution he had gone to war to maintain. In the Gettysburg Address in 1863 he declared the aims of preserving a 'nation conceived in liberty, and dedicated to the proposition that all men are created equal'. With the war turning in favour of the North, he was re-elected in 1864 with a large majority on a National Union ticket, having advocated a reconciliatory policy towards the South 'with malice towards none, with charity for all'.

Five days after General Lee's surrender, Lincoln was shot in a theatre audience by an actor and Confederate sympathizer, John Wilkes ▷Booth.

Related Web site: Abraham Lincoln – sixteenth president 1861–1865 http://www.whitehouse.gov/WH/glimpse/presidents/html/al16.html

> **Abraham Lincoln**
> *The ballot is stronger than the bullet.*
> Speech, 19 May 1856

Lincolnshire county of eastern England.
area 5,890 sq km/2,274 sq mi **towns and cities** ▷Lincoln (administrative headquarters), Skegness, Boston, Stamford **physical** hills of Lincoln Edge and the Wolds; marshy coastline; the Fens in the southeast; rivers Trent, Welland, Witham **features** Belton House, a Restoration mansion; Gibraltar Point National Nature Reserve **agriculture** cattle, sheep, horses; cereals (mainly barley); flower bulbs (largest bulb-growing industry in the UK, around Spalding); vegetables **population** (1996) 615,900 **famous people** Isaac Newton, Alfred Tennyson, Margaret Thatcher, John Wesley

Lincs abbreviation for ▷Lincolnshire, an English county.

Lindbergh, Charles A(ugustus) (1902–1974) US aviator. He made the first solo nonstop flight in 33.5 hours across the Atlantic (Roosevelt Field, Long Island, New York, to Le Bourget airport, Paris) in 1927 in the *Spirit of St Louis*, a Ryan monoplane designed by him.

Lindbergh was born in Detroit, Michigan. He was a barnstorming pilot before attending the US Army School in Texas 1924 and becoming an officer in the Army Air Service Reserve 1925. Learning that Raymond B Orteig had offered a prize of £25,000 for the person who first made a nonstop air flight between New York and Paris, he appealed to some St Louis businessmen who agreed to finance him.

Related Web site: American Experience: Lindbergh http://www.pbs.org/wgbh/pages/amex/lindbergh/

linden another name for the ▷lime tree.

Lindisfarne Gospels (or St Cuthbert's Evangelistarium) Celtic manuscript conceived as a memorial volume to St Cuthbert, who died in 687, held in the British Museum, London. It was produced at the Anglo-Irish monastery of Lindisfarne on Holy Island, Northumberland. Its decorative interlaced ornament is similar in style to that of the Book of Kells, now in Trinity College, Dublin (see ▷Kells, Book of).

linear accelerator (or linac) in physics, a type of particle ▷accelerator in which the particles move along a straight tube.

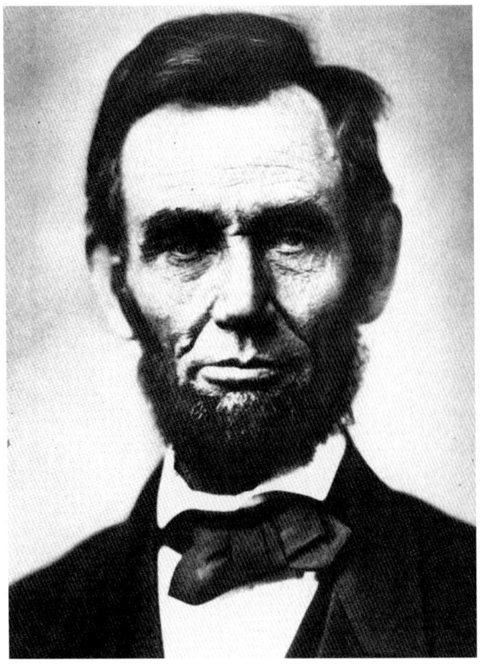

ABRAHAM LINCOLN US president Abraham Lincoln. Lincoln, a Republican, was the 16th president of the USA. He was assassinated in 1865, five days after the surrender of the Confederate forces in the American Civil War. *Archive Photos*

Particles pass through a linear accelerator only once – unlike those in a cyclotron or synchrotron (ring-shaped accelerators), which make many revolutions, gaining energy each time.

linear equation in mathematics, a relationship between two variables that, when plotted on Cartesian axes produces a straight-line graph; the equation has the general form $y = mx + c$, where m is the slope of the line represented by the equation and c is the y-intercept, or the value of y where the line crosses the y-axis in the ▷Cartesian coordinate system. Sets of linear equations can be used to describe the behaviour of buildings, bridges, trusses, and other static structures.

linear motor type of electric motor, an induction motor in which the fixed stator and moving armature are straight and parallel to each other (rather than being circular and one inside the other as in an ordinary induction motor). Linear motors are used, for example, to power sliding doors. There is a magnetic force between the stator and armature; this force has been used to support a vehicle, as in the experimental ▷maglev linear motor train.

Lineker, Gary (1960–) English footballer and television presenter. He scored over 250 goals in 550 games for Leicester, Everton, Barcelona, and Tottenham. With 48 goals in 80 internationals he failed by one goal to equal Bobby Charlton's record of 49 goals for England. Lineker was elected Footballer of the Year in 1986 and 1992, and was leading scorer at the 1986 World Cup finals. In 1993 he moved to Japan to play for Nagoya Grampus Eight but retired a year later. Turning to television, he has appeared as a contestant on several series of the game show *They Think It's All Over*, and as a presenter on the football highlights programme *Match of the Day*, for the BBC.

linen yarn spun and the textile woven from the fibres of the stem of the ▷flax plant. Used by the ancient Egyptians, linen was introduced by the Romans to northern Europe, where production became widespread. Religious refugees from the Low Countries in the 16th century helped to establish the linen industry in England, but here and elsewhere it began to decline in competition with cotton in the 18th century.

line printer computer ▷printer that prints a complete line of characters at a time. Line printers can achieve very high printing speeds of up to 2,500 lines a minute, but can print in only one typeface, cannot print graphics, and are very noisy. Today, most users prefer ▷laser printers.

ling any of several deepwater long-bodied fishes of the cod family found in the North Atlantic. (Genus *Molva*, family Gadidae.)

ling another name for common ▷heather.

lingua franca (Italian 'Frankish tongue') any language that is used as a means of communication by groups who do not themselves normally speak that language; for example, English is a lingua franca used by Japanese doing business in Finland, or by Swedes in Saudi Arabia. The term comes from the mixture of French, Italian, Spanish, Greek, Turkish, and Arabic that was spoken around the Mediterranean from the time of the Crusades until the 18th century.

linguistics scientific study of language. Linguistics has many branches, such as origins (historical linguistics), the changing way language is pronounced (phonetics), derivation of words through various languages (etymology), development of meanings (semantics), and the arrangement and modifications of words to convey a message (grammar).

linkage in genetics, the association between two or more genes that tend to be inherited together because they are on the same chromosome. The closer together they are on the chromosome, the less likely they are to be separated by crossing over (one of the processes of ▷recombination) and they are then described as being 'tightly linked'.

Linköping industrial town in southeastern Sweden; 172 km/107 mi southwest of Stockholm; population (1994) 130,500. Industries include hosiery, aircraft and engines, and tobacco. It has a 12th-century cathedral.

> **Carolus Linnaeus**
> *Nature does not make jumps.*
> Philosophia Botanica

Linnaeus, Carolus (1707–1778) (Latinized form of Carl von Linné) Swedish naturalist and physician. His botanical work *Systema naturae* (1735) contained his system for classifying plants into groups depending on shared characteristics (such as the number of stamens in flowers), providing a much-needed framework for identification. He also devised the concise and precise system for naming plants and animals, using one Latin (or Latinized) word to represent the genus and a second to distinguish the species.

For example, in the Latin name of the daisy, *Bellis perennis*, *Bellis* is the name of the genus to which the plant belongs, and *perennis* distinguishes the species from others of the same genus. By tradition the generic name always begins with a capital letter. The author who first described a particular species is often indicated after the name, for example, *Bellis perennis* Linnaeus, showing that the author was Linnaeus.

linnet small seed-eating bird belonging to the finch family, which is very abundant in Europe, Asia, and northwestern Africa. The male has a chestnut back with a pink breast and grey head, and a red breast and forehead during the breeding season; the female is mainly a dull brown. The linnet measures barely 13 cm/5 in length, begins to breed in April, and generally chooses low-lying bush for its home. The eggs, ranging from four to six in number, are a delicate pale blue streaked with a purplish brown. (Species *Acanthis cannabina*, family Fringillidae, order Passeriformes.)

linoleum (Latin *lini oleum* 'linseed oil') floor covering made from linseed oil, tall oil, rosin, cork, woodflour, chalk, clay, and pigments, pressed into sheets with a jute backing. Oxidation of the oil is accelerated by heating, so that the oil mixture solidifies into a tough, resilient material. Linoleum tiles have a backing made of polyester and glass.

Linotype trademark for a typesetting machine once universally used for newspaper work, which sets complete lines (slugs) of hot-metal type as operators type the copy at a keyboard. It was invented in the USA in 1884 by German-born Ottmar Mergenthaler. It has been replaced by phototypesetting.

Lin Piao alternative transliteration of ▷Lin Biao.

linseed seeds of the ▷flax plant, from which linseed oil is produced, the residue being used as cattle feed. The oil is used in paint, wood treatments, and varnishes, and in the manufacture of linoleum floor coverings.

Linz capital and industrial river port of Upper Austria, in northern Austria, on the River Danube; population (1995) 201,500. Iron and steel production is a major industry powered by locally-sourced hydroelectricity. Other activities include metalworking, furnituremaking, and the manufacture of electrochemicals and clothing.

lion large wild cat with a tawny coat. The young have darker spot markings to camouflage them; these usually disappear in the adult. The male has a heavy mane and a tuft at the end of the tail. Head and body measure about 2 m/6 ft, plus 1 m/3 ft of tail; lionesses are slightly smaller. Lions produce litters of two to six cubs, and often live in groups (prides) of several adult males and females with young. They are carnivores (meat-eaters) and are found only in Africa, south of the Sahara desert, and in the Gir Forest of northwest India.

Behaviour Capable of short bursts of speed, lionesses do most of the hunting, working together to run down grazing animals. Females remain with the pride permanently; young males remain until they about three years old and one or more adult males (usually brothers) stay a couple of years or so until they are supplanted by a competing coalition of males. The incoming males, or male, kill all the cubs in a pride so that the lionesses become ready to breed again. When not hunting, lions spend most of their time dozing and sleeping. The average lifespan of a lion is 15–20 years in the wild and 20–25 years in captivity.

The Asiatic lion is listed on ▷CITES Appendix 1 (endangered); its total population numbered only 250–300 in 1996. 'Mountain lion' is a name for the ▷puma.

Classification Lions belong to the animal phylum Chordata, subphylum Vertebrata, class Mammalia (mammals), order Carnivora (carnivores). They belong to the cat family, Felidae, genus *Panthera* (which also includes tigers, leopards, and jaguars), species *P. Leo*.

Related Web site: African lion
http://www.seaworld.org/
animal_bytes/lionab.html

Lipari Islands (or Aeolian Islands) volcanic group of seven islands off northeastern Sicily, including **Lipari** (on which is the capital of the same name), **Stromboli** (active volcano 926 m/3,038 ft high), and **Vulcano** (also with an active volcano); area 114 sq km/44 sq mi. In Greek mythology, the god Aeolus kept the winds imprisoned in a cave on the Lipari Islands.

lipase enzyme responsible for breaking down fats into fatty acids and glycerol. It is produced by the ▷pancreas and requires a slightly alkaline environment. The products of fat digestion are absorbed by the intestinal wall.

Lipchitz, Jacques (1891–1973) Lithuanian-born sculptor. He was active in Paris from 1909 and emigrated to the USA in 1941. He was one of the first cubist sculptors, his best-known piece being *Man with a Guitar* (1916; Museum of Modern Art, New York). In the 1920s he experimented with small open forms he called 'transparents'. His later works, often political allegories, were characterized by heavy, contorted forms.

Li Peng (1928–) Chinese communist politician, a member of the Politburo from 1985, and prime minister 1987–98. During the prodemocracy demonstrations of 1989 he supported the massacre of students by Chinese troops and the subsequent execution of others. He sought improved relations with the USSR before its demise, and has favoured maintaining firm central and party control over the economy. In March 1998 Li stepped down as prime minister, being replaced by the more reformist Zhu Rongji. He was elected chairman of the National People's Congress (China's parliament), although an unprecedented 200 of the 2,950 delegates voted against his nomination.

Li was born at Chengdu in Sichuan province, the son of the writer Li Shouxun (who took part in the Nanchang rising in 1927

LINOLEUM Linoleum manufacturing in Kirkcaldy, Scotland. The various ingredients of linoleum are mixed, then pressed into sheet form by rollers and applied to a backing material such as jute or hardened canvas. This is then heated, which hardens the linoleum. *Image Bank*

LION The colour of an adult male lion's mane can range from a light beige to a brown so dark as to be almost black. On an adult male lion in captivity, the mane is generally far more extensive over the head and shoulders than on a wild lion. No satisfactory explanation has been provided for such variations. *Image Bank*

and was executed in 1930), and was adopted by the communist leader Zhou Enlai. He studied at the communist headquarters of Yan'an 1941–47 and trained as a hydroelectric engineer at the Moscow Power Institute from 1948. He was appointed minister of the electric power industry in 1981, a vice premier in 1983, and prime minister in 1987. In 1989 he launched the crackdown on demonstrators in Beijing that led to the massacre in ▷Tiananmen Square.

lipid any of a large number of esters of fatty acids, commonly formed by the reaction of a fatty acid with glycerol (see ▷glyceride). They are soluble in alcohol but not in water. Lipids are the chief constituents of plant and animal waxes, fats, and oils.

Phospholipids are lipids that also contain a phosphate group, usually linked to an organic base; they are major components of biological cell membranes.

Li Po (*c.* 705–762) Taoist Chinese poet of the Tang dynasty (618–907). He used traditional literary forms, but his exuberance, the boldness of his imagination, and the intensity of his feeling have won him recognition as perhaps the greatest of all Chinese poets. Although he was mostly concerned with higher themes, he is also remembered for his celebratory verses on drinking.

Lippershey, Hans (*c.* 1570–*c.* 1619) Dutch lensmaker, credited with inventing the telescope in 1608.

Lippi, Filippino (*c.* 1457–1504) Florentine painter. He was trained by his father Filippo ▷Lippi and ▷Botticelli. His most important works are frescoes in the Strozzi Chapel of Sta Maria Novella in Florence, painted in a graceful but also dramatic and at times bizarre style.

Lippi, Fra Filippo (*c.* 1406–1469) Florentine painter. His most important works include frescoes depicting the lives of St Stephen and St John the Baptist (1452–66; Prato Cathedral), which in their use of perspective and grouping of figures show the influence of ▷Masaccio. He also painted many altarpieces featuring the Madonna.

Lippmann, Gabriel (1845–1921) French doctor. He invented the direct colour process in photography. He was awarded the Nobel Prize for Physics in 1908 for his photographic reproduction of colours by interference.

liquefaction the process of converting a gas to a liquid, normally associated with low temperatures and high pressures (see ▷condensation).

liquefaction in earth science, the conversion of a soft deposit, such as clay, to a jellylike state by severe shaking. During an earthquake buildings and lines of communication built on materials prone to liquefaction will sink and topple. In the Alaskan earthquake of 1964 liquefaction led to the destruction of much of the city of Anchorage.

liquefied petroleum gas (LPG) liquid form of butane, propane, or pentane, produced by the distillation of petroleum during oil refining. At room temperature these substances are gases, although they can be easily liquefied and stored under pressure in metal containers. They are used for heating and cooking where other fuels are not available: camping stoves and cigarette lighters, for instance, often use liquefied butane as fuel.

liquid state of matter between a ▷solid and a ▷gas. A liquid forms a level surface and assumes the shape of its container. Its atoms do not occupy fixed positions as in a crystalline solid, nor do they have freedom of movement as in a gas. Unlike a gas, a liquid is difficult to compress since pressure applied at one point is equally transmitted throughout (Pascal's principle). ▷Hydraulics makes use of this property.

liquid air air that has been cooled so much that it has liquefied. This happens at temperatures below about −196°C/−321°F. The various constituent gases, including nitrogen, oxygen, argon, and neon, can be separated from liquid air by the technique of ▷fractionation.

liquidation in economics, the winding up of a company by converting all its assets into money to pay off its liabilities.

liquid-crystal display (LCD) display of numbers (for example, in a calculator) or pictures (such as on a pocket television screen) produced by molecules of a substance in a semiliquid state with some crystalline properties, so that clusters of molecules align in parallel formations. The display is a blank until the application of an electric field, which 'twists' the molecules so that they reflect or transmit light falling on them. There two main types of LCD are **passive matrix** and **active matrix**.

Related Web site: Polymers and liquid crystals http://plc.cwru.edu/

liquidity in economics, the state of possessing sufficient money and/or assets to be able to pay off all liabilities. **Liquid assets** are those such as shares that may be converted quickly into cash, as opposed to property.

liquorice perennial European herb belonging to the ▷legume family. The long sweet root yields an extract that is made into a hard black paste and used in confectionery and medicines. (*Glycyrrhiza glabra*, family Leguminosae.)

Lisbon (Portuguese **Lisboa**) capital of Portugal, and of the Lisboa district, in the southwest of the country, situated on a tidal lake and estuary formed by the River Tagus; population (1991) 677,800. It is a major commercial and industrial centre, and industries include steel, textiles, chemicals, pottery, shipbuilding, and fishing. Lisbon has been Portugal's capital since 1260 and reached its peak of prosperity in the period of Portugal's empire during the 16th century. In 1755 an earthquake accompanied by a tidal wave killed 30,000–60,000 people (the estimates vary) and destroyed much of the city.

Lisbon has been an important centre since Roman times. The fortress of São Jorge was taken from the Moors by Alfonso I in 1147. Points of interest include the cathedral, a Moorish citadel founded in 1150, the nearby 15th-century Batalha Abbey, the palace of the National Assembly (formerly a Benedictine monastery), the Palacio das Necessidades (formerly the royal palace), the museums of ancient and contemporary art, and the English cemetery, where the novelist Henry Fielding is buried. The present university dates from 1911; the university founded in 1290 was transferred to Coimbra in 1537. In 1998 Lisbon hosted the international trade fair Expo '98.

Related Web site: Lisbon http://www.EUnet.pt/Lisboa/i/lisboa.html

LISP (contraction of list processing) high-level computer-programming language designed for manipulating lists of data items. It is used primarily in research into ▷artificial intelligence (AI).

Lister, Joseph (1827–1912) 1st Baron Lister. English surgeon. He was the founder of antiseptic surgery, influenced by Louis ▷Pasteur's work on bacteria. He introduced dressings soaked in carbolic acid and strict rules of hygiene to combat wound sepsis in hospitals. He was made a baronet in 1883, and a baron in 1897.

The number of surgical operations greatly increased following the introduction of anaesthetics, but death rates were more than 40%. Under Lister's regime they fell dramatically.

listeriosis disease of animals that may occasionally infect humans, caused by the bacterium *Listeria monocytogenes*. The bacteria multiply at temperatures close to 0°C/32°F, which means they may flourish in precooked frozen meals if the cooking has not been thorough. Listeriosis causes flulike symptoms and inflammation of the brain and its surrounding membranes. It can be treated with penicillin.

Liszt, Franz (1811–1886) Hungarian pianist and composer. An outstanding virtuoso of the piano, he was an established concert artist by the age of 12. His expressive, romantic, and frequently chromatic works include piano music (*Transcendental Studies*, 1851), Masses and oratorios, songs, organ music, and a symphony. Much of his music is programmatic; he also originated the symphonic poem. Liszt was taught by his father, then by Carl Czerny. He travelled widely in Europe, producing an operetta *Don Sanche* in Paris, France, at the age of 14. As musical director and conductor at Weimar, Germany, 1848–59, he championed the music of Hector Berlioz and Richard Wagner.

Retiring to Rome, Italy, he turned again to his early love of religion, and in 1865 became a secular priest (adopting the title abbé), while continuing to teach and give concert tours for which he also made virtuoso piano arrangements of orchestral works by Beethoven, Schubert, and Wagner. He died in Bayreuth, Germany.

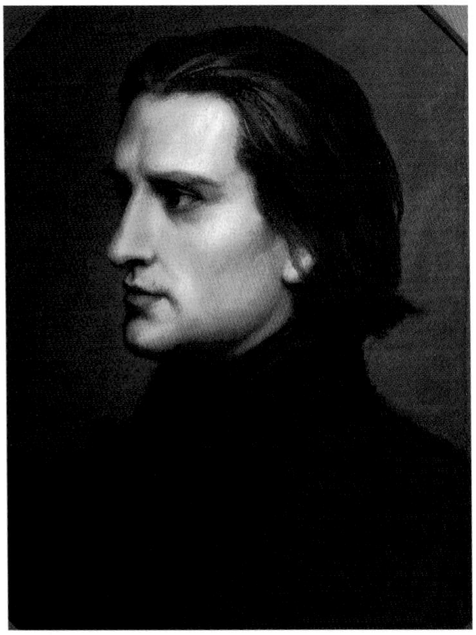

FRANZ LISZT A portrait of the Hungarian composer Franz Liszt, aged 29 years, by Charles Laurent Marechal.
The Art Archive/Richard Wagner Museum Bayreuth/Dagli Orti

litany in the Christian church, a form of prayer or supplication led by a priest with set responses by the congregation. It was introduced in the 4th century.

litchi (or **lychee**) evergreen tree belonging to the soapberry family. The delicately flavoured egg-shaped fruit has a rough brownish outer skin and a hard seed. The litchi is native to southern China, where it has been cultivated for 2,000 years. (*Litchi chinensis*, family Sapindaceae.)

literacy ability to read and write. The level at which functional literacy is set rises as society becomes more complex, and it becomes increasingly difficult for an illiterate person to find work and cope with the other demands of everyday life.

Related Web site: Literacy http://www.literacytrust.org.uk/Database/index.html

literary criticism the assessment and interpretation of literary works. The term 'criticism' is often taken to mean exclusively adverse comment, but in fact it refers to all literary assessment, whether positive or negative. Contemporary criticism offers analyses of literary works from structuralist, semiological, feminist, Marxist, and psychoanalytical perspectives, whereas earlier criticism tended to deal with moral or political ideas, or with a literary work as a formal object independent of its creator.

literature words set apart in some way from ordinary everyday communication. In the ancient oral traditions, before stories and poems were written down, literature had a mainly public function – mythic and religious. As literary works came to be preserved in writing, and, eventually, printed, their role became more private, serving as a vehicle for the exploration and expression of emotion and the human situation.

Poetry and prose In the development of literature, aesthetic criteria have come increasingly to the fore, although these have been challenged on ideological grounds by some recent cultural critics. The English poet and critic Coleridge defined **prose** as words in their best order, and **poetry** as the 'best' words in the best order. The distinction between poetry and prose is not always clear-cut, but in practice poetry tends to be metrically formal (making it easier to memorize), whereas prose corresponds more closely to the patterns of ordinary speech. Poetry therefore had an early advantage over prose in the days before printing, which it did not relinquish until comparatively recently.

Over the centuries poetry has taken on a wide range of forms, from the lengthy narrative such as the ▷epic, to the lyric, expressing personal emotion in songlike form; from the ▷ballad and the 14-line ▷sonnet, to the extreme conciseness of the 17-syllable Japanese ▷haiku.

Prose came into its own in the West as a vehicle for imaginative literature with the rise of the novel in the 18th century, and ▷fiction has since been divided into various genres such as the historical novel, detective fiction, fantasy, and science fiction. See also the literature of particular countries, under ▷English literature, ▷French literature, ▷United States literature, and so on.

Related Web site: BBC A–Z of authors http://www.bbc.co.uk/education/bookcase/authors/index.shtml

lithification the conversion of an unconsolidated sediment into solid sedimentary rock by **compaction** of mineral grains that make up the sediment, **cementation** by crystallization of new minerals from percolating aqueous solutions, and new growth of the original mineral grains. The term is less commonly used to refer to solidification of magma to form igneous rock.

lithium (Greek *lithos* 'stone') soft, ductile, silver-white, metallic element, symbol Li, atomic number 3, relative atomic mass 6.941. It is one of the ▷alkali metals, has a very low density (far less than most woods), and floats on water (specific gravity 0.57); it is the lightest of all metals. Lithium is used to harden alloys, and in batteries; its compounds are used in medicine to treat manic depression.

Lithium was named in 1818 by Swedish chemist Jöns Berzelius, having been discovered the previous year by his student Johan A Arfwedson (1792–1841). Berzelius named it after 'stone' because it is found in most igneous rocks and many mineral springs.

lithography printmaking technique invented in 1798 by Aloys Senefelder, based on the mutual repulsion of grease and water. A drawing is made with greasy crayon on an absorbent stone, which is then wetted. The wet stone repels ink (which is greasy) applied to the surface and the crayon absorbs it, so that the drawing can be printed. Lithographic printing is used in book production, posters, and prints, and this basic principle has developed into complex processes.

lithosphere upper rocky layer of the Earth that forms the jigsaw of plates that take part in the movements of ▷plate tectonics. The lithosphere comprises the ▷crust and a portion of the upper ▷mantle. It is regarded as being rigid and brittle and moves about on the more plastic and less brittle ▷asthenosphere.
The lithosphere ranges in thickness from 2–3 km/1–2 mi at mid-ocean ridges to 150 km/93 mi beneath old ocean crust, to 250 km/155 mi under ▷cratons.

Lithuania see country box.

Lithuanian language Indo-European language spoken by the people of Lithuania, which through its geographical isolation has retained many ancient features of the Indo-European language family. It acquired a written form in the 16th century, using the Latin alphabet, and is currently spoken by some 3–4 million people.

litmus dye obtained from various ▷lichens and used in chemistry as an indicator to test the acidic or alkaline nature of aqueous solutions; it turns red in the presence of acid, and blue in the presence of alkali.

litotes the use of understatement for effect ('He is no Einstein' = 'He is a bit dim'). It is the opposite of ▷hyperbole.

litre metric unit of volume (symbol l), equal to one cubic decimetre (1.76 imperial pints/2.11 US pints). It was formerly defined as the volume occupied by one kilogram of pure water at 4°C at standard pressure, but this is slightly larger than one cubic decimetre.

Little Bighorn, Battle of the (or Custer's Last Stand) engagement on a tributary of the Bighorn River in Montana, USA, on 25 June 1876, in which Lt-Col George ▷Custer suffered a crushing defeat by ▷Sioux, Cheyenne, and ▷Arapaho Indians, under chiefs ▷Sitting Bull, ▷Crazy Horse, and Gall. The battle was the greatest defeat inflicted on the US Army in the Plains Wars.

Little Richard (1932–) Stage name of Richard Wayne Penniman. US rock singer and pianist. He was one of the creators of rock and roll with his wildly uninhibited renditions of 'Tutti Frutti' (1956), 'Long Tall Sally' (1956), and 'Good Golly Miss Molly' (1957). His subsequent career in soul and rhythm and blues was interrupted by periods as a Seventh-Day Adventist cleric.

> **Little Richard**
> *I am the real King of rock'n'roll. I was singing before anybody knew what rock was . . . People like Elvis Presley were the builders of rock'n'roll, but I was the architect.*
> Interview in *Los Angeles Times* 1984

Little Rock largest city and capital of ▷Arkansas, USA, a port of entry on the Arkansas River, 215 km/133 mi west of Memphis, Tennessee; seat of Pulaski County; population (1994 est) 178,000. It is the centre of a rich agricultural, mining, timber, natural gas, and oil region; products include metal goods, oilfield and electronic equipment, valves and pipes, aircraft, ammunition, watches, chemicals, clothing, and processed food.

Littlewood, Joan Maud (1914–2002) English theatre director. She established the Theatre Workshop in 1945 and was responsible for many vigorous productions at the Theatre Royal, Stratford, London, 1953–75, such as *A Taste of Honey* (1959), Brendan Behan's *The Hostage* (1959–60), and *Oh, What a Lovely War* (1963).

liturgy in the Christian church, any written, authorized version of a service for public worship, especially the Roman Catholic ▷Mass.

Liu Shaoqi (or Liu Shao-chi) (1898–1969) Chinese communist politician, president 1960–65 and the most prominent victim of the 1966–69 leftist ▷Cultural Revolution. A Moscow-trained labour organizer, he was a firm proponent of the Soviet style of government based around disciplined one-party control, the use of incentive gradings, and priority for industry over agriculture. This was opposed by ▷Mao Zedong, but began to be implemented by Liu while he was state president 1960–65. Liu was brought down during the ▷Cultural Revolution.

liver large organ of vertebrates, which has many regulatory and storage functions. The human liver is situated in the upper abdomen, and weighs about 2 kg/4.5 lb. It is divided into four lobes. The liver receives the products of digestion, converts glucose to glycogen (a long-chain carbohydrate used for storage), and then back to glucose when needed. In this way the liver regulates the level of glucose in the blood (see ▷homeostasis). It removes excess amino acids from the blood, converting them to urea, which is excreted by the kidneys. The liver also synthesizes vitamins, produces bile and blood-clotting factors, and removes damaged red cells and toxins such as alcohol from the blood.

Liverpool city, seaport, and metropolitan borough in Merseyside, northwest England; population (1998 est) 461,500. Liverpool is the UK's chief Atlantic port with miles of specialized, mechanized quays on the River Mersey, and 2,100 ha/5,187 acres of dockland. The port handles 27.8 million tonnes/28.25 million tons of cargo annually. Imports include crude oil, grain, ores, edible oils, timber, and containers. There are ferries to Ireland and the Isle of Man. Traditional industries, such as ship-repairing, have declined. Liverpool's manufacturing sector is dominated by a small number of large firms. Manufacturing has declined in importance, while employment in the service sector in areas such as education, health, insurance, banking, and tourism has increased. There are industrial estates at Aintree, Kirkby, and Speke. A rail tunnel and Queensway Tunnel (1934) link Liverpool and Birkenhead; Kingsway Tunnel (1971), also known as the Mersey Tunnel, links Liverpool and Wallasey.
Features The Albert Dock on the waterfront comprises a number of restored dock buildings. It also hosts the Museum of Liverpool Life. Landmarks include the Bluecoat Chambers (1717); the Town Hall (1754); St George's Hall (1838–54), a good example of classical architecture; the Brown Library and Museum (1860); the Picton Library (1879); the Anglican Cathedral, designed by George Gilbert Scott (begun 1904, completed 1980); the Roman Catholic Metropolitan Cathedral of Christ the King, designed by Frederick ▷Gibberd, consecrated in 1967; and the Tate Gallery in the North in the Albert Dock (opened in 1987). The Walker Art Gallery (1877) and the Liverpool Philharmonic Orchestra, (founded in 1840, the Royal LPO since 1957), are here. The Grand National steeplechase takes place at ▷Aintree. Outstanding buildings include the 16th-century Speke Hall, the Victoria Building of the University of Liverpool, the Dock Offices, the Port of Liverpool building (1907), Royal Liver Building (1911), and the Cunard Building (1916) on Pier Head. In the Canning Conservation Area, 600 Georgian and Victorian houses are being restored.
The Central Libraries (a conglomerate of several libraries) constitute one of the best public libraries in the country; the Picton Library (1879) for the humanities is a 19th-century building. There are two universities: the University of Liverpool (opened in 1903) and John Moores University. Britain's first International Garden Festival was held here in 1984. The ▷Beatles were born here. The Liverpool Institute for the Performing Arts, set up by former Beatle Paul McCartney and opened in 1995, occupies the old Liverpool Institute for Boys, where Paul McCartney and George Harrison went to school. It offers a bachelor's degree in the performing arts.
History Liverpool grew in importance during the 18th century as a centre of the slave trade, and until the early 20th century through the export of textiles from Lancashire and Yorkshire.

Liverpool, Robert Banks Jenkinson 2nd Earl Liverpool (1770–1828) British Tory politician. He entered Parliament in 1790 and was foreign secretary 1801–03, home secretary 1804–06 and 1807–09, war minister 1809–12, and prime minister 1812–27. His government conducted the Napoleonic Wars to a successful conclusion, but its ruthless suppression of freedom of speech and of the press aroused such opposition that during 1815–20 revolution frequently seemed imminent. He became an earl in 1808.

liverwort nonvascular plant (with no 'veins' to carry water and food), related to ▷hornworts and mosses; it is found growing in damp places. (Class Hepaticae, order Bryophyta.)

Livingstone, David (1813–1873) Scottish missionary explorer. In 1841 he went to Africa, reaching Lake Ngami in 1849. He followed the Zambezi to its mouth, saw the Victoria Falls in 1855, and went to East and Central Africa 1858–64, reaching Lakes Shirwa and Nyasa. From 1866, he tried to find the source of the River Nile, and reached Ujiji in Tanganyika in November 1871. British explorer Henry Stanley joined Livingstone in Ujiji.

Livingstone not only mapped a great deal of the African continent but also helped to end the Arab slave trade.

He died in Old Chitambo (now in Zambia) and was buried in Westminster Abbey, London.

Related Web site: Livingstone – Man of Africa http://atschool.eduweb.co.uk/blantyre/living/livmenu.html

Livingstone, Ken(neth) (1945–) British left-wing Labour politician, leader of the Greater London Council (GLC) 1981–86, member of Parliament for Brent East from 1987, and mayor of London from 2000. He stood as a candidate for the Labour Party leadership elections in 1992. He ran as an independent candidate for election as Mayor of London, in opposition to Frank Dobson, the candidate endorsed by the Labour Party. The decision ended Livingstone's 30-year allegiance to the party and his subsequent election was a setback for Tony Blair's leadership. He was expelled from the Labour Party for five years.

Livonia (German **Livland**) one of the former ▷Baltic States, divided in 1918 between the modern states of Estonia and Latvia. Livonia belonged to the Teutonic Knights from the 13th to 16th centuries, to Poland from 1561, Sweden from 1629, and Russia from 1721.

Related Web site: Virtual Livonia http://www.geocities.com/tuksnesis/livonia/livonia.html

Livorno (English **Leghorn**) industrial port and resort in Tuscany, western Italy, 75 km/47 mi southwest of Florence; population (1992) 166,400. Industries include shipbuilding, distilling, oil-refining, and motor vehicle manufacture. A fortress town since the 12th century, it was developed by the Medici family in the 16th century. It is the site of a naval academy.

Livy (59 BC–AD 17) Adopted name of Titus Livius. Roman historian. He was the author of a *History of Rome* from the city's foundation to 9 BC, based partly on legend. It was composed of 142 books, of which 35 survive, covering the periods from the arrival of Aeneas in Italy to 293 BC and from 218 to 167 BC.

Li Xiannian (1909–1992) Chinese communist politician, member of the Chinese Communist Party (CCP) Politburo from 1956, and state president 1983–88. He fell from favour during the 1966–69 Cultural Revolution, but was rehabilitated as finance minister in 1973, by ▷Zhou Enlai, and proceeded to implement cautious economic reform.

During the 1950s and early 1960s Li was vice premier to the State Council and minister for finance and was inducted into the CCP Politburo and Secretariat in 1956 and 1958 respectively. He was elected to the Politburo's controlling Standing Commitee in 1977, where he was to remain until 1987, and he was state president in June 1983. As part of a general move to retire the CCP's ageing 'old guard', Li stepped down as president in April 1988 and became chairman of the Chinese People's Political Consultative Conference, a broad-based discussion forum. The father-in-law of ▷Jiang Zemin, Li remained influential as a 'party elder' until his death in 1992, establishing himself as a critic of destabil excessive liberalization.

lizard reptile generally distinguishable from snakes, which belong to the same order, by having four legs, moveable eyelids, eardrums, and a fleshy tongue, although some lizards are legless and snakelike in appearance. There are over 3,000 species of lizard worldwide. (Suborder Lacertilia, order Squamata.)

Like other reptiles, lizards are abundant in the tropics, although some species live as far north as the Arctic circle. There are about 20 families of lizards, including geckos, chameleons, skinks, monitors, agamas, and iguanas. The **common** or **viviparous lizard** (*Lacerta vivipara*), about 15 cm/6 in long, is found throughout Europe; in the far north, it hibernates through the long winter. Like many other species, it can shed its tail as a defence, later regrowing it. The **frilled lizard** (*Chlamydosaurus kingi*) of Australia has an erectile collar to frighten its enemies. There are two poisonous species of lizard, the **Mexican bearded lizard** and the **gila monster**. (For flying lizard see ▷flying dragon.)

Lizard Point southernmost point of mainland England in Cornwall. The coast is broken into small bays, overlooked by two cliff lighthouses.

Ljubljana (German **Laibach**) capital and industrial city of Slovenia, near the

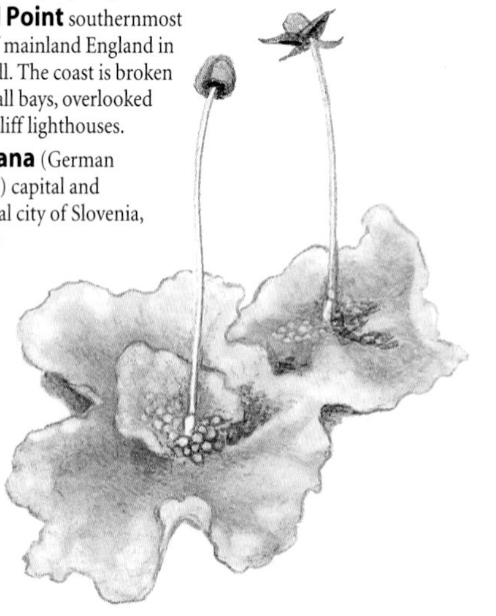

LIVERWORT Liverworts belong to a group of plants called the Bryophyta, which also includes the mosses. Neither mosses nor liverworts possess true roots and both require water to enable the male gametes to swim to the female sex organs to fertilize the eggs. Unlike mosses most liverwort have no, or only very frail, leaves.

Lithuania

Lithuania country in northern Europe, bounded north by Latvia, east by Belarus, south by Poland and the Kaliningrad area of Russia, and west by the Baltic Sea.

NATIONAL NAME *Lietuvos Respublika/Republic of Lithuania*
AREA 65,200 sq km/25,173 sq mi
CAPITAL Vilnius
MAJOR TOWNS/CITIES Kaunas, Klaipeda, Siauliai, Panevezys
PHYSICAL FEATURES central lowlands with gentle hills in west and higher terrain in southeast; 25% forested; some 3,000 small lakes, marshes, and complex sandy coastline; River Nemunas

Government

HEAD OF STATE Rolandas Paksas from 2003
HEAD OF GOVERNMENT Algirdas Brazauskas from 2001
POLITICAL SYSTEM emergent democracy
POLITICAL EXECUTIVE dual executive
ADMINISTRATIVE DIVISIONS 10 districts subdivided into 60 municipalities
ARMED FORCES 13,500 (2002 est)
CONSCRIPTION military service is compulsory for 12 months
DEATH PENALTY abolished in 1998
DEFENCE SPEND (% GDP) 1.8 (2002 est)
EDUCATION SPEND (% GDP) 2.1 (2001 est)
HEALTH SPEND (% GDP) 6 (2000 est)

Economy and resources

CURRENCY litas
GPD (US$) 13.8 billion (2002 est)
REAL GDP GROWTH (% change on previous year) 5.9 (2001)
GNI (US$) 12.7 billion (2002 est)
GNI PER CAPITA (PPP) (US$) 9,880 (2002 est)
CONSUMER PRICE INFLATION 2.1% (2003 est)
UNEMPLOYMENT 17% (2001)
FOREIGN DEBT (US$) 2.9 billion (2001 est)
MAJOR TRADING PARTNERS Russia, UK, Germany, Latvia, Poland, France, Italy, EU
RESOURCES small deposits of petroleum, natural gas, peat, limestone, gravel, clay, sand
INDUSTRIES petroleum refining and petroleum products, cast iron and steel, textiles, mineral fertilizers, fur coats, refrigerators, TV sets, bicycles, paper
EXPORTS mineral products, textiles, machinery and equipment, non-precious metals, chemicals, animal products, timber and wood products. Principal market: UK 13.8% (2001)
IMPORTS mineral products, machinery and transport equipment, chemicals, fertilizers, textiles and clothing, consumer goods. Principal source: Russia 25.3% (2001)
ARABLE LAND 45.3% (2001 est)
AGRICULTURAL PRODUCTS cereals, sugar beet, potatoes, vegetables; livestock rearing and dairy farming

Population and society

POPULATION 3,444,000 (2003 est)
POPULATION GROWTH RATE –0.2% (2000–15)
POPULATION DENSITY (per sq km) 53 (2003 est)
URBAN POPULATION (% of total) 69 (2003 est)
AGE DISTRIBUTION (% of total population) 0–14 18%, 15–59 63%, 60+ 19% (2002 est)
ETHNIC GROUPS 80% Lithuanian ethnic descent, 9% ethnic Russian, 8% Polish, 2% Belarussian, 1% Ukrainian
LANGUAGE Lithuanian (official)
RELIGION predominantly Roman Catholic; Evangelical Lutheran, also Russian Orthodox, Evangelical Reformist, and Baptist
EDUCATION (compulsory years) 9
LITERACY RATE 99% (men); 99% (women) (2003 est)
LABOUR FORCE 20.2% agriculture, 26.9% industry, 52.9% services (1999)
LIFE EXPECTANCY 68 (men); 78 (women) (2000–05)
CHILD MORTALITY RATE (under 5, per 1,000 live births) 9 (2001)
PHYSICIANS (per 1,000 people) 4 (1999 est)
HOSPITAL BEDS (per 1,000 people) 9.2 (1999 est)
TV SETS (per 1,000 people) 422 (2000 est)
RADIOS (per 1,000 people) 524 (2000 est)
INTERNET USERS (per 10,000 people) 1,445.1 (2002 est)
PERSONAL COMPUTER USERS (per 100 people) 11.0 (2002 est)

See also ▷Landsbergis, Vytautas; ▷Union of Soviet Socialist Republics.

Chronology

late 12th century: Became a separate nation.
1230: Mindaugas united Lithuanian tribes to resist attempted invasions by German and Livonian Teutonic Knights, and adopted Christianity.
14th century: Strong Grand Duchy formed by Gediminas, founder of Vilnius and Jogaila dynasty, and his son, Algirdas; absorbing Ruthenian territories to east and south, it stretched from the Baltic to the Black Sea and east, nearly reaching Moscow.
1410: Led by Duke Vytautas, and in alliance with Poland, the Teutonic Knights were defeated decisively at the Battle of Tannenberg.
1569: Joined Poland in a confederation, under the Union of Lublin, in which Poland had the upper hand and Lithuanian upper classes were Polonized.
1795: Came under control of Tsarist Russia, following partition of Poland; 'Lithuania Minor' (Kaliningrad) fell to Germany.
1831 and 1863: Failed revolts for independence.
1880s: Development of organized nationalist movement.
1914–18: Occupied by German troops during World War I.
1918–19: Independence declared and, after uprising against attempted imposition of Soviet Union (USSR) control, was achieved as a democracy.
1920–39: Province and city of Vilnius occupied by Poles.
1926: Democracy overthrown in authoritarian coup by Antanas Smetona, who became president.
1934: Baltic Entente mutual-defence pact signed with Estonia and Latvia.
1939–40: Secret German–Soviet agreement brought most of Lithuania under Soviet influence as a constituent republic.
1941: Lithuania revolted and established own government, but during World War II Germany again occupied the country and 210,000, mainly Jews, were killed.
1944: USSR resumed rule.

1944–52: Lithuanian guerrillas fought USSR, which persecuted the Catholic Church, collectivized agriculture, and deported half a million Balts to Siberia.
1972: Demonstrations against Soviet government.
1980s: There was a growth in nationalist dissent, influenced by the Polish Solidarity movement and the *glasnost* ('openness') initiative of reformist Soviet leader Mikhail Gorbachev.
1988: An independence movement, the Sajudis, was formed to campaign for increased autonomy; the parliament declared Lithuanian the state language and readopted the flag of the interwar republic.
1989: The Communist Party split into pro-Moscow and nationalist wings, and lost the local monopoly of power; over 1 million took part in nationalist demonstrations.
1990: Nationalist Sajudis won elections; their leader, Vytautas Landsbergis, became the president; a unilateral declaration of independence was rejected by the USSR, who imposed an economic blockade.
1991: Soviet paratroopers briefly occupied key buildings in Vilnius, killing 13; the Communist Party was outlawed; Lithuanian independence was recognized by the USSR and Western nations; the country was admitted into the United Nations.
1992: Economic restructuring caused a contraction in GDP.
1993: A free-trade agreement was reached with other Baltic States. The last Russian troops departed.
1994: A friendship and cooperation treaty was signed with Poland.
1994: A trade and cooperation agreement was reached with the European Union.
1997: A border treaty was signed with Russia.
1998: Valdas Adamkus became president.
1999: Andrius Kubelius became prime minister following the resignation of Rolandas Paksas.
2000: Paksas was returned to power, leading a centre-left coalition.
2004: Lithuania was set to join the EU 1 May.

LITHUANIA Vilnius, the capital of Lithuania, stands on the banks of the Neris River, only a few miles from the border with Belarus. *Lithuanian tourist board*

confluence of the rivers Ljubljanica and Sava; population (1991) 276,100. Products include textiles, chemicals, paper, and leather goods. It has a nuclear research centre and is linked with southern Austria by the Karawanken road tunnel under the Alps (1979–83).

Related Web site: Ljubljana
http://www.ijs.si/slo/ljubljana/

llama South American even-toed hoofed mammal belonging to the camel family, about 1.2 m/4 ft high at the shoulder. Llamas can be white, brown, or dark, sometimes with spots or patches. They are very hardy, and require little food or water. They spit when annoyed. (Species *Lama glama*, family Camelidae.)

Llamas are used in Peru as beasts of burden, and also for their wool, milk, and meat. Llamas and alpacas are both domesticated forms of the ▷guanaco.

Lleida (formerly **Lérida**) capital of Lleida province in Cataluña, northeast Spain, situated on the River Segre, 132 km/82 mi west of Barcelona; population (1991) 111,900. Industries include leather, paper, glass, and cloth production. It has Roman remains and the ruins of a 13th-century cathedral.

Llewelyn two princes of Wales:

Llewelyn I (1173–1240) Prince of Wales from 1194. He extended his rule to all Wales not in Norman hands, driving the English from northern Wales in 1212, and taking Shrewsbury in 1215. During the early part of Henry III's reign, he was several times attacked by English armies. He was married to Joanna, the illegitimate daughter of King John.

Llewelyn II ap Gruffydd (*c*. 1225–1282) Prince of Wales from 1246, grandson of Llewelyn I. In 1277 Edward I of England compelled Llewelyn to acknowledge him as overlord and to surrender southern Wales. His death while leading a national uprising ended Welsh independence.

Lloyd, Harold (Clayton) (1893–1971) US film comedian. He wore thick horn-rimmed glasses and a straw hat, and performed daring stunts in cliffhanger serials. He appeared from 1913 in silent and talking films. His silent films include *Grandma's Boy* (1922), *Safety Last* (1923), and *The Freshman* (1925). His first talkie was *Movie Crazy* (1932).

Lloyd George, David 1st Earl Lloyd-George of Dwyfor (1863–1945) British Liberal politician, born in Manchester of Welsh parentage, prime minister 1916–22. A pioneer of social reform and the ▷welfare state, as chancellor of the Exchequer 1908–15 he introduced old-age pensions in 1908 and health and unemployment insurance in 1911. High unemployment, intervention in the Russian Civil War, and use of the military police force, the ▷Black and Tans, in Ireland eroded his support as prime minister, and the creation of the Irish Free State in 1921 and his pro-Greek policy against the Turks caused the collapse of his coalition government.

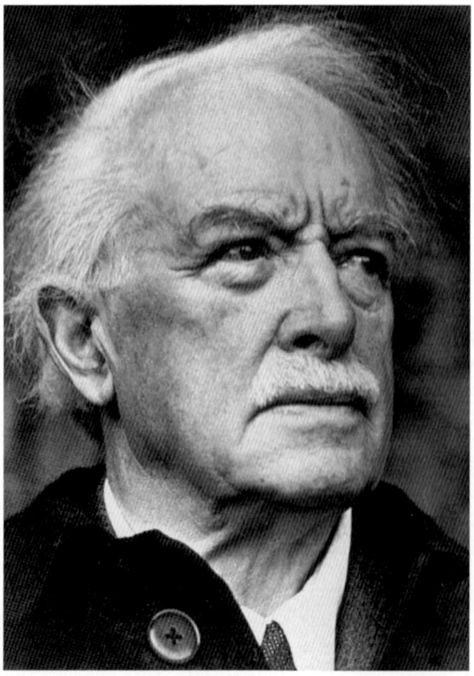

DAVID LLOYD GEORGE British statesman David Lloyd George, Liberal prime minister 1916–22. *Archive Photos*

Lloyd George was brought up in north Wales, became a solicitor, and was member of Parliament for Caernarvon Boroughs from 1890. During the Boer War, he was prominent as a pro-Boer. His 1909 budget (with graduated direct taxes and taxes on land values) provoked the Lords to reject it, and resulted in the Act of 1911 limiting their powers. He held ministerial posts during World War I until 1916 when there was an open breach between him and Prime Minister ▷Asquith, and he became prime minister of a coalition government. Securing a unified Allied command, he enabled the Allies to withstand the last German offensive and achieve victory. After World War I he had a major role in the Versailles peace treaty. In the 1918 elections, he achieved a huge majority over Labour and Asquith's followers. He had become largely distrusted within his own party by 1922, and never regained power. He was made an earl in 1945.

David Lloyd George
What is our task? To make Britain a fit country for heroes to live in.
Speech at Wolverhampton, 24 November 1918

Lloyd's Register of Shipping international society for the survey and classification of merchant shipping, which provides rules for the construction and maintenance of ships and their machinery. It was founded in 1760.

Lloyd Webber, Andrew (1948–) English composer and theatre owner. His early musicals, with lyrics by Tim Rice, include *Joseph and the Amazing Technicolor Dreamcoat* (1968), *Jesus Christ Superstar* (1971), and *Evita* (1978), based on the life of the Argentine leader Eva Perón. He also wrote *Cats* (1981), based on T S Eliot's *Old Possum's Book of Practical Cats*, *Starlight Express* (1984), *The Phantom of the Opera* (1986), and *Aspects of Love* (1989). In January 2000 Lloyd Webber bought Stoll Moss, the British theatre company, which owned ten of London's theatres. Lloyd Webber joined his company, the Really Useful Group, with City financiers NatWest Equity Partners, to buy the ten theatres, and to put the three London theatres already owned by the Really Useful Group into the partnership. His musical play *The Beautiful Game* (2000) won him a London Theatre Critics Circle Award.

Llull, Ramon (*c*. 1232–1316) Catalan scholar and mystic. He began his career at the court of James I of Aragón (1212–1276) in Mallorca. He produced treatises on theology, mysticism, and chivalry in Catalan, Latin, and Arabic. His *Ars magna* was a mechanical device, a kind of prototype computer, by which all problems could be solved by manipulating fundamental Aristotelian categories.

loa spirit in ▷voodoo. Loas may be male or female, and include Maman Brigitte, the loa of death and cemeteries, and Aida-Wedo, the rainbow snake. Believers may be under the protection of one particular loa.

loach carplike freshwater fish with a long narrow body and no teeth in the small downward-pointing mouth, which is surrounded by barbels (sensitive bristles). Loaches are native to Asian and European waters. (Family Cobitidae.)

loam type of fertile soil, a mixture of sand, silt, clay, and organic material. It is porous, which allows for good air circulation and retention of moisture.

loan form of borrowing by individuals, businesses, and governments. Individuals and companies usually obtain loans from banks. The loan with interest is typically paid back in fixed monthly instalments over a period of between one and five years in the UK, although longer-term loans and different repayment conditions may be negotiated. Debentures and ▷mortgages are specific forms of loan. In business, loans are the second most important way after retained profit in which firms finance their expansion.

lobby individual or pressure group that sets out to influence government action. The lobby is prevalent in the USA, where the term originated in the 1830s from the practice of those wishing to influence state policy waiting for elected representatives in the lobby of the Capitol.

lobelia any of a group of temperate and tropical plants with white to mauve flowers. Lobelias may grow to shrub size but are mostly small annual plants. (Genus *Lobelia*, family Lobeliaceae.)

lobotomy another name for the former brain operation, ▷leucotomy.

lobster any of various large marine ▷crustaceans. Lobsters are grouped with freshwater ▷crayfish in the suborder Reptantia ('walking'), although both lobsters and crayfish can also swim, using their fanlike tails. Lobsters have eyes on stalks and long antennae, and are mainly nocturnal. They scavenge and eat dead or dying fish. (Family Homaridae, order Decapoda.)

True lobsters are distinguished by having very large 'claws' or pincers on their first pair of legs, and smaller ones on their second and third pairs. Spiny lobsters (family Palinuridae) have no large pincers. They communicate by means of a serrated pad at the base of their antennae, the 'sound' being picked up by sensory nerves located on hairlike outgrowths on their fellow lobsters up to 60 m/180 ft away.

Species include the **common lobster** (*Homarus gammarus*) found off Britain, which is bluish-black, the closely related **American lobster** (*H. americanus*), the spiny lobster (*Palinurus vulgaris*) found off Britain, and the **Norwegian lobster** (*Nephrops norvegicus*), a small orange species.

local government that part of government dealing mainly with matters concerning the inhabitants of a particular area or town, usually financed at least in part by local taxes. In the USA and UK, local government has comparatively large powers and responsibilities.

Related Web site: Oultwood Local Government Web Site Index
http://www.oultwood.com/localgov/

Locarno, Pact of series of diplomatic documents initialled in Locarno, Switzerland, on 16 October 1925 and formally signed in London on 1 December 1925. The pact settled the question of French security, and the signatories – Britain, France, Belgium, Italy, and Germany – guaranteed Germany's existing frontiers with France and Belgium. Following the signing of the pact, Germany was admitted to the League of Nations.

loc. cit. abbreviation for **loco citato** (Latin 'at the place cited'), used in reference citation.

Lochner, Stephan (*c*. 1400–1451) German painter. Active in Cologne from 1442, where most of his work still remains, notably the *Virgin in the Rose Garden* (*c*. 1440; Wallraf-Richartz Museum) and *Adoration of the Magi*, (1448; Cologne Cathedral). His work combines the indigenous German style with the naturalism of Flemish painting.

Loch Ness Scottish lake; see ▷Ness, Loch.

lock construction installed in waterways to allow boats or ships to travel from one level to another. The earliest form, the **flash lock**, was first seen in the East in 1st-century-AD China and in the West in 11th-century Holland. By this method barriers temporarily dammed a river and when removed allowed the flash flood to propel the waiting boat through or over any obstacle. This was followed in 12th-century China and 14th-century Holland by the **pound lock**. In this system the lock has gates at each end. Boats enter through one gate when the levels are the same both outside and inside. Water is then allowed in (or out of) the lock until the level rises (or falls) to the new level outside the other gate.

Locks are important to shipping where canals link oceans of differing levels, such as the Panama Canal, or where falls or rapids are replaced by these adjustable water 'steps'.

lock and key devices that provide security, usually fitted to a door of some kind. In 1778 English locksmith Robert Barron made the forerunner of the **mortise lock**, which contains levers that the key must raise to an exact height before the bolt can be moved. The **Yale lock**, a pin-tumbler cylinder design, was invented by US locksmith Linus Yale, Jr, in 1865. More secure locks include **combination locks**, with a dial mechanism that must be turned certain distances backwards and forwards to open, and **time locks**, which are set to be opened only at specific times.

Locke, John (1632–1704) English philosopher. His *Essay concerning Human Understanding* (1690) maintained that experience is the only source of knowledge (empiricism), and that 'we can have knowledge no farther than we have ideas' prompted by such experience. *Two Treatises on Government* (1690) helped to form contemporary ideas of liberal democracy.

For Locke, the physical universe was a mechanical system of material bodies, composed of corpuscules, or 'invisible particles'. He believed that at birth the mind was a blank, and that all ideas came from sense impressions.

His *Two Treatises on Government* supplied the classical statement of Whig theory and enjoyed great influence in America and France. It supposed that governments derive their authority from popular consent (regarded as a 'contract'), so that a government may be rightly overthrown if it infringes such fundamental rights of the people as religious freedom.

Related Web site: Debate between Thomas Hobbes and John Locke: A Creative Essay http://www.yucc.yorku.ca/~rickg/academics/hobesvlo.html

lockjaw former name for ▷tetanus, a type of bacterial infection.

locomotive engine for hauling railway trains. In 1804 Cornish engineer Richard Trevithick built the first steam engine to run on rails. Locomotive design did not radically improve until English engineer George Stephenson built the *Rocket* in 1829, which featured a multitube boiler and blastpipe, standard in all following **steam locomotives**. Today most locomotives are diesel or electric: **diesel locomotives** have a powerful diesel engine, and **electric**

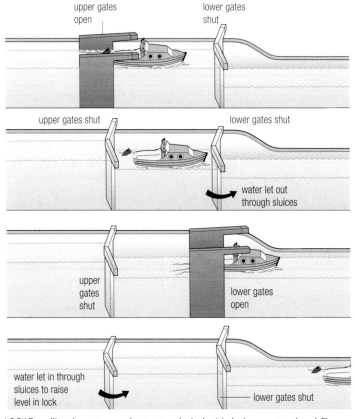

LOCK Travelling downstream, a boat enters the lock with the lower gates closed. The upper gates are then shut and the water level lowered by draining through sluices. When the water level in the lock reaches the downstream level, the lower gates are opened.

locomotives draw their power from either an overhead cable or a third rail alongside the ordinary track.

In a steam locomotive, fuel (usually coal, sometimes wood) is burned in a furnace. The hot gases and flames produced are drawn through tubes running through a huge water-filled boiler and heat up the water to steam. The steam is then fed to the cylinders, where it forces the pistons back and forth. Movement of the pistons is conveyed to the wheels by cranks and connecting rods. Diesel locomotives have a powerful diesel engine, burning oil.

The engine may drive a generator to produce electricity to power electric motors that turn the wheels, or the engine drives the wheels mechanically or through a hydraulic link. A number of **gas-turbine locomotives** are in use, in which a turbine spun by hot gases provides the power to drive the wheels.

locus (Latin 'place') in mathematics, traditionally the path traced out by a moving point, but now defined as the set of all points on a curve satisfying given conditions. For example, the locus of a point that moves so that it is always at the same distance from another fixed point is a circle; the locus of a point that is always the same distance from two fixed points is a straight line that perpendicularly bisects the line joining them. The locus of points a fixed distance from a line is two parallel lines running either side.

locust swarming grasshopper with short feelers, or antennae, and hearing organs on the abdomen (rear segment of the body). As winged adults, flying in swarms, locusts may be carried by the wind hundreds of miles from their breeding grounds; on landing they devour all vegetation. Locusts occur in nearly every continent. (Family Acrididae, order Orthoptera.)

locust tree another name for the ▷carob, a small tree of the Mediterranean region. It is also the name of several North American trees of the ▷legume family (Leguminosae).

lode geological deposit rich in certain minerals, generally consisting of a large vein or set of veins containing ore minerals. A system of veins that can be mined directly forms a lode, for example the mother lode of the California gold rush.
Lodes form because hot hydrothermal liquids and gases from magmas penetrate surrounding rocks, especially when these are limestones; on cooling, veins of ores formed from the magma then extend from the igneous mass into the local rock.

lodestar (or **loadstar**) star used in navigation or astronomy, often ▷Polaris, the Pole Star.

Lodge, David John
(1935–) English novelist, short-story writer, dramatist, and critic. Much of his fiction concerns the role of Catholicism in mid-20th-century England, exploring the situation both through broad comedy and parody, as in *The British Museum is Falling Down* (1967), and realistically, as in *How Far Can You Go?* (1980). *Nice Work* (1988) was short-listed for the Booker Prize.

Łódź industrial city (textiles, machinery, dyes) in central Poland, 120 km/75 mi southwest of Warsaw; population (1993) 844,900.

loess yellow loam, derived from glacial meltwater deposits and accumulated by wind in periglacial regions during the ▷ice ages. Loess usually attains considerable depths, and the soil derived from it is very fertile. There are large deposits in central Europe (Hungary), China, and North America. It was first described in 1821 in the Rhine area, and takes its name from a village in Alsace.

Loewe, Frederick (1904–1988) German-born US composer. He worked on Broadway from the 1930s and began a collaboration with the lyricist Alan Jay Lerner in 1942. Their joint successes include *Brigadoon* (1947), *Paint Your Wagon* (1951), *My Fair Lady* (1956), *Gigi* (1958), and *Camelot* (1960).

log any apparatus for measuring the speed of a ship; also the daily record of events on board a ship or aircraft.

JOHN LOCKE A contemporary portrait of the 17th-century English philosopher John Locke. *Image Bank*

loganberry hybrid between a ▷blackberry and a ▷raspberry with large, tart, dull-red fruit. It was developed in 1881 by US judge James H Logan.

logarithm (or **log**) the ▷exponent or index of a number to a specified base – usually 10. For example, the logarithm to the base 10 of 1,000 is 3 because $10^3 = 1,000$; the logarithm of 2 is 0.3010 because $2 = 10^{0.3010}$. The whole-number part of a logarithm is called the **characteristic**; the fractional part is called the **mantissa**.

Before the advent of cheap electronic calculators, multiplication and division could be simplified by being replaced with the addition and subtraction of logarithms. For any two numbers x and y (where $x = b^a$ and $y = b^c$) $x \times y = b^a \times b^c = b^{a+c}$; hence we would add the logarithms of x and y, and look up this answer in antilogarithm tables.

Tables of logarithms and antilogarithms are available that show conversions of numbers into logarithms, and vice versa. For example, to multiply 6,560 by 980, one looks up their logarithms (3.8169 and 2.9912), adds them together (6.8081), then looks up the antilogarithm of this to get the answer (6,428,800). **Natural** or **Napierian logarithms** are to the base e, an ▷irrational number equal to approximately 2.7183.

The principle of logarithms is also the basis of the slide rule. With the general availability of the electronic pocket calculator, the need for logarithms has been reduced. The first log tables (to base e) were published by the Scottish mathematician John Napier in 1614. Base-ten logs were introduced by the Englishman Henry Briggs (1561–1631) and Dutch mathematician Adriaen Vlacq (1600–1667).

logic branch of philosophy that studies valid reasoning and argument. It is also the way in which one thing may be said to follow from, or be a consequence of, another (deductive logic). Logic is generally divided into the traditional formal logic of Aristotle and the symbolic logic derived from Friedrich Frege and Bertrand Russell.

logical positivism doctrine that the only meaningful propositions are those that can be verified empirically. Metaphysics, religion, and aesthetics are therefore meaningless. However, the doctrine itself cannot be verified empirically and so is self-refuting.

LOGO (Greek *logos* 'word') high-level computer programming language designed to teach mathematical concepts. Developed in about 1970 at the Massachusetts Institute of Technology, it became popular in schools and with home computer users because of its 'turtle graphics' feature. This allows the user to write programs that create line drawings on a computer screen, or drive a small mobile robot (a 'turtle' or 'buggy') around the floor.

> **David Lodge**
> *Literature is mostly about having sex and not much about having children. Life is the other way round.*
> The British Museum is Falling Down

LOCK AND KEY A photograph of Joseph Bramah's 'unpickable' lock, which he patented in 1784, and which bears his name. *The Art Archive/Eileen Tweedy*

LOCOMOTIVE High-speed steam locomotive. The first successful steam locomotive was built by English engineer George Stephenson. In 1825, his engine *Locomotion* opened the world's first passenger railway, the Stockton–Darlington Railway, in northeast England. *Archive Photos*

Loire longest river in France, rising in the Cévennes Mountains in the *département* of Ardèche at 1,350 m/4,430 ft near Mont Gerbier de Jonc, and flowing for over 1,000 km/620 mi north through Nevers to Orléans, then west through Tours and Nantes until it reaches the Bay of Biscay at St Nazaire. The Loire drains 116,550 sq km/45,000 sq mi of land, more than a fifth of France, and there are many châteaux and vineyards along its banks. The Loire gives its name to the *départements* of Loire, Haute-Loire, Loire-Atlantique, Indre-et-Loire, Maine-et-Loire, and Saône-et-Loire.

Loki in Norse mythology, the giant-born god and blood-brother of Odin, companion of the Aesir (principal warrior gods), but a source of trickery and evil, and the cause of dissension among the gods. Instrumental in the slaying of ▷Balder, he hastened the coming of ▷Ragnarök, the final battle of the gods. His children by the giantess Angrboda were the Midgard serpent Jörmungander, which girdles the Earth; the wolf Fenris; and ▷Hel, goddess of death.

Lollard follower of the English religious reformer John Wycliffe in the 14th century. The Lollards condemned the doctrine of the transubstantiation of the bread and wine of the Eucharist, advocated the diversion of ecclesiastical property to charitable uses, and denounced war and capital punishment. They were active from about 1377; after the passing of the statute *De heretico comburendo* ('The Necessity of Burning Heretics') in 1401 many Lollards were burned, and in 1414 they raised an unsuccessful revolt in London, known as Oldcastle's Rebellion.

The name is derived from the Dutch *lollaert* (mumbler), applied to earlier European groups accused of combining pious pretensions with heretical belief. Lollardy lingered on in London and East Anglia, and in the 16th century became absorbed into the Protestant movement.

Related Web site: Lollards http://www.newadvent.org/cathen/09333a.htm

Lombard (or **Langobard**) member of a Germanic people who invaded Italy in 568 and occupied Lombardy (named after them) and central Italy. Their capital was Monza. They were conquered by the Frankish ruler Charlemagne in 774.

Lombardy (Italian **Lombardia**) region of northern Italy, between the Alps and the River Po, comprising the provinces of Bergamo, Brescia, Como, Cremona, Mantua, Milan, Pavia, Sondrio, and Varese; area 23,900 sq km/9,225 sq mi; population (2001 est) 8,922,500. Its capital is ▷Milan. It is the country's chief industrial area with chemical, pharmaceutical, textile, and engineering operations, and its most productive agricultural region yielding wheat, maize, wine, meat, and dairy products.

Related Web site: Sites of Lombardy http://www.initaly.com/~initaly/regions/lombardy/sites.htm

Lombardy League, The Italian regional political party, committed to federalism. It models itself on the 12th–13th century Lombard League. In 1993 it became the core of a new conservative-populist political grouping, the Northern League, led by Umberto Bossi, and fought the 1994 general election as part of the right-wing Freedom Alliance.

Lomé capital, port, and administrative centre of ▷Togo, on the Bight of Benin; population (1995 est) 501,000. It is a centre for gold, silver, and marble crafts. Industries include steel production, oil refining, brewing, plastics, cement, paper manufacturing, and food processing. Main exports include cacao, palm nuts, cotton, and coffee. There is an international airport and tourism is growing in importance. Lomé became capital of the independent Togo in 1960.

In 1975 a trade agreement known as the ▷Lomé Convention was reached here, establishing economic cooperation between the European Economic Community (now the European Union) and 46 African, Caribbean, and Pacific countries. The University of Benin was founded here in 1965.

Lomé Convention convention in 1975 that established economic cooperation between the European Economic Community (now the European Union) and developing countries of Africa, the Caribbean, and the Pacific (ACP). It was renewed in 1979, 1985, 1989, and 2000. At the end of 1996, 70 ACP states were parties to the convention.

Lomond, Loch largest freshwater Scottish lake, 37 km/23 mi long, area 70 sq km/27 sq mi. It is overlooked by the mountain **Ben Lomond** (973 m/3,192 ft) and is linked to the Clyde estuary.

London city in southwestern Ontario, Canada, on the Thames River, 198 km/123 mi southwest of Toronto and 200 km/124 mi west of the Niagara Falls; seat of Middlesex County; population (1991) 303,200; population of metropolitan area 381,500. The centre of a farming district, it has tanneries, breweries, and factories making hosiery, radio and electrical equipment, leather, and footwear.

London capital of England and the United Kingdom, located on the River Thames. Since 1965 its metropolitan area has been known as ▷Greater London, consisting of the City of London and 32 boroughs; total area 1,580 sq km/610 sq mi; combined population (2000 est) 7,375,000. London is the biggest city in Western Europe at the heart of the most populous region – 18 million people live in London and the South East. The **City of London**, known as the 'square mile', is the financial and commercial centre of the UK; area 2.7 sq km/1 sq mi. Over 25 million people visited London in 1999. Popular tourist attractions include the **Tower of London**, St Paul's Cathedral, Buckingham Palace, and Westminster Abbey. The ▷Millennium Dome at Greenwich was the centrepiece of Britain's millennium celebrations.

History Roman **Londinium** was established soon after the Roman invasion in AD 43; in the 2nd century London became a walled city; by the 11th century it was the main city of England and gradually extended beyond the walls to link with the originally separate Westminster. Throughout the 19th century London had the largest city-based population in the world.

Features The **Tower of London** was built by William the Conqueror on a Roman site, and now houses the crown jewels and the royal armouries; it is a World Heritage Site. Other features include the 15th-century Guildhall; the Monument, a column designed by Christopher Wren, which marks the site in Pudding Lane where the Fire of London began in 1666; Mansion House, the residence of the lord mayor; the Barbican arts and conference centre; the Houses of ▷Parliament and Big Ben; the Old Bailey (Central Criminal Court); and the Inns of Court. Covent Garden, once a vegetable market, is now a tourist, shopping, and entertainment area.

Architecture London contains buildings in all styles of English architecture dating back to the 11th century.

Norman: the White Tower, Tower of London; St Bartholomew's, Smithfield; the Temple Church.

Gothic: Westminster Abbey; Westminster Hall; Lambeth Palace; Southwark Cathedral.

Tudor: St James's Palace; Staple Inn.

17th century: Banqueting Hall, Whitehall (Inigo Jones); St Paul's; Kensington Palace; many City churches (Sir Christopher Wren).

18th century: Somerset House (Chambers); St Martin-in-the-Fields; Buckingham Palace.

19th century: British Museum (neoclassical); Houses of Parliament; Law Courts (neo-Gothic); Westminster Cathedral (Byzantine style).

20th century: Lloyd's of London (High Tech); Millennium Dome.

Between 1986, when the Greater London Council was abolished, and the year 2000, when the Greater London Authority (GLA) was established, there was no central authority for Greater London. Responsibility is now divided between the Greater London Authority and 32 London boroughs. The Greater London Authority (GLA) is a new form of strategic citywide government for London. It is made up of a directly elected Mayor – the Mayor of London – and a separately elected Assembly – the London Assembly. Ken Livingstone formally took over as the first directly-elected Mayor of London on 3 July 2000. He was declared Mayor on 5 May 2000, and two months later at the headquarters of the GLA at Romney House in Westminster he officially took control of the first city-wide government in London for 14 years. The Mayor prepares strategies to deal with London issues, and co-ordinates action on a London basis. The Assembly scrutinises the Mayor's activities, questioning the Mayor about his or her decisions. The GLA has taken over control of a number of existing government programmes in London. Its main areas of responsibilities are: transport, planning, economic development, environment, policing, fire and emergency planning, culture, and health.

LONDON A view of London, England, from a manuscript of the poems of Charles, Duke of Orléans (1394–1465). The principal building is the White Tower in the Tower of London. *The Art Archive/British Museum/Harper Collins Publishers*

The Corporation of the City of London is the local authority for the City of London, and dates back to the 12th century. Among local authorities the Corporation of London is unique. Not only is it the oldest in the country, combining its ancient traditions and ceremonial functions with the role of a modern authority, but it operates on a non-party political basis. It is governed by the Court of the Common Council, comprising the lord mayor, 24 aldermen, and 130 common councilmen. The lord mayor and two sheriffs are nominated annually by the councillors and elected by the aldermen in November (although in the late 1990s it was proposed that London's mayor should be elected by the people of London). After being sworn in at the Guildhall, he or she is presented the next day to the lord chief justice at the Royal Courts of Justice in Westminster, an event marked by the ceremonial procession of the Lord Mayor's Show. There are over 100 city guilds (livery companies) covering an array of occupations, including, in order of civic precedence, mercers, grocers, drapers, fishmongers, goldsmiths, merchant taylors, skinners, haberdashers, salters, ironmongers, vintners (wine merchants), and clothworkers. The original purpose of the guilds was to administer apprenticeships and oversee production. Although many of the professions are now in decline, there are still more than 23,000 liverymen entitled to vote at Common Hall, the ruling body of the Corporation of the City of London. The Corporation has the same functions as the boroughs and also runs the **City of London Police** and the health authority for the Port of London. It is also responsible for health controls on animal imports throughout Greater London, including Heathrow airport, runs the Central Criminal Court and the large markets, and owns and manages public open spaces throughout Greater London.

Commerce and industry From Saxon times the **Port of London** dominated the Thames from Tower Bridge to Tilbury. Its activity is now centred outside the metropolitan area, and downstream Tilbury has been extended to cope with container traffic. The prime economic importance of modern London is as a financial centre. There are various industries, mainly on the outskirts. There are also recording, broadcasting, television, and film studios; publishing companies; and the works and offices of the national press. Tourism is important.

Some of the docks in the East End of London, once the busiest in the world, were sold to the Docklands Development Corporation, which has built offices, houses, factories, and a railway. The world's largest office development project is at ▷Canary Wharf. The City Thameslink station, the first mainline railway station to be built in London for nearly a century, opened in 1991.

Education and entertainment London has many museums, including the British Museum, the Victoria and Albert Museum, the Natural History Museum, and the Science Museum. Galleries include the National Gallery, National Portrait Gallery, Tate Britain, Hayward Gallery, Wallace Collection, and Courtauld Institute. The former Bankside power station, opposite St Paul's Cathedral, has been converted into Tate Modern, a gallery of modern art. London University is the largest in Britain. The Inns of Court have been the training school for lawyers since the 13th century. London has been the centre of English drama since its first theatre was built by James Burbage in 1576. A re-creation of the Globe Theatre opened in Southwark in 1996.

Boroughs The inner London boroughs of Greater London are Camden, Hackney, Hammersmith and Fulham, Haringey, Islington, Kensington and Chelsea, Lambeth, Lewisham, Newham, Southwark, Tower Hamlets, Wandsworth, and the City of Westminster. The outer London boroughs of Greater London are Barking and Dagenham, Barnet, Bexley, Brent, Bromley, Croydon, Ealing, Enfield, Greenwich, Harrow, Havering, Hillingdon, Hounslow, Kingston upon Thames, Merton, Redbridge, Richmond upon Thames, Sutton, and Waltham Forest.

Related Web site: LondonNet – The Net Magazine Guide to London http://www.londonnet.co.uk/

London, Jack (John Griffith Chaney) (1876–1916) US novelist. He was a prolific author of naturalistic novels, adventure

JACK LONDON US writer Jack London based many of his stories on his own experiences in the wild and unfriendly Yukon region of northern Canada. His writing often carries contrasting messages since he believed in socialist equalities, but also in the rule of survival of the fittest. *Archive Photos*

stories, and socialist reportage. His works, which are often based on his own life, typically concern the human struggle for survival against extreme natural forces, as dramatized in such novels as *The Call of the Wild* (1903), *The Sea Wolf* (1904), and *White Fang* (1906). By 1906 he was the most widely read writer in the USA and had been translated into 68 languages.

Londonderry (or Derry; formerly **Derry-Calgaich** (until the 10th century); Irish 'oak wood'; *Derry-Calgaich* 'the oak wood of Calgaich' (a fierce warrior)) historic city and port on the River Foyle, 35 km/22 mi from Lough Foyle, county town of County ▷Londonderry, Northern Ireland; population (1991) 95,400. Industries include textiles, chemicals, food processing, shirt manufacturing, and acetylene from naphtha.

Features the Protestant Cathedral of St Columba dating from 1633; the Gothic revival Roman Catholic Cathedral of St Eugene (completed in 1833); the Guildhall (rebuilt in 1912), containing stained glass windows presented by livery companies of the City of London; the city walls, on which are modern iron statues by Anthony Gormley; four gates into the city still survive.

History Londonderry dates from the foundation of a monastery there by St Columba in AD 546. The city was subject to a number of sieges by the Danes between the 9th and 11th centuries, and by the Anglo-Normans in the 12th century; however, these were unsuccessful until James I of England captured the city in 1608. The king granted the borough and surrounding land to the citizens of

London. The Irish Society was formed to build and administer the city and a large colony of English Protestants was established. The city, then governed by Major Henry Baker and the Reverend George Walker, was unsuccessfully besieged in 1689 by the armies of James II, who had fled England when William of Orange was declared joint sovereign with James' daughter Mary. James' army was led by Richard Talbot, Earl of Tyrconnell, in a conflict known as the **Siege of Derry**, when 13 Derry apprentices and citizens loyal to William of Orange locked the city gates against the Jacobite army. The siege lasted 15 weeks, during which many of the inhabitants died of starvation and disease because of the blockade.

Londonderry (or Derry) county of Northern Ireland.
  area 2,070 sq km/799 sq mi   **towns and cities** ▷Londonderry (county town), Coleraine, Portstewart, Limavady   **physical** hilly moorland, coniferous forest; Sperrin Mountains; rivers Foyle, Bann, Roe, and Faughan; borders Lough Neagh   **industries** stone and lime quarrying, food processing, textiles and synthetic fibres, shirt manufacturing, light engineering, chemicals   **agriculture** farming is hindered by the very heavy rainfall; flax, cattle, sheep grazing on moorland, salmon and eel fisheries on the Bann   **population** (1981) 187,000   **famous people** Joyce Cary, Seamus ▷Heaney, William Massey, former prime minister of New Zealand

London Eye a 151 m/495 ft diameter vertical wheel with glass enclosed pods, located beside the River Thames in London, England, near Waterloo Station and County Hall, opposite the Houses of Parliament. The construction of a wheel to symbolize the turning of the century and create a monument in which people could participate was the idea of architects David Marks and Julia Barfield, and is said to have been inspired by other celebratory structures such as the Ferris Wheel built for Chicago's World's Colombian Exposition (1893) and the Eiffel Tower built for the Paris Exposition (1889). The construction was sponsored by the airline company British Airways, but due to technical problems the Eye could not be opened on 31 December 1999 as scheduled, and was opened to advance ticket holders on 1 February 2000 and to the public on 1 March.

London, Greater metropolitan area of ▷London, England, comprising the City of London, which forms a self-governing enclave, and 32 surrounding boroughs. Certain powers were exercised over this whole area by the Greater London Council (GLC) 1974–86.
  area 1,580 sq km/610 sq mi   **population** (1996) 7,074,200

London, Treaty of secret treaty signed on 26 April 1915 between Britain, France, Russia, and Italy. It promised Italy territorial gains (at the expense of Austria-Hungary) on condition that it entered World War I on the side of the Triple Entente (Britain, France, and Russia). Italy's intervention did not achieve the rapid victories expected, and the terms of the treaty (revealed by Russia 1918) angered the USA. Britain and France refused to honour the treaty and, in the post-war peace treaties, Italy received far less territory than promised.

lone pair in chemistry, a pair of electrons in the outermost shell of an atom that are not used in bonding. In certain circumstances, they will allow the atom to bond with atoms, ions, or molecules (such as boron trifluoride, BF_3) that are deficient in electrons, forming coordinate covalent (dative) bonds in which they provide both of the bonding electrons.

long. abbreviation for **longitude**; see ▷latitude and longitude.

Long, Huey (Pierce) 'the Kingfish' (1893–1935) US Democratic politician. As governor of Louisiana 1928–32 and senator for Louisiana 1932–35, he became legendary for his political rhetoric. He was popular with poor white voters for his programme of social and economic reform, which he called the 'Share Our Wealth' programme. It represented a significant challenge to F D Roosevelt's ▷New Deal economic programme.

Long Beach port and industrial city in southwestern California, USA; population (1994 est) 434,000. Long Beach forms part of Greater ▷Los Angeles and adjoins the San Pedro harbour of Los Angeles. Manufactured goods include aircraft, ships, petroleum products, chemicals, fabricated metals, electronic equipment, and processed food; the city also has oil wells and a naval shipyard, and is a convention centre. Long Beach was laid out in the 1880s and incorporated in 1888; the port was opened in 1909. Oil was discovered here in 1921, and the aircraft industry dates from World War II.

Longfellow, Henry Wadsworth (1807–1882) US poet. He is remembered for his ballads ('Excelsior', 'The Village Blacksmith', 'The Wreck of the Hesperus') and the mythic narrative epics *Evangeline* (1847), *The Song of Hiawatha* (1855), and *The Courtship of Miles Standish* (1858).

Longfellow was born in Portland, Maine. He graduated from Bowdoin College and taught modern languages there and at Harvard University 1835–54, after which he travelled widely. The most popular US poet of the 19th century, Longfellow was also an adept translator. His other works include six sonnets on Dante, a translation of Dante's *Divine Comedy*, and *Tales of a Wayside Inn* (1863), which includes the popular poem 'Paul Revere's Ride'.

HENRY WADSWORTH LONGFELLOW The US poet Henry Wadsworth Longfellow was Smith Professor of Modern Languages at Harvard from 1834 to 1854. His poems, which were widely appreciated in the 1800s, have lost popularity, although many schoolchildren are still familiar with *Paul Revere's Ride* (1863). *Archive Photos*

Longford county of the Republic of Ireland, in the province of Leinster; county town Longford; area 1,040 sq km/401 sq mi; population (1996) 30,200. The county is low-lying (the highest point is Carn Clonhugh 279 m/916 ft), and the western border is formed of the River Shannon and part of Lough Ree, one of several lakes. Other rivers are the Camlin, a tributary of the Shannon, and the Inny, which flows into Lough Ree. Agricultural activities include cattle and sheep rearing, and the production of oats and potatoes.

longhorn beetle beetle with extremely long antennae, usually equalling the length of the entire body, and often twice its length. Their bodies are 2–150 mm/0.1–6 in long, usually cylindrical, and often mimic wasps, moss, or lichens. The larvae, white or yellow

LONDON EYE The London Eye formed an important part of the UK's millennium celebrations. Big Ben can be seen in the background. *Image Bank*

grubs, are wood-borers, mostly attacking decaying or dead wood, but they may bore into healthy trees causing much damage. (Order Coleoptera, class Insecta, phylum Arthropoda.)

Long Island island east of Manhattan and southeast of Connecticut, USA, separated from the mainland by Long Island Sound and the East River; 193 km/120 mi long by about 48 km/30 mi wide; area 3,627 sq km/1,400 sq mi; population (2000 est) 7,448,600. It is mainly a residential district with farming in the east. Henry Hudson discovered the island in 1609, and it was settled by the Dutch from New Amsterdam (in the west) and the English from New England (in the east) from the 1640s.

Related Web site: Welcome to Destination Long Island, NY http://www.licvb.com/

LOOSESTRIFE The tall spikes of the purple loosestrife (*Lythrum saclicaria*) appear in abundance along riverbanks and ditches from June to August in temperate regions. *Premaphotos Wildlife*

longitude see ▷latitude and longitude.

long jump field event in athletics in which competitors sprint and jump as far as possible into a sandpit from a take-off board. The take-off board is one metre from the landing area and the sandpit measures nine metres in length. Each competitor usually has six attempts, and the winner is the one with the longest jump.

Related Web site: Long jump http://www.iaaf.org/TrainingTips/Sport/LJ/intro.html

Long March in Chinese history, the 10,000-km/6,000-mi trek undertaken from 1934 to 1935 by ▷Mao Zedong and his communist forces from southeast to northwest China, under harassment from the Guomindang (nationalist) army. Some 100,000 communists left Mao's first headquarters in Jiangxi province in October 1934, and only 8,000 lasted the journey to arrive about a year later in Shanxi, which became their new base. The march cemented Mao Zedong's control of the movement.

Long Parliament English Parliament 1640–53 and 1659–60, that continued through the English Civil War. After the Royalists withdrew in 1642 and the Presbyterian right was excluded in 1648, the remaining ▷Rump ruled England until expelled by Oliver ▷Cromwell in 1653. Reassembled in 1659–60, the Long Parliament initiated the negotiations for the ▷Restoration of the monarchy.

Longshan (or Lung-shan) site of a sophisticated late Neolithic culture 2500–1700 BC in northern China now situated in the province of Shandong in the lower Huang He (Yellow River) valley. More advanced than Yangshao, the culture was the immediate precursor of the bronze-using ▷Shang civilization. Its distinctive burnished black ceramics were kiln-fired and the first in the Far East to be made on the fast wheel.

longshore drift the movement of material along a ▷beach. When a wave breaks obliquely, pebbles are carried up the beach in the direction of the wave (swash). The wave draws back at right angles to the beach (backwash), carrying some pebbles with it. In this way, material moves in a zigzag fashion along a beach. Longshore drift is responsible for the erosion of beaches and the formation of spits (ridges of sand or shingle projecting into the water). Attempts are often made to halt longshore drift by erecting barriers, or groynes, at right angles to the shore.

long-sightedness nontechnical term for ▷hypermetropia, a vision defect.

loom any machine for weaving yarn or thread into cloth. The first looms were used to weave sheep's wool in about 5000 BC. A loom is a frame on which a set of lengthwise threads (warp) is strung. A second set of threads (weft), carried in a shuttle, is inserted at right angles over and under the warp.

loop in computing, short for ▷program loop.

Loos, Adolf (1870–1933) Austrian architect. His buildings include private houses on Lake Geneva (1904) and the Steiner House in Vienna (1910). In his article 'Ornament and Crime' (1908) he rejected the ornamentation and curved lines of the Viennese *Jugendstil* movement (see ▷Art Nouveau).

Loos, Anita (1893–1981) US writer. She was the author of the humorous fictitious diary *Gentlemen Prefer Blondes* (1925). She became a screenwriter in 1912 and worked on more than 60 films, including D W ▷Griffith's *Intolerance* (1916).

loosestrife any of several plants belonging to the primrose family, including the yellow loosestrife (*L. vulgaris*), with spikes of yellow flowers, and the low-growing creeping jenny (*L. nummularia*). The striking purple loosestrife (*Lythrum saclicaria*) belongs to a different family. (Genus *Lysimachia*, family Primulaceae; purple loosestrife family Lythraceae.)

Lope de Vega, (Carpio) Felix Spanish poet and dramatist; see ▷Vega, Lope de.

López, Francisco Solano (1827–1870) Paraguayan dictator in succession to his father Carlos López. He involved the country in a war with Brazil, Uruguay, and Argentina, during which approximately 80% of the population died.

loquat evergreen tree native to China and Japan, also known as the Japan medlar. The golden pear-shaped fruit has a delicate sweet-sour taste. (*Eriobotrya japonica*, family Rosaceae.)

Lorca, Federico García (1898–1936) Spanish poet and playwright. His plays include *Bodas de sangre/Blood Wedding* (1933), *Yerma* (1934), and *La casa de Bernarda Alba/The House of Bernarda Alba* (1936). His poems include the collection *Romancero gitano/Gypsy Ballad-book* (1928) and the 'Lament' written for the bullfighter Ignacio Sánchez Mejías. Lorca was shot by the Falangists during the Spanish Civil War.

He was born in Fuente Vaqueros, near Granada. Early collections of poetry were *Libros de poemas/Books of Poems* (1921) and *Canciones/Gypsy Songs* (1927). He established himself with the *Romancero gitano*, a collection of mysterious and beautiful ballads of gypsy life and Andalusian folklore. In 1929–30 he visited New York, and his experiences there are reflected in *Poeta en Nuevo York/Poet in New York* (published posthumously in 1940).

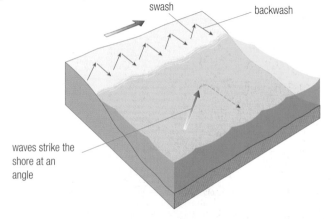

LONGSHORE DRIFT The diagram above shows the direction of longshore drift and therefore of movement along the beach. Waves sometimes hit the beach at an angle. The incoming waves (swash) carry sand and shingle up onto the shore and the outgoing wave takes some material away with it. Gradually material is carried down the shoreline in the same direction as the longshore current.

Returning to Spain, he founded a touring theatrical company and began to write plays.

Lord (Old English *hlaford* 'bread keeper') in the UK, prefix used informally as a less formal alternative to the full title of a marquess, earl, or viscount, for example 'Lord Salisbury' instead of 'the Marquess of Salisbury'. Barons are normally referred to as lords, the term baron being used for foreign holders of that rank. 'Lord' is also used as a courtesy title before the forename and surname of younger sons of dukes and marquesses.

Lord Advocate chief law officer of the crown in Scotland who has ultimate responsibility for criminal prosecutions in Scotland. The Lord Advocate does not usually act in inferior courts, where prosecution is carried out by procurators-fiscal acting under the Lord Advocate's instructions.

Lord Chamberlain in the UK, chief officer of the royal household who engages staff and appoints retail suppliers. Until 1968 the Lord Chamberlain licensed and censored plays before their public performance. The office is temporary, and appointments are made by the government.

Lord Chancellor (Latin *cancellarius*) UK state official, originally the royal secretary, today a member of the cabinet, whose office ends with a change of government. The Lord Chancellor acts as Speaker of the House of Lords, may preside over the Court of Appeal, and is head of the judiciary.

Lords, House of upper chamber of the UK ▷Parliament. In 1998 there were 1,134 members: 631 hereditary peers, 477 life peers, two archbishops and 24 bishops. The Lords Temporal consist of 762 hereditary peers, and 435 life peers, of whom 26 are 'law lords'. In total there are 86 women peers. 304 of the hereditary peers are Conservatives and only 17 Labour. In contrast, 169 of the life peers are Conservatives, 139 are Labour, 42 are Liberal Democrats and 127 are independent 'cross-benchers'. The Labour government elected in May 1997 intends to introduce legislation to end the right of hereditary peers to sit and vote in the chamber. This will be the first stage in its democratization. The legislative powers of the Lords will not be changed. In 1998 the government, led by Tony Blair, introduced legislation to abolish the right of peers to sit and vote in the House of Lords. A compromise allowed 92 (elected by their fellow peers) to remain as temporary members.

Its members are unelected and comprise the **temporal peers**: all hereditary peers of England created to 1707, all hereditary peers of Great Britain created 1707–1800, and all hereditary peers of the UK from 1801 onwards; all hereditary Scottish peers (under the Peerage Act 1963); all peeresses in their own right (under the same act); all life peers (both the ▷law lords and those created under the Life Peerages Act 1958); and the **spiritual peers**: the two archbishops and 24 of the bishops (London, Durham, and Winchester by right, and the rest by seniority). Since the Parliament Act of 1911 the powers of the Lords have been restricted in that they may delay a bill passed by the Commons but not reject it. The Lords are presided over by the Lord Chancellor.

HOUSE OF LORDS A 16th-century manuscript depicting Edward I in Parliament. The king is flanked by Alexander II of Scotland on his right and Llewellyn ap Gruffyd of Wales on his left. In front of him the justices and law officers are sitting on woolsacks. *Philip Sauvain Picture Collection*

Lorelei in Germanic folklore, a river ▷nymph of the Rhine who lures sailors onto the rock where she sits combing her hair. She features in several poems, including 'Die Lorelei' by the German Romantic writer Heinrich Heine. The **Lurlei** rock south of Koblenz is 130 m/430 ft high.

Loren, Sophia (1934–) Stage name of Sofia Scicolone. Italian film actor. Her boldly sensual appeal was promoted by her husband, the producer Carlo Ponti. She won an Academy Award for *La Ciociara/Two Women* (1960).

SOPHIA LOREN The 29-year-old Italian actor at the Academy Awards ceremony in Los Angeles, California, USA, in April 1963. *Image Bank*

Lorenz, Konrad Zacharias (1903–1989) Austrian ethologist who was awarded a Nobel Prize for Physiology or Medicine in 1973 with Nikolaas ▷Tinbergen and Karl von Frisch for their work on animal behaviour patterns. He studied the relationship between instinct and behaviour, particularly in birds, and described the phenomenon of ▷imprinting in 1935. His books include *King Solomon's Ring* (1952) on animal behaviour, and *On Aggression* (1966) on human behaviour.

Lorestan alternative form of ▷Luristan, a province of Iran.

lorikeet any of various small, brightly coloured parrots found in Southeast Asia and Australasia.

Lorimer, Robert Stodart (1864–1929) Scottish architect. The most prolific architect representative of the Scottish Arts and Crafts Movement, Lorimer drew particularly from Scottish vernacular buildings of the 16th and 17th centuries to create a series of mansions and houses, practically planned, with picturesque, turreted exteriors.

loris any of a group of small prosimian ▷primates native to Southeast Asia. Lorises are slow-moving, tree-dwelling, and nocturnal. They have very large eyes; true lorises have no tails. They climb without leaping, gripping branches tightly and moving on or hanging below them. (Family Lorisidae.)

    The **slender loris** (*Loris tardigradus*) of southern India and Sri Lanka is about 20 cm/8 in long. The tubbier **slow loris** (*Nycticebus coucang*) of Southeast Asia is 30 cm/1 ft.

    The **angwantibo** (genus *Arctocebus*), **potto** (genus *Perodicticus*), and **galagos** or **bushbabies** (genera *Galago* and *Euoticus*) are similar African forms.

Lorrain, Claude French painter; see ▷Claude Lorrain.

Lorraine (German **Lothringen**) region and former province of northeast France in the upper reaches of the Meuse and Moselle rivers; bounded in the north by Belgium, Luxembourg, and Germany, and in the east by Alsace; area 23,600 sq km/9,095 sq mi; population (1990) 2,305,700. It comprises the *départements* of Meurthe-et-Moselle, Meuse, Moselle, and Vosges, and its chief cities are Metz, ▷Nancy (the capital), Luneville, and Epinal. There are deposits of coal, iron ore, and salt; grain, fruit, and livestock are farmed. In 1871, after the Franco-Prussian War, the northern part of the region was ceded to Germany as part of ▷Alsace-Lorraine. The whole area saw heavy fighting in World War I.

Lorre, Peter (1904–1964) Stage name of Lazlo Löwenstein. Hungarian character actor. He made his international reputation

---

LORIS The two species of loris are primitive primates related to bush babies and pottos. The slow loris lives among the trees of the rainforests in South and Southeast Asia where it feeds at night, mainly on insects and plant material, although it will take small birds and their eggs. It gets its name from its slow, deliberate movements.

as the whistling child-murderer in Fritz Lang's thriller *M* (1930). Becoming one of Hollywood's best-loved villains, he played opposite Humphrey Bogart in *The Maltese Falcon* (1941), *Casablanca* (1942), and *Beat the Devil* (1954), and in several films with the portly British actor Sydney Greenstreet.

lory any of various small Australasian ▷parrots. Lories are very brightly coloured and characterized by a tongue with a brushlike tip adapted for feeding on pollen and nectar from flowers. (Subfamily Loriinae, order Psittaciformes.)

Los Angeles city and port in southwestern California, USA; population (2000 est) 3,694,800; Los Angeles–Riverside–Orange County consolidated metropolitan area (also known as Greater Los Angeles) (1994) 15,302,000. In size of population it is the second-largest city and the second-largest metropolitan area in the USA. The city occupies 1,204 sq km/465 sq mi. Industries include aerospace, electronics, motor vehicles, chemicals, clothing, building materials, printing, food processing, and films. Los Angeles was established as a Spanish settlement in 1781.

Losey, Joseph (Walton) (1909–1984) US film director. Blacklisted in the USA for political reasons, he settled in the UK, where he made a series of subtle if sometimes wilfully mannered studies of personal relationships as shaped and distorted by class and other social factors. These include *The Servant* (1963), *Accident* (1966), and *The Go-Between* (1971).

Lost Generation, the disillusioned US literary generation of the 1920s, members of which went to live in Paris. The phrase is attributed to the writer Gertrude Stein in Ernest Hemingway's early novel of 1920s Paris, 'Fiesta' (*The Sun Also Rises*) (1927).

Lot French river; see ▷Gironde.

Lothair (825–869) King of Lotharingia from 855, when he inherited the region from his father, the Holy Roman Emperor Lothair I.

Lothair two Holy Roman emperors:

Lothair I (795–855) Holy Roman Emperor from 817 in association with his father Louis I. On Louis's death in 840, the empire was divided between Lothair and his brothers; Lothair took northern Italy and the valleys of the rivers Rhône and Rhine.

Lothair II (c. 1070–1137) Holy Roman Emperor from 1133 and German king from 1125. His election as emperor, opposed by the ▷Hohenstaufen family of princes, was the start of the feud between the ▷Guelph and Ghibelline factions, who supported the papal party and the Hohenstaufens' claim to the imperial throne respectively.

Lotharingia medieval region west of the Rhine, between the Jura mountains and the North Sea; the northern portion of the lands assigned to Lothair I when the Carolingian empire was divided. It was called after his son King Lothair, and later corrupted to Lorraine; it is now part of Alsace-Lorraine, France.

Lothian former region of Scotland (1975–96), which was replaced by East Lothian, Midlothian, West Lothian, and City of Edinburgh unitary authorities.

Konrad Lorenz
Historians will have to face the fact that natural selection determined the evolution of cultures in the same manner as it did that of species.
On Aggression (1966)

Lotto, Lorenzo (c. 1480–1556) Venetian painter active in Bergamo, Treviso, Venice, Ancona, and Rome. His early works were influenced by Giovanni Bellini. He painted religious works but is best known for his portraits, which often convey a sense of unease or an air of melancholy.

lotus any of several different plants, especially the **water lily** (*Nymphaea lotus*), frequent in Egyptian art, and the pink **Asiatic lotus** (*Nelumbo nucifera*), a sacred symbol in Hinduism and Buddhism, whose flower head floats erect above the water.

    Others are those of the genus *Lotus* (family Leguminosae), including the **bird's foot trefoil** (*L. corniculatus*); the ▷**jujube shrub** (*Zizyphus lotus*), known to the ancient Greeks who used its fruit to make a type of bread and also a wine supposed to induce happy oblivion – hence **lotus-eaters**; and the **American lotus** (*Nelumbo lutea*), a pale yellow water lily of the southern USA.

Lotus Sūtra scripture of Mahāyāna Buddhism. The original is in Sanskrit (*Saddharmapundarīka Sūtra*) and is thought to date from some time after 100 BC.

Louangphrabang (or Louang Prabang) Buddhist religious centre in Laos, on the Mekong River at the head of river navigation; population (1998 est) 110,400. It was the capital of the kingdom of Louangphrabang, incorporated in Laos in 1946, and the royal capital of Laos 1946–75.

loudspeaker electromechanical device that converts electrical signals into sound waves, which are radiated into the air. The most common type of loudspeaker is the **moving-coil speaker**. Electrical signals from, for example, a radio are fed to a coil of fine wire wound around the top of a cone. The coil is surrounded by a magnet. When signals pass through it, the coil becomes an electromagnet, which by moving causes the cone to vibrate, setting up sound waves.

Loughborough industrial town in Leicestershire, central England, 18 km/11 mi northwest of Leicester, on the River Soar; population (1995 est) 55,300. Industries include engineering, bell-founding, children's book publishing, brickmaking, and the manufacture of heavy duty electrical goods and power generators, knitwear, hosiery, pharmaceuticals, and medical supplies.

Louis eighteen kings of France, including:

Louis (I) the Pious (788–840) Holy Roman Emperor from 814, when he succeeded his father Charlemagne.

Louis III (c. 863–882) King of northern France from 879, while his brother Carloman (866–884) ruled southern France. He was the son of Louis II. Louis countered a revolt of the nobility at the beginning of his reign, and his resistance to the Normans made him a hero of epic poems.

Louis IV (c. 921–954) Called 'Louis d'Outremer'. King of France from 936. His reign was marked by the rebellion of nobles who refused to recognize his authority. As a result of his liberality they were able to build powerful feudal lordships.

Louis (VI) the Fat (1081–1137) King of France from 1108. He led his army against feudal brigands, the English (under Henry I), and the Holy Roman Empire, temporarily consolidating his realm and extending it into Flanders. He was a benefactor to the church, and his advisers included Abbot Suger.

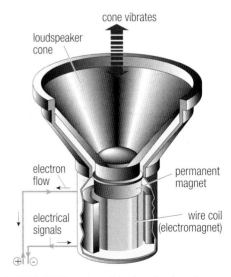

LOUDSPEAKER A moving-coil loudspeaker shows how electrical signals flowing through the wire coil turn it into an electromagnet, which moves as the signals vary. The attached cone vibrates, producing sound waves.

Louis VII (c. 1120–1180) King of France from 1137, who led the Second ▷Crusade. He annulled his marriage to Eleanor of Aquitaine 1152, whereupon Eleanor married Henry of Anjou, later Henry II of England. Louis was involved in a bitter struggle with Henry 1152–74.

Louis VIII (1187–1226) King of France from 1223, who was invited to become king of England in place of ▷John by the English barons, and unsuccessfully invaded England 1215–17.

Louis IX, St (1214–1270) King of France from 1226, leader of the 7th and 8th ▷Crusades. He was defeated in the former by the Muslims, spending four years in captivity. He died in Tunis. He was canonized in 1297.

Louis (X) the Stubborn (1289–1316) King of France who succeeded his father Philip IV in 1314. His reign saw widespread discontent among the nobles, which he countered by granting charters guaranteeing seignorial rights, although some historians claim that by using evasive tactics, he gave up nothing.

Louis XI (1423–1483) King of France from 1461. He broke the power of the nobility (headed by ▷Charles the Bold) by intrigue and military power.

Louis XII (1462–1515) King of France from 1498. He was Duke of Orléans until he succeeded his cousin Charles VIII to the throne. His reign was devoted to Italian wars.

Louis XIII (1601–1643) King of France from 1610 (in succession to his father Henry IV), he assumed royal power in 1617. He was under the political control of Cardinal ▷Richelieu 1624–42.

Louis XIV (1638–1715) Called 'the Sun King'. King of France from 1643, when he succeeded his father Louis XIII; his mother was Anne of Austria. Until 1661 France was ruled by the chief minister, Jules Mazarin, but later Louis took absolute power, summed up in his saying *L'Etat c'est moi* ('I am the state'). Throughout his reign he was engaged in unsuccessful expansionist wars – 1667–68, 1672–78, 1688–97, and 1701–13 (the War of the ▷Spanish Succession) – against various European alliances, always including Britain and the Netherlands. He was a patron of the arts.

Foreign policy Following the death of his father-in-law, Philip II of Spain, Louis claimed the Spanish Netherlands and attempted 1667–68 to annex the territory, but was frustrated by an alliance of the Netherlands, Britain, and Sweden. Having detached Britain from the alliance, he invaded the Netherlands in 1672, but the Dutch stood firm (led by ▷William of Orange) and despite the European alliance formed against France, achieved territorial gains at the Peace of Nijmegen (1678).

Hostilities were renewed in the war of the League of Augsburg 1688–97 between Louis and the Grand Alliance (including Britain), formed by William of Orange. The French were victorious on land, but the French fleet was almost destroyed at the Battle of La Hogue

LOUIS XII King Louis XII of France leaving Alexandria on 24 April 1507. *Philip Sauvain Picture Collection*

LOUIS XVI The execution of Louis XVI on 21 January 1793 (Musée Carnavalet, Paris). *The Art Archive*

in 1692 and the Treaty of Ryswick forced Louis to give up all his conquests since 1678. The acceptance by Louis of the Spanish throne in 1700 (for his grandson) precipitated the War of the Spanish Succession, with England encouraged to join against the French by Louis' recognition of the Old Pretender as James III. Although the Treaty of Utrecht (1713) gave Spain to Louis' grandson, the war effectively ended French supremacy in Europe, and left France virtually bankrupt.

In 1660 Louis married the Infanta Maria Theresa of Spain, but he was greatly influenced by his mistresses, including Louise de La Vallière, Madame de Montespan, and Madame de Maintenon.

Related Web site: L'Age d'Or – The Age of the Sun King http://www.geocities.com/Paris/Rue/1663/index.html

Louis XV (1710–1774) King of France from 1715, with the Duke of Orléans as regent until 1723. He was the great-grandson of Louis XIV. Indolent and frivolous, Louis left government in the hands of his ministers, the Duke of Bourbon and Cardinal Fleury (1653–1743). On the latter's death he attempted to rule alone but became entirely dominated by his mistresses, Madame de Pompadour and Madame Du Barry. His foreign policy led to French possessions in Canada and India being lost to England.

Louis XVI (1754–1793) King of France from 1774, grandson of Louis XV, and son of Louis the Dauphin. He was dominated by his queen, ▷Marie Antoinette, and French finances fell into such confusion that in 1789 the ▷States General (parliament) had to be summoned, and the ▷French Revolution began. Louis lost his personal popularity in June 1791 when he attempted to flee the country, and in August 1792 the Parisians stormed the Tuileries palace and took the royal family prisoner. Deposed in September 1792, Louis was tried in December, sentenced for treason in January 1793, and guillotined.

Louis XVII (1785–1795) nominal king of France, the son of Louis XVI. During the French Revolution he was imprisoned with his parents in 1792 and probably died in prison.

Louis XVIII (1755–1824) King of France 1814–24, the younger brother of Louis XVI. He assumed the title of king in 1795, having fled into exile in 1791 during the French Revolution, but became king only on the fall of Napoleon I in April 1814. Expelled during Napoleon's brief return (the 'hundred days') in 1815, he resumed power after Napoleon's final defeat at Waterloo, pursuing a policy of calculated liberalism until ultra-royalist pressure became dominant after 1820.

Louis, Joe (1914–1981) Adopted name of Joseph Louis Barrow. US boxer, nicknamed 'the Brown Bomber'. He was world heavyweight champion 1937–49 and made a record 25 successful defences (a record for any weight). Louis announced his retirement, undefeated, in 1949, but made a comeback and lost to US boxer Ezzard Charles in a world title fight in 1950.

In the first round of his first fight, Louis achieved his first knockout. He suffered his first defeat, and knockout, at the hands of German boxer Max Schmeling in 1936. Two years later, in a contest that was seen as a battle of race and ideologies, he turned the tables, and defeated Schmeling with a knockout.

Louisiana state in southern USA, nicknamed the Pelican State. Louisiana was admitted to the Union in 1818 as the 18th US state. It has been in the hands of the Spanish, French, and Americans since the 16th century, and its culture also has been influenced by African slaves and their descendants, and Caribbean and French-Canadian immigrants; the Creoles of southern parishes were originally a mix of French and Spanish descendants; the Cajuns of the southwest were originally French immigrants who had been expelled from Acadia in modern-day Nova Scotia, Canada. Musically, the state is associated with the development of jazz and the blues, particularly in the city of New Orleans. Louisiana is bordered to the north by Arkansas, to the west by Texas, with the Sabine River and Toledo Bend Reservoir forming much of the boundary, and to the east by Mississippi, with the Mississippi and Pearl rivers forming much of

the boundary. To the south, the state extends into the Gulf of Mexico, its area expanding continuously through the accretional growth of the delta of the Mississippi River; much of Louisiana consists literally of fragments of other states in the Mississippi-Missouri system.

population (1995) 4,342,300; including Cajuns, descendants of 18th-century religious exiles from Canada, who speak a French dialect **area** 135,900 sq km/52,457 sq mi **capital** ▷Baton Rouge **towns and cities** New Orleans, Shreveport, Lafayette, Metairie **industries and products** rice, cotton, sugar, soybeans, oil, natural gas, chemicals, sulphur, fish and shellfish, salt, processed foods, petroleum products, timber, paper, tourism, music industry

Louisiana Purchase purchase by the USA from France in 1803 of an area covering about 2,144,000 sq km/828,000 sq mi, including the present-day states of Louisiana, Missouri, Arkansas, Iowa, Nebraska, North Dakota, South Dakota, and Oklahoma. The purchase, which doubled the size of the USA, marked the end of Napoleon's plans for a colonial empire and ensured free navigation on the Mississippi River for the USA.

Related Web site: Louisiana Purchase and Associated Documents http://www.yale.edu/lawweb/avalon/diplomacy/fr1803m.htm

Louis-Napoleon name by which ▷Napoleon III was known.

Louis Philippe (1773–1850) King of France 1830–48. Son of Louis Philippe Joseph, Duke of Orléans 1747–93; both were known as **Philippe Egalité** from their support of the 1792 Revolution. Louis Philippe fled into exile 1793–1814, but became king after the 1830 revolution with the backing of the rich bourgeoisie. Corruption discredited his regime, and after his overthrow, he escaped to the UK and died there.

Lourdes town in the *département* of Hautes-Pyrénées in the Midi-Pyrénées region of southwest France, on the Gave de Pau River; population (1991) 15,600. Its Christian shrine to St ▷Bernadette has a reputation for miraculous cures, and Lourdes is an important Roman Catholic pilgrimage centre. In 1858 a young peasant girl, Bernadette Soubirous, claimed to have been shown the healing springs of the Grotte de Massabielle by a vision of the Virgin Mary.

Related Web site: Notre-Dame de Lourdes http://www.newadvent.org/cathen/09389b.htm

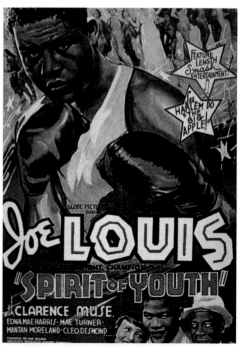

JOE LOUIS A film poster of US boxer Joe Louis in *Spirit of Youth* (1938), a classic tale of a poor boy making good, which was the only feature film Louis ever made. *Archive Photos*

louse parasitic insect that lives on mammals. It has a flat, segmented body without wings, and a tube attached to the head, used for sucking blood from its host. (Order Anoplura.)

Some lice occur on humans, including the **head louse** (*Pediculus capitis*) and the **body louse** (*P. corporis*), a typhus carrier. Pediculosis is a skin disease caused by infestation of lice. Most mammals have a species of lice adapted to living on them. Biting lice belong to a different order of insects (Mallophaga) and feed on the skin, feathers, or hair. Each year 14 million children in the USA alone suffer from head lice.

Related Web site: Louse http://www.ent.iastate.edu/Imagegal/phthiraptera/

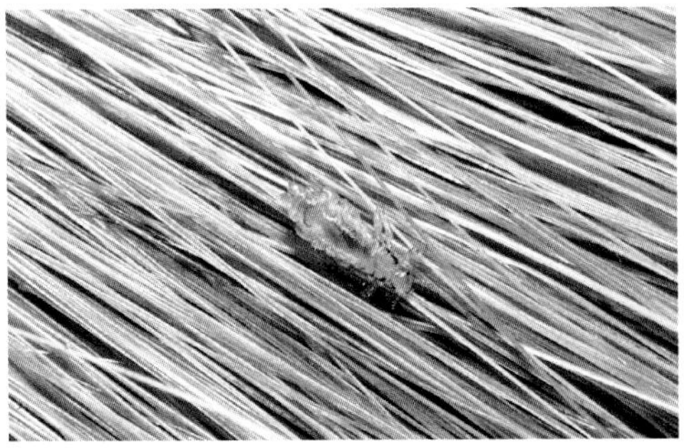

LOUSE The human head louse *Pediculus capitis* spends its entire life cycle on the human head, though it may change hosts. *Ken Preston-Mafham/Premaphotos Wildlife*

Louth smallest county of the Republic of Ireland, in the province of Leinster; county town Dundalk; area 820 sq km/317 sq mi; population (1996) 92,200. It is mainly fertile and low-lying. The chief towns are Dundalk at the north end of Dundalk bay, Drogheda, and Ardee, and the chief rivers are the Fane, Lagan, Glyde, and Dee. There is cattle rearing and fishing; oats and potatoes are grown. Greenore on Carlingford Lough is a container shipping port. Louth is rich in ancient buildings and remains, and was of strategic importance during the 12th–18th centuries. Important monastic sites with extensive remains include Monasterboice (founded in the 5th century), and Mellifont Abbey (founded in the 12th century).

lovebird any of a group of birds belonging to the ▷parrot family, found in Africa south of the Sahara. They take their name from the affection the male displays towards the female. Lovebirds are generally just larger than sparrows (about 16 cm/6 in) and coloured green with red, yellow, and black markings on the head. (Genus *Agapornis*, family Psittacidae, order Psittaciformes.)

love-in-a-mist perennial plant of southern Europe with fine leaves that create a soft haze around the delicate blue or white flowers; these are followed by large seedheads and, later, a profusion of new plants. (*Nigella damascena*, family Ranunculaceae.)

Lovelace, Richard (1618–1657) English poet. Imprisoned in 1642 for petitioning for the restoration of royal rule, he wrote 'To Althea, from Prison', and during a second term in jail in 1648 arranged the publication of his collection *Lucasta* (1649). His poetry is varied in style and content, some in the 'metaphysical' style of conceits, some more courtly and graceful.

Richard Lovelace
Stone walls do not a prison make /
Nor iron bars a cage.
'To Althea, From Prison'

Low Countries region of Europe that consists of ▷Belgium and the ▷Netherlands, and usually includes ▷Luxembourg.

Lowell, Amy Lawrence (1874–1925) US poet. She began her career by publishing the conventional *A Dome of Many-Colored Glass* (1912) but eventually succeeded Ezra Pound as leader of the Imagists (see ▷Imagism). Her works, in free verse, include *Sword Blades and Poppy Seed* (1916).

Lowell, Robert Traill Spence, Jr (1917–1977) US poet. His brutal yet tender verse stressed the importance of individualism, especially during times of war. His works include *Lord Weary's Castle* (1946; Pulitzer prize), *Life Studies* (1959), and *For the Union Dead* (1964).

Much of his poetry is confessional. During World War II he was imprisoned for five months for conscientious objection. Several of his poems, notably 'Memories of West Street and Lepke', reflect on this experience. 'Skunk Hour', included in the acclaimed volume *Life Studies*, is another example of his autobiographical poetry. In the 1960s he was again a war protester and also a civil-rights activist.

Lower Austria (German **Niederösterreich**) largest federal state of Austria, bordered on the north by the Czech Republic, drained by the River Danube; area 19,200 sq km/7,411 sq mi; population (1994) 1,511,600. Its capital is St Pölten. The main towns are Wiener Neustadt and Krems. ▷Vienna is a provincial enclave within the province. In addition to wine, sugar beet, and grain, there are reserves of oil and natural gas. Manufactured products include textiles, chemicals, and metal goods. Agriculture and forestry are important.

Lower Saxony (German **Niedersachsen**) administrative region (German *Land*) in northern Germany, bordered to the north by Schleswig-Holstein and the city-state of Hamburg, to the northeast by Mecklenburg-West Pomerania, to the south by North Rhine-Westphalia and Hesse, on the east and southeast by Saxony-Anhalt and Thuringia respectively, and on the west by the Netherlands; area 47,400 sq km/18,296 sq mi; population (1995) 7,823,000. The capital is ▷Hannover, and other towns and cities include Braunschweig (Brunswick), Osnabrück, Oldenburg, Göttingen, Wolfsburg, Salzgitter, and Hildesheim. The region includes the Lüneburg Heath, the Harz Mountains, and the Elbe, Weser, Jade, and Ems rivers. Industries include cars (the Volkswagen plant at Wolfsburg is in the east of the state), machinery, electrical engineering, and iron and steel production. Agriculture includes cereals, oats, potatoes, and livestock farming.

low-level language in computing, a programming language designed for a particular computer and reflecting its internal ▷machine code; low-level languages are therefore often described as **machine-oriented** languages. They cannot easily be converted to run on a computer with a different central processing unit, and they are relatively difficult to learn because a detailed knowledge of the internal working of the computer is required. Since they must be translated into machine code by an assembler program, low-level languages are also called ▷assembly languages.

Lowry, L(aurence) S(tephen) (1887–1976) English painter. His works depict life in the industrial towns of the north of England. In the 1920s he developed a naive style characterized by matchstick figures, often in animated groups, and gaunt simplified factories and terraced houses, painted in an almost monochrome palette. *The Pond* (1950; Tate Gallery, London) is an example. The Lowry Arts Centre in Salford, near Manchester, England, opened in 2000 with exhibits of almost 100 Lowry works.

He also painted remote seascapes, lonely hill landscapes and some striking portraits, for example *A Manchester Man* (1936).

Born in Manchester, where he studied at the Art College, he spent the rest of his life in nearby Salford, earning his living as a rent collector. He concentrated entirely on the life around him, his paintings sometimes inspired by a humorous anecdote, as in *The Arrest* (1927; Castle Museum, Nottingham).

Although he was a legend in his lifetime, he remained an elusive, retiring figure, rarely venturing beyond his native towns.

Loyalist member of approximately 30% of the US population who remained loyal to Britain in the ▷American Revolution. Many Loyalists went to eastern Ontario, Canada, after 1783.

Loyola founder of the Jesuits. See ▷Ignatius Loyola.

Loyola, St Ignatius (1491–1556) Born Iñigo López de Recalde. Spanish noble who founded the ▷Jesuit order in 1534, also called the Society of Jesus.

Related Web site: Loyola, St Ignatius http://www.newadvent.org/cathen/07639c.htm

LSD (abbreviation for lysergic acid diethylamide) psychedelic drug, a ▷hallucinogen. Colourless, odourless, and easily synthesized, it is nonaddictive and nontoxic, but its effects are unpredictable. Its use is illegal in most countries.

The initials are from the German *lyserg-säure-diäthylamid*; the drug was first synthesized by a German chemist, Albert Hofmann, in 1943. In 1947 the US Central Intelligence Agency began experiments with LSD, often on unsuspecting victims. Many psychiatrists in North America used it in treatment in the 1950s. Its use as a means to increased awareness and enhanced perception was popularized in the 1960s by US psychologist Timothy Leary (1920–1996), novelist Ken Kesey, and chemist Augustus Owsley Stanley III. A series of laws to ban LSD were passed in the USA from 1965 (by which time 4 million Americans were estimated to have taken it) and in the UK in 1966; other countries followed suit. The drug had great influence on the ▷hippie movement.

LSI (abbreviation for large-scale integration) technology that enables whole electrical circuits to be etched into a piece of semiconducting material just a few millimetres square.

By the late 1960s a complete computer processor could be integrated on a single chip, or ▷integrated circuit, and in 1971 the US electronics company Intel produced the first commercially available ▷microprocessor. Very large-scale integration (VLSI) results in even smaller chips.

Ltd abbreviation for **Limited**; see ▷private limited company.

Luanda (formerly **Loanda**) capital and industrial port of Angola; population (1995) 2,250,000. Products include cotton, sugar, tobacco, timber, textiles, paper, fuel oil, and lubricants. Founded in 1575 by Portuguese settlers, it became a Portuguese colonial administrative centre as well as an outlet for slaves transported to Brazil.

Lubbers, Rudolph Franz Marie (Ruud) (1939–) Dutch politician, prime minister of the Netherlands 1982–94. Leader of the right-of-centre Christian Democratic Appeal (CDA), he became minister for economic affairs in 1973. In October 2000, he was appointed United Nations High Commissioner for Refugees.

Lübeck (Wendish Slavonic 'lovely one') seaport and resort of Schleswig-Holstein, Germany, 24 km/15 mi from the Baltic Sea, 60 km/37 mi northeast of Hamburg; population (1995) 216,900. Manufactured goods include machinery, aeronautical and space equipment, steel, and ironwork; there are also marine engineering, ship-repairing, and fish-canning industries. Lübeck is known for its wine trade and its marzipan. The Elbe–Lübeck Canal (1900) links the city with the main waterways of Europe and the docks at Travemunde have ferry connections to Scandinavia.

Lubetkin, Berthold Romanovich (1901–1990) Russian-born architect. He settled in the UK in 1930 and formed, with six young architects, a group called **Tecton**. His pioneering designs include Highpoint I (1933–35), a block of flats in Highgate, London; and the curved lines of the Penguin Pool (1933) at London Zoo, which employ ▷reinforced concrete to sculptural effect.

Lubitsch, Ernst (1892–1947) German film director. He worked in the USA from 1921 and became known for the 'Lubitsch touch' – a combination of incisive social critique, witty humour, sophistication, and visual understatement, seen in, for example, *Ninotchka* (1939) and *Heaven Can Wait* (1943).

Lublin city in Poland, on the Bystrzyca River, 150 km/95 mi southeast of Warsaw; population (1993) 352,500. Industries include textiles, engineering, aircraft, and electrical goods. A trading centre from the 10th century, it has an ancient citadel, a 16th-century cathedral, and a university (1918). A council of workers and peasants proclaimed Poland's independence at Lublin 1918, and a Russian-sponsored committee of national liberation, which proclaimed itself the provincial government of Poland at Lublin on 31 December 1944, was recognized by Russia five days later.

lubricant substance used between moving surfaces to reduce friction. Carbon-based (organic) lubricants, commonly called grease and oil, are recovered from petroleum distillation.

Extensive research has been carried out on chemical additives to lubricants, which can reduce corrosive wear, prevent the accumulation of 'cold sludge' (often the result of stop-start driving in city traffic jams), keep pace with the higher working temperatures of aviation gas turbines, or provide radiation-resistant greases for nuclear power plants. Silicon-based spray-on lubricants are also used; they tend to attract dust and dirt less than carbon-based ones.

A solid lubricant is graphite, an allotropic form of carbon, either flaked or emulsified (colloidal) in water or oil.

Lucan (AD 39–65) Born Marcus Annaeus Lucanus. Latin poet. Born in Córdoba, Spain, he was a nephew of the writer Seneca and favourite of Nero until the emperor became jealous of his verse. Lucan then joined a republican conspiracy and committed suicide on its failure. His epic poem *Pharsalia*, in ten books (the last incomplete), deals with the civil wars of Caesar and Pompey 49–48 BC, and was influential in the Middle Ages and Renaissance.

Lucas, George (1944–) US film director. He wrote and directed *Star Wars* (1977), wrote and produced *The Empire Strikes Back* (1980) and *Return of the Jedi* (1983), and produced a trilogy of adventure films beginning with *Raiders of the Lost Ark* (1981). He wrote and produced *Star Wars Episode I: The Phantom Menace* (1999), and *Star Wars Episode II: Attack of the Clones* (2002); *Episode III* is due to be released in 2005. See picture on p. 572.

Lucas van Leyden (1494–1533) Dutch painter and engraver. Active in Leiden and Antwerp, he was a pioneer of Netherlandish genre scenes, for example *The Chess Players* (*c.* 1510; Staatliche Museen, Berlin). His woodcuts and engravings, often more highly regarded than his paintings, were inspired by Albrecht ▷Dürer.

Lucca (ancient **Luca**) town in Tuscany, northwest Italy, on the River Serchio, 60 km/37 mi northwest of Florence; population (1990) 86,400. Industries include weaving, food-processing, engineering, and the manufacture of chemicals. It was an independent republic from 1160 until its absorption into Tuscany in 1847. The composer Giacomo Puccini was born here.

Luce, (Ann) Clare Boothe (1903–1987) US journalist, playwright, and politician. She was managing editor of *Vanity Fair* magazine 1933–34, and wrote several successful plays, including *The Women* (1936) and *Margin for Error* (1940), both of which were made into films. She served as a Republican member of Congress 1943–47 and as ambassador to Italy 1953–57.

Luce, Henry Robinson (1898–1967) US publisher, founder of Time, Inc, which publishes the weekly news magazine *Time* (from 1923), the business magazine *Fortune* (from 1930), the pictorial magazine *Life* (from 1936), and the sports magazine *Sports Illustrated* (from 1954). He married Clare Boothe Luce in 1935.

Lucerne (German **Luzern**) capital and tourist centre of Lucerne canton, Switzerland, 45 km/28 mi southwest of Zürich, on the River Reuss where it flows out of Lake Lucerne; population (1994) city 61,700; canton 337,700. Manufactured goods include chemicals, metal products, and textiles. The city developed around a Benedictine monastery established in about 750, and owes its prosperity to its position on the St Gotthard road and railway.

lucerne another name for the plant ▷alfalfa.

Lucerne, Lake (German **Vierwaldstättersee**, 'lake of the four forest cantons') scenic lake surrounded by mountains in north-central Switzerland; area 114 sq km/44 sq mi. It lies at an altitude of 437 m/1,434 ft and its greatest depth is 215 m/705 ft. It has four main basins, connected by narrow channels. The lake is subject to sudden storms whipped up by the ▷föhn wind.

Lucian (*c.* 125–*c.* 190) Greek writer. In his satirical dialogues, he pours scorn on religions and mocks human pretensions. His 65 genuine works also include rhetorical declamations, literary criticism, biography, and romance. Among the most interesting of his works are *Dialogues of the Gods*, *Dialogues of the Dead*, *Zeus Confounded*, and *Zeus Tragedian*. His *True History* inspired ▷Rabelais's *Voyage of Pantagruel*, Swift's *Gulliver's Travels*, and ▷Cyrano de Bergerac's *Journey to the Moon*.

Lucifer (Latin 'bearer of light') in Christian theology, another name for the ▷devil, the leader of the angels who rebelled against God. In Greek mythology, Lucifer is another name for the morning star (the planet ▷Venus).

Lucknow capital of the state of ▷Uttar Pradesh, India, on the Gumti River, 70 km/46 mi northeast of Kanpur on a railway junction; population (1991) 1,669,200. Industries include engineering, chemicals, textiles, and many handicrafts. The city has many beautiful mosques including the Great Mosque and the Pearl Mosque. It was capital of the Nawabs of ▷Oudh in the 18th century. During the ▷Indian Mutiny against British rule, the British residency was besieged 2 July–16 November 1857.

Lucretia in Roman legend, the wife of Collatinus, said to have committed suicide after being raped by Sextus, son of ▷Tarquinius Superbus, the last king of Rome. According to tradition, this incident led to the dethronement of Tarquinius and the establishment of the Roman Republic in 509 BC.

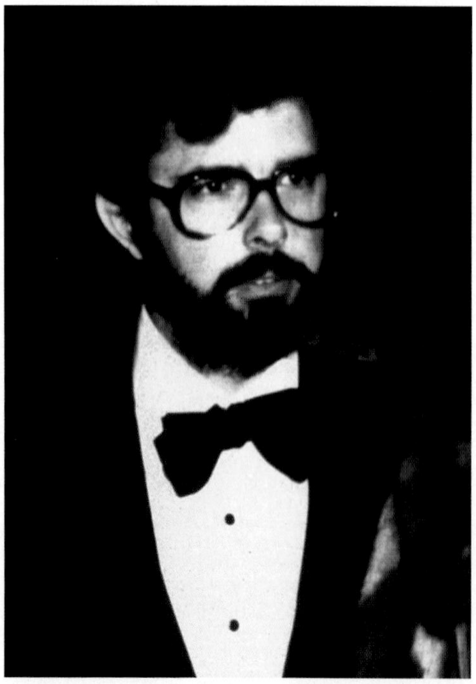

GEORGE LUCAS The US film director at the Directors Guild of America annual awards dinner in Beverly Hills, California, in 1978. See entry on p. 571. *Archive Photos*

Lucretius (*c.* 99–55 BC) Born Titus Lucretius Carus. Roman poet and ▷Epicurean philosopher. His *De Rerum natura/On the Nature of The Universe*, a didactic poem in six books, envisaged the whole universe as a combination of atoms, and had some concept of evolutionary theory.

Related Web site: Lucretius http://www.utm.edu/research/iep/l/lucretiu.htm

Lucretius
Nothing can be created out of nothing.
De Rerum Natura

Lucullus, Lucius Licinius (*c.* 110–*c.* 56 BC) Roman general and consul. As commander against ▷Mithridates of Pontus 74–66 BC he proved to be one of Rome's ablest generals and administrators, until superseded by Pompey. He then retired from politics.

Luddite one of a group of people involved in machine-wrecking riots in northern England 1811–16. The organizer of the Luddites was referred to as **General Ludd**, but may not have existed. Many Luddites were hanged or transported to penal colonies, such as Australia.

The movement, which began in Nottinghamshire and spread to Lancashire, Cheshire, Derbyshire, Leicestershire, and Yorkshire, was primarily a revolt against the unemployment caused by the introduction of machines in the Industrial Revolution.

Ludendorff, Erich von (1865–1937) German general, chief of staff to ▷Hindenburg in World War I, and responsible for the eastern-front victory at the Battle of Tannenberg in 1914. After Hindenburg's appointment as chief of general staff and Ludendorff's as quartermaster-general in 1916, he was also politically influential and the two were largely responsible for the conduct of the war from then on. After the war he propagated the myth of the 'stab in the back', according to which the army had been betrayed by the politicians in 1918. He took part in the Nazi rising in Munich in 1923 and sat in the Reichstag (parliament) as a right-wing Nationalist.

Ludwig three kings of Bavaria.

Ludwig I (1786–1868) King of Bavaria 1825–48, succeeding his father Maximilian Joseph I. He made Munich an international cultural centre, but his association with the dancer Lola Montez, who dictated his policies for a year, led to his abdication in 1848.

Ludwig II (1845–1886) King of Bavaria from 1864, when he succeeded his father Maximilian II. He supported Austria during the Austro-Prussian War of 1866, but brought Bavaria into the Franco-Prussian War as Prussia's ally and in 1871 offered the German crown to the king of Prussia. He was the composer Richard Wagner's patron and built the Bayreuth theatre for him. Declared insane in 1886, he drowned himself soon after.

Ludwig III (1845–1921) King of Bavaria 1913–18, when he abdicated upon the formation of a republic.

Luftwaffe German air force used both in World War I and (as reorganized by the Nazi leader Hermann Goering in 1933) in World War II. The Luftwaffe also covered anti-aircraft defence and the launching of the flying bombs ▷V1 and V2.

Lugano, Lake lake partly in Italy, between lakes Maggiore and Como, and partly in the canton of Ticino, Switzerland; area 49 sq km/19 sq mi. Noted for its beautiful scenery, it lies at an altitude of 271 m/890 ft and its greatest depth is 288 m/945 ft.

Lugosi, Bela (1884–1956) Stage name of Bela Ferenc Denzso Blasko. Hungarian-born US film actor. Acclaimed for his performance in *Dracula* on Broadway (1927), Lugosi began acting in feature films in 1930. His appearance in the film version of *Dracula* (1931) marked the start of Lugosi's long career in horror films – among them, *Murders in the Rue Morgue* (1932), *The Raven* (1935), and *The Wolf Man* (1941).

lugworm any of a group of marine ▷annelid worms that grow up to 10 in/25 cm long. They are common burrowers between tidemarks and are useful for their cleansing and powdering of the beach sand, of which they may annually bring to the surface about 5,000 tonnes per hectare/2,000 tons per acre. (Genus *Arenicola*.)

Lu Hsün alternative transliteration of Chinese writer ▷Lu Xun.

Lukács, Georg (1885–1971) Hungarian philosopher and literary critic, one of the founders of 'Western' or 'Hegelian' Marxism, a philosophy opposed to the Marxism of the official communist movement. He also wrote on aesthetics and the sociology of literature.

In *History and Class Consciousness* (1923), he discussed the process of reification, reintroducing alienation as a central concept, and argued that bourgeois thought was 'false consciousness'. Rejected by official socialist literati, he was also an outsider to the dominant literary movements of the West. He argued for realism in literature and opposed modernism, particularly the work of James Joyce and Franz Kafka.

Luke, St (lived 1st century AD) traditionally the compiler of the third Gospel and of the Acts of the Apostles in the New Testament. He is the patron saint of painters; his emblem is a winged ox, and his feast day 18 October.

Luke is supposed to have been a Greek physician born in Antioch (Antakiyah, Turkey) and to have accompanied Paul after the ascension of Jesus.

Related Web site: Luke, St http://www.newadvent.org/cathen/09420a.htm

Lully, Jean-Baptiste (1632–1687) Adopted name of Giovanni Battista Lulli. French composer of Italian origin. He was court composer to Louis XIV of France. He composed music for the ballet and for Molière's plays, and established French opera with such works as *Alceste* (1674) and *Armide et Rénaud* (1686). He was also a ballet dancer.

lumbago pain in the lower region of the back, usually due to strain or faulty posture. If it occurs with ▷sciatica, it may be due to pressure on spinal nerves from a slipped disc. Treatment includes rest, application of heat, and skilled manipulation. Surgery may be needed in rare cases.

lumbar puncture (or **spinal tap**) insertion of a hollow needle between two lumbar (lower back) vertebrae to withdraw a sample of cerebrospinal fluid (CSF) for testing. Normally clear and colourless, the CSF acts as a fluid buffer around the brain and spinal cord. Changes in its quantity, colour, or composition may indicate neurological damage or disease.

Lumbee ▷American Indian people numbering about 48,500 (1990) and living in Robeson county, North Carolina. The Lumbee are named after Lumber River (which they call Lumbee), and claim to be descendants of several Siouan- and Algonquian-speaking people who lived in the area in the 18th century, although no trace of their original language remains. Even in 1732, when the first land grants were made, the only language they spoke was English. Although they were recognized as American Indians in 1956 and are the ninth-largest American Indian group in the USA, they lack status as a federally recognized American Indian ethnic group.

Lumbini birthplace of ▷Buddha in the foothills of the Himalayas near the Nepalese-Indian frontier. A sacred garden and shrine were established here in 1970 by the Nepalese government.

lumen SI unit (symbol lm) of luminous flux (the amount of light passing through an area per second).

lumen in biology, the space enclosed by an organ, such as the bladder, or a tubular structure, such as the gastrointestinal tract.

Lumet, Sidney (1924–) US film director. His films are concerned with social issues, and he evoked powerful performances from his actors in, for example, *12 Angry Men* (1957), *Dog Day Afternoon* (1975), *Network* (1976), *Running on Empty* (1988), and *Q & A* (1990).

Lumière Auguste Marie Louis Nicolas (1862–1954) and Louis Jean (1864–1948). French brothers who pioneered cinematography. In February 1895 they patented their cinematograph, a combined camera and projector operating at 16 frames per second, screening short films for the first time on 22 March, and in December opening the world's first cinema in Paris. Among their first films were the simple documentaries *La Sortie des usines Lumière/Workers Leaving the Lumière Factory* (1895) and *L'Arrivée d'un train en gare de La Ciotat/The Arrival of a Train at Ciotat Station* (1895), and the comedy *L'Arroseur arrosé/The Hoser Hosed* (1895).

Between 1896 and 1900, the Lumiéres employed a number of camera operators to travel around the world and both demonstrate their invention and film new documentary shorts. Production was abandoned in 1900 after their films were displayed at the Paris Exposition. The brothers withdrew from film-making itself to concentrate on developing film technology and marketing their inventions.

luminescence emission of light from a body when its atoms are excited by means other than raising its temperature. Short-lived luminescence is called fluorescence; longer-lived luminescence is called phosphorescence.

When exposed to an external source of energy, the outer electrons in atoms of a luminescent substance absorb energy and 'jump' to a higher energy level. When these electrons 'jump' back to their former level they emit their excess energy as light. Many different exciting mechanisms are possible: visible light or other forms of electromagnetic radiation (ultraviolet rays or X-rays), electron bombardment, chemical reactions, friction, and ▷radioactivity. Certain living organisms produce ▷bioluminescence.

luminosity (or brightness) in astronomy, the amount of light emitted by a star, measured in ▷magnitudes. The apparent brightness of an object decreases in proportion to the square of its distance from the observer. The luminosity of a star or other body can be expressed in relation to that of the Sun.

lumpsucker marine bony fish so called from the frequent presence of a sucking disc formed from the united ventral fins. It is also distinguished by an absence of scales and the presence of spined plates along its side. Lumpsuckers feed mainly on small crustaceans and jellyfish. Genus *Cyclopterus*, family Cyclopteridae, order Scorpaeniformes, class Osteichthyes.

Lumumba, Patrice Emergy (1925–1961) Congolese politician, prime minister of the Republic of the Congo (now the Democratic Republic of Congo) in 1960. Founder of the National Congolese Movement in 1958, he led his party to victory in the elections following independence in 1960. However, the country collapsed into civil war, and Lumumba was ousted in a coup led by Mobutu in September 1960, and murdered a few months later.

Lundy Island rocky, granite island at the entrance to the Bristol Channel; 19 km/12·mi northwest of Hartland Point, Devon, southwest England; area 9.6 sq km/3.7 sq mi; population (1981) 52. Formerly used by pirates and privateers as a lair, it is now the site of a bird sanctuary and the first British Marine Nature Reserve (1986). It has Bronze and Iron Age field systems, which can be traced by their boundaries which stand up above the surface.

lung large cavity of the body, used for gas exchange. It is essentially a sheet of thin, moist membrane that is folded so as to occupy less space. Most tetrapod (four-limbed) vertebrates have a pair of lungs occupying the thorax. The lung tissue, consisting of multitudes of air sacs and blood vessels, is very light and spongy, and functions by bringing inhaled air into close contact with the blood so that oxygen can pass into the organism and waste carbon dioxide can be passed out. The efficiency of lungs is enhanced by ▷breathing movements, by the thinness and moistness of their surfaces, and by a constant supply of circulating blood.

In humans, the principal diseases of the lungs are tuberculosis, pneumonia, bronchitis, emphysema, and cancer.

lung cancer in medicine, cancer of the lung. The main risk factor is smoking, with almost nine out of ten cases attributed to it. Other risk factors include workspace exposure to carcinogenic substances such as asbestos, and radiation. Warning symptoms include a persistent and otherwise unexplained cough, breathing difficulties, and pain in the chest or shoulder. Treatment is with chemotherapy, radiotherapy, and surgery.

lungfish any of a group of fleshy-finned bony fishes found in South America, Australia, and Africa. They have elongated bodies, and grow to about 2 m/6 ft, and in addition to gills have 'lungs' with which they can breathe air during periods of drought conditions. (Genera *Lepidosiren*, *Neoceratodus*, and *Protopterus*, subclass Dipnoi.)

Luo (or Lwoo or Kavirondo) member of the second-largest ethnic group of Kenya, living in the Lake Victoria region and numbering around 2,650,000 (1987). The Luo are a Nilotic people who traditionally lived by farming livestock. Many, however, now work as wage labourers throughout East Africa. Traditionally they had a strong clan system without centralized political authority. Their religion includes beliefs in a supreme creator, Nyasi, and ancestor worship. The Luo language is of the Nilo-Saharan family.

Luo Guan Zhong (or Luo Kuan-chung) (lived 14th century) Chinese novelist who reworked popular tales into *The Romance of the Three Kingdoms* and *The Water Margin*.

Luo Kuan-chung alternative transliteration of Chinese writer ▷Luo Guan Zhong.

Luoyang (or Loyang) city in Henan province, China, south of the Huang He River; population (1994) 1,340,000. Industries include oil-refining and the production of glass, machinery, and tractors. Luoyang was the capital of China for nearly eight centuries under the Eastern Zhou (8th–3rd century BC) and other dynasties, and an important Buddhist centre in the 5th and 6th centuries.

Lupercalia annual Roman festival of purification celebrated on 15 February. It has been associated with the Greek Lycaean ▷Pan, god of flocks and herds (identified with the Roman ▷Faunus), and the wolf (*lupus*) who supposedly suckled Romulus and Remus, the twin founders of Rome. Goats and dogs were sacrificed at the Lupercal at the foot of the Palatine Hill, near the cave of Lupercus, the wolf's lair.

lupin any of a group of leguminous plants (see ▷legume) that comprises about 300 species. Lupins are native to Mediterranean regions and parts of North and South America, and some species are naturalized in Britain. Their spikes of pealike flowers may be white, yellow, blue, or pink. *L. albus* is cultivated in some places for cattle fodder and for green manuring; other varieties are cultivated in Europe as cottage garden plants. (Genus *Lupinus*, family Leguminosae.)

lupus in medicine, any of various diseases characterized by lesions of the skin. One form (lupus vulgaris) is caused by the tubercle bacillus (see ▷tuberculosis). The organism produces ulcers that spread and eat away the underlying tissues. Treatment is primarily with standard antituberculous drugs, but ultraviolet light may also be used.

Lupus erythematous (LE) has two forms: **discoid** LE, seen as red, scaly patches on the skin, especially the face; and **disseminated** or **systemic** LE, which may affect connective tissue anywhere in the body, often involving the internal organs. The latter is much more serious. Treatment is with ▷corticosteroids. LE is an ▷autoimmune disease.

Luria, Salvador Edward (1912–1991) Italian-born US physician who was awarded a Nobel Prize for Physiology or Medicine in 1969 for his work on the replication mechanism and genetic structure of viruses. Luria was a pacifist and was identified with efforts to keep science humanistic.

Luristan (or Lorestan) mountainous province in western Iran; area 28,800 sq km/11,120 sq mi; population (1991) 1,501,800. The capital is Khorramabad. The province is primarily inhabited by the Lur people who herd sheep and cattle. Excavation in the area has revealed a culture of the 8th–7th century BC with bronzes decorated with animal forms; its origins are uncertain.

Lusaka capital of ▷Zambia from 1964 (of Northern Rhodesia 1935–64), 370 km/230 mi northeast of Livingstone; population (1995 est) 1,041,000. With good communications by rail, road, and air, it is Zambia's chief centre of trade, industry, banking, and administration, as well as a manufacturing and agricultural centre. Industries include chemicals, including insecticides and fertilizers, flour mills, tobacco factories, vehicle assembly, plastics, printing, cement, iron and steel, food processing, paints, plastics, furniture, and clothing.

The cathedral dates from 1957 and the university from 1965. Other important institutions include the geological survey museum and the national archives.

Lusitania ancient area of the Iberian peninsula, roughly equivalent to Portugal. Conquered by Rome in 139 BC, the province of Lusitania rebelled periodically until it was finally conquered by Pompey (73–72 BC).

lute member of a family of plucked stringed musical instruments of the 14th–18th centuries, including the mandore, theorbo, and chitarrone. Lutes are pear-shaped with up to seven courses of strings (single or double), plucked with the fingers. Music for lutes is written in special notation called tablature and chords are played simultaneously, not arpeggiated as for guitar. Modern lutenists include Julian Bream and Anthony Rooley.

luteinizing hormone ▷hormone produced by the pituitary gland. In males, it stimulates the testes to produce androgens (male sex hormones). In females, it works together with follicle-stimulating hormone to initiate production of egg cells by the ovary. If fertilization occurs, it plays a part in maintaining the pregnancy by controlling the levels of the hormones oestrogen and progesterone in the body.

lutetium (Latin *Lutetia* 'Paris') silver-white, metallic element, the last of the ▷lanthanide series, symbol Lu, atomic number 71, relative atomic mass 174.97. It is used in the 'cracking', or breakdown, of petroleum and in other chemical processes. It was named by its discoverer, French chemist Georges Urbain, (1872–1938) after his native city.

Luther, Martin (1483–1546) German Christian church reformer, a founder of Protestantism. While he was a priest at the University of Wittenberg, he wrote an attack on the sale of ▷indulgences (remissions of punishment for sin). The Holy Roman emperor Charles V summoned him to the Diet (meeting of dignitaries of the Holy Roman Empire) of Worms in Germany, in 1521, where he refused to retract his objections. Originally intending reform, his protest led to schism, with the emergence, following the ▷Augsburg Confession in 1530 (a statement of the Protestant faith), of a new Protestant church. Luther is regarded as the instigator of the Protestant revolution, and ▷Lutheranism is now the predominant religion of many northern European countries, including Germany, Sweden, and Denmark. See also the ▷Reformation: Lutheranism.

Luther was born in Eisleben, the son of a miner; he studied at the University of Erfurt, spent three years as a monk in the Augustinian convent there, and in 1507 was ordained priest. Shortly afterwards he attracted attention as a teacher and preacher at the University of Wittenberg.

On a trip to Rome in 1511, Luther had been horrified by the wealth and luxury of the Roman Catholic Church, compared to the poverty of the people in Germany. Further, his study of the Bible, particularly the books of the Psalms, Romans, Galatians, and Hebrews, convinced him that good works and confession could not earn salvation, but that justification was by faith alone and was the gift of God. He came to believe that the church's teaching – that pilgrimages, relics, and penances could earn salvation – was wrong. When, in 1516–17, the Dominican friar Johann Tetzell (1455–1519) was sent round Germany selling indulgences (payments to secure remissions of punishment for sin) to raise funds for the rebuilding of St Peter's Basilica in Rome, Luther was horrified that the church seemed to be trying to sell salvation to raise money for itself. On 31 October 1517 Luther nailed on the church door in Wittenberg a statement of '95 theses' attacking these practices and suggesting that religion was an inward relation with God, and the following year he was summoned to Rome to defend his action. His reply was to attack the papal system even more strongly, and in 1520 he published his three greatest works. In the first, *Address to the German Nobility*, he attacked the authority of the pope and called on Germans to unite against papal exploitation and to reform the church. In the second, *On Christian Liberty*, he expounded the nature of Christian faith and argued that 'the soul . . . is justified by

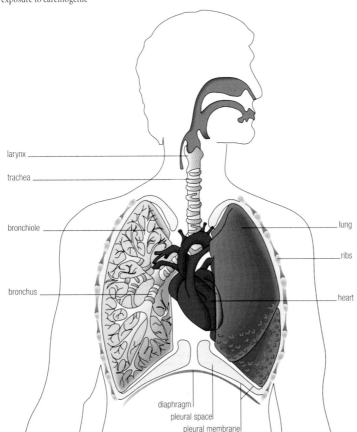

larynx

trachea

bronchiole

bronchus

lung

ribs

heart

diaphragm
pleural space
pleural membrane

LUNG The human lungs contain 300,000 million tiny blood vessels which would stretch for 2,400 km/1,500 mi if laid end to end. A healthy adult at rest breathes 12 times a minute; a baby breathes at twice this rate. Each breath brings 350 millilitres of fresh air into the lungs, and expels 150 millilitres of stale air from the nose and throat.

LUTHERANISM Lutherans from the Tirol journeying to Georgia, USA, in 1732. *Art Archive*

faith alone, and not by any works' – the doctrine that became the founding principle of Reformation theology. In the third, *On the Babylonish Captivity of the Church*, he rejected five of the seven contemporary sacraments and the doctrine of ▷transubstantiation (the transformation of bread and water into the body and blood of Christ during the Eucharist). When a papal bull (edict) was published against him, he publicly burned it.

At the Diet of Worms in 1521 the Holy Roman Emperor Charles V demanded that he retract his objections – Luther's reply: 'Here I stand', marked the start of the Reformation. On his way home from Worms he was taken into 'protective custody' by the elector of Saxony in the castle of Wartburg. Originally intending reform, his protest led to a split in the church, the Augsburg Confession (1530) leading to the foundation of a new Protestant church. Later Luther became estranged from the Dutch theologian ▷Erasmus, who had formerly supported him in his attacks on papal authority, and engaged in violent controversies with political and religious opponents. After the Augsburg Confession, Luther gradually retired from the Protestant leadership. His translation of the scriptures is generally regarded as the beginning of modern German literature.

Related Web site: Luther's 95 Theses http://www.fordham.edu/halsall/source/luther95.txt

Lutheranism form of Protestant Christianity derived from the life and teaching of Martin ▷Luther; it is sometimes called Evangelical to distinguish it from the other main branch of European Protestantism, the Reformed. The most generally

---

> ## Martin Luther
> *My conscience is taken captive by God's word, I cannot and will not recant anything. . . . Here I stand. I can do no other. God help me. Amen.*
> Speech at the Diet of Worms, 18 April 1521

MARTIN LUTHER The German Christian church reformer pictured in about 1522. *Philip Sauvain Picture Collection*

---

accepted statement of Lutheranism is that of the Confession of ▷Augsburg in 1530 but Luther's Shorter Catechism also carries great weight. It is the largest Protestant body, including some 80 million persons, of whom 40 million are in Germany, 19 million in Scandinavia, 8.5 million in the USA and Canada, with most of the remainder in central Europe.

Luthuli (or Lutuli)**, Albert John** (*c.* 1898–1967) South African politician, president of the ▷African National Congress 1952–67. Luthuli, a ▷Zulu tribal chief, preached nonviolence and multiracialism. He was awarded the Nobel Prize for Peace in 1960 for his advocacy of a nonviolent struggle against ▷apartheid.

Arrested in 1956, he was never actually tried for treason, although he suffered certain restrictions from 1959. He was under suspended sentence for burning his pass (an identity document required for non-white South Africans) when awarded the 1960 Nobel prize.

Related Web site: Lutuli, Albert John http://www.nobel.se/peace/laureates/1960/lutuli-bio.html

Luton industrial town and unitary authority in south-central England, 48 km/30 mi north of London. It was part of the county of Bedfordshire to 1997.

area 43 sq km/17 sq mi **features** the Luton Hoo mansion (1767), designed and built by Robert Adam and with a park laid out by Capability Brown, is located south of the town; large church of St Mary (13th–15th centuries) is a cruciform building largely in the Decorated and Perpendicular styles **industries** cars and trucks, chemicals, engineering components, and electrical goods. Luton airport is a secondary airport for London **population** (1996) 181,400

Lutosławski, Witold (1913–1994) Polish composer and conductor. His output includes three symphonies, *Paroles tissées/Teased Words* (1965) for tenor and chamber orchestra, dedicated to the singer Peter Pears, and *Chain I* for orchestra (1981). For 30 years he conducted most of the world's leading orchestras in his own compositions, and was greatly influential both within and beyond his native land.

Lutyens, Edwin Landseer (1869–1944) English architect. His designs ranged from the picturesque, such as Castle Drogo (1910–30), Devon, to Renaissance-style country houses, and ultimately evolved into a classical style as seen in the Cenotaph, London (1919), and the Viceroy's House, New Delhi, India (1912–31). His complex use of space, interest in tradition, and distorted classical language have proved of great interest to a number of postmodern architects, especially Robert Venturi.

Lutyens, (Agnes) Elizabeth (1906–1983) English composer. Her works, using the twelve-tone system, are expressive and tightly organized, and include chamber music, stage, and orchestral works. Her choral and vocal works include a setting of the Austrian philosopher Ludwig Wittgenstein's *Tractatus* and a cantata *The Tears of Night* (1971). She also composed much film and incidental music.

lux SI unit (symbol lx) of illuminance or illumination (the light falling on an object). It is equivalent to one ▷lumen per square metre or to the illuminance of a surface one metre distant from a point source of one ▷candela.

Luxembourg capital of the country of Luxembourg, on the Alzette and Pétrusse rivers, south of the Ardennes uplands; population (1997) 78,300. The 16th-century Grand Ducal Palace, European Court of Justice, and European Parliament secretariat are situated here, but plenary sessions of the parliament are now held only in Strasbourg, France. Industries include steel, chemicals, textiles, and processed food.

Luxembourg see country box.

Luxembourg province of southeastern Belgium; area 4,400 sq km/1,698 sq mi; population (1995) 240,300. The capital is Arlon and other towns and cities include Bastogne, St Hubert, and Bouillon. Industries include dairy products, iron and steel, and tobacco. The province is situated in the southeastern Ardennes and is widely forested. It includes the rivers Ourthe, Semois, and Lesse. The province was formerly part of the Grand Duchy of Luxembourg, and became a Belgian province in 1831.

Luxemburg, Rosa (1870–1919) Polish-born German communist. She helped found the Polish Social Democratic Party in the 1890s, the forerunner of the Polish Communist Party. She was a leader of the left wing of the German Social Democratic

---

> ## Rosa Luxemburg
> *Freedom is always and exclusively freedom for the one who thinks differently.*
> The Russian Revolution

Party from 1898 where she collaborated with Karl ▷Liebknecht in founding the Spartacus League in 1918 (see ▷Spartacist).

Imprisoned during World War I for opposing the continuation of the war, she was also critical of the decision to launch an uprising in November 1918. She disagreed with leading Polish left-wing ideologists on the issue of Polish nationalism. Luxemburg was also the author of a Marxist critique of capitalist imperialism, *The Accumulation of Capital*. She was murdered, together with Liebknecht, in January 1919 by the Frei Corps who put down the Spartacist uprising.

ROSA LUXEMBURG German communist Rosa Luxemburg was leader of the Social Democratic Party and the Spartacus Party in the late 1890s–early 1900s. *Archive Photos*

Luxembourg Accord French-initiated agreement of 1966 that a decision of the Council of Ministers of the European Community (now the European Union) may be vetoed by a member whose national interests are at stake.

Luxor (Arabic **al-Uqsur**) town in Egypt on the east bank of the River Nile; population (1992) 146,000. The temple of Luxor, built by Amenhotep III (*c.* 1411–1375 BC) is found here, and tombs of the pharaohs in the Valley of the Kings can be found on the west side of the Nile.

Lu Xun (1881–1936) Pen-name of Chon Shu-jêu. Chinese short-story writer. His three volumes of satirically realistic stories, *Call to Arms, Wandering*, and *Old Tales Retold*, reveal the influence of the Russian writer Nicolai Gogol. He was also an important polemical essayist and literary critic.

Luzern German name of ▷Lucerne, a city in Switzerland.

Luzon largest island of the ▷Philippines; area 108,130 sq km/41,750 sq mi; capital Quezon City; population (1995 est) 32,558,000. The chief city is Manila, capital of the Philippines. Industries include rice, timber, minerals, sugar cane, and hemp. It has US military bases.

Lviv (Russian **Lvov**; Polish **Lwów**; German **Lemberg**) capital and industrial city of Lviv region (oblast), western Ukraine, 450 km/280 mi southwest of Kiev; population (1990) 798,000. Lviv is an important manufacturing centre and transport junction. There are chemical, metallurgical, and engineering industries in the city; manufactured goods include motor vehicles, agricultural equipment, textiles, and electronics. Lviv was the principal city of the historical region known as ▷Galicia. The Ivan Franko University was founded in 1661. The city was the centre of the revival of Ukrainian nationalism and the resurgence of the Ukrainian Catholic Church in the 1980s.

Lviv was formerly a trade and transit centre on the Black Sea–Baltic and east–west routes. Founded as a fortress town against Mongol invasion in 1256 by a Galician prince (the name means

Luxembourg

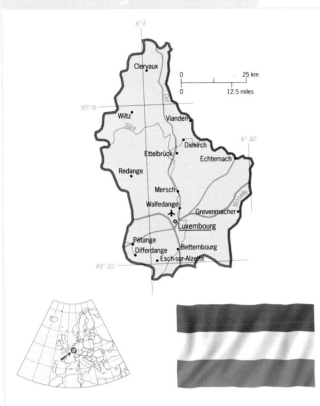

Luxembourg landlocked country in Western Europe, bounded north and west by Belgium, east by Germany, and south by France.

NATIONAL NAME *Grand-Duché de Luxembourg/Grand Duchy of Luxembourg*
AREA 2,586 sq km/998 sq mi
CAPITAL Luxembourg
MAJOR TOWNS/CITIES Esch-sur-Alzette, Differdange, Dudelange, Pétange
PHYSICAL FEATURES on the River Moselle; part of the Ardennes (Oesling) forest in north

Government

HEAD OF STATE Grand Duke Henri from 2000
HEAD OF GOVERNMENT Jean-Claude Juncker from 1995
POLITICAL SYSTEM liberal democracy
POLITICAL EXECUTIVE parliamentary
ADMINISTRATIVE DIVISIONS 12 cantons within three districts
ARMED FORCES 900; plus gendarmerie of 600 (2002 est)
CONSCRIPTION military service is voluntary
DEATH PENALTY abolished in 1979
DEFENCE SPEND (% GDP) 0.9 (2002 est)
EDUCATION SPEND (% GDP) 3.7 (2000 est)
HEALTH SPEND (% GDP) 5.8 (2000 est)

Economy and resources

CURRENCY euro (Luxembourg franc until 2002)
GPD (US$) 20.1 billion (2002 est)
REAL GDP GROWTH (% change on previous year) 1 (2001)
GNI (US$) 17.7 billion (2002 est)
GNI PER CAPITA (PPP) (US$) 51,060 (2002 est)
CONSUMER PRICE INFLATION 2.1% (2003 est)
UNEMPLOYMENT 2.6% (2001)
MAJOR TRADING PARTNERS EU (principally Belgium, Germany, and France), USA, Japan
RESOURCES iron ore
INDUSTRIES steel and rolled steel products, chemicals, rubber and plastic products, metal and machinery products, paper and printing products, food products, financial services
EXPORTS machinery and transport equipment, base metals and manufactures, mechanical and electrical equipment, rubber and related products, plastics, textiles and clothing. Principal market: Germany 24.6% (2001)
IMPORTS machinery and electrical apparatus, transport equipment, mineral products, chemicals, plastics, food, beverages, tobacco. Principal source: Belgium 34.3% (2001)
ARABLE LAND 25% (2000 est)
AGRICULTURAL PRODUCTS maize, roots and tubers, wheat, forage crops, grapes; livestock rearing and dairy farming

Population and society

POPULATION 453,000 (2003 est)
POPULATION GROWTH RATE 1.2% (2000–05)
POPULATION DENSITY (per sq km) 175 (2003 est)
URBAN POPULATION (% of total) 93 (2003 est)
AGE DISTRIBUTION (% of total population) 0–14 19%, 15–59 62%, 60+ 19% (2002 est)
ETHNIC GROUPS majority descended from the Moselle Franks (French and German blend), Portuguese, Italian, and other European guest and resident workers
LANGUAGE Letzeburgisch (a German-Moselle-Frankish dialect; official), English
RELIGION Roman Catholic about 95%, Protestant and Jewish 4%
EDUCATION (compulsory years) 9
LITERACY RATE 99% (men); 99% (women) (2003 est)
LABOUR FORCE 2.1% agriculture, 25.2% industry, 72.7% services (1998)
LIFE EXPECTANCY 75 (men); 81 (women) (2000–05)
CHILD MORTALITY RATE (under 5, per 1,000 live births) 5 (2001)
PHYSICIANS (per 1,000 people) 2.5 (2001 est)
HOSPITAL BEDS (per 1,000 people) 6.9 (2001 est)
TV SETS (per 1,000 people) 599 (1999 est)
RADIOS (per 1,000 people) 683 (1997)
INTERNET USERS (per 10,000 people) 3,674.8 (2002 est)
PERSONAL COMPUTER USERS (per 100 people) 59.0 (2000)

See also ▷Belgium; ▷Netherlands, The.

Chronology

963: Luxembourg became autonomous within Holy Roman Empire under Siegfried, Count of Ardennes.
1060: Conrad, descendent of Siegfried, took the title Count of Luxembourg.
1354: Emperor Charles IV promoted Luxembourg to the status of duchy.
1441: Luxembourg ceded to dukes of Burgundy.
1482: Luxembourg came under Habsburg control.
1555: Luxembourg became part of Spanish Netherlands on division of Habsburg domains.
1684–97: Much of Luxembourg occupied by France.
1713: Treaty of Utrecht transferred Spanish Netherlands to Austria.
1797: Conquered by revolutionary France.
1815: Congress of Vienna made Luxembourg a grand duchy, under King William of the Netherlands.
1830: Most of Luxembourg supported Belgian revolt against the Netherlands.
1839: Western part of Luxembourg assigned to Belgium.
1842: Luxembourg entered the Zollverein (German customs union).
1867: Treaty of London confirmed independence and neutrality of Luxembourg to allay French fears about possible inclusion in a unified Germany.
1870s: Development of iron and steel industry.
1890: Link with Dutch crown ended on accession of Queen Wilhelmina, since Luxembourg's law of succession did not permit a woman to rule.
1912: Revised law of succession allowed Marie-Adelaide to become grand duchess.
1914–18: Occupied by Germany.
1919: Plebiscite overwhelmingly favoured continued independence; Marie-Adelaide abdicated after allegations of collaboration with Germany; Charlotte became grand duchess.
1921: Entered into close economic links with Belgium.
1940: Invaded by Germany.
1942–44: Annexed by Germany.
1948: Luxembourg formed Benelux customs union with Belgium and the Netherlands.
1949: Luxembourg became founding member of North Atlantic Treaty Organization (NATO).
1958: Luxembourg became founding member of European Economic Community (EEC).
1964: Grand Duchess Charlotte abdicated in favour of her son Jean.
1994: Former premier Jacques Santer became the president of the European Commission (EC).
1995: Jean-Claude Juncker became prime minister.
2000: Grand Duke Jean abdicated in favour of his son Henri.

LUXEMBOURG High-technology industries have kept Luxembourg's economy strong, and the capital city, also called Luxembourg, is very wealthy. *Leonardo.com*

'city of Leo' or 'city of Lev'), it was Polish from 1340 until 1772, Austrian (1772–1918), Polish (1919–39), and under German administration from 1941 to 1944. During the Nazi occupation, the Jewish community that had been present in the city since 1349 was wiped out. Lviv, which had been seized by Soviet troops in 1939, was finally annexed by the USSR in 1945.

Related Web site: Welcome to Lviv http://www.lviv.ua/

LW abbreviation for **long wave**, a radio wave with a wavelength of over 1,000 m/3,300 ft; one of the main wavebands into which radio frequency transmissions are divided.

Lwów Polish form of ▷Lviv, a historic city in western Ukraine.

lycanthropy (Greek *lukos* 'wolf' *anthropos* 'human') in folk belief, the transformation of a human being into a wolf (▷werewolf); or, in psychology, a delusion involving this belief.

Lyceum ancient Athenian gymnasium and garden, with covered walks, where the philosopher Aristotle taught. It was southeast of the city and named after the nearby temple of Apollo Lyceus.

lychee alternative spelling of ▷litchi, a fruit-bearing tree.

lycra synthetic fibre composed mainly of elastomer and other stretch fibres. It was introduced as a fabric for underwear, such as girdles, bras, and support stockings, but it became a popular material for sports and casual wear such as stretch leggings in the 1980s–90s.

Lycurgus Spartan lawgiver. He was believed to have been a member of the royal house of the ancient Greek city-state of Sparta, who, while acting as regent, gave the Spartans their constitution and system of education. Many modern scholars believe him to be at least partly legendary.

Lydgate, John (*c.* 1370–1449) English poet. He was a Benedictine monk and later prior. His numerous works, including poems, moral tales, legends of the saints, and histories, were often translations or adaptations. His chief works are *Troy Book*, written during 1412–21 at the request of Henry V when Prince of Wales, *The Siege of Thebes* (1420–22), and *The Fall of Princes* (1431–38).

Lydia ancient kingdom in Anatolia (7th–6th centuries BC), with its capital at Sardis. The Lydians were the first Western people to use standard coinage. Their last king, Croesus, was defeated by the Persians in 546 BC.

Lyell, Charles (1797–1875) Scottish geologist. In his *Principles of Geology* (1830–33), he opposed the French anatomist Georges ▷Cuvier's theory that the features of the Earth were formed by a series of catastrophes, and expounded the Scottish geologist James ▷Hutton's view, known as ▷uniformitarianism, that past events were brought about by the same processes that occur today – a view that influenced Charles ▷Darwin's theory of ▷evolution. He was knighted in 1848.

Lyly, John (*c.* 1553–1606) English dramatist and author. His romance *Euphues, or the Anatomy of Wit* (1578), with its elaborate stylistic devices, gave rise to the word euphuism for a mannered rhetorical style. It was followed by a second part, *Euphues and his England* (1580).

> **John Lyly**
> *Night hath a thousand eyes.*
> Maides Metamorphose

JOHN LYDGATE English poet and Benedictine monk John Lydgate was a friend and admirer of the poet Geoffrey Chaucer. *Archive Photos*

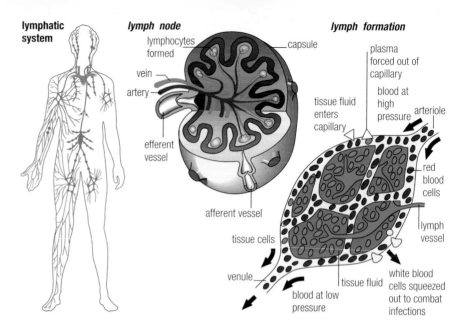

lymphatic system

lymph node
lymphocytes formed
capsule
vein
artery
efferent vessel
afferent vessel

lymph formation
plasma forced out of capillary
blood at high pressure
tissue fluid enters capillary
arteriole
red blood cells
lymph vessel
tissue cells
venule
blood at low pressure
tissue fluid
white blood cells squeezed out to combat infections

LYMPH Lymph is the fluid that carries nutrients and white blood cells to the tissues. Lymph enters the tissue from the capillaries (right) and is drained from the tissues by lymph vessels. The lymph vessels form a network (left) called the lymphatic system. At various points in the lymphatic system, lymph nodes (centre) filter and clean the lymph.

lymph fluid found in the lymphatic system of vertebrates.

Lymph is drained from the tissues by lymph capillaries, which empty into larger lymph vessels (lymphatics). These lead to lymph nodes (small, round bodies chiefly situated in the neck, armpit, groin, thorax, and abdomen), which process the ▷lymphocytes produced by the bone marrow, and filter out harmful substances and bacteria. From the lymph nodes, vessels carry the lymph to the thoracic duct and the right lymphatic duct, which drain into the large veins in the neck. Some vertebrates, such as amphibians, have a lymph heart, which pumps lymph through the lymph vessels.

Lymph carries some nutrients, and white blood cells to the tissues, and waste matter away from them. It exudes from capillaries into the tissue spaces between the cells and is similar in composition to blood plasma.

lymph nodes small masses of lymphatic tissue in the body that occur at various points along the major lymphatic vessels. Tonsils and adenoids are large lymph nodes. As the lymph passes through them it is filtered, and bacteria and other micro-organisms are engulfed by cells known as macrophages.

lymphocyte type of white blood cell with a large nucleus, produced in the bone marrow. Most occur in the ▷lymph and blood, and around sites of infection. **B lymphocytes** or B cells are responsible for producing ▷antibodies. **T lymphocytes** or ▷T cells have several roles in the mechanism of ▷immunity.

lymphokines chemical messengers produced by lymphocytes that carry messages between the cells of the immune system (see ▷immunity). Examples include interferon, which initiates defensive reactions to viruses, and the interleukins, which activate specific immune cells.

Lynch, Jack (John Mary) (1917–1999) Irish politician, Taoiseach (prime minister) 1966–73 and 1977–79, and leader of Fianna Fáil 1966–79.

Lynch entered the Dáil (lower chamber of the Irish parliament) in 1948 and served in various ministerial capacities, before emerging as the surprise winner of the contest to succeed Lemass as Fianna Fáil leader in 1966. Lynch continued the conciliatory policies of his predecessor towards Northern Ireland, visiting O'Neill in Belfast in December 1967, and receiving the Northern Irish premier in Dublin the following month. The renewed violence in the North however destabilized Lynch's government, and its internal conflicts burst into the public arena in May 1970, when Lynch sacked his finance minister, Charles Haughey, and his minister of agriculture and fisheries, Neil Blaney, for allegedly using government money to import arms for the IRA. There was also a political aspect to the affair, since both Haughey and Blaney harboured leadership aspirations, and hoped to reveal Lynch's weakness on the Northern Ireland issue. Lynch narrowly lost the election of 1973, but regained power in 1977. However, serious economic mismanagement by his government, and the reemergence of personal and political tensions within the party led to Lynch's sudden decision to resign in 1979.

lynching killing of an alleged offender by an individual or group having no legal authority. In the USA it originated in 1780 with creation of a 'committee of vigilance' in Virginia; it is named after a member of that committee, Captain William Lynch, to whom is attributed 'Lynch's law'. Later examples occurred mostly in the Southern states after the Civil War, and were racially motivated. During 1882–1900 the annual number of lynchings in the USA varied between 96 and 231, but today it is an exceptional occurrence.

Lynn, Vera Margaret Lewis (1917–) English singer. Known during World War II as the 'Forces' Sweetheart', she became famous with such songs as 'We'll Meet Again', 'White Cliffs of Dover', and in 1952 'Auf Wiederseh'n, Sweetheart'. She was made a DBE in 1975.

lynx wild cat found in rocky and forested regions of North America and Europe. About 1 m/3 ft in length, it has a short tail

Temple of Luxor

Dedicated to the god Amon (king of the gods), the goddess Mut, and their son Khons, the Temple of Luxor in Egypt was commissioned by Amenhotep III and built between 1411 and 1375 BC. Tutankhamen and Horemheb completed the building of the temple. It was linked to the Great Temple of Amon, in Karnak just over 2 km/1.3 mi away, by a road lined with statues of sphinxes.

The temple comprised a large pillared courtyard with a complex of rooms beyond. Typically the tops of columns in Egyptian buildings were decorated to look like plants, to serve as a reminder of the myth that Egypt was the first land to rise from the sea. The tops of the columns surrounding the courtyard of the Temple of Luxor were decorated to look like papyrus. Another prominent feature of the temple is a colonnade of 14 pillars 16 m/52 ft high. Additions of an outer court, a pylon (tall tower) and obelisks were made by Ramses II (1279–13).

Later in history, a Roman legion used the temple for its headquarters, Coptic churches were built in and around the temple, and during the Fatimid period (AD 909–1171) a mosque was built over the foundations of one of the churches. See entry on p. 574.

and tufted ears, and the long, silky fur is reddish brown or grey with dark spots. The North American **bobcat** or **bay lynx** (*Felix rufus*) looks similar but is smaller. Some zoologists place the lynx, the bobcat, and the ▷caracal in a separate genus, *Lynx*. (Species *Felis lynx*, family Felidae.)

Lynxes are nocturnal and solitary and need a large range, but the size of the range varies depending on the population size of the prey animal, from 300 sq km/115 sq mi to up to 1,900 sq km/734 sq mi. They feed mainly on small deer but are capable of killing prey much larger than themselves. Lynxes do not have dens, but mothers place cubs under a tree or close to rocks. Gestation lasts 9–10 weeks and litters contain 1–4 cubs. They reach independence at around 10 months and usually live for 10–15 years. There were only an estimated 1,000 Iberian lynx left in the wild in 2000.

Lyon (English **Lyons**) industrial city and administrative centre of Rhône *département* in the Rhône-Alpes region, part of which lies on the long tongue of land between the Rivers Rhône and Saône, 275 km/170 mi north of Marseille; population (2002 est) 444,100, conurbation 1,665,700. Lyon is France's third-largest city and most important educational centre after Paris; its main industries are textiles, chemicals, machinery, and printing. Formerly a chief fortress of France, it was the ancient **Lugdunum**, taken by the Romans in 43 BC.

    Related Web site: Discovering Lyon http://www.ec-lyon.fr/tourisme/Lyon/index.html.en

Lyra small but prominent constellation of the northern hemisphere, represented as the harp of Orpheus. Its brightest star is ▷Vega.

lyre stringed musical instrument of great antiquity. It consists of a hollow soundbox with two curved arms extended upwards to a crosspiece to which four to ten strings are attached. It is played with a plectrum or the fingers. It originated in Asia, and was widespread in ancient Greece and Egypt.

lyrebird either of two species of large birds found in southeastern Australia. They have very stout beaks and short, rounded wings; the tail has 16 feathers, and in the males the exterior pair of feathers are curved in the shape of a lyre; the tail of the female is long, broad, and normal in shape. Lyrebirds nest on the ground, and feed on insects, worms, and snails. (Genus *Menura*, family Menuridae, order Passeriformes.)

lyretail African freshwater fish, 6 cm/2.4 in long, whose tail has two outward-curving fin supports for a central fin area which looks like the strings of a lyre. The male is bright blue with red markings; the less brightly coloured female has plainer fins. (Species *Aphyosemion australe.*)

lyric poem any short, personal, and passionate form of verse. Lyric poetry is a genre; it does not imply a particular rhyme scheme or technique. Sonnets, odes, and elegies are lyric poems, for example, since they express strong feeling or ideas. Originally, a lyric was a song sung to a lyre, and song texts are still called lyrics.

Lysander (died 395 BC) Spartan politician and admiral. He brought the ▷Peloponnesian War between Athens and Sparta to a successful conclusion by capturing the Athenian fleet at Aegospotami in 405 BC, and by starving Athens into surrender in the following year. He set up puppet governments in Athens and its former allies, and tried to secure for himself the Spartan kingship, but was killed in battle with the Thebans 395 BC.

Lysenko, Trofim Denisovich (1898–1976) Soviet biologist who believed in the inheritance of acquired characteristics (changes acquired in an individual's lifetime) and used his position under Joseph Stalin officially to exclude Gregor ▷Mendel's theory of inheritance. He was removed from office after the fall of Nikita Khrushchev in 1964.

Lysippus (or Lysippos) (lived 4th century BC) Greek sculptor. He made a series of portraits of Alexander the Great (Roman copies survive, including examples in the British Museum and the Louvre) and also sculpted the *Apoxyomenos*, an athlete (copy in the Vatican), and a colossal *Hercules* (lost).

lysis in biology, any process that destroys a cell by rupturing its membrane or cell wall (see ▷lysosome).

lysosome membrane-enclosed structure, or organelle, inside a ▷cell, principally found in animal cells. Lysosomes contain enzymes that can break down proteins and other biological substances. They play a part in digestion, and in the white blood cells known as phagocytes the lysosome enzymes attack ingested bacteria.

Lytton, Edward George Earle Lytton Bulwer (1803–1873) 1st Baron Lytton. English writer. His novels successfully followed every turn of the public taste of his day and include the Byronic *Pelham* (1828), *The Last Days of Pompeii* (1834), and *Zanoni* 1842. His plays include *Richelieu* (1838). He had a keen sense of character, fair knowledge of historical lore, and a wide knowledge of life and society. His works were voraciously read by the Victorians. He was created a baronet in 1838; baron in 1866.

M

M Roman numeral for 1,000.

MA abbreviation for the degree of Master of Arts; the state of ▷Massachusetts.

MA abbreviation for ▷mechanical advantage.

Maas Dutch or Flemish name for the River ▷Meuse.

Maastricht industrial city and capital of Limburg province, the Netherlands, on the River Maas, near the Dutch-Belgian frontier; population (1997) 118,900. Industries include metallurgy, textiles, and pottery. Maastricht dates from Roman times. It was the site of the Maastricht summit (see ▷Maastricht Treaty) in December 1991.

Maastricht Treaty treaty establishing the ▷European Union (EU). Agreed in 1991 and signed in 1992, the treaty took effect on 1 November 1993, following ratification by member states. It advanced the commitment of member states to ▷economic and monetary union (but included an opt-out clause for the United Kingdom); provided for intergovernmental arrangements for a common foreign and security policy; increased cooperation on justice and home affairs policy issues (though the ▷Social Chapter was rejected by the UK until a change of government in 1997); introduced the concept of EU citizenship (as a supplement to national citizenship); established new regional development of bodies; increased the powers of the ▷European Parliament; and accepted the principle of ▷subsidiarity (a controversial term defining the limits of European Community involvement in national affairs).

Denmark initially rejected the treaty, and then accepted it, in national referenda in June 1992 and May 1993. The original 'no' vote, together with the UK's and Italy's subsequent enforced withdrawal from the European ▷Exchange Rate Mechanism, caused repercussions throughout the European Community. The French only narrowly voted in favour in September 1992 and a British government proposal to go ahead with ratification in November 1992 was passed by only a small parliamentary majority, prompting the then British prime minister, John Major, to delay ratification until after a second Danish national referendum. These results contrasted with a clear 'yes' vote in lower-income countries such as Spain and Ireland, which stood to benefit substantially from the treaty.

By the end of 1992, all parliaments, apart from those of Denmark and Britain, had completed ratification, and at a summit in Edinburgh in December 1992, a series of compromises was agreed, including limited Danish participation. Denmark subsequently ratified the treaty in May 1993, followed by the UK in July.

Mabuse, Jan (*c.* 1478–*c.* 1533) Adopted name of Jan Gossaert. Flemish painter. His visit to Italy in 1508 started a new vogue in Flanders for Italianate ornament and classical detail in painting, including sculptural nude figures, as in his *Neptune and Amphitrite* (*c.* 1516, Staatliche Museen, Berlin).

McAdam, John Loudon (1756–1836) Scottish engineer, inventor of the **macadam** road surface. It originally consisted of broken granite bound together with slag or gravel, raised for drainage. Today, it is bound with tar or asphalt.

macadamia edible nut of a group of trees native to Australia (especially *M. ternifolia*), and cultivated in Hawaii, South Africa, Zimbabwe, and Malawi. The nuts are slow-growing; they are harvested when they drop. (Genus *Macadamia*, family Proteaceae.)

McAleese, Mary Patricia (1951–) Irish lawyer and academic, president from 1997. When President Mary Robinson announced her resignation, McAleese was nominated by the ruling Fianna Fáil and Progressive Democrats as their candidate in preference to former prime minister Albert Reynolds. She asserted her opposition to violence and secured a clear victory over the Fine Gael nominated candidate, Mary Bannotti.

macaque any of a group of medium-sized Old World monkeys. Various species live in forests from the Far East to North Africa. The ▷rhesus monkey and the ▷Barbary ape belong to this group. (Genus *Macaca.*)

Macaques range from long-tailed to tailless types, and have well-developed cheek pouches to carry food.

MACAQUE Bonnet macaques *Macaca radiata* from southern India usually spend the hottest part of the day grooming each other. *Premaphotos Wildlife*

MacArthur, Douglas (1880–1964) US general in World War II, commander of US forces in the Far East and, from March 1942, of the Allied forces in the southwestern Pacific. After the surrender of Japan he commanded the Allied occupation forces there. During 1950 he commanded the UN forces in Korea, but in April 1951, after expressing views contrary to US and UN policy, he was relieved of all his commands by President Truman.

Born in Arkansas, Macarthur was the son of an army officer. He graduated from West Point 1903, distinguished himself in World War I, and rose to become chief of staff 1930–35. He defended the Philippines against the Japanese forces 1941–42 and escaped to Australia, where he based his headquarters. He was responsible for the reconquest of New Guinea 1942–45 and of the Philippines 1944–45, being appointed general of the army in 1944. As commander of the UN forces in the Korean War, he invaded the North in 1950 until beaten back by Chinese troops; his threats to bomb China were seen as liable to start World War III and he was removed from command, but received a hero's welcome on his return to the USA.

Macassar another name for ▷Ujung Pandang, a port in Sulawesi, Indonesia.

Macau (or Macao) former Portuguese possession on the south coast of China, about 65 km/40 mi west of Hong Kong, from which it is separated by the estuary of the Pearl River; it consists of a peninsula and the islands of Taipa and Colôane; area 17 sq km/7 sq mi; population (1994 est) 395,300. The capital is Macau, on the peninsula. On 31 December 1999 Portugese rule ended and Macau was reintegrated into China, though, like Hong Kong, with a guarantee of 50 years' non-interference in its political system.

Related Web site: Macau http://www.cityguide.gov.mo/

Macaulay, (Emilie) Rose (1881–1958) English novelist. The serious vein of her early novels changed to light satire in *Potterism* (1920) and *Keeping up Appearances* (1928). Her later books include *The World My Wilderness* (1950) and *The Towers of Trebizond* (1956; Tait Black Memorial Prize). Her work reflects the contemporary scene with wit and a shrewd understanding. She was made a DBE in 1958.

> **Thomas Macaulay**
> *Now who will stand on either hand, / And keep the bridge with me?*
> Lays of Ancient Rome, 'Horatius' 29

Macaulay, Thomas Babington (1800–1859) 1st Baron Macaulay. British historian, essayist, poet, and politician, secretary of war 1839–41. His *History of England* in five volumes (1849–61) celebrates the Glorious Revolution of 1688 as the crowning achievement of the Whig party. He was made a baron in 1857.

His works include an essay on Milton (1825) published in the *Edinburgh Review*; a volume of verse, *Lays of Ancient Rome* (1842); and the *History of England* covering the years up to 1702.

He entered Parliament as a liberal Whig 1830. In India 1834–38, he redrafted the Indian penal code. He sat again in Parliament 1839–47 and 1852–56, and in 1857 accepted a peerage.

Related Web site: Selected poetry of Thomas Babington Macaulay (1800–1859) http://www.library.utoronto.ca/utel/rp/authors/macaulay.html

macaw any of a group of large, brilliantly coloured, long-tailed tropical American ▷parrots, such as the blue and yellow macaw *Ara ararauna*. They can be recognized by the massive beak, about half the size of the head, and by the extremely long tail. (Genera *Ara*, *Aratinga*, and *Anodorhynchus.*)

Macbeth (*c.* 1005–1057) King of Scotland from 1040. The son of Findlaech, hereditary ruler of Moray and Ross, he was commander of the forces of Duncan I, King of Scotland, whom he killed in battle in 1040. His reign was prosperous until Duncan's son Malcolm III led an invasion and killed him at Lumphanan in Aberdeenshire.

He was probably the grandson of Kenneth II and married Gruoch, the granddaughter of Kenneth III.

Shakespeare's tragedy *Macbeth* was based on the 16th-century historian ▷Holinshed's *Chronicles.*

Macbeth, George Mann (1932–1992) Scottish poet and novelist. His early poetry, such as *A Form of Words* (1954), often focused on violent or macabre events. *The Colour of Blood* (1967) and *Collected Poems 1958–1970* (1971) show mastery of both experimental and traditional styles and a playful wit. Committed to performance poetry, he produced poetry programmes for BBC radio 1955–76. There are strong erotic elements in his eight novels, which include *The Seven Witches* (1978) and *Dizzy's Woman* (1986).

Maccabee Also known as **Hasmonaean.** member of an ancient Hebrew family founded by the priest Mattathias (died 166 BC) who, with his sons, led the struggle for independence against the Syrians in the 2nd century BC. Judas (died 161) reconquered Jerusalem in 164 BC, and Simon (died 135) established its independence in 142 BC. The revolt of the Maccabees lasted until the capture of Jerusalem by the Romans in 63 BC. The story is told in four books of the ▷Apocrypha.

McCarran, Patrick (1876–1954) US Democrat politician. He became senator for Nevada in 1932, and as an isolationist strongly opposed ▷lend-lease during World War II. He sponsored the McCarran–Walter Immigration and Nationality Act of 1952, which severely restricted entry and immigration to the USA; the act was amended in 1965.

McCarthy, Joe (Joseph Raymond) (1908–1957) US right-wing Republican politician. His unsubstantiated claim in 1950 that the State Department had been infiltrated by communists started a wave of anticommunist hysteria, wild accusations, and blacklists, which continued until he was discredited in 1954. He was censured by the Senate for misconduct.

> **Joe McCarthy**
> *McCarthyism is Americanism with its sleeves rolled.*
> Speech in Wisconsin, 1952

A lawyer, McCarthy became senator for his native Wisconsin in 1947, and in February 1950 caused a sensation by claiming to hold a list of about 200 Communist Party members working in the State Department. This was in part inspired by the Alger ▷Hiss case. McCarthy continued a witch-hunting campaign against, among others, members of the Harry Truman administration. When he turned his attention to the army, and it was shown that he and his aides had been falsifying evidence, President Eisenhower denounced his tactics. By this time, however, many people in public life and the arts had been unofficially blacklisted as suspected communists or fellow travellers (communist sympathizers). **McCarthyism** came to represent the practice of using innuendo and unsubstantiated accusations against political adversaries.

Related Web site: Fight for America – Senator Joseph McCarthy http://mccarthy.cjb.net/

McCartney, (James) Paul (1942–) English rock singer, songwriter, and bass guitarist. He was a member of the ▷Beatles, and leader of the pop group Wings 1971–81, in which his wife, Linda, also performed. His subsequent albums include *Off the Ground* (1993) and *Flaming Pie* (1997). Solo hits have included collaborations with Michael Jackson and Elvis Costello. Together with composer Carl Davis, McCartney wrote the *Liverpool Oratorio* (1991), his first work of classical music. Another classical composition, *Standing Stones*, achieved considerable success in the USA in the same year. He was knighted in 1997 and inducted into the US Rock and Roll Hall of Fame in March 1999.

McClellan, George Brinton (1826–1885) US soldier. In the Civil War he was made general in chief of the Union forces 1861–62, but was dismissed by President Abraham Lincoln when he delayed five weeks in following up his victory over the Confederate General Robert E Lee at Antietam (see under ▷Civil War, American). He was the unsuccessful Democratic presidential candidate against Lincoln in 1864.

McClintock, Barbara (1902–1992) US geneticist who was awarded a Nobel Prize for Physiology or Medicine in 1983 for her discovery of mobile genetic elements, meaning she discovered 'jumping' ▷genes (genes that can change their position on a chromosome from generation to generation). This would explain how originally identical cells take on the specialized functions of skin, muscle, bone, and nerve, and also how evolution could give rise to the multiplicity of species.

McColgan, Elizabeth (1964–) Scottish long-distance runner who became the 1992 world 10,000-metre champion. She won consecutive gold medals at the Commonwealth Games in 1986 and 1990 at the same distance.

McCullers, (Lula) Carson (1917–1967) Born Lula Carson Smith. US novelist. Most of her writing, including the novels *The Heart is a Lonely Hunter* (1940) and *Reflections in a Golden Eye* (1941), is set in her native South. Her work, like that of Flannery ▷O'Connor, has been characterized as 'Southern Gothic' for its images of the grotesque, using physical abnormalities to project the spiritual and psychological distortions of Southern experience.

McCullin, Don(ald) (1935–) English war photographer. He started out as a freelance photojournalist for the Sunday newspapers. His coverage of hostilities in the Congo in 1967, Vietnam in 1968, Biafra in 1968 and 1970, and Cambodia in 1970 is notable for its pessimistic vision. He has published several books of his work, among them *Destruction Business.*

MacDiarmid, Hugh (1892–1978) Pen-name of Christopher Murray Grieve. Scottish poet. A nationalist and Marxist, he was one of the founders in 1928 of the National Party of Scotland. His works include 'A Drunk Man Looks at the Thistle' (1926) and the collections *First Hymn to Lenin* (1931) and *Second Hymn to Lenin* (1935), in which poetry is made relevant to politics. He developed a form of modern poetic Scots, based on an amalgam of Middle and Modern Scots, and was the leader of the Scottish literary renaissance of the 1920s and 1930s. *Complete Poems 1920–1976* was published in 1978 and *Selected Poems* in 1992.

Niccolò Machiavelli

One of the most powerful safeguards a prince can have against conspiracies is to avoid being hated by the populace.

The Prince (1513)

Macdonald, Flora (1722–1790) Scottish heroine. She rescued Prince ▷Charles Edward Stuart, the Young Pretender, after the ▷Jacobite defeat at the Battle of ▷Culloden in 1746. Disguising him as her maid, she escorted him from her home on South Uist in the Hebrides, to France. She was arrested and imprisoned in the Tower of London, but released in 1747.

Macdonald, George (1824–1905) Scottish novelist and children's writer. *David Elginbrod* (1863) and *Robert Falconer* (1868) are characteristic novels but his children's stories, including *At the Back of the North Wind* (1871) and *The Princess and the Goblin* (1872), are now better known. He was much influenced by the German Romantics, and mystical imagination pervades all his books, most notably *Lilith* (1895). His work inspired later writers including G K ▷Chesterton, C S ▷Lewis, and J R R ▷Tolkien.

Macdonald, John Alexander (1815–1891) Canadian Conservative politician, prime minister 1867–73 and 1878–91. He was born in Glasgow, Scotland, but taken to Ontario as a child. In 1857 he became prime minister of Upper Canada. He took the leading part in the movement for federation, and in 1867 became the first prime minister of Canada. He was defeated in 1873 but returned to office in 1878 and retained it until his death. He was knighted in 1867.

MacDonald, (James) Ramsay (1866–1937) British politician, first Labour prime minister January–October 1924 and 1929–31, born in Morayshire, Scotland. He left the party to form a coalition government in 1931, which was increasingly dominated by Conservatives, until he was replaced by Stanley Baldwin in 1935.

MacDonald was born in Lossiemouth, the son of a labourer. He joined the Independent Labour Party in 1894, and became first secretary of the new Labour Party in 1900. He was elected to Parliament in 1906, and led the party until 1914, when his opposition to World War I lost him the leadership. This he recovered in 1922, and in January 1924 he formed a government dependent on the support of the Liberal Party. When this was withdrawn in October the same year, he was forced to resign. He returned to office in 1929, again as leader of a minority government, which collapsed in 1931 as a result of the economic crisis. MacDonald left the Labour Party to form a national government with backing from both Liberal and Conservative parties. He resigned the premiership in 1935.

Macdonnell Ranges mountain range in Northern Territory, central Australia, running east to west in parallel ridges for 644 km/400 mi. The highest peaks are Mount Liebig (1,524m/5,000 ft) and Mount Zeil (1,510 m/4,955 ft). The town of Alice Springs is situated in the middle of the Macdonnell Ranges. The spectacular scenery, with its deep gorges and red rocks, attracts many tourists.

Macedonia ancient region of Greece, forming parts of modern Greece, Bulgaria, and the Former Yugoslav Republic of Macedonia. Macedonia gained control of Greece after Philip II's victory at Chaeronea in 338 BC. His son, Alexander the Great, conquered a vast empire. Macedonia became a Roman province in 146 BC.

Macedonia see country box.

Macedonia (Greek Makedhonia) mountainous region of northern Greece, part of the ancient country of Macedonia which was divided between Serbia, Bulgaria, and Greece after the Balkan Wars of 1912–13. Greek Macedonia is bounded west and north by Albania and the Former Yugoslav Republic of Macedonia; area 34,177 sq km/13,200 sq mi; population (1991) 2,263,000. There are two regions, Macedonia Central, and Macedonia East and Thrace. The chief city is Thessaloniki.

McEnroe, John Patrick (1959–) US tennis player whose brash behaviour and fiery temper on court dominated the men's game in the early 1980s. He was three times winner of Wimbledon in 1981 and 1983–84. He also won three successive US Open titles 1979–81 and again in 1984. A fine doubles player, McEnroe also won ten Grand Slam titles, seven in partnership with Peter Fleming. After his retirement, he became a tennis commentator for television, with his notoriously outspoken remarks proving very popular among viewers in both the US and the UK.

McEwan, Ian Russell (1948–) English novelist and short-story writer. His works often have sinister or macabre undertones and contain elements of violence and bizarre sexuality, as in the short stories in *First Love, Last Rites* (1975). His novels include *The Comfort of Strangers* (1981), *The Child in Time* (1987), *Black Dogs* (1992; short-listed for the Booker Prize), and *Enduring Love* (1997). *The Daydreamer* (1994) is a novel for children. He has also published *Short Stories* (1995). His novel *Amsterdam* was awarded the 1998 Booker Prize.

McGough, Roger (1937–) English poet, dramatist, songwriter, and performer, and, with Adrian Henri and Brian Patten, one of the group known as the 'Liverpool Poets'. He came to prominence in the late 1960s as a singer in the pop group Scaffold, and he wrote many of their songs (including their 1968 hit 'Lily the Pink'). His poems were strongly influenced by the pop culture of the 1960s, and he later became noted for his poetry readings. His poetry collections include *Gig* (1973) and *Waving at Trains* (1982). He has also written several plays, often with music, and a range of children's books.

McGrath, John Peter (1935–) Scottish dramatist and director. He founded the socialist 7:84 Theatre Companies in England in 1971 and Scotland in 1973, and is the author of such plays as *Events Guarding the Bofors Gun* (1966); *The Cheviot, the Stag, and the Black, Black Oil* (1973), a musical account of the economic exploitation of the Scottish highlands; and *The Garden of England* (1985).

Machado de Assis, Joaquim Maria (1839–1908) Brazilian writer and poet. He is generally regarded as the greatest Brazilian novelist. His sceptical, ironic wit is well displayed in his 30 volumes of novels and short stories, including *Epitaph for a Small Winner* (1880) and *Dom Casmurro* (1900).

Elbert Hubbard
US writer

One machine can do the work of fifty ordinary men. No machine can do the work of one extraordinary man.

A Thousand and One Epigrams

Machel, Samora Moises (1933–1986) Mozambique nationalist leader, president 1975–86. Machel was active in the liberation front Frelimo from its conception in 1962, fighting for independence from Portugal. He became Frelimo leader in 1966, and Mozambique's first president from independence in 1975 until his death in a plane crash near the South African border.

Machiavelli, Niccolò (1469–1527) Italian politician and author. His name is synonymous with cunning and cynical statecraft. In his chief political writings, *Il principe/The Prince* (1513) and *Discorsi/Discourses* (1531), he discussed ways in which rulers can advance the interests of their states (and themselves) through an often amoral and opportunistic manipulation of other people.

Machiavelli was born in Florence and was second chancellor to the republic (1498–1512). On the accession to power of the ▷Medici family in 1512, he was arrested and imprisoned on a charge of conspiracy, but in 1513 was released to exile in the country. *The Prince*, based on his observations of Cesare ▷Borgia, is a guide for the future prince of a unified Italian state (which did not occur until the Risorgimento in the 19th century). In *L'Arte della guerra/The Art of War* (1520), Machiavelli outlined the provision of an army for the prince, and in *Historie fiorentine/History of Florence* he analysed the historical development of Florence until 1492. Among his later works are the comedies *Clizia* (1515) and *La Mandragola/The Mandrake* (1524).

Related Web site: Machiavelli, Niccolò http://www.utm.edu/research/iep/m/machiave.htm

NICCOLÒ MACHIAVELLI A contemporary, 16th-century portrait of Niccolò Machiavelli, Italian politician and author. *Image Bank*

machine in mechanics, device that allows a small force (the effort) to overcome a larger one (the load). There are three basic machines: the inclined plane (ramp), the lever, and the wheel and axle. All other machines are combinations of these three basic types. Simple machines derived from the inclined plane include the wedge, the gear, and the screw; the spanner is derived from the lever; the pulley from the wheel.

The principal features of a machine are its ▷mechanical advantage, which is the ratio of load to effort, its velocity ratio, and its ▷efficiency, which is the work done by the load divided by the work done by the effort; the latter is expressed as a percentage. In a perfect machine, with no friction, the efficiency would be 100%. All practical machines have efficiencies of less than 100%.

machine code in computing, a set of instructions that a computer's central processing unit (CPU) can understand and obey directly, without any translation. Each type of CPU has its own machine code. Because machine-code programs consist entirely of binary digits (bits), most programmers write their programs in an easy-to-use ▷high-level language. A high-level program must be translated into machine code – by means of a ▷compiler or ▷interpreter program – before it can be executed by a computer.

machine gun rapid-firing automatic gun. The Maxim (named after its inventor, US-born British engineer H S Maxim (1840–1916)) of 1884 was recoil-operated, but some later types have been gas-operated (Bren) or recoil assisted by gas (some versions of the Browning).

machine tool automatic or semi-automatic power-driven machine for cutting and shaping metals. Machine tools have powerful electric motors to force cutting tools into the metal: these are made from hardened steel containing heat-resistant metals such as tungsten and chromium. The use of precision machine tools in mass-production assembly methods ensures that all duplicate parts produced are virtually identical.

Mach number ratio of the speed of a body to the speed of sound in the undisturbed medium through which the body travels. Mach 1 is reached when a body (such as an aircraft) has a velocity greater than that of sound ('passes the sound barrier'), namely 331 m/1,087 ft per second at sea level. It is named after Austrian physicist Ernst Mach (1838–1916).

MACHU PICCHU The ruined Inca city of Machu Picchu, northwest of Cuzco in Peru. *Image Bank*

Machu Picchu ruined Inca city in the Peruvian Andes, northwest of Cuzco. This settlement and stronghold stands at the top of 300-m/1,000-ft-high cliffs above the Urabamba River and covers an area of 13 sq km/5 sq mi. Built in about AD 1500, the city's remote location saved it from being found and destroyed by the Spanish conquistadors, and the remains of its houses and temples are well preserved. Machu Picchu was discovered in 1911 by the US archaeologist Hiram L Bingham.

Macintosh range of microcomputers originally produced by Apple Computer. The Apple Macintosh, introduced in 1984, was the first popular microcomputer with a ▷graphical user interface. The success of the Macintosh prompted other manufacturers and software companies to create their own graphical user interfaces. Most notable of these are Microsoft Windows, which runs on IBM PC-compatible microcomputers, and OSF/Motif, from the Open Software Foundation, which is used with many Unix systems.

Macintosh, Charles (1766–1843) Scottish manufacturing chemist who invented a waterproof fabric, lined with rubber, that was used for raincoats – hence **mackintosh**. Other waterproofing processes have now largely superseded this method.

Macke, August (1887–1914) German expressionist painter. He was a founding member of the ▷*Blaue Reiter* group in Munich. With Franz ▷Marc he developed a semi-abstract style, and became noted for his simple, brightly coloured paintings of park and street scenes. He was killed in World War I.

McKellen, Ian Murray (1939–) English actor. He has been acclaimed as the leading Shakespearean player of his generation. His stage roles include Richard II (1968), Macbeth (1977), Max in Martin Sherman's *Bent* (1979), Platonov in Chekhov's *Wild Honey* (1986), Iago in *Othello* (1989), and Richard III (1990); he has also appeared in *Uncle Vanya* (1992) and *Enemy of the People* (1998). His films include *Priest of Love* (1982), *Plenty* (1985), *Scandal* (1990), *The Ballad of Little Jo* (1991), *Last Action Hero* (1993), *Gods and Monsters* (1998), *X-Men* (2000) and *The Fellowship of the Ring* (2001). He was knighted in 1991.

Mackenzie, Alexander (1764–1820) British explorer and fur trader. In 1789, he was the first European to see the river, now part of northern Canada, named after him. In 1792–93 he crossed the Rocky Mountains to the Pacific coast of what is now British Columbia, making the first known crossing north of Mexico.

Mackenzie, Compton (1883–1972) Adopted name of Edward Montague Compton. Scottish writer. He published his first novel, *The Passionate Elopement*, in 1911. Subsequent novels included *Carnival* (1912), a melodrama of stage life, the semi-autobiographical *Sinister Street* (1913–14), the sequence *The Four Winds of Love* (1937–45), and the comedy *Whisky Galore!* (1947; filmed in 1949).

Mackenzie River river in the Northwest Territories, northwestern Canada; about 1,705 km/1,060 mi long (from the Great Slave Lake to the Beaufort Sea). It originates as the Athabasca River in British Columbia and flows over 966 km/600 mi to Lake Athabasca; it then flows northwest from the Great Slave Lake until it enters the Beaufort Sea (part of the Arctic Ocean). The Mackenzie River is navigable from June to October, when it eventually freezes over. It is the main channel of the Finlay-Peace-Mackenzie system (4,241 km/2,635 mi long), the second longest system in North America.

mackerel any of various fishes of the mackerel family, especially the **common mackerel** (*Scomber scombrus*) found in the North Atlantic and Mediterranean. It weighs about 0.7 kg/1.5 lb, and is blue with irregular black bands down its sides, the sides and under surface having a metallic sheen. Like all mackerels, it has a deeply forked tail, and a sleek, streamlined body form. (Family Scombroidia.)

The largest of the mackerels is the **tuna**, which weighs up to 700 kg/1,550 lb.

Mackerras, (Alan) Charles (MacLaurin) (1925–) Australian conductor. He has helped to make the music of the Czech composer Leoš Janáček more widely known. He was conductor of the English National Opera 1970–78.

McKinley, William (1843–1901) 25th president of the USA 1897–1901, a Republican. His term as president was marked by the USA's adoption of an imperialist foreign policy, as exemplified by the Spanish-American War in 1898 and the annexation of the Philippines. He sat in Congress 1876–91, apart from one term.

Throughout his political life, McKinley was a trusted friend of business interests, supporting high tariffs for fledgling US industries. He sat in the House of Representatives 1877–83 and 1885–91, and was governor of Ohio 1892–96. As president he presided over a period of prosperity and was drawn into foreign conflicts largely against his will. He annexed the Philippine Islands and implemented the open-door policy with China.

He was assassinated by an anarchist, Leon Czolgosz, in Buffalo, New York State, and was succeeded by his vice-president Theodore Roosevelt.

Related Web site: William McKinley – Twenty-fifth President 1897–1901 http://www.whitehouse.gov/WH/glimpse/presidents/html/wm25.html

McKinley, Mount (or Denali) highest peak in North America, situated in the ▷Rocky Mountains, Alaska; height 6,194 m/20,320 ft. It was named after US president William McKinley.

mackintosh waterproof coat created in the 19th century, made from a waterproof woollen fabric, patented in 1823 by Charles Macintosh, and Charles Goodyear's vulcanized rubber, created in 1839. The first mackintoshes of the late 19th century were neck-to-ankle garments. In the 20th century the mackintosh was redesigned to create styles such as the trenchcoat, a belted calf-length coat based on military coats, and raincoat, a lightweight version of the mackintosh. Fabric inventions have since enabled manufacturers to create waterproof coats from synthetic blends.

Mackintosh, Charles Rennie (1868–1928) Scottish architect, designer, and painter, whose highly original work represents a dramatic break with the late Victorian style. He worked initially in the ▷Art Nouveau idiom but later developed a unique style, both rational and expressive, that is more angular and stylized than the flowing, full-blown art nouveau style.

Influenced by the ▷Arts and Crafts Movement, he designed furniture and fittings, cutlery, and lighting to go with his interiors. Mackintosh was initially influential, particularly on Austrian architects such as Joseph Maria Olbrich and Josef Hoffman. However, he was not successful in his lifetime, and has only recently come to be regarded as a pioneer of modern design.

Mackintosh was born and educated in Glasgow, and also travelled in Italy. In 1896 he won the competition for the Glasgow School of Art (completed 1909). Other major works include the Cranston tea rooms, Glasgow (1897–1909); Hill House, Helensburgh (1902–03); the Scottish pavilion at the Turin exhibition in 1902; and Queen's Cross Church, Glasgow (1899). After 1913 he devoted himself to painting and eventually abandoned architecture and design altogether.

Maclean, Fitzroy Hew (1911–1996) Scottish writer and diplomat whose travels in the USSR and Central Asia inspired his books *Eastern Approaches* (1949) and *A Person from England* (1958). His other works include *To the Back of Beyond* (1974), *Holy Russia* (1979), and *Bonnie Prince Charlie* (1988).

McLuhan, (Herbert) Marshall (1911–1980) Canadian theorist of communication who emphasized the effects of technology on modern society. He coined the phrase 'the medium is the message', meaning that the form rather than the content of information has become crucial. His works include *The Gutenberg Galaxy* (1962) – in which he coined the phrase 'the global village' for the worldwide electronic society then emerging; *Understanding Media* (1964); and *The Medium is the Massage* (sic, 1967).

> **Marshall McLuhan**
> *The medium is the message.*
> Understanding Media ch. 1

Macmillan, (Maurice) Harold (1894–1986) 1st Earl of Stockton. British Conservative politician, prime minister 1957–63; foreign secretary 1955 and chancellor of the Exchequer 1955–57. In 1963 he attempted to negotiate British entry into the European Economic Community (EEC), but was blocked by the French president Charles de Gaulle. Much of his career as prime minister was spent defending the UK's retention of a nuclear weapon, and he was responsible for the purchase of US Polaris missiles in 1962.

Macmillan was MP for Stockton 1924–29 and 1931–45, and for Bromley 1945–64. As minister of housing 1951–54 he achieved the construction of 300,000 new houses a year. He became prime minister on the resignation of Anthony Eden after the ▷Suez Crisis, and led the Conservative Party to victory in the 1959 elections on the slogan 'You've never had it so good' (the phrase was borrowed from a US election campaign). Internationally, his realization of the 'wind of change' in Africa advanced the independence of former colonies. Macmillan's nickname **Supermac** was coined by the cartoonist Vicky.

MacNeice, (Frederick) Louis (1907–1963) Northern Irish poet, born in Belfast. He made his debut with *Blind Fireworks* (1929) and developed a polished ease of expression, reflecting his classical training, as in the autobiographical and topical *Autumn Journal* (1939). He is noted for his low-key, socially committed but politically uncommitted verse; and his ability to reflect the spirit of his times in his own emotional experience earned him an appreciative public.

Mâcon capital of the French *département* of Saône-et-Loire, on the River Saône, 72 km/45 mi north of Lyon; population (1990) 38,500. It produces wine. Mâcon dates from ancient Gaul, when it was known as **Matisco**. The French writer Alphonse Lamartine was born here.

Macpherson, James (1736–1796) Scottish writer. He published *Fragments of Ancient Poetry Collected in the Highlands of Scotland* in 1760, followed by the epics *Fingal* in 1761 and *Temora* in 1763, which he claimed as the work of the 3rd-century bard ▷Ossian. After his death they were shown largely, but not entirely, to be forgeries.

Macquarie, Lachlan (1762–1824) Scottish administrator in Australia. He succeeded Admiral ▷Bligh as governor of New South Wales in 1809, raised the demoralized settlement to prosperity, and did much to rehabilitate ex-convicts. In 1821 he returned to Britain in poor health, exhausted by struggles with his opponents. Lachlan River and Macquarie River and Island are named after him.

Macquarie Island outlying Australian territorial possession, a Tasmanian dependency, some 1,370 km/850 mi southeast of Hobart; area 170 sq km/65 sq mi; it is uninhabited except for an Australian government research station.

McQueen, (Terrence) Steve(n) (1930–1980) US film actor. He was admired for his portrayals of the strong, silent loner, and noted for performing his own stunt work. After television success in the 1950s, he became a film star with *The Magnificent Seven* (1960). His films include *The Great Escape* (1963), *Bullitt* (1968), *Papillon* (1973), and *The Hunter* (1980).

macramé art of making decorative fringes and lacework with knotted threads. The name comes from the Arabic word for 'striped cloth', which is often decorated in this way.

macro in computer programming, a new command created by combining a number of existing ones. For example, a word processing macro might create a letterhead or fax cover sheet, inserting words, fonts, and logos with a single keystroke or mouse click. Macros are also useful to automate computer communications – for example, users can write a macro to ask their computer to dial an Internet Service Provider (ISP), retrieve e-mail and Usenet articles, and then disconnect. A **macro key** on the keyboard combines the effects of pressing several individual keys.

macro- a prefix meaning on a very large scale, as opposed to micro.

macroeconomics division of economics concerned with the study of whole (aggregate) economies or systems, including such aspects as government income and expenditure, the balance of payments, fiscal policy, investment, inflation, and unemployment. It seeks to understand the influence of all relevant economic factors on each other and thus to quantify and predict aggregate national income.

Modern macroeconomics takes much of its inspiration from the work of Maynard Keynes, whose *General Theory of Employment, Interest, and Money* (1936) proposed that governments could prevent financial crises and unemployment by adjusting demand through control of credit and currency. **Keynesian macroeconomics** thus analyses aggregate supply and demand and holds that markets do not continuously 'clear' (quickly attain equilibrium between supply and demand) and may require intervention if objectives such as full employment are thought desirable. Keynesian macroeconomic formulations were generally accepted well into the post-war era and have been refined and extended by the **neo-Keynesian school**, which contends that in a recession the market will clear only very slowly and that full employment equilibrium may never return without significant demand management (by government). At the same time, however, **neoclassical economics** has experienced a resurgence, using tools from ▷microeconomics to challenge the central Keynesian assumption that resources may be underemployed and that full employment equilibrium requires state intervention. Another important school is **new classical**

Macedonia

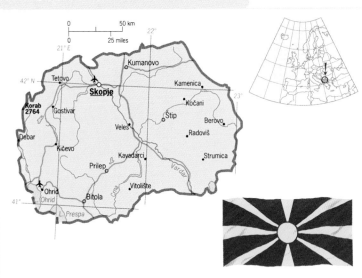

Macedonia landlocked country in southeast Europe, bounded north by Serbia, west by Albania, south by Greece, and east by Bulgaria.

NATIONAL NAME *Republika Makedonija/Republic of Macedonia* (official internal name); *Poranesna Jugoslovenska Republika Makedonija/Former Yugoslav Republic of Macedonia* (official international name)
AREA 25,700 sq km/9,922 sq mi
CAPITAL Skopje
MAJOR TOWNS/CITIES Bitola, Prilep, Kumanovo, Tetovo
PHYSICAL FEATURES mountainous; rivers: Struma, Vardar; lakes: Ohrid, Prespa, Scutari; partly Mediterranean climate with hot summers

Government

HEAD OF STATE Ljupco Jordanovski from 2004

MACEDONIA The wood carving on this stamp, which was produced for the first anniversary of Macedonian independence, shows two figures from Montenegrin history: the poet Bishop Petar II and the monk Makarije, a pioneer of the printing press. *Stanley Gibbons*

HEAD OF GOVERNMENT Branco Crvenkovski from 2002
POLITICAL SYSTEM emergent democracy
POLITICAL EXECUTIVE limited presidency
ADMINISTRATIVE DIVISIONS 123 municipalities
ARMED FORCES 12,300; plus paramilitary forces of 7,600 (2002 est)
CONSCRIPTION military service is compulsory for six months
DEATH PENALTY laws do not provide for the death penalty for any crime
DEFENCE SPEND (% GDP) 2.7 (2002 est)
EDUCATION SPEND (% GDP) 4.1 (2002 est)
HEALTH SPEND (% GDP) 6 (2000 est)

Economy and resources

CURRENCY Macedonian denar
GPD (US$) 3.7 billion (2002 est)
REAL GDP GROWTH (% change on previous year) –4.6 (2001)
GNI (US$) 3.5 billion (2002 est)
GNI PER CAPITA (PPP) (US$) 6,210 (2002 est)
CONSUMER PRICE INFLATION 3% (2003 est)
UNEMPLOYMENT 32% (2000)
FOREIGN DEBT (US$) 1.25 billion (2001 est)
MAJOR TRADING PARTNERS Germany, Serbia and Montenegro, Ukraine, USA, Greece, Italy, Russia
RESOURCES coal, iron, zinc, chromium, manganese, lead, copper, nickel, silver, gold
INDUSTRIES metallurgy, chemicals, textiles, buses, refrigerators, detergents, medicines, wood pulp, wine
EXPORTS tobacco, manufactured goods, machinery and transport equipment, metals, miscellaneous manufactured articles, sugar

beet, vegetables, cheese, lamb. Principal market: Serbia and Montenegro 25.3% (2000)
IMPORTS mineral fuels and lubricants, manufactured goods, machinery and transport equipment, food and live animals, chemicals. Principal source: Germany 12.1% (2000)
ARABLE LAND 21.8% (2001 est)
AGRICULTURAL PRODUCTS rice, wheat, barley, sugar beet, fruit and vegetables, tobacco, sunflowers, potatoes, grapes (wine industry is important); livestock rearing and dairy farming

Population and society

POPULATION 2,056,000 (2003 est)
POPULATION GROWTH RATE 0.4% (2000–15)
POPULATION DENSITY (per sq km) 80 (2003 est)
URBAN POPULATION (% of total) 59 (2003 est)
AGE DISTRIBUTION (% of total population) 0–14 22%, 15–59 63%, 60+ 15% (2002 est)
ETHNIC GROUPS 67% Macedonian ethnic descent, 23% ethnic Albanian, 4% Turkish, 2% Romanian, 2% Serb, and 2% Muslim, comprising Macedonian Slavs who converted to Islam during the Ottoman era, and are known as Pomaks. This ethnic breakdown is disputed by Macedonia's ethnic Albanian population, who claim that they form 40% of the population, and seek autonomy and by ethnic Serbs, who claim that they form 11.5%
LANGUAGE Macedonian (related to Bulgarian; official), Albanian
RELIGION Christian, mainly Orthodox 67%; Muslim 30%
EDUCATION (compulsory years) 8
LITERACY RATE 99% (men); 99% (women) (2003 est)
LABOUR FORCE 13.4% agriculture, 33.7% industry, 52.9% services (1997 est)
LIFE EXPECTANCY 71 (men); 76 (women) (2000–05)
CHILD MORTALITY RATE (under 5, per 1,000 live births) 26 (2001)
HOSPITAL BEDS (per 1,000 people) 5 (1999 est)
TV SETS (per 1,000 people) 282 (2001 est)
RADIOS (per 1,000 people) 206 (1998)
INTERNET USERS (per 10,000 people) 484.5 (2002 est)

See also ▷Alexander (III) the Great; ▷Byzantine Empire; ▷Balkan Wars; ▷Ottoman Empire.

Chronology

4th century BC: Part of ancient great kingdom of Macedonia, which included northern Greece and southwest Bulgaria and, under Alexander the Great, conquered a vast empire; Thessaloniki founded.
146 BC: Macedonia became a province of the Roman Empire.
395 AD: On the division of the Roman Empire, came under the control of Byzantine Empire, with its capital at Constantinople.
6th century: Settled by Slavs, who later converted to Christianity.
9th–14th centuries: Under successive rule by Bulgars, Byzantium, and Serbia.
1371: Became part of Islamic Ottoman Empire.
late 19th century: The 'Internal Macedonian Revolutionary Organization', through terrorism, sought to provoke Great Power intervention against Turks.
1912–13: After First Balkan War, partitioned between Bulgaria, Greece, and the area that constitutes the current republic of Serbia.
1918: Serbian part included in what was to become Yugoslavia; Serbian imposed as official language.
1941–44: Occupied by Bulgaria.
1945: Created a republic within Yugoslav Socialist Federation.
1967: The Orthodox Macedonian archbishopric of Skopje, forcibly abolished 200 years earlier by the Turks, was restored.
1980: The rise of nationalism was seen after the death of Yugoslav leader Tito.

1990: Multiparty elections produced an inconclusive result.
1991: Kiro Gligorov became president. A referendum supported independence.
1992: Independence was declared, and accepted by Serbia/Yugoslavia, but international recognition was withheld because of Greece's objections to the name.
1993: Sovereignty was recognized by the UK and Albania; United Nations membership was won under the provisional name of the Former Yugoslav Republic of Macedonia; Greece blocked full European Union (EU) recognition.
1994: Independence was recognized by the USA; a trade embargo was imposed by Greece.
1995: Independence was recognized by Greece and the trade embargo lifted. President Gligorov survived a car bomb assassination attempt.
1998: The UN extended the mandate of UNPREDEP. A general election resulted in Ljubco Georgievski, the VRMO-DPMNE leader, becoming prime minister. A 1,700-strong NATO force was deployed in Macedonia to safeguard the 2,000 ceasefire verification monitors in neighbouring Kosovo, Yugoslavia.
1999: Boris Trajkovski was elected president.
2001: Heavy fighting broke out between Macedonian security forces and ethnic Albanians.
2002: Albanian was recognized as an official language. Macedonia joined the World Trade Organization (WTO).

economics, which seeks to show the futility of Keynesian demand-management policies and stresses instead the importance of **supply-side economics**, believing that the principal factor influencing growth of national output is the efficient allocation and use of labour and capital. A related school is that of the **Chicago monetarists**, led by Milton ▷Friedman, who have revived the old idea that an increase in money supply leads inevitably to an increase in prices rather than in output; however, whereas the new classical school contends that wage and price adjustment are almost instantaneous and so the level of employment at any time must be the natural rate, the Chicago monetarists are more gradualist, believing that such adjustment may take some years.

macromolecule in chemistry, a very large molecule, generally a ▷polymer.

macrophage type of ▷white blood cell, or leucocyte, found in all vertebrate animals. Macrophages specialize in the removal of bacteria and other micro-organisms, or of cell debris after injury. Like phagocytes, they engulf foreign matter, but they are larger than phagocytes and have a longer life span. They are found throughout the body, but mainly in the lymph and connective tissues, and especially the lungs, where they ingest dust, fibres, and other inhaled particles.

> **Madonna**
> *Ever since my daughter was born I feel the fleetingness of time, and I don't want to waste it in getting the perfect lip colour.*
> Interview in the *Daily Telegraph*, 3 February 1998

Madagascar see country box.

mad cow disease common name for ▷bovine spongiform encephalopathy, an incurable brain condition in cattle.

madder any of a group of plants bearing small funnel-shaped flowers, especially the perennial vine *R. tinctorum* which grows in Europe and Asia, the red root of which yields a red dye called alizarin (now made synthetically from coal tar). (Genus *Rubia*, family Rubiaceae.)

Madeira river of northwest Brazil; length 3,250 km/2,020 mi. It is the longest tributary of the Amazon, and is formed by the rivers Beni and Mamoré. It flows northeast through the state of Amazonas to join the Amazon east of the city of Manaus. It is navigable by ocean-going vessels for 1,144 km/711 miles as far as Pôrto Velho. Gold-prospecting still occurs near the Bolivian border.

Madeira Islands group of islands forming an autonomous region of Portugal, off the northwest coast of Africa, about 420 km/260 mi north of the Canary Islands; area 796 sq km/308 sq mi; population (1994 est) 256,000. Madeira, the largest, and Porto Santo are the only inhabited islands. The Desertas and Selvagens are uninhabited islets. Their mild climate makes them a popular, year-round tourist destination. The capital is ▷Funchal, on Madeira. Pico Ruivo, also on Madeira, is the highest mountain at 1,861 m/6,106 ft. Industries include Madeira (a fortified wine), sugar cane, fruit, fish, handicrafts, and tourism.

The islands were Portuguese from the 15th century, and occupied by Britain in 1801 and 1807–14. In 1980 Madeira gained partial autonomy but remains a Portuguese overseas territory.

Related Web site: Madeira Web http://www.madeira-web.com/PagesUK/index.html

Madhya Bharat state of India 1950–56. It was a union of 24 states of which Gwalior and Indore were the most important. In 1956 Madhya Bharat was absorbed in ▷Madhya Pradesh.

Madhya Pradesh state of central India, the largest of the Indian states; area 443,400 sq km/171,200 sq mi; population (2001 est) 64,920,000; about 20% are from tribes (Gonds, Bhils, Baigas, Korkus, Kols, Kamars, and Marias). The capital is ▷Bhopal, and other towns and cities are Indore, Jabalpur, Gwalior, Durg-Bhilainagar, Raipur, and Ujjain. The state is land-locked and mainly upland. It includes the northern part of the Deccan plateau, drained by the rivers Narmada and Mahanadi, as well as the Betwa, Chambal, Tapti, and Son. Vindhya and Satpura mountain ranges (rising to 600 m/2,000 ft) are found in the state, which is heavily forested, particularly in the east. Industries include textiles, engineering, iron ore, steel (at Bhilai complex), coal, bauxite, manganese, paper, aluminium, limestone, diamonds, and cement. Hydroelectric power comes from the Chambal, ▷Narmada, and Mahanadi rivers. Main agricultural products include rice in the wetter regions of the east, cotton, millet, wheat, oilseed, sugar, groundnuts, and soya. In 2000 a new state, ▷Chhattisgarh, was created from Madya Pradesh.

Madison state capital of ▷Wisconsin, USA, 193 km/120 mi northwest of Chicago and 120 km/74 mi west of Milwaukee, on an isthmus between lakes Mendota and Monona; seat of Dane County; population (1994 est) 195,000. It is the centre of a rich agricultural region; industries include agricultural machinery, meat packing, battery production, and medical equipment.

Madison, James (1751–1836) 4th president of the USA 1809–17. In 1787 he became a member of the Philadelphia Constitutional Convention and took a leading part in drawing up the US Constitution and the Bill of Rights. In the struggle between the more democratic views of Thomas ▷Jefferson and the aristocratic, upper-class sentiments of Alexander ▷Hamilton, he allied himself firmly with Jefferson. As secretary of state in Jefferson's government 1801–09, Madison completed the ▷Louisiana Purchase negotiated by James Monroe. During his period of office the War of 1812 with Britain took place.

Madison Square Garden venue in New York, built as a boxing arena and also used for concerts. The current 'Garden' is the fourth to bear the name and staged its first boxing match in 1968. It is situated over Pennsylvania Station on 7th Avenue, New York City, and has a capacity of 20,000.

Madonna Italian name for the Virgin ▷Mary, meaning 'my lady'.

Madonna (1958–) Stage name of Madonna Louise Veronica Ciccone. US pop singer and actor who is arguably the most successful female artist in popular music. Her first hit was 'Like a Virgin' (1984); others include 'Material Girl' (1985) and 'Like a Prayer' (1989). Her albums *Ray of Light* (1998) and *Music*, influenced by dance and electronic music more than her previous releases, were both immediate commercial and critical successes. Her films include *Desperately Seeking Susan* (1985) and *Evita* (1996).

Related Web site: Madonna MIDI Files http://www.geocities.com/Hollywood/Set/2804/

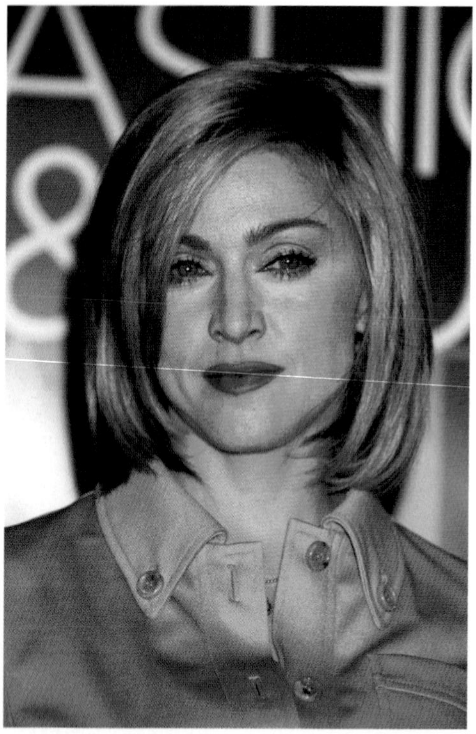

MADONNA US singer and actor Madonna. For some, the frank eroticism of her songs and stage acts is a spirited refusal to pander to the prevalent submissive image of female sexuality. For others, it is a cynical manipulation of sexual stereotypes. © *Mitchell Gerber/CORBIS*

Madras former name, to 1996, of ▷Chennai, an industrial port and capital of the state of Tamil Nadu, India, and the former name of the state of Tamil Nadu itself.

Madrid autonomous community of central Spain; area 8,000 sq km/3,088 sq mi; population (2001 est) 5,372,400. Bounded by the Sierra de Guadarrama mountains in the northwest, and by the River Tagus in the southeast, it is arid plateau country. It is crossed by several rivers, including the Jarama, a tributary of the Tagus. Products include fruit and vegetables, grown in the south; timber from the forests in the northeast, and granite and gypsum from quarries in the mountains. The ▷Escorial palace lies in the northwest; Aranjuez in the south has contained a royal palace since the 15th century and has luxurious gardens. The capital is ▷Madrid.

> **Maurice Maeterlinck**
> *We possess only the happiness we are able to understand.*
> Wisdom and Destiny

Madrid city and capital of Spain and of ▷Madrid autonomous community, on the Manzanares River; population (2001 est) 5,372,400. Built on an elevated plateau in the centre of the country, at 655 m/2,183 ft it is the highest capital in Europe and has excesses of heat and cold. Industries include the production of food, electronics, pharmaceuticals, leather, chemicals, furniture, tobacco, and paper, and there is engineering and publishing.

Features The Real Academia de Bellas Artes (1752); the Prado museum (1785); the royal palace (1764), built for Philip V; the 15th-century Retiro Park; the Plaza Mayor (1617–20); the Puerta de Alcalá arch; and the basilica of San Francisco el Grande (1761–84).

History Madrid began as the Moorish city of Magerit. It was captured in 1083 by King Alfonso VI of Castile. It remained a small provincial town until Philip II made it his capital in 1561 because of its position at the centre of the Iberian peninsula; it became the national capital in 1607. In 1808 there was an uprising here against Napoleon's army of occupation. Madrid was the centre of opposition to Franco during the Spanish Civil War, and was besieged by the Nationalists 1936–39.

madrigal form of secular song in four or five parts, usually sung without instrumental accompaniment. It originated in 14th-century Italy. Madrigal composers include Andrea Gabrieli, Monteverdi, Thomas Morley, and Orlando Gibbons.

Maecenas, Gaius Cilnius (*c.* 69–8 BC) Roman patron of the arts, and close friend and diplomatic agent of ▷Augustus. He was influential in providing encouragement and material support for the Augustan poets Horace and Virgil.

maenad in Greek mythology, one of the women participants in the orgiastic rites of ▷Dionysus; maenads were also known as Bacchae.

Maestricht alternative form of ▷Maastricht, a city in the Netherlands.

Maeterlinck, Maurice Polydore Marie Bernard (1862–1949) Count Maeterlinck. Belgian poet and dramatist. His plays include *Pelléas et Mélisande* (1892) (on which Debussy based his opera), *L'Oiseau bleu/The Blue Bird* (1908), and *Le Bourgmestre de Stilmonde/The Burgomaster of Stilemonde* (1918). This last celebrates Belgian resistance in World War I, a subject that led to his exile in the USA in 1940. His philosophical essays include 'Le Trésor des humbles/The Treasure of the Humble' (1896) and 'La vie des abeilles/The Life of the Bee' (1901). He was awarded the Nobel Prize for Literature in 1911.

Mafeking former name of ▷Mafikeng, a town in South Africa.

Mafia (Italian 'swank') secret society reputed to control organized crime such as gambling, loansharking, drug traffic, prostitution, and protection; connected with the ▷Camorra of Naples. It originated in Sicily in the late Middle Ages and now operates chiefly there and in countries to which Italians have emigrated, such as the USA and Australia. During the early 1990s many centre and right-wing Italian politicians, such as the former Christian Democrat prime minister Giulio Andreotti, became discredited when it emerged that they had had dealings with the Mafia.

mafic rock plutonic rock composed chiefly of dark-coloured minerals such as olivine and pyroxene that contain abundant magnesium and iron. It is derived from **magnesium** and **ferric** (iron). The term **mafic** also applies to dark-coloured minerals rich in iron and magnesium as a group. 'Mafic rocks' usually refers to dark-coloured igneous rocks such as basalt, but can also refer to their metamorphic counterparts.

Magadha kingdom of ancient northeastern India, roughly corresponding to the middle and southern parts of modern ▷Bihar. It was the scene of many incidents in the life of the Buddha and was the seat of the ▷Mauryan dynasty founded in the 3rd century BC. Its capital Pataliputra was a great cultural and political centre.

magazine publication brought out periodically, typically containing articles, essays, short stories, reviews, and illustrations. It is thought that the first magazine was *Le Journal des savants*, published in France in 1665. The first magazine in the UK was a penny weekly, the *Athenian Gazette*, better known later as the *Athenian Mercury* (1690–97). This was produced by a London publisher, John Dunton, to resolve 'all the most Nice and Curious Questions'. The US *Reader's Digest*, first published in 1922, with editions in many different countries and languages, was the world's best-selling magazine until overtaken by a Soviet journal in the mid-1980s.

Related Web site: Good Housekeeping http://goodhousekeeping.women.com/gh/index.htm

Magdeburg industrial city and capital of ▷Saxony-Anhalt, Germany, on the River Elbe; population (1995) 263,000. Products include chemicals, precision instruments, paper, textiles, and machinery. A former capital of Saxony, Magdeburg became capital of Saxony-Anhalt on German reunification in 1990. In 1938 the city was linked by canal with the Rhine and Ruhr rivers.

Magellan, Ferdinand (c. 1480–1521) Portuguese navigator. In 1519 he set sail in the *Victoria* from Seville with the intention of reaching the East Indies by a westerly route. He sailed through the **Strait of Magellan** at the tip of South America, crossed an ocean he named the Pacific, and in 1521 reached the Philippines, where he was killed in a battle with the islanders. His companions returned to Seville in 1522, completing the voyage under del ▷Cano.

Magellan was brought up at court and entered the royal service, but later transferred his services to Spain. He and his Malay slave, Enrique de Malacca, are considered the first circumnavigators of the globe, since they had once sailed from the Philippines to Europe.

    Related Web site: Magellan, Ferdinand http://www.mariner.org/age/magellan.html

Magellanic Clouds in astronomy, the two galaxies nearest to our own galaxy. They are irregularly shaped, and appear as detached parts of the ▷Milky Way, in the southern constellations Dorado, Tucana, and Mensa.

    The Large Magellanic Cloud spreads over the constellations of Dorado and Mensa. The Small Magellanic Cloud is in Tucana. The Large Magellanic Cloud is 169,000 light years from Earth, and about a third the diameter of our Galaxy; the Small Magellanic Cloud, 180,000 light years away, is about a fifth the diameter of our Galaxy. They are named after the early-16th-century Portuguese navigator Ferdinand Magellan, who first described them.

Madagascar

MADAGASCAR Zebu carts are widely used in Madagascar for carrying all kinds of loads. Zebus represent wealth for many farmers in Africa and Madagascar, but cause far more damage to fragile habitats than the equivalent native animals of the area, such as (in Africa) antelope. *Premaphotos Wildlife*

Madagascar island country in the Indian Ocean, off the coast of East Africa, about 400 km/280 mi from Mozambique.

NATIONAL NAME *Repoblikan'i Madagasikara/République de Madagascar/Republic of Madagascar*
AREA 587,041 sq km/226,656 sq mi
CAPITAL Antananarivo
MAJOR TOWNS/CITIES Antsirabe, Mahajanga, Fianarantsoa, Toamasina, Ambatondrazaka
MAJOR PORTS Toamasina, Antsiranana, Toliara, Mahajanga
PHYSICAL FEATURES temperate central highlands; humid valleys and tropical coastal plains; arid in south

Government

HEAD OF STATE Marc Ravalomanana from 2002
HEAD OF GOVERNMENT Jacques Sylla from 2002
POLITICAL SYSTEM emergent democracy
POLITICAL EXECUTIVE limited presidency
ADMINISTRATIVE DIVISIONS six provinces
ARMED FORCES 13,500; plus paramilitary gendarmerie of 8,100 (2002 est)
DEATH PENALTY retains the death penalty for ordinary crimes but can be considered abolitionist in practice; date of last known execution 1958

Economy and resources

CURRENCY Malagasy franc
GPD (US$) 4.5 billion (2002 est)
REAL GDP GROWTH (% change on previous year) 6.7 (2001)
GNI (US$) 3.9 billion (2002 est)
GNI PER CAPITA (PPP) (US$) 720 (2002 est)

CONSUMER PRICE INFLATION 3.5% (2003 est)
UNEMPLOYMENT 6% (1995 est)
FOREIGN DEBT (US$) 4.1 billion (2001 est)
MAJOR TRADING PARTNERS France, Japan, Germany, USA, UK, China, Singapore, Mauritius, Iran
RESOURCES graphite, chromite, mica, uranium, titanium ore, small quantities of precious stones, bauxite and coal deposits, petroleum reserves
INDUSTRIES food products, textiles and clothing, beverages, chemical products, cement, fertilizers, pharmaceuticals
EXPORTS fish, coffee, shrimps and prawns, cloves, vanilla, petroleum products, chromium, cotton fabrics. Principal market: France 39.3% (2000)
IMPORTS minerals (crude petroleum), chemicals, machinery, vehicles and parts, base metal, electrical equipment. Principal source: France 24% (2000)
ARABLE LAND 5% (2000 est)
AGRICULTURAL PRODUCTS rice, cassava, mangoes, bananas, potatoes, sugar cane, seed cotton, sisal, vanilla, cloves, coconuts, tropical fruits; cattle-farming; sea-fishing

Population and society

POPULATION 17,404,000 (2003 est)
POPULATION GROWTH RATE 2.5% (2000–15)
POPULATION DENSITY (per sq km) 30 (2003 est)
URBAN POPULATION (% of total) 31 (2003 est)

AGE DISTRIBUTION (% of total population) 0–14 45%, 15–59 50%, 60+ 5% (2002 est)
ETHNIC GROUPS 18 main Malagasy tribes of Malaysian–Polynesian origin; also French, Chinese, Indians, Pakistanis, and Comorans
LANGUAGE Malagasy, French (both official), local dialects
RELIGION over 50% traditional beliefs, Roman Catholic, Protestant about 40%, Muslim 7%
EDUCATION (compulsory years) 5
LITERACY RATE 75% (men); 64% (women) (2003 est)
LABOUR FORCE 75.5% agriculture, 7% industry, 17.5% services (1997 est)

LIFE EXPECTANCY 53 (men); 55 (women) (2000–05)
CHILD MORTALITY RATE (under 5, per 1,000 live births) 136 (2001)
PHYSICIANS (per 1,000 people) 0.1 (1998 est)
HOSPITAL BEDS (per 1,000 people) 0.9 (1994 est)
TV SETS (per 1,000 people) 23 (1999)
RADIOS (per 1,000 people) 198 (1998)
INTERNET USERS (per 10,000 people) 28.3 (2002 est)
PERSONAL COMPUTER USERS (per 100 people) 0.3 (2002 est)

Chronology

c. 6th–10th centuries AD: Settled by migrant Indonesians.

1500: First visited by European navigators.

17th century: Development of Merina and Sakalava kingdoms in the central highlands and west coast.

1642–74: France established a coastal settlement at Fort-Dauphin, which they abandoned after a massacre by local inhabitants.

late 18th–early 19th century: Merinas, united by their ruler Andrianampoinimerina, became dominant kingdom; court converted to Christianity.

1861: Ban on Christianity (imposed in 1828) and entry of Europeans lifted by Merina king, Radama II.

1885: Became French protectorate.

1895: Merina army defeated by French and became a colony; slavery abolished.

1942–43: British troops invaded to overthrow French administration allied to the pro-Nazi Germany Vichy regime and install anti-Nazi Free French government.

1947–48: Nationalist uprising brutally suppressed by French.

1960: Independence achieved from France, with Philibert Tsiranana, the leader of the Social Democratic Party (PSD), as president.

1972: Merina-dominated army overthrew Tsiranana's government, dominated by the cotier (coastal tribes), as the economy deteriorated.

1975: Martial law imposed; new one-party state Marxist constitution adopted, with Lt-Commander Didier Ratsiraka as president.

1978: More than 1,000 people were killed in race riots in Majunga city in the northwest.

1980: Ratsiraka abandoned the Marxist experiment, which had involved nationalization and the severing of ties with France.

1990: Political opposition was legalized and 36 new parties were created.

1991: Antigovernment demonstrations were held. Ratsiraka formed a new unity government, which included opposition members.

1992: Constitutional reform was approved by a referendum.

1995: A referendum backed the appointment of a prime minister by the president, rather than the assembly.

1996: Didier Ratsiraka was elected president again.

2002: Ratsiraka fled the country, ending a dispute with his rival, Marc Ravalomanana, over the 2001 presidential election and averting civil war. Ravalomanana had earlier been confirmed as the legitimate president in a court-supervised recount.

Magellan, Strait of (Spanish **Estrecho de Magallanes**) channel at the southern tip of Chile; it separates the South American mainland from Tierra del Fuego, and joins the South Pacific and South Atlantic oceans. It is 595 km/370 mi long with a maximum width of 32 km/20 mi. The strait is named after the Portuguese navigator Ferdinand ▷Magellan who discovered it in 1520. It provided a safer passage than that around Cape Horn, but its importance declined following the opening of the Panama Canal in 1914, an international waterway within Chile's territorial waters.

Maggiore, Lake (ancient **Verbanus Lacus**) lake largely in Italy, bounded on the west by Piedmont and on the east by Lombardy; its northern end is in the Swiss canton of Ticino. It is 63 km/39 mi long and up to 9 km/5.5 mi wide, with an area of 212 sq km/82 sq mi.

maggot soft, plump, limbless ▷larva of flies, a typical example being the larva of the blowfly which is deposited as an egg on fles

magi (singular **magus**) priests of the Zoroastrian religion of ancient Persia, noted for their knowledge of astrology. The term i used in the New Testament of the Latin Vulgate Bible where the Authorized Version gives 'wise men'. The magi who came to visit t infant Jesus with gifts of gold, frankincense, and myrrh (the **Adoration of the Magi**) were in later tradition described as 'the three kings' – Caspar, Melchior, and Balthazar.

> **Related Web site: Magi** http://www.newadvent.org/cathen/09527a.htm

magic art of controlling the forces of nature by supernatural means such as charms and ritual. The central ideas are that like produces like (**sympathetic magic**) and that influence carries by contagion or association; for example, by the former principle an enemy could be destroyed through an effigy, and by the latter principle through personal items such as hair or nail clippings. See also ▷witchcraft.

magic bullet term sometimes used for a drug that is specifically targeted on certain cells or tissues in the body, such as a small collection of cancerous cells (see ▷cancer) or cells that have been invaded by a virus. Such drugs can be made in various ways, but ▷monoclonal antibodies are increasingly being used to direct the drug to a specific target.

magic realism in 20th-century literature, a fantastic situation realistically treated, as in the works of many Latin American writers such as Isabel Allende, Jorge Luis ▷Borges, and Gabriel ▷García Márquez.

magic square in mathematics, a square array of numbers in which the rows, columns, and diagonals add up to the same total. A simple example employing the numbers 1 to 9, with a total of 15, has a first row of 6, 7, 2, a second row of 1, 5, 9, and a third row of 8, 3, 4.

A **pandiagonal magic square** is one in which all the broken diagonals also add up to the magic constant.

Maginot Line French fortification system along the German frontier from Switzerland to Luxembourg built 1929–36 under the direction of the war minister, André Maginot. It consisted of semi-underground forts joined by underground passages, and was protected by antitank defences; lighter fortifications continued the line to the sea. In 1940 German forces pierced the Belgian frontier line and outflanked the Maginot Line.

magistrate in English law, a person who presides in a magistrates' court: either a justice of the peace (with no legal qualifications, and unpaid) or a stipendiary magistrate. Stipendiary magistrates are paid, qualified lawyers working mainly in London and major cities.

magistrates' court in England and Wales, a local law court that mainly deals with minor criminal cases. A magistrates' court consists of between two and seven lay justices of the peace (who are advised on the law by a clerk to the justices), or a single paid lawyer called a stipendiary magistrate.

maglev (acronym for **magnetic levitation**) high-speed surface transport using the repellent force of superconductive magnets (see ▷superconductivity) to propel and support, for example, a train above a track.

magma molten rock (either beneath or on a planetary surface) from which ▷igneous rocks are formed. ▷Lava is magma that has extruded on to the surface.

Magna Carta (Latin 'great charter') in English history, the charter granted by King ▷John (I) Lackland in 1215, traditionally seen as guaranteeing human rights against the excessive use of royal power. As a reply to the king's demands for feudal dues and attacks on the privileges of the medieval church, Archbishop Stephen ▷Langton proposed to the barons the drawing-up of a binding document in 1213. John was forced to accept this at Runnymede (now in Surrey) on 15 June 1215.

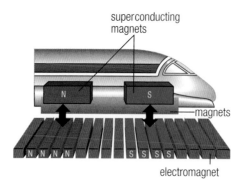

superconducting magnets

magnets

electromagnet

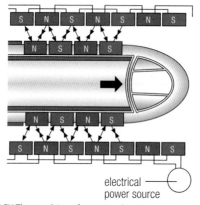

electrical power source

MAGLEV The repulsion of superconducting magnets and electromagnets in the track keeps a maglev train suspended above the track. By varying the strength and polarity of the track electromagnets, the train can be driven forward.

Magna Carta begins by reaffirming the rights of the medieval church. Certain clauses guard against infringements of feudal custom: for example, Clause 2 limits the relief payable by an heir to inherit his father's barony. Others are designed to check extortions or maladministration of justice by royal officials. The privileges of London and the cities were also guaranteed.

As feudalism declined, Magna Carta lost its significance, and under the Tudors was almost forgotten. During the 17th century it was rediscovered and reinterpreted by the Parliamentary party as a document of democracy, guaranteeing the rights of the people. Such rights were particularly seen to be enshrined in Clause 12, which appeared to forbid taxation without consent, and Clause 39, which states that 'no freeman shall be...imprisoned...except by lawful judgement of his peers or by the law of the land'. In this way, a direct link has been claimed from Magna Carta through to the UK ▷Bill of Rights (1689), US ▷Declaration of Independence (1776), and the United Nations' Universal Declaration of ▷Human Rights (1948).

Four original copies of Magna Carta exist, one each in Salisbury and Lincoln cathedrals and two in the British Library.

> **Related Web site: Calvin Coolidge – Thirtieth President 1923–1929** http://www.whitehouse.gov/WH/glimpse/presidents/html/cc30.html

magnesia common name for ▷magnesium oxide.

magnesium lightweight, very ductile and malleable, silver-white, metallic element, symbol Mg, atomic number 12, relative atomic mass 24.305. It is one of the ▷alkaline-earth metals, and the lightest of the commonly used metals. Magnesium silicate, carbonate, and chloride are widely distributed in nature. The metal is used in alloys and flash photography. It is a necessary trace element in the human diet, and green plants cannot grow without it since it is an essential constituent of the photosynthetic pigment ▷chlorophyll ($C_{55}H_{72}MgN_4O_5$).

It was named after the ancient Greek city of Magnesia, near where it was first found. It was first recognized as an element by Scottish chemist Joseph Black 1755 and discovered in its oxide by English chemist Humphry ▷Davy 1808. Pure magnesium was isolated in 1828 by French chemist Antoine-Alexandre-Brutus Bussy.

magnesium oxide (or **magnesia**) MgO white powder or colourless crystals, formed when magnesium is burned in air or oxygen; a typical basic oxide. It is used to treat acidity of the stomach, and in some industrial processes; for example, as a lining brick in furnaces, because it is very stable when heated (refractory oxide).

magnet any object that forms a magnetic field (displays ▷magnetism), either permanently or temporarily through induction, causing it to attract materials such as iron, cobalt, nickel, and alloys of these. It always has two ▷magnetic poles, called north and south.

The world's most powerful magnet was built in 1997 at the Lawrence Berkeley National Laboratory, California. It produces a field 250,000 times stronger than the Earth's magnetic field (13.5 teslas). The coil magnet is made of an alloy of niobium and tin.

magnetic compass device for determining the direction of the horizontal component of the Earth's magnetic field. It consists of a magnetized needle with its north-seeking pole clearly indicated, pivoted so that it can turn freely in a plane parallel to the surface of the Earth (in a horizontal circle). The needle will turn so that its north-seeking pole points towards the Earth's magnetic north pole. See also ▷compass.

magnetic dipole the pair of north and south magnetic poles, separated by a short distance, that makes up all magnets. Individual magnets are often called 'magnetic dipoles'. Single magnetic poles, or monopoles, have never been observed despite being searched for. See also magnetic ▷domain.

magnetic field region around a permanent magnet, or around a conductor carrying an electric current, in which a force acts on a moving charge or on a magnet placed in the field. The field can be represented by lines of force parallel at each point to the direction of a small compass needle placed on them at that point. A magnetic field's magnitude is given by the ▷magnetic flux density, expressed in ▷teslas. See also ▷polar reversal.

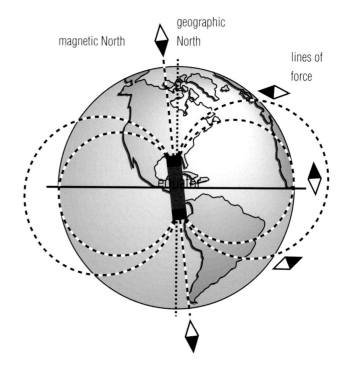

geographic North

magnetic North

lines of force

equator

MAGNETIC FIELD The Earth's magnetic field is similar to that of a bar magnet with poles near, but not exactly at, the geographic poles. Compass needles align themselves with the magnetic field, which is horizontal near the equator and vertical at the magnetic poles.

magnetic flux measurement of the strength of the magnetic field around electric currents and magnets. Its SI unit is the ▷weber; one weber per square metre is equal to one tesla.

magnetic-ink character recognition (MICR) in computing, a technique that enables special characters printed in magnetic ink to be read and input rapidly to a computer. MICR is used extensively in banking because magnetic-ink characters are difficult to forge and are therefore ideal for marking and identifying cheques.

magnetic material one of a number of substances that are strongly attracted by magnets and can be magnetized. These include iron, nickel, and cobalt, and all those ▷alloys that contain a proportion of these metals.

magnetic pole region of a magnet in which its magnetic properties are strongest. Every magnet has two poles, called north and south. The north (or north-seeking) pole is so named because a freely suspended magnet will turn so that this pole points towards the Earth's magnetic north pole. The north pole of one magnet will be attracted to the south pole of another, but will be repelled by its north pole. So unlike poles attract, like poles repel.

magnetic resonance imaging (MRI) diagnostic scanning system based on the principles of nuclear magnetic resonance. MRI yields finely detailed three-dimensional images of structures within the body without exposing the patient to harmful radiation. The technique is invaluable for imaging the soft tissues of the body, in particular the brain and the spinal cord.

Claimed as the biggest breakthrough in diagnostic imaging since the discovery of X-rays, MRI is a noninvasive technique based on a magnet which is many thousands of times stronger than the Earth's magnetic field. It causes nuclei within the atoms of the body to align themselves in one direction. When a brief radio pulse is beamed at the body the nuclei spin, emitting weak radio signals as they realign themselves to the magnet. These signals, which are characteristic for each type of tissue, are converted electronically into images on a viewing screen.

Also developed around magnetic technology, **magnetic resonance spectroscopy (MRS)** is a technique for investigating conditions in which there is a disturbance of the body's energy metabolism, including ischaemia and toxic damage due to drugs or other chemicals. MRS is also of value in diagnosing some cancers.

magnetic storm in meteorology, a sudden disturbance affecting the Earth's magnetic field, causing anomalies in radio transmissions and magnetic compasses. It is probably caused by ▷sunspot activity.

magnetic strip (or **magnetic stripe**) thin strip of magnetic material attached to a plastic card and used for recording data. Magnetic strips are used on credit cards, bank cards (as used at cash dispensing machines), telephone cards, and railway tickets.

magnetic tape narrow plastic ribbon coated with an easily magnetizable material on which data can be recorded. It is used in sound recording, audiovisual systems (videotape), and computing. For mass storage on commercial mainframe computers, large reel-to-reel tapes are still used, but cartridges are becoming popular. Various types of cartridge are now standard on minis and PCs, while audio cassettes are sometimes used with home computers.

Magnetic tape was first used in **sound recording** in 1947, and made overdubbing possible, unlike the direct-to-disc system it replaced. Two-track tape was introduced in the 1950s and four-track in the early 1960s; today, studios use 16-, 24-, or 32-track tape, from which the tracks are mixed down to a stereo master tape.

In computing, magnetic tape was first used to record data and programs in 1951 as part of the UNIVAC 1 system. It was very popular as a storage medium for external memory in the 1950s and 1960s. Since then it has been largely replaced by magnetic ▷disks as a working medium, although tape is still used to make backup copies of important data. Information is recorded on the tape in binary form, with two different strengths of signal representing 1 and 0.

magnetism phenomena associated with ▷magnetic fields. Magnetic fields are produced by moving charged particles: in electromagnets, electrons flow through a coil of wire connected to a battery; in permanent magnets, spinning electrons within the atoms generate the field.

Susceptibility Substances differ in the extent to which they can be magnetized by an external field (susceptibility). Materials that can be strongly magnetized, such as iron, cobalt, and nickel, are said to be **ferromagnetic**; this is due to the formation of areas called ▷domains in which atoms, weakly magnetic because of their spinning electrons, align to form areas of strong magnetism. Magnetic materials lose their magnetism if heated to the Curie temperature. Most other materials are **paramagnetic**, being only weakly pulled towards a strong magnet. This is because their atoms have a low level of magnetism and do not form domains. **Diamagnetic** materials are weakly repelled by a magnet since electrons within their atoms act as electromagnets and oppose the applied magnetic force. **Antiferromagnetic** materials have a very low susceptibility that increases with temperature; a similar phenomenon in materials such as ferrites is called **ferrimagnetism**.

Application Apart from its universal application in dynamos, electric motors, and switch gears, magnetism is of considerable importance in advanced technology – for example, in particle ▷accelerators for nuclear research, memory stores for computers, tape recorders, and ▷cryogenics.

magnetite black, strongly magnetic opaque mineral, Fe_3O_4, of the spinel group, an important ore of iron. Widely distributed, magnetite is found in nearly all igneous and metamorphic rocks. Some deposits, called lodestone, are permanently magnetized. Lodestone has been used as a compass since the first millennium BC. Today the orientations of magnetite grains in rocks are used in the study of the Earth's magnetic field (see ▷palaeomagnetism).

magneto simple electric generator, often used to provide the electricity for the ignition system of motorcycles and used in early cars.

It consists of a rotating magnet that sets up an electric current in a coil, providing the spark.

magnetometer device for measuring the intensity and orientation of the magnetic field of a particular rock or of a certain area. In geology, magnetometers are used to determine the original orientation of a rock formation (or the orientation when the magnetic signature was locked in), which allows for past plate reconstruction. They are also used to delineate 'magnetic striping' on the sea floor in order to make plate reconstruction and to prospect for ore bodies such as iron ore, which can disrupt the local magnetic field.

magnetosphere volume of space, surrounding a planet, in which the planet's magnetic field has a significant influence. The Earth's magnetosphere extends 64,000 km/40,000 mi towards the Sun, but many times this distance on the side away from the Sun. That of Jupiter is much larger, and, if it were visible, from the Earth it would appear to have roughly the same extent as the full moon.

magnetron thermionic ▷valve (electron tube) for generating very high-frequency oscillations, used in radar and to produce microwaves in a microwave oven. The flow of electrons from the tube's cathode to one or more anodes is controlled by an applied magnetic field.

Magnificat in the New Testament, the song of praise sung by Mary, the mother of Jesus, on her visit to her cousin Elizabeth shortly after the Annunciation. It is used in the liturgy of some Christian churches in the form of a canticle based on text from St Luke's gospel 1:46–55 ('My soul doth magnify the Lord ...'). It is sung at Roman Catholic vespers and Anglican evensong, either in plainsong or to a composer's setting, as in works by Monteverdi, Johann Sebastian Bach, Palestrina, and Vaughan Williams.

magnification measure of the enlargement or reduction of an object in an imaging optical system. **Linear magnification** is the ratio of the size (height) of the image to that of the object. **Angular magnification** is the ratio of the angle subtended at the observer's eye by the image to the angle subtended by the object when viewed directly.

magnitude in astronomy, measure of the brightness of a star or other celestial object. The larger the number denoting the magnitude, the fainter the object. Zero or first magnitude indicates some of the brightest stars. Still brighter are those of negative magnitude, such as Sirius, whose magnitude is -1.46. **Apparent magnitude** is the brightness of an object as seen from Earth; **absolute magnitude** is the brightness at a standard distance of 10 parsecs (32.616 light years).

Each magnitude step is equal to a brightness difference of 2.512 times. Thus a star of magnitude 1 is $(2.512)^5$ or 100 times brighter than a sixth-magnitude star just visible to the naked eye. The apparent magnitude of the Sun is -26.8, its absolute magnitude $+4.8$.

magnolia any of a group of trees or shrubs belonging to the magnolia family, native to North America and East Asia, and cultivated as ornamentals. Magnolias vary in height from 60 cm/2 ft to 30 m/150 ft. The large, fragrant single flowers are white, pink, or purple. The southern magnolia (*M. grandiflora*) of the USA grows up to 24 m/80 ft tall and has white flowers 23 cm/9 in across. (Genus *Magnolia*, family Magnoliaceae.)

magpie any of various birds belonging to the crow family. They feed on insects, snails, young birds, and carrion, and are found in Europe, Asia, North Africa, and western North America. (Genus *Pica*, family Corvidae, order Passeriformes.)

The **common magpie** (*P. pica*) is about 45 cm/18 in long, and has black and white plumage, the long tail having a metallic gloss. It prefers relatively open areas for feeding with trees for roosting and as lookout posts.

Magritte, René François Ghislain (1898–1967) Belgian painter, one of the major figures in Surrealism. His work focuses on visual paradoxes and everyday objects taken out of context. Recurring motifs include bowler hats, apples, and windows, for example *Golconda* (1953; private collection), in which men in bowler hats are falling from the sky to a street below.

Influenced by de ▷Chirico, Magritte joined the other Surrealists in Paris 1927, returning to Brussels 1930. His most influential works are those that question the relationship between image and reality, as in *The Treason of Images* 1928–29 (Los Angeles County Museum of Art), in which a picture of a smoker's pipe appears with the words 'Ceci n'est pas une pipe' (This is not a pipe).

Related Web site: Magritte Art Gallery http://www.magritte.com/

Maguire Seven seven Irish victims of a miscarriage of justice. In 1976 Annie Maguire, five members of her family, and a family friend were imprisoned in London for possessing explosives. All seven of the convictions were overturned in June 1991.

Magyar (or **Hungarian**) member of the largest ethnic group in Hungary, comprising 92% of the population. Most are Roman Catholic. The ▷Hungarian language belongs to the Uralic group.

Mahādeva (Sanskrit 'great god') title given to the Hindu god ▷Siva.

Mahādevī (Sanskrit 'great goddess') title given to Sakti, the consort of the Hindu god Siva. She is worshipped in many forms, including her more active manifestations as Kali or Durga and her peaceful form as Parvati.

Maharashtra state in west central India; area 307,700 sq km/ 118,800 sq mi; population (2001 est) 97,663,000. The capital is ▷Mumbai (formerly Bombay), and other towns and cities include Pune, Nagpur, Ulhasnagar, Sholapur, Nasik, Thana, Kolhapur, Aurangabad, Sangli, and Amravati. The state is divided by the heavily forested Western ▷Ghats into the Konkan coastal plain and the Deccan plateau. The plain is subject to the southwest monsoon from June to September. Inland is in a rain shadow receiving only half the coastal rainfall. The Godavari and Krishna rivers rise in the Western Ghats and flow eastwards across the Deccan. The Marathi language is spoken by 50% of the population. 80% of the population are Hindu, with Parsee, Jain, and Sikh minorities. The state was formed in 1960 from the southern part of the former Bombay state.

maharishi (Sanskrit *mahā* 'great', *rishi* 'sage') Hindu guru (teacher), or spiritual leader. The Maharishi Mahesh Yogi influenced the Beatles and other Westerners in the 1960s.

Mahathir bin Muhammad (1925–) Malaysian politician, prime minister from 1981. Leader of the New United Malays' National Organization (UMNO Baru), his 'look east' economic policy, which emulated Japanese industrialization, met with considerable success, but faced its first serious challenge in 1997 when the Malaysian currency came under attack from international speculators. This forced austerity measures in 1998, including the repatriation of many foreign workers.

Mahathir bin Muhammad was elected to the house of representatives in 1964 and gained the support of the radical youth wing of the then dominant United Malays' National Organization (UMNO) as an advocate of economic help to bumiputras (ethnic

MAGNOLIA In the magnolia's large flowers, the sepals are often indistinguishable from the petals and leaves. The earliest flowering plants must have looked like these about 160 million years ago.

Malays) and as a proponent of a more Islamic social policy. Mahathir held a number of ministerial posts from 1974 before being appointed prime minister and UMNO leader in 1981. He was re-elected 1986, but alienated sections of UMNO by his authoritarian leadership and from 1988 led a reconstituted UMNO Baru (New UMNO). In 1994 he temporarily suspended all forthcoming trade deals with the UK after allegations in the British press that aid for Malaysia's Pergau dam had been given in exchange for an arms contract in 1988. In the 1995 elections, his UMNO-Baru-led coalition achieved a landslide victory. At the end of November 1999, his ruling coalition party kept power in the general elections, even though the newly united opposition doubled its number of seats and won control of two state assemblies.

mahatma (Sanskrit 'great soul') title conferred on Mohandas ▷Gandhi by his followers as the first great national Indian leader.

Mahāyāna (Sanskrit 'greater vehicle') one of the two major forms of ▷Buddhism, found in China, Korea, Japan, and Tibet. Veneration of bodhisattvas (those who achieve enlightenment but remain on the human plane in order to help other living beings) is a fundamental belief in Mahāyāna, as is the idea that everyone has within them the seeds of Buddhahood.

Mahdi (Arabic 'he who is guided aright') in Islam, the title of a coming messiah who will establish a reign of justice on Earth. The title has been assumed by many Muslim leaders, notably the Sudanese sheikh Muhammad Ahmed (1848–1885), who headed a revolt in 1881 against Egypt and in 1885 captured Khartoum.

Mahfouz, Naguib (1911–) Egyptian novelist and playwright. His novels, which deal with the urban working class, include the semi-autobiographical *Khan al-Kasrain/The Cairo Trilogy* (1956–57). His *Children of Gebelawi* (1959) was banned in Egypt because of its treatment of religious themes. He was awarded the Nobel Prize for Literature in 1988.

He was seriously wounded in a knife attack by Islamic militants outside his home in Cairo in October 1994.

> **Related Web site: Mahfouz, Naguib** http://www.sis.gov.eg/egyptinf/culture/html/nmahfouz.htm

Mahler, Gustav (1860–1911) Austrian composer and conductor. His epic symphonies express a world-weary Romanticism in visionary tableaux incorporating folk music and pastoral imagery. He composed nine large-scale symphonies, many with voices, including *Symphony No 2, the 'Resurrection'* (1884–86). He revised it 1893–96, but left a tenth unfinished. He also composed orchestral lieder (songs) including *Das Lied von der Erde/The Song of the Earth* (1909) and *Kindertotenlieder/Dead Children's Songs* (1901–04).

The second movement of his *Resurrection* symphony, based on a *Ländler* (folk dance in three time), is reinterpreted in stream-of-consciousness mode by Luciano Berio in *Sinfonia* (1968), into which Berio inserts a history of musical references from J S Bach to Stockhausen. The *Adagietto* slow movement from *Symphony No 5* provided a perfect foil for Luchino Visconti's film *Death in Venice* (1971).

> **Related Web site: Gustav Mahler** http://www.netaxs.com/~jgreshes/mahler/

Mahmud two sultans of the Ottoman Empire:

Mahmud I (1696–1754) Ottoman sultan from 1730. After restoring order to the empire in Istanbul in 1730, he suppressed the ▷janissary rebellion in 1731 and waged war against Persia 1731–46. He led successful wars against Austria and Russia, concluded by the Treaty of Belgrade in 1739. He was a patron of the arts and also carried out reform of the army.

Mahmud II (1785–1839) Ottoman sultan from 1808 who attempted to Westernize the declining empire, carrying out a series of far-reaching reforms in the civil service and army. The pressure for Greek independence after 1821 led to conflict with Britain, France, and Russia, and he was forced to recognize Greek independence in 1830.

In 1826 Mahmud destroyed the elite ▷janissary army corps. Wars against Russia 1807–12 resulted in losses of territory. The Ottoman fleet was destroyed at the Battle of Navarino in 1827, and the Ottoman forces suffered defeat in the Russo-Turkish war 1828–29. There was further disorder with the revolt in Egypt of ▷Mehmet Ali 1831–32, which in turn led to temporary Ottoman-Russian peace. Attempts to control the rebellious provinces failed in 1839, resulting in effect in the granting of Egyptian autonomy.

mahogany timber from any of several trees found in the Americas and Africa. Mahogany is a tropical hardwood obtained chiefly by rainforest logging. It has a warm red colour and can be highly polished. True mahogany comes mainly from *S. mahogoni* and *S. macrophylla*, but other types come from the Spanish and Australian cedars, the Indian redwood, and other trees of the mahogany family, native to Africa and the East Indies. (True mahogany genus *Swietenia*, family Meliaceae.)

Mahón (or **Port Mahon**) capital and port of the Spanish island of Menorca; population (1990) 24,400. Probably founded by the Carthaginians, it was under British occupation 1708–56 and 1762–82.

Mahratta rivals of the Mogul emperors in the 17th and 18th centuries; see ▷Maratha.

Maia in Greek mythology, eldest and most beautiful of the Pleiades, daughters of ▷Atlas and Pleione, and mother of ▷Hermes by Zeus. Identified by the Romans with an ancient Italian goddess of spring, also Maia (or **Maiesta**), she was celebrated in May, the month reputedly named after her.

maidenhair any of a group of ferns, especially *A. capillus-veneris*, with delicately hanging hairlike fronds ending in small kidney-shaped spore-bearing lobes. It is widely distributed in the Americas, and is sometimes found in the British Isles. (Genus *Adiantum*, family Polypodiaceae.)

maidenhair tree another name for the ▷ginkgo, a surviving member of an ancient group of plants.

Maidstone town and administrative headquarters of ▷Kent, southeast England, on the River Medway; population (1991) 90,900. Industries include the manufacture of agricultural machinery, and paper and card for packaging. There are a number of medieval buildings, among them the parish church of All Saints', the late 14th-century Archbishop's Palace (a former residence of the archbishops of Canterbury), and the College of Priests (1395–98) built of Kentish ragstone from quarries to the west of the town. The Elizabethan Chillington Manor is an art gallery and museum.

Maikop (or **Maykop**) capital city of the ▷Adygeya (Adygei) Republic in the southwestern Russian Federation, 150 km/93 mi southwest of Stavropol on the River Bielaia; population (1996 est) 166,000. The main industries are the production of foodstuffs and tobacco, leather, and furniture. Maikop lies at the centre of an oil-producing region. Nearby oilfields, discovered in 1900, are linked by pipeline with Tuapse on the Black Sea. There is a famous Bronze-Age burial mound nearby.

Mailer, Norman Kingsley (1923–) US writer and journalist. One of the most prominent figures of post-war American literature, he gained wide attention with his first, best-selling book *The Naked and the Dead* (1948), a naturalistic war novel. His later works, which use sexual and scatological material, show his personal engagement with history, politics, and psychology. Always a pugnacious and controversial writer, his polemics on the theory and practice of violence-as-sex brought him into direct conflict with feminist Kate Millet in a series of celebrated debates during the 1970s.

His essay 'White Negro' in *Advertisements for Myself* (1959), defining the 'hipster' hero, was a seminal statement of the artistic need to rebel against cultural conformity. His other books include his dark thriller of sex and power *An American Dream* (1965), the fictionalized antiwar journalism of *The Armies of the Night* (1968, Pulitzer prize), *The Executioner's Song* (1979, Pulitzer prize), about convicted murderer Gary Gilmore, and two massive novels, *Ancient Evenings* (1983), dealing with Egyptian life and mythologies, and *Harlot's Ghost* (1991), about the CIA. A combative public figure, Mailer cofounded the magazine *Village Voice* in the 1950s, edited *Dissent*, and in 1969 ran for mayor of New York City. *Pablo and Fernande* appeared 1994.

> **Related Web site: Norman Mailer: His Life and Works** http://www.iol.ie/~kic/

Maimonides, Moses (Ben Maimon) (1135–1204) Spanish-born Jewish rabbi and philosopher, one of the greatest Hebrew scholars. He attempted to reconcile faith and reason. His codification of Jewish law is known as the *Mishneh Torah/Torah Reviewed* (1180); he also formulated the **Thirteen Principles**, which summarize the basic beliefs of Judaism.

Maimonides was born in Córdoba, but left Spain 1160 to escape the persecution of the Jews and settled in Fez, and later in Cairo, where he was personal physician to Sultan Saladin. His philosophical classic *More nevukhim/The Guide to the Perplexed* 1176–91 helped to introduce Aristotelian thought into medieval philosophy.

mainboard new (and more politically correct) name for a ▷motherboard.

Maine northeasternmost state of the USA and the largest of the New England states. It is nicknamed the Pine Tree State. Maine was admitted to the Union in 1820 as the 23rd US state. It is bordered to the northwest by Québec, Canada, to the north and east by New Brunswick, Canada, to the east and south by the Atlantic Ocean, and to the west by New Hampshire; it is the sole US state to be contiguous with only one other US state. Maine's West Quoddy Head is the easternmost US point; the state (and region) is popularly known as 'Down East'.

> **population** (1995) 1,241,400 **area** 86,200 sq km/33,300 sq mi **capital** Augusta **towns and cities** Portland, Lewiston, Bangor **industries and products** blueberries, dairy and market garden produce, paper, pulp, timber, footwear, leather, textiles, fish, lobster; tourism, shipbuilding

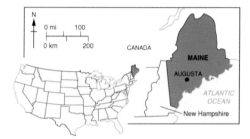

mainframe large computer used for commercial data processing and other large-scale operations. Because of the general increase in computing power, the differences between the mainframe, ▷supercomputer, ▷minicomputer, and ▷microcomputer (personal computer) are becoming less marked.

Mainframe manufacturers include IBM, Amdahl, Fujitsu, and Hitachi. Typical mainframes have from 128 MB to 4 GB of memory and hundreds of gigabytes of disk storage.

maintenance in law, payments to support children or a spouse, under the terms of an agreement, or by a court order. In Britain, financial provision orders are made on divorce, but a court action can also be brought for maintenance without divorce proceedings. Applications for maintenance of illegitimate children are now treated in the same way as for legitimate children. Under the Child Support Act 1991 the Department of Social Security can assess suitable levels of maintenance and enforce payment.

Mainz (French **Mayence**) river port and capital of ▷Rhineland-Palatinate, Germany, on the left bank of the Rhine, 37 km/23 mi

NORMAN MAILER The US writer Norman Mailer, US poet Allen Ginsberg, and US anthropologist Ashley Montagu appearing on a US television show in about 1970. *Archive Photos*

southwest of Frankfurt-am-Main; population (1995) 184,500. It is a major centre of the wine trade. Industries include computers (IBM), metal goods, precision instruments, chemicals, machinery, telecommunications, television broadcasting, and printed fabrics. In Roman times it was a fortified camp and became the capital of Germania Superior. Printing was possibly invented here in about 1448 by Johann ▷Gutenberg.

maize (North American **corn**) tall annual ▷cereal plant (Genus *Zea mays*) that produces spikes of yellow grains that are widely used as an animal feed. Grown extensively in all subtropical and warm temperate regions, its range has been extended to colder zones by hardy varieties developed in the 1960s. It was domesticated by 6500 BC in Mesoamerica, where it grew wild.

Majapahit empire last Hindu empire of eastern ▷Java from *c.* 1293 to *c.* 1520. Based in the fertile Brantas River valley, it encompassed much of Malaya, Borneo, Sumatra, and Bali, and reached its peak under the ruler Hayam Wuruk (reigned 1350–1389).

majolica (or **maiolica**) tin-glazed ▷earthenware and the richly decorated enamel pottery produced in Italy in the 15th to 18th centuries. The name derives from the Italian form of Mallorca, the island from where Moorish lustreware made in Spain was shipped to Italy. During the 19th century the word was used to describe moulded earthenware with relief patterns decorated in coloured glazes.

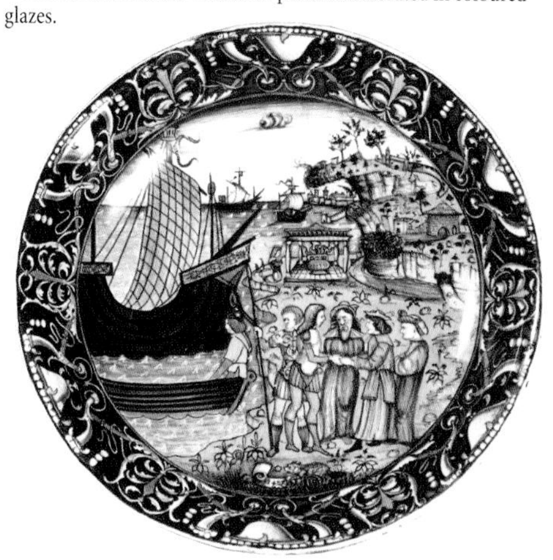

MAJOLICA A majolica dish made in Faenza, Italy, in 1497, decorated with the mythical scene of the arrival of Aeneas at Delos, Greece. *The Art Archive/Musmadee Ceramique Sevres*

major one of the two predominant ▷scales (the other being minor) of the tonal system, characterized by the presence of a major third between the 1st and 3rd degrees. A major key is one based on the major scale.

Major, John (1943–) British Conservative politician, prime minister 1990–97. He was foreign secretary in 1989 and chancellor of the Exchequer 1989–90.

John Major was born in Merton, southwest London. Formerly a banker, he became MP for Huntingdonshire in 1979 and become deputy to chancellor of the Exchequer Nigel Lawson in 1987. Within the space of six months in 1989, he was appointed foreign secretary and, after Lawson's resignation, chancellor. As chancellor he led the UK into the European ▷Exchange Rate Mechanism (ERM) in October 1990. The following month he became prime minister on winning the Conservative Party leadership election in a contest with Michael Heseltine and Douglas Hurd, after the resignation of Margaret Thatcher. Despite continuing public dissatisfaction with the poll tax, the decline of the National Health Service, and the recession, Major was returned to power in the April 1992 general election. He subsequently faced mounting pressure over a range of issues, including the sudden withdrawal of the pound from the ERM, a drastic pit-closure programme, and past sales of arms to Iraq. In addition, Major had to deal with 'Euro-sceptics' within his own party who fiercely opposed any moves that they saw as ceding national sovereignty to Brussels. His success in negotiating a Northern Ireland ceasefire in 1994 did much to improve his standing, but delays in the progress of peace talks resulted in criticism of his cautious approach. On the domestic front, local and European election defeats and continuing divisions within the Conservative Party led to his dramatic and unexpected resignation of the party leadership in June 1995 in a desperate bid for party unity. He was narrowly re-elected to the post the following month. Criticized for weak leadership of his divided party, he resigned as leader of the Conservative Party after a crushing defeat in the 1997 general election. In March 2000 he announced his retirement from the House of Commons.

Majorca alternative spelling of ▷Mallorca.

Makarios III (1913–1977) Born Mikhail Christodoulou Mouskos. Cypriot politician and Greek Orthodox archbishop 1950–77. A leader of the Greek-Cypriot resistance organization EOKA, he was exiled by the British to the Seychelles 1956–57 for supporting armed action to achieve union with Greece (*enosis*). He was president of the republic of Cyprus 1960–77 (briefly deposed by a Greek military coup July–Dec 1974).

Makhachkala (formerly **Petrovsk** (1844–1922)) city in northern Caucasia, capital, economic and cultural centre of the Dagestan Republic, in the southwestern Russian Federation; population (1996 est) 347,000. Makhachkala is a major port on the Caspian Sea; oil is piped here for export from Groznyy and Izberbash. The city has aerospace, shipbuilding, oil-refining, textile, and food industries. It was founded as a Russian fort in 1844, and became a town in 1857. Makhachkala gained its present name (after the local Bolshevik leader Makhach) and was made the capital of Dagestan in 1922.

Makua a people living to the north of the Zambezi River in Mozambique. With the Lomwe people, they make up the country's largest ethnic group. The Makua are mainly farmers, living in villages ruled by chiefs. The Makua language belongs to the Niger-Congo family, and has about 5 million speakers.

Malabo port and capital of ▷Equatorial Guinea, on the north coast of the volcanic island of Bioko; population (1992) 35,000. It trades in cocoa, coffee, copra, and other agricultural products. It was founded in the 1820s by the British as **Port Clarence** (also **Clarencetown**). Under Spanish rule it was known as **Santa Isabel** (until 1973). It became the capital in 1968.

Malacca (or **Melaka**) state of west Peninsular Malaysia; capital Malacca; area 1,700 sq km/656 sq mi; population (1993) 583,400 (about 70% Chinese). Products include rubber, tin, and wire. The town originated in the 13th century as a fishing village frequented by pirates, and later developed into a trading port. Portuguese from 1511, then Dutch from 1641, it was ceded to Britain in 1824, becoming part of the Straits Settlements.

Malacca, Strait of channel between Sumatra and the Malay Peninsula; length 965 km/600 mi; it narrows to less than 38 km/24 mi wide. It carries all shipping between the Indian Ocean and the South China Sea.

malachite common ▷copper ore, basic copper carbonate, $Cu_2CO_3(OH)_2$. It is a source of green pigment and is used as an antifungal agent in fish farming, as well as being polished for use in jewellery, ornaments, and art objects.

Málaga industrial seaport and capital of Málaga province in Andalusia, southern Spain, situated at the mouth of the River Guadalmedina on the Mediterranean coast; population (1991) 512,100. Industries include sugar refining, distilling, brewing, and olive-oil pressing; it is also a holiday resort. Crude oil is unloaded from tankers offshore into a pipeline that transports it to Puertollano in the province of Ciudad Real.

Malamud, Bernard (1914–1986) US novelist and short-story writer. He first attracted attention with *The Natural* (1952), a mythic story about a baseball hero. It established Malamud's central concern of moral redemption and transcendence, which was more typically dealt with in books set in Jewish immigrant communities. These drew on the magical elements and mores of the European Yiddish tradition and include such novels as, *The Assistant* (1957), *The Fixer* (1966), *Dubin's Lives* (1979), and *God's Grace* (1982).

> **Bernard Malamud**
> *The past exudes legend: one can't make pure clay of time's mud.*
> Dubin's Lives

malapropism amusing slip of the tongue, arising from the confusion of similar-sounding words; for example, 'the pineapple [pinnacle] of politeness'. The term derives from the French *mal à propos* (inappropriate); historically, it is associated with Mrs Malaprop, a character in Richard Sheridan's play *The Rivals* (1775).

malaria infectious parasitic disease of the tropics transmitted by mosquitoes, marked by periodic fever and an enlarged spleen. When a female mosquito of the *Anopheles* genus bites a human who has malaria, it takes in with the human blood one of four malaria protozoa of the genus *Plasmodium*. This matures within the insect and is then transferred when the mosquito bites a new victim. Malaria affects around 300–500 million people each year, in 103 countries, and in 1995 around 2.1 million people died of the disease. In sub-Saharan Africa alone between 1.5 and 2 million children die from malaria and its consequences each year. In November 1998, an agreement was reached to establish a multi-agency programme for research and control of the disease. The agencies involved include the World Health Organization (WHO), the World Bank, the United Nations Children's Fund, and the United Nations Development Programme. The Roll Back Malaria campaign aims to halve deaths from malaria by 2010.

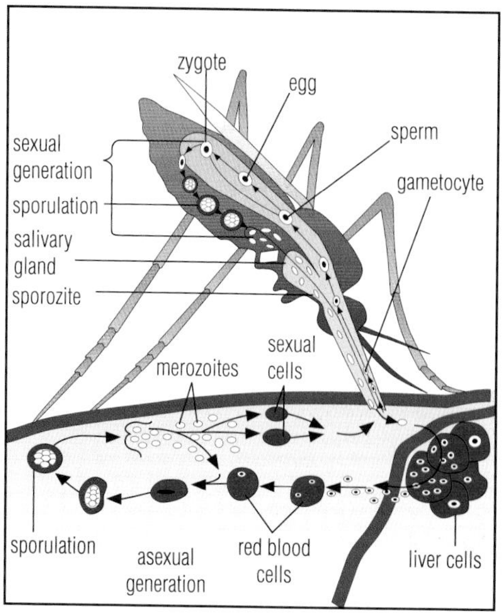

MALARIA The life cycle of the malaria parasite is split between mosquito and human hosts. The parasites are injected into the human bloodstream by an infected *Anopheles* mosquito and carried to the liver. Here they attack red blood cells, and multiply asexually. The infected blood cells burst, producing spores, or merozoites, which reinfect the bloodstream. After several generations, the parasite develops into a sexual form. If the human host is bitten at this stage, the sexual form of the parasite is sucked into the mosquito's stomach. Here fertilization takes place, the zygotes formed reproduce asexually and migrate to the salivary glands ready to be injected into another human host, completing the cycle.

Infection Inside the human body the parasite settles first in the liver, then multiplies to attack the red blood cells. Within the red blood cells the parasites multiply, eventually causing the cells to rupture and other cells to become infected. The cell rupture tends to be synchronized, occurring every 2–3 days, when the symptoms of malaria become evident.

On the increase Global warming is causing a worldwide increase in malaria, for example in 1998 in Nairobi, where previously malaria cases have been limited to individuals who have travelled to lowland areas of Kenya, doctors were regularly reporting cases in people who have not left the city. In Irian Jaya, New Guinea, thousands of people who have never been exposed to malaria are now affected. According to a WHO report released in September 1999, cases of malaria in Europe rose from 2,882 in 1981 to 12,328 in 1997. African leaders met in Nigeria in April 2000 to discuss ways of fighting the disease, which was spreading across the continent, and according to a WHO report, which had cost Africa £160 billion/$100 billion in productivity over the past 35 years.

Treatment ▷Quinine, the first drug used against malaria, has now been replaced by synthetics, such as chloroquine, used to prevent or treat the disease. However, chloroquine-resistant strains of the main malaria parasite, *Plasmodium fulciparum*, are spreading rapidly in many parts of the world.

The drug mefloquine (Lariam) is widely prescribed for use in areas where chloroquine-resistant malaria prevails. It is surrounded by controversy, however, as it has been linked to unpleasant side effects, including psychiatric disturbances such as anxiety and hallucinations, epileptic seizures, and memory loss.

Another drug, artemether, derived from the shrub wormwood, was found in 1996 trials to be as effective as quinine in the treatment of cerebral malaria.

The insecticide ▷DDT remains one of the most effective means of controlling malaria, and consequently is still used despite its persistence in the environment and subsequent danger to wildlife.

Vaccine An experimental malaria vaccine SPf66, developed by Colombian scientist Manuel Patarroyo, was trialled in 1994 in rural

Tanzania, where villagers are bitten an average of 300 times a year by infected mosquitoes. It reduced the incidence of malaria by one third. However, further trials of SPf66 in the Gambia concluded that the vaccine provided only 8% protection for young children. A further trial in Thailand in 1996 failed to provide any evidence of its effectiveness. A new vaccine was successfully trialled in rabbits in 1999, with human trials anticipated in 2000. The vaccine attacks *Plasmodium falciparum*, the parasite that causes the symptoms of the disease, at each stage of the four main stages of its life cycle.

The last recorded outbreak of malaria in the UK occurred in Kent in the early 1950s. However, 2,500 cases are reported each year in people who have contracted the disease elsewhere.

   Related Web site: Malaria http://www.malaria.org/whatismalaria.html

Malawi see country box.

Malawi, Lake (or Lake Nyasa) lake, bordered by Malawi, Tanzania, and Mozambique, formed in a section of the Great ▷Rift Valley. It is about 500 m/1,650 ft above sea level and 560 km/350 mi long, with an area of 28,749 sq km/11,100 sq mi and a depth of 700 m/2,296 ft, making it the ninth biggest lake in the world. It is intermittently drained to the south by the River Shire into the Zambezi.

Malay member of any of a large group of peoples comprising the majority population of the Malay Peninsula and archipelago, and also found in southern Thailand and coastal Sumatra and Borneo. Their language belongs to the western branch of the Austronesian family.

Malayalam southern Indian language, the official language of the state of Kerala. Malayalam is closely related to Tamil, also a member of the Dravidian language family; it is spoken by about 20 million people. Written records in Malayalam date from the 9th century AD.

Malay language member of the Western or Indonesian branch of the Malayo-Polynesian language family, used in the Malay Peninsula and many of the islands of Malaysia and Indonesia. The Malay language can be written in either Arabic or Roman scripts. The dialect of the southern Malay peninsula is the basis of both Bahasa Malaysia and Bahasa Indonesia, the official languages of Malaysia and Indonesia. Bazaar Malay is a widespread pidgin variety used for trading and shopping.

Malayo-Polynesian family of languages spoken in Malaysia, better known as ▷Austronesian.

Malay Peninsula southern projection of the continent of Asia, lying between the Strait of Malacca, which divides it from Sumatra, and the China Sea. The northern portion is partly in Myanmar (formerly Burma), partly in Thailand; the south forms part of Malaysia. The island of Singapore lies off its southern extremity.

Malaysia see country box.

Malcolm four Celtic kings of Scotland, including:

Malcolm III (*c.* 1031–1093) Called 'Canmore'. King of Scotland from 1058, the son of Duncan I. He fled to England in 1040 when the throne was usurped by ▷Macbeth, but recovered southern Scotland and killed Macbeth in battle in 1057. In 1070 he married Margaret (*c.* 1045–1093), sister of Edgar Atheling of England; their

Malawi

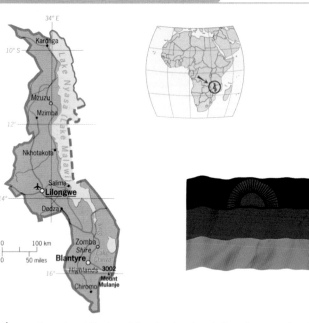

Malawi country in southeast Africa, bounded north and northeast by Tanzania; east, south, and west by Mozambique; and west by Zambia.

NATIONAL NAME *Republic of Malawi*
AREA 118,484 sq km/45,735 sq mi
CAPITAL Lilongwe
MAJOR TOWNS/CITIES Blantyre, Mzuzu, Zomba
PHYSICAL FEATURES landlocked narrow plateau with rolling plains; mountainous west of Lake Nyasa

Government

HEAD OF STATE AND GOVERNMENT Bakili Muluzi from 1994
POLITICAL SYSTEM emergent democracy
POLITICAL EXECUTIVE limited presidency
ADMINISTRATIVE DIVISIONS three regions, subdivided into 24 districts
ARMED FORCES 5,300 (2002 est)
DEATH PENALTY retained and used for ordinary crimes

Economy and resources

CURRENCY Malawi kwacha
GPD (US$) 1.9 billion (2002 est)
REAL GDP GROWTH (% change on previous year) –1.5 (2001)
GNI (US$) 1.7 billion (2002 est)
GNI PER CAPITA (PPP) (US$) 570 (2002 est)
CONSUMER PRICE INFLATION 5% (2003 est)
UNEMPLOYMENT 1.1% (1998)
FOREIGN DEBT (US$) 2.5 billion (2001 est)

MAJOR TRADING PARTNERS South Africa, USA, Germany, India, Zimbabwe, Zambia, Japan
RESOURCES marble, coal, gemstones, bauxite and graphite deposits, reserves of phosphates, uranium, glass sands, asbestos, vermiculite
INDUSTRIES food products, chemical products, textiles, beverages, cement
EXPORTS tobacco, tea, sugar, cotton, coffee, groundnuts. Principal market: South Africa 19.5% (2000)
IMPORTS petroleum products, fertilizers, coal, machinery and transport equipment, miscellaneous manufactured articles. Principal source: South Africa 41.9% (2000)
ARABLE LAND 22.3% (2000 est)
AGRICULTURAL PRODUCTS maize, cassava, groundnuts, pulses, tobacco, tea, sugar cane, coffee

Population and society

POPULATION 12,105,000 (2003 est)
POPULATION GROWTH RATE 1.8% (2000–15)
POPULATION DENSITY (per sq km) 102 (2003 est)
URBAN POPULATION (% of total) 16 (2003 est)
AGE DISTRIBUTION (% of total population) 0–14 46%, 15–59 44%, 60+ 5% (2002 est)

ETHNIC GROUPS almost all indigenous Africans, divided into numerous ethnic groups, such as the Chewa, Nyanja, Tumbuka, Yao, Lomwe, Sena, Tonga, and Ngoni. There are also Asian and European minorities
LANGUAGE English, Chichewa (both official), other Bantu languages
RELIGION Protestant 50%, Roman Catholic 20%, Muslim 2%, animist
EDUCATION (compulsory years) 8
LITERACY RATE 76% (men); 50% (women) (2003 est)
LABOUR FORCE 84.1% agriculture, 5.9% industry, 10% services (1997 est)
LIFE EXPECTANCY 37 (men); 38 (women) (2000–05)
CHILD MORTALITY RATE (under 5, per 1,000 live births) 183 (2001)
PHYSICIANS (per 1,000 people) 0.06 (1998 est)
HOSPITAL BEDS (per 1,000 people) 1.3 (1998 est)
TV SETS (per 1,000 people) 4 (2001 est)
RADIOS (per 1,000 people) 250 (1998)
INTERNET USERS (per 10,000 people) 25.9 (2002 est)

Chronology

1st–4th centuries AD: Immigration by Bantu-speaking peoples.
1480: Foundation of Maravi (Malawi) Confederacy, which covered much of central and southern Malawi and lasted into the 17th century.
1530: First visited by the Portuguese.
1600: Ngonde kingdom founded in northern Malawi by immigrants from Tanzania.
18th century: Chikulamayembe state founded by immigrants from east of Lake Nyasa; slave trade flourished and Islam introduced in some areas.
mid-19th century: Swahili-speaking Ngoni peoples, from South Africa, and Yao entered the region, dominating settled agriculturists; Christianity introduced by missionaries, such as David Livingstone.
1891: Became British protectorate of Nyasaland; cash crops, particularly coffee, introduced.
1915: Violent uprising, led by Rev John Chilembwe, against white settlers who had moved into the fertile south, taking land from local population.
1953: Became part of white-dominated Central African Federation, which included South Rhodesia (Zimbabwe) and North Rhodesia (Zambia).
1958: Dr Hastings Kamuzu Banda returned to the country after working abroad and became head of the conservative-nationalist Nyasaland/Malawi Congress Party (MCP), which spearheaded the campaign for independence.
1963: Central African Federation dissolved.

1964: Independence achieved within Commonwealth as Malawi, with Banda as prime minister.
1966: Became one-party republic, with Banda as president.
1967: Banda became pariah of Black Africa by recognizing racist, white-only republic of South Africa.
1971: Banda was made president for life.
1970s: There were reports of human-rights violations and the murder of Banda's opponents.
1980s: The economy began to deteriorate after nearly two decades of expansion.
1986–89: There was an influx of nearly a million refugees from Mozambique.
1992: There were calls for a multiparty political system. Countrywide industrial riots caused many fatalities. Western aid was suspended over human-rights violations.
1993: A referendum overwhelmingly supported the ending of one-party rule.
1994: A new multiparty constitution was adopted. Bakili Muluzi, of the United Democratic Front (UDF), was elected president in the first free elections for 30 years.
1995: Banda and the former minister of state John Tembo were charged with conspiring to murder four political opponents in 1983, but were cleared.
1999: Violent protests followed the announcement that Muluzi had been re-elected as president.
2000: Muluzi sacked his entire cabinet after high-ranking officials were accused of corruption. However, his new government included many of the same people.

MALAWI Produced in commemoration of the 18th Commonwealth Parliamentary Conference, held in Malawi in 1972, this stamp bears the coat of arms and motto of the country. *Stanley Gibbons*

Malaysia

Malaysia country in southeast Asia, comprising the Malay Peninsula, bounded north by Thailand, and surrounded east and south by the South China Sea and west by the Strait of Malacca; and the states of Sabah and Sarawak in the northern part of the island of Borneo (southern Borneo is part of Indonesia).

NATIONAL NAME *Persekutuan Tanah Malaysia/Federation of Malaysia*
AREA 329,759 sq km/127,319 sq mi
CAPITAL Kuala Lumpur
MAJOR TOWNS/CITIES Johor Bahru, Ipoh, George Town (on Penang island), Kuala Terengganu, Kota Bahru, Petaling Jaya, Kelang, Kuching (on Sarawak), Kota Kinabalu (on Sabah)
MAJOR PORTS Kelang
PHYSICAL FEATURES comprises peninsular Malaysia (the nine Malay states – Johore, Kedah, Kelantan, Negeri Sembilan, Pahang, Perak, Perlis, Selangor, Terengganu – plus Melaka and Penang); states of Sabah and Sarawak on the island of Borneo; and the federal territory of Kuala Lumpur; 75% tropical rainforest; central mountain range; Mount Kinabalu, the highest peak in southeast Asia, is in Sabah; swamps in east; Niah caves (Sarawak)

Government

HEAD OF STATE Syed Sirajuddin bin al-Marhum Syed Putra Jamalullail from 2001
HEAD OF GOVERNMENT Datuk Badawi from 2003
POLITICAL SYSTEM liberal democracy
POLITICAL EXECUTIVE parliamentary
ADMINISTRATIVE DIVISIONS 13 states
ARMED FORCES 100,000; plus paramilitary forces of 20,100 (2002 est)
CONSCRIPTION military service is voluntary
DEATH PENALTY retained and used for ordinary crimes
DEFENCE SPEND (% GDP) 3.6 (2002 est)
EDUCATION SPEND (% GDP) 6.2 (2001 est)
HEALTH SPEND (% GDP) 2.5 (2002 est)

Economy and resources

CURRENCY ringgit
GPD (US$) 95.2 billion (2002 est)
REAL GDP GROWTH (% change on previous year) 0.5 (2001)
GNI (US$) 86.0 billion (2002 est)
GNI PER CAPITA (PPP) (US$) 8,280 (2002 est)

CONSUMER PRICE INFLATION 2.5% (2003 est)
UNEMPLOYMENT 3.6% (2001)
FOREIGN DEBT (US$) 36.3 billion (2001 est)
MAJOR TRADING PARTNERS Japan, USA, Singapore, China, South Korea, the Netherlands, Thailand, Germany
RESOURCES tin, bauxite, copper, iron ore, petroleum, natural gas, forests
INDUSTRIES electrical and electronic appliances (particularly radio and TV receivers), food processing, rubber products, industrial chemicals, wood products, petroleum refinery, motor vehicles, tourism
EXPORTS electronics and electrical machinery, palm oil, rubber, crude petroleum, machinery and transport equipment, timber, tin, textiles, chemicals. Principal market: USA 20.5% (2001)
IMPORTS machinery and transport equipment, chemicals, foodstuffs, crude petroleum, consumer goods. Principal source: Japan 19.7% (2001)

MALAYSIA The Sultan Samad Building in Kuala Lumpur, the capital of Malaysia. It was built by the British in the 1890s as a government secretariat; it reflects the area's mixed culture, with Islamic arcades and a very British clock tower. *Malaysian Tourist Board*

ARABLE LAND 5.5% (2000 est)
AGRICULTURAL PRODUCTS rice, cocoa, palm, rubber, pepper, coconuts, tea, pineapples

Population and society

POPULATION 24,425,000 (2003 est)
POPULATION GROWTH RATE 1.5% (2000–15)
POPULATION DENSITY (per sq km) 74 (2003 est)
URBAN POPULATION (% of total) 59 (2003 est)
AGE DISTRIBUTION (% of total population) 0–14 34%, 15–59 59%, 60+ 7% (2002 est)

Chronology

1st century AD: Peoples of Malay peninsula influenced by Indian culture and Buddhism.
8th–13th centuries: Malay peninsula formed part of Buddhist Srivijaya Empire based in Sumatra.
14th century: Siam (Thailand) expanded to include most of Malay peninsula.
1403: Muslim traders founded port of Malacca, which became a great commercial centre, encouraging the spread of Islam.
1511: The Portuguese attacked and captured Malacca.
1641: The Portuguese were ousted from Malacca by the Dutch after a seven-year blockade.
1786: The British East India Company established a trading post on island of Penang.
1795–1815: Britain occupied the Dutch colonies after France conquered the Netherlands.
1819: Stamford Raffles of East India Company obtained Singapore from Sultan of Johore.
1824: Anglo-Dutch Treaty ceded Malacca to Britain in return for territory in Sumatra.
1826: British possessions of Singapore, Penang, and Malacca formed the Straits Settlements, ruled by the governor of Bengal; ports prospered and expanded.
1840: The Sultan of Brunei gave Sarawak to James Brooke, whose family ruled it as an independent state until 1946.
1851: Responsibility for Straits Settlements assumed by the governor general of India.
1858: British government, through India Office, took over administration of Straits Settlements.
1867: Straits Settlements became crown colony of British Empire.
1874: British protectorates established over four Malay states of Perak, Salangor, Pahang, and Negri Sembilan, which federated in 1896.
1888: Britain declared protectorate over northern Borneo (Sabah).
late 19th century: Millions of Chinese and thousands of Indians migrated to Malaya to work in tin mines and on rubber plantations.
1909–14: Britain assumed indirect rule over five northern Malay states after agreement with Siam (Thailand).
1941–45: Japanese occupation.

ETHNIC GROUPS 56% of the population is Malay, four-fifths of whom live in rural areas; 34% is Chinese, four-fifths of whom are in towns; 9% is Indian, mainly Tamil
LANGUAGE Bahasa Malaysia (Malay; official), English, Chinese, Tamil, Iban, many local dialects
RELIGION Muslim (official) about 53%, Buddhist 19%, Hindu, Christian, local beliefs
EDUCATION (compulsory years) 11
LITERACY RATE 92% (men); 85% (women) (2003 est)
LABOUR FORCE 18.4% agriculture, 31.7% industry, 49.9% services (1999)
LIFE EXPECTANCY 71 (men); 76 (women) (2000–05)
CHILD MORTALITY RATE (under 5, per 1,000 live births) 8 (2001)
PHYSICIANS (per 1,000 people) 0.7 (1999 est)
HOSPITAL BEDS (per 1,000 people) 2 (1999 est)
TV SETS (per 1,000 people) 201 (2001 est)
RADIOS (per 1,000 people) 420 (2001 est)
INTERNET USERS (per 10,000 people) 3,196.9 (2002 est)
PERSONAL COMPUTER USERS (per 100 people) 14.7 (2002 est)

See also ▷Borneo; ▷Singapore.

1946: United Malay National Organization (UMNO) founded to oppose British plans for centralized Union of Malaya.
1948: Britain federated nine Malay states with Penang and Malacca to form the single colony of the Federation of Malaya.
1948–60: Malayan emergency: British forces suppressed insurrection by communist guerrillas.
1957: Federation of Malaya became independent with Prince Abdul Rahman (leader of UMNO) as prime minister.
1963: Federation of Malaya combined with Singapore, Sarawak, and Sabah to form Federation of Malaysia.
1963–66: 'The Confrontation' – guerrillas supported by Indonesia opposed federation with intermittent warfare.
1965: Singapore withdrew from the Federation of Malaysia.
1968: Philippines claimed sovereignty over Sabah.
1969: Malay resentment of Chinese economic dominance resulted in race riots in Kuala Lumpur.
1971: *Bumiputra* policies which favoured ethnic Malays in education and employment introduced by Tun Abul Razak of UMNO.
1981: Mahathir bin Muhammad (UMNO) became the prime minister; the government became increasingly dominated by Muslim Malays.
1987: Malay–Chinese relations deteriorated; over 100 opposition activists were arrested.
1991: An economic development policy was launched which aimed at 7% annual growth.
1997: The currency was allowed to float. Parts of Borneo and Sumatra were covered by thick smog for several weeks following forest-clearing fires.
1998: The repatriation of foreign workers commenced. Currency controls were introduced as the GDP contracted sharply.
1999: Mahathir bin Muhammad's ruling coalition party was elected to retain power.
2000: Ex-deputy prime minister Anwar Ibrahim was found guilty of charges of sodomy by the high court and sentenced to nine-years' imprisonment, to be served in addition to the six-year sentence he received in April 1999 for corruption. The International Commission of Jurists condemned the verdict as politically motivated.
2003: Prime Minister Muhammad stepped down after 22 years, and was succeeded by his deputy prime minister Abdullah Badawi.

MALCOLM X The leader of the Organization of Afro-American Unity. *Archive Photos*

daughter Matilda (d. 1118) married Henry I of England. Malcolm was killed at Alnwick while invading Northumberland, England.

Malcolm X (1926–1965) Adopted name of Malcolm Little. US black nationalist leader. Malcolm Little was born in Omaha, Nebraska, but grew up in foster homes in Michigan, Massachusetts, and New York. In 1952 he officially changed his name to Malcolm X, the X representing his lost African ancestral surname. While serving a prison sentence for burglary 1946–53, he joined the ▷Black Muslims sect and converted to Islam. On his release he campaigned for black separatism, condoning violence in self-defence, but in 1964 modified his views to found the Islamic, socialist Organization of Afro-American Unity, preaching racial solidarity. A year later he was assassinated by ▷Nation of Islam opponents while addressing a rally in Harlem, New York City. His *Autobiography of Malcolm X*, written with Alex Haley, was published in 1964.

> **Malcolm X**
> *You can't separate peace from freedom because no one can be at peace unless he has his freedom.*
> Speech, New York City, 7 January 1965

Maldini, Paolo (1968–   ) Italian footballer. A tall, left-sided defender, he made his international debut in 1988 at the age of 18, and by July 2000 had won 111 Italian caps, scoring 7 goals. One of the game's greatest defenders, he was a member of the Italian side which reached the 1994 World Cup final, and he also played in the 1990 and 1998 finals. An AC Milan first team player since the age of 16, he has won the Italian league championship six times and the European Cup three times.

Maldives see country box.

Maldon English market town in Essex, at the mouth of the River Chelmer. It was the scene of a battle commemorated in a 325-line fragment of an Anglo-Saxon poem *The Battle of Maldon*, describing the defeat and death of Ealdorman Byrhtnoth by the Vikings in 991.

Malé capital and chief atoll of the Maldives in the Indian Ocean; population (1995 est) 64,800. It lies 700 km/435 mi southwest of Sri Lanka and has an airport which has helped the development of the tourist industry in recent decades. It trades in copra, breadfruit, fish, and palm products.

Maldives

Maldives group of 1,196 islands in the north Indian Ocean, about 640 km/400 mi southwest of Sri Lanka; only 203 of them are inhabited.

NATIONAL NAME *Divehi Raajjeyge Jumhuriyya*/Republic of the Maldives
AREA 298 sq km/115 sq mi
CAPITAL Malé
PHYSICAL FEATURES comprises 1,196 coral islands, grouped into 12 clusters of atolls, none bigger than 13 sq km/5 sq mi, average elevation 1.8 m/6 ft; 203 are inhabited

Government

HEAD OF STATE AND GOVERNMENT Maumoon Abd Gayoom from 1978
POLITICAL SYSTEM authoritarian nationalist
POLITICAL EXECUTIVE unlimited presidency
ADMINISTRATIVE DIVISIONS 20 districts and the capital (Malé)
ARMED FORCES no standing army; plus paramilitary forces of 5,000 (2000)
DEATH PENALTY retained for ordinary crimes but can be considered abolitionist in practice; date of last known execution 1952

Economy and resources

CURRENCY rufiya
GPD (US$) 618 million (2002 est)
REAL GDP GROWTH (% change on previous year) 7 (1999 est)

GNI (US$) 598 million (2002 est)
GNI PER CAPITA (PPP) (US$) 2,740 (2002 est)
CONSUMER PRICE INFLATION 2.5% (2003 est)
UNEMPLOYMENT 0.9% (1997 est)
FOREIGN DEBT (US$) 238 million (2001 est)
MAJOR TRADING PARTNERS UK, Singapore, USA, India, Sri Lanka, Thailand, Malaysia, Germany, Japan, United Arab Emirates
RESOURCES coral (mining was banned as a measure against the encroachment of the sea)
INDUSTRIES fish canning, clothing, soft-drink bottling, shipping, lacquer work, shell craft, tourism
EXPORTS marine products, (tuna bonito ('Maldive Fish')) clothing. Principal market: USA 44.2% (2000)
IMPORTS consumer manufactured goods, petroleum products, food, intermediate and capital goods. Principal source: Singapore 25.5% (2000)
ARABLE LAND 3.3% (2000 est)
AGRICULTURAL PRODUCTS coconuts, maize, cassava, sweet potatoes, chillies; fishing

Population and society

POPULATION 318,000 (2003 est)
POPULATION GROWTH RATE 3.0% (2000–05)
POPULATION DENSITY (per sq km) 1,068 (2003 est)
URBAN POPULATION (% of total) 29 (2003 est)
AGE DISTRIBUTION (% of total population) 0–14 43%, 15–59 52%, 60+ 5% (2002 est)
ETHNIC GROUPS four main groups: Dravidian in the northern islands, Arab in the middle islands, Sinhalese in the southern islands, and African
LANGUAGE Divehi (a Sinhalese dialect; official), English, Arabic

Chronology

12th century AD: Islam introduced by seafaring Arabs, who displaced the indigenous Dravidian population.
14th century: Ad-Din sultanate established.
1558–73: Under Portuguese rule.
1645: Became a dependency of Ceylon (Sri Lanka), which was ruled by the Dutch until 1796 and then by the British, with Sinhalese and Indian colonies being established.
1887: Became an internally self-governing British protectorate, which remained a dependency of Sri Lanka until 1948.
1932: The sultanate became an elected position when the first constitution was introduced.
1953: Maldive Islands became a republic within the Commonwealth.
1954: Sultan restored.

RELIGION Sunni Muslim
EDUCATION not compulsory
LITERACY RATE 97% (men); 97% (women) (2003 est)
LABOUR FORCE 14% agriculture, 19% industry, 67% services (2000)
LIFE EXPECTANCY 68 (men); 67 (women) (2000–05)
CHILD MORTALITY RATE (under 5, per 1,000 live births) 77 (2001)
PHYSICIANS (per 1,000 people) 0.5 (1998 est)
TV SETS (per 1,000 people) 38 (1999 est)
RADIOS (per 1,000 people) 129 (1997)
INTERNET USERS (per 10,000 people) 533.8 (2002 est)
PERSONAL COMPUTER USERS (per 100 people) 7.1 (2002 est)

1959–60: Secessionist rebellion in Suvadiva (Huvadu) and Addu southern atolls.
1965: Achieved full independence.
1968: Sultan deposed after referendum; republic reinstated with Ibrahim Nasir as president.
1975: The closure of a British airforce staging post on the southern island of Gan led to a substantial loss in income.
1978: The autocratic Nasir retired and was replaced by the progressive Maumoon Abd Gayoom.
1980s: Economic growth was boosted by the rapid development of the tourist industry.
1982: Rejoined the Commonwealth.
1985: Became a founder member of the South Asian Association for Regional Cooperation.
1988: A coup attempt by Sri Lankan mercenaries, thought to have the backing of former president Nasir, was foiled by Indian paratroops.
2003: Gayoom was re-elected for a record sixth presidential term.

MALDIVES Motorized water taxis, called *dhonis*, are a common form of transportation in the Maldives. *PhotoDisk*

Mali

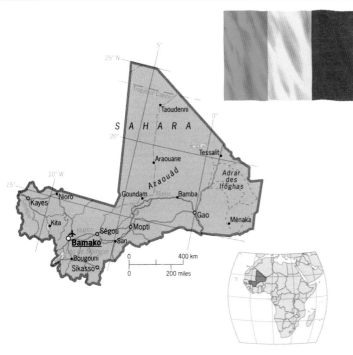

Mali landlocked country in northwest Africa, bounded to the northeast by Algeria, east by Niger, southeast by Burkina Faso, south by Côte d'Ivoire, southwest by Senegal and Guinea, and west and north by Mauritania.

NATIONAL NAME *République du Mali/Republic of Mali*
AREA 1,240,142 sq km/478,818 sq mi
CAPITAL Bamako
MAJOR TOWNS/CITIES Mopti, Kayes, Ségou, Tombouctou, Sikasso
PHYSICAL FEATURES landlocked state with River Niger and savannah in south; part of the Sahara in north; hills in northeast; Senegal River and its branches irrigate the southwest

Government

HEAD OF STATE Amadou Toumani Touré from 2002
HEAD OF GOVERNMENT Ahmed Mohamed Ag Hamani from 2002
POLITICAL SYSTEM emergent democracy
POLITICAL EXECUTIVE limited presidency
ADMINISTRATIVE DIVISIONS capital district of Bamako and eight regions
ARMED FORCES 7,400; plus paramilitary forces of 7,800 (2002 est)
CONSCRIPTION selective conscription for two years
DEATH PENALTY retains the death penalty for ordinary crimes but can be considered abolitionist in practice; date of last known execution 1980
DEFENCE SPEND (% GDP) 2.3 (2002 est)
EDUCATION SPEND (% GDP) 2.8 (2000 est)
HEALTH SPEND (% GDP) 4.9 (2000 est)

Economy and resources

CURRENCY franc CFA
GPD (US$) 3.2 billion (2002 est)
REAL GDP GROWTH (% change on previous year) 6.2 (2001)
GNI (US$) 2.8 billion (2002 est)
GNI PER CAPITA (PPP) (US$) 840 (2002 est)
CONSUMER PRICE INFLATION 5.1% (2003 est)
FOREIGN DEBT (US$) 3 billion (2001 est)
MAJOR TRADING PARTNERS Côte d'Ivoire, Italy, Thailand, France, Brazil, Senegal, Germany, South Korea
RESOURCES iron ore, uranium, diamonds, bauxitè, manganese, copper, lithium, gold
INDUSTRIES food processing, cotton processing, textiles, clothes, cement, pharmaceuticals
EXPORTS gold, cotton, livestock, miscellaneous manufactured articles. Principal market: Thailand 17% (2001)
IMPORTS machinery and transport equipment, food products, petroleum products, other raw materials, chemicals, miscellaneous manufactured articles. Principal source: Côte d'Ivoire 17.5% (2001)
ARABLE LAND 3.8% (2000 est)
AGRICULTURAL PRODUCTS seed cotton, cotton lint, groundnuts, millet, sugar cane, rice, sorghum, sweet potatoes, mangoes, vegetables; livestock rearing (cattle, sheep, and goats); fishing

Population and society

POPULATION 13,007,000 (2003 est)
POPULATION GROWTH RATE 2.2% (2000–15)
POPULATION DENSITY (per sq km) 10 (2003 est)
URBAN POPULATION (% of total) 32 (2003 est)
AGE DISTRIBUTION (% of total population) 0–14 46%, 15–59 48%, 60+ 6% (2002 est)
ETHNIC GROUPS around 50% belong to the Mande group, including the Bambara, Malinke, and Sarakole; other significant groups include the Fulani, Minianka, Senutu, Songhai, and the nomadic Tuareg in the north
LANGUAGE French (official), Bambara, other African languages
RELIGION Sunni Muslim 80%, animist, Christian
LITERACY RATE 48% (men); 18% (women) (2003 est)
LABOUR FORCE 82.6% agriculture, 2.4% industry, 15% services (1997 est)
LIFE EXPECTANCY 48 (men); 49 (women) (2000–05)
CHILD MORTALITY RATE (under 5, per 1,000 live births) 231 (2001)
PHYSICIANS (per 1,000 people) 0.1 (1998 est)
HOSPITAL BEDS (per 1,000 people) 0.2 (1998 est)
TV SETS (per 1,000 people) 17 (2001 est)
RADIOS (per 1,000 people) 180 (2001 est)
INTERNET USERS (per 10,000 people) 30.1 (2002 est)
PERSONAL COMPUTER USERS (per 100 people) 0.1 (2002 est)

See also ▷Ghana, ancient; ▷Mali Empire.

Chronology

5th–13th centuries: Ghana Empire founded by agriculturist Soninke people, based on the Saharan gold trade for which Timbuktu became an important centre. At its height in the 11th century it covered much of the western Sahel, comprising parts of present-day Mali, Senegal, and Mauritania. Wars with Muslim Berber tribes from the north led to its downfall.

13th–15th centuries: Ghana Empire superseded by Muslim Mali Empire of Malinke (Mandingo) people of southwest, from which Mali derives its name. At its peak, under Mansa Musa in the 14th century, it covered parts of Mali, Senegal, Gambia, and southern Mauritania.

15th–16th centuries: Muslim Songhai Empire, centred around Timbuktu and Gao, superseded Mali Empire. It covered Mali, Senegal, Gambia, and parts of Mauritania, Niger, and Nigeria, and included a professional army and civil service.

1591: Songhai Empire destroyed by Moroccan Berbers, under Ahmad al-Mansur, who launched an invasion to take over western Sudanese gold trade and took control over Timbuktu.

18th–19th centuries: Niger valley region was divided between the nomadic Tuareg, in the area around Gao in the northeast, and the Fulani and Bambara kingdoms, around Macina and Bambara in the centre and southwest.

late 18th century: Western Mali visited by Scottish explorer Mungo Park.

mid-19th century: The Islamic Tukolor, as part of a jihad (holy war) conquered much of western Mali, including Fulani and Bambara kingdoms, while in the south, Samori Ture, a Muslim Malinke (Mandingo) warrior, created a small empire.

1880–95: Region conquered by French, who overcame Tukolor and Samori resistance to establish colony of French Sudan.

1904: Became part of the Federation of French West Africa.

1946: French Sudan became an overseas territory within the French Union, with its own territorial assembly and representation in the French parliament; the pro-autonomy Sudanese Union and Sudanese Progressive Parties founded in Bamako.

1959: With Senegal, formed the Federation of Mali.

1960: Separated from Senegal and became independent Republic of Mali, with Modibo Keita, an authoritarian socialist of the Sudanese Union party, as president.

1968: Keita replaced in army coup by Lt Moussa Traoré, as economy deteriorated: constitution suspended and political activity banned.

1974: A new constitution made Mali a one-party state, dominated by Traoré's nationalistic socialist Malian People's Democratic Union (UDPM), formed in 1976.

1979: More than a dozen were killed after a student strike was crushed.

1985: There was a five-day conflict with Burkina Faso over a long-standing border dispute which was mediated by the International Court of Justice.

late 1980s: Closer ties developed with the West and free-market economic policies were pursued, including privatization.

1991: Violent demonstrations and strikes against one-party rule led to 150 deaths; Traoré was ousted in a coup.

1992: A referendum endorsed a new democratic constitution. The opposition Alliance for Democracy in Mali (ADEMA) won multiparty elections; Alpha Oumar Konare was elected president.

1993–94: Ex-president Traoré was sentenced to death for his role in suppressing the 1991 riots.

1997: President Konare was re-elected.

2000: Mande Sidibe became prime minister.

2002: Amadou Toumani Touré was sworn in as president. It was the first time in Mali history that one constitutionally elected president handed over to another.

MALI Mali is populated by various different peoples who have maintained many traditional customs, such as the costume worn by this tribeswoman. Among the different peoples of this country are the Songhai, the Dogon, and Senoufa. *Image Bank*

MALLARD A pair of mallard ducks (*Anas platyrhynchos*), common throughout Europe, northern areas of North America, and most of Asia. The drake (male) has distinctive metallic head plumage of green and purple feathers, whilst the hen (female) is a duller yellowish-brown. *Image Bank*

MALLOW The musk mallow *Malva moschata* is widespread in dry grassy places throughout most of Europe, the British Isles, and North Africa. *Premaphotos Wildlife*

Mali see country box.

malic acid HOOCCH₂CH(OH)COOH organic crystalline acid that can be extracted from apples, plums, cherries, grapes, and other fruits, but occurs in all living cells in smaller amounts, being one of the intermediates of the ▷Krebs cycle.

Mali Empire Muslim state in northwestern Africa during the 7th–15th centuries. Thriving on its trade in gold, it reached its peak in the 14th century under Mansa Musa (reigned 1312–37), when it occupied an area covering present-day Senegal, the Gambia, Mali, and southern Mauritania. Mali's territory was similar to (though larger than) that of the Ghana Empire (see ▷Ghana, ancient), and gave way in turn to the ▷Songhai Empire.

mallard common wild duck from which domestic ducks were bred, found almost worldwide. The male can grow to a length of 60 cm/2 ft and usually has a glossy green head, white collar, and chestnut brown breast with a pale grey body, while the female is mottled brown. Mallards are omnivorous dabbling ducks. (Species *Anas platyrhynchos*, subfamily Anatinae, order Anseriformes.)

Mallarmé, Stéphane (1842–1898) French poet. A leader of the Symbolist school, he became known as a poet's poet for his condensed, hermetic verse and unorthodox syntax, reaching for the ideal world of the intellect. His belief that poetry should be evocative and suggestive was reflected in *L'Après-midi d'un faune/Afternoon of a Faun* (1876; illustrated by Manet), which inspired the composer Debussy. Later works are *Poésies complètes/Complete Poems* (1887), *Vers et prose/Verse and Prose* (1893), and the prose *Divagations/Digressions* (1897).

After 1863 he composed mindfully and looked for the ideal essence of things beyond everyday reality, a movement symbolized by the heroine of the poem 'Hérodiade' 1864 and the satyr of *L'Après-midi d'un faune* (first composed 1865) and their attitudes of withdrawal and refusal. Mallarmé's important poems do not progress by images or by plot and narrative; instead they are self-contained verbal artifacts built around a central object (a room, a chair, stars), symbol, or idea. He devoted his life to the creation of a language capable of transmuting everyday realities onto a higher level. He also experimented with the visual impact of written verse, notably 'Un Coup de dés/A Cast of the Dice' 1914, in which the words are irregularly placed on the page and differing typefaces are used.

Malle, Louis (1932–1995) French film director. His early work anticipated the New Wave. Working in both France and the USA, he made such films as *Le Feu follet/A Time to Live and a Time to Die* (1963), *Atlantic City* (1980), and *Damage* (1993).

mallee any of a group of small eucalyptus trees and shrubs with many small stems and thick underground roots that retain water. Before irrigation farming began, dense thickets of mallee characterized most of northwestern Victoria, Australia, known as the mallee region. (Genus *Eucalyptus*, family Myrtaceae.)

Mallorca (or **Majorca**) largest of the ▷Balearic Islands, belonging to Spain, in the western Mediterranean; area 3,640 sq km/1,405 sq mi; population (2001 est) 702,100. The capital is Palma. The highest mountain on the island is Puig Mayor (1,445 m/4,741 ft). Industries include olives, figs, oranges, wine, brandy, timber, and sheep farming. Tourism is the mainstay of the economy.

Related Web site: Mallorca online http://www.mallorcaonline.com/malhomu.htm

mallow any flowering plant of the mallow family, including the European common mallow (*M. sylvestris*), the tree mallow (*L. arborea*), marsh mallow (*A. officinalis*), and hollyhock (*A. rosea*). Most mallows have pink or purple flowers. (Genera *Malva*, *Lavatera*, and *Althaea*, family Malvaceae.)

Malmö industrial port (shipbuilding, engineering, textiles) in southwestern Sweden, situated across the Øresund from Copenhagen, Denmark; population (1994 est) 242,700. Founded in the 12th century, Malmö is Sweden's third-largest city.

Related Web site: Welcome to Malmö http://www.malmo.com/

malnutrition condition resulting from a defective diet where certain important food nutrients (such as proteins, vitamins, or carbohydrates) are absent. It can lead to deficiency diseases. A related problem is ▷undernourishment. A high global death rate linked to malnutrition has arisen from famine situations caused by global warming, droughts, and the greenhouse effect, as well as by sociopolitical factors, such as alcohol and drug abuse, poverty, and war.

In 1998 there was an estimated 180 million malnourished children in the world and malnutrition contributed to 6 million deaths annually, mainly amongst children.

Malory, Thomas (c. 1410–1471) English author. He is known for the prose romance *Le Morte D'Arthur* (c. 1470), printed in 1485, which relates the exploits of King Arthur's knights of the Round Table and the quest for the ▷Holy Grail. He was knight of the shire from 1445.

Malory is thought to have been the Warwickshire landowner of that name who was member of Parliament for Warwick in 1445 and was subsequently charged with rape, theft, and attempted murder. If that is so, he must have compiled *Le Morte D'Arthur* during his 20 years in and out of prison. Based on an unidentified 'French book',

MALLEE Typical mallee country in Wyperfeld National Park in the Australian state of Victoria. All the surrounding land has been converted to agricultural use. The endangered mallee fowl *Leipoa ocellata* still builds its nest mounds within the sanctuary of the reserve. *Premaphotos Wildlife*

with imaginative additions from other sources, it is the fullest version of the legends of King Arthur, and a notable contribution to English prose.

Related Web site: Thomas Malory's 'Morte d'Arthur' http://www.hti.umich.edu/bin/me-idx?type=header&idno=MaloryWks2

> **Thomas Malory**
> *The joy of love is too short,*
> *and the sorrow thereof, and*
> *what cometh thereof,*
> *dureth over long.*
> *Le Morte d'Arthur bk 10, ch. 56*

Malouf, David George Joseph (1934–) Australian poet, novelist, and short-story writer. He is of Lebanese and English extraction. His poetry collections include *Neighbours in a Thicket* (1974), which won several awards, *Wild Lemons* (1980), and *First Things Last* (1980). Malouf's first novel *Johnno* (1975) deals with his boyhood in Brisbane. It was followed by *An Imaginary Life* (1978) and other novels, including *Fly Away Peter* (1982), *Remembering Babylon* (1993), and *Dream Stuff* (2000).

malpractice in law, ▷negligence by a professional person, usually a doctor, that may lead to an action for damages by the client.

Malraux, André (Georges) (1901–1976) French writer, art critic, and politician. An active antifascist, he gained international renown for his novel *La Condition humaine/Man's Estate* (1933), set during the nationalist/communist revolution in China in the 1920s. *L'Espoir/Days of Hope* (1937) is set in Civil War Spain, where he was a bomber pilot in the International Brigade. In his revolutionary novels he frequently depicts individuals in situations where they are forced to examine the meaning of their own life. He also made an outstanding contribution to aesthetics with *La Psychologie de l'art* (1947–49), revised as *Les Voix du silence/The Voices of Silence* (1951).

Political career Malraux rejected communism and supported the Gaullist resistance during World War II, becoming minister of information in de Gaulle's government 1945–46 and minister of cultural affairs 1960–69.

malt in brewing, grain (barley, oats, or wheat) artificially germinated and then dried in a kiln. Malts are fermented to make beers or lagers, or fermented and then distilled to produce spirits such as whisky.

Malta see country box.

Malta, Knights of another name for members of the military-religious order of the Hospital of ▷St John of Jerusalem.

maltase enzyme found in plants and animals that breaks down the disaccharide maltose into glucose.

Maltese dog breed of long-coated lap dog. Its white coat is straight and silky and parted from head to tail and the short tail is doubled into the coat on the back. Maltese dogs have dark eyes, long drooping ears, and small feet. The ideal maximum height is 25 cm/10 in, and the weight is 3–4 kg/6.5–9 lb.

Malthus, Thomas Robert (1766–1834) English economist. His *Essay on the Principle of Population* (1798; revised 1803) argued for population control, since populations increase in geometric ratio and food supply only in arithmetic ratio, and influenced Charles ▷Darwin's thinking on natural selection as the driving force of evolution.

Malthus saw war, famine, and disease as necessary checks on population growth. Later editions of his work suggested that 'moral restraint' (delaying marriage, with sexual abstinence before it) could also keep numbers from increasing too quickly, a statement seized on by later birth-control pioneers (the 'neo-Malthusians').

Related Web site: Malthus 'Essay on the Principle of Population' http://www.ac.wwu.edu/~stephan/malthus/malthus.0.html

Malthus theory projection of population growth made by Thomas Malthus. He based his theory on the ▷population explosion that was already becoming evident in the 18th century, and argued that the number of people would increase faster than the food supply. Population would eventually reach a resource limit (▷overpopulation). Any further increase would result in a population crash, caused by famine, disease, or war.

maltose $C_{12}H_{22}O_{11}$ a ▷disaccharide sugar in which both monosaccharide units are glucose.

Maluku (or Moluccas) group of Indonesian islands; area 74,500 sq km/28,764 sq mi; population (1995 est) 2,094,700. The capital is Ambon, on Ambon. As the Spice Islands, they were formerly part of the Dutch East Indies; the southern Moluccas attempted secession from the newly created Indonesian republic from 1949, with sectarian fighting continuing into 2000.

Malvern English spa town in Worcester, on the east side of the Malvern Hills, which extend for about 16 km/10 mi and have their high point in Worcester Beacon 425 m/1,395 ft; population (1991) 31,500. The Malvern Festival (1929–39), associated with the playwright G B Shaw and the composer Edward Elgar, was revived in 1977. Elgar lived and was buried here.

Malvinas, Islas Argentine name for the ▷Falkland Islands.

mamba either of two venomous snakes belonging to the cobra family, found in Africa south of the Sahara. Unlike cobras, they are not hooded. (Genus *Dendroaspis*, family Elapidae.)

The green mamba (*D. angusticeps*) is 1.5 m/5 ft long or more and lives in trees, feeding on birds and lizards. The black mamba (*D. polylepis*) is the largest venomous snake in Africa, occasionally as long as 3.4 m/11 ft, and spends more time on the ground.

Mameluke member of a powerful political class that dominated Egypt from the 13th century until their massacre in 1811 by Mehmet Ali.

Mamet, David (Alan) (1947–) US dramatist, writer, and director. His plays use vivid, freewheeling language and urban settings. *American Buffalo* (1975), about a gang of hopeless robbers, was his first major success. *Glengarry Glen Ross* (1983) was a dark depiction of US business ethics. He made his directorial debut with *House of Games* (1987), which used gambling as a metaphor for relationships. He also directed *The Spanish Prisoner* (1997) and *State and Main* (2000). In 2000 he published a collection of essays, *Jafsie and John Henry*, and a novel, *Wilson: A Consideration of the Sources*. He wrote the screenplay for, and directed, *Heist* in 2001.

mammal any of a large group of warm-blooded vertebrate animals characterized by having ▷mammary glands in the female; these are used for suckling the young. Other features of mammals are ▷hair (very reduced in some species, such as whales); a middle ear formed of three small bones (ossicles); a lower jaw consisting of

Malta

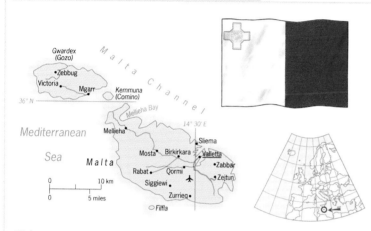

Malta island in the Mediterranean Sea, south of Sicily, east of Tunisia, and north of Libya.

NATIONAL NAME *Repubblika ta'Malta*/Republic of Malta
AREA 320 sq km/124 sq mi
CAPITAL Valletta (and chief port)
MAJOR TOWNS/CITIES Rabat, Birkirkara, Qormi, Sliema, Zejtun, Zabor
MAJOR PORTS Marsaxlokk, Valletta
PHYSICAL FEATURES includes islands of Gozo 67 sq km/26 sq mi and Comino 3 sq km/1 sq mi

Government

HEAD OF STATE Guido de Marco from 1999
HEAD OF GOVERNMENT Edward Fenech Adami from 1998
POLITICAL SYSTEM liberal democracy
POLITICAL EXECUTIVE parliamentary
ADMINISTRATIVE DIVISIONS 68 local councils (Malta and Gozo)
ARMED FORCES 2,100 (2002 est)
CONSCRIPTION military service is voluntary
DEATH PENALTY abolished in 2000

Economy and resources

CURRENCY Maltese lira
GPD (US$) 3.8 billion (2002 est)
REAL GDP GROWTH (% change on previous year) –0.4 (2001)
GNI (US$) 3.9 billion (2002 est)
GNI PER CAPITA (PPP) (US$) 16,790 (2002 est)
CONSUMER PRICE INFLATION 2% (2003 est)
UNEMPLOYMENT 5.1% (2001)
FOREIGN DEBT (US$) 8.3 billion (2001 est)
MAJOR TRADING PARTNERS USA, France, Italy, Germany, UK, Libya, the Netherlands
RESOURCES stone, sand; offshore petroleum reserves were under exploration 1988–95
INDUSTRIES transport equipment and machinery, food and beverages, textiles and clothing, chemicals, ship repair and shipbuilding, tourism
EXPORTS machinery and transport equipment, manufactured articles (including clothing), beverages, chemicals, tobacco. Principal market: USA 20.2% (2001)
IMPORTS machinery and transport equipment, basic manufactures (including textile yarn and fabrics), food and live animals, mineral fuels, tobacco. Principal source: France 15% (2001)
ARABLE LAND 25% (2000 est)
AGRICULTURAL PRODUCTS potatoes, tomatoes, peaches, plums, nectarines, apricots, melons, strawberries, wheat, barley; livestock rearing (cattle, pigs, and poultry) and livestock products (chicken eggs, pork, and dairy products)

Population and society

POPULATION 394,000 (2003 est)
POPULATION GROWTH RATE 0.4% (2000–05)
POPULATION DENSITY (per sq km) 1,248 (2003 est)
URBAN POPULATION (% of total) 92 (2003 est)
AGE DISTRIBUTION (% of total population) 0–14 19%, 15–59 64%, 60+ 17% (2002 est)
ETHNIC GROUPS essentially European, supposedly originated from ancient North African kingdom of Carthage
LANGUAGE Maltese, English (both official)
RELIGION Roman Catholic 98%
EDUCATION (compulsory years) 10
LITERACY RATE 92% (men); 94% (women) (2003 est)
LABOUR FORCE 2% agriculture, 27% industry, 71% services (1998)
LIFE EXPECTANCY 76 (men); 81 (women) (2000–05)
CHILD MORTALITY RATE (under 5, per 1,000 live births) 5 (2001)
PHYSICIANS (per 1,000 people) 2.6 (1998 est)
HOSPITAL BEDS (per 1,000 people) 5.3 (1996 est)
TV SETS (per 1,000 people) 549 (1997)
RADIOS (per 1,000 people) 669 (1997)
INTERNET USERS (per 10,000 people) 2,525.5 (2002 est)
PERSONAL COMPUTER USERS (per 100 people) 25.5 (2002 est)

Chronology

7th century BC: Invaded and subjugated by Carthaginians from North Africa.
218 BC: Came under Roman control.
AD 60: Converted to Christianity by the apostle Paul.
395: On the division of the Roman Empire, became part of Eastern (Byzantine) portion, dominated by Constantinople.
870: Came under Arab rule.
1091: Arabs defeated by Norman Count Roger I of Sicily; Roman Catholic Church re-established.
1530: Handed over by Holy Roman Emperor Charles V to a religious military order, the Hospitallers (Knights of St John of Jerusalem).
1798–1802: Occupied by French.
1814: Annexed to Britain by the Treaty of Paris on condition that Roman Catholic Church was maintained and Maltese Declaration of Rights honoured.
later 19th century–early 20th century: Became vital British naval base, with famous dockyard that developed as the island's economic mainstay.
1942: Awarded the George Cross for valour in resisting severe Italian aerial attacks during World War II.
1947: Achieved self-government.
1956: Referendum approved MLP's proposal for integration with UK. Plebiscite opposed and boycotted by right-of-centre Nationalist Party (PN).
1958: MLP rejected final British integration proposal.
1964: Independence achieved from Britain, within Commonwealth. A ten-year defence and economic-aid treaty with the UK was signed.
1971: Prime Minister Mintoff adopted a policy of nonalignment and declared the 1964 treaty invalid; negotiations began for leasing NATO base in Malta.
1972: Seven-year NATO agreement signed.
1974: Became a republic.
1979: British military base closed; closer links were established with communist and Arab states, including Libya.
1987: Edward Fenech Adami (PN) was narrowly elected prime minister; he adopted a more pro-European and pro-American policy stance than the preceding administration.
1990: A formal application was made for European Community membership.
1998: The PN was returned to power after a snap election, with Edward Fenech Adami returning as prime minister.
1999: Guido de Marco was elected president.
2004: Malta was set to join the EU 1 May.

MALTA The Mediterranean island of Gozo is the second largest of the main islands that form the state of Malta. The others are Malta and Comino. *Image Bank*

MAMMAL An elephant in Hwange National Park, Zimbabwe, southern Africa. *Corel*

Classification of Mammals		
Order	**Number of species**	**Examples**
Leading class: Mammalia		
Subclass: Prototheria (egg-laying mammals)		
Monotremata	3	echidna, platypus
Subclass: Theria		
Infraclass: Metatheria (pouched mammals)		
Marsupiala	266	kangaroo, koala, opossum
Infraclass: Eutheria (placental mammals)		
Rodentia	1,700	rat, mouse, squirrel, porcupine
Chiroptera	970	all bats
Insectivora	378	shrew, hedgehog, mole
Carnivora	230	cat, dog, weasel, bear
Primates	180	lemur, monkey, ape, human
Artiodactyla	145	pig, deer, cattle, camel, giraffe
Cetacea	79	whale, dolphin
Lagomorpha	58	rabbit, hare, pika
Pinnipedia	33	seal, walrus
Edentata	29	anteater, armadillo, sloth
Perissodactyla	16	horse, rhinoceros, tapir
Hyracoidea	11	hyrax
Pholidota	7	pangolin
Sirenia	4	dugong, manatee
Dermoptera	2	flying lemur
Proboscidea	2	elephant
Tubulidentata	1	aardvark

two bones only; seven vertebrae in the neck; and no nucleus in the red blood cells. (Class Mammalia.)

Mammals are divided into three groups:

placental mammals, where the young develop inside the mother's body, in the ▷uterus, receiving nourishment from the blood of the mother via the ▷placenta;

marsupials, where the young are born at an early stage of development and develop further in a pouch on the mother's body where they are attached to and fed from a nipple; and

monotremes, where the young hatch from an egg outside the mother's body and are then nourished with milk.

The monotremes are the least evolved and have been largely displaced by more sophisticated marsupials and placentals, so that there are only a few types surviving (platypus and echidna). Placentals have spread to all parts of the globe, and where placentals have competed with marsupials, the placentals have in general displaced marsupial types. However, marsupials occupy many specialized niches in South America and, especially, Australasia.

According to the Red List of endangered species published by the ▷World Conservation Union for 1996, 25% of mammal species are threatened with extinction.

The theory that marsupials succeed only where they do not compete with placentals was shaken 1992, when a tooth, 55 million years old and belonging to a placental mammal, was found in Murgon, Australia, indicating that placental animals appeared in Australia at the same time as the marsupials. The marsupials, however, still prevailed.

There are over 4,000 species of mammals, adapted to almost every way of life. The smallest shrew weighs only 2 g/0.07 oz, the largest whale up to 140 tonnes. A 50 million year-old jaw discovered in 1998 is from the smallest mammal ever to have lived, *Batodonoides* was an insectivore weighing only 1.3 g/0.046 oz.

mammary gland in female mammals, a milk-producing gland derived from epithelial cells underlying the skin, active only after the production of young. In all but monotremes (egg-laying mammals), the mammary glands terminate in teats which aid infant suckling. The number of glands and their position vary between species. In humans there are 2, in cows 4, and in pigs between 10 and 14.

The hatched young of monotremes simply lick milk from a specialized area of skin on the mother's abdomen.

mammography X-ray procedure used to screen for breast cancer. It can detect abnormal growths at an early stage, before they can be seen or felt.

Mammon evil personification of wealth and greed; originally a Syrian god of riches, cited in the New Testament as opposed to the Christian god.

mammoth extinct elephant, remains of which have been found worldwide. Some were 50% taller than modern elephants; others were much smaller. (Genus *Mammuthus* (or **Elephas**).)

The **woolly mammoth** (*M. primigenius*) of northern zones, the size of an Indian elephant, had long fur and large inward-curving tusks. Various species of mammoth were abundant in both the Old World and the New World in Pleistocene times, and were hunted by humans for food.

management buyout purchase of control of a company by its management, generally with debt funding, making it a ▷leveraged buyout.

managing director director of a company who is also its most senior manager. The managing director is therefore responsible for the day-to-day running of the company but has a seat on the board of the company. The managing director may also be the chairman of the company, but in large companies the role of chairman is likely to be separate from that of managing director.

Managua capital and chief industrial city of Nicaragua, and capital of a department of the same name; it is situated on the southern shore of Lake Managua 45km/28 mi from the Pacific coast and 138 km/86 mi from the main port of Corinto; population (1995 est) 1,240,000. One-fifth of the nation's population is resident here. It is Nicaragua's largest city and main industrial and commercial centre. Managua produces 60% of the nation's goods by value including tobacco, textiles, cement, cotton, drinks, and processed foods. Surrounding lowlands are very fertile, supporting maize, beans, sugar cane, and banana plantations. The city's university was founded in 1961.

Founded as the capital in 1858, it was destroyed by an earthquake in 1931, and again in 1972; it was also badly damaged during the civil war of 1978–79. The major earthquake of 1972 (6.2 on the Richter scale) killed 5,000 people. Near the lakeshore are the preserved **Huellas de Acahualinca**, prehistoric animal and human footprints.

manatee any of a group of plant-eating aquatic mammals found in marine bays and sluggish rivers, usually in thick, muddy water. They have flippers as forelimbs, no hindlimbs, and a short rounded and flattened tail used for swimming. The marine manatees can grow up to about 4.5 m/15 ft long and weigh up to 600 kg/1,323 lb. (Genus *Trichechus*, family Trichechidae, order Sirenia.)

All three species of manatee are in danger of becoming extinct as a result of pollution and because they are hunted for food. They are the **Amazonian manatee** (*T. Inunguis*), found in the River Amazon; the **African manatee** (*T. Senegalensis*), which lives in the rivers and coastal areas of West Africa; and the **West Indian manatee** (*T. manatus*), which lives in the Caribbean Sea and along the east coasts of tropical North and South America. Only about 2,400 West Indian manatees remain in the main population around Florida; more than 200 died in 1996, poisoned by an algal toxin.

Related Web site: Save the Manatee Club http://www.objectlinks. com/manatee/

Manaus capital of Amazonas federal unit (state), northwest Brazil, on the Río Negro, 16 km/10 mi from its confluence with the River Solimó which forms the River Amazon; population (1991) 996,700. It is the industrial trading and commercial centre of the state, and its chief port, although 1,600 km/1,000 mi from the Atlantic. Timber and rubber are the main exports, and there are sawmills and an oil refinery. Manaus is an important free-trade zone (established in 1966) that distributes products nationwide. It specializes in electrical goods.

Manchester metropolitan district of Greater Manchester, and city in northwest England, on the River Irwell, 50 km/31 mi east of Liverpool; population (1998 est) 429,800. A financial and manufacturing centre, its industries include banking and insurance; the production of cotton and man-made textiles, petro-chemicals, rubber, paper, machine tools, and processed foods; and heavy, light, and electrical engineering, also printing. It is linked to the River Mersey and the Irish Sea by the **Manchester Ship Canal**, opened in 1894. Only one dock is now open.

Features Manchester is the home of the Hallé Orchestra, the Royal Northern College of Music, Chetham's School of Music, and Bridgewater Hall; Manchester Grammar School (1515), and four universities (the University of Manchester, UMIST, Manchester Metropolitan University, and the University of Salford); Manchester United Football Club and Manchester Arena (the largest indoor arena in Europe); the Royal Exchange (built in 1869, now a theatre); the Town Hall (1877) designed by Alfred Waterhouse, and the Free Trade Hall (1856); Liverpool Road station (the world's oldest surviving passenger station); the Whitworth Art Gallery, the Cotton Exchange (now a leisure centre), the Central Library (designed by Frank Lloyd ▷Wright in 1934, the world's largest municipal library), and the John Rylands Library (1900). The Castlefield Urban Heritage Park includes the Granada television studios, including the set of the soap opera *Coronation Street*, open to visitors, and also the Museum of Science and Industry.

History Originally a Roman camp (**Mancunium** or **Mamucium**), Manchester is mentioned in the Domesday Book, and by the 13th century was already a centre for the wool trade. Its damp climate and many waterways made it ideal for the production of cotton, introduced in the 16th century, and from the mid-18th century onwards the Manchester area was a world centre of manufacture, using cotton imported from North America and India. Unrest after the Napoleonic Wars led to the ▷Peterloo Massacre in 1819 when troops charged a political meeting at St Peter's Fields. In the 19th century Manchester was the centre for a school of political economists, including John Bright and Richard Cobden, who campaigned for the repeal of the Corn Laws in the first half of the century. Manchester was also the original home of *The Guardian* newspaper (founded as the *Manchester Guardian* in 1821).

After 1945 there was a sharp decline in the cotton industry, and many disused mills have been refurbished to provide alternative industrial uses. The pop music scene flourished in the 1960s and 1980s. Metrolink, a light rail system, was opened in 1992. An Irish study (1993–95) found Manchester to be the European city worst affected by ▷acid rain. The Commonwealth Games are to be held in Manchester in 2002. New sports facilities include the National Cycling Centre.

Related Web site: Virtual Manchester http://www.manchester.com/ home.html

Manchester, Greater metropolitan county of northwest England, created in 1974; in 1986 most of the functions of the former county council were transferred to metropolitan district councils.

area 1,290 sq km/498 sq mi **towns and cities** Manchester, Bolton, Bury, Oldham, Rochdale, Salford, Stockport, Tameside, Trafford, Wigan **features** Manchester Ship Canal links it with the River Mersey and the sea; Old Trafford cricket ground at Stretford, and the football ground of Manchester United **industries** engineering, textiles, textile machinery, chemicals, plastics, electrical goods, electronic equipment, paper, printing, rubber, and asbestos **population** (2000 est) 2,585,800 **famous people** Anthony Burgess, John Dalton, Gracie Fields, James Joule, Emmeline Pankhurst

Manchester terrier breed of smooth-haired black-and-tan terrier. Manchester terriers have a long, wedge-shaped head, small dark eyes, and V-shaped ears, hanging close to the head. The usual weight is 8 kg/17.5 lb and the height 38–41 cm/15–16 in.

Manchu (also known as **Qing**) Last ruling dynasty in China, from 1644 until its overthrow in 1912; its last emperor was the infant ▷P'u-i. Originally a nomadic people from Manchuria, they established power through a series of successful invasions from the north, then granted trading rights to the USA and Europeans, which eventually brought strife and the ▷Boxer Rebellion.

Related Web site: Historical Facts about the Ch'ing Dynasty
http://www.uni-koeln.de/phil-fak/ostas/sinol/manfacts.html

Manchukuo former Japanese puppet state in Manchuria and Jehol 1932–45, ruled by the former Chinese emperor Henry ▷P'u-i.

Manchuria European name for the northeastern region of China, comprising the provinces of Heilongjiang, Jilin, and Liaoning. It was united with China by the Manchu dynasty in 1644, but as the Chinese Empire declined, Japan and Russia were rivals for its control.

The Russians were expelled after the ▷Russo-Japanese War 1904–05, and in 1932 Japan consolidated its position by creating a puppet state, **Manchukuo**, nominally led by the Chinese pretender to the throne Henry P'u-i. At the end of World War II the Soviets occupied Manchuria in a two-week operation in August 1945. Japanese settlers were expelled when the region was returned to Chinese control.

Mandalay chief city of the Mandalay division of Myanmar (formerly Burma), on the River Irrawaddy, about 495 km/370 mi north of Yangon (Rangoon); population (1998 est) 370,000. It is a river port, with a university founded in 1964.

MANDALAY Tapestry weaving in Mandalay, Myanmar. Mandalay is the handicrafts centre of the country, and a *kalaga* or embroidered hand-woven tapestry is a popular purchase by tourists. Kalagas are heavily studded with sequins and glass beads, with gold- or silver-coloured threads woven into the cloth. *Image Bank*

Mandarin (Sanskrit *mantrin* 'counsellor') standard form of the ▷Chinese language. Historically it derives from the language spoken by **mandarins**, Chinese imperial officials, from the 7th century onwards. It is used by 70% of the population and taught in schools of the People's Republic of China.

mandarin type of small ▷orange.

mandate in history, a territory whose administration was entrusted to Allied states by the League of Nations under the Treaty of Versailles after World War I. Mandated territories were former German and Turkish possessions (including Iraq, Syria, Lebanon, and Palestine). When the United Nations replaced the League of Nations in 1945, mandates that had not achieved independence became known as ▷trust territories.

Mandela, Nelson (Rolihlahla) (1918–   ) South African politician and lawyer, president 1994–99. He was president of the ▷African National Congress (ANC) 1991–97. Imprisoned from 1964, as organizer of the then banned ANC, he became a symbol of unity for the worldwide anti-▷apartheid movement. In February 1990 he was released, the ban on the ANC having been lifted, and entered into negotiations with the government about a multiracial future for South Africa. In May 1994 he was sworn in as South Africa's first post-apartheid president after the ANC won 62.65% of the vote in universal-suffrage elections. He shared the Nobel Prize for Peace in 1993 with South African president F W ▷de Klerk for their work towards dismantling apartheid and negotiating the transition to a nonracial democracy. In June 1999 he stepped down as president and was succeeded by ANC president, Thabo Mbeki.

> **Nelson Mandela**
> *Never, never and never again shall it be that this beautiful land will again experience the oppression of one by another.*
> Inaugural speech as president of South Africa, May 1994

NELSON MANDELA South African president Nelson Mandela after receiving the Congressional Gold Medal at a ceremony in the US Capitol Rotunda, Washington, DC, in September 1998. *Archive Photos*

Mandela was born near Umtata, south of Lesotho, the son of a local chief. In a trial of several ANC leaders, he was acquitted of treason in 1961, but was once more arrested in 1964 and given a life sentence on charges of sabotage and plotting to overthrow the government. In February 1990 he was released from prison on the orders of state president F W de Klerk and in July 1991 was elected, unopposed, to the presidency of the ANC. In December 1991 the ANC began constitutional negotiations with the government and in February 1993 Mandela and President de Klerk agreed to the formation of a government of national unity after free, nonracial elections (that took place in 1994). Relations between Mandela and de Klerk deteriorated when former members of de Klerk's security forces were prosecuted in March 1996. He stepped down as ANC president in December 1997 and was replaced by his former deputy Thabo Mbeki. He was appointed as UN mediator for the seven-year civil war in Burundi in January 2000.

Mandela married the South African civil-rights activist Winnie ▷Mandela in 1958. They separated in 1992 and were divorced in 1996. In 1998 he married Graca Machel, the widow of the Mozambique nationalist leader. His autobiography, *Long Walk to Freedom* (1994) was widely acclaimed, and his state visit to Britain in July 1996 was a resounding success.

Related Web site: Akkadian Language http://saturn.sron.ruu.nl/
~jheise/akkadian/index.html

Mandela, Winnie Madikizela (Nomzamo) (1934–   ) South African civil-rights activist, former wife of Nelson Mandela. A leading spokesperson for the African National Congress (ANC) during Nelson Mandela's imprisonment 1964–90, in 1991 she received a six-year prison sentence for her role in the kidnapping and assault of four youths. Her sentence was later waived and in May 1994, following the ANC's victory in the country's first universal-suffrage elections, she was given a deputy ministerial post in the new government. In 1995 she was dismissed from her cabinet post, following allegations of dereliction of duty. In April 2003 she was found guilty of fraud and theft, and was sentenced to five years in prison.

Mandelstam, Osip Emilevich (1891–1938) Russian poet. He was a leader of the Acmeist movement. The son of a Jewish merchant, he was sent to a concentration camp by the communist authorities in the 1930s, and died there. His posthumously published work, with its classic brevity, established his reputation as one of the greatest 20th-century Russian poets.

mandolin plucked string instrument which flourished 1600–1800. It has four to six pairs of strings (courses) and is tuned like a violin. The fingerboard is fretted to regulate intonation. It takes its name from its almond-shaped body (Italian *mandorla* 'almond'). Vivaldi composed two concertos for the mandolin in about 1736.

mandragora (or **mandrake**) any of a group of almost stemless Old World plants with narcotic (pain-killing and sleep-inducing) properties, belonging to the nightshade family. They have large leaves, pale blue or violet flowers, and round berries known as devil's apples. (Genus *Mandragora*, family Solanaceae.)

mandrake another name for the plant ▷mandragora.

mandrill large West African forest-living baboon, active mainly on the ground. It has large canine teeth like the drill (*M. leucophaeus*), to which it is closely related. The nose is bright red and the cheeks are striped with blue; the thick skin of the buttocks is also red, and the fur is brown, apart from a yellow beard. (Species *Mandrillus sphinx*.)

Males are much larger than females, showing greater sexual dimorphism than any other primate. Males weigh up to 35 kg/77 lb and females usually less than 12 kg/26 lb. Females exhibit none of the bright coloration of the male. A single infant is born after 5 months' gestation; it is weaned at 6 months. Females reach sexual maturity at about three years; males at around ten years.

Manes in ancient Rome, the spirits of the dead, worshipped as divine and sometimes identified with the gods of the underworld (Dis and Proserpine), hence the inscription DMS (*dis manibus sacrum*) on many Roman tombs.

Manet, Edouard (1832–1883) French painter. One of the foremost French artists of the 19th century, he is often regarded as the father of modern painting. Rebelling against the academic tradition, he developed a clear and unaffected realist style that was one of the founding forces of ▷Impressionism. His subjects were mainly contemporary, such as *A Bar at the Folies-Bergère* (1882; Courtauld Art Gallery, London).

Manet received a very traditional academic art education under a history painter; his real influences were Goya, Velázquez and Courbet. His *Déjeuner sur l'herbe/Picnic on the Grass* 1863 and *Olympia* 1865 (both Musée d'Orsay, Paris), though both based on Renaissance masterpieces, offended conservative tastes in their matter-of-fact treatment of the nude body.

Though he never exhibited with the Impressionists – he had a classical sense of order and composition – many of them were were strongly influenced by his pioneering works, and he in turn,from the early 1870s, was influenced by figures such as Berthe ▷Morisot, his works becoming lighter in both touch and colour.

manganese hard, brittle, grey-white metallic element, symbol Mn, atomic number 25, relative atomic mass 54.9380. It resembles iron (and rusts), but it is not magnetic and is softer. It is used chiefly in making steel alloys, also alloys with aluminium and copper. It is used in fertilizers, paints, and industrial chemicals. It is a necessary trace element in human nutrition. The name is old, deriving from the French and Italian forms of Latin for *magnesia* (MgO), the white tasteless powder used as an antacid from ancient times.

manganese ore any mineral from which manganese is produced. The main ores are the oxides, such as **pyrolusite**, MnO_2; **hausmannite**, Mn_3O_4; and **manganite**, $MnO(OH)$.

mangelwurzel (or **mangold**) variety of the common beet *Beta vulgaris* used chiefly as feed for cattle and sheep.

mango evergreen tree belonging to the cashew family, native to India but now widely cultivated for its large oval fruits in other tropical and subtropical areas, such as the West Indies. (*Mangifera indica*, family Anacardiaceae.)

mangold another name for ▷mangelwurzel.

mangrove any of several shrubs and trees, especially of the mangrove family, found in the muddy swamps of tropical and subtropical coastlines and estuaries. By sending down aerial roots from their branches, they rapidly form close-growing mangrove thickets. Their timber is resistant to water penetration and damage

MANGROVE Trees of the Sonneratiaceae family, such as these *Sonnerata alba* from Borneo, are also known as mangroves, and often grow intermixed with the more familiar *Rhizophora* mangroves. *Premaphotos Wildlife*

by marine worms. Mangrove swamps are rich breeding grounds for fish and shellfish, but these habitats are being destroyed in many countries. (Genera *Rhizophora* and *Avicennia*, families Rhizophoraceae (mangrove) and Avicenniaceae (related).)

Manhattan island of the city of ▷New York, USA, forming most of a borough; population (2000 est) 1,537,200. It is 20 km/12.5 mi long and 4 km/2.5 mi wide, and lies between the Hudson and East rivers. The rocks from which it is formed rise to a height of more than 73 m/240 ft in the north of the island. Manhattan Island is bounded on the north and northeast by the Harlem River and Spuyten Duyvil Creek (which separate it from the Bronx); on the south by Upper New York Bay; on the west by the Hudson River (which separates it from New Jersey); and on the east by the East River (which separates it from Queens and Brooklyn). The borough of Manhattan also includes a small port at the Bronx mainland and several islands in the East River. Manhattan is the economic hub of New York City, although there are large residential and industrial areas here also. It includes the Wall Street business centre, Broadway and its theatres, Carnegie Hall (1891), the Empire State Building (1931), the United Nations headquarters (1952), Madison Square Garden, and Central Park. The twin towers of the World Trade Center (1973) collapsed on 11 September 2001, minutes after each was struck by hijacked aircraft piloted by terrorists. The death toll was estimated at around 3,000.

MANHATTAN The skyline of the island of Manhattan, New York, before the twin towers of the World Trade Center fell on 11 September 2001. *Image Bank*

Manhattan Project code name for the development of the ▷atom bomb in the USA in World War II, to which the physicists Enrico Fermi and J Robert Oppenheimer contributed.

manic depression (or **bipolar disorder**) mental disorder characterized by recurring periods of either ▷depression or mania (inappropriate elation, agitation, and rapid thought and speech) or both. Sufferers may be genetically predisposed to the condition.

Manichaeism religion founded by the Persian prophet Mani (Latinized as Manichaeus, *c.* 216–276). Despite persecution, Manichaeism spread and flourished until about the 10th century. Based on the concept of dualism, it held that the material world is evil, an invasion of the spiritual realm of light by the powers of darkness; particles of divine light imprisoned in evil matter were to be rescued by messengers such as Jesus, and finally by Mani himself.

Manila industrial port (textiles, tobacco, distilling, chemicals, shipbuilding) and capital of the Philippines, in the southwest of the island of Luzon, where the River Pasig enters Manila Bay; population of the metropolitan area (including ▷Quezon City) 9,286,000 (1996); city (1998 est) 1,761,900. Other industries include timber and food processing.

manioc another name for the plant ▷cassava.

Manipur state of northeast India; bordered south and east by Myanmar; area 22,300 sq km/8,610 sq mi; population (2001 est) 2,373,000 (30% are hill tribes such as Nagas and Kukis). The capital is ▷Imphal. The state is mostly wooded and mountainous (mainly over 2,000 m/6,500 ft), with a central valley containing Imphal. Features include Loktak Lake, and the state is the original Indian home of polo. Industries include textiles, cement, and handloom weaving. Agricultural products include rice, grain, fruit, vegetables, and sugar. Languages spoken in the state are Manipuri and English. 70% of the population are Hindu.

Man, Isle of (Gaelic **Ellan Vannin**) island in the Irish Sea, a dependency of the British crown, but not part of the UK; area 570 sq km/220 sq mi; population (2001 est) 76,300, almost 50% of which lives in the capital ▷Douglas and nearby Onchan. Other towns and cities include Ramsey, Peel, and Castletown. Industries include light engineering products, agriculture, and fishing. Tourism has declined in importance and has been replaced by financial services as the island's principal industry. The Isle of Man

was Norwegian until 1266, when it was ceded to Scotland. It came under UK administration in 1765.

Manitoba (Algonquian *Manitou* 'great spirit') province in central Canada, the easternmost of the Prairie provinces. Bounded to the south, on the 49th Parallel, by the US states of Minnesota (in the east) and North Dakota (in the west); to the west by Saskatchewan; to the north, on the 60th Parallel, by the Northwest Territories and Hudson Bay; and to the east by Ontario; area 650,000 sq km/251,000 sq mi; population (1996) 1,113,900. The capital is ▷Winnipeg, and other towns and cities include Brandon, Thompson, St Boniface, Churchill, Flin Flon, Portage La Prairie, and The Pas. Lakes Winnipeg, Winnipegosis, and Manitoba (area 4,700 sq km/1,814 sq mi) are in the province, which is 50% forested. Industries include production of grain and food-processing; manufacture of machinery; fur-trapping; fishing; mining of nickel, zinc, copper, and the world's largest deposits of caesium (a metallic element used in the manufacture of photocells).

Manley, Michael (Norman) (1924–1997) Jamaican trade unionist, centre-left politician, leader of the socialist People's National Party from 1969, and prime minister (1972–80 and 1989–92). A charismatic orator, he was the son of Norman Manley, founder of the socialist People's National Party (PNP), and became leader of the PNP on his father's death in 1969. After a landslide victory in 1972, his 'democratic socialist' programme was beset by economic depression, losing him the election in 1980. He was re-elected on a more moderate manifesto in 1989, but ill health forced his resignation as prime minister in March 1992 and retirement from politics. He was succeeded as premier by Percival ▷Patterson.

Mann, Heinrich (1871–1950) German novelist. He left Nazi Germany in 1937 with his brother Thomas ▷Mann and went to the USA. His books include *Im Schlaraffenland/In the Land of Cockaigne* (1901) and *Professor Unrat/The Blue Angel* (1904; widely known as a film), depicting the sensual downfall of a schoolteacher. His novels show Germany in its new, vulgar prosperity from the end of the 19th century to the period just before World War I, and his best works were suppressed for a time.

Mann, Thomas (1875–1955) German novelist and critic. A largely subjective artist, he drew his themes from his own experiences and inner thoughts. He was constantly preoccupied with the idea of death in the midst of life and with the position of the artist in relation to society. His first novel was *Buddenbrooks* (1901), a saga of a merchant family which traces through four generations the gradual growth of decay as culture slowly saps virility. *Der Zauberberg/The Magic Mountain* (1924), a vast symbolic work on the subject of disease in sick minds and bodies, and also the sickness of Europe, probes the question of culture in relation to life. Notable among his works of short fiction is 'Der Tod in Venedig/Death in Venice' (1913). He was awarded the Nobel Prize for Literature in 1929.

He was born in Lübeck, the younger brother of Heinrich ▷Mann. He worked in an insurance office in Munich and became a reader on the staff of the periodical *Simplicissimus*, in which some of his stories were published. His opposition to the Nazi regime forced him to leave Germany and in 1940 he became a US citizen, but he returned to Europe in 1954. Among his other works are a biblical tetralogy *Joseph und seine Brüde/Joseph and his Brothers* (1933–43); *Doktor Faustus, das Leben des deutschen Tonsetzers Adrian Leverkuehn, erzählt von einem Freund/Dr Faustus: the Life of the German Composer Adrian Leverkuehn, as told by a Friend* (1947), the Faust legend brought up to date with a background of pre- and post-war Germany; *Die Bekenntnisse des Hochstaplers Felix Krull/Confessions of Felix Krull, Confidence Man* (1954), widely considered to be the greatest comic novel in German literature; and a number of short stories, including 'Tonio Kröger' (1903) which exemplifies the conflict between the ordinary person and the artist.

THOMAS MANN German novelist Thomas Mann. *Archive Photos*

manna sweetish exudation obtained from many trees such as the ash and larch, and used in medicine. The Old Testament (Exodus ch. 16) relates that God provided manna for the Israelites in the desert when there was no other food. The manna of the Bible is thought to have been from the tamarisk tree, or a form of lichen.

Mannerism in a general sense some idiosyncrasy, extravagance, or affectation of style or manner in art, though it has more specific reference to Italian painting in the 16th century and represents a distinct phase between the art of the High Renaissance and the rise of baroque. It was largely based on an admiration for Michelangelo and a consequent exaggeration of the emphasis of his composition and the expressive distortion of his figures.

Mannheim, Karl (1893–1947) Hungarian sociologist who settled in the UK in 1933. In *Ideology and Utopia* (1929) he argued that all knowledge, except in mathematics and physics, is ideological, a reflection of class interests and values; that there is therefore no such thing as objective knowledge or absolute truth.

Manning, Olivia Mary (1908–1980) English novelist. Among her books are the semi-autobiographical series set during World War II. These include *The Great Fortune* (1960), *The Spoilt City* (1962), and *Friends and Heroes* (1965), forming the 'Balkan trilogy', and a later 'Levant trilogy'.

manometer instrument for measuring the pressure of liquids (including human blood pressure) or gases. In its basic form, it is a U-tube partly filled with coloured liquid. Greater pressure on the liquid surface in one arm will force the level of the liquid in the other arm to rise. A difference between the pressures in the two arms is therefore registered as a difference in the heights of the liquid in the arms.

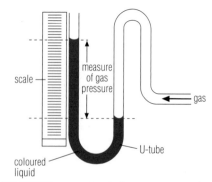

MANOMETER The manometer indicates gas pressure by the rise of liquid in the tube.

manor basic economic unit in ▷feudalism in Europe, established in England under the Norman conquest. It consisted of the lord's house and cultivated land, land rented by free tenants, land held by villagers, common land, woodland, and waste land.

Man Ray US photographer, painter, and sculptor; see Man ▷Ray.

Mansfield industrial town in Nottinghamshire, England, on the River Maun, 22 km/14 mi north of Nottingham; population (1991) 71,900. It is a retail centre for the area. The most important industries are brewing and light engineering, especially the production of car components, while minor industries include quarrying, moulding sand and sand lime bricks, and the manufacture of coal tar products.

Mansfield, Katherine (1888–1923) Pen-name of Kathleen Beauchamp. New Zealand writer. She lived most of her life in England. Her delicate artistry emerges not only in her volumes of short stories – such as *In a German Pension* (1911), *Bliss* (1920), and *The Garden Party* (1923) – but also in her 'Letters' and *Journal*. She developed the technique of the short story much in the same way as James Joyce and Virginia Woolf developed the novel: in particular she recognized that fiction survives if it recreates life, and she was a pioneer of the central character as narrator.

Born near Wellington, New Zealand, she was educated in London. She returned to London after a two-year visit home, where she published her earliest stories. She married the critic John Middleton Murry in 1913.

manslaughter in English law, the unlawful killing of a human being in circumstances less culpable than murder – for example, when the killer suffers extreme provocation, is in some way mentally ill (diminished responsibility), did not intend to kill but did so accidentally in the course of another crime or by behaving with criminal recklessness, or is the survivor of a genuine suicide pact that involved killing the other person.

Mansur (lived *c.* 1700) Mogul painter. He started work at the court of ▷Akbar, contributing several miniatures to the *Akbar-nama*, and later painted court scenes and portraits at the court of ▷Jahangir. He is best known for his animal paintings, which combine close observation and highly decorative stylization.

manta another name for the ▷devil ray, a large fish.

Mantegna, Andrea (*c.* 1431–1506) Italian painter and engraver. He painted religious and mythological subjects, his works noted for their *all'antica* style taking elements from Roman antique architecture and sculpture, and for their innovative use of perspective.

ANDREA MANTEGNA *The Duke's Grooms*, from the fresco of the *Family of Ludovico Gonzaga*, by Italian painter and engraver Andrea Mantegna, in the Camera degli Sposi in the Ducal Palace, Mantua, Italy. *The Art Archive/British Museum/Eileen Tweedy*

Mantel, Hilary (1952–) English writer. She lived in Botswana for five years from 1977, and then in Saudi Arabia for three years. Her writing covers a varied subject matter from historical fiction tales to true-to-life tales from both modern Saudi Arabia (as in *Eight Months on Ghazzah Street* (1988)) and Africa (as in *A Change of Climate* (1994)).

mantis any of a group of carnivorou insects related to cockroaches. There are about 2,000 species of mantis,

MAORI Traditional ceremonies remain an important part of Maori culture. The *marae*, or meeting house, is still the main focus of the Maori community. Visitors are welcomed with a strict formal protocol and traditional welcome, which includes the *haka* (challenge) and a *hongi* (pressing of noses). This Maori meeting house is on the Otago Peninsula, New Zealand. *Image Bank*

mainly tropical; some can reach a length of 20 cm/8 in. (Family Mantidae, order Dictyoptera.)

Mantises are often called 'praying mantises' because of the way they hold their front legs, adapted for grasping prey, when at rest. The eggs are laid in September and hatch early the following summer.

Related Web site: Praying Mantis
http://www.insect-world.com

mantissa in mathematics, the decimal part of a ▷logarithm. For example, the logarithm of 347.6 is 2.5411; in this case, the 0.5411 is the mantissa, and the integral (whole number) part of the logarithm, the 2, is the characteristic.

mantle intermediate zone of the Earth between the ▷crust and the ▷core, accounting for 82% of Earth's volume. The boundary between the mantle and the crust above is the ▷Mohorovičić discontinuity, located at an average depth of 32 km/20 mi. The lower boundary with the core is the Gutenburg discontinuity at an average depth of 2,900 km/1813 mi.

mantra in Hindu or Buddhist belief, a word repeatedly intoned to assist concentration and develop spiritual power; for example, *om*, which represents the names of Brahma, Vishnu, and Siva. Followers of a guru may receive their own individual mantra.

Mantua (Italian **Mantova**) capital of Mantua province, Lombardy, Italy, on an island in a lagoon of the River Mincio, southwest of Verona; population (1990) 54,200. It is the market and service centre of a prosperous agricultural region. Industries include petrochemicals, engineering, plastics, brewing, and printing. The town, which dates from Etruscan times, has Gothic palaces and a cathedral founded in the 10th century. The Roman poet Virgil was born nearby in 70 BC.

Manu in Hindu mythology, the founder of the human race, who was saved by ▷Brahma from a deluge.

manufacturing base share of the total output in a country's economy contributed by the manufacturing sector. This sector has greater potential for productivity growth than the service sector, which is labour-intensive; in manufacturing, productivity can be increased by replacing workers with technically advanced capital equipment. It is also significant because of its contribution to exports.

manumission in medieval England, the act of freeing a villein or serf from his or her bondage. The process took place in a county court and freedom could either be bought or granted as a reward for services rendered. The term was used in the USA when slaves were freed.

Manx Gaelic ▷Gaelic language of the Isle of Man.

Maoism form of communism based on the ideas and teachings of the Chinese communist leader ▷Mao Zedong. It involves an

> ## Mao Zedong
> *Letting a hundred flowers blossom and a hundred schools of thought contend is the policy for promoting progress in the arts and the sciences and a flourishing socialist culture in our land.*
>
> Speech, Beijing, 27 February 1957

adaptation of ▷Marxism to suit conditions in China and apportions a much greater role to agriculture and the peasantry in the building of socialism, thus effectively bypassing the capitalist (industrial) stage envisaged by Marx. In addition, Maoism stresses ideological, as well as economic, transformation, based on regular contact between party members and the general population.

Maori (New Zealand *Maui* 'native' or 'indigenous') member of the Polynesian people of ▷New Zealand. They number 435,000, about 15% of the total population, and around 89% live in the North Island. Maori civilization had particular strengths in warfare, cultivation, navigation, and wood- and stonework. Speechmaking and oral history, as well as woodcarving, were the main cultural repositories before the European introduction of writing, and Maori mythology and cosmology were highly developed. Their language, Maori, belongs to the eastern branch of the Austronesian family. The Maori Language Act 1987 recognized Maori as an official language of New Zealand.

Mao Tse-tung alternative transcription of ▷Mao Zedong.

Mao Zedong (or Mao Tse-tung) (1893–1976) Chinese communist politician and theoretician, leader of the Chinese Communist Party (CCP) 1935–76. Mao was a founder of the CCP in 1921, and became its leader in 1935. He organized the ▷Long March 1934–35 and the war of liberation 1937–49, following which he established a People's Republic and communist rule in China. He was state president until 1959, and headed the CCP until his death. His influence diminished with the failure of his 1958–60 ▷Great Leap Forward, but he emerged dominant again during the 1966–69 ▷Cultural Revolution, which he launched in order to promote his own anti-bureaucratic line and to purge the party of 'revisionism'.

MAO ZEDONG Chairman Mao Zedong was one of the founders of the Chinese Communist Party and the leader of the People's Republic of China from 1949 until his death in 1976. *Archive Photos*

MANTIS The praying mantis is a superbly designed predator. It waits motionless or slightly swaying as if in a breeze until prey appears. Many species are effectively camouflaged to look like dead leaves.

Mao adapted communism to Chinese conditions, as set out in the *Little Red Book* (1960), in which he stressed the need for rural rather than urban-based revolutions in Asia; for reducing rural–urban differences; and for perpetual revolution to prevent the emergence of new elites. He advocated a 'mass line' form of leadership, involving the broad mobilization of the people in economic, social, and political movements. He was also an advocate of a non-aligned Third World strategy, and helped to precipitate the Sino-Soviet split of 1960, which arose when the USSR withdrew military and technical support from China. His writings and thoughts dominated the functioning of the People's Republic 1949–76, and some 740 million copies of his *Quotations* have been printed to date, while his works as a whole total over 2,000 publications.

Related Web site: Mao Zedong http://www.pathfinder.com/time/time100/leaders/profile/mao.html

map diagrammatic representation of an area – for example, part of the Earth's surface or the distribution of the stars. Modern maps of the Earth are made using satellites in low orbit to take a series of overlapping stereoscopic photographs from which a three-dimensional image can be prepared. The earliest accurate large-scale maps appeared about 1580 (see ▷atlas).

Conventional aerial photography, laser beams, microwaves, and infrared equipment are also used for land surveying. Many different kinds of ▷map projection (the means by which a three-dimensional body is shown in two dimensions) are used in map-making. Detailed maps requiring constant updating are kept in digital form on computer so that minor revisions can be made without redrafting.

The ▷Ordnance Survey is the official body responsible for the mapping of Britain; it produces maps in a variety of scales, such as the Landranger series (scale 1:50,000). Large-scale maps – for example, 1:25,000 – show greater detail at a local level than small-scale maps; for example, 1:100,000.

Related Web site: Great Globe Gallery http://hum.amu.edu.pl/~zbzw/glob/glob1.htm

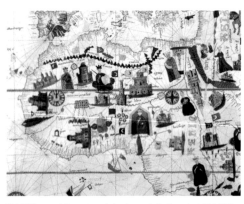

MAP The world map made by Juan de la Cosa in 1500. This section shows the Mediterranean and North Africa, and demonstrates the increasing accuracy with which cartographers were able to depict the coastlines of Europe and the known shores of Africa. *The Art Archive/Naval Museum Genoa*

maple any of a group of deciduous trees with lobed leaves and green flowers, followed by two-winged fruits, or samaras. There are over 200 species, chiefly in northern temperate regions. (Genus *Acer*, family Aceraceae.)

Mapplethorpe, Robert (1946–1989) US art photographer. He was known for his use of racial and homo-erotic imagery in chiefly fine platinum prints. He developed a style of polished elegance in his gallery art works, whose often culturally forbidden subject matter caused controversy.

map projection way of showing the Earth's spherical surface on a flat piece of paper. The most common approach has been to redraw the Earth's surface within a rectangular boundary. The main weakness of this is that countries in high latitudes are shown disproportionately large. The most famous cylindrical projection is the ▷Mercator projection, which dates from 1569. Although it gives an exaggerated view of the size of northern continents, it is the best map for navigation as a constant bearing appears as a straight line.

In 1973 German historian Arno Peters devised the **Peters projection** in which the countries of the world retain their relative areas. In other projections, lines of longitude and latitude appear distorted, or the Earth's surface is shown as a series of segments joined along the Equator. In 1992 the US physicist Mitchell

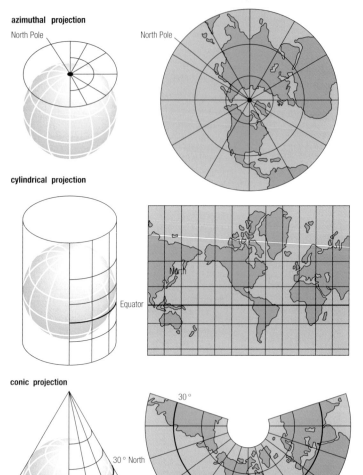

azimuthal projection
North Pole
North Pole

cylindrical projection
North
Equator

conic projection
30°
30° North

MAP PROJECTION The diagrams show three widely used map projections. If a light were placed at the centre of a transparent Earth, the shapes of the countries would be thrown as shadows on a sheet of paper. If the paper is flat, the azimuthal projection results; if it is wrapped around a cylinder or in the form of a cone, the cylindrical or conic projections result.

Feigenbaum devised the **optimal conformal** projection, using a computer program designed to take data about the boundary of a given area and calculate the projection that produces the minimum of inaccuracies.

Maputo (formerly **Lourenço Marques** (until 1975)) capital of ▷Mozambique, and Africa's second-largest port, on Delagoa Bay; population (1993 est) 2,000,000. Linked by road and rail with

MAPLE Maples are typically deciduous; with lobed leaves and winged fruit, or keys. They grow throughout the north temperate regions of the world. The leaves are often strikingly coloured in the autumn.

Zimbabwe, Swaziland, and South Africa, it is a major outlet for minerals, steel, textiles, processed foods, and furniture.

Maquis French ▷resistance movement that fought against the German occupation during World War II.

maquis general term for a large evergreen type of vegetation common in many Mediterranean countries, consisting of scrub woodland with many low-growing tangled bushes and shrubs, typically including species of broom, gorse, and heather.

marabou African stork, about 120 cm/4 ft tall, with a bald head, long heavy bill, black back and wings and white underparts, and an inflatable throat pouch. It eats snakes, lizards, insects, and carrion. The bald head avoids blood clogging the plumage when the stork feeds on carcasses left by predators such as lions. (Species *Leptoptilos crumeniferus*, family Ciconiidae, order Ciconiiformes.)

Marat, Jean Paul (1743–179) Swiss-born French Revolutionary leader, physician, and journalist. He was elected to the National Convention in 1792, where, as leader of the radical Montagnard faction, he carried on a long struggle with the right-wing ▷Girondins, which resulted in their overthrow in May 1793. In July he was murdered in his bath by Charlotte Corday, a Girondin supporter.

Marat was born in Boudry, Neuchâtel, in Switzerland. After studying medicine in Bordeaux, France, he lived in the Netherlands and practised as a doctor in England. During the Revolution, he founded the radical paper *L'Ami du Peuple* and also edited *Le Journal de la République française*. Marat was a fervent anti-royalist, and led demands for the execution of the king.

Maratha (or **Mahratta**) member of a people living mainly in Maharashtra, western India. There are about 40 million speakers of Marathi, a language belonging to the Indo-European family. The Marathas are mostly farmers, and practise Hinduism. In the 17th and 18th centuries the Marathas formed a powerful military confederacy in rivalry with the Mogul emperors. The latter's Afghan allies defeated the Marathas at Panipat in 1761, and, after a series of wars with the British 1779–1871, most of their territory was annexed. During the ▷Indian Mutiny and the rise of the movement of independence, the Marathas became a symbol of Hindu revival.

MARABOU With its naked head, inflatable throat pouch, and large bill, the marabou, one of the world's largest storks, is easily recognized. *Premaphotos Wildlife*

JEAN PAUL MARAT A violent leader of the French Revolution, from the earliest days of the Revolution, Jean Paul Marat demanded the death penalty for all supporters of the monarchy, and his views encouraged violence in the streets of Paris, France, in 1792. *Archive Photos*

marathon athletics endurance race over 42.195 km/26 mi 385 yd. It was first included in the Olympic Games in Athens in 1896. The distance varied until it was standardized in 1924. More recently, races have been opened to wider participation, including social runners as well as those competing at senior level.
> **Related Web site: Marathon** http://www.iaaf.org/TrainingTips/Sport/Mar/intro.html

Marathon, Battle of battle fought in September 490 BC at the start of the Persian Wars in which the Athenians and their allies from Plataea resoundingly defeated the Persian king Darius' invasion force. Fought on the Plain of Marathon about 40 km/25 mi northeast of Athens, it is one of the most famous battles of antiquity.

Marbella port and tourist resort in the province of Málaga in Andalusia, southern Spain, on the Costa del Sol between Málaga and Algeciras; population (2003 est) 103,400. There are three bullrings, a Moorish castle, and the remains of a medieval defensive wall.

marble rock formed by metamorphosis of sedimentary ▷limestone. It takes and retains a good polish, and is used in building and sculpture. In its pure form it is white and consists almost entirely of calcite $CaCO_3$. Mineral impurities give it various colours and patterns. Carrara, Italy, is known for white marble.

Marble Arch triumphal arch in London in the style of the Arch of Constantine. It was designed by John ▷Nash and John Flaxman (1755–1826) in 1828 to commemorate Nelson's and Wellington's victories, and was originally intended as a ceremonial entry to ▷Buckingham Palace. In 1851, after the completion of Buckingham Palace, it was moved by Edward Blore to the northeast corner of Hyde Park at the end of Oxford Street.

Marc, Franz (1880–1916) German expressionist painter. He was associated with Wassily Kandinsky in founding the ▷*Blaue Reiter* movement. Animals played an essential part in his view of the world, and bold semi-abstracts of red and blue animals, particularly horses, are characteristic of his work.

He studied at Munich, and after travel to Italy and Paris was influenced by post-Impressionist art, applying its lessons of colour and design to animal painting and in particular a series of horses. Acquaintance with Kandinsky and Macke in 1910 led to his adopting their free use of brilliant colour, and in 1912 a meeting with Delaunay in Paris added a cubist influence, as in his *Roes in the Wood* (1913–14; Karlsruhe). His animals were subjective and symbolic creations rather than studies of nature and in this sense he was an expressionist. The trend of his development, cut short by war, was towards abstraction.

Marceau, Marcel (1923–) French mime artist. He is the creator of the clown-harlequin Bip and mime sequences such as 'Youth, Maturity, Old Age, and Death'.

Marches boundary areas of England with Wales, and England with Scotland. For several centuries from the time of William the Conqueror, these troubled frontier regions were held by lords of the Marches, those on the Welsh frontier called Marcher Lords, sometimes called *marchiones*, and those on the Scottish border known as earls of March. The first Marcher Lord was Roger de Mortimer (about 1286–1330); the first earl of March, Patrick Dunbar (died in 1285).

March on Rome, the means by which fascist leader Benito Mussolini came to power in Italy in 1922. A protracted crisis in government and the threat of civil war enabled him to demand the formation of a fascist government to restore order. On 29 October 1922, King Victor Emmanuel III invited Mussolini to come to Rome to take power. The 'march' was a propaganda myth: Mussolini travelled overnight by train from Milan to Rome, where he formed a government the following day, 30 October. Some 25,000 fascist Blackshirts were also transported to the city, where they marched in a ceremonial parade on 31 October.

Marcian (396–457) Eastern Roman emperor 450–457. He was a general who married Pulcheria, sister of Theodosius II; he became emperor on Theodosius' death. He convened the Council of ▷Chalcedon (the fourth Ecumenical Council of the Christian Church) in 451 and refused to pay tribute to Attila the Hun.

Marconi, Guglielmo (1874–1937) Italian electrical engineer and pioneer in the invention and development of radio. In 1895 he achieved radio communication over more than a mile, and in England in 1896 he conducted successful experiments that led to the formation of the company that became Marconi's Wireless Telegraph Company Ltd. He shared the Nobel Prize for Physics in 1909 for the development of wireless telegraphy.

After reading about radio waves, Marconi built a device to convert them into electrical signals. He then tried to transmit and receive radio waves over increasing distances. In 1898 he successfully transmitted signals across the English Channel, and in 1901 established communication with St John's, Newfoundland, from Poldhu in Cornwall, and in 1918 with Australia.

Marconi was an Italian delegate to the Versailles peace conference in 1919 after World War I.
> **Related Web site: Biography of G Marconi** http://www.nobel.se/physics/laureates/1909/marconi-bio.html

> ### Marcel Marceau
> *I have spent more than half a lifetime trying to express the tragic moment.*
> The Guardian, August 1988

> ### Zoe Koplowitz
> Multiple sclerosis sufferer who completed the 1999 London Marathon in 30 hours 10 minutes
> *I've always believed that the race belongs not only to the swift, but also to those who keep on running.*
> Daily Telegraph, 20 April 1999

MARBLE The floor of one of the many marble quarries at Carrara, Italy. *Image Bank*

Marco Polo Venetian traveller and writer; see Marco ▷Polo.

Marcos, Ferdinand Edralin (1917–1989) Filipino right-wing politician, dictator-president 1965–86, when he was forced into exile in Hawaii by a popular front led by Corazon ▷Aquino.

Born in Sarrat, Marcos was convicted, while a law student in 1939, of murdering a political opponent of his father, but eventually secured his own acquittal. His claim that during World War II he was a guerrilla fighter against the Japanese invaders was subsequently discredited. He worked as a special assistant to President Roxas during the 1940s and was a member of the house of representatives 1949–59 and senate 1959–61, representing the Liberal Party until 1964, before becoming president in 1965. He was elected as the candidate of the right-wing Nationalist Party, defeating Diosdado Macapagal.

During his first term, Marcos launched military campaigns against communist insurgents and Muslim rebels on Mindanao, and made a reputation as a reformer. He was re-elected in 1969, but, with civil strife increasing, declared martial law in 1972. The Marcos regime became increasingly repressive, with secret pro-Marcos groups terrorizing, arresting, and executing opponents and press censorship being imposed. The new 1973 constitution made Marcos a virtual dictator. With corruption, nepotism, and electoral fraud rife, Marcos was finally overthrown and exiled in February 1986, following a nonviolent 'people's power' movement, led by Corazon Aquino, the widow of a murdered opposition leader, which obtained international and army support. Marcos was backed by the USA when in power, but in 1988 US authorities indicted him and his wife, Imelda ▷Marcos, for racketeering and embezzlement.

GUGLIELMO MARCONI The Italian wireless pioneer Guglielmo Marconi beside the telegraph on board his yacht *Elettra* in the early 1930s. *Archive Photos*

Marcos, Imelda Romualdez (1930–) Filipino politician and socialite, wife of the dictator-president Ferdinand ▷Marcos, and known as the 'Iron Butterfly'.

Born into poverty, Imelda began her career as a singer and, with her striking looks, won the title of Miss Manila in 1953. A year later, she married Ferdinand Marcos, who was then a member of the Philippines House of Representatives. When he was elected president in 1965, she became an unusually politically active first lady. She took a leading role in prestige cultural projects and served as governor of the National Capital Region, from 1975, and as minister of human settlements and ecology, from 1978. Her influence increased during the 1980s, as her husband's health deteriorated, but she became accused of using her public position improperly to amass private wealth. Following her husband's overthrow as president in February 1986, the Marcos' lived in exile and her enormous collection of shoes, clothes, and art was put on display in the Malacanang Palace.

After her husband's death in 1989, Imelda Marcos stood trial in New York in answer to charges of concealing ownership of US property and other goods, purchased with stolen Philippine-government funds. She was acquitted, her lawyer claiming the responsibility had lain solely with her husband. In 1991, the government of the Philippines lifted its ban on Imelda Marcos returning to her homeland in the hope of recouping an estimated $350 million from frozen Marcos accounts in Swiss banks. She returned to Manila in November 1991 and was an unsuccessful candidate in the 1992 presidential elections. In 1993 she was convicted of corruption and sentenced to 18–24 years imprisonment, but remained free on bail pending an appeal. This succeeded, in October 1998.

Marcus Aurelius (AD 121–180) Adopted name of Marcus Annius Verus. Roman emperor from 161 and Stoic philosopher who wrote the philosophical *Meditations*. He fought a series of campaigns against the Germanic tribes on the Rhine–Danube frontier, known collectively as the Marcomannic Wars, and died in Pannonia where he had gone to drive back the invading Marcomanni.

Related Web site: Works by Marcus Aurelius Antoninus http://classics.mit.edu/Browse/browse-Antoninus.html

Marcuse, Herbert (1898–1979) German-born US political philosopher. His theories combining Marxism and Freudianism influenced radical thought in the 1960s and 1970s. He preached the overthrow of the existing social order by using the system's very tolerance to ensure its defeat; he was not an advocate of violent revolution.

Mardonius Persian general who in 492 BC took command of Ionia in western Asia Minor, following the Ionian Revolt. He eased local unrest by replacing tyrants with democracy. The nephew and son-in-law of ▷Darius I, he acted as a leading counsellor and general for Xerxes in the second invasion of Greece in 480 BC. He stayed with the army after its defeat by the Greeks at Salamis, and was killed at the Battle of Plataea.

Marengo, Battle of during the Napoleonic Wars, defeat of the Austrians on 14 June 1800 by the French army under Napoleon Bonaparte, as part of his Italian campaign, near the village of Marengo in Piedmont, Italy. It was one of Napoleon's greatest victories which resulted in the Austrians ceding northern Italy to France.

Margaret, St (c. 1045–1093) Queen of Scotland, the granddaughter of King Edmund Ironside of England. She went to Scotland after the Norman Conquest, and soon after married Malcolm III. The marriage of her daughter Matilda to Henry I united the Norman and English royal houses.

Margaret of Anjou (1430–1482) Queen of England from 1445, wife of ▷Henry VI of England. After the outbreak of the Wars of the ▷Roses in 1455, she acted as the leader of the Lancastrians, but was defeated and captured at the battle of Tewkesbury in 1471 by Edward IV.

Margaret, Rose (1930–2002) Princess of the UK, younger daughter of George VI and sister of Elizabeth II. In 1960 she married Anthony Armstrong-Jones, later created Lord Snowdon, but they were divorced in 1978. Their children are David, Viscount Linley (1961–) and Lady Sarah Chatto (1964–).

margay small wild cat living in forested areas from the southern USA to South America, where it hunts birds and small mammals. It is about 60 cm/2 ft long with a 40 cm/1.3 ft tail, and has a rounded head and yellowish-brown fur marked with black spots and blotches. (Species *Felis wiedi*, family Felidae.)

marginal cost pricing in economics, the setting of a price based on the additional cost to a firm of producing one more unit of output (the marginal cost), rather than the actual average cost per unit (total production costs divided by the total number of units produced). In this way, the price of an item is kept to a minimum, reflecting only the extra cost of labour and materials.

marginal theory in economics, the study of the effect of increasing a factor by one more unit (known as the marginal unit). For example, if a firm's production is increased by one unit, its costs will increase also; the increase in costs is called the marginal cost of production. Marginal theory is a central tool of microeconomics.

marginal utility in economics, the measure of additional satisfaction (utility) gained by a consumer who receives one additional unit of a product or service. The concept is used to explain why consumers buy more of a product when the price falls.

margrave German title (equivalent of marquess) for the 'counts of the march', who guarded the frontier regions of the Holy Roman Empire from Charlemagne's time. Later the title was used by other territorial princes. Chief among these were the margraves of Austria and of Brandenburg.

Margrethe II (1940–) Queen of Denmark from 1972, when she succeeded her father Frederick IX. In 1967, she married the French diplomat Count Henri de Laborde de Monpezat, who took the title Prince Hendrik. Her heir is Crown Prince Frederick (1968–).

marguerite European plant belonging to the daisy family. It is a shrubby perennial with white daisylike flowers. Marguerite is also the name of a cultivated variety of ▷chrysanthemum. (*Leucanthemum vulgare*, family Compositae.)

Marguerite of Navarre (1492–1549) Also known as **Margaret d'Angoulême**. Queen of Navarre from 1527, French poet, and author of the 'Heptaméron' (1558), a collection of stories in imitation of Boccaccio's 'Decameron'. The sister of Francis I of France, she was born in Angoulême. Her second husband (1527) was Henri d'Albret, King of Navarre.

Mariana Islands (or Marianas) archipelago in the northwest Pacific, east of the Philippines, divided politically into ▷Guam (an unincorporated territory of the USA) and the ▷Northern Mariana Islands (a commonwealth of the USA with its own internal government).

Mariana Trench lowest region on the Earth's surface; the deepest part of the sea floor. The trench is 2,400 km/1,500 mi long and is situated 300 km/200 mi east of the Mariana Islands, in the northwestern Pacific Ocean. Its deepest part is the gorge known as the Challenger Deep, which extends 11,034 m/36,210 ft below sea level.

Maria Theresa (1717–1780) Empress of Austria from 1740, when she succeeded her father, the Holy Roman Emperor Charles VI; her claim to the throne was challenged and she became embroiled, first in the War of the ▷Austrian Succession 1740–48, then in the ▷Seven Years' War 1756–63; she remained in possession of Austria but lost Silesia. The rest of her reign was peaceful and, with her son Joseph II, she introduced social reforms.

Marie Antoinette (1755–1793) Queen of France from 1774. She was the fourth daughter of Empress Maria Theresa of Austria and the Holy Roman Emperor Francis I, and married ▷Louis XVI of France in 1770. Her devotion to the interests of Austria, reputation for extravagance, and supposed connection with the scandal of the Diamond Necklace made her unpopular, and helped to provoke the ▷French Revolution of 1789. She was tried for treason in October 1793 and guillotined.

Marie Antoinette influenced her husband to resist concessions in the early days of the Revolution – for example, ▷Mirabeau's plan

MARIGOLD The corn marigold *Chrysanthemum segetum* is found widely in Europe and Asia, but less frequently in the British Isles, usually on sandy soils. *Premaphotos Wildlife*

for a constitutional settlement. She instigated the disastrous flight to Varennes, which discredited the monarchy, and sought foreign intervention against the Revolution, betraying French war strategy to the Austrians in 1792.

Related Web site: Life of Marie Antoinette http://www.geocities.com/Athens/Aegean/7545/MarieAntoinette.html

Marie de' Medici (1573–1642) Queen of France, wife of Henry IV from 1600, and regent (after his murder) for their son Louis XIII. She left the government to her favourites, the Concinis, until Louis XIII seized power and executed them in 1617. She was banished but, after she led a revolt in 1619, ▷Richelieu effected her reconciliation with her son. When she attempted to oust him again in 1630, she was exiled.

Mari El (or Mariy El) autonomous republic of the Russian Federation; area 23,200 sq km/8,950 sq mi; population (1990) 754,000 (47% Russian, 43% ethnic Mari). The capital is Yoshkar-Ola. The Volga flows through the middle of the republic, 60% of which is forested. It lies west of the Ural Mountains. Industries include timber, paper, grain, flax, potatoes, fruit; metalworking, food processing, machine tool production, and the manufacture of artificial leather.

marigold any of several plants belonging to the daisy family, including pot marigold (*C. officinalis*) and the tropical American *T. patula*, commonly known as French marigold. (Genera *Calendula* and *Tagetes*, family Compositae.)

marijuana dried leaves and flowers of the hemp plant ▷cannabis, used as a drug; it is illegal in most countries. It is eaten or inhaled and causes euphoria, distortion of time, and heightened sensations of sight and sound. Mexico is the world's largest producer.

A report released in March 1999 by the Institute of Medicine in the USA said that marijuana should have clinical tests because it helps fight pain and nausea. A US study involving 3,882 people who had survived heart attacks revealed that smoking marijuana may increase the risk of a heart attack, by as much as five times for an hour after smoking. The risk may increase because marijuana increases the heart rate by about 40 beats a minute. On 29 January 2004, cannabis was reclassified from a Class B to a Class C drug in the UK. Production, supply and possession remain illegal, but the maximum sentence for posession has been reduced from 5 to 2 years imprisonment.

marimba musical instrument, a bass ▷xylophone, a Mexican variant of an instrument originating in Africa, with wooden rather than metal tubular resonators.

Mariner spacecraft series of US space probes that explored the planets Mercury, Venus, and Mars 1962–75.

marines fighting force that operates both on land and at sea. The **US Marine Corps** (1775) is constituted as an arm of the US Navy. It is made up of infantry and air support units trained and equipped for amphibious landings under fire.

Marinetti, (Emilio) Filippo Tommaso (1876–1944) Italian author. In 1909 he published *Manifesto del Futurismo*, the first manifesto of ▷Futurism, exhorting the youth of Italy to break with tradition in art, poetry, and the novel and face the challenges of a new machine age. He illustrated his theories in *Mafarka le futuriste: Roman africaine/Mafarka the Futurist: African Novel* (1909). His best-known work is the *Manifesto technico della letteratura futuristica/Technical Manifesto of Futurist Literature* (1912; translated 1971). He also wrote plays, a volume on theatrical

> **Marcus Aurelius**
> *Men exist for the sake of one another. Either teach them or bear with them.*
> Meditations

> **Marie Antoinette**
> *Courage! I have shown it for years. Do you think I shall lose it at the moment when my sufferings are to end?*
> Remark as she was taken to the guillotine, October 1793. Attributed

MARIE ANTIONETTE As the indulged 18-year-old daughter of the Holy Roman Emperor Francis I, Marie Antoinette was totally unfit to take the throne as queen of France in 1774. Her heedless extravagance and lack of perception have been blamed for helping to cause the French Revolution. *Archive Photos*

practice (1916), and a volume of poems *Guerra sola igiene del mondo/War the Only Hygiene of the World* (1915).

marionette type of ▷puppet, a jointed figure controlled from above by wires or strings. Intricately crafted marionettes were used in Burma (now Myanmar) and Ceylon (now Sri Lanka) and later at the courts of Italian princes in the 16th–18th centuries.

maritime law that part of the law dealing with the sea: in particular, fishing areas, ships, and navigation. Seas are divided into **internal waters** governed by a state's internal laws (such as harbours, inlets); ▷territorial waters (the area of sea adjoining the coast over which a state claims rights); the **continental shelf** (the seabed and subsoil that the coastal state is entitled to exploit beyond the territorial waters); and the **high seas**, where international law applies.

Marius, Gaius (*c.* 157–86 BC) Roman general and politician. He was elected consul seven times, the first time in 107 BC. He defeated the Cimbri and the Teutons (Germanic tribes attacking Gaul and Italy) 102–101 BC. Marius tried to deprive Sulla of the command in the east against ▷Mithridates and, as a result, civil war broke out in 88 BC. Sulla marched on Rome, and Marius fled to Africa, but later returned and created a reign of terror in Rome.

Marivaux, Pierre Carlet de Chamblain de (1688–1763) French novelist and dramatist. His sophisticated comedies deal primarily with love and include *Le Jeu de l'amour et du hasard/The Game of Love and Chance* (1730) and *Les Fausses Confidences/False Confidences* (1737). He wrote two novels: *La Vie de Marianne/The Life of Marianne* (1731–41), the study of a young girl written with much psychological insight, which has autobiographical elements; and *Le Paysan parvenu/The Fortunate Villager* (1735–36), which gives a broader picture of French society. Both were left incomplete.

Marivaux was a master of brilliant dialogue, full of veiled avowals and subtle indications, and he gave the word *marivaudage* (oversubtle lovers' conversation) to the French language.

marjoram aromatic herb belonging to the mint family. Wild marjoram (*O. vulgare*) is found in both Europe and Asia and has become naturalized in the Americas; the sweet marjoram (*O. majorana*) used in cooking is widely cultivated. (Genus *Origanum* or *Marjorana*, family Labiatae.)

Mark in Celtic legend, king of Cornwall, uncle of ▷Tristan, and suitor and husband of ▷Isolde.

Mark, St (lived 1st century AD) In the New Testament, Christian apostle and evangelist whose name is given to the second Gospel. It was probably written AD 65–70, and used by the authors of the first and third Gospels. He is the patron saint of Venice, and his emblem is a winged lion. His feast day is 25 April.

Mark Antony (*c.* 83–30 BC) (Latin **Marcus Antonius**) Roman politician and soldier who was the last serious rival to Octavian's (later Augustus) domination of the Roman world. He served under Julius ▷Caesar in Gaul and during the civil war when he commanded the left wing at the final battle of Pharsalus. He was consul with Caesar in 44 when he tried to secure for him the title of king. After Caesar's assassination, he formed the Second Triumvirate with Octavian and Lepidus. In 42 he defeated Brutus and Cassius at Philippi. He took Egypt as his share of the empire and formed a liaison with the Egyptian queen Cleopatra, but returned to Rome in 40 to marry Octavia, the sister of Octavian. In 32 the Senate declared war on Cleopatra, and Antony, who had combined forces with Cleopatra, was defeated by Octavian at the Battle of Actium in 31. He returned to Egypt and committed suicide.

market capitalization market value of a company, based on the market price of all its issued securities – a price that would be unlikely to apply, however, if a bid were actually made for control of them.

market forces in economics, the forces of demand (a want backed by the ability to pay) and supply (the willingness and ability to supply).

marketing promoting goods and services to consumers. In the 20th century, marketing has played an increasingly larger role in determining company policy, influencing product development, pricing, methods of distribution, advertising, and promotion techniques.

marketing mix the factors that help a firm to sell its products. Four elements – the **four Ps** – are normally distinguished: getting the right **product** to the market, at the right **price**; ensuring that the **promotion** in terms of advertising and marketing for the product is right; and ensuring that the product is distributed to the most convenient **place** for customers to buy it.

market research process of gaining information about customers in a market through field research or desk research. **Field research** involves collecting **primary data** by interviewing customers or completing questionnaires. **Desk research** involves collecting **secondary data** by looking at information and statistics collected by others and published, for example, by the government.

Markievicz, Constance Georgina, Countess Markievicz (1868–1927) Born Constance Georgina Gore Booth. Irish socialist, revolutionary, and politician. Founder of Na Fianna, the republican youth organization, in 1909, she joined the Irish Citizen Army and took part in the ▷Easter Rising of 1916; her resulting death sentence was commuted. In 1918 she was elected to Westminster as a Sinn Fein candidate (technically the first British woman MP), but did not take her seat, instead serving as minister for labour in the first Dáil Éireann (then the illegal republican parliament) 1919–22.

Markova, Alicia (1910–) Adopted name of Lilian Alicia Marks. English ballet dancer. She danced with ▷Diaghilev's company 1925–29, was the first resident ballerina of the Vic-Wells Ballet 1933–35, partnered Anton ▷Dolin in their own Markova–Dolin Ballet Company 1935–38, and danced with the Ballets Russes de Monte Carlo 1938–41, American Ballet Theater 1941–46, and the London Festival Ballet 1950–52. A dancer of delicacy and lightness, she is associated with the great classical ballets such as *Giselle*. She was made a DBE in 1963.

MARJORAM Wild marjoram is a perennial growing up to 70 cm/2 ft 4 in high.

Marks, Simon, 1st Baron Marks of Broughton (1888–1964) English chain-store magnate. His father, Polish immigrant Michael Marks, had started a number of 'penny bazaars' with Yorkshireman Tom Spencer in 1887. Simon Marks entered the business in 1907 and, with his brother-in-law Israel (later Lord) Seiff (1899–1972), he built up a national chain of ▷Marks & Spencer stores.

Marks & Spencer UK chain store. The company was founded in 1884 by **Michael Marks** (1863–1907). In 1894 he was joined by **Thomas Spencer** (1852–1905), cashier at one of his suppliers. Simon ▷Marks, the founder's son, became chairman in 1916 and with his brother-in-law, Israel Sieff, developed the company from a 'Penny Bazaar' to a national and international chain store.

mark sensing in computing, a technique that enables pencil marks made in predetermined positions on specially prepared forms to be rapidly read and input to a computer. The technique makes use of the fact that pencil marks contain graphite and therefore conduct electricity. A **mark sense reader** scans the form by passing small metal brushes over the paper surface. Whenever a brush touches a pencil mark a circuit is completed and the mark is detected.

marl crumbling sedimentary rock, sometimes called **clayey limestone**, including various types of calcareous ▷clays and fine-grained ▷limestones. Marls are often laid down in freshwater lakes and are usually soft, earthy, and of a white, grey, or brownish colour. They are used in cement-making and as fertilizer.

Marlborough House mansion in Pall Mall, London, opposite St James's Palace. It was designed by Christopher ▷Wren for the 1st Duke of Marlborough in 1709–10 as his London home.

Marlborough, John Churchill, 1st Duke of Marlborough (1650–1722) English soldier, created a Duke in 1702 by Queen Anne. He was granted Blenheim Palace in Oxfordshire in recognition of his services, which included defeating the French army outside Vienna in the Battle of Blenheim in 1704, during the War of the ▷Spanish Succession.

In 1688 he deserted his patron, James II, for William of Orange, but in 1692 fell into disfavour for ▷Jacobite intrigue.

He had married Sarah Jennings (1660–1744), confidante of the future Queen Anne, who created him a duke on her accession. He achieved further victories in Belgium at the battles of Ramillies (1706) and Oudenaarde (1708), and in France at Malplaquet in 1709. However, the return of the Tories to power and his wife's quarrel with the queen led to his dismissal in 1711, and his flight to Holland to avoid charges of corruption. He returned in 1714.

Marley, Bob (Robert Nesta) (1945–1981) Jamaican reggae singer and songwriter. A Rastafarian, his songs, many of which were topical and political, popularized reggae worldwide in the 1970s. They include 'Get Up, Stand Up' (1973) and 'No Woman No Cry' (1974); his albums include *Natty Dread* (1975) and *Exodus* (1977).

BOB MARLEY Jamaican reggae singer and songwriter Bob Marley. His style of reggae came to be increasingly influenced by rock and African music. *Archive Photos*

marlin (or **spearfish**) any of several open-sea fishes known as billfishes. Some 2.5 m/7 ft long, they are found in warmer waters and have elongated snouts and high-standing dorsal (back) fins. Members of the family include the **sailfish** (*Istiophorus platypterus*), the fastest of all fishes over short distances – reaching speeds of 100 kph/62 mph – and the **blue marlin** (*Makaira nigricans*), highly prized as a 'game' fish. (Family Istiophoridae, order Perciformes.)

Marlowe, Christopher (1564–1593) English poet and dramatist. His work includes the blank-verse plays *Tamburlaine the Great* in two parts (1587–88), *The Jew of Malta* (about 1591), *Edward II* (about 1592) and *Dr Faustus* (about 1594), the poem *Hero and Leander* (1598), and a translation of parts of ▷Ovid's *Amores*. Marlowe transformed the new medium of English blank verse into a powerful, melodic form of expression.

He was born in Canterbury and educated at Cambridge University, where he is thought to have become a government agent. His life was turbulent, with a brief imprisonment in connection with a man's death in a brawl (of which he was cleared), and a charge of atheism (following statements by the dramatist Thomas ▷Kyd under torture). He was murdered in a Deptford tavern, allegedly in a dispute over the bill, but it may have been a political killing.

Marlowe's work, considered as a whole, is remarkable for its varied, and even conflicting moods. *Hero and Leander* and the early play *Dido, Queen of Carthage* exhibit a sensuous sweetness and charm which is as peculiarly Marlovian as the mighty rhetoric and over-reaching egotism of *Tamburlaine* or *Dr Faustus*. Even within individual plays there are striking and often confusing contrasts: in *The Jew of Malta* Machiavellian heroism stands side by side with farcical melodrama, while in *Dr Faustus* comic slapstick is followed by the thrilling poetry of the hero's final speeches. There has been much critical controversy about Marlowe's true intentions and real merits as a dramatist, but modern audiences continue to be intrigued and provoked by his major plays, and there can be no doubt of his formative influence on his Elizabethan contemporaries, including Shakespeare.

> **Christopher Marlowe**
> *Who ever loved that loved not at first sight?*
> *Hero and Leander* I

Related Web site: Complete Works of Christopher Marlowe
http://www.perseus.tufts.edu/Texts/Marlowe.html

Marmara, Sea of small inland sea separating Turkey in Europe from Turkey in Asia, connected through the Bosporus with the Black Sea, and through the Dardanelles with the Aegean; length 275 km/170 mi, breadth up to 80 km/50 mi. In parts it reaches depths of over 1,200 m/3,936 ft. The chief island is Marmara, on which there are marble quarries.

marmoset any of a group of small tree-dwelling monkeys found in South and Central America; some reach a body length of only

MARMOSET The golden lion tamarin, a member of the marmoset family, is one of three species of tamarin found in the rainforests of southeast Brazil.

15 cm/6 in. Most species have characteristic tufted ears, clawlike nails, and a handsome tail, which is not prehensile (it cannot be used to grip branches in the same way as the arms and legs). Some marmosets are known as tamarins. (Genus *Callithrix* and related genera, family Callithricidae.)

Best-known is the **common marmoset** *C. jacchus* of Brazil, often kept there as a pet. The discovery of a new species of Brazilian marmoset, *C. saterei*, was announced in 1996. The black-capped dwarf marmoset was discovered in Brazil in 1997. Another new species was discovered in Brazil in 1998. It is the world's second smallest monkey and weighs 160 g/5.6 oz with a body length of 15 cm/6 in (excluding tail) and has been named dwarf marmoset *Callithrix humilis*. Two new species of marmoset were discovered in northwestern Brazil in 2000: the Manicore marmoset *Callithrix manicorensis* and the Acari marmoset *C. acariensis*.

marmot any of several large burrowing rodents belonging to the squirrel family. There are about 15 species, distributed throughout Canada and the USA, and from the Alps to the Himalayas. They eat plants and some insects, and live in colonies, make burrows (one to each family), and hibernate in winter (alpine marmots hibernate for six months of the year). In North America they are called **woodchucks** or **groundhogs**. (Genus *Marmota*, family Sciuridae.)

The rarest marmot is the Vancouver Island marmot which is found only in a limited area on Vancouver Island. The marmots are threatened by logging, and fewer than 100 remain.

The alpine marmot *M. marmota* is the typical marmot of the Central European Alps. Adults weigh up to 5.70 kg/12.6 lb and live in family groups of up to 20. Only the territorial (dominant) female reproduces. The other females may become pregnant as the dominant female does not prevent them mating, but she subsequently fights them repeatedly and interferes with feeding until they are so stressed they abort or the embryo is reabsorbed, according to German and Austrian ecologists in 1999. The litter usually consists of four pups.

Marne river in France which rises in the plateau of Langres and joins the Seine at Charenton near Paris; length 525 km/326 mi. It gives its name to the *départements* of Marne, Haute-Marne, Seine-et-Marne, and Val-de-Marne, and to two battles of World War I (see ▷Marne, Battles of the).

Marne, Battles of the in World War I, two unsuccessful German offensives in northern France. In the **First Battle** 6–9 September 1914, German advance was halted by French and British troops under the overall command of the French general Jospeh Joffre; in the **Second Battle** 15 July–4 August 1918, the German advance was defeated by British, French, and US troops under the French general Henri Pétain, and German morale crumbled.
Related Web site: Report on the Marne http://www.lib.byu.edu/~rdh/wwi/1914/joffre.html

Maronite member of a Christian sect deriving from refugee Monothelites (Christian heretics) of the 7th century. They were subsequently united with the Roman Catholic Church and number about 400,000 in Lebanon and Syria, with an equal number scattered in southern Europe and the Americas.

maroon (Spanish *cimarrón* 'wild, untamed') in the West Indies and Suriname, a freed or escaped African slave. Maroons were organized and armed by the Spanish in Jamaica in the late 17th century and early 18th century. They harried the British with guerrilla tactics.

Marquesas Islands (French **Iles Marquises**) island group in ▷French Polynesia, lying 1184 km/736 mi northeast of Tahiti; area 1,270 sq km/490 sq mi; population (1995 est) 8,600. The administrative headquarters is Atuona on Hiva Oa. The largest settlement is Taiohae on Hiva Oa; other islands include Kuku Hiva, Ua Pa, Ua Huka, Tahuata, and Fatu Hiva. The islands were annexed by France in 1842. The main products are copra and vanilla.

marquess (or **marquis**) title and rank of a nobleman who in the British peerage ranks below a duke and above an earl. The wife of a marquess is a marchioness.

marquetry inlaying of various woods, bone, or ivory, usually on furniture, to create ornate patterns and pictures. **Parquetry** is the term used for geometrical inlaid patterns. The method is thought to have originated in Germany or Holland.

Márquez, Gabriel García Colombian novelist; see Gabriel ▷García Márquez.

Marquises, Iles French form of ▷Marquesas Islands, part of ▷French Polynesia.

Marrakesh (or **Marrakech**) historic imperial city in Morocco in the foothills of the Atlas Mountains, about 210 km/130 mi south of Casablanca; population (1994) 672,500; urban area (1993) 602,000. It is a tourist centre, and has textile, leather, and food processing industries. Founded in 1062, it has a medieval palace and mosques, and was formerly the capital of Morocco.

marram grass coarse perennial grass that flourishes in sandy areas. Because of its tough, creeping roots, it is widely used to hold coastal dunes in place. (*Ammophila arenaria*, family Gramineae.)

marriage legally or culturally sanctioned union of one man and one woman (monogamy); one man and two or more women (polygamy); one woman and two or more men (polyandry). The basis of marriage varies considerably in different societies (romantic love in the West; arranged marriages in some other societies), but most marriage ceremonies, contracts, or customs involve a set of rights and duties, such as care and protection, and there is generally an expectation that children will be born of the union to continue the family line and maintain the family property. In the 1990s the concept of marriage was extended in some countries to include the blessing or registration of homosexual relationships.
Related Web site: Weddings UK http://www.weddings.co.uk/

marrow (or **vegetable marrow**) trailing vine that produces large pulpy fruits, used as vegetables and in preserves; the young fruits of one variety are known as courgettes (US zucchini). (*Cucurbita pepo*, family Cucurbitaceae.)

Marryat, Frederick (Captain) (1792–1848) English naval officer and writer. He was the originator of the British sea story. His adventure stories, taken from personal experience, are full of life, humour, and stirring narrative; they include *Peter Simple* (1834) and *Mr Midshipman Easy* (1836). He also wrote children's books, including *The Children of the New Forest* (1847).

Mars fourth planet from the Sun. It is much smaller than Venus or Earth, with a mass 0.11 that of Earth. Mars is slightly pear-shaped, with a low, level northern hemisphere, which is comparatively uncratered and geologically 'young', and a heavily cratered 'ancient' southern hemisphere.

There are four enormous volcanoes near the equator, of which the largest is Olympus Mons 24 km/15 mi high, with a base 600 km/375 mi across, and a crater 65 km/40 mi wide. To the east of the four volcanoes lies a high plateau cut by a system of valleys, Valles Marineris, some 4,000 km/2,500 mi long, up to 200 km/120 mi wide and 6 km/4 mi deep; these features are apparently caused by faulting and wind erosion. Recorded temperatures vary from −100°C/−148°F to 0°C/32°F.

Mars may approach Earth to within 54.7 million km/34 million mi. The first human-made object to orbit another planet was *Mariner 9*. *Viking 1* and *Viking 2*, which landed, also provided much information. Studies in 1985 showed that enough water might exist to sustain prolonged missions by space crews.

In December 1996, US National Aeronautics and Space Administration (NASA) launched the *Mars Pathfinder*, which made a successful landing on Mars in July 1997 on a flood plain called Ares Vallis. After initial technical problems, its 0.3-m rover, *Sojourner*, began to explore the Martian landscape and to transmit data back to Earth. Photographs from the *Mars Pathfinder* indicate that the planet is rusting. NASA announced this in July 1997 and said that a supercorrosive force was eroding rocks on the surface due to iron oxide in the soil.

In May 1997 US scientists announced that Mars is becoming increasingly cold and cloudy. Images from the Hubble Space Telescope showed that dust storms had covered areas of the planet that had been dark features in the early century, including one section as large as California.

The *Global Surveyor*, launched 7 November 1996, entered Martian orbit in September 1997. Its data revealed that Mars' magnetic field is a mere 800th that of the Earth. In February 1999 the spacecraft established its orbit for mapping the surface of the planet.

NASA's *Mars Climate Orbiter* to monitor weather on Mars was launched from Cape Canaveral, Florida, in December 1998. It was expected to reach its destination in September 1999. However, a measurement error caused the probe to fly too close to Mars and break up. NASA officals said that the failure of the ship was caused by 'English measurements' being used instead of metric ones. Workers at Lockheed Martin Astronautics in Colorado had given acceleration data in pounds of force, but navigators at NASA's Jet Propulsion Laboratory had assumed the numbers were metric newtons.

NASA launched its *Mars Polar Lander* in January 1999, which was designed to search for ice with a shovel and send back sounds from an attached microphone. It arrived near Mars on schedule, but in December 1999 it had apparently burned up or crashed, ending the $165 million mission, and provoking criticism of NASA's Mars exploration programme. In May 2001, the head of NASA predicted crewed flights to Mars within 20 years.

The European Space Agency's (ESA) *Mars Express* was given the go-ahead in June 2003. Launched in June 2003, it carried a lander, *Beagle 2* that was to search for ice, water, and chemicals under the surface. Communication was lost and its fate was unknown, though the orbiter survived and detected methane in the atmosphere, which could indicate present-day life.

NASA launched the Mars Exploration Rover mission in June 2003. The mission aim was to land on Mars and look for signs of water and life by examining different aspects of the planet's geology. In March, 2004, the rover *Opportunity* found evidence that rocks on its landing site, Meridiani Planum, were formed at the bottom of a salty sea. Three days later the rover *Spirit* uncovered signs that water had once seeped up into the soil of its landing site, Gusev Crater, which might have been a lake. The rovers completed their primary mission in April 2004, but NASA added five months to the original three-month mission.

mean distance from the Sun 227.9 million km/141.6 million mi **equatorial diameter** 6,780 km/4,210 mi **rotation period** 24 hr 37 min **year** 687 Earth days **atmosphere** 95% carbon dioxide, 3% nitrogen, 1.5% argon, and 0.15% oxygen. Red atmospheric dust from the surface whipped up by winds of up to 450 kph/280 mph accounts for the light pink sky. The surface pressure is less than 1% of the Earth's atmospheric pressure at sea level **surface** The landscape is a dusty, red, eroded lava plain. Mars has white polar caps (water ice and frozen carbon dioxide) that advance and retreat with the seasons **satellites** two small satellites: Phobos and Deimos

IMAGE from the Mars Rover.
© NASA/JPL/Cornell University/ZUMA/CORBIS

Mars (or **Mavors** or **Mamers**) in Roman mythology, the god of war (**Mars Gradivus**), depicted as a fearless warrior. The month of March is named after him. He was identified with the Greek ▷Ares, but achieved greater status.

Marsala (ancient **Lilybaeum**; Arab **Marsah-el-Allah** 'port of Allah') port in western Sicily, Italy, on the Mediterranean coast 30 km/19 mi south of Trapani; population (1990) 80,800. The nationalist leader Giuseppe ▷Garibaldi landed here in 1860 at the start of his campaign to capture Sicily for Italy. The town produces the sweet wine of the same name; there is also trade in agricultural produce and olive oil.

Marsalis, Wynton (1961–) US trumpet player. He has recorded both classical and jazz music. He was a member of Art Blakey's Jazz Messengers 1980–82 and also played with Miles Davis before forming his own quintet. At one time this included his brother Branford Marsalis on saxophone.

Marseille (English **Marseilles**) chief seaport and second city of France, and administrative centre of the *département* of Bouches-du-Rhône and of the ▷Provence-Alpes-Côte d'Azur region, situated on the Golfe du Lion on the Mediterranean Sea; population (2002 est) 815,100. Industries include chemicals, metallurgy, shipbuilding, and food processing, as well as oil-refining at the massive industrial complex of Fos-sur-Mer to the west.

Marseille is surrounded by hills and is connected with the River Rhône by a canal, and there are several offshore islands including If. In 1991 a grotto was discovered nearby, accessible only by an underwater passage. It contains prehistoric wall paintings showing people and animals, which may date from 20,000–12,000 BC; at that time the cave would have been accessible by land as the sea-level was much lower.

History   Marseille was founded by mariners of Phocaea in Asia Minor around 600 BC. Under the Romans it was a free city, and then, after suffering successive waves of invaders, became in the 13th century an independent republic, until included in France in 1481. Much of the old quarter was destroyed by the Germans in 1943.

Related Web site: Marseille http://www.mairie-marseille.fr/

marsh low-lying wetland. Freshwater marshes are common wherever groundwater, surface springs, streams, or run-off cause frequent flooding, or more or less permanent shallow water. A marsh is alkaline whereas a ▷bog is acid. Marshes develop on inorganic silt or clay soils. Rushes are typical marsh plants. Large marshes dominated by papyrus, cattail, and reeds, with standing water throughout the year, are commonly called ▷swamps. Near the sea, ▷salt marshes may form.

Marsh, (Edith) Ngaio (1899–1982) New Zealand detective fiction writer. Her first detective novel *A Man Lay Dead* (1934) introduced her protagonist Chief Inspector Roderick Alleyn. She was made a DBE in 1966.

Marshall, George Catlett (1880–1959) US general and diplomat. He was army chief of staff in World War II, secretary of state 1947–49, and secretary of defence September 1950–September 1951. He was awarded the Nobel Prize for Peace in 1953 for initiating the ▷Marshall Plan for European economic recovery in 1947.

Marshall Islands see country box.

Marshall Plan programme of US economic aid to Europe, set up at the end of World War II, totalling $13,000 billion between 1948 and 1952. Post-war Europe was in a state of economic collapse and physical ruin and the USA, as the world's richest nation, intended to resurrect the European economy and combat the perceived danger of a communist takeover in Europe. Officially known as the European Recovery Programme, it was announced by Secretary of State George C ▷Marshall in a speech at Harvard in June 1947, but it was in fact the work of a State Department group led by Dean ▷Acheson. See also ▷United States of America, the Truman Doctrine.

Related Web site: Marshall Plan http://www.loc.gov/exhibits/marshall/

marsh gas gas consisting mostly of ▷methane. It is produced in swamps and marshes by the action of bacteria on dead vegetation.

marsh marigold plant belonging to the buttercup family, known as the kingcup in the UK and as the cowslip in the USA. It grows in moist, sheltered places and has brilliant yellow five-sepalled flowers. (*Caltha palustris*, family Ranunculaceae.)

MARSH MARIGOLD The marsh marigold is widely found by streams and water meadows in Europe, Asia, and the USA.

Marshall Islands

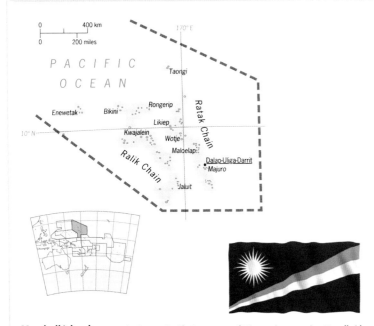

Marshall Islands country in the west Pacific Ocean, part of Micronesia, occupying 31 atolls (the Ratak and Ralik chains).

NATIONAL NAME *Majol/Republic of the Marshall Islands*
AREA 181 sq km/70 sq mi
CAPITAL Dalap-Uliga-Darrit (on Majuro atoll)
MAJOR TOWNS/CITIES Ebeye (the only other town)
PHYSICAL FEATURES comprises the Ratak and Ralik island chains in the West Pacific, which together form an archipelago of 31 coral atolls, 5 islands, and 1,152 islets

Government

HEAD OF STATE AND GOVERNMENT Kessai Note from 2000
POLITICAL SYSTEM liberal democracy
POLITICAL EXECUTIVE limited presidency
ADMINISTRATIVE DIVISIONS each of the 24 inhabited atolls has a local government

ARMED FORCES the USA maintains a military presence on the Kwajalein Atoll (the Compact of Free Association gave the USA responsibility for defence in return for US assistance)
DEATH PENALTY abolished in 1991

Economy and resources

CURRENCY US dollar
GPD (US$) 108 million (2002 est)
REAL GDP GROWTH (% change on previous year) 1.7 (2001)
GNI (US$) 125 million (2002 est)
GNI PER CAPITA (PPP) (US$) 4,820 (2002 est)
CONSUMER PRICE INFLATION 2% (2001)
UNEMPLOYMENT 31.5% (2000)
FOREIGN DEBT (US$) 79.2 million (2001 est)

MAJOR TRADING PARTNERS USA, Japan, Australia
RESOURCES phosphates
INDUSTRIES processing of agricultural products, handicrafts, fish products and canning, tourism
EXPORTS coconut products, trochus shells, copra, handicrafts, fish, live animals. Principal market: USA 71.2% (2000)
IMPORTS mineral fuels, food and live animals, beverages and tobacco, building materials, machinery and transport equipment, chemicals. Principal source: USA 61.4% (2000)
AGRICULTURAL PRODUCTS coconuts, tomatoes, melons, breadfruit, cassava, sweet potatoes, copra; fishing; seaweed and pearl oysters

Population and society

POPULATION 53,000 (2003 est)
POPULATION GROWTH RATE 1.3% (2000–05)
POPULATION DENSITY (per sq km) 293 (2003 est)
URBAN POPULATION (% of total) 66 (2003 est)
AGE DISTRIBUTION (% of total population) 0–14 49%, 15–59 47%, 60+ 4% (2002 est)
ETHNIC GROUPS 90% Marshallese, of predominantly Micronesian descent; remainder European origin, Indian, Chinese, Lebanese
LANGUAGE Marshallese, English (both official)

RELIGION Christian (mainly Protestant) and Baha'i
EDUCATION (compulsory years) 8
LITERACY RATE 91% (men); 90% (women) (1994 est)
LABOUR FORCE 25.6% agriculture, 9.4% industry, 65% services (1996)
LIFE EXPECTANCY 64 (men); 68 (women) (2001 est)
CHILD MORTALITY RATE (under 5, per 1,000 live births) 66 (2001)
PHYSICIANS (per 1,000 people) 0.4 (1998 est)

See also ▷Bikini Atoll; ▷Pacific Islands.

Chronology

after c. 1000 BC: Micronesians first settled the islands.
1529: Came under Spanish influence.
1875: Spanish rule formally declared in face of increasing encroachment by German traders.
1885: German protectorate established.
1914: Seized by Japan on the outbreak of World War I.
1920–44: Administered under League of Nations mandate by Japan and vigorously colonized.
1944: Japanese removed after heavy fighting with US troops during World War II.
1946–63: Eniwetok and Bikini atolls used for US atom-bomb tests; islanders later demanded rehabilitation and compensation for the damage.
1947: Became part of United Nations (UN) Pacific Islands Trust Territory, administered by USA.
1979: Amata Kabua was elected president as internal self-government was established.
1986: The Compact of Free Association with the USA granted the islands self-government, with the USA retaining the responsibility for defence and security until 2001.
1990: UN trust status was terminated.
1991: Independence was agreed with Kabua as president; UN membership was granted.

MARSHALL ISLANDS This German five-pfennig stamp, over-printed with the German name for the islands, reflects the period when the Marshall Islands were a protectorate of Germany. *Stanley Gibbons*

marsh rose shrub native to South Africa, which grows to 1–4 m/3–13 ft high. It is under threat, partly because its beautiful flowers are frequently picked, but also because of fungi, probably introduced by footwear or equipment, and by changes in management practice that have prevented periodic fires which are necessary for seed germination. Ironically, numbers of the shrub are now so low that uncontrolled fires could wipe out the remaining adult specimens. Although protected, they remain highly threatened. (*Orothamnus zeyheri*.)

Marston, John (1576–1634) English satirist and dramatist. His early plays, the revenge tragedies *Antonio and Mellida* and *Antonio's Revenge* (1599), were followed by a number of satirical comedies including *What You Will* (1601), *The Malcontent* (1604), and *The Dutch Courtesan* (1605).

Marston Moor, Battle of battle fought in the English Civil War on 2 July 1644 on Marston Moor, 11 km/7 mi west of York. The Royalists were conclusively defeated by the Parliamentarians and Scots. The Royalist forces were commanded by Prince Rupert and William Cavendish (later Duke of Newcastle); their opponents by Oliver Cromwell and Lord Leven. Lord Fairfax, on the right of the Parliamentarians, was routed, but Cromwell's cavalry charges were decisive.

marsupial (Greek *marsupion* 'little purse') mammal in which the female has a pouch where she carries her young (born tiny and immature) for a considerable time after birth. Marsupials include omnivorous, herbivorous, and carnivorous species, among them the kangaroo, wombat, opossum, phalanger, bandicoot, dasyure, and wallaby.

The Australian marsupial anteater known as the ▷numbat is an exception to the rule in that it has no pouch.
   Related Web site: Marsupial Cooperative Research Centre http://www.newcastle.edu.au/marsupialcrc/

Marsyas in Greek mythology, a Phrygian ▷satyr who found the flute discarded by the goddess ▷Athena and challenged ▷Apollo to a musical contest judged by the ▷Muses. On losing, he was flayed alive, his blood sourcing the River Marsyas.

marten small bushy-tailed carnivorous mammal belonging to the weasel family. Martens live in North America, Europe, and temperate regions of Asia, and are agile tree climbers. (Genus *Martes*, family Mustelidae.)

Martens, Wilfried (1936–) Belgian politician; prime minister 1979–92. He was president of the Dutch-speaking Social Christian Party (CVP) 1972–79 and, as prime minister, headed several coalition governments in the period 1979–92, when he was replaced by Jean-Luc ▷Dehaene heading a new coalition.

Martí, José Julian (1853–1895) Cuban revolutionary. Active in the Cuban independence movement from boyhood, he was deported to Spain in 1871, returning in 1878. Exiled again for continued opposition, he fled to the USA in 1880, from where he organized resistance to Spanish rule. He was killed in battle at Dos Ríos, soon after proclaiming the uprising which led to Cuban independence.

Martial, (Marcus Valerius Martialis) (*c.* AD 41–*c.* 104) Latin poet and epigrammatist. Born in Bilbilis, Spain, Martial settled in Rome AD 64, where he lived a life of poverty and dependence. His poetry, often obscene, is keenly observant of all classes in contemporary Rome. Of his works the following survive: about 33 poems from *Liber Spectaculorum*, published AD 80 to commemorate the opening of the Colosseum; two collections of short mottoes entitled *Xenia* and *Apophoreta* (AD 84–85); and 12 books of *Epigrams*, published AD 86–102.

martial arts any of several styles of armed and unarmed combat developed in the East from ancient techniques and arts. Common martial arts include aikido, ▷judo, jujitsu, ▷karate, kendo, and ▷kung fu.

martial law replacement of civilian by military authorities in the maintenance of order.

Martin five popes, including:

Martin V (1368–1431) Born Oddone Colonna. Pope from 1417. A member of the Roman family of Colonna, he was elected during the Council of Constance, and ended the Great Schism between the rival popes of Rome and Avignon.

Martin, St (*c.* 316–*c.* 400) Bishop of Tours, France, from about 371, and founder of the first monastery in Gaul. He is usually represented as tearing his cloak to share it with a beggar. His feast day is Martinmas, 11 November.

martin any of several species of birds belonging to the swallow family. (Family Hirundinidae, order Passeriformes.)

Martin, Dean (1917–1995) Stage name of Dino Paul Crocetti. US singer and actor. He met US comedian Jerry ▷Lewis in 1946; they became a top comedy-singing nightclub attraction and went on to make several films together 1949–56, the first of which was *My Friend Irma*. After the duo broke up, Martin went on to have his own television show during the late 1960s and early 1970s. His many hit records include 'That's Amore' (1953), 'Memories are made of this' (1955), and 'Everybody Loves Somebody' (1964).

> **Harriet Martineau**
> *Any one must see at a glance that if men and women marry those whom they do not love, they must love those whom they do not marry.*
> *Society in America* vol. III 'Marriage'

Martineau, Harriet (1802–1876) English journalist, economist, and novelist. She wrote popular works on economics; several novels, including *Deerbrook* (1839); children's stories, including *Feats on the Fiord* (1844); and articles in favour of the abolition of slavery. Her *Illustrations of Political Economy* (1832–34) consist of theoretical tracts roughly disguised as stories which reveal her passion for social reform. *Poor Laws and Paupers Illustrated* followed in 1833–34. Other works include *Society in America* (1837).

Martinique French island in the West Indies (Lesser Antilles); area 1,079 sq km/417 sq mi; population (1996 est) 399,200. The capital is ▷Fort-de-France. The island features several active volcanoes; a major eruption of the volcano Mont Pelée in 1902 destroyed the city of Saint-Pierre, which was the largest city on the island. Agricultural products include sugar, cocoa, rum, bananas, pineapples, vanilla, and tobacco, although the tourist industry is now more important than agriculture. Petroleum products, cement, and processed foods are also manufactured. The official language is French, with Creole also spoken.

History Martinique was reached by Spanish navigators in 1493, became a French colony in 1635, an overseas department in 1946, and from 1974 also an administrative region of France. Napoleon's wife ▷Josephine was born in Martinique, and her childhood home is now a museum.

Martinmas in the Christian calendar, the feast of St Martin, 11 November.

Martins, Peter (1946–) Danish-born US dancer, choreographer, and ballet director. He was principal dancer with the New York City Ballet (NYCB) from 1969, its joint ballet master (with Jerome ▷Robbins) from 1983, and its director from 1990. He is especially noted for his partnership with Suzanne Farrell, with whom he danced Balanchine's *Jewels* (1967). He retired from performing in 1983, after partnering Farrell in *The Nutcracker*, to concentrate on choreography.

HARRIET MARTINEAU The 19th-century English author and economist Harriet Martineau was an energetic woman who was deaf from an early age. She later suffered from heart disease and at the age of 44 years she became so ill that she was obliged to retire to comparative seclusion for the rest of her life. *Image Bank*

Martinů, Bohuslav Jan (1890–1959) Czech composer. He settled in New York after the Nazi occupation of Czechoslovakia in 1939. His music is voluble, richly expressive, and has great vitality. His works include the operas *Julietta* (1937) and *The Greek Passion* (1959), symphonies, and chamber music.

martyr (Greek 'witness') one who voluntarily suffers death for refusing to renounce a religious faith. The first recorded Christian martyr was St Stephen, who was killed in Jerusalem shortly after the apostles began to preach.

Marvell, Andrew (1621–1678) English metaphysical poet and satirist. In 'To His Coy Mistress' (1650–52) and 'An Horatian Ode upon Cromwell's Return from Ireland' (1650) he produced, respectively, the most searching seduction and political poems in the language. He was committed to the Parliamentary cause, and was Member of Parliament for Hull from 1659. He devoted his last years mainly to verse satire and prose works attacking repressive aspects of the state and government.

ANDREW MARVELL English metaphysical poet and satirist Andrew Marvell was unofficial poet laureate to Oliver Cromwell. His poem 'Upon the Death of his Late Highness the Lord Protector' (1658) mourns the death of Cromwell. *Archive Photos*

BATTLE OF MARSTON MOOR *Battle of Marston Moor* by James Ward. At this major battle of the English Civil War, fought near York on 2 July 1644, the Royalists were defeated by the Parliamentarians, led by Oliver Cromwell (Cromwell Museum, England). *Art Archive*

His reputation in his own day was as a champion of liberty and toleration, and as a polemicist. Today his reputation rests mainly on a small number of skilful and graceful but perplexing and intriguing poems, which were published posthumously as *Miscellaneous Poems* (1681). They include love lyrics, pastorals, and religious poems, executed with a compelling mixture of lyric grace and dialectical urgency and complexity. His prose works include *An Account of the Growth of Popery and Arbitrary Government* (1677), a scathing review of Charles II's reign.

Related Web site: Marvell, Andrew http://www.luminarium.org/sevenlit/marvell/index.html

Marvin, Lee (1924–1987) US film actor. An accomplished performer, with a tough, violent screen persona, he worked with such film-makers as Fritz Lang, John Ford, Don Siegel, and John Boorman on *The Big Heat* (1953), *The Man Who Shot Liberty Valance* (1962), *The Killers* (1964), and *Point Blank* (1967) respectively.

Marx, Karl Heinrich (1818–1883) German philosopher, economist, and social theorist whose account of change through conflict is known as historical, or dialectical, materialism (see ▷Marxism). His *Das* ▷*Kapital/Capital* (1867–95) is the fundamental text of Marxist economics, and his systematic theses on class struggle, history, and the importance of economic factors in politics have exercised an enormous influence on later thinkers and political activists.

In 1844 Marx began his lifelong collaboration with Friedrich ▷Engels, with whom he developed the Marxist philosophy, first formulated in their joint works *Die heilige Familie/The Holy Family* (1844) and *Die deutsche Ideologie/German Ideology* (1846) (which contains the theory demonstrating the material basis of all human activity: 'Life is not determined by consciousness, but consciousness by life'). Both joined the Communist League, a German refugee organization, and in 1847–48 they prepared its programme, *The Communist Manifesto*. In the wake of the 1848 revolution, Marx was expelled from Prussia in 1849.

He then settled in London, where he wrote *Die Klassenkämpfe in Frankreich/Class Struggles in France* (1849), *Die Achtzehnte Brumaire des Louis Bonaparte/The 18th Brumaire of Louis Bonaparte* (1852), *Zur Kritik der politischen Ökonomie/Critique of Political Economy* (1859), and his monumental work *Das Kapital/Capital*. In 1864 the International Working Men's Association was formed, whose policy Marx, as a member of the general council, largely controlled. Although he showed extraordinary tact in holding together its diverse elements, it collapsed in 1872 owing to Marx's disputes with the anarchists, including the Russian ▷Bakunin.

Related Web site: Marx/Engels Archive http://csf.colorado.edu/psn/marx

Marx Brothers Team of US film comedians: the silent **Harpo** (from the harp he played) (1888–1964); Julius **Groucho** (from his temper) (1890–1977); Leonard **Chico** (from the 'chicks' – women – he chased) (1891–1961); Adolph, Milton **Gummo** (from his gumshoes, or galoshes) (*c.* 1892–1977), who left the team before they began making films; and Herbert **Zeppo** (born at the time of the first zeppelins) (1901–1979), part of the team until 1935. They made a total of 13 zany films 1929–49 including *Animal Crackers* (1930), *Monkey Business* (1931), *Duck Soup* (1933), *A Day at the Races* (1937), *A Night at the Opera* (1935), and *Go West* (1940).

The Marx Brothers made their reputation on Broadway in *Cocoanuts* (1926; later filmed). After the team disbanded in 1948, Groucho Marx continued to make films and appeared on his own television quiz show, *You Bet Your Life* 1947–62.

Marxism philosophical system, developed by the 19th-century German social theorists ▷Marx and ▷Engels, also known as **dialectical materialism**, under which matter gives rise to mind (materialism) and all is subject to change (from dialectic; see ▷Hegel). As applied to history, it supposes that the succession of feudalism, capitalism, socialism, and finally the classless society is inevitable. The stubborn resistance of any existing system to change necessitates its complete overthrow in the **class struggle** – in the case of capitalism, by the proletariat – rather than gradual modification.

Related Web site: Marxism Page http://www.anu.edu.au/polsci/marx/marx.html

Marxism–Leninism term used by the Soviet dictator Stalin and his supporters to define their own views as the orthodox position of ▷Marxism as a means of refuting criticism. It has subsequently been employed by other communist parties as a yardstick for ideological purity.

Mary In the New Testament, the mother of Jesus through divine intervention (see ▷Annunciation), wife of ▷Joseph. The Roman Catholic Church maintains belief in her ▷Immaculate Conception and bodily assumption into heaven, and venerates her as a mediator. The feast day of the Assumption is 15 August.

Traditionally her parents were elderly and named Joachim and Anna. Mary (Hebrew **Miriam**) married Joseph and accompanied him to Bethlehem. Roman Catholic doctrine assumes that the brothers of Jesus were Joseph's sons by an earlier marriage, and that she remained a virgin. Pope Paul VI proclaimed her 'Mother of the Church' 1964.

Mary two queens of England:

Mary I (1516–1558) Called 'Bloody Mary'. Queen of England from 1553. She was the eldest daughter of Henry VIII by Catherine of Aragón. When Edward VI died, Mary secured the crown without difficulty in spite of the conspiracy to substitute Lady Jane ▷Grey. In 1554 Mary married Philip II of Spain, and as a devout Roman Catholic obtained the restoration of papal supremacy and sanctioned the persecution of Protestants (see ▷Reformation, **England**). She was succeeded by her half-sister Elizabeth I.

Mary II (1662–1694) Queen of England, Scotland, and Ireland from 1688. She was the Protestant elder daughter of the Catholic ▷James II, and in 1677 was married to her cousin ▷William of Orange. After the ▷Glorious Revolution of 1688 she accepted the crown jointly with William.

During William's absences from England she took charge of the government, and showed courage and resource when invasion seemed possible in 1690 and 1692.

Mary, Duchess of Burgundy (1457–1482) Daughter of Charles the Bold, Duke of Burgundy. She married Maximilian of Austria in 1477, thus bringing the Low Countries into the possession of the Habsburgs and, ultimately, of Spain.

Maryland state of eastern USA. It was nicknamed Old Line State or Free State. Maryland ratified the US Constitution in 1788, becoming the 7th state to join the Union. It is bordered to the north by Pennsylvania, along the old ▷Mason-Dixon Line, to the east by Delaware, with which it shares most of the Delmarva Peninsula, to the south by Virginia and West Virginia, with the latter of which it also shares a western boundary. At the Fall Line, where the Anacostia River joins the Potomac River, is the District of Columbia, which was carved out of Maryland and Virginia in 1790. **population** (1995) 5,042,400 **area** 31,600 sq km/12,198 sq mi **capital** ▷Annapolis **towns and cities** Baltimore, Silver Spring, Dundalk, Bethesda **industries and products** poultry, dairy products, machinery, steel, cars and parts, boatbuilding, electric and electronic equipment, chemicals, fish and shellfish, tourism

Mary Magdalene, St (lived 1st century AD) in the New Testament, a woman whom Jesus cured of possession by evil spirits. She was present at the Crucifixion and burial, and was the first to meet the risen Jesus. She is often identified with the woman of St Luke's gospel who anointed Jesus' feet, and her symbol is a jar of ointment. Her feast day is 22 July.

Mary of Guise (1515–1560) Also known as **Mary of Lorraine**. French-born second wife of James V of Scotland from 1538, and 1554–59 regent of Scotland for her daughter ▷Mary Queen of Scots. A Catholic, she moved from reconciliation with Scottish Protestants to repression, and died during a Protestant rebellion in Edinburgh.

Daughter of Claude, Duke of Guise, she was first married in 1534 to the Duke of Lorraine, who died in 1537. After James V died in 1542 she played a leading role in Scottish politics, seeking a close union with France, but she was unpopular, and was deposed as regent in 1559.

Mary of Modena (1658–1718) Born Marie Beatrice d'Este. Queen consort of England and Scotland. She was the daughter of the Duke of Modena, Italy, and second wife of James, Duke of York, later James II, whom she married in 1673. The birth of their son James Francis Edward Stuart was the signal for the revolution of 1688 that overthrew James II. Mary fled to France.

Mary Queen of Scots (1542–1587) Queen of Scotland (1542–67). Also known as **Mary Stuart**, she was the daughter of James V. Mary's connection with the English royal line from Henry VII made her a threat to Elizabeth I's hold on the English throne, especially as she represented a champion of the Catholic cause. She was married three times. After her forced abdication she was imprisoned but escaped in 1568 to England. Elizabeth I held her prisoner, while the Roman Catholics, who regarded Mary as rightful queen of England, formed many conspiracies to place her on the throne, and for complicity in one of these she was executed.

Mary's mother was the French Mary of Guise. Born in Linlithgow (now in Lothian region, Scotland), Mary was sent to France, where she married the dauphin, later Francis II. After his death she returned to Scotland in 1561, which, during her absence, had become Protestant. She married her cousin, the Earl of ▷Darnley in 1565, but they soon quarrelled, and Darnley took part in the murder of Mary's secretary, ▷Rizzio. In 1567 Darnley, staying alone in Kirk o'Field House in Edinburgh, was killed in an explosion, the result of a conspiracy formed by the Earl of ▷Bothwell, possibly with Mary's connivance. When, shortly after this Bothwell married Mary, the Scots rebelled. Defeated at Carberry Hill, Mary abdicated and was imprisoned. She escaped in 1568, raised an army, and after its defeat at Langside fled to England, only to be imprisoned again. The discovery by Francis ▷Walsingham of a plot against Elizabeth I, devised by Anthony ▷Babington, led to her trial and execution at Fotheringay Castle in 1587.

Masaccio, Tommaso di Giovanni di Simone Guidi (1401–*c.* 1428) Florentine painter, one of the major figures of the early Italian Renaissance. His frescoes in the Brancacci Chapel of Santa Maria del Carmine, Florence (1425–28) show a decisive break with traditional styles. He was the first painter to apply the scientific laws of perspective, newly discovered by the architect Brunelleschi, and achieved a sense of space and volume that gives his pictures a sculptural quality.

Masada rock fortress 396 m/1,300 ft above the western shore of the Dead Sea, Israel. Site of the Hebrews' final stand in their revolt against the Romans (AD 66–73). After withstanding a year-long siege, the Hebrew population of 953 committed mass suicide rather than be conquered and enslaved.

Masai (or **Maasai**) member of an East African people whose territory is divided between Tanzania and Kenya. They number about 250,000, and speak a Nilotic language belonging to the Nilo-Saharan family. Traditionally they are

---

Groucho Marx
I never forget a face but in your case I'll be glad to make an exception.
Leo Rosten *People I have loved, known or admired*

MASAI A girl from the Masai tribe of East Africa. *Image Bank*

warriors and pastoral nomads, but much of their land was taken over by European colonists and today there is considerable pressure on them from the Kenyan government to settle as farmers.

Masaryk, Tomáš Garrigue (1850–1937) Czechoslovak nationalist politician. He directed the revolutionary movement against the Austrian Empire, founding with Edvard ▷Beneš and Milan Stefanik the Czechoslovak National Council. In 1918 he was elected first president of the newly formed Czechoslovak Republic. Three times re-elected, he resigned in 1935 in favour of Beneš.

After the communist coup in 1948, Masaryk was systematically removed from public memory in order to reverse his semi-mythological status as the forger of the Czechoslovak nation.

Masefield, John (1878–1967) English poet and novelist. His early years in the merchant navy inspired *Salt Water Ballads* (1902) and two further volumes of poetry, and several adventure novels; he also wrote children's books, such as *The Midnight Folk* (1927) and *The Box of Delights* (1935), and plays. *The Everlasting Mercy* (1911), characterized by its forcefully colloquial language, and *Reynard the Fox* (1919) are long verse narratives. He was poet laureate from 1930.

> **John Masefield**
> *I must go down to the seas again, to the lonely sea and the sky, / And all I ask is a tall ship and a star to steer her by.*
> 'Sea Fever'

His other works include the novels *Jim Davis* (1911) and *Sard Harker* (1924), and the play *The Tragedy of Nan* (1908). *Collected Poems* was first published in 1923.

maser (acronym for microwave amplification by stimulated emission of radiation) in physics, a high-frequency microwave amplifier or oscillator in which the signal to be amplified is used to stimulate excited atoms into emitting energy at the same frequency. Atoms or molecules are raised to a higher energy level and then allowed to lose this energy by radiation emitted at a precise frequency. The principle has been extended to other parts of the electromagnetic spectrum as, for example, in the ▷laser.

The two-level ammonia-gas maser was first suggested in 1954 by US physicist Charles Townes at Columbia University, New York, and independently the same year by Nikolai Basov and Aleksandr Prokhorov in Russia. The solid-state three-level maser, the most sensitive amplifier known, was envisaged by Nicolaas Bloembergen at Harvard in 1956. The ammonia maser is used as a frequency standard oscillator, and the three-level maser as a receiver for satellite communications and radio astronomy.

Maseru capital of ▷Lesotho, on the Caledon River at the border with Free State in South Africa; population (1992 est) 367,000. Founded in 1869 by the Basotho chief Mshweshwe I, it is a centre for trade, light manufacturing, and food processing. The National University of Lesotho (1975) is at nearby Roma.

Mashraq (Arabic 'east') the Arab countries of the eastern Mediterranean: Egypt, Jordan, Syria, Lebanon, Palestine, and Iraq. The term is contrasted with ▷Maghreb, comprising the Arab countries of northwest Africa.

Masire, Quett Ketumile Joni (1925–) Botswanan politician; president 1980–98. In 1962, with Seretse ▷Khama, he founded the Botswana Democratic Party (BDP) and in 1965 was made deputy prime minister. After independence in 1966, he became vice-president and, on Khama's death in 1980, president, continuing a policy of nonalignment. He retired in March 1998 and was succeeded by Festus Mogae of the BDP.

mask artificial covering for part or all of the face, or for the whole head, associated with ritual or theatrical performances in many cultures. Theatrical traditions using masks include ancient Greek drama (full head masks), Japanese Nō (facial masks), and the Italian commedia dell'arte (caricatured half-masks). In the 20th century masked performance was re-explored in experimental and mainstream theatrical productions.

Maskelyne, Nevil (1732–1811) English astronomer. He made observations to investigate the reliability of the lunar distance method for determining longitude at sea. In 1774 he estimated the mass of the Earth by noting the deflection of a plumb line near Mount Schiehallion in Perthshire, Scotland.

masochism desire to subject oneself to physical or mental pain, humiliation, or punishment, for erotic pleasure, to alleviate guilt, or out of destructive impulses turned inward. The term is derived from Leopold von Sacher-Masoch.

Mason, James (Neville) (1909–1984) English film actor. He portrayed romantic villains in British films of the 1940s. After *Odd Man Out* (1947) he worked in the USA, often playing intelligent but troubled, vulnerable men, notably in *A Star Is Born* (1954). In 1960 he returned to Europe, where he made *Lolita* (1962).

Mason–Dixon Line in the USA, the boundary line between Maryland and Pennsylvania (latitude 39° 43' 26.3' N), named after Charles Mason (1730–1787) and Jeremiah Dixon (died 1777), English astronomers and surveyors who surveyed it 1763–67. It is popularly seen as dividing the North from the South.

masonry the craft of constructing stonework walls. The various styles of masonry include **random rubblework**, irregular stones arranged according to fit; **coursed rubblework**, irregular stones placed in broad horizontal bands, or courses; **ashlar masonry**, smooth, square-cut stones arranged in courses; **Cyclopean masonry**, large polygonal stones cut to fit each other; and **rustification**, large stones separated by deep joints and chiselled or hammered into a variety of styles. Rustification is usually employed at the base of buildings, on top of an ashlar base, to give an appearance of added strength.

masque spectacular court entertainment with a fantastic or mythological theme in which music, dance, and extravagant costumes and scenic design figured larger than plot. Originating in Italy, where members of the court actively participated in the performances, the masque reached its height of popularity at the English court between 1600 and 1640, with the collaboration of Ben ▷Jonson as writer and Inigo ▷Jones as stage designer. John Milton also wrote masque verses. Composers included Thomas Campion, John Coperario, Henry Lawes, William ▷Byrd, and Henry Purcell.

Mass in Christianity, the celebration of the ▷Eucharist.

mass in physics, the quantity of matter in a body as measured by its inertia. Mass determines the acceleration produced in a body by a given force acting on it, the acceleration being inversely proportional to the mass of the body. The mass also determines the force exerted on a body by ▷gravity on Earth, although this attraction varies slightly from place to place. In the SI system, the base unit of mass is the kilogram.

At a given place, equal masses experience equal gravitational forces, which are known as the weights of the bodies. Masses may, therefore, be compared by comparing the weights of bodies at the same place. The standard unit of mass to which all other masses are compared is a platinum-iridium cylinder of 1 kg, which is kept at the International Bureau of Weights and Measures in Sèvres, France.

Massachusetts state of northeast USA. It is nicknamed the Bay State or the Old Colony State. Massachusetts ratified the US Constitution in 1788, becoming the 6th state to join the Union. It is a region of great significance to US history, being the point of disembarkation for the *Mayflower* Pilgrims, as well as the site of key conflicts in the American Revolution. Massachusetts is bordered to the north by Vermont and New Hampshire, to the west by New York, to the south by Connecticut and Rhode Island, and to the southeast and east by the Atlantic Ocean.

population (1995) 6,073,600 **area** 21,500 sq km/8,299 sq mi **capital** ▷Boston **towns and cities** Worcester, Springfield, Lowell, New Bedford, Brockton, Cambridge **industries and products** electronic, communications, and optical equipment, precision instruments, non-electrical machinery, fish, cranberries, dairy products, tourism, academia and research, finance sector. Massachussets outranked all other states, in 1999, in building its economy on the Internet and exports. Massachusetts ranked first in managerial/professional jobs as a share of the workforce and in venture capital invested as a share of the gross domestic product (GDP).

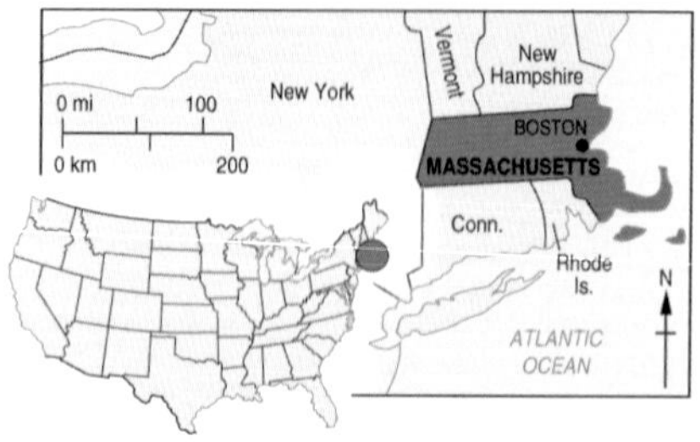

MASK Masks made by villagers along the Sepik River in New Guinea are generally carved from soft wood (though some are made of clay moulded over a coconut shell) and decorated with shells, pig tusks, and feathers. There are no holes for eyes as few of these masks are meant to be worn directly over the face – some are used for dance costumes, others mainly for display (Museum of African and Oceanic Art, Paris). *Art Archive*

massage manipulation of the soft tissues of the body, the muscles, ligaments, and tendons, either to encourage the healing of specific injuries or to produce the general beneficial effects of relaxing muscular tension, stimulating blood circulation, and improving the tone and strength of the skin and muscles.

Massawa (or Mesewa or Massaua) second biggest town and main port in Eritrea, situated on a small sterile coral island in the Red Sea, 200 m/656 ft from the mainland; population (1995 est) 49,300. It lies 65 km/40 mi northeast of Asmara, the largest town of Eritrea. Activities within the port include salt production, fishing, fish and meat processing, and cement manufacture. Exports include oil seed, coffee, and cattle. It is one of the hottest inhabited places in the world, the temperature reaching 46°C/115°F in May.

mass–energy equation Albert ▷Einstein's equation $E = mc^2$, denoting the equivalence of mass and energy. In SI units, E is the energy in joules, m is the mass in kilograms, and c, the speed of light in a vacuum, is in metres per second.

Massenet, Jules Emile Frédéric (1842–1912) French composer of operas. His work is characterized by prominent roles for females, sincerity, and sentimentality. Notable works are *Manon* (1884), *Le Cid* (1885), and *Thaïs* (1894); among other works is the orchestral suite *Scènes pittoresques* (1874). He was professor of composition at the Paris Conservatory 1878–96.

mass extinction an event that produces the extinction of many species at about the same time. One notable example is the boundary between the Cretaceous and Tertiary periods (known as the ▷K-T boundary) that saw the extinction of the dinosaurs and other large reptiles, and many of the marine invertebrates as well. Mass extinctions have taken place frequently during Earth's history.

There have been five major mass extinctions, in which 75% or more of the world's species have been wiped out: End Ordovician period (440 million years ago) in which about 85% of species were destroyed (second most severe); Late Devonian period (365 million years ago) which took place in two waves a million years apart, and was the third most severe, with marine species particularly badly hit; Late Permian period (251 million years ago), the gravest mass Late Triassic (205 million years ago), in which about 76% of species were destroyed, mainly marine; Late Cretaceous period (65 million years ago), in which 75–80 of species became extinct, including dinosaurs.

Massif Central upland region of south-central France with mountains and plateaux; area 93,000 sq km/36,000 sq mi, highest peak Puy de Sancy, 1,886 m/6,188 ft. It is a source of hydroelectricity.

Massine, Léonide (1895–1979) Adopted name of Leonid Fyodorovich Miassin. Russian choreographer and dancer with the Ballets Russes. He was a creator of comedy in ballet and also symphonic ballet using concert music. His works include the first cubist-inspired ballet, *Parade* (1917), *La Boutique fantasque* (1919), and *The Three-Cornered Hat* (1919).

Massinger, Philip (1583–1640) English dramatist. He was the author of *A New Way to Pay Old Debts* (*c.* 1625). He collaborated with John ▷Fletcher and Thomas ▷Dekker, and has been credited with a share in writing Shakespeare's *Two Noble Kinsmen* and *Henry VIII*.

mass number (or nucleon number) sum (symbol *A*) of the numbers of protons and neutrons in the nucleus of an atom. It is used along with the ▷atomic number (the number of protons) in ▷nuclear notation: in symbols that represent nuclear isotopes, such as $^{14}_{6}$C, the lower number is the atomic number, and the upper number is the mass number.

Massorah collection of philological notes on the Hebrew text of the Old Testament. It was at first an oral tradition, but was committed to writing in the Aramaic language at Tiberias, Palestine, between the 6th and 9th centuries.

mass production manufacture of goods on a large scale, a technique that aims for low unit cost and high output. In factories mass production is achieved by a variety of means, such as division and specialization of labour and mechanization. These speed up production and allow the manufacture of near-identical, interchangeable parts. Such parts can then be assembled quickly into a finished product on an assembly line.

mass spectrometer in physics, an apparatus for analysing chemical composition. Positive ions (charged particles) of a substance are separated by an electromagnetic system, designed to focus particles of equal mass to a point where they can be detected. This permits accurate measurement of the relative concentrations of the various ionic masses present, particularly isotopes.

Master of the King's/Queen's Music(k) honorary appointment to the British royal household, the holder composing appropriate music for state occasions. The first was Nicholas Lanier, appointed by Charles I in 1626; later appointments have included Edward Elgar and Arthur Bliss. The present holder, Malcolm Williamson, was appointed in 1975.

Master of the Rolls English judge who is the president of the civil division of the Court of Appeal, besides being responsible for ▷Chancery records and for the admission of solicitors.

Masters, John (1914–1983) British novelist. Born in Calcutta, he served in the Indian army 1934–47. He wrote a series of books dealing with the Savage family throughout the period of the Raj – for example, *Nightrunners of Bengal* (1951), *The Deceivers* (1952), and *Bhowani Junction* (1954).

mastiff breed of powerful dog, usually fawn in colour, that was originally bred in Britain for hunting purposes. It has a large head, wide-set eyes, and broad muzzle. It can grow up to 90 cm/36 in at the shoulder, and weigh 100 kg/220 lb.
>   Related Web site: Mastiff http://www.akc.org/breeds/recbreeds/mastif.cfm

mastodon any of an extinct family of mammals belonging to the elephant order. They differed from elephants and mammoths in the structure of their grinding teeth. There were numerous species, among which the **American mastodon** (*Mastodon americanum*), about 3 m/10 ft high, of the Pleistocene era, is well known. They were hunted by humans for food. (Family Mastodontidae, order Proboscidae.)

Mastroianni, Marcello (1924–1996) Italian film actor. He was popular for his carefully understated roles as an unhappy romantic lover in such films as Michelangelo Antonioni's *La notte/The Night* (1961). He starred in several films with Sophia Loren, including *Una giornata speciale/A Special Day* (1977), and

MASS PRODUCTION A worker in a toaster manufacturing company in the 1940s tests the final product. *Image Bank*

worked with Federico Fellini in *La dolce vita* (1960), *8½* (1963), and *Ginger and Fred* (1986).

Masur, Kurt (1927–) German conductor. He has been music director of the New York Philharmonic from 1990. His speciality is late Romantic and early 20th-century repertoire, in particular Mendelssohn, Liszt, Bruch, and Prokofiev.

Matabeleland western portion of Zimbabwe between the Zambezi and Limpopo rivers, inhabited by the Ndebele people. It is divided into two administrative regions (Matabeleland North and Matabeleland South); area 181,605 sq km/70,118 sq mi. Towns and cities include Bulawayo and Hwange. The region features rich plains watered by tributaries of the Zambezi and Limpopo rivers. Industries include gold and other mineral mines, and engineering. Agricultural products include cotton, sugar, maize, and cattle. The language spoken is Ndebele.

Matadi chief river port of the Democratic Republic of Congo on the south bank of the Congo River, 115 km/70 mi from its mouth, linked by rail with the capital Kinshasa; population (1994 est) 172,700. Matadi is the distribution point for all the country's oil products (except fuel oil), which are pumped via a 350 km/217 mi pipeline to Kinshasa.

Mata Hari (1876–1917) Stage name of Margaretha Geertruida Zelle. Dutch courtesan, dancer, and probable spy. In World War I she had affairs with highly placed military and government officials on both sides and told Allied secrets to the Germans. She may have been a double agent, in the pay of both France and Germany. She was shot by the French on espionage charges.

maté dried leaves of the Brazilian ▷holly (*Ilex paraguayensis*), an evergreen shrub that grows in Paraguay and Brazil. The roasted, powdered leaves are made into a tea. (Family Aquifoliaceae.)

materialism philosophical theory that there is nothing in existence over and above matter and matter in motion. Such a theory excludes the possibility of deities. It also sees mind as an attribute of the physical, denying idealist theories that see mind as something independent of body; for example, Descartes' theory of 'thinking substance'.

mathematical induction formal method of proof in which the proposition $P(n + 1)$ is proved true on the hypothesis that the proposition $P(n)$ is true. The proposition is then shown to be true for a particular value of n, say k, and therefore by induction the proposition must be true for $n = k + 1, k + 2, k + 3, \ldots$. In many cases $k = 1$, so then the proposition is true for all positive integers.

mathematics science of relationships between numbers, between spatial configurations, and abstract structures. The main divisions of **pure mathematics** include geometry, arithmetic, algebra, calculus, and trigonometry. Mechanics, statistics, numerical analysis, computing, the mathematical theories of astronomy, electricity, optics, thermodynamics, and atomic studies come under the heading of **applied mathematics**.

Early history Prehistoric humans probably learned to count at least up to ten on their fingers. The ancient Egyptians (3rd millennium BC), Sumerians (2000–1500 BC), and Chinese (1500 BC) had systems for writing down numbers and could perform calculations using various types of ▷abacus. They used some fractions. Mathematicians in ancient Egypt could solve simple problems which involved finding a quantity that satisfied a given linear relationship. Sumerian mathematicians knew how to solve problems that involved quadratic equations. The fact that, in a right-angled triangle, the square of the longest side is equal to the sum of the squares of the other two sides (Pythagoras' theorem) was known in various forms in these cultures and also in Vedic India (1500 BC).

The first theoretical mathematician is held to be Thales of Miletus (*c.* 580 BC) who is believed to have proposed the first theorems in plane geometry. His disciple ▷Pythagoras established geometry as a recognized science among the Greeks. Pythagoras began to

MATA HARI A portrait of Dutch-born German World War I spy Mata Hari, *c.* 1915. *Archive Photos*

insist that mathematical statements must be proved using a logical chain of reasoning starting from acceptable assumptions. Undoubtedly the impetus for this demand for logical proof came from the discovery by this group of the surprising fact that the square root of 2 is a number which cannot be expressed as the ratio of two whole numbers. The use of logical reasoning, the methods of which were summarized by Aristotle, enabled Greek mathematicians to make general statements instead of merely solving individual problems as earlier mathematicians had done.

The spirit of Greek mathematics is typified in one of its most lasting achievements, the *Elements* by Euclid. This is a complete treatise on geometry in which the entire subject is logically deduced from a handful of simple assumptions. The ancient Greeks lacked a simple notation for numbers and nearly always relied on expressing problems geometrically. Although the Greeks were extremely successful with their geometrical methods they never developed a general theory of equations or any algebraic ideas of structure. However, they made considerable advances in techniques for solving particular kinds of equations and these techniques were summarized by Diophantus of Alexandria.

Medieval period When the Hellenic civilization declined, Greek mathematics (and the rest of Greek science) was kept alive by the Arabs, especially in the scientific academy at the court of the caliphs of Baghdad. The Arabs also learned of the considerable scientific achievements of the Indians, including the invention of a system of numerals (now called 'arabic' numerals) which could be used to write down calculations instead of having to resort to an abacus. One mathematician can be singled out as a bridge between the ancient and medieval worlds: al-▷Khwārizmī summarized Greek and Indian methods for solving equations and wrote the first treatise on the Indian numerals and calculating with them. Al-Khwarizmi's books and other Arabic works were translated into Latin and interest in mathematics in Western Europe began to increase in the 12th century. It was the demands of commerce which gave the major impetus to mathematical development and north Italy, the centre of trade at the time, produced a succession of important mathematicians beginning with Italian mathematician Leonardo Fibonacci who introduced Arabic numerals. The Italians made considerable advances in elementary arithmetic which was needed for money-changing and for the technique of double-entry bookkeeping invented in Venice. Italian mathematicians began to express equations in symbols instead of words. This algebraic notation made it possible to shift attention from solving individual equations to investigating the relationship between equations and their solutions, and led eventually to the discovery of methods of solving cubic equations (about 1515) and quartic equations. They began to use the square roots of negative numbers (complex numbers) in their solutions to equations.

Early modern period In the 17th century the focus of mathematical activity moved to France and Britain though continuing with the major themes of Italian mathematics:

(continued on p. 610)

The Origins of Mathematics

by Peter Higgins

I t is often said that people first encountered mathematics when they began to count their livestock or tried to measure the size of a field. The two sides of the mathematical coin, discrete mathematics based on counting, and continuous mathematics that arises through measurement, still form the basis of modern mathematics.

A 19TH-CENTURY ABACUS from China. Abacuses were one of the earliest calculating devices invented and were used for many centuries. They have now been superseded by electronic calculators and computers. © *Museum of the History of Science, Oxford*

inventing names for numbers

Counting and arithmetic did not come about easily for a variety of reasons. To count we just need tally marks; but in order to talk about counting, we need a name for each number we use. Every language combined names of small numbers as a way of expressing larger ones, as in the French word for 80, *quatre-vingt*, literally 'four twenties'. The ancient Greeks used letters to represent numbers so that α was 1 while κ stood for 20 and in that way would write κα for 21. They could equally have written ακ to convey the same meaning, 'one-and-twenty'.

Roman numerals were based on ten with the basic symbols being I, X, C, and M for 1, 10, 100, and 1,000 respectively, although they also introduced V to stand

for 5, L for 50, and D for 500. The symbols were generally written in descending order, so that 1,944 = MDCCCCXXXXIIII.

Sometimes they made use of **position**: a smaller unit placed before a larger one indicated subtraction of the smaller from the larger – for instance 9 was written as IX instead of VIIII. So 1,944 = MCMXLIV. But this representation is not always as easy to understand or employ in arithmetic, which may be why the Romans did not always make use of it.

positional systems and '0'

In our number system, unlike the Greek system, **order** matters. Take 21. Swapping the places of the numerals 2 and 1 gives 12, a different number, for the 1 now represents 1 ten, while the 2 means two units.

No ancient European society devised a complete positional numbering system in which the meaning of a numeral depends on its position within the number and full use is made of a zero symbol. The idea of a zero symbol was used by the Mesopotamians and Babylonians, and was employed in the way that we do to distinguish between 74 and 704. The full potential of the system was not embraced, however, as the zero was seldom used in the final place, the way we show the difference between 74 and 740.

There were, nonetheless, many practical and sophisticated counting systems in the ancient world. Commercial and trading societies often constructed good systems of arithmetic and the peoples of ancient Mesopotamia did have a sexagesimal

positional system, one based on 60, over 4,000 years ago. Numbers exceeding 60 were written according to the positional principle, while combinations of the symbols from one to ten were used to make the basic numbers of their system which ran from 1 to 59. For instance, the ancient clay tablets reveal examples like:

$$524,551 = 2 \times 60^3 + 25 \times 60^2 + 42 \times 60 + 31.$$

The first complete positional system came into use in India around the 1st century AD. The symbol for zero was called *sunya*, the Hindu word for 'empty'. It is the basis of our number system, called Hindu-Arabic, as it passed to Europe via medieval Arabic scholars. A positional system, complete with zero, was also invented by the Mayan civilization of Central America by the 6th century AD, based on multiples of powers of 20 instead of 10.

early computing

Throughout Asia and Europe, arithmetic was carried out on the calculator of the ancient world, the **abacus** (Greek 'sand tray'). The main obstacle to written arithmetic was lack of cheap writing materials. The first example of long division is by Calandri in 1491. The decimal system of fractions did not firmly take root until planted by force after the French Revolution of 1789.

A typical abacus consisted of a wooden rectangular frame in which a series of parallel rods were housed. Along each were a number of identical beads. Cutting across the rods was a counting bar. One rod represented the units column and the beads on rods to its left each represented multiples of 10, 100, 1,000, and so on. Beads above the counting bar counted for five while those below represented one. Addition using an abacus is easy, as we need only count the number of each bead type and carry over to higher units as the need arises, although to carry out subtractions may require borrowing from the next highest rod.

A great advantage of the pen and paper methods that emerged in the Renaissance is one of communication, for they allowed working to be shown and checked. The scribes of the ancient Babylonian tablets left descriptions of numerous problems and their answers, but we would need to see the clerks of the ancient world in action on their counting frames to appreciate exactly how they did their sums.

geometry and paradox

An early use of geometry and measurement arose in Egypt where the ancient Greek historian Herodotus tells us that the Nile's annual flood regularly washed away boundaries and landmarks so that a system of accurate surveying was needed in order to reaffirm who owned what: indeed the Greek word 'geometry' means 'Earth measure'. The founder of geometry was the Greek philosopher and scientist Thales of Miletus, who is said to have impressed the Egyptians by measuring the height of the Great Pyramid of Cheops through the use of shadows.

His successor was the Greek mathematician and philosopher Pythagoras of Samos, best known for his theorem that says that the square of the longest side (hypotenuse) of a right-angled triangle has an area equal to the sum of the area of the squares of the other two sides. Pythagoras is also said to have discovered irrational numbers. If a right-angled triangle has two sides which are both 1 in length, the hypotenuse will be the square root of 2. Pythagoras proved this number was irrational, that is to say that it cannot be represented by any ordinary fraction $\frac{a}{b}$. Up to this point, it was taken as self-evident that, *in principle*, any constructed line could be measured *exactly* using a standard ruler, provided that we marked the ruler with a sufficiently fine scale. Pythagoras proved this to be false.

This and some other paradoxes in classical mathematics were eventually resolved in the 4th century BC by the Greek mathematician and astronomer Eudoxus with his *Theory of Proportions*, an account of which is to be found in *The Elements*, the classical texts written by the Greek mathematician Euclid of Alexandria. Eudoxus introduced a theory that applied equally well to all lengths by making subtle use of inequalities to deal with equalities.

later achievements

Euclid's Alexandrian School remained the leading centre of thought during the later classical period. Its greatest genius was the Greek mathematician Archimedes, who took both geometry and mechanics to new heights. He died in 212 BC, probably killed by the Roman invaders of his home city of Syracuse, which he brilliantly defended through the use of devastating war machines that capsized the vessels of the invaders. In his tract, *The Method*, Archimedes allied mathematics and physics by insisting on rigorous standards of proof while emphasizing the importance of physical intuition as a guide to the truth.

The Greek mathematician Apollonius of Perga, a younger contemporary of Archimedes, gave the definitive description of curves arising from cones that proved to be a major ingredient of the theory devised by English physicist and mathematician Isaac Newton nearly 2,000 years later to explain planetary orbits. The Greek mathematician and engineer Hero of Alexandria (lived AD 62) invented the first working steam engine, made a primitive thermometer, and proved the formula for the area of a triangle in terms of its three sides. Other outstanding figures were Greek geographer and mathematician Eratosthenes, who calculated the diameter of the earth in 230 BC through the difference in the Sun's elevation at Syrene and Alexandria at the summer solstice, and Greek mathematician Diophantus, whose treatise on number theory inspired French mathematician Fermat's last theorem, while *The Collection* of Greek mathematician, astronomer, and geographer Pappus was the final great intellectual work of classical times.

Arabic	Egyptian	Ionic (Greek)	Hebrew	Chinese	Mayan	Babylonian	Roman
1	I	α	א	一	•	𒁹	I
2	II	β	ב	二	••	𒐖	II
3	III	γ	ג	三	•••	𒐗	III
4	IIII	δ	ד	四	••••	𒐘	IV
5	IIIII	ε	ה	五	—	𒐙	V
6	IIIIII	Γ	ו	六	•̄	𒐚	VI
7	IIIIIII	ζ	ז	七	••̄	𒐛	VII
8	IIIIIIII	η	ח	八	•••̄	𒐜	VIII
9	IIIIIIIII	θ	ט	九	••••̄	𒐝	IX
10	∩	Ι	׳	十	=	𒌋	X

EARLY NUMBER SYSTEMS shown in a comparative chart. In the Middle Ages Greek mathematics was kept alive by the Arabs, who also used a system of numerals devised in India (now called 'Arabic' numerals), which could be used to write down calculations instead of having to resort to an abacus. The Arab scholar al-Khwārizmī summarized Greek and Indian methods for solving equations and wrote the first treatise on the Indian numerals and calculating with them.

decline and fall

Despite its success and staggering sophistication, Greek mathematics remained wedded to the geometric style of Euclid, in which even common algebraic facts about numbers were demonstrated in what appears to us a strange and unnatural fashion through areas of geometrical figures. Even the Ancient Babylonians, 1,000 years before the birth of Pythagoras, seemed more at home with algebra. Although they did not use symbols to represent numbers as we would today, they demonstrated how to solve quadratic equations (in which the unknown quantity x appears through its square, x^2) and compiled astonishingly extensive tables of number triples such as (3, 4, 5) and (4961, 6480, 8161) where the sum of the squares of the two smaller numbers equals the square of the larger. The precursors of modern algebraic methods are to be found in societies such as Mesopotamia, India, and China.

After the 4th century AD classical Greek mathematics entered terminal decline. Mathematics was not revived until the dawn of the modern age, when the need to solve problems in navigation and the physical world ushered in a fresh and progressive epoch.

(continued from p. 607)

improvements in methods of calculation, development of algebraic symbolism, and the development of mathematical methods for use in physics and astronomy. Geometry was revitalized by the invention of coordinate geometry by René Descartes 1637; Blaise Pascal and Pierre de Fermat developed probability theory; John Napier invented logarithms; and Isaac Newton and Gottfried Leibniz invented calculus, later put on a more rigorous footing by Augustin Cauchy. In Russia, Nikolai Lobachevsky rejected Euclid's parallelism and developed a non-Euclidean geometry; this was subsequently generalized by Bernhard Riemann and later utilized by Einstein in his theory of relativity. In the mid-19th century a new major theme emerged: investigation of the logical foundations of mathematics. George Boole showed how logical arguments could be expressed in algebraic symbolism. Friedrich Frege and Giuseppe Peano considerably developed this symbolic logic.

The present In the 20th century, mathematics became much more diversified. Each specialist subject is being studied in far greater depth and advanced work in some fields may be unintelligible to researchers in other fields. Mathematicians working in universities have had the economic freedom to pursue the subject for its own sake. Nevertheless, new branches of mathematics have been developed which are of great practical importance and which have basic ideas simple enough to be taught in secondary schools. Probably the most important of these is the mathematical theory of statistics in which much pioneering work was done by Karl Pearson. Another new development is operations research, which is concerned with finding optimum courses of action in practical situations, particularly in economics and management. As in the late medieval period, commerce began to emerge again as a major impetus for the development of mathematics.

Higher mathematics has a powerful tool in the high-speed electronic computer, which can create and manipulate mathematical 'models' of various systems in science, technology, and commerce.

Modern additions to school syllabuses such as sets, group theory, matrices, and graph theory are sometimes referred to as 'new' or 'modern' mathematics. See also The Origins of Mathematics Focus Feature on pp. 608–609.

> **Related Web sites: Babylonian and Egyptian Mathematics** http://www-history.mcs.st-and.ac.uk/~history/HistTopics/Babylonian_and_Egyptian.html
> **History of Mathematics** http://www-groups.dcs.st-andrews.ac.uk/history/HistTopics/History_overview.html

Matilda, the Empress Maud (1102–1167) claimant to the throne of England as daughter of Henry I. In 1127 Henry forced the barons to accept Matilda, his only surviving legitimate child since the death of his son, as his successor as monarch of England. However, there had never been a woman ruler in either England or Normandy, and most of the barons, supported by the church, elected her cousin ▷Stephen to be king on Henry's death in 1135. Matilda invaded England in 1139 and captured Stephen at Lincoln in 1141. She entered London to be crowned, but was driven out when she demanded money from the Londoners. Civil war followed until Stephen acknowledged Matilda's son, the future Henry II, as his successor in 1153.

On one occasion during the civil war, Matilda was trapped in Oxford Castle in 1142 but escaped over the ice of the frozen River Thames.

Matilda was married to the Holy Roman Emperor Henry V in 1114 and returned to England as the 'Empress Maud' after his death in 1125. In 1128 she married Geoffrey Plantagenet, Count of Anjou (1113–1151) in northwest France, by whom she had a son, the future Henry II. Having returned to England to lay claim to the throne, she rejoined her son in Normandy in 1148.

Matilda's case is sometimes used to suggest that medieval women could not rule a medieval kingdom, but in fact Matilda retained control of Normandy after 1148, and ruled the duchy effectively on behalf of her son when he became king of England in 1154.

Matisse, Henri Emile Benoît (1869–1954) French painter, sculptor and illustrator. Matisse was one of the most original creative forces in early 20th-century art. He was a leading figure in ▷fauvism and later developed a style characterized by strong, sinuous lines, surface pattern, and brilliant colour. *The Dance* (1910; The Hermitage, St Petersburg) is characteristic. Later works include pure abstracts, as in his collages of coloured paper shapes (*gouaches découpées*).

Influenced by Impressionism and then post-Impressionism, by 1905 he had developed his fauvist style of strong, expressive colours. Largely unaffected by cubism and other strident forms of modern art, he concentrated on the decorative effects of colour, line and form, a vivid example being *The Red Room* (1908–09; The Hermitage, St Petersburg).

As early as 1899 he made sculptures and in later years resumed the practice of free and unconventional modelling, his best-known

works being the series in bronze relief, *The Back* (1909–29). As a graphic artist he produced etchings, lithographs and wood-engravings and illustrated Mallarmé's poems, James Joyce's *Ulysses* and other works. As a designer he produced sets and costumes for Diaghilev's Ballets Russes. He also designed and built the chapel for the Dominicans of Vence, near Nice, consecrated in 1951, a late work of importance in applying an entirely modern decorative sense to a religious interior.

matriarchy form of society where domestic and political life is dominated by women, where kinship is traced exclusively through the female line, and where religion is centred around the cult of a mother goddess. A society dominated by men is known as a patriarchy.

matrix in biology, usually refers to the ▷extracellular matrix.

matrix in mathematics, a square ($n \times n$) or rectangular ($m \times n$) array of elements (numbers or algebraic variables) used to facilitate the study of problems in which the relation between the elements is important. They are a means of condensing information about mathematical systems and can be used for, among other things, solving simultaneous linear equations (see ▷simultaneous equations and ▷transformation).

Matsuoka, Yosuke (1880–1946) Japanese politician, foreign minister 1940–41. A fervent nationalist, Matsuoka led Japan out of the League of Nations in 1933 when it condemned Japan for the seizure of Manchuria. As foreign minister, he allied Japan with Germany and Italy. At the end of World War II, he was arrested as a war criminal but died before his trial was concluded.

Matsuyama largest city of Ehime prefecture, Shikoku island, Japan, facing the Inland Sea; population (1994) 456,000. Industries include agricultural machinery, textiles, and chemicals. Traditional cotton cloth is also produced locally. The Dogo hot spring attracts visitors to its public bath house, built in 1894. The castle, built in 1602–3, has been restored or rebuilt five times, most recently in 1986.

matter in physics, anything that has mass. All matter is made up of ▷atoms, which in turn are made up of ▷elementary particles; it ordinarily exists in one of three physical states: solid, liquid, or gas.

States of matter Whether matter exists as a solid, liquid, or gas depends on its temperature and the pressure on it. ▷Kinetic theory describes how the state of a material depends on the movement and arrangement of its atoms or molecules. In a solid the atoms or molecules vibrate in a fixed position. In a liquid, they do not occupy fixed positions as in a solid, and yet neither do they have the freedom of random movement that occurs within a gas, so the atoms or molecules within a liquid will always follow the shape of their container. The transition between states takes place at definite temperatures, called melting point and boiling point.

Conservation of matter In chemical reactions matter is conserved, so no matter is lost or gained and the sum of the mass of the reactants will always equal the sum of the end products.

> **Related Web site: States of Matter** http://ull.chemistry.uakron.edu/genobc/Chapter_06/

HENRI MATISSE French artist Henri Matisse working on a charcoal sketch. *Archive Photos*

MATTERHORN The Matterhorn, in the Pennine Alps on the Swiss–Italian border, is snow-covered all year round. *Image Bank*

Matterhorn (French *le Cervin*; Italian *il Cervino*) mountain peak in the Alps on the Swiss-Italian border; 4,478 m/14,690 ft. It was first climbed in 1865 by English mountaineer Edward Whymper (1840–1911); four members of his party of seven were killed when a rope broke during their descent.

Matthau, Walter (1920–2000) Born Walter Matuschanskavasky. US actor. He was impressive in both comedy and dramatic roles. He gained film stardom after his stage success in *The Odd Couple* (1965), and won an Academy Award for *The Fortune Cookie* (1966). In *Grumpy Old Men* (1993) and *Grumpy Old Men II* (1995), he was reunited with his frequent 1960s co-star Jack ▷Lemmon.

> *Somerset Maugham*
> *No married man's ever made up his mind till he's heard what his wife has got to say about it.*
> *Lady Frederick*

Matthew, St (lived 1st century AD) Christian apostle and evangelist, the traditional author of the first Gospel. He is usually identified with Levi, who was a tax collector in the service of Herod Antipas, and was called by Jesus to be a disciple as he sat by the Lake of Galilee receiving customs dues. His emblem is a man with wings. His feast day is 21 September.

Matthews, Stanley (1915–2000) English footballer who played for Stoke City, Blackpool, and England. He played nearly 700 Football League games, and won 54 international caps. He was the first Footballer of the Year in 1948 (and again in 1963), the first European Footballer of the Year in 1956, and the first footballer to be knighted for services to the game in 1965.

Matthias Corvinus (c. 1440–1490) King of Hungary from 1458. His aim of uniting Hungary, Austria, and Bohemia involved him in long wars with Holy Roman emperor Frederick III and the kings of Bohemia and Poland, during which he captured Vienna (1485) and made it his capital. His father was János Hunyadi.

Maugham, W(illiam) Somerset (1874–1965) English writer. His work includes the novels *Of Human Bondage* (1915), *The Moon and Sixpence* (1919), and *Cakes and Ale* (1930); the short-story collections *Ashenden* (1928) and *Rain and Other Stories* (1933); and the plays *Lady Frederick* (1907) and *Our Betters* (1917). There were new editions of *Collected Stories* in 1900 and *Selected Plays* in 1991. A penetrating observer of human behaviour, his writing is essentially anti-romantic and there is a vein of cynicism running through his work.

Maugham was born in Paris. He studied medicine at St Thomas's Hospital, London. He drew upon his medical experiences in his first novel, *Liza of Lambeth* (1897), and the success of that novel, and of *Mrs Craddock* (1902), made him decide upon a literary career. *Of Human Bondage* is once again set in the familiar world of the medical student; *The Moon and Sixpence* is partly based on the life of the artist Paul Gauguin; *Cakes and Ale* is about a famous novelist; and *The Razor's Edge* (1944) is the story of a young US war veteran. During World War I Maugham was a secret agent in Switzerland and Russia, and his *Ashenden* spy stories are based on this experience. Of his numerous other volumes of short stories, those with a Malayan or Pacific background are particularly well known.

Mau Mau Kenyan secret guerrilla movement 1952–60, an offshoot of the Kikuyu Central Association banned in World War II. Its aim was to end British colonial rule. This was achieved in 1960 with the granting of Kenyan independence and the election of Jomo Kenyatta as Kenya's first prime minister.

Mauna Loa active volcano on the Pacific island of Hawaii, rising to a height of 4,169 m/13,678 ft. It has numerous craters, including the second-largest active crater in the world. Since the early 19th century there have been lava flows from the crater covering about half the island of Hawaii; averaging one eruption every 3½ years, it is considered an effusive, rather than an explosive, volcano, with eruptions along fissures in its flank as well as in its central crater.

Maundy Thursday in the Christian church, the Thursday before Easter. The ceremony of washing the feet of pilgrims on that day was instituted in commemoration of Jesus' washing of the apostles' feet and observed from the 4th century to 1754.

Maupassant, (Henry René Albert) Guy de (1850–1893) French author. He established a reputation with the short story 'Boule de suif/Ball of Fat' (1880) and wrote some 300 short stories in all. His novels include *Une Vie/A Woman's Life* (1883) and *Bel-Ami* (1885). He was encouraged as a writer by Gustave ▷Flaubert.

Related Web site: Maupassant's Short Stories of the Tragedy and Comedy of Life http://etext.lib.virginia.edu/etcbin/ browse-mixed-new?id=MauStor&images=images/ modeng&data=/texts/english/modeng/parsed&tag=public

Mauriac, François (1885–1970) French novelist. His novels are studies, from a Roman Catholic standpoint, of the psychological and moral problems of the Catholic and provincial middle class, usually set in his native city of Bordeaux and the Landes region of southwestern France. *Le Baiser au lépreux/A Kiss for the Leper* (1922) describes the conflict of an unhappy marriage, while the irreconcilability of Christian practice and human nature is examined in *Fleuve de feu/River of Fire* (1923), *Le Désert de l'amour/The Desert of Love* (1925), and *Thérèse Desqueyroux* (1927). He was awarded the Nobel Prize for Literature in 1952.

Mauritania see country box.

Mauritius see country box.

Maurois, André (1885–1967) Pen-name of Emile Herzog. French writer and biographer. During World War I he was attached to the British Army as a liaison officer, and the essays in *Les Silences du Colonel Bramble* (1918) and *Les Discours du Docteur O'Grady* (1920) offer humorously sympathetic observations on the British character. His other works include the semi-autobiographical *Bernard Quesnay* (1926) and distinguished biographies intended to read as novels, such as *Ariel, ou la vie de Shelley* (1923), *La Vie de Disraëli* (1927), *Byron* (1930), *Voltaire* (1932), *Dickens* (1934), *Lélia, ou la vie de George Sand* (1952), *Olympia, ou la vie de Victor Hugo* (1953), and *Les Trois Dumas* (1957).

Mauritania

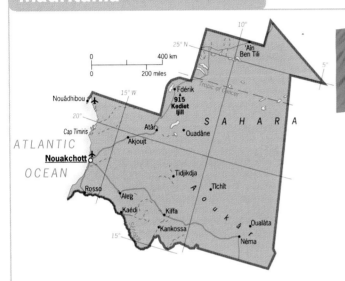

ETHNIC GROUPS over 80% of the population is of Moorish or Moorish-black origin; about 18% is black African (concentrated in the south); there is a small European minority
LANGUAGE Hasaniya Arabic (official), Pulaar, Soninke, Wolof (all national languages), French (particularly in the south)
RELIGION Sunni Muslim (state religion)
EDUCATION not compulsory
LITERACY RATE 52% (men); 32% (women) (2003 est)
LABOUR FORCE 53% agriculture, 15% industry, 32% services (1997 est)
LIFE EXPECTANCY 51 (men); 54 (women) (2000–05)
CHILD MORTALITY RATE (under 5, per 1,000 live births) 183 (2001)
INTERNET USERS (per 10,000 people) 37.3 (2002 est)
PERSONAL COMPUTER USERS (per 100 people) 1.1 (2002 est)

Population and society

POPULATION 2,893,000 (2003 est)
POPULATION GROWTH RATE 2.5% (2000–15)
POPULATION DENSITY (per sq km) 3 (2003 est)
URBAN POPULATION (% of total) 62 (2003 est)
AGE DISTRIBUTION (% of total population) 0–14 44%, 15–59 51%, 60+ 5% (2002 est)

Mauritania country in northwest Africa, bounded northeast by Algeria, east and south by Mali, southwest by Senegal, west by the Atlantic Ocean, and northwest by Western Sahara.

NATIONAL NAME *Al-Jumhuriyya al-Islamiyya al-Mawritaniyya/République Islamique Arabe et Africaine de Mauritanie/Islamic Republic of Mauritania*
AREA 1,030,700 sq km/397,953 sq mi
CAPITAL Nouakchott (and chief port)
MAJOR TOWNS/CITIES Nouâdhibou, Kaédi, Zouerate, Kiffa, Rosso, Atar
MAJOR PORTS Nouâdhibou
PHYSICAL FEATURES valley of River Senegal in south; remainder arid and flat

Government

HEAD OF STATE Maaoya Sid'Ahmed Ould Taya from 1984
HEAD OF GOVERNMENT Sghair Ould Mbureck from 2003
POLITICAL SYSTEM emergent democracy
POLITICAL EXECUTIVE limited presidency
ADMINISTRATIVE DIVISIONS 12 regions and one capital district
ARMED FORCES 15,700; plus paramilitary forces of 5,000 (2002 est)
DEATH PENALTY retained and used for ordinary crimes

Economy and resources

CURRENCY ouguiya
GPD (US$) 983 million (2002 est)
REAL GDP GROWTH (% change on previous year) 4.6 (2001)
GNI (US$) 1.2 billion (2002 est)
GNI PER CAPITA (PPP) (US$) 1,740 (2002 est)
CONSUMER PRICE INFLATION 4% (2003 est)
UNEMPLOYMENT 23% (1995 est)

FOREIGN DEBT (US$) 2.3 billion (2001 est)
MAJOR TRADING PARTNERS Japan, France, Spain, Italy, Belgium, Algeria, Germany
RESOURCES copper, gold, iron ore, gypsum, phosphates, sulphur, peat
INDUSTRIES fish products, cheese and butter, processing of minerals (including imported petroleum), mining
EXPORTS iron ore, fish and fish products. Principal market: Italy 15% (2001)
IMPORTS machinery and transport equipment, foodstuffs, consumer goods, building materials, mineral fuels. Principal source: France 23% (2001)
ARABLE LAND 0.5% (2000 est)
AGRICULTURAL PRODUCTS millet, sorghum, dates, maize, rice, pulses, groundnuts, sweet potatoes; livestock rearing (the principal occupation of rural population); fishing (providing 41.4% of export earnings in 1999). Only 1% of Mauritania receives enough rain to grow crops

MAURITANIA This Mauritanian stamp depicts the development of the iron-ore mining industry, centred around the town of Zouerate. *Stanley Gibbons*

Chronology

early Christian era: A Roman province with the name Mauritania, after the Mauri, its Berber inhabitants who became active in the long-distance salt trade.

7th–11th centuries: Eastern Mauritania was incorporated in the larger Ghana Empire, centred on Mali to the east, but with its capital at Kumbi in southeast Mauritania. The Berbers were reduced to vassals and converted to Islam in the 8th century.

11th–12th centuries: The area's Sanhadja Berber inhabitants, linked to the Morocco-based Almoravid Empire, destroyed the Ghana Empire and spread Islam among neighbouring peoples.

13th–15th centuries: Southeast Mauritania formed part of the Muslim Mali Empire, which extended to the east and south.

1441: Coast visited by Portuguese, who founded port of Arguin and captured Africans to sell as slaves.

15th–16th centuries: Eastern Mauritania formed part of Muslim Songhai Empire, which spread across western Sahel, and Arab tribes migrated into the area.

1817: Senegal Treaty recognized coastal region (formerly disputed by European nations) as French sphere of influence.

1903: Formally became French protectorate.

1920: Became French colony, within French West Africa.

1960: Independence achieved, with Moktar Ould Daddah, leader of Mauritanian People's Party (PPM), as president. New capital built at Nouakchott.

1968: Underlying tensions between agriculturalist black population of south and economically dominant semi-nomadic Arabo-Berber peoples,

or Moors, of desert north became more acute after Arabic was made an official language (with French).

1976: Western Sahara, to the northwest, ceded by Spain to Mauritania and Morocco. Mauritania occupied the southern area and Morocco the mineral-rich north. Polisario Front formed in Sahara to resist this occupation and guerrilla war broke out, with the Polisario receiving backing from Algeria and Libya.

1979: A peace accord was signed with the Polisario Front in Algiers, in which Mauritania renounced its claims to southern Western Sahara and recognized the Polisario regime; diplomatic relations were restored with Algeria.

1981: Diplomatic relations with Morocco were broken after it annexed southern Western Sahara.

1984: Col Maaoya Sid'Ahmed Ould Taya became president.

1985: Relations with Morocco were restored.

1989: There were violent clashes in Mauritania and Senegal between Moors and black Africans, chiefly of Senegalese origins; over 50,000 Senegalese were expelled.

1991: An amnesty was called for political prisoners. Political parties were legalized and a new multiparty constitution was approved in a referendum.

1992: The first multiparty elections were largely boycotted by the opposition; Taya and his Social Democratic Republican Party (DSRP) were re-elected. Diplomatic relations with Senegal resumed.

2003: President Taya was re-elected with 67% of the vote. His main opposition rival, former president Khouna Ould Haidalla, won 19% and rejected the poll as fraudulent. Haidalla was later arrested and accused of plotting to overthrow Taya.

Mauryan dynasty Indian dynasty *c.* 321–*c.* 185 BC, founded by **Chandragupta Maurya** (321–*c.* 297 BC). Under Emperor ▷Asoka most of India was united for the first time, but after his death in 232 the empire was riven by dynastic disputes. Reliant on a highly organized aristocracy and a centralized administration, it survived until the assassination of Emperor Brihadratha in 185 BC and the creation of the Sunga dynasty.

mausoleum large, free-standing, sumptuous tomb. The term derives from the magnificent sepulchral monument built for King Mausolus of Caria (died 353 BC) by his wife Artemisia at Halicarnassus in Asia Minor (modern-day Bodrum in Anatolia, Turkey); it was considered one of the ▷Seven Wonders of the World. Today, little remains at the site of the original monument, although some fragmentary sculptures from it are kept in the British Museum, London.

maxim saying or proverb that gives moral guidance or a piece of advice on the way to live ('First come, first served'; 'Better late than never').

Maximilian (1832–1867) Emperor of Mexico 1864–67. He accepted that title when the French emperor Napoleon III's troops occupied the country, but encountered resistance from the deposed president Benito ▷Juárez. In 1866, after the French troops withdrew on the insistence of the USA, Maximilian was captured by Mexican republicans and shot.

Maximilian I (1459–1519) German king from 1486, Holy Roman Emperor from 1493. He was the son of the emperor Frederick III (1415–93). Through a combination of dynastic marriages and diplomacy backed up by military threats, Maximilian was able to build up the Habsburg inheritance. He married Mary of Burgundy in 1477, and after her death in 1582 held onto Burgundian lands. He married his son, Philip the Handsome, to Joanna, the daughter of ▷Ferdinand and ▷Isabella, and undertook long wars with Italy and Hungary in attempts to extend Habsburg power. The eventual legatee of these arrangements was Maximilian's grandson, Charles V.

maximum and minimum in ▷coordinate geometry, points at which the slope of a curve representing a ▷function changes from positive to negative (maximum), or from negative to positive (minimum). A tangent to the curve at a maximum or minimum has zero gradient.

Maxwell, James Clerk (1831–1879) Scottish physicist. His main achievement was in the understanding of ▷electromagnetic waves: **Maxwell's equations** bring together electricity, magnetism, and light in one set of relations. He studied gases, optics, and the sensation of colour, and his theoretical work in magnetism prepared the way for wireless telegraphy and telephony. In developing the kinetic theory of gases, Maxwell gave the final proof that heat resides in the motion of molecules. Studying colour vision, Maxwell explained how all colours could be built up from mixtures of the primary colours red, green, and blue. Maxwell confirmed English physicist Thomas ▷Young's theory that the eye has three kinds of receptors sensitive to the primary colours, and showed that colour blindness is due to defects in the receptors. In 1861 he produced the first colour photograph to use a three-colour process.

Related Web site: Maxwell, James Clerk http://www-history.mcs. st-and.ac.uk/history/Mathematicians/Maxwell.html

Maya member of an American Indian civilization originating in the Yucatán Peninsula in Central America about 2600 BC, with later sites in Mexico, Guatemala, and Belize, and enjoying a classical period AD 325–925, after which it declined as Toltecs from the

Mauritius

Mauritius island country in the Indian Ocean, east of Madagascar.

Government

NATIONAL NAME *Republic of Mauritius*
AREA 1,865 sq km/720 sq mi
CAPITAL Port Louis (and chief port)
MAJOR TOWNS/CITIES Beau Bassin-Rose Hill, Curepipe, Quatre Bornes, Vacaos-Phoenix
PHYSICAL FEATURES mountainous, volcanic island surrounded by coral reefs; the island of Rodrigues is part of Mauritius; there are several small island dependencies

HEAD OF STATE Aneerood Jugnauth from 2003
HEAD OF GOVERNMENT Paul Bérenger from 2003
POLITICAL SYSTEM liberal democracy
POLITICAL EXECUTIVE parliamentary
ADMINISTRATIVE DIVISIONS five municipalities and four district councils
ARMED FORCES no standing defence forces; 2,000-strong police mobile unit (2002 est)
DEATH PENALTY abolished in 1995

Economy and resources

CURRENCY Mauritian rupee
GPD (US$) 4.5 billion (2002 est)
REAL GDP GROWTH (% change on previous year) 5.8 (2001)
GNI (US$) 4.7 billion (2002 est)
GNI PER CAPITA (PPP) (US$) 10,530 (2002 est)
CONSUMER PRICE INFLATION 5.8% (2003 est)
UNEMPLOYMENT 8% (2001)
FOREIGN DEBT (US$) 1.4 billion (2001 est)
MAJOR TRADING PARTNERS UK, France, South Africa, USA, India, Australia, Germany
INDUSTRIES textiles and clothing, footwear and other leather products, food products, diamond cutting, jewellery, electrical components, chemical products, furniture, tourism
EXPORTS raw sugar, clothing, tea, molasses, jewellery. Principal market: UK 25.8% (2000)
IMPORTS textile yarn and fabrics, petroleum products, industrial machinery, food products, mineral fuels, manufactured goods. Principal source: France 20% (2000)
ARABLE LAND 49.3% (2000 est)
AGRICULTURAL PRODUCTS sugar cane, tea, tobacco, potatoes, maize; poultry farming; fishing; forest resources

Population and society

POPULATION 1,221,000 (2003 est)
POPULATION GROWTH RATE 0.9% (2000–15)
POPULATION DENSITY (per sq km) 599 (2003 est)
URBAN POPULATION (% of total) 42 (2003 est)
AGE DISTRIBUTION (% of total population) 0–14 25%, 15–59 66%, 60+ 9% (2002 est)
ETHNIC GROUPS five principal ethnic groups: French, black Africans, Indians, Chinese, and Mulattos (or Creoles). Indo-Mauritians predominate, constituting 68% of the population, followed by Creoles (27%), Sino-Mauritians (3%), Franco-Mauritians (2%), and Europeans (0.5%)
LANGUAGE English (official), French, Creole (36%), Bhojpuri (32%), other Indian languages
RELIGION Hindu over 50%, Christian (mainly Roman Catholic) about 30%, Muslim 17%
EDUCATION (compulsory years) 7
LABOUR FORCE 11.1% agriculture, 39% industry, 49.9% services (2001)

See also ▷Berber; ▷Ghana, ancient; ▷Mali Empire; ▷Western Sahara.

Chronology

1598: Previously uninhabited, the island was discovered by the Dutch and named after Prince Morris of Nassau.

1710: Dutch colonists withdrew.

1721: Reoccupied by French East India Company, who renamed it Île de France, and established sugar cane and tobacco plantations worked by imported African slaves.

1814: Ceded to Britain by the Treaty of Paris.

1835: Slavery abolished; indentured Indian and Chinese labourers imported to work the sugar-cane plantations, which were later hit by competition from beet sugar.

1903: Formerly administered with Seychelles, it became a single colony.

1936: Mauritius Labour Party (MLP) founded, drawing strong support from sugar workers.

1957: Internal self-government granted.

1968: Independence achieved from Britain within Commonwealth, with Seewoosagur Ramgoolam of centrist Indian-dominated MLP as prime minister.

1971: A state of emergency was temporarily imposed as a result of industrial unrest.

1982: Aneerood Jugnauth, of the moderate socialist Mauritius Socialist Movement (MSM), became prime minister, pledging a programme of nonalignment, nationalization, and the creation of a republic.

1992: Became a republic within the Commonwealth, with Cassam Uteem elected as president.

1995: The MLP and the cross-community Mauritian Militant Movement (MMM) coalition won election victory; Navin Ramgoolam (MLP) became the prime minister.

2000: General elections in mid-September 2000 were won by an opposition alliance, led by a former prime minister, Aneerood Jugnauth.

2003: Prime Minister Jugnauth stepped down and was replaced by deputy prime minister and finance minister Paul Bérenger.

MAURITIUS The island's beaches, such as this one at St Garav, are becoming increasingly popular with tourists. *Leonardo.com*

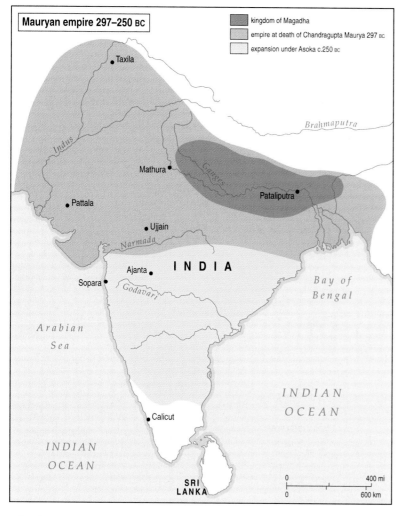

Mauryan empire 297–250 BC

kingdom of Magadha

empire at death of Chandragupta Maurya 297 BC

expansion under Asoka c.250 BC

MAYFLY *Ephemera danica*, the largest British species of mayfly, which swarms on fast-flowing streams. *Premaphotos Wildlife*

Valley of Mexico moved south into the area, building new ceremonial centres and dominating the local people. Nevertheless, Maya sovereignty was maintained, for the most part, until late in the Spanish conquest (1560s) in some areas. Today the Maya are Roman Catholic, and number 8–9 million (1994 est). They live in Yucatán, Guatemala, Belize, and western Honduras. Many still speak Maya, a member of the Totonac-Mayan (Penutian) language family, as well as Spanish. In the 1980s more than 100,000 Maya fled from Guatemala to Mexico.

> **Related Web site: Mayan Folktales** http://www.folkart.com/ ~latitude/folktale/folktale.htm

maya (Sanskrit 'illusion') in Hindu philosophy, mainly in the *Vedānta*, the cosmos which Isvara, the personal expression of Brahman, or the ▷atman, has called into being. This is real, yet also an illusion, since its reality is not everlasting.

Mayan art see ▷pre-Columbian art.

Mayapán ancient Mayan city 55 km/35 mi southeast of Mérida, in modern Mexico. Mayapán was the dominant religious and political centre of the Yucatán region from 1200 to 1450. Ruled by the despotic Cocon, it was abandoned when they were overthrown in the mid-15th century.

MAYA A terracotta vase made by the Maya people during what is now known as their late classical period, AD 600–900. *The Art Archive/Museum San Pedro de Sula Honduras/Dagli Orti*

May Day first day of May. In many countries it is a national holiday in honour of labour; see also ▷Labour Day.

Mayer, Louis B(urt) (1885–1957) Adopted name of Eliezer Mayer. Russian-born US film producer. One of the founders of ▷Metro-Goldwyn-Mayer (MGM) studios in 1924, he was largely responsible for MGM's lavish style. He retired in 1951.

mayfly any of a group of insects whose adult form lives only very briefly in the spring. The larval stage, which can last a year or

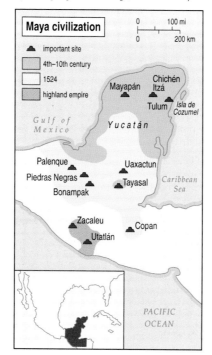

Maya civilization

▲ important site

4th–10th century

1524

highland empire

more, is passed in water, the adult form developing gradually from the nymph through successive moults. The adult has transparent, net-veined wings. (Order Ephemerida.)

May 4th Movement Chinese student-led nationalist movement ignited by demonstrations in Beijing in 1919. It demanded that China's unpopular warlord government reject the decision by the Versailles peace conference to confirm Japan's rights over the Shandong peninsula that had been asserted in the Twenty-one demands in 1915.

Maynard Smith, John (1920–) English geneticist and evolutionary biologist. He applied ▷game theory to animal behaviour and developed the concept of the ▷evolutionary stable strategy as a mathematical technique for studying the evolution of behaviour.

Mayo county of the Republic of Ireland, in the province of Connacht; county town Castlebar; area 5,400 sq km/2,084 sq mi; population (1996) 111,500. Its wild Atlantic coastline is about 400 km/249 mi long. The principal towns are Ballina, Ballinrobe, and Westport, and the principal rivers are the Moy, the Robe, and the Owenmore. Loughs Conn and Mask lie within the county. Agriculture includes pig, sheep, and cattle farming, and salmon fishing (particularly in the River Moy). The soil of the central plain is fertile, and crops include potatoes and oats. An excellent marble is found in the northwest district.

> **Related Web site: History of Magh Eó (Mayo Abbey) in County Mayo in the West of Ireland** http://www.mayo-ireland.ie/Mayo/Towns/ MayAbbey/HistMAbb/HistMAbb.htm

mayor title of the head of urban administration. In England, Wales, and Northern Ireland, the mayor is the principal officer of a district council that has been granted district-borough status under royal charter. In the USA a mayor is the elected head of a city or town. In 1996 the Labour Party floated proposals for directly elected mayors in Britain, which it confirmed when it came into power in 1997. A referendum in May 1998 approved establishing an elected mayor of London. A July 1998 government White Paper proposed allowing local authorites to introduce directly elected mayors, working in tandem with assemblies or executive committees, as a way of reviving local democracy. In 2000 Ken Livingstone was elected Mayor of London.

Mayotte (or Mahore) island group of the ▷Comoros, off the east coast of Africa, a *collectivité territoriale* of France by its own wish; area 374 sq km/144 sq mi; population (1994 est) 109,600. The two main islands are Grande Terre and Petite Terre. The capital is Dzaoudzi. Industries include coffee, copra, vanilla, fishing, cloves, cocoa, and ylang-ylang (oil-yielding tree). The languages spoken are French and Swahili.

mayweed any of several species of the daisy family native to Europe and Asia and naturalized elsewhere, including the European dog fennel or stinking daisy (*Anthemis cotula*), naturalized in North America, and the pineapple mayweed (*Matricaria matricarioides*), found in Europe and Asia. All have finely divided leaves. (Family Compositae.)

Mazarin, Jules (1602–1661) Born Giulio Raimondo Mazzarini. French politician who succeeded Richelieu as chief minister of France in 1642. His attack on the power of the nobility led to the ▷Fronde and his temporary exile, but his diplomacy achieved a successful conclusion to the Thirty Years' War, and, in alliance with Oliver Cromwell during the British protectorate, he gained victory over Spain.

Mazowiecki, Tadeusz (1927–) Polish politician, adviser to the ▷Solidarity trade-union movement and Poland's first post-war non-communist prime minister 1989–90. In the presidential elections of November 1990 he lost to Lech ▷Wałęsa. In April 1994 he formed the Freedom Union (UW). In the late 1990s he moved away from direct involvement in Polish internal politics. In 1992 he was appointed special reporter to the United Nations (UN) over conflicts in former Yugoslavia.

mazurka any of a family of traditional Polish dances from the 16th century, characterized by foot-stamping and heel-clicking, together with a turning movement. The music for the mazurka is in triple time (3/4), with dotted rhythms and the accentuation of weak beats, on which phrases also begin and end. It is found at a variety of speeds, but is usually not as fast as the waltz, which is also formally a more rigid dance than the mazurka. During the 18th and 19th centuries, it spread throughout Europe and was made famous by Chopin's approximately 60 works in the genre. Other composers of the mazurka include Karol Szymanowski, Glinka, and Mussorgsky.

Mazzini, Giuseppe (1805–1872) Italian nationalist. He was a member of the revolutionary society, the Carbonari, and founded in exile the nationalist movement Giovane Italia (Young Italy) in 1831. Returning to Italy on the outbreak of the 1848 revolution, he headed a republican government established in Rome, but was forced into exile again on its overthrow in 1849. He acted as a focus for the movement for Italian unity (see ▷Risorgimento).

Mbabane administrative capital of ▷Swaziland, in the north-west of the country, near the South African border; population (2001 est) 74,800. It is situated in the Hhohho District of the Highveld, and is connected by rail to nearby coal mines and to the Indian Ocean port of Maputo, in Mozambique, 160 km/100 mi to the east. The legislative capital, **Lobamba**, is nearby to the south. In addition to mining and local crafts, industries include cement manufacture, finance, and banking. Aided by the development of a hotel and casino complex in the Ezulwini valley, about 11 km/7 mi from Mbabane, tourism has become a major industry.

mbalax pop music of West Africa with polyrhythmic percussion and dramatic vocal harmonies. Evolving from the traditional rhythms of the Mandinka people, and absorbing a Cuban influence, it incorporated electric guitars and other Western instruments in the 1970s.

mbaqanga (or **township jive**) South African pop music, an urban style that evolved in the 1960s, with high-pitched, choppy guitar and a powerful bass line; it draws on funk, reggae, and (vocally) on South African choral music. Mahlathini (1937–1999) and the Mahotella Queens were long-established exponents.

Mbeki, Thabo (1942–) South African politician, first executive deputy president from 1994 and president from 1999. As chair of the ▷African National Congress (ANC) from 1989, he played an important role in the constitutional talks with the de Klerk government that eventually led to the adoption of a nonracial political system. In December 1997 he replaced Nelson Mandela as ANC President, and in June 1999 succeeded him as president.

MCC abbreviation for **Marylebone Cricket Club**.

MD abbreviation for ▷Maryland, a state of the USA.

MDMA (3,4-methylenedio-xymethamphetamine) psychedelic drug, also known as ▷ecstasy.

ME abbreviation for ▷Maine, a state of the USA.

Mead, Margaret (1901–1978) US anthropologist who popularized cultural relativity and challenged the conventions of Western society with *Coming of Age in Samoa* (1928) and subsequent works. Her fieldwork was later criticized. She was a popular speaker on civil liberties, ecological sanity, feminism, and population control.

> **Margaret Mead**
> *Human beings do not carry civilization in their genes.*
> The New York Times Magazine, April 1964

meal-worm any larva of the beetle genus *Tenebrio*, especially *T. molitor*. Meal-worms are slender and round, about 2.5 cm/1 in long, and tawny with bright rusty bands. They are pests of stored grain.

mealy bug kind of ▷scale insect.

mean in mathematics, a measure of the average of a number of terms or quantities. The simple **arithmetic mean** is the average value of the quantities, that is, the sum of the quantities divided by their number. The **weighted mean** takes into account the frequency of the terms that are summed; it is calculated by multiplying each term by the number of times it occurs, summing the results and dividing this total by the total number of occurrences. The **geometric mean** of n quantities is the nth root of their product. In statistics, it is a measure of central tendency of a set of data.

meander loop-shaped curve in a mature ▷river flowing sinuously across flat country. As a river flows, any curve in its course is accentuated by the current. On the outside of the curve the velocity, and therefore the erosion, of the current is greatest. Here the river cuts into the outside bank, producing a **cutbank** or **river cliff** and the river's deepest point, or **thalweg**. On the curve's inside the current is slow and deposits any transported material, building up a gentle slip-off slope. As each meander migrates in the direction of its cutbank, the river gradually changes its course across the flood plain.

mean deviation in statistics, a measure of the spread of a population from the ▷mean.

mean free path in physics, the average distance travelled by a particle, atom, or molecule between successive collisions. It is of importance in the ▷kinetic theory of gases.

means test method of assessing the amount to be paid in ▷social security benefits, (for example the ▷income support and housing benefits) which takes into account all sources of personal or family income.

measles acute virus disease (rubeola), spread by airborne infection. Symptoms are fever, severe catarrh, small spots inside the mouth, and a raised, blotchy red rash appearing for about a week after two weeks' incubation. Prevention is by vaccination.

In industrialized countries measles is not usually a serious disease, but serious complications may develop, so most developed countries have a vaccination programme. More than 1 million children a year die of measles (1995); a high percentage of them are Third World children.

In the UK, the MMR (measles, mumps, and rubella) vaccine is given to children at 12 to 15 months, with a reinforcing dose (a booster) before school, usually between 3 and 5 years.

Meath county of the Republic of Ireland, in the province of Leinster; county town Navan; area 2,340 sq km/903 sq mi; population (1996) 109,700. The chief river is the Boyne, of which the Blackwater is a tributary. The principal towns are Kells, Trim, Athboy, Bettystown, and Laytown. Cattle and sheep are reared, and oats and potatoes are grown. The largest working lead mine in Europe is located near Navan. ▷Tara Hill, 155 m/509 ft high, was the site of a palace and was the coronation place of many kings of Ireland; St Patrick also preached here. The Book of Kells (now held in the Trinity College Library) was produced at Kells in the early 9th century.

Mecca (Arabic **Makkah**) city in Saudi Arabia and, as birthplace of Muhammad, the holiest city of the Islamic world; population (1992 est) 965,700. In the centre of Mecca is the Great Mosque, in the courtyard of which is the ▷Kaaba, the sacred shrine containing the black stone believed to have been given to Abraham by the angel Gabriel.

mechanical advantage (MA) in physics, the ratio by which the load moved by a machine is greater than the effort applied to that machine. In equation terms: MA = load/effort.

mechanical equivalent of heat in physics, a constant factor relating the calorie (the c.g.s. unit of heat) to the joule (the unit of mechanical energy), equal to 4.1868 joules per calorie. It is redundant in the SI system of units, which measures heat and all forms of energy in ▷joules.

mechanics branch of physics dealing with the motions of bodies and the forces causing these motions, and also with the forces acting on bodies in ▷equilibrium. It is usually divided into ▷dynamics and ▷statics.

Quantum mechanics is the system based on the ▷quantum theory, which has superseded Newtonian mechanics in the interpretation of physical phenomena on the atomic scale.

mechanization the use of machines in place of manual labour or the use of animals. Until the 1700s there were few machines available to help people in the home, on the land, or in industry. There were no factories, only cottage industries, in which people carried out work, such as weaving, in their own homes for other people. The 1700s saw a long series of inventions, initially in the textile industry, that ushered in a machine age and brought about the ▷Industrial Revolution.

mechanized infantry combat vehicle (MICV) tracked military vehicle designed to fight as part of an armoured battle group; that is, with tanks. It is armed with a quick-firing cannon and one or more machine guns. MICVs have replaced armoured personnel carriers.

Meciar, Vladimír (1942–) Slovak politician, prime minister of the Slovak Republic January 1993–March 1994 and again October 1994–September 1998. He held a number of posts under the Czechoslovak communist regime until, as a dissident, he was expelled from the party in 1970. He joined the Public Against Violence (PAV) movement in 1989, campaigning for a free Czechoslovakia, then, as leader of the Movement for a Democratic Slovakia (HZDS) from 1990, sought an independent Slovak state. Under the federal system, Meciar became prime minister of the Slovak Republic in 1990 and the new state's first prime minister in January 1993. He resigned in March 1994 after a no-confidence vote in parliament, but was returned as premier in October 1994

following a general election victory. In 1999 he was defeated by Rudolf Schuster in the country's first direct presidential elections. In April 2000, Meciar was arrested on charges of corruption.

Mecklenburg–West Pomerania (German **Mecklenburg-Vorpommern**) administrative *Land* (state) of Germany; area 22,887 sq km/8,837 sq mi; population (1995) 1,825,000; the capital is ▷Schwerin and other towns and cities include Rostock, Wismar, Stralsund, and Neubrandenburg. Products include fish, ships, diesel engines, electronics, plastics, and chalk.

Medan seaport and economic centre of the island of Sumatra, Indonesia; population (1990) 1,885,000. The largest city on the island, its industries include tobacco and tea processing, and manufacture of machinery, rope, ceramics, bricks, tiles, and soap. Some of its products are rubber, tobacco, and palm oil.

Medawar, Peter Brian (1915–1987) Brazilian-born British immunologist who was awarded a Nobel Prize for Physiology or Medicine in 1960 with Macfarlane Burnet for their work on acquired immunological tolerance of transplanted tissues. They discovered that the body's resistance to grafted tissue is undeveloped in the newborn child, and studied the way it is acquired. Medawar was knighted in 1965.

Mede member of a people of northwestern Iran who in the 9th century BC were tributaries to Assyria, with their capital at Ecbatana (now Hamadán), in the ancient southwestern Asian country of Media. Allying themselves with Babylon, they destroyed the Assyrian capital of ▷Nineveh in 612 BC, and extended their conquests into central Anatolia. In 550 BC they were overthrown by the Persians, with whom they rapidly merged.

Medea in Greek mythology, the sorceress daughter of the king of Colchis. When ▷Jason reached Colchis, she fell in love with him, helped him acquire the ▷Golden Fleece, and they fled together. When Jason later married Creusa, daughter of the king of Corinth, Medea killed his bride with the gift of a poisoned garment, and then killed her own two children by Jason.

Medellín industrial city and capital of Antioquia department, northwest Colombia; situated at 1,538 m/5,048 ft above sea level in the Aburrá Valley, Central Cordillera of the Andes; population (1994) 1,608,000. It is the second city and main textile centre of Colombia, producing over 80% of the country's total output. Other main industries include gold and silver mining, chemicals, coffee-growing, and engineering. Medellín has also had a reputation for cocaine production.

median in mathematics and statistics, the middle number of an ordered group of numbers. If there is no middle number (because there is an even number of terms), the median is the ▷mean (average) of the two middle numbers. For example, the median of the group 2, 3, 7, 11, 12 is 7; that of 3, 4, 7, 9, 11, 13 is 8 (the average of 7 and 9).

In geometry, the term refers to a line from the vertex of a triangle to the midpoint of the opposite side.

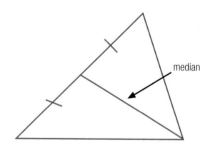

median

MEDIAN The median is the name given to a line from the vertex (corner) of a triangle to the mid-point of the opposite side.

medical ethics moral guidelines for doctors governing good professional conduct. The basic aims are considered to be doing good, avoiding harm, preserving the patient's autonomy, telling the truth, and pursuing justice. Ethical issues provoke the most discussion in medicine where these five aims cannot be simultaneously achieved – for example, what is 'good' for a child may clash with his or her autonomy or that of the parents.

Medici (family) noble family that ruled the Italian city-state of Florence from the 15th to the 18th centuries. The Medici arrived in Florence in the 13th century and made their fortune in banking. The first family member to control the city, from 1434 to 1464, was Cosimo de' Medici ('the Elder'); he and his grandson Lorenzo ('the Magnificent'), who ruled from 1469 to 1492, made Florence the

LORENZO DE' MEDICI A member of the influential Medici family, Lorenzo de' Medici became ruler of Florence, Italy, at the age of 20 years, with his younger brother, Giuliano. After his brother's assassination in 1478, Lorenzo ruled alone for a further 14 years, bringing great prosperity to the city. *Archive Photos*

foremost city-state in ▷Renaissance Italy, and were famed as patrons of the arts and ▷humanist thought. Four Medici were elected pope, and others married into the royal families of Europe.

Medici, Cosimo de' (1389–1464) Italian politician and banker. Regarded as the model for Machiavelli's *The Prince*, he dominated the government of Florence from 1434 and was a patron of the arts. He was succeeded by his inept son **Piero de' Medici** (1416–1469).

Medici, Cosimo de' (1519–1574) Italian politician, ruler of Florence; duke of Florence from 1537 and 1st grand duke of Tuscany from 1569.

Medici, Ferdinand de' (1549–1609) Italian politician, grand duke of Tuscany from 1587.

Medici, Giovanni de' (1360–1429) Italian entrepreneur and banker, with political influence in Florence as a supporter of the popular party. He was the father of Cosimo de' Medici.

Medici, Lorenzo de', the Magnificent (1449–1492) Italian politician, ruler of Florence from 1469. He was also a poet and a generous patron of the arts.

medicine the practice of preventing, diagnosing, and treating disease, both physical and mental; also any substance used in the treatment of disease. The basis of medicine is anatomy (the structure and form of the body) and physiology (the study of the body's functions).

In the West, medicine increasingly relies on new drugs and sophisticated surgical techniques, while diagnosis of disease is more and more by noninvasive procedures. The time and cost of Western-type medical training makes it inaccessible to many parts of the Third World; where health care of this kind is provided it is often by auxiliary medical

ALTERNATIVE MEDICINE Gingko seed pods and leaves are an old naturopathic remedy for bad circulation, particularly in the brain. They may play a major role in slowing down some of the mental aspects of ageing. *Image Bank*

helpers trained in hygiene and the administration of a limited number of standard drugs for the prevalent diseases of a particular region. See Medicine, Western: Key Events on p. 616.

Related Web site: MedicineNet
http://www.medicinenet.com/

medicine, alternative forms of medical treatment that do not use synthetic drugs or surgery in response to the symptoms of a disease, but aim to treat the patient as a whole (holism). The emphasis is on maintaining health (with diet and exercise) and on dealing with the underlying causes rather than just the symptoms of illness. It may involve the use of herbal remedies and techniques like ▷acupuncture, ▷homeopathy, and ▷chiropractic. Some alternative treatments are increasingly accepted by orthodox medicine, but the absence of enforceable standards in some fields has led to the proliferation of eccentric or untrained practitioners.

medicine, history medical science has developed by gradual steps from very early times. There is evidence of trepanning (cutting holes in the skull to relieve pressure) being practised in the prehistoric medicine of Stone Age peoples. In the earliest societies, medical practice was part of the duties of the priests; it relied more on the influence of the gods than on the value of the methods adopted. In ancient Greek medicine, even the priests of Asclepius, the god of healing, relied mainly on religious exercises to effect a cure. The main advances in medical practice came in the 1800s and 1900s, and today physicians and surgeons have a record of some success in treating and curing disease and injuries.

medieval art painting and sculpture of the Middle Ages in Europe and parts of the Middle East, dating roughly from the 3rd century to the emergence of the Renaissance in Italy in the 1400s. This includes early Christian, Byzantine, Celtic, Anglo-Saxon, and Carolingian art. The Romanesque style was the first truly international style of medieval times, superseded by Gothic in the late 12th century. Religious sculpture, frescoes, and manuscript illumination proliferated; panel painting was introduced only towards the end of the Middle Ages.

Early Christian art (4th–5th centuries AD) In AD 313 Constantine the Great formally recognized Christianity as the official religion of the Roman Empire. In response, churches were built and commissioned art took on the subject matter of the Christian saints and symbols. Roman burial chests (*sarcophagi*) were adopted by the Christians and the imagery of pagan myths gradually gave way to biblical themes.

Byzantine art (4th–15th centuries) ▷Byzantine art developed in the Eastern Roman Empire, centred on Byzantium (renamed Constantinople 330; Istanbul 1453). The use of mosaic associated with Byzantine art also appears in church decoration in the West. In Ravenna, for example, churches of the 5th and 6th centuries present powerful religious images on walls and vaults in brilliant, glittering colour and a bold, linear style. The Byzantine style continued for many centuries in ▷icon painting in Greece and Russia.

Celtic and Anglo-Saxon art (4th–9th centuries) Stemming from the period when southern Europe was overrun by Germanic tribes from the north, this early medieval art consists mainly of portable objects, such as articles for personal use or adornment. Among the invading tribes, the Anglo-Saxons, particularly those who settled in the British Isles, excelled in metalwork and jewellery, often in gold

with garnet or enamel inlays, ornamented with highly stylized, plant-based interlace patterns with animal motifs. The ornament of ▷Celtic art and ▷Anglo-Saxon art was translated into stone-carving, from simple engraved monoliths to elaborate sculpted crosses, as well as the illuminated manuscripts produced in Christian monasteries, such as the decorated pages of the Northumbrian 7th-century *Lindisfarne Gospels* (British Museum, London) or the Celtic 8th-century Book of Kells (Trinity College, Dublin, Ireland). Illumination usually included a large, decorated initial to mark the opening of a gospel or passage, sometimes with an elaborate facing or 'carpet page'.

Romanesque or Norman art (10th–12th centuries) This is chiefly evident in church architecture and church sculpture, on capitals and portals, and in manuscript illumination. Romanesque art was typified by the rounded arch, and combined naturalistic elements with the fantastic, poetical, and pattern-loving Celtic and Germanic traditions. Imaginary beasts and medieval warriors mingle with biblical themes. Fine examples remain throughout Europe, from northern Spain and Italy to France, the Germanic lands of the Holy Roman Empire, England, and Scandinavia. although in Italy, the classical influence remained strong.

Gothic art (late 12th–15th centuries) ▷Gothic art developed as large cathedrals were built in Europe. Sculptural decoration in stone became more monumental, and stained glass filled the tall windows, as at Chartres Cathedral, France. Figures were also carved in wood. Court patronage produced exquisite small ivories, goldsmiths' work, devotional books illustrated with miniatures, and tapestries depicting romantic tales. Panel painting, initially on a gold background, evolved in northern Europe into the more realistic ▷International Gothic style. In Italy fresco painting made great advances; a seminal figure in this development was the artist ▷Giotto di Bondone, whose work is seen as proto-Renaissance.

Related Web site: Guide to Medieval and Renaissance Instruments
http://www.s-hamilton.k12.ia.us/antiqua/instrumt.html

Medina Saudi Arabian city, about 355 km/220 mi north of Mecca; population (1991 est) 400,000. It is the second holiest city in the Islamic world, and contains the tomb of ▷Muhammad. It produces grain and fruit.

meditation act of spiritual contemplation, practised by members of many religions or as a secular exercise. It is a central practice in Buddhism (the Sanskrit term is *samādhi*) and the movement for ▷transcendental meditation.

Mediterranean Sea inland sea separating Europe from north Africa, with Asia to the east; extreme length 3,700 km/2,300 mi; area 2,966,000 sq km/1,145,000 sq mi. It is linked to the Atlantic Ocean (at the Strait of Gibraltar), Red Sea and Indian Ocean (by the Suez Canal), and the Black Sea (at the Dardanelles and Sea of Marmara). The main subdivisions are the Adriatic, Aegean, Ionian, and Tyrrhenian seas. It is highly polluted.

The Mediterranean is almost tideless, and is saltier and warmer than the Atlantic, with a constant deep-water temperature of 12°C; shallows from Sicily to Cape Bon (Africa) divide it into an east and a west basin, which reach depths of 3,400 m/11,155 ft and 4,200 m/13,780 ft, respectively. Dense salt water forms a permanent deep current out into the Atlantic. The main rivers draining into the sea are the Ebro, Rhône, Po, Arno, Tiber, and Nile. The chief

MEDIEVAL ART *Calendar for October*, from an 11th-century English manuscript. Farm workers are gathering in the hay crop with scythes and pitchforks. *The Art Archive/British Library*

Medicine, Western: Key Events

c. 400 BC	The Greek physician Hippocrates of Cos recognizes that diseases have natural causes. The Hippocratic oath, still taken by doctors today, is attributed to him.
c. AD 200	The Greek physician Galen consolidates the work of the Alexandrian doctors and introduces the theory of the four humours, which remains the foundation of western medicine throughout the Middle Ages.
1530	The Swiss doctor and alchemist Paracelsus advocates the use of chemicals and minerals in the treatment of illness. In 1536 he publishes *Die grosse Wundartzney/Great Surgery Book*, challenging the precepts of Galen.
1543	Andreas Vesalius of Flanders gives the first accurate account of the human body.
1628	English doctor William Harvey discovers the circulation of the blood.
1768	Scottish surgeon John Hunter lays the foundation of experimental and surgical pathology.
1785	English doctor William Withering reports his discovery of the use of digitalis in treating heart disease; the active ingredient, derived from the foxglove, is isolated in 1904.
1798	English doctor Edward Jenner publishes his work on vaccination.
1877	Scottish doctor Patrick Manson studies animal carriers of infectious diseases.
1882	German bacteriologist Robert Koch isolates the bacillus responsible for tuberculosis.
1884	German doctor and bacteriologist Edwin Klebs isolates the diphtheria bacillus.
1885	French bacteriologist Louis Pasteur produces a vaccine against rabies.
1890	English surgeon Joseph Lister demonstrates antiseptic surgery.
1895	German physicist Wilhelm Röntgen discovers X-rays.
1897	Dutch botanist and chemist Martinus Beijerinck discovers viruses.
1899	Aspirin is introduced in general medical use as an analgesic.
1900	Austrian biochemist Karl Landsteiner identifies the first three blood groups, later designated A, B, and O; Sigmund Freud publishes *The Interpretation of Dreams* and profoundly influences modern psychiatry.
1905	US doctor George Washington Crile performs the first blood transfusion.
1910	German bacteriologist Paul Ehrlich develops the first specific antibacterial agent, Salvarsan, a cure for syphilis.
1922	Insulin is first used to treat diabetes.
1928	Scottish bacteriologist Alexander Fleming discovers penicillin.
1932	Gerhard Domagk of Germany discovers the first antibacterial sulphonamide drug, Prontosil.
1937	Electro-convulsive therapy (ECT) is developed by the Italian doctors Ugo Cerlutti and Lucio Bini.
1940s	Lithium treatment for manic-depressive illness is developed.
1950s	Antidepressant drugs and beta-blockers for heart disease are developed. Manipulation of the molecules of synthetic chemicals becomes the main source of new drugs. Peter Medawar studies the body's tolerance of transplanted organs and skin grafts. First kidney transplants.
1950	Proof of a link between cigarette smoking and lung cancer is established.
1953	Francis Crick of England and James Watson of the USA announce the structure of DNA. US microbiologist Jonas Salk develops a vaccine against polio.
1958	Scottish doctor Ian Donald pioneers diagnostic ultrasound.
1960s	A new generation of minor tranquillizers called benzodiazepines is developed.
1964	First pig heart valve transplant in the UK.
1967	South African surgeon Christiaan Barnard performs the world's first human heart transplant operation in Cape Town.
1971	Viroids, disease-causing organisms even smaller than viruses, are isolated outside the living body.
1972	The CAT scan, pioneered by Godfrey Hounsfield of England, is first used to image the human brain.
1975	French microbiologist César Milstein develops monoclonal antibodies.
1978	Louise Brown, the world's first 'test-tube baby' is born in the UK.
1980s	AIDS (acquired immune deficiency syndrome) is recognized in the USA (later research suggests that the first death from AIDS took place in Africa in 1959). US microbiologist Barbara McClintock's discovery of the transposable gene is recognized.
1980	The World Health Organization reports the eradication of smallpox.
1983	The virus responsible for AIDS, now known as human immunodeficiency virus (HIV), is identified by French microbiologist Luc Montagnier at the Institut Pasteur, Paris; A US scientist, Robert Gallo, at the National Cancer Institute, Maryland, USA, discovers the virus independently in 1984.
1984	The first vaccine against leprosy is developed.
1987	English microbiologist Walter Bodmer and others announce the discovery of a marker for the gene that causes cancer of the colon.
1989	Grafts of fetal brain tissue are first used to treat Parkinson's disease.
1990s	Cochlear implants for very young children achieve a success rate of more than 90% in alleviating profound deafness. Scientists discover that bovine spongiform encephalopathy (BSE), a fatal brain disease of cattle, can be transmitted to other species, including humans. The human form of BSE is believed to manifest itself as a variant form of Creutzfeldt-Jakob disease (CJD). Both these and other fatal brain-wasting disorders are thought to be caused by a self-replicating protein called a prion. A strain of typhoid fever that is resistant to all known antibiotics emerges in the late 1990s.
1990	The gene for maleness is discovered by UK researchers.
1991	First successful use of gene therapy (to treat severe combined immune deficiency) is reported in the USA.
1993	First trials of gene therapy against cystic fibrosis take place in the USA.
1996	An Australian man, Ben Dent, is the first person to end his life by legally sanctioned euthanasia.
1998	French surgeons at Lyons, France, perform the first arm transplant by sewing the hand and forearm of a brain-dead patient onto the arm stump of a living patient, New Zealand-born Clint Hallam.
1999	The UK Department of Health announces that all pregnant women in England and Wales will be offered an HIV test. HIV transmission to newborns can be cut from 15% to 2% by antiviral therapy, Caesarean section delivery, and bottle feeding but at present most infected mothers are unaware that they carry the virus.
2000	A UK study shows that women suffering from breast cancer are surviving longer than ever before because of improvements in treatment and especially the use of the drug tamoxifen.

WESTERN MEDICINE An exhibition of surgical instruments used by the Etruscans. *The Art Archive*

islands are Sicily and Malta in the centre; Cyprus, Crete, and the Ionian Islands in the east; and Sardinia, Corsica, and the Balearic Islands in the west.

The Mediterranean is severely endangered by human and industrial waste pollution; 130 million people live along the coast and another 100 million visit each summer. More than 500 million tonnes of sewage per year is discharged into the Mediterranean without treatment, and it is regularly crossed by oil tankers.

The Barcelona Convention of 1976 to clean up the Mediterranean was signed by 17 countries and led to a ban on dumping of mercury, cadmium, persistent plastics, DDT, crude oil, and hydrocarbons.

medlar small shrub or tree native to southeastern Europe. It is widely cultivated for its fruits, resembling small brown-green pears or quinces. These are palatable when they have begun to decay. (*Mespilus germanica*, family Rosaceae.)

Médoc French district bordering the Gironde in Aquitaine region, north of Bordeaux. It is famed for its claret wines, Margaux and St Julien being two well-known names. Lesparre and Pauillac are the chief towns.

medulla central part of an organ. In the mammalian kidney, the medulla lies beneath the outer cortex and is responsible for the reabsorption of water from the filtrate. In plants, it is a region of packing tissue in the centre of the stem. In the vertebrate brain, the medulla is the posterior region responsible for the coordination of basic activities, such as breathing and temperature control.

Medusa in Greek mythology, a mortal woman who was transformed into a snake-haired ▷Gorgon by Athena for defiling the goddess's temple with the god Poseidon. She was slain by the hero ▷Perseus who watched her reflection in his shield, as her head was so hideous – even in death – that a direct beholder was turned to stone.

The winged horse ▷Pegasus and warrior Chrysaor were said to have sprung from her blood; offspring of Medusa and Poseidon.

medusa the free-swimming phase in the life cycle of a coelenterate, such as a ▷jellyfish or ▷coral. The other phase is the sedentary **polyp**.

Medway river of southeast England; length about 96 km/60 mi. It rises in Sussex and flows through Kent and **Medway Towns** unitary authority, becoming an estuary at Rochester, before entering the Thames at Sheerness. In local tradition it divides the 'Men of Kent', who live to the east, from the 'Kentish Men', who live to the west. It is polluted by industrial waste.

Medway Towns unitary authority in southeast England, created in 1998 by combining the former city council of Rochester upon Medway with Gillingham borough council, both formerly in Kent.

area 194 sq km/75 sq mi **towns and cities** Rochester, Chatham, Gillingham, Strood (administrative headquarters) **features** River Medway flows through Rochester; River Thames forms northern border of authority; reclaimed estuarine mudflats form the Isle of Grain; Charles Dickens Centre (Rochester) is housed in a 16th-century mansion; Royal Naval Dockyard (Chatham); Royal Engineers Museum (Chatham); Upnor Castle (16th century) at Upper Upnor **industries** education and health, distribution, manufacturing, banking, financial services, insurance, transport and communications, engineering, Thamesport (privately-owned deep-water container port), avionics, information technology **population** (1996) 240,000 **famous people** William Jenner

meerkat (or suricate) small mammal with long soft grey fur, which is found in southern Africa, and belongs to the mongoose family. A third of its length of 35 cm/14 in is occupied by the tail. It feeds on succulent bulbs, insects, and small vertebrates, and is sociable, living in large extended family groups. Meerkat groups have a dominant breeding pair and up to 23 helpers to assist in the rearing of the babies. The dominant female produces 75% of the young. The Madagascar cat and *Cynictis penicillata* are also termed meerkats.
Classification Meerkats *Suricata suricatta* are in family Viverridae, order Carnivora.

MEERKAT Yellow meerkats *Cynictis penicillata* on sentry duty just outside their burrow. The open savannah where they live and the large number of their predators, including snakes, jackals, and birds of prey, requires constant vigilance. *K G Preston-Mafham/Premaphotos Wildlife*

meerschaum aggregate of minerals, usually the soft white clay mineral **sepiolite**, hydrous magnesium silicate. It floats on water and is used for making pipe bowls.

mega- prefix denoting multiplication by a million. For example, a megawatt (MW) is equivalent to a million watts.

megabyte (MB) in computing, a unit of memory equal to 1,024 ▷kilobytes. It is sometimes used, less precisely, to mean 1 million bytes.

megalith (Greek *megas* 'great', *lithos* 'stone') prehistoric stone monument of the late Neolithic (New Stone Age) or early Bronze Age. Most common in Europe, megaliths include single large uprights or ▷menhirs (for example, the Five Kings, Northumberland, England); rows or **alignments** (for example, Carnac, Brittany, France); stone circles; and the hutlike remains of burial chambers after the covering earth has disappeared, known as dolmens (for example, Kits Coty, Kent, England, where only the entrance survives).

megamouth deep-sea shark that feeds on plankton. It has a bulbous head with protruding jaws and blubbery lips, is 4.5 m/15 ft long, and weighs 750 kg/1,650 lb. Although first discovered in 1976, the first live specimen was found in 1992 off the coast of Los Angeles. The first female was found in 1994 in Hakata Bay, Kyushu, Japan; she was 4.8 m/16 ft long and weighed 790 kg/1,740 lb. (Species *Megachasma pelagios*.)

megapode (or mound-builder) any of a group of chickenlike birds found in the Malay Archipelago and Australia. They pile up large mounds of vegetable matter, earth, and sand 4 m/13 ft across, in which to deposit their eggs, then cover the eggs and leave them to be incubated by the heat produced by the rotting vegetation. There are 19 species, all large birds, 50–70 cm/20–27.5 in in length, with very large feet. They include brush turkeys. (Family Megapodiidae, order Galliformes.)

megaton one million (10^6) tons. Used with reference to the explosive power of a nuclear weapon, it is equivalent to the explosive force of one million tons of trinitrotoluene (TNT).

megavitamin therapy the administration of large doses of vitamins to combat conditions considered wholly or in part due to their deficiency.

Meghalaya state of northeast India, bordered to the north by Assam, to the south by Bangladesh; area 22,400 sq km/8,648 sq mi; population (2001 est) 2,324,000, mainly Khasi, Jaintia, and Garo. The capital is Shillong. The state is upland with hills reaching 2,000 m/6,500 ft, rising steeply in the south away from its border with Bangladesh. There is heavy monsoon rainfall. Minerals in the area include coal, limestone, white clay, and corundum, which are mainly unexploited. Industries include mineral extraction, which includes 95% of India's sillimanite. Agricultural products include cotton, potatoes, fruit, rice, maize, timber, and jute. 70% of the population are Hindu.

Megiddo site of a fortress town in northern Israel, where Thutmose III defeated the Canaanites; the Old Testament figure Josiah was killed in battle in about 609 BC; and in World War I the British field marshal Allenby broke the Turkish front in 1918. It is identified with ▷Armageddon.

Mehmet Ali (or Muhammad Ali) (1769–1849) Pasha (governor) of Egypt from 1805, and founder of the dynasty that ruled until 1953. An Albanian in the Ottoman service, he had originally been sent to Egypt to fight the French. As pasha, he established a European-style army and navy, fought his Turkish overlord in 1831 and 1839, and conquered Sudan.

Mehta, Zubin (1936–) Indian-born US conductor. He has been music director of the New York Philharmonic from 1978. He specializes in robust, polished interpretations of 19th- and 20th-century repertoire, including contemporary US composers.

Meiji, Mutsuhito (1852–1912) Emperor of Japan from 1867, under the regnal era name Meiji ('enlightened'). During his reign Japan became a world industrial and naval power. His ministers abolished the feudal system and discrimination against the lowest caste, established state schools, reformed the civil service, and introduced conscription, the Western calendar, and other measures to modernize Japan, including a constitution in 1889.

meiosis in biology, a process of cell division in which the number of ▷chromosomes in the cell is halved. It only occurs in ▷eukaryotic cells, and is part of a life cycle that involves sexual reproduction because it allows the genes of two parents to be combined without the total number of chromosomes increasing.

Meir, Golda (1898–1978) Born Golda Mabovitch, later Golda Myerson. Israeli Labour politician; foreign minister 1956–66 and prime minister 1969–74. Criticism of the Israelis' lack of preparation for the 1973 Arab-Israeli War led to election losses for Labour and, unable to form a government, she resigned.
    Born in Russia, she emigrated to the USA in 1906, and in 1921 went to Palestine.

Meistersinger (German 'master singer') one of a group of German lyric poets, singers, and musicians of the 14th–16th centuries, who formed guilds for the revival of minstrelsy. Hans Sachs was a Meistersinger, and Wagner's opera *Die Meistersinger von Nürnberg/The Mastersingers of Nuremberg* (1868) depicts the tradition.

meitnerium synthesized radioactive element of the ▷transactinide series, symbol Mt, atomic number 109, relative atomic mass 266. It was first produced in 1982 at the Laboratory for Heavy Ion Research in Darmstadt, Germany, by fusing bismuth and iron nuclei; it took a week to obtain a single new, fused nucleus. It was named in 1997 after the Austrian-born Swedish physicist ▷Lise Meitner. Its temporary name was unnilennium.

Mek'elē capital of Tigré region, northern Ethiopia; population (1992) 113,000. It trades in salt, incense, and resin. It is the centre of Ethiopia's inland salt trade, based on the Danakil Plain.

Mekong river of China, rising as the Za Qu in Qinghai province, flowing through Tibet autonomous region and Yunnan province as the Lancang Jiang, and then through Laos, where part of its course forms the border with Thailand, Cambodia, and Vietnam; length 4,425 km/2,750 mi. The Mekong empties into the South China Sea through a vast delta, covering about 200,000 sq km/77,000 sq mi. It is being developed for irrigation and hydroelectricity by Cambodia, Laos, Thailand, and Vietnam.

melaleuca tree (or paperbark) tropical tree belonging to the myrtle family. The leaves produce **cajuput oil**, which is used in medicine. (*Melaleuca leucadendron*, family Myrtaceae.)

melamine $C_3H_6N_6$ ▷thermosetting ▷polymer based on urea–formaldehyde. It is extremely resistant to heat and is also scratch-resistant. Its uses include synthetic resins.

Melanchthon, Philip (1497–1560) Adopted name of Philip Schwarzerd. German theologian who helped Martin Luther prepare a German translation of the New Testament. In 1521 he issued the first systematic formulation of Protestant theology, reiterated in the Confession of ▷Augsburg (1530).

Melanesia islands in the southwestern Pacific between Micronesia to the north and Polynesia to the east, embracing all the islands from the New Britain archipelago to the Fiji Islands.

Melanesian the indigenous inhabitants of Melanesia; any of the Pacific peoples of Melanesia. The Melanesian languages belong to the Austronesian family.

Melanesian languages see ▷Austronesian languages.

melanin brown pigment that gives colour to the eyes, skin, hair, feathers, and scales of many vertebrates. In humans, melanin helps protect the skin against ultraviolet radiation from sunlight. Both genetic and environmental factors determine the amount of melanin in the skin.

melanoma highly malignant tumour of the melanin-forming cells (melanocytes) of the skin. It develops from an existing mole in up to two-thirds of cases, but can also arise in the eye or mucous membranes.

MEIOSIS Meiosis is a type of cell division that produces gametes (sex cells, sperm and egg). This sequence shows an animal cell but only four chromosomes are present in the parent cell (1). There are two stages in the division process. In the first stage (2–6), the chromosomes come together in pairs and exchange genetic material. This is called crossing over. In the second stage (7–9), the cell divides to produce four gamete cells, each with only one copy of each chromosome from the parent cell.

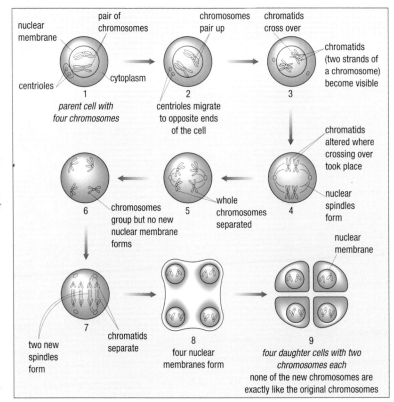

Malignant melanoma is the most dangerous of the skin cancers; it is associated with brief but excessive exposure to sunlight. It is easily treated if caught early but deadly once it has spread. There is a genetic factor in some cases.

Once rare, this disease is increasing at the rate of 7% in most countries with a predominantly fair-skinned population, owing to the increasing popularity of holidays in the sun. Most at risk are those with fair hair and light skin, and those who have had a severe sunburn in childhood. Cases of melanoma are increasing by 4% a year worldwide.

It strikes about 3,000 people a year in the UK, killing 1,250.

Related Web site: Melanoma Skin Cancer http://www3.cancer.org/cancerinfo/load_cont.asp.ct=50

Melbourne capital of the state of ▷Victoria, Australia; population (2001 est) 3,366,500. Australia's second-largest city, Melbourne is situated on the southeast coast of Australia, on Port Philip Bay, at the mouth of the River Yarra. It is separated from Tasmania by the Bass Strait. Industries include engineering, shipbuilding, electronics, printing, oil refining, food processing, brewing, flour-milling, and the manufacture of chemicals, cars, furniture, plastics, textiles, and clothing. It is an important port and the largest receiver of container vessels in Australia. Melbourne has seven universities, including the University of Melbourne (1853), Monash University (1961, the largest university in Australia), and La Trobe University (1964).

Melbourne was founded in 1835 and named, in 1837, after the British prime minister, Lord Melbourne. It grew rapidly after the discovery of gold at ▷Ballarat and Bendigo in the early 1850s, and was the capital of Australia from 1901 to 1927. It was the site of the 1956 Olympic Games.

Related Web site: Melbourne City Search http://www.melbourne.vic.gov.au//

Melbourne, (Henry) William Lamb (1779–1848) 2nd Viscount Melbourne. British Whig politician. Home secretary 1830–34, he was briefly prime minister in 1834 and again in 1835–41. Accused in 1836 of seducing Caroline Norton, he lost the favour of William IV. Viscount 1829.

Melchite (or Melkite; Syriac 'royalist') member of a Christian church in Syria, Egypt, Lebanon, and Israel. The Melchite Church was founded in Syria in the 6th–7th centuries and is now part of the Eastern Orthodox Church.

Melgarejo, Mariano (*c.* 1820–1871) Bolivian dictator and most notorious of the caudillos who dominated 19th-century Bolivia. Melgarejo seized power in 1864 and survived a series of rebellions before he was overthrown by the last in a series of military uprisings seven years later.

Méliès, Georges (1861–1938) French film pioneer. From 1896 to 1912 he made over 1,000 films, mostly fantasies (including *Le Voyage dans la lune/A Trip to the Moon* 1902). He developed trick effects, slow motion, double exposure, and dissolves, and in 1897 built Europe's first film studio in Montreuil, northern France.

Mellon, Andrew William (1855–1937) US financier who donated his art collection to found the National Gallery of Art, Washington, DC, in 1937. He was secretary of the Treasury 1921–32, pursuing tax-cutting policies.

melodrama play or film with romantic and sensational plot elements, often concerned with crime, vice, or catastrophe. Originally a melodrama was a play with an accompaniment of music contributing to the dramatic effect. It became popular in the late 18th century, due to works like *Pygmalion* (1770), with pieces written by the French philosopher Jean-Jacques Rousseau. The early melodramas used extravagant theatrical effects to heighten violent emotions and actions artificially. By the end of the 19th century, melodrama had become a popular genre of stage play.

melody (Greek *melos* 'song') in music, a recognizable series of notes played or sung one after the other, a tune. Melody is one of the three main elements of music, the others being rhythm and ▷harmony. In Western music a melody is usually formed from the notes of a ▷scale or mode. A melody, with or without accompaniment, may be a complete piece on its own – such as a simple song. In classical music it is more often used as a theme within a longer piece of music.

melon any of several large, juicy (95% water), thick-skinned fruits of trailing plants of the gourd family. The muskmelon (*Cucumis melo*), of which the honeydew melon is a variety, and the large red ▷watermelon (*Citrullus vulgaris*) are familiar edible varieties. (Family Cucurbitaceae.)

Related Web site: Cucumbers, Melons, and Squash http://www.ext.vt.edu/pubs/envirohort/426-406/426-406.html

meltdown the melting of the core of a nuclear reactor, due to overheating.

To prevent such accidents all reactors have equipment intended to flood the core with water in an emergency. The reactor is housed in a strong containment vessel, designed to prevent radiation escaping into the atmosphere. The result of a meltdown would be an area radioactively contaminated for 25,000 years or more.

melting point temperature at which a substance melts, or changes from solid to liquid form. A pure substance under standard conditions of pressure (usually one atmosphere) has a definite melting point. If heat is supplied to a solid at its melting point, the temperature does not change until the melting process is complete. The melting point of ice is 0°C or 32°F.

Melville, Herman (1819–1891) US writer. His novel *Moby-Dick* (1851) was inspired by his whaling experiences in the South Seas and is considered to be one of the masterpieces of American literature. *Billy Budd, Sailor*, completed just before his death and published in 1924, was the basis of an opera by Benjamin ▷Britten (1951). Although most of his works were unappreciated during his lifetime, today he is one of the most highly regarded of US authors.

Melville's experiences as a sailor were also the basis for earlier fiction, such as the adventure narratives of *Typee* 1846 and *Omoo* 1847. He explored the dark, troubled side of American experience in novels of unusual form and great philosophical power. He was a friend of the novelist Nathaniel Hawthorne.

Related Web site: Herman Melville: Life and Works http://www.melville.org/

membrane in living things, a continuous layer, made up principally of fat molecules, that encloses a ▷cell or ▷organelles within a cell. Small molecules, such as water and sugars, can pass through the cell membrane by ▷diffusion. Large molecules, such as proteins, are transported across the membrane via special channels, a process often involving energy input. The ▷Golgi apparatus within the cell is thought to produce certain membranes.

Memel German name for ▷Klaipeda, the main port in Lithuania.

Memling (or Memlinc), **Hans** (*c.* 1430–1494) Flemish painter. He was probably a pupil of van der ▷Weyden, but his style is calmer and softer. He painted religious subjects and also portraits, including *Tommaso Portinari and His Wife* (about 1480; Metropolitan Museum of Art, New York).

memorandum (or memo) written note or message giving information or issuing instructions. It is usually short and details who is sending the memo and to whom it should be distributed.

Memorial Day in the USA, a day of remembrance (formerly Decoration Day) instituted in 1868 for those killed in the US Civil War. Since World War I it has been observed as a national holiday on the last Monday in May, traditionally falling on 30 May, in remembrance of all Americans killed in war.

memory in computing, the part of a system used to store data and programs either permanently or temporarily. There are two main types: immediate access memory and backing storage. Memory capacity is measured in ▷bytes or, more conveniently, in kilobytes (units of 1,024 bytes) or megabytes (units of 1,024 kilobytes).

memory ability to store and recall observations and sensations. Memory does not seem to be based in any particular part of the brain; it may depend on changes to the pathways followed by nerve impulses as they move through the brain. Memory can be improved by regular use as the connections between ▷nerve cells (neurons) become 'well-worn paths' in the brain. Events stored in **short-term memory** are forgotten quickly, whereas those in **long-term memory** can last for many years, enabling recall of information and recognition of people and places over long periods of time.

H L Mencken

Conscience is the inner voice which warns us that someone may be looking.

A Mencken Chrestomathy, 'Sententiae: the Mind of Men'

MELON The tsamma melon *Citrullus lunatus*. These variegated melons are a common sight in the Kalahari Desert and other dry regions of Africa. When ripe they turn yellow and are much relished by antelopes. *Premaphotos Wildlife*

Memphis ruined city beside the Nile, 19 km/12 mi southwest of Cairo, Egypt. Once the centre of the worship of Ptah, it was the earliest capital of a united Egypt under King Menes in about 3050 BC, and acted intermittently as capital until around 1300 BC.

Memphis industrial city and port on the Mississippi River, in southwestern Tennessee, USA, linked by a bridge with West Memphis, Arkansas, across the river; seat of Shelby County; population (2000) 650,100. It is a major cotton market, and one of the leading centres in the USA for the production of hardwood lumber; other industries include food processing and the manufacture of pharmaceuticals, chemicals, medical supplies, furniture, and tobacco products. A 1980s industry of handmade ultramodern furniture is called Memphis style and copied by Italian and French firms.

Menai Strait (Welsh Afon Menai) channel of the Irish Sea dividing ▷Anglesey from the Welsh mainland; about 22 km/14 mi long and up to 3 km/2 mi wide. It is crossed by two bridges. Thomas Telford's suspension bridge (521 m/1,710 ft long) was opened in 1826 but was reconstructed to the original design in 1940, and freed from tolls. Robert Stephenson's tubular rail bridge (420 m/1,378 ft long) was opened in 1850, and is known as the Britannia Bridge.

MENAI STRAIT The Menai road bridge links the mainland of Wales to the island of Anglesey. Built by Thomas Telford between 1819 and 1826, this suspension bridge is 521 m/1,710 ft long. Its central span measures 176 m/579 ft. *Image Bank*

Menam another name for the River ▷Chao Phraya, Thailand.

Menander (*c.* 342–291 BC) Greek comic dramatist. Previously only known by reputation and some short fragments, Menander's comedy *Bad-Tempered Man* (316 BC), was discovered in 1957 on Egyptian papyrus. Substantial parts of *The Samian Woman, The Arbitration, The Unkindest Cut*, and *The Shield* are also extant. His comedies, with their wit and ingenuity of plot often concerning domestic intrigue, were adapted by the Roman comic dramatists ▷Plautus and ▷Terence.

Mencius (*c.* 372–*c.* 289 BC) Chinese **Mengzi**. Chinese philosopher and moralist in the tradition of orthodox Confucianism. He considered human nature innately good, although this goodness required cultivation, and based his conception of morality on this conviction.

Mencken, H(enry) L(ouis) (1880–1956) US essayist and critic. He was known as 'the sage of Baltimore'. His unconventionally phrased, satiric contributions to the periodicals *The Smart Set* and *American Mercury* (both of which he edited) aroused controversy.

Mende a West African people living in the rainforests of central east Sierra Leone and western Liberia. They number approximately 1 million. The Mende are farmers as well as hunter-gatherers, and each of their villages is led by a chief and a group of elders. The Mende language belongs to the Niger-Congo family.

Mendel, Gregor Johann (1822–1884) Austrian biologist, founder of ▷genetics. His experiments with successive generations of peas gave the basis for his theory of particulate inheritance rather than blending, involving dominant and recessive characters; see ▷Mendelism. His results, published 1865–69, remained unrecognized until the early 20th century.

mendelevium synthesized, radioactive metallic element of the ▷actinide series, symbol Md, atomic number 101, relative atomic mass 258. It was first produced by bombardment of Es-253 with helium nuclei. Its longest-lived isotope, Md-258, has a half-life of about two months. The element is chemically similar to thulium. It was named by the US physicists at the University of California at

Berkeley who first synthesized it in 1955 after the Russian chemist Mendeleyev, who in 1869 devised the basis for the periodic table of the elements.

Mendeleyev, Dmitri Ivanovich (1834–1907) Russian
chemist who framed the periodic law in chemistry in 1869, which states that the chemical properties of the elements depend on their relative atomic masses. This law is the basis of the ▷periodic table of the elements, in which the elements are arranged by atomic number and organized by their related groups.

Mendeleyev was the first chemist to understand that all elements are related members of a single ordered system. From his table he predicted the properties of elements then unknown, of which three (gallium, scandium, and germanium) were discovered in his lifetime. Meanwhile Lothar Meyer in Germany presented a similar but independent classification of the elements.

Related Web site: Mendeleyev, Dmitri Ivanovich http://www.chem.msu.su/eng/misc/mendeleev/welcome.html

Mendelism in genetics, the theory of inheritance originally
outlined by Austrian biologist Gregor Mendel. He suggested that, in sexually reproducing species, all characteristics are inherited through indivisible 'factors' (now identified with ▷genes) contributed by each parent to its offspring.

Mendelssohn(-Bartholdy), (Jakob Ludwig) Felix
(1809–1847) German composer, also a pianist and conductor. His music has the lightness and charm of classical music, applied to Romantic and descriptive subjects. Among his best-known works are *A Midsummer Night's Dream* (1827); the *Fingal's Cave* overture (1832); and three symphonies, which include the 'Reformation' (1830), the 'Italian' (1833), and the 'Scottish' (1842). He was instrumental in promoting the revival of interest in J S Bach's music.

Mendes, Chico (Filho Francisco) (1944–1988) Brazilian
environmentalist and labour leader. Opposed to the destruction of Brazil's rainforests, he organized itinerant rubber tappers into the Workers' Party (PT) and was assassinated by Darci Alves, a cattle rancher's son. Of 488 similar murders in land conflicts in Brazil 1985–89, his was the first to come to trial.

mendicant order religious order dependent on alms. In the
Roman Catholic Church there are four orders of mendicant friars: Franciscans, Dominicans, Carmelites, and Augustinians. Buddhism has similar orders.

Mendip Hills (or Mendips) range of limestone hills in southern
England, stretching nearly 40 km/25 mi southeast–northwest from Wells in Somerset towards the Bristol Channel. There are many cliffs, scars, and caverns, notably Cheddar Gorge. The highest peak is Blackdown (326 m/1,068 ft).

Mendoza capital of Mendoza federal district, western Argentina,
in the foothills of the Andes, 760 m/2,500 ft above sea level; population (1991) 121,700; metropolitan area (1992 est) 801,900. It is the commercial centre of an irrigated wine-producing and fruit-growing region. The city has an important university, and because of a nearby oilfield, a growing industrial base. The city was founded in 1561 on the site of an Inca fort by the Spaniard Garcí

Hurtado de Mendoza, after whom it is named. It developed because of its position on the Trans-Andean railway where the Argentine and Chilean rail lines link.

Mendoza, Antonio de (c. 1490–1552) First Spanish viceroy
of New Spain (Mexico) (1535–51). He attempted to develop agriculture and mining and supported the church in its attempts to convert the Indians. The system he established lasted until the 19th century. He was subsequently viceroy of Peru (1551–52).

Menelaus in Greek mythology, a king of Sparta; son of Atreus;
brother of ▷Agamemnon; husband of ▷Helen, and father of Hermione. With his brother he ousted ▷Thyestes from the throne of Mycenae and was joint leader of the Greek expedition against ▷Troy.

Menem, Carlos (Saul) (1930–) Argentine politician,
president 1989–99; leader of the Peronist Justicialist Party. As president, he introduced sweeping privatization and cuts in public spending to address Argentina's economic crisis and stimulate the free market; released hundreds of political prisoners jailed under the Alfonsin regime; and sent two warships to the Gulf to assist the USA against Iraq in the 1992 Gulf War (the only Latin American country to offer support to the USA). He also improved relations with the UK.

The son of Syrian immigrants to La Rioja province in the 1920s, Menem joined the Justicialist Party while training to be a lawyer. He was arrested in June 2001 for illegal arms trafficking during his administration, along with two former ministers, and a former chief of the armed forces. In July they were charged with conspiracy to ship government guns and explosives illegally to Croatia and Ecuador. Officially destined for Panama and Venezuela, around 6,500 tonnes of weapons ended up in Croatia and Ecuador between 1991 and 1995. At the time, Argentina was bound by international arms embargoes on both countries. Menem faced a ten-year jail sentence if found guilty but in fact was placed under house arrest for five months.

Mengistu, Haile Mariam (1937–) Ethiopian soldier and
socialist politician, head of state 1977–91 (president 1987–91). He seized power in a coup, and instituted a regime of terror to stamp out any effective opposition. Confronted with severe problems of drought and secessionist uprisings, he survived with help from the USSR and the West until his violent overthrow by rebel forces.

menhaden (or hardhead or mossbunker) marine bony fish
allied to ▷shads and common on the Atlantic coast of North America. It is chiefly valuable for its rich oil. The residue remaining after extraction is used as a fertilizer. The menhaden *Brevoortia tyrannus* is in order Clupeiformes, class Osteichthyes.

menhir (Breton 'long stone') prehistoric tall, upright stone
monument or ▷megalith. Menhirs may be found singly as ▷monoliths or in groups. They have a wide geographical distribution in the Americas (mainly as monoliths), and in Europe, Asia, and Africa, and belong to many different periods. Most European examples were erected in the late Neolithic (New Stone Age) or early Bronze Age.

MENHIR A prehistoric standing stone near Dol de Bretagne, France. *Philip Sauvain Picture Collection*

Ménière's disease (or Ménière's syndrome) recurring
condition of the inner ear caused by an accumulation of fluid in the labyrinth of the ear that affects mechanisms of both hearing and balance. It usually develops in the middle or later years. Symptoms, which include deafness, ringing in the ears (▷tinnitus), nausea, vertigo, and loss of balance, may be eased by drugs, but there is no cure.

Menindee village and sheep centre on the Darling River in New
South Wales, Australia. It is the centre of a scheme for conserving the waters of the Darling in Menindee Lake (155 sq km/60 sq mi) and other lakes nearby.

meningitis inflammation of the meninges (membranes)
surrounding the brain, caused by bacterial or viral infection. Bacterial meningitis, though treatable by antibiotics, is the more serious threat. Diagnosis is by ▷lumbar puncture.

Bacterial meningitis is caused by *Neisseria meningitidis*, a bacterium that colonizes the lining of the throat and is carried by 2–10% of the healthy population. Illness results if the bacteria enters the bloodstream, but normally the epithelial lining of the throat is a sufficient barrier.

Many common viruses can cause the occasional case of meningitis, although not usually in its more severe form. The treatment for viral meningitis is rest.

There are three strains of bacterial meningitis: serogroups A, B, and C. Vaccines exist only for A and C. However, they do not provide long-term protection nor are they suitable for children under the age of two. B is the most prevalent of the groups, causing over 50% of cases in Europe and the USA.

The severity of the disease varies from mild to rapidly lethal, and symptoms include fever, headache, nausea, neck stiffness, delirium, and (rarely) convulsions.

Around 3,000 cases are recorded in the UK each year, mostly in children and teenagers. By January 2001, Britain succeeded in virtually eradicating meningitis C after an extensive vaccination programme involving 18 million children and teenagers.

Related Web site: Childhood Infections – Meningitis http://kidshealth.org/parent/infections/lung/meningitis.html

meniscus in physics, the curved shape of the surface of a liquid
in a thin tube, caused by the cohesive effects of ▷surface tension (capillary action). When the walls of the container are made wet by the liquid, the meniscus is concave, but with highly viscous liquids (such as mercury) the meniscus is convex. Also, a meniscus lens is a concavo-convex or convexo-concave ▷lens.

Mennonite member of a Protestant Christian sect, originating
as part of the ▷Anabaptist movement in Zürich, Switzerland in 1523. Members refuse to hold civil office or do military service, and reject infant baptism. They were named Mennonites after Menno Simons (1496–1559), leader of a group in Holland.

Persecution drove other groups to Russia and North America.

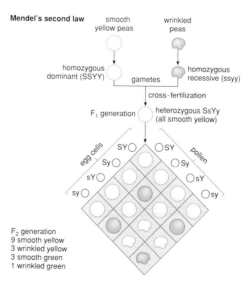

Mendel's first law

smooth peas — homozygous dominant (SS)

wrinkled peas — homozygous recessive (ss)

gametes

cross-fertilization

F₁ generation — heterozygous Ss (all smooth)

self-fertilization

F₂ generation (smooth and wrinkled in a ratio of 3:1; SS, Ss, Ss,ss)

Mendel's second law

smooth yellow peas — homozygous dominant (SSYY)

wrinkled peas — homozygous recessive (ssyy)

gametes

cross-fertilization

F₁ generation — heterozygous SsYy (all smooth yellow)

egg cells — SY, Sy, sY, sy — pollen — SY, Sy, sY, sy

F₂ generation
9 smooth yellow
3 wrinkled yellow
3 smooth green
1 wrinkled green

MENDELISM Mendel's laws explain the proportion of offspring having various characteristics. When pea plants having smooth yellow peas are crossed with plants with wrinkled green peas, the first-generation offspring all have smooth yellow peas. The second-generation offspring, however, contain smooth yellow, wrinkled green, smooth green, and wrinkled yellow peas. This can be understood by tracing the passage of alleles Y, S, s, y throughout the generations. S and Y are dominant genes.

menopause in women, the cessation of reproductive ability, characterized by menstruation (see ▷menstrual cycle) becoming irregular and eventually ceasing. The onset is at about the age of 50, but varies greatly. Menopause is usually uneventful, but some women suffer from complications such as flushing, excessive bleeding, and nervous disorders. Since the 1950s, ▷hormone-replacement therapy (HRT), using ▷oestrogen alone or with progestogen, a synthetic form of ▷progesterone, has been developed to counteract such effects.

Long-term use of HRT was previously associated with an increased risk of cancer of the uterus, and of clot formation in the blood vessels, but newer formulations using natural oestrogens are not associated with these risks. Without HRT there is increased risk of ▷osteoporosis (thinning of the bones) leading to broken bones, which may be indirectly fatal, particularly in the elderly.

The menopause is also known as the 'change of life'.
Related Web site: Menopause Information and Resources http://www.pslgroup.com/MENOPAUSE.HTM

menorah nine-branched candlestick used on the Jewish festival of ▷Hanukkah.

Menorca second largest of the ▷Balearic Islands in the Mediterranean; area 689 sq km/266 sq mi; population (2001 est) 75,300. The capital is ▷Mahón, and other towns and cities are Ciudadela, Mercadal, Ferrerias, and Fornells. Leather goods, costume jewellery, and cheese and dairy products are produced on the island, and tourism is also important.

Menshevik (Russian *menshinstvo* 'minority') member of the minority of the Russian Social Democratic Party, who split from the ▷Bolsheviks in 1903. The Mensheviks believed in a large, loosely organized party and that, before socialist revolution could occur in Russia, capitalist society had to develop further. During the Russian Revolution they had limited power and set up a government in Georgia, but were suppressed in 1922.

menstrual cycle cycle that occurs in female mammals of reproductive age, in which the body is prepared for pregnancy. At the beginning of the cycle, a Graafian (egg) follicle develops in the ovary, and the inner wall of the uterus forms a soft spongy lining. The egg is released from the ovary, and the uterus lining (endometrium) becomes vascularized (filled with blood vessels). If fertilization does not occur, the corpus luteum (remains of the Graafian follicle) degenerates, and the uterine lining breaks down, and is shed. This is what causes the loss of blood that marks menstruation. The cycle then begins again. Human menstruation takes place from puberty to menopause, except during pregnancy, occurring about every 28 days.

The cycle is controlled by a number of ▷hormones, including ▷oestrogen and ▷progesterone. If fertilization occurs, the corpus luteum persists and goes on producing progesterone.

mental disability arrested or incomplete development of mental capacities. It can be very mild, but in more severe cases is associated with social problems and difficulties in living independently. A person may be born with a mental disability

(for example, ▷Down's syndrome) or may acquire it through brain damage. Between 90 and 130 million people in the world suffer from such disabilities.

mental illness disordered functioning of the mind. Since normal working cannot easily be defined, the borderline between mild mental illness and normality is a matter of opinion (not to be confused with normative behaviour). It is broadly divided into two categories: ▷neurosis, in which the patient remains in touch with reality; and ▷psychosis, in which perception, thought, and belief are disordered.
Related Web site: Mental Health http://www.mentalhealth.com/

Mentor in Homer's *Odyssey*, an old man, adviser to ▷Telemachus in the absence of his father ▷Odysseus. His form is often taken by the goddess Athena.

menu in computing, a list of options, displayed on screen, from which the user may make a choice – for example, the choice of services offered to the customer by a bank cash dispenser: withdrawal, deposit, balance, or statement. Menus are used extensively in ▷graphical user interface (GUI) systems, where the menu options are often selected using a pointing device called a ▷mouse.

Menuhin, Yehudi, Baron Menuhin (1916–1999) US-born violinist and conductor. His solo repertoire extended from Vivaldi to George Enescu. He recorded the Elgar *Violin Concerto* in 1932 with the composer conducting, and commissioned the *Sonata* for violin solo in 1944 from an ailing Bartók. He appeared in concert with sitar virtuoso Ravi Shankar, and with jazz violinist Stéphane Grappelli. In March 1997 he was awarded Germany's highest honour, the Great Order of Merit. He first played in Berlin in 1928, and was the first Jewish artist to play with the Berlin Philharmonic after World War II. He was also noted for his humanitarian activities.

He made his debut with an orchestra at the age of 11 in New York. A child prodigy, he achieved great depth of interpretation, and was often accompanied on the piano by his sister Hephzibah (1921–1981). In 1959 he moved to London, becoming a British subject in 1985. He founded the Yehudi Menuhin School of Music, Stoke d'Abernon, Surrey, in 1963.

Menzies, Robert Gordon (1894–1978) Australian conservative politician, leader of the United Australia (now Liberal) Party and prime minister 1939–41 and 1949–66.

Meo (or Miao) another name (sometimes considered derogatory) for the ▷Hmong, a Southeast Asian people.

MEP abbreviation for member of the ▷European Parliament.

Mephistopheles (or Mephisto) another name for the ▷devil, or an agent of the devil, associated with the ▷Faust legend.

Mequinez Spanish name for ▷Meknès, a city in Morocco.

Mercalli scale a qualitative scale of the intensity of an ▷earthquake. It differs from the ▷Richter scale, which indicates earthquake **magnitude** and is quantitative. It is named after the Italian seismologist Giuseppe Mercalli (1850–1914).

mercantilism economic theory, held in the 16th–18th centuries, that a nation's wealth (in the form of bullion or treasure) was the key to its prosperity. To this end, foreign trade should be regulated to create a surplus of exports over imports, and the state should intervene where necessary (for example, subsidizing exports and taxing imports). The bullion theory of wealth was demolished by Adam ▷Smith in Book IV of *The Wealth of Nations* (1776).

Mercator, Gerardus (1512–1594) Flemish Gerhard Kremer. Flemish mapmaker who devised **Mercator's projection** in which the parallels and meridians on maps are drawn uniformly at 90°. The projection continues to be used, in particular for navigational charts, because compass courses can be drawn as straight lines, but the true area of countries is increasingly distorted the further north or south they are from the Equator. For other types, see ▷map projection.
Related Web site: Mercator, Gerardus http://www-groups.dcs.st-and.ac.uk/history/Mathematicians/Mercator_Gerardus.html

mercenary soldier hired by the army of another country or by a private army. Mercenary military service originated in the 14th century, when cash payment on a regular basis was the only means of guaranteeing soldiers' loyalty. In the 20th century mercenaries have been common in wars and guerrilla activity in Asia, Africa, and Latin America.

Merchant, Ismail (1936–) Indian film producer, known for his stylish collaborations with James ▷Ivory on films including *Shakespeare Wallah* (1965), *The Europeans* (1979), *Heat and Dust* (1983), *A Room with a View* (1987), *Maurice* (1987), *Howards End* (1992), and *The Remains of the Day* (1993). In 2000 he directed *Cotton Mary*.

merchant bank financial institution that specializes in corporate finance and financial and advisory services for business. Originally developed in the UK in the 19th century, merchant banks now offer many of the services provided by the commercial banks.

merchant navy the passenger and cargo ships of a country. Most are owned by private companies. To avoid strict regulations on safety, union rules on crew wages, and so on, many ships are today registered under 'flags of convenience', that is, flags of countries that do not have such rules.

Merchants Adventurers English trading company founded in 1407, which controlled the export of cloth to continental Europe. It comprised guilds and traders in many northern European ports. In direct opposition to the Hanseatic League, it came to control 75% of English overseas trade by 1550. In 1689 it lost its charter for furthering the traders' own interests at the expense of the English economy. The company was finally dissolved in 1806.

Mercia Anglo-Saxon kingdom that emerged in the 6th century. By the late 8th century it dominated all England south of the Humber, but from about 825 came under the power of ▷Wessex. Mercia eventually came to denote an area bounded by the Welsh border, the River Humber, East Anglia, and the River Thames.

Mercosur (or **South American Common Market**; Portuguese **Mercosul**; Spanish *Mercado del Sur* 'Market of the South') free-trade organization, founded in March 1991 on signature of the Asunción Treaty by Argentina, Brazil, Paraguay, and Uruguay, and formally inaugurated on 1 January 1995. With a GNP of $800,000 million and a population of more than 190 million, Mercosur constitutes the world's fourth-largest free-trade bloc after the ▷European Economic Area, the ▷North American Free Trade Agreement, and the Asia-Pacific Economic Cooperation Conference.

Mercury in astronomy, the closest planet to the Sun. Its mass is 0.056 that of Earth. On its sunward side the surface temperature reaches over 400°C/752°F, but on the 'night' side it falls to −170°C/−274°F.

mean distance from the Sun 58 million km/36 million mi
equatorial diameter 4,880 km/3,030 mi **rotation period** 59 Earth days **year** 88 Earth days **atmosphere** Mercury's small mass and high daytime temperature mean that it is impossible for an atmosphere to be retained. **surface** composed of silicate rock often in the form of lava flows. In 1974 the US space probe *Mariner 10* showed that Mercury's surface is cratered by meteorite impacts. **satellites** none In 1999 NASA approved a $286 million mission to send the spacecraft *Messenger* into orbit around Mercury in 2008 (launching in 2004), to photograph the planet's surface, analyse its atmospheric composition, and map its magnetic field. Its largest known feature is the Caloris Basin, 1,400 km/870 mi wide. There are also cliffs hundreds of kilometres long and up to 4 km/2.5 mi high, thought to have been formed by the cooling of the planet billions of years ago. Inside is an iron core three-quarters of the planet's diameter, which produces a magnetic field 1% the strength of Earth's.

menstruation   ovulation   egg dies if not fertilized

womb lining (endometrium is shed)   egg released from ovary   womb lining continues to thicken

follicle maturing   ovulation   corpus luteum developing   corpus luteum breaks down

oestrogens   progesterone

menstruation   end of menstruation   menstruation
days

1 2 3 4 5 6 7 8 9 10 11 12 13 14 15 16 17 18 19 20 21 22 23 24 25 26 27 28 1 2 3

start of menstruation   intercourse could result in fertilization

MENSTRUAL CYCLE From puberty to the menopause, most women produce a regular rhythm of hormones that stimulate the various stages of the menstrual cycle. The change in hormone levels may cause premenstrual tension. This diagram shows an average menstrual cycle. The dates of each stage vary from woman to woman.

Mercury (or Mercurius; Latin *merx* 'merchandise') in Roman mythology, a god of commerce and gain, and messenger of the gods. He was identified with the Greek ▷Hermes, and similarly represented with winged sandals and a winged staff entwined with snakes.

mercury (or **quicksilver**; Latin *mercurius*) heavy, silver-grey, metallic element, symbol Hg (from Latin *hydrargyrum*), atomic number 80, relative atomic mass 200.59. It is a dense, mobile liquid with a low melting point (−38.87°C/−37.96°F). Its chief source is the mineral cinnabar, HgS, but it sometimes occurs in nature as a free metal.

Uses Its alloys with other metals are called amalgams (a silver–mercury amalgam is used in dentistry for filling cavities in teeth). Industrial uses include drugs and chemicals, mercury-vapour lamps, arc rectifiers, power-control switches, barometers, and thermometers.

Hazards Mercury is a cumulative poison that can contaminate the food chain, and cause intestinal disturbance, kidney and brain damage, and birth defects in humans. The World Health Organization's 'safe' limit for mercury is 0.5 milligrams of mercury per kilogram of muscle tissue. The US Environmental Protection Agency recommended a maximum safe level for mercury of 0.1 mg per kilogram of body weight in January 1998 (a fifth of that recommended by WHO).The discharge into the sea by industry of organic mercury compounds such as dimethylmercury is the chief cause of mercury poisoning in the latter half of the 20th century. Between 1953 and 1975, 684 people in the Japanese fishing village of Minamata were poisoned (115 fatally) by organic mercury wastes that had been dumped into the bay and had accumulated in the bodies of fish and shellfish.

In a landmark settlement, a British multinational chemical company in April 1997 agreed to pay £1.3 million in compensation to 20 South African workers who were poisoned by mercury. Four of the black workers had died and a number of others were suffering severe brain and other neurological damage. The workers had accused Thor Chemical Holdings of adopting working practices in South Africa which would not have been allowed in Britain. The claimants had all worked at Thor's mercury plant at Cato Ridge in Natal. Thor had operated a mercury plant at Margate, in Kent, which during the 1980s was repeatedly criticised by the Health and Safety Executive (HSE) for bad working practices and over-exposure of British workers to mercury. Under pressure from the HSE, Thor closed down its mercury operations in Britain in 1987 and expanded them in South Africa.

History The element was known to the ancient Chinese and Hindus, and is found in Egyptian tombs of about 1500 BC. It was named by the alchemists after the fast-moving god, for its fluidity.

mercury fulminate highly explosive compound used in detonators and percussion caps. It is a grey, sandy powder and extremely poisonous.

Meredith, George (1828–1909) English novelist and poet. His realistic psychological novel *The Ordeal of Richard Feverel* (1859) engendered both scandal and critical praise. His best-known novel, *The Egoist* (1879), is superbly plotted and dissects the hero's self-centredness with merciless glee. The sonnet sequence *Modern Love* (1862) reflects the failure of his own marriage to the daughter of Thomas Love ▷Peacock. Other novels include *Evan Harrington* (1861), *Diana of the Crossways* (1885), and *The Amazing Marriage* (1895). His verse also includes *Poems and Lyrics of the Joy of Earth* (1883).

> **George Meredith**
> *Speech is the small change of silence.*
> *The Ordeal of Richard Feverel* ch. 34

merengue Latin American dance music with a lively 2/4 beat. Accordion and saxophone are prominent instruments, with ethnic percussion. It originated in the Dominican Republic and became popular in New York in the 1980s.

merganser any of several diving ducks with long, slender, serrated bills for catching fish, widely distributed in the northern hemisphere. Most have crested heads. (Genus *Mergus*, family Anatidae.)

merger the linking of two or more companies, either by creating a new organization by consolidating the original companies or by absorption by one company of the others. Unlike a takeover, which is not always a voluntary fusion of the parties, a merger is the result of an agreement.

Mérida capital of Yucatán state, Mexico, a centre of the sisal industry; population (1990) 556,800. It was founded in 1542, and has a cathedral dating from 1598. Its port on the Gulf of Mexico is Progreso.

meridian half a ▷great circle drawn on the Earth's surface passing through both poles and thus through all places with the same longitude. Terrestrial longitudes are usually measured from the Greenwich Meridian.

An astronomical meridian is a great circle passing through the celestial pole and the zenith (the point immediately overhead).

Mérimée, Prosper (1803–1870) French author. Among his works are the short novels *Mateo Falcone* (1829), *Colomba* (1841), *Carmen* (1846) (the basis for Bizet's opera), and the *Lettres à une inconnue/Letters to an Unknown Girl* (1873). Romantically set in foreign countries, his stories nevertheless have a realistic background of local colour and atmosphere.

merino breed of sheep. Its close-set, silky wool is highly valued. Originally from Spain, the merino is now found all over the world, and is the breed on which the Australian wool industry is built.

Merionethshire (Welsh **Sir Feirionnydd**) former county of north Wales, now part of ▷Gwynedd.

meristem region of plant tissue containing cells that are actively dividing to produce new tissues (or have the potential to do so). Meristems found in the tip of roots and stems, the apical meristems, are responsible for the growth in length of these organs.

Merit, Order of British order (see ▷knighthood, order of), instituted in 1902 and limited in number to 24 men and women of eminence. It confers no precedence or knighthood.

Merlin (Welsh **Myrddin**) legendary magician and seer Arthur. Welsh bardic literature has a cycle of poems attributed to him, and he may have been a real person. His legend is related in *Vita Merlini* by the 12th-century chronicler Geoffrey of Monmouth.

merlin small ▷falcon of Europe, Asia, and North America, where it is also called a **pigeon hawk**. The male, 26 cm/10 in long, has a grey-blue back and reddish-brown barred front; the female, 32 cm/13 in long, has a dark brown back and lighter front with streaks. Merlins fly relatively low over the ground when hunting and 'stoop' quickly onto their prey, which consists mainly of small birds. (Species *Falco columbarius*, order Falconiformes.)

They are found mainly on rocks and moors. On moorland the nest is generally built on a slope among the heather, and in other localities on rock ledges. The eggs are bluish-white, blotched with brown markings; four or five are laid.

mermaid (Old English *mere* 'lake', *maegth* 'maid') mythical sea creature (the male is a **merman**), having a human head and torso, often of great beauty, and a fish's tail. Suggested animals behind the myth include the dugong or manatee and seal.

mermaid's purse purse-shaped egg case of the ▷skates and many ▷sharks.

Meroë ancient city in Sudan, on the Nile near Khartoum, capital of Nubia from about 600 BC to AD 350. Tombs and inscriptions have been excavated, and iron-smelting slag heaps have been found.

Merovingian dynasty (lived 5th–8th centuries) Frankish dynasty, named after its founder, **Merovech** (5th century AD). His descendants ruled France from the time of Clovis (481–511) to 751.

Mersey river in northwest England; length 112 km/70 mi. Formed by the confluence of the Goyt and Tame rivers at Stockport, it flows west through the south of Manchester, is joined by the Irwell at Flixton and by the Weaver at Runcorn, and enters the Irish Sea at Liverpool Bay. It drains large areas of the Lancashire and Cheshire plains. The Mersey is linked to the Manchester Ship Canal. Although plans were announced in 1990 to build a 1,800-m/5,907-ft barrage across the Mersey estuary to generate electricity from tides, these were abandoned in 1992 for financial reasons.

Mersey beat pop music of the mid-1960s that originated in the northwest of England. It was also known as the Liverpool sound or ▷beat music in the UK. It was almost exclusively performed by all-male groups, the most popular being the Beatles.

Merseyside metropolitan county of northwest England, created in 1974; in 1986, most of the functions of the former county council were transferred to metropolitan borough councils (The Wirral, Sefton, Liverpool, Knowsley, St Helens).

area 650 sq km/251 sq mi **towns and cities** Liverpool, Bootle, Birkenhead, St Helens, Wallasey, Southport **physical** River Mersey **features** Merseyside Innovation Centre (MIC), linked with Liverpool and John Moores Universities; Prescot Museum of clock- and watch-making; Speke Hall (Tudor), and Croxteth Hall and Country Park (a working country estate open to the public) **industries** brewing, chemicals, electrical goods, glassmaking, metal-working, pharmaceutical products, tanning, vehicles **population** (1996) 1,420,400 **famous people** the Beatles, William Ewart Gladstone, George Stubbs

Merthyr Tydfil unitary authority in south Wales, created in 1996 from part of the former county of Mid Glamorgan.

area 111 sq km/43 sq mi **towns** ▷Merthyr Tydfil (administrative headquarters) **features** area includes part of Brecon Beacons National Park **industries** light engineering, electrical goods **population** (1996) 60,000

Merton outer borough of southwest Greater London comprising the suburbs of Wimbledon, Mitcham, and Morden; population (1991) 168,500. Features include the Augustinian priory, founded in 1114, where Thomas à Becket and Walter de Merton, founder of Merton College, Oxford, were educated (it was demolished at the dissolution and the stones used by Henry VIII to build Nonsuch Palace); Merton Place, where Admiral Nelson lived; Merton Park, laid out in the mid-19th century, claimed as the forerunner of garden suburbs; Wimbledon Common, includes Caesar's Camp – an Iron Age fort; and the All England Lawn Tennis Club (founded 1877). Merton was created as a borough on 1 April 1965.

Merv oasis in Turkmenistan, a centre of civilization from at least 1200 BC, and site of a town founded by Alexander the Great. Old Merv was destroyed by the emir of Bokhara in 1787, and the modern town of Mary, founded by the Russians in 1885, lies 29 km/18 mi to its west.

mesa (Spanish 'table') flat-topped, steep-sided plateau, consisting of horizontal weak layers of rock topped by a resistant formation; in particular, those found in the desert areas of the USA and Mexico. A small mesa is called a butte.

mescaline psychedelic drug derived from a small, spineless cactus *Lophophora williamsii* of northern Mexico and the southwest USA, known as ▷peyote. The tops (called mescal buttons), which scarcely appear above ground, are dried and chewed, or added to alcoholic drinks. Mescaline is a crystalline alkaloid $C_{11}H_{17}NO_3$. It is used by some North American Indians in religious rites.

Meskhetian a community of Turkish descent that formerly inhabited Meskhetia, on the then Turkish–Soviet border. They were deported by Stalin in 1944 to Kazakhstan and Uzbekistan, and have campaigned since then for a return to their homeland. In June 1989 at least 70 were killed in pogroms directed against their community in the Fergana Valley of Uzbekistan by the ethnic Uzbeks.

Mesmer, Friedrich Anton (or **Franz**) (1734–1815) Austrian physician, an early experimenter in ▷hypnosis, which was formerly (and popularly) called 'mesmerism' after him.

Mesolithic the Middle Stone Age developmental stage of human technology and of ▷prehistory.

meson in physics, a group of unstable subatomic particles made up of a ▷quark and an antiquark. It is found in cosmic radiation, and is emitted by nuclei under bombardment by very high-energy particles.

The mesons form a subclass of the hadrons and include the kaons and pions. Their existence was predicted in 1935 by Japanese physicist Hideki Yukawa.

mesophyll the tissue between the upper and lower epidermis of a leaf blade (▷lamina), consisting of parenchyma-like cells containing numerous ▷chloroplasts.

Mesopotamia the land between the Tigris and Euphrates rivers, now part of Iraq. The civilizations of Sumer and Babylon flourished here. The ▷Sumerian civilization (3500 BC) may have been the earliest urban civilization.

Mesopotamian art the art of the ancient civilizations which grew up in the area around the Tigris and Euphrates rivers, now in Iraq. Mesopotamian art, which was largely used to glorify powerful dynasties, achieved great richness and variety.

Sumerian (3500–2300 BC) The first of the powerful Mesopotamian civilizations, Sumer was concentrated in the cities of Ur, Eridu, and Uruk in southern Mesopotamia. The Sumerians built temples on top of vast ziggurats (stepped towers) and also vast, elaborately decorated palaces. Sculptures include erect, stylized figures carved in marble and characterized by clasped hands and huge eyes; those found in the Abu Temple, Tell Asmar, date from 2700 BC. Earlier sculptures in alabaster, such as the *Female Head* (3000 BC; Iraq Museum, Baghdad), show a greater naturalism and sensitivity. Inlay work is seen in the *Standard of Ur* (2500 BC), a box decorated with pictures in lapis lazuli, shell, and red sandstone. The Sumerians, who invented writing about 3000 BC, produced many small, finely carved cylindrical seals made of marble, alabaster, carnelian, lapis lazuli, and stone.

Akkadian (2300–2150 BC) The Akkadian invaders quickly assimilated Sumerian styles. The stele (decorated upright slab) *Victory of Naram-Sin* (2200 BC; Louvre, Paris), carved in relief, depicts a military campaign of the warlike Akkadians. The technical and artistic sophistication of bronze sculpture is illustrated by the *Head of an Akkadian King* (2200 BC; Iraq Museum, Baghdad).

Assyrian (1400–600 BC) The characteristic Assyrian art form was narrative relief sculpture, which was used to decorate palaces, for example, the Palace of Ashurbanipal (7th century BC). Its dramatic and finely carved reliefs, including dramatic scenes of a lion hunt, are in the British Museum, London. Winged bulls with

human faces, carved partially in the round, stood as sentinels at the royal gateways (Louvre, Paris).
Babylonian (625–538 BC) Babylon, although it had ancient traditions, came to artistic prominence in the 6th century BC, when it flourished under King Nebuchadnezzar II. He built the ▷Hanging Gardens of Babylon, a series of terraced gardens. The Babylonians practised all the Mesopotamian arts and excelled in brightly coloured glazed tiles, used to create relief sculptures. An example is the Ishtar Gate (about 575 BC) from the Temple of Bel, the biblical Tower of Babel (Pergamon Museum, Berlin, and Metropolitan Museum of Art, New York).

MESOPOTAMIAN ART An alabaster statuette from the far northern Mesopotamian kingdom of Kish, dating from early in the 3rd millennium BC, which was found at Tell Chuera, Syria. *The Art Archive/Damascus Museum Syria/Dagli Orti*

mesosphere layer in the Earth's ▷atmosphere above the stratosphere and below the thermosphere. It lies between about 50 km/31 mi and 80 km/50 mi above the ground.

Mesozoic era of geological time 245–65 million years ago, consisting of the Triassic, Jurassic, and Cretaceous periods. At the beginning of the era, the continents were joined together as Pangaea; dinosaurs and other giant reptiles dominated the sea and air; and ferns, horsetails, and cycads thrived in a warm climate worldwide. By the end of the Mesozoic era, the continents had begun to assume their present positions, flowering plants were dominant, and many of the large reptiles and marine fauna were becoming extinct.

Messalina, Valeria (*c.* AD 25–48) Third wife of the Roman emperor ▷Claudius I. She was notorious for her immorality, persuading a noble to marry her in AD 48, although still married to Claudius. Claudius was then persuaded (with some difficulty), by his secretary Narcissus, to have her executed.

Messerschmitt, Willy (Wilhelm Emil) (1898–1978) German aeroplane designer. His Me-109 was a standard Luftwaffe fighter in World War II, and his Me-262 (1944) was the first mass-produced jet fighter.

Messiaen, Olivier Eugène Prosper Charles (1908–1992) French composer, organist, and teacher. His music is mystical in character, vividly coloured, and incorporates transcriptions of birdsong. Among his works are the *Quartet for the End of Time* (1941), the large-scale *Turangalîla Symphony* (1949), and solo organ and piano pieces. As a teacher at the Paris Conservatoire from 1942, he influenced three generations of composers.

His theories of melody, harmony, and rhythm, drawing on medieval and oriental music, have inspired contemporary composers such as Boulez and Stockhausen.

Messiah (from Hebrew *māshīach* 'anointed') in Judaism and Christianity, the saviour or deliverer. Jews from the time of the Old Testament exile in Babylon have looked forward to the coming of the Messiah. Christians believe that the Messiah came in the person of ▷Jesus, and hence called him the Christ.

Messier, Charles (1730–1817) French astronomer. He discovered 15 comets and in 1784 published a list of 103 star clusters and nebulae. Objects on this list are given M (for Messier) numbers, which astronomers still use today, such as M1 (the Crab nebula) and M31 (the Andromeda galaxy).

Messina, Strait of (ancient **Siculum Fretum**) channel in the central Mediterranean separating Sicily from mainland Italy, joining the Tyrrhenian and Ionian seas; it is 35 km/22 mi long, and its width varies from 17 km/11 mi in the south to 3 km/2 mi in the north. In Greek legend the monster Scylla devoured sailors from a rock on the Italian shore, while another, Charybdis, created a whirlpool on the Sicilian side which sank ships. The classical hero Odysseus passed safely between them.

metabolism the chemical processes of living organisms enabling them to grow and to function. It involves a constant alternation of building up complex molecules (**anabolism**) and breaking them down (**catabolism**). For example, green plants build up complex organic substances from water, carbon dioxide, and mineral salts (▷photosynthesis); by digestion animals partially break down complex organic substances, ingested as food, and subsequently resynthesize them for use in their own bodies (see ▷digestive system). Within cells, complex molecules are broken down by the process of ▷respiration. The waste products of metabolism are removed by ▷excretion.

metal any of a class of chemical elements with specific physical and chemical characteristics. Metallic elements compose about 75% of the 112 elements in the ▷periodic table of the elements.

Physical properties include a sonorous tone when struck, good conduction of heat and electricity, opacity but good reflection of light, malleability, which enables them to be cold-worked and rolled into sheets, ductility, which permits them to be drawn into thin wires, and the possible emission of electrons when heated (thermionic effect) or when the surface is struck by light (▷photoelectric effect).

The majority of metals are found in nature in a combined form only, as compounds or mineral ores; about 16 of them also occur in the elemental form, as ▷native metals. Their chemical properties are largely determined by the extent to which their atoms can lose one or more electrons and form positive ions (cations).

Commercial use The following are widely used in commerce: **precious metals** – gold, silver, and platinum, used principally in jewellery; **heavy metals** – iron, copper, zinc, tin, and lead, the common metals of engineering; **rarer heavy metals** – nickel, cadmium, chromium, tungsten, molybdenum, manganese, cobalt, vanadium, antimony, and bismuth, used principally for alloying with the heavy metals; **light metals** – aluminium and magnesium; **alkali metals** – sodium, potassium, and lithium; and **alkaline-earth metals** – calcium, barium, and strontium, used principally for chemical purposes.

Other metals have come to the fore because of special nuclear requirements – for example, technetium, produced in nuclear reactors, is corrosion-inhibiting; zirconium may replace aluminium and magnesium alloy in canning uranium in reactors.

metal detector electronic device for detecting metal, usually below ground, developed from the wartime mine detector. In the head of the metal detector is a coil, which is part of an electronic circuit. The presence of metal causes the frequency of the signal in the circuit to change, setting up an audible note in the headphones worn by the user.

metal fatigue condition in which metals fail or fracture under relatively light loads, when these loads are applied repeatedly. Structures that are subject to flexing, such as the airframes of aircraft, are prone to metal fatigue.

metallic bond the force of attraction operating in a metal that holds the atoms together. In the metal the ▷valency electrons are able to move within the crystal and these electrons are said to be delocalized (see ▷electrons, delocalized). Their movement creates short-lived, positively charged ions. The electrostatic attraction between the delocalized electrons and the ceaselessly forming ions constitutes the metallic bond.

metallic character chemical properties associated with those elements classed as metals. These properties, which arise from the element's ability to lose electrons, are: the displacement of hydrogen from dilute acids; the formation of basic oxides; the formation of ionic chlorides; and their reducing reaction, as in the ▷thermite process (see ▷reduction). In the periodic table of the elements, metallic character increases down any group and across a period from right to left.

metalloid (or **semimetal**) any chemical element having some of but not all the properties of metals; metalloids are thus usually electrically semiconducting. They comprise the elements germanium, arsenic, antimony, and tellurium.

metallurgy the science and technology of producing metals, which includes extraction, alloying, and hardening. **Extractive**, or **process, metallurgy** is concerned with the extraction of metals from their ▷ores and refining and adapting them for use. **Physical metallurgy** is concerned with their properties and application. **Metallography** establishes the microscopic structures that contribute to hardness, ductility, and strength.

metamorphic rock a rock that has been changed from its original form, texture, and/or mineral assemblage by pressure or heat. For example, limestone can be metamorphosed by heat into marble, and shale by pressure into slate. The term was coined in 1833 by Scottish geologist Charles ▷Lyell.

There are two main types of metamorphism. **Thermal metamorphism**, or contact metamorphism, is brought about by the baking of solid rocks in the vicinity of an igneous intrusion (molten rock, or magma, in a crack in the Earth's crust). It is responsible, for example, for the conversion of limestone to marble. **Regional metamorphism** results from the heat and intense pressures associated with burial and the movements and collision of tectonic plates (see ▷plate tectonics). It brings about the conversion of shale to slate, for example. A third type, **shock metamorphism**, occurs when a rock is very quickly subjected to high pressures such as those brought about by a meteorite impact.

Metamorphic rocks have essentially the same chemical composition as their protoliths, but because different mineral are stable at different temperatures and pressures, they are commonly composed of different, metamorphic minerals. Metamorphism also produces changes in the texture of the rock, for example, rocks become foliated (or layered), and crystals grow larger.

metamorphism geological term referring to the changes in rocks of the Earth's crust caused by increasing pressure and temperature. The resulting rocks are metamorphic rocks. All metamorphic changes take place in solid rocks. If the rocks melt and then harden, they are considered ▷igneous rocks.

metamorphosis period during the life cycle of many invertebrates, most amphibians, and some fish, during which the individual's body changes from one form to another through a major reconstitution of its tissues. For example, adult frogs are produced by metamorphosis from tadpoles, and butterflies are produced from caterpillars following metamorphosis within a pupa.

In classical thought and literature, metamorphosis is the transformation of a living being into another shape, either living or inanimate (for example Niobe). The Roman poet ▷Ovid wrote about this theme.

metaphor (Greek 'transfer') figure of speech using an analogy or close comparison between two things that are not normally treated as if they had anything in common. Metaphor is a common means of extending the uses and references of words. See also ▷simile.

metaphysical painting (Italian *pittura metafisica*) Italian painting style, conceived in 1917 by Giorgio de ▷Chirico and Carlo Carrà, which sought to convey a sense of mystery through the use of dreamlike imagery. Reacting against both ▷cubism and ▷Futurism, it anticipated ▷surrealism in the techniques it employed, notably the incongruous juxtaposition of familiar objects. Though short-lived – it had disbanded by the early 1920s – its influence was considerable.

metaphysical poets group of early 17th-century English poets whose work is characterized by ingenious, highly intricate wordplay and unlikely or paradoxical imagery. They used rhetorical and literary devices, such as paradox, hyperbole, and elaborately developed conceits, in such a way as to engage the reader by their humour, strangeness, or sheer outrageousness. Among the exponents of this genre are John ▷Donne, George ▷Herbert, Andrew ▷Marvell, Richard Crashaw, and Henry Vaughan. As originally used, the term 'metaphysical' implied a criticism of these poets; Samuel ▷Johnson, for example, complained that their poetry was laden with too much far-fetched learning. Their reputation declined after the ▷Restoration but underwent a dramatic revival in the 20th century, prompted by T S ▷Eliot's essay 'The Metaphysical Poets' (1921).

metaphysics branch of philosophy that deals with first principles, in particular 'being' (ontology) and 'knowing' (▷epistemology), and that is concerned with the ultimate nature of reality. It has been maintained that no certain knowledge of metaphysical questions is possible.

Related Web site: Revealing Word: A Dictionary of Metaphysics
http://websyte.com/unity/RVLS2.HTM

Metchnikoff, Elie (1845–1916) Russian **Ilya Ilich Mechnikov**. Russian zoologist and immunologist who was a pioneer of cellular immunology and shared the Nobel Prize for Physiology or Medicine in 1908 with Paul ▷Ehrlich for his discovery of the innate immune response.

meteor flash of light in the sky, popularly known as a **shooting** or **falling star**, caused by a particle of dust, a **meteoroid**, entering the atmosphere at speeds up to 70 kps/45 mps and burning up by friction at a height of around 100 km/60 mi. On any clear night, several **sporadic meteors** can be seen each hour.

Several times each year the Earth encounters swarms of dust shed by comets, which give rise to a **meteor shower**. This appears to radiate from one particular point in the sky, after which the shower is named; the **Perseid** meteor shower in August appears in the constellation Perseus. The **Leonids** shoot out from the constellation Leo and are caused by dust from Comet Tempel-Tuttle, which orbits the Sun every 33 years. The Leonid shower reaches its peak when the comet is closest to the Sun.

Related Web site: Meteors, Meteorites, and Impacts http://www.seds.org/billa/tnp/meteorites.html

meteorite piece of rock or metal from space that reaches the surface of the Earth, Moon, or other body. Most meteorites are thought to be fragments from asteroids, although some may be pieces from the heads of comets. Most are stony, although some are made of iron and a few have a mixed rock-iron composition.

Stony meteorites can be divided into two kinds: **chondrites** and **achondrites**. Chondrites contain chondrules, small spheres of the silicate minerals olivine and orthopyroxene, and comprise 85% of meteorites. Achondrites do not contain chondrules. Meteorites provide evidence for the nature of the Solar System and may be similar to the Earth's core and mantle, neither of which can be observed directly.

Thousands of meteorites hit the Earth each year, but most fall in the sea or in remote areas and are never recovered. The largest known meteorite is one composed of iron, weighing 60 tonnes, which lies where it fell in prehistoric times at Grootfontein, Namibia. Meteorites are slowed down by the Earth's atmosphere, but if they are moving fast enough they can form a ▷crater on impact. Meteor Crater in Arizona, about 1.2 km/0.7 mi in diameter and 200 m/650 ft deep, is the site of a meteorite impact about 50,000 years ago.

meteorology scientific observation and study of the ▷atmosphere, so that ▷weather can be accurately forecast.

Data from meteorological stations and weather satellites are collated by computer at central agencies, and forecast and weather maps based on current readings are issued at regular intervals. Modern analysis, employing some of the most powerful computers, can give useful forecasts for up to six days ahead.

At meteorological stations readings are taken of the factors determining weather conditions: atmospheric pressure, temperature, humidity, wind (using the ▷Beaufort scale), cloud cover (measuring both type of cloud and coverage), and precipitation such as rain, snow, and hail (measured at 12-hour intervals). ▷Satellites are used either to relay information transmitted from the Earth-based stations, or to send pictures of cloud development, indicating wind patterns, and snow and ice cover.

History Apart from some observations included by Aristotle in his book *Meteorologia*, meteorology did not become a precise science until the end of the 16th century, when Galileo and the Florentine academicians constructed the first thermometer of any importance, and when Evangelista Torricelli in 1643 discovered the principle of the barometer. Robert ▷Boyle's work on gases, and that of his assistant, Robert ▷Hooke, on barometers, advanced the physics necessary for the understanding of the weather. Gabriel ▷Fahrenheit's invention of a superior mercury thermometer provided further means for temperature recording.

Weather maps In the early 19th century a chain of meteorological stations was established in France, and weather maps were constructed from the data collected. The first weather map in England, showing the trade winds and monsoons, was made in 1688, and the first telegraphic weather report appeared 31 August 1848. The first daily telegraphic weather map was prepared at the Great Exhibition in 1851, but the Meteorological Office was not established in London until 1855. The first regular daily collections of weather observations by telegraph and the first British daily weather reports were made in 1860, and the first daily printed maps appeared 1868.

Collecting data Observations can be collected not only from land stations, but also from weather ships, aircraft, and self-recording and automatic transmitting stations, such as the ▷radiosonde. ▷Radar may be used to map clouds and storms. Satellites have played an important role in televising pictures of global cloud distribution.

As well as supplying reports for the media, the Meteorological Office in Bracknell, near London, does specialist work for industry, agriculture, and transport. Kew is the main meteorological observatory in the British Isles, but other observatories are at Eskdalemuir in the southern uplands of Scotland, Lerwick in the Shetlands, and Valentia in southwestern Ireland. Climatic information from British climatological reporting stations is published in the Monthly Weather Report, and periodically in tables of averages and frequencies.

The British Meteorological Office's Daily Weather Report contains a detailed map of the weather over the British Isles and a less detailed map of the weather over the northern hemisphere, and the Daily Aerological Record contains full reports of radiosonde ascents made over the British Isles and from some of the ocean weather ships, together with maps of the heights of the 700 mb, 500 mb, and 300 mb pressure surfaces, giving a picture of the winds at 3,048 m/10,000 ft, 5,182 m/18,000 ft, and 9,144 m/30,000 ft; there is also a map of the height of the tropopause. Ships' reports are plotted on the same charts using the same symbolic form. Data from radiosondes and aircraft are plotted on upper-air charts and on temperature–height diagrams, the diagram in use in Britain being the tephigram. With the help of this diagram it is possible to predict the formation or otherwise of clouds, showers, or thunderstorms, and sometimes to identify the source region of the air mass.

meter any instrument used for measurement. The term is often compounded with a prefix to denote a specific type of meter: for example, ammeter, voltmeter, flowmeter, or pedometer.

methanal (or **formaldehyde**) HCHO gas at ordinary temperatures, condensing to a liquid at −21°C/−5.8°F. It has a powerful, penetrating smell. Dissolved in water, it is used as a biological preservative. It is used in the manufacture of plastics, dyes, foam (for example urea-formaldehyde foam, used in insulation), and in medicine.

Related Web site: Formaldehyde http://www.nsc.org/EHC/indoor/formald.htm

methane CH_4 the simplest hydrocarbon of the paraffin series. Colourless, odourless, and lighter than air, it burns with a bluish flame and explodes when mixed with air or oxygen. It is the chief constituent of natural gas and also occurs in the explosive firedamp of coal mines. Methane emitted by rotting vegetation forms marsh gas, which may ignite by spontaneous combustion to produce the pale flame seen over marshland and known as ▷will-o'-the-wisp.

Methane causes about 38% of the warming of the globe through the ▷greenhouse effect; weight for weight it is 60–70 times more potent than carbon dioxide at trapping solar radiation in the atmosphere and so heating the planet. The rate of increase of atmospheric methane is declining and global emissions have remained relatively constant over the period 1984–96, so atmospheric levels were predicted, in 1998, to stabilize by the 2020s. An estimated 15% of all methane gas into the atmosphere is produced by cattle and other cud-chewing animals, and 20% is produced by termites that feed on soil.

Britain discharges about 4 million tonnes of methane each year (of which about 1.5 million tonnes is produced by agriculture).

methanoic acid (or **formic acid**) HCOOH, a colourless, slightly fuming liquid that freezes at 8°C/46.4°F and boils at 101°C/213.8°F. It occurs in stinging ants, nettles, sweat, and pine needles, and is used in dyeing, tanning, and electroplating.

methanol (common name **methyl alcohol**) CH_3OH the simplest of the alcohols. It can be made by the dry distillation of wood (hence it is also known as wood alcohol), but is usually made from coal or natural gas. When pure, it is a colourless, flammable liquid with a pleasant odour, and is highly poisonous.

Method US adaptation of ▷Stanislavsky's teachings on acting and direction, in which importance is attached to the psychological building of a role rather than the technical side of its presentation. Emphasis is placed on improvisation, aiming for a spontaneous and realistic style of acting. One of the principal exponents of the Method was the US actor and director Lee Strasberg, who taught at the Actors Studio in New York.

Methodism evangelical Protestant Christian movement that was founded by John ▷Wesley in 1739 within the Church of England, but became a separate body in 1795. The Methodist Episcopal Church was founded in the USA in 1784. There are over 50 million Methodists worldwide.

Methodius, St (*c.* 825–884) Greek Christian bishop, who with his brother ▷Cyril translated much of the Bible into Slavonic. Feast day 14 February.

Methuselah in the Old Testament, Hebrew patriarch who lived before the Flood; his lifespan of 969 years makes him a byword for longevity.

methyl alcohol common name for ▷methanol.

methylated spirit alcohol that has been rendered undrinkable, and is used for industrial purposes, as a fuel for spirit burners or a solvent. It is nevertheless drunk by some individuals, resulting eventually in death. One of the poisonous substances in it is ▷methanol, or methyl alcohol, and this gives it its name. (The 'alcohol' of alcoholic drinks is ethanol.)

methyl benzene alternative name for ▷toluene.

methyl orange $C_{14}H_{14}N_3NaO_3S$ orange-yellow powder used as an acid–base indicator in chemical tests, and as a stain in the preparation of slides of biological material. Its colour changes with pH; below pH 3.1 it is red, above pH 4.4 it is yellow.

metre SI unit (symbol m) of length, equivalent to 1.093 yards or 39.37 inches. It is defined by scientists as the length of the path travelled by light in a vacuum during a time interval of 1/299,792,458 of a second.

metric system system of weights and measures developed in France in the 18th century and recognized by other countries in the 19th century.

In 1960 an international conference on weights and measures recommended the universal adoption of a revised International System (Système International d'Unités, or SI), with seven prescribed 'base units': the metre (m) for length, kilogram (kg) for mass, second (s) for time, ampere (A) for electric current, kelvin (K) for thermodynamic temperature, candela (cd) for luminous intensity, and mole (mol) for quantity of matter.

metropolitan (Greek 'mother-state, capital') in the Christian church generally, a bishop who has rule over other bishops (termed **suffragans**). In the Eastern Orthodox Church, a metropolitan has a rank between an archbishop and a ▷patriarch.

Metternich, Klemens Wenzel Nepomuk Lothar, Prince von Metternich (1773–1859) Austrian politician, the leading figure in European diplomacy after the fall of Napoleon. As foreign minister 1809–48 (as well as chancellor from 1821), he tried to maintain the balance of power in Europe, supporting monarchy and repressing liberalism.

Related Web site: Memoirs of Prince Metternich http://www.h-net.msu.edu/~habsweb/sourcetexts/mettsrc.htm

KLEMENS METTERNICH In the face of revolutionary movements throughout Europe in 1848, Metternich, Austrian minister of foreign affairs, was forced to retire, as shown in this cartoon. *The Art Archive/Dagli Orti*

Meuse (Dutch **Maas**) river flowing through France, Belgium, and the Netherlands; length 900 km/559 mi. It was an important line of battle in both world wars. It gives its name to a French *département*.

Mexicali city in northwestern Mexico; population (1990) 601,900. It produces soap and cottonseed oil. The availability of cheap labour attracts many US companies (Hughes Aerospace, Rockwell International, and others).

Mexican Empire short-lived empire 1822–23 following the liberation of Mexico from Spain. The empire lasted only eight months, under the revolutionary leader Agustín de Iturbide.

When the French emperor Napoleon I put his brother Joseph on the Spanish throne in 1808, links between Spain and its colonies weakened and an independence movement grew in Mexico.

There were several unsuccessful uprisings until, in 1821, General Agustín de Iturbide published a plan promising independence, protection for the church, and the establishment of a monarchy. As no European came forward, he proclaimed himself emperor in 1822. Forced to abdicate, he went into exile; on his return to Mexico he was shot by republican leaders Guadalupe Victoria and Santa Anna. Victoria became the first president of Mexico.

Mexican War war between the USA and Mexico 1846–48, begun in territory disputed between Texas (annexed by the USA in 1845 but claimed by Mexico) and Mexico. It began when General Zachary Taylor invaded New Mexico after efforts to purchase what are now California and New Mexico failed. Mexico City was taken in 1847, and, under the Treaty of Guadaloupe Hidalgo that ended the war, the USA acquired New Mexico and California, as well as clear title to Texas in exchange for $15 million.

Tensions were high between the USA and Mexico as a result of continuing border disputes and the annexation of Texas. President James ▷Polk determined to pursue his notion of manifest destiny for the USA and dispatched Taylor to add the disputed territories, by force if necessary. After repeated defeats and invasion of its home territory, a Mexican government was formed that was willing to negotiate a settlement. Presidential envoy Nicholas Trist was ordered home, but he ignored his orders and negotiated the pact ceding vast Mexican territories to the USA. Polk was enraged but had little choice but to submit the exceptionally favourable treaty to the Senate, which ratified it.

Mexico see country box.

Mexico City (Spanish **Ciudad de México**) capital, industrial (iron, steel, chemicals, textiles) and cultural centre of Mexico, 2,255 m/7,400 ft above sea level on the southern edge of the central plateau; population (1994) 15,500,000. It is thought to be one of the world's most polluted cities because of its position in a volcanic basin 2,000 m/7,400 ft above sea level. Pollutants gather in the basin causing a smog cloud.

Notable buildings include the 16th-century cathedral, the national palace, national library, Palace of Justice, and national university; the Ministry of Education has murals (1923–27) by Diego Rivera.

The city dates from about 1325, when the Aztec capital Tenochtitlán was founded on an island in Lake Texcoco. This city was levelled in 1521 by the Spaniards, who in 1522 founded a new city on the site. It was the location of the 1968 Summer Olympics. In 1984, the explosion of a liquefied gas tank caused the deaths of over 450 people, and in 1985, over 2,000 were killed by an earthquake.

Related Web site: The US–Mexican War 1846–1848 http://www.pbs.org/kera/usmexicanwar/

Meyerbeer, Giacomo (1791–1864) Adopted name of Jakob Liebmann Meyer Beer. German composer. His spectacular operas include *Robert le Diable* (1831) and *Les Huguenots* (1836). From 1826 he lived mainly in Paris, returning to Berlin after 1842 as musical director of the Royal Opera.

Meynell, Alice Christiana Gertrude (1847–1922) Born Alice Christiana Gertrude Thompson. English poet and essayist. She published *Preludes* (1875) and several other slim volumes of poetry, concluding with *Last Poems* (1923). Her writing is similar to that of Christina ▷Rossetti in its delicate craftsmanship. Her essays were collected in *The Rhythm of Life* (1893), *The Colour of Life* (1896), and *The Spirit of Place* (1898). She married the author and journalist Wilfrid Meynell (1852–1948).

mezuza in Judaism, a small box containing a parchment scroll inscribed with a prayer, the Shema from Deuteronomy 6:4–9; 11:13–21, which is found on the doorpost of every home and every room in a Jewish house, except the bathroom.

Mezzogiorno (Italian 'midday') hot, impoverished area of southern Italy, comprising the regions of Molise, Campania, Apulia, Basilicata, and Calabria, and the islands of Sardinia and Sicily. Agriculture is the chief mainstay of a generally poor economy; the main products are grains, vegetables, grapes, and olives. The region's economic, educational, and income levels are much lower than those of northern Italy.

mezzo-soprano female singing voice with an approximate range A4–F5, between contralto and soprano. It is commonly abbreviated to just 'mezzo'.

mezzotint (Italian 'half tint') print produced by a method of etching in density of tone rather than line, popular in the 18th and 19th centuries when it was largely used for the reproduction of paintings, especially portraits. A copper or steel plate is roughened with a finely-toothed tool known as a 'rocker' to raise an even, overall burr (rough edge), which will hold ink. At this point the plate would print a rich, even black, so areas of burr are carefully smoothed away with a 'scraper' to produce a range of lighter tones. Primarily a reproductive technique, mezzotint declined rapidly with the invention of photography.

Mfecane in African history, a series of disturbances in the early 19th century among communities in what is today the eastern part of South Africa. They arose when chief ▷Shaka conquered the Nguni peoples between the Tugela and Pongola rivers, then created by conquest a centralized, militaristic Zulu kingdom from several communities, resulting in large-scale displacement of people.

MI abbreviation for ▷Michigan, a state of the USA.

MI5 (or the **Security Service**) abbreviation for **Military Intelligence, section five**, the counter-intelligence agency of the British ▷intelligence services. Its role is to prevent or investigate espionage, subversion, and sabotage. The headquarters of MI5 are at Thames House, Millbank, London.

MI6 (or the **Secret Intelligence Service**) abbreviation for **Military Intelligence, section six**, the secret intelligence agency of the British ▷intelligence services which operates largely under Foreign Office control.

Miami industrial city and port in southeastern Florida, USA, on the Atlantic coast of the Florida peninsula about 70 km/43 mi from its southern tip; seat of Dade County; population (1995 est) 365,500. 60% of the population is of Hispanic origin, many of whom are Cubans who live in the Little Havana area; African-Americans comprise 21%, whites 12%. Miami is the hub of finance, trade, and transport in the region, with air connections to Latin America and the Caribbean; industries include food processing, transportation and electronic equipment, clothing, furniture, and machinery. Major employers are the state and federal governments. With its subtropical climate Miami is also a major tourist resort (tourism is the city's major industry) and a centre for oceanographic research. The city of Miami beach is situated on a barrier island, and is linked to Miami by bridges. The first permanent European settlement dates from the 1870s; Miami was incorporated in 1896.

Tourism is the mainstay of the local economy; each year millions of visitors use the hotels and tourist facilities of the city and its offshore island beaches. In 1995 there were 9,379,200 arrivals in Miami; 4,317,600 were domestic and 5,061,600 foreign.

Related Web site: Miami Information Access http://miami.info-access.com/

mica group of silicate minerals that split easily into thin flakes along lines of weakness in their crystal structure (perfect basal cleavage). They are glossy, have a pearly lustre, and are found in many igneous and metamorphic rocks. Their good thermal and electrical insulation qualities make them valuable in industry.

Micah (lived 8th century BC) In the Old Testament, a Hebrew prophet whose writings denounced the oppressive ruling class of Judah and demanded justice.

Michael (1921–) King of Romania 1927–30 and 1940–47. The son of Carol II, he succeeded his grandfather as king in 1927 but was displaced when his father returned from exile in 1930. In 1940 he was proclaimed king again on his father's abdication, overthrew in 1944 the fascist dictatorship of Ion Antonescu (1882–1946), and enabled Romania to share in the victory of the Allies at the end of World War II. He abdicated and left Romania in 1947.

Michael, George (1963–) Born Georgios Kyriacos Panayiotou. UK pop singer. His career began in the early 1980s as a member of the pop duo Wham! with Andrew Ridgeley (1963–). He has also achieved great success in a subsequent solo career with a more diverse following and a range of musical styles, from slow ballads to up-tempo pop to jazz- and soul-influenced songs.

Michael, Mikhail Fyodorovich Romanov (1596–1645) Tsar of Russia from 1613. He was elected tsar by a national assembly, at a time of chaos and foreign invasion, and was the first of the Romanov dynasty, which ruled until 1917.

Michaelmas daisy popular name for a species of ▷aster, and also for the sea aster or starwort.

Michaelmas Day in Christian church tradition, the festival of St Michael and all angels, observed 29 September.

Michaux, André (1746–1802) French botanist and explorer. As manager of a royal farm, he was sent by the French government in 1782 and 1785 on expeditions to collect plants and select timber for shipbuilding. Together with his son François (1770–1852), he travelled to Carolina, Florida, Georgia, and, in 1792, to Hudson's Bay. On his return to France, he compiled the first guide to the flora of eastern America.

François Michaux wrote the first book on American forest trees in 1810–13.

Michelangelo (1475–1564) Born Michelangelo di Lodovico Buonarroti. Italian sculptor, painter, architect, and poet. He was active in his native Florence and in Rome. His giant talent dominated the High Renaissance.

Michelangelo was born in Caprese, though the family was from Florence, and returned soon after his birth. At 13 he was apprenticed to the successful painter Domenico Ghirlandaio. He also studied Giotto and the frescoes of Masaccio in the Brancacci Chapel. He was encouraged to develop his natural gift and liking for sculpture. In rivalry with the antique, he produced the *Head of a Faun* (*c.* 1489; Palazzo Vecchio, Florence) and the relief, *Battle of Centaurs and Lapiths* (Casa Buonarroti, Florence).

He spent a year in Bologna and, in 1496, went to Rome, aged 21. During five years' stay he produced two famous works of sculpture, *Bacchus* (1496–98; Museo Nazionale del Bargello, Florence) and *Pietà* (1498–99; St Peter's, Rome). He returned to Florence in 1501, and carved the colossal *David* (1501–04; Accademia, Florence), from a block of Carrara marble that had been discarded as spoilt.

MICHELANGELO The *Goddess of the Dawn*, on the tomb of Italian statesman and scholar Lorenzo de' Medici, dated *c.* 1525, by the Italian sculptor and painter Michelangelo. *The Art Archive/San Lorenzo Florence/Dagli Orti*

Michelangelo had not abandoned painting altogether. Works from this time include the *Madonna and Child with St John and Angels* (*c.* 1495) and *Entombment* (*c.* 1501; both National Gallery, London); and the Holy Family (Uffizi Gallery, Florence) of 1503 was a masterpiece executed for his and Raphael's patron Angelo Doni. In 1504 he was commissioned to paint a large fresco in the council hall of the new Florentine Republic as a companion piece to the *Battle of Anghiari* by Leonardo da Vinci. Neither artist finished their frescoes. Michelangelo, however, was summoned to Rome by Pope Julius II to work on his now famous tomb on which Michelangelo was to toil at intervals during 40 years.

The Pope then decided that the vaulting of the Sistine Chapel should be decorated. The architect Bramante suggested that the commission should be given to Michelangelo. It was presumed this was out of jealousy, Bramante hoping that Michelangelo would fail in the undertaking or produce a minor work. Though reluctant, Michelangelo accepted the challenge, and in an astonishingly short space of time, working without assistants and under difficult conditions, painted the famous ceiling (1508–12). A tremendous biblical symphony, it interprets the Creation of the World and of Man, the Fall, and the Flood in nine great compositions flanked by the figures of prophets and sibyls, and with supporting 'slaves' or 'atlases'. The conception is conveyed with the utmost force and lucidity by the human figure and gesture alone, as in the magnificent *Creation of Adam*.

He went back to working on Pope Julius's tomb, but it was not until 1545 that it was finished, on a less ambitious scale than had been planned, only the figure of Moses being the artist's own work. He was commissioned in 1520 by Pope Clement VII, to design the Medici sepulchral chapel in San Lorenzo, Florence. This, with its famous figures of Day and Night, Morning and Evening, was finished in 1535. In 1534 he was required by Clement VII to devote himself to painting the altar wall of the Sistine Chapel, which had previously been decorated by Perugino, a commission urgently affirmed by Clement's successor, Pope Paul III. He took the Last Judgement as his subject and in six years (1535–41) produced his overwhelming masterpiece. It is sombrely majestic and tells of torture and martyrdom, stern retribution and tragic fate.

The architectural designs of Michelangelo's later years in Rome (which included the magnificent dome of St Peter's) had a great influence on the emergence of the baroque style. Two frescoes in the Capella Paolina representing the Martyrdom of St Peter and the Conversion of St Paul, 1549, were his last paintings.

Michelson, Albert Abraham (1852–1931) German-born US physicist. With his colleague Edward Morley, he performed in 1887 the **Michelson–Morley experiment** to detect the motion of the Earth through the postulated ether (a medium believed to be necessary for the propagation of light). The failure of the experiment indicated the nonexistence of the ether, and led Albert ▷Einstein to his theory of ▷relativity. Michelson was awarded the Nobel Prize for Physics in 1907 for his measurement of the speed of light through the design and application of precise optical

Mexico

MEXICO A sardine fisherman casting a net in the Sea of Cortez, Mexico. *Corel*

Mexico country in the North American continent, bounded north by the USA, east by the Gulf of Mexico, southeast by Belize and Guatemala, and southwest and west by the Pacific Ocean. It is the northernmost country in ▷Latin America.

NATIONAL NAME *Estados Unidos Mexicanos/United States of Mexico*
AREA 1,958,201 sq km/756,061 sq mi
CAPITAL Mexico City
MAJOR TOWNS/CITIES Guadalajara, Monterrey, Puebla, Netzahualcóyotl, Ciudad Juárez, Tijuana
MAJOR PORTS 49 ocean ports
PHYSICAL FEATURES partly arid central highlands; Sierra Madre mountain ranges east and west; tropical coastal plains; volcanoes, including Popocatepetl; Rio Grande

Government

HEAD OF STATE AND GOVERNMENT Vicente Fox Quesada from 2000
POLITICAL SYSTEM liberal democracy
POLITICAL EXECUTIVE limited presidency
ADMINISTRATIVE DIVISIONS 31 states and a Federal District
ARMED FORCES 192,800; plus rural defence militia of 11,000 (2002 est)
CONSCRIPTION one year, part-time (conscripts selected by lottery)
DEATH PENALTY retained for exceptional crimes only; last execution 1937
DEFENCE SPEND (% GDP) 0.9 (2002 est)
EDUCATION SPEND (% GDP) 4.4 (2000 est)
HEALTH SPEND (% GDP) 5.4 (2000 est)

Economy and resources

CURRENCY Mexican peso
GPD (US$) 673.2 billion (2002 est)
REAL GDP GROWTH (% change on previous year) 6.6 (2001)
GNI (US$) 596.7 billion (2002 est)
GNI PER CAPITA (PPP) (US$) 8,540 (2002 est)
CONSUMER PRICE INFLATION 4.3% (2003 est)
UNEMPLOYMENT 2.5% (2001)
FOREIGN DEBT (US$) 133.7 billion (2001 est)
MAJOR TRADING PARTNERS USA, Japan, Canada, Spain, France, Germany, Italy, Brazil
RESOURCES petroleum, natural gas, zinc, salt, silver, copper, coal, mercury, manganese, phosphates, uranium, strontium sulphide
INDUSTRIES motor vehicles, food processing, iron and steel, chemicals, beverages,

electrical machinery, electronic goods, petroleum refining, cement, metals and metal products, tourism
EXPORTS petroleum and petroleum products, engines and spare parts for motor vehicles, motor vehicles, electrical and electronic goods, fresh and preserved vegetables, coffee, cotton. Principal market: USA 88.7% (2001)
IMPORTS motor vehicle chassis, industrial machinery and equipment, iron and steel, telecommunications apparatus, organic chemicals, cereals and cereal preparations, basic manufactures. Principal source: USA 67.7% (2001)
ARABLE LAND 13% (2000 est)
AGRICULTURAL PRODUCTS maize, wheat, sorghum, barley, rice, beans, potatoes, coffee, cotton, sugar cane, fruit and vegetables; livestock raising and fisheries

Population and society

POPULATION 103,457,000 (2003 est)
POPULATION GROWTH RATE 1.4% (2000–15)
POPULATION DENSITY (per sq km) 53 (2003 est)
URBAN POPULATION (% of total) 75 (2003 est)
AGE DISTRIBUTION (% of total population) 0–14 32%, 15–59 61%, 60+ 7% (2002 est)
ETHNIC GROUPS around 60% mestizo (mixed American Indian and Spanish descent), 30% American Indians, remainder mainly of European origin
LANGUAGE Spanish (official), Nahuatl, Maya, Zapoteco, Mixteco, Otomi
RELIGION Roman Catholic about 90%
EDUCATION (compulsory years) 6
LITERACY RATE 94% (men); 90% (women)
LABOUR FORCE 21.0% agriculture, 25.2% industry, 53.8% services (1999)
LIFE EXPECTANCY 70 (men); 76 (women) (2000–05)
CHILD MORTALITY RATE (under 5, per 1,000 live births) 29 (2001)
PHYSICIANS (per 1,000 people) 1.9 (1998 est)
HOSPITAL BEDS (per 1,000 people) 1.1 (1998 est)

Chronology

c. 2600 BC: Mayan civilization originated in Yucatán peninsula.

1000–500 BC: Zapotec civilization developed around Monte Albán in southern Mexico.

4th–10th centuries AD: Mayan Empire at its height.

10th–12th centuries: Toltecs ruled much of Mexico from their capital at Tula.

12th century: Aztecs migrated south into the valley of Mexico.

c. 1325: Aztecs began building their capital Tenochtitlán on site of present-day Mexico City.

15th century: Montezuma I built up the Aztec Empire in central Mexico.

1519–21: Hernán Cortes conquered Aztec Empire and secured Mexico for Spain.

1520: Montezuma II, last king of the Aztecs, was killed.

1535: Mexico became Spanish viceroyalty of New Spain; plantations and mining developed with Indian labour.

1519–1607: Indigenous population reduced from 21 million to 1 million, due mainly to lack of resistance to diseases transported from Old World.

1810: Father Miguel Hidalgo led unsuccessful revolt against Spanish.

1821: Independence proclaimed by Augustín de Iturbide with support of Church and landowners.

1822: Iturbide overthrew provisional government and proclaimed himself Emperor Augustín I.

1824: Federal republic established amid continuing public disorder.

1824–55: Military rule of Antonio López de Santa Anna, who imposed stability (he became president in 1833).

1846–48: Mexican War: Mexico lost California and New Mexico to USA.

1848: Revolt of Mayan Indians suppressed.

1855: Benito Juárez aided overthrow of Santa Anna's dictatorship.

1857–60: Sweeping liberal reforms and anti-clerical legislation introduced by Juárez led to civil war with conservatives.

1861: Mexico suspended payment on foreign debt leading to French military intervention; Juárez resisted with US support.

1864: Supported by conservatives, France installed Archduke Maximilian of Austria as emperor of Mexico.

1867: Maximilian shot by republicans as French troops withdrew; Juárez resumed presidency.

1872: Death of Juárez.

TV SETS (per 1,000 people) 283 (2001 est)
RADIOS (per 1,000 people) 330 (2001 est)
INTERNET USERS (per 10,000 people) 457.7 (2002 est)
PERSONAL COMPUTER USERS (per 100 people) 8.2 (2002 est)

See also ▷Aztec; ▷Maya; ▷Yucatán.

1876: Gen Porfirio Diaz established dictatorship; Mexican economy modernized through foreign investment.

1911: Revolution overthrew Diaz; liberal president Francisco Madero introduced radical land reform but political disorder increased.

1914 and 1916–17: US military intervened to quell disorder.

1917: New constitution, designed to ensure permanent democracy, adopted.

1924–35: Government dominated by anti-clerical Gen Plutarco Calles, who introduced further social reforms.

1929: Foundation of National Revolutionary Party (PRFN), renamed the Institutional Revolutionary Party (PRI) in 1946.

1938: President Lázaro Cárdenas nationalized all foreign-owned oil wells in face of US opposition.

1942: Mexico declared war on Germany and Japan (and so regained US favour).

1946–52: Miguel Alemán first of succession of authoritarian PRI presidents to seek moderation and stability rather than further radical reform.

1960s: Rapid industrial growth.

1976: Huge oil reserves were discovered in the southeastern state of Chiapas; oil production tripled in six years.

1982: Falling oil prices caused a grave financial crisis; Mexico defaulted on debt.

1985: An earthquake in Mexico City killed thousands.

1994: There was an uprising in Chiapas by the Zapatista National Liberation Army (EZLN), seeking rights for the Mayan Indian population; Mexico formed the North American Free Trade Area (NAFTA) with the USA and Canada.

1995: The government agreed to offer greater autonomy to Mayan Indians in Chiapas.

1996: There were short-lived peace talks with the EZLN; and violent attacks against the government by the new leftist Popular Revolutionary Army (EPR) increased.

1997: The PRI lost its assembly majority. A civilian counterpart to the Zapatista rebels, the Zapatista National Liberation Front (EZLN), was formed.

1998: A lapsed peace accord with Zapatist rebels was reactivated, but talks between the government and the rebels broke down.

2000: After 71 years, the PRI lost power, and Vicente Fox of the conservative National Action Party was elected president. He signed a bill on indigenous rights, in response to which the leader of the rebels offered to open peace talks.

2001: The Zapatista leader, Subcomandante Marcos, led a peaceful march from Chiapas to Mexico City to ask Congress to ratify the indigenous rights bill.

2002: Mexico withdrew from the Rio Pact, a mutual-defence treaty for the Americas dating back to the Cold War era.

instruments such as the interferometer. He was the first American to be awarded a Nobel prize.

Michigan state in north-central USA. It is nicknamed the Wolverine State or the Great Lakes State. Michigan was admitted to the Union in 1837 as the 26th US state. It is situated in the Midwest and Great Lakes regions, and is comprised of two major peninsulas. The mitten-shaped, north–south oriented **Lower Peninsula** is bordered to the south by Ohio and Indiana, and faces Ontario, Canada, to the north and east across the Great Lakes. The east–west oriented **Upper Peninsula** is bordered to the south by Wisconsin, and also faces Ontario to the north and east across the lakes.

> **population** (1995) 9,549,400 **area** 151,600 sq km/58,518 sq mi **capital** Lansing **towns and cities** Detroit, Grand Rapids, Flint, Warren, Sterling Heights, Ann Arbor, Livonia **industries and products** motor vehicles and equipment, non-electrical machinery, iron and steel, chemicals, pharmaceuticals, dairy products, fruit and beans, salt, coal, oil, natural gas, music industry, tourism

Michigan, Lake (Algonquian 'big lake'.) lake in north-central USA, the third largest of the ▷Great Lakes and the only one lying entirely within the USA, it is bordered by Michigan to the north and east, Indiana to the south, and Wisconsin and Illinois to the west; area 58,000 sq km/22,390 sq mi. The lake is 517 km/321 mi long, 190 km/118 mi at its widest point, has a maximum depth of 282 m/925 ft, and lies 176 m/577 ft above sea level. Lake Michigan is joined to Lake Huron by the Straits of Mackinac in the north. Green Bay is its largest inlet, and Chicago and Milwaukee are its main ports. The first European to see the Lake Michigan was the French explorer Jean Nicolet, in 1634.

Mickey Mouse cartoon character created in 1928 by US animator Walt Disney, characterized by black disc-shaped ears and white gloves. He made his film debut in *Plane Crazy* and starred in the first synchronized sound cartoon, *Steamboat Willie* (1928). The comic book *Mickey Mouse Weekly* started in 1936 and ran 920 issues. Mickey Mouse also appeared in the feature-length animated films *Fantasia* (1940), *Fun and Fancy Free* (1947), and *The Simple Things* (1953).

Mickiewicz, Adam Bernard (1798–1855) Polish revolutionary poet. His *Pan Tadeusz* (1832–34) is Poland's national epic. He died in Constantinople while raising a Polish corps to fight against Russia in the Crimean War.

MICR abbreviation for ▷magnetic-ink character recognition.

micro- prefix (symbol μ) denoting a one-millionth part (10^{-6}). For example, a micrometre, μm, is one-millionth of a metre.

microbe another name for ▷micro-organism.

microbiological warfare use of harmful micro-organisms as a weapon. See ▷biological warfare.

microbiology the study of micro-organisms, mostly viruses and single-celled organisms such as bacteria, protozoa, and yeasts. The practical applications of microbiology are in medicine (since many micro-organisms cause disease); in brewing, baking, and other food and beverage processes, where the micro-organisms carry out fermentation; and in genetic engineering, which is creating increasing interest in the field of microbiology.

microchip popular name for the silicon chip, or ▷integrated circuit.

microclimate the climate of a small area, such as a woodland, lake, or even a hedgerow. Significant differences can exist between the climates of two neighbouring areas – for example, a town is usually warmer than the surrounding countryside (forming a heat island), and a woodland cooler, darker, and less windy than an area of open land.

Microclimates play a significant role in agriculture and horticulture, as different crops require different growing conditions.

microcomputer (or **micro** or **personal computer**) small desktop or portable ▷computer, typically designed to be used by one person at a time, although individual computers can be linked in a network so that users can share data and programmes.

Its central processing unit is a ▷microprocessor, contained on a single integrated circuit.

microeconomics the division of economics concerned with the study of individual decision-making units within an economy: a consumer, firm, or industry. Unlike macroeconomics, it looks at how individual markets work and how individual producers and consumers make their choices and with what consequences. This is done by analysing how relevant prices of goods are determined and the quantities that will be bought and sold.

microfiche sheet of film on which printed text is photographically reduced. See ▷microform.

microform generic name for media on which text or images are photographically reduced. The main examples are **microfilm** (similar to the film in an ordinary camera) and **microfiche** (flat sheets of film, generally 105 mm/4 in × 148 mm/6 in, holding the equivalent of 420 standard pages). Microform has the advantage of low reproduction and storage costs, but it requires special devices for reading the text. It is widely used for archiving and for storing large volumes of text, such as library catalogues.

micrometer instrument for measuring minute lengths or angles with great accuracy; different types of micrometer are used in astronomical and engineering work.

micrometre one-millionth of a ▷metre (symbol μm).

Micronesia, Federated States of see country box.
> **Related Web site: Welcome to the Federated States of Micronesia**
> http://www.fsmgov.org/

Micronesian any of the indigenous Australoid and Polynesian peoples of Micronesia, including Pacific islands north of the Equator, such as the Caroline, Marshall, Mariana, and Gilbert islands. Their languages belong to the Austronesian family.

micro-organism (or **microbe**) living organism invisible to the naked eye but visible under a microscope. Micro-organisms include viruses and single-celled organisms such as bacteria, protozoa, yeasts, and some algae. The term has no taxonomic significance in biology. The study of micro-organisms is known as microbiology.

microphone primary component in a sound-reproducing system, whereby the mechanical energy of sound waves is converted into electrical signals by means of a ▷transducer. One of the simplest is the telephone receiver mouthpiece, invented by Scottish–US inventor Alexander Graham Bell in 1876; other types of microphone are used with broadcasting and sound-film apparatus.

microprocessor complete computer ▷central processing unit contained on a single ▷integrated circuit, or chip. The appearance of the first microprocessor in 1971 designed by Intel for a pocket calculator manufacturer heralded the introduction of the microcomputer. The microprocessor has led to a dramatic fall in the size and cost of computers, and ▷dedicated computers can now be found in washing machines, cars, and so on. Examples of microprocessors are the Intel Pentium family and the IBM/Motorola PowerPC, used by Apple Computer.

Texas Instruments introduced in January 1997 a digital-signal microprocessor chip that can process 1.6 billion instructions a second. This is about 40 times more powerful than a chip now found in today's computer modem. The new chip can reduce the time needed to download a file from the Internet from ten minutes to less than five seconds.

micropropagation the mass production of plants by placing tiny pieces of plant tissue in sterile glass containers along with nutrients. Perfect clones of superplants are produced in sterile cabinets, with filtered air and carefully controlled light, temperature, and humidity. The system is used for the house-plant industry and for forestry – micropropagation gives immediate results, whereas obtaining

genetically homogeneous tree seed by traditional means would take over a hundred years.

microscope instrument for forming magnified images with high resolution for detail. Optical and electron microscopes are the ones chiefly in use; other types include acoustic, scanning tunnelling, and ▷atomic force microscopes.
> **Related Web site: Dennis Kunkel's Microscopy**
> http://www.pbrc.hawaii.edu/~kunkel/

microsurgery part or all of an intricate surgical operation – rejoining a severed limb, for example – performed with the aid of a binocular microscope, using miniaturized instruments. Sewing of the nerves and blood vessels is done with a nylon thread so fine that it is only just visible to the naked eye.

microwave ▷electromagnetic wave with a wavelength in the range 0.3 to 30 cm/0.1 in to 12 in, or 300–300,000 megahertz (between radio waves and ▷infrared radiation). Microwaves are used in radar, in radio broadcasting, and in microwave heating and cooking.

microwave heating heating by means of microwaves. Microwave ovens use this form of heating for the rapid cooking or reheating of foods, where heat is generated throughout the interior of the food. If food is not heated completely, there is a danger of bacterial growth that may lead to food poisoning. Industrially, microwave heating is used for destroying insects in grain and enzymes in processed food, pasteurizing and sterilizing liquids, and drying timber and paper.

Midas in Greek mythology, a king of Phrygia who was granted the ability to convert all he touched to gold by ▷Dionysus, god of wine and excess; the gift became a curse when his food and drink also turned to metal. In another story he was given ass's ears by Apollo for preferring the music of Pan in a contest between the two gods.

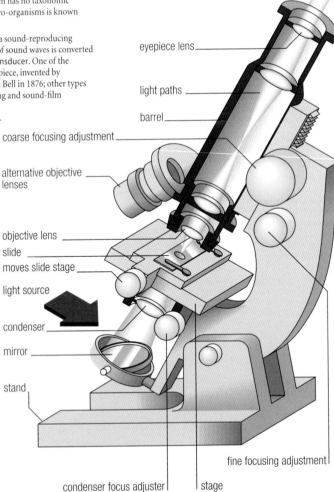

eyepiece lens
light paths
barrel
coarse focusing adjustment
alternative objective lenses
objective lens
slide
moves slide stage
light source
condenser
mirror
stand
condenser focus adjuster
stage
fine focusing adjustment

MICROSCOPE In essence, the optical microscope consists of an eyepiece lens and an objective lens, which are used to produce an enlarged image of a small object by focusing light from a light source. Optical microscopes can achieve magnifications of up to 1,500–2,000. Higher magnifications and resolutions are obtained by electron microscopes.

THE MIDDLE AGES A typical weapon of the Middle Ages, the ballista is a development from the Roman weapon. It is a type of crossbow, on a larger scale, which is used for throwing objects such as stones or dead animals over town or castle walls during sieges. *The Art Archive*

Mid-Atlantic Ridge ▷ocean ridge that runs along the centre of the Atlantic Ocean, parallel to its edges, for some 14,000 km/ 8,800 mi – almost from the Arctic to the Antarctic. Like other ocean ridges, the Mid-Atlantic Ridge is essentially a linear, segmented volcano.

Middle Ages, the (or the **medieval period**) term used by Europeans to describe the period between ancient history and the Renaissance. It is not a precise term, but is often taken to cover the time from the fall of the western Roman Empire in AD 476 to the fall of Constantinople (Istanbul) and the end of the Eastern Roman Empire in 1453, or alternatively Columbus's voyage to the Americas in 1492. The term Dark Ages is sometimes used to cover the period from AD 476 to AD 1000, because it was a time when learning and the rule of law were at a low ebb in Europe. During this period Germanic and Scandinavian tribes overran Europe, bringing with them changes in language and culture.

Middle East indeterminate area now usually taken to include Egypt and the Arab states of the eastern Mediterranean and Arabian Peninsula, sometimes extended to the states of northwest Africa, Turkey, Iran and Afghanistan. See also The History of the Conflict in the Middle East Focus Feature on pp. 628–629.

Middle English the period of the ▷English language from about 1050 to 1550.

Middle Kingdom period of Egyptian history embracing the 11th and 12th dynasties (roughly 2040–1640 BC); Chinese term for China and its empire until 1912, describing its central position in the Far East.

> **Ehud Barak**
> Former Israeli prime minister
>
> *I never pretended to have magic solutions to solve a conflict of 100 years in three weeks or three months.*
>
> On peace negotiations in the Middle East

Middlesbrough industrial town, port, and unitary authority, on the estuary of the River Tees, northeast England, created in 1996 from part of the former county of Cleveland. The town was the administrative headquarters of the county of Cleveland to 1996. It is the commercial centre of the Teesside industrial area, which also includes Stockton-on-Tees, Redcar, Billingham, Thornaby, and Eston.
area 54 sq km/21 sq mi   **features** Transporter Bridge (1911) transports cars and passengers across the Tees to Hartlepool in a cable car; Newport Bridge (1934) was the first vertical lift bridge in England; the University of Teesside, formerly Teesside Polytechnic, was established in 1992; the Captain Cook Birthplace Museum commemorates the life of the naval explorer James Cook; the 18th-century National Trust-owned Ormesby Hall is located nearby
industries formerly a centre of heavy industry, it diversified its products in the 1960s; there are constructional, electronics, engineering, and shipbuilding industries, and iron, steel, and chemicals are produced   **famous people** James Cook   **population** (1996) 146,000

Middleton, Thomas (1580–1627) English dramatist. He produced numerous romantic plays, tragedies, and realistic comedies, both alone and in collaboration, including *A Fair Quarrel* (1617), *The Changeling* (1622), and *The Spanish Gypsy* (1623) with William ▷Rowley; *The Roaring Girl* (1611) with Thomas ▷Dekker; and (alone) *Women Beware Women* (1621). He also composed many pageants and masques.

Middle Way the path to enlightenment, taught by the Buddha, which avoids the extremes of indulgence and asceticism.

Micronesia, Federated States of

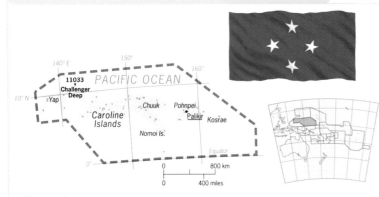

Micronesia country in the west Pacific Ocean, forming part of the archipelago of the Caroline Islands, 800 km/497 mi east of the Philippines.

NATIONAL NAME *Federated States of Micronesia (FSM)*
AREA 700 sq km/270 sq mi
CAPITAL Palikir (in Pohnpei island state)
MAJOR TOWNS/CITIES Kolonia (in Pohnpei), Weno (in Truk), Lelu (in Kosrae)
MAJOR PORTS Teketik, Lepukos, Okak
PHYSICAL FEATURES an archipelago of 607 equatorial, volcanic islands in the West Pacific

Government

HEAD OF STATE AND GOVERNMENT Joseph Urusemal from 2003
POLITICAL SYSTEM liberal democracy
POLITICAL EXECUTIVE limited presidency
ADMINISTRATIVE DIVISIONS four states
DEATH PENALTY laws do not provide for the death penalty for any crime

Economy and resources

CURRENCY US dollar
GPD (US$) 232 million (2002 est)
REAL GDP GROWTH (% change on previous year) 1.7 (2001)
GNI (US$) 242 million (2002 est)
GNI PER CAPITA (PPP) (US$) 4,760 (2002 est)
CONSUMER PRICE INFLATION 2.5% (2001 est)
UNEMPLOYMENT 2.6% (2000)
FOREIGN DEBT (US$) 66.5 million (2001 est)

MAJOR TRADING PARTNERS USA, Japan, Guam
INDUSTRIES coconut products, tourism
EXPORTS fish and fish products, copra, pepper. Principal market: Japan 91.9% (1999)
IMPORTS food and live animals, manufactured goods, machinery and transport equipment, mineral fuels. Principal source: USA 43.9% (1999)
AGRICULTURAL PRODUCTS mainly subsistence farming; coconuts, cassava, sweet potatoes, breadfruit, bananas, copra, citrus fruits, taro, peppers; fishing

Population and society

POPULATION 109,000 (2003 est)
POPULATION GROWTH RATE 2.4% (2000–05)
POPULATION DENSITY (per sq km) 156 (2003 est)
URBAN POPULATION (% of total) 29 (2003 est)
AGE DISTRIBUTION (% of total population) 0–14 44%, 15–59 51%, 60+ 5% (2002 est)
ETHNIC GROUPS main ethnic groups are the Trukese (41%) and Pohnpeian (26%)
LANGUAGE English (official), eight officially recognized local languages (including Trukese, Pohnpeian, Yapese, and Kosrean), a number of other dialects
RELIGION Christianity (mainly Roman Catholic in Yap state, Protestant elsewhere)

FEDERATED STATES OF MICRONESIA Tropical foliage on the island of Pohnpei. With an area of 334 sq km/129 sq mi, Pohnpei is the largest island in the Federated States of Micronesia. Mangrove swamps grow in the fertile soil of the coast, while rainforest clads the hills of the interior. *PhotoDisk*

EDUCATION (compulsory years) 8
LITERACY RATE 91% (men); 88% (women) (1980 est)
LABOUR FORCE 55.3% agriculture, 2.8% industry, 41.9% services (2000)

LIFE EXPECTANCY 68 (men); 69 (women) (2000–05)
CHILD MORTALITY RATE (under 5, per 1,000 live births) 24 (2001)

See also ▷Pacific Islands.

Chronology

c. 1000 BC: Micronesians first settled the islands.
1525: Portuguese navigators first visited Yap and Ulithi islands in the Carolines (Micronesia).
later 16th century: Fell under Spanish influence.
1874: Spanish rule formally declared in face of increasing encroachment by German traders.
1885: Yap seized by German naval forces, but was restored to Spain after arbitration by Pope Leo XIII on the condition that Germany was allowed freedom of trade.
1899: Purchased for $4.5 million by Germany from Spain, after the latter's defeat in the Spanish–American War.
1914: Occupied by Japan at the outbreak of World War I.
1919: Administered under League of Nations mandate by Japan, and vigorously colonized.
1944: Occupied by USA after Japanese forces defeated in World War II.

1947: Administered by USA as part of the United Nations (UN) Trust Territory of the Pacific Islands, under the name of the Federated States of Micronesia (FSM).
1979: A constitution was adopted that established a federal system for its four constituent states (Yap, Chuuk, Pohnpei, and Kosrae) and internal self-government.
1986: The Compact of Free Association was entered into with the USA, granting the islands self-government with the USA retaining responsibility for defence and security until 2001.
1990: UN trust status was terminated.
1991: Independence agreed, with Bailey Olter as president. Entered into United Nations (UN) membership.
1997: Jacob Nena was sworn in as president after the existing president, Bailey Olter, was incapacitated by a stroke.

The History of the Conflict in Palestine

by Charles Messenger

Palestine is the historic homeland of the Jewish community. For five centuries – between around 1200 BC, when the Israelites, an immigrant Semitic group claiming descent from Abraham of Ur and led by the prophet Moses, settled in the area, and 722 BC, when conquered by the Assyrian king Sargon II – Palestine (Canaan) was the centre of Israeli kingdoms. In 1020 BC, the Jewish people were united for the first time under Saul and their kingdom achieved greatness under his successor, David, 1006–966 BC. The capital, Jerusalem, became the Jews' holy city. From 587 BC, after the Babylonians' conquest of Jerusalem, the diaspora ('dispersal') of Jews began, which accelerated after 135 AD, when the Romans dissolved the province of Judea and barred Jews from entering Jerusalem. However, the dream of a return to the historic homeland lived on.

historic homelands

Palestine is also an Arab homeland. As early as the 2nd century BC Arab tribes began to settle in the area. With the rise of Islam in the 7th century, a distinctive Arab culture developed. This led to the building in Jerusalem of the al Aqsa mosque. One of the three holiest places of Islam, it is from where, Muslims believe, Muhammad rode on his magic steed to

PALESTINIAN WOMEN CROSSING SAND BARRIERS that block the entrance to Bethlehem in the West Bank. Following attacks on Israelis, the Israeli army sealed off all Palestinian cities in the West Bank and Gaza Strip with sand barriers such as this, stopping people moving freely to and from the areas. *PA Photos/EPA European Press Agency*

heaven. For centuries, Arabs in the region were subjected to foreign empires. However, during the late 19th century Arab national consciousness reawakened. This occurred at the same time as an organized Zionist movement was developing and there was increasing immigration of Jews into Palestine, with many fleeing persecution in Europe. In 1914 the Arab population in Palestine numbered 650,000, but the number of Jewish colonists had risen to 85,000. Arabs feared that further immigration and a Jewish conquest of Palestine would shatter the territorial unity of the Arab world and weaken their cause. The two communities, with irreconcilable goals, were headed on a collision course.

Balfour declaration

Many of the seeds of current Middle East tensions were sown during World War I. Conscious of the need to safeguard Britain's interest in the Suez Canal and of the growing Zionist agitation to establish a Jewish state in Palestine, British foreign secretary Arthur Balfour wrote to leading British Zionist Lord Rothschild on 2 November 1917. Balfour assured him that the British government would use 'its best endeavours' to establish 'a National Home for the Jewish people in Palestine', while ensuring that civil and religious rights of non-Jews in the country were not prejudiced. At the time, Palestine was part of the Turkish Ottoman empire, but on 9 December 1917, British forces took Jerusalem. After World War I, the League of Nations made Palestine a British-administered mandate territory.

The British were conscious that the existing population was predominantly Arab, but allowed increasing Jewish immigration. Jewish purchase of land provoked resentment among the Palestinian Arabs, culminating in open revolt in 1936. It took the British three years to quell the violence, which only ended after they promised an independent Palestine, with equal rights for both Jews and Arabs and restricted Jewish immigration. By this time World War II had broken out, which postponed the creation of a Palestinian state.

creation of Israel

An underground Zionist movement grew up during the war, determined to create an independent Jewish state, if necessary by force. A terrorist campaign erupted in Palestine in October 1945. It was accompanied by a further surge in Jewish immigration as Holocaust survivors settled in the region. The British reaction was to revoke their 1939 promise to set up an independent Palestine and to turn away Jewish refugee ships. This provoked international condemnation and, combined with the growing violence within Palestine, led the British to present the problem before the United Nations (UN). In spite of Arab and British objections, the UN decided that the only solution was to create separate Arab and Jewish states, with Jerusalem being administered by the UN itself. The British mandate was to end in May 1948, with their troops departing Palestine by 1 August 1948.

During the summer of 1948, violence between Arabs and Jews grew. The British troops left and the Jews unilaterally declared the state of Israel. The neighbouring Arab countries sent in troops and almost overwhelmed the infant state before a UN ceasefire was implemented. It failed to hold, however, and the Israelis eventually succeeded in defeating the Arab countries. A UN armistice was brokered in 1949, but Israel was left in possession of all of former Palestine except the Gaza Strip in the southwest (held by Egypt) and Jordanian territory west of the River Jordan (known as the West Bank). Control of Jerusalem was split between Israel (holding the west) and Jordan (holding the east). Rather than accept Jewish rule, some 725,000 Arabs left Israel, marking the beginning of the Palestinian refugee problem.

Suez crisis

On 11 May 1949 the State of Israel became a member of the UN. However, the Arab nations refused to recognize Israel. During the subsequent few years, internal coups brought in governments that were not only anti-Israel, but also turned against the West for supporting the Israelis. This culminated in the Egyptian nationalization of the Suez Canal in July 1956. That October, the Israelis invaded Sinai in Egypt, quickly overrunning it. A few days later, British and French forces attacked Egypt, determined to regain control of the canal by force. UN pressure brought a halt to the fighting and by the end of the year the Anglo-French forces had withdrawn, with Israel evacuating Sinai shortly afterwards.

the creation of the Palestine Liberation Organization

The Suez affair increased the standing of Egyptian leader Gamal Nasser in the Middle East, and he sought to bind the Arab states more closely in an alliance against Israel. In 1964, at an Arab summit in Cairo, the Palestinian Liberation Organization (PLO) was set up to coordinate terrorist action against Israel. Feeling increasingly threatened, the Israelis launched a pre-emptive strike against Egypt in June 1967. In just six days, they overran Sinai once more, and seized the Golan Heights across the Syrian border, the Gaza Strip, east Jerusalem, and the entire West Bank. These successes doubled the size of the territory Israel controlled. This time Israel refused UN demands to withdraw. The best the UN could do was to pass Resolution 242 which called for Israel to vacate the occupied regions in exchange for a recognition by all states in the Middle East of each other's sovereignty.

However, the UN failed to address the Palestinian refugee problem. The PLO increased its terrorist activities, attacking Israeli property abroad and hijacking airliners. It was operating from Jordan, but King Hussein of Jordan became concerned that the PLO would overthrow him, and provoke another Arab–Israeli war. In 1970 his army turned on the PLO, which was forced to move to Lebanon. That same year Nasser died. His successor, Anwar Sadat, was keen to regain Sinai and reopen the Suez Canal, which had been closed since the 1967 'Six-Day War'. He opened up a dialogue with US president Richard Nixon, recognizing that only the US could bring pressure to bear on Israel. The negotiations came to nothing. On 6 October 1973, on the Jewish fast of Yom Kippur, Sadat launched a sudden assault across the Suez Canal. Once again the UN organized a ceasefire, but, in retaliation, the Organization of Arab Petroleum Exporting Countries (OAPEC) radically raised oil prices, instituting a boycott on countries supporting Israel.

Camp David Agreement

During the next five years, the US took the lead in attempting to bring peace to the region. Tensions were gradually reduced, culminating in the 1978 Camp David Agreement, brokered by US president Jimmy Carter. This finally brought peace between the two countries, with the Israelis withdrawing from Sinai, apart from the Gaza Strip. The plight of the Palestinian Arabs had not improved, however, and was compounded by a fresh problem.

In January 1979, the Shah of Iran was overthrown by elements resentful of the growing westernization of the country. In 1980 Iraqi forces invaded Iran, beginning a costly eight-year war between the two countries. The following year fundamentalists assassinated President Sadat.

Fundamentalist factions within the PLO intensified terrorism against Israel to such an extent that, in June 1982, the Israelis launched a full-scale invasion of southern Lebanon. It took almost three months to bring in a ceasefire, which included the PLO being forced to leave Lebanon and setting up a new headquarters in Tunis. The civil war resumed and a multinational force (MNF) was deployed to Lebanon in a vain attempt to halt the violence, but was forced to withdraw in early 1984. Thereafter, fundamentalist groups seized a number of westerners in Beirut and held them hostage. The Israeli occupation of southern Lebanon was, however, becoming increasingly costly and during 1985 they began a phased withdrawal, but insisted on retaining a 'security zone' along the Lebanese border. The PLO soon crept back into the refugee camps and the civil war continued.

Oslo Accord

The Palestinian problem remained. The Arabs living in the Gaza Strip and on the West Bank resented the influx of Jewish settlers and in 1987 rose against Israeli military rule in what they called the *Intifada* (uprising). But the following year, the PLO recognized that they would have to negotiate with Israel if they were to achieve their dream of an independent Palestinian state. This was reinforced by the dissolution of the Soviet Union, their main international backer, in 1991. Israel and the PLO opened a Norwegian-sponsored dialogue in 1993, signing an agreement, the Oslo Accord, that September. The PLO recognized Israel's right to exist, while the latter accepted that the PLO was the official representative of the Palestinian people and gave the Palestinians limited autonomy in the occupied territories. In July 1994 the PLO leader, Yassir Arafat, made a triumphal return to Gaza to became head of the new self-rule Palestinian Authority. These positive steps encouraged Jordan to finally sign a peace agreement with Israel in October 1994, but not all welcomed the new atmosphere of compromise.

On 4 November 1995, an orthodox Jewish student assassinated Israeli moderate prime minister Yitzhak Rabin. Islamic fundamentalists among the Palestinians also opposed the deal, declaring that Israel must be destroyed. Even so, Palestinian autonomy in the occupied territories was gradually increased. Simultaneously, more extreme Jews, often with the support of the Israeli government, established further settlements in the West Bank, especially around Jerusalem. In retaliation, Palestinian fundamentalist groups continued to perpetrate terrorist atrocities within Israel itself. In the meantime, efforts to achieve a lasting peace

THE DOME OF THE ROCK and the Wailing Wall, two sacred places in Jerusalem. The Dome stands on the legendary site of Muhammad's journey to heaven and is the third holiest place of Islam after Mecca and Medina. The Wailing (or Western) Wall is the only remaining part of the original temple of King Solomon, and is the holiest place of pilgrimage and prayer for Jews. © *Image Bank*

between Israel and its other Arab neighbour, Syria, failed. Throughout this period the US remained the principal broker, supported by Egypt.

no foreseeable resolution

On 23 October 1998 Israel's prime minister Binjamin Netanyahu signed the Wye River Accord, outlining further Israeli withdrawal from the West Bank. This followed 18 months of stagnation in the peace process. Further West Bank territory was handed over by Israel, now led by Ehud Barak, to the Palestinians in early 2000 and Israel withdrew from its Lebanon security zone. However, negotiations over the final Israeli withdrawal from remaining parts of the West Bank stalled, largely because of the creation of new Jewish settlements. The problem over who should govern Jerusalem, with its sacred Arab and Jewish shrines, proved intractable. It was aggravated in September 2000, when Palestinian resentment boiled over after a visit by an Israeli right-wing politician, Ariel Sharon, to the city. A new *Intifada* erupted. In February 2001 the hardline Sharon was swept to power as prime minister.

The 1917 Balfour Declaration had attempted to satisfy Jewish aspirations towards an independent state in their historic land, while placating the Palestinian Arabs, who largely populated the region at the time. Almost 90 years later, and after much bloodshed, peace in the Middle East still appears elusive.

Middx abbreviation for ▷Middlesex, former county of England.

midge common name for many insects resembling ▷gnats, generally divided into biting midges (family Ceratopogonidae) that suck blood and non-biting midges (family Chironomidae).

Mid Glamorgan (Welsh **Morgannwg Ganol**) former county of south Wales, 1974–1996, now divided between ▷Rhondda Cynon Taff, ▷Merthyr Tydfil, ▷Bridgend, and Vale of Glamorgan unitary authorities.

MIDI (acronym for musical instrument digital interface) manufacturer's standard allowing different pieces of digital music equipment used in composing and recording to be freely connected.

Midi-Pyrénées region of southwest France, comprising the *départements* of Ariège, Aveyron, Haute-Garonne, Gers, Lot, Hautes-Pyrénées, Tarn, and Tarn-et-Garonne; the capital is ▷Toulouse; area 45,300 sq km/17,500 sq mi; population (1990) 2,430,700. The region includes several spa towns (including ▷Lourdes), winter resorts, and prehistoric caves. It produces fruit, wine, and livestock, and industries include aerospace. There are two large universities. Other notable towns include Montauban, Cahors, and Rodez.

Midlands area of central England corresponding roughly to the Anglo-Saxon kingdom of ▷Mercia. The **East Midlands** comprises Derbyshire, Leicestershire, Northamptonshire, and Nottingham-shire. The **West Midlands** covers the metropolitan district of ▷West Midlands created from parts of Staffordshire, Warwickshire, and Worcestershire, and split into the metropolitan boroughs of Dudley, Sandwell, Coventry, Birmingham, Walsall, Solihull, and Wolverhampton; and (often included) the **South Midlands** comprising Bedfordshire, Buckinghamshire, and Oxfordshire.

Midlothian unitary authority in southeast Scotland, south of the Firth of Forth, which was previously a district within Lothian region (1975–96) and a county until 1974.

> **area** 363 sq km/140 sq mi **towns** Dalkeith (administrative headquarters), Penicuik, Bonnyrigg **physical** inland area rising toward the Moorfoot Hills in the south; River Esk **features** Crichton Castle, Roslin Castle, Rosslyn Chapel, Newtongrange Mining Museum **industries** glass and crystal, coalmining (declining), light manufacturing, food processing **agriculture** productive agriculturally to the north (arable and dairy), less productive and intensive toward the hills in the south **population** (1996) 79,900 **history** historically important mining area, with Scottish Mining Museum at Newtongrange

mid-ocean ridge a long submarine mountain range that winds along the middle of the ocean floor for roughly 60,000 km. The mid-ocean ridge system is essentially a segmented, linear shield volcano. There are a number of major ridges, including the ▷Mid-Atlantic Ridge, which runs down the centre of the Atlantic; the East Pacific Rise in the south-east Pacific; and the Southeast Indian Ridge. Ridges are now known to be spreading centres, or divergent margins, where two plates of oceanic lithosphere are moving away from one another (see ▷plate tectonics). Ocean ridges can rise thousands of metres above the surrounding seabed.

Midway Islands two coral islands in the Pacific, near the northwestern end of the Hawaiian Islands chain, USA, 1,800 km/1,120 mi northwest of Honolulu; area 5 sq km/2 sq mi. They used to be a naval base with no indigenous population. The islands are individually known as Eastern and Sand; they were annexed by the USA in 1867, and are now administered by the US Navy. The naval Battle of Midway (3–6 June 1942), between the USA and Japan, was a turning point in the Pacific in World War II; the US victory marked the end of Japanese expansion in the region.

MIGRATION
The map shows animal migratory patterns.

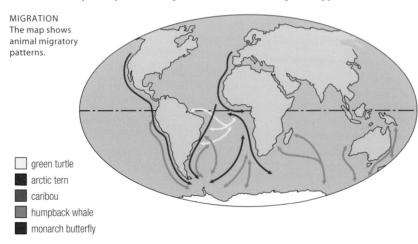

☐ green turtle
■ arctic tern
■ caribou
■ humpback whale
■ monarch butterfly

Midwest (or **Middle West**) large area of the north-central USA. It is loosely defined geographically, but is generally taken to comprise the states of Illinois, Iowa, Wisconsin, Minnesota, Nebraska, Kansas, Missouri, North Dakota, and South Dakota, and the portions of Montana, Wyoming, and Colorado that lie east of the Rocky Mountains. Ohio, Michigan, and Indiana are often variously included as well. In its broadest sense, the Midwest has an area of 986,800 sq mi/2,556,000 sq km and a population of about 61.5 million – roughly a quarter of the national total. The region is generally flat and well-watered, with good transportation links. Traditionally its economy is divided between agriculture and heavy industry. The main urban Midwest centre is Chicago. In the summer of 1993 the Midwest was devastated by floods, which left tens of thousands of people homeless.

midwifery assistance of women in childbirth. Traditionally, it was undertaken by experienced specialists; in modern medical training it is a nursing speciality for practitioners called midwives.

Mies van der Rohe, Ludwig (1886–1969) German architect. A leading exponent of the ▷international style, he practised in the USA from 1937. He succeeded Walter ▷Gropius as director of the ▷Bauhaus 1929–33. He designed the bronze-and-glass Seagram building in New York City 1956–59 and numerous apartment buildings.

mifepristone (RU486) anti-progesterone drug used, in combination with a ▷prostaglandin, to procure early ▷abortion (up to the tenth week in pregnancy). It is administered only in hospitals or recognized clinics and a success rate of 95% is claimed. Also known as RU486, it was developed and first used in France in 1989. It was licensed in the UK in 1991, and became available in the USA from October 2000.

Mifune, Toshirō (1920–1997) Japanese film actor. He appeared in many films directed by Akira ▷Kurosawa, including *Rashōmon* (1950), *Shichinin no samurai/Seven Samurai* (1954), and *Kumonosu-jō/Throne of Blood* (1957). He also occasionally appeared in European and American films, such as *Grand Prix* (1966) or *Hell in the Pacific* (1969).

mignonette sweet-scented plant, native to North Africa, with yellowish-green flowers in racemes (along the main stem) and abundant foliage; it is widely cultivated. (*Reseda odorata*, family Resedaceae.)

migraine acute, sometimes incapacitating headache (generally only on one side), accompanied by nausea, that recurs, often with advance symptoms such as flashing lights. No cure has been discovered, but ergotamine normally relieves the symptoms. Some sufferers learn to avoid certain foods, such as chocolate, which suggests an allergic factor.

The bacterium *Helicobacter pylori* has been linked to migraine by Italian researchers who found, in 1998, that 48% of migraine sufferers harboured the bacterium and that their migraine symptoms were greatly alleviated following antibiotics to eradicate *H. pylori*.

migration movement of population away from its home, either occurring from one country to another (**international** migration) or from one region in a country to another (**internal** migration). Migrations may be temporary (for example, holidaymakers), seasonal (transhumance), or permanent (people moving to cities to find employment); local, national, or international.

migration the movement, either seasonal or as part of a single life cycle, of certain animals, chiefly birds and fish, to distant breeding or feeding grounds.

Mihailovič, Draza (Dragoljub) (1893–1946) Yugoslav soldier, leader of the guerrilla ▷Chetniks of World War II, a nationalist resistance movement against the German occupation. His feud with Tito's communists led to the withdrawal of Allied support and that of his own exiled government from 1943. He turned for help to the Italians and Germans, and was eventually shot for treason.

mikado (Japanese 'honourable palace gate') title until 701 of the Japanese emperor, when it was replaced by the term *tennō* ('heavenly sovereign').

Milan (Italian **Milano**; Roman **Mediolanum**) second-largest city in Italy, situated in Lombardy, 120 km/75 mi northeast of Genoa; population (1992) 1,358,600. Industries include printing, engineering, and the manufacture of aircraft, cars, locomotives, chemicals, clothing, and textiles. Milan is Italy's chief commercial and industrial centre: the main stock exchange, and the headquarters of banks and insurance companies are here. It is also the country's most important publishing centre.
Features The Gothic cathedral, built about 1450, crowned with pinnacles, can hold 40,000 worshippers; the Pinacoteca di Brera art gallery; Leonardo da Vinci's *Last Supper* (1495–97) in the refectory of Sta Maria della Grazie; La Scala opera house (*Teatro alla Scala*) opened in 1778; an annual trade fair.

MILAN The Vittorio Emanuele gallery is an arcade of shops in the heart of Milan, Italy. Named after Victor Emmanuel II, first king of a united Italy in 1861, it is noted for its mosaic floor. The roof is louvred to admit natural light. *Image Bank*

Milankovitch hypothesis the combination of factors governing the occurrence of ▷ice ages proposed in 1930 by the Yugoslav geophysicist M Milankovitch (1879–1958). These include the variation in the angle of the Earth's axis, and the geometry of the Earth's orbit around the Sun.

mildew any ▷fungus that appears as a destructive growth on plants, paper, leather, or wood when they become damp for a certain length of time; such fungi usually form a thin white coating on the surface.

mile imperial unit of linear measure. A statute mile is equal to 1,760 yards (1.60934 km), and an international nautical mile is equal to 2,026 yards (1,852 m).

Miles, Bernard James, Baron Miles (1907–1991) English actor and producer. He appeared on stage as Briggs in *Thunder Rock* (1940) and Iago in *Othello* (1942), and his films include *Great Expectations* (1947). He founded a trust that in 1959 built the City of London's first new theatre for 300 years, the Mermaid, which presents a mixed classical and modern repertoire. He was knighted in 1969 and was made a baron in 1979.

milfoil another name for the herb ▷yarrow. Water milfoils are unrelated; they have whorls of fine leaves and grow underwater. (Genus *Miriophyllum*, family Haloragidaceae.)

Militant Tendency in British politics, left-wing faction originally within the Labour Party, aligned with the publication *Militant*. It became active in the 1970s, with radical socialist policies based on Trotskyism (see ▷Trotsky), and gained some success in local government, for example in the inner-city area of Liverpool. In the mid-1980s the Labour Party considered it to be a separate organization within the party and banned it.

military-industrial complex conjunction of the military establishment and the arms industry, both inflated by Cold War demands. The phrase was first used by US president and former general Dwight D Eisenhower in 1961 to warn Americans of the potential misplacement of power.

militia body of civilian soldiers, usually with some military training, who are on call in emergencies, distinct from professional soldiers. In Switzerland, the militia is the national defence force, and every able-bodied man is liable for service in it. In the UK the ▷Territorial Army and in the USA the ▷National Guard have supplanted earlier voluntary militias.

milk secretion of the ▷mammary glands of female mammals, with which they suckle their young (during ▷lactation). Over 85% is water, the remainder comprising protein, fat, lactose (a sugar), calcium, phosphorus, iron, and vitamins. The milk of cows, goats, and sheep is often consumed by humans, but regular drinking of milk after infancy is principally a Western practice.

Milk composition varies among species, depending on the nutritional requirements of the young; human milk contains less protein and more lactose than that of cows.

Skimmed milk is what remains when the cream has been separated from milk. It is readily dried and is available in large quantities at low prices, so it is often sent as food aid to Third World countries. **Evaporated milk** is milk reduced by heat until it reaches about half its volume. **Condensed milk** is concentrated to about a third of its original volume with added sugar.

The average consumption of milk in the UK is about 2.5–3 l/ 4–5 pt per week.

Milky Way faint band of light crossing the night sky, consisting of stars in the plane of our Galaxy. The name Milky Way is often used for the Galaxy itself. It is a spiral ▷galaxy, 100,000 light years in diameter and 2,000 light years thick, containing at least 100 billion ▷stars. The Sun is in one of its spiral arms, about 25,000 light years from the centre, not far from its central plane.

The densest parts of the Milky Way, towards the Galaxy's centre, lie in the constellation ▷Sagittarius. In places, the Milky Way is interrupted by lanes of dark dust that obscure light from the stars beyond, such as the Coalsack ▷nebula in Crux (the Southern Cross). It is because of these that the Milky Way is irregular in width and appears to be divided into two between Centaurus and Cygnus.

Mill, James (1773–1836) Scottish philosopher and political thinker who developed the theory of ▷utilitarianism. He is remembered for his political articles, and for the rigorous education he gave his son John Stuart Mill.

Mill, John Stuart (1806–1873) English philosopher and economist who wrote *On Liberty* (1859), the classic philosophical defence of liberalism, and *Utilitarianism* (1863), a version of the 'greatest happiness for the greatest number' principle in ethics. His progressive views inspired *On the Subjection of Women* (1869).

He was born in London, the son of James Mill. In 1822 he entered the East India Company, where he remained until retiring in 1858. In 1826, as described in his *Autobiography* (1873), he passed through a mental crisis; he found his father's bleakly intellectual utilitarianism emotionally unsatisfying and abandoned it for a more human philosophy influenced by the poet S T Coleridge. Mill sat in Parliament as a Radical 1865–68 and introduced a motion for women's suffrage.

In *Utilitarianism*, he states that actions are right if they bring about happiness and wrong if they bring about the reverse of happiness. *On Liberty* moved away from the utilitarian notion that individual liberty was necessary for economic and governmental efficiency and advanced the classical defence of individual freedom as a value in itself and the mark of a mature society; this change can be traced in the later editions of *Principles of Political Economy* (1848). His philosophical and political writings include *A System of Logic* (1843) and *Considerations on Representative Government* (1861).

> **John Stuart Mill**
> *The worth of a State, in the long run, is the worth of the individuals composing it.*
> On Liberty ch. 5

Millais, John Everett (1829–1896) English painter, a founder member of the ▷Pre-Raphaelite Brotherhood in 1848. By the late 1860s he had left the Brotherhood, developing a more fluid and conventional style which appealed strongly to Victorian tastes.

Precocious in talent, he was a student at the Royal Academy Schools at the age of 11. Early acquaintanceship with Holman ▷Hunt and Dante Gabriel ▷Rossetti led to the founding of the Pre-Raphaelite Brotherhood and, inspired by its doctrine of 'truth to nature', he produced some of his best works during the 1950s, among them the painting of Miss Siddell as Ophelia and *Christ in the House of His Parents* (1850; Tate Gallery, London); the latter caused an outcry on its first showing, since its realistic detail was considered unfitting to a sacred subject.

His marriage to Euphemia Gray in 1855 after the annulment of her marriage to John Ruskin estranged him from that early mentor and the *milieu* of Pre-Raphaelite idealism. His illustrations for the Moxon Tennyson (1857) and Trollope's *Orley Farm* (1863) show the change from Pre-Raphaelite principle to mid-Victorian Academicism. Though appealing to popular sentiment, his original style and quality disappeared from his later subject pictures and portraits, which include *The Boyhood of Raleigh* (1870; Tate Gallery, London) and the hugely successful *Bubbles* (1885), used as an advertisement by the Pears soap company. He became a baronet in 1885, and president of the Royal Academy in 1896.

Other works *Lorenzo and Isabella* (1849; Walker Gallery, Liverpool), depicting the banquet scene from Keat's 'Isabella', was Millais' first painting on Pre-Raphaelite principles. With more or less strict adherence to the Pre-Raphaelite style, Millais then produced *The Return of the Dove to the Ark* (1851); *Mariana of the Moated Grange* (1851); *Ophelia*; and the popular *The Order of Release* (1853).

In his latter days he turned to portraits (his sitters including Gladstone, Tennyson, and Cardinal Newman); landscapes, such as *Chill October* (1871); and single figures, such as the hugely popular child portraits and *Cherry Ripe*, *Little Miss Muffet*, and *Bubbles*, for which the model was Admiral Sir William James as a boy.

JOHN EVERETT MILLAIS Portrait of the English painter John Everett Millais. *Archive Photos*

millefiore (Italian 'a thousand flowers') ornamental glassmaking technique. Coloured glass rods are arranged in bundles so that the cross-section forms a pattern.

When the bundle is heated and drawn out thinly, the design becomes reduced in scale. Slices of this are used in glass-bead manufacture and can be set side by side and fused into metalware.

Millennium Bug crisis that faced computer professionals and users at the end of the year 1999. The crisis arose because it was feared that computers would be unable to operate normally when faced with the unfamiliar date format of the year 2000. Information about the year was typically stored in a two-digit instead of a four-digit field in order to save memory space, which without remedial work would have meant that after the year 1999 ended the year could have appeared as '00', interpreted as 1900 or not recognized at all. The turn of the century itself passed without significant breakdowns of normal services. However, it was stressed that problems could continue to surface throughout 2000.

Millennium Dome giant structure serving as the centrepiece of Great Britain's celebrations of the year 2000. Located on a 732,483 sq m/181-acre festival site in Greenwich, southeast London, the Dome is on the Greenwich Prime Meridian (0° longitude). It is 320 m/1,050 ft in diameter, 50 m/164 ft in height, and covers an area of 80,425 sq m/19.86 acres. The dome canopy is made of panels of teflon-coated PTFE, supported by 12 steel masts, each 100 m/328 ft long. It was designed by the Richard Rogers Partnership (architects of another London landmark, the Lloyd's Building), and is twice as big as the world's former largest dome, the Georgia Dome in Atlanta, USA. It was the central venue on 31 December 1999 for London's official millennium celebrations and remained open to the public throughout 2000.

The Dome and exhibition were dogged by controversy from the start: the Greenwich site, the cost of the Dome itself (£700 million to build, with £400 million from lottery funds and £160 million from commercial backers), and the contents all caused disagreement. Its forecast, made in its business plan, that it would attract 12 million paying visitors during 2000, proved to be wildly optimistic. It attracted fewer than half this number of visitors and barely 4 million paying visitors, and became technically insolvent. It closed on 1 January 2001, and much of its contents were sold in auction in February 2001, while the government undertook to try to sell it to property consortia.

Miller, Arthur (1915–) US dramatist. His plays deal with family relationships and contemporary American values, and include *Death of a Salesman* (1949, Pulitzer Prize), and *The Crucible* (1953), based on the Salem witch trials and reflecting the communist witch-hunts of Senator Joe ▷McCarthy. He was married from 1956 to 1961 to the film star Marilyn Monroe, for whom he wrote the film *The Misfits* (1960).

Miller was born in New York and educated at the University of Michigan. His first Broadway play *The Man Who Had All the Luck* (1944) was a failure, but his second *All My Sons* (1947), won the Drama Critics' Award. Among his other plays are *A View from the Bridge* (1955), and *After the Fall* (1964), based on his relationship with Monroe. He also wrote a novel *Focus* (1945), and *Situation Normal*, an account of army life. More recent work includes *The American Clock* (1979) on the 1930s depression, *The Ride Down Mount Morgan* (1991), and *Broken Glass* (1994), on anti-semitism in the 1930s. In 1999 Miller received a Special Tony Award, honouring his achievement in Broadway theatre. He published a collection of his essays *The Crucible in History* (2000) and received the Medal for Distinguished Contribution to American Letters in November 2001. His play *Resurrection Blues* was published in 2002.

> **Arthur Miller**
> *A good newspaper, I suppose, is a nation talking to itself.*
> The Observer 26 November 1962

Miller, (Alton) Glenn (1904–1944) US trombonist and bandleader. He was an exponent of the big-band swing sound from 1938. He composed his signature tune 'Moonlight Serenade' (a hit 1939). Miller became leader of the US Army Air Force Band in Europe 1942, made broadcasts to troops throughout the world during World War II, and disappeared without trace on a flight between England and France.

Miller, Henry Valentine (1891–1980) US writer. From 1930 to 1940 he lived a bohemian life in Paris, where he wrote his fictionalized, sexually explicit, autobiographical trilogy *Tropic of Cancer* (1934), *Black Spring* (1936), and *Tropic of Capricorn* (1938). They were banned in the USA and England until the 1960s.

> **Henry Miller**
> *The aim of life is to live, and to live means to be aware, joyously, drunkenly, serenely, divinely aware.*
> The Wisdom of the Heart, 'Creative Death'

miller's thumb another name for ▷bullhead, a small fish.

millet any of several grasses of which the grains are used as a cereal food and the stems as animal fodder. Species include *Panicum miliaceum*, extensively cultivated in the warmer parts of Europe, and *Sorghum bicolor*, also known as durra. (Family Gramineae.)

Millet, Jean François (1814–1875) French artist. A leading member of the ▷Barbizon School, he painted scenes of peasant life and landscapes. *The Angelus* (1859; Musée d'Orsay, Paris) and *The Gleaners* (1857; Louvre, Paris) were widely reproduced in his day.

JEAN FRANÇOIS MILLET *The Wood Sawyers* is one of French painter Jean François Millet's paintings ennobling the hard labour of rural life. *The Art Archive*

Millett, Kate (1934–) US radical feminist lecturer, writer, and sculptor whose book *Sexual Politics* (1970) was a landmark in feminist thinking. She was a founding member of the National Organisation of Women (NOW).

milli- prefix (symbol m) denoting a one-thousandth part (10^{-3}). For example, a millimetre, mm, is one thousandth of a metre.

millibar unit of pressure, equal to one-thousandth of a ▷bar.

millilitre one-thousandth of a litre (ml), equivalent to one cubic centimetre (cc).

millimetre of mercury unit of pressure (symbol mmHg), used in medicine for measuring blood pressure defined as the pressure exerted by a column of mercury one millimetre high, under the action of gravity.

millionaire city (or **million city**) city with more than 1 million inhabitants. In 1985 there were 273 millionaire cities in the world, compared with just two in 1850. Most of these are now found in the Third World, whereas before 1970 most were in industrialized countries.

millipede any of a group of ▷arthropods that have segmented bodies, each segment usually bearing two pairs of legs, and a pair of short clubbed antennae on the distinct head. Most millipedes are no more than 2.5 cm/1 in long; a few in the tropics are 30 cm/12 in. (Class Diplopoda.)

Millipedes live in damp, dark places, feeding mainly on rotting vegetation. Some species injure crops by feeding on tender roots, and some produce a poisonous secretion in defence. Certain orders have silk glands.

MILLIPEDE Giant millipedes can reach lengths of 20 cm/ 8 in and live in East Africa. *K G Preston-Mafham/Premaphotos Wildlife*

Mills, John (Lewis Ernest Watts) (1908–) English actor. A very versatile performer, he appeared in films such as *In Which We Serve* (1942), *The Rocking Horse Winner* (1949), *The Wrong Box* (1966), and *Oh! What a Lovely War* (1969). He received an Academy Award for *Ryan's Daughter* (1970).

Milne, A(lan) A(lexander) (1882–1956) English writer. He is best known as the author of *Winnie-the-Pooh* (1926) and *The House at Pooh Corner* (1928), based on the teddy bear and other toys of his son Christopher Robin, with illustrations by E H Shepard. He also wrote children's verse, including *When We Were Very Young* (1924) and *Now We Are Six* (1927). He was an accomplished dramatist whose plays included *Wurzel-Flummery* (1917), *Mr Pim Passes By* (1920), *The Dover Road* (1922), and *Toad of Toad Hall* (1929), an adaptation of Kenneth ▷Grahame's *The Wind in the Willows*.

Milošević, Slobodan (1941–) Serbian communist politician; party chief and president of Serbia 1986–97, and president of Yugoslavia 1997–2000. Widely believed to be the instigator of the conflict in ▷Bosnia-Herzegovina 1992–94, Milošević changed tactics from 1994, adopting the public persona of peacemaker and putting pressure on his allies, the Bosnian Serbs, to accept negotiated peace terms; this contributed to the Dayton peace accord for Bosnia-Herzegovina in November 1995. As president of Yugoslavia, Milošević faced international condemnation for the brutal treatment of ethnic Albanians by Serbian forces in ▷Kosovo. In March 1999, NATO aircraft began a bombing campaign in an attempt to force the Yugoslav government to end the persecution. In June 1999 Milošević accepted NATO's peace agreement. He was replaced by Vojislav ▷Koštunica in October 2000, and arrested in April 2001 and charged with abuse of power, corruption, and fraud. He was extradited to The Hague to face trial for war crimes in June 2001.

Milošević wielded considerable influence over the Serb-dominated Yugoslav federal army during the 1991–92 civil war and continued to back Serbian militias in Bosnia-Herzegovina 1992–94, although publicly disclaiming any intention to carve up the newly independent republic.

One of his first acts as president of Serbia in 1989 was to repeal the autonomy enjoyed by the province of Kosovo since 1974. In 1998 there was fierce fighting between Serbian forces and Albanian separatist guerrillas in Kosovo. In February 1999, representatives of the separatists agreed to attend Western-sponsored talks in Paris, France. A peace plan was accepted by the separatists but rejected by Serbia.

Following Milošević's rejection of the Rambouillet peace plan which had been formulated in Paris, NATO began a bombing campaign. In April, President Milošević dismissed his deputy, Vuk Draskovic, following his criticisms of the programme of 'ethnic cleansing' in Kosovo. He agreed to peace in June.

Milošević was beaten in elections held on 24 September 2000 by Vojislav Koštunica, leader of the Democratic Opposition of Serbia (DOS). Despite initially refusing to accept the election results, Milošević was forced out of power by a campaign of civil disobedience organized by the incoming opposition. President Koštunica initially ruled out extraditing Milošević to the United Nations (UN) war crimes tribunal, but was persuaded by the threat of losing much-needed Western aid money. Milošević's trial opened on 12 February 2002.

Related Web site: Serbian Nationalism, Slobodan Milošević, and the Origins of the Yugoslav War http://www.suc.org/politics/papers/history/vujacic.html

Milton, John (1608–1674) English poet and prose writer. His epic *Paradise Lost* (1667) is one of the landmarks of English literature. Early poems, including *Comus* (a masque performed 1634) and *Lycidas* (an elegy, 1638), showed Milton's superlative lyric gift. He also wrote many pamphlets and prose works, including *Areopagitica* (1644), which opposed press censorship, and he was Latin secretary to Oliver ▷Cromwell and the Council of State from 1649 until the restoration of Charles II.

Born in Cheapside, London, and educated at St Paul's School and Christ's College, Cambridge, Milton was a scholarly poet, ambitious to match the classical epics, and with strong theological views. Of polemical temperament, he published prose works on republicanism and church government. His middle years were devoted to the Puritan cause and writing pamphlets, including *The Doctrine and Discipline of Divorce* (1643), which may have been based on his own experience of marital unhappiness. During his time as secretary to Cromwell and the Council of State his assistants, as his sight failed, included Andrew ▷Marvell. *Paradise Lost* and the less successful sequel *Paradise Regained* (1671) were written when he was blind and in some political danger (after the restoration of Charles II), as was the dramatic poem *Samson Agonistes* (1671).

Milton's early poems have a baroque exuberance, a rich and sensuous use of imagery and cadence, while his later works are more sober, the blank verse more measured in its mixture of classical and English diction. His stated intention in writing *Paradise Lost* was to 'assert eternal Providence/And justify the ways of God to men'. He does not so much imitate the classical epics as demonstrate the supremacy of the Christian revelation over their pagan truths by redefining and reinterpreting the epic conventions. In *Lycidas*, too, Christian values finally supplant the range of thought available to the classical elegists, and *Samson Agonistes* reinterprets the values of Greek tragedy.

> **John Milton**
> *The mind is its own place, and in itself / Can make a Heav'n of Hell, a Hell of Heav'n.*
> *Paradise Lost* I. 254

Related Web site: Milton, John http://www.luminarium.org/sevenlit/milton/index.html

Milton Keynes unitary authority in central England, formerly part of Buckinghamshire.

area 311 sq km/120 sq mi **towns and cities** Milton Keynes (administrative headquarters), Newport Pagnell, Olney, Bletchley, Stony Stratford, Woburn Sands, Wolverton **features** Grand Union Canal; River Great Ouse; River Tove; Open University (established in Milton Keynes in 1971); Milton Keynes National Bowl (venue for outdoor events); National Badminton Centre (Milton Keynes); Bletchley Park, government centre of code-breaking during World War II; Ouse Valley Park with wetland habitats; Peace Pagoda (Milton Keynes), first to be built in northern hemisphere and surrounded by a thousand cherry and cedar trees planted in memory of all war victims; Milton Keynes' famous concrete cows, constructed in 1978 by a community artist and local school children **industries** financial services, telecommunications, soft drinks, high technology industries, motor vehicle parts and manufacture (Aston Martin-Lagonda, Mercedes-Benz, Volkswagen-Audi), education (Open University and De Montfort University campuses), vellum and parchment **population** (1996) 198,600

Milwaukee industrial city and port in southeastern Wisconsin, USA, at the mouth of the Milwaukee River, on the western shore of Lake Michigan, 128 km/79 mi north of Chicago; seat of Milwaukee County; population (1994 est) 617,000. It is the centre of a dairying and beef-producing region, and an important port of entry on the Great Lakes–St Lawrence Seaway system; industries include brewing (there are two major breweries, including Millers, the second largest brewery in the USA), engineering, machinery, motorcyles (the Harley-Davidson factory was founded here in 1906), electronic and electrical equipment, and chemicals.

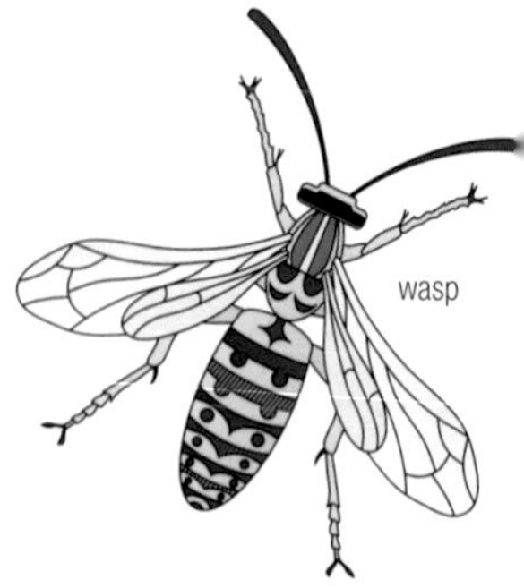

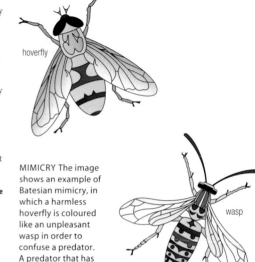

MIMICRY The image shows an example of Batesian mimicry, in which a harmless hoverfly is coloured like an unpleasant wasp in order to confuse a predator. A predator that has tried to eat a wasp will avoid the hoverfly.

mime type of acting in which gestures, movements, and facial expressions replace speech. It has developed as a form of theatre, particularly in France, where Marcel ▷Marceau and Jean Louis ▷Barrault have continued the traditions established in the 19th century by Deburau and the practices of the ▷commedia dell'arte in Italy. In ancient Greece, mime was a crude, realistic comedy with dialogue and exaggerated gesture.

mimicry imitation of one species (or group of species) by another. The most common form is **Batesian mimicry** (named after English naturalist H W ▷Bates), where the mimic resembles a model that is poisonous or unpleasant to eat, and has aposematic, or warning, coloration; the mimic thus benefits from the fact that predators have learned to avoid the model. Hoverflies that resemble bees or wasps are an example. Appearance is usually the basis for mimicry, but calls, songs, scents, and other signals can also be mimicked.

Mimosa (or **Becrux** or **Beta Crucis**) second-brightest star in the southern-hemisphere constellation of Crux, marking one of the four corners of the Southern Cross, and the 19th-brightest star in the night sky. It is a blue-white giant star of magnitude 0.8 around 460 light years from the Sun.

mimosa any of a group of leguminous trees, shrubs, or herbs belonging to the mimosa family, found in tropical and subtropical regions. They all have small, fluffy, golden, ball-like flowers. A similar but unrelated plant, *Acacia dealbata*, is sold as mimosa by European florists. (True mimosa genus *Mimosa*, family Mimosaceae.)

min. abbreviation for **minute** (time); **minimum**.

Minamoto Also known as **Genji**. ancient Japanese clan, the members of which were the first ruling shoguns 1192–1219. Their government was based in Kamakura, near present-day Tokyo. After the death of the first shogun, Minamoto Yoritomo (1147–1199), the real power was exercised by the regent for the shogun; throughout the Kamakura period (1192–1333), the regents were of the Hōjō family, a branch of the ▷Taira.

Minangkabau an Indonesian people of western Sumatra. In addition to approximately 3 million Minangkabau in western Sumatra, there are sizeable communities in the major Indonesian cities. The Minangkabau language belongs to the Austronesian family.

Minas Gerais (Portuguese **general mines**) inland federal unit (state) of southeast Brazil; area 586,624 sq km/226,,495 sq mi; population (1991) 16,956,900; capital Belo Horizonte. The region is rich in mineral deposits (iron ore, manganese, bauxite, nickel) and is the centre of the country's iron ore, coal, diamond, and gold mining industries. Cattle are raised in the northwest of the region, and coffee, maize, dairy products, fruit, and sugar are produced. The ports of Rio de Janeiro, Vitoria, and Santos are used for its external trade. The Rio São Francisco flows through the northern part of the region. Other towns include Juiz de Fora, Governador Valadares, Uberaban, and Uberlândia. Gold was discovered at the end of the 17th century.

mind in philosophy, the presumed mental or physical being or faculty that enables a person to think, will, and feel; the seat of the intelligence and of memory; sometimes only the cognitive or intellectual powers, as distinguished from the will and the emotions.

Mindanao second-largest island of the Philippines. The indigenous peoples are the Lumad and Moro; area 94,627 sq km/ 36,536 sq mi; population (1990) 14,298,250. Towns and cities include Davao and Zamboanga. Industries include pineapples, coffee, rice, coconut, rubber, hemp, timber, nickel, gold, steel, chemicals, and fertilizer. The island is mainly mountainous rainforest; the active volcano Apo reaches 2,954 m/9,600 ft, and the island is subject to severe earthquakes.

There is a Muslim guerrilla resistance movement, the Moro Islamic Liberation Front.

mine explosive charge on land or sea, or in the atmosphere, designed to be detonated by contact, vibration (for example, from an enemy engine), magnetic influence, or a timing device. Countermeasures include metal detectors (useless for plastic types), specially equipped helicopters, and (at sea) ▷minesweepers. Mines were first used at sea in the early 19th century, during the Napoleonic Wars; landmines came into use during World War I to disable tanks.

mineral naturally formed inorganic substance with a particular chemical composition and a regularly repeating internal structure. Either in their perfect crystalline form or otherwise, minerals are the constituents of ▷rocks. In more general usage, a mineral is any substance economically valuable for mining (including coal and oil, despite their organic origins).

Related Web site: Mineral Gallery http://mineral.galleries.com/

mineral extraction recovery of valuable ores from the Earth's crust. The processes used include open-cast mining, shaft mining, and quarrying, as well as more specialized processes such as those used for oil and sulphur (see, for example, ▷Frasch process).

mineralogy study of minerals. The classification of minerals is based chiefly on their chemical composition and the kind of chemical bonding that holds these atoms together. The mineralogist also studies their crystallographic and physical characters, occurrence, and mode of formation.

Related Web site: Mineralogy Database http://webmineral.com

mineral oil oil obtained from mineral sources, for example coal or petroleum, as distinct from oil obtained from vegetable or animal sources.

mineral salt in nutrition, a simple inorganic chemical that is required by living organisms. Plants usually obtain their mineral salts from the soil, while animals get theirs from their food. Important mineral salts include iron salts (needed by both plants and animals), magnesium salts (needed mainly by plants, to make chlorophyll), and calcium salts (needed by animals to make bone or shell). A ▷trace element is required only in tiny amounts.

Minerva in Roman mythology, the goddess of wisdom and war, and of handicrafts and the arts, equivalent to the Greek ▷Athena. From the earliest days of ancient Rome, there was a temple to her on the Capitoline Hill, near the Temple of Jupiter.

minesweeper small naval vessel for locating and destroying mines at sea. A typical minesweeper weighs about 725 tonnes, and is built of reinforced plastic (immune to magnetic and acoustic mines). Remote-controlled miniature submarines may be used to lay charges next to the mines and destroy them.

Ming dynasty (lived 14th–17th centuries) Chinese dynasty 1368–1644, based in Nanjing. During the rule 1402–24 of Yongle (or Yung-lo), there was territorial expansion into Mongolia and Yunnan in the southwest. The administrative system was improved, public works were carried out, and foreign trade was developed. Art and literature flourished and distinctive blue and white porcelain was produced.

Mingus, Charles (1922–1979) US jazz bassist and composer. He played with Louis Armstrong, Duke Ellington, and Charlie Parker. His experimentation with ▷atonality and dissonant effects opened the way for the new style of free collective jazz improvisation of the 1960s.

miniature painting painting on a very small scale, notably early manuscript illumination, and later miniature portraits, sometimes set in jewelled cases, and Islamic paintings. Hans Holbein the Younger introduced miniature portrait painting into England, the form reaching its height in the works of ▷Hilliard in the 16th century, though continuing well into the 19th century. There was also a very strong tradition of miniature portrait painting in France. Miniatures by Islamic artists flourished in India and Persia, their subjects often bird and flowers, or scenes from history and legend, rather than portraits (▷Islamic art).

minicomputer multiuser computer with a size and processing power between those of a ▷mainframe and a ▷microcomputer. Nowadays almost all minicomputers are based on ▷microprocessors.

minimalism movement in abstract art (mostly sculpture) and music towards severely simplified composition. Minimal art developed in the USA in the 1950s in reaction to ▷abstract expressionism, shunning its emotive approach in favour of impersonality and elemental, usually geometric, shapes. It has found its fullest expression in sculpture, notably in the work of Carl Andre, who employs industrial materials in modular compositions. In music, from the 1960s, it manifested itself in large-scale statements, usually tonal or even diatonic, and highly repetitive, based on a few 'minimal' musical ideas. Major minimalist composers are Steve ▷Reich and Philip ▷Glass.

Related Web site: Minimalism http://www.artcyclopedia.com/history/minimalism.html

minimum wage minimum level of pay for workers, usually set by government. In the UK, minimum pay for many groups of workers has been fixed by wages councils. Minimum wages are set to prevent low-paid workers from being exploited by employers who would otherwise pay them even lower wages. However, minimum wages are argued by some economists to cause unemployment because if wages were allowed to fall below the minimum wage level, some employers would be prepared to take on more workers.

mining extraction of minerals from under the land or sea for industrial or domestic uses. Exhaustion of traditionally accessible resources has led to development of new mining techniques; for example, extraction of oil from offshore deposits and from land shale reserves. Technology is also under development for the exploitation of minerals from entirely new sources such as mud deposits and mineral nodules from the sea bed.

mink either of two species of carnivorous mammals belonging to the weasel family, usually found in or near water. They have rich brown fur, and are up to 50 cm/1.6 ft long with bushy tails 20 cm/8 in long. They live in Europe and Asia (*M. lutreola*) and North America (*M. vison*). (Genus *Mustela*.)

They produce an annual litter of six in their riverbank burrows. The demand for their fur led to the establishment from the 1930s of mink ranches for breeding of the animals in a wide range of fur colours. In 1997 world production of mink skins was 26 million, which represented a 36% decline since 1986.

Although not indigenous to the UK, there is now a well-established feral mink population due to escapes from mink farms and many mink being released from the 1940s onwards as farms went out of business. The mink is generally accepted as filling a niche for a generalist riverside predator, although it is still persecuted in some areas.

In 1998 the UK had 15 licensed mink farms.

Minneapolis (American Indian *minne* 'water', Greek *polis* 'town') city in southeastern Minnesota, USA, 13 km/8 mi from ▷St Paul, with which it forms the 'Twin Cities' area; seat of Hennepin County; population (1994 est) 355,000; metropolitan area (1992) 2,618,000. It is at the head of navigation of the Mississippi River, and is the centre of one of the richest agricultural areas in the USA. Industries include food processing and the manufacture of machinery, electrical and electronic equipment, precision instruments, transport machinery, and metal and paper products. Cray computers – used for long-range weather forecasting, spacecraft design, and code-breaking – are built here.

Minnelli, Liza (May) (1946–) US actor and singer. The daughter of Judy ▷Garland and the director Vincente ▷Minnelli, she achieved stardom in the Broadway musical *Flora, the Red Menace* (1965) and in the film *Cabaret* (1972). Her subsequent films include *New York, New York* (1977) and *Arthur* (1981).

Minnelli, Vincente (1910–1986) US film director. His colourfully stylish musicals include *Meet Me in St Louis* (1944), *An American in Paris* (1951), and *Gigi* (1958) (Academy Award for best direction). He also directed a number of powerful dramas, including *The Bad and the Beautiful* (1952), *The Cobweb* (1955), and *Two Weeks in Another Town* (1962).

Minnesinger (German 'love-singer') any of a group of 12th- to 14th-century German lyric poets and musicians. They represent a continuation of the French ▷troubadour tradition, their songs dealing mainly with the theme of courtly love, but their musical and literary styles diverged. Many were of noble birth, unlike the later ▷Meistersingers (German 'master singers') who were from the middle classes. Dietmar von Aist, Friedrich von Hausen, Heinrich von Morungen, Reinmar, and Walther von der Vogelweide were well-known Minnesingers.

Minnesota state in north Midwest USA. It is nicknamed the Gopher State or the North Star State. Minnesota was admitted to the Union in 1858 as the 32nd US state. One of the Great Lakes states, it is bordered to the south by Iowa, to the west by North and South Dakota, to the north by the Canadian states of Ontario and Manitoba, and to the east by Wisconsin.

population (1995) 4,609,500 **area** 218,700 sq km/84,418 sq mi **capital** ▷St Paul **towns and cities** Minneapolis, Duluth, Bloomington, Rochester **industries and products** cereals, soybeans, livestock, meat and dairy products, iron ore (about two-thirds of US output), non-electrical machinery, electronic equipment, pulp, finance sector

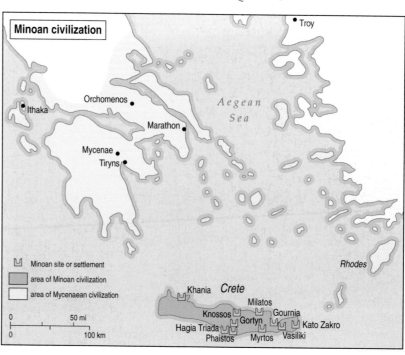

Minoan civilization

Minoan site or settlement
area of Minoan civilization
area of Mycenaean civilization

See Minoan civilization on p. 634.

minnow any of various small freshwater fishes of the carp family, found in streams and ponds worldwide. Most species are small and dull in colour, but some are brightly coloured. They feed on larvae and insects. (Family Cyprinidae.)

Minoan civilization Bronze Age civilization on the Aegean island of Crete. The name is derived from Minos, the legendary king of Crete. The civilization is divided into three main periods: early Minoan, about 3000–2000 BC; middle Minoan, about 2000–1550 BC; and late Minoan, about 1550–1050 BC. See map on p. 633.

Minogue, Kylie (Anne) (1968–) Australian pop singer and actor. She started her career as an actress, achieving her first major on the popular Australian soap opera *Neighbours*. After initial musical success in the late 1980s she struggled to find her place in the industry. However her return in 2001 with the worldwide hit single 'Can't Get You Out of My Head' and the accompanying album *Fever*, propelled her to a peak of international success. She appeared in several films, including *Moulin Rouge* (2001).

minor legal term for those under the age of majority, which varies from country to country but is usually between 18 and 21. In the USA (from 1971 for voting, and in some states for nearly all other purposes) and certain European countries (in Britain since 1970) the age of majority is 18.

Minority Rights Group international human-rights organization established in 1965 to increase awareness of minority issues. It publishes reports on minority groups worldwide, produces educational material for schools, and makes representations at the United Nations. Its headquarters are in London.

Minos in Greek mythology, a king of Crete, who demanded a yearly tribute of seven youths and seven girls from Athens for the ▷Minotaur, the offspring of his wife ▷Pasiphaë and a bull. After his death, he became a judge in ▷Hades.

Minotaur in Greek mythology, a monster with a man's body and bull's head, offspring of Pasiphaë, wife of King Minos of Crete, and a bull sent by Poseidon. It was housed in a Labyrinth designed by ▷Daedalus at Knossos, and its victims were seven girls and seven youths sent in annual tribute by Athens. The beast was killed by ▷Theseus with the aid of Ariadne, daughter of Minos.

Minsk (Belorussian **Mensk**) industrial city and capital of Belarus (also capital of the Minsk oblast); population (1990) 1,612,800. Motor vehicles, machinery, textiles, leather are produced here; Minsk is also a centre of the computer industry. The city's large pre-war Jewish community, which comprised over half of its inhabitants, was deported and murdered during the Nazi occupation. The headquarters of the Commonwealth of Independent States (CIS) is located here.

Minsk dates from the 11th century and has in turn been held by Lithuania, Poland, Sweden, and Russia before Belarus became an independent republic in 1991.

mint in botany, any aromatic plant of the mint family, widely distributed in temperate regions. The plants have square stems, creeping roots, and spikes of usually pink or purplish flowers. The family includes garden mint (*M. spicata*) and peppermint (*M. piperita*). (Genus *Mentha*, family Labiatae.)

MINT The water mint *Mentha aquatica*. As its name suggests, water mint grows in marshes and fens, producing small pink flowers from July to October. *Premaphotos Wildlife*

mint in economics, a place where coins are made under government authority. In Britain, the official mint is the **Royal Mint**; the US equivalent is the **Bureau of the Mint**. The UK Royal Mint also manufactures coinages, official medals, and seals for Commonwealth and foreign countries.

Mintoff, Dom(inic) (1916–) Maltese Labour politician; prime minister of Malta 1955–58 and 1971–84. He negotiated the removal of British and other foreign military bases 1971–79 and made treaties with Libya.

Minton, Thomas (1765–1836) English potter. After an apprenticeship as an engraver for transfer printing at Caughley and working for the potter Josiah Spode, he established himself at Stoke-on-Trent as an engraver of designs in 1789. The Chinese-style blue and white 'willow pattern' was reputedly originated by Minton. In 1796 he founded a pottery, producing a cream-base blue-decorated earthenware and (from 1798) high-quality porcelain and bone china, decorated with flowers and fruit. Chinaware became the chief production under his son Herbert Minton (1792–1858).

minuet French country dance in three time adapted as a European courtly dance of the 17th century. The music was later used as the third movement of a classical four-movement symphony where its gentle rhythm provides a foil to the slow second movement and fast final movement.

minute unit of time consisting of 60 seconds; also a unit of angle equal to one sixtieth of a degree.

Miocene ('middle recent') fourth epoch of the Tertiary period of geological time, 23.5–5.2 million years ago. At this time grasslands spread over the interior of continents, and hoofed mammals rapidly evolved.

Mir (Russian 'peace' or 'world') Soviet space station, the core of which was launched on 20 February 1986. It was permanently occupied until 1999. In November 2000, the Russian government announced that it would crash the space station into the Pacific Ocean in February 2001.

Mira (or Omicron Ceti) brightest long-period pulsating ▷variable star, located in the constellation ▷Cetus. Mira was the first star discovered to vary periodically in brightness.

In 1596 Dutch astronomer David Fabricus noticed Mira as a third-magnitude object. Because it did not appear on any of the star charts available at the time, he mistook it for a ▷nova. The German astronomer Johann Bayer included it on his star atlas in 1603 and designated it Omicron Ceti. The star vanished from view again, only to reappear within a year. It was named 'Stella Mira', 'the wonderful star', by Hevelius, who observed it 1659–82.

Mirabeau, Honoré Gabriel Riqueti, comte de (1749–1791) French politician, leader of the National Assembly in the French Revolution. He wanted to establish a parliamentary monarchy on the English model. From May 1790 he secretly acted as political adviser to the king.

miracle play another name for ▷mystery play.

mirage illusion seen in hot weather of water on the horizon, or of distant objects being enlarged. The effect is caused by the ▷refraction, or bending, of light.

Miranda, Carmen (1909–1955) Stage name of Maria de Carmo Miranda da Cunha. Portuguese dancer and singer. She lived in Brazil from childhood, moving to Hollywood in 1939. Her Hollywood musicals include *Down Argentine Way* (1940) and *The Gang's All Here* (1943). Her hallmarks were extravagant costumes and headgear adorned with tropical fruits, a staccato singing voice, and fiery temperament.

Miró, Joan (1893–1983) Spanish painter and sculptor, a major figure in ▷surrealism. In the mid-1920s he developed an abstract style, lyrical and often witty, with amoeba shapes, some linear, some highly coloured, generally floating on a plain background. *Birth of the World* (1925; Museum of Modern Art, New York) is typical of his more abstract works.

His paintings before 1922 combine the influence of ▷cubism with an emblematic treatment of detail. In 1924 he joined the surrealists, and increasingly a strong element of fantasy entered his work, as in the painting *The Hunter* (1923–24; Museum of Modern Art, New York), an elaborate composition full of strange creatures and erotic imagery. He also made more abstract paintings in which rudimentary signs are set against a background of drips and splashes, anticipating ▷abstract expressionism.

During the 1930s he was deeply affected by the Spanish Civil War and his style became more sober, probing, and at times savage. After World War II he produced larger abstracts, experimented with printmaking and sculpture (sometimes using everyday objects), and produced ceramic murals (including two in the UNESCO building in Paris, 1958). He also designed stained glass and sets for the ballet impresario Sergei Diaghilev.

mirror any polished surface that reflects light; often made from 'silvered' glass (in practice, a mercury-alloy coating of glass). A plane (flat) mirror produces a same-size, erect 'virtual' image located behind the mirror at the same distance from it as the object is in front of it. A spherical concave mirror produces a reduced, inverted real image in front or an enlarged, erect virtual image behind it (as in a shaving mirror), depending on how close the object is to the mirror. A spherical convex mirror produces a reduced, erect virtual image behind it (as in a car's rear-view mirror).

miscarriage spontaneous expulsion of a fetus from the womb before it is capable of independent survival. Miscarriage is believed to occur in 15% of pregnancies. Possible causes include fetal abnormality, abnormality of the uterus or cervix, infection, shock, underactive thyroid, and cocaine use.

misdemeanour in US law, an offence less serious than a felony. A misdemeanour is an offence punishable by a relatively insevere penalty, such as a fine or short term in prison or a term of community service, while a felony carries more severe penalties, such as a term of imprisonment of a year or more up to the death penalty.

Mishima, Yukio (1925–1970) Pen-name of Hiraoka Kimitake. Japanese novelist. His work often deals with sexual desire and perversion, as in *Confessions of a Mask* (1949) and *The Temple of the Golden Pavilion* (1956). He committed hara-kiri (ritual suicide) as a protest against what he saw as the corruption of the nation and the loss of the samurai warrior tradition.

Mishnah (or Mishna; Hebrew '(teaching by) repetition') collection of commentaries on written Hebrew law, consisting of discussions between rabbis, handed down orally from their inception in AD 70 until about 200, when, with the *Gemara* (the main body of rabbinical debate on interpretations of the Mishnah), it was committed to writing to form the *Talmud*.

misrepresentation in law, an untrue statement of fact, made in the course of negotiating a contract, that induces one party to enter into the contract. The remedies available for misrepresentation depend on whether the representation is found to be fraudulent, negligent, or innocent.

missal in the Roman Catholic Church, a service book containing the complete office of Mass for the entire year. A simplified missal in the vernacular was introduced in 1969 (obligatory from 1971): the first major reform since 1570.

missel thrush bird belonging to the ▷thrush family.

missile rocket-propelled weapon, which may be nuclear-armed (see ▷nuclear warfare). Modern missiles are often classified as surface-to-surface missiles (SSM), air-to-air missiles (AAM), surface-to-air missiles (SAM), or air-to-surface missiles (ASM). A **cruise missile** is in effect a pilotless, computer-guided aircraft; it can be sea-launched from submarines or surface ships, or launched from the air or the ground.

MISSILE Missiles awaiting their final checks before being loaded onto a transporter and delivered to a military base. *Image Bank*

mission organized attempt to spread a religion. Throughout its history Christianity has been the most assertive of missionary religions. During the 20th century, sects such as the Mormons and Jehovah's Witnesses proselytized regularly and systematically. Islam also has a history of militant missionizing, but in the 20th century found ready converts in the Black Muslim movement of the USA. Buddhism was spread both historically and recently by the teaching spirit of the wandering Buddha and his followers.

Missionary activity in the Third World has frequently been criticized for its disruptive effects on indigenous peoples and their traditional social, political, and cultural systems.

Mississippi (American Indian **missi** 'big', **sipi** 'river') river in the USA, the main arm of the great river system draining the USA between the Appalachian and the Rocky mountain ranges. The length of the Mississippi is 3,778 km/2,348 mi; with its tributary the Missouri it totals 6,020 km/3,740 mi. The Mississippi rises in the lake region of northern Minnesota in the basin of Lake Itasca, and drops 20 m/65 ft over the St Anthony Falls at Minneapolis. Below the tributaries of the Minnesota, Wisconsin, Des Moines, and Illinois rivers, the confluence of the Missouri and Mississippi occurs at St Louis. Turning at the Ohio junction, it passes Memphis, and takes in the St Francis, Arkansas, Yazoo, and Red tributaries before reaching its delta on the Gulf of Mexico, beyond New Orleans. Altogether the Mississippi has 42 tributary streams and the whole Mississippi river system has a navigable length in excess of 25,900 km/16,100 mi.

Related Web site: Mississippi Village Home Page: Towns and Villages
http://www.greatriver.com/maps/mrpc.htm

Mississippi state in southeast USA. It is nicknamed the Magnolia State or the Bayou State. Mississippi was admitted to the Union in 1817 as the 20th US state. Part of the Deep South, it was historically associated with the cotton plantations, slavery, and the blues. Mississippi is bordered to the east by Alabama, to the north by Tennessee, and to the west by Arkansas and Louisiana. To the south the state has a coast *c.* 115 km/70 mi long on the Gulf of Mexico, with a number of islands in the Mississippi Sound.

population (1995) 2,697,200 **area** 123,600 sq km/47,710 sq mi **capital** ▷Jackson **towns and cities** Biloxi, Greenville, Meridian, Hattiesburg **industries and products** cotton, rice, soybeans, chickens, fish and shellfish, lumber and wood products, petroleum and natural gas, transportation equipment, chemicals

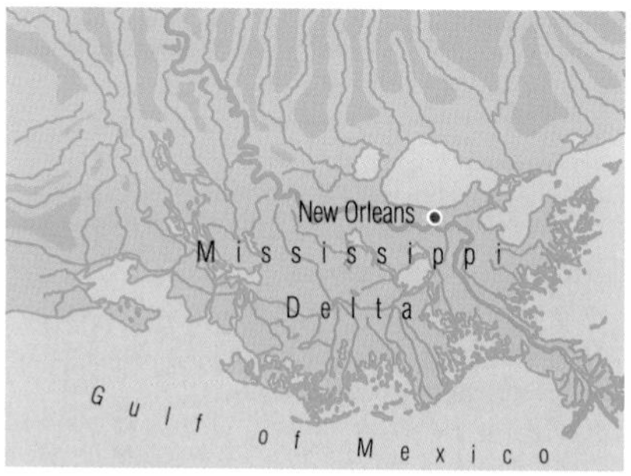

Mississippian US term for the Lower or Early ▷Carboniferous period of geological time, 363–323 million years ago. It is named after the state of Mississippi.

Missolonghi (Greek **Mesolóngion**) town in western central Greece and Eubrea region, on the north shore of the Gulf of Patras; population (1991) 10,900. It was several times under siege by the Turks in the wars of 1822–26 and it was here that the British poet Byron died.

Missouri major river in central USA, largest tributary of the ▷Mississippi, which it joins north of St Louis; length 3,969 km/2,466 mi; drainage area 1,370,000 sq km/529,000 sq mi. It rises among the Rocky Mountains in Montana, and passes northwards through a 366 m/1,200 ft gorge known as the 'Gate of the Mountains'. The river is formed by the confluence of the Jefferson, Gallatin, and Madison rivers near Gallatin City, southwestern Montana, and flows southeast through the states of Montana, North Dakota, and South Dakota to Sioux City, Iowa. It then turns south to form the borders between Iowa and Nebraska and between Kansas and Missouri, and enters the Mississippi channel 32 km/20 mi north of St Louis. Kansas City, Missouri, is the largest city on its banks.

Missouri state in central USA. It is nicknamed Show Me State or the Bullion State. Missouri was admitted ot the Union in 1821 as the 24th US state. Part of the Midwest, it is bordered to the south by Arkansas, to the west by Oklahoma, Kansas, and Nebraska, to the north by Iowa, and to the east by Illinois and, in the extreme southeast, by parts of Kentucky and Tennessee.

population (1995) 5,323,500 **area** 180,600 sq km/69,712 sq mi **capital** Jefferson City **towns and cities** St Louis, Kansas City, Springfield, Independence **industries and products** meat and other processed food, aerospace and transport equipment, lead, zinc, tourism

Missouri Compromise in US history, the solution by Congress (1820–21) of a sectional crisis caused by the 1819 request from Missouri for admission to the Union as a slave state, despite its proximity to existing nonslave states. The compromise was the simultaneous admission of Maine as a nonslave state to keep the same ratio.

mistletoe parasitic evergreen plant, native to Europe. It grows on trees as a small bush with translucent white berries. Used in many Western countries as a Christmas decoration, it also featured in the pagan religion ▷Druidism. (*Viscum album*, family Loranthaceae.)

Mitchell, James Leslie real name of Scottish novelist Lewis Grassic ▷Gibbon.

Mitchell, Joni (1943–) Adopted name of Roberta Joan Anderson. Canadian singer, songwriter, and guitarist. She started her career in the 1960s folk style and subsequently incorporated elements of rock and jazz with sophisticated confessional lyrics. Her albums include *Blue* (1971), *For the Roses* (1972), and *Court and Spark* (1974).

Margaret Mitchell
Death and taxes and childbirth! There's never any convenient time for any of them.
Gone with the Wind ch. 38

Mitchell, Margaret (1900–1949) US novelist. She was born in Atlanta, Georgia, which is the setting for her one book, the best-seller *Gone With the Wind* (1936; Pulitzer prize), a story of the US Civil War. It was filmed in 1939 and starred Vivien Leigh and Clark Gable.

Mitchum, Robert (Charles Duran) (1917–1997) US film actor. His career spanned more than 50 years of film-making, and embraced more than 100 film and television roles. As one of Hollywood's most enduring stars, he was equally at home as the relaxed modern hero or psychopathic villain. Mitchum's hard-boiled performances in a series of war films, melodramas, *films noirs*, and Westerns of the 1940s and early 1950s established him firmly in the pantheon of Hollywood's leading male performers. His films include *Out of the Past* (1947), *The Night of the Hunter* (1955), and *The Friends of Eddie Coyle* (1973).

Robert Mitchum
People think I have an interesting walk. Hell, I'm just trying to keep my gut in.
Quoted in Leslie Halliwell's *Filmgoer's Companion* 1965

mite minute ▷arachnid related to the ▷ticks. Some mites are free-living scavengers or predators. Some are parasitic, such as the **itch mite** (*Sarcoptes scabiei*), which burrows in skin causing scabies in humans and mange in dogs, and the **red mite** (*Dermanyssus gallinae*), which sucks blood from poultry and other birds. Others parasitize plants. (Order Acarina.)

Mitford sisters The six daughters of British aristocrat 2nd Lord Redesdale, including: **Nancy** (1904–1973), author of the semi-autobiographical *The Pursuit of Love* (1945) and *Love in a Cold Climate* (1949), and editor and part author of the satirical essays collected in *Noblesse Oblige* (1956) elucidating 'U' (upper-class) and 'non-U' behaviour; **Diana** (1910–2003), who married British fascist Oswald ▷Mosley; **Unity** (1914–1948), who became an admirer of Hitler; and **Jessica** (1917–1996), author of the autobiographical *Hons and Rebels* (1960) and *The American Way of Death* (1963).

Mithradates alternative spelling of ▷Mithridates VI Eupator, King of Pontus (on the Black Sea coast of modern Turkey).

Mithras (or Mithra) in Persian mythology, the god of light, son of the sublime god, Ahura Mazda. Mithras represented the power of morality and goodness against Ahriman, the personification of evil, and promised his followers compensation for present evil after death. Mithraism was introduced into the Roman Empire in 68 BC and spread rapidly, gaining converts especially among soldiers; by about AD 250, it rivalled Christianity in strength.

Mithridates VI Eupator the Great (*c.* 120–60 BC) King of Pontus (on the Black Sea coast of modern Turkey), who became the greatest obstacle to Roman expansion in the east. He massacred 80,000 Romans while overrunning Asia Minor and went on to invade Greece. He was defeated by ▷Sulla during the first Mithridatic War in 88–84 BC, by Lucullus in the second 83–81, and by Pompey the Great in the third 74–64.

mitochondria (singular **mitochondrion**) membrane-enclosed organelles within ▷eukaryotic cells, containing enzymes responsible for energy production during ▷aerobic respiration. Mitochondria absorb O_2 and glucose and produce energy in the form of ▷ATP by breaking down the glucose to CO_2 and H_2O. These rod-like or spherical bodies are thought to be derived from free-living bacteria that, at a very early stage in the history of life, invaded larger cells and took up a symbiotic way of life inside. Each still contains its own small loop of DNA called mitochondrial DNA, and new mitochondria arise by division of existing ones. Mitochondria each have 37 genes.

mitosis in biology, the process of cell division by which identical daughter cells are produced. During mitosis the DNA is duplicated and the chromosome number doubled, so new cells contain the same amount of DNA as the original cell.

The genetic material of ▷eukaryotic cells is carried on a number of ▷chromosomes. To control movements of chromosomes during cell division so that both new cells get the correct number, a system of protein tubules, known as the spindle, organizes the chromosomes into position in the middle of the cell before they replicate. The spindle then controls the movement of chromosomes as the cell goes through the stages of division: **interphase**, **prophase**, **metaphase**, **anaphase**, and **telophase**. See also ▷meiosis. See diagram on p. 636.

Mitre, Bartólomé (1821–1906) Argentine president 1862–68. In 1852 he helped overthrow the dictatorial regime of Juan Manuel de Rosas, and in 1861 helped unify Argentina. Mitre encouraged immigration and favoured growing commercial links with Europe. He is seen as a symbol of national unity.

Mitsotakis, Constantine (1918–) Greek politician, leader of the conservative New Democracy Party (ND) 1984–93, prime minister 1990–93. Minister for economic coordination in 1965 (a post he held again 1978–80), he was arrested by the military junta in 1967, but escaped from house arrest and lived in exile until 1974. In 1980–81 he was foreign minister. He resigned the leadership of the ND after its 1993 election defeat; in January 1996 proposed corruption charges against him were dropped.

Mitterrand, François (1916–1996) French socialist politician. After a successful ministerial career under the Fourth Republic, holding posts in 11 governments 1947–58, Mitterrand joined the new Parti Socialiste (PS; English Socialist Party) in 1971, establishing it as the most popular party in France before winning two successive terms

MITE The African giant red velvet mite (family Trombidiidae) can be found wandering around in semi-arid areas after rains. *Premaphotos Wildlife*

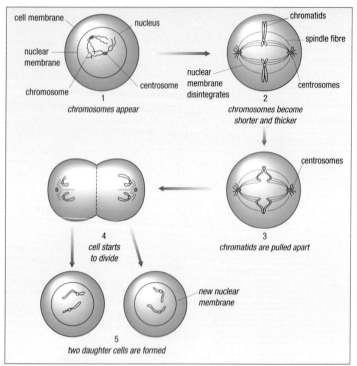

MITOSIS The stages of mitosis, the process of cell division that takes place when a plant or animal cell divides for growth or repair. The two daughter cells each receive the same number of chromosomes as were in the original cell. See entry on p. 635.

as president, 1981–88 and 1988–95. From 1982 his administrations reverted from redistributive and reflationary policies to economic orthodoxy and maintenance of the 'strong franc' (linked to the Deutschmark), despite the high levels of unemployment this entailed, and vigorously pursued further European integration.

Mitterrand studied law and politics in Paris. During World War II he came to prominence in the resistance after initially working in Marshal ▷Pétain's Vichy adminstration. In 1945 he was elected as deputy for Nièvre, as the member of a small centre-left Resistance-based party. Opposed to General Charles ▷de Gaulle's creation of the Fifth Republic in 1958, he formed a Federation of the Left and as its candidate challenged de Gaulle unsuccessfully for the presidency in 1965. In 1971, as leader of the PS, he negotiated an electoral pact and Common Programme of Government with the Communist Party, 1972–77, but again failed to win the presidency in 1974, this time against Valéry ▷Giscard d'Estaing. He was finally elected president in 1981.

His ambitious programme of social, economic and institutional reforms was hampered by deteriorating economic conditions after 1983. When the socialists lost their majority in March 1986, he was compelled to work with the Gaullist Jacques ▷Chirac as prime minister, and grew in popularity, defeating Chirac's bid for the presidency in May 1988. In 1993 he entered a second term of 'cohabitation' with the conservative prime minister Edouard ▷Balladur. Towards the end of his presidency his failing health weakened his hold on power. Whereas he was able to enhance his reputation when 'cohabiting' with Chirac, the successful elements of Balladur's premiership contrasted with Mitterrand's waning popularity and weakened influence.

mixed economy type of economic structure that combines the private enterprise of capitalism with a degree of state monopoly. In mixed economies, governments seek to control the public services, the basic industries, and those industries that cannot raise sufficient capital investment from private sources. Thus a measure of economic planning can be combined with a measure of free enterprise. A notable example was US President Franklin D Roosevelt's ▷New Deal in the 1930s.

Mixtec ancient civilization of pre-colonial Mexico. The Mixtecs succeeded the ▷Zapotecs in the valley of Oaxaca. They founded new towns, including Tilatongo and Teozacualco, and partially rebuilt some Zapotec cities. The Mixtecs produced historical records which contain biographies of rulers and noblemen and trace Mixtec history back to AD 692. They were skilled in the use of metals, including gold and silver.

mixture in chemistry, a substance containing two or more compounds that retain their separate physical and chemical properties. There is no chemical bonding between them and they can be separated from each other by physical means (▷compound).

Miyake, Issey (1938–) Japanese fashion designer. Active in Paris from 1965, he showed his first collection in New York and Tokyo 1971, and has been showing in Paris since 1973. His 'anti-fashion' looks combined Eastern and Western influences: a variety of textured and patterned fabrics were layered and wrapped round the body to create linear and geometric shapes.

Mizoram state of northeast India, lying between Bangladesh and Myanmar; area 21,100 sq km/ 8,150 sq mi; population (2001 est) 976,000. The capital is Aizawl. The state features north–south ranges in the east that rise to over 2,000 m/6,500 ft. The state is densely forested. Products include rice, maize, and hand-loom weaving. 84% of the population are Christian.

m.k.s. system system of units in which the base units metre, kilogram, and second replace the centimetre, gram, and second of the ▷c.g.s. system. From it developed the SI system (see ▷SI units).

Mladic, Ratko (1943–) Bosnian Serb general, leader of the Bosnian Serb army 1992–96. His ruthless conduct in the civil war in Bosnia, including the widespread maltreatment of prisoners and the disappearance of many more, led to his being indicted for war crimes by the United Nations War Crimes Commission in 1995.

Mmabatho capital of North West Province, South Africa, and former capital of the former independent homeland of Bophuthatswana; population (1991) 13,300. Many of the major buildings were built from revenues of the Sun City casino-resort.

MN abbreviation for ▷Minnesota, a state of the USA.

MO abbreviation for ▷Missouri, a state of the USA.

moa any of a group of extinct flightless kiwi-like birds that lived in New Zealand. There were 19 species; they varied from 0.5 to 3.5 m/ 2 to 12 ft, with strong limbs, a long neck, and no wings. The largest species was *Dinornis maximus*. The last moa was killed in the 1800s. (Order Dinornithiformes.)

Moab ancient country in Jordan, east of the southern part of the River Jordan and the Dead Sea. The inhabitants were closely akin to the Hebrews in culture, language, and religion, but were often at war with them, as recorded in the Old Testament.

Moab eventually fell to Arab invaders. The **Moabite Stone**, discovered in 1868 at Dhiban, dates from the 9th century BC and records the rising of Mesha, king of Moab, against Israel.

Mobile industrial city and administrative headquarters of Mobile County, southwest Alabama, at the mouth of the Mobile River, on the northwest shore of Mobile Bay, 48 km/30 mi from the Gulf of Mexico; population (2000 est) 198,900. It is the only seaport in Alabama. Industries include meatpacking and the manufacture of wood products, aircraft engines, chemical and petroleum products, computer equipment, and textiles. It is home to Spring Hill College (1830), Mobile College (1961), and the University of South Alabama (1963). A tourist centre, it is noted for its Mardi Gras and for its 60-km/37-mi Azalea Trail.

mobile ion in chemistry, an ion that is free to move; such ions are only found in the aqueous solutions or melts (molten masses) of an ▷electrolyte. The mobility of the ions in an electrolyte is what allows it to conduct electricity.

mobile phone in computing, cordless telephone linked to a digital cellular radio network. Early cellular networks used analogue technology, but since the late 1990s most services use a digital system. Mobile phones can connect to the Internet via a datacard, which converts computer data into a form that can be passed over the network and vice versa. Users can connect them to a ▷laptop computer, and others incorporate a full pocket organizer. A trend for greater integration of phone and computer emerged in 1996, leading to the arrival of ▷WAP (wireless application protocol) phones in 1999.

Möbius strip structure made by giving a half twist to a flat strip of paper and joining the ends together. It has certain remarkable properties, arising from the fact that it has only one edge and one side. If cut down the centre of the strip, instead of two new strips of paper, only one long strip is produced. It was invented by the German mathematician August Möbius.

Mobutu, Sese Seko Kuku Ngbeandu Wa Za Banga (1930–1997) Adopted name of Joseph Desire Mobutu. President of Zaire (now the Democratic Republic of Congo) 1965–97. The harshness of some of his policies and charges of corruption attracted widespread international criticism.

Mobutu, Lake alternative name of Lake ▷Albert in central Africa.

Moçambique Portuguese name for ▷Mozambique.

Moche (or **Mochica**) pre-Inca civilization on the coast of Peru AD 100–800. Remains include cities, massive platform tombs (*adobe*), and pottery that details daily and ceremonial life.

mockingbird North American songbird of the mimic thrush family, found in the USA and Mexico. About 25 cm/10 in long, it is brownish grey, with white markings on the black wings and tail. It is remarkable for its ability to mimic the songs of other species. (Species *Mimus polyglottos*, family Mimidae, order Passeriformes.)

mock orange (or **syringa**) any of a group of deciduous shrubs, including *P. coronarius*, which has white, strongly scented flowers similar to those of the orange tree. (Genus *Philadelphus*, family Philadelphaceae.)

mode in mathematics, the element that appears most frequently in a given set of data. For example, the mode for the data 0, 0, 9, 9, 9, 12, 87, 87 is 9.

model simplified version of some aspect of the real world. Models are produced to show the relationships between two or more factors, such as land use and the distance from the centre of a town (for example, concentric-ring theory). Because models are idealized, they give only a general guide to what may happen.

Model Parliament English parliament set up in 1295 by ▷Edward I; it was the first to include representatives from outside the clergy and aristocracy, and was established because Edward needed the support of the whole country against his opponents: Wales, France, and Scotland. His sole aim was to raise money for military purposes, and the parliament did not pass any legislation.

The parliament comprised archbishops, bishops, abbots, earls, and barons (all summoned by special writ, and later forming the basis of the House of Lords); also present were the lower clergy (heads of chapters, archdeacons, two clerics from each diocese, and one from each cathedral) and representatives of the shires, cities, and boroughs (two knights from every shire, two representatives from each city, and two burghers from each borough).

modem (contraction of modulator/demodulator) device for transmitting computer data over telephone lines. Such a device is used to convert the ▷digital signals produced by computers to ▷analogue signals compatible with the telephone network. The modem converts the digital signals to analogue, and back again.

Modena (ancient **Mutina**) town in Emilia-Romagna, Italy, capital of the province of Modena, 37 km/23 mi northwest of Bologna; population (1992) 177,000. Industries include engineering and the production of vehicles (Ferrari), glass, textiles, shoes, pasta, and sausages. The town has a 12th-century cathedral, a 17th-century ducal palace, and a university (1175), with medical and legal faculties.

Moderator in the Church of Scotland, the minister chosen to act as president of the annual General Assembly.

moderator in a ▷nuclear reactor, a material such as graphite or heavy water used to reduce the speed of high-energy neutrons. Neutrons produced by nuclear fission are fast-moving and must be slowed to initiate further fission so that nuclear energy continues to be released at a controlled rate.

modern dance 20th-century dance idiom that evolved in opposition to traditional ballet by those seeking a freer and more immediate means of dance expression. Leading exponents include Martha ▷Graham and Merce ▷Cunningham in the USA, Isadora ▷Duncan and Mary Wigman in Europe.

Modern dance was pioneered by US women seeking individual freedom but it is from Ruth St Denis and Ted Shawn's Denishawn School of Dancing and Related Arts in Los Angeles (1915) that the first generation of modern dance – Martha Graham, Doris Humphrey, and Charles Weidman – emerged. In the UK, the London Contemporary Dance Theatre and school was set up in 1966–67 and flourished under the artistic direction of Graham's pupil, Robert Cohan. The school is the only European institute authorized to teach the Graham Technique. In 1966, the Ballet Rambert became a modern-dance company.

Related Web site: Place, The http://www.theplace.org.uk/

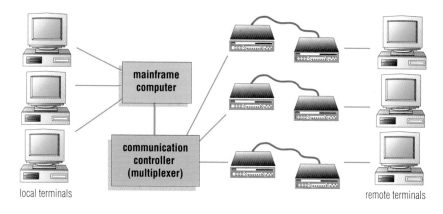

local terminals   remote terminals

MODEM Remote computer terminals communicate with the central mainframe via modems and telephone lines. The controller allocates computer time to the terminals according to predetermined priority rules. The multiplexer allows more than one terminal to use the same communications link at the same time (multiplexing).

modernism in the arts, a general term used to describe the 20th century's conscious attempt to break with the artistic traditions of the 19th century; it is based on a concern with form and the exploration of technique as opposed to content and narrative. In the visual arts, direct representationalism gave way to abstraction (see ▷abstract art); in literature, writers experimented with alternatives to orthodox sequential storytelling, such as ▷stream of consciousness; in music, the traditional concept of key was challenged by ▷atonality; and in architecture, Functionalism ousted decorativeness as a central objective (see ▷Modern Movement).

Modern Movement the dominant movement in 20th-century architecture, which grew out of the technological innovations of 19th-century Industrial architecture, crystallized in the ▷international style of the 1920s and 1930s, and has since developed various regional trends, such as Brutalism. 'Truth to materials' and 'form follows function' are its two most representative dicta, although neither allows for the modernity of large areas of contemporary architecture, concerned with proportion, human scale, and attention to detail. Currently, architectural ▷postmodernism, a reaction to the movement, is developing alongside such modernist styles as ▷high-tech.

Modigliani, Amedeo (1884–1920) Italian painter and sculptor, active in France from 1906. He is best known for graceful nudes and portraits. His paintings – for example, the portrait of his mistress Jeanne Hébuterne (1919; Guggenheim Museum, New York) – have a distinctive style, the forms elongated and sensual.

Born in Livorno of an Italian-Jewish family, he first studied art in Florence and Venice, but settled in Paris 1906. He was encouraged to sculpt by Constantin ▷Brancusi, the study of African tribal masks suggesting the bold elongation and simplification of his sculptured heads, as in *Stone Head* 1911 (Philadelphia Museum of Art, Pensylvania). His paintings showed the same influences, though in their subtle colour and their sensitive linear design they show his sympathy with Italian Renaissance art, particularly that of ▷Botticelli. Typical are the portrait *Lunia Czechowska* 1916 (Musée de Peinture, Grenoble), and the nude *Standing Nude (Elvira)* 1918 (Kunstmuseum, Bern).

After years of poverty he had some little success towards 1918, but privations, drugs, alcohol, and tuberculosis combined to cut short his life.

modulation in music, movement from one ▷key to another. In classical dance music, modulation is a guide to phrasing rhythm to the step pattern.

modulation in radio transmission, the variation of frequency, or amplitude, of a radio carrier wave, in accordance with the audio characteristics of the speaking voice, music, or other signal being transmitted.

See also ▷pulse-code modulation, ▷amplitude modulation (AM), and ▷frequency modulation (FM).

module in construction, a standard or unit that governs the form of the rest. For example, Japanese room sizes are traditionally governed by multiples of standard tatami floor mats; today prefabricated buildings are mass-produced in a similar way. The components of a spacecraft are designed in coordination; for example, for the Apollo Moon landings the craft comprised a command module (for working, eating, sleeping), service module (electricity generators, oxygen supplies, manoeuvring rocket), and lunar module (to land and return the astronauts).

modulus in mathematics, a number that divides exactly into the difference between two given numbers. Also, the multiplication factor used to convert a logarithm of one base to a logarithm of another base. Also, another name for ▷absolute value.

Mogadishu (or **Muqdisho**) capital and chief port of Somalia; population (1995 est) 525,000. The city lies on the Indian Ocean coast of Somalia and is a centre for oil refining, food processing, and chemical production; there are uranium reserves nearby. During the civil war 1991–92, much of the city was devastated and many thousands killed. The population has decreased since the civil war because of famine and the movement of refugees.

The city has mosques dating from the 13th century; the cathedral, built 1925–28, was destroyed during the civil war. There is an airport and a university, which was founded in 1954. Mogadishu orginated as an Arab settlement in the 10th century, but was in decline by the 16th century. In 1871 it was controlled by the sultan of Zanzibar. The site was leased to Italy in 1892 and became the headquarters of Italian Somaliland.

Mogul dynasty northern Indian dynasty 1526–1858, established by ▷Babur, Muslim descendant of Tamerlane, the 14th-century Mongol leader. The Mogul emperors ruled until the last one, ▷Bahadur Shah II, was dethroned and exiled by the British; they included ▷Akbar, ▷Aurangzeb, and ▷Shah Jahan. The Moguls established a more extensive and centralized empire than their Delhi sultanate forebears, and the Mogul era was one of great artistic achievement as well as urban and commercial development.

Mogul empire	empire under Zahir 1526

expansion
by Akbar to 1605
by Shah Jahan and Aurangzeb to 1707

LAHORE
Delhi
Agra
AJMER
BENGAL
AURANGABAD GONDWANA
HYDERABAD
Goa
Bay of Bengal
Ceylon
INDIAN OCEAN

0   500 mi
0   800 km

mohair (Arabic *mukhayyar* 'goat') yarn made from the long, lustrous hair of the ▷Angora goat or rabbit, loosely woven with cotton, silk, or wool to produce a fuzzy texture. It became popular for jackets, coats, and sweaters in the 1950s. Commercial mohair is now obtained from cross-bred animals, pure-bred supplies being insufficient to satisfy demand.

Mohammed alternative form of ▷Muhammad, founder of Islam.

Mohave Desert arid region in southern California, USA; see ▷Mojave Desert.

Mohawk member of an ▷American Indian people, part of the ▷Iroquois confederation, who lived in the Mohawk Valley, New York, and now live on reservations in Ontario, Québec, and New York State, as well as among the general population, and number about 10,000 (1990). Their language belongs to the Macro-Siouan group. In 1990 Mohawks south of Montréal mounted a blockade in a dispute over land with the government of Québec province.

Mohegan member of an Algonquian-speaking ▷American Indian people. Traditionally their economy was based on the cultivation of corn, and hunting and fishing. They are closely related to the ▷Mohican.

Mohenjo Daro ('mound of the dead') site of a city about 2500–1600 BC on the lower Indus River, northwestern Pakistan, where excavations from the 1920s have revealed the ▷Indus Valley civilization, to which the city of Harappa also belongs.

Mohican (or **Mahican**) member of an Algonquian-speaking ▷American Indian people. Traditionally their economy was based on the cultivation of corn, and hunting and fishing. They are closely related to the Mohegan.

Moholy-Nagy, Laszlo (1895–1946) Hungarian-born painter, sculptor and photographer. Inspired by ▷constructivism, he made abstract sculptures from the early 1920s, and from 1923 to 1929 taught at the Bauhaus school in Weimar and later in the USA. He experimented with a wide range of media, materials, and techniques, including the use of photographic techniques to achieve non-naturalistic effects.

Mohorovičić discontinuity (or **Moho** or **M-discontinuity**) a seismic discontinuity, marked by a rapid increase in the speed of earthquake waves, that is taken to represent the boundary between the Earth's crust and mantle. It follows the variations in the thickness of the crust and is found approximately 35–40 km/ 22–25 mi below the continents and about 10 km/6 mi below the oceans. It is named after the Croatian geophysicist Andrija Mohorovičić, who suspected its presence after analysing seismic waves from the Kulpa Valley earthquake in 1909. The 'Moho' is as deep as 70 km beneath high mountain ranges.

Mohs scale scale of hardness for minerals (in ascending order): 1 talc; 2 gypsum; 3 calcite; 4 fluorite; 5 apatite; 6 orthoclase; 7 quartz; 8 topaz; 9 corundum; 10 diamond.

Moi, Daniel arap (1924–   ) Kenyan politician, president 1978–2002. Leader of the Kenya African National Union (KANU), he became minister of home affairs in 1964, vice-president in 1967, and succeeded Jomo Kenyatta as president. He enjoyed the support of Western governments but was widely criticized for Kenya's poor human-rights record. His administration, first challenged by a coup attempt in 1982, became increasingly authoritarian. In 1991, in the face of widespread criticism, he promised the eventual introduction of multiparty politics. In 1992 he was elected president in the first free elections amid widespread accusations of vote rigging.

Moi was first nominated to the legislative council in 1955. In 1960 he became chair of the Kenya Africa Democratic Union (KADU) and opposition leader after independence in 1963. KADU merged with the ruling KANU party in 1964, and he was appointed vice-president of the party in 1966.

Moirai (or **Moerae**) in Greek mythology, the title of the three ▷Fates; the name refers to the 'portions' of life they allotted to each human being, a destiny represented by a thread, although they sometimes appeared as goddesses of inevitability. **Lachesis** assigned the length of a life from her distaff, **Clotho** spun its existence, and **Atropos** broke the thread to signify its termination.

Mojave Desert (or **Mohave Desert** or **High Desert**) arid region in southern California, USA, part of the Great Basin; average height above sea-level 600 m/2,000 ft; area 38,500 sq km/ 15,000 sq mi. It lies to the northeast of Los Angeles, and to the southeast of the ▷Sierra Nevada.

molar one of the large teeth found towards the back of the mammalian mouth. The structure of the jaw, and the relation of the muscles, allows a massive force to be applied to molars. In herbivores the molars are flat with sharp ridges of enamel and are used for grinding, an adaptation to a diet of tough plant material. Carnivores have sharp powerful molars called carnassials, which are adapted for cutting meat.

molarity in chemistry, ▷concentration of a solution expressed as the number of ▷moles in grams of solute per cubic decimetre of solution.

molar volume volume occupied by one ▷mole (the molecular mass in grams) of any gas at standard temperature and pressure, equal to 2.24136×10^{-2} m³.

Moldavia former principality in southeastern Europe, situated on the River Danube, and occupying an area divided today between the states of Moldova and Romania. Moldavia was independent between the 14th and 16th centuries, when it became part of the Ottoman Empire. In 1861, it was united with its neighbouring principality Wallachia to form the kingdom of Romania. In 1940 the eastern part, ▷Bessarabia, became part of the USSR (the Moldavian SSR), while the western part remained in Romania. See also ▷Bukovina.

Moldova (or **Moldavia**) see country box.

mole SI unit (symbol mol) of the amount of a substance. It is defined as the amount of a substance that contains as many elementary entities (atoms, molecules, and so on) as there are atoms in 12 g of the ▷isotope carbon-12.

mole person working subversively within an organization. The term has come to be used broadly for someone who gives out ('leaks') secret information in the public interest; it originally

Moldova

Moldova country in east-central Europe, bounded north, south, and east by Ukraine, and west by Romania.

NATIONAL NAME *Republica Moldova/Republic of Moldova*
AREA 33,700 sq km/13,011 sq mi
CAPITAL Chisinau (Russian Kishnev)
MAJOR TOWNS/CITIES Tiraspol, Balti, Tighina
PHYSICAL FEATURES hilly land lying largely between the rivers Prut and Dniester; northern Moldova comprises the level plain of the Balti Steppe and uplands; the climate is warm and moderately continental

Government

HEAD OF STATE Vladimir Voronin from 2001
HEAD OF GOVERNMENT Vasile Tarlev from 2001
POLITICAL SYSTEM emergent democracy
POLITICAL EXECUTIVE limited presidency
ADMINISTRATIVE DIVISIONS 11 counties, one municipality (Chisinau), and two autonomous regions – Gauguz (Gagauzi Yeri) and Trans-Dniestr
ARMED FORCES 7,200 (2002 est)
CONSCRIPTION military service is compulsory for 12 months
DEATH PENALTY abolished in 1995
DEFENCE SPEND (% GDP) 1.7 (2002 est)
EDUCATION SPEND (% GDP) 4 (2001 est)
HEALTH SPEND (% GDP) 3.5 (2000 est)

Economy and resources

CURRENCY leu
GPD (US$) 1.6 billion (2002 est)
REAL GDP GROWTH (% change on previous year) 6.1 (2001)
GNI (US$) 1.7 billion (2002 est)
GNI PER CAPITA (PPP) (US$) 1,560 (2002 est)
CONSUMER PRICE INFLATION 4.6% (2003 est)
UNEMPLOYMENT 2.1% (2000)
FOREIGN DEBT (US$) 915 million (2001 est)
MAJOR TRADING PARTNERS Russia, Ukraine, Romania, Germany, Italy

RESOURCES lignite, phosphorites, gypsum, building materials; petroleum and natural gas deposits discovered in the early 1990s were not yet exploited in 2001 (although exploration was underway)
INDUSTRIES food processing, wine, tobacco, metalworking, light industry, machine building, cement, textiles, footwear
EXPORTS wine, food and agricultural products, machinery and equipment, textiles, clothing. Principal market: Russia 44.5% (2000)
IMPORTS mineral fuels, energy and mineral products, mechanical engineering products, foodstuffs, chemicals, textiles, clothing. Principal source: Romania 16.3% (2000)
ARABLE LAND 55.3% (2000 est)
AGRICULTURAL PRODUCTS grain, sugar beet, potatoes, vegetables, wine grapes and other fruit, tobacco; livestock products (milk, pork, and beef)

Population and society

POPULATION 4,267,000 (2003 est)
POPULATION GROWTH RATE –0.1% (2000–15)

MOLDOVA Showing the Moldovan flag, this stamp was printed to commemorate the first anniversary of the country's declaration of independence.
Stanley Gibbons

POPULATION DENSITY (per sq km) 127 (2003 est)
URBAN POPULATION (% of total) 42 (2003 est)
AGE DISTRIBUTION (% of total population) 0–14 21%, 15–59 65%, 60+ 14% (2002 est)
ETHNIC GROUPS 65% ethnic Moldovan (Romanian), 14% Ukrainian, 13% ethnic Russian, 4% Gagauzi, 2% Bulgarian, 2% Jewish
LANGUAGE Moldovan (official), Russian, Gaganz (a Turkish dialect)
RELIGION Eastern Orthodox 98.5%; remainder Jewish
EDUCATION (compulsory years) 11
LITERACY RATE 99% (men); 99% (women) (2003 est)

LABOUR FORCE 48.9% agriculture, 13.6% industry, 37.5% services (1999)
LIFE EXPECTANCY 66 (men); 72 (women) (2000–05)
CHILD MORTALITY RATE (under 5, per 1,000 live births) 32 (2001)
PHYSICIANS (per 1,000 people) 3.5 (1999 est)
HOSPITAL BEDS (per 1,000 people) 12.1 (1999 est)
TV SETS (per 1,000 people) 296 (2001 est)
RADIOS (per 1,000 people) 758 (20001 est)
INTERNET USERS (per 10,000 people) 136.7 (2002 est)
PERSONAL COMPUTER USERS (per 100 people) 1.8 (2002 est)

See also ▷Bessarabia; ▷Ottoman Empire; ▷Union of Soviet Socialist Republics.

Chronology

AD 106: The current area covered by Moldova, which lies chiefly between the Prut River, bordering Romania in the west, and the Dniestr River, with Ukraine in the east, was conquered by the Roman Emperor Trajan and became part of the Roman province of Dacia. It was known in earlier times as Bessarabia.

mid-14th century: Formed part of an independent Moldovan principality, which included areas, such as Bukovina to the west, that are now part of Romania.

late 15th century: Under Stephen IV the Great the principality reached the height of its power.

16th century: Became a tributary of the Ottoman Turks.

1774–75: Moldovan principality, though continuing to recognize Turkish overlordship, was placed under Russian protectorship; Bukovina was lost to Austria.

1812: Bessarabia ceded to tsarist Russia.

1856: Remainder of Moldovan principality became largely independent of Turkish control.

1859: Moldovan Assembly voted to unite with Wallachia, to the southwest, to form the state of Romania, ruled by Prince Alexandru Ion Cuza. The state became fully independent in 1878.

1918: Following the Russian Revolution, Bessarabia was seized and incorporated within Romania.

1924: Moldovan autonomous Soviet Socialist Republic (SSR) created, as part of Soviet Union, comprising territory east of Dniestr River.

1940: Romania returned Bessarabia, east of Prut River, to Soviet Union, which divided it between Moldovan SSR and Ukraine, with Trans-Dniestr region transferred from Ukraine to Moldova.

1941: Moldovan SSR occupied by Romania and its wartime ally Germany.

1944: Red Army reconquered Bessarabia.

1946–47: Widespread famine as agriculture was collectivized; rich farmers and intellectuals were liquidated.

1950: Immigration by settlers from Russia and Ukraine as industries were developed.

late 1980s: There was an upsurge in Moldovan nationalism, encouraged by the *glasnost* initiative of reformist Soviet leader Mikhail Gorbachev.

1988: The Moldovan Movement in Support of Perestroika (economic restructuring) campaigned for accelerated political reform.

1989: There were nationalist demonstrations in Kishinev (now Chişinău). The Moldovan Popular Front (MPF) was founded; Moldovan was made the state language. There were campaigns for autonomy among ethnic Russians.

1990: The MPF polled strongly in parliamentary elections and Mircea Snegur, a reform-nationalist communist, became president. Economic and political sovereignty was declared.

1991: Independence was declared and the Communist Party outlawed after a conservative coup in Moscow against Gorbachev; joined Commonwealth of Independent States (CIS). There was insurrection in the Trans-Dniestr region.

1992: Admitted into United Nations and the Conference on Security and Cooperation in Europe; a peace agreement was signed with Russia to end the civil war in Trans-Dniestr, giving special status to the region. The MPF-dominated government fell; A 'government of national accord' was formed, headed by Andrei Sangheli and dominated by the ADP.

1993: A new currency, the leu, was introduced. A privatization programme was launched and closer ties were established with Russia.

1994: Parliamentary elections were won by the ADP. Plebiscite rejected nationalist demands for a merger with Romania. Russia agreed to withdraw Trans-Dniestr troops by 1997.

1995: Joined Council of Europe; economic growth resumed.

1996: Petru Lucinschi was elected president.

1997: A cooperation agreement was signed with the Dniestr region. A law was passed that provided for elections using proportional representation.

1999: A new coalition government was formed, headed by Ion Sturza. It fell in November, and Vladimir Voronin, a communist, succeeded as prime minister.

2000: Constitutional changes increased the powers of the Parlamentul (legislature) and the president was now to be elected by the legislature rather than the people. However, the incumbent president Lucinschi refused to stand, and neither of the two presidential candidates in the December contest were able to secure the required majority.

2001: The Communist Party regained power in parliamentary elections. Vladimir Voronin became president, and Vasile Tarlev became prime minister.

meant a person who spends several years working for a government department or a company with the intention of passing secrets to an enemy or a rival.

mole small burrowing mammal with typically dark, velvety fur. Moles grow up to 18 cm/7 in long, and have acute senses of hearing, smell, and touch, but poor eyesight. They have short, muscular forelimbs and shovel-like, clawed front feet for burrowing in search of insects, grubs, and worms. Their fur lies without direction so that they can move forwards or backwards in their tunnels without discomfort. Moles are greedy eaters; they cannot live more than a few hours without food. (Family Talpidae, order Insectivora.)

North American moles differ from those of the Old World in having tusklike front upper incisor teeth. The same ecological role is taken in Africa by the **golden moles** (family Chrysochloridae), and in Australia by **marsupial moles** (genus *Notoryctes*, order Marsupialia).

Some members of the Talpidae family are aquatic, such as the **Russian desman** (*Desmana moschata*) and the North American **star-nosed mole** (*Condylura cristata*).

The **common mole** of Europe (*Talpa europaea*) has a thickset body about 18 cm/7 in long with soft dark fur, a long pointed muzzle, short tail, broad, powerful five-clawed forelimbs and long, narrow hindlimbs. Practically blind, it lives underground in circular grass-lined nests, dug usually under banks or among the roots of trees, and excavates extensive tunnels, throwing up the earth at intervals in molehills.

mole cricket dark brown burrowing insect about 35–50 mm/1.5–2 in long, covered with soft hairs. Over 50 species of mole crickets have been identified. They feed mainly on worms and other insects.

molecular biology study of the molecular basis of life, including the biochemistry of molecules such as DNA, RNA, and proteins, and the molecular structure and function of the various parts of living cells.

molecular clock use of rates of ▷mutation in genetic material to calculate the length of time elapsed since two related species diverged from each other during evolution. The method can be based on comparisons of the DNA or of widely occurring proteins, such as haemoglobin.

molecular formula in chemistry, formula indicating the actual number of atoms of each element present in a single molecule of a chemical compound. This is determined by two pieces of information: the empirical ▷formula and the ▷relative molecular mass, which is determined experimentally.

molecular mass (or **relative molecular mass**) the mass of a molecule, calculated relative to one-twelfth the mass of an atom of carbon-12. It is found by adding the relative atomic masses of the atoms that make up the molecule.

molecular solid in chemistry, solid composed of molecules that are held together by relatively weak ▷intermolecular forces. Such solids are low-melting and tend to dissolve in organic solvents. Examples of molecular solids are sulphur, ice, sucrose, and solid carbon dioxide.

molecular weight see ▷relative molecular mass.

molecule molecules are the smallest particles of an element or compound that can exist independently. Hydrogen ▷atoms, at room temperature, do not exist independently. They are bonded in pairs to form hydrogen molecules. A molecule of a compound consists of two or more different atoms bonded together. Molecules vary in size and complexity from the hydrogen molecule (H_2) to the large ▷macromolecules of proteins. They may be held together by ionic bonds, in which the atoms gain or lose electrons to form ▷ions, or by covalent bonds, where electrons from each atom are shared in a new molecular orbital. Each compound is represented by a chemical symbol, indicating the elements into which it can be broken down and the number of each type of atom present. The symbolic representation of a molecule is known as its formula. For example, one molecule of the compound water, having two atoms of hydrogen and one atom of oxygen, is shown as H_2O.

Kinetic theory of matter According to the molecular or ▷kinetic theory of matter, matter is made up of molecules that are in a state of constant motion, the extent of which depends on their ▷temperature. Molecules also exert forces on one another. The nature and strength of these forces depends on the temperature and state of the matter (solid, liquid, or gas). The existence of molecules was first inferred from the Italian physicist Amedeo ▷Avogadro's hypothesis in 1811. He observed that when gases combine, they do so in simple proportions. For example, exactly one volume of oxygen and two volumes of hydrogen combine to produce water. He hypothesized that equal volumes of gases at the same temperature and ▷pressure contain equal numbers of molecules. Avogadro's hypothesis only became generally accepted in 1860 when proposed by the Italian chemist Stanislao ▷Cannizzaro. The movement of some molecules can be observed in a microscope. As early as 1827, Robert ▷Brown observed that very fine pollen grains suspended in water move about in a continuously agitated manner. This continuous, random motion of particles in a fluid medium (gas or liquid) as they are subjected to impact from the molecules of the medium is known as ▷Brownian movement. The spontaneous and random movement of molecules or particles in a fluid can also be observed as ▷diffusion occurs from a region in which they are at a high concentration to a region of lower concentration, until a uniform concentration is achieved throughout. No mechanical mixing or stirring is involved. For example, if a drop of ink is added to water, its molecules will diffuse until the colour becomes evenly distributed.

Kinetic theory of gases The effects of pressure, temperature, and ▷volume on a gas were investigated during the seventeenth and eighteenth centuries. ▷Boyle's law states that for a fixed mass of gas the volume of the gas is inversely proportional to the pressure at constant temperature. ▷Charles's law states that for a fixed mass of gas the volume of the gas is proportional to the absolute temperature at constant pressure. The pressure law states that the pressure of a fixed mass of gas at constant volume is directly proportional to its absolute temperature. These statements together give the ▷gas laws which can be expressed as:

$$(\text{pressure} \times \text{volume})/\text{temperature} = \text{constant}$$

A plot of the volume of a gas against its temperature gives a straight line, showing that the two are proportional. The line intercepts the x axis at −273°C/−459°F. This suggests that, if the gas did not liquefy first, it would occupy zero volume at a temperature of −273°C. This temperature is referred to as ▷absolute zero, or zero Kelvin (0K) on the ▷kelvin scale, and is the lowest temperature theoretically possible. This behaviour applies only to ideal gases, which are assumed to occupy negligible volume and contain negligible forces between particles. A real gas often behaves rather differently, and the ▷van der Waals' law contains a correction to the gas laws to account for the non-ideal behaviour of real gases.

> **Molière**
> *I assure you that a learned fool is more foolish than an ignorant fool.*
> Les Femmes Savantes IV. iii

Change of state As matter is heated its temperature may rise or it may cause a ▷change of state. As the internal energy of matter increases the energy possessed by each particle increases too. This can be visualized as the ▷kinetic energy of the molecules increasing, causing them to move more quickly. This movement includes both vibration within the molecule (assuming the substance is made of more than one atom) and rotation. A solid is made of particles that are held together by forces. As a solid is heated, the particles vibrate more vigorously, taking up more space, and causing the material to expand. As the temperature of the solid increases, it reaches its ▷melting point and turns into a liquid. The particles in a liquid can move around more freely but there are still forces between them. As further energy is added, the particles move faster until they are able to overcome the forces between them. When the ▷boiling point is reached the liquid boils and becomes a gas. Gas particles move around independently of one another except when they collide. Different objects require different amounts of heat energy to change their temperatures by the same amount. The ▷heat capacity of an object is the quantity of heat required to raise its temperature by one degree. The ▷specific heat capacity of a substance is the heat capacity per unit of mass, measured in joules per kilogram per Kelvin. As a substance is changing state while being heated, its temperature remains constant, provided that thermal energy is being added. For example, water boils at a constant temperature as it turns to steam. The energy required to cause the change of state is called ▷latent heat. This energy is used to break down the forces holding the particles together so that the change in state can occur. ▷Specific latent heat is the thermal energy required to change the state of a certain mass of that substance without any temperature change. ▷Evaporation causes cooling as a liquid vaporizes. Heat is transferred by the movement of particles (that possess kinetic energy) by conduction, convection, and radiation. ▷Conduction involves the movement of heat through a solid material by the movement of free electrons. ▷Convection involves the transfer of energy by the movement of fluid particles. ▷Convection currents are caused by the expansion of a liquid or gas as its temperature rises. The expanded material, being less dense, rises above colder and therefore denser material.

The size and shape of molecules The shape of a molecule profoundly affects its chemical, physical, and biological properties. Optical ▷isomers (molecules that are mirror images of each other) rotate plane ▷polarized light in opposite directions; isomers of drug molecules may have different biological effects; and ▷enzyme reactions are crucially dependent on the shape of the enzyme and the substrate on which it acts. A wheel-shaped molecule containing 700 atoms and with a relative molecular mass of about 24,000 was built by German chemists in 1995. Containing 154 ▷molybdenum atoms surrounded by oxygen atoms, it belongs to the class of compounds known as metal clusters.

Related Web site: Molecule of the Month http://www.bris.ac.uk/Depts/Chemistry/MOTM/motm.htm

mole rat, naked small underground mammal, almost hairless, with a disproportionately large head. The mole rat is of importance to zoologists as one of the very few mammals that are eusocial, that is, living in colonies with sterile workers and one fertile female. (Species *Heterocephalus glaber*.)

Its underground colonies comprise one breeding female and up to three breeding males in a colony of approximately 75 closely related animals, most being functionally sterile workers of either sex. The breeding female produces litters of around 25 pups.

Tool use has been observed in naked mole rats by US researchers in 1998. The animals hold a piece of tuber or wood in their mouths when gnawing anything that produces dust. This 'mask' lessens the amount of dust inhaled.

Molière (1622–1673) Pen-name of Jean-Baptiste Poquelin. French satirical dramatist and actor. Modern French comedy developed from his work. After the collapse of the Paris-based Illustre Théâtre (of which he was one of the founders), Molière performed in the provinces 1645–58. In 1655 he wrote his first play, *L'Etourdi/The Blunderer*, and on his return to Paris produced *Les Précieuses ridicules/The Affected Ladies* (1659). His satires include *L'Ecole des femmes/The School for Wives* (1662), *Le Misanthrope* (1666), *Le Bourgeois Gentilhomme/The Would-Be Gentleman* (1670), and *Le Malade imaginaire/The Imaginary Invalid* (1673). Other satiric plays include *Tartuffe* (1664) (banned for attacking the hypocrisy of the clergy; revised in 1667; banned again until 1699), *Le Médecin malgré lui/Doctor in Spite of Himself* (1666), and *Les Femmes savantes/The Learned Ladies* (1672).

Molière's art marked a new departure in the French theatre away from reliance on classical Greek themes. In his comedies the ideal hero of classical tragedy gave way to the flawed human individual with all his or her foibles and vices. Molière presents his characters firmly planted in their surroundings, not detached from them, and thus illuminates the whole group to which the character belongs. His chief aim seems to have been to amuse by depicting things as they really were, in strict truthfulness to life. It is uncertain whether he had any deliberate moral designs on his audiences by his exposure of hypocrisy and cant. However, there is little room for sympathy in the amusement evoked by his characters, and this made Molière vulnerable to many attacks (from which he was protected by Louis XIV).

mollusc any of a group of invertebrate animals, most of which have a body divided into three parts: a head, a central mass containing the main organs, and a foot for movement; the more

MOLLUSC Prior to mating, Roman snails *Helix pomatia* engage in a courtship dance during which each participant shoots a 'love dart' into the other's body. *Premaphotos Wildlife*

sophisticated octopuses and related molluscs have arms to capture their prey. The majority of molluscs are marine animals, but some live in fresh water, and a few live on dry land. They include clams, mussels, and oysters (bivalves), snails and slugs (gastropods), and cuttlefish, squids, and octopuses (cephalopods). The body is soft, without limbs (except for the cephalopods), and cold-blooded. There is no internal skeleton, but many species have a hard shell covering the body. (Phylum Mollusca.)

Molluscs have varying diets, the carnivorous species feeding mainly on other molluscs. Some are vegetarian. Reproduction is by means of eggs and is sexual; many species are hermaphrodite (having both male and female reproductive organs). The shells of molluscs take a variety of forms: single or univalve (like the snail), double or bivalve (like the clam), chambered (like the nautilus), and many other variations. In some cases (for example cuttlefish and squid), the shell is internal. Every mollusc has a fold of skin, the mantle, which covers either the whole body or only the back, and secretes the chalky substance that forms the shell. The lower ventral surface (belly area) of the body forms the foot, which enables the mollusc to move about.

Shellfish (oysters, mussels, clams) are commercially valuable, especially when artificially bred and 'farmed'. The Romans, and in the 17th century the Japanese, experimented with advanced methods of farming shellfish, and raft culture of oysters is now widely practised. The cultivation of pearls, pioneered by Kokichi Mikimoto, began in the 1890s and became an important export industry after World War I.

Molly Maguires, the in US history, a secret Irish coalminers' organization in the 1870s that staged strikes and used violence against coal-company officials and property in the anthracite fields of Pennsylvania, prefiguring a long period of turbulence in industrial relations. The movement was infiltrated by ▷Pinkerton agents (detectives), and in 1876 trials led to convictions and executions.

Moloch (or **Molech**) in the Old Testament, a Phoenician deity worshipped in Jerusalem in the 7th century BC, to whom live children were sacrificed by fire.

Molotov, Vyacheslav Mikhailovich (1890–1986) Adopted name of Vyacheslav Mikhailovich Skriabin. Soviet communist politician. He was chair of the Council of People's Commissars (prime minister) 1930–41 and foreign minister 1939–49 and 1953–56. He negotiated the 1939 non-aggression treaty with Germany (the ▷Ribbentrop–Molotov pact), and, after the German invasion in 1941, the Soviet partnership with the Allies. His post-war stance prolonged the Cold War and in 1957 he was expelled from the government for Stalinist activities.

VYACHESLAV MOLOTOV Vyacheslav Molotov (seated) signs the Soviet–German non-aggression treaty, the Ribbentrop–Molotov Pact, in August 1939, in the company of the Soviet leader, Joseph Stalin (right), and the German foreign minister, Joachim von Ribbentrop. Two years later, Germany invaded the USSR. *Archive Photos*

Molotov cocktail (or **petrol bomb**) home-made weapon consisting of a bottle filled with petrol, plugged with a rag as a wick, ignited, and thrown as a grenade. Resistance groups during World War II named them after the Soviet foreign minister Molotov.

Moltke, Helmuth Carl Bernhard, Count von Moltke (1800–1891) Prussian general. He became chief of the general staff in 1857, and was responsible for devising the highly effective strategy that brought Prussia swift victories in the wars with Denmark in 1863 to 1864, Austria in 1866 (the 'Seven Weeks' War'), and France in 1870 to 1871. He was made a count in 1870 and a field marshal in 1871.

Moluccas another name for ▷Maluku, a group of Indonesian islands.

molybdenite molybdenum sulphide, MoS_2, the chief ore mineral of molybdenum. It possesses a hexagonal crystal structure similar to graphite, has a blue metallic lustre, and is very soft (1–1.5 on Mohs scale).

molybdenum (Greek *molybdos* 'lead') heavy, hard, lustrous, silver-white, metallic element, symbol Mo, atomic number 42, relative atomic mass 95.94. The chief ore is the mineral molybdenite. The element is highly resistant to heat and conducts electricity easily. It is used in alloys, often to harden steels. It is a necessary trace element in human nutrition. It was named in 1781 by Swedish chemist Karl Scheele, after its isolation by P J Hjelm (1746–1813), for its resemblance to lead ore.

It has a melting point of 2,620°C, and is not found in the free state. As an aid to lubrication, molybdenum disulphide (MoS_2) greatly reduces surface friction between ferrous metals. Producing countries include Canada, the USA, and Norway.

Mombasa industrial port and tourist resort in Kenya (the port also serves Uganda and Tanzania); population (1998 est) 838,700. It stands on Mombasa Island and the adjacent mainland (the island of Mombasa is linked to the mainland by the Mukapa causeway). As well as tourism, current industries include car assembly. Mombasa was founded by Arab traders in the 11th century and was an important centre for ivory and slave trading until the 16th century. One of the oldest buildings, Fort Jesus, was set up by the Portugese and is now a museum.

moment of a force in physics, measure of the turning effect, or torque, produced by a force acting on a body. It is equal to the product of the force and the perpendicular distance from its line of action to the point, or pivot, about which the body will turn. Its unit is the newton metre.

moment of inertia in physics, the sum of all the point masses of a rotating object multiplied by the squares of their respective distances from the axis of rotation.

momentum the product of the mass of a body and its velocity. If the mass of a body is m kilograms and its velocity is v m s^{-1}, then its momentum is given by:

$$\text{momentum} = mv$$

Its unit is the kilogram metre-per-second (kg m s^{-1}) or the newton second. The momentum of a body does not change unless a resultant or unbalanced force acts on that body (see ▷Newton's laws of motion).

Mon (or **Talaing**) a minority ethnic group living in the Irrawaddy delta region of lower Myanmar (Burma) and Thailand. The Mon founded the city of Bago in 573 and established kingdoms in the area in the 7th century, but much of their culture was absorbed by invaders such as the Toungoo in 1539, and Alaungpaya, founder of the Konbaung dynasty, in 1757.

Mona Latin name for ▷Anglesey, an island off the northeast coast of Wales.

Monaco see country box.

Monagas, José Tadeo (1784–1868) Venezuelan president 1847–51 and 1855–58, a hero of the independence movement. Monagas wanted to create a separate state in eastern Venezuela called Oriente, leading an uprising against President José Antonio Páez 1831. He called it off in return for a pardon for his rebels. The Liberal Monagas clan gained power after the fall in 1847 of Páez's Conservative oligarchy. Monagas's brother José Gregorio was president 1851–55, and their 'Liberal oligarchy' was marked by a series of revolts led by Páez's supporters and by the disillusionment of their Liberal backers. José Tadeo was forced to resign in 1858.

Monaghan (Irish **Mhuineachain**) county of the Republic of Ireland, in the province of Ulster; county town Monaghan; area 1,290 sq km/498 sq mi; population (1996) 51,300. The county is low and rolling, with hills in the northwest, the highest point being Slieve Beagh (381 m/1,217 ft). The principal towns are Clones, Carrickmacross, and Castleblayney. Rivers include the Finn and the Glyde in the south, and the Blackwater in the north. Much of the county is fertile. The main form of agriculture is dairy farming, but cattle and pigs are also raised, and cereals and potatoes grown. Industries include leather, linen, knitwear, footwear, furniture, and lacemaking.

Mona Lisa, the (or ***La Gioconda***) oil painting by ▷Leonardo da Vinci (1503–05; Louvre, Paris), a portrait of the wife of a Florentine official, Francesco del Giocondo, which, according to ▷Vasari, Leonardo worked on for four years. It was the first Italian portrait to extend below waist level, setting a precedent for composition that was to dominate portraiture until the 19th century. In the *Mona Lisa* Leonardo brought his technique of *sfumato* (avoiding sharp outlines through gentle gradations of colour) to perfection.

monasticism devotion to religious life under vows of poverty, chastity, and obedience, known to Judaism (for example ▷Essenes), Buddhism, and other religions, before Christianity. In Islam, the Sufis formed monastic orders from the 12th century.

monazite mineral, $(Ce,La,Th)PO_4$, yellow to red, valued as a source of ▷lanthanides or rare earths, including cerium and europium; generally found in placer deposit (alluvial) sands.

Monck, George (1608–1670) 1st Duke of Albemarle; or **Monk**. English soldier. During the English Civil War he fought for King Charles I, but after being captured changed sides and took command of the Parliamentary forces in Ireland. Under Oliver ▷Cromwell he became commander-in-chief in Scotland, and in 1660 he led his army into England and brought about the ▷Restoration of ▷Charles II. He became duke in 1660.

Mondale, Walter Frederick (1928–) US Democrat politician, unsuccessful presidential candidate In 1984. He was a senator 1965–77 for his home state of Minnesota, and vice president to Jimmy Carter 1977–81. After losing the 1984 presidential election to Ronald Reagan, Mondale retired from national politics to resume his law practice.

Mondrian, Piet (Pieter Cornelis Mondriaan) (1872–1944) Dutch painter. A founder member of the De ▷Stijl movement, he was the chief exponent of neoplasticism, a rigorous abstract style based on the use of simple geometric forms and pure colours. Typically his works are frameworks of horizontal and vertical lines forming rectangles of white, red, yellow, and blue, as in *Composition in Red, Yellow and Blue* (1920; Stedelijk, Amsterdam).

Born in Amersfoort, he studied art in Amsterdam and in 1911 went to Paris where he was strongly influenced by ▷cubism. Returning to the Netherlands during World War I, he executed a series of still lifes and landscapes to refine his ideas, ultimately developing a pure abstract style. He lived in Paris 1919–38, then in London, and from 1940 in New York. His aesthetic theories – which were in part based on the spiritualist theories of the Theosophists – were published in the journal *De Stijl* from 1917, in *Neo-Plasticism* (1920), and in the essay 'Plastic Art and Pure Plastic Art' (1937). From the New York period his *Broadway Boogie-Woogie* (1942–43; Museum of Modern Art, New York) reflects a late preoccupation with jazz rhythms.

Monet, Claude (1840–1926) French painter. He was a pioneer of Impressionism and a lifelong exponent of its ideals; his painting *Impression, Sunrise* (1872) gave the movement its name. In the 1870s he began painting the same subjects at different times of day to explore the ever-changing effects of light on colour and form; the *Haystacks* and *Rouen Cathedral* series followed in the 1890s, and from 1899 he painted a series of *Water Lilies* in the garden of his house at Giverny, Normandy (now a museum).

He spent his youth at Le Havre, where he was diverted from caricature to open-air landscape painting by the encouragement of ▷Boudin. Boudin and Jongkind, with whom Monet became friendly in 1860, had taught him much about atmosphere before he went in 1862 to Gleyre's studio in Paris, where he met Renoir, Sisley, and Bazille. He painted with them in the forest of Fontainebleau and until 1870 was engaged in perfecting a new approach to which the realism of Courbet and the direct method of Manet both contributed, as may be seen in the beautiful *Femmes au Jardin* (1867; Louvre), and the Manetesque *Plage à Trouville.* (1870; Tate). A wartime interlude followed, spent in Holland and London, where he admired the works of Turner. He worked at Argenteuil 1872–78, where he had a floating studio, his mature method of rendering light in colour being now fully developed. His *Impression* in the exhibition of 1874, in which he and his friends appeared as a fairly homogeneous group, brought the term Impressionism into currency for the first time. He painted at Vétheuil 1878–83, and afterwards settled at Giverny, where in the garden of his house he painted his last remarkable studies of water lilies. Almost abstract visions of colour, these studies were long regarded dubiously as the most formless of his works, but have been hailed in recent years as outstanding examples of pure painting.

monetarism economic policy that proposes control of a country's money supply to keep it in step with the country's ability to produce goods, with the aim of curbing inflation. Cutting

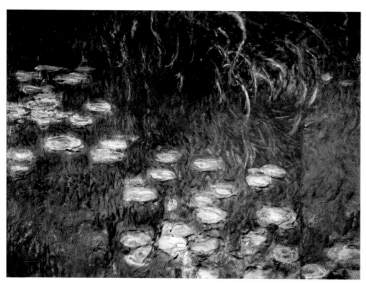

CLAUDE MONET For the last 27 years or so of his life, Monet painted virtually nothing but studies of water lilies, of which this is an example. As Monet's eyesight gradually failed, so the average size of the paintings increased and the water lilies became progressively less realistic. The majority of these works now form a special collection in Paris, France. *The Art Archive/ JW and P Guillaume Coll Paris/Dagli Orti*

AD 800). Developments such as the cheque and credit card fulfil many of the traditional functions of money. In 1994 Mondex electronic money was introduced experimentally in Swindon, Wiltshire, England.

Related Web site: History of Money from Ancient Times to the Present Day http://www.ex.ac.uk/~RDavies/arian/llyfr.html

money market institution that deals in gold and foreign exchange, and securities in the short term. Long-term transactions are dealt with on the capital market. There is no physical marketplace, and many deals are made by telephone or telex.

money supply quantity of money in circulation in an economy at any given time. It can include notes, coins, and clearing-bank and other deposits used for everyday payments. Changes in the quantity of lending are a major determinant of changes in the money supply. One of the main principles of ▷monetarism is that increases in the money supply in excess of the rate of economic growth are the chief cause of inflation.

In Britain there are several definitions of money supply. M0 was defined as notes and coins in circulation, together with the operational balance of clearing banks with the Bank of England. The M1 definition encompasses M0 plus current account deposits; M2, now rarely used, covers the M1 items plus deposit accounts; M3 covers M2 items plus all other deposits held by UK citizens and companies in the UK banking sector. In May 1987 the Bank of England introduced new terms including M4 (M3 plus building society deposits) and M5 (M4 plus Treasury bills and local authority deposits).

Mongol member of any of the various Mongol (or Mongolian) ethnic groups of central Asia. Mongols live in Mongolia, Russia, Inner Mongolia (China), Tibet, and Nepal. The Mongol language

government spending is advocated, and the long-term aim is to return as much of the economy as possible to the private sector, allegedly in the interests of efficiency. Monetarism was first advocated by the economist Milton Friedman and the Chicago school of economists.

monetary policy economic policy aimed at controlling the amount of money in circulation, usually through controlling the level of lending or credit. Increasing interest rates is an example of a contractionary monetary policy, which aims to reduce inflation by reducing the rate of growth of spending in the economy.

money any common medium of exchange acceptable in payment for goods or services or for the settlement of debts; legal tender. Money is usually coinage (invented by the Chinese in the second millennium BC) and paper notes (used by the Chinese from about

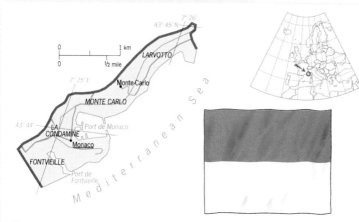

Monaco small sovereign state forming an enclave in southern France, with the Mediterranean Sea to the south.

ETHNIC GROUPS 47% French; 10% Monégasque; 20% Italian and other European
LANGUAGE French (official), Monégasgne

1191: The Genoese took control of Monaco, formerly part of the Holy Roman Empire.
1297: Came under the rule of the Grimaldi dynasty, the current ruling family, who initially allied themselves to the French.
1524–1641: Came under Spanish protection.
1793: Annexed by France during French Revolutionary Wars. One member of the ruling family was guillotined; the rest imprisoned.
1815: Placed under protection of Sardinia.
1848: The towns of Menton and Roquebrune, which had formed the greater part of the principality, seceded and later became part of France.
1861: Franco-Monegasque treaty restored Monaco's independence under French protection; the first casino was built.
1865: Customs union established with France.

(a mixture of the French Provençal and Italian Ligurian dialects), Italian
RELIGION Roman Catholic about 90%
EDUCATION (compulsory years) 10

1918: France given veto over succession to throne and established that if a reigning prince dies without a male heir, Monaco is to be incorporated into France.
1941–45: Occupied successively by Italians and Germans during World War II.
1949: Prince Rainier III ascended the throne.
1956: Prince Rainier married US actor Grace Kelly.
1958: Birth of male heir, Prince Albert.
1962: A new, more liberal constitution was adopted.
1982: Princess Grace died in a car accident.
1993: Joined United Nations.
1998: Michel Leveque was appointed head of government.
2000: Patrick Leclerq replaced Michel Leveque as minister of state. France threatened to take punitive measures against Monaco unless it took action against money-laundering and tax-evasion.

NATIONAL NAME *Principauté de Monaco/Principality of Monaco*
AREA 1.95 sq km/0.75 sq mi
PHYSICAL FEATURES steep and rugged; surrounded landwards by French territory; being expanded by filling in the sea

Government

HEAD OF STATE Prince Rainier III from 1949
HEAD OF GOVERNMENT Patrick Leclercq from 2000
POLITICAL SYSTEM liberal democracy
POLITICAL EXECUTIVE parliamentary
ADMINISTRATIVE DIVISIONS four districts: Monaco-Ville, Monte Carlo, La Condamine, Fontvieille
ARMED FORCES no standing defence forces; defence is the responsibility of France
DEATH PENALTY abolished in 1962

Economy and resources

CURRENCY euro
GPD (US$) 890 million (2001)
REAL GDP GROWTH (% change on previous year) 2.2 (2001)
GNI PER CAPITA (PPP) (US$) 27,500 (2001)

UNEMPLOYMENT 3.2% (2000)
MAJOR TRADING PARTNERS full customs integration with France (for external trade figures, see France)
INDUSTRIES chemicals, pharmaceuticals, plastics, microelectronics, electrical goods, paper, textiles and clothing, gambling, banking and finance, real estate, tourism (which provides an estimated 25% of Monaco's annual revenue)
IMPORTS AND EXPORTS largely dependent on imports from France; full customs integration with France
AGRICULTURAL PRODUCTS no agricultural land; some fish farming

Population and society

POPULATION 34,000 (2003 est)
POPULATION GROWTH RATE 0.9% (2000–05)
POPULATION DENSITY (per sq km) 23,090 (2003 est)
URBAN POPULATION (% of total) 100 (2003 est)
AGE DISTRIBUTION (% of total population) 0–14 15%, 15–59 62%, 60+ 23% (2002 est)

MONACO A view over the principality of Monaco from the grounds of the royal palace. *Corel*

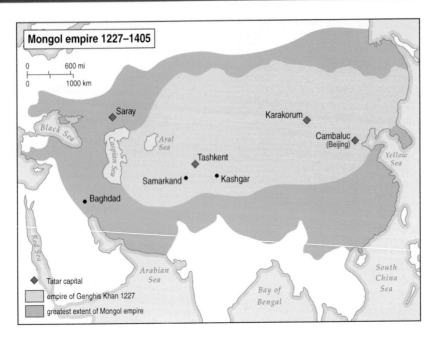

Mongol empire 1227–1405

| 0 | 600 mi |
| 0 | 1000 km |

◆ Tatar capital

☐ empire of Genghis Khan 1227

▨ greatest extent of Mongol empire

belongs to the Altaic family, although some groups of Mongol descent speak languages in the Sino-Tibetan family.

Mongol Empire empire established by ▷Genghis Khan, a loosely constructed federation of tribal groups extending from Russia to northern China; see ▷Mongol.

History Genghis became khan of the Mongol tribes in 1206. Divided by his sons at his death in 1227, Ogotai overcame the Jin and Sun dynasties of China in 1234, and another son, Batu, occupied Russia, parts of Hungary, and Georgia and Armenia, establishing the Kipchak Empire and other khanates. The Western Kipchaks, known as the ▷Golden Horde terrorized Europe from 1237. Genghis's grandson ▷Kublai Khan conquered China and used foreigners (such as the Venetian traveller Marco Polo) as well as subjects to administer his empire. Another grandson, Hulagu, conquered Baghdad and Syria. The Mongols lost China in 1367 and suffered defeats in the west in 1380; the empire broke up soon afterwards, fragmenting into separate chiefdoms.

    Related Web site: Mongol Invasion of Europe
    http://www.thehistorynet.
    com/MilitaryHistory/articles/1997/06972_text.htm

Mongolia see country box.

Mongolia, Inner (Chinese Nei Mongol) autonomous region of north China from 1947; bounded to the north by Mongolia and Russia; to the east by Heilongjiang and Jilin; to the southeast by Liaoning; to the south by Hebei, Shanxi, Shaanxi, and Ningxia Hui Autonomous Region; and to the west by Gansu; area 1,200,00 sq km/463,300 sq mi; population (1996) 23,070,000; less than one-sixth are Mongols. The capital is ▷Hohhot, and Baotou is a town in the region. The region is characterized by grassland and desert. Industries include coal; reserves of iron ore, rare earth oxides europium, and yttrium at Bayan Obo; woollen textiles; dairy-processing; and leather. Agricultural products include cereals under irrigation, animal husbandry, and forestry.

mongolism former name (now considered offensive) for ▷Down's syndrome.

mongoose any of a group of carnivorous tropical mammals. The **Indian mongoose** (*H. mungo*) is greyish in colour and about 50 cm/1.5 ft long, with a long tail. It can be tamed and is often kept

MONGOOSE The ring-tailed mongoose *Galidia elegans* is found in Madagascar where it is active by day in both wet and dry forests. *Premaphotos Wildlife*

for its ability to kill snakes. Like the snakes themselves, the acetylcholine receptors connecting the mongooses' nerves and muscle cells are unaffected by the venom. (Genera *Herpestes*, *Ichneumia*, and other related genera, family Viverridae.)

    Most mongooses are solitary, but the **banded mongoose** *Mungos mungo* is highly gregarious, living in groups of 15–40 individuals. They feed on small reptiles and invertebrates and spend about 60% of their day foraging.

    The **white-tailed mongoose** (*I. albicauda*) of central Africa has a distinctive grey or white bushy tail.

monism in philosophy, the theory that reality is made up of only one substance. This view is usually contrasted with ▷dualism, which divides reality into two substances, matter and mind. The Dutch philosopher Baruch Spinoza saw the one substance as God or Nature. Monism is also sometimes used as a description of a political system in which only one party is permitted to operate.

monitor any of various lizards found in Africa, South Asia, and Australasia. Monitors are generally large and carnivorous, with well-developed legs and claws and a long powerful tail that can be swung in defence. (Family Varanidae.)

    Monitors include the **Komodo dragon** (*Varanus komodoensis*), the largest of all lizards, and also the slimmer **Salvador's monitor** (*V. salvadorii*), which may reach 2.5 m/8 ft. Several other monitors, such as the **lace monitor** (*V. varius*), the **perentie** (*V. giganteus*) of Australia, and the **Nile monitor** (*V. niloticus*) of Africa, are up to 2 m/6 ft long.

monk man belonging to a religious order under the vows of poverty, chastity, and obedience, and living under a particular rule; see ▷monasticism.

Monk, Thelonious Sphere (1917–1982) US jazz pianist and composer. He took part in the development of ▷bebop. He had a highly idiosyncratic style, but numbers such as 'Round Midnight' and 'Blue Monk' have become standards. Monk worked in Harlem, New York, during the Depression, and became popular in the 1950s.

monkey any of the various smaller, mainly tree-dwelling anthropoid ▷primates, excluding humans and the ▷apes. There are 125 species, living in Africa, Asia, and tropical Central and South America. Monkeys eat mainly leaves and fruit, and also small animals. Several species are endangered due to loss of forest habitat, for example the woolly spider monkey and black saki of the Amazonian forest.

    Old World monkeys (family Cercopithecidae) of tropical Africa and Asia are distinguished by their close-set nostrils and differentiated thumbs, some also having cheek pouches and rumps with bare patches (callosities) of hardened skin. They include ▷baboons, ▷langurs, ▷macaques, and guenons.

    New World monkeys of Central and South America are characterized by wide-set nostrils, and some have highly sensitive prehensile tails that can be used as additional limbs, to grasp and hold branches or objects. They include two families:

    (1) the family Cebidae, which includes the larger species saki, ▷capuchin, squirrel, howler, and spider monkeys;

    (2) the family Callithricidae, which includes the small ▷marmosets and tamarins.

    Related Web site: Heather's Wild World http://members.
primary.net/~heather/

monkey puzzle (or Chilean pine) coniferous evergreen tree, native to Chile; its branches, growing in circular arrangements (whorls) around the trunk and larger branches, are covered in prickly, leathery leaves. (*Araucaria araucana*, family Araucariaceae.)

Monmouth, James Scott, 1st Duke of Monmouth (1649–1685) Claimant to the English crown, the illegitimate son of Charles II and Lucy Walter. After James II's accession in 1685, Monmouth landed in England at Lyme Regis, Dorset, claimed the crown, and raised a rebellion, which was crushed at ▷Sedgemoor in Somerset. He was executed with 320 of his accomplices. He was made duke in 1663.

    When ▷James II converted to Catholicism, the Whig opposition attempted unsuccessfully to secure Monmouth the succession to the crown by the Exclusion Bill, and having become implicated in a Whig conspiracy, the ▷Rye House Plot in 1683, he fled to Holland.

Monmouthshire (Welsh Trefynwy) unitary authority in southeast Wales. A former county, between 1974 and 1996 it became (except for a small area on the border with Mid Glamorgan) the county of Gwent.

    area 851 sq km/328 sq mi **towns** Cwmbran (administrative headquarters), ▷Chepstow **physical** rivers ▷Wye and Usk; mountainous in north **features** ▷Chepstow and Raglan castles, Tintern Abbey, salmon and trout fishing; peak of Pen-y-Fal or Sugar Loaf (596 m/1,955 ft) **agriculture** lowlands have rich mixed farming, with arable crops, including wheat, being important **population** (1996) 80,400

monocarpic (or hapaxanthic) describing plants that flower and produce fruit only once during their life cycle, after which they die. Most ▷annual plants and ▷biennial plants are monocarpic, but there are also a small number of monocarpic ▷perennial plants that flower just once, sometimes after as long as 90 years, dying shortly afterwards, for example, century plant *Agave* and some species of bamboo *Bambusa*. The general biological term related to organisms that reproduce only once during their lifetime is ▷semelparity.

monoclonal antibody (MAB) antibody produced by fusing an antibody-producing lymphocyte with a cancerous myeloma (bone-marrow) cell. The resulting fused cell, called a hybridoma, is immortal and can be used to produce large quantities of a single, specific antibody. By choosing antibodies that are directed against antigens found on cancer cells, and combining them with cytotoxic drugs, it is hoped to make so-called magic bullets that will be able to pick out and kill cancers.

monocotyledon angiosperm (flowering plant) having an embryo with a single cotyledon, or seed leaf (as opposed to ▷dicotyledons, which have two). Monocotyledons usually have narrow leaves with parallel veins and smooth edges, and hollow or soft stems. Their flower parts are arranged in threes. Most are small plants such as orchids, grasses, and lilies, but some are trees such as palms.

Monod, Jacques Lucien (1910–1976) French biochemist who was awarded a Nobel Prize for Physiology or Medicine in 1965 with his co-workers André Lwoff and François ▷Jacob for research into the genetic control of enzyme and virus synthesis.

MONKEY Snow monkeys in Nagano, Japan. *Image Bank*

monoecious having separate male and female flowers on the same plant. Maize (*Zea mays*), for example, has a tassel of male flowers at the top of the stalk and a group of female flowers (on the ear, or cob) lower down. Monoecism is a way of avoiding self-fertilization.

    Dioecious plants have male and female flowers on separate plants.

monogamy practice of having only one husband or wife at a time in ▷marriage.

monolith (Greek *monos* 'sole', *lithos* 'stone') single isolated stone or column, usually standing and of great size, used as a form of monument. Some are natural features, such as the Buck Stone in the Forest of Dean, England. Other monoliths may be quarried, resited, finished, or carved; those in Egypt of about 3000 BC take the form of ▷obelisks. They have a wide distribution including Europe, South America, North Africa, and the Middle East.

monologue one person speaking, though the term is generally understood to mean a virtuoso solo performance. Literary monologues are often set pieces in which a character reveals his or her personality, sometimes unintentionally (as in the dramatic monologue); in drama the soliloquy performs a similar function.

A monologue can occur in a dialogue; for example, in a conversation where one person suddenly launches into a lengthy anecdote.

monomer chemical compound composed of simple molecules from which ▷polymers can be made. Under certain conditions the simple molecules (of the monomer) join together (polymerize) to form a very long chain molecule (macromolecule) called a polymer. For example, the polymerization of ethene (ethylene) monomers produces the polymer polyethene (polyethylene).

$$2n\text{CH}_2 = \text{CH}_2 \rightarrow (\text{CH}_2-\text{CH}_2-\text{CH}_2-\text{CH}_2)_n$$

monophonic music in a single melodic part, without harmony, as distinct from homophonic, which is melodic music accompanied by harmony, or polyphonic, which is music in a number of melodic parts moving simultaneously.

Monophysite (Greek 'one-nature') member of a group of Christian heretics of the 5th–7th centuries who taught that Jesus had one nature, in opposition to the orthodox doctrine (laid down at the Council of Chalcedon in 451) that he had two natures, the human and the divine. Monophysitism developed as a reaction to ▷Nestorianism and led to the formal secession of the Coptic and

Mongolia

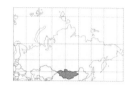

Mongolia formerly Outer Mongolia (until 1924), People's Republic of Mongolia (1924–91) country in east-Central Asia, bounded north by Russia and south by China.

NATIONAL NAME *Mongol Uls/State of Mongolia*
AREA 1,565,000 sq km/604,246 sq mi
CAPITAL Ulaanbaatar
MAJOR TOWNS/CITIES Darhan, Choybalsan, Erdenet
PHYSICAL FEATURES high plateau with desert and steppe (grasslands); Altai Mountains in southwest; salt lakes; part of Gobi desert in southeast; contains both the world's southernmost permafrost and northernmost desert

Government

HEAD OF STATE Natsagiyn Bagabandi from 1997
HEAD OF GOVERNMENT Nambaryn Enkhbayar from 2000
POLITICAL SYSTEM emergent democracy
POLITICAL EXECUTIVE limited presidency
ADMINISTRATIVE DIVISIONS 21 provinces and one municipality (Ulaanbaatar)
ARMED FORCES 9,100; plus paramilitary forces of 7,200 (2002 est)
CONSCRIPTION military service is compulsory for 12 months
DEATH PENALTY retained and used for ordinary crimes
DEFENCE SPEND (% GDP) 2.2 (2002 est)
EDUCATION SPEND (% GDP) 8.7 (2002 est)
HEALTH SPEND (% GDP) 6.6 (2000 est)

Economy and resources

CURRENCY tugrik
GPD (US$) 1.3 billion (2002 est)
REAL GDP GROWTH (% change on previous year) 1.1 (2001)
GNI (US$) 1.1 billion (2002 est)
GNI PER CAPITA (PPP) (US$) 1,650 (2002 est)
CONSUMER PRICE INFLATION 5% (2003 est)
UNEMPLOYMENT 4.6% (2001)
FOREIGN DEBT (US$) 887 million (2001 est)
MAJOR TRADING PARTNERS Russia, China, Japan, South Korea, Germany, USA, Italy
RESOURCES copper, nickel, zinc, molybdenum, phosphorites, tungsten, tin, fluorospar, gold, lead; reserves of petroleum discovered in 1994
INDUSTRIES mostly small-scale; food products, copper and molybdenum

concentrates, cement, lime, wood and metal-worked products, beverages, leather articles
EXPORTS minerals and metals (primarily copper concentrate), consumer goods, foodstuffs, agricultural products. Principal market: China 58.9% (2000)
IMPORTS mineral fuels and products, engineering goods, vehicles, industrial consumer goods, foodstuffs. Principal source: Russia 33.6% (2000)
ARABLE LAND 0.8% (2000 est)
AGRICULTURAL PRODUCTS wheat, oats, barley, potatoes, vegetables; animal herding (particularly cattle rearing) is country's main economic activity (there were 28.6 million

MONGOLIA A Mongolian woman in traditional costume at the Nadam Fair. This fair takes place every autumn and people gather to compete in traditional Mongolian arts such as archery, horse racing, and wrestling. It is also known as the Yurt fair, a yurt being a type of tent used by nomadic peoples of Central Asia. *Image Bank*

cattle, sheep, goats, horses, and camels in 1995)

Population and society

POPULATION 2,594,000 (2003 est)
POPULATION GROWTH RATE 1.3% (2000–15)
POPULATION DENSITY (per sq km) 2 (2003 est)
URBAN POPULATION (% of total) 57 (2003 est)
AGE DISTRIBUTION (% of total population) 0–14 33%, 15–59 61%, 60+ 6% (2002 est)
ETHNIC GROUPS 91% Mongol, 6% Kazakh;

Chronology

AD 1206: Nomadic Mongol tribes united by Genghis Khan to form nucleus of vast Mongol Empire which, stretching across central Asia, reached its zenith under Genghis Khan's grandson, Kublai Khan.
late 17th century: Conquered by China to become province of Outer Mongolia.
1911: Independence proclaimed by Mongolian nationalists after Chinese 'republican revolution'; tsarist Russia helped Mongolia to secure autonomy, under a traditionalist Buddhist monarchy in the form of a reincarnated lama.
1915: Chinese sovereignty reasserted.
1921: Chinese rule overthrown with Soviet help.
1924: People's Republic proclaimed on death of king, when the monarchy was abolished; defeudalization programme launched, entailing collectivization of agriculture and suppression of lama Buddhism.
1932: Armed antigovernment uprising suppressed with Soviet assistance; 100,000 killed in political purges.
1946: China recognized Mongolia's independence.
1952: Death of Marshal Horloogiyn Choybalsan, the dominant force in the ruling communist Mongolian People's Revolutionary Party (MPRP) since 1939.
1958: Yumjaagiyn Tsedenbal became the dominant figure in MPRP and country.
1962: Joined Comecon.
1966: 20-year friendship, cooperation, and mutual-assistance pact signed with Soviet Union (USSR). Relations with China deteriorated.
1987: There was a reduction in the number of Soviet troops; Mongolia's external contacts broadened. The tolerance of traditional social customs encouraged a nationalist revival.

very small groups of Russian (2,000) and Chinese (1,500)
LANGUAGE Khalkha Mongolian (official), Kazakh (in the province of Bagan-Ölgiy), Chinese, Russian, Turkic languages
RELIGION there is no state religion, but traditional lamaism (Mahayana Buddhism) is gaining new strength; the Sunni Muslim Kazakhs of Western Mongolia have also begun the renewal of their religious life, and Christian missionary activity has increased
EDUCATION (compulsory years) 8
LITERACY RATE 99% (men); 98% (women) (2003 est)
LABOUR FORCE 48.7% agriculture, 14.1% industry, 37.2% services (2000)
LIFE EXPECTANCY 62 (men); 66 (women) (2000–05)
CHILD MORTALITY RATE (under 5, per 1,000 live births) 76 (2001)
PHYSICIANS (per 1,000 people) 2.7 (2001 est)
HOSPITAL BEDS (per 1,000 people) 7.4 (2001 est)
TV SETS (per 1,000 people) 72 (2001 est)
RADIOS (per 1,000 people) 50 (2001 est)
INTERNET USERS (per 10,000 people) 205.9 (2002 est)
PERSONAL COMPUTER USERS (per 100 people) 2.8 (2002 est)

See also ▷Genghis Khan; ▷Lamaism; ▷Mongol.

1989: Further Soviet troop reductions.
1990: A demonstrations and democratization campaign was launched, influenced by events in Eastern Europe. Ex-communist MPRP elected in the first free multiparty elections; Punsalmaagiyn Ochirbat was indirectly elected president. Mongolian script was readopted.
1991: A privatization programme was launched. GDP declined by 10%.
1992: The MPRP returned to power in assembly elections held under a new, noncommunist constitution. The economic situation worsened; GDP again declined by 10%.
1993: Ochirbat won the first direct presidential elections.
1996: The economy showed signs of revival. The Union Coalition won assembly elections, defeating the MPRP and ending 75 years of communist rule. A defence cooperation agreement was signed with the USA.
1997: The ex-communist Natsagiyn Bagabandi was elected MPRP chairman and then became president. An economic shock therapy programme, supervised by IMF and World Bank, created unemployment and made the government unpopular. All taxes and tariffs on trade were abolished.
1998: The National Democratic Party (DU) government was toppled after losing a no-confidence vote. Attempts to form a new DU-led government, led by Rinchinnyamiyn Amarjargal, failed, and Janlaviyn Narantsatsralt of the MNDP became prime minister.
1999: Rinchinnyamiyn Marajargal became prime minister.
2000: Mongolia's former communists, the MPRP, now branding themselves a centre-left party, won a landslide victory in parliamentary elections, led by Nambariin Enkhbayar.

Armenian churches from the rest of the Christian church. Monophysites survive today in Armenia, Syria, and Egypt.

Monopolies and Mergers Commission (MMC) UK government body re-established in 1973 under the Fair Trading Act and, since 1980, embracing the Competition Act. Its role is to investigate and report when there is a risk of creating a monopoly by a company merger or takeover, or when a newspaper or newspaper assets are transferred. It also investigates companies, nationalized industries, or local authorities that are suspected of operating in a noncompetitive way.

Monopoly the world's biggest-selling copyrighted game, a board game of buying properties, building houses on them, and charging rent. It was devised in the USA in 1934 by Charles B Darrow (1889–1967), with street names from Atlantic City, New Jersey, where he spent his holidays; he sold the game in 1935 to Parker Brothers, US game manufacturers, for a royalty.

monopoly in economics, the domination of a market for a particular product or service by a single company, which can therefore restrict competition and keep prices high. In practice, a company can be said to have a monopoly when it controls a significant proportion of the market (technically an ▷oligopoly). In a communist country the state itself has the overall monopoly; in capitalist countries some services, such as transport or electricity supply, may be state monopolies.

monorail railway that runs on a single rail; the cars can be balanced on it or suspended from it. It was invented in 1882 to carry light loads, and when run by electricity was called a **telpher**.

monosaccharide (or **simple sugar**) ▷carbohydrate that cannot be hydrolysed (split) into smaller carbohydrate units. Examples are glucose and fructose, both of which have the molecular formula $C_6H_{12}O_6$.

monosodium glutamate (MSG) $NaC_5H_8NO_4$ a white, crystalline powder, the sodium salt of glutamic acid (an ▷amino acid found in proteins that plays a role in the metabolism of plants and animals). It has no flavour of its own, but enhances the flavour of foods such as meat and fish. It is used to enhance the flavour of many packaged and 'fast foods', and in Chinese cooking. Ill effects may arise from its overconsumption, and some people are very sensitive to it, even in small amounts. It is commercially derived from vegetable protein. It occurs naturally in soybeans and seaweed.

monotheism (Greek *monos* 'sole', *theos* 'god') belief or doctrine that there is only one God; the opposite of polytheism.

Monotheism is also opposed to all systems of moral dualism, asserting the ultimate supremacy of good over evil. The Jewish, Muslim, and Christian religions are strictly monotheistic. Monotheism differs from Deism in that it asserts that God is not only the creator of the universe and the source of the laws of nature, but is also constantly active and concerned in the world.

It is the unifying theme of the Old Testament. See also ▷religion.

Monothelite member of a group of Christian heretics of the 7th century who sought to reconcile the orthodox and ▷Monophysite theologies by maintaining that, while Christ possessed two natures, he had only one will. Monothelitism was condemned as a heresy by the Third Council of Constantinople in 680.

monotreme any of a small group of primitive egg-laying mammals, found in Australasia. They include the ▷echidnas (spiny anteaters) and the ▷platypus. (Order Monotremata.)

In 1995 Australian palaeontologists announced a new (extinct) family of monotreme, the Kollikodontidae, following the discovery of a 120-million-year-old jawbone in New South Wales.

Monroe, James (1758–1831) 5th president of the USA 1817–25, a Democratic Republican. He served in the American Revolution, was minister to France 1794–96, and in 1803 negotiated the ▷Louisiana Purchase. He was secretary of state 1811–14 and 1815–17, and secretary of war 1814–15. His name is associated with the ▷Monroe Doctrine.

Monroe served in the legislature of his native Virginia in 1782, and represented Virginia along with Thomas ▷Jefferson in the Continental Congress 1783–86. Monroe opposed ratification of the constitution when it came before the Virginia ratifying convention in 1788, fearing a central government with excessive power. He was a member of the US Senate 1790–94 and governor of Virginia 1799–1802. As president, he presided over the so-called Era of Good Feeling, a period of domestic tranquillity. He took no firm stand on the question of slavery, making his mark in foreign policy.

Related Web site: James Monroe – Fifth President 1817–1825 http://www.whitehouse.gov/WH/glimpse/presidents/html/jm5.html

Monroe, Marilyn (1926–1962) Stage name of Norma Jean Mortenson. US film actor. The voluptuous blonde sex symbol of the 1950s, she made adroit comedies such as *Gentlemen Prefer Blondes* (1953), *How to Marry a Millionaire* (1953), *The Seven Year Itch* (1955), *Bus Stop* (1956), and *Some Like It Hot* (1959).

In *Niagara* (1953) she had one of her first starring roles, as a *femme fatale* who plans to murder her husband; *River of No Return* (1954) was a Western; and in *The Prince and the Showgirl* (1957) she co-starred with Laurence Olivier. Her third husband was the playwright Arthur ▷Miller, who wrote *The Misfits* (1960) for her, a serious film that became her last. She died as a result of an overdose of sleeping pills.

Related Web site: Marilyn Pages http://www.ionet.net/~jellenc/marilyn.html

Monroe Doctrine declaration by US president James ▷Monroe in 1823 that any further European colonial ambitions in the Western hemisphere would be regarded as threats to US peace and security, made in response to proposed European intervention against newly independent former Spanish colonies in South America. In return for the quietening of such European ambitions, the USA would not interfere in European affairs. The doctrine, subsequently broadened, has been a recurrent theme in US foreign policy, although it has no basis in US or international law.

At the time of the declaration, the USA was militarily incapable of enforcing its sweeping proclamations. The impetus for and the power behind the doctrine came from the British, whose commercial interests were at risk in the event of a Franco-Spanish reassertion of colonial influence. President Theodore ▷Roosevelt drew on the doctrine to proclaim a US right to intervene in the internal affairs of Latin American states.

Related Web site: Monroe Doctrine http://odur.let.rug.nl/~usa/D/1801-1825/jmdoc.htm

Monrovia capital and port of ▷Liberia; population (1992) 490,000. Industries include iron ore, rubber, cement, and petrol processing. Civil war damaged much of the infrastructure in and around Monrovia in the 1990s. The National Museum and the University of Liberia are here.

Mons (Flemish **Bergen**) industrial city and capital of the province of Hainaut, Belgium, 52 km/32 mi southwest of Brussels; population (1997) 92,000. Industries include coal mining, textiles, and sugar refining. The military headquarters of NATO is at nearby Chièvres-Casteau. It stands on the site of a Roman camp.

monsoon wind pattern that brings seasonally heavy rain to South Asia; it blows towards the sea in winter and towards the land in summer. The monsoon may cause destructive flooding all over India and Southeast Asia from April to September, leaving thousands of people homeless each year.

The monsoon cycle is believed to have started about 12 million years ago with the uplift of the Himalayas.

monstera (or **Swiss cheese plant**) evergreen climbing plant belonging to the arum family, native to tropical America. *M. deliciosa* is grown as a house plant. Areas between the veins of the leaves dry up, forming deep notches and eventually holes. (Genus *Monstera*, family Araceae.)

montage in cinema, the juxtaposition of several images or shots to produce an independent meaning. The term is also used more generally to describe the whole process of editing or a rapidly edited series of shots. It was coined by the Russian director Sergei ▷Eisenstein.

Montagu, Lady Mary Wortley (1689–1762) Born Mary Wortley Pierrepont. English society hostess. She was well known in literary circles, associating with writers such as the English poet Alexander Pope, with whom she later quarrelled. Her witty and erudite letters were renowned. She introduced the practice of inoculation against smallpox into Britain from Turkey in 1721.

Montagu-Chelmsford reforms changes to the constitution of India in 1919, whereby Indians obtained greater control in local and some provincial matters such as health, education, and agriculture, while British administrators still controlled finance and law and order. Arguing that the reforms did not go far enough, Indian nationalists organized a concerted ▷noncooperation campaign 1920–22 in protest.

Montaigne, Michel Eyquem de (1533–1592) French writer. He is regarded as the creator of the essay form. In 1580 he published the first two volumes of his *Essais*; the third volume appeared in 1588, and the definitive edition was issued posthumously in 1595. In his writings Montaigne considers all aspects of life from an urbanely sceptical viewpoint. He is critical of human pride and suspicious of philosophy and religion, seeking his own independent path to self-knowledge. Francis ▷Bacon was among the thinkers who have been challenged and stimulated by his work, and through the translation by John Florio in 1603, he influenced Shakespeare and other English writers.

He was born at the Château de Montaigne near Bordeaux, studied law, and in 1554 became a counsellor of the Bordeaux *parlement*. Little is known of his earlier life, except that he regularly visited Paris and the court of Francis II. In 1569 he published his translation of the *Theologia Naturalis* of Raymond Sebond (a 15th-century professor of Toulouse), and in the same year edited the works of his friend Etienne de La Boétie. In 1571 he retired to his estates, relinquishing his magistracy, and began to write his *Essais* (1572). The ironical *Apologie de Raymond Sebond* (*c.* 1576) reveals the full extent of his sceptical philosophy, refusing to trust the reasoning and rationality of other philosophies. He toured Germany, Switzerland, and Italy 1580–81, returning upon his election as mayor of Bordeaux, a post he held until 1585.

Related Web site: Montaigne, Michel Eyquem de http://www.orst.edu/instruct/phl302/philosophers/montaigne.html

Montana state in western USA, on the Canadian border. It is nicknamed the Treasure State. Montana was admitted to the Union in 1889 as the 41st US state. One of the Mountain States, it is bordered to the east by North Dakota and South Dakota, to the north by the Canadian states of Saskatchewan, Alberta, and British Columbia, to the west by Idaho, and to the south by Idaho and Wyoming.

population (1995) 870,300 **area** 380,847 sq km/147,045 sq mi **capital** Helena **towns and cities** Billings, Great Falls, Butte **industries and products** wheat, cattle, coal, copper, oil, natural gas, lumber, wood products, oil, natural gas, and strip-mined coal, tourism

Montand, Yves (1921–1991) Stage name of Ivo Livi. Italian-born French actor and singer. Popular in France from the 1950s, he also appeared in such US films as *Let's Make Love* in 1960 (with Marilyn Monroe). Later films include *Z* (1968), *Le Sauvage/The Savage* (1976), *Jean de Florette* (1986), and *Manon des Sources* (1986).

Montanism movement within the early Christian church that strove to return to the purity of primitive Christianity. It originated in Phrygia in about 156 with the teaching of a prophet named Montanus, and spread to Anatolia, Rome, Carthage, and Gaul. The theologian ▷Tertullian was a Montanist.

Mont Blanc (Italian **Monte Bianco**) the highest mountain in the ▷Alps, on the border between France and Italy, and one of the highest points in Europe at 4,807 m/15,772 ft. Lying 10 km/6 mi south of ▷Chamonix, it forms part of the Mont Blanc range.

MONT BLANC Situated on the French–Italian border, Mont Blanc is the highest peak in the Alps. *Image Bank*

MONTE CARLO The resort town of Monte Carlo, in the principality of Monaco, on the south coast of France. *Image Bank*

The peak was first climbed in 1786 by Jacques Balmat and Michel Paccard of Chamonix. In 1965 the longest road tunnel in the world (12 km/7.5 mi) was opened under the mountain, linking Chamonix to Courmayeur in Italy.

montbretia plant belonging to the iris family, native to South Africa, with orange or reddish flowers on long stems. They are grown as ornamental pot plants. (*Tritonia crocosmiflora*, family Iridaceae.)

Montcalm-Gozon, Louis-Joseph de (1712–1759) Marquis de Montcalm. French general, appointed military commander in Canada in 1756. He won a succession of victories over the British during the French and Indian War, but was defeated in 1759 by James ▷Wolfe at Québec on the Plains of Abraham, where both he and Wolfe were killed; this battle marked the end of French rule in Canada.

Monte Carlo town and luxury resort in the principality of ▷Monaco, situated on a rocky promontory northeast of Monaco town; population (1998 est) 14,000. It is a popular summer resort known for its casino (1878) designed by architect Charles Garnier; the Monte Carlo car rally and Monaco Grand Prix motor races; and its international television festival.

Montego Bay port and resort on the northwest coast of Jamaica; population (1991) 83,400. The fine beaches and climate attract tourists.

Montenegro (Serbo-Croatian **Crna Gora**) constituent republic, with the far larger ▷Serbia, of Serbia and Montenegro (previously Yugoslavia); area 13,800 sq km/5,300 sq mi; population (1991) 615,300, including *c.* 397,000 Montenegrins, 79,500 Muslims, and 39,500 Albanians. The capital is ▷Podgorica; other towns and cities include Kotor and Cetinje. The republic is mountainous and Mount Lovéen rises to 1,749 m/5,738 ft. There is a ▷karst region in the southwest, and there are forests and grasslands in the east. Skadarska Jezero (Late Scutari) is shared with Albania. A Serbian variant of Serbo-Croat is spoken, and the religion is predominantly Serbian Orthodox Christianity.

Montessori, Maria (1870–1952) Italian educationist. Working with mentally disabled

> ### Maria Montessori
> *If help and salvation are to come, they can only come from the children, for the children are the makers of men.*
>
> The Absorbent Mind ch. 1

children, she developed the **Montessori method**, an educational system for all children based on an informal approach, incorporating instructive play and allowing children to develop at their own pace.

Monteverdi, Claudio Giovanni Antonio (1567–1643) Italian composer. He contributed to the development of the opera with *La favola d'Orfeo/The Legend of Orpheus* (1607) and *L'incoronazione di Poppea/The Coronation of Poppea* (1642). He also wrote madrigals, motets, and sacred music, notably the *Vespers* (1610). Born in Cremona, he was in the service of the Duke of Mantua about 1591–1612, and was director of music at St Mark's, Venice, from 1613. He was first to use an orchestra and to reveal the dramatic possibilities of the operatic form. His first opera *Orfeo* was produced for the carnival at Mantua in 1607.

Montevideo capital and chief port of ▷Uruguay, situated on the northen shore of the Río de la Plata estuary; 210 km/130 mi east of Buenos Aires; population (1992) 1,383,700. It is Uruguay's chief industrial and commercial centre, and handles almost 90% of the country's imports and exports. Industries include meat packing, tanning, footwear, flour milling, and textiles. The main exports are grain, meat products, and hides. All Uruguay's railways converge on the city, and a large fishing fleet is based here. Montevideo is also a tourist resort with extensive beaches.

Features include a cathedral, (built 1790–1804) on the Plaza Constitución; the University of Uruguay, founded in 1849; the Teatro Solís; the Palacio Legislativo, built (1908–1925) from local marble; museums of fine art and history in the park El Prado.

Founded by the Spanish in 1726 as a defence against the attacks by the Portuguese from Brazil, it has been the capital of Uruguay since 1830; it is also the capital of a department of the same name.

Montezuma II (1466–1520) Aztec emperor of Mexico. He succeeded his uncle in 1502. Although he was a great warrior and legislator, heavy centralized taxation provoked resentment in outlying areas. When the Spanish conquistador Hernán ▷Cortés landed at Veracruz in 1519 and attempted to march on Tenochtitlán, he was well received by the inhabitants and made Montezuma his prisoner. The emperor was restored to his throne as a vassal of Spain, but dissident groups among his subjects rebelled and killed him.

Montfort, Simon de (*c.* 1208–1265) Called 'the Younger'. English politician and soldier. From 1258 he led the baronial opposition to Henry III's misrule during the second ▷Barons' War, and in 1264 defeated and captured the king at Lewes, Sussex. In 1265, as head of government, he summoned the first parliament in which the towns were represented; he was killed at the Battle of Evesham during the last of the Barons' Wars.

Initially one of Henry III's favourites, he married the king's sister Eleanor in 1238. He later disagreed with the king's administrative policies, and in 1258 Montfort and his baronial supporters forced Henry to accept the **Provisions of Oxford**, by which the king's powers were in effect transferred to a committee of barons. These provisions were annulled by the **Dictum of Kenilworth** in 1266, after the final defeat of Montfort's followers, and their lands and titles were confiscated.

Born in Normandy, the son of **Simon de Montfort** (*c.* 1160–1218) who led a crusade against the Albigenses, he arrived in England in 1230, and was granted the earldom of Leicester.

Montgolfier Joseph Michel (1740–1810) and Jacques Etienne (1745–1799). French brothers whose hot-air balloon was used for the first successful human flight 21 November 1783.

On 5 June 1783 they first sent up a balloon filled with hot air. After further experiments with wood-fuelled fabric-and-paper balloons, and one crewed ascent in a tethered balloon, they sent up two people who travelled for 20 minutes above Paris, a

CLAUDIO MONTEVERDI This picture of the Italian composer is in the 17th-century *Gravenbrock* manuscript. *The Art Archive/Museo Correr Venice/Dagli Orti*

journey of 9 km/6 mi. The Montgolfier experiments greatly stimulated scientific interest in aviation.

Montgomery state capital of ▷Alabama, USA, on the Alabama River; population (1996 est) 196,400. Linked to the port of ▷Mobile by river, it is a long-established administrative and commercial centre with diverse light industries. Two major air force bases are located nearby. Montgomery was the capital of the Confederacy in the first months of the American Civil War. The 1955 Montgomery Bus Boycott was a landmark in the civil-rights campaign against segregation laws. Black residents make up one-third of the population.

Montgomery, Bernard Law (1887–1976) 1st Viscount Montgomery of Alamein; called 'Monty'. English field marshal. In World War II he commanded the 8th Army in North Africa in the Second Battle of El ▷Alamein in 1942. As commander of British troops in northern Europe from 1944, he received the German surrender in 1945.

At the start of World War II Montgomery commanded part of the British Expeditionary Force in France 1939–40 and took part in the evacuation from Dunkirk. In August 1942 he took command of the 8th Army, then barring the German advance on Cairo. The victory of El ▷Alamein in October turned the tide in North Africa; it was followed by the expulsion of Field Marshal Rommel from Egypt and rapid Allied advance into Tunisia. In February 1943 Montgomery's forces came under US general Eisenhower's command, and they took part in the conquest of Tunisia and Sicily and the invasion of Italy. Montgomery was promoted to field marshal in 1944. In 1948 he became permanent military chair of the Commanders-in-Chief Committee for Western European defence, and 1951–58 was deputy Supreme Commander Europe. He was created 1st Viscount Montgomery of Alamein in 1946.

Montgomery commanded the Allied armies during the opening phase of the invasion of France in June 1944, and from August the British and imperial troops that liberated the Netherlands, overran northern Germany, and entered Denmark. At his 21st Army Group headquarters on Lüneburg Heath, he received the German surrender on 4 May 1945. He was in command of the British occupation force in Germany until February 1946, when he was appointed chief of the Imperial General Staff.

Montgomeryshire former county of north Wales, included in Powys between 1974 and 1996; now part of ▷Powys unitary authority.

month unit of time based on the motion of the Moon around the Earth. The time from one new or full Moon to the next (the **synodic** or **lunar month**) is 29.53 days. The time for the Moon to complete one orbit around the Earth relative to the stars (the **sidereal month**) is 27.32 days. The **solar month** equals 30.44 days, and is exactly one-twelfth of the solar or tropical year, the time taken for the Earth to orbit the Sun. The **calendar month** is a human invention, devised to fit the calendar year.

Montmartre district of ▷Paris, France, dominated by the basilica of Sacré-Coeur, completed in 1919. It is situated in the north of the city on a hill 120 m/400 ft high. It is known for its night-life and artistic associations and is a popular tourist site.

MONTMARTRE The church of Sacré-Coeur in Montmartre, Paris, France. *Image Bank*

Montparnasse district of ▷Paris, France, formerly frequented by artists and writers. It is situated in the southwest of the city. The Pasteur Institute is also here.

Montpelier capital of ▷Vermont, USA, and county seat of Washington county, on the Winooski River, in the Green Mountains; population (1996 est) 7,900. Settled in 1787, it is the smallest state capital. The city is a long-established centre for granite production, sourced from the world's largest granite quarry, the Rock of Ages. Service industries include insurance and tourism.

Montpellier industrial city and administrative centre of the *département* of Hérault and of the ▷Languedoc-Roussillon region of southern France; population (1990) 210,900. It is situated on the River Lez 130 km/80 mi northwest of Marseille. Industries include electronics, medical research, engineering, textiles, and food processing, and there is a trade in wine and brandy. It is the birthplace of the philosopher Auguste Comte.

Montréal inland port and commercial centre of Québec, Canada, on Montréal Island at the junction of the Ottawa and St Lawrence rivers; population of metropolitan area (1996 est) 3,326,500. It is the second-largest port on the North American east coast, the chief port of the St Lawrence–Great Lakes waterway system, and the world's farthest inland port, situated 1,600 km/1,000 mi from the Atlantic. Industries include oil-refining, engineering, food-processing, distilling, brewing, and the manufacture of steel, aircraft, ships, petrochemicals, tobacco products, clothing, pulp, and paper. Founded by the French in 1642, Montréal became a British possession in 1763.

The city was badly affected by the great ice storm of January 1998 which coated electricity pylons with ice and the weight brought many of them down, blacking out parts of Montréal and Québec.

Montréal Protocol international agreement, signed in 1987, to stop the production of chemicals that are ▷ozone depleters by the year 2000.

Montrose, James Graham, 1st Marquess and 5th Earl of Montrose (1612–1650) Scottish soldier, son of the 4th Earl of Montrose. He supported the ▷Covenanters against Charles I, but after 1640 changed sides. As lieutenant general in 1644, he rallied the loyalist Highland clans to Charles, defeating the Covenanters' forces at Tippermuir and Aberdeen, but his subsequent attempt to raise the Royalist standard in the Lowlands ended in failure at Philiphaugh in 1645, and he escaped to Holland. Returning in 1650 to raise a revolt, he survived shipwreck only to have his weakened forces defeated, and (having been betrayed to the Covenanters) was hanged in Edinburgh.

Montserrat volcanic island in the West Indies, one of the Leeward group, a British crown colony; capital Plymouth; area 110 sq km/42 sq mi; population (1991) 11,957. Practically all buildings were destroyed by Hurricane Hugo in September 1989. The eruption of the Soufrière volcano in July 1997 buried the capital, Plymouth, under rock and ashes. Around 7,000 islanders were evacuated.

Montserrat produces cotton, cotton-seed, coconuts, citrus and other fruits, and vegetables. Its first European visitor was Christopher ▷Columbus in 1493, who named it after the mountain in Spain.

It was first colonized by English and Irish settlers who moved from St Christopher in 1632. It was held by the French until ceded to Britain in 1783. It became part of the colony of the Leeward Islands in 1871, and a British crown colony in 1956.

Montserrat (Spanish *monte serrado* 'serrated mountain') isolated mountain in Cataluña, northeast Spain, on the right bank of the River Llobregat, 37 km/23 mi north of Barcelona; so called because its uneven outline of eroded pinnacles resembles the edge of a saw. Its highest point is 1,240 m/4,070 ft.

Mont St-Michel granite islet in the bay of St-Michel, northwest France, situated in the *département* of Manche near the mouth of the River Couesnon, 24 km/15 mi southeast of Granville. It was converted to a peninsula in 1875 with the construction of a 2 km/1.2 mi long causeway. It has a Benedictine monastery, the abbey being founded in the 10th century in the place of an oratory built in 708.

Montt, Manuel (1809–1900) Chilean president 1851–61. He was a hardliner who promoted economic development, especially railway building, the telegraph, postal services, and gas lighting. His final years in office saw economic recession and political turmoil, including clashes between church and state.

Monument, the stone column commemorating the ▷Fire of London in 1666, situated near the north approach to London Bridge and the site of the house in Pudding Lane where the conflagration began. It was designed by Christopher ▷Wren and Robert Hooke, and erected 1671–77.

THE MONUMENT The Monument, in the City of London, England, was built 67 m/220 ft from where the Fire of London started, and is 67 m/220 ft tall. *The Art Archive*

MOON US astronauts landed on the Moon in July and November 1969. *Corel*

Moon natural satellite of Earth, 3,476 km/2,160 mi in diameter, with a mass 0.012 (approximately one-eightieth) that of Earth.

Its surface gravity is only 0.16 (one-sixth) that of Earth. Its average distance from Earth is 384,400 km/238,855 mi, and it orbits in a west-to-east direction every 27.32 days (the **sidereal month**). It spins on its axis with one side permanently turned towards Earth. The Moon has no atmosphere and was thought to have no water till ice was discovered on its surface in 1998.

Phases The Moon is illuminated by sunlight, and goes through a cycle of phases of shadow, waxing from **new** (dark) via **first quarter** (half Moon) to **full**, and waning back again to new every 29.53 days (the **synodic month**, also known as a **lunation**). On its sunlit side, temperatures reach 110°C/230°F, but during the two-week lunar night the surface temperature drops to −170°C/−274°F.

Origins The origin of the Moon is still open to debate. Scientists suggest the following theories: that it split from the Earth; that it was a separate body captured by Earth's gravity; that it formed in orbit around Earth; or that it was formed from debris thrown off when a body the size of Mars struck Earth.

Research The far side of the Moon was first photographed from the Soviet *Lunik 3* in October 1959. Much of our information about the Moon has been derived from this and other photographs and measurements taken by US and Soviet Moon probes, from geological samples brought back by US Apollo astronauts and by Soviet Luna probes, and from experiments set up by the US astronauts in 1969–72. The US probe *Lunar Prospector*, launched in January 1998, examined the composition of the lunar crust, recorded gamma rays, and mapped the lunar magnetic field. It was the *Lunar prospector* that discovered the Ice on the moon in March 1988.

Composition The Moon's composition is rocky, with a surface heavily scarred by ▷meteorite impacts that have formed craters up to 240 km/150 mi across. Seismic observations indicate that the Moon's surface extends downwards for tens of kilometres; below this crust is a solid mantle about 1,100 km/688 mi thick, and below that a silicate core, part of which may be molten. Rocks brought back by astronauts show the Moon is 4.6 billion years old, the same age as Earth. It is made up of the same chemical elements as Earth, but in different proportions, and differs from Earth in that most of the Moon's surface features were formed within the first billion years of its history when it was hit repeatedly by meteorites.

The youngest craters are surrounded by bright rays of ejected rock. The largest scars have been filled by dark lava to produce the lowland plains called seas, or **maria** (plural of mare). These dark patches form the so-called 'man-in-the-Moon' pattern. Inside some craters that are permanently in shadow is up to 300 million metric tons/330 million tons of ice existing as a thin layer of crystals.

One of the Moon's easiest features to observe is the mare **Plato**, which is about 100 km/62 mi in diameter and 2,700 m/8,860 ft deep, and at times is visible with the naked eye alone.

moon in astronomy, any natural ▷satellite that orbits a planet. Mercury and Venus are the only planets in the Solar System that do not have moons.

Moon, Sun Myung (1920–) Korean industrialist and founder of the ▷Unification Church (**Moonies**) 1954. From 1973 he launched a major mission in the USA and elsewhere. The church has been criticized for its manipulative methods of recruiting and keeping members. He was convicted of tax fraud in the USA 1982.

Moon probe crewless spacecraft used to investigate the Moon. Early probes flew past the Moon or crash-landed on it, but later ones achieved soft landings or went into orbit. Soviet probes included the Luna/Lunik series. US probes (Ranger, Surveyor, Lunar Orbiter) prepared the way for the Apollo crewed flights.

moonstone translucent, pearly variety of potassium sodium ▷feldspar, found in Sri Lanka and Myanmar, and distinguished by a blue, silvery, or red opalescent tint. It is valued as a gem.

Moor any of the northwestern African Muslims, of mixed Arab and Berber origin, who conquered Spain and ruled its southern part from 711 to 1492, when they were forced to renounce their faith and became Christian (they were then known as *Moriscos*). The name (English form of Latin *Maurus*) was originally applied to an inhabitant of the Roman province of Mauritania, in northwestern Africa.

moor in earth science, a stretch of land, usually at a height, which is characterized by a vegetation of heather, coarse grass, and bracken. A moor may be poorly drained and contain boggy hollows. More than 50% of Scotland is regarded as moorland.

Moorcock, Michael John (1939–) English writer. Associated with the 1960s new wave in science fiction, he was editor of the magazine *New Worlds* (1964–69). He wrote the Jerry Cornelius novels, collected as *The Cornelius Chronicles* (1977), and *Gloriana* (1978). Among later novels are *The Revenge of the Rose* (1989) and *Blood* (1994).

Moore, Bobby (Robert Frederick) (1941–1993) English footballer who led the England team to victory against West Germany in the 1966 World Cup final. A superb defender, he played 108 games for England 1962–70 (until 1978, a world-record number of international appearances) and was captain 90 times. His Football League career, spent at West Ham 1968–74 and Fulham 1974–77, spanned 19 years and 668 matches.

Related Web site: Moore, Bobby http://www.geocities.com/Colosseum/Field/3163/moore.html

Moore, Henry (Spencer) (1898–1986) English sculptor. His subjects include the reclining nude, mother-and-child groups, the warrior, and interlocking abstract forms. Many of his post-1945 works are in bronze or marble, including monumental semi-abstracts such as *Reclining Figure* (1957–58; outside the UNESCO building in Paris), and are often designed to be placed in landscape settings. He is considered one of the leading artists of the 20th century.

Moore claimed to have learned much from archaic South and Central American sculpture, and this is reflected in his work of the 1920s which laid stress on truth to material and the original block, as in *Reclining Figure* (1929; Leeds City Art Gallery). By the early 1930s most of his main themes had emerged, and the surrealists' preoccupation with organic forms in abstract works proved a strong influence, particularly that of Alberto Giacometti. Moore's hollowed biomorphic wooden shapes strung with wires, such as *The Bride* (1940; Museum of Modern Art, New York), show affinities with sculpture by Hans Arp and Barbara ▷Hepworth. Semi-abstract work suggesting organic structures recurs after World War II, for example in the interwoven bonelike forms of the *Hill Arches* and the bronze *Sheep Pieces* (1970s), set in fields by his studio in Perry Green, Hertfordshire.

Moore, John (1761–1809) Scottish-born British general. In 1808 he commanded the British army sent to Portugal in the Peninsular War. After advancing into Spain he had to retreat to Coruña in the northwest, and was killed in the battle fought to cover the embarkation. He was knighted in 1804.

moorhen marsh bird belonging to the rail family, common in swamps, lakes, and ponds throughout Europe, Asia, Africa, and North and South America. It is about 33 cm/13 in long, brown above and dark grey below, with a red bill and forehead, a white stripe along the edge of the folded wings, a vivid white underside to the tail, and green legs. Its big feet are not webbed or lobed, but the moorhen can swim well. The nest is built by the waterside, and the eggs are buff-coloured with orange-brown spots. (Species *Gallinula chloropus*, family Rallidae, order Gruiformes.)

moose North American name for the ▷elk.

mopane worm caterpillar of the southern African emperor moth *Gonimbrasia belina* which is eaten in South Africa, either dried as a snack or rehydrated in stews. They grow to around 10 cm/4 in in length and are very high in protein.

moquette textile woven in the same manner as velvet (with cut or uncut pile) from coarse wool and linen yarns, usually for upholstery or carpeting. By introducing rods during weaving, the thread is raised in loops.

moraine rocky debris or ▷till carried along and deposited by a ▷glacier. Material eroded from the side of a glaciated valley and carried along the glacier's edge is called a **lateral moraine**; that worn from the valley floor and carried along the base of the glacier is called a **ground moraine**. Rubble dropped at the snout of a melting glacier is called a **terminal moraine**.

morality play didactic medieval European verse drama, in part a development of the ▷mystery play (or miracle play), in which human characters are replaced by personified virtues and vices, the limited humorous elements being provided by the Devil. In England, morality plays, such as *Everyman*, flourished in the 15th century. They exerted an influence on the development of Elizabethan drama and comedy.

Moral Rearmament (MRA) international movement calling for 'moral and spiritual renewal', founded by the Christian evangelist F N D Buchman in the 1920s as the **Oxford Group**. It based its teachings on the 'Four Absolutes' (honesty, purity, unselfishness, love).

Moravia (Czech **Morava**) area of central Europe, forming two regions of the Czech Republic: **South Moravia** (Czech Jihomoravský) and **North Moravia** (Czech Severomoravský). South Moravia has an area of 15,030 sq km/5,800 sq mi and a population (1991) of 2,048,900. Its capital is ▷Brno. North Moravia has an area of 11,070 sq km/4,273 sq mi and a population (1991) of 1,961,500. Its capital is ▷Ostrava. The River Morava is found in the region. 25% of the region is forested. Products include maize, grapes, and wine in the south; wheat, barley, rye, flax, and sugar beet in the north; and coal and iron.

Moravia, Alberto (1907–1991) Pen-name of Alberto Pincherle. Italian novelist. His first successful novel was *Gli indifferenti/The Time of Indifference* (1929), but its criticism of Mussolini's regime led to the government censoring his work until after World War II. Later books include *Agostino* (1944), *La romana/Woman of Rome* (1947), *Racconti Romani/Roman Tales* (1954), *La ciociara/Two Women* (1957), *La noia/The Empty Canvas* (1961; a study of an artist's obsession with his model), *L'attenzione/The Lie* (1965), and *La vita interiore/Time of Desecration* (1978).

Moravian member of a Christian Protestant sect, the **Moravian Brethren**. An episcopal church that grew out of the earlier Bohemian Brethren, it was established by the Lutheran Count Zinzendorf in Saxony in 1722.

Moray another spelling of ▷Murray, regent of Scotland 1567–70.

Moray unitary authority in northeast Scotland, created in 1996 from the Moray district of Grampian region.

area 2,224 sq km/859 sq mi **towns** Elgin (administrative headquarters), Forres, Buckie, Lossiemouth **physical** the land gradually slopes from the Grampian Mountains in the south (Cairn Gorm 1,245 m/4,085 ft) towards the Moray Firth; extensive coastal lowlands fringe an area of sand-dune formation; part of this land was reclaimed from the sea and is now covered by the Culbin forest. The River Spey reaches the North Sea near Buckie **features** Elgin cathedral; Brodie and Duffus castles; Gordonstoun school **industries** whisky distilling, food processing **agriculture** some fishing (Buckie, Lossiemouth); trout and salmon fishing in rivers; cereals in lowland plain **population** (1996) 85,000 **history** numerous royal residences and setting for Shakespeare's *Macbeth*

Mordoviya another name for ▷Mordvinia, an autonomous republic of the Russian Federation.

Mordred in Arthurian legend, nephew and final opponent of King Arthur. What may be an early version of his name (Medraut) appears with Arthur in annals from the 10th century, listed under the year AD 537.

Mordvinia (or **Mordoviya**) autonomous republic of central Russian Federation; area 26,200 sq km/10,100 sq mi; population (1990) 964,000 (60% Russian, 35% Mordvinians). The capital is Saransk. The republic is about 350 km/217 mi southeast of Moscow. The River Sura is in the east, and there are forests in the west. Industries include sugar beet, grains, hemp, and potatoes; sheep and dairy farming; commercial vehicles, timber, furniture, and textiles. Languages spoken are Russian and Mordvin.

More, Kenneth Gilbert (1914–1982) English actor. A wholesome film star of the 1950s, he was cast as leading man in adventure films and light comedies such as *Genevieve* (1953), *Doctor in the House* (1954), and *Northwest Frontier* (1959). He played war hero Douglas Bader in *Reach for the Sky* (1956).

More, (St) Thomas (1478–1535) English politician and author. From 1509 he was favoured by ▷Henry VIII and employed on foreign embassies. He was a member of the privy council from 1518 and Lord Chancellor from 1529 but resigned over Henry's break with the pope. For refusing to accept the king as head of the church, he was executed. The title of his political book *Utopia* (1516) has come to mean any supposedly perfect society.

Son of a London judge, More studied Greek, Latin, French, theology, and music at Oxford, and law at Lincoln's Inn, London, and was influenced by the humanists John Colet and ▷Erasmus, who became a friend. In Parliament from 1504, he was made Speaker of the House of Commons in 1523. He was knighted in 1521, and on the fall of Cardinal Wolsey became Lord Chancellor, but resigned in 1532 because he could not agree with the king on his ecclesiastical policy and marriage with Anne Boleyn. In 1534 he refused to take the oath of supremacy to Henry VIII as head of the church, and after a year's imprisonment in the Tower of London he was executed.

Among Thomas More's writings are the Latin *Utopia* (1516), sketching an ideal commonwealth; the English *Dialogue* (1528), a theological argument against the Reformation leader Tyndale; and a *History of Richard III*. He was also a patron of artists, including ▷Holbein. More was canonized in 1935, and in November 2000, the pope declared him patron saint of politicians.

Related Web site: Thomas More Web Site http://www.d-holliday.com/tmore/

Moreau, Jeanne (1928–) French actor. She has appeared in international films, often in passionate, intelligent roles. Her work includes *Les Amants/The Lovers* (1958), François Truffaut's *Jules et Jim/Jules and Jim* (1962), Orson Welles's *Chimes at Midnight* (1966), and *Querelle* (1982).

morel any of a group of edible ▷mushrooms. The common morel (*M. esculenta*) grows in Europe and North America. The yellowish-brown cap is pitted with holes like a sponge and is about 2.5 cm/1 in long. It is used for seasoning gravies, soups, and sauces and is second only to the ▷truffle as the world's most sought-after mushroom. (Genus *Morchella*, order Pezizales.)

Morelos, José María (1765–1815) Mexican priest and revolutionary. A mestizo (person with Spanish American and American Indian parents), Morelos followed independence campaigner Miguel Hidalgo y Costilla, intending to be an army chaplain, but he displayed military genius and came to head his own forces. The independence movement was stalled for five years after his death.

Morgan, Henry (c. 1635–1688) Welsh buccaneer in the Caribbean. He made war against Spain, capturing and sacking Panama in 1671. In 1675 he was knighted and appointed lieutenant governor of Jamaica.

Morgan, J(ohn) P(ierpont) (1837–1913) US financier and investment banker whose company (sometimes criticized as 'the money trust') became the most influential private banking house after the Civil War, being instrumental in the formation of many trusts which stifled competition. He set up the US Steel Corporation in 1901 and International Harvester in 1902.

Morgan, Thomas Hunt (1866–1945) US geneticist who was awarded a Nobel Prize for Physiology or Medicine in 1933 for his work on the role of chromosomes in heredity. He helped establish that ▷genes are located on the chromosomes, discovered sex chromosomes, and invented the techniques of genetic mapping. He was the first to work on the fruit fly *Drosophila*, which has since become a major subject of genetic studies.

Morgan horse breed of riding and driving show horse originating in the USA in the 1780s from a single stallion named *Justin Morgan* after his owner. They are marked by high, curved necks and a high-stepping action. The breed is valued for its strength, endurance, and speed.

Morgan le Fay in the romance and legend of the English king Arthur, an enchantress and healer, ruler of ▷Avalon and sister of the king, whom she tended after his final battle. In *Le Morte d'Arthur* (completed in 1470) she revealed the intrigue between ▷Guinevere and ▷Lancelot to her brother.

Morisot, Berthe Marie Pauline (1841–1895) French painter, the first woman to join the Impressionist movement. Taught by ▷Corot, she was also much influenced by ▷Manet and, in the 1880s, ▷Renoir. She specialized in sensitive pictures of women and children, as in *The Cradle* (1872; Impressionist Museum, Paris).

Morley, Robert (1908–1992) English actor and dramatist. He was active both in Britain and the USA. His film work consisted mainly of character roles, in such movies as *Marie Antoinette* (1938), *The African Queen* (1952), and *Oscar Wilde* (1960).

Morley, Thomas (*c.* 1557–*c.* 1602) English composer. He wrote consort music, madrigals, and airs including the lute song 'It was a lover and his lass' for Shakespeare's play *As You Like It* (1599). He edited a collection of Italian madrigals *The Triumphs of Oriana* (1601), and published an influential keyboard tutor *A Plaine and Easie Introduction to Practicall Musicke* (1597). He was also organist at St Paul's Cathedral, London.

Morley-Minto reforms measures announced in 1909 to increase the participation of Indians in their country's government. Introduced by John Morley (1838–1923), secretary of state for India, and Lord Minto (1845–1914), viceroy of India, they did not affect the responsibility of government, which remained in British hands, but did give Indians wider opportunities to be heard.

Mormon (or **Latter-day Saint**) member of a Christian sect, the **Church of Jesus Christ of Latter-day Saints**, founded at Fayette, New York, in 1830 by Joseph ▷Smith. According to Smith, Mormon was an ancient prophet in North America whose *Book of Mormon*, which Smith claimed was divinely revealed to him, is accepted by Mormons as part of the Christian scriptures. Originally persecuted, the Mormons migrated west to ▷Salt Lake City, Utah, under Brigham ▷Young's leadership and prospered; their headquarters are here. The Mormon Church is a missionary church with a worldwide membership of about 6 million.

Related Web site: Trail of Hope: Story of the Mormon Trail
http://www.pbs.org/trailofhope/

morning glory any of a group of twining or creeping plants native to tropical America, especially *I. purpurea*, with dazzling blue flowers. (Genus *Ipomoea*, family Convolvulaceae.)

MORNING GLORY The seeds of certain species of morning glory were once used by the Central American Indians, the Aztecs, to induce hallucinations during religious ceremonies. Nowadays, it is grown as an ornamental.

Moro, Aldo (1916–1978) Italian Christian Democrat politician. Prime minister 1963–68 and 1974–76, he was expected to become Italy's president, but he was kidnapped and shot by Red Brigade urban guerrillas.

Moroccan Crises two periods of international tension in 1905 and 1911 following German objections to French expansion in Morocco. Their wider purpose was to break up the Anglo-French entente of 1904, but both crises served to reinforce the entente and isolate Germany. The first was resolved at the Algeciras Conference. The second brought Europe to the brink of war and is known as the Agadir Incident.

Morocco see country box.

Moroni capital of the ▷Comoros Republic, on Njazidja (Grand Comore); population (1992) 22,000. It has a small natural harbour from which coffee, cacao, and vanilla are exported. Local agricultural markets trade in coconuts, cassava, bananas, and rice.

Morpheus in Greek and Roman mythology, the god of dreams, son of Hypnos or Somnus, god of sleep.

morphine narcotic alkaloid $C_{17}H_{19}NO_3$ derived from ▷opium and prescribed only to alleviate severe pain. Its use produces serious side effects, including nausea, constipation, tolerance, and addiction, but it is highly valued for the relief of the terminally ill.

The risk of addiction arising from the use of morphine for pain relief is much lower than for recreational use (about 1 in 3,000) as the drug is processed differently by the body when pain is present.

It is a controlled substance in Britain.

morphogen in medicine, one of a class of substances believed to be present in the growing embryo, controlling its growth pattern.

It is thought that variations in the concentration of morphogens in different parts of the embryo cause them to grow at different rates.

morphology in biology, the study of the physical structure and form of organisms, in particular their soft tissues.

Morricone, Ennio (1928–) Italian composer of film music. His atmospheric scores for 'spaghetti westerns', notably the Sergio ▷Leone movies *Per un pugno di dollari/A Fistful of Dollars* (1964) and *Il buono, il brutto, il cattivo/The Good, the Bad, and the Ugly* (1966), were widely imitated. His highly ritualized, incantatory style pioneered the use of amplified instruments and solo voices, using studio special effects.

Morrigan in Celtic mythology, a goddess of war and death who could take the shape of a crow.

Morris, Jan (1926–) English travel writer and journalist. Her books display a zestful, witty, and knowledgeable style and offer deftly handled historical perspectives. They include *Coast to Coast* (1956), *Venice* (1960), *Oxford* (1965), *Farewell the Trumpets* (1978), and *Among the Cities* (1985). *Fisher's Face* (1995) is a biography of Admiral of the Fleet Lord Fisher. Born James Morris, her adoption of female gender is described in *Conundrum* (1974), and *Pleasures of a Tangled Life* (1989) is a further autobiographical study.

Morris, William (1834–1896) English designer, socialist, and writer. A founder of the ▷Arts and Crafts Movement, he condemned 19th-century mechanization and sought a revival of traditional crafts, such as furnituremaking, book illustration, fabric design, and so on. He linked this to a renewal of society based on Socialist principles.

Morris was born in London and educated at Oxford, where he formed a lasting friendship with the Pre-Raphaelite artist Edward ▷Burne-Jones and was influenced by the art critic John Ruskin and the painter and poet Dante Gabriel ▷Rossetti. He abandoned his first profession, architecture, to study painting, but had a considerable influence on such architects as William Lethaby and Philip Webb. In 1861 he cofounded Morris, Marshall, Faulkner and Company ('the Firm') which designed and produced stained glass, furniture, fabric, carpets, and decorative wallpapers; many of the designs, inspired by medieval, classical, and oriental sources, are still produced today.

Morris's first book of verse was *The Defence of Guenevere* (1858). He published several verse romances, notably *The Life and Death of Jason* (1867) and *The Earthly Paradise* (1868–70). A visit to Iceland in 1871 inspired the epic poem *Sigurd the Volsung* (1876) and general interest in the sagas. His Kelmscott Press, set up in 1890 to print beautifully designed books, influenced printing and book design.

A leading Socialist, his prose romances *A Dream of John Ball* (1888) and utopian *News from Nowhere* (1891) reflected his socialist ideology. He joined the Social Democratic Federation in 1883, but left in 1884 because he found it too moderate, and set up the Socialist League. To this period belong the critical and sociological studies *Signs of Change* (1888) and *Hopes and Fears for Art* (1892). He also lectured on socialism.

Design work After being articled as an architect he was for some years a painter, before jointly founding 'the Firm', in which Rossetti, Burne-Jones, and other artists were partners. Famous designs include his 'Daisy' (1864) and 'Vine' (1873) wallpapers; the 'Woodpecker' tapestry (1880s); and his 'Honeysuckle' chintz (1876). He also designed windows for Middleton Cheney Parish Church in 1864, and centralized his weaving and dyeing works at Merton Abbey in 1880, where William de Morgan joined him to produce tiles and ruby-lustre ware. As a founder of the Arts and Crafts Movement, Morris did much to raise British craft standards.

Verse and prose He was one of the originators of the *Oxford and Cambridge Magazine*, to which he contributed poems, tales, and essays. Following *The Defence of Guenevere and other Poems*, he published *The Life and Death of Jason* (1867), *The Earthly Paradise*, and *Love is Enough* (1875), in which year he also made a translation in verse of Virgil's *Aeneid*. *Three Northern Love Stories* was inspired by his travels in Iceland. His translation of the *Odyssey* in verse appeared in 1887. A series of prose romances include the *House of Wolfings* (1889), and *The Well at the World's End* (1896). The most notable product of the Kelmscott Press was the *Kelmscott Chaucer*.

Morris was born at Walthamstow, and educated at Marlborough and at Exeter College, Oxford.

Related Web site: Selected Poetry of William Morris (1834–1896)
http://www.library.utoronto.ca/utel/rp/authors/morris.html

morris dance English folk dance. The dances take different forms and various theories about the origin of morris dancing have been put forward. These include the claim that it originated in pagan fertility rites, that it was imported to England in the 15th century as a European court entertainment, and that it was a staple of springtime church and village festivals. Shakespeare refers to it as a dance for festivals, as well as referring to the dancers as 'Moriscos', which may indicate a moorish influence via Spain. Today morris dancers still appear at public and local festivals, and may have bells, handkerchiefs, or sticks as their props.

Morrison, Herbert Stanley (1888–1965) Baron Morrison of Lambeth. British Labour politician. He was a founder member and later secretary of the London Labour Party 1915–45, and a member of the London County Council 1922–45. He entered Parliament in 1923, representing South Hackney in 1923, 1929–31, and 1935–45, and East Lewisham 1945–59. He organized the Labour Party's general election victory in 1945. He was twice defeated in the contest for leadership of the party, once by Clement Attlee in 1932, and then by Hugh Gaitskell in 1955. A skilful organizer, he lacked the ability to unite the party. He was created baron in 1959.

Morrison was born in Brixton, London. He was minister of transport 1929–31, home secretary 1940–45, Lord President of the Council and leader of the House of Commons 1945–51, and foreign secretary March–October 1951 and was instrumental in Labour's post-war social revolution.

Morrison, Toni (1931–) Born Chloe Anthony Wofford. US novelist. Her fiction records African-American life in the South, including *Song of Solomon* (1978), *Tar Baby* (1981), *Beloved* (1987), based on a true story about infanticide in Kentucky, which won a Pulitzer Prize in 1988 and was made into a film in 1998, and *Jazz* (1992). She was awarded the Nobel Prize for Literature in 1993. Her novel *Love* was published in 2003.

Morrison, Van (1945–) Stage name of George Ivan Morrison. Northern Irish singer, songwriter, and saxophonist. His jazz-inflected Celtic soul style was already in evidence on *Astral Weeks* (1968) and has been highly influential. Among other albums are *Tupelo Honey* (1971), *Veedon Fleece* (1974), and *Avalon Sunset* (1989). He continued to release albums throughout the 1990s, with a consistently retrospective tone, one of the finest being *Hymns to the Silence* (1991). In 1994 he was awarded a Brit Award for his outstanding contribution to music.

Morrissey (1959–) Stage name of Steven Patrick Morrissey. English rock singer and lyricist. He was a founder member of the Smiths 1982–87 and subsequently a solo artist. His lyrics reflect on everyday miseries or glumly celebrate the England of his childhood. Solo albums include *Viva Hate* (1987) and *Your Arsenal* (1992). His popularity declined in the UK in the 1990s and he moved to the USA.

Morse, Samuel Finley Breese (1791–1872) US inventor. In 1835 he produced the first adequate electric telegraph (see ▷telegraphy), and in 1843 was granted $30,000 by Congress for an experimental line between Washington, DC, and Baltimore. With his assistant Alexander Bain (1810–1877) he invented the Morse code.

Morse code international code for transmitting messages by wire or radio using signals of short (dots) and long (dashes) duration, originated by US inventor Samuel Morse for use on his invention, the telegraph (see ▷telegraphy).

mortar method of projecting a bomb via a high trajectory at a target up to 6–7 km/3–4 mi away. A mortar bomb is stabilized in flight by means of tail fins. The high trajectory results in a high angle of attack and makes mortars more suitable than artillery for use in built-up areas or mountains; mortars are not as accurate, however. Artillery also differs in firing a projectile through a rifled barrel, thus creating greater muzzle velocity.

mortgage transfer of property, usually a house, as a security for repayment of a loan. The loan is normally repaid to a bank or building society over a period of years.

Mortimer, John Clifford (1923–) English barrister and writer. His works include the plays *The Dock Brief* (1958) and *A Voyage Round My Father* (1970), and numerous stories about the fictional barrister who first appeared in the volume *Rumpole of the Bailey* (1978) and then in several television series. Subsequent satirical fiction has tended to be developed alongside television, and includes *Paradise Postponed* (1985) and *Summer's Lease* (1988). *Dunster* (1992) is a mystery story featuring a libel case.

Mortimer, Roger de (*c.* 1287–1330) 8th Baron of Wigmore and 1st Earl of March. English politician and adventurer. He opposed Edward II and with Edward's queen, Isabella, led a rebellion against him in 1326, bringing about his abdication. From 1327 Mortimer ruled England as the queen's lover, until Edward III had him executed. Knighted 1306, Earl 1328.

Morton, Jelly Roll (1885–1941) Stage name of Ferdinand Joseph La Menthe Morton. US New Orleans-style jazz pianist, singer, and composer. Influenced by Scott Joplin, he was a pioneer in the development of jazz from ragtime to swing by improvising and imposing his own personality on the music. His 1920s band was called the Red Hot Peppers. In 1997 Morton was chosen for the Rock and Roll Hall of Fame.

Morton, William Thomas Green (1819–1868) US dentist who in 1846, with Charles Thomas Jackson (1805–1880), a chemist and physician, introduced ▷ether as an anaesthetic. They were not the first to use it but they patented the process and successfully publicized it.

mosaic design or picture, usually for a floor or wall, produced by setting small pieces (*tesserae*) of marble, glass, or other materials in a cement ground. The ancient Greeks were the first to use large-scale mosaic (in the Macedonian royal palace at Pella, for example).

Morocco

Morocco country in northwest Africa, bounded to the north and northwest by the Mediterranean Sea, to the east and southeast by Algeria, and to the south by Western Sahara.

NATIONAL NAME *Al-Mamlaka al-Maghribyya/Kingdom of Morocco*
AREA 458,730 sq km/177,115 sq mi (excluding Western Sahara)
CAPITAL Rabat
MAJOR TOWNS/CITIES Casablanca, Marrakesh, Fès, Oujda, Kenitra, Tétouan, Meknès
MAJOR PORTS Casablanca, Tangier, Agadir
PHYSICAL FEATURES mountain ranges, including the Atlas Mountains northeast–southwest; fertile coastal plains in west

Government

HEAD OF STATE Sayyid Muhammad VI ibn-Hassan from 1999
HEAD OF GOVERNMENT Driss Jettou from 2002
POLITICAL SYSTEM emergent democracy
POLITICAL EXECUTIVE dual executive
ADMINISTRATIVE DIVISIONS 43 provinces, nine wilayas, and 22 prefectures
ARMED FORCES 196,300; plus paramilitary forces of 50,000 (2002 est)
CONSCRIPTION 18 months authorized; most enlisted personnel are volunteers
DEATH PENALTY retained and used for ordinary crimes
DEFENCE SPEND (% GDP) 3.6 (2002 est)
EDUCATION SPEND (% GDP) 5.5 (2001 est)

HEALTH SPEND (% GDP) 4.5 (2000 est)

Economy and resources

CURRENCY dirham
GPD (US$) 37.3 billion (2002 est)
REAL GDP GROWTH (% change on previous year) 6.5 (2001)
GNI (US$) 35.4 billion (2002 est)
GNI PER CAPITA (PPP) (US$) 3,690 (2002 est)
CONSUMER PRICE INFLATION 2% (2003 est)
UNEMPLOYMENT 19.5% (2001)
FOREIGN DEBT (US$) 16.6 billion (2001 est)
MAJOR TRADING PARTNERS France, Spain, USA, UK, Saudi Arabia, Italy, Germany, India
RESOURCES phosphate rock and phosphoric acid, coal, iron ore, barytes, lead, copper, manganese, zinc, petroleum, natural gas, fish
INDUSTRIES phosphate products (chiefly fertilizers), petroleum refining, food processing, textiles, clothing, leather goods, paper and paper products, tourism
EXPORTS phosphates and phosphoric acid, mineral products, seafoods and seafood products, citrus fruit, tobacco, clothing, hosiery. Principal market: France 33.6% (2000)
IMPORTS crude petroleum, textiles, raw materials, wheat, chemicals, sawn wood,

consumer goods. Principal source: France 24.3% (2000)
ARABLE LAND 19.6% (2000 est)
AGRICULTURAL PRODUCTS wheat, barley, sugar beet, citrus fruits, tomatoes, olives, dates, potatoes; fishing (seafoods)

Population and society

POPULATION 30,566,000 (2003 est)
POPULATION GROWTH RATE 1.4% (2000–15)

Chronology

10th–3rd centuries BC: Phoenicians from Tyre settled along north coast.

1st century AD: Northwest Africa became Roman province of Mauritania.

5th–6th centuries: Invaded by Vandals and Visigoths.

682: Start of Arab conquest, followed by spread of Islam.

8th century: King Idris I established small Arab kingdom.

1056–1146: The Almoravids, a Berber dynasty based at Marrakesh, built an empire embracing Morocco and parts of Algeria and Spain.

1122–1268: After a civil war, the Almohads, a rival Berber dynasty, overthrew the Almoravids; Almohads extended empire but later lost most of Spain.

1258–1358: Beni Merin dynasty supplanted Almohads.

14th century: Moroccan Empire fragmented into separate kingdoms, based in Fez and Marrakesh.

15th century: Spain and Portugal occupied Moroccan ports; expulsion of Muslims from Spain in 1492.

16th century: Saadian dynasty restored unity of Morocco and resisted Turkish invasion.

1649: Foundation of current Alaouite dynasty of sultans; Morocco remained an independent and isolated kingdom.

1856: Under British pressure, the sultan opened Morocco to European commerce.

1860: Spain invaded Morocco, which was forced to cede the southwestern region of Ifni.

1905: A major international crisis was caused by German objections to increasing French influence in Morocco.

1911: Agadir Crisis: further German objections to French imperialism in Morocco were overcome by territorial compensation in central Africa.

1912: Morocco was divided into French and Spanish protectorates; the sultan was reduced to puppet ruler.

POPULATION DENSITY (per sq km) 68 (2003 est)
URBAN POPULATION (% of total) 57 (2003 est)
AGE DISTRIBUTION (% of total population) 0–14 34%, 15–59 60%, 60+ 6% (2002 est)
ETHNIC GROUPS majority indigenous Berbers (99%); sizeable Jewish minority
LANGUAGE Arabic (75%) (official), Berber dialects (25%), French, Spanish
RELIGION Sunni Muslim; Christian and Jewish minorities
EDUCATION (compulsory years) 6
LITERACY RATE 63% (men); 39% (women) (2003 est)
LABOUR FORCE 5.7% agriculture, 33.4% industry, 60.9% services (1999)
LIFE EXPECTANCY 67 (men); 71 (women) (2000–05)
CHILD MORTALITY RATE (under 5, per 1,000 live births) 44 (2001)
PHYSICIANS (per 1,000 people) 0.5 (1998 est)
HOSPITAL BEDS (per 1,000 people) 1 (1998 est)
TV SETS (per 1,000 people) 159 (2001)
RADIOS (per 1,000 people) 243 (2001)
INTERNET USERS (per 10,000 people) 168.7 (2002 est)
PERSONAL COMPUTER USERS (per 100 people) 1.5 (2002 est)

See also ▷Almoravid; ▷Western Sahara.

1921: Moroccan rebels, the Riffs, led by Abd el-Krim, defeated a large Spanish force at Anual.

1923: The city of Tangier was separated from Spanish Morocco and made a neutral international zone.

1926: French forces crushed Riff revolt.

1944: A nationalist party, Istiqlal, was founded to campaign for full independence.

1948: Consultative assemblies introduced.

1953–55: Serious anti-French riots.

1956: French and Spanish forces withdrew; Morocco regained effective independence under Sultan Muhammad V, who took title of king in 1957.

1961: Muhammad V succeeded by Hassan II.

1962: First constitution adopted; replaced in 1970 and 1972.

1965–77: King Hassan suspended the constitution and ruled by decree.

1969: Spanish overseas province of Ifni returned to Morocco.

1975: Spain withdrew from Western Sahara, leaving Morocco and Mauritania to divide it between themselves.

1976: Polisario Front, supported by Algeria, began guerrilla war in Western Sahara with the aim of securing its independence as the Sahrahwi Arab Democratic Republic.

1979: Mauritania withdrew from its portion of Western Sahara, which Morocco annexed after major battles with Polisario.

1984: Morocco signed mutual defence with Libya, which had previously supported Polisario.

1991: A UN-sponsored ceasefire came into effect in the Western Sahara.

1992: The constitution was amended in an attempt to increase the influence of parliament.

1996: A new two-chamber assembly was approved.

1998: Prime Minister Abderrahmane Youssoufi formed a centre–left coalition.

1999: King Hassan II died and was succeeded by his son, Muhammad VI.

2000: King Muhammad VI embarked on a programme of social and political reform, including strengthening the rights of women.

MOROCCO The Kasbah Valley in southern Morocco. Tinghir, once a garrison of the French Foreign Legion, is set amid the outstanding scenery of the Drâa Valley, with its red-earthern *kasbahs* (citadels) and surrounding mountains and gorges. *Image Bank*

MOSAIC The famous 'Alexander mosaic' at Pompeii, Italy, dating from the early 1st century BC and depicting the Battle of Issus between Alexander the Great and the Persian King Darius III. *The Art Archive/Archaeological Museum Naples/Dagli Orti*

Mosaic was commonly used by the Romans for their baths and villas (a well-known example being at Hadrian's Villa in Tivoli) and reached its highest development in the early Byzantine period (for example, in the church of San Vitale, Ravenna).

Moscow (Russian **Moskva**) industrial and commercial city, capital of the Russian Federation and of the Moscow region, and formerly (1922–91) of the USSR; population (1990) 8,801,000. Moscow lies on the Moskva River 640 km/400 mi southeast of St Petersburg, and covers an area of some 880 sq km/340 sq mi. It is the main political, economic, and cultural centre of Russia. A major manufacturing city, its industries include aerospace technology and vehicle assembly, machine and precision tool manufacture, and the production of such diverse goods as electrical equipment, textiles, chemicals, and many food products. Moscow's State University was founded in 1755; other cultural institutions include the extensive Russian State Library and the Academy of Sciences. The city is home to the renowned Bolshoi Theatre of Opera and Ballet, the Pushkin Fine Arts Museum, the Tretyakov Gallery, and the Exhibition of Economic Achievements.

Landmarks The 12th-century Kremlin ('Citadel'), at the centre of the city on the north bank of the river, is Moscow's main landmark. It is a walled enclosure containing several historic buildings, including three cathedrals, one of them the burial place of the tsars; the 90 m-/300 ft-high Ivan Veliki tower, a famine-relief work commissioned by Boris Godunov in 1600; various palaces, including the former imperial palace; museums; and the Tsar Kolokol, the world's largest bell (200 tonnes), cast in 1735. The Kremlin walls are crowned by 18 towers and have five gates. Red Square, adjoining the Kremlin on the northeast, contains St Basil's Cathedral and Lenin's tomb and was formerly the scene of Soviet military parades. To the southwest of the city centre lie the Central Lenin Stadium, a huge sports complex, and Gorky Park. The seat of the prime minister and national government of the Russian Federation, the marble 'White House', stands near the Kutuzovsky Bridge over the Moskva River. This building was a key location in the two failed coup attempts in 1991 and 1993.

History Moscow was first mentioned in chronicles in 1147 as a settlement near the southern frontier of the Rostov-Suzdal principality. The town was sacked by Mongols under Batu Khan in 1238, but was rebuilt by Daniel, the son of ▷Alexander Nevski, and established as the capital of his independent principality of Muscovy in 1294. During the 14th century, under the rule of Ivan I (1304–1341) and Dmitri Donskai (1350–1389), Moscow became the foremost political power in Russia and its religious capital. It also continued to develop as an important commercial and manufacturing centre, attracting a large artisan population. In 1712, Tsar Peter the Great transferred the Russian capital to St Petersburg, and Moscow was reduced to the role of a second capital throughout the imperial period. In 1812 the inhabitants of Moscow, having fled under the approach of Napoleon's troops, returned to find their city in ruins, with over two-thirds of the

buildings burned to the ground. Rebuilding was a major operation that took many decades to complete. With the collapse of the Tsarist regime during the 1917 October Revolution, Moscow regained its status as Russia's principal city, being made capital of the Russian Soviet Federated Social Republic (RSFSR) in 1918, and of the Union of Soviet Socialist Republics (USSR) in 1922. In 1941, Nazi forces advanced to within 32 km/20 mi of Moscow, but were defeated by a fierce Russian defence and severe weather conditions. In the turmoil that preceded and followed the demise of the Soviet Union in the early 1990s, Moscow was the scene of two abortive coup attempts, the first in 1991 by hardline communists attempting to overthrow Mikhail Gorbachev, and the second, in 1993, by conservative parliamentary leaders opposed to the constitutional reforms of President Boris Yeltsin.

Related Web site: Exploring Moscow http://www.interknowledge.com/russia/moscow01.htm

MOSCOW Situated in the Kremlin, Moscow, Russia, the Cathedral of the Assumption is one of the most holy places in the Russian Orthodox church. The tsars of Russia were crowned here. *Image Bank*

Moselle (German **Mosel**) river in Western Europe, some 515 km/320 mi long. It rises in the Vosges Mountains, France, in two headwaters uniting near St-Maurice. It flows north past Metz and is canalized from Thionville to its confluence with the ▷Rhine at Koblenz in Germany. It gives its name to the *départements* of Moselle and Meurthe-et-Moselle in France. Vineyards along the Moselle in Germany produce popular white wines.

Moses (lived *c.* 13th century BC) Hebrew lawgiver and judge who led the Israelites out of Egypt to the promised land of Canaan. On Mount Sinai he claimed to have received from Jehovah the oral and written Law, including the **Ten Commandments** engraved on tablets of stone. The first five books of the Old Testament – in Judaism, the *Torah* – are ascribed to him.

According to the Torah, the infant Moses was hidden among the bulrushes on the banks of the Nile when the pharaoh commanded that all newborn male Hebrew children should be destroyed. He was found by a daughter of the pharaoh, who reared him. Eventually he became the leader of the Israelites in their **Exodus** from Egypt and their 40 years' wandering in the wilderness. He died at the age of 120, after having been allowed a glimpse of the Promised Land from Mount Pisgah.

MOSES Orazio Gentileschi's *Moses Rescued from the River Nile*, painted in 1630–33. *The Art Archive/Prado Museum Madrid*

Moses, 'Grandma' (1860–1961) Born Anna Mary Robertson. US painter. Born in Washington County, New York, she began full-time painting about 1927, after many years as a farmer's wife. She was self-taught, and painted naive and colourful scenes from rural American life. Her first solo exhibition *What a Farmwife Painted* was held in New York in 1940. Her work was subsequently seen in many exhibitions in the USA, Canada, and Europe.

Moskva Russian name for ▷Moscow, the capital of the Russian Federation.

Moslem alternative spelling of **Muslim**, a follower of ▷Islam.

Mosley, Oswald (Ernald) (1896–1980) British politician, founder of the British Union of Fascists (BUF) in 1932. He was a member of Parliament 1918–31. A Conservative MP for Harrow 1918–22, he joined the Labour party in 1924 and represented Shetwick 1926–31. He resigned in 1931 and founded the New Party. He then led the BUF until his internment 1940–43 during World War II. In 1946 Mosley was denounced when it became known that Italy had funded his prewar efforts to establish ▷fascism in the UK, but in 1948 he resumed fascist propaganda with his Union Movement, the revived BUF.

mosque (Arabic *mesjid*) in Islam, a place of worship. Chief features are: the dome; the minaret, a balconied turret from which the faithful are called to prayer; the *mihrab*, or prayer niche, in one of the interior walls, showing the direction of the holy city of Mecca; and an open court surrounded by porticoes.

mosquito any of a group of flies in which the female has needlelike mouthparts and sucks blood before laying eggs. The males feed on plant juices. Some mosquitoes carry diseases such as ▷malaria. (Family Culicidae, order Diptera.)

Related Web site: Mosquito Bytes http://whyfiles.news.wisc.edu/016skeeter/index.html

Mosquito Coast Caribbean coast of Honduras and Nicaragua, characterized by swamp, lagoons, and tropical rainforest. The territory is inhabited by Miskito Indians, Garifunas, and Zambos, many of whom speak English. Between 1823 and 1860 Britain maintained a protectorate over the Mosquito Coast which was ruled by a succession of 'Mosquito Kings'.

moss small nonflowering plant of the class Musci (10,000 species), forming with the ▷liverworts and the ▷hornworts the order Bryophyta. The stem of each plant bears rhizoids that anchor it; there are no true roots. Leaves spirally arranged on its lower portion have sexual organs at their tips. Most mosses flourish best in damp conditions where other vegetation is thin. There are 1,000 British species of moss and more than 1,200 North American species.

MOSS Antheridia of the moss *Bryum schleicheri*. The antherozoids (male gametes) are formed in the antheridia. *K G Preston-Mafham/Premaphotos Wildlife*

Mossi member of the majority ethnic group living in Burkina Faso. Their social structure, based on a monarchy, aristocracy, commoners, and slaves, was established in the 13th–14th centuries. There are about 4 million speakers of Mossi, a language belonging to the Gur branch of the Niger–Congo family.

Mostar industrial town (aluminium, tobacco) in Bosnia-Herzegovina, known for its grapes and wines; population (1991) 126,000. The eastern, mainly Muslim sector of the town was under siege by Bosnian Croat forces 1993–94.

moth any of a large number of mainly night-flying insects closely related to butterflies. Their wings are covered with microscopic scales. Most moths have a long sucking mouthpart (proboscis) for feeding on the nectar of flowers, but some have no functional mouthparts and rely instead upon stores of fat and other reserves built up during the caterpillar stage. At least 100,000 different species of moth are known. (Order Lepidoptera.)

Moths feed chiefly on nectar and other fluid matter; some, like the ▷hawk moths, frequent flowers and feed while hovering. The females of some species (such as bagworm moths) have no wings at all or wings that are reduced to tiny flaps. Moths vary greatly in size: the minute Nepticulidae sometimes have a wingspread less than 3 mm/0.1 in, while the giant Noctuid or owlet moth (*Erebus agrippina*) measures about 280 mm/11 in across. In many cases the males are smaller and more brightly coloured than the females.

The larvae (caterpillars) have a well-developed head and three thoracic (middle) and ten abdominal (end) segments. Each

MOTH Not all moths are night-flying. The burnet moths (family Zygaenidae), such as this *Zygaena praslini* from Israel, are active exclusively by day when they can exhibit their aposematic (warning) colours. *Premaphotos Wildlife*

thoracic segment has a pair of short legs, ending in single claws; a pair of suckerlike feet is present on segments three to six and ten of the end part of the body. In the family Geometridae the caterpillars have abdominal feet only on segments six and ten of the end part of the body. They move in a characteristic looping way and are known as 'loopers', 'inchworms', or geometers. Projecting from the middle of the lower lip of a caterpillar is a tiny tube or spinneret, through which silk is produced to make a cocoon within which the change to the pupa or chrysalis occurs. Silk glands are especially large in the ▷silkworm moth. Many caterpillars, including the geometers, which are hunted by birds, are protected by their resemblance in both form and colour to their immediate surroundings. Others, which are distasteful to such enemies, are brightly coloured or densely hairy.

The feeding caterpillars of many moths cause damage: the codling moth, for example, attacks fruit trees; and several species of clothes moth eat natural fibres.

The winter moth attacks fruit trees; the Mediterranean flour moth infects flour mills. The largest British moths are the death's head and convolvulus hawk moths, which have a wingspread ranging from 114 mm/4.5 in to 133 mm/5.25 in.

motherboard ▷printed circuit board that contains the main components of a microcomputer. The power, memory capacity, and capability of the microcomputer may be enhanced by adding expansion boards to the motherboard, now more commonly called a mainboard.

mother-of-pearl (or nacre) the smooth lustrous lining in the shells of certain molluscs – for example pearl oysters, abalones, and mussels. When this layer is especially thick it is used commercially for jewellery and decorations. Mother-of-pearl consists of calcium carbonate. See ▷pearl.

Mother's Day day set apart in the USA, UK, and many European countries for honouring mothers. It is thought to have originated in Grafton, West Virginia, USA, in 1908 when Anna Jarvis observed the anniversary of her mother's death.

Related Web site: Story of Mother's Day http://www.holidays.net/mother/story.htm

motion picture US term for film; see ▷cinema.

motor anything that produces or imparts motion; a machine that provides mechanical power – for example, an electric motor. Machines that burn fuel (petrol, diesel) are usually called engines, but the internal-combustion engine that propels vehicles has long been called a motor, hence 'motoring' and 'motor car'. Actually the motor is a part of the car engine.

motorcycle (or motorbike) two-wheeled vehicle propelled by a ▷petrol engine. The first successful motorized bicycle was built in France in 1901, and British and US manufacturers first produced motorbikes in 1903.

History In 1868 Ernest and Pierre Michaux in France experimented with a steam-powered bicycle, but the steam-power unit was too heavy and cumbersome. Gottlieb ▷Daimler, a German engineer, created the first motorcycle when he installed his lightweight petrol engine in a bicycle frame in 1886. Daimler soon lost interest in two wheels in favour of four and went on to pioneer the ▷car.

The first really successful two-wheel design was devised by Michael and Eugene Werner in France in 1901. They adopted the classic motorcycle layout with the engine low down between the wheels.

Harley Davidson in the USA and Triumph in the UK began manufacture in 1903. Road races like the Isle of Man TT (Tourist Trophy), established in 1907, helped improve motorcycle design and it soon evolved into more or less its present form. British bikes included the Vincent, BSA, and Norton.

Industry In the 1970s British manufacturers were overtaken by Japanese ones, and such motorcycles as Honda, Kawasaki, Suzuki, and Yamaha now dominate the world market. They make a wide variety of machines, from mopeds (lightweights with pedal assistance) to streamlined superbikes capable of speeds up to 250 kph/160 mph. There is still a smaller but thriving Italian motorcycle industry, making more specialist bikes. Laverda, Moto Guzzi, and Ducati continue to manufacture in Italy.

Technical description The lightweight bikes are generally powered by a two-stroke petrol engine (see ▷two-stroke cycle), while bikes with an engine capacity of 250 cc or more are generally four-strokes (see ▷four-stroke cycle). However, many special-use larger bikes (such as those developed for off-road riding and racing) are two-stroke. Most motorcycles are air-cooled – their engines are surrounded by metal fins to offer a large surface area – although some have a water-cooling system similar to that of a car. Most small bikes have single-cylinder engines, but larger machines can have as many as six. The single-cylinder engine is economical and was popular in British manufacture; the Japanese developed multiple-cylinder models, but there has recently been some return to single-cylinder engines. A revived British Norton racing motorcycle uses a Wankel (rotary) engine. In the majority of bikes a chain carries the drive from the engine to the rear wheel, though some machines are now fitted with shaft drive.

Related Web site: Harley Davidson http://www.harley-davidson-london.co.uk/

motorcycle racing speed contests on motorcycles. It has many different forms: **road racing** over open roads; **circuit racing** over purpose-built tracks; **speedway** over oval-shaped dirt tracks; **motocross** over natural terrain, incorporating hill climbs; and **trials**, also over natural terrain, but with the addition of artificial hazards.

Related Web site: AMA Superbike http://www.amasuperbike.com/

MOTORCYCLE RACING A rider cornering in a motocross event in Norway. *Image Bank*

motor effect tendency of a wire carrying an electric current in a magnetic field to move. The direction of the movement is given by the left-hand rule (see ▷Fleming's rules). This effect is used in the ▷electric motor. It also explains why streams of electrons produced, for instance, in a television tube can be directed by electromagnets.

motoring law legislation affecting the use of vehicles on public roads. It covers the licensing of vehicles and drivers, and the criminal offences that can be committed by the owners and drivers of vehicles.

motor nerve in anatomy, any nerve that transmits impulses from the central nervous system to muscles or organs. Motor nerves cause voluntary and involuntary muscle contractions, and stimulate glands to secrete hormones.

motor neuron disease (MND or amyotrophic lateral sclerosis) chronic disease in which there is progressive degeneration of the nerve cells which instigate movement. It leads to weakness, wasting, and loss of muscle function and usually proves fatal within two to three years of onset. Motor neuron disease occurs in both familial and sporadic forms but its causes remain unclear. A gene believed to be implicated in familial cases was discovered in 1993.

motor racing competitive racing of motor vehicles. It has forms as diverse as hill-climbing, stock-car racing, rallying, sports-car racing, and Formula 1 Grand Prix racing. The first organized race was from Paris to Rouen, France, in 1894. Outside of Formula 1, other events include the Le Mans Grand Prix d'Endurance and the Indianapolis 500. Rally-driving events include the Monte Carlo Rally, the Acropolis Rally, and the Rally of Great Britain, first held in 1932.

Related Web site: Sky Sports Online Motor Sports http://www.sky.com/sports/motorsports/

motorway main road for fast motor traffic, with two or more lanes in each direction, and with special access points (junctions) fed by slip roads. After World War II motorways were built in a growing number of countries, for example the USA, France, and the UK. The most ambitious building programme was in the USA, which by 1974 had 70,800 km/44,000 mi of 'expressway'. Construction of new motorways causes much environmental concern.

MOTORWAY A section of the M8 motorway between Edinburgh and Glasgow in Scotland. *Aerofilms*

Motown first black-owned US record company, founded in Detroit (Mo[tor] Town) in 1959 by Berry Gordy, Jr (1929–   ). Its distinctive, upbeat sound (exemplified by the Four Tops and the ▷Supremes) was a major element in 1960s pop music.

mouflon wild sheep found in mountain areas of Cyprus, Corsica, and Sardinia. It has woolly underfur in winter, but this is covered by heavy guard hairs. The coat is brown with a white belly and rump. Males have strong, curving horns. (Species *Ovis ammon*, family Bovidae.)

mould furlike growth caused by any of a group of fungi (see ▷fungus) living on foodstuffs and other organic matter; a few are parasitic on plants, animals, or each other. Many moulds are of medical or industrial importance; for example, the antibiotic penicillin comes from a type of mould.

moulding use of a pattern, hollow form, or matrix to give a specific shape to something in a plastic or molten state. It is

The First Motorways

The world's first motorway (85 km/53 mi) ran from Milan to Varese, Italy, and was completed in 1924; by 1939 some 500 km/300 mi of motorway had been built, although these did not attain the standards of later express highways. In Germany some 2,100 km/1,310 mi of Autobahnen had been completed by 1942.

The first motorway in the UK, the Preston by-pass (now part of the M6) was opened in 1958, and the first section of the M1 was opened in 1959.

commonly used for shaping plastics, clays, and glass. When metals are used, the process is called ▷casting.

Moulins administrative centre of the *département* of Allier in the Auvergne region of central France, situated on the River Allier; population (1990) 23,400. It is a market town for the surrounding agricultural region, and its main industries are cutlery, textiles, glass, leather, electrical products, and food processing. Moulins was capital of the old province of Bourbonnais from 1368 to 1527.

moulting periodic shedding of the hair or fur of mammals, feathers of birds, or skin of reptiles. In mammals and birds, moulting is usually seasonal and is triggered by changes of day length.

The term is also often applied to the shedding of the ▷exoskeleton of arthropods, but this is more correctly called ▷ecdysis.

Moundbuilder member of any of the various American Indian peoples of the Midwest and the South who built earth mounds, from about 300 BC. Some mounds were linear and pictographic in form, such as the Great Serpent Mound in Ohio, with truncated pyramids and cones for the platforms of chiefs' houses and temples. The ▷Hopewell and ▷Natchez were Moundbuilders.

mountain natural upward projection of the Earth's surface, higher and steeper than a hill. Mountains are at least 330 m/1000 ft above the surrounding topography. The existing rock is also subjected to high temperatures and pressures causing metamorphism. Plutonic activity also can accompany mountain building.

mountain ash (or rowan) European flowering tree. It grows to 15 m/50 ft and has pinnate leaves (leaflets growing either side of the stem) and large clusters of whitish flowers, followed by scarlet berries in autumn. (*Sorbus aucuparia*, family Rosaceae.)

MOUNTAIN ASH The mountain ash, or rowan, is native to Europe and West Asia. The tree has divided leaves with small toothed leaflets and red berries and grows to a height of 18 m/60 ft.

mountain biking recreational sport that enjoyed increasing popularity in the 1990s. Mountain bikes were developed from the rugged 'clunkers' ridden by a small group of off-road riders on the steep, rocky hillsides of Marin County, California, in the mid-70s. The fashion spread and the first mass-produced model appeared in the USA in 1981, and in the UK in 1984.

mountaineering art and practice of mountain climbing. For major peaks of the Himalayas it was formerly thought necessary to have elaborate support from Sherpas (local people), fixed ropes, and oxygen at high altitudes (**siege-style** climbing). In the 1980s the **Alpine style** was introduced. This dispenses with these aids, and relies on human ability to adapt, Sherpa-style, to high altitude.

mountain gorilla highly endangered ape found in bamboo and rainforest on the Rwanda, Democratic Republic of Congo (formerly Zaire), and Uganda borders in central Africa, with a total population of around 600 (1995). It is threatened by deforestation and illegal hunting for skins and the zoo trade. (Subspecies *Gorilla gorilla beringei*.)

mountain lion another name for the ▷puma.

Mountbatten, Louis Francis Albert Victor Nicholas (1900–1979) 1st Earl Mountbatten of Burma. English admiral and administrator, a great-grandson of Queen Victoria. In World War II he became chief of combined operations in 1942 and commander-in-chief in southeast Asia in 1943. As last viceroy and governor

general of India 1947–48, he oversaw that country's transition to independence. He was killed by an Irish Republican Army (IRA) bomb aboard his yacht at Mullaghmore, County Sligo, in the Republic of Ireland. He was knighted in 1922, became a viscount in 1945, and an earl in 1947.

As chief of combined operations he was criticized for the heavy loss of Allied lives in the disastrous Dieppe raid. In southeast Asia he concentrated on the reconquest of Burma, although the campaign was actually conducted by General ▷Slim. Mountbatten accepted the surrender of 750,000 Japanese troops in his area of command at a formal parade in Singapore in September 1945. He was chief of UK Defence Staff 1959–65.

Mounties popular name for the **Royal Canadian Mounted Police**, known for their uniform of red jacket and broad-brimmed hat. Their Security Service, established 1950, was disbanded 1981 and replaced by the independent Canadian Security Intelligence Service.

Mount Palomar astronomical observatory, near Pasedena, California. Its telescopes include the 5-m/200-in diameter reflector called the Hale, and the 1.2-m/48-in Schmidt Telescope. Completed in 1948, it was the world's premier observatory during the 1950s.

Mount Stromlo Observatory astronomical observatory established in Canberra, Australia, in 1923. Important observations have been made there on the Magellanic Clouds, which can be seen clearly from southern Australia.

Mount Wilson site near Los Angeles, California, of the 2.5 m/100 in Hooker telescope, opened in 1917, with which Edwin Hubble discovered the expansion of the universe. Two solar telescopes in towers 18.3 m/60 ft and 45.7 m/150 ft tall, and a 1.5 m/60 in reflector opened in 1908, also operate there.

Mourning Becomes Electra trilogy of plays by Eugene ▷O'Neill in 1931 that retells the Orestes legend, dramatized by Aeschylus (see ▷Oresteia), setting it in the world of 19th-century New England. The three are considered among the greatest of modern US plays.

mouse in computing, an input device used to control a pointer on a computer screen. It is a feature of ▷graphical user interface (GUI) systems. The mouse is about the size of a pack of playing cards, is connected to the computer by a wire, and incorporates one or more buttons that can be pressed. Moving the mouse across a flat surface causes a corresponding movement of the pointer. In this way, the operator can manipulate objects on the screen and make menu selections.

mouse in zoology, one of a number of small rodents with small ears and a long, thin tail. The **house mouse** (*Mus musculus*) is distributed worldwide. It is 75 mm/3 in long, with a naked tail of the same length, and has a grey-brown body. (Family Muridae.)

Common in Britain is the **wood mouse** (*Apodemus sylvaticus*), richer in colour, and normally shy of human habitation. The tiny **harvest mouse** (*Micromys minutus*), 65–75 mm/2.5–3 in long, makes spherical nests of straw supported on grass stems. It is threatened with extinction: a survey conducted in 1997 by the Mammal Society showed that harvest mice had disappeared from 71% of the nest sites they occupied in the 1970s. **Jumping mice** (family Zapodidae), with enlarged back legs, live across the northern hemisphere, except in Britain.

mousebird any of a family of small crested birds found only in Africa. They have hairlike feathers, long tails, and move with a mouselike agility. The largest is the **blue-naped mousebird** (*Colius macrourus*), about 35 cm/14 in long. (Family Coliidae, order Coliiformes.)

Moustier, Le rock shelter in the Dordogne, southwestern France, with prehistoric remains. It gave the name Mousterian to a type of flint-tool culture associated with Neanderthal sites of 100,000–40,000 years ago.

mouth cavity forming the entrance to the digestive tract. In land vertebrates, air from the nostrils enters the mouth cavity to pass down the trachea. The mouth in mammals is enclosed by the jaws, cheeks, and palate.

mouth organ any of a family of small portable free-reed wind instruments originating in Eastern and South Asia. The compact **harmonica**, or European mouth organ, developed by Charles Wheatstone in 1829, has tuned metal free reeds of variable length contained in a narrow rectangular box and is played by blowing and sucking air while moving the instrument from side to side through the lips.

movement in music, a self-contained composition of specific character, usually a constituent piece of a ▷suite, ▷symphony, or similar work, with its own tempo, distinct from that of the other movements.

Mozambique see country box.

Mozart, (Johann Chrysostom) Wolfgang Amadeus (1756–1791) Austrian composer and performer who showed astonishing precocity as a child and was an adult virtuoso. He was trained by his father, **Leopold Mozart** (1719–1787). From an early age he composed prolifically, and his works include 27 piano concertos, 23 string quartets, 35 violin sonatas, and 41 symphonies including the E♭ K543, G minor K550, and C major K551 ('Jupiter') symphonies, all composed in 1788. His operas include *Idomeneo* (1780), *Entführung aus dem Serail/The Abduction from the Seraglio* (1782), *Le Nozze di Figaro/The Marriage of Figaro* (1786), *Don Giovanni* (1787), *Così fan tutte/Thus Do All Women* (1790), and *Die Zauberflöte/The Magic Flute* (1791). Together with the work of Haydn, Mozart's music marks the height of the classical age in its purity of melody and form.

> **Wolfgang Amadeus Mozart**
> *Neither a lofty degree of intelligence nor imagination nor both together go to the making of genius. Love, love, love, that is the soul of genius.*
> Attributed remark

Mozart's career began when, with his sister, Maria Anna, he was taken on a number of tours 1762–79, visiting Vienna, the Rhineland, Holland, Paris, London, and Italy. He had already begun to compose. In 1772 he was appointed master of the archbishop of Salzburg's court band, but found the post uncongenial and in 1781 was suddenly dismissed. He married Constanze Weber in 1782, settled in Vienna, and embarked on a punishing freelance career as a concert pianist, composer, and teacher that brought lasting fame but only intermittent financial security. His *Requiem*, unfinished at his death, was completed by a pupil.

His works were catalogued chronologically in 1862 by the musicologist Ludwig von Köchel (1800–1877) whose system of numbering – giving each work a 'Köchel number' – for example K354 – remains in use in modified form.

WOLFGANG AMADEUS MOZART The young musical genius Wolfgang Amadeus Mozart playing at a recital for the French aristocracy (c. 1763). *Philip Sauvain Picture Collection*

MP abbreviation for **member of Parliament**.
  Related Web site: House of Commons – Members, Ministers, and Committees 1997–1998 http://www.parliament.uk/commons/lib/lists.htm

MP3 (contraction of MPEG-1 Audio Layer 3) specification for a way of compressing digital sound files with very little loss of quality. This allows files, particularly music files such as pop songs, to be distributed via the Internet at low cost. MP3 is Layer 3 of the MPEG-2 video compression system developed by the Moving Pictures Expert Group (MPEG).

mpg abbreviation for **miles per gallon**.

mph abbreviation for **miles per hour**.

MPLA (abbreviation for Movimento Popular de Libertaçaõ de Angola/Popular Movement for the Liberation of Angola) socialist organization founded in the early 1950s that sought to free Angola from Portuguese rule 1961–75 before being involved in the civil war against its former allies ▷UNITA and FNLA 1975–76. The MPLA gained control of the country in 1976 and in 1977 renamed itself the People's Movement for the Liberation of Angola-Workers' Party (**MPLA-PT**). It won the first multiparty elections in 1992, but UNITA disputed the result and guerrilla activity continued, escalating into full-scale civil war in 1993. A peace agreement was signed with UNITA in 1994.

Mpumalanga (formerly **Eastern Transvaal**) province of the Republic of South Africa from 1994, formerly part of Transvaal

MP3

The Internet is set to have a profound influence on recorded music. Already, CDs can be bought more cheaply from Web sites outside the UK than from high street shops. According to a Mintel report published in August 1999, the value of music sales online is expected to soar from a 1998 figure of $29 million to $3.9 billion in 2005. However, the development of even cheaper ways of acquiring music threatens to undermine the traditional recording industry.

MP3 (short for Motion Picture Experts Group Audio Level 3) is a technology that allows the storage of CD-quality digital sound in a compact file format; it can be replayed on a computer or on a special MP3 player, and can be copied onto compact disc. MP3 compresses each minute of music into one megabyte of computer-readable digital data, so downloading a five-minute pop track can be done quickly, especially on a modern Pentium processor. MP3 could pose a challenge to big record producers and famous labels, because the ease with which MP3 tracks can be transmitted over the Internet is an open invitation to piracy and copyright infringement, or at least to the free acquisition of music. But many artists, especially those lesser known, may welcome MP3 as a means of promoting themselves or reaping more directly the profits of their talents.

province; area 81,816 sq km/31,589 sq mi; population (1995 est) 3,007,100. The capital is Nelspruit. Features of the province include Limpopo River, Vaal River, Kruger National Park, Blyde River Canyon Nature Reserve, and Mpumalanga Drakensberg Mountains. Industries include farming and coal. Languages spoken in the province are Siswati, Zulu, and Afrikaans.

Mr abbreviation for **mister**, title used before a name to show that the person is male.

Mrs title used before a name to show that the person is married and female; partly superseded by Ms, which does not indicate marital status. Mrs was originally an abbreviation for **mistress**.

MS abbreviation for ▷Mississippi, a state of the USA.

Ms title used before a woman's name; pronounced 'miz'. Unlike Miss or Mrs, it can be used by married or unmarried women, and was introduced by the women's movement in the 1970s to parallel Mr, which also does not distinguish marital status.

MSc in education, abbreviation for the degree of **Master of Science**. The US abbreviation is **MS**.

MS-DOS (abbreviation for Microsoft Disk Operating System) computer ▷operating system produced by Microsoft Corporation, widely used on ▷microcomputers with Intel x 86 and Pentium family microprocessors. A version called PC-DOS is sold by IBM specifically for its personal computers. MS-DOS and PC-DOS are usually referred to as DOS. MS-DOS first appeared in 1981, and was similar to an earlier system from Digital Research called CP/M.

MT abbreviation for ▷Montana, a state of the USA.

MTBF abbreviation for **mean time between failures**, the statistically average time a component can be used before it goes wrong. The MTBF of a computer hard disk, for example, is around 150,000 hours.

Mubarak, Hosni (1928–) Egyptian politician, president from 1981. Vice-president to Anwar Sadat from 1975, Mubarak succeeded him on his assassination. He continued to pursue Sadat's moderate policies, and significantly increased the freedom of the press and of political association, while trying to repress the growing Islamic fundamentalist movement. He was re-elected (uncontested) in 1987 and 1993. He survived an assassination attempt in 1995. Mubarak, was re-elected in September 1999 to a fourth six-year term after taking nearly 94% of the vote in a poll whose result was never in doubt. Mubarak faced no challenger in the referendum. He began his term by replacing his prime minister, Kamal Ganzouri, with an economist, Atef Obeid, who headed Egypt's privatization programme.

Mubarak commanded the air force 1972–75 and was responsible for the initial victories in the Egyptian campaign of 1973 against Israel. He led Egypt's opposition to Iraq's invasion of Kuwait in 1990 and played an instrumental role in arranging the Middle East peace conference in November 1991.

Mucha, Alphonse Maria (1860–1939) Czech painter and designer, one of the leading figures of ▷art nouveau. His posters and decorative panels brought him international fame, presenting idealized images of young women with long, flowing hair, within a patterned flowered border. His early theatre posters were done for the actor Sarah Bernhardt, notably the lithograph *Gismonda* (1894).

Muckrakers, the movement of US writers and journalists about 1880–1914 who aimed to expose political, commercial, and corporate corruption, and record frankly the age of industrialism, urban poverty, and conspicuous consumption. Novelists included Frank ▷Norris, Theodore Dreiser, Jack ▷London, and Upton Sinclair. The muckrakers were closely associated with ▷Progressivism.

mucous membrane thin skin lining all animal body cavities and canals that come into contact with the air (for example, eyelids, breathing and digestive passages, genital tract). It secretes mucus, a moistening, lubricating, and protective fluid.

mucus lubricating and protective fluid, secreted by mucous membranes in many different parts of the body. In the gut, mucus smooths the passage of food and keeps potentially damaging digestive enzymes away from the gut lining. In the lungs, it traps airborne particles so that they can be expelled.

mudfish another name for the ▷bowfin.

mudnester any of an Australian group of birds that make their nests from mud, including the **apostle bird** (*Struthidea cinerea*) (so called from its appearance in little flocks of about 12), the **white-winged chough** (*Corcorax melanorhamphos*), and the **magpie lark** (*Grallina cyanoleuca*).

mudpuppy any of five species of brownish ▷salamanders, living in fresh water in North America. They all breathe in water using external gills. The species *N. maculatus* is about 20 cm/8 in long. Mudpuppies eat fish, snails, and other invertebrates. (Genus *Necturus*, family Proteidae.)

mudskipper any of a group of fishes belonging to the goby family, found in brackish water and shores in the tropics, except for the Americas. It can walk or climb over mudflats, using its strong pectoral (chest) fins as legs, and has eyes set close together on top of the head. It grows up to 30 cm/12 in long. (Genus *Periophthalmus*, family Gobiidae.)

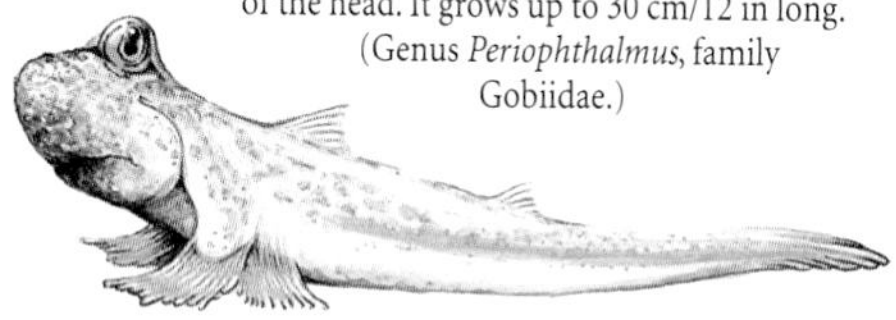

MUDSKIPPER Mudskippers often leave the waters of the mangrove swamps and tidal flats of the Indian and Pacific Oceans where they live, to lie on the mud or climb on exposed mangrove roots. Alert to danger, they quickly skip away when disturbed.

mudstone fine-grained sedimentary rock made up of clay- to silt-sized particles (up to 0.0625 mm/0.0025 in).

muezzin (Arabic) a person whose job is to perform the call to prayer five times a day from the minaret of a Muslim mosque.

Mugabe, Robert (Gabriel) (1925–) Zimbabwean politician, prime minister from 1980 and president from 1987. He was in detention in Rhodesia for nationalist activities 1964–74, then carried on guerrilla warfare from Mozambique. As leader of ▷ZANU(Zimbabwe African National Union) he was in an uneasy alliance with Joshua ▷Nkomo of ZAPU (Zimbabwe African People's Union) from 1976 until 1987, when the two parties merged under Mugabe's leadership. His one-party rule came under criticism in the 1990s and in 2000 as Zimbabwe suffered economic decline and increased political violence.

Mugabe is a member of the Shona people, and was educated at Fort Hare University, South Africa. In 1985 he postponed the introduction of a multiparty state for five years. His failure to anticipate and respond to the 1991–92 drought in southern Africa adversely affected his popularity, but he was re-elected, unchallenged, in February 1996. In May 1998 he faced student demonstrations against alleged government corruption and in November there were violent protests in Harare at the rise in fuel prices and the country's involvement in the Congo war. In February 1999 there were more violent protests against Mugabe. In June the human rights group African Rights produced a scathing report on his government, accusing it of corruption, human rights abuse, and lack of respect for the rule of law.

Criticism of his leadership multiplied in 2000 following Mugabe's role as an aggressor in the repossession of white farms for land redistribution, and his invoking of special presidential powers in order to seize land without compensation. Human rights group Amnesty International announced in June 2000 that owing to state-sponsored terrorism, a free and fair election was no longer possible in imminent parliamentary elections in Zimbabwe. Mugabe was re-elected as president in 2002.

mugwump (from Algonquin 'chief') in US political history, a colloquial name for the reform Republicans who voted in the 1884 presidential election for Grover Cleveland, the Democratic candidate, rather than for the Republican nominee James G Blaine. Blaine was accused of financial improprieties, and the reform-minded mugwumps were partly responsible for his defeat. The term has come to mean a politician who remains neutral on divisive issues.

Muhammad (or **Mohammed** or **Mahomet**) (*c.* 570–632) (Arabic 'praised') Founder of Islam, born in Mecca on the Arabian peninsula. In about 616 he began to preach the worship of one God, who allegedly revealed to him the words of the Koran (it was later written down by his followers) through the angel Jibra'el (Gabriel). Muhammad fled from persecution to the town now known as Medina in 622: the flight, **Hijrah** or **Hegira**, marks the beginning of the Islamic era.

Muhammad was originally a shepherd and trader. He married Khadija, a widow, in 595, spent time in meditation, and received his first revelation in 610. The series of revelations continued throughout his life. At first he doubted their divine origin but later he began to teach others, who wrote down the words of his revelations; they were collected after his death to form the Koran.

The move to Medina resulted in the first Islamic community, which for many years fought battles against fierce opposition from Mecca and from neighbouring tribes. In 630 the Muslim army defeated that of Mecca and the city came under Muslim rule. By the time of Muhammad's death in 632, Islam had spread throughout the Arabian peninsula. After his death, the leadership of the Muslims was disputed.

Muslims believe that Muhammad was the final prophet, although they recognize other, earlier prophets, including Ibrahim (Abraham) and Isa (Jesus). Muhammad is not worshipped, but honoured by the words 'Peace be upon him' whenever Muslims mention his name.

Muir, Edwin (1887–1959) Scottish poet. He drew mystical inspiration from his Orkney childhood. *First Poems* (1925) was published after an extended period of travel and residence in Europe, which also resulted in translations from German of Franz Kafka and Lion Feuchtwanger, in collaboration with his wife, the novelist Willa Anderson (1890–1970). Dreams, myths, and menaces coexist in his poetry and his *Autobiography* (1954) explores similar themes.

Mujahedin (Arabic *mujahid* 'fighters', from *jihad* 'holy war') Islamic fundamentalist guerrillas of contemporary Afghanistan and Iran.

Mukden, Battle of Japanese victory over the Russians during the ▷Russo-Japanese War, February–March 1905, outside Mukden (now called Shenyang), capital city of Manchuria. This was the last major battle of the war – the Russian defeat finally persuaded the tsar to accept US mediation in June 1905.

mulberry any of a group of trees consisting of a dozen species, including the black mulberry (*M. nigra*). It is native to western Asia and has heart-shaped, toothed leaves and spikes of whitish flowers. It is widely cultivated for its compound fruits, which resemble raspberries. The leaves of the Asiatic white mulberry (*M. alba*) are those used in feeding silkworms. (Genus *Morus*, family Moraceae.)

Muldoon, Robert David (1921–1992) New Zealand National Party right-of-centre politician, prime minister 1975–84. He pursued austere economic policies such as a wage-and-price policy to control inflation, sought to introduce curbs on trade unions, was a vigorous supporter of the Western alliance, and was a proponent of reform of the international monetary system. A traditionalist and somewhat authoritarian conservative, Muldoon sought to maintain close links with the UK and the USA, gave state assistance to farmers and industrialists, and promoted traditional social values. He came into conflict with feminists, Maori rights campaigners, and anti-nuclear campaigners, who

Mozambique

Mozambique country in southeast Africa, bounded north by Zambia, Malawi, and Tanzania; east and south by the Indian Ocean; southwest by South Africa and Swaziland; and west by Zimbabwe.

NATIONAL NAME *República de Moçambique/Republic of Mozambique*
AREA 799,380 sq km/308,640 sq mi
CAPITAL Maputo (and chief port)
MAJOR TOWNS/CITIES Beira, Nampula, Nacala, Chimoio
MAJOR PORTS Beira, Nacala, Quelimane
PHYSICAL FEATURES mostly flat tropical lowland; mountains in west; rivers Zambezi and Limpopo

Government

HEAD OF STATE Joaquim Alberto Chissano from 1986
HEAD OF GOVERNMENT Luisa Diogo from 2004
POLITICAL SYSTEM emergent democracy
POLITICAL EXECUTIVE limited presidency
ADMINISTRATIVE DIVISIONS 11 provinces
ARMED FORCES 11,000 (2002 est)
CONSCRIPTION two years

AIDS educators perform an educational song in Bobole, Mozambique.
© Gideon Mendel/CORBIS

DEATH PENALTY abolished in 1990
DEFENCE SPEND (% GDP) 2 (2002 est)
EDUCATION SPEND (% GDP) 2.4 (2000 est)
HEALTH SPEND (% GDP) 4.3 (2000 est)

Economy and resources

CURRENCY metical
GPD (US$) 3.9 billion (2002 est)
REAL GDP GROWTH (% change on previous year) 13.9 (2001)
GNI (US$) 3.9 billion (2002 est)
GNI PER CAPITA (PPP) (US$) 1,180 (2002 est)
CONSUMER PRICE INFLATION 8.5% (2003 est)
FOREIGN DEBT (US$) 7.1 billion (2001 est)
MAJOR TRADING PARTNERS South Africa, Spain, USA, Japan, Zimbabwe, Portugal, UK
RESOURCES coal, salt, bauxite, graphite; reserves of iron ore, gold, precious and semi-precious stones, marble, natural gas (all largely unexploited in 1996)
INDUSTRIES aluminium smelting (one of the world's top producers), food products, steel, engineering, textiles and clothing, beverages, tobacco, chemical products
EXPORTS alumimium, shrimps, lobsters, and other crustaceans, cashew nuts, raw cotton, coal, sugar, sisal, copra. Principal market: Spain 15.3% (2001)
IMPORTS machinery and equipment, foodstuffs, capital goods, crude petroleum and petroleum products, textiles, metal products, chemicals. Principal source: South Africa 40.5% (2001)
ARABLE LAND 5% (2000 est)
AGRICULTURAL PRODUCTS cassava, maize, bananas, rice, groundnuts, copra, cashew nuts, cotton, sugar cane; fishing (shrimps, prawns, and lobsters) is principal export

Chronology

1st–4th centuries AD: Bantu-speaking peoples settled in Mozambique.
8th–15th century: Arab gold traders established independent city-states on the coast.
1498: Portuguese navigator Vasco da Gama was the first European visitor; at this time the most important local power was the Maravi kingdom of the Mwene Matapa peoples, who controlled much of the Zambezi basin.
1626: The Mwene Matapa formally recognized Portuguese sovereignty. Portuguese soldiers set up private agricultural estates and used slave labour to exploit gold and ivory resources.
late 17th century: Portuguese temporarily pushed south of Zambezi by the ascendant Rozwi kingdom.
1752: First Portuguese colonial governor appointed; slave trade outlawed.
late 19th century: Concessions given by Portugal to private companies to develop and administer parts of Mozambique.
1930: Colonial Act established more centralized Portuguese rule, ending concessions to monopolistic companies and forging closer integration with Lisbon.
1951: Became an overseas province of Portugal and, economically, a cheap labour reserve for South Africa's mines.
1962: Frelimo (National Front for the Liberation of Mozambique) established in exile in Tanzania by Marxist guerrillas, including Samora Machel, to fight for independence.
1964: Fighting broke out between Frelimo forces and Portuguese invaders, starting a ten-year liberation war; Portugal despatched 70,000 troops to Mozambique.
1969: Eduardo Mondlane, leader of Frelimo, was assassinated.

activity; forest resources (eucalyptus, pine, and rare hardwoods)

Population and society

POPULATION 18,863,000 (2003 est)
POPULATION GROWTH RATE 1.7% (2000–15)
POPULATION DENSITY (per sq km) 24 (2003 est)
URBAN POPULATION (% of total) 36 (2003 est)
AGE DISTRIBUTION (% of total population) 0–14 44%, 15–59 51%, 60+ 5% (2002 est)
ETHNIC GROUPS the majority belong to local groups, the largest being the Makua-Lomue, who comprise about 38% of the population; the other significant group is the Tsonga (24%)
LANGUAGE Portuguese (official), 16 African languages
RELIGION animist 48%, Muslim 20%, Roman Catholic 16%, Protestant 16%
EDUCATION (compulsory years) 7
LITERACY RATE 63% (men); 33% (women) (2003 est)
LABOUR FORCE 53% of population: 83% agriculture, 8% industry, 9% services (1990)
LIFE EXPECTANCY 37 (men); 40 (women) (2000–05)
CHILD MORTALITY RATE (under 5, per 1,000 live births) 197 (2001)
HOSPITAL BEDS (per 1,000 people) 1 (1994 est)
TV SETS (per 1,000 people) 5 (2001 est)
RADIOS (per 1,000 people) 44 (2001 est)
INTERNET USERS (per 10,000 people) 17.0 (2002 est)
PERSONAL COMPUTER USERS (per 100 people) 0.5 (2002 est)

1975: Following revolution in Portugal, independence was achieved as a socialist republic, with Machel as president, Joaquim Chissano as prime minister, and Frelimo as the sole legal party; Portuguese settlers left the country. Lourenço Marques renamed Maputo. Key enterprises were nationalized.
1977: Renamo resistance group formed, with covert backing of South Africa.
1979: Machel encouraged Patriotic Front guerrillas in Rhodesia to accept Lancaster House Agreement, creating Zimbabwe.
1983: Good relations were restored with Western powers.
1984: The Nkomati Accord of nonaggression was signed with South Africa.
1986: Machel was killed in air crash near the South African border and was succeeded by Chissano.
1988: Tanzanian troops withdrawn from Mozambique.
1989: Renamo continued attacks on government facilities and civilians.
1990: One-party rule officially ended, and Frelimo abandoned Marxist–Leninism and embraced market economy.
1992: A peace accord was signed with Renamo.
1993: There were price riots in Maputo as a result of the implementation of IMF-promoted reforms to restructure the economy, which was devastated by war and drought.
1994: The demobilization of contending armies was completed. Chissano and Frelimo were re-elected in the first multiparty elections; Renamo (now a political party) agreed to cooperate with the government. Pascoal Mocumbi was appointed prime minister by President Chissano.
1995: Admitted to Commonwealth.
2000: Severe flooding was estimated to involve the loss of 10,000 lives and 1 million homes. The Paris Club of rich countries agreed to suspend Mozambique's repayment of foreign debts.

sought to prevent US nuclear-powered and nuclear-armed ships visiting New Zealand harbours. With the economy deteriorating, he was defeated in the general election of 1984 by the Labour Party, led by David ▷Lange. He stood down as National Party leader in 1984 and was knighted, but was to remain shadow foreign affairs spokesperson.

mule hybrid animal, usually the offspring of a male ass and a female horse.

Mull second-largest island of the Inner ▷Hebrides, Argyll and Bute, Scotland; area 950 sq km/367 sq mi; population (1991) 2,700. It is mountainous, and is separated from the mainland by the Sound of Mull and the Firth of Lorne; it lies 11 km/7 mi west of Oban. The main town is Tobermory, from which there are ferry connections to Oban; Craignure is also connected by ferry to Oban. The economy is based on fishing, forestry, tourism, and stock rearing.

mullein any of a group of ▷herbaceous plants belonging to the figwort family. The great mullein (*V. thapsus*) has lance-shaped leaves 30 cm/12 in or more in length, covered in woolly down, and a large spike of yellow flowers. It is found in Europe and Asia and is naturalized in North America. (Genus *Verbascum*, family Scrophulariaceae.)

Muller, Hermann Joseph (1890–1967) US geneticist who was awarded a Nobel Prize for Physiology or Medicine in 1946 for his discovery, in 1926, that X-ray irradiation can cause mutation. This showed that mutations are nothing more than chemical changes.

mullet either of two species of fish. The red mullet (*Mullus surmuletus*) is found in the Mediterranean and warm Atlantic as far north as the English Channel. It is about 40 cm/16 in long, red with yellow stripes, and has long barbels (sensitive bristles) round the mouth. (Family Mullidae.) The grey mullet (*Crenimugil labrosus*) lives in ponds and estuaries. It is greyish above, with horizontal dark stripes, and grows to 60 cm/24 in. (Family Mugilidae.)

Mullingar county town of County ▷Westmeath, Republic of Ireland, on the River Brosna; population (1996) 8,000. It is an important road and rail junction and was a harbour on the (now disused) Royal Canal that links Dublin and the River Shannon. It is a cattle market and trout-fishing centre. Industries include tobacco, vinyl, furniture, and pencils.

Mulroney, Brian (1939–) Canadian politician, Progressive Conservative Party leader 1983–93, prime minister 1984–93. He achieved a landslide victory in the 1984 election, and won the 1988 election on a platform of free trade with the USA, but with a reduced majority. Opposition within Canada to the 1987 Meech Lake agreement, a prerequisite to signing the 1982 Constitution, continued to plague Mulroney in his second term. A revised reform package in October 1992 failed to gain voters' approval, and in February 1993 he was forced to resign the leadership of the Conservative Party, though he remained prime minister until Kim Campbell was appointed his successor in June.

multicultural education education aimed at preparing children to live in a multiracial society by giving them an understanding of the culture and history of different ethnic groups.

multilateralism trade among more than two countries without discrimination over origin or destination and regardless of whether a large trade gap is involved.

multimedia computerized method of presenting information by combining audio and video components using text, sound, and graphics (still, animated, and video sequences). For example, a multimedia database of musical instruments may allow a user not only to search and retrieve text about a particular instrument but also to see pictures of it and hear it play a piece of music. Multimedia applications emphasize interactivity between the computer and the user.

multinational corporation company or enterprise operating in several countries, usually defined as one that has 25% or more of its output capacity located outside its country of origin.

multiple birth in humans, the production of more than two babies from one pregnancy. Multiple births can be caused by more than two eggs being produced and fertilized (often as the result of hormone therapy to assist pregnancy), or by a single fertilized egg dividing more than once before implantation. See also ▷twin.

multiple independently targeted re-entry vehicle (MIRV) nuclear-warhead-carrying part of a ballistic ▷missile that splits off in midair from the main body. Since each is individually steered and controlled, MIRVs can attack separate targets over a wide area.

multiple proportions, law of in chemistry, the principle that if two elements combine with each other to form more than one compound, then the ratio of the masses of one of them that combine with a particular mass of the other is a small whole number.

multiple sclerosis (MS or disseminated sclerosis) incurable chronic disease of the central nervous system, occurring in young or middle adulthood. Most prevalent in temperate zones, it affects more women than men. It is characterized by degeneration of the myelin sheath that surrounds nerves in the brain and spinal cord.

Depending on where the demyelination occurs – which nerves are affected – the symptoms of MS can mimic almost any neurological disorder. Typically seen are unsteadiness, ataxia (loss of muscular coordination), weakness, speech difficulties, and rapid involuntary movements of the eyes. The course of the disease is episodic, with frequent intervals of ▷remission. Its cause is unknown, but it may be initiated in childhood by some environmental factor, such as infection, in genetically susceptible people. It has been shown that there is a genetic component: identical twins of MS sufferers have a 1 in 4 chance of developing the disease, compared to the 1 in 1,000 chance for the general population.

In 1993 interferon beta 1b became the first drug to be approved in the USA for treating MS. It reduces the number and severity of relapses, and slows the formation of brain lesions giving hope that it may slow down the progression of the disease. In December 1999 the British Medical Research Council approved a three-year study to assess the benefits of cannabis in alleviating some of the symptoms of multiple sclerosis.

Related Web site: World of Multiple Sclerosis http://www.ifmss.org.uk/

> **Lewis Mumford**
> *The chief function of the city is to convert power into form, energy into culture, dead matter into the living symbols of art, biological reproduction into social creativity.*
> *The City in History* ch. 18

multiplexer in telecommunications, a device that allows a transmission medium to carry a number of separate signals at the same time – enabling, for example, several telephone conversations to be carried by one telephone line, and radio signals to be transmitted in stereo.

multiplier in economics, the theoretical concept, formulated by John Maynard Keynes, of the effect on national income or employment by an adjustment in overall demand. For example, investment by a company in a new plant will stimulate new income and expenditure, which will in turn generate new investment, and so on, so that the actual increase in national income may be several times greater than the original investment.

multistage rocket rocket launch vehicle made up of several rocket stages (often three) joined end to end. The bottom stage fires first, boosting the vehicle to high speed, then it falls away. The next stage fires, thrusting the now lighter vehicle even faster. The remaining stages fire and fall away in turn, boosting the vehicle's payload (cargo) to an orbital speed that can reach 28,000 kph/17,500 mph.

multitasking (or multiprogramming) in computing, a system in which one processor appears to run several different programs (or different parts of the same program) at the same time. All the programs are held in memory together and each is allowed to run for a certain period.

For example, one program may run while other programs are waiting for a peripheral device to work or for input from an operator. The ability to multitask depends on the ▷operating system rather than the type of computer. Unix is one of the commonest.

multiuser system (or multiaccess system) in computing, an operating system that enables several users to access centrally-stored data and programs simultaneously over a network. Each user has a terminal, which may be local (connected directly to the computer) or remote (connected to the computer via a modem and a telephone line).

Muluzi, Bakili (1943–) Malawi politician, president from 1994. Muluzi formed the United Democratic Front (UDF) in 1992 when President ▷Banda agreed to end one-party rule, and went on to win almost half of the presidential votes. After taking office, he applied his business experience to the task of liberalizing trade and reviving the economy. He was re-elected in June 1999.

Mumbai (formerly Bombay (until 1995)) Indian city, industrial port, and commercial centre; population (2001 est) 11,914,400. Previously known as Bombay, the city was once the capital of Bombay Presidency and Bombay State and in 1960 became the capital of ▷Maharashtra, a newly created state. By a decision of the Maharashtra government implemented in 1995, the city was renamed Mumbai. Industries include textiles, engineering, pharmaceuticals, and diamonds. It is the centre of the Hindi film industry.

Features World Trade Centre (1975); National Centre for the Performing Arts (1969). The port handles half of India's foreign trade. Its factories generate 30% of India's GDP.

History The site was originally seven islands occupied by Koli fishermen, but silting and land reclamation have created a narrow isthmus on which Mumbai now stands. The city was founded in the 13th century, came under Mogul rule, was occupied by Portugal in 1530, and passed to Britain in 1662 as part of Catherine of Braganza's dowry. It was the headquarters of the ▷East India Company from 1685 to 1708. The city expanded rapidly with the development of the cotton trade and the railway in the 1860s. In 1995 the city was renamed Mumbai after the goddess Mumba, the name in the local Marathi language for Parvati, the wife of the Hindu god Shiva.

Mumford, Lewis (1895–1990) US urban planner and social critic, concerned with the adverse effect of technology on contemporary society.

mummers' play (or St George play) British folk drama enacted in dumb show by a masked cast, performed on Christmas Day to celebrate the death of the old year and its rebirth as the new year. The plot usually consists of a duel between St George and an infidel knight, in which one of them is killed but later revived by a doctor. Mummers' plays are still performed in some parts of Britain, often by Morris dance teams.

mummy any dead body, human or animal, that has been naturally or artificially preserved. Natural mummification can occur through freezing (for example, mammoths in glacial ice from 25,000 years ago), drying, or preservation in bogs or oil seeps. Artificial mummification may be achieved by embalming (for example, the mummies of ancient Egypt) or by freeze-drying.

Related Web site: Mysterious Mummies of China http://www.pbs.org/wgbh/nova/chinamum/

mumps (or infectious parotitis) virus infection marked by fever, pain, and swelling of one or both parotid salivary glands (situated in front of the ears). It is usually shortlived in children, although meningitis is a possible complication. In adults the symptoms are more serious and it may cause sterility in men.

Mumps is the most common cause of ▷meningitis in children, but it follows a much milder course than bacterial meningitis, and a complete recovery is usual. Rarely, mumps meningitis may lead to deafness. An effective vaccine against mumps, measles, and rubella (MMR vaccine) is now offered for children aged 18 months.

Munch, Edvard (1863–1944) Norwegian painter and graphic artist, a major influence on ▷expressionism. His highly charged paintings, characterized by strong colours and distorted forms, often focus on intense emotional states, as in one of his best-known works *The Scream* (1893). His works brought a new urgency and power to the two themes that dominated late 19th-century decadence, death and sexuality.

He studied in Paris and Berlin, and his major works date from the period 1892–1908, when he lived mainly in Germany. Influenced first by the Symbolists and then by van Gogh and Gauguin, he soon developed his own expressive style, reducing his compositions to broad areas of strong colour with sinuous contours emphasized by heavy brushstrokes, distorting faces and figures. His first show in Berlin 1892 made a great impact on young German artists. The *Frieze of Life* 1890s, a sequence of symbolic paintings, includes some of his most characteristic images.

In 1908 he suffered a nervous breakdown and returned to Norway. Later works include a series of murals 1910–15 in the assembly halls of Oslo University.

München German name of ▷Munich, a city in Germany.

Münchhausen's syndrome emotional disorder in which a patient feigns or invents symptoms to secure medical treatment. It is the chronic form of factitious disorder, which is more common, and probably underdiagnosed. In some cases the patient will secretly ingest substances to produce real symptoms. It was named after the exaggerated tales of Baron Münchhausen. Some patients invent symptoms for their children, a phenomenon known as Münchhausen's by proxy.

Munda any one of several groups living in northeastern and central India, numbering about 5 million (1983). Their most widely spoken languages are Santali and Mundari, languages of the Munda group, an isolated branch of the Austro-Asiatic family. The Mundas were formerly nomadic hunter-gatherers, but now practise shifting cultivation. They are Hindus but retain animist beliefs.

Mungo, St another name for St ▷Kentigern, first bishop of Glasgow.

Munich (German München) capital of Bavaria, Germany, on the River Isar, about 520 m/1,706 ft above sea level, some 45 km/28 mi from the edge of the Alps; population (1995) 1,240,600. The main industries are brewing, printing, precision instruments, machinery, electrical goods, computers, telecommunications, fashion, and food processing.

Features Munich owes many of its buildings and art treasures to the kings ▷Ludwig I and Maximilian II of Bavaria. The cathedral is late 15th century. Art galleries such as the Alte Pinakothek contain paintings by old masters, and the Neue Pinakothek, modern paintings. The Glyptothek also has important art collections. There is the Bavarian National Museum, the Bavarian State Library, and the Deutsches Museum (science and technology). The Ludwig Maximilian University, founded at Ingolstadt in 1472, was transferred to Munich in 1826; there are also two newer universities. To the northeast at Garching there is a nuclear research centre.

History Dating from the 12th century, Munich became the residence of the dukes of Wittelsbach in the 13th century, and the capital of independent Bavaria. It was the scene of the November revolution of 1918, the 'Soviet' republic of 1919, and the Hitler putsch of 1923. It became the centre of the Nazi movement, and the Munich Agreement of 1938 was signed here. When the 1972 Summer Olympics were held in Munich, 11 Israeli athletes were killed by Palestine Liberation Organization terrorists. The World Cup football championship was held here in 1974.

Related Web site: Munich http://www.city.net/countries/germany/munich/

Munich Agreement pact signed on 29 September 1938 by the leaders of the UK (Neville ▷Chamberlain), France (Edouard ▷Daladier), Germany (Adolf ▷Hitler), and Italy (Benito ▷Mussolini), under which Czechoslovakia was compelled to surrender its Sudeten-German districts (the **Sudeten**) to Germany. Chamberlain claimed it would guarantee 'peace in our time', but it did not prevent Hitler from seizing the rest of Czechoslovakia in March 1939.

Related Web site: Munich Pact http://www.yale.edu/lawweb/avalon/imt/munich1.htm

Munro, H(ector) H(ugh) British author who wrote under the pen-name ▷Saki.

Munster historic southern province of the Republic of Ireland, comprising the counties of Clare, Cork, Kerry, Limerick, North and South Tipperary, and Waterford; area 24,140 sq km/9,320 sq mi; population (1996) 1,033,900.

Münster industrial city in North Rhine-Westphalia, northwest Germany, 100 km/62 mi northeast of Düsseldorf on the Dortmund-Ems Canal; population (1995) 264,500. There are wire, cement, chemicals, steel, brewing, and distilling industries. It was formerly the capital of Westphalia. The Treaty of Westphalia was signed simultaneously here and at Osnabrück in 1648, ending the Thirty Years' War.

Munternia Romanian name of ▷Wallachia, a former province of Romania.

muntjac any of about nine species of small deer found in Southeast Asia. They live mostly in dense vegetation and do not form herds. The males have short spiked antlers and two sharp canine teeth forming tusks. They are sometimes called 'barking deer' because of their voices. (Genus *Muntiacus*.)

muon an ▷elementary particle similar to the electron except for its mass which is 207 times greater than that of the electron. It has a half-life of 2 millionths of a second, decaying into electrons and ▷neutrinos. The muon was originally thought to be a ▷meson but is now classified as a ▷lepton. See also ▷tau.

Murakami, Haruki (1949–) Japanese novelist and translator. He is one of Japan's best-selling writers, influenced by 20th-century US writers and popular culture. His dreamy, gently surrealist novels include *A Wild Sheep Chase* (1982) and *Norwegian Wood* (1987).

Iris Murdoch
One doesn't have to get anywhere in a marriage. It's not a public conveyance.
A Severed Head ch. 3

mural painting (Latin *murus* 'wall') decoration of the wall either by painting on the surface, or on a canvas which is subsequently affixed in position, the latter being a method frequently used in modern times. In painting directly on the wall, various media have been used, principal among them being fresco, though tempera, encaustic and oil also have their examples. Mural painting is found in all periods of art, but mainly, as distinct from the domestic easel picture, in palaces, churches, or the interiors of buildings of public use or significance.

Shikibu Murasaki
There are those who do not dislike wrong rumours if they are about the right men.
The Tale of Genji

Murasaki, Shikibu (*c.* 978–*c.* 1015) Japanese writer. She was a lady at the court. Her masterpiece of fiction, *The Tale of Genji* (*c.* 1010), is one of the classic works of Japanese literature, and may be the world's first novel.

She was a member of the Fujiwara clan, but her own name is not known; scholars have given her the name Murasaki after a character in the book. It deals with upper-class life in Heian Japan, centring on the affairs of Prince Genji. A portion of her diary and a number of poems also survive.

Related Web site: Murasaki Shikibu http://home.earthlink.net/~womenwhist/heroine9.html

Murat, Joachim (1767–1815) King of Naples 1808–15. An officer in the French army, he was made king by Napoleon, but deserted him in 1813 in the vain hope that Austria and Great Britain would recognize him. In 1815 he attempted unsuccessfully to make himself king of all Italy, but when he landed in Calabria in an attempt to gain the throne he was captured and shot.

Murayama, Tomiichi (1924–) Japanese trade unionist and politician, leader of the Social Democratic Party (SDPJ) 1993–96, prime minister 1994–96. At the age of 70, Murayama, who had held no previous political office, became Japan's first socialist prime minister for more than 40 years. His emergence as a major figure followed months of virtual chaos in Japanese politics, during which two prime ministers resigned. Despite losses for the SDPJ in upper-house elections in 1995, his administration survived until January 1996; he resigned from the SDPJ leadership in September 1996.

Murchison, Roderick Impey (1792–1871) Scottish geologist responsible for naming the ▷Silurian period, the subject of his book *The Silurian System* (1839). Expeditions to Russia 1840–45 led him to define another worldwide system, the Permian, named after the strata of the Perm region. He was knighted in 1846, and became a baronet in 1866.

MURAL PAINTING Situated in a part of the city known as the Mission, Potrero and neighbouring streets in San Francisco, California, USA, are decorated with a large number of murals. *Image Bank*

Murcia autonomous community of southeast Spain, with a coastline on the Mediterranean Sea; area 11,300 sq km/4,362 sq mi; population (2001 est) 1,190,400. The River Segura and its tributaries (the Sangonera and the Quipar) flow through the region, which is very mountainous in the south and east. The irrigated area, the huerta of Murcia, is one of the most intensively farmed areas in Spain and is especially important for citrus fruits. Products include esparto grass (for weaving into simple products such as sandals), iron, olives, and fruit. There are large deposits of salt and minerals, especially lead and zinc. The main port is ▷Cartagena and the capital is ▷Murcia.

Murcia industrial city (silk, metal, glass, textiles, pharmaceuticals), capital of the Spanish province of Murcia, on the River Segura; population (1994) 342,000. Murcia was founded in 825 on the site of a Roman colony by 'Abd-ar-Rahman II, caliph of Córdoba. It has a university and a 14th-century cathedral.

Murdoch, (Jean) Iris (1919–1999) English novelist, born in Dublin. Her novels combine philosophical speculation with often outrageous situations and tangled human relationships. They include *The Sandcastle* (1957), *The Bell* (1958), *The Sea, The Sea* (1978; Booker Prize), *Nuns and Soldiers* (1980), *The Message to the Planet* (1989), *The Green Knight* (1993), and *Jackson's Dilemma* (1995). Her husband, John Bayley, wrote *Iris: A Memoir* (1999), recording her decline with Alzheimer's disease.

Murdoch, (Keith) Rupert (1931–) Australian-born US media magnate with worldwide interests. His UK newspapers, generally right-wing, include the *Sun*, the *News of the World*, and *The Times*; in the USA, he has a 50% share of 20th Century Fox, six Metromedia TV stations, and newspaper and magazine publishing companies. He purchased a 50% stake in a Hungarian tabloid, *Reform*, in 1989. His newspapers (which also include *Today* and the *Sunday Times*) and 50% of Sky Television, the UK's first satellite television service, are controlled by News International, a wholly owned subsidiary of the Australian-based News Corporation. In November 1990 Sky Television and its rival company British Satellite Broadcasting merged to form British Sky Broadcasting (BSkyB).

Murillo, Bartolomé Esteban (*c.* 1618–1682) Spanish painter. Active mainly in Seville, he painted sentimental pictures of the Immaculate Conception, and also specialized in studies of street urchins. His *Self-Portrait* (*c.* 1672; National Gallery, London) is generally considered to be one of his finest works.

Murmansk seaport and capital of the Murmansk oblast located 1000 km/624 mi north of St Petersburg on the Kola Peninsula in the northwest of the Russian Federation; population (1990) 472,000. Situated on an estuary 50 km/31 mi inland from the Barents Sea, it is the largest city in the Arctic, Russia's principal fishing port, and a base for icebreakers that keep the ▷Northeast Passage open. Shipbuilding is a major industry, and polar research institutes are located here.

Murphy, Eddie (Edward Regan) (1951–) US film actor and comedian. His first film, *48 Hours* (1982), introduced the street-wise, cocksure character that has become his speciality. With his next two films, *Trading Places* (1983) and *Beverly Hills Cop* (1984), he became one of the biggest box-office draws of the 1980s. In the late 1990s he had success with the films *The Nutty Professor* (1996), *Dr Dolittle* (1998), and *Bowfinger* (1999).

Murray principal river of Australia, which rises in the Snowy Mountains of the Australian Alps near Mount Kosciusko, in New South Wales; length 2,540 km/1,578 mi. The Murray flows west and northwest, for most of its length forming the boundary between New South Wales and Victoria, then turns south to reach the Southern Ocean at Encounter Bay, southeast of Adelaide in South Australia. The River Murray is an important source of hydroelectric power and irrigation. With its main tributary, the ▷Darling, it is 3,750 km/2,330 mi long. Together they produce 40% of the country's agricultural wealth.

Murray, (George) Gilbert (Aimé) (1866–1957) Australian-born British scholar. Author of *History of Ancient Greek Literature* (1897), he became known for verse translations of the Greek dramatists, notably of Euripides.

Murray, James Augustus Henry (1837–1915) Scottish philologist. He was the first editor of the *Oxford English Dictionary* (originally the *New English Dictionary*) from 1878 until his death.

Murray, James Stuart (1531–1570) 1st Earl of Murray; or **Moray**. Regent of Scotland from 1567, an illegitimate son of James V by Lady Margaret Erskine, daughter of the 4th Earl of Mar. He became chief adviser to his half-sister ▷Mary Queen of Scots on her return to Scotland in 1561, but lost her favour when he opposed her marriage in 1565 to Henry, Lord Darnley. He was one of the leaders of the Scottish Reformation, and after the deposition of Mary he became regent. He was assassinated by one of her supporters.

Murray cod Australian freshwater fish that grows to about 2 m/6 ft. It is is named after the river in which it is found. (Species *Maccullochella macquariensis*.)

Murrayfield Scottish rugby football ground and home of the national team. It staged its first international in 1925 when Scotland beat England 14–11. The capacity is approximately 70,000.

Murrumbidgee river in New South Wales, Australia; length 1,609 km/1,000 mi. The Murrumbidgee rises in the Australian Alps, then flows north and west to meet the River ▷Murray on the Victoria border. It is a major tributary of the Murray. The Murrumbidgee is navigable for 807 km/501 mi to Wagga Wagga during the winter months. The Murrumbidgee Irrigation Area is a large, fertile region irrigated by the waters of the Murrumbidgee.

Murry, John Middleton (1889–1957) English writer. His writings largely consist of literary criticism and criticism of existing social institutions, and include *Aspects of Literature* (1920) and *Son of Woman* (a study of the writer D H Lawrence; 1931). In 1918 he married the writer Katherine ▷Mansfield, whose biography he wrote.

Muscat (or **Masqat**) capital and port of Oman; lying in the Gulf of Oman; population (2001 est) 57,600. The Muscat region has a population of 621,500 (1998 est). With the advantage of a deepwater harbour at Matrah, in the western part of the city, Muscat handles the bulk of the country's foreign trade, especially the export of crude oil and the import of food. Mina, with a terminal for loading supertankers, and Riyam, which handles incoming refined petroleum products, are both nearby. Natural gas and chemical industries are also important. Muscat is served by an international airport, As-sib, and is linked to Salalah, a former capital, by a 1,000 km/625 mi trunk road completed in 1984.

muscle contractile animal tissue that produces locomotion and power, and maintains the movement of body substances. Muscle is made of long cells that can contract to between one-half and one-third of their relaxed length.

    Striped (or striated) muscles are activated by ▷motor nerves under voluntary control; their ends are usually attached via tendons to bones.

    Involuntary or **smooth** muscles are controlled by motor nerves of the ▷autonomic nervous system, and are located in the gut, blood vessels, iris, and various ducts.

    Cardiac muscle occurs only in the heart, and is also controlled by the autonomic nervous system.

muscovite white mica, $KAl_2Si_3AlO_{10}(OH,F)_2$, a common silicate mineral. It is colourless to silvery white with shiny surfaces, and like all micas it splits into thin flakes along its one perfect cleavage. Muscovite is a metamorphic mineral occurring mainly in schists; it is also found in some granites, and appears as shiny flakes on bedding planes of some sandstones.

muscular dystrophy any of a group of inherited chronic muscle disorders marked by weakening and wasting of muscle. Muscle fibres degenerate, to be replaced by fatty tissue, although the nerve supply remains unimpaired. Death occurs in early adult life.

    The commonest form, Duchenne muscular dystrophy, strikes boys (1 in 3,000), usually before the age of four. The child develops a waddling gait and an inward curvature (lordosis) of the lumbar spine. The muscles affected by dystrophy and the rate of progress vary. There is no cure, but physical treatments can minimize disability. Death usually occurs before the age of 20.

Muse in Greek mythology, one of the nine inspiring deities of the creative arts: Clio, Euterpe, Thalia, Melpomene, Terpsichore, Erato, Polyhymnia, Urania, and Calliope; daughters of Zeus and Mnemosyne, goddess of memory. Reputedly born in Pieria, at the foot of Mount Olympus, they were originally only three in number, but became nine from the time of Hesiod.
    Related Web site: Muses from Greek Mythology http://www.eliki.com/portals/fantasy/circle/define.html

Musée D'Orsay museum of 19th- and early 20th-century painting, sculpture, decorative arts, and photography, opened at the former Gare du Quai d'Orsay (Orsay quayside railway station), Paris, France, in 1986. The museum includes collections from leading artists, mostly French, from the Romantic, neoclassical, realist, Impressionist, post-Impressionist, and pointillist schools.

Museum of Modern Art, New York leading US art museum devoted to art of the late 19th and early 20th centuries. Opened in 1929, it has amassed an exceptional collection of modern works, including collections of films and photographs.

Museveni, Yoweri Kaguta (1945–) Ugandan general and politician, president from 1986. He led the opposition to Idi ▷Amin's regime 1971–79, and became minister of defence 1979–80. Unhappy with Milton Obote's autocratic leadership, he formed the National Resistance Army (NRA). When Obote was ousted in a coup in 1985, Museveni entered into a brief power-sharing agreement with his successor, Tito Okello, before taking over as president. Museveni led a broad-based coalition government.

    Until Amin's removal Museveni led the anti-Amin Front for National Salvation, and he supported the invasion of Uganda by the Tanzanian army in 1979. In the 1980 elections he led the Uganda Patriotic Movement and subsequently the NRA, which helped to remove Obote from power. In 1993 he reinstated the country's four tribal monarchies. In 2001 he was re-elected as president, a result that, despite some voting irregularities, international observers felt reflected voters' wishes.

Musgrave, Thea (1928–) Scottish composer. Her music, in a conservative modern idiom, include concertos, chamber music, and operas, including *Mary, Queen of Scots* (1977), and *Harriet, the Woman Called Moses* (1985). Recent works include the bass clarinet concerto *Autumn Sonata* (1995), and the orchestral piece *Phoenix Rising* (1998).

Musgrave Ranges Australian mountain ranges on the border between South Australia and the Northern Territory; the highest peak is Mount Woodruffe at 1,525 m/5,000 ft. The area is an Aboriginal reserve.

mushroom fruiting body of certain fungi (see ▷fungus), consisting of an upright stem and a spore-producing cap with radiating gills on the undersurface. There are many edible species belonging to the genus *Agaricus*, including the field mushroom (*A. campestris*). See also ▷toadstool.
    Related Web site: Edible and Poisonous Mushrooms http://www.conservation.state.mo.us/nathis/mushrooms/mushroom/index.htm

music art of combining sounds into a coherent perceptual experience, typically in accordance with conventional patterns and for an aesthetic purpose. Music is generally categorized as classical, ▷jazz, ▷pop music, ▷country and western, and so on. See Music, Western: Key Events on p. 658.
    Related Web sites: Glossary of Musical Terms http://www.hnh.com/mgloss.htm
    Musicianship Basics http://www.dragnet.com.au/~donovan/mb/music.html

musical 20th-century form of dramatic musical performance, combining elements of song, dance, and the spoken word, often characterized by lavish staging and large casts. It developed from the operettas and musical comedies of the 19th century.

musical instrument digital interface manufacturer's standard for digital music equipment; see ▷MIDI.

music hall British light theatrical entertainment, in which singers, dancers, comedians, and acrobats perform in 'turns'. The music hall's heyday was at the beginning of the 20th century, with such artistes as Marie Lloyd, Harry Lauder, and George Formby. The US equivalent is vaudeville.

music therapy use of music as an adjunct to relaxation therapy, or in ▷psychotherapy to elicit expressions of suppressed emotions by prompting patients to dance, shout, laugh, cry, or other, in response.

musique concrète (French 'concrete music') music created by reworking natural sounds recorded on disk or tape, developed in 1948 by Pierre Schaeffer and Pierre Henry in the drama studios of Paris Radio. The term was used to differentiate the process from ▷electronic music, which used synthesized tones and sounds. From the mid-1950s the two techniques were usually combined, and the term is now purely historic.

musk in botany, perennial plant whose small oblong leaves give off the musky scent from which it takes its name; it is also called **monkey flower**. The name 'musk' is also given to several other plants with a similar scent, including the musk mallow (*Malva moschata*) and the musk rose (*Rosa moschata*). (*Mimulus moschatus*, family Scrophulariaceae.)

musk deer any of three species of small deer native to the mountains of central and northeastern Asia. A solitary animal, the musk deer is about 80–100 cm/30–40 in, sure-footed, and has large ears and no antlers. Males have long tusklike upper canine teeth. They are hunted and farmed for their musk (a waxy substance secreted by the male from a gland in the stomach area), which is used as medicine or perfume. (Genus *Moschus*.)

musk ox ruminant (cud-chewing) mammal native to the Arctic regions of North America. It has characteristics of both sheep and

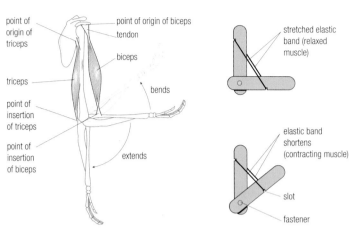

MUSCLE The movements of the arm depend on two muscles, the biceps and the triceps. To lift the arm, the biceps shortens and the triceps lengthens. To lower the arm, the opposite occurs: the biceps lengthens and the triceps shortens.

MUSCLE Muscles make up 35–45% of our body weight; there are over 650 skeletal muscles. Muscle cells 20 cm/0.8 in long. They are arranged in bundles, fibres, fibrils, and myofilaments.

fibres

capillary

myofibril

myosin

actin

Music, Western: Key Events

AD 590	St Gregory the Great is elected pope. Under his rule, music attains new heights, initiating Gregorian chant.
600s	The system of notation known as 'neumes' is devised, giving the approximate pitch and rhythm of plainchant.
800s	Early medieval polyphony known as 'organum' consists of two voice parts singing parallel lines.
1000s	Composers begin using polyphony involving two independent voice parts.
1026	The Italian monk Guido d'Arezzo completes his treatise *Micrologus*. He founds modern notation and tonic sol-fa.
1207	Minnesingers (singer songwriters) Walther von der Vogelweide, Tannhäuser, and Wolfram von Eschenbach compete in a song contest at Wartburg Castle, later celebrated in Richard Wagner's opera *Die Meistersinger von Nürnberg*.
1240	The earliest known canon, *Sumer is Icumen In*, is composed around this year.
1280	*Carmina Burana*, a collection of students' songs, is compiled in Benediktbuern, Bavaria; Carl Orff is later inspired by their subject matter.
1288	France's greatest troubadour, Adam de la Halle, dies in Naples, Italy.
1300s	*Musica ficta*, the practice of altering the notated pitch in order to prevent dissonance, becomes widespread.
1320	*Ars nova*, a tract by the French composer Philippe de Vitry, gives its name to a new, more graceful era in music.
1364	Music's first large-scale masterpiece, the *Notre Dame Mass* of Guillaume de Machaut, is performed in Reims to celebrate the coronation of Charles V of France.
1452	Ockeghem, the great Flemish composer, joins the French court; he also serves as teacher to Josquin Desprez.
1453	John Dunstable, England's first composer of significance, dies in London.
1473	The earliest known printed music, the *Collectorium super Magnificat* by Johannes Gerson, is published in Esslingen, near Stuttgart, Germany.
1474	Guillaume Dufay, who pioneered the four-voice style popular in the 16th century, dies in Cambrai.
1521	Josquin Desprez, the leading musician of his time, dies in Condé-sur-Escaut, Burgundy.
1550s	Production of violins begins at the workshop of Andrea Amati in Cremona.
1561	Palestrina composes the *Missa Papae Marcelli* in line with the period reforms of church music
1575	Thomas Tallis and William Byrd jointly publish their *Cantiones sacrae*, a collection of 34 motets.
1576	Hans Sachs, the most famous of the Meistersinger (mastersinger) poets and composers, dies in Nuremberg.
1597	The first opera, *La Dafne* by Jacopo Peri, is staged privately at the Corsi Palazzo in Florence.
1610	Claudio Monteverdi's *Vespers* is published in Venice.
1637	The world's first opera house opens in Venice.
1644	Antonio Stradivari is born. More than 600 of his violins, made in Cremona, survive into the 20th century.
1672	The violinist John Banister inaugurates the first season of public concerts in London.
1673	Lully's first opera, *Cadmus et Hermione*, is produced after the composer is granted a monopoly by Louis XIV on such works.
1709	Bartolemmeo Cristofori unveils the first fortepiano in Florence.
1721	J S Bach completes his six *Brandenburg Concertos* for baroque orchestra.
1722	Jean-Philippe Rameau's book *Traité de l'harmonie* is published, founding modern harmonic theory.
1725	Antonio Vivaldi's set of four violin concertos *The Four Seasons* is published in Amsterdam.
1732	Covent Garden Theatre opens in London.
1742	Georg Friedrich Handel's *Messiah* receives its world premiere in Dublin, Ireland.
1753	C P E Bach writes his influential treatise 'The Essay on the True Art of Playing Keyboard Instruments'.
1757	Johann Stamitz dies in Mannheim, Rhine Palatinate, where he has made important contributions to the development of the symphony and raised the status of the orchestra.
1761	Franz Joseph Haydn takes up liveried service as vice kapellmeister with the aristocratic Esterházy family, to whom he is connected until his death in 1809.
1788	Wolfgang Amadeus Mozart completes his last three symphonies, numbers 39–41, in six weeks.
1798	The *Allgemeine Musikalische Zeitung*, a journal of music criticism, is first published in Leipzig, Germany.
1805	Ludwig van Beethoven's 'Eroica' Symphony is first performed; it vastly expands the horizons of orchestral music.
1810	The pianist/composer Frédéric Chopin is born in Zelazowa Wola, Poland.
1814	Johann Maelzel invents the metronome.
1815	Franz Schubert's output for this year includes two symphonies, two masses, 20 waltzes, and 145 songs.
1821	Carl Weber's *Der Freischütz/The Marksman* introduces heroic German Romanticism to opera.
1828	The limits of instrumental virtuosity are redefined by the violinist Niccolò Paganini's Vienna debut.
1830	Hector Berlioz's dazzlingly avant-garde and programmatic *Symphonie fantastique* startles Paris concertgoers.
1831	Grand opera is inaugurated with *Robert le diable* by Giacomo Meyerbeer.
1839	Verdi's first opera, *Oberto*, is produced at La Scala, Milan.
1840	Robert Schumann marries the pianist Clara Wieck.
1851	Jenny Lind, a singer managed by P T Barnum, earns $176,675 from nine months of concerts in the USA.
1842	The Vienna Philharmonic Orchestra gives its first concerts.
1854	In Weimar, Germany, Franz Liszt conducts the premieres of his first symphonic poems.
1855	Like most orchestras around this date, the New York Philharmonic for the first time sits down while playing (cellists are already seated).
1865	Richard Wagner's opera *Tristan and Isolde* scales new heights of expressiveness using unprecedented chromaticism. Schubert's *Unfinished Symphony* (1822) is premiered in Vienna.
1875	The first of a series of collaborations between Arthur Sullivan and the librettist W S Gilbert, *Trial by Jury*, is given its premiere.
1876	Wagner's *The Ring of the Nibelung* is produced in Bayreuth. Johannes Brahms's *First Symphony* is performed in Karlsruhe.
1877	Thomas Alva Edison invents the cylindrical tin-foil phonograph.
1883	The Metropolitan Opera House opens in New York with a production of Charles Gounod's *Faust*.
1885	Liszt composes *Bagatelle without Tonality* (his *Faust Symphony* of 1857 opened with a 12-note row).
1894	Claude Debussy's *Prélude à l'après-midi d'un faune* anticipates 20th-century composition with its use of the whole-tone scale.
1895	Henry Wood conducts the first Promenade Concert at the Queen's Hall in London.
1897	Mahler becomes director of the Vienna Court Opera.
1899	Scott Joplin's *Maple Leaf Rag* is published in Sedalia, Missouri.
1900	Elgar's oratorio *Dream of Gerontius* is produced at the Birmingham Festival.
1902	Enrico Caruso records ten arias in a hotel room in Milan, the success of which establishes the popularity of the phonograph. By the time of his death 1921 he has earned $2 million from sales of his recordings.
1906	Agnostic Vaughan Williams becomes editor of the *English Hymnal*.
1907	Avant-garde composer Charles Ives sets up his own insurance agency while continuing his art.
1908	Camille Saint-Saëns becomes the first leading composer to write a film score, for *L'Assassinat du duc de Guise*.
1911	Irving Berlin has his first big success as a songwriter with 'Alexander's Ragtime Band'.
1912	Arnold Schoenberg's atonal *Pierrot lunaire*, for reciter and chamber ensemble, foreshadows many similar small-scale quasi-theatrical works.
1913	Igor Stravinsky's ballet *The Rite of Spring* precipitates a riot at its premiere in Paris.
1917	Rakhmaninov flees Russia following the Revolution, and turns his attentions away from composition to performance as a pianist.
1919	Schoenberg, who is experimenting with serial technique, sets up the Society for Private Musical Performances in Vienna, which lasts until 1921.
1921	Schoenberg writes the first works based entirely on 12-note serial technique.
1922	Alessandro Moreschi, last of the castrati, dies in Rome.
1924	Puccini dies, leaving his opera *Turandot* unfinished (completed by Alfano 1926). Gershwin's *Rhapsody in Blue* is premiered.
1925	Louis Armstrong makes his first jazz records with the Hot Five. Duke Ellington's Washingtonians also starts recording.
1927	Jerome Kern's *Show Boat*, with libretto by Oscar Hammerstein II, lays the foundations of the US musical.
1930	The BBC Symphony Orchestra is founded in London under Adrian Boult.
1937	Arturo Toscanini, one of the greatest conductors in the history of music, begins his 17-year association with the NBC Symphony Orchestra.
1938	Sergei Prokofiev's score for Sergei Eisenstein's *Alexander Nevsky* raises film music to new levels. Big-band music becomes popular.
1939	Elisabeth Lutyens is one of the first English composers to use 12-note composition in her *Chamber Concerto No 1* for nine instruments.
1940	Walt Disney's *Fantasia* introduces classical music, conducted by Leopold Stokowski, to a worldwide audience of filmgoers.
1940s	Bebop jazz is initiated. The jazz greats Charlie Parker and Dizzy Gillespie first record together. Big bands, such as those led by Duke Ellington and Glen Miller, reach their height of popularity.
1941	The 'Proms' move to the Royal Albert Hall, London.
1942	In Chicago, John Cage conducts the premiere of his *Imaginary Landscape No 3*, scored for marimbula, gongs, tin cans, buzzers, plucked coil, electric oscillator, and generator.
1945	Bartók composes his final work, the *Third Piano Concerto*, and dies later the same year in New York. Britten's *Peter Grimes* is premiered.
1953	The death of Stalin heralds an era of greater artistic freedom in the Soviet Union.
1954	Karlheinz Stockhausen's *Electronic Studies* for magnetic tape are broadcast in Cologne. Edgard Varèse's *Déserts*, the first work to combine instruments and prerecorded magnetic tape, is performed in Paris. Elvis Presley makes his first rock-and-roll recordings in Memphis, Tennesee.
1955	Pierre Boulez's *Le Marteau sans maître*, for contralto and chamber ensemble, is performed in Baden-Baden. Its formidable serial technique and exotic orchestration is acclaimed by the avant-garde. The Miles Davis Quintet with John Coltrane unites two of the most important innovators in jazz.
1956	The first annual Warsaw autumn festival of contemporary music is held. This becomes important for the promotion of Polish composers such as Witold Lutosławski and Krzystof Penderecki.
1957	Leonard Bernstein's *West Side Story* is premiered in New York. A computer, programmed at the University of Illinois by Lejaren Hiller and Leonard Isaacson, composes the *Illiac Suite* for string quartet.
1961	Ligeti composes *Atmosphères*, later popularized by the film *2001: A Space Odyssey* 1968.
1963	Dmitry Shostakovich's opera *Lady Macbeth of Mezensk*, earlier banned and condemned in the Soviet newspaper *Pravda* 1936, is produced in a revised version as *Katerina Ismaylova*.
1965	Robert Moog invents a synthesizer that considerably widens the scope of electronic music. The film soundtrack of *The Sound of Music*, with music by Rodgers and lyrics by Hammerstein, is released, and stays in the sales charts for the next two years. Bob Dylan turns to electric instrumentation on *Highway 61 Revisited*.
1967	The Beatles' album *Sgt Pepper's Lonely Hearts Club Band*, which took over 500 hours to record, is released. The first Velvet Underground album is released. Psychedelic rock spreads from San Francisco, and hard rock develops in the UK and the USA.
1968	Walter Carlos uses the Moog synthesizer to produce *Switched-on Bach*.
1969	Peter Maxwell Davies's theatre piece *Eight Songs for a Mad King*, for vocalist and six instruments, is premiered under his direction in London by the Pierrot Players, later to become the Fires of London ensemble.
1970s	Minimalism becomes popular, led by composers Steve Reich and Philip Glass.
1970	Jimi Hendrix, who discovered the full potential of the electric guitar's effects, dies from an overdose of drugs and alcohol.
1971	B B King's popular *Live at the Regal* proves the continuing tradition of the blues.
1972	Bob Marley's LP *Catch a Fire* begins the popularization of reggae beyond Jamaica.

Music, Western: Key Events (cont'd)

1976	Philip Glass's opera *Einstein on the Beach*, using the repetitive techniques of minimalism, is given its first performance in Paris. Punk rock arrives with the Sex Pistols' 'Anarchy in the UK'.
1977	The Institute for Research and Coordination of Acoustics and Music (IRCAM) is founded in Paris under the direction of Pierre Boulez, for visiting composers to make use of advanced electronic equipment. Jean-Michel Jarre's *Oxygène* is the first album of synthesized music to be a hit.
1980s	Digital techniques and the use of computers revolutionize the recording industry. Digital synthesizers transform electronic instruments and sound production.
1981	MTV (Music Television) starts broadcasting nonstop pop videos on cable in the USA, growing into a worldwide network in the following decade.
1983	Olivier Messiaen's only opera, *Saint François d'Assise*, is given its first performance in Paris. Lutosławski's *Third Symphony* is premiered to worldwide acclaim by the Chicago Symphony Orchestra under Georg Solti. Compact discs are launched.
1986	Paul Simon's *Graceland* album draws on and popularized world music.
1989	The conductor Herbert von Karajan and the pianist Vladimir Horowitz die.

1990	Many record chain stores cease to stock seven-inch singles, accelerating the decline of vinyl records' share of the market.
1991	US rap group NWA is declared not obscene by a UK court. Various attempts, especially in the USA, to limit freedom of speech in popular music are generally unsuccessful.
1992	DCC (digital compact cassettes) and MiniDisc (MD), two new audio formats, are launched by Philips and Sony, respectively.
1996	La Fenice opera house in Venice burns down; arson is suspected.
1998	Harrison Birtwistle's orchestral work *Exody*, completed earlier in the year, is performed at the Proms in London, England.
2000	New data-compression techniques allow music to be copied and transferred over the Internet easily and without paying duplication fees or royalties. This provokes vociferous complaints from some artists and record companies who want copyright law changed and such Web sites as napster.com banned.

oxen, is about the size of a small domestic cow, and has long brown hair. At certain seasons it has a musky smell. (Species *Ovibos moschatus*, family Bovidae.)

Its underwool (**qiviut**) is almost as fine as that of the vicuna, and musk-ox farms have been established in Alaska, Québec, and Norway to harvest this wool.

muskrat North American rodent, about 30 cm/12 in long, that lives beside streams, rivers, and lakes. It has webbed hind feet, a side-to-side flattened tail, and shiny, light-brown fur. It builds up a store of food, plastering it over with mud, for winter consumption. It is hunted for its fur. (Species *Ondatra zibethicus*, family Cricetidae.)

Muslim (or **Moslem**) a follower of the religion of ▷Islam.

Muslim Brotherhood Sunni Islamic movement founded in Egypt in 1928, active throughout the Arab world although banned in most countries. It aims at the establishment of a Muslim state governed by Islamic law.

Muslim League Indian political organization. The All India Muslim League was founded in 1906 under the leadership of the Aga Khan. In 1940 the league, led by Muhammad Ali ▷Jinnah, demanded an independent Muslim state. The ▷Congress Party and the Muslim League won most seats in the 1945 elections for an Indian central legislative assembly. In 1946 the Indian constituent assembly was boycotted by the Muslim League. It was partly the activities of the League that led to the establishment of Pakistan.

mussel any of a group of shellfish, some of which are edible, such as the **common mussel** (*Mytilus edulis*) which has a blue-black hinged shell and is found in clusters attached to rocks around the North Atlantic and American coasts. Mussels are bivalve ▷molluscs. (Class Bivalvia, phylum Mollusca.)

Freshwater pearl mussels, such as the species *Unio margaritiferus*, are found in some North American and European rivers. The larvae of the North American freshwater mussel *Lampsilis perovalis* are parasitic, living on the gills or fins of freshwater bass. The larvae of the British **swan mussel** (*Anodonta cygnea*) are also parasitic. *Margaritifera margaritifera* became a protected species in 1991 having suffered from pollution and from amateur fishers who, unlike professionals, are not able to extract the pearl without killing the mussel itself. The **green-lipped mussel**, found only off New Zealand, produces an extract that is used in the treatment of arthritis.

MUSSEL Living as it does on the surface of rocks and piers along the coast, the common mussel *Mytilus edulis* is one of the most familiar bivalves. *Premaphotos Wildlife*

Mussolini, Benito Amilcare Andrea (1883–1945) Italian dictator 1925–43. As founder of the Fascist Movement (see ▷fascism) in 1919 and prime minister from 1922, he became known as *Il Duce* ('the leader'). He invaded Ethiopia 1935–36, intervened in the Spanish Civil War 1936–39 in support of Franco, and conquered Albania in 1939. In June 1940 Italy entered World War II supporting Hitler. Forced by military and domestic setbacks

to resign in 1943, Mussolini established a breakaway government in northern Italy 1944–45, but was killed trying to flee the country.

Mussolini was born in the Romagna, the son of a blacksmith, and worked in early life as a teacher and journalist. He became active in the socialist movement, notably as editor of the party newspaper *Avanti* 1912–14. He was expelled in 1914 for advocating Italian intervention in World War I. He served in the army 1915–17, and in 1919 founded the Fascist Movement, whose programme combined violent nationalism with demagogic republican and anticapitalist slogans, and launched a campaign of terrorism against the socialists. Though anti-capitalist in origin, the movement was backed by agrarian and industrial elites in the context of post-war popular unrest. In October 1922 Mussolini came to power by semi-constitutional means as prime minister at the head of a coalition government. In 1925 he assumed dictatorial powers, and in 1926 all opposition parties were banned. During the years that followed, the political, legal, and education systems were remodelled on fascist lines. Fascism prefigured other 'totalitarian' regimes, in that it aspired to be an all-embracing ideology, but Mussolini faced constraints on his power – from monarch, church, and industrial elites – which had no real parallel in Hitler's Germany.

Mussolini's Blackshirt followers were the forerunners of Hitler's Brownshirts, and his career of conquest drew him into close cooperation with Nazi Germany. Italy and Germany formed the ▷Axis alliance in 1936. During World War II Italian defeats in North Africa and Greece, the Allied invasion of Sicily, and discontent at home destroyed Mussolini's prestige, and in July 1943 he was compelled to resign by his own Fascist Grand Council. He was released from prison by German parachutists in September 1943 and set up a 'Republican Fascist' government in northern Italy. In April 1945 he and his mistress, Clara Petacci, were captured by partisans at Lake Como while heading for the Swiss border, and shot. Their bodies were taken to Milan and hung upside down in a public square.

Related Web site: Mussolini, Benito http://library.thinkquest.org/17120/data/bios/mussolini/

Mussorgsky, Modest Petrovich (1839–1881) Russian composer. He was a member of the group of five composers ('The Five'). His opera masterpiece *Boris Godunov* (1869, revised 1871–72), touched a political nerve and employed realistic transcriptions of speech patterns. Many of his works, including *Pictures at an Exhibition* (1874) for piano, were 'revised' and orchestrated by others, including Rimsky-Korsakov, Ravel, and Shostakovich, and some have only recently been restored to their original harsh beauty.

Mussorgsky, born in Karevo (Pskov, Russia), resigned his commission in the army in 1858 to concentrate on music while working as a government clerk. He was influenced by both folk music and literature. Among his other works are the incomplete operas *Khovanshchina* and *Sorochintsy Fair*, the orchestral *Night on the Bare Mountain* (1867), and many songs. He died in poverty, from alcoholism.

BENITO MUSSOLINI Fascist leaders Adolf Hitler and Benito Mussolini inspect damage to Hitler's headquarters after an assassination attempt in 1944. Mussolini had hoped to limit Italy's participation in World War II to the Mediterranean area, but was forced by the more powerful Hitler to send his armies to defeat in Russia. *Archive Photos*

Mustafa Kemal Pasha Turkish leader who assumed the name ▷Atatürk.

mustard any of several annual plants belonging to the cress family, with seed-bearing pods and sweet-smelling yellow flowers. Brown and white mustard are cultivated as an accompaniment to food in Europe and North America. The seeds of brown mustard (*B. juncea*) and white mustard (*Sinapis alba*) are used in the preparation of table mustard. (Genus mainly *Brassica*, family Cruciferae.)

Mustique island in the Caribbean; see ▷St Vincent and the Grenadines.

mutagen any substance that increases the rate of gene ▷mutation. A mutagen may also act as a ▷carcinogen.

mutation in biology, a change in the genes produced by a change in the ▷DNA that makes up the hereditary material of all living organisms. Mutations, the raw material of evolution, result from mistakes during replication (copying) of DNA molecules. Due to the redundancy built into genetic code many mutations have no effect upon DNA functions. Only a few improve the organism's performance and are therefore favoured by ▷natural selection. Mutation rates are increased by certain chemicals and by radiation.

mute in music, any device used to dampen the vibration of an instrument and so affect the tone. Orchestral strings apply a form of clamp to the bridge – the change is used to dramatic effect by Bartók in the opening bars of *Music for Strings, Percussion, and Celesta* (1936). Brass instruments use the hand or a plug of metal or cardboard inserted in the bell.

Muti, Riccardo (1941–) Italian conductor. Artistic director of La Scala, Milan, from 1986, he was previously conductor of the Philharmonia Orchestra, London, 1973–82 and the Philadelphia Orchestra from 1981. He is equally at home with opera or symphonic repertoire performed with bravura, energy, and scrupulous detail, and is known as a purist.

Mutsuhito personal name of the Japanese emperor ▷Meiji.

> **Benito Mussolini**
> *Fascism is a religion; the twentieth century will be known as the century of fascism.*
> February 1933

mutton bird any of various shearwaters and petrels that breed in burrows on Australasian islands. Each parent feeds the chick for 2–3 days and then leaves for up to three weeks in search of food. These foraging trips can cover a distance of 15,000 km/9,300 mi and mean the chick may be left unattended for over a week. By the time the chicks have reached independence they weigh around 900 g/32 lb, twice as heavy as their parents. The young are killed for food and oil.

mutual fund another name for ▷unit trust, used in the USA.

mutual induction in physics, the production of an electro-motive force (emf) or voltage in an electric circuit caused by a changing ▷magnetic flux in a neighbouring circuit. The two circuits are often coils of wire, as in a ▷transformer, and the size of the induced emf depends largely on the numbers of turns of wire in each of the coils.

mutualism an association between two organisms of different species whereby both profit from the relationship; see ▷symbiosis.

Muybridge, Eadweard (1830–1904) Adopted name of Edward James Muggeridge. English-born US photographer. He made a series of animal locomotion photographs in the USA in the 1870s and proved that, when a horse trots, there are times when all its feet are off the ground. He also explored motion in birds and humans.

Muzorewa, Abel (Tendekayi) (1925–) Zimbabwean politician and Methodist bishop. He was president of the African National Council 1971–85 and prime minister of Rhodesia/ Zimbabwe 1979–80. He was detained for a year in 1983–84. Muzorewa was leader of the minority United Africa National Council, which merged with the Zimbabwe Unity Movement (ZUM) in 1994. He pulled out of the 1996 presidential election contest at the last minute, claiming the electoral process was unfairly tilted in President Mugabe's favour.

Myanmar (formerly **Burma** (until 1989)) see country box.

myasthenia gravis in medicine, an uncommon condition characterized by loss of muscle power, especially in the face and neck. The muscles tire rapidly and fail to respond to repeated nervous stimulation. ▷Autoimmunity is the cause.

mycelium interwoven mass of threadlike filaments or hyphae, forming the main body of most fungi. The reproductive structures, or 'fruiting bodies', grow from the mycelium.

Mycenae ancient Greek city in the eastern Peloponnese, which gave its name to the Mycenaean (Bronze Age) civilization. Its peak was 1400–1200 BC, when the Cyclopean walls (using close-fitting stones) were erected. The city ceased to be inhabited after about 1120 BC.

Mycenaean civilization Bronze Age civilization that flourished in Crete, Cyprus, Greece, the Aegean Islands, and western Anatolia about 3000–1000 BC. During this period, magnificent architecture and sophisticated artefacts were produced.

mycorrhiza mutually beneficial (mutualistic) association occurring between plant roots and a soil fungus. Mycorrhizal roots take up nutrients more efficiently than non-mycorrhizal roots, and the fungus benefits by obtaining carbohydrates from the plant or tree.

myelin sheath insulating layer that surrounds nerve cells in vertebrate animals. It serves to speed up the passage of nerve impulses.

Myelin is made up of fats and proteins and is formed from up to a hundred layers, laid down by special cells, the **Schwann cells**.

Myers, F(rederic) W(illiam) H(enry) (1843–1901)
English psychic researcher, classical scholar, and poet. He coined the word 'telepathy' and was a founder in 1882 and one of the first presidents, in 1900, of the Society for Psychical Research. His main works include *Essays Classical and Modern* (1883), *Phantasms of the Living* (1886), *Science and a Future Life* (1893), and the posthumous *Human Personality and its Survival of Bodily Death* (1903). His best-known poem is 'St Paul' (1867), and his *Collected Poems* were published in 1921.

My Lai massacre killing of 109 civilians in My Lai, a village in South Vietnam, by US troops in March 1968. An investigation in 1969 produced enough evidence to charge 30 soldiers with war crimes, but the only soldier convicted was Lt William Calley, commander of the platoon.

mynah any of various tropical starlings found in Southeast Asia. The glossy black **hill mynah** (*Gracula religiosa*) of India can realistically mimic sounds and human speech. It is up to 40 cm/16 in long with yellow wattles (loose folds of skin) on the head, and a yellow bill and legs. (Family Sturnidae, order Passeriformes.)

myoglobin globular protein, closely related to ▷haemoglobin and located in vertebrate muscle. Oxygen binds to myoglobin and is released only when the haemoglobin can no longer supply adequate oxygen to muscle cells.

myopia (or **short-sightedness**) defect of the eye in which a person can see clearly only those objects that are close up. It is caused either by the eyeball being too long or by the cornea and lens system of the eye being too powerful, both of which cause the images of distant objects to be formed in front of the retina instead of on it. Nearby objects are sharply perceived. Myopia can be corrected by suitable glasses or contact lenses.

myopia, low-luminance poor night vision. About 20% of people have poor vision in twilight and nearly 50% in the dark. Low-luminance myopia does not show up in normal optical tests, but in 1989 a method was developed of measuring the degree of blurring by projecting images on a screen using a weak laser beam.

myrmecophyte plant that lives in association with a colony of ants and possesses specialized organs in which the ants live. For example, *Myrmecodia*, an epiphytic plant from Malaysia, develops root tubers containing a network of cavities inhabited by ants.

Myrmidon in Greek mythology, a member of a legendary race, subjects of the Greek warrior ▷Achilles, whom he commanded at the siege of Troy in Homer's *Iliad*. Originally from Aegina, many Myrmidones followed Achille's father Peleus to Phthiotis in Thessaly, northern Greece.

MYRTLE *Leptospermum juniperinum* in flower in the state of Victoria, Australia. It is a member of the myrtle family Myrtaceae, which is well represented in Australia. *Premaphotos Wildlife*

Myron (c. 500–440 BC) Greek sculptor. A late contemporary of ▷Phidias, he is known to have made statues of the athletes Timanthes (456 BC) and Lycinus (448 BC), excelling in the representation of movement. His bronze *Discobolus/Discus-Thrower* and *Athene and Marsyas*, much admired in his time, are known through Roman copies, which confirm his ancient reputation for brilliant composition and naturalism.

myrrh gum ▷resin produced by several small trees belonging to the bursera family, especially *C. myrrha*, found in Ethiopia and Arabia. In ancient times it was used for incense and perfume and in embalming dead bodies. (Genus *Commiphora*, family Burseraceae.)

myrtle any of a group of Old World evergreen shrubs belonging to the myrtle family. The commonly cultivated Mediterranean myrtle (*M. communis*) has oval opposite leaves and white flowers followed by purple berries, all of which are fragrant. (Genus *Myrtus*, family Myrtaceae.)

mystery play (or **miracle play**) medieval religious drama based on stories from the Bible. Mystery plays were performed around the time of church festivals, reaching their height in Europe during the 15th and 16th centuries. A whole cycle running from the Creation to the Last Judgement was performed in separate scenes on mobile wagons by various town guilds, usually on the festival of Corpus Christi in midsummer.

mystery religion any of various cults of the ancient world that were open only to the initiated; for example, the cults of Demeter (see ▷Eleusinian Mysteries), Dionysus, Cybele, Isis, and Mithras. Underlying some of them is a fertility ritual, in which a deity undergoes death and resurrection and the initiates feed on the flesh and blood to attain communion with the divine and ensure their own life beyond the grave. The influence of mystery religions on early Christianity was considerable.

mysticism religious belief or spiritual experience based on direct, intuitive communion with the divine or apprehension of truths beyond the understanding. It does not always involve an orthodox deity, though it is found in all the main religions – for example, kabbalism in Judaism, Sufism in Islam, and the bhakti movement in Hinduism.
Related Web site: Mysticism in World Religions http://www.digiserve.com/mystic/

mythology (Greek *mythos*, *logos* 'story-telling' or a 'rationale of stories') body of traditional stories symbolically underlying a given culture. These stories describe gods and other supernatural beings with whom humans may have relationships, and are often intended to explain the workings of the universe, nature, or human history. Mythology is sometimes distinguished from ▷legend as being entirely fictitious and imaginary, legend being woven around an historical figure or nucleus such as the tale of Troy, but such division is difficult as myth and legend are often closely interwoven.
Related Web site: Mythmedia http://www-lib.haifa.ac.il/www/art/MYTHOLOGY_WESTART.HTML

myxoedema thyroid-deficiency disease developing in adult life, most commonly in middle-aged women. The symptoms include loss of energy and appetite, weight gain, inability to keep warm, mental dullness, and dry, puffy skin. It is reversed by giving the thyroid hormone thyroxine.

myxomatosis contagious, usually fatal, virus infection of rabbits which causes much suffering. It has been deliberately introduced in the UK and Australia since the 1950s to reduce the rabbit population.

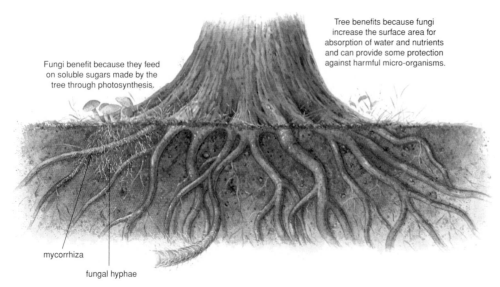

Tree benefits because fungi increase the surface area for absorption of water and nutrients and can provide some protection against harmful micro-organisms.

Fungi benefit because they feed on soluble sugars made by the tree through photosynthesis.

mycorrhiza

fungal hyphae

MYCORRHIZA The tree and fungus both benefit from their symbiotic relationship.

Myanmar

Myanmar formerly Burma (until 1989) country in Southeast Asia, bounded northwest by India and Bangladesh, northeast by China, southeast by Laos and Thailand, and southwest by the Bay of Bengal.

NATIONAL NAME *Pyedawngsu Myanma Naingngan/Union of Myanmar*
AREA 676,577 sq km/261,226 sq mi
CAPITAL Yangon (formerly Rangoon) (and chief port)
MAJOR TOWNS/CITIES Mandalay, Mawlamyine, Bago, Pathein, Taunggyi, Sittwe, Manywa
PHYSICAL FEATURES over half is rainforest; rivers Irrawaddy and Chindwin in central lowlands ringed by mountains in north, west, and east

Government

HEAD OF STATE Than Shwe from 1992
HEAD OF GOVERNMENT Khin Nyunt from 2003
POLITICAL SYSTEM military
POLITICAL EXECUTIVE military
ADMINISTRATIVE DIVISIONS seven states and seven divisions
ARMED FORCES 440,000; plus two paramilitary units totalling 100,300 (2002 est)
CONSCRIPTION military service is voluntary
DEATH PENALTY retained and used for ordinary crimes
DEFENCE SPEND (% GDP) 5 (2002 est)
EDUCATION SPEND (% GDP) 1.4 (2001 est)
HEALTH SPEND (% GDP) 2.2 (2000 est)

Economy and resources

CURRENCY kyat
GPD (US$) 4.8 billion (2002 est)
REAL GDP GROWTH (% change on previous year) 5.3 (2001)
GNI PER CAPITA (PPP) (US$) 1,570 (2002 est)
CONSUMER PRICE INFLATION 40% (2003 est)
UNEMPLOYMENT 2.8% (1999)
FOREIGN DEBT (US$) 5.8 billion (2001 est)
MAJOR TRADING PARTNERS India, Singapore, China, Thailand, Japan, Malaysia, USA, South Korea

RESOURCES natural gas, petroleum, zinc, tin, copper, tungsten, coal, lead, gems, silver, gold
INDUSTRIES food processing, beverages, cement, fertilizers, plywood, petroleum refining, textiles, paper, motor cars, tractors, bicycles
EXPORTS gas, teak, rice, pulses and beans, rubber, hardwood, prawns, fish and fish products, base metals, gems, cement. Principal market: Thailand 31.2% (2001)
IMPORTS crude oil, raw materials, machinery and transport equipment, tools and spares, construction materials, electrical machinery, chemicals, consumer goods. Principal source: Singapore 21.3% (2001)
ARABLE LAND 15.1% (2000 est)
AGRICULTURAL PRODUCTS rice, sugar cane, maize, groundnuts, pulses, rubber, tobacco; fishing; forest resources (teak and hardwood) – teak is frequently felled illegally and smuggled into Thailand; cultured pearls and oyster shells are part of aquacultural fish production

Population and society

POPULATION 49,485,000 (2003 est)
POPULATION GROWTH RATE 1.0% (2000–15)
POPULATION DENSITY (per sq km) 73 (2003 est)
URBAN POPULATION (% of total) 29 (2003 est)
AGE DISTRIBUTION (% of total population) 0–14 33%, 15–59 60%, 60+ 7% (2001 est)
ETHNIC GROUPS Burmans, who predominate in the fertile central river valley and southern coastal and delta regions, constitute the ethnic majority, comprising 72% of the total population. Out of more than 100 minority communities, the most important are the Karen (7%), Shan (6%), Indians (6%), Chinese (3%), Kachin (2%), and Chin (2%). The indigenous minority communities, who predominate in mountainous border regions, show considerable hostility towards the culturally and politically dominant Burmans, undermining national unity. There are also minority groups of Indians, Tamils, and Chinese
LANGUAGE Burmese (official), English, tribal dialects
RELIGION Hinayana Buddhist 89%, Christian 5%, Muslim 4%, animist 1.5%
EDUCATION (compulsory years) 5
LITERACY RATE 89% (men); 82% (women) (2003 est)
LABOUR FORCE 62.7% agriculture, 12.2% industry, 25.1% services (1998)
LIFE EXPECTANCY 55 (men); 60 (women) (2000–05)
CHILD MORTALITY RATE (under 5, per 1,000 live births) 109 (2001)
PHYSICIANS (per 1,000 people) 0.3 (1999 est)
HOSPITAL BEDS (per 1,000 people) 0.3 (1999 est)
TV SETS (per 1,000 people) 8 (2001 est)
RADIOS (per 1,000 people) 65 (2001 est)
INTERNET USERS (per 10,000 people) 2.1 (2002 est)
PERSONAL COMPUTER USERS (per 100 people) 0.1 (2002 est)

MYANMAR A unique method of fishing, on Lake Inle in Myanmar. The conical trap, which contains a net, is pushed down to the shallow lake's bottom, catching any fish that get in the way. The Intha people have been fishing in this fashion since they migrated to the lake in the 18th century. To propel his boat, the fisherman wraps one leg around a long stern-oar. *Image Bank*

See also ▷Aung San; ▷Burman; ▷Suu Kyi, Aung San.

Chronology

3rd century BC: Sittoung valley settled by Mons; Buddhism introduced by missionaries from India.

3rd century AD: Arrival of Burmans from Tibet.

1057: First Burmese Empire established by King Anawrahta, who conquered Thaton, established capital inland at Pagan, and adopted Theravāda Buddhism.

1287: Pagan sacked by Mongols.

1531: Founding of Toungoo dynasty, which survived until mid-18th century.

1755: Nation reunited by Alaungpaya, with port of Rangoon as capital.

1824–26: First Anglo-Burmese war resulted in Arakan coastal strip, between Chittagong and Cape Negrais, being ceded to British India.

1852: Following defeat in second Anglo-Burmese war, Lower Burma, including Rangoon, was annexed by British.

1886: Upper Burma ceded to British after defeat of Thibaw in third Anglo-Burmese war; British united Burma, which was administered as a province of British India.

1886–96: Guerrilla warfare waged against British in northern Burma.

early 20th century: Burma developed as a major rice, teak and, later, oil exporter, drawing in immigrant labourers and traders from India and China.

1937: Became British crown colony in Commonwealth, with a degree of internal self-government.

1942: Invaded and occupied by Japan, who installed anti-British nationalist puppet government headed by Ba Maw.

1945: Liberated from Japanese control by British, assisted by nationalists Aung San and U Nu, formerly ministers in puppet government, who had formed the socialist Anti Fascist People's Freedom League (AFPFL).

1947: Assassination of Aung San and six members of interim government by political opponents.

1948: Independence achieved from Britain as Burma, with U Nu as prime minister. Left Commonwealth. Quasi-federal state established.

1958–60: Administered by emergency government, formed by army chief of staff Gen Ne Win.

1962: Gen Ne Win reassumed power in left-wing army coup; he proceeded to abolish federal system and follow the 'Burmese way to socialism', involving sweeping nationalization and international isolation, which crippled the economy.

1973–74: Adopted presidential-style 'civilian' constitution.

1975: The opposition National Democratic Front was formed by regionally-based minority groups, who mounted guerrilla insurgencies.

1987: There were student demonstrations in Rangoon as food shortages worsened.

1988: The government resigned after violent student demonstrations and workers' riots. Gen Saw Maung seized power in a military coup; over 2,000 were killed.

1989: Martial law was declared; thousands were arrested including advocates of democracy and human rights. The country was renamed Myanmar, and its capital Yangon.

1990: The landslide general election victory for opposition National League for Democracy (NLD) was ignored by the military junta; NLD leaders U Nu and Suu Kyi, the daughter of Aung San, were placed under house arrest.

1991: Martial law and human-rights abuses continued. Suu Kyi, still imprisoned, was awarded the Nobel Peace Prize. There was a pogrom against the Muslim community in the Arakan province in southwest Myanmar. Western countries imposed sanctions.

1992: Saw Maung was replaced as head of state by Than Shwe. Several political prisoners were liberated. Martial law was lifted, but restrictions on political freedom remained.

1993: A ceasefire was agreed with Kachin rebels in the northeast.

1995: Suu Kyi was released from house arrest, but her appointment as NLD leader was declared illegal.

1996: Suu Kyi held the first party congress since her release; 200 supporters were detained by the government. There were major demonstrations in support of Suu Kyi.

1997: Admission to Association of South East Asian Nations (ASEAN) granted, despite US sanctions for human-rights abuses.

1998: Japan resumed a flow of aid, which had been stopped in 1988. The military junta ignored pro-democracy roadside protests by Suu Kyi and broke up student demonstrations. 300 members of the opposition NLD were released from detention.

2000: Aung San Suu Kyi was forced to give up a pro-democracy roadside protest after nine days and was placed under house arrest for two weeks.

2001: The government began talks with Suu Kyi and released 84 members of the NLD from prison.

2002: The government released Suu Kyi from almost 20 months of house arrest. Her release was widely seen as a move to get US and European Union (EU) sanctions against the regime eased.

N abbreviation for ▷newton, a unit of force; the chemical symbol for **nitrogen**.

NAACP abbreviation for ▷National Association for the Advancement of Colored People, a US civil-rights organization.

Nabokov, Vladimir Vladimirovich (1899–1977) US writer. He left his native Russia in 1917 and began writing in English in the 1940s. His most widely known book is *Lolita* (1955), the story of the middle-aged Humbert Humbert's infatuation with a precocious girl of 12. His other books, remarkable for their word play and ingenious plots, include *Laughter in the Dark* (1938), *The Real Life of Sebastian Knight* (1945), *Pnin* (1957), and his memoirs *Speak, Memory* (1947).

Born in St Petersburg, Nabokov settled in the USA in 1940, and became a US citizen in 1945. He was professor of Russian literature at Cornell University 1948–59, producing a translation and commentary on Pushkin's *Eugene Onegin* (1963). He was also a lepidopterist (a collector of butterflies and moths), a theme used in his book *Pale Fire* (1962).

nacre another name for ▷mother-of-pearl.

nadir point on the celestial sphere vertically below the observer and hence diametrically opposite the **zenith**.

naevus mole, or patch of discoloration on the skin which has been present from birth. There are many different types of naevi, including those composed of a cluster of small blood vessels, such as the 'strawberry mark' (which usually disappears early in life) and the 'port-wine stain'.

Naga member of any of the various peoples who inhabit the highland region near the Indian-Myanmar (Burma) border; they number approximately 800,000. These peoples do not possess a common name; some of the main groups are Ao, Konyak, Sangtam, Lhota, Sema, Rengma, Chang, and Angami. They live by farming, hunting, and fishing, with rice as the staple diet. Some peoples are egalitarian, others are stratified into aristocrats and commoners. Their languages belong to the Sino-Tibetan family.

Nagaland state of northeast India, bordering Myanmar on the east, and the Indian states of Manipur to the south, and Assam to the north and west; area 16,600 sq km/6,409 sq mi; population (2001 est) 1,817,000, which is made up of many different tribal groups. The capital is Kohima. The state is mainly upland, averaging over 1,500 m/4,900 ft, and densely forested. Wildlife includes tigers and elephants. Industries in the state include timber and paper, and petroleum at Dikhu. Agricultural products include tea, sugar, coffee, rice, millet, maize, and vegetables. The population is mainly Christian.

Nagasaki industrial port (coal, iron, shipbuilding) on Kyushu island, Japan; population (2000 est) 438,600. Nagasaki was the only Japanese port open to European trade from the 16th century until 1859. The first modern Japanese shipyard opened here 1855–61. On 9 August 1945, an atom bomb was dropped on Nagasaki by the USA, killing an estimated 40,000.

Nagorno-Karabakh (Russian 'mountainous Qarabagh') autonomous region of ▷Azerbaijan; area 4,400 sq km/1,700 sq mi; population (1996 est) 200,000 (77% Armenian, 23% Azeri), the Christian Armenians forming an enclave within the predominantly

Shiite Muslim Azerbaijan. The capital is Xankändi. The region lies on the eastern slopes of the Lesser ▷Caucasus Mountains, partly covered with oak and beech forests. Main agricultural products include cotton, grapes, wheat, silk, and livestock (sheep, cattle, pigs, and horses). Since 1989 the region has experienced conflict between local Armenian troops and Azeri forces. By 1998, Nagorno-Karabakh was effectively an independent state. In March 2000, President Arkady Gukasyan (elected in 1997) survived an assassination attempt.

The region formed part of Armenia until the 7th century, but was subsequently taken by the Arabs, and ruled by them for 300 years. In the 11th century, the region came under the rule of the Bagratid kings of Georgia, who held the area until the Mongol invasion. After a century of Mongol rule, Karabakh fell into Turkish hands. In the early 1600s, Persia gained control of the region, and ▷Abbas I allowed the local khan to rule in Karabakh. This line of khans was overthrown in 1805 by the Russians, who created a province of the region in 1822.

An autonomous protectorate following the Russian Revolution of 1917, Nagorno-Karabakh subsequently saw heavy fighting in the Civil War (1918–20), and was annexed to Azerbaijan in 1923 against the wishes of the largely Christian-Armenian population. From 1989, when the local council declared its intention to transfer control of the region to Armenia, the enclave was racked by fighting between local Armenian troops (reputedly backed by Armenia) and Azeri forces, both attempting to assert control. After a declaration of independence on 6 January 1992 by the region's parliament (following a referendum on 10 December 1991), the conflict intensified. In May 1994 a ceasefire was agreed between Azerbaijan and Armenia. Border fighting between Azerbaijan and Armenia continued through 1997 and, in November 1998, the Azerbaijan government announced the rejection of the OSCE peace plan for the Nagoro-Karabakh dispute.

Nagoya industrial seaport, seat of Aichi prefecture, and capital of the ▷Chubu region, Honshu island, Japan; population (1994) 2,091,000. Situated at the head of Ise Bay, 260 km/162 mi west of Tokyo and 140 km/87 mi east of Osaka, Nagoya is the fourth-largest city of Japan and is a major port. Manufactured products include cars, textiles, and clocks. It has a shogun fortress, built 1610–14 and rebuilt in 1959, and a notable Shinto shrine, Atsuta Jingu.

Related Web site: Nagoya http://www.city.nagoya.jp/indexe.html

Nagpur industrial city in Maharashtra, India, 710 km/440 mi east of Mumbai (formerly Bombay); population (2000 est) 2,123,000. Industries include textiles, metal goods, pharmaceuticals, cotton goods, and hosiery; oranges are traded. Nagpur was the centre of the Chanda ▷Gond dynasty in the 10th–11th centuries, and was the former capital of ▷Central Provinces and Berar, and Madhya Pradesh states. In 1956 it alternated with Mumbai as capital of Maharashtra state.

> **Vladimir Nabokov**
> *The cradle rocks above an abyss, and common sense tells us that our existence is but a brief crack of light between two eternities of darkness.*
> Speak, Memory ch. 1, 1

Nagy, Imre (1895–1958) Hungarian politician, prime minister 1953–55 and 1956. He led the Hungarian revolt against Soviet domination in 1956, for which he was executed.

Nahayan, Sheikh Sultan bin Zayed al- (1918–) Emir of Abu Dhabi from 1969, when he deposed his brother, Sheikh Shakhbut. He was elected president of the supreme council of the United Arab Emirates in 1971. In 1991 he was implicated, through his majority ownership, in the international financial scandals associated with the Bank of Commerce and Credit International (BCCI), and in 1994 approved a payment by Abu Dhabi of $1.8 billion to BCCI creditors.

Nahuatl any of a group of Mesoamerican Indian peoples (Mexico and Central America), of which the best-known group were the Aztecs. The Nahuatl are the largest ethnic group in Mexico, and their languages, which belong to the Uto-Aztecan (Aztec-Tanoan) family, are spoken by over a million people today.

naiad in classical mythology, a water nymph. Naiads lived in rivers and streams; ▷nereids in the sea.

nail in biology, a hard, flat, flexible outgrowth of the digits of primates (humans, monkeys, and apes). Nails are composed of ▷keratin.

Naipaul, V(idiadhar) S(urajprasad) (1932–) Trinidadian novelist and travel writer living in Britain. His novels include *A House for Mr Biswas* (1961), *The Mimic Men* (1967), *In a Free State* (1971; for which he won the Booker Prize), *A Bend in the River* (1979), *Finding the Centre* (1984), *A Way in the World* (1994),

and *Letters Between a Father and Son* (1999) – letters between him and his family back in India while he was at Oxford. He was knighted in 1990.

Nairobi capital of ▷Kenya, in the central highlands at 1,660 m/5,450 ft; population (1993 est) 1,758,900. Industries include engineering, paints, brewing, and food processing. It is the headquarters of the United Nations Environment Programme, and has the UN Centre for Human Settlements. It is one of Africa's largest and fastest-growing cities.

Nairobi was founded in 1899. It has the International Louis Leakey Institute for African Prehistory (1977), the University of Nairobi, and the National Museum; the International Primate Research Institute is nearby.

naive art fresh, childlike style of painting, employing bright colours and strong, rhythmic designs, usually the work of artists with no formal training. Outstanding naive artists include Henri Rousseau and Camille Bombois (1883–1970) in France, and Alfred Wallis (1855–1942) in England. The term is also used to describe the work of trained artists who employ naive techniques and effects, for example, L S Lowry.

Najibullah, Ahmadzai (1947–1996) Afghan communist politician, leader of the People's Democratic Party of Afghanistan (PDPA) from 1986, and state president 1986–92. Although his government initially survived the withdrawal of Soviet troops in February 1989, continuing pressure from the Mujahedin forces resulted in his eventual overthrow. He was executed in September 1996 by the Talibaan (Islamic student army), who had seized control of most of Afghanistan.

> **V S Naipaul**
> *I'm the kind of writer that people think other people are reading.*
> Radio Times 1979

Nakasone, Yasuhiro (1917–) Japanese conservative politician, leader of the Liberal Democratic Party (LDP) and prime minister 1982–87. He increased military spending and Japanese participation in international affairs, with closer ties to the USA. He was forced to resign his party post in May 1989 as a result of having profited from insider trading in the ▷Recruit scandal. After serving a two-year period of atonement, he rejoined the LDP in April 1991.

Nakhichevan autonomous region of Azerbaijan, an enclave within the neighbouring state of Armenia, located on the Iranian frontier and separated from the rest of Azerbaijan by a narrow strip of Armenian territory; area 5,500 sq km/2,124 sq mi; population (1997 est) 333,200. The capital is ▷Nakhichevan, and Paragachay is another city in the enclave. The region is extremely arid, a mountainous country with large salt deposits. Industries include irrigated agriculture (cotton, tobacco, grain), horticulture, and sheep raising; mining of salt, molybdenum, and lead; cotton ginning, silk spinning, fruit canning, meat packing, and tobacco manufacture.

Namib Desert coastal desert region between the Kalahari Desert and the Atlantic Ocean, extending some 2,800 km/1,740 mi from Luanda in Angola to St Helena Bay in South Africa. Its aridity is caused by the descent of dry air cooled by the cold Benguela current along the coast. The sand dunes of the Namib Desert are among the tallest in the world, reaching heights of 370 m/1,200 ft. In some parts rainfall can be as little as 23 mm/0.9 in per year.

Related Web site: Namib: Africa's Burning Shore http://www.pbs.org/edens/namib/

NAMIB DESERT The sand dunes of the Namib Desert, which stretches 1,290 km/800 mi along the coast and covers one-third of Namibia. *Premaphotos Wildlife*

Namibia (formerly South West Africa (to 1968)) see country box.

Nanak (1469–c. 1539) Indian guru and founder of Sikhism, a religion based on the unity of God and the equality of all human beings. He was strongly opposed to caste divisions.

Namibia

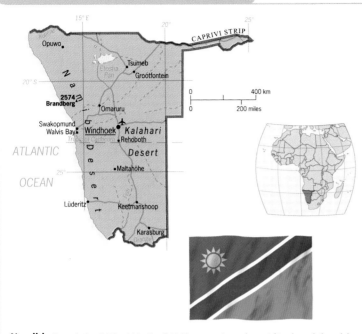

Namibia formerly South West Africa (until 1968) country in southwest Africa, bounded north by Angola and Zambia, east by Botswana and South Africa, and west by the Atlantic Ocean.

NATIONAL NAME *Republic of Namibia*
AREA 824,300 sq km/318,262 sq mi
CAPITAL Windhoek
MAJOR TOWNS/CITIES Swakopmund, Rehoboth, Rundu
MAJOR PORTS Walvis Bay
PHYSICAL FEATURES mainly desert (Namib and Kalahari); Orange River; Caprivi Strip links Namibia to Zambezi River; includes the enclave of Walvis Bay (area 1,120 sq km/432 sq mi)

Government

HEAD OF STATE Samuel Nujoma from 1990
HEAD OF GOVERNMENT Theo-Ben Gurirab from 2002
POLITICAL SYSTEM emergent democracy
POLITICAL EXECUTIVE limited presidency
ADMINISTRATIVE DIVISIONS 13 regions
ARMED FORCES 9,000 (2002 est)
CONSCRIPTION military service is voluntary
DEATH PENALTY abolished in 1990
DEFENCE SPEND (% GDP) 2.8 (2002 est)

EDUCATION SPEND (% GDP) 8.6 (1999)
HEALTH SPEND (% GDP) 7.1 (2000 est)

Economy and resources

CURRENCY Namibian dollar
GPD (US$) 2.8 billion (2002 est)
REAL GDP GROWTH (% change on previous year) 2.4 (2001)
GNI (US$) 3.3 billion (2002 est)
GNI PER CAPITA (PPP) (US$) 6,650 (2002 est)
CONSUMER PRICE INFLATION 9.5% (2003 est)
UNEMPLOYMENT 38% (1997 est)
FOREIGN DEBT (US$) 465 million (2001 est)
MAJOR TRADING PARTNERS South Africa, UK, Germany, France, Spain, USA
RESOURCES uranium, copper, lead, zinc, silver, tin, gold, salt, semi-precious stones, diamonds (one of the world's leading producers of gem diamonds), hydrocarbons, lithium, manganese, tungsten, cadmium, vanadium

INDUSTRIES food processing (fish), mining and quarrying, metal and wooden products, brewing, meat processing, chemicals, textiles, cement, leather shoes
EXPORTS diamonds, fish and fish products, live animals and meat, uranium, copper, karakul pelts. Principal market: UK 43% (2000)
IMPORTS transport equipment, food and live animals, beverages, tobacco, mineral fuels, chemicals, rubber and plastic products, electrical and other machinery. Principal source: South Africa 80% (2000)
ARABLE LAND 1% (2000 est)
AGRICULTURAL PRODUCTS wheat, maize, sunflower seed, sorghum, vegetables (crop farming is greatly limited by scarcity of water and poor rainfall); fishing; principal agricultural activity is livestock rearing (cattle, sheep, and goats); beef and karakul sheepskin are also produced

Population and society

POPULATION 1,987,000 (2003 est)
POPULATION GROWTH RATE 1.2% (2000–15)
POPULATION DENSITY (per sq km) 2 (2003 est)
URBAN POPULATION (% of total) 32 (2003 est)
AGE DISTRIBUTION (% of total population) 0–14 43%, 15–59 51%, 60+ 6% (2002 est)

ETHNIC GROUPS 85% black African, of which 51% belong to the Ovambo tribe; the remainder includes the pastoral Nama and hunter-gatherer groups. There is a 6% white minority
LANGUAGE English (official), Afrikaans, German, Ovambo (51%), Nama (12%), Kavango (10%), other indigenous languages
RELIGION about 90% Christian (Lutheran, Roman Catholic, Dutch Reformed Church, Anglican)
EDUCATION (compulsory years) 7
LITERACY RATE 84% (men); 84% (women) (2003 est)
LABOUR FORCE 53.4% agriculture, 17.6% industry, 29.0% services (1991)
LIFE EXPECTANCY 43 (men); 46 (women) (2000–05)
CHILD MORTALITY RATE (under 5, per 1,000 live births) 67 (2001)
PHYSICIANS (per 1,000 people) 0.3 (1998 est)
HOSPITAL BEDS (per 1,000 people) 4.8 (1994 est)
TV SETS (per 1,000 people) 38 (1999 est)
RADIOS (per 1,000 people) 144 (1997)
INTERNET USERS (per 10,000 people) 266.7 (2002 est)
PERSONAL COMPUTER USERS (per 100 people) 7.1 (2002 est)

See also ▷apartheid; ▷Khoikhoi; ▷League of Nations; ▷SWAPO; ▷Walvis Bay.

Chronology

1480s: Coast visited by European explorers.

16th century: Bantu-speaking Herero migrated into northwest and Ovambo settled in northernmost areas.

1840s: Rhenish Missionary Society began to spread German influence; Jonkar Afrikaner conquest state dominant in southern Namibia.

1884: Germany annexed most of the area, calling it South West Africa, with Britain incorporating a small enclave around Walvis Bay in the Cape Colony of South Africa.

1892: German farmers arrived to settle in the region.

1903–04: Uprisings by the long-settled Nama (Khoikhoi) and Herero peoples brutally repressed by Germans, with over half the local communities slaughtered.

1908: Discovery of diamonds led to a larger influx of Europeans.

1915: German colony invaded and seized by South Africa during World War I and the Ovambo, in the north, were conquered.

1920: Administered by South Africa, under League of Nations mandate.

1946: Full incorporation in South Africa refused by United Nations (UN).

1949: White voters in South West Africa given representation in the South African parliament.

1958: South West Africa People's Organization (SWAPO) formed to campaign for racial equality and full independence.

1960: Radical wing of SWAPO, led by Sam Nujoma, forced into exile.

1964: UN voted to end South Africa's mandate, but South Africa refused to relinquish control or soften its policies towards the economically disenfranchised black majority.

1966: South Africa's apartheid laws extended to the country; 60% of land was allocated to whites, who formed 10% of the population.

1968: South West Africa redesignated Namibia by UN; SWAPO, drawing strong support from the Ovambo people of the north, began armed guerrilla struggle against South African rule, establishing People's Liberation Army of Namibia (PLAN).

1971: Prolonged general strike by black Namibian contract workers.

1973: The UN recognized SWAPO as the 'authentic representative of the Namibian people'.

1975–76: The establishment of a new Marxist regime in independent Angola strengthened the position of SWAPO guerrilla movement, but also led to the increased military involvement of South Africa in the region.

1978: UN Security Council Resolution 435 for the granting of full independence was accepted by South Africa, and then rescinded.

1983: Direct rule was reimposed by Pretoria after the resignation of the Democratic Turnhalle Alliance (DTA), a conservative administration dominated by whites.

1985: South Africa installed a new puppet administration, the Transitional Government of National Unity (TGNU), which tried to reform the apartheid system, but was not recognized by the UN.

1988: Peace talks between South Africa, Angola, and Cuba led to an agreement on troop withdrawals and full independence for Namibia.

1989: UN peacekeeping force were stationed to oversee free elections to the assembly to draft a new constitution; SWAPO won the elections.

1990: A liberal multiparty constitution was adopted and independence was achieved. Sam Nujoma, SWAPO's former guerrilla leader, was elected president. Joined the Commonwealth. Hage Geingob was appointed prime minister.

1993: South Africa, with its new multiracial government, relinquished its claim to Walvis Bay sovereignty. Namibia dollar was launched with South African rand parity.

1994: SWAPO won assembly elections; Nujoma was re-elected president.

NAMIBIA A view of the Namib Desert, Namibia, southwest Africa. A chaotic mass of barren rocks such as this one is known as moonscape. *Corel*

Nanchang capital of ▷Jiangxi province, China, on the River Gan, about 260 km/160 mi southeast of Wuhan; population (1994) 1,465,400. Motor vehicles, aircraft, tractors, textiles, glass, porcelain, soap, and lumber are produced. There is a considerable trade in rice, beans, linen, timber, paper, and tobacco.

Nancy administrative centre of the *département* of Meurthe-et-Moselle and of the region of ▷Lorraine, France, on the River Meurthe and the Rhine and Marne Canal, 280 km/175 mi east of Paris; population (1990) 102,400, conurbation 300,000. Nancy dates from the 11th century. It has a university (founded in 1572, transferred here in 1797) and is the seat of a bishopric; building of the cathedral was began in 1703 by J H Mansart.

Nanda Devi peak in the Himalayas, Uttar Pradesh, northern India; height 7,817 m/25,645 ft. Until Kanchenjunga was absorbed into India, Nanda Devi was the country's highest mountain.

Nanga Parbat peak in the Himalayan Karakoram Mountains of Kashmir; height 8,126 m/26,660 ft.

Nanjing (or Nanking; 'southern capital') inland port and capital of ▷Jiangsu province, China, 270 km/165 mi northwest of Shanghai; population (1993) 2,430,000. It is a commercial centre and communications hub, with engineering, electronics, shipbuilding, chemical, and oil-refining industries. Textiles are a traditional manufacture. The bridge over the Chang Jiang River, built in 1968, is the longest in China at 6,705 m/22,000 ft.

Related Web site: WWW Memorial Hall of the Victims in the Nanjing Massacre (1937–38) http://www.arts.cuhk.edu.hk/NanjingMassacre/NM.html

Nanning river port and capital of ▷Guangxi Zhuang Autonomous Region, China, on the Yong Jiang River; population (1994) 1,181,200. It is an important trading centre, particularly in spices. Industries include sugar-refining, food-processing, and the manufacture of chemicals, machines, and cotton. It was a supply town during the Vietnam War and the Sino-Vietnamese confrontation of 1979. Almost a third of the population is of Zhuang cultural background.

nano- prefix used in ▷SI units of measurement, equivalent to a one-billionth part (10^{-9}). For example, a nanosecond is one-billionth of a second.

nanotechnology experimental technology using individual atoms or molecules as the components of minute machines, measured by the nanometre, or millionth of a millimetre. Nanotechnology research in the 1990s focused on testing molecular structures and refining ways to manipulate atoms using a scanning tunnelling microscope. The ultimate aim is to create very small computers and molecular machines which could perform vital engineering or medical tasks.

The ▷scanning electron microscope can be used to see and position single atoms and molecules, and to drill holes a nanometre (billionth of a metre) across in a variety of materials. The instrument can be used for ultrafine etching; the entire 28 volumes of the *Encyclopedia Britannica* could be engraved on the head of a pin. In the USA a complete electric motor has been built, which is less than 0.1 mm across with a top speed of 600,000 rpm. It is etched out of silicon, using the ordinary methods of chip manufacturers.

Nansen, Fridtjof (1861–1930) Norwegian explorer and scientist. In 1893 he sailed to the Arctic in the *Fram*, which was deliberately allowed to drift north with an iceflow. Nansen, accompanied by F Hjalmar Johansen (1867–1923), continued north on foot and reached 86° 14′ N, the highest latitude then attained. After World War I, Nansen became League of Nations high commissioner for refugees. He was awarded the Nobel Prize for Peace in 1922 for his relief work after World War I.

Nanshan Islands Chinese name for the ▷Spratly Islands.

Nantes industrial port and administrative centre of the *département* of Loire-Atlantique and the ▷Pays de la Loire region in western France, situated on the right bank of the River Loire, 50 km/31 mi from its mouth; population (1990) 252,000. Industries include oil, sugar refining, metal goods, textiles, soap, biscuits, and tobacco. The city has many splendid buildings, including a cathedral constructed between 1434 and 1884 and a castle founded in 938.

Nantes, Edict of decree by which Henry IV of France granted religious freedom to the ▷Huguenots in 1598. It was revoked in 1685 by Louis XIV.

Nantucket (called 'the Little Grey Lady') resort island and county in southeast Massachusetts, USA, 40 km/25 mi south of Cape Cod across Nantucket Sound; population of town (1997 est) 7,500. Extending over 120 sq km/46 sq mi, its beaches have made it a popular summer vacation area. The island was explored by the English in 1602, settled in 1659 by Quaker and Presbyterian families, and became part of Massachusetts in 1692. In the 18th–19th centuries, Nantucket Town was a whaling port.

Napa city and administrative headquarters of Napa County, north-central California; population (1992) 63,300. It is situated on the Napa River, 58 km/38 mi northeast of San Francisco on San Pablo Bay. It is a major trading centre for wine produced in the surrounding Napa Valley vineyards; other products include fruit, clothing, steel pipe, and leather goods. The city has also served as a shipping point for cattle, lumber, and minerals. Tourism is important to the regional economy. Napa State Hospital and Napa Valley College (1940) are both in the city.

NAPA Irrigation of vineyards in Napa Valley, California, USA. The town of Napa first developed in the 19th century as a port for shipping goods to San Francisco, California, and later as an agricultural centre for the area. Today it is best known for the wines produced in the vineyards of Napa Valley. *Image Bank*

napalm fuel used in flamethrowers and incendiary bombs. Produced from jellied petrol, it is a mixture of **na**phthenic and **palm**itic acids. Napalm causes extensive burns because it sticks to the skin even when aflame. It was widely used by the US Army during the Vietnam War, and by Serb forces in the civil war in Bosnia-Herzegovina.

naphtha the mixtures of hydrocarbons obtained by destructive distillation of petroleum, coal tar, and shale oil. It is a raw material for the petrochemical and plastics industries. The term was originally applied to naturally occurring liquid hydrocarbons.

naphthalene $C_{10}H_8$ solid, white, shiny, aromatic hydrocarbon obtained from coal tar. The smell of moth-balls is due to their naphthalene content. It is used in making indigo and certain azo dyes, as a mild disinfectant, and as a pesticide.

Napier, John (1550–1617) 8th Laird of Merchiston. Scottish mathematician who invented ▷logarithms in 1614 and 'Napier's bones', an early mechanical calculating device for multiplication and division. It was Napier who first used and then popularized the decimal point to separate the whole number part from the fractional part of a number.

Related Web site: Napier, John http://www-groups.dcs.st-and.ac.uk/history/Mathematicians/Napier.html

Naples (Italian **Napoli**; Greek *Neapolis* 'new city') industrial port and capital of Campania, Italy, on the Tyrrhenian Sea; population (2001 est) 993,400. Industries include shipbuilding, food-processing, and the manufacture of cars, textiles, and paper. To the south is the Isle of Capri, and behind the city is Mount Vesuvius, with the ruins of Pompeii at its foot. Naples is the third-largest city of Italy, and as a port second in importance only to Genoa. Buildings include the royal palace (17th–19th centuries), the San Carlo opera house (18th century), the Castel Nuovo (1283), and the university (1224). The city began as the Greek colony **Neapolis** in the 6th century BC and was taken over by Romans in 326 BC; it became part of the Kingdom of the Two ▷Sicilies in 1140 and capital of the Kingdom of Naples in 1282.

Naples, Kingdom of the southern part of Italy, alternately independent and united with ▷Sicily in the Kingdom of the Two Sicilies.

Napoleon I (1769–1821) Also known as **Napoleon Bonaparte**. Emperor of the French 1804–14 and 1814–15. A general from 1796 in the ▷Revolutionary Wars, in 1799 he overthrew the ruling Directory (see ▷French Revolution) and made himself dictator. From 1803 he conquered most of Europe (the **Napoleonic Wars**) and installed his brothers as puppet kings (see ▷Bonaparte). After the Peninsular War and retreat from Moscow in 1812, he was forced to abdicate in 1814 and was banished to the island of Elba. In March 1815 he reassumed power but was defeated by British and Prussian forces at the Battle of ▷Waterloo and exiled to the island of St Helena. His internal administrative reforms and laws are still evident in France.

Napoleon, born in Ajaccio, Corsica, received a commission in the artillery in 1785 and first distinguished himself at the siege of ▷Toulon in 1793. Having suppressed a royalist uprising in Paris in 1795, he was given command against the Austrians in Italy and defeated them at Lodi, Arcole, and Rivoli 1796–97. Egypt, seen as a halfway house to India, was overrun and Syria invaded, but his fleet was destroyed by the British admiral ▷Nelson at the Battle of the Nile. Napoleon returned to France and carried out a coup against the government of the Directory to establish his own dictatorship, nominally as First Consul. The Austrians were again defeated at Marengo in 1800 and the coalition against France shattered, a truce being declared in 1802. A plebiscite the same year made him consul for life. In 1804 a plebiscite made him emperor.

While retaining and extending the legal and educational reforms of the Jacobins, Napoleon replaced the democratic constitution established by the Revolution with a centralized despotism, and by his ▷concordat with Pius VII conciliated the Catholic Church. The **Code Napoléon** remains the basis of French law.

War was renewed by Britain in 1803, aided by Austria and Russia from 1805 and Prussia from 1806. Prevented by the British navy from invading Britain, Napoleon drove Austria out of the war by victories at Ulm and Austerlitz in 1805, and Prussia by the victory at Jena in 1806. Then, after the battles of Eylau and Friedland, he formed an alliance with Russia at Tilsit in 1807. Napoleon now forbade entry of British goods to Europe, attempting an economic blockade known as the ▷Continental System, occupied Portugal, and in 1808 placed his brother Joseph on the Spanish throne. Both countries revolted, with British aid, and Austria attempted to re-enter the war but was defeated at Wagram. In 1796 Napoleon had married ▷Josephine de Beauharnais, but in 1809, to assert his equality with the Habsburgs, he divorced her to marry the Austrian emperor's daughter, Marie Louise.

When Russia failed to enforce the Continental System, Napoleon marched on and occupied Moscow, but his army's retreat in the bitter winter of 1812 encouraged Prussia and Austria to declare war again in 1813. He was defeated at Leipzig and driven from Germany. Despite his brilliant campaign on French soil, the Allies invaded Paris and compelled him to abdicate in April 1814; he was banished to the island of Elba, off the west coast of Italy. In March 1815 he escaped and took power for a hundred days, with the aid of Marshal ▷Ney, but Britain and Prussia led an alliance against him at Waterloo, Belgium, in June. Surrendering to the British, he again abdicated, and was exiled to the island of St Helena, 1,900 km/1,200 mi west of Africa, where he died. His body was brought back in 1840 to be interred in the Hôtel des Invalides, Paris.

Related Web site: Napoleon Series – Life and Times of Napoleon Bonaparte http://www.historyserver.org/napoleon.series/

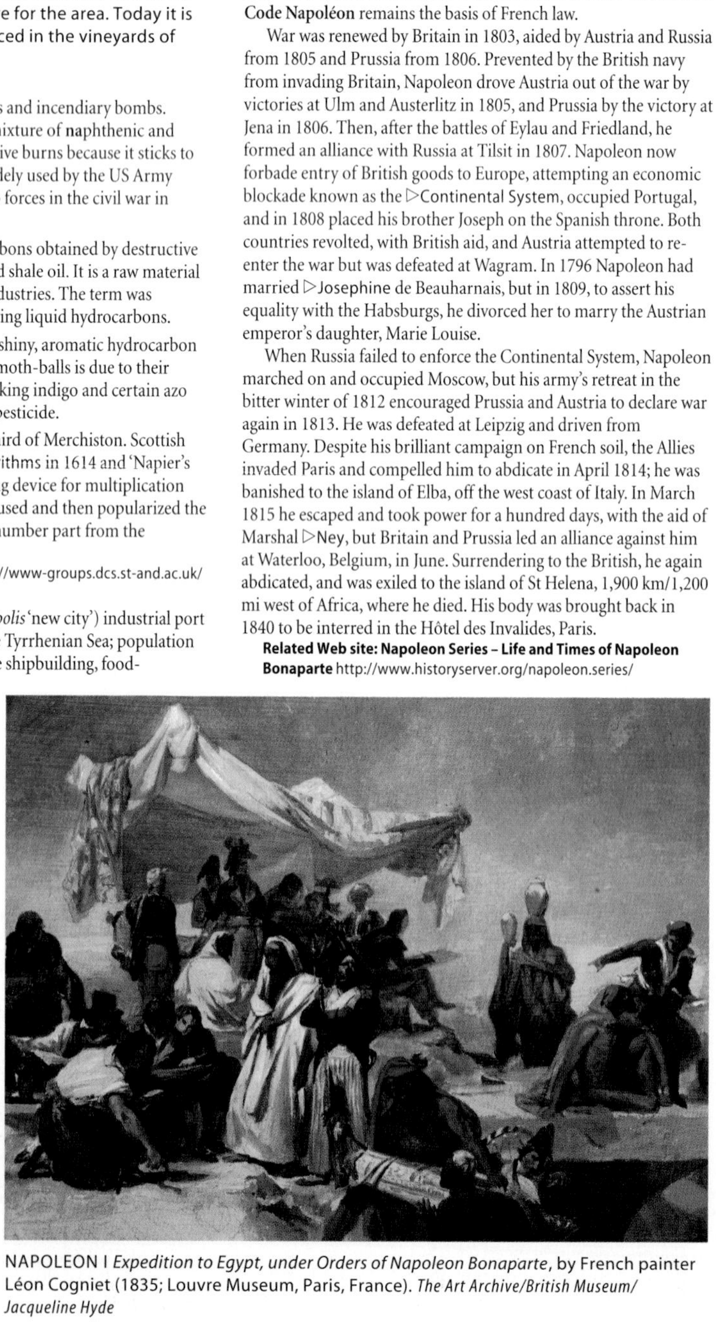

NAPOLEON I *Expedition to Egypt, under Orders of Napoleon Bonaparte*, by French painter Léon Cogniet (1835; Louvre Museum, Paris, France). *The Art Archive/British Museum/Jacqueline Hyde*

Napoleon II (1811–1832) Born François Charles Joseph Bonaparte. Title given by the Bonapartists to the son of Napoleon I and Marie Louise; until 1814 he was known as the king of Rome and after 1818 as the duke of Reichstadt. After his father's abdication in 1814 he was taken to the Austrian court, where he spent the rest of his life.

Napoleon III (1808–1873) Born Charles Louis Napoleon Bonaparte. Emperor of the French 1852–70, known as **Louis-Napoleon**. After two attempted coups (1836 and 1840) he was jailed, then went into exile, returning for the revolution of 1848, when he became president of the Second Republic but proclaimed himself emperor in 1852. In 1870 he was manoeuvred by the German chancellor Bismarck into war with Prussia (see ▷Franco-Prussian war); he was forced to surrender at Sedan, northeastern France, and the empire collapsed.

The son of Louis Bonaparte and Hortense de Beauharnais, brother and step-daughter respectively of Napoleon I, he led two unsuccessful revolts against the French king Louis Philippe, at Strasbourg in 1836 and at Boulogne in 1840. After the latter he was imprisoned. Escaping in 1846, he lived in London until 1848. He was elected president of the newly established French republic in December, and set himself to secure a following by posing as the champion of order and religion against the revolutionary menace. He secured his re-election by a military coup d'état in 1851, and a year later was proclaimed emperor. Hoping to strengthen his regime by military triumphs, he joined in the Crimean War (1854–55), waged war with Austria in 1859, winning the Battle of Solferino, annexed Savoy and Nice in 1860, and attempted unsuccessfully to found a vassal empire in Mexico 1863–67. In so doing he aroused the mistrust of Europe and isolated France.

At home, his regime was discredited by its notorious corruption; republican and socialist opposition grew, in spite of severe repression, and forced Napoleon, after 1860, to make concessions in the direction of parliamentary government. After losing the war with Prussia he withdrew to England, where he died. His son by Empress ▷Eugénie, **Eugène Louis Jean Joseph Napoleon**, Prince Imperial (1856–79), was killed fighting with the British army against the Zulus in Africa.

Napoleonic Wars series of European wars (1803–15) conducted by ▷Napoleon I of France against an alliance of Britain, the German states, Spain, Portugal, and Russia, following the ▷Revolutionary Wars, and aiming for French conquest of Europe. At one time nearly all of Europe was under Napoleon's domination. He was finally defeated at the ▷Battle of Waterloo in 1815.

During the Napoleonic Wars, the annual cost of the British army was between 60% and 90% of total government income. About half of Napoleon's army was made up of foreign mercenaries, mainly Swiss and German.

Admiral Horatio ▷Nelson's victory over a combined French and Spanish fleet at the Battle of ▷Trafalgar (1805) confirmed British naval supremacy during the wars.

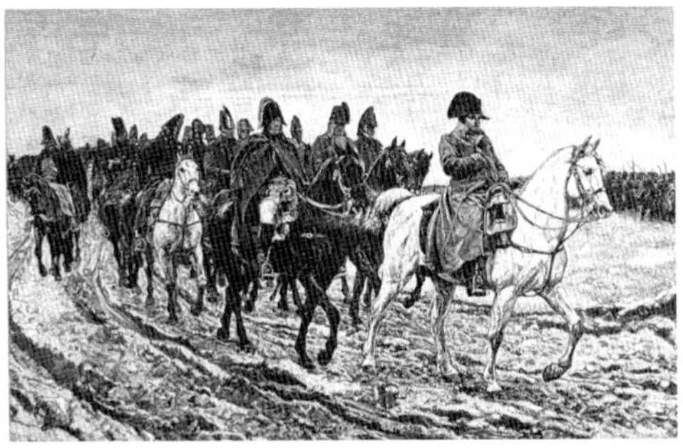

NAPOLEONIC WARS This picture shows Napoleon's retreat from Moscow following the disastrous invasion of Russia. Of the 500,000 men he led to Moscow, nearly 400,000 died in the severe cold of the Russian winter. *Philip Sauvain Picture Collection*

Napoli Italian form of ▷Naples, a city in Italy.

Narayanan, Kocheril Raman (1920–) Indian politician and public servant, president from 1997. A *dalit* ('untouchable') from the southern state of Kerala, after a career chiefly as a diplomat, he became vice-president in 1992 and, in July 1997, was indirectly elected, with cross-party support, as the country's first ever *dalit* president.

narcissism in psychology, an exaggeration of normal self-respect and self-involvement which may amount to mental disorder when it precludes relationships with other people.

Narcissus in late Greek mythology, a beautiful youth who rejected the love of the nymph ▷Echo and was condemned by Nemesis, goddess of retribution, to fall in love with his reflection in a pool. He pined away, and a flower which appeared at the spot was named after him.

narcissus any of a group of bulbous plants belonging to the amaryllis family. Species include the daffodil, jonquil, and narcissus. All have flowers with a cup or trumpet projecting from the centre. (Genus *Narcissus*, family Amaryllidaceae.)

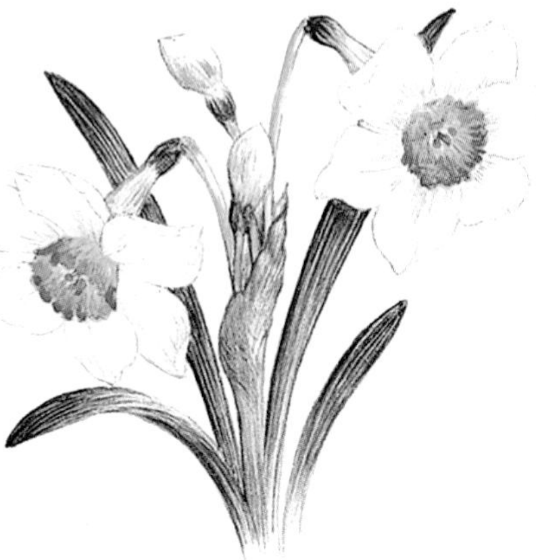

NARCISSUS In the true narcissus, the petals form a small bowl rather than the long trumpet of the daffodil.

narcotic pain-relieving and sleep-inducing drug. The term is usually applied to heroin, morphine, and other opium derivatives, but may also be used for other drugs which depress brain activity, including anaesthetic agents and ▷hypnotics.

Thomas Nashe
Brightness falls from the air; / Queens have died young and fair; / Dust hath closed Helen's eye.
'In Time of Pestilence'

Narmada river that rises in the Maikala range in Madhya Pradesh state, central India, and flows 1,245 km/778 mi west and southwest to the Gulf of Khambat, an inlet of the Arabian Sea. Forming the traditional boundary between Hindustan and Deccan, the Narmada is a holy river of the Hindus.

Narváez, Pánfilo de (*c.* 1480–1525) Spanish conquistador and explorer. Narváez was largely responsible for bringing Cuba under Spanish control in 1511. The governor of Cuba sent him to Mexico in 1520 to reassert authority over Hernán ▷Cortés. Defeated, he was held captive for two years. He drowned during an expedition to Florida after a fruitless detour for gold split his party.

narwhal toothed whale found only in the Arctic Ocean. It grows to 5 m/16 ft long, has a grey and black body, a small head, and short flippers. The male has a single spiral tusk growing straight out in front of its upper lip that can measure up to 2.7 m/9 ft long. (Species *Monodon monoceros*, family Monodontidae.)

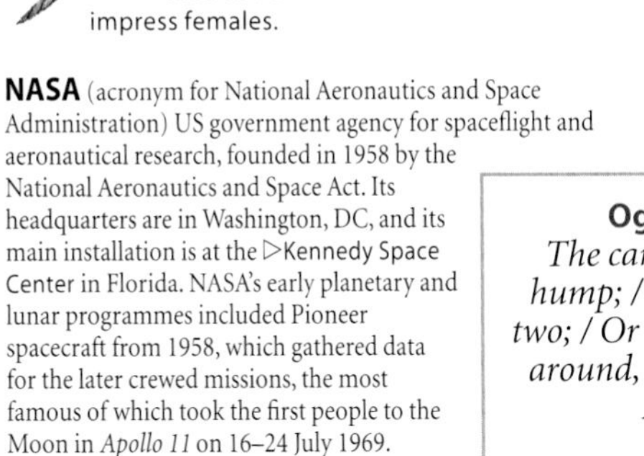

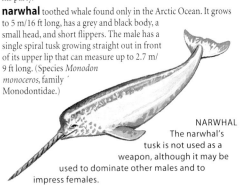

NARWHAL The narwhal's tusk is not used as a weapon, although it may be used to dominate other males and to impress females.

NASA (acronym for National Aeronautics and Space Administration) US government agency for spaceflight and aeronautical research, founded in 1958 by the National Aeronautics and Space Act. Its headquarters are in Washington, DC, and its main installation is at the ▷Kennedy Space Center in Florida. NASA's early planetary and lunar programmes included Pioneer spacecraft from 1958, which gathered data for the later crewed missions, the most famous of which took the first people to the Moon in *Apollo 11* on 16–24 July 1969.

In the early 1990s, NASA moved towards lower-budget missions, called 'Discovery', which were intended not to exceed a budget of about $200 million (excluding launch costs). The first missions were the Near Earth Asteroid Rendezvous craft and the *Lunar Projector*. Following the loss of the Mars Climate Orbiter and another Mars probe in 1999, a report published in 2000 found that NASA's funds and overview were inadequate for the projects that were being undertaken, and recommended that the organization found clearer goals, responsible management, and more economical programmes.

Related Web site: NASA Home Page http://www.nasa.gov/

Ogden Nash
The camel has a single hump; / The dromedary, two; / Or else the other way around, / I'm never sure. Are you?
'The Camel'

Naseby, Battle of decisive battle of the English Civil War on 14 June 1645, when the Royalists, led by Prince Rupert, were defeated by the Parliamentarians ('Roundheads') under Oliver ▷Cromwell and General ▷Fairfax. It is named after the nearby village of Naseby, 32 km/20 mi south of Leicester.

Both armies drew up in similar formation, infantry in the centre, cavalry on the flanks, and reserves behind. The Royalists opened the battle by dashing downhill, across the intervening valley, and up the facing hill to where the Roundheads were massed. Prince Rupert's cavalry broke the Parliamentary right wing and then recklessly pursued them toward the village of Naseby. On the other wing, however, Cromwell's cavalry routed the force opposing them and then turned inward to take the Royalist infantry in the flank. King ▷Charles I ordered his last reserves to charge, but the Earl of Carnwath, seeing this to be a futile move, turned his horse away and led his troops off the field; the Parliamentarians took heart from this, rallied, and completed the victory. Prince Rupert, returning from his chase, found the battle over and could do nothing but follow the king to Leicester. About 1,000 loyalists were killed and 5,000 taken prisoner, together with all their artillery.

Related Web site: Battle of Naseby 1645
http://easyweb.easynet.co.uk/~crossby/ECW/battles/naseby.html

Nash, John (1752–1835) English architect. His large country-house practice, established about 1796 with the landscape gardener Humphry Repton, used a wide variety of styles, and by 1798 he was enjoying the patronage of the Prince of Wales (afterwards George IV). Later he laid out Regent's Park, London, and its approaches, as well as Trafalgar Square and St James's Park. Between 1811 and 1821 he planned Regent Street (later rebuilt), repaired and enlarged ▷Buckingham Palace (for which he designed Marble Arch), and rebuilt the Royal Pavilion, Brighton, in flamboyant oriental style. For himself he built East Cowes Castle (1798) which greatly influenced the early Gothic Revival.

Nash, (Frederic) Ogden (1902–1971) US poet and wit. He published numerous volumes of humorous, quietly satirical light verse, characterized by unorthodox rhymes and puns. They include *I'm a Stranger Here Myself* (1938), *Versus* (1949), and *Bed Riddance* (1970). Most of his poems first appeared in the *New Yorker* magazine, where he held an editorial post and did much to establish the magazine's tone.

Nash, Paul (1889–1946) English painter. He was an official war artist in World Wars I and II. In the 1930s he was one of a group of artists promoting avant-garde style, and was deeply influenced by surrealism. Two works which illustrate the visionary quality of his paintings are *Totes Meer/Dead Sea* (1940–41; Tate Gallery, London); and *Solstice of the Sunflower* (1945; National Gallery of Canada, Ottawa). 'Structural purpose' was an aim which led him into many forms of design, for textiles, ceramics, the stage and the book, but the surrealist trend of the 1930s and the exhibition of 1936 brought out an imaginative and poetic feeling already apparent in his oils and watercolours.

Nashe, Thomas (1567–1601) English poet, satirist, and anti-Puritan pamphleteer. He was drawn into the Martin ▷Marprelate controversy and wrote at least three attacks on the Martinists. Among his later works are the satirical *Pierce Pennilesse, his Supplication to the Divell* (1592) and the religious *Christes Teares over Jerusalem* (1593); *The Unfortunate Traveller* (1594) is a picaresque narrative mingling literary parody and mock-historical fantasy.

Nashville capital and river port of ▷Tennessee, USA, on the Cumberland River; population (1996 est) 511,300. It is a banking and commercial centre, a major processing point for timber and agricultural produce, and has large car-manufacturing, printing, music-publishing, and recording industries. Nashville was settled in 1779 as Fort Nashborough.

Nassau capital and port of the Bahamas, on New Providence Island; population (1998 est) 205,400. It is a popular tourist resort, especially in winter, and was the scene in 1994 of an international conference on biological diversity. A series of forts was built there (Fort Nassau, 1697; Fort Charlotte, 1787–94; Fort Fincastle, 1793) as protection against the dangers of Spanish invasion and of piracy. English settlers founded it in the 17th century, and it was a supply base for Confederate blockade runners during the American Civil War.

Nassau agreement treaty signed on 18 December 1962 whereby the USA provided Britain with Polaris missiles, marking a strengthening in Anglo-American relations.

Nasser, Gamal Abdel (1918–1970) Egyptian politician, prime minister 1954–56 and from 1956 president of Egypt (the United Arab Republic 1958–71). In 1952 he was the driving power behind the Neguib coup, which ended the monarchy. His nationalization of the Suez Canal in 1956 led to an Anglo-French invasion and the ▷Suez Crisis, and his ambitions for an Egyptian-led union of Arab states led to disquiet in the Middle East (and in the West). Nasser was also an early and influential leader of the nonaligned movement.

Nasser entered the army from Cairo Military Academy, and was wounded in the Palestine War of 1948–49. Initially unpopular after the 1952 coup, he took advantage of demands for change by initiating land reform and depoliticizing the army. His position was secured by an unsuccessful assassination attempt in 1954 and his handling of the Suez Crisis in 1956.

nastic movement plant movement that is caused by an external stimulus, such as light or temperature, but is directionally independent of its source, unlike ▷tropisms. Nastic movements occur as a result of changes in water pressure within specialized cells or differing rates of growth in parts of the plant. Examples include the opening and closing of crocus flowers following an increase or decrease in temperature (**thermonasty**), and the opening and closing of evening-primrose *Oenothera* flowers on exposure to dark and light (**photonasty**).

nasturtium any of a group of plants that includes watercress (*N. officinale*), a perennial aquatic plant of Europe and Asia, grown as a salad crop. Belonging to a different family altogether, the South American trailing nasturtiums include the cultivated species *T. majus*, with orange, scarlet, or yellow flowers, and *T. minus*, which has smaller flowers. (Genus *Nasturtium*, family Cruciferae; South American genus *Tropaeolum*, family Tropaeolaceae.)

Natal seaport and capital of Rio Grande do Norte federal unit (state), northeast Brazil; situated on the banks of the Potengi River on the Atlantic coast 410 km/255 mi southeast of the port of Fortaleza; population (1991) 606,600. There are textile and salt-refining industries, and cotton, sugar, salt, and hides are exported. Tourism is important. The Fort of the Three Kings is a pentagonal monument, so named because of the founding of the city in 1597 on 6 January, the Epiphany. There is also a cathedral (1768) and a university, founded in 1958.

Nataraja ('Lord of the Dance') in Hinduism, a title of ▷Siva.

Natchez member of an ▷American Indian people whose original territory extended along the Gulf of Mexico. They were one of the ▷Moundbuilder group of peoples. In 1700 the Natchez numbered about 6,000, but were almost exterminated by wars with French settlers in 1716, 1723, and 1729. Those who survived took refuge with the Chickasaw and ▷Cherokee whom they accompanied to Oklahoma in the 1830s when they were forced to relocate. Only a few Natchez now survive in Oklahoma. Their Muskogean language is extinct.

National Assembly for Wales devolved parliamentary body for Wales, comprising 60 members and based in Cardiff. The Assembly was created by the July 1998 Government of Wales Act, which was passed following the Welsh electorate's narrow approval of government proposals in an 18 September 1997 referendum on devolution. Its temporary base is the Cardiff University Council Chamber and Crickhowell House on Cardiff Bay. A new building, designed by the architect Richard ▷Rogers, is to be built at Cardiff Bay to house the assembly from 2001.

The assembly has taken over virtually all of the functions of the Secretary of State for Wales, spending the Welsh Office's £7 billion budget. Foreign affairs, defence, taxation, social security, broadcasting, and overall economic policy remain with the government in London. The assembly may pass secondary legislation, but, unlike the Scottish Parliament, does not have primary law-making powers, even in areas such as the Welsh language. It implements Westminster legislation and oversees quangos, making them more accountable. The English and Welsh languages are treated equally in the assembly's work.

Its members are elected for four-year terms through a semi-proportional electoral system; 40 are returned on a first-past-the-post basis from single-member constituencies, comprising Wales' existing Westminster constituencies, and an additional 20 members are selected on a proportional basis from party lists based on Wales' five European Parliament constituencies. The assembly's first elections were held on 6 May 1999. A first secretary (*Prif Ysgrifennydd y Cynulliad*) is elected by majority vote from within the assembly, to act as its leader and to appoint a cabinet comprising assembly secretaries.

National Association for the Advancement of Colored People (NAACP) US civil-rights organization dedicated to ending inequality and segregation for African-Americans through nonviolent protest. Founded in 1910, its first aim was to eradicate lynching. The NAACP campaigned to end segregation in state schools; it funded test cases that eventually led to the Supreme Court decision, in 1954, outlawing school segregation, although it was only through the ▷civil-rights movement of the 1960s that desegregation was achieved. In 1987 the NAACP had about 500,000 members, black and white. Its chairman from 1998 is Julian Bond, an early civil-rights leader.

NATIONAL ASSOCIATION FOR THE ADVANCEMENT OF COLORED PEOPLE Poster produced by the National Association for the Advancement of Colored People (NAACP) to show the horrors of lynching. Figures for reported lynchings show that, between 1882 and 1951, 3,437 African-Americans were lynched in the USA. *Archive Photos*

National Curriculum in England and Wales from 1988, a course of study in ten subjects common to all primary and secondary state schools. The National Curriculum is divided into three core subjects – English, maths, and science – and seven foundation subjects: geography, history, technology, a foreign language (for secondary school pupils), art, music, and physical education (plus Welsh in Wales). There are four key stages, on completion of which the pupil's work is assessed. The stages are for ages 5–7, 7–11, 11–14, and 14–16.

The National Curriculum and the linked assessment system (see ▷SATs) was set up through the Education Reform Act 1988 and first reviewed in 1993 by Ron Dearing following teachers' complaints of overload and a boycott of the first year of tests. Content was cut back and the tests finally introduced in 1994. The incoming Labour government instituted a further review and in 1999 confirmed a greater emphasis on literacy and numeracy skills in primary schools, with greater flexibility for teachers in other subjects, and introduced compulsory lessons in citizenship for the first time.

Related Web site: National Curriculum http://www.nc.uk.net/

national debt debt incurred by the central government of a country to its own people and institutions and also to overseas creditors. A government can borrow from the public by means of selling interest-bearing bonds, for example, or from abroad. Traditionally, a major cause of national debt was the cost of war but in recent decades governments have borrowed heavily in order to finance development or nationalization, to support an ailing currency, or to avoid raising taxes.

National Economic Development Council (NEDC; called 'Neddy') the UK forum for economic consultation between government, management, and trade unions. It examines the country's economic and industrial performance, in both the public and private sectors, and seeks agreement on ways to improve efficiency. It was established in 1962; its role diminished during the 1980s.

National Endowment for Democracy US political agency founded in 1983 with government backing. It has funded a range of political organizations abroad, with over 95% of its $114 million annual income coming from the US government after 1984.

National Front in the UK, extreme right-wing political party founded in 1967. In 1991 the party claimed 3,000 members. Some of its members had links with the National Socialist Movement of the 1960s (see ▷Nazism). It attracted attention during the 1970s through the violence associated with its demonstrations in areas with large black and Asian populations and in, response, the left-wing Anti Nazi League was formed to mount counter protests.

National Gallery London art gallery housing the British national collection of pictures by artists no longer living, founded in 1824. Its collection covers all major pre-20th-century periods and schools, but it is unique in its collection of Italian Gothic and Renaissance works, which is more comprehensive than any other collection outside Italy.

national grid the network of cables, carried overhead on pylons or buried under the ground, that connects consumers of electrical power to power stations, and interconnects the power stations. It ensures that power can be made available to all customers at any time, allowing demand to be shared by several power stations, and particular power stations to be shut down for maintenance work from time to time.

NATIONAL GRID A view of a switching centre, part of an electricity grid or network. This allows for power to be distributed from one area to another, where the need may be greater. *Image Bank*

National Guard ▷militia force recruited by each state of the USA. The volunteer National Guard units are under federal orders in emergencies, and under the control of the governor in peacetime, and are now an integral part of the US Army. The National Guard has been used against demonstrators; in May 1970 at Kent State University, Ohio, they killed four students who were protesting against the bombing of Cambodia by the USA.

National Health Service (NHS) UK government medical scheme; see ▷health service.

national income the total income of a state in one year, including both the wages of individuals and the profits of companies. It is equal to the value of the output of all goods and services during the same period. National income is equal to gross national product (the value of a country's total output) minus an allowance for replacement of ageing capital stock.

national insurance in the UK, state social-security scheme that provides child allowances, maternity benefits, and payments to the unemployed, sick, and retired, and also covers medical treatment. It is paid for by weekly or monthly contributions from employees and employers.

nationalism in music, the adoption by 19th-century composers of folk idioms with which an audience untrained in the classics could identify. Nationalism was encouraged by governments in the early 20th century for propaganda purposes in times of war and political tension. Composers of nationalist music include Bedřich ▷Smetana, Jean ▷Sibelius, Edvard ▷Grieg, Antonín ▷Dvořák, Carl ▷Nielsen, Zoltán ▷Kodály, Aaron ▷Copland, Edward ▷Elgar, Dmitri ▷Shostakovich, and Stephen ▷Foster.

nationalism in politics, a movement that consciously aims to unify a nation, create a state, or liberate it from foreign or imperialistic rule. Nationalist movements became a potent factor in European politics during the 19th century; since 1900 nationalism has become a strong force in Asia and Africa and in the late 1980s revived strongly in Eastern Europe.

In the second half of the 20th century a strongly national literary and political movement developed in Scotland and Wales. See also Nationalism and Citizenship Focus Feature on pp. 668–669.

nationalization policy of bringing a country's essential services and industries under public ownership. It was pursued, for example, by the UK Labour government 1945–51. Subsequently the trend towards nationalization has slowed and in many countries (the UK, France, and Japan) reversed (▷privatization). Assets in the hands of foreign governments or companies may also be nationalized; for example, Iran's oil industry (see ▷Abadan), the ▷Suez Canal, and US-owned fruit plantations in Guatemala, all in the 1950s.

National Party of Australia Australian political party, favouring free enterprise and seeking to promote the interests of people outside the major metropolitan areas. It holds the balance of power between Liberals and Labor. It was formed in 1916 as the **Country Party of Australia** and adopted its present name in 1982. It gained strength following the introduction of proportional representation in 1918 and was in coalition with the Liberals 1949–83. Its leader from 1990 is Tim Fischer and its federal president John Paterson. In 1996 it entered into a coalition with the Liberal Party led by Prime Minister John Howard.

National Portrait Gallery London art gallery containing portraits of distinguished British men and women. It was founded in 1856 and moved to its present building in St Martin's Place, Trafalgar Square, in 1896. In addition to paintings, there are drawings, cartoons, sculptures, and photographs on display.

National Rivers Authority (NRA) UK government agency launched in 1989. It had responsibility for managing water resources, investigating and regulating pollution, and taking over flood controls and land drainage from the former ten regional water authorities of England and Wales. In April 1996 the NRA was replaced by the Environment Agency, having begun to establish a reputation for being supportive to wildlife projects and tough on polluters.

National Security Agency (NSA) largest and most secret of US intelligence agencies. Established in 1952 to intercept foreign communications as well as to safeguard US transmissions, the NSA collects and analyses computer communications, telephone signals, and other electronic data, and gathers intelligence. Known as the Puzzle Palace, its headquarters are at Fort Meade, Maryland (with a major facility at Menwith Hill, England).

National Security Council US federal executive council that was established under the National Security Act of 1947. The statutory membership includes the president, vice-president, and secretaries of state and defence. Other officials, such as the directors of foreign operations administration and emergency planning, may attend by invitation of the president. Their special advisers include the head of the joint chiefs of staff and the director of the ▷Central Intelligence Agency. The operations coordinating board also reports to the council. The special assistant to the president for national security affairs is the chief staff officer, and the national security adviser heads the council's staff.

national security directive in the USA, secret decree issued by the president that can establish national policy and commit federal funds without the knowledge of Congress, under the National Security Act 1947. The National Security Council alone decides whether these directives may be made public; most are not. The directives have been criticized as unconstitutional, since they enable the executive branch of government to make laws.

national service ▷conscription into the armed services in peacetime.

national socialism official name for the ▷Nazi movement in Germany; see also ▷fascism.

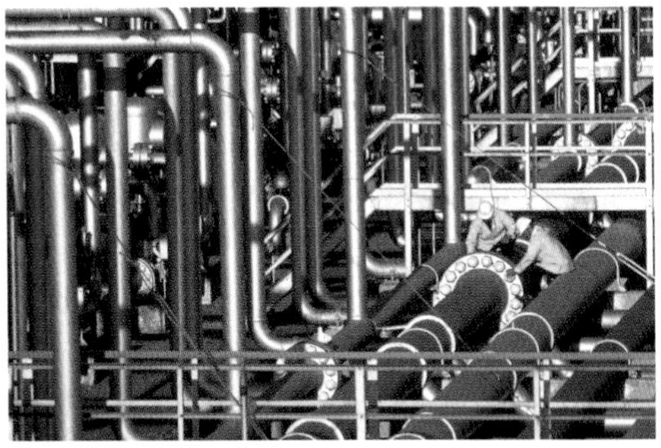

NATURAL GAS A factory to which natural gas is piped for liquefying. *Image Bank*

National Theatre, Royal British national theatre company established in 1963, and the complex, opened in 1976, that houses it on London's South Bank. From 1988 it has been formally called the Royal National Theatre of Great Britain. Nicholas Hytner became the artistic director in 2003. The national theatre of France is the ▷Comédie Française, founded in 1680.

National Trust British trust founded in 1895 for the preservation of land and buildings of historic interest or beauty, incorporated by an act of Parliament in 1907. It is the largest private landowner in Britain. The National Trust for Scotland was established in 1931.

Related Web site: About the National Trust http://www.nationaltrust.org.uk/aboutnt.htm

national vocational qualification (NVQ) in the UK, a certificate of attainment of a standardized level of skill and competence. A national council for NVQs was set up 1986 in an effort by the government in cooperation with employers to rationalize the many unrelated vocational qualifications then on offer. The Scottish equivalent is SVQ.

National Westminster Tower building designed by Richard Seifert, located in the City of London, England. It is 183 m/600 ft high and has 49 storeys. Seen from above it resembles the National Westminster Bank's logo. It was completed in 1979 at a cost of £72 million, and was London's tallest building until 1991.

Nation of Islam original name of the group popularly known as the ▷Black Muslims, now the title of a 100,000-member splinter group faithful to the Black Muslims' original principles led by Louis ▷Farrakhan. Members strive to improve their social and religious position in society, and the group has won praise for its work in deprived areas, although its reputation has been tarnished by Farrakhan's anti-Semitic and anti-white beliefs. In October 1995 the group demonstrated its political strength by organizing the 'Million Man March' – a march of around 400,000 black men in Washington.

native companion another name for the ▷brolga, so called because these birds are often seen in pairs.

native metal (or **free metal**) any of the metallic elements that occur in nature in the chemically uncombined or elemental form (in addition to any combined form). They include bismuth, cobalt, copper, gold, iridium, iron, lead, mercury, nickel, osmium, palladium, platinum, ruthenium, rhodium, tin, and silver. Some are commonly found in the free state, such as gold; others occur almost exclusively in the combined state, but under unusual conditions do occur as native metals, such as mercury. Examples of native nonmetals are carbon and sulphur.

nativity Christian festival celebrating a birth: **Christmas** has been celebrated on 25 December from AD 336 in memory of the birth of Jesus in Bethlehem; **Nativity of the Virgin Mary** is celebrated on 8 September by the Catholic and Eastern Orthodox churches; **Nativity of John the Baptist** is celebrated on 24 June by the Catholic, Eastern Orthodox, and Anglican churches.

NATO abbreviation for ▷North Atlantic Treaty Organization.

natural (♮) in music, a sign cancelling a sharp or flat. A **natural trumpet** or **horn** is an instrument without valves, thus restricted to playing natural harmonics.

Natural Environment Research Council (NERC) UK organization established by royal charter in 1965 to undertake and support research in the earth sciences, to give advice both on exploiting natural resources and on protecting the environment, and to support education and training of scientists in these fields of study. Research areas include geothermal energy, industrial pollution, waste disposal, satellite surveying, acid rain, biotechnology, atmospheric circulation, and climate. Research is carried out principally within the UK but also in Antarctica and in many developing countries. It comprises 13 research bodies.

natural frequency the frequency at which a mechanical system will vibrate freely. A pendulum, for example, always oscillates at the same frequency when set in motion. More complicated systems, such as bridges, also vibrate with a fixed natural frequency. If a varying force with a frequency equal to the natural frequency is applied to such an object the vibrations can become violent, a phenomenon known as ▷resonance.

natural gas mixture of flammable gases found in the Earth's crust (often in association with petroleum). It is one of the world's three main fossil fuels (with coal and oil). Natural gas is a mixture of ▷hydrocarbons, chiefly methane (80%), with ethane, butane, and propane. Natural gas is usually transported from its source by pipeline, although it may be liquefied for transport and storage and is, therefore, often used in remote areas where other fuels are scarce and expensive. Prior to transportation, butane and propane are removed and liquefied to form 'bottled gas'.

natural justice the concept that there is an inherent quality in law that compares favourably with arbitrary action by a government. It is largely associated with the idea of the rule of law. For natural justice to be present, it is generally argued that no one should be a judge in his or her own case, and that each party in a dispute has an unalienable right to be heard and to prepare their case thoroughly (the rule of *audi alterem partem*).

natural logarithm in mathematics, the ▷exponent of a number expressed to base e, where e represents the ▷irrational number 2.71828.... Natural ▷logarithms are also called Napierian logarithms, after their inventor, the Scottish mathematician John Napier.

natural radioactivity radioactivity generated by those radioactive elements that exist in the Earth's crust. All the elements from polonium (atomic number 84) to uranium (atomic number 92) are radioactive. ▷Radioisotopes of some lighter elements are also found in nature (for example potassium-40). See ▷background radiation.

natural selection the process whereby gene frequencies in a population change through certain individuals producing more

(*continued on p. 670*)

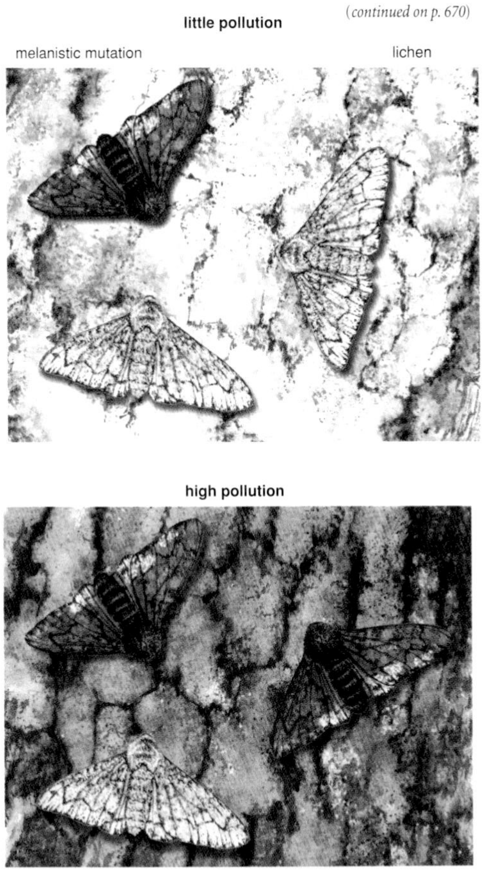

NATURAL SELECTION Industrial melanism in the peppered moth was first noticed by English geneticist Henry Kettlewell. Kettlewell observed that whereas in rural areas peppered moths were light in colour to camouflage them against the lichens, in industrial areas where the tree trunks were dirtied with soot, peppered moths were darker. Natural selection favoured the darker mutation in industrial areas because it offered better camouflage there, so it had become widespread, whereas in rural areas the darker mutant was highly visible against the lighter tree trunks and so was easy prey to insect feeders.

KURDISH WOMEN DEMONSTRATE in Germany, October 1999, demanding the release of Kurdish rebel leader Abdullah Ocalan. The march through the streets of Frankfurt am Main involved some 10,000 Kurds and is symbolic of the increasing nationalist sentiment witnessed in Europe in recent years. The banner reads 'Freedom for Abdullah Ocalan. Peace in Kurdistan'. *PA Photos/EPA European Press Agency*

Nationalism and Citizenship

by Ian Derbyshire

Nationalism is the world's most potent political ideology and lies at the heart of many of the world's most enduring, bitter, and intractable conflicts. Nationalism is founded on the belief that inhabitants of a geographically delimited 'nation' form a 'natural community', derived from a unique shared ethnic, linguistic, cultural, and historical heritage. According to nationalism, the nation should be the focus of citizens' identity and loyalty and should form an independent nation state. During the 1950s and 1960s, with the development of internationalist sentiment and pan-national regional groupings, nationalism began to be viewed as outdated in the developed world.

nationalism and its contribution to modern world conflicts

Since the 1970s, however, there has been an unexpected revival in nationalist politics, particularly within Europe and Asia. From Euskadi (the Basque country, straddling northwest Spain and southwest France) to East Timor, Corsica to Chechnya, Kosovo to Korea, nationalist issues now dominate the political agenda and nationalist movements generate armed conflict, terrorist outrages, and 'ethnic cleansing' genocide. Notwithstanding the unprecedented growth in the number of independent nation states, from 33 in 1914, to 50 in 1945, 173 in 1989, and 192 in 2000, there exists considerable scope for further nation-building. Globally, there are at least 6,000 linguistic groups

and several hundred aspirant 'nations without states'. Three-quarters of the world's 127 largest states contain at least one sizeable national minority that aspires to self-determination.

concept of nationalism

The common symbols of a nation state are a flag, national anthem, head of state, passport, and currency. However, the feeling of national identity resides in the imagination and emotions of citizens. It is for this reason that nations are often referred to as 'invented' communities. A nation can live on in the minds and hearts of its people even when it no longer formally exists on the world political map – this is the case today with Kurdistan, whose people live in parts

of southern Turkey and northern Iraq. At the heart of nationalist sentiment is a sense of belonging to a distinct ethnic group, separate from others. The sense of 'separateness' can arise from differences in language and religion, reinforced by a distinctive common historical experience, underpinned by a shared culture and mythology.

emergence of nationalism

Ethnic and regional traditions have deep roots. However, identification with a nation is a more recent phenomenon. English national identity was forged early by the Tudor aristocracy in the 16th century. After the Act of Union (1707) with Scotland, a British identity developed gradually. However, not until the late 18th century, with the philosophical writings of the German nationalist Johann Herder and the French Revolution, did nationalism spread more widely across Europe. Previously, the focus of allegiance had been more local and personal, towards a fiefdom, a city, a guild, and/or a religious group. Early modern European states were based typically on dynastic alliances and embraced a range of ethnic communities, as exemplified by the Habsburg empire; while the orientation of the Christian (and Muslim) community was supra-national, aiming to embrace the whole of humanity.

Nationalism's emergence was made possible by several interconnected political, social, economic, and technological developments:

- the destruction of feudal structures by large centralized states ruled, at first, by absolute monarchs
- the growing secularization of life and rupturing of Christian unity by the Reformation
- the creation by industrialization of a rising middle class anxious to participate in government and of an urban working class searching for a common identity
- revived interest in national languages and traditions, following study by intellectuals, and its dissemination through the printing press
- the spread of literacy through public education
- inter-state military conflicts, leading to national conscription
- the revolution in communications.

Early stirrings of nationalism were seen in the anti-colonial revolts in the Americas in the late 18th and early 19th centuries and in the European nationalist uprisings of 1830 and 1848, which were led by political liberals. With the founding of an Italian kingdom in 1861 and unification of Germany in 1871, a system of competing European nation states came into being. This provoked military rivalries in Europe and overseas, where colonial empires were established. As representative democracy spread, nationalism became an increasingly conservative ideology, drawn upon by right-wing parties to court support from sections of the newly enfranchised lower classes.

20th century's three nationalist waves

The 20th century saw three main waves of nation-building associated with nationalism. The first wave came at the end of World War I, which had been triggered by ethnic rivalries in the Balkans. The war was followed by dismemberment of the empires of the defeated Habsburg and Ottoman (Turkish) powers. Consequently, new states emerged in central and southern Europe, including Poland and Yugoslavia, while boundaries were also redrawn at the expense of Germany. A new international body, the League of Nations, was set up in 1920, with the intention of arbitrating future international disputes. However, it lacked teeth and proved unable to prevent territorial expansion from the mid-1930s by Nazi Germany and Mussolini's Italy – states motivated by an extreme form of nationalism known as **fascism**, which was based on claims of national superiority.

THE PALAIS DES NATIONS, Geneva, Switzerland. This was the headquarters of the League of Nations until 1946, when it became the European office of the United Nations. © *Corel*

The second, and most significant, nationalist wave followed the end of World War II, which began an unfolding process of decolonization by the European powers. New nation states were created in Asia, Africa, and Oceania, typically in response to pressure from national liberation movements, some of which had a socialist orientation. However, across central and southern Europe an '**Iron Curtain**' of domination by Russia resulted in the smothering of nationalism and the incorporation of a number of nations, including the Baltic states, as parts of the Soviet Union.

The third, and still continuing, wave of new nation-building commenced from 1989, with the collapse of Soviet communism. Nationalist sentiment was unleashed in central and southern Europe and in central Asia. New states were created in which political parties drew on nationalism to attract democratic support, while violent ethnic conflicts and insurgencies erupted in the Balkans (Bosnia-Herzegovina and Kosovo) and Caucasus (Chechnya, Georgia, and Nagorno-Karabakh).

nationalism as a source of ethnic conflict

Nationalism can take a range of forms. It can drive a state into expansionist military conflicts in an attempt to increase the nation's power or to bring within the nation's borders national groups living outside. The latter is known as 'irredentist nationalism'. It is what initially motivated Nazi German expansion during the late 1930s and what has been behind the contemporary Armenian and Azerbaijani dispute over Nagorno-Karabakh. Nationalism can also lead to persecution or, at its extreme, genocide of ethnic minorities, as occurred in the Holocaust and has been seen in recent 'ethnic cleansing' in Rwanda and Burundi. However, nationalism can also be benign, motivating economic progress through pride in the nation.

Nationalism arises as a source of conflict most commonly when large numbers of people identify with a different 'nation' from that in which they live. Their domination by 'foreign' rulers may be the result of conquest, partition, or an earlier agreement. Reactions to this domination can vary. In many cases, it leads to peaceful, law-abiding demands for increased cultural or political autonomy (as seen in the nationalist movements in Catalonia in northeast Spain and in Wales) or political agitation for independence (for example in Québec, Canada, and in Scotland, with the Scottish Nationalist Party). However, in other cases it can lead to militant insurgency or terrorist movements, such as Euskadi ta Askatasuna (ETA) in the Basque country and the Irish Republican Army (IRA) in Northern Ireland. Many recent civil wars, for example the Tamil separatist conflict in northern Sri Lanka and the Kosovo conflict within Yugoslavia, were triggered by such armed insurgency movements, reacting to what they perceive as discrimination against their national community. In such cases, differences in religion intensified the conflict. It is not typical, however, for insurgencies to succeed. It often takes a crisis in the legitimacy of the ruling regime, as occurred for example in Indonesia (with respect to East Timor) in 1999, to make the achievement of independence possible.

During the last 50 years, the course of nation-building has been typically two-staged. Ruling colonial powers have been overthrown by a broad-based national liberation front, which has then inherited a state whose borders have not always matched those of its constituent national groups. Consequently, many newly liberated states have faced the problem of insurrection by national minorities within. This has been a particularly acute problem in Africa, where colonial states were artificial constructions set over more enduring tribal structures. Civil wars have been endemic in the region, from the 1967–70 Biafran civil war in Nigeria through to contemporary Angola, Congo, Somalia, and Sudan. In Asia, multi-ethnic India, Indonesia, and Myanmar also continue to face armed insurgencies. Meanwhile, as a legacy of the collapsed Soviet empire, scattered across central Asia, the Caucasus region, and eastern Europe, are some 20 million formerly dominant ethnic Russians – a source of potential 'irredentist nationalist' unrest.

future for nationalism

Nationalism is an ascendant ideology at the beginning of the 21st century. Within Europe, far-right nationalist parties have made electoral gains in Austria and France, while power has been devolved recently in Belgium, Spain, and the United Kingdom. Concurrently, symbolized by the introduction of the Euro currency and EU passports, the sovereignty of Europe's traditional nation states has been diminished. This has created confusion in national identities. For example, in multi-ethnic Britain, citizens now claim a range of identities from European, Commonwealth, British, English/Scottish/Welsh through to regional and separate ethnic identities.

It is likely that in the developing world national tensions will remain a source of bitter and bloody conflicts, as dominant groups attempt to resist the formation of new secessionist states. Looking forward 20 or 50 years, it is likely that the number of nation states will have increased still further – to 250 or more. New nation states such as Chechnya, Kosovo, Ossetia, Somaliland, and Tibet are likely to have become established. They will form part of an increasingly economically integrated 'New World Order', which will be dominated by a relatively small number of broader regional political and economic groupings.

STORMING OF THE BASTILLE Paris, France, on 14 July 1789, during the French Revolution. The uprising in France helped the spread of nationalism across Europe. © Archive Photos

(continued from p. 667)

descendants than others because they are better able to survive and reproduce in their environment. The accumulated effect of natural selection is to produce ▷adaptations such as the insulating coat of a polar bear or the spadelike forelimbs of a mole. The process is slow, relying firstly on random variation in the genes of an organism being produced by ▷mutation and secondly on the genetic ▷recombination of sexual reproduction. It was recognized by Charles Darwin and English naturalist Alfred Russel Wallace as the main process driving ▷evolution.

Nature Conservancy Council (NCC) former name of UK government agency divided in 1991 into English Nature, Scottish Natural Heritage, and the Countryside Council for Wales.

nature–nurture controversy (or environment–heredity controversy) long-standing dispute among philosophers and psychologists over the relative importance of environment, that is, upbringing, experience, and learning ('nurture'), and heredity, that is, genetic inheritance ('nature'), in determining the make-up of an organism, as related to human personality and intelligence.

nature reserve area set aside to protect a habitat and the wildlife that lives within it, with only restricted admission for the public. A nature reserve often provides a sanctuary for rare species and rare habitats, such as marshland. The world's largest is Etosha Reserve, Namibia; area 99,520 sq km/38,415 sq mi.

naturopathy in alternative medicine, facilitating of the natural self-healing processes of the body. Naturopaths are the general practitioners (GPs) of alternative medicine and often refer clients to other specialists, particularly in manipulative therapies, to complement their own work of seeking, through diet, the prescription of natural medicines and supplements, and lifestyle counselling, to restore or augment the vitality of the body and thereby its optimum health.

Nauru see country box.

nautical mile unit of distance used in navigation, an internationally agreed-on standard (since 1959) equalling the average length of one minute of arc on a great circle of the Earth, or 1,852 m/6,076.12 ft. The term formerly applied to various units of distance used in navigation.

nautilus sea animal related to octopuses and squids, with many short, grasping tentacles surrounding a sharp beak, but different in that it has an outer shell. It is a ▷cephalopod, a type of ▷mollusc, and is found in the Indian and Pacific oceans. The well-known **pearly nautilus** (*N. pompilius*) has a chambered spiral shell about 20 cm/8 in in diameter. Its body occupies the outer chamber. (Genus *Nautilus*, class Cephalopoda.)

Navaho alternative spelling of ▷Navajo.

Navajo (or Navaho; Tena *Navahu* 'large planted field') member of the second-largest group of ▷American Indian people, numbering about 220,000 (1990) and living in Arizona, New Mexico, and Utah. They are related to the ▷Apache, and speak an Athabaskan language, belonging to the Na-Dené family. The Navajo were traditionally cultivators, although many now herd sheep, which they acquired from the Spanish. They are renowned for their artistry and earn an income from tourism, selling their painted pottery, woven rugs and blankets, and silver and turquoise jewellery.

Navarino, Battle of during the Greek war of liberation, destruction on 20 October 1827 of a joint Turkish–Egyptian fleet by the combined fleets of the British, French, and Russians under Vice-Admiral Edward Codrington (1770–1851). The destruction of their fleet left the Turks highly vulnerable in Greece as they had no protection to their rear and no supply line, and this proved to be the decisive battle of the war. Navarino is the Italian and historic name of Pylos Bay, Greece, on the southwest coast of the Peloponnese.

Navarre (Spanish **Navarra**) autonomous community of northern Spain, bordered by France on the north; area 10,400 sq km/4,000 sq mi; population (1991) 516,300. The region is mountainous, containing spurs of the Pyrenees, and includes Monte Adi (1,503 m/4,933 ft high); the rivers Arga, Aragón, and Ebro flow through the area. Cereals and wine are produced in the lowlands. The capital is Pamplona.

Navarre, Kingdom of former kingdom comprising the Spanish province of Navarre and part of what is now the French *département* of Basses-Pyrénées. It resisted the conquest of the ▷Moors and was independent until it became French in 1284 on the marriage of Philip IV to the heiress of Navarre. In 1479 Ferdinand of Aragón annexed Spanish Navarre, with French Navarre going to Catherine of Foix (1483–1512), who kept the royal title. Her grandson became Henry IV of France, and Navarre was absorbed in the French crown lands in 1620.

nave (Latin *navis* 'a ship') in architecture, the central area of a church extending from the entrance to the crossing, if any; otherwise, up to the altar. It was developed by the early Christian builders out of the Roman hall of justice. The central space became flanked by side aisles and the early flat timber roofs gave way to stone vaulting. It is the section of the building used by the laity.

navel (or umbilicus) small indentation in the centre of the abdomen of mammals, marking the site of attachment of the ▷umbilical cord, which connects the fetus to the ▷placenta.

navigation the science and technology of finding the position, course, and distance travelled by a ship, plane, or other craft. Traditional methods include the magnetic ▷compass and ▷sextant. Today the gyrocompass is usually used, together with highly sophisticated electronic methods, employing beacons of radio signals, such as Decca, Loran, and Omega. Satellite navigation uses satellites that broadcast time and position signals.

The US global positioning system (GPS) was introduced in 1992. When complete, it will feature 24 Navstar satellites that will enable users (including eventually motorists and walkers) to triangulate their position (from any three satellites) to within 15 m/50 ft.

In 1992, 85 nations agreed to take part in trials of a new navigation system which makes use of surplus military space technology left over from the Cold War. The new system, known as FANS or Future Navigation System, will make use of the 24 Russian Glonass satellites and the 24 US GPS satellites. Small computers will gradually be fitted to civil aircraft to process the signals from the satellite, allowing aircraft to navigate with pinpoint accuracy anywhere in the world. The signals from at least three satellites will guide the craft to within a few metres of accuracy. FANS will be used in conjunction with four Inmarsat satellites to provide worldwide communications between pilots and air-traffic controllers.

Navigation Acts in British history, a series of acts of Parliament passed from 1381 to protect English shipping from foreign competition and to ensure monopoly trading between Britain and its colonies. The last was repealed in 1849 (coastal trade exempt until 1853). The Navigation Acts helped to establish England as a major sea power, although they led to higher prices. They ruined the Dutch merchant fleet in the 17th century, and were one of the causes of the ▷American Revolution.

Nauru

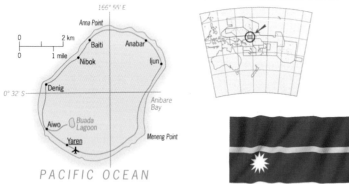

Nauru island country in Polynesia, southwest Pacific, west of Kiribati.

NATIONAL NAME *Republic of Nauru*
AREA 21 sq km/8.1 sq mi
CAPITAL Yaren District (seat of government)
PHYSICAL FEATURES tropical coral island in southwest Pacific; plateau encircled by coral cliffs and sandy beaches

Government

HEAD OF STATE AND GOVERNMENT René Harris from 2001
POLITICAL SYSTEM liberal democracy
POLITICAL EXECUTIVE limited presidency
ADMINISTRATIVE DIVISIONS 14 districts
ARMED FORCES no standing army; Australia is responsible for Nauru's defence
DEATH PENALTY retained for ordinary crimes but abolitionist in practice

Economy and resources

CURRENCY Australian dollar
GPD (US$) 60 million (2002 est)
REAL GDP GROWTH (% change on previous year) 0.8 (2001)
GNI (US$) 220 million (2002 est)
GNI PER CAPITA (PPP) (US$) 5,120 (2002 est)
CONSUMER PRICE INFLATION 4% (2001 est)
UNEMPLOYMENT 0% (1996)
FOREIGN DEBT (US$) 145 million (2000 est)
MAJOR TRADING PARTNERS Australia, New Zealand, Philippines, Japan
RESOURCES phosphates
INDUSTRIES phosphate mining, financial services
EXPORTS phosphates. Principal market: Australia
IMPORTS food and live animals, building construction materials, petroleum, machinery, medical supplies, water. Principal source: Australia
AGRICULTURAL PRODUCTS small-scale production; coconuts, bananas, pineapples, screw-pines, livestock rearing (pigs and chickens)

Population and society

POPULATION 13,000 (2003 est)
POPULATION GROWTH RATE 2.3% (2000–05)
POPULATION DENSITY (per sq km) 622 (2003 est)
URBAN POPULATION (% of total) 100 (2003 est)
AGE DISTRIBUTION (% of total population) 0–14 42%, 15–59 54%, 60+ 4% (2001 est)
ETHNIC GROUPS about 68% indigenous Nauruan (mixture of Micronesian, Polynesian, and Melanesian descent), about 18% Pacific Islander, 8% European, 6% Chinese
LANGUAGE Nauruan, English (both official)
RELIGION majority Protestant, Roman Catholic
EDUCATION (compulsory years) 10
LITERACY RATE 99% (men); 99% (women) (2003 est)

See also ▷Pacific Islands.

NAURU A stamp from Nauru showing how the island is divided into 14 administrative provinces. *Stanley Gibbons*

Chronology

1798: British whaler Capt John Fearn first visited Nauru and named it Pleasant Island.

1830s–80s: The island was a haven for white runaway convicts and deserters.

1888: Annexed by Germany at the request of German settlers who sought protection from local clan unrest.

1899: Phosphate deposits discovered; mining began eight years later, with indentured Chinese labourers brought in to work British Australian-owned mines.

1914: Occupied by Australia on the outbreak of World War I.

1920: Administered by Australia on behalf of itself, New Zealand, and the UK until independence, except 1942–43, when occupied by Japan, and two-thirds of the population were deported briefly to Micronesia.

1951: Local Government Council set up to replace Council of Chiefs.

1956: Hammer DeRoburt became head chief.

1968: Independence achieved, with 'special member' British Commonwealth status. Hammer DeRoburt elected president.

1976: Bernard Dowiyogo elected president.

1987: Kennan Adeang established the Democratic Party of Nauru.

1994: Australia agreed to an out-of-court settlement of A$107 million, payable over 20 years, for environmental damage caused by phosphate mining which had left 80% of land agriculturally barren.

2000: Bernard Dowiyogo was elected president for the sixth time. General elections saw Rene Harris win the popular vote, but he resigned and Dowiyogo was installed.

2001: Dowiyogo was ousted in a parliamentary vote, and Harris was re-elected president.

1650 'Commonwealth Ordinance' forbade foreign ships to trade in English colonies.

1651 Forbade the importation of goods except in English vessels or in vessels of the country of origin of the goods. This act led to the Anglo-Dutch War 1652–54.

1660 All colonial produce was required to be exported in English vessels.

1663 Colonies were prohibited from receiving goods in foreign (rather than English) vessels.

navigation, biological the ability of animals or insects to navigate. Although many animals navigate by following established routes or known landmarks, many animals can navigate without such aids; for example, birds can fly several thousand miles back to their nest site, over unknown terrain. Such feats may be based on compass information derived from the position of the Sun, Moon, or stars, or on the characteristic patterns of Earth's magnetic field.

Navratilova, Martina (1956–) Czech tennis player who became a naturalized US citizen in 1981. The most outstanding woman player of the 1980s, she had 55 Grand Slam victories by 1991, including 18 singles titles. She won the Wimbledon singles title a record nine times, including six in succession 1982–87. She was defeated by Conchita Martinez in the final of her last Wimbledon as a singles player in 1994. She became a tennis coach in February 1997, and made her debut as captain of the defending champion US Fed Cup team, replacing Billie Jean King. In 2003, at the age of 46, she won the Australian Open mixed doubles title with Leander Paes.

navy fleet of ships, usually a nation's ▷warships and the organization to maintain them. In the early 1990s, the UK had a force of small carriers, destroyers, frigates, and submarines.

Nazarbayev, Nursultan (1940–) Kazakh politician, president of Kazakhstan from 1990. In the Soviet period he was prime minister of the republic 1984–89 and leader of the Kazakh Communist Party 1989–91, which established itself as the independent Socialist Party of Kazakhstan in September 1991. He was an advocate of free-market policies, and yet also enjoyed the support of the environmentalist lobby.

Nazareth city in Galilee, northern Israel, 30 km/19 mi southeast of Haifa; population (1993) 53,500. According to the New Testament it was the boyhood home of Jesus.

Related Web site: Nazareth – The Flower of Galilee http://198.62.75.1/www1/ofm/san/TSnzmain.html

Nazi member of the *Nationalsozialistische Deutsche Arbeiterpartei*, usually abbreviated to the **Nazi Party**. The party was based on the ideology of ▷Nazism.

Related Web site: Nazi Gold http://www.pbs.org/wgbh/pages/frontline/shows/nazis/

Nazism ideology based on racism, nationalism, and the supremacy of the state over the individual. The German Nazi party, the *Nationalsozialistische Deutsche Arbeiterpartei* (National Socialist German Workers' Party), was formed from the German Workers' Party (founded in 1919) and led by Adolf ▷Hitler from 1921 to 1945.

During the 1930s many similar parties were created throughout Europe and the USA, such as the British Union of Fascists (BUF) founded in the UK in 1932 by Oswald ▷Mosley. However, only those of Austria, Hungary, and Sudeten were of major importance. These parties collaborated with the German occupation of Europe from 1939 to 1945. After the Nazi atrocities of World War II (see ▷SS, ▷concentration camp, ▷Holocaust), the party was banned in Germany, but today parties with Nazi or neo-Nazi ideologies exist in many countries.

Nazism in pre-war Germany The Nazi party's ideology was based on extreme German nationalism, ▷anti-Semitism, and opposition to German communism. Overlaying this thinking was the concept of unquestioning loyalty to Hitler, the Führer (leader). The National Socialist German Workers' Party used these views to force its way to power in Germany by 1933.

The various aspects of Nazi ideology were combined to form a political programme, the concepts merging and supporting each other. Nationalist feelings linked with the racial prejudices of Nazi ideology. Nazi belief in a master race of ▷Aryans, represented by people of 'pure' German stock, supported Hitler's policy of ▷*Lebensraum* ('living space'). As the Nazis considered that Aryan Germans were superior to other races, such as the Slavs of Eastern Europe, they felt justified in annexing neighbouring states to reduce the overpopulation of Germany. Anti-Semitism was a key principle of Nazism; any failure on the part of Aryan Germans was blamed on the Jews. They were accused of being part of a worldwide conspiracy to destroy Germany, in league with the communists. To save the purity of the Aryan race and the strength of the German nation, the Nazis believed that the Jews would have to be removed from German society.

Also crucial to Nazi party ideology was the role of Hitler as party leader. To the Nazis, Hitler was the guiding visionary who would lead the German nation to a glorious future as the master race of the world. He was, therefore, to be followed without question. The concept of a single master and goal reflected Nazi belief that the needs of the nation were more important than those of the individual. Only if the Germans worked together as one nation, following an absolute leader, would they be able to fulfill their destiny as the master race.

On a practical level Nazi party ideology meant opposition to the Treaty of ▷Versailles (1919) and the democratic ▷Weimar Republic. The Nazis blamed the Weimar politicians for ceding German territory and destroying Germany's economy in the 1920s. Under the Treaty Germany had surrendered Alsace–Lorraine to France, and large areas in the east to Poland, as well as making smaller cessions to Czechoslovakia, Lithuania, Belgium, and Denmark. A ▷Polish Corridor to the Baltic had been created, cutting off East Prussia from the rest of Germany. The Rhineland had been demilitarized, German rearmament restricted, and the Germans forced to make large reparations. The Nazis wanted to unite Germany with Austria in an *Anschluss* (union), bringing the German people into one nation, but this, too, had been banned under the Treaty of Versailles. The Nazis sought to overturn the Treaty in order to achieve their stated goal of a united and powerful Germany.

> **Nebuchadnezzar**
> *Is not this Babylon the great, which I have built as a royal residence by my own mighty power and for the honour of my majesty.*
> Daniel 4:30

Post-war Nazism In the USA the American Nazi Party was founded in 1958 by George Lincoln Rockwell. In the UK Colin Jordan founded the National Socialist Movement in 1962 and in 1967 the ▷National Front was formed. In 1993 there was a political storm after Derek Beackon of the British National Party (BNP; founded in 1982 after a split from the National Front) won a council by-election in the East London borough of Millwall. There were allegations of intimidation of Asian voters by BNP supporters at the polling stations. In a determined attempt to curb right-wing violence, the German government banned six neo-Nazi groups between 1994 and 1995.

Nazi–Soviet pact another name for the ▷Ribbentrop–Molotov pact.

NC abbreviation for ▷North Carolina, a state of the USA.

ND abbreviation for ▷North Dakota, a state of the USA.

Ndjamena (formerly **Fort Lamy** (until 1973)) capital of ▷Chad, in the southwest of the country, at the confluence of the Chari and Logone rivers, on the Cameroon border; population (1993) 531,000. Industries include cotton, textiles, and meat packing. The city's agricultural markets trade in livestock, salt, dates, and grain. The Great Mosque built 1974–78 is an important landmark. It is a staging point for many pilgrims from West Africa to Mecca.

Ndola mining centre and capital of Western Province in the copperbelt region of central Zambia; population (1995 est) 466,000. It lies 275 km/171 mi north of Lusaka, the capital of Zambia, and is the commercial centre of the copperbelt, with good communications by rail and air. There is a copper refinery, a cobalt treatment plant, an oil refinery, a sugar refinery, and sawmills.

Neagh, Lough lake in Northern Ireland, 25 km/15 mi west of Belfast; area 396 sq km/153 sq mi. It is the largest lake in the British Isles, being 27 km/17 mi long, 16 km/10 mi wide, with an average depth of 12 m/39 ft. The shores are mostly flat and marshy; there are a few islands of which Ram's Island is the largest, on which is an early round tower. The lake is famous for trout and eel fishing, and breeding waterbirds.

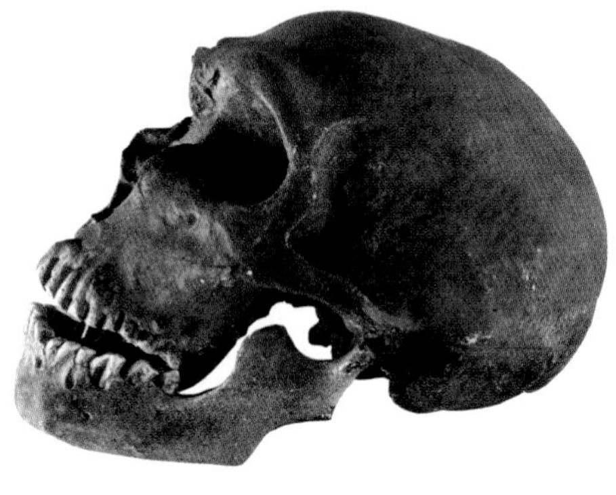

NEANDERTHAL Neanderthal skull from La Ferrassie, France, dating to approximately 35,000 years ago.
The Art Archive/UnterlindenMuseum Colmar/Album/Joseph Martin

Neanderthal hominid of the Mid-Late Palaeolithic, named after the Neander Tal (valley) near Düsseldorf, Germany, where a skeleton was found in 1856. *Homo sapiens neanderthalensis* lived from about 150,000 to 35,000 years ago and was similar in build to present-day people, but slightly smaller, stockier, and heavier-featured with a strong jaw and prominent brow ridges on a sloping forehead. The condition of the Neanderthal teeth that have been found suggests that they were used as clamps for holding objects with the hands.

Neath Port Talbot unitary authority in south Wales, created in 1996 from part of the former county of West Glamorgan.

area 442 sq km/171 sq mi **towns** Port Talbot (administrative headquarters) **physical** the terrain is dominated by the alternation of river valleys and high moorland interfluves **features** Roman fort of Nidum is near Neath **industries** coal mining, chemicals, various metalworks, variety of light industry **population** (1996) 139,400

Neave, Airey Middleton Sheffield (1916–1979) British intelligence officer and Conservative member of Parliament 1953–79. He was a close adviser to Conservative Party leader (later prime minister) Margaret Thatcher. During World War II he escaped from Colditz, a German high-security prison camp. As shadow undersecretary of state for Northern Ireland from 1975, he became a target for extremist groups and was assassinated by an Irish terrorist bomb.

Nebraska state in central USA. It is nicknamed the Cornhusker State or the Blackwater State. Nebraska was admitted to the Union in 1867 as the 37th US state. Part of the Midwest, and one of the Great Plains states, it is bordered to the west by Wyoming, to the north by South Dakota, to the east by Iowa and Missouri, to the south by Kansas, and to the southwest by Colorado.

population (1995) 1,637,100 **area** 200,400 sq km/77,354 sq mi **capital** Lincoln **towns and cities** Omaha, Grand Island, North Platte **industries and products** cereals, livestock, processed foods, fertilizers, oil, natural gas, finance sector

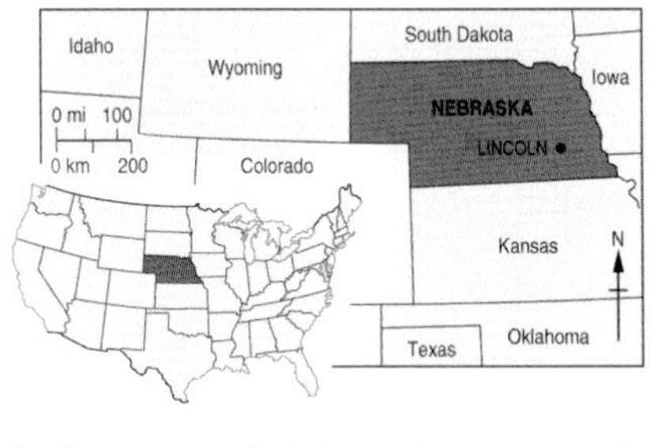

Nebuchadnezzar (or Nebuchadrezzar II) (*c.* 630–*c.* 562 BC) King of Babylonia from 604 BC. Shortly before his accession he defeated the Egyptians at Carchemish and brought Palestine and Syria into his empire. Judah revolted, with Egyptian assistance, in 596 and 587–586 BC; on both occasions he captured Jerusalem and took many Hebrews into captivity. He largely rebuilt Babylon and constructed the hanging gardens.

nebula cloud of gas and dust in space. Nebulae are the birth-places of stars, but some nebulae are produced by gas thrown off from dying stars (see ▷planetary nebula; ▷supernova). Nebulae are classified depending on whether they emit, reflect, or absorb light.

An **emission nebula**, such as the ▷Orion nebula, glows brightly because its gas is energized by stars that have formed within it. In a **reflection nebula**, starlight reflects off grains of dust in the nebula, such as surround the stars of the ▷Pleiades cluster. A **dark nebula** is a dense cloud, composed of molecular hydrogen, which partially or completely absorbs light behind it. Examples include the Coalsack nebula in Crux and the Horsehead nebula in Orion.

Related Web site: Web Nebulae http://www.rog.nmm.ac.uk/astroweb/twn/intro.html

neck structure between the head and the trunk in animals. In the back of the neck are the upper seven vertebrae of the spinal column, and there are many powerful muscles that support and move the head. In front, the neck region contains the ▷pharynx and ▷trachea, and behind these the oesophagus. The large arteries (carotid, temporal, maxillary) and veins (jugular) that supply the brain and head are also located in the neck. The ▷larynx (voice box) occupies a position where the trachea connects with the pharynx, and one of its cartilages produces the projection known as Adam's apple. The ▷thyroid gland lies just below the larynx and in front of the upper part of the trachea.

Necker, Jacques (1732–1804) French politician. As finance minister 1776–81, he attempted reforms, and was dismissed through Queen Marie Antoinette's influence. Recalled in 1788, he persuaded Louis XVI to summon the States General (parliament), which earned him the hatred of the court, and in July 1789 he was banished. The outbreak of the French Revolution with the storming of the Bastille forced his reinstatement, but he resigned in September 1790.

nectar sugary liquid secreted by some plants from a nectary, a specialized gland usually situated near the base of the flower. Nectar often accumulates in special pouches or spurs, not always in the same location as the nectary. Nectar attracts insects, birds, bats, and other animals to the flower for ▷pollination and is the raw material used by bees in the production of honey.

nectarine smooth, shiny-skinned variety of ▷peach, usually smaller than other peaches and with firmer flesh. It arose from a natural variation of the original form.

needlefish any of a group of bony marine fishes with an elongated body and long jaws lined with many sharp teeth. They live in warm, tropical seas. (Family Belonidae.)

Needles, the group of rocks in the sea, rising to 30 m/100 ft, off the western extremity of the Isle of Wight, southern England.

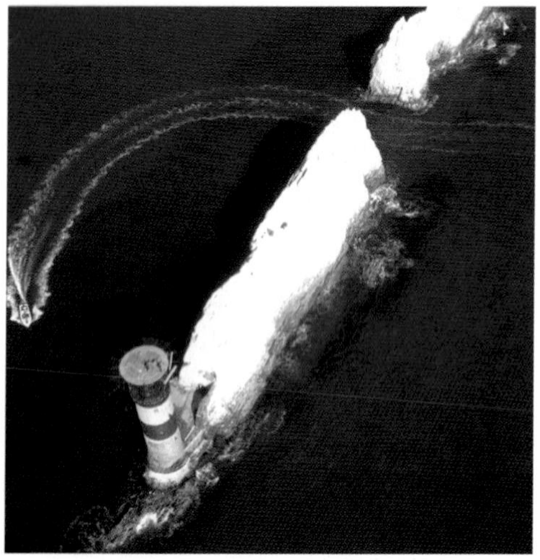

THE NEEDLES An aerial view of the lighthouse at the Needles, a group of rocks at the most western point of the Isle of Wight, England. The lighthouse rises to 218 m/715 ft above the sea. *Image Bank*

Nefertiti (or Nofretete) Queen of Egypt and wife of the pharaoh ▷Akhenaton.

negative/positive in photography, a reverse image, which when printed is again reversed, restoring the original scene. It was invented by Fox ▷Talbot in about 1834.

Negev triangular desert region in southern Israel that tapers to the port of Elat, 120 km/75 mi wide at Beersheba, 13 km/8 mi at Elat; area 12,215 sq km/4,716 sq mi. It is fertile under irrigation, and minerals include oil and copper.

negligence in law, doing some act that a 'prudent and reasonable' person would not do, or omitting to do some act that such a person would do. Negligence may arise in respect of a person's duty towards an individual or towards other people in general. Breach of the duty of care that results in reasonably foreseeable damage is a tort.

Negrito (or Negrillo) member of any of several peoples living on various islands in Southeast Asia. The Negritos are long-established inhabitants of the region and have affinities with Australoid groups. They include the cave-dwelling Vedda of Sri Lanka, the Andamanese of the Andaman Islands, and the Semang of Malaysia.

Negro term formerly used to refer to the indigenous people of Africa south of the Sahara, today distributed around the world. The term generally preferred today is black.

Negroid former racial classification, based on physical features, used to describe the indigenous peoples of sub-Saharan Africa and some of the nearby islands in the Indian Ocean and the western Pacific. See ▷race.

Negro, Río river in South America, rising in eastern Colombia and joining the Amazon at Manáus, Brazil; length 2,250 km/ 1,400 mi.

Nehru, Jawaharlal (1889–1964) Indian nationalist politician, prime minister from 1947 until his death. Before the partition (the division of British India into India and Pakistan), he led the socialist wing of the nationalist ▷Congress Party, and was second in influence only to Mahatma Gandhi. He was imprisoned nine times by the British 1921–45 for political activities. As prime minister from the creation of the dominion (later republic) of India in August 1947, he originated the idea of nonalignment (neutrality towards major powers). His daughter was Prime Minister Indira Gandhi. His sister, Vijaya Lakshmi Pandit was the UN General Assembly's first female president 1953–54.

Nehru Report constitution drafted for India in 1928. After Indian nationalists rejected the Simon Commission in 1927, an all-party committee was set up, chaired by Motilal Nehru (1861–1931), to map out a constitution. Established to counter British charges that Indians could not find a constitutional consensus among themselves, it advocated that India be given dominion status of complete internal self-government. Many members of the Congress preferred complete independence to dominion status, and in 1929 announced a campaign of ▷civil disobedience to support their demands.

neighbourhood unit in the UK, an area within a ▷new town planned to serve the local needs of families. These units typically have a primary school, a low order shopping centre, a church, and a public house. Main roads form the boundaries. Neighbourhood units were designed to give a sense of community to people migrating to the new towns.

Nelson, Horatio (1758–1805) 1st Viscount Nelson. English admiral. He joined the navy in 1770. During the Revolutionary Wars against France he lost the sight in his right eye in 1794, and lost his right arm in 1797. He became a rear admiral and a national hero after the victory off Cape St Vincent, Portugal. In 1798 he tracked the French fleet to Aboukir Bay where he almost entirely destroyed it. In 1801 he won a decisive victory over Denmark at the Battle of ▷Copenhagen, and in 1805, after two years of blockading Toulon, he defeated the Franco-Spanish fleet at the Battle of ▷Trafalgar, near Gibraltar. He was knighted in 1797, made a baron in 1798, and a viscount in 1801.

Nelson was almost continuously on active service in the Mediterranean 1793–1800; he lingered at Naples for a year, during which he helped to crush a democratic uprising, and fell completely under the influence of Lady ▷Hamilton. In 1800 he returned to England and soon after separated from his wife, Frances Nisbet (1761–1831). He was promoted to vice admiral in 1801, and sent to the Baltic to operate against the Danes, nominally as second in command; in fact, it was Nelson who was responsible for the victory of Copenhagen and for negotiating peace with Denmark. In 1803 he received the Mediterranean command and for nearly two years blockaded Toulon. When in 1805 his opponent, the French admiral Pierre de Villeneuve (1763–1806), eluded him, Nelson pursued him to the West Indies and back, and on 21 October defeated the combined French and Spanish fleets off Cape Trafalgar, capturing 20 of the enemy ships; Nelson himself was mortally wounded. He is buried in St Paul's Cathedral, London.

Related Web site: Letters and Dispatches of Lord Horatio Nelson
http://www.wtj.com/pl/pages/nelson2.htm

> **Horatio Nelson**
> *England expects every man will do his duty.*
> At the Battle of Trafalgar 1805

nematode any of a group of unsegmented ▷worms that are pointed at both ends, with a tough, smooth outer skin. They include many free-living species found in soil and water, including the sea, but a large number are parasites, such as the roundworms and pinworms that live in humans, or the eelworms that attack plant roots. They differ from ▷flatworms in that they have two openings to the gut (a mouth and an anus). (Phylum Nematoda.) The group includes *caenorhabditis elegans* which is a model genetic organism and the first multicellular animal to have its complete genome sequenced.

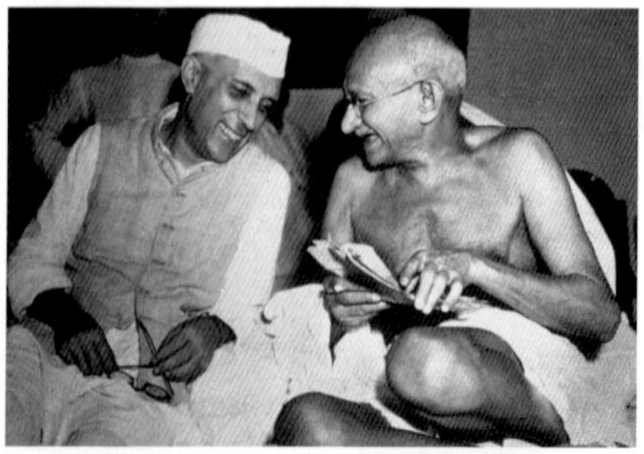

JAWAHARLAL NEHRU Jawaharlal Nehru and Mahatma Gandhi during an intermission on the opening day of the All India Congress Committee meeting in Bombay, 6 July 1946. *Archive Photos*

Most nematode species are found in deep-sea sediment. Around 13,000 species are known, but a 1995 study by the Natural History Museum, London, based on the analysis of sediment from 17 seabed sites worldwide, estimated that nematodes may make up as much as 75% of all species, with there being an estimated 100 million species. Some are anhydrobiotic, which means they can survive becoming dehydrated, entering a state of suspended animation until they are rehydrated.

Nemesis in late Greek mythology, the goddess of retribution, who especially punished hubris (Greek *hybris*), violent acts carried through in defiance of the gods and human custom.

neo- (Greek *neos* 'new') prefix used to indicate a revival or development of an older form, often in a different spirit. Examples include neo-Marxism and neo-Darwinism.

neoclassicism movement in art, architecture, and design in Europe and North America about 1750–1850, characterized by a revival of classical Greek and Roman styles. Leading figures of the movement were the architects Claude-Nicolas Ledoux and Robert Adam; the painters Jacques-Louis David, Jean Ingres, and Anton Mengs; the sculptors Antonio Canova, John Flaxman, Bertel Thorvaldsen, and Johann Sergel; and the designers Josiah Wedgwood, George Hepplewhite, and Thomas Sheraton.

neocolonialism disguised form of ▷imperialism, by which a country may grant independence to another country but continue to dominate it by control of markets for goods or raw materials. Examples of countries that have used economic pressure to secure and protect their interests internationally are the USA and Japan.

neo-Darwinism the modern theory of ▷evolution, built up since the 1930s by integrating the 19th-century English scientist Charles ▷Darwin's theory of evolution through natural selection with the theory of genetic inheritance founded on the work of the Austrian biologist Gregor ▷Mendel.

Neo-Darwinism asserts that evolution takes place because the environment is slowly changing, exerting a selection pressure on the individuals within a population. Those with characteristics that happen to adapt to the new environment are more likely to survive and have offspring and hence pass on these favourable characteristics. Over time the genetic make-up of the population changes and ultimately a new species is formed.

neodymium yellowish metallic element of the ▷lanthanide series, symbol Nd, atomic number 60, relative atomic mass 144.24. Its rose-coloured salts are used in colouring glass, and neodymium is used in lasers. It was named in 1885 by Austrian chemist Carl von Welsbach (1858–1929), who fractionated it away from didymium (originally thought to be an element but actually a mixture of rare-earth metals consisting largely of neodymium, praesodymium, and cerium).

Neo-Expressionism style of modern painting in which the artist handles the materials in a rough and raw way, typically expressing violent emotion. It developed in the late 1970s and became a dominant force in avant-garde art during the 1980s, especially in the USA, Germany, and Italy. Pablo Picasso's late paintings, which are often aggressively sexual in subject and almost frenzied in brushwork, were a major source for the style. Neo-expressionist paintings often feature the human figure, but they are sometimes virtually abstract. In Italy neo-expressionism is sometimes known as the *Transavantgarde* ('beyond the avant-garde'), and in Germany its exponents are sometimes called *Neue Wilden* ('new wild ones'). Various alternative names have been used in the USA, including new fauvism, punk art, and bad painting (the latter because, in spite of the commercial success enjoyed by several exponents, many critics find the work crude and ugly, flaunting a lack of conventional skills).

Neo-Impressionism movement in French painting that developed from ▷Impressionism in the 1880s and flourished until the early years of the 20th century. The name was coined in 1886 in a review of the eighth and last Impressionist exhibition, held in Paris that year. Among the artists who exhibited there was Georges Seurat, who was the chief creator and outstanding exponent of Neo-Impressionism.

Neolithic literally 'New Stone', the last period of the ▷Stone Age. It was characterized by settled agricultural communities who kept domesticated animals, and made pottery and sophisticated, finely finished stone tools. The Neolithic period began and ended at different times in different parts of the world. For example, the earliest Neolithic communities appeared about 9000 BC in the Middle East, and were followed by those in Egypt, India, and China. In Europe farming began in about 6500 BC in the Balkans and

NEOLITHIC Polished axe-head, dating from about 1800 BC (Devizes Museum, Wiltshire, England). *The Art Archive*

Aegean Sea areas, spreading north and east by 1000 BC. The Neolithic period ended with the start of the ▷Bronze Age, when people began using metals. Some Stone Age cultures persisted into the 20th century, notably in remote parts of New Guinea.

neon (Greek *neos* 'new') colourless, odourless, nonmetallic, gaseous element, symbol Ne, atomic number 10, relative atomic mass 20.183. It is grouped with the ▷inert gases, is nonreactive, and forms no compounds. It occurs in small quantities in the Earth's atmosphere. Tubes containing neon are used in electric advertising signs, giving off a fiery red glow; it is also used in lasers. Neon was discovered by the Scottish chemist William Ramsay and the Englishman Morris Travers.

neo-Nazism the upsurge in racial and political intolerance in Eastern and Western Europe of the early 1990s. In Austria, Belgium, France, Germany, Russia, and Italy, the growth of extreme right-wing political groupings, coupled with racial violence, particularly in Germany, has revived memories of the Nazi period in Hitler's Germany. Ironically, the liberalization of politics in the post-Cold War world has unleashed anti-liberal forces hitherto checked by authoritarian regimes. The most significant parties in Western Europe described by the media as 'neo-nazi' were the National Front in France, led by Jean-Marie ▷Le Pen, and the National Alliance in Italy (although, by 1998, the National Alliance claimed to be a mainstream conservative party).

neoplasm (Greek 'new growth') any lump or tumour, which may be benign or malignant (cancerous).

neoplatonism school of philosophy that flourished during the declining centuries of the Roman Empire (3rd–6th centuries AD). Neoplatonists argued that the highest stage of philosophy is attained not through reason and experience, but through a mystical ecstasy. Many later philosophers, including Nicholas of Cusa, were influenced by neoplatonism.

neoprene synthetic rubber, developed in the USA in 1931 from the polymerization of chloroprene. It is much more resistant to heat, light, oxidation, and petroleum than is ordinary rubber.

neo-realism movement in Italian cinema that emerged in the 1940s. It is characterized by its naturalism, social themes, frequent use of nonprofessional actors, and the visual authenticity achieved through location filming. Exponents include the directors Vittorio de Sica, Luchino Visconti, and Roberto Rossellini.

NEP abbreviation for the Soviet leader Lenin's ▷New Economic Policy.

Nepal see country box.

nephritis (or Bright's disease) general term used to describe inflammation of the kidney. The degree of illness varies, and it may be acute (often following a recent streptococcal infection), or chronic, requiring a range of treatments from antibiotics to ▷dialysis or transplant.

nephron microscopic unit in vertebrate kidneys that forms urine. A human kidney is composed of over a million nephrons. Each nephron consists of a knot of blood capillaries called a glomerulus, contained in the Bowman's capsule, and a long narrow tubule enmeshed with yet more capillaries. Waste materials and water pass from the bloodstream into the tubule, and essential minerals and some water are reabsorbed from the tubule back into the bloodstream. The remaining filtrate (urine) is passed out from the body.

Neptune in astronomy, the eighth planet in average distance from the Sun. It is a giant gas (hydrogen, helium, methane) planet, with a mass 17.2 times that of Earth. It has the highest winds in the Solar System.

> **mean distance from the Sun** 4.4 billion km/2.794 billion mi
> **equatorial diameter** 48,600 km/30,200 mi   **rotation period** 16 hr 7 min   **year** 164.8 Earth years   **atmosphere** methane in its atmosphere absorbs red light and gives the planet a blue colouring. Consists primarily of hydrogen (85% with helium (13%) and methane (1–2%)   **surface** hydrogen, helium and methane. Its interior is believed to have a central rocky core covered by a layer of ice   **satellites** of Neptune's eight moons, two (▷Triton and Nereid) are visible from Earth. Six were discovered by the *Voyager 2* probe in 1989, of which Proteus (diameter 415 km/260 mi) is larger than Nereid

(300 km/200 mi)   **rings** there are four faint rings: Galle, Le Verrier, Arago, and Adams (in order from Neptune). Galle is the widest at 1,700 km/1,060 mi. Le Verrier and Arago are divided by a wide diffuse particle band called the plateau

Neptune was located in 1846 by German astronomers Johan Galle and Heinrich d'Arrest (1822–1875), after calculations by English astronomer John Couch Adams and French mathematician Urbain Le Verrier, had predicted its existence from disturbances in the movement of Uranus. *Voyager 2*, which passed Neptune in August 1989, revealed various cloud features, notably an Earth-sized oval storm cloud, the Great Dark Spot, similar to the Great Red Spot on Jupiter, but images taken by the Hubble Space Telescope in 1994 show that the Great Dark Spot has disappeared. A smaller dark spot DS2 has also gone.

Neptune in Roman mythology, god of water, who became god of the sea only after his identification with the Greek ▷Poseidon.

neptunium silvery, radioactive metallic element of the ▷actinide series, symbol Np, atomic number 93, relative atomic mass 237.048. It occurs in nature in minute amounts in ▷pitchblende and other uranium ores, where it is produced from the decay of neutron-bombarded uranium in these ores. The longest-lived isotope, Np-237, has a half-life of 2.2 million years. The element can be produced by bombardment of U-238 with neutrons and is chemically highly reactive. It was first synthesized in 1940 by US physicists E McMillan (1907–) and P Abelson (1913–), who named it after the planet Neptune (since it comes after uranium as the planet Neptune comes after Uranus). Neptunium was the first ▷transuranic element to be synthesized.

Nereid in Greek mythology, any of 50 sea goddesses, or ▷nymphs, who sometimes mated with mortals. Their father was Nereus, a sea god, and their mother was Doris.

Nero (AD 37–68) Adopted name of Lucius Domitius Ahenobarbus. Roman emperor from 54. In 59 he had his mother Agrippina and his wife Octavia put to death. The great fire at Rome in 64 was blamed on the Christians, whom he subsequently persecuted. In 65 a plot against Nero was discovered. Further revolts followed in 68, and he committed suicide. Son of Domitius Ahenobarbus and Agrippina, Nero was adopted by Claudius, and succeeded him as emperor. He was a poet and connoisseur of art, and performed publicly as an actor and a singer.

> **Nero**
> *What an artist dies with me!*
> On his deathbed, quoted in Suetonius *Life of Nero*

Neruda, Pablo (1904–1973) Pen-name of Neftalí Ricardo Reyes y Basoalto. Chilean poet and diplomat. His work includes lyrics and the epic poem of the American continent *Canto General* (1950). He was awarded the Nobel Prize for Literature in 1971. He served as consul and ambassador to many countries during the period 1927–44.

Nerva, Marcus Cocceius (AD c. 30–98) Roman emperor. He was proclaimed emperor on Domitian's death in AD 96, and introduced state loans for farmers, family allowances, and allotments of land to poor citizens in his sixteen-month reign.

Nerval, Gérard de (1808–1855) Pen-name of Gérard Labrunie. French writer and poet. He was a precursor of French ▷symbolism and ▷surrealism. His writings include the travelogue *Le Voyage en Orient* (1851); short stories, including the collection *Les Filles du feu* (1854); poetry, including *Les Chimères* (1854), a sequence of 12 sonnets; a novel *Aurélia* (1855), containing episodes of visionary psychosis; and several plays, in collaboration with others.

nerve bundle of nerve cells enclosed in a sheath of connective tissue and transmitting nerve impulses to and from the brain and spinal cord. A single nerve may contain both ▷motor and sensory nerve cells, but they function independently.

nerve cell (or **neuron**) elongated cell, the basic functional unit of the ▷nervous system that transmits information rapidly between different parts of the body. Each nerve cell has a cell body, containing the nucleus, from which trail processes called dendrites, responsible for receiving incoming signals. The unit of information is the **nerve impulse**, a travelling wave of chemical and electrical changes involving the membrane of the nerve cell. The cell's longest process, the ▷axon, carries impulses away from the cell body. See picture on p. 675.

Nervi, Pier Luigi (1891–1979) Italian engineer. He used soft steel mesh within ▷concrete to give it flowing form; for example, the Turin exhibition hall 1948–49, consisting of a single undulating large-span roof, the UNESCO building in Paris 1953–58, with Marcel Breuer and Bernard-Louis Zehrfuss, and the cathedral at New Norcia, near Perth, Australia, (1960). He was the structural engineer on Gio Ponti's Pirelli skyscraper project in Milan in 1958. See picture on p. 675.

nervous breakdown popular term for a reaction to overwhelming psychological stress. There is no equivalent medical term. People said to be suffering from a nervous breakdown may be suffering from a neurotic illness, such as depression or anxiety, or a psychotic illness, such as schizophrenia.

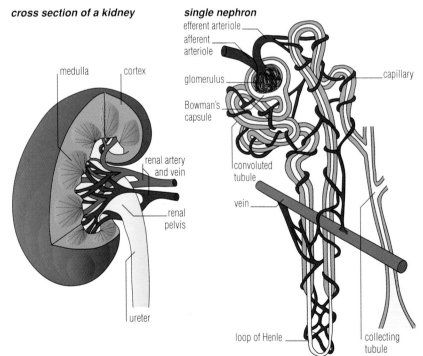

cross section of a kidney   **single nephron**

NEPHRON The kidney (left) contains more than a million filtering units, or nephrons (right), consisting of the glomerulus, Bowman's capsule, and the loop of Henle. Blood flows through the glomerulus – a tight knot of fine blood vessels from which water and metabolic wastes filter into the tubule. This filtrate flows through the convoluted tubule and loop of Henle where most of the water and useful molecules are reabsorbed into the blood capillaries. The waste materials are passed to the collecting tubule as urine.

Nepal

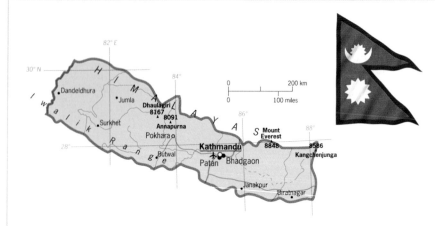

Nepal landlocked country in the Himalayan mountain range in Central Asia, bounded north by Tibet (an autonomous region of China), east, south, and west by India.

NATIONAL NAME *Nepál Adhirajya/Kingdom of Nepal*
AREA 147,181 sq km/56,826 sq mi
CAPITAL Kathmandu
MAJOR TOWNS/CITIES Moráng, Biratnagar, Lalitpur, Bhaktapur, Pokhara, Birganj
PHYSICAL FEATURES descends from the Himalayas in the north through foothills to the River Ganges plain in the south; Mount Everest, Mount Kanchenjunga

Government

HEAD OF STATE King Gyanendra Bir Bikram Shah Dev from 2001
HEAD OF GOVERNMENT Surya Bahadur Thapa from 2003
POLITICAL SYSTEM emergent democracy
POLITICAL EXECUTIVE parliamentary
ADMINISTRATIVE DIVISIONS 14 zones and 75 districts
ARMED FORCES 51,000 (2002 est)
CONSCRIPTION military service is voluntary
DEATH PENALTY abolished in 1997
DEFENCE SPEND (% GDP) 1.9 (2002 est)
EDUCATION SPEND (% GDP) 3.7 (2001 est)
HEALTH SPEND (% GDP) 5.4 (2000 est)

Economy and resources

CURRENCY Nepalese rupee
GPD (US$) 5.5 billion (2002 est)
REAL GDP GROWTH (% change on previous year) 4.8 (2001)
GNI (US$) 5.6 billion (2002 est)
GNI PER CAPITA (PPP) (US$) 1,350 (2002 est)
CONSUMER PRICE INFLATION 4% (2003 est)
UNEMPLOYMENT 4.9% (2000)
FOREIGN DEBT (US$) 3.1 billion (2001 est)
MAJOR TRADING PARTNERS India, China, Germany, Japan, Singapore, USA, Switzerland, France, Kuwait
RESOURCES lignite, talcum, magnesite, limestone, copper, cobalt
INDUSTRIES bricks and tiles, carpets, clothing, paper, cotton fabrics, cement, leather, jute goods, electrical cable, soap, edible oils, sugar, tourism
EXPORTS clothing, woollen carpets, hides and skins, food grains, jute goods, timber, toothpaste, oil seeds, ghee, potatoes, medicinal herbs, cattle. Principal market: India 47.7% (2001)

IMPORTS petroleum products, textiles, gold, silver, basic manufactures, machinery and transport equipment, chemicals, pharmaceuticals. Principal source: India 41.2% (2001)
ARABLE LAND 20.3% (2000 est)
AGRICULTURAL PRODUCTS rice, maize, wheat, sugar cane, millet, potatoes, barley, tobacco, cardamoms, fruits, oil seeds; livestock rearing (cattle and pigs)

Population and society

POPULATION 25,164,000 (2003 est)
POPULATION GROWTH RATE 2.0% (2000–15)
POPULATION DENSITY (per sq km) 179 (2003 est)
URBAN POPULATION (% of total) 13 (2003 est)
AGE DISTRIBUTION (% of total population) 0–14 41%, 15–59 53%, 60+ 6% (2002 est)
ETHNIC GROUPS 80% of Indo-Nepalese origin, including the Gurkhas, Paharis, Newars, and Tharus; 20% of Tibeto-Nepalese descent (concentrated in the north and east)
LANGUAGE Nepali (official), Tibetan, numerous local languages
RELIGION Hindu 90%; Buddhist 5%, Muslim 3%, Christian
EDUCATION (compulsory years) 5
LITERACY RATE 63% (men); 28% (women) (2003 est)
LABOUR FORCE 78.5% agriculture, 5.5% industry, 21.0% services (1995)
LIFE EXPECTANCY 60 (men); 60 (women) (2000–05)

See also ▷caste; ▷Gurkha; ▷Hinduism.

Chronology

8th century BC: Kathmandu Valley occupied by Ahirs (shepherd kings), Tibeto-Burman migrants from northern India.

***c.* 563 BC:** In Lumbini in far south, Prince Siddhartha Gautama, the historic Buddha, was born.

AD 300: Licchavis dynasty immigrated from India and introduced caste system.

13th–16th centuries: Dominated by Malla dynasty, great patrons of the arts.

1768: Nepal emerged as a unified kingdom after the ruler of the principality of the Gurkhas in the west, King Prithwi Narayan Shah, conquered Kathmandu Valley.

1792: Nepal's expansion halted by defeat at the hands of Chinese in Tibet; commercial treaty signed with Britain.

1815–16: Anglo-Nepali 'Gurkha War'; Nepal became British-dependent buffer state with British resident stationed in Kathmandu.

1846: Fell under sway of Rana family, who became hereditary chief ministers, dominating powerless monarchy and isolating Nepal from outside world.

1923: Full independence formally recognized by Britain.

1951: Monarchy restored to power and Ranas overthrown in 'palace revolution' supported by Nepali Congress Party (NCP).

1959: Constitution created an elected legislature.

1960–61: Parliament dissolved by King Mahendra; political parties banned after NCP's pro-India socialist leader B P Koirala became prime minister.

1962: New constitution provided for tiered, traditional system of indirectly elected local councils (*panchayats*) and an appointed prime minister.

1972: King Mahendra died; succeeded by his son, King Birendra Bikram Shah Dev.

1980: A constitutional referendum was held, following popular agitation led by B P Koirala, resulted in the introduction of direct, but nonparty, elections to the National Assembly.

1983: The monarch-supported prime minister was overthrown by directly elected deputies to the National Assembly.

1986: New assembly elections returned a majority opposed to the *panchayat* system of partyless government.

1988: Strict curbs were placed on opposition activity; over 100 supporters of the banned NCP were arrested, and censorship was imposed.

1989: A border blockade was imposed by India during a treaty dispute.

1990: The *panchayat* system collapsed after mass NCP-led violent prodemocracy demonstrations; a new democratic constitution was introduced, and the ban on political parties lifted.

1991: The Nepali Congress Party, led by Girija Prasad Koirala, won the general election.

1992: Communists led antigovernment demonstrations in Kathmandu and Pátan.

1994: Koirala's government was defeated on a no-confidence motion; parliament was dissolved. A minority communist government was formed under Man Mohan Adhikari.

1995: Parliament was dissolved by King Birendra at Prime Minister Adhikari's request; fresh elections were called but the Supreme Court ruled the move unconstitutional.

1998: Krishna Prasad Bhattarai became prime minister and formed a new coalition government.

2000: A vote of no confidence in Prime Minister Krishna Prasad Bhattarai, who had been in power since 1999 led to his replacement by Girija Prasad Koirala of the NCP.

2001: King Birendra and nine other members of the royal family were shot dead by Crown Prince Dipendra, who later also died in hospital. Gyarendra, Birendra's brother, was subsequently crowned.

2002: In an ongoing Maoist rebellion against the constitutional monarchy, over 150 people were killed in Mangelsen in the far west of the country. In response a government offensive targeted rebel bases, killing more than 150 insurgents.

2003: Maoist insurgents agreed a ceasefire with the government designed to lead to peace talks and an end to fighting that had claimed over 7,000 lives.

NEPAL A valley in Nepal with terraced hillsides for growing rice, and the Annapurna range in the distance. The highest of the Annapurna peaks, Annapurna 1, was first climbed in 1950 by a French expedition led by Maurice Herzog. *Corel*

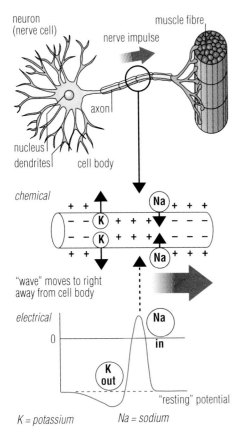

NERVE CELL The anatomy and action of a nerve cell. The nerve cell, or neuron, consists of a cell body with a nucleus and projections called dendrites which pick up messages. An extension of the cell, the axon, connects one cell to the dendrites of the next. When a nerve cell is stimulated, waves of sodium (Na^+) and potassium (K^+) ions carry an electrical impulse down the axon. See entry on p. 673.

nervous system the system of interconnected ▷nerve cells of most invertebrates and all vertebrates. It is composed of the ▷central and ▷autonomic nervous systems. It may be as simple as the nerve net of coelenterates (for example, jellyfishes) or as complex as the mammalian nervous system, with a central nervous system comprising ▷brain and ▷spinal cord and a peripheral nervous system connecting up with sensory organs, muscles, and glands.

Human nervous system The human nervous system represents the product of millions of years of evolution, particularly in the degree of **encephalization** or brain complexity. It can be divided into central and peripheral parts for descriptive purposes, although there is both anatomical and functional continuity between the two parts. The central nervous system consists of the brain and the spinal cord. The peripheral nervous system is not so clearly subdivided, but its anatomical parts are: (1) the spinal nerves; (2) the cranial nerves; and (3) the autonomic nervous system.

Nesbit, E(dith) (1858–1924) English author of children's books. She wrote *The Story of the Treasure Seekers* (1899) and *The Railway Children* (1906). Her stories often have a humorous magical element, as in *Five Children and It* (1902) and *The Phoenix and the Carpet* (1904). *The Treasure Seekers* is the first of several books about the realistically squabbling Bastable children; it was followed by *The Would-be Goods* (1901) and *The New Treasure Seekers* (1904). Nesbit was a Fabian socialist and supported her family by writing.

Ness, Loch lake in the Highland unitary authority, Scotland, extending northeast to southwest. Forming part of the Caledonian Canal, it is 36 km/22.5 mi long, 2 km/1 mi wide (on average), 229 m/754 ft deep, and is the greatest expanse of fresh water in Europe. There have been unconfirmed reports of a Loch Ness monster since the 6th century.
    Related Web site: Cryptozoo Archives: Lake Monsters http://www.ncf.carleton.ca/~bz050/HomePage.lm.html

nest place chosen or constructed by a bird or other animal for incubation of eggs, hibernation, and shelter. Nests vary enormously, from saucerlike hollows in the ground, such as the scrapes of hares, to large and elaborate structures, such as the 4-m/13-ft diameter mounds of the ▷megapode birds.

Nestlé multinational corporation, the world's largest packaged-food company, best known for producing chocolate, coffee, and baby milk (the marketing of which in the Third World has been criticized as inappropriate). The company's market value in 1999 was estimated at US$66.3 billion, and it employed 230,000 people.

Nestorianism Christian doctrine held by the Syrian ecclesiastic Nestorius (died *c.* 451), patriarch of Constantinople 428–431. He asserted that Jesus had two natures, human and divine. He was banished for maintaining that Mary was the mother of the man Jesus only, and therefore should not be called the mother of God. Today the Nestorian Church is found in small communities in Syria, Iraq, Iran, and India.

net of a particular figure or price, calculated after the deduction of specific items such as commission, discounts, interest, and taxes. The opposite is ▷gross.

net assets either the total ▷assets of a company less its current liabilities (that is, the capital employed) or the total assets less current liabilities, debt capital, long-term loans and provisions, which would form the amount available to ordinary shareholders if the company were to be wound up.

Netherlands Antilles two groups of Caribbean islands, overseas territories of the Netherlands with full internal autonomy, comprising ▷Curaçao and Bonaire off the coast of Venezuela (▷Aruba is considered separately), and St Eustatius, Saba, and the southern part of St Maarten in the Leeward Islands, 800 km/500 mi to the northeast; area 797 sq km/308 sq mi; population (1993 est) 197,100. The capital is Willemstad on Curaçao. Oil from Venezuela is refined here. Other industries include rum, some manufacturing, and tourism is also important. Dutch is the official language, and Papiamento and English are also spoken.

Netherlands, The see country box.

nettle any of a group of weedy plants with stinging hairs on oval, tooth-edged leaves; the hairs contain nerve poisons that penetrate the skin and cause a rash. The flowers are small and greenish, carried on spikes emerging at the same point where the leaves join the stem. The common nettle (*U. dioica*) grows on waste ground in Europe and North America, where it was introduced. (Genus *Urtica*, family Urticaceae.)
    Related Web site: Nettles http://www.botanical.com/botanical/mgmh/n/nettle03.html

nettle rash popular name for the skin disorder ▷urticaria.

network in computing, a method of connecting computers so that they can share data and peripheral devices, such as printers. The main types are classified by the pattern of the connections – star or ring network, for example – or by the degree of geographical spread allowed; for example, local area networks (LANs) for communication within a room or building, and ▷wide area networks (WANs) for more remote systems. Internet is the computer network that connects major English-speaking institutions throughout the world; by 2004 there were around 650 million users. JANET (joint academic network), a variant of Internet, is used in Britain. SuperJANET, launched in 1992, is an extension of this that can carry 1,000 million bits of information per second.

neuralgia sharp or burning pain originating in a nerve and spreading over its area of distribution. Trigeminal neuralgia, a common form, is a severe pain on one side of the face.

neural network artificial network of processors that attempts to mimic the structure of nerve cells (neurons) in the human brain. Neural networks may be electronic, optical, or simulated by computer software.

neurology medical speciality concerned with the study and treatment of disorders of the brain, spinal cord, and peripheral nerves.

neuron another name for a ▷nerve cell.

neurosis in psychology, a general term referring to emotional disorders, such as anxiety, depression, and phobias. The main disturbance tends to be one of mood; contact with reality is relatively unaffected, in contrast to ▷psychosis.

neurotransmitter chemical that diffuses across a ▷synapse, and thus transmits impulses between ▷nerve cells, or between

PIER NERVI Italian engineer Pier Luigi Nervi, photographed in the 1960s. See entry on p. 673. *Archive Photos*

nerve cells and effector organs (for example, muscles). Common neurotransmitters are noradrenaline (which also acts as a hormone) and acetylcholine, the latter being most frequent at junctions between nerve and muscle. Nearly 50 different neurotransmitters have been identified.

neutrality the legal status of a country that decides not to choose sides in a war. Certain states, notably Switzerland and Austria, have opted for permanent neutrality. Neutrality always has a legal connotation. In peacetime, neutrality towards the big power alliances is called **nonalignment** (see ▷nonaligned movement).

neutralization in chemistry, a process occurring when the excess acid (or excess base) in a substance is reacted with added base (or added acid) so that the resulting substance is neither acidic nor basic. In theory neutralization involves adding acid or base as required to achieve ▷pH 7. When the colour of an ▷indicator is used to test for neutralization, the final pH may differ from pH7 depending upon the indicator used. It will also differ from 7 in reactions between strong acids and weak bases and weak acids and strong bases, as the salt formed will have acid or basic properties respectively.

neutrino in physics, any of three uncharged ▷elementary particles (and their antiparticles) of the ▷lepton class, having a mass that is very small (possibly zero). The most familiar type, the antiparticle of the electron neutrino, is emitted in the beta decay of a nucleus. The other two are the muon and tau neutrinos.

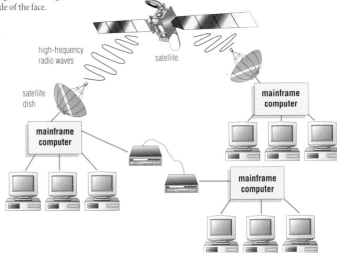

NETWORK A wide area network is used to connect remote computers via telephone lines or satellite links. The ISDN (Integrated Services Digital Network) telecommunications network allows high-speed transfer of digital data. See also local area network on p. 677.

Netherlands, The

THE NETHERLANDS Windmills and tulips are characteristic features of the Dutch landscape. The Netherlands produces 60% of the world's commercially grown flowers. *Image Bank*

EDUCATION (compulsory years) 11
LITERACY RATE 99% (men); 99% (women) (2003 est)
LABOUR FORCE 3.2% agriculture, 21.8% industry, 75.0% services (1998)
LIFE EXPECTANCY 76 (men); 81 (women) (2000–05)
CHILD MORTALITY RATE (under 5, per 1,000 live births) 6 (2001)
PHYSICIANS (per 1,000 people) 3.2 (1998 est)
HOSPITAL BEDS (per 1,000 people) 10.8 (1998 est)
TV SETS (per 1,000 people) 553 (2001 est)
RADIOS (per 1,000 people) 981 (1998)
INTERNET USERS (per 10,000 people) 5,304.1 (2002 est)
PERSONAL COMPUTER USERS (per 100 people) 46.7 (2002 est)

See also ▷Belgium; ▷East India Company, Dutch; ▷Luxembourg; ▷Orange, House of.

Netherlands, The (or Holland) country in Western Europe on the North Sea, bounded east by Germany and south by Belgium.

NATIONAL NAME *Koninkrijk der Nederlanden/Kingdom of the Netherlands*
AREA 41,863 sq km/16,163 sq mi
CAPITAL Amsterdam (official), the Hague (legislative and judicial)
MAJOR TOWNS/CITIES Rotterdam, Utrecht, Eindhoven, Groningen, Tilburg, Maastricht, Apeldoorn, Nijmegen, Breda
MAJOR PORTS Rotterdam
PHYSICAL FEATURES flat coastal lowland; rivers Rhine, Schelde, Maas; Frisian Islands
TERRITORIES Aruba, Netherlands Antilles (Caribbean)

Government

HEAD OF STATE Queen Beatrix Wilhelmina Armgard from 1980
HEAD OF GOVERNMENT Jan Peter Balkenende from 2002
POLITICAL SYSTEM liberal democracy
POLITICAL EXECUTIVE parliamentary
ADMINISTRATIVE DIVISIONS 12 provinces
ARMED FORCES 49,600 (2002 est)
CONSCRIPTION military service is voluntary
DEATH PENALTY abolished in 1982
DEFENCE SPEND (% GDP) 1.6 (2002 est)
EDUCATION SPEND (% GDP) 4.8 (2000 est)
HEALTH SPEND (% GDP) 8.1 (2000 est)

Economy and resources

CURRENCY euro (guilder until 2002)
GPD (US$) 413.7 billion (2002 est)
REAL GDP GROWTH (% change on previous year) 1.3 (2001)
GNI (US$) 386.8 billion (2002 est)
GNI PER CAPITA (PPP) (US$) 27,470 (2002 est)
CONSUMER PRICE INFLATION 2% (2003 est)
UNEMPLOYMENT 2% (2001)
MAJOR TRADING PARTNERS EU (principally Germany,

Belgium–Luxembourg, UK, France, and Italy), USA
RESOURCES petroleum, natural gas
INDUSTRIES electrical machinery, metal products, food processing, electronic equipment, chemicals, rubber and plastic products, petroleum refining, dairy farming, horticulture, diamond cutting
EXPORTS machinery and transport equipment, foodstuffs, live animals, petroleum and petroleum products, natural gas, chemicals, plants and cut flowers, plant-derived products. Principal market: Germany 26% (2001)
IMPORTS electrical machinery, cars and other vehicles, mineral fuels, metals and metal products, plastics, paper and cardboard, clothing and accessories. Principal source: Germany 19% (2001)
ARABLE LAND 26.8% (2000 est)
AGRICULTURAL PRODUCTS sugar beet, potatoes, wheat, barley, flax, fruit, vegetables, flowers; dairy farming

Population and society

POPULATION 16,149,000 (2003 est)
POPULATION GROWTH RATE 0.4% (2000–15)
POPULATION DENSITY (per sq km) 395 (2003 est)
URBAN POPULATION (% of total) 90 (2003 est)
AGE DISTRIBUTION (% of total population) 0–14 18%, 15–59 63%, 60+ 19% (2002 est)
ETHNIC GROUPS primarily Dutch (Germanic, with some Gallo-Celtic mixtures); sizeable Indonesian, Surinamese, and Turkish minorities
LANGUAGE Dutch (official)
RELIGION atheist 39%, Roman Catholic 31%, Dutch Reformed Church 14%, Calvinist 8%

Chronology

55 BC: Julius Caesar brought lands south of River Rhine under Roman rule.
4th century AD: Region overrun by Franks and Saxons.
7th–8th centuries: Franks subdued Saxons north of Rhine and imposed Christianity.
843–12th centuries: Division of Holy Roman Empire: the Netherlands repeatedly partitioned.
12th–14th centuries: Local feudal lords, led by count of Holland and bishop of Utrecht, became practically independent; Dutch towns became prosperous trading centres, usually ruled by small groups of merchants.
15th century: Low Countries (Holland, Belgium, and Flanders) came under rule of dukes of Burgundy.
1477: Low Countries passed by marriage to Habsburgs.
1555: The Netherlands passed to Spain upon division of Habsburg domains.
1568: Dutch rebelled under leadership of William the Silent, Prince of Orange, and fought a long war of independence.
1579: Union of Utrecht: seven northern rebel provinces formed United Provinces.
17th century: 'Golden Age': Dutch led world in trade, art, and science, and founded colonies in East and West Indies, primarily through Dutch East India Company, founded in 1602.
1648: Treaty of Westphalia: United Provinces finally recognized as independent Dutch Republic.
1652–54: Commercial and colonial rivalries led to naval war with England.
1652–72: Johann de Witt ruled Dutch Republic as premier after conflict between republicans and House of Orange.
1665–67: Second Anglo-Dutch war.
1672–74: Third Anglo-Dutch war.
1672: William of Orange became stadholder (ruling as chief magistrate) of the Dutch Republic, an office which became hereditary in the Orange family.
1672–78: The Netherlands fought to prevent domination by King Louis XIV of France.
1688–97 and 1701–13: War with France resumed.
18th century: Exhausted by war, the Netherlands ceased to be a Great Power.
1795: Revolutionary France conquered the Netherlands and established Batavian Republic.

1806: Napoleon made his brother Louis king of Holland.
1810: France annexed the Netherlands.
1815: Northern and southern Netherlands (Holland and Belgium) unified as Kingdom of the Netherlands under King William I of Orange.
1830: Southern Netherlands rebelled and declared independence as Belgium.
1848: Liberal constitution adopted.
1890: Queen Wilhelmina succeeded to throne; dynastic link with Luxembourg broken.
1894–96: Dutch suppressed colonial revolt in Java.
1914–18: The Netherlands neutral in World War I.
1940–45: Occupied by Germany in World War II.
1948: The Netherlands formed Benelux customs union with Belgium and Luxembourg; Queen Wilhelmina abdicated her daughter Juliana.
1949: Became a founding member of the North Atlantic Treaty Organization (NATO).
1953: Dykes breached by storm; nearly 2,000 people and tens of thousands of cattle died in flood.
1954: Remaining Dutch colonies achieved internal self-government.
1958: The Netherlands became a founding member of the European Economic Community (EEC).
1963: The Dutch colony of Western New Guinea was ceded to Indonesia.
1975: Dutch Guiana became independent as Suriname.
1980: Queen Juliana abdicated in favour of her daughter Beatrix.
1994: Following an inconclusive general election, a three-party coalition was formed under PvdA leader Wim Kok.
1999: The coalition government resigned in May after the smallest party, Democrats 66 (D-66), withdrew.
2000: The Netherlands became the first country to legalize euthanasia.
2001: The country became the first to legalize homosexual marriages.
2002: The government resigned in response to a critical report on the inaction of Dutch peacekeeping troops in the Bosnian town of Srebrenica, where a massacre of Muslims took place during the Balkan war in 1995. Pim Fortuyn, a far-right populist Dutch politician, was assassinated in Hilversum. His party, List Pim Fortuyn (LPF) came second in general elections, but the subsequent ruling coalition collapsed after only four months.

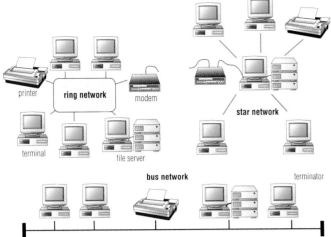

NETWORK Local area networks can be connected together in a ring circuit or in a star arrangement. In the ring arrangement, signals from a terminal or peripheral circulate around the ring to reach the terminal or peripheral addressed. In the star arrangement, signals travel via a central controller. In a bus network, all elements are connected off a single cable that is terminated at each end. See article on p. 675.

neutron one of the three main subatomic particles, the others being the ▷proton and the ▷electron. The neutron is a composite particle, being made up of three ▷quarks, and therefore belongs to the ▷baryon group of the ▷hadrons. Neutrons have about the same mass as protons but no electric charge, and occur in the nuclei of all atoms except hydrogen. They contribute to the mass of atoms but do not affect their chemistry.

For instance, the ▷isotopes of a single element differ only in the number of neutrons in their nuclei but have identical chemical properties. Outside a nucleus, a free neutron is unstable, decaying with a half-life of 11.6 minutes into a proton, an electron, and an antineutrino. The neutron was discovered by the British chemist James Chadwick in 1932. Neutrons and protons have masses 2000 times those of electrons. The process by which a neutron changes into a proton is called ▷beta decay.

neutron beam machine nuclear reactor or accelerator producing a stream of neutrons, which can 'see' through metals. It is used in industry to check molecular changes in metal under stress.

neutron bomb (or enhanced radiation weapon) small hydrogen bomb for battlefield use that kills by radiation, with minimal damage to buildings and other structures. See ▷nuclear warfare.

neutron star very small, 'superdense' star composed mostly of ▷neutrons. They are thought to form when massive stars explode as ▷supernovae, during which the protons and electrons of the star's atoms merge, owing to intense gravitational collapse, to make neutrons. A neutron star has the mass of 2-3 suns, compressed into a globe only 20 km/12 mi in diameter. If its mass is any greater, its gravity will be so strong that it will shrink even further to become a ▷black hole. Being so small, neutron stars can spin very quickly. The rapidly flashing radio stars called ▷pulsars are believed to be neutron stars. The flashing is caused by a rotating beam of radio energy similar in behaviour to a lighthouse beam of light.

Nevada state in western USA. It is nicknamed the Silver State or the Sagebrush State. Nevada was admitted to the Union in 1864 as the 36th US state. It is famous as a gambling centre and, historically, especially in Reno, as a state in which marriages and divorces could be expedited. Nevada is bordered to the east by Utah and Arizona, to the west and southwest by California, and to the north by Oregon and Idaho.

> **population** (1995) 1,530,100   **area** 286,400 sq km/110,550 sq mi   **capital** Carson City   **towns and cities** Las Vegas, Reno   **industries and products** mercury, barite, gold; tourism and gambling now generate more than half of the state's income

new age movement of the late 1980s characterized by an emphasis on the holistic view of body and mind, alternative (or complementary) medicines, personal growth therapies, and a loose mix of theosophy, ecology, oriental mysticism, and a belief in the dawning of an astrological age of peace and harmony.

Related Web site: New Age Dictionary http://mysticplanet.com/8diction.htm

Newark largest city and port of New Jersey, USA, on Newark Bay, 15 km/9 mi west of lower Manhattan; population (1996 est) 268,500. It is a commercial, financial, and industrial centre, with an international airport. Electrical equipment, machinery, chemicals, paints, beer, and canned meats are produced. Port Newark, a deep-water facility under the New York Port Authority, handles some aspects of New York harbour business. It was founded as Milford in 1666 by Puritans. The city is the seat of Essex county.

New Britain largest island in the ▷Bismarck Archipelago, part of Papua New Guinea; capital Rabaul; population (1995 est) 285,000. It has an area of 37,800 sq km/14,600 sq mi, an average width of 80 km/50 mi and is 482 km/300 mi long. The highest mountain is Mount Sinewit, 2,438 m/7,999 ft. Copra is the chief product; coffee, cocoa, palm oil, timber, and iron are also produced. Gold, copper, and coal are mined. The population is Melanesian.

New Brunswick largest maritime province of eastern Canada; area 73,400 sq km/28,332 sq mi; population (1991) 762,500; 33% French-speaking; 52% rural inhabitants. It is bounded on the north by Québec, with the Matapédia and Restigouche rivers forming part of the border; in the northeast Chaleur Bay separates New Brunswick's north shore from Québec's Gaspé Peninsula. Off its eastern coast is the Gulf of St Lawrence and in the southeast the Northumberland Strait, on the far side of which lies Prince Edward Island. Nova Scotia province is situated to its south and southeast, across the Bay of Fundy and the narrow land bridge known as the Chignecto Isthmus. To the southwest lies the US state of Maine, with the Saint John and Saint Croix rivers forming parts of the

boundary. The capital of the province is Fredericton, and Saint John and Moncton are other towns.

Grand Lake, Saint John River, Bay of Fundy, and Hopewell Cape are features found in the province. Industries include the production of wood, pulp, and paper; mining (lead, zinc, copper, nickel, silver, tungsten, gypsum, bismuth, antimony, coal, and potash), and oil and natural-gas extraction. Manufacturing includes heavy engineering, light industries (electronics, footwear), and production of building materials (bricks and tiles). There is also arable farming (cereals, potatoes, and apples), plus livestock-rearing and dairy industry, and fishing (herring and lobsters).

Newby, (George) Eric (1919–) English travel writer and sailor. His books include *A Short Walk in the Hindu Kush* (1958), *The Big Red Train Ride* (1978), *Slowly Down the Ganges* (1966), and *A Traveller's Life* (1985).

New Caledonia island group in the South Pacific, a French overseas territory between Australia and the Fiji Islands; area 18,576 sq km/7,170 sq mi; population (1997 est) 191,000 (45% Kanak (Melanesian), 34% European, 9% Wallisian, 4% Vietnamese and Indonesian, 8% Polynesian). The capital is ▷Nouméa. The islands are surrounded by a barrier reef, and are the world's third-largest producer of nickel. Other industries include chrome, iron, chlorine, oxygen, and cement works; agricultural products include beef, pork, coffee, and maize; and tourism is also an important industry. The currency used is the CFP franc. French is the official language, although English is widely spoken. 60% of the population are Roman Catholic, and 30% are Protestant.

Newcastle industrial city and port in New South Wales, Australia, on the Hunter River, 157 km/98 mi north of Sydney; population (1996) 270,324. Newcastle is the second-largest city in the state after Sydney, and is dependent mainly on coalmining and alumina production. Other industries include shipbuilding and the manufacture of electronic equipment, textiles, chemicals, fertilizers, and wine products. Newcastle has a university (1965).

Newcastle, Thomas Pelham-Holles, 1st Duke of Newcastle (1693–1768) British Whig politician, prime minster 1754–56 and 1757–62. He served as secretary of state for 30 years from 1724, then succeeded his younger brother, Henry ▷Pelham, as prime minister in 1754. In 1756 he resigned as a result of setbacks in the Seven Years' War, but returned to office in 1757 with ▷Pitt the Elder (1st Earl of Chatham) taking responsibility for the conduct of the war. He was made an earl in 1714, and a duke in 1715.

Newcastle upon Tyne city and metropolitan borough in Tyne and Wear in northeast England on the River Tyne opposite Gateshead, 17 km/10 mi from the North Sea; population (1999 est) 273,000. It is the administrative centre of Tyne and Wear and regional centre of northeast England, as well as a centre for retail, commerce, communications, and the arts. Industries include engineering (including offshore technology), food processing, brewing, and the manufacture of electronics. Only 1% of the workforce is now in heavy industry, 80% are in the public or service sectors. The University of Newcastle was founded in 1963, and the University of Northumbria in 1992.

Features Parts are preserved of a castle built by Henry II 1172–77 on the site of an older castle (1080). Other landmarks include the cathedral, formerly the parish church, which is chiefly 14th-century; a 12th-century church, and the Guildhall (1658); the Metro underground; the Laing Art Gallery; the Newcastle Discovery Museum; the Hancock Museum; fine 19th-century classical buildings. The quayside area with its historic buildings has

Neural Networks

Neural networks are interconnected webs of computer processing units. They are loosely modelled on the networks of neurons (nerve cells) that make up brains.

Conventional computers have distinct processing and memory units, controlled by programs, but in neural networks (as in animal nervous systems and brains), there are no specific memory locations, information instead being stored as patterns of interconnections between processing units. Neural networks are not programmed, they are trained by example and can therefore learn things that cannot easily be stated in programs. They have the potential to offer solutions to problems that have proved difficult to solve using conventional computers.

Such problems include the identification of visual or audio patterns, for example character, voice, and handwriting recognition, machine learning (where machines recognize patterns that have occurred repeatedly and improve their performance based on this experience), and robot control.

A famous example of a neural network application was the development by T J Sejnowski and C R Rosenberg at Johns Hopkins University in the USA, of a neural network called NET-talk. It was trained to recognize speech and was linked to a computer that could produce synthetic speech so that its progress could be heard.

been restored, and is now a fashionable waterside area known for its nightlife, with clubs and pubs here, as well as in Bigg Market. Newcastle is connected with the neighbouring town of Gateshead by eight bridges and a tunnel.

History Newcastle stands on the site of a Roman settlement, **Pons Aelius**. Newcastle first began to trade in coal in the 13th century, and was an important centre for coal and ship-building until the 1980s. In 1826 ironworks were established by George ▷Stephenson, and the first engine used on the Stockton and Darlington railway was made in Newcastle.

Newcomen, Thomas (1663–1729) English inventor of an early steam engine. His 'fire engine' of 1712 was used for pumping water from mines until James ▷Watt invented one with a separate condenser.

new country US ▷country and western movement of the 1980s–90s away from the overproduction associated with the Nashville record industry. New country generated successful crossover performers like Garth Brooks (1961–) and Ricky Skaggs (1954–).

New Criticism in literature, a US movement dominant in the 1930s and 1940s, stressing the autonomy of the text without biographical and other external interpolation, but instead requiring close readings of its linguistic structure. The major figures of New Criticism include Allen Tate, John Crowe Ransom, and Robert Penn Warren. The term was coined by J E Spingarn in 1910.

New Deal in US history, the programme introduced by President Franklin D Roosevelt in 1933 to tackle the Great Depression, including employment on public works, farm loans at low rates, and social reforms such as old-age and unemployment insurance, prevention of child labour, protection of employees against unfair practices by employers, and loans to local authorities for slum clearance.

The centrepiece of the New Deal was the Social Security Act of 1935, which introduced a comprehensive federal system of insurance for the elderly and unemployed. The **Public Works Administration** was given $3.3 billion to spend on roads, public buildings, and similar developments (the ▷Tennessee Valley Authority was a separate project). The **Agricultural Adjustment Administration** raised agricultural prices by restriction of output. In 1935 Harry L Hopkins was put in charge of a new agency, the **Works Progress Administration** (WPA), which in addition to taking over the public works created something of a cultural revolution with its federal theatre, writers', and arts projects. When the WPA was disbanded in 1943 it had found employment for 8.5 million people.

Some of the provisions of the New Deal were declared unconstitutional by the Supreme Court (1935–36). The New Deal encouraged the growth of trade-union membership, brought previously unregulated areas of the US economy under federal control, and revitalized cultural life and community spirit. Although full employment did not come until the military-industrial needs of World War II, the New Deal did bring political stability to the industrial-capitalist system. It also transformed the political landscape, making the Democratic Party the natural majority party and breaking Republican dominance since 1806.

Related Web site: New Deal Network http://newdeal.feri.org/

New Delhi capital of India, situated in the north of the country on the Yamuna River in the Union Territory of ▷Delhi; population (1991) 301,000. It lies near the old city of ▷Delhi, some 5 km/3 mi south of the Red Fort. Predominantly an administrative centre, it also produces chemicals, textiles, machine tools, electrical goods, and footwear.

New Democratic Party (NDP) Canadian political party, moderately socialist, formed in 1961 by a merger of the Labour Congress and the Cooperative Commonwealth Federation. Its leader is Alexa McDonough.

New Economic Policy (NEP) economic policy of the USSR 1921–29 devised by the Soviet leader Vladimir Ilyich ▷Lenin. Rather than requisitioning all agricultural produce above a stated subsistence allowance, the state requisitioned only a fixed proportion of the surplus; the rest could be traded freely by the peasant. The NEP thus reinstated a limited form of free-market trading, although the state retained complete control of major industries.

New England district of northern New South Wales, Australia, especially the tableland area of Glen Innes and Armidale.

New England region of northeast USA, comprising the states of Maine, New Hampshire, Vermont, Massachusetts, Rhode Island, and Connecticut. It is a geographic region rather than a political entity, with an area of 172,681 sq km/66,672 sq mi. Boston is the principal urban centre of the region, and Harvard and Yale are its major universities. First inhabited by the American Indian Algonquin peoples, New England was named by the explorer John Smith in 1614, and settled by Pilgrims and Puritans from England in the 17th century.

New Forest ancient forest in southwest Hampshire, southern England, and the largest stretch of semi-natural vegetation in lowland Britain. Lying between the River Avon on the west and Southampton Water on the east, its legal boundary encloses 38,000 ha/93,898 acres (1995). Of this area 8,400 ha/20,756 acres is enclosed plantation, and 20,000 ha/49,420 acres is common land, including ancient woodland, heath, grassland, and bog. The remainder is privately owned land and villages. More than six million tourists visit annually.

Newfoundland breed of large, gentle dog said to have originated in Newfoundland, Canada. Males can grow to 70 cm/27.5 in tall, and weigh 65 kg/145 lb; the females are slightly smaller. They have a dense, flat coat, usually dull black, and an oily, water-repellent undercoat, and they are excellent swimmers.

Newfoundland Canadian province on the Atlantic Ocean, the country's most easterly administrative region, comprising the island of ▷Newfoundland and mainland ▷Labrador, separated by the Strait of Belle Isle; area 405,700 sq km/156,600 sq mi; population (1996 est) 570,700. It is bounded on the west by Québec, while to the southwest lie the Gulf of St Lawrence and the provinces of Nova Scotia and Prince Edward Island. The capital is ▷St John's, and other towns and cities are Corner Brook, Gander, and Goose Bay (Labrador). Industries include offshore oil extraction; fishing and fish-processing; mining (iron, copper, zinc, and uranium); wood-processing and paper manufacture; and hydroelectric power generation.

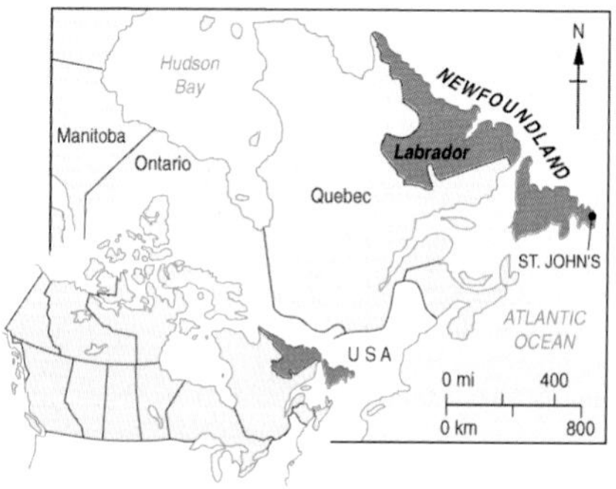

New Guinea island in the southwest Pacific, north of Australia, comprising ▷Papua New Guinea and the Indonesian province of ▷Irian Jaya; total area about 885,780 sq km/342,000 sq mi. Part of the Dutch East Indies from 1828, West Irian was ceded by the United Nations to Indonesia in 1963 and renamed Irian Jaya ('victorious Irian') in 1973.

Newham inner borough of east Greater London, north of the River Thames; population (1991) 200,200. It includes the districts of East and West Ham and the northern part of Woolwich.

Features Site of former Royal Docks: Victoria (1855), Albert (1880), and King George V (1921); post-war tower blocks (collapse of Ronan Point in 1968 led to official enquiry); Stratford has been chosen as an International Passenger Station for the Channel Tunnel Rail Link.

New Hampshire state in northeastern USA. It is nicknamed the Granite State. New Hampshire ratified the US Constitution in 1788, becoming the 9th state to join the Union. Part of New England, it is bordered to the east by Maine, to the north by Québec, Canada, to the west by Vermont, and to the south by Massachusetts.

population (1995) 1,148,300 **area** 24,000 sq km/9,264 sq mi **capital** Concord **towns and cities** Manchester, Nashua **industries and products** dairy, poultry, fruits and vegetables, electrical and other machinery, pulp and paper, tourism, leisure industry

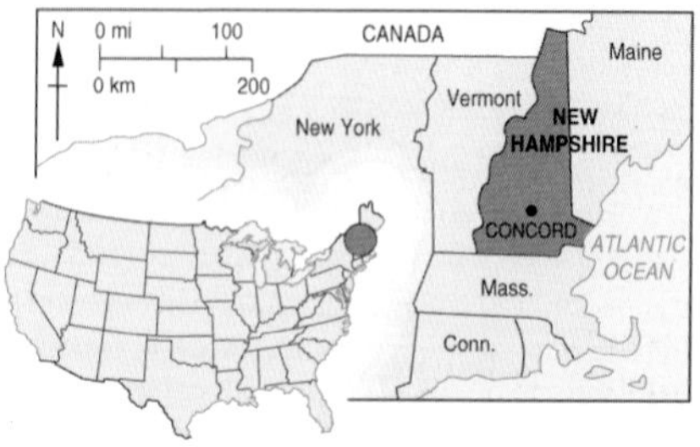

Newhaven city and port in Connecticut, USA, at the mouth of the Quinnipiac River on Long Island Sound; population (1996 est) 124,700. Metal goods, rubber goods, ammunition, and clothing are manufactured. Yale University, third oldest in the USA, was founded here in 1701 and named after Elihu Yale (1648–1721), an early benefactor. Newhaven was settled in 1638 by English Protestants from Massachusetts.

New Hebrides former name (to 1980) of ▷Vanuatu, a country in the South Pacific.

Ne Win (1911–) Adopted name of Maung Shu Maung. ('Brilliant Sun') Myanmar (Burmese) politician, prime minister 1958–60, ruler from 1962 to 1974, president 1974–81, and chair until 1988 of the ruling Burma Socialist Programme Party (BSPP). His domestic 'Burmese Way to Socialism' policy programme brought the economy into serious decline.

New Jersey state in northeastern USA. It is nicknamed the Garden State. New Jersey ratified the US Constitution in 1787, becoming the 3rd state to join the Union. The most densely populated US state, it lies within the suburban orbits of the cities of New York and Philadelphia. The New Jersey Turnpike, traversing a zone of heavy development, is the busiest highway in the country. New Jersey is bordered to the north by New York state. It lies largely between two rivers, the Hudson to the east and the Delaware to the west, with the Atlantic Ocean along its southeastern and southern boundaries. New York faces it across the Hudson River, Pennsylvania lies to the west, across the Delaware River, and to the southwest, across the river's mouth and Delaware Bay, is the state of Delaware.

population (1995) 7,945,300 **area** 20,200 sq km/7,797 sq mi **capital** Trenton **towns and cities** Newark, Jersey City, Paterson, Elizabeth **industries and products** fruits and vegetables, fish and shellfish, chemicals, pharmaceuticals, soaps and cleansers, transport equipment, petroleum refining, research centres, finance sector, tourism

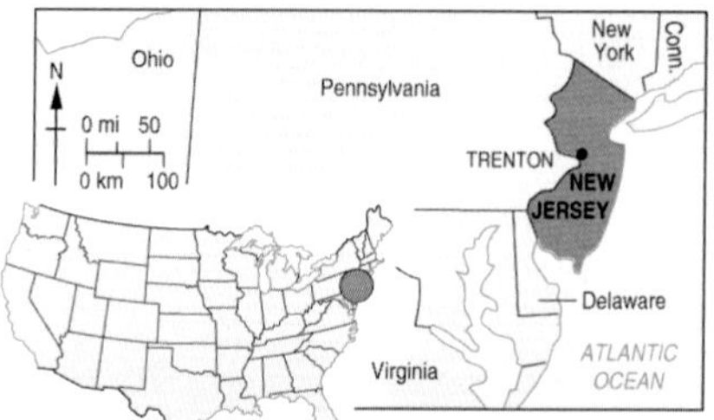

Newlands, John Alexander Reina (1837–1898) English chemist who worked as an industrial chemist; he prepared in 1863 the first ▷periodic table of the elements arranged in order of relative atomic masses, and pointed out in 1865 the 'law of octaves' whereby every eighth element has similar properties. He was ridiculed at the time, but five years later the Russian chemist Dmitri ▷Mendeleyev published a more developed form of the table, also based on atomic masses, which forms the basis of the one used today (arranged by atomic number).

newly industrialized country (NIC) country formerly classified as less developed, but which is becoming rapidly industrialized. The first wave of countries to be identified as newly-industrializing included Hong Kong, South Korea, Singapore, and Taiwan. These countries underwent rapid industrial growth in the 1970s and 1980s, attracting significant financial investment, and are now associated with high-technology industries. More recently, Thailand, China, and Malaysia have been classified as newly-industrializing countries.

Newman, John Henry (1801–1890) English Roman Catholic theologian. While still an Anglican, he wrote a series of *Tracts for the Times*, which gave their name to the Tractarian Movement (subsequently called the ▷Oxford Movement) for the revival of Catholicism. He became a Catholic in 1845 and was made a cardinal in 1879. In 1864 his autobiography, *Apologia pro vita sua*, was published.

Newman, born in London, was ordained in the Church of England in 1824, and in 1827 became vicar of St Mary's, Oxford. There he was influenced by the historian R H Froude and the Anglican priest ▷Keble, and in 1833 published the first of the *Tracts for the Times*. They culminated in *Tract 90* (1841) which found the Thirty-Nine Articles of the Anglican church compatible with Roman Catholicism. He was rector of Dublin University 1854–58 and published his lectures on education as *The Idea of a University* (1873). His poem *The Dream of Gerontius* appeared in 1866, the words of which were used in Edward Elgar's *The Dream of Gerontius*, and *The Grammar of Assent*, an analysis of the nature of belief, in 1870. He wrote the hymn 'Lead, kindly light' (1833).

Related Web site: Selected Poetry of John Henry Newman (Cardinal; 1801–1890) http://www.library.utoronto.ca/utel/rp/authors/newman.html

Newman, Paul (1925–) US actor and director. He was one of Hollywood's leading male stars of the 1960s and 1970s, in such films as *The Hustler* (1961), *Sweet Bird of Youth* (1962), *Hud* (1963), *Butch Cassidy and the Sundance Kid* (1969), and *The Sting* (1973). He won an Academy Award for *The Color of Money* (1986). Initially he often played an alienated figure, and later appeared in character roles of many kinds. His films include *Somebody Up There Likes Me* (1956), *Cat on a Hot Tin Roof* (1958), *Cool Hand Luke* (1967), *The Verdict* (1983), *Mr and Mrs Bridge* (1991), and *The Hudsucker Proxy* (1994). He directed his wife Joanne Woodward in *Rachel, Rachel* (1968) and other films.

The profits from his Newman's Own speciality foods are donated to charity. He is also noted as a race-car driver and for his philanthropic activities.

PAUL NEWMAN US actor Paul Newman, pictured here in the 1960s, frequently played outsiders and rebels in his films. *Archive Photos*

New Mexico state in southwestern USA. It is nicknamed the Land of Enchantment. New Mexico was admitted to the Union in 1912 as the 47th US state. One of the Mountain States, it is bordered to the east by Texas and the Oklahoma panhandle, and to the north by Colorado. In the northwest, at the 'Four Corners', it meets Colorado, Utah, and Arizona. Arizona also lies along its western border. To the south, it is bordered by the Mexican states of Sonora and Chihuahua, and by the Trans-Pecos section of Texas.

    population (1995) 1,685,400   **area** 315,000 sq km/121,590 sq mi   **capital** Santa Fe   **towns and cities** Albuquerque, Las Cruces, Roswell   **industries and products** uranium, potash, copper, oil, natural gas, petroleum and coal products, sheep farming, cotton, pecans, vegetables, chilli peppers, tourism
    Related Web site: Chetro Ketl Great Kiva http://sipapu.ucsb.edu/html/kiva.html

New Model Army army created in 1645 by Oliver ▷Cromwell to support the cause of Parliament during the English ▷Civil War. It was characterized by organization and discipline. Thomas ▷Fairfax was its first commander.

New Orleans (called 'the Big Easy') city and river port in southeast Louisiana, USA, on the Mississippi River, and the Gulf of Mexico; population (1996 est) 476,600; metropolitan area (1992) 1,303,000. It is a commercial and manufacturing centre with shipbuilding, oil-refining, and petrochemical industries. Tourism is a major activity. New Orleans is regarded as the traditional birthplace of jazz, believed to have developed from the singing and

voodoo rhythms of the weekly slave gatherings in Congo Square, during the 18th and 19th centuries. The city was founded by the French in 1718.
    Related Web site: Welcome to New Orleans http://www.nawlins.com/

Newport unitary authority in south Wales, created in 1996 from part of the former county of Gwent.
    area 190 sq km/73 sq mi   **towns** ▷Newport (administrative headquarters)   **physical** rivers Usk Ebbw, Afon Llwyd   **features** Legionary Museum and Roman amphitheatre at Caerleon   **industries** steel and aluminium production, engineering, chemicals, fertilizers, electronics   **population** (1996) 133,300

Newport river port, administrative headquarters of the ▷Isle of Wight unitary authority, southern England, on the River Medina; population (1991) 25,000. Newport is the retail centre for the island, and Parkhurst Prison and Camp Hill Prison, in the nearby residential district of Parkhurst, are important sources of employment. Products include electronic current boards and computer parts. Charles I was imprisoned 1647–1648 in nearby Carisbrooke Castle.

Newport (Welsh Casnewydd) seaport and administrative centre of ▷Newport unitary authority, southeast Wales, situated on the River Usk 30 km/19 mi northwest of Bristol; population (1994 est) 111,000. There is a steelworks at nearby Llanwern, and a high-tech complex at Cleppa Park. Other industries include engineering, and the manufacture of chemicals, fertilizers, aluminium, and electronics.

news agency business handling news stories and photographs that are then sold to newspapers and magazines. International agencies include the Associated Press (AP, 1848), *Agence France-Presse* (AFP, 1944), United Press International (UPI, 1907), and Reuters.

New South Wales state of southeast Australia, including the dependency of Lord Howe Island; area 801,600 sq km/309,500 sq mi; population (1996) 6,038,700 (about 54% in the capital, ▷Sydney). The state is bounded by Queensland on the north, the Tasman Sea on the east, Victoria on the south, and South Australia on the west. Other towns and cities in the state are Newcastle, Wollongong, Wagga Wagga, Broken Hill, Goulburn, Bathurst, Armidale, Coffs Harbour, Albury, and Tamworth.

Physical features include the ▷Great Dividing Range (including Blue Mountains) and part of the Australian Alps (including Snowy Mountains and Mount Kosciusko); the rivers Murray, Darling, and Murrumbidgee; the ▷Riverina district, irrigated by the Murray-Darling-Murrumbidgee river system; the Hunter Valley wine-producing area; and the Snowy River Scheme. ▷Canberra forms an enclave within the state.

There is a radio telescope at Parkes. Siding Spring Mountain (859 m/2,817 ft), northwest of Sydney, has telescopes that can observe the central sector of the Galaxy.

Products include cereals, fruit, wine, sugar, tobacco, dairy products, meat, wool, gold, silver, copper, zinc, lead, coal, iron and steel, machinery, electrical appliances, cars, furniture, textiles and textile goods, hides and leather, tobacco, chemicals, paint, oil, paper, hydroelectric power from the Snowy River, mineral sands, glassware, timber, poultry, opals, fish and other seafood.

New South Wales was visited by Captain James ▷Cook in 1770 and was a convict settlement 1788–1850. It was opened to free settlement by 1819 and achieved self-government in 1855, becoming a state of the Commonwealth of Australia in 1901.

newspaper daily or weekly publication in the form of folded sheets containing news and comment. News-sheets became commercial undertakings after the invention of printing and were introduced in 1609 in Germany and 1616 in the Netherlands. In

NEW ORLEANS A float in the Mardi Gras parade, New Orleans, Louisiana, USA. Held at the beginning of Lent, this festival has become a celebration of music, particularly jazz, and dance, with exotic costumes on show. *Archive Photos*

1622 the first newspaper appeared in English, the *Weekly News*, edited by Nicholas Bourne and Thomas Archer. Improved ▷printing (steam printing in 1814, the rotary press in 1846 in the USA and in 1857 in the UK), newsprint (paper made from wood-pulp), and a higher literacy rate led to the growth of newspapers. In the 20th century production costs fell with the introduction of new technology.

The oldest national newspaper currently printed in the UK is *The Observer* (1791); the highest circulation UK newspaper is the Sunday *News of the World* (nearly 5 million copies weekly). The world's most widely read newspaper is Japan's *Yomiuri Shimbun*, with a daily circulation of 10 million.

newt small ▷salamander found in Europe, Asia, northwestern Africa, and North America. (Family Salamandridae, order Urodela.) The European newts, such as the **smooth newt** (*Triturus vulgaris*), live on land for part of the year but enter a pond or lake to breed in the spring. Britain has three native species: the **common** or **smooth newt** (*Triturus vulgaris*); the **palmate newt** (*T. helveticus*); and the endangered **great crested** or **warty newt** (*T. cristatus*).

The **smooth newt** is about 5 cm/2 in long with a 4 cm/1.6 in tail. It is olive, spotted in the breeding male, and the underside is orange with blotches. It eats small invertebrates and fish. The **crested newt** is the most aquatic. Its head is flat and the upper lip overhangs the lower one. The upper parts of the body are blackish-brown with darker brown spots. The underparts are reddish-orange, with black spots, and the sides are dotted with white. In the spring the colours of the rough skin brighten and the male, which can reach 15 cm/6 in long, develops a notched crest.
    Related Web site: Tappaboy Newt Page http://www.ultranet.com/~vail/newt/index.html

New Testament the second part of the ▷Bible, recognized by the Christian church from the 4th century as sacred doctrine. The New Testament includes the Gospels, which tell of the life and teachings of Jesus, the history of the early church, the teachings of St Paul, and mystical writings. It was written in Greek during the 1st and 2nd centuries AD, and the individual sections have been ascribed to various authors by biblical scholars.

newton SI unit (symbol N) of ▷force. One newton is the force needed to accelerate an object with mass of one kilogram by one metre per second. The weight of a medium size (100 g/3 oz) apple is one newton.

Newton, Isaac (1642–1727) English physicist and mathematician who laid the foundations of physics as a modern discipline. During 1665–66, he discovered the binomial theorem, differential and integral calculus, and that white light is composed of many colours. He developed the three standard laws of motion (see ▷Newton's laws of motion) and the universal law of gravitation, set out in *Philosophiae naturalis principia mathematica* (1687), usually referred to as the *Principia*. He was knighted in 1705.

Newton's greatest achievement was to demonstrate that scientific principles are of universal application. He clearly defined the nature of mass, weight, force, inertia, and acceleration.

In 1679 Newton calculated the Moon's motion on the basis of his theory of gravity and also found that his theory explained the laws of planetary motion that had been derived by German astronomer Johannes ▷Kepler on the basis of observations of the planets.

Newton's laws of motion in physics, three laws that form the basis of Newtonian mechanics. (1) Unless acted upon by an unbalanced force, a body at rest stays at rest, and a moving body continues moving at the same speed in the same straight line. (2) An unbalanced force applied to a body gives it an acceleration proportional to the force (and in the direction of the force) and inversely proportional to the mass of the body. (3) When a body A exerts a force on a body B, B exerts an equal and opposite force on A; that is, to every action there is an equal and opposite reaction.

Newton's rings in optics, an ▷interference phenomenon seen (using white light) as concentric rings of spectral colours where light passes through a thin film of transparent medium, such as the wedge of air between a large-radius convex lens and a flat glass plate. With monochromatic light (light of a single wavelength), the rings take the form of alternate light and dark bands. They are caused by interference (interaction) between light rays reflected from the plate and those reflected from the curved surface of the lens.

new town in the UK, centrally planned urban area. New towns such as Milton Keynes and Stevenage were built after World War II to accommodate the overspill from cities and large towns, at a time when the population was rapidly expanding and inner-city centres had either decayed or been destroyed. In 1976 the policy, which had been criticized for disrupting family groupings and local communities, destroying small shops and specialist industries, and furthering the decay of city centres, was abandoned.

New Wave in pop music, a style that evolved parallel to punk in the second half of the 1970s. It shared the urban aggressive spirit of punk but was musically and lyrically more sophisticated; examples are the early work of Elvis Costello and Talking Heads. New Wave underwent a revival in the 1990s.

New World the Americas, so called by the first Europeans who reached them. The term also describes animals and plants of the Western hemisphere.

Related Web site: Ordinance and Constitution of the Virginia Company in England http://odur.let.rug.nl/~usa/D/1601-1650/virginia/ordi.htm

New York the most populous city in the USA, located on an inlet of the Atlantic Ocean in the far southeastern corner of ▷New York State; population (2000 est excluding suburban metropolitan areas under separate administration) 8,008,300. New York is composed of five city boroughs that are also counties of New York State: ▷Manhattan (New York County); the ▷Bronx (Bronx County); ▷Queens (Queens County); ▷Brooklyn (Kings County); and Staten Island (Richmond County). As well as being the main port in North America, New York is one of the world's principal commercial and cultural centres. The many industries and services operating here include banking and other financial activities, publishing and printing, the electronic media, advertising, clothing manufacture and the fashion industry, and the production of food, chemicals, machinery, and textiles. The city also attracts a large number of tourists each year. New York is also known as the 'Big Apple'.

Features The Statue of Liberty stands on Liberty Island in the inner harbour of New York Bay. Manhattan skyscrapers include the Empire State Building (381 m/1,250 ft), and the Chrysler Building; the headquarters of the United Nations is also here. The twin towers of the World Trade Center (412m/1,350 ft) were the city's highest buildings until they were destroyed by terrorists in September 2001. Central Park is New York's largest park. ▷Wall Street in Lower Manhattan is the home of the New York stock exchange. There are a number of art galleries, including the Frick Collection, the Metropolitan Museum of Art, the Museum of Modern Art, and the Guggenheim. Columbia University is one of a number of institutions of higher education.

History The Italian navigator Giovanni da Verrazano (*c.* 1485–*c.* 1528) reached New York Bay in 1528, and Henry Hudson explored it in 1609. The Dutch established a settlement on Manhattan in 1624, named New Amsterdam from 1626; this was captured by the English in 1664 and renamed New York. British troops occupied New York 1776–84; it was the capital of the USA 1785–90. The five boroughs were linked in 1898 to give the city its present extent.

Isaac Newton
If I have seen farther it is by standing on the shoulders of giants.
Letter to Robert Hooke, February 1675

New York state in northeast USA. It is nicknamed the Empire State. New York ratified the US Constitution in 1788, becoming the 11th state to join the Union. It is bordered to the north by the Canadian states of Québec and Ontario, to the east by Vermont, Massachusetts, and Connecticut, and to the south by Pennsylvania and New Jersey. In the west is a strip of Pennsylvania that reaches north to Lake Erie. New York has shores on both Lakes Erie and Lake Ontario, between which it faces part of the state of Ontario across the Niagara River. In the southeast it faces New Jersey across the lower Hudson River. Long Island extends east from New York Bay into the Atlantic Ocean, with Connecticut and Rhode Island lying to the north across Long Island Sound.

population (1995) 18,136,100 **area** 127,200 sq km/49,099 sq mi **capital** Albany **towns and cities** New York City, Buffalo, Rochester, Yonkers, Syracuse **industries and products** dairy products, apples, clothing, periodical and book printing and publishing, electronic components and accessories, office machines and computers, communications equipment, motor vehicles and equipment, pharmaceuticals, aircraft and parts, finance sector, tourism

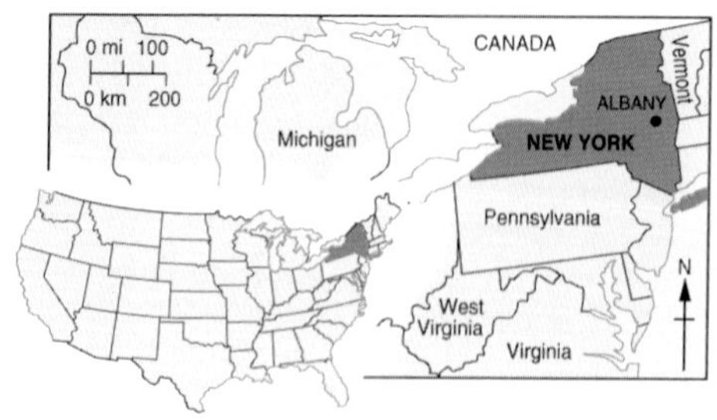

New Zealand (or Aotearoa; Maori 'long daylight') see country box.

New Zealand literature prose and poetry of New Zealand. The short stories of Katherine Mansfield in the early 20th century became internationally known, and in 1985 Keri Hulme won the UK-based Booker Prize for her novel *The Bone People*.

19th century Among interesting pioneer records of the mid- to late 19th century are those of Edward Jerningham Wakefield and F E Maning; and *A First Year in Canterbury Settlement* by Samuel ▷Butler. Earliest of the popular poets was Thomas Bracken, author of the New Zealand national song, followed by native-born Jessie Mackay and W Pember Reeves, though the latter is better known as the author of the prose account of New Zealand *The Long White Cloud*; and Ursula Bethell (1874–1945).

20th century Mansfield's stories were written in Europe, but she drew on her New Zealand background. *Tutira, the Story of a New Zealand Sheep Station* (1926), by W H Guthrie Smith (1861–1940), struck a specifically New Zealand note. The 1930s saw the debut of an exponent of detective fiction, Dame Ngaio Marsh. Poetry of a new quality was written by R A K Mason (1905–1971) in the 1920s, and in the 1930s by a group of which A R D Fairburn (1904–1957), with a witty conversational turn, and Allen Curnow, poet, critic, and anthologist, are the most striking. In fiction, the 1930s were remarkable for the short stories of Frank Sargeson and Roderick Finlayson (1904–1992), and the talent of John Mulgan (1911–1945), who is remembered both for his novel *Man Alone* and for his posthumous factual account of World War II, in which he died, *Report on Experience* (1947). Kendrick Smithyman (1922–) struck a metaphysical note in poetry, James K Baxter (1926–1972) published fluent lyrics, and Janet Frame has a brooding depth of meaning in such novels as *The Rainbirds* (1968) and *Intensive Care* (1970).

Brendan Behan
Irish dramatist
New York is my Lourdes, where I go for spiritual refreshment – a place where you're least likely to be bitten by a wild goat.
New York Post, 22 March 1964

Ney, Michel (1769–1815) Duke of Elchingen, Prince of Ney. Marshal of France under ▷Napoleon I, who commanded the rearguard of the French army during the retreat from Moscow, and for his personal courage was called 'the bravest of the brave'. When Napoleon returned from Elba, Ney was sent to arrest him, but instead deserted to him and fought at Waterloo. He was subsequently shot for treason.

Ngugi wa Thiong'o (1938–) Born James Ngugi. Kenyan writer. His work includes essays, plays, short stories, and novels. Imprisoned after the performance of the play *Ngaahika Ndeenda/I Will Marry When I Want* (1977), he lived in exile from 1982. His novels, written in English and Kikuyu, include *The River Between* (1965), *Petals of Blood* (1977), *Caitaani Mutharaba-ini/Devil on the Cross* (1982), and *Matigari* (1989), and deal with colonial and post-independence oppression.

NH abbreviation for ▷New Hampshire, a state of the USA.

NHS abbreviation for **National Health Service**, the UK state-financed ▷health service.

niacin one of the 'B group' vitamins; see ▷nicotinic acid.

Niagara Falls two waterfalls on the Niagara River, on the Canada–USA border, between lakes Erie and Ontario and separated by Goat Island. The **American Falls** are 51 m/167 ft high, 330 m/1,080 ft wide; **Horseshoe Falls**, in Canada, are 49 m/160 ft high, 790 m/2,600 ft across.

On the west bank of the river is **Niagara Falls**, a city in Ontario, Canada; population (1981) 71,000; on the east bank is **Niagara Falls**, a city in New York State, USA; population (1990) 61,800. Their economies are based on hydroelectric generating plants, diversified industry, and tourism. The use of hydroelectric power in North America was pioneered here in 1881.

Related Web site: Niagara Falls Convention and Visitors Bureau http://www.nfcvb.com/

Niamey port, capital, and administrative centre of ▷Niger, in the southwest of the country, on the northeast bank of the Niger River; population (1995 est) 495,000. It produces textiles, chemicals, pharmaceuticals, ceramics, plastics, and foodstuffs. It replaced Zinder as the capital in 1926. It has an international airport and railway terminus. A French fort was established at Niamey in 1902. It was selected as an administrative centre in 1922. The population grew rapidly from 30,000 in 1960 when independence was gained from France. The city grew again in the 1970s following the discovery of uranium in Niger in 1968. The university was established in 1971. The city has the National Museum, botanical gardens, and a zoo.

Nicaea, Council of Christian church council held in Nicaea (now Iznik, Turkey) in 325, called by the Roman emperor Constantine. It condemned ▷Arianism as heretical and upheld the doctrine of the Trinity in the Nicene Creed.

Nicaragua see country box.

Nicaragua, Lake lake in southwest Nicaragua, the largest in Central America; area 8,250 sq km/3,185 sq mi. It is 24 km/15 mi from the Pacific Ocean and drains into the Caribbean at San Juan del Norte via the Río San Juan. It is a freshwater lake inhabited by a variety of salt-water fish including shark and swordfish. The lake contains about 310 small islands, most of which are inhabited. The largest island, Ometepe, has two volcanoes: Concepción (1,610 m/ 5,282 ft), and Madera (1,394 m/4,573 ft). Lake Managua to the north drains into Lake Nicaragua via the River Tipitapa. The area is ecologically important for many rare and colourful birds.

Nicaraguan Revolution the revolt 1978–79 in Nicaragua, led by the socialist **Sandinistas** against the US-supported right-wing dictatorship established by Anastasio ▷Somoza. His son, President Anastasio (Debayle) Somoza (1925–1980), was forced into exile in 1979 and assassinated in Paraguay. The Sandinista National Liberation Front (FSLN) was named after Augusto César Sandino, a guerrilla leader killed by the US-trained National Guard in 1934.

Nice city on the French ▷Riviera and administrative centre of the *département* of Alpes-Maritimes, situated at the mouth of the River Paillon on the Baie des Anges, near the Italian frontier; population (1999 est) 345,900. Founded in the 3rd century BC, it repeatedly changed hands between France and the Duchy of Savoy from the 14th to the 19th century. In 1860 it was finally transferred to France after a plebiscite. Nice is the fifth-largest city in France. Nice is situated on the Cote d'Azur which is a centre for information technology industries and has a world-renowned reputation. Employment is concentrated in business and services and 83% of the labour force in Nice is involved in the service industry.

Related Web site: Welcome to Nice French Riviera http://www.nice-coteazur.org/americain/index.html

Nicene Creed one of the fundamental ▷creeds of Christianity, promulgated by the Council of ▷Nicaea in 325.

niche in ecology, the 'place' occupied by a species in its habitat, including all chemical, physical, and biological components, such as what it eats, the time of day at which the species feeds, temperature, moisture, the parts of the habitat that it uses (for example, trees or open grassland), the way it reproduces, and how it behaves.

Nichiren (1222–1282) Japanese Buddhist monk, founder of the sect that bears his name. The sect bases its beliefs on the *Lotus Sa tra*, which Nichiren held to be the only true revelation of the teachings of Buddha, and on repetition of the sūtra's title to attain enlightenment.

Nicholas two tsars of Russia:

Nicholas I (1796–1855) tsar of Russia from 1825. His Balkan ambitions led to war with Turkey 1827–29 and the Crimean War 1853–56.

Nicholas II (1868–1918) tsar of Russia 1894–1917. He was dominated by his wife, Tsarina ▷Alexandra, who was under the influence of the religious charlatan ▷Rasputin. His mismanagement of the Russo-Japanese War and of internal affairs led to the revolution of 1905, which he suppressed, although he was forced to grant limited constitutional reforms. He took Russia into World War I in 1914, was forced to abdicate in 1917 after the ▷Russian Revolution, and was executed with his family. See picture on p. 682.

Related Web site: Alexander Palace Time Machine http://www.alexanderpalace.org/palace/index.html

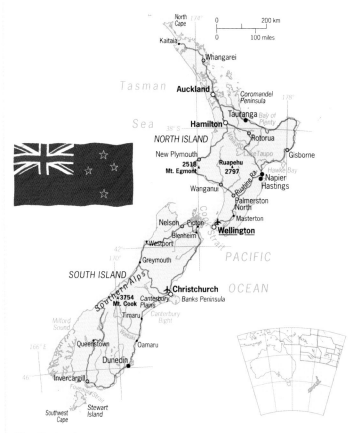

New Zealand country in the southwest Pacific Ocean, southeast of Australia, comprising two main islands, North Island and South Island, and other small islands.

NATIONAL NAME *Aotearoa/New Zealand*
AREA 268,680 sq km/103,737 sq mi
CAPITAL Wellington
MAJOR TOWNS/CITIES Auckland, Hamilton, Christchurch, Manukau, North Shore, Waitakere
MAJOR PORTS Auckland, Wellington
PHYSICAL FEATURES comprises North Island, South Island, Stewart Island, Chatham Islands, and minor islands; mainly mountainous; Ruapehu in North Island, 2,797 m/9,180 ft, highest of three active volcanoes; geysers and hot springs of Rotorua district; Lake Taupo (616 sq km/238 sq mi), source of Waikato River; Kaingaroa state forest. In South Island are the Southern Alps and Canterbury Plains

TERRITORIES Tokelau (three atolls transferred in 1926 from former Gilbert and Ellice Islands colony); Niue Island (one of the Cook Islands, separately administered from 1903: chief town Alafi); Cook Islands are internally self-governing but share common citizenship with New Zealand; Ross Dependency in Antarctica

Government

HEAD OF STATE Queen Elizabeth II from 1952, represented by Governor General Silvia Cartwright from 2001
HEAD OF GOVERNMENT Helen Clark from 1999
POLITICAL SYSTEM liberal democracy
POLITICAL EXECUTIVE parliamentary

ADMINISTRATIVE DIVISIONS 93 counties, nine districts and three town districts
ARMED FORCES 8,700 (2000)
CONSCRIPTION military service is voluntary
DEATH PENALTY abolished in 1989
DEFENCE SPEND (% GDP) 1.2 (2002 est)
EDUCATION SPEND (% GDP) 6.1 (2001 est)
HEALTH SPEND (% GDP) 8 (2000 est)

Economy and resources

CURRENCY New Zealand dollar
GPD (US$) 58.2 billion (2002 est)
REAL GDP GROWTH (% change on previous year) 1.4 (2001)
GNI (US$) 53.1 billion (2002 est)
GNI PER CAPITA (PPP) (US$) 20,020 (2002 est)
CONSUMER PRICE INFLATION 1.5% (2003 est)
UNEMPLOYMENT 5.3% (2001)
MAJOR TRADING PARTNERS Australia, USA, Japan, UK
RESOURCES coal, clay, limestone, dolomite, natural gas, hydroelectric power, pumice, iron ore, gold, forests
INDUSTRIES food processing, machinery, textiles and clothing, fisheries, wood and wood products, paper and paper products, metal products; farming, particularly livestock and dairying, cropping, fruit growing, horticulture
EXPORTS meat, dairy products, wool, fish, timber and wood products, fruit and vegetables, aluminium, machinery. Principal market: Australia 19% (2001)
IMPORTS machinery and mechanical appliances, vehicles and aircraft, petroleum, fertilizer, consumer goods. Principal source: Australia 22.2% (2001)
ARABLE LAND 5.8% (2000 est)

AGRICULTURAL PRODUCTS barley, wheat, maize, fodder crops, exotic timber, fruit (kiwi fruit and apples); livestock and dairy farming

Population and society

POPULATION 3,875,000 (2003 est)
POPULATION GROWTH RATE 0.5% (2000–15)
POPULATION DENSITY (per sq km) 14 (2003 est)
URBAN POPULATION (% of total) 86 (2003 est)
AGE DISTRIBUTION (% of total population) 0–14 23%, 15–59 61%, 60+ 16% (2002 est)
ETHNIC GROUPS around 75% of European origin, 15% Maori, 3% Pacific Islander
LANGUAGE English (official), Maori
RELIGION Christian (Anglican 18%, Roman Catholic 14%, Presbyterian 13%)
EDUCATION (compulsory years) 11
LITERACY RATE 99% (men); 99% (women) (2003 est)
LABOUR FORCE 8.7% agriculture, 23.2% industry, 68.1% services (2000)
LIFE EXPECTANCY 76 (men); 81 (women) (2000–05)
CHILD MORTALITY RATE (under 5, per 1,000 live births) 6 (2001)
PHYSICIANS (per 1,000 people) 2.2 (1998)
HOSPITAL BEDS (per 1,000 people) 6.2 (1998 est)
TV SETS (per 1,000 people) 557 (2001 est)
RADIOS (per 1,000 people) 997 (2001 est)
INTERNET USERS (per 10,000 people) 4,843.8 (2002 est)
PERSONAL COMPUTER USERS (per 100 people) 41.4 (2002 est)

See also ▷Maori.

1916: Labour Party of New Zealand established.

1931: Statute of Westminster affirmed equality of status between Britain and dominions, effectively granting independence to New Zealand.

1935–49: Labour governments of Michael Savage and Peter Fraser introduced social reforms and encouraged state intervention in industry.

1936: Liberal Party merged with Reform Party to create National Party.

1939–45: New Zealand troops fought in World War II, notably in Crete, North Africa, and Italy.

1947: Parliament confirmed independence of New Zealand within British Commonwealth.

1951: New Zealand joined Australia and USA in ANZUS Pacific security treaty.

1965–72: New Zealand contingent took part in Vietnam War.

1973: British entry into European Economic Community (EEC) forced New Zealand to seek closer trading relations with Australia.

1985: Non-nuclear military policy led to disagreements with France and USA.

1986: The USA suspended defence obligations to New Zealand after it banned the entry of US warships.

1988: A free-trade agreement was signed with Australia.

1991: The Alliance Party was formed to challenge the two-party system.

1998: The government was ordered to return more than £2 million worth of land confiscated from its Maori owners more than 30 years earlier.

1999: The conservative government was replaced by a centre-left coalition of the Labour Party and New Zealand Alliance, with Helen Clark, leader of the Labour Party, as the new prime minister.

2000: Dame Silvia Cartwright was named as next governor-general, and took office in April 2001, making all top political offices held by women.

1642: Dutch explorer Abel Tasman reached New Zealand but indigenous Maori prevented him from going ashore.

1769: English explorer James Cook surveyed coastline of islands.

1773 and 1777: Cook again explored coast.

1815: First British missionaries arrived in New Zealand.

1826: New Zealand Company founded in London to establish settlement.

1839: New Zealand Company relaunched, after initial failure, by Edward Gibbon Wakefield.

1840: Treaty of Waitangi: Maori accepted British sovereignty; colonization began and large-scale sheep farming developed.

1845–47: Maori revolt against loss of land.

1851: Became separate colony (was originally part of the Australian colony of New South Wales).

1852: Colony procured constitution after dissolution of New Zealand Company; self-government fully implemented in 1856.

1860–72: Second Maori revolt led to concessions, including representation in parliament.

1891: New Zealand took part in Australasian Federal Convention in Sydney but rejected the idea of joining the Australian Commonwealth.

1893: Became the first country to give women the right to vote in parliamentary elections.

1898: Liberal government under Richard Seddon introduced pioneering old-age pension scheme.

1899–1902: Volunteers from New Zealand fought alongside imperial forces in Boer War.

1907: New Zealand achieved dominion status within British Empire.

1912–25: Government of Reform Party, led by William Massey, reflected interests of North Island farmers and strongly supported imperial unity.

1914–18: 130,000 New Zealanders fought for the British Empire in World War I.

NEW ZEALAND The precipitous sides of the dramatic, narrow inlet Milford Sound, which is part of the Fiordland National Park, New Zealand. *Image Bank*

NICHOLAS II The last tsar of Russia, Nicholas II, pictured in July 1917. See entry on p. 680. *Archive Photos*

Nicholas, St (lived 4th century) Also known as **Santa Claus**. In the Christian church, patron saint of Russia, children, merchants, sailors, and pawnbrokers; bishop of Myra (now in Turkey). His legendary gifts of dowries to poor girls led to the custom of giving gifts to children on the eve of his feast day, 6 December, still retained in some countries, such as the Netherlands; elsewhere the custom has been transferred to Christmas Day. His emblem is three balls.

Nicholson, Ben(jamin Lauder) (1894–1982) English abstract artist. After early experiments influenced by ▷cubism and the Dutch ▷De Stijl group, Nicholson developed an elegant style of geometrical reliefs, notably a series of white reliefs (1933–38). He won the first Guggenheim Award in 1957.

Nicholson, Jack (1937–) US film actor and director. Films in which he has appeared include *One Flew Over the Cuckoo's Nest* (Academy Award, 1975), *The Shining* (1979), *Terms of Endearment* (Academy Award, 1983), *Batman* (1989), and *About Schmidt* (2002). In 1994 Nicholson received the American Film Institute's life achievement award. He was presented with an Academy Award for *As Good As It Gets* in 1998, and in the 1999 Golden Globe awards he received the Cecil B DeMille Lifetime Achievement Award.

In the late 1960s, Nicholson captured the mood of nonconformist, uncertain young Americans in such films as *Easy Rider* (1969) and *Five Easy Pieces* (1970). He subsequently became a mainstream Hollywood star, in films ranging from *Chinatown* (1974) to *A Few Good Men* (1992). He has directed several films, including *The Two Jakes* (1990), a sequel to *Chinatown*.

nickel hard, malleable and ductile, silver-white metallic element, symbol Ni, atomic number 28, relative atomic mass 58.71. It occurs in igneous rocks and as a free metal (▷native metal), occasionally occurring in fragments of iron-nickel meteorites. It is a component of the Earth's core, which is held to consist principally of iron with some nickel. It has a high melting point, low electrical and thermal conductivity, and can be magnetized. It does not tarnish and therefore is much used for alloys, electroplating, and for coinage.

It was discovered in 1751 by Swedish mineralogist Axel Cronstedt (1722–1765) and the name given as an abbreviated form of *kopparnickel*, Swedish 'false copper', since the ore in which it is found resembles copper but yields none.

Nicklaus, Jack William (1940–) US golfer, nicknamed 'the Golden Bear' and widely regarded as the game's greatest ever player. He won a record 20 major titles, including 18 professional majors between 1962 and 1986. In 1999, the US magazine *Sports Illustrated* named him 'Best Individual Male Athlete of the 20th Century'. He played his last major championships in 2000 and planned to play on the US Seniors Tour.

Nicobar Islands group of Indian islands, part of the Union Territory of ▷Andaman and Nicobar Islands.

Nicolle, Charles Jules Henri (1866–1936) French bacteriologist who was awarded a Nobel Prize for Physiology or Medicine in 1928 for his work on the role of the body louse in transmitting typhus. In 1909 he discovered that typhus is transmitted by the body louse and delousing was made a compulsory part of the military routine for the armies of World War I.

Nicolson, Harold George (1886–1968) English author and diplomat. His works include biographies – *Lord Carnock* (1930), *Curzon: The Last Phase* (1934), and *King George V* (1952) – and studies such as *Monarchy* (1962), as well as the 'Diaries and Letters' (1930–62) for which he is best known. He married Vita ▷Sackville-West in 1913. He was knighted in 1953.

Nicosia (Greek **Lefkosia**; Turkish **Lefkosha**) capital of Cyprus, with leather, textile, and pottery industries; population (1993) 177,000. Nicosia was the residence of Lusignan kings of Cyprus 1192–1475. The Venetians, who took Cyprus in 1489, surrounded Nicosia with a high wall, which still exists; the city fell to the Turks in 1571. It was again partly taken by the Turks in the invasion in 1974.

nicotine $C_{10}H_{14}N_2$ ▷alkaloid (nitrogenous compound) obtained from the dried leaves of the tobacco plant *Nicotiana tabacum* and used as an insecticide. A colourless oil, soluble in water, it turns brown on exposure to the air.

Nicotine in its pure form is one of the most powerful poisons known. It is the component of cigarette smoke that causes physical addiction. It is named after a 16th-century French diplomat, Jacques Nicot, who introduced tobacco to France.

nicotinic acid (or **niacin**) water-soluble ▷vitamin ($C_5H_5N.COOH$) of the B complex, found in meat, fish, and cereals; it can also be formed in small amounts in the body from the essential ▷amino acid tryptophan. Absence of nicotinic acid from the diet leads to the disease ▷pellagra.

Niebuhr, Reinhold (1892–1971) US Protestant theologian, a Lutheran minister. His *Moral Man and Immoral Society* (1932) attacked depersonalized modern industrial society but denied the possibility of fulfilling religious and political utopian aspirations, a position that came to be known as Christian realism. Niebuhr was a pacifist, activist, and socialist but advocated war to stop totalitarianism in the 1940s.

niello black substance made by melting powdered silver, copper, sulphur, and often borax. It is used as a filling for incised decoration on silver and fixed by the application of heat.

Nielsen, Carl August (1865–1931) Danish composer. His works combine an outward formal strictness with an inner waywardness of tonality and structure, best exemplified by his six programmatic symphonies 1892–1925.

Niemeyer, (Soares Filho) Oscar (1907–) Brazilian architect. He was joint designer of the United Nations headquarters in New York in 1947 and from 1957 architect of many public buildings in the capital, Brasília. His idiosyncratic interpretation of the modernist idiom uses symbolic form to express the function of a building; for example, the Catholic cathedral in Brasília.

Nietzsche, Friedrich Wilhelm (1844–1900) German philosopher who rejected the accepted absolute moral values and the 'slave morality' of Christianity. He argued that 'God is dead' and therefore people were free to create their own values. His ideal was the *Übermensch*, or 'Superman', who would impose his will on the weak and worthless. Nietzsche claimed that knowledge is never objective but always serves some interest or unconscious purpose. His insights into the relation between thought and language were a major influence on philosophy. Although he has been claimed as a precursor by Nazism, many of his views are incompatible with totalitarian ideology. He is a profoundly ambivalent thinker whose philosophy can be appropriated for many purposes. He published *Morgenröte/The Dawn* (1880–81), *Die fröhliche Wissenschaft/The Gay Science* (1881–82), *Also sprach Zarathustra/Thus Spoke Zarathustra* (1883–85), *Jenseits von Gut und Böse/Between Good and Evil* (1885–86), *Zur Genealogie der Moral/Towards a Genealogy of Morals* (1887), and *Ecce Homo* (1888).

Related Web site: Nietzsche, Friedrich http://www.usc.edu/dept/annenberg/thomas/nietzsche.html

Niger see country box.

Niger (Semitic **Nihal**) third-longest river in Africa, 4,185 km/2,600 mi. It rises in the highlands bordering Sierra Leone and Guinea, flows northeast through Mali, then southeast through Niger and Nigeria to an inland delta on the Gulf of Guinea. Its total catchment area is 1.5 million sq km/579,150 sq mi. The flow is sluggish and the river frequently floods its banks. It was explored by the Scot Mungo Park 1795–1806, who was drowned in the river near Bussa.

Niger-Congo languages the largest group of languages in Africa. It includes about 1,000 languages and covers a vast area south of the Sahara desert, from the west coast to the east, and down the east coast as far as South Africa. It is divided into groups and subgroups; the most widely spoken Niger-Congo languages are Swahili (spoken on the east coast), the members of the Bantu group (southern Africa), and Yoruba (Nigeria).

Nigeria see country box.

nightingale songbird belonging to the thrush family; it sings with remarkable beauty by night as well as during the day. About 16.5 cm/6.5 in long, it is dull brown with a reddish-brown rounded tail; the breast is dull greyish-white, tinting to brown. It migrates in summer to Europe and winters in Africa. It feeds on insects, small animals, and occasionally fruit. It has a huge musical repertoire, built from about 900 melodic elements. (Species *Luscinia megarhyncos*, family Muscicapidae.) The female is slightly smaller than the male, but the plumage is very similar. The nest is often built on the ground, made of dry grass and leaves, and four to six olive-green eggs are laid in it. The male's song continues until the young are hatched.

The **thrush nightingale** (*L. luscinia*) of eastern Europe, is a louder but less sweet songster. Both species also sing in their winter ranges in Africa.

The male nightingale arrives in Britain from central Africa in the middle of April, a few days before the female, and settles in woods or copses. Distribution is very local, being confined to the southern and Midland counties, though nightingales are sometimes found in the west. The winter migration begins as early as July, and is completed before the end of August. The nightingale is becoming increasingly rare.

Nightingale, Florence (1820–1910) English nurse, the founder of nursing as a profession. She took a team of nurses to Scutari (now Üsküdar, Turkey) in 1854 and reduced the ▷Crimean War hospital death rate from 42% to 2%. In 1856 she founded the Nightingale School and Home for Nurses in London, attached to St Thomas's Hospital, London. Born in Florence, Italy, she trained in Germany and France. She was the author of the classic *Notes on Nursing* (1860), the first textbook for nurses. In 1907 she was awarded the Order of Merit.

Related Web site: Country Joe McDonald's Florence Nightingale Tribute http://www.dnai.com/~borneo/nightingale/

nightjar any of about 65 species of night-hunting birds. They have wide, bristly mouths for catching flying insects. Their distinctive calls have earned them such names as 'whippoorwill' and 'church-will's-widow'. Some US species are called nighthawks. (Family Caprimulgidae, order Caprimulgiformes.)

Night Journey (or **al-Miraj** (Arabic 'the ascent')) in Islam, the journey of the prophet Muhammad, guided by the archangel Gabriel, from Mecca to Jerusalem, where he met the earlier prophets, including Adam, Moses, and Jesus; he then ascended to paradise, where he experienced the majesty of Allah, and was also shown hell.

> **Reinhold Niebuhr**
> *God grant me the serenity to accept the things I cannot change, courage to change the things I can, and wisdom to know the difference.*
> Attributed to, but never claimed by, Niebuhr; adopted motto of Alcoholics Anonymous

> **Friedrich Nietzsche**
> *In every ascetic morality man worships a part of himself as God and for that he needs to diabolize the other part.*
> Human, All Too Human 137

NIGHTJAR A tropical nightjar shows a gaping and wing-flapping 'injury' display to lead a predator away from its nest on the ground. *K G Preston-Mafham/Premaphotos Wildlife*

Nicaragua

Nicaragua country in Central America, between the Pacific Ocean and the Caribbean Sea, bounded north by Honduras and south by Costa Rica.

NATIONAL NAME *República de Nicaragua/Republic of Nicaragua*
AREA 127,849 sq km/49,362 sq mi
CAPITAL Managua
MAJOR TOWNS/CITIES León, Chinandega, Masaya, Granada, Estelí
MAJOR PORTS Corinto, Puerto Cabezas, El Bluff
PHYSICAL FEATURES narrow Pacific coastal plain separated from broad Atlantic coastal plain by volcanic mountains and lakes Managua and Nicaragua; one of the world's most active earthquake regions

Government

HEAD OF STATE AND GOVERNMENT Enrique Bolaños Geyer from 2002
POLITICAL SYSTEM emergent democracy
POLITICAL EXECUTIVE limited presidency
ADMINISTRATIVE DIVISIONS 15 departments and two autonomous regions
ARMED FORCES 14,000 (2002 est)
CONSCRIPTION military service is voluntary (since 1990)
DEATH PENALTY abolished in 1979
DEFENCE SPEND (% GDP) 1.3 (2002 est)
EDUCATION SPEND (% GDP) 2.4 (1999)
HEALTH SPEND (% GDP) 4.4 (2000 est)

Economy and resources

CURRENCY cordoba
GPD (US$) 2.4 billion (2002 est)
REAL GDP GROWTH (% change on previous year) 3 (2001)
GNI (US$) 2 billion (2002 est)
GNI PER CAPITA (PPP) (US$) 1,970 (2002 est)
CONSUMER PRICE INFLATION 6% (2003 est)
UNEMPLOYMENT 10.7% (2001)
FOREIGN DEBT (US$) 5.98 billion (2001 est)
MAJOR TRADING PARTNERS USA, El Salvador, Mexico, France, Honduras, Japan, Germany, Costa Rica, Venezuela, Guatemala
RESOURCES gold, silver, copper, lead, antimony, zinc, iron, limestone, gypsum, marble, bentonite
INDUSTRIES food products, beverages, petroleum refining, chemicals, metallic products, processed leather, cement
EXPORTS coffee, meat, cotton, sugar, seafood, bananas, chemical products. Principal market: USA 28.2% (2001)
IMPORTS machinery and transport equipment, food and live animals, consumer goods, mineral fuels and lubricants, chemicals, and related products. Principal source: USA 27.4% (2001)
ARABLE LAND 20.2% (2000 est)
AGRICULTURAL PRODUCTS coffee, cotton, sugar cane, bananas, maize, rice, beans, green tobacco; livestock rearing (cattle and pigs); fishing; forest resources

Population and society

POPULATION 5,466,000 (2003 est)
POPULATION GROWTH RATE 2.1% (2000–15)
POPULATION DENSITY (per sq km) 42 (2003 est)
URBAN POPULATION (% of total) 57 (2003 est)
AGE DISTRIBUTION (% of total population) 0–14 42%, 15–59 53%, 60+ 5% (2002 est)

ETHNIC GROUPS about 70% of mixed American Indian and Spanish origin; about 15% European origin; about 9% African; 5% American Indian; mixed American Indian and black origin
LANGUAGE Spanish (official), English, American Indian languages
RELIGION Roman Catholic 95%
EDUCATION (compulsory years) 6
LITERACY RATE 67% (men); 68% (women) (2003 est)
LABOUR FORCE 42% agriculture, 15% industry, 43% services (2000)
LIFE EXPECTANCY 67 (men); 72 (women) (2000–05)
CHILD MORTALITY RATE (under 5, per 1,000 live births) 43 (2001)
PHYSICIANS (per 1,000 people) 0.9 (1998 est)
HOSPITAL BEDS (per 1,000 people) 1.5 (1998 est)
TV SETS (per 1,000 people) 69 (1999)
RADIOS (per 1,000 people) 277 (1998)
INTERNET USERS (per 10,000 people) 167.6 (2002 est)
PERSONAL COMPUTER USERS (per 100 people) 2.8 (2002 est)

See also ▷Contra; ▷Nicaraguan Revolution.

Chronology

10th century: Indians from Mexico and Mesoamerica migrated to Nicaragua's Pacific lowlands.

1522: Visited by Spanish explorer Gil Gonzalez de Avila, who named the area Nicaragua after local Indian chief, Nicarao.

1523–24: Colonized by the Spanish, under Francisco Hernandez de Cordoba, who was attracted by local gold deposits and founded the cities of Granada and León.

17th–18th centuries: Britain was the dominant force on the Caribbean side of Nicaragua, while Spain controlled the Pacific lowlands.

1821: Independence achieved from Spain; Nicaragua was initially part of Mexican Empire.

1823: Became part of United Provinces (Federation) of Central America, also embracing Costa Rica, El Salvador, Guatemala, and Honduras.

1838: Became fully independent when it seceded from the Federation.

1857–93: Ruled by succession of Conservative Party governments.

1860: The British ceded control over the Caribbean ('Mosquito') Coast to Nicaragua.

1893: Liberal Party leader, José Santos Zelaya, deposed the Conservative president and established a dictatorship which lasted until overthrown by US marines in 1909.

1912–25: At the Nicaraguan government's request, with the political situation deteriorating, the USA established military bases and stationed marines.

1927–33: Re-stationed US marines faced opposition from the anti-American guerrilla group led by Augusto César Sandino, who was assassinated in 1934 on the orders of the commander of the US-trained National Guard, Gen Anastasio Somoza Garcia.

1937: Gen Somoza was elected president; start of near-dictatorial rule by the Somoza family, which amassed a huge personal fortune.

1961: Left-wing Sandinista National Liberation Front (FSLN) formed to fight the Somoza regime.

1978: The Nicaraguan Revolution: Pedro Joaquin Chamorro, a popular publisher and leader of the anti-Somoza Democratic Liberation Union (UDEL), was assassinated, sparking a general strike and mass movement in which moderates joined with the FSLN to overthrow the Somoza regime.

1979: The Somoza government was ousted by the FSLN after a military offensive.

1980: A FSLN junta took power in Managua, headed by Daniel Ortega Saavedra; lands held by Somozas were nationalized and farming cooperatives established.

1982: There was subversive activity against the government by right-wing Contra guerrillas, promoted by the USA, attacking from bases in Honduras. A state of emergency was declared.

1984: US troops mined Nicaraguan harbours. The action was condemned by the World Court in 1986 and $17 billion in reparations ordered. FSLN won the assembly elections.

1985: The US president Ronald Reagan denounced the Sandinista government, vowing to 'remove it', and imposed a US trade embargo.

1987: A Central American peace agreement was cosigned by Nicaraguan leaders.

1988: The peace agreement failed. Nicaragua held talks with the Contra rebel leaders. A hurricane left 180,000 people homeless.

1989: Demobilization of rebels and release of former Somozan supporters; the ceasefire ended but the economy was in ruins after the Contra war; there was 60% unemployment.

1990: The FSLN was defeated by right-of-centre National Opposition Union (UNO), a US-backed coalition; Violeta Barrios de Chamorro, widow of the murdered Pedro Joaquin Chamorro, was elected president. There were antigovernment riots.

1992: Around 16,000 people were made homeless by an earthquake.

1994: A peace accord was made with the remaining Contra rebels.

1996: Right-wing candidate Arnoldo Aleman won the presidential elections.

1998: Daniel Ortega was re-elected FSLN leader.

NICARAGUA Farmland adjacent to the town of Jinotega in the north-central highlands, just south of Lake Apanas. This is the main coffee-producing region of Nicaragua, and coffee processing is one of the core industries of the town. In the fertile soil of the valley many other crops are also grown, including tobacco, maize, and beans. *Photodisk*

nightshade any of several plants in the nightshade family. They include the annual herbaceous black nightshade (*S. nigrum*), with white flowers similar to those of the potato plant and black berries; the perennial shrubby bittersweet or woody nightshade (*S. dulcamara*), with purple, potatolike flowers and scarlet berries; and, belonging to a different genus, deadly nightshade or ▷belladonna (*A. belladonna*). (Genera *Solanum* and *Atropa*, family Solanaceae.)

    Related Web site: Nightshade, Woody http://www.botanical.com/botanical/mgmh/n/nighwo06.html

Nihilist member of a group of Russian revolutionaries in the reign of Alexander II 1855–81. Despairing of reform, they saw change as possible only through the destruction of morality, justice, marriage, property, and the idea of God. In 1878 the Nihilists launched a guerrilla campaign leading to the murder of the tsar in 1881.

Nijinksa, Bronislava (1891–1972) Russian choreographer and dancer. Nijinksa was the first major female choreographer to work in classical ballet, creating several dances for Diaghilev's Ballets Russes, including *Les Noces* (1923), a landmark in 20th-century modernist dance. She was the sister of Vaslav ▷Nijinsky, continuing his revolutionary ideas of kinetic movement in dance. Other pieces include *Les Biches* (1924).

Nijinsky, Vaslav Fomich (1890–1950) Russian dancer and choreographer. Noted for his powerful but graceful technique, he was a legendary member of ▷Diaghilev's Ballets Russes, for whom he choreographed Debussy's *Prélude à l'après-midi d'un faune* (1912) and *Jeux* (1913), and Stravinsky's *Le Sacre du printemps/ The Rite of Spring* (1913). Nijinsky also took lead roles in ballets such as *Petrushka* (1911). He rejected conventional forms of classical ballet in favour of free expression. His sister was the choreographer Bronislava Nijinska.

Nile (Semitic *nihal* 'river') river in Africa, the world's longest, 6,695 km/4,160 mi. The **Blue Nile** rises in Lake Tana, Ethiopia, the **White Nile** at Lake Victoria, and they join at Khartoum, Sudan. The river enters the Mediterranean Sea at a vast delta in northern Egypt.

NILE View of the River Nile, with the Cairo Tower and city behind. *Image Bank*

Niger

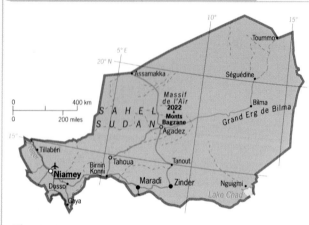

Niger landlocked country in northwest Africa, bounded north by Algeria and Libya, east by Chad, south by Nigeria and Benin, and west by Burkina Faso and Mali.

NATIONAL NAME *République du Niger/Republic of Niger*
AREA 1,186,408 sq km/458,072 sq mi
CAPITAL Niamey
MAJOR TOWNS/CITIES Zinder, Maradi, Tahoua, Agadez, Birnin Konni, Arlit
PHYSICAL FEATURES desert plains between hills in north and savannah in south; River Niger in southwest, Lake Chad in southeast

Government

HEAD OF STATE Mamadou Tandja from 1999
HEAD OF GOVERNMENT Hama Amadou from 2000
POLITICAL SYSTEM military
POLITICAL EXECUTIVE military
ADMINISTRATIVE DIVISIONS seven regions and the municipality of Niamey
ARMED FORCES 5,300; plus paramilitary forces of 5,400 (2002 est)
DEATH PENALTY retains the death penalty for ordinary crimes but can be considered abolitionist in practice; date of last known execution 1976

Economy and resources

CURRENCY franc CFA
GPD (US$) 2.2 billion (2002 est)
REAL GDP GROWTH (% change on previous year) 7.6 (2001)
GNI (US$) 2 billion (2002 est)
GNI PER CAPITA (PPP) (US$) 770 (2002 est)
CONSUMER PRICE INFLATION 0.3% (2003 est)
FOREIGN DEBT (US$) 1.5 billion (2001 est)
MAJOR TRADING PARTNERS France, South Korea, Germany, USA, Côte d'Ivoire, Nigeria
RESOURCES uranium (one of world's leading producers), phosphates, gypsum, coal, cassiterite, tin, salt, gold; deposits of other minerals (including petroleum, iron ore,

copper, lead, diamonds, and tungsten) have been confirmed
INDUSTRIES processing of agricultural products, textiles, furniture, chemicals, brewing, cement
EXPORTS uranium ore, live animals, hides and skins, cow-peas, cotton. Principal market: France 33.5% (2000)
IMPORTS machinery and transport equipment, miscellaneous manufactured articles, cereals and food products, chemicals, refined petroleum products. Principal source: France 18.6% (2000)
ARABLE LAND 3.5% (2000 est)
AGRICULTURAL PRODUCTS millet, maize, sorghum, groundnuts, cassava, sugar cane, sweet potatoes, cotton; livestock rearing (cattle and sheep) is especially important among the nomadic population; agricultural production is dependent upon adequate rainfall

Population and society

POPULATION 11,972,000 (2003 est)
POPULATION GROWTH RATE 2.9% (2000–15)
POPULATION DENSITY (per sq km) 9 (2003 est)
URBAN POPULATION (% of total) 22 (2003 est)
AGE DISTRIBUTION (% of total population) 0–14 50%, 15–59 47%, 60+ 3% (2002 est)
ETHNIC GROUPS two ethnic groups make up over 75% of the population: the Hausa (mainly in central areas and the south), and the Djerma-Songhai (southwest); the other principal ethnic groups are the Fulani, Tuareg, and Beriberi-Manga
LANGUAGE French (official), Hausa (70%), Djerma, other ethnic languages
RELIGION Sunni Muslim 95%; also Christian, and traditional animist beliefs

EDUCATION (compulsory years) 8
LITERACY RATE 26% (men); 10% (women) (2003 est)
LABOUR FORCE 88.5% agriculture, 4.2% industry, 7.3% services (1997 est)
LIFE EXPECTANCY 46 (men); 47 (women) (2000–05)
CHILD MORTALITY RATE (under 5, per 1,000 live births) 265 (2001)
PHYSICIANS (per 1,000 people) 0.04 (1998 est)
HOSPITAL BEDS (per 1,000 people) 0.1 (1998 est)
TV SETS (per 1,000 people) 37 (2001 est)
RADIOS (per 1,000 people) 121 (2001 est)
INTERNET USERS (per 10,000 people) 10.7 (2002 est)
PERSONAL COMPUTER USERS (per 100 people) 0.1 (2002 est)

Chronology

10th–13th centuries: Kanem-Bornu Empire flourished in southeast, near Lake Chad, spreading Islam from the 11th century.
15th century: Tuareg sultanate of Agades dominant in the north.
17th century: Songhai-speaking Djerma established an empire on Niger River.
18th century: Powerful Gobir kingdom founded by Hausa people, who had migrated from the south in the 14th century.
late 18th–early 19th centuries: Visited by European explorers, including the Scottish explorer, Mungo Park; Sultanate of Sokoto formed by Islamic revivalist Fulani, who had defeated the Hausa in a jihad (holy war).
1890s: French conquered the region and ended the local slave trade.
1904: Became part of French West Africa, although Tuareg resistance continued until 1922.
1946: Became French overseas territory, with its own territorial assembly and representation in the French parliament.
1958: Became an autonomous republic within the French community.
1960: Achieved full independence; Hamani Diori of Niger Progressive Party (NPP) elected president, but maintained close ties with France.
1971: Uranium production commenced.
1974: Diori was ousted in an army coup; the military government launched a drive against corruption.
1977: A cooperation agreement was signed with France.

NIGER A Wodaabe girl in traditional dress, in Niger, Africa. *Image Bank*

1984: There was a partial privatization of state firms due to further drought and increased government indebtedness as world uranium prices slumped.
1989: Ali Saibu was elected president without opposition.
1991: Saibu was stripped of executive powers, and a transitional government was formed amid student and industrial unrest.
1992: The transitional government collapsed amid economic problems and ethnic unrest among secessionist Tuareg in the north. A referendum approved of a new multiparty constitution.
1993: The Alliance of the Forces for Change (AFC), a left-of-centre coalition, won an absolute majority in assembly elections. Mahamane Ousmane, a Muslim Hausa, was elected president in the first free presidential election.
1994: A peace agreement was signed with northern Tuareg.
1996: President Ousmane was ousted in a military coup led by Ibrahim Barre Mainassara. Civilian government was restored with Boukary Adji as premier; Mainassara was formally elected president.
1997: Ibrahim Hassane Mayaki was appointed prime minister.
1999: President Mainassara was assassinated in a coup; Major Daouda Mallam Wanke, the commander of Niger's presidential guard, assumed power. In the elections which followed, Tandja Mamadou was elected president, and Hama Amadou was appointed prime minister.

Nile, Battle of the alternative name for the Battle of ▷Aboukir Bay.

Nîmes administrative centre of Gard *département*, in the Languedoc-Roussillon region of southern France, 100 km/62 mi northwest of Marseille; population (1990) 133,600. Its Roman remains include an amphitheatre dating from the 2nd century and the nearby aqueduct known as the Pont du Gard. The city gives its name to the cloth known as denim (*de Nîmes*).

Nineteen Propositions demands presented by the English Parliament to Charles I in 1642. They were designed to limit the powers of the crown, and their rejection represented the beginning of the Civil War.

Nineveh capital of the Assyrian Empire from the 8th century BC until its destruction by the Medes under King Cyaxares in 612 BC. It was situated on the River Tigris (opposite the present city of Mosul, Iraq) and was adorned with palaces.

Ningxia Hui Autonomous Region (or **Ningxia**; formerly **Ninghsia**) administrative area of northwest China, bounded to the north by Inner Mongolia, to the east by Shaanxi, and to the south by Gansu; area 66,400 sq km/25,600 sq mi; population (1996) 5,210,000; one-third are Hui (Chinese Muslims) and there is a large Mongolian population in the north. The capital is ▷Yinchuan. It is a desert plateau, and the Huang He River is in the area. Industries include coal and chemicals, and agricultural products include cereals and rice under irrigation, and animal herding.

niobium soft, grey-white, somewhat ductile and malleable, metallic element, symbol Nb, atomic number 41, relative atomic mass 92.906. It occurs in nature with tantalum, which it resembles in chemical properties. It is used in making stainless steel and other alloys for jet engines and rockets and for making superconductor magnets. Niobium was discovered in 1801 by the English chemist Charles Hatchett (1765–1847), who named it columbium (symbol Cb), a name that is still used in metallurgy. In 1844 it was renamed after Niobe by the German chemist Heinrich Rose (1795–1864) because of its similarity to tantalum (Niobe is the daughter of Tantalus in Greek mythology).

Nippon (or **Nihon**) English transliteration of the Japanese name for ▷Japan.

Nirvana US rock group 1986–94 who popularized a hard-driving, dirty sound, a tuneful ▷grunge, exemplified by their second album, *Nevermind* (1991), and its hit single 'Smells Like Teen Spirit'.

nirvana (Sanskrit 'a blowing out') in Buddhism, and other Indian religions, the ultimate religious goal characterized by the attainment of perfect serenity, compassion, and wisdom by the eradication of all desires. When nirvana is attained, the cycle of life and death, known as transmigration, is broken and a state of liberty, free from pain and desire, is reached.

Nissan Motor Company Japanese car manufacturer founded in 1934. Its production of motor vehicles, initially marketed under the name of Datsun and then as Nissan, was more than 1.5 million in 1988.

nit egg case of the ▷louse, which is glued to the base of the host's hair.

nitrate salt or ester of nitric acid, containing the NO_3^- ion. Nitrates are used in explosives, in the chemical and pharmaceutical industries, in curing meat (see ▷nitre), and as fertilizers. They are the most water-soluble salts known and play a major part in the nitrogen cycle. Nitrates in the soil, whether naturally occurring or from inorganic or organic fertilizers, can be used by plants to make proteins and nucleic acids. However, runoff from fields can result in ▷nitrate pollution.

nitrate pollution the contamination of water by nitrates. Increased use of artificial fertilizers and land cultivation means that higher levels of nitrates are being washed from the soil into rivers, lakes, and aquifers. There they cause an excessive enrichment of the water (▷eutrophication), leading to a rapid growth of algae, which in turn darkens the water and reduces its oxygen content. The water is expensive to purify and many plants and animals die. High levels are now found in drinking water in arable areas. These may be harmful to newborn babies, and it is possible that they contribute to stomach cancer, although the evidence for this is unproven.

nitre (or **saltpetre**) potassium nitrate, KNO_3, a mineral found on and just under the ground in desert regions; used in explosives. Nitre occurs in Bihar, India, Iran, and Cape Province, South Africa. The salt was formerly used for the manufacture of gunpowder, but the supply of nitre for explosives is today largely met by making the salt from nitratine (also called Chile saltpetre, $NaNO_3$). Saltpetre is a ▷preservative and is widely used for curing meats.

NIRVANA Grunge band Nirvana at the MTV Video Music Awards in 1993, receiving the Best Alternative Video Award for 'In Bloom'. *Archive Photos*

nitric acid (or **aqua fortis**) HNO_3 fuming acid obtained by the oxidation of ammonia or the action of sulphuric acid on potassium nitrate. It is a highly corrosive acid, dissolving most metals, and a strong oxidizing agent. It is used in the nitration and esterification of organic substances, and in the making of sulphuric acid, nitrates, explosives, plastics, and dyes.

nitrification process that takes place in soil when bacteria oxidize ammonia, turning it into nitrates. Nitrates can be absorbed by the roots of plants, so this is a vital stage in the ▷nitrogen cycle.

nitrite salt or ester of nitrous acid, containing the nitrite ion (NO_2^-). Nitrites are used as preservatives (for example, to prevent the growth of botulism spores) and as colouring agents in cured meats such as bacon and sausages.

nitrogen (Greek *nitron* 'native soda', sodium or potassium nitrate) colourless, odourless, tasteless, gaseous, nonmetallic element, symbol N, atomic number 7, relative atomic mass 14.0067. It forms almost 80% of the Earth's atmosphere by volume and is a constituent of all plant and animal tissues (in proteins and nucleic acids). Nitrogen is obtained for industrial use by the liquefaction and fractional distillation of air. Its compounds are used in the manufacture of foods, drugs, fertilizers, dyes, and explosives.

Nitrogen has been recognized as a plant nutrient, found in manures and other organic matter, from early times, long before the complex cycle of ▷nitrogen fixation was understood. It was isolated in 1772 by the English chemist Daniel Rutherford (1749–1819) and named in 1790 by the French chemist Jean Chaptal (1756–1832).

Nitrogen is used in the Haber process to make ammonia, NH_3, and to provide an inert atmosphere for certain chemical reactions.

nitrogen cycle the process of nitrogen passing through the ecosystem. Nitrogen, in the form of inorganic compounds (such as nitrates) in the soil, is absorbed by plants and turned into organic compounds (such as proteins) in plant tissue. A proportion of this nitrogen is eaten by ▷herbivores, with some of this in turn being

passed on to the carnivores, which feed on the herbivores. The nitrogen is ultimately returned to the soil as excrement and when organisms die and are converted back to inorganic form by ▷decomposers.

nitrogen fixation the process by which nitrogen in the atmosphere is converted into nitrogenous compounds by the action of micro-organisms, such as cyanobacteria (see ▷blue-green algae) and bacteria. Several chemical processes duplicate nitrogen fixation to produce fertilizers; see ▷nitrogen cycle.

NITROGEN FIXATION Root nodules containing nitrogen-fixing bacteria on the roots of the lupin. *K G Preston-Mafham/Premaphotos Wildlife*

nitrogen oxide any chemical compound that contains only nitrogen and oxygen. All nitrogen oxides are gases. Nitrogen monoxide and nitrogen dioxide contribute to air pollution.

nitroglycerine $C_3H_5(ONO_2)_3$ flammable, explosive oil produced by the action of nitric and sulphuric acids on glycerol. Although poisonous, it is used in cardiac medicine. It explodes with great violence if heated in a confined space and is used in the preparation of dynamite, cordite, and other high explosives.

It was invented by the Italian Ascanio Soberro in 1846, and is unusual among explosives in that it is a liquid. Nitroglycerine is an effective explosive because it has low ▷activation energy, and produces little smoke when burned. However, it was initially so reactive it was virtually unusable. Alfred ▷Nobel's innovation was to purify nitroglycerine (using water, with which it is immiscible, to dissolve the impurities), and thereby make it more stable.

nitrous oxide (or **dinitrogen oxide**) N_2O colourless, nonflammable gas that, used in conjunction with oxygen, reduces sensitivity to pain. In higher doses it is an anaesthetic. Well tolerated, it is often combined with other anaesthetic gases to enable them to be self-administered in lower doses. It may be self-administered; for example, in childbirth. It is a greenhouse gas; about 10% of nitrous oxide released into the atmosphere comes from the manufacture of nylon. It used to be known as 'laughing gas'.

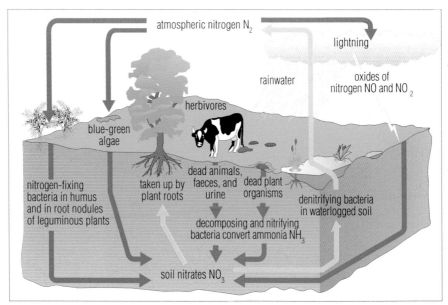

NITROGEN CYCLE The nitrogen cycle is one of a number of cycles during which the chemicals necessary for life are recycled. The carbon, sulphur, and phosphorus cycles are others. Since there is only a limited amount of these chemicals in the Earth and its atmosphere, the chemicals must be continuously recycled if life is to go on.

Nigeria

Nigeria country in west Africa on the Gulf of Guinea, bounded north by Niger, east by Chad and Cameroon, and west by Benin.

NATIONAL NAME *Federal Republic of Nigeria*
AREA 923,773 sq km/356,668 sq mi
CAPITAL Abuja
MAJOR TOWNS/CITIES Ibadan, Lagos, Ogbomosho, Kano, Oshogbo, Ilorin, Abeokuta, Zaria, Port Harcourt
MAJOR PORTS Lagos, Port Harcourt, Warri, Calabar
PHYSICAL FEATURES arid savannah in north; tropical rainforest in south, with mangrove swamps along coast; River Niger forms wide delta; mountains in southeast

Government

HEAD OF STATE AND GOVERNMENT Olusegun Obasanjo from 1999
POLITICAL SYSTEM emergent democracy
POLITICAL EXECUTIVE limited presidency
ADMINISTRATIVE DIVISIONS 36 states and a Federal Capital Territory
ARMED FORCES 78,500 (2002 est)
CONSCRIPTION military service is voluntary
DEATH PENALTY retained and used for ordinary crimes

DEFENCE SPEND (% GDP) 1.2 (2002 est)
EDUCATION SPEND (% GDP) 1.3 (2001 est)
HEALTH SPEND (% GDP) 2.2 (2000 est)

Economy and resources

CURRENCY naira
GPD (US$) 43.5 billion (2002 est)
REAL GDP GROWTH (% change on previous year) 3.8 (2001)
GNI (US$) 38.7 billion (2002 est)
GNI PER CAPITA (PPP) (US$) 780 (2002 est)
CONSUMER PRICE INFLATION 15.3% (2003 est)
UNEMPLOYMENT 4.5% (1997)
FOREIGN DEBT (US$) 18 billion (2001 est)
MAJOR TRADING PARTNERS USA, UK, France, Germany, Spain, India
RESOURCES petroleum, natural gas, coal, tin, iron ore, uranium, limestone, marble, forest
INDUSTRIES food processing, brewing, petroleum refinery, iron and steel, motor vehicles (using imported components), textiles, cigarettes, footwear, pharmaceuticals, pulp and paper, cement

EXPORTS petroleum, cocoa beans, rubber, palm products, cotton and yarn, urea and ammonia, fish and shrimps. Principal market: USA 40.1% (2001)
IMPORTS machinery and transport equipment, basic manufactures, cereals, chemicals, food and live animals. Principal source: UK 9.8% (2001)
ARABLE LAND 31% (2000 est)
AGRICULTURAL PRODUCTS cocoa, groundnuts, oil palm, rubber, rice, maize, taro, yams, cassava, sorghum, millet, plantains; livestock (principally goats, sheep, cattle, and poultry) and fisheries

Population and society

POPULATION 124,009,000 (2003 est)
POPULATION GROWTH RATE 1.9% (2000–15)

POPULATION DENSITY (per sq km) 134 (2003 est)
URBAN POPULATION (% of total) 47 (2003 est)
AGE DISTRIBUTION (% of total population) 0–14 45%, 15–59 50%, 60+ 5% (2002 est)
ETHNIC GROUPS over 250 tribal groups, ten of which account for over 80% of population: the Hausa-Fulani (in the north), Yoruba (in the south) Ibo (in the east), Tiv, Nupe, Kanuri, Ibibio, Ijaw, and Edo
LANGUAGE English, French (both official), Hausa, Ibo, Yoruba
RELIGION Sunni Muslim 50% (in north), Christian 35% (in south), local religions 15%
EDUCATION (compulsory years) 6
LITERACY RATE 75% (men); 60% (women) (2003 est)
LABOUR FORCE 2.9% agriculture, 22.0% industry, 75.1% services (1995)
LIFE EXPECTANCY 51 (men); 52 (women) (2000–05)
CHILD MORTALITY RATE (under 5, per 1,000 live births) 183 (2001)
PHYSICIANS (per 1,000 people) 0.2 (1996 est)
HOSPITAL BEDS (per 1,000 people) 1.8 (1994 est)
TV SETS (per 1,000 people) 68 (2001 est)
RADIOS (per 1,000 people) 224 (1998)
INTERNET USERS (per 10,000 people) 16.7 (2002 est)
PERSONAL COMPUTER USERS (per 100 people) 0.7 (2002 est)

See also ▷Benin; ▷Biafra, Republic of.

Chronology

4th century BC–2nd century AD: Highly organized Nok culture flourished in northern Nigeria.

9th century: Northeast Nigeria became part of empire of Kanem-Bornu, based around Lake Chad.

11th century: Creation of Hausa states, including Kano and Katsina.

13th century: Arab merchants introduced Islam in the north.

15th century: Empire of Benin at its height in south; first contact with European traders.

17th century: Oyo Empire dominant in southwest; development of slave trade in Niger delta.

1804–17: Islamic Fulani (or Sokoto) Empire established in north.

1861: British traders procured Lagos; spread of Christian missionary activity in south.

1884–1904: Britain occupied most of Nigeria by stages.

1914: North and south protectorates united; growth of railway network and trade.

1946: Nigerians allowed a limited role in decision-making in three regional councils.

1951: The introduction of elected representation led to the formation of three regional political parties.

1954: New constitution increased powers of the regions.

1958: Oil discovered in the southeast.

1960: Achieved independence from Britain, within the Commonwealth.

1963: Became a republic, with Nnamdi Azikiwe as president.

1966: Gen Aguiyi-Ironsi of Ibo tribe seized power and imposed unitary government; massacre of Ibo by Hausa in north; Gen Gowon seized power and restored federalism.

1967: Conflict over oil revenues led to secession of eastern region as independent Ibo state of Biafra; ensuing civil war claimed up to a million lives.

1970: Surrender of Biafra and end of civil war; development of the oil industry financed more effective central government.

1975: Gowon ousted in military coup; second coup put Gen Olusegun Obasanjo in power.

1979: Civilian rule restored under President Shehu Shagari.

1983: A bloodless coup was staged by Maj-Gen Muhammadu Buhari.

1985: Buhari was replaced by Maj-Gen Ibrahim Babangida; Islamic northerners were dominant in the regime.

1992: Multiparty elections were won by Babangida's SDP.

1993: Moshood Abiola (SDP) won the first free presidential election; the results were suspended. Gen Sani Abacha restored military rule and dissolved political parties.

1995: Commonwealth membership was suspended in protest at human-rights abuses by the military regime.

1998: General Abdulsalam Abubakar took over as president. Nigeria's most prominent political prisoner, Moshood Abiola, died suddenly on the eve of his expected release. There were moves towards political liberalization, with the formation of new political parties and the release of some dissidents.

1999: The People's Democratic Party won a Senate majority. Olusegun Obasanjo was elected president. Nigeria rejoined the Commonwealth.

2000: Throughout the year, violent clashes between Christians and Muslims accompanied the adoption of Islamic law (sharia) in a number of states throughout Nigeria. Ethnic violence erupted between the militant Yoruba separatists' group Odua People's Congress (OPC) and the Hausas in October. The OPC was outlawed.

NIGERIA A fisherman in traditional dress prepares his nets in Lekki Lagoon. It is usual for such catches to be taken to market in nearby Lagos. *Corel*

Niven, (James) David (Graham) (1910–1983) Scottish-born US film actor. A suave and sophisticated leading man, he made films in Hollywood and Britain from the 1930s, often featuring in witty comedies and war films. His films include *Wuthering Heights* (1939), *Around the World in 80 Days* (1956), *Separate Tables* (1958, Academy Award), *The Guns of Navarone* (1961), and *The Pink Panther* (1964).

Nixon, Richard M(ilhous) (1913–1994) 37th president of the USA 1969–74, a Republican. He attracted attention as a member of the ▷House Un-American Activities Committee in 1948, and was vice-president to Eisenhower 1953–61. As president he was responsible for US withdrawal from Vietnam, and the normalization of relations with communist China, but at home his culpability in the cover-up of the ▷Watergate scandal and the existence of a 'slush fund' for political machinations during his re-election campaign of 1972 led him to resign in 1974 when threatened with ▷impeachment.

Political career Nixon, a Californian, entered Congress in 1947, and rose to prominence during the McCarthyite era of the 1950s. As a member of the Un-American Activities Committee, he pressed for the investigation of Alger ▷Hiss, accused of being a spy. Nixon was senator for California from 1951 until elected vice-president. He played a more extensive role in government than previous vice-presidents, in part because of the poor health of President Dwight D Eisenhower. He narrowly lost the 1960 presidential election to J F Kennedy, partly because televised electoral debates put him at a disadvantage.

Presidency He did not seek presidential nomination in 1964, but in a 'law and order' campaign defeated vice-president Hubert Humphrey in 1968. Facing a Democratic Congress, Nixon sought to extricate the USA from the war in Vietnam. He formulated the Nixon Doctrine in 1969, abandoning close involvement with Asian countries, but escalated the war in Cambodia by massive bombing, although the USA was not officially at war with neutral Cambodia.

Resignation Nixon was re-elected in 1972 in a landslide victory over George McGovern, and immediately faced allegations of irregularities and illegalities conducted on his behalf in his re-election campaign and within the White House. Despite his success in extricating the USA from Vietnam, congressional and judicial investigations, along with press exposures of the Watergate affair, undermined public support. He resigned in 1974, the first and only US president to do so, under threat of impeachment on three counts: obstruction of the administration of justice in the investigation of Watergate; violation of constitutional rights of citizens – for example, attempting to use the Internal Revenue Service, Federal Bureau of Investigation, and Central Intelligence Agency as weapons against political opponents; and failure to produce 'papers and things' as ordered by the Judiciary Committee.

He was granted a pardon in 1974 by President Ford and turned to lecturing and writing.

Related Web site: Richard Nixon Library and Birthplace Foundation
http://www.nixonfoundation.org/

Nizhniy Novgorod (formerly **Gorky** (1932–90)) city and river port in the central Russian Federation, 375 km/233 mi east of Moscow; population (1990) 1,443,000. The city is situated at the confluence of the ▷Volga and Oka rivers, and is a major transportation centre; six railway lines converge here, and large quantities of freight and passengers are carried by river traffic. Motor vehicles, locomotives, aircraft, and ships are manufactured here, making its transport industry the largest in the Russian Federation. There are also diesel motor and machine-tool works, oil processing, glass, woodworking, and various light and food industries. An International Trade Fair is held annually in Nizhniy Novgorod.

NJ abbreviation for ▷New Jersey, a state of the USA.

Nkomati Accord nonaggression treaty between South Africa and Mozambique concluded in 1984, under which they agreed not to give material aid to opposition movements in each other's countries, which in effect meant that South Africa pledged itself not to support the Mozambique National Resistance (Renamo), while Mozambique was committed not to help the then outlawed African National Congress (ANC).

Nkomo, Joshua (1917–1999) Zimbabwean trade unionist and politician, vice president 1990–99. As president of ZAPU (Zimbabwe African People's Union) from 1961, he was a leader of the black nationalist movement against the white Rhodesian regime. He was a member of Robert ▷Mugabe's cabinet 1980–82 and from 1987.

After completing his education in South Africa, Joshua Nkomo became a welfare officer on Rhodesian Railways and later organizing secretary of the Rhodesian African Railway Workers' Union. He entered politics in 1950, and was president of the African National Congress (ANC) in southern Rhodesia 1957–59. In 1961 he created ZAPU, of which he was president.

Arrested along with other black African politicians, he was kept in detention 1963–74. After his release he joined forces with Robert Mugabe as a joint leader of the Patriotic Front in 1976, opposing the white-dominated regime of Ian Smith. Nkomo took part in the Lancaster House Conference, which led to Rhodesia's independence as the new state of Zimbabwe, and became a cabinet minister and vice president.

Nkrumah, Kwame (1909–1972) Ghanaian nationalist politician, prime minister of the Gold Coast (Ghana's former name) 1952–57 and of newly independent Ghana 1957–60. He became Ghana's first president in 1960 but was overthrown in a coup in 1966. His policy of 'African socialism' led to links with the communist bloc.

Originally a teacher, he studied later in both the UK and the USA, and on returning to Africa formed the Convention People's Party (CPP) in 1949 with the aim of immediate self-government. He was imprisoned in 1950 for inciting illegal strikes, but was released the same year. As president he established an authoritarian regime and made Ghana a one-party (CPP) state in 1964. He then dropped his stance of nonalignment and drew closer to the USSR and other communist countries. Deposed from the presidency while on a visit to Beijing (Peking) in 1966, he remained in exile in Guinea, where he was made a co-head of state until his death, but was posthumously 'rehabilitated' in 1973.

NM abbreviation for ▷New Mexico, a state of the USA.

Nō (or **Noh**) classical, aristocratic Japanese drama which developed from the 14th to the 16th centuries and is still performed. There is a repertoire of some 250 pieces, of which five, one from each of the several classes devoted to different subjects, may be put on in a performance lasting a whole day. Dance, mime, music, and chanting develop the mythical or historical themes. All the actors are men, some of whom wear masks and elaborate costumes; scenery is limited. Nō influenced kabuki drama.

Related Web site: Background to Noh-Kyogen
http://www.iijnet.or.jp/NOH-KYOGEN/english/english.html

RICHARD NIXON Richard Nixon announcing his resignation in 1974. *Archive Photos*

Noah in the Old Testament, the son of Lamech and father of Shem, Ham, and Japheth, who, according to God's instructions, built a ship, the ark, so that he and his family and specimens of all existing animals might survive the ▷Flood. There is also a Babylonian version of the tale, the *Epic of* ▷*Gilgamesh*.

Related Web site: Noah
http://www.newadvent.org/cathen/11088a.htm

Nobel, Alfred Bernhard (1833–1896) Swedish chemist and engineer. He invented ▷dynamite in 1867, gelignite in 1875, and ballistite, a smokeless gunpowder, in 1887. Having amassed a large fortune from the manufacture of explosives and the exploitation of the Baku oilfields in Azerbaijan, near the Caspian Sea, he left this in trust for the endowment of five ▷Nobel prizes.

Related Web site: Alfred Nobel – His Life and Work http://www.nobel.se/nobel/alfred-nobel/biographical/life-work/index.html

nobelium synthesized, radioactive, metallic element of the ▷actinide series, symbol No, atomic number 102, relative atomic mass 259. It is synthesized by bombarding curium with carbon nuclei. It was named in 1957 after the Nobel Institute in Stockholm, Sweden, where it was claimed to have been first synthesized. Later evaluations determined that this was in fact not so, as the successful 1958 synthesis at the University of California at Berkeley produced a different set of data. The name was not, however, challenged. In 1992 the International Unions for Pure and Applied Chemistry and Physics (IUPAC and IUPAP) gave credit to Russian scientists in Dubna for the discovery of nobelium.

Nobel prize annual international prize, first awarded in 1901 under the will of Alfred Nobel, Swedish chemist, who invented dynamite. The interest on the Nobel endowment fund is divided annually among the persons who have made the greatest contributions in the fields of physics, chemistry, medicine, literature, and world peace. The first four are awarded by academic committees based in Sweden, while the peace prize is awarded by a committee of the Norwegian parliament. A sixth prize, for economics, financed by the Swedish National Bank, was first awarded in 1969. The prizes have a large cash award and are given to organizations – such as the United Nations peacekeeping forces, which received the Nobel Peace Prize in 1988 – as well as individuals.

Related Web site: Nobel Prize Internet Archive
http://www.nobelprizes.com/

noble gas alternative name for ▷inert gas.

nocturne in music, a reflective character piece, often for piano, introduced by John Field (1782–1837) and adopted by Frédéric ▷Chopin.

node in physics, a position in a ▷standing wave pattern at which there is no vibration. Points at which there is maximum vibration are called **antinodes**. Stretched strings, for example, can show nodes when they vibrate. Guitarists can produce special effects (▷harmonics) by touching a sounding string lightly to produce a node.

nodule in geology, a lump of mineral or other matter found within rocks or formed on the seabed surface; ▷mining technology is being developed to exploit them.

Nofretete alternative name for ▷Nefertiti, queen of Egypt.

noise in pop music, a style that relies heavily on feedback, distortion, and dissonance. A loose term that came into use in the 1980s with the slogan 'noise annoys', it has been applied to hardcore punk, ▷grunge, and ▷industrial music, among others.

noise unwanted sound. Permanent, incurable loss of hearing can be caused by prolonged exposure to high noise levels (above 85 decibels). Over 55 decibels on a daily outdoor basis is regarded as an unacceptable level. In scientific and engineering terms, a noise is any random, unpredictable signal.

Nolan, Sidney Robert (1917–1992) Australian artist. Largely self-taught, he created atmospheric paintings of the outback, exploring themes from Australian history such as the life of the outlaw Ned Kelly. His work, along with that of ▷Drysdale and others, marked the beginning of modernism in Australian art. He was knighted in 1981.

Noland, Kenneth Clifton (1927–) US painter. He is associated with the colour-stain painters Helen ▷Frankenthaler and Morris Louis. In the 1950s and early 1960s he painted targets, or concentric circles of colour, in a clean, hard-edged style on unprimed canvas. His work centred on geometry, colour, and symmetry. His paintings of the 1960s experimented with the manipulation of colour vision and afterimages, pioneering the field of ▷op art.

Nolde, Emil (1867–1956) Adopted name of Emil Hansen. German expressionist painter and graphic artist. Nolde studied in Paris and Dachau, joined the group of artists known as *die* ▷*Brücke* 1906–07, and visited Polynesia in 1913; he then became almost a recluse in northeastern Germany.

nomad (Greek *nomas* 'roaming') person whose way of life involves freely moving from place to place according to the state of pasturage or food availability. Nomads believe that land is not an object of property. Nomads fall into two main groups: herders and hunter-gatherers. Those who move from place to place selling their skills or trading are also nomads; for example, the ▷Romany people.

Nomura Securities the world's largest financial institution, an investment house handling about 20% of all transactions on the Tokyo stock exchange. In 1991 Nomura admitted to paying

¥16.5 billion in compensation to favoured clients (including companies in London and Hong Kong) for losses sustained on the stock market since the beginning of 1990, resulting in tax evasion of ¥9 billion. It was also shown to have links with organized crime.

nonaligned movement countries adopting a strategic and political position of neutrality ('nonalignment') towards major powers, specifically the USA and former USSR. The movement emerged in the 1960s during the ▷Cold War between East and West 1949–89. Although originally used by poorer states, the nonaligned position was later adopted by oil-producing nations. Its 113 members hold more than half the world's population and 85% of oil resources, but only 7% of global GDP (1995).

Nonconformist in religion, originally a member of the Puritan section of the Church of England clergy who, in the Elizabethan age, refused to conform to certain practices, for example the wearing of the surplice and kneeling to receive Holy Communion.

noncooperation movement (or satyagraha) in India, a large-scale civil disobedience campaign orchestrated by Mahatma ▷Gandhi in 1920 following the ▷Amritsar Massacre in April 1919. Based on a policy of peaceful non-cooperation, the strategy was to bring the British administrative machine to a halt by the total withdrawal of Indian support. British-made goods were boycotted, as were schools, courts of law, and elective offices. The campaign made little impression on the British government, since they could ignore it when it was peaceful; when it became violent, Gandhi felt obliged to call off further demonstrations. Its most successful aspect was that it increased political awareness among the Indian people.

Nonjuror any of the priests of the Church of England who, after the revolution of 1688, refused to take the oaths of allegiance to William and Mary. They continued to exist as a rival church for over a century, and consecrated their own bishops, the last of whom died in 1805.

nonmetal one of a set of elements (around 20 in total) with certain physical and chemical properties opposite to those of metals. Nonmetals accept electrons (see ▷electronegativity) and are sometimes called electronegative elements.

Their typical reactions are as follows.

With acids and alkalis Nonmetals do not react with dilute acids but may react with alkalis.

$$2NaOH + Cl_2 \rightarrow NaCl + NaOCl + H_2O$$

With air or oxygen They form acidic or neutral oxides.

$$S + O_2 \rightarrow SO_2$$

With chlorine They react with chlorine gas to form covalent chlorides.

$$2P_{(s)} + 3Cl_2 \rightarrow 2PCl_3$$

With reducing agents Nonmetals act as oxidizing agents.

$$2FeCl_2 + Cl_2 \rightarrow 2FeCl_3$$

Nono, Luigi (1924–1990) Italian composer. He wrote attenuated pointillist works such as *Il canto sospeso/Suspended Song* (1955–56) for soloists, chorus, and orchestra, in which influences of Webern and Gabrieli are applied to issues of social conscience. After the opera *Intolleranza/Intolerance* (1960) his style became more richly expressionist, and his causes more overtly polemical.

nonrenewable resource natural resource, such as coal or oil, that takes millions of years to form naturally and can therefore not be replaced once it is consumed. The main energy sources used by humans are nonrenewable; ▷renewable resources, such as solar, tidal, and geothermal power, have so far been less exploited.

nonvolatile memory in computing, ▷memory that does not lose its contents when the power supply to the computer is disconnected.

noradrenaline in the body, a catecholamine that acts directly on specific receptors to stimulate the sympathetic nervous system. Released by nerve stimulation or by drugs, it slows the heart rate mainly by constricting arterioles (small arteries) and so raising blood pressure. It is used therapeutically to treat ▷shock.

Nordenskjöld, Nils Adolf Erik (1832–1901) Swedish explorer. He made voyages to the Arctic with the geologist Torell and in 1878–79 discovered the Northeast Passage. He published the results of his voyages in a series of books, including *Voyage of the Vega round Asia and Europe* (1881).

Nordic ethnic designation for any of the various Germanic peoples, especially those of Scandinavia. The physical type of Caucasoid described under that term is tall, long-headed, blue-eyed, fair of skin and hair. The term is no longer in current scientific use.

Nord-Pas-de-Calais region of northern France; area 12,400 sq km/4,800 sq mi; population (1990) 3,965,100. Its administrative centre is ▷Lille, and it consists of the *départements* of Nord and Pas-de-Calais.

Norfolk county of eastern England.

area 5,360 sq km/2,069 sq mi **towns and cities** ▷Norwich (administrative headquarters), King's Lynn, Great Yarmouth (ports); Cromer, Hunstanton (resorts) **physical** low-lying with the Fens in the west and the ▷Norfolk Broads in the east; rivers Bure, Ouse, Waveney, Yare **features** the Broads (a series of lakes famous for fishing and water fowl, and for boating); Halvergate Marshes wildlife area; traditional reed thatching; Grime's Graves (Neolithic flint mines); shrine of Our Lady of Walsingham, a medieval and present-day centre of pilgrimage; Blickling Hall (Jacobean, built 1619–24, situated 14 km/7 mi south of Cromer); residence of Elizabeth II at Sandringham (built 1869–71) **agriculture** cereals (wheat and barley); fruit and vegetables (beans, sugar beets, swedes, turnips); turkeys, geese, cattle; fishing centred on Great Yarmouth **industries** agricultural implements; boots and shoes; brewing and malting; offshore natural gas; tanning; there are flour mills and mustard works **population** (1996) 777,000 **famous people** Fanny Burney, John Sell Cotman, John Crome ('Old Crome'), Diana, Princess of Wales, Rider Haggard, Horatio Nelson, Thomas Paine

Norfolk Broads area of interlinked shallow freshwater lakes in East Anglia, eastern England, between Norwich, Sea Palling, and Lowestoft. The area has about 200 km/125 mi of navigable waterways, and the region is a popular tourist destination for boating and fishing.

Norfolk terrier breed of dog identical to the ▷Norwich terrier except that the ears drop forward rather than being pricked.

Noriega Morena, Manuel (Antonio) (1940–) Panamanian soldier and politician, effective ruler of Panama from 1983, as head of the National Guard, until deposed by the USA in 1989. An informer for the US Central Intelligence Agency (CIA) from the late 1960s, he was known to be involved in drug trafficking as early as 1972.

He enjoyed US support until 1987. In the December 1989 US invasion of Panama, he was forcibly taken to the USA. He was tried and convicted of cocaine trafficking and money laundering in 1992.

normal distribution curve the bell-shaped curve that results when a normal distribution is represented graphically by plotting the distribution $f(x)$ against x. The curve is symmetrical about the mean value.

Norman any of the descendants of the Norsemen (to whose chief, Rollo, Normandy was granted by Charles III of France in 911) who adopted French language and culture. During the 11th and 12th centuries they conquered England in 1066 (under William the Conqueror), Scotland in 1072, parts of Wales and Ireland, southern Italy, Sicily, and Malta, and took a prominent part in the Crusades.

They introduced feudalism, Latin as the language of government, and Norman French as the language of literature. Church architecture and organization were also influenced by the Normans, although they ceased to exist as a distinct people after the 13th century.

Norman architecture style of architecture used in England in the 11th and 12th centuries, also known as ▷Romanesque. Norman buildings are massive, with round arches (although trefoil arches are sometimes used for small openings). Buttresses are of slight projection, and vaults are barrel-roofed. Examples in England include the Keep of the Tower of London and parts of the cathedrals of Chichester, Gloucester, and Ely.

Norman Conquest invasion and settlement of England by the ▷Normans, following the victory of William (I) the Conqueror at the Battle of ▷Hastings in 1066. The story of the conquest from the Norman point of view is told in the ▷Bayeux Tapestry.

Normandy (French Normandie) former duchy of northwest France now divided into two regions: ▷Haute-Normandie and ▷Basse-Normandie; area 29,900 sq km/11,544 sq mi; population (both parts, 1999 est) 3,202,400. Normandy was named after the Viking Norsemen (Normans) who conquered and settled in the area in the 9th century. As a French duchy it reached its peak under William the Conqueror and was renowned for its centres of learning established by Lanfranc and St Anselm. Normandy was united with England from 1100 to 1135. England and France fought over it during the Hundred Years' War, England finally losing it in 1449 to Charles VII. In World War II the Normandy beaches were the site of the Allied invasion on D-day, 6 June 1944.

Related Web site: Welcome to Normandy http://www.normandy-tourism.org/gb/index.html

Normandy landings alternative name for ▷D-day.

Norman French form of French used by the Normans in Normandy from the 10th century, and by the Norman ruling class in England after the Conquest in 1066. It remained the language of the English court until the 15th century, and the official language of the law courts until the 17th century.

Norris, Frank (Benjamin Franklin) (1870–1902) US novelist. A naturalist writer, he wrote *McTeague* (1899), about a brutish San Francisco dentist and the love of gold (filmed as *Greed* in 1923). He completed only two parts of his projected trilogy, the *Epic of Wheat*: *The Octopus* (1901), dealing with the struggles between wheat farmers, and *The Pit* (1903), describing the Chicago wheat exchange.

Norse early inhabitant of ▷Norway or ▷Scandinavia; also referring to their language and culture.

North, Frederick (1732–1792) 2nd Earl of Guilford; or Lord North. English Tory politician. He entered Parliament in 1754, became chancellor of the Exchequer in 1767, and was prime minister in a government of Tories and 'king's friends' from 1770. His hard line against the American colonies was supported by George III, but in 1782 he was forced to resign by the failure of his policy. In 1783 he returned to office in a coalition with Charles ▷Fox. After its defeat, he retired from politics. He became an earl in 1790.

North, Oliver (1943–) US Marine lieutenant colonel. In 1981 he joined the staff of the National Security Council (NSC), where he supervised the mining of Nicaraguan harbours in 1983, an air-force bombing raid on Libya in 1986, and an arms-for-hostages deal with Iran in 1985, which, when uncovered in 1986 (▷Irangate), forced his dismissal and trial.

North, Thomas (*c.* 1535–*c.* 1601) English translator. His translations include ▷Plutarch's *Lives*, which appeared in 1579 as *Lives of the Noble Grecians and Romans*. ▷Shakespeare drew heavily on this translation for his Roman plays (*Julius Caesar*, *Antony and Cleopatra*, and *Coriolanus*).

North America third largest of the continents (including Greenland and Central America), and over twice the size of Europe.

area 24,000,000 sq km/9,400,000 sq mi **largest cities** (population over 1 million) Mexico City, New York, Chicago, Toronto, Los Angeles, Montréal, Guadalajara, Monterrey, Philadelphia, Houston, Guatemala City, Vancouver, Detroit, San Diego, Dallas **physical** occupying the northern part of the landmass of the Western hemisphere between the Arctic Ocean and the tropical southeast tip of the isthmus that joins Central America to South America; the northernmost point on the mainland is the tip of Boothia Peninsula in the Canadian Arctic; the northernmost point on adjacent islands is Cape Morris Jesup on Greenland; the most westerly point on the mainland is Cape Prince of Wales, Alaska; the most westerly point on adjacent islands is Attu Island in the Aleutians; the most easterly point on the mainland lies on the southeast coast of Labrador; the highest point is Mount McKinley, Alaska, 6,194 m/20,320 ft; the lowest point is Badwater in Death Valley −86 m/−282 ft. Perhaps the most dominating characteristic is the western cordillera running parallel to the coast from Alaska to Panama; it is called the ▷Rocky Mountains in the USA and Canada and its continuation into Mexico is called the ▷Sierra Madre. The cordillera is a series of ranges divided by intermontane plateaus and takes up about one-third of the continental area. To the east of the cordillera lie the Great Plains, the agricultural heartland of North America, which descend in a series of steps to the depressions occupied by the ▷Great Lakes in the east and the Gulf of Mexico coastal lowlands in the southeast. The Plains are characterized by treeless expanses crossed by broad, shallow river valleys. To the north and east of the region lie the Laurentian Highlands of Canada, an ancient plateau or shield area. Glaciation has deeply affected its landscape. In the east are the Appalachian Mountains, flanked by the narrow coastal plain which widens further south. Erosion here has created a line of planed

Norman invasion of England

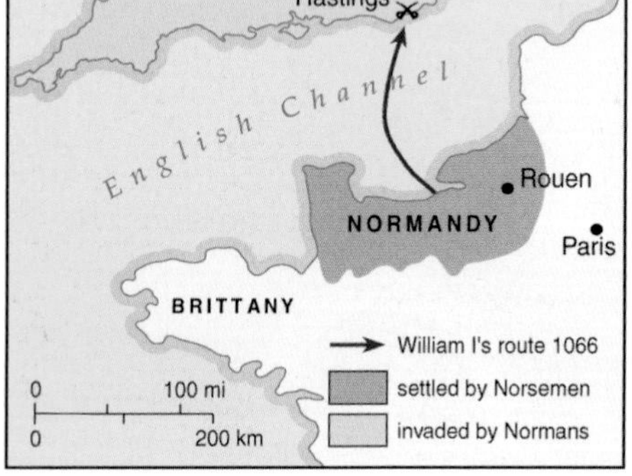
SCOTLAND
North Sea
York
ENGLAND
WALES
London
Hastings
English Channel
Rouen
NORMANDY
Paris
BRITTANY
William I's route 1066
settled by Norsemen
invaded by Normans
0
100 mi
0
200 km

crests, or terraces, at altitudes between 300–1,200 m/985–3,935 ft. This has also formed a ridge-and-valley topography which was an early barrier to continental penetration. The Fall Line is the abrupt junction of plateau and coastal plain in the east. Low plains on the Atlantic coast are indented by the Gulf of St Lawrence, Bay of Fundy, Delaware Bay, and Chesapeake Bay; the St Lawrence and Great Lakes form a rough crescent (with Lake Winnipeg, Lake Athabasca, the Great Bear, and the Great Slave lakes) around the exposed rock of the great Canadian/Laurentian shield, into which Hudson Bay breaks from the north; Greenland (the largest island in the world next to Australia) is a high, ice-covered plateau with a deeply indented coastline of fjords. North America has one of the longest rivers in the world (the Mississippi) and also a drainage system with one of the greatest water capacities (the St Lawrence–Great Lakes). The chief continental divide is the western cordillera and because rivers rising on the east slopes have a long way to go to the sea, it follows that the drainage basins of these large rivers (such as the Mackenzie) are enormous. Whilst the rivers flowing east are the largest, the rivers flowing west (the Colorado, Columbia, and the Frazer), cutting through the western cordillera, are the most spectacular. They are also an important source of hydroelectric power. Lakes also abound, mainly as a result of glaciation. Arctic Canada is covered with the remains of an immense glacial lake (Lake Agassiz) and also the results of ice damming the drainage of water to the open sea, such as the Great Slave and Bear lakes. The ice sheet deepened the basins but the early lakes drained south into the Mississippi–Ohio system, and not until the final retreat of the ice did the lakes seek the lowest outlet east through the St Lawrence **features** Lake Superior (the largest body of fresh water in the world); Grand Canyon on the Colorado River; Redwood National Park, California, has some of the world's tallest trees; San Andreas Fault, California; deserts: Death Valley, Mojave, Sonoran; rivers (over 1,600 km/1,000 mi) include Mississippi, Missouri, Mackenzie, Rio Grande, Yukon, Arkansas, Colorado, Saskatchewan-Bow, Columbia, Red, Peace, Snake **population** (1990 est) 395 million, rising to an estimated 450 million by the year 2000; annual growth rate from 1980 to 1985: Canada 1.08%, USA 0.88%, Mexico 2.59%, Honduras 3.39%; the American Indian, Inuit, and Aleut peoples are now a minority within a population predominantly of European immigrant origin. Many Africans were brought in as part of the slave trade **language** English predominates in Canada, the USA, and Belize; Spanish is the chief language of the countries of Latin America and a sizeable minority in the USA; French is spoken by about 25% of the population of Canada, and by people of the French *département* of St Pierre and Miquelon; indigenous non-European minorities, including the Inuit of Arctic Canada, the Aleuts of Alaska, North American Indians, and the Maya of Central America, have their own languages and dialects **religion** Christian and Jewish religions predominate; 97% of Latin Americans, 47% of Canadians, and 21% of those living in the USA are Roman Catholic **climate** with a north–south length of over 8,000 km/4,970 mi, North America has a wide range of climates, and resultant soil and vegetation zoning. About one-third of the continent has a dry climate, chiefly in the southwest, where the tropical continental air mass and the rainshadow effect of the western cordillera coincide. The Great Plains area can be classed as semi-arid. The larger rivers act as funnels for storms. The Arctic zone includes the Canadian Shield and Alaska and is dominated by polar air masses; only in June–September do temperatures rise above freezing. The cool temperate zone stretches south of this from Newfoundland to Alaska and is dominated by the polar continental air mass bringing long, severe winters. Spring and autumn frosts are hazardous to crops. The warm temperate zone covers the Mississippi lowlands and the southeastern USA and is dominated by the Gulf tropical air mass. Winters are mild and the frost-free season lasts over 200 days. The southwestern USA experiences a Mediterranean-type climate, with dry summers and mild winters **products** with abundant resources and an ever-expanding home market, the USA's fast-growing industrial and technological strength has made it less dependent on exports and a dominant economic power throughout the continent. Canada is the world's leading producer of nickel, zinc, uranium, potash, and linseed, and the world's second-largest producer of asbestos, silver, titanium, gypsum, sulphur, and molybdenum; Mexico is the world's leading producer of silver and the fourth-largest oil producer; the USA is the world's leading producer of salt and the second-largest producer of oil and cotton; nearly 30% of the world's beef and veal is produced in North America.

North American Free Trade Agreement (NAFTA) trade agreement between the USA, Canada, and Mexico, agreed in August 1992 and effective from January 1994. The first trade pact of its kind to link two highly-industrialized countries to a developing one, it created a free market of 375 million people, with a total GDP of $6.8 trillion (equivalent to 30% of the world's GDP). Tariffs were to be progressively eliminated over a 10–15 year period and investment into low-wage Mexico by Canada and the USA progressively increased. Chile was invited to join in December 1994.

Northampton market town and administrative headquarters of ▷Northamptonshire, central England, on the River Nene, 108 km/67 mi northwest of London; population (1996 est) 192,400. The major employers are public administration, financial services, and the distribution trade. The manufacture of boots and shoes was historically important, but engineering has taken over as the key industry; other industries include food processing, brewing, and the manufacture of shoe machinery, cosmetics, leather goods, and car accessories.

Northamptonshire county of central England.

area 2,370 sq km/915 sq mi **towns and cities** ▷Northampton (administrative headquarters), Kettering, Corby, Daventry, Wellingborough **physical** rivers Avon, Cherwell, Leam, Nene, Ouse, and Welland **features** Althorp Park, Spencer family home and burial place of Diana, Princess of Wales; Canons Ashby, Tudor house, home of the Drydens for 400 years; churches with broached spires (an octagonal spire on a square tower) **agriculture** cereals (wheat and barley), sugar beet, sheep rearing; cattle rearing, especially in the Nene and Welland valleys, where there is rich pasture **industries** engineering, food processing, printing, shoemaking; Northampton is the centre of the leather trade in England **population** (1996) 604,300 **famous people** Robert Browne, John Dryden, Charles Kingsley, Richard III; the family of George Washington, first president of the USA, originated at Sulgrave Manor

North Atlantic Drift warm ▷ocean current in the North Atlantic Ocean; an extension of the ▷Gulf Stream. It flows east across the Atlantic and has a mellowing effect on the climate of northwestern Europe, particularly the British Isles and Scandinavia.

North Atlantic Treaty Agreement signed on 4 April 1949 by Belgium, Canada, Denmark, France, Iceland, Italy, Luxembourg, the Netherlands, Norway, Portugal, the UK, and the USA, in response to the Soviet blockade of Berlin June 1948–May 1949. They agreed that 'an armed attack against one or more of them in Europe or North America shall be considered an attack against them all'. The ▷North Atlantic Treaty Organization (NATO), which other countries have joined since, is based on this agreement.

North Atlantic Treaty Organization (NATO) Military association of major Western European and North American states set up under the ▷North Atlantic Treaty of 4 April 1949. The original signatories were Belgium, Canada, Denmark, France, Iceland, Italy, Luxembourg, Netherlands, Norway, Portugal, the UK, and the USA. Greece and Turkey were admitted to NATO in 1952, West Germany in 1955, Spain in 1982, and Poland, Hungary, and the Czech Republic in 1999. NATO has been the basis of the defence of the Western world since 1949. During the ▷Cold War (1945–89), NATO stood in opposition to the perceived threat of communist Eastern Europe, led by the USSR and later allied under the military ▷Warsaw Pact (1951–91). Having outlasted the Warsaw Pact, NATO has increasingly redefined itself as an agent of international peace keeping and enforcement.

Institutional structure NATO's chief body is the Council of Foreign Ministers (who have representatives in permanent session). There is an international secretariat in Brussels, Belgium, and also a Military Committee consisting of the Chiefs of Staff. The military headquarters SHAPE (Supreme Headquarters Allied Powers, Europe) is in Chièvres, near Mons, Belgium. In August 1999, George Robertson, then the UK defence secretary, was elected secretary general of NATO, replacing Javier Solana.

Both the Supreme Allied Commanders (Europe and Atlantic) are from the USA, but there is also an Allied Commander, Channel (a British admiral). In 1960 a permanent multinational **Allied Mobile Force** (AMF) was established with headquarters in Heidelberg, Germany, to move immediately to any NATO country under threat of attack. In May 1991, a meeting of NATO defence ministers endorsed the creation of a UK-commanded, 100,000-strong 'rapid-reaction corps' as the core of a new, streamlined military structure, based on mobile, multinational units adaptable to post-Cold War contingencies. The new force was to be used solely inside NATO territory, unless otherwise agreed by all members of the alliance. In 1992 it was agreed that the ▷Organization for Security and Cooperation in Europe (OSCE) would in future authorize all NATO's military responses within Europe.

The Cold War NATO was formed at the start of the Cold War, at a time when the capitalist nations of the West were fearful of the potential for a communist Soviet invasion of Western Europe following the Soviet blockade of Berlin. The Soviet leader Joseph ▷Stalin appeared to harbour expansionist ambitions and to be intent on forcing his rule on to the whole of Europe, not just the eastern portion that the Soviets had conquered in World War II. In response to the establishment of NATO, Stalin set up the Warsaw Pact in 1951 as the defensive alliance of the communist Eastern bloc nations.

Throughout the Cold War NATO had at its disposal the combined military force of all its members, including the nuclear weapons of the USA, the UK, and France. But throughout this time, not a single shot was fired in war. This fact is viewed as a great success by NATO's supporters, as it indicates that NATO acted as a strong deterrent to the perceived ambitions of the USSR in Europe.

NATO has encountered numerous problems since its inception over such issues as the dominant position of the USA, the presence in Europe of US nuclear weapons, burden sharing, and standardization of weapons.

After the Cold War The collapse of communism in eastern Europe from 1989 prompted the most radical review of NATO's policy and defence strategy since its inception in 1949. After the Warsaw Pact was disbanded in 1991, an adjunct to NATO, the **North Atlantic Cooperation Council** (NACC), was established. This included all the former Soviet republics, with the aim of building greater security in Europe.

At the 1994 Brussels summit a 'partnership for peace' (PFP) programme was formally launched, inviting former members of the Warsaw Pact and ex-Soviet republics to take part in a wide range of military cooperation arrangements, including training alongside NATO members and opening up defence plans. Romania was the first to join, followed by Estonia, Lithuania, Poland, and Russia the following year. By 1996 the partnership included 27 countries, comprising the 15 former Soviet republics, Austria, Hungary, the Slovak Republic, Bulgaria, Malta, Albania, the Czech Republic, Macedonia, Finland, and Sweden.

In May 1997, a NATO–Russia security pact, called the Founding Act on Mutual Relations, Cooperation and Security, was signed in Paris by all 16 NATO heads of government and Russian president Yeltsin. The charter gave Russia an assurance that NATO had no intention of siting nuclear weapons or allowing major troop deployments on the territories of new Eastern European member states. It also created a Russian–NATO advisory council, which, however, would have no veto over NATO actions.

In July 1997, Poland, Hungary, and the Czech Republic, who were former members of the Warsaw Pact, were invited to join the alliance, which they did at the Madrid summit in March 1999. The decision meant NATO's territory expanded by 14%.

The Balkans NATO engaged in its first major combat action in August–September 1995 in Bosnia-Herzegovina. In December, a 60,000-strong, NATO-led 'International Implementation Force' was sent to police the Dayton peace settlement. The USA supplied one-third of the troops for the mission, termed 'Joint Endeavour'. In June 1999, NATO mounted the biggest military operation in Europe since World War II, when its forces took over the Serbian province of Kosovo to keep the peace in the region.

Related Web site: NATO http://www.nato.int/

North Ayrshire unitary authority in western Scotland, created in 1996 from Cunninghame district in Strathclyde region.

area 889 sq km/343 sq mi **towns** Irvine (administrative headquarters), Kilwinning, Saltcoats, Largs, Kilbirnie **physical** low-lying coastal plain on the mainland, rising inland to a plateau of over 305 m/1,000 ft; the islands of the Firth of Clyde are Arran,

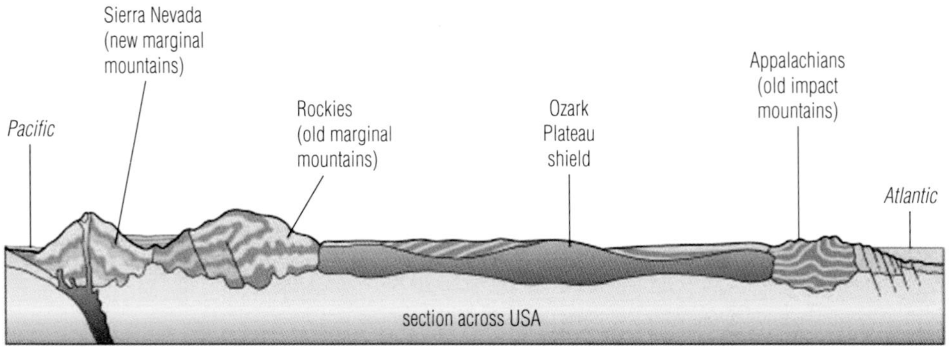

NORTH AMERICA The North American continent is growing in the west as a result of collision with the Pacific plate. On the east of the wide area of the Ozark Plateau shield lie the Appalachian Mountains, showing where the continent once collided with another continent. The eastern coastal rifting formed when the continents broke apart. On the western edge, new impact mountains have formed.

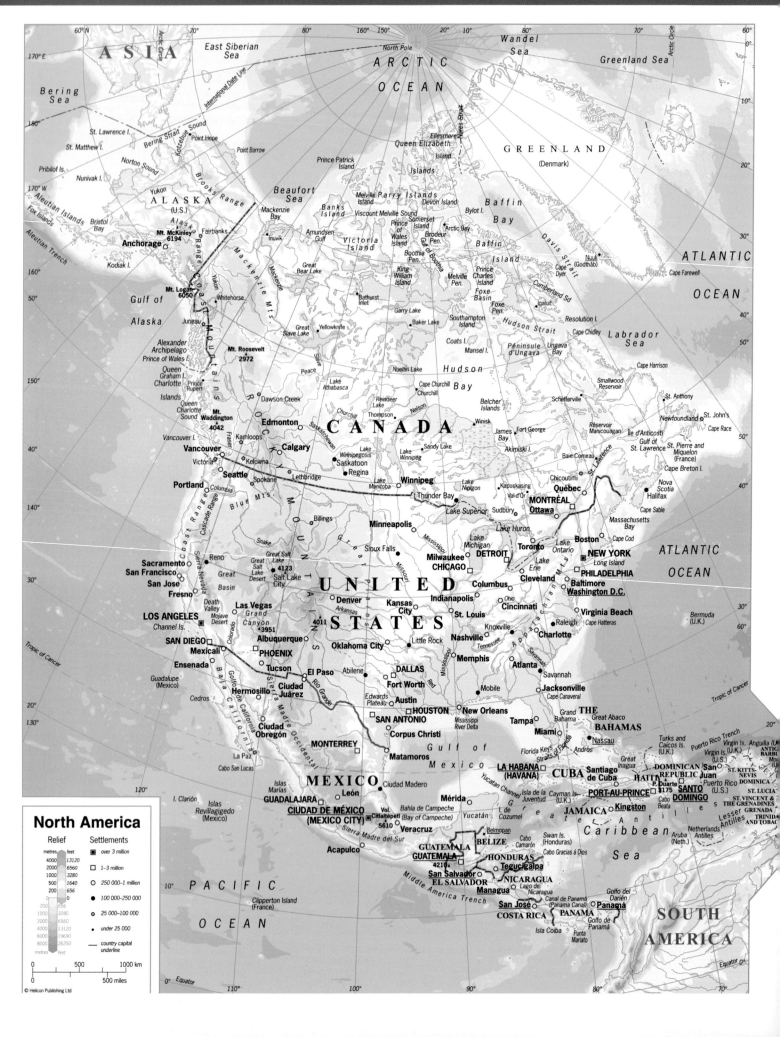

North America

Relief

metres	feet
4000	13120
2000	6560
1000	3280
500	1640
200	656
0	0
200	656
1000	3280
2000	6560
4000	13120
6000	19690
8000	26250
metres	feet

Settlements

- ◼ over 3 million
- ☐ 1–3 million
- ○ 250 000–1 million
- ● 100 000–250 000
- ◉ 25 000–100 000
- • under 25 000
- ── country capital underline

0 500 1000 km
0 500 miles

© Helicon Publishing Ltd

Holy Isle, Cumbraes; the rivers Irvine and Garnock reach the sea at Irvine; Goat Fell (874 m/2,867 ft) **features** Pencil Monument, Largs; Scottish Maritime Museum, Irvine; Hunterston nuclear power station **industries** chemicals, electronics, computer manufacturing **agriculture** dairying, potatoes **population** (1996) 139,200 **history** Eglinton Tournament (19th century); Battle of Largs (1263), when the Scots captured the Hebrides from the Norwegians

North Brabant (Dutch **Noord Brabant**) largest province of the Netherlands, located in the south of the country, lying between the Maas River (Meuse) and Belgium; area 4,940 sq km/1,907 sq mi; population (1997) 2,304,100. The capital is ▷'s-Hertogenbosch. Industries include brewing, tobacco, engineering, microelectronics, and textiles. There is cattle farming, and wheat and sugar beet are grown.

North Cape (Norwegian **Nordkapp**) cape in the Norwegian county of Finnmark; the most northerly point of Europe.

North Carolina state in eastern USA. It is nicknamed the Tar Heel State or Old North State. North Carolina ratified the US Constitution in 1789, becoming the 12th state to join the Union. It is bordered to the north by Virginia, to the west and northwest by Tennessee, to the south by Georgia and South Carolina, and to the east by the Atlantic Ocean.

population (1995) 7,195,100 **area** 136,400 sq km/52,650 sq mi **capital** Raleigh **towns and cities** Charlotte, Greensboro, Winston-Salem, Durham **industries and products** tobacco, corn, soya beans, livestock, poultry, textiles, clothing, cigarettes, furniture, chemicals, machinery, tourism, finance sector, research

Related Web site: North Carolina Encyclopedia http://statelibrary.dcr.state.nc.us/NC/COVER.HTM

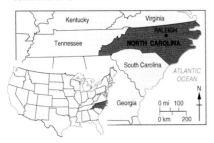

Northcliffe Alfred Charles William Harmsworth, 1st Viscount Northcliffe (1865–1922) British newspaper proprietor, born in Dublin. Founding the *Daily Mail* in 1896, he revolutionized popular journalism, and with the *Daily Mirror* in 1903 originated the picture paper. In 1908 he also obtained control of *The Times*.

Northd abbreviation for ▷Northumberland, an English county.

North Dakota state in the northern USA. It is nicknamed the Peace Garden State. North Dakota was admitted to the Union in 1889 as the 39th US state. Part of the Midwest, and one of the Great Plains states, it is bordered to the south by South Dakota, to the west by Montana, to the north by the Canadian states of Saskatchewan and Manitoba, and to the east by Minnesota. North Dakota remains the most rural of all the US states.

population (1995) 641,400 **area** 183,100 sq km/70,677 sq mi **capital** Bismarck **towns and cities** Fargo, Grand Forks, Minot **industries and products** cereals, meat products, farm equipment, oil, coal, tourism

North-East India (or **North-East Hill States**) area of India (Meghalaya, Assam, Mizoram, Tripura, Manipur, Nagaland, and Arunachal Pradesh) linked with the rest of India only by a narrow corridor, and bounded by Myanmar (Burma), China, Bhutan, and Bangladesh. There is opposition to immigration from Bangladesh and the rest of India, and demand for secession.

North East Lincolnshire unitary authority in eastern England created in 1996 from part of the former county of Humberside.

area 192 sq km/74 sq mi **towns and cities** ▷Grimsby (administrative headquarters), Immingham, Cleethorpes, Humberston, New Waltham, Waltham, Healing, Laceby **features** Humber Estuary forms east border of authority; River Freshney; Immingham Museum; National Fishing Heritage Centre (Grimsby)

industries fishing and associated industries, docks and shipping services at Immingham and Grimsby, chemical manufacture, heavy engineering, marine engineering, oil refining, tourism (Cleethorpes) **population** (1996) 164,000

Northeast Passage sea route from the North Atlantic, around Asia, to the North Pacific, pioneered by the Swedish explorer Nils ▷Nordenskjöld 1878–79 and developed by the USSR in settling Northern Siberia from 1935.

Northern Cape province of the Republic of South Africa from 1994, formerly part of Cape Province; area 363,389 sq km/140,305 sq mi; population (1995 est) 742,000. The capital is ▷Kimberley. Diamonds are mined in the province.

Northern Ireland constituent part of the United Kingdom. See also Northern Ireland: Key Events from 1967 on p. 692.

area 13,460 sq km/5,196 sq mi **capital** Belfast **towns and cities** Londonderry, Enniskillen, Omagh, Newry, Armagh, Coleraine **features** Mourne Mountains; Belfast Lough and Lough Neagh; Giant's Causeway; comprises the six counties (Antrim, Armagh, Down, Fermanagh, Londonderry, and Tyrone) that form part of Ireland's northernmost province of Ulster **exports** engineering, shipbuilding, textile machinery, aircraft components; linen and synthetic textiles; processed foods, especially dairy and poultry products; rubber products, chemicals **currency** pound sterling **population** (2001 est) 1,727,900 **language** English; 5.3% Irish-speaking **religion** Protestant 51%, Roman Catholic 38% **government** direct rule from the UK from 1972 to devolution in 1998. Northern Ireland is entitled to send 18 members to the Westminster Parliament. Local government: 26 district councils. Under the terms of the 1998 Good Friday agreement, Northern Ireland has a 108-member assembly, elected by proportional representation, exercising devolved executive and legislative authority in areas including health, social security, education, and agriculture. There are provisions to ensure that all sections of the community participate in the government and that minority rights are protected

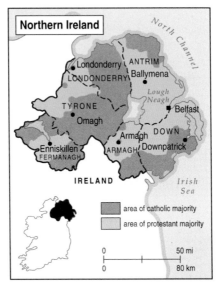

Northern Ireland Assembly in the UK, power-sharing assembly based in Belfast, Northern Ireland, suspended from October 2002. The assembly came into being as a result of the 10 April 1998 Good Friday Peace Agreement between the contending Unionist and Irish Nationalist communities in Northern Ireland. The agreement negotiated the devolution of a range of executive and legislative powers – in areas such as agriculture, economic development, education, the environment, finance, health, and social security – from the secretary of state for Northern Ireland to an elected assembly. The assembly effectively took over much of the work of the Northern Ireland Office, although the post of secretary of state for Northern Ireland remained. Elections were first held on 25 June 1998. The Assembly met for the first time on 1 July 1998, but was not to become fully operational until later in 1999. It was suspended 11 Feb–29 May 2000; 11–12 August and 21 September 2001, and from 14 October 2002.

Related Web site: Northern Ireland Assembly http://www.ni-assembly.gov.uk/index.htm

Northern Mariana Islands archipelago in the northwestern Pacific, with ▷Guam known collectively as the Mariana Islands; area 471 sq km/182 sq mi; population (1995 est) 47,200. The Northern Marianas are a commonwealth in union with the USA. The capital is

Garapan on Saipan. The archipelago consists of 16 islands and atolls extending 560 km/350 mi north of Guam. The main language is English, and the principal religion is Roman Catholicism.

Related Web site: Hafa Adai and Welcome to the Commonwealth of the Northern Mariana Islands http://www.saipan.com/

Northern Province (formerly **Northern Transvaal**) province of the Republic of South Africa from 1994, formerly part of Transvaal; area 119,606 sq km/46,180 sq mi; population (1995 est) 5,397,200. The capital is Pietersburg. Diamonds are mined, and there are copper, asbestos, and iron industries. Tourism is important. Wheat, maize, tobacco, and groundnuts are grown.

Northern Rhodesia former name (to 1964) of ▷Zambia, a country in Africa.

Northern Territory territory of north-central Australia, bounded on the north by the Timor and Arafura seas, on the east by Queensland, on the south by South Australia, and on the west by Western Australia; area 1,346,200 sq km/519,770 sq mi; population (1996) 195,100. The capital is ▷Darwin. The main products are beef, bauxite, gold, copper, uranium, manganese, tropical fruits, and fish. Tourism is important.

Government Northern Territory has an administrator and a Legislative Assembly (25 elected members). It is represented in the federal parliament.

History The area was part of New South Wales from 1827, it was annexed to South Australia in 1863, and was under the control of the Commonwealth of Australia government 1911–78. Self-government was introduced in 1978. Mineral discoveries on land occupied by Aborigines led to a royalty agreement in 1979.

Population distribution Northern Territory is sparsely populated, concentrated in Darwin and, to a lesser extent, Alice Springs. Almost one half of the land belongs to Aboriginal people who constitute more than 25% of the population. Arnhem Land, in the eastern section of the northern peninsula, and Groote Eylandt, in the Gulf of Carpentaria, are Aboriginal reserves.

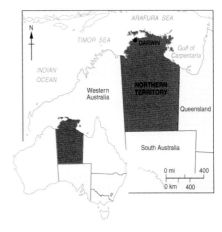

Northern Transvaal former name of ▷Northern Province, a province of the Republic of South Africa.

North Holland (Dutch **Noord Holland**) low-lying coastal province of the Netherlands occupying the peninsula jutting northward between the North Sea and the IJsselmeer, bounded on the south by the provinces of South Holland and Utrecht, and includes the island of Texel to the north; area 2,670 sq km/1,031 sq mi; population (1997) 2,474,800. The capital is ▷Haarlem. There are iron and steel works in the province, and agriculture includes dairying and the growing of flower bulbs, grain, and vegetables.

North Island smaller of the two main islands of ▷New Zealand.

North Korea see country box.

North Lanarkshire unitary authority in central Scotland, created in 1996 from three districts of Strathclyde region.

area 475 sq km/183 sq mi **towns** Airdrie, Coatbridge, Cumbernauld, Motherwell (administrative headquarters) **physical** low-lying, heavily urbanized area; River Clyde **industries** paper, pharmaceuticals, engineering, electronics, light manufacturing, food and drink processing **agriculture** dairying (around urban environment) **population** (1995) 326,700 **history** former industrial region of central Scotland

---

Tony Blair
UK Prime Minister

The entire civilized world will not understand if we cannot put this together and make this work.

On the peace negotiations in Northern Ireland;
Radio 5 Live, 1 July 1999

Northern Ireland: Key Events from 1967

1967	Northern Ireland Civil Rights Association is set up to press for equal treatment for Catholics in the provinces.
1968	Series of civil rights marches spark off rioting and violence, especially in Londonderry.
1969	Election results weaken Terence O'Neil's Unionist government. Further rioting leads to call-up of (Protestant-based) B-Specials to Royal Ulster Constabulary. Chichester-Clark replaces O'Neil. Irish Republican Army (IRA) splits into 'official' and more radical 'provisional' wings. Resumption of IRA activities: urban guerrilla warfare in the north and kidnap and murder in the south. RUC is disarmed and B-Specials is replaced by nonsectarian Ulster Defence Regiment (UDR). British Army is deployed in Belfast and Londonderry.
1971	First British soldier is killed. Brian Faulkner replaces Chichester-Clark. IRA steps up bombing campaign. Internment of people suspected of IRA membership is introduced.
1972	'Bloody Sunday' in Londonderry when British troops fire on demonstrators: 13 killed. Direct rule from Westminster is introduced. Constitution is suspended. IRA extends bombing campaign to mainland England. Seven soldiers are killed in bomb attack in Aldershot.
1973	Sunningdale Agreement, to establish Council of Ireland with representatives from north and south.
1974	'Power sharing' between Protestant and Catholic groups is tried but fails. Bombs in Guildford and Birmingham cause a substantial number of fatalities.
1976	British Ambassador in Dublin, Christopher Ewart Biggs, is assassinated. Ulster Peace Movement is founded by Betty Williams and Mairead Corrigan, later awarded Nobel Prize for Peace.
1979	British MP Airey Neave is assassinated by Irish National Liberation Army (INLA) at the House of Commons. Earl Mountbatten and three others are killed by IRA bomb.
1980	Meeting of British Prime Minister Margaret Thatcher and Irish premier Charles Haughey on a peaceful settlement to the Irish question. Hunger strikes and 'dirty protests' started by Republican prisoners in pursuit of political status.
1981	Hunger strikes by detainees of Maze Prison lead to deaths of Bobby Sands and nine other hunger strikers; Anglo-Irish Intergovernmental Council formed.
1982	Northern Ireland Assembly is created to devolve legislative and executive powers back to the province. Social Democratic Labour Party (19%) and Sinn Fein (10%) boycott the assembly.
1983	Six killed in IRA bomb attack outside Harrods, London.
1984	Series of reports from various groups on the future of the province. IRA bomb at Conservative Party conference in Brighton kills five people. Second Anglo-Irish Intergovernmental Council summit meeting agrees to oppose violence and cooperate on security; Britain rejects ideas of confederation or joint sovereignty.
1985	Meeting of Margaret Thatcher and Irish premier Garrett Fitzgerald at Hillsborough produces Anglo-Irish agreement on the future of Ulster; regarded as a sell-out by Unionists.
1986	Unionist opposition to Anglo-Irish agreement includes protests and strikes. Loyalist violence against police. Unionist MPs boycott Westminster.
1987	IRA bombs British Army base in West Germany. Unionist boycott of Westminster ends. Extradition clauses of Anglo-Irish Agreement are approved in Eire. IRA bombs Remembrance Day service at Enniskillen, killing 11 people – and later admits it to be a 'mistake'.
1988	Three IRA bombers are killed by security forces on Gibraltar.
1989	After serving 14 years in prison, the 'Guildford Four' are released when their convictions are ruled unsound by the Court of Appeal.
1990	Anglo-Irish Agreement is threatened when Eire refuses extraditions. Convictions of 'Birmingham Six' are also called into question and sent to the Court of Appeal. Murder of Ian Gow, MP.
1991	IRA renews bombing campaign on British mainland, targeting a meeting of the cabinet in Downing Street and mainline railway stations. Formal talks on political future of Northern Ireland are initiated by Peter Brooke, Secretary of State for Northern Ireland.
1992	Leaders of four main political parties as well as British and Irish government ministers hold round-table talks for first time in 70 years; they end without agreement. UDA is officially proscribed as an illegal organization. The 3,000th death since 1969 as a result of terrorist activity in Northern Ireland occurs.
1993	May: Northern Ireland Secretary, Sir Patrick Mayhew, denies secret talks with IRA, but it emerges that there has been clandestine contact between the government and Sinn Fein/IRA representatives on a possible end to the conflict. June: Irish president Mary Robinson meets Sinn Fein leader Gerry Adams during visit to Belfast. August: talks begin between John Hulme, leader of SDLP, and Gerry Adams, president of Sinn Fein. December: John Major and the Irish prime minister Albert Reynolds issue joint Anglo-Irish peace proposal for Northern Ireland, the Downing Street Declaration. Gerry Adams calls for 'direct and unconditional talks' between Britain and Ireland and Sinn Fein/IRA.
1994	Total dead now 3,169, with 38,680 injured. There are 18,000 troops in Northern Ireland. IRA announces ceasefire.
1995	February: Framework document forming a basis for peace negotiations is issued. May: Sinn Fein engages in the first public talks with British government officials since 1973.
1996	Deadlock on all-party talks continues over the decommissioning of arms by the IRA. British government-Unionist proposals for elections to select representatives to the talks are opposed by Sinn Fein and SDLP. February: The peace process is disrupted when the ceasefire is broken by an IRA bombing campaign. Firm date given for the start of all-party talks by UK and Irish governments. IRA bombing campaign continues.
1997	July: second IRA ceasefire announced; UK Labour government resumes contact with Sinn Fein.
1998	January: multi-party talks resume at Stormont Castle, Belfast. April: the Northern Ireland Political Talks Document (also known as the Good Friday agreement) is released. May: the Good Friday agreement is accepted in parallel referenda by the people of Northern Ireland and the Republic of Ireland. July: Orangemen protest at the government prohibition on the route of their traditional march at Drumcree. August: the Real IRA explodes a car bomb at Omagh, killing 28; worst terrorist act to date. September: Gerry Adams and David Trimble (Ulster Unionist leader) meet and talk for the first time. October: David Trimble and John Hume (SDLP leader) share Nobel peace prize.
1999	March: dispute over IRA failure to decommission weapons causes postponement of inauguration of the Northern Ireland Executive (the cabinet) of the proposed National Assembly. July: inauguration of the Executive boycotted by Ulster Unionists. November: final cross-party agreement on power-sharing following devolution. December: the Assembly and its Executive begin work.
2000	February: the Assembly and its Executive are suspended by the UK Parliament after failure of IRA still to decommission weapons and consequent threat to resign by First Minister Trimble, but resume operation in May. July: ten days of civil disturbance at Drumcree after Orangemen's march route is again banned. October: IRA offers again to reveal privately to independent authorities exactly what weapons they hold.

North Lincolnshire unitary authority in eastern England created in 1996 from part of the former county of Humberside.
area 850 sq km/328 sq mi   **towns and cities** Scunthorpe (administrative headquarters), Brigg, Barton-upon-Humber, Barrow upon Humber, Epworth   **features** Humber Estuary forms north border; River Trent; Isle of Axholme; Stainforth and Keadby Canal; River Torne; Humber Bridge southern landfall at Barton upon Humber; Julian's Bower (near Alkborough) – medieval maze cut in turf; wetland nature reserves at Barton Waterside and Blackroft Sands; Sandtoft Transport Centre with 60 trolley buses running on own circuit; Old Rectory (Epworth) where John Wesley, founder of Methodism, was born   **industries** steelworks and manufacture of steel products, computer equipment and electronics, food processing (Golden Wonder)   **population** (1996) 153,000   **famous people** Thomas Dunhill, David Hogarth, John Wesley
Related Web site: Welcome to North Lincolnshire http://www.northlincs.gov.uk/

North Ossetia former name for ▷Alania.

North Pole the northern point where an imaginary line penetrates the Earth's surface by the axis about which it revolves; see also ▷pole and ▷Arctic.

North Rhine-Westphalia (German Nordrhein-Westfalen) administrative region (German Land) in northwestern Germany, bounded to the north and northeast by Lower Saxony, on the east by Hesse, on the south by the Rhineland-Palatinate, and on the west by Belgium and the Netherlands; area 34,100 sq km/13,200 sq mi; population (1995) 17,920,000. The capital is ▷Düsseldorf. Industries include iron, steel, coal, lignite, electrical goods, fertilizers, and synthetic textiles. There is dairying, and cereals and vines are grown.

North Sea sea to the east of Britain and bounded by the coasts of Belgium, The Netherlands, Germany, Denmark, and Norway; part of the Atlantic Ocean; area 523,000 sq km/202,000 sq mi; average depth 55 m/180 ft, greatest depth 660 m/2,165 ft. The Dogger Bank extends east to west with shallows of as little as 11 m/36 ft, forming a traditionally well-stocked fishing ground. A deep channel follows the coast of Scandinavia reaching as far as the Skagerrak. In the northeast the North Sea joins the Norwegian Sea, and in the south it meets the Strait of Dover. It has 300 oil platforms, 10,000 km/6,200 mi of gas pipeline (gas was discovered in 1965), and fisheries (especially mackerel and herring).

North Somerset unitary authority in southwest England created in 1996 from part of the former county of Avon.
area 372 sq km/144 sq mi   **towns and cities** Weston-Super-Mare (administrative headquarters), Clevedon, Portishead, Yatton, Congresbury   **features** Severn Estuary forms northwest border of authority; River Yea; River Avon forms northeast border; west end of the Mendips including Bleadon Hill (134 m/440 ft); Clevedon Court – 14th/15th century manor house owned by Elton family; Weston Woods and Worlebury Hill iron age sites (Weston-Super-Mare); International Helicopter Museum (Weston-Super-Mare)   **industries** automotive components, rubber and plastics manufacture   **population** (1996) 177,000   **famous people** Hartley Coleridge, Portishead

North–South divide geographical division of the world that theoretically demarcates the rich from the poor. The South includes all of Asia except Japan, Australia, New Zealand, Brunei, and the South East Asian 'dragons' of Hong Kong, South Korea, Malaysia, Singapore, Taiwan, and Thailand; all of Africa; the Middle East, except the oil-rich UAE, Qatar, Saudi Arabia, and Bahrain; and Central and South America. The North includes Europe; the USA, except Bermuda and the Bahamas; Canada; and the European republics of the former Soviet Union. Newly industrialized countries such as South Korea and Taiwan now have more in common with the industrialized North and fast-developing Argentina, Mexico, Brazil, Peru, and Chile than with ▷Third World countries.

Northumberland county of northern England.
area 5,030 sq km/1,942 sq mi   **towns and cities** Morpeth (administrative headquarters), Berwick-upon-Tweed, Hexham   **physical** Cheviot Hills; rivers Aln, Coquet, Rede, Till, Tweed, upper Tyne; Northumberland National Park in the west   **features** Holy Island (Lindisfarne); the Farne island group 8 km/5 mi east of Bamburgh, home to seal and bird colonies; part of Hadrian's Wall (a World Heritage site), including Housesteads Fort; Alnwick and Bamburgh castles; Thomas Bewick museum; Hexham Abbey; the walls of Berwick-upon-Tweed; large moorland areas used for military manoeuvres; Longstone Lighthouse from which Grace Darling rowed to rescue the crew of the Forfarshire; wild white cattle of Chillingham; Kielder Water (1982), the largest artificial lake in northern Europe   **agriculture** sheep, cattle; fishing   **industries** manufacturing of computer monitors (Cramlington); coal was formerly mined at several locations   **population** (1996) 307,400   **famous people** Thomas Bewick, Jack and Bobby Charlton, Grace Darling

Northumberland, John Dudley, Duke of (c. 1502–1553) English politician. He was chief minister from 1551 until ▷Edward VI's death in 1553. He tried to place his daughter-in-law Lady Jane ▷Grey on the throne, and was executed on ▷Mary I's accession.

Northumbria Anglo-Saxon kingdom that covered northeast England and southeast Scotland. Comprising the 6th-century kingdoms of Bernicia (Forth–Tees) and Deira (Tees–Humber), united in the 7th century, it accepted the supremacy of Wessex in 827 and was conquered by the Danes in the late 9th century. It was not until the reign of William the Conqueror that Northumbria became an integral part of England. Influenced by Irish missionaries, it was a cultural and religious centre until the 8th century with priests such as Bede, Cuthbert, and Wilfrid.

North West province of the Republic of South Africa from 1994; area 118,710 sq km/45,834 sq mi; population (1995 est) 3,351,800. The capital is ▷Mmabatho. There are platinum, chrome, and iron industries; groundnuts are grown.

North-West Frontier Province province of Pakistan; capital ▷Peshawar; area 74,500 sq km/28,800 sq mi; population (1993 est) 20,090,000. It was a province of British India 1901–47. It includes the strategic Khyber Pass, the site of constant struggle between the British Raj and the ▷Pathan warriors. In the 1980s it had to accommodate a stream of refugees from neighbouring Afghanistan.

Northwest Ordinances US Congressional legislation 1784–87 setting out procedures for the sale and settlement of lands still occupied by American Indians. The land, between the Great Lakes and the Mississippi and Ohio rivers, was to be formed into townships and sold at minimum $1 per acre. The sales revenue was the first significant source of income for the new federal government.

Northwest Passage Atlantic–Pacific sea route around the north of Canada. Canada, which owns offshore islands, claims it as an internal waterway; the USA insists that it is an international waterway and sent an icebreaker through without permission in 1985.

Northwest rebellion revolt against the Canadian government March–May 1885 by the métis (people of mixed French Canadian and American Indian descent). Led by their political leader Louis Riel and his military lieutenant Gabriel Dumont (1838–1906), the métis population of what is now Saskatchewan rebelled after a number of economic and political grievances were ignored by the government.

Northwest Territories large administrative area of Canada, extending into the ▷Arctic Circle. Covering one-eighth of the total area of the country, it comprises the mainland lying north of the 60th parallel (latitude 60° north) and some islands between the Canadian mainland and the North Pole. It is bounded by Yukon Territory to the west, Nunavut to the east, the Beaufort Sea and the Arctic Ocean to the north, and the provinces of British Columbia, Alberta, and Saskatchewan to the south; area 1,299,070 sq km/ 501,441 sq mi; population (1997 est) 40,300 (with substantial numbers of indigenous peoples: Inuvialuit, Slavey, Dene, Métis, Inuit). The capital is ▷Yellowknife. Industries include oil and natural gas extraction and mining of zinc, lead, and gold; other activities are fur-trapping and fishing.

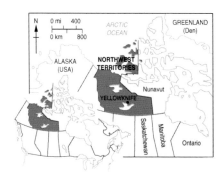

North Korea

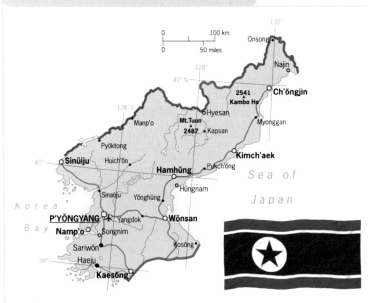

North Korea country in East Asia, bounded northeast by Russia, north and northwest by China, east by the Sea of Japan, south by South Korea, and west by the Yellow Sea.

NATIONAL NAME *Chosun Minchu-chui Inmin Konghwa-guk/Democratic People's Republic of Korea*
AREA 120,538 sq km/46,539 sq mi
CAPITAL Pyongyang
MAJOR TOWNS/CITIES Hamhung, Chongjin, Nampo, Wonsan, Sinuiji
PHYSICAL FEATURES wide coastal plain in west rising to mountains cut by deep valleys in interior

Government

HEAD OF STATE Kim Jong Il from 1994
HEAD OF GOVERNMENT Hong Song Nam from 1997
POLITICAL SYSTEM communist
POLITICAL EXECUTIVE communist
ADMINISTRATIVE DIVISIONS nine provinces and three cities
ARMED FORCES 1,082,000; plus paramilitary forces of 189,000 (2002 est)
CONSCRIPTION conscription is selective; 5–12 years (army), 5–10 years (navy), 3–4 years (air force), followed by compulsory part-time service to age 40, then service in the Worker/Peasant Red Guard to age 60
DEATH PENALTY retained and used for ordinary crimes

Economy and resources

CURRENCY won
GPD (US$) 15.7 billion (2001)
REAL GDP GROWTH (% change on previous year) 3.7 (2001)
GNI PER CAPITA (PPP) (US$) 820 (2001)
FOREIGN DEBT (US$) 7.7 billion (2001 est)
MAJOR TRADING PARTNERS China, Japan, Russia, South Korea, Germany, Italy, Iran
RESOURCES coal, iron, lead, copper, zinc, tin, silver, gold, magnesite (has 40–50% of world's deposits of magnesite)
INDUSTRIES mining, metallurgy, electricity, machine-building, textiles, cement, chemicals, cotton, silk and rayon weaving, foods
EXPORTS textiles, base metals, vegetable products, machinery and electronic goods. Principal market: Japan 36.3% (2000)
IMPORTS petroleum and petroleum products, machinery and equipment, grain, textiles, coal, foodstuffs. Principal source: China 26.7% (2000)

NORTH KOREA This North Korean stamp from 2000 depicts a foundry worker. Metallic ores are a vital natural resourse for the republic, helping to support its large military forces and providing metals for export. *Stanley Gibbons*

ARABLE LAND 14.1% (2000 est)
AGRICULTURAL PRODUCTS rice, maize, sweet potatoes, soybeans; livestock rearing (cattle and pigs); forestry; fishing

Population and society

POPULATION 22,664,000 (2003 est)
POPULATION GROWTH RATE 0.6% (2000–15)
POPULATION DENSITY (per sq km) 188 (2003 est)
URBAN POPULATION (% of total) 61 (2003 est)

Chronology

2333 BC: Legendary founding of Korean state by Tangun dynasty.
1122 BC–4th century AD: Period of Chinese Kija dynasty.
668–1000: Peninsula unified by Buddhist Shilla kingdom, with capital at Kyongju.
1392–1910: Period of Chosun, or Yi, dynasty, during which Korea became a vassal of China and Confucianism became the dominant intellectual force.
1910: Korea formally annexed by Japan.
1920s and 1930s: Heavy industries developed in the coal-rich north, with Koreans forcibly conscripted as low-paid labourers; suppression of Korean culture led to the development of a resistance movement.
1945: Russian and US troops entered Korea at the end of World War II, forced surrender of Japanese, and divided the country in two at the 38th parallel. Soviet troops occupied North Korea.
1946: Soviet-backed provisional government installed, dominated by Moscow-trained Korean communists, including Kim Il Sung; radical programme of land reform and nationalization launched.
1948: Democratic People's Republic of Korea declared after pro-USA Republic of Korea founded in the south; Soviet troops withdrew.
1950: North Korea invaded South Korea to unite the nation, beginning the Korean War.
1953: Armistice agreed to end the Korean War, which had involved US participation on the side of South Korea, and Chinese on that of North Korea. The war ended in stalemate, at a cost of 2 million lives.
1961: Friendship and mutual assistance treaty signed with China.
1972: A new constitution, with an executive president, was adopted. Talks were held with South Korea about possible reunification.

AGE DISTRIBUTION (% of total population) 0–14 26%, 15–59 63%, 60+ 11% (2002 est)
ETHNIC GROUPS entirely Korean, with the exception of a 50,000 Chinese minority
LANGUAGE Korean (official)
RELIGION Buddhist (predominant religion), Chondoist, Christian, traditional beliefs
EDUCATION (compulsory years) 10
LITERACY RATE 99% (men); 99% (women) (2003 est)
LABOUR FORCE 50% of population: 32.4% agriculture, 32% industry, 35.6% services (1997 est)
LIFE EXPECTANCY 61 (men); 66 (women) (2000–05)
CHILD MORTALITY RATE (under 5, per 1,000 live births) 55 (2001)
PHYSICIANS (per 1,000 people) 3 (1998 est)
TV SETS (per 1,000 people) 59 (2001 est)
RADIOS (per 1,000 people) 154 (2001 est)

See also ▷Korean War; ▷South Korea.

1983: Four South Korean cabinet ministers were assassinated in Rangoon, Burma (Myanmar), by North Korean army officers.
1985: Relations improved with the Soviet Union.
1990: Diplomatic contacts with South Korea and Japan suggested a thaw in North Korea's relations with the rest of the world.
1991: North Korea became a member of the United Nations (UN). A nonaggression agreement with South Korea was signed.
1992: The Nuclear Safeguards Agreement was signed, allowing international inspection of nuclear facilities. A pact was also signed with South Korea for inspection of nuclear facilities.
1994: Kim Il Sung died and was succeeded by his son, Kim Jong Il. An agreement was made to halt the nuclear-development programme in return for US aid, resulting in the easing of a 44-year-old US trade embargo.
1996: US aid was sought in the face of famine.
1997: Kang Song San was replaced as prime minister by Hong Song Nam.
1998: A UN food-aid operation was instituted. A ballistic missile test was fired over Japan. Deceased former leader Kim Il Sung was declared 'president for perpetuity'. Relations with the US deteriorated when they demanded access to an underground site in Kumchangri suspected of being part of a nuclear weapons program.
1999: Japan lifted sanctions against North Korea.
2000: North Korea forged diplomatic links with Japan, the US, Italy, and the UK. At a first summit meeting between Kim Jong Il and King Dae Jung of South Korea, the two leaders agreed to South Korean economic investment in North Korea.
2002: In the worst clash between North and South Korea in three years, naval vessels fired on each other in disputed coastal waters in the Yellow Sea. The government admitted that it had been pursuing a secret nuclear weapons development programme in contravention of a 1994 agreement with the US government.

North Yorkshire county of northeast England, created in 1974 from most of the North Riding and parts of the East and West Ridings of Yorkshire (since April 1996 York has been a separate unitary authority).

area 8,037 sq km/3,103 sq mi **towns and cities** Northallerton (administrative headquarters); resorts: Harrogate, Scarborough, Whitby **physical** England's largest county; rivers Derwent, Esk, Ouse; includes part of the Pennines; the Vale of York (a vast plain); the Cleveland Hills; North Yorkshire Moors, which form a national park (within which is Fylingdales radar station to give early warning – 4 minutes – of nuclear attack) **features** Rievaulx Abbey; Yorkshire Dales National Park (including Swaledale, Wensleydale, and Bolton Abbey in Wharfedale); Fountains Abbey near Ripon, with Studley Royal Gardens (a World Heritage site); Castle Howard, designed by Vanbrugh; largest accessible cavern in Britain, the Battlefield Chamber, Ingleton **agriculture** cereals, dairy products (Vale of York, Pickering); wool and meat from sheep (North York Moors) **industries** coal, footwear, clothing, vehicles, plastics, foodstuffs, high technology industries, light industry **population** (2000 est) 576,000 **famous people** Alcuin, W H Auden, Guy Fawkes

Norway see country box.

Norwegian people of Norwegian culture. There are 4–4.5 million speakers of Norwegian (including some in the USA), a Germanic language belonging to the Indo-European family. The seafaring culture of the Norwegians can be traced back to the Viking age from about AD 800–1050, when people of Norwegian descent settled Iceland and Greenland, and voyaged to Vinland (coast of Newfoundland).

Norwich cathedral city and administrative headquarters of ▷Norfolk, eastern England, on the River Wensum, 160 km/100 mi northeast of London; population (1991) 172,600. Industries include financial services and insurance, tourism, television and radio broadcasting, engineering, printing, high-technology and biotechnology industries, and the manufacture of shoes, mustard, clothing, chemicals, and confectionery. It is the largest medieval walled city in England.

Features Norwich has a Norman castle, a cathedral founded in 1096, a 15th-century guildhall, over 30 medieval churches, Tudor houses, and a Georgian assembly house. Its city hall dates from 1938. The University of East Anglia (established in 1963) includes the Sainsbury Centre for Visual Arts (1978), designed by Norman Foster, and the Sainsbury Laboratory for Molecular Research (1987) designed by Denys Lasdun. New Technopolis, a business and education centre, is a Millennium Commission Landmark Project which is scheduled to open in 2001.

History First fortified by the Saxons in the 9th century, Norwich was settled in medieval times by Flemish weavers and it became the centre of the worsted trade in the 14th century. As northern manufacturing towns expanded during the Industrial Revolution, Norwich lost some of its importance. During World War II Norwich was heavily damaged.

Norwich School English regional school of landscape painters, inspired by the 17th-century Dutch realist tradition of landscape painting, notably the work of ▷Ruisdael. Founded in 1803, the school was made up of both professional and amateur artists and flourished until the 1830s. Its leading members were John Sell Cotman and John ▷Crome.

Norwich terrier small compact breed of terrier. It has a hard and wiry coat, that is close-lying and straight, and is coloured red, black, and tan; red grizzle; or grizzle and tan. Its head is rather foxlike, the muzzle being rather short and the skull wide between the erect ears. The legs are short, straight, and strong; the tail is traditionally docked. The height is usually 25 cm/10 in and the weight 5–6 kg/11–13 lb.

nose in humans, the upper entrance of the respiratory tract; the organ of the sense of smell. The external part is divided down the middle by a septum of ▷cartilage. The nostrils contain plates of cartilage that can be moved by muscles and have a growth of stiff hairs at the margin to prevent foreign objects from entering. The whole nasal cavity is lined with a ▷mucous membrane that warms and moistens the air as it enters and ejects dirt. In the upper parts of the cavity the membrane contains 50 million olfactory receptor cells (cells sensitive to smell).

nosebleed (or *epistaxis*) bleeding from the nose. It may be caused by injury, infection, high blood pressure, or some disorders of the blood. Although usually minor and easily controlled, the loss of blood may occasionally be so rapid as to be life-threatening, particularly in small children. Most nosebleeds can be stopped by simply squeezing the nose for a few minutes with the head held forwards, but in exceptional cases transfusion may be required and the nose may need to be packed with ribbon gauze or cauterized.

Nostradamus, Michael (1503–1566) (French Michel de Nôtredame) French physician and astrologer who was consulted by Catherine de' Medici and Charles IX of France. His book of prophecies in verse, *Centuries* (1555), makes cryptic predictions about world events up to the year 3797.

Related Web site: Nostradamus: Could he See the Future?
http://www.activemind.com/Mysterious/Topics/Nostradamus/

nostril in vertebrates, the opening of the nasal cavity, in which cells sensitive to smell are located. (In fish, these cells detect water-borne chemicals, so they are effectively organs of taste.) In vertebrates with lungs, the nostrils also take in air. In humans, and most other mammals, the nostrils are located on the ▷nose.

notary public legal practitioner who attests or certifies deeds and other documents. British diplomatic and consular officials may exercise notarial functions outside the UK.

notation in dance, the codification and recording of dances by symbols. There are several dance notation systems; prominent among them is ▷Labanotation.

notation system of signs and symbols for writing music, either for performers to read from, or to make a permanent record. Early systems of music notation were developed in China in the 3rd century BC, and by the ancient Sumerians, and later by the ancient Greeks and Romans for their music dramas. The Greeks were the first to name the notes of the ▷scale with letters of the alphabet.

notebook computer in computing, a small battery-powered portable about A4 in size and about 50 mm/2 in thick. The first notebook computers, such as the Epson HX-20 and Tandy 100, became available in the early 1980s, with the first PC-compatible notebook, the Toshiba T1100, following in 1985. In the 1990s, the notebook format became the standard for portable PCs and Apple PowerBooks.

Nottingham City industrial city and unitary authority in central England, on the River Trent, 200 km/124 mi northwest of London. It was the administrative headquarters of the county of Nottinghamshire to April 1998.

area 74 sq km/29 sq mi **features** Nottingham Playhouse (1963), the Theatre Royal (1866), the Royal Concert Hall (1982), and the Castle Museum; University of Nottingham (1881) and Nottingham Trent University (1992), formerly Trent Polytechnic; the Goose Fair, dating from the Middle Ages, is held every October; Nottingham has a racecourse, and test matches are played on the Trent Bridge cricket

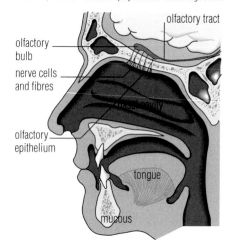

detail of olfactory epithelium

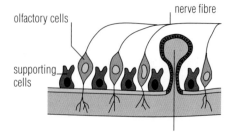

NOSE The structure of the nose. The organs of smell are confined to a small area in the roof of the nasal cavity. The olfactory cells are stimulated when certain molecules reach them. Smell is one of our most subtle senses: tens of thousands of smells can be distinguished. By comparison, taste, although closely related to smell, is a crude sensation. All the subtleties of taste depend upon smell.

ground; the Harvey Haddon sports stadium opened in 1964; the National Water Sports Centre is to the east of the city, near the village of Holme Pierrepont; a Tudor mansion, Holme Pierrepont Hall, is also in the village **industries** tourism, engineering, and the manufacture of bicycles, textiles, knitwear, pharmaceuticals, tobacco, lace, hosiery, and electronics **population** (1996) 285,000 **famous people** William Booth, Alan Sillitoe

Nottinghamshire county of central England, which has contained the unitary authority Nottingham City since April 1998.

area 2,160 sq km/834 sq mi **towns and cities** West Bridgford (administrative headquarters), Mansfield, Newark, Worksop **physical** rivers: Erewash Idle, Soar, Trent **features** the remaining areas of Sherwood Forest (home of ▷Robin Hood) are included in the Dukeries, an area of estates; originally 32 km/20 mi long and 12 km/7 mi wide, the forest was formerly a royal hunting ground; Cresswell Crags (remains of prehistoric humans); D H Lawrence commemorative walk from Eastwood (where he lived) to Old Brinsley Colliery **agriculture** cereals (barley, wheat), market gardening (potatoes), sugar beet; cattle, sheep; there are many orchards **industries** cigarettes, coal mining, engineering, footwear, furniture, gravel, gypsum, ironstone, light engineering, limestone, oil, pharmaceuticals, sandstone, textiles **population** (2000 est) 743, 800 **famous people** Robin Hood, D H Lawrence

Nouakchott capital of ▷Mauritania, 270 mi/435 km northeast of Dakar, Senegal; population (1992) 600,000. It is the largest city in the Sahara. Products include salt, cement, insecticides, rugs, carpets, embroidery, and crafts. Exports include copper, petroleum, and phosphates. There is some light engineering.

Nouméa port and capital on the southwest coast of New Caledonia; population (1992) 65,000.

nouveau roman (French 'new novel') experimental literary form produced in the 1950s by French novelists including Alain Robbe-Grillet and Nathalie Sarraute. In various ways, these writers seek to eliminate character, plot, and authorial subjectivity in order to present the world as a pure, solid 'thing in itself'.

nova (plural **novae**) faint star that suddenly erupts in brightness by 10,000 times or more, remains bright for a few days, and then fades away and is not seen again for very many years, if at all. Novae are believed to occur in close ▷binary star systems, where gas from one star flows to a companion ▷white dwarf. The gas ignites and is thrown off in an explosion at speeds of 1,500 kps/930 mps or more. Unlike a ▷supernova, the star is not completely disrupted by the outburst. After a few weeks or months it subsides to its previous state; it may erupt many more times.

Although the name comes from the Latin 'new', photographic records show that such stars are not really new, but faint stars undergoing an outburst of radiation that temporarily gives them an absolute magnitude in the range −6–10, at least 100,000 times brighter than the Sun. They fade away, rapidly at first and then more slowly over several years. Two or three such stars are detected in our Galaxy each year, but on average one is sufficiently close to us to become a conspicuous naked-eye object only about once in ten years.

Novalis (1772–1801) Pen-name of Friedrich Leopold von Hardenberg. Pioneer German Romantic poet. He wrote *Hymnen an die Nacht/Hymns to the Night* (1800), prompted by the death of his fiancée Sophie von Kühn. Feeling himself ecstatically united with his dead beloved, he tried to free his spirit from material things, and many of his poems contain a note of mysticism. He left two unfinished romances, *Die Lehrlinge zu Sais/The Novices of Sais* and *Heinrich von Ofterdingen*.

Nova Scotia maritime province of eastern Canada, comprising the peninsula of Nova Scotia, extending southeast from New Brunswick into the Atlantic Ocean, and Cape Breton Island, which is separated from the northeastern end of the mainland by the Canso Strait; area 55,500 sq km/21,400 sq mi; population (1996 est) 942,800. The capital (and chief port) is ▷Halifax. Industries include mineral extraction (coal, barite, gypsum), lumbering, paper-milling, and fishing. Agricultural products include dairy produce, poultry, eggs, vegetables, and fruit. Tourism is important.

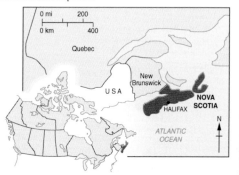

Norway

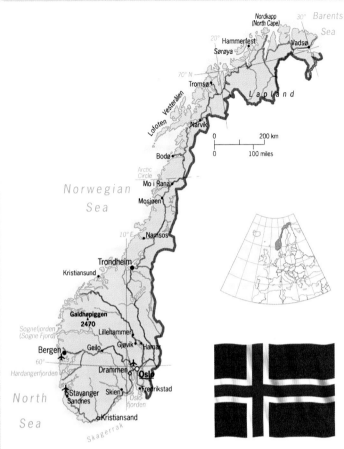

Norway country in northwest Europe, on the Scandinavian peninsula, bounded east by Sweden, northeast by Finland and Russia, south by the North Sea, west by the Atlantic Ocean, and north by the Arctic Ocean.

NATIONAL NAME *Kongeriket Norge/Kingdom of Norway*
AREA 387,000 sq km/149,420 sq mi (including Svalbard and Jan Mayen)
CAPITAL Oslo
MAJOR TOWNS/CITIES Bergen, Trondheim, Stavanger, Kristiansand, Drammen
PHYSICAL FEATURES mountainous with fertile valleys and deeply indented coast; forests cover 25%; extends north of Arctic Circle
TERRITORIES dependencies in the Arctic (Svalbard and Jan Mayen) and in Antarctica (Bouvet and Peter I Island, and Queen Maud Land)

Government

HEAD OF STATE King Harald V from 1991
HEAD OF GOVERNMENT Kjell Magne Bondevik from 2001
POLITICAL SYSTEM liberal democracy
POLITICAL EXECUTIVE parliamentary
ADMINISTRATIVE DIVISIONS 19 counties and 439 municipalities
ARMED FORCES 26,600 (2002 est)
CONSCRIPTION 12 months, with 4–5 refresher training periods
DEATH PENALTY abolished in 1979
DEFENCE SPEND (% GDP) 1.9 (2002 est)
EDUCATION SPEND (% GDP) 6.8 (2001 est)
HEALTH SPEND (% GDP) 7.8 (2002 est)

Economy and resources

CURRENCY Norwegian krone
GPD (US$) 189.4 billion (2002 est)
REAL GDP GROWTH (% change on previous year) 1.2 (2001)

GNI (US$) 171.8 billion (2002 est)
GNI PER CAPITA (PPP) (US$) 35,840 (2002 est)
CONSUMER PRICE INFLATION 2.1% (2003 est)
UNEMPLOYMENT 3.6% (2001)
MAJOR TRADING PARTNERS UK, Sweden, Germany, the Netherlands, USA, France, Denmark
RESOURCES petroleum, natural gas, iron ore, iron pyrites, copper, lead, zinc, forests
INDUSTRIES mining, fishery, food processing, non-electrical machinery, metals and metal products, paper products, printing and publishing, shipbuilding, chemicals
EXPORTS petroleum, natural gas, fish products, non-ferrous metals, wood pulp and paper. Principal market: UK 19.8% (2001)
IMPORTS machinery and transport equipment, chemicals, clothing, mineral fuels, iron and steel, office machines and computers, manufactured goods, crude materials, ships. Principal source: Sweden 15.5% (2001)
ARABLE LAND 2.9% (2000 est)
AGRICULTURAL PRODUCTS wheat, barley, oats, potatoes, fruit; fishing industry, including fish farming

Population and society

POPULATION 4,533,000 (2003 est)
POPULATION GROWTH RATE 0.4% (2000–15)
POPULATION DENSITY (per sq km) 14 (2003 est)

URBAN POPULATION (% of total) 76 (2003 est)
AGE DISTRIBUTION (% of total population) 0–14 20%, 15–59 60%, 60+ 20% (2002 est)
ETHNIC GROUPS majority of Nordic descent; Saami minority in far north (approximately 30,000)
LANGUAGE Norwegian (official), Saami (Lapp), Finnish
RELIGION Evangelical Lutheran (endowed by state) 88%; other Protestant and Roman Catholic 4%
EDUCATION (compulsory years) 9
LITERACY RATE 99% (men); 99% (women) (2003 est)
LABOUR FORCE 4.2% agriculture, 21.9% industry, 73.9% services (2000)
LIFE EXPECTANCY 76 (men); 82 (women) (2000–05)
CHILD MORTALITY RATE (under 5, per 1,000 live births) 4 (2001)
PHYSICIANS (per 1,000 people) 4.1 (1998 est)
HOSPITAL BEDS (per 1,000 people) 14.6 (1998 est)
TV SETS (per 1,000 people) 883 (2001 est)
RADIOS (per 1,000 people) 3,324 (2001 est)
INTERNET USERS (per 10,000 people) 5,048.3 (2002 est)
PERSONAL COMPUTER USERS (per 100 people) 52.8 (2002 est)

See also ▷Denmark; ▷Sweden; ▷Viking.

See also ▷Denmark; ▷Sweden; ▷Viking.

NORWAY This wooden church in Norway dates from the medieval period. The use of wood (a good thermal insulating material), with a steeply pitched roof for the snow to slide off easily, is typical of many older Scandinavian buildings. *Image Bank*

Chronology

5th century: First small kingdoms established by Goths.
c. 900: Harald Fairhair created united Norwegian kingdom; it dissolved after his death.
8th–11th centuries: Vikings from Norway raided and settled in many parts of Europe.
c. 1016–28: Olav II (St Olav) reunited the kingdom and introduced Christianity.
1217–63: Haakon VI established royal authority over nobles and church and made the monarchy hereditary.
1263: Iceland submitted to the authority of the king of Norway.
1397: Union of Kalmar: Norway, Denmark, and Sweden united under a single monarch.
15th century: Norway, the weakest of the three kingdoms, was increasingly treated as an appendage of Denmark.
1523: Secession of Sweden further undermined Norway's status.
16th century: Introduction of the sawmill precipitated the development of the timber industry and the growth of export trade.
1661: Denmark restored formal equality of status to Norway as a twin kingdom.
18th century: Norwegian merchants profited from foreign wars which increased demand for naval supplies.
1814: Treaty of Kiel: Denmark ceded Norway (minus Iceland) to Sweden; Norway retained its own parliament but cabinet appointed by the king of Sweden.
19th century: Economic decline followed slump in timber trade due to Canadian competition; expansion of merchant navy and whaling industry.
1837: Democratic local government introduced.
1884: Achieved internal self-government when the king of Sweden made the Norwegian

cabinet accountable to the Norwegian parliament.
1895: Start of constitutional dispute over control of foreign policy: Norway's demand for a separate consular service refused by Sweden.
1905: Union with Sweden dissolved; Norway achieved independence under King Haakon VII.
1907: Norway became first the European country to grant women the right to vote in parliamentary elections.
early 20th century: Development of industry based on hydroelectric power; long period of Liberal government committed to neutrality and moderate social reform.
1940–45: German occupation with Vidkun Quisling as puppet leader.
1945–65: Labour governments introduced economic planning and permanent price controls.
1949: Became a founding member of the North Atlantic Treaty Organization (NATO).
1952: Joined the Nordic Council.
1957: Olaf V succeeded his father King Haakon VII.
1960: Joined European Free Trade Association (EFTA).
1972: A national referendum rejected membership of European Economic Community (EEC).
1975: The export of North Sea oil began.
1981: Gro Harlem Brundtland (Labour) became Norway's first woman prime minister.
1986: Falling oil prices caused a recession.
1991: Olaf V was succeeded by his son Harald V.
1994: A national referendum rejected membership of European Union (EU).
1997: Kjell Magne Bondevik (KrF) became prime minister.
1998: There was a decline in the state of the economy.
2000: Bondevik resigned as prime minister and was succeeded by Jens Stoltenberg.

novel extended fictional prose narrative, usually between 30,000 and 100,000 words, that deals imaginatively with human experience through the psychological development of the central characters and of their relationship with a broader world. The modern novel took its name and inspiration from the Italian *novella*, the short tale of varied character which became popular in the late 13th century. As the main form of narrative fiction in the 20th century, the novel is frequently classified according to genres and subgenres such as the ▷historical novel, ▷detective fiction, ▷fantasy, and ▷science fiction.

Novello, Ivor (1893–1951) Stage name of Ivor Novello Davies. Welsh composer and actor-manager. He wrote popular songs, such as 'Keep the Home Fires Burning', in World War I, and musicals in which he often appeared as the romantic lead, including *Glamorous Night* (1925), *The Dancing Years* (1939), and *Gay's the Word* (1951).

Noverre, Jean-Georges (1727–1810) French choreographer, writer, and ballet reformer. He promoted *ballet d'action* (with a plot) and simple, free movement, and is often considered the creator of modern classical ballet. *Les Petits Riens* (1778) was one of his works.

Novgorod city on the Volkhov River in the northwest Russian Federation and capital of Novgorod oblast, 500 km/311 mi northwest of Moscow; population (1990) 232,000. Novgorod is one of the oldest cities in Russia, and was the capital of the Russian state before the ascendancy of Moscow. Chemicals, clothing, electrical goods, furniture, and beer are manufactured.

Related Web site: Novgorod the Great http://www.adm.nov.ru/web.nsf/pages/englishhome

Novgorod school Russian school of icon and mural painters active from the late 14th to the 16th century in Novgorod, inspired by the work of the refugee Byzantine artist Theophanes the Greek. Russian artists imitated his linear style, but their work became increasingly stilted and mannered.

Novi Sad industrial and commercial city (pottery and cotton), capital of the autonomous province of Vojvodina in northern Serbia, on the River Danube; population (1991) 179,600. Products include leather, textiles, and tobacco.

Novosibirsk (formerly **Novonikolayevsk** (1893–1925)) capital city, economic and cultural centre of Novosibirsk oblast (region) in southwestern Siberia, Russian Federation; population (1996 est) 1,368,000. Sited on the River Ob and the Trans-Siberian Railway, it is the largest city in Siberia and one of the main industrial centres of the Russian Federation. It is at the hub of an extensive transport network; the Turksib (Turkestan–Siberian) Railway runs from here to Almaty, former capital of Kazakhstan. Novosibirsk has large engineering industries and varied light and food industries. Since the collapse of communism in 1991, there has been considerable development of financial, business, and other services.

NSPCC abbreviation for National Society for the Prevention of Cruelty to Children (UK).

NT abbreviation for ▷Northern Territory, Australia.

Nuba member of a minority ethnic group forming many small autonomous groups in southern Sudan, and numbering about 1 million (1991). They are primarily agriculturalists, and go in for elaborate body painting. They speak related dialects of Nubian, which belongs to the Chari-Nile family. Forced Islamization threatens their cultural identity, and thousands were killed in the Sudan civil war.

Nubia former African country now divided between Egypt and Sudan; it gives its name to the **Nubian Desert** south of Lake Nasser. Ancient Egypt, which was briefly ruled by Nubian kings in the 8th–7th centuries BC, knew the north as Wawat and the south as Kush, with the dividing line roughly at Dongola. Egyptian building work in the area included temples at ▷Abu Simbel, Philae, and a defensive chain of forts that established the lines of development of medieval fortification. Nubia's capital about 600 BC–AD 350 was Meroe, near Khartoum. About AD 250–550 most of Nubia was occupied by the X-group people, of whom little is known; their royal mound tombs (mistaken by earlier investigations for natural mounds created by wind erosion) were excavated in the 1930s by W B ▷Emery, and many horses and attendants were found to have been slaughtered to accompany the richly jewelled dead.

nuclear arms verification the process of checking the number and types of nuclear weapons held by a country in accordance with negotiated limits. The chief means are: **reconnaissance satellites** that detect submarines or weapon silos, using angled cameras to give three-dimensional pictures of installations, penetrating camouflage by means of scanners, and partially seeing through cloud and darkness by infrared devices; **telemetry** or radio transmission of instrument readings; **interception** to get information on performance of weapons under test; **on-site inspection** by experts visiting bases, launch sites, storage facilities, and test sites in another country; **radar tracking** of missiles in flight; **seismic monitoring** of underground tests, in the same way as with earthquakes. This is not accurate and on-site inspection is needed. Tests in the atmosphere, space, or the oceans are forbidden, and the ban is accepted because explosions are not only dangerous to all but immediately detectable.

nuclear energy (or **atomic energy**) energy released from the inner core, or ▷nucleus, of the atom. Energy produced by nuclear ▷fission (the splitting of uranium or plutonium nuclei) has been harnessed since the 1950s to generate electricity, and research continues into the possible controlled use of ▷nuclear fusion (the fusing, or combining, of atomic nuclei).

In nuclear power stations, fission takes place in a ▷nuclear reactor. The nuclei of uranium or, more rarely, plutonium are induced to split, releasing large amounts of heat energy. The heat is then removed from the core of the reactor by circulating gas or water, and used to produce the steam that drives alternators and turbines to generate electrical power. Unlike fossil fuels, such as coal and oil, which must be burned in large quantities to produce energy, nuclear fuels are used in very small amounts and supplies are therefore unlikely to be exhausted in the foreseeable future. However, the use of nuclear energy has given rise to concern over safety. Anxiety has been heightened by accidents such as the one at Chernobyl, Ukraine, in 1986. There has also been mounting concern about the production and disposal of toxic nuclear waste, which may have an active life of several thousand years, and the cost of maintaining nuclear power stations and decommissioning them at the end of their lives.

Despite concerns over its safety, in 1997 nuclear power overtook coal as the number one source for UK's electricity for the first time. In the second quarter of 1997 the UK's nuclear plants generated 36% of the nation's power, while coal-fired stations were responsible for 33% and gas for 33%.

Related Web site: Nuclear Energy: Frequently Asked Questions http://www-formal.stanford.edu/jmc/progress/nuclear-faq.html

nuclear fusion process whereby two atomic nuclei are fused, with the release of a large amount of energy. Very high temperatures and pressures are required for the process. Under these conditions the atoms involved are stripped of all their electrons so that the remaining particles, which together make up a **plasma**, can come close together at very high speeds and overcome the mutual repulsion of the positive charges on the atomic nuclei. At very close range the strong nuclear force will come into play, fusing the particles to form a larger nucleus. As fusion is accompanied by the release of large amounts of energy, the process might one day be harnessed to form the basis of commercial energy production. Methods of achieving controlled fusion are therefore the subject of research around the world.

nuclear physics study of the properties of the nucleus of the ▷atom, including the structure of nuclei; nuclear forces; the interactions between particles and nuclei; and the study of radioactive decay. The study of elementary particles is ▷particle physics.

nuclear reaction reaction involving the nuclei of atoms. Atomic nuclei can undergo changes either as a result of radioactive decay, as in the decay of radium to radon (with the emission of an alpha particle):

$$^{226}_{88}Ra \rightarrow ^{222}_{86}Rn + ^{4}_{2}He$$

NUBIA Pottery jars from the tomb of the Nubian queen Nefertari, wife of Ramses II of Egypt (19th dynasty) (Egyptian Museum, Turin, Italy). *The Art Archive/Victoria and Albert Museum London*

or as a result of particle bombardment in a machine or device, as in the production of cobalt-60 by the bombardment of cobalt-59 with neutrons:

$$^{59}_{27}Co + ^{1}_{0}n \rightarrow ^{60}_{27}Co + \gamma$$

Nuclear ▷fission and nuclear ▷fusion are examples of nuclear reactions. The enormous amounts of energy released arise from the mass–energy relation put forward by Einstein, stating that $E = mc^2$ (where E is energy, m is mass, and c is the velocity of light).

NUCLEAR ENERGY Chapelcross Nuclear Power Station, Dumfriesshire, Scotland, opened in 1959 and was built at the same time as the Calder Hall plant at Sellafield in West Cumbria, England. Its four carbon-dioxide-cooled reactors were once used to produce plutonium for nuclear weapons, and are currently used to produce tritium. Accidents in the handling of nuclear waste at Chapelcross, and concern about the transportation of nuclear waste in the UK, led to public protests at the plant in 1999. *Image Bank*

nuclear reactor device for producing ▷nuclear energy in a controlled manner. There are various types of reactor in use, all using nuclear ▷fission. In a **gas-cooled reactor**, a circulating gas under pressure (such as carbon dioxide) removes heat from the core of the reactor, which usually contains natural uranium. The efficiency of the fission process is increased by slowing neutrons in the core by using a ▷moderator such as carbon. The reaction is controlled with neutron-absorbing rods made of boron. An **advanced gas-cooled reactor** (AGR) generally has enriched uranium as its fuel. A **water-cooled reactor**, such as the steam-generating heavy water (deuterium oxide) reactor, has water circulating through the hot core. The water is converted to steam, which drives turbo-alternators for generating electricity. The most widely used reactor is the **pressurized-water reactor** (PWR), which contains a sealed system of pressurized water that is heated to form steam in heat exchangers in an external circuit. The **fast reactor** has no moderator and uses fast neutrons to bring about fission. It uses a mixture of plutonium and uranium oxide as fuel. When operating, uranium is converted to plutonium, which can be extracted and used later as fuel. It is also called the fast breeder or breeder reactor because it produces more plutonium than it consumes. Heat is removed from the reactor by a coolant of liquid sodium.

Related Web site: Advanced Reactors http://www.uic.com.au/nip16.htm

nuclear safety measures to avoid accidents in the operation of nuclear reactors and in the production and disposal of nuclear weapons and of ▷nuclear waste. There are no guarantees of the safety of any of the various methods of disposal. Nuclear safety is a controversial subject since governments will not recognize the hazards of ▷atomic radiation and ▷radiation sickness.

nuclear warfare war involving the use of nuclear weapons. Nuclear-weapons research began in Britain in 1940, but was transferred to the USA after it entered World War II. The research programme, known as the ▷Manhattan Project, was directed by J Robert Oppenheimer. The development of technology that could destroy the Earth by the two major superpowers, the USA and USSR, as well as by Britain, France, and China, has since become a source of contention and heated debate. The worldwide total of nuclear weapons in 1990 was about 50,000, and the number of countries possessing nuclear weapons stood officially at five – USA, USSR, UK, France, and China; South Africa developed nuclear weapons in the 1980s but gave them up voluntarily in 1991. India and Pakistan exploded nuclear devices in 1998. Countries suspected of possessing or developing nuclear capability in the 1990s include Israel, North Korea, Iraq, and Iran.

nuclear waste the radioactive and toxic by-products of the nuclear-energy and nuclear-weapons industries. Nuclear waste may have an active life of several thousand years. Reactor waste is of three types: **high-level** spent fuel, or the residue when nuclear fuel has been removed from a reactor and reprocessed; **intermediate**, which may be long-or short-lived; and **low-level**, but bulky, waste from reactors, which has only short-lived radioactivity. Disposal, by burial on land or at sea, has raised problems of safety, environmental pollution, and security.

nucleic acid complex organic acid made up of a long chain of nucleotides, present in the nucleus and sometimes the cytoplasm of the living cell. The two types, known as ▷DNA (deoxyribonucleic acid) and ▷RNA (ribonucleic acid), form the basis of heredity. The nucleotides are made up of a sugar (deoxyribose or ribose), a phosphate group, and one of four purine or pyrimidine bases. The order of the bases along the nucleic acid strand contains the genetic code.

nucleon in particle physics, either a ▷proton or a ▷neutron, when present in the atomic nucleus. **Nucleon number** is an alternative name for the ▷mass number of an atom.

nucleus in biology, the central, membrane-enclosed part of a eukaryotic cell, containing threads of DNA. During cell division these coil up to form chromosomes. The nucleus controls the function of the cell by determining which proteins are produced within it (see ▷DNA for details of this process). Because proteins are the chief structural molecules of living matter and, as enzymes, regulate all aspects of metabolism, it may be seen that the genetic code within the nucleus is effectively responsible for building and controlling the whole organism.

The nucleus contains the **nucleolus**, the part of the cell where ribosomes are produced. Movement of molecules into and out of the nucleus occurs through the nuclear pores. An average mammalian nucleus has approximately 3,000 pores.

nucleus in physics, the positively charged central part of an ▷atom, which constitutes almost all its mass. Except for hydrogen nuclei, which have only protons, nuclei are composed of both protons and neutrons. Surrounding the nuclei are electrons, of equal and opposite charge to that of the protons, thus giving the atom a neutral charge.

The nucleus was discovered by the New Zealand physicist Ernest Rutherford in 1911 as a result of experiments in passing alpha particles through very thin gold foil. A few of the particles were deflected back, and Rutherford, astonished, reported: 'It was almost as if you fired a 15-inch shell at a piece of tissue paper and it came back and hit you!' The deflection, he deduced, was due to the positively charged alpha particles being repelled by approaching a small but dense positively charged nucleus.

nuclide in physics, a species of atomic nucleus characterized by the number of protons (Z) and the number of neutrons (N). Nuclides with identical ▷proton number but differing neutron number are called ▷isotopes.

Nuffield, William Richard Morris, 1st Viscount Nuffield (1877–1963) English manufacturer and philanthropist. Starting with a small cycle-repairing business, in 1910 he designed a car that could be produced cheaply, and built up **Morris Motors Ltd** at Cowley, Oxford.

nuisance in law, interference with enjoyment of, or rights over, land. There are two kinds of nuisance. **Private nuisance** affects a particular occupier of land, such as noise from a neighbour; the aggrieved occupier can apply for an ▷injunction and claim ▷damages. **Public nuisance** affects an indefinite number of members of the public, such as obstructing the highway; it is a criminal offence. In this case, individuals can claim damages only if they are affected more than the general public.

Nujoma, Sam (1929–) Namibian left-wing politician, founder and leader of ▷SWAPO (the South West Africa People's Organization) from 1959, president from 1990. He was exiled in 1960, and controlled SWAPO's armed struggle against South Africa

NUCLEAR WARFARE The first US intercontinental ballistic missile (ICBM) goes on show. This photograph was taken on 15 May 1959, at the Aquarium Compound on Coney Island, New York, USA. *Archive Photos*

from Angolan bases in 1966. When the first free elections were held in 1989 under the United Nations peace plan, he returned to lead his party to victory, taking office in March 1990.

Nujoma was exiled after SWAPO appointed him to present the case for Namibian independence before the UN in 1960. He set up SWAPO provisional headquarters in Tanzania in 1961 and, apart from a brief return home in 1966 when he was arrested, he remained in exile until 1989. SWAPO was recognized as the legitimate authority by the Organization of African Unity in 1968 and the UN in 1973, but South African opposition delayed the implementation of the UN peace plan.

Nuku'alofa capital and port of Tonga on Tongatapu Island; population (1998 est) 30,400.

numbat (or banded anteater) Australian ▷marsupial anteater. It is brown with white stripes on the back and has a long tubular tongue to gather termites and ants. The body is about 25 cm/10 in long, and the tongue can be extended 10 cm/4 in. It is different from other marsupials in that it has no pouch. (Species *Myrmecobius fasciatus.*)

number symbol used in counting or measuring. In mathematics, there are various kinds of number. The everyday number system is the decimal ('proceeding by tens') system, using the base ten. ▷Real numbers include all rational numbers (integers, or whole numbers, and fractions) and irrational numbers (those not expressible as fractions). ▷Complex numbers include the real and imaginary numbers (real-number multiples of the square root of −1). The ▷binary number system, used in computers, has two as its base. The natural numbers, 0, 1, 2, 3, 4, 5, 6, 7, 8, and 9, give a counting system that, in the decimal system, continues 10, 11, 12, 13, and so on. These are whole numbers (integers), with fractions represented as, for example, $\frac{1}{4}$, $\frac{1}{2}$, $\frac{3}{4}$, or as decimal fractions (0.25, 0.5, 0.75). They are also **rational numbers**.

Irrational numbers cannot be represented in this way and require symbols, such as $\sqrt{2}$, π, and e. They can be expressed numerically only as the (inexact) approximations 1.414, 3.142, and 2.718 (to three places of decimals) respectively. The symbols π and e are also examples of **transcendental numbers**, because they (unlike $\sqrt{2}$) cannot be derived by solving a ▷polynomial equation (an equation with one ▷variable quantity) with rational ▷coefficients (multiplying factors). Complex numbers, which include the real numbers as well as imaginary numbers, take the general form $a + bi$, where $i = \sqrt{-1}$ (that is, $i^2 = -1$), and a is the real part and bi the imaginary part.

Evolution of number systems The ancient Egyptians, Greeks, Romans, and Babylonians all evolved number systems, although none had a zero, which was introduced from India by way of Arab mathematicians in about the 8th century and allowed a place-value system to be devised on which the decimal system is based. Other number systems have since evolved and have found applications. For example, numbers to base two (binary numbers), using only 0 and 1, are commonly used in digital computers to represent the

two-state 'on' or 'off' pulses of electricity. Binary numbers were first developed by German mathematician Gottfried Leibniz in the late 17th century.

Related Web site: Arabic Numerals http://www.islam.org/ Mosque/ihame/Ref6.htm

nun (Latin *nonna* 'elderly woman') woman belonging to a religious order under the vows of poverty, chastity, and obedience, and living under a particular rule. Christian convents are ruled by a superior (often elected), who is subject to the authority of the bishop of the diocese or sometimes directly to the pope. See ▷monasticism.

Nunavut (Inuit 'our land') semi-autonomous Inuit homeland, established as a territory of Canada on 1 April 1999. It consists of former parts of the ▷Northwest Territories, Canada, including Keewatin and Kitikmeot, the Arctic Islands of Baffin, Ellesmere, Devon, Prince of Wales and Banks, and the eastern areas of Victoria and Melville Islands, as well as Southampton and smaller islands in Hudson Bay. Nunavut extends to 1,994,000 sq km/769,846 sq mi, one-fifth of the total land area of Canada. Its creation was approved by a narrow majority in a regional plebiscite in 1992, though the measure was opposed by representatives of the Dene people from the western Arctic, where 74% voted against (the Dene claimed that the homeland cut across their traditional hunting grounds). In the eastern Arctic where most Inuit live, 84% voted in favour. Representatives of the Initio had earlier negotiated hunting and fishing rights in the area, and a final land claims agreement, signed in 1993 on Baffin Island (where Iqaluit, the capital of Nunavut is located), gave the Inuit outright ownership of 353,610 sq km/ 136,493 sq mi of the land, and mineral rights to 36,257 sq km/ 13,995 sq mi. The remainder is Crown Land over which the Inuit have joint control with the Federal Government.

In spite of its vast size, Nunavut has only 27,200 inhabitants (1999 est), over 80% of whom are Inuit. The government structure for Nunavut is being established in phases to 2009. Iqaluit became

WILLIAM NUFFIELD English car manufacturer and philanthropist Lord Nuffield. *Philip Sauvain Picture Collection*

the home of the legislative assembly of 19 members in 1999 and transfer of administration for culture, public housing, and health is planned to be completed by 2009. In order to spread decision-making and economic benefits, government will be decentralized in the three regions of Qikiqtaaluk, Kivalliq, and Kitikmeot, and 28 communities. Government activity is expected to continue as a major economic sector in Nunavut, as in the Northwest Territories.

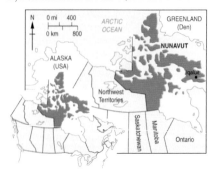

Núñez, Rafael (1825–1894) Colombian president 1880–82 and 1884–94, responsible for a new, authoritarian constitution in 1886. A doctrinaire Liberal in the 1850s, he held several government posts, and was a foreign diplomat 1863–74. During his terms in office he restored the church's influential position and tried to stimulate economic development with a protective tariff. He also established a central bank, and concluded a concordat with the Vatican in 1887.

Nunn, Trevor Robert (1940–) English stage director. He was artistic director of the Royal Shakespeare Company 1968–86 and artistic director of the Royal National Theatre in London, England, 1997–2003. He received a Tony award (with John Caird (1948–)) for his production of *Nicholas Nickleby* (1982) and for the musical *Les Misérables* (1985). He directed Andrew Lloyd Webber's musical *Cats* (1981), followed by *Starlight Express* (1984), *Chess* (1986), and *Aspects of Love* (1989). *Oklahoma!*, directed by Nunn, won the Best Musical award in the 1998 *Evening Standard* Drama Awards. In 1999 he won the *Evening Standard* best director award for *The Merchant of Venice* and *Summerfolk*.

Nuremberg (German **Nürnberg**) city in Bavaria, Germany, on the River Pegnitz, 149 km/92 mi northwest of Munich; population (1995) 494,100. Industries include electrical and other machinery, precision instruments, toys, and food processing. From 1933 the Nuremberg rallies were held here, and in 1945 the Nuremberg trials of war criminals.

Nuremberg rallies annual meetings 1933–38 of the German ▷Nazi Party. They were characterized by extensive torchlight parades, marches in party formations, and mass rallies addressed by Nazi leaders such as Hitler and Goebbels.

Nuremberg trials after World War II, the trials of the 24 chief ▷Nazi war criminals November 1945–October 1946 by an international military tribunal consisting of four judges and four prosecutors: one of each from the USA, UK, USSR, and France. An appendix accused the German cabinet, general staff, high command, Nazi leadership corps, ▷SS, ▷Sturmabteilung, and ▷Gestapo of criminal behaviour.

The main charges in the indictment were: (1) conspiracy to wage wars of aggression; (2) crimes against peace; (3) war crimes: for example, murder and ill-treatment of civilians and prisoners of war, deportation of civilians for slave labour, and killing of hostages; (4) crimes against humanity: for example, mass murder of the Jews and other peoples, and murder and ill-treatment of political opponents. Of the accused, Krupp was too ill to be tried; Ley (1890–1945) committed suicide during the trial; and Bormann, who had fled, was sentenced to death in his absence. Fritsche (1899–1953), Schacht (1877–1970), and Papen were acquitted. The other 18 were found guilty on one or more counts. Hess, Walther Funk (1890–1960), and Raeder were sentenced to life imprisonment; Shirach (1907–1974) and Speer (1905–1981) to 20 years; Neurath (1873–1956) to 15 years; and Dönitz to 10 years. The remaining 11 men, sentenced to death by hanging, were Hans Frank (1900–1946), Wilhelm Frick (1877–1946), Goering (who committed suicide before he could be executed), Jodl, Kaltenbrunner, Keitel, Ribbentrop, Rosenberg, Fritz Sauckel (1894–1946), Arthur Seyss-Inquart (1892–1946), and Julius Streicher (1885–1946). The SS and Gestapo were declared criminal organizations.

Related Web site: Nuremberg War Crimes Trials
http://www.yale.edu/lawweb/avalon/imt/imt.htm

Nureyev, Rudolf Hametovich (1938–1993)

Russian dancer and choreographer. A soloist with the Kirov Ballet, he defected to the West during a visit to Paris in 1961. Mainly associated with the Royal Ballet (London) and as Margot ▷Fonteyn's principal partner, he was one of the most brilliant dancers of the 1960s and 1970s. Nureyev danced in such roles as Prince Siegfried in *Swan Lake* and Armand in *Marguerite and Armand*, which was created especially for Fonteyn and Nureyev. He also danced and acted in films and on television and choreographed several ballets. It was due to his enormous impact on the ballet world that the male dancer's role was elevated to the equivalent of the ballerina's.

nursery school
(or **kindergarten**) educational establishment for children aged three to five. The first was established in Germany in 1836 by Friedrich ▷Froebel. Provision of nursery education varies widely between countries. In the UK, fewer than half of three- and four-year olds have nursery education. In France, all children attend a state-run *école maternelle* from the age of three. In Japan, education is compulsory only from the age of six, but 90% of children attend a private nursery school from the age of three.

RUDOLF NUREYEV Dancers Maria Tallchief and Rudolf Nureyev, 1965. Tallchief helped form the New York City Ballet with George Balanchine in 1948. Here, a young Nureyev, who had defected to the west only four years before, is practising in the dance studio with her. *Archive Photos*

nursing care of the sick, the very young, the very old, and the disabled. Organized training originated in 1836 in Germany, and was developed in Britain by the work of Florence ▷Nightingale, who, during the Crimean War, established standards of scientific, humanitarian care in military hospitals. Nurses give day-to-day care and carry out routine medical and surgical duties under the supervision of doctors.

In ancient times very limited care was associated with some temples, and in Christian times nursing became associated with the religious orders until the Reformation brought it into secular hands in Protestant countries. Other early pioneers of nursing included the English prison reformer Elizabeth ▷Fry, who set up the first training school for nurses in the UK; the Jamaican nurse Mary Seacole, who worked among the wounded of the Crimean War; and the US health worker Clara Barton, founder of the American Red Cross in 1881. Many specialities and qualifications now exist in Western countries, standards being maintained by professional bodies and boards.

In the UK there are four National Boards (England, Scotland, Wales, and Northern Ireland) for Nursing, Midwifery, and Health Visiting, and the Royal College of Nursing (1916) is the professional body.

nut any dry, single-seeded fruit that does not split open to release the seed, such as the chestnut. A nut is formed from more than one carpel, but only one seed becomes fully formed, the remainder aborting. The wall of the fruit, the pericarp, becomes hard and woody, forming the outer shell.

Examples of true nuts are the acorn and hazelnut. The term also describes various hard-shelled fruits and seeds, including almonds and walnuts, which are really the stones of ▷drupes, and brazil nuts and shelled peanuts, which are seeds. The kernels of most nuts provide a concentrated, nutritious food, containing vitamins, minerals, and enzymes, about 50% fat, and 10–20% protein, although a few, such as chestnuts, are high in carbohydrates and have only a moderate protein content of 5%. Nuts also provide edible and industrial oils. Most nuts are produced by perennial trees and shrubs. Whereas the majority of nuts are obtained from plantations, considerable quantities of pecans and brazil nuts are still collected from the wild. World production in the mid-1980s was about 4 million tonnes per year.

nutation in botany, the spiral movement exhibited by the tips of certain stems during growth; it enables a climbing plant to find a suitable support. Nutation sometimes also occurs in tendrils and flower stalks.

nutcracker either of two species of bird similar to a jay, belonging to the crow family. One species is found in the Old World

and the other in the New World. (Genus *Nucifraga*, family Corvidae, order Passeriformes.)

nuthatch any of a group of small birds with short tails and pointed beaks. Nuthatches climb head first up, down, and around tree trunks and branches, foraging for insects and their larvae. (Family Sittidae, order Passeriformes.)

nutmeg kernel of the hard aromatic seed of the evergreen nutmeg tree, native to the Maluku Islands, Indonesia. Both the nutmeg and its secondary covering, known as **mace**, are used as spices in cookery. (*Myristica fragrans*, family Myristicaceae.)

nutrition the strategy adopted by an organism to obtain the chemicals it needs to live, grow, and reproduce. Also, the science of food, and its effect on human and animal life, health, and disease. Nutrition involves the study of the basic nutrients required to sustain life, their bioavailability in foods and overall diet, and the effects upon them of cooking and storage. It is also concerned with dietary deficiency diseases.

There are six classes of nutrients: water, carbohydrates, proteins, fats, vitamins, and minerals.

Related Web site: Reference Guide for Vitamins
http://www.realtime.net/anr/vitamins.html

Nu, U (Thakin) (1907–1995) Myanmar politician, prime minister of Burma (now Myanmar) for most of the period from 1947 to the military coup of 1962. He was the country's first democratically elected prime minister. Exiled from 1966, U Nu returned to the country in 1980 and, in 1988, helped found the National League for Democracy opposition movement.

Nuuk Greenlandic for ▷Godthåb, the capital of Greenland.

NV abbreviation for ▷Nevada, a state of the USA.

NVQ abbreviation for ▷national vocational qualification.

NY abbreviation for ▷New York, a city and state of the USA.

NUTHATCH The European nuthatch is one of about 25 species of nuthatch. They are robust little birds, with strong legs and sharp claws to help them climb.

Nyanja a central African people living mainly in Malawi, and numbering about 400,000 (1984). The Nyanja are predominantly farmers, living in villages under a hereditary monarchy. They speak a Bantu language belonging to the Niger-Congo family.

Nyasa, Lake alternative name for Lake ▷Malawi.

Nyasaland former name (to 1964) for ▷Malawi.

Nyerere, Julius Kambarage (1922–1999) Tanzanian socialist politician, president 1964–85. He devoted himself from 1954 to the formation of the Tanganyika African National Union and subsequent campaigning for independence. He became chief minister in 1960, was prime minister of Tanganyika 1961–62, president of the newly formed Tanganyika Republic 1962–64, and first president of Tanzania 1964–85. He became head of the Organization of African Unity in 1984.

Nyers, Rezso (1923–   ) Hungarian socialist leader. A member of the politburo from 1966 and the architect of Hungary's liberalizing economic reforms in 1968, he was ousted from power by hardliners in 1974. In 1988 he was brought back into the politburo, and was head of the newly formed Hungarian Socialist Party 1989–90.

Nykvist, Sven (1924–   ) Swedish director of photography. He was associated with the director Ingmar Bergman. From the mid-1970s onwards he worked frequently in the USA. His films include *The Virgin Spring* (1960) (for Bergman), *Pretty Baby* (1978) (for Louis Malle), and *Fanny and Alexander* (1982) (for Bergman). He directed *Oxen/The Ox* in 1992.

nylon synthetic long-chain polymer similar in chemical structure to protein. Nylon was the first all-synthesized fibre, made from petroleum, natural gas, air, and water by the Du Pont firm in 1938. It is used in the manufacture of moulded articles, textiles, and medical sutures. Nylon fibres are stronger and more elastic than silk and are relatively insensitive to moisture and mildew. Nylon is used for hosiery and woven goods, simulating other materials such as silks and furs; it is also used for carpets. It was developed in 1937 by the US chemist W H Carothers and his associates.

Nyman, Michael (1944–   ) English composer. His highly stylized music is characterized by processes of gradual modification by repetition of complex musical formulae (known as minimalism). His compositions include scores for the English film-maker Peter Greenaway and the New Zealand film-maker Jane Campion (*The Piano*, 1993); a chamber opera, *The Man Who Mistook His Wife for a Hat* (1989); and three string quartets.

nymph in entomology, the immature form of insects that do not have a pupal stage; for example, grasshoppers and dragonflies. Nymphs generally resemble the adult (unlike larvae), but do not have fully formed reproductive organs or wings.

nymph in Greek mythology, a guardian spirit of nature. ▷Dryads or **hamadryads** guarded trees; **naiads**, springs and pools; **oreads**, hills and rocks; **oceanids**, the open sea; and ▷Nereids, the Aegean.

O

oak any of a group of trees or shrubs belonging to the beech family, with over 300 known species widely distributed in temperate zones. Oaks are valuable for timber, the wood being durable and straight-grained. Their fruits are called ▷acorns. (Genus *Quercus*, family Fagaceae.)

OAK The English oak is the most common oak species in Northern Europe.

Oakland industrial port in central California, USA, on the eastern, inland coast of San Francisco Bay; population (1996 est) 367,200. It is linked by the Bay Bridge (opened 1936) with San Francisco. Industries include food processing, shipbuilding, and the manufacture of vehicles, textiles, and chemicals. The community was laid out in 1852 and became a terminus of the first transcontinental railroad in 1869. Extensive port facilities handle much of the freight traffic of the bay area, and include a naval yard and naval air station. The city was damaged by earthquake in 1989.

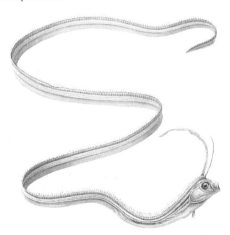

OARFISH The oarfish is a silver-bodied deep-sea fish found in warm parts of the Atlantic, Pacific, and Indian oceans.

oarfish any of a group of deep-sea bony fishes, found in warm parts of the Atlantic, Pacific, and Indian oceans. Oarfish are large, up to 9 m/30 ft long, elongated, and compressed, with a fin along the back and a manelike crest behind the head. They have a small mouth, no teeth or scales, and large eyes. They are often described as sea serpents. (Genus *Regalecidae*.)

oarweed (or **tangleweed**) any of several large, coarse, brown seaweeds found on the lower shore and below the low-tide mark, especially *L. digitata*. This species has fronds 1–2 m/3–6 ft long, a thick stalk, and a frond divided into flat fingers. In Japan and Korea it is cultivated and harvested commercially (especially genus *Laminaria*.)

OAS abbreviation for ▷Organization of American States.

oasis area of land made fertile by the presence of water near the surface in an otherwise arid region. The occurrence of oases affects the distribution of plants, animals, and people in the desert regions of the world.

oat type of annual grass, a ▷cereal crop. The plant has long narrow leaves and a stiff straw stem; the panicles of flowers (clusters around the main stem), and later of grain, hang downwards. The cultivated oat (*A. sativa*) is produced for human and animal food. (Genus *Avena*.)

Oates, Laurence Edward Grace (1880–1912) English Antarctic explorer who accompanied Robert Falcon ▷Scott on his second expedition to the South Pole. On the return journey, suffering from frostbite, he went out alone into the blizzard to die rather than delay the others.

Oates, Titus (1648–1705) English conspirator. A priest, he entered the Jesuit colleges at Valladolid, Spain, and St Omer, France, as a spy in 1677–78, and on his return to England announced he had discovered a 'Popish Plot' to murder Charles II and re-establish Catholicism. Although this story was almost entirely false, many innocent Roman Catholics were executed during 1678–80 on Oates's evidence.

oath solemn promise to tell the truth or perform some duty, combined with a declaration naming a deity or something held sacred. In English courts, witnesses normally swear to tell the truth holding a ▷New Testament in their right hand. In the USA, witnesses raise their right hand in taking the oath. People who object to the taking of oaths, such as ▷Quakers and atheists, give a solemn promise (affirmation) to tell the truth. Jews swear holding the Torah (Pentateuch), with their heads covered. Muslims and Hindus swear by their respective sacred books.

OAU abbreviation for ▷Organization of African Unity.

Oaxaca capital of a state of the same name in the Sierra Madre del Sur mountain range, central Mexico; population (1990) 212,900. Industries include food processing, textiles, and handicrafts.

Ob major river in Asian Russia, flowing 3,380 km/2,100 mi from the Altai Mountains through the western Siberian Plain to the Gulf of Ob in the Kara Sea (an inlet of the Arctic Ocean). With its main tributary, the **Irtysh**, the Ob is 5,600 km/3,480 mi long, and drains a total area of 2,990,000 sq km/1,150,000 sq mi.

obelisk tall, tapering column of stone, much used in ancient Egyptian and Roman architecture. Examples are Cleopatra's Needles (1475 BC), one of which is in London, another in New York.

Oberammergau village in Bavaria, Germany, 72 km/45 mi southwest of Munich. A Christian ▷passion play has been performed here every ten years since 1634 (except during the world wars) to commemorate the ending of the Black Death plague.

obesity condition of being overweight (generally, 20% or more above the medically recommended weight for one's sex, build, and height). Obesity increases susceptibility to disease, strains the vital organs, and reduces life expectancy; it is usually remedied by controlled weight loss, healthy diet, and exercise.

In 2000, 23% of US adults and 20% of British adults were considered to be obese. In some countries, such as Samoa, 50% of adults are obese.

obi (or **obeah**) form of witchcraft practised in the West Indies. It combines elements of Christianity and African religions, such as snake worship.

oboe musical instrument of the woodwind family, a refined treble shawm of narrow tapering bore and exposed double reed. The oboe was developed by the Hotteterre family of instrument-makers about 1700 and was incorporated in the court ensemble of Louis XIV. In C, with a normal compass of about $2\frac{1}{2}$ octaves, it has a rich tone of elegant finish. Oboe concertos have been composed by Vivaldi, Albinoni, Richard Strauss, Martinů, and others. Heinz Holliger is a modern virtuoso oboist.

Obote, (Apollo) Milton (1924–) Ugandan politician, prime minister 1962–66, and president 1966–71 and 1980–85. After forming the Uganda People's Congress (UPC) in 1959, he led the independence movement from 1961. As prime minister, his rule became increasingly authoritarian, and in 1966 he suspended the constitution and declared himself president. He was ousted by Idi ▷Amin in 1971, fleeing to exile in Tanzania. Returning in 1979 after the collapse of the Amin regime, he was re-elected president in 1980 but failed to restore order and was deposed by Lieutenant General Tito Okello in 1985.

obscenity law law established by the Obscene Publications Act 1959 prohibiting the publishing of any material that tends to deprave or corrupt. In Britain, obscene material can be, for example, pornographic or violent, or can encourage drug taking. Publishing includes distribution, sale, and hiring of the material. There is a defence in support of the public good if the defendant can produce expert evidence to show that publication was in the interest of, for example, art, science, or literature.

observatory site or facility for observing astronomical or meteorological phenomena. The modern observatory dates from the invention of the telescope. Observatories may be ground-based, carried on aircraft, or sent into orbit as satellites, in space stations, and on the space shuttle.

The erection of observatories was revived in West Asia about AD 1000, and extended to Europe. The observatory built on the island of Hven (now Ven) in Denmark in 1576 for Tycho Brahe (1546–1601) was elaborate, but survived only to 1597. Later, observatories were built in Paris in 1667, Greenwich (the ▷Royal Greenwich Observatory) in 1675, and Kew, England. Most early observatories were near towns, but with the advent of big telescopes, clear skies with little background light, and hence high, remote sites, became essential.

The most powerful optical telescopes covering the sky are at Mauna Kea, Hawaii; ▷Mount Palomar, California; Kitt Peak National Observatory, Arizona; La Palma, Canary Islands; Cerro Tololo Inter-American Observatory, and the European Southern Observatory, Chile; Siding Spring Mountain, Australia; and ▷Zelenchukskaya in the Caucasus.

Radio astronomy observatories include ▷Jodrell Bank, Cheshire, England; the Mullard Radio Astronomy Observatory, Cambridge, England; ▷Arecibo, Puerto Rico; ▷Effelsberg, Germany; and Parkes, Australia. The ▷Hubble Space Telescope was launched into orbit in 1990. The Very Large Telescope is under construction by the European Southern Observatory in the mountains of northern Chile, at the Cerro Paranal Space Obsevatory, and will transmit it first images in 2001.

obsession persistently intruding thought, emotion, or impulse, often recognized by the sufferer as irrational, but nevertheless causing distress. It may be a brooding on destiny or death, or chronic doubts interfering with everyday life (such as fearing the gas is not turned off and repeatedly checking), or an impulse leading to repetitive action, such as continually washing one's hands.

obsessive-compulsive disorder (OCD) in psychiatry, anxiety disorder that manifests itself in the need to check constantly that certain acts have been performed 'correctly'. Sufferers may, for example, feel compelled to wash themselves repeatedly or return home again and again to check that doors have been locked and appliances switched off. They may also hoard certain objects and insist in these being arranged in a precise way, or be troubled by intrusive and unpleasant thoughts. In extreme cases, normal life is disrupted through the hours devoted to compulsive actions. Treatment involves ▷cognitive therapy and drug therapy with serotonin-blocking drugs such as Prozac.

Related Web site: Obsessive-Compulsive Disorder http://ocd.mentalhelp.net/

obsidian black or dark-coloured glassy volcanic rock, chemically similar to ▷granite, but formed by cooling rapidly on the Earth's surface at low pressure.

obstetrics medical speciality concerned with the management of pregnancy, childbirth, and the immediate postnatal period.

O'Casey, Seán (1884–1964) Adopted name of John Casey. Irish dramatist, born in Dublin. His early plays are tragicomedies, blending realism with symbolism and poetic with vernacular speech: *The Shadow of a Gunman* (1923), *Juno and the Paycock* (1924), and *The Plough and the Stars* (1926). Later plays include *Red Roses for Me* (1946) and *The Drums of Father Ned* (1959).

> **Seán O'Casey**
> *There's no reason to bring religion into it. I think we ought to have as great a regard for religion as we can, so as to keep it out of as many things as possible.*
> The Plough and the Stars

Occam (or **Ockham**), **William of** (*c.* 1300–1349) English philosopher and scholastic logician who revived the fundamentals of nominalism. As a Franciscan monk he defended evangelical poverty against Pope John XXII, becoming known as the Invincible Doctor. He was imprisoned in Avignon, France, on charges of heresy in 1328 but escaped to Munich, Germany, where he died. The principle of reducing assumptions to the absolute minimum is known as **Occam's razor**.

occluded front weather ▷front formed when a cold front catches up with a warm front. It brings clouds and rain as air is forced to rise upwards along the front, cooling and condensing as it does so.

occult (Latin 'hidden from general view') vague term describing a wide range of activities connected with the supernatural, from seances to black magic. The term has come to have largely sinister overtones and an association with Satanism and witchcraft.

occupation in law, the physical possession and control of land. In the UK, under the Land Registration Act 1925, the rights of a person in actual occupation may be an overriding interest binding a purchaser of registered land, unless the rights are disclosed on inquiry.

ocean great mass of salt water. Geographically speaking three oceans exist – the Atlantic, Indian, and Pacific – to which the Arctic is often added; but they are often considered a single entity. They cover approximately 70% or 363,000,000 sq km/140,000,000 sq mi of the total surface area of the Earth. Water levels recorded in the world's oceans have shown an increase of 10–15 cm/4–6 in over the past 100 years.

Depth (average) 3,660 m/12,000 ft, but shallow ledges (continental shelves) 180 m/600 ft run out from the continents, beyond which the continental slope reaches down to the ▷abyssal zone, the largest area, ranging from 2,000–6,000 m/6,500–19,500 ft. Only the ▷deep-sea trenches go deeper, the deepest recorded being 11,034 m/36,201 ft (by the *Vityaz*, USSR) in the Mariana Trench of the western Pacific in 1957.

Features Deep trenches (off eastern and southeast Asia, and western South America), volcanic belts (in the western Pacific and eastern Indian Ocean), and ocean ridges (in the mid-Atlantic, eastern Pacific, and Indian Ocean).

Temperature Varies on the surface with latitude (−2°C to +29°C); decreases rapidly to 370 m/1,200 ft, then more slowly to 2,200 m/7,200 ft; and hardly at all beyond that.

Water contents Salinity averages about 3%; minerals commercially extracted include bromine, magnesium, potassium, salt; those potentially recoverable include aluminium, calcium, copper, gold, manganese, silver.

Pollution Oceans have always been used as a dumping area for human waste, but as the quantity of waste increases, and land areas for dumping it diminish, the problem is exacerbated. Today ocean pollutants include airborne emissions from land (33% by weight of total marine pollution); oil from both shipping and land-based sources; toxins from industrial, agricultural, and domestic uses; sewage; sediments from mining, forestry, and farming; plastic litter; and radioactive isotopes. Thermal pollution by cooling water from power plants or other industry is also a problem, killing coral and other temperature-sensitive sedentary species. See Major Oceans and Seas of the World on p. 702.

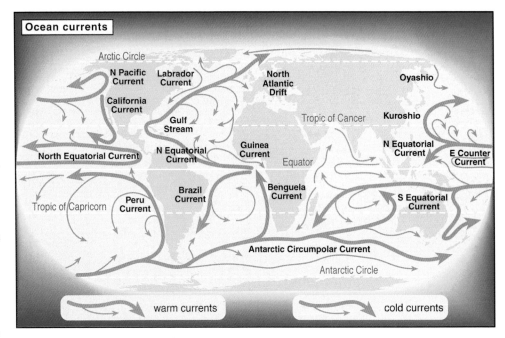

Ocean currents

Arctic Circle
N Pacific Current
Labrador Current
North Atlantic Drift
Oyashio
California Current
Tropic of Cancer
Kuroshio
Gulf Stream
Guinea Current
N Equatorial Current
North Equatorial Current
N Equatorial Current
E Counter Current
Equator
Brazil Current
Benguela Current
S Equatorial Current
Tropic of Capricorn
Peru Current
Antarctic Circumpolar Current
Antarctic Circle

warm currents   cold currents

OCEAN CURRENT Ocean currents are the movements of surface water in the oceans. Their direction is influenced by many factors, including the rotation of the Earth, the size and shapes of the continents, the prevailing winds, and even water density. Ocean currents caused by prevailing winds are called drift currents. In the northern hemisphere the circulation of the oceans is clockwise, in the southern hemisphere, the currents are anticlockwise. Currents originating from the polar regions carry cold water. Currents originating from the equatorial regions carry warm water.

ocean current fast-flowing body of seawater forced by the wind or by variations in water density (as a result of temperature or salinity variations) between two areas. Ocean currents are partly responsible for transferring heat from the Equator to the poles and thereby evening out the global heat imbalance.

Oceania the groups of islands in the southern and central Pacific Ocean, comprising all those intervening between the southeastern shores of Asia and the western shores of America. See ▷Australasia and Oceania.

Oceanic art the art of the native peoples of Australia and the South Pacific Islands, including New Guinea and New Zealand, have little historical depth, despite the classifying work of modern anthropology. Of the little that remains from the prehistoric period, an outstanding example is the sculpture of ▷Easter Island, huge standing figures, possibly representing ancestors. Most Oceanic arts are considered primitive in that until recently the indigenous cultures possessed no metal, and cutting tools were of stone or shell. For Australian aboriginal art, see ▷Australian art.

Melanesian art The most striking of all the Oceanic arts. Associated with ancestor and spirit cults, headhunting, and cannibalism, it is typified by exaggerated natural forms with prominent sexual motifs. Ritual masks made for use in the islands' elaborate festivals are both colourful and disturbing. Many of the carved figures are demonic in appearance, at least to Western eyes. The ancestor

figures, known as *uli*, from New Ireland have been amassed by Western collectors; *Soul Boat* is in the Linden Museum, Stuttgart. Melanesian art – little of which remains in the islands – has inspired such Western artists as ▷Ernst, ▷Brancusi, ▷Giacometti, and Henry ▷Moore, among others.

Polynesian art More decorative than that of Melanesia, characterized by the featherwork of Hawaii, the curvilinear surface ornament of the Maori carvers of New Zealand, and tattooing. Traditionally, cult objects were made to contain or conduct 'mana', a supernatural power.

Micronesian art Typically combines extreme functional simplicity with a high-quality finish. Surface decoration is rare. Few examples of Micronesian art have found their way into Western collections.

oceanography study of the oceans. Its subdivisions deal with each ocean's extent and depth, the water's evolution and composition, its physics and chemistry, the bottom topography, currents and wind, tidal ranges, biology, and the various aspects of human use. Computer simulations are widely used in oceanography to plot the possible movements of the waters, and many studies are carried out by remote sensing.

Oceanography involves the study of water movements – currents, waves, and tides – and the chemical and physical properties of the seawater. It deals with the origin and topography of the ocean floor – ocean trenches and ridges formed by ▷plate tectonics, and continental shelves from the submerged portions of the continents.

Related Web site: OceanLink http://oceanlink.island.net/index.html

ocean trench a submarine valley. Ocean trenches are characterized by the presence of a volcanic arc on the concave side of the trench. Trenches are now known to be related to subduction zones, places where a plate of oceanic ▷lithosphere dives beneath another plate of either oceanic or continental lithosphere. Ocean trenches are found around the edge of the Pacific Ocean and the northeastern Indian Ocean; minor ones occur in the Caribbean and near the Falkland Islands.

ocelot wild cat of the southwestern USA, Mexico, and Central and South America. It is up to 1 m/3 ft long, with a 45 cm/1.5 ft tail, weighs about 18 kg/40 lb, and has a pale yellowish coat marked with horizontal stripes and blotches. As a result of being hunted for its fur, it is close to extinction. (Species *Felis pardalis*, family Felidae.)

Ockham, William English philosopher; see ▷Occam.

O'Connell, Daniel (1775–1847) Irish lawyer and politician, known as 'the Liberator'. In 1823 he formed the Catholic Association, to campaign for Catholic emancipation and the repeal of the 1801 Act of Union between Britain and Ireland. He achieved the first objective in 1829, but failed in the second.

O'Connell's influence began to wane when his reserved and vacillating leadership and conservative outlook on social questions alienated his most active supporters. They broke away to form the more radical nationalist ▷Young Ireland movement.

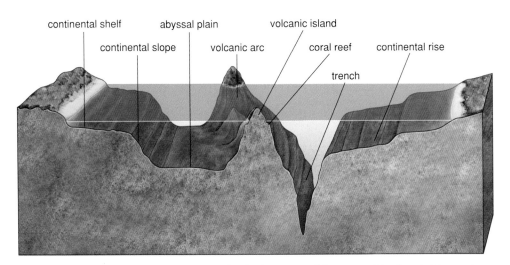

continental shelf   abyssal plain   volcanic island
continental slope   volcanic arc   coral reef   continental rise
trench

OCEAN The profile of an ocean floor. The ocean trench is the deepest part of the ocean and the abyssal plains constitute most of the ocean bed.

Major Oceans and Seas of the World

Ocean/sea	Area[1]		Average depth	
	sq km	sq mi	m	ft
Pacific Ocean	166,242,000	64,186,000	3,939	12,925
Atlantic Ocean	86,557,000	33,420,000	3,575	11,730
Indian Ocean	73,429,000	28,351,000	3,840	12,598
Arctic Ocean	13,224,000	5,106,000	1,038	3,407
South China Sea	2,975,000	1,149,000	1,464	4,802
Caribbean Sea	2,754,000	1,063,000	2,575	8,448
Mediterranean Sea	2,510,000	969,000	1,501	4,926
Bering Sea	2,261,000	873,000	1,491	4,893
Sea of Okhotsk	1,580,000	610,000	973	3,192
Gulf of Mexico	1,544,000	596,000	1,614	5,297
Sea of Japan	1,013,000	391,000	1,667	5,468
Hudson Bay	730,000	282,000	93	305
East China Sea	665,000	257,000	189	620
Andaman Sea	565,000	218,000	1,118	3,667
Black Sea	461,000	178,000	1,190	3,906
Red Sea	453,000	175,000	538	1,764
North Sea	427,000	165,000	94	308
Baltic Sea	422,000	163,000	55	180
Yellow Sea	294,000	114,000	37	121
Persian Gulf	230,000	89,000	100	328
Gulf of California	153,000	59,000	724	2,375
English Channel	90,000	35,000	54	177
Irish Sea	89,000	34,000	60	197

[1] All figures are approximate as boundaries of oceans and seas cannot be exactly determined.

See entry on p. 701.

O'Connor, (Mary) Flannery (1925–1964) US novelist and short-story writer. Her works have a great sense of evil and sin, and often explore the religious sensibility of the Deep South, as in her novels *Wise Blood* (1952) and *The Violent Bear It Away* (1960). Her work exemplifies the post-war revival of the ▷gothic novel in southern US fiction.

octane rating numerical classification of petroleum fuels indicating their combustion characteristics.

octave in music, a span of eight notes as measured on the white notes of a piano keyboard. It corresponds to the consonance of first and second harmonics.

Octavian original name of ▷Augustus, the first Roman emperor.

October Revolution second stage of the ▷Russian Revolution 1917, when, on the night of 24 October (6 November in the Western calendar), the Bolshevik forces under Trotsky, and on orders from Lenin, seized the Winter Palace and arrested members of the Provisional Government. The following day the Second All-Russian Congress of Soviets handed over power to the Bolsheviks.

Octobrists group of Russian liberal constitutional politicians who accepted the reforming October Manifesto instituted by Tsar Nicholas II after the 1905 revolution and rejected more radical reforms.

octopus soft-bodied sea animal with a round or oval body and eight slender arms (tentacles) in a ring surrounding its mouth. They are solitary creatures, living alone in rocky dens. They feed on crabs and other small animals. There are about 50 different species of octopus living in all the oceans of the world. Some are small, having bodies only 8 cm/3 in long, but the largest deep-sea species can grow to lengths of 20 m/64 ft.

Behaviour Octopuses can change colour to blend in with their surroundings and can swim using their arms or by a form of jet propulsion by squirting out water from their bodies. The octopus has rows of suckers along the length of each arm (or tentacle) which, as well as helping it swim and crawl around the ocean floor, allows it to search in cracks and crevices and grab prey. The octopus is a carnivore (flesh-eater), usually feeding on crabs, shrimps, and mussels, but the larger species of octopus have been known to hunt small sharks and dogfish. They trap the prey in their arms and drag it towards their powerful beaklike jaws. Once it has bitten its prey, the octopus injects it with a poisonous saliva to kill it. Sometimes, when frightened or to avoid enemies, they squirt out a black ink from their bodies which hides them and allows them to escape. If they lose an arm, they can grow another in its place. Octopuses are highly intelligent with two well developed eyes, similar to those of vertebrates (animals with backbones). They breathe using gills as fish do, but are unique in that they have three hearts.

Classification Octopuses belong to the phylum Mollusca (▷molluscs), class Cephalopoda (▷cephalopods), subclass Coleoidea. They belong to the genus *Octopus* and there are about 50 known species including the **common octopus** (*O. vulgaris*), which may reach 2 m/6 ft in length; the Australian blue-ringed octopus (genus *Hapalochlaena*) that can kill a human being in 15 minutes as a result of its venomous bite; and the giant deep-sea octopus (*Architeuthis dux*) that can grow to 20 m/64 ft.

Related Web site: Cephalopod Page http://is.dal.ca/~ceph/TCP/index.html

ode lyric poem of complex form. Odes originated in ancient Greece, where they were chanted to a musical accompaniment. Classical writers of odes include Sappho, Pindar, Horace, and Catullus. English poets who adopted the form include Spenser, Milton, Dryden, and Keats.

Oder (Polish **Odra**) European river flowing north from the Czech Republic to the Baltic Sea (the Neisse River is a tributary); length 885 km/550 mi.

Odessa principal seaport of Ukraine, on the Black Sea, and capital of the Odessa region (oblast); population (1990) 1,106,400. Odessa is a commercial port, naval base, and tourist resort. The principal industries here are shipbuilding, fishing, steelmaking, and food processing. Products manufactured in the city include chemicals, pharmaceuticals, and machinery. Among the main goods handled in the port are grain, sugar, timber, and oil.

The site of Odessa was under Turkish Ottoman control from 1526 to 1789. The city was founded by Catherine (II) the Great in 1795 near what was believed to be the ancient Greek settlement of Odessos, from which it took its name. It was bombarded during the ▷Crimean War. In the Revolution of 1905, Odessa was the site of a mutiny by sailors of the battleship *Potemkin*. It changed hands several times during the Russian Civil War 1918–20. Taken by German and Romanian forces in 1941, the city suffered severe damage from its three-year occupation and its recapture.

Related Web site: Odessa Web http://www.odessit.com/tours/tours/english/overview.htm

Odin (German **Woden** or **Wotan**; 'the raging one') chief god of Norse mythology, god of war, and the source of wisdom. A sky god, he lived in Asgard at the top of the world-tree ▷Yggdrasil. From the ▷Valkyries, his divine maidens, he received the souls of half those heroes slain in battle, feasting with them in his great hall Valhalla; the remainder were feasted by ▷Freya. His son was ▷Thor, god of thunder. Wednesday or Woden's day is named after him.

Odysseus (Latin **Ulysses**; 'son of wrath') chief character of Homer's *Odyssey*, king of the island of Ithaca (modern Thiaki or Levkas); he is also mentioned in the *Iliad* as one of the leaders of the Greek forces at the siege of Troy. Odysseus was distinguished among Greek leaders for his cleverness and cunning. He appears in other later tragedies, but his ten years' odyssey by sea after the fall of Troy is the most commonly known tradition.

OECD abbreviation for ▷Organization for Economic Cooperation and Development.

oedema any abnormal accumulation of fluid in tissues or cavities of the body; waterlogging of the tissues due to excessive loss of ▷plasma through the capillary walls. It may be generalized (the condition once known as dropsy) or confined to one area, such as the ankles.

Oedipus in Greek mythology, king of Thebes who unwittingly killed his father, Laius, and married his mother, Jocasta, in fulfilment of a prophecy. When he learned what he had done, he put out his eyes. His story was dramatized by the Greek tragedian ▷Sophocles.

Oedipus complex in psychology, the unconscious antagonism of a son to his father, whom he sees as a rival for his mother's affection. For a girl antagonistic to her mother as a rival for her father's affection, the term is **Electra complex**. The terms were coined by Sigmund ▷Freud.

oesophagus muscular tube by which food travels from the mouth to the stomach. The human oesophagus is about 23 cm/9 in long. It extends downwards from the ▷pharynx, immediately behind the windpipe. It is lined with a mucous membrane which secretes lubricant fluid to assist the downward movement of food (▷peristalsis).

oestrogen any of a group of hormones produced by the ▷ovaries of vertebrates; the term is also used for various synthetic hormones that mimic their effects. The principal oestrogen in mammals is oestradiol. Oestrogens control female sexual development, promote the growth of female secondary sexual characteristics, stimulate egg production, and, in mammals, prepare the lining of the uterus for pregnancy.

Oestrogens are used therapeutically for some hormone disorders and to inhibit lactation; they also form the basis of oral contraceptives. US researchers in 1995 observed that oestrogen plays a role in the healing of damaged blood vessels. It has also been found that women recover more quickly from strokes if given a low oestrogen dose.

oestrus in mammals, the period during a female's reproductive cycle (also known as the oestrus cycle or ▷menstrual cycle) when mating is most likely to occur. It usually coincides with ovulation.

Offa (died c. 796) King of the Anglo-Saxon kingdom of Mercia (west-central England) 757–97. He conquered Essex, Kent, Sussex, and Surrey; defeated the Welsh and the West Saxons; and established Mercian supremacy over all England south of the River Humber. He built the earthwork known as Offa's Dyke along the Welsh border to defend his frontier in the west.

Offaly county of the Republic of Ireland, in the province of Leinster, between Galway and Roscommon in the west and Kildare in the east; county town Tullamore; area 2,000 sq km/772 sq mi; population (1996) 59,100. It is low-lying, with part of the Bog of Allen to the north.

Offa's Dyke defensive earthwork dyke along the English–Welsh border, of which there are remains from the mouth of the River Dee to that of the River ▷Severn. It was built about AD 785 by King ▷Offa of Mercia, England, and represents the boundary secured by his wars with Wales.

Offenbach, Jacques (1819–1880) Adopted name of Jakob Levy Eberst. French composer. He wrote light opera, initially for presentation at the Bouffes Parisiens. Among his works are *Orphée aux enfers/Orpheus in the Underworld* (1858, revised 1874), *La belle Hélène* (1864), and *Les contes d'Hoffmann/The Tales of Hoffmann* (1881).

Official Secrets Act UK act of Parliament 1989, prohibiting the disclosure of confidential material from government sources by employees; it remains an absolute offence for a member or former member of the security and intelligence services (or those working closely with them) to disclose information about their work. There is no public-interest defence, and disclosure of information already in the public domain is still a crime. Journalists who repeat disclosures may also be prosecuted.

offset printing the most common method of ▷printing, which works on the principle of ▷lithography: that is, that grease and water repel one another.

O'Flaherty, Liam (1896–1984) Irish author. He is best known for his short stories published in volumes such as *Spring Sowing* (1924), *The Tent* (1926), and *Two Lovely Beasts* (1948). His novels, set in Dublin, are less poetic and more violent than his stories; they include *Thy Neighbour's Wife* (1923), *The Informer* (1925), winner of the Tait Black Memorial Prize, *Skerrett* (1932), and *Famine* (1937). *The Short Stories* (new edition) was published in 1986. O'Flaherty's writings have a strength acquired from his sense of primeval humanity beneath the layers of civilization.

Oflot the Office of the National Lottery. It was established in 1993 by the then Secretary of State for National Heritage, Peter Brooke. Its first task was to issue a licence to the National Lottery operator and thereafter to monitor its performance. In May 1994, a seven-year licence was issued to the Camelot Group, a consortium that included Cadbury-Schweppes, Racal Electronics, the bank note printers De La Rue, ICL, and an experienced US lottery group, G-Tech. The licence was renewed for a further seven years in December 2000.

Ogaden desert region in southeastern Ethiopia, between the Ethiopian Highlands and the border with Somalia. It is a desert plateau, rising to 1,000 m/3,280 ft, inhabited mainly by Somali nomads practising arid farming.

Ogbomosho industrial city and commercial centre in Oyo State, western Nigeria, 80 km/50 mi northeast of Ibadan; population (1992 est) 660,600. It is one of Nigeria's largest cities. Products include cattle, staple crops, cotton, and palm oil. There are tobacco and craft industries, and shoe, textile, and food-processing factories.

Oglethorpe, James Edward (1696–1785) English soldier and colonizer of Georgia, USA. He served in parliament for 32 years and in 1732 obtained a charter for the colony of Georgia, intended as a refuge for debtors and European Protestants.

Ogoni an ethnic minority of about 500,000 (1990) occupying an impoverished area of about 350 sq mi in the Niger river delta of Nigeria. The Ogoni speak Khana, Gokama, and Eleme languages that form a distinct branch of the Benue-Congo language family. They are fishermen and farmers, yams being the principal crop. In 1958 oil was discovered under their land. In protest at the pollution from the oil wells and their lack of any benefit from oil revenues, the Movement for the Survival of the Ogoni People (MOSOP) was founded in 1990 to seek both political autonomy and compensation for the destruction of their environment from the Nigerian government.

Ogun state of southwestern Nigeria; area 16,762 sq km/ 6,474 sq mi; capital Abeokuta; population (1991) 2,338,600.

OH abbreviation for the state of ▷Ohio, USA.

O Henry see ▷Henry, O, US author.

O'Higgins, Bernardo (1778–1842) Chilean revolutionary, known as 'the Liberator of Chile'. He was a leader of the struggle for independence from Spanish rule 1810–17 and head of the first permanent national government 1817–23.

Ohio river in east-central USA, 1,580 km/980 mi long and 365–1,220 m/1,200–4,005 ft wide; the second-largest tributary of the Mississippi; navigable throughout its length. It is formed by the union of the Allegheny and Monongahela rivers at Pittsburgh, Pennsylvania, and flows southwest to join the Mississippi at Cairo, Illinois.

Ohio state in northern central USA. It is nicknamed the Buckeye State. It was admitted to the Union in 1803 as the 17th US state. Part of the Midwest, it is bordered to the east by Pennsylvania, to the east and southeast by West Virginia, to the southwest by Kentucky, to the west by Indiana, to the northwest by Michigan's Lower Peninsula, and to the north by Lake Erie. Ohio comprises the eastern section of the US Corn Belt; heavily industrialized, it is also a quintessential Rust Belt state, today struggling with pollution and the need to diversify industrially.

> **population** (1995) 11,150,500 **area** 107,100 sq km/41,341 sq mi **capital** Columbus **towns and cities** Cleveland, Cincinnati, Dayton, Akron, Toledo, Youngstown, Canton **industries and products** coal, cereals, livestock, dairy foods, machinery, chemicals, steel, motor vehicles, automotive and aircraft parts, rubber products, office equipment, refined petroleum, tourism

ohm SI unit (symbol Ω) of electrical ▷resistance (the property of a conductor that restricts the flow of electrons through it).

Ohm, Georg Simon (1789–1854) German physicist who studied electricity and discovered the fundamental law that bears his name (see ▷Ohm's law). The SI unit of electrical resistance, the ohm, is named after him, and the unit of conductance (the inverse of resistance) was formerly called the mho, which is 'ohm' spelled backwards.

Ohm's law law that states that, for many materials over a wide range of conditions, the current flowing in a conductor maintained at constant temperature is directly proportional to the potential difference (voltage) between its ends. The law was discovered by German physicist Georg Ohm in 1827.

oil flammable substance, usually insoluble in water, and composed chiefly of carbon and hydrogen. Oils may be solids (fats and waxes) or liquids. The three main types are: **essential oils**, obtained from

---

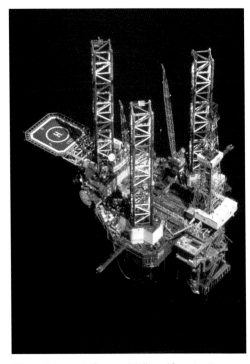

OIL An oil rig – a platform and drill used for extracting crude oil from the seabed – in the Mediterranean Sea. *Image Bank*

plants; **fixed oils**, obtained from animals and plants; and **mineral oils**, obtained chiefly from the refining of ▷petroleum.

Essential oils are volatile liquids that have the odour of their plant source and are used in perfumes, flavouring essences, and ▷aromatherapy. Fixed oils are mixtures of ▷lipids of varying consistency, found in both animals (for example, fish oils) and plants (in nuts and seeds); they are used as foods and lubricants, and in the making of soaps, paints, and varnishes. Mineral oils are composed of a mixture of hydrocarbons, and are used as fuels and lubricants.

Eight of the 14 top-earning companies in the USA in 1990 (led by Exxon with $7 billion in sales) were in the global petroleum industry.

The crude oil (unrefined petroleum) found beneath the Earth's surface was formed from the remains of dead plants and animals. As these plants and animals died they were buried with mud near the sea floor. Over millions of years, heat from the Earth's interior and pressure from overlying rocks slowly changed the dead remains into hydrocarbons (substances containing hydrogen and carbon). The hydrocarbons, being light molecules, moved upwards and became trapped beneath impermeable rocks. Oil reservoirs are often found beneath the seabed and drilling technology is used to locate these supplies of oil. Crude oil extracted from the ground is refined in fractional distillation columns to produce more useful products such as petrol, diesel, kerosene, plastics, and chemicals for pharmaceuticals.

oil, cooking fat that is liquid at room temperature, extracted from the seeds or fruits of certain plants and used for frying, salad dressings, and sauces and condiments such as mayonnaise and mustard. Plants used for cooking oil include sunflower, olive, maize (corn), soya, peanut, and rape. Vegetable oil is a blend of more than one type of oil. Most oils are hot-pressed and refined, a process that leaves them without smell or flavour. Cold-pressed, unrefined oils keep their flavour. Oils are generally low in cholesterol and contain a high proportion of polyunsaturated or

OKAPI The okapi has a prehensile tongue that is used to pick tasty leaves. The tongue is so long that the animal uses it to clean its eyes and eyelids.

---

monounsaturated fatty acids, although all except soya and corn oil become saturated when heated.

oil crop plant from whose seeds vegetable oils are pressed. Cool temperate areas grow rapeseed and linseed; warm temperate regions produce sunflowers, olives, and soybeans; tropical regions produce groundnuts (peanuts), palm oil, and coconuts.

oil paint painting medium in which ground pigment is bound with oil, usually linseed.

oil palm African ▷palm tree, the fruit of which yields valuable oils, used as food or processed into margarine, soaps, and livestock feeds. (*Elaeis guineensis*.)

oil spill oil released by damage to or discharge from an ocean-going tanker, pipeline, or oil installation. An oil spill kills shore life, clogging the feathers of birds and suffocating other creatures. At sea, toxic chemicals leach into the water below, poisoning sea life. Mixed with dust, the oil forms globules that sink to the seabed, poisoning sea life there as well. Oil spills are broken up by the use of detergents but such chemicals can themselves damage wildlife. The annual spillage of oil is 8 million barrels a year. At any given time tankers are carrying 500 million barrels.

Oise European river that rises in the Ardennes plateau, Belgium, and flows southwest through France for 300 km/186 mi to join the Seine at Conflans-Sainte-Honorine, about 65 km/40 mi south of Paris. It gives its name to the French *département* of Oise in Picardy.

OK abbreviation for the state of ▷Oklahoma, USA.

okapi ruminant (cud-chewing) mammal related to the giraffe, although with a much shorter neck and legs, found in the tropical rainforests of central Africa. Its purplish brown body, creamy face, and black and white stripes on the legs and hindquarters provide excellent camouflage. Okapis have remained virtually unchanged for millions of years. (Species *Okapia johnstoni*, family Giraffidae.)

The okapi was unknown to Europeans until 1901; now only a few hundred are thought to survive.

Okavango Delta marshy area in northwest Botswana covering about 20,000 km/7,722 sq mi, fed by the Okavango River, which rises in Angola and flows southeast about 1,600 km/1,000 mi. It is an important area for wildlife as it provides the main area of permanently available water in the Kalahari Desert.

Okayama industrial port and old castle town in the southwest of Honshu island, Japan, 120 km/75 mi west of Kobe; population (1994) 598,000. The main industries are cotton spinning and the manufacture of rubber, chemicals, agricultural implements, and 'tatami' and 'hanamushiro', types of Japanese matting. The Korakuen is one of the three most important traditional gardens in Japan. The others are in Mito and Kanazawa.

Okeechobee, Lake lake in the northern Everglades, south-central Florida; roughly circular, it is 65 km/40 mi long and 40 km/ 25 mi wide, and reaches a depth of 6 m/20 ft. It is the largest lake in the southern USA, about 1,800 sq km/700 sq mi. There are numerous small islands in the lake, which receives the Kissimmee River from the northwest. Since the 1930s, diking around the south shore has prevented overflow; drainage canals are used for light navigation to the Atlantic Ocean. The lake is a fishing resort with some commercial fisheries.

O'Keeffe, Georgia (1887–1986) US painter. She is known chiefly for her large, semi-abstract studies of flowers and bones, such as *Black Iris* (1926; Metropolitan Museum of Art, New York) and the *Pelvis Series* of the 1940s. She was married 1924–46 to photographer and art exhibitor Alfred ▷Stieglitz, in whose gallery her work was first shown.

Born in Sun Prairie, Wisconsin, she studied art in Chicago. Her mature style stressed contours and subtle tonal transitions, which often transformed the subject into a powerful and erotic abstract image. In 1946 she settled in New Mexico, where the desert landscape inspired many of her paintings.

Related Web site: O'Keeffe, Georgia http://www.ionet.net/~jellenc/okeeffe1.html

Okhotsk, Sea of arm of the North Pacific Ocean between the Kamchatka Peninsula and Sakhalin, and bordered to the south by the Kuril Islands, and the northern Japanese island of Hokkaido; area 937,000 sq km/361,700 sq mi, average depth 777 m/2,550 ft, maximum depth 3,372 m/11,062 ft. It is free of ice only in summer, and is often fog-bound. Magadan is the chief port, and the River Amur flows into it.

Okinawa group of islands, 520 km/323 mi from the Japanese mainland, forming part of the Japanese ▷Ryukyu Islands in the west Pacific; Okinawa is also the name of the largest island, and of a city on Okinawa; area 2,250 sq km/869 sq mi; population (1995) 1,274,000. The capital is ▷Naha.

Oklahoma state in southern central USA. It is nicknamed the Sooner State. Oklahoma was admitted to the Union in 1907 as the 46th US state. It is bordered to the south by Texas, to the west, at the extreme of the Oklahoma panhandle, by New Mexico, to the north by Colorado and Kansas, and to the east by Missouri and Arkansas. Oklahoma is the US state most associated with American Indians; its name is a Choctaw coinage meaning 'red people'.

population (1995) 3,277,700 **area** 181,100 sq km/69,900 sq mi **capital** Oklahoma City **towns and cities** Tulsa, Lawton, Norman, Enid **industries and products** cereals, peanuts, cotton, livestock, oil, natural gas, helium, machinery and other metal products

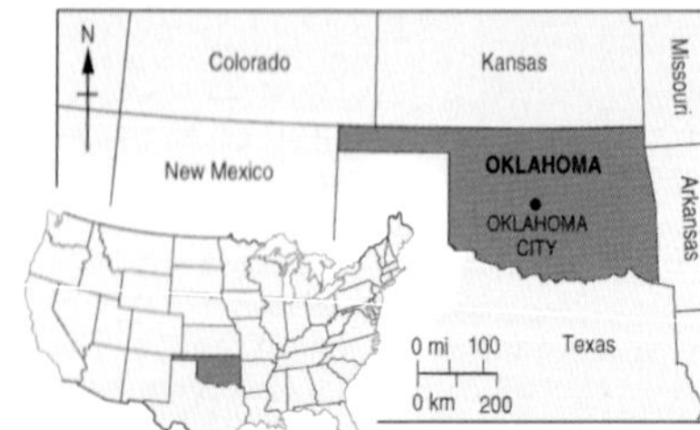

Oklahoma City capital of ▷Oklahoma, USA, on the North Canadian River; population (1998 est) 472,200. It is a major commercial, service, and distribution centre for a rich oil-producing and agricultural area; its cattle markets are among the largest and busiest in the world. Industries include oil refining, food processing (meat and cereals), car hire, and the manufacture of iron, steel, machinery, cars, tyres, aircraft, electronic equipment, and cotton. Manufacturing makes up more than 10% of employment in the region (1999), and the health sector is also a significant employer. A right-wing terrorist bomb attack occurred in 1995, killing 168 people. Timothy McVeigh, who had links with anti-government militia groups, was found guilty of the bombing in 1997 and was executed in June 2001.

On 22 April 1889, a tent city of nearly 10,000 inhabitants appeared overnight when the area was opened to settlement. It became state capital in 1910. Oil was discovered in 1928, and derricks are situated even on the state capitol grounds. A General Motors car plant was established in 1979. Several military installations are located within the area. These include the Tinker airforce base, which employs almost 8,000 military personnel and 13,500 civilians (1999). In May 1999, Oklahoma City was hit by a category 5 tornado with the strongest wind speeds ever recorded – over 300 mph/480 kmph. The damage trail reached for 19 × 1 mi/30.6 × 1.6 km; 22 people in the city died, with further deaths outside the city.

Related Web site: Oklahoma City http://www.okccvb.org/

okra plant belonging to the Old World hibiscus family. Its red-and-yellow flowers are followed by long, sticky, green fruits known as **ladies' fingers** or **bhindi**. The fruits are cooked in soups and stews. (*Hibiscus esculentus*, family Malvaceae.)

Okri, Ben (1959–) Nigerian novelist, short-story writer, broadcaster, and journalist. His novel *The Famished Road* won the UK Booker Prize in 1991. Short-story collections include 'Incidents at the Shrine' (1987) and 'Stars of the New Curfew' (1988). His first book of poems, *An African Elegy* (1992), is based on contemporary Africa. More recent work includes *Astonishing the Gods* (1995) and a collection of essays *A Way of Being* (1997).

Olaf five kings of Norway, including:

Olaf (I) Tryggvesson (*c.* 969–1000) King of Norway from 995. He began the conversion of Norway to Christianity and was killed in a sea battle against the Danes and Swedes.

Olaf (II) Haraldsson (*c.* 995–1030) King of Norway from 1015. He offended his subjects by his centralizing policy and zeal for Christianity, and was killed in battle by Norwegian rebel chiefs backed by ▷Canute of Denmark. He was declared the patron saint of Norway in 1164.

Olaf V (1903–1991) King of Norway from 1957, when he succeeded his father, Haakon VII.

Old Catholic one of various breakaway groups from Roman Catholicism, including those in the Netherlands (such as the **Church of Utrecht**, which separated from Rome in 1724 after accusations of ▷Jansenism); and groups in Austria, Czechoslovakia, Germany, and Switzerland, which rejected the proclamation of ▷papal infallibility of 1870. Old Catholic clergy are not celibate.

Oldenburg, Claes Thure (1929–) US pop artist. He organized happenings and made assemblages, but is best known for 'soft sculptures', gigantic replicas of everyday objects and foods, made of stuffed canvas or vinyl. One characteristic work is *Lipstick* (1969; Yale University, Connecticut, USA).

Old English general name for the range of dialects spoken by Germanic settlers in England between the 5th and 12th centuries AD, also known as Anglo-Saxon. The literature of the period includes 'Beowulf', an epic in West Saxon dialect. See also ▷Old English literature and ▷English language.

Related Web site: Modern English to Old English Vocabulary http://www.mun.ca/Ansaxdat/vocab/wordlist.html

Old English literature poetry and prose in the various dialects of Old English written between AD 449 and 1066. Poetry (alliterative, without rhyme) was composed and delivered orally; much has therefore been lost. What remains owes its survival to monastic scribes who favoured verse with a Christian motivation or flavour. Prose in Old English was a later achievement, essentially beginning in the reign of Alfred the Great.

The greatest surviving epic poem is 'Beowulf' (*c.* 700), which recounts the hero's battles with mythical foes such as the man-eating Grendel and his mother. 'Widsith', 'The Wanderer', 'Finnsburgh' (about a tragic battle), and 'Waldhere' (fragments of a lost epic), all written in the mid-7th century, also belong to the earlier centuries and express the bleakness and melancholy of life. 'The Battle of Maldon', written soon after the event in 991, extols heroic values of courage in defeat.

One of the earliest attributed short poems consists of six lines by ▷Caedmon the herder, reputedly inspired to sing about the Creation by a vision. 'The Dream of the Rood' (*c.* 698) shows the cult of the Cross, as does ▷Cynewulf's 'Elene'. Elegies, including 'The Seafarer', written before 940, express the sense of loneliness in exile and an inflexible Fate.

Prose in Old English dates from Alfred the Great's translations of St Gregory, Boethius, and Bede's *History of the English Peoples* (first published in Latin in 731, translated between 871 and 899). Historical writing began with the ▷*Anglo-Saxon Chronicle*, at first brief notes of yearly events but later a dignified and even poetic narrative. The existing version of the Chronicle dates from King Alfred's reign and was compiled from earlier records (now lost) purporting to go back to the time of Adam. Dating from the 10th and 11th centuries are sermons by ▷Aelfric, a Dorset monk who also translated the Old Testament, and those by the prelate Wulfstan (died 1023). Some spells and riddles have also survived.

> **Laurence Olivier**
> *What is acting but lying and what is good acting but convincing lying?*
> Autobiography

Old Pretender nickname of ▷James Edward Stuart, the son of James II of England.

Old Testament Christian term for the Hebrew ▷Bible, which is the first part of the Christian Bible. It contains 39 (according to Christianity) or 24 (according to Judaism) books, which include the origins of the world, the history of the ancient Hebrews and their covenant with God, prophetical writings, and religious poetry. The first five books (*The five books of Moses*) are traditionally ascribed to Moses and known as the Pentateuch (by Christians) or the ▷Torah (by Jews).

Olduvai Gorge deep cleft in the Serengeti steppe, Tanzania, where Louis and Mary ▷Leakey found prehistoric stone tools in the 1930s. They discovered Pleistocene remains of prehumans and gigantic animals 1958–59. The gorge has given its name to the **Olduvai culture**, a simple stone-tool culture of prehistoric hominids, dating from 2–0.5 million years ago.

Old World the continents of the eastern hemisphere, so called because they were familiar to Europeans before the Americas. The term is used as an adjective to describe animals and plants that live in the eastern hemisphere.

oleander (or **rose bay**) evergreen Mediterranean shrub belonging to the dogbane family, with pink or white flowers and aromatic leaves that produce and release the poison oleandrin. (*Nerium oleander*, family Apocynaceae.)

olefin common name for ▷alkene.

oligarchy (Greek *oligarchia* 'government of the few') rule of the few, in their own interests. It was first identified as a form of government by the Greek philosopher Aristotle. In modern times there have been a number of oligarchies, sometimes posing as democracies; the paramilitary rule of the ▷Duvalier family in Haiti, 1957–86, is an example.

Oligocene epoch third epoch of the Tertiary period of geological time, 35.5–3.25 million years ago. The name, from Greek, means 'a little recent', referring to the presence of the remains of some modern types of animals existing at that time.

oligopoly in economics, a situation in which a few companies control the major part of a particular market. For example, in the UK the two largest soap-powder companies, Procter & Gamble and Unilever, control over 85% of the market. In an oligopolistic market, firms may well join together in a ▷cartel, colluding to fix high prices. This collusion, an example of a ▷restrictive trade practice, is illegal in the UK and the European Union.

oligosaccharide ▷carbohydrate comprising a few ▷monosaccharide units linked together. It is a general term used to indicate that a carbohydrate is larger than a simple di- or trisaccharide but not as large as a polysaccharide.

olive evergreen tree belonging to the olive family. Native to Asia but widely cultivated in Mediterranean and subtropical areas, it grows up to 15 m/50 ft high and has twisted branches and lance-shaped silvery leaves that grow opposite each other. The white flowers are followed by small green oval fruits that turn bluish-black when ripe. They are preserved in brine or oil, dried, or pressed to make olive oil. (*Olea europaea*, family Oleaceae.)

olive branch ancient symbol of peace; in the Bible (Genesis 9), an olive branch is brought back by the dove to Noah to show that the flood has abated.

olivenite basic copper arsenate, $Cu_2AsO_4(OH)$, occurring as a mineral in olive-green prisms.

Olives, Mount of range of hills east of Jerusalem, associated with the Christian religion: a former chapel (now a mosque) marks the traditional site of Jesus' ascension to heaven, with the Garden of Gethsemane at its foot.

Olivier, Laurence (Kerr) (1907–1989) English actor and director. For many years associated with the Old Vic Theatre, he was director of the National Theatre company 1962–73 (see ▷National Theatre, Royal). His stage roles include Henry V, Hamlet, Richard III, and Archie Rice in John Osborne's *The Entertainer* (1957; filmed 1960). He directed and starred in filmed versions of Shakespeare's plays; for example, *Henry V* (1944) and *Hamlet* (1948) (Academy Award). He was knighted in 1947 and created a baron in 1970.

Olivier appeared in many films, including *Wuthering Heights* (1939), *Rebecca* (1940), *Sleuth* (1972), *Marathon Man* (1976), and *The Boys from Brazil* (1978).

Related Web site: Olivier, Laurence http://www.reelclassics.com/Actors/Olivier/olivier.htm

olivine greenish mineral, magnesium iron silicate, $(Mg,Fe)_2SiO_4$. It is a rock-forming mineral, present in, for example, peridotite, gabbro, and basalt. Olivine is called **peridot** when pale green and transparent, and used in jewellery.

olm cave-dwelling aquatic ▷salamander. Olms are found in underground caves along the Adriatic seaboard in Italy and Croatia. The adult is permanently larval in form, about 25 cm/10 in long, almost blind, with external gills and underdeveloped limbs. See ▷neoteny. (Species *Proteus anguinus*, family Proteidae.)

Olmec first civilization of Mesoamerica and thought to be the mother culture of the Mayans. It developed in the coastal zone south of Vera Cruz and in adjacent Tabasco 1200–400 BC. The Olmecs built a large clay pyramid and several smaller mounds on the island of La Venta. Some gigantic stone heads, vestiges of their religion, also remain. The naturalistic Olmec art had a distinctive and influential style, often using the 'were-jaguar' motif of a sexless figure with fangs.

Olympia ancient sanctuary in the western Peloponnese, Greece, with a temple of Zeus, stadium (for foot races, boxing, and wrestling) and hippodrome (for chariot and horse races), where the original Olympic Games, founded 776 BC, were held every four years. The gold and ivory statue of Zeus that stood here, made by ▷Phidias, was one of the ▷Seven Wonders of the World. It was removed to Constantinople, where it was destroyed in a fire. The face of Zeus may have served as a model for the face of Christ Pantocrator in the dome of St Sophia.

Olympic Games sporting contests originally held in Olympia, ancient Greece, every four years during a sacred truce; records were kept from 776 BC. Women were forbidden to be present, and the male contestants were naked. The ancient Games were abolished in AD 394. The present-day games have been held every four years since 1896. Since 1924 there has been a separate winter Games programme; since 1994 the winter and summer Games have been

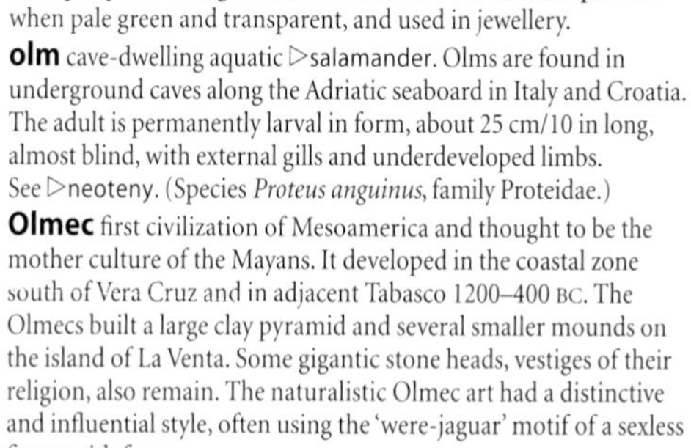

OLYMPIC GAMES The sports stadium built in Sydney, New South Wales, Australia, for the 2000 Olympic Games, designed by Bligh Lobb Sports Architects. *Image Bank*

held two years apart. Athens is scheduled to host the 2004 Games, and Beijing, China, will host the 2008 Games.

Olympus (Greek *Olimbos*) any of several mountains in Greece and elsewhere, one of which is **Mount Olympus** in northern Thessaly, Greece, which is 2,918 m/9,577 ft high. In ancient Greece it was considered the home of the gods.

Om sacred word in Hinduism, used to begin prayers and placed at the beginning and end of books. It is composed of three syllables, symbolic of the Hindu Trimurti, or trinity of gods.

Oman see country box.

Omar alternative spelling of ▷Umar, 2nd caliph of Islam.

Omar Khayyám (*c.* 1050–*c.* 1123) Persian astronomer, mathematician, and poet. In the West, he is chiefly known as a poet through Edward ▷Fitzgerald's version of 'The Rubaiyat of Omar Khayyám' (1859).

Khayyám was born in Nishapur. He founded a school of astronomical research and assisted in reforming the calendar. The result of his observations was the *Jalali* era, begun 1079. He wrote a study of algebra, which was known in Europe as well as in the East.
Related Web site: Khayyam, Omar http://www.history.mcs.st-and. ac.uk/history/Mathematicians/Khayyam.html

Omayyad dynasty alternative spelling of ▷Umayyad dynasty.

ombudsman (Swedish 'commissioner') official who acts on behalf of the private citizen in investigating complaints against the government. The post is of Scandinavian origin; it was introduced in Sweden in 1809, Denmark in 1954, and Norway in 1962, and spread to other countries from the 1960s.

Omdurman city in Khartoum State, Sudan, on the west bank of the White Nile, now considered a major suburb of Khartoum; population (1995 est) 719,000. It trades in hides, textiles, livestock, and handicrafts. It is connected to Khartoum by a bridge over the White Nile. Omdurman was built as a new city to be the residence of the Sudanese ruler known as the Mahdi, and his successor Khalifa Abdullah el Taaisha. The city is a religious and cultural centre for the majority Muslim population of the Sudan, and at the city centre is the tomb of the ▷Mahdi (Muhammad Ahmed).

Omdurman, Battle of victory 2 September 1898 of British and Egyptian troops under General Horatio Kitchener over Sudanese tribesmen (Dervishes) led by the Khalifa Abdullah el Taashi. The Khalifa escaped, to be pursued and later brought to battle and killed.

BATTLE OF OMDURMAN *The Battle of Omdurman, September 2, 1898* by A Sutherland. *Art Archive*

Omega Workshops group of early 20th-century English artists (1913–20), led by Roger ▷Fry, who brought them together to design and make interiors, furnishings, and craft objects. The workshops included members of the ▷Bloomsbury Group,

Oman

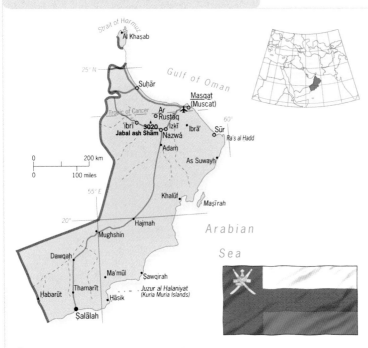

Oman country at the southeastern end of the Arabian peninsula, bounded west by the United Arab Emirates, Saudi Arabia, and Yemen, southeast by the Arabian Sea, and northeast by the Gulf of Oman.

NATIONAL NAME *Saltanat `Uman/Sultanate of Oman*
AREA 272,000 sq km/105,019 sq mi
CAPITAL Muscat
MAJOR TOWNS/CITIES Salalah, Ibri, Sohar, Al-Buraimi, Nizwa, Sur, Matrah
MAJOR PORTS Mina Qaboos, Mina Raysut
PHYSICAL FEATURES mountains to the north and south of a high arid plateau; fertile coastal strip; Jebel Akhdar highlands; Kuria Muria Islands

Government

HEAD OF STATE AND GOVERNMENT Qaboos bin Said from 1970
POLITICAL SYSTEM absolutist
POLITICAL EXECUTIVE absolute
ADMINISTRATIVE DIVISIONS eight regional governorates, subdivided into 59 districts
ARMED FORCES 41,700 (2002 est)
DEATH PENALTY retained and used for ordinary crimes

Economy and resources

CURRENCY Omani rial
GPD (US$) 20.1 billion (2002 est)
REAL GDP GROWTH (% change on previous year) 5.9 (2001)
GNI (US$) 19.1 billion (2002 est)
GNI PER CAPITA (PPP) (US$) 12,910 (2002 est)
CONSUMER PRICE INFLATION 2.7% (2003 est)
FOREIGN DEBT (US$) 6.1 billion (2001 est)
MAJOR TRADING PARTNERS United Arab Emirates, Japan, South Korea, China, Thailand, USA, UK
RESOURCES petroleum, natural gas, copper, chromite, gold, salt, marble, gypsum, limestone
INDUSTRIES mining, petroleum refining, cement, construction materials, copper smelting, food processing, chemicals, textiles
EXPORTS petroleum and gas, metals and metal goods, textiles, animals and products. Principal market: China 22.3% (2001)
IMPORTS machinery and transport equipment, basic manufactures, food and live animals, beverages, tobacco. Principal source: United Arab Emirates 28.4% (2001)

ARABLE LAND 0.1% (2000 est)
AGRICULTURAL PRODUCTS dates, tomatoes, limes, alfalfa, mangoes, melons, bananas, coconuts, cucumbers, onions, peppers, frankincense (agricultural production is mainly at subsistence level); livestock; fishing

Population and society

POPULATION 2,851,000 (2003 est)
POPULATION GROWTH RATE 2.2% (2000–15)
POPULATION DENSITY (per sq km) 13 (2003 est)
URBAN POPULATION (% of total) 78 (2003 est)
AGE DISTRIBUTION (% of total population) 0–14 43%, 15–59 53%, 60+ 4% (2002 est)
ETHNIC GROUPS predominantly Arab, with substantial Iranian, Baluchi, Indo-Pakistani, and East African minorities
LANGUAGE Arabic (official), English, Urdu, other Indian languages
RELIGION Muslim 75% (predominantly Ibadhi Muslim), about 25% Hindu
EDUCATION not compulsory
LITERACY RATE 81% (men); 64% (women) (2003 est)
LABOUR FORCE 9.4% agriculture, 27.8% industry, 62.8% services (1993)
LIFE EXPECTANCY 71 (men); 74 (women) (2000–05)
CHILD MORTALITY RATE (under 5, per 1,000 live births) 13 (2001)
PHYSICIANS (per 1,000 people) 1.3 (1998 est)
HOSPITAL BEDS (per 1,000 people) 2.2 (1998 est)
TV SETS (per 1,000 people) 575 (1999)
RADIOS (per 1,000 people) 598 (1998)
INTERNET USERS (per 10,000 people) 664.0 (2002 est)

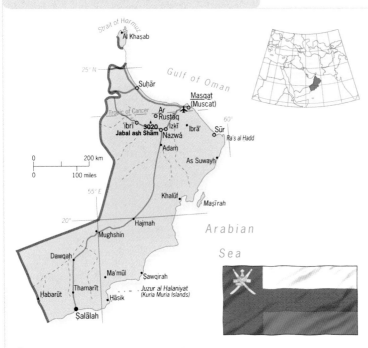

OMAN The satellite photograph shows the Jebel Samhan mountain range. *Photodisc*

PERSONAL COMPUTER USERS (per 100 people) 3.5 (2002 est)

Chronology

c. **3000 BC**: Archaeological evidence suggests Oman may have been the semilegendary Magan, a thriving seafaring state at the time of the Sumerian Civilization of Mesopotamia (the Tigris and Euphrates region of Iraq).

9th century BC: Migration of Arab clans to Oman, notably the Qahtan family from southwest Arabia and the Nizar from northwest Arabia, between whom rivalry has continued.

4th century BC–AD 800: North Oman under Persian control.

AD 630: Converted to Islam.

751: Julanda ibn Masud was elected imam (spiritual leader); Oman remained under imam rule until 1154.

1151: Dynasty established by Banu Nabhan.

1428: Dynastic rule came under challenge from the imams.

1507: Coastal area, including port city of Muscat, fell under Portuguese control.

1650: Portuguese ousted by Sultan ibn Sayf, a powerful Ya'ariba leader.

early 18th century: Civil war between the Hinawis (descendents of the Qahtan) and the Ghafiris (descendents of the Nizar).

1749: Independent Sultanate of Muscat and Oman established by Ahmad ibn Said, founder of the Al Bu Said dynasty that still rules Oman.

first half of 19th century: Muscat and Oman was the most powerful state in Arabia, ruling Zanzibar until 1861, and coastal parts of Persia, Kenya, and Pakistan; came under British protection.

1951: The Sultanate of Muscat and Oman achieved full independence from Britain. Treaty of Friendship with Britain signed.

1964: Discovery of oil led to the transformation of the undeveloped kingdom into a modern state.

1970: After 38 years' rule, Sultan Said bin Taimur was replaced in a bloodless coup by his son Qaboos bin Said. Name was changed to the Sultanate of Oman and a modernization programme was launched.

1975: Left-wing rebels in Dhofar in the south, who had been supported by South Yemen, defeated with UK military assistance, ending a ten-year insurrection.

1981: The Consultative Council was set up; Oman played a key role in the establishment of a six-member Gulf Cooperation Council.

1982: The Memorandum of Understanding with the UK was signed, providing for regular consultation on international issues.

1991: Joined the US-led coalition opposing Iraq's occupation of Kuwait.

such as Vanessa Bell, Duncan Grant, Wyndham Lewis, and Henri Gaudier-Brzeska.

omnivore animal that feeds on both plant and animal material. Omnivores have digestive adaptations intermediate between those of ▷herbivores and ▷carnivores, with relatively unspecialized digestive systems and gut micro-organisms that can digest a variety of foodstuffs. Omnivores include humans, the chimpanzee, the cockroach, and the ant.

OMR abbreviation for ▷optical mark recognition.

Omsk capital city, economic and cultural centre of Omsk oblast (region), Russian Federation; population (1996 est) 1,160,000. Omsk is located at the junction of the Om and Irtysh rivers and lies on the Trans-Siberian Railway, 900 km/559 mi east of Yekaterinburg. The city is a major industrial and commercial centre of west Siberia. It contains engineering works, oil refineries (linked with Tuimazy in Bashkortostan by a 1,600-km/1,000-mi pipeline), wood-processing plants, and various food and other light industrial factories.

onager wild ass found in western Asia. Onagers are sandy brown, lighter underneath, and about the size of a small horse. (Species *Equus hemionus.*)

onchocerciasis (or **river blindness**) disease found in tropical Africa and Central America. It is transmitted by bloodsucking black flies, which infect the victim with parasitic filarial worms (genus *Onchocerca*), producing skin disorders and intense itching; some invade the eyes and may cause blindness.

oncogene gene carried by a virus that induces a cell to divide abnormally, giving rise to a cancer. Oncogenes arise from mutations in genes (proto-oncogenes) found in all normal cells. They are usually also found in viruses that are capable of transforming normal cells to tumour cells. Such viruses are able to insert their oncogenes into the host cell's DNA, causing it to divide uncontrollably. More than one oncogene may be necessary to transform a cell in this way.

oncology medical speciality concerned with the diagnosis and treatment of ▷neoplasms, especially cancer.

onco-mouse mouse that has a human ▷oncogene (gene that can cause certain cancers) implanted into its cells by genetic engineering. Such mice are used to test anticancer treatments and were patented within the USA by Harvard University in 1988, thereby protecting its exclusive rights to produce the animal and profit from its research.

Onega, Lake (Russian **Onezhskoye Ozero**) lake in the far northwestern Russian Federation, near the Finnish border. With an area of some 9,600 sq km/3,700 sq mi (excluding islands), it is the second-largest lake in Europe. Lake Onega is connected by the River Svir with Lake Ladoga (the largest lake in Europe) and the Baltic Sea, and by artificial waterways with the White Sea and the Volga (the 'Mariinsk' system).

O'Neill, Eugene Gladstone (1888–1953) US playwright. He is widely regarded as the greatest US dramatist. His plays, although tragic, are characterized by a down-to-earth quality and are often experimental in form, influenced by German expressionism, Strindberg, and Freud. They were a radical departure from the romantic and melodramatic American theatre entertainments. They include *Beyond the Horizon* (1920) and *Anna Christie* (1921), both of which won a Pulitzer prize, as well as *The Emperor Jones* (1920), *The Hairy Ape* (1922), *Desire Under the Elms* (1924), *The Iceman Cometh* (1946), and the posthumously produced autobiographical drama *A Long Day's Journey into Night* (1956; written 1941), also a Pulitzer prize winner. He was awarded the Nobel Prize for Literature in 1936.

O'Neill was born in New York City, the son of stage actors James O'Neill and Ella Quinlan. His tumultuous family relationships would later provide much material for his plays. He had varied experience as gold prospector, sailor, and actor. Other plays include *The Great God Brown* (1925), *Strange Interlude* (1928; which lasts five hours), ▷*Mourning Becomes Electra* (1931; a trilogy on the theme of Orestes from Greek mythology), and *A Moon for the Misbegotten* (1947; written 1943).

Related Web site: Beyond the Horizon http://www.bartleby.com/132/index.html

one-party state state in which one political party dominates, constitutionally or unofficially, to the point where there is no effective opposition. There may be no legal alternative parties, as, for example, in Cuba. In other instances, a few token members of an opposition party may be tolerated, or one party may be permanently in power, with no elections. The one-party state differs from the 'dominant-party' state, where one party controls government for an extended period, as the Liberal Democrats did in Japan 1955–93, but where there are openly democratic competitive elections.

onion plant belonging to the lily family, whose bulb has a strong, distinctive smell and taste. Cultivated from ancient times, it may have originated in Asia. The bulb is edible; its pale concentric layers of leaf bases contain an oil that is released into the air when the onion is cut open, causing the eyes to water. Onions are used extensively in cooking. (*Allium cepa*, family Liliaceae.)

Related Web site: Onions, Garlic, and Shallots http://www.ext.vt.edu/pubs/envirohort/426-411/426-411.html#L1

online system in computing, originally a system that allows the computer to work interactively with its users, responding to each instruction as it is given and prompting users for information when necessary. As almost all the computers used now work this way, 'online system' is now used to refer to large database, electronic mail, and conferencing systems accessed via a dial-up modem. These often have tens or hundreds of users from different places – sometimes from different countries – 'on line' at the same time.

onomatopoeia (Greek 'name-making') ▷figure of speech that copies natural sounds. For example, the word 'cuckoo' imitates the sound that the cuckoo makes.

Ontario province of southeastern–central Canada, in area the country's second-largest province, and its most populous. It is bounded to the north and northeast by Hudson Bay and James Bay, to the east by Québec (with the Ottawa River forming most of the boundary), and by Manitoba to the west. On the south, it borders on, and extends into, all of the Great Lakes except Lake Michigan. From west to east along Ontario's southern boundary lie the US states of Minnesota, Wisconsin, Michigan, Ohio, Pennsylvania, and New York; area 1,068,600 sq km/412,600 sq mi; population (1996) 11,252,400. The capital is ▷Toronto (Canada's largest city). Industries include mining (nickel, iron, gold, copper, uranium) and the production of cars, aircraft, iron, steel, high-tech goods, pulp, paper, oil, and chemicals; agriculture includes livestock rearing, and cultivation of fruit, vegetables, and cereals.

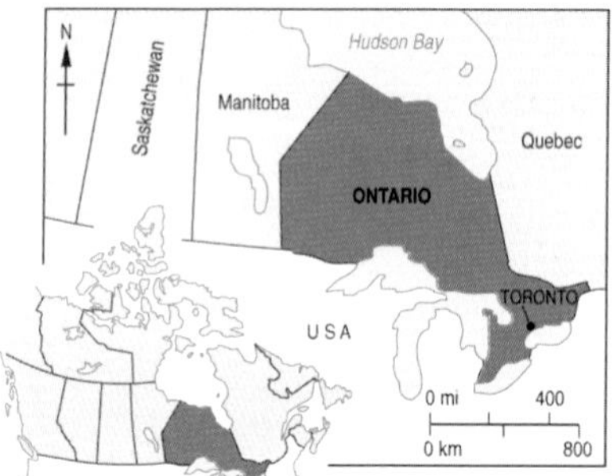

Ontario, Lake smallest and easternmost of the ▷Great Lakes, on the US–Canadian border; area 19,200 sq km/7,400 sq mi. Extending for 310 km/194 mi, it has an average width of about 80 km/50 mi, and maximum depth of 244m/800 ft. It is connected to Lake Erie in the southeast by the ▷Welland Ship Canal and the Niagara River, and drains into the ▷St Lawrence River to the northeast. The opening of the ▷St Lawrence Seaway in 1959 made the lake accessible to large ocean-going vessels. Its main port is Toronto, Canada.

ontogeny process of development of a living organism, including the part of development that takes place after hatching or birth. The idea that 'ontogeny recapitulates phylogeny' (the development of an organism goes through the same stages as its evolutionary history), proposed by the German scientist Ernst Heinrich Haeckel, is now discredited.

onyx semiprecious variety of chalcedonic ▷silica (SiO_2) in which the crystals are too fine to be detected under a microscope, a state known as cryptocrystalline. It has straight parallel bands of different colours: milk-white, black, and red.

oolite limestone made up of tiny spherical carbonate particles, called **ooliths**, cemented together. Ooliths have a concentric structure with a diameter up to 2 mm/0.08 in. They were formed by chemical precipitation and accumulation on ancient sea floors.

Oort, Jan Hendrik (1900–1992) Dutch astronomer. In 1927, he calculated the mass and size of our Galaxy, the ▷Milky Way, and the Sun's distance from its centre, from the observed movements of stars around the Galaxy's centre. In 1950 Oort proposed that comets exist in a vast swarm, now called the ▷Oort cloud, at the edge of the Solar System.

In 1944 Oort's student Hendrik van de Hulst (1918–) calculated that hydrogen in space would emit radio waves at 21 cm/8.3 in wavelength, and in the 1950s Oort's team mapped the spiral structure of the Milky Way from the radio waves given out by interstellar hydrogen.

Oort cloud spherical cloud of comets beyond Pluto, extending out to about 100,000 astronomical units (approximately 1.0 light years) from the Sun. The gravitational effect of passing stars and the rest of our Galaxy disturbs comets from the cloud so that they fall in towards the Sun on highly elongated orbits, becoming visible from Earth. As many as 10 trillion comets may reside in the Oort cloud, named after Dutch astronomer Jan Oort who postulated it in 1950.

oosphere another name for the female gamete, or ▷ovum, of certain plants such as algae.

ooze sediment of fine texture consisting mainly of organic matter found on the ocean floor at depths greater than 2,000 m/6,600 ft. Several kinds of ooze exist, each named after its constituents.

opah (or **moonfish**) large marine bony fish. These fish may be up to 2 m/6.6 ft long and weigh approximately 200 kg/440 lb. They are widely distributed in warm seas, and feed on squids, crustaceans, and small fish.

opal form of hydrous ▷silica ($SiO_2.nH_2O$), often occurring as stalactites and found in many types of rock. The common opal is translucent, milk-white, yellow, red, blue, or green, and lustrous. Precious opal is opalescent, the characteristic play of colours being caused by close-packed silica spheres diffracting light rays within the stone.

op art (abbreviation for optical art) type of abstract art, mainly painting, in which patterns are used to create the impression that the image is flickering or vibrating. This type of art began to emerge in about 1960 and the name was coined in 1964; it is a pun on ▷pop art, a dominant style in the art world at the time.

OPEC acronym for ▷Organization of Petroleum-Exporting Countries.

opencast mining (or **open-pit mining** or **strip mining**) mining at the surface rather than underground. Coal, iron ore, and phosphates are often extracted by opencast mining. Often the mineral deposit is covered by soil, which must first be stripped off, usually by large machines such as walking draglines and bucket-wheel excavators. The ore deposit is then broken up by explosives.

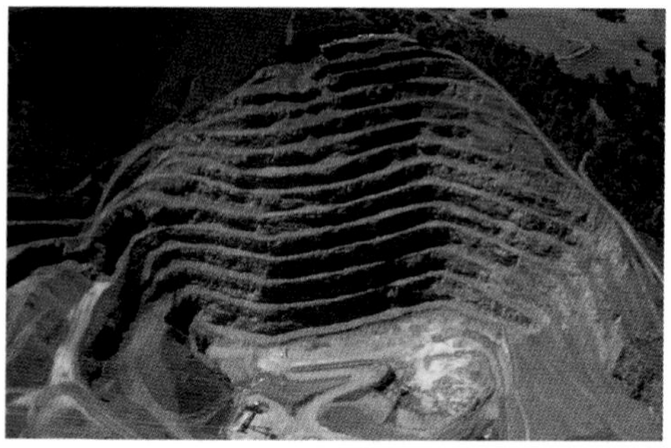

OPENCAST MINING An aerial view of a quarry in California, USA that clearly shows the terraces formed by the opencast mining process. Limestone is being dug out to form the basis of cement – the stone is heat-processed with clay, producing a powdery mixture of calcium and silicates (including aluminium). *Image Bank*

Open College in the UK, a network launched in 1987 by the Manpower Services Commission (now the Training Agency) to enable people to gain and update technical and vocational skills by means of distance teaching, such as correspondence, radio, and television.

open-hearth furnace method of steelmaking, now largely superseded by the ▷basic-oxygen process. It was developed in 1864 in England by German-born William and Friedrich Siemens, and improved by Pierre and Emile Martin in France in the same year. In the furnace, which has a wide, saucer-shaped hearth and a low roof, molten pig iron and scrap are packed into the shallow hearth and heated by overhead gas burners using preheated air.

open shop factory or other business employing men and women not belonging to trade unions, as opposed to the ▷closed shop, which employs trade unionists only.

Open University institution established in the UK in 1969 to enable mature students without qualifications to study to degree level without regular attendance. Open University teaching is based on a mixture of correspondence courses, television and radio lectures and demonstrations, personal tuition organized on a regional basis, and summer schools.

Related Web site: Open University http://www.open.ac.uk/

opera dramatic musical work in which singing takes the place of speech. In opera, the music accompanying the action has paramount importance, although dancing and spectacular staging may also play their parts. Opera originated in late 16th-century Florence when the musical declamation, lyrical monologues, and choruses of classical Greek drama were reproduced in current forms.

Early development One of the earliest opera composers was Jacopo Peri, whose *Euridice* influenced Claudio Monteverdi, the first great master of the operatic form. Initially solely a court entertainment, opera soon became popular, and in 1637 the first public opera house was opened in Venice. It spread to other Italian towns, to Paris (about 1645), and to Vienna and Germany, where it remained Italian at the courts but became partly German at Hamburg from about 1680.

In the later 17th century the elaborately conventional aria, designed to display the virtuosity of the singer, became predominant, overshadowing the dramatic element. Composers of this type of opera included Pier Cavalli, Pietro Antonio Cesti (1623–1669), and Alessandro Scarlatti. In France, opera was developed by Jean-Baptiste Lully and Jean-Philippe Rameau, and in England by Henry Purcell, but the Italian style retained its ascendancy, as exemplified by Georg Handel.

J Robert Oppenheimer
The atomic bomb . . . made the prospect of future war unendurable. It has led us up those last few steps to the mountain pass; and beyond there is a different country.
Quoted in R Rhodes *The Making of the Atomic Bomb* 1987

Comic opera (opera buffa) was developed in Italy by such composers as Giovanni Battista Pergolesi (1710–1736), while in England *The Beggar's Opera* (1728) by John Gay started the vogue of the **ballad opera**, using popular tunes and spoken dialogue. **Singspiel** was the German equivalent (although its music was newly composed). A lessening of artificiality began with Christoph Willibald von Gluck, who insisted on the pre-eminence of the dramatic over the purely vocal element. Wolfgang Mozart learned much from Gluck in writing his serious operas, but excelled in Italian opera buffa (humerous opera). In works such as *The Magic Flute*, he laid the foundations of a purely German-language opera, using the *Singspiel* as a basis. This line was continued by Ludwig van Beethoven in *Fidelio* and by the work of Carl Weber, who introduced the Romantic style for the first time in opera.

Developments into the 19th century The Italian tradition, which placed the main stress on vocal display and melodic suavity (*bel canto*), continued unbroken into the 19th century in the operas of Gioacchino Rossini, Gaetano Donizetti, and Vincenzo Bellini. It is in the Romantic operas of Weber and Giacomo Meyerbeer that the work of Richard Wagner has its roots. Dominating the operatic scene of his time, Wagner attempted to create, in his 'music-dramas', a new art form, and completely transformed the 19th-century conception of opera. In Italy, Giuseppe Verdi assimilated, in his mature work, much of the Wagnerian technique, without sacrificing the Italian virtues of vocal clarity and melody. This tradition was continued by Giacomo Puccini. In French opera in the mid-19th century, represented by such composers as Léo Delibes, Charles Gounod, Camille Saint-Saëns, and Jules Massenet, the drama was subservient to the music. Comic opera (*opéra comique*), as represented in the works of André Gréry (1741–1813) and, later, Daniel Auber, became a popular genre in Paris. More serious artistic ideals were put into practice by Hector Berlioz in *The Trojans*, but the merits of his work were largely unrecognized in his own time.

George Bizet's *Carmen* began a trend towards realism in opera; his lead was followed in Italy by Pietro Mascagni, Ruggero Leoncavallo, and Puccini. Claude Debussy's *Pelléas et Mélisande* represented a reaction against the over-emphatic emotionalism of Wagnerian opera. National operatic styles were developed in Russia by Mikhail Glinka, Nikolai Rimsky-Korsakov, Modest Mussorgsky, Alexander Borodin, and Pyotr Ilyich Tchaikovsky, and in Bohemia by Bedřich Smetana and, later, Dvořák and Janáček. Several composers of light opera emerged, including Arthur Sullivan, Franz Lehár, Jacques Offenbach, and Johann Strauss.

20th-century opera In the 20th century the Viennese school produced an outstanding opera in Alban Berg's *Wozzeck*, and the Romanticism of Wagner was revived by Richard Strauss in *Der Rosenkavalier*. Other 20th-century composers of opera include George Gershwin, Leonard Bernstein, and John Adams in the USA; Roberto Gerhard, Michael Tippett, Benjamin Britten, and Harrison Birtwistle in the UK; Arnold Schoenberg, Paul Hindemith, and Hans Henze in Germany; Luigi Dallapiccola and Goffreddo Petrassi in Italy; and the Soviet composers Sergey Prokofiev and Dmitry Shostakovich. The operatic form has developed in many different directions, for example, towards oratorio in Igor Stravinsky's *Oedipus Rex* (1925), and towards cabaret and music-theatre, as represented by the works of Kurt Weill.

operating system (OS) in computing, a program that controls the basic operation of a computer. A typical OS controls the peripheral devices such as printers, organizes the filing system, provides a means of communicating with the operator, and runs other programs.

Many operating systems were written to run on specific computers, but some are available from third-party software houses and will run on machines from a variety of manufacturers. Examples include Apple's OS 9, Microsoft's ▷Windows, and Unix.

Unix (developed at AT&T's Bell Laboratories) is the standard on workstations, minicomputers, and supercomputers; it is also used on desktop PCs and mainframes. Windows is the standard on desktop PCs.

operational amplifier (or **op-amp**) electronic circuit that is used as a basic building block in electronic design. Operational amplifiers are used in a wide range of electronic measuring instruments. The name arose because they were originally designed to carry out mathematical operations and solve equations.

operetta light form of opera, with music, dance, and spoken dialogue. The story line is romantic and sentimental, often employing farce and parody. Its origins lie in the 19th-century *opéra comique* and it is intended to amuse. Examples of operetta are Jacques Offenbach's *Orphée aux enfers/Orpheus in the Underworld* (1858), Johann Strauss' *Die Fledermaus/The Flittermouse* (1874), and Gilbert and Sullivan's *The Pirates of Penzance* (1879) and *The Mikado* (1885).

operon group of genes that are found next to each other on a chromosome, and are turned on and off as an integrated unit. They usually produce enzymes that control different steps in the same biochemical pathway by a single operator gene. Operons were discovered in 1961 (by the French biochemists François Jacob and Jacques Monod) in bacteria.

ophthalmia neonatorum form of ▷conjunctivitis mostly contracted during delivery by an infant whose mother is infected with ▷gonorrhoea. It can lead to blindness unless promptly treated.

ophthalmology medical speciality concerned with diseases of the eye and its surrounding tissues.

Ophüls, Max (1902–1957) Adopted name of Max Oppenheimer, German film director. His style is characterized by an ironic, bittersweet tone and intricate camera movement. He worked in Europe and the USA, attracting much critical praise for such films as *Letter from an Unknown Woman* (1948), *Caught* (1949), *The Reckless Moment* (1949), *La Ronde* (1950), *The Earrings of Madame de ...* (1953), and *Lola Montès* (1955).

opiate, endogenous naturally produced chemical in the body which has effects similar to morphine and other opiate drugs; a type of neurotransmitter.

Examples include ▷endorphins and encephalins.

opinion poll attempt to measure public opinion by taking a survey of the views of a representative sample of the electorate; the science of opinion sampling is called **psephology**. Most standard polls take random samples of around a thousand voters, which give results that should be accurate to within three percentage points, 95% of the time. The first accurately sampled opinion poll was carried out by George ▷Gallup during the US presidential election in 1936.

opium drug extracted from the unripe seeds of the opium poppy (*Papaver somniferum*) of southwestern Asia. An addictive ▷narcotic, it contains several alkaloids, including **morphine**, one of the most powerful natural painkillers and addictive narcotics known, and **codeine**, a milder painkiller.

Opium Wars two wars, the First Opium War 1839–42 and the Second Opium War 1856–60, waged by Britain against China to enforce the opening of Chinese ports to trade in opium. Opium from British India paid for Britain's imports from China, such as porcelain, silk, and, above all, tea.

The **First Opium War** resulted in the cession of Hong Kong to Britain and the opening of five treaty ports. Other European states were also subsequently given concessions. The **Second Opium War** followed, with Britain and France in alliance against China, when there was further Chinese resistance to the opium trade. China was forced to give the European states greater trading privileges, at the expense of its people.

Oporto English form of ▷Porto, a city in Portugal.

opossum any of a family of marsupials (mammals that carry their young in a pouch) native to North and South America. Most opossums are tree-living, nocturnal animals, with prehensile tails that can be used as an additional limb, and hands and feet well adapted for grasping. They range from 10 cm/4 in to 50 cm/20 in in length and are insectivorous, carnivorous, or, more commonly, omnivorous. (Family Didelphidae.)

The name is also popularly applied to some of the similar-looking phalangers found in Australia.

However, the **common opossum** (*Didelphis marsupialis*), with yellowish-grey fur, has spread its range into North America.

Oppenheimer, J(ulius) Robert (1904–1967) US physicist. As director of the Los Alamos Science Laboratory 1943–45, he was in charge of the development of the atom bomb (the Manhattan Project). He objected to the development of the hydrogen bomb, and was alleged to be a security risk in 1953 by the US Atomic Energy Commission (AEC).

opposition in astronomy, the moment at which a body in the Solar System lies opposite the Sun in the sky as seen from the Earth and crosses the ▷meridian at about midnight.

Although the ▷inferior planets cannot come to opposition, it is the best time for observation of the superior planets as they can then be seen all night.

Opposition, Leader of His/Her Majesty's in UK politics, official title (from 1937) of the leader of the largest opposition party in the House of Commons. Since 1989 the post has received a government salary, starting at £98,000 (from 1997).

optical character recognition (OCR) in computing, a technique for inputting text to a computer by means of a document reader. First, a ▷scanner produces a digital image of the text; then character-recognition software makes use of stored knowledge about the shapes of individual characters to convert the digital image to a set of internal codes that can be stored and processed by computer.

optical disk in computing, a storage medium in which laser technology is used to record and read large volumes of digital data. Types include ▷CD-ROM, ▷WORM, and erasable optical disk.

optical fibre very fine, optically pure glass fibre through which light can be reflected to transmit images or data from one end to the other. Although expensive to produce and install, optical fibres can carry more data than traditional cables, and are less susceptible to interference. Standard optical fibre transmitters can send up to 10 billion bits of information per second by switching a laser beam on and off.

Optical fibres are increasingly being used to replace metal communications cables, the messages being encoded as digital pulses of light rather than as fluctuating electric current. Current research is investigating how optical fibres could replace wiring inside computers.

Bundles of optical fibres are also used in endoscopes to inspect otherwise inaccessible parts of machines or of the living body (see ▷endoscopy).

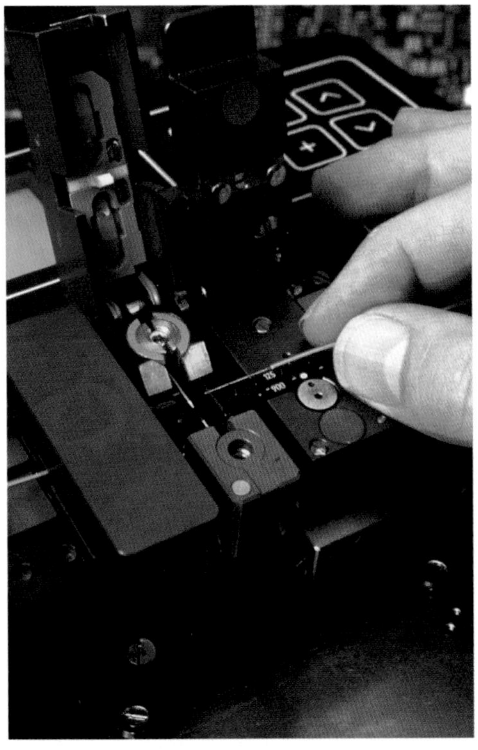

OPTICAL FIBRE Fibre-optic splicing. *Image Bank*

optical illusion scene or picture that fools the eye. An example of a natural optical illusion is that the Moon appears bigger when it is on the horizon than when it is high in the sky, owing to the ▷refraction of light rays by the Earth's atmosphere.

optical mark recognition (OMR) in computing, a technique that enables marks made in predetermined positions on computer-input forms to be detected optically and input to a computer. An **optical mark reader** shines a light beam onto the input document and is able to detect the marks because less light is reflected back from them than from the paler, unmarked paper.

optic nerve large nerve passing from the eye to the brain, carrying visual information. In mammals, it may contain up to a million nerve fibres, connecting the sensory cells of the retina to the optical centres in the brain. Embryologically, the optic nerve develops as an outgrowth of the brain.

optics branch of physics that deals with the study of ▷light and vision – for example, shadows and mirror images, lenses, microscopes, telescopes, and cameras. On striking a surface, light rays are reflected or refracted with some absorption of energy, and the study of this is known as geometrical optics.

opting out in UK education, schools that choose to be funded directly from the Department for Education and Employment are said to be opting out of local-authority control. The Education Reform Act 1988 gave this option to all secondary schools and the larger primary schools, and in 1990 it was extended to all primary schools. However, by 1995 only 1,040 of 27,000 schools had opted out.

option in business, a contract giving the owner the right (as opposed to the obligation, as with futures contracts; see ▷futures trading) to buy or sell a specific quantity of a particular commodity or currency at a future date and at an agreed price, in return for a premium. The buyer only can decide not to exercise the option if it would prove disadvantageous, but in this case would lose the premium paid.

optoelectronics branch of electronics concerned with the development of devices (based on the ▷semiconductor gallium arsenide) that respond not only to the ▷electrons of electronic data transmission, but also to ▷photons.

opuntia any ▷cactus belonging to the same group of plants as the ▷prickly pear. They all have showy flowers and fleshy, jointed stems. (Genus *Opuntia*, family Cactaceae.)

OR abbreviation for ▷Oregon, a state of the USA.

oracle (Latin *orare* 'to speak') sacred site where a deity gives answers or oracles, through the mouth of its priest, to a supplicant's questions about personal affairs or state policy. These were often ambivalent. There were more than 250 oracular seats in the Greek world. The earliest example was probably at Dodona (in ▷Epirus), where priests interpreted the sounds made by the sacred oaks of ▷Zeus, but the most celebrated was that of ▷Apollo, god of prophecy, at ▷Delphi.

oral literature stories that are or have been transmitted in spoken form, such as public recitation, rather than through writing or printing. Most pre-literate societies have had a tradition of oral literature, including short folk tales, legends, myths, proverbs, and riddles, as well as longer narrative works; and most of the ancient epics – such as the Greek *Odyssey* and the Mesopotamian *Gilgamesh* – seem to have been composed and added to over many centuries before they were committed to writing.

Oran (Arabic *Wahran*) fortified seaport and commercial and manufacturing centre in Algeria, 5 km/3 mi from the port of Mers-el-Kebir; population (1998 est) 850,500. Products include cigarettes, iron, plastics, textiles, footwear, and processed food; the port trades in grain, wool, vegetables, and native esparto grass. Natural gas is brought to the city via a pipeline from the Sahara, and hydrocarbons are exported. There is an international airport. A university was established in 1965.

Orange river in South Africa, rising at the Mont-aux-Sources in the Maluti Mountains in Lesotho and flowing west to the Atlantic Ocean; length 2,100 km/1,300 mi. It runs along the southern boundary of the Free State Province. Water from the Orange is diverted via the Orange-Fish River Tunnel (1975) to irrigate the semi-arid Eastern Cape Province. It was named in 1779 after William of Orange.

orange round orange-coloured juicy citrus fruit of several species of evergreen trees, which bear white blossom and fruits at the same time. Thought to have originated in Southeast Asia, orange trees are commercially cultivated in Spain, Israel, the USA, Brazil, South Africa, and elsewhere. The sweet orange (*C. sinensis*) is commonly eaten fresh; the Jaffa, blood, and navel orange are varieties of this species. (Genus *Citrus*, family Rutaceae.)

ORANGE Oranges growing in Valencia, Spain. The first orange groves in California, USA, were set up by the Spanish in the 18th century. *Image Bank*

Orange, House of royal family of the Netherlands. The title is derived from the small principality of Orange in southern France, held by the family from the 8th century to 1713. They held considerable possessions in the Netherlands, to which, after 1530, was added the German county of Nassau.

Orangeman in Northern Ireland, a member of one of the Ulster Protestant **Orange Societies** established within the ▷Orange Order (founded 1795).

Orange Order in Northern Ireland, solely Protestant organization founded in County Armagh in 1795 in opposition to the Defenders, a Catholic secret society. It was a revival of the Orange Institution founded in 1688 to support ▷William (III) of Orange, whose victory over the Catholic James II at the Battle of the ▷Boyne in 1690 has been commemorated annually by Protestants in parades since 1796. The new order was organized into **Orange Societies** in a similar way to freemasonry, with a system of lodges. It has institutional ties with the Ulster Unionist Party.

orang-utan large ape found only in Borneo and Sumatra. Up to 1.65 m/5.5 ft in height, it is covered with long, red-brown hair and lives a largely solitary life in the trees, feeding mainly on fruit. Now an endangered species, it is officially protected because its habitat is being systematically destroyed by ▷deforestation. In 1998 there were fewer than 27,000 orang-utans in the wild, with an estimated 5,000–7,000 in Sumatra, 3,000–5,000 in Sabah (northeast Borneo), and 12,000–15,000 in Kalimantan (Indonesia). (Species *Pongo pygmaeus*.)

There are two subspecies: *P. p. pygmaeus* found in Borneo, and the smaller *P. p. abelli* on the island of Sumatra. Their rate of reproduction is very slow, with an eight-year gap between births. Orang-utans are slow-moving and have been hunted for food, as well as by animal collectors. The name means 'man of the forest'.

Oratorian member of the Roman Catholic order of secular priests, called in full **Congregation of the Oratory of St Philip Neri**, formally constituted by Philip Neri in 1575 in Rome, and characterized by the degree of freedom allowed to individual communities.

oratorio dramatic, nonscenic musical setting of religious texts, scored for orchestra, chorus, and solo voices. Its origins lie in the *Laude spirituali* performed by St Philip Neri's Oratory in Rome in the 16th century, followed by the first definitive oratorio in the 17th century by Cavalieri. The form reached perfection in such works as J S Bach's *Christmas Oratorio*, and Handel's *Messiah*.

orbit path of one body in space around another, such as the orbit of Earth around the Sun, or the Moon around Earth. When the two bodies are similar in mass, as in a ▷binary star, both bodies move around their common centre of mass. The movement of objects in orbit follows Johann ▷Kepler's laws, which apply to artificial satellites as well as to natural bodies.

As stated by the laws, the orbit of one body around another is an ellipse. The ellipse can be highly elongated, as are comet orbits around the Sun, or it may be almost circular, as are those of some planets. The closest point of a planet's orbit to the Sun is called **perihelion**; the most distant point is **aphelion**. (For a body orbiting the Earth, the closest and furthest points of the orbit are called **perigee** and **apogee**.)

orbital, atomic region around the nucleus of an atom (or, in a molecule, around several nuclei) in which an ▷electron is likely to be found. According to ▷quantum theory, the position of an electron is uncertain; it may be found at any point. However, it is more likely to be found in some places than in others, and this pattern of probabilities makes up the orbital.

orchestra group of musicians playing together on different instruments. In Western music, an orchestra is typically based on the bowed, stringed instruments of the violin family, but often contains wind, brass, and percussion sections. The size and format may vary according to the requirements of composers.
History The term was originally used in Greek theatre for the semicircular space in front of the stage, and was adopted in 17th-century France to refer first to the space in front of the stage where musicians sat, and later to the musicians themselves.
Western instruments The string section is commonly divided into two groups of violins (first and second), violas, cellos, and double basses. During the 18th century, the most common additions to the strings were pairs of horns and oboes. The woodwind section became standardized by the end of the 18th century, when it consisted of two each of flutes, oboes, clarinets, and bassoons, to which were later added piccolo, ▷cor anglais, bass clarinet, and double bassoon. At that time, two timpani and two horns were also standard, and two trumpets were occasionally added. During the 19th century, the brass section was gradually expanded to include four horns, three trumpets, three trombones, and tuba. To the percussion section a third timpano was added, and from Turkey came the bass drum, side drum, cymbals, and triangle. One or more harps became common and, to maintain balance, the number of string instruments to a part also increased. Other instruments used in the orchestra include xylophone, ▷celesta, ▷glockenspiel, piano (which superseded the harpsichord in the late 18th century), and organ. In the 20th century, composers have often preferred smaller groupings of instruments, often in unconventional combinations.
Non-Western ensembles The term may also be applied to non-Western ensembles such as the Indonesian ▷gamelan orchestra, founded on families of percussion instruments, mainly tuned gongs and bells.

orchestration scoring of a composition for orchestra; the choice of instruments of a score expanded for orchestra (often by another hand). A work may be written for piano, then transferred to an orchestral score.

orchid any plant of a large family that contains at least 15,000 species and 700 genera, distributed throughout the world except in the coldest areas, and most numerous in damp equatorial regions. The flowers are the most highly evolved of the plant kingdom; they have three ▷sepals and three petals and sometimes grow singly, but more usually appear with other flowers on spikes, growing up one side of the main stem, or all around the main stem, which may be upright or drooping. (Family Orchidaceae.)

ORCHID The orchid has evolved complex mechanisms and structures to ensure pollination by insects.

ordeal, trial by in tribal societies and in Europe in medieval times, a method of testing the guilt of an accused person based on the belief in heaven's protection of the innocent. Examples of such ordeals include walking barefoot over heated iron, dipping the hand into boiling water, and swallowing consecrated bread (causing the guilty to choke).

order in classical architecture, the ▷column (including capital, shaft, and base) and the ▷entablature, considered as an architectural whole. The five orders are Doric, Ionic, Corinthian, Tuscan, and Composite.

order in biological classification, a group of related ▷families. For example, the horse, rhinoceros, and tapir families are grouped in the order Perissodactyla, the odd-toed ungulates, because they all have either one or three toes on each foot. The names of orders are not shown in italic (unlike genus and species names) and by convention they have the ending '-formes' in birds and fish; '-a' in mammals, amphibians, reptiles, and other animals; and '-ales' in fungi and plants. Related orders are grouped together in a ▷class.

order in council in the UK, an order issued by the sovereign with the advice of the ▷Privy Council; in practice it is issued only on the advice of the cabinet. Acts of Parliament often provide for the issue of orders in council to regulate the detailed administration of their provisions.

ordinal number in mathematics, one of the series first, second, third, fourth, … . Ordinal numbers relate to order, whereas ▷cardinal numbers (1, 2, 3, 4, …) relate to quantity, or count.

ordinate in ▷coordinate geometry, the *y* coordinate of a point; that is, the vertical distance of the point from the horizontal or *x*-axis. For example, a point with the coordinates (3,4) has an ordinate of 4. See ▷abscissa.

ordination religious ceremony by which a person is accepted into the priesthood or monastic life in various religions. Within the Christian church, ordination authorizes a person to administer the sacraments.

Ordnance Survey (OS) official body responsible for the mapping of Britain. It was established in 1791 as the **Trigonometrical Survey** to continue work initiated in 1784 by Scottish military surveyor General William Roy (1726–1790). Its first accurate maps appeared in 1830, drawn to a scale of 1 in to the mile (1:63,000). In 1858 the OS settled on a scale of 1:2,500 for the mapping of Great Britain and Ireland (higher for urban areas, lower for uncultivated areas).

Ordovician period period of geological time 510–439 million years ago; the second period of the ▷Palaeozoic era. Animal life was confined to the sea: reef-building algae and the first jawless fish are characteristic. The period is named after the Ordovices, an ancient Welsh people, because the system of rocks formed in the Ordovician period was first studied in Wales.

ore body of rock, a vein within it, or a deposit of sediment, worth mining for the economically valuable mineral it contains. The term is usually applied to sources of metals. Occasionally metals are found uncombined (native metals), but more often they occur as compounds such as carbonates, sulphides, or oxides.

oregano any of several perennial herbs belonging to the mint family, especially the aromatic *O. vulgare*, also known as wild marjoram. It is native to Mediterranean countries and western Asia and naturalized in the Americas. (Genus *Origanum*, family Labiatae.)

Oregon state in northwestern USA, on the Pacific coast. It is nicknamed Beaver State. Oregon was admitted to the Union in 1859 as the 33rd US state. It is bordered to the east by Idaho, to the north by Washington, to the south by California and Nevada, and to the west by the Pacific Ocean.

population (1995) 3,140,600 **area** 251,500 sq km/97,079 sq mi **capital** Salem **towns and cities** Portland, Eugene, Gresham, Beaverton **industries and products** wheat, fruit, dairy farming, livestock, salmon and tuna, timber, electronics, tourism, leisure industry

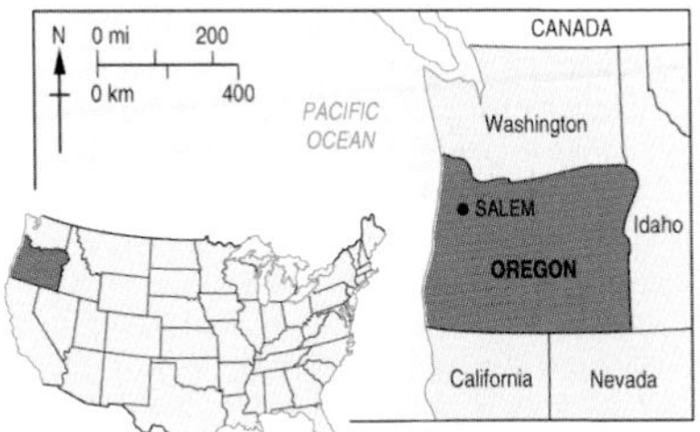

Orenburg (formerly **Chkalov** (1938–57)) capital city, economic and cultural centre of Orenburg oblast (region), west-central Russian Federation; population (1996 est) 532,000. Orenburg is situated on the River Ural, 350 km/217 mi southeast of Samara. It has extensive oil refineries, together with engineering, flour, meat, leather, and clothing industries, and is an important trading and transportation centre.

Orestes in Greek mythology, the son of ▷Agamemnon and ▷Clytemnestra, who killed his mother on the instructions of Apollo because she and her lover Aegisthus had murdered his father. He was subsequently hounded by the ▷Furies until he was purified, and acquitted of the crime of matricide.

Øresund strait leading from the ▷Kattegat to the Baltic Sea, between Sweden on the east and the Danish island of Sjaelland on the west. Its length is 113 km/70 mi; its narrowest point, between Helsingor and Hälsingborg, is 5 km/3 mi; its widest point is 60 km/37 mi; and its deepest part is about 25 m/80 ft. In English it is called the Sound.

orfe freshwater fish belonging to the carp family. It grows up to 50 cm/1.7 ft in length, and feeds on small aquatic animals. The species is generally greyish-black, but an ornamental variety is orange. It lives in rivers and lakes of Europe and northwestern Asia. (Species *Leuciscus idus*, family Cyprinidae.)

Orff, Carl (1895–1982) German composer. An individual stylist, his work is characterized by sharp dissonances and percussion. Among his compositions are the cantata *Carmina Burana* (1937) and the opera *Antigone* (1949).

Orford, 1st Earl of, title of the British politician Robert ▷Walpole.

organ in biology, part of a living body that has a distinctive function or set of functions. Examples include the liver or brain in animals, or the leaf in plants. An organ is composed of a group of coordinated ▷tissues. A group of organs working together to perform a function is called an **organ system**, for example, the ▷digestive system comprises a number of organs including the stomach, the small intestine, the colon, the pancreas, and the liver.

organ musical wind instrument of ancient origin, in which sound is produced when a depressed key opens a valve, allowing compressed air to pass through a single pipe or a series of pipes; the number of pipes in total may vary, according to the size of the instrument. Apart from its continued use in serious compositions and for church music, the organ has been adapted for light entertainment.

organelle discrete and specialized structure in a living cell; organelles include mitochondria, chloroplasts, lysosomes, ribosomes, and the nucleus.

organic chemistry branch of chemistry that deals with carbon compounds. Organic compounds form the chemical basis of life and are more abundant than inorganic compounds. In a typical organic compound, each carbon atom forms bonds covalently with each of its neighbouring carbon atoms in a chain or ring, and additionally with other atoms, commonly hydrogen, oxygen, nitrogen, or sulphur.

The basis of organic chemistry is the ability of carbon to form long chains of atoms, branching chains, rings, and other complex structures. Compounds containing only carbon and hydrogen are known as **hydrocarbons**.

Related Web site: Introduction To Organic chemistry: Frequently Asked Questions http://antoine.frostburg.edu/chem/senese/101/organic/faq.shtml

organic farming farming without the use of synthetic fertilizers (such as ▷nitrates and phosphates) or ▷pesticides (herbicides, insecticides, and fungicides) or other agrochemicals (such as hormones, growth stimulants, or fruit regulators). Food produced by genetic engineering cannot be described as organic.

In place of artificial fertilizers, compost, manure, seaweed, or other substances derived from living things are used (hence the name 'organic'). Growing a crop of a nitrogen-fixing plant such as lucerne, then ploughing it back into the soil, also fertilizes the ground. Some organic farmers use naturally occurring chemicals such as nicotine or pyrethrum to kill pests, but control by non-chemical methods is preferred. Those methods include removal by hand, intercropping (planting with companion plants which deter pests), mechanical barriers to infestation, crop rotation, better cultivation methods, and ▷biological control. Weeds can be controlled by hoeing, mulching (covering with manure, straw, or black plastic), or burning off. Organic farming methods produce food with minimal pesticide residues and greatly reduce pollution of the environment. They are more labour intensive, and therefore more expensive, but use less fossil fuel. Soil structure is greatly improved by organic methods, and recent studies show that a conventional farm can lose four times as much soil through erosion as an organic farm, although the loss may not be immediately obvious. In 2003, surveys predicted 10% of European food production would be organics by 2010.

Related Web site: International Federation of Organic Farming Movements http://ecoweb.dk/ifoam/

Organization for Economic Cooperation and Development (OECD) international organization of 29 industrialized countries that provides a forum for discussion and coordination of member states' economic and social policies. Founded in 1961, with its headquarters in Paris, the OECD superseded the Organization for European Economic Cooperation (OEEC), which had been established in 1948 to implement the ▷Marshall Plan. The Commission of the European Union also participates in the OECD's work.

Related Web site: OECD – Organization for Economic Cooperation and Development http://www.oecd.org/

Organization for Security and Cooperation in Europe (OSCE); formerly the Conference on Security and Cooperation in Europe (CSCE). International forum to reach agreement in security, economics, science, technology, and human rights. It was founded in 1975 as the Conference on Security and Cooperation in Europe (CSCE). At the ▷Helsinki Conference in Finland in 1975 it produced the Helsinki Act on East-West Relations, committing members to increasing consultation and cooperation. By mid-1995, having admitted the former republics of the USSR, as well as other new nations from the former communist bloc (including Yugoslavia, whose membership was suspended July 1992–November 2000), its membership had risen to 55 states. In 1994 it was renamed the Organization for Security and Cooperation in Europe.

A second conference in Paris in November 1990 was hailed as marking the formal end of the ▷Cold War. A third conference in Helsinki in July 1992 debated the Yugoslav problem and gave the CSCE the power to authorize military responses of the ▷North Atlantic Treaty Organization (NATO), the Western European Union (WEU), and the European Community (now the ▷European Union) within Europe. A revised version of the 1990 Conventional Forces in Europe (CFE) treaty was signed at the summit, but awaited ratification by Armenia and Belarus.

A summit in Istanbul in November 1999 saw OSCE's 54 members sign a European Security Charter (ESC) which strengthened OSCE's ability to send teams of civilian experts to intervene in countries' internal crises, and which formalised existing agreements on security cooperation and human rights. Again a revised version of the CFE treaty was signed, which forbids the deployment of forces in another state without the host country's permission and specifies quantitative limits, state-by-state, for different types of military equipment, along with verification procedures. The summit also saw the signing by US President Clinton and Russian President Yeltsin of a revised treaty limiting conventional (non-nuclear) forces. The western governments of OSCE also used the summit to repeat their call on Russia to find a political end to the fighting in Chechnya.

Organization of African Unity (OAU) association established in 1963 to eradicate colonialism and improve economic, cultural, and political cooperation in Africa. The secretary general is Salim Ahmed Salim of Tanzania. Its headquarters are in Addis Ababa, Ethiopia. There are now 53 members representing virtually the whole of central, southern, and northern Africa.

Organization of American States (OAS) association founded in 1948 at Bogotá, Colombia by a charter signed by representatives of North, Central, and South American states. It aims to maintain peace and solidarity within the hemisphere, and is also concerned with the social and economic development of Latin America.

Related Web site: Organization of American States http://www.oas.org/

Organization of Arab Petroleum Exporting Countries (OAPEC) body established in 1968 to safeguard the interests of its members and encourage economic cooperation within the petroleum industry. Its members are Algeria, Bahrain, Egypt, Iraq, Kuwait, Libya, Qatar, Saudi Arabia, Syria, and the United Arab Emirates; together they account for more than 25% of the world's oil output. The organization's headquarters are in Kuwait.

Organization of Petroleum-Exporting Countries (OPEC) body established in 1960 to coordinate price and supply policies of oil-producing states. Its concerted action in raising prices in the 1970s triggered worldwide recession but also lessened demand so that its influence was reduced by the mid-1980s. However, continued reliance on oil re-strengthened its influence in the late 1990s. OPEC members are: Algeria, Gabon, Indonesia, Iran, Iraq, Kuwait, Libya, Nigeria, Qatar, Saudi Arabia, the United Arab Emirates, and Venezuela. Ecuador, formerly a member, withdrew in 1993. OPEC's secretary general is Rilwanu Lukman of Nigeria.

Related Web site: OPEC Online http://www.opec.org/

Organization of the Islamic Conference (OIC) association of 44 states in the Middle East, Africa, and Asia, established in 1971 in Rabat, Morocco, to promote Islamic solidarity between member countries, and to consolidate economic, social, cultural, and scientific cooperation. Its headquarters are in Jeddah, Saudi Arabia.

organizer in embryology, a part of the embryo that causes changes to occur in another part, through ▷induction, thus 'organizing' development and ▷differentiation.

orienteering sport of cross-country running and route-finding. Competitors set off at one-minute intervals and have to find their way, using map and compass, to various checkpoints (approximately 0.8 km/0.5 mi apart), where their control cards are marked. World championships have been held since 1966.

original sin Christian doctrine that the ▷Fall of Man rendered humanity predisposed to sin and unable to achieve salvation except through divine grace and the redemptive power of Jesus.

Orinoco river in northern South America; it rises in the Sierra Parima range in southern Venezuela near the Brazilian border and flows north for about 2,400 km/1,500 mi through Venezuela, forming the boundary with Colombia for about 320 km/200 mi; tributaries include the Guaviare, Meta, Apure, Ventuari, Caura, Arauca, and Caroni rivers. It is navigable by large steamers for 1,125 km/700 mi from its Atlantic delta; rapids obstruct the upper river. The Orinoco is South America's third-largest river; its drainage basin area is 962,000 sq km/371500 sq mi.

oriole any of several brightly coloured songbirds belonging to two families: New World orioles belong to the family Icteridae, and Old World orioles are members of the family Oriolidae. They eat insects, seeds, and fruit.

Orion in astronomy, a very prominent constellation in the equatorial region of the sky (see ▷celestial sphere), identified with the hunter of Greek mythology.

The bright stars Alpha (▷Betelgeuse), Gamma (Bellatrix), Beta (▷Rigel), and Kappa Orionis mark the shoulders and legs of Orion. Between them the belt is formed by Delta, Epsilon, and Zeta, three second-magnitude stars equally spaced in a straight line. Beneath the belt is a line of fainter stars marking Orion's sword. One of these, Theta, is not really a star but the brightest part of the ▷Orion nebula. Nearby is one of the most distinctive dark nebulae, the Horsehead.

Orion nebula luminous cloud of gas and dust 1,500 light years away, in the constellation Orion, from which stars are forming. It is about 15 light years in diameter, and contains enough gas to make a cluster of thousands of stars.

Orissa state of northeast India; area 155,700 sq km/60,100 sq mi; population (2001 est) 37,557,000. The capital is Bhubaneshwar. Industries include chemicals, paper, steel, aluminium smelting, and mineral extraction. Rice, wheat, oilseed, and sugar are grown. Oriya is the official language, and 90% of the population is Hindu.

Oriya the majority ethnic group living in the Indian state of Orissa. Oriya is Orissa's official language; it belongs to the Eastern group of the Indo-Iranian branch of the Indo-European family.

Orkney Islands island group and unitary authority off the northeast coast of Scotland.

area 1,014 sq km/391 sq mi **towns** ▷Kirkwall (administrative headquarters), Stromness, both on Mainland (Pomona) **physical** there are 90 islands and inlets in the group. The surface of the islands is irregular and indented by many arms of the sea. Next to Mainland, the most important of the islands are North and South Ronaldsay, Hoy, Rousay, Stronsay, Flotta, Shapinsay, Eday, Sanday, and Westray. The highest peak is Ward Hill in Hoy, which has an elevation of 479 m/1,572 ft. The Old Man of Hoy is an isolated stack of red sandstone 137 m/450 ft high, off Hoy's northwest coast **features** Skara Brae Neolithic village, and Maes Howe burial chamber; Scapa Flow; oil terminal on Flotta **industries** offshore oil, woollen weaving, wind-powered electricity generation, distilling, boat-building, fish curing **agriculture** fishing, beef cattle, dairy products **population** (1996) 19,600 **famous people** Edwin Muir, John Rae **history** population of Scandinavian descent; Harald I (Fairhair) of Norway conquered the islands in 876; pledged to James III of Scotland in 1468 for the dowry of Margaret of Denmark; Scapa Flow, between Mainland and Hoy, was a naval base in both world wars, the German fleet scuttled itself here on 21 June 1919

Related Web site: Online Guide to Orkney http://www.orknet.co.uk/tourism/ork_map.htm

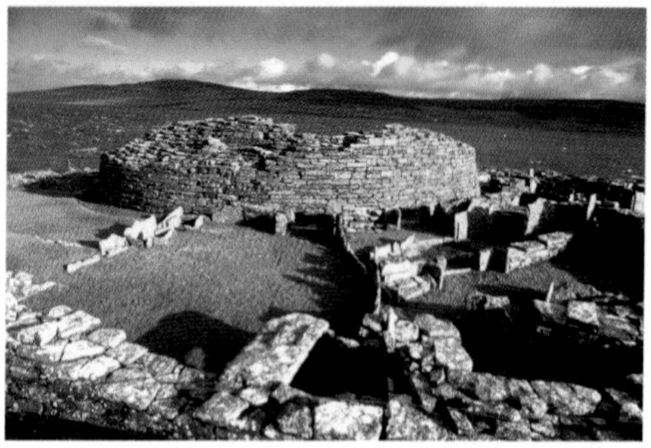

ORKNEY ISLANDS Iron Age remains at Broch of Gurness in the Orkney Islands, Scotland. Dating from the 1st century AD, the broch (a high, round, stone tower) was originally built as a defensive structure. The stone dwellings surrounding the broch are among the most well-preserved of their kind in Scotland, and contain prime examples of Pict architecture. *Image Bank*

Orlando industrial city and administrative headquarters of Orange County, Florida; population (1992) 174,200. It is a winter resort and tourist centre, with Walt Disney World and the Epcot Center nearby. Electronic and aerospace equipment are manufactured in the city, and citrus-fruit products are processed here. Educational institutions include the University of Central Florida. The city is also the site of the Orlando Naval Training Center (1968), a major basic-training facility.

Orléans administrative centre of Loiret *département* in central France, situated on the right bank of the River Loire, 115 km/70 mi southwest of Paris; population (1990) 108,000, conurbation 243,000. Industries include engineering, textiles and food processing; there is also an extensive trade in agricultural produce and wine. Orléans is of pre-Roman origin. Joan of Arc, known as the Maid of Orléans, liberated the town from the English in 1429.

Orly suburb of Paris in the *département* of Val-de-Marne; population (1990) 21,800. Orly international airport is the busiest in France.

Ormuzd another name for **Ahura Mazda**, the good god of ▷Zoroastrianism.

ornamentation in music, decorative filling-in of a melody, or accentuation of a structural feature such as the end of a phrase, by rhetorical flourishes or cascades of notes, indicated by special notational signs. Examples of ornament are the turn, a form of melodic pirouette around a note, the trill, the appoggiatura, an upward or downward inflection, arpeggio, and the mordent, a form of accented trill.

ornithology study of birds. It covers scientific aspects relating to their structure and classification, and their habits, song, flight, and value to agriculture as destroyers of insect pests. Worldwide scientific banding (or the fitting of coded rings to captured specimens) has resulted in accurate information on bird movements and distribution. There is an International Council for Bird Preservation with its headquarters at the Natural History Museum, London.

Interest in birds has led to the formation of societies for their protection, of which the Society for the Protection of Birds 1889 in Britain was the first; it received a royal charter 1904. The Audubon Society 1905 in the USA has similar aims; other countries now have similar societies. The headquarters of the British Trust for Ornithology is at The Nunnery, Thetford, Norfolk. Migration, age, and pollution effects on birds are monitored by ringing (trained government-licensed operators fit numbered metal rings to captured specimens with a return address). Legislation in various countries to protect wild birds followed from a British act of Parliament in 1880.

ornithophily ▷pollination of flowers by birds. Ornithophilous flowers are typically brightly coloured, often red or orange. They produce large quantities of thin, watery nectar, and are scentless because most birds do not respond well to smell. They are found mostly in tropical areas, with hummingbirds being important pollinators in North and South America, and the sunbirds in Africa and Asia.

orogenesis in its original, literal sense, orogenesis means 'mountain building', but today it more specifically refers to the tectonics of mountain building (as opposed to mountain building by erosion).

Orogenesis is brought about by the movements of the rigid plates making up the Earth's crust and upper-most mantle (described by ▷plate tectonics). Where two plates collide at a destructive margin rocks become folded and lifted to form chains of mountains (such as the Himalayas). Processes associated with orogeny are faulting and thrusting (see ▷fault), folding, metamorphism, and plutonism (see ▷plutonic rock). However, many topographical features of mountains – cirques, u-shaped valleys – are the result of *non-orogenic* processes, such as weathering, erosion, and glaciation. ▷Isostasy (uplift due to the buoyancy of the Earth's crust) can also influence mountain physiography.

Orpheus mythical Greek poet and musician of Thrace; the son of ▷Apollo and the Muse ▷Calliope. Orpheus ventured into Hades, the underworld, to bring back his wife ▷Eurydice, who had died from a snakebite. His lyre playing was so charming that Pluto granted her return to life, but on condition that Orpheus walked ahead without looking back. He turned at the entrance and Eurydice was irretrievably lost. In his grief, he offended the ▷maenad women of Thrace, and they tore him to pieces.

Orphism ancient Greek ▷mystery religion of which the Orphic hymns, poems attributed to the legendary poet ▷Orpheus, formed a part. The cult dates from the 6th or 7th century BC, but the poems are of a later date. Secret rites of purification and initiation, accompanied by a harsh lifestyle, were aimed at securing immortality in the Islands of the Blessed.

orrery mechanical device for demonstrating the motions of the heavenly bodies. Invented about 1710 by George Graham, it was named after his patron, the 4th Earl of Orrery. It is the forerunner of the planetarium.

orris root underground stem of a species of ▷iris grown in southern Europe. It is violet-scented and is used in perfumery and herbal medicine.

Ortega Saavedra, Daniel (1945–) Nicaraguan socialist politician, head of state 1979–90. He was a member of the Marxist Sandinista Liberation Front (FSLN), which overthrew the regime of Anastasio ▷Somoza Debayle in 1979, later becoming its secretary general. US-sponsored ▷Contra guerrillas opposed his government from 1982.

Ortega left law studies at the Central American University in Managua at the age of 18 to join the FSLN, and soon became head of the underground urban resistance activities against the Somoza regime. He was imprisoned and tortured several times, and was temporarily exiled to Cuba in 1974. He became a member of the national directorate of the FSLN and fought in the two-year campaign for the ▷Nicaraguan Revolution. Ortega became a member of the junta of national reconstruction, and its coordinator two years later. The FSLN won the free 1984 elections and Ortega became president, but in February 1990, with the economy in tatters, Ortega lost the presidency to US-backed Violeta ▷Barrios de Chamorro. Despite repackaging himself as a more moderate democratic socialist, he was also defeated in the 1996 presidential election, by Arnoldo Alemán.

orthochromatic photographic film or paper of decreased sensitivity, which can be processed with a red safelight. Using it, blue objects appear lighter and red ones darker because of increased blue sensitivity.

orthodontics branch of ▷dentistry concerned with ▷dentition, and with treatment of any irregularities, such as correction of malocclusion (faulty position of teeth).

Orthodox Church (or **Eastern Orthodox Church** or **Greek Orthodox Church**) federation of self-governing Christian churches mainly found in Eastern Europe and parts of Asia. The centre of worship is the Eucharist. There is a married clergy, except for bishops; the Immaculate Conception is not accepted. The highest rank in the church is that of ecumenical patriarch, or bishop of Istanbul.

There are (1990) about 130 million adherents.

orthopaedics (Greek *orthos* 'straight'; *pais* 'child') medical speciality concerned with the correction of disease or damage in bones and joints.

ortolan songbird belonging to the bunting family, common in Europe and West Asia, migrating to Africa in the winter. It is about 15 cm/6 in long and reddish-brown with black streaks on top, pinkish-buff below, and has an olive-green head and chest and a yellow throat; the female is paler with small dark streaks on the chest. The nest is built in the undergrowth, on the ground, or on banks. Long considered a delicacy among gourmets, it has become rare and is now a protected species. (Species *Emberiza hortulana*, family Emberizidae, order Passeriformes.)

Orton, Joe (John Kingsley) (1933–1967) English dramatist. In his black comedies, surreal and violent action takes place in genteel and unlikely settings. Plays include *Entertaining Mr Sloane* (1964), *Loot* (1966), and *What the Butler Saw* (1968). His diaries deal frankly with his personal life. He was murdered by his lover Kenneth Halliwell.

Orvieto (Etruscan *Volsinii*; Latin *Urbs Vetus* 'old town') town in Umbria, Italy, on a high plateau overlooking the River Tiber; population (1990) 22,600. Built on the site of an Etruscan town destroyed by the Romans in 280 BC, Orvieto has many Etruscan remains. The district produces white wine of the same name, and tourism is an important industry.

Orwell, George (1903–1950) Pen-name of Eric Arthur Blair. English writer. His books include the satirical fable *Animal Farm* (1945), an attack on the Soviet Union and its leader, Stalin, which includes such slogans as 'All animals are equal, but some are more equal than others'; and the prophetic ▷*Nineteen Eighty-Four* (1949), targeting Cold War politics, which portrays the catastrophic excesses of state control over the individual. He also wrote numerous essays. Orwell was distrustful of all political parties and ideologies, and a deep sense of social conscience and antipathy towards political dictatorship characterizes his work.

Orwell was born in Motihari, Bengal, India, and educated in England at Eton. He served in Burma (now Myanmar) with the Indian Imperial Police 1922–27, an experience reflected in the novel *Burmese Days* (1934). In horrified retreat from imperialism, he moved towards socialism and even anarchism. A period of poverty, during which he was successively tutor, teacher, dishwasher, tramp, and bookshop assistant, is described in *Down and Out in Paris and London* (1933), and also provided him with material for *The Road to Wigan Pier* (1937) and *Keep the Aspidistra Flying* (1936). In 1936 he fought on the Republican side in the Spanish Civil War and was wounded; these experience are related in *Homage to Catalonia* (1938). Orwell reacted strongly against his exposure to the brutally practical politics of the communists in Spain. He was forced to flee the country, and the experience made him an active opponent both of communism and fascism. *Coming up for Air* appeared in 1939. During World War II, Orwell worked for the BBC, writing and monitoring propaganda.

Related Web site: Orwell, George http://www.k-1.com/Orwell/

oryx any of a group of large antelopes native to Africa and Asia. The **Arabian oryx** (*O. leucoryx*), at one time extinct in the wild, was successfully reintroduced into its natural habitat using stocks bred in captivity in 1982. By 1998 the oryx reintroduction project was seriously reduced through poaching. The population fell to 138, and 40 animals were returned to captivity as the population was believed to be no longer viable. By January 1999 there were fewer than 100 oryx remaining in the wild and only 11 of these were female. (Genus *Oryx*, family Bovidae.)

The **scimitar-horned oryx** (*O. tao*) of the Sahara is also rare. The **Beisa oryx** (*O. beisa*) in East Africa and **gemsbok** (*O. gazella*) in the Kalahari are more common. In profile the two long horns appear as one, which may have given rise to the legend of the unicorn.

Osaka industrial port on the Pacific coast of Honshu island, Japan, 24 km/15 mi from Kobe; population (1994) 2,481,000. It is Japan's third-largest city. Industries include iron, steel, shipbuilding, chemicals, and textiles. Emperor Kotoku established it as a capital in 645. **Osaka castle**, built in 1583, was the scene of a siege in 1614–15. The city is the home of the *bunraku* puppet theatre.

Osborne, John James (1929–1994) English dramatist. He became one of the first ▷Angry Young Men (anti-establishment writers of the 1950s) of British theatre with his debut play, *Look Back in Anger* (1956). Other plays include *The Entertainer* (1957), *Luther* (1960), *Inadmissible Evidence* (1964), and *A Patriot for Me* (1965).

Oscar two kings of Sweden and Norway, including:

Oscar II (1829–1907) King of Sweden and Norway 1872–1905, king of Sweden until 1907. He was the younger son of Oscar I, and succeeded his brother Charles XV. He tried hard to prevent the separation of his two kingdoms but relinquished the throne of Norway to Haakon VII in 1905.

oscillating universe in astronomy, a theory that states that the gravitational attraction of the mass within the universe will eventually slow down and stop the expansion of the universe. The outward motions of the galaxies will then be reversed, eventually resulting in a 'Big Crunch' where all the matter in the universe will be contracted into a small volume of high density. This could undergo a further ▷Big Bang, thereby creating another expansion phase. The theory suggests that the universe would alternately expand and collapse through alternate Big Bangs and Big Crunches.

oscillation one complete to-and-fro movement of a vibrating object or system. For any particular vibration, the time for one oscillation is called its period and the number of oscillations in one second is called its ▷frequency. The maximum displacement of the vibrating object from its rest position is called the ▷amplitude of the oscillation.

oscillator any device producing a desired oscillation (vibration). There are many types of oscillator for different purposes, involving various arrangements of thermionic ▷valves or components such as ▷transistors, ▷inductors, ▷capacitors, and ▷resistors.

oscillograph instrument for displaying or recording rapidly changing oscillations, electrical or mechanical.

oscilloscope another name for ▷cathode-ray oscilloscope.

osier any of several willow trees and shrubs, cultivated for their supple branches which are used in basket making; in particular, *S. viminalis*. (Genus *Salix*.)

Osiris ancient Egyptian god, the embodiment of goodness, who ruled the underworld after being killed by ▷Set. The pharaohs were believed to be his incarnation. The sister-wife of Osiris was ▷Isis or Hathor; she miraculously conceived their son ▷Horus after the death of Osiris, and he eventually captured his father's murderer.

Oslo industrial port and capital of Norway; population (1996) 731,600. The main industries are shipbuilding, textiles, electrical equipment, engineering, machine tools, timber, and food processing. The first recorded settlement was made in the 11th century by Harald III Hardrada, but after a fire in 1624, it was entirely replanned by the Danish king Christian IV and renamed **Christiania** from 1624 to 1924. Following Norway's separation from Denmark (1814) and then Sweden (1905), the city reverted in 1925 to its original Norwegian name of Oslo.

Osman I (or Uthman I) (1259–1326) Turkish ruler from 1299. He began his career in the service of the Seljuk Turks, but in 1299 he set up a kingdom of his own in Bithynia, northwestern Asia, and assumed the title of sultan. He conquered a great part of Anatolia, so founding a Turkish empire. His successors were known as 'sons of Osman', from which the term ▷Ottoman Empire is derived.

osmium (Greek *osme* 'odour') hard, heavy, bluish-white, metallic element, symbol Os, atomic number 76, relative atomic mass 190.2. It is the densest of the elements, and is resistant to tarnish and corrosion. It occurs in platinum ores and as a free metal (see ▷native metal) with iridium in a natural alloy called osmiridium, containing traces of platinum, ruthenium, and rhodium. Its uses include pen points and light-bulb filaments; like platinum, it is a useful catalyst.

It was discovered in 1803 and named in 1804 by English chemist Smithson Tennant (1761–1815) after the irritating smell of one of its oxides.

osmosis movement of water through a selectively permeable membrane separating solutions of different concentrations. Water passes by ▷diffusion from a **weak solution** (high water concentration) to a **strong solution** (low water concentration) until the two concentrations are equal. The selectively permeable membrane allows the diffusion of water but not of the solute (for example, sugar molecules). Many cell membranes behave in this way, and osmosis is a vital mechanism in the transport of fluids in living organisms – for example, in the transport of water from soil (weak solution) into the roots of plants (stronger solution of cell sap).

Osmoregulation Excessive flow of water into a cell by osmosis can burst the cell. Cells protect against this using processes of osmoregulation. If external pressure is applied to the stronger solution, osmosis is arrested. By this mechanism plant cells can osmoregulate, since the cell wall of a fully turgid cell exerts pressure on the solution within the cell. Animal cells such as the red blood cell cannot osmoregulate in this way since they have no cell wall. Instead, the correct concentration of plasma is maintained by the kidneys.

osprey bird of prey, sometimes called 'fish hawk' because it plunges feet first into the water to catch fish. It is dark brown above and a striking white below, and measures 60 cm/2 ft with a 2 m/6 ft wingspan. The nest is often built in trees near the seashore or

OSLO The famous Holmenkollen ski jump. Every skiing season, between November and March, the World Championships spend five days ay Holmenkollen. *Image Bank*

> ## George Orwell
> *To see what is in front of one's nose needs a constant struggle.*
> *Tribune, 22 March 1946*

lakeside, and two or three white eggs, blotched with crimson, are laid. Ospreys occur on all continents except Antarctica and have faced extinction in several areas. (Species *Pandion haliaetus*, family Pandionidae, order Falconiformes.)

Once extinct in Britain, they are now breeding again; in 1994 there were 69 successful broods with 146 surviving young at the RSPB's Operation Osprey protected nest site in Speyside, Scotland. In July 1996 seven of the Scottish chicks were transferred to a nature reserve near Leicester as part of a programme to re-establish ospreys in England, where they have been absent since 1843.

The 'osprey plumes' of the milliner are in fact ▷egret feathers.

OSS abbreviation for Office of Strategic Services.

Ossa, Mount the highest peak on the island of Tasmania, Australia; height 1,617 m/5,250 ft.

Ossetia region in the Caucasus, on the border between Russia and Georgia, comprising the autonomous republic of ▷Alania, formerly North Ossetia, and ▷South Ossetia, an autonomous region of Georgia. It is inhabited by the Ossetes, descendants of the Alani people who speak the Iranian language Ossetic, and who were conquered by the Russians in 1801–6.

Ossian (Irish Oisin) Legendary Gaelic hero and bard, claimed by both Ireland and Scotland. He is sometimes represented as the son of ▷Finn Mac Cumhaill, in about AD 250, and as having lived to tell the tales of Finn and the Ulster heroes to St Patrick, in about 400. The publication in 1760 of James ▷Macpherson's poems, attributed to Ossian, made Ossian's name familiar throughout Europe.

ossification (or osteogenesis) process whereby bone is formed in vertebrate animals by special cells (**osteoblasts**) that secrete layers of ▷extracellular matrix on the surface of the existing ▷cartilage.

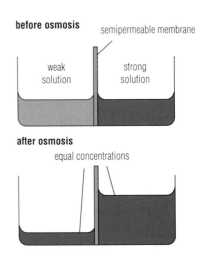

before osmosis

semipermeable membrane

weak solution | strong solution

after osmosis

equal concentrations

OSMOSIS In 1877 German physicist Wilhelm Pfeffer used this apparatus to make the first ever measurement of osmotic pressure and to show that osmotic pressure varies according to temperature and the strength of the solute (dissolved substance).

Conversion to bone occurs through the deposition of calcium phosphate crystals within the matrix.

Ostend (Flemish **Oostende**; French **Ostende**) seaport and pleasure resort in West Flanders, Belgium; 108 km/67 mi northwest of Brussels; population (1997) 68,000. There are large docks, and the Belgian fishing fleet has its headquarters here. There are ferry links to Dover and Folkestone, England. It was occupied by the Germans 1914–18 and developed as an important naval base.

osteomyelitis infection of bone, with spread of pus along the marrow cavity. Now quite rare, it may follow from a compound fracture (where broken bone protrudes through the skin), or from infectious disease elsewhere in the body. It is more common in children whose bones are not yet fully grown.

osteopathy system of alternative medical practice that relies on physical manipulation to treat mechanical stress. It was developed over a century ago by US physician Andrew Taylor Still, who maintained that most ailments can be prevented or cured by techniques of spinal manipulation.

> Related Web site: British Osteopathic Association http://www.osteopathy.org/main/index.htm

osteoporosis disease in which the bone substance becomes porous and brittle. It is common in older people, affecting more women than men. It may be treated with calcium supplements and etidronate. Approximately 1.7 million people worldwide, mostly women, suffer hip fractures, mainly due to osteoporosis. A single gene was discovered in 1993 to have a major influence on bone thinning.

> Related Web site: MEdiC – Heath Explorer – Osteoporosis http://medic.med.uth.tmc.edu/ptnt/00000767.htm

Ostia ancient Roman town near the mouth of the Tiber. Founded about 330 BC, it was the port of Rome and had become a major commercial centre by the 2nd century AD. It was abandoned in the 9th century. The present-day seaside resort **Ostia Mare** is situated nearby.

ostracon in ancient Egypt, a piece of limestone or pottery used as a cheap alternative to ▷papyrus. It was also used for voting tablets in Athens.

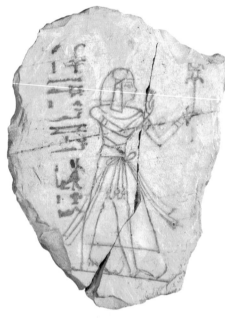

OSTRACON Limestone ostracon from Deir el-Medina, Egypt (New Kingdom, *c.* 1300–1200 BC), now in the Egyptian Museum, Turin, Italy. *The Art Archive/Victoria and Albert Museum London/Eileen Tweedy*

ostrich large flightless bird. There is only one species, found in Africa. The male may be about 2.5 m/8 ft tall and weigh 135 kg/300 lb, and is the largest living bird. It has exceptionally strong legs and feet (two-toed) that enable it to run at high speed, and are also used in defence. It lives in family groups of one cock with several hens, each of which lays about 14 eggs. (Species *Struthio camelus*, order Struthioniformes.)

The adult male's body is covered with black feathers, the plumes of the wings and tail being white; females and young males have grey feathers. The bill is wide and flat, the small head has large eyes, and the long neck has a sparse covering of downy feathers. The male incubates the eggs at night, but the female may sit on them during the day. Their eggs are the smallest in relation to the adult's

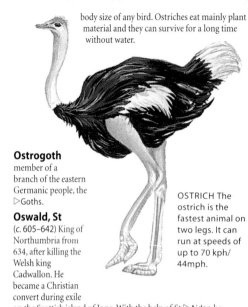

body size of any bird. Ostriches eat mainly plant material and they can survive for a long time without water.

Ostrogoth member of a branch of the eastern Germanic people, the ▷Goths.

Oswald, St (*c.* 605–642) King of Northumbria from 634, after killing the Welsh king Cadwallon. He became a Christian convert during exile on the Scottish island of Iona. With the help of St ▷Aidan he furthered the spread of Christianity in northern England. Feast day 9 August.

OSTRICH The ostrich is the fastest animal on two legs. It can run at speeds of up to 70 kph/44mph.

Othman alternative spelling of ▷Uthman, third caliph of Islam.

Othman I another name for the Turkish sultan ▷Osman I.

Otho I (1815–1867) King of Greece 1832–62. As the 17-year-old son of King Ludwig I of Bavaria, he was selected by the European powers as the first king of independent Greece. He was overthrown by a popular revolt.

Otis, Elisha Graves (1811–1861) US engineer who developed a lift that incorporated a safety device, making it acceptable for passenger use in the first skyscrapers. The device, invented in 1852, consisted of vertical ratchets on the sides of the lift shaft into which spring-loaded catches would engage and lock the lift in position in the event of cable failure.

otitis inflammation of the ear. *Otitis externa*, occurring in the outer ear canal, is easily treated with antibiotics. Inflamed conditions of the middle ear (*otitis media*) or inner ear (*otitis interna*) are more serious, carrying the risk of deafness and infection of the brain. Treatment is with antibiotics or, more rarely, surgery. A 1999 US survey of childrens' middle-ear problems indicated that the risk is, to a large extent, hereditary.

O'Toole, Peter (Seamus) (1932–) Irish-born British actor. He made his name in the title role of *Lawrence of Arabia* (1962), and then starred in such films as *Becket* (1964) and *The Lion in Winter* (1968), moving effortlessly from comic to dramatic roles – from the philanderer of *What's New Pussycat?* (1965) to his King Henry II of *The Lion in Winter* (1968). Subsequent appearances include *The Ruling Class* (1972), *The Stuntman* (1980), and *High Spirits* (1988).

otosclerosis overgrowth of bone in the middle ear causing progressive deafness. This inherited condition is gradual in onset, developing usually before middle age. It is twice as common in women as in men.

Ottawa capital of ▷Canada, in eastern Ontario, on the hills overlooking the Ottawa River, and divided by the Rideau Canal into the Upper (western) and Lower (eastern) towns; population (1996 est) of metropolitan area (with adjoining Hull, Québec) 1,030,500. Industries include engineering, food processing, publishing, lumber, and the manufacture of pulp, paper, textiles, and leather products. Government, and community and health services employ a large section of the workforce. Ottawa was founded 1826–32 as Bytown, in honour of John By (1781–1836), whose army engineers were building the Rideau Canal. In 1854 it was renamed after the Ottawa River, the name deriving from the Outaouac, Native Canadian Algonquin people of the area.

Features include the National Art Gallery, the Parliament Buildings, Rideau Hall (the governor general's residence), and the National Arts Centre 1969 (with an orchestra and English/French theatre). In 1858 it was chosen by Queen Victoria as the country's capital.

otter any of various aquatic carnivores belonging to the weasel family, found on all continents except Australia. Otters have thick brown fur, short limbs, webbed toes, and long, compressed tails. They are social, playful, and agile.

Otters produce 1–2 cubs per litter. The cubs are totally dependent on their mother for food for the first 13–14 months.

The otter of Europe and Asia (*Lutra lutra*) has a broad head, an elongated body covered with grey-brown fur, short legs, and webbed feet. Including a 45 cm/1.5 ft tail, it measures over 1 m/3.5 ft and lives on fish. There are a number of American species, including the larger *L. canadensis* of North America, the sea otter (*Enhydra lutris*) of the North Pacific, and the giant otter (*Pteronura brasiliensis*) of South America. The hairy-nosed otter *Lutra sumatrana* was sighted in Thailand in early 2000 for the first time in a number of years. It was feared that it had become extinct. There are 13 species of otter worldwide.

In the UK, otters have been hunted to near extinction for their fur, but are slowly making a recovery with the aid of protective legislation.

> Related Web site: Sea Otter http://www.seaworld.org/animal_bytes/sea_otterab.html

Otto four Holy Roman emperors, including:

Otto I (912–973) Holy Roman Emperor from 962. He restored the power of the empire and asserted his authority over the pope and the nobles. His son, Liudolf, led a German rebellion allied with the Magyars, but Otto drew them from the siege of Augsburg (Bavaria) and ended the Magyar menace by his victory at Lechfeld in 955. He refounded the East Mark, or Austria, as a barrier against them.

Otto IV (*c.* 1174–1218) Holy Roman Emperor, elected in 1198. He was the son of Henry the Lion (1129–95), and was made Count of Poitou by his uncle, Richard (I) the Lionheart (1157–99). He clashed with Philip, Duke of Swabia, in rivalry for the empire. He engaged in controversy with Pope Innocent III (*c.* 1160–1216), and was defeated by the pope's ally Philip (II) Augustus of France at Bouvines in 1214. Otto lost the throne to Holy Roman Emperor ▷Frederick II, and retired to Brunswick (Germany).

OTTO IV An illustration from the *Manesse codex* (1305–1340) of the German emperor Otto IV playing chess. The emperor's opponent is a woman, and as they play they are accompanied by musicians. *The Art Archive/University Library Heidelberg/Dagli Orti*

Otto cycle alternative name for the ▷four-stroke cycle, introduced by the German engineer Nikolaus Otto (1832–1891) in 1876.

Ottoman Empire Muslim empire of the Turks from 1300 to 1920, the successor of the ▷Seljuk Empire. It was founded by ▷Osman I and reached its height with ▷Suleiman in the 16th century. Its capital was Istanbul (formerly Constantinople).

At its greatest extent the Ottoman Empire's boundaries were: in Europe as far north as Hungary and part of southern Russia; Iran; the Palestinian coastline; Egypt; and North Africa. From the 1600s the empire was in decline. There was an attempted revival and reform under the Young Turk party in 1908, but the regime

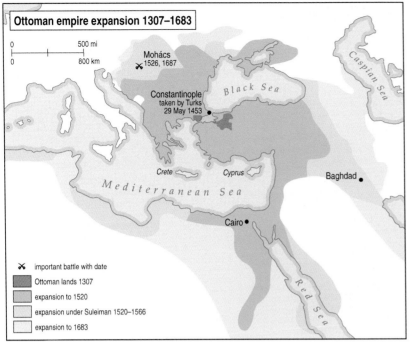

Ottoman empire expansion 1307–1683

important battle with date
Ottoman lands 1307
expansion to 1520
expansion under Suleiman 1520–1566
expansion to 1683

crumbled when Turkey sided with Germany in World War I. The sultanate was abolished by Kemal Atatürk in 1922; the last sultan was Muhammad VI.

OU abbreviation for ▷Open University.

Ouagadougou (or **Wagadugu**) capital and industrial centre of ▷Burkina Faso, and of Kadiogo Province; population (1991 est) 634,000. Products include textiles, vegetable oil, beverages, and soap. Its pre-eminence as a commercial centre is challenged by Bobo-Dioulasso. The city has the palace of Moro Naba, emperor of the Mossi people, a neo-Romanesque cathedral, and a central avenue called the Champs Elysées. It was the capital of the Mossi empire from the 15th century.

Oudh region of north India, now part of Uttar Pradesh. An independent kingdom before it fell under Mogul rule, Oudh regained independence 1732–1856, when it was annexed by Britain. Its capital was Lucknow, centre of the ▷Indian Mutiny 1857–58. In 1877 it was joined with Agra, from 1902 as the United Provinces of Agra and Oudh, renamed Uttar Pradesh in 1950.

Oughtred, William (1575–1660) English mathematician, credited as the inventor of the slide rule in 1622. His major work *Clavis mathematicae/The Key to Mathematics* (1631) was a survey of the entire body of mathematical knowledge of his day. It introduced the 'x' symbol for multiplication, as well as the abbreviations 'sin' for *sine* and 'cos' for *cosine*.

ounce another name for the snow ▷leopard.

ounce unit of mass, one-sixteenth of a pound ▷avoirdupois, equal to 437.5 grains (28.35 g); also one-twelfth of a pound troy, equal to 480 grains.

Ouse, Great (Celtic 'water') river that rises near Brackley in Northamptonshire, central England, and flows eastwards through Buckinghamshire, Bedfordshire, Cambridgeshire, and Norfolk, before entering the Wash north of King's Lynn; length 250 km/160 mi. A large sluice across the Great Ouse, near King's Lynn, was built as part of extensive flood-control works in 1959.

outback the inland region of Australia. Its main inhabitants are Aborigines, miners (including opal miners), and cattle ranchers. Its harsh beauty has been recorded by such artists as Sidney Nolan.

outlawry in medieval England, a declaration that a criminal was outside the protection of the law, with his or her lands and goods forfeited to the crown, and all civil rights being set aside. It was a lucrative royal 'privilege'; ▷Magna Carta restricted its use, and under Edward III it was further modified. Some outlaws, such as ▷Robin Hood, became popular heroes.

output device in computing, any device for displaying, in a form intelligible to the user, the results of processing carried out by a computer.

The most common output devices are the ▷VDU (visual display unit, or screen) and the ▷printer. Other output devices include graph plotters, speech synthesizers, and COM (computer output on microfilm/microfiche).

onset of the menopause, an ovum is released from the ovary. This is called ovulation, and forms part of the ▷menstrual cycle. In botany, an ovary is the expanded basal portion of the ▷carpel of flowering plants, containing one or more ▷ovules. It is hollow with a thick wall to protect the ovules. Following fertilization of the ovum, it develops into the fruit wall or pericarp.

The ovaries of female animals secrete the hormones responsible for the secondary sexual characteristics of the female, such as smooth, hairless facial skin and enlarged breasts. An ovary in a half-grown human fetus contains 5 million eggs, and so the unborn baby already possesses the female genetic information for the next generation.

In botany, the relative position of the ovary to the other floral parts is often a distinguishing character in classification; it may be either inferior or superior, depending on whether the petals and sepals are inserted above or below.

overdraft in banking, a loan facility on a current account. It allows the account holder to overdraw on his or her account up to a certain limit and for a specified time, and interest is payable on the amount borrowed. An overdraft is a cheaper form of borrowing than the credit options that major credit-card companies offer.

overfishing fishing at rates that exceed the sustained-yield cropping of fish species, resulting in a net population decline. For example, in the North Atlantic, herring has been fished to the verge of extinction, and the cod and haddock populations are severely depleted. In the developing world, use of huge factory ships, often by fisheries from industrialized countries, has depleted stocks for local people who cannot obtain protein in any other way.

Overijssel province of the east central Netherlands, extending from the IJsselmeer to the German border; area 3,340 sq km/1,290 sq mi; population (1997) 1,057,900. The capital is ▷Zwolle. Industries include textile production (cotton-spinning in the district of Twente). Other activities are livestock rearing, dairying, and fishing.

overlander one of the Australian drovers in the 19th century who opened up new territory by driving their cattle through remote areas to new stations, or to market, before the establishment of regular stock routes.

overpopulation too many people for the resources available in an area (such as food, land, and water). The consequences were first set out by English economist Thomas ▷Malthus at the start of the population explosion.
Related Web site: Paul Ehrlich and the Population Bomb http://www.pbs.org/kqed/population_bomb/

overtone note that has a frequency or pitch that is a multiple of the fundamental frequency, the sounding body's ▷natural frequency. Each sound source produces a unique set of overtones, which gives the source its quality or timbre.

overture in music, the opening piece of a concert or opera, having the dual function of settling the audience and allowing the conductor and musicians to become acquainted with the ▷acoustic of a concert auditorium. See also ▷prelude.

ouzel (or **ousel**) ancient name for the blackbird. The **ring ouzel** (*Turdus torquatus*) is similar to a blackbird, but has a white band across the breast. It is found in Europe in mountainous and rocky country. **Water ouzel** is another name for the ▷dipper.

ovary in female animals, the organ that generates the ▷ovum. In humans, the ovaries are two whitish rounded bodies about 25 mm/1 in by 35 mm/1.5 in, located in the lower abdomen to either side of the uterus. Every month, from puberty to the

Ovid (43 BC–AD 17) Born Publius Ovidius Naso. Latin poet. His poetry deals mainly with the themes of love (*Amores* (20 BC), *Ars amatoria/The Art of Love* (1 BC)), mythology (*Metamorphoses* (AD 2)), and exile (*Tristia* (AD 9–12)). Born at Sulmo, Ovid studied rhetoric in Rome in preparation for a legal career, but soon turned to literature. In AD 9 he was banished by Augustus to Tomis, on the Black Sea, where he died. Sophisticated, ironical, and self-pitying, his work was highly influential during the Middle Ages and Renaissance.

oviparous method of animal reproduction in which eggs are laid by the female and develop outside her body, in contrast to ovoviviparous and viviparous. It is the most common form of reproduction.

ovoviviparous method of animal reproduction in which fertilized eggs develop within the female (unlike oviparous), and the embryo gains no nutritional substances from the female (unlike viviparous). It occurs in some invertebrates, fishes, and reptiles.

ovulation in female animals, the process of releasing egg cells (ova) from the ▷ovary. In mammals it occurs as part of the ▷menstrual cycle.

ovule structure found in seed plants that develops into a seed after fertilization. It consists of an embryo sac containing the female gamete (▷ovum or egg cell), surrounded by nutritive tissue, the nucellus. Outside this there are one or two coverings that provide protection, developing into the testa, or seed coat, following fertilization.

ovum (plural **ova**) female gamete (sex cell) before fertilization. In animals it is called an egg, and is produced in the ovaries. In plants, where it is also known as an egg cell or oosphere, the ovum is produced in an ovule. The ovum does not move by itself. It must be fertilized by a male gamete before it can develop further, except in cases of ▷parthenogenesis.

Owen, Robert (1771–1858) British socialist, born in Wales. In 1800 he became manager of a mill at New Lanark in Scotland, where, by improving working and housing conditions and providing schools, he created a model community. His ideas stimulated the ▷cooperative movement (the pooling of resources for joint economic benefit).

Owen, Wilfred Edward Salter (1893–1918) English poet. His verse, owing much to the encouragement of Siegfried ▷Sassoon, is among the most moving of World War I poetry; it shatters the illusion of the glory of war, revealing its hollowness and cruel destruction of beauty. Only four poems were published during his lifetime; he was killed in action a week before the Armistice. After Owen's death, Sassoon collected and edited his *Poems* (1920). Among the best known are 'Dulce et Decorum Est' and 'Anthem for Doomed Youth', published in 1921. Benjamin ▷Britten used several of the poems in his *War Requiem* (1962). In technique Owen's work is distinguished by the extensive use of ▷assonance in place of rhyme, anticipating the later school of W H ▷Auden and Stephen ▷Spender.
Related Web site: Selected Poetry of Wilfred Owen (1893–Nov. 4, 1918) http://www.library.utoronto.ca/utel/rp/authors/owen.html

Owens, Jesse (1913–1980) Born James Cleveland Owens. US track and field athlete who excelled in sprints, hurdles, and the long jump. At the 1936 Berlin Olympics he won four gold medals.
Related Web site: Owens, Jesse http://www.cmgww.com/sports/owens/

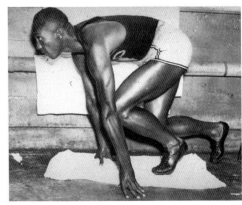

JESSE OWENS An outstanding athlete, Jesse Owens broke many world records, including a long jump record that stood for 25 years. His supremacy at the Berlin Olympics in 1936 dealt a blow to Adolf Hitler's attempts to use the Olympics as a demonstration of Aryan racial superiority. *Archive Photos*

owl any of a group of mainly nocturnal birds of prey found worldwide. They have hooked beaks, heads that can turn quickly and far round on their very short necks, and forward-facing immobile eyes, surrounded by 'facial discs' of rayed feathers; they fly silently and have an acute sense of hearing. Owls comprise two families: typical owls (family Strigidae), of which there are about 120 species, and barn owls (family Tytonidae), of which there are 10 species. (Order Strigiformes.)

They feed mainly on rodents, but sometimes also eat reptiles, fish, and insects, and some species have been seen feeding on carrion. All species lay white eggs, and begin incubation as soon as the first egg is laid. They regurgitate indigestible remains of their prey in pellets (castings).

The **tawny owl** (*Strix aluco*) is a brown-flecked species of Europe and the Middle East; the **little owl** (*Athene noctua*) is the Greek symbol of wisdom and bird of ▷Athena, found widely near human homes; the **snowy owl** (*Nyctea scandiaca*) lives in the Arctic; the largest of the owls are the **eagle owl** (*Bubo bubo*) of Europe and Asia, and the **powerful owl** (*Ninox strenua*) of Australia, both up to 0.75 m/2.25 ft long. The worldwide **barn owl** (*Tyto alba*) was formerly common in Britain, but is now diminished by pesticides and loss of habitat. In Malaysia, it is used for rat control. The **long-eared owl** (*Asio otus*) is distinguished by its ear tufts, which are about 3 cm/1 in long. It feeds on small rodents and frequently birds up to thrush size, and is notorious for its habit of occupying other birds' nests.

OWL A snowy owl, from British Columbia in Canada. *Image Bank*

ox castrated male of domestic cattle, used in developing countries for ploughing and other agricultural work. Also the extinct wild ox or ▷aurochs of Europe, and surviving wild species such as buffaloes and yaks.

OX Since the earliest days of civilization, oxen have been used for a wide variety of tasks requiring strength and stamina. Here, in India, they are being used to dehusk the rice crop with a concrete roller. *Premaphotos Wildlife*

oxalic acid ((COOH)$_2$.2H$_2$O) white, poisonous solid, soluble in water, alcohol, and ether. Oxalic acid is found in rhubarb, and its salts (oxalates) occur in wood sorrel (genus *Oxalis*, family Oxalidaceae) and other plants. It also occurs naturally in human body cells. It is used in the leather and textile industries, in dyeing and bleaching, ink manufacture, metal polishes, and for removing rust and ink stains.

oxbow lake curved lake found on the flood plain of a river. Oxbows are caused by the loops of ▷meanders being cut off at times of flood and the river subsequently adopting a shorter course. In the USA, the term bayou is often used.

Oxfam (abbreviation for Oxford Committee for Famine Relief) charity working to relieve poverty and famine worldwide. It was established in the UK in 1942 by Canon Theodore Richard Milford (1896–1987), initially to assist the starving people of Greece. Its director since 1992 has been David Bryer (1944–   ).

Oxford university city and administrative centre of ▷Oxfordshire in south central England, at the confluence of the rivers Thames (called the Isis around Oxford) and Cherwell, 84 km/52 mi northwest of London; population (1994 est) 121,000. ▷Oxford University has 36 colleges, the oldest being University College (1249). Industries include steel products, electrical goods, car production, publishing (Oxford University Press, Blackwells), and English language schools. Tourism is important.

Features these include Christ Church Cathedral (12th century); the Divinity School and Duke Humphrey's Library (1488); the Sheldonian Theatre, designed by Christopher ▷Wren (1663–69); the Ashmolean Museum (1845); and the 17th-century Bodleian Library. Other museums include the University Museum (1855–60), designed by Benjamin Woodward, the Pitt-Rivers Museum, and the Museum of Modern Art. Features of the colleges include the 14th-century Mob Quad and library at Merton College; the Canterbury Quad (1636) and gardens laid out by 'Capability' Brown at St John's College; and Holman Hunt's *The Light of the World* in Keble College. The Bate Collection of Historical Instruments is housed in the Faculty of Music. The Botanic Gardens (laid out in 1621) are the oldest in Britain. On 1 May (May morning) ▷madrigals are sung at the top of Magdalen College tower. St Giles Fair takes place every September.

History the town was first occupied in Saxon times as a fording point, and is first mentioned in written records in the Anglo-Saxon Chronicle of 912. The University of Oxford, the oldest in England, is first mentioned in the 12th century, when its growth was encouraged by the influx of English students expelled from Paris in 1167. The fame of the university grew steadily, until by the 14th century it was the equal of any in Europe. As the university grew, there was increasing antagonism between it and the town. Most of the university's buildings were built during the 15th, 16th, and 17th centuries. Oxford's earliest colleges were University College (1249), Balliol (1263), and Merton (1264).

During the Civil War, the university supported the Royalist cause while the city declared for Parliament. Oxford became the headquarters of the king and court in 1642, but yielded to the Parliamentary commander-in-chief, General Fairfax, in 1646.

By the beginning of the 20th century, the city had experienced rapid expansion and industrialization, and printing and publishing industries had become firmly established. In the 1920s the English industrial magnate William Morris (1877–1963), later Lord ▷Nuffield, began a motor-car industry at Cowley, just outside the city, which became the headquarters of the Austin-Rover group. The group was sold to German car manufacturer BMW in 1994; the plant received a £230 million investment to produce a new model Mini in 2001.

Oxford and Asquith, Earl of, title of British Liberal politician Herbert Henry ▷Asquith.

Oxford Movement (or Tractarian Movement or Catholic Revival) movement that attempted to revive Catholic religion in the Church of England. Cardinal Newman dated the movement from ▷Keble's sermon in Oxford in 1833. The Oxford Movement by the turn of the century had transformed the Anglican communion, and survives today as Anglo-Catholicism.

> **Related Web site: Oxford Movement** http://www.newadvent.org/cathen/11370a.htm

Oxfordshire county of south central England.

> **area** 2,610 sq km/1,007 sq mi **towns and cities** ▷Oxford (administrative headquarters), Abingdon, Banbury, Goring, Henley-on-Thames, Wallingford, Witney, Woodstock, Wantage, Chipping Norton, Thame **physical** River Thames and tributaries (the Cherwell, Evenlode, Ock, Thame, and Windrush); Cotswold Hills (in the north) and Chiltern Hills (in the southeast) **features** Vale of the White Horse (with a chalk hill figure 114 m/374 ft, below the hill camp known as Uffington Castle); Oxford University; Blenheim Palace (a World Heritage site), Woodstock, started in 1705 by Vanbrugh with help from Nicholas Hawksmoor, completed in 1722, with landscaped grounds by Capability ▷Brown; early 14th-century Broughton Castle; Rousham Park (1635), remodelled by William ▷Kent (1738–40), with

OXFORD *Seige of Oxford* in 1646, by Jan Wyck. During the English Civil War, Oxford University supported the Royalist cause and became the headquarters of King Charles I and his court. The city was besieged by Parliamentary forces under Thomas Fairfax in May 1646 and surrendered the following month. *Art Archive*

> landscaped garden; Ditchley Park, designed by James ▷Gibbs in 1720; Europe's major fusion project JET (Joint European Torus) at the UK Atomic Energy Authority's fusion laboratories at Culham; the Manor House, Kelmscott (country house of William Morris, leader of the Arts and Crafts Movement); Henley Regatta **agriculture** cereals, sheep, dairy farming **industries** agricultural implements (at Banbury); aluminium (at Banbury); bricks; cars (Cowley); cement; iron ore (in the north); high technology industries; medical electronic equipment; paper; publishing; nuclear research (Harwell); biotechnology **population** (1996) 603,100 **famous people** Winston Churchill, William Davenant, Stephen Hawking, William Morris, Flora Thompson
> **Related Web site: Oxfordshire County Council** http://www.oxfordshire.gov.uk/

Oxford University oldest British university, established during the 12th century, the earliest existing college being founded in 1249. After suffering from land confiscation during the Reformation, it was reorganized by Elizabeth I in 1571. In 1996–97 there were 15,641 undergraduates in residence. All colleges, with the exception of St Hilda's (women only), are now coeducational.

oxidation in chemistry, the loss of ▷electrons, gain of oxygen, or loss of hydrogen by an atom, ion, or molecule during a chemical reaction.

Oxidation may be brought about by reaction with another compound (oxidizing agent), which simultaneously undergoes ▷reduction, or electrically at the anode (positive electrode) of an electrolytic cell.

oxidation in earth science, a form of ▷chemical weathering caused by the chemical reaction that takes place between certain iron-rich minerals in rock and the oxygen in water. It tends to result in the formation of a red-coloured soil or deposit. The inside walls of canal tunnels and bridges often have deposits formed in this way.

oxide compound of oxygen and another element, frequently produced by burning the element or a compound of it in air or oxygen.

Oxides of metals are normally ▷bases and will react with an acid to produce a ▷salt in which the metal forms the cation (positive ion). Some of them will also react with a strong alkali to produce a salt in which the metal is part of a complex anion (negative ion; see ▷amphoteric). Most oxides of nonmetals are acidic (dissolve in water to form an ▷acid). Some oxides display no pronounced acidic or basic properties.

oxlip plant closely related to the ▷cowslip.

Oxon. abbreviation for Oxoniensis (Latin 'of Oxford').

oxpecker (or tick-bird) either of two species of African birds belonging to the starling family. They were thought to climb around on the bodies of large mammals, feeding on ticks and other parasites and on cattle earwax, but in a British study, published in April 2000, of red-billed oxpeckers on oxen in Zimbabwe, researchers found that the oxpeckers were not eating the oxen ticks, but were feeding on blood by pecking at existing wounds. Oxpeckers are usually seen in groups of seven or eight, attending a herd of buffaloes or antelopes, and may help to warn the host of approaching dangers.

oxyacetylene torch gas torch that burns ethyne (acetylene) in pure oxygen, producing a high-temperature flame (3,000°C/5,400°F). It is widely used in welding to fuse metals. In the cutting torch, a jet of oxygen burns through metal already melted by the flame.

oxygen (Greek *oxys* 'acid'; *genes* 'forming') colourless, odourless, tasteless, nonmetallic, gaseous element, symbol O, atomic number 8, relative atomic mass 15.9994. It is the most abundant element in the Earth's crust (almost 50% by mass), forms about 21% by volume of the atmosphere, and is present in combined form in water and many other substances. Oxygen is a by-product of ▷photosynthesis and the basis for ▷respiration in plants and animals.

Oxygen is very reactive and combines with all other elements except the ▷inert gases and fluorine. It is present in carbon dioxide, silicon dioxide (quartz), iron ore, calcium carbonate (limestone). In nature it exists as a molecule composed of two atoms (O_2); single atoms of oxygen are very short-lived owing to their reactivity. They can be produced in electric sparks and by the Sun's ultraviolet radiation in space, where they rapidly combine with molecular oxygen to form ozone (an allotrope of oxygen).

Oxygen is obtained for industrial use by the fractional distillation of liquid air, by the electrolysis of water, or by heating manganese (IV) oxide with potassium chlorate. It is essential for combustion, and is used with ethyne (acetylene) in high-temperature oxyacetylene welding and cutting torches.

The element was first identified by English chemist Joseph Priestley in 1774 and independently in the same year by Swedish chemist Karl Scheel. It was named by French chemist Antoine Lavoisier in 1777.

oxygen debt physiological state produced by vigorous exercise, in which the lungs cannot supply all the oxygen that the muscles need.

oxymoron (Greek 'sharply dull' or 'pointedly foolish') ▷figure of speech involving the combination of two or more words that are normally opposites, in order to startle. *Bittersweet* is an oxymoron, as are *cruel to be kind* and *beloved enemy*.

oyster edible shellfish with a rough, irregular hinged shell, found on the sea bottom in coastal areas. Oysters are bivalve ▷molluscs; the upper valve (shell) is flat, the lower hollow, like a bowl, and the two are hinged by an elastic ligament. The mantle, a protective layer of skin, lies against the shell, shielding the inner body, which includes the organs for breathing, digesting food, and reproduction. Oysters commonly change their sex once a year, sometimes more often; females can release up to one million eggs during a spawning period. (Family Ostreidae.)

Oysters have been considered a delicacy since ancient times. Among the species commercially exploited for food today are the North American eastern oyster (*Crassostrea virginica*) of the Atlantic coast and the European oyster (*Ostrea edulis*). The former is oviparous (eggs are discharged straight into the water) and the latter is larviparous (eggs and larvae remain in the mantle cavity for a period before release). Oyster farming is increasingly practised, the beds being specially cleansed for the easy setting of the free-swimming larvae (known as 'spats'), and the oysters later properly spaced for growth and fattened.

Valuable ▷pearls are not obtained from members of the true oyster family; they occur in pearl oysters (family Pteriidae). There are also tree oysters (family Isognomonidae) and thorny oysters (family Spondylidae).

In England, there are oyster beds at Colchester, Essex, and Whitstable, Kent. The Pacific oyster is now bred at Whitstable in warm water before being hardened and transported to Northern Ireland to continue growing for a further three to four years. This species has eggs which hatch outside the oyster, allowing it to be eaten all year round.

oyster catcher any of several quite large, chunky shorebirds, with a long, heavy bill which is flattened at the sides and used to prise open the shells of oysters, mussels, and other shellfish. (Family Haematopodidae, order Charadriiformes.)

Özal, Turgut (1927–1993) Turkish Islamic right-wing politician, prime minister 1983–89, and president 1989–93. He was responsible for improving his country's relations with Greece, but his prime objective was to strengthen Turkey's alliance with the USA.

Ozalid process trademarked copying process used to produce positive prints from drawn or printed materials or film, such as printing proofs from film images. The film is placed on top of chemically treated paper and then exposed to ultraviolet light. The image is developed dry using ammonia vapour.

Ozark Mountains highland plateau region in south-central USA (shared by Arkansas, Illinois, Kansas, Missouri, Oklahoma) with ridges, valleys, and streams; area 130,000 sq km/50,000 sq mi.

Extending between the Missouri and Arkansas rivers, it contains the **Ozark** and Springfield plateaux, the Boston Mountains, and the Salem uplands. Generally low in elevation, 300 m/400 m–984 ft/1,312 ft, the highlands crest in the Boston Mountains at 800 m/2,625 ft. The area is heavily forested, with lead and zinc mining, agricultural, and recreational activities.

ozone O_3 highly reactive pale-blue gas with a penetrating odour. Ozone is an allotrope of oxygen (see ▷allotropy), made up of three atoms of oxygen. It is formed when the molecule of the stable form of oxygen (O_2) is split by ultraviolet radiation or electrical discharge. It forms the ▷ozone layer in the upper atmosphere, which protects life on Earth from ultraviolet rays, a cause of skin cancer.

ozone depleter any chemical that destroys the ozone in the stratosphere. Most ozone depleters are chemically stable compounds containing chlorine or bromine, which remain unchanged for long enough to drift up to the upper atmosphere. The best known are ▷chlorofluorocarbons (CFCs), but many other ozone depleters are known, including halons, used in some fire extinguishers; methyl chloroform and carbon tetrachloride, both solvents; some CFC substitutes; and the pesticide methyl bromide.

ozone layer thin layer of the gas ▷ozone in the upper atmosphere that shields the Earth from harmful ultraviolet rays. A continent-sized hole has formed over Antarctica as a result of damage to the ozone layer. This has been caused in part by ▷chlorofluorocarbons (CFCs), but many reactions destroy ozone in the stratosphere: nitric oxide, chlorine, and bromine atoms are implicated.

    Related Web site: Chemistry of the Ozone Layer http://pooh.chem. wm.edu/chemWWW/courses/chem105/projects/group2/page1.html

Ozu, Yasujirō (1903–1963) Japanese film director. He made silent films until 1936, by which time his basic style and themes were clear: an absorption in family life, in the interrelationships of its characters, and the use of comedy to reveal character. His *Tōkyō monogatari/Tokyo Story* (1953) is widely regarded as one of the great classics of world cinema.

P

p(p). abbreviation for page(s).

p.a. abbreviation for **per annum** (Latin 'yearly').

PA abbreviation for the state of ▷Pennsylvania, USA.

paca large, tailless, nocturnal, burrowing ▷rodent, related to the agoutis. The paca, about 60 cm/2 ft long, is native to Central and South America. (Genus *Cuniculus*, family Dasyproctidae.)

pacemaker (or **sinoatrial node (SA node)**) in vertebrates, a group of muscle cells in the wall of the heart that contracts spontaneously and rhythmically, setting the pace for the contractions of the rest of the heart. The pacemaker's intrinsic rate of contraction is increased or decreased, according to the needs of the body, by stimulation from the ▷autonomic nervous system. The term also refers to a medical device implanted under the skin of a patient whose heart beats inefficiently. It delivers minute electric shocks to stimulate the heart muscles at regular intervals and restores normal heartbeat.

The latest pacemakers are powered by radioactive isotopes for long life and weigh no more than 15 g/0.5 oz.

Pacific Community (PC; formerly **South Pacific Commission** until 1998) organization to promote economic and social cooperation in the region, including dialogue between Pacific countries and those, such as France and the UK, that have dependencies in the region. It was established in February 1947. Its members include American Samoa, Australia, Cook Islands, Federated States of Micronesia, Fiji Islands, France, French Polynesia, Guam, Kiribati, Marshall Islands, Nauru, New Caledonia, New Zealand, Niue, Northern Marianas, Palau, Papua New Guinea, Pitcairn Islands, Samoa, Solomon Islands, Tokelau, Tonga, Tuvalu, United Kingdom, United States of America, Vanuatu, and Wallis and Futuna; headquarters are in Nouméa, New Caledonia. See also Pacific Islanders Past and Present Focus Feature on pp. 718–719.

Pacific Islands former (1947–1990) United Nations ▷trust territory in the western Pacific captured from Japan during World War II. The territory comprised over 2,000 islands and atolls and was assigned to the USA in 1947. The islands were divided into four governmental units: the **Northern Mariana Islands** (except Guam) which became a self-governing commonwealth in union with the USA in 1975 (inhabitants granted US citizenship 1986); the ▷Marshall Islands, the Federated States of ▷Micronesia, and the Republic of ▷Palau (formerly also known as Belau) became self-governing 1979–80, signing agreements of free association with the USA in 1986. In December 1990 the United Nations Security Council voted to dissolve its trusteeship over the islands with the exception of Palau. The Marshall Islands and the Federated States of Micronesia were granted UN membership in 1991.

Pacific Islands Forum (PIF; formerly called **South Pacific Forum** until 2000) association of states in the region to discuss common interests and develop common policies, created in 1971 as an offshoot of the South Pacific Commission, now the ▷Pacific Community. Its 26 member countries include Australia, Cook Islands, Fiji Islands, Kiribati, Marshall Islands, the Federated States of Micronesia, Nauru, New Zealand, Niue, Papua New Guinea, Samoa, Solomon Islands, Tonga, Tuvalu, and Vanuatu, with New Caledonia an observer since 1999.

Pacific Ocean world's largest ocean, extending from Antarctica to the Bering Strait; area 166,242,500 sq km/64,186,500 sq mi; greatest breadth 16,000 km/9,942 mi; length 11,000 km/6,835 mi; average depth 4,188 m/13,749 ft; greatest depth of any ocean 11,524 m/37,808 ft in the Mindanao Trench, east of the Philippines.

Depth The Pacific is the deepest ocean; the western and northern areas are deeper than the east and south. Some of the greater depths lie alongside islands, such as the Mariana Trench (11,034 m/36,200 ft), alongside the Mariana Islands, the Tuscarora Deep (8,500 m/27,886 ft), alongside Japan and the Kurils and extending for 640 km/397 mi, and the Aldrich Deep, east of New Zealand (9,400 m/30,840 ft).

Islands There are over 2,500 islands in the central and western regions, of volcanic or coral origin, many being atolls. The Pacific is ringed by an area of volcanic activity, with accompanying earthquakes.

Currents Winds in the northern Pacific produce generally clockwise currents; a northward current from the equator flows past the Philippines and is joined by currents from the East Indies and China Sea at Taiwan to form the Kuroshio. This branches opposite Vancouver to flow south as the California current, and north around the Alaskan coast. A cold current from the Bering Sea enters the Okhotsk and Japan seas, causing freezing in winter. In the South Pacific the trade winds cause anticlockwise equatorial currents which branch opposite southern Chile, to flow north as the cooling Peru or Humboldt Current, and south round Cape Horn.

European exploration Vasco Núñez de Balboa was the first European to see the Pacific Ocean from Panama in 1513. Ferdinand Magellan sailed through the Strait of Magellan in 1520, and gave the name to the ocean (because of its calmness during his voyage). In 1577 Francis Drake, the first Englishman to enter the Pacific, sailed north to California and across to the Moluccas. The Australasian region was explored by Europeans in the 17th century.

Pacific Security Treaty military alliance agreement between Australia, New Zealand, and the USA, signed in 1951. Military cooperation between the USA and New Zealand has been restricted by the latter's policy of banning ships that might be carrying nuclear weapons or nuclear power sources.

Pacific War war 1879–83 fought by an alliance of Bolivia and Peru against Chile. Chile seized Antofagasta and the coast between the mouths of the rivers Loa and Paposo, rendering Bolivia landlocked, and also annexed the south Peruvian coastline from Arica to the mouth of the Loa, including the nitrate fields of the Atacama Desert.

pacifism belief that violence, even in self-defence, is unjustifiable under any conditions and that arbitration is preferable to war as a means of solving disputes. In the East, pacifism has roots in Buddhism, and nonviolent action was used by Mahatma ▷Gandhi in the struggle for Indian independence.

Pacino, Al(fredo James) (1940–) US film actor. He has played powerful, introverted but violent roles in such films as *The Godfather* (1972), *Serpico* (1973), and *Scarface* (1983). *Dick Tracy* (1990) added comedy to his range. He won an Academy Award for his role in *Scent of a Woman* (1992). His recent films include *Donnie Brasco* (1997), *The Insider* (1999), and *Insomnia* (2002).

Packer, Kerry Francis Bullmore (1937–) Australian media proprietor. He is chair of Consolidated Press Holdings (CPH), which he privatized in 1983, a conglomerate founded by his father which produces such magazines as the *Australian Women's Weekly* and the *Bulletin*. CPH also has interests in radio and television stations. In 1977 Packer created World Series Cricket, which introduced one-day matches and coloured kit to the game. The *Business Review Weekly* named him in 1998 as Australia's richest man, worth $A5.2 billion.

packet switching a method of transmitting data between computers connected in a ▷network. Packet switched networks do not provide a dedicated connection between two locations, as with a circuit switched network. Packet switched networks make more effective use of bandwidth than circuit switched networks, and are more resilient to breaks in network links because there are always multiple routes from source to destination.

Paderewski, Ignacy Jan (1860–1941) Polish pianist, composer, and politician. After his debut in Vienna in 1887, he became celebrated in Europe and the USA as an interpreter of the piano music of Chopin and as composer of the *Polish Fantasy* (1893) for piano and orchestra and the *'Polonia' Symphony* (1903–09).

During World War I he helped organize the Polish army in France; in 1919 he became prime minister of the newly independent Poland, which he represented at the Peace Conference, but continuing opposition forced him to resign the same year. He resumed a musical career in 1922, was made president of the Polish National Council in Paris in 1940, and died in New York.

Padua (Italian **Padova**; ancient **Patavium**) town in Veneto, northern Italy, on the canalized section of the River Bacchiglione, 38 km/24 mi west of Venice; population (1992) 213,700. Industries include engineering, and the manufacture of clothing and man-made fibres. The astronomer Galileo taught at the university, founded in 1222.

PAGAN The site of Pagan, Myanmar (formerly Burma). *Image Bank*

paediatrics medical speciality concerned with the care of children. Paediatricians treat childhood diseases such as measles, chicken pox, and mumps, and immunize children against more serious infections such as diptheria. Their role also includes treating and identifying disorders caused by lack of proper nutrition or child abuse.

Pagan archaeological site in Myanmar, on the Irrawaddy River, with the ruins of the former capital (founded 847, taken by the Mongol leader Kublai Khan 1287). These include Buddhist pagodas, shrines, and temples with wall paintings of the great period of Burmese art (11th–13th centuries), during which the Pagan state controlled much of Burma (now Myanmar).

pagan (Latin *paganus* 'a person from the countryside') usually, a member of one of the pre-Christian cultures of northern Europe, primarily Celtic or Norse, linked to the stone circles and to an agricultural calendar of which the main festivals are the summer and winter solstices and Beltane, the spring festival.

Paganini, Niccolò (1782–1840) Italian violinist and composer. He was a concert soloist from the age of nine. A prodigious technician, he drew on folk and gypsy idioms to create the modern repertoire of virtuoso techniques.

His dissolute appearance, wild love life, and amazing powers of expression, even on a single string, fostered rumours of his being in league with the devil. His compositions include six concertos and various sonatas and variations for violin and orchestra, sonatas for violin and guitar, and guitar quartets.

page printer computer ▷printer that prints a complete page of text and graphics at a time. Page printers use electrostatic techniques, very similar to those used by photocopiers, to form images of pages, and range in size from small ▷laser printers designed to work with microcomputers to very large machines designed for high-volume commercial printing.

paging method of increasing a computer's apparent memory capacity. See ▷virtual memory.

Pagnol, Marcel (Paul) (1895–1974) French film director, producer, writer, and dramatist. His work includes the novels *Fanny* (1932) and *Manon des sources* (1952; filmed 1986). His autobiographical *La Gloire de mon père/My Father's Glory* (1957) was filmed in 1991. He regarded the cinema as recorded theatre; thus his films, although strong on character and background, fail to exploit the medium fully as an independent art form.

pagoda Buddhist structure common in China, Japan, and Korea, built to contain a relic or sutra (collection of recorded Buddhist dialogues and discourses). Pagodas have three, five, or seven storeys (in exceptional cases more), crowned by a tall spire (*sōrin*). There is generally no room inside, so that a pagoda is essentially just a stack of roofs, not a functioning building. Deriving from the Indian ▷stupa, the pagoda came to resemble a Chinese watchtower; the shape also has symbolic meaning.

Pahang state of east Peninsular Malaysia; capital Kuantan; area 36,000 sq km/14,000 sq mi; population (1993) 1,056,100. It is mountainous and forested and produces rubber, tin, gold, and timber. There is a port at Tanjung Gelang. Pahang is ruled by a sultan.

Pahlavi dynasty Iranian dynasty founded by Reza Khan (1877–1944), an army officer who seized control of the government in 1921 and was proclaimed shah in 1925. During World War II, Britain and the USSR were nervous about his German sympathies and occupied Iran 1941–46. They compelled him to abdicate in 1941 in favour of his son Muhammad Reza Shah Pahlavi who was deposed in the Islamic revolution of 1979.

Pahsien alternative name of ▷Chongqing, a city in Sichuan province, China.

pain sense that gives an awareness of harmful effects on or in the body. It may be triggered by stimuli such as trauma, inflammation, and heat. Pain is transmitted by specialized nerves and also has psychological components controlled by higher centres in the brain. Drugs that control pain are known as painkillers or ▷analgesics.

Paine, Thomas (1737–1809) English left-wing political writer. He was active in the American and French revolutions. His pamphlet *Common Sense* (1776) ignited passions in the American Revolution; others include *The Rights of Man* (1791) and *The Age of Reason* (1793). He advocated republicanism, deism, the abolition of slavery, and the emancipation of women.

Paine, born in Thetford, Norfolk, was a friend of US scientist and politician Benjamin Franklin and went to America in 1774, where he published several republican pamphlets and fought for the colonists in the revolution. In 1787 he returned to Britain. *The Rights of Man* is an answer to the conservative theorist Burke's *Reflections on the Revolution in France*. In 1792, Paine was indicted for treason and escaped to France, to represent Calais in the National Convention. Narrowly escaping the guillotine, he regained his seat after the fall of Robespierre. Paine returned to the USA in 1802 and died in New York.

Related Web site: Thomas Paine: American Crisis, 1780–1783
http://odur.let.rug.nl/~usa/D/1776-1800/paine/AC/crisisxx.htm

paint any of various materials used to give a protective and decorative finish to surfaces or for making pictures. A paint consists of a pigment suspended in a vehicle, or binder, usually with added solvents. It is the vehicle that dries and hardens to form an adhesive film of paint. Among the most common kinds are cellulose paints (or lacquers), oil-based paints, emulsion (water-based) paints, and special types such as enamels and primers.

painted lady brownish-red and black butterfly that migrates to Britain from North Africa. The caterpillar feeds on thistles and other plants.

painting the application of coloured pigment to a surface. The chief methods of painting are: **tempera** emulsion painting, with a gelatinous (for example, egg yolk) rather than oil base – known in ancient Egypt; **fresco** watercolour painting on plaster walls – the palace of Knossos, Crete, contains examples from about 2,000 BC; **ink** developed in China for calligraphy in the Sung period and highly popular in Japan from the 15th century; **oil** ground pigments in linseed, walnut, or other oil, it spread from northern to southern Europe in the 15th century; **watercolour** pigments combined with gum arabic and glycerol, which are diluted with water – the method was developed in the 15th–17th centuries for wash drawings; **acrylic** synthetic pigments developed after World War II, the colours are very hard and brilliant. High-resolution video cameras and computers are now being used to help art experts identify damage to paintings in some of the world's major galleries, including the Louvre and the National Gallery in the UK. The system identifies damage by comparing 'before' and 'after' images in order to highlight changes in the craquelure (a network of fine cracks on a painting's surface that are due to age – they are an authentic sign of age and, where artifically induced in forged works of art, are usually detectable).

For the history of painting see ▷medieval art; ▷Chinese art and so on. Individual painters and art movements are listed

(continued on p. 720)

Painting: Key Dates of Western Painting

27000–13000 BC	Cave art in southwest Europe expresses the concerns of hunters.
3000–100	Egyptian wall paintings combine front, three-quarter, and side views of the human body in a flat 'diagrammatic' style.
2000–1450	The Minoan civilization, based at Knossos in Crete, has bright wall paintings.
1000–400	Greek painting by the finest artists survives mainly as vase decorations.
AD 79	Volcanic ash from Vesuvius preserves fine examples of Roman domestic painting and mosaics.
230–450	Early Christian murals are painted in catacombs and as mosaics in churches.
330–1453	Byzantine art expresses Orthodox Christian values in formalized mosaics and painted icons.
680–800	Celtic Christian art develops in illuminated religious texts such as the *Lindisfarne Gospel* and the *Book of Kells*.
1290–1337	Italian painting emerges from the Byzantine style with the new depth and realism of Giotto, the first great painter of the Italian Renaissance period.
1315–1425	Italian Gothic and then International Gothic evolve an elegant and decorative style.
1420–92	Fra Angelico, Piero della Francesca, and Botticelli bring a new freshness of vision to Italian painting.
1425–50	A new and vivid realism, owing much to the established use of high-quality oil paints, appears in the work of early Renaissance painters such as Jan van Eyck.
c. 1428	Masaccio incorporates Brunelleschi's laws of perspective in his grand and austere *Holy Trinity*, creating an illusion of depth never seen before in painting.
1470–1569	The Northern Renaissance produces a series of disparate geniuses, including Dürer, Bosch, and Brueghel, who expressed the religious anxieties of the age.
1472–1519	Leonardo da Vinci brings a new sense of mystery and psychological depth to painting.
1500–64	Michelangelo rediscovers classical grandeur and harnesses it to Christian subjects, for example in the Sistine Chapel frescoes.
1504–20	Raphael's short career expresses Florentine Renaissance ideals with an unsurpassed harmony.
1506–94	The Venetian Renaissance is manifested in the warm sensuality of Titian, Giorgione, Tintoretto, and Veronese.
1520–1600	Mannerists, such as Romano, Pontormo, and Parmigianino, apply the discoveries of the High Renaissance in more stylized forms.
1525–1792	The tradition of portrait painting in Britain begins with Holbein and is continued by Reynolds and Gainsborough.
1560–1609	Caravaggio, a master of dramatic light and shade, leads the way towards the baroque style.
1570–1682	The great age of Spanish painting lasts from the tortured religious idealism of El Greco through to Velázquez.
1577–1640	Rubens is the supreme master of the baroque grand style.
1620–70	Dutch genre painting produces masters of portraiture, interiors, landscapes, and still life.
1624–82	Poussin and Claude Lorraine establish the idealized classical landscape painting.
1626–69	Rembrandt brings an unparalled psychological and emotional depth to biblical scenes and portraits.
1706–1806	The elegance of French rococo is captured by Watteau, Boucher, and Fragonard.
1780–1851	The Romantic spirit is expressed in the vision of painters such as Goya, Turner, Constable, and Delacroix.
1780–1867	Ingres and David sustain the classicism of the French revolutionary and post-revolutionary periods.
1840–77	Courbet develops a radical realism in his work.
1863	By his use of flat colour and avoidance of realist conventions, Manet is a forerunner of Impressionism, heralding a new era in art.
1870–90	The Symbolists and Pre-Raphaelites portray visionary ideas through the use of symbols and rich colours.
1874	Monet, Renoir, and Degas exhibit at the first Impressionist exhibiton with paintings composed of broken surfaces of light.
1883–91	Seurat carries the discoveries of the Impressionists further with his pointillist techniques of dots of colour.
1883–1903	Gauguin's spiritual and sensual odyssey to the Pacific island of Tahiti foreshadows Expressionism and Fauvism.
1885–90	Van Gogh's personal vision invests ordinary scenes with unparalleled emotion and spirituality through broad strokes of bright colour.
1886–1906	Cézanne creates a new kind of painting with solid forms built with a mosaic of brush strokes. His concentration on geometric forms inspires the Cubism.
1892–1926	Munch, and later the Expressionists, use colour and form to express emotions.
1905	Matisse and the Fauves create compositions where form is defined by subjective choice of colour.
1907	*Les Demoiselles d'Avignon* by Picasso heralds the Cubist movement by rejecting conventional naturalistic representation from only one viewpoint and conventional ideas of beauty.
1910–14	Kandinsky develops a purely abstract art.
1913	The Armory Show, often regarded as the beginning of public interest in progressive art in the USA, takes place in New York.
1913–44	A geometrical abstract art is developed by Malevitch, Tatlin, Rodchenko, and Mondrian.
1914	Duchamp and the Dadaists bring an anarchist element to painting that questions traditional notions of art.
1914–40	Klee develops figurative painting out of abstract patterns.
From 1924	Surrealist painters, notably Dalí, Magritte, and Miro, use the unconscious, such as dreams, as a source of inspiration.
1940s	Abstract expressionism is developed in New York by Jackson Pollock and Arshile Gorky, and adds an element of uninhibited expression to pure abstraction.
1940s–1950s	European post-war anxiety finds expression in the Art Brut of Jean Dubuffet, and the expressionism of the COBRA group, including Karel Appel.
1950s–1960s	Pop art returns to a representative style, drawing on popular images, for example from comic books, and commercial techniques.
From late 1950s	The broadly based 'London School' continues the British figurative tradition.
1960s	In the USA, super-realist artists (Malcolm Morley and Richard Estes) strive for a photographic realism. Op art extends the range of abstraction, with Bridget Riley a leading figure.
1970s–1980s	In the USA, graffiti, seen as an urban folk art, is exploited by artists such as Keith Haring and Jean-Michel Basquiat.
Late 1970s–1980s	Neo-expressionism flourishes in Germany (Anselm Keifer and Georg Baselitz), Italy (Francesco Clemente and Enzo Cucchi), and the USA (Julian Schnabel).
1980s–1990s	A multiplicity of styles are popular with no dominant tendency. The self-conscious use of styles and images from a broad range of sources – from pop culture to old masters – is common.
1997	The controversial and provocative *Sensation* exhibition is held at the Royal Acadamy, London. It includes works such as 'pickled animal' sculptures by Damien Hirst, and a portrait of child murderer, Myra Hindley.
1999	The exhibition *Monet in the 20th Century* is held at the Royal Academy, London, England. Tickets cost a record £9 each, and a record 813,000 people visit the exhibition.

PAINTING *The Picnic*, by the Spanish painter and etcher Goya, is in the Prado Museum, Madrid, Spain. *The Art Archive/Prado Museum Madrid/Dagli Orti*

Pacific Islanders – Past and Present

by Eugene Ogan

HULI TRIBESMAN, New Guinea. The Huli are the largest ethnic group in the Southern Highlands of Papua New Guinea. The tribesmen wear traditional face paint, nose quills, and intricate decorated wigs. © *Corel*

Humans first settled the Pacific islands between 40,000 and 60,000 years ago. As glaciers expanded and contracted during the Ice Age, sea levels fell and rose. When the first settlers entered the islands, low sea levels had created land bridges linking Australia and the large island of New Guinea, and had expanded the land mass of Southeast Asia. Even so, these first settlers must have been able to travel by sea for some distances in order to eventually populate the islands as far east as New Britain and New Ireland by about 35,000 years ago. This migration may represent the earliest purposive voyaging in human history.

settling the islands

About 5,000 years ago, people with advanced seafaring skills began a second migration out of Asia. Though they lacked the compass, sextant, and other devices used much later by Europeans, their knowledge of the stars and the motion of waves and ocean swells formed a system of navigation that enabled them to travel across thousands of miles of open sea. Their larger outrigger canoes were able to sail into the wind and to carry people, pigs, and new plants. Beginning with the Caroline and Marshall Islands, the settlers populated the rest of the previously uninhabited Pacific islands, including New Zealand, Hawaii, the Society Islands, and the far-flung smaller islands of what is now called Polynesia. Such skills of navigation have only recently been relearned, by modern Hawaiians among others.

These later settlers made a distinctive kind of pottery, called Lapita, by which their migration can be traced. They are generally believed to have spoken languages that are now classed as Austronesian. Such languages are the most widespread in the world, spoken from Madagascar to Rapa Nui (Easter Island). The settlers travelled back and forth between islands, adding to the populations of New Guinea, the largest Pacific island, and the Bismarck Archipelago as they moved east, and linking Fiji, Samoa, and Tonga about 3,000 years ago.

arrival of Europeans

The Spanish and Portuguese entered the Pacific in the 16th century, followed by Dutch, British, and French explorers and adventurers. It was not until the 18th century that the development of navigational tools like the sextant and chronometer permitted accurate mapping of the islands. The English seafarer Captain James Cook played a vital role in this effort. His three voyages from 1768 to 1779 greatly increased European knowledge of the Pacific and its peoples. Another landmark was the establishment of a British penal colony in Australia, which gave incentive for trade and travel in the region.

The European presence in the Pacific islands in the 19th century brought rapid change, often in forms so disastrous that some writers refer to a 'fatal impact'. Introduced diseases, to which islanders had no immunity, led to loss of life, and warfare was made more deadly by the use of European firearms. Crews from whaling vessels operating in Polynesia and Micronesia created social disruption. Christian missionaries attempted to ease the problems faced by islanders but inevitably undermined much of their traditional culture.

Polynesia, Micronesia, and Melanesia

In 1832 the French voyager Dumont d'Urville gave the names Polynesia (Greek for 'many islands'), Micronesia ('little islands'), and Melanesia ('black islands') to regions of the Pacific. These names are still in popular use today.

Polynesia remains the most meaningful of d'Urville's classifications. The term covers the vast area bounded by a triangle with its points at New Zealand in the southwest, the Hawaiian Archipelago in the northeast, and Rapa Nui at the easternmost point. Polynesians speak closely related languages and shared many cultural traits. Their traditional societies were more stratified than others in the Pacific, and chiefs with real power were found in Tonga, Tahiti, and Hawaii.

Micronesian islands, in the northwestern region of the Pacific, are indeed small; but although all inhabitants speak Austronesian languages, there is more linguistic variation than in Polynesia. Micronesian social stratification varies according to island size. A large island like Yap could demand tribute from smaller nearby isles.

ONE OF THE MARQUESAS ISLANDS, French Polynesia, in the central southern Pacific. They have magnificent scenery, with verdant forests, rugged peaks, and turquoise seas. The French artist Paul Gauguin is buried on the largest island, Hiva Oa. © *Image Bank*

The term Melanesia encompasses a great variety of peoples, languages, and cultures. Melanesia stretches from New Guinea in the west to New Caledonia in the east. (Fiji is sometimes grouped with Melanesia, though its language and culture would seem to link it more closely to Polynesia.) D'Urville's term 'black islands' reflected the darker skin colour of the people, but even this is inaccurate, as some are no darker-skinned than Polynesians. Some Melanesians speak Austronesian languages, but a bewildering variety of tongues is spoken by a majority. When first contacted by Europeans, most Melanesians lived in small political units, quite different from Polynesian chiefdoms.

20th century

By 1900, European nations had established control over most of the Pacific. Germany held most of Micronesia, as well as the Bismarck Archipelago, part of the Solomons, and Western Samoa. Germany, Britain, and the Netherlands each claimed portions of the large island of New Guinea. Britain controlled Fiji as a crown colony, and most of the Solomons as a protectorate. France ruled New Caledonia and the Society Islands, and joined Britain in an unusual kind of government over the New Hebrides. In Polynesia, only Tonga remained politically independent. Hawaii had been annexed by the United States, which also held eastern Samoa, Guam, and the Marianas.

GOLD AND COPPER MINING in quarries in the Star Mountains, Papua New Guinea, provides some of the country's main exports and revenue. These mines, situated in the high altitude rainforests in the Western Highlands, also pose a significant threat to this sensitive environment, however. *Wayne Lawler, Ecoscene/Corbis*

A GOLD MINER from the Mount Kare region of Papua New Guinea. Mining is an important source of employment in Papua New Guinea. *Arne Hodalic, Corbis*

Beginning with Samoa in 1962, many of the islands have emerged from colonial domination to become independent nation states. These range in size from Papua New Guinea (including the eastern half of New Guinea, the Bismarck Archipelago, and Bougainville Island) to tiny Kiribati (formerly the Gilbert Islands). Twelve of the new countries are members of the United Nations (UN). The major exceptions to independent political status are west New Guinea, which has become the West Irian province of Indonesia; New Caledonia and French Polynesia (France); and Guam, the Marianas, and American Samoa (USA). New Zealand and Hawaii are special cases, in which the original Polynesian inhabitants have become minorities within larger nations.

Pacific islands today

Pacific islanders now live in a complex mixture of old versus new, of rural versus urban, of political independence versus minority status in their own islands, and of all the entanglements of a global economy offering both potential enrichment and 'fourth world' poverty.

Independence has not always brought political or economic stability. Since 1987, Fiji has endured two military coups, Bougainville fought from 1988 to 1998 in an attempt to secede from Papua New Guinea, and most recently, ethnic conflict has threatened to tear apart the Solomon Islands. Polynesian countries like Tonga and Samoa have suffered less political unrest but, like the smaller nations in Micronesia, are heavily dependent on economic aid from the industrialized world to survive. Many islanders have left their homes to settle throughout the world; for example, there are now more Samoans in New Zealand and the United States than in their original homeland. Desire for a better economic future is a major motivation to migrate, and those who are successful send substantial sums to those who remain behind.

Papua New Guinea

Papua New Guinea, by far the largest country in the Pacific, demonstrates some of the complexities of the island-world today. The Melanesian inhabitants speak an estimated 800 different languages (most of which are not Austronesian). When the Germans and English claimed parts of the area in the 1880s, they found people still living with Stone-Age technology. There were no large political units. Leaders, generally described as 'big men' rather than chiefs, had limited authority, often over no more than a small group of kinsmen. Traditional religion took the form of ancestral or spirit cults, and a belief in magic was widespread. Many of these old cultural patterns are still in evidence, despite the changes brought by more than a century of western contact. Traditional beliefs have mixed with early missionary work and more recent evangelism to produce a world view sometimes loosely labelled 'cargo cult'.

Although television sets and other modern conveniences are common in towns like the capital Port Moresby, more than 80% of Papua New Guinea's citizens live in a rural environment. Village houses still have thatched roofs, and plumbing and electricity are rare. The striking gap between town and village is echoed by the social distance between a small elite and the majority of citizens. Gold mining, hydroelectric, and natural-gas projects produce great wealth; yet infant and maternal mortality rates are among the highest in the world, and AIDS threatens to replace malaria as the country's greatest health problem.

tradition and the future

Nationalist sentiment is leading to a revival of traditional cultural ideas in some parts of the Pacific. For instance, in Hawaii, where Polynesian culture was once thought to have died out, the Hawaiian language is being revived and taught in public schools.

At the beginning of the 21st century, islanders are also learning to face new challenges. For example, tiny Tuvalu has successfully negotiated the sale of its .tv Internet domain name extension. This kind of creative approach to modernity may reflect the spirit of the Pacific peoples who once sent canoes sailing across uncharted seas to settle their island world.

(*continued from p. 717*)

alphabetically. For the major style of Western painters, see ▷Mannerism, ▷baroque, ▷rococo, ▷neoclassicism, ▷Romanticism, ▷realism, ▷impressionism, and ▷abstract art.

Related Web site: Fineart Forum Online WWW Resources Directory
http://www.msstate.edu/Fineart_Online/art-resources/museums.html

PAINTING A fresco of 'Europa and the bull', from a house in Pompeii, Italy, which was buried for over a thousand years under volcanic ash. *The Art Archive/Archaeological Museum Naples/Dagli Orti*

Paisley, Ian (Richard Kyle) (1926–   ) Northern Ireland politician, cleric, and leader of the Democratic Unionist Party (DUP) from 1971. An imposing and deeply influential member of the Protestant community, he remains staunchly committed to the union with Britain. His political career was one of high drama, marked by protests, resignations, fierce oratory, and a pugnacious and forthright manner.

Paisley was born in Armagh, the son of a Baptist minister, and was educated at the Model School and Technical High School in Ballymena, the South Wales Bible College, and the Reformed Presbyterian Theological College in Belfast. He preached his first sermon at the age of 16, and in 1951 established the Free Presbyterian Church of Ulster in Belfast. When Catholic civil-rights agitation began to flourish in the 1960s, Paisley organized numerous marches and speeches in opposition, which led to his imprisonment for six weeks in 1968 for unlawful assembly. In April 1970, one year into 'the Troubles' in Northern Ireland, Paisley won the seat for Bannside in Northern Ireland's Stormont assembly, and he went on to win the North Antrim seat two months later. The following year, he established the DUP as a more hardline rival to the ruling dominant Ulster Unionist Party. He was influential in the actions of the Ulster Workers' Council and their general strike, which destroyed the Sunningdale Power Sharing Initiative in 1974. Paisley's powerful speeches and image of strength won him great support within the Protestant community and he scored huge victories in both the 1979 and 1984 European elections, polling around one-third of the first-preference votes each time.

Throughout the 1980s, Paisley stuck rigidly to his 'no surrender' policies, resigning his seat in 1985 in protest at the Anglo-Irish Agreement. He re-entered Parliament early the following year. His Presbyterian beliefs were inextricably bound up with his political aims, and in 1988 he was ejected from the European Parliament for interrupting an address by Pope John Paul II. Paisley was sceptical of the various initiatives to solve the problems of Northern Ireland, particularly those involving any 'sellout', in his view, to the Dublin government or Sinn Fein and the Irish Republican Army (IRA).

He opposed the 1998 Good Friday Agreement on power-sharing in Northern Ireland and in the May 1998 referendum his North Antrim constituency was the only one of Northern Ireland's 18 seats in which there was a majority against the accord. He went on to lead the opposition to the agreement within the new Northern Ireland Assembly.

Pakaraima Mountains mountain range in the Guiana Highlands along the border between Brazil, Venezuela, and Guyana, extending from west to east for over 800 km/497 mi. Its highest peak is Mount Roraima at 2,810 m/9,222 ft above sea level, surrounded by cliffs 300 m/1,000 ft high, at the conjunction of the three countries.

Pakistan see country box.

Pala dynasty (lived 8th–13th centuries) northeastern Indian hereditary rulers, influential between the 8th and 13th centuries. Based in the agriculturally rich region of Bihar and Bengal, the dynasty was founded by Gopala, who had been elected king, and reached its peak under his son Dharmapala (reigned *c.* 770–810).

Palaeocene epoch (Greek 'old' + 'recent') first epoch of the Tertiary period of geological time, 65–56.5 million years ago. Many types of mammals spread rapidly after the disappearance of the great reptiles of the Mesozoic. Flying mammals replaced the flying reptiles, swimming mammals replaced the swimming reptiles, and all the ecological niches vacated by the reptiles were adopted by mammals.

At the end of the Palaeocene there was a mass extinction that caused more than half of all bottom-dwelling organisms to disappear worldwide, over a period of around one thousand years. Surface-dwelling organisms remained unaffected, as did those on land. The cause of this extinction remains unknown, though US palaeontologists have found evidence (released 1998) that it may have been caused by the Earth releasing tonnes of methane into the oceans causing increased water temperatures.

Palaeolithic the Old Stone Age period, the earliest stage of human technology; see ▷prehistory.

palaeomagnetism the study of the magnetic properties of rocks in order to reconstruct the Earth's ancient magnetic field and the former positions of the continents, using traces left by the Earth's magenetic field in igneous rocks before they cool. Palaeomagnetism shows that the Earth's magnetic field has reversed itself – the magnetic north pole becoming the magnetic south pole, and vice versa – at approximate half-million-year intervals, with shorter reversal periods in between the major spans.

palaeontology in geology, the study of ancient life, encompassing the structure of ancient organisms and their environment, evolution, and ecology, as revealed by their ▷fossils and the rocks those fossils are found in. The practical aspects of palaeontology are based on using the presence of different fossils to date particular rock strata and to identify rocks that were laid down under particular conditions; for instance, giving rise to the formation of oil.

The use of fossils to trace the age of rocks was pioneered in Germany by Johann Friedrich Blumenbach (1752–1830) at Göttingen, followed by Georges ▷Cuvier and Alexandre Brongniart in France in 1811.

Related Web site: Museum of Palaeontology http://www.ucmp.berkeley.edu/exhibit/exhibits.html

Palaeozoic era era of geological time 570–245 million years ago. It comprises the Cambrian, Ordovician, Silurian, Devonian, Carboniferous, and Permian periods. The Cambrian, Ordovician, and Silurian constitute the Lower or Early Palaeozoic; the Devonian, Carboniferous, and Permian make up the Upper or Late Palaeozoic. The era includes the evolution of hard-shelled multicellular life forms in the sea; the invasion of land by plants and animals; and the evolution of fish, amphibians, and early reptiles.

Palatinate (German Pfalz) historic division of Germany, dating from before the 8th century. It was ruled by a **count palatine** (a count with royal prerogatives) and varied in size.

Palau (or Belau) see country box.

Palembang oil-refining city in Indonesia, capital of southern Sumatra province; population (1990) 1,084,500. Products include rubber and palm oil.

Palermo capital and seaport of Sicily; population (1992) 696,700. It is also capital of Palermo province. Palermo is situated on the northern coastal plain of the Conca d'Oro, on a bay of the Tyrrhenian Sea. Industries include shipbuilding, steel, glass, textiles, and chemicals. Palermo is the most important industrial centre and port with shipbuilding facilities in southern Italy after Naples. It was founded by the Phoenicians in the 8th century BC.

Palestine: Key Events

c. 1000 BC	Hebrew leader King David forms a united Kingdom of Israel.
922	Kingdom of Israel splits into Israel in the north and Judah in the south after the death of King Solomon.
722	Israel is conquered by Assyrians.
586	Judah is conquered by Babylonians who destroy Jerusalem and force many Jews into exile in Babylon.
539	Palestine becomes part of Persian empire.
536	Jews are allowed to return to Jerusalem.
332	Conquest by Alexander the Great.
168	Maccabean revolt against Seleucids restores independence.
63	Conquest by Roman empire.
AD 70	Romans destroy Jerusalem following Jewish revolt.
636	Conquest by the Muslim Arabs makes Palestine a target for the Crusades.
1516	Conquest by the Ottoman Turks.
1880–1914	Jewish immigration increases sharply as a result of pogroms in Russia and Poland.
1897	At the first Zionist Congress, Jews call for a permanent homeland in Palestine.
1909	Tel Aviv, the first all-Jewish town in Palestine, is founded.
1917	The Balfour Declaration expresses the British government's support for the establishment of a Jewish national homeland in Palestine.
1917–18	The Turks are driven out by the British under field marshal Allenby in World War I.
1922	A League of Nations mandate (which incorporates the Balfour Declaration) places Palestine under British administration.
1936–39	Arab revolt takes place, fuelled by Jewish immigration (300,000 people 1920–39).
1937	The Peel Commission report recommends the partition of Palestine into Jewish and Arab states.
1939–45	Arab and Jewish Palestinians serve in the Allied forces in World War II.
1946	Resentment of immigration restrictions leads to acts of anti-British violence by Jewish guerrilla groups.
1947	The United Nations (UN) approves Britain's plan for partition.
1948	A Jewish state of Israel is proclaimed 14 May (eight hours before Britain's renunciation of the mandate is due). A series of Arab-Israeli Wars results in Israeli territorial gains and the occupation of other parts of Palestine by Egypt and Jordan. Many Palestinian Arabs are displaced.
1964	The Palestinian Liberation Organization (PLO) is formed and a guerrilla war is waged against the Jewish state.
1974	The PLO becomes the first nongovernmental delegation to be admitted to a plenary session of the UN General Assembly.
1987	The Intifada, a popular uprising against Israeli occupation, begins.
1988	PLO leader Yassir Arafat renounces terrorism; the USA agrees to meetings.
1989	Israeli prime minister Yitzhak Shamir proposes Palestinian elections in the West Bank/Gaza Strip.
1991	Gulf War against Iraq's annexation of Kuwait causes diplomatic reconsideration of a Palestinian state in an effort to stabilize the Middle East. A peace conference in Spain in November includes Israel and Arab states.
1993	Historic accord of mutual recognition is signed by Israel and PLO (the Oslo Accord), outlining plans for interim Palestinian self-rule in Gaza Strip and West Bank town of Jericho and for phased withdrawal of Israeli troops from occupied territories.
1995	By the end of December Israeli troops have withdrawn from six West Bank cities.
1996	January: Yassir Arafat is elected president of the self-governing Palestinian National Council. Violent protests erupt when Israel opens to tourists an archaeological site an ancient tunnel beneath the al-Asqa Mosque. The Peace Protest falters as Israeli strong-arm tactics are countered by Palestinian terrorism.
1997	Jewish settlement recommences in areas considered by Palestinians to be their responsibility.
1998	Peace talks resume and a truce brokered by US president Clinton is agreed. However, Israel shows little commitment to the terms of the agreement.
1999	Under pressure from the USA Arafat postpones declaration of Palestinian independence. Violence continues.
2000	Arafat again postpones declaration of Palestinian independence. Violence escalates.

See entry on p. 722.

Pakistan

Pakistan country in southern Asia, stretching from the Himalayas to the Arabian Sea, bounded to the west by Iran, northwest by Afghanistan, and northeast and east by India.

NATIONAL NAME *Islami Jamhuriyya e Pakistan/Islamic Republic of Pakistan*
AREA 803,940 sq km/310,321 sq mi
CAPITAL Islamabad
MAJOR TOWNS/CITIES Lahore, Rawalpindi, Faisalabad, Karachi, Hyderabad, Multan, Peshawar, Gujranwala, Quetta
MAJOR PORTS Karachi, Port Qasim
PHYSICAL FEATURES fertile Indus plain in east, Baluchistan plateau in west, mountains in north and northwest; the 'five rivers' (Indus, Jhelum, Chenab, Ravi, and Sutlej) feed the world's largest irrigation system; K2 mountain; Khyber Pass

Government

HEAD OF STATE Pervez Musharraf from 2001
HEAD OF GOVERNMENT Zafarullah Khan Jamali from 2002
POLITICAL SYSTEM military
POLITICAL EXECUTIVE military
ADMINISTRATIVE DIVISIONS four provinces, the Federal Capital Territory, and the federally administered tribal areas
ARMED FORCES 620,000; plus paramilitary forces of 289,000 (2002 est)
CONSCRIPTION military service is voluntary
DEATH PENALTY retained and used for ordinary crimes
DEFENCE SPEND (% GDP) 3.9 (2002 est)
EDUCATION SPEND (% GDP) 1.8 (2001 est)
HEALTH SPEND (% GDP) 4.1 (2000 est)

Economy and resources

CURRENCY Pakistan rupee
GPD (US$) 60.5 billion (2002 est)
REAL GDP GROWTH (% change on previous year) 3.9 (2003 est)
GNI (US$) 59.2 billion (2002 est)
GNI PER CAPITA (PPP) (US$) 1,940 (2002 est)
CONSUMER PRICE INFLATION 3.2% (2001)
UNEMPLOYMENT 5.9% (2000)
FOREIGN DEBT (US$) 31.7 billion (2001 est)
MAJOR TRADING PARTNERS United Arab Emirates, Japan, USA, Hong Kong, Germany, UK, Saudi Arabia, Kuwait

RESOURCES iron ore, natural gas, limestone, rock salt, gypsum, silica, coal, petroleum, graphite, copper, manganese, chromite
INDUSTRIES textiles (principally cotton), food processing, petroleum refining, leather production, soda ash, sulphuric acid, bicycles
EXPORTS garments and hosiery, cotton, textiles, leather, rice, food and live animals. Principal market: USA 24.4% (2001)
IMPORTS petroleum and petroleum products, machinery and transport equipment, chemicals and related products, grains, pulses and flours, edible oils. Principal source: United Arab Emirates 13.1% (2001)
ARABLE LAND 27.6% (2000 est)
AGRICULTURAL PRODUCTS cotton, rice, wheat, maize, sugar cane

Population and society

POPULATION 153,578,000 (2003 est)
POPULATION GROWTH RATE 2.2% (2000–15)
POPULATION DENSITY (per sq km) 193 (2003 est)
URBAN POPULATION (% of total) 34 (2003 est)
AGE DISTRIBUTION (% of total population) 0–14 41%, 15–59 53%, 60+ 6% (2002 est)
ETHNIC GROUPS four principal, regionally based, antagonistic communities: Punjabis

PAKISTAN Ruins of a stupa, a shrine to the Buddha and his disciples, at the important archaeological site of Taxila.
Philip Baird/www.anthroach.eart.org

in the Punjab; Sindhis in Sind; Baluchis in Baluchistan; and the Pathans (Pushtans) in the Northwest Frontier Province
LANGUAGE Urdu (official), English, Punjabi, Sindhi, Pashto, Baluchi, other local dialects
RELIGION Sunni Muslim 90%, Shiite Muslim 5%; also Hindu, Christian, Parsee, Buddhist
EDUCATION (years) 5–12 (not compulsory, but free)
LITERACY RATE 60% (men); 31% (women) (2003 est)

Chronology

2500–1600 BC: The area was the site of the Indus Valley civilization, a sophisticated, city-based ancient culture.

327 BC: Invaded by Alexander the Great of Macedonia.

1st–2nd centuries: North Pakistan was the heartland of the Kusana Empire, formed by invaders from Central Asia.

8th century: First Muslim conquests, in Baluchistan and Sind, followed by increasing immigration by Muslims from the west, from the 10th century.

1206: Establishment of Delhi Sultanate, stretching from northwest Pakistan and across northern India.

16th century: Sikh religion developed in Punjab.

16th–17th centuries: Lahore served intermittently as a capital city for the Mogul Empire, which stretched across the northern half of the Indian subcontinent.

1843–49: Sind and Punjab annexed by British and incorporated within empire of 'British India'.

late 19th century: Major canal irrigation projects in West Punjab and the northern Indus Valley drew in settlers from the east, as wheat and cotton production expanded.

1933: The name 'Pakistan' (Urdu for 'Pure Nation') invented by Choudhary Rahmat Ali, as Muslims within British India began to campaign for the establishment of an independent Muslim territory that would embrace the four provinces of Sind, Baluchistan, Punjab, and the Northwest Frontier.

1940: The All-India Muslim League (established in 1906), led by Karachi-born Muhammad Ali Jinnah, endorsed the concept of a separate nation for Muslims in the Lahore Resolution.

1947: Independence achieved from Britain, as a dominion within the Commonwealth. Pakistan, which included East Bengal, a Muslim-dominated province more than 1,600 km/1,000 mi from Punjab, was formed following the partition of British India. Large-scale and violent cross-border migrations of Muslims, Hindus, and Sikhs followed, and a brief border war with India over disputed Kashmir.

1956: Proclaimed a republic.

1958: Military rule imposed by Gen Ayub Khan.

1965: Border war with India over disputed territory of Kashmir.

1969: Power transferred to Gen Yahya Khan following strikes and riots.

1970: A general election produced a clear majority in East Pakistan for the pro-autonomy Awami League, led by Sheikh Mujibur Rahman, and in West Pakistan for Islamic socialist Pakistan People's Party (PPP), led by Zulfiqar Ali Bhutto.

1971: East Pakistan secured independence, as Bangladesh, following a civil war in which it received decisive military support from India. Power was transferred from the military to the populist Bhutto in Pakistan.

1977: Bhutto overthrown in military coup by Gen Zia ul-Haq following months of civil unrest; martial law imposed.

1979: Bhutto executed for alleged murder; tight political restrictions imposed by Zia regime.

1980: 3 million refugees fled to the Northwest Frontier Province and Baluchistan as a result of the Soviet invasion of Afghanistan.

LABOUR FORCE 47.3% agriculture, 17.1% industry, 35.6% services (1999)
LIFE EXPECTANCY 61 (men); 61 (women) (2000–05)
CHILD MORTALITY RATE (under 5, per 1,000 live births) 109 (2001)
INTERNET USERS (per 10,000 people) 102.8 (2002 est)
PERSONAL COMPUTER USERS (per 100 people) 0.4 (2002 est)

See also ▷Bangladesh; ▷India; ▷Kashmir.

1981: The broad-based Opposition Movement for the Restoration of Democracy was formed. The Islamization process was pushed forward by the government.

1985: Martial law and the ban on political parties was lifted.

1986: Agitation for free elections was launched by Benazir Bhutto, the daughter of Zulfiqar Ali Bhutto.

1988: An Islamic legal code, the Shari'a, was introduced; Zia was killed in a military plane crash. Benazir Bhutto became prime minister after the (now centrist) PPP won the general election.

1989: Tension with India was increased by outbreaks of civil war in Kashmir. Pakistan rejoined the Commonwealth.

1990: Bhutto was dismissed as prime minister by President Ghulam Ishaq Khan on charges of incompetence and corruption. The conservative Islamic Democratic Alliance (IDA), led by Nawaz Sharif, won the election and launched a privatization and economic deregulation program.

1993: Khan and Sharif resigned. Benazir Bhutto and PPP were re-elected.

1994: There was regional sectarian violence between Shia and Sunni Muslims, centred in Karachi.

1996: Benazir Bhutto was dismissed amid allegations of corruption.

1997: The right-of-centre Pakistan Muslim League won the general election, returning Sharif to power as prime minister.

1998: Rafiq Tarar became president. Pakistan conducted its first ever nuclear tests, provoking international condemnation and sanctions by the US. Benazir Bhutto and her husband were charged with corruption. A $5.5 billion economic bailout package was agreed with the IMF and World Bank.

1999: Benazir Bhutto and her husband were found guilty of corruption, sentenced to five years in prison, and fined £5.3 million. India agreed to enter peace talks on Kashmir. Pakistan's army overthrew the government after Sharif tried to sack General Pervez Musharraf from the top military job. General Musharraf, who appointed himself the country's chief executive, declared a state of emergency, and assumed all power, although he maintained Tarar as president.

2000: Relations with India worsened as India accused Pakistan of involvement in the hijacking of an Indian airliner by Kashmiri militants. Pakistan denied any involvement. Sharif was given two life sentences for hijacking and terrorism, and was also sentenced for corruption. He was later freed and fled to Saudi Arabia. Musharraf announced local elections from December, but decreed that anyone convicted of a criminal offence or of corruption would be disqualified from standing.

2002: Musharraf claimed endorsement in a referendum for an extensin of his presidency for a further five years. The longstanding quarrel with India about disputed sovereignty over the territory of Kashmir erupted again, prompting international concern.

2003: Pakistan and India began their first formal ceasefire in the disputed territory of Kashmir in 20 years. President Musharraf narrowly survived a second assassination attempt in less than two weeks as two car bombs exploded near his motorcade at Rawalpindi.

Palestine (Arabic *Falastin*, 'Philistine') historic geographical area at the eastern end of the Mediterranean sea, also known as the Holy Land because of its historic and symbolic importance for Jews, Christians, and Muslims. Early settlers included the Canaanites, Hebrews, and Philistines. Over the centuries it became part of the Egyptian, Assyrian, Babylonian, Macedonian, Ptolemaic, Seleucid, Roman, Byzantine, Arab, Ottoman, and British empires. Today it comprises parts of modern Israel and Jordan.

Palestinian Arabs include 1,300,000 in the West Bank, 900,000 in the Gaza Strip, 850,000 in Israel, and 160,000 in Jerusalem (1996). In 1993 more than 750,000 Palestinian children under the age of 16 were living in refugee camps. There are millions of Palestinian refugees outside Israel–Palestine in Jordan, Syria, Lebanon, USA, and Europe.

The 1993 Oslo Accord marked the beginning of the Israel–Palestine peace process, under which interim Palestinian self-rule was introduced in the Gaza Strip and West Bank town of Jericho; an agreement signed in May 1995 in Cairo marked the beginning of what was intended to be a permanent pact on Palestinian self-rule. In January 1996, Yassir ▷Arafat, the leader of the ▷Palestine Liberation Organization (PLO), was elected president of the Palestinian National Authority.

Setbacks to peace The assassination of Yitzhak ▷Rabin in November 1995, and the election in 1996 of a Likud government with a reduced commitment to the peace process, delayed the envisaged timetable for a permanent solution to the Israeli–Palestinian conflict. In May 1998, talks between Israeli prime minister Binyamin Netanyahu and Yassir ▷Arafat, held in London following a US initiative, failed to reach agreement on the deployment of Israeli troops in the ▷West Bank, and in the following month the Israeli government defied international criticism by announcing an expansion of its West Bank occupation. In April 1996, the Palestinian parliament-in-exile voted to remove from its charter clauses calling for armed struggle to replace Israel with a Palestinian state. Israel had made this a condition for the final phase of peace talks with the Palestinians and their partial withdrawal from the West Bank city of ▷Hebron. However, the peace process was set back in September 1996 by Palestinian protests against the Israeli reopening of a tunnel next to a disputed holy site, Haram al-Sharif (Temple Mount). Further setbacks occurred in 1997 when the construction of a Jewish settlement at Har Homa on the southern outskirts of Jerusalem was against Palestinian demands, as was the Israeli refusal to allow a port and airport to be opened in Gaza.

Hebron remained a flashpoint, with 20% of the city remaining under Israeli control to provide protection for 400 militant settlers living in its old town. The 50th anniversary of the establishment of the state of Israel in 1998 was met with violent clashes with Israeli troops, mainly in Gaza and the West Bank towns of Hebron, Bethlehem, and Ramallah.

Talks in the USA Although an agreement at Wye Plantation, in Maryland, USA, in July 1998, brokered by US president ▷Clinton, was reached to commence the withdrawal of Israelis from the West Bank, it began to be typified by delays and postponed deadlines on the part of Israel.

Yassir Arafat and other Palestinian leaders meeting in Gaza in April 1999 postponed the long-promised declaration of an independent Palestinian state. Arafat was under pressure from the USA not to declare Palestinian independence.

Withdrawal from the West Bank Following an initial failure to implement the Wye agreement, and Arafat leaving the talks in protest, in August 1999, Israel began to cede percentages of its land to Palestine, while Arafat pledged to combat terrorism against Israel. Further concessionary measures were taken, including the ending of a policy which stripped Palestinians of their right to live in Jerusalem if they left the city for seven years. It was announced that negotiations regarding a permanent status treaty would resume in November.

In November 1999, Arafat's Palestinian Authority reacted angrily to internal problems with the West Bank when a petition signed by 20 prominent West Bankers accused the authority of corruption, and levelled the responsibility at Arafat. The parliamentarians among them were immune from arrest, but other signatories were detained without charge. Outrage at Arafat's reaction increased when one of the signatories was shot. The West Bank remained a site of dispute between Israel and Palestine, and in April 2000 it was proposed by Israel that it would be divided into a majority Palestinian area, with an Israeli annex; this offer and the refusal by Israelis to release Palestinian prisoners held in Israel, sparked riots.

Declaration of an independent state In July 2000, Palestinian leader Yassir Arafat announced that he would declare Palestine an independent state on 13 September 2000, with or without Israel's agreement. This announcement was backed by the PLO. It was within this atmosphere that Arafat went into peace talks with Israeli prime minister Ehud ▷Barak at ▷Camp David, Maryland, USA. However, the talks finished in a deadlock after no agreement could be made over the future of Jerusalem. Upon his return home, Arafat was praised for refusing to abandon his demand for sovereignty over east Jerusalem. The Palestinian Central Council, caving in to US and Israeli pressure, on 10 September 2000 put back the 13 September deadline to continue talks with Israel which were stalling over the Haram al-Sharif (Temple Mount) in Jerusalem's Old City.

Breakdown of peace process Following a controversial visit of the Likud leader, Ariel Sharon, to Haram al-Sharif (Temple Mount), clashes between Palestinians and Israeli security forces spread to other disputed areas including the West Bank and Gaza. Despite international pleas for restraint on both sides, and peace talks between Barak and Arafat, it seemed impossible to prevent popular violence, in which Palestinians suffered greater death tolls. Barak was forced to include the Likud party in his coalition government, which would make future peace negotiations more difficult. Arafat appealed for 2,000 United Nations peacekeepers to be deployed in

Palau

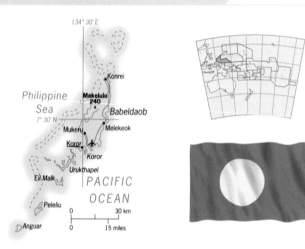

Palau or Belau country comprising more than 350 islands and atolls (mostly uninhabited) in the west Pacific Ocean.

NATIONAL NAME *Belu'u era Belau/Republic of Palau*
AREA 508 sq km/196 sq mi
CAPITAL Koror (on Koror island)
PHYSICAL FEATURES more than 350 (mostly uninhabited) islands, islets, and atolls in the west Pacific; warm, humid climate, susceptible to typhoons

Government

HEAD OF STATE AND GOVERNMENT Tommy Remengesau from 2001
POLITICAL SYSTEM liberal democracy
POLITICAL EXECUTIVE limited presidency
ADMINISTRATIVE DIVISIONS 18 states
ARMED FORCES no defence forces of its own; under the Compact of Free Association, the USA is responsible for the defence of Palau; two US military bases operate on the islands
DEATH PENALTY laws do not provide for the death penalty for any crime

Economy and resources

CURRENCY US dollar
GPD (US$) 130 million (2002 est)
REAL GDP GROWTH (% change on previous year) 1 (2001)
GNI (US$) 142 million (2002 est)
GNI PER CAPITA (PPP) (US$) 7,460 (2002 est)
UNEMPLOYMENT 2.3% (2000)
MAJOR TRADING PARTNERS USA, UK, Japan
INDUSTRIES processing of agricultural products, fish products, handicrafts, tourism
EXPORTS copra, coconut oil, handicrafts, trochus, tuna
IMPORTS food and live animals, crude materials, mineral fuels, beverages, tobacco, chemicals, basic manufactures, machinery and transport equipment
AGRICULTURAL PRODUCTS coconuts, cassava, bananas, sweet potatoes; farming and fishing are mainly on a subsistence level

Population and society

POPULATION 20,000 (2003 est)
POPULATION GROWTH RATE 2.1% (2000–05)
POPULATION DENSITY (per sq km) 45 (2003 est)
URBAN POPULATION (% of total) 69 (2003 est)
AGE DISTRIBUTION (% of total population)

Chronology

c. 1000 BC: Micronesians first settled the islands.
AD 1543: First visited by Spanish navigator Ruy Lopez de Villalobos.
16th century: Colonized by Spain.
1899: Purchased from Spain by Germany.
1914: Occupied by Japan at the outbreak of World War I.
1920: Administered by Japan under League of Nations mandate.
1944: Occupied by USA after Japanese removed during World War II.
1947: Became part of United Nations (UN) Pacific Islands Trust Territory, administered by USA.
1981: Acquired autonomy as the Republic of Belau (Palau) under a constitution which prohibited the

0–14 27%, 15–59 65%, 60+ 8% (2001 est)
ETHNIC GROUPS predominantly Micronesian
LANGUAGE Palauan, English (both official in most states)
RELIGION Christian, principally Roman Catholic; Modekngei (indigenous religion)
EDUCATION (compulsory years) 8

See also ▷Pacific Islands.

entry, storage, or disposal of nuclear or biological weapons.
1982: The Compact of Free Association signed with the USA, providing for the right to maintain US military facilities in return for economic aid. The compact could not come into force since it contradicted the constitution, which could only be amended by a 75% vote in favour.
1992: Kuniwo Nakamura was elected president, taking office in 1993.
1993: A referendum approved a constitutional amendment allowing the implementation of the Compact of Free Association with the USA.
1994: Independence was achieved and UN membership granted.
2001: Tommy Remengesau became president.

PALAU An aerial view of some of the islands of Palau. The five major populated islands are Bablethuap, Koror, Malakal, Arakabesan, and Peleliu. *Photodisk*

the West Bank and Gaza, while Barak proposed extending the interim peace accords, recognizing a Palestinian state, and withdrawing from more of the West Bank. But the two sides were unable to reach agreement on a ceasefire.

The conflict intensified in late November 2000, leaving more than 300 people dead since the end of September. A US-led commission into the violence, agreed at a summit held in Sharm el-Sheikh, Egypt, on 17 October, made its first visit to the region on 11 December. A planned summit for late December was called off after the Palestinians rejected an Israeli demand that Palestinian refugees abandon their long-standing dream of returning to their homes inside what was now Israel, from which they were expelled in 1948. See also The History of The Conflict in The Middle East Focus Feature on pp. 628–629, and Palestine: Key Events on p. 720.

Related Web site:History of Palestine http://www.thestraightpath.net/path/misc/Al-Quds_modern.htm

Palestine Liberation Organization (PLO) Arab organization founded in 1964 to bring about an independent state in Palestine. It consists of several distinct groupings, the chief of which is al-▷Fatah, led by Yassir ▷Arafat, the president of the PLO from 1969.

Palestine Wars another name for the ▷Arab-Israeli Wars.

Palestrina, Giovanni Pierluigi da (c. 1525–1594) Italian composer. He wrote secular and sacred choral music, and is regarded as the outstanding exponent of Renaissance ▷counterpoint. Apart from motets and madrigals, he also wrote 105 Masses, including *Missa Papae Marcelli*.

Paley, William (1743–1805) English Christian theologian and philosopher. He put forward the argument for design theory, which reasons that the complexity of the universe necessitates a superhuman creator and that the existence of this being (God) can be deduced from a 'design' seen in all living creatures. His views were widely held until challenged by Charles ▷Darwin.

Pali ancient Indo-European language of northern India, related to Sanskrit, and a classical language of Buddhism.

Palikir capital of the Federated States of Micronesia, on the island of Pohnpei; population (1998 est) 9,885.

Palikur an American Indian people living in northern Brazil and numbering about 1 million (1980). Formerly a warlike people, they occupied a vast area between the Amazon and Orinoco rivers.

palindrome word, sentence, or verse that reads the same backwards as forwards (ignoring word breaks and punctuation). 'Madam, in Eden, I'm Adam.' 'Ten animals I slam in a net.'

palisade cell cylindrical cell lying immediately beneath the upper epidermis of a leaf. Palisade cells normally exist as one closely packed row and contain many chloroplasts. During the hours of daylight palisade cells are photosynthetic, using the energy of the sun to create carbohydrates from water and carbon dioxide.

Palk Strait channel separating southeast India from the island of Sri Lanka, lying north of the sandbanks known as Adam's Bridge, which separates it from the Gulf of Mannar; it is 53 km/33 mi at the narrowest point. It was named by the Dutch after Governor Palk.

Palladian style of revivalist architecture influenced by the work of the great Italian Renaissance architect Andrea ▷Palladio. Inigo ▷Jones introduced Palladianism to England with his Queen's House, Greenwich (1616–35), but the true Palladian revival began in the early 18th century when Richard Boyle ▷Burlington and Colen ▷Campbell 'rediscovered' the Palladio–Jones ideal. Campbell's Mereworth Castle, Kent, (1722–25) is an example of the style. The revival, which spread to Russia and the USA, often involved little more than the reuse of Palladian decorative features.

Palladio, Andrea (1508–1580) Italian architect who created harmonious and balanced classical structures. He designed numerous palaces and country houses in and around Vicenza, making use of Roman classical forms, symmetry, and proportion. The Villa Malcontenta and the Villa Rotonda are examples of houses designed from 1540 for patrician families of the Venetian Republic. He also designed churches in Venice and published his studies of classical form in several illustrated books.

His ideas were initiated in England in the early 17th century by Inigo ▷Jones.

Related Web site: Palladio, Andrea http://www.newadvent.org/cathen/11423c.htm

palladium lightweight, ductile and malleable, silver-white, metallic element, symbol Pd, atomic number 46, relative atomic mass 106.4. It is one of the so-called platinum group of metals, and is resistant to tarnish and corrosion. It often occurs in nature as a free metal (see ▷native metal) in a natural alloy with platinum. Palladium is used as a catalyst, in alloys of gold (to make white gold) and silver, in electroplating, and in dentistry. It was discovered in 1803 by British physicist William Wollaston (1766–1828), and named after the asteroid Pallas (found 1802).

Pallas in Greek mythology, a title of the goddess ▷Athena, possibly meaning virgin.

Pallava dynasty (lived 4th–9th centuries) hereditary Hindu rulers who dominated southeastern India between the 4th and 9th centuries. The dynasty's greatest kings were Simhavisnu (ruled c. 575–600) and Narasimhavarman I (ruled 630–668). Their capital was Kanchi, southwest of Madras (now Chennai).

palliative in medicine, any treatment given to relieve symptoms rather than to cure the underlying cause. In conditions that will resolve of their own accord (for instance, the common cold) or that are incurable, the entire treatment may be palliative.

palm any of a group of large treelike plants with a single tall stem that has a thick cluster of large palmate (five-lobed) leaves or pinnate leaves (leaflets either side of the stem) at the top. Most of the numerous species are tropical or subtropical. Some, such as the coconut, date, sago, and oil palms, are important economically. (Family Palmae.)

Palma de Mallorca port and capital of the ▷Balearic Islands, an autonomous community of Spain, situated on a wide bay on the southwest coast of the island of ▷Mallorca, population (1994) 322,000. Industries include textiles, cement, paper, pottery, and tourism. Palma was founded as a Roman colony in 276 BC. It has a Gothic cathedral, begun in 1229; the 14th-century Almudaina palace, a former royal residence; and the 13th-century church of St Francis of Assisi, which contains the tomb of the Mallorcan scholar Ramon ▷Llull.

Palmas, Las port in the Canary Islands; see ▷Las Palmas.

Palme, (Sven) Olof Joachim (1927–1986) Swedish social-democratic politician, prime minister 1969–76 and 1982–86. As prime minister he carried out constitutional reforms, turning the Riksdag into a single-chamber parliament and stripping the monarch of power, and was widely respected for his support of Third World countries. He was assassinated in February 1986.

Palmer, Samuel (1805–1881) English landscape painter and etcher. His early works, small pastoral scenes mostly painted in watercolour and sepia, have an intense, visionary quality, greatly

PALM Collecting palm oil in Myanmar (Burma).
Image Bank

influenced by a meeting with the aged William Blake, and the latter's engravings for Thornton's *Virgil*. From 1826 to 1835 he lived in Shoreham, Kent, with a group of artists who followed Blake, styling themselves 'the Ancients'.

Palmerston, Henry John Temple, 3rd Viscount Palmerston (1784–1865) British politician. He was prime minister 1855–58 (when he rectified Aberdeen's mismanagement of the Crimean War, suppressed the ▷Indian Mutiny, and carried through the Second Opium War) and 1859–65 (when he almost involved Britain in the American Civil War on the side of the South). Initially a Tory, in Parliament from 1807, he was secretary-at-war 1809–28. He broke with the Tories in 1830 and sat in the Whig cabinets of 1830–34, 1835–41, and 1846–51 as foreign secretary. He became viscount in 1802.

Palmerston succeeded to an Irish peerage in 1802. He served under five Tory prime ministers before joining the Whigs. His foreign policy was marked by distrust of France and Russia, against whose designs he backed the independence of Belgium and Turkey. He became home secretary in the coalition government of 1852, and prime minister on its fall, and was responsible for the warship *Alabama* going to the Confederate side in the American Civil War. He was popular with the people and made good use of the press, but his high-handed attitude annoyed Queen Victoria and other ministers.

Palm Sunday in the Christian calendar, the Sunday before Easter and first day of Holy Week, commemorating Jesus' entry into Jerusalem, when the crowd strewed palm leaves in his path.

Palmyra (Arabic Tidmor) ancient city and oasis in the desert of Syria, about 240 km/150 mi northeast of Damascus. Palmyra, the biblical **Tadmor**, was flourishing by about 300 BC. It was destroyed in AD 272 after Queen Zenobia led a revolt against the Romans. Extensive temple ruins exist, and on the site is a town called Tadmor.

Pamir central Asian plateau mainly in Tajikistan, but extending into China and Afghanistan, traversed by mountain ranges. Its highest peak is Kommunizma Pik (Communism Peak, 7,495 m/24,600 ft) in the Akademiya Nauk range.

Pampas flat treeless plains in central Argentina, lying between the foothills of the Andes and the Atlantic coast, and stretching north from the Río Colorado to the Gran Chaco; area 750,000 sq km/290,000 sq mi; it incorporates the provinces of Buenos Aires, La Pampa, Santa Fé, and Cordobá. The eastern Pampas consist of grasslands which support large cattle ranches and produce flax and over half the nation's output of grain; the western Pampas are arid and unproductive. The characteristic vegetation is the **pampas grass** which grows to a height of 2–3m/6–10 ft.

Figure labels (palisade cell diagram):
xylem vessel
sunlight
epidermis
palisade cell
chloroplast
guard cell
water diffuses from xylem
stoma
carbon dioxide from air

PALISADE CELL Palisade cells are closely packed, columnar cells, lying in the upper surfaces of leaves. They contain many chloroplasts (where photosynthesis takes place) and are well adapted to receive and process the components necessary for photosynthesis – carbon dioxide, water, and sunlight. For instance, their vertical arrangement means that there are few cross-walls to interfere with the passage of sunlight.

pampas grass any of a group of large grasses native to South America, especially *C. argentea*, which is grown in gardens and has tall leaves and large clusters of feathery white flowers growing around the tips of the flower-bearing stems. (Genus *Cortaderia*.)

Pan (Greek 'all') in Greek mythology, the god of flocks and herds. He is depicted as a man with the horns, ears, and hoofed legs of a goat, and plays a shepherd's syrinx or **panpipes**; an instrument he reputedly invented. Later he was regarded as the personification of nature, the existing order of things. The Romans identified him with ▷Faunus and Silvanus.

Pan-Africanist Congress (PAC) South African political party, formed as a militant black nationalist group in 1959, when it broke away from the African National Congress (ANC), promoting a black-only policy for Africa. PAC was outlawed 1960–90; its

military wing was called Poqo ('we alone'). It suspended its armed struggle in 1994, and transformed itself into a political party to contest the first multiracial elections. It is more radical than the ANC, advocating a radical redistribution of land and a state-run economy.

Panama see country box.

Panamá capital of the Republic of Panama, on the east bank of the Pacific entrance to the Panama Canal, with its port at Balboa in the Canal Zone; population (1995 est) 663,000. It became capital in 1903 following independence from Colombia. The city developed rapidly following the completion of the Canal. Its good communications by air and rail, as well as by the Pan-American Highway, have enabled the city to become the main transport and industrial centre of Panama. Products include oil, plastics, leather, food, and drink.

PAMPAS GRASS Fronds of pampas grass growing in Japan. *Image Bank*

Panama

Panama country in Central America, on a narrow isthmus between the Caribbean and the Pacific Ocean, bounded west by Costa Rica and east by Colombia.

NATIONAL NAME *República de Panamá/Republic of Panama*
AREA 77,100 sq km/29,768 sq mi
CAPITAL Panamá
MAJOR TOWNS/CITIES San Miguelito, Colón, David, La Chorrera, Santiago, Chitré, Changuinola
MAJOR PORTS Colón, Cristóbal, Balboa
PHYSICAL FEATURES coastal plains and mountainous interior; tropical rainforest in east and northwest; Archipelago de las Perlas in Gulf of Panama; Panama Canal

Government

HEAD OF STATE AND GOVERNMENT Mireya Moscoso Rodríguez from 1999
POLITICAL SYSTEM liberal democracy
POLITICAL EXECUTIVE limited presidency
ADMINISTRATIVE DIVISIONS nine provinces and three Autonomous Indian Reservations
ARMED FORCES no active army; paramilitary forces of 11,800 (2002 est)
DEATH PENALTY laws do not provide for the death penalty for any crime

Economy and resources

CURRENCY balboa
GPD (US$) 12.3 billion (2002 est)
REAL GDP GROWTH (% change on previous year) 0.3 (2001)
GNI (US$) 11.8 billion (2002 est)
GNI PER CAPITA (PPP) (US$) 5,870 (2002 est)
CONSUMER PRICE INFLATION 1.1% (2003 est)
UNEMPLOYMENT 14.4% (2001)
FOREIGN DEBT (US$) 7.3 billion (2001 est)
MAJOR TRADING PARTNERS USA, Japan, Costa Rica, Ecuador, Germany, Italy, Venezuela
RESOURCES limestone, clay, salt; deposits of coal, copper, and molybdenum have been discovered
INDUSTRIES food processing, petroleum refining and petroleum products, chemicals, paper and paper products, beverages, textiles and clothing, plastic products, light assembly, tourism

EXPORTS bananas, shrimps and lobsters, sugar, clothing, coffee. Principal market: USA 49.6% (2001)
IMPORTS machinery and transport equipment, petroleum and mineral products, chemicals and chemical products, electrical and electronic equipment, foodstuffs. Principal source: USA 33.1% (2001)
ARABLE LAND 6.7% (2001 est)
AGRICULTURAL PRODUCTS rice, maize, dry beans, bananas, sugar cane, coffee, oranges, mangoes, cocoa; cattle rearing; tropical timber; fishing (particularly shrimps for export)

Population and society

POPULATION 3,120,000 (2003 est)
POPULATION GROWTH RATE 1.3% (2000–15)

POPULATION DENSITY (per sq km) 41 (2003 est)
URBAN POPULATION (% of total) 57 (2003 est)
AGE DISTRIBUTION (% of total population) 0–14 30%, 15–59 62%, 60+ 8% (2001 est)
ETHNIC GROUPS about 70% mestizos (of Spanish–American and American–Indian descent), 14% West Indian, 10% white American or European, and 6% Indian
LANGUAGE Spanish (official), English
RELIGION Roman Catholic 93%
EDUCATION (compulsory years) 8
LITERACY RATE 93% (men); 92% (women) (2003 est)
LABOUR FORCE 17.4% agriculture, 18.2% industry, 64.4% services (1999)
LIFE EXPECTANCY 72 (men); 77 (women) (2000–05)
CHILD MORTALITY RATE (under 5, per 1,000 live births) 25 (2001)
PHYSICIANS (per 1,000 people) 1.7 (1998 est)
HOSPITAL BEDS (per 1,000 people) 2.2 (1998 est)
TV SETS (per 1,000 people) 194 (2000 est)
RADIOS (per 1,000 people) 300 (1998)
INTERNET USERS (per 10,000 people) 413.9 (2002 est)
PERSONAL COMPUTER USERS (per 100 people) 3.8 (2002 est)

Chronology

1502: Visited by Spanish explorer Rodrigo de Bastidas, at which time it was inhabited by Cuna, Choco, Guaymi, and other Indian groups.

1513: Spanish conquistador Vasco Núñez de Balboa explored Pacific Ocean from Darien isthmus; he was made governor of Panama (meaning 'abundance of fish').

1519: Spanish city established at Panama, which became part of the Spanish viceroyalty of New Andalucia (later New Granada).

1572–95 and 1668–71: Spanish settlements sacked by British buccaneers Francis Drake and Henry Morgan.

1821: Achieved independence from Spain; joined confederacy of Gran Colombia, which included Colombia, Venezuela, Ecuador, Peru, and Bolivia.

1830: Gran Colombia split up and Panama became part of Colombia.

1846: Treaty signed with USA, allowing it to construct a railway across the isthmus.

1880s: French attempt to build a Panama canal connecting the Atlantic and Pacific Oceans failed as a result of financial difficulties and the death of 22,000 workers from yellow fever and malaria.

1903: Full independence achieved with US help on separation from Colombia; USA bought rights to build Panama Canal, and were given control of a 10-mile strip, the Canal Zone, in perpetuity.

1914: Panama Canal opened.

1939: Panama's status as a US protectorate was terminated by mutual agreement.

1968–81: Military rule of Gen Omar Torrijos Herrera, leader of the National Guard, who deposed the

elected president and launched a costly programme of economic modernization.

1977: USA–Panama treaties transferred the canal o Panama (effective from 2000), with the USA guaranteeing protection and annual payment.

1987: Gen Manuel Noriega (head of the National Guard and effective ruler since 1983) resisted calls for his removal, despite suspension of US military and economic aid.

1988: Noriega, charged with drug smuggling by the USA, declared a state of emergency after a coup against him failed.

1989: 'State of war' with USA announced, and US invasion (codenamed 'Operation Just Cause') deposed Noriega; 4,000 Panamanians died in the fighting. Guillermo Endara, who had won earlier elections, was installed as president in December.

1991: Constitutional reforms were approved by the assembly, including the abolition of the standing army; a privatization programme was introduced.

1992: Noriega was found guilty of drug offences and given a 40-year prison sentence in USA. A referendum rejected the proposed constitutional reforms.

1994: The constitution was amended by assembly; the army was formally abolished.

1998: Voters rejected a proposed constitutional change to allow the president to run for a second term.

1999: Mireya Moscoso, widow of former president Arnulfo Arias, became Panama's first female head of state. Panama formally took control of its canal.

PANAMA The Panama Canal bisects the Isthmus of Panama, connecting the Atlantic and Pacific oceans. Its construction ended the need for long shipping journeys around South America. *Corel*

The original old city was founded by the Spaniard Pedro Arias de Avila in 1519, on the site of an Indian fishing village; it was destroyed in 1671 by the Welsh buccaneer Henry Morgan, and rebuilt on its present site, 8 km/5 mi to the southwest, in 1673. The city has two universities, founded in 1935 and 1965, and a cathedral, built 1688–1794. The Palacio Presidencial, built in 1673 to house successive colonial governors, is the official residence of Panama's presidents.

Panama Canal canal across the Panama isthmus in Central America, connecting the Pacific and Atlantic oceans; length 80 km/ 50 mi, with 12 locks; average width 150 m/492 ft. It was built by the USA 1904–14, after an unsuccessful attempt by the French. The **Panama Canal Zone** was acquired 'in perpetuity' by the USA in 1903, comprising land extending about 5 km/3 mi on either side of the canal. The zone passed to Panama in 1979, and under a treaty signed by President Carter in 1978, control of the canal was ceded to Panama at the end of 1999. In December 1999 all US military bases in the Canal Zone were closed, and the control changeover went into effect on 31 December 1999.

The route through the Canal from the Pacific entrance passes under the Puente de las Americas, past Balboa on the eastern bank to the Miraflores Locks, which raise the water level in preparation for entry to Lake Miraflores. The Pedro Miguel Locks raise the level again for entry to the Gaillard Cut (13 km/8 mi long), which leads to Lake Gatún, one of the largest artificial lakes of this type in the world. Vessels proceed through the lake under their own steam; it is the longest section of the passage (37 km/23 mi). The Gatú Locks at the north end of the lake form the final stage of passage to the Caribbean; they have double flights, enabling simultaneous passage in opposite directions.

The Gatún Dam, the largest in the world at the time of construction, was built in 1906 in order to conserve enough water to operate the locks during dry seasons. It supplies 296 million litres of water each time the locks are opened.

Pan-American Highway road linking the USA with Central and South America; length 25,300 km/15,700 mi. Starting from the US-Canadian frontier (where it links with the Alaska Highway), it runs through San Francisco, Los Angeles, and Mexico City to Panamá, then down the west side of South America to Valparaiso, Chile, where it crosses the Andes and goes to Buenos Aires, Argentina. The road was first planned in 1923, and work began in 1928. Completion of the final section, across the Darien Gap in Panama, will lead to a major ecological transformation of the region.

Panchen Lama (1995–) Tibetan spiritual leader, second in importance to the ▷Dalai Lama. China installed the present Panchen Lama, the 11th incarnation, seven-year-old Gyantsen Norpo, in December 1995, after rejecting the Dalai Lama's choice, another seven-year-old boy, Gedhun Choekyo Nyima.

panchromatic in photography, a term describing highly sensitive black-and-white film made to render all visible spectral colours in correct grey tones. Panchromatic film is always developed in total darkness.

pancreas in vertebrates, an accessory gland of the digestive system located close to the duodenum. When stimulated by the hormone secretin, it releases enzymes into the duodenum that digest starches, proteins, and fats. In humans, it is about 18 cm/7 in long, and lies behind and below the stomach. It contains groups of cells called the **islets of Langerhans**, which secrete the hormones insulin and glucagon that regulate the blood sugar level.

panda one of two carnivores of different families, native to northwestern China and Tibet. The **giant panda** *Ailuropoda melanoleuca* has black-and-white fur with black eye patches and feeds mainly on bamboo shoots, consuming about 8 kg/17.5 lb of bamboo per day. It can grow up to 1.5 m/4.5 ft long, and weigh up to 140 kg/300 lb. It is an endangered species. In 2000 there were only 1,000 remaining in the wild, and a further 120 in zoos. The **lesser**, or **red**, **panda** *Ailurus fulgens*, of the raccoon family, is about 50 cm/1.5 ft long, and is black and chestnut, with a long tail.

Pandas' bamboo diet is of low nutritional value, being about 90% water. This makes it impossible for them to hibernate, since although they spend about 12 hours of every day eating, they cannot accumulate the necessary reserves of fat. There is some dispute about whether they should be included in the bear family or the raccoon family, or classified as a family of their own.

Destruction of the giant pandas' natural habitats threatens to make them extinct in the wild, and they are the focus of conservation efforts. In July 1998 China's national Academy of Sciences announced a project to clone the panda by 2003. They plan to transfer the nucleus of a panda cell into that of another bear species, with the same species being used as a surrogate mother. In 1999 Chinese scientists succeeded in cloning hybrid embryos using the nucleus from a panda cell transferred into a rabbit ovum. The scientists will now attempt to implant an embryo into another bear species, probably a black bear.

Related Web site: Giant Panda Facts http://www.panda. org/resources/ factsheets/species/ fct_panda.htm

Pandora (Greek 'all gifts') in Greek mythology, the first mortal woman. Zeus sent her to Earth with a box containing

PANDA A giant panda. It is possible that the current population of pandas is already too small to avoid extinction. *Image Bank*

every human woe to counteract the blessings brought to mortals by ▷Prometheus, whose gift of fire was stolen from the gods. In the most common tradition, she opened the box, and the evils flew out; only hope was left inside as a consolation.

Pandya dynasty (lived 3rd century BC–16th century AD) southern Indian hereditary rulers based in the region around Madurai (its capital). The dynasty extended its power into Kerala (southwestern India) and Sri Lanka during the reigns of kings Kadungon (ruled 590–620), Arikesar Maravarman (670–700), Varagunamaharaja I (765–815), and Srimara Srivallabha (815–862). Pandya influence peaked in Jatavarman Sundara's reign 1251–1268. After Madurai was invaded by forces from the Delhi sultanate in 1311, the Pandyas declined into merely local rulers.

Pangaea (or **Pangea**; Greek 'all-land') single land mass, made up of all the present continents, believed to have existed between 300 and 200 million years ago; the rest of the Earth was covered by the Panthalassa ocean. Pangaea split into two land masses – ▷Laurasia in the north and ▷Gondwanaland in the south – which subsequently broke up into several continents. These then moved slowly to their present positions (see ▷plate tectonics).

pangolin (or **scaly anteater**) toothless mammal of tropical Africa and Southeast Asia. They are long-tailed and covered with large, overlapping scales, except on the muzzle, sides of the head, throat, chest, and belly. They have an elongated skull and a long, extensible tongue. Pangolins measure 30–100 cm/12–39 in long, exclusive of the prehensile tail, which is about twice as long as the body.

Some are arboreal and others are terrestrial. All live on ants and termites. Pangolins comprise the order Pholidota. There is only one genus (*Manis*) and family Manidae, with seven species.

The lower gums of the mouth form two thickened horny ridges separated by a groove along which the cylindrical wormlike tongue slips in and out. The feet are strongly clawed, especially on the third toe of the forefoot, which is used in burrowing and in climbing. The extreme tip of the tail is free from scales and padded with thick skin. To deter predators, a powerful stench is emitted by the entire surface of the skin, and its bony overlapping scales protect it when it rolls up into a ball.

Panipat, Battles of three decisive battles in the vicinity of this Indian town, about 120 km/75 mi north of Delhi: 1526, when ▷Babur, great-grandson of the Mongol conqueror Tamerlane, defeated the emperor of Delhi and founded the Mogul empire; 1556, won by his descendant ▷Akbar; 1761, when the ▷Marathas were defeated by ▷Ahmad Shah Durrani of Afghanistan.

Panjshir Valley valley of the River Panjshir, which rises in the Panjshir range to the north of Kabul, eastern Afghanistan. It was the chief centre of Mujahedin rebel resistance against the Soviet-backed Najibullah government in the 1980s.

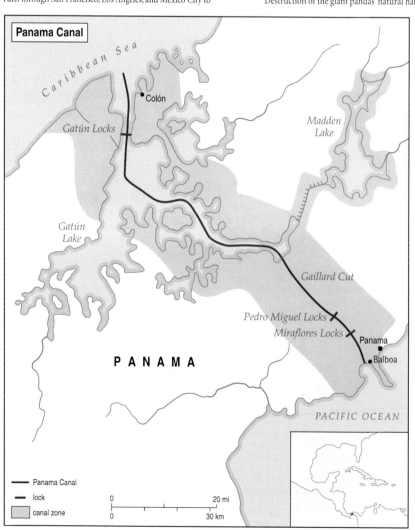

Panama Canal

Caribbean Sea

Colón

Gatún Locks

Madden Lake

Gatún Lake

Gaillard Cut

Pedro Miguel Locks

Miraflores Locks

Panama

Balboa

PANAMA

PACIFIC OCEAN

—— Panama Canal
- lock
▨ canal zone

0   20 mi
0   30 km

Pankhurst, Emmeline (1858–1928) Born Emmeline Goulden. English ▷suffragette. Founder of the ▷Women's Social and Political Union (WSPU) in 1903, she launched the militant suffragette campaign in 1905. In 1926 she joined the Conservative Party and was a prospective Parliamentary candidate for Whitechapel.

Mrs Pankhurst was born in Manchester, the daughter of Robert Goulden, a calico-printer and early advocate of women's suffrage. In 1879 she married **Richard Marsden Pankhurst** (died 1898), a lawyer, and they served together on the committee that promoted the Married Women's Property Act. From 1906, as a militant, she was frequently arrested and in 1913 was sentenced to three years' penal servitude in connection with the blowing up of Lloyd George's house at Walton.

She was supported by her daughters **Christabel Pankhurst** (1880–1958), political leader of the movement, and **Sylvia Pankhurst** (1882–1960). The latter was imprisoned nine times under the 'Cat and Mouse Act', and was a pacifist in World War I.

> **Emmeline Pankhurst**
> *We women suffragists have a great mission – the greatest mission the world has ever known. It is to free half the human race, and through that freedom save the rest.*
> Speech, published in 'Votes for Women', 25 October 1912

pansy cultivated plant derived from the European wild pansy (*Viola tricolor*) and including many different varieties and strains. The flowers are usually purple, yellow, or cream, or a mixture of these colours, and there are many highly developed varieties bred for size, colour, or special markings. Several of the 400 different species are scented. (Family Violaceae.)

Panthalassa ocean that covered the surface of the Earth not occupied by the world continent ▷Pangaea between 300 and 200 million years ago.

pantheism (Greek *pan* 'all'; *theos* 'God') doctrine that regards all of reality as divine, and God as present in all of nature and the universe. It is expressed in Egyptian religion and Brahmanism; Stoicism, neo-Platonism, Judaism, Christianity, and Islam can be interpreted in pantheistic terms. Pantheistic philosophers include Giordano Bruno, Baruch Spinoza, J G Fichte, F W J Schelling, and G W F Hegel.

    Related Web site: Pantheism http://plato.stanford.edu/entries/pantheism/

Pantheon temple in the Campus Martius at Rome, now the church of Santa Maria della Rotunda. It was built, and most probably designed, by the emperor ▷Hadrian on the site of an earlier temple dedicated to Mars and Venus by Marcus Vipsanius ▷Agrippa in 27 BC. The name derives from a much later tradition that it was a temple 'of all the gods' (Greek *panton ton theon*).

pantheon originally a temple for worshipping all the gods, such as that in ancient Rome, rebuilt by the emperor Hadrian between AD 118 and about 128, and still used as a church. In more recent times, the name has been used for a building where famous people are buried (as in the Panthéon, Paris).

panther another name for the ▷leopard.

pantomime in the British theatre, a traditional Christmas entertainment. It has its origins in the harlequin spectacle of the 18th century and burlesque of the 19th century, which gave rise to the tradition of the principal boy being played by a woman and the dame by a man. The harlequin's role diminished altogether as themes developed on folk tales such as 'The Sleeping Beauty' and 'Cinderella', and with the introduction of additional material such as popular songs, topical comedy, and audience participation. Popular television stars regularly feature in modern pantomime.

pantothenic acid water-soluble ▷vitamin ($C_9H_{17}NO_5$) of the B complex, found in a wide variety of foods. Its absence from the diet can lead to dermatitis, and it is known to be involved in the breakdown of fats and carbohydrates.

panzer (German 'armour') German mechanized units in World War II created by Heinz Guderain. A Panzer army was a mechanized unit based on a core of tanks and supported by infantry, artillery, and service troops in vehicles capable of accompanying the tanks.

Paolozzi, Eduardo Luigi (1924–) Scottish sculptor and graphic artist. He was an important figure in the Pop-art movement in London in the 1950s and 1960s. In his early sculptures he typically assembled bronze casts of machinery to create sinister, robotlike figures; *Cyclops* (1957; Tate Gallery, London) and *Jason* (1956; Museum of Modern Art, New York) are examples. From the 1960s his work became more abstract and lighter in mood.

Papa Doc nickname of François ▷Duvalier, president of Haiti 1957–71.

papal infallibility doctrine formulated by the Roman Catholic Vatican Council in 1870, which stated that the pope, when speaking officially on certain doctrinal or moral matters, was protected from error by God, and therefore such rulings could not be challenged.

Papal States area of central Italy in which the pope was temporal ruler from 756 until the unification of Italy in 1870.

Papandreou, Andreas (1919–1996) Greek socialist politician, founder of the Pan-Hellenic Socialist Movement (PASOK); prime minister 1981–89, and again 1993–96. He lost the 1989 election after being implicated in an alleged embezzlement scandal, involving the diversion of funds to the Greek government from the Bank of Crete, headed by George Koskotas. In January 1992 a trial cleared Papandreou of all corruption charges.

papaya tropical evergreen tree, native from Florida to South America. Varieties are grown throughout the tropics. The edible fruits are like melons, with orange-coloured flesh and large numbers of blackish seeds in the centre; they can weigh up to 9 kg/20 lb. (*Carica papaya*, family Caricaceae.)

Papeete capital and port of French Polynesia on the northwest coast of Tahiti; population (1992) 24,200. Products include vanilla, copra, and mother-of-pearl.

paper thin, flexible material made in sheets from vegetable fibres (such as wood pulp) or rags and used for writing, drawing, printing, packaging, and various household needs. The name comes from papyrus, a form of writing material made from water reed, used in ancient Egypt. The invention of true paper, originally made of pulped fishing nets and rags, is credited to Tsai Lun, Chinese minister of agriculture, in AD 105.

    Related Web site: You Can Make Paper http://www.beakman.com/paper/paper.html

paper nautilus another name for the ▷argonaut.

papier mâché (French 'chewed paper') craft technique that involves building up layer upon layer of pasted paper, which is then baked or left to harden. Used for trays, decorative objects, and even furniture, it is often painted, lacquered, or decorated with mother-of-pearl.

Papineau, Louis Joseph (1786–1871) Canadian politician. He led a mission to England to protest against the planned union of Lower Canada (Québec) and Upper Canada (Ontario), and demanded economic reform and an elected provincial legislature. In 1835 he gained the cooperation of William Lyon Mackenzie in Upper Canada, and in 1837 organized an unsuccessful rebellion of the French against British rule in Lower Canada. He fled the country, but returned in 1847 to sit in the United Canadian legislature until 1854.

Papp, Joseph (1921–1991) Born Joseph Papirofsky. US theatre director. He was the founder of the New York Shakespeare Festival 1954 held in an open-air theatre in the city's Central Park. He also founded the New York Public Theater 1967, an off-Broadway forum

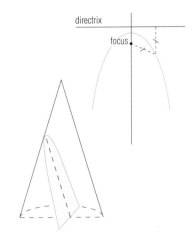

PARABOLA The parabola is a curve produced when a cone is cut by a plane. It is one of a family of curves called conic sections that also includes the circle, ellipse, and hyperbole. These curves are produced when the plane cuts the cone at different angles and positions.

for new talent, which staged the first productions of the musicals *Hair* (1967) and *A Chorus Line* (1975).

Pap test (or **Pap smear**) common name for ▷cervical smear.

Papua New Guinea see country box.

papyrus type of paper made by the ancient Egyptians. Typically papyrus was made by gluing together some 20 sheets of the pith of the papyrus or paper reed plant *Cyperus papyrus*, family Cyperaceae. These sheets were arranged in alternating layers aligned vertically, followed by horizontally. The strips were then covered with linen and beaten with a mallet. Finally, the papyrus was polished with a stone. Papyrus was in use before the First Dynasty.

Pará state of northern Brazil, bounded in the north by Guyana and Suriname, and in the northeast by the Atlantic; area 1,246,833 sq km/481,405 sq mi; population (1991) 5,181,570; capital ▷Belém. It is the second-largest state in Brazil; the Amazon delta lies wholly within it. There are dense rain forests and the area is well watered by the Amazon, Pará, Tocatins, Xingu, and Tapajos rivers. Timber, rubber, and brazilnuts are produced, and cattle are raised. Chief towns include Obidos, Santarém, Marabá and Cameta.

parabola in mathematics, a curve formed by cutting a right circular cone with a plane parallel to the sloping side of the cone. A parabola is one of the family of curves known as ▷conic sections. The graph of $y = x^2$ is a parabola.

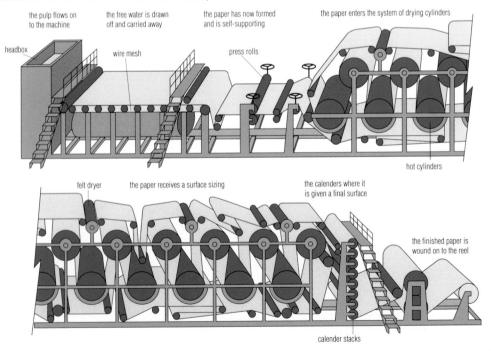

the pulp flows on to the machine   the free water is drawn off and carried away   the paper has now formed and is self-supporting   the paper enters the system of drying cylinders

headbox   wire mesh   press rolls   hot cylinders

felt dryer   the paper receives a surface sizing   the calenders where it is given a final surface   the finished paper is wound on to the reel

calender stacks

PAPER Today's fully automatic papermaking machines can be 200 m/640 ft long and produce over 1,000 m/3,200 ft of paper in a minute. The most common type of papermaking machine is the Fourdrinier, named after two British stationer brothers who invented it in 1803. Their original machine deposited the paper on pieces of felt, after which it was finished by hand.

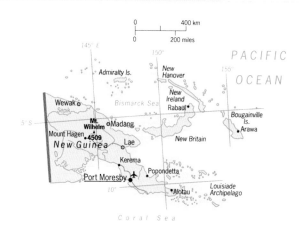

Papua New Guinea country in the southwest Pacific, comprising the eastern part of the island of New Guinea, the Bismarck Archipelago, and part of the Solomon Islands.

NATIONAL NAME *Gau Hedinarai ai Papua-Matamata Guinea/Independent State of Papua New Guinea*
AREA 462,840 sq km/178,702 sq mi
CAPITAL Port Moresby (on East New Guinea)
MAJOR TOWNS/CITIES Lae, Madang, Arawa, Wewak, Goroka, Rabaul
MAJOR PORTS Port Moresby, Rabaul
PHYSICAL FEATURES mountainous; swamps and plains; monsoon climate; tropical islands of New Ireland, New Britain, and Bougainville; Admiralty Islands, D'Entrecasteaux Islands, and Louisiade Archipelago; active volcanoes Vulcan and Tavurvur

Government

HEAD OF STATE Queen Elizabeth II from 1975, represented by Governor General Silas Atopare from 1997
HEAD OF GOVERNMENT Michael Somare from 2002
POLITICAL SYSTEM liberal democracy
POLITICAL EXECUTIVE parliamentary
ADMINISTRATIVE DIVISIONS 20 provinces including the National Capital District (administered by an Interim Commission)
ARMED FORCES 3,100 (2002 est)

CONSCRIPTION military service is voluntary
DEATH PENALTY retains the death penalty for ordinary crimes but can be considered abolitionist in practice; date of last known execution 1950
DEFENCE SPEND (% GDP) 0.5 (2002 est)
EDUCATION SPEND (% GDP) 2.3 (2001 est)
HEALTH SPEND (% GDP) 4.1 (2000 est)

Economy and resources

CURRENCY kina
GPD (US$) 2.8 billion (2002 est)
REAL GDP GROWTH (% change on previous year) –2.6 (2001)
GNI (US$) 2.8 billion (2002 est)
GNI PER CAPITA (PPP) (US$) 2,080 (2002 est)
CONSUMER PRICE INFLATION 4.7% (2003 est)
UNEMPLOYMENT 16% (1998)
FOREIGN DEBT (US$) 1.5 billion (2001 est)
MAJOR TRADING PARTNERS Australia, Japan, USA, Singapore, Germany, South Korea, UK, New Zealand, Malaysia
RESOURCES copper, gold, silver; deposits of chromite, cobalt, nickel, quartz; substantial reserves of petroleum and natural gas (petroleum production began in 1992)

INDUSTRIES food processing, beverages, tobacco, timber products, metal products, machinery and transport equipment, fish canning
EXPORTS gold, copper ore and concentrates, crude petroleum, timber, coffee beans, coconut and copra products. Principal market: Australia 23.9% (2001)
IMPORTS machinery and transport equipment, manufactured goods, food and live animals, miscellaneous manufactured articles, chemicals, mineral fuels. Principal source: Australia 50.4% (2001)
ARABLE LAND 0.5% (2001 est)
AGRICULTURAL PRODUCTS coffee, cocoa, coconuts, pineapples, palm oil, rubber, tea, pyrethrum, peanuts, spices, potatoes, maize, taro, bananas, rice, sago, sweet potatoes; livestock; poultry; fishing; timber production

Population and society

POPULATION 5,711,000 (2003 est)
POPULATION GROWTH RATE 2.0% (2000–15)
POPULATION DENSITY (per sq km) 12 (2003 est)
URBAN POPULATION (% of total) 18 (2003 est)
AGE DISTRIBUTION (% of total population) 0–14 40%, 15–59 56%, 60+ 4% (2002 est)
ETHNIC GROUPS mainly Melanesian (95%), particularly in coastal areas; inland (on New Guinea and larger islands), Papuans predominate. On the outer archipelagos and islands, mixed Micronese-Melanesians and Polynesian groups are found. A small Chinese minority also exists
LANGUAGE English (official), pidgin English, over 700 local languages
RELIGION Christian 97%, of which 3% Roman Catholic; local pantheistic beliefs
EDUCATION not compulsory
LITERACY RATE 72% (men); 59% (women) (2003 est)
LABOUR FORCE 76% agriculture, 6% industry, 18% services (1997 est)
LIFE EXPECTANCY 57 (men); 59 (women) (2000–05)
CHILD MORTALITY RATE (under 5, per 1,000 live births) 94 (2001)
PHYSICIANS (per 1,000 people) 0.07 (1998 est)
HOSPITAL BEDS (per 1,000 people) 4.5 (1994 est)
TV SETS (per 1,000 people) 19 (2001 est)
RADIOS (per 1,000 people) 95 (1998)
INTERNET USERS (per 10,000 people) 137.3 (2002 est)
PERSONAL COMPUTER USERS (per 100 people) 5.9 (2002 est)

See also ▷Australasia and Oceania.

Chronology

c. 3000 BC: New settlement of Austronesian (Melanesian) immigrants.

AD 1526: Visited by Portuguese navigator Jorge de Menezes, who named the main island the Ilhos dos Papua.

1545: Spanish navigator Ynigo Ortis de Retez gave the island the name of New Guinea, as a result of a supposed resemblance of the peoples with those of the Guinea coast of Africa.

17th century: Regularly visited by Dutch merchants.

1828: Dutch East India Company incorporated the western part of New Guinea into Netherlands East Indies (becoming Irian Jaya, in Indonesia).

1884: Northeast New Guinea annexed by Germany; the southeast was claimed by Britain.

1870s: Visits by Western missionaries and traders increased.

1890s: Copra plantations developed in German New Guinea.

1906: Britain transferred its rights to Australia, which renamed the lands Papua.

1914: German New Guinea occupied by Australia at the outbreak of World War I; from the merged territories Papua New Guinea was formed.

1920–42: Held as League of Nations mandate by Australia.

1942–45: Occupied by Japan, who lost 150,000 troops resisting Allied counterattack.

1947: Held as United Nations Trust Territory by Australia.

1951: Legislative Council established.

1964: Elected House of Assembly formed.

1967: Pangu Party (Pangu Pati; PP) formed to campaign for home rule.

1975: Independence achieved from Australia, within Commonwealth, with Michael Somare (PP) as prime minister.

1985: Somare challenged by deputy prime minister Paias Wingti, who later left the PP and formed the People's Democratic Movement (PDM); he became head of a five-party coalition government.

1988: Joined Solomon Islands and Vanuatu to form the Spearhead Group, aiming to preserve Melanesian cultural traditions.

1989: State of emergency imposed on copper-rich Bougainville in response to separatist violence.

1990: The Bougainville Revolutionary Army (BRA) issued a unilateral declaration of independence.

1991: There was an economic boom as gold production doubled.

1994: There was a short-lived peace agreement with the BRA.

1996: The prime minister of Bougainville was murdered, jeopardizing the peace process. Gerard Sinato was elected president of the transitional Bougainville government.

1997: The army and police mutinied following the government's use of mercenaries against secessionist rebels. Silas Atopare was appointed governor general.

1998: There was a truce with Bougainville secessionists. At least 1,500 people died and thousands were left homeless when tidal waves destroyed villages on the north coast.

1999: A coalition of parties headed by Mekere Morauta won a parliamentary majority to form a new government. Bougainville Transitional Government (BTG) was replaced by the new interim Bougainville Reconciliation Government (BRG), headed by former rebel leader Joseph Kabui and BTG leader Gerard Sinato.

PAPUA NEW GUINEA The Huli tribesmen are the largest ethnic group in the Southern Highlands of Papua New Guinea. They wear traditional face paint, nose quills, and intricate decorated wigs. *Corel*

Paracelsus, Philippus Aureolus (1493–1541) Adopted name of Theophrastus Bombastus von Hohenheim. Swiss physician, alchemist, and scientist who developed the idea that minerals and chemicals might have medical uses (iatrochemistry). He introduced the use of ▷laudanum (which he named) for pain-killing purposes.

Overturning the contemporary view of illness as an imbalance of the four humours (see ▷humours, theory of), Paracelsus sought an external agency as the source of disease. This encouraged new modes of treatment, supplanting, for example, bloodletting, and opened the way for new ideas on the source of infection.

Paracelsus was extremely successful as a doctor. His descriptions of miners' diseases first identified silicosis and tuberculosis as occupational hazards. He recognized goitre as endemic and related to minerals in drinking water, and originated a medical account of chorea, rather than believing this nervous disease to be caused by possession by spirits. Paracelsus was the first to distinguish the congenital from the infectious form of syphilis, and showed that it could be treated with carefully controlled doses of a mercury compound.

paracetamol analgesic, particularly effective for musculoskeletal pain. It is as effective as aspirin in reducing fever, and less irritating to the stomach, but has little anti-inflammatory action. An overdose can cause severe, often irreversible or even fatal, liver and kidney damage.

parachute any canopied fabric device strapped to a person or a package, used to slow down descent from a high altitude, or returning spent missiles or parts to a safe speed for landing, or sometimes to aid (through braking) the landing of a plane or missile. Modern designs enable the parachutist to exercise considerable control of direction, as in skydiving.

paradigm all those factors, both scientific and sociological, that influence the research of the scientist. The term, first used by the US historian of science Thomas ▷Kuhn, has subsequently spread to social studies and politics.

paradise (Persian 'pleasure garden') in various religions, a place or state of happiness. Examples are the Garden of ▷Eden and the Messianic kingdom; the Islamic paradise of the Koran is a place of sensual pleasure.

paradox statement that seems contradictory but contains an element of truth. The truth is emphasized by the unexpected form of expression. The Bible is a rich source of paradox: 'Love your enemies'; 'The first shall be last and the last shall be first.'

paraffin common name for ▷alkane, any member of the series of hydrocarbons with the general formula C_nH_{2n+2}. The lower members are gases, such as methane (marsh or natural gas). The middle ones (mainly liquid) form the basis of petrol, kerosene, and lubricating oils, while the higher ones (paraffin waxes) are used in ointment and cosmetic bases. The fuel commonly sold as paraffin in Britain is more correctly called kerosene.

Paraguay see country box.

parakeet any of various small long-tailed ▷parrots, order Psittaciformes, with a moderate beak. They include the **ring-necked parakeets**, genus *Psittacula*, which are very common in India and Africa, and ▷cockatiels, and ▷budgerigars, natives of Australia. The **king parakeet** is about the size of a magpie and has a red head and breast and green wings.

Paraguay

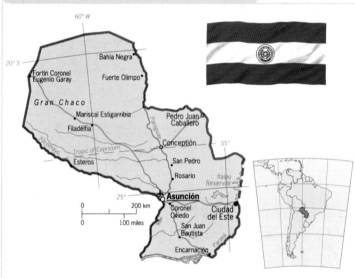

Paraguay landlocked country in South America, bounded northeast by Brazil, south by Argentina, and northwest by Bolivia.

NATIONAL NAME *República del Paraguay/Republic of Paraguay*
AREA 406,752 sq km/157,046 sq mi
CAPITAL Asunción (and chief port)
MAJOR TOWNS/CITIES Ciudad del Este, Pedro Juan Caballero, San Lorenzo, Fernando de la Mora, Lambare, Luque, Capiatá
MAJOR PORTS Concepción
PHYSICAL FEATURES low marshy plain and marshlands; divided by Paraguay River; Paraná River forms southeast boundary

Government

HEAD OF STATE AND GOVERNMENT Oscar Duarte Frutos from 2003
POLITICAL SYSTEM emergent democracy
POLITICAL EXECUTIVE limited presidency
ADMINISTRATIVE DIVISIONS 17 departments and the capital district of Asunción
ARMED FORCES 18,600; plus paramilitary forces of 14,800 (2002 est)
CONSCRIPTION 12 months (army) or 24 months (navy)
DEATH PENALTY abolished in 1992
DEFENCE SPEND (% GDP) 1 (2002 est)
EDUCATION SPEND (% GDP) 5 (2001 est)
HEALTH SPEND (% GDP) 7.9 (2000 est)

Economy and resources

CURRENCY guaraní
GPD (US$) 5.4 billion (2002 est)
REAL GDP GROWTH (% change on previous year) 0.8 (2001)

GNI (US$) 6.4 billion (2002 est)
GNI PER CAPITA (PPP) (US$) 4,450 (2002 est)
CONSUMER PRICE INFLATION 19.2% (2003 est)
UNEMPLOYMENT 17.8% (2001)
FOREIGN DEBT (US$) 2.6 billion (2001 est)
MAJOR TRADING PARTNERS Brazil, Argentina, Uruguay, the Netherlands, Japan, USA, France, UK
RESOURCES gypsum, kaolin, limestone, salt; deposits (not commercially exploited) of bauxite, iron ore, copper, manganese, uranium; deposits of natural gas discovered in 1994; exploration for petroleum deposits ongoing mid-1990s
INDUSTRIES food processing, beverages, tobacco, wood and wood products, textiles (cotton), clothing, leather, chemicals, metal products, machinery
EXPORTS soybeans (and other oil seeds), cotton, timber and wood manufactures, hides and skins, meat. Principal market: Brazil 28.1% (2001)
IMPORTS machinery, vehicles and parts, mineral fuels and lubricants, beverages, tobacco, chemicals, foodstuffs. Principal source: Brazil 28.3% (2001)
ARABLE LAND 5.8% (2000 est)
AGRICULTURAL PRODUCTS cassava, soybeans, maize, cotton, wheat, rice, tobacco, sugar cane, 'yerba maté' (strongly flavoured tea); livestock rearing; forest resources

Population and society

POPULATION 5,878,000 (2003 est)
POPULATION GROWTH RATE 2.1% (2000–15)
POPULATION DENSITY (per sq km) 14 (2003 est)

PARAGUAY Medicinal plants illustrate this stamp from Paraguay, where natural medicine continues to be practised extensively.

URBAN POPULATION (% of total) 58 (2003 est)
AGE DISTRIBUTION (% of total population) 0–14 39%, 15–59 56%, 60+ 5% (2002 est)
ETHNIC GROUPS predominantly mixed-race mestizos (94%); Asian 5%, foreigners and Indian 1%
LANGUAGE Spanish (official), Guaraní (an indigenous Indian language)
RELIGION Roman Catholic (official religion) 85%; Mennonite, Anglican
EDUCATION (compulsory years) 6
LITERACY RATE 95% (men); 93% (women) (2003 est)
LABOUR FORCE 5.2% agriculture, 22.0% industry, 72.8% services (1996)
LIFE EXPECTANCY 69 (men); 73 (women) (2000–05)
CHILD MORTALITY RATE (under 5, per 1,000 live births) 30 (2001)
TV SETS (per 1,000 people) 218 (2001 est)
RADIOS (per 1,000 people) 182 (1997)
INTERNET USERS (per 10,000 people) 173.0 (2002 est)
PERSONAL COMPUTER USERS (per 100 people) 3.5 (2002 est)

Chronology

1526: Visited by Italian navigator Sebastian Cabot, who travelled up the Paraná River; at this time the east of the country had long been inhabited by Guaraní-speaking Amerindians, who gave the country its name, which means 'land with an important river'.

1537: Spanish made an alliance with Guaraní Indians against hostile Chaco Indians, enabling them to colonize interior plains; Asunción founded by Spanish.

1609: Jesuits arrived from Spain to convert local population to Roman Catholicism and administer the country.

1767: Jesuit missionaries expelled.

1776: Formerly part of Spanish Viceroyalty of Peru, which covered much of South America, became part of Viceroyalty of La Plata, with capital at Buenos Aires (Argentina).

1808: With Spanish monarchy overthrown by Napoleon Bonaparte, La Plata Viceroyalty became autonomous, but Paraguayans revolted against rule from Buenos Aires.

1811: Independence achieved from Spain.

1814: Under dictator Gen José Gaspar Rodriguez Francia ('El Supremo'), Paraguay became an isolated state.

1840: Francia was succeeded by his nephew, Carlos Antonio Lopez, who opened country to foreign trade and whose son, Francisco Solano Lopez, as president from 1862, built up a powerful army.

1865–70: War with Argentina, Brazil, and Uruguay over access to sea; more than half the population died and 150,000 sq km/58,000 sq mi of territory were lost.

late 1880s: Conservative Colorado Party and Liberal Party founded.

1912: Liberal leader Edvard Schaerer came to power, ending decades of political instability.

1932–35: Territory in west won from Bolivia during Chaco War (settled by arbitration in 1938).

1940–48: Presidency of autocratic Gen Higinio Morínigo.

1948–54: Political instability; six different presidents.

1954: Gen Alfredo Stroessner seized power in a coup. He ruled as a ruthless autocrat, suppressing civil liberties; the country received initial US backing as the economy expanded.

1989: Stroessner was ousted in a coup led by Gen Andrés Rodríguez. Rodríguez was elected president; the right-of-centre military-backed Colorado Party won assembly elections.

1992: A new democratic constitution was adopted.

1993: The Colorado Party won the most seats in the first free multiparty elections, but no overall majority; its candidate, Juan Carlos Wasmosy, won the first free presidential elections.

1999: Luis Gonzalez Macchi became president.

2000: An attempted anti-government coup, led by supporters within the military of the ex-army chief Lino Oviedo, failed after the USA and Brazil put pressure on the army's commanders. The opposition candidate, Julio César Franco, of the Authentic Liberal Radical Party, won the vice-presidential elections, the first national defeat for the Colorado Party. Congress approved the start of a programme of privatization.

2003: Oscar Duarte Frutos of the authoritarian Colorado Party won the presidential election, but with only 38% of the vote.

parallax change in the apparent position of an object against its background when viewed from two different positions. In astronomy, nearby stars show a shift owing to parallax when viewed from different positions on the Earth's orbit around the Sun. A star's parallax is used to deduce its distance from the Earth.

parallel lines and parallel planes in mathematics, straight lines or planes that always remain a constant distance from one another no matter how far they are extended. This is a principle of Euclidean geometry. Some non-Euclidean geometries, such as elliptical and hyperbolic geometry, however, reject Euclid's parallel axiom.

parallelogram in mathematics, a quadrilateral (four-sided plane figure) with opposite pairs of sides equal in length and parallel, and opposite angles equal. The diagonals of a parallelogram bisect each other. Its area is the product of the length of one side and the perpendicular distance between this and the opposite side. In the special case when all four sides are equal in length, the parallelogram is known as a rhombus, and when the internal angles are right angles, it is a rectangle or square.

(i) opposite sides and angles are equal

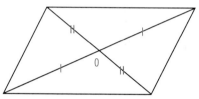

(ii) diagonals bisect each other at 0

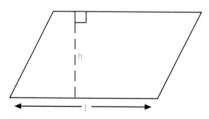

(iii) area of a parallelogram l x h

PARALLELOGRAM Some properties of a parallelogram.

parallelogram of forces in physics and applied mathematics, a method of calculating the resultant (combined effect) of two different forces acting together on an object. Because a force has both magnitude and direction it is a ▷vector quantity and can be represented by a straight line. A second force acting at the same point in a different direction can be represented by another line drawn at an angle to the first. By completing the parallelogram (of which the two lines are sides) a diagonal may be drawn from the original angle to the opposite corner to represent the resultant force vector.

parallel processing emerging computer technology that allows more than one computation at the same time. Although in the 1990s this technology enabled only a small number of computer processor units to work in parallel, in theory thousands or millions of processors could be used at the same time. Parallel processing, which involves breaking down computations into small parts and performing thousands of them simultaneously, rather than in a linear sequence, offers the prospect of a vast improvement in working speed for certain repetitive applications.

Paralympic Games an international sporting competition for athletes with disabilities, held every four years since 1948 in 'parallel' with the Olympic Games. The Games were the creation of Dr Ludwig Guttmann, neurologist at Stoke Mandeville hospital in Buckinghamshire, England, as an extension of his rehabilitation programme for World War II veterans with spinal injuries.

paralysis loss of voluntary movement due to failure of nerve impulses to reach the muscles involved. It may result from almost any disorder of the nervous system, including brain or spinal cord injury, poliomyelitis, stroke, and progressive conditions such as a tumour or multiple sclerosis. Paralysis may also involve loss of sensation due to sensory nerve disturbance.

Paramaribo chief port and capital of ▷Suriname, on the west bank of the Suriname River near its mouth on the Atlantic coast; population (1996) 150,000. Products include coffee, fruit, timber, and bauxite.

Features Dutch colonial architecture; 17th-century Fort Zeelandia; Peter and Paul Cathedral, built in 1885 entirely of wood.

History Originally an American Indian village, it was settled by the French in about 1640. The British Lord Willoughby of Parham founded the first successful colony on the west bank of the River Suriname in 1651 with the establishment of a sugar and tobacco plantation economy. Following the second Anglo-Dutch war, Paramaribo was ceded to the Dutch in the Treaty of Breda of 1667 in exchange for the North American settlement of New Amsterdam, now New York, and remained under Dutch rule until 1975 except for two periods during the Napoleonic Wars (1799–1802 and 1804–15).

paramilitary uniformed, armed force found in many countries, occupying a position between the police and the military. In France such a force is called the Gendarmerie and in Germany the Federal Border Guard. In recent years the term has been extended to include illegal organizations of a terrorist or guerrilla nature.

paranoia mental disorder marked by delusions of grandeur or persecution. In popular usage, paranoia means baseless or exaggerated fear and suspicion.

paranormal not within the range of, or explicable by, established science. Paranormal phenomena include extrasensory perception (ESP) which takes in clairvoyance, precognition, and telepathy; **telekinesis**, the movement of objects from one position to another by human mental concentration; and **mediumship**, supposed contact with the spirits of the dead, usually via an intermediate 'guide' in the other world. ▷Parapsychology is the study of such phenomena.

paraplegia paralysis of the lower limbs, involving loss of both movement and sensation; it is usually due to spinal injury.

parapsychology (Greek *para* 'beyond') study of ▷paranormal phenomena, which are generally subdivided into two types: ▷extrasensory perception (ESP), or the paracognitive; and psychokinesis (PK), telekinesis, or the paraphysical – movement of an object without the use of physical force or energy.

paraquat $CH_3(C_5H_4N)_2CH_3.2CH_3SO_4$ (technical name 1, 1-dimethyl-4,4-**dipyridylium**) nonselective herbicide (weedkiller). Although quickly degraded by soil micro-organisms, it is deadly to human beings if ingested.

parasite organism that lives on or in another organism (called the host) and depends on it for nutrition, often at the expense of the host's welfare. Parasites that live inside the host, such as liver flukes and tapeworms, are called **endoparasites**; those that live on the exterior, such as fleas and lice, are called **ectoparasites**.

parathyroid one of a pair of small ▷endocrine glands. Most tetrapod vertebrates, including humans, possess two such pairs, located behind the ▷thyroid gland. They secrete parathyroid hormone, which regulates the amount of calcium in the blood.

Paré, Ambroise (c. 1509–1590) French surgeon who introduced modern principles to the treatment of wounds. As a military surgeon, Paré developed new ways of treating wounds and amputations, which greatly reduced the death rate among the wounded. He abandoned the practice of cauterization (sealing with heat), using balms and soothing lotions instead, and used ligatures to tie off blood vessels.

parenchyma plant tissue composed of loosely packed, more or less spherical cells, with thin cellulose walls. Although parenchyma often has no specialized function, it is usually present in large amounts, forming a packing or ground tissue. It usually has many intercellular spaces.

parent governor elected parent representative on the governing body of a state school. The 1980 Education Act in the UK made it mandatory for all state schools to include parent governors, in line with the existing practice of some local education authorities. The 1986 Education (No.2) Act increased parental representation.

parent–teacher association (PTA) group attached to a school consisting of parents and teachers who support the school by fund-raising and other activities.

Pareto, Vilfredo (1848–1923) Italian economist and political philosopher. A vigorous opponent of socialism and liberalism, he justified inequality of income and rule by elites on the grounds of his empirical observation (**Pareto's law**) that income distribution remained constant whatever efforts were made to change it. In some ways a classical liberal, his ideas nevertheless influenced Mussolini, who appointed him senator in 1922.

Paris port and capital of France, on the River Seine; *département* (*Ville de Paris*) in the Île-de-France region; area of the *agglomération parisienne* (comprising the *Ville de Paris* and 379 *communes* surrounding it) 105 sq km/40.5 sq mi; population *Ville de Paris* (2002 est) 2,113,000; *agglomération parisienne* (2002 est) 11,293,200. The city is the core of a highly centralized national administration, a focus of European transport networks, and France's leading centre for education, research, finance, and industry. Manufactured products include metal, electrical and luxury goods, chemicals, glass, and tobacco. As one of the world's principal historic and cultural centres, Paris attracts enormous numbers of tourists throughout the year.

> **Vilfredo Pareto**
> *Give me fruitful error any time, full of seeds, bursting with its own corrections. You can keep your sterile truth for yourself.*
> *Mind and Society*

Features The River Seine is spanned by 32 bridges, the oldest of which is the Pont Neuf (1578). Churches include Notre Dame cathedral (built 1163–1250); the Hôtel des Invalides, housing the tomb of Napoleon; the Gothic Sainte-Chapelle; and the late 19th-century basilica of Sacré-Cœur, 125 m/410 ft high, consecrated in 1919. Notable buildings include the Palais de Justice, the Hôtel de Ville, and the Palais du Luxembourg and its gardens. The former palace of the Louvre (with its glass pyramid entrance by I M Pei 1989) is one of the world's major art galleries; the Musée d'Orsay (opened in 1986) has Impressionist and other paintings from the period 1848–1914; the Pompidou Centre (the Centre National d'Art et de Culture Georges Pompidou, 1977) in the Beaubourg *quartier* exhibits modern art.

Other landmarks are the Tuileries (the gardens in front of the Louvre), the Place de la Concorde, the Eiffel Tower, and the Champs-Élysées avenue leading to the Arc de Triomphe. To the west is the Bois de Boulogne and, beyond the river, La Défense business centre with the Grande Arche (1989) by Danish architect Johan Otto von Spreckelsen; Montmartre is in the north of the city; to the northeast is the cemetery of Père-Lachaise, and in the northern suburbs is the abbey of St-Denis containing the royal tombs. The university, founded about 1150, is on the Left Bank. Work began in 1990 on the New Bibliothèque Nationale (opened in 1997), designed by French architect Dominique Perrault. Euro Disney, renamed Disneyland Paris in 1995, opened 32 km/20 mi to the east of the city centre in 1992.

History The Île de la Cité, the largest of the Seine islands and the nucleus of modern Paris, was the capital of the Parisii, a Gaulish people. It was occupied by Julius Caesar in 53 BC, and became known as **Lutetia Parisiorum**. In AD 451 Attila attempted to enter the city but is said to have been halted by the prayer of St Geneviève, who became the city's patron saint. The Merovingian king Clovis made Paris the capital in about AD 508, and the city became important under the Capetian kings 987–1328. Paris was occupied by the English 1420–36, and was besieged by Henry IV of France 1590–94.

The Bourbon kings did much to beautify the city. Louis XIV built many magnificent buildings but lost the loyalty of the

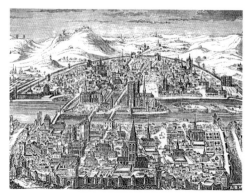

PARIS An aerial impression of Paris showing the Île de la Cité including Notre Dame, 1607. *Philip Sauvain Picture Collection*

populace by moving the court to Versailles. The French Revolution began in Paris in 1789 with the storming and destruction of the Bastille. Napoleon I, as emperor from 1804, undertook to modernize the city and added new boulevards, bridges, and triumphal arches, as did Napoleon III (emperor 1852–70). Paris was the centre of the revolutions of 1789–94, 1830, and 1848. The medieval heart of the city was redesigned by the French administrator Baron Haussmann 1853–70 and the modern layout of boulevards, avenues, and parks established. It was besieged by Prussia 1870–71, and by government troops during the Commune period (a local socialist government) March–May 1871.

During World War I Paris suffered from air raids and bombardment, and in World War II it was occupied by German troops from June 1940 until August 1944. The German commandant, General Cholitz, ignored Hitler's order to defend Paris at all costs to avoid causing large-scale damage to the city. Aerial bombardment mainly affected suburban railway installations and some factory sites. Large-scale architectural projects of note were again undertaken during the presidency of François Mitterrand (1981–95).

Related Web site: Paris Pages http://www.paris.org/

Paris in Greek mythology, a Trojan prince whose abduction of ▷Helen, wife of ▷Menelaus, caused the Trojan wars. Helen had been promised to him by the goddess Aphrodite as a bribe, during his judgement between her beauty and that of the goddesses, Hera and Athena. During the wars, he killed the Greek hero ▷Achilles by shooting an arrow into his heel, but was later mortally wounded by the archer Philoctetes.

Paris Commune name given to two separate periods in the history of Paris:

The **Paris municipal government of 1789–94** was established after the storming of the ▷Bastille and remained powerful in the French Revolution until the fall of Robespierre in 1794.

The **provisional national government of 18 March–May 1871** was formed while Paris was besieged by the German troops during the Franco-Prussian War. It consisted of socialists and left-wing republicans, and is often considered the first socialist government in history. Elected after the right-wing National Assembly at Versailles tried to disarm the National Guard, it fell when the Versailles troops captured Paris and massacred 20,000–30,000 people during 21–28 May.

Related Web site: Siege and Commune of Paris http://www.library. nwu.edu/spec/siege/

parish council lowest neighbourhood unit of local government in England and Wales, based on church parishes. They developed as units for local government with the introduction of the Poor Law in the 17th century. In Wales and Scotland they are commonly called **community councils**.

Paris, Treaty of any of various peace treaties signed in Paris, including: **1763** ending the ▷Seven Years' War; **1783** (also known as the Peace of Versailles) recognizing American independence; **1814** and **1815** following the abdication and final defeat of ▷Napoleon I; **1856** ending the ▷Crimean War; **1898** ending the ▷Spanish-American War; **1919–20** the conference preparing the Treaty of ▷Versailles at the end of World War I was held in Paris; **1947** after World War II, the peace treaties between the ▷Allies and Italy, Romania, Hungary, Bulgaria, and Finland; **1951** treaty signed by France, West Germany, Italy, Belgium, Netherlands, and Luxembourg, embodying the Schuman Plan to set up a single coal and steel authority; **1973** ending US participation in the ▷Vietnam War.

parity of a number, the state of being either even or odd. In computing, the term refers to the number of 1s in the binary codes used to represent data. A binary representation has **even parity** if it contains an even number of 1s and **odd parity** if it contains an odd number of 1s.

For example, the binary code 1000001, commonly used to represent the character 'A', has even parity because it contains two 1s, and the binary code 1000011, commonly used to represent the character 'C', has odd parity because it contains three 1s. A **parity bit** (0 or 1) is sometimes added to each binary representation to give all the same parity so that a ▷validation check can be carried out each time data are transferred from one part of the computer to another. So, for example, the codes 1000001 and 1000011 could have parity bits added and become 01000001 and 11000011, both with even parity. If any bit in these codes should be altered in the course of processing the parity would change and the error would be quickly detected.

parity in economics, equality of price, rate of exchange, wages, and buying power. Parity ratios may be used in the setting of wages to establish similar status to different work groups. Parity in international exchange rates means that those on a par with each other share similar buying power. In the USA, agricultural output prices are regulated by a parity system.

Park, Mungo (1771–1806) Scottish explorer who traced the course of the Niger River 1795–97. He disappeared and probably drowned during a second African expedition 1805–06. He published *Travels in the Interior of Africa* (1799).

Park, Nick (1958–) English animator, specializing in stop-motion animation using clay figures. His creation of the much-loved characters Wallace and Gromit earned him international fame. He met with early success with his first two shorts, *A Grand Day Out* (1989) – the first to star Wallace and his faithful canine side-kick Gromit – and *Creature Comforts* (1990), for which he won an Academy Award. The next two Wallace and Gromit instalments, *The Wrong Trousers* (1993) and *A Close Shave* (1995), both earned him further Academy Awards. In 2000 *Chicken Run* was released, starring Mel Gibson and Jane Horrocks.

Park Chung Hee (1917–1979) South Korean politician, president 1963–79. Under his rule South Korea had one of the world's fastest-growing economies, but recession and his increasing authoritarianism led to his assassination in 1979.

Parker, Bonnie US criminal; see ▷Bonnie and Clyde.

Parker, Charlie (1920–1955) Born Charles Christopher Parker; called 'Bird' or 'Yardbird'. US alto saxophonist and jazz composer. He was associated with the trumpeter Dizzy Gillespie in developing the ▷bebop style. His skilful improvisations inspired performers on all jazz instruments.

Parker was born in Kansas City, a hub of jazz music. The young Parker studied the work of saxophonist Lester ▷Young and played in several conventional jazz and dance bands. Joining the Earl Hines Orchestra 1942–43 brought him into collaboration with Gillespie, and in their early recordings together ('Salt Peanuts', 'Groovin' High' (1945)) bebop began to take shape. 'Ko-Ko' and 'Billie's Bounce' (1945) were recorded with a group that included Miles Davis on trumpet. Among other Parker compositions are 'Yardbird Suite' and 'Ornithology' (late 1940s). Parker was also very influential as a live performer; primitive bootleg tapes were made by fans, and live albums include *Quintet of the Year* (1953), again with Gillespie.

Related Web site: Tribute to Charlie 'Yardbird' Parker http://www. geocities.com/BourbonStreet/5066/

Parker, Dorothy (1893–1967) Born Dorothy Rothschild. US writer and wit. She was a leading member of the literary circle known as the Algonquin Round Table. She reviewed for the magazines *Vanity Fair* and the *New Yorker*, and wrote wittily ironic verses, collected in several volumes including *Enough Rope* (1927), and *Not So Deep as a Well* (1936). Her short stories include the collections 'Laments for Living' (1930), and 'Here Lies' (1939). She also wrote screenplays in Hollywood, having moved there from New York City along with other members of her circle.

> **Dorothy Parker**
> *There's a hell of a distance between wise-cracking and wit. Wit has truth in it; wise-cracking is simply callisthenics with words.*
> Paris Review, 1956

Parkinson's disease (or parkinsonism or paralysis agitans) degenerative disease of the brain characterized by a progressive loss of mobility, muscular rigidity, tremor, and speech difficulties. The condition is mainly seen in people over the age of 50.

Parkinson's law formula invented by the English political analyst Cecil Northcote Parkinson (1909–1993), which states that 'work expands so as to fill the time available for its completion'.

parliament (French 'speaking') legislative body of a country. The world's oldest parliament is the Icelandic Althing, which dates from about 930. The UK Parliament is usually dated from 1265. The legislature of the USA is called ▷Congress and comprises the ▷House of Representatives and the ▷Senate.

Related Web site: Houses of Parliament Home Page http://www. parliament.uk/

Parliament, European governing body of the European Union (formerly the European Community); see ▷European Parliament.

Parliament, Houses of building where the UK legislative assembly meets. The present Houses of Parliament in London, designed in Gothic Revival style by the architects Charles ▷Barry and A W N ▷Pugin, were built 1840–60, the previous building having burned down in 1834. It incorporates portions of the medieval Palace of Westminster.

Parma town in Emilia-Romagna, northern Italy, on the River Parma, 85 km/53 mi northwest of Bologna; population (1992) 170,600. It is the second largest in the region after Bologna. Industries include food-processing, oil-refining, engineering, and the production of textiles. Founded by the Etruscans, it was the capital of the duchy of Parma 1545–1860. It has given its name to a type of ham, and to Parmesan cheese.

Parnassus mountain in central Greece, height 2,457 m/8,200 ft, revered by the ancient Greeks as the abode of Apollo and the Muses. The sacred site of Delphi lies on its southern flank.

Parnell, Charles Stewart (1846–1891) Irish nationalist politician. He supported a policy of obstruction and violence to attain ▷home rule, and became the president of the Nationalist Party in 1877. In 1879 he approved the ▷Land League, and his attitude led to his imprisonment in 1881. His career was ruined in 1890 when he was cited as co-respondent in a divorce case. Because of his great influence over his followers, he was called 'the uncrowned king of Ireland'.

Parnell, born in Avondale, County Wicklow, was elected member of Parliament for Meath in 1875. He welcomed Gladstone's Home Rule Bill, and continued his agitation after its defeat in 1886. In 1887 his reputation suffered from an unfounded accusation by *The Times* of complicity in the murder of Lord Frederick ▷Cavendish, chief secretary to the Lord Lieutenant of Ireland. Three years later came the adultery scandal, and for fear of losing the support of Gladstone, Parnell's party deposed him. He died suddenly of rheumatic fever at the age of 45.

parody in literature and the other arts, a work that imitates the style of another work, usually with mocking or comic intent; it is related to ▷satire.

parole conditional release of a prisoner from jail. The prisoner remains on licence until the date release would have been granted, and may be recalled if the authorities deem it necessary.

parquetry geometric version of ▷marquetry: a decorative veneer applied to furniture and floors, composed of shaped pieces of wood or other suitable materials, such as bone, horn, or ivory, to form a geometric pattern or mosaic.

Parr, Catherine (1512–1548) Sixth wife of Henry VIII of England. She had already lost two husbands when in 1543 she married Henry. She survived him, and in 1547 married the Lord High Admiral Thomas Seymour of Sudeley (1508–1549).

Parramatta river inlet, western arm of Sydney Harbour, New South Wales, Australia. It is 24 km/15 mi long and is lined with industrial suburbs of Sydney: Balmain, Drummoyne, Concord, Parramatta, Ermington and Rydalmere, Ryde, and Hunter's Hill.

parrot tropical bird found mainly in Australia and South America. These colourful birds have been valued as pets in the Western world for many centuries. Parrots have the ability to imitate human speech. They are mainly vegetarian, and range in size from the 8.5 cm/3.5 in pygmy parrot to the 100 cm/40 in Macaw. The smaller species are commonly referred to as ▷parakeets. The plumage is often very colourful, and the call is usually a harsh screech. In most species the sexes are indistinguishable. Several species are endangered. Parrots are members of the family Psittacidae, of the order Psittaciformes.

Parrots all have powerful hooked bills and feet adapted for tree climbing. The bill, with its elongated tip, is well adapted in most parrots for tearing up fruit and cracking nuts, and in a number of species the tongue is highly specialized for extracting honey by means of a brushlike tip.

The talent for imitating human speech is marked in the grey parrot *Psittacus erithacus* of Africa. Alex, a 20-year-old African grey taking part in a long-term language project at the University of Arizona during 1996, can count up to six, name 100 objects and describe their colour, texture, and shape. Parrots were among the first items to be traded between natives and European settlers and merchants.

Under threat Many parrot species are threatened: of the 350 species, more than 90 were under threat of extinction and a further 40 species were vulnerable in 1998. The most serious threat is caused by destruction of the rainforest, although trapping for the pet trade is also a major threat to many species.

Unusual parrots The ▷kakapo of New Zealand is flightless and usually lives on the ground, though it can still climb trees. The ▷kea, another New Zealand parrot, differs from the rest of the group in having developed carnivorous habits.

Related Web site: Parrot http://www.seaworld.org/animal_bytes/ parrotsab.html

parrot fish (or parrot wrasse) member of a family of marine bony fish. The teeth of this group have fused to form extremely hard beaks that are able to bite off pieces of coral; these, with seaweed and molluscs, form the principal food. The fish are all brilliantly coloured, and some may grow up to 1 m/3.3 ft in length. Parrot fish comprise the family Scaridae, order Perciformes, class Osteichthyes.

Parry, William Edward (1790–1855) English admiral and Arctic explorer. He made detailed charts during explorations of the Northwest Passage (the sea route between the Atlantic and Pacific oceans) 1819–20, 1821–23, and 1824–25. Knighted 1829.

parsec in astronomy, a unit (symbol pc) used for distances to stars and galaxies. One parsec is equal to 3.2616 ▷light years, 2.063×10^5 ▷astronomical units, and 3.857×10^{13} km.

Parsee (or Parsi; Persian *parsi* 'Persian') follower of the religion ▷Zoroastrianism. The Parsees fled from Persia after its conquest by the Arabs, and settled in India in the 8th century AD. About 100,000 Parsees now live mainly in the former Bombay State.

Parsifal in Germanic mythology, one of the knights who sought the ▷Holy Grail; the father of ▷Lohengrin.

parsley herb belonging to the carrot family, cultivated for flavouring and garnishing in cookery and for its nutrient value, being rich in vitamin C and minerals. It can grow up to 45 cm/1.5 ft high and has aromatic, curled or flat pinnate leaves (leaflets either side of the stem) and delicate open clusters of yellow flowers. It is a biennial plant. (*Petroselinum crispum*, family Umbelliferae.)

PARSLEY The hardy biennial parsley has been cultivated for so long that its origin is uncertain, but it may have originated in southeast Europe.

parsnip temperate biennial plant belonging to the carrot family, found in Europe and Asia, and cultivated for its tapering, creamy-white, aromatic root, which is much used as a winter vegetable. (*Pastinaca sativa*, family Umbelliferae.)

parthenocarpy in botany, the formation of fruits without seeds. This phenomenon, of no obvious benefit to the plant, occurs naturally in some plants, such as bananas. It can also be induced in some fruit crops, either by breeding or by applying certain plant hormones.

parthenogenesis development of an ovum (egg) without any genetic contribution from a male. Parthenogenesis is the normal means of reproduction in a few plants (for example, dandelions) and animals (for example, certain fish). Some sexually reproducing species, such as aphids, show parthenogenesis at some stage in their life cycle to accelerate reproduction to take advantage of good conditions.

In most cases, there is no fertilization at all, but in a few the stimulus of being fertilized by a sperm is needed to initiate development, although the male's chromosomes are not absorbed into the nucleus of the ovum. Parthenogenesis can be artificially induced in many animals (such as rabbits) by cooling, pricking, or applying acid to an egg.

Parthenon temple of Athena Parthenos ('the Virgin') on the Acropolis at Athens; built 447–438 BC by Callicrates and Ictinus under the supervision of the sculptor ▷Phidias, and the most perfect example of Doric architecture. In turn a Christian church and a Turkish mosque, it was then used as a gunpowder store, and reduced to ruins when the Venetians bombarded the Acropolis in 1687. The ▷Elgin marbles were removed from the Parthenon in the early 19th century and are now in the British Museum, London, England.

PARTHENOGENESIS During spring and summer female aphids such as this *Macrosiphum cholodkovskyi* produce a continuous succession of offspring by parthenogenesis, but mate and lay eggs before the onset of winter. *Premaphotos Wildlife*

Parthia ancient country in western Asia in what is now northeastern Iran, capital Ctesiphon. Parthian ascendancy began with the Arsacid dynasty in 248 BC, and reached the peak of its power under Mithridates I in the 2nd century BC; the region was annexed to Persia under the Sassanians AD 226.

particle detector one of a number of instruments designed to detect subatomic particles and track their paths; they include the ▷cloud chamber, ▷bubble chamber, ▷spark chamber, and multiwire chamber.

particle physics study of the particles that make up all atoms, and of their interactions. More than 300 subatomic particles have now been zidentified by physicists, categorized into several classes according to their mass, electric charge, spin, magnetic moment, and interaction. Subatomic particles include the ▷elementary particles (▷quarks, ▷leptons, and ▷gauge bosons), which are indivisible, so far as is known, and so may be considered the fundamental units of matter; and the ▷hadrons (baryons, such as the proton and neutron, and mesons), which are composite particles, made up of two or three quarks. Quarks, protons, electrons, and neutrinos are the only stable particles (the neutron being stable only when in the atomic nucleus). The unstable particles decay rapidly into other particles, and are known from experiments with particle accelerators and cosmic radiation. See ▷atomic structure.

Pioneering research took place at the Cavendish laboratory, Cambridge, England. In 1897 the English physicist Joseph John Thomson discovered that all atoms contain identical, negatively charged particles (▷electrons), which can easily be freed. By 1911 the New Zealand physicist Ernest Rutherford had shown that the electrons surround a very small, positively-charged ▷nucleus. In the case of hydrogen, this was found to consist of a single positively charged particle, a ▷proton. The nuclei of other elements are made up of protons and uncharged particles called ▷neutrons. 1932 saw the discovery of a particle (whose existence had been predicted by the British theoretical physicist Paul Dirac in 1928) with the mass of an electron, but an equal and opposite charge – the ▷positron. This was the first example of ▷antimatter; it is now believed that all particles have corresponding antiparticles. In 1934 the Italian-born US physicist Enrico Fermi argued that a hitherto unsuspected particle, the ▷neutrino, must accompany electrons in beta-emission.

Particles and fundamental forces By the mid-1930s, four types of fundamental ▷force interacting between particles had been identified. The ▷electromagnetic force (1) acts between all particles with electric charge, and is related to the exchange between these particles of ▷gauge bosons called ▷photons, packets of electromagnetic radiation. In 1935 the Japanese physicist Hideki Yukawa suggested that the ▷strong nuclear force (2) (binding protons and neutrons together in the nucleus) was transmitted by the exchange of particles with a mass about one-tenth of that of a proton; these particles, called ▷pions (originally pi mesons), were found by the British physicist Cecil Powell in 1946. Yukawa's theory was largely superseded from 1973 by the theory of ▷quantum chromodynamics, which postulates that the strong nuclear force is transmitted by the exchange of gauge bosons called ▷gluons between the ▷quarks and antiquarks making up protons and neutrons. Theoretical work on the ▷weak nuclear force (3) began with Enrico Fermi in the 1930s. The existence of the gauge bosons that carry this force, the ▷weakons (W and Z particles), was confirmed in 1983 at CERN, the European nuclear research organization. The fourth fundamental force, ▷gravity (4), is experienced by all matter; the postulated carrier of this force has been named the ▷graviton.

Leptons The electron, muon, tau, and their neutrinos comprise the ▷leptons – particles with half-integral spin that 'feel' the weak nuclear and electromagnetic force but not the strong force. The muon (found by the US physicist Carl Anderson in cosmic radiation in 1937) produces the muon neutrino when it decays; the tau, a surprise discovery of the 1970s, produces the tau neutrino when it decays.

Mesons and baryons The hadrons (particles that 'feel' the strong nuclear force) were found in the 1950s and 1960s. They are classified into ▷mesons, with whole-number or zero spins, and ▷baryons (which include protons and neutrons), with half-integral spins. It was shown in the early 1960s that if hadrons of the same spin are represented as points on suitable charts, simple patterns are formed. This symmetry enabled a hitherto unknown baryon, the omega-minus, to be predicted from a gap in one of the patterns; it duly turned up in experiments.

Quarks In 1964 the US physicists Murray Gell-Mann and George Zweig suggested that all hadrons were built from three 'flavours' of a new particle with half-integral spin and a charge of magnitude either $\frac{1}{3}$ or $\frac{2}{3}$ that of an electron; Gell-Mann named the particle the **quark**. Mesons are quark–antiquark pairs (spins either add to one or cancel to zero), and baryons are quark triplets. To account for new mesons such as the psi (J) particle the number of quark flavours had risen to six by 1985.

Related Web site: Particle Physics http://www.pparc.ac.uk/

particle, subatomic in physics, a particle that is smaller than an atom; see ▷particle physics.

partisan member of an armed group that operates behind enemy lines or in occupied territories during wars. The name 'partisans' was first given to armed bands of Russians who operated against Napoleon's army in Russia during 1812, but has since been used to describe Russian, Yugoslav, Italian, Greek, and Polish Resistance groups against the Germans during World War II. In Yugoslavia the communist partisans under their leader, Tito, played a major role in defeating the Germans.

part of speech grammatical function of a word, described in the grammatical tradition of the Western world, based on Greek and Latin. The four major parts of speech are the noun, verb, adjective, and adverb; the minor parts of speech vary according to schools of grammatical theory, but include the article, conjunction, preposition, and pronoun.

partridge any of various medium-sized ground-dwelling fowl of the family Phasianidae, order Galliformes, that also includes pheasants, quail, and chickens. Partridges are Old World birds, some of which have become naturalized in North America.

Partridges pair very early in the year, the males, like the males of most gallinaceous species, being very pugnacious. The nest is made with a minimum of trouble on the ground in fields or hedgerows, and contains 10–20 olive brown eggs. The hen hatches them, but the male is attentive to her during incubation. The young are fed chiefly on ant pupae, and other insects when these are not available; these and snails and slugs form a considerable proportion of the food of older birds, but in addition grain and other seeds are consumed in great quantity when obtainable. The young remain with their parents for some months, forming coveys of about 20 birds. In the morning and evening they search the stubble and pastures for food, but during the day they hide wherever safe cover may be found.

Two species common in the UK are the grey partridge *Perdix perdix*, with mottled brown back, grey speckled breast, and patches of chestnut on the sides, and the French partridge *Alectoris rufa*, distinguished by its red legs, bill, and eyelids. The back is plain brown, the throat white edged with black, and the sides barred chestnut and black. The wings are rounded and short.

During the period 1960–99 the grey partridge *Perdix perdix* has declined by 90% in Britain. Reasons for decline include increased herbicide use and infection by parasites.

Parvati in Hindu mythology, the consort of Siva in one of her gentler manifestations, and the mother of Ganesa, the god of prophecy; she is said to be the daughter of the Himalayas.

Pascal (French acronym for *program appliqué à la selection et la compilation automatique de la littérature*) high-level computer-programming language. Designed by Niklaus Wirth in the 1960s as an aid to teaching programming, it is still widely used as such in universities, and as a good general-purpose programming language. Most professional programmers, however, now use ▷C or C++. Pascal was named after the 17th-century French mathematician Blaise ▷Pascal.

pascal SI unit (symbol Pa) of pressure, equal to one newton per square metre. It replaces ▷bars and millibars (10^5 Pa equals one bar). It is named after the French mathematician Blaise Pascal.

Pascal, Blaise (1623–1662) French philosopher and mathematician. He contributed to the development of hydraulics, ▷calculus, and the mathematical theory of ▷probability.
Mathematics Pascal's work in mathematics widened general understanding of conic sections, introduced an algebraic notational system that rivalled that of ▷Descartes and made use of the arithmetical triangle (called ▷Pascal's triangle) in the study of probabilities.

Together with ▷Fermat, Pascal studied two specific problems of probability: the first concerned the probability that a player will obtain a certain face of a dice in a given number of throws; and the second was to determine the portion of the stakes returnable to each player of several if a game is interrupted. Pascal used the arithmetical triangle to derive combinational analysis. **Pascal's triangle** is a triangular array of numbers in which each number is the sum of the pair of numbers above it. In general the *n*th ($n = 0, 1, 2, ...$) row of the triangle gives the binomial coefficients ^nC_r, with $r = 0, 1, ..., n$.

In 1657–59, Pascal also perfected his 'theory of indivisibles' – the forerunner of integral calculus – which enabled him to study problems involving infinitesimals, such as the calculations of areas and volumes.
Hydrostatics, Pascal's principle and hydraulics Pascal's work in hydrostatics involved repeating the experiment by Italian physicist Evangelista ▷Torricelli to prove that air pressure supports a column of mercury. He confirmed that a vacuum must exist in the space at the top of the tube, and set out to prove that the column of mercury is held up by the weight of air exerted on the container of liquid at the base of the tube. Pascal suggested that at high altitudes there would be less air above the tube and that the column would be lower. Poor health prevented him from undertaking the experiment himself, so he entrusted it to his brother-in-law who obtained the expected results using a mercury column in the mountains of the Puy de Dôme in 1648. This led rapidly to investigations of the use of the mercury barometer in weather forecasting.

Pascal then turned to a study of pressure in liquids and gases, and found that pressure is transmitted equally in all directions throughout a fluid and is always exerted perpendicular to any surface in or containing the fluid. Propounded in a treatise on hydrostatics in 1654, **Pascal's principle** is fundamental to applications of hydrostatics and governs the operation of hydraulic machines, such as the hydraulic press and jack.
Calculating machine Between 1642 and 1645, Pascal constructed a machine to carry out the processes of addition and subtraction, and then organized the manufacture and sale of these first calculating machines. At least seven of these 'computers' still exist. One was presented to Queen Christina of Sweden in 1652.

Pascal's triangle triangular array of numbers (with 1 at the apex), in which each number is the sum of the pair of numbers above it. It is named after French mathematician Blaise Pascal, who used it in his study of probability. When plotted at equal distances along a horizontal axis, the numbers in the rows give the binomial probability distribution (with equal probability of success and failure) of an event, such as the result of tossing a coin.

pas de deux (French 'step for two') dance for two performers. Codified by Marius ▷Petipa into the *grand pas de deux*, the dance opens with the ballerina and her male partner dancing together. It continues with display solos, firstly for the man and then the woman, and ends with the two dancing together again.

Pasolini, Pier Paolo (1922–1975) Italian film director, poet, and novelist. From his Marxist viewpoint, he illustrated the decadence and inequality of society, set in a world ravaged by violence and sexuality. Among his films are *Il vangelo secondo Mateo/The Gospel According to St Matthew* (1964), *The Decameron* (1970), and *I racconti de Canterbury/The Canterbury Tales* (1972).

pasqueflower plant belonging to the buttercup family. A low-growing hairy perennial, it has feathery leaves and large purple bell-shaped flowers that are upright at first, then droop. Found in Europe and Asia, it grows on grassland on limy soil. (*Pulsatilla vulgaris*, family Ranunculaceae.)

Passchendaele, Battle of in World War I, successful but costly British operation to capture the Passchendaele ridge in western Flanders, part of the third Battle of ▷Ypres October–November 1917; British casualties numbered nearly 400,000. The name is often erroneously applied to the whole of the battle of Ypres, but Passchendaele was in fact just part of that battle.

Passfield, Baron Passfield, title of the Fabian socialist Sidney ▷Webb.

passion flower any of a group of tropical American climbing plants. They have distinctive flowers consisting of a saucer-shaped petal base, a fringelike corona or circle of leafy outgrowths inside

PASSION FLOWER These climbing, vinelike plants derive their names from the 'passion' or sufferings of Jesus at the crucifixion. Spanish missionaries to South America, where many species grow, thought the flowers resembled the crown of thorns and the wounds on Jesus' body. Some species are cultivated for their edible fruits or decorative flowers.

the ring of petals, and a central stalk bearing five pollen-producing ▷stamens and three pollen-receiving ▷stigmas. The flowers can be yellow, greenish, purple, or red. Some species produce edible fruit. (Genus *Passiflora*, family Passifloraceae.)

passion play play representing the death and resurrection of Jesus, performed on Good Friday throughout medieval Europe. It has its origins in medieval ▷mystery plays. Traditionally, a passion play takes place every ten years at ▷Oberammergau, Germany.

passive margin in plate tectonics, a region on the Earth's surface in which one plate slides past another. An example is the San Andreas Fault, California, where the movement of the plates is irregular and sometimes takes the form of sudden jerks, which cause the ▷earthquakes common in the San Francisco–Los Angeles area.

passive smoking inhalation of tobacco smoke from other people's cigarettes; see ▷smoking.

pass laws South African laws that required the black population to carry passbooks (identity documents) at all times and severely restricted freedom of movement. The laws, a major cause of discontent, formed a central part of the policies of ▷apartheid. They were repealed in 1986.

Passover (or Pesach) in Judaism, an eight-day spring festival which commemorates the exodus of the Israelites from Egypt and the passing over by the Angel of Death of the Jewish houses, so that only the Egyptian firstborn sons were killed, in retribution for Pharaoh's murdering of all Jewish male infants.
Related Web site: Passover on the Net http://www.holidays.net/passover/

pastel sticklike drawing or painting material consisting of ground pigment bound with gum; also works produced in this medium. Pastel is a form of painting in dry colours and produces a powdery surface, which is delicate and difficult to conserve. Exponents include Rosalba Carriere (1675–1785), La Tour, Chardin, Degas, and Mary Cassatt.

Pasternak, Boris Leonidovich (1890–1960) Russian poet and novelist. His novel *Dr Zhivago* (1957) was banned in the USSR as a 'hostile act', and was awarded the Nobel prize for Literature in 1957 (which Pasternak declined). The ban on *Dr Zhivago* has since been lifted and Pasternak has been posthumously rehabilitated.

Pasteur, Louis (1822–1895) French chemist and microbiologist who discovered that fermentation is caused by micro-organisms and developed the germ theory of disease. He also created a vaccine for ▷rabies, which led to the foundation of the Pasteur Institute in Paris in 1888.

Pasteur first gained recognition through his early work on the optical activity of stereo ▷isomers.

A query from an industrialist about wine- and beer-making prompted Pasteur's research into fermentation. Using a microscope he found that properly aged wine contains small spherical globules of yeast cells whereas sour wine contains elongated yeast cells. He proved that fermentation does not require oxygen, yet it involves living micro-organisms, and that, to produce the correct type of fermentation (alcohol-producing rather than lactic acid-producing), it is necessary to use the correct type of yeast. Pasteur also realized that, after wine has formed, it must be gently heated to about 50°C/122°F – pasteurized – to kill the yeast and thereby prevent souring during the ageing process.

Pasteur then turned his attention to the question of ▷spontaneous generation of life. Pasteur showed that dust in the air contains spores of living organisms that reproduce when introduced into a nutrient broth. Then he boiled the broth in a container with a U-shaped tube that allowed air to reach the broth but trapped dust in the U-bend. He found that the broth remained free of living organisms, disproving the theory of spontaneous generation.

In the mid-1860s, the French silk industry was seriously threatened by a disease that killed silkworms and Pasteur was commissioned by the government to investigate the disease. He announced in 1868 that he had found a minute parasite that infects the silkworms, and recommended that all infected silkworms be destroyed. His advice was followed and the disease eliminated. Pasteur developed the **germ theory of disease**. This theory was probably the most important single medical discovery of all time, because it provided both a practical method of combating disease by disinfection and a theoretical foundation for further research.

In 1881 Pasteur developed a method for reducing the virulence of certain pathogenic micro-organisms. By heating a preparation of anthrax bacilli he attenuated their virulence but found that they still brought about the full immune response when injected into sheep. Using a similar method, Pasteur then inoculated fowl against chicken cholera, following the work of Edward ▷Jenner (who first vaccinated against cowpox in 1796).

In 1882 Pasteur began what proved to be his most spectacular research: the prevention of rabies. He demonstrated that the causative micro-organism (actually a virus, although the existence of viruses was not known at that time) infects the nervous system and then, using the dried tissues of infected animals, he succeeded in obtaining an attenuated form of the virus suitable for the inoculation of human beings. The culmination of this work came on 6 July 1885, when Pasteur used his vaccine to save the life of a young boy who had been bitten by a rabid dog. The success of this experiment brought Pasteur even greater acclaim and led to the establishment of the Pasteur Institute in 1888.

Louis Pasteur

When meditating over a disease, I never think of finding a remedy for it, but, instead, a means of preventing it.

Address to the Fraternal Association of Former Students of the Ecole Centrale des Arts et Manufactures, Paris, 15 May 1884

pasteurization treatment of food to reduce the number of micro-organisms it contains and so protect consumers from disease. Harmful bacteria are killed and the development of others is delayed. For milk, the method involves heating it to 72°C/161°F for 15 seconds followed by rapid cooling to 10°C/50°F or lower. The process also kills beneficial bacteria and reduces the nutritive property of milk.

Patagonia geographic region of South America, in southern Argentina and Chile; area 780,000 sq km/301,000 sq mi. A thinly populated vast plateau area, it stretches from the Río Colorado in central Argentina to the Magellan Straits in the south, and slopes eastwards from the Andes to the Atlantic coast. It consists of the provinces of Neuquén, Rio Negro, Chubut, and Santa Cruz. The main towns are the port of Comodoro Rivadavia (Argentina) and Punta Arenas (Chile).
Related Web site: Patagonia: Life at the End of the Earth http://www.pbs.org/edens/patagonia/

Pataliputra ancient northern Indian city, founded *c.* 490 BC as a small fort (Pataligrama) near the River Ganges within the kingdom of ▷Magadha *janapada*. It became the capital for both the Mauryan dynasty under Chandragupta and, later, of the imperial Guptas. During the reign of Emperor Asoka in the 3rd century BC, it was the world's largest city, with a population of 150,000–300,000. As **Patna**, it remains an important regional centre.

patella (or **kneecap**) flat bone embedded in the knee tendon of birds and mammals, which protects the joint from injury.

Pater, Walter Horatio (1839–1894) English scholar, essayist, and art critic. He published *Studies in the History of the Renaissance* (1873), which expressed the idea of 'art for art's sake' that influenced the ▷Aesthetic Movement.

Pathan (or Pathkun) member of a people of northwestern Pakistan and Afghanistan, numbering about 14 million (1984). The majority are Sunni Muslims. The Pathans speak Pashto, a member of the Indo-Iranian branch of the Indo-European family.

Pathé, Charles (1863–1957) French film pioneer. He began his career selling projectors in 1896 and with the profits formed Pathé Frères with his brothers. In 1901 he embarked on film production and by 1908 had become the world's biggest producer, with branches worldwide. He also developed an early colour process and established a weekly newsreel, *Pathé Journal*.

pathogen (Greek 'disease producing') in medicine, any micro-organism that causes disease. Most pathogens are ▷parasites, and the diseases they cause are incidental to their search for food or shelter inside the host. Nonparasitic organisms, such as soil bacteria or those living in the human gut and feeding on waste foodstuffs, can also become pathogenic to a person whose immune system or liver is damaged. The larger parasites that can cause disease, such as nematode worms, are not usually described as pathogens.

pathology medical speciality concerned with the study of disease processes and how these provoke structural and functional changes in the body.

patina effect produced on bronze by oxidation, which turns the surface green, and by extension any lacquering or finishing technique, other than gilding, applied to bronze objects. Patina can also mean the surface texture of old furniture, silver, and antique objects.

Patmos Greek island in the Aegean Sea, one of the Dodecanese; the chief town is Hora. St John is said to have written the New Testament Book of Revelation while in exile here.

Patna capital of ▷Bihar state, India, on the River Ganges, 450 km/280 mi northwest of Calcutta; population (1991) 917,000. It has remains of a hall built by the emperor ▷Asoka in the 3rd century BC; it was capital of several kingdoms in the succeeding centuries, under the name of ▷Pataliputra.

Patou, Jean (1880–1936) French clothes designer. He opened a fashion house in 1919 and was an overnight success. His swimsuits and innovative designs were popular in the 1920s and he dominated both the couture and the ready-to-wear sectors of the fashion world until his death. He had a great influence on the designers he employed, many of whom went on to make names for themselves.

Patras (Greek *Pátrai*) industrial city (hydroelectric installations, textiles, paper) in the northwestern Peloponnese region, Greece, on the Gulf of Patras; population (1991) 155,200. The ancient **Patrai**, it is the only one of the 12 cities of the ancient Greek province of ▷Achaea to survive.

patriarch (Greek 'ruler of a family') in the Old Testament, one of the ancestors of the human race, and especially those of the ancient Hebrews, from Adam to Abraham, Isaac, Jacob, and his sons (who became patriarchs of the Hebrew tribes). In the Eastern Orthodox Church, the term refers to the leader of a national church.

patriarchy (Greek 'rule of the father') form of social organization in which a man heads and controls the family unit. By extension, in a patriarchal society men also control larger social and working groups as well as government. The definition has been broadened by feminists to describe the dominance of male values throughout society.

patrician member of a privileged class in ancient Rome, which originally dominated the ▷Senate. During the 5th and 4th centuries BC many of the rights formerly exercised by the patricians alone were extended to the plebeians, and patrician descent became a matter of prestige.

Patrick, St (*c.* 389–*c.* 461) Patron saint of Ireland. Born in Britain, probably in South Wales, he was carried off by pirates to six years' slavery in Antrim, Ireland, before escaping either to Britain or Gaul – his poor Latin suggests the former – to train as a missionary. He is variously said to have landed again in Ireland in 432 or 456, and his work was a vital factor in the spread of Christian influence there. His symbols are snakes and shamrocks; feast day 17 March.

Patrick is credited with founding the diocese of Armagh, of which he was bishop, though this was probably the work of a 'lost apostle' (Palladius or Secundinus). Of his writings only his *Confessio* and an *Epistola* survive.

Related Web site: Patrick, St http://www.newadvent.org/cathen/11554a.htm

patronage power to give a favoured appointment to an office or position in politics, business, or the church; or sponsorship of the arts. Patronage was for centuries bestowed mainly by individuals (in Europe often royal or noble) or by the church. In the 20th century, patrons have tended to be political parties, the state, and – in the arts – private industry and foundations.

In Britain, where it was nicknamed 'Old Corruption', patronage existed in the 16th century, but was most common from the

2Restoration of 1660 to the 19th century, when it was used to manage elections and ensure party support. Patronage was used not only for the preferment of friends, but also as a means of social justice, often favouring, for example, the families of those in adversity. Political patronage has largely been replaced by a system of meritocracy (in which selection is by open competition rather than by personal recommendation).

Ecclesiastical patronage was the right of selecting a person to a living or benefice, termed an advowson.

Salaried patronage was the nomination to a salaried post: at court, in government, the Church of England, the civil service, the armed services, or to the East India Company. The Northcote-Trevelyan report of 1854 on the civil service advised the replacement of patronage in the civil service by open competitive examination, although its recommendations were carried out only later in the century. Commissions in the British army were bought and sold openly until the practice was abolished in 1871. Church livings were bought and sold as late as 1874.

Patronage survives today in the political honours system (awards granted to party supporters) and the appointment of university professors, leaders of national corporations, and government bodies or ▷quangos, which is often by invitation rather than by formal application. Selection on grounds other than solely the basis of ability lives on today with the practice of positive ▷discrimination.

Patten, Chris(topher Francis) (1944–) British Conservative politician, governor of Hong Kong 1992–97. He was MP for Bath 1979–1992 and Conservative Party chair 1990–92, orchestrating the party's campaign for the 1992 general election, in which he lost his parliamentary seat. He accepted the governorship of Hong Kong for the crucial five years prior to its transfer to China in 1997. He went on to take part in the reform of the Royal Ulster Constabulary.

Patterson, P(ercival) J(ames) (1935–) Jamaican centre-left politician and lawyer; prime minister from 1992. Having lost his seat in the crushing defeat of the People's National Party (PNP) by the Jamaican Labour Party (JLP) in 1980, he oversaw the PNP's successful reorganization as a moderate centre-left force. Re-elected in 1989, he was chosen to succeed Michael ▷Manley as prime minister by an overwhelming majority in 1992, despite having resigned his post of finance minister amidst financial scandal the previous year. He pursued a moderate, free-market economic strategy and achieved an increased majority for the PNP in 1993, and an unprecedented third consecutive term in 1997.

Patton, George Smith (1885–1945) US general in World War II, known as 'Old Blood and Guts'. During World War I, he formed the first US tank force and led it in action in 1918. He was appointed to command the 2nd Armored Division in 1940 and became commanding general of the First Armored Corps in 1941. In 1942 he led the Western Task Force that landed at Casablanca, Morocco. After commanding the 7th Army in the invasion of Sicily, he led the 3rd Army across France and into Germany, and in 1945 took over the 15th Army.

Paul six popes, including:

Paul VI, Giovanni Battista Montini (1897–1978) Pope from 1963. His encyclical *Humanae Vitae/Of Human Life* (1968) reaffirmed the church's traditional teaching on birth control, thus following the minority report of the commission originally appointed by Pope John rather than the majority view.

Paul, St (*c.* AD 3–*c.* AD 68) Christian missionary and martyr; in the New Testament, one of the apostles and author of 13 epistles. Originally opposed to Christianity, he took part in the stoning of St Stephen. He is said to have been converted by a vision on the road to Damascus. After his conversion he made great missionary journeys, for example to Philippi and Ephesus, becoming known as the Apostle of the Gentiles (non-Jews). His emblems are a sword and a book; feast day 29 June.

The Jewish form of his name is Saul. He was born in Tarsus (now in Turkey), son of well-to-do Pharisees, and had Roman citizenship. On his return to Jerusalem after his missionary journeys, he was arrested, appealed to Caesar, and (as a citizen) was sent to Rome for trial about 57 or 59. After two years in prison, he may have been released before his final arrest and execution under the emperor Nero.

St Paul's theology was rigorous on such questions as sin and atonement, and his views on the role of women were adopted by the Christian church generally.

Paul, Les (1915–) Adopted name of Lester Polfuss. US inventor of the solid-body electric guitar in the early 1940s. He was also a pioneer of recording techniques including overdubbing and electronic echo. The Gibson Les Paul guitar was first marketed in 1952 (the first commercial solid-body guitar was made by Leo

▷Fender). As a guitarist in the late 1940s and 1950s he recorded with the singer Mary Ford (1928–1977).

Pauling, Linus Carl (1901–1994) US theoretical chemist and biologist. He was awarded the Nobel Prize for Chemistry in 1954 for his study of the nature of chemical bonds, especially in complex substances. His ideas are fundamental to modern theories of molecular structure. He also investigated the properties and uses of vitamin C as related to human health. He was awarded the Nobel Prize for Peace in 1962 for having campaigned for the control of nuclear weapons and nuclear testing. Pauling's work on the nature of the chemical bond included much new information about interatomic distances. Applying his knowledge of molecular structure to proteins in blood, he discovered that many proteins have structures held together with hydrogen bonds, giving them helical shapes.

He was a pioneer in the application of quantum-mechanical principles to the structures of molecules, relating them to interatomic distances and bond angles by X-ray and electron diffraction, magnetic effects, and thermochemical techniques. In 1928, Pauling introduced the concept of hybridization of bonds. This provided a clear, basic insight into the framework structure of all carbon compounds – in effect, of the whole of organic chemistry. He also studied electronegativity of atoms and polarization (location of electrons) in chemical bonds. Electronegativity values can be used to show why certain substances, such as hydrochloric acid, are acid, whereas others, such as sodium hydroxide, are alkaline. Much of this work was consolidated in his book *The Nature of the Chemical Bond* (1939).

Related Web site: Dr Linus Pauling Profile http://www.achievement.org/autodoc/page/pau0pro-1

Pavarotti, Luciano (1935–) Italian tenor. He has an impressive dynamic range. His operatic roles have included Rodolfo in *La Bohème*, Cavaradossi in *Tosca*, the Duke of Mantua in *Rigoletto*, and Nemorino in *L'Elisir d'amore*. He achieved much in popularizing opera, performing to wide audiences outside the opera houses including open-air concerts in New York and London city parks. He collaborated with José Carreras and Placido Domingo in a recording of operatic hits coinciding with the World Cup soccer series in Rome in 1990, calling themselves the Three Tenors. Pavarotti's rendition of 'Nessun Dorma' from Puccini's *Turandot* was adopted as the theme music for the series.

Pavlov, Ivan Petrovich (1849–1936) Russian physiologist who was awarded a Nobel Prize for Physiology or Medicine in 1904 for his discovery of the physiology of digestion. Pavlov studied conditioned reflexes in animals (see ▷conditioning). His work had a great impact on behavioural theory (see ▷behaviourism) and learning theory.

Pavlova, Anna (1881–1931) Russian dancer. Prima ballerina of the Imperial Ballet from 1906, she left Russia in 1913, and went on to become one of the world's most celebrated exponents of classical ballet. With London as her home, she toured extensively with her own company, influencing dancers worldwide with roles such as Mikhail ▷Fokine's *The Dying Swan* solo (1907). She was opposed to the modern reforms of Diaghilev's Ballets Russes, adhering strictly to conservative aesthetics.

pawpaw (or papaw) small tree belonging to the custard-apple family, native to the eastern USA. It produces oblong fruits 13 cm/5 in long with yellowish edible flesh. The name 'pawpaw' is also used for the ▷papaya. (*Asimina triloba*, family Annonaceae.)

Paxton, Joseph (1801–1865) English architect. He was also garden superintendent to the Duke of Devonshire from 1826. He designed the Great Exhibition building 1851 (the Crystal Palace), which was revolutionary in its structural use of glass and iron. He was knighted in 1851.

Pay-As-You-Earn (PAYE) system of tax collection in the UK in which income tax is deducted on a regular basis by the employer from wages before they are paid.

Pays de la Loire agricultural region of western France, comprising the *départements* of Loire-Atlantique, Maine-et-Loire, ▷Mayenne, Sarthe, and Vendée; area 32,100 sq km/12,400 sq mi; population (1999 est) 3,222,100. The administrative centre is ▷Nantes. Industries include shipbuilding and wine production. See picture on p. 735.

Paz, Octavio (1914–1998) Mexican poet, essayist, and political thinker. His works reflect many influences, including Marxism, surrealism, and Aztec mythology. *El laberinto de la soledad/The Labyrinth of Solitude* (1980), the book which brought him to world attention, explores Mexico's heritage. His long poem *Piedra del sol/Sun Stone* (1957) uses contrasting images, centring on the Aztec Calendar Stone (representing the Aztec universe), to symbolize the loneliness of individuals and their search for union with others.

PAYS DE LA LOIRE Chenonceau castle (or château) in the Loire Valley, France, a region famous for its castles. See entry on p. 733. *Image Bank*

He was awarded the Nobel Prize for Literature in 1990. In 1962 Paz was appointed Mexican ambassador to India, but resigned in 1968 in protest against the Mexican government's killing of 200 student demonstrators on the eve of the Olympic Games. In 1971 he founded the monthly magazine *Plural* (later called *Vuelta*), which he used to analyse socialism and liberalism, urging Mexico to become independent of communist and US influences. His publications include *Collected Poems: 1957–87* (1988) and *One Earth, Four or Five Worlds/Tiempo Nublado* (1984).

> **Related Web site: Paz, Octavio** http://www.nobel.se/literature/laureates/1990/paz-bio.html

> **Octavio Paz**
> *We are condemned to kill time: Thus we die little by little.*
> Cuento de los Jardines

Paz, (Estenssoro) Victor (1907–2001) Bolivian president 1952–56, 1960–64, and 1985–89. He founded and led the Movimiento Nacionalista Revolucionario (MNR), which seized power in 1952. His regime extended the vote to Indians, nationalized the country's largest tin mines, embarked on a programme of agrarian reform, and brought inflation under control.

PC abbreviation for ▷Pacific Community.

PC abbreviation for **personal computer; politically correct; police constable; Privy Councillor.**

PCB abbreviation for ▷polychlorinated biphenyl; ▷printed circuit board.

PCP abbreviation for **phencyclidine hydrochloride**, a drug popularly known as angel dust.

pea climbing leguminous plant (see ▷legume) with pods of round green edible seeds, grown since prehistoric times for food. The pea is a popular vegetable and is eaten fresh, canned, frozen, or dried. The **sweet pea** (*Lathyrus odoratus*) of the same family is grown for its scented red, purple, pink, and white butterfly-shaped flowers; it is a popular cottage garden plant. (Edible pea *Pisum sativum*, family Leguminosae.)

Peace Corps US organization of trained men and women, established by President Kennedy in 1961. The Peace Corps provides skilled volunteer workers for Third World countries, especially in the fields of teaching, agriculture, and health, for a period of two years.

peace movement collective opposition to war. The Western peace movements of the late 20th century can trace their origins to the pacifists of the 19th century and conscientious objectors during World War I (see ▷pacifism). The campaigns after World War II have tended to concentrate on nuclear weapons, but there are numerous organizations devoted to peace, some wholly pacifist, some merely opposed to escalation.

peach yellow-reddish round edible fruit of the peach tree, which is cultivated for its fruit in temperate regions and has oval leaves and small, usually pink, flowers. The fruits have thick velvety skins; nectarines are a smooth-skinned variety. (*Prunus persica*, family Rosaceae.)

peacock technically, the male of any of various large ▷pheasants, order Galliformes. The name is most often used for the common peacock *Pavo cristatus*, a bird of the pheasant family, native to South Asia. It is rather larger than a pheasant. The male has a large fan-shaped tail, brightly coloured with blue, green, and purple 'eyes' on a chestnut background, that is raised during courtship displays. The female (peahen) is brown with a small tail.

The hen lays 4–8 eggs in the spring, and incubation takes 30 days. She remains with her chicks eight months. The green peacock, *P. muticus*, native to Southeast Asia, breeds freely with the common peacock. A third species, *Afropavus congensis*, was discovered in the late 1930s in the forests of the Congo. These are much smaller than the common peacock and do not have erectile tail coverts.

Peacock, Thomas Love (1785–1866) English satirical novelist and poet. His unique whimsical novels are full of paradox, prejudice, curious learning, and witty dialogue, interspersed with occasional poems, and he satirizes contemporary ideas, outlooks, and attitudes in a prevailing comic tone. They include *Headlong Hall* (1816), *Melincourt* (1817), and *Nightmare Abbey* (1818), which has very little plot, consisting almost entirely of conversation expressing points of view on contemporary controversies and society.

peacock butterfly butterfly measuring about 5 cm/2 in across the wings, which are a dull deep or brownish-red, and each of which bears an 'eye' rather like those in the peacock's tail. The peacock butterfly *Vanessa io* is in family Nymphalidae, order Lepidoptera, class Insecta, phylum Arthropoda.

Peak District elevated plateau of the south ▷Pennines in northwest Derbyshire, central England; area 1,438 sq km/555 sq mi. It is a tourist region and part of it forms a national park. The highest point is Kinder Scout (636 m/2,087 ft), part of High Peak. In the surrounding area the main cities are Manchester, Sheffield, and Derby, and the town of Bakewell is located within the Peak District.

> **Thomas Love Peacock**
> *Marriage may often be a stormy lake, but celibacy is almost always a muddy horsepond.*
> Melincourt

Peake, Mervyn Laurence (1911–1968) English writer and illustrator. His novels include the grotesque fantasy trilogy *Titus Groan* (1946), *Gormenghast* (1950), and *Titus Alone* (1959), together creating an allegory of the decline of modern civilization. He illustrated most of his own work and produced drawings for an edition of *Treasure Island* (1949), and other works. Among his collections of verse are *The Glassblowers* (1950) and the posthumous *A Book of Nonsense* (1972). He also wrote a play, *The Wit to Woo* (1957).

PEANUT The peanut is a leguminous perennial plant belonging to the pea family.

peanut (or **groundnut** or **monkey nut**) South American vinelike annual plant. After flowering, the flower stalks bend and force the pods into the earth to ripen underground. The nuts are a staple food in many tropical countries and are widely grown in the southern USA. They provide a valuable edible oil and are the basis for a large number of processed foods. (*Arachis hypogaea*, family Leguminosae.)

pear succulent, gritty-textured edible fruit of the pear tree, native to temperate regions of Europe and Asia. White flowers precede the fruits, which have a greenish-yellow and brown skin and taper towards the stalk. Pear trees are cultivated for their fruit which are eaten fresh or canned; a wine known as perry is made from pear juice. (*Pyrus communis*, family Rosaceae.)

pearl shiny, hard, rounded abnormal growth composed of nacre (or mother-of-pearl), a chalky substance. Nacre is secreted by many molluscs, and deposited in thin layers on the inside of the shell around a parasite, a grain of sand, or some other irritant body. After several years of the mantle (the layer of tissue between the shell and the body mass) secreting this nacre, a pearl is formed.

Although commercially valuable pearls are obtained from freshwater mussels and oysters, most precious pearls come from the various species of the family Pteriidae (the pearl oysters) found in tropical waters off northern and western Australia, off the Californian coast, in the Persian Gulf, and in the Indian Ocean. Because of their rarity, large mussel pearls of perfect shape are worth more than those from oysters.

Artificial pearls were first cultivated in Japan in 1893. A tiny bead of shell from a clam, plus a small piece of membrane from another pearl oyster's mantle (to stimulate the secretion of nacre) is inserted in oysters kept in cages in the sea for three years, and then the pearls are harvested.

The UK government in 1998 imposed a total ban on fishing for freshwater pearl mussels, under the Wildlife and Countryside Act of 1981.

Pearl Harbor US Pacific naval base on Oahu island, Hawaii, USA, the scene of a Japanese aerial attack on 7 December 1941, which brought the USA into World War II. The attack took place while Japanese envoys were holding so-called peace talks in Washington. More than 2,000 members of the US armed forces were killed, and a large part of the US Pacific fleet was destroyed or damaged.

The local commanders Admiral Kimmel and Lt-Gen Short were relieved of their posts and held responsible for the fact that the base was totally unprepared at the time of the attack, but recent information indicates that warnings of the attack given to the USA (by British intelligence and others) were withheld from Kimmel and Short by President Franklin D Roosevelt. US public opinion

PEA The Fyfield pea *Lathyrus tuberosus* is one of a number of large-flowered peas that are now widely grown as ornamental flowers. *Premaphotos Wildlife*

PEARL HARBOR An aerial view of the Arizona Memorial, Oahu, Hawaii, USA, which floats above the half-submerged wreck of the USS *Arizona*. The battleship was sunk by Japanese forces on 7 December, 1941, at Pearl Harbor, Hawaii, during World War II. *Image Bank*

was very much against entering the war, and Roosevelt wanted an excuse to change popular sentiments and take the USA into the war. The Japanese, angered by US embargoes of oil and other war material and convinced that US entry into the war was inevitable, had hoped to force US concessions. Instead, the attack galvanized public opinion and raised anti-Japanese sentiment to fever pitch; war was declared shortly thereafter.

Related Web site: Pearl Harbor http://www.execpc.com/~dschaaf/mainmenu.html

Pears, Peter Neville Luard (1910–1986) English tenor. He
was the life companion of Benjamin ▷Britten and with him co-founded the Aldeburgh Festival. He inspired and collaborated with Britten in a rich catalogue of song cycles and operatic roles, exploiting a distinctively airy and luminous tone, from the title role in *Peter Grimes* (1947) to Aschenbach in *Death in Venice* (1973).

Pearse, Patrick Henry (1879–1916) Irish writer,
educationalist and revolutionary. He was prominent in the Gaelic revival, and a leader of the ▷Easter Rising in 1916. Proclaimed president of the provisional government, he was court-martialled and shot after its suppression.

Pearse was a founding member of the Irish Volunteers, and was inducted into the Irish Republican Brotherhood (the Irish wing of the ▷Fenian movement) in 1913. He came to believe that a 'blood sacrifice' was needed to awaken the slumbering Irish nation. In a famous graveside oration in 1915, he declared that 'Ireland unfree shall never be at peace'.

He was commander-in-chief of the Volunteers during the Easter Rising in 1916, and read the declaration of the Irish Republic. The rebellion that he led emerged in short order as a defining moment in modern Irish history, its authors as founding martyrs of modern Ireland, and the words of the declaration as the sacred text of modern Irish republicanism.

Pearson, Lester Bowles (1897–1972) Canadian politician,
leader of the Liberal Party from 1958, prime minister 1963–68. He was awarded the Nobel Prize for Peace in 1957 for playing a key role in settling the ▷Suez Crisis of 1956 when as foreign minister 1948–57, he represented Canada at the United Nations (UN).

Peary, Robert Edwin (1856–1920) US polar explorer who,
after several unsuccessful attempts, became the first person to reach the North Pole on 6 April 1909. In 1988 an astronomer claimed Peary's measurements were incorrect.

Peasants' Revolt the rising of the English peasantry in June
1381, the result of economic, social, and political disillusionment. It was sparked off by the attempt to levy a new poll tax in the village of Fobbing, Essex, three times the rates of those imposed in 1377

and 1379. Led by Wat ▷Tyler and John ▷Ball, rebels from southeast England marched on London and demanded reforms. The authorities put down the revolt by pretending to make concessions and then using force.

Following the ▷Black Death, an epidemic of plague in the mid–14th century, a shortage of agricultural workers had led to higher wages. However, the government attempted to return wages to pre-plague levels by passing the Statute of Labourers (1351). Other causes of discontent were the youthfulness of King Richard II, who was only 14 years old; the poor conduct of the Hundred Years' War, which England was losing to France; and complaints about the church led by John ▷Wycliffe and the ▷Lollards. When a third poll tax was enforced in 1381, three times higher than previous levies, riots broke out all over England, especially in Essex and Kent. Wat Tyler and John Ball emerged as leaders and the rebels marched on London to demand reforms. They plundered the city, including John of Gaunt's palace at the Savoy, and freed the prisoners from the prisons at Newgate and Fleet. The young king ▷Richard II attempted to appease the mob, who demanded an end to villeinage and ▷feudalism. The rebels then took the Tower of London and murdered Archbishop Sudbury. The king attempted to make peace at Smithfield, but Tyler was stabbed to death by William Walworth, the lord mayor of London. The young king rode bravely forward and offered to be the rebels' leader. He made concessions to the rebels, and they dispersed, but the concessions were revoked immediately and a fierce repression followed. Nevertheless, many lords realised that the revolt was a 'warning to beware', and began to commute their feudal dues to money rents.

Related Web site: Conflagration: The Peasants' Revolt http://historymedren.about.com/education/historymedren/library/weekly/aa071798.htm

peat fibrous organic substance found in bogs and formed by the incomplete decomposition of plants such as sphagnum moss. Northern Asia, Canada, Finland, Ireland, and other places have large deposits, which have been dried and used as fuel from ancient times. Peat can also be used as a soil additive.

Peat bogs began to be formed when glaciers retreated, about 9,000 years ago. They grow at the rate of only a millimetre a year,

ROBERT PEARY Wearing his Arctic furs, US explorer Robert Peary stands proudly on the deck of his ship, the *Roosevelt*. *Archive Photos*

PEAT Peat cutters at the Ring of Kerry, County Kerry, Republic of Ireland. *Image Bank*

and large-scale digging can result in destruction both of the bog and of specialized plants growing there. The destruction of peat bogs is responsible for diminishing fish stocks in coastal waters; the run off from the peatlands carries high concentrations of iron, which affects the growth of the plankton on which the fish feed.

Approximately 60% of the world's wetlands are peat, and in May 1999 the Ramsar Convention on the Conservation of Wetlands approved a peatlands action plan that should have a major impact on the conservation of peat bogs. In 1999, only 6% of UK peat bogs were undamaged by peat extraction for sale at garden centres. Half of UK peat comes from just three sites (Wedholme Flow, Hatfield Moor, and Thorne Moor), all of which are Sites of Special Scientific Interest (SSSIs). In 1999 there were only 6,270 ha of untouched raised bog remaining in the UK, 3,000 ha in Scotland.

A number of ancient corpses, thought to have been the result of ritual murders, have been found preserved in peat bogs, mainly in Scandinavia. In 1984, Lindow Man, dating from about 500 BC, was found in mainland Britain, near Wilmslow, Cheshire.

pecan nut-producing ▷hickory tree (*C. illinoensis* or *C. pecan*), native to the central USA and northern Mexico and now widely cultivated. The trees grow to over 45 m/150 ft, and the edible nuts are smooth-shelled, the kernel resembling a smooth, oval walnut. (Genus *Carya*, family Juglandaceae.)

peccary one of two species of the New World genus *Tayassu* of piglike hoofed mammals. A peccary has a gland in the middle of its back which secretes a strong-smelling substance. Peccaries are blackish in colour, covered with bristles, and have tusks that point downwards. Adults reach a height of 40 cm/16 in, and a weight of 25 kg/60 lb.

Peck, (Eldred) Gregory (1916–2003) US film actor. He
specialized in strong, upright characters, but also had a gift for light comedy. His films include *Spellbound* (1945), *Duel in the Sun* (1946), *Gentleman's Agreement* (1947), *Roman Holiday* (1953), *To Kill a Mockingbird* (1962), for which he won an Academy Award, and (cast against type as a Nazi doctor) *The Boys from Brazil* (1974). In 1998 he was awarded the National Medal of Arts.

Peckinpah, (David) Sam(uel) (1926–1984) US film
director. Mainly westerns, his films usually featured slow-motion, blood-spurting violence. His best work, such as *The Wild Bunch* (1969), exhibits a magisterial grasp of staging and construction.

pectoral relating to the upper area of the thorax associated with the muscles and bones used in moving the arms or forelimbs, in vertebrates. In birds, the *pectoralis major* is the very large muscle used to produce a powerful downbeat of the wing during flight.

pedicel the stalk of an individual flower, which attaches it to the main floral axis, often developing in the axil of a bract.

pediment in architecture, the triangular structure crowning the portico of a classical building. The pediment was a distinctive feature of Greek temples.

Pedro two emperors of Brazil:

Pedro I (1798–1834) Emperor of Brazil 1822–31. The son of
John VI of Portugal, he escaped to Brazil on Napoleon's invasion, and was appointed regent in 1821. He proclaimed Brazil

independent in 1822 and was crowned emperor, but abdicated in 1831 and returned to Portugal.

Pedro II (1825–1891) Emperor of Brazil 1831–89. He proved an enlightened ruler, but his antislavery measures alienated the landowners, who compelled him to abdicate.

Peel, Robert (1788–1850) British Conservative politician. As home secretary 1822–27 and 1828–30, he founded the modern police force and in 1829 introduced Roman Catholic emancipation. He was prime minister 1834–35 and 1841–46, when his repeal of the ▷Corn Laws caused him and his followers to break with the party. He became 2nd baronet in 1830.

Peel, born in Lancashire, entered Parliament as a Tory in 1809. After the passing of the Reform Bill of 1832, which he had resisted, he reformed the Tories under the name of the Conservative Party, on a basis of accepting necessary changes and seeking middle-class support. He fell from prime ministerial office because his repeal of the Corn Laws in 1846 was opposed by the majority of his party. He and his followers then formed a third party standing between the Liberals and Conservatives; the majority of the Peelites, including Gladstone, subsequently joined the Liberals.

peepul another name for the ▷bo tree.

ROBERT PEEL Shown here in a contemporary illustration, Robert Peel was the founder in 1834 of the modern Conservative Party. *Philip Sauvain Picture Collection*

peerage the high nobility; in the UK, holders, in descending order, of the titles of duke, marquess, earl, viscount, and baron. In the late 19th century the peerage was augmented by the Lords of Appeal in Ordinary (the nonhereditary life peers) and, from 1958, by a number of specially created life peers of either sex (usually long-standing members of the House of Commons). Since 1963 peers have been able to disclaim their titles, usually to enable them to take a seat in the Commons (where peers are disqualified from membership).

peer group in the social sciences, people who have a common identity based on such characteristics as similar social status, interests, age, or ethnic group. The concept has proved useful in analysing the power and influence of co-workers, school friends, and ethnic and religious groups in socialization and social behaviour.

Pegasus in astronomy, a constellation of the northern hemisphere, near Cygnus, and represented as the winged horse of Greek mythology.

Pegasus in Greek mythology, the winged horse that sprang from the blood of the ▷Gorgon Medusa when she was decapitated by the hero Perseus. He carried ▷Bellerophon in his fight with the ▷chimera, and was later transformed into a constellation.

pegmatite extremely coarse-grained ▷igneous rock of any composition found in veins; pegmatites are usually associated with large granite masses.

Pei, I(eoh) M(ing) (1917–   ) Chinese-born US modernist architect. He is noted for his innovative high-tech structures, particularly the use of glass walls. His projects include the 70-storey Bank of China, Hong Kong (1987; Asia's tallest building at 368 m/1,209 ft), the glass pyramid in front of the Louvre, Paris, France (1989), and the Miho Museum (1997), in a nature reserve near Kyoto, Japan.

Pei became a US citizen in 1948. His buildings in the USA include the Mile High Center, Denver; Dallas City Hall, Texas; East Building, National Gallery of Art, Washington, DC (1978); John F Kennedy Library Complex and the John Hancock Tower, Boston (1979); and the National Airlines terminal (now owned by TWA) at Kennedy Airport, New York.

Peiping ('northern peace') name of ▷Beijing in China from 1928 to 1949.

pekan (or fisher marten) North American marten (carnivorous mammal) *Martes penanti* about 1.2 m/4 ft long, with a doglike face, and brown fur with white patches on the chest. It eats porcupines.

Peking alternative transcription of ▷Beijing, the capital of China.

pekingese breed of small long-haired dog first bred at the Chinese court as the 'imperial lion dog'. It has a flat skull and flat face, is typically less than 25 cm/10 in tall, and weighs less than 5 kg/11 lb.

Peking man Chinese representative of an early species of human, found as fossils, 500,000–750,000 years old, in the cave of Choukoutien in 1927 near Beijing (Peking). Peking man used chipped stone tools, hunted game, and used fire. Similar varieties of early human have been found in Java and East Africa. Their classification is disputed: some anthropologists classify them as *Homo erectus*, others as *Homo sapiens pithecanthropus*.

Pelagius (*c.* 360–*c.* 420) British theologian. He taught that each person possesses free will (and hence the possibility of salvation), denying Augustine's doctrines of predestination and original sin. Cleared of heresy by a synod in Jerusalem 415, he was later condemned by the pope and the emperor.

pelargonium (or geranium) any of a group of shrubby, tender flowering plants belonging to the geranium family, grown extensively for their colourful white, pink, scarlet, and black-purple flowers. They are the familiar summer bedding and pot 'geraniums'. Ancestors of the garden hybrids came from southern Africa. (Genus *Pelargonium*, family Geraniaceae.)

Pelé (1940–   ) Adopted name of Edson Arantes do Nascimento. Brazilian soccer player. A prolific goal scorer, he appeared in four World Cup competitions 1958–70 and led Brazil to three championships (1958, 1962, 1970).

He spent most of his playing career with the Brazilian team Santos, before ending it with the New York Cosmos in the USA. In a poll conducted by the International Soccer Hall of Fame in 1997 he was voted the world's greatest footballer. Also in 1997 he received an honorary knighthood from Queen Elizabeth II of the UK. In 2000, he was awarded jointly with Diego Maradona the title of FIFA Footballer of the Century.

PELÉ Brazilian soccer player Pelé, who led the national team to victory in the World Cup in 1958, 1962, and 1970. In 1980 he was named athlete of the century. *Archive Photos*

Pelham, Henry (1696–1754) English Whig politician. He held a succession of offices in Robert Walpole's cabinet 1721–42, and was prime minister 1743–54. His influence in the House of Commons was based on systematic corruption rather than ability. He concluded the War of the Austrian Succession and was an able financier.

pelican large water bird of family Pelecanidae, order Pelecaniformes, remarkable for the pouch beneath the bill, which is used as a fishing net and temporary store for catches of fish. Some species grow up to 1.8 m/6 ft and have wingspans of 3 m/10 ft.

The legs are short and the feet large, with four webbed toes; the tail is short and rounded, and the neck long. The wings are long and expansive, and the birds are capable of rapid flight. The species are widely distributed, frequenting the seashore and margins of lakes,

PELICAN A brown pelican in flight. *Image Bank*

and feeding almost exclusively on fish, which are deposited in the pouch for subsequent digestion.

Pelion mountain in Thessaly, Greece, near Mount Ossa; height 1,548 m/5,079 ft. In Greek mythology it was the home of the centaurs, creatures half-human and half-horse.

Pella capital of the ancient kingdom of ▷Macedonia. It was the birthplace of ▷Philip II of Macedon and Alexander the Great. Excavations began in 1957 and many elaborate mosaics have been revealed at the site, 40 km/25 mi northwest of Thessaloniki. It declined after the defeat of Macedonia by Rome 168 BC, and later became a Roman colony.

pellagra chronic disease mostly seen in subtropical countries in which the staple food is maize. It is caused by deficiency of ▷nicotinic acid (one of the B vitamins), which is contained in protein foods, beans and peas, and yeast. Symptoms include diarrhoea, skin eruptions, and mental disturbances.

pellitory-of-the-wall plant belonging to the nettle family, found growing in cracks in walls and rocks and also on banks in western and southern Europe; it is widely cultivated in gardens. The stems are up to 1 m/3 ft tall and reddish, the leaves are lance-shaped, and the greenish male and female flowers grow separately but on the same plant. (*Parietaria judaica*, family Urticaceae.)

Peloponnese (Greek **Peloponnesos**) peninsula forming the southern part of Greece; area 21,549 sq km/8,320 sq mi; population (1991) 1,077,000. It is joined to the mainland by the narrow isthmus of Corinth and is divided into the nomes (administrative areas) of Argolis, Arcadia, Achaea, Elis, Corinth, Lakonia, and Messenia, representing its seven ancient states. It is divided into two regions; Greece West (including Achaea and Elis), and Peloponnese (including Argolis, Arcadia, Corinth, Lakonia, and Messenia).

Peloponnesian War war fought 431–404 BC between Athens and Sparta and their respective allies, involving most of the Greek world from Asia Minor to Sicily and from Byzantium (present-day Istanbul, Turkey) to Crete. Sparked by Spartan fears about the growth of Athenian power, it continued until the Spartan general Lysander captured the Athenian fleet in 405 at Aegospotami and starved the Athenians into surrender in 404. As a result of this victory, Athens' political power collapsed.
Related Web site: Epic of the Peloponnesian War: Historical Commentary http://www.warhorsesim.com/epw_hist.html

Peltier effect in physics, a change in temperature at the junction of two different metals produced when an electric current flows through them. The extent of the change depends on what the conducting metals are, and the nature of change (rise or fall in temperature) depends on the direction of current flow. It is the reverse of the ▷Seebeck effect. It is named after the French physicist Jean Charles Peltier (1785–1845) who discovered it in 1834.

pelvis in vertebrates, the lower area of the abdomen featuring the bones and muscles used to move the legs or hindlimbs. The **pelvic girdle** is a set of bones that allows movement of the legs in relation to the rest of the body and provides sites for the attachment of relevant muscles.

Pembrokeshire (Welsh **Sir Benfro**) unitary authority in southwest Wales; a former county, from 1974 to 1996 it was part of the county of Dyfed.
area 1,588 sq km/613 sq mi **towns** Haverfordwest (administrative headquarters), ▷Milford Haven **physical** bounded on the south by the Bristol Channel; valleys and hills inland; rivers East and West Cleddau **features** Pembrokeshire Coast National Park **industries** oil refinery at ▷Milford Haven, agriculture, fishing, woollen milling **population** (1996) 117,700
Related Web site: Pembrokeshire Coast National Park http://www.pembrokeshirecoast.org.uk/

penal colony settlement established to receive transported convicts and built in part by convict labour. The first examples of penal colonies were those established by the British in New South Wales, Australia, which began European encroachment on the continent; these included Sydney (Port Jackson; 1788–1840), Newcastle (1804–23), and Port Macquarie (1821–36). The prison regime in these settlements was frequently brutal, leading to many deaths and attempted breakouts and revolts. Other notorious penal colonies were Devil's Island, a French institution off the coast of South America, and the vast network of Soviet forced labour camps (or 'gulags') set up under Stalin in remote areas of the Soviet Union, in which millions perished.

penance Roman Catholic sacrament, involving confession of sins and receiving absolution, and works performed (or punishment self-inflicted) in atonement for sin. Penance is worked out nowadays in terms of good deeds rather than routine repetition of prayers.

Penang (Malay **Pulau Pinang**) state in west Peninsular Malaysia, formed of **Penang Island**, Province Wellesley, and the Dindings on the mainland; area 1,030 sq km/398 sq mi; capital Penang (George Town); population (1993) 1,141,500. Penang Island was bought by Britain from the ruler of Kedah in 1785; Province Wellesley was acquired in 1800.

Penda (c. 577–654) King of Mercia, an Anglo-Saxon kingdom in England, from about 632. He raised Mercia to a powerful kingdom, and defeated and killed two Northumbrian kings, Edwin in 632 and ▷Oswald in 642. He was killed in battle by Oswy, king of Northumbria.

Penderecki, Krzysztof (1933–) Polish composer. His expressionist works, such as the *Threnody for the Victims of Hiroshima* (1961) for strings, employ cluster and percussion effects. He later turned to religious subjects and a more orthodox style, as in the *Magnificat* (1974) and the *Polish Requiem* (1980–83). His opera *The Black Mask* (1986) uncovered a new vein of surreal humour.

pendulum weight (called a 'bob') swinging at the end of a rod or cord. The regularity of a pendulum's swing was used in making the first really accurate clocks in the 17th century. Pendulums can be used for measuring the acceleration due to gravity (an important constant in physics).

Penelope in Greek mythology, the wife of ▷Odysseus, king of Ithaca; their son was ▷Telemachus. She represented wifely faithfulness. While Odysseus was absent at the siege of Troy, she kept her many suitors at bay by asking them to wait while she completed a shroud for Laertes, her father-in-law; every night she unravelled her weaving. When Odysseus returned after 20 years, he and Telemachus killed her suitors.

Penfield, Wilder Graves (1891–1976) Canadian neurosurgeon who, while developing surgical options for the treatment of ▷epilepsy, located several functional areas of the cerebral cortex by stimulating the patient's brain electrically while he or she was conscious. He demonstrated that sensations and memories, including memories that could not be recalled except by electrical stimulation, had specific locations in the brain that remained constant. He devised the homunculus, a schematic representation showing the site and relative proportions of the cortical areas specialized for motor and sensory functions.

penguin marine flightless bird, family Spheniscidae, order Sphenisciformes, mostly black and white, found in the southern hemisphere. They comprise 18 species in six genera. Males are usually larger than the females. Penguins range in size from 40 cm/1.6 ft to 1.2 m/4 ft tall, and have thick feathers to protect them from the intense cold. They are awkward on land (except on snow slopes down which they propel themselves at a rapid pace), but their wings have evolved into flippers, making them excellent swimmers. Penguins congregate to breed in 'rookeries', and often spend many months incubating their eggs while their mates are out at sea feeding. They feed on a mixture of fish, squid, and krill.

The wing is long and has no covert or quill feathers, and always remains open.

The feathers are tiny, with very broad shafts and little vane or web. The legs of the birds are placed far back, and in the water the feet are stretched out straight behind and held motionless, the wings working rapidly as if being used in flight. Moult in penguins is general and areas of feathers are lost all at once. It is usually a rapid process unlike the ordered progressive moult of flying birds. Penguins generally moult once a year, and have to stay out of the water during this time, without feeding.

The nest is often no more than a slight hollow in the ground, but some penguins, especially the Adelie penguins *Pygoscelis adeliae*, collect stones, with which they bank the nest round. One or two eggs are laid, and both birds, but chiefly the male, attend to their incubation. Both parents are very devoted to the young, one always staying to guard them, the other bringing them sea crustaceans and other small animals, which the young take by pushing their beaks far down the parent's throat.

They are very social birds, living together, and usually breed in vast colonies, always returning to the same rookery (breeding group). The young gather in groups while the parents are foraging for food. When the parents return, the chicks often have to chase for food, with the stronger chick being fed first. They spend much time preening themselves and each other (allopreening).

It was estimated in 1997 that the penguin population fell 20% in 10 years. Zoologists blame over-fishing, particularly by large trawling fleets.

Related Web site: Penguin Page http://www.vni.net/~kwelch/penguins/

penicillin any of a group of ▷antibiotic (bacteria killing) compounds obtained from filtrates of moulds of the genus *Penicillium* (especially *P. notatum*) or produced synthetically. Penicillin was the first antibiotic to be discovered (by Alexander ▷Fleming); it kills a broad spectrum of bacteria, many of which cause disease in humans.

The use of the original type of penicillin is limited by the increasing resistance of ▷pathogens and by allergic reactions in patients. Since 1941, numerous other antibiotics of the penicillin family have been discovered which are more selective against, or resistant to, specific micro-organisms.

Peninsular War war of 1808–14 caused by the French emperor Napoleon's invasion of Portugal and Spain. British expeditionary forces under Sir Arthur Wellesley (Duke of ▷Wellington), combined with Spanish and Portuguese resistance, succeeded in defeating the French at Vimeiro in 1808, Talavera in 1809, Salamanca in 1812, and Vittoria in 1813. The results were inconclusive, and the war was ended by Napoleon's forced abdication in 1814.

penis male reproductive organ containing the ▷urethra, the channel through which urine and semen are voided. It transfers sperm to the female reproductive tract to fertilize the ovum. In mammals, the penis is made erect by vessels that fill with blood, and in most mammals (but not humans) is stiffened by a bone.

Snakes and lizards have a paired structure that serves as a penis; other reptiles have a single organ. A few birds, mainly ducks and geese, also have a type of penis, as do snails, barnacles, and some other invertebrates. Many insects have a rigid, nonerectile male organ, usually referred to as an intromittent organ.

Penn, William (1644–1718) English member of the Society of Friends (Quakers) and founder of the American colony of ▷Pennsylvania. Born in London, he joined the Society in 1667 and was imprisoned several times for his beliefs. In 1681 he obtained a grant of land in America (in settlement of a ebt owed by King Charles II to his father) on which he established Pennsylvania as a refuge for persecuted Quakers.

> **William Penn**
> *It is a reproach to religion and government to suffer so much poverty and excess.*
> Reflexions and Maxims pt 1, no. 52

Pennines, the range of hills in northern England, known as the 'the backbone of England'; length (from the Scottish border to the Peaks in Derbyshire) 400 km/250 mi. The highest peak in the Pennines (which are sometimes referred to as mountains rather than hills) is Cross Fell (893 m/2,930 ft). It is the watershed for the main rivers of

PENINSULAR WAR This satirical cartoon depicts French emperor Napoleon with his brother Joseph Bonaparte, king of Spain, pondering the events of 1808. *Philip Sauvain Picture Collection*

northeast England. The rocks are carboniferous limestone and millstone grit, the land high moorland and fell.

Pennsylvania state in northeastern USA. It is nicknamed the Keystone State. Pennsylvania ratified the US Constitution in 1787, becoming the 2nd state to join the Union. It is bordered to the north by New York, with a small coastal strip on Lake Erie, to the west by Ohio and the West Virginia panhandle, to the south, on what was the ▷Mason-Dixon Line, by West Virginia, Maryland, and Delaware, and to the east by New Jersey, across the Delaware River. Pennsylvania was the hub of US industry in the late 19th and early 20th century.

population (1995) 12,071,800　**area** 117,400 sq km/45,316 sq mi **capital** Harrisburg　**towns and cities** Philadelphia, Pittsburgh, Erie, Allentown, Scranton　**industries and products** hay, cereals, mushrooms, cattle, poultry, dairy products, cement, limestone, coal, steel, petroleum products, pharmaceuticals, chemicals, motor vehicles and equipment, electronic components, textiles, tourism **Related Web site: Pennsylvania History** http://www.ushistory.org/pennsylvania/index.html

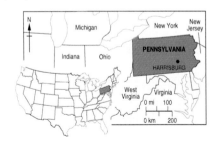

Pennsylvanian period US term for the Upper or Late ▷Carboniferous period of geological time, 323–290 million years ago; it is named after the US state, which contains vast coral deposits.

pennyroyal European perennial plant belonging to the mint family, with oblong leaves and clusters or whorls of purplish flowers growing around the stem at intervals. It is found in wet places on sandy soil. (*Mentha pulegium*, family Labiatae.)

pension organized form of saving for retirement. Pension schemes, which may be government-run or privately administered, involve regular payment for a qualifying period; when the person retires, a payment is made each week or month from the invested pension fund. Pension funds have today become influential investors in major industries; 44% of UK shares are owned by pension funds (1995).

PENGUIN Magellanic penguins (*Spheniscus magellanicus*) heading for the sea. They are found on the Pacific and Atlantic coasts around South America and are medium-sized penguins, reaching about 71 cm/ 28 in in size. *K G Preston-Mafham/Premaphotos Wildlife*

pentadactyl limb typical limb of the mammals, birds, reptiles, and amphibians. These vertebrates (animals with backbone) are all descended from primitive amphibians whose immediate ancestors were fleshy-finned fish. The limb which evolved in those amphibians had three parts: a 'hand/foot' with five digits (fingers/toes), a lower limb containing two bones, and an upper limb containing one bone.

Pentagon the headquarters of the US Department of Defense, Arlington, Virginia from 1947, situated on the Potomac River opposite Washington DC. One of the world's largest office buildings (five storeys high and five-sided, with a pentagonal central court), it houses the administrative and command headquarters for the US armed forces and has become synonymous with the military establishment bureaucracy. On ▷September 11th 2001 it was damaged by an aircraft flown by terrorists.

pentagon five-sided plane figure. The regular pentagon has ▷golden section proportions between its sides and diagonals. The five-pointed star formed by drawing all the diagonals of a regular pentagon is called a **pentagram**. This star has further golden sections.

pentanol $C_5H_{11}OH$ (common name **amyl alcohol**) clear, colourless, oily liquid, usually having a characteristic choking odour. It is obtained by the fermentation of starches and from the distillation of petroleum.

Pentateuch Greek (and Christian) name for the first five books of the Bible, ascribed to Moses, and called the ▷Torah by Jews.

pentathlon five-sport competition. Pentathlon consists of former military training pursuits: swimming, fencing, running, horsemanship, and shooting. It has been an Olympic event for men since 1912, but the Sydney 2000 Games were the first Olympics to include a women's event. The first modern pentathlon world championships for men took place in 1949, and for women in 1981.

Pentecost in Judaism, the festival of *Shavuot*, celebrated on the 50th day after ▷Passover in commemoration of the giving of the Ten Commandments to Moses on Mount Sinai, and the end of the grain harvest; in the Christian church, Pentecost is the day on which the apostles experienced inspiration of the Holy Spirit, commemorated on Whit Sunday.

Related Web site: Pentecost (Whitsunday) http://www.newadvent.org/cathen/15614b.htm

Pentecostal movement Christian revivalist movement that was inspired by the experience of the apostles after the resurrection of Christ. The apostles were baptized in the Holy Spirit and were able to speak in tongues. The Pentecostal Movement represents a reaction against the rigid theology and formal worship of the traditional churches. It originated in the USA in 1906.

Pentecostalists believe in the literal word of the Bible and faith healing; glossalia, or speaking in tongues, often occurs. It is an intensely missionary faith, and recruitment has been rapid since the 1960s: worldwide membership is more than 10 million.

peony any of a group of perennial plants native to Europe, Asia, and North America, remarkable for their large, round, brilliant white, pink, or red flowers. Most popular in gardens are the common peony (*P. officinalis*), the white peony (*P. lactiflora*), and the taller tree peony (*P. suffruticosa*). (Genus *Paeonia*, family Paeoniaceae.)

Related Web site: Peonies – Glorious in Bloom http://www.munchkinnursery.com/newsletter/peonies/index.html

Pepin the Short (*c.* 714–*c.* 768) King of the Franks from 751. The son of Charles Martel, he acted as Mayor of the Palace to the last Merovingian king, Childeric III, deposed him and assumed the royal title himself, founding the ▷Carolingian dynasty. He was ▷Charlemagne's father.

pepper climbing plant native to the East Indies. When gathered green, the berries are crushed to release the seeds for the spice called black pepper. When the berries are ripe, the seeds are removed and their outer skin is discarded, to produce white pepper. Chilli pepper, cayenne or red pepper, and the sweet peppers used as a vegetable come from ▷capsicums native to the New World. (*Piper nigrum*, family Piperaceae.)

peppermint perennial herb of the mint family, native to Europe, with oval aromatic leaves and purple flowers. Oil of peppermint is used in medicine and confectionery. (*Mentha piperita*, family Labiatae.)

pepsin enzyme that breaks down proteins during digestion. It requires a strongly acidic environment and is present in the stomach.

peptide molecule comprising two or more ▷amino acid molecules (not necessarily different) joined by **peptide bonds**, whereby the acid group of one acid is linked to the amino group of the other (–CO.NH). The number of amino acid molecules in the peptide is indicated by referring to it as a di-, tri-, or polypeptide (two, three, or many amino acids).

Proteins are built up of interacting polypeptide chains with various types of bonds occurring between the chains. Incomplete hydrolysis (splitting up) of a protein yields a mixture of peptides, examination of which helps to determine the sequence in which the amino acids occur within the protein.

Pepys, Samuel (1633–1703) English naval administrator and diarist. His *Diary* (1660–69) is a unique record of the daily life of the period, the historical events of the Restoration, the manners and scandals of the court, naval administration, and Pepys's own interests, weaknesses, and intimate feelings. Written in shorthand, it was not deciphered until 1825.

Pepys entered the Navy Office in 1660 and was secretary to the Admiralty from 1672–79. He was imprisoned in 1679 in the Tower of London on suspicion of being connected with the Popish Plot (see Titus ▷Oates). He was reinstated as secretary to the Admiralty in 1684, but was finally deprived of his post after the 1688 Revolution. He published *Memoires of the Navy* in 1690. Pepys abandoned writing his diary because he believed, mistakenly, that his eyesight was about to fail – in fact, it continued to serve him for 30 or more years of active life.

> **Samuel Pepys**
> *Strange to see how a good dinner and feasting reconciles everybody.*
> *Diary*, 9 November 1665

The original manuscript of the *Diary*, preserved in Cambridge together with other papers, is in six volumes, containing more than 3,000 pages. It is closely written in cipher (a form of shorthand), which Pepys probably used in case his journal should fall into unfriendly hands during his life or be rashly published after his death. Highlights include his accounts of the Great Plague of London in 1665, the Fire of London in 1666, and the sailing up the Thames of the Dutch fleet in 1667.

Perak state of west Peninsular Malaysia; capital Ipoh; area 21,000 sq km/8,000 sq mi; population (1993) 2,222,400. It produces tin and rubber. The government is a sultanate. The other principal city is Taiping.

percentage way of representing a number as a ▷fraction of 100. Thus 45 percent (45%) equals $\frac{45}{100}$, and 45% of 20 is $\frac{45}{100} \times 20 = 9$.

In general, if a quantity x changes to y, the percentage change is $100(x - y)/x$. Thus, if the number of people in a room changes from 40 to 50, the percentage increase is $(100 \times 10)/40 = 25\%$. To express a fraction as a percentage, its denominator must first be converted to 100 – for example, $\frac{1}{8} = 12.5/100 = 12.5\%$. The use of percentages often makes it easier to compare fractions that do not have a common denominator.

To convert a fraction to a percentage on a calculator, divide numerator by denominator. The percentage will correspond to the first figures of the decimal, for example $\frac{7}{12} = 0.5833333 = 58.3\%$ correct to three decimal places.

The percentage sign is thought to have been derived as an economy measure when recording in the old counting houses; writing in the numeric symbol for $\frac{25}{100}$ of a cargo would take two lines of parchment, and hence the '100' denominator was put alongside the 25 and rearranged to '%'.

perch any of the largest order of spiny-finned bony fishes, the Perciformes, with some 8,000 species. This order includes the sea basses, cichlids, damselfishes, mullets, barracudas, wrasses, and gobies. Perches of the freshwater genus *Perca* are found in Europe, Asia, and North America. They have varied shapes and are usually a greenish colour. They are very prolific, spawning when about three years old, and have voracious appetites.

percussion instrument musical instrument played by being struck with the hand or a beater. Percussion instruments can be divided into those that can be tuned to produce a sound of definite pitch, such as the timpani, tubular bells, glockenspiel, xylophone, and piano, and those of indefinite pitch, including the bass drum, tambourine, triangle, cymbals, and castanets.

Percy, Henry 'Hotspur' (1364–1403) English soldier, son of the 1st Earl of Northumberland. In repelling a border raid, he defeated the Scots at Homildon Hill, Durham, in 1402. He was killed at the Battle of Shrewsbury while in revolt against Henry IV.

perennating organ in plants, that part of a ▷biennial plant or herbaceous perennial that allows it to survive the winter; usually a root, tuber, rhizome, bulb, or corm.

perennial plant plant that lives for more than two years. Herbaceous perennials have aerial stems and leaves that die each autumn. They survive the winter by means of an underground storage (perennating) organ, such as a bulb or rhizome. Trees and shrubs or woody perennials have stems that persist above ground throughout the year, and may be either ▷deciduous or ▷evergreen. See also ▷annual plant, ▷biennial plant.

Peres, Shimon (1923–) Israeli Labour politician, prime minister 1984–86 and 1995–96. He was prime minister, then foreign minister, under a power-sharing agreement with the leader of the Likud Party, Yitzhak ▷Shamir. From 1989 to 1990 he was finance minister in a Labour–Likud coalition. As foreign minister in Yitzhak Rabin's Labour government from 1992, he negotiated the 1993 peace agreement with the ▷Palestine Liberation Organization (PLO). He shared the Nobel Prize for Peace in 1994 with Yitzhak ▷Rabin and PLO leader Yassir ▷Arafat for their agreement of an accord on Palestinian self-rule.

Following the assassination of Rabin in November 1995, Peres succeeded him as prime minister, and pledged to continue the peace process in which they had both been so closely involved, but in May 1996 he was defeated in Israel's first direct elections for prime minister.

Peres emigrated from Poland to Palestine in 1934, but was educated in the USA. In 1959 he was elected to the Knesset (Israeli parliament). He was leader of the Labour Party 1977–92, when he was replaced by Rabin.

perestroika (Russian 'restructuring') in Soviet politics, the wide-ranging economic and political reforms initiated from 1985 by Mikhail Gorbachev, finally leading to the demise of the Soviet Union. Originally, in the economic sphere, *perestroika* was conceived as involving 'intensive development' concentrating on automation and improved labour efficiency. It evolved to attend increasingly to market indicators and incentives ('market socialism') and the gradual dismantling of the Stalinist central-planning system, with decision-taking being devolved to self-financing enterprises.

Pérez de Cuéllar, Javier (1920–) Peruvian politician and diplomat, fifth secretary general of the United Nations 1982–91 and prime minister of Peru from 2000. He raised the standing of the UN by his successful diplomacy in ending the Iran–Iraq War in 1988 and in securing the independence of Namibia in 1989. He was a candidate in the Peruvian presidential elections of 1995, but was defeated by his opponent Alberto Fujimori, who resigned in 2000. He was unable to resolve the Gulf conflict resulting from Iraq's invasion of Kuwait in 1990 before combat against Iran by the UN coalition began in January 1991, but later in 1991 he negotiated the release of Western hostages held in Beirut. A delegate to the first UN General Assembly 1946–47, he subsequently held several ambassadorial posts, including ambassador to Switzerland and the USSR. Between 1971 and 1975, he was Peru's permanent representative to the UN, becoming an undersecretary in 1979.

perfect competition in economics, a market in which there are many potential and actual buyers and sellers, each being too small to be an individual influence on the price; the market is open to all and the products being traded are homogeneous. At the same time, the producers are seeking the maximum profit and consumers the best value for money. There are many economic, social, and political barriers to perfect competition, not least because the underlying assumptions are unrealistic and in conflict. Nevertheless some elements are applicable in free trade.

performance art type of modern art combining elements of the visual arts and the theatrical arts (sometimes including music) that flourished in the late 1960s and early 1970s. It often overlaps with other avant-garde forms of expression, particularly body art. The term happening is sometimes used synonymously with performance art, but happenings are often more informal and improvised than performance art, which is usually carefully planned.

performing right permission to perform ▷copyright musical or dramatic works in public; this is subject to licence and the collection of fees. The first performing right society was established in 1851 in France. In the UK the Copyright Act 1842 was the first to encompass musical compositions. The agent for live performances is the Performing Right Society, founded in 1914; the rights for recorded or broadcast performance are administered by the Mechanical Copyright Protection Society, founded in 1924.

Pergamum ancient Greek city in Mysia in western Asia Minor, which became the capital of an independent kingdom in 283 BC under the Attalid dynasty. As the ally of Rome it achieved great political importance in the 2nd century BC, and became a centre of art and culture. It had a famous library, the contents of which were transported to Alexandria when they were given by ▷Mark Antony to Cleopatra, queen of Egypt. Pergamum was the birthplace of the physician ▷Galen. Most of its territory became the Roman province of Asia in 133 BC, when the childless King Attalus III bequeathed it to Rome. Close to its site is the modern Turkish town of Bergama.

Pergau Dam hydroelectric dam on the Pergau River in Malaysia, near the Thai border. Building work began in 1991 with money from the UK foreign aid budget. Concurrently, the Malaysian government bought around £1 billion worth of arms from the UK. The suggested linkage of arms deals to aid became the subject of a UK government enquiry from March 1994. In November 1994 a High Court ruled as illegal British foreign secretary Douglas ▷Hurd's allocation of £234 million towards the funding of the dam, on the grounds that it was not of economic or humanitarian benefit to the Malaysian people.

perianth in botany, a collective term for the outer whorls of the flower, which protect the reproductive parts during development. In most ▷dicotyledons the perianth is composed of two distinct whorls, the calyx of ▷sepals and the corolla of ▷petals, whereas in many ▷monocotyledons the sepals and petals are indistinguishable and the segments of the perianth are then known individually as tepals.

Peri, Jacopo (1561–1633) Italian composer who lived in Florence in the service of the Medici. His experimental melodic opera *Euridice* (1600) established the opera form and influenced Monteverdi. His first opera, *Dafne* (1597), believed to be the earliest opera, is now lost.

pericarp wall of a ▷fruit. It encloses the seeds and is derived from the ▷ovary wall. In fruits such as the acorn, the pericarp becomes dry and hard, forming a shell around the seed. In fleshy fruits the pericarp is typically made up of three distinct layers. The **epicarp**, or **exocarp**, forms the tough outer skin of the fruit, while the **mesocarp** is often fleshy and forms the middle layers. The innermost layer or **endocarp**, which surrounds the seeds, may be membranous or thick and hard, as in the ▷drupe (stone) of cherries, plums, and apricots.

Pericles (c. 495–429 BC) Athenian politician under whom Athens reached the height of power. He persuaded the Athenians to reject Sparta's ultimata in 432 BC, and was responsible for Athenian strategy in the opening years of the Peloponnesian War. His policies helped to transform the Delian League into an empire, but the disasters of the ▷Peloponnesian War led to his removal from office in 430 BC. Although quickly reinstated, he died soon after.

peridot pale-green, transparent gem variety of the mineral ▷olivine.

peridotite rock consisting largely of the mineral olivine; pyroxene and other minerals may also be present. Peridotite is an ultramafic rock containing less than 45% silica by weight. It is believed to be one of the rock types making up the Earth's upper mantle, and is sometimes brought from the depths to the surface by major movements, or as inclusions in lavas.

perigee point at which an object, travelling in an elliptical orbit around the Earth, is at its closest to the Earth. The point at which it is furthest from the Earth is the apogee.

periglacial bordering a glacial area but not actually covered by ice, or having similar climatic and environmental characteristics, such as mountainous areas. Periglacial areas today include parts of Siberia, Greenland, and North America. The rock and soil in these areas is frozen to a depth of several metres (▷permafrost) with only the top few centimetres thawing during the brief summer. The vegetation is characteristic of ▷tundra.

perihelion point at which an object, travelling in an elliptical orbit around the Sun, is at its closest to the Sun. The point at which it is furthest from the Sun is the aphelion.

periodic table of the elements in chemistry, a table in which the elements are arranged in order of their atomic number. The table summarizes the major properties of the elements and enables predictions to be made about their behaviour.

There are striking similarities in the chemical properties of the elements in each of the ▷groups (vertical columns), which are numbered I–VII and 0 to reflect the number of electrons in the outermost unfilled shell and hence the maximum ▷valency. Reactivity increases down the group. A gradation (trend) of properties may be traced along the horizontal rows (called **periods**). Metallic character increases across a period from right to left, and down a group. A large block of elements, between groups II and III, contains the transition elements, characterized by displaying more than one valency state.

Related Web sites: Modelling the Periodic Table: An Interactive Simulation http://www.genesismission.org/educate/scimodule/cosmic/ptable.html

Table of Elements Drill Game http://www.edu4kids.com/chem/

periodontal disease (formerly **pyorrhoea**) disease of the gums and bone supporting the teeth, caused by the accumulation of plaque and micro-organisms; the gums recede, and the teeth eventually become loose and may drop out unless treatment is sought. Bacteria can eventually erode the bone that supports the teeth, so that surgery becomes necessary.

peripheral device in computing, any item connected to a computer's ▷central processing unit (CPU). Typical peripherals include keyboard, mouse, monitor, and printer. Users who enjoy playing games might add a ▷joystick or a trackball; others might connect a ▷modem, ▷scanner, or ▷integrated services digital network (ISDN) terminal to their machines.

periscope optical instrument designed for observation from a concealed position such as from a submerged submarine. In its basic form it consists of a tube with parallel mirrors at each end, inclined at 45° to its axis. The periscope attained prominence in naval and military operations of World War I.

peristalsis wavelike contractions, produced by the contraction of smooth muscle, that pass along tubular organs, such as the intestines. The same term describes the wavelike motion of earthworms and other invertebrates, in which part of the body contracts as another part elongates.

peristyle in architecture, a range of columns surrounding a building or open courtyard.

peritoneum membrane lining the abdominal cavity and digestive organs of vertebrates. **Peritonitis**, inflammation within the peritoneum, can occur due to infection or other irritation. It is sometimes seen following a burst appendix and quickly proves fatal if not treated.

periwinkle in botany, any of several trailing blue-flowered evergreen plants of the dogbane family, native to Europe and Asia. They range in length from 20 cm/8 in to 1 m/3 ft. (Genus *Vinca*, family Apocynaceae.)

PERIWINKLE A plant native to central and south Europe and north Africa, the greater periwinkle *Vinca major* is now widespread in the British Isles. *Premaphotos Wildlife*

periwinkle in zoology, any marine snail of the family Littorinidae, found on the shores of Europe and eastern North America. Periwinkles have a conical spiral shell, and feed on algae.

PERIWINKLE Periwinkles *Littorina littoralis* in an English rockpool, showing the variations of colour within a population (genetic polymorphism). *Dr Rod Preston-Mafham/Premaphotos Wildlife*

perjury the offence of deliberately making a false statement on ▷oath (or affirmation) when appearing as a witness in legal proceedings, on a point material to the question at issue. In Britain and the USA it is punishable by a fine, imprisonment, or both.

Perkins, Anthony (1932–1992) US film actor. He played the mother-fixated psychopath Norman Bates in Alfred Hitchcock's *Psycho* (1960) and *Psycho II* (1982), and played shy but subtle roles in *Friendly Persuasion* (1956), *The Trial* (1962), and *The Champagne Murders* (1967). He also appeared on the stage in London and New York.

Perlis border state of Peninsular Malaysia, northwest Malaysia; capital Kangar; area 800 sq km/309 sq mi; population (1993) 187,600. It produces rubber, tin, coconuts, and tin. Perlis is ruled by a raja. It was transferred by Siam (Thailand) to Britain in 1909.

Perm (formerly Molotov (1940–57)) capital city, economic and cultural centre of Perm oblast (region), in the west-central Russian Federation, in the southern foothills of the Urals; population (1996 est) 1,028,000. Perm, which lies on the River Kama 475 km/295 mi northeast of Kazan, is a major centre of commerce and transportation. It is also an important industrial centre, producing machinery, chemicals, oil by-products, and timber.

permafrost condition in which a deep layer of soil does not thaw out during the summer. Permafrost occurs under ▷periglacial conditions. It is claimed that 26% of the world's land surface is permafrost.

Permafrost gives rise to a poorly drained form of grassland typical of northern Canada, Siberia, and Alaska known as ▷tundra.

Permian period of geological time 290–245 million years ago, the last period of the Palaeozoic era. Its end was marked by a dramatic change in marine life – the greatest mass extinction in geological history – including the extinction of many corals and trilobites. Deserts were widespread, terrestrial amphibians and mammal-like reptiles flourished, and cone-bearing plants (gymnosperms) came to prominence. In the oceans, 49% of families and 72% of genera vanished in the late Permian. On land, 78% of reptile families and 67% of amphibian families disappeared.

Pernambuco federal unit (state) of northeast Brazil, on the Atlantic coast; area 101,000 sq km/39,000 sq mi; population (1991) 7,122,500; capital Recife (former name Mauritzstaadt). The state is situated mainly on the northeastern plateau, with a narrow fertile coastal belt. The River San Francisco flows along much of its southern border. Sugar cane, cotton, coffee, and sisal are grown in the east and cattle are raised in the west. There are steel and sugar refining industries.

Perón, Eva ('Evita') Duarte de (1919–1952) Born María Eva Duarte. Argentine populist leader. A successful radio actor, she became the second wife of Juan ▷Perón in 1945. When he became president the following year, she became his chief adviser and virtually ran the health and labour ministries, devoting herself to helping the poor, improving education, and achieving women's suffrage. She founded a social welfare organization called the Eva Perón Foundation. She was politically astute and sought the vice-presidency in 1951, but was opposed by the army and withdrew. After her death from cancer in 1952, Juan Perón's political strength began to decline.

EVA PERÓN Wife of the president of Argentina, speaking at the celebrations of the festival of the Virgin of Paloma in Madrid, during her visit to Spain in June 1947. Beside her, on the far right, is General Franco. *Archive Photos*

Perón, (María Estela) Isabel (1931–) Born María Estela Isabel Martínez. Argentine president 1974–76, and third wife of Juan Perón. She succeeded him after he died in office in 1974 (she had been elected vice president in 1973), but labour unrest, inflation, and political violence pushed the country to the brink of chaos. Accused of corruption in 1976, she was held under house arrest for five years. She went into exile in Spain in 1981.

Perón, Juan Domingo (1895–1974) Argentine politician, dictator 1946–55 and from 1973 until his death. His populist appeal to the poor was enhanced by the charisma and political work of his second wife Eva ('Evita') Perón. After her death in 1952 his popularity waned and, with increasing economic difficulties and labour unrest, he was deposed in a military coup in 1955. He fled to Paraguay and, in 1960, to Spain. He returned from exile to the presidency in 1973, but died in office in 1974, and was succeeded by his third wife, Isabel Perón.

A professional army officer, Perón took part in the right-wing military coup that toppled Argentina's government in 1943. As secretary of labour and social welfare in the new government, he developed a pro-labour programme that won him popularity with the *descamisados* ('shirtless ones') – former trade unions that were converted into militant organizations. With their support and the aid of his wife Eva, he was elected president in 1946.

Perón instituted social reforms, but encountered economic difficulties, and his increasingly dictatorial methods caused him to lose the support of the Roman Catholic Church. He was instrumental in initiating long-lasting changes in the national political arena, and today Peronism remains a powerful political force.

perovskite a yellow, brown or greyish-black orthorhombic mineral, $CaTiO_3$, which sometimes contains cerium. Other minerals that have a similar structure are said to have the **perovskite structure**. The term also refers to $MgSiO_3$ with the perovskite structure, the principle mineral that makes up the Earth's lower ▷mantle.

Perpendicular period of English Gothic architecture lasting from the end of the 14th century to the mid-16th century. It is characterized by window tracery consisting chiefly of vertical members, two or four arc arches, lavishly decorated vaults, and the use of traceried panels. Examples include the choir, transepts, and cloister of Gloucester Cathedral (about 1331–1412); and King's College Chapel, Cambridge, built in three phases: 1446–61, 1477–85, and 1508–15.

perpendicular in mathematics, at a right angle; also, a line at right angles to another or to a plane. For a pair of skew lines (lines in three dimensions that do not meet), there is just one common perpendicular, which is at right angles to both lines; the nearest points on the two lines are the feet of this perpendicular.

perpetual motion the idea that a machine can be designed and constructed in such a way that, once started, it will do work indefinitely without requiring any further input of energy (motive power). Such a device would contradict at least one of the two laws of thermodynamics that state that (1) energy can neither be created nor destroyed (the law of conservation of energy) and (2) heat cannot by itself flow from a cooler to a hotter object. As a result, all practical (real) machines require a continuous supply of energy, and no heat engine is able to convert all the heat into useful work.

Perrault, Charles (1628–1703) French writer who published a collection of fairy tales, *Contes de ma mère l'oye/Mother Goose's Fairy Tales* (1697). These are based on traditional stories and include 'The Sleeping Beauty', 'Little Red Riding Hood', 'Blue Beard', 'Puss in Boots', and 'Cinderella'.

Perry, Matthew Calbraith (1794–1858) US naval officer, commander of the expedition of 1853 that reopened communication between Japan and the outside world after 250 years' isolation. A show of evident military superiority, the use of steamships (thought by the Japanese to be floating volcanoes), and an exhibition of US technical superiority enabled him to negotiate the Treaty of Kanagawa in 1854, granting the USA trading rights with Japan.

Persephone (Roman **Proserpina**) in Greek mythology, the goddess and queen of the underworld; the daughter of Zeus and ▷Demeter, goddess of agriculture. She was carried off to the underworld by ▷Pluto, also known as Hades, although Zeus

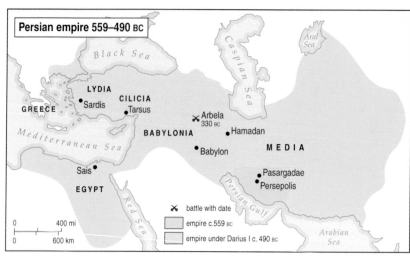

Persian empire 559–490 BC

battle with date
empire c.559 BC
empire under Darius I c. 490 BC

later ordered that she should spend six months of the year above ground with her mother. The myth symbolizes the growth and decay of vegetation and the changing seasons.

Persepolis ancient royal city of the Persian Empire, 65 km/40 mi northeast of Shiraz. It was burned down after its capture in 331 BC by Alexander the Great.

Perseus in astronomy, a bright constellation of the northern hemisphere, near ▷Cassiopeia. It is represented as the mythological hero; the head of the decapitated Gorgon, Medusa, is marked by ▷Algol (Beta Persei), the best known of the eclipsing binary stars.

Perseus in Greek mythology, the son of Zeus and Danaë. He beheaded the ▷Gorgon Medusa, watching the reflection in his shield to avoid being turned to stone. Having rescued and married Andromeda, he later became king of Tiryns. He used the Gorgon's head, set on his shield, to turn the tyrant Polydectes and, in some traditions, the Titan ▷Atlas, to stone.

Persia, ancient kingdom in southwestern Asia. The early Persians were a nomadic Aryan people who migrated through the Caucasus to the Iranian plateau. Cyrus organized the empire into provinces which were each ruled by Satraps. The royal house is

known as the Achaemenids after the founder of the line. The administrative centre was Susa, with the royal palace at Persepolis. Expansion led the Persians into conflicts with Greek cities, notably in the Ionian Revolt, Darius I's campaign that ended at the Athenian victory of Marathon (490 BC), and Xerxes I's full-blown invasion of the Greek mainland in 480. For modern history see ▷Iran.

Related Web site: History of Persia http://www.fordham.edu/halsall/ancient/asbook05.html

Persian inhabitant of or native to Persia, now Iran, and referring to the culture and the language (see also ▷Farsi). The Persians claim descent from central Asians of southern Russia (Aryans) who are thought to have migrated south into the region around 2000 BC.

Persian art the arts of Persia (now Iran) from the 6th century BC. Subject to invasions from both east and west, Persia has over the centuries blended many influences to create a rich diversity of arts, styles, and techniques. Persian art is particularly noted for its architecture and production of exquisite miniatures, although perhaps best known today for ornate carpets. Although the wide diversity of outside influences make it difficult to pin down distinct characteristics, Persian art is generally characterized by its firm lines, extensive detail, and bold use of colour.

PERSEUS The myth of Perseus and Andromeda, as illustrated on the peristyle (colonnade) of a building in Pompeii, Italy, around AD 50–79. *The Art Archive/Archaeological Museum Naples/Dagli Orti*

PERSIAN ART An example of Persian art from the palace at Susa, the capital of the Persian Empire under Darius I. The enamelled brick wall shows spear-carriers forming the bodyguard of King Darius I. *Philip Sauvain Picture Collection*

Persian Gulf (or **Arabian Gulf**) large shallow inlet of the Arabian Sea; area 233,000 sq km/90,000 sq mi. It divides the Arabian peninsula from Iran and is linked by the Strait of Hormuz and the Gulf of Oman to the Arabian Sea. Oilfields producing about one-third of the world's oil surround it in the Gulf States of Bahrain, Iran, Iraq, Kuwait, Oman, Qatar, Saudi Arabia, and the United Arab Emirates.

Persian language language belonging to the Indo-Iranian branch of the Indo-European family; see ▷Farsi.

Persian literature prose and poetry of Iran, in Persian or Arabic, with ancient roots. The 11th-century poet Omar Khayyám, who is well known outside Iran, is considered less important there. Censorship has been a problem at various times.

Persian Wars series of conflicts between Greece and Persia in 499–479 BC. Greek involvement with Persia began when ▷Cyrus (II) the Great (reigned 559–530 BC) conquered the Greek cities of western Asia Minor and ended with ▷Alexander (III) the Great's conquest of Persia, but the term 'Persian Wars' usually refers to the two Persian invasions of mainland Greece in 490 and 480–79. The Greek victory marked the end of Persian domination of the ancient world and the beginning of Greek supremacy.

persicaria any of a group of plants belonging to the dock family, found growing in waste places and arable land, often near water. Common persicaria (*P. persicaria*) is sprawling in shape and has lance-shaped, black-spotted leaves and spikes of pink flowers. Pale persicaria (*P. lapathifolium*) is slightly larger, with pale dots on the leaves, and heads of usually white flowers. Both are found throughout much of the northern hemisphere. (Genus *Polygonum*, family Polygonaceae.)

PERSICARIA Common persicaria or redleg *Polygonum persicaria* produces spikes of pink flowers from June onwards. For the nonbotanist it is difficult to distinguish from pale persicaria, *P. lapathifolium*, which is almost as common. *Premaphotos Wildlife*

persimmon any of a group of tropical trees belonging to the ebony family, especially the common persimmon (*D. virginiana*) of the southeastern USA. Growing up to 19 m/60 ft high, the persimmon has alternate oval leaves and yellow-green flowers. The small, sweet, orange fruits are edible. (Genus *Diospyros*, family Ebenaceae.)

personal computer (PC) another name for ▷microcomputer. The term is also used, more specifically, to mean the IBM Personal Computer and computers compatible with it. The first IBM PC was introduced in the USA in 1981; it had 64 kilobytes of random access memory (RAM) and one floppy-disk drive. It was followed in 1983 by the XT (with a hard drive disk drive) and in 1984 by the AT. Many manufacturers have copied the basic design, which is now regarded as a standard for business microcomputers. Computers designed to function like an IBM PC were orignally known as **IBM-compatible computers**, but are now more usually called Windows PCs. The power of personal computers has increased year by year, as their ability to handle sophisticated tasks, such as desktop video editing.

personal equity plan (PEP) investment scheme introduced in the UK in 1987. Shares of public companies listed on the UK stock exchange are purchased by PEP managers on behalf of their clients. Up to certain limits, individuals may purchase such shares and, provided they hold them for at least a year, enjoy any capital gains and reinvested dividends tax-free.

personality individual's characteristic way of behaving across a wide range of situations. Two broad dimensions of personality are ▷extroversion and neuroticism. A number of more specific personal traits have also been described, including ▷psychopathy (antisocial behaviour).

personality cult practice by which a leader is elevated to a pre-eminent status through a propaganda campaign. In the USSR, the cult of personality was developed by Joseph Stalin in the 1930s. Later, both Mao Zedong in China and Kim Il Sung in North Korea used similar techniques to reinforce their leadership and power. Current leaders who developed personality cults include Saddam ▷Hussein in Iraq and Saparmurad Niyazov in Turkmenistan.

personification ▷figure of speech (poetic or imaginative expression) in which animals, plants, objects, and ideas are treated as if they were human or alive ('Clouds chased each other across the face of the Moon'; 'Nature smiled on their work and gave it her blessing'; 'The future beckoned eagerly to them').

perspective the realistic representation of a three-dimensional object in two dimensions. In a perspective drawing, vertical lines are drawn parallel from the top of the page to the bottom. Horizontal lines, however, are represented by straight lines which meet at one of two perspective points. These perspective points lie to the right and left of the drawing at a distance which depends on the view being taken of the object.

Perspex trade name for a clear, lightweight, tough plastic first produced in 1930. It is widely used for watch glasses, advertising signs, domestic baths, motorboat windscreens, aircraft canopies, and protective shields. Its chemical name is polymethyl-methacrylate (PMMA). It is manufactured under other names: Plexiglas, Lucite, Acrylite, and Rhoplex (in the USA), and Oroglas (in Europe).

perspiration excretion of water and dissolved substances from the ▷sweat glands of the skin of mammals. Perspiration has two main functions: body cooling by the evaporation of water from the skin surface, and excretion of waste products such as salts.

Perth capital of the state of ▷Western Australia; population (1996) 1,096,829. Perth is situated on the southwest coast of Australia, on the River Swan, 19 km/12 mi inland. Its port is at Fremantle, to the southwest at the mouth of the Swan. Industries include oil refining, electronics, food processing, shipbuilding, banking and finance, and tourism; products include textiles, nickel, alumina, fertilizers, cement, furniture, and motor vehicles. Perth is an important centre for the export of primary products: refined oil, minerals, wool, wheat, meat, fruit, timber, and dairy produce. Perth has four universities: the University of Western Australia (founded 1911); Murdoch University (1975); Curtin University of Technology (1987); Edith Cowan University (1990).

Perth was founded in 1829 and grew rapidly after the discovery of gold in 1893 at Kalgoorlie, 545 km/340 mi to the northeast, and the opening of the harbour at Fremantle in 1897. It is Australia's fourth-largest city.

Related Web site: Destination Perth http://www.lonelyplanet.com/dest/aust/perth.htm

Perth town and administrative headquarters of ▷Perth and Kinross, central Scotland, on the River Tay, 70 km/43 mi northwest of Edinburgh; population (1991) 41,500. It is known as the 'fair city'. Industries include dyeing, textiles, whisky distilling, and light engineering. It is an important agricultural centre, noted for the sale of pedigree livestock, particularly young beef cattle. It was the capital of Scotland from the 12th century until 1452. James I of Scotland was assassinated here in 1437.

Perth and Kinross unitary authority in central Scotland, created in 1996 from the district bearing the same name in Tayside region.

area 5,388 sq km/2,080 sq mi **towns** Blairgowrie, Crieff, Kinross, ▷Perth (administrative headquarters), Pitlochry, Aberfeldy **physical** the geological fault that gives the distinctive character to lowland and highland Scotland passes southwest–northeast through the area. The population is largely centred in the lowlands, along wide fertile valleys such as Strathearn, and the Carse of Gowrie. To the north and west are the Grampians intersected by narrow glens with lochs in their valley floors. Among the highest elevations in the Grampians are Ben Lawers (1,214 m/3,984 ft) and Schiehallion (1,083 m/3,554 ft); in the south are the lower Ochil and Sidlaw Hills **features** Highland Games at Pitlochry; Dunkeld Cathedral; Scone Palace; Glenshee Ski Development **industries** woollen manufacture, whisky distilling and blending **agriculture** highly productive and varied agricultural area with soft fruit (Carse of Gowrie), arable crops (to the south), livestock, salmon fisheries (to the north) **population** (1996) 131,800

pertussis medical name for ▷whooping cough, an infectious disease mainly seen in children.

Peru see country box.

Peru Current (formerly **Humboldt Current**) cold ocean ▷current flowing north from the Antarctic along the west coast of South America to southern Ecuador, then west. It reduces the coastal temperature, making the western slopes of the Andes arid because winds are already chilled and dry when they meet the coast.

Perugia (ancient **Perusia**) capital of Umbria, Italy, 520 m/1,700 ft above the River Tiber, about 137 km/85 mi north of Rome; population (1992) 146,200. Textiles, liqueurs, and chocolate are produced. One of the 12 cities of the ancient country of Etruria, it surrendered to Rome in 309 BC.

Perugino, Pietro (*c.* 1450–1523) Also known as **Pietro di Cristoforo Vannucci**. Painter from Perugia. Early in his career, he was employed by Sixtus IV, most notably on the frescoes for the Sistine Chapel. Later he was based in his hometown where ▷Raphael was his pupil. But, with his skills continually in demand, he also ran a studio in Florence and accepted commissions from Orvieto, Mantua, Siena, and Naples.

Pesach Jewish name for the ▷Passover festival.

Peshawar capital of ▷North-West Frontier Province, Pakistan, 18 km/11 mi east of the Khyber Pass, on the Bara River; population (1998) 988,000. It has long been a major centre of trade because the Khyber Pass provides the easiest route between the Indian subcontinent and Afghanistan. Products include fruit, textiles, leather, and copper.

pessary medical device designed to be inserted into the vagina either to support a displaced womb or as a contraceptive. The word is also used for a vaginal suppository used for administering drugs locally, made from glycerol or oil of theobromine, which melts within the vagina to release the contained substance – for example, a contraceptive, antibiotic, antifungal agent, or ▷prostaglandin (to induce labour).

pest in biology, any insect, fungus, rodent, or other living organism that has a harmful effect on human beings, other than those that directly cause human diseases. Most pests damage crops or livestock, but the term also covers those that damage buildings, destroy food stores, and spread disease.

pesticide any chemical used in farming, gardening, or indoors to combat pests. Pesticides are of three main types: **insecticides** (to kill insects), **fungicides** (to kill fungal diseases), and **herbicides** (to kill plants, mainly those considered weeds). Pesticides cause a number of pollution problems through spray drift on to surrounding areas, direct contamination of users or the public, and as residues on food. The World Health Organization (WHO) estimated in 1999 that 20,000 people die annually worldwide from pesticide poisoning incidents.

The safest pesticides include those made from plants, such as the insecticides pyrethrum and derris.

Pyrethrins are safe and insects do not develop resistance to them. Their impact on the environment is very small as the ingredients break down harmlessly.

More potent are synthetic products, such as chlorinated hydrocarbons. These products, including DDT and dieldrin, are highly toxic to wildlife and often to human beings, so their use is now restricted by law in some areas and is declining. Safer pesticides such as malathion are based on organic phosphorus compounds, but they still present hazards to health. The aid organization Oxfam estimates that pesticides cause about 10,000 deaths worldwide every year.

Pesticides were used to deforest South-East Asia during the Vietnam War, causing death and destruction to the area's ecology and lasting health and agricultural problems.

Many pesticides remain in the soil, since they are not biodegradable, and are then passed on to foods. In the UK, more than half of all potatoes sampled in 1995 contained residues of a storage pesticide; seven different pesticides were found in carrots, with concentrations up to 25 times the permitted level; and 40% of bread contained pesticide residues.

There are around 4,000 cases of acute pesticide poisoning a year in the UK.

The Pesticide Safety Directorate, an executive agency of the Ministry of Agriculture, Fisheries and Food (MAFF) is responsible for the evaluation and approval of pesticides in Great Britain and provides policy advice.

Related Web site: Molecular Expressions: The Pesticide Collection http://micro.magnet.fsu.edu/pesticides/index.html

Pétain, (Henri) Philippe Benoni Omer Joseph (1856–1951) French general and head of state. Voted in as prime minister in June 1940, Pétain signed an armistice with Germany on 22 June before assuming full powers on 16 July. His authoritarian regime, established at Vichy, collaborated with the Germans and proposed a reactionary 'National Revolution' for France under the slogan 'Work, Family, Fatherland'. Convinced in 1940 of Britain's imminent defeat, Pétain accepted Germany's terms for peace, including the occupation of northern France. In December 1940 he

Peru

Peru country in South America, on the Pacific, bounded north by Ecuador and Colombia, east by Brazil and Bolivia, and south by Chile.

NATIONAL NAME *República del Perú/Republic of Peru*
AREA 1,285,200 sq km/496,216 sq mi
CAPITAL Lima
MAJOR TOWNS/CITIES Arequipa, Iquitos, Chiclayo, Trujillo, Huancayo, Piura, Chimbote
MAJOR PORTS Callao, Chimbote, Salaverry
PHYSICAL FEATURES Andes mountains running northwest–southeast cover 27% of Peru, separating Amazon river-basin jungle in northeast from coastal plain in west; desert along coast north–south (Atacama Desert); Lake Titicaca

Government

HEAD OF STATE Alejandro Toledo Manrique from 2001
HEAD OF GOVERNMENT Carlos Ferrero Costa from 2003
POLITICAL SYSTEM liberal democracy
POLITICAL EXECUTIVE limited presidency
ADMINISTRATIVE DIVISIONS 24 departments and the constitutional province of Callao
ARMED FORCES 110,000; plus paramilitary forces of 77,000 (2002 est)
CONSCRIPTION conscription is selective for two years
DEATH PENALTY abolished for ordinary crimes in 1979; laws provide for the death penalty for exceptional crimes, such as crimes committed in wartime
DEFENCE SPEND (% GDP) 1.6 (2002 est)
EDUCATION SPEND (% GDP) 3.3 (2000 est)
HEALTH SPEND (% GDP) 4.8 (2000 est)

Economy and resources

CURRENCY nuevo sol
GPD (US$) 56.9 billion (2002 est)
REAL GDP GROWTH (% change on previous year) 0.2 (2001)
GNI (US$) 54.7 billion (2002 est)
GNI PER CAPITA (PPP) (US$) 4,800 (2002 est)

CONSUMER PRICE INFLATION 2.5% (2003 est)
UNEMPLOYMENT 8.2% (2001)
FOREIGN DEBT (US$) 21.9 billion (2001 est)
MAJOR TRADING PARTNERS USA, Japan, China, Chile, Venezuela, Colombia
RESOURCES lead, copper, iron, silver, zinc (world's fourth-largest producer), petroleum
INDUSTRIES food processing, textiles and clothing, petroleum refining, metals and metal products, chemicals, machinery and transport equipment, beverages, tourism
EXPORTS gold, copper, fishmeal, zinc, refined petroleum products. Principal market: USA 27.2% (2001)
IMPORTS machinery and transport equipment, basic foodstuffs, basic manufactures, chemicals, mineral fuels, consumer goods. Principal source: USA 20% (2001)
ARABLE LAND 2.9% (2000 est)
AGRICULTURAL PRODUCTS potatoes, wheat, seed cotton, coffee, rice, maize, beans, sugar cane; fishing (particularly for South American pilchard and the anchovetta)

Population and society

POPULATION 27,167,000 (2003 est)

PERU A member of one of the indigenous Indian peoples of Loreto, Peru, who live along the rivers of the Amazon basin.
Image Bank

POPULATION GROWTH RATE 1.3% (2000–15)
POPULATION DENSITY (per sq km) 21 (2003 est)
URBAN POPULATION (% of total) 74 (2003 est)
AGE DISTRIBUTION (% of total population) 0–14 32%, 15–59 61%, 60+ 7% (2002 est)
ETHNIC GROUPS about 50% South American Indian, 40% mestizo, 7% European, and 3% African origin
LANGUAGE Spanish, Quechua (both official), Aymara, many indigenous dialects

See also ▷Bolívar, Simón; ▷Inca.

Chronology

4000 BC: Evidence of early settled agriculture in Chicama Valley.
AD 700–1100: Period of Wari Empire, first expansionist militarized empire in Andes.
1200: Manco Capac became the first emperor of South American Indian Quechua-speaking Incas, who established a growing and sophisticated empire centred on the Andean city of Cuzco, and believed their ruler was descended from the Sun.
late 15th century: At its zenith, the Inca Empire stretched from Quito in Ecuador to beyond Santiago in southern Chile. It superseded the Chimu civilization, which had flourished in Peru 1250–1470.
1532–33: Incas defeated by Spanish conquistadores, led by Francisco Pizarro. Empire came under Spanish rule, as part of the Viceroyalty of Peru, with capital in Lima, founded in 1535.
1780: Tupac Amaru, who claimed to be descended from the last Inca chieftain, led a failed native revolt against Spanish.
1810: Peru became the headquarters for the Spanish government as European settlers rebelled elsewhere in Spanish America.
1820–22: Fight for liberation from Spanish rule led by Gen José de San Martín and Army of Andes which, after freeing Argentina and Chile, invaded southern Peru.
1824: Became last colony in Central and South America to achieve independence from Spain after attacks from north by Field Marshal Sucre, acting for freedom fighter Simón Bolívar.
1836–39: Failed attempts at union with Bolivia.
1849–74: Around 80,000–100,000 Chinese labourers arrived in Peru to fill menial jobs such as collecting guano.
1866: Victorious naval war fought with Spain.
1879–83: Pacific War fought in alliance with Bolivia and Chile over nitrate fields of the Atacama Desert in the south; three provinces along coastal south lost to Chile.
1902: Boundary dispute with Bolivia settled.
mid-1920s: After several decades of civilian government, a series of right-wing dictatorships held power.
1927: Boundary dispute with Colombia settled.
1929: Tacna province, lost to Chile in 1880, was returned.
1941: A brief war with Ecuador secured Amazonian territory.
1945: Civilian government, dominated by left-of-centre American Popular Revolutionary Alliance (APRA, formed 1924), came to power after free elections.
1948: Army coup installed military government led by Gen Manuel Odría, who remained in power until 1956.

RELIGION Roman Catholic (state religion) 95%
EDUCATION (compulsory years) 11
LITERACY RATE 95% (men); 87% (women) (2003 est)
LABOUR FORCE 5.8% agriculture, 18.7% industry, 75.5% services (1999)
LIFE EXPECTANCY 67 (men); 72 (women) (2000–05)
CHILD MORTALITY RATE (under 5, per 1,000 live births) 39 (2001)
PHYSICIANS (per 1,000 people) 0.9 (1998 est)
HOSPITAL BEDS (per 1,000 people) 1.5 (1998 est)
TV SETS (per 1,000 people) 148 (2000 est)
RADIOS (per 1,000 people) 273 (1997)
INTERNET USERS (per 10,000 people) 934.6 (2002 est)
PERSONAL COMPUTER USERS (per 100 people) 5.6 (2002 est)

1963: Return to civilian rule, with centrist Fernando Belaúnde Terry as president.
1968: Return of military government in bloodless coup by Gen Juan Velasco Alvarado, following industrial unrest. Populist land reform programme introduced.
1980: Return to civilian rule, with Fernando Belaúnde as president; agrarian and industrial reforms pursued. Sendero Luminoso ('Shining Path') Maoist guerrilla group active.
1981: Boundary dispute with Ecuador renewed.
1985: Belaúnde succeeded by Social Democrat Alan García Pérez, who launched campaign to remove military and police 'old guard'.
1988: García was pressured to seek help from International Monetary Fund (IMF) as the economy deteriorated. Sendero Luminoso increased its campaign of violence.
1990: Right-of-centre Alberto Fujimori defeated ex-communist writer Vargas Llosa in presidential elections. Inflation rose to 400%; a privatization programme was launched.
1992: Fujimori allied himself with the army and suspended the constitution, provoking international criticism. The Sendero Luminoso leader was arrested and sentenced to life imprisonment. A new single-chamber legislature was elected.
1993: A new constitution was adopted.
1994: 6,000 Sendero Luminoso guerrillas surrendered to the authorities.
1995: A border dispute with Ecuador was resolved after armed clashes. Fujimori was re-elected. A controversial amnesty was granted to those previously convicted of human-rights abuses.
1996: Hostages were held in the Japanese embassy by Marxist Tupac Amaru Revolutionary Movement (MRTA) guerrillas.
1997: The hostage siege ended.
1998: A border dispute that had lasted for 157 years was settled with Ecuador.
1999: Alberto Bustamante was made prime minister.
2000: Fujimori was re-elected as president for a third term in July. In September, the head of the national intelligence service, Vladimiro Montesinos, was proved to have bribed a member of congress. He fled to Panama, which refused to accept him, and returned to Peru, where his arrest was ordered on charges of corruption and abusing human rights. Fujimori sent his resignation from Japan, from where he could not be extradited, and Valentin Paniagua became president. He appointed former United Nations (UN) secretary general Javier Pérez de Cuélla as prime minister.
2001: Paniagua set up a commission to investigate the disappearance of 4,000 people during the fighting in the 1980s and 1990s. Alejandro Toledo was elected president.

dismissed his deputy Pierre ▷Laval, who wanted to side with the Axis powers, but bowed to German pressures to reinstate him in April 1942. With Germany occupying the whole of France from that November, Pétain found himself head, in name only, of a puppet state. Removed from France by the German army in 1944, he returned voluntarily and was tried and condemned to death for treason in August 1945. He died in prison on the Ile d'Yeu, his sentence having been commuted to life imprisonment.

A career soldier from northern France, Pétain's defence of Verdun in 1916 had made him, at the age of 60, a national hero. Promoted in 1917 to commander-in-chief, he came under Marshal ▷Foch's supreme command in 1918. Subsequently, as a leading member of the Higher Council for War, his advocacy of a purely defensive military policy culminated in France's reliance on the Maginot Line as protection from German attack.

petal part of a flower whose function is to attract pollinators such as insects or birds. Petals are frequently large and brightly coloured and may also be scented. Some have a nectary at the base and markings on the petal surface, known as honey guides, to direct pollinators to the source of the nectar. In wind-pollinated plants, however, the petals are usually small and insignificant, and sometimes absent altogether. Petals are derived from modified leaves, and are known collectively as a corolla.

Peter three tsars of Russia, including:

Peter (I) the Great (1672–1725) Tsar of Russia from 1682 on the death of his half-brother Tsar Feodor III; he assumed control of the government in 1689. He attempted to reorganize the country on Western lines. He modernized the army, had a fleet built, remodelled the administrative and legal systems, encouraged education, and brought the Russian Orthodox Church under state control. On the Baltic coast, where he had conquered territory from Sweden, Peter built a new city, St Petersburg, and moved the capital there from Moscow.

When Feodor III died in 1682 without an heir, the patriarch of Moscow and leading noblemen chose the ten-year-old Peter to be tsar rather than his 16-year-old half-brother Ivan, who was mentally deficient. Ivan's older sister Sophia organized a coup by the palace guards that resulted in the coronation of Ivan and Peter as joint tsars, with Sophia as regent.

Taking power Peter spent the next seven years with his mother in a village near Moscow. Although he received no formal education, he was physically and mentally far in advance of his years. He acquired a mass of knowledge and technical skills, mainly from foreigners in Russian service who lived nearby. In 1689, having been warned that Sophia was plotting against him, Peter forced her to resign. He left nominal precedence to Ivan, but ruled the country himself. Peter's first task was to form an army on Western European lines. He also strove to create a navy and a merchant fleet. Thinking that the possession of a portion of the Black Sea coast would best give Russia a seaboard and port, he declared war on Turkey and took the city of Azov in 1696, after a long siege.

In 1712 he married his mistress, a Lithuanian peasant woman named Catherine. She later succeeded him on the throne as ▷Catherine I the Great. In 1716-17 Peter made another tour of Europe. Soon afterwards he ordered the execution of Alexei, his son by his first wife, for suspected treason, but Alexei died before the sentence could be carried out.

Peter did much to develop Russia's trade and industry, and encouraged scholarship. Though personally cruel and barbaric in many of his habits, he was a great monarch who transformed Russia and made it one of Europe's major powers.

Peter, St (lived 1st century) Christian martyr, the author of two epistles in the New Testament and leader of the apostles. He is regarded as the first bishop of Rome, whose mantle the pope inherits. His real name was Simon, but he was nicknamed Kephas ('Peter', from the Greek for 'rock') by Jesus, as being the rock upon which he would build his church. His emblem is two keys; his feast day is 29 June.

Originally a fisherman of Capernaum, on the Sea of Galilee, Peter may have been a follower of John the Baptist, and was the first to acknowledge Jesus as the Messiah. Tradition has it that he later settled in Rome; he was martyred during the reign of the emperor Nero, perhaps by crucifixion. Bones excavated from under the Basilica of St Peter's in the Vatican in 1968 were accepted as those of St Peter by Pope Paul VI.

Related Web site: Peter, St http://www.newadvent.org/cathen/11744a.htm

Peterborough unitary authority in eastern England, created in 1998 from part of Cambridgeshire.

area 334 sq km/129 sq mi **towns and cities** ▷Peterborough (administrative headquarters), Wittering, Old Fletton, Thorney, Glinton, Northborough, Peakirk **features** River Nene; western margins of the Fens; St Peter's Cathedral (Peterborough), 12th century, containing Catherine of Aragon's tomb; Wildfowl and Wetlands Centre at Peakirk **industries** aluminium founding and manufacture, electronics, domestic appliances, plastics and rubber manufacture, precision engineering, telecommunications equipment, food manufacture and processing **population** (1996) 156,900 **famous people** John Clare, L P Hartley

Peterborough city in eastern England, on the River Nene, 64 km/40 mi northeast of Northampton, and from April 1998 administrative headquarters of ▷Peterborough unitary authority; population (1994 est) 139,000. Situated on the edge of the ▷Fens in the centre of an agricultural area, it is one of the fastest growing cities in Europe. Industries include sugar-beet refining, foodstuffs, aluminium founding and manufacturing, agricultural machinery, engineering, brick-making, diesel engines, and refrigerators. It has an advanced electronics industry. It is noted for its 12th-century cathedral. Nearby Flag Fen disclosed in 1985 a well-preserved Bronze Age settlement of 660 BC. The 17th-century Thorpe Hall is a cultural and leisure centre.

The plans for Hampton Township (formerly known as Peterborough Southern Township), the largest town in Europe built by the private sector, threatened the world's largest colony of great crested newts in old clay pits. Work has begun on the town, and the first people moved in in 1997.

Peterloo massacre the events in St Peter's Fields in Manchester, England, on 16 August 1819, when an open-air meeting in support of parliamentary reform was charged by yeomanry (voluntary cavalry soldiers) and hussars (regular cavalry soldiers). Eleven people were killed and 500 wounded. The name was given in analogy with the Battle of Waterloo.

The well-known radical politician Henry Hunt was to speak at the meeting. The crowd, numbering some 60,000 and including many women and children, was unarmed and entirely peaceful. The magistrates, who had brought in special constables from Lancashire and the Cheshire Yeomanry, nevertheless became nervous and ordered Hunt's arrest. As the yeomanry attempted to obey them, they were pressed by the mob. The hussars were sent in to help, and, in the general panic which followed, 11 people were killed and about 500 injured. The 'massacre' aroused great public indignation, but the government stood by the magistrates and passed the Six Acts to control future agitation.

Related Web site: Peterloo Massacre http://www.spartacus.schoolnet.co.uk/peterloo.html

Petipa, Marius (1822–1910) French choreographer. He created some of the most important ballets in the classical repertory. For the Imperial Ballet in Russia he created masterpieces such as *Don Quixote* (1869), *La Bayadère* (1877), *The Sleeping Beauty* (1890), *Swan Lake* (1895) (with Ivanov), and *Raymonda* (1898).

petit Brabançon smooth-haired form of the ▷griffon Bruxelloise.

petition of right in British law, the procedure whereby, before the passing of the Crown Proceedings Act 1947, a subject petitioned for legal relief against the crown, for example for money due under a contract, or for property of which the crown had taken possession.

Petra (Arabic **Wadi Musa**) ancient city carved out of the red rock at a site in Jordan, on the eastern slopes of the Wadi el Araba, 90 km/56 mi south of the Dead Sea. An Edomite stronghold and capital of the Nabataeans in the 2nd century, it was captured by the Roman emperor Trajan in 106 and destroyed by the Arabs in the 7th century. It was forgotten in Europe until 1812 when the Swiss traveller Johann Ludwig Burckhardt (1784–1817) came across it.

Petrarch (1304–1374) Born Francesco Petrarca. Italian poet, humanist, and leader of the revival of classical learning. His *Il canzoniere/Songbook* (also known as *Rime Sparse/Scattered Lyrics*) contains madrigals, songs, and ▷sonnets in praise of his idealized love, 'Laura', whom he first saw in 1327 (she was a married woman and refused to become his mistress). These were Petrarch's greatest contributions to Italian literature; they shaped the lyric poetry of the Renaissance and greatly influenced French and English love poetry. Although he did not invent the sonnet form, he was its finest early practitioner and the 'Petrarchan sonnet' was admired as an ideal model by later poets.

petrel any of various families of seabirds in the order Procellariiforme, including the worldwide **storm petrels** (family Hydrobatidae), which include the smallest seabirds (some only 13 cm/5 in long), and the **diving petrels** (family Pelecanoididae) of the southern hemisphere. All have a hooked bill, rudimentary hind toes, tubular nostrils, and feed by diving underwater. They include ▷fulmars and ▷shearwaters.

Like other ground-nesting or burrow-nesting seabirds, petrels are vulnerable to predators such as rats that take eggs and nestlings. Several island species are in danger of extinction, including the **Bermuda petrel** *Pterodroma cahow* and the **Freira petrel** of Madeira *P. madeira*.

PETRARCH A portrait of the Italian poet and Renaissance humanist Francesco Petrarch, by Andrea del Castagno (1421–1457). *The Art Archive/Galleria degli Uffizi Florence/Dagli Orti*

Petrie, (William Matthew) Flinders (1853–1942) English archaeologist who excavated sites in Egypt (the pyramids at Giza, the temple at Tanis, the Greek city of Naucratis in the Nile delta, Tell el Amarna, Naqada, Abydos, and Memphis) and Palestine from 1880. He was knighted in 1923.

petrochemical chemical derived from the processing of petroleum (crude oil).

Petrochemical industries are those that obtain their raw materials from the processing of petroleum and natural gas. Polymers, detergents, solvents, and nitrogen fertilizers are all major products of the petrochemical industries. Inorganic chemical products include carbon black, sulphur, ammonia, and hydrogen peroxide.

petrodollars in economics, dollar earnings of nations that make up the ▷Organization of Petroleum-Exporting Countries (OPEC).

Petrograd former name (1914–24) of ▷St Petersburg, a city in Russia. It adopted this Russian-style name as a patriotic gesture at the outbreak of World War I, but was renamed Leningrad on the death of the USSR's first leader.

petrol mixture of hydrocarbons derived from petroleum, mainly used as a fuel for internal-combustion engines. It is colourless and highly volatile. **Leaded petrol** contains antiknock (a mixture of tetraethyl lead and dibromoethane), which improves the combustion of petrol and the performance of a car engine. The lead from the exhaust fumes enters the atmosphere, mostly as simple lead compounds. There is strong evidence that it can act as a nerve poison on young children and cause mental impairment. This has prompted a gradual switch to the use of **unleaded petrol** in the UK.

The changeover from leaded petrol gained momentum from 1989 owing to a change in the tax on petrol, making it cheaper to buy unleaded fuel. Unleaded petrol contains a different mixture of hydrocarbons, and has a lower ▷octane rating than leaded petrol. Leaded petrol cannot be used in cars fitted with a ▷catalytic converter.

In the USA, petrol is called gasoline, and unleaded petrol has been used for some years.

PETREL Like all petrels, the Madeiran fork-tailed petrel has globular salt glands close to the eyes. Petrels are highly social birds, nesting in large colonies and feeding together in large, floating 'rafts'.

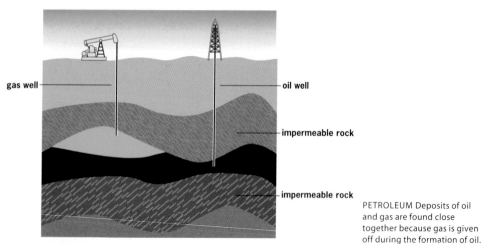

gas well
oil well
impermeable rock
impermeable rock

PETROLEUM Deposits of oil and gas are found close together because gas is given off during the formation of oil.

petrol engine the most commonly used source of power for motor vehicles, introduced by the German engineers Gottlieb Daimler and Karl Benz in 1885. The petrol engine is a complex piece of machinery made up of about 150 moving parts. It is a reciprocating piston engine, in which a number of pistons move up and down in cylinders. A mixture of petrol and air is introduced to the space above the pistons and ignited. The gases produced force the pistons down, generating power. The engine-operating cycle is repeated every four strokes (upward or downward movement) of the piston, this being known as the ▷four-stroke cycle. The motion of the pistons rotate a crankshaft, at the end of which is a heavy flywheel. From the flywheel the power is transferred to the car's driving wheels via the transmission system of clutch, gearbox, and final drive.

petroleum (or **crude oil**) natural mineral oil, a thick greenish-brown flammable liquid found underground in permeable rocks. Petroleum consists of hydrocarbons mixed with oxygen, sulphur, nitrogen, and other elements in varying proportions. It is thought to be derived from ancient organic material that has been converted by, first, bacterial action, then heat, and pressure (but its origin may be chemical also).

From crude petroleum, various products are made by distillation and other processes; for example, fuel oil, petrol, kerosene, diesel, and lubricating oil. Petroleum products and chemicals are used in large quantities in the manufacture of detergents, artificial fibres, plastics, insecticides, fertilizers, pharmaceuticals, toiletries, and synthetic rubber.

petrology branch of geology that deals with the study of rocks, their mineral compositions, their textures, and their origins.

Pevsner, Nikolaus Bernhard Leon (1902–1983) Anglo-German art historian. Born in Leipzig, he fled from the Nazis to England. He became an authority on architecture, especially English. His *Outline of European Architecture* was published in 1942, followed by numerous other editions. In his series *The Buildings of England* (46 volumes; 1951–74), he built up a first-hand report on every notable building in the country.

pewter any of various alloys of mostly tin with varying amounts of lead, copper, or antimony. Pewter has been known for centuries and was once widely used for domestic utensils but is now used mainly for ornamental ware.

peyote spineless cactus of northern Mexico and the southwestern USA. It has white or pink flowers. Its buttonlike tops contain **mescaline**, which causes hallucinations and is used by American Indians in religious ceremonies. (*Lophophora williamsii*, family Cactaceae.)

Pfalz German name of the historic division of Germany, the ▷Palatinate.

pH scale from 0 to 14 for measuring acidity or alkalinity. A pH of 7.0 indicates neutrality, below 7 is acid, while above 7 is alkaline. Strong acids, such as those used in car batteries, have a pH of about 2; strong alkalis such as sodium hydroxide are pH 13.

Acidic fruits such as citrus fruits are about pH 4. Fertile soils have a pH of about 6.5 to 7.0, while weak alkalis such as soap are 9 to 10.

The pH of a solution can be measured by using a broad-range indicator, either in solution or as a paper strip. The colour produced by the indicator is compared with a colour code related to the pH value. An alternative method is to use a pH meter fitted with a glass electrode.

Related Web site: Acid and Base pH Tutorial http://www.science.ubc.ca/~chem/tutorials/pH/launch.html

Phaethon (Greek 'shining one') in Greek mythology, the son of ▷Helios, god of the Sun, and Clymene. He was allowed to drive his father's chariot for one day, but lost control of the horses and almost set the Earth on fire, whereupon he was killed by Zeus with a thunderbolt and hurled into the River Eridanos.

phage another name for a ▷bacteriophage, a virus that attacks bacteria.

phagocyte type of ▷white blood cell, or leucocyte, that can engulf a bacterium or other invading micro-organism. Phagocytes are found in blood, lymph, and other body tissues, where they also ingest foreign matter and dead tissue. A ▷macrophage differs in size and life span.

Phalangist member of a Lebanese military organization (**Phalanges Libanaises**), since 1958 the political and military force of the ▷Maronite Church in Lebanon. The Phalangists' unbending right-wing policies and resistance to the introduction of democratic institutions were among the contributing factors to the civil war in Lebanon.

phalanx in ancient Greece and Macedonia, a battle formation using up to 16 lines of infantry with pikes about 4 m/13 ft long, protected to the sides and rear by cavalry. It was used by Philip II and Alexander the Great of Macedonia, and though more successful than the conventional hoplite formation, it proved inferior to the Roman legion.

phalarope any of a genus *Phalaropus* of small, elegant shorebirds in the sandpiper family (Scolopacidae). They have the habit of spinning in the water to stir up insect larvae. They are native to North America, the UK, and the polar regions of Europe.

Phanerozoic eon (Greek *phanero* 'visible') eon in Earth history, consisting of the most recent 570 million years. It comprises the Palaeozoic, Mesozoic, and Cenozoic eras. The vast majority of fossils come from this eon, owing to the evolution of hard shells and internal skeletons. The name means 'interval of well-displayed life'.

Pharaoh Hebrew form of the Egyptian royal title Per-'o. This term, meaning 'great house', was originally applied to the royal household, and after about 950 BC to the king.

distillation tower for separating components of crude oil

crude oil fractionating tower
low temperature
crude oil
high temperature
gas
gas oil
heavy gas oil
lubricating oil stock
fuel oil
crude oil
bitumen

gases to refinery fuel and for chemical manufacture
liquified petroleum gases
aviation spirit
petrol/gasoline
turbo jet fuel
kerosene
diesel oil
further fractionated
lubricating oil
paraffin
residual fuel oil
bitumen

PETROLEUM This diagram shows how to refine petroleum using a distillation column. The crude petroleum is fed in at the bottom of the column where the temperature is high. The gases produced rise up the column, cooling as they travel. At different heights up the column different gases condense to liquids called fractions and are drawn off.

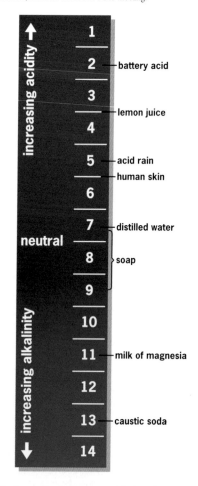

increasing acidity
1
2 — battery acid
3
4 — lemon juice
5 — acid rain
— human skin
6
7 — distilled water
neutral
8 — soap
9
10
11 — milk of magnesia
12
13 — caustic soda
14
increasing alkalinity

pH The lower the pH, the more acidic the substance; the higher the pH, the more alkaline the substance.

Pharisee (Hebrew 'separatist') member of a conservative Jewish sect that arose in Roman-occupied Palestine in the 2nd century BC in protest against all movements favouring compromise with Hellenistic culture. The Pharisees were devout adherents of the law, both as found in the Torah and in the oral tradition known as the Mishnah.

pharmacology study of the properties of drugs and their effects on the human body.

pharynx muscular cavity behind the nose and mouth, extending downwards from the base of the skull. Its walls are made of muscle strengthened with a fibrous layer and lined with mucous membrane. The internal nostrils lead backwards into the pharynx, which continues downwards into the oesophagus and (through the epiglottis) into the windpipe. On each side, a Eustachian tube enters the pharynx from the middle ear cavity.

phase in chemistry, a physical state of matter: for example, ice and liquid water are different phases of water; a mixture of the two is termed a two-phase system.

phase in physics, a stage in an oscillatory motion, such as a wave motion: two waves are in phase when their peaks and their troughs coincide. Otherwise, there is a **phase difference**, which has consequences in ▷interference phenomena and ▷alternating current electricity.

pheasant any of various large, colourful Asiatic fowls of the family Phasianidae, order Galliformes, which also includes grouse, quail, and turkey. The typical pheasants are in the genus *Phasianus*, which has two species: the Japanese pheasant, *P. versicolor*, found in Japan, and the Eurasian ring-necked or common pheasant, *P. colchicus*, also introduced to North America. The genus is distinguished by the very long wedge-shaped tail and the absence of a crest. The plumage of the male common pheasant is richly tinted with brownish-green, yellow, and red markings, but the female is a camouflaged brownish colour. The nest is made on the ground. The male is polygamous.

In Britain approximately 20 million pheasants are raised annually for shooting.

phenol member of a group of aromatic chemical compounds with weakly acidic properties, which are characterized by a hydroxyl (OH) group attached directly to an aromatic ring. The simplest of the phenols, derived from benzene, is also known as phenol and has the formula C_6H_5OH. It is sometimes called **carbolic acid** and can be extracted from coal tar.

Pure phenol consists of colourless, needle-shaped crystals, which take up moisture from the atmosphere. It has a strong and characteristic smell and was once used as an antiseptic. It is, however, toxic by absorption through the skin.

phenomenalism philosophical position that argues that statements about objects can be reduced to statements about what is perceived or perceivable. Thus English philosopher John Stuart Mill defined material objects as 'permanent possibilities of sensation'. Phenomenalism is closely connected with certain forms of ▷empiricism.

phenomenology the philosophical perspective, founded by the German philosopher Edmund ▷Husserl, that concentrates on phenomena as objects of perception (rather than as facts or occurrences that exist independently) in attempting to examine the ways people think about and interpret the world around them. It has been practised by the philosophers Martin Heidegger, Jean-Paul Sartre, and Maurice Merleau-Ponty.

PHEROMONE This male *Mechanitis lysimnia* butterfly in a Brazilian rainforest is releasing pheromones from fringes of hairs which are erected along the leading edge of the hind wings. *Premaphotos Wildlife*

phenotype in genetics, visible traits, those actually displayed by an organism. The phenotype is not a direct reflection of the ▷genotype because some alleles are masked by the presence of other, dominant alleles (see ▷dominance). The phenotype is further modified by the effects of the environment (for example, poor nutrition stunts growth).

pheromone chemical signal (such as an odour) that is emitted by one animal and affects the behaviour of others. Pheromones are used by many animal species to attract mates.

Phidias (or Pheidias) (lived mid-5th century BC) Greek sculptor. Active in Athens, he supervised the sculptural programme for the Parthenon (most of it is preserved in the British Museum, London, and known as the ▷Elgin marbles). He also executed the colossal statue of Zeus at Olympia, one of the ▷Seven Wonders of the World. No surviving sculptures can be credited to him with certainty.

Philadelphia (Greek 'the city of brotherly love') river port and chief city in Pennsylvania, USA, on the Delaware River at the junction with the Schuykill River; population (1996 est) 1,478,000; metropolitan area (1992) 5,939,000. It is the world's largest freshwater port, the fifth largest city in the USA, and a financial, business, and research centre. Industries include oil-refining, food-processing, electronics, printing, publishing, and the production of iron, steel, chemicals, textiles, carpets, and transportation equipment, although manufacturing is less important than it was, now employing about 12% of the workforce. It was originally settled by Swedish settlers in 1682, and was the capital of the USA 1790–1800.

philanthropy love felt by an individual towards humankind. It is expressed through acts of generosity and ▷charity and seeks to promote the greater happiness and prosperity of humanity.

philately the collection and study of postage stamps. It originated as a hobby in France about 1860.
Related Web site: Stamp Collecting for Beginners http://www.geocities.com/Heartland/2769/

Philby, Kim (Harold Adrian Russell) (1912–1988) British intelligence officer from 1940 and Soviet agent from 1933. He was liaison officer in Washington 1949–51, when he was confirmed to be a double agent and asked to resign. Named in 1963 as having warned Guy Burgess and Donald Maclean (also double agents) that their activities were known, he fled to the USSR and became a Soviet citizen and a general in the KGB. A fourth member of the ring was Anthony Blunt.

Philip six kings of France, including:

Philip II (1165–1223) Also known as **Philip Augustus**. King of France from 1180. As part of his efforts to establish a strong monarchy and evict the English from their French possessions, he waged war in turn against the English kings ▷Henry II, Richard (I) the Lionheart (with whom he also went on the Third Crusade), and John (1167–1216).

Philip IV the Fair (1268–1314) King of France from 1285. He engaged in a feud with Pope Boniface VIII and made him a prisoner 1303. Clement V (1264–1314), elected pope through Philip's influence in 1305, moved the papal seat to Avignon in 1309 and collaborated with Philip to suppress the ▷Templars, a powerful order of knights. Philip allied with the Scots against England and invaded Flanders.

Philip VI (1293–1350) King of France from 1328, first of the house of Valois, elected by the barons on the death of his cousin, Charles IV. His claim was challenged by Edward III of England, who defeated him at Crécy in 1346.

Philip II of Macedon (382–336 BC) King of ▷Macedonia from 359 BC. He seized the throne from his nephew, for whom he was regent, defeated the Greek city states at the battle of Chaeronea (in central Greece) in 338 and formed them into a league whose forces could be united against Persia. He was assassinated while he was planning this expedition, and was succeeded by his son Alexander the Great.

Philip's tomb was discovered at Vergina, northern Greece, in 1978.

Philip five kings of Spain, including:

PHILIP II A 16th-century engraving of the tournament to celebrate the marriage of Philip II of Spain to Isabella, daughter of Henry II of France. *The Art Archive/Dagli Orti*

Philip II (1527–1598) King of Spain from 1556. He was born at Valladolid, the son of the Habsburg emperor Charles V, and in 1554 married Queen ▷Mary I of England. In 1559, after Mary's death, he pursued his ambitions on England by offering to marry her sister ▷Elizabeth I, who had succeeded to the English throne. On his father's abdication in 1556 he inherited Spain, the Netherlands, and the Spanish possessions in Italy and the Americas, and in 1580 he annexed Portugal. His intolerance and lack of understanding of the Netherlanders drove them into revolt. He tried to conquer England in 1588, sending the unsuccessful ▷Spanish Armada, and in 1589 he claimed the throne of France for his daughter Isabella.

Philip V (1683–1746) King of Spain from 1700. A grandson of Louis XIV of France, he was the first Bourbon king of Spain. He was not recognized by the major European powers until 1713. See ▷Spanish Succession, War of the.

Philip, St (lived 1st century AD) In the New Testament, one of the 12 apostles. He was an inhabitant of Bethsaida (northern Israel), and is said to have worked as a missionary in Anatolia. Feast day 3 May.

Philip, Duke of Edinburgh (1921–) Prince of the UK, husband of Elizabeth II, a grandson of George I of Greece and a great-great-grandson of Queen Victoria. He was born in Corfu, Greece, but brought up in England.

He was educated at Gordonstoun and Dartmouth Naval College. During World War II he served in the Mediterranean, taking part in the battle of Matapan, and in the Pacific. A naturalized British subject, taking the surname Mountbatten in March 1947, he married Princess Elizabeth in Westminster Abbey on 20 November 1947, having the previous day received the title Duke of Edinburgh. In 1956 he founded the Duke of Edinburgh's Award Scheme to encourage creative achievement among young people. He was created a prince of the UK in 1957, and awarded the Order of Merit in 1968.

Philip Neri, St (1515–1595) (Italian **Filippo Neri**) Florentine cleric who organized the Congregation of the Oratory. He built the oratory over the Church of St Jerome, Rome, where prayer meetings were held and scenes from the Bible performed with music, originating the musical form ▷oratorio. Feast day 26 May.

PHILIP II OF MACEDON A gold quiver from the royal tomb of King Philip II of Macedon (Verghina), dating from 350–340 BC, depicting warriors in battle (Archaeological Museum, Thessalonika, Greece). *The Art Archive/Victoria and Albert Museum London*

Philippines

Philippines country in southeast Asia, on an archipelago of more than 7,000 islands west of the Pacific Ocean and south of the Southeast Asian mainland.

NATIONAL NAME *Republika Ng Pilipinas/Republic of the Philippines*
AREA 300,000 sq km/115,830 sq mi
CAPITAL Manila (on Luzon island) (and chief port)
MAJOR TOWNS/CITIES Quezon City, Davao, Cebu, Bacolod, Cagayan de Oro, Iloilo City
MAJOR PORTS Cebu, Davao (on Mindanao), Iloilo City, Zamboanga (on Mindanao)
PHYSICAL FEATURES comprises over 7,000 islands; volcanic mountain ranges traverse main chain north–south; 50% still forested. The largest islands are Luzon 108,172 sq km/41,754 sq mi and Mindanao 94,227 sq km/36,372 sq mi; others include Samar, Negros, Palawan, Panay, Mindoro, Leyte, Cebu, and the Sulu group; Pinatubo volcano (1,759 m/5,770 ft); Mindanao has active volcano Apo (2,954 m/9,690 ft) and mountainous rainforest

Government

HEAD OF STATE AND GOVERNMENT Gloria Macapagal Arroyo from 2001
POLITICAL SYSTEM liberal democracy
POLITICAL EXECUTIVE limited presidency
ADMINISTRATIVE DIVISIONS 73 provinces and the National Capital Region
ARMED FORCES 106,000; plus reserve forces of 131,000 and paramilitary forces of 44,000 (2002 est)
CONSCRIPTION military service is voluntary
DEATH PENALTY retained and used for ordinary crimes
DEFENCE SPEND (% GDP) 2.1 (2002 est)
EDUCATION SPEND (% GDP) 3.5 (2001 est)
HEALTH SPEND (% GDP) 3.4 (2000 est)

Economy and resources

CURRENCY peso
GPD (US$) 77.1 billion (2002 est)
REAL GDP GROWTH (% change on previous year) 3.2 (2001)
GNI (US$) 81.5 billion (2002 est)
GNI PER CAPITA (PPP) (US$) 4,280 (2002 est)
CONSUMER PRICE INFLATION 4% (2003 est)
UNEMPLOYMENT 10.3% (2002)
FOREIGN DEBT (US$) 51.6 billion (2001 est)
MAJOR TRADING PARTNERS USA, Japan, EU, Singapore, Taiwan, South Korea, Hong Kong
RESOURCES copper ore, gold, silver, chromium, nickel, coal, crude petroleum, natural gas, forests
INDUSTRIES food processing, petroleum refining, textiles, chemical products, pharmaceuticals, electrical machinery (mainly telecommunications equipment), metals and metal products, tourism
EXPORTS electrical and electronic products (notably semiconductors and microcircuits),

PHILIPPINES Fuente Osmeña, an impressive circular park in the heart of Cebu city, on the island of Cebu. The park is named after Sergio Osmeña Sr, the second president of the Philippine Commonwealth and a native of Cebu. Situated in the Visayas region, Cebu is a major port and the second city of the Philippines, after Manila. *Embassy of the Philippines*

machinery and transport equipment, garments, agricultural products (particularly fruit and seafood), woodcraft and furniture, lumber, chemicals, coconut oil. Principal market: USA 30.4% (2001)
IMPORTS semi-processed raw materials, machinery and transport equipment, telecommunications equipment and electrical machinery, mineral fuels, basic manufactures, chemicals, power generation equipment and specialized machines. Principal source: USA 23.2% (2001)
ARABLE LAND 18.6% (2000 est)
AGRICULTURAL PRODUCTS rice, maize, cassava, coconuts, sugar cane, bananas, pineapples; livestock (chiefly pigs, buffaloes, goats, and poultry) and fisheries

Population and society

POPULATION 79,999,000 (2003 est)
POPULATION GROWTH RATE 1.7% (2000–15)
POPULATION DENSITY (per sq km) 267 (2003 est)
URBAN POPULATION (% of total) 61 (2003 est)
AGE DISTRIBUTION (% of total population) 0–14 37%, 15–59 57%, 60+ 6% (2002 est)
ETHNIC GROUPS comprises more than 50 ethnic communities, although 95% of the population is designated 'Filipino', an Indo-Polynesian ethnic grouping
LANGUAGE Filipino, English (both official), Spanish, Cebuano, Ilocano, more than 70 other indigenous languages
RELIGION Christian 94%, mainly Roman Catholic (84%), Protestant; Muslim 4%, local religions
EDUCATION (compulsory years) 6
LITERACY RATE 96% (men); 95% (women) (2003 est)
LABOUR FORCE 39.1% agriculture, 15.6% industry, 45.3% services (1999)
LIFE EXPECTANCY 68 (men); 72 (women) (2000–05)
CHILD MORTALITY RATE (under 5, per 1,000 live births) 38 (2001)
PHYSICIANS (per 1,000 people) 1.2 (1998 est)
HOSPITAL BEDS (per 1,000 people) 1.1 (1994 est)
TV SETS (per 1,000 people) 173 (2001 est)
RADIOS (per 1,000 people) 161 (2001 est)
INTERNET USERS (per 10,000 people) 440.4 (2002 est)
PERSONAL COMPUTER USERS (per 100 people) 2.8 (2002 est)

Chronology

14th century: Traders from Malay peninsula introduced Islam and created Muslim principalities of Manila and Jolo.
1521: Portuguese navigator Ferdinand Magellan reached the islands, but was killed in battle with islanders.
1536: Philippines named after Charles V's son (later Philip II of Spain) by Spanish navigator Ruy López de Villalobos.
1565: Philippines conquered by Spanish army led by Miguel López de Lagazpi.
1571: Manila was made capital of the colony, which was part of the Viceroyalty of Mexico.
17th century: Spanish missionaries converted much of the lowland population to Roman Catholicism.
1762–63: British occupied Manila.
1834: End of Spanish monopoly on trade; British and American merchants bought sugar and tobacco.
1896–97: Emilio Aguinaldo led a revolt against Spanish rule.
1898: Spanish-American War: US navy destroyed Spanish fleet in Manila Bay; Aguinaldo declared independence, but Spain ceded Philippines to USA.
1898–1901: Nationalist uprising suppressed by US troops; 200,000 Filipinos killed.
1907: Americans set up elected legislative assembly.
1916: Bicameral legislature introduced based on the US model.
1935: Philippines gained internal self-government with Manuel Quezon as president.
1942–45: Occupied by Japan.
1946: Philippines achieved independence from USA under President Manuel Roxas; USA retained military bases and supplied economic aid.
1957–61: 'Filipino First' policy introduced by President Carlos García to reduce economic power of Americans and Chinese; official corruption increased.
1972: President Ferdinand Marcos declared martial law and ended the freedom of the press; economic development financed by foreign loans, of which large sums were diverted by Marcos for personal use.
1981: Martial law officially ended but Marcos retained sweeping emergency powers, ostensibly needed to combat long-running Muslim and communist insurgencies.
1983: Opposition leader Benigno Aquino was murdered at Manila airport while surrounded by government troops.
1986: Corazon Aquino (widow of Benigno Aquino) used 'people's power' to force Marcos to flee the country.
1987: A 'Freedom constitution' was adopted; Aquino's People's Power won congressional elections.
1989: A state of emergency was declared after the sixth coup attempt was suppressed with US aid.
1991: The Philippine senate called for the withdrawal of US forces; US renewal of Subic Bay naval base lease was rejected.
1992: Fidel Ramos was elected to succeed Aquino; a 'Rainbow Coalition' government was formed.
1995: Imelda Marcos (the widow of Ferdinand Marcos) was elected to the House of Representatives while on bail from prison on a sentence for corruption.
1996: The LDP withdrew from the LDP–DFSP coalition. A peace agreement was made between the government and the Moro National Liberation Front (MNLF) after 25 years of civil unrest on Mindanao.
1997: Preliminary peace talks took place between the government and the secessionist Moro Islamic Liberation Front (MILF). The Supreme Court rejected a proposal to allow a second presidential term.
1998: Joseph Estrada was inaugurated as president and Gloria Macapagal Arroyo as vice-president. Imelda Marcos was acquitted of corruption charges. A dispute with China over the mineral-rich Spratly Islands was resolved with an agreement on the joint use of the resources.
2000: The worst fighting since 1996 erupted between government troops and the MILF, fighting for an independent Muslim state on Mindanao. In April, another Islamic separatist group, Abu Sayyaf, took 21 foreign hostages from holiday resorts in Malaysia. They were slowly released, the last few in September when Libya paid $4 million/£2.8 million to the captors. However, further hostages continued to be taken throughout the year. Some were rescued by the Philippine army in September. In November, President Estrada was impeached on corruption charges.
2001: Estrada's trial was suspended after senators blocked the presentation of vital evidence, and Estrada left office. Former vice-president Gloria Macapagal Arroyo, who had led the call for Estrada's impeachment, became president.

Philippines see country box.

Philistine member of a seafaring people of non-Semitic origin who founded city-states on the Palestinian coastal plain in the 12th century BC, adopting a Semitic language and religion.
  Related Web site: Philistine http://www.newadvent.org/cathen/12021c.htm

philology (Greek 'love of language') in historical ▷linguistics, the study of the development of languages. It is also an obsolete term for the study of literature.

philosophy (Greek 'love of wisdom') systematic analysis and critical examination of fundamental problems such as the nature of reality, mind, perception, self, free will, causation, time and space, and moral judgements. Traditionally, philosophy has three branches: metaphysics (the nature of being), epistemology (theory of knowledge), and logic (study of valid inference). Modern philosophy also includes ethics, aesthetics, political theory, the philosophy of science, and the philosophy of religion.
  Related Web site: The Talk.Origins Archive http://www.talkorigins.org/

phlebitis inflammation of the wall of a vein. It is sometimes associated with ▷varicose veins or with a blockage by a blood clot (▷thrombosis), in which case it is more accurately described as thrombophlebitis.

phloem tissue found in vascular plants whose main function is to conduct sugars and other food materials from the leaves, where they are produced, to all other parts of the plant.

phlox any of a group of plants native to North America and Siberia. Phloxes are small with alternate leaves and clusters of showy white, pink, red, or purple flowers. (Genus *Phlox*, family Polemoniaceae.)

Phnom Penh capital of Cambodia, on the Mekong River, 210 km/130 mi northwest of Saigon; population (1994) 920,000. Industries include textiles and food-processing. It has been Cambodia's capital since the 15th century, and has royal palaces, museums, and pagodas.
  On 17 April 1975 the entire population (about 3 million) was forcibly evacuated by the ▷Khmer Rouge communist movement as they captured the city; survivors later returned. In 1979 it was taken by the Vietnamese, who ousted ▷Pol Pot and the Khmer Rouge; they withdrew in 1989, and were banned in 1994.

phobia excessive irrational fear of an object or situation – for example, agoraphobia (fear of open spaces and crowded places), acrophobia (fear of heights), and claustrophobia (fear of enclosed places). ▷Behaviour therapy is one form of treatment.

Phoenicia ancient Greek name for northern ▷Canaan on the east coast of the Mediterranean. The Phoenician civilization flourished from about 1200 until the capture of Tyre by Alexander the Great in 332 BC. Seafaring traders and artisans, they are said to have circumnavigated Africa and established colonies in Cyprus, North Africa (for example, Carthage), Malta, Sicily, and Spain. Their cities (Tyre, Sidon, and Byblos were the main ones) were independent states ruled by hereditary kings but dominated by merchant ruling classes.
  The Phoenicians occupied the seaboard of Lebanon and Syria, north of Mount Carmel. Their exports included Tyrian purple dye and cloth, furniture (from the timber of Lebanon), and jewellery. Documents found in 1929 at Ugarit on the Syrian coast give much information on their civilization; their deities included ▷Baal, Astarte or ▷Ishtar, and ▷Moloch. Competition from the colonies combined with attacks by the Sea Peoples, the Assyrians, and the Greeks on the cities in Phoenicia led to their ultimate decline.

Phoenix capital and largest city of ▷Arizona, USA, located on the Salt River; population (1996 est) 1,159,200. It is a commercial and industrial centre, an agricultural distribution point for the irrigated Salt River valley, and a popular winter resort. Products include steel, aluminium, aviation equipment, computers, electrical goods, cosmetics, clothing, and processed foods.

phoenix in Egyptian and Oriental mythology, a sacred bird born from the sun. The Egyptians believed it was also connected with the soul and the obelisk. In China the phoenix signified good and its appearance prosperity; its departure boded calamity. According to the Greek historian Herodotus, the creature visited the temple of the sun at Heliopolis every 500 years to bury its dead father, embalmed in a ball of myrrh. In another version, the phoenix placed itself on the city's burning altar or built a nest as a funeral pyre, and rose rejuvenated from the ashes. Only one phoenix existed at a time.

phon unit of loudness, equal to the value in decibels of an equally loud tone with frequency 1,000 Hz. The higher the frequency, the louder a noise sounds for the same decibel value; thus an 80-decibel tone with a frequency of 20 Hz sounds as loud as 20 decibels at 1,000 Hz, and the phon value of both tones is 20. An aircraft engine has a loudness of around 140 phons.

phoneme distinctive unit of sound from which a language is formed. For example, /t/ and /d/ are phonemes in English because they can be used to distinguish between two words, for example 'bad' and 'bat'.

phonetics the identification, description, and classification of sounds used in articulate speech. These sounds are codified in the International Phonetic Alphabet (IPA), a highly modified version of the Roman alphabet.

phosphate salt or ester of ▷phosphoric acid. Incomplete neutralization of phosphoric acid gives rise to acid phosphates (see ▷acid salts and ▷buffer). Phosphates are used as fertilizers, and are required for the development of healthy root systems. They are involved in many biochemical processes, often as part of complex molecules, such as ▷ATP.

phospholipid any ▷lipid consisting of a glycerol backbone, a phosphate group, and two long chains. Phospholipids are found everywhere in living systems as the basis for biological membranes.

phosphor any substance that is phosphorescent, that is, gives out visible light when it is illuminated by a beam of electrons or ultraviolet light. The television screen is coated on the inside with phosphors that glow when beams of electrons strike them. Fluorescent lamp tubes are also phosphor-coated. Phosphors are also used in Day-Glo paints, and as optical brighteners in detergents.

phosphorescence in physics, the emission of light by certain substances after they have absorbed energy, whether from visible light, other electromagnetic radiation such as ultraviolet rays or X-rays, or cathode rays (a beam of electrons). When the stimulating energy is removed phosphorescence ceases, although it may persist for a short time after (unlike ▷fluorescence, which stops immediately).

phosphoric acid acid derived from phosphorus and oxygen. Its commonest form (H_3PO_4) is also known as orthophosphoric acid, and is produced by the action of phosphorus pentoxide (P_2O_5) on water. It is used in rust removers and for rust-proofing iron and steel.

phosphorus (Greek *phosphoros* 'bearer of light') highly reactive, nonmetallic element, symbol P, atomic number 15, relative atomic mass 30.9738. It occurs in nature as phosphates (commonly in the form of the mineral ▷apatite), and is essential to plant and animal life. Compounds of phosphorus are used in fertilizers, various organic chemicals, for matches and fireworks, and in glass and steel.
  Phosphorus was first identified in 1674 by German alchemist Hennig Brand (born c. 1630), who prepared it from urine. The element has three allotropic forms: a black powder; a white-yellow, waxy solid that ignites spontaneously in air to form the poisonous gas phosphorus pentoxide; and a red-brown powder that neither ignites spontaneously nor is poisonous.

photocell (or **photoelectric cell**) device for measuring or detecting light or other electromagnetic radiation, since its electrical state is altered by the effect of light. In a **photoemissive** cell, the radiation causes electrons to be emitted and a current to flow (▷photoelectric effect); a **photovoltaic** cell causes an ▷electromotive force to be generated in the presence of light across the boundary of two substances. A **photoconductive** cell, which contains a semiconductor, increases its conductivity when exposed to electromagnetic radiation.

photochemical reaction any chemical reaction in which light is produced or light initiates the reaction. Light can initiate reactions by exciting atoms or molecules and making them more reactive: the light energy becomes converted to chemical energy. Many photochemical reactions set up a ▷chain reaction and produce ▷free radicals.
  This type of reaction is seen in the bleaching of dyes or the yellowing of paper by sunlight. It is harnessed by plants in ▷photosynthesis and by humans in ▷photography.

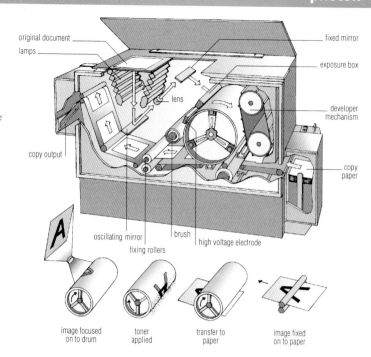

PHOTOCOPIER At the heart of the photocopier is a metal drum on which an image is formed. The toner is attracted to the image by static electricity. As the paper moves past the drum, the image is transferred to the paper. The image is fixed by heating and pressing the toner into the paper.

Chemical reactions that produce light are most commonly seen when materials are burned. Light-emitting reactions are used by living organisms in ▷bioluminescence. One photochemical reaction is the action of sunlight on car exhaust fumes, which results in the production of ▷ozone. Some large cities, such as Los Angeles, and Santiago, Chile, now suffer serious pollution due to photochemical smog.

photocopier machine that uses some form of photographic process to reproduce copies of documents or illustrations. Most modern photocopiers, as pioneered by the Xerox Corporation, use electrostatic photocopying, or ▷xerography ('dry writing').

photoelectric cell alternative name for ▷photocell.

photoelectric effect in physics, the emission of ▷electrons from a substance (usually a metallic surface) when it is struck by ▷photons (quanta of electromagnetic radiation), usually those of visible light or ultraviolet radiation.

photography process for reproducing images on sensitized materials by various forms of radiant energy, including visible light, ultraviolet, infrared, X-rays, atomic radiations, and electron beams.
  Photography was developed in the 19th century; among the pioneers were Louis ▷Daguerre in France and ▷Fox Talbot in the UK. Colour photography dates from the early 20th century. See Photography: Key Dates on p. 748.
  Related Web sites: Exposure: A Beginners Guide to Photography http://www.88.com/exposure/index.htm
  History of Photography http://www.rleggat.com/photohistory/
  Photo.net http://photo.net/photo/

photogravure ▷printing process that uses a plate prepared photographically, covered with a pattern of recessed cells in which the ink is held. See ▷gravure.

photometer instrument that measures luminous intensity, usually by comparing relative intensities from different sources. Bunsen's grease-spot photometer of 1844 compares the intensity of a light source with a known source by each illuminating one half of a translucent area. Modern photometers use ▷photocells, as in a photographer's exposure meter. A photomultiplier can also be used as a photometer.

photon in physics, the ▷elementary particle or 'package' (quantum) of energy in which light and other forms of electromagnetic radiation are emitted. The photon has both particle and wave properties; it has no charge, is considered massless but possesses momentum and energy. It is one of the ▷gauge bosons, and is the carrier of the ▷electromagnetic force, one of the fundamental forces of nature.
  According to ▷quantum theory the energy of a photon is given by the formula $E = hf$, where h is Planck's constant and f is the frequency of the radiation emitted.

Photography: Key Dates

1515	Leonardo da Vinci describes the camera obscura.
1750	The painter Canaletto uses a camera obscura as an aid to his painting in Venice.
1790	Thomas Wedgwood in England makes photograms –placing objects on leather, sensitized using silver nitrate.
1826	Nicéphore Niepce, a French doctor, produces the world's first photograph from nature on pewter plates with a camera obscura and an eight-hour exposure.
1838	As a result of his earlier collaboration with Niepce, L J M Daguerre produces the first daguerreotype camera photograph.
1839	Daguerre is awarded an annuity by the French government and his process is given to the world.
1840	Invention of the Petzval lens, which reduces exposure time by 90%. John Herschel uses sodium thiosulphate as a fixer for silver halides.
1841	William Henry Fox Talbot's calotype process is patented – the first multicopy method of photography using a negative/positive process, sensitized with silver iodide.
1844–46	Fox Talbot publishes the first photographic book, *The Pencil of Nature*.
1845	David Hill and Robert Adamson begin to use calotypes for portraits in Edinburgh, Scotland.
1851	Fox Talbot uses a one-thousandth of a second exposure to demonstrate high-speed photography. Invention of the wet-collodion-on-glass process and the waxed-paper negative. Photographs are displayed at the Great Exhibition in London, England.
1852	The London Society of Arts exhibits 779 photographs.
1855	Roger Fenton makes documentary photographs of the Crimean War from a specially constructed caravan with portable darkroom.
1858	Nadar takes the first aerial photographs from a balloon.
1859	Nadar in Paris makes photographs underground using battery-powered arc lights.
1860	Queen Victoria is photographed. Abraham Lincoln is photographed for political campaigning purposes.
1861	The single-lens reflex plate camera is patented by Thomas Sutton. The principles of three-colour photography are demonstrated by Scottish physicist James Clerk Maxwell.
1870	Julia Margaret Cameron uses long lenses for her distinctive portraits.
1871	Gelatin-silver bromide is developed.
1878	In the USA Eadweard Muybridge analyses the movements of animals through sequential photographs, using a series of cameras.
1879	The photogravure process is invented.
1880	A silver bromide emulsion is fixed with hypo. Photographs are first reproduced in newspapers in New York using the half-tone engraving process. The first twin-lens reflex camera is produced in London. Gelatin-silver chloride paper is introduced.
1884	George Eastman produces flexible negative film.
1889	The Eastman Company in the USA produces the Kodak No 1 camera and roll film, facilitating universal, hand-held snapshots.
1891	The first telephoto lens. The interference process of colour photography is developed by the French doctor Gabriel Lippmann.
1897	The first issue of Alfred Stieglitz's *Camera Notes* in the USA.
1904	The autochrome colour process is patented by the Lumière brothers.
1905	Alfred Stieglitz opens the gallery '291' in New York, USA, promoting photography. Lewis Hine uses photography to expose the exploitation of children in US factories – as a result, laws to protect them are passed.
1907	The autochrome process begins to be factory-produced.
1914	Oskar Barnack designs a prototype Leica camera for Leitz in Germany.
1924	Leitz launches the first 35-mm camera, the Leica, delayed because of World War I. It becomes very popular with photojournalists because it is quiet, small, dependable, and has a range of lenses and accessories.
1929	Rolleiflex produces a twin-lens reflex camera in Germany.
1935	In the USA, Mannes and Godowsky invent Kodachrome transparency film, which produces sharp images and rich colour quality. Electronic flash is invented in the USA.
1936	*Life* magazine, significant for its photojournalism, is first published in the USA.
1940	Multigrade enlarging paper by Ilford is made available in the UK.
1942	Kodacolour negative film is introduced.
1945	The zone system of exposure estimation is published in the book *Exposure Record* by Ansel Adams.
1947	Polaroid black and white instant process film is invented by Dr Edwin Land, who sets up the Polaroid corporation in Boston, Massachusetts. The principles of holography are demonstrated in England by Dennis Gabor.
1955	Kodak introduces Tri-X, a black and white 200 ISO film.
1959	The zoom lens is invented by the Austrian firm of Voigtlander.
1960	The laser is invented in the USA, making holography possible. Polacolor, a self-processing colour film, is introduced by Polaroid, using a 60-second colour film and dye diffusion technique.
1963	Cibachrome, paper and chemicals for printing directly from transparencies, is made available by Ciba-Geigy of Switzerland. One of the most permanent processes, it is marketed by Ilford in the UK.
1966	The International Center of Photography is established in New York.
1969	Photographs are taken on the Moon by US astronauts.
1970	A charge-coupled device is invented at Bell Laboratories in New Jersey, USA, to record very faint images (for example in astronomy). Rencontres Internationales de la Photographie, the annual summer festival of photography with workshops, is founded in Arles, France.
1971	Opening of the Photographers' Gallery, London, and the Photo Archive of the Bibliothéque Nationale, Paris.
1972	The SX70 system, a single-lens reflex camera with instant prints, is produced by Polaroid.
1975	The Center for Creative Photography is established at the University of Arizona.
1980	Ansel Adams sells an original print, *Moonrise: Hernandez*, for $45,000, a record price, in the USA. *Voyager 1* sends photographs of Saturn back to Earth across space.
1983	The National Museum of Photography, Film and Television opens in Bradford, England.
1985	The Minolta Corporation in Japan introduces the Minolta 7000 – the world's first body-integral autofocus single-lens reflex camera.
1988	The electronic camera, which stores pictures on magnetic disc instead of on film, is introduced in Japan.
1990	Kodak introduces PhotoCD, which converts 35-mm camera pictures (on film) into digital form and stores them on compact disc (CD) for viewing on TV.
1992	Japanese company Canon introduces a camera with autofocus controlled by the user's eye. The camera focuses on whatever appears at the centre of the image in the viewfinder. *Girl with a Leica* by Russian photographer Aleksandr Rodchenko sells for £115,500 at Christie's, London – a world-record price for a photograph.
1996	Corbis, a company owned by Bill Gates, buys the exclusive rights to 2,500 photographs by Ansel Adams. Kodak produces its first 'point-and-shoot' digital camera.
2001	Kodak introduces 'easy-dock' digital cameras, simplifying the processes of downloading pictures and charging batteries.

See entry on p. 747.

Photorealism (or **Superrealism** or **Hyperrealism**) style of painting and sculpture popular in the late 1960s and 1970s, especially in the USA, characterized by intense, photographic realism and attention to minute detail. The Photorealists' aim was to create a record of peoples, places, and objects that was dispassionate to the extent of being almost surreal. Leading exponents were US painters Chuck Close (1940–) and Richard Estes (1936–) and US sculptor Duane Hanson (1925–).

photosphere visible surface of the Sun, which emits light and heat. About 300 km/200 mi deep, it consists of incandescent gas at a temperature of 5,800 K (5,530°C/9,980°F).

photosynthesis process by which green plants trap light energy from the Sun. This energy is used to drive a series of chemical reactions which lead to the formation of carbohydrates. The carbohydrates occur in the form of simple sugar, or glucose, which provides the basic food for both plants and animals. For photosynthesis to occur, the plant must possess ▷chlorophyll and must have a supply of carbon dioxide and water. Photosynthesis takes place inside ▷chloroplasts which are found mainly in the leaf cells of plants.

The by-product of photosynthesis, oxygen, is of great importance to all living organisms, and virtually all atmospheric oxygen has originated by photosynthesis.

Chloroplasts contain the enzymes and chlorophyll necessary for photosynthesis, and the leaf structure of plants is specially adapted to this purpose.

Leaf structure In the lower epidermis on the leaf underside are stomata (pores; see ▷stoma), each of which is surrounded by a pair of ▷guard cells that control their opening and closing. These guard cells contain chloroplasts. The central layer of the leaf between the layers of epidermis is called the mesophyll, and all the cells in this tissue contain chloroplasts. Running through the mesophyll are the veins, each of which contains large, thick-walled ▷xylem vessels for carrying water, and smaller, thin-walled ▷phloem tubes for transporting the food produced by the leaf. Most of the glucose that forms during photosynthesis is stored in the chloroplasts as starch. As plant-eating animals eat the leaves they too are dependent on plant photosynthesis to supply their basic energy needs.

Chemical process The chemical reactions of photosynthesis occur in two stages. During the **light reaction** sunlight is used to split water (H_2O) into oxygen (O_2), protons (hydrogen ions, H^+), and electrons, and oxygen is given off as a by-product. In the **dark reaction**, for which sunlight is not required, the protons and electrons are used to convert carbon dioxide (CO_2) into carbohydrates ($C_m(H_2O)_n$) . So the whole process can be summarized by the equation

$$CO_2 + 2H_2O \rightarrow C_m(H_2O)_n + H_2O + O_2$$

Photosynthesis depends on the ability of chlorophyll to capture the energy of sunlight and to use it to split water molecules. The initial charge separation occurs in less than a billionth of a second, a speed that compares with current computers.

Plant pigments Photosynthetic pigments are the plant pigments responsible for capturing light energy during photosynthesis. The primary pigment is chlorophyll, which absorbs blue and red light. Other pigments, such as ▷carotenoids, are accessory pigments which also capture light energy and pass it on to chlorophyll. Photosynthesis by cyanobacteria was responsible for the appearance of oxygen in the Earth's atmosphere 2 billion years ago, and photosynthesis by plants maintains the oxygen levels today.

phototropism movement of part of a plant toward or away from a source of light. Leaves are positively phototropic, detecting the source of light and orientating themselves to receive the maximum amount.

phrase-structure grammar theory of language structure that proposes that a given language has several different potential sentence patterns, consisting of various sorts of phrases, which can be expanded in various ways.

Phrygia former kingdom of western Asia covering the Anatolian plateau. It was inhabited in ancient times by an Indo-European people and achieved great prosperity in the 8th century BC under a line of kings bearing in turn the names Gordius and Midas, but then fell under Lydian rule. From Phrygia the cult of the Earth goddess Cybele was introduced into Greece and Rome.

Related Web site: Phrygia http://www.focusmm.com/civcty/phyr_00.htm

phylacteries in Judaism, another name for ▷tefillin.

phylloxera plant-eating insect of the family Phylloxeridae, closely related to the aphids.

phylogeny historical sequence of changes that occurs in a given species during the course of its evolution. It was once erroneously associated with ontogeny (the process of development of a living organism).

phylum (plural **phyla**) major grouping in biological classification. Mammals, birds, reptiles, amphibians, fishes, and tunicates belong to the phylum Chordata; the phylum Mollusca consists of snails, slugs, mussels, clams, squid, and octopuses; the phylum Porifera contains sponges; and the phylum Echinodermata includes starfish, sea urchins, and sea cucumbers. In classifying plants (where the term 'division' often takes the place of 'phylum'), there are between four and nine phyla depending on the criteria used; all flowering plants belong to a single phylum, Angiospermata, and all conifers to another, Gymnospermata. Related phyla are grouped together in a ▷kingdom; phyla are subdivided into ▷classes.

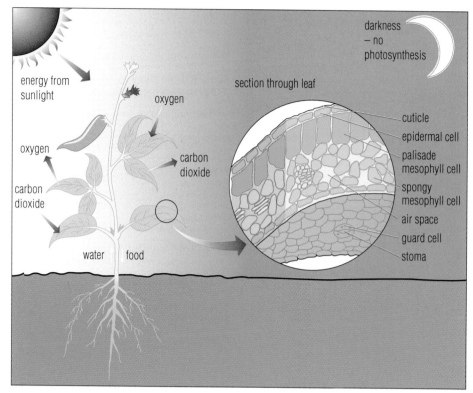

PIANO Austrian pianist Carl Czerny (1791–1857) was a pupil of the German composer Beethoven, and later became piano tutor to Beethoven's nephew. A composer of many works for the piano, he is remembered for his graded piano lessons. He published several other works for the teaching of the piano, which include a *School of the Left Hand*, and a *School of Virtuosity*. *The Art Archive/Society Friends Music Vienna/Dagli Orti*

PHOTOSYNTHESIS Process by which green plants and some bacteria manufacture carbohydrates from water and atmospheric carbon dioxide, using the energy of sunlight. Photosynthesis depends on the ability of chlorophyll molecules within plant cells to trap the energy of light, in order to split water molecules, giving off oxygen as a by-product. The hydrogen of the water molecules is then used to reduce carbon dioxide to simple carbohydrates.

There are 36 different phyla. The most recently identified is the Cyclophora described in 1995. It contains a single known species, *Symbion pandora*, that lives on lobsters.

physical chemistry branch of chemistry concerned with examining the relationships between the chemical compositions of substances and the physical properties that they display. Most chemical reactions exhibit some physical phenomenon (change of state, temperature, pressure, or volume, or the use or production of electricity), and the measurement and study of such phenomena has led to many chemical theories and laws.

physics branch of science concerned with the laws that govern the structure of the universe, and the investigation of the properties of matter and energy and their interactions. For convenience, physics is often divided into branches such as atomic physics, nuclear physics, particle physics, solid-state physics, molecular physics, electricity and magnetism, optics, acoustics, heat, thermodynamics, quantum theory, and relativity. Before the 20th century, physics was known as **natural philosophy**. See Physics: Key Dates on p. 750.
Related Web site: How Things Work http://howthingswork.virginia.edu/

physiocrat member of a school of 18th-century French economists, including François Quesnay (1694–1774) and Mirabeau, who believed in the bounty of nature and the inherent goodness of man. They held that governments should intervene in society only where individuals' liberties were infringed. Otherwise there should be a *laissez-faire* system with free trade between states. The Scottish economist Adam Smith was much influenced by their ideas.

physiology branch of biology that deals with the functioning of living organisms, as opposed to anatomy, which studies their structures.

physiotherapy treatment of injury and disease by physical means such as exercise, heat, manipulation, massage, and electrical stimulation.

phytomenadione one form of vitamin K, a fat-soluble chemical found in green vegetables. It is involved in the production of prothrombin, which is essential in blood clotting. It is given to newborns to prevent potentially fatal brain haemorrhages.

pi symbol π, the ratio of the circumference of a circle to its diameter. Pi is an irrational number; it cannot be expressed as the ratio of two integers, and its expression as a decimal never terminates and never starts recurring. The value of pi is 3.1415926, correct to seven decimal places. Common approximations to pi are 22/7 and 3.14, although the value 3 can be used as a rough estimation.

Pi is also a transcendental number (a number that cannot be expressed as a root or as the solution of an algebraic equation with rational coefficients). This was proved in 1882 by German mathematician Ferdinand von Lindemann, and it means that from a line segment drawn to represent the diameter of a circle it is impossible to construct another straight-line segment to represent the circumference of the circle using straight edge and compasses only.
Related Web site: Pi Through The Ages http://www-history.mcs.st-and.ac.uk/history/HistTopics/Pi_through_the_ages.html

Piaf, Edith (1915–1963) Stage name of Edith Giovanna Gassion. French singer and songwriter, a cabaret singer in Paris, France, from the late 1930s. She is remembered for her powerful voice and for the songs 'Je ne regrette rien/I Regret Nothing' and 'La Vie en rose' (1946).

piano (or **pianoforte**; originally **fortepiano**) stringed musical instrument played by felt-covered hammers activated from a keyboard. It is therefore a form of mechanized ▷dulcimer, a percussion instrument, unlike the earlier ▷harpsichord, a mechanized harp in which the strings are plucked. It is capable of dynamic gradation between soft (Italian *piano*) and loud (Italian *forte*) tones, hence its name. The first piano was constructed in 1704 and introduced in 1709 by Bartolommeo Cristofori, a harpsichord maker from Padua. It uses a clever mechanism to make the keyboard touch-sensitive. Extensively developed during the 18th century, the piano attracted admiration among many composers, although it was not until 1768 that Johann Christian ▷Bach gave one of the first public recitals on the instrument.
Related Web site: Piano Page http://www.ptg.org/

Piano, Renzo (1937–) Italian high-tech architect. With Richard ▷Rogers, he designed the Pompidou Centre, Paris, France (1970–77). Among his other buildings are Kansai Airport, Osaka, Japan and a sports stadium in Bari, Italy (1989), both employing new materials and making imaginative use of civil engineering techniques.

Picardy (French **Picardie**) region of northern France, including Aisne, Oise, and Somme *départements*; area 19,400 sq km/ 7,500 sq mi; population (1999 est) 1,857,800. Its industries include chemicals and metals. Principal towns include Abbeville and ▷Amiens; the latter is the administrative centre and was capital of the old province.

picaresque (Spanish *picaro* 'rogue') genre of novel that takes a rogue or villain for its central character, telling his or her story in episodic form. The genre originated in Spain and was popular in the 18th century in Britain. Daniel Defoe's *Moll Flanders* (1722), Tobias Smollett's *Roderick Random* (1748), Henry Fielding's *Tom Jones* (1749), and Mark Twain's *Huckleberry Finn* (1885) are typical picaresque novels. The device of using an outsider gave the author the opportunity to give fresh moral insights into society.

Picasso, Pablo Ruiz y (1881–1973) Spanish artist, chiefly active in France. He was one of the most inventive and prolific talents in 20th-century art. His Blue Period 1901–04 and Rose Period 1905–06 preceded the revolutionary *Les Demoiselles d'Avignon* (1907; Museum of Modern Art, New York), which paved the way for ▷cubism. In the early 1920s he was considered a leader of the surrealist movement. From the 1930s his work included sculpture, ceramics, and graphic works in a wide variety of media. Among his best-known paintings is ▷*Guernica* (1937), a comment on the bombing of civilians in the Spanish Civil War.

He first went to Paris in 1900 and settled there permanently in 1904. To begin with his work was concerned with the social scene, after the fashion of Degas and Toulouse-Lautrec, but between 1901 and 1904 he turned to austere figure studies, blue being the dominant colour (Blue Period). Circus pictures followed, delicate and more varied in colour (Rose Period, 1905–06).

An epoch-making change in his art followed when between 1907 and 1909, together with Georges ▷Braque, he developed cubism, from the study of Cézanne combined with that of Negro sculpture and primitive art. *Les Demoiselles d'Avignon* (1907) marks the birth of the cubist movement, to which Picasso adhered until 1914. Like Braque, he practised successively its 'analytic' form (construction in depth) and its 'synthetic' form (more decorative and two-dimensional in effect). A feature of his cubist still life, 1912–14, was the use of 'collage'.

He reverted to a neoclassical style 1920–24, in painting and in outline etchings of classical themes. He met Diaghilev and designed the *décor* of a number of ballets 1917–1927. A new and imaginative phase of his art began in about 1925, and coincided with the development of surrealism. The bull, a traditional Spanish emblem of conflict and tragedy, began to appear in paintings and etchings, and the *Guernica*, painted in 1937 during the Spanish Civil War, was a fierce pictorial comment on a deplorable bombing incident, making use

David Hilbert
German mathematician
He who seeks for methods without having a definite problem in mind for the most part seeks in vain.
Quoted in J R Oppenheimer *Physics in the Contemporary World*

Pablo Picasso
I paint objects as I think them, not as I see them.
Quoted in J Golding *Cubism*

Physics: Key Dates

c. 400 BC	The first 'atomic' theory is put forward by the Greek philosopher Democritus.
c. 340	Arisotle adapts and elaborates an earlier theory of his earlier Greek compatriot Empedocles that all matter consists of four elements – earth, air, fire, and water – with a fifth element, ether, making up the heavens. He also develops ideas about motion.
c. 250	Archimedes' principle of buoyancy is established. Archimedes also discovers the principle of the lever.
c. 60	The Roman poet Lucretius writes *De rerum natura / On the nature of the Universe*, which includes an exposition of the atomic theory of Democritus.
AD 1600	Magnetism is described by William Gilbert of England.
c. 1610	The principle of falling bodies descending to earth at the same speed is established by the Italian astronomer and physicist Galileo Galilei.
1642	The principles of hydraulics are put forward by French physicist and mathematician Blaise Pascal.
1662	Boyle's law concerning the behaviour of gases is established by Irish physicist and chemist Robert Boyle.
c. 1665	The English physicist and mathematician Isaac Newton works out that the Earth exerts a constant force on falling bodies. This force is called gravitation or gravity.
1685	Newton publishes his *Principia mathematica philosophiae naturalis / Principles of natural philosophy*, containing an outline of his system of mechanics and including his law of universal gravitation and his three laws of motion.
1690	The wave theory of light is propounded by Christiaan Huygens.
1704	The corpuscular theory of light is put forward by Newton.
1714	Polish-born Dutch physicist Daniel Fahrenheit invents a temperature scale that is later refined to register the freezing point of water at 32° and its boiling point at 212°.
1724	Fahrenheit describes the phenomenon of supercooled water.
1729	English physicist Stephen Gray discovers that static electric charges exist on the surfaces of objects, not within them, and that electricity can pass from one object to another and over distances by means of conductors.
1733	French physicist Charles François de Cisternay du Fay discovers that there are two kinds of static electric charge and that like charges repel, while unlike charges attract.
1742	Anders Celsius, a Swedish astronomer, invents a centigrade temperature scale, fixing 0° as the boiling point of water and 100° as the freezing point. In 1743, these points are swapped to give the centigrade scale still in use.
1751	The American polymath Benjamin Franklin describes electricity as a fluid, differentiates between positive and negative electricity, and shows that electricity can magnetize and demagnetize iron. In 1752 he performs his famous experiment, flying a kite into a thunder cloud and proving that lightning is a form of electricity.
1764	Specific and latent heats are described by the Scottish chemist Joseph Black.
1771	The link between nerve action and electricity is discovered by the Italian physicist Luigi Galvani.
c. 1787	Charles's law relating the pressure, volume, and temperature of a gas is established by French physicist and chemist Jacques Charles.
1795	The metric system is adopted in France.
1798	The link between heat and friction is discovered by the American-born physicist Benjamin Thompson, Count Rumford.
1801	Interference of light is discovered by the English physicist Thomas Young.
1808	The 'modern' atomic theory is propounded by the English chemist John Dalton.
1811	Avogadro's hypothesis relating volumes and numbers of molecules of gases is proposed by Italian chemist Amedeo Avogadro.
1814	Dark lines in the solar spectrum are mapped by the German physicist and optician Joseph von Fraunhofer, from whom they receive their name.
1815	Refraction of light is explained by French physicist Augustin Fresnel.
1820	The discovery of electromagnetism is made by Danish physicist Hans Oersted.
1821	The dynamo principle is described by the English physicist Michael Faraday.
1822	The laws of electrodynamics are established by the French physicist André Ampère.
1826	French physiologist Henri Dutrochet discovers and explains osmosis.
1827	Ohm's law of electrical resistance is established by the German physicist Georg Ohm; Brownian movement (rapid movement resulting from molecular vibrations) is observed by the Scottish botanist Robert Brown in pollen grains suspended in a liquid.
1829	The law of gaseous diffusion is established by Scottish chemist and physicist Thomas Graham.
1831	Electromagnetic induction is discovered independently by Michael Faraday and US physicist Joseph Henry.
1842	The principle of conservation of energy is observed by German physicist Julius von Mayer.
c. 1847	The mechanical equivalent of heat is described by the English physicist James Joule.
1849	A measurement of the velocity of light is put forward by French physicist Armand Fizeau. Fizeau discovers in 1851 that light travels slower in water when the direction of the light beam is against the current of water than when it is following the current. Scottish mathematician and physicist William Thomson, later Lord Kelvin, invents the term 'thermodynamics' in an article on the theory of heat developed by Sadi Carnot.
1850	Rudolf Clausius publishes the first generalized statement of the second law of thermodynamics, later restated by him as 'In a closed system entropy tends to increase'.
1851	The rotation of the Earth is demonstrated by French physicist Jean Foucault using a pendulum. William Thomson, later Lord Kelvin, proposes the concept of absolute zero, the temperature at which all molecular movement stops.
1859	Spectrographic analysis carried out by Robert Bunsen and Gustav Kirchhoff of Germany reveals that each chemical element is uniquely associated with a specific spectral line or set of lines.
1864	Scottish physicist James Clerk Maxwell presents the first mathematical treatment of electricity and magnetism using Faraday's idea of a field as a set of lines of force.
1873	Maxwell conceives light as electromagnetic radiation.
1877	A theory of sound as vibrations in an elastic medium is propounded by the English physicist John Strutt, 3rd Baron Rayleigh.
1880	Piezoelectricity is discovered by the French physicist Pierre Curie.
1887	The existence of radio waves is predicted by the German physicist Heinrich Hertz. The US physicists Albert Michelson and Edward Morley measure the velocity of light in two different directions in an attempt to detect the Earth's motion through the ether, the supposed medium allowing the propagation of light. They find no difference in the two measurements, proving that the speed of light is constant and independent of the motion of the observer and that the ether does not exist.
1895	X-rays are discovered by the German physicist Wilhelm Röntgen.
1896	The French physicist Antoine Becquerel discovers that uranium gives off rays. This is the first observation of natural radioactivity.
1897	The English physicist Joseph Thomson discovers the electron.
1898	French physicists Marie and Pierre Curie discover that the element thorium gives off rays like uranium. Marie Curie names the phenomenon radioactivity.
1899	New Zealand-born physicist Ernest Rutherford discovers alpha and beta rays. Becquerel discovers in 1900 that beta rays in fact consist of electrons.
1900	Quantum theory is propounded by Max Planck of Germany; the discovery of gamma rays is made by French physicist Paul-Ulrich Villard.
1904	The theory of radioactivity is put forward by Rutherford and English chemist Frederick Soddy.
1905	The German-born physicist Albert Einstein propounds his special theory of relativity.
1911	Rutherford discovers the atomic nucleus.
1911	The Dutch physicist Heike Kamerlingh Onnes observes that mercury, when cooled to just above absolute zero, loses its electrical resistance. The phenomenon becomes known as superconductivity.
1913	The orbiting electron atomic theory is propounded by Danish physicist Niels Bohr.
1915	X-ray crystallography is discovered by the English physicists William and Lawrence Bragg.
1916	Einstein puts forward his general theory of relativity; mass spectrography is discovered by the Englishman William Aston.
1926	Wave mechanics is introduced by the Austrian physicist Erwin Schrödinger.
1927	The uncertainty principle of quantum physics is established by the German physicist Werner Heisenberg.
1932	James Chadwick of England discovers the neutron.
1933	The positron, the antiparticle of the electron, is discovered by US physicist Carl Anderson.
1934	Artificial radioactivity is developed by the French physicists Frédéric and Irène Joliot-Curie.
1939	The discovery of nuclear fission is made by the German physicists Otto Hahn and Fritz Strassmann.
1942	The first controlled nuclear chain reaction is achieved by the Italian-born US physicist Enrico Fermi.
1956	The neutrino, an elementary particle, is discovered by Clyde Cowan and Fred Reines of the USA.
1960	The Mössbauer effect of atom emissions is discovered by German physicist Rudolf Mössbauer; the first laser and the first maser are developed by US physicist Theodore Maiman.
1964	Murray Gell-Mann and George Zweig of the USA discover and name the quark.
1979	The discovery of the asymmetry of elementary particles is made by US physicists James W Cronin and Val L Fitch.
1983	Evidence of the existence of weakons (W and Z particles) is confirmed at CERN, the European centre for nuclear research, validating the link between the weak nuclear force and the electromagnetic force.
1986	The first high-temperature superconductor is discovered, able to conduct electricity without resistance at a temperature of −238°C/−396°F.
1996	CERN physicists create the first atoms of antimatter (nine atoms of antihydrogen). The Lawrence Livermore National Laboratory, California, USA, produces a laser of 1.3 petawatts (130 trillion watts).
1999	Scientists succeed in slowing down the speed of light from its normal speed of 299,792 km/186,282 mi per second to 61 km/38 mi per hour, opening up potential for the development of high-precision computer and telecommunications technologies, as well as for the advanced study of quantum mechanics.
2000	CERN scientists announce a new state of matter produced when lead atoms are made to collide in a particle accelerator. It is 20 times as dense as nuclear matter and is believed to have existed about 10 microseconds after the Big Bang. In this new state of matter, quarks are not bound together but roam freely.

See entry on p. 749.

of this symbolism. In later works he moved freely from one style and one medium to another, using all with astonishing freedom and virtuosity.

Related Web site: Picasso Project http://www.tamu.edu/mocl/picasso/

Piccard, Auguste Antoine (1884–1962) Swiss scientist. In 1931–32, he and his twin brother, **Jean Félix** (1884–1963), made ascents to 17,000 m/55,000 ft in a balloon of his own design, resulting in useful discoveries concerning stratospheric phenomena such as ▷cosmic radiation. He also built and used, with his son **Jacques Ernest** (1922–   ), bathyscaphs for research under the sea.

piccolo woodwind instrument, the smallest member of the ▷flute family, for which Vivaldi composed three concertos. It sounds an octave higher than the flute, and for this reason is sometimes known as the *ottavino* (Italian, 'octave'). Used adjectivally, piccolo is also an alternative term for sopranino.

Pickford, Mary (1893–1979) Stage name of Gladys Mary Smith. Canadian-born US actor. The first star of the silent screen, she was known as 'America's Sweetheart,' and played innocent ingenue roles into her thirties. She and her second husband (from 1920), Douglas ▷Fairbanks Sr, were known as 'the world's sweethearts'. With her

husband, Charlie ▷Chaplin, and D W ▷Griffith she founded United Artists studio in 1919. For many years she was the wealthiest and most influential woman in Hollywood.

Pict Roman term for a member of the peoples of northern Scotland, possibly meaning 'painted' (tattooed). Of pre-Celtic origin, and speaking a Celtic language which died out in about the 10th century, the Picts are thought to have inhabited much of England before the arrival of the Celtic Britons. They were united with the Celtic Scots under the rule of Kenneth MacAlpin in 844. Their greatest monument is a series of carved stones, whose symbols remain undeciphered.

pidgin language any of various trade jargons, contact languages, or ▷lingua francas arising in ports and markets where people of different linguistic backgrounds meet for commercial and other purposes. Usually a pidgin language is a rough blend of the vocabulary of one (often dominant) language with the syntax or grammar of one or more other (often dependent) groups. Pidgin English in various parts of the world, *français petit negre*, and Bazaar Hindi or Hindustani are examples of pidgins that have served long-term purposes to the extent of being acquired by children as one of their everyday languages. At this point they become ▷creole languages.

Piedmont (Italian **Piemonte**) region of northern Italy, comprising the provinces of Alessandria, Asti, Cuneo, Novara, Turin, and Vercelli; area 25,400 sq km/9,800 sq mi; population (1992 est) 4,303,800. It borders Switzerland to the north and France to the west, and is surrounded, except to the east, by the Alps and the Apennines. The regional capital is ▷Turin. Piedmont also includes the fertile Po Valley. Products include rice, fruit, grain, cattle, cars, and textiles. The movement for the unification of Italy started in the 19th century in Piedmont, under the House of Savoy.

Pierce, Franklin (1804–1869) 14th president of the USA, 1853–57. He sat as a Democrat in the House of Representatives 1833–37 and the Senate 1837–42. Chosen as a compromise candidate of the Democratic Party, he was elected president in 1852. His presidency was marked by territorial and commercial expansion, including the ▷Gadsden Purchase, but also by escalating North–South tensions.

Piero della Francesca (*c.* 1420–1492) Painter from Borgo San Sepulcro in Umbria. Active in Arezzo and Urbino, he was one of the major artists of the 15th century. His work has a solemn stillness and unusually solid figures, luminous colour, and carefully calculated compositional harmonies. It includes several important fresco series and panel paintings such as the *Flagellation of Christ* (*c.* 1455; Ducal Palace, Urbino), which is remarkable for its use of perspective.

Formal and austere, all his works, of whatever size or medium, show in their use of colour, perspective, and composition a fascination with mathematical order. His largest-scale work is the fresco series *The Legend of the True Cross* (1452–60; the Church of San Francesco, Arezzo); other works include the fresco *The Resurrection of Christ* (Pinacoteca, Borgo San Sepulcro) and the panel altarpiece *Madonna with the Duke of Urbino as Donor* (Brera, Milan). The two famous panel paintings in the National Gallery, London, the *Baptism of Christ* and the *Nativity*, though closely related in style, are considered to be an early and late work respectively.

His portraits include *Federigo da Montefeltro* (*c.* 1470) and *Battista Sforza* (*c.* 1470; both Uffizi, Florence).

The oil method of these portraits suggests some acquaintance with Netherlandish painting, but in general the art of Piero is strongly individual in its poetry and contemplative spirit, and the feeling of intellectual force conveyed by its abstract treatment of space and form.

Piero di Cosimo (*c.* 1462–*c.* 1521) Florentine, idiosyncratic (if not mentally unstable) painter. As well as religious paintings, he produced inventive pictures of mythological subjects, often featuring fauns and centaurs, like the *Forest Fire* (*c.* 1505; Ashmolean Museum, Oxford).

Pietism religious movement within Lutheranism in the 17th century that emphasized spiritual and devotional faith rather than theology and dogma. It was founded by Philipp Jakob Spener (1635–1705), a minister in Frankfurt, Germany, who emphasized devotional meetings for 'groups of the Elect' rather than biblical learning; he wrote the *Pia Desideria* (1675).

Pietro da Cortona (1596–1669) Born Pietro Berrettini. Italian painter and architect. He was a major influence in the development of the high baroque. His enormous fresco *Allegory of Divine Providence* (1633–39; Barberini Palace, Rome) glorifies his patron the pope and the Barberini family, and gives a convincing illusion of reality.

piezoelectric effect property of some crystals (for example, quartz) to develop an electromotive force or voltage across opposite faces when subjected to tension or compression, and, conversely, to expand or contract in size when subjected to an electromotive force. Piezoelectric crystal ▷oscillators are used as frequency standards (for example, replacing balance wheels in watches), and for producing ultrasound.

The crystals are also used in gramophone pickups, transducers in ultrasonics, and certain gas lighters.

PIF abbreviation for ▷Pacific Islands Forum.

pig any even-toed hoofed mammal of the family Suidae. They are omnivorous, and have simple, non-ruminating stomachs and thick hides. The Middle Eastern **wild boar** *Sus scrofa* is the ancestor of domesticated breeds; it is 1.5 m/4.5 ft long and 1 m/3 ft high, with formidable tusks, but not naturally aggressive. The smallest member of the pig family is the **pygmy hog** *Sus salvanus*. Males are 65 cm long (25 cm at the shoulder) and weigh 8–9 kg.

Wild pigs include the ▷babirusa and the ▷wart hog. The farming of domesticated pigs was practised during the Neolithic period in the Middle East and China at least 11,000 years ago and the pig was a common farm animal in ancient Greece and Rome. Over 400 breeds evolved over the centuries, many of which have all but disappeared in more recent times with the development of intensive rearing systems; however, different environments and requirements have ensured the continuation of a variety of types. The Berkshire, Chester White, Poland, China, Saddleback, Yorkshire, Duroc, and Razorback are the main surviving breeds. Modern indoor rearing methods favour the large white breeds, such as the Chester White and the originally Swedish Landrace, over coloured varieties, which tend to be hardier and can survive better outdoors. Since 1960, hybrid pigs, produced by crossing two or more breeds, have become popular for their heavy but lean carcasses.

The Berkshire and Tamworth are now rare in the UK, but still widespread in Australia and New Zealand. Only a quarter of Britain's pigs are raised outside (1998), the remainder are confined in indoor intensive piggeries. About 30% of the pork and bacon consumed in the UK is imported from intensive farms in the Netherlands and Denmark.

pigeon (or **dove**) bird of the family Columbidae, order Columbiformes, distinguished by its large crop, which becomes glandular in the breeding season and secretes a milky fluid ('pigeon's milk') that aids digestion of food for the young. There are many species and they are found worldwide.

New World species include the mourning-doves, which live much of the time on the ground. The fruit pigeons of Australasia and the Malay regions are beautifully coloured. In the USA, there were once millions of passenger pigeons *Ectopistes migratorius*, but they have been extinct since 1914.

Species The **collared dove** *Streptopelia decaocto* has multiplied greatly in Europe since it first arrived from central Asia 1930. It is a sandy coloured bird with a black collar, edged in white around the back of the head, and lives in urban areas as well as the countryside. The **stock-dove** *Columba oenas* is similar to the rock dove, but the wood-pigeon, or ring-dove, *C. palumbus* is much larger and has white patches on the neck. The **carrier pigeon** is remarkable for the huge white wattle round the eyes and at the base of the beak. Other varieties of domesticated pigeon include pouter, fantail, and homer. The European turtle dove, with brown speckled wings and a long, dark tail, lives mostly on the ground.

pigeon hawk another name for the merlin, a small ▷falcon.

Piggott, Lester Keith (1935–) English jockey. He adopted a unique high riding style and is renowned as a brilliant tactician. A champion jockey 11 times between 1960 and 1982, he rode a record nine Derby winners. Piggott retired from riding in 1985 and took up training. In 1987 he was imprisoned for tax evasion. He returned to racing in 1990 and has ridden 4,460 winners, including a record 30 classics to the start of the 1994 season. He retired as a jockey for the second time in September 1995.

pig iron (or **cast iron**) the quality of iron produced in a ▷blast furnace. It contains around 4% carbon plus some other impurities.

Pigs, Bay of inlet on the south coast of Cuba about 145 km/90 mi southwest of Havana. It was the site of an unsuccessful invasion attempt by 1,500 US-sponsored Cuban exiles 17–20 April 1961; 1,173 were taken prisoner.

The creation of this antirevolutionary force by the CIA had been authorized by the Eisenhower administration, and the project was executed under that of J F Kennedy. In 1962 most of the Cuban prisoners were ransomed for $53 million in food and medicine. The incident served to strengthen Cuba's links with the USSR. The CIA internal investigation report in the 1960s into the Bay of Pigs disaster was released for the first time after 36 years in February 1998, and it blamed the agency, not J F Kennedy, for the failure. It said it had been CIA's ignorance and incompetence that caused the disaster. The report was released under the Freedom of Information Act after a request by the National Security Archive, a nonprofit organization in Washington, DC.

Related Web site: Bay of Pigs Invasion http://www.parascope.com/articles/1296/bayofpigs.htm

pika (or **mouse-hare**) any small mammal of the family Ochotonidae, belonging to the order Lagomorpha (rabbits and hares). The single genus *Ochotona* contains about 15 species, most of which live in mountainous regions of Asia, although two species are native to North America.

Pikas have short, rounded ears, and most species are about 20 cm/8 in long, with greyish-brown fur and no visible tail. Their warning call is a sharp whistle. They are vegetarian and in late summer cut grasses and other plants and place them in piles to dry as hay, which is then stored for the winter.

Pikas can be divided into rock pikas and burrowing pikas. Rock pikas live in rocky territory alone or in pairs. Population densities are low and lifespan is about six years. Females have two or three young per year. Burrowing pikas are social animals and live in family groups at high densities in meadows or steppes, with a much shorter lifespan, of less than two years. Females have as many as twenty young per year, in several large litters.

Pikas do not hibernate, but stay mostly in their burrows, feeding on the hay piles that they have stocked up during the summer.

pike any of a family Esocidae in the order Salmoniformes, of slender, freshwater bony fishes with narrow pointed heads and sharp, pointed teeth. The northern pike *Esox lucius*, of North America and Eurasia, may reach a length of 2.2 m/7 ft and a weight of 9 kg/20 lb.

Other kinds of pike include muskellunges, up to 2.2 m/7 ft long, and the smaller pickerels, both in the genus *Esox*.

pikeperch any of various freshwater members of the perch family, resembling pikes, especially the walleye *Stizostedion vitreum*, common in Europe, western Asia, and North America. It reaches over 1 m/3 ft.

Pik Pobedy highest peak in the Tian Shan mountain range on the Kyrgyz-Chinese border, at 7,439 m/24,406 ft.

Pilate, Pontius (died *c.* AD 36) Roman procurator of Judea AD 26–36. The New Testament Gospels describe his reluctant ordering of Jesus' crucifixion, but there has been considerable debate about his actual role in it.

Pilate was unsympathetic to the Jews; his actions several times provoked riots, and in AD 36 he was recalled to Rome to account for the brutal suppression of a Samaritan revolt. The Greek historian Eusebius says Pilate committed suicide after Jesus' crucifixion, but another tradition says he became a Christian, and he is regarded as a saint and martyr in the Ethiopian Coptic and Greek Orthodox churches.

Related Web site: Pilate, Pontius http://www.newadvent.org/cathen/12083c.htm

pilchard any of various small, oily members of the herring family, Clupeidae, especially the commercial sardine of Europe *Sardina pilchardus*, and the California sardine *Sardinops sagax*.

In March 1995 a mystery virus or toxin began causing the deaths of millions of pilchards in the oceans south of Australia, killing adults over 12 cm/4.7 in long, but not appearing to harm fish feeding on the pilchards. In April a slick of dead pilchards 40 km/25 mi long was observed off Tasmania.

Bluish-green above and silvery beneath, the European sardine grows to 25 cm/10 in long. It is most abundant in the western Mediterranean.

pilgrimage journey to sacred places inspired by religious devotion. For Hindus, the holy places include Varanasi and the

PILGRIMAGE A fresco by Italian painter Domenico di Bartolo showing pilgrims receiving treatment from monks and doctors at the Santa Maria della Scala Hospital, Siena, Italy (1443). Behind the pilgrims, through the arch, are the general wards. *The Art Archive/Santa Maria della Scala Hospital Siena/Dagli Orti*

purifying River Ganges; for Buddhists, the places connected with the crises of Buddha's career; for the ancient Greeks, shrines such as those at Delphi and Ephesus; for Jews, the Western Wall in Jerusalem; for Muslims, Mecca and Medina; and for Roman Catholics, Lourdes in France, among others.

Related Web site: Places of Peace and Power http://www.sacredsites.com/

Pilgrimage of Grace rebellion against ▷Henry VIII of England 1536–37, originating in Yorkshire and Lincolnshire. The uprising was directed against the policies of the monarch (such as the Dissolution of the Monasteries during the ▷Reformation and the effects of the ▷enclosure of common land).

At the height of the rebellion, the rebels controlled York and included the archbishop of York among their number. A truce was arranged in December 1536 and the rebels dispersed, but their demands were not met, and a further revolt broke out in 1537, which was severely suppressed, with the execution of over 200 of the rebels, including the leader, Robert Aske.

Pilgrims (or Pilgrim Fathers) the emigrants who sailed from Plymouth, Devon, England, in the *Mayflower* on 16 September 1620 to found the first colony in New England, North America, at New Plymouth, Massachusetts. Of the 102 passengers about a third were Puritan refugees.

The Pilgrims originally set sail for Virginia in the *Mayflower* and *Speedwell* from Southampton on 5 August 1620, but had to put into Dartmouth when the *Speedwell* needed repair. Bad weather then drove them into Plymouth Sound, where the *Speedwell* was abandoned. They landed at Cape Cod in December and decided to stay, moving on to find New Plymouth harbour and founding the Massachusetts colony. Considerable religious conflict had erupted between the 35 Puritans and the other, largely Anglican, passengers. Open mutiny was averted by the Mayflower Compact, which established the rights of the non-Puritans. About half the Pilgrims died over the winter before they received help from the Indians; the survivors celebrated the first ▷Thanksgiving in the autumn of 1621.

Pill, the commonly used term for the contraceptive pill, based on female hormones. The combined pill, which contains synthetic hormones similar to oestrogen and progesterone, stops the production of eggs, and makes the mucus produced by the cervix hostile to sperm. It is the most effective form of contraception apart from sterilization, being more than 99% effective.

The **minipill** or progesterone-only pill prevents implantation of a fertilized egg into the wall of the uterus. The minipill has a slightly higher failure rate, especially if not taken at the same time each day, but has fewer side effects and is considered safer for long-term use. Possible side effects of the Pill include migraine or headache and high blood pressure. More seriously, oestrogen-containing pills can slightly increase the risk of a clot forming in the blood vessels. This risk is increased in women over 35 if they smoke. Controversy surrounds other possible health effects of taking the Pill. The evidence for a link with cancer is slight (and the Pill may protect women from some forms of cancer). Once a woman ceases to take it, there is an increase in the likelihood of conceiving identical twins.

pilotfish small marine fish *Naucrates ductor* of the family Carangidae, which also includes pompanos. It hides below sharks, turtles, or boats, using the shade as a base from which to prey on smaller fish. It is found in all warm oceans and grows to about 36 cm/1.2 ft.

Piłsudski, Józef (Klemens) (1867–1935) Polish nationalist politician, dictator from 1926. Born in Russian Poland, he founded the Polish Socialist Party in 1892 and was twice imprisoned for anti-Russian activities. During World War I he commanded a Polish force to fight for Germany and evicted the Russians from eastern Poland but fell under suspicion of intriguing with the Allies and was imprisoned by the Germans in 1917–18. When Poland became independent in 1919, he was elected chief of state, and led a Polish attack on invading Soviet forces in 1920, driving the Soviets out of Poland. He retired in 1923, but in 1926 led a military coup that established his dictatorship until his death.

Piltdown man (or *Eoanthropus dawsoni*) fossil skull and jaw fragments 'discovered' by Charles Dawson at Piltdown, East Sussex, England, between 1908 and 1912, and believed to be the earliest European human remains until proved a hoax in 1953. The jaw was that of an orang-utan with the teeth filed flat, and the skull bones were human but from an ancient deposit; both had been stained to match the Piltdown gravel deposits.

pimento (or **allspice**) any of several evergreen trees belonging to the myrtle family, found in tropical parts of the New World. The dried berries of the species *P. dioica* are used as a spice (see ▷allspice). Also, a sweet variety of ▷capsicum pepper (more correctly spelled **pimiento**). (Pimento genus *Pimenta*, family Myrtaceae.)

pimpernel any of a group of plants belonging to the primrose family, comprising about 30 species mostly native to Western Europe. The European scarlet pimpernel (*A. arvensis*) grows in cornfields, the small star-shaped flowers opening only in full sunshine. It is naturalized in North America. (Genus *Anagallis*, family Primulaceae.)

PIN (acronym for personal identification number) in banking, a unique number used as a password to establish the identity of a customer using an automatic cash dispenser. The PIN is normally encoded into the magnetic strip of the customer's bank card and is known only to the customer and to the bank's computer. Before a cash dispenser will issue money or information, the customer must insert the card into a slot in the machine (so that the PIN can be read from the magnetic strip) and enter the PIN correctly at a keyboard. This helps to prevent stolen cards from being used to obtain money from cash dispensers.

Pinatubo, Mount active volcano on Luzon Island, the Philippines, 88 km/55 mi north of Manila. Dormant for 600 years, it erupted in June 1991, killing 343 people and leaving as many as 200,000 homeless. Surrounding rice fields were covered with 3 m/10 ft of volcanic ash.

Related Web site: Volcanic Crisis in the Philippines: the 1991 Eruption of Mount Pinatubo http://vulcan.wr.usgs.gov/Volcanoes/Philippines/Pinatubo/framework.html

Pindling, Lynden (Oscar) (1930–2000) Bahamian politician, prime minister 1967–92. In the 1960s he became leader of the centrist Progressive Liberal Party (PLP), formed in 1953. Attracting support from the islands' demographically dominant black community, the PLP won the 1967 House of Assembly elections, the first to be held on a full adult voting register, and Pindling became the Bahamas' first black prime minister. He led the country to independence, within the British Commonwealth, in 1973 and successfully expanded the tourist industry, but accusations of government corruption grew in the 1980s and the PLP lost power in 1992. After further electoral defeat in 1997, Pindling retired as PLP leader.

pine any of a group of coniferous, ▷resin-producing trees with evergreen needle-shaped leaves; there are about 70–100 species of pines, making them the largest family of ▷conifers. (Genus *Pinus*, family Pinaceae.)

Related Web site: Ancient Bristlecone Pine http://www.sonic.net/bristlecone/intro.html

pineal body (or **pineal gland**) a cone-shaped outgrowth of the vertebrate brain. In some lower vertebrates, it develops a rudimentary lens and retina, which show it to be derived from an eye, or pair of eyes, situated on the top of the head in ancestral vertebrates. In fishes that can change colour to match their background, the pineal perceives the light level and controls the colour change. In birds, the pineal detects changes in daylight and stimulates breeding behaviour as spring approaches. Mammals also have a pineal gland, but it is located deeper within the brain. It secretes a hormone, melatonin, thought to influence rhythms of activity. In humans, it is a small piece of tissue attached by a stalk to the rear wall of the third ventricle of the brain.

pineapple large, juicy fruit of the pineapple plant, which belongs to the bromeliad family and is native to South and Central America but now cultivated in many other tropical areas, such as Hawaii and Queensland, Australia. The plant's mauvish flowers are produced in the second year, and afterwards join with their bracts (specialized leaves protecting the buds) to form the fleshy fruit, which looks like a giant cone. (Genus *Ananas comosus*, family Bromeliaceae.)

Pinero, Arthur Wing (1855–1934) English dramatist. A leading exponent of the 'well-made' play, he enjoyed great contemporary success with his farces, beginning with *The Magistrate* (1885). More substantial social drama followed with *The Second Mrs Tanqueray* (1893), and comedies including *Trelawny of the 'Wells'* (1898). He was knighted in 1909.

pink any of a group of annual or perennial plants that have stems with characteristic swellings (nodes) and scented flowers ranging in colour from white through pink to purple. Members of the pink family include carnations, sweet williams, and baby's breath (*Gypsophila paniculata*). (Genus *Dianthus*, family Carophyllaceae.)

Pinkerton, Allan (1819–1884) US detective, born in Glasgow, Scotland. He founded Pinkerton's National Detective Agency in 1852 and built up the federal secret service from the espionage system he developed during the American Civil War.

Pink Floyd British psychedelic rock group, formed in 1965. The original members were Syd Barrett (1946–), Roger Waters (1944–), Richard Wright (1945–), and Nick Mason (1945–). Dave Gilmour (1946–) joined the band in 1968. Their albums include *The Dark Side of the Moon* (1973) and *The Wall* (1979), with its spin-off film starring Bob Geldof.

PINEAPPLE With its large pineapple-like fruit, *Ananas ananassoides* from central Brazil is very closely related to the ancestor of the true pineapple, which is native to the same region. *Premaphotos Wildlife*

pinnate leaf leaf that is divided up into many small leaflets, arranged in rows along either side of a midrib, as in ash trees (*Fraxinus*). It is a type of compound leaf. Each leaflet is known as a **pinna**, and where the pinnae are themselves divided, the secondary divisions are known as pinnules.

Pinochet (Ugarte), Augusto (1915–) Chilean military dictator 1973–89. He came to power when a coup backed by the US Central Intelligence Agency (CIA) ousted and killed President Salvador Allende. Pinochet took over the presidency as the result of the coup and governed ruthlessly, crushing all political opposition (including more than 3,000 people who 'vanished' or were killed) but also presiding over the country's economic expansion in the 1980s, stimulated further by free-market reforms. In 1988 he called and lost a plebiscite to ratify him as sole nominee for the presidency. He was voted out of power when general elections were held in December 1989, but remained head of the armed forces until March 1998 when he became senator-for-life, which gave him instant legal immunity. In October 1998, he was arrested in London, England, where he was undergoing medical treatment. However, he was found unfit for trial by a team of British doctors, and allowed to return to Chile in March 2000. The Chilean courts stripped Pinochet of his immunity from prosecution, and he was arrested in January 2001 on the charge of organizing the killings of 77 left-wing activists and union leaders. However, in July 2001 the trial was halted, as Pinochet was ruled mentally unfit by a Chilean court.

Pinsent, Matthew (1970–) English oarsman who has won three Olympic gold medals and seven World Championship gold medals. In 1990 he joined Steve ▷Redgrave in the coxless pair and they won a bronze medal at the World Championships. During the following year they were unbeaten and became world champions. Pinsent won his first Olympic gold medal a year later. The pair retained their title at the 1993 World Championships in Prague, before winning another two consecutive world titles, and retaining their Olympic crown in Atlanta in 1996. In 1997, Redgrave and Pinsent switched to a coxless four and were unbeaten in the 1997 World Cup series, winning another World Championship gold medal. They retained their title at the 1998 and 1999 World Championships. Pinsent won his third Olympic gold medal in succession – Redgrave his fifth – in Sydney in 2000.

pint imperial dry or liquid measure of capacity equal to 20 fluid ounces, half a quart, one-eighth of a gallon, or 0.568 litre. In the USA, a liquid pint is equal to 0.473 litre, while a dry pint is equal to 0.550 litre.

Pinter, Harold (1930–) English dramatist, originally an actor. He specializes in the tragicomedy of the breakdown of communication, broadly in the tradition of the Theatre of the ▷Absurd – for example, *The Birthday Party* (1958) and *The Caretaker* (1960). Later plays include *The Homecoming* (1965), *Old Times* (1971), *Betrayal* (1978), *Moonlight* (1993), and *Celebration* (2000), which opened at the Almeida theatre, London, in March 2000. His anthology *Various Voices: Prose, Poetry, Politics, 1948–1998* was published in 1998. Born in East London, Pinter's work is known for its pauses, allowing the audience to read between the lines. He writes for radio and television, and his screenplays include *The Go-Between* (1969), *The French Lieutenant's Woman* (1982) and *Mountain Language* (1988).

    Related Web site:Pinter, Harold http://www.kirjasto.sci.fi/hpinter.htm

Pinturicchio (or **Pintoricchio**) (*c.* 1454–1513) Born Bernardino di Betto. Painter from Perugia. He produced fresco series for both the Borgia Apartments in the Vatican, painted in the 1490s, and in the Piccolomini Library of Siena Cathedral, 1503–08, illustrating the history of Pius II.

pinworm ▷nematode worm *Enterobius vermicularis*, an intestinal parasite of humans.

Pinyin Chinese phonetic alphabet approved in 1956 by the People's Republic of China, and used since 1979 in transcribing all names of people and places from Chinese ideograms into other languages using the English/Roman alphabet. For example, the former transcription Chou En-lai becomes Zhou Enlai, Hua Kuo-feng became Hua Guofeng, Teng Hsiao-ping became Deng Xiaoping, and Peking became Beijing.

pion (or **pi meson**) in physics, a subatomic particle with a neutral form (mass 135 MeV) and a charged form (mass 139 MeV). The charged pion decays into muons and neutrinos and the neutral form decays into gamma-ray photons. They belong to the ▷hadron class of ▷elementary particles.

pipefish any of various long-snouted, thin, pipelike marine fishes in the same family (Syngnathidae) as seahorses. The great pipefish *Syngnathus acus* grows up to 50 cm/1.6 ft. The male has a brood pouch for eggs and developing young, in which he carries the eggs from three to four different females. The eggs hatch in five to six weeks as tiny versions of the adults; there is no larval stage.

piping crow (or **Australian magpie**) Australian crowlike bird *Gymnorhina tibicen*, family Cracticidae, order Passeriformes, with black and white plumage. Their diet consists of insects and a variety of small animals such as reptiles, amphibians or mammals. They are skilful mimics.

PIPING CROW The Australian piping crow *Gymnorhina tibicen*. *K G Preston-Mafham/Premaphotos Wildlife*

pipit any of various sparrow-sized ground-dwelling songbirds of the genus *Anthus* of the family Motacillidae, order Passeriformes.

piracy the taking of a ship, aircraft, or any of its contents, from lawful ownership, punishable under international law by the court of any country where the pirate may be found or taken. When the craft is taken over to alter its destination, or its passengers held to ransom, the term is ▷hijacking. Piracy is also used to describe infringement of ▷copyright.

Piraeus port of both ancient and modern Athens and main port of Greece, on the Gulf of Aegina; population (1991) 169,600. Constructed as the port of Athens about 493 BC, it was linked with that city by the Long Walls, a fortification protecting the approaches to Athens comprising three walls built 496–456 BC. After the destruction of Athens by Sulla 86 BC, Piraeus declined. Piraeus is now an industrial suburb of Athens.

Pirandello, Luigi (1867–1936) Italian dramatist, novelist, and short-story writer. His plays, which often deal with the themes of illusion and reality, and the tragicomic absurdity of life, include *Sei personaggi in cerca d'autore/Six Characters in Search of an Author* (1921), and *Enrico IV/Henry IV* (1922). Among his novels are *L'esclusa/The Outcast* (1901), *Il fu Mattia Pascal/The Late Mattia Pascal* (1904), and *I vecchi e i giovani/The Old and the Young* (1909). He was awarded the Nobel Prize for Literature in 1934.

Piranesi, Giambattista (Giovanni Battista) (1720–1778) Italian architect and graphic artist. He made powerful etchings of Roman antiquities and was an influential theorist of architecture, advocating imaginative use of Roman models. His series of etchings *Carceri d'Invenzione/Prisons of Invention* (*c.* 1745–61) depicts imaginary prisons, vast and gloomy.

piranha any South American freshwater fish of the genus *Serrusalmus*, in the same order as cichlids. They can grow to 60 cm/ 2 ft long, and have razor-sharp teeth; some species may rapidly devour animals, especially if attracted by blood.

Pisa (ancient **Pisae**) town in Tuscany, Italy, on the River Arno, 70 km/43 mi southwest of Florence; population (2001) 85,400. Industries include tourism, engineering, and the production of glass and textiles. Its famous campanile (bell-tower), the **Leaning Tower of Pisa** (repaired 1990 and again in 2001), is 55 m/180 ft high and about 4.1 m/13.5 ft out of perpendicular, the foundations being only about 3 m/10 ft deep and built on unstable ground.

PISA The cathedral of Pisa, Italy, and its campanile (bell-tower), the Leaning Tower. The tower was repaired in 2001, stabilizing it for the foreseeable future. *Image Bank*

Pisanello (*c.* 1395–*c.* 1455) Born Antonio Pisano. Italian painter and medallist. He painted religious works and portraits in a style untouched by recent Florentine innovations, as in *Madonna and Child with St George and St Anthony Abbot* (*c.* 1445; National Gallery, London). He was also an outstanding portrait medallist. His frescoes in the Palazzo Ducale in Mantua were rediscovered after World War II.

Pisces inconspicuous zodiac constellation, mainly in the northern hemisphere between ▷Aries and ▷Aquarius, near ▷Pegasus. It is represented as two fish tied together by their tails. The Circlet, a delicate ring of stars, marks the head of the western fish in Pisces. The constellation contains the **vernal equinox**, the point at which the Sun's path around the sky (the **ecliptic**) crosses the celestial equator (see ▷celestial sphere). The Sun reaches this point around 21 March each year as it passes through Pisces from mid-March to late April. In astrology, the dates for Pisces are between about 19 February and 20 March (see ▷precession).

Pisistratus (or **Peisistratos**) (*c.* 605–527 BC) Athenian tyrant. Although of noble family, he became the leader of the anti-aristocratic party, and seized power in 561 BC. He was twice expelled, but recovered power securely from 546 BC until his death. Ruling as a tyrant under constitutional forms (the historians Herodotus and Thucydides both attest that he left the rules and regulations of ▷Solon as he found them), Pisistratus was a patron of the arts and literature and the first to have the poems of ▷Homer written down. He introduced the Dionysiac rural festivals into Athens. He was succeeded by his sons Hippias and Hipparchus.

Pissarro, Camille (1830–1903) French painter. A leading member of the Impressionists, he experimented with various styles, including ▷pointillism, in the 1880s. Though he is closely linked with pictures of the French countryside and peasant life, he also painted notable street scenes, as in *Boulevard Montmartre* (1897; Hermitage, St Petersburg).

Born in the West Indies, he went to Paris in 1855. He studied at the Académie Suisse, where he met Claude Monet, and was influenced, like most young painters of the time, by Corot and Courbet. His early work, subdued in tone and simple in composition, already showed the feeling of open air which he developed in country retreat at Pontoise and Louveciennes before 1870.

During the Franco-Prussian war 1870–71, when his house was occupied and most of his pictures destroyed, he was in England with Monet, living in south London and painting pictures of the Crystal Palace, Sydenham and Upper Norwood. On his return he pursued a course parallel to Monet's, rendering light with colour, with blues, purples and greens prevailing.

He settled at Eragny in 1884, but made frequent visits to Le Havre, Rouen, and Paris, resulting in pictures of the boulevards of the capital and waterfronts, though his most typical paintings represent the quiet countryside and its peasants.

He was consistent in style, though under the influence of Seurat he practised a systematic division of colour 1886–88.

pistachio deciduous tree of the cashew family, native to Europe and Asia, whose green nuts are eaten salted or used to enhance and flavour food, especially ice cream. (Genus *Pistacia vera*, family Anacardiaceae.)

pistil general term for the female part of a flower, either referring to one single ▷carpel or a group of several fused carpels.

pistol any small ▷firearm designed to be fired with one hand. Pistols were in use from the early 15th century.

piston barrel-shaped device used in reciprocating engines (steam, petrol, diesel oil) to harness power. Pistons are driven up and down in cylinders by expanding steam or hot gases. They pass on their motion via a connecting rod and crank to a crankshaft, which turns the driving wheels. In a pump or compressor, the role of the piston is reversed, being used to move gases and liquids. See also ▷internal-combustion engine.

PISTOL Two of Samuel Colt's single-action army cavalry model revolvers (barrel length $7\frac{1}{2}$ in/19 cm, calibre .45) or 'revolving pistols'. The standard military issue had a plain, unornamented butt. *The Art Archive/Gunshots*

pit bull terrier (or **American pit bull terrier**) variety of dog that was developed in the USA solely as a fighting dog. It usually measures about 50 cm/20 in at the shoulder and weighs roughly 23 kg/50 lb, but there are no established criteria since it is not recognized as a breed by either the American or British Kennel Clubs. Selective breeding for physical strength and aggression has created a dog unsuitable for life in the modern community.

Pitcairn Islands British colony in Polynesia, 5,300 km/3,300 mi northeast of New Zealand; area 47 sq km/18 sq mi; population (1996) 58. The capital is Adamstown. Products are coconuts, bananas, breadfruit, yams, pineapples, tomatoes, oranges, and pineapples; souvenirs are sold to passing ships.

pitch in chemistry, a black, sticky substance, hard when cold, but liquid when hot, used for waterproofing, roofing, and paving. It is made by the destructive distillation of wood or coal tar, and has been used since antiquity for caulking wooden ships.

pitch in mechanics, the distance between the adjacent threads of a screw or bolt. When a screw is turned through one full turn it moves a distance equal to the pitch of its thread. A screw thread is a simple type of machine, acting like a rolled-up inclined plane, or ramp (as may be illustrated by rolling a long paper triangle around a pencil). A screw has a ▷mechanical advantage greater than one.

pitch in music, how high or low a note is. This depends on the frequency of vibration of the sound and is measured in Hertz (Hz), or cycles per second. It also means the standard to which instruments are tuned, nowadays using the A above middle C (A4 or a') with a frequency of 440Hz as a reference tone. This is often known as **concert pitch**.

Pitch can now be measured accurately by electronic tuning devices, which are beginning to replace the traditional tuning fork, but it is still normal practice for orchestras to tune to an oboe playing A4, despite the inherent inaccuracy of this practice.

pitchblende (or **uraninite**) brownish-black mineral, the major constituent of uranium ore, consisting mainly of uranium oxide (UO_2). It also contains some lead (the final, stable product of uranium decay) and variable amounts of most of the naturally occurring radioactive elements, which are products of either the decay or the fissioning of uranium isotopes. The uranium yield is 50–80%; it is also a source of radium, polonium, and actinium. Pitchblende was first studied by Pierre and Marie ▷Curie, who found radium and polonium in its residues in 1898.

pitcher plant any of various ▷insectivorous plants, the leaves of which are shaped like a pitcher and filled with a fluid that traps and digests insects. (Genera especially *Nepenthes* and *Sarracenia*, family Sarraceniaceae.)

Pitman, Isaac (1813–1897) English teacher and inventor of Pitman's shorthand. He studied Samuel Taylor's scheme for shorthand writing, and in 1837 published his own system, *Stenographic Soundhand*, fast, accurate, and adapted for use in many languages. He was knighted in 1894.

Pitot tube instrument that measures fluid (gas and liquid) flow. It is used to measure the speed of aircraft, and works by sensing pressure differences in different directions in the airstream. It was invented in the 1730s by the French scientist Henri Pitot (1695–1771).

Related Web site: Pitot Tube http://www.grc.nasa.gov/WWW/K-12/airplane/pitot.html

Pitt, William, the Elder (1708–1778) 1st Earl of Chatham. British Whig politician, 'the Great Commoner'. As paymaster of the forces 1746–55, he broke with tradition by refusing to enrich himself; he was dismissed for attacking the Duke of Newcastle, the prime minister. He served effectively as prime minister in coalition governments 1756–61 (successfully conducting the Seven Years' War) and 1766–68. He was created an earl in 1766.

Entering Parliament in 1735, Pitt led the Patriot faction opposed to the Whig prime minister Robert Walpole and attacked Walpole's successor, Carteret, for his conduct of the War of the Austrian Succession. Recalled by popular demand to form a government on the outbreak of the Seven Years' War in 1756, he was forced to form a coalition with Newcastle in 1757. A 'year of victories' ensued in 1759, and the French were expelled from India and Canada. In 1761 Pitt wished to escalate the war by a declaration of war on Spain, George III disagreed, and Pitt resigned, but was again recalled to form an all-party government in 1766. He championed the Americans against the king, though rejecting independence, collapsed during his last speech in the House of Lords – opposing the withdrawal of British troops – and died a month later.

Related Web site: William Pitt: Speech on the Stamp Act http://odur.let.rug.nl/~usa/D/1751-1775/stampact/sapitt.htm

Pitt, William, the Younger (1759–1806) British Tory prime minister 1783–1801 and 1804–06. He raised the importance of the House of Commons, clamped down on corruption, carried out fiscal reforms, and effected the union with Ireland. He attempted to keep Britain at peace but underestimated the importance of the French Revolution and became embroiled in wars with France from 1793; he died on hearing of Napoleon's victory at Austerlitz.

The son of William Pitt the Elder, he entered Cambridge University at the age of 14 and Parliament at the age of 22. He was the Whig Shelburne's chancellor of the Exchequer 1782–83, and with the support of the Tories and king's friends became Britain's youngest prime minister in 1783. He reorganized the country's finances and negotiated reciprocal tariff reduction with France. In 1793, however, the new French republic declared war and England fared badly. Pitt's policy in Ireland led to the 1798 revolt, and he tried to solve the Irish question by the Act of Union of 1800, but George III rejected the Catholic emancipation Pitt had promised as a condition, and Pitt resigned in 1801.

On his return to office in 1804, he organized an alliance with Spain, Austria, Russia, and Sweden against Napoleon, which was shattered at the battles of Ulm and Austerlitz. In declining health, he died on hearing the news, saying: 'Oh, my country! How I leave my country!' He was buried in Westminster Abbey.

> **William Pitt the Younger**
> *Necessity is the plea for every infringement of human freedom.*
> *It is the argument of tyrants; it is the creed of slaves.*
> Speech, House of Commons, 18 November 1783

pitta tropical bird of order Passeriformes, genus *Pitta*, forming the family Pittidae. Some 20 species are native to Southeast Asia, West Africa, and Australia. They have round bodies, big heads, are often brightly coloured, and are silent. They live on the ground and in low undergrowth, and can run from danger. They feed on insects.

Pittsburgh (called 'City of Bridges') second-largest city in Pennsylvania, USA, at the confluence of the Allegheny and Monongahela rivers, forming the Ohio River; population (1996 est) 350,400; metropolitan area (1992) 2,406,000. It is a business and financial centre with one of the largest river ports in the world. High technology and healthcare services dominate an economy formerly based on iron, steel, heavy engineering, and glass industries.

pituitary gland major ▷endocrine gland of vertebrates, situated in the centre of the brain. It is attached to the ▷hypothalamus by a stalk. The pituitary consists of two lobes. The posterior lobe is an extension of the hypothalamus, and is in effect nervous tissue. It stores two hormones synthesized in the hypothalamus: ADH and oxytocin. The anterior lobe secretes six hormones, some of which control the activities of other glands (thyroid, gonads, and adrenal cortex); others are direct-acting hormones affecting milk secretion and controlling growth.

Piura capital of Piura department, in the arid coastal region of northwest Peru, situated on the Piura River 160 km/100 mi southwest of Punta Pariñas; population (1993) 278,000. It is an agricultural centre for the surrounding region (made viable with irrigation systems) which produces rice, cotton, and corn. The first colonial settlement in Peru, Piura was founded in 1532 by the Spanish conquistadors left behind by Francisco Pizarro, and moved to its present site in 1588.

Pius 12 popes, including:

Pius IV (1499–1565) Pope from 1559, of the ▷Medici family. He reassembled the Council of Trent (see Counter-Reformation under ▷Reformation) and completed its work in 1563.

Pius V, Antonio Etrislieri (1504–1572) Pope from 1566. His early career was in the Inquisition, a role which brought him the support of Paul IV who made him a cardinal in 1558. From the beginning of his own pontificate, he stressed his determination to carry out the reforms of the Council of Trent. He also excommunicated Elizabeth I of England, and organized the expedition against the Turks that won the victory of ▷Lepanto.

Related Web site: Pope St Pius V http://www.newadvent.org/cathen/12130a.htm

Pius VI (1717–1799) Born Giovanni Angelo Braschi. Pope from 1775. He strongly opposed the French Revolution, and died a prisoner in French hands.

Pius VII (1742–1823) Born Gregorio Barnaba Chiaramonte. Pope from 1800. He concluded a concordat (papal agreement) with France in 1801 and took part in Napoleon's coronation, but relations became strained. Napoleon annexed the papal states, and Pius was imprisoned 1809–14. After his return to Rome in 1814, he revived the Jesuit order.

Pius IX (1792–1878) Pope from 1846. He never accepted the incorporation of the papal states and of Rome in the kingdom of Italy. He proclaimed the dogmas of the Immaculate Conception of the Virgin in 1854 and papal infallibility in 1870; his pontificate was the longest in history.

Pius XII (1876–1958) Born Eugenio Pacelli. Pope from 1939. He was conservative in doctrine and politics, and condemned modernism. In 1950 he proclaimed the dogma of the bodily assumption of the Virgin Mary, and in 1951 restated the doctrine (strongly criticized by many) that the life of an infant must not be sacrificed to save a mother in labour. He was criticized for failing to speak out against atrocities committed by the Germans during World War II and has been accused of collusion with the Nazis.

pixel (derived from picture element) single dot on a computer screen. All screen images are made up of a collection of pixels, with each pixel being either off (dark) or on (illuminated, possibly in colour). The number of pixels available determines the screen's resolution. Typical resolutions of microcomputer screens vary from 320 × 200 pixels to 800 × 600 pixels, but screens with 1,024 × 768 pixels or more are now common for high-quality graphic (pictorial) displays.

Pizarro, Francisco (1475–1541) Spanish conquistador. He took part in the expeditions of Vasco Núñez de ▷Balboa and others. He began exploring the northwest coast of South America in 1524, and, with the permission of the king of Spain, conquered Peru in 1531 with 180 followers. The Inca king Atahualpa was seized and murdered. In 1535 Pizarro founded the Peruvian city of Lima. Internal feuding led to his assassination.

pizzicato (Italian 'pinched') in music, an instruction to pluck a bowed stringed instrument (such as the violin) with the fingers. It is frequently abbreviated to 'pizz'.

PKK abbreviation for ▷Workers' Party of Kurdistan, a Kurdish guerrilla organization.

Plaatje, Solomon Tshekiso (1875–1932) South African black community leader, the founder and first secretary general of the South African National Congress (SANNC) in 1912. Later the ▷African National Congress (ANC), the SANNC campaigned against the Land Act of 1913. Plaatje led a protest delegation to the UK in 1914 and remained there until 1917, lecturing and writing. In 1919 he joined another unsuccessful SANNC delegation to the Versailles peace conference and later participated in the pan-African congress organized by the US educator and social critic W E B Du Bois. He returned to South Africa in 1923 and continued to write until his death in 1932.

placenta organ that attaches the developing ▷embryo or ▷fetus to the ▷uterus in placental mammals (mammals other than marsupials, platypuses, and echidnas). Composed of maternal and embryonic tissue, it links the blood supply of the embryo to the blood supply of the mother, allowing the exchange of oxygen, nutrients, and waste products. The two blood systems are not in direct contact, but are separated by thin membranes, with materials diffusing across from one system to the other. The placenta also produces hormones that maintain and regulate pregnancy. It is shed as part of the afterbirth.

It is now understood that a variety of materials, including drugs and viruses, can pass across the placental membrane. HIV, the virus that causes ▷AIDS, can be transmitted in this way.

The tissue in plants that joins the ovary to the ovules is also called a placenta.

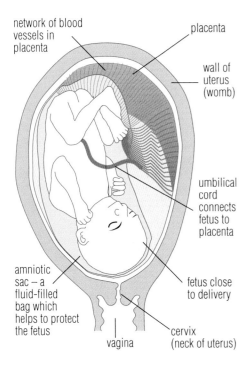

network of blood vessels in placenta
placenta
wall of uterus (womb)
umbilical cord connects fetus to placenta
amniotic sac – a fluid-filled bag which helps to protect the fetus
fetus close to delivery
vagina
cervix (neck of uterus)

PLACENTA The placenta is a disc-shaped organ about 25 cm/10 in in diameter and 3 cm/1 in thick. It is connected to the fetus by the umbilical cord.

plague term applied to any epidemic disease with a high mortality rate, but it usually refers to the bubonic plague. This is a disease transmitted by fleas (carried by the black rat) which infect the sufferer with the bacillus *Yersinia pestis*. An early symptom is swelling of lymph nodes, usually in the armpit and groin; such swellings are called 'buboes'. It causes virulent blood poisoning and the death rate is high.

plaice fish *Pleuronectes platessa* belonging to the flatfish group, abundant in the North Atlantic. It is white beneath and brownish with orange spots on the 'eyed' side. It can grow to 75 cm/2.5 ft long and weigh about 2 kg/4.5 lb.

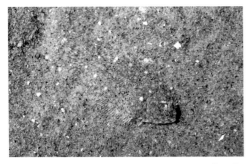

PLAICE A young plaice *Pleuronectes platessa* camouflaged on a sandy estuary bed in North Wales. *Dr Rod Preston-Mafham/Premaphotos Wildlife*

Plaid Cymru (Welsh 'Party of Wales') Welsh nationalist political party established in 1925, dedicated to an independent Wales. In 1966 the first Plaid Cymru member of Parliament was elected. Four Plaid Cymru MPs were returned in the 1997 general election. The Labour Party's 1997 devolution proposals for Wales were criticized by Plaid Cymru as being too cautious. Nevertheless, the party supported the 'Yes' vote in the subsequent referendum.
    Related Web site: Plaid Cymru, the Party of Wales http://www.plaidcymru.org/

plain (or **grassland**) land, usually flat, upon which grass predominates. The plains cover large areas of the Earth's surface, especially between the deserts of the tropics and the rainforests of the Equator, and have rain in one season only. In such regions the climate belts move north and south during the year, bringing rainforest conditions at one time and desert conditions at another. Temperate plains include the North European Plain, the High Plains of the USA and Canada, and the Russian Plain also known as the steppe.

Plains Indian member of any of the ▷American Indian peoples of the ▷Great Plains, which extend over 3,000 km/2,000 mi from Alberta to Texas. The Plains Indians were drawn from diverse linguistic stocks fringing the Plains but shared many cultural traits, especially the nomadic hunting of the North American buffalo (bison) herds once horses became available early in the 18th century. It is the Plains Indians who provide the traditional image of American Indians as war-painted warrior-horseriders, living in tepees, and dressed in buffalo robes, and eagle-feather bonnets. The various peoples include ▷Arapaho, Blackfoot, Cheyenne, Comanche, Pawnee, and the ▷Sioux or Lakota.

plaintiff in law, a person who brings a civil action in a court of law seeking relief (for example, damages).

Planck, Max Karl Ernst Ludwig (1858–1947) German physicist who was awarded the Nobel Prize for Physics in 1918 for his formulation of the ▷quantum theory in 1900. His research into the manner in which heated bodies radiate energy led him to report that energy is emitted only in indivisible amounts, called 'quanta', the magnitudes of which are proportional to the frequency of the radiation. His discovery ran counter to classical physics and is held to have marked the commencement of the modern science.
    Measurements of the frequency distribution of black-body radiation by Wilhelm Wien in 1893 showed the peak value of energy occurring at a higher frequency with greater temperature. This may be observed in the varying colour produced by a glowing object. At low temperatures, it glows red but as the temperature rises the peak energy is emitted at a greater frequency, and the colour become yellow and then white.
    Wien attempted to derive a radiation law that would relate the energy to frequency and temperature but discovered a radiation law in 1896 that was valid only at high frequencies. Lord ▷Rayleigh later found a similar equation that held for radiation emitted at low frequencies. Planck was able to combine these two radiation laws,

arriving at a formula for the observed energy of the radiation at any given frequency and temperature. This entailed making the assumption that the energy consists of the sum of a finite number of discrete units of energy that he called quanta, and that the energy ϵ of each quantum is given by the equation:

$$\epsilon = h\nu$$

where ν is the frequency of the radiation and h is a constant now recognized to be a fundamental constant of nature, called ▷Planck's constant. By directly relating the energy of a radiation to its frequency, an explanation was found for the observation that radiation of greater energy has a higher frequency distribution.
    Planck's idea that energy must consist of indivisible particles, not waves, was revolutionary because it totally contravened the accepted belief that radiation consisted of waves. It soon found rapid acceptance: Albert ▷Einstein in 1905 used Planck's quantum theory as an explanation for photoelectricity and in 1913 Danish physicist Niels ▷Bohr successfully applied the quantum theory to the atom. This was later developed into a full system of quantum mechanics in the 1920s, when it also became clear that energy and matter have both a particle and a wave nature.
    Planck's constant, a fundamental constant (symbol h), is the energy of one quantum of electromagnetic radiation divided by the frequency of its radiation.
    Related Web site: Planck, Max Karl Ernst Ludwig http://www-history.mcs.st-and.ac.uk/history/Mathematicians/Planck.html

Planck's constant in physics, a fundamental constant (symbol h) that relates the energy (E) of one quantum of electromagnetic radiation (a 'packet' of energy; see ▷quantum theory) to the frequency (f) of its radiation by $E = hf$. Its value is 6.6262×10^{-34} joule seconds.

plane in botany, any of several trees belonging to the plane family. Species include the oriental plane (*P. orientalis*), a favourite plantation tree of the Greeks and Romans, and the American plane

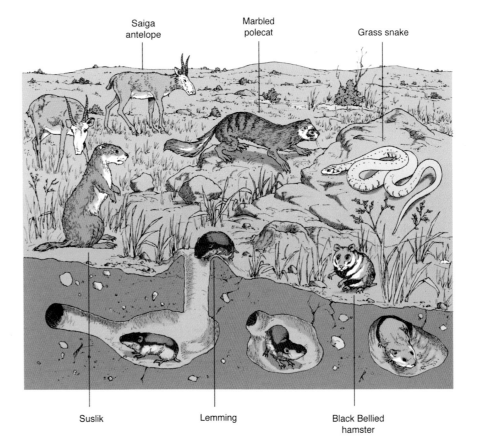

Saiga antelope
Marbled polecat
Grass snake

Suslik
Lemming
Black Bellied hamster

PLAIN The Eurasian steppe or plain is largely treeless and characterized by a climate ranging from extreme winter cold to great summer heat. The larger animals found here overcome this problem by being nomadic and the smaller ones by burrowing. At one time the steppe carried immense herds of herbivores including wild ass, wild horse, wild camel, and saiga, but owing to human intervention these species have declined, some almost to the point of extinction.

or buttonwood (*P. occidentalis*). A hybrid of these two is the London plane (*P. × acerifolia*), with palmate, usually five-lobed leaves, which is widely planted in cities for its resistance to air pollution. (Genus *Platanus*, family Platanaceae.)

PLANE The plane tree is very tolerant of pollution and is widely grown in towns. It has flaky bark and burrlike fruit resembling drumsticks.

planet (Greek 'wanderer') large celestial body in orbit around a star, composed of rock, metal, or gas. There are nine planets in the ▷Solar System: Mercury, Venus, Earth, Mars, Jupiter, Saturn, Neptune, Uranus, and Pluto. The inner four, called the **terrestrial planets**, are small and rocky, and include the planet Earth. The outer planets, with the exception of Pluto, are called the **major planets**, and consist of large balls of rock, liquid, and gas; the largest is Jupiter, which contains a mass greater than all the other planets combined. Planets do not produce light, but reflect the light of their parent star.

As seen from the Earth, all the historic planets are conspicuous naked-eye objects moving in looped paths against the stellar background. The size of these loops, which are caused by the Earth's own motion round the Sun, are inversely proportional to the planet's distance from the Earth.

New discoveries In 1995 Italian astronomers believed they had detected a new planet around 51 Pegasi in the constellation Pegasus.

PLANET Venus, the planet nearest to Earth, photographed from the *Mariner 10* space probe in 1974. When the Sun was cooler, Venus may have had oceans and life may have appeared, but as the Sun grew hotter the planet's surface became scorched and covered by dense clouds of carbon dioxide. *National Aeronautical Space Agency*

It was named 51 Pegasi B and is thought to have a mass comparable to that of Jupiter. The gravitational pull thought to be that of the planet may be caused by pulsation in the parent star.

The discovery of three further new planets was announced at the American Astronomical Society meeting in January 1996. All are outside the Solar System, but two are only about 35 light years from Earth and orbit stars visible with the naked eye. One, 70 Vir B, is in the constellation Virgo, and the other, 47 UMa B, is in Ursa Major. The third, β Pictoris, is about 50 light years away in the southern constellation Pictor.

In April 1996 another planet was discovered, orbiting Rho Cancri in the constellation Cancer. Yet another was found in June 1996, this time orbiting the star Tau Bootis.

The discovery of a new planet with an orbit which is more irregular than that of any other was discovered by US astronomers in October 1996. The new planet has 1.6 times the mass of Jupiter and orbits the star 16 Cygni B. Its distance from the star 16 Cygni B varies from 90 million km/55.9 million mi to 390 million km/242 million mi.

In 1998 six planets were discovered beyond our Solar System. Australian and New Zealand astronomers discovered a planet 25,000 light years away. The planet is known as 98-35. The Mount Stromlo observatory in Australia and the Mount John observatory in New Zealand were involved in making the discovery. By August 2000 astronomers had located 50 planets outside the solar system, nine of which were spotted in 2000.

planetary nebula shell of gas thrown off by a star at the end of its life. Planetary nebulae have nothing to do with planets. They were named by William Herschel, who thought their rounded shape resembled the disc of a planet. After a star such as the Sun has expanded to become a ▷red giant, its outer layers are ejected into space to form a planetary nebula, leaving the core as a ▷white dwarf at the centre.

plankton small, often microscopic, forms of plant and animal life that live in the upper layers of fresh and salt water, and are an important source of food for larger animals. Marine plankton is concentrated in areas where rising currents bring mineral salts to the surface.

plant organism that carries out ▷photosynthesis, has cellulose cell walls and complex cells, and is immobile. A few parasitic plants have lost the ability to photosynthesize but are still considered to be plants. Plants are ▷autotrophs, that is, they make carbohydrates from water and carbon dioxide, and are the primary producers in all food chains, so that all animal life is dependent on them. They play a vital part in the carbon cycle, removing carbon dioxide from the atmosphere and generating oxygen. The study of plants is known as ▷botany.

Levels of complexity The simplest plants consist of a body, or thallus, on which the organs of reproduction are borne. Simplest of all are the threadlike algae, for example *Spirogyra*, which consist of a chain of cells.

The seaweeds (algae) and mosses and liverworts (bryophytes) represent a further development, with simple, multicellular bodies that have specially modified areas in which the reproductive organs are carried. Higher in the morphological scale are the ferns, club mosses, and horsetails (pteridophytes). Ferns produce leaflike fronds bearing sporangia on their undersurface in which the spores are carried. The spores are freed and germinate to produce small independent bodies carrying the sexual organs; thus the fern, like other pteridophytes and some seaweeds, has two quite separate generations in its life cycle (see ▷alternation of generations).

The pteridophytes have special supportive water-conducting tissues, which identify them as vascular plants, a group which includes all seed plants, that is the gymnosperms (conifers, yews, cycads, and ginkgos) and the angiosperms (flowering plants).

Seed plants The seed plants are the largest group, and structurally

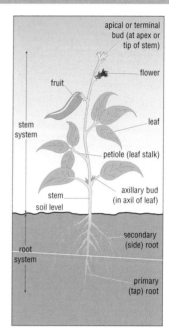

PLANT The external anatomy a typical flowering plant.

the most complex. They are usually divided into three parts: root, stem, and leaves. Stems can grow above or below ground. Their cellular structure is designed to carry water and salts from the roots to the leaves in the ▷xylem, and sugars from the leaves to the roots in the ▷phloem. The leaves manufacture the food of the plant by means of photosynthesis, which occurs in the ▷chloroplasts they contain. Flowers and cones are modified leaves arranged in groups, enclosing the reproductive organs from which the fruits and seeds result.

Conservation status The ▷World Conservation Union published a world list of threatened plants in 1998. The list includes 33,798 species of vascular plants (flowering plants, ferns, cycads, and conifers); in other words, 1 in 8 of the estimated 270,000 species of vascular plants are now endangered.

Plantagenet English royal house, which reigned from 1154 to 1399, and whose name comes from the nickname of Geoffrey, Count of Anjou (1113–1151), father of Henry II, who often wore in his hat a sprig of broom, *planta genista*. In the 1450s, Richard, Duke of York, took 'Plantagenet' as a surname to emphasize his superior claim to the throne over that of Henry VI.

plantain any of a group of northern temperate plants. The great plantain (*P. major*) is low-growing with large oval leaves close to the ground, grooved stalks, and spikes of green flowers with purple anthers (in which the pollen matures) followed by seeds, which are used in bird food. (Genus *Plantago*, family Plantaginaceae.)

plant classification taxonomy or classification of plants. Originally the plant kingdom included bacteria, diatoms, dinoflagellates, fungi, and slime moulds, but these are not now thought of as plants. The groups that are always classified as plants are the bryophytes (mosses and liverworts), pteridophytes (ferns, horsetails, and club mosses), gymnosperms (conifers, yews, cycads, and ginkgos), and angiosperms (flowering plants). The angiosperms are split into monocotyledons (for example, orchids, grasses, lilies) and dicotyledons (for example, oak, buttercup, geranium, and daisy).

The basis of plant classification was established by the Swedish naturalist Carolus ▷Linnaeus. Among the angiosperms, it is largely based on the number and arrangement of the flower parts.

The Planets

Planet	Main constituents	Atmosphere	Average distance from the Sun		Orbital period (Earth yrs)	Diameter		Average density (water = 1 unit)
			km (millions)	mi (millions)		km (thousands)	mi (thousands)	
Mercury	rock, ferrous	–	58	36	0.241	4.88	3.03	5.4
Venus	rock, ferrous	carbon dioxide	108	67	0.615	12.10	7.51	5.2
Earth	rock, ferrous	nitrogen, oxygen	150	93	1.000	12.76	7.92	5.5
Mars	rock	carbon dioxide	228	141	1.880	6.78	4.21	3.9
Jupiter	liquid hydrogen, helium	–	778	483	11.860	142.80	88.73	1.3
Saturn	hydrogen, helium	–	1,427	886	29.460	120.00	74.56	0.7
Uranus	ice, hydrogen, helium	hydrogen, helium	2,870	1,783	84.000	50.80	31.56	1.3
Neptune	ice, hydrogen, helium	hydrogen, helium	4,497	2,794	164.800	48.60	30.20	1.6
Pluto	ice, rock	methane	5,900	3,666	248.50	2.27	1.41	~2.0
(– = not applicable)								

The unicellular algae, such as *Chlamydomonas*, are often now put with the protists (single-celled organisms) instead of the plants. Some classification schemes even classify the multicellular algae (seaweeds and freshwater weeds) in a new kingdom, the Protoctista, along with the protists.

plant hormone substance produced by a plant that has a marked effect on its growth, flowering, leaf fall, fruit ripening, or some other process. Examples include ▷auxin, ▷gibberellin, ▷ethene, and cytokinin.

plaque any abnormal deposit on a body surface, especially the thin, transparent film of sticky protein (called mucin) and bacteria on tooth surfaces. If not removed, this film forms tartar (calculus), promotes tooth decay, and leads to gum disease. Another form of plaque is a deposit of fatty or fibrous material in the walls of blood vessels causing atheroma.

plasma in biology, the liquid component of the ▷blood. It is a straw-coloured fluid, largely composed of water (around 90%), in which a number of substances are dissolved. These include a variety of proteins (around 7%) such as fibrinogen (important in ▷blood clotting), inorganic mineral salts such as sodium and calcium, waste products such as ▷urea, traces of ▷hormones, and ▷antibodies to defend against infection.

plasma in physics, an ionized gas produced at extremely high temperatures, as in the Sun and other stars. It contains positive and negative charges in equal numbers. It is a good electrical conductor. In thermonuclear reactions the plasma produced is confined through the use of magnetic fields.

plasmapheresis technique for acquiring plasma from blood. Blood is withdrawn from the patient and separated into its components (plasma and blood cells) by centrifugal force in a continuous-flow cell separator. Once separated, the plasma is available for specific treatments. The blood cells are transfused back into the patient.

plasmid small, mobile piece of ▷DNA found in bacteria that, for example, confers antibiotic resistance, used in ▷genetic engineering. Plasmids are separate from the bacterial chromosome but still multiply during cell growth. Their size ranges from 3% to 20% of the size of the chromosome. Some plasmids carry 'fertility genes' that enable them to move from one bacterium to another and transfer genetic information between strains. Plasmid genes determine a wide variety of bacterial properties including resistance to antibiotics and the ability to produce toxins.

plaster of Paris form of calcium sulphate, obtained from gypsum; it is mixed with water for making casts and moulds.

plastic any of the stable synthetic materials that are fluid at some stage in their manufacture, when they can be shaped, and that later set to rigid or semi-rigid solids. Plastics today are chiefly derived from petroleum. Most are polymers, made up of long chains of identical molecules.

Environmental influence Since plastics have afforded an economical replacement for ivory in the manufacture of piano keys and billiard balls, the industrial chemist may well have been responsible for the survival of the elephant.

Most plastics cannot be broken down by micro-organisms, so cannot easily be disposed of. Incineration leads to the release of toxic fumes, unless carried out at very high temperatures.
Related Web site: Plastics http://www.plasticsusa.com/polylist.html

plastic surgery surgical speciality concerned with the repair of congenital defects and the reconstruction of tissues damaged by disease or injury, including burns. If a procedure is undertaken solely for reasons of appearance, for example, the removal of bags under the eyes or a double chin, it is called **cosmetic surgery**.

plastid general name for a cell ▷organelle of plants that is enclosed by a double membrane and contains a series of internal membranes and vesicles. Plastids contain ▷DNA and are produced by division of existing plastids. They can be classified into two main groups: the **chromoplasts**, which contain pigments such as carotenes and chlorophyll, and the **leucoplasts**, which are colourless; however, the distinction between the two is not always clear-cut.

Plataea, Battle of battle in 479 BC, in which the Greeks defeated the Persians during the ▷Persian Wars.

plate (or **tectonic plate** or **lithospheric plate**) one of several relatively distinct sections of ▷lithosphere approximately 100 km/60 mi thick, which together comprise the outermost layer of the Earth like the pieces of the cracked shell of a hard-boiled egg.

The plates are made up of two types of crustal material: oceanic crust (sima) and continental crust (sial), both of which are underlain by a solid layer of ▷mantle. Dense **oceanic crust** lies beneath Earth's oceans and consists largely of ▷basalt. **Continental crust**, which underlies the continents and their continental shelves, is thicker, less dense, and consists of rocks rich in silica and aluminium.

Due to convection in the Earth's mantle (see ▷plate tectonics) these pieces of lithosphere are in motion, riding on a more plastic layer of the mantle, called the asthenosphere. Mountains, volcanoes, earthquakes, and other geological features and phenomena all come about as a result of interaction between the plates.

plateau elevated area of fairly flat land, or a mountainous region in which the peaks are at the same height. An **intermontane plateau** is one surrounded by mountains. A **piedmont plateau** is one that lies between the mountains and low-lying land. A **continental plateau** rises abruptly from low-lying lands or the sea. Examples are the Tibetan Plateau and the Massif Central in France.

platelet tiny disc-shaped structure found in the blood, which helps it to clot. Platelets are not true cells, but membrane-bound cell fragments without nuclei that bud off from large cells in the bone marrow.

plate tectonics theory formulated in the 1960s to explain the phenomena of ▷continental drift and seafloor spreading, and the formation of the major physical features of the Earth's surface. The Earth's outermost layer, the ▷lithosphere, is regarded as a jigsaw puzzle of rigid major and minor plates that move relative to each other, probably under the influence of convection currents in the mantle beneath. At the margins of the plates, where they collide or move apart or slide past one another, major landforms such as ▷mountains, ▷rift valleys, ▷volcanoes, ▷ocean trenches, and **ocean ridges** are created. The rate of plate movement is at most 15 cm/6 in per year.

The concept of plate tectonics brings together under one unifying theory many phenomena observed in the Earth's crust that were previously thought to be unrelated. The size of the crust plates is variable, as they are constantly changing, but six or seven large plates now cover much of the Earth's surface, the remainder being occupied by a number of smaller plates. Each large plate may include both continental and ocean lithosphere. As a result of seismic studies it is known that the lithosphere is a rigid layer extending to depths of 50–100 km/30–60 mi, overlying the upper part of the mantle (the ▷asthenosphere), which is composed of rocks very close to melting point, with a low shear strength. This zone of mechanical weakness allows the movement of the overlying plates. The margins of the plates are defined by major earthquake zones and belts of volcanic and tectonic activity, which have been well known for many years. Almost all earthquake, volcanic, and tectonic activity is confined to the margins of plates, and shows that the plates are in constant motion.
Related Web site: Plate Tectonics http://www.seismo.unr.edu/ftp/pub/louie/class/100/plate-tectonics.html

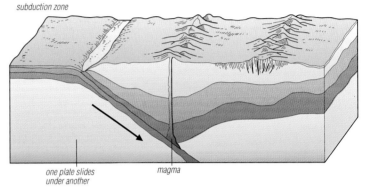

PLATE TECTONICS The diagrams show the constructive and destructive action in plate tectonics. In seafloor spreading, the upwelling of magma forces apart the crust plates, producing new crust at the joint. Rapid extrusion of magma produces a domed ridge; more gentle spreading produces a central valley. The drawing downwards of an oceanic plate beneath a continent produces a range of volcanic fold mountains parallel to the plate edge. Collision of continental plates produces immense fold mountains, such as the Himalayas.

Plath, Sylvia (1932–1963) US poet and novelist. Her powerful, highly personal poems, often expressing a sense of desolation, are distinguished by their intensity and sharp imagery. Her *Collected Poems* (1981) was awarded a Pulitzer prize. Her autobiographical novel *The Bell Jar* (1961) deals with the events surrounding a young woman's emotional breakdown.

Plath was born in Boston, Massachusetts, attended Smith College, and was awarded a Fulbright scholarship to study at Cambridge University, England. Here she met the poet Ted ▷Hughes, whom she married in 1956; they separated in 1962. She committed suicide while living in London. Collections of her poems include *The Colossus* (1960) and *Ariel* (1965), published after her death.

platinum (Spanish *platina* 'little silver' (*plata* 'silver') heavy, soft, silver-white, malleable and ductile, metallic element, symbol Pt, atomic number 78, relative atomic mass 195.09. It is the first of a group of six metallic elements (platinum, osmium, iridium, rhodium, ruthenium, and palladium) that possess similar traits, such as resistance to tarnish, corrosion, and attack by acid, and that often occur as free metals (▷native metals). They often occur in natural alloys with each other, the commonest of which is osmiridium. Both pure and as an alloy, platinum is used in dentistry, jewellery, and as a catalyst.

> ### Sylvia Plath
> *Out of the ash /*
> *I rise with my red hair /*
> *And I eat men like air.*
> 'Lady Lazarus'

Plato (c. 427–347 BC) Greek philosopher. He was a pupil of Socrates, teacher of Aristotle, and founder of the Academy school of philosophy. He was the author of philosophical dialogues on such topics as metaphysics, ethics, and politics. Central to his teachings is the notion of Forms, which are located outside the everyday world – timeless, motionless, and absolutely real.

Plato's philosophy has influenced Christianity and European culture, directly and, through Augustine, the Florentine Platonists during the Renaissance, as well as countless others.

Of his work, some 30 dialogues survive, intended for performance either to his pupils or to the public. The principal figure in these ethical and philosophical debates is Socrates and the early ones employ the Socratic method, in which he asks questions and traps the students into contradicting themselves; for example, *Iron*, on poetry. Other dialogues include the *Symposium*, on love, *Phaedo*, on immortality, and *Apology* and *Crito*, on Socrates' trial and death. It is impossible to say whether Plato's Socrates is a faithful representative of the real man or an articulation of Plato's own thought.

Plato's philosophy rejects scientific rationalism (establishing facts through experiment) in favour of arguments, because mind, not matter, is fundamental, and material objects are merely imperfect copies of abstract and eternal 'ideas'. His political philosophy is expounded in two treatises, *The Republic* and *The Laws*, both of which describe ideal states. Platonic love is inspired by a person's best qualities and seeks their development.

Related Web site: Works by Plato http://classics.mit.edu/Browse/browse-Plato.html

platoon in the army, the smallest infantry subunit. It contains 30–40 soldiers and is commanded by a lieutenant or second lieutenant. There are three or four platoons in a company.

platypus monotreme, or egg-laying, mammal *Ornithorhynchus anatinus*, found in Tasmania and eastern Australia. Semiaquatic, it has small eyes and no external ears, and jaws resembling a duck's beak. It lives in long burrows along river banks, where it lays two eggs in a rough nest. It feeds on water worms and insects, and when full-grown is 60 cm/2 ft long.

Platypuses locate their prey by detecting the small electric fields produced by their nerve and muscle activity. Males have sharp venomous spurs on their hind legs that they use for defence. The spurs administer (by way of a kick) a cocktail of at least four different toxins that cause intense pain that may last for several weeks.

Related Web site: Platypus World http://library.thinkquest.org/11420/

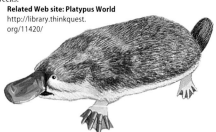

PLATYPUS When the platypus was discovered 200 years ago, scientists thought the first specimens were fakes.

Plautus, Titus Maccius (*c.* 250–*c.* 184 BC) Roman comic dramatist. Born in Umbria, he settled in Rome and began writing plays about 224 BC. Twenty-one comedies survive in his name; 35 other titles are known. Many of his plays are based on Greek originals by playwrights such as ▷Menander, to which Plautus added his own brand of native wit and sharp character-drawing. He had a perfect command of language and metre, and enjoyed unrivalled popularity in his day; since the Renaissance he has been acknowledged as one of the greatest of ancient playwrights.

playa temporary lake in a region of interior drainage. Such lakes are common features in arid desert basins fed by intermittent streams. The streams bring dissolved salts to the lakes, and when the lakes shrink during dry spells, the salts precipitate as evaporite deposits.

plc abbreviation for ▷public limited company.

pleadings in law, documents exchanged between the parties to court actions, which set out the facts that form the basis of the case they intend to present in court, and (where relevant) stating what damages or other remedy they are claiming.

plebeian Roman citizen who did not belong to the privileged class of the ▷patricians. During the 5th–4th centuries BC, plebeians waged a long struggle to win political and social equality with the patricians, eventually securing admission to the offices formerly reserved for patricians.

plebiscite (Latin *plebiscitium* 'ordinance, decree') ▷referendum or direct vote by all the electors of a country or district on a specific question. Since the 18th century plebiscites have been employed on many occasions to decide to what country a particular area should belong; for example, in Upper Silesia and elsewhere after World War I, and in the Saar in 1935. The term fell into disuse during the 1930s, after the widespread abuse by the Nazis in Germany to legitimize their regime.

Pleiades in astronomy, an open star cluster about 400 light years away from Earth in the constellation Taurus, represented as the Seven Sisters of Greek mythology. Its brightest stars (highly luminous, blue-white giants only a few million years old) are visible to the naked eye, but there are many fainter ones.

It is a young cluster, and the stars of the Pleiades are still surrounded by traces of the reflection ▷nebula from which they formed, visible on long-exposure photographs.

Pleistocene Epoch first epoch of the Quaternary period of geological time, beginning 1.64 million years ago and ending 10,000 years ago. The polar ice caps were extensive and glaciers were abundant during the ice age of this period, and humans evolved into modern *Homo sapiens sapiens* about 100,000 years ago.

Related Web site: Late Pleistocene Extinctions http://www.museum.state.il.us/exhibits/larson/LP_extinction.html

PLINY THE ELDER A 15th-century manuscript from Siena, Italy, of the *Historia Naturalis*, an immense encyclopedia probably completed in AD 77 by the Roman writer Pliny the Elder. *The Art Archive/Victoria and Albert Museum London/Graham Brandon*

Plekhanov, Georgi Valentinovich (1857–1918) Russian Marxist revolutionary and theorist, founder of the ▷Menshevik party. He led the first populist demonstration in St Petersburg, became a Marxist and, with Lenin, edited the newspaper *Iskra* ('Spark'). In 1903 his opposition to Lenin led to the Bolshevik–Menshevik split.

plesiosaur prehistoric carnivorous marine reptile of the Jurassic and Cretaceous periods, which reached a length of 12 m/36 ft, and had a long neck and paddlelike limbs. The pliosaurs evolved from the plesiosaurs.

pleurisy inflammation of the pleura, the thin, secretory membrane that covers the lungs and lines the space in which they rest. Pleurisy is nearly always due to bacterial or viral infection, but may also be a complication of other diseases.

Plimsoll line loading mark painted on the hull of merchant ships, first suggested by the 19th-century English politician Samuel Plimsoll. It shows the depth to which a vessel may be safely (and legally) loaded.

Pliny the Elder (*c.* AD 23–79) Born Gaius Plinius Secundus. Roman scientific encyclopedist and historian. Many of his works have been lost, but in *Historia naturalis/Natural History*, probably completed AD 77, Pliny surveys all the known sciences of his day, notably astronomy, meteorology, geography, mineralogy, zoology, and botany.

Pliny the Younger (*c.* AD 61–113) Born Gaius Plinius Caecilius Secundus. Roman administrator. He was the nephew of Pliny the Elder. His correspondence is of great interest; among his surviving letters are those describing the eruption of Vesuvius, his uncle's death, and his correspondence with the emperor ▷Trajan.

Pliocene Epoch ('almost recent') fifth and last epoch of the Tertiary period of geological time, 5.2–1.64 million years ago. The earliest hominid, the humanlike ape *Australopithecines*, evolved in Africa.

pliosaur prehistoric carnivorous marine reptile, descended from the plesiosaurs, but with a shorter neck, and longer head and jaws. It was approximately 5 m/15 ft long. In 1989 the skeleton of one of a previously unknown species was discovered in northern Queensland, Australia. A hundred million years ago, it lived in the sea that once covered the Great Artesian Basin.

Plisetskaya, Maya Mikhailovna (1925–) Soviet ballerina and actor. She attended the Moscow Bolshoi Ballet School and became prima ballerina of the Bolshoi Ballet In 1945. An extremely strong yet supple dancer of flamboyant exuberance, she is noted for her fast spins, scissor-like jumps, and head-to-heel backward kicks, which she displayed to best advantage in the role of Kitri in *Don Quixote*. Her other noted classical role is Odette/Odile in *Swan Lake*. She is also associated with *Carmen Suite* (1967).

PLO abbreviation for ▷Palestine Liberation Organization, founded in 1964 to bring about an independent state of Palestine.

plotter (or **graph plotter**) device that draws pictures or diagrams under computer control. Plotters are often used for producing business charts, architectural plans, and engineering drawings.

Flatbed plotters move a pen up and down across a flat drawing surface, whereas **roller plotters** roll the drawing paper past the pen as it moves from side to side.

plough agricultural implement used for tilling the soil. The plough dates from about 3500 BC, when oxen were used to pull a simple wooden blade, or ard. In about 500 BC the iron ploughshare came into use. By about AD 1000 horses as well as oxen were being used to pull wheeled ploughs, equipped with a ploughshare for cutting a furrow, a blade for forming the walls of the furrow (called a coulter), and a mouldboard to turn the furrow. In the 18th century an innovation introduced in England by Robert Ransome (1753–1830), led to a reduction in the number of animals used to draw a plough: from 8–12 oxen, or 6 horses, to a 2- or 4-horse plough.

Plough, the in astronomy, a popular name for the most prominent part of the constellation ▷Ursa Major.

Plovdiv industrial city (textiles, chemicals, leather, tobacco) in Bulgaria, on the River Maritsa; population (1991) 379,000. Conquered by Philip of Macedon in the 4th century BC, it was known as **Philippopolis** ('Philip's city'). It was the capital of Roman Thrace.

plover any shore bird of the family Charadriidae, order Charadriiformes, found worldwide. Plovers are usually black or brown above and white below, and have short bills. The European **golden plover** *Pluviatilis apricaria*, of heathland and sea coast, is about 28 cm/11 in long. In winter the upper parts are a sooty black with large yellow spots, and white throat and underparts, changing to black in the spring. It nests on the ground, laying four yellowish eggs blotched with brown.

The **ringed plover** *Charadrius hiaticula*, with a black and white face, and black band on the throat, is found on British shores, nesting in a scrape on a beach or amongst shingle. The largest of the ringed plovers is the **killdeer** *Charadrius vociferus*, so called because of its cry.

PLOVER The crowned plover *Vanellus coronatus* in the desert in South Africa. It is a large plover (30 cm/12 in) and lives in pairs or small flocks in open country. *K G Preston-Mafham/Premaphotos Wildlife*

plucking in earth science, a process of glacial erosion. Water beneath a glacier will freeze fragments of loose rock to the base of the ice. When the ice moves, the rock fragment is 'plucked' away from the underlying bedrock. Plucking is thought to be responsible for the formation of steep, jagged slopes such as the backwall of the corrie and the downslope-side of the *roche moutonnée*.

plum smooth-skinned, oval, reddish-purple or green edible fruit of the plum tree. There are many varieties, including the Victoria, czar, egg-plum, greengage, and damson; the wild sloe (*P. spinosa*), which is the fruit of the ▷blackthorn, is closely related. Dried plums are known as prunes. (Genus *Prunus domestica*, family Rosaceae.)

plumule part of a seed embryo that develops into the shoot, bearing the first true leaves of the plant. In most seeds, for example the sunflower, the plumule is a small conical structure without any leaf structure. Growth of the plumule does not occur until the ▷cotyledons have grown above ground. This is epigeal germination. However, in seeds such as the broad bean, a leaf structure is visible on the plumule in the seed. These seeds develop by the plumule growing up through the soil with the cotyledons remaining below the surface. This is known as ▷hypogeal germination.

pluralism in political science, the view that decision-making in contemporary liberal democracies is the outcome of competition among several interest groups in a political system characterized by free elections, representative institutions, and open access to the organs of power. This concept is opposed by corporatism and other approaches that perceive power to be centralized in the state and its principal elites (the Establishment).

Plutarch (*c.* AD 46–*c.* 120) Greek biographer and essayist. He is best remembered for his *Lives*, a collection of short biographies of famous figures from Greek and Roman history arranged in contrasting pairs (for example, Alexander the Great and Julius Caesar are paired). He also wrote *Moralia*, a collection of essays on moral and social themes.

Related Web site: Works by Plutarch http://classics.mit.edu/Browse/browse-Plutarch.html

Pluto in astronomy, the smallest and, usually, outermost planet of the Solar System. The existence of Pluto was predicted by calculation by Percival Lowell and the planet was located by US astronomer Clyde Tombaugh in 1930. Its highly elliptical orbit occasionally takes it within the orbit of Neptune, as in 1979–99. Pluto has a mass about 0.002 of that of Earth.

mean distance from the Sun 5.8 billion km/3.6 billion mi **equatorial diameter** 2,300 km/1,438 mi **rotation period** 6.39 Earth days **year** 248.5 Earth years **atmosphere** thin atmosphere with small amounts of methane gas **surface** low density, composed of rock and ice, primarily frozen methane; there is an ice cap at Pluto's north pole **satellites** one moon, Charon, discovered in 1978 by US astronomer James Walter Christy (1938–). It is about 1,200 km/750 mi in diameter, half the size of Pluto, making it the largest moon in relation to its parent planet in the Solar System. It orbits about 20,000 km/12,500 mi from the planet's centre every 6.39 days – the same time that Pluto takes to spin on its axis. Charon is composed mainly of ice. Some astronomers have suggested that Pluto was a former moon of Neptune that escaped, but it is more likely that it was an independent body that was captured. The Hubble Space Telescope photographed Pluto's surface in 1996.

Pluto (or Hades) in Greek mythology, lord of ▷Hades, the underworld and also his original name. His Roman counterpart was Dis (also Orcus). He was the son of the Titans ▷Kronos and ▷Rhea; and brother of Zeus, Poseidon, Hera, Hestia, and Demeter. He abducted and married ▷Persephone, daughter of the goddess of agriculture ▷Demeter, causing winter on Earth; Persephone was eventually allotted six months of each year in Hades, and six with her mother.

plutonic rock igneous rock derived from magma that has cooled and solidified deep in the crust of the Earth; granites and gabbros are examples of plutonic rocks.

plutonium silvery-white, radioactive, metallic element of the ▷actinide series, symbol Pu, atomic number 94, relative atomic mass 239.13. It occurs in nature in minute quantities in ▷pitchblende and other ores, but is produced in quantity only synthetically. It has six allotropic forms (see ▷allotropy) and is one of three fissile elements (elements capable of splitting into other elements – the others are thorium and uranium). Plutonium dioxide, PuO_2, a yellow crystalline solid, is the compound most widely used in the nuclear industry. It was believed to be inert until US researchers discovered in 1999 that it reacts very slowly with oxygen and water to form a previously unknown green crystalline compound that is soluble in water.

Because Pu-239 is so easily synthesized from abundant uranium, it has been produced in large quantities by the weapons industry. It has a long half-life (24,000 years) during which time it remains highly toxic. Plutonium is dangerous to handle, difficult to store, and impossible to dispose of.

It was first synthesized in 1940 by Glenn Seaborg and his team at the University of California at Berkeley, by bombarding uranium with deuterons; this was the second transuranic element to be synthesized, the first being neptunium.

Plymouth city, seaport, and unitary authority in southwest England, at the mouth of the River Plym; until April 1998 it was part of the county of Devon.

area 79 sq km/31 sq mi **features** dockyard and naval base at Devonport; three harbours, Sutton Pool, Catwater (Cattewater), and the Hamoaze, which unite in Plymouth Sound, a bay with a breakwater over 1 km/0.6 mi in length across the entrance; ferry links with France and Spain; Plymouth University, formerly South West Polytechnic, established in 1992; ramparts of a 17th-century citadel, built to guard the harbour soon after the Civil War; Eddystone Rocks lighthouse 22 km/14 mi to the south; the Hoe, an esplanade overlooking Plymouth Sound, with many monuments including a statue of Sir Francis Drake, and Smeaton's Tower, originally erected in 1759 on the Eddystone Rocks and replaced in 1882; Plymouth Dome illustrates the history of the city; aquarium of the Marine Biological Association, which has its headquarters in Plymouth **industries** marine and machine tools industries, and clothing, radio equipment, and processed foods are produced **population** (1996) 257,000

Related Web site: Welcome to the Plymouth Pages http://www.plymouth.gov.uk/

Plymouth Brethren fundamentalist Christian Protestant sect characterized by extreme simplicity of belief, founded in Dublin in about 1827 by the Reverend John Nelson Darby (1800–1882). The Plymouth Brethren have no ordained priesthood, affirming the ministry of all believers, and maintain no church buildings. They hold prayer meetings and Bible study in members' houses.

Edgar Allan Poe
All that we see or seem / Is but a dream within a dream.
A Dream within a Dream

plywood manufactured panel of wood widely used in building. It consists of several thin sheets, or plies, of wood, glued together with the grain (direction of the wood fibres) of one sheet at right angles to the grain of the adjacent plies. This construction gives plywood equal strength in every direction.

pneumatic drill drill operated by compressed air, used in mining and tunnelling, for drilling shot holes (for explosives), and in road repairs for breaking up pavements. It contains an air-operated piston that delivers hammer blows to the drill bit many times a second. The French engineer Germain Sommeiller (1815–1871) developed the pneumatic drill in 1861 for tunnelling in the Alps.

pneumatophore erect root that rises up above the soil or water and promotes gas exchange. Pneumatophores, or breathing roots, are formed by certain swamp-dwelling trees, such as mangroves, since there is little oxygen available to the roots in waterlogged conditions. They have numerous pores or lenticels over their surface, allowing gas exchange.

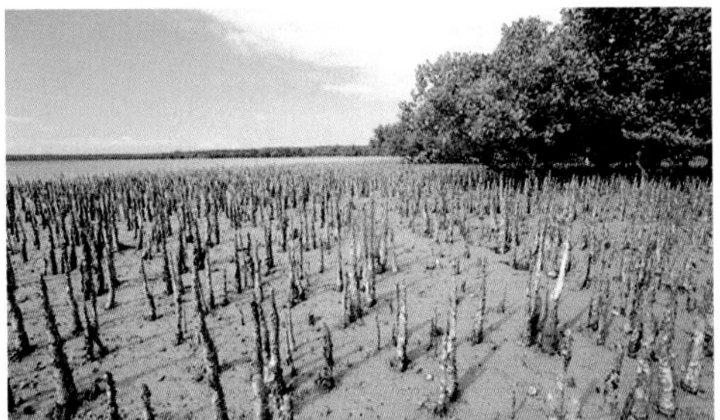

PNEUMATOPHORE Pneumatophoric mangrove roots exposed at low tide in Madagascar. *K G Preston-Mafham/Premaphotos Wildlife*

pneumoconiosis disease of the lungs caused by an accumulation of dust, especially from coal, asbestos, or silica. Inhaled particles make the lungs gradually fibrous and the victim has difficulty breathing. Over many years the condition causes severe disability.

pneumonia inflammation of the lungs, generally due to bacterial or viral infection but also to particulate matter or gases. It is characterized by a build-up of fluid in the alveoli, the clustered air sacs (at the ends of the air passages) where oxygen exchange takes place.

Symptoms include fever and pain in the chest. With widespread availability of antibiotics, infectious pneumonia is much less common than it was. However, it remains a dire threat to patients whose immune systems are suppressed (including transplant recipients and AIDS and cancer victims) and to those who are critically ill or injured. Pneumocystis pneumonia is a leading cause of death in AIDS.

pneumothorax the presence of air in the pleural cavity, between a lung and the chest wall. It may be due to a penetrating injury of the lung or to lung disease, or it may occur without apparent cause (spontaneous pneumothorax) in an otherwise healthy person. Prevented from expanding normally, the lung is liable to collapse.

Pnom Penh alternative form of ▷Phnom Penh, the capital of Cambodia.

PO abbreviation for Post Office.

Po (Greek Eridanos; Latin Padus) longest river in Italy, flowing from the Cottian Alps to the Adriatic Sea; length 668 km/415 mi. Its valley is fertile and contains natural gas. The river is heavily polluted with nitrates, phosphates, and arsenic.

poaching illegal hunting of game and fish on someone else's property. Since the creation of hunting grounds in the early Middle Ages, poaching has attracted heavy punishments.

Pocahontas, Matoaka (*c.* 1595–1617) American Indian alleged to have saved the life of the English colonist John Smith when he was captured by her father, the Indian chief Powhatan. She was kidnapped in 1613 by an Englishman, Samuel Argall, and later married the colonist John Rolfe (1585–1622) and was entertained as a princess at the English court of James I.

pochard any of various diving ducks found in Europe and North America, especially the genus *Aythya*. They feed largely on water plants. Their nest is made in long grass on the borders of lakes and pools.

pocket borough a borough in the UK before the ▷Reform Act of 1832, where all the houses were owned by one man, whose vote returned two members of Parliament. An example was Gatton in Surrey. See also ▷rotten borough.

pod in botany, a type of fruit that is characteristic of legumes (plants belonging to the Leguminosae family), such as peas and beans. It develops from a single ▷carpel and splits down both sides when ripe to release the seeds.

Podgorica (formerly Titograd (1946–92)) capital of Montenegro, a republic within Serbia and Montenegro; population (1993 est) 135,000. Industries include metalworking, furniture-making, and tobacco. It was damaged in World War II and after rebuilding was renamed in honour of Marshal Tito; it reverted to its original name with the collapse of communism. It was the birthplace of the Roman emperor Diocletian.

podzol (or podsol) type of light-coloured soil found predominantly under coniferous forests and on moorlands in cool regions where rainfall exceeds evaporation. The constant downward movement of water leaches nutrients from the upper layers, making podzols poor agricultural soils.

Poe, Edgar Allan (1809–1849) US writer and poet. His short stories are renowned for their horrific atmosphere, as in 'The Fall of the House of Usher' (1839) and 'The Masque of the Red Death' (1842), and for their acute reasoning (ratiocination), as in 'The Gold Bug' (1843) and 'The Murders in the Rue Morgue' (1841; in which the investigators Legrand and Dupin anticipate Conan Doyle's Sherlock Holmes). His poems include 'The Raven' (1845). His novel *The Narrative of Arthur Gordon Pym of Nantucket* (1838) has attracted critical attention.

Poe, born in Boston, was orphaned in 1811 and joined the army in1827 but was court-martialled in 1830 for deliberate neglect of duty. He failed to earn a living by writing, became an alcoholic, and in 1847 lost his wife (commemorated in his poem 'Annabel Lee'). His verse, of haunting lyric beauty (for example, 'Ulalume' and 'The Bells'), influenced the French Symbolists. The cause of his death has been debated. Poe had a history of opiate and alcohol abuse, though his family maintained that he had recently abstained from both. In 1996 a US doctor suggested that he may have died of rabies. See picture on p. 760.

Related Web site: Selected Poetry of Edgar Allan Poe (1809–1849) http://www.library.utoronto.ca/utel/rp/authors/poe.html

poet laureate poet of the British royal household or of the USA, so called because of the laurel wreath awarded to eminent poets in the Greco-Roman world. Early UK poets with unofficial status were John Skelton, Samuel Daniel, Ben ▷Jonson, and

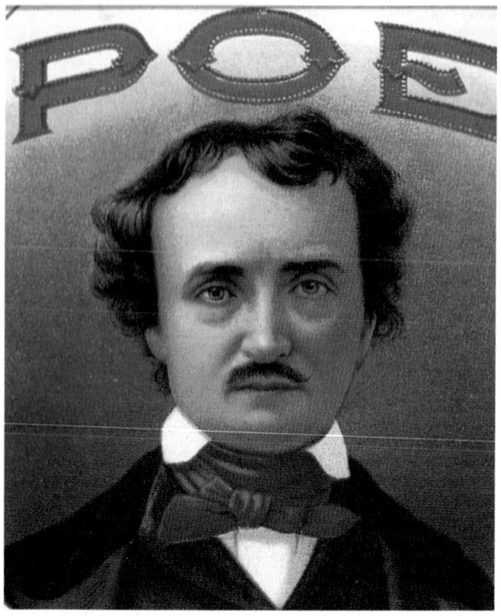

EDGAR ALLAN POE His fictional detective, Inspector Dupin, was an original creation, and the forerunner of many other investigators in this genre. See entry on p. 759. *Archive Photos*

William Davenant. John ▷Dryden was the first to receive the title by letters-patent in 1668 and from then on the post became a regular institution. Andrew Motion was appointed UK poet laureate in 1999. His was the first appointment to the post to be made for ten years, rather than for life.

There is a stipend of £70 a year, plus £27 in lieu of the traditional butt of sack (cask of wine).

poetry the imaginative expression of emotion, thought, or narrative, frequently in metrical form and often using figurative language. Poetry has traditionally been distinguished from prose (ordinary written language) by rhyme or the rhythmical arrangement of words (metre), the employment of the line as a formal unit, heightened vocabulary, and freedom of syntax.

Poetic images are presented using a variety of techniques, of which the most universal is the use of metaphor and simile to evoke a range of associations through implicit or explicit comparison. Although not frequently encountered in modern verse, alliteration has been used, chiefly for rhetoric or emphasis, in works dating back to Old English.

Related Web site: Poetry Zone http://www.poetryzone.ndirect.co.uk/index2.htm

pogrom (Russian 'destruction') unprovoked violent attack on an ethnic group, particularly Jews, carried out with official sanction. The Russian pogroms against Jews began in 1881, after the assassination of Tsar Alexander II, and again in 1903–06; persecution of the Jews remained constant until the Russian Revolution. Later there were pogroms in Eastern Europe, especially in Poland after 1918, and in Germany under Hitler (see ▷Holocaust).

poikilothermy the condition in which an animal's body temperature is largely dependent on the temperature of the air or water in which it lives. It is characteristic of all animals except birds and mammals, which maintain their body temperatures by ▷homeothermy (they are 'warm-blooded').

Poikilotherms have behavioural means of temperature control; they can warm themselves up by basking in the sun, or shivering, and can cool themselves down by sheltering from the Sun under a rock or by bathing in water.

Poikilotherms are often referred to as 'cold-blooded animals', but this is not correct: their internal temperatures, regulated by behavioural means, are often as high as those of birds and mammals during the times they need to be active for feeding and reproductive purposes, and may be higher, for example in very hot climates. The main difference is that their body temperatures fluctuate more than those of homeotherms.

Poindexter, John Marlane (1936–) US rear admiral and Republican government official. In 1981 he joined the Reagan administration's National Security Council (NSC) and became national security adviser in 1985. As a result of the ▷Irangate scandal, Poindexter was forced to resign in 1986, along with his assistant, Oliver North.

poinsettia (or **Christmas flower**) winter-flowering shrub with large red leaves encircling small greenish-yellow flowers. It is native to Mexico and tropical America and is a popular houseplant in North America and Europe. (Genus *Euphorbia pulcherrima*, family Euphorbiaceae.)

pointe (French 'toe of shoe') in dance, the tip of the toe. A dancer *sur les pointes* is dancing on her toes in blocked shoes, as popularized by the Italian dancer Marie Taglioni in 1832.

Pointe-Noire chief port and second-largest city of the Republic of the Congo, formerly (1950–58) the capital; population (1995 est) 576,200. It is on the Atlantic coast and is the terminus of the railway from Brazzaville. Industries include oil refining, shipbuilding, potash processing, brewing, and food exporting. Tourism is also important here.

pointer any of several breeds of gun dog, bred especially to scent the position of game and indicate it by standing, nose pointed towards it, often with one forefoot raised, in silence. English pointers have smooth coats, mainly white mixed with black, tan, or dark brown. They stand about 60 cm/24 in tall and weigh 28 kg/62 lb.

pointillism (or **Divisionism**) technique in oil painting developed in the 1880s by the Neo-Impressionist Georges Seurat. He used small dabs of pure colour laid side by side to create form and an impression of shimmering light when viewed from a distance.

poison (or **toxin**) any chemical substance that, when introduced into or applied to the body, is capable of injuring health or destroying life.

The liver removes some poisons from the blood. The majority of poisons may be divided into **corrosives**, such as sulphuric, nitric, and hydrochloric acids; **irritants**, including arsenic and copper sulphate; **narcotics** such as opium and carbon monoxide; and **narcotico-irritants** from any substances of plant origin including carbolic acid and tobacco.

poison pill in business, a tactic to avoid hostile takeover by making the target unattractive. For example, a company may give a certain class of shareholders the right to have their shares redeemed at a very good price in the event of the company being taken over, thus involving the potential predator in considerable extra cost.

Poitevin in English history, relating to the reigns of King John and King Henry III. The term is derived from the region of France south of the Loire (Poitou), which was controlled by the English for most of this period.

Poitier, Sidney (1924–) US actor and film director. He was a major black star in Hollywood. His won acclaim in *No Way Out* (1950), and later films include *Something of Value* (1957), *Lilies of the Field* (1963), *In the Heat of the Night* (1967), *Sneakers* (1992), and *The Jackal* (1997). He has directed *Stir Crazy* (1980) and *Ghost Dad* (1990).

Poitiers administrative centre of the *département* of Vienne and of the ▷Poitou-Charentes region in western France, at the confluence of the Rivers Clain and Boivre; population (1990) 82,500. Products include chemicals, electrical and metal goods, and clothing. The theme park of Mirapolis is nearby. The Merovingian king Clovis I defeated the Visigoths, for whom it was an important town, under Alaric II here in 507; ▷Charles Martel stemmed the Saracen advance in 732; and ▷Edward the Black Prince of England, with English and Gascon forces, defeated the French troops of Jean le Bon (John II) here in 1356, and took him prisoner.

Poitou-Charentes region of west-central France, comprising the *départements* of Charente, Charente-Maritime, Deux-Sèvres, and Vienne; area 25,800 sq km/9,950 sq mi; population (1990) 1,595,100. Its administrative centre is ▷Poitiers. Industries include dairy products, wheat, chemicals, and metal goods; brandy is made at Cognac.

Poland see country box.

Polanski, Roman (1933–) Polish film director. His films include *Repulsion* (1965), *Cul de Sac* (1966), *Rosemary's Baby* (1968), *Tess* (1979), *Frantic* (1988), *Bitter Moon* (1992), *Death and the Maiden* (1995), *The Ninth Gate* (2000), and *The Pianist* (2002), which won the Palme d'Or at the Cannes film festival.

He suffered a traumatic childhood in Nazi-occupied Poland, and later his wife, the actor Sharon Tate, was the victim of murder by the Charles Manson 'family'. He left the USA for Europe and his tragic personal life is reflected in his work.

polar bear large white-coated bear that lives in the Arctic. Polar bears are normally solitary, except for females when rearing cubs. They feed mainly on seals but will eat berries and scavenge when food is scarce. Males weigh 400–800 kg/880–1,760 lb and are up to 2.5 m/8.25 ft in length (twice as large as females, 200–400 kg). The estimated world population in 1997 was 20,000–30,000 bears.

Polar bears mate in spring, but egg implantation is delayed until autumn to ensure that when the cubs emerge from the den in the following March, the weather is milder and food more plentiful. Two or sometimes three cubs are born after a short gestation, weighing only 500 g/17.6 oz each. Cubs remain with their mother for 2.5 years.

Single species *Thalarctos maritimus*, in the bear family Ursidae, order Carnivora.

polar coordinates in mathematics, a way of defining the position of a point in terms of its distance r from a fixed point (the origin) and its angle θ to a fixed line or axis. The coordinates of the point are (r,θ).

Polaris (or **Pole Star** or **North Star**) bright star closest to the north celestial pole, and the brightest star in the constellation ▷Ursa Minor. Its position is indicated by the 'pointers' in ▷Ursa Major. Polaris is a yellow ▷supergiant about 500 light years away from the Sun. It is also known as **Alpha Ursae Minoris**.

It currently lies within 1° of the north celestial pole; ▷precession (Earth's axial wobble) will bring Polaris closest to the celestial pole (less than 0.5° away) in about AD 2100. Then its distance will start to increase, reaching 1° in 2205 and 47° in 28000. Other bright stars that have been, or will be close to the north celestial pole are Alpha Draconis (2800 BC), Gamma Cephei (AD 4000), Alpha Cephei (AD 7000), and ▷Vega (AD 14000).

polarized light light in which the electromagnetic vibrations take place in one particular plane. In ordinary (unpolarized) light, the electric fields vibrate in all planes perpendicular to the direction of propagation. After reflection from a polished surface or transmission through certain materials (such as Polaroid), the electric fields are confined to one direction, and the light is said to be **linearly polarized**. In **circularly polarized** and **elliptically polarized** light, the electric fields are confined to one direction, but the direction rotates as the light propagates. Polarized light is used to test the strength of sugar solutions and to measure stresses in transparent materials.

Polaroid camera instant-picture camera, invented by Edwin Land in the USA in 1947. The original camera produced black-and-white prints in about one minute. Modern cameras can produce black-and-white prints in a few seconds, and colour prints in less than a minute. An advanced model has automatic focusing and exposure. It ejects a piece of film on paper immediately after the picture has been taken.

Polar Regions see ▷Antarctica, ▷Antarctic Ocean, ▷Arctic, the, ▷Arctic Ocean.

polar reversal (or **magnetic reversal**) change in polarity of Earth's magnetic field. Like all magnets, Earth's magnetic field has two opposing regions, or poles, positioned approximately near geographical North and South Poles. During a period of normal polarity the region of attraction corresponds with the North Pole. Today, a compass needle, like other magnetic materials, aligns itself parallel to the magnetizing force and points to the North Pole. During a period of reversed polarity, the region of attraction would change to the South Pole and the needle of a compass would point south.

Studies of the magnetism retained in rocks at the time of their formation (like little compasses frozen in time) have shown that the polarity of the magnetic field has reversed repeatedly throughout geological time.

The reason for polar reversals is not known. Although the average time between reversals over the last ten million years has been 250,000 years, the rate of reversal has changed continuously over geological time. The most recent reversal was 780,000 years ago; scientists have no way of predicting when the next reversal will occur. The reversal process probably takes a few thousand years. Dating rocks using distinctive sequences of magnetic reversals is called magnetic stratigraphy.

polder area of flat reclaimed land that used to be covered by a river, lake, or the sea. Polders have been artificially drained and protected from flooding by building dykes. They are common in the Netherlands, where the total land area has been increased by nearly one-fifth since AD 1200. Such schemes as the Zuider Zee project have provided some of the best agricultural land in the country.

Pole people of Polish culture from Poland and the surrounding area. There are 37–40 million speakers of Polish (including some in the USA), a Slavic language belonging to the Indo-European family. The Poles are predominantly Roman Catholic, though there is an Orthodox Church minority. They are known for their distinctive cooking, folk festivals, and folk arts.

pole either of the geographic north and south points of the axis about which the Earth rotates. The geographic poles differ from the

Poland

URBAN POPULATION (% of total) 63
(2003 est)

AGE DISTRIBUTION (% of total population)
0–14 18%, 15–59 65%, 60+ 17% (2002 est)

ETHNIC GROUPS 98% ethnic Western-Slav
ethnic Poles; small ethnic German,
Ukrainian, and Belarussian minorities

LANGUAGE Polish (official)

RELIGION Roman Catholic 95%

EDUCATION (compulsory years) 8

LITERACY RATE 99% (men); 99% (women)
(2003 est)

LABOUR FORCE 19.2% agriculture, 32.1%
industry, 48.7% services (1998)

LIFE EXPECTANCY 70 (men); 78 (women)
(2000–05)

CHILD MORTALITY RATE (under 5, per 1,000
live births) 9 (2001)

PHYSICIANS (per 1,000 people) 2.4 (1998 est)

HOSPITAL BEDS (per 1,000 people) 4.9
(1998 est)

TV SETS (per 1,000 people) 401 (2001 est)

RADIOS (per 1,000 people) 523 (2001 est)

INTERNET USERS (per 10,000 people) 983.7
(2002 est)

PERSONAL COMPUTER USERS (per 100
people) 10.6 (2002 est)

See also ▷Solidarity; ▷Union of Soviet
Socialist Republics; ▷Warsaw ghetto.

Poland country in eastern Europe, bounded north by the Baltic Sea, northeast by Lithuania, east by Belarus and Ukraine, south by the Czech Republic and the Slovak Republic, and west by Germany.

NATIONAL NAME *Rzeczpospolita
Polska/Republic of Poland*

AREA 312,683 sq km/120,726 sq mi

CAPITAL Warsaw

MAJOR TOWNS/CITIES Lódz, Kraków,
Wroclaw, Poznan, Gdansk, Szczecin,
Katowice, Bydgoszcz, Lublin

MAJOR PORTS Gdansk (Danzig), Szczecin
(Stettin), Gdynia (Gdingen)

PHYSICAL FEATURES part of the great plain
of Europe; Vistula, Oder, and Neisse rivers;
Sudeten, Tatra, and Carpathian mountains
on southern frontier

Government

HEAD OF STATE Aleksander Kwasniewski
from 1995

HEAD OF GOVERNMENT Leszek Miller from
2001

POLITICAL SYSTEM liberal democracy

POLITICAL EXECUTIVE limited presidency

ADMINISTRATIVE DIVISIONS 16 provinces
and three city governments (Warsaw,
Kraków, and Lódz)

ARMED FORCES 163,000 (2002 est)

CONSCRIPTION 12 months (to be nine
months from 2004)

DEATH PENALTY abolished in 1997

DEFENCE SPEND (% GDP) 1.9 (2002 est)

EDUCATION SPEND (% GDP) 5.2
(2001 est)

HEALTH SPEND (% GDP) 6 (2000 est)

Economy and resources

CURRENCY zloty

GPD (US$) 187.7 billion (2002 est)

REAL GDP GROWTH (% change on previous
year) 1 (2001)

GNI (US$) 176.6 billion (2002 est)

GNI PER CAPITA (PPP) (US$) 10,130
(2002 est)

CONSUMER PRICE INFLATION 1.1%
(2003 est)

UNEMPLOYMENT 16.2% (2001)

FOREIGN DEBT (US$) 39.8 billion (2001 est)

MAJOR TRADING PARTNERS Germany, Italy,
the Netherlands, Russia, UK, France, USA,
Ukraine

RESOURCES coal (world's fifth-largest
producer), copper, sulphur, silver, petroleum
and natural gas reserves

INDUSTRIES machinery and transport
equipment, food products, metals,
chemicals, beverages, tobacco, textiles and
clothing, petroleum refining, wood and
paper products, tourism

EXPORTS machinery and transport
equipment, textiles, chemicals, coal, coke,
copper, sulphur, steel, food and agricultural
products, clothing and leather products,
wood and paper products. Principal market:
Germany 34.3% (2001)

IMPORTS electro-engineering products, fuels
and power (notably crude petroleum and
natural gas), textiles, food products, iron ore,
fertilizers. Principal source: Germany 23.9%
(2001)

ARABLE LAND 46% (2000 est)

AGRICULTURAL PRODUCTS wheat, rye,
barley, oats, maize, potatoes, sugar beet;
livestock rearing; forest resources

Population and society

POPULATION 38,587,000 (2003 est)

POPULATION GROWTH RATE –0.0%
(2000–15)

POPULATION DENSITY (per sq km) 119
(2003 est)

POLAND The town square of old Warsaw, Poland. Though known as the 'old' part of the city of Warsaw, this square is a reconstruction of the town square that was dynamited by German troops in World War II. *Image Bank*

Chronology

966: Polish Slavic tribes under Mieszko I, leader of Piast dynasty, adopted Christianity and united region around Poznań to form first Polish state.

1241: Devastated by Mongols.

13th–14th centuries: German and Jewish refugees settled among Slav population.

1386: Jagellonian dynasty came to power: golden age for Polish culture.

1569: Poland united with Lithuania to become the largest state in Europe.

1572: Jagellonian dynasty became extinct; future kings were elected by nobility and gentry, who formed 10% of the population.

mid-17th century: Defeat in war against Russia, Sweden, and Brandenburg (in Germany) set in a process of irreversible decline.

1772–95: Partitioned between Russia, which ruled the northeast; Prussia, the west, including Pomerania; and Austria in the south-centre, including Galicia, where there was greatest autonomy.

1815: After Congress of Vienna, Russian eastern portion of Poland re-established as kingdom within Russian Empire.

1830 and 1863: Uprisings against repressive Russian rule.

1892: Nationalist Polish Socialist Party (PPS) founded.

1918: Independent Polish republic established after World War I, with Marshal Józef Piłsudski, founder of the PPS, elected president.

1919–21: Abortive advance into Lithuania and Ukraine.

1926: Piłsudski seized full power in coup and established an autocratic regime.

1935: On Piłsudski's death, a military regime held power under Marshal Śmigły-Rydz.

1939: Invaded by Germany; western Poland incorporated into Nazi Reich (state) and the rest became a German colony; 6 million Poles – half of them Jews – were slaughtered in the next five years.

1944–45: Liberated from Nazi rule by Soviet Union's Red Army; boundaries redrawn westwards at the Potsdam Conference. One half of 'old Poland', 180,000 sq km/70,000 sq mi in the east, was lost to the USSR; 100,000 sq km/40,000 sq mi of ex-German territory in Silesia, along the Oder and Neisse rivers, was added, shifting the state 240 km/150 mi westwards; millions of Germans were expelled.

1947: Communist people's republic proclaimed after manipulated election.

1949: Joined Comecon.

early 1950s: Harsh Stalinist rule under communist leader Bolesław Bierut: nationalization; rural collectivization; persecution of Catholic Church members.

1955: Joined Warsaw Pact defence organization.

1956: Poznań strikes and riots. The moderate Władysław Gomułka installed as Polish United Workers' Party (PUWP) leader.

1960s: Private farming reintroduced and Catholicism tolerated.

1970: Gomułka replaced by Edward Gierek after Gdańsk riots against food price rises.

1970s: Poland heavily indebted to foreign creditors after a failed attempt to boost economic growth.

1980: Solidarity, led by Lech Wałęsa, emerged as free trade union following Gdańsk disturbances.

1981: Martial law imposed by General Wojciech Jaruzelski, trade-union activity banned, and Solidarity leaders and supporters arrested.

1983: Martial law ended.

1984: Amnesty for 35,000 political prisoners.

1988: Solidarity-led strikes and demonstrations for pay increases. Reform-communist Mieczysław Rakowski became prime minister.

1989: Agreement to relegalize Solidarity, allow opposition parties, and adopt a more democratic constitution, after round-table talks involving Solidarity, the Communist Party, and the Catholic Church. Widespread success for Solidarity in first open elections for 40 years; noncommunist 'grand coalition' government was formed, headed by Tadeusz Mazowiecki of Solidarity; an economic austerity and free-market restructuring programme began.

1990: The PUWP was dissolved and re-formed as the Democratic Left Alliance (SLD). Wałęsa was elected president and Jan Bielecki became prime minister.

1991: A shock-therapy economic restructuring programme, including large-scale privatization, produced a sharp fall in living standards and a rise in the unemployment rate to 11%. The unpopular Bielecki resigned and, after inconclusive elections, Jan Olszewski formed a fragile centre–right coalition government.

1992: The political instability continued.

1993: The economy became the first in Central Europe to grow since the collapse of communism.

1994: Poland joined the NATO 'partnership for peace' programme; the last Russian troops left the country.

1995: Aleksander Kwaśniewski, leader of the SLD, was elected president.

1997: Further structural reform and privatization took place and a new constitution was approved. Poland was invited to join NATO and begin negotiations to join the European Union (EU). A general election was won by Solidarity Electoral Action (AWS). A coalition government was formed, led by Jerzy Buzek.

1998: Full EU membership negotiations began.

1999: Poland became a full member of NATO.

2000: Alexander Kwaśniewski was elected for a further five years as president.

2002: The first direct local elections since the fall of communism were held.

2004: Poland was set to join the EU 1 May.

magnetic poles, which are the points towards which a freely suspended magnetic needle will point.

In 1985 the magnetic north pole was some 350 km/218 mi northwest of Resolute Bay, Northwest Territories, Canada. It moves northwards about 10 km/6 mi each year, although it can vary in a day about 80 km/50 mi from its average position. It is relocated every decade in order to update navigational charts.

It is thought that periodic changes in the Earth's core cause a reversal of the magnetic poles (see ▷polar reversal, ▷magnetic field). Many animals, including migrating birds and fish, are believed to orient themselves partly using the Earth's magnetic field. A permanent scientific base collects data at the South Pole.

polecat Old World weasel *Mustela putorius* with a brown back and dark belly and two yellow face patches. The body is about 50 cm/20 in long and it has a strong smell from anal gland secretions. It is native to Asia, Europe, and North Africa. In North America, ▷skunks are sometimes called polecats. A ferret is a domesticated polecat. Almost extinct in Britain around 1915, the polecat has since increased in numbers. It breeds once or twice a year, producing up to eight young.

Pole Star another name for ▷Polaris, the northern pole star. There is no bright star near the southern celestial pole.

police civil law-and-order force. In the UK, it is responsible to the Home Office, with 56 autonomous police forces, generally organized on a county basis; mutual aid is given in circumstances such as mass picketing in the 1984–85 miners' strike, but there is no national police force or police riot unit (such as the French CRS riot squad). The predecessors of these forces were the ineffective medieval watch and London's Bow Street runners, introduced in 1749 by Henry ▷Fielding, which formed a model for the London police force established by Robert ▷Peel's government in 1829 (hence 'peelers' or 'bobbies'); the system was introduced throughout the country from 1856.

Related Web site: Met Police http://www.met.police.uk/

polio (or poliomyelitis) viral infection of the central nervous system affecting nerves that activate muscles. The disease used to be known as infantile paralysis since children were most often affected. Two kinds of vaccine are available, one injected (see ▷Salk) and one given by mouth. The Americas were declared to be polio-free by the Pan American Health Organization in 1994. In 1997 the World Health Organization (WHO) reported that causes of polio had dropped by nearly 90% since 1988 when the organization began its programme to eradicate the disease by the year 2000. Most remaining cases were in Africa and southeast Asia in early 2000.

polis (Greek 'city') in ancient Greece, a city-state, the political and social centre of most larger Greek communities. Membership of a polis as a citizen, participation in its cults and festivals, and the protection of its laws formed the basis of classical Greek civilization, which was marked by intense intercity rivalries and conflicts until the Hellenistic period.

Polish language member of the Slavonic branch of the Indo-European language family, spoken mainly in Poland. Polish is written in the Roman and not the Cyrillic alphabet and its standard form is based on the dialect of Poznań in western Poland.

Polish literature a vernacular literature that began to emerge in the 14th century and enjoyed a golden age in the 16th and 17th centuries under Renaissance influences, particularly apparent in the poetry of Jan Kochanowski (1530–1584). The tradition revived in the later 18th century, the era of the Enlightenment poet and pioneer novelist Ignacy Krasicki (1735–1801), and a Polish national theatre was opened in 1765.

The domination of Poland by Austria, Russia, and Prussia towards the end of the 18th century and during the 19th century, and particularly the failure of the 1830 Polish insurrection, stimulated romantically tragic nationalism in major writers such as Adam ▷Mickiewicz, Juliusz Słowacki (1809–1849), and Zygmunt Krasiński. This theme also affected historical novelists such as Henryk Sienkiewicz. At the end of the 19th century there was a reaction against Naturalism and other orthodoxies in the 'Young Poland' movement (1890–1918), in theatre and fiction as well as poetry.

In the 20th century, political independence in the interwar years fostered writers as bewilderingly varied as the exuberant 'Skamander' group of poets and the fantastic, pessimistic philosopher and dramatist Stanisław Witkiewicz (1885–1939). Poland's tragic wartime and post-war experiences have given rise to poetry and prose registering social trauma and survival. Important writers include the veteran poet and scholar Czesław Miłosz (Nobel prize winner), Zbigniew Herbert, Witold Gombrowicz, the poet Tadeusz Różewicz, and the satirical dramatist Sławomir Mrozek.

Politburo contraction of 'political bureau', the executive committee (known as the Presidium 1952–66) of the Supreme Soviet in the USSR, which laid down party policy. It consisted of about 12 voting and 6 candidate (nonvoting) members.

political action committee (PAC) in the USA, any lobbying organization that raises funds for political candidates and in return seeks to commit them to a particular policy. PACs also spend money on changing public opinion through media campaigns. In 1990, there were about 4,300 PACs, controlling 30% of all funds spent in elections for ▷Congress. Donations to candidates amounted to $358.1 million, the largest PACs being the National Association of Realtors and the American Medical Association.

political correctness (or PC) shorthand term for a set of liberal attitudes about education and society, and the terminology associated with them. To be politically correct is to be sensitive to unconscious racism and sexism and to display environmental awareness. However, the real or alleged enforcement of PC speech codes ('people of colour' instead of 'coloured people', 'differently abled' instead of 'disabled', and so on) at more than 130 US universities by 1991 attracted derision and was criticized as a form of thought-policing.

politics ruling by the consent of the governed; an activity whereby solutions to social and economic problems are arrived at and different aspirations are met by the process of discussion and compromise rather than by the application of decree or force.

Polk, James Knox (1795–1849) 11th president of the USA 1845–49, a Democrat. Presiding over a period of westward expansion, he allowed Texas admission to the Union, and forced the war on Mexico that resulted in the annexation of California and New Mexico.

Related Web site: James K Polk – Eleventh President 1845–1849 http://www.whitehouse.gov/WH/glimpse/presidents/html/jp11.html

polka Bohemian dance in quick duple time (2/4). Originating in the 19th century, it became popular throughout Europe. The basic step is a hop followed by three short steps. The polka spread with German immigrants to the USA, becoming a style of Texas country music. It was also used by European composers, including Bedřich Smetana in *The Bartered Bride* (1866) and *Bohemian Dances* (1878), Antonín Dvořák, and others.

pollack marine fish *Pollachius virens* of the cod family, growing to 75 cm/2.5 ft, and found close to the shore on both sides of the North Atlantic.

Pollack, Sydney (1934–) US director, actor, and producer. He directed *Out of Africa*, which won the Academy Awards for best picture and best director in 1985. He also directed *The Way We Were* (1973), *The Electric Horseman* (1979), *Absence of Malice* (1981), *Tootsie* (1982), *The Firm* (1993), *Sabrina* (1995), and *Random Hearts* (1999). He appeared in such films as *Husbands and Wives* (1992), *The Player* (1992), and *Eyes Wide Shut* (1999).

Pollaiuolo Antonio del (*c.* 1432–1498) and Piero (*c.* 1441–1496). Two Italian artists, brothers. They ran an artistic workshop in their hometown Florence and later in Rome. Both were painters, sculptors, goldsmiths, engravers, and designers. Antonio, widely considered the better artist, is said to have been the first Renaissance artist to make a serious study of anatomy. *The Martyrdom of St Sebastian* (1475; National Gallery, London) is a joint work.

pollen the grains of ▷seed plants that contain the male gametes. In ▷angiosperms (flowering plants) pollen is produced within ▷anthers; in most ▷gymnosperms (cone-bearing plants) it is produced in male cones. A pollen grain is typically yellow and, when mature, has a hard outer wall. Pollen of insect-pollinated plants (see ▷pollination) is often sticky and spiny and larger than the smooth, light grains produced by wind-pollinated species.

The outer wall of pollen grains from both insect-pollinated and wind-pollinated plants is often elaborately sculptured with ridges or spines so distinctive that individual species or genera of plants can be recognized from their pollen. Since pollen is extremely resistant to decay, useful information on the vegetation of earlier times can be gained from the study of fossil pollen. The study of pollen grains is known as palynology.

pollen tube outgrowth from a pollen grain that grows towards the ▷ovule, following germination of the grain on the ▷stigma. In ▷angiosperms (flowering plants) the pollen tube reaches the ovule by growing down through the ▷style, carrying the male gametes inside. The gametes are discharged into the ovule and one fertilizes the egg cell.

pollination the process by which pollen is transferred from one plant to another. The male ▷gametes are contained in pollen grains, which must be transferred from the anther to the stigma in ▷angiosperms (flowering plants), and from the male cone to the female cone in ▷gymnosperms (cone-bearing plants). Fertilization

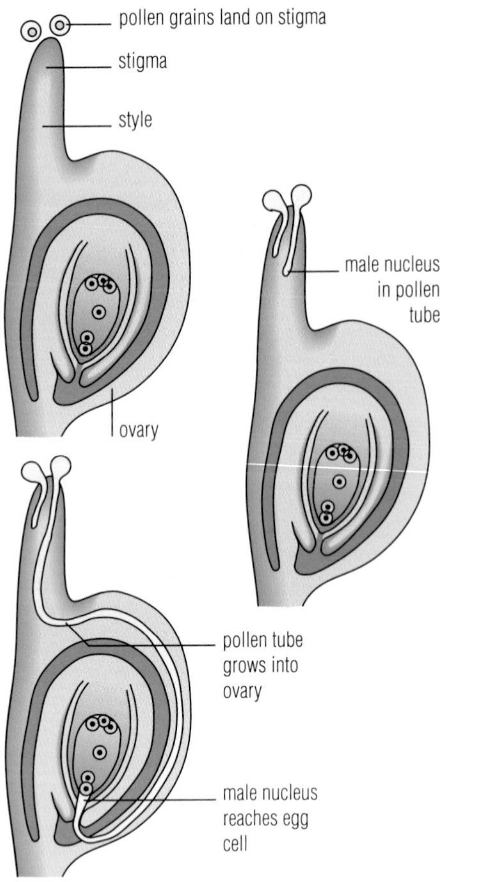

POLLEN Pollination is the process by which pollen grains transfer their male nuclei (gametes) to the ovary of a flower. The pollen grains land on the stigma and form a pollen tube that grows down into the ovary. The male nuclei travel along the pollen tube.

(not the same as pollination) occurs after the growth of the pollen tube to the ovary. Self-pollination occurs when pollen is transferred to a stigma of the same flower, or to another flower on the same plant; cross-pollination occurs when pollen is transferred to another plant. This involves external pollen-carrying agents, such as wind (see ▷anemophily), water (see ▷hydrophily), insects, birds (see ▷ornithophily), bats, and other small mammals.

Pollock, (Paul) Jackson (1912–1956) US painter. He was a pioneer of abstract expressionism and one of the foremost exponents of ▷action painting. His style is characterized by complex networks of swirling, interwoven lines of great delicacy and rhythmic subtlety.

In the early 1940s Pollock moved from a vivid expressionist style, influenced by Mexican muralists such as Siqueiros and by surrealism, towards a semi-abstract style. The paintings of this period are colourful and vigorous, using enigmatic signs and mysterious forms. From 1947 he developed his more violently expressive abstracts, placing large canvases on the studio floor and dripping or hurling paint across them. He was soon recognized as the leading abstract expressionist and continued to develop his style, producing even larger canvases in the 1950s.

poll tax tax levied on every individual, without reference to income or property. Being simple to administer, it was among the earliest sorts of tax (introduced in England in 1379), but because of its indiscriminate nature (it is a regressive tax, in that it falls proportionately more heavily on poorer people) it has often proved unpopular.

polluter-pays principle the idea that whoever causes pollution is responsible for the cost of repairing any damage. The principle is accepted in British law but has in practice often been ignored; for example, farmers causing the death of fish through slurry pollution have not been fined the full costs of restocking the river.

pollution the harmful effect on the environment of by-products of human activity, principally industrial and agricultural processes – for example, noise, smoke, car emissions, chemical and radioactive effluents in air, seas, and rivers, pesticides, radiation, sewage (see ▷sewage disposal), and household waste. Pollution contributes to the ▷greenhouse effect. See also ▷air pollution.

Pollution control involves higher production costs for the industries concerned, but failure to implement adequate controls may result in irreversible environmental damage and an increase in the incidence of diseases such as cancer. Radioactive pollution results from inadequate ▷nuclear safety.

Transboundary pollution is when the pollution generated in one country affects another, for example as occurs with ▷acid rain. Natural disasters may also cause pollution; volcanic eruptions, for example, cause ash to be ejected into the atmosphere and deposited on land surfaces.

In the UK in 1987 air pollution caused by carbon monoxide emission from road transport was measured at 5.26 million tonnes. In February 1990 the UK had failed to apply 21 European Community (now European Union) laws on air and water pollution and faced prosecution before the European Court of Justice on 31 of the 160 EU directives in force.

The existence of 1,300 toxic waste tips in the UK in 1990 posed a considerable threat of increased water pollution.

polo stick-and-ball game played between two teams of four on horseback. It originated in Iran, spread to India, and was first played in England in 1869. Polo is played on the largest field of any game, measuring up to 274 m/300 yd by 182 m/200 yd. A small solid ball is struck with the side of a longhandled mallet through goals at each end of the field. A typical match lasts about an hour, and is divided into 'chukkas' of 7½ minutes each. No pony is expected to play more than two chukkas in the course of a day.

Polo, Marco (1254–1324) Venetian traveller and writer. He joined his father (Niccolo) and uncle (Maffeo), who had travelled to China as merchants (1260–69), when they began a journey overland back to China (1271). Once there, he learned Mongolian and served the emperor Kubla Khan until he returned to Europe by sea 1292–95.

He was captured while fighting for Venice against Genoa, and, while in prison 1296–98, dictated an account of his travels. These accounts remained the primary source of information about the Far East until the 19th century.

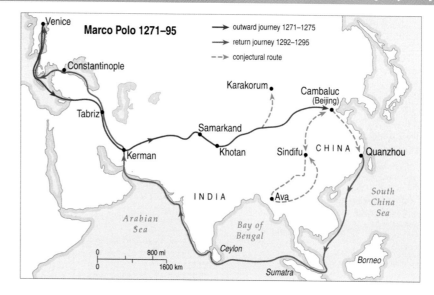

Marco Polo 1271–95

→ outward journey 1271–1275
→ return journey 1292–1295
--→ conjectural route

> **Marco Polo**
> *I have not told half of what I saw.*
> Last words

MARCO POLO The title page of the first printed edition of *The Travels of Marco Polo* (1477). Known in the original as *Il milione* (*The Million*), the book provided a wealth of new geographical information that was widely used during the great age of European exploration in the late 15th and 16th centuries. *The Art Archive/Victoria and Albert Museum London*

polonaise Polish dance in stately 3/4 time that was common in 18th-century Europe. The composer Frédéric ▷Chopin developed the polonaise as a pianistic form.

polonium radioactive, metallic element, symbol Po, atomic number 84, relative atomic mass 210. Polonium occurs in nature in small amounts and was isolated from ▷pitchblende. It is the element having the largest number of isotopes (27) and is 5,000 times as radioactive as radium, liberating considerable amounts of heat. It was the first element to have its radioactive properties recognized and investigated.

Polonium was isolated in 1898 from the pitchblende residues analyzed by French scientists Pierre and Marie ▷Curie, and named after Marie Curie's native Poland.

Pol Pot (*c.* 1925–1998) Also known as **Saloth Sar, Tol Saut,** or **Pol Porth**. Cambodian politician and leader of the Khmer Rouge communist movement that overthrew the government in 1975. After widespread atrocities against the civilian population, his regime was deposed by a Vietnamese invasion in 1979. Pol Pot continued to help lead the Khmer Rouge despite officially resigning from all positions in 1989. He was captured in 1997 but escaped from Cambodia, reportedly to Thailand, in January 1998 to avoid facing an international court for his crimes against humanity. The Cambodian government announced mid-April 1998 that he had been captured inside Thailand. However, a few days later reports of Pol Pot's death were confirmed. He died following a heart attack, in a Cambodian village two miles from the Thai border.

Pol Pot was a member of the anti-French resistance under Ho Chi Minh in the 1940s. In 1975 he proclaimed Democratic Kampuchea with himself as premier. His policies were to evacuate cities and put people to work in the countryside. The Khmer Rouge also carried out a systematic extermination of the Western-influenced educated and middle classes (1–4 million people).

Related Web site: Key Events in Pol Pot's Life http://www.washingtonpost.com/wp-srv/inatl/longterm/cambodia/stories/polpottimeline.htm

polyandry system whereby a woman has more than one husband at the same time. It is found in various parts of the world, for example, in Madagascar, Malaysia, and certain Pacific isles, and among certain Inuit and American Indian groups. In Tibet and parts of India, polyandry takes the form of the marriage of one woman to several brothers, as a means of keeping intact a family's heritage and property.

polyanthus cultivated variety of ▷primrose, with several flowers on one stalk, bred in a variety of colours. (Family Primulaceae, *Primula* × *polyantha*.)

Polybius (*c.* 200–*c.* 118 BC) Greek politician and historian of Rome. He was a senior politician of the ▷Achaean League against the Romans and, following the defeat of the Macedonians at Pydna in 168 BC, he was taken, together with other Achaean aristocrats, as a political hostage to Italy. He was allowed to settle in Rome, became a valued member of the circle of ▷Scipio Africanus Minor, and gained access to the public records. He returned to Greece in 151 and was present at the capture of Carthage by Scipio in 146. His history of Rome, in 40 books, covers the years 220–146. The first five books remain intact and of the rest fragments and abstracts have survived. He conscientiously sought to emulate the historian Thucydides and his history is of great value.

polychlorinated biphenyl (PCB) any of a group of chlorinated isomers of biphenyl (C_6H_5)$_2$. They are dangerous industrial chemicals, valuable for their fire-resistant qualities. They constitute an environmental hazard because of their persistent toxicity. Since 1973 their use had been limited by international agreement. In December 2000, 122 nations agreed a treaty to ban the toxic chemicals known as persistent organic polluters (POPs), which include PCBs, although they are unlikely to be totally eliminated until about 2025.

polyester synthetic resin formed by the condensation of polyhydric alcohols (alcohols containing more than one hydroxyl group) with dibasic acids (acids containing two replaceable hydrogen atoms). Polyesters are thermosetting ▷plastics, used in making synthetic fibres, such as Dacron and Terylene, and constructional plastics. With glass fibre added as reinforcement, polyesters are used in car bodies and boat hulls.

POLYESTER Spinning polyester in a plant in Egypt. *Image Bank*

polyethylene (or polyethene) polymer of the gas ethylene (technically called ethene, C_2H_4). It is a tough, white, translucent, waxy thermoplastic (which means it can be repeatedly softened by heating). It is used for packaging, bottles, toys, wood preservation, electric cable, pipes, and tubing.

Polyethylene is produced in two forms: low-density polyethylene, made by high-pressure polymerization of ethylene gas, and high-density polyethylene, which is made at lower pressure by using catalysts. This form, first made in 1953 by German chemist

Karl Ziegler, is more rigid at low temperatures and softer at higher temperatures than the low-density type. Polyethylene was first made in the 1930s at very high temperatures by ICI.

In the UK it is better known under the trademark Polythene.

POLYETHYLENE Manufactured in vast rolls under the supervision of one or more technical engineers, polythene is the trade name of a variety of polyethylene (or polyethene). *Image Bank*

polygamy the practice of having more than one spouse at the same time. It is found among many peoples. Normally it has been confined to the wealthy and to chiefs and nobles who can support several women and their offspring, as among ancient Egyptians, Teutons, Irish, and Slavs. Islam limits the number of legal wives a man may have to four. Certain Christian sects for example, the Anabaptists of Münster, Germany, and the Mormons – have practised polygamy because it was the norm in the Old Testament.

polygon in geometry, a plane (two-dimensional) figure with three or more straight-line sides. Common polygons have names which define the number of sides (for example, triangle (3), quadrilateral (4), pentagon (5), hexagon (6), heptagon (7), octagon (8), and so on. **Regular polygons** have sides of the same length and all the exterior angles are equal.

polyhedron in geometry, a solid figure with four or more plane faces. The more faces there are on a polyhedron, the more closely it approximates to a sphere. Knowledge of the properties of polyhedra is needed in crystallography and stereochemistry to determine the shapes of crystals and molecules.

Polykleitos (or Polyclitus) (lived 5th century BC) Greek sculptor. His *Spear Carrier* (450–440 BC; only Roman copies survive) exemplifies the naturalism and harmonious proportions of his work. He created the legendary colossal statue of Hera in Argos, in ivory and gold.

polymer compound made up of a large long-chain or branching matrix composed of many repeated simple units (**monomers**) linked together by ▷polymerization. There are many polymers, both natural (cellulose, chitin, lignin) and synthetic (polyethylene and nylon, types of plastic). Synthetic polymers belong to two groups: thermosoftening and thermosetting (see ▷plastic).

The size of the polymer matrix is determined by the amount of monomer used; it therefore does not form a molecule of constant molecular size or mass.

Related Web site: Polymers: They're Everywhere http://www. nationalgeographic.com/resources/ngo/education/plastics/index.html

polymerization chemical union of two or more (usually small) molecules of the same kind to form a new compound. **Addition polymerization** produces simple multiples of the same compound. **Condensation polymerization** joins molecules together with the elimination of water or another small molecule.

polymorphism in genetics, the coexistence of several distinctly different types in a ▷population (groups of animals of one

species). Examples include the different blood groups in humans, different colour forms in some butterflies, and snail shell size, length, shape, colour, and stripiness.

polymorphism in mineralogy, the ability of a substance to adopt different internal structures and external forms, in response to different conditions of temperature and/or pressure. For example, diamond and graphite are both forms of the element carbon, but they have very different properties and appearance.

Polynesia islands of Oceania east of 170° E latitude, including Hawaii, Kiribati, Tuvalu, Fiji Islands, Tonga, Tokelau, Samoa, Cook Islands, and French Polynesia.

Related Web site: Polynesian Voyaging Society http://leahi.kcc.hawaii.edu/org/pvs/

Polynesian any of the seafaring peoples of Polynesia. They migrated by canoe from South Asia in about 2000 BC, peopling the islands of the South Pacific for about 2,000 years, and settling Hawaii last, from Tahiti. The Polynesian languages belong to the Oceanic branch of the Austronesian family.

Polynesian languages see ▷Malayo-Polynesian languages.

polynomial in mathematics, an algebraic expression that has one or more ▷variables (denoted by letters). A polynomial of degree one, that is, whose highest ▷power of x is 1, as in $2x + 1$, is called a linear polynomial; $3x^2 + 2x + 1$ is quadratic; $4x^3 + 3x^2 + 2x + 1$ is cubic.

polyp (or polypus) small 'stalked' benign tumour, usually found on mucous membrane of the nose or bowels. Intestinal polyps are usually removed, since some have been found to be precursors of cancer.

polyphony music combining two or more 'voices' or parts, each with an individual melody. A polyphony of widely separated groups is called antiphony.

polyploid in genetics, possessing three or more sets of chromosomes in cases where the normal complement is two sets (▷diploid). Polyploidy arises spontaneously and is common in plants (mainly among flowering plants), but rare in animals. Many crop plants are natural polyploids, including wheat, which has four sets of chromosomes per cell (durum wheat) or six sets (common wheat).

Plant breeders can induce the formation of polyploids by treatment with a chemical, colchicine.

polysaccharide long-chain ▷carbohydrate made up of hundreds or thousands of linked simple sugars (monosaccharides) such as glucose and closely related molecules.

The polysaccharides are natural polymers. They either act as energy-rich food stores in plants (starch) and animals (glycogen), or have structural roles in the plant cell wall (cellulose, pectin) or the tough outer skeleton of insects and similar creatures (chitin). See also ▷carbohydrate.

polystyrene type of ▷plastic used in kitchen utensils or, in an expanded form, in insulation and ceiling tiles. CFCs are used to produce expanded polystyrene so alternatives are being sought.

MARQUISE DE POMPADOUR A portrait of the infamous Jeanne Antoinette Poisson Pompadour by François Boucher. *Archive Photos*

polytechnic formerly, in the UK, an institution for higher education offering courses mainly at degree level and concentrating on full-time vocational courses, although many polytechnics provided a wide range of part-time courses at advanced levels.

In April 1989 the polytechnics in England and Wales became independent corporations. In 1992 all polytechnics and some colleges of higher education became universities, and from 1993 all universities began to compete for funding on an equal basis.

polytetrafluoroethene (PTFE) polymer made from the monomer tetrafluoroethene (CF_2CF_2). It is a thermosetting plastic with a high melting point that is used to produce 'nonstick' surfaces on pans and to coat bearings. Its trade name is Teflon.

polytheism (Greek *polus* 'many', *theos* 'god') the worship of many gods, as opposed to monotheism (belief in one god). Examples are the religions of ancient Egypt, Babylon, Greece, Rome, and Mexico. Modern Hinduism, while worshipping God in many forms, teaches an underlying unity of the godhead.

Polythene trade name for a variety of ▷polyethylene.

polyvinyl chloride (PVC) type of ▷plastic used for drainpipes, floor tiles, audio discs, shoes, and handbags. It is derived from vinyl chloride ($CH_2=CHCl$).

pome type of ▷pseudocarp, or false fruit, typical of certain plants belonging to the Rosaceae family. The outer skin and fleshy tissues are developed from the ▷receptacle (the enlarged end of the flower stalk) after fertilization, and the five ▷carpels (the true fruit) form the pome's core, which surrounds the seeds. Examples of pomes are apples, pears, and quinces.

pomegranate round, leathery, reddish-yellow fruit of the pomegranate tree, a deciduous shrub or small tree native to southwestern Asia but cultivated widely in tropical and subtropical areas. The fruit contains a large number of seeds that can be eaten fresh or made into wine. (Genus *Punica granatum*, family Punicaceae.)

Related Web site: Pomegranates in California http://fruitsandnuts.ucdavis.edu/pomeg.html

Pomerania (Polish Pomorze; German **Pommern**) region along the southern shore of the Baltic Sea, including the island of Rügen, divided between Poland and (west of the Oder–Neisse line) East Germany 1945–90, and the Federal Republic of Germany after reunification in 1990. The chief port is Gdańsk. It was formerly a province of Germany.

pomeranian breed of toy dog, about 15 cm/6 in high, weighing about 3 kg/6.5 lb. It has long straight hair with a neck frill, and the tail is carried over the back.

Pommern German form of ▷Pomerania, a region of northern Europe, now largely in Poland.

Pompadour, Jeanne Antoinette Poisson, Marquise de Pompadour (1721–1764) Also known as **Madame de Pompadour**. Mistress of ▷Louis XV of France from 1744, born in Paris. She largely dictated the government's ill-fated policy of reversing France's anti-Austrian policy for an anti-Prussian one. She acted as the patron of the Enlightenment philosophers Voltaire and Diderot.

○ hydrogen atom

● carbon atom

━━━ double covalent bond

━━━ single covalent bond

POLYMERIZATION In polymerization, small molecules (monomers) join together to make large molecules (polymers). In the polymerization of ethene to polyethene, electrons are transferred from the carbon–carbon double bond of the ethene molecule, allowing the molecules to join together as a long chain of carbon–carbon single bonds.

Pompeii ancient city in Italy, near the volcano ▷Vesuvius, 21 km/13 mi southeast of Naples. In AD 63 an earthquake destroyed much of the city, which had been a Roman port and pleasure resort; it was completely buried beneath volcanic ash when Vesuvius, a composite – and therefore explosive – ▷volcano erupted in AD 79. Over 2,000 people were killed. Pompeii was rediscovered in 1748 and the systematic excavation begun in 1763 still continues.

Related Web site: Pompeii Forum Project http://jefferson.village.virginia.edu/pompeii/forummap.html

POMPEII A mural in the Villa of the Mysteries just outside the walls to the northwest of old Pompeii, Italy. The villa was evidently a religious establishment devoted to the worship of the god Pan, for in the mural a priest plays the syrinx (panpipes) in the presence of Pan's animals, the goats, while a priestess enacts terror, thus explaining the derivation of the English word 'panic'. *The Art Archive/Villa of the Mysteries Pompeii/Dagli Orti*

Pompey the Great (106–48 BC) Born Gnaeus Pompeius Magnus. Roman soldier and politician. From 60 BC to 53 BC, he was a member of the First Triumvirate with Julius Caesar and Marcus Livius Crassus. Originally a supporter of Sulla, Pompey became consul with Crassus in 70 BC. He defeated ▷Mithridates VI Eupator of Pontus, and annexed Syria and Palestine. He married Caesar's daughter Julia (died 54 BC) in 59 BC. When the Triumvirate broke down after 53 BC, Pompey was drawn into leadership of the senatorial faction. On the outbreak of civil war in 49 BC he withdrew to Greece, was defeated by Caesar at Pharsalus in 48 BC, and was murdered in Egypt.

> **Georges Pompidou**
> *A statesman is a politician who places himself at the service of the nation. A politician is a statesman who places the nation at his service.*
> *The Observer*, December 1973

Pompidou, Georges Jean Raymond (1911–1974) French Gaullist politician and head of state, President ▷de Gaulle's second prime minister 1962–68 and his successor as president 1969–74. As prime minister he played a key role in managing the Gaullist party but his moderate and pragmatic conservativism brought a rift with de Gaulle in May–June 1968, when he negotiated the Grenelle Agreement with employers and unions to end the strike movement. Their political divergences were confirmed when, during his own presidency, he authorized a devaluation of the franc (which de Gaulle had vetoed in 1968), agreed to British entry into the European Community (which de Gaulle had twice vetoed in the 1960s), and approved initial steps towards a European Monetary System. Pompidou died in office before completing his full seven-year presidential term.

Ponce de León, Juan (c. 1460–1521) Spanish soldier and explorer. He is believed to have sailed to the Americas with Christopher Columbus in 1493, and served in Hispaniola 1502–04. He conquered Puerto Rico in 1508, and was made governor in 1509. In 1513 he was the first European to reach Florida.

Pondicherry Union Territory of southeast India; area 492 sq km/190 sq mi; population (2001 est) 1,052,000. Its capital is Pondicherry which lies on the Coromandel Coast, 196 km/122 mi south of Chennai (formerly Madras). Its products include rice, millet, groundnuts, cotton, and sugar; industry is based on textiles and coastal trade.

pond-skater water ▷bug (insect of the Hemiptera order with piercing mouth parts) that rows itself across the surface by using its middle legs. It feeds on smaller insects.

pondweed any of a group of aquatic plants that either float on the surface of the water or are submerged. The leaves of floating pondweeds are broad and leathery, whereas leaves of the submerged forms are narrower and translucent; the flowers grow in green spikes. (Genus *Potamogeton*, family Potamogetonaceae.)

Pontefract (or Pomfret) industrial town in West Yorkshire, northern England, 34 km/21 mi southwest of York, near the junction of the rivers Aire and Calder; population (1991) 28,400. Industries include coalmining, iron founding, engineering, tanning, brewing, corn milling, market gardening, and the manufacture of furniture and confectionery. The town gives its name to liquorice Pontefract or Pomfret cakes. Features include the remains of the Norman castle (built in 1069) where Richard II was murdered in 1399.

Pontiac (c. 1720–1769) American Indian, chief of the Ottawa from 1755. Allied with the French forces during the French and Indian War (the American branch of the Seven Years' War), Pontiac was hunted by the British after the French withdrawal. He led the 'Conspiracy of Pontiac' 1763–64 in an attempt to resist British persecution. He achieved remarkable success against overwhelming odds, but eventually signed a peace treaty in 1766.

pony small ▷horse under 1.47 m/4.5 ft (14.2 hands) shoulder height. Although of Celtic origin, all the pony breeds have been crossed with thoroughbred and Arab stock, except for the smallest – the hardy Shetland, which is less than 105 cm/42 in shoulder height.

poodle breed of gun dog, including standard (above 38 cm/15 in at shoulder), miniature (below 38 cm/15 in), and toy (below 28 cm/11 in) varieties. The dense curly coat, usually cut into an elaborate style, is often either black or white, although greys and browns are also bred.

Poole unitary authority in southwest England, created in 1997 from part of Dorset.

area 64 sq km/25 sq mi **towns and cities** ▷Poole (administrative headquarters), Broadstone, Hillbournes, Sandbanks **features** River Stour formers northern border of authority; Poole Harbour; Holes Bay; Pergins Island; Maritime Museum (Poole); Compton Acres themed gardens (including water, rock, heather, Japanese, Roman, Italian); Canford Heath, tumuli field; Sandbanks spit guarding entrance to harbour; ferry from Poole to Brownsea Island and the Channel Islands **industries** boat building and repair, tourism, electro-mechanical engineering, marine engineering and marine electronics, electrical systems, aeronautical instruments **population** (1996) 138,100

Poona former spelling of ▷Pune, a city in India; after independence in 1947 the form Poona was gradually superseded by Pune.

poor law English system for poor relief, established by the Poor Relief Act of 1601. Each parish was responsible for its own poor, paid for by a parish tax. The care of the poor was transferred to the Ministry of Health in 1918, but the poor law remained in force until 1930.

Elizabethan poor law Before the reign of Elizabeth I the approach to poverty in England was punitive. In 1495 a law had ordered beggars to be put in the stocks. In 1547 beggars and vagrants had been ordered to be branded with a 'V' and made a slave for two years. A law of 1572 continued this approach, declaring that beggars should be whipped and, for a third offence, executed. The only help for poor people was private charity. However, steady inflation and rural economic problems, caused by ▷enclosure and the move from tillage to sheep farming, were exacerbated in the 1570s and the 1590s by a series of poor harvests. The government was worried that the growing numbers of beggars and vagrants might lead to social disorder, and also came to realize that poverty was not always the fault of the victim – a distinction was made between the 'deserving' and the 'undeserving' poor. The Poor Relief Act of 1601 allowed each parish to collect a poor rate to give a little money to the 'impotent poor', such as the elderly and the blind; and to provide workhouses for the 'poor by casualty', such as the sick and the senile. Orphans were to be given an apprenticeship. Only the 'idle poor', the so-called 'sturdy beggars', were to be whipped and returned to their place of birth. The 1601 Poor Relief Act did not end poverty, but it remained the basis of England's poor law system for two centuries, and supplied for the first time a basic 'safety-net' for those who had fallen on hard times.

Poor Law Amendment Act, 1834 The old poor law was substantially adapted in the 18th century to meet changing needs.

POND-SKATER Toothed pond-skaters *Gerris odontogaster* feeding on a common blue damselfly. *Dr Rod Preston-Mafham/Premaphotos Wildlife*

The Workhouse Act of 1722 required parishes to build ▷workhouses to accommodate the poor; it was largely ignored, because it was far more expensive to build a workhouse than it was to allow 'outdoor relief'. Instead, in 1762 Gilbert's Act tried to make the administration of the poor law more professional; it also laid down that the 'able-bodied' poor were to receive outdoor relief. In response to changing agricultural practices in the south of England, the system was further liberalized in the late 18th century by the Speenhamland system and the Roundsman system.

The poor law system certainly prevented many families from starving in times of poor harvests, and outdoor relief was well-suited to the industrial regions of the north, where unemployment fluctuated according to the trade cycle, and an economic depression might throw a large number of people out of work for a short time. However, the system was very expensive, especially in times of economic depression when ratepayers had least money. A Royal Commission, set up in 1834 to investigate the poor law, also reported that it encouraged labourers to be lazy, since their wages were made up to a fixed level however hard they worked; that it encouraged them to have more children than they could afford, since the system gave them an amount per child; and that it allowed farmers to pay low wages, which they knew would be made up from the parish rates. The system also failed to prevent the Swing Riots of 1830–31.

The Poor Law Amendment Act of 1834 set up large poor law unions, administered by elected boards of guardians, and controlled by a central Poor Law Commission. Outdoor relief for able-bodied paupers was abolished and replaced by workhouses run by unions of parishes. The principle applied was that of 'less eligibility': conditions in such workhouses were designed to act as a deterrent for all but the genuinely destitute. The level of provision was supposed to be worse than that which would be afforded by the lowest-paying job, and husbands, wives, and children were to be split up. The Act was implemented quickly in the south, but it provoked riots in the north, where it proved impossible to implement, and some workhouses were burned down. Conditions in some of the workhouses were terrible, but after the Andover workhouse scandal of 1847 (where it was found that workhouse inmates were so hungry that they were eating scraps from the bones they were meant to be crushing for bonemeal fertilizer), the government removed some of the greatest corruptions and evils of the system.

By the end of the century, local councils began to take over the work of the Guardians, and although the Act remained in force until 1929, it was gradually superseded by other forms of welfare.

pop art movement in modern art that took its imagery from the glossy world of advertising and from popular culture such as comic strips, films, and television; it developed in the 1950s and flourished in the 1960s, notably in Britain and the USA. The term was coined by the British critic Lawrence Alloway (1926–1990) in about 1955, to refer to works of art that drew upon popular culture. Richard Hamilton, one of the leading British pioneers and exponents of pop art, defined it in 1957 as 'popular, transient, expendable, low-cost, mass-produced, young, witty, sexy, gimmicky, glamorous, and Big Business'. In its eclecticism and sense of irony and playfulness, pop art helped to prepare the way for the ▷postmodernism that has been a feature of Western culture since the 1970s.

pope the bishop of Rome, head of the Roman Catholic Church, which claims he is the spiritual descendant of St Peter. Elected by the Sacred College of Cardinals, a pope dates his pontificate from his coronation with the tiara, or triple crown, at St Peter's Basilica, Rome. The pope had great political power in Europe from the early Middle Ages until the Reformation.

Pope, Alexander (1688–1744) English poet and satirist. He established his poetic reputation with the precocious *Pastorals* (1709) and *An Essay on Criticism* (1711), which were followed by a

parody of the heroic epic, *The Rape of the Lock* (1712–14), *The Temple of Fame* (1715), and 'Eloisa to Abelard' (1717). The highly neoclassical translations of Homer's *Iliad* and *Odyssey* (1715–26) were very successful but his edition of Shakespeare (1725) attracted scholarly ridicule, which led Pope to write a satire on scholarly dullness, *The Dunciad* (1728). His finest mature works are his *Imitations of the Satires of Horace* (1733–38) and his personal letters.

Pope had a biting wit, expressed in the heroic couplet, of which he was a master. His couplets have an epigrammatic quality ('True wit is nature to advantage dressed/What oft was thought, but ne'er so well expressed'), and many of his observations have passed into the language as proverbs, for example 'A little learning is a dang'rous thing'. His philosophical verse, including *An Essay on Man* (1733–34) and *Moral Essays* (1731–35), was influenced by the political philosopher Henry ▷Bolingbroke. As a Catholic, he was subject to discrimination, and he was embittered by a deformity of the spine caused by childhood illness. Among his friends were the writers Jonathan ▷Swift, John ▷Arbuthnot, and John ▷Gay, and with them he was a member of the Scriblerus Club.

His position as a poet has been the subject of much contention among critics. There was a reaction against the neoclassicism of his poetry as Romantic tastes began to prevail later in the 18th century, and in the 19th century Pope was often inaccurately dismissed as bitter, malicious, and 'unpoetic'. More recently the quality of his verse has again been recognized. In the polish and perfection of his heroic couplets he aimed to reflect the qualities of the true poet, a man of taste and dedication, committed to the preservation of human and social standards. These positive qualities lie behind the spleen and bitterness of much of his work.

Related Web site: Selected Poetry and Prose of Alexander Pope (1688–1744) http://www.library.utoronto.ca/utel/rp/authors/pope.html

poplar any of a group of deciduous trees with characteristically broad leaves. The white poplar (*P. alba*) has a smooth grey trunk and leaves with white undersides. (Genus *Populus*, family Salicaceae.)

pop music any contemporary music not categorizable as jazz or classical.

Characterized by strong rhythms of African origin, simple harmonic structures often repeated to strophic melodies, and the use of electrically amplified instruments, pop music generically includes the areas of rock, country and western, rhythm and blues, soul, and others. Pop became distinct from folk music with the advent of sound-recording techniques; electronic amplification and other technological innovations have played a large part in the creation of new styles. The traditional format is a song of roughly three minutes with verse, chorus, and middle eight bars.

Related Web site: Rockmine Archives http://www.rockmine.music.co.uk/Rockmn.html

POP MUSIC The Spice Girls were a late 1990s phenomenon. Their funk rhythms and 'girl power' ethos struck a chord with young fans, especially with pre-teen girls. *Archive Photos*

Popper, Karl Raimund (1902–1994) British philosopher of science, who was born in Austria and became a naturalized British subject in 1945. His theory of falsificationism states that although scientific generalizations cannot be conclusively verified, they can be conclusively falsified by a counterinstance; therefore, science is not certain knowledge but a series of 'conjectures and refutations', approaching, though never reaching, a definitive truth. For Popper, psychoanalysis and Marxism are falsifiable and therefore unscientific.

Popper is one of the most widely read philosophers of the 20th century. His book *The Open Society and its Enemies* (1945) became a modern classic. In it he investigated the long history of attempts to formulate a theory of the state. Animated by a dislike of the views of Freud and Marx, Popper believed he could show that their hypotheses about hidden social and psychological processes were falsifiable.

POP MUSIC Tin Pan Alley, 28th Street, New York, USA, where many famous musicians sold their first songs. *Archive Photos*

His major work on the philosophy of science is *The Logic of Scientific Discovery* (1935). Other works include *The Poverty of Historicism* (1957) (about the philosophy of social science), *Conjectures and Refutations* (1963), and *Objective Knowledge* (1972).

Popper was professor of logic and scientific method at the London School of Economics (LSE) 1949–69. He was knighted in 1965.

poppy any of a group of plants belonging to the poppy family. They have brightly coloured mainly red and orange flowers, often with dark centres, and yield a milky sap. Species include the crimson European field poppy (*P. rhoeas*) and the Asian opium poppy (*P. somniferum*), source of the drug ▷opium. Closely related are the California poppy (*Eschscholtzia californica*) and the yellow horned or sea poppy (*Glaucium flavum*). (Poppy genus *Papaver*, family Papaveraceae.)

POPPY The opium poppy *Papaver somniferum*, native to Asia, has been widely cultivated since antiquity. *Premaphotos Wildlife*

popular front political alliance of liberals, socialists, communists, and other centre and left-wing parties. This policy was propounded by the Communist International in 1935 against fascism and was adopted in France and Spain, where popular-front governments were elected in 1936; that in France was overthrown in 1938 and the one in Spain fell with the defeat of the Republic in the Spanish Civil War in 1939.

population in biology and ecology, a group of animals of one species, living in a certain area and able to interbreed; the members of a given species in a ▷community of living things.

population the number of people living in a specific area or region, such as a town or country, at any one time. The study of populations, their distribution and structure, resources, and patterns of ▷migration, is called ▷demography. Information on population is obtained in a number of ways, such as through the registration of births and deaths. These figures are known as 'vital statistics'. However, more detailed information on population distribution, density, and change is necessary to enable governments to plan for education, health, housing, and transport on local and national levels. This information is usually obtained from ▷censuses (population counts), which provide data on sex, age, occupation, and nationality.

Related Web site: Facing The Future: People and the Planet http://www.popinfo.org/

population control measures taken by some governments to limit the growth of their countries' populations by trying to reduce ▷birth rates. Propaganda, freely available contraception, and tax disincentives for large families are some of the measures that have been tried.

population cycle in biology, regular fluctuations in the size of a population, as seen in lemmings, for example. Such cycles are often caused by density-dependent mortality: high mortality due to overcrowding causes a sudden decline in the population, which then gradually builds up again. Population cycles may also result from an interaction between a predator and its prey.

population explosion the rapid and dramatic rise in world population that has occurred over the last few hundred years. Between 1959 and 1995, the world's population increased from 2.5 billion to 5.6 billion people. It was estimated to reach 6 billion by the end of the 20th century.

Populism in US history, a late 19th-century political movement that developed out of farmers' protests against economic hardship. The Populist (or People's) Party was founded in 1892 and ran several presidential candidates. It failed, however, to reverse increasing industrialization and the relative decline of agriculture in the USA.

porbeagle medium-sized ▷shark.

porcelain (or hardpaste) translucent ceramic material with a shining finish, see ▷pottery and porcelain.

porcupine any ▷rodent with quills on its body, belonging to either of two families: Old World porcupines (family Hystricidae), terrestrial in habit and having long black-and-white quills; or New World porcupines (family Erethizontidae), tree-dwelling, with prehensile tails and much shorter quills.

pornography obscene literature, pictures, photos, or films considered to be of no artistic merit and intended only to arouse sexual desire. Standards of what is obscene and whether a particular work has artistic value are subjective, hence there is often difficulty in determining whether a work violates the ▷obscenity laws. Opponents of pornography claim that it is harmful and incites violence to women and children.

porphyria group of rare genetic disorders caused by an enzyme defect. Porphyria affects the digestive tract, causing abdominal distress; the nervous system, causing psychotic disorder, epilepsy, and weakness; the circulatory system, causing high blood pressure; and the skin, causing extreme sensitivity to light. No specific treatments exist.

porphyry any ▷igneous rock containing large crystals in a finer matrix.

porpoise any small whale of the family Delphinidae that, unlike dolphins, have blunt snouts without beaks. Common porpoises of the genus *Phocaena* can grow to 1.8 m/6 ft long; they feed on fish and crustaceans.

The harbour porpoise is in danger of extinction in the Celtic Sea (between southern Ireland and northern Cornwall) as the result of the animals being caught and killed in fishing nets.

port in computing, a socket that enables a computer processor to communicate with an external device. It may be an **input port** (such as a joystick port), or an **output port** (such as a printer port), or both (an **i/o port**).

port point where goods are loaded or unloaded from a water-based to a land-based form of transport. Most ports are coastal, though inland ports on rivers also exist. Ports often have specialized equipment to handle cargo in large quantities (for example, container or roll-on/roll-off facilities).

Port Arthur former name (to 1905) of the port and naval base of Lüshun in northeast China, now part of ▷Dalian.

Port-au-Prince capital and industrial port (sugar, rum, textiles, plastics) of Haiti; population (1992) 1,255,100.

Founded by the French 1749, it was destroyed by earthquakes 1751 and 1770.

Port Elizabeth industrial port in Eastern Cape Province, South Africa, about 710 km/440 mi east of Cape Town, on Algoa Bay; population (urban area, 1991) 853,200. Local industries include motor assembly plants, shoemaking, foundries, sawmills, flour mills, canning factories, engineering, food processing, and the production of soap, tyres, furniture, chemicals, safety glass, electrical goods, cable, steel, textiles, plastics, and paints. The port also exports manganese ore and has large pre-cooling plants for fruit.

Fort Frederick, a former British fort, dates from 1799. The Addo Elephant National Park is nearby. The University of Port Elizabeth (1964) is the only dual-language university in South Africa.

> **Cole Porter**
> *In olden days a glimpse of stocking / Was looked on as something shocking / Now, heaven knows, / Anything goes.*
> 'Anything Goes'

Porter, Cole (Albert) (1892–1964) US composer and lyricist. He wrote mainly musical comedies. His witty, sophisticated songs like 'Let's Do It' (1928), 'I Get a Kick Out of You' (1934), and 'Don't Fence Me In' (1944) have been widely recorded and admired. His shows, many of which were made into films, include *The Gay Divorce* (1932, filmed 1934 as *The Gay Divorcee*) and *Kiss Me Kate* (1948). He also wrote movie musicals, such as *Born to Dance* (1936) and *High Society* (1956).

Related Web site: Cole Porter Wide Web http://www.coleporter.org/

Porter, William Sydney real name of the US author O ▷Henry.

Portillo, Michael (Denzil Xavier) (1953–) British Conservative politician, employment secretary 1994–95, and defence secretary 1995–97. Representative of the right wing of the party in John Major's government, his progress up the ministerial ladder was swift. He lost his House of Commons seat of Enfield Southgate in the 1997 general election, but in February 2000, having regained a seat in Parliament, he was promoted to shadow chancellor.

Portland, William Henry Cavendish Bentinck (1738–1809) 3rd Duke of Portland. English Whig politician. He was prime minister in 1783 and 1807–09, each time as titular leader of a government dominated by stronger characters. He served as home secretary in William Pitt's Tory administration 1794–1801.

Port Louis capital of Mauritius, on the island's northwest coast; population (1995) 145,600. Exports include sugar, textiles, and electronic goods. Industries include chemicals, plastics, fertilizers, and sugar and food processing.

Port Moresby capital and port of Papua New Guinea, on the south coast of New Guinea; population (1995 est) 215,000. The port trades in coffee, copper, gold, copra, palm oil, and timber. There is an airport; the town is the country's centre for national broadcasting and for overseas telecommunications.

Porto (English **Oporto**) industrial city and capital of Porto district, northwest Portugal, 280 km/174 mi north of Lisbon, on the River Douro, 5 km/3 mi from its mouth on the Atlantic coast; population (1998 est) 293,500. Port wine is exported, and industries include textiles, leather, and pottery. Porto is built on terraces cut into the steep northern slopes of the Douro gorge. It is connected to the southern suburb of Vila Nova de Gaia by the two-storey bridge of Dom Luis I, built by ▷Eiffel, and which crosses the river in a single span of 160 m/525 ft at a height of 36 m/118 ft.

Pôrto Alegre industrial port and capital of Río Grande do Sul federal unit (state), southeast Brazil; population (1991) 1,254,600; (metropolitan area 3,757,500). The port is situated on the eastern bank of Río Guaíba (formed by the confluence of five rivers), at the northwestern end of Lagôa dos Patos, a freshwater lagoon which flows into the Atlantic; the lagoon is accessible to ocean-going vessels via the port of Río Grande. It is southern Brazil's chief industrial and commercial centre. Chief exports include pinewood, meat, rice, wheat, hides, and wool. The city has a cathedral, whose foundations are built over a church that dates back to 1772, and two universities. It was founded in 1755.

Port-of-Spain port and capital of Trinidad and Tobago, on the island of Trinidad; population (1990) 58,400. It has a cathedral (1813–28) and the San Andres Fort (1785).

Porto-Novo port and capital of ▷Benin, on Porto-Novo lagoon; population (1994) 179,000. It trades in palm oil, palm kernels, and cotton. A former Portuguese centre for the slave and tobacco trade with Brazil, it became a French protectorate in 1863. The National Museum of Ethnography is here.

Although Porto-Novo is the official capital, most political and commercial activity in Benin takes place in Cotonou. Porto-Novo is linked by railway with other parts of Benin and with Lagos by internal waterway.

portraiture in the visual arts, the creation of a likeness of someone. Such likenesses appear in many cultures but first flourished in the West in ancient Rome as statues and coins of the rich and the powerful. The portrait complete in itself was produced both in Italy and the Netherlands from the 15th century, and flourished in England especially in the 18th century. Before the invention of photography, portraiture in the form of a ▷miniature painting also became a strong tradition in England and France.

Port Said port in Egypt, on reclaimed land at the north end of the ▷Suez Canal; population (1992) 460,000. During the 1967 Arab–Israeli War the city was damaged and the canal blocked; Port Said was evacuated by 1969 but by 1975 had been largely reconstructed.

Related Web site: Port Said http://www.idsc.gov.eg/govern/PSD.htm

PORT SAID Port Said, the Egyptian port at the north entrance to the Suez Canal, in a photograph taken in about 1880. *Philip Sauvain Picture Collection*

Portsmouth city, naval port, and unitary authority in southern England, 118 km/73 mi southwest of London, on the peninsula of Portsea Island, opposite the Isle of Wight; it was part of the county of Hampshire until 1997.

area 42 sq km/16 sq mi **features** 12th-century cathedral; UK headquarters of IBM (UK) Ltd, Pall Europe Ltd, and Zurich Insurance Group; Portsmouth University, formerly Portsmouth Polytechnic, was established in 1992; the city has won a Millennium Award for a harbour development that will create a maritime leisure complex; Tudor warship *Mary Rose* and Admiral Horatio Nelson's flagship HMS *Victory* are exhibited here **industries** high-technology and manufacturing industries, including aircraft engineering, electronics, shipbuilding, and ship maintenance; naval dockyard was closed in 1981, although some naval facilities remain; it is a continental ferry port **population** (1996) 189,300 **famous people** Walter Besant, Isambard Kingdom Brunel, Charles Dickens, Jonas Hanway, Captain Frederick Marryat, George Meredith

Portugal see country box.

Portuguese language member of the Romance branch of the Indo-European language family; spoken by 120–135 million people worldwide, it is the national language of Portugal, closely related to Spanish and strongly influenced by Arabic. Portuguese is also spoken in Brazil, Angola, Mozambique, Cape Verde, and other former Portuguese colonies.

Portuguese literature under Provençal influence, medieval Portuguese literature produced popular ballads and troubadour songs.

The Renaissance provided a stimulus for the outstanding work of the dramatist Gil Vicente and of the lyric and epic poet ▷Camoëns. In the 17th and 18th centuries there was a decline towards mere formality, but the *Letters of a Portuguese Nun*, attributed to Marianna Alcoforado (1640–1723), were a poignant exception and found echoes in the modern revolutionary period. The outstanding writer of the 20th century was the poet Fernando Pessoa. There is a lively tradition of writing in Brazil, and Angola has developed its own school of Portuguese-African poetry.

Portuguese man-of-war any of a genus *Physalia* of phylum *Coelenterata* (see ▷coelenterate). They live in the sea, in colonies, and have a large air-filled bladder (or 'float') on top and numerous hanging tentacles made up of feeding, stinging, and reproductive individuals. The float can be 30 cm/1 ft long.

Port-Vila port and capital of Vanuatu, on the southwest of Efate Island; population (1996 est) 31,800. Local industries include meat canning.

Poseidon (Roman **Neptune**) in Greek mythology the chief god of the sea, brother of Zeus and Pluto. The brothers dethroned their father, ▷Kronos, and divided his realm, Poseidon taking the sea. Husband of Amphitrite, his sons were the merman sea god ▷Triton and the Cyclops ▷Polyphemus.

positivism theory that confines genuine knowledge within the bounds of science and observation. The theory is associated with the French philosopher Auguste Comte and ▷empiricism. **Logical positivism** developed in the 1920s. It rejected any metaphysical world beyond everyday science and common sense, and confined statements to those of formal logic or mathematics.

positron in physics, the antiparticle of the electron; an ▷elementary particle having the same mass as an electron but exhibiting a positive charge. The positron was discovered in 1932 by US physicist Carl Anderson at the California Institute of Technology, USA, its existence having been predicted by the British physicist Paul Dirac in 1928.

positron emission tomography (PET) an imaging technique which enables doctors to observe the metabolic activity of the human body by following the progress of a radioactive chemical that has been inhaled or injected, detecting ▷gamma radiation given out when ▷positrons emitted by the chemical are annihilated. The technique has been used to study a wide range of conditions, including schizophrenia, Alzheimer's disease and Parkinson's disease.

possum another name for the ▷opossum, a marsupial animal with a prehensile tail found in North, Central and South America. The name is also used for many of the smaller marsupials found in Australia.

postal service system for delivering mail. In Britain regular permanent systems were not created until the emergence of the modern nation state. In 1516 Henry VIII appointed Sir Brian Tuke as Master of the Posts, to maintain a regular service on the main roads from London. Postmasters (usually innkeepers) passed the mail to the next post, and supplied horses for the royal couriers. In 1635 a royal proclamation established the first public service. Private services were discouraged to avoid losing revenue for the state service and assisting treasonable activities, the latter point being stressed by the act establishing the Post Office, passed under Oliver ▷Cromwell in 1657. Mail coaches first ran in 1784, and in 1840 Rowland Hill's prepaid penny postage stamp, for any distance within the UK, led to a massive increase in use. Services were extended to registered post in 1841; post boxes in 1855; savings bank in 1861; postcards in 1870; postal orders in 1881; parcel post in 1883; air mail in 1911; telephone in 1912; data processing by computer in 1967; and giro in 1968. The Post Office also has responsibility for paying out social security and collecting revenue for state insurance schemes. In 1969 the original General Post Office ceased to be a government department, and in 1981 it split into two, the Post Office and the telecommunications corporation British Telecom (privatized in 1984). The Post Office lost its monopoly in 1987. International cooperation is through the Universal Postal Union (1875) at Bern, Switzerland.

poster public notice used for advertising or propaganda, often illustrated. Ancestors of the modern poster were **handbills** with

POSTER Poster publicizing the government's 'one family one child' policy in Chengdu, Sichuan Province, China. Under this policy families were offered incentives to have only one child in order to slow the population increase. *Corel*

Portugal

ETHNIC GROUPS most of the population is descended from Caucasoid peoples who inhabited the whole of the Iberian peninsula in classical and pre-classical times; there are a number of minorities from Portugal's overseas possessions and former possessions

LANGUAGE Portuguese (official)

RELIGION Roman Catholic 97%

EDUCATION (compulsory years) 9

LITERACY RATE 95% (men); 91% (women) (2003 est)

LABOUR FORCE 12.7% agriculture, 35.0% industry, 52.3% services (1999)

LIFE EXPECTANCY 73 (men); 80 (women) (2000–05)

CHILD MORTALITY RATE (under 5, per 1,000 live births) 6 (2001)

PHYSICIANS (per 1,000 people) 3.2 (1999 est)

HOSPITAL BEDS (per 1,000 people) 4 (1999 est)

TV SETS (per 1,000 people) 567 (2000 est)

RADIOS (per 1,000 people) 306 (2000 est)

INTERNET USERS (per 10,000 people) 3,554.6 (2002 est)

PERSONAL COMPUTER USERS (per 100 people) 13.9 (2002 est)

See also ▷Azores; ▷Peninsular War.

Chronology

2nd century BC: Romans conquered Iberian peninsula.

5th century AD: Iberia overrun by Vandals and Visigoths after fall of Roman Empire.

711: Visigoth kingdom overthrown by Muslims invading from North Africa.

997–1064: Christians resettled northern area, which came under rule of Léon and Castile.

1139: Afonso I, son of Henry of Burgundy, defeated Muslims; the area became an independent kingdom.

1340: Final Muslim invasion defeated.

15th century: Age of exploration: Portuguese mariners surveyed coast of Africa, opened sea route to India (Vasco da Gama), and reached Brazil (Pedro Cabral).

16th century: 'Golden Age': Portugal flourished as commercial and colonial power.

1580: Philip II of Spain took throne of Portugal.

1640: Spanish rule overthrown in bloodless coup; Duke of Braganza proclaimed as King John IV.

1668: Spain recognized Portuguese independence.

1755: Lisbon devastated by earthquake.

1807: Napoleonic France invaded Portugal; Portuguese court fled to Brazil.

1807–11: In the Peninsular War British forces played a leading part in liberating Portugal from the French.

1820: Liberal revolution forced King John VI to return from Brazil and accept constitutional government.

1822: First Portuguese constitution adopted.

1828: Dom Miguel blocked the succession of his niece, Queen Maria, and declared himself absolute monarch; civil war ensued between liberals and conservatives.

1834: Queen Maria regained the throne with British, French, and Brazilian help; constitutional government restored.

1840s: Severe disputes between supporters of radical 1822 constitution and more conservative 1826 constitution.

late 19th century: Government faced severe financial difficulties; rise of socialist, anarchist, and republican parties.

1908: Assassination of King Carlos I.

1910: Portugal became republic after a three-day insurrection forced King Manuel II to flee.

1911: New regime adopted liberal constitution, but republic proved unstable, violent, and corrupt.

1916–18: Portugal fought in World War I on Allied side.

1926–51: Popular military coup installed Gen António de Fragoso Carmona as president.

1933: Authoritarian 'Estado Novo' ('New State') constitution adopted.

1949: Portugal became founding member of North Atlantic Treaty Organization (NATO).

1974: Army seized power to end stalemate situation in African colonial wars.

1975: Portuguese colonies achieved independence.

1976: First free elections in 50 years.

1986: Soares became the first civilian president in 60 years; Portugal joined the European Community (EC).

1989: The Social Democrat government started to dismantle the socialist economy and privatize major industries.

1995: Antonio Gutteres was elected prime minister in the legislative elections.

1996: Jorge Sampaio (PS) was elected president.

2001: Sampaio was re-elected president.

Portugal country in southwestern Europe, on the Atlantic Ocean, bounded north and east by Spain.

NATIONAL NAME *República Portuguesa/Republic of Portugal*

AREA 92,000 sq km/35,521 sq mi (including the Azores and Madeira)

CAPITAL Lisbon

MAJOR TOWNS/CITIES Porto, Coimbra, Amadora, Setúbal, Funchal, Braga, Vila Nova de Gaia

MAJOR PORTS Porto, Setúbal

PHYSICAL FEATURES mountainous in the north (Serra da Estrêla mountains); plains in the south; rivers Minho, Douro, Tagus (Tejo), Guadiana

Government

HEAD OF STATE Jorge Branco de Sampaio from 1996

HEAD OF GOVERNMENT José Manuel Durão Barroso from 2002

POLITICAL SYSTEM liberal democracy

POLITICAL EXECUTIVE dual executive

ADMINISTRATIVE DIVISIONS 18 districts and two autonomous regions

ARMED FORCES 43,600 (2002 est)

CONSCRIPTION four months

DEATH PENALTY abolished in 1976

DEFENCE SPEND (% GDP) 2.3 (2002 est)

EDUCATION SPEND (% GDP) 5.8 (2001 est)

HEALTH SPEND (% GDP) 8.2 (2000 est)

Economy and resources

CURRENCY euro (escudo until 2002)

GPD (US$) 121.3 billion (2002 est)

REAL GDP GROWTH (% change on previous year) 1.8 (2001)

GNI (US$) 108.7 billion (2002 est)

GNI PER CAPITA (PPP) (US$) 17,350 (2002 est)

CONSUMER PRICE INFLATION 3.1% (2003 est)

UNEMPLOYMENT 4.1% (2001)

MAJOR TRADING PARTNERS EU (principally Spain, Germany, France, Italy, UK, Belgium–Luxembourg), USA, Japan

RESOURCES limestone, granite, marble, iron, tungsten, copper, pyrites, gold, uranium, coal, forests

INDUSTRIES textiles and clothing, footwear, paper pulp, cork items (world's largest producer of cork), chemicals, petroleum refining, fish processing, viticulture, electrical appliances, ceramics, tourism

EXPORTS textiles, clothing, footwear, pulp and waste paper, wood and cork manufactures, tinned fish, electrical equipment, wine, refined petroleum. Principal market: Germany 19.2% (2001)

IMPORTS foodstuffs, machinery and transport equipment, crude petroleum, natural gas, textile yarn, coal, rubber, plastics, tobacco. Principal source: Spain 26.5% (2001)

ARABLE LAND 21.7% (2000 est)

AGRICULTURAL PRODUCTS wheat, maize, rice, potatoes, tomatoes, grapes, olives, fruit; fishing (1993 sardine catch was the world's largest at 89,914 tonnes)

Population and society

POPULATION 10,062,000 (2003 est)

POPULATION GROWTH RATE –0.1% (2000–15)

POPULATION DENSITY (per sq km) 109 (2003 est)

URBAN POPULATION (% of total) 68 (2003 est)

AGE DISTRIBUTION (% of total population) 0–14 17%, 15–59 62%, 60+ 21% (2002 est)

PORTUGAL Both pruning and harvesting of port wine grapes is often still carried out by hand in the Douro Valley, Portugal. *Image Bank*

woodcut illustrations, which were posted up in public places. The French artist Jules Chéret pioneered the medium of colour lithography in his posters of the early 1860s, but the 1890s were the classic age of the poster, notable exponents being Toulouse-Lautrec, Aubrey Beardsley, and the 'Beggarstaff Brothers' (William Nicholson and James Pryde). Poster design flourished again in the 1960s with the advent of Psychedelic art, and artists such as Rick Griffin (1944–1991) and Stanley Mouse (1921–) in the USA, and Michael English (1942–) in the UK.

post-Impressionism broad term covering various developments in French painting that developed out of ▷Impressionism in the period from about 1880 to about 1905. Some of these developments built on the achievements of Impressionism, but others were reactions against its concentration on surface appearances, seeking to reintroduce a concern with emotional and symbolic values.

The term was coined in 1910 by the British art critic Roger Fry, in the title of 'Manet and the Post-Impressionists', an exhibition he organized at the Grafton Galleries, London. Fry also organized a second post-Impressionist exhibition two years later.

The artists who were best represented at the first exhibition were ▷Cézanne, ▷Gauguin, and van ▷Gogh, and these three are regarded as the most important and influential of the post-Impressionists, closely followed by Georges ▷Seurat. Seurat was the founder of the movement called ▷Neo-Impressionism, in which artists attempted to treat colour and light with the same affection as the Impressionists, but in a more rational and consistent way.

Fry's post-Impressionist exhibitions, especially the first, attracted a huge amount of publicity. It was the first time that the work of Cézanne, Gauguin, and van Gogh had been seen in such strength in Britain (there were more than 20 paintings by each of them in the first exhibition) and many people with conservative views thought that their pictures were childish and degenerate; some people thought that Fry was insane. However, many artists were greatly impressed with the exhibitions and they had a particularly strong influence on several members of the Camden Town Group, encouraging them to use strong, flat colour.

postmodernism late 20th-century movement in architecture and the arts that rejects the preoccupation of ▷modernism with purity of form and technique. Postmodernists use an amalgam of style elements from the past, such as the classical and the baroque, and apply them to spare modern forms, often with ironic effect. Their slightly off-key familiarity creates a more immediate appeal than the austerities of modernism.

Exponents include the architects Robert Venturi and Michael Graves and the novelists David ▷Lodge and Thomas ▷Pynchon. In literary criticism and critical theory, postmodernism denotes a differently conceived resumption rather than a repudiation of modernist radicalism.

Related Web site: 'What is Post-Modernism?' http://www.naciente.com/essay15.htm

postnatal depression mood change occurring in many mothers a few days after the birth of a baby, also known as 'baby blues'. It is usually a shortlived condition but can sometimes persist; one in five women suffer a lasting depression after giving birth. The most severe form of post-natal depressive illness, **puerperal psychosis**, requires hospital treatment.

Post Office (PO) government department or authority with responsibility for postal services; see ▷postal service. The Post Office in the UK also has responsibility for paying out social security and collecting revenue for state insurance schemes. Post Office activities were divided in 1981 and in 1984 telecommunications activities were privatized, forming a new company, British Telecom. Plans to privatize the Royal Mail, including customer services and parcel deliveries, were revived in 1996 by the Conservatives before they lost the general election.

potash general name for any potassium-containing mineral, most often applied to potassium carbonate (K_2CO_3) or potassium hydroxide (KOH). Potassium carbonate, originally made by roasting plants to ashes in earthenware pots, is commercially produced from the mineral sylvite (potassium chloride, KCl) and is used mainly in making artificial fertilizers, glass, and soap.

The potassium content of soils and fertilizers is also commonly expressed as potash, although in this case it usually refers to potassium oxide (K_2O).

POTASH An aerial view of a potash mine in Utah, USA. *Image Bank*

potassium (Dutch *potassa* 'potash') soft, waxlike, silver-white, metallic element, symbol K (Latin *kalium*), atomic number 19, relative atomic mass 39.0983. It is one of the ▷alkali metals and has a very low density – it floats on water, and is the second lightest metal (after lithium). It oxidizes rapidly when exposed to air and reacts violently with water. Of great abundance in the Earth's crust, it is widely distributed with other elements and found in salt and mineral deposits in the form of potassium aluminium silicates.

Potassium is the main base ion of the fluid in the body's cells. Along with ▷sodium, it is important to the electrical potential of the nervous system and, therefore, for the efficient functioning of nerve and muscle. Shortage, which may occur with excessive fluid loss (prolonged diarrhoea, vomiting), may lead to muscular paralysis; potassium overload may result in cardiac arrest. It is also required by plants for growth. The element was discovered and named in 1807 by English chemist Humphry Davy, who isolated it from potash in the first instance of a metal being isolated by electric current.

potato perennial plant with edible tuberous roots that are rich in starch and are extensively eaten as a vegetable. Used by the Andean Indians for at least 2,000 years before the Spanish Conquest, the potato was introduced to Europe by the mid-16th century, and reputedly to England by the explorer Walter Raleigh. (Genus *Solanum tuberosum*, family Solanaceae.)

Related Web site: Potatoes, Peppers, and Eggplants http://www.ext.vt.edu/pubs/envirohort/426-413/426-413.html

potato blight disease of the potato caused by a parasitic fungus *Phytophthora infestans*. It was the cause of the 1845 potato famine in Ireland. New strains of *P. infestans* continue to arise. The most virulent version so far is *P. infestans US-8*, which arose in Mexico in 1992 , spreading to North America in 1994.

Potemkin, Grigory Aleksandrovich (1739–1791) Prince Potemkin. Russian politician. He entered the army and attracted the notice of Catherine II, whose friendship he kept throughout his life. He was an active administrator who reformed the army, built the Black Sea Fleet, conquered the Crimea in 1783, developed southern Russia, and founded the Kherson arsenal in 1788 (the first Russian naval base on the Black Sea).

potential difference (PD) difference in the electrical potential (see ▷potential, electric) of two points, being equal to the electrical energy converted by a unit electric charge moving from one point to the other. The SI unit of potential difference is the volt (V). The potential difference between two points in a circuit is commonly referred to as voltage. See also ▷Ohm's law.

In equation terms, potential difference *V* may be defined by:

$$V = W/Q$$

here *W* is the electrical energy converted in joules and *Q* is the charge in coulombs. The unit of potential difference is the volt.

potential, electric in physics, energy required to bring a unit electric charge from infinity to the point at which potential is defined. The SI unit of potential is the volt (V). Positive electric charges will flow 'downhill' from a region of high potential to a region of low potential.

potential energy (PE) in physics, ▷energy possessed by an object by virtue of its relative position or state (for example, as in a compressed spring or a muscle). It is contrasted with kinetic energy, the form of energy possessed by moving bodies. An object that has been raised up is described as having gravitational potential energy.

potentiometer in physics, an electrical ▷resistor that can be divided so as to compare, measure, or control voltages. In radio circuits, any rotary variable resistance (such as volume control) is referred to as a potentiometer.

Potomac river of the eastern USA, forming the boundaries between West Virginia, Virginia, and Maryland states. Rising in the Allegheny Mountains, it flows 459 km/285 mi southeast into Chesapeake Bay. It is created by the confluence of the North Potomac, 153 km/95 mi long, and South Potomac, 209 km/130 mi long, and its chief tributaries are the Shenandoah and the Monocacy. At ▷Washington, DC, 185 km/116 mi from its mouth, the Potomac becomes tidal and navigable for large ships.

Potsdam capital of the *Land* of Brandenburg, Germany, on the River Havel southwest of Berlin; population (1995) 137,600. Products include textiles, pharmaceuticals, and electrical goods. A leading garrison town and Prussian military centre, Potsdam was restored to its position of capital of Brandenburg with the reunification of Germany in 1990.

POTSDAM CONFERENCE British prime minister Winston Churchill (left) is pictured here at the beginning of the Potsdam Conference in Berlin, Germany, on 23 July 1945, with US president Harry S Truman (centre) and the Soviet leader Josef Stalin (right). *Archive Photos*

Potsdam Conference conference held in Potsdam, Germany, 17 July–2 August 1945, between representatives of the USA, the UK, and the USSR. They established the political and economic principles governing the treatment of Germany in the initial period of Allied control at the end of World War II, and sent an ultimatum to Japan demanding unconditional surrender on pain of utter destruction.

Potter, (Helen) Beatrix (1866–1943) English writer and illustrator of children's books. Her first book was *The Tale of Peter Rabbit* (1900), followed by *The Tailor of Gloucester* (1902), based on her observation of family pets and wildlife. Other books in the series include *The Tale of Mrs Tiggy-Winkle* (1904), *The Tale of Jeremy Fisher* (1906), and a sequel to Peter Rabbit, *The Tale of the Flopsy Bunnies* (1909). Her tales are told with a childlike wonder, devoid of sentimentality, and accompanied by delicate illustrations.

Potter was also an accomplished mycologist. She was the first person to report the symbiotic relationship between lichen and fungi, and to catalogue the fungi of the British Isles. She was excluded from professional scientific societies because of her sex.

Related Web site:Kids' Corner – Beatrix Potter http://www.tcom.ohiou.edu/books/kids.htm

> **Dennis Potter**
> *The trouble with words is that you never know whose mouths they have been in.*
> Remark

Potter, Dennis Christopher George (1935–1994) English dramatist and journalist. His most important works were television plays, extending the boundaries of the art form. Plays include *Pennies from Heaven* (1978; feature film 1981), *Brimstone and Treacle* (1976; transmitted 1987, feature film 1982), and *The Singing Detective* (1986).

Potteries, the home of the china and earthenware industries, in central England. Wedgwood and Minton are factory names associated with the Potteries.

pottery and porcelain ceramics in domestic and ornamental use, including ▷earthenware, stoneware, and **bone china** (or softpaste porcelain). Made of 5% bone ash and china clay, bone china was first made in the West in imitation of Chinese porcelain. The standard British bone china was developed about 1800, with a body of clay mixed with ox bones; a harder version, called **parian**, was developed in the 19th century and was used for figurine ornaments.

Hardpaste **porcelain** is characterized by its hardness, ringing sound when struck, translucence, and shining finish, like that of a cowrie shell (Italian *porcellana*). It is made of kaolin and petuntse (fusible feldspar consisting chiefly of silicates reduced to a fine white powder); it is high-fired at 1,400°C/2,552°F. Porcelain first evolved from stoneware in China in about the 6th century AD. A formula for making porcelain was developed in the 18th century in Germany, also in France, Italy, and Britain. It was first produced in the USA in the early 19th century.

POTTERY AND PORCELAIN A jar with cover 'flambé glazed in Sung style', made at the Doulton factory during the 1930s and marked 'Royal Doulton'. *The Art Archive/Eileen Tweedy*

potto arboreal, nocturnal, African prosimian primate *Perodicticus potto* belonging to the ▷loris family. It has a thick body, strong limbs, and grasping feet and hands, and grows to 40 cm/16 in long, with horny spines along its backbone, which it uses in self-defence. It climbs slowly, and eats insects, snails, fruit, and leaves.

POULTRY At this egg-packing factory in Minnesota, USA eggs are graded and sorted mechanically into trays and then packed into boxes or other containers for delivery to retail outlets. *Image Bank*

Poulenc, Francis Jean Marcel (1899–1963) French composer and pianist. A self-taught composer of witty and irreverent music, he was a member of the group of French composers known as ▷*Les Six*. Among his many works are the operas *Les Mamelles de Tirésias/The Breasts of Tiresias* (1947) and *Dialogues des Carmélites/Dialogues of the Carmelites* (1957), and the ballet *Les Biches/The Little Darlings* (1923).

poultry domestic birds such as chickens, turkeys, ducks, and geese. They were domesticated for meat and eggs by early farmers in China, Europe, Egypt, and the Americas. Chickens were domesticated from the Southeast Asian jungle fowl *Gallus gallus* and then raised in the East as well as the West. Turkeys are New World birds, domesticated in ancient Mexico. Geese and ducks were domesticated in Egypt, China, and Europe.

Related Web site: Poultry Breeds
http://www.ansi.okstate.edu/poultry/

pound imperial unit (abbreviation lb) of mass. The commonly used avoirdupois pound, also called the **imperial standard pound** (7,000 grains/0.45 kg), differs from the **pound troy** (5,760 grains/0.37 kg), which is used for weighing precious metals. It derives from the Roman *libra*, which weighed 0.327 kg.

pound British standard monetary unit, issued as a gold sovereign before 1914, as a note 1914–83, and as a circular yellow metal-alloy coin from 1983. The pound is also the name given to the unit of currency in Egypt, Lebanon, Malta, Sudan, and Syria.

Pound, Ezra Loomis (1885–1972) US poet and cultural critic. He is regarded as one of the most important figures of 20th-century literature. His *Personae* and *Exultations* (1909) established and promoted the principles of ▷Imagism, and influenced numerous poets, including T S ▷Eliot. His largest work was his series of *Cantos* (1925–69), a highly complex, eclectic collage that sought to create a unifying, modern cultural tradition.

Born in Idaho, Pound was educated at Pennsylvania University and settled in Europe from 1907. He lived in London 1909–21 and then moved to Paris 1921–25, where he became a friend of the writers Gertrude Stein and Ernest Hemingway. He then settled in Rapallo, Italy. His anti-Semitism and sympathy with the fascist dictator Mussolini led him to broadcast from Italy in World War II, and he was arrested by US troops in 1945. Found unfit to stand trial, he was confined in a mental hospital until 1958.

Related Web site: Pound, Ezra http://www.lit.kobe-u.ac.jp/~hishika/pound.htm

EZRA LOOMIS POUND The US poet Ezra Pound revolutionized modern poetry *Archive Photos*

Poussin, Nicolas (1594–1665) French painter. Active chiefly in Rome, he was the foremost exponent of 17th-century baroque classicism. He painted several major religious works, but is best known for his mythological and literary scenes executed in an austere classical style, for example, *Et in Arcadia Ego* (1638–39; Louvre, Paris). His style had a profound effect on the development of French art.

poverty condition in which the basic needs of human beings (shelter, food, and clothing) are not being met. Over one-fifth of the world's population was living in extreme poverty in 1995, of which around 70% were women. Nearly 13.5 million children under five die each year from poverty-related illness (measles, diarrhoea, malaria, pneumonia, and ▷malnutrition). In its annual report, the UN Children's Fund (UNICEF) said that 600 million children continue to live in poverty. There are different definitions of the standard of living considered to be the minimum adequate level (known as the **poverty level**). The European Union (EU) definition of poverty is an income of less than half the EU average (£150 a

week in 1993). By this definition, there were 50 million poor in the EU in 1993.

poverty cycle set of factors or events by which poverty, once started, is likely to continue unless there is outside intervention. Once an area or a person has become poor, this tends to lead to other disadvantages, which may in turn result in further poverty. The situation is often found in inner city areas and shanty towns. Applied to countries, the poverty cycle is often called the **development trap**.

poverty trap situation where a person reduces his or her net income by taking a job, or gaining a higher wage, which disqualifies him/her from claiming social security benefits or raises his/her tax liability.

Powell, Anthony Dymoke (1905–2000) English novelist and critic. He wrote the series of 12 volumes *A Dance to the Music of Time* (1951–75) that begins shortly after World War I and chronicles a period of 50 years in the lives of Nicholas Jenkins and his circle of upper- and middle-class friends and acquaintances. It is written in an elegant style which sets off the blend of the comic, the melancholic, and the tragic in the situations he describes.

Powell, Colin (Luther) (1937–) US general, chair of the Joint Chiefs of Staff 1989–93, and US Secretary of State from 2001. A Vietnam War veteran, he first worked in government in 1972 and was national security adviser 1987–89. As chair of the Joint Chiefs of Staff, he was responsible for the overall administration of the Allied forces in Saudi Arabia during the ▷Gulf War of 1991. Following intense media speculation, in November 1995 Powell announced that he would not seek the Republican party's presidential nomination in 1996, citing family reasons. In December 2000 he was appointed the first black Secretary of State by president-elect George W Bush.

Related Web site: General Colin L Powell Profile
http://www.achievement.org/autodoc/page/pow0pro-1

Powell, (John) Enoch (1912–1998) British Conservative politician. He was minister of health (1960–63), and contested the party leadership in 1965. In 1968 he made a speech against immigration that led to his dismissal from the shadow cabinet. He resigned from the party in 1974, and was Official Unionist Party member for South Down, Northern Ireland (1974–1987).

Powell, Michael (Latham) (1905–1990) English film director and producer. In collaboration with the Hungarian-born screenwriter Emeric ▷Pressburger, he produced a succession of ambitious and richly imaginative films, including *I Know Where I'm Going!* (1945), *A Matter of Life and Death* (1946), and *The Red Shoes* (1948).

power in mathematics, that which is represented by an ▷exponent or index, denoted by a superior small numeral. A number or symbol raised to the power of 2 – that is, multiplied by itself – is said to be squared (for example, 3^2, x^2), and when raised to the power of 3, it is said to be cubed (for example, 2^3, y^3). Any number to the power zero always equals 1.

Powers can be negative. Negative powers produce fractions, with the numerator as one, as a number is divided by itself, rather than being multiplied by itself, so for example $2^{-1} = \frac{1}{2}$ and $3^{-3} = \frac{1}{27}$.

power in optics, a measure of the amount by which a lens will deviate light rays. A powerful converging lens will converge parallel rays strongly, bringing them to a focus at a short distance from the lens. The unit of power is the **dioptre**, which is equal to the reciprocal of focal length in metres. By convention, the power of a converging (or convex) lens is positive and that of a diverging (or concave) lens negative.

power in physics, the rate of doing work or consuming energy. It is measured in watts (joules per second) or other units of work per unit time.

If the work done or energy consumed is W joules and the time taken is t seconds, then the power P is given by the formula:

$$P = W/t$$

power station building where electrical energy is generated from a fuel or from another form of energy. Fuels used include fossil fuels such as coal, gas, and oil, and the nuclear fuel uranium. Renewable sources of energy include gravitational potential energy, used to produce ▷hydroelectric power, and ▷wind power.

The energy supply is used to turn ▷turbines either directly by means of water or wind pressure, or indirectly by steam pressure, steam being generated by burning fossil fuels or from the heat released by the fission of uranium nuclei. The turbines in their turn spin alternators, which generate electricity at very high voltage.

The world's largest power station is Turukhansk, on the Lower Tunguska River, Russia, with a capacity of 20,000 megawatts.

The largest power station in Europe is the Drax power station near Selby, North Yorkshire, which supplies 10% of Britain's electricity.

According to a report by the Office of National Statistics in 1996, power stations produce a quarter of all greenhouse emissions, and nearly half of the acid rain emissions, in the UK.

Powys unitary authority in central Wales, created in 1996 from the former county of Powys.

area 5,179 sq km/1,999 sq mi **towns** Llandrindod Wells (administrative headquarters), Brecon, Builth Wells, Newtown, Welshpool **physical** mountainous to the north, Black Mountains, rivers ▷Wye and ▷Severn, which both rise on the eastern slopes of Plynlimon **features** the Brecon Beacons National Park, Lake Vyrnwy (an artificial reservoir supplying Liverpool and Birmingham), alternative-technology centre near Machynlleth **industries** agriculture, tourism **agriculture** arable and dairy farming, sheep-rearing **population** (1996) 123,600

Powys, John Cowper (1872–1963) English novelist. His mystic and erotic books include *Wolf Solent* (1929) and *A Glastonbury Romance* (1933); *Owen Glendower* (1940) is the most successful of his historical novels. He was one of six brothers, including **Theodore Francis Powys** (1875–1953) who is best known for the novel *Mr Weston's Good Wine* (1927), and **Llewelyn Powys** who wrote essays, novels, and autobiographical works.

Poznań (German **Posen**) industrial city (machinery, aircraft, beer) in western Poland; population (1993) 590,000. Founded 970, it was settled by German immigrants in 1253 and passed to Prussia in 1793; it was restored to Poland in 1919.

PPP abbreviation for ▷purchasing-power parity.

Prado (or **Real Museo de Pintura del Prado**) Spanish art gallery containing the national collection of pictures. The building was designed as a natural history museum and begun in 1785; it became an art gallery in 1818 under Ferdinand VII.

praetor in ancient Rome, a magistrate, elected annually, who assisted the ▷consuls (the chief magistrates) and presided over the civil courts. After a year in office, a praetor would act as a provincial governor for a further year. The number of praetors was finally increased to eight. The office declined in importance under the emperors.

pragmatism philosophical tradition that interprets truth in terms of the practical effects of what is believed and, in particular, the usefulness of these effects. The US philosopher Charles Peirce is often accounted the founder of pragmatism; it was further advanced by William James.

Prague (Czech **Praha**) city and capital of the Czech Republic on the River Vltava; population (1993) 1,217,300. Industries include cars, aircraft, chemicals, paper and printing, clothing, brewing, and food processing. It was the capital of Czechoslovakia 1918–93.

Features Charles University, founded in 1348 by Emperor Charles IV; Gothic cathedral of St Vitus; Prague castle (Prásky-Hrad); Malá Strana, with 17th- and 18th-century mansions; Old Town.

History In the 14th century Prague became important during the reign of Charles IV, king of Bohemia and Moravia, and Holy Roman Emperor; he established the university and laid out the New Town. In the 15th century the Hussite wars held back development. The Battle of the White Mountain took place near Prague in 1620; the Czechs were defeated, and were ruled by the Habsburgs until 1918, when Czechoslovakia was created and Prague became the national capital. Between 1939 and 1945 during World War II Prague was occupied by the Nazis. The ▷Prague Spring in 1968 led to occupation by Soviet troops. In 1989 protests in Prague led to the fall of the Communist regime.

PRAGUE Houses in the Old Town Square, Prague, Czech Republic. *Image Bank*

Prague Spring the 1968 programme of liberalization, begun under a new Communist Party leader in Czechoslovakia. In August 1968 Soviet tanks invaded Czechoslovakia and entered the capital Prague to put down the liberalization movement initiated by the prime minister Alexander Dubček, who had earlier sought to assure the Soviets that his planned reforms would not threaten socialism. Dubček was arrested but released soon afterwards. Most of the Prague Spring reforms were reversed. See also ▷Czechoslovakia.

PRAGUE SPRING A group of boys paint pro-Czech slogans on a bus. The word *svoboda* means 'freedom' in the Czech language. This demonstration occurred during the Soviet-led invasion by Warsaw Pact forces into Czechoslovakia in August 1968. *Archive Photos*

Praha Czech name for Prague, the capital of the Czech Republic.

Praia port and capital of the Republic of Cape Verde, on the island of São Tiago (Santiago); population (2001 est) 96,300. Industries include fishing, shipping, and tourism.

prairie the central North American plain, formerly grass-covered, extending over most of the region between the Rocky Mountains, to the west, and the Great Lakes and Ohio River, to the east.

prairie dog any of the North American genus *Cynomys* of burrowing rodents in the squirrel family (Sciuridae). They grow to 30 cm/12 in, plus a short 8 cm/3 in tail. Their 'towns' can contain up to several thousand individuals. Their barking cry has given them their name. Persecution by ranchers has brought most of the five species close to extinction.

The prairie dog is also another term for the ▷marmot, a large burrowing rodent.

Prakrit general name for the ancient Indo-European dialects of northern India, contrasted with the sacred classical language Sanskrit. The word is itself Sanskrit, meaning 'natural', as opposed to *Sanskrit*, which means 'perfected'. The Prakrits are considered to be the ancestors of such modern northern Indian languages as Hindi, Punjabi, and Bengali.

Prasad, Rajendra (1884–1963) Indian politician. He was president of the Indian National Congress several times between 1934 and 1948 and India's first president after independence 1950–62.

praseodymium (Greek *prasios* 'leek-green' + *didymos* 'twin') silver-white, malleable, metallic element of the ▷lanthanide series, symbol Pr, atomic number 59, relative atomic mass 140.907. It occurs in nature in the minerals monzanite and bastnaesite, and its green salts are used to colour glass and ceramics. It was named in 1885 by Austrian chemist Carl von Welsbach (1858–1929).

He fractionated it from dydymium (originally thought to be an element but actually a mixture of rare-earth metals consisting largely of neodymium, praseodymium, and cerium), and named it for its green salts and spectroscopic line.

prawn any of various ▷shrimps of the suborder Natantia ('swimming'), of the crustacean order Decapoda, as contrasted with lobsters and crayfishes, which are able to 'walk'. Species called prawns are generally larger than species called shrimps.

PRAWN The common prawn in a rockpool in England. *Dr Rod Preston-Mafham/Premaphotos Wildlife*

The **common prawn** *Leander serratus*, of temperate seas has a long saw-edged spike or rostrum just in front of its eyes, and antennae much longer than its body length. It is pinkish-orange when cooked. The larger **Norway lobster** or **Dublin Bay prawn** *Nephrops norwegicus* is sold as 'scampi'.

Praxiteles (lived mid-4th century BC) Greek sculptor. His *Aphrodite of Cnidus* of about 350 BC is thought to have initiated the tradition of life-size free-standing female nudes in Greek sculpture. It was destroyed by fire in AD 475, but a Roman copy exists in the Vatican.

prayer address to divine power, ranging from a ritual formula to attain a desired end, to selfless communication in meditation.

Within Christianity, the Catholic and Orthodox churches sanction prayer to the Virgin Mary, angels, and saints as intercessors, whereas Protestantism limits prayer to God alone. Muslims pray only to God (see ▷salat).

praying mantis another name for ▷mantis.

Precambrian in geology, the time from the formation of Earth (4.6 billion years ago) up to 570 million years ago. Its boundary with the succeeding Cambrian period marks the time when animals first developed hard outer parts (exoskeletons) and so left abundant fossil remains. It comprises about 85% of geological time and is divided into two eons: the Archaean and the Proterozoic.

precession slow wobble of the Earth on its axis, like that of a spinning top. The gravitational pulls of the Sun and Moon on the Earth's equatorial bulge cause the Earth's axis to trace out a circle on the sky every 25,800 years. The position of the celestial poles (see ▷celestial sphere) is constantly changing owing to precession, as are the positions of the equinoxes (the points at which the celestial equator intersects the Sun's path around the sky). The **precession of the equinoxes** means that there is a gradual westward drift in the ecliptic – the path that the Sun appears to follow – and in the coordinates of objects on the celestial sphere.

This is why the dates of the astrological signs of the zodiac no longer correspond to the times of year when the Sun actually passes through the constellations. For example, the Sun passes through Leo from mid-August to mid-September, but the astrological dates for Leo are between about 23 July and 22 August.

Precession, first detected in 1891, was finally explained by a US researcher at NASA in 2000. The wobble is caused by changes in ocean pressure, brought about by fluctuations in winds and salinity (salt levels), on the Earth's crust. The pressure change exaggerates the Earth's natural resonance.

Precession also occurs in other planets. Uranus has the Solar System's fastest known precession (264 days) determined in 1995.

precipitation in chemistry, the formation of an insoluble solid in a liquid as a result of a reaction within the liquid between two or more soluble substances. If the solid settles, it forms a **precipitate**; if the particles of solid are very small, they will remain in suspension, forming a **colloidal precipitate** (see ▷colloid).

precipitation in meteorology, water that falls to the Earth from the atmosphere. It is part of the ▷hydrological cycle. Forms of precipitation include ▷rain, snow, sleet, ▷hail, ▷dew, and ▷frost.

pre-Columbian architecture the architecture of the Central and South American civilizations that existed prior to the arrival of European colonizers in the 16th century.

Central American architecture Little evidence remains of pre-Mayan buildings, but the distinctive form of the pyramid – the focus of pre-Columbian ceremonial architecture – was in evidence by the 4th century BC, for example, at Cuicuilco, and well developed by AD 100, as in the Pyramid of the Sun at Teotihuacán, Mexico. Mesoamerican pyramids were different in form and function to those of the Egyptians. Instead of tombs, they were sites for ritual, usually topped by altars and with steeply sloping, stepped sides and rectangular or circular planforms. The Maya civilization, AD 300–900, left many imposing monuments, significant for their regular, symmetric form, stylized external decoration, and use of corbel arches and internal vaulting. Mayan sites include Chichén Itzá, Mexico, and Tikal, Guatemala. The Totonac, 5th–11th centuries, and Zapotec, 6th–7th centuries, were active during the latter part of the Mayan era and left their own monuments at Tajin and Monte Alban respectively. Arriving from the north in the 10th century, the Toltecs, 10th–12th centuries, took over Chichén Itzá and added many of their own structures, including the nine-tiered pyramid, the Castillo. At Tula, thought to be the Toltec capital, they employed free-standing columns – huge, sculpted figures of warriors and hunters – to support the roof of the temple of the god Quetzalcoatl. The architecture of the Aztecs, 14th–16th centuries, was influenced by Toltec culture but the sculpture that surrounded it had a more fluid and less stylized form. Their capital, Tenochtitlán, was levelled by the Spanish and is now the site of Mexico City, but they left many important buildings such as the double pyramid of Tenayuca, about 1450–1500. There was also a

Mixtec civilization that evolved independently of the Aztecs. Few of their buildings remain but the Palace of the Columns at Mitla, AD 1000, is notable for the geometric patterns that cover its interior and exterior walls.

South American architecture Some monuments remain that predate Inca rule, such as the Temple of the Sun at Moche, about 200–600, a pyramidal stepped structure built by the Chavin peoples, and the Gateway of the Sun, Tiahuanaco, about 500–700, a richly carved monolithic structure. Between 1300–1400, a number of local cultures developed including those centred around Chan Chan and Cajamarquilla, towns laid out on a complex grid system composed of streets, pyramids, and reservoirs. The Inca civilization was formed about 1440 and came to dominate the region. Their architecture is best known for its use of huge masonry, laid without cement. The ancient capital of ▷Cuzco, 1200 onwards, has examples of this, as has the spectacularly sited ▷Machu Picchu, about 1500, high in the Andes. This late Inca city follows the typical pattern of the culture: a Sun Temple and palace situated on either side of a central plaza, a water system servicing baths and fountains, and terraced fields for step-cultivation descending the mountainside.

pre-Columbian art the art of the Central and South American civilizations that existed prior to the arrival of European colonizers in the 16th century.

Central American art The art of the Mesoamerican and Mexican cultures up to the Spanish conquest. The Olmec civilization, of about 1200–600 BC, is characterized by jade figurines and heavy featured, colossal heads, resting mysteriously in the landscape. During the classic period, about AD 200–900, the dominant culture was Mayan, AD 300–900, of Yucatan, southern Mexico, and Guatemala. Its sculpture, mostly in relief, combined glyphs and stylized figures and was used to decorate architecture, such as the pyramid temple of Chichén Itzá; murals dating from about AD 750 were discovered when the city of Bonampak was excavated in 1946. The Mayans were succeeded by more warlike, brutal societies governed by deities which demanded human sacrifice. The Toltecs, 10th–12th centuries, made colossal, blocklike sculptures, for example those employed as free-standing columns at Tula, Mexico. The Mixtecs developed a style of painting called 'Mixtec-Puebla', as seen in their murals and manuscripts ('codices'), in which all available space is covered by flat figures in geometric designs. The Aztec culture in Mexico produced some dramatically expressive work, such as the decorated skulls of captives and stone sculpture, a good example of which is *Tlazolteotl* (Woods Bliss Collection, Washington), a goddess in childbirth, AD 1300–1500.

South American art The art of the indigenous peoples of South America. The Chavin culture flourished in the Andean area (modern-day Peru) about 1000 BC, producing small sculpture and pottery, often human in form but with animal attributes, such as bird feet, reptilian eyes, or feline fangs. The Andean Mochicha peoples, about 100 BC–AD 700, were among the best artisans of the New World, producing delightful portrait vases (Moche ware), which, while realistic, are steeped in religious references, the significance of which is lost to us. They were also goldsmiths and weavers of outstanding talent. The short-lived Inca culture, about AD 1400–1580, of Peru and Bolivia, sculpted animal and human figurines, but is best known for its architecture at Andean sites such as Cuzco and Machu Picchu (see ▷pre-Columbian architecture).

predestination in Christian theology, the doctrine asserting that God has determined all events beforehand, including the ultimate salvation or damnation of the individual human soul.

Today Christianity in general accepts that humanity has free will, though some forms, such as Calvinism, believe that salvation can only be attained by the gift of God. The concept of predestination is also found in Islam.

pre-eclampsia (or toxaemia of pregnancy) potentially serious condition developing in the third trimester and marked by high blood pressure and fluid retention. Arising from unknown causes, it disappears when pregnancy is over. It may progress to ▷eclampsia if untreated. Pre-eclampsia affects 5–10% of pregant women globally.

preference share in finance, a share in a company with rights in various ways superior to those of ordinary shares; for example, priority to a fixed dividend and priority over ordinary shares in the event of the company being wound up.

pregnancy in humans, the process during which a developing embryo grows within the woman's womb. It begins at conception and ends at birth, and the normal length is 40 weeks, or around nine months.

Menstruation usually stops on conception. About one in five pregnancies fails, but most of these failures occur very early on, so the woman may notice only that her period is late. After the second month, the breasts become tender, and the areas round the nipples become darker. Enlargement of the uterus can be felt at about the end of the third month, and after this the abdomen enlarges progressively. Fetal movement can be felt at about 18 weeks; a heartbeat may be heard during the sixth month. Pregnancy in animals is called ▷gestation.

prehistoric life the diverse organisms that inhabited Earth from the origin of life about 3.5 billion years ago to the time when humans began to keep written records, about 3500 BC. During the course of evolution, new forms of life developed and many other forms, such as the dinosaurs, became extinct. Prehistoric life evolved over this vast timespan from simple bacteria-like cells in the oceans to algae and protozoans and complex multicellular forms such as worms, molluscs, crustaceans, fishes, insects, land plants, amphibians, reptiles, birds, and mammals. On a geological timescale human beings evolved relatively recently, about 4 million years ago, although the exact dating is a matter of some debate. See also ▷geological time.

prehistory human cultures before the use of writing. The study of prehistory is mainly dependent on archaeology. General chronological dividing lines between prehistoric eras, or history and prehistory, are difficult to determine because communities have developed at differing rates. The Three Age System of classification (published in 1836 by the Danish archaeologist Christian Thomsen) is based on the predominant materials used by early humans for tools and weapons: ▷Stone Age, ▷Bronze Age, and ▷Iron Age.

Human prehistory begins with the emergence of early modern hominids (see ▷human species, origins of). *Homo habilis*, the first tool user, was in evidence around 2 million years ago, and found at such sites as Koobi Fora, Kenya and Olduvai Gorge, Tanzania.

Stone Age Stone was the main material used for tools and weapons. The Stone Age is divided into:

Old Stone Age (Palaeolithic) 3,500,000–8500 BC. Stone and bone tools were chipped into shape by early humans or hominids from Africa, Asia, the Middle East, and Europe, as well as later ▷Neanderthal and ▷Cro-Magnon people; the only domesticated animals were dogs. Some Asians crossed the Bering land bridge to inhabit the Americas. Prehistoric art was being produced 20,000 years ago in many parts of the world; for example, at Altamira in Spain, Lascaux in France, in southern Africa, and in Australia.

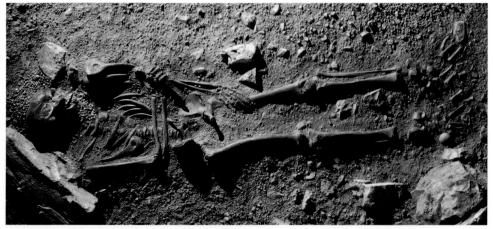

PREHISTORIC LIFE A neolithic burial from the grotto of Arene Candide, near Finale Ligure (Liguria, Italy). *The Art Archive/ San Angelo in Formis Capua Italy/Dagli Orti*

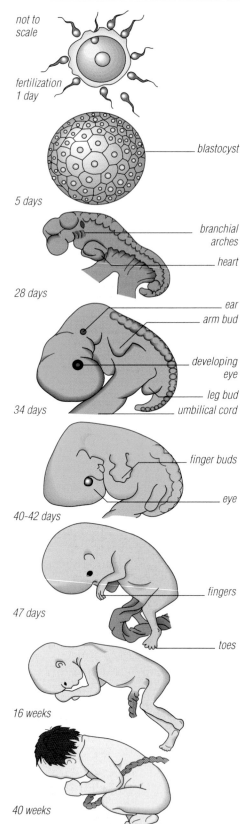

not to scale

fertilization 1 day

blastocyst

5 days

branchial arches

heart

28 days

ear

arm bud

developing eye

leg bud

umbilical cord

34 days

finger buds

eye

40-42 days

47 days

fingers

toes

16 weeks

40 weeks

PREGNANCY Division of the fertilized egg, or ovum, begins within hours of conception. Within a week a ball of cells – a blastocyst – has developed. After the third week, the embryo has changed from a mass of cells into a recognizable shape. At four weeks, the embryo is 3 mm/0.1 in long, with a large bulge for the heart and small pits for the ears. At six weeks, the embryo is 1.5 cm/0.6 in, with a pulsating heart and ear flaps. At the eighth week, the embryo is 2.5 cm/1 in long and recognizably human, with eyelids, small fingers, and toes. From the end of the second month, the embryo is almost fully formed and further development is mainly by growth. After this stage, the embryo is termed a fetus.

Middle Stone Age (Mesolithic) and **New Stone Age** (Neolithic). Bone tools and stone or flint implements were used. In Neolithic times, agriculture and the domestication of goats, sheep, and cattle began. Stone Age cultures survived in the Americas, Asia, Africa, Oceania, and Australia until the 19th and 20th centuries.

Bronze Age Bronze tools and weapons appeared approximately 5000 BC in the Far East, and continued in the Middle East until about 1200 BC; in Europe this period lasted from about 2000 to 500 BC.

Iron Age Iron was hardened (alloyed) by the addition of carbon, so that it superseded bronze for tools and weapons; in the Old World generally from about 1000 BC.

In Britain the Roman conquest in AD 43 is usually considered the dividing line between prehistory and history.

British Heritage announced in 1997 the discovery of the largest prehistoric building ever found anywhere in the world at a sacred stone age site in southwestern England, at Stanton Drew, near Bristol. The structure dates from *c.* 3000 BC.

prelude in music, a composition intended as the preface to further music, especially preceding a ▷fugue, forming the opening piece of a ▷suite, or setting the mood for a stage work, as in Richard Wagner's *Lohengrin*. As used by Frédéric Chopin, a prelude is a short self-contained piano work.

Premadasa, Ranasinghe (1924–1993) Sri Lankan right-wing politician, prime minister 1978–88, president from 1988, having gained popularity through overseeing a major house-building and poverty-alleviation programme. He sought peace talks with the Tamil Tiger guerrillas. He was assassinated in office by a suicide bomber in the centre of Colombo; the Tamil Tigers denied responsibility.

prematurity the condition of an infant born before the full term. In obstetrics, an infant born before 37 weeks' gestation is described as premature.

premenstrual tension (PMT or premenstrual syndrome) medical condition caused by hormone changes and comprising a number of physical and emotional features that occur cyclically before menstruation and disappear with its onset. Symptoms include mood changes, breast tenderness, a feeling of bloatedness, and headache.

Preminger, Otto (Ludwig) (1906–1986) Austrian-born US film producer, director, and actor. His films include *Margin for Error* (1942), *The Man with the Golden Arm* (1955), *Advise and Consent* (1962), and *The Human Factor* (1980). His work is characterized by an intricate technique of storytelling and a masterly use of the wide screen and the travelling camera.

premium price difference between the current market price of a security and its issue price (where the current price is the greater).

preparatory school fee-paying independent school. In the UK, it is a junior school that prepares children for entry to a senior school at about age 13. In the USA, it is a school that prepares students for university entrance at about the age of 18.

Pre-Raphaelite Brotherhood (PRB) group of British painters (1848–53); Dante Gabriel ▷Rossetti, John Everett ▷Millais, and Holman Hunt – at this time young students at the Royal Academy – were the leading figures among the seven founders. They aimed to paint serious subjects, to study nature closely, and to return to the sincerity of spirit of painters before the time of ▷Raphael Sanzio (1483–1520). Their subjects were mainly biblical and literary, painted with obsessive naturalism and attention to detail. The group was short-lived but added a new realism to the art of the 1850s, and influenced many painters.

In his later work only Hunt remained true to Pre-Raphaelite ideals, but the name stuck to Rossetti, the least committed of the original group, and was applied to his later dreamily romantic pictures although these had moved away from the movement's founding ideas. A 'second wave' of Pre-Raphaelitism in the late 19th century, stimulated by Ruskin and Rossetti, was associated with the revival of handicrafts and the art of design. William Morris and Edward Burne-Jones were among the many artists influenced at this time.

Related Web site: Pre-Raphaelite Critic http://www.engl.duq.edu/servus/PR_Critic/

presbyopia vision defect, an increasing inability with advancing age to focus on near objects. It is caused by thickening and loss of elasticity in the lens, which is no longer able to relax to the near-spherical shape required for near vision.

Presbyterianism system of Christian Protestant church government, expounded during the Reformation by John Calvin in Geneva, Switzerland, which gives its name to the established Church of Scotland, and is also practised in England, Wales, Ireland, Switzerland, North America, and elsewhere. There is no compulsory form of worship and each congregation is governed by presbyters or elders (clerical or lay), who are of equal rank. Congregations are grouped in presbyteries, synods, and general assemblies.

Prescott, John Leslie (1938–) British Labour politician, deputy leader from 1994, deputy prime minister from 1997. He unsuccessfully contested the party leadership in 1988 and 1992. After the 1997 Labour victory, he was given a key appointment in Tony Blair's new government, combining the role of deputy prime minister with responsibility for transport, the environment, and the regions. This broad department was broken up after the 2001 election, and Prescott was moved to the Cabinet Office.

preservative substance (additive) added to a food in order to inhibit the growth of bacteria, yeasts, moulds, and other micro-organisms, and therefore extend its shelf life. The term sometimes refers to anti-oxidants (substances added to oils and fats to prevent their becoming rancid) as well. All preservatives are potentially damaging to health if eaten in sufficient quantity. Both the amount used, and the foods in which they can be used, are restricted by law.

PRE-RAPHAELITE BROTHERHOOD A Pre-Raphaelite painting *Girlhood of Mary Virgin*, painted in 1849 by Dante Gabriel Rossetti. *The Art Archive/British Museum/Eileen Tweedy*

president in government, the usual title of the head of state in a republic; the power of the office may range from the equivalent of a constitutional monarch to the actual head of the government. For presidents of the USA, see ▷United States of America.

Presidential Medal of Freedom highest peacetime civilian award in the USA, instituted in 1963, conferred annually on Independence Day by the president on those making significant contributions to the 'quality of American life'. It replaced the Medal of Freedom awarded from 1945 for acts and service aiding US security.

Presley, Elvis Aron (1935–1977) US singer and guitarist, the most influential performer of the rock-and-roll era. With his recordings for Sun Records in Memphis, Tennessee, 1954–55 and early hits such as 'Heartbreak Hotel', 'Hound Dog' and 'Love Me Tender' (all 1956), he created an individual vocal style, influenced by southern blues, gospel music, country music, and rhythm and blues. His records continue to sell in their millions.

Presley was born in Tupelo, Mississippi. His first records were regional hits in the south, and he became a nationwide star in 1956, Sun Records having sold his recording contract to RCA at the instigation of his new manager, the self-styled Colonel Tom Parker (1909–97), a former carnival huckster. Of the four films Presley made in the 1950s, *Loving You* (1957) and *Jailhouse Rock* (1957) offer glimpses of the electrifying stage performer he then was. After his army service 1958–60, the album *Elvis Is Back* (1960) and some gospel-music recordings made the same year were outstanding, but from then on his work deteriorated quickly. Parker pushed him into a demeaning career divided between Hollywood and Las Vegas. By the time of his death, Presley had long been a caricature. His early contribution to rock music was, however, inestimable, and his Memphis home, Graceland, draws millions of visitors each year.

Related Web site: Elvis Presley Home Page http://sunsite.unc.edu/elvis/elvishom.html

Pressburger, Emeric (1902–1988) Adopted name of Imre József Pressburger. Hungarian-born film producer, screenwriter, and novelist. He worked on films in Germany, France, and Britain. Together with Michael ▷Powell, he made 14 films between 1942 and 1956, including such classics of the British cinema as *The Life and Death of Colonel Blimp* (1943), *A Canterbury Tale* (1944), and *The Red Shoes* (1948).

Press Complaints Commission non-statutory UK body formed in 1991 to replace the former Press Council and oversee the effective self-regulation of the press. It was set up on the basis of the recommendations of the Committee on Privacy and Related Matters. Its role is to promote a code of practice for newspaper and magazine editors and to deal with readers' complaints.

Press Council in the UK, an organization (1953–91) founded to preserve the freedom of the press, maintain standards, consider complaints, and report on monopoly developments. The Press Council was replaced by the Press Complaints Commission, which began operations in January 1991.

press, freedom of the absence of political censorship in the press or other media, a concept regarded as basic to Western democracy. Access to and expression of views are, however, in practice restricted by the commercial interests of the owners and advertisers.

press gang method used to recruit soldiers and sailors into the British armed forces in the 18th and early 19th centuries. In effect it was a form of kidnapping carried out by the services or their agents, often with the aid of armed men. This was similar to the practice of 'shanghaiing' sailors for duty in the merchant marine, especially in the Far East.

pressure in a fluid, the force that would act normally (at right angles) per unit surface area of a body immersed in the fluid. The SI unit of pressure is the pascal (Pa), equal to a pressure of one newton per square metre. In the atmosphere, the pressure declines with height from about 100 kPa at sea level to zero where the atmosphere fades into space. Pressure is commonly measured with a ▷barometer, ▷manometer, or ▷Bourdon gauge. Other common units of pressure are the bar and the torr.

Absolute pressure is measured from a vacuum; gauge pressure is the difference between the absolute pressure and the local ▷atmospheric pressure. In a liquid, the pressure at a depth h is given by $\rho g h$ where ρ is the density and g is the acceleration of free fall.

pressure cooker closed pot in which food is cooked in water under pressure, where water boils at a higher temperature than normal boiling point (100°C/212°F) and therefore cooks food quickly. The modern pressure cooker has a quick-sealing lid and a safety valve that can be adjusted to vary the steam pressure inside.

pressure group association that puts pressure on governments, businesses, or parties to ensure laws and treatment favourable to its own interest. Pressure groups have played an increasingly prominent role in contemporary Western democracies.

In general they fall into two types: groups concerned with a single issue, such as nuclear disarmament, and groups attempting to promote their own interest, such as oil producers.

pressurized water reactor

(PWR) ▷nuclear reactor design used in nuclear power stations in many countries, and in nuclear-powered submarines. In the PWR, water under pressure is the coolant and ▷moderator. It circulates through a steam generator, where its heat boils water to provide steam to drive power ▷turbines.

Prestel

▷viewdata service that provides information on the television screen via the telephone network. The service was first offered to the public by British Telecom – then a division of the General Post Office – in 1979. It never lived up to expectations and British Telecom sold off what remained in 1995.

Prestel On-Line is now a subsidiary of Thus (formerly Scottish Telecom) specializing in Internet access and content provision.

Preston

industrial town and administrative headquarters of ▷Lancashire, northwest England, on the River Ribble, 34 km/21 mi south of Lancaster, at the highest navigable point of the Irish Sea estuary; population (1991) 126,100. Industries include textiles, chemicals, electrical goods, aircraft, plastics, and engineering; it is also an agricultural market centre. Oliver Cromwell defeated the Royalists at Preston in 1648. It is the birthplace of Richard Arkwright, inventor of cotton-spinning machinery, and was a centre of the cotton industry in the 18th century.

prestressed concrete

developed form of ▷reinforced concrete in which tensioned steel cables enclosed in ducts take the place of steel reinforcement. This allows the most efficient use of the tensile strength of steel with the compressive strength of concrete. Its use was pioneered by the French engineer Eugène Freysinnet in the 1920s.

Pretoria

city in Gauteng Province, South Africa, and the country's administrative capital; population (1991) 1,080,200. Industries include engineering, chemicals, iron, steel, cement, diamonds, granite quarrying, chemicals, and food processing. Founded in 1855, it was named after Boer leader Andries Pretorius (1799–1853). It was the administrative capital of the Union of South Africa from 1910 and capital of Transvaal Province 1860–1994.

Previn, André George

(1929–) German-born US conductor and composer. He was principal conductor of the London Symphony Orchestra 1968–79 and was appointed music director of Britain's Royal Philharmonic Orchestra in 1985 (a post he relinquished the following year, staying on as principal conductor until 1991). He was also principal conductor of the Los Angeles Philharmonic 1986–89 and is now a guest conductor of many orchestras in Europe and the USA. He was one of the recipients of the 1998 Kennedy Center Honors.

After early success as a composer and arranger for film, he studied conducting with Pierre Monteux in 1951. His compositions include concertos for piano (1971) and guitar (1984); he has conducted Gershwin and Mozart concertos from the keyboard and recorded many US and British composers.

Priapus

in Greek mythology, the god of fertility, son of Dionysus and Aphrodite, represented as grotesquely ugly, with an exaggerated phallus. He was later a Roman god of gardens, where his image was frequently used as a scarecrow.

price

value put on a commodity at the point of exchange. In a free market it is determined by the market forces of demand and supply. In an imperfect market, firms face a trade-off between charging a higher price and losing sales, or charging a lower price and gaining sales.

price/earnings ratio

(or p/e ratio) company's share price divided by its earnings per share after tax.

prices and incomes policy

governmental strategy to curb inflation; see ▷incomes policy.

prickly pear

any of several cacti (see ▷cactus) native to Central and South America, mainly Mexico and Chile, but naturalized in

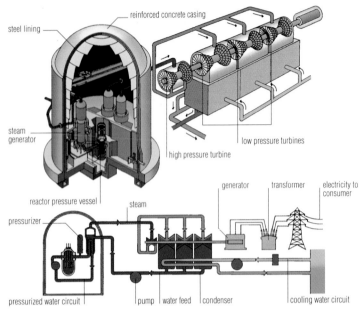

PRESSURIZED WATER REACTOR At a pressurized water nuclear power station, water at high pressure is circulated around the reactor vessel, where it is heated. The hot water is pumped to the steam generator where it boils in a separate circuit; the steam drives the turbines coupled to the electricity generator.

southern Europe, North Africa, and Australia, where it is a pest. The common prickly pear (*O. vulgaris*) is low-growing, with flat, oval stem joints, bright yellow flowers, and prickly, oval fruit; the flesh and seeds of the peeled fruit have a pleasant taste. (Genus *Opuntia*, family Cactaceae.)

Pride's purge

the removal of about 100 Royalists and Presbyterians of the English House of Commons from Parliament by a detachment of soldiers led by Col Thomas Pride (died 1658) in 1648. They were accused of negotiating with Charles I and were seen by the army as unreliable. The remaining members were termed the ▷Rump and voted in favour of the king's trial.

Priestley, J(ohn) B(oynton)

(1894–1984) English novelist and dramatist. His first success was a novel about travelling theatre, *The Good Companions* (1929). He followed it with a realist novel about London life, *Angel Pavement* (1930). His career as a dramatist began with *Dangerous Corner* (1932), one of several plays in which time is a preoccupation. His best-known plays are the enigmatic *An Inspector Calls* (1945) and *The Linden Tree* (1948), a study of post-war social issues.

Priestley had a gift for family comedy; for example, the play *When We Are Married* (1938). He was also known for his wartime BBC broadcasts and literary criticism, such as *Literature and Western Man* (1960). Later novels include *Festival at Farbridge* (1951) and *The Image Men* (1968). He was a stern critic of the social effects of 20th-century modernization, and in his work he fondly reflects his youth in Edwardian Yorkshire.

Primakov, Yevgeny Maksimovich

(1928–) Russian politician, prime minister 1998–99. He was appointed foreign minister in 1995 to appease the communists and nationalists who approved of his championing of Russia's interests and his willingness to use anti-Western rhetoric. Yeltsin appointed him prime minister in 1998 with what seemed to be a surprisingly conservative mandate. Primakov, though far from an old-fashioned communist and relatively subtle in his private diplomacy, still saw the achievement of consensus as more important than reform, and refused to adopt an economic programme that could attract the support of the IMF. The result was that political peace was preserved, at the cost of a disastrously declining economy. Primakov was sacked by Yeltsin in a surprise move in May 1999.

primary

in presidential election campaigns in the USA, a statewide ballot in which voters indicate their candidate preferences for the two main parties. Held in 41 states, primaries begin with New Hampshire in February and continue until June; they operate under varying complex rules. primaries are also held to choose candidates for other posts, such as Congressional seats.

primate

in zoology, any member of the order of mammals that includes monkeys, apes, and humans (together called **anthropoids**), as well as lemurs, bushbabies, lorises, and tarsiers (together called **prosimians**).

Generally, they have forward-directed eyes, gripping hands and feet, opposable thumbs, and big toes. They tend to have nails rather than claws, with gripping pads on the ends of the digits, all adaptations to the arboreal, climbing mode of life.

In 1996 a new primate genus (probably extinct) was identified by a US anthropologist from a collection of bones believed to belong to a ▷potto. The animal has been named *Pseudopotto martini*.

In the same year, the Red List of endangered species published by the ▷World Conservation Union indicated that 46% of the world's 310 primate species are threatened with extinction. Four years later, this figure had increased to 50% and at least 10% of primate species are likely to become extinct in the wild over the next two decades. The first to be declared extinct, in autumn 2000, was Miss Waldron's red colobus, *Procolobus badius waldroni*.

In June 2000 the number of recognized species of primate was increased from 275 to 310 following a meeting of primatologists, conservationists, and taxonomists in Orlando, Florida. A number of species were reclassified using molecular genetic research, behavioural observations, and anatomical evidence. Brazil has 77 species of primate, far more than any other country. By means of a fossil discovered in China in 2000, it has been established that the smallest primate that ever lived was a prosimian that weighed only 10 g and lived about 45 million years ago.

prime minister

(or premier) head of a parliamentary government, usually the leader of the largest party. In countries with an executive president, the prime minister is of lesser standing, whereas in those with dual executives, such as France, power is shared with the president. In federal countries, such as Australia, the head of the federal government has the title prime minister, while the heads of government of the states are called premiers. In Germany, the equivalent of the prime minister is known as the chancellor.

> ### J B Priestley
> *Most of us could do with a smaller, plainer, more companionable world.*
> Delight ch. 105

prime number

number that can be divided only by 1 and itself, that is, having no other factors. There is an infinite number of primes, the first ten of which are 2, 3, 5, 7, 11, 13, 17, 19, 23, and 29 (by definition, the number 1 is excluded from the set of prime numbers). The number 2 is the only even prime number because all other even numbers have 2 as a factor.

Over the centuries mathematicians have sought general methods (algorithms) for calculating primes, from ▷Eratosthenes' sieve to programs on powerful computers.

Mersenne primes are in the form 2^q-1, where q is also a prime. The thirty-eighth Mersenne prime was discovered in 1999. It is 2 million digits long and was discovered as part of the Great Internet

PRIMATE A young female grey langur *Presbytis entellus* with an infant. Like most primates, langurs are adapted to living in trees and have forward-looking eyes and well-developed sight and hearing. Unlike most other mammals, primates are relatively unspecialized, depending instead on their brains for survival. *Premaphotos Wildlife*

Prime Numbers

All the prime numbers between 1 and 1,000

2	3	5	7	11	13	17	19	23	29
31	37	41	43	47	53	59	61	67	71
73	79	83	89	97	101	103	107	109	113
127	131	137	139	149	151	157	163	167	173
179	181	191	193	197	199	211	223	227	229
233	239	241	251	257	263	269	271	277	281
283	293	307	311	313	317	331	337	347	349
353	359	367	373	379	383	389	397	401	409
419	421	431	433	439	443	449	457	461	463
467	479	487	491	499	503	509	521	523	541
547	557	563	569	571	577	587	593	599	601
607	613	617	619	631	641	643	647	653	659
661	673	677	683	691	701	709	719	727	733
739	743	751	757	761	769	773	787	797	809
811	821	823	827	829	839	853	857	859	863
877	881	883	887	907	911	919	929	937	941
947	953	967	971	977	983	991	997		

Prime Search, where volunteers download software to search for primes whilst their computers are idle.

> **Related Web site: Great Internet Mersenne Prime Search**
> http://www.mersenne.org/prime.htm

prime rate the interest rate charged by commercial banks to their best customers. It is the lowest interest or base rate on which other rates are calculated according to the risk involved. Only borrowers who have the highest credit rating qualify for the prime rate.

Primo de Rivera, Miguel, Marqués de Estella (1870–1930) Spanish soldier and politician, dictator from 1923 as well as premier from 1925. He was captain general of Cataluña when he led a coup against the ineffective monarchy and became virtual dictator of Spain with the support of Alfonso XIII. He resigned in 1930.

primrose any of a group of plants belonging to the primrose family, with showy five-lobed flowers. The common primrose (*P. vulgaris*) is a woodland plant, native to Europe, with abundant pale yellow flowers in spring. Related to it is the ▷cowslip. (Genus *Primula*, family Primulaceae.)

> **Related Web site: Primrose** http://www.botanical.com/botanical/mgmh/p/primro69.html

Prince (1958–   ) Former stage name of Prince Rogers Nelson; called 'the artist formerly known as Prince (TAFKAP)'. US pop musician. He composes, arranges, and produces his own records and often plays all the instruments. His albums, including *1999* (1982) and *Purple Rain* (1984), contain elements of rock, funk, and jazz. His stage shows are energetic and extravagant. Prince has now changed his name to a symbol.

> **Related Web site: (The Artist Formally Known As) Prince**
> http://www.geocities.com/SunsetStrip/1131/index.htm

Prince Edward Island smallest province of Canada, situated in the Gulf of St Lawrence, separated from Nova Scotia (to the south and east) and New Brunswick (to the west) by the Northumberland Strait; area 5,700 sq km/2,200 sq mi; population (1996) 137,300. The capital is ▷Charlottetown. Industries include fishing, food processing, and farm vehicle manufacture. Potatoes are grown and there is also dairying.

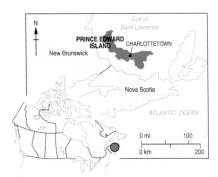

Princeton town and borough in west-central New Jersey, USA, 80 km/50 mi southwest of New York; population (1996 est) 11,900. It is the seat of **Princeton University**, fourth oldest in the USA, which was founded as the College of New Jersey at Elizabethtown in 1746, and relocated to Princeton in 1756. The town is a centre for business and research.

Prince William Sound island-filled inlet of the Gulf of Alaska, to the east of the Kenai Peninsula and south of the Chugach Mountains in south-central Alaska. It extends 200 km/125 mi northwest from Kayak Island. Cordova and Valdez are major ports

on the 130 km/80 mi–wide sound. Montague and Hinchinbrook are its largest islands. The area is a fishing, mining, and oil shipment centre. In March 1989 the oil tanker *Exxon Valdez* ran aground here, spilling 42 million litres of crude oil in one of the world's greatest oil-pollution disasters. Commercial fishing, birds, sea mammals, and hundreds of miles of shoreline were devastated.

printed circuit board (PCB) electrical circuit created by laying (printing) 'tracks' of a conductor such as copper on one or both sides of an insulating board. The PCB was invented in 1936 by Austrian scientist Paul Eisler, and was first used on a large scale in 1948.

Components such as integrated circuits (chips), resistors, and capacitors can be soldered to the surface of the board (surface-mounted) or, more commonly, attached by inserting their connecting pins or wires into holes drilled in the board. PCBs include ▷motherboards, expansion boards, and adaptors.

printer in computing, an output device for producing printed copies of text or graphics. Types include the ▷daisywheel printer, which produces good-quality text but no graphics; the ▷dot matrix printer, which produces text and graphics by printing a pattern of small dots; the ▷ink-jet printer, which creates text and graphics by spraying a fine jet of quick-drying ink onto the paper; and the ▷laser printer, which uses electrostatic technology very similar to that used by a photocopier to produce high-quality text and graphics.

Printers may be classified as **impact printers** (such as daisywheel and dot-matrix printers), which form characters by striking an inked ribbon against the paper, and **nonimpact printers** (such as ink-jet and laser printers), which use a variety of techniques to produce characters without physical impact on the paper.

A further classification is based on the basic unit of printing, and categorizes printers as character printers, line printers, or page printers, according to whether they print one character, one line, or a complete page at a time.

printing reproduction of multiple copies of text or illustrative material on paper, as in books or newspapers, or on an increasing variety of materials; for example, on plastic containers. The first printing used woodblocks, followed by carved wood type or moulded metal type and hand-operated presses. Modern printing is effected by electronically controlled machinery. Current printing processes include electronic phototypesetting with ▷offset printing, and ▷gravure print.

PRINTING A reconstruction of an early printing press.
The Art Archive

printmaking creating a picture or design by printing from a plate (woodblock, stone, or metal sheet) that holds ink or colour. The oldest form of print is the woodcut, common in medieval Europe, followed by line ▷engraving (from the 15th century), and ▷etching (from the 17th century); coloured woodblock prints flourished in Japan from the 18th century. ▷Lithography was invented in 1796.

prion (acronym for proteinaceous infectious particle) infectious agent, a hundred times smaller than a virus. Composed of protein, and without any detectable nucleic acid (genetic material), it is strongly linked to a number of fatal degenerative brain diseases in mammals, such as bovine spongiform encephalopathy (BSE) in cattle, scrapie in sheep, and Creutzfeldt-Jakob disease (CJD) and kuru in humans.

prism in mathematics, a solid figure whose cross section is constant in planes drawn perpendicular to its axis. A cube, for example, is a rectangular prism with all faces (bases and sides) the same shape and size.

prism in optics, a triangular block of transparent material (plastic, glass, silica) commonly used to 'bend' a ray of light or split a beam into its spectral colours. Prisms are used as mirrors to define the optical path in binoculars, camera viewfinders, and periscopes. The dispersive property of prisms is used in the ▷spectroscope.

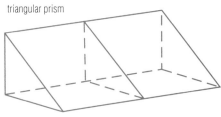

triangular prism

cross section is the same throughout the prism's length

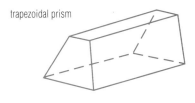

trapezoidal prism

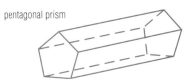

pentagonal prism

PRISM The volume of a prism is determined by multiplying the area of the cross section by the length of the prism.

prison place of confinement for those accused or convicted of contravening the laws of the state; after conviction, most countries claim to aim also at rehabilitation and deterrence as well as punishment. For major crimes, life imprisonment (or death in some countries or US states) may be the sentence. The average number of people in prison in the UK in 1995 was 58,375; 12,669 on ▷remand (awaiting trial or sentence), 45,052 sentenced, and 654 other. Of these, 56,189 were male and 2,186 female.

prisoner of war (POW) person captured in war, who has fallen into the hands of, or surrendered to, an opponent. Such captives may be held in prisoner-of-war camps. The treatment of POWs is governed by the ▷Geneva Convention.

Priština capital of Kosovo autonomous province within Serbia and Montenegro; population (1991) 108,000. Once capital of the medieval Serbian empire, it is now a trading centre.

Pritchett, V(ictor) S(awdon) (1900–1997) English short-story writer, novelist, and critic. His style was often witty and satirical. Many of his short stories were set in London and southeast England, among them *The Spanish Virgin* (1930), *Blind Love* (1969), and *The Camberwell Beauty* (1974). His critical works included *The Living Novel* (1946) and biographies of the Russian writers ▷Turgenev (1977) and ▷Chekhov (1988).

privacy the right of the individual to be free from secret surveillance (by scientific devices or other means) and from the disclosure to unauthorized persons of personal data, as accumulated in computer data banks. Always an issue complicated by considerations of state security, public welfare (in the case of criminal activity), and other factors, it has been rendered more complex by present-day technology.

privateer privately owned and armed ship commissioned by a state to attack enemy vessels. The crews of such ships were, in effect, legalized pirates; they were not paid but received a share of the spoils. Privateering existed from ancient times until the 19th century, when it was declared illegal by the Declaration of Paris in 1856.

private finance initiative (PFI) an idea floated by the UK Labour Party when in opposition before 1997, particularly by the deputy leader, John ▷Prescott, who argued that the country's infrastructure could be improved by combining public expenditure with private finance. Since assuming office in May 1997 the Labour government has kept the initiative alive by gaining the support of major companies for its investment plans and inviting prominent industrialists to work in or with the administration.

private limited company a registered company which has limited liability (the shareholders cannot lose more than their original shareholdings), and a minimum of two shareholders and a maximum of fifty. It cannot offer its shares or debentures to the public and their transfer is restricted.

private school alternative name in the UK for a fee-paying ▷independent school.

private sector the part of the economy that is owned and controlled by private individuals and business organizations such as private and public limited companies. In a ▷free enterprise economy, the private sector is responsible for allocating most of the resources within the economy. This contrasts with the ▷public sector, where economic resources are owned and controlled by the state.

privatization policy or process of selling or transferring state-owned or public assets and services (notably nationalized industries) to private investors. Privatization of services involves the government contracting private firms to supply services previously supplied by public authorities.

privet any of a group of evergreen shrubs with dark green leaves, belonging to the olive family. They include the European common privet (*L. vulgare*) with white flowers and black berries, naturalized in North America, and the native North American California privet (*L. ovalifolium*), also known as hedge privet. (Genus *Ligustrum*, family Oleaceae.)

privilege in law, a special right or immunity in connection with legal proceedings. **Public-interest privilege** may be claimed by the government seeking to preserve the confidentiality of state documents. **Private privilege** can only attach to an individual by virtue of rank or office; for example, for members of Parliament in defence of defamation proceedings.

Privy Council council composed originally of the chief royal officials of the Norman kings in Britain; under the Tudors and early Stuarts it became the chief governing body. It was replaced from 1688 by the ▷cabinet, originally a committee of the council, and the council itself now retains only formal powers in issuing royal proclamations and orders in council.

In 1998 there were over 200 Privy Counsellors. Cabinet ministers are automatically members, and it is presided over by the Lord President of the Council.

privy purse personal expenditure of the British sovereign, which derives from his/her own resources (as distinct from the ▷civil list, which now finances only expenses incurred in pursuance of official functions and duties). The office that deals with this expenditure is also known as the Privy Purse.

Prix Goncourt French literary prize for fiction, given by the Académie Goncourt (founded by Edmond de ▷Goncourt in 1903).

probability likelihood, or chance, that an event will occur, often expressed as odds, or in mathematics, numerically as a fraction or decimal.

In general, the probability that n particular events will happen out of a total of m possible events is n/m. A certainty has a probability of 1; an impossibility has a probability of 0. Empirical probability is defined as the number of successful events divided by the total possible number of events.

In tossing a coin, the chance that it will land 'heads' is the same as the chance that it will land 'tails', that is, 1 to 1 or even; mathematically, this probability is expressed as $\frac{1}{2}$ or 0.5. The odds against any chosen number coming up on the roll of a fair die are 5 to 1; the probability is $\frac{1}{6}$ or 0.1666... . If two dice are rolled there are $6 \times 6 = 36$ different possible combinations. The probability of a double (two numbers the same) is $\frac{6}{36}$ or $\frac{1}{6}$ since there are six doubles in the 36 events: (1,1), (2,2), (3,3), (4,4), (5,5), and (6,6).

Independent events are those which do not affect each other, for example rolling two dice are independent events, as the rolling of the first die does not effect the outcome of the rolling of the second die. If events are described as **mutually exclusive** it means that if one happens, then it prevents the other from happening. So tossing a coin is a mutually exclusive event as it can result in a head or a tail but not both. The sum of the probabilities of mutually exclusive events is always equal to one. For example, if one has a bag containing three marbles, each of a different colour, the probability of selecting each colour would be $\frac{1}{3}$.

$$\tfrac{1}{3} + \tfrac{1}{3} + \tfrac{1}{3} = 1$$

To find out the probability of two or more mutually exclusive events occurring, their individual probabilities are added together. So, in the above example, the probability of selecting either a blue marble or a red marble is

$$\tfrac{1}{3} + \tfrac{1}{3} = \tfrac{2}{3}$$

The probability of two independent events both occurring is smaller than the probability of one such event occurring. For example, the probability of throwing a three when rolling a die is $\frac{1}{6}$,

but the probability of throwing two threes when rolling two dice is $\frac{1}{36}$.

Probability theory was developed by the French mathematicians Blaise Pascal and Pierre de Fermat in the 17th century, initially in response to a request to calculate the odds of being dealt various hands at cards. Today probability plays a major part in the mathematics of atomic theory and finds application in insurance and statistical studies.

probate formal proof of a will. In the UK, if a will's validity is unquestioned, it is proven in 'common form'; the executor, in the absence of other interested parties, obtains at a probate registry a grant upon his or her own oath. Otherwise, it must be proved in 'solemn form': its validity established at a probate court (in the Chancery Division of the High Court), those concerned being made parties to the action.

probation in law, the placing of offenders under supervision of probation officers in the community, as an alternative to prison.

procedure in computing, a small part of a computer program that performs a specific task, such as clearing the screen or sorting a file. A **procedural language**, such as BASIC, is one in which the programmer describes a task in terms of how it is to be done, as opposed to a **declarative language**, such as PROLOG, in which it is described in terms of the required result. See ▷programming.

processor in computing, another name for the ▷central processing unit or ▷microprocessor of a computer.

Proconsul prehistoric ape skull found on Rusinga Island in Lake Victoria (Nyanza), East Africa, by Mary ▷Leakey. It is believed to be 20 million years old.

Procrustes (or Damastes or Polypemon; Greek 'the stretcher') in Greek mythology, a robber of Attica who tied his victims to a bed and adjusted them to its length by amputating their legs or racking (stretching) their bodies. He was killed by the hero ▷Theseus.

procurator fiscal officer of a Scottish sheriff's court who (combining the role of public prosecutor and coroner) inquires into suspicious deaths and carries out the preliminary questioning of witnesses to crime.

Procyon (or Alpha Canis Minoris) brightest star in the constellation ▷Canis Minor and the eighth-brightest star in the night sky. Procyon is a white star 11.4 light years from the Sun, with a mass of 1.7 Suns. It has a ▷white dwarf companion that orbits it every 40 years.

The name, derived from Greek, means 'before the dog', and reflects the fact that in midnorthern latitudes Procyon rises shortly before ▷Sirius, the Dog Star. Procyon and Sirius are sometimes called 'the Dog Stars'. Both are relatively close to us and have white dwarf companions.

productivity in economics, the output produced by a given quantity of labour, usually measured as output per person employed in the firm, industry, sector, or economy concerned. Productivity is determined by the quality and quantity of the fixed ▷capital used by labour, and the effort of the workers concerned.

profit amount by which total revenue exceeds total cost. It is the reward for risk-taking for shareholders in a business organization. **Gross profit** is the difference between sales revenue and the direct cost of production. **Net profit** is total revenue minus total direct and indirect cost (for example, overheads, the cost of running the business).

progesterone ▷steroid hormone that occurs in vertebrates. In mammals, it regulates the menstrual cycle and pregnancy. Progesterone is secreted by the corpus luteum (the ruptured Graafian follicle of a discharged ovum).

program in computing, a set of instructions that controls the operation of a computer. There are two main kinds: ▷applications programs, which carry out tasks for the benefit of the user – for example, word processing; and ▷systems programs, which control the internal workings of the computer. A ▷utility program is a systems program that carries out specific tasks for the user. Programs can be written in any of a number of ▷programming languages but are always translated into machine code before they can be executed by the computer.

program loop part of a computer program that is repeated several times. The loop may be repeated a fixed number of times (**counter-controlled loop**) or until a certain condition is satisfied (**condition-controlled loop**). For example, a counter-controlled loop might be used to repeat an input routine until exactly ten numbers have been input; a condition-controlled loop might be used to repeat an input routine until the ▷data terminator 'XXX' is entered.

programme music instrumental music that interprets a story, depicts a scene or painting, or illustrates a literary or philosophical idea. The term was first used by Franz ▷Liszt in the 19th century, when programme music was especially popular with composers of Romantic music (see ▷Romanticism), but there had been a great

deal of descriptive music before then. Examples include Antonio Vivaldi's *Four Seasons* concertos, Ludwig van Beethoven's *Eroica* and *Pastoral* symphonies, Felix Mendelssohn's *Hebrides Overture* ('Fingal's Cave'), and the ▷symphonic poems of Liszt and Richard Strauss.

programming writing instructions in a programming language for the control of a computer. **Applications programming** is for end-user programs, such as accounts programs or word-processing packages. **Systems programming** is for operating systems and the like, which are concerned more with the internal workings of the computer.

There are several programming styles. **Procedural programming**, in which programs are written as lists of instructions for the computer to obey in sequence, is by far the most popular. It is the 'natural' style, closely matching the computer's own sequential operation. **Declarative programming**, as used in the programming language PROLOG, does not describe how to solve a problem, but rather describes the logical structure of the problem. Running such a program is more like proving an assertion than following a procedure. **Functional programming** is a style based largely on the definition of functions. There are very few functional programming languages, HOPE and ML being the most widely used, though many more conventional languages (for example C) make extensive use of functions. **Object-oriented programming**, the most recently developed style, involves viewing a program as a collection of objects that behave in certain ways when they are passed certain 'messages'. For example, an object might be defined to represent a table of figures, which will be displayed on screen when a 'display' message is received.

programming language in computing, a special notation in which instructions for controlling a computer are written. Programming languages are designed to be easy for people to write and read, but must be capable of being mechanically translated (by a ▷compiler or an ▷interpreter) into the ▷machine code that the computer can execute. Programming languages may be classified as ▷high-level languages or ▷low-level languages. See also ▷source language.

progression sequence of numbers each occurring in a specific relationship to its predecessor. An **arithmetic progression** has numbers that increase or decrease by a common sum or difference (for example, 2, 4, 6, 8); a **geometric progression** has numbers each bearing a fixed ratio to its predecessor (for example, 3, 6, 12, 24); and a **harmonic progression** has numbers whose ▷reciprocals are in arithmetical progression, for example $1, \frac{1}{2}, \frac{1}{3}, \frac{1}{4}$.

progressive education teaching methods that take as their starting point children's own aptitudes and interests, and encourage them to follow their own investigations and lines of inquiry.

progressive tax tax such that the higher the income of the taxpayer the greater the proportion or percentage paid in that tax. This contrasts with ▷regressive taxes where the proportion paid falls as income increases, and ▷proportional taxes where the proportion paid remains the same at all levels of income. Examples of progressive taxes in the UK include ▷income tax and capital gains tax.

Progressivism in US history, a reform movement in the two decades before World War I. Mainly middle-class and urban-based, progressives secured legislation at national, state, and local levels to improve the democratic system, working conditions, and welfare provision.

Prohibition in US history, the period 1920–33 when the 18th Amendment to the US Constitution was in force, and the manufacture, transportation, and sale of alcohol was illegal. This led to ▷bootlegging (the illegal distribution of liquor, often illicitly distilled), to the financial advantage of organized crime.

The 18th Amendment was enforced by the Volstead Act in 1919. It represented the culmination of a long campaign by church and women's organizations, Populists, progressives, temperance societies, and the Anti-Saloon League. The result was widespread disdain for the law; speakeasies for illicit drinking sprang up, and organized crime activity increased, especially in Chicago and towns near the Canadian border. Public opinion insisted on repeal in 1933 (the 21st Amendment).

Related Web site: Temperance and Prohibition http://www.cohums. ohio-state.edu/history/projects/prohibition/Contents.htm

projection of the earth on paper, see ▷map projection.

projector any apparatus that projects a picture on to a screen. In a **slide projector**, a lamp shines a light through the photographic slide or transparency, and a projection ▷lens throws an enlarged image of the slide onto the screen. A **film projector** has similar optics, but incorporates a mechanism that holds the film still while light is transmitted through each frame (picture). A shutter covers the film when it moves between frames. A **television projector**, often used at sports events, produces an enlarged image of the television screen. It shines an intense light through a small LCD (liquid crystal display) throwing the television picture onto a large screen.

prokaryote in biology, an organism whose cells lack organelles (specialized segregated structures such as nuclei, mitochondria, and chloroplasts). Prokaryote DNA is not arranged in chromosomes but forms a coiled structure called a **nucleoid**. The prokaryotes comprise only the **bacteria** and **cyanobacteria** (see ▷blue-green algae); all other organisms are eukaryotes.

Prokofiev, Sergey Sergeyevich (1891–1953) Russian composer. His music includes operas such as *The Love for Three Oranges* (1921); ballets for Sergei Diaghilev, including *Romeo and Juliet* (1935); seven symphonies including the *Classical Symphony* (1916–17); music for film, including Eisenstein's *Alexander Nevsky* (1938); piano and violin concertos; songs and cantatas (for example, that composed for the 30th anniversary of the October Revolution); and *Peter and the Wolf* (1936) for children, to his own libretto after a Russian folk tale.

Prokofiev was essentially a classicist in his use of form, but his extensive and varied output demonstrates great lyricism, humour, and skill. His music in his earlier years was distinguished by its hard brilliance, his later works showing a mellowing and maturity of style. Born near Ekaterinoslav (now Dnipropetrovs'k), he studied at St Petersburg under Rimsky-Korsakov and achieved fame as a pianist. He left Russia in 1918 and lived for some time in the USA and in Paris, but returned in 1927 and again in 1935.

Related Web site: Prokofiev http://www.siue.edu/~aho/musov/sergei.html

prolapse displacement of an organ due to the effects of strain in weakening the supporting tissues. The term is most often used with regard to the rectum (due to chronic bowel problems) or the uterus (following several pregnancies).

proletariat (Latin *proletarii* 'the class possessing no property') in Marxist theory, those classes in society that possess no property, and therefore depend on the sale of their labour or expertise (as opposed to the capitalists or bourgeoisie, who own the means of production, and the petty bourgeoisie, or working small-property owners). They are usually divided into the industrial, agricultural, and intellectual proletariat.

PROLOG (contraction of programming in logic) high-level computer programming language based on logic. Invented in 1971 at the University of Marseille, France, it did not achieve widespread use until more than ten years later. It is used mainly for ▷artificial intelligence programming.

PROM (acronym for programmable read-only memory) in computing, a memory device in the form of an integrated circuit (chip) that can be programmed after manufacture to hold information permanently. PROM chips are empty of information when manufactured, unlike ROM (read-only memory) chips, which have information built into them. Other memory devices are ▷EPROM (erasable programmable read-only memory) and ▷RAM (random-access memory).

Prometheus (Greek 'forethought') in Greek mythology, a ▷Titan who stole fire from heaven for the human race. In revenge, Zeus chained him to a rock and sent an eagle to gnaw at his liver by day; the organ grew back each night. ▷Heracles rescued him from the torture.

promethium radioactive, metallic element of the ▷lanthanide series, symbol Pm, atomic number 61, relative atomic mass 145. It occurs in nature only in minute amounts, produced as a fission product/by-product of uranium in ▷pitchblende and other uranium ores; for a long time it was considered not to occur in nature. The longest-lived isotope has a half-life of slightly more than 20 years.

Promethium is synthesized by neutron bombardment of neodymium, and is a product of the fission of uranium, thorium, or plutonium; it can be isolated in large amounts from the fission-product debris of uranium fuel in nuclear reactors. It is used in phosphorescent paints and as an X-ray source.

It was named in 1949 after the Greek Titan Prometheus.

prominence bright cloud of gas projecting from the Sun into space 100,000 km/60,000 mi or more. **Quiescent prominences** last for months, and are held in place by magnetic fields in the Sun's corona. **Surge prominences** shoot gas into space at speeds of 1,000 kps/600 mps. **Loop prominences** are gases falling back to the Sun's surface after a solar ▷flare.

pronghorn ruminant mammal *Antilocapra americana* constituting the family Antilocapridae, native to the western USA. It is not a true antelope. It is light brown and about 1 m/3 ft high. It sheds its horns annually and can reach speeds of 100 kph/60 mph. The loss of prairies to agriculture, combined with excessive hunting, has brought this unique animal close to extinction.

Related Web site: Pronghorn http://www.geocities.com/Athens/Forum/3807/features/pronghorn.html

pronunciation the way in which words are rendered into human speech sounds; either a language as a whole ('French pronunciation') or a particular word or name ('what is the pronunciation of 'controversy'?'). The pronunciation of languages forms the academic subject of ▷phonetics.

proof spirit numerical scale used to indicate the alcohol content of an alcoholic drink. Proof spirit (or 100% proof spirit) acquired its name from a solution of alcohol in water which, when used to moisten gunpowder, contained just enough alcohol to permit it to burn.

propaganda systematic spreading (propagation) of information or disinformation, usually to promote a religious or political doctrine with the intention of instilling particular attitudes or responses. As a system of disseminating information it was considered a legitimate instrument of government, but became notorious through the deliberate distortion of facts or the publication of falsehoods by totalitarian regimes, notably Nazi Germany.

Related Web site: Propaganda http://carmen.artsci.washington.edu/propaganda/contents.htm

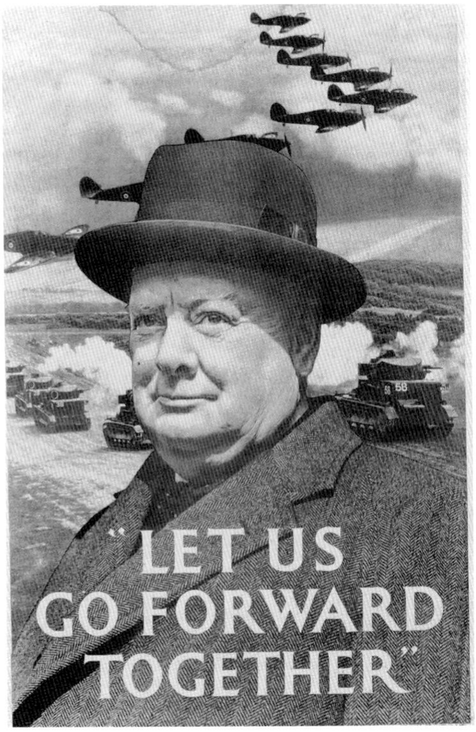

PROPAGANDA A World War II propaganda poster showing a steadfast image of Winston Churchill, backed by the armed forces, supporting his view that the nation would 'go forward'. *The Art Archive/Eileen Tweedy*

propane C_3H_8 gaseous hydrocarbon of the ▷alkane series, found in petroleum and used as fuel.

propanol (or **propyl alcohol**) third member of the homologous series of ▷alcohols. Propanol is usually a mixture of two isomeric compounds (see ▷isomer): propan-1-ol ($CH_3CH_2CH_2OH$) and propan-2-ol ($CH_3CHOHCH_3$). Both are colourless liquids that can be mixed with water and are used in perfumery.

propanone CH_3COCH_3 (common name **acetone**) colourless flammable liquid used extensively as a solvent, as in nail-varnish remover. It boils at 56.5°C/133.7°F, mixes with water in all proportions, and has a characteristic odour.

propellant substance burned in a rocket for propulsion. Two propellants are used: oxidizer and fuel are stored in separate tanks and pumped independently into the combustion chamber. Liquid oxygen (oxidizer) and liquid hydrogen (fuel) are common propellants, used, for example, in the space-shuttle main engines. The explosive charge that propels a projectile from a gun is also called a propellant.

propeller screwlike device used to propel some ships and aeroplanes. A propeller has a number of curved blades that describe a helical path as they rotate with the hub, and accelerate fluid (liquid or gas) backwards during rotation. Reaction to this backward movement of fluid sets up a propulsive thrust forwards. The marine screw propeller was developed by Francis Pettit Smith in the UK and Swedish-born John Ericson in the USA and was first used in 1839.

propene $CH_3CH{=}CH_2$ (common name **propylene**) second member of the alkene series of hydrocarbons. A colourless, flammable gas, it is widely used by industry to make organic chemicals, including polypropylene plastics.

proper motion gradual change in the position of a star that results from its motion in orbit around our Galaxy, the Milky Way. Proper motions are slight and undetectable to the naked eye, but can be accurately measured on telescopic photographs taken many years apart.

Barnard's Star is the star with the largest proper motion, 10.3 arc seconds per year.

Propertius, Sextus (*c.* 47–15 BC) Roman elegiac poet. A member of the literary circle of ▷Maecenas, he is best known for his highly personal love poems addressed to his mistress 'Cynthia'.

property the right to control the use of a thing (such as land, a building, a work of art, or a computer program). In English law, a distinction is made between **real property**, which involves a degree of geographical fixity, and **personal property**, which does not. Property is never absolute, since any society places limits on an individual's property (such as the right to transfer that property to another). Different societies have held widely varying interpretations of the nature of property and the extent of the rights of the owner of that property.

prophet person thought to speak from divine inspiration or one who foretells the future. Prophets whose words and actions are recorded in the Bible include Moses, Samuel, Elijah, Isaiah, and Jeremiah. In Islam, ▷Muhammad is believed to be the last and greatest of a long line of prophets beginning with Adam and including Moses and Jesus.

prophylaxis any measure taken to prevent disease, including exercise and ▷vaccination. Prophylactic (preventive) medicine is an aspect of public-health provision that is receiving increasing attention.

proportion the relation of a part to the whole (usually expressed as a fraction or percentage). In mathematics two variable quantities x and y are proportional if, for all values of x, $y = kx$, where k is a constant. This means that if x increases, y increases in a linear fashion.

proportional representation (PR) electoral system in which distribution of party seats corresponds to their proportion of the total votes cast, and minority votes are not wasted (as opposed to a simple majority, or 'first past the post', system). Forms of proportional representation include:

party list system (PLS) or **additional member system** (AMS). As recommended by the Hansard Society in 1976 for introduction in the UK, three-quarters of the members would be elected in single-member constituencies on the traditional majority-vote system, and the remaining seats be allocated according to the overall number of votes cast for each party (a variant of this, the additional member system, is used in Germany, where half the members are elected from lists by proportional representation, and half compete for single-member 'first past the post' constituencies). Proportional representation is used for the new Scottish Parliament and National Assembly for Wales, both first elected in 1999, and, also since 1999, for European Parliament elections in Britain. For the European Parliament elections, 'closed' regional party lists (in which voters cannot change the order of candidates on a party's list) are used and seats allocated in proportion to each party's regional vote. The system allowed the environmentalist Green Party and the anti-European Union UK Independence Party to win European Parliament seats for the first ever time, in June 1999. For the Scottish Parliament and Welsh National Assembly elections, more than half of the members are returned by first-past-the-post from single-member constituencies, with the remainder being drawn, by means of 'top-up' proportional representation from regional party lists. This 'additional member system', which gives electors two votes, is similar to that used in German elections. It has also been used, since May 2000, for elections to the Greater London Assembly.

single transferable vote (STV). Candidates are numbered in order of preference by the voter, and any votes surplus to the minimum required for a candidate to win are transferred to second preferences, as are second-preference votes from the successive candidates at the bottom of the poll until the required number of elected candidates is achieved. This is in use in the Republic of Ireland and for European Parliament elections in Northern Ireland. It has also been used since June 1998 for elections to the Northern Ireland Assembly.

alternative vote (AV). Not strictly a form of proportional representation, since it cannot guarantee a close relationship between votes and seats, the AV is a system which is simple and can make the voting system fairer. It is based on single-member constituencies in which the elector receives two votes: a first vote, to be marked '1', for the preferred candidate, and a second, to be marked '2', for a second choice. If no one candidate collects more than 50% of the 'first preference' votes, the candidate with the fewest of first choice votes is eliminated and his or her 'second preference' votes are allocated among the remaining candidates. This process continues until one candidate emerges with 50+%. The system is used in Australian House of Representatives elections. Termed the Supplementary Vote (SV), it has also been used since May 2000 to elect the Greater London mayor.

proportional tax tax such that the proportion or percentage paid in tax remains constant as income of the taxpayer changes. This contrasts with ▷regressive tax where the proportion paid falls as income increases, and ▷progressive tax where the proportion paid increases. ▷Value-added tax is often said to be an example of a proportional tax.

prop root (or **stilt root**) modified root that grows from the lower part of a stem or trunk down to the ground, providing a plant with extra support. Prop roots are common on some woody plants, such as mangroves, and also occur on a few herbaceous plants, such as maize. **Buttress roots** are a type of prop root found at the base of tree trunks, extended and flattened along the upper edge to form massive triangular buttresses; they are common on tropical trees.

propyl alcohol common name for ▷propanol.

propylene common name for ▷propene.

prose spoken or written language without metrical regularity; in literature, prose corresponds more closely to the patterns of everyday speech than ▷poetry.

prosecution in law, the party instituting legal proceedings. In the UK, the prosecution of a criminal case is begun by bringing the accused (defendant) before a magistrate, either by warrant or summons, or by arrest without warrant. Most criminal prosecutions are conducted by the ▷Crown Prosecution Service, although other government departments may also prosecute some cases; for example, the Department of Inland Revenue. An individual may bring a private prosecution, usually for assault.

Prosecution Service, Crown see ▷Crown Prosecution Service.

Proserpina in Roman mythology, the goddess of the underworld. Her Greek equivalent is ▷Persephone.

prostaglandin any of a group of complex fatty acids present in the body that act as messenger substances between cells. Effects include stimulating the contraction of smooth muscle (for example, of the womb during birth), regulating the production of stomach acid, and modifying hormonal activity. In excess, prostaglandins may produce inflammatory disorders such as arthritis. Synthetic prostaglandins are used to induce labour in humans and domestic animals.

Prost, Alain Marie Pascal (1955–) French motor-racing driver who was world champion in 1985, 1986, 1989, and 1993, and the first French world drivers' champion. To the end of the 1993 season he had won 51 Grand Prix from 199 starts. He retired in 1993.

Related Web site: Alain Prost Grand Prix Home Page http://www.glink.net.uk/~alanw/welcome.html

prostate cancer ▷cancer of the ▷prostate gland. It is a slow progressing cancer, and about 60% of cases are detected before metastasis (spreading), so it can be successfully treated by surgical removal of the gland and radiotherapy. It is, however, the second commonest cancer-induced death in males (after lung cancer). It kills 32,000 men a year in the USA alone.

prostatectomy surgical removal of the ▷prostate gland. In many men over the age of 60 the prostate gland enlarges, causing obstruction to the urethra. This causes the bladder to swell with retained urine, leaving the sufferer more prone to infection of the urinary tract.

prostate gland gland surrounding and opening into the ▷urethra at the base of the ▷bladder in male mammals.

The prostate gland produces an alkaline fluid that is released during ejaculation; this fluid activates sperm, and prevents their clumping together. Older men may develop **benign prostatic hyperplasia** (BPH), a painful condition in which the prostate becomes enlarged and restricts urine flow. This can cause further problems of the bladder and kidneys. It is treated by ▷prostatectomy.

prosthesis artificial device used to substitute for a body part which is defective or missing. Prostheses include artificial limbs, hearing aids, false teeth and eyes, heart ▷pacemakers and plastic heart valves and blood vessels.

Prostheses in the form of artificial limbs, such as wooden legs and metal hooks for hands, have been used for centuries, although artificial limbs are now more natural-looking and comfortable to wear. The comparatively new field of ▷bionics has developed myoelectric, or bionic, arms, which are electronically operated and worked by minute electrical impulses from body muscles.

prostitution receipt of money for sexual acts. Society's attitude towards prostitution varies according to place and period. In some countries, tolerance is combined with licensing of brothels and health checks on the prostitutes (both male and female).

protactinium (Latin *protos* 'before' + *aktis* 'first ray') silver–grey, radioactive, metallic element of the ▷actinide series, symbol Pa, atomic number 91, relative atomic mass 231.036. It occurs in nature in very small quantities, in ▷pitchblende and other uranium ores. It has 14 known isotopes; the longest-lived, Pa-231, has a half-life of 32,480 years.

The element was discovered in 1913 (Pa-234, with a half-life of only 1.2 minutes) as a product of uranium decay. Other isotopes were later found and the name was officially adopted in 1949, although it had been in use since 1918.

protease general term for a digestive enzyme capable of splitting proteins. Examples include pepsin, found in the stomach, and trypsin, found in the small intestine.

protectionism in economics, the imposition of heavy duties or import ▷quotas by a government as a means of discouraging the import of foreign goods likely to compete with domestic products. Price controls, quota systems, and the reduction of surpluses are among the measures taken for agricultural products in the European Union. The opposite practice is ▷free trade.

protectorate formerly in international law, a small state under the direct or indirect control of a larger one. The 20th-century equivalent was a ▷trust territory. In English history the rule of Oliver and Richard ▷Cromwell 1653–59 is referred to as the ▷Protectorate.

protein complex, biologically important substance composed of amino acids joined by ▷peptide bonds. Proteins are essential to all living organisms. As ▷enzymes they regulate all aspects of metabolism. Structural proteins such as **keratin** and **collagen** make up the skin, claws, bones, tendons, and ligaments; **muscle** proteins produce movement; **haemoglobin** transports oxygen; and **membrane** proteins regulate the movement of substances into and out of cells. For humans, protein is an essential part of the diet, and is found in greatest quantity in soy beans and other grain legumes, meat, eggs, and cheese.

Other types of bond, such as sulphur–sulphur bonds, hydrogen bonds, and cation bridges between acid sites, are responsible for creating the protein's characteristic three-dimensional structure, which may be fibrous, globular, or pleated. Protein provides 4 kcal of energy per gram (60 g per day is required).

Related Web site: Introduction to Proteins http://biotech.icmb.utexas.edu/pages/science/protein_intro.html

Marcel Proust

A work of art that contains theories is like an object on which the price tag has been left.

Remembrance of Things Past: Time Regained

protein engineering the creation of synthetic proteins designed to carry out specific tasks. For example, an enzyme may be designed to remove grease from soiled clothes and remain stable at the high temperatures in a washing machine.

Proterozoic Eon eon of geological time, 3.5 billion to 570 million years ago, the second division of the Precambrian. It is defined as the time of simple life, since many rocks dating from this eon show traces of biological activity, and some contain the fossils of bacteria and algae.

Protestantism one of the main divisions of Christianity, which emerged from Roman Catholicism at the ▷Reformation. The chief denominations are the Anglican Communion (Church of England in the UK and Episcopal Church in the USA), Baptists, Christian Scientists, Congregationalists (United Church of Christ), Lutherans, Methodists, Pentecostals, and Presbyterians, with a total membership of about 300 million.

Proteus in Greek mythology, the warden of the sea beasts of ▷Poseidon; his flocks were usually said to comprise of seals. He possessed the gift of prophecy but could transform himself into many forms to evade questioning.

protist in biology, a single-celled organism which has a eukaryotic cell, but which is not a member of the plant, fungal, or animal kingdoms. The main protists are ▷protozoa.

Single-celled photosynthetic organisms, such as diatoms and dinoflagellates, are classified as protists or algae. Recently the term has also been used for members of the kingdom Protista, which features in certain five-kingdom classifications of the living world (see also ▷plant classification). This kingdom may include slime moulds, all algae (seaweeds as well as unicellular forms), and protozoa.

proton (Greek 'first') in physics, a positively charged subatomic particle, a constituent of the nucleus of all atoms. It belongs to the ▷baryon group of ▷hadrons. A proton is extremely long-lived, with a lifespan of at least 10^{32} years. It carries a unit positive charge equal to the negative charge of an ▷electron. Its mass is almost 1,836 times that of an electron, or 1.67×10^{-27} kg. Protons are composed of two up ▷quarks and one down quark held together by ▷gluons. The number of protons in the atom of an element is equal to the atomic number of that element.

proton number alternative name for ▷atomic number.

protoplasm contents of a living cell. Strictly speaking it includes all the discrete structures (organelles) in a cell, but it is often used simply to mean the jellylike material in which these float. The contents of a cell outside the nucleus are called ▷cytoplasm.

prototype in technology, any of the first few machines of a new design. Prototypes are tested for performance, reliability, economy, and safety; then the main design can be modified before full-scale production begins.

protozoa group of single-celled organisms without rigid cell walls. Some, such as amoeba, ingest other cells, but most are ▷saprotrophs or parasites. The group is polyphyletic (containing organisms which have different evolutionary origins).

protractor instrument used to measure a flat ▷angle.

Proudhon, Pierre Joseph (1809–1865) French anarchist, born in Besançon. He sat in the Constituent Assembly of 1848, was imprisoned for three years, and had to go into exile in Brussels. He published *Qu'est-ce que la propriété/What is Property?* (1840) and *Philosophie de la misère/Philosophy of Poverty* (1846).

Proust, Marcel (1871–1922) French novelist and critic. His immense autobiographical work *A la Recherche du temps perdu/Remembrance of Things Past* (1913–27), consisting of a series of novels, is the expression of his childhood memories coaxed from his subconscious; it is also a precise reflection of life in France at the end of the 19th century.

Born in Auteuil, Paris, Proust was a delicate, asthmatic child; until he was 35 he moved in the fashionable circles of Parisian society, but after the death of his parents 1904–05 he went into seclusion in a cork-lined room in his Paris apartment, and devoted the rest of his life to writing his masterpiece. Posthumous publications include the novel *Jean Santeuil* (1957), which seems to have been an early sketch for *A la recherche*, and *Contre Sainte-Beuve/By Way of Sainte-Beuve* (1954).

Related Web site: Kolb-Proust Archive for Research http://www.library.uiuc.edu/kolbp/

Provençal language member of the Romance branch of the Indo-European language family, spoken in and around Provence in southeastern France. It is now regarded as a dialect or patois.

Provence-Alpes-Côte d'Azur region of southeast France, comprising the *départements* of Alpes-de-Haute-Provence, Hautes-Alpes, Alpes-Maritimes, Bouches-du-Rhône, Var, and Vaucluse; area 31,400 sq km/12,120 sq mi; the administrative centre is

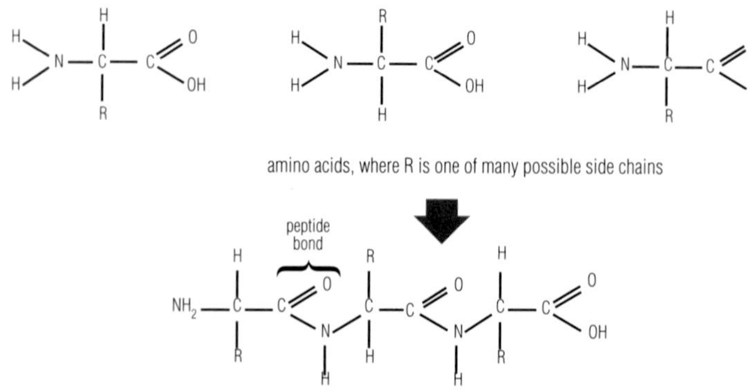

peptide – this is one made of just three amino acid units. Proteins consist of very large numbers of amino acid units in long chains, folded up in specific ways

PROTEIN A protein molecule is a long chain of amino acids linked by peptide bonds. The properties of a protein are determined by the order, or sequence, of amino acids in its molecule, and by the three-dimensional structure of the molecular chain. The chain folds and twists, often forming a spiral shape.

▷Marseille; population (1990) 4,257,900. The Côte d'Azur, on the Mediterranean, is a tourist centre. Provence was an independent kingdom in the 10th century, and the area still has its own traditional language, Provençal.

Related Web site: Touring Guide of Provence http://www.provenceweb.fr/e/provpil.htm

provincia in ancient Rome, region of authority of a magistrate holding power in Italy or elsewhere. In the Republic, provinces were determined by the ▷Senate for the consuls and praetors. Under the empire, they were divided into senatorial and imperial; for the latter the emperor himself made the appointments. Additions to the provinces of the Roman empire effectively stopped after ▷Trajan died in AD 117.

proviso in law, a clause in a statute, deed, or some other legal document introducing a qualification or condition to some other provision, frequently the one immediately preceding the proviso itself.

provitamin any precursor substance of a vitamin. Provitamins are ingested substances that become converted to active vitamins within the organism. One example is ergosterol (provitamin D_2), which through the action of sunlight is converted to calciferol (vitamin D_2); another example is beta-carotene, which is hydrolysed in the liver to vitamin A.

Proxima Centauri closest star to the Sun, 4.2 light years away from the Sun. It is a faint ▷red dwarf, visible only with a telescope, and is a member of the Alpha Centauri triple-star system.

proxy in law, a person authorized to stand in another's place; also the document conferring this right. The term usually refers to voting at meetings, but marriages by proxy are possible.

Prud'hon, Pierre Paul (1758–1823) French painter. One of the minor Romantic artists, opposed to the neoclassicism of Jacques-Louis ▷David, he is best known for his portraits and his mythological and allegorical subjects, such as *Love and Friendship* (*c.* 1793; Minneapolis Institute of Arts). He was patronized by Napoleon.

Prussia northern German state 1618–1945 on the Baltic coast. It was an independent kingdom until 1867, when it became, under Otto von ▷Bismarck, the military power of the North German Confederation and part of the German Empire in 1871 under the Prussian king Wilhelm I. West Prussia became part of Poland under the Treaty of ▷Versailles, and East Prussia was largely incorporated into the USSR after 1945.

prussic acid former name for ▷hydrocyanic acid.

Prut (or **Pruc** or **Prutul**) river in eastern Europe; length 900 km/565 mi. The Prut rises in the Carpathian Mountains in south-western Ukraine, and flows south to meet the Danube at Reni. For most of its course it forms the frontier between Romania and Moldova.

Prypyat' (or **Pripet**) river in eastern Europe, flowing through southern Belarus and northern Ukraine; length 775 km/482 mi. The Pripyat' is a tributary of the River ▷Dnieper, which it joins 80 km/50 mi above Kiev. The **Pripyat' marshes**, which lie near the river's source in a forested area called Polesye, near Pinsk, were of strategic importance in both World Wars.

Przhevalsky, Nikolai Mikhailovitch (1839–1888) Russian explorer and soldier. In 1870 he crossed the Gobi Desert to Beijing and then went on to the upper reaches of the Chang Jiang River. His attempts to penetrate Tibet as far as Lhasa failed on three occasions, but he continued to explore the mountain regions between Tibet and Mongolia, where he made collections of plants and animals, including a wild camel and a wild horse (the species is now known as **Przhevalsky's horse**).

PS abbreviation for **post scriptum** (Latin 'after writing').

psalm sacred poem or song of praise. The Book of Psalms in the Old Testament is divided into five books containing 150 psalms, traditionally ascribed to David, the second king of Israel. In the Christian church they may be sung antiphonally in plainsong or set by individual composers to music in a great variety of styles, from Josquin Desprez's *De profundis* to Igor Stravinsky's *Symphony of Psalms* (1930).

pseudocarp in botany, a fruitlike structure that incorporates tissue that is not derived from the ovary wall. The additional tissues may be derived from floral parts such as the ▷receptacle and ▷calyx. For example, the coloured, fleshy part of a strawberry develops from the receptacle and the true fruits are small ▷achenes – the 'pips' embedded in its outer surface. Rose hips are a type of pseudocarp that consists of a hollow, fleshy receptacle containing a number of achenes within. Different types of pseudocarp include pineapples, figs, apples, and pears.

pseudocopulation attempted copulation by a male insect with a flower. It results in ▷pollination of the flower and is common in the orchid family, where the flowers of many species resemble a particular species of female bee. When a male bee attempts to mate with a flower, the pollinia (groups of pollen grains) stick to its body. They are transferred to the stigma of another flower when the insect attempts copulation again.

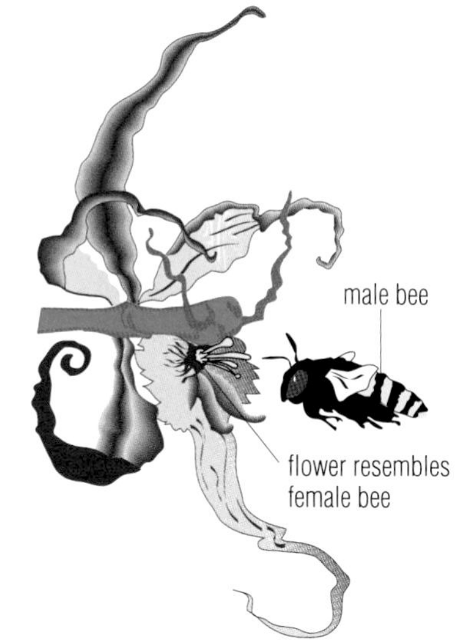

PSEUDOCOPULATION The male bee, attracted to the orchid because of its resemblance to a female bee, attempts to mate with the flower. The bee's efforts cover its body with pollen, which is carried to the next flower it visits.

pseudomorph mineral that has replaced another *in situ* and has retained the external crystal shape of the original mineral.

pseudoscorpion member of the order Pseudoscorpiones, class Arachnida. They are very small, usually less than 8 mm/0.3 in long, and resemble scorpions in having pincers (pedipalps); the rear end, however, is not narrowed and there is no sting. Book scorpions, genus *Chelifer*, are often found in old books, but most pseudoscorpions live as predators in decaying leaf mould.

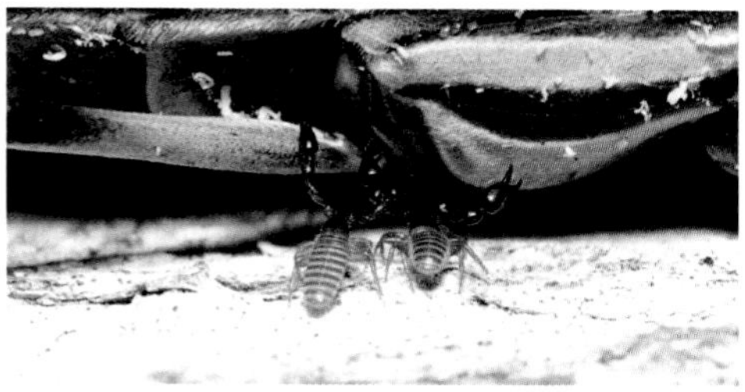

PSEUDOSCORPION Male pseudoscorpions *Cordylochernes scorpioides* heading towards the corpse of a harlequin beetle for scavenging, in Trinidad. *K G Preston-Mafham/ Premaphotos Wildlife*

psi in parapsychology, a hypothetical faculty common to humans and other animals, said to be responsible for ▷extrasensory perception, telekinesis, and other paranormal phenomena.

psoriasis chronic, recurring skin disease characterized by raised, red, scaly patches, on the scalp, elbows, knees, and elsewhere. Tar preparations, steroid creams, and ultraviolet light are used to treat it, and sometimes it disappears spontaneously. Psoriasis may be accompanied by a form of arthritis (inflammation of the joints). Psoriasis affects 100 million people worldwide.

Psyche late Greek personification of the soul as a winged girl or young woman. In Greek mythology, she was the youngest and most beautiful of three princesses. Incensed by her beauty, Aphrodite ordered her son Eros, the god of love, to inspire Psyche with desire for the vilest creatures. Instead, he fell in love with her, in some traditions by accidently grazing himself with his arrow.

psychedelic drug any drug that produces hallucinations or altered states of consciousness. Such sensory experiences may be in the auditory, visual, tactile, olfactory, or gustatory fields or in any combination. Among drugs known to have psychedelic effects are LSD (lysergic acid diethylamide), mescaline, and, to a mild degree, marijuana, along with a number of other plant-derived or synthetically prepared substances.

psychiatry branch of medicine dealing with the diagnosis and treatment of mental disorder, normally divided into the areas of **neurotic conditions**, including anxiety, depression, and hysteria, and **psychotic disorders**, such as schizophrenia. Psychiatric treatment consists of drugs, analysis, or electroconvulsive therapy.

psychoanalysis theory and treatment method for neuroses, developed by Sigmund ▷Freud in the 1890s. Psychoanalysis asserts that the impact of early childhood sexuality and experiences, stored in the ▷unconscious, can lead to the development of adult emotional problems. The main treatment method involves the free association of ideas, and their interpretation by patient and analyst, in order to discover these long-buried events and to grasp their significance to the patient, linking aspects of the patient's historical past with the present relationship to the analyst. Psychoanalytic treatment aims to free the patient from specific symptoms and from irrational inhibitions and anxieties.

psychology systematic study of human and animal behaviour. The first psychology laboratory was founded in 1879 by Wilhelm ▷Wundt at Leipzig, Germany. The subject includes diverse areas of study and application, among them the roles of instinct, heredity, environment, and culture; the processes of sensation, perception, learning, and memory; the bases of motivation and emotion; and the functioning of thought, intelligence, and language. Significant psychologists have included Gustav Fechner, founder of psychophysics; Wolfgang Köhler, one of the ▷Gestalt or 'whole' psychologists; Sigmund Freud and his associates Carl Jung and Alfred Adler; William James, Jean Piaget; Carl Rogers; Hans Eysenck; J B Watson; and B F Skinner.

Related Web site: Experimental Psychology Lab http://www.psych.unizh.ch/genpsy/Ulf/Lab/WebExpPsyLab.html

Karl Kraus
Austrian dramatist and critic

My unconscious knows more about the consciousness of the psychologist than his consciousness knows about my unconscious.

Die Fackel, 18 January 1917

psychopathy personality disorder characterized by chronic antisocial behaviour (violating the rights of others, often violently) and an absence of feelings of guilt about the behaviour.

psychosis (or **psychotic disorder**) general term for a serious mental disorder in which the individual commonly loses contact with reality and may experience hallucinations (seeing or hearing things that do not exist) or delusions (fixed false beliefs). For example, in a paranoid psychosis, an individual may believe that others are plotting against him or her. A major type of psychosis is ▷schizophrenia.

psychosurgery operation to relieve severe mental illness. See ▷leucotomy.

psychotherapy any treatment for psychological problems that involves talking rather than surgery or drugs. Examples include ▷cognitive therapy and ▷psychoanalysis.

psychotic disorder another name for ▷psychosis.

Ptah Egyptian god, the divine potter, a personification of the creative force. Worshipped at ▷Memphis, he was portrayed as a primitive human statue or mummy holding an ankh, symbol of life. He was said to be the father of ▷Imhotep, the physician and architect.

ptarmigan hardy, northern ground-dwelling bird of genus *Lagopus*, family Phasianidae (which also includes ▷grouse), with feathered legs and feet.

pteridophyte simple type of ▷vascular plant. The pteridophytes comprise four classes: the Psilosida, including the most primitive vascular plants, found mainly in the tropics; the Lycopsida, including the club mosses; the Sphenopsida, including the horsetails; and the Pteropsida, including the ferns. They do not produce seeds.

pterodactyl genus of ▷pterosaur.

pterosaur extinct flying reptile of the order Pterosauria, existing in the Mesozoic age. They ranged from the size of a starling to the 12 m/39 ft wingspan of *Arambourgiania philadelphiae*; the largest of the pterosaurs discovered so far. Some had horns on their heads that, when in flight, made a whistling to roaring sound.

Pterosaurs were formerly assumed to be smooth-skinned gliders, but recent discoveries show that at least some were furry, probably warm-blooded, and may have had muscle fibres and blood vessels on their wings, stiffened by moving the hind legs, thus allowing controlled and strong flapping flight.

Ptolemy (*c.* AD 100–*c.* AD 170) Born Claudius Ptolemaeus. Egyptian astronomer and geographer. His *Almagest* developed the theory that Earth is the centre of the universe, with the Sun, Moon, and stars revolving around it. In 1543 the Polish astronomer ▷Copernicus proposed an alternative to the **Ptolemaic system**.

Ptolemy's *Geography* was a standard source of information until the 16th century.

The *Almagest* (he called it *Syntaxis*) contains all his works on astronomical themes, the only authoritative works until the time of ▷Copernicus. Probably inspired by ▷Plato, Ptolemy began with the premise that the Earth was a perfect sphere; all planetary orbits were circular, but those of Mercury and Venus, and possibly Mars (Ptolemy was not sure), were epicyclic (the planets orbited a point that itself was orbiting the Earth); and the sphere of the stars formed a dome with points of light attached or pricked through.

> **Related Web site: Ptolemy, The Man** http://seds.lpl.arizona.edu/billa/psc/theman.html

Ptolemy dynasty of kings of Macedonian origin who ruled Egypt over a period of 300 years; they included:

Ptolemy I (*c.* 367–283 BC) Called 'Soter' (Saviour). Ruler of Egypt from 323 BC, king from 304 BC. One of Alexander the Great's most valued generals, he was given Egypt as his share of Alexander's conquests. His capital, ▷Alexandria, became a centre of trade and learning; here, the mathematician Euclid worked under his patronage, and construction of the great library and museum began. Ptolemy's rule established a dynasty of Macedonian kings that governed Egypt until 30 BC.

Ptolemy II (308–246 BC) Ruler of Egypt 283–246 BC. He consolidated Greek control and administration, constructing a canal from the Red Sea to the Nile as well as the museum, library, and the Pharos (lighthouse) at Alexandria, one of the ▷Seven Wonders of the World. He was the son of Ptolemy I.

Ptolemy XIII (63–47 BC) Joint ruler of Egypt with his sister-wife ▷Cleopatra in the period preceding the Roman annexation of Egypt. He was killed fighting against Julius Caesar.

puberty stage in human development when the individual becomes sexually mature. It may occur from the age of ten upwards. The sexual organs take on their adult form and pubic hair grows. In girls, menstruation begins, and the breasts develop; in boys, the voice breaks and becomes deeper, and facial hair develops.

pubes lowest part of the front of the human trunk, the region where the external generative organs are situated. The underlying bony structure, the pubic arch, is formed by the union in the midline of the two pubic bones, which are the front portions of the hip bones. In women this is more prominent than in men, to allow more room for the passage of the child's head at birth, and it carries a pad of fat and connective tissue, the *mons veneris* (mount of Venus), for its protection.

public corporation company structure that is similar in organization to a public limited company but with no shareholder rights. Such corporations are established to carry out state-owned activities, but are financially independent of the state and are run by a board. The first public corporation to be formed in the UK was the Central Electricity Board in the 1920s.

public inquiry in English law, a legal investigation where witnesses are called and evidence is produced in a similar fashion to a court of law. Inquiries may be held as part of legal procedure, or into a matter of public concern.

public lending right (PLR) method of paying a royalty to authors when books are borrowed from libraries, similar to a royalty on performance of a play or piece of music. Payment to the copyright holder for such borrowings was introduced in Australia in 1974 and in the UK in 1984.

public limited company (plc) registered company in which shares and debentures may be offered to the public. It must have a minimum of two shareholders and there is no upper limit. The company's financial records must be available for any member of the public to scrutinize, and the company's name must carry the words 'public limited company' or initials 'plc'. A public company can raise large sums of money to fuel its development and expansion by inviting the public to buy shares.

Public Order Act UK act of Parliament in 1986 that abolished the common-law offences of riot, rout, unlawful assembly, and affray, and created a new expanded range of statutory offences: riot, violent disorder, affray, threatening behaviour, and disorderly conduct. These are all arrestable offences that may be committed in both private and public places. Prosecution for riot requires the consent of the Director of Public Prosecutions.

public school in England and Wales, a prestigious fee-paying independent school such as Eton, Harrow, Roedean or Benenden. In Scotland, the USA, and many other English-speaking countries, a 'public' school is a state-maintained school, and independent schools are generally known as 'private' schools.

public sector the part of the economy that is owned and controlled by the state, namely central government, local government, and government enterprises. In a ▷command economy, the public sector allocates most of the resources in the economy. The opposite of the public sector is the ▷private sector, where resources are allocated by private individuals and business organizations.

public sector borrowing requirement (PSBR) amount of money needed by a government to cover any deficit in financing its own activities.

public sector debt repayment (PSDR) amount left over when government expenditure (▷public spending) is subtracted from government receipts. This occurs only when government spending is less than government receipts. A PSDR enables a government to repay some of the ▷national debt. A PSDR enables a government to repay some of the ▷national debt.

public spending expenditure by government, covering the military, health, education, infrastructure, development projects, and the cost of servicing overseas borrowing.

Puccini, Giacomo (Antonio Domenico Michele Secondo Maria) (1858–1924) Italian opera composer. His music shows a strong gift for melody and dramatic effect and his operas combine exotic plots with elements of *verismo* (realism). They include *Manon Lescaut* (1893), *La Bohème* (1896), *Tosca* (1900), *Madama Butterfly* (1904), and the unfinished *Turandot* (1926).

GIACOMO PUCCINI Sketch of a costume design, by Umberto Brunelleschi, for the first production of Italian composer Giacomo Puccini's *Turandot* in 1926. *The Art Archive/Puccini Foundation Lucca/Dagli Orti*

puddle clay clay, with sand or gravel, that has had water added and mixed thoroughly so that it becomes watertight. The term was coined in 1762 by the canal builder James Brindley, although the use of such clay in dams goes back to Roman times.

pueblo (Spanish 'village') settlement of flat-roofed stone or adobe houses that are the communal dwelling houses of the Hopi, Zuni, and other American Indians of Arizona and New Mexico. The word has also come to refer to the pueblo-dwelling American Indians of the southwest themselves.

Puerto Rico (in full, the **Commonwealth of Puerto Rico**) easternmost island of the Greater Antilles, situated between the US Virgin Islands and the Dominican Republic; area 9,000 sq km/3,475 sq mi; population (1992 est) 3,336,000. The capital is ▷San Juan. Exports include sugar, tobacco, rum, pineapples, textiles, plastics, chemicals, processed foods, vegetables, and coffee.

puff adder variety of ▷adder, a poisonous snake.

puffball ball-shaped fruiting body of certain fungi (see ▷fungus) that cracks open when it ripens, releasing the enclosed spores in the form of a brown powder; for example, the common puffball (*L. perlatum*). (Genera *Lycoperdon* and *Calvatia*.)

puffer fish fish of the family Tetraodontidae. As a means of defence it inflates its body with water until it becomes spherical and the skin spines become erect. Puffer fish are mainly found in warm waters, where they feed on molluscs, crustaceans, and coral.

puffin any of various sea birds of the genus *Fratercula* of the ▷auk family, found in the northern Atlantic and Pacific. The puffin

PUFFER FISH The spiny puffer fish *Diodon holocanthus* in its alarmed state, in the Caribbean. *Cliff Nelson ARPS/Premaphotos Wildlife*

is about 35 cm/14 in long, with a white face and front, red legs, and a large deep bill, very brightly coloured in summer. Having short wings and webbed feet, puffins are poor fliers but excellent swimmers. They nest in rock crevices, or make burrows, and lay a single egg.

The Atlantic, or common, puffin *F. arctica* has a distinctive striped bill. It breeds in the spring in colonies on islands, and spends the winter at sea.

pug breed of small dog with short wrinkled face, hanging ears, chunky body, and tail curled over the hip. It weighs 6–8 kg/13–18 lb. Its short coat may be black, beige or grey; the beige or grey dogs have black on the face and ears.

Puget Sound inlet of the Pacific Ocean on the west coast of Washington State, USA, extending southwards for about 160 km/100 mi, from the eastern end of the Strait of Juan de Fuca to Olympia, the state capital. It covers an area of about 5,180 sq km/1,990 sq mi, and contains a number of islands; Whidbey, Vashon, and Bainbridge are the largest. The major port of ▷Seattle lies on its eastern shore, and a government naval yard is situated at Bremerton. The sound contains two main branches, Admiralty Inlet and Hood Canal, and receives rivers from the Cascade Range. Its waterways serve a rich industrial and agricultural area, and timber is rafted from its well-wooded shores to lumber and paper mills along the coast.

Pugin, Augustus Welby Northmore (1812–1852) English architect and designer. He collaborated with Charles ▷Barry in the detailed design of the New Palace of Westminster (Houses of Parliament). He did much to instigate the Gothic Revival in England, largely through his books *Contrasts: or a Parallel between the Architecture of the 15th and 19th Centuries* (1836) and *Gothic Ornaments from Ancient Buildings in England and France* (1828–31).

Pugin was born in London and educated at Christ's Hospital. While a boy, he designed some of the furniture of Windsor Castle in 1827. Subsequently he undertook a variety of commissions (especially ecclesiastical), before working on the Houses of Parliament from 1836 to 1852. He became a Roman Catholic, and designed many Roman Catholic churches, including the cathedral of St George at Southwark in London (severely damaged during World War II).

In *Contrasts* and *The Principles of Christian Architecture* (1841), Pugin set out his belief in a close connection between Christianity and Gothic architecture, and attacked what he held to be the 'pagan' methods of classical architecture of his immediate predecessors and some of his contemporaries. His churches include St Giles, Cheadle, Staffordshire (1841-46); St Thomas of Canterbury, Fulham, London; and St Augustine, Ramsgate, England (1846–51), which he paid for himself.

> **Related Web site: Pugin, Augustus** http://www.hubcom.com/pugin/

PUFFIN The puffin's scientific (Latin) name relates to its overall black and white appearance, and describes it as a 'little friar' (*Fratercula*). *Image Bank*

Puglia Italian form of ▷Apulia, a region of Italy.

P'u-i (or Pu-Yi) **Henry** (1906–1967) Last Manchu Qing emperor of China (as Hsuan Tung) from 1908 until he was deposed in the republican revolution of 1912; he was restored for a week in 1917. After his deposition he chose to be called Henry. He was president 1932–34 and emperor 1934–45 of the Japanese puppet state of Manchukuo (see ▷Manchuria).

Captured by Soviet troops, he was returned to China in 1949 after the 1949 communist revolution and put on trial in the new People's Republic of China in 1950. Pardoned by Mao Zedong in 1959, he became a worker in a botanical garden in Beijing. His life is captured in Bernardo Betrolucci's 1987 Academy Award-winning film, *The Last Emperor*.

Pulitzer, Joseph (1847–1911) Hungarian-born US newspaper publisher. He acquired *The World* in 1883 in New York City and, as a publisher, his format set the style for the modern newspaper. After his death, funds provided in his will established in 1912 the school of journalism at Columbia University and the annual Pulitzer Prizes in journalism, literature, and music (from 1917).

Pulitzer came to the USA in 1864 and became a citizen in 1867. A Democrat, he merged two St Louis newspapers and published in 1878 the successful St Louis *Post-Dispatch*. He made *The World* into a voice of the Democratic Party. During a circulation battle with rival publisher William Randolph ▷Hearst's papers, he and Hearst were accused of resorting to 'yellow journalism', or sensationalism.

pulley simple machine consisting of a fixed, grooved wheel, sometimes in a block, around which a rope or chain can be run. A simple pulley serves only to change the direction of the applied effort (as in a simple hoist for raising loads). The use of more than one pulley results in a mechanical advantage, so that a given effort can raise a heavier load.

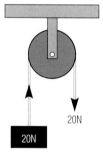

20N

20N

simple pulley (above)

pulley system used for heavy weights (below)

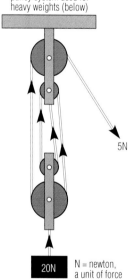

5N

20N   N = newton, a unit of force

PULLEY The mechanical advantage of a pulley increases with the number of rope strands.

pulmonary pertaining to the ▷lungs.

pulsar celestial source that emits pulses of energy at regular intervals, ranging from a few seconds to a few thousandths of a second. Pulsars are thought to be rapidly rotating ▷neutron stars, which flash at radio and other wavelengths as they spin. They were discovered in 1967 by Jocelyn ▷Bell-Burnell and Antony ▷Hewish at the Mullard Radio Astronomy Observatory, Cambridge,

England. By 1998 1,000 pulsars had been discovered since the initial identification in 1967.

Pulsars slow down as they get older, and eventually the flashes fade. Of the 500 known radio pulsars, 20 are millisecond pulsars (flashing 1,000 times a second). Such pulsars are thought to be more than a billion years old. Two pulsars, one (estimated to be 1,000 years old) in the Crab nebula and one (estimated to be 11,000 years old) in the constellation Vela, give out flashes of visible light.

pulse impulse transmitted by the heartbeat throughout the arterial systems of vertebrates. When the heart muscle contracts, it forces blood into the ▷aorta (the chief artery). Because the arteries are elastic, the sudden rise of pressure causes a throb or sudden swelling through them. The actual flow of the blood is about 60 cm/ 2 ft a second in humans. The average adult pulse rate is generally about 70 per minute. The pulse can be felt where an artery is near the surface, for example in the wrist or the neck.

pulse crop such as peas and beans. Pulses are grown primarily for their seeds, which provide a concentrated source of vegetable protein, and make a vital contribution to human diets in poor countries where meat is scarce, and among vegetarians. Soybeans are the major temperate protein crop in the West; most are used for oil production or for animal feed. In Asia, most are processed into soymilk and beancurd. Peanuts dominate pulse production in the tropical world and are generally consumed as human food.

pulse-code modulation (PCM) in physics, a form of digital ▷modulation in which microwaves or light waves (the carrier waves) are switched on and off in pulses of varying length according to a binary code. It is a relatively simple matter to transmit data that are already in binary code, such as those used by computer, by these means. However, if an analogue audio signal is to be transmitted, it must first be converted to a **pulse-amplitude modulated** signal (PAM) by regular sampling of its amplitude. The value of the amplitude is then converted into a binary code for transmission on the carrier wave.

puma (or **cougar** or **mountain lion**) large wild cat *Felis concolor* found in North and South America. Tawny-coated, it is 1.5 m/4.5 ft long with a 1-m/3-ft tail. Pumas live alone, with each male occupying a distinct territory; they eat deer, rodents, and cattle. Pumas need large territories, with females maintaining up to 100 sq km and males even more. Two to four cubs are born and will remain with the mother till they are 18–24 months old (they are completely weaned at six months).

Although in some areas they have been hunted nearly to extinction, in California puma populations have grown, with numbers reaching an estimated 5,000–6,000 by 1996.

pumice light volcanic rock produced by the frothing action of expanding gases during the solidification of lava. It has the texture of a hard sponge and is used as an abrasive.

pump any device for moving liquids and gases, or compressing gases.

Some pumps, such as the traditional **lift pump** used to raise water from wells, work by a reciprocating (up-and-down) action. Movement of a piston in a cylinder with a one-way valve creates a partial vacuum in the cylinder, thereby sucking water into it.

pumped storage hydroelectric plant that uses surplus electricity to pump water back into a high-level reservoir. In normal working conditions the water flows from this reservoir through the ▷turbines to generate power for feeding into the grid. At times of low power demand, electricity is taken from the grid to turn the turbines into pumps that then pump the water back again. This ensures that there is always a maximum 'head' of water in the reservoir to give the maximum output when required.

pumpkin creeping plant whose large round fruit has a thick orange rind, pulpy flesh, and many seeds. Pumpkins are used in cookery (especially pies and soups) and are hollowed out to form candle lanterns at Halloween. (Genus *Cucurbita pepo*, family Cucurbitaceae.)

pun ▷figure of speech, a play on words, or double meaning that is technically known as **paronomasia** (Greek 'adapted meaning'). Double meaning can be accidental, often resulting from homonymy, or the multiple meaning of words; puns, however, are deliberate, intended as jokes or as clever and compact remarks.

Related Web site: Pun Page http://punpunpun.com/

punctuated equilibrium model evolutionary theory developed by Niles Eldredge and US palaeontologist Stephen Jay Gould in 1972 to explain discontinuities in the fossil record. It claims that evolution continues through periods of rapid change alternating with periods of relative stability (stasis), and that the appearance of new lineages is a separate process from the gradual evolution of adaptive changes within a species.

punctuation system of conventional signs (punctuation marks) and spaces employed to organize written and printed language in order to make it as readable, clear, and logical as possible.

Related Web site: Punctuation Made Simple http://www.cas.usf.edu/ JAC/pms/

Pune (formerly **Poona**) city in Maharashtra, India, 100 km/60 mi southeast of Mumbai (formerly Bombay) on the Mutha River; population (1991) 2,494,000. Products include chemicals, rubber, rice, sugar, cotton, paper, and jewellery. Industries include cars, trucks, scooters, and motorbikes; pumps, cables, machinery, arms and ammunitions, cutting tools, televisions, boilers, and generators.

Punic (Latin *Punicus* 'a Phoenician') relating to ▷Carthage, ancient city in North Africa founded by the Phoenicians.

Punic Wars three wars between ▷Rome and ▷Carthage: **First Punic War** 264–241 BC, resulted in the defeat of the Carthaginians under ▷Hamilcar Barca and the cession of Sicily to Rome; **Second Punic War** 218–201 BC, Hannibal invaded Italy, defeated the Romans at Trebia, Trasimene, and at Cannae (under ▷Fabius Maximus), but was finally defeated himself by Scipio Africanus Major at Zama (now in Algeria); **Third Punic War** 149–146 BC, ended in the destruction of Carthage, and its possessions becoming the Roman province of Africa.

Punjab (Sanskrit 'five rivers': the Indus tributaries Jhelum, Chenab, Ravi, Beas, and Sutlej) former state of British India, now divided between India and Pakistan. Punjab was annexed by Britain in 1849 after the Sikh Wars (1845–46 and 1848–49), and formed into a province with its capital at Lahore. Under the British, West Punjab was extensively irrigated, and land was granted to Indians who had served in the British army.

Punjab state of northwest India, bordering Pakistan; area 50,400 sq km/19,454 sq mi; population (2001 est) 24,475,000. The capital is ▷Chandigarh. Textiles and sewing machines are produced; wheat, rice, sugar, maize, millet, barley, and cotton are grown.
Geography The rivers Sutlej and Beas, tributaries of the ▷Indus, flow through the gently sloping alluvial plain that makes up most of the state.
Features The region is mainly agricultural, with crops chiefly grown under irrigation through schemes such as the Bhakra Nangal dam on the Sutlej. There are ruins from the ▷Indus Valley civilization (2500 to 1600 BC). Towns and cities include Amritsar, Jalandhar, Faridkot, and Ludhiana.
Language and religion The main language is Punjabi. Religions are Sikh (60%) and Hindu (30%); there is friction between the two groups.
History In 1919 unrest led to the Punjab riots (known as the ▷Amritsar Massacre). The present state was formed at the partition of India in 1947 (see ▷Punjab massacres). The Indian Punjab was further divided into three areas: Himachal Pradesh, the Patiala and East Punjab States Union, and the state of East Punjab. In 1956 the latter two were merged to form Punjab (India), which was again divided in 1966 along linguistic lines to create three states: the predominantly Hindu states of Himachal Pradesh and Haryana (which shares the capital Chandigarh with Punjab); and the remaining Punjab state, 60% of which are Punjabi-speaking Sikhs.

Punjab state of northeast Pakistan; area 205,344 sq km/79,263 sq mi; population (1993 est) 72,300,000. The capital is ▷Lahore. Wheat is cultivated (by irrigation). The state contains a semi-arid alluvial plain, drained by the ▷Indus River and its tributaries, the Jhelum, Chenab, Ravi and Sutlej rivers. To the north are the Himalayan foothills, and the Salt Range mountains (containing oil) are between the Indus and Jhelum valleys. There are ruins from the ▷Indus Valley civilization (2500 to 1600 BC). The main languages are Punjabi and Urdu; the principal religion is Islam. The state was formed as West Punjab in 1947 upon partition of India and the formation of ▷Pakistan.

Punjabi the majority ethnic group living in the Punjab. Approximately 37 million live in the Pakistan half of Punjab, while another 14 million live on the Indian side of the border. In addition to Sikhs, there are Rajputs in Punjab, some of whom have adopted Islam. The Punjabi language belongs to the Indo-Iranian branch of the Indo-European family. It is considered by some to be a variety of Hindi, by others to be a distinct language.

Punjab massacres in the violence occurring after the partition of India in 1947, more than a million people died while relocating in the Punjab. The eastern section became an Indian state, while the western area, dominated by the Muslims, went to Pakistan. Violence occurred as Muslims fled from eastern Punjab, and Hindus and Sikhs moved from Pakistan to India.

punk movement of disaffected youth of the late 1970s, manifesting itself in fashions and music designed to shock or intimidate. **Punk rock** began in the UK and stressed aggressive performance within a three-chord, three-minute format, as exemplified by the Sex Pistols. The punk aesthetic continued to be revived periodically with the nostalgia boom of the 1990s, supported by the growth of a neo-punk movement in the USA and by groups such as the Clash being accorded the status of rock 'n' roll 'classics'.

Related Web site: Punk Page http://www.thepunkpage.com/

pupa nonfeeding, largely immobile stage of some insect life cycles, in which larval tissues are broken down, and adult tissues and structures are formed.

In many insects, the pupa is **exarate**, with the appendages (legs, antennae, wings) visible outside the pupal case; in butterflies and moths, it is called a chrysalis, and is **obtect**, with the appendages developing inside the case.

PUPA The pupae or chrysalises produced by many butterflies inhabiting tropical rainforests often bear a striking resemblance to a large drop of water. In an environment where water drips almost constantly from leaves, this makes them less conspicuous to predators. *Premaphotos Wildlife*

puppet figure manipulated on a small stage, usually by an unseen operator. The earliest known puppets are from 10th-century BC China. The types include **finger** or **glove puppets** (such as Punch); **string marionettes** (which reached a high artistic level in ancient Burma and Sri Lanka and in Italian princely courts from the 16th to 18th centuries, and for which the composer Franz Joseph Haydn wrote his operetta *Dido* in 1778); **shadow silhouettes** (operated by rods and seen on a lit screen, as in Java); and **bunraku** (devised in Osaka, Japan), in which three or four black-clad operators on stage may combine to work each puppet about 1 m/3 ft high.

Purcell, Henry (*c.* 1659–1695) English baroque composer. His music balances high formality with melodic expression of controlled intensity, for example, the opera *Dido and Aeneas* (1689) and music for Dryden's *King Arthur* (1691) and for *The Fairy Queen* (1692). He wrote more than 500 works, ranging from secular operas and incidental music for plays to cantatas and church music.

purchasing-power parity (PPP) system for comparing standards of living between different countries. Comparing the gross domestic product of different countries involves first converting them to a common currency (usually US dollars or pounds sterling), a conversion which is subject to large fluctuations with variations in exchange rates. Purchasing-power parity aims to overcome this by measuring how much money in the currency of those countries is required to buy a comparable range of goods and services.

purdah (Persian and Hindu 'curtain') seclusion of women practised by some Islamic and Hindu peoples. It had begun to disappear with the adoption of Western culture, but the fundamentalism of the 1980s revived it; for example, the wearing of the chador (an all-enveloping black mantle) in Iran.

Pure Land Buddhism dominant form of Buddhism in China and Japan. It emphasizes faith in and love of the Buddha Amitābha (Amida in Japan, Amituofo in China), the ideal 'Buddha of boundless light', who has vowed that all believers who call on his name will be reborn in his Pure Land, or Western Paradise, Sukhāvati. There are over 16 million Pure Land Buddhists in Japan.

purgatory in Roman Catholic belief, a purificatory state or place where the souls of those who have died in a state of grace can expiate their venial sins, with a limited amount of suffering.

purge removal (for example, from a political party) of suspected opponents or persons regarded as undesirable (often by violent means). During the 1930s purges were conducted in the USSR under Joseph ▷Stalin, carried out by the secret police against political opponents, Communist Party members, minorities, civil servants, and large sections of the armed forces' officer corps. Some 10 million people were executed or deported to labour camps from 1934 to 1938.

Purim Jewish festival celebrated in February or March (the 14th of Adar in the Jewish calendar), commemorating Esther, who saved the Jews from destruction in 473 BC during the Persian occupation.

Puritan from 1564, a member of the Church of England who wished to eliminate Roman Catholic survivals in church ritual, or substitute a presbyterian for an episcopal form of church government. Activities included the ▷Marprelate controversy, a pamphleteering attack carried out under the pseudonym 'Martin Marprelate'. The term also covers the separatists who withdrew from the church altogether. The Puritans were characterized by a strong conviction of human sinfulness and the wrath of God and by a devotion to plain living and hard work.

purple emperor handsome high-flying butterfly, with rusty black wings, lustrous in the male, and with seven white spots and a transverse white band. The purple emperor *Apatura iris* is in order Lepidoptera, class Insecta, phylum Arthropoda.

purpura condition marked by purplish patches on the skin or mucous membranes due to localized spontaneous bleeding. It may be harmless, as sometimes with the elderly, or linked with disease, allergy, or drug reactions.

pus yellowish fluid that forms in the body as a result of bacterial infection; it includes white blood cells (leucocytes), living and dead bacteria, dead tissue, and serum. An enclosed collection of pus is called an abscess.

Pusan (or Busan) chief industrial port (textiles, rubber, salt, fishing) of Korea; population (2002 est) 4,085,300. It was invaded by the Japanese in 1592 and opened to foreign trade in 1883.

Related Web site: Welcome to Pusan http://pusanweb.com/

Pusey, Edward Bouverie (1800–1882) English Church of England priest and theologian. In 1835 he joined J H ▷Newman in the ▷Oxford Movement, and contributed to the series *Tracts for the Times*. After Newman's conversion to Roman Catholicism in 1845, Pusey became leader of the High Church Party, or Puseyites, striving until his death to keep them from conversion.

Pushkin, Aleksandr Sergeyevich (1799–1837) Russian poet and writer. His works include the novel in verse *Eugene Onegin* (1823–31) and the tragic drama *Boris Godunov* (1825). Pushkin's range was wide, and his willingness to experiment freed later Russian writers from many of the archaic conventions of the literature of his time.

Pushkin was born in Moscow. He was exiled in 1820 for his political verse and in 1824 was in trouble for his atheistic opinions. He wrote ballads such as *The Gypsies* (1827), and the prose pieces *The Captain's Daughter* (1836) and *The Queen of Spades* (1834). He was mortally wounded in a duel with his brother-in-law.

Pushtu another name for the ▷Pashto language of Afghanistan and northern Pakistan.

Puttnam, David (Terence) (1941–) English film producer. He played a major role in reviving the British film industry internationally in the 1980s, and has been involved in an eclectic range of films with a variety of film-makers. They include *Midnight Express* (1978), *Chariots of Fire* (1981) (Academy Award for best film), *The Killing Fields* (1984), and *Memphis Belle* (1990). He was head of Columbia Pictures 1986–87.

In the 1990s he produced *Meeting Venus* (1991), *Le Confessional* (1995), and *The World of Moss* (1998).

He was made a life peer in 1997.

Pu-Yi alternative transliteration of the name of the last Chinese emperor, Henry ▷P'u-i.

PVC abbreviation for ▷polyvinyl chloride.

> **Henry Purcell**
> *Musick is yet in its nonage, a forward child, which gives hope of what it may be hereafter in England . . . 'Tis now learning Italian, which is its best master, and studying a little of the French air, to give it somewhat more of gayety and fashion.*
> On himself, in the preface to his semi-opera *The Prophetess, or the History of Dioclesian* (1690)

PURITAN English Puritan family *c.* 1563. *Philip Sauvain Picture Collection*

pyelitis inflammation of the renal pelvis, the central part of the kidney where urine accumulates before discharge. It is caused by bacterial infection and is more common in women than in men.

Pygmalion in Greek mythology, a king of Cyprus who fell in love with an ivory statue he had carved. When Aphrodite breathed life into it, he married the woman and named her Galatea. Their children were Paphos and Metharme.

Pygmy (or **Negrillo**) member of any of several groups of small-statured, dark-skinned peoples living in the equatorial jungles of Africa. The most important groups are the Twa, Aka, Mbuti, Binga, Baka, Gelli Efé; their combined population is less than 200,000. They were probably the aboriginal inhabitants of the region, before the arrival of farming peoples from elsewhere. They live nomadically in small groups, as hunter-gatherers; they also trade with other, settled people in the area.

Pym, John (1584–1643) English Parliamentarian, largely responsible for the ▷Petition of Right in 1628. As leader of the Puritan opposition in the ▷Long Parliament from 1640, he moved the impeachment of Charles I's advisers the Earl of Strafford and William Laud, drew up the ▷Grand Remonstrance, and was the chief of five members of Parliament Charles I wanted arrested in 1642. The five hid themselves and then emerged triumphant when the king left London.

Pynchon, Thomas (1937–) US novelist. With great stylistic verve, he created a bizarre, labyrinthine world in his books, the first of which was *V* (1963), a parodic detective story in pursuit of the endlessly elusive Lady V. It was followed by the shorter comic quest novel, *The Crying of Lot 49* (1966), before his gargantuan tour-de-force *Gravity's Rainbow* (1973), which represents a major achievement in 20th-century literature, with its fantastic imagery and esoteric language, drawn from mathematics and science.

Pyongyang capital and industrial city of North Korea; population (1996 est) 2,500,000. The oldest city in Korea, it was the capital of the Choson kingdom in the 3rd century BC. Industries include aircraft manufacture, coal, iron, steel, textiles, and chemicals. The university was founded in 1946.

pyramid four-sided building with triangular sides. Pyramids were used in ancient Egypt to enclose a royal tomb; for example, the Great Pyramid of Khufu/Cheops at El Giza, near Cairo, 230 m/ 755 ft square and 147 m/481 ft high. The three pyramids at Giza were considered one of the ▷Seven Wonders of the World. In Babylon and Assyria, broadly stepped pyramids (▷ziggurats) were used as the base for a shrine to a god: the Tower of ▷Babel was probably one of these.

Related Web site: Pyramids – The Inside Story http://www.pbs.org/wgbh/nova/pyramid/

PYRAMID The Step Pyramid at Sakkara, Egypt is over 60 m/197 ft high. Built around 2737–2717 BC from blocks of stone, this was the first pyramid ever constructed, and at the time was the largest monumental stone structure in the world. *Corel*

pyramid in geometry, a three-dimensional figure with triangular side-faces meeting at a common vertex (point) and with a ▷polygon as its base. The volume V of a pyramid is given by $V = \frac{1}{3} Bh$, where B is the area of the base and h is the perpendicular height.

pyramidal peak angular mountain peak with concave faces found in glaciated areas; for example, the Matterhorn in Switzerland. It is formed when three or four ▷corries (steep-sided hollows) are eroded, back-to-back, around the sides of a mountain, leaving an isolated peak in the middle.

Pyrenees (French **Pyrénées**; Spanish **Pirineos**) mountain range in southwest Europe between France and Spain; length about 435 km/270 mi; highest peak Aneto (French Néthon) 3,404 m/ 11,172 ft. ▷Andorra lies entirely within the range. Hydroelectric power has encouraged industrial development in the foothills.

pyrethrum popular name for several cultivated chrysanthemums. The ornamental species *C. coccineum*, and hybrids derived from it, are commonly grown in gardens. Pyrethrum powder, made from the dried flower heads of some species, is a powerful pesticide for aphids and mosquitoes. (Genus *Chrysanthemum*, family Compositae.)

pyridine C_5H_5N a heterocyclic compound (see ▷cyclic compounds). It is a liquid with a sickly smell and occurs in coal tar. It is soluble in water, acts as a strong ▷base, and is used as a solvent, mainly in the manufacture of plastics.

pyridoxine (or vitamin B_6) $C_8H_{11}NO_3$ water-soluble ▷vitamin of the B complex. There is no clearly identifiable disease associated with deficiency but its absence from the diet can give rise to malfunction of the central nervous system and general skin disorders. Good sources are liver, meat, milk, and cereal grains. Related compounds may also show vitamin B_6 activity.

pyrite iron sulphide FeS_2; also called **fool's gold** because of its yellow metallic lustre. Pyrite has a hardness of 6–6.5 on the Mohs scale. It is used in the production of sulphuric acid.

pyroclastic deposit deposit made up of fragments of rock, ranging in size from fine ash to large boulders, ejected during an explosive volcanic eruption.

pyrometer in physics, any instrument used for measuring high temperatures by means of the thermal radiation emitted by a hot object. In a **radiation pyrometer** the emitted radiation is detected by a sensor such as a thermocouple. In an **optical pyrometer** the colour of an electrically heated filament is matched visually to that of the emitted radiation. Pyrometers are especially useful for measuring the temperature of distant, moving or inaccessible objects.

pyroxene any one of a group of minerals, silicates of calcium, iron, and magnesium with a general formula X,YSi_2O_6, found in igneous and metamorphic rocks. The internal structure is based on single chains of silicon and oxygen. Diopside ($X = Ca$, $Y = Mg$) and augite ($X = Ca$, $Y = Mg,Fe,Al$) are common pyroxenes.

Pyrrho (c. 360–c. 270 BC) Greek philosopher, founder of ▷Scepticism, who maintained that since certainty was impossible, peace of mind lay in renouncing all claims to knowledge.

Pyrrhus (319–272 BC) King of Epirus (an area of northwestern Greece and southern Albania) from 307 BC. In the early years of his reign he struggled to maintain his throne and retain independence from Macedonian control. In 280 BC he invaded Italy as an ally of the Tarentines against Rome. He twice defeated the Romans, but with such heavy losses that a 'Pyrrhic victory' has come to mean a victory not worth winning. He returned to Epirus in 275 after his defeat at Beneventum and was killed in street fighting at Argos.

Pythagoras (c. 580–500 BC) Greek mathematician and philosopher who formulated ▷Pythagoras' theorem.

Much of Pythagoras' work concerned numbers, to which he assigned mystical properties. For example, he classified numbers into triangular ones (1, 3, 6, 10, ...), which can be represented as a triangular array, and square ones (1, 4, 9, 16, ...), which form squares. He also observed that any two adjacent triangular numbers added together form a square number (for example, 1 + 3 = 4; 3 + 6 = 9; 6 + 10 = 16).

Related Web sites:Pythagoras http://www.utm.edu/research/iep/p/pythagor.htm
Pythagoras' Theorem http://www-groups.dcs.st-and.ac.uk/~history/Diagrams/PythagorasTheorem.gif

Pythagoras' theorem in geometry, a theorem stating that in a right-angled triangle, the square of the hypotenuse (the longest side) is equal to the sum of the squares of the other two sides. If the hypotenuse is h units long and the lengths of the other sides are a and b, then $h^2 = a^2 + b^2$.

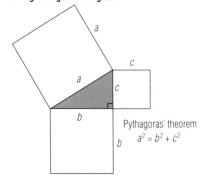

for right-angled triangles

Pythagoras' theorem
$a^2 = b^2 + c^2$

PYTHAGORAS' THEOREM The theorem is likely to have been known long before the time of Pythagoras. It was probably used by the ancient Egyptians to lay out the pyramids.

The theorem provides a way of calculating the length of any side of a right-angled triangle if the lengths of the other two sides are known. It is also used to determine certain trigonometrical relationships such as $\sin^2 \theta + \cos^2 \theta = 1$.

python any constricting snake of the Old World subfamily Pythoninae of the family Boidae, which also includes ▷boas and the ▷anaconda. Pythons are found in the tropics of Africa, Asia, and Australia. Unlike boas, they lay eggs rather than produce living young. Some species are small, but the reticulated python *Python reticulatus* of Southeast Asia can grow to 10 m/33 ft.

A healthy adult can survive from six to twelve months without food. When food is scarce females do not ovulate so energy is not used up in reproducing.

Related Web site: Carpet Python http://www.seaworld.org/animal_bytes/carpet_pythonab.html

Q

Qaboos bin Said (1940–) Sultan of Oman, the 14th descendant of the Albusaid family. Opposed to the conservative views of his father, he overthrew him in 1970 in a bloodless coup and assumed the sultanship. Since then he has followed more liberal and expansionist policies, while maintaining his country's position of international nonalignment.

Qaddafi alternative form of ▷Khaddhafi, Libyan leader.

Qaraghandy (formerly **Karaganda** (1857–1991)) industrial city and capital of the Qaraghandy oblast (region) in central-eastern Kazakhstan; population (1996) 1,339,900. The city lies at the centre of an area rich in minerals, where coal, copper, tungsten, and manganese are mined. Iron and steel mills are located here, and food-processing also takes place. Qaraghandy is joined by canal with the Irtysh River and lies on the railway line linking Almaty with the Trans-Siberian Railway.

qat (or **kat** or **khat**) evergreen shrub with white flowers belonging to the staff-tree family, native to Africa and Asia. The leaves are chewed as a mild narcotic drug in some Arab countries. Its use was banned in Somalia 1983. (Genus *Catha edulis*, family Celastraceae.)

Qatar see country box.

QC abbreviation for ▷Queen's Counsel.

QED abbreviation for **quod erat demonstrandum** (Latin 'which was to be proved'), added at the end of a geometry proof.

Qin dynasty China's first imperial dynasty 221–206 BC. It was established by ▷Shi Huangdi, ruler of the Qin, the most powerful of the Zhou era warring states. The power of the feudal nobility was curbed and greater central authority exerted over north central China, which was unified through a bureaucratic administrative system.

Qinghai (or **Tsinghai**; Mongolian **Koko Nor**; Tibetan **Amdo**) province of northwest China, bounded to the north by Gansu, to the south by Sichuan, to the west by Tibet, and to the northwest by Xinjiang Uygur Autonomous Region; area 721,000 sq km/ 278,400 sq mi; population (1996) 4,448,000. The capital is ▷Xining. Industries include minerals, chemicals, livestock, oil, and medical products. There is animal rearing and bee-keeping.

Qom (or **Qum**, or **Kom**, or **Kum**) holy city of Shiite Muslims, in central Iran, 145 km/90 mi south of Tehran on the Qom River; population (1991) 681,300. Pottery, textiles, shoes, and glass are the main industries. The Islamic academy of Madresseh Faizieh in 1920 became the headquarters of Ayatollah ▷Khomeini.

quadratic equation in mathematics, a polynomial equation of second degree (that is, an equation containing as its highest power the square of a variable, such as x^2). The general formula of such equations is

$$ax^2 + bx + c = 0$$

in which a, b, and c are real numbers, and only the coefficient a cannot equal 0.

In ▷coordinate geometry, a quadratic function represents a ▷parabola.

quadrilateral plane (two-dimensional) figure with four straight sides. The following are all quadrilaterals, each with distinguishing properties: **square** with four equal angles and sides, four axes of symmetry; **rectangle** with four equal angles, opposite sides equal, two axes of symmetry; **rhombus** with four equal sides, two axes of symmetry; **parallelogram** with two pairs of parallel sides, rotational symmetry; **kite** with two pairs of adjacent equal sides and one axis of symmetry; and **trapezium** one pair of parallel sides.

Quadruple Alliance in European history, three military alliances of four nations:
The Quadruple Alliance 1718 Austria, Britain, France, and the United Provinces (Netherlands) joined forces to prevent Spain from annexing Sardinia and Sicily;
The Quadruple Alliance 1813 Austria, Britain, Prussia, and Russia allied to defeat the French emperor Napoleon; renewed in 1815 and 1818. See Congress of ▷Vienna.
The Quadruple Alliance 1834 Britain, France, Portugal, and Spain guaranteed the constitutional monarchies of Spain and Portugal against rebels in the Carlist War.

quaestor junior Roman magistrate whose primary role was to oversee the finances of individual provinces under the Republic. Quaestors originated as assistants to the consuls. They often commanded units in the army when the governor of the province fought a campaign.

quagga South African zebra that became extinct in the 1880s. It was brown, with a white tail and legs, and unlike surviving zebra species, had stripes only on its head, neck, and forequarters.

quail any of several genera of small ground-dwelling birds of the family Phasianidae, which also includes grouse, pheasants, bobwhites, and prairie chickens. Species are found in Africa, India, Australia, North America, and Europe. The **common** or **European quail** *Coturnix coturnix* is about 18 cm/7 in long, reddish-brown, with a white throat with a black patch at the bottom, and a yellowish belly. It is found in Europe, Asia, and Africa, and has been introduced to North America. The nest is a small hollow in the ground, and in it are laid about ten yellowish-white eggs blotched with brown. The bird feeds upon grain seeds and insects.

Quaker popular name, originally derogatory, for a member of the Society of ▷Friends.

qualitative analysis in chemistry, a procedure for determining the identity of the component(s) of a single substance or mixture. A series of simple reactions and tests can be carried out on a compound to determine the elements present.

quango (acronym for quasi-autonomous nongovernmental organization) any administrative body that is nominally independent but relies on government funding; for example, the British Council (1935), the Equal Opportunities Commission (1975) in the UK, and the Environmental Protection Agency (1970) in the USA.

Quant, Mary (1934–) English fashion designer. She popularized the miniskirt in the UK and was one of the first designers to make clothes specifically for the teenage and early twenties market, producing bold, simple outfits which were in tune with the 'swinging London' of the 1960s. Her designs were sharp, angular, and streetwise, and she combined spots, stripes, and checks in an original way. Her boutique in Chelsea's King's Road, opened in 1955, was named Bazaar. In the 1970s she extended into cosmetics and textile design.

Born in London, Quant studied at Goldsmith's College of Art. An exhibition, **Mary Quant's London**, was held at the Museum of London in 1973–74. In 1990 she won the British Fashion Council's Hall of Fame award. Her cosmetics company became part of the Max Factor empire.

quantitative analysis in chemistry, a procedure for determining the precise amount of a known component present in a single substance or mixture. A known amount of the substance is subjected to particular procedures.

Gravimetric analysis determines the mass of each constituent present; ▷volumetric analysis determines the concentration of a solution by ▷titration against a solution of known concentration.

quantum chromodynamics (QCD) in physics, a theory describing the interactions of ▷quarks, the ▷elementary particles that make up all ▷hadrons (subatomic particles such as protons and neutrons). In quantum chromodynamics, quarks are considered to interact by exchanging particles called gluons, which carry the ▷strong nuclear force, and whose role is to 'glue' quarks together.

quantum electrodynamics (QED) in physics, a theory describing the interaction of charged subatomic particles within electric and magnetic fields. It combines ▷quantum theory and ▷relativity, and considers charged particles to interact by the

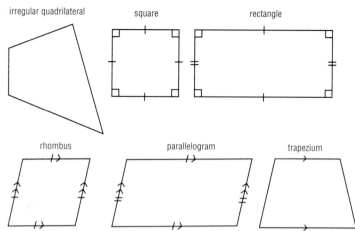

QUADRILATERAL The diagram shows different types of quadrilateral, each with distinguishing properties.

exchange of photons. QED is remarkable for the accuracy of its predictions; for example, it has been used to calculate the value of some physical quantities to an accuracy of ten decimal places, a feat equivalent to calculating the distance between New York and Los Angeles to within the thickness of a hair. The theory was developed by US physicists Richard Feynman and Julian Schwinger and by Japanese physicist Sin-Itiro Tomonaga in 1948.

quantum mechanics branch of physics dealing with the interaction of ▷matter and ▷radiation, the structure of the ▷atom, the motion of atomic particles, and with related phenomena (see ▷elementary particle and ▷quantum theory).

quantum number in physics, one of a set of four numbers that uniquely characterize an ▷electron and its state in an ▷atom. The **principal quantum number** n defines the electron's main energy level. The **orbital quantum number** l relates to its angular momentum. The **magnetic quantum number** m describes the energies of electrons in a magnetic field. The **spin quantum number** m_s gives the spin direction of the electron.

quantum theory (or **quantum mechanics**) in physics, the theory that ▷energy does not have a continuous range of values, but is, instead, absorbed or radiated discontinuously, in multiples of definite, indivisible units called quanta. Just as earlier theory showed how light, generally seen as a wave motion, could also in some ways be seen as composed of discrete particles (▷photons), quantum theory shows how atomic particles such as electrons may also be seen as having wavelike properties. Quantum theory is the basis of particle physics, modern theoretical chemistry, and the solid-state physics that describes the behaviour of the silicon chips used in computers.

The theory began with the work of Max Planck in 1900 on radiated energy, and was extended by Albert Einstein to electromagnetic radiation generally, including light. Danish physicist Niels Bohr used it to explain the ▷spectrum of light emitted by excited hydrogen atoms. Later work by Erwin Schrödinger, Werner Heisenberg, Paul Dirac, and others elaborated the theory to what is called quantum mechanics (or wave mechanics).

Related Web site: Quantum Age Begins http://www-history. mcs.st-and.ac.uk/history/HistTopics/The_Quantum_age_begins.html

quarantine (from French *quarantine* '40 days') any period for which people, animals, plants, or vessels may be detained in isolation to prevent the spread of contagious disease.

In the UK, imported animals are quarantined to prevent the spread of ▷rabies.

In September 1998 Britain announced that its quarantine regulations would be changing from April 2000, to allow animals from the European Union, and rabies-free islands, such as Australia and New Zealand, into the country without a period of quarantine. This applies only to microchipped animals with vaccination certificates.

quark in physics, the ▷elementary particle that is the fundamental constituent of all ▷hadrons (subatomic particles that experience the strong nuclear force and divided into baryons, such as neutrons and protons, and mesons). Quarks have electric charges that are fractions of the electronic charge ($+\frac{2}{3}$ or $-\frac{1}{3}$ of the electronic charge). There are six types, or 'flavours': up, down, top, bottom, strange, and charmed, each of which has three varieties, or 'colours': red, green, and blue (visual colour is not meant, although the analogy is useful in many ways). To each quark there is an antiparticle, called an antiquark. See ▷quantum chromodynamics (QCD).

quart imperial liquid or dry measure, equal to two pints or 1.136 litres. In the USA, a liquid quart is equal to 0.946 litre, while a dry quart is equal to 1.101 litres.

quarter day in the financial year, any of the four dates on which such payments as ground rents become due: in England 25 March (Lady Day), 24 June (Midsummer Day), 29 September (Michaelmas), and 25 December (Christmas Day).

quartz crystalline form of ▷silica SiO₂, one of the most abundant minerals of the Earth's crust (12% by volume). Quartz occurs in many different kinds of rock, including sandstone and granite. It ranks 7 on the Mohs scale of hardness and is resistant to chemical or mechanical breakdown. Quartzes vary according to the size and purity of their crystals. Crystals of pure quartz are coarse, colourless, transparent, show no cleavage, and fracture unevenly; this form is usually called rock crystal. Impure coloured varieties, often used as gemstones, include ▷agate, citrine quartz, and ▷amethyst. Quartz is also used as a general name for the cryptocrystalline and noncrystalline varieties of silica, such as chalcedony, chert, and opal.

Quartz is used in ornamental work and industry, where its reaction to electricity makes it valuable in electronic instruments (see ▷piezoelectric effect). Quartz can also be made synthetically.

quartzite ▷metamorphic rock consisting of pure quartz sandstone that has recrystallized under increasing heat and pressure.

quasar (from 'quasi-stellar object' or QSO) one of the most distant extragalactic objects known, discovered in 1963. Quasars appear starlike, but each emits more energy than 100 giant galaxies. They are thought to be at the centre of galaxies, their brilliance emanating from the stars and gas falling towards an immense ▷black hole at their nucleus. Most quasars are found in elliptical galaxies.

Quasar light shows a large ▷red shift, indicating that the quasars are very distant. Some quasars emit radio waves (see ▷radio astronomy), which is how they were first identified, but most are radio-quiet. The furthest are over 10 billion light years away.

QUARTZITE Quartzite rocks in Maglaliesberg, Transvaal, Southern Africa. *K G Preston-Mafham/Premaphotos Wildlife*

quassia any of a group of tropical American trees with bitter bark and wood. The heartwood of *Q. amara* is a source of quassiin, an infusion of which was formerly used as a tonic; it is now used in insecticides. (Genus *Quassia*, family Simaroubaceae.)

Quaternary Period period of geological time from 1.64 million years ago through to the present. It is divided into the ▷Pleistocene and ▷Holocene epochs.

Quatre Bras, Battle of battle fought on 16 June 1815 during the Napoleonic Wars, in which the British commander Wellington defeated French forces under Marshal Ney. It is named after a hamlet in Brabant, Belgium, 32 km/20 mi southeast of Brussels.

Quayle, (James) Dan(forth) (1947–   ) US Republican politician, vice president 1989–93. A congressman for Indiana 1977–81, he became a senator in 1981.

Québec (Iroquois *Kebec*, 'a place where waters narrow') capital and port of ▷Québec province, Canada, at the junction of the Saint-Charles and St Lawrence rivers, Canada; population (2001 est) 169,100, metropolitan area (1996) 697,600. It is a major inland seaport, and a commercial, financial, and administrative centre. Industries include printing and publishing; and the production of paper, pulp, wood products, electronic goods, textiles, and leather. Lumber and wheat are exported. It is a centre of French culture, and most of its inhabitants are French-speaking.

Growth of the city Québec was founded by the French explorer Samuel de ▷Champlain as a fur-trading post in 1608. The British, under General ▷Wolfe, captured Québec in 1759 after a battle on the nearby Plains of Abraham; both Wolfe and the French commander ▷Montcalm were killed. Québec was capital of Lower Canada 1791–1841; capital of the United Provinces of Canada 1851–55 and 1859–67; and at the formation of the Dominion in 1867, became capital of Québec province. The opening of the ▷St Lawrence Seaway in 1959 reduced the volume of shipping, although it remains a major port. There are two universities: Laval (1663), the oldest in North America; and Québec (1969). The picturesque old town survives below the Citadel, which is perched on a 110 m/360 ft cliff above the St Lawrence River.

Québec province of eastern Canada; the largest province, second only in area among the nation's administrative subdivisions to the Northwest Territories. Québec is bordered on the northeast by Labrador, on the east by Newfoundland, on the southeast by New Brunswick and Nova Scotia, and on the west and southwest by Ontario. On its southern border lie (west–east) the US states of New York, Vermont, New Hampshire, and Maine; area 1,540,700 sq km/594,900 sq mi; population (1991) 6,811,800. The capital is ▷Québec. Industries include mining (iron, copper, gold, zinc), fishing, and the production of paper, textiles, and maple syrup (70% of world output). Cereals and potatoes are grown. See picture on p. 786.

Québec Conference two conferences of Allied leaders in the city of Québec during World War II. The **first conference** in 1943 approved British admiral Mountbatten as supreme Allied commander in Southeast Asia and made plans for the invasion of France, for which US general Eisenhower was to be supreme commander. The **second conference** in September 1944 adopted plans for intensified air attacks on Germany, created a unified

Qatar

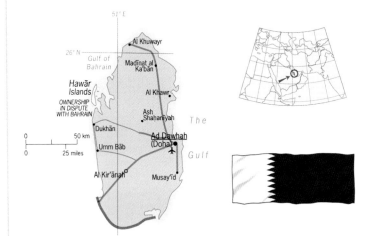

Qatar country in the Middle East, occupying Qatar peninsula in the Arabian Gulf, bounded southwest by Saudi Arabia and south by United Arab Emirates.

NATIONAL NAME *Dawlat Qatar/State of Qatar*
AREA 11,400 sq km/4,401 sq mi
CAPITAL Doha (and chief port)
MAJOR TOWNS/CITIES Dukhan, Wakra, ad-Dawhah, ar-Rayyan, Umm Salal, Musay'id, Ash Shahaaniyah
PHYSICAL FEATURES mostly flat desert with salt flats in south

Government

HEAD OF STATE Sheikh Hamad bin Khalifa al-Thani from 1995
HEAD OF GOVERNMENT Sheikh 'Abd Allah ibn Khalifah Al Thani from 1996
POLITICAL SYSTEM absolutist
POLITICAL EXECUTIVE absolute
ADMINISTRATIVE DIVISIONS nine municipalities

ARMED FORCES 12,400 (2002 est)
CONSCRIPTION military service is voluntary
DEATH PENALTY retained and used for ordinary crimes

Economy and resources

CURRENCY Qatari riyal
GPD (US$) 16.5 billion (2002 est)
REAL GDP GROWTH (% change on previous year) 5.2 (2001)
CONSUMER PRICE INFLATION 2.9% (2003 est)
UNEMPLOYMENT dependent on immigrant workers – shortage of indigenous labour
FOREIGN DEBT (US$) 9.5 billion (2001 est)
MAJOR TRADING PARTNERS Japan, France, Italy, USA, South Korea, Singapore, UK, United Arab Emirates, Germany, Thailand

RESOURCES petroleum, natural gas, water
INDUSTRIES petroleum refining and petroleum products, industrial chemicals, iron and steel, flour, cement, concrete, plastics, paint
EXPORTS petroleum, liquefied natural gas, petrochemicals. Principal market: Japan 43.5% (2001)
IMPORTS machinery and transport equipment, basic manufactures, food and live animals, miscellaneous manufactured articles, chemicals. Principal source: France 17.9% (2001)
ARABLE LAND 6.1% (2000 est)
AGRICULTURAL PRODUCTS cereals, vegetables, fruits; livestock rearing; fishing

Population and society

POPULATION 610,000 (2003 est)
POPULATION GROWTH RATE 1.5% (2000–05)
POPULATION DENSITY (per sq km) 55 (2003 est)
URBAN POPULATION (% of total) 93 (2003 est)

QATAR Doha, the capital of Qatar is half way down the east coast of the peninsula. Al Corniche, a panoramic seafront boulevard typical of many Gulf cities, stretches 7 km/4.4 mi along Doha Bay. *British Embassy for the State of Qatar*

Chronology

7th century AD: Islam introduced.

8th century: Developed into important trading centre during time of Abbasid Empire.

1783: The al-Khalifa family, who had migrated to northeast Qatar from west and north of the Arabian Peninsula, foiled Persian invasion and moved their headquarters to Bahrain Island, while continuing to rule the area of Qatar.

1867–68: After the Bahrain-based al-Khalifa had suppressed a revolt by their Qatari subjects, destroying the town of Doha, Britain intervened and installed Muhammad ibn Thani al-Thani, from the leading family of Qatar, as the ruling sheikh (or emir). A British Resident was given power to arbitrate disputes with Qatar's neighbours.

1871–1914: Nominally part of Turkish Ottoman Empire, although in 1893 sheik's forces inflicted a defeat on Ottomans.

1916: Qatar became British protectorate after treaty signed with Sheikh Abdullah al-Thani.

1949: Oil production began at onshore Dukhan field in west.

1960: Sheikh Ahmad al-Thani became new emir.

1968: Britain's announcement that it would remove its forces from the Persian Gulf by 1971 led Qatar to make an abortive attempt to arrange a federation of Gulf states.

1970: Constitution adopted, confirming emirate as absolute monarchy.

1971: Independence achieved from Britain.

1991: Qatar forces joined the United Nations (UN) coalition in the Gulf War against Iraq.

1995: Sheikh Khalifa was ousted by his son, Crown Prince Sheikh Hamad bin Khalifa al-Thani.

1996: The announcement of plans to introduce democracy were followed by an assassination attempt on Sheikh Hamad. Sheikh 'Abd Allah ibn Khalifah Al Thani was appointed prime minister.

2001: The ruling of the International Court of Justice on a long-standing territorial dispute with Bahrain was accepted.

QUÉBEC The interior of the church of Notre Dame in Old Montreal, Québec, Canada. See entry on p. 785. *Image Bank*

quenching ▷heat treatment used to harden metals. The metals are heated to a certain temperature and then quickly plunged into cold water or oil.

quetzal long-tailed Central American bird *Pharomachus mocinno* of the ▷trogon family, order Trogoniformes. The male is brightly coloured, with green, red, blue, and white feathers. It has a train of blue-green plumes (tail coverts) that hang far beyond the true tail feathers. There is a crest on the head and decorative drooping feathers on the wings. It is about 1.3 m/4.3 ft long including tail. The female is smaller and lacks the tail and plumage.

The quetzal eats fruit, insects, and small frogs and lizards. It is the national emblem of Guatemala, and was considered sacred by the Mayans and the Aztecs. The quetzal's forest habitat is rapidly being destroyed, and hunting of birds for trophies or souvenirs also threatens its survival.

QUETZAL The long-tailed quetzal of Mexico and Central America was associated by the ancient Maya and Aztecs with the plumed serpent god Quetzalcoatl, and they used its magnificent tail feathers in religious ceremonies.

strategy against Japan, and established a post-war policy for a defeated Germany.

quebracho any of several South American trees belonging to the cashew family, with very hard, tannin-rich wood; chiefly the red quebracho (*S. lorentzii*), used in the tanning of leather. (Genus *Schinopsis*, family Anacardiaceae.)

Quechua (or Quichua or Kechua) the largest group of American Indians living in South America. The Quechua live in the Andean region. Their ancestors included the Inca, who established the Quechua language in the region, now the second official language of Peru and widely spoken as a lingua franca in Ecuador, Bolivia, Colombia, Argentina, and Chile; it belongs to the Andean-Equatorial family.

Queen British glam-rock group 1971–91 credited with making the first successful pop video, for their hit 'Bohemian Rhapsody' (1975). The operatic flamboyance of lead singer Freddie Mercury (1946–1991) was the cornerstone of their popularity. Among their other hits are 'We Will Rock You' (1977) and the rockabilly pastiche 'Crazy Little Thing Called Love' (1980). They were inducted into the Rock and Roll Hall of Fame in the USA in 2001.
Related Web site: **Queen Home Page** http://queen-fip.com/

Queen Anne style decorative art style in England (1700–20), characterized by plain, simple lines, mainly in silver and furniture.

Queens largest borough and county of New York City, USA; population (1996 est) 1,980,600. Situated at the west end of ▷Long Island, it covers an area of 280 sq km/108 sq mi. Mainly residential, its districts include Jackson Heights, Forest Hills, and Flushing. Industries are concentrated in Long Island City, a railroad and shipping terminus, and Maspeth. Products include processed foods, metalware, paint, furniture, stonemasonry, clothes, and electronic and office equipment.

Queen's Counsel (QC) in England, a barrister appointed to senior rank by the Lord Chancellor. When the monarch is a king the term is **King's Counsel** (KC). A QC wears a silk gown and takes precedence over a junior member of the Bar.

Queen's English see ▷English language.

Queensland state in northeast Australia, including the adjacent islands in the Pacific Ocean and in the Gulf of ▷Carpentaria; bordered on the west by Northern Territory, on the southwest by South Australia, on the south by New South Wales, on the east by the Pacific Ocean, and on the extreme northwest by the Gulf of Carpentaria; area 1,727,200 sq km/666,900 sq mi; population (1996) 3,368,850, concentrated in the southeast. The capital is ▷Brisbane. Products include sugar, wheat, pineapples, beef, cotton, wool, tobacco, copper, gold, silver, lead, zinc, coal, nickel, bauxite, uranium, natural gas, oil, and fish.

Queensland is predominantly agricultural; the main crops are sugar cane, wheat, oats, peanuts, bananas, and pineapples. Cattle (beef and dairy) and sheep are raised. The state has rich mineral reserves; coal, lead, silver, zinc, copper, gold, and bauxite are mined, and there are deposits of oil and natural gas. Industries are mainly connected with the processing of primary produce: sugar refining, food processing, oil refining. Other industries include engineering, textile manufacture, and shipbuilding. Many tourists are attracted to the ▷Great Barrier Reef and the beaches of the southeast coast, especially the Gold Coast, a 32-km/20-mi long stretch south of Brisbane and running into Queensland, and the Sunshine Coast, a 100-km/60-mi stretch of coast north of Brisbane, between Rainbow Beach and Bribie Island, including the resorts of Noosa Heads, Coolum Beach, and Caloundra.
Related Web site: **Destination Queensland** http://www.qttc.com.au/

Queen's Proctor in England, the official representing the crown in matrimonial, probate, and admiralty cases. The Queen's Proctor's chief function is to intervene in divorce proceedings if it is discovered that material facts have been concealed from the court or that there has been collusion. When the monarch is a king the term is **King's Proctor**.

Quetzalcoatl in pre-Columbian cultures of Central America, a feathered serpent god of air and water. In his human form, he was said to have been fair-skinned and bearded and to have reigned on Earth during a golden age. He disappeared across the eastern sea, with a promise to return; the Spanish conquistador Hernán ▷Cortés exploited the myth in his own favour when he invaded. Ruins of Quetzalcoatl's temples survive in various ancient Mesoamerican ceremonial centres, including the one at Teotihuacán in Mexico. (See also ▷Aztec, ▷Mayan, and ▷Toltec civilizations).

Quezon City former capital of the Philippines 1948–76, northeastern part of metropolitan ▷Manila (the present capital), on Luzon Island; population (2000) 2,173,800. It was named after the Philippines' first president, Manuel Luis Quezon (1878–1944).

quicksilver another name for the element ▷mercury.

quietism religious attitude, displayed periodically in the history of Christianity, consisting of passive contemplation and meditation to achieve union with God. The founder of modern quietism was the Spanish priest Molinos who published a *Guida Spirituale/Spiritual Guide* (1675).

Quiller-Couch, Arthur (Thomas) (1863–1944) English scholar and writer, who wrote under the pseudonym Q. He edited several anthologies, including the original edition of *The Oxford Book of English Verse* (1900), and wrote a number of critical studies, such as *On the Art of Writing* (1916) and *On the Art of Reading* (1920). He was professor of English literature at Cambridge University from 1912 until his death. He was knighted in 1910.

Quimby, Fred(erick) (1886–1965) US film producer. He was head of MGM's short films department 1926–56. Among the cartoons produced by this department were the *Tom and Jerry* series and those directed by Tex Avery.

quince small tree native to western Asia but widely cultivated elsewhere. The bitter, yellow, pear-shaped fruit is used in preserves. Flowering quinces are cultivated mainly for their attractive flowers. (*Cydonia oblonga*; flowering quince; genus *Chaenomeles*; family Rosaceae.)

quinine antimalarial drug extracted from the bark of the cinchona tree. Peruvian Indians taught French missionaries how to use the bark in 1630, but quinine was not isolated until 1820. It is a bitter alkaloid, with the formula $C_{20}H_{24}N_2O_2$.

QUINCE The quince is related to the japonica and other plants of the rose family.

Quinn, Anthony (Rudolph Oaxaca) (1916–2001)
Mexican-born US actor. His roles frequently displayed volatile machismo and he often played larger-than-life characters, such as the title role in *Zorba the Greek* (1964). Other films include *Viva Zapata!* (1952; Academy Award for Best Supporting Actor) and Federico Fellini's *La strada* (1954).

Quintana Roo
state of Mexico, on the ▷Yucatán Peninsula; area 50,350 sq km/ 19,440 sq mi; population (1990) 493,300. Its capital is Chetumal. The chief products are chicle and copra, and there is sponge and turtle fishing. Most of the inhabitants are descendents of Maya Indians, and there are important archaeological remains of the Pre-Columbian Mayan Empire.

Quintero, Serafin Alvárez and Joaquin Alvárez
Spanish dramatists; see ▷Alvárez Quintero.

Quintilian (*c.* AD 35–*c.* 100) Born Marcus Fabius Quintilianus. Roman rhetorician. Born at Calagurris, Spain, he was educated in Rome, but left early in Nero's reign. He returned to Rome in AD 68, where he quickly achieved fame and wealth as a teacher of rhetoric. He composed the *Institutio Oratoria/The Education of an Orator*, in which he advocated a simple and sincere style of public speaking. His moral tone is in striking contrast with the general degradation of his age.

Quirinal one of the seven hills on which ancient Rome was built. Its summit is occupied by a palace built in 1574 as a summer residence for the pope and occupied 1870–1946 by the kings of Italy. The name Quirinal is derived from that of Quirinus, local god of the ▷Sabines.

Quisling, Vidkun Abraham Lauritz Jonsson
(1887–1945) Norwegian politician. Leader from 1933 of the Norwegian Fascist Party, he aided the Nazi invasion of Norway in 1940 by delaying mobilization and urging nonresistance. He was made premier by Hitler in 1942, and was arrested and shot as a traitor by the Norwegians in 1945. His name became a generic term for a traitor who aids an occupying force.

Quito industrial city, capital of ▷Ecuador and of Pichincha province; situated on a plateau in the Andes, 22 km/14 mi south of the equator, at an altitude of 2,850 m/9,350 ft; population (1995 est) 1,1246,000. Industries include textiles, chemicals, leather, gold, silver, pharmaceuticals, and motor vehicles. Quito lies at the foot of the volcano Pichincha (4,794 m/15,728 ft), which last erupted in 1666, in an area prone to earthquakes. It has a temperate climate all year round. The city, which is the oldest capital in South America, has been declared a World Cultural Heritage Site by UNESCO.

History Quito was an ancient Indian settlement, taken by the Incas in about 1470, and became the capital of the Inca Kingdom of Quito until it was captured by the Spaniard Sebastián de Benalcázar in 1534.

Features Many old colonial buildings survive in the old quarter. These include Spanish houses with balconies and fountains, and churches with wooden sculptures. Many display Moorish architectural influences, although their overall style is baroque. The old city has been designated a World Cultural Heritage Site by UNESCO, and its buildings include the oldest astronomical observatory in South America in the Parque Alameda, La Compañía Jesuit church, and the church and monastery of La Merced, which has a clock identical to that of Big Ben in London. Religious buildings occupy a quarter of the space in the city. The cathedral was built 1550–62. The oldest colonial church in Quito, the Monasterio de San Francisco, was constructed shortly after the city's foundation and completed 70 years later. The art school, established by Franciscans in 1535, led to the flourishing of religious art throughout the Spanish colonial period. The burial place of Antonio José de Sucre is here. There are three universities, dating from 1769, 1869, and 1946.

Qum alternative spelling of ▷Qom, a city in Iran.

Qumran (or Khirbet Qumran) archaeological site in Jordan, excavated from 1951, in the foothills northwest of the Dead Sea. Originally an Iron Age fort (6th century BC), it was occupied in the late 2nd century BC by a monastic community, the ▷Essenes, until the buildings were burned by Romans in AD 68. The monastery library once contained the ▷Dead Sea Scrolls, which had been hidden in caves for safekeeping and were discovered in 1947.

quod vide (abbreviation qv; Latin 'which see') term indicating a cross-reference.

Quorn mycoprotein, a tiny relative of mushrooms, that feeds on carbohydrates and grows prolifically in culture using a form of liquid fermentation. It is moist, looks like meat, and is used in cooking. It is rich in protein (12.3 g/100 g) and fibre (3.6 g/100 g) and low in fat (0.49 g/100 g).

quorum minimum number of members required to be present for the proceedings of an assembly to be valid. The actual number of people required for a quorum may vary.

quota in international trade, a limitation on the amount of a commodity that may be exported, imported, or produced. Restrictions may be imposed forcibly or voluntarily.

R

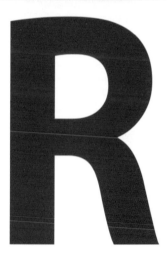

Rabat capital and industrial port of ▷Morocco, on the Atlantic coast, 177 km/110 mi west of Fès; population (city, 1994) 787,700; Rabat-Salé (urban area, 1998 est) 1,453,400. It is situated on the Bou Regreg River, opposite Salé. Industries include textiles, asbestos, carpets, pottery, leather goods, fishing; other exports include skins, wax, cork, slippers, and beans. Founded in 1190, it is named after its original *ribat* or fortified monastery.

rabbi in Judaism, the chief religious leader of a synagogue or the spiritual leader (not a hereditary high priest) of a Jewish congregation; also, a scholar of Judaic law and ritual from the 1st century AD.

rabbit any of several genera of hopping mammals of the order Lagomorpha, which together with ▷hares constitute the family Leporidae. Rabbits differ from hares in bearing naked, helpless young and in occupying burrows.

The Old World rabbit (*Oryctolagus cuniculus*), originally from southern Europe and North Africa, has now been introduced worldwide. It is bred for meat and for its fur, which is usually treated to resemble more expensive furs. It lives in interconnected burrows called 'warrens', unlike cottontails (genus *Sylvilagus*), of which 13 species are native to North and South America.

The common rabbit is greyish-brown, long-eared, has legs and feet adapted for running and hopping, and large front teeth. It can grow up to 40 cm/16 in long. Each female can produce several large litters in a year. Introduced into England in the 11th century, rabbits were originally delicate animals but they subsequently flourished until the virus disease myxomatosis was introduced in 1953 as a means of controlling the population by ▷biological control.

Related Web site: Paulson's Rabbit World http://www.rabbitworld.com/

Rabelais, François (*c.* 1495–1553) French satirist, monk, and physician. His name has become synonymous with bawdy humour. He was educated in the humanist tradition and was the author of satirical allegories, including a cycle known as Gargantua and Pantagruel which included *La Vie estimable du grand Gargantua, père de Pantagruel/The Inestimable Life of the Great Gargantua, Father of Pantagruel*, the first to be written, but published in 1534, two years after *Les Horribles et Épouvantables Faits et prouesses du très renommé Pantagruel/The Horrible and Dreadful Deeds and Prowess of the Very Renowned Pantagruel* (1532).

rabies (or **hydrophobia**; Greek 'fear of water') viral disease of the central nervous system that can afflict all warm-blooded creatures. It is caused by a lyssavirus. It is almost invariably fatal once symptoms have developed. Its transmission to humans is generally by a bite from an infected animal. Rabies continues to kill hundreds of thousands of people every year; almost all these deaths occur in Asia, Africa, and South America.

After an incubation period, which may vary from ten days to more than a year, symptoms of fever, muscle spasm, and delirium develop. As the disease progresses, the mere sight of water is enough to provoke convulsions and paralysis. Death is usual within four or five days from the onset of symptoms. Injections of rabies vaccine and antiserum may save those bitten by a rabid animal from developing the disease. Louis ▷Pasteur was the first to produce a preventive vaccine, and the Pasteur Institute was founded to treat the disease.

As a control measure for foxes and other wild animals, vaccination (by bait) is recommended. In France, Germany, and the border areas of Austria and the Czech Republic, foxes are now vaccinated against rabies with capsules distributed by helicopter; as a result, rabies has been virtually eradicated in Western Europe, and no-one has died of the disease in the European Union since 1973. In 1999 Switzerland became the first country to completely eradicate rabies by vaccinating foxes in this way.

In Britain, no human rabies has been transmitted since 1902. Britain and Ireland are the only countries in the European Union to ▷quarantine all incoming pets (for a six-month period), following the decisions of Sweden and Norway to replace their four-month quarantine period with a vaccination scheme in 1994. In September 1998 Britain announced that its quarantine regulations would be changing to allow animals from the European Union, and rabies-free islands, such as Australia and New Zealand, into the country without a period of quarantine.

Rabin, Yitzhak (1922–1995) Israeli Labour politician, prime minister 1974–77 and 1992–95. As a former soldier, he was a national hero in the Arab-Israeli Wars. His policy of favouring Palestinian self-government in the occupied territories contributed to the success of the centre-left party in the 1992 elections. In September 1993 he signed a historic peace agreement with the Palestinian Liberation Organization (PLO), providing for a phased withdrawal of Israeli forces. He shared the Nobel Prize for Peace in 1994 with Israeli foreign minister Shimon ▷Peres and PLO leader Yassir ▷Arafat for their agreement of an accord on Palestinian self-rule. He was shot and killed by a young Israeli extremist while attending a peace rally in Tel Aviv in November 1995.

Rabin was minister for defence under the conservative Likud coalition government 1984–90.

Rabuka, Sitiveni (1948–) Fijian soldier and politician, prime minister from 1992. When the April 1987 elections produced a new left-of-centre government, headed by Timoci Bavadra, which was determined to end discrimination against the country's ethnic Indian community, Rabuka staged two successive coups, in May and September 1987. Within months of the second coup, he stepped down, allowing a civilian government headed by Kamisese Mara, to take over. In 1992 Rabuka was nominated as the new Fijian premier. He was re-elected to the post in 1994 and, after revising the constitution so as not to discriminate against the ethnic Indian community, secured Fiji's re-admission to the Commonwealth in October 1997.

> **François Rabelais**
> *I go to seek a great perhaps.*
> Attributed remark on his deathbed

raccoon any of several New World species of carnivorous mammals of the genus *Procyon*, in the family Procyonidae. The common raccoon *P. lotor* is about 60 cm/2 ft long, with a grey-brown body, a black-and-white ringed tail, and a black 'mask' around its eyes. The crab-eating raccoon *P. cancrivorus* of South America is slightly smaller and has shorter fur.

Related Web site: Raccoons http://www.loomcom.com/raccoons

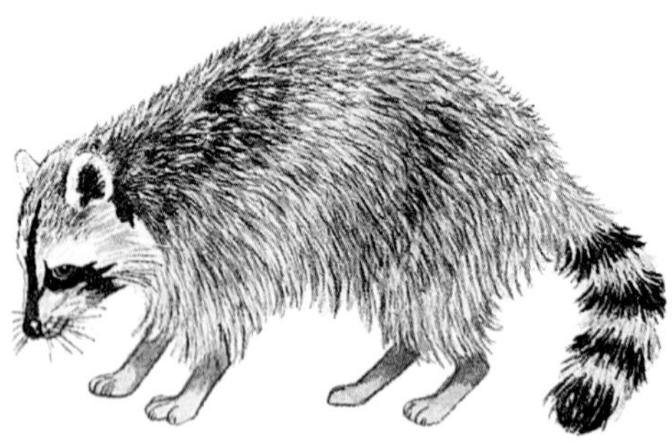

RACCOON Raccoons are good climbers and spend much of their time in trees, usually near water. Their varied diet includes small aquatic animals such as frogs, crayfish, and fish. The common raccoon, found in North America from southern Canada to the Panama Canal, was adopted as a pet by the early settlers.

race term sometimes applied to a physically distinctive group of people, on the basis of their difference from other groups in skin colour, head shape, hair type, and physique. Formerly, anthropologists divided the human race into three hypothetical racial groups: Caucasoid, Mongoloid, and Negroid. Others postulated from 6 to 30 races. Scientific studies, however, have produced no proof of definite genetic racial divisions. Race is a cultural, political, and economic concept, not a biological one. Genetic differences do exist between populations but they do not define historical lineages, and are minimal compared to the genetic variation between individuals. Most anthropologists today, therefore, completely reject the concept of race, and social scientists tend to prefer the term 'ethnic group' (see ▷ethnicity).

Rachmaninov, Sergei Vasilevich (1873–1943) Russian composer, conductor, and pianist. After the 1917 Revolution he emigrated to the USA. His music is melodious and emotional and includes operas, such as *Francesca da Rimini* (1906), three symphonies, four piano concertos, piano pieces, and songs. Among his other works are the *Prelude in C-Sharp Minor* (1892) and *Rhapsody on a Theme of Paganini* (1934) for piano and orchestra.

Racine, Jean Baptiste (1639–1699) French dramatist. He was an exponent of the classical tragedy in French drama, taking his subjects from Greek mythology and observing the rules of classical Greek drama. Most of his tragedies have women in the title role, for example *Andromaque* (1667), *Iphigénie* (1674), and *Phèdre* (1677).

An orphan, Racine was educated by Jansenists at Port Royal (see ▷Jansenism), but later moved away from an ecclesiastical career to success and patronage at court. His ingratiating flattery won him the success he craved in 1677 when he was appointed royal historiographer. After the failure of *Phèdre* in the theatre he no longer wrote for the secular stage but, influenced by Madame de Maintenon, wrote two religious dramas, *Esther* (1689) and *Athalie* (1691), which achieved posthumous success.

racism belief in, or set of implicit assumptions about, the superiority of one's own ▷race or ethnic group, often accompanied by prejudice against members of an ethnic group different from one's own. Racism may be used to justify ▷discrimination, verbal or physical abuse, or even genocide, as in Nazi Germany, or as practised by European settlers against American Indians in both North and South America.

rad unit of absorbed radiation dose, now replaced in the SI system by the ▷gray (one rad equals 0.01 gray), but still commonly used. It is defined as the dose when one kilogram of matter absorbs 0.01 joule of radiation energy (formerly, as the dose when one gram absorbs 100 ergs).

radar (acronym for radio direction and ranging) device for locating objects in space, direction finding, and navigation by means of transmitted and reflected high-frequency radio waves.

The direction of an object is ascertained by transmitting a beam of short-wavelength (1–100 cm/0.5–40 in), short-pulse radio waves, and picking up the reflected beam. Distance is determined by timing the journey of the radio waves (travelling at the speed of light) to the object and back again. Radar is also used to detect objects underground, for example service pipes, and in archaeology. Contours of remains of ancient buildings can be detected down to 20 m/66 ft below ground. Radar is essential to navigation in darkness, cloud, and fog, and is widely used in warfare to detect enemy aircraft and missiles. To avoid detection, various devices, such as modified shapes (to reduce their radar cross-section), radar-absorbent paints and electronic jamming are used. To pinpoint small targets ▷laser 'radar', instead of microwaves, has been developed. Developed independently in Britain, France, Germany, and the USA in the 1930s, it was first put to practical use for aircraft detection by the British, who had a complete coastal chain of radar stations installed by September 1938. It proved invaluable in the Battle of Britain 1940, when the ability to spot incoming German aircraft did away with the need to fly standing patrols. Chains of ground radar stations are used to warn of enemy attack – for example, North Warning System 1985, consisting of 52 stations across the Canadian Arctic and northern Alaska. Radar is also used in ▷meteorology and ▷astronomy.

Related Web site: History of Radar http://www.fi.edu/weather/radar/history.html

radar astronomy bouncing of radio waves off objects in the Solar System, with reception and analysis of the 'echoes'. Radar contact with the Moon was first made in 1945 and with Venus in 1961. The travel time for radio reflections allows the distances of objects to be determined accurately. Analysis of the reflected beam reveals the rotation period and allows the object's surface to be mapped. The rotation periods of Venus and Mercury were first determined by radar. Radar maps of Venus were obtained first by Earth-based radar and subsequently by orbiting space probes.

radian SI unit (symbol rad) of plane angles, an alternative unit to the ▷degree. It is the angle at the centre of a circle when the centre is joined to the two ends of an arc (part of the circumference) equal in length to the radius of the circle. There are 2π (approximately 6.284) radians in a full circle (360°).

One radian is approximately 57°, and 1° is $\pi/180$ or approximately 0.0175 radians. Radians are commonly used to specify angles in ▷polar coordinates.

radiation in physics, emission of radiant ▷energy as particles or waves – for example, heat, light, alpha particles, and beta particles (see ▷electromagnetic waves and ▷radioactivity). See also ▷atomic radiation.

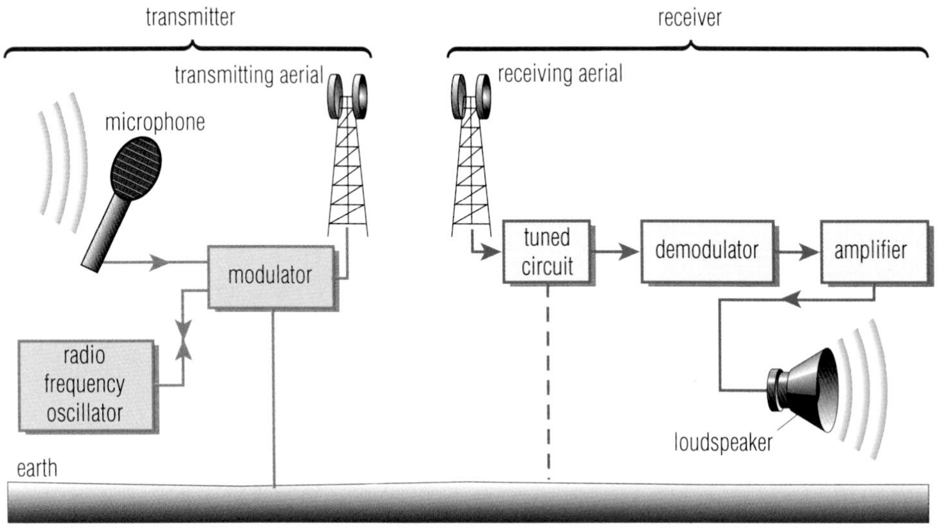

RADIO The diagram shows how a radio transmits and receives. The radio frequency oscillator generates rapidly varying electrical signals, which are sent to the transmitting aerial. In the aerial, the signals produce radio waves (the carrier wave), which spread out at the speed of light. The sound signal is added to the carrier wave by the modulator. When the radio waves fall on the receiving aerial, they induce an electrical current in the aerial. The electrical current is sent to the tuning circuit, which picks out the signal from the particular transmitting station desired. The demodulator separates the sound signal from the carrier wave and sends it, after amplification, to the loudspeaker.

Of the radiation given off by the Sun, only a tiny fraction of it, called insolation, reaches the Earth's surface; much of it is absorbed and scattered as it passes through the ▷atmosphere. The radiation given off by the Earth itself is called **ground radiation**.

Related Web site: Radiation Reassessed http://whyfiles.news.wisc.edu/020radiation/index.html

radiation sickness sickness resulting from exposure to radiation, including X-rays, gamma rays, neutrons, and other nuclear radiation, as from weapons and fallout. Such radiation ionizes atoms in the body and causes nausea, vomiting, diarrhoea, and other symptoms. The body cells themselves may be damaged even by very small doses, causing leukaemia and other cancers.

radiation units units of measurement for radioactivity and radiation doses. In SI units, the activity of a radioactive source is measured in becquerels (symbol Bq), where one becquerel is equal to one nuclear disintegration per second (an older unit is the curie). The exposure is measured in coulombs per kilogram ($C\ kg^{-1}$); the amount of ionizing radiation (X-rays or gamma rays) which produces one coulomb of charge in one kilogram of dry air (replacing the roentgen). The absorbed dose of ionizing radiation is measured in grays (symbol Gy) where one gray is equal to one joule of energy being imparted to one kilogram of matter (the rad is the previously used unit). The dose equivalent, which is a measure of the effects of radiation on living organisms, is the absorbed dose multiplied by a suitable factor which depends upon the type of radiation. It is measured in sieverts (symbol Sv), where one sievert is a dose equivalent of one joule per kilogram (an older unit is the rem).

Radical in Britain, supporter of parliamentary reform before the Reform Bill of 1832. As a group the Radicals later became the progressive wing of the Liberal Party. During the 1860s (led by Cobden, Bright, and J S Mill) they campaigned for extension of the franchise, free trade, and ▷*laissez-faire*, but after 1870, under the leadership of Joseph Chamberlain and Charles Dilke, they adopted a republican and semi-socialist programme. With the growth of ▷socialism in the later 19th century, Radicalism ceased to exist as an organized movement.

In France, the Radical Party was a major force in the politics of the Third Republic, 1871–1940.

radical in chemistry, a group of atoms forming part of a molecule, which acts as a unit and takes part in chemical reactions without disintegration, yet often cannot exist alone for any length of time; for example, the methyl radical $-CH_3$, or the carboxyl radical $-COOH$.

radical in politics, anyone with opinions more extreme than the main current of a country's major political party or parties. It is more often applied to those with left-wing opinions, although the radical right also exists.

radicle part of a plant embryo that develops into the primary root. Usually it emerges from the seed before the embryonic shoot, or ▷plumule, its tip protected by a root cap, or calyptra, as it pushes through the soil. The radicle may form the basis of the entire root system, or it may be replaced by adventitious roots (positioned on the stem).

radio transmission and reception of radio waves. In radio transmission a microphone converts sound waves (pressure variations in the air) into ▷electromagnetic waves that are then picked up by a receiving aerial and fed to a loudspeaker, which converts them back into sound waves.

The theory of electromagnetic waves was first developed by Scottish physicist James Clerk ▷Maxwell 1864, given practical confirmation in the laboratory in 1888 by German physicist Heinrich ▷Hertz, and put to practical use by Italian inventor Guglielmo ▷Marconi, who in 1901 achieved reception of a signal in Newfoundland, Canada, transmitted from Cornwall, England.

To carry the transmitted electrical signal, an ▷oscillator produces a carrier wave of high frequency; different stations are allocated different transmitting carrier frequencies. A modulator superimposes the audiofrequency signal on the carrier. There are two main ways of doing this: ▷amplitude modulation (AM), used for long- and medium-wave broadcasts, in which the strength of the carrier is made to fluctuate in time with the audio signal; and ▷frequency modulation (FM), as used for VHF broadcasts, in which the frequency of the carrier is made to fluctuate. The transmitting aerial emits the modulated electromagnetic waves, which travel outwards from it.

In radio reception a receiving aerial picks up minute voltages in response to the waves sent out by a transmitter. A tuned circuit selects a particular frequency, usually by means of a variable ▷capacitor connected across a coil of wire. A demodulator disentangles the audio signal from the carrier, which is now discarded, having served its purpose. An amplifier boosts the audio signal for feeding to the loudspeaker. In a ▷superheterodyne receiver, the incoming signal is mixed with an internally-generated signal of fixed frequency so that the amplifier circuits can operate near their optimum frequency.

Related Web site: Radio Days http://www.otr.com/index.shtml

radioactive decay process of disintegration undergone by the nuclei of radioactive elements, such as radium and various isotopes of uranium and the transuranic elements. This changes the element's atomic number, thus transmuting one element into another, and is accompanied by the emission of radiation. Alpha and beta decay are the most common forms.

In **alpha decay** (the loss of a helium nucleus – two protons and two neutrons) the atomic number decreases by two and a new nucleus is formed, for example, an atom of uranium isotope of mass 238, on emitting an alpha particle, becomes an atom of thorium, mass 234. In **beta decay** the loss of an electron from an atom is accomplished by the transformation of a neutron into a proton, thus resulting in an increase in the atomic number of one. For example, the decay of the carbon-14 isotope results in the formation of an atom of nitrogen (mass 14, atomic number 7) and the emission of an electron. Gamma emission usually occurs as part of alpha or beta emission. In gamma emission high-speed electromagnetic radiation is emitted from the nucleus, making it more stable during the loss of an alpha or beta particle. Certain lighter artificially created isotopes also undergo radioactive decay. The associated radiation consists of alpha rays, beta rays, or gamma rays (or a combination of these), and it takes place at a constant rate expressed as a specific half-life, which is the time taken for half of any mass of that particular isotope to decay completely. Less commonly occurring decay forms include heavy-ion emission, electron capture, and spontaneous fission (in each of these the atomic number decreases). The original nuclide is known as the parent substance, and the product is a daughter nuclide (which may or may not be radioactive). The final product in all modes of decay is a stable element.

radioactive tracer any of various radioactive ▷isotopes used in labelled compounds. See ▷tracer.

radioactive waste any waste that emits radiation in excess of the background level. See ▷nuclear waste.

radioactivity spontaneous alteration of the nuclei of radioactive atoms, accompanied by the emission of radiation. It is the property exhibited by the radioactive ▷isotopes of stable elements and all isotopes of radioactive elements, and can be either natural or induced. See ▷radioactive decay.

The discovery of radioactivity Radioactivity was first discovered in 1896, when French physicist Henri Becquerel observed that some photographic plates, although securely wrapped up, became blackened when placed near certain uranium compounds. A closer investigation showed that thin metal coverings were unable to prevent the blackening of the plates. It was clear that the uranium compounds emitted radiation that was able to penetrate the metal coverings. Pierre and Marie ▷Curie soon succeeded in isolating other radioactive elements. One of these was radium, which was found to be over 1 million times more radioactive than uranium.

Radioactive radiations Further investigation of the nature of ▷radiation by Ernest Rutherford revealed that there are three types of radiation: ▷alpha particles, ▷beta particles, and gamma rays. Alpha particles are positively charged, high-energy particles emitted from the nucleus of a radioactive atom. They consist of two neutrons and two protons and are thus identical to the nucleus of a helium atom. Because of their large mass, alpha particles have a short range of only a few centimetres in air, and can be stopped by a sheet of paper. Beta particles are more penetrating and can travel through a 3-mm/0.1-in sheet of aluminium or up to 1 m/3 ft of air. They consist of high-energy electrons emitted at high velocity from a radioactive atom that is undergoing spontaneous disintegration. Gamma rays comprise very high-frequency electromagnetic radiation. Gamma rays are stopped only by direct collision with an atom and are therefore very penetrating; they can, however, be stopped by about 4 cm/1.5 in of lead. When alpha, beta, and gamma radiation pass through matter they tend to knock electrons out of atoms, ionizing them. They are therefore called ionizing radiation. Alpha particles are the most ionizing, being heavy, slow moving and carrying two positive charges. Gamma rays are weakly ionizing as they carry no charge. Beta particles fall between alpha and gamma radiation in ionizing potential.

Detection of radioactivity Detectors of ionizing radiation make use of the ionizing properties of radiation to cause changes that can be detected and measured. A ▷Geiger counter detects the momentary current that passes between electrodes in a suitable gas when ionizing radiation causes the ionization of that gas. The device is named after the German physicist Hans ▷Geiger. The activity of a radioactive source describes the rate at which nuclei are disintegrating within it. One ▷becquerel (1 Bq) is defined as a rate of one disintegration per second.

Radioactive decay Radioactive decay occurs when an unstable nucleus emits alpha, beta, or gamma radiation in order to become more stable. The energy given out by disintegrating atoms is called ▷atomic radiation. An alpha particle consists of two protons and two neutrons. When ▷alpha decay occurs (the emission of an alpha particle from a nucleus) it results in the formation of a new nucleus. An atom of uranium isotope of mass 238, on emitting an alpha particle, becomes an atom of thorium, mass 234. ▷Beta decay, the loss of an electron from an atom, is accomplished by the transformation of a neutron into a proton, thus resulting in an increase in the atomic number of one. For example, the decay of the carbon 314 isotope results in the formation of an atom of nitrogen (mass 14, atomic number 7) and the emission of an electron. Gamma emission usually occurs as part of alpha or beta emission. High-speed electromagnetic radiation is emitted from the nucleus in order to make it more stable during the loss of an alpha or beta particle. ▷Isotopes of an element have different atomic masses. They have the same number of protons but different numbers of neutrons in the nucleus. For example, uranium 235 and uranium 238 both have 92 protons but the latter has three more neutrons than the former. Some isotopes are naturally radioactive (see ▷radioisotopes) while others are not. Radioactive decay can take place either as a one-step decay, or through a series of steps that transmute one element into another. This is called a decay series or chain, and sometimes produces an element more radioactive than its predecessor. For example, uranium 238 decays by alpha emission to thorium 234; thorium 234 is a beta emitter and decays to give protactinium 234. This emits a beta particle to form uranium 234, which in turn undergoes alpha decay to form thorium 230. A further alpha decay yields the isotope radium 226.

The rate of radioactive decay The emission of radioactivity by an atom occurs spontaneously and quite unpredictably. However, in a sample containing many radioactive atoms, the overall rate of decay appears to be governed by the number of nuclei left undecayed. The time taken for half the radioactive atoms in a sample to decay remains constant and is called the ▷half-life. Radioactive substances decay exponentially with time, and the value of the half-life for a substance can vary from a fraction of a second to billions of years.

Health hazards We are surrounded by radioactive substances. Our food contains traces of radioactive isotopes and our own bodies are made of naturally radioactive matter. In addition, we are bombarded by streams of high-energy charged particles from outer space. Radiation present in the environment is known as ▷background radiation and we should take this into account when considering the risk of exposure to other sources. Alpha, beta, and gamma radiation are dangerous to body tissues because of their ionizing properties, especially if a radioactive substance is ingested or inhaled. Illness resulting from exposure to radioactive substances can take various forms, which are collectively known as ▷radiation sickness.

Radioactivity in use Radioactivity has a number of uses in modern science, but its use should always be carefully controlled and monitored to minimize the risk of harm to living things. In science, a small quantity of a radioactive tracer can be used to follow the path of a chemical reaction or a physical or biological process. ▷Radiocarbon dating is a technique for measuring the age of organic materials. Another application is in determining the age of rocks. This is based on the fact that in many uranium and thorium ores, all of which have been decaying since the formation of the rock, the alpha particles released during decay have been trapped as helium atoms in the rock. The age of the rock can be assessed by calculating the relative amounts of helium, uranium, and thorium in it. This calculation can help to estimate the age of the Earth at around 4.6 billion years. In medicine, radioactive emissions and electromagnetic radiation can be used therapeutically; for example, to treat cancer, when the radiation dose is very carefully controlled (see ▷radiotherapy).

Nuclear fission and fusion ▷Fission of a nucleus occurs when the nucleus splits into two approximately equal fragments. The fission of the nucleus results in the release of neutrons and a large amount of energy. In a nuclear reactor, the fission of uranium 235 is caused by bombarding it with neutrons. A nuclear ▷chain reaction is caused as neutrons released by the splitting of atomic nuclei themselves go on to split other nuclei, releasing even more neutrons. In a nuclear reactor this process is carefully controlled to release ▷nuclear energy. In ▷nuclear fusion, two light nuclei combine to form a bigger nucleus. As fusion is accompanied by the release of large amounts of energy, the process might one day be harnessed to form the basis of commercial energy production. So far, no successful fusion reactor has been built.

Related Web site: Radioactivity in Nature http://www.physics.isu.edu/radinf/natural.htm

radio astronomy study of radio waves emitted naturally by objects in space, by means of a ▷radio telescope. Radio emission comes from hot gases (**thermal radiation**); electrons spiralling in magnetic fields (**synchrotron radiation**); and specific wavelengths (**lines**) emitted by atoms and molecules in space, such as the 21-cm/8.3-in line emitted by hydrogen gas.

Radio astronomy began in 1932 when US radio astronomer Karl Jansky detected radio waves from the centre of our Galaxy, but the subject did not develop until after World War II. Radio astronomy has greatly improved our understanding of the evolution of stars, the structure of galaxies, and the origin of the universe. Astronomers have mapped the spiral structure of the Milky Way from the radio waves given out by interstellar gas, and they have detected many individual radio sources within our Galaxy and beyond.

Among radio sources in our Galaxy are the remains of ▷supernova explosions, such as the ▷Crab nebula and ▷pulsars. Short-wavelength radio waves have been detected from complex molecules in dense clouds of gas where stars are forming. Searches have been undertaken for signals from other civilizations in the Galaxy, so far without success.

Strong sources of radio waves beyond our Galaxy include ▷radio galaxies and ▷quasars. Their existence far off in the universe demonstrates how the universe has evolved with time. Radio astronomers have also detected weak cosmic **background radiation** thought to be from the ▷Big Bang explosion that marked the birth of the universe.

radio beacon radio transmitter in a fixed location, used in marine and aerial ▷navigation. Ships and aircraft pinpoint their positions by reference to continuous signals given out by two or more beacons.

radiocarbon dating (or **carbon dating**) method of dating organic materials (for example, bone or wood), used in archaeology. Plants take up carbon dioxide gas from the atmosphere and incorporate it into their tissues, and some of that carbon dioxide contains the radioactive isotope of carbon, ^{14}C or carbon-14. As this decays at a known rate (half of it decays every 5,730 years), the time elapsed since the plant died can be measured in a laboratory. Animals take carbon-14 into their bodies from eating plant tissues and their remains can be similarly dated. After 120,000 years so little carbon-14 is left that no measure is possible (see ▷half-life).

Related Web site: Radiocarbon WEB-info http://www2.waikato.ac.nz/c14/webinfo/index.html

radio, cellular portable telephone system; see ▷cellular phone.

radiochemistry chemical study of radioactive isotopes and their compounds (whether produced from naturally radioactive or irradiated materials) and their use in the study of other chemical processes.

When such isotopes are used in labelled compounds, they enable the biochemical and physiological functioning of parts of the living body to be observed. They can help in the testing of new drugs, showing where the drug goes in the body and how long it stays there. They are also useful in diagnosis – for example cancer, fetal abnormalities, and heart disease.

radio frequencies and wavelengths see ▷electromagnetic waves.

radio galaxy galaxy that is a strong source of electromagnetic waves of radio wavelengths. All galaxies, including our own, emit some radio waves, but radio galaxies are up to a million times more powerful.

In many cases the strongest radio emission comes not from the visible galaxy but from two clouds, invisible through an optical telescope, that can extend for millions of light years either side of the galaxy. This double structure at radio wavelengths is also shown by some ▷quasars, suggesting a close relationship between the two types of object. In both cases, the source of energy is thought to be a massive black hole at the centre. Some radio galaxies are thought to result from two galaxies in collision or recently merged.

radiography branch of science concerned with the use of radiation (particularly ▷X-rays) to produce images on photographic film or fluorescent screens. X-rays penetrate matter according to its nature, density, and thickness. In doing so they can cast shadows on photographic film, producing a radiograph. Radiography is widely used in medicine for examining bones and tissues and in industry for examining solid materials; for example, to check welded seams in pipelines.

radioisotope (or **radioactive isotope**) in physics, a naturally occurring or synthetic radioactive form of an element. Most radioisotopes are made by bombarding a stable element with neutrons in the core of a nuclear reactor (see ▷fission). The radiations given off by radioisotopes are easy to detect (hence their use as ▷tracers), can in some instances penetrate substantial thicknesses of materials, and have profound effects (such as genetic ▷mutation) on living matter.

Most natural isotopes of relative atomic mass below 208 are not radioactive. Those from 210 and up are all radioactive.

Radioisotopes have many uses in medicine, for example in ▷radiotherapy and ▷radioisotope scanning. The use of radioactive isotopes in the diagnosis, investigation, and treatment of disease is called **nuclear medicine**.

radioisotope scanning use of radioactive materials (radioisotopes or radionucleides) to pinpoint disease. It reveals the size and shape of the target organ and whether any part of it is failing to take up radioactive material, usually an indication of disease.

radiology medical speciality concerned with the use of radiation, including X-rays, and radioactive materials in the diagnosis and treatment of injury and disease.

radiometric dating method of dating rock by assessing the amount of ▷radioactive decay of naturally occurring ▷isotopes. The dating of rocks may be based on the gradual decay of uranium into lead. The ratio of the amounts of 'parent' to 'daughter' isotopes in a sample gives a measure of the time it has been decaying, that is, of its age. Different elements and isotopes are used depending on the isotopes present and the age of the rocks to be dated. Once-living matter can often be dated by ▷radiocarbon dating, employing the half-life of the isotope carbon-14, which is naturally present in organic tissue.

Radiometric methods have been applied to the decay of long-lived isotopes, such as potassium-40, rubidium-87, thorium-232, and uranium-238, which are found in rocks. These isotopes decay very slowly and this has enabled rocks as old as 3,800 million years to be dated accurately. Carbon dating can be used for material between 1,000 and 100,000 years old. **Potassium** dating is used for material more than 100,000 years old, **rubidium** for rocks more than 10 million years old, and **uranium** and **thorium** dating is suitable for rocks older than 20 million years.

radiosonde balloon carrying a compact package of meteorological instruments and a radio transmitter, used to 'sound', or measure, conditions in the atmosphere. The instruments measure temperature, pressure, and humidity, and the information gathered is transmitted back to observers on the ground. A radar target is often attached, allowing the balloon to be tracked.

radio telescope instrument for detecting radio waves from the universe in ▷radio astronomy. Radio telescopes usually consist of a metal bowl that collects and focuses radio waves the way a concave mirror collects and focuses light waves. Radio telescopes are much larger than optical telescopes, because the wavelengths they are detecting are much longer than the wavelength of light. The largest single dish is 305 m/1,000 ft across, at Arecibo, Puerto Rico.

A large dish such as that at ▷Jodrell Bank, Cheshire, England, can see the radio sky less clearly than a small optical telescope sees the visible sky. **Interferometry** is a technique in which the output from two dishes is combined to give better resolution of detail than with a single dish. **Very long baseline interferometry** (VBLI) uses radio telescopes spread across the world to resolve minute details of radio sources.

In **aperture synthesis**, several dishes are linked together to simulate the performance of a very large single dish. This technique was pioneered by English radio astronomer Martin ▷Ryle at the Mullard Radio Astronomy Observatory, Cambridge, England, site of a radio telescope consisting of eight dishes in a line 5 km/3 mi long. The ▷Very Large Array in New Mexico, USA, consists of 27 dishes arranged in a Y-shape, which simulates the performance of a single dish 27 km/17 mi in diameter. Other radio telescopes are shaped like long troughs, and some consist of simple rod-shaped aerials.

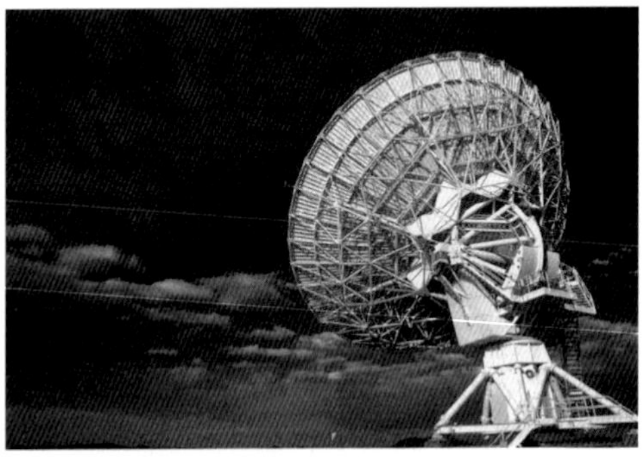

RADIO TELESCOPE A radio telescope dish at Soccorro, New Mexico, USA. This particular site contains the VLA. *Image Bank*

radiotherapy treatment of disease by ▷radiation from X-ray machines or radioactive sources. Radiation, which reduces the activity of dividing cells, is of special value for its effect on malignant tissues, certain nonmalignant tumours, and some diseases of the skin.

radio wave electromagnetic wave possessing a long wavelength (ranging from about 10^{-3} to 10^4 m) and a low frequency (from about 10^5 to 10^{11} Hz). Included in the radio wave part of the spectrum are ▷microwaves, used for both communications and for cooking; ultra high- and very high-frequency waves, used for television and FM (▷frequency modulation) radio communications; and short, medium, and long waves, used for AM (▷amplitude modulation) radio communications. Radio waves that are used for communications have all been modulated (see ▷modulation) to carry information. Certain astronomical objects emit radio waves, which may be detected and studied using ▷radio telescopes.

radish annual herb native to Europe and Asia, and cultivated for its fleshy, pungent, edible root, which is usually reddish but sometimes white or black; it is eaten raw in salads. (Genus *Raphanus sativus*, family Cruciferae.)

radium (Latin *radius* 'ray') white, radioactive, metallic element, symbol Ra, atomic number 88, relative atomic mass 226.02. It is one of the ▷alkaline-earth metals, found in nature in ▷pitchblende and other uranium ores. Of the 16 isotopes, the commonest,

Ra-226, has a half-life of 1,620 years. The element was discovered and named in 1898 by Pierre and Marie ▷Curie, who were investigating the residues of pitchblende.

Radium decays in successive steps to produce radon (a gas), polonium, and finally a stable isotope of lead. The isotope Ra-223 decays through the uncommon mode of heavy-ion emission, giving off carbon-14 and transmuting directly to lead. Because radium luminesces, it was formerly used in paints that glowed in the dark; when the hazards of radioactivity became known its use was abandoned, but factory and dump sites remain contaminated and many former workers and neighbours contracted fatal cancers.

radius a straight line from the centre of a circle to its circumference, or from the centre to the surface of a sphere.

radon colourless, odourless, gaseous, radioactive, nonmetallic element, symbol Rn, atomic number 86, relative atomic mass 222. It is grouped with the ▷inert gases and was formerly considered nonreactive, but is now known to form some compounds with fluorine. Of the 20 known isotopes, only three occur in nature; the longest half-life is 3.82 days (Rn-222).

Raffles, (Thomas) Stamford (1781–1826) British colonial administrator, born in Jamaica. He served in the British ▷East India Company, took part in the capture of Java from the Dutch in 1811, and while governor of Sumatra 1818–23 was responsible for the acquisition and founding of Singapore in 1819. He was knighted in 1817.

rafflesia (or **stinking corpse lily**) any of a group of parasitic plants without stems, native to Malaysia, Indonesia, and Thailand. There are 14 species, several of which are endangered by the destruction of the forests where they grow. The fruit is used locally for medicine. The largest flowers in the world are produced by *R. arnoldiana*. About 1 m/3 ft across, they exude a smell of rotting flesh, which attracts flies to pollinate them. (Genus *Rafflesia*, family Rafflesiaceae.)

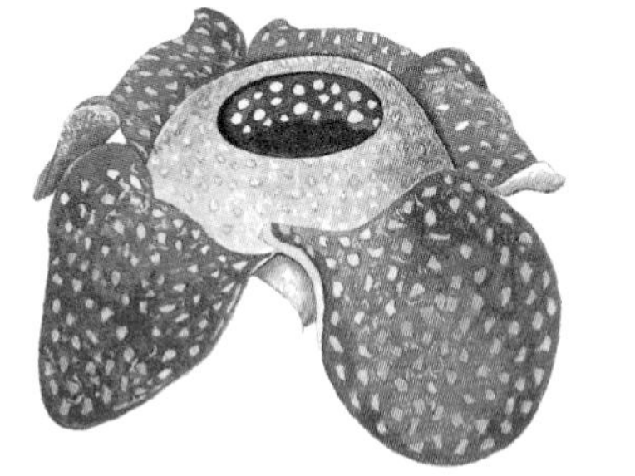

RAFFLESIA The rafflesia, or stinking corpse lily, is the largest known flower, about 1 m/3 ft across and weighing 7 kg/15 lb.

Rafsanjani, Hojatoleslam Ali Akbar Hashemi (1934–) Iranian politician and cleric, president 1989–97. When his former teacher Ayatollah ▷Khomeini returned after the revolution of 1979–80, Rafsanjani became the speaker of the Iranian parliament and, after Khomeini's death, state president and effective political leader. He was succeeded in 1997 by Seyyed Muhammad Khatami. In parliamentary elections in late February 2000 Rafsanjani failed to win a seat, while supporters of President Khatami and their reformist allies won a convincing majority. Following the pro-reformist election, it was disclosed that Rafsanjani was allegedly linked to government officials who had committed human rights abuses and executions of dissidents, intellectuals, and criminals during his presidency.

raga (Sanskrit *rāga* 'tone' or 'colour') in Indian music, a scale of notes and style of ornament for music associated with a particular mood or time of day; the equivalent term in rhythm is tala. A choice of raga and tala forms the basis of improvised music; however, a written composition may also be based on (and called) a raga.

ragga type of ▷reggae music with a rhythmic, rapid-fire, semi-spoken vocal line. A macho swagger is a common element in the lyrics. Ragga developed around 1990 from 'toasting', itself an offshoot of reggae. Ragga performers include the Jamaicans Shabba Ranks, Anthony Red Rose, and Ninja Man.

Raglan, FitzRoy James Henry Somerset (1788–1855) 1st Baron Raglan. English general. He took part in the Peninsular War under Wellington, and lost his right arm at Waterloo. He commanded the British forces in the Crimean War from 1854. The **raglan sleeve**, cut right up to the neckline with no shoulder seam, is named after him.

Ragnarök in Norse mythology, the ultimate cataclysmic battle that would be fought between the gods and forces of evil, and from which a new order would come. In Germanic mythology, this is known as Götterdämmerung.

ragtime syncopated music ('ragged time') in 2/4 rhythm, usually played on piano. It developed in the USA among black musicians in the late 19th century; it was influenced by folk tradition, minstrel shows, and marching bands, and was later incorporated into jazz. Scott ▷Joplin was a leading writer of ragtime pieces, called 'rags'.

ragworm marine bristle-worm (polychaete), characterized by its prominent parapodia (lateral, paired 'paddles' found on each of its segments). Ragworms are usually well adapted to an active existence, with large muscle blocks and stout parapodia for swimming as well as crawling and burrowing, and a large head complete with complex sense organs. Some, such as *Nereis virens*, reach several metres in length, but most are 2–10 cm/1–4 in long.

ragwort any of several European perennial plants, usually with yellow flower heads; some are poisonous. (Genus *Senecio*, family Compositae.)

Rahman, Tunku (Prince) Abdul (1903–1990) Malaysian politician, first prime minister of independent Malaya 1957–63 and of Malaysia 1963–70.

raï Algerian pop music developed in the 1970s from the Bedouin song form *melhoun*, using synthesizers and electronic drums. Singers often take the name Cheb or Cheba ('young'), for example, Cheb Khaled, Cheb Mami.

rail any wading bird of the family Rallidae, including the rails proper (genus *Rallus*), coots, moorhens, and gallinules. Rails have dark plumage, a short neck and wings, and long legs. They are 10–45 cm/4–18 in long.

Many oceanic islands have their own species of rail, often flightless, such as the Guam rail *R. owstoni* and Auckland Island rail *R. muelleri*. Several of these species have declined sharply, usually because of introduced predators such as rats and cats.

Railtrack British company responsible for the commercial operation of the railway network in Britain. In May 1996 it was privatized, and the 20 British Rail service companies that had previously provided Railtrack's infrastructure support functions were sold into the private sector. There are three rolling stock companies, which lease locomotives and passenger coaches; 25 train operating companies; four freight service providers; seven infrastructure maintenance companies; and six track renewal companies. Railtrack does not operate train services, but is responsible for timetabling and signalling, and owns the freehold of stations. Fatal accidents at London in 1999, at Hatfield in 2000, and at Selby in 2001, led to increased financial difficulties for Railtrack, and demands for greater investment in the railways. Miles of track were relaid in efforts to improve safety, but the Cullen Report of June 2001 made a number of further recommendations, focusing in particular on signal failures.

Related Web site: Railtrack – The Heart of the Railway http://www.railtrack.co.uk/

railway method of transport in which trains convey passengers and goods along a twin rail track. Following the work of British steam pioneers such as the Scottish engineer James ▷Watt, English engineers such as George ▷Stephenson, developed the steam locomotive and built the first railways; Stephenson built the first public steam railway, from Stockton to Darlington, England, in 1825. This heralded extensive railway building in Britain, continental Europe, and North America, providing a fast and economical means of transport and communication. After World War II, steam engines were replaced by electric and diesel engines. At the same time, the growth of road building, air services, and car ownership brought an end to the supremacy of the railways.

Gauge Railway tracks were at first made of wood but later of iron or steel, with ties wedging them apart and keeping them parallel. The distance between the wheels is known as the gauge. Since much of the early development of the railway took place in Tyneside, England, the gauge of local coal wagons, 1.24 m/4 ft 8.5 in, was adopted in 1824 for the Stockton–Darlington railway, and most other early railways followed suit. The main exception was the Great Western Railway (GWR) of Isambard Kingdom ▷Brunel, opened in 1841, with a gauge of 2.13 m/7 ft. The narrow gauge won legal backing in the UK in 1846, but parts of GWR carried on with Brunel's broad gauge until 1892. British engineers building railways overseas tended to use the narrow gauge, and it became the standard in the USA from 1885. Other countries, such as Ireland and Finland, favoured the broad gauge. Although expensive, it offers a more comfortable journey.

Social and economic impact The railways quickly helped spread the ▷Industrial Revolution in Britain. Building the railways increased demand for bricks, stone, wood, iron, and coal. Civil engineering developed and the mechanical engineering industry grew up to supply the precision parts needed by the locomotives. The large amounts of finance needed to construct the railways led to the further development of the ▷stock exchange. Raw materials such as coal could be delivered more promptly, in far greater quantities, and significantly more cheaply than by canal, and manufactured goods distributed more efficiently. Trade, and the velocity of transactions, speeded up, increasing prosperity. The wages of more than a quarter of a million employees went into the British economy, stimulating demand. The expanding railway network contributed to the rise of major towns by bringing ever more people to work in mills and factories. They were the first means of mass passenger transport, and the 1844 Railways Act (the so-called Cheap Trains Act) required railway companies to provide third-class travel on all lines at a cost of no more than a penny (1d) a mile, stopping at every station. The railways were also to play a large part in the growth of mass leisure. Resorts such as Blackpool in the northwest of England grew up to cater for railway holiday excursions by workers from the Lancashire cotton mills. Later, suburbs on the outskirts of London were actively promoted by railway companies – notably the Metropolitan Line, part of the capital's underground system – as pleasant dormitory towns for city commuters. Even time was changed; the demands of accurate timetabling saw the introduction of standard 'railway time' (▷Greenwich Mean Time) to replace a confusing variety of local times. The size and problems of the railway network also required government intervention, even though the government principle of the time was *laissez faire*. After 1840 the Board of Trade appointed inspectors and investigated accidents. In 1842 the government set up the Railway Clearing House to try to co-ordinate the activities of the various companies, and in 1871 the Regulation of Railways Act set up a commission to decide upon amalgamations.

In the huge expanses of the USA, where four standard time zones were fixed, the railways played a key role in spreading settler culture across the continent. Carried by train, white hunters quickly exterminated the vast herds of buffalo on which Native American Plains peoples depended. Ranching and farming took their place, as the railway companies attracted immigrant farmers from Europe. Railheads established along the cattle trails meant that livestock could be transported direct to the slaughterhouses in cities such as Kansas City and Chicago. In Canada, the creation of a unified country was directly linked to railway expansion; in 1871 British Columbia, in the far west, only agreed to join the federation on the promise that a transcontinental railway would be built across its territory.

Decline of the railways With the increasing use of private cars and government-encouraged road haulage after World War II, and the demise of steam, rising costs on the railways meant higher fares, fewer passengers, and declining freight traffic. In the UK many rural rail services closed down on the recommendations of the Beeching Report of 1963, reducing the size of the network by more than 20% between 1965 and 1970, from a peak of 24,102 km/14,977 mi. In the 1970s national railway companies began investing in faster intercity services: in the UK, the diesel high-speed train (HST) was introduced. Elsewhere such trains run on specially built tracks; for example, the Shinkansen (Japan) and TGV (France) networks.

Rail privatization in Britain The process of rail privatization in Britain, which began in 1992, was formally completed in April 1997 when the British Rail chairman signed papers handing over ScotRail to National Express. National Express, with five of the 25 franchises, extending from London to the Highlands, became the biggest single buyer of BR.

The British company ▷Railtrack is now responsible for the track and infrastructure. See also Railways: Key Dates on p. 792.

rain form of ▷precipitation in which separate drops of water fall to the Earth's surface from clouds. The drops are formed by the accumulation of fine droplets that condense from water vapour in the air. The condensation is usually brought about by rising and subsequent cooling of air.

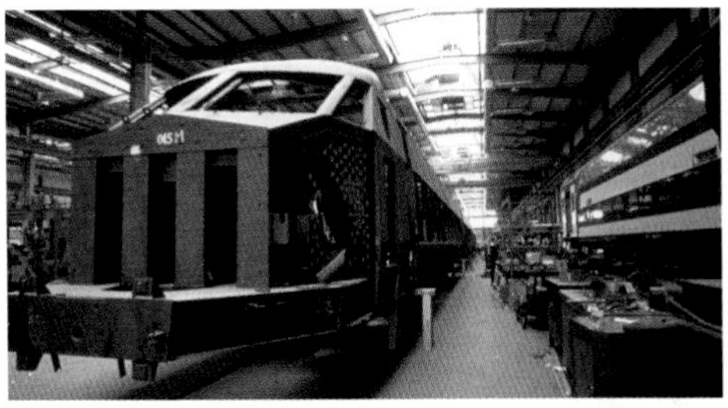

RAILWAY An assembly line for the TGV (*train à grande vitesse*) in Spain. These high-speed trains can reach an average speed of 214 kph/133 mph, which compares well with the Japanese Shinkansen, or bullet train. High-speed trains use less energy per passenger than aeroplanes or cars. *Image Bank*

Railways: Key Dates

1500s	Tramways – wooden tracks along which trolleys run – are in use in European mines.
1785	English engineer William Jessop develops cast-iron rails upon which flanged wheels may run; cars are still horse-drawn.
1797	Some roads in Shropshire, England, are converted to iron railways along which horse-drawn trams may run.
1804	An English engineer, Richard Trevithick, builds the first steam locomotive and runs it on the track at the Pen-y-darren ironworks at Merthyr Tydfil, South Wales.
1820	An English inventor, John Birkinshaw, begins making rails out of wrought iron.
1825	The English engineer George Stephenson builds the first public railway to carry steam trains – the Stockton and Darlington line – using his engine *Locomotion*.
1829	Stephenson designs his locomotive *Rocket*.
1830	Stephenson completes the Liverpool and Manchester Railway, the first steam passenger line. The first US-built locomotive, *Best Friend of Charleston*, goes into service on the South Carolina Railroad.
1832	The German engineer Franz Anton von Gerstner designs the first railway passenger carriages.
1835	Germany pioneers steam railways in Europe, using *Der Adler/The Eagle*, a locomotive built by Stephenson.
1863	Scottish inventor Robert Fairlie patents a locomotive with pivoting driving bogies, allowing tight curves in the track (this is later applied in the Garratt locomotives). London opens the world's first underground railway, powered by steam.
1869	The first US transcontinental railway is completed at Promontory, Utah, when the Union Pacific and the Central Pacific railroads meet. George Westinghouse of the USA invents the compressed-air brake.
1879	German inventor Werner von Siemens demonstrates an electric train at an exhibition in Berlin.
1881	Siemens begins the world's first public electric streetcar service at Lichterfelde, Berlin, Germany.
1883	Volk's Electric Railway begins operating a public service along the Brighton seafront in England and is still in business at the start of the 21st century. French engineer Charles Lartique builds the first monorail, in Ireland. The Orient Express, a luxury steam train running from Paris, France, to Constantinople (later Istanbul), Turkey, enters service. It continues operation until 1977.
1885	The trans-Canada continental railway is completed, from Montréal in the east to Port Moody in the west.
1890	The first electric underground railway opens in London.
1891	Construction of the Trans-Siberian Railway begins. It is completed in 1904. A section of line built in 1916 around Lake Baikal allows passengers to make the journey from Moscow in the west to Vladivostok in the east without changing trains.
1901	The world's longest-established monorail, the Wuppertal Schwebebahn, goes into service in Germany.
1912	The first diesel locomotive takes to the rails in Germany.
1921	The 250 private railway companies that provide the UK's rail services are reorganized into four regional systems.
1938	The British steam locomotive *Mallard* sets a steam-rail speed record of 203 kph/126 mph.
1941	Swiss Federal Railways introduce a gas-turbine locomotive.
1948	A Labour government brings the UK railways into public ownership. The rail services are nationalized under the name British Railways. This name is changed to British Rail in 1965, three years after the setting up of the supervisory British Railways Board.
1955	Steam locomotives begin to be replaced by diesel trains in the UK.
1960s	Electric trains begin to come into regular service in the UK.
1963–65	Richard Beeching, head of the British Railways Board, implements most of the recommendations made in his government report to close down the loss-making parts of the UK rail network. He reduces it from 21,000 km/13,000 mi to 17,000 km/11,000 mi, shutting down many branch lines and closing more than 2,000 stations.
1964	Japan National Railways inaugurates the 515 km/320 mi New Tokaido line between Osaka and Tokyo, on which the 210 kph/130 mph 'bullet' trains run.
1973	British Rail's High Speed Train (HST) sets a diesel-rail speed record of 229 kph/142 mph.
1979	Japan National Railways' maglev test vehicle ML-500 attains a speed of 517 kph/321 mph.
1981	France's Train à Grande Vitesse (TGV) superfast trains begin operation between Paris and Lyons, regularly attaining a peak speed of 270 kph/168 mph.
1987	British Rail sets a new diesel-traction speed record of 238.9 kph/148.5 mph, on a test run between Darlington and York; France and the UK begin work on the Channel Tunnel, a railway link connecting the two countries, running beneath the English Channel.
1988	The West German Intercity Experimental train reaches 405 kph/252 mph on a test run between Würzburg and Fulda.
1990	A new rail-speed record of 515 kph/320 mph is established by a French TGV train, on a stretch of line between Tours and Paris.
1991	The British and French twin tunnels meet 23 km/14 mi out to sea to form the Channel Tunnel.
1993	British Rail privatization plans are announced, separating the management of the infrastructure from the provision of train services and placing the running of the rail system under a regulatory regime; government investment is further reduced.
1994	In the UK's newly privatized rail system, a new company called Railtrack takes over ownership and management of all 17,000 km/11,000 mi of railway lines, signalling and other infrastructure. Rail services start through the Channel Tunnel.
1996	After being awarded franchises under the government's rail privatization programme, the first private companies to offer train services in the UK since 1948 begin operating. Railtrack is floated on the London Stock Exchange.
1998	A Labour government seeks greater regulatory powers over the private rail companies through its proposed Strategic Rail Authority (SRA). The SRA will have power to guide future planning for the UK rail industry, encourage greater rail travel and penalize underperforming franchise-holders.
1999	The government passes legislation to establish the SRA by late 2000.
2000	Railtrack, with the service operator South West Trains, announces a feasibility study for the introduction of double-decker trains to cope with a 25% rise in commuter traffic using London's Waterloo station.

RAINFOREST This picture of typical tropical rainforest vegetation shows giant ferns in the Braulio Carrillo National Park, Costa Rica. *Image Bank*

rainbow arch in the sky displaying the colours of the ▷spectrum formed by the refraction and reflection of the Sun's rays through rain or mist. Its cause was discovered by Theodoric of Freiburg in the 14th century.

rainbow coalition (or **rainbow alliance**) in politics, from the mid-1980s, a loose, left-of-centre alliance of people from several different sections of society that are traditionally politically underrepresented, such as nonwhite ethnic groups. Its aims include promoting minority rights and equal opportunities.

rainforest dense forest usually found on or near the ▷Equator where the climate is hot and wet. Moist air brought by the converging tradewinds rises because of the heat producing heavy rainfall. Over half the tropical rainforests are in Central and South America, primarily the lower Amazon and the coasts of Ecuador and Columbia. The rest are in Southeast Asia (Malaysia, Indonesia, and New Guinea) and in West Africa and the Congo.

Tropical rainforest once covered 14% of the Earth's land surface, but are now being destroyed at an increasing rate as their valuable timber is harvested and the land cleared for agriculture, causing problems of ▷deforestation. Although by 1991 over 50% of the world's rainforest had been removed, they still comprise about 50% of all growing wood on the planet, and harbour at least 40% of the Earth's species (plants and animals).

The vegetation in tropical rainforests typically includes an area of dense forest called **selva**; a **canopy** formed by high branches of tall trees providing shade for lower layers; an intermediate layer of shorter trees and tree roots; ▷lianas; and a ground cover of mosses and ferns. The lack of **seasonal rhythm** causes adjacent plants to flower and shed leaves simultaneously. Chemical weathering and leaching take place in the iron-rich soil due to the high temperatures and humidity.

Rainforests comprise some of the most complex and diverse ecosystems on the planet, deriving their energy from the sun and photosynthesis. In a hectare (10,000 sq m) of rainforest there an estimated 200–300 tree species compared with 20–30 species in a hectare of temperate forest. The trees are the main **producers**. ▷Herbivores such as insects, caterpillars, and monkeys feed on the plants and trees and in turn are eaten by the ▷carnivores, such as ocelots and puma. Fungi and bacteria, the primary **decomposers**, break down the dead material from the plants, herbivores, and carnivores with the help of heat and humidity. This decomposed material provides the **nutrients** for the plants and trees.

The rainforest ecosystem helps to regulate global weather patterns – especially by taking up CO_2 (carbon dioxide) from the atmosphere – and stabilizes the soil. Rainforests provide the bulk of the oxygen needed for plant and animal respiration. When deforestation occurs, the microclimate of the mature forest disappears; soil erosion and flooding become major problems since rainforests protect the shallow tropical soils. Once an area is cleared it is very difficult for shrubs and bushes to re-establish because soils are poor in nutrients. This causes problems for plans to convert rainforests into agricultural land – after two or three years the crops fail and the land is left bare. Clearing of the rainforests may lead to a global warming of the atmosphere, and contribute to the ▷greenhouse effect. See also The Fate of The Rainforests Focus Feature on pp. 794–795.

Related Web site: Rainforests of the World http://www.eco-portal.com/

Rainier, Mount (or Mount Tacoma; American Indian **Tacoma** 'mountain that was God') highest mountain in the Cascade Range, Washington State, USA. Rising to 4,392 m/14,415 ft, it is a dormant volcano, crowned by 5 major and 20 minor glaciers. Dense forests cover the slopes below the treeline, which is located at about 1,520 m/5,000 ft. Mount Rainier National Park was created in 1899.

raison d'être (French) reason for existence.

RAILWAY The first transcontinental railway in the USA was completed on 10 May 1869, when the Union Pacific line from Omaha, Nebraska joined up with the Central Pacific line from Sacramento, California. Workers from each company surrounded the two proprietors (Harriman and Huntington) as they solemnly shook hands for the camera. *Image Bank*

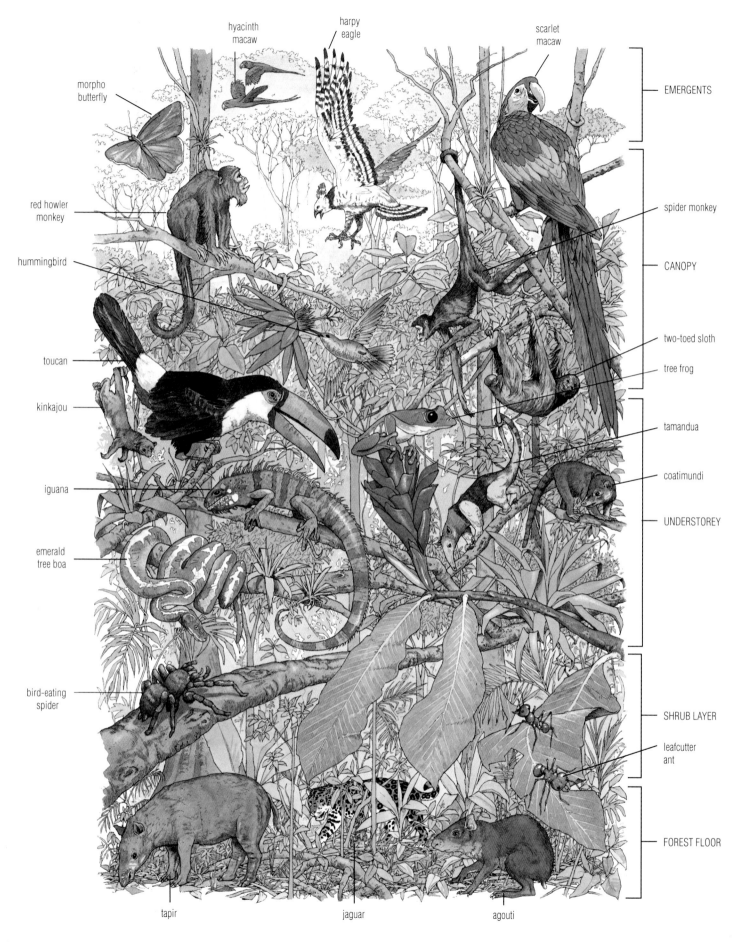

morpho
butterfly

hyacinth
macaw

harpy
eagle

scarlet
macaw

EMERGENTS

red howler
monkey

spider monkey

CANOPY

hummingbird

two-toed sloth

tree frog

toucan

kinkajou

tamandua

coatimundi

iguana

UNDERSTOREY

emerald
tree boa

bird-eating
spider

SHRUB LAYER

leafcutter
ant

FOREST FLOOR

tapir

jaguar

agouti

RAINFOREST A cross section of a South American rainforest, showing the different horizontal layers of vegetation, and the animals and plants found in each layer. To a certain extent the separate layers provide unique microhabitats, with animals and plants found only in one stratum and being adapted to life there, so for example the tapir occupies only the forest floor and some butterfly species always fly at specific heights. Other animals and plants move across strata, for example many of the monkeys and birds.

The Fate of the Rainforests

by Jon Turney

MALAYSIAN RAINFORESTS, being burned as part of a land clearance programme. Human and economic pressures are resulting in encroachment into rainforests, causing widespread deforestation and habitat loss. Despite international efforts to protect such areas, logging and burning has continued and the environmental effects can be felt far outside the immediate area. *Sally Morgan, Ecoscene*

The English naturalist Charles Darwin, who went on to devise the theory of evolution, was greatly impressed by his first sight of the Brazilian rainforest in 1832: 'The elegance of the grasses, the novelty of the parasitical plants, the beauty of the flowers, the glossy green of the foliage, but above all the general luxuriance of the vegetation, filled me with admiration… The noise from the insects is so loud, that it may be heard even in a vessel anchored several hundred yards from the shore.'

rainforests: the richest natural habitat

Today, you can still see what Darwin saw. But it is getting more difficult. We are as likely to agonize about the rainforests as admire them. These richest of all natural habitats are the focus of intense conflicts between developers and conservationists, international agencies and local inhabitants. And their continual erosion concerns people around the world interested in biodiversity and climate change.

no ordinary forest

What Darwin saw was tropical rainforest, the richest kind, which grows in a belt 4° either side of the Earth's equator. It flourishes where it is hottest and wettest, needing mean monthly temperatures of 20–28°C/68–82°F and annual rainfall of 1.5–10 m/ 5–33 ft, spread evenly through the year. This happens in 30 different countries, mainly in South America, the islands of the Malay Archipelago in Asia, and the Congo basin in Africa. The country with the largest area of tropical rainforest is Brazil, with Indonesia second.

Visitors, like Darwin, have always found the rainforest fascinating. The tallest trees soar 45–55 m/ 150–180 ft aloft. Beneath them, several other layers of trees and plants vie for a share of food and energy. Although the tropical sun beats down on the canopy, only 1–3% of the light ever reaches the forest floor. Most of the biological activity takes place well above the ground.

The combination of high rainfall and humidity, high temperatures and abundant energy from sunlight sustains a profusion of competing plant and animal species unlike any other ecosystem. Scientists don't really know how many species there are on the planet. However, the best estimates suggest that around half of them are found in tropical rainforests, even though they only cover 7% of the land area.

This is true for all types of living things. Whatever you sample, the chances are there are more kinds in the rainforest than anywhere else, especially trees, of course. The temperate forests of northern Europe have only 50 native tree species. North America has 171. A single 50-hectare plot of Malayan rainforest yielded 830 species. Tropical trees and plants in turn support thousands of other kinds of creatures. Insects are the most varied by far. A single tree at Tambopata, Peru, hosted 43 different species of ant. You would have to survey the whole of the British Isles to find as many. The plants and insects support many birds and animals. One survey at Maraca in Brazil recorded 450 different species of birds and 45 kinds of bats. Further up the evolutionary scale, rainforest dwellers include 90% of all non-human primates. At the other end of the scale, there may be as many as one and a half million kinds of fungi.

past and future harvest

This vast natural hothouse has yielded many plants vital to humans. In the past, these included rice, potatoes, cassava, tomatoes, peanuts, and bananas for food. We also use bamboo, rubber, coffee, and cocoa.

New edible plants may yet be cultivated, although tropical forests are more likely to yield genetic variants of existing crops that have greater resistance to pests or disease. It is also possible that some plants not yet tested by scientists will contain compounds useful in medicine. Plants were the original source for many valuable drugs, including digitoxin, used to treat heart disease, and quinine, which has antimalarial properties. Many forest peoples, like the Penan in Sarawak, Malaysia, use dozens of medicinal plants.

felling the forest

Human use of the forest lands is changing. Some indigenous peoples, notably groups of American Indians and central African Pygmies, still live as hunter-gatherers, much as they have done for thousands of years. For them, the forest is a kind of natural supermarket. The Chacabo Indians of Bolivia use 82% of the plant species that are known to grow in their foraging grounds.

The forest has limited stocks, though, and supports relatively small populations. Most forest dwellers are farmers, who cultivate the shallow soils in cleared patches, then move on. This so-called 'shifting cultivation' often goes along with planting useful crops in the forest itself, which may even increase its diversity. All this leaves its traces. Around 12% of the vast Amazonian rainforest in Brazil shows signs of past human occupation, such as the relative abundance of particular trees.

But this is nothing compared to the imprint left by modern exploitation. Growing populations, and improved technologies for road-building and for cutting and processing the giant trees, have encouraged incursions into the rainforest. Shifting cultivation is only sustainable when population densities are relatively low, and migrations along new roads increase clearance. Larger agricultural clearances for ranching and commercial logging are also eating into tropical forests wherever they flourish, not to mention mining, dams for hydroelectric power, and oil prospecting.

In many countries, the rainforests are already considerably reduced. In Costa Rica, for example, primary forest cover fell from 67% of the land area to a mere 17% between 1940 and 1983. Losses in other, larger countries are typically less startling. But the largest forest tract of all, in Amazonia, has already shrunk by around 15%.

A TOMATO FROG on Madagascar in the Indian Ocean, where many unusual rainforest species have been able to survive because of the very isolated location of the island. Its bright colours are a signal of its toxicity. © *Image Bank*

A TROPICAL RAINFOREST in St Lucia, which is typical of such environments around the world. Tropical rainforests are found in a narrow geographical band either side of the Equator and are home to a diverse range of species. *Andrew Brown, Ecoscene*

In some ways, this fits a historical pattern. Early 20th-century ecologists saw the rainforest as a stable system, carrying on unchanged for tens of thousands of years. But later studies reveal a more dynamic picture, with widespread traces of damage by volcanoes, storms, droughts, and, most importantly, fires. It is not so long in geological terms, 12,000–18,000 years ago, since Ice-Age climates limited most of the lands where rainforests can grow now to seasonal savannah grasslands.

The other effects we now see in the tropics are not really new either. The temperate forests which once covered much of Europe and China were mostly felled by humans thousands of years ago. European colonists then set about felling the trees of North and South America and Australia. But perhaps rainforests are different. Their remarkable biodiversity, their little-understood effects on atmosphere and climate, to say nothing of their beauty, may mean there is a greater global interest in conserving more of the tropical forest than ever occurred to earlier generations of forest-fellers. For example, there is evidence that rainforests grow faster as atmospheric carbon dioxide increases, which might just slow down global warming.

a future for rainforests?

Whatever the case for preservation, there is no doubt that contemporary rainforests are under threat. Estimates from the United Nations Food and Agriculture Organization, based on a combination of ground-based surveys and remote sensing from space, show a net loss of 65.1 million hectares of forest in developing countries between 1990 and 1995. This is a smaller number than in the decade 1980–90 (13.7 million hectares per year compared with 15.5 million

per year). The net result is that total forestation in the developing world, much of it rainforest, declined by just over 9% between 1980 and 1995.

More local studies show why concern about the future of the forests does not translate easily into successful conservation. Outside activists have often focused on logging for export, for example, but more than three-quarters of Amazon timber is used in Brazil. Estimates based on satellite images indicate that 1.7 million hectares of Amazon forest were lost in 1999. Although government regulations are tightening, and this is slightly smaller than the loss registered the previous year, much illegal felling still takes place.

In central Africa, where an estimated 4 million hectares a year of forest are succumbing to chainsaws, the Worldwide Fund for Nature has teamed up with the World Bank to try and press governments to grant logging concessions to companies that will use known techniques to improve the chances of forest regeneration. A 'forest summit' in Yaoundé, capital of Cameroon, in 2000 saw the presidents of five central African countries pledge to protect remaining forests and harvest timber sustainably. However, such measures reduce production in the short term, and local people lose money and sometimes jobs. Someone then has to explain to these people why they should suffer to preserve biodiversity. Telling them that there are hundreds of species of birds or 1,200 species of termites is not persuasive. They need other sources of income, other ways to buy food. If outsiders want to help preserve the forest, they will probably need to find some way to pay for it. Tourism may be one answer, but it still has a long way to go to compete with the wood trade.

Rajasthan state of northwest India; area 342,200 sq km/ 132,100 sq mi; population (2001 est) 56,728,000. The capital is ▷Jaipur. Industries include textiles, cement, glass, asbestos, chemicals, and mineral extraction. Millet, wheat, and barley are grown; oilseed, cotton, and sugar are produced; and cattle, sheep, and camels are raised.

Related Web site: Rajasthan http://www.bayarea.net/~emerald/ raja1.html

Rajneesh meditation meditation based on the teachings of the Indian Shree Rajneesh (born Chaadra Mohan Jain), established in the early 1970s. Until 1989 he called himself **Bhagwan** (Hindi 'God'). His followers, who number about 0.5 million worldwide, regard themselves as ▷sannyasin, or Hindu ascetics; they wear orange robes and carry a string of prayer beads. They are not expected to observe any specific prohibitions but to be guided by their instincts.

Rajput (or Thakur) member of a Hindu people, predominantly soldiers and landowners, widespread over northern India. The Rajput states of northwestern India are now merged in Rajasthan. The Rana family (ruling aristocracy of Nepal until 1951) was also Rajput. Rajastani languages belong to the Indo-Iranian branch of the Indo-European family.

Raj, the the period of British rule in India before independence in 1947.

Rakhmaninov alternative spelling for Russian composer Sergei ▷Rachmaninov.

Raleigh (or Ralegh), **Walter** (*c.* 1552–1618) English adventurer, writer, and courtier to Queen Elizabeth I. He organized expeditions to colonize North America 1584–87, all unsuccessful, and made exploratory voyages to South America in 1595 and 1616. His aggressive actions against Spanish interests, including attacks on Spanish ports, brought him into conflict with the pacific James I. He was imprisoned for treason 1603–16 and executed on his return from an unsuccessful final expedition to South America. He is traditionally credited with introducing the potato to Europe and popularizing the use of tobacco.

Born in Devon, England, Raleigh became a confidant of Queen Elizabeth I and was knighted in 1584. He led a gold-seeking expedition to the Orinoco River in South America in 1595 (described in his *Discoverie of Guiana* of 1596).

After James I's accession to the English throne in 1603, Raleigh was condemned to death on a charge of conspiracy, but was reprieved and imprisoned in the Tower of London, where he wrote his unfinished *History of the World*. Released in 1616 to lead a second expedition to the Orinoco, which failed disastrously, he was beheaded on his return under the charges of his former sentence.

Related Web site: Raleigh, Sir Walter http://www.luminarium.org/ renlit/ralegh.htm

RAM (acronym for random-access memory) in computing, a memory device in the form of a collection of integrated circuits (chips), frequently used in microcomputers. Unlike ▷ROM (read-only memory) chips, RAM chips can be both read from and written to by the computer, but their contents are lost when the power is switched off.

Many modern commercial programs require a great deal of RAM to work efficiently. By 2004, most PCs were supplied with 512 megabytes (MB) of RAM.

Ram Das (1534–1581) Indian religious leader, fourth guru (teacher) of Sikhism 1574–81, who founded the Sikh holy city of Amritsar.

Rama incarnation of ▷Vishnu, the supreme spirit of Hinduism. He is the hero of the epic poem the ▷*Rāmāyana*, and he is regarded as an example of morality and virtue.

Ramadan in the Muslim ▷calendar, the ninth month of the year. Throughout Ramadan a strict fast is observed during the hours of daylight; Muslims are encouraged to read the whole Koran in commemoration of the Night of Power (which falls during the month) when, it is believed, Muhammad first received his revelations from the angel Gabriel.

Related Web site: Ramadhan and Eid ul Fitr http://www. ummah.org.uk/ramadhan/

Ramakrishna (1836–1886) Adopted name of Gadadhar Chatterjee. Hindu sage, teacher, and mystic (dedicated to achieving oneness with or a direct experience of God or some force beyond the normal world). Ramakrishna claimed that mystical experience was the ultimate aim of religions, and that all religions which led to this goal were equally valid.

Rambert, Marie (1888–1982) Adopted name of Cyvia Myriam Rambam. Polish-born British ballet dancer and teacher. One of the major innovative and influential figures in modern ballet, she worked with Vaslav Nijinsky on *The Rite of Spring* for the Diaghilev ballet in Paris 1912–13, opened the Rambert School in London in 1920, and in 1926 founded the Ballet Rambert which she directed.

JEAN-PHILIPPE RAMEAU French organist and composer, Jean-Phillipe Rameau wrote many varied works. *The Art Archive/Victoria and Albert Museum London*

It became a modern-dance company from 1966 and was renamed the Rambert Dance Company in 1987. Rambert became a British citizen in 1918. She was created a DBE in 1962.

Rameau, Jean-Philippe (1683–1764) French organist and composer. His *Traité de l'harmonie/Treatise on Harmony* (1722) established academic rules for harmonic progression, and his varied works include keyboard and vocal music and many operas, such as *Castor and Pollux* (1737).

Rameses alternative spelling of ▷Ramses, name of kings of ancient Egypt.

ramjet simple jet engine (see under ▷jet propulsion) used in some guided missiles. It only comes into operation at high speeds. Air is then 'rammed' into the combustion chamber, into which fuel is sprayed and ignited.

Ramos, Fidel (Eddie) (1928–) Filipino centre-right politician, president 1992–98. He launched a commission to consult with Muslim secessionist rebel groups on Mindanao, which produced a peace deal with one of the rebel groups in September 1996. In addition, as part of a government move to end corruption and human-rights abuses, he purged the police force. These and other initiatives won him popular support, and in the May 1995 congressional elections, with the economy booming, his supporters won a sweeping victory. However, from 1997 the economic situation deteriorated, with the peso being devalued in July 1997. Ramos was prevented, by the constitution, from seeking a second term in 1998 and he was succeeded by the former vice president Joseph Estrada.

Ramsay, Allan (1713–1784) Scottish painter. Having studied in Edinburgh and then in Italy, he settled in London, becoming one of the most successful portraitists of his day, his works valued for their charm and elegance. He became artist to George III in 1760 and played an active role in London's literary and intellectual life.

Ramsay, Allan (1685–1758) Scottish anthologist and poet. He was chiefly responsible for the renaissance of Scottish literature in the 18th century. *The Ever Green* (1724) was an anthology of mainly edited versions of pre-1600 Scottish poetry, including the work of William ▷Dunbar and Robert Henryson. The several volumes of *The Tea-Table Miscellany* (1724–37) comprised songs and ballads.

Ramsay, William (1852–1916) Scottish chemist who, with Lord Rayleigh, discovered argon in 1894. In 1895 Ramsay produced helium and in 1898, in cooperation with Morris Travers, identified neon, krypton, and xenon. In 1903, with Frederick ▷Soddy, he noted the transmutation of radium into helium, which led to the discovery of the density and relative atomic mass of radium. He was awarded the Nobel Prize for Chemistry in 1904 for his discovery of inert gases in air and their locations in the periodic table. He was made a KCB in 1902.

In his book *The Gases of the Atmosphere* (1896), Ramsay repeated a suspicion he had stated in 1892 that there was an eighth group of new elements at the end of the periodic table. During the next decade Ramsay and Travers sought the remaining rare gases by the fractional distillation of liquid air.

Ramses (or Rameses) 11 kings (pharaohs) of ancient Egypt, including:

Ramses II (or Rameses II) Called 'Ramses the Great'. King (pharaoh) of ancient Egypt about 1279–1213 BC, the son of Seti I. He campaigned successfully against the Hittites, and built two rock temples at ▷Abu Simbel in southern Egypt.

RAMSES II The face of the pharaoh Ramses II, king of ancient Egypt. His was the face on the colossi (huge seated statues) that were carefully moved, with international cooperation, from Abu Simbel to higher ground before the building of the Aswan Dam. *Image Bank*

Ramses III (or Rameses III) King (pharaoh) of ancient Egypt about 1187–1156 BC. He won victories over the Libyans and the ▷Sea Peoples and asserted his control over Palestine.

Ramsey, Alf(red) Ernest (1920–1999) English football player and manager. England's most successful manager ever, he won the 1966 World Cup. Of the 113 matches in which he was in charge of the national side between 1963 and 1974, England had 69 victories, 27 draws, and only 17 defeats. Shrewd, pragmatic, and single-minded, he was not afraid to go against traditional football wisdom, most notably in 1966 when he decided to play without wingers; a step which was greeted with widespread scepticism, but subsequently was hailed as a masterstroke when England won the World Cup. He led England to the quarter-finals of the 1970 World Cup, but was sacked four years later after the team failed to qualify for the 1974 finals.

As a player for Southampton and then Tottenham, he was capped 32 times by England, before becoming the manager of Ipswich Town in 1955. He took the club up from the Third Division in 1957, and in 1961–62 won the Second and First Division titles in consecutive seasons. He retired from football management after he was sacked as the national team manager, but returned for a brief spell with Birmingham City in 1977.

random access in computing, an alternative term for ▷direct access.

random number one of a series of numbers having no detectable pattern. Random numbers are used in ▷computer simulation and ▷computer games. It is impossible for an ordinary computer to generate true random numbers, but various techniques are available for obtaining pseudo-random numbers – close enough to true randomness for most purposes.

rangefinder instrument for determining the range or distance of an object from the observer; used to focus a camera or to sight a gun accurately. A **rangefinder camera** has a rotating mirror or prism that alters the image seen through the viewfinder, and a secondary window. When the two images are brought together into one, the lens is sharply focused.

Rangoon former name (to 1989) of ▷Yangon, the capital of Myanmar (Burma).

Ranjit Singh (1780–1839) Indian maharajah. He succeeded his father as a minor Sikh leader In 1792, and created a Sikh army that conquered Kashmir and the Punjab. In alliance with the British, he established himself as 'Lion of the Punjab', ruler of the strongest of the independent Indian states.

Rank, J(oseph) Arthur, 1st Baron Rank (1888–1972) English film magnate. Having entered films in 1933 to promote the Methodist cause, by the mid-1940s he controlled, through the Rank Organization, half the British studios and more than 1,000 cinemas. The Rank Organization still owns the Odeon chain of cinemas, although film is now a minor part of its activities. He was created a baron in 1957.

Ransome, Arthur (Michell) (1884–1967) English writer of adventure stories for children. A journalist, he was correspondent in Russia for the *Daily News* during World War I and the Russian Revolution. His children's novels feature sailing and include *Swallows and Amazons* (1930) and *Peter Duck* (1932).

Rao, P(amulaparti) V(enkata) Narasimha (1921–) Indian politician, prime minister 1991–96 and Congress leader 1991–96. He governed the state of Andhra Pradesh as chief minister 1971–73, and served in the cabinets of Indira and Rajiv Gandhi as minister of external affairs 1980–85 and 1988–90 and of human resources 1985–88. He took over the Congress party leadership after the assassination of Rajiv Gandhi. Elected prime minister the following month, he instituted a market-centred and outward-looking reform of the economy. He survived a vote of no confidence in 1993. After Congress was defeated in national elections in May 1996, Rao resigned as prime minister and dissolved parliament. He resigned as Congress leader in September 1996 as allegations mounted over his alleged involvement in political bribery. Along with his home minister, Buta Singha, he was sentenced in October 2000 to three years imprisonment, having been found guilty of bribing opposition MPs to swing a vote the government's way in a crucial confidence vote in 1993.

> **Arthur Ransome**
> *Grab a chance and you won't be sorry for a might-have-been.*
> *We Didn't Mean to Go to Sea* ch. 2

rape in law, sexual intercourse without the consent of the subject. Most cases of rape are of women by men. In Islamic law a rape accusation requires the support of four independent male witnesses.

Rape and sexual abuse are systematically used in many countries, such as Pakistan, against women in police custody; and in warfare, to intimidate civilian populations and force ethnic groups to flee. Tens of thousands of women have been raped in the conflicts in former Yugoslavia.

In the UK from 1976 the victim's name may not be published, her sex history should not be in question, and her 'absence of consent' rather than (as previously required) proof of her 'resistance to violence' is the criterion of the crime. The anonymity of the accused is also preserved unless he is convicted. In 1985, there were 22,900 reported cases of sexual assault in the UK. However, since victims are often unwilling to report what has happened, it is thought that there are perhaps ten times as many rapes as the reported figure. In 1991 rape within marriage became a criminal offence (as was already the case in Scotland, the Republic of Ireland, New Zealand, Israel, and some states in the USA and Australia).

rape in botany, either of two plant species of the mustard family grown for their seeds, which yield a pungent edible oil. The common turnip is a variety of *B. rapa* and the swede turnip is a variety of of *B. napus*. (Genus *Brassica rapa* and *B. napus*, family Cruciferae.)

Raphael Sanzio (1483–1520) Born Raffaello Sanzio. Painter and architect born in Urbino and eventually settled in Rome. He painted portraits and mythological and religious works, noted for their harmony of colour and composition. He was active in Perugia, Florence, and (from 1508) Rome, where he painted frescoes in the Vatican. Among his best-known works are *The Marriage of the Virgin* (1504; Brera, Milan) and the fresco *The School of Athens* (1509–11; Vatican, Rome).

Raphael was the son of Giovanni Santi (died 1494), a painter at the court of Urbino. In 1499 he went to Perugia, where he worked with ▷Perugino, whose graceful style is reflected in Raphael's *Marriage of the Virgin*. This work also shows his early concern for harmonious disposition of figures in the pictorial space.

In Florence 1504–08 he studied the works of Leonardo da Vinci, Michelangelo, Masaccio, and Fra Bartolommeo. His paintings of this period include the *Ansidei Madonna*. Pope Julius II commissioned him to decorate the papal apartments (the Stanze della Segnatura) in the Vatican. Raphael's first fresco series there, *The School of Athens*, is a complex but classically composed grouping of Greek philosophers and mathematicians, centred on the figures of Plato and Aristotle. A second series of frescoes 1511–14 includes the dramatic and richly coloured *Mass of Bolsena*.

Raphael received many commissions and within the next few years he produced mythological frescoes in the Villa Farnesina in Rome 1511–12; cartoons for tapestries for the Sistine Chapel in the Vatican; the *Sistine Madonna* about 1512; and portraits, for example of Baldassare Castiglione about 1515.

He inspired many of his contemporaries and later the Caracci, Rubens, Poussin, and Rembrandt, the neoclassicists and the Romantics.

rap music rapid, rhythmic chant over a prerecorded repetitive backing track. Rap emerged in New York 1979 as part of the ▷hip-hop culture, although the macho, swaggering lyrics that initially predominated have roots in ritual boasts and insults. Different styles were flourishing by the 1990s, such as jazz rap, ▷gangsta rap, and reggae rap.

rare-earth element alternative name for ▷lanthanide.

rare gas alternative name for ▷inert gas.

Rarotonga Treaty agreement that formally declares the South Pacific a nuclear-free zone. The treaty came into effect in December 1986, having been signed by members of the ▷Pacific Islands Forum. China and the USSR later signed protocols concerning nuclear-armed powers. The treaty takes its name from Rarotonga, in the Cook Islands, where an anti-nuclear Declaration on Natural Resources and the Environment was adopted at an international conference in 1982.

Ras al Khaimah (or Ra's al Khaymah) emirate on the Gulf; area 1,690 sq km/652 sq mi; population (1995) 144,400. Products include oil, pharmaceuticals, and cement. It is one of the seven members of the ▷United Arab Emirates.

Related Web site: Ras al Khaimah http://www.uaeforever.com/RasAlKhaimah/

rash in medicine, eruption on the surface of the skin. It is usually raised and red or it may contain vesicles filled with fluid. It may also be scaly or crusty. Characteristic rashes are produced by infectious diseases, such as chickenpox, measles, German measles, and scarlet fever. The severity of the rash usually reflects the severity of the disease. Rashes are also produced as an allergic response to stings from insects and plants. These are often alleviated by antihistamines and they usually resolve within a few days.

raspberry any of a group of prickly cane plants native to Europe, Asia, and North America, and widely cultivated. They have white flowers followed by hollow red composite fruits, which are eaten fresh as a delicacy and used for making jam and wine. (Genus *Rubus*, family Rosaceae.)

RASPBERRY The wild raspberry *Rubus idaeus* grows in woods and on heathland, especially in hilly districts, throughout much of Europe (including Iceland) and Asia. *Premaphotos Wildlife*

Rasputin (1871–1916) Born Grigory Efimovich Novykh. (Russian 'dissolute') Siberian Eastern Orthodox mystic. He acquired influence over the Tsarina ▷Alexandra, wife of ▷Nicholas II, and was able to make political and ecclesiastical appointments. His abuse of power and notorious debauchery (reputedly including the tsarina) led to his murder by a group of nobles.

Rasputin, the illiterate son of a peasant, began as a wandering 'holy man'. Through the tsarina's faith in his power to ease her son's suffering from haemophilia, he became a favourite at the court, where he instigated wild parties under the slogan 'Sin that you may obtain forgiveness'. A larger-than-life character, he even proved hard to kill: when poison had no effect, his assassins shot him and dumped him in the River Neva.

Related Web site: Rasputin http://www.stlawu.edu/rkre:http/indv5/rasp.htm

Rastafarianism religion originating in the West Indies, based on the ideas of Marcus ▷Garvey, who called on black people to return to Africa and set up a black-governed country there. When Haile Selassie (**Ras Tafari**, 'Lion of Judah') was crowned emperor of Ethiopia in 1930, this was seen as a fulfilment of prophecy and some Rastafarians acknowledged him as an incarnation of God (**Jah**), others as a prophet. The use of ganja (marijuana) is a sacrament. There are no churches. In 2000 it was estimated that there were 700,000 Rastafarians worldwide.

raster graphics computer graphics that are stored in the computer memory by using a map to record data (such as colour and intensity) for every ▷pixel that makes up the image. When transformed (enlarged, rotated, stretched, and so on), raster graphics become ragged and suffer loss of picture resolution, unlike ▷vector graphics. Raster graphics are typically used for painting applications, which allow the user to create artwork on a computer screen much as if they were painting on paper or canvas.

rat any of numerous long-tailed ▷rodents (especially of the families Muridae and Cricetidae) larger than mice and usually with scaly, naked tails. The genus *Rattus* in the family Muridae includes the rats found in human housing.

The **brown rat** *R. norvegicus* is about 20 cm/8 in long with a tail of almost equal length. It is believed to have originated in central Asia, and is now found worldwide after being transported from Europe by ships. Female brown rats become sexually receptive at the age of 8–12 weeks. If food is plentiful, litters of up to 12 are born every few months. The **black rat** *R. rattus*, responsible for the ▷plague, is smaller than the brown rat, but has larger ears and a

RAT A cotton rat *Sigmodon hispidus* at night in dry tropical rainforest in Costa Rica. *K G Preston-Mafham/Premaphotos Wildlife*

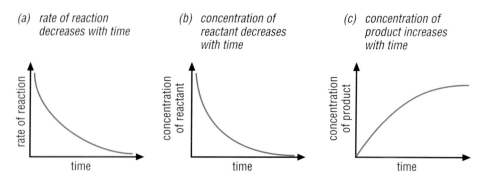

(a) rate of reaction decreases with time

(b) concentration of reactant decreases with time

(c) concentration of product increases with time

RATE OF REACTION The rate of reaction decreases with time whilst the concentration of product increases.

longer, more pointed snout. It does not interbreed with brown rats. The **pack rat** or **wood rat**, genus *Neotoma*, is common throughout North America and there are seven different species. Their dens, made of partly eaten plants, dung, and miscellaneous objects, are known as middens and can be up to 2 m/6.5 ft across and 20–30 cm/8–12 in high. The rats' crystallized urine preserves the midden, in some cases for up to 40,000 years.

rate of reaction the speed at which a chemical reaction proceeds. It is usually expressed in terms of the concentration (usually in ▷moles per litre) of a reactant consumed, or product formed, in unit time; so the units would be moles per litre per second (mol l^{-1} s^{-1}). The rate of a reaction may be affected by the concentration of the reactants, the temperature of the reactants (or the amount of light in the case of a photochemical reaction), and the presence of a ▷catalyst. If the reaction is entirely in the gas state, the rate is affected by pressure, and, where one of the reactants is a solid, it is affected by the particle size.

rates in the UK, a local government tax levied on industrial and commercial property (business rates) and, until the introduction of the community charge (see ▷poll tax) 1989–90, also on residential property to pay for local amenities such as roads, footpaths, refuse collection and disposal, and community and welfare activities. The water companies also use a rating system to charge most householders for water supply.

ratio measure of the relative size of two quantities or of two measurements (in similar units), expressed as a proportion. For example, the ratio of vowels to consonants in the alphabet is 5:21; the ratio of 500 m to 2 km is 500:2,000, or 1:4. Ratios are normally expressed as whole numbers, so 2:3.5 would become 4:7 (the ratio remains the same provided both numbers are multiplied or divided by the same number).

rationalism in theology, the belief that human reason rather than divine revelation is the correct means of ascertaining truth and regulating behaviour. In philosophy, rationalism takes the view that self-evident ▷a priori propositions (deduced by reason alone) are the sole basis of all knowledge. It is usually contrasted with ▷empiricism, which argues that all knowledge must ultimately be derived from the senses.

rational number in mathematics, any number that can be expressed as an exact fraction (with a denominator not equal to 0), that is, as $a \div b$ where a and b are integers; or an exact decimal. For example, $\frac{2}{7}, \frac{1}{4}, 1\frac{5}{4}, -\frac{3}{5}$ are all rational numbers, whereas π (which represents the constant 3.141592 ...) is not. Numbers such as π are called ▷irrational numbers.

Ratisbon English name for the German city of ▷Regensburg.

ratite flightless bird that has a breastbone without the keel to which flight muscles are attached. Examples are ▷ostrich, ▷rhea, ▷emu, ▷cassowary, and ▷kiwi.

rat-tail (or **grenadier**) any fish of the family Macrouridae of deep-sea bony fishes. They have stout heads and bodies, and long tapering tails. They are common in deep waters on the continental slopes. Some species have a light-emitting organ in front of the anus.

Rattle, Simon (1955–) English conductor, principal conductor of the City of Birmingham Symphony Orchestra (CBSO) 1979–98. He built the CBSO into a world-class orchestra, with a core repertoire of early 20th-century music; he also commissioned new works. A popular and dynamic conductor, he achieves a characteristically clear and precise sound. In 1999 he was appointed artistic director of the Berlin Philharmonic Orchestra, seen as one of the most prestigious posts in the classical music world. He is expected to take up the post in 2002, when the present conductor, Claudio Abbado, steps down.

rattlesnake any of various New World pit ▷vipers of the genera *Crotalus* and *Sistrurus* (the massasaugas and pygmy rattlers), distinguished by horny flat segments of the tail, which rattle when vibrated as a warning to attackers. They can grow to 2.5 m/8 ft long. The venom injected by some rattlesnakes can be fatal.

There are 31 species distributed from southern Canada to central South America. The eastern diamondback *C. adamanteus* 0.9–2.5 m/2.8–8 ft long, is found in the flat pinelands of the southern USA.

Rauschenberg, Robert (1925–) Born Milton Rauschenberg. US pop artist. He has created happenings and multimedia works, called 'combined painting', such as *Monogram* (1959; Moderna Museet, Stockholm), a stuffed goat daubed with paint and wearing a car tyre around its body. In the 1960s he returned to painting and used the silk-screen printing process to transfer images to canvas.

Ravel, (Joseph) Maurice (1875–1937) French composer and pianist. His work is characterized by its sensuousness, exotic harmonics, and dazzling orchestral effects. His opera *L'enfant et les sortilèges* (1924) illustrates most of the various styles which influenced him at different times. Other works include the piano pieces *Pavane pour une infante défunte/Pavane for a Dead Infanta* (1899) and *Jeux d'eau/Waterfall* (1901), and the ballets *Daphnis et Chloë* (1912) and *Boléro* (1928).

raven any of several large ▷crows, genus *Corvus*, of the Corvidae family, order Passeriformes. The common raven *C. corax* is about 60 cm/2 ft long with a wingspan of nearly 1 m/3 ft, and has black, lustrous plumage; the beak and mouth, tongue, legs, and feet are also black. It is a scavenger and is found only in the northern hemisphere.

The nest is built in cliffs or in the fork of a tall tree, and is a bulky structure. In it are laid four or five pale-green eggs spotted with brown. Incubation by the female lasts about 21 days.

Ravens are traditionally associated with death, probably from their practice of gathering in large numbers around a carcass, despite being by habit a solitary species.

Ravenna industrial port in Emilia-Romagna, Italy, about 65 km/ 40 mi east of Bologna; population (1992) 137,100. It is connected to the Adriatic Sea by the Corsini Canal. Industries include oil-refining, and the production of petrochemicals, synthetic rubber, and fertilizers. It lies in a marshy plain and methane deposits have been discovered nearby. The town has several Byzantine churches with superb mosaics.

RAVENNA One of the mosaics for which Ravenna is famous is a depiction of the Roman port of Classis, showing the castle battlements and ships in the harbour, 6th century AD (San Apollinare Nuovo, Ravenna). *Art Archive*

Rawalpindi city in Punjab province, Pakistan, on the north bank of the River Leh, 175 km/110 mi southeast of Peshawar in the foothills of the Himalayas; population (1998) 1,406,200. Industries include oil refining, iron, chemicals, locomotives and furniture. There is a considerable trade in grain, wool, and timber. It has good communications by rail and by air and is both a commercial and a military centre which is strategically important because it controls routes into Kashmir. It was the temporary capital of Pakistan 1959–67 during the construction nearby of the new capital, ▷Islamabad.

ray any of several orders (especially Ragiformes) of cartilaginous fishes with a flattened body, winglike pectoral fins, and a whiplike tail.

Ray, John (1627–1705) English naturalist who devised a classification system accounting for some 18,000 plant species. It was the first system to divide flowering plants into ▷monocotyledons and ▷dicotyledons, with additional divisions made on the basis of leaf and flower characters and fruit types.

Ray, Man (1890–1976) Adopted name of Emmanuel Rabinovich Rudnitsky. US photographer, painter, and sculptor. He was active mainly in France and was associated with the ▷Dada movement and then ▷surrealism. One of his best-known sculptures is *Gift* (1921), a surrealist ▷ready-made consisting of an iron on to which a row of nails has been glued.

Man Ray was born in Philadelphia, but lived mostly in Paris from 1921. He began as a painter and took up photography in 1915, the year he met the Dada artist Marcel ▷Duchamp in New York. In 1922 he invented the **rayograph**, a black-and-white image obtained without a camera by placing objects on sensitized photographic paper and exposing them to light. He also used the technique of **solarization** (partly reversing the tones on a photograph). Among his photographs is *Le Violon d'Ingres* (1924), a nude woman viewed from the back so as to suggest a violin. His photographs include portraits of many artists and writers.

His autobiography, *Self Portrait*, appeared in 1963.

Related Web site: Ray, Man http://www.icp.org/exhibitions/ man_ray/mr_bio.html

> ## Man Ray
> *It has never been my object to record my dreams, just the determination to realize them.*
> Quoted in N Baldwin, *Man Ray*

Ray, Nicholas (1911–1979) Adopted name of Raymond Nicholas Kienzle. US film director. He was critically acclaimed for socially aware dramas that concentrated on the individual as an outsider, such as *They Live by Night* (1948) and *Rebel Without a Cause* (1955). Other films include *In a Lonely Place* (1950) and *55 Days at Peking* (1963).

Ray, Satyajit (1921–1992) Indian film director. He became internationally known with his trilogy of life in his native Bengal: *Pather Panchali*, *Unvanquished*, and *The World of Apu* (1955–59). Later films include *The Music Room* (1963), *Charulata* (1964), *The Chess Players* (1977), and *The Home and the World* (1984).

rayon any of various shiny textile fibres and fabrics made from ▷cellulose. It is produced by pressing whatever cellulose solution is used through very small holes and solidifying the resulting filaments. A common type is ▷viscose, which consists of regenerated filaments of pure cellulose. Acetate and triacetate are kinds of rayon consisting of filaments of cellulose acetate and triacetate.

razorbill North Atlantic sea bird *Alca torda* of the auk family, order Charadriiformes, which breeds on cliffs and migrates south in winter. It is about 40 cm/16 in long, has a large curved beak, and is black above and white below. It uses its wings as paddles when diving. Razorbills make no nest; the female lays a single egg, which is white with brown markings. They are common off Newfoundland.

razor-shell (or **razor-fish**; US name **razor clam**) any bivalve mollusc in two genera *Ensis* and *Solen* with narrow, elongated shells, resembling an old-fashioned razor handle and delicately coloured. They can burrow rapidly into sand and are good swimmers.

reaction in chemistry, the coming together of two or more atoms, ions, or molecules with the result that a chemical change takes place; that is, a change that occurs when two or more substances interact with each other, resulting in the production of different substances with different chemical compositions. The nature of the reaction is portrayed by a ▷chemical equation.

Chemical equations show the reactants and products of a chemical reaction by using chemical symbols and formulae. State symbols and the energy symbol (ΔH) can be used to show whether reactants and products are solids, liquids, or gases, and whether energy has been released or absorbed during the reaction.

reactivity series chemical series produced by arranging the metals in order of their ease of reaction with reagents such as oxygen, water, and acids. This arrangement aids the understanding of the properties of metals, helps to explain differences between them, and enables predictions to be made about a metal's behaviour, based on a knowledge of its position or properties. It also allows prediction of the relative stability of the compounds formed by an element: the more reactive the metal, the more stable its compounds are likely to be.

Read, Herbert (Edward) (1893–1968) English critic and poet. His reputation as an art critic was established in the 1930s and 1940s, when he was a keen supporter of such artists as Henry ▷Moore, Barbara ▷Hepworth, and Ben ▷Nicholson. His many books and essays, which helped to make modern art accessible to a wider public, include *The Meaning of Art* (1931) and the influential *Education through Art* (1943). He was knighted in 1953.

Reading industrial town and unitary authority in southern England, on the River Thames where it meets the Kennet, 61 km/38 mi west of London; it was the administrative headquarters of the county of Berkshire until April 1998.

area 37 sq km/14 sq mi **features** remains of a 12th-century Benedictine abbey where Henry I is buried; the Museum of Reading includes Roman and Saxon relics, and a full-size Victorian reproduction of the Bayeaux Tapestry; the Museum of English Rural Life is also here; Reading hosts an annual pop festival **industries** biscuits, brewing, boats, engineering, printing, and electronics; it is an agricultural and horticultural centre with seed-testing grounds, and is a major bulb producer **population** (1996) 131,000 **famous people** William Laud, archbishop of Canterbury from 1633; the writer Oscar Wilde spent two years in Reading jail (1895–97) **history** reading was a Danish encampment in 871. By the time of the Domesday survey of 1086, 'Radynges', as it was then known, had 30 religious houses. The Benedictine abbey was founded in 1121 and consecrated in 1164. In the 16th century the town was important in the cloth industry. The university was established in 1892 as a college affiliated to the University of Oxford and gained independent university status in 1926. The city was extensively rebuilt after World War II.

ready-made in the visual arts, an object chosen at random by the artist, as opposed to being selected for any presumed aesthetic merit, and presented as a work of art. The concept was first launched by Marcel ▷Duchamp when he exhibited a bicycle wheel set on a stool in 1913. Popular among Dadaists, ready-mades have been used to challenge the elitist qualities of fine art.

Reagan, Ronald (Wilson) (1911–) 40th president of the USA 1981–89, a Republican. He was governor of California 1966–74, and a former Hollywood actor. Reagan was a hawkish and popular president. He adopted an aggressive policy in Central America, attempting to overthrow the government of Nicaragua, and invading Grenada in 1983. In 1987, ▷Irangate was investigated by the Tower Commission; Reagan admitted that USA–Iran negotiations had become an 'arms for hostages deal', but denied knowledge of resultant funds being illegally sent to the Contras guerrillas in Nicaragua. He increased military spending (sending the national budget deficit to record levels), cut social programmes, introduced the deregulation of domestic markets, and cut taxes. His ▷Strategic Defense Initiative, announced in 1983, proved controversial owing to the cost, unfeasibility, and opposition of the USSR. Leaving office in 1988 at the age of 78, he was the oldest president in US history. He was succeeded by Vice-President George Bush.

Reagan was born in Tampico, Illinois, the son of a shoe salesman who was bankrupted during the Depression. He graduated from Eureka College, Illinois, and was a sports announcer in Davenport and Des Moines, Iowa 1932–37. He became a Hollywood actor in 1937 and appeared in 50 films, including *Bedtime for Bonzo* (1951) and *The Killers* (1964). He is best remembered for the films *Knute Rockne, All American* (1940), where he used the film line 'Win one for the Gipper', and for *Kings Row* (1942).

As president of the Screen Actors' Guild 1947–52, he became a conservative, critical of the bureaucratic stifling of free enterprise, and named names before the ▷House Un-American Activities Committee. He joined the Republican Party in 1962, and his term as governor of California was marked by battles against student protesters.

Having lost the Republican presidential nomination in 1968 and 1976 to Richard Nixon and Gerald Ford respectively, Reagan won it in 1980 and defeated President Jimmy Carter. He was wounded in an assassination attempt in 1981. The invasion of Grenada, following a coup there, generated a revival of national patriotism, and this, along with his record of tax cutting, was one of the various causes of his landslide re-election in 1984. His last years in office were dominated by friction with the USSR over the USA's ▷Strategic Defense Initiative, popularly called Star Wars because incoming missiles would be intercepted in space.

Related Web site: Ronald Reagan – Fortieth President 1981–1989
http://www.whitehouse.gov/WH/glimpse/presidents/html/rr40.html

realism in the arts and literature generally, an unadorned, naturalistic approach to subject matter. More specifically, realism refers to a movement in mid-19th-century European art and literature, a reaction against Romantic and classical idealization and a rejection of conventional academic themes (such as mythology, history, and sublime landscapes) in favour of everyday life and carefully observed social settings. The movement was particularly important in France, where it had political overtones; the painters Gustave ▷Courbet and Honoré ▷Daumier, two leading realists, both used their art to expose social injustice.

realism in philosophy, the theory that ▷universals (properties such as 'redness') have an existence independent of the human mind. Realists hold that the essence of things is objectively given in nature, and that our classifications are not arbitrary. As such, realism is contrasted with nominalism, the theory that universals are merely names or general terms.

real number in mathematics, any of the ▷rational numbers (which include the integers) or ▷irrational numbers. Real numbers exclude ▷imaginary numbers, found in ▷complex numbers of the general form $a + bi$ where $i = \sqrt{-1}$, although these do include a real component a.

realpolitik (German *Realpolitik* 'politics of realism') belief that the pragmatic pursuit of self-interest and power, backed up by force when convenient, is the only realistic option for a great state. The term was coined in 1859 to describe the German chancellor ▷Bismarck's policies.

real tennis racket and ball game played in France, from about the 12th century, over a central net in an indoor court, but with a sloping roof let into each end and one side of the court, against which the ball may be hit. The term 'real' here means 'royal', not 'genuine'. Basic scoring is as for lawn ▷tennis, but with various modifications.

REAL TENNIS Beyond the Fountain Gardens at Hampton Court, near Richmond, England, are the indoor real tennis courts, where King Henry VIII first played. Real tennis courts are a rarity in England. *Image Bank*

real-time system in computing, a program that responds to events in the world as they happen. For example, an automatic-pilot program in an aircraft must respond instantly in order to correct deviations from its course. Process control, robotics, games, and many military applications are examples of real-time systems.

received pronunciation (RP) in the UK, a term used to describe national and international English accents which are associated with ▷Standard English. Spoken by royalty and representatives of the church, the government, and the law courts, RP is the language of official authority.

receiver in law, a person appointed by a court to collect and manage the assets of an individual, company, or partnership in serious financial difficulties. In the case of bankruptcy, the assets may be sold and distributed by a receiver to creditors.

receptacle the enlarged end of a flower stalk to which the floral parts are attached. Normally the receptacle is rounded, but in some plants it is flattened or cup-shaped. The term is also used for the region on that part of some seaweeds which becomes swollen at certain times of the year and bears the reproductive organs.

recession in economics, a fall in business activity lasting more than a few months, causing stagnation in a country's output. A serious recession is called a **slump**.

recessive gene in genetics, an ▷allele (alternative form of a gene) that will show in the ▷phenotype (observed characteristics of an organism) only if its partner allele on the paired chromosome is similarly recessive. Such an allele will not show if its partner is dominant, that is if the organism is ▷heterozygous for a particular characteristic. Alleles for blue eyes in humans and for shortness in pea plants are recessive. Most mutant alleles are recessive and therefore are only rarely expressed (see ▷haemophilia).

reciprocal in mathematics, the result of dividing a given quantity into 1. Thus the reciprocal of 2 is $\frac{1}{2}$; of $\frac{2}{3}$ is $\frac{3}{2}$; of x^2 is $\frac{1}{x^2}$ or x^{-2}. Reciprocals are used to replace division by multiplication, since multiplying by the reciprocal of a number is the same as dividing by that number.

recitative in opera and oratorio, sung narration partly modelled on the rhythms and inflections of natural speech. It is usually sparingly accompanied by harpsichord or organ.

recombination in genetics, any process that recombines, or 'shuffles', the genetic material, thus increasing genetic variation in the offspring. The two main processes of recombination both occur during meiosis (reduction division of cells). One is **crossing over**, in which chromosome pairs exchange segments; the other is the random reassortment of chromosomes that occurs when each gamete (sperm or egg) receives only one of each chromosome pair.

Reconquista (Spanish 'reconquest') Christian defeat of the ▷Moors 9th–15th centuries, and their expulsion from Spain.

Reconstruction in US history, the period 1865–77 after the Civil War during which the nation was reunited under the federal government after the defeat of the Southern Confederacy.

Amendments to the US constitution, and to Southern state constitutions, conferred equal civil and political rights on blacks, although many Southern states, opposed to these radical Republican measures, still practised discrimination and segregation. During Reconstruction, industrial and commercial projects restored the economy of the South but failed to ensure racial equality, and the former slaves remained, in most cases, landless labourers, although emancipated slaves were assisted in finding work, shelter, and lost relatives through federal agencies. Reconstruction also resulted in an influx of Northern profiteers known as ▷carpetbaggers. Both the imposition of outside military authority and the equal status conferred on former slaves combined to make Southerners bitterly resentful. Although Radical Republicans sought punitive measures against the South, they were restrained by President Abraham ▷Lincoln. When President Andrew ▷Johnson refused to agree to their programme, the Radicals contrived to bring about his impeachment, failing by one vote to convict him.

Related Web site: Report of the Joint Committee on Reconstruction
http://odur.let.rug.nl/~usa/D/1851-1875/reconstruction/repojc.htm

recorder in the English legal system, a part-time judge who usually sits in the ▷crown courts in less serious cases but may also sit in the county courts or the High Court. Recorders are chosen from barristers of standing and also, since the Courts Act of 1971, from solicitors. They may eventually become circuit judges.

recorder any of a widespread range of woodwind instruments of the whistle type which flourished in consort ensembles in the Renaissance and baroque eras, along with viol consorts, as an instrumental medium for polyphonic music. Unlike the flute, the recorder is held vertically and blown into through a mouthpiece in which the air is diverted by an obstructive block called the 'fipple' and produces a milder tone than that of the flute. A modern consort may include a sopranino in F5, soprano (descant) in C4, alto (treble) in F3, tenor in C3, bass in F2, and great bass in C2.

recording any of a variety of techniques used to capture, store, and reproduce music, speech, and other information carried by sound waves. A microphone first converts the sound waves into an electrical signal which varies in proportion to the loudness of the sound. The signal can be stored in digital or analogue form, or on magnetic tape.

record player device for reproducing recorded sound stored as a spiral groove on a vinyl disc. A motor-driven turntable rotates the record at a constant speed, and a stylus or needle on the head of a pick-up is made to vibrate by the undulations in the record groove. These vibrations are then converted to electrical signals by a ▷transducer in the head (often a ▷piezoelectric crystal). After amplification, the signals pass to one or more loudspeakers, which convert them into sound. Alternative formats are ▷compact disc and magnetic ▷tape recording.

Recruit scandal in Japanese politics, the revelation in 1988 that a number of politicians and business leaders had profited from insider trading. It led to the resignation of several cabinet ministers, including Prime Minister Takeshita, whose closest aide committed suicide, and to the arrest of 20 people. It set in motion the breakaway from the ruling Liberal Democratic Party (LDP) of important factions in 1993 to form the nucleus of the new Shinshinto (New Frontier Party) opposition force.

rectangle quadrilateral (four-sided plane figure) with opposite sides equal and parallel and with each interior angle a right angle (90°). Its area A is the product of the length l and height h; that is, $A = l \times h$. A rectangle with all four sides equal is a ▷square.

rectifier in electrical engineering, a device used for obtaining one-directional current (DC) from an alternating source of supply (AC). (The process is necessary because almost all electrical power is generated, transmitted, and supplied as alternating current, but many devices, from television sets to electric motors, require direct current.) Types include plate rectifiers, thermionic ▷diodes, and ▷semiconductor diodes.

rectum lowest part of the large intestine of animals, which stores faeces prior to elimination (defecation).

recursion in computing and mathematics, a technique whereby a ▷function or ▷procedure calls itself into use in order to enable a complex problem to be broken down into simpler steps. For example, a function that finds the factorial of a number n (calculates the product of all the whole numbers between 1 and n) would obtain its result by multiplying n by the factorial of $n - 1$.

recycling processing of industrial and household waste (such as paper, glass, and some metals and plastics) so that the materials can be reused. This saves expenditure on scarce raw materials, slows down the depletion of ▷nonrenewable resources, and helps to reduce pollution. Aluminium is frequently recycled because of its value and special properties that allow it to be melted down and re-pressed without loss of quality, unlike paper and glass, which deteriorate when recycled.

Related Web site: Recycle City http://www.epa.gov/recyclecity/

RECYCLING A glass recycling mountain in Stuttgart, Germany. *Image Bank*

red admiral butterfly the best-known of the ▷admiral butterflies.

Red Army the army of the USSR until 1946; it later became known as the Soviet Army. Founded by the revolutionary Leon ▷Trotsky, it developed from the Red Guards, volunteers who were in the vanguard of the Bolshevik revolution. The force took its name from its rallying banner, the red flag. At its peak, during World War II, it reached a strength of around 12 million men and women. The revolutionary army that helped the communists under ▷Mao Zedong win power in China in 1949 was also popularly known as the Red Army.

red blood cell (or **erythrocyte**) the most common type of blood cell, responsible for transporting oxygen around the body. It contains haemoglobin, which combines with oxygen from the lungs to form oxyhaemoglobin. When transported to the tissues, these cells are able to release the oxygen because the oxyhaemoglobin splits into its original constituents.

Mammalian erythrocytes are disc-shaped with a depression in the centre and no nucleus; they are manufactured in the bone marrow and, in humans, last for only four months before being destroyed in the liver and spleen. Those of other vertebrates are oval and nucleated.

Red Brigades (Italian **Brigate rosse**) extreme left-wing guerrilla groups active in Italy during the 1970s and early 1980s. They were implicated in many kidnappings and killings, some later attributed to right-wing *agents provocateurs*, including that of Christian Democrat leader Aldo Moro in 1978.

Redcar and Cleveland unitary authority in northeast England created in 1996 from part of the former county of Cleveland.

area 240 sq km/93 sq mi **towns and cities** Redcar (administrative headquarters), Skelton, Guisborough, Marske-by-the-Sea, Saltburn-by-the-Sea, Brotton, Loftus **features** North Sea coast; River Tees forms northwest border; Boulby Cliffs are highest cliffs on England's east coast (203 m/666 ft); 12th-century Priory at Guisborough; Cleveland Way long-distance path reaches coast at Saltburn; RNLI Zetland Lifeboat Museum (Redcar); Ironstone Mining Museum (Saltburn-by-the-Sea) **industries** manufacture of steel products (British Steel), engineering, fertilizers and potash products, textiles **population** (1996) 144,000

RED CROSS Members of the US Red Cross international relief organization caring for a group of orphans during World War I. *Image Bank*

Red Cross (or **International Federation of the Red Cross**) international relief agency founded by the Geneva Convention in 1863 at the instigation of the Swiss doctor Henri Dunant to assist the wounded and prisoners in war. Its symbol is a symmetrical red cross on a white ground. In addition to dealing with associated problems of war, such as refugees and the care of the disabled, the Red Cross is concerned with victims of natural disasters – floods, earthquakes, epidemics, and accidents. It was awarded the Nobel Prize for Peace in 1917, 1944, and 1963.

Related Web site: International Committee of the Red Cross http://www.icrc.org/

red deer large deer widely distributed throughout Europe, Asia and North Africa. A full-grown male (stag or hart) stands 1.2 m/4 ft at the withers, and typical antlers measure about 80 cm/31 in in length with a spread of about the same. During the breeding season the colour is a rich brown, turning grey at the approach of winter. The young are spotted with white.

Redditch industrial town in Worcestershire, 19 km/12 mi south of Birmingham; population (1991) 72,700. It was designated a ▷new town in 1964 to take overspill population from Birmingham. Industries include engineering, electronics, and the production of electrical equipment, car and aircraft components, motorcycles, and fishing tackle.

red dwarf any star that is cool, faint, and small (about one-tenth the mass and diameter of the Sun). Red dwarfs burn slowly, and have estimated lifetimes of 100 billion years. They may be the most abundant type of star, but are difficult to see because they are so faint. Two of the closest stars to the Sun, ▷Proxima Centauri and ▷Barnard's Star, are red dwarfs.

> **Robert Redford**
> *I have a very low regard for cynics. I think it's the beginning of dying.*
> Time 29 March 1976

Redford, (Charles) Robert (1937–) US actor and film director. His blond good looks and versatility earned him his first starring role in *Barefoot in the Park* (1967), followed by *Butch Cassidy and the Sundance Kid* (1969) and *The Sting* (1973), both with Paul ▷Newman.

His other films as an actor include *All the President's Men* (1976), *Out of Africa* (1985), *Indecent Proposal* (1993), and *The Horse Whisperer* (1998; also directed by Redford). He directed *Ordinary People* (1980), *The Milagro Beanfield War* (1988), *A River Runs Through It* (1992), *Quiz Show* (1994), and *The Legend of Bagger Vance* (2000). He established the Sundance Institute in Utah for the development of film-making in 1981.

red giant any large bright star with a cool surface. It is thought to represent a late stage in the evolution of a star like the Sun, as it runs out of hydrogen fuel at its centre and begins to burn heavier elements, such as helium, carbon, and silicon. Because of more complex nuclear reactions that then occur in the red giant's interior, it eventually becomes gravitationally unstable and begins to collapse and heat up. The result is either explosion of the star as a ▷supernova, leaving behind a ▷neutron star, or loss of mass by more gradual means to produce a ▷white dwarf.

Red giants have diameters between 10 and 100 times that of the Sun. They are very bright because they are so large, although their surface temperature is lower than that of the Sun, about 2,000–3,000K (1,700–2,700°C/3,000–5,000°F). See also red ▷supergiants.

Redgrave, Michael (Scudamore) (1908–1985) English actor. His stage roles included Hamlet and Lear (Shakespeare), Uncle Vanya (Chekhov), and the schoolmaster in Terence Rattigan's *The Browning Version* (filmed 1951). On screen he appeared in *The Lady Vanishes* (1938), *The Importance of Being Earnest* (1952), and *Goodbye Mr Chips* (1969). He was knighted in 1959.

Redgrave, Steve(n Geoffrey) (1962–) English rower and gold medallist at five successive Olympics (1984–2000), winning the coxed fours in 1984, the coxless pairs in 1988 and 1992, and the coxless fours in 1996. He also won nine gold medals at the World Championships 1986–99, a gold at the World Indoor Championships in 1991, and was a member of the winning four-man bobsleigh team at the national bobsleigh championships in 1989. He announced his retirement from rowing in November 2000. In December 2000, he received the BBC Sports Personality of the Year award, and was elected vice-president of the British Olympic Association (BOA).

Redgrave, Vanessa (1937–) English actor. She has played Shakespeare's Lady Macbeth and Cleopatra on the stage, Ellida in Ibsen's *Lady From the Sea* (1976 and 1979), and Olga in Chekhov's *Three Sisters* (1990). She won an Academy Award for Best Supporting Actress for the title role in the film *Julia* (1976); other films include *Wetherby* (1985), *Howards End* (1992), *A Month by the Lake* (1995), and *Girl, Interrupted* (2000). She won a Tony Award for her stage performance in *Long Day's Journey into Night* (2003). She is active in left-wing politics.

Red Guard one of the militant school and college students, wearing red armbands, who were the shock-troops of the ▷Cultural Revolution in China from 1966 to 1969. After killing many party officials and plunging the country into chaos, the Red Guards were outlawed and suppressed by the Chinese leader ▷Mao Zedong.

red-hot poker any of a group of perennial plants native to Africa, in particular *K. uvaria*, with a flame-coloured spike of flowers. (Genus *Kniphofia*, family Liliaceae.)

Redmond, John Edward (1856–1918) Irish nationalist politician, leader of the Irish Parliamentary Party (IPP) 1900–18. He rallied his party after Charles Stewart ▷Parnell's imprisonment in 1881, and came close to achieving home rule for all Ireland in 1914. However, the pressure of World War I, Unionist intransigence, and the fallout of the 1916 ▷Easter Rising destroyed both his career and his party.

Redon, Odilon (1840–1916) French painter and graphic artist. One of the major figures of ▷Symbolism, he is famous for his fantastic and dreamlike images. From 1890 onwards he produced oil paintings and pastels, brilliant in colour, including numerous flower pieces. His works anticipated ▷surrealism.

redox reaction chemical change where one reactant is reduced and the other reactant oxidized. The reaction can only occur if both reactants are present and each changes simultaneously. For example, hydrogen reduces copper(II) oxide to copper while it is itself oxidized to water. The corrosion of iron and the reactions taking place in electric and electrolytic cells are just a few instances of redox reactions.

Red River (or **Red River of the South**) western tributary of the ▷Mississippi River 1,638 km/1,018 mi long; so called because of the reddish soil sediment it carries. Formed in Oklahoma by the confluence of the North Fork and the Prairie Dog Town Fork, it flows through Texas, Arkansas, and Louisiana, before entering the Mississippi near Baton Rouge, about 500 km/310 mi above the Gulf of Mexico. The stretch that forms the Texas–Oklahoma border is called Tornado Alley because of the storms caused by the collision in spring of warm air from the Gulf of Mexico with cold fronts from the north. The largest city on its course is Shreveport, Louisiana.

Red River river in north Vietnam, 500 km/310 mi long, that flows into the Gulf of Tonkin. Its extensive delta is a main centre of population.

Red Scare in US history, campaign against radicals and dissenters which took place in the aftermath of World War I and the Russian Revolution, during a period of labour disorders in the USA. A wave of strikes in 1919 was seen as a prelude to revolution and violently suppressed. Thousands of people were arrested on suspicion, and communists were banned from entry to the country.

Red Sea branch of the Indian Ocean, formed from a submerged section of the Great ▷Rift Valley, extending northwest from the Gulf of Aden. It is 2,000 km/1,200 mi long and up to 320 km/200 mi wide, reaching depths of over 2,300 m/7,545 ft. Egypt, Sudan, Ethiopia, and Eritrea (in Africa) and Saudi Arabia (Asia) are on its shores. At its northern end, it divides into the gulfs of Suez and Aqaba, separated by the Sinai peninsula.

red setter breed of dog. See ▷setter.

redshank wading bird *Tringa totanus* of northern Europe and Asia, a type of sandpiper. It nests in swampy areas, rarely in Europe, since most redshanks winter in the south. It is greyish and speckled black, and has long red legs.

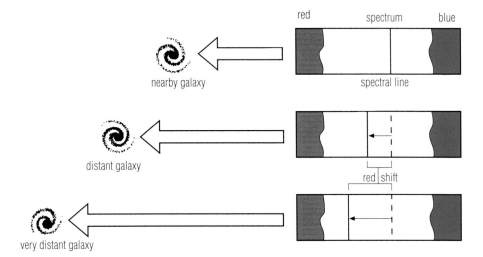

red   spectrum   blue

spectral line

nearby galaxy

distant galaxy

red shift

very distant galaxy

RED SHIFT The red shift causes lines in the spectra of galaxies to be shifted towards the red end of the spectrum. More distant galaxies have greater red shifts than closer galaxies. The red shift indicates that distant galaxies are moving apart rapidly, as the universe expands.

red shift in astronomy, the lengthening of the wavelengths of light from an object as a result of the object's motion away from us. It is an example of the ▷Doppler effect. The red shift in light from galaxies is evidence that the universe is expanding.

Lengthening of wavelengths causes the light to move or shift towards the red end of the ▷spectrum, hence the name. The amount of red shift can be measured by the displacement of lines in an object's spectrum. By measuring the amount of red shift in light from stars and galaxies, astronomers can tell how quickly these objects are moving away from us. A strong gravitational field can also produce a red shift in light; this is termed **gravitational red shift**.

redstart any bird of the genus *Phoenicurus*, a member of the thrush family Muscicapidae, order Passeriformes. It winters in Africa and spends the summer in Eurasia. The **American redstart** *Setophaga ruticulla* belongs to the family Parulidae.

reduction in chemistry, the gain of electrons, loss of oxygen, or gain of hydrogen by an atom, ion, or molecule during a chemical reaction.

Reduction may be brought about by reaction with another compound, which is simultaneously oxidized (reducing agent), or electrically at the cathode (negative electrode) of an electric cell. Examples include the reduction of iron(III) oxide to iron by carbon monoxide:

$$Fe_2O_3 + 3CO \rightarrow 2Fe + 3CO_2$$

the hydrogenation of ethene to ethane:

$$CH_2=CH_2 + H_2 \rightarrow CH_3-CH_3$$

and the reduction of a sodium ion to sodium.

$$Na^+ + e^- \rightarrow Na$$

redwing type of thrush *Turdus iliacus*, family Muscicapidae, order Passeriformes. It is smaller than the song thrush, with reddish wing and body markings, and there is a distinct white line over the eye. It breeds in the north of Europe and Asia, flying south in winter.

redwood giant coniferous tree, one of the two types of ▷sequoia.

reed any of various perennial tall, slender grasses found growing in wet or marshy environments; also the hollow, jointed stalks of any of these plants. The common reed (*P. australis*) reaches a height of 3 m/10 ft, having stiff, upright leaves and straight stems with a plume of purplish flowers at the top. (Especially species of the genera *Phragmites* and *Arundo*, family Gramineae.)

Reed, Carol (1906–1976) English film producer and director. He was an influential figure in the British film industry of the 1940s. His films include *Odd Man Out* (1946), *The Fallen Idol* (1948), *The Third Man* (1949), *Our Man in Havana* (1959), and the Academy Award-winning musical *Oliver!* (1968).

Reed, Lou(is Firbank) (1942–) US rock singer, songwriter, and guitarist. He was a member (1965–70 and 1993) of the New York avant-garde group the Velvet Underground, one of the most influential bands of the period. His solo work deals largely with urban alienation and angst, and includes the albums *Berlin* (1973), *Street Hassle* (1978), and *New York* (1989). His best-known recording is 'Walk on the Wild Side' from the album *Transformer* (1972).

    Related Web site: Lou Reed and the Velvet Underground http://www.rocknroll.net/loureed/

reel in cinema, a plastic or metal spool used for winding and storing film. As the size of reels became standardized, the word came to refer to the running time of the film: a standard 35-mm reel holds 313 m/900 ft of film, which runs for ten minutes when projected at 24 frames per second, so a two-reeler was a film lasting 20 minutes. Today's projectors, however, hold bigger reels.

referendum procedure whereby a decision on proposed legislation is referred to the electorate for settlement by direct vote of all the people. It is most frequently employed in Switzerland, the first country to use it, but has become increasingly widespread.

refining any process that purifies or converts something into a more useful form. Metals usually need refining after they have been extracted from their ores by such processes as ▷smelting. Petroleum, or crude oil, needs refining before it can be used; the process involves fractional ▷distillation, the separation of the substance into separate components or 'fractions'.

reflection the throwing back or deflection of waves, such as ▷light or sound waves, when they hit a surface. The **law of reflection** states that the angle of incidence (the angle between the ray and a perpendicular line drawn to the surface) is equal to the angle of reflection (the angle between the reflected ray and a perpendicular to the surface).

When light passes from a dense medium to a less dense medium, such as from water to air, both ▷refraction and reflection can occur. If the angle of incidence is small, the reflection will be relatively weak compared to the refraction. But as the angle of incidence increases the relative degree of reflection will increase. At some **critical angle of incidence** the angle of refraction is 90°. Since refraction cannot occur above 90°, the light is totally reflected at angles above this critical angle of incidence. This condition is known as **total internal reflection**. Total internal reflection is used in ▷fibre optics to transmit data over long distances, without the need of amplification.

reflex in animals, a very rapid involuntary response to a particular stimulus. It is controlled by the ▷nervous system. A reflex involves only a few nerve cells, unlike the slower but more complex responses produced by the many processing nerve cells of the brain.

reflex camera camera that uses a mirror and prisms to reflect light passing through the lens into the viewfinder, showing the photographer the exact scene that is being shot. When the shutter button is released the mirror springs out of the way, allowing light to reach the film. The most common type is the single-lens reflex (▷SLR) camera. The twin-lens reflex (TLR) camera has two lenses: one has a mirror for viewing, the other is used for exposing the film.

reflexology in alternative medicine, manipulation and massage of the feet to ascertain and treat disease or dysfunction elsewhere in the body.

Reform Acts in the UK, acts of Parliament in 1832, 1867, and 1884 that extended voting rights and redistributed parliamentary seats; also known as ▷Representation of the People Acts.

Reformation religious and political movement in 16th-century Europe to reform the Roman Catholic Church, which led to the establishment of the Protestant churches. Anticipated by medieval movements such as the ▷Waldenses, ▷Lollards, and ▷Hussites, it was started by the German priest Martin ▷Luther in 1517, and became effective when local princes gave it support by challenging the political power of the papacy and confiscating church wealth.

REFORMATION A woodcarving by Lucas Cranach, showing the contrast between the Protestant and Roman Catholic churches. The Protestants, on the left, are described as following the true religion by believing in salvation through Jesus Christ. *Philip Sauvain Picture Collection*

refraction the bending of a wave when it passes from one medium into another. It is the effect of the different speeds of wave propagation in two substances that have different densities. The amount of refraction depends on the densities of the media, the angle at which the wave strikes the surface of the second medium, and the amount of bending and change of velocity corresponding to the wave's frequency (dispersion). Refraction occurs with all types of progressive waves – ▷electromagnetic waves, sound waves, and water waves – and differs from ▷reflection, which involves no change in velocity.

Refraction of light The degree of refraction depends in part on the angle at which the light hits the surface of a material. A line perpendicular to that surface is called the **normal**. The angle between the incoming light ray and the normal to the surface is called the **angle of incidence**. The angle between the refracted ray and the normal is called the **angle of refraction**. The angle of refraction cannot exceed 90°. An example of refraction is light hitting a glass pane. When light in air enters the denser medium, it is bent toward the normal. When light passes out of the glass into the air, which is less dense, it is bent away from the normal. The incident light will be parallel to the emerging light because the two faces of the glass are parallel. However, if the two faces are not parallel, as with a prism, the emerging light will not be parallel to the incident light. The angle between the incident ray and the emerging ray is called the **angle of deviation**. The amount of bending and change in velocity of the refracted wave is due to the amount of ▷dispersion corresponding to the wave's frequency, and the **refractive index** of the material. When light hits the denser material, its ▷frequency remains constant, but its velocity decreases due to the influence of electrons in the denser medium. Constant frequency means that the same number of light waves must pass by in the same amount of time. If the waves are slowing down, wavelength must also decrease to maintain the constant frequency. The waves become more closely spaced, bending toward the normal as if they are being dragged. The refractive index of a

Reformation: Key Dates	
1517	Martin Luther's protest against the sale of indulgences begins the Reformation in Europe.
1519	Ulrich Zwingli leads the Reformation in Switzerland.
1529	The term 'Protestant' is first used.
1533	Henry VIII renounces papal supremacy and proclaims himself head of the Church of England.
1541	The French theologian John Calvin establishes Presbyterianism in Geneva, Switzerland.
1559	The Protestant John Knox returns from exile to found the Church of Scotland.
1545–1563	The Counter-Reformation is initiated by the Roman Catholic Church at the **Council of Trent**. It aims at reforming abuses and regaining the lost ground by using moral persuasion and extending the Spanish Inquisition to other countries.
1648	By the end of the Thirty Years' War, the present European alignment has been reached, with the separation of Catholic and Protestant churches.

material indicates by how much a wave is bent. It is found by dividing the velocity of the wave in the first medium by the velocity of the wave in the second medium. The **absolute refractive index** of a material is the velocity of light in that material relative to the velocity of light in a vacuum. See also ▷apparent depth.

Refraction of sound Sound waves, unlike light, travel faster in denser materials, such as solids and liquids, than they travel in air. When sound waves enter a solid, their velocity and wavelength *increase* and they are bent away from the normal to the surface of the solid.

Water waves Water waves are refracted when their velocity decreases. Water waves slow down as water becomes shallower. A good example of this is a wavefront approaching a shore that is shallower in one place and deeper in another. When the wavefront approaches, the part of the wave in shallower water will slow down and its wavelength will decrease, causing it to lag behind the part of the wave in the deeper water.

refractive index measure of the refraction of a ray of light as it passes from one transparent medium to another. If the angle of incidence is i and the angle of refraction is r, the ratio of the two refractive indices is given by $n_1/n_2 = \sin i/\sin r$. It is also equal to the speed of light in the first medium divided by the speed of light in the second, and it varies with the wavelength of the light.

refractory (of a material) able to resist high temperature, for example ▷ceramics made from clay, minerals, or other earthy materials. Furnaces are lined with refractory materials such as silica and dolomite.

refrigeration use of technology to transfer heat from cold to warm, against the normal temperature gradient, so that a body can remain substantially colder than its surroundings. Refrigeration equipment is used for the chilling and deep-freezing of food in food technology, and in air conditioners and industrial processes.

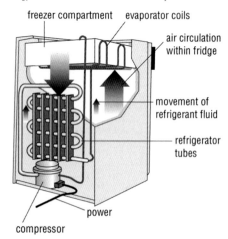

REFRIGERATION The constituent parts of a refrigerator and the flow of air and refrigerant fluid around the system.

refugee according to international law, a person fleeing from oppressive or dangerous conditions (such as political, religious, or military persecution) and seeking refuge in a foreign country. In 1995 there were an estimated 27 million refugees worldwide; their resettlement and welfare is the responsibility of the United Nations High Commission for Refugees (UNHCR). An estimated average of 10,000 people a day become refugees. Women and children make up 75% of all refugees and displaced persons. Many more millions are 'economic' or 'environmental' refugees, forced to emigrate because of economic circumstances, lack of access to land, or environmental disasters.

Related Web site: Disaster Relief http://www.disasterrelief.org/

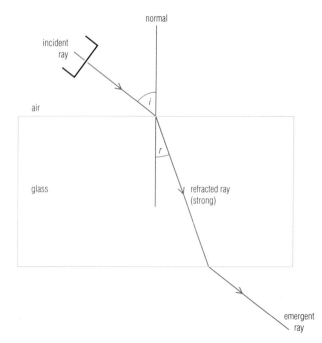

REFRACTION The diagram shows the refraction of light through glass. When the light ray strikes the glass (a denser medium than the air) it is bent towards the normal. When it leaves the glass and re-enters the less dense medium it is bent away from the normal.

regelation phenomenon in which water refreezes to ice after it has been melted by pressure at a temperature below the freezing point of water. Pressure makes an ice skate, for example, form a film of water that freezes once again after the skater has passed.

Regency in Britain, the years 1811–20 during which ▷George IV (then Prince of Wales) acted as regent for his father ▷George III, who was finally declared insane and unfit to govern in December 1810. The Regency was marked by the Prince Regent's turbulent private life, his dissolute public image, and the fashionable society he patronized.

In 1795 George had been forced to marry his cousin Caroline of Brunswick after his earlier, illegal union with a Roman Catholic was annulled; his contemptuous treatment of Caroline in this loveless marriage lost him much public sympathy. His friendship with the dandy and notorious gambler Beau Brummel further boosted his reputation for extravagance. The Regency gave its name to an elegant style of architecture and decorative arts characterized by borrowings from classical Greece and Rome, as well as from ancient Egypt, China, and India. The most famous building commissioned by the Prince Regent was the flamboyant summer residence in Brighton known as the Royal Pavilion, built in the style of an Indian palace by the architect John Nash between 1815 and 1823.

Related Web site: Regency Fashion Page http://locutus.ucr.edu/~cathy/reg3.html

Regency style style of architecture and interior furnishings popular in England during the late 18th and early 19th centuries. It is characterized by restrained simplicity and the imitation of ancient classical elements, often Greek.

regeneration in biology, regrowth of a new organ or tissue after the loss or removal of the original. It is common in plants, where a new individual can often be produced from a 'cutting' of the original. In animals, regeneration of major structures is limited to lower organisms; certain lizards can regrow their tails if these are lost, and new flatworms can grow from a tiny fragment of an old one. In mammals, regeneration is limited to the repair of tissue in wound healing and the regrowth of peripheral nerves following damage.

Regensburg (English **Ratisbon**) historic and commercial city in Bavaria, Germany, on the River Danube at its confluence with the Regen, 100 km/63 mi northeast of Munich; population (1995) 126,000. It has mechanical and electrical engineering, pharmaceutical, and food-processing industries. It has many medieval buildings, including a Gothic cathedral (1275–1530), and is a 'living museum' of German culture and architecture from the early Middle Ages.

History Regensburg stands on the site of a Celtic settlement dating from 500 BC. It became the Roman **Castra Regina** AD 179, the capital of the Eastern Frankish Empire, a free imperial city in 1245, and seat of the German *Diet* (parliament) 16th century–1806. It was included in Bavaria in 1810.

regent person who carries out the duties of a sovereign during the sovereign's minority, incapacity, or lengthy absence from the country. In England since the time of Henry VIII, Parliament has always appointed a regent or council of regency when necessary.

reggae predominant form of West Indian popular music of the 1970s and 1980s, characterized by a heavily accented offbeat and a thick bass line. The lyrics often refer to ▷Rastafarianism. Musicians include Bob Marley, Lee 'Scratch' Perry (performer and producer), and the group Black Uhuru. Reggae is also popular in the UK, South Africa, and elsewhere.

register in computing, a memory location that can be accessed rapidly; it is often built into the computer's central processing unit.

Some registers are reserved for special tasks – for example, an **instruction register** is used to hold the machine-code command that the computer is currently executing, while a **sequence-control register** keeps track of the next command to be executed. Other registers are used for holding frequently used data and for storing intermediate results.

regolith the surface layer of loose material that covers most bedrock. It consists of eroded rocky material, volcanic ash, river alluvium, vegetable matter, or a mixture of these known as ▷soil.

regressive tax tax such that the higher the income of the taxpayer the smaller the proportion or percentage paid in that tax. This contrasts with progressive taxes where the proportion paid rises as income increases, and proportional taxes where the proportion paid remains the same at all levels of income. Examples of regressive taxes in the UK are the ▷council tax and ▷excise duties.

Rehnquist, William (1924–) US lawyer, associate justice 1972–86, and chief justice of the US ▷Supreme Court from 1986. Under his leadership the Court established a reputation for conservative rulings on such issues as abortion and capital punishment.

Rehoboam King of Judah about 932–915 BC, son of Solomon. Under his rule the Jewish nation split into the two kingdoms of **Israel** and **Judah**. Ten of the tribes revolted against him and took Jeroboam as their ruler, leaving Rehoboam only the tribes of Judah and Benjamin.

Reich (German 'empire') three periods in European history. The First Reich was the Holy Roman Empire (962–1806), the Second Reich the German Empire (1871–1918), and the ▷Third Reich Nazi Germany (1933–45).

Reich, Steve (1936–) US composer. His minimalist music employs simple patterns carefully superimposed and modified to highlight constantly changing melodies and rhythms; examples are *Phase Patterns* for four electronic organs (1970), *Music for Mallet Instruments, Voices, and Organ* (1973), and *Music for Percussion and Keyboards* (1984).

Reich, Wilhelm (1897–1957) Austrian physician who emigrated to the USA in 1939. He combined ▷Marxism and ▷psychoanalysis to advocate the positive effects of directed sexual energies and sexual freedom. His works include *Die Sexuelle Revolution/The Sexual Revolution* (1936–45) and *Die Funktion des Orgasmus/The Function of the Orgasm* (1948).

Reichstadt, Duke of title of ▷Napoleon II, son of Napoleon I.

Reichstag German parliament building and lower legislative house during the German Empire 1871–1918 and Weimar Republic 1919–33. It was burned down in February 1933. Following the MPs' decision after reunification in 1991, German parliament was brought back to Berlin, and the Reichstag officially reopened in April 1999.

Reichstag Fire burning of the German parliament building in Berlin 27 February 1933, less than a month after the Nazi leader Hitler became chancellor. The fire was used as a justification for the suspension of many constitutional guarantees and also as an excuse to attack the communists. There is still debate over whether the Nazis were involved in this crime, of which they were the main beneficiaries.

Reigate town in Surrey, southeast England, at the foot of the North Downs; population (1991, with Redhill) 46,300. Situated 30 km/19 mi south of London, it is primarily a commuter town.

Reims (English **Rheims**) city in the *département* of Marne, and largest commercial centre of the ▷Champagne-Ardenne region, France, situated 130 km/80 mi northeast of Paris on the right bank of the River Vesle, a tributary of the Aisne; population

(1990) 185,200, conurbation 206,000. From 987 all but six French kings were crowned here. The western facade of its cathedral, Notre Dame, is one of the masterpieces of the Middle Ages. In World War II the German High Command formally surrendered here to US general Eisenhower on 7 May 1945. Reims is the centre of the ▷champagne trade and has textile, chemical, mechanical, metallurgical, and foodstuff manufactures.

reincarnation (or **transmigration** or **metempsychosis**) belief that after death the human soul or the spirit of a plant or animal may live again in another human or animal. It is part of the teachings of many religions and philosophies; for example, ancient Egyptian and Greek (the philosophies of Pythagoras and Plato), Buddhism, Hinduism, Jainism, Sikhism, certain Christian heresies (such as the Cathars), and theosophy.

reindeer (or **caribou**) deer *Rangifer tarandus* of Arctic and subarctic regions, common to North America and Eurasia. About 1.2 m/4 ft at the shoulder, it has a thick, brownish coat and broad hooves well adapted to travel over snow. It is the only deer in which both sexes have antlers; these can grow to 1.5 m/5 ft long, and are shed in winter.

The Old World reindeer have been domesticated by the Lapps of Scandinavia for centuries. There are two types of North American caribou: the large woodland caribou of the more southerly regions, and the barren-ground caribou of the far north. Reindeer migrate south in winter, moving in large herds. They eat grass, small plants, and lichens.

reinforced concrete material formed by casting ▷concrete in timber or metal formwork around a cage of steel reinforcement. The steel gives added strength by taking up the tension stresses, while the concrete takes up the compression stresses. Its technical potential was first fully demonstrated by François Hennebique in the facade of the Charles VI Mill at Tourcoing, France, 1895.

REINFORCED CONCRETE Construction workers in Argentina check out the steel rods that will form the framework for another storey in a predominantly concrete building. *Image Bank*

Reinhardt, Django (Jean Baptiste) (1910–1953) Belgian jazz guitarist and composer. He was co-leader, with Stéphane ▷Grappelli, of the Quintet du Hot Club de France 1934–39. He had a lyrical acoustic style and individual technique, and influenced many US musicians.

relative atomic mass the mass of an atom relative to one-twelfth the mass of an atom of carbon-12. It depends primarily on the number of protons and neutrons in the atom, the electrons having negligible mass. If more than one ▷isotope of the element is present, the relative atomic mass is calculated by taking an average that takes account of the relative proportions of each isotope, resulting in values that are not whole numbers. The term **atomic weight**, although commonly used, is strictly speaking incorrect.

relative density the density (at 20°C/68°F) of a solid or liquid relative to (divided by) the maximum density of water (at 4°C/39.2°F). The relative density of a gas is its density divided by the density of hydrogen (or sometimes dry air) at the same temperature and pressure.

relative humidity the concentration of water vapour in the air. It is expressed as the ratio of the partial pressure of the water vapour to its saturated vapour pressure at the same temperature. The higher the temperature, the higher the saturated vapour pressure.

relative molecular mass the mass of a molecule, calculated relative to one-twelfth the mass of an atom of carbon-12. It is found by adding the relative atomic masses of the atoms that make up the molecule. The term **molecular weight** is often used, but strictly this is incorrect.

relativism philosophical position that denies the possibility of objective truth independent of some specific social or historical context or conceptual framework.

relativity in physics, the theory of the relative rather than absolute character of mass, time, and space, and their interdependence, as developed by German-born US physicist Albert ▷Einstein in two phases:

Special theory of relativity (1905) Starting with the premises that (1) the laws of nature are the same for all observers in unaccelerated motion, and (2) the speed of light is independent of the motion of its source, Einstein arrived at some rather unexpected consequences. Intuitively familiar concepts, like mass, length, and time, had to be modified. For example, an object moving rapidly past the observer will appear to be both shorter and more massive than when it is at rest (that is, at rest relative to the observer), and a clock moving rapidly past the observer will appear to be running slower than when it is at rest. These predictions of relativity theory seem to be foreign to everyday experience merely because the changes are quite negligible at speeds less than about 1,500 km s^{-1}, and they only become appreciable at speeds approaching the speed of light.

General theory of relativity (1915) The geometrical properties of space-time were to be conceived as modified locally by the presence of a body with mass. A planet's orbit around the Sun (as observed in three-dimensional space) arises from its natural trajectory in modified space-time. Einstein's general theory accounts for a peculiarity in the behaviour of the motion of the perihelion of the orbit of the planet Mercury that cannot be explained in Newton's theory. The new theory also said that light rays should bend when they pass by a massive object. The predicted bending of starlight was observed during the eclipse of the Sun in 1919. A third corroboration is found in the shift towards the red in the spectra of the Sun and, in particular, of stars of great density – white dwarfs such as the companion of Sirius.

Einstein showed that, for consistency with the above premises (1) and (2), the principles of dynamics as established by Newton needed modification; the most celebrated new result was the equation $E = mc^2$, which expresses an equivalence between mass (m) and ▷energy (E), c being the speed of light in a vacuum. In 'relativistic mechanics', conservation of mass is replaced by the new concept of conservation of 'mass-energy'. General relativity is central to modern ▷astrophysics and ▷cosmology; it predicts, for example, the possibility of ▷black holes. General relativity theory was inspired by the simple idea that it is impossible in a small region to distinguish between acceleration and gravitation effects (as in a lift one feels heavier when the lift accelerates upwards), but the mathematical development of the idea is formidable. Such is not the case for the special theory, which a nonexpert can follow up to $E = mc^2$ and beyond.

Related Web site: Light Cone http://www.phy.syr.edu/courses/modules/LIGHTCONE/

relay in electrical engineering, an electromagnetic switch. A small current passing through a coil of wire wound around an iron core attracts an ▷armature whose movement closes a pair of sprung contacts to complete a secondary circuit, which may carry a large current or activate other devices. The solid-state equivalent is a thyristor switching device.

relief in sculpture, particularly architectural sculpture, carved figures and other forms that project from the background. The Italian terms *basso-rilievo* (low relief), *mezzo-rilievo* (middle relief), and *alto-rilievo* (high relief) are used according to the extent to which the sculpture projects. The French term *bas-relief* is commonly used to mean low relief.

religion (Latin *religare* 'to bind'; bond of humans to God) code of belief or philosophy that often involves the worship of a ▷God or gods. Belief in a supernatural power is not essential (absent in, for example, Buddhism and Confucianism), but faithful adherence is usually considered to be rewarded; for example, by escape from human existence (Buddhism), by a future existence (Christianity, Islam), or by worldly benefit (Sōka Gakkai Buddhism). Religions include: **ancient and pantheist** religions of Babylonia, Assyria, Egypt, Greece, and Rome; **animist** or **polytheistic** traditional central African religions, voodoo and related beliefs in Latin America and

Religion: Followers of Major Faiths

2000 figures	
Christianity	2,015,000,000
Islam	1,215,000,000
Hinduism	786,000,000
Buddhism	362,000,000
Judaism	18,000,000
Sikhism	16,000,000
Confucianism	5,000,000
Baha'ism	4,000,000
Jainism	3,000,000
Shinto	3,000,000

the Caribbean, traditional faiths of American Indians, Maoris, Australian Aborigines, and Javanese; **oriental** Hinduism, Buddhism, Jainism, Zoroastrianism, Confucianism, Taoism, and Shinto; **'religions of a book'** Judaism, Christianity (the principal divisions are Roman Catholic, Eastern Orthodox, and Protestant), and Islam (the principal divisions are Sunni and Shiite); **combined derivation** these include Baha'ism, the Unification church, and Mormonism.

Related Web site: Multifaithnet http://www.multifaith.org/

Religion, Wars of series of civil wars 1562–89 in France between Catholics and (Protestant) Huguenots. Each side was led by noble families which competed for influence over a weakened monarchy. The most infamous event was the Massacre of ▷St Bartholomew in 1572, carried out on the orders of the Catholic faction led by ▷Catherine de' Medici and the Duke of Guise. After 1584, the heir apparent to the French throne was the Huguenot Henry of Navarre. This prompted further hostilities, but after his accession as Henry IV in 1589, he was able to maintain his hold on power, partly through military victory and partly by converting to Catholicism in 1593.

He introduced the Edict of Nantes in 1598, guaranteeing freedom of worship throughout his kingdom.

REM US rock group. Their songs are characterized by melodic bass lines, driving guitar, and evocative lyrics. The album *Out of Time* (1991) included the worldwide hit single 'Losing My Religion', and further successes include *Automatic For The People* (1992) and *Monster* (1994). *New Adventures in Hi-Fi* followed in 1996 to disappointing commercial success. Bill Berry left the band in 1997 and the three remaining members released the album *Up* in 1998.

rem (acronym for roentgen equivalent man) unit of radiation dose equivalent.

remand in law, the committing of an accused but not convicted person into custody or to release on bail pending a court hearing.

Remarque, Erich Maria (1898–1970) German novelist. He was a soldier in World War I. His *All Quiet on the Western Front* (1929), one of the first anti-war novels, led to his being deprived of German nationality. He lived in Switzerland 1929–39, and then in the USA.

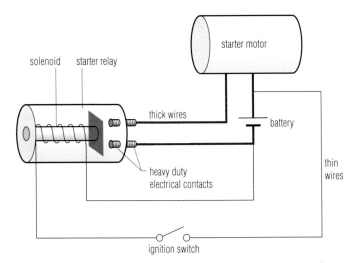

RELAY A relay is a device that allows a small amount of electrical current to control a large amount of current. A car starter motor uses a relay to solve the problem that a car has in needing a large amount of current to start the engine. A starter relay is installed in series between the battery and the starter. Some cars use a starter solenoid (as shown here) to accomplish the same purpose of allowing a small amount of current from the ignition switch to control a high current flow from the battery to the starter.

Rembrandt, Harmensz van Rijn (1606–1669) Dutch painter and etcher. He was one of the most prolific and significant artists in Europe in the 17th century. Between 1629 and 1669 he painted about 60 penetrating self-portraits. He also painted religious subjects, and produced about 300 etchings and over 1,000 drawings. His major group portraits include *The Anatomy Lesson of Dr Tulp* (1632; Mauritshuis, The Hague) and *The Night Watch* (1642; Rijksmuseum, Amsterdam).

After studying in Leiden and for a few months in Amsterdam (with a history painter), Rembrandt began his career in 1625 in Leiden, where his work reflected knowledge of Adam Elsheimer and ▷Caravaggio, among others. He settled permanently in Amsterdam in 1631 and obtained many commissions for portraits from wealthy merchants. The *Self-Portrait with Saskia* (his wife, Saskia van Uylenburgh) (*c.* 1634; Gemäldegalerie, Dresden) displays prosperity in warm tones and rich, glittering textiles.

Saskia died in 1642, and that year Rembrandt's fortunes began to decline (he eventually became bankrupt in 1656). His work became more sombre, revealing a deeper emotional content, and his portraits were increasingly melancholy; for example, *Jan Six* (1654; Six Collection, Amsterdam). From 1660 onwards he lived with Hendrickje Stoffels, but he outlived her, and in 1668 his only surviving child, Titus, died too. Rembrandt had many pupils, including Gerard Dou and Carel Fabritius. He was buried in the Wester Kerk in Amsterdam, and his house in the city is now a Rembrandt museum.

Related Web site: Rembrandt http://amsterdam.park.org/ Netherlands/pavilions/culture/rembrandt/

HARMENSZ VAN RIJN REMBRANDT A self-portrait in his later years by the Dutch painter. Though the greatest portrait artist of his time, Rembrandt died in poverty, and in his later studies of his own face he appears tense and sad. *The Art Archive/Prado Museum Madrid/Dagli Orti*

Remembrance Sunday (formerly **Armistice Day** (until 1945)) in the UK, national day of remembrance for those killed in both world wars and later conflicts, on the second Sunday of November. In Canada 11 November is **Remembrance Day**. The US equivalent is ▷Veterans Day.

Remington, Philo (1816–1889) US inventor and businessman. He designed the breech-loading rifle that bears his name. He began manufacturing typewriters in 1873, using the patent of Christopher ▷Sholes, and made improvements that resulted five years later in the first machine with a shift key, thus providing lower-case letters as well as capital letters.

The Remington rifle and carbine, which had a falling block breech and a tubular magazine, were developed in collaboration with his father Eliphalet Remington.

remission in medicine, temporary disappearance of symptoms during the course of a disease.

remix in pop music, the studio practice of reassembling a recording from all or some of its individual components, often with the addition of new elements. As a commercial concept, remixes accompanied the rise of the 12-inch single in the 1980s.

remora any of a family of warm-water fishes that have an adhesive disc on the head, by which they attach themselves to whales, sharks, and turtles. These provide the remora with shelter and transport, as well as food in the form of parasites on the host's skin.

remote sensing gathering and recording information from a distance. Space probes have sent back photographs and data about planets as distant as Neptune. In archaeology, surface survey techniques provide information without disturbing subsurface deposits.

REM sleep (acronym for **rapid-eye-movement sleep**) phase of sleep that recurs several times nightly in humans and is associated with dreaming. The eyes flicker quickly beneath closed lids.

Renaissance (or **Revival of Learning**) period in European cultural history that began in Italy around 1400 and lasted there until the end of the 1500s. Elsewhere in Europe it began later, and lasted until the 1600s. One characteristic of the Renaissance was the rediscovery of classical literature, led by the writers Giovanni ▷Boccaccio and Francesco ▷Petrarch. A central theme of the Renaissance was ▷humanism, the belief in the active rather than the contemplative life, and a faith in the republican ideal. The greatest expression of the Renaissance was in the arts and learning. The term 'Renaissance' (French for 'rebirth') to describe this period of cultural history was invented by historians in the 1800s.

Leon ▷Alberti, in his writings on painting, created both a method of painting – using perspective to create an illusion of a third dimension – and the idea of using classically-inspired, nonreligious subjects. In architecture, by his writing and his buildings, Alberti created a system of simple proportion that was followed for hundreds of years. Alberti's contemporaries Masaccio and Filippo Brunelleschi exemplified these ideas in painting and architecture respectively.

In the arts, critics regard the years 1490–1520 (the 'High Renaissance') as a peak, with the work of ▷Leonardo da Vinci, ▷Raphael Sanzio, and ▷Michelangelo Buonarotti in painting, and Michelangelo and Donato ▷Bramante in architecture being of paramount importance. The high-point of Venetian painting came some years later, with the work of ▷Titian, Paolo ▷Veronese, and ▷Tintoretto. Leonardo has been described as a 'universal man' for his enormously wide-ranging studies, including painting, architecture, science, and engineering.

The enormous achievements of creative artists during the Renaissance were made possible by the ▷patronage of wealthy ruling families such as the ▷Sforza in Milan and the ▷Medici in Florence; by the ruling doge of Venice; and by popes, notably ▷Julius II and ▷Leo X.

In literature, both Boccaccio and Petrarch wrote major works in Italian rather than Latin, a trend that was continued by the creation of epic poems in the vernacular by Ludovico ▷Ariosto and Torquato ▷Tasso. Progress from the religious to the secular was seen in the creation of the first public libraries, and in the many translations from the classics published in Venice in the 16th century. In philosophy, the rediscovery of Greek thought took the form of ▷neo-Platonism in the work of such people as Marsilio Ficino. Niccolò ▷Machiavelli in *The Prince* 1513 founded the modern study of politics.

Spread of the Renaissance Outside Italy, Renaissance art and ideas became widespread throughout Europe. The Dutch scholar Desiderius ▷Erasmus embodied humanist scholarship for northern Europe; Dutch painters included Albrecht ▷Dürer and Hans ▷Holbein. In France, Renaissance writers included François ▷Rabelais, Joaquim Du Bellay, and Michel Eyquem de ▷Montaigne; in Spain, Miguel de ▷Cervantes; in Portugal, Luís Vaz de ▷Camoëns; and in England William ▷Shakespeare.

In the visual arts, the end of the High Renaissance is marked by a movement in the late 1400s known as ▷Mannerism, a tendency to deliberate elongation of the body, and a wilful distortion of perspective. The true end of the Renaissance ideal came with the ▷enlightenment movement in the late 1600s.

Renault, Mary (1905–1983) Pen-name of (Eileen) Mary Challans. English historical novelist. She specialized in stories about ancient Greece, with two novels on the mythical hero Theseus: *The King Must Die* (1958) and *The Bull from the Sea* (1962); and two on Alexander the Great: *Fire from Heaven* (1970) and *The Persian Boy* (1972).

Rendell, Ruth Barbara (1930–   ) English novelist and short-story writer. She is the author of a popular detective series featuring Chief Inspector Wexford, of which *Harm Done* (1999) was the 17th. Her psychological crime novels explore the minds of people who commit murder, often through obsession or social inadequacy, as in *A Demon in my View* (1976), *Heartstones* (1987), *The Keys to the Street* (1996), and *A Sight for Sore Eyes* (1998). Many of her works have been adapted for television. She sometimes writes under the pseudonym Barbara Vine.

René, France-Albert (1935–   ) Seychelles left-wing politician. He became the country's first prime minister after independence, and president from 1977 after a coup. He followed a nonnuclear policy of nonalignment. In 1993 René and his party, the People's Progressive Front, won the country's first free elections in 16 years.

renewable energy power from any source that replenishes itself. Most renewable systems rely on ▷solar energy directly or through the weather cycle as ▷wave power, ▷hydroelectric power, or wind power via ▷wind turbines, or solar energy collected by plants (alcohol fuels, for example). In addition, the gravitational force of the Moon can be harnessed through tidal power stations, and the heat trapped in the centre of the Earth is used via ▷geothermal energy systems.

renewable resource natural resource that is replaced by natural processes in a reasonable amount of time. Soil, water, forests, plants, and animals are all renewable resources as long as they are properly conserved. Solar, wind, wave, and geothermal energies are based on renewable resources.

Renfrewshire unitary authority in west central Scotland, bordering the Firth of Clyde, which was formed from the northern and western parts of Renfrew district in Strathclyde region (1975–96), which in turn was formed from the former county of Renfrewshire (until 1974).

RENAISSANCE *Flemish Madonna and Child with Canon George van der Poele, 1436, with Saint George and Saint Donatus*, by Flemish painter Jan van Eyck. *The Art Archive/ Groeningen Museum Bruges*

area 260 sq km/100 sq mi **towns** Paisley (administrative headquarters), Renfrew, Johnstone, Erskine **physical** mainly low lying, but hilly in the west, rising to Hill of Stake (525 m/1,723 ft); rivers Clyde, Gryfe, White Cart, Black Cart **features** sculptural stones at Inchinnan, near Erskine; Glasgow International Airport **industries** engineering, computers, electronics, chemicals **agriculture** sheep on grassy uplands; dairy farming on lowlands **population** (1995) 178,300 **history** once part of the ancient kingdom of Strathclyde; name given to Stuart heirs since Robert III made his son Baron of Renfrew

Reni, Guido
(1575–1642) Italian painter. He was an important figure in the development of the ▷baroque style. His best-known work is the fresco *Aurora* (1613–14; Casino Rospigliosi, Rome), a work which shows the strong influence of the classicism of the ▷Carracci.

GUIDO RENI The Biblical story of David and Goliath, illustrated by an example of the work of the Bolognese painter Guido Reni. *The Art Archive/Musmadee du Louvre Paris/ Dagli Orti*

Rennes
(*Redones*, a Celtic tribe) administrative centre of Ille-et-Vilaine *département*, western France, 60 km/37 mi southeast of St Malo at the confluence of the Ille and Vilaine rivers; population (1990) 203,500, conurbation 245,000. It is the main commercial centre for western France and produces chemicals, electronics, cars, railway equipment, agricultural machinery and food products. There are printing works and nearby Vern-sur-Seiche has an oil refinery. It was the capital of the former province of ▷Brittany. It was destroyed by fire in 1720 and had to be almost wholly rebuilt.

rennet extract, traditionally obtained from a calf's stomach, that contains the enzyme rennin, used to coagulate milk in the cheesemaking process. The enzyme can now be chemically produced.

Renoir, Jean
(1894–1979) French film director. His films, characterized by their humanism and naturalistic technique, include *Boudu sauvé des eaux/Boudu Saved from Drowning* (1932), *La Grande Illusion* (1937), and *La Règle du jeu/The Rules of the Game* (1939).

Renoir, Pierre-Auguste
(1841–1919) French Impressionist painter. He met Claude ▷Monet and Alfred ▷Sisley in the early 1860s, and together they formed the nucleus of ▷Impressionism. He developed a lively, colourful painting style with feathery brushwork (known as his 'rainbow style') and painted many scenes of everyday life, such as *The Luncheon of the Boating Party* (1881; Phillips Collection, Washington, DC), and also female nudes, such as *The Bathers* (about 1884–87; Philadelphia Museum of Art).

His early pictures show the influence of Gustave ▷Courbet, but after the Franco-Prussian War (in which he served as *cuirassier*), with Monet at the Paris suburb of Argenteuil, he produced riverscapes completely Impressionist in their atmospheric colour, such as the *Regatta, Argenteuil* (1874).

While associated with Impressionism, and exhibiting at the Impressionist exhibitions in the 1870s, many of Renoir's works show that his main delight was in human life and the female model. *La Loge/The Theatre Box* (1874; Courtauld Gallery, London), a work painted in the studio, *Dancing at the Moulin de la Galette* (1876; Louvre, Paris), and *Madame Charpentier and her Daughters* (1879; Metropolitan Museum, New York) are good examples. He also produced about 150 lithographs.

His reaction against Impressionism began in the 1880s after he had visited Italy, where he was influenced by the Graeco-Roman paintings from Pompeii at Naples, and by a stay at L'Estaque with ▷Cézanne (who was also concerned with solid and permanent qualities in painting). He now began to take a closer interest in ▷Ingres. A harder, linear manner resulted, as in *The Umbrellas* (1884; National Gallery, London) and *The Bathers*.

repellent anything whose smell, taste, or other properties discourages nearby creatures. **Insect repellent** is usually a chemical substance that keeps, for example, mosquitoes at bay; natural substances include citronella, lavender oil, and eucalyptus oils. A device that emits ultrasound waves is also claimed to repel insects and small mammals.

repetitive strain injury
(RSI) inflammation of tendon sheaths, mainly in the hands and wrists, which may be disabling. It is found predominantly in factory workers involved in constant repetitive movements, and in those who work with computer keyboards. The symptoms include aching muscles, weak wrists, tingling fingers and in severe cases, pain and paralysis. Some victims have successfully sued their employers for damages. In 1999 RSI affected more than a million people annually in Britain and the USA.

> **Related Web site: Repetitive Strain Injury** http://home.clara.net/ ruegg/index.htm

replication in biology, production of copies of the genetic material DNA; it occurs during cell division (▷mitosis and ▷meiosis). Most mutations are caused by mistakes during replication.

Representation of the People Acts
series of UK acts of Parliament from 1867 that extended voting rights, creating universal suffrage in 1928. The 1867 and 1884 acts are known as the second and third ▷Reform Acts.

repression in psychology, a mental process that ejects and excludes from consciousness ideas, impulses, or memories that would otherwise threaten emotional stability.

reprieve legal temporary suspension of the execution of a sentence of a criminal court. It is usually associated with the death penalty. It is distinct from a pardon (extinguishing the sentence) and commutation (alteration) of a sentence (for example, from death to life imprisonment).

reproduction in biology, the process by which a living organism produces other organisms more or less similar to itself. The ways in which species reproduce differ, but the two main methods are by ▷asexual reproduction and ▷sexual reproduction. Asexual reproduction involves only one parent without the formation of ▷gametes: the parent's cells divide by ▷mitosis to produce new cells with the same number and kind of ▷chromosomes as its own. Thus offspring produced asexually are clones of the parent and there is no variation. Sexual reproduction involves two parents, one male and one female. The parents' sex cells divide by ▷meiosis producing gametes, which contain only half the number of chromosomes of the parent cell. In this way, when two sets of chromosomes combine during ▷fertilization, a new combination of genes is produced. Hence the new organism will differ from both parents, and variation is introduced. The

REPTILE One of the rarest reptiles is the gavial (also known as the gharial), a relative of the crocodile. It inhabits rivers in northern India and Myanmar, and has an exceptionally long nose and jaw. *Image Bank*

ability to reproduce is considered one of the fundamental attributes of living things.

Sexual reproductive systems The plant organs concerned with sexual reproduction are found in the flowers. These consist of the ▷stamens (male organ) and ▷carpels (female organ). In male mammals the reproductive system consists of the ▷testes, which produce sperm, epididymis, sperm duct, and ▷penis, and in the females the ▷ovaries, which produce eggs, ▷Fallopian tubes, and ▷uterus.

Hermaphrodites These are bisexual organisms, such as earthworms, that have both male and female reproductive organs, or plants whose flowers contain both stamens and carpels. This is the normal arrangement in most plants. Some plant species, such as maize and birch, which have separate male and female flowers on the same plants are described as **monoecious**; in dioecious species, such as willow and holly, the male and female flowers are on separate plants.

reptile any member of a class (Reptilia) of vertebrates. Unlike amphibians, reptiles have hard-shelled, yolk-filled eggs that are laid on land and from which fully formed young are born. Some snakes and lizards retain their eggs and give birth to live young. Reptiles are cold-blooded, and their skin is usually covered with scales. The metabolism is slow, and in some cases (certain large snakes) intervals between meals may be months. Reptiles date back over 300 million years.

Many extinct forms are known, including the orders Pterosauria, Plesiosauria, Ichthyosauria, and Dinosauria. The chief living orders are the Chelonia (tortoises and turtles), Crocodilia (alligators and crocodiles), and Squamata, divided into three suborders: Lacertilia (lizards), Ophidia or Serpentes (snakes), and Amphisbaenia (worm lizards). The order Rhynchocephalia has one surviving species, the lizardlike tuatara of New Zealand.

A four-year study of rainforest in eastern Madagascar revealed 26 new reptile species in 1995.

republic (Latin *res publica* 'the state'; from *res* 'affair', and *publica* 'public') country where the head of state is not a monarch, either hereditary or elected, but usually a president, whose role may or may not include political functions.

Republican Party
one of the two main political parties of the USA, formed in 1854. It is more right-wing than the Democratic Party, favouring capital and big business and opposing state subvention and federal controls. In the late 20th century most presidents have come from the Republican Party, but in Congress Republicans were generally outnumbered until 1994. In 1992 Republican George Bush lost the presidency to Democrat Bill Clinton, who in 1996 was re-elected for a second term, although the Republicans retained control of Congress. In 2000, Republican George W ▷Bush was elected president, giving Republicans control of both Congress and the White House.

> **Related Web site: Welcome to Republican Mainstreet** http:// www.rnc.org/

requiem (from Latin *Requiem aeternam dona eis, Domine*, 'Give them eternal rest, O Lord') in the Roman Catholic Church, a Mass for the dead. Musical settings include those by Palestrina, Mozart, Berlioz, Verdi, Fauré, and Britten.

reredos in church architecture, an ornamented wall or screen at the back of the high altar. It usually consists of a screen detached from the wall, and is elaborately adorned with sculpture and tracery or painting. Originally the reredos was a hanging of tapestry or silk; later it became more substantial, but could still be moved, and was used only at certain festivals. See also ▷altarpiece.

research the primary activity in science, a combination of theory and experimentation directed towards finding scientific explanations of phenomena. It is commonly classified into two types: **pure research**, involving theories with little apparent relevance to human concerns; and **applied research**, concerned with finding solutions to problems of social or commercial importance – for instance in medicine and engineering. The two types are linked in that theories developed from pure research may eventually be found to be of great value to society.

reserve currency in economics, a country's holding of internationally acceptable means of payment (major foreign currencies or gold); central banks also hold the ultimate reserve of money for their domestic banking sector. On the asset side of company balance sheets, undistributed profits are listed as reserves.

residue in chemistry, a substance or mixture of substances remaining in the original container after the removal of one or more components by a separation process.

resin substance exuded from pines, firs, and other trees in gummy drops that harden in air. Varnishes are common products of the hard resins, and ointments come from the soft resins.

standard potential divider

potentiometer used as a potential divider

R_{in}

V_{in}

R_{in}

V_{out}

contact

V_{out}

RESISTOR A potential divider is a resistor or a chain of resistors connected in series in an electrical circuit. It is used to obtain a known fraction of the total voltage across the whole resistor or chain. When a variable resistor, or potentiometer, is used as a potential divider, the output voltage can be varied continuously by sliding a contact along the resistor. Devices like this are used in electronic equipment to to vary volume, tone, and brightness control.

Rosin is the solid residue of distilled turpentine, a soft resin. The name 'resin' is also given to many synthetic products manufactured by polymerization; they are used in adhesives, plastics, and varnishes.

resistance in physics, that property of a conductor that restricts the flow of electricity through it, associated with the conversion of electrical energy to heat; also the magnitude of this property. Resistance depends on many factors, such as the nature of the material, its temperature, dimensions, and thermal properties; degree of impurity; the nature and state of illumination of the surface; and the frequency and magnitude of the current. The SI unit of resistance is the ▷ohm.

resistance = voltage/current

The statement that current is proportional to voltage (resistance is constant) at constant temperature is known as ▷Ohm's law. It is approximately true for many materials that are accordingly described as 'ohmic'.

A ▷rheostat is a variable resistor.

resistance movement opposition movement in a country occupied by an enemy or colonial power, especially in the 20th century; for example, the French resistance to Nazism in World War II.

resistivity in physics, a measure of the ability of a material to resist the flow of an electric current. It is numerically equal to the ▷resistance of a sample of unit length and unit cross-sectional area, and its unit is the ohm metre (symbol Ωm). A good conductor has a low resistivity (1.7×10^{-8} Ωm for copper); an insulator has a very high resistivity (10^{15} Ωm for polyethane).

resistor in physics, any component in an electrical circuit used to introduce ▷resistance to a current. Resistors are often made from wire-wound coils or pieces of carbon. ▷Rheostats and ▷potentiometers are variable resistors.

resolution in computing, the number of dots per unit length in which an image can be reproduced on a screen or printer. A typical screen resolution for colour monitors is 75 dpi (dots per inch). A ▷laser printer will have a printing resolution of 600 dpi upwards, and an ▷ink-jet printer typically has a resolution of 300 dpi. Photographs in books and magazines have a resolution of 1,200 dpi or 2,400 dpi.

resolution of forces in mechanics, the division of a single force into two parts that act at right angles to each other. The two parts of a resolved force, called its **components**, have exactly the same effect when acting together on an object as the single force which they replace.

resonance rapid amplification of a vibration when the vibrating object is subject to a force varying at its ▷natural frequency. In a trombone, for example, the length of the air column in the instrument is adjusted until it resonates with the note being sounded. Resonance effects are also produced by many electrical circuits. Tuning a radio, for example, is done by adjusting the natural frequency of the receiver circuit until it coincides with the frequency of the radio waves falling on the aerial.

Resonance has many physical applications. Children use it to increase the size of the movement on a swing, by giving a push at the same point during each swing. Soldiers marching across a bridge in step could cause the bridge to vibrate violently if the frequency of their steps coincided with its natural frequency. Resonance caused the collapse of the Tacoma Narrows Bridge, USA, 1940, when the frequency of the wind gusts coincided with the natural frequency of the bridge.

resources materials that can be used to satisfy human needs. Because human needs are diverse and extend from basic physical requirements, such as food and shelter, to ill-defined aesthetic needs, resources encompass a vast range of items. The intellectual resources of a society – its ideas and technologies – determine which aspects of the environment meet that society's needs, and therefore become resources. For example, in the 19th century, uranium was used only in the manufacture of coloured glass. Today, with the advent of nuclear technology, it is a military and energy resource. Resources are often categorized into **human resources**, such as labour, supplies, and skills, and **natural resources**, such as climate, fossil fuels, and water. Natural resources are divided into ▷nonrenewable resources and ▷renewable resources.

respiration metabolic process in organisms in which food molecules are broken down to release energy. The cells of all living organisms need a continuous supply of energy, and in most plants and animals this is obtained by **aerobic** respiration. In this process, oxygen is used to break down the glucose molecules in food. This releases energy in the form of energy-carrying molecules (▷ATP), and produces carbon dioxide and water as by-products. Respiration sometimes occurs without oxygen, and this is called **anaerobic** respiration. In this case, the end products are energy and either lactose acid or ethanol (alcohol) and carbon dioxide; this process is termed ▷fermentation.

The exchange of oxygen and carbon dioxide between body tissues and the environment is termed 'external respiration', or ventilation (see ▷gas exchange). In air-breathing vertebrates the exchange takes place in the alveoli of the ▷lungs, aided by the muscular movements of ▷breathing. Respiration at the cellular level is termed **internal respiration**, and in all higher organisms occurs in the ▷mitochondria. This takes place in two stages: the first stage, which does not require oxygen, is a form of ▷anaerobic respiration; the second stage is the main energy-producing stage and does require oxygen. This is termed the ▷Krebs cycle. In some bacteria the oxidant is the nitrate or sulphate ion.

Related Web site: Structure of the Human Respiratory System
http://www.stemnet.nf.ca/~dpower/resp/main.htm

rest mass in physics, the mass of a body when its velocity is zero or considerably below that of light. According to the theory of ▷relativity, at very high velocities, there is a relativistic effect that increases the mass of the particle.

Restoration In English history, the period when the monarchy, in the person of ▷Charles II, was re-established after the English ▷Civil War and the fall of the ▷Protectorate in 1660.

In literature, the term 'Restoration' is often applied generally to writers active at this period, most notably John ▷Dryden, John ▷Bunyan, and Samuel ▷Pepys. 'Restoration comedy', popular drama played in the theatres newly reopened since Cromwell's time, was characterized by its bawdiness and wit.

Restoration comedy style of English theatre, dating from the Restoration (1660). It witnessed the first appearance of women on the English stage, most notably in the 'breeches part', specially created in order to costume the actor in male attire, thus revealing her figure to its best advantage. The genre placed much emphasis on wit and sexual intrigues. Examples include Wycherley's *The Country Wife* (1675), Congreve's *The Way of the World* (1700), and Farquhar's *The Beaux' Stratagem* (1707).

restrictive trade practice any agreement between people in a particular trade or business that restricts free trade in a market. For example, several producers may join together to form a ▷cartel and fix prices; or a manufacturer may refuse to supply goods to a retailer if the retailer stocks the products of a rival company.

resurrection in Christian, Jewish, and Muslim belief, the rising from the dead that all souls will experience at the Last Judgement. The Resurrection also refers to Jesus rising from the dead on the third day after his crucifixion, a belief central to Christianity and celebrated at Easter.

resuscitation steps taken to revive anyone on the brink of death. The most successful technique for life-threatening emergencies, such as electrocution, near-drowning, or heart attack, is mouth-to-mouth resuscitation. Medical and paramedical staff are trained in cardiopulmonary resuscitation (CPR): the use of specialized equipment and techniques to attempt to restart the

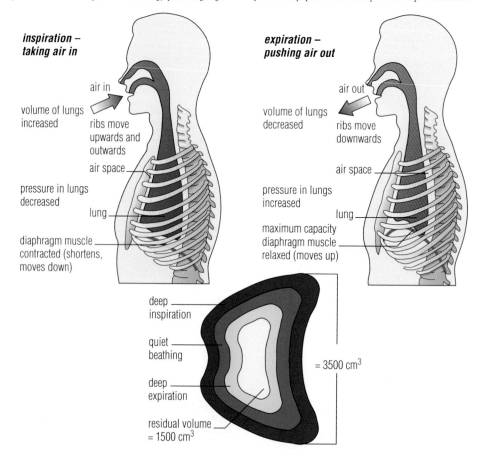

inspiration – taking air in

air in

volume of lungs increased

ribs move upwards and outwards

air space

pressure in lungs decreased

lung

diaphragm muscle contracted (shortens, moves down)

expiration – pushing air out

air out

volume of lungs decreased

ribs move downwards

air space

pressure in lungs increased

lung

maximum capacity diaphragm muscle relaxed (moves up)

deep inspiration

quiet breathing

deep expiration

residual volume = 1500 cm³

= 3500 cm³

subdivisions of lung air

RESPIRATION The diagrams show the two phases of the process of respiration. Gas exchange occurs in the alveoli, tiny air tubes in the lungs.

breathing and/or heartbeat and stabilize the patient long enough for more definitive treatment. CPR has a success rate of less than 30%.

retail sale of goods and services to a consumer. The retailer is the last link in the distribution chain. A retailer's purchases are usually made from a wholesaler, who in turn buys from a manufacturer.

retail-price index (RPI) indicator of variations in the ▷cost of living, superseded in the USA by the consumer price index.

retail-price maintenance (RPM) exceptions to the general rule that shops can charge whatever price they choose for goods. The main areas where RPM applies in the UK are books (where the Net Book Agreement prevents booksellers charging less than the publisher's price) and some pharmaceutical products.

retina light-sensitive area at the back of the ▷eye connected to the brain by the optic nerve. It has several layers and in humans contains over a million rods and cones, sensory cells capable of converting light into nervous messages that pass down the optic nerve to the brain.

The **rod cells**, about 120 million in each eye, are distributed throughout the retina. They are sensitive to low levels of light, but do not provide detailed or sharp images, nor can they detect colour. The **cone cells**, about 6 million in number, are mostly concentrated in a central region of the retina called the **fovea**, and provide both detailed and colour vision. The cones of the human eye contain three visual pigments, each of which responds to a different primary colour (red, green, or blue). The brain can interpret the varying signal levels from the three types of cone as any of the different colours of the visible spectrum.

The image actually falling on the retina is highly distorted; research into the eye and the optic centres within the brain has shown that this poor quality image is processed to improve its quality. The retina can become separated from the wall of the eyeball as a result of a trauma, such as a boxing injury. It can be reattached by being 'welded' into place by a laser.

retinol (or **vitamin A**) fat-soluble chemical derived from β-carotene and found in milk, butter, cheese, egg yolk, and liver. Lack of retinol in the diet leads to the eye disease **xerophthalmia**.

retriever any of several breeds of hunting dogs, often used as guide dogs for the blind. The commonest breeds are the **Labrador retriever**, large, smooth-coated, and usually black or yellow; and the **golden retriever**, with either flat or wavy coat. They can grow to 60 cm/2 ft high and weigh 40 kg/90 lb.

retrovirus any of a family of ▷viruses (Retroviridae) containing the genetic material ▷RNA rather than the more usual ▷DNA.

For the virus to express itself and multiply within an infected cell, its RNA must be converted to DNA. It does this by using a built-in enzyme known as reverse transcriptase (since the transfer of genetic information from DNA to RNA is known as ▷transcription, and retroviruses do the reverse of this). Retroviruses include those causing ▷AIDS and some forms of leukaemia. See ▷immunity.

Retroviruses are used as vectors in ▷genetic engineering, but they cannot be used to target specific sites on the chromosome. Instead they incorporate their genes at random sites.

Réunion French island of the Mascarenes group, in the Indian Ocean, 650 km/400 mi east of Madagascar and 180 km/110 mi southwest of Mauritius; area 2,512 sq km/970 sq mi; population (1995 est) 653,400. The capital is St Denis. Produce includes sugar, maize, vanilla, tobacco, and rum.

reuse multiple use of a product (often a form of packaging), by returning it to the manufacturer or processor each time. Many such returnable items are sold with a deposit which is reimbursed if the item is returned. Reuse is usually more energy- and resource-efficient than ▷recycling unless there are large transport or cleaning costs.

Reuter, (Paul) Julius de (1816–1899) Baron Reuter; adopted name of Israel Beer. German founder of the international news agency ▷Reuters. He began a continental pigeon post in 1849 at Aachen, Germany, and in 1851 set up a news agency in London. In 1858 he persuaded the press to use his news telegrams, and the service became worldwide.

Reuters London-based international news agency. General, political, economic, and sports news is provided by 1,200 journalists and photographers based in 75 countries. Reuters' television news agency, Visinews, acquired in 1992, is the largest of its kind in the world, serving 650 broadcasters in more than 80 countries.

revenge tragedy form of Elizabethan and Jacobean drama in which revenge provides the mainspring of the action. It is usually characterized by bloody deeds, intrigue, and high melodrama. It was pioneered by Thomas Kyd with *The Spanish Tragedy* (*c.* 1588), Shakespeare's *Titus Andronicus* (*c.* 1593), and Cyril Tourneur's *The Revenger's Tragedy* (1607). Its influence is apparent in tragedies such as Shakespeare's *Hamlet* and *Macbeth*.

reverberation in acoustics, the multiple reflections, or echoes, of sounds inside a building that merge and persist a short time (up to a few seconds) before fading away. At each reflection some of the sound energy is absorbed, causing the amplitude of the sound wave and the intensity of the sound to reduce a little.

Revere, Paul (1735–1818) American revolutionary, a Boston silversmith, who carried the news of the approach of British troops to Lexington and Concord (see ▷American Revolution) on the night of 18 April 1775. On the next morning the first shots of the Revolution were fired at Lexington. Henry Wadsworth Longfellow's poem 'Paul Revere's Ride' (1863) commemorates the event.

reverse osmosis the movement of solvent (liquid) through a semipermeable membrane from a more concentrated solution to a more dilute solution. The solvent's direction of movement is opposite to that which it would experience during ▷osmosis, and is achieved by applying an external pressure to the solution on the more concentrated side of the membrane. The technique is used in desalination plants, when water (the solvent) passes from brine (a salt solution) into fresh water via a semipermeable filtering device.

reverse takeover in business, a ▷takeover where a company sells itself to another (a ▷white knight) to avoid being the target of a purchase by an unwelcome predator.

reversible reaction chemical reaction that proceeds in both directions at the same time, as the product decomposes back into reactants as it is being produced. Such reactions do not run to completion, provided that no substance leaves the system. Examples include the manufacture of ammonia from hydrogen and nitrogen, and the oxidation of sulphur dioxide to sulphur trioxide.

revisionism political theory derived from Marxism that moderates one or more of the basic tenets of Karl Marx, and is hence condemned by orthodox Marxists.

revolution any rapid, far-reaching, or violent change in the political, social, or economic structure of society. It is usually applied to political change: examples include the American Revolution, where the colonists broke free from their colonial ties and established a sovereign, independent nation; the ▷French Revolution, where an absolute monarchy was overthrown by opposition from inside the country and a popular uprising; and the ▷Russian Revolution, where a repressive monarchy was overthrown by those seeking to institute widespread social and economic changes based on a socialist model. In 1989–90 the Eastern Bloc nations demonstrated against and voted out the Communist Party, in many cases creating a pro-democracy revolution.

While political revolutions are often associated with violence, other types of change can have just as much impact on society. Most notable is the ▷Industrial Revolution of the mid-18th century, which caused massive economic and social changes. In the 1970s and 1980s a high-tech revolution based on the silicon chip took place, facilitating the widespread use of computers.

Revolutionary Wars series of wars from 1791 to 1802 between France and the combined armies of England, Austria, Prussia, and others, during the period of the ▷French Revolution and ▷Napoleon's campaign to conquer Europe.

Revolutionary Wars

1791	Emperor Leopold II and Frederick William II of Prussia issue the Declaration of Pillnitz inviting the European powers to restore the French king Louis XVI to power.
1792	France declares war on Austria, which forms a coalition with Prussia, Sardinia, and (from 1793) Britain, Spain, and the Netherlands; victories for France at Valmy and Jemappes.
1793	French reverses until the reorganization by Lazare Carnot.
1795	Prussia, the Netherlands, and Spain make peace with France.
1796	Sardinia is forced to make peace by the Italian campaign of Napoleon I, then a commander.
1797	Austria is compelled to make peace with France under the Treaty of Campo-Formio.
1798	Napoleon's fleet, after its capture of Malta, is defeated by the British admiral Nelson in Egypt at the Battle of Aboukir Bay (Battle of the Nile), and Napoleon has to return to France without his army; William Pitt the Younger, Britain's prime minister, organizes a new coalition with Russia, Austria, Naples, Portugal, and Turkey.
1798–99	The coalition mounts its major campaign in Italy (under the Russian field marshal Suvorov), but dissension leads to the withdrawal of Russia.
1799	Napoleon, on his return from Egypt, reorganizes the French army.
1800	Austrian army defeated by Napoleon at Marengo in northwest Italy on 14 June, and again on 3 December (by General Moreau) at Hohenlinden near Munich; the coalition collapses.
1801	Austria makes peace under the Treaty of Lunéville; Sir Ralph Abercromby defeats the French army by land in Egypt at the Battle of Alexandria, but is himself killed.
1802	Treaty of Amiens truce between France and Britain, followed by the Napoleonic Wars.

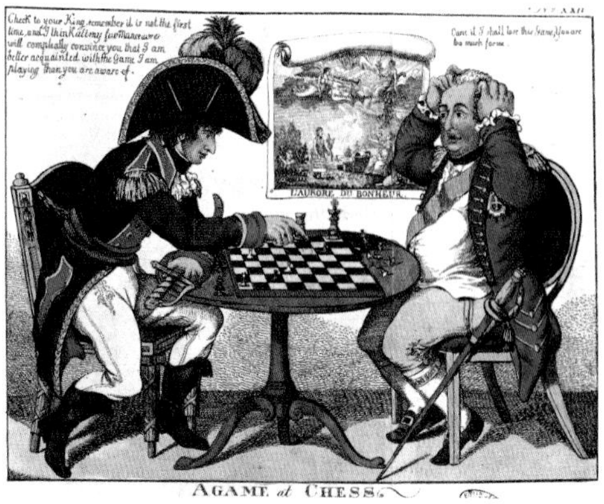

REVOLUTIONARY WARS The cartoon shows French emperor Napoleon Bonaparte playing chess with King George III of Great Britain and Ireland. The caption, *A Game at Chess*, is in English, and it can therefore be presumed that the cartoon has been drawn by an English artist. George III looks decidedly worried, and his king appears to be cornered as Napoleon moves forward. The inference may be that the Frenchman is too wily and clever for the British king. *The Art Archive/Dagli Orti*

revolutions of 1848 series of revolts in various parts of Europe against monarchical rule. Although some of the revolutionaries had republican ideas, many more were motivated by economic grievances. The revolution began in France with the overthrow of Louis Philippe and then spread to Italy, the Austrian Empire, and Germany, where the short-lived Frankfurt Parliament put forward ideas about political unity in Germany. None of the revolutions enjoyed any lasting success, and most were violently suppressed within a few months.

Related Web site: Revolutions of 1848 http://www.pvhs.chico.k12.ca.us/~bsilva/projects/revs/1848essy.html

revolutions of 1989 popular uprisings in many countries of Eastern Europe against communist rule, prompted by internal reforms in the USSR that permitted dissent within its sphere of influence. By 1990 nearly all the Warsaw Pact countries had moved from one-party to pluralist political systems, in most cases peacefully but with growing hostility between various nationalist and ethnic groups.

revue stage presentation involving short satirical and topical items in the form of songs, sketches, and monologues; it originated in the late 19th century.

Reykjavik chief port and capital (from 1918) of Iceland, on the southwest coast on Faxa Bay; population (1994) 103,000. Fish processing is the main industry. Most of the city is heated by an underground water mains system, built in 1945, the source of the hot water being volcanic springs and geysers. It was a seat of Danish administration from 1801 to 1918, and has been the seat of the Parliament since 1843. Reykjavik is the world's most northerly capital.

Related Web site: Reykjavik – Next Door to Nature http://www.rvk.is/vefur/owa/disp.birta?pk=542

Reynolds, Albert (1932–) Irish Fianna Fáil politician, Taoiseach (prime minister) 1992–94. He was minister for industry and commerce 1987–88 and minister of finance 1988–92. In December 1993 Reynolds and UK prime minister John Major issued a joint peace initiative for Northern Ireland, the Downing Street Declaration, which led to a ceasefire by both the Irish Republican Army (IRA) and the loyalist paramilitaries the following year.

Reynolds became party leader and prime minister in January 1992, but his government was defeated on a vote of confidence in

November 1992. He succeeded in forming a Fianna Fáil–Labour coalition, but resigned as premier and party leader in November 1994 after Labour disputed a judicial appointment he had made and withdrew from the coalition.

Reynolds saw the advantages of European Community membership, and after a referendum in 1992 ratified the Maastricht Treaty for closer union.

Reynolds, Joshua (1723–1792) English painter. One of the greatest portraitists of the 18th century, he displayed a facility for striking and characterful compositions in the 'Grand Manner', a style based on classical and Renaissance art. He often borrowed classical poses, for example *Mrs Siddons as the Tragic Muse* (1784; San Marino, California). His elegant portraits are mostly of wealthy patrons, though he also painted such figures as the writers Laurence Sterne and Dr Johnson, and the actor David Garrick. Active in London from 1752, he became the first president of the Royal Academy in 1768 and founded the Royal Academy schools. He was knighted in 1769.

> **Joshua Reynolds**
> *If you have great talents, industry will improve them: if you have but moderate abilities, industry will supply their deficiency.*
> Discourse to Students of the Royal Academy 11 December 1769

Reynolds was particularly influenced by classical antiquity and the High Renaissance masters, Michelangelo, Raphael, Titian, and Leonardo da Vinci. In his *Discourses on Art*, based on lectures given at the Royal Academy from 1769 to 1791, he argued that art should be of the Grand Manner, presenting the ideal rather than the mundane and realistic. Some of his finest portraits, however, combine classical form with a keen awareness of individuality, as in his *Lord Heathfield* (1787; National Gallery, London) and *Admiral Keppel* (1753–54; National Maritime Museum, London). Certain works – such as his *Self-Portrait* (about 1773; Royal Academy, London) – appear closer to ▷Rembrandt than to Renaissance artists.

JOSHUA REYNOLDS Samuel Foote, in a portrait from the studio of Joshua Reynolds, painted in about 1767.

rhapsody in music, an instrumental ▷fantasia, often based on folk melodies, such as Franz Liszt's *Hungarian Rhapsodies* (1853–54).

rhea one of two flightless birds of the family Rheidae, order Rheiformes. The common rhea *Rhea americana* is 1.5 m/5 ft high and is distributed widely in South America. The smaller Darwin's rhea *Pterocnemia pennata* occurs only in the south of South America and has shorter, feathered legs, and mottled plumage. Rheas differ from the ostrich in their smaller size and in having a feathered neck and head, three-toed feet, and no plumelike tail feathers.

Rhee, Syngman (1875–1965) Korean right-wing politician. A rebel under Chinese and Japanese rule, he became president of South Korea from 1948 until riots forced him to resign and leave the country in 1960. He established a repressive dictatorship and was an embarrassing ally for the USA.

Rheims English form of ▷Reims, a city in France.

Rheinland-Pfalz German name for the ▷Rhineland-Palatinate region of Germany.

rhenium (Latin *Rhenus* 'Rhine') heavy, silver-white, metallic element, symbol Re, atomic number 75, relative atomic mass 186.2. It has chemical properties similar to those of manganese and a very high melting point (3,180°C/5,756°F), which makes it valuable as an ingredient in alloys.

It was identified and named in 1925 by German chemists W Noddack (1893–1960), I Tacke, and O Berg from the Latin name for the River Rhine.

rheostat in physics, a variable ▷resistor, usually consisting of a high-resistance wire-wound coil with a sliding contact. It is used to vary electrical resistance without interrupting the current (for example, when dimming lights). The circular type, which can be used, for example, as the volume control of an amplifier, is also known as a ▷potentiometer.

rhesus factor group of ▷antigens on the surface of red blood cells of humans which characterize the rhesus blood group system. Most individuals possess the main rhesus factor (Rh+), but those without this factor (Rh−) produce ▷antibodies if they come into contact with it. The name comes from rhesus monkeys, in whose blood rhesus factors were first found.

If an Rh− mother carries an Rh+ fetus, she may produce antibodies if fetal blood crosses the ▷placenta. This is not normally a problem with the first infant because antibodies are only produced slowly. However, the antibodies continue to build up after birth, and a second Rh+ child may be attacked by antibodies passing from mother to fetus, causing the child to contract anaemia, heart failure, or brain damage. In such cases, the blood of the infant has to be changed for Rh− blood; a badly affected fetus may be treated in the womb (see ▷fetal therapy). The problem can be circumvented by giving the mother anti-Rh globulin just after the first pregnancy, preventing the formation of antibodies.

rhesus monkey macaque monkey *Macaca mulatta* found in northern India and Southeast Asia. It has a pinkish face, red buttocks, and long, straight, brown-grey hair. It can grow up to 60 cm/2 ft long, with a 20 cm/8 in tail.

rhetoric (Greek *rhetor* 'orator') traditionally, the art of public speaking and debate. Rhetorical skills are valued in such occupations as politics, teaching, law, religion, and broadcasting.
Related Web site: Glossary of Rhetorical Terms With Examples
http://www.uky.edu/ArtsSciences/Classics/rhetoric.html

rhetorical question question, often used by public speakers and debaters, that either does not require an answer or for which the speaker intends to provide his or her own answer ('Does this government know what it is doing?'). Such a question is used as a striking substitute for a statement.

rheumatic fever (or acute rheumatism) acute or chronic illness characterized by fever and painful swelling of joints. Some victims also experience involuntary movements of the limbs and head, a form of ▷chorea. It is now rare in the developed world.

rheumatism nontechnical term for a variety of ailments associated with inflammation and stiffness of the joints and muscles.

rheumatoid arthritis inflammation of the joints; a chronic progressive disease, it begins with pain and stiffness in the small joints of the hands and feet and spreads to involve other joints, often with severe disability and disfigurement. There may also be damage to the eyes, nervous system, and other organs. The disease is treated with a range of drugs and with surgery, possibly including replacement of major joints.

rhim (or sand gazelle) smallish gazelle *Gazella leptocerus* that has already disappeared over most of its former range of north Africa. Populations are fragmented and often isolated. It is one of several highly threatened gazelle species in northern Africa and the Sahara.

Rhine (German Rhein; French Rhin; Dutch Rijn) European river rising in Switzerland and reaching the North Sea via Germany and the Netherlands; length 1,320 km/820 mi. It drains an area of some 220,000 sq km/85,000 sq mi and is navigable for 805 km/500 mi. Tributaries include the Moselle and the Ruhr. The Rhine is linked with the Mediterranean by the Rhine–Rhône Waterway, and with the Black Sea by the Rhine–Main–Danube Waterway.

Rhineland province of Prussia from 1815. Its unchallenged annexation by Nazi Germany in 1936 was a harbinger of World War II.

Under the terms of the Treaty of Versailles (1919), following World War I, the Rhineland was to be occupied by Allied forces for 15 years, with a permanent demilitarized zone. Demilitarization

RHINE The River Rhine, at the border between Germany and Switzerland, broadens to form Lake Constance.
Image Bank

was reaffirmed by the Treaties of Locarno, but German foreign minister Gustav Stresemann achieved the removal of the British forces in 1926 and French forces in 1930. Both treaties were violated when Adolf Hitler's troops marched into the demilitarized zone of the Rhineland in 1936. Britain and France merely protested, and it remained under German occupation. It was the scene of heavy fighting in 1944, and was recaptured by US troops in 1945, becoming one of the largest states of West Germany after the end of the war.

Rhineland-Palatinate (German Rheinland-Pfalz) administrative region (German *Land*) of Germany, bordered on the north by North Rhine-Westphalia, on the east by Hesse and Baden-Württemberg, on the south by France, on the southwest by the Saarland, and on the west by Luxembourg and Belgium; area 19,800 sq km/7,650 sq mi; population (1995) 4,015,000. The capital is ▷Mainz. There are motor vehicle, mechanical and electrical engineering, chemical, machinery, leather goods, pottery, glass, and beverage industries. Wine (75% of German output), potatoes, cereals, sugar beet, fruit, and tobacco are produced, and there is stock rearing.

rhinoceros large grazing mammal with one or more horns on its snout. Rhinoceroses have thick, loose skin with little hair, stumpy, powerful legs with three toes on each foot. The largest species (the one-horned Indian rhinoceros) can grow up to 2 m/6 ft high at the shoulder and weigh 2,300–4,000 kg/5,060–8,800 lb. Rhinoceroses eat grass, leafy twigs, and shrubs, and are solitary. They have poor eyesight but excellent hearing and smell. Although they look clumsy, rhinos can reach speeds of 56 kph/35 mph. In the wild they are thought to live for about 25 years, and up to 47 in captivity. There are five species: three Asian and two African, all in danger of extinction.

Species The largest rhinoceros is the **one-horned Indian rhinoceros** *Rhinoceros unicornis*, which has a rough skin, folded into shieldlike pieces; the African rhinoceroses are smooth-skinned and two-horned. The African **black rhinoceros** *Diceros bicornis* is 1.5 m/5 ft high, with a prehensile (grasping) upper lip for feeding on shrubs, and sometimes a smaller third horn. The **broad-lipped** ('white') rhinoceros *Ceratotherium simum* is actually slaty-grey, with a squarish mouth for browsing grass. The **Javan rhinoceros** *R. sondaicus* is near extinction, as is the **two-horned Sumatran rhinoceros** *Dicerorhinus sumatrensis*.

In danger The Javan rhino is now one of the world's rarest mammals, and is included on the ▷CITES list of endangered species. In 1998 there were 50–60 Javan rhino *Rhinoceros sondaicus sondaicus* in Ujing Kulon National Park, Java, and an estimated five of the subspecies *R. s. annamiticus* in Vietnam. The total population of Indian rhinoceros (1995) consists of about 2,000 animals.

Huge ancestor An extinct hornless species, the baluchithere (genus *Baluchitherium*), reached 4.5 m/15 ft high.

Classification Rhinoceroses belong to the phylum Chordata, subphylum Vertebrata, class Mammalia (mammal), order Perissodactyla (odd-toed ungulates), suborder Ceratomorpha, family Rhinocerotidae. Today there are four genera with five remaining species: the great Indian rhinoceros (*Rhinoceros unicornis*), the Javan or lesser one-horned rhinoceros (*R. sondaicus*), the Sumatran or Asiatic two-horned or hairy rhinoceros (*Dicerorhinus sumatrensis*), the African black rhinoceros (*Diceros bicornis*) and the African white rhinoceros (*Ceratotherium simum*).

rhizome (or rootstock) horizontal underground plant stem. It is a ▷perennating organ in some species, where it is generally thick

RHINOCEROS The white rhinoceros, now on the list of endangered species, deliberately stamps its feet in its own dung in order to spread its personal scent wherever it goes. This is sometimes used as a device for staking a claim to territory, but it is primarily a means by which the animal can track where it is. *Image Bank*

and fleshy, while in other species it is mainly a means of ▷vegetative reproduction, and is therefore long and slender, with buds all along it that send up new plants. The potato is a rhizome that has two distinct parts, the tuber being the swollen end of a long, cordlike rhizome.

rhm (abbreviation of roentgen-hour-metre) the unit of effective strength of a radioactive source that produces gamma rays. It is used for substances for which it is difficult to establish radioactive disintegration rates.

Rhode Island smallest state of the USA, located in New England. It is nicknamed Little Rhody or the Ocean State, and is officially known as **Rhode Island and Providence Plantations**. Rhode Island ratified the US Constitution in 1790, becoming the 13th state to join the Union. It is bordered to the north and east by Massachusetts, to the west by Connecticut, and to the south by the Atlantic Ocean.

> **population** (1995) 989,800   **area** 3,100 sq km/1,197 sq mi   **capital** Providence   **towns and cities** Warwick, Cranston, Newport, Woonsocket   **industries and products** electronics, machine tools, jewellery, textiles, silverware, rubber, and plastics. Agriculture is limited by the rocky terrain but is important in rural areas, the main crops being apples and potatoes. Rhode Island Red hens were developed here from the 19th century

Rhodes (Greek *Ródhos*) Greek island, largest of the Dodecanese, in the eastern Aegean Sea; area 1,412 sq km/545 sq mi; population (1991) 98,200. The capital is Rhodes. Grapes and olives are grown.
> **Related Web site: Rhodes** http://rhodes.helios.gr/

Rhodes, Cecil John (1853–1902) South African politician, born in the UK, prime minister of Cape Colony 1890–96. Aiming at the formation of a South African federation and the creation of a block of British territory from the Cape to Cairo, he was responsible for the annexation of Bechuanaland (now Botswana) in 1885. He formed the British South Africa Company in 1889, which occupied Mashonaland and Matabeleland, thus forming Rhodesia (now Zambia and Zimbabwe).

Rhodes went to Natal in 1870. As head of De Beers Consolidated Mines and Goldfields of South Africa Ltd, he amassed a large fortune. He entered the Cape legislature in 1881, and became prime minister in 1890, but the discovery of his complicity in the ▷Jameson Raid forced him to resign in 1896. Advocating

Anglo-Afrikaner cooperation, he was less alive to the rights of black Africans, despite the final 1898 wording of his dictum: 'Equal rights for every civilized man south of the Zambezi.'

The **Rhodes scholarships** were founded at Oxford University, UK, under his will, for students from the Commonwealth, the USA, and Germany.

Rhodesia former name of ▷Zambia (Northern Rhodesia) and ▷Zimbabwe (Southern Rhodesia), in southern Africa.

rhodium (Greek *rhodon* 'rose') hard, silver-white, metallic element, symbol Rh, atomic number 45, relative atomic mass 102.905. It is one of the so-called platinum group of metals and is resistant to tarnish, corrosion, and acid. It occurs as a free metal in the natural alloy osmiridium and is used in jewellery, electroplating, and thermocouples.

rhododendron any of numerous, mostly evergreen shrubs belonging to the heath family. The leaves are usually dark and leathery, and the large funnel-shaped flowers, which grow in tight clusters, occur in all colours except blue. They thrive on acid soils. ▷Azaleas belong to the same genus. (Genus *Rhododendron*, family Ericaceae.)

Rhodope Mountains range of mountains on the frontier between Greece and Bulgaria, rising to 2,925 m/9,497 ft at Musala.

rhombus in geometry, an equilateral (all sides equal) ▷parallelogram. Its diagonals bisect each other at right angles, and its area is half the product of the lengths of the two diagonals. A rhombus whose internal angles are 90° is called a ▷square.

Rhondda Cynon Taff unitary authority in south Wales, created in 1996 from part of the former county of Mid Glamorgan.
> **area** 440 sq km/170 sq mi   **towns** Clydach Vale (administrative headquarters)   **physical** rivers Rhondda Fawr and Rhondda Fach   **industries** light industries   **population** (1996) 232,600

Rhône river of southern Europe; length 810 km/500 mi. It rises at the Rhône Glacier (altitude 1,825 m/5,987 ft) in the canton of Valais in Switzerland and flows through Lake Geneva to Lyon in France, where, at its confluence with the ▷Saône, the upper limit of navigation is reached. The river then turns due south and passes Vienne and Avignon. Near Arles it divides into the **Grand** and **Petit Rhône**, flowing respectively southeast and southwest into the Mediterranean west of Marseille. Here it forms a two-armed delta; the area between the tributaries is the marshy region known as the ▷Camargue.

Rhône-Alpes region of eastern France in the upper reaches of the ▷Rhône; area 43,700 sq km/16,868 sq mi; population (1992) 5,344,000. It consists of the *départements* of Ain, Ardèche, Drôme, Isère, Loire, Rhône, Savoie, and Haute-Savoie. The capital is ▷Lyon. There are several wine-producing areas, including Chenas, Fleurie, and Beaujolais. Industrial products include chemicals, textiles, and motor vehicles.

rhubarb perennial plant grown for its pink edible leaf stalks. The large leaves contain ▷oxalic acid, and are poisonous. There are also wild rhubarbs native to Europe and Asia. (Genus *Rheum rhaponticum*, family Polygonaceae.)
> **Related Web site: Rhubarb Compendium** http://www.rhubarbinfo.com/

rhyme identity of sound, usually in the endings of lines of verse, such as *wing* and *sing*. Avoided in Japanese, it is a common literary device in other Asian and European languages. Rhyme first appeared in Europe in late Latin poetry but was not used in classical Latin or Greek.

rhyolite ▷igneous rock, the fine-grained volcanic (extrusive) equivalent of granite.

Rhys, Jean (1894–1979) Adopted name of Ella Gwendolen Rees Williams. Dominican-born English novelist. Her works include *Wide Sargasso Sea* (1966), a recreation, set in a Caribbean island, of the life of the mad wife of Rochester from Charlotte Brontë's *Jane Eyre*.

rhythm and blues (R & B) US popular music of the 1940s–60s, which drew on swing and jump-jazz rhythms and blues vocals, and was an important influence on rock and roll. It diversified into soul, funk, and other styles. R & B artists include Bo Diddley, Jackie Wilson, and Etta James.

rhythm method method of natural contraception that relies on refraining from intercourse during ▷ovulation.

The time of ovulation can be worked out by the calendar (counting days from the last period), by temperature changes, or by inspection of the cervical mucus. All these methods are unreliable because it is possible for ovulation to occur at any stage of the menstrual cycle.

RI abbreviation for the state of ▷Rhode Island, USA.

ria long narrow sea inlet, usually branching and surrounded by hills. A ria is deeper and wider towards its mouth, unlike a ▷fjord. It is formed by the flooding of a river valley due to either a rise in sea level or a lowering of a landmass.

> **Jean Rhys**
> *The perpetual hunger to be beautiful and that thirst to be loved which is the real curse of Eve.*
> The Left Bank, 'Illusion'

rib long, usually curved bone that extends laterally from the ▷spine in vertebrates. Most fishes and many reptiles have ribs along most of the spine, but in mammals they are found only in the chest area. In humans, there are 12 pairs of ribs. The ribs protect the lungs and heart, and allow the chest to expand and contract easily.

Ribbentrop, Joachim von (1893–1946) German Nazi politician and diplomat. As foreign minister 1938–45, he negotiated the nonaggression pact between Germany and the USSR (the Ribbentrop–Molotov pact of 1939). He was tried at Nürnberg as a war criminal in 1946 and hanged.

RHODODENDRON Native to Asia, rhododendrons are now widely cultivated in northern temperate regions as ornamentals. This *Rhododendron stenophyllum* is one of many members of the genus found on the shady forested slopes of Mount Kinabalu in Borneo. *Premaphotos Wildlife*

Ribbentrop–Molotov pact (or Nazi–Soviet pact) nonaggression treaty signed by Germany and the USSR on 23 August 1939. The pact is named after the German foreign minister Joachim von ▷Ribbentrop and Russian foreign minister Vyacheslav ▷Molotov, working under German Nazi dictator Adolf Hitler and Soviet dictator Joseph Stalin respectively. Under the terms of the treaty both countries agreed to remain neutral and to refrain from acts of aggression against each other if either went to war. Secret clauses allowed for the partition of Poland – Hitler was to acquire western Poland, Stalin the eastern part. On 1 September 1939 Hitler invaded Poland. The pact ended when Hitler invaded Russia on 22 June 1941 during ▷World War II.

Ribble river in northern England, formed by the confluence of the Gayle and Cam; length 120 km/75 mi. From its source in the Pennine hills, North Yorkshire, it flows south and southwest past Preston, Lancashire, to join the Irish Sea.

ribbonfish member of a family of marine fish. They have elongated and compressed bodies which have a ribbonlike appearance. They are pelagic (open sea) fishes.

ribbon lake long, narrow lake found on the floor of a ▷glacial trough. A ribbon lake will often form in an elongated hollow carved out by a glacier, perhaps where it came across a weaker band of rock. Ribbon lakes can also form when water ponds up behind a terminal moraine or a landslide. The English Lake District is named after its many ribbon lakes, such as Lake Windermere and Coniston Water.

Ribera, José (Jusepe) de (1591–1652) Spanish painter. He was active in Italy from 1616 under the patronage of the viceroys of Naples. His early work shows the impact of Caravaggio, but his colours gradually lightened. He painted many full-length versions of saints as well as mythological figures and genre scenes, which he produced without preliminary drawing.

riboflavin (or vitamin B₂) ▷vitamin of the B complex important in cell respiration. It is obtained from eggs, liver, and milk. A deficiency in the diet causes stunted growth.

ribonucleic acid full name of ▷RNA.

ribosome in biology, the protein-making machinery of the cell. Ribosomes are located on the endoplasmic reticulum (ER) of eukaryotic cells, and are made of proteins and a special type of ▷RNA, ribosomal RNA. They receive messenger RNA (copied from the ▷DNA) and ▷amino acids, and 'translate' the messenger RNA by using its chemically coded instructions to link amino acids in a specific order, to make a strand of a particular protein.

Ricardo, David (1772–1823) English economist. Among his discoveries were the principle of **comparative advantage** (that countries can benefit by specializing in goods they produce efficiently and trading internationally to buy others), and the **law of diminishing returns** (that continued increments of capital and labour applied to a given quantity of land will eventually show a declining rate of increase in output). He wrote *Principles of Political Economy* (1817).

Ricci, Sebastiano (1659–1734) Venetian painter. Working in the style of ▷Veronese, he became one of the leading decorative painters of his day, working throughout Italy as well as in Vienna and London 1712–16. His *Resurrection* is in the chapel of the Royal Hospital, Chelsea, London.

rice principal ▷cereal of the wet regions of the tropics, derived from wild grasses probably native to India and Southeast Asia. Rice is unique among cereal crops in that it is grown standing in water. The yield is very large, and rice is said to be the staple food of one-third of the world's population. (Genus *Oryza sativa*.)

Richard three kings of England:

Richard (I) the Lion-Heart (1157–1199) (French Coeur-de-Lion) King of England 1189–99. He spent all but six months of his reign abroad. He was the third son of Henry II, against whom he twice rebelled. In the third ▷Crusade 1191–92 he won victories at Cyprus, Acre, and Arsuf (against ▷Saladin), but failed to recover Jerusalem. While returning overland he was captured by the Duke of Austria, who handed him over to the emperor Henry VI, and he was held prisoner until a large ransom was raised. He then returned

briefly to England, where his brother John had been ruling in his stead. His later years were spent in warfare in France, where he was killed by a crossbow bolt while besieging Châlus-Chabrol in 1199. He left no heir.

Richard's experience in warfare came from controlling his rebellious vassals in Poitou in the 1170s and against his father, ▷Henry II, in 1183. He took up Henry's plans to recover Jerusalem on his accession in 1189 and set out to establish bases for crusades in Sicily in 1190 and Cyprus, which he took in 1191. Engaging in the Siege of Acre, which he brought to a swift conclusion, he set off down the coast to Jaffa, conducting a fighting march against Saladin. Once ransomed from the Germans, Richard recovered lands in France taken by Philip. In the Vexin, where he built Chateau Gaillard, the great castle on the Seine, and in the Touraine and Poitou, he thwarted the French king's every manoeuvre.

Himself a poet, he became a hero of legends after his death. He was succeeded by his brother John I.

RICHARD (I) THE LION-HEART The Great Seal of King Richard I, who spent most of his reign away from England. *Philip Sauvain Picture Collection*

Richard II (1367–1400) Also known as **Richard of Bordeaux**. King of England from 1377, effectively from 1389, son of Edward the Black Prince. He reigned in conflict with Parliament; they executed some of his associates in 1388, and he executed some of the opposing barons in 1397, whereupon he made himself absolute. Two years later, forced to abdicate in favour of ▷Henry IV, he was jailed and probably assassinated.

Richard III (1452–1485) King of England from 1483. The son of Richard, Duke of York, he was created Duke of Gloucester by his brother Edward IV, and distinguished himself in the Wars of the ▷Roses. On Edward's death in 1483 he became protector to his nephew Edward V, and soon secured the crown for himself on the plea that Edward IV's sons were illegitimate. He proved a capable ruler, but the suspicion that he had murdered Edward V and his brother undermined his popularity. In 1485 Henry, Earl of Richmond (later ▷Henry VII), raised a rebellion, and Richard III was defeated and killed at ▷Bosworth.

Scholars now tend to minimize the evidence for his crimes as Tudor propaganda.

Related Web site: Ricardian Studies Primer
http://www.r3.org/basics/index.html

Richard, Cliff (1940–) Stage name of Harry Roger Webb. English pop singer. Initially influenced by Elvis Presley, he soon became a Christian family entertainer. One of his best-selling early records was 'Livin' Doll' (1959); it was followed by a string of other successful singles. His original backing group was the Shadows (1958–68 and later re-formed). During the 1960s he starred in a number of musical films including *The Young Ones* (1962) and *Summer Holiday* (1963). Fulfilling a personal ambition, he produced the musical *Heathcliff* (1997) in which he played the title role.

Richards, Viv (Isaac Vivian Alexander) (1952–) West Indian cricketer. He was captain of the West Indies team 1986–91. He has played for the Leeward Islands and, in the UK, for Somerset and Glamorgan. A prolific run-scorer, he holds the record for the greatest number of runs made in Test cricket in one calendar year (1,710 runs in 1976). He retired from international cricket after the West Indies tour of England in 1991 and from first-class cricket at the end of the 1993 season.

Richardson, Dorothy (Miller) (1873–1957) English novelist. Her sequence of 12 autobiographical novels was published together as *Pilgrimage* in 1938. It began with *Pointed Roofs* (1915), in which she was one of the first English novelists to use the 'stream of consciousness' technique.

Richardson, Ralph (David) (1902–1983) English actor. He played many stage parts, including Falstaff (Shakespeare), Peer Gynt (Ibsen), and Cyrano de Bergerac (Rostand). He shared the management of the Old Vic Theatre with Laurence ▷Olivier 1944–50. In later years he revealed himself as an accomplished deadpan comic.

Richardson, Samuel (1689–1761) English novelist. He was one of the founders of the modern novel. *Pamela* (1740–41), written in the form of a series of letters and containing much dramatic conversation, was sensationally popular all across Europe, and was followed by *Clarissa* (1747–48) and *Sir Charles Grandison* (1753–54).

Richardson, Tony (Cecil Antonio) (1928–1991) English director and producer. With George Devine he established the English Stage Company in 1955 at the Royal Court Theatre, London, with such productions as John Osborne's *Look Back in Anger* (1956). He was a leading figure in the English realist cinema of the late 1950s and early 1960s, with such films as *Look Back in Anger* (1958), his feature debut, *Saturday Night and Sunday Morning* (1960), *A Taste of Honey* (1961), and *Tom Jones* (1963; Academy Award).

RICHARD II An illustration from a 14th-century manuscript of French historian Jean Froissart's *Chronicles*. The picture shows Richard II of England as a prisoner in the Tower of London, England. The king is relinquishing his crown and sceptre to Henry, Duke of Lancaster, who subsequently became King Henry IV. *The Art Archive/British Museum*

Richelieu, Armand Jean du Plessis de (1585–1642) French cardinal and politician, chief minister from 1624. He aimed to make the monarchy absolute; he ruthlessly crushed opposition by the nobility and destroyed the political power of the ▷Huguenots, while leaving them religious freedom. Abroad, he sought to establish French supremacy by breaking the power of the Habsburgs; he therefore supported the Swedish king Gustavus Adolphus and the German Protestant princes against Austria and in 1635 brought France into the Thirty Years' War.

Born in Paris of a noble family, he entered the church and was created bishop of Luçon in 1606 and a cardinal in 1622. Through the influence of ▷Marie de' Medici he became ▷Louis XIII's chief minister in 1624, a position he retained until his death. His secretary Père Joseph was the original Grey Eminence.

Richmond capital and seaport of ▷Virginia, USA, on the James River, 209 mi from its mouth on the Atlantic, 160 km/100 mi south of Washington, DC; population (1996 est) 198,300. It is a major tobacco market and a distribution, commercial, and financial centre for the surrounding region. Industries include the manufacture of tobacco products, processed foods, chemicals, metalware, paper and print, and textiles. Established in 1637, Richmond was the site of the first permanent colonial American settlement. The city became the capital of Virginia in 1779, and the ▷Confederacy 1861–65; several Civil War battles were fought for its possession. The cigarette-rolling machine was invented here in the 1870s.

RICE Flooded rice terraces are common in rural areas of the Guanxi province of China. Water from the topmost level makes its way, under the force of gravity, to all the succeeding levels, in a carefully controlled, intermittent flow. *Image Bank*

Richter scale a quantitative scale of earthquake magnitude based on measurement of seismic waves, used to indicate the magnitude of an ▷earthquake at its epicentre. The magnitude of an earthquake differs from its intensity, measured by the ▷Mercalli scale, which is qualitative and varies from place to place for the same earthquake. The scale is named after US seismologist Charles Richter.

An earthquake's magnitude is a function of the total amount of energy released, and each point on the Richter scale represents a thirtyfold increase in energy over the previous point. The greatest earthquake ever recorded, in 1920 in Gansu, China, measured 8.6 on the Richter scale.

Related Web site: Story of the Richter Scale http://www.dkonline.com/science/private/earthquest/contents/hall2.html

Richthofen, Manfred, Freiherr von (1892–1918) Called 'the Red Baron'. German aviator. In World War I he commanded the 11th Chasing Squadron, known as **Richthofen's Flying Circus**, and shot down 80 aircraft before being killed in action.

ricin extremely poisonous extract from the seeds of the castor-oil plant. When incorporated into ▷monoclonal antibodies, ricin can attack cancer cells, particularly in the treatment of lymphoma and leukaemia.

rickets defective growth of bone in children due to an insufficiency of calcium deposits. The bones, which do not harden adequately, are bent out of shape. It is usually caused by a lack of vitamin D and insufficient exposure to sunlight. Renal rickets, also a condition of malformed bone, is associated with kidney disease.

ridge of high pressure elongated area of high atmospheric pressure extending from an anticyclone. On a synoptic weather chart it is shown as a pattern of lengthened isobars. The weather under a ridge of high pressure is the same as that under an anticyclone.

Ridley, Nicholas (*c.* 1500–1555) English Protestant bishop. He became chaplain to Henry VIII in 1541, and bishop of London in 1550. He took an active part in the ▷Reformation and supported Lady Jane Grey's claim to the throne. After ▷Mary I's accession he was arrested and burned as a heretic.

Riff a ▷Berber people of northern Morocco, who under Abd al-Karim long resisted the Spanish and French.

rifle ▷firearm that has spiral grooves (rifling) in its barrel. When a bullet is fired, the rifling makes it spin, thereby improving accuracy. Rifles were first introduced in the late 18th century.

rift valley valley formed by the subsidence of a block of the Earth's ▷crust between two or more parallel ▷faults. Rift valleys are steep-sided and form where the crust is being pulled apart, as at ▷ocean ridges, or in the Great Rift Valley of East Africa.

Rift Valley, Great longest 'split' in the Earth's surface; see ▷Great Rift Valley.

Riga capital and port of Latvia; population (1995) 840,000. Industries include engineering, brewing, food processing, and the manufacture of textiles and chipboard.

A member of the ▷Hanseatic League from 1282, Riga has belonged in turn to Poland (1582), Sweden (1621), and Russia (1710). It was occupied by the Germans in 1917 and then, after being seized by both Russian and German troops in the aftermath of World War I, became the capital of independent Latvia 1919–40. It was again occupied by Germany 1941–44, before being annexed by the USSR. It again became independent Latvia's capital in 1991.

Rigel (or **Beta Orionis**) brightest star in the constellation Orion. It is a blue-white supergiant, with an estimated diameter 50 times that of the Sun. It is 910 light years from Earth, and is intrinsically the brightest of the first-magnitude stars, its true luminosity being about 100,000 times that of the Sun. It is the seventh-brightest star in the night sky.

right-angled triangle triangle in which one of the angles is a right angle (90°). It is the basic form of triangle for defining trigonometrical ratios (for example, sine, cosine, and tangent) and for which ▷Pythagoras' theorem holds true. The longest side of a right-angled triangle is called the hypotenuse; its area is equal to half the product of the lengths of the two shorter sides.

right of way the right to pass over land belonging to another. Other rights of way are licences (where personal permission is given) and ▷easements.

rights an individual's automatic entitlement to certain freedoms and other benefits, usually, in liberal democracies such as the USA and UK, in the context of the individual's relationship with the government of the country. The struggle to assert political and civil rights against arbitrary government has been a major theme of Western political history.

rights issue in finance, new shares offered to existing shareholders to raise new capital. Shareholders receive a discount on the market price while the company benefits from not having the costs of a relaunch of the new issue.

Rights of Man and the Citizen, Declaration of the historic French document. According to the statement of the French National Assembly in 1789, these rights include representation in the legislature; equality before the law; equality of opportunity; freedom from arbitrary imprisonment; freedom of speech and religion; taxation in proportion to ability to pay; and security of property. In 1946 were added equal rights for women; right to work, join a union, and strike; leisure, social security, and support in old age; and free education.

right wing the more conservative or reactionary section of a political party or spectrum. It originated in the French national assembly in 1789, where the nobles sat in the place of honour on the president's right, whereas the commons were on his left (hence ▷left wing).

Rigil Kent (or **Alpha Centauri**) brightest star in the constellation Centaurus and the third-brightest star in the night sky. It is actually a triple star (see ▷binary star); the two brighter stars orbit each other every 80 years, and the third, Proxima Centauri, is the closest star to the Sun, 4.2 light years away from the sun, 0.1 light years closer than the other two.

rigor medical term for shivering or rigidity. **Rigor mortis** is the stiffness that ensues in a corpse soon after death, owing to chemical changes in muscle tissue.

Rig-Veda oldest of the ▷*Vedas*, the chief sacred writings of Hinduism. It consists of hymns to the Aryan gods, such as Indra, and to nature gods.

Riley, Bridget Louise (1931–) English painter. A pioneer of ▷op art, she developed her characteristic style in the early 1960s, arranging hard-edged black lines in regular patterns to create disturbing effects of scintillating light and movement. *Fission* (1963; Museum of Modern Art, New York) is an example.

Rilke, Rainer Maria (1875–1926) Austrian writer. His prose works include the semi-autobiographical *Die Aufzeichnungen des Malte Laurids Brigge/The Notebook of Malte Laurids Brigge* (1910). His verse is characterized by a form of mystic pantheism that seeks to achieve a state of ecstasy in which existence can be apprehended as a whole.

Rimbaud, (Jean Nicolas) Arthur (1854–1891) French Symbolist poet. His verse was chiefly written before the age of 20, notably *Les Illuminations* (published 1886). From 1871 he lived with the poet Paul ▷Verlaine.

Although the association ended after Verlaine attempted to shoot him, it was Verlaine's analysis of Rimbaud's work in 1884 that first brought him recognition. Rimbaud then travelled widely, working as a trader in North Africa 1880–91.

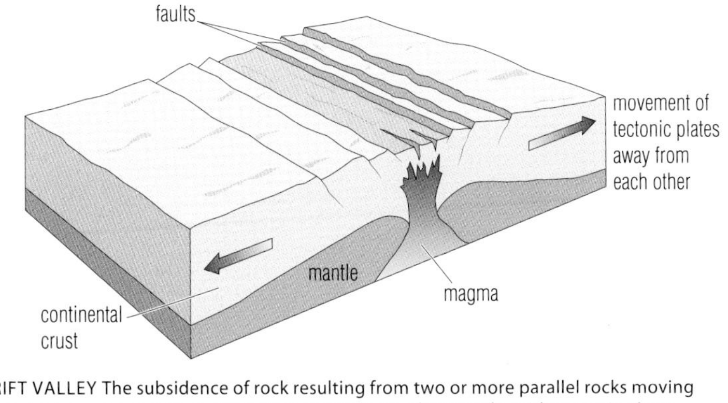

RIFT VALLEY The subsidence of rock resulting from two or more parallel rocks moving apart is known as a graben. When this happens on a large scale, with tectonic plates moving apart, a rift valley is created.

Rimsky-Korsakov, Nikolai Andreievich (1844–1908) Russian composer. He composed many operas and works for orchestra, He also wrote an influential text on orchestration. His opera *The Golden Cockerel* (1907) was a satirical attack on despotism that was banned until 1909. He also completed works by other composers, for example, Mussorgsky's *Boris Godunov* (1868–69).

ring circuit household electrical circuit in which appliances are connected in series to form a ring with each end of the ring connected to the power supply. It superseded the radial circuit.

ring ouzel mountain songbird *Turdus torquatus* with brownish-black plumage and a broad white patch on the throat. It nests in heather or on banks in moorland districts. It belongs to the thrush family Muscicapidae, order Passeriformes.

ringworm any of various contagious skin infections due to related kinds of fungus, usually resulting in circular, itchy, discoloured patches covered with scales or blisters. The scalp and feet (athlete's foot) are generally involved. Treatment is with antifungal preparations.

Rio de Janeiro (Portuguese 'river of January') port and resort in southeast Brazil; capital of Rio de Janeiro federal unit (state), and former national capital (1763–1960); population (1991) 5,480,800 (metropolitan area 10,389,400). It is situated on the southwest shore of Guanabara Bay, an inlet of the Atlantic Ocean; Sugar Loaf Mountain (a huge cone-shaped rock outcrop, composed of granite, quartz and feldspar) stands at the entrance to the harbour, and the city is dominated by the 30 m/100 ft-high figure of Christ on the top of Corcovado, a jagged peak 690 m/2,264 ft high. Industries include ship-repair, sugar refining, textiles, and the manufacture of foodstuffs; coffee, sugar, and iron ore are exported.

Features Some colonial churches and other buildings survive; there are modern boulevards, including Avenida Rio Branco and Avenida Presidente Vargas. The neighbourhoods of Rio de Janeiro include the middle-class residential beach resorts of Copacabana, Ipanema, and Leblon; more recent urban sprawl has resulted in the new suburbs of São Conrado, Barra da Tijuca and Itanhanga to the south. Tourists are attracted by the renowned annual carnival. One-third of the population lives in shanty towns, with an income of less than $70 a month per person. Rocinha is the largest squatter settlement in South America and is located on the south side of the city in the neighbourhood of São Conrado.

History Portuguese explorers landed on the site on 1 January 1502. The city was founded by the Portuguese in 1567 as São Sebastião de Rio de Janeiro (although the site was occupied by the French as early as 1555 under Nicolas de Villecagnon). The name commemorates the arrival of the Portuguese, but there is in fact no river.

Related Web site: Rio de Janeiro, Brazil http://www.if.ufrj.br/general/tourist.html

Rio Grande (Mexican **Río Bravo del Norte**) river of the USA and Mexico, rising in the Rocky Mountains in southern Colorado, it flows southeast, through New Mexico and Texas, to the Gulf of Mexico near Brownsville; length 3,050 km/1,900 mi. From El Paso, the river forms the US-Mexican border for the last 2,400 km/1,500 mi of its course. Insufficient water is carried for the demands of irrigation both sides of the border, and the Rio Grande is eventually reduced to a trickle in its lower reaches. Its rate of flow is subject to international agreements.

Rio Grande do Norte federal unit (state) of northeast Brazil, bounded on the north and east by the Atlantic Ocean; area 53,100 sq km/20,500 sq mi; population (1991) 2,414,100; capital Natal. Apart from a narrow coastal zone with abundant rainfall, most of the state lies on a semi-arid plateau, crossed by several rivers, where there is stock-raising, and cotton, sugar, and cassava are grown. There are oil, textile, and agricultural industries. It produces 90% of the nation's salt. Carnauba wax is extensively produced from the carnauba palm.

Rio Grande do Sul southernmost federal unit (state) of Brazil, to the east of the Uruguay River, bounded on the east by the Atlantic Ocean, on the west by Argentina, and on the south by Uruguay; area 282,184 sq km/108,993 sq mi; population (1991) 9,138,700; capital ▷Porto Alegre. The region consists mainly of vast grasslands where there is extensive stock-raising (cattle, sheep, pigs); wine, rice, and soybeans are produced, and industries are centred around agricultural production and processing. The state produces 90% of the national wine production.

Rioja, La see ▷La Rioja, a region of Spain.

riot disturbance caused by a potentially violent mob. In the UK, riots formerly suppressed under the Riot Act are now governed by the Public Order Act 1986. Methods of riot control include plastic bullets, stun bags (soft canvas pouches filled with buckshot which spread out in flight), water cannon, and CS gas (tear gas).

RIP abbreviation for **requiescat in pace** (Latin 'may he/she rest in peace').

Ripon city and market centre in North Yorkshire, northern England, on the River Ure; population (1991) 14,200. Agricultural produce is traded here. Features include a cathedral (1154–1520), and nearby are the 12th-century ruins of ▷Fountains Abbey, among the finest monastic ruins in Europe.

ripple tank in physics, shallow water-filled tray used to demonstrate various properties of waves, such as reflection, refraction, diffraction, and interference.

RISC (acronym for reduced instruction-set computer) in computing, a microprocessor (processor on a single chip) that carries out fewer instructions than other (▷CISC) microprocessors in common use in the 1990s. Because of the low number and the regularity of ▷machine code instructions, the processor carries out those instructions very quickly.

RISC microprocessors became commercially available in the mid 1980s and were used mainly in Unix workstations and servers. They are now widely used in games consoles and laser printers, as well as in microcomputers made by Acorn and Apple Computer.

risk capital (or venture capital) finance provided by venture capital companies, individuals, and merchant banks for medium- or long-term business ventures that are not their own and in which there is a strong element of risk.

Risorgimento 19th-century movement for Italian national unity and independence, begun 1815. Leading figures in the movement included ▷Cavour, ▷Mazzini, and ▷Garibaldi. Uprisings 1848–49 failed, but with help from France in a war against Austria – to oust it from Italian provinces in the north – an Italian kingdom was founded in 1861. Unification was finally completed with the addition of Venetia in 1866 and the Papal States in 1870.

rite of passage ritual that accompanies any of the most significant moments or transitions (birth, puberty, marriage, and so on) in an individual's life. In Hinduism there are 14, called samskaras.

ritualization in ethology, a stereotype that occurs in certain behaviour patterns when these are incorporated into displays. For example, the exaggerated and stylized head toss of the goldeneye drake during courtship is a ritualization of the bathing movement used to wet the feathers; its duration and form have become fixed. Ritualization may make displays clearly recognizable, so ensuring that individuals mate only with members of their own species.

Rivadavia, Bernardino (1780–1845) Argentine politician, first president of Argentina 1826–27. During his rule he made a number of social reforms including extending the franchise to all males over 20 and encouraging freedom of the press. Unable to control the provincial caudillos, he was forced to resign and spent most of his remaining years in exile in Europe.

river large body of water that flows down a slope along a channel restricted by adjacent banks and ▷levées. A river originates at a point called its **source**, and enters a sea or lake at its **mouth**. Along its length it may be joined by smaller rivers called **tributaries**; a river and its tributaries are contained within a drainage basin. The point at which two rivers join is called the confluence.

Rivers are formed and moulded over time chiefly by the processes of ▷erosion, and by the **transport** and **deposition** of ▷sediment. Rivers are able to work on the landscape because the energy stored in the water, or potential energy, is converted as it flows downhill into the kinetic energy used for erosion, transport, and deposition. The amount of potential energy available to a river is proportional to its initial height above sea level. A river follows the path of least resistance downhill, and deepens, widens and lengthens its channel by erosion.

One way of classifying rivers is by their stage of development. A youthful stream is typified by a narrow V-shaped valley with numerous ▷waterfalls, lakes, and rapids. Because of the steep gradient of the topography and the river's height above sea level, the rate of erosion is greater than the rate of deposition, and downcutting occurs by **vertical corrasion**. These characteristics may also be said to typify a river's **upper course**.

In a mature river, the topography has been eroded down over time and the river's course has a shallow gradient. Such a river is said to be graded. Erosion and deposition are delicately balanced as the river meanders (gently curves back and forth) across the extensive ▷flood plain (sometimes called an inner ▷delta). **Horizontal corrasion** is the dominant erosive process. The flood plain is an area of periodic ▷flooding along the course of river valleys made up of fine silty material called alluvium deposited by the flood water. Features of a the mature river (or the **lower course** of a river) include extensive ▷meanders, ▷ox-bow lakes, and braiding.

Many important flood plains, such as the inner Niger delta in Mali, occur in arid areas where their exceptional fertility is of great importance to the local economy. However, using flood plains as the site of towns and villages involves a certain risk, and it is safer to use flood plains for other uses, such as agriculture and parks. Water engineers can predict when flooding is likely and take action to prevent it by studying ▷hydrographs, graphs showing how the discharge of a river varies with time. Major rivers of the world include the ▷Ganges, the ▷Mississippi, and the ▷Nile, the world's longest river.

Rivera, Diego (1886–1957) Mexican painter. He was one of the most important muralists of the 20th century. An exponent of social realism, he received many public commissions for murals depicting the Mexican revolution, his vivid style influenced by Mexican folk art. A vast cycle on historical themes (National Palace, Mexico City) was begun in 1929.

Rivera, José Fructuoso (c. 1788–1854) Uruguayan general and politician, president 1830–34, 1839–43. Rivera fought under José Artigas and submitted to Brazilian occupation before rejoining the revolution in 1825. When he became president his financial mismanagement and favouritism provoked open dissent.

Rivera, Primo de Spanish politician; see ▷Primo de Rivera.

riveting method of joining metal plates. A hot metal pin called a rivet, which has a head at one end, is inserted into matching holes in two overlapping plates, then the other end is struck and formed into another head, holding the plates tight. Riveting is used in building construction, boilermaking, and shipbuilding.

Riviera the Mediterranean coast of France and Italy from Hyères to La Spezia. The most exclusive stretch of the Riviera, with the

DIEGO RIVERA Mexican artist Diego Rivera, shown working on a large mural in 1945. *Archive Photos*

finest climate, is the ▷Côte d'Azur, from Menton to St-Tropez, which includes Monaco.

Riyadh (Arabic **Ar Riyad**) capital of Saudi Arabia and of the Riyadh region, situated in an oasis and connected by rail with Dammam 450 km/280 mi away on the Arabian Gulf; population (1992 est) 2,776,100.

RNA (abbreviation for ribonucleic acid) nucleic acid involved in the process of translating the genetic material ▷DNA into proteins. It is usually single-stranded, unlike the double-stranded DNA, and

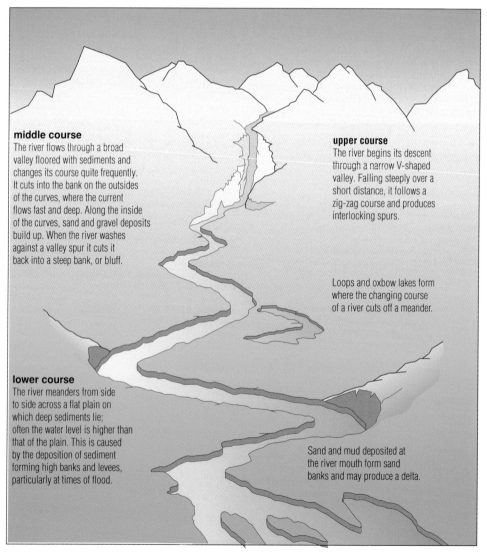

middle course
The river flows through a broad valley floored with sediments and changes its course quite frequently. It cuts into the bank on the outsides of the curves, where the current flows fast and deep. Along the inside of the curves, sand and gravel deposits build up. When the river washes against a valley spur it cuts it back into a steep bank, or bluff.

upper course
The river begins its descent through a narrow V-shaped valley. Falling steeply over a short distance, it follows a zig-zag course and produces interlocking spurs.

Loops and oxbow lakes form where the changing course of a river cuts off a meander.

lower course
The river meanders from side to side across a flat plain on which deep sediments lie; often the water level is higher than that of the plain. This is caused by the deposition of sediment forming high banks and levees, particularly at times of flood.

Sand and mud deposited at the river mouth form sand banks and may produce a delta.

RIVER The course of a river from its source of a spring or melting glacier, through to maturity where it flows into the sea.

Rivets

round head (snap head)   flat head (Tiriman's rivet)   countersunk   bifurcated rivet   pop rivet

steel pin

rivet

RIVETING Rivets are a quick method of permanently joining metal sheets together. Pop rivets are useful as they enable riveting from just one side.

consists of a large number of nucleotides strung together, each of which comprises the sugar ribose, a phosphate group, and one of four bases (uracil, cytosine, adenine, or guanine). RNA is copied from DNA by the formation of ▷base pairs, with uracil taking the place of thymine.

RNA occurs in three major forms, each with a different function in the synthesis of protein molecules. **Messenger RNA (mRNA)** acts as the template for protein synthesis. Each ▷codon (a set of three bases) on the RNA molecule is matched up with the corresponding amino acid, in accordance with the ▷genetic code. This process (translation) takes place in the ribosomes, which are made up of proteins and **ribosomal RNA (rRNA)**. **Transfer RNA (tRNA)** is responsible for combining with specific amino acids, and then matching up a special 'anticodon' sequence of its own with a codon on the mRNA. This is how the genetic code is translated.

RIVER Some of the animals and plants that are likely to be found in a slow-moving British river.

Although RNA is normally associated only with the process of protein synthesis, it makes up the hereditary material itself in some viruses, such as ▷retroviruses.

roach any freshwater fish of the Eurasian genus *Rutilus*, of the carp family, especially *R. rutilus* of northern Europe. It is dark green above, whitish below, with reddish lower fins; it grows to 35 cm/1.2 ft.

Roach, Hal (Harald Eugene) (1892–1992) US film producer. He was active from the 1910s to the 1940s, producing many comedies. He worked with ▷Laurel and Hardy, and also produced films for Harold Lloyd and Charley Chase. His work includes *The Music Box* (1932), *Way Out West* (1936), and *Of Mice and Men* (1939).

road specially constructed route for wheeled vehicles to travel on. Reinforced tracks became necessary with the invention of wheeled vehicles in about 3000 BC and most ancient civilizations had some form of road network.

Early history The first major road was the Persian Royal Road from the Persian Gulf to the Aegean Sea, more than 2,800 km/4,480 mi long, used from 3500 BC. Ancient China also had an extensive road network. The Romans developed engineering techniques that were not equalled for another 1,400 years. Roman roads were usually straight, and composed of large flat stones, topped with a layer of gravel and a hard surface. During the Middle Ages, the quality of roads deteriorated. By the late 18th century most European roads were haphazardly maintained, making winter travel difficult. In England the Statute for Mending the Highways (1555) required all members of the parish to spend four days a year working on mending the roads, but the work was poorly done or not done at all, and travellers complained of ruts, mud, accidents, and highwaymen. Roads were particularly impracticable for heavy or bulk transport, and iron-rimmed wagon wheels broke up the road surface, despite legislation to try to increase the width of wheels.

Improvements after 1700 General George Wade, commander of the English army in Scotland, improved many of the roads in the highlands between 1726 and 1737, so that troops could be moved to areas of disturbance more quickly. In the 18th century in the UK, the increasing pace of trade required a corresponding improvement in the roads. The turnpike road system of collecting tolls created some improvement – although the turnpikes met with some opposition, notably the Rebecca Riots in South Wales. The Scottish engineers Thomas ▷Telford and John ▷McAdam introduced sophisticated construction methods in the late 18th and early 19th century. The years from around 1750 to 1835 have been called 'the Coaching Age', as improved road transport allowed reduced journey times, stagecoaches, coaching inns, haulage firms, and a national postal service. The advent of the railways, however, drove most coaching firms into bankruptcy.

Modern roads The bicycling craze of the late 19th century and the development of the internal combustion engine and motor car led to the improvement of road systems after 1900. Road builders began to use asphalt to create a smooth, durable surface that would not create dust. The first ▷motorway was built in New York in 1925, and Hitler initiated a system of autobahns in Germany in the 1930s.

roadrunner crested North American ground-dwelling bird *Geococcyx californianus* of the ▷cuckoo family, found in the southwestern USA and Mexico. It can run at a speed of 25 kph/15 mph. See also fact box on p. 814.

Robbe-Grillet, Alain (1922–) French writer. He was the leading theorist of *le nouveau roman* ('the new novel'), for example his own *Les Gommes/The Erasers* (1953), *La Jalousie/Jealousy* (1957), and *Dans le Labyrinthe/In the Labyrinth* (1959), which concentrates on the detailed description of physical objects. He also wrote the script for the film *L'Année dernière à Marienbad/Last Year at Marienbad* (1961).

Robben Island island in Table Bay, Cape Town, South Africa. It was used by the South African government to house political prisoners. Nelson ▷Mandela was imprisoned here 1964–82.

robbery in law, a variety of theft: stealing from a person, using force, or the threat of force, to intimidate the victim.

Robbins, Jerome (1918–1998) US dancer and choreographer. He was co-director of the New York City Ballet 1969–83 (with George ▷Balanchine). His ballets were internationally renowned and he was considered the greatest US-born ballet choreographer. He also choreographed the musicals *The King and I* (1951), *West Side Story* (1957), and *Fiddler on the Roof* (1964).

Robert two dukes of Normandy:

Robert (I) the Devil Duke of Normandy from 1027. Also known as **the Magnificent**, he was the father of William the Conqueror, and was legendary for his cruelty. He became duke after the death of his brother Richard III, in which he may have been implicated.

Robert (II) Curthose (c. 1054–1134) Duke of Normandy 1087–1106. He was the son of William the Conqueror, and a noted crusader 1096–1100. When the English throne passed to his younger brother William II in 1087, Robert was unable to recover it by war. In 1106 Robert again attempted to recover England from Henry I, but was defeated at Tinchebrai and imprisoned until his death.

Robert three kings of Scotland:

Robert (I) the Bruce (1274–1329) King of Scots from 1306, successful guerrilla fighter, and grandson of Robert de Bruce. In 1307 he displayed his tactical skill in the Battle of Loudun Hill against the English under Edward I, and defeated the English again under Edward II at Bannockburn in 1314. In 1328 the Treaty of Northampton recognized Scotland's independence and Robert the Bruce as king.

Large English expeditions of 1322 and 1327 were beaten by Robert's 'scorched earth' policy, apparently his deathbed advice on how best to conduct warfare.

Robert II (1316–1390) King of Scotland from 1371. He was the son of Walter (1293–1326), steward of Scotland, and Marjory, daughter of Robert the Bruce. He acted as regent during the exile and captivity of his uncle David II, whom he eventually succeeded. He was the first king of the house of Stuart.

Robert III (c. 1340–1406) King of Scotland from 1390, son of Robert II. He was unable to control the nobles, and the government fell largely into the hands of his brother, Robert, Duke of Albany (c. 1340–1420).

Robert Guiscard (c. 1015–1085) Norman adventurer and duke of Apulia. Robert, also known as 'the Wizard', carved out a fiefdom centred on Apulia in southern Italy, of which he became duke in 1059. By 1071 he had expelled the ▷Byzantines from southern Italy and the ▷Arabs from Sicily, establishing his younger brother Roger as count and laying the foundations for the Norman kingdom of Sicily. He imposed a centralized feudal state over an ethnically diverse realm, and was a great patron of the Catholic Church.

Robeson, Paul Bustill (1898–1976) US singer, actor, lawyer, and activist. From the 1930s he was a staunch fighter against anti-semitism and racism against black people, and he was a supporter of the various national liberation movements that came to prominence in Africa after World War II. Robeson appeared in Eugene O'Neill's play *The Emperor Jones* (1924) and the Jerome Kern musical *Show Boat* (1927), in which he sang 'Ol' Man River', and took the title role in *Othello* in 1930.

Robespierre, Maximilien François Marie Isidore de (1758–1794) French politician in the ▷French Revolution. As leader of the ▷Jacobins in the National Convention (1792), he supported the execution of Louis XVI and the overthrow of the right-wing republican Girondins, and in July 1793 was elected to the Committee of Public Safety. A year later he was guillotined; many believe that he was a scapegoat for the Reign of ▷Terror since he ordered only 72 executions personally.

Robespierre, a lawyer, was elected to the National Assembly from 1789 to 1791. His defence of democratic principles made him popular in Paris, while his disinterestedness won him the nickname of 'the sea-green Incorruptible'. His zeal for social reform and his attacks on the excesses of the extremists made him enemies on both right and left; a conspiracy was formed against him, and in July 1794 he was overthrown and executed by those who actually perpetrated the Reign of Terror.

> **Maximilien de Robespierre**
> *Any institution which does not suppose the people good, and the magistrate corruptible, is evil.*
> Déclaration des Droits de l'homme/Declaration of the Rights of Man 24 April 1793

robin migratory songbird *Erithacus rubecula* of the thrush family Muscicapidae, order Passeriformes, found in Europe, West Asia, Africa, and the Azores. About 13 cm/5 in long, both sexes are olive brown with a red breast. Two or three nests are constructed during the year in sheltered places, and from five to seven white freckled eggs are laid.

The larger North American robin *Turdus migratorius* belongs to the same family. In Australia members of several unrelated genera are called robins, and may have white, yellowish, or red breasts.

The robin's song is continued through most of the year, and is especially noticeable in winter. The young birds are yellowish olive-brown on the upper parts, and the underparts are a strongly mottled buff and brown. There were approximately four million breeding pairs in Britain in 1997.

ROBIN Both sexes of the European robin *Erithacus rubecula* sport the characteristic red breast and it is impossible to distinguish between them. *Premaphotos Wildlife*

Robin Hood in English legend, an outlaw and champion of the poor against the rich, said to have lived in Sherwood Forest, Nottinghamshire, during the reign of Richard I (1189–99). He feuded with the sheriff of Nottingham, accompanied by Maid Marian and a band of followers known as his 'merry men'. He appears in many popular ballads from the 13th century, but his first datable appearance is in William Langland's *Piers Plowman* in the late 14th century. He became popular in the 15th century.

Traditionally he is a nobleman who remained loyal to Richard during his exile and opposed the oppression of King John. His companions included Little John, so-called because of his huge stature, Friar Tuck, a jovial cleric, and Alan a Dale. There may be some historical basis for the legend, but many of the customs and practices associated with his name suggest that he is a character of May Day celebrations. He is claimed to have been buried at Kirklees Hall, Yorkshire.

Related Web site: Robin Hood Project
http://www.lib.rochester.edu:80/camelot/rh/rhhome.stm

Robinson, Edward G (1893–1973) Stage name of Emmanuel Goldenberg. US film actor, born in Romania. He typically played gangster roles, as in *Little Caesar* (1930), but also gave strong performances in psychological dramas such as *Scarlet Street* (1945).

Robinson, Edwin Arlington (1869–1935) US poet. His verse, dealing mainly with psychological themes in a narrative style, is collected in volumes such as *The Children of the Night* (1897), which established his reputation. He was awarded three Pulitzer Prizes for poetry: *Collected Poems* (1922), *The Man Who Died Twice* (1925), and *Tristram* (1928).

Robinson, Mary (1944–) Irish Labour politician, president 1990–97. She became a professor of law at the age of 25. A strong supporter of women's rights, she campaigned for the liberalization of Ireland's laws prohibiting divorce and abortion.

Robinson won a seat in the Irish senate (Seanad Éireann) in 1969 and held it for 20 years. As a lawyer she achieved an international reputation in the field of human rights. She tried unsuccessfully to enter the Dáil Éireann (lower house of parliament) in 1990, and then surprisingly won the presidency of her country. In 1997 she became the UN High Commissioner for Human Rights.

Robinson, Smokey (William) (1940–) US singer, songwriter, and record producer. He was associated with ▷Motown records from its conception. He was lead singer of the Miracles 1957–72 hits include 'Shop Around' (1961) and 'The Tears of a Clown' (1970) and his solo hits include 'Cruisin' (1979) and 'Being With You' (1981). His light tenor voice and wordplay characterize his work.

Robinson, Sugar Ray (1920–1989) Adopted name of Walker Smith. US boxer. He was world welterweight champion 1945–51; he defended his title five times. Defeating Jake LaMotta in 1951, he took the middleweight title. He lost the title six times and won it seven times. He retired at the age of 45.

Robinson, W(illiam) Heath (1872–1944) English cartoonist and illustrator. He made humorous drawings of bizarre machinery for performing simple tasks, such as raising one's hat. A clumsily designed apparatus is often described as a 'Heath Robinson' contraption.

robot any computer-controlled machine that can be programmed to move or carry out work. Robots are often used in industry to transport materials or to perform repetitive tasks. For instance, robotic arms, fixed to a floor or workbench, may be used to paint machine parts or assemble electronic circuits. Other robots are designed to work in situations that would be dangerous to humans – for example, in defusing bombs or in space and deep-sea exploration.

Some robots are equipped with sensors, such as touch sensors and video cameras, and can be programmed to make simple decisions based on the sensory data received. As robots do not suffer from fatigue or become distracted, researchers in robotics aim to produce robots that can carry out sophisticated tasks more efficiently than humans, for example a voice-operated robot able to carry out some heart operations was tested successfully on a cow in the USA in 1998.

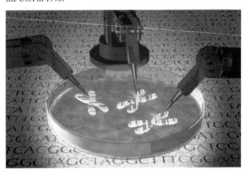

ROBOT These tiny robotic arms are being used in a genetic-engineering laboratory. Safety precautions are very strict and any possible contamination must be avoided. *Image Bank*

Rochdale industrial town in Greater Manchester, northwest England, on the River Roch, 16 km/10 mi northeast of Manchester; population (1994 est) 138,000. It was formerly an important cotton-spinning town; industries now include textiles and the manufacture of machinery and asbestos. The Rochdale Pioneers founded the first Cooperative Society in England here in 1844.

Rochester city in southeastern England, on the Medway estuary, in Medway Towns unitary authority; population (1991) 24,000. Rochester upon Medway district joined with Gillingham to form the Medway Towns unitary authority in April 1998. Rochester was a Roman town, **Durobrivae**. It has a 12th-century Norman castle keep (the largest in England), a 12th–15th-century cathedral (containing a memorial to Charles Dickens), and many timbered buildings. Industries include aeronautical, electrical, and mechanical engineering; cement; paper; and paint and varnish. The Charles Dickens Centre (1982) commemorates the town's links with the novelist Charles Dickens, whose home was at Gad's Hill.

Roadrunner

Although roadrunners can fly, they prefer to run. They are often seen on roads, as their name implies, and they run rapidly away if disturbed. They frequently run at speeds of up to 25 kph/15 mph and have been known to reach speeds of over 38 kph/23 mph.

Description: slender with brown, heavily streaked plumage, long tail, powerful legs, bushy crest, long pointed bill; length 51–61 cm/20–24 in

Habitat: the semi-arid open country of the southwestern USA

Diet: ground-dwelling insects, lizards, snakes, scorpions, mice, and tarantulas; the roadrunner kills its prey with a sudden pounce

Nest and eggs: nests in small trees, bushes, or cactus clumps, and lays between two and eight white eggs.

ROADRUNNER The greater roadrunner is often seen on roads, as its name implies, and runs rapidly away if disturbed. It inhabits the semi-arid open country of the southwestern USA, and feeds on ground-dwelling insects, which it kills by a sudden pounce.

Rochester, John Wilmot, 2nd Earl of Rochester, (1647–1680) English poet and courtier. He fought gallantly at sea against the Dutch, but chiefly led a debauched life at the court of Charles II. He wrote graceful (but often obscene) lyrics, and his *A Satire against Mankind* (1675) rivals Swift. He was a patron of the English poet John Dryden. He was made an earl in 1658.

rock a solid piece of the Earth or any other inorganic body in the Solar System. Rocks are composed of ▷minerals or materials of organic origin. There are three basic types of rocks: ▷igneous, ▷sedimentary, or ▷metamorphic rocks. Because rocks are composed of a combination (or aggregate) of minerals, the property of a rock will depend on its components. Where deposits of economically valuable minerals occur they are termed ▷ores. As a result of ▷weathering, rock breaks down into very small particles that combine with organic materials from plants and animals to form ▷soil. In ▷geology the term 'rock' can also include unconsolidated materials such as ▷sand, mud, ▷clay, and ▷peat.

Igneous rock is formed by the cooling and solidification of ▷magma, the molten rock material that originates in the lower part of the Earth's crust, or ▷mantle, where it reaches temperatures as high as 1,000°C. The rock may form on or below the Earth's surface and is usually crystalline in texture. Larger ▷crystals are more common in rocks such as ▷granite which have cooled slowly within the Earth's crust; smaller crystals form in rocks such as ▷basalt which have cooled more rapidly on the surface. Because of their acidic composition, igneous rocks such as granite are particularly susceptible to ▷acid rain.

Sedimentary rocks are formed by the compression of particles deposited by water, wind, or ice. They may be created by the erosion of older rocks, the deposition of organic materials, or they may be formed from chemical precipitates. For example, ▷sandstone is derived from sand particles, ▷limestone from the remains of sea creatures, and gypsum is precipitated from evaporating sea water. Sedimentary rocks are typically deposited in distinct layers or strata and many contain ▷fossils.

Metamorphic rocks are formed through the action of high pressure or heat on existing igneous or sedimentary rocks, causing changes to the composition, structure, and texture of the rocks. For example, ▷marble is formed by the effects of heat and pressure on limestone, while granite may be metamorphosed into ▷gneiss, a coarse-grained foliated rock.

Related Web site: Composition of Rocks http://www.geog. ouc.bc.ca/physgeog/contents/10d.html

rockabilly the earliest style of ▷rock and roll as it developed in the US South with a strong country (hillbilly) element. The typical rockabilly singer was young, white, male, working class, and recorded for the Sun label in Memphis; among them were Elvis Presley, Johnny Cash, Roy Orbison, Jerry Lee Lewis, and Carl Perkins. Many rockabilly performers later became country singers.

rock and roll pop music born of a fusion of rhythm and blues and country and western and based on electric guitar and drums. In the mid-1950s, with the advent of Elvis Presley, it became the heartbeat of teenage rebellion in the West and also had considerable impact on other parts of the world. It found perhaps its purest form in late-1950s ▷rockabilly, the style of white Southerners in the USA; the blanket term 'rock' later came to comprise a multitude of styles.

Related Web site: Rock and Roll http://www.pbs.org/wgbh/ pages/rocknroll/

rock climbing sport originally an integral part of mountaineering. It began as a form of training for Alpine expeditions and is now divided into three categories: the **outcrop climb** for climbs of up to 30 m/100 ft; the **crag climb** on cliffs of 30–300 m/100–1,000 ft, and the **big wall climb**, which is the nearest thing to Alpine climbing, but without the hazards of snow and ice.

Rockefeller, John D(avison) (1839–1937) US millionaire. He was the founder of Standard Oil in 1870 (which achieved control of 90% of US refineries by 1882). He also founded the philanthropic **Rockefeller Foundation** in 1913, to which his son John D(avison) Rockefeller Jr (1874–1960) devoted his life.

The activities of the Standard Oil Trust led to an outcry against monopolies and the passing of the Sherman Anti-Trust Act of 1890. A lawsuit of 1892 prompted the dissolution of the trust, only for it to be refounded 1899 as a holding company. In 1911, this was also declared illegal by the Supreme Court.

rocket projectile driven by the reaction of gases produced by a fast-burning fuel. Unlike jet engines, which are also reaction engines, rockets carry their own oxygen supply to burn their fuel and do not require any surrounding atmosphere. For warfare, rocket heads carry an explosive device.

Rockets have been valued as fireworks since the middle ages, but their intensive development as a means of propulsion to high

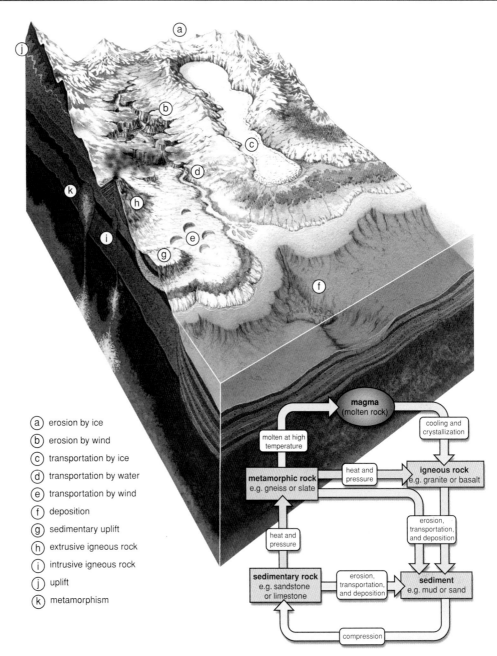

(a) erosion by ice
(b) erosion by wind
(c) transportation by ice
(d) transportation by water
(e) transportation by wind
(f) deposition
(g) sedimentary uplift
(h) extrusive igneous rock
(i) intrusive igneous rock
(j) uplift
(k) metamorphism

magma (molten rock)

cooling and crystallization

molten at high temperature

metamorphic rock e.g. gneiss or slate → heat and pressure → **igneous rock** e.g. granite or basalt

erosion, transportation, and deposition

heat and pressure

sedimentary rock e.g. sandstone or limestone → erosion, transportation, and deposition → **sediment** e.g. mud or sand

compression

ROCK Rocks are not as permanent as they seem but are being constantly destroyed and renewed. When a rock becomes exposed on the Earth's surface, it starts to break down through weathering and erosion. The resulting debris is washed or blown away and deposited, for example in sea or river beds, or in deserts, where it eventually becomes buried by yet more debris. Over time, this debris is compressed and compacted to form sedimentary rock, which may in time become exposed and eroded once more. Alternatively the sedimentary rock may be pushed further towards the Earth's centre where it melts and solidifies to form igneous rock or is heated and crushed to such a degree that its mineral content alters and it becomes metamorphic rock. Igneous and metamorphic rock may also become exposed and eroded by the same processes as sedimentary rock, and the cycle continues.

altitudes, carrying payloads, started only in the interwar years with the state-supported work in Germany (primarily by German-born US rocket engineer Wernher ▷von Braun) and the work of US inventor Robert Hutchings Goddard (1882–1945) in the USA. Being the only form of propulsion available that can function in a vacuum, rockets are essential to exploration in outer space. ▷Multistage rockets have to be used, consisting of a number of rockets joined together.

Two main kinds of rocket are used: one burns liquid propellants, the other solid propellants. The fireworks rocket uses gunpowder as a solid propellant. The ▷space shuttle's solid rocket boosters use a mixture of powdered aluminium in a synthetic rubber binder. Most rockets, however, have liquid propellants, which are more powerful and easier to control. Liquid hydrogen and kerosene are common fuels, while liquid oxygen is the most common oxygen provider, or oxidizer. One of the biggest rockets ever built, the Saturn V Moon rocket, was a three-stage design, standing 111 m/365 ft high. It weighed more than 2,700 tonnes/3,000 tons on the launch pad, developed a takeoff thrust of some 3.4 million kg/7.5 million lb, and could place almost 140 tonnes/150 tons into low Earth orbit.

In the early 1990s, the most powerful rocket system was the Soviet Energiya, capable of placing 190 metric tonnes/210 tons into low Earth orbit. The US space shuttle can only carry up to 29 metric tonnes/32 tons of equipment into orbit. See ▷nuclear warfare and ▷missile. See picture on p. 816.

rock music another term for ▷pop music; sometimes, another term for ▷rock and roll. When a distinction is made between rock and pop, rock is generally perceived as covering the less commercial and more adult end of the spectrum.

Rocky Mountain goat species of ruminant that occurs in North America. It is intermediate in position between a goat and an antelope. It resembles a goat in size and has long white hair with woolly undercoat, black, hollow horns, compressed at the base, and short ears. The Rocky Mountain goat *Oreamnos americanus* is a member of the family Bovidae, order Artiodactyla.

Rocky Mountains (or Rockies) largest North American mountain system, extending for 4,800 km/3,000 mi from the Mexican plateau near Sante Fe, north through the west-central states of the USA, and through Canada to the Alaskan border. It forms part of the Continental Divide, which separates rivers draining into the Atlantic or Arctic oceans from those flowing toward the Pacific Ocean. To the east lie the Great Plains, and to the west, the plateaux separating the Rocky Mountains from parallel Pacific coast ranges. Mount Elbert is the highest peak, 4,400 m/ 14,433 ft. Some geographers consider the Yukon and Alaskan ranges as part of the system, making the highest point Mount McKinley (Denali) 6,194 m/20,320 ft, and its total length 5,150 km/ 3,219 mi.

Many large rivers rise in the Rocky Mountains, including the ▷Missouri. **Rocky Mountain National Park** (1915) in Colorado has more than 107 named peaks over 3,350 m/10,000 ft. Because of the rugged terrain, the Rocky Mountains are sparsely populated. The mountains' chief economic asset is their minerals, including coal, petroleum, natural gas, copper, and gold. Lumbering is found in the northern Rockies, and cattle and sheep are raised. The Rockies have US and Canadian national parks, which attract many tourists.

rococo movement in the arts and architecture in 18th-century Europe, tending towards lightness, elegance, delicacy, and decorative charm. The term 'rococo' is derived from the French *rocaille* (rock- or shell-work), a style of interior decoration based on S-curves and scroll-like forms. Jean-Antoine Watteau's paintings

ROCKY MOUNTAINS Reflections in Lake Louise in the province of Alberta, in the Canadian Rockies. *Corel*

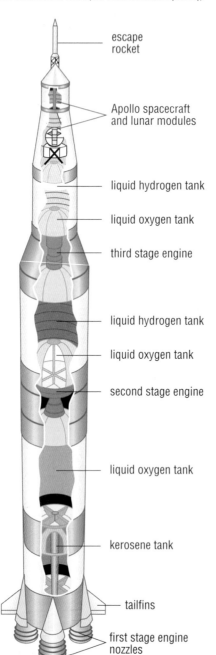

escape rocket

Apollo spacecraft and lunar modules

liquid hydrogen tank

liquid oxygen tank

third stage engine

liquid hydrogen tank

liquid oxygen tank

second stage engine

liquid oxygen tank

kerosene tank

tailfins

first stage engine nozzles

ROCKET A diagram of the three-stage Saturn V rocket, which was used in the Apollo moonshots of the 1960s and 1970s. See entry on p. 815.

and Sèvres porcelain belong to the French rococo vogue. In the 1730s the movement became widespread in Europe, notably in the churches and palaces of southern Germany and Austria. Chippendale furniture is an English example of the French rococo style.

Roddick, Anita (1943–) Born Anita Lucia Perilli. English entrepreneur, founder of the Body Shop, which now has branches worldwide. Roddick started with one shop in Brighton, England, in 1976, selling only natural toiletries which were not tested on animals, and sold them in refillable plastic containers. She campaigns on green issues and is an advocate of 'caring capitalism'.

rodent any mammal of the worldwide order Rodentia, making up nearly half of all mammal species. Besides ordinary 'cheek teeth', they have a single front pair of incisor teeth in both upper and lower jaw, which continue to grow as they are worn down.

They are often subdivided into three suborders: Sciuromorpha, including primitive rodents, with squirrels as modern representatives; Myomorpha, rats and mice and their relatives; and Hystricomorpha, including the Old World and New World porcupines and guinea pigs.

Rodgers, Richard Charles (1902–1979) US composer. He collaborated with librettist Lorenz Hart (1895–1943) on songs like 'Blue Moon' (1934) and musicals like *On Your Toes* (1936). With Oscar Hammerstein II, he wrote many musicals, including *Oklahoma!* (1943), *South Pacific* (1949), *The King and I* (1951), and *The Sound of Music* (1959).

Ródhos Greek name for the island of ▷Rhodes.

Rodin, (René François) Auguste (1840–1917) French sculptor. He is considered the greatest of his day. He freed sculpture from the idealizing conventions of the time by his realistic treatment of the human figure, introducing a new boldness of style and expression. Examples are *Le Penseur/The Thinker* (1904; Musée Rodin, Paris), *Le Baiser/The Kiss* (1886; marble version in the Louvre, Paris), and *The Burghers of Calais* (1884–86; copy in Embankment Gardens, Westminster, London).

Rodin failed the entrance examination for the Ecole des Beaux Arts, and never attended. He started as a mason, began to study in museums, and in 1875 visited Italy, where he was inspired by the work of Michelangelo. His early statue *The Age of Bronze* (1877; Musée Rodin, Paris) was criticized for its total naturalism and accuracy. In 1880 he began the monumental bronze *Gates of Hell* for the Ecole des Arts Décoratifs in Paris (inspired by Ghiberti's bronze doors in Florence), a project that occupied him for many years and was unfinished at his death. Many of the figures designed for the gate became independent sculptures. During the 1890s he received two notable commissions, for statues of the writers *Balzac* 1893–97 and *Victor Hugo* 1886–90 (both Musée Rodin, Paris). He also produced many drawings.

roebuck male of the Eurasian roe ▷deer.

roe deer (or roebuck) small deer (the buck stands about 66 cm/ 26 in at the shoulder, and is 1.2 m/ 4 ft in length from the nose to the tiny tail). Roe deer are reddish-brown in summer (in winter the redness disappears), and the underparts are yellowish-grey. The horns average about 20 cm/8 in in length.

Roeg, Nicolas (Jack) (1928–) English film director and writer. He was initially a cinematographer. His striking visual style is often combined with fractured, disturbing plots, as in

Performance (1970), *Don't Look Now* (1973), *The Man Who Fell to Earth* (1976), and *The Witches* (1989). In the 1990s he directed *Cold Heaven* (1992), *Two Deaths* (1995), *Hotel Paradise* (1995), and the television features *Heart of Darkness* (1994), *Full Body Massage* (1995), and *Samson and Delilah* (1996).

roentgen (or röntgen) unit (symbol R) of radiation exposure, used for X-rays and gamma rays. It is defined in terms of the number of ions produced in one cubic centimetre of air by the radiation. Exposure to 1,000 roentgens gives rise to an absorbed dose of about 870 rads (8.7 grays), which is a dose equivalent of 870 rems (8.7 sieverts).

Roe v. Wade US Supreme Court decision in 1973 dealing with the constitutionality of state anti-abortion laws. The case challenged a Texas statute prohibiting the abortion of pregnancies that did not threaten the mother's life. The Court struck down the Texas law, ruling that state prohibition of abortion is unconstitutional on two grounds: (1) women are guaranteed the right to privacy by the 14th Amendment, and (2) unborn fetuses are not persons with the right to equal protection of the law. The highly controversial ruling limited state regulation to the prohibition of third-trimester abortions.

Roger II (1095–1154) King of Sicily from 1130, the second son of Count Roger I of Sicily (1031–1101). By the time he was crowned king on the authority of Pope Innocent II (died 1143), he had achieved mastery over the whole of Norman Italy. He used his navy

AUGUSTE RODIN *The Thinker* (dated 1905) by the French sculptor Auguste Rodin, developed from a design for a large sculptured door for the Ecole des Arts Décoratifs, Paris, France, which was commissioned in 1880. *The Art Archive/Album/Joseph Martin*

to conquer Malta and territories in north Africa, and to harass Byzantine possessions in the eastern Mediterranean. His Palermo court was a cultural centre where Latin, Greek, and Arab scholars mixed freely.

Rogers, Carl Ransom (1902–1987) US psychologist who developed the client-centred approach to counselling and psychotherapy. This stressed the importance of clients making their own decisions and developing their own potential (self-actualization).

Rogers, Ginger (1911–1995) Stage name of Virginia Katherine McMath. US actor, dancer, and singer. She worked from the 1930s to the 1950s, often starring with Fred ▷Astaire in such films as *Top Hat* (1935) and *Swing Time* (1936). Her other film work includes *Bachelor Mother* (1939) and *Kitty Foyle* (1940; Academy Award). She later appeared in stage musicals.

Rogers, Richard George (1933–) English high-tech architect. His works include the Pompidou Centre in Paris (1977), with Renzo ▷Piano; the Lloyd's of London building in London (1986); and the Reuters building at Blackwall Yard, London (1992), which won him a RIBA award. He was knighted in 1991.

Roget, Peter Mark (1779–1869) English physician and scholar, one of the founders of the University of London, and author of a *Thesaurus of English Words and Phrases* (1852), a text constantly revised and still in print, offering a range of words classified according to underlying concepts and meanings, as an aid to more effective expression and communication.

Röhm, Ernst (1887–1934) German leader of the Nazi Brownshirts, the SA (▷Sturmabteilung). On the pretext of an intended SA putsch (uprising) by the Brownshirts, the Nazis had some hundred of them, including Röhm, killed 29–30 June 1934. The event is known as the Night of the Long Knives.

Rohmer, Eric (1920–) Adopted name of Jean-Maurice Henri Schérer. French film director, screenwriter, and critic. Part of the French New Wave, his films are often concerned with the psychology of self-deception. They include *Ma Nuit chez Maud/ My Night at Maud's* (1969), *Le Genou de Claire/Claire's Knee* (1970), *Die Marquise von O/The Marquise of O* (1976), and *Conte d'été/ A Tale of Summer* (1996).

Roland (died *c.* 778) French hero. His real and legendary deeds of valour and chivalry inspired many medieval and later romances, including the 11th-century *Chanson de Roland* and Ariosto's *Orlando furioso*. A knight of ▷Charlemagne, Roland was killed in 778 with his friend Oliver and the 12 peers of France at Roncesvalles (in the Pyrenees) by Basques. He headed the rearguard during Charlemagne's retreat from his invasion of Spain.

role in the social sciences, the part(s) a person plays in society, either in helping the social system to work or in fulfilling social responsibilities towards others. **Role play** refers to the way in which children learn adult roles by acting them out in play (mothers and fathers, cops and robbers). Everyone has a number of roles to play in a society: for example, a woman may be an employee, mother, and wife at the same time.

roller any brightly coloured bird of the Old World family Coraciidae, resembling crows but in the same order as kingfishers and hornbills. Rollers grow up to 32 cm/13 in long. The name is derived from the habit of some species of rolling over in flight.

rolling common method of shaping metal. Rolling is carried out by giant mangles, consisting of several sets, or stands, of heavy rollers positioned one above the other. Red-hot metal slabs are rolled into sheet and also (using shaped rollers) girders and rails. Metal sheets are often cold-rolled finally to impart a harder surface.

ROLLER The lilac-breasted roller *Coracias caudata* is a common sight in thorn veld savannas from Natal province in South Africa northwards to Ethiopia and Somalia. *Premaphotos Wildlife*

Rolling Stones, the British band formed in 1962, once notorious as the 'bad boys' of rock. Original members were Mick Jagger (1943–), Keith Richards (1943–), Brian Jones (1942–1969), Bill Wyman (1936–), Charlie Watts (1941–), and the pianist Ian Stewart (1938–1985). A rock-and-roll institution, the Rolling Stones were still performing and recording in the 1990s.

Related Web site: Official Rolling Stones Web Site http://www. stones.com/retro/

ROLLING STONES, An early shot (1963) of English rock star Mick Jagger performing as lead singer of the Rolling Stones. *Image Bank*

Rollins, Sonny (Theodore Walter) (1930–) US tenor saxophonist and jazz composer. A leader of the hard-bop school, he is known for the intensity and bravado of his music and for his skilful improvisation.

Rollo (*c.* 860–*c.* 932) 1st Duke of Normandy; or Hrolfr. First Viking ruler and Duke of Normandy (although he never used the title). He founded the duchy of Normandy and established the dynasty of ▷William (I) the Conqueror. The city of Rouen is named after him.

Rolls, Master of the British judge; see ▷Master of the Rolls.

ROM (acronym for read-only memory) in computing, a memory device in the form of a collection of integrated circuits (chips), frequently used in microcomputers. ROM chips are loaded with data and programs during manufacture and, unlike ▷RAM (random-access memory) chips, can subsequently only be read, not written to, by computer. However, the contents of the chips are not lost when the power is switched off, as happens in RAM.

ROM is used to form a computer's permanent store of vital information, or of programs that must be readily available but protected from accidental or deliberate change by a user. For example, a microcomputer ▷operating system is often held in ROM memory.

Romagna area of Italy on the Adriatic coast, under papal rule 1278–1860 and now part of the region of ▷Emilia-Romagna.

Roman architecture, ancient the architecture of the Roman Empire, spanning the period 4th century BC– 5th century AD. The Romans' mastery of concrete (used in combination with bricks) freed the ▷orders from their earlier structural significance and enabled the development of such rounded forms as the arch, vault, and dome.

Roman art sculpture and painting of ancient Rome, from the 4th century BC to the fall of the Western Empire in the 5th century AD. Much Roman art was intended for public education, notably the sculpted triumphal arches and giant columns, such as Trajan's Column AD 106–113, and portrait sculptures of soldiers, politicians, and emperors. Surviving mural paintings (in Pompeii, Rome, and Ostia) and mosaic decorations show Greek influence. Roman art was to prove of lasting inspiration in the West.

Roman Britain period in British history from the two expeditions by Julius Caesar in 55 and 54 BC to the early 5th century AD. Roman relations with Britain began with Caesar's expeditions, but the actual conquest was not begun until AD 43. During the reign of the emperor Domitian, the governor of the province, Agricola, campaigned in Scotland. After several unsuccessful attempts to conquer Scotland, the northern frontier was fixed between the Solway and the Tyne at ▷Hadrian's Wall.

The process of Romanization was enhanced by the establishment of Roman colonies and other major urban centres. Most notable was the city of Colchester (Camulodunum), which was the location of the temple dedicated to the Divine Claudius, and the focus of the revolt of Boudicca. Other settlements included London, York, Chester, St Albans, Lincoln, and Gloucester, as well as the spa at Bath, dedicated to the worship of Sulis Minerva, a combination of local and Roman deities. England was rapidly Romanized, but north of York few remains of Roman civilization have been found.

Related Web site: Roman Military Sites in Britain http://www. morgue.demon.co.uk/index.htm

Roman Catholicism one of the main divisions of the Christian religion, separate from the Eastern Orthodox Church from 1054, and headed by the pope. For history and beliefs, see ▷Christianity. Membership is concentrated in southern Europe, Latin America, and the Philippines. In February 2000 Rome reported the number of baptized Roman Catholics to be 1.045 billion, an increase of 40 million since 1998.

The Protestant churches separated from the Catholic church with the ▷Reformation in the 16th century. In Germany, Switzerland, and other European countries, this came about as a result of fundamental divisions on matters of church doctrine and practice. However, in England, the Reformation was sparked primarily by disagreement over questions of royal marriage and succession. The Tudor monarch ▷Henry VIII – once a staunch 'defender of the faith', who had written a pamphlet attacking the German Protestant reformer Martin Luther – established a separate Anglican Church with its own doctrine and liturgy after the pope had refused to sanction his divorce of Catherine of Aragon in order to marry Anne Boleyn.

In response to the Reformation, in the 16th and 17th centuries, the Catholic Church undertook the campaign of education and coercion known as the ▷Counter-Reformation. An attempt to update Catholic doctrines was condemned by Pope Pius X in 1907, and more recent moves towards reform have been rejected by John Paul II.

Doctrine The focus of liturgical life is the Mass, or Eucharist, and attendance is obligatory on Sundays and Feasts of Obligation such as Christmas and Easter. The Roman Catholic Church differs from the other Christian churches in that it acknowledges the supreme jurisdiction of the pope, infallible when he speaks *ex cathedra* ('from the throne'); in the doctrine of the Immaculate Conception (which states that the Virgin Mary, the mother of Jesus, was conceived without the original sin with which all other human beings are born); and in according a special place to the Virgin Mary.

Organization Since the Second Vatican Council 1962–66, major changes have taken place. They include the use of vernacular or everyday language instead of Latin in the liturgy, and increased

ROMAN ART A terracotta ex-voto of the head of a woman, 2nd century BC, from the Via Prenestina in Rome. Ex-votos in the shape of the body part affected by illness were offered to the gods in the hope of a cure (National Railway Museum, York, England). *Art Archive*

freedom among the religious and lay orders. The pope has an episcopal synod of 200 bishops elected by local hierarchies to collaborate in the government of the church. The priesthood is celibate and there is a strong emphasis on the monastic orders. Great importance is also attached to ▷missionary work.

In England, for more than two centuries after the Reformation, scattered Catholics were served by missionary priests, whose activities were subject to penal laws. Toleration was officially extended to Catholics by the Catholic Emancipation Act 1829, and a Roman Catholic episcopate was restored in England and Wales in 1850, and in Scotland in 1878.

Irish immigration (chiefly as a result of the potato famine in the mid-19th century) played a major role in determining the subsequent development and character of English Roman Catholicism. Today, its demonstrative worship and apostolic fervour contrast forcibly with the sober and unobtrusive English Catholicism of penal times.

In March 2000 the Most Reverend Cormac Murphy-O'Conner became the 10th Archbishop of Westminster, leader of the Catholic Church in Britain, succeeding Cardinal Basil Hume who died in 1999.

romance in literature, tales of love and chivalric adventure, in verse or prose, that became popular in France about 1200 and spread throughout Europe.

Romance languages branch of Indo-European languages descended from the Latin of the Roman Empire ('popular' or 'vulgar' as opposed to 'classical' Latin). The present-day Romance languages with national status are French, Italian, Portuguese, Romanian, and Spanish.

Roman Empire from 27 BC to the 5th century AD; see ▷Rome, ancient.

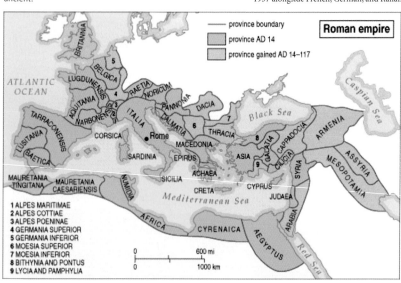

Romanesque architecture style of Western European ▷architecture of the 10th to 12th centuries, marked by rounded arches, solid volumes, and emphasis on perpendicular elements. In England the style is also known as ▷Norman architecture.

Romanesque art European art of the 10th to 12th centuries; see ▷medieval art.

Romania see country box.

Romanian people of Romanian culture from Romania, Yugoslavia, Moldova, and the surrounding area. There are 20–25 million speakers of the Romanian language.

Romanian language member of the Romance branch of the Indo-European language family, spoken in Romania, Macedonia, Albania, and parts of northern Greece. It has been strongly influenced by the Slavonic languages and by Greek. The Cyrillic alphabet was used until the 19th century, when a variant of the Roman alphabet was adopted.

Roman law legal system of ancient Rome that is now the basis of ▷civil law, one of the main European legal systems.

It originated under the republic, was developed under the empire, and continued in use in the Byzantine Empire until 1453. The first codification was that of the 12 Tables (450 BC), of which only fragments survive. Roman law assumed its final form in the codification of Justinian AD 528–34. An outstanding feature of Roman law was its system of international law (*jus gentium*), applied in disputes between Romans and foreigners or provincials, or between provincials of different states.

Roman numerals ancient European number system using symbols different from Arabic numerals (the ordinary numbers 1, 2, 3, 4, 5, and so on). The seven key symbols in Roman numerals, as represented today, are I (1), V (5), X (10), L (50), C (100), D (500), and M (1,000). There is no zero, and therefore no place-value as is fundamental to the Arabic system. The first ten Roman numerals are I, II, III, IV (or IIII), V, VI, VII, VIII, IX, and X. When a Roman symbol is preceded by a symbol of equal or greater value, the values of the symbols are added (XVI = 16).

When a symbol is preceded by a symbol of less value, the values are subtracted (XL = 40). A horizontal bar over a symbol indicates a multiple of 1,000 ($\bar{X}$ = 10,000). Although addition and subtraction are fairly straightforward using Roman numerals, the absence of a zero makes other arithmetic calculations (such as multiplication) clumsy and difficult.

Romanov dynasty rulers of Russia from 1613 to the ▷Russian Revolution in 1917. Under the Romanovs, Russia developed into an absolutist empire.

Related Web site: Nicholas and Alexandra Romanov http://www. geocities.com/Vienna/9463/

Roman religion religious system that retained early elements of animism (with reverence for stones and trees) and totemism (see ▷Romulus and Remus), and had a strong domestic base in the ▷lares and penates, the cult of Janus and Vesta. It also had a main pantheon of gods derivative from the Greek one, which included Jupiter and Juno, Mars and Venus, Minerva, Diana, Ceres, and many lesser deities.

Romansch member of the Romance branch of the Indo-European language family, spoken by some 50,000 people in the eastern cantons of Switzerland. It was accorded official status in 1937 alongside French, German, and Italian. It is also known among scholars as Rhaeto-Romanic.

Romanticism in literature and the visual arts, a style that emphasizes the imagination, emotions, and creativity of the individual artist. Romanticism also refers specifically to late-18th- and early-19th-century European culture, as contrasted with 18th-century ▷classicism.

Inspired by the ideas of Jean Jacques ▷Rousseau and by contemporary social change and revolution (American and French), Romanticism emerged as a reaction to 18th-century values, asserting emotion and intuition over rationalism, the importance of the individual over social conformity, and the exploration of natural and psychic wildernesses over classical restraint. Major themes of Romantic art and literature include a love of atmospheric landscapes; nostalgia for the past, particularly the Gothic; a love of the primitive, including folk traditions; cult of the hero figure, often an artist or political revolutionary; romantic passion; mysticism; and a fascination with death.

In literature, Romanticism is represented by Novalis, Clemens Brentano, Joseph Eichendorff, and Johann Tieck in Germany, who built on the work of the ▷*Sturm und Drang* movement; William Wordsworth, Samuel Taylor Coleridge, Percy Bysshe Shelley, Byron, and Walter Scott in Britain; and Victor Hugo, Alfonse de Lamartine, George Sand, and Alexandre Dumas *père* in France. The work of the US writers Edgar Allan Poe, Herman Melville, Henry Wadsworth Longfellow, and Walt Whitman reflects the influence of Romanticism.

In art, Caspar David Friedrich in Germany and J M W Turner in England are outstanding landscape painters of the Romantic tradition, while Henry Fuseli and William Blake represent a mystical and fantastic trend. The French painter Eugène Delacroix is often cited as the quintessential Romantic artist.

Related Web site: Romanticism on the Net http://users.ox.ac.uk/ ~scat0385/

Romanticism in music, a preoccupation with subjective emotion expressed primarily through melody, a use of folk idioms, and a cult of the musician as visionary artist and hero (virtuoso).

Often linked with nationalistic feelings, the Romantic movement reached its height in the late 19th century, as in the works of Robert ▷Schumann and Richard ▷Wagner.

ROMANTICISM *Sadak in Search of the Waters of Oblivion*, by English Romantic painter John Martin. *The Art Archive/Southampton Art Gallery*

Romany (or Gypsy) member of a nomadic people believed to have originated in northwestern India and now living throughout the world. They used to be thought of as originating in Egypt, hence the name Gypsy (a corruption of 'Egyptian'). The Romany language, spoken in several different dialects, belongs to the Indic branch of the Indo-European family.

Rome (Italian Roma) capital of Italy and of Lazio region, on the River Tiber, 27 km/17 mi from the Tyrrhenian Sea; population (2001 est) 2,459,800.

Rome is an important road, rail, and cultural centre. A large section of the population finds employment in government and other offices: the headquarters of the Roman Catholic Church (the ▷Vatican City State, a separate sovereign area within Rome) and other international bodies, such as the Food and Agriculture Oranization (FAO), are here; it is also a destination for many tourists and pilgrims. Industries have developed, mainly to the south and east of the city; these include engineering, printing, food-processing, electronics, and the manufacture of chemicals, pharmaceuticals, plastics, and clothes. The city is a centre for the film and fashion industries. Among the remains of the ancient city (see ▷Rome, ancient) are the Forum, ▷Colosseum, and Pantheon.

Features East of the river are the seven hills on which Rome was originally built (Quirinal, Aventine, Caelian, Esquiline, Viminal, Palatine, and Capitol); to the west are the quarter of Trastevere, the residential quarters of the Prati, and the Vatican. Among ancient buildings and monuments are Castel Sant'Angelo (the mausoleum of the emperor Hadrian), the baths of Caracalla (206), the Colosseum, and the Arch of Constantine (c. 315). The Appian Way, bordered by ancient tombs, retains long sections of the old paving. Among the Renaissance palaces are the Lateran, Quirinal, Colonna, Borghese (now the Villa Umberto I), Barberini, and Farnese. The Trevi Fountain (1762) fronts the palace of the dukes of Poli, near the Quirinal.

The many churches of different periods include the five greater or patriarchal basilicas: S Giovanni; St Peter's (S Pietro), the largest church in the world, within the Vatican; S Paolo, founded by the emperor Constantine on St Paul's grave; Sta Maria Maggiore, with the city's highest campanile; and S Lorenzo. The Vatican Palace, which adjoins St Peter's, is the residence of the pope. Other ancient churches of interest are S Pietro in Vincoli, which houses the chains that fettered St Peter; Sta Maria in Cosmedin, built before the 6th century on the remains of a pagan temple; and the Pantheon, also built on pagan edifices.

Several important routeways date from the era of Mussolini, notably the Via dei Fori Imperiali (formerly the Via dell'Impero) and the Via della Conciliazione, running from St Peter's to the Castel Sant'Angelo. The house where the English poet John Keats died is near the Piazza di Spagna, known for the Spanish Steps.

The city has numerous museums, including the vast papal collections (dating from the 15th century) of the Vatican, the Lateran museum, the Capitol, and the Thermae. The Sistine

Romania

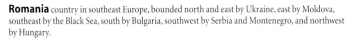

Romania country in southeast Europe, bounded north and east by Ukraine, east by Moldova, southeast by the Black Sea, south by Bulgaria, southwest by Serbia and Montenegro, and northwest by Hungary.

NATIONAL NAME *România/Romania*
AREA 237,500 sq km/91,698 sq mi
CAPITAL Bucharest
MAJOR TOWNS/CITIES Brasov, Timisoara, Cluj-Napoca, IasI, Constanta, Galati, Craiova
MAJOR PORTS Galati, Constanta, Braila
PHYSICAL FEATURES mountains surrounding a plateau, with river plains in south and east. Carpathian Mountains, Transylvanian Alps; River Danube; Black Sea coast; mineral springs

Government

HEAD OF STATE Ion Iliescu from 2000
HEAD OF GOVERNMENT Adrian Nastase from 2000
POLITICAL SYSTEM liberal democracy
POLITICAL EXECUTIVE limited presidency
ADMINISTRATIVE DIVISIONS 41 counties and the municipality of Bucharest
ARMED FORCES 99,200 (2002 est)
CONSCRIPTION military service is compulsory for 12 months
DEATH PENALTY abolished in 1989
DEFENCE SPEND (% GDP) 2.3 (2002 est)
EDUCATION SPEND (% GDP) 3.5 (2000 est)
HEALTH SPEND (% GDP) 2.9 (2000 est)

Economy and resources

CURRENCY leu
GPD (US$) 44.4 billion (2002 est)
REAL GDP GROWTH (% change on previous year) 5.3 (2001)
GNI (US$) 41.3 billion (2002 est)
GNI PER CAPITA (PPP) (US$) 6,290 (2002 est)
CONSUMER PRICE INFLATION 16.2% (2003 est)
UNEMPLOYMENT 8.6% (2001)
FOREIGN DEBT (US$) 8.7 billion (2001 est)
MAJOR TRADING PARTNERS Italy, Germany, France, Russia, Iran, China, Turkey
RESOURCES brown coal, hard coal, iron ore, salt, bauxite, copper, lead, zinc, methane gas, petroleum

(reserves expected to be exhausted by mid-to late 1990s)
INDUSTRIES metallurgy, mechanical engineering, chemical products, timber and wood products, textiles and clothing, food processing
EXPORTS base metals and metallic articles, textiles and clothing, machinery and equipment, mineral products, foodstuffs. Principal market: Italy 24.9% (2001)
IMPORTS mineral products, machinery and transport equipment, textiles, clothing and footwear, chemicals, plastics and rubber. Principal source: Italy 19.9% (2001)
ARABLE LAND 40.7% (2000 est)
AGRICULTURAL PRODUCTS wheat, maize, potatoes, sugar beet, barley, apples, grapes, sunflower seeds; wine production; forestry; fish breeding

Population and society

POPULATION 22,334,000 (2003 est)
POPULATION GROWTH RATE –0.3% (2000–15)

ROMANIA The Orthodox Cathedral in Cluj–Napoca, Transylvania was built in the Neo–Byzantine style during the early 20th century. In the square in front of the cathedral is a statue of Avram Iancu (1824–72), a democratic revolutionary who led local intellectuals and an army of peasants during an attempted revolution in 1848. He studied law in the town. *Photodisc*

Chronology

106: Formed heartland of ancient region of Dacia, which was conquered by Roman Emperor Trajan and became a province of Roman Empire; Christianity introduced.

275: Taken from Rome by invading Goths, a Germanic people.

4th–10th centuries: Invaded by successive waves of Huns, Avars, Bulgars, Magyars, and Mongols.

c. 1000: Transylvania, in north, became an autonomous province under Hungarian crown.

mid-14th century: Two Romanian principalities emerged, Wallachia in south, around Bucharest, and Moldova in northeast.

15th–16th centuries: The formerly autonomous principalities of Wallachia, Moldova, and Transylvania became tributaries to Ottoman Turks, despite peasant uprisings and resistance from Vlad Tepes ('the Impaler'), ruling prince of Wallachia.

late 17th century: Transylvania conquered by Austrian Habsburgs.

1829: Wallachia and Moldova brought under tsarist Russian suzerainty.

1859: Under Prince Alexandru Ion Cuza, Moldova and Wallachia united to form Romanian state.

1878: Romania's independence recognized by Great Powers in Congress of Berlin.

1881: Became kingdom under Carol I.

1916–18: Fought on Triple Entente side (Britain, France, and Russia) during World War I; acquired Transylvania and Bukovina, in north, from dismembered Austro-Hungarian Empire, and Bessarabia, in east, from Russia. This made it the largest state in Balkans.

1930: King Carol II abolished democratic institutions and established dictatorship.

1940: Forced to surrender Bessarabia and northern Bukovina, adjoining Black Sea, to Soviet Union, and northern Transylvania to Hungary; King Carol II abdicated, handing over effective power to Gen Ion Antonescu, who signed Axis Pact with Germany.

1941–44: Fought on Germany's side against Soviet Union; thousands of Jews massacred.

POPULATION DENSITY (per sq km) 94 (2003 est)
URBAN POPULATION (% of total) 56 (2003 est)
AGE DISTRIBUTION (% of total population) 0–14 17%, 15–59 64%, 60+ 19% (2002 est)
ETHNIC GROUPS 89% non-Slavic ethnic Romanian; substantial Hungarian (7%), Romany (2%), German (0.5%), and Serbian minorities
LANGUAGE Romanian (official), Hungarian, German
RELIGION Romanian Orthodox 87%; Roman Catholic and Uniate 5%, Reformed/Lutheran 3%, Unitarian 1%
EDUCATION (compulsory years) 8
LITERACY RATE 99% (men); 98% (women) (2003 est)
LABOUR FORCE 41.8% agriculture, 27.6% industry, 30.6% services (1999)
LIFE EXPECTANCY 67 (men); 74 (women) (2000–05)
CHILD MORTALITY RATE (under 5, per 1,000 live births) 21 (2001)
HOSPITAL BEDS (per 1,000 people) 7.6 (1998 est)
TV SETS (per 1,000 people) 379 (2001 est)
RADIOS (per 1,000 people) 358 (2001 est)
INTERNET USERS (per 10,000 people) 806.1 (2002 est)
PERSONAL COMPUTER USERS (per 100 people) 4.0 (2002 est)

See also ▷Ceauşescu, Nicolae; ▷Moldavia; ▷Ottoman Empire.

1944: Romania joined war against Germany.

1945: Occupied by Soviet Union; communist-dominated government installed.

1947: Paris Peace Treaty reclaimed Transylvania for Romania, but lost southern Dobruja to Bulgaria and northern Bukovina and Bessarabia to Soviet Union; King Michael, son of Carol II, abdicated and People's Republic proclaimed.

1955: Romania joined Warsaw Pact.

1958: Soviet occupation forces removed.

1965: Nicolae Ceauşescu became Romanian Communist Party leader, and pursued foreign policy autonomous of Moscow.

1975: Ceauşescu made president.

1985–87: Winter of austerity and power cuts as Ceauşescu refused to liberalize the economy. Workers' demonstrations against austerity programme are brutally crushed at Braşov.

1989: Bloody overthrow of Ceauşescu regime in 'Christmas Revolution'; Ceauşescu and wife tried and executed; estimated 10,000 dead in civil war. Power assumed by NSF, headed by Ion Iliescu.

1990: Securitate secret police was replaced by new Romanian Intelligence Service; Eastern Orthodox Church and private farming were re-legalized.

1994: A military cooperation pact was made with Bulgaria. Far-right parties were brought into the governing coalition.

1996: There were signs of economic growth; parliamentary elections were won by the DCR, who formed a coalition government with the SDU.

1997: An economic reform programme and drive against corruption were announced; there was a sharp increase in inflation. Former King Michael returned from exile.

1998: The Social Democrats withdrew support from ruling coalition, criticizing the slow pace of reform. Full EU membership negotiations commenced. The economy deteriorated sharply.

1999: Roadblocks were imposed by tanks north of Bucharest to prevent 10,000 striking miners entering Bucharest.

2000: Former communist president Ion Iliescu was elected president, and his Social Democrats won the largest share of the vote in parliamentary elections.

Chapel, with frescoes by Michelangelo, lies within the Vatican. Other public art collections are the Corsini and Galleria d'Arte; private collections include the Barberini, Doria, Albani, and Collona. The University of Rome was founded in 1303 by Pope Boniface VIII.

History (For early history see ▷Rome, ancient.) After the deposition of the last emperor, Romulus Augustulus, in 476, the papacy became the real ruler of Rome and from the 8th century was recognized as such. The Sack of Rome (1527) led to an era of rebuilding, and most of the great palaces and churches were built in the 16th and 17th centuries. As a result of the French Revolution, Rome temporarily became a republic (1798–99), and was annexed to the French Empire (1808–14) until the pope returned on Napoleon's fall. During the 1848–49 revolution a republic was established under Giuseppe Mazzini's leadership, but, in spite of Giuseppe Garibaldi's defence, was overthrown by French troops.

In 1870 Rome became the capital of Italy, the pope retiring into the Vatican until 1929 when the Vatican City was recognized as a sovereign state. The occupation of Rome by the Fascists (1922) marked the beginning of Mussolini's rule, but in 1943 Rome was occupied by Germany and then captured by the Allies in 1944.

Related Web site: Rome, Italy http://www.geocities.com/ Athens/Forum/2680/

Rome, ancient history ancient Rome was a civilization based on the city of Rome. It lasted for about 800 years. Traditionally founded as a kingdom in 753 BC, Rome became a republic in 510 BC following the expulsion of its last king, Tarquinius Superbus. From then, its history is one of almost continual expansion until the murder of Julius Caesar and the foundation of the empire in 27 BC under ▷Augustus and his successors. At its peak under ▷Trajan, the Roman Empire stretched from Britain to Mesopotamia and the Caspian Sea. A long line of emperors ruling by virtue of military, rather than civil, power marked the beginning of Rome's long decline; under Diocletian the empire was divided into two parts – East and West – although it was temporarily reunited under ▷Constantine, the first emperor to formally adopt Christianity. The end of the Roman Empire is generally dated by the deposition of the last emperor in the west in AD 476. The Eastern Empire continued until 1453 with its capital at Constantinople (modern Istanbul).

The civilization of ancient Rome occupied first the Italian peninsula, then most of Europe, the Middle East, and North Africa. It influenced the whole of Western Europe throughout the Middle Ages, the Renaissance, and beyond, in the fields of art and architecture, literature, law, and engineering, and through the continued use by scholars of its language, ▷Latin.

ROME A view looking up into the dome of the Pantheon, in Rome, Italy, which, although it dates from the ancient Roman period, is still in almost perfect condition. *Image Bank*

Rome, Treaties of two international agreements signed 25 March 1957 by Belgium, France, West Germany, Italy, Luxembourg, and the Netherlands, which established the European Economic Community (now ▷European Union) and the European Atomic Energy Commission (EURATOM).

The terms of the economic treaty, which came into effect 1 January 1958, provided for economic cooperation, reduction (and eventual removal) of customs barriers, and the free movement of capital, goods, and labour between the member countries, together with common agricultural and trading policies. Subsequent new members of the European Union have been obliged to accept these terms.

Related Web site: Treaty Establishing the European Community http://europa.eu.int/abc/obj/treaties/en/entoc05.htm

Rommel, Erwin Johannes Eugen (1891–1944) German field marshal. He served in World War I, and in World War II he played an important part in the invasions of central Europe and France. He was commander of the North African offensive from 1941 (when he was nicknamed 'Desert Fox') until defeated in the Battles of El ▷Alamein and he was expelled from Africa in March 1943.

Rommel was commander-in-chief for a short time against the Allies in Europe in 1944 but (as a sympathizer with the ▷Stauffenberg plot against Hitler) was forced to commit suicide.

Romney, George (1734–1802) English painter. Active in London from 1762, he became, with Thomas Gainsborough and Joshua Reynolds, one of the most successful portrait painters of the late 18th century. His best work is to be found in the straightforward realism of *The Beaumont Family* (1777–79; National Gallery, London) or the simple charm of *The Parson's Daughter* (c. 1785; Tate Gallery, London).

Romulus in Roman legend, the founder and first king of Rome; the son of Mars and Rhea Silvia, daughter of Numitor, king of Alba Longa.

Romulus and his twin brother Remus were thrown into the Tiber by their great-uncle Amulius, who had deposed Numitor, but the infants were saved and suckled by a she-wolf, and later protected by the shepherd Faustulus. On reaching adulthood they killed Amulius, restored Numitor, and founded the city of Rome on the River Tiber.

Roman Emperors 27 BC–AD 395

In 27 BC Julius Caesar's nephew Octavian proclaimed the restoration of the republic, but effectively became sole ruler, receiving the name Augustus. The empire was frequently split from AD 305, and was divided for the last time between the sons of Theodosius (I) the Great in 395.

Reign	Name
Julio-Claudian Emperors	
27 BC–AD 14	Augustus
14–37	Tiberius I
37–41	Caligula (Gaius Caesar)
41–54	Claudius I
54–68	Nero
Civil Wars	
68–69	Galba
69	Otho
69	Vitellius
Flavian Emperors	
69–79	Vespasian
79–81	Titus
81–96	Domitian
96–98	Nerva
98–117	Trajan
117–38	Hadrian
Antonine Emperors	
138–61[1]	Antoninus Pius
161–69[1]	Lucius Verus
Despotic Emperors	
161–80	Marcus Aurelius
180–92[2]	Commodus
193	Pertinax
193	Didius Julianus
The Severi	
193–211	Septimus Severus
193–97	Clodius Albinus
193–94	Pescennius Niger
211–217	Caracalla
209–12	Geta
217–18	Macrinus
218	Diadumenianus
218–22	Elagabalus
222–35	Alexander Severus
The Soldier Emperors	
235–38	Maximinus
238	Gordian I
238	Gordian II
238	Balbinus
238	Pupienus
238–44	Gordian III
244–49	Philip (I) the Arab
249–51	Trajan Decius
251–53	Trebonianus Gallus
251–53	Volusianus
253–60	Valerian
253–68	Gallienus
268–70	Claudius II
270	Quintillus
270–75	Aurelian
275–76	Tacitus

Reign	Name
276	Florianus
276–82	Probus
282–83	Carus
283–85	Carinus
283–84	Numerianus
284–305	Diocletian[3]
286–305	Maximianus
293–306	Constantius I
293–311	Galerius
305–337	Constantine I[4]
337–361	Constantius[5]
337–350	Constans I
361–363	Julian the Apostate
364–375	Valentinian I
375–383	Gratian
375–392	Valentinian II
379–395	Theodosius (I) the Great[6]

[1] Divided voluntarily between two brothers.

[2] Between 180 and 284 there was a succession of emperors placed on the throne by their respective armies or factions. Therefore, dates of emperors' reigns in this period often overlap.

[3] The end of Diocletian's reign marked the first split of the Roman empire. Whereas Diocletian retained supreme power, Maximianus ruled Italy and Africa, Constantius I ruled Gaul and Spain, and Galerius ruled Thrace.

[4] Emperor of the west from 305, sole emperor from 324.

[5] Emperor of the east from 337, sole emperor from 350.

[6] Appointed emperor of the east; sole emperor from 393.

ROMAN EMPERORS A marble bust of Roman emperor Commodus as a boy. *The Art Archive/Capitoline Museum Rome/Dagli Orti*

Rome, Ancient: Key Dates

753 BC	According to tradition, Rome is founded.
510	The Etruscan dynasty of the Tarquins is expelled and a republic established, with power concentrated in patrician hands.
450	Publication of the law code contained in the Twelve Tables.
396	Capture of Etruscan Veii, 15 km/9 mi north of Rome.
387	Rome is sacked by Gauls.
367	Plebeians gain the right to be consuls (the two chief magistrates, elected annually).
343–290	Sabines to the north, and the Samnites to the southeast, are conquered.
338	Cities of Latium form into a league under Roman control.
280–272	Greek cities in southern Italy are subdued.
264–241	First Punic War against Carthage, ending in a Roman victory and the annexation of Sicily.
238	Sardinia is seized from Carthage.
226–222	Roman conquest of Cisalpine Gaul (Lombardy, Italy). More conflict with Carthage, which is attempting to conquer Spain.
218	Second Punic War. Hannibal crosses the Alps and invaded Italy, winning a series of brilliant victories.
202	Victory of General Scipio Africanus Major over Hannibal at Zama is followed by the surrender of Carthage and the relinquishing of its Spanish colonies.
188	Peace of Apamea confines the rule of the Seleucid king Antiochus the Great to Asia.
168	Final defeat of Macedon by Rome.
146	After a revolt, Greece becomes in effect a Roman province. Carthage is destroyed and its territory annexed.
133	Tiberius Gracchus suggests agrarian reforms and is murdered by the senatorial party. Roman province of Asia is formed from the kingdom of Pergamum, bequeathed to Rome by the Attalid dynasty.
123	Tiberius' policy is adopted by his brother Gaius Gracchus, who is likewise murdered.
91–88	Social War: revolt by the Italian cities forces Rome to grant citizenship to all Italians.
87	While Sulla is repelling an invasion of Greece by King Mithridates of Pontus (in Asia Minor), Marius seizes power.
82–79	Sulla returns and establishes a dictatorship ruled by terror.
70	Sulla's constitutional changes are reversed by Pompey and Crassus.
66–63	Pompey defeats Mithridates and annexes Syria.
60	The First Triumvirate is formed, an alliance between Pompey and the democratic leaders Crassus and Caesar.
51	Caesar conquers Gaul as far as the Rhine.
49	Caesar crosses the Rubicon and returns to Italy, and a civil war between him and Pompey's senatorial party begins.
48	Pompey is defeated at Pharsalus.
44	Caesar's dictatorship is ended by his assassination.
43	Second Triumvirate formed by Octavian, Mark Antony, and Lepidus.
32	War between Octavian and Mark Antony.
31	Mark Antony is defeated at Actium.
30	Egypt is annexed after the deaths of Mark Antony and Cleopatra.
27	Octavian takes the name Augustus. He is by now absolute ruler, though in title he is only 'princeps' (first citizen).
AD 14	Augustus dies. Tiberius is proclaimed as his successor.
43	Claudius adds Britain to the empire.
70	Jerusalem is sacked by Titus.
96–180	The empire enjoys a golden age under the Flavian and Antonine emperors Nerva, Trajan, Hadrian, Antoninus Pius, and Marcus Aurelius Antoninus.
115	Trajan conquers Parthia, achieving the peak of Roman territorial expansion.
180	Marcus Aurelius dies, and a century of war and disorder follows, with a succession of generals being put on the throne by their armies.
212	Caracalla grants citizenship to the communities of the empire.
284–305	Diocletian reorganizes the empire, dividing power between himself and three others (the Tetrarchy).
313	Constantine the Great recognizes the Christians' right to freedom of worship by the Edict of Milan.
330	Constantine makes Constantinople his new imperial capital.
395	The empire is divided into eastern and western parts.
410	Visigoths sack Rome. Roman legions withdraw from Britain.
451–52	Huns raid Gaul and Italy.
455	Vandals sack Rome.
476	Last Western emperor, Romulus Augustulus, is deposed.

Romulus Augustulus (born *c.* AD 461) Last Roman emperor in the western Roman empire. He was made emperor, while still a child, by his father the patrician Orestes about 475. He was compelled to abdicate 476 by Odoacer, leader of the barbarian mercenaries, who nicknamed him Augustulus (meaning 'little Augustus'). Orestes was executed and Romulus Augustulus was sent to live on a pension in Campania. His subsequent fate and the date of his death are unknown.

Ronaldo (1976–) Born Luiz de Nazario de Lima Ronaldo. Brazilian footballer who was voted FIFA World Player of the Year in 1996 and 1997. A prolific goalscorer, he has twice been transferred for world record fees, moving from PSV Eindhoven to Barcelona for £13.25 million in 1996, then a year later to Inter Milan for an estimated £21 million. He was top scorer at the 2002 World Cup, with eight goals.

rondo (or **rondeau**) antique musical form in which verses alternate with a refrain. Often festive in character, the form with its recurring theme is also a popular final movement of a sonata, concerto, or symphony.

Rondônia federal unit (state) of northwest Brazil, within the drainage basin of the Amazon River, and bordered on the southwest by Bolivia; the centre of Amazonian tin and gold mining and a frontier region of agricultural colonization; area 238,400 sq km/ 92,000 sq mi; population (1991) 1,130,900; capital Pôrto Velho. Its principal products are rubber and brazil nuts. Known as the Federal Territory of **Guaporé** until 1956, Rondônia became a state in 1981.

Ronsard, Pierre de (1524–1585) French poet. He was the leader of the *Pléiade* group of poets. Under the patronage of Charles IX, he published original verse in a lightly sensitive style, including odes and love sonnets, such as *Odes* (1550), *Les Amours/Lovers* (1552–53), and the 'Marie' cycle, *Continuation des amours/Lovers Continued* (1555–56). He also produced a theoretical treatise *Art poétique* (1565).

röntgen alternative spelling for ▷roentgen, unit of X- and gamma-ray exposure.

Röntgen (or **Roentgen**), **Wilhelm Konrad** (1845–1923) German physicist. He was awarded the Nobel Prize for Physics in 1901 for his discovery of ▷X-rays in 1895. While investigating the passage of electricity through gases, he noticed the ▷fluorescence of a barium platinocyanide screen. This radiation passed through some substances opaque to light, and affected photographic plates. Developments from this discovery revolutionized medical diagnosis.

Related Web site: Röntgen, Wilhelm Konrad http://www.nobel.se/physics/laureates/1901/rontgen-bio.html

rook gregarious European ▷crow *Corvus frugilegus*. The plumage is black and lustrous and the face bare; the legs, toes, and claws are also black. A rook can grow to 45 cm/18 in long. Rooks nest in colonies (rookeries) at the tops of trees. They feed mainly on invertebrates found just below the soil surface. The last 5 mm/0.2 in of beak tip is mostly cartilage containing lots of nerve endings to enable the rook to feel for hidden food.

The nest is a large structure made of twigs and straw, and in it are laid four to six bluish-green eggs blotched with greenish-brown. Feathers round the base of the beak are present in young birds but do not grow again after the second moult.

Rooney, Mickey (1922–) Stage name of Joe Yule. US actor. He began his career aged two in his parents' stage act. He played Andy Hardy in the Hardy family series of B films (1937–47) and starred opposite Judy ▷Garland in several musicals, including *Babes in Arms* (1939). He also gave memorable performances in *Boys' Town* (1935), as Puck in *A Midsummer Night's Dream* (1935), and in the title role of *Baby Face Nelson* (1957).

Roosevelt, (Anna) Eleanor (1884–1962) US social worker, lecturer, and first lady. Her newspaper column 'My Day', started in 1935, was widely syndicated. She influenced ▷New Deal policies, especially those supporting desegregation. She was a delegate to the United Nations general assembly and chair of the UN commission on human rights 1946–51, and helped to draw up the Declaration of Human Rights at the UN in 1945. She was married to her cousin President Franklin D Roosevelt, and was the niece of Theodore ▷Roosevelt.

> **Eleanor Roosevelt**
> *No one can make you feel inferior without your consent.*
> Catholic Digest

Roosevelt, Franklin D(elano) (1882–1945) 32nd president of the USA 1933–45, a Democrat. He served as governor of New York 1929–33. Becoming president during the Great ▷Depression, he launched the ▷New Deal economic and social reform programme, which made him popular with the people. After the outbreak of World War II he introduced ▷lend-lease for the supply of war materials and services to the Allies and drew up the Atlantic Charter of solidarity. Once the USA had entered the war in 1941, he spent much time in meetings with Allied leaders.

> **Franklin D Roosevelt**
> *We must be the great arsenal of democracy.*
> Speech 1940

Born in Hyde Park, New York, of a wealthy family, Roosevelt was educated in Europe and at Harvard and Columbia universities, and became a lawyer. In 1910 he was elected to the New York state senate. He held the assistant secretaryship of the navy in Wilson's administrations 1913–21, and did much to increase the efficiency of the navy during World War I. He suffered from polio from 1921 but returned to politics, winning the governorship of New York State in 1929. When he became president in 1933, Roosevelt inculcated a new spirit of hope by his skilful 'fireside chats' on the radio and his inaugural-address statement: 'The only thing we have to fear is fear itself.' Surrounding himself by a 'Brain Trust' of experts, he immediately launched his reform programme. Banks were reopened, federal credit was restored, the gold standard was abandoned, and the dollar devalued. During the first 100 days of his administration, major legislation to facilitate industrial and agricultural recovery was enacted. In 1935 he introduced the Utilities Act, directed against abuses in the large holding companies, and the ▷Social Security Act, providing for disability and retirement insurance. The presidential election of 1936 was won entirely on the record of the New Deal. During 1935–36 Roosevelt was involved in a conflict over the composition of the Supreme Court, following its nullification of major New Deal measures as unconstitutional. In 1938 he introduced measures for farm relief and the improvement of working conditions.

In his foreign policy, Roosevelt endeavoured to use his influence to restrain Axis aggression, and to establish 'good neighbour' relations with other countries in the Americas. Soon after the outbreak of war, he launched a vast rearmament programme, introduced conscription, and provided for the supply of armaments to the Allies on a 'cash-and-carry' basis. In spite of strong isolationist opposition, he broke a long-standing precedent in running for a third term; he was re-elected in 1940. He announced that the USA would become the 'arsenal of democracy'. Roosevelt was eager for US entry into the war on behalf of the Allies. In addition to his revulsion for Hitler, he wanted to establish the USA as a world power, filling the vacuum he expected to be left by the break-up of the British Empire. He was restrained by isolationist forces in Congress.

Public opinion, however, was in favour of staying out of the war, so Roosevelt and the military chiefs deliberately kept back the intelligence reports received from the British and others concerning the imminent Japanese attack on the naval base at Pearl Harbor in Hawaii. The deaths at Pearl Harbor on 7 December 1941 incited public opinion, and the USA entered the war. From this point on, Roosevelt concerned himself solely with the conduct of the war. He participated in the Washington (1942) and Casablanca (1943) conferences to plan the Mediterranean assault, and the conferences in ▷Québec, Cairo, and Tehran in 1943, and ▷Yalta in 1945, at which the final preparations were made for the Allied victory. He was re-elected for a fourth term in 1944, but died in 1945.

Related Web site: Franklin D Roosevelt – Thirty-second President 1933–1945 http://www.whitehouse.gov/WH/glimpse/presidents/html/fr32.html

Roosevelt, Theodore (1858–1919) 26th president of the USA 1901–09, a Republican. After serving as governor of New York 1898–1900 he became vice president to ▷McKinley, whom he succeeded as president on McKinley's assassination in 1901. He campaigned against the great trusts (associations of enterprises that reduce competition), while carrying on a jingoist foreign policy designed to enforce US supremacy over Latin America. He was awarded the Nobel Prize for Peace in 1906 for his mediation at the end of the Russo-Japanese war in 1904.

As president, Roosevelt became more liberal. He tackled business monopolies, initiated measures for the conservation of national resources, and introduced the Pure Food and Drug Act. In 1904 he announced the Roosevelt Corollary to the ▷Monroe Doctrine, to the effect that the USA would intervene in Latin America in order to prevent European intervention. Alienated after his retirement by the conservatism of his successor W H Taft, Roosevelt formed the Progressive or 'Bull Moose' Party. He unsuccessfully ran for the presidency in 1912. During World War I he strongly advocated US intervention.

Related Web site: TR: The Story of Teddy Roosevelt http://www.pbs.org/wgbh/pages/amex/tr/index.html

root the part of a plant that is usually underground, and whose primary functions are anchorage and the absorption of water and dissolved mineral salts. Roots usually grow downwards and towards water (that is, they are positively geotropic and hydrotropic; see ▷tropism). Plants such as epiphytic orchids, which grow above ground, produce aerial roots that absorb moisture from the atmosphere. Others, such as ivy, have climbing roots arising from the stems, which serve to attach the plant to trees and walls.

The absorptive area of roots is greatly increased by the numerous slender root hairs formed near the tips. A calyptra, or root cap, protects the tip of the root from abrasion as it grows through the soil.

Symbiotic associations occur between the roots of certain plants, such as clover, and various bacteria that fix nitrogen from the air (see ▷nitrogen fixation). Other modifications of roots include ▷contractile roots, ▷pneumatophores, ▷taproots, and ▷prop roots.

Evolution The evolution of root systems by land plants was very fast, in evolutionary terms. The earliest plants (410 million years ago) had tiny roots only a few millimetres in length, but within 20 million years roots were as long as 50 cm/20 in.

root of an equation, a value that satisfies the equality. For example, $x = 0$ and $x = 5$ are roots of the equation $x^2 - 5x = 0$.

root in language, the basic element from which a word is derived. The root is a morpheme, a unit that cannot be subdivided. The Latin word *dominus* ('master'), for example, is a root from which many English words are derived, such as 'dominate', 'dominion', and 'domino'.

root crop plant cultivated for its swollen edible root (which may or may not be a true root). Potatoes are the major temperate root crop; the major tropical root crops are cassava, yams, and sweet potatoes. Root crops are second in importance only to cereals as human food. Roots have a high carbohydrate content, but their protein content rarely exceeds 2%. Consequently, communities relying almost exclusively upon roots may suffer from protein deficiency. Food production for a given area from roots is greater than from cereals.

root hair tiny hairlike outgrowth on the surface cells of plant roots that greatly increases the area available for the absorption of water and other materials. It is a delicate structure, which survives for a few days only and does not develop into a root.

roots music term originally denoting ▷reggae, later encompassing any music indigenous to a particular culture; see ▷world music.

rootstock another name for ▷rhizome, an underground plant organ.

rorqual any of a family (Balaenopteridae) of baleen ▷whales, especially the genus *Balaenoptera*, which includes the blue whale *B. musculus*, the largest of all animals, measuring 30 m/100 ft and more. The common rorqual or fin whale *B. physalus* is slate-coloured and not quite so long.

Rorschach test in psychology, a method of diagnosis involving the use of inkblot patterns that subjects are asked to interpret, to help indicate personality type, degree of intelligence, and emotional stability. It was invented by the Swiss psychiatrist Hermann Rorschach.

rosary string of beads used in a number of religions, including Buddhism, Christianity, and Islam. The term also refers to a form of prayer used by Catholics, consisting of 150 ▷Ave Marias and 15 Paternosters and Glorias, or to a string of 165 beads for keeping count of these prayers; it is linked with the adoration of the Virgin Mary.

Rosas, Juan Manuel de (1793–1877) Argentine soldier, gaucho (cowboy), and dictator 1835–52. Rosas used his private gaucho army to overthrow the Liberal regime of Bernardino ▷Rivadavia in 1827. A Buenos Aires Federalist, he was governor of that city 1829–32 and, when he was also dictator of Argentina, presided over a reign of terror. While appealing to the urban masses, he allowed huge land sales at absurdly low prices that benefited the landed aristocracy, including Rosas's wealthy Creole family.

Roscommon (formerly **Ros-Comain**; 'wood around a monastery') county of the Republic of Ireland, in the province of Connacht; county town **Roscommon**; area 2,460 sq km/950 sq mi; population (1996) 52,000. It has rich pastures and is bounded on the east by the River Shannon, with bogs and lakes, including Lough Key and Lough Gara. The three largest lakes (loughs Allen, Boderg, and Ree) lie only partly within the county. There is agriculture, especially cattle rearing. Roscommon was established as a county in about 1580. Other important towns are Castlerea, Elphin, and Boyle.

rose any shrub or climbing plant belonging to the rose family, with prickly stems and fragrant flowers in many different colours. Numerous cultivated forms have been derived from the sweetbrier or eglantine (*R. rubiginosa*) and dogrose (*R. canina*) native to Europe and Asia. There are many climbing varieties, but the forms most commonly grown in gardens are bush roses and standards (cultivated roses grafted on to a brier stem). (Genus *Rosa*, family Rosaceae.)

Related Web site: Yesterday's Rose http://www.country-lane.com/yr/

Roseau (formerly **Charlotte Town**) capital of ▷Dominica, West Indies, on the southwest coast of the island; population (1991) 15,900. It is a sea port, with a trade in tropical fruit and vegetables. The town suffered severe damage in a hurricane in 1979.

rosebay willowherb common perennial weed. See ▷willowherb.

Rosebery, Archibald Philip Primrose, 5th Earl of Rosebery (1847–1929) British Liberal politician. He was foreign secretary in 1886 and 1892–94, when he succeeded Gladstone as prime minister, but his government survived less than a year. After 1896 his imperialist views gradually placed him further from the mainstream of the Liberal Party. He was made an Earl in 1868.

rosemary evergreen shrub belonging to the mint family, native to the Mediterranean and western Asia, with small, narrow, scented leaves and clusters of pale blue or purple flowers. It is widely cultivated as a herb for use in cooking and for its aromatic oil, used in perfumery and pharmaceuticals. Rosemary is a traditional symbol of remembrance. (*Rosmarinus officinalis*, family Labiatae.)

ROSEMARY Rosemary is a bushy perennial shrub, often growing to a height of over 180 cm/6 ft. It has evergreen needles, dark green on top and silver underneath. It produces light-blue or purple flowers in early summer.

Rosenberg, Alfred (1893–1946) German politician, born in Tallinn, Estonia. He became the chief Nazi ideologist and was minister for eastern occupied territories 1941–44. He was tried at ▷Nuremberg in 1946 as a war criminal and hanged.

Rosenberg, Julius (1918–1953) and Ethel Greenglass (1915–1953). US married couple, convicted of being leaders of an atomic-espionage ring passing information from Ethel's brother via courier to the USSR. The Rosenbergs were executed after much public controversy and demonstration. They were the only Americans executed for espionage during peacetime.

Roses, Wars of the civil wars in England 1455–85 between the houses of ▷Lancaster (badge, red rose) and ▷York (badge, white rose), both of whom claimed the throne through descent from the sons of Edward III. As a result of ▷Henry VI's lapse into insanity in 1453, Richard, Duke of York, was installed as protector of the realm. Upon his recovery, Henry forced York to take up arms in self-defence.

Rosetta Stone slab of basalt with inscriptions from 197 BC, found near the town of Rosetta, Egypt, 1799. Giving the same text in three versions – Greek, hieroglyphic, and demotic script – it became the key to deciphering other Egyptian inscriptions.

Rosh Hashanah two-day holiday that marks the start of the Jewish New Year (first new Moon after the autumn equinox), traditionally announced by blowing a ram's horn (a shofar).

Related Web site: New Year's Day http://www.geocities.com/Heartland/Plains/7214/newyear.htm

Rosicrucians group of early 17th-century philosophers who claimed occult powers and employed the terminology of ▷alchemy to expound their mystical doctrines (said to derive from ▷Paracelsus). The name comes from books published in 1614 and 1615, attributed to Christian Rosenkreutz ('rosy cross'), most probably a pen-name but allegedly a writer living around 1460. Several societies have been founded in Britain and the USA that claim to be their successors, such as the Rosicrucian Fraternity (1614 in Germany, 1861 in the USA).

Ross, James Clark (1800–1862) English explorer. He discovered the north magnetic pole in 1831. He also went to the Antarctic 1839; Ross Island, Ross Sea, and Ross Dependency are named after him. He was knighted in 1843.

Ross, Ronald (1857–1932) Indian-born British physician and bacteriologist who was awarded a Nobel Prize for Physiology or Medicine in 1902 for his work on the role of the *Anopheles*

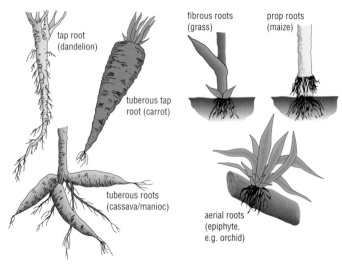

tap root (dandelion)

tuberous tap root (carrot)

tuberous roots (cassava/manioc)

fibrous roots (grass)

prop roots (maize)

aerial roots (epiphyte, e.g. orchid)

ROOT Many flowers (dandelion) and vegetables (carrot) have swollen tap roots with smaller lateral roots. The tuberous roots of the cassava are swollen parts of an underground stem modified to store food. The fibrous roots of the grasses are all of equal size. Prop roots grow out from the stem and then grow down into the ground to support a heavy plant. Aerial roots grow from stems but do not grow into the ground; many absorb moisture from the air.

mosquito in transmitting malaria. From 1881 to 1899 he served in the Indian Medical Service, and during 1895–98 identified mosquitoes of the genus *Anopheles* as being responsible for the spread of malaria. He was knighted in 1911.

Ross Dependency all the Antarctic islands and territories between 160° east and 150° west longitude, and situated south of 60° south latitude; it includes Edward VII Land, the Ross Sea and its islands (including the Balleny Isles), and parts of Victoria Land. It is claimed by New Zealand; area 450,000 sq km/173,745 sq mi.

Rossellini, Roberto (1906–1977) Italian film director. His World War II trilogy, *Roma città aperta/Rome, Open City* (1945), *Paisà/Paisan* (1946), and *Germania anno zero/Germany Year Zero* (1947), reflects his humanism and is considered a landmark of European cinema.

Rossetti, Christina Georgina (1830–1894) English poet and a devout High Anglican (see ▷Oxford movement). Her best-known work is *Goblin Market and Other Poems* (1862); among others are *The Prince's Progress* (1866), *Annus Domini* (1874), and *A Pageant* (1881). She was the sister of Dante Gabriel ▷Rossetti.

Her verse expresses unfulfilled spiritual yearning and frustrated love. She was a skilful technician and made use of irregular rhyme and line length.

Related Web site: Selected Poetry of Christina Rossetti (1830–1894) http://www.library.utoronto.ca/utel/rp/authors/rossettc.html

Rossetti, Dante Gabriel (1828–1882) English painter and poet. He was a founding member of the ▷Pre-Raphaelite Brotherhood (PRB) in 1848. As well as romantic medieval scenes, he produced many idealized portraits of women, including the *Beata Beatrix* (1864). His verse includes 'The Blessed Damozel' (1850). His sister was the poet Christina ▷Rossetti.

He formed the PRB with the painters John Everett Millais and Holman Hunt but produced only two deliberately Pre-Raphaelite pictures, *The Girlhood of Mary Virgin* (1849) and *Ecce Ancilla Domini* (1850), both in the Tate Gallery, London. Afterwards he refused to exhibit, and developed a broader style and a personal subject matter, related to his poetry. He was a friend of the critic John ▷Ruskin, who helped establish his reputation as a painter, and of William Morris and his wife Jane, who became Rossetti's lover and the subject of much of his work. From 1857 to 1858 he worked on the Arthurian frescoes for the Oxford Union with Edward Burne-Jones and William Morris, and initiated a second phase of Pre-Raphaelitism associated with the Arts and Crafts Movement.

His *Poems* (1870) were recovered from the grave of his wife Elizabeth Siddal (1834–1862), also a painter, whom he had married in 1860, and were attacked as being of 'the fleshly school of poetry'.

Related Web site: Rossetti Archive http://jefferson.village.virginia.edu/rossetti/rossetti.html

> **Dante Gabriel Rossetti**
> *My name is Might-have-been; / I am also called No-more, Too-late, Farewell.*
> 'A Superscription'

Rossini, Gioacchino Antonio (1792–1868) Italian composer. His first success was the opera *Tancredi* in 1813. In 1816 his opera buffa *Il barbiere di Siviglia/The Barber of Seville* was produced in Rome. He was the most successful opera composer of his time, producing 20 operas in the period 1815–23. He also created (with Gaetano Donizetti and Bellini) the 19th-century Italian operatic style.

After *Guillaume Tell/William Tell* (1829), Rossini gave up writing opera and his later years were spent in Bologna and Paris. Among the works of this period are the *Stabat Mater* (1842) and the piano music arranged for ballet by Respighi as *La boutique fantasque/The Fantastic Toyshop* (1919).

Rostand, Edmond (1868–1918) French poetic dramatist. He wrote *Cyrano de Bergerac* (1898) and *L'Aiglon* (1900) (based on the life of Napoleon III), in which Sarah Bernhardt played the leading role.

Rostock industrial port in the *Land* of Mecklenburg–West Pomerania, Germany, on the River Warnow, 13 km/8 mi south of the Baltic; population (1995) 231,300. Industries include shipbuilding, ship repair, electronics, and fish processing. There is a technical university here.

Rostov-na-Donu capital of Rostov oblast (region), southwestern Russian Federation; population (1996 est) 1,025,000. A major industrial and commercial city and the centre of a fertile agricultural region, it lies on the River Don, 46 km/29 mi from its mouth. Rostov is home to many large engineering concerns manufacturing chemicals, agricultural machinery, aircraft, and ships; there are also tobacco and food-processing plants, shoe factories, and textile mills. The city is an important transportation centre; railway lines from Moscow and Kiev converge here, and river cruises run up the Don and Volga. Rostov has been called the 'Gateway to the Caucasus'.

Rostropovich, Mstislav (Leopoldovich) (1927–) Russian cellist and conductor. He left the USSR in 1974 and was deprived of his Soviet citizenship in 1978 because of his sympathies with political dissidents. Prokofiev, Shostakovich, Khachaturian, and Britten wrote pieces for him. From 1977 he directed the National Symphony Orchestra, Washington, DC.

Roth, Philip Milton (1933–) US novelist. His witty, sharply satirical, and increasingly fantastic novels depict the moral and sexual anxieties of 20th-century Jewish-American life, most notably in *Goodbye Columbus* (1959) and *Portnoy's Complaint* (1969). In 1998 he was awarded the National Medal of Arts.

Rotherham industrial town in South Yorkshire, northern England, at the confluence of the rivers Don and Rother, 10 km/6 mi northeast of Sheffield; population (1994) 154,000. Industries include engineering, pottery, glass, iron and steel, brassware, machinery, and coal.

Rothermere, Vere Harold Esmond Harmsworth, 3rd Viscount Rothermere (1925–1998) British newspaper proprietor. He became chair of Associated Newspapers in 1971, controlling the right-wing *Daily Mail* (founded by his great-uncle Lord ▷Northcliffe) and *Mail on Sunday* (launched in 1982), the London *Evening Standard*, and a string of regional newspapers.

Rothko, Mark (1903–1970) Adopted name of Marcus Rothkovich. Russian-born US painter. He was a leading exponent of ▷abstract expressionism and a pioneer, towards the end of his life, of Colour Field painting. Typically, his works are canvases covered in large hazy rectangles of thin paint, the colours subtly modulated, as in *Light Red over Black* (1957; Tate Gallery, London).

Born in Dvinsk, Russia, he went to the USA with his parents 1913. He received his only training at New York City's Art Students League. During the 1930s he painted for the Federal Arts Project and, with Adolph Gottlieb, founded the expressionist group The Ten. During the mid-1940s he painted in a style influenced by surrealism but by the end of the decade he had evolved his distinctive manner employing flat areas of matt colour spread over large-scale canvases. These paintings strongly influenced younger painters in the USA and Britain.

Rothschild European family active in the financial world for two centuries. **Mayer Amschel** (1744–1812) set up as a moneylender in Frankfurt-am-Main, Germany, and business houses were established throughout Europe by his ten children.

rotifer any of the tiny invertebrates, also called 'wheel animalcules', of the phylum Rotifera. Mainly freshwater, some marine, rotifers have a ring of ▷cilia that carries food to the mouth and also provides propulsion. They are the smallest of multicellular animals – few reach 0.05 cm/0.02 in.

rotten borough English parliamentary constituency, before the Great Reform Act of 1832, that returned members to Parliament in spite of having small numbers of electors. Such a borough could easily be manipulated by those with sufficient money or influence.

Rotterdam industrial city and port in South Holland province, the Netherlands, in the Rhine-Maas delta, 90 km/56 mi southwest of Amsterdam; population (1997) 590,000. The Rotterdam-Europoort complex is the biggest oil refining centre in the world, and one of its foremost ocean cargo ports. Other industries include brewing, distilling, shipbuilding, sugar and petroleum refining, margarine, and tobacco. A canal, the New Waterway (*Nieuwe Waterweg*), links Rotterdam with the North Sea.

Rottweiler breed of dog originally developed in Rottweil, Germany, as a herding and guard dog, and subsequently used as a police dog. Powerfully built, the dog is about 63–66 cm/25–27 in high at the shoulder, black with tan markings. It has a short coat and docked tail.

Rouault, Georges Henri (1871–1958) French painter, etcher, illustrator, and designer. He was one of the major religious artists of the 20th century. Early in his career he was associated with the ▷Fauves, but created his own highly distinctive style using rich, dark colours and heavy outlines. His subjects include clowns, prostitutes, lawyers, and religious figures, as in *Christ Mocked* (1932; Museum of Modern Art, New York).

Roubiliac (or Roubillac)**, Louis François** (*c.* 1705–1762) French sculptor. A Huguenot, he fled religious persecution to settle in England in 1732. He became a leading sculptor of the day, creating a statue of German composer Georg Handel for Vauxhall Gardens, London, in 1737.

Rouen industrial port and administrative centre of the Seine-Maritime *département* in France, situated on the River Seine 120 km/75 mi northwest of Paris; population (1999 est) 106,600, conurbation 380,000. Rouen is an important commercial city whose industries include textiles, particularly cotton, electronics, distilling, and oil refining. It is the seat of an archbishopric and has a 13th–16th-century cathedral. As the capital of ▷Normandy from 912, it was ruled by England for periods of time in the Middle Ages; the English burned Joan of Arc in the city square in 1431. The novelist Gustave Flaubert was born here in 1821.

roughage alternative term for dietary ▷fibre, material of plant origin that cannot be digested by enzymes normally present in the human ▷gut.

rounders bat-and-ball game similar to ▷baseball but played on a much smaller pitch. The first reference to rounders was in 1744.

Roundhead member of the Parliamentary party during the English Civil War 1640–60, opposing the Royalist Cavaliers. The term referred to the short hair then worn only by men of the lower classes.

Men at the court of Charles I fashionably wore their hair in long ringlets, so the Parliamentarians chose to wear theirs short in contrast. Many Parliamentarians were also Puritans, who thought they should live and dress simply and austerely. 'Roundhead' was originally a derogatory term and is thought to have first been used in 1641, possibly by Queen Henrietta Maria.

Rousseau, Henri Julien Félix (1844–1910) Called 'Le Douanier'. French painter. A self-taught naive artist, he painted scenes of the Parisian suburbs, portraits, and exotic scenes with painstaking detail, as in *Tropical Storm with a Tiger* (1891; National Gallery, London). He was much admired by artists such as Gauguin and Picasso, and writers such as the poet Apollinaire.

Rousseau served in the army for some years, then became a toll collector (hence *Le Douanier* 'the customs official'), and finally took up full-time painting in 1885. He exhibited at the Salon des Indépendants 1886–1910 and was associated with the group led by Picasso and Apollinaire. His work has been seen as an anticipation of ▷surrealism.

Among his best-known works are *The Sleeping Gypsy* (1897; Museum of Modern Art, New York), *The Snake Charmer* (1907; Musée d'Orsay, Paris), and *The Football Players* (1908; Guggenheim Museum, New York).

> **Jean-Jacques Rousseau**
> *We are born, so to speak, twice over; born into existence, and born into life; born a human being, and born a man.*
> Emile bk 4

Rousseau, Jean-Jacques (1712–1778) French social philosopher and writer. His book *Du Contrat social/Social Contract* (1762), emphasizing the rights of the people over those of the government, was a significant influence on the French Revolution. In the novel *Emile* (1762), he outlined a new theory of education. Rousseau was born in Geneva, Switzerland. *Discourses on the Origins of Inequality* (1754) made his name: he denounced civilized society and postulated the paradox of the superiority of the 'noble savage'. In *Social Contract* he argued that government is justified only if sovereignty stays with the people. He thereby rejected representative democracy in favour of direct democracy, modelled on the Greek polis and the Swiss canton, and stated that a government could be legitimately overthrown if it failed to express the general will of the people. *Emile* was written as an example of how to elicit the unspoiled nature and abilities of children, based on natural development and the power of example.

Rousseau's ideas were condemned by philosophers, the clergy, and the public, and he lived in exile in England for a year, being helped by Scottish philosopher David Hume until they fell out. He was a contributor to the *Encyclopédie* and also wrote operas. *Confessions*, published posthumously in 1782, was a frank account of his occasionally immoral life and was a founding work of autobiography.

rove bettle any of a number of beetles with characteristic very short elytra (wing cases) that conceal large, well developed wings that are intricately folded away. When required the wings can unfold very rapidly, for almost instantaneous flight. The family includes some 20,000 species. The rove beetle is in family Staphylinidae, in order Coleoptera, class Insecta, phylum Arthropoda.

rowan another name for the European ▷mountain ash tree.

rowing propulsion of a boat by oars, either by one rower with two oars (sculling) or by crews (two, four, or eight persons) with one oar each, often with a coxswain (the nonrowing member who steers and determines rowing speed). Major events include the world championship, first held in 1962 for men and 1974 for women, and the Boat Race (between England's Oxford and Cambridge universities), first held in 1829.

> **Related Web site: Rowing FAQ** http://riceinfo.rice.edu/~hofer/Rowingfaq.html

Rowland, Tiny (1917–1998) Adopted name of Roland Walter Fuhrhop. British entrepreneur, co-chief executive and managing director of Lonrho 1961–1994, and owner of the *Observer* Sunday newspaper from 1981 to 1993.

Rowlandson, Thomas (1757–1827) English painter and illustrator. One of the greatest caricaturists of 18th-century England, his fame rests on his humorous, often bawdy, depictions of the vanities and vices of Georgian social life. He illustrated many books, including *Tour of Dr Syntax in Search of the Picturesque* (1809), which was followed by two sequels between 1812 and 1821.

Rowley, William (c. 1585–c. 1642) English actor and dramatist. He collaborated with Thomas ▷Middleton on *The Changeling* (1622) and with Thomas ▷Dekker and John ▷Ford on *The Witch of Edmonton* (1621).

Rowling, J(oanne) K (1965–) English children's novelist. Her novels *Harry Potter and the Philosopher's Stone* (US edition: *Harry Potter and the Sorcerer's Stone*; 1997), *Harry Potter and the Chamber of Secrets* (1998), *Harry Potter and the Prisoner of Azkaban* (1999), *Harry Potter and the Goblet of Fire* (2000) and *Harry Potter and the Order of the Phoenix* (2003) are the first five of a planned series of seven books about a schoolboy wizard. They hit the top of the (adult) best-seller lists in both the UK and the USA, making Rowling the highest paid woman in the UK in 2000.

When the fourth book in the series was published in 2000, it was the fastest-selling book ever published, with shoppers queuing as bookshops opened, and purchasing 372,000 books in the first weekend of availability. Preorders for the fifth book in the series meant that it was, in July 2000, already on a best-sellers list, despite the fact that it had not been written at the time.

Rowntree, B(enjamin) Seebohm (1871–1954) English entrepreneur and philanthropist. He used much of the money he acquired as chair (1925–41) of the family firm of confectioners, H I Rowntree, to fund investigations into social conditions. His writings include *Poverty, A Study of Town Life* (1900), a landmark in empirical sociology. The three **Rowntree Trusts**, which were founded by his father **Joseph Rowntree** (1836–1925) in 1904, fund research into housing, social care, and social policy, support projects relating to social justice, and give grants to pressure groups working in these areas.

Rowse, A(lfred) L(eslie) (1903–1997) English historian. He published a biography of Shakespeare in 1963, and in *Shakespeare's Sonnets: The Problems Solved* (1973) controversially identified the 'Dark Lady' of Shakespeare's sonnets as Emilia Lanier, half-Italian daughter of a court musician, with whom the Bard is alleged to have had an affair in 1593–95.

Royal Academy of Arts (RA) British society founded by George III in London in 1768 to encourage painting, sculpture, and architecture; its first president was Joshua ▷Reynolds. It is now housed in Old Burlington House, Piccadilly. There is an annual summer exhibition for contemporary artists, and tuition is provided at the Royal Academy schools.

Royal Air Force (RAF) the ▷air force of Britain. The RAF was formed 1918 by the merger of the Royal Naval Air Service and the Royal Flying Corps.

royal antelope small nocturnal African antelope, inhabitants of dense jungle. They are the smallest of all antelopes, being no more than 30 cm/12 in high, and are slenderly built with very thin legs, no thicker than a pencil; they are generally brown in colour. The royal antelope *Neotragus pygmaeus* is in family Bovidae, in order Artiodactyla.

royal assent in the UK, formal consent given by a British sovereign to the passage of a bill through Parliament, after which it becomes an ▷act of Parliament. The last instance of a royal refusal was the rejection of the Scottish Militia Bill of 1702 by Queen Anne.

Royal Ballet leading British ballet company and school, based at the Royal Opera House, Covent Garden, London. Until 1956 it was known as the Sadler's Wells Ballet. It was founded in 1931 by Ninette ▷de Valois, who established her school and company at the Sadler's Wells Theatre. It moved to Covent Garden in 1946. Frederick ▷Ashton became principal choreographer in 1935, providing the company with its uniquely English ballet style. Leading dancers included Margot Fonteyn, Rudolf Nureyev, Alicia Markova, and Antoinette Sibley. The artistic director is Monica Mason, from 2003. In 1990 the ballet's touring company became the Birmingham Royal Ballet.

Royal Botanic Gardens, Kew botanic gardens in Richmond, Surrey, England, popularly known as ▷Kew Gardens.

Royal Canadian Mounted Police (RCMP or Mounties) Canadian national police force, known as the ▷Mounties, and the sole police force operating in the Northwest and Yukon territories. Founded as the North West Mounted Police in 1873, it was renamed in 1920 with the extension of its territory. It is administered by the solicitor general of Canada, and its headquarters are in Ottawa, Ontario.

royal commission in the UK and Canada, a group of people appointed by the government (nominally by the sovereign) to investigate a matter of public concern and make recommendations on any actions to be taken in connection with it, including changes in the law. In cases where agreement on recommendations cannot be reached, a minority report can be submitted by dissenters.

Royal Doulton British pottery firm. See Henry ▷Doulton.

Royal Greenwich Observatory originally one of the two UK national astronomical observatories run by the Particle Physics and Astronomy Research Council (PPARC). It was founded in 1675 at Greenwich, East London, to provide navigational information to sailors. After World War II it moved to Herstmonceux Castle in Sussex, where the 2.5-m/8.2-ft Isaac Newton Telescope (INT) was constructed in 1967. Following the relocation of the INT to the island of La Palma, in the Canary Islands, RGO was relocated to Cambridge in 1988–90. In 1998 the Cambridge site was closed and the RGO merged with the Royal Observatory Edinburgh to form a new Astronomy Technology Centre on the Edinburgh site.

Royal Horticultural Society (RHS) British society established in 1804 for the improvement of horticulture. The annual Chelsea Flower Show, held in the grounds of the Royal Hospital, London, is also a social event, and another flower show is held at Vincent Square, London. There are gardens, orchards, and trial grounds at Wisley, Surrey, and the Lindley Library has one of the world's finest horticultural collections. The RHS also has a rose garden at Rosemoor in Devon.

Royalist term often used to describe monarchist factions. In England, it is used especially for those who supported Charles I during the English ▷Civil War. They are also known as 'Cavaliers', and their opponents as 'Parliamentarians' or ▷Roundheads.

The Royalists first appeared as a distinct group in Parliament during the debates on the Root and Branch Petition in the House of Commons in 1641. As the Civil War progressed it was obvious that the Royalists were strongest in the northwest, and the Parliamentarians in the southeast, though there were several exceptions to this, such as Royalist Colchester in the southeast and Parliamentarian Gloucester in the west. Royalists were drawn from all classes, though their steadiest support came from the lesser gentry. They embraced a wide range of religious opinions: Catholics and Arminians were all Royalist, but the party included moderate Anglicans and, after 1649, many Presbyterians and some of the Independents. This diverse group was, in fact, held together solely by its allegiance to the king.

Royal Marines British military force trained for amphibious warfare. See ▷marines.

royal prerogative powers, immunities, and privileges recognized in common law as belonging to the crown. Most prerogative acts in the UK are now performed by the government on behalf of the crown. The royal prerogative belongs to the Queen as a person as well as to the institution called the crown, and the award of some honours and dignities remain her personal choice. As by prerogative 'the king can do no wrong', the monarch is immune from prosecution.

Royal Shakespeare Company (RSC) British professional theatre company that performs Shakespearean and other plays. It was founded in 1961 from the company at the Shakespeare Memorial Theatre (1932, now the Royal Shakespeare Theatre) in Stratford-upon-Avon, Warwickshire, England, and produces plays in Stratford and the Barbican Centre in London.

The RSC initially presented mainly Shakespeare at Stratford; these productions were usually transferred to the Aldwych Theatre, London, where the company also performed modern plays and non-Shakespearean classics. In 1982 it moved into a permanent London headquarters at the Barbican. A second large theatre in Stratford, the Swan, opened in 1986 with an auditorium similar to theatres of Shakespeare's day.

The first director of the RSC was Peter Hall. In 1968 Trevor Nunn replaced him, and in 1986 Nunn was succeeded by Terry Hands. Adrian Noble has been director since 1990.

Royal Society oldest and premier scientific society in Britain, originating in 1645 and chartered in 1662; Robert Boyle, Christopher ▷Wren, and Isaac ▷Newton were prominent early members. Its Scottish equivalent is the **Royal Society of Edinburgh** (1783).

The headquarters of the Royal Society is in Carlton House Terrace, London; the Royal Society of Edinburgh is in George Street.

THOMAS ROWLANDSON *Camelford Fair*, one of English artist Thomas Rowlandson's scenes of English country life. Rowlandson was better known as a caricaturist and many of his engravings were produced at great speed. His designs were initially made with a reed pen and then washed with colour. *The Art Archive/Tate Gallery London*

Royal Society for the Prevention of Cruelty to Animals (RSPCA)

British organization formed 1824 to safeguard the welfare of animals; it promotes legislation, has an inspectorate to secure enforcement of existing laws, and runs clinics.

Royal Society for the Protection of Birds (RSPB)

UK charity, founded in 1889, aiming to conserve and protect wild birds, both in the UK and overseas. It has a network of reserves in all types of habitat (73,000 ha/180,000 acres), and is the largest voluntary wildlife-conservation body in Europe, with a membership of 827,000 (1990).

royalty in law, payment to the owner for rights to use or exploit literary or artistic copyrights and patent rights in new inventions of all kinds.

Rozwi empire (or Changamire) highly advanced empire in southeastern Africa, located south of the Zambezi River and centred on the stone city of Great Zimbabwe. It replaced the gold-trading empire of Mwene Mutapa from the 15th century. The Rozwi empire survived until the ▷Mfecane of the 1830s, when overpopulation to the south drove the Nguni and Ndebele people northwards into Rozwi territory in search of more land.

rpm abbreviation for **revolutions per minute**.

RSI abbreviation for ▷repetitive strain injury, a condition that can affect people who repeatedly perform certain movements with their hands and wrists for long periods of time, such as typists, musicians, or players of computer games.

RSPB abbreviation for ▷Royal Society for the Protection of Birds.

RSVP abbreviation for *répondez s'il vous plaît* (French 'please reply').

Rt Hon abbreviation for **Right Honourable**, title of members of the Privy Council (including all present and former UK Cabinet members).

RU486 another name for ▷mifepristone, an abortion pill.

Ruanda part of the former Belgian territory of Ruanda-Urundi until it achieved independence as ▷Rwanda, a country in central Africa.

Rub' al Khālī (Arabic 'empty quarter') vast sandy desert in southern Saudi Arabia and Yemen; area 650,000 sq km/ 250,000 sq mi. In 1930–31 the British explorer Bertram Thomas became the first European to cross it.

rubber coagulated ▷latex of a variety of plants, mainly from the New World. Most important is Para rubber, which comes from the tree *Hevea brasiliensis*, belonging to the spurge family. It was introduced from Brazil to Southeast Asia, where most of the world supply is now produced, the chief exporters being Peninsular Malaysia, Indonesia, Sri Lanka, Cambodia, Thailand, Sarawak, and Brunei. At about seven years the tree, which may grow to 20 m/60 ft, is ready for tapping. Small cuts are made in the trunk and the latex drips into collecting cups. In pure form, rubber is white and has the formula $(C_5H_8)_n$.

RUBBER A rubber tapper in Indonesia makes a partial, diagonal cut through the bark of the *Hevea* tree to recover a milky liquid, or latex. *Image Bank*

rubber plant Asiatic tree belonging to the mulberry family, native to Asia and North Africa, which produces ▷latex in its stem. It has shiny, leathery, oval leaves, and young specimens are grown as house plants. (*Ficus elastica*, family Moraceae.)

Rubbra, Edmund (1901–1986) English composer. He studied under the composer Gustav Holst and specialized in contrapuntal writing, as exemplified in his study *Counterpoint* (1960). His compositions include 11 symphonies, chamber music, and songs. In 1948 he became a Roman Catholic and his later music shows the influence of Catholic mysticism.

rubella technical term for ▷German measles.

Rubens, Peter Paul (1577–1640) Flemish painter. He was one of the greatest figures of the ▷baroque period. Bringing the exuberance of Italian baroque to northern Europe, he created innumerable religious and allegorical paintings for churches and palaces. These show mastery of drama and movement in large compositions, and a love of rich colour and texture. He also painted portraits and, in his last years, landscapes. *The Rape of the Daughters of Leucippus* (1617; Alte Pinakothek, Munich) is typical.

Rubens's energy was prodigious. In less than 40 years he produced more than 3,000 paintings. He created masterpieces in every genre: religious, for example *The Descent from the Cross* (c. 1611–14; Antwerp Cathedral); portraiture, the so-called *Chapeau de pailles* (c. 1620; National Gallery, London); peasant life, the *Kermesse* (c. 1622; Louvre, Paris); allegory, *War and Peace* (c. 1629–30; National Gallery, London); and landscape, the *Château de Steen* (c. 1635–37; National Gallery, London).

As a colourist and technician he was remarkable; he devised a classic oil method of thinly painted shadow and loaded highlight. His studio-factory was a model of efficient administration, his assistants so able and his supervision so well directed, that the standard of works not due to his hand alone is consistently high. He summoned into being a whole school of engravers, occupied in reproducing his works. His influence on other painters – Velázquez, Watteau, Delacroix, and Constable among them – was enormous.

He was also a great collector (of ancient marbles and gems, pictures, manuscripts, and books), a classical scholar who knew and corresponded with people of learning throughout Europe, and a diplomat who spoke five languages.

Rubicon ancient name of the small river flowing into the Adriatic that, under the Roman Republic, marked the boundary between Italy proper and Cisalpine Gaul. When Caesar led his army across it 49 BC, he therefore declared war on the Republic; hence to 'cross the Rubicon' means to take an irrevocable step.

rubidium (Latin *rubidus* 'red') soft, silver-white, metallic element, symbol Rb, atomic number 37, relative atomic mass 85.47. It is one of the ▷alkali metals, ignites spontaneously in air, and reacts violently with water. It is used in photocells and vacuum-tube filaments.

Rubidium was discovered spectroscopically by German physicists Robert Bunsen and Gustav Kirchhoff in 1861 and named after the red lines in its spectrum.

Rubinstein, Artur (1887–1982) Polish-born US pianist. Considered by many to be the greatest 20th-century piano virtuoso, he played with an intellectual and commanding tone, appeared in films, and made many distinctive recordings. He was a supreme interpreter of Chopin and was also acclaimed for his reading of modern Spanish composers. His early encounters with Joseph Joachim and the Belgian v iolinist, conductor, and composer Eugène Ysaÿe (1858–1931) link his interpretations of Beethoven, Mozart, and Chopin with the virtuoso Romantic tradition. He was also a noted interpreter of de Falla.

Rublev (or Rublyov), **Andrei** (c. 1360–c. 1430) Russian icon painter. He is considered the greatest exponent of the genre in Russia. Only one documented work of his survives, the *Old Testament Trinity* (c. 1411; Tretyakov Gallery, Moscow). This shows a basically Byzantine style, but with a gentler expression.

PETER PAUL RUBENS Rubens' famous painting known as *The Three Graces*. Women with full figures are sometimes described as 'Rubenesque'. A full figure was a sign of wealth and social status. *The Art Archive/Prado Museum Madrid/Dagli Orti*

ruby the red transparent gem variety of the mineral ▷corundum Al_2O_3, aluminium oxide. Small amounts of chromium oxide, Cr_2O_3, substituting for aluminium oxide, give ruby its colour. Natural rubies are found mainly in Myanmar (Burma), but rubies can also be produced artificially and such synthetic stones are used in ▷lasers.

rudd (or **red eye**) freshwater bony fish allied to the ▷roach. It is tinged with bronze, and has reddish fins, the dorsal being farther back than that of the roach. It is found in British and European lakes and sluggish streams. The largest weigh over 1 kg/2.2 lb and may be as much as 45 cm/18 in long. The rudd *Scardinius erythrophthalmus* belongs to the order Cypriniformes, class Osteichthyes.

Rudolf, Lake former name (to 1979) of Lake ▷Turkana in eastern Africa.

Rudolph two Holy Roman Emperors:

Rudolph I (1218–1291) Holy Roman Emperor from 1273. Originally count of Habsburg, he was the first Habsburg emperor and expanded his dynasty by investing his sons with the duchies of Austria and Styria.

Rudolph II (1552–1612) Holy Roman Emperor from 1576, when he succeeded his father Maximilian II. His policies led to unrest in Hungary and Bohemia, which led to the surrender of Hungary to his brother Matthias in 1608 and religious freedom for Bohemia.

rue shrubby perennial herb native to southern Europe and temperate Asia. It bears clusters of yellow flowers. An oil extracted from the strongly scented blue-green leaves is used in perfumery. (*Ruta graveolens*, family Rutaceae.)

ruff bird *Philomachus pugnax* of the sandpiper family Scolopacidae. The name is taken from the frill of erectile purple-black feathers developed in the breeding season around the neck of the male. The females (reeves) have no ruff; they lay four spotted green eggs in a nest of coarse grass made amongst reeds or rushes. The ruff is found across northern Europe and Asia, and migrates south in winter. It is a casual migrant throughout North America.

rug small ▷carpet.

Rugby market town and railway junction in Warwickshire, central England, on the River Avon, 19 km/12 southeast of Coventry; population (1991) 60,500. Industries include engineering and the manufacture of cement, and the town has a cattle market. Rugby School (1567), a private school for boys, established its reputation under headmaster Thomas Arnold; it was described in Thomas Hughes' semi-autobiographical classic *Tom Brown's Schooldays*. ▷Rugby football originated at the school in 1823.

rugby contact sport that is traditionally believed to have originated at Rugby School, England, in 1823 when a boy, William Webb Ellis, picked up the ball and ran with it while playing football (now soccer). It is now played in two forms: ▷Rugby League and ▷Rugby Union.

Rugby League professional form of rugby football founded in England in 1895 as the Northern Union when a dispute about pay caused northern clubs to break away from the Rugby Football Union. The game is similar to ▷Rugby Union, but the number of players was reduced from 15 to 13 in 1906, and other rule changes have made the game more open and fast-moving.

Related Web site: Sky Sports Online Rugby League http://www.sky.com/sports/rugbyleague/

RUGBY A scrum during a rugby match between England and Russia. A scrum is used to restart play after a knock-on or forward pass. The forwards from either side bind together and then the two packs come together to allow the scrum half to put the ball into the scrum. A scrum can also be awarded or chosen in different circumstances by the referee. *Image Bank*

Rugby Union form of rugby in which there are 15 players on each side. Points are scored by 'tries', scored by 'touching down' the ball beyond the goal line or by kicking goals from penalties. The Rugby Football Union was formed in 1871 and has its headquarters in England (Twickenham, Middlesex).

Formerly an amateur game, the game's status was revoked in August 1995 by the International Rugby Football Board, which lifted restrictions on players moving between Rugby Union and Rugby League.

Related Web site: Planet Rugby http://www.planet-rugby.com/

Ruhr river in Germany, length 235 km/146 mi. It rises in the Rothaargebirge Mountains at the eastern boundary of North Rhine-Westphalia, and flows west to join the Rhine at Duisburg. The Ruhr Valley, a metropolitan industrial area, produces petrochemicals, cars, iron, and steel at Duisburg and Dortmund; it is also a coal-mining area.

Ruisdael (or **Ruysdael**), **Jacob Isaakszoon van** (c. 1628–1682) Dutch artist. He is widely considered the greatest of the Dutch landscape painters. He painted scenes near his native town of Haarlem and in Germany, his works often concentrating on the dramatic aspects of nature. A notable example of his atmospheric style is *The Jewish Cemetery* (c. 1660; Gemäldegalerie, Dresden).

rule of law doctrine that no individual, however powerful, is above the law. The principle had a significant influence on attempts to restrain the arbitrary use of power by rulers and on the growth of legally enforceable human rights in many Western countries. It is often used as a justification for separating legislative from judicial power.

rule of the road convention or law that governs the side of the road on which traffic drives. In Britain, this states that vehicles should be kept to the left of the road or be liable for any ensuing damage. The reverse applies nearly everywhere else in the world, all traffic keeping to the right, which is also the rule at sea and for two ships crossing, when the one having the other on its starboard must give way.

Rumania alternative spelling of ▷Romania.

ruminant any even-toed hoofed mammal with a rumen, the 'first stomach' of its complex digestive system. Plant food is stored and fermented before being brought back to the mouth for chewing (chewing the cud) and then is swallowed to the next stomach. Ruminants include cattle, antelopes, goats, deer, and giraffes, all with a four-chambered stomach. Camels are also ruminants, but they have a three-chambered stomach.

Rump, the English parliament formed between December 1648 and November 1653 after ▷Pride's purge of the ▷Long Parliament to ensure a majority in favour of trying Charles I. It was dismissed in 1653 by Cromwell, who replaced it with the ▷Barebones Parliament.

Reinstated after the Protectorate ended in 1659 and the full membership of the Long Parliament was restored in 1660, the Rump dissolved itself shortly afterwards and was replaced by the Convention Parliament, which brought about the restoration of the monarchy.

Runcie, Robert Alexander Kennedy, Baron Runcie (1921–2000) English cleric, archbishop of Canterbury 1980–91, the first to be appointed on the suggestion of the Church Crown Appointments Commission (formed in 1977) rather than by political consultation. He favoured cooperation with Roman Catholicism and was successful in organizing visits between Canterbury and Rome, although he came under attack for this from some quarters. He presided over General Synods on homosexuality, ecclesiastical remarriage for the divorced, and the ordination of women. He was widely attacked for his liberalism,

but believed himself that such changes would come eventually and that delay should be avoided. He was created Baron in 1991.

Rundstedt, (Karl Rudolf) Gerd von (1875–1953) German field marshal in World War II. Largely responsible for the German breakthrough in France in 1940, he was defeated on the Ukrainian front in 1941. As commander-in-chief in France from 1942, he resisted the Allied invasion in 1944 and in December launched the temporarily successful Ardennes offensive.

After his defeat in the Ukraine he resigned in November 1941 because of Hitler's order that there should be no withdrawals. He was rehabilitated in 1942 and was responsible for the construction of the Atlantic Wall and the defence of 'Fortress Europe'. He had his hands tied in resisting the Allied invasion of Europe by having to have every decision approved by Hitler. Recognizing the position as hopeless, he advocated peace and was dismissed but again recalled in September 1944. He was captured in 1945, but war-crime charges were dropped in 1949 owing to his ill health.

runner (or **stolon**) in botany, aerial stem that produces new plants.

running racing on foot as a sport. There are various kinds of running event: sprinting, middle distance, cross country, road running (e.g. ▷marathons), hurdles, and steeplechase.

Runyon, (Alfred) Damon (1880–1946) US journalist. Primarily a sports reporter, his short stories in 'Guys and Dolls' (1932) deal wryly with the seamier side of New York City life in his own invented jargon.

Rupert, Prince (1619–1682) Called 'Rupert of the Rhine'. English Royalist general and admiral, born in Prague, son of the Elector Palatine Frederick V and James I's daughter Elizabeth. Defeated by Cromwell at ▷Marston Moor and ▷Naseby in the Civil War, he commanded a privateering fleet 1649–52, until routed by Admiral Robert Blake, and, returning after the Restoration, was a distinguished admiral in the Dutch Wars. He founded the ▷Hudson's Bay Company. He was created Duke of Cumberland and Earl of Holderness in 1644.

rupture in medicine, another name for ▷hernia.

rush any of a group of grasslike plants found in wet places in cold and temperate regions. The round stems and flexible leaves of some species have been used for making mats and baskets since ancient times. (Genus *Juncus*, family Juncaceae.)

Rushdie, (Ahmed) Salman (1947–) British writer. He was born in India of a Muslim family. His book *Midnight's Children* (1981) deals with India from the date of independence and won the Booker Prize. His novel *The Satanic Verses* (1988) (the title refers to verses deleted from the Koran) offended many Muslims with alleged blasphemy. In 1989 the Ayatollah Khomeini of Iran placed a religious *fatwa* on Rushdie, calling for him and his publishers to be killed.

In September 1998 the Iranian government pledged formally to dissociate itself from the *fatwa* placed on Rushdie by the late Ayatollah Khomeini; the *fatwa*, however, continued to stand. The agreement, which had been under secret negotiation between the two governments since early 1989 ended nearly ten years of diplomatic chill between Britain and Iran. Both sides agreed on the normalization of diplomatic relations and the imminent exchange of ambassadors.

Rusk, (David) Dean (1909–1994) US Democrat politician. He was secretary of state to presidents J F Kennedy and L B Johnson 1961–69, and became unpopular through his involvement with the ▷Vietnam War.

Ruskin, John (1819–1900) English art and social critic. Much of his finest art criticism appeared in two widely influential works, *Modern Painters* (1843–60) and *The Seven Lamps of Architecture* (1849). He was a keen advocate of painters considered unorthodox at the time, such as J M W ▷Turner and members of the ▷Pre-Raphaelite Brotherhood. His later writings were concerned with social and economic problems.

Ruskin was one of the major figures of 19th-century British intellectual life. Like his contemporaries Thomas ▷Carlyle and Matthew ▷Arnold, he was an outspoken critic of Victorian society, and, like them, called for a renewal of British moral, intellectual, and artistic life. His early works were concerned with architecture and painting: his support both for the Pre-Raphaelite Brotherhood and the Gothic Revival had a profound effect on Victorian art, architecture, and crafts.

From these aesthetic concerns he increasingly drew social and moral views, and from the 1860s he devoted himself to political and economic problems, condemning *laissez-faire* economics, and extolling both the dignity of labour and the moral and aesthetic value of 'craftsmanship'. His beliefs took a practical turn, and he played a leading role in providing education and decent housing for working people.

Russell, Bertrand Arthur William (1872–1970) 3rd Earl

Russell. English philosopher, mathematician, and peace campaigner. He contributed to the development of modern mathematical logic and wrote about social issues. His works include *Principia Mathematica* (1910–13; with A N Whitehead), in which he attempted to show that mathematics could be reduced to a branch of logic; *The Problems of Philosophy* (1912); and *A History of Western Philosophy* (1946). He was an outspoken liberal pacifist. He was awarded the Nobel Prize for Literature in 1950. He was made an Earl in 1931.

    Related Web site: Bertrand Russell Society
    http://www.users.drew.edu/~jlenz/brs.html

Russell, Jane (1921–) US actor. She was discovered by the

producer Howard Hughes, and promoted as a 'pin-up girl'. Her first film *The Outlaw* (1943), was not properly released for several years because of censorship problems. Other films include *The Paleface* (1948), *Gentlemen Prefer Blondes* (1953), and *The Revolt of Mamie Stover* (1957).

Russell, John (1792–1878) 1st Earl Russell; known until 1861

as Lord John Russell. British Liberal politician, son of the 6th Duke of Bedford. He entered the House of Commons in 1813 and supported Catholic emancipation and the Reform Bill. He held cabinet posts 1830–41, became prime minister 1846–52, and was again a cabinet minister until becoming prime minister again 1865–66. He retired after the defeat of his Reform Bill in 1866.

As foreign secretary in Aberdeen's coalition government in 1852 and in Palmerston's second government 1859–65, Russell assisted Italy's struggle for unity, although his indecisive policies on Poland, Denmark, and the American Civil War provoked much criticism. He had a strained relationship with Palmerston. He was created Earl in 1861.

> **John Ruskin**
> *Life without industry is guilt, and industry without art is brutality.*
> Lectures on Art 3, 'The Relation of Art to Morals' 23 February 1870

Russell, Ken (Henry Kenneth

Alfred) (1927–) English film director. His work, typified by stylistic extravagance, includes *Women in Love* (1969), *The Music Lovers* (1971), *Tommy* (1975), *Lisztomania* (1975), and *Gothic* (1986),. His work is often criticized for self-indulgence, containing gratuitous sex and violence, but is also regarded for its vitality and imagination.

Russell, William, Lord (1639–1683) British Whig politician. Son of the 1st Duke of Bedford, he was among the founders of the Whig Party and actively supported attempts in Parliament to exclude the Roman Catholic James II from succeeding to the throne. In 1683 he was accused, on dubious evidence, of complicity in the Rye House Plot to murder Charles II, and was executed. He used the courtesy title Lord Russell from 1678.

Russia country name originally designating the prerevolutionary Russian Empire (until 1917), now used to refer informally to the ▷Russian Federation.

Russian art painting and sculpture of Russia, including art from the USSR 1917–91. For centuries Russian art was dominated by an unchanging tradition of church art inherited from Byzantium, responding slowly and hesitantly to Western influences. Briefly, in the early 20th century, it assumed a leading and influential role in European avant-garde art. However, official Soviet disapproval of this trend resulted in its suppression in favour of art geared to the glorification of workers.

Russian civil war bitter conflict in Russia (1918–21), which followed Russian setbacks in World War I and the upheavals of the 1917 ▷Russian Revolution. In December 1917 counter-revolutionary armies, the ▷Whites, began to organize resistance to the October Revolution of 1917. The ▷Red Army (Bolsheviks), improvised by Leon ▷Trotsky, opposed them and civil war resulted. The Bolsheviks eventually emerged victorious.

The war was fought in the regions of the Caucasus and southern Russia, the Ukraine, the Baltic, northern Russia, and Siberia.

Foreign involvement The Bolsheviks also had to fight against the armies of Latvia, Lithuania, Estonia, and Finland. In northern Russia the British and French landed troops at Murmansk in June 1918, seized Archangel, and set up a puppet government. They continued outbursts of fighting against the Bolsheviks until

October 1919. In Siberia, Admiral Kolchak, with the assistance of a Czech legion (composed of prisoners of war) and of Japanese forces that had landed at Vladivostok, established a White government in Omsk, western Siberia. Kolchak was captured and executed by the Bolsheviks in February 1920.

Bolshevik victory While each of the White armies was engaged in an isolated operation, the Soviet forces were waging a single war. Trotsky was an active agent for the Bolsheviks in all the crucial operations of the war. The Bolsheviks put down peasant risings in 1920 and the ▷Kronstadt rising, a mutiny by sailors of the Russian Baltic Fleet at Kronstadt, outside Petrograd (St Petersburg), in March 1921. Bolshevik leaders ▷Lenin and Trotsky used severe measures to achieve the suppression of the peasant risings. Whole villages were burnt to the ground and their populations executed, while the inhabitants of local villages were forced to watch as a warning not to oppose the Bolsheviks. The Bolsheviks were far superior to the Whites in both organization and propaganda. The last foreign forces left Soviet soil in 1922 when the Japanese evacuated Vladivostok. The Soviet government was recognized by Britain in 1924 and by the USA in 1933.

Russian Federation (or **Russia**) see country box.

Russian literature literary works produced in Russia and later in the USSR. Religious works and oral tradition in Slavonic survive from the 11th–17th centuries. The golden age of the 19th century produced the poetry of Alexander Pushkin and novels by such literary giants as Fyodor Dostoevsky and Leo Tolstoy, and in drama the innovative genius of Anton Chekhov. During the Soviet era many writers, among them Alexander Solzhenitsyn, were imprisoned or exiled.

Russian Orthodox Church another name for the ▷Orthodox Church.

Russian Revolution two revolutions of February and October 1917 (Julian ▷calendar) that began with the overthrow of the Romanov dynasty and ended with the establishment of a communist soviet (council) state, the Union of Soviet Socialist Republics (USSR). In October Bolshevik workers and sailors, led by Vladimir Ilyich ▷Lenin, seized government buildings and took over power.

The **February Revolution** (March by the Western calendar) arose because of food and fuel shortages, continuing repression by the tsarist government, and military incompetence in World War I. Riots broke out in Petrograd (as St Petersburg was known 1914–24), which led to the abdication of Tsar Nicholas II and the

---

Russian Tsars

In 1547 Ivan the Terrible was the first ruler to take the title of tsar.

Reign	Name
House of Rurik	
1547–84	Ivan the Terrible
1584–98	Theodore (Fyodor) I
1598	Irina
House of Godunov	
1598–1605	Boris Godunov
1605	Theodore (Fyodor) II
Usurpers	
1605–06	Dimitri III
1606–10	Basil IV
1610–13	interregnum
House of Romanov	
1613–45	Michael Romanov
1645–76	Alexis
1676–82	Theodore III
1682–96	Peter (I) the Great and Ivan V (brothers)
1689–1721	Peter I, as tsar
1721–25	Peter I, as emperor
1725–27	Catherine I
1727–30	Peter II
1730–40	Anna Ivanovna
1740–41	Ivan VI
1741–62	Elizabeth
1762	Peter III
1762–96	Catherine (II) the Great
1796–1801	Paul
1801–25	Alexander I
1825–55	Nicholas I
1855–81	Alexander II
1881–94	Alexander III
1894–1917	Nicholas II (abdicated)

Russian Revolution: Key Dates (Western Calendar)

1894	Beginning of the reign of Tsar Nicholas II.
1898	Formation of the Social Democratic Party among industrial workers under the influence of Georgi Plekhanov and Lenin.
1901	Formation of the Socialist Revolutionary Party.
1903	Split in Social Democratic Party at the party's second congress (London Conference) into Bolsheviks and Mensheviks.
1905	(January) 'Bloody Sunday', where repression of workers in St Petersburg leads to widespread strikes and the '1905 Revolution'.
	(October) Strikes and the first 'soviet' (local revolutionary council) in St Petersburg. October constitution provides for new parliament (Duma).
	(December) Insurrection of workers in Moscow. Punitive repression by the 'Black Hundreds'.
1914	(July) Outbreak of war between Russia and the Central Powers.
1917	(March) Outbreak of riots in Petrograd (St Petersburg). Tsar Nicholas abdicates. Provisional government is established under Prince Lvov. Power struggles between government and Petrograd soviet.
	(April) Lenin arrives in Petrograd. He demands the transfer of power to soviets; an end to the war; the seizure of land by the peasants; control of industry by the workers.
	(July) Bolsheviks attempt to seize power in Petrograd. Trotsky is arrested and Lenin is in hiding. Alexandr Kerensky becomes head of a provisional government.
	(September) Lavr Kornilov coup fails owing to strike by workers. Kerensky's government weakens.
	(November) Bolshevik Revolution. Military revolutionary committee and Red Guards seize government offices and the Winter Palace, arresting all the members of the provisional government. Second All-Russian Congress of Soviets creates the Council of Peoples Commissars as new governmental authority. It is led by Lenin, with Trotsky as commissar for war and Stalin as commissar for national minorities. Land Decree orders immediate distribution of land to the peasants. Banks are nationalized and national debt repudiated. Elections to the Constituent Assembly give large majority to the Socialist Revolutionary Party. Bolsheviks a minority.
1918	(January) Constituent Assembly meets in Petrograd but is almost immediately broken up by Red Guards.
	(March) Treaty of Brest-Litovsk marks the end of the war with the Central Powers but with massive losses of territory.
	(July) Murder of the tsar and his family.
1918–20	Civil War in Russia between Red Army led by Trotsky and White Russian force. Red Army ultimately victorious.
1923	(6 July) Constitution of USSR adopted.

RUSSIAN REVOLUTION Russian workers fill the streets to listen to a speaker in 1917. *Image Bank*

formation of a provisional government, made up of liberals and a few social democrats, under Prince Gyorgy Yevgenevich Lvov (1861–1925). Lvov was then replaced as head of government by Alexander Kerensky, a respected orator who was concerned to stabilize the revolution. The government had little support, however, as troops, communications, and transport were controlled by the Petrograd Soviet of Workers, Peasants, and Soldiers, which was originally formed during the failed revolution of 1905. In April Lenin returned to Russia (after having been exiled since 1905) as head of the Bolsheviks, and under his command the Bolsheviks gained control of the soviets; advocated land reform (under the slogan 'All power to the Soviets'); and appealed for an end to Russian involvement in World War I, which Lenin characterized as an 'Imperialist' war.

The **October Revolution** was a coup on the night of 25–26 October (6–7 November by the Western calendar). Bolshevik workers and sailors seized the government buildings and the Winter Palace, Petrograd, where they arrested the ministers of the provisional government in the name of the people. The second All-Russian Congress of Soviets, which met the following day, proclaimed itself the new government of Russia, and Lenin became leader. In his speech to the Congress he announced an immediate end to Russian involvement in the war and advocated the return of the land to the peasants. The Bolsheviks soon took control of the cities, established worker control in factories, and nationalized the banks. They also set up the Cheka (secret police) to silence the opposition, and, in 1918, concluded peace with Germany through the Treaty of ▷Brest-Litovsk. In the same year the ▷Russian civil war broke out, when anti-Bolshevik elements within the army attempted to seize power. The war lasted until 1922, when the Red Army, organized by Leon ▷Trotsky, finally overcame ▷White (tsarist) opposition, but with huge losses, after which communist control was complete. Some 2 million refugees fled from Russia during these years.

Related Web site: Russian Revolution http://www.barnsdle.demon.co.uk/russ/rusrev.html

Russian revolution, 1905 political upheaval centred in and around St Petersburg, Russia (1905–06), leading up to the February and October revolutions of 1917. On 22 January 1905 thousands of striking unarmed workers marched to Tsar Nicholas II's Winter Palace in St Petersburg to ask for reforms. Government troops fired on the crowd, killing many people. After this 'Bloody Sunday' slaughter the revolution gained strength, culminating in a general strike which paralysed the whole country in October 1905. Revolutionaries in St Petersburg formed a 'soviet' (council) called the Soviet of Workers' Deputies. Nicholas II then granted the Duma (parliament) the power to pass or reject proposed laws. Although these measures satisfied the liberal element, the revolution continued to gain ground and came to a head when the army crushed a serious uprising in December 1905.

Russian Soviet Federal Socialist Republic (RSFSR) the largest republic of the former Soviet Union; it became independent as the ▷Russian Federation in 1991.

Russo-Japanese War war between Russia and Japan 1904–05, which arose from conflicting ambitions in Korea and ▷Manchuria, specifically, the Russian occupation of Port Arthur (modern Lüshun) in 1897 and of the Amur province in 1900. Japan successfully besieged Port Arthur May 1904–January 1905, took Mukden (modern Shenyang, see ▷Mukden, Battle of) on 29 February–10 March, and on 27 May defeated the Russian Baltic fleet, which had sailed halfway around the world to Tsushima Strait. A peace treaty was signed on 23 August 1905. Russia surrendered its lease on Port Arthur, ceded southern Sakhalin to Japan, evacuated Manchuria, and recognized Japan's interests in Korea.

russula any of a large group of fungi (see ▷fungus), containing many species. They are medium-to-large mushrooms with flattened caps and many are brightly coloured. (Genus *Russula*.)

rust in botany, common name for a group of minute parasitic fungi (see ▷fungus) that appear on the leaves of their hosts as orange-red spots, later becoming darker. The commonest is the wheat rust (*Puccinia graminis*, order Uredinales.)

rust reddish-brown oxide of iron formed by the action of moisture and oxygen on the metal. It consists mainly of hydrated iron(III) oxide ($Fe_2O_3.H_2O$) and iron(III) hydroxide ($Fe(OH)_3$). Rusting is the commonest form of ▷corrosion.

Rust prevention There are two main approaches to protect against rusting. **Barrier methods** introduce a barrier between the metal and the air and moisture to minimize the reaction. This is the commonest method of rust prevention and the barrier may consist of a layer of grease, paint, plastic, or an unreactive metal, such as tin, copper, or chromium.

In **sacrificial protection**, the iron is actually covered by a more reactive metal, such a zinc (galvanization), or connected to a more

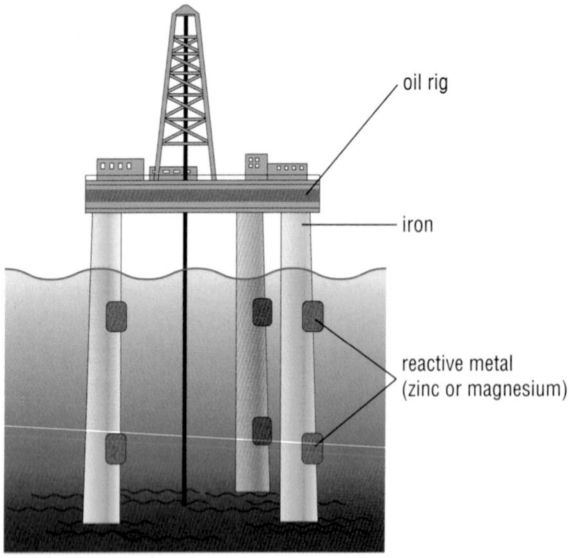

RUST Sacrificial metal is used to protect pipes and other exposed metal on oil rigs from corrosion by rust.

reactive metal, such as magnesium, so that as long as the 'sacrificial' metal is present it will corrode first.

Ruthenia (or **Carpathian Ukraine**) region of central Europe, on the southern slopes of the Carpathian Mountains, home of the Ruthenes or Russniaks. Dominated by Hungary from the 10th century, it was part of Austria-Hungary until World War I. In 1918 it was divided between Czechoslovakia, Poland, and Romania; independent for a single day in 1938, it was immediately occupied by Hungary, captured by the USSR in 1944 and incorporated 1945–47 (as the Transcarpathian Region) into Ukraine Republic, which became independent as Ukraine in 1991.

ruthenium hard, brittle, silver-white, metallic element, symbol Ru, atomic number 44, relative atomic mass 101.07. It is one of the so-called platinum group of metals; it occurs in platinum ores as a free metal and in the natural alloy osmiridium. It is used as a hardener in alloys and as a catalyst; its compounds are used as colouring agents in glass and ceramics.It was discovered in 1827 and named in 1828 after its place of discovery, the Ural Mountains in Ruthenia (now part of Ukraine). Pure ruthenium was not isolated until 1845.

Rutherford, Ernest (1871–1937) 1st Baron Rutherford of Nelson. New Zealand-born British physicist. He was a pioneer of modern atomic science. His main research was in the field of ▷radioactivity, and he discovered alpha, beta, and gamma rays. He was the first to recognize the nuclear nature of the atom in 1911. He was awarded the Nobel Prize for Chemistry in 1908 for his work in atomic disintegration and the chemistry of radioactive substances.

Rutherford produced the first artificial transformation, changing one element to another (1919) by bombarding nitrogen with alpha particles and getting hydrogen and oxygen. After further research he announced that the nucleus of any atom must contain hydrogen nuclei; at Rutherford's suggestion, the name 'proton' was given to the hydrogen nucleus in 1920. He speculated that uncharged particles (neutrons) must also exist in the nucleus. In 1934, using heavy water, Rutherford and his co-workers bombarded deuterium with deuterons and produced tritium. This may be considered the first ▷nuclear fusion reaction. He was knighted in 1914, and created Baron in 1931.

Ernest Rutherford

When we have found how the nuclei of atoms are built up we shall have found the greatest secret of all – except life. We shall have found the basis of everything – of the earth we walk on, of the air we breathe, of the sunshine, of our physical body itself, of everything in the world, however great or however small – except life.

Passing Show 24

Rutherford, Margaret (1892–1972) English film and theatre actor. She specialized in formidable yet jovially eccentric roles. She played Agatha Christie's Miss Marple in four films in the early 1960s and won an Academy Award for her role in *The VIPs* (1963). She was made a DBE in 1967.

rutherfordium synthesized, radioactive, metallic element, symbol Rf. It is the first of the ▷transactinide series, atomic number 104, relative atomic mass 262. It is produced by bombarding californium with carbon nuclei and has ten isotopes, the longest-lived of which, Rf-262, has a half-life of 70 seconds. Two institutions claim to be the first to have synthesized it: the Joint Institute for Nuclear Research in Dubna, Russia, in 1964; and the University of California at Berkeley, USA, in 1969.

rutile titanium oxide mineral, TiO_2, a naturally occurring ore of titanium. It is usually reddish brown to black, with a very bright (adamantine) surface lustre. It crystallizes in the tetragonal system. Rutile is common in a wide range of igneous and metamorphic rocks and also occurs concentrated in sands; the coastal sands of eastern and western Australia are a major source. It is also used as a pigment that gives a brilliant white to paint, paper, and plastics.

Rutland unitary authority in central England, formerly the smallest English county, which was part of ▷Leicestershire 1974–1997.
area 394 sq km/152 sq mi **towns and cities** Oakham (administrative headquarters), Uppingham **physical** rivers Chater, Eye, Gwash, and Welland **features** Rutland Water, a large reservoir in the valley of the Gwash at Empingham, with outdoor leisure facilities (sailing, cycling, birdwatching); historic villages and churches, including Braunston-in-Rutland, Preston, Wing, and Exton **agriculture** cereals (barley, wheat), sugar beet, potatoes; sheep and cattle are reared, and Stilton cheese is produced **industries** clothing, engineering, and plastics; limestone and ironstone are quarried **population** (1996) 34,600 **famous people** Charles Boys, Robert of Ketton

Rutskoi, Aleksander (1947–) Russian politician, founder of the reformist Communists for Democracy group, and vice president of the Russian Federation 1991–93. During the abortive August 1991 coup he led the Russian delegation to rescue Soviet leader Mikhail Gorbachev from his forced confinement in the Crimea. In September 1993, with Ruslan Khasbulatov, he led the insurrection against Russian president Boris Yeltsin. Both men were arrested and imprisoned but then released in 1994 on the instructions of the federal assembly. Shortly after his release, Rutskoi, as leader of the Russian Social Democratic People's Party, professed his support for a reconstituted Soviet Union. In August 1996 Rutskoi became a leading member of the communist-led Patriotic Popular Union of Russia. He was elected governor of Kursk in southwestern Russia in October 1996.

Ruysdael, Jacob van Dutch painter; see Jacob van ▷Ruisdael.

Ruyter, Michiel Adriaanszoon de (1607–1676) Dutch admiral who led his country's fleet in the wars against England. On 1–4 June 1666 he forced the British fleet under Rupert and Albemarle to retire into the Thames, but on 25 July was heavily defeated off the North Foreland, Kent. In 1667 he sailed up the Medway, burning three men-of-war at Chatham, and capturing others.

Rwanda see country box.

Ryazan (formerly **Pereyaslav-Ryazanski** (1237–1778)) capital city of Ryazan oblast (region), Russian Federation, 175 km/109 mi southeast of Moscow; population (1996 est) 536,000. Industries include engineering, oil refining, food processing, and a variety of light industries.

Rydberg constant in physics, a constant that relates atomic spectra to the ▷spectrum of hydrogen. Its value is 1.0977×10^7 per metre.

Ryder, Albert Pinkham (1847–1917) US painter. He was one of the most original US artists of the 19th century. His romantic landscapes, moonlit seascapes, and depictions of scenes from Shakespeare and Wagner are intense, poetic, and dreamlike. His best-known work, *Death on a Pale Horse* (*c.* 1910; Cleveland Museum of Art), has an eerie, haunted quality.

Russia

Russia formerly Russian Soviet Federal Socialist Republic (RSFSR; within the Soviet Union USSR) (until 1991) country in northern Asia and eastern Europe, bounded north by the Arctic Ocean; east by the Bering Sea and the Sea of Okhotsk; west by Norway, Finland, the Baltic States, Belarus, and Ukraine; and south by China, Mongolia, Georgia, Azerbaijan, and Kazakhstan.

NATIONAL NAME *Rossiiskaya Federatsiya/Russian Federation*

AREA 17,075,400 sq km/6,592,811 sq mi

CAPITAL Moscow

MAJOR TOWNS/CITIES St Petersburg, Nizhniy Novgorod, Samara, Yekaterinburg, Novosibirsk, Chelyabinsk, Kazan, Omsk, Perm, Ufa

PHYSICAL FEATURES fertile Black Earth district; extensive forests; the Ural Mountains with large mineral resources; Lake Baikal, world's deepest lake

Government

HEAD OF STATE Vladimir Putin from 2000

HEAD OF GOVERNMENT Mikhail Fradkov from 2004

POLITICAL SYSTEM emergent democracy

POLITICAL EXECUTIVE limited presidency

ADMINISTRATIVE DIVISIONS 21 republics, 6 provinces, 49 regions, 10 autonomous districts, two cities with federal status (Moscow and St Petersburg), and one autonomous area

ARMED FORCES 988,100; plus paramilitary forces of 409,100 (2002 est)

CONSCRIPTION 18–24 months

DEATH PENALTY retained and used for ordinary crimes

DEFENCE SPEND (% GDP) 4.8 (2002 est)

EDUCATION SPEND (% GDP) 2.9 (2001 est)

HEALTH SPEND (% GDP) 5.3 (2000 est)

Economy and resources

CURRENCY rouble

GPD (US$) 346.5 billion (2002 est)

REAL GDP GROWTH (% change on previous year) 5 (2001)

GNI (US$) 307.9 billion (2002 est)

GNI PER CAPITA (PPP) (US$) 7,820 (2002 est)

CONSUMER PRICE INFLATION 13.4% (2003 est)

UNEMPLOYMENT 8.7% (2001)

FOREIGN DEBT (US$) 116.9 billion (2001 est)

MAJOR TRADING PARTNERS Ukraine, Germany, Belarus, Ukraine, Kazakhstan, USA, Italy

RESOURCES petroleum, natural gas, coal, peat, copper (world's fourth-largest producer), iron ore, lead, aluminium, phosphate rock, nickel, manganese, gold, diamonds, platinum, zinc, tin

INDUSTRIES cast iron, steel, rolled iron, synthetic fibres, soap, cellulose, paper, cement, machinery and transport equipment, glass, bricks, food processing, confectionery

EXPORTS mineral fuels, ferrous and non-ferrous metals and derivatives, precious stones, chemical products, machinery and transport equipment, weapons, timber and paper products. Principal market: Germany 9.2% (2001)

IMPORTS machinery and transport equipment, grain and foodstuffs, chemical products, textiles, clothing, footwear, pharmaceuticals, metals. Principal source: Germany 13.8% (2001)

ARABLE LAND 7.4% (2000 est)

AGRICULTURAL PRODUCTS grain, potatoes, flax, sunflower seed, vegetables, fruit and berries, tea; livestock and dairy farming

Population and society

POPULATION 143,246,000 (2003 est)

POPULATION GROWTH RATE –0.5% (2000–15)

POPULATION DENSITY (per sq km) 8 (2003 est)

URBAN POPULATION (% of total) 73 (2003 est)

AGE DISTRIBUTION (% of total population) 0–14 16%, 15–59 66%, 60+ 18% (2002 est)

ETHNIC GROUPS predominantly ethnic Russian (eastern Slav); significant Tatar, Ukranian, Chuvash, Belarussian, Bashkir, and Chechen minorities; over 130 nationalities

LANGUAGE Russian (official) and many East Slavic, Altaic, Uralic, Caucasian languages

RELIGION traditionally Russian Orthodox; significant Muslim and Buddhist communities

EDUCATION (compulsory years) 9

LITERACY RATE 99% (men); 99% (women) (2003 est)

LABOUR FORCE 11.8% agriculture, 29.4% industry, 58.8% services (1999)

LIFE EXPECTANCY 61 (men); 73 (women) (2000–05)

CHILD MORTALITY RATE (under 5, per 1,000 live births) 21 (2001)

PHYSICIANS (per 1,000 people) 4.2 (1999 est)

HOSPITAL BEDS (per 1,000 people) 12.1 (1999 est)

TV SETS (per 1,000 people) 538 (2001 est)

RADIOS (per 1,000 people) 418 (1997)

INTERNET USERS (per 10,000 people) 409.3 (2002 est)

PERSONAL COMPUTER USERS (per 100 people) 8.9 (2002 est)

See also ▷Cold War; ▷Commonwealth of Independent States; ▷Russian Revolution; ▷Union of Soviet Socialist Republics.

Russia (cont.)

Chronology

9th–10th centuries: Viking chieftains established own rule in Novgorod, Kiev, and other cities.

10th–12th centuries: Kiev temporarily united Russian peoples into its empire. Christianity introduced from Constantinople 988.

13th century: Mongols (Golden Horde) overran the southern steppes in 1223, compelling Russian princes to pay tribute.

14th century: Byelorussia and Ukraine came under Polish rule.

1462–1505: Ivan the Great, grand duke of Muscovy, threw off Mongol yoke and united lands in the northwest.

1547–84: Ivan the Terrible assumed title of tsar and conquered Kazan and Astrakhan; colonization of Siberia began.

1613: First Romanov tsar, Michael, elected after period of chaos.

1667: Following Cossack revolt, eastern Ukraine reunited with Russia.

1682–1725: Peter the Great modernized the bureaucracy and army; he founded a navy and a new capital, St Petersburg, introduced Western education, and wrested the Baltic seaboard from Sweden. By 1700 colonization of Siberia had reached the Pacific.

1762–96: Catherine the Great annexed the Crimea and part of Poland and recovered western Ukraine and Byelorussia.

1798–1814: Russia intervened in Revolutionary and Napoleonic Wars (1798–1801, 1805–07); repelled Napoleon, and took part in his overthrow (1812–14).

1827–29: Russian attempts to dominate the Balkans led to a war with Turkey.

1853–56: Crimean War.

1856–64: Caucasian War of conquest completed the annexation of northern Caucasus, causing more than a million people to emigrate.

1858–60: Treaties of Aigun (1858) and Peking (1860) imposed on China, annexing territories north of the Amur and east of the Ussuri rivers; Vladivostok founded on Pacific coast.

1861: Serfdom abolished. Rapid growth of industry followed, a working-class movement developed, and revolutionary ideas spread, culminating in the assassination of Alexander II in 1881.

1877–78: Russo-Turkish War

1898: Social Democratic Party founded by Russian Marxists; split into Bolshevik and Menshevik factions in 1903.

1904–05: Russo-Japanese War caused by Russian expansion in Manchuria.

1905: A revolution, though suppressed, forced tsar to accept parliament (Duma) with limited powers.

1914: Russo-Austrian rivalry in Balkans was a major cause of outbreak of World War I; Russia fought in alliance with France and Britain.

1917: Russian Revolution: tsar abdicated, provisional government established; Bolsheviks seized power under Vladimir Lenin.

1918: Treaty of Brest-Litovsk ended war with Germany; murder of former tsar; Russian Empire collapsed; Finland, Poland, and Baltic States seceded.

1918–22: Civil War between Red Army, led by Leon Trotsky, and White Russian forces with foreign support; Red Army ultimately victorious; control regained over Ukraine, Caucasus, and Central Asia.

1922: Former Russian Empire renamed Union of Soviet Socialist Republics.

1924: Death of Lenin.

1928: Joseph Stalin emerged as absolute ruler after ousting Trotsky.

1928–33: First five-year plan collectivized agriculture by force; millions died in famine.

1936–38: The Great Purge: Stalin executed his critics and imprisoned millions of people on false charges of treason and sabotage.

1939: Nazi-Soviet nonaggression pact; USSR invaded eastern Poland and attacked Finland.

1940: USSR annexed Baltic States.

1941–45: 'Great Patriotic War' against Germany ended with Soviet domination of eastern Europe and led to 'Cold War' with USA and its allies.

1949: Council for Mutual Economic Assistance (Comecon) created to supervise trade in Soviet bloc.

1953: Stalin died; 'collective leadership' in power.

1955: Warsaw Pact created.

1956: Nikita Khrushchev made 'secret speech' criticizing Stalin; USSR invaded Hungary.

1957–58: Khrushchev ousted his rivals and became effective leader, introducing limited reforms.

1960: Rift between USSR and Communist China.

1962: Cuban missile crisis: Soviet nuclear missiles installed in Cuba but removed after ultimatum from USA.

1964: Khrushchev ousted by new 'collective leadership' headed by Leonid Brezhnev and Alexei Kosygin.

1968: USSR and allies invaded Czechoslovakia.

1970s: 'Détente' with USA and western Europe.

1979: USSR invaded Afghanistan; fighting continued until Soviet withdrawal ten years later.

1985: Mikhail Gorbachev became leader and announced wide-ranging reform programme (*perestroika*).

1986: Chernobyl nuclear disaster.

1988: Special All-Union Party Congress approved radical constitutional changes and market reforms; start of open nationalist unrest in Caucasus and Baltic republics.

1989: Multi-candidate elections held in move towards 'socialist democracy'; collapse of Soviet satellite regimes in eastern Europe; end of Cold War.

1990: Baltic and Caucasian republics defied central government; Boris Yeltsin became president of Russian Federation and left the Communist Party.

1991: There was an unsuccessful coup by hardline communists; republics declared independence; communist rule dissolved in the Russian Federation; the USSR was replaced by a loose Commonwealth of Independent States (CIS). Mikhail Gorbachev, president of the USSR, resigned, leaving power to Yeltsin.

1992: Russia assumed former USSR seat on the United Nations (UN) Security Council; a new constitution was devised; end of price controls.

1993: There was a power struggle between Yeltsin and the Congress of People's Deputies; congress was dissolved; an attempted coup was foiled; a new parliament was elected.

1994: Russia joined NATO 'Partnership for Peace'; Russian forces invaded the breakaway republic of Chechnya.

1997: A peace treaty was signed with Chechnya. Yeltsin signed an agreement on cooperation with NATO. Russia gained effective admission to the G-7 group.

1998: President Yeltsin sacked the government and appointed Sergei Kiriyenko as prime minister. The rouble was heavily devalued. Yevgeny Primakov replaced Kiriyenko as prime minister and market-centred reform was abandoned. The USA pledged aid of over 3 million tonnes of grain and meat, after a 5% contraction in GDP in 1998.

1999: Yeltsin dismissed first Primakov's government, and then in August, Stepashin's government, appointing Vladimir Putin as prime minister. Troubles with Chechnya continued and Russian forces claimed to have surrounded the capital, Groznyy, and issued an ultimatum to civilians that they must leave or die. After western protests the Russian ultimatum was deferred by a week. President Yeltsin resigned on 31 December, and Putin took over as acting president.

2000: Vladimir Putin was elected president and sought to reassert central control. He installed Mikhail Kasyanov as his prime minister. The Russian army in Chechnya declared it had secured control of the region, despite continuing rebel activity. In August a nuclear-powered submarine, the *Kursk*, sank after an explosion caused by the misfire of a torpedo. Putin was slow to request Western help in the abortive rescue mission, and all 118 crew died.

2001: Putin announced that control of the war in Chechnya would be transferred to the secret police.

2002: The 1972 Anti-Ballistic Missile (ABM) Treaty between the US and the then Soviet Union lapsed when the US withdrew. US President George Bush visited Moscow to sign a Strategic Offensive Reduction Treaty (SORT), to reduce US and Russian strategic nuclear arsenals by two-thirds by the end of 2012.

RUSSIA The Kremlin (left), the centre of government in Russia and the seat of the Russian Orthodox church, and 16th century St Basil's Cathedral (right) in the centre of Moscow. *Corel*

Ryle, Martin (1918–1984) English radio astronomer. At the Mullard Radio Astronomy Observatory, Cambridge, he developed the technique of sky-mapping using 'aperture synthesis', combining smaller dish aerials to give the characteristics of one large one. His work on the distribution of radio sources in the universe brought confirmation of the ▷Big Bang theory. He was awarded with his co-worker, the English radio astronomer Antony ▷Hewish, the Nobel Prize for Physics in 1974 for his work on the development of radio astronomy, particularly the aperture-synthesis technique, and the discovery of ▷pulsars, rapidly rotating neutron stars that emit pulses of energy. He was knighted in 1966.

Rysbrack, Jan Michiel (1694–1770) Dutch-born sculptor, settled in England from 1720. Working in a style of restrained baroque, he established an extensive practice in monumental sculpture, his work being found in many English churches. Some of his portraits and tombs are in Westminster Abbey, London, including the monument to the scientist Isaac Newton (1731).

Ryukyu Islands (or **Riukiu** or **Nansei**) southernmost island group of Japan, stretching towards Taiwan and including ▷Okinawa, Miyako, and Ishigaki; area 2,254 sq km/870 sq mi; population (1995 est) 1,260,000. The capital is ▷Naha (on Okinawa). Produce includes sugar, pineapples, and fish.

Ryzhkov, Nikolai Ivanovich (1929–) Russian politician. He held governmental and party posts from 1975 before being brought into the Politburo and serving as prime minister 1985–90 under Gorbachev. A low-profile technocrat, Ryzhkov was the author of unpopular economic reforms. In August 1996 he became a leading member of the communist-led Patriotic Popular Union of Russia, one of the main left-wing factions in Russia's Duma.

Rwanda

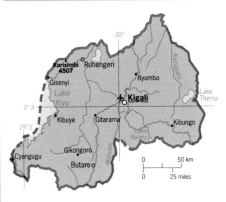

Rwanda formerly Ruanda (until 1962) landlocked country in central Africa, bounded north by Uganda, east by Tanzania, south by Burundi, and west by the Democratic Republic of Congo (formerly Zaire).

NATIONAL NAME *Republika y'u Rwanda/Republic of Rwanda*
AREA 26,338 sq km/10,169 sq mi
CAPITAL Kigali
MAJOR TOWNS/CITIES Butare, Ruhengeri, Gisenyi, Kibungo, Cyangugu
PHYSICAL FEATURES high savannah and hills, with volcanic mountains in northwest; part of lake Kivu; highest peak Mount Karisimbi 4,507 m/14,792 ft; Kagera River (whose headwaters are the source of the Nile)

Government

HEAD OF STATE Paul Kagame from 2000
HEAD OF GOVERNMENT Bernard Makuza from 2000
POLITICAL SYSTEM authoritarian nationalist
POLITICAL EXECUTIVE unlimited presidency
ADMINISTRATIVE DIVISIONS 12 prefectures

ARMED FORCES 70,000 (2002 est)
CONSCRIPTION military service is voluntary
DEATH PENALTY retains and used for ordinary crimes
DEFENCE SPEND (% GDP) 4.1 (2002 est)
EDUCATION SPEND (% GDP) 2.8 (2001 est)
HEALTH SPEND (% GDP) 5.2 (2000 est)

Economy and resources

CURRENCY Rwandan franc
GPD (US$) 1.7 billion (2002 est)
REAL GDP GROWTH (% change on previous year) 6.7 (2001)
GNI (US$) 1.9 billion (2002 est)
GNI PER CAPITA (PPP) (US$) 1,210 (2002 est)
CONSUMER PRICE INFLATION 3% (2003 est)
FOREIGN DEBT (US$) 1.2 billion (2001 est)
MAJOR TRADING PARTNERS Germany, Kenya, Belgium, France, India, Tanzania, UK, USA

RESOURCES cassiterite (a tin-bearing ore), wolframite (a tungsten-bearing ore), natural gas, gold, columbo-tantalite, beryl
INDUSTRIES food processing, beverages, tobacco, mining, chemicals, rubber and plastic products, metals and metal products, machinery
EXPORTS coffee, tea, tin ores and concentrates, pyrethrum, quinquina, hides. Principal market: Germany 39.4% (2001)
IMPORTS food, clothing, mineral fuels and lubricants, construction materials, transport equipment, machinery, tools, consumer goods. Principal source: Kenya 25.7% (2001)
ARABLE LAND 36.5% (2000 est)
AGRICULTURAL PRODUCTS sweet potatoes, cassava, dry beans, sorghum, plantains, coffee, tea, pyrethrum; livestock rearing (long-horned Ankole cattle and goats)

Population and society

POPULATION 8,387,000 (2003 est)
POPULATION GROWTH RATE 1.8% (2000–15)

Chronology

10th century onwards: Hutu peoples settled in region formerly inhabited by hunter-gatherer Twa Pygmies, becoming peasant farmers.

14th century onwards: Majority Hutu community came under dominance of cattle-owning Tutsi peoples, immigrants from the east, who became a semi-aristocracy and established control through land and cattle contracts.

15th century: Ruganzu Bwimba, a Tutsi leader, founded kingdom near Kigali.

17th century: Central Rwanda and outlying Hutu communities subdued by Tutsi mwami (king) Ruganzu Ndori.

late 19th century: Under the great Tutsi king, Kigeri Rwabugiri, a unified state with a centralized military structure was established.

1890: Known as Ruandi, the Tutsi kingdom, along with neighbouring Burundi, came under nominal German control, as Ruanda-Urundi.

1916: Occupied by Belgium during World War I.

1923: Belgium granted League of Nations mandate to administer Ruanda-Urundi; they were to rule 'indirectly' through Tutsi chiefs.

1959: Inter-ethnic warfare between Hutu and Tutsi, forcing mwami Kigeri V into exile.

1961: Republic proclaimed after mwami deposed.

1962: Independence from Belgium achieved as Rwanda, with Hutu Grégoire Kayibanda as president; many Tutsis left the country.

1963: 20,000 killed in inter-ethnic clashes, after Tutsis exiled in Burundi had launched a raid.

1973: Kayibanda ousted in military coup led by Hutu Maj-Gen Juvenal Habyarimana; this was caused by resentment of Tutsis, who held some key government posts.

1981: Elections created civilian legislation, but dominated by Hutu socialist National Revolutionary Development Movement (MRND), in a one-party state.

POPULATION DENSITY (per sq km) 318 (2003 est)
URBAN POPULATION (% of total) 7 (2003 est)
AGE DISTRIBUTION (% of total population) 0–14 44%, 15–59 52%, 60+ 4% (2002 est)
ETHNIC GROUPS 85% belong to the Hutu tribe, most of the remainder being Tutsis (14%); there are also Twa (1%) and Pygmy minorities
LANGUAGE Kinyarwanda, French (both official), Kiswahili
RELIGION about 50% animist; about 40% Christian, mainly Roman Catholic; 9% Muslim
EDUCATION (compulsory years) 7
LITERACY RATE 76% (men); 65% (women) (2003 est)
LABOUR FORCE 90% agriculture, 2% industry, 8% services (2000)
LIFE EXPECTANCY 39 (men); 40 (women) (2000–05)
CHILD MORTALITY RATE (under 5, per 1,000 live births) 183 (2001)

See also ▷Burundi; ▷Hutu; ▷Tutsi.

1988: Hutu refugees from Burundi massacres streamed into Rwanda.

1990: The government was attacked by the Rwanda Patriotic Front (FPR), a Tutsi refugee military-political organization based in Uganda, which controlled parts of northern Rwanda.

1993: UN mission was sent to monitor the peace agreement made with the FPR in 1992.

1994: President Habyarimana and Burundian Hutu president Ntaryamira were killed in an air crash; involvement of FPR was suspected. Over 800,000 people were killed in the ensuing civil war, with many Tutsi massacred by Hutu death squads and the exodus of 2 million refugees. The government fled. An interim coalition government was installed, with moderate Hutu and FPR leader, Pasteur Bizimungu, as president.

1995: A war-crimes tribunal opened and government human-rights abuses were reported. Pierre Rwigema was appointed prime minister.

1996–97: Rwanda and Zaire (Democratic Republic of Congo) were on the brink of war after Tutsi killings of Hutu in Zaire. A massive Hutu refugee crisis was narrowly averted as thousands were allowed to return to Rwanda.

1998: 378 rebels were killed by the Rwandan army.

2000: Bizimungu resigned after disagreeing with his party. Paul Kagame, the vice-president, was inaugurated as president. Bernard Makuza became prime minister.

2002: A peace deal was struck with the Democratic Republic of Congo. Rwanda promised to withdraw its troops from the east of the country if the Congolese government disarmed or expelled the Hutu militias who had been hiding there since the early 1990s.

2003: In the first multiparty presidential elections since the genocide of 1994, President Kagame won with 95% of the vote. The main challenger, former prime minister Faustin Twagiramungu, won just 3.7% and claimed that voters were intimidated.

RWANDA A child waits in a queue for food at one of the refugee camps organized by the French in Rwanda. Initially, adults can withstand hunger better than children, but for the adults in most of the camps security from attack is an equal priority. *Image Bank*

S

Saami (or **Lapp**) an indigenous people numbering over 60,000 (1996) and living in northern Finland (7,000), Norway (36,000), Sweden (17,000) and Russia (2,000). Traditionally fishermen, hunter-gatherers, and nomadic reindeer herders, the Saami have lost large areas of pasture since 1965 due to forestry, mining and other economic activities. Today many are settled and have entered the professions. Their religion was originally animist, but most Saami now belong either to the Russian Orthodox or Lutheran churches. Their language belongs to the Finno-Ugric group.

Saarinen, Eero (1910–1961) Finnish-born US architect. He was renowned for his wide range of innovative modernist designs, experimenting with different structures and shapes. His works include the US embassy, London (1955–61); the TWA terminal at John F Kennedy Airport, New York City (1956–62); and Dulles Airport, Washington, DC (1958–63). He collaborated on a number of projects with his father, Eliel ▷Saarinen.

> **Eero Saarinen**
> *Always design a thing by considering it in its larger context – a chair in a room, a room in a house, a house in an environment, an environment in a city plan.*
> *Time* July 1956

Saarinen, (Gottlieb) Eliel (1873–1950) Finnish-born US architect and town planner. He founded the Finnish Romantic school. His best-known European project is the Helsinki railway station (1905–14). In 1923 he emigrated to the USA, where he is remembered for his designs for the Cranbrook Academy of Art in Bloomfield Hills, Michigan (1926–43), and Christ Church, Minneapolis (1949).

Saarland (French **Sarre**) administrative region (German *Land*) in southwest Germany, bordered by Rhineland-Palatinate and the French *département* of Moselle; area 2,570 sq km/992 sq mi; population (1995) 1,103,000. The capital is Saarbrücken. There are motor vehicle, mechanical and electrical engineering, coal, and steel industries. Cereals are grown, and cattle, pigs, and poultry are raised.

Sabah self-governing state of the federation of Malaysia, occupying northeast Borneo, forming (with Sarawak) East Malaysia; area 73,613 sq km/28,415 sq mi; population (1990) 1,736,900. The capital is Kota Kinabalu (formerly Jesselton). Products include oil (from offshore rigs), hardwoods, rubber, fish, cocoa, palm oil, copper, copra, and hemp.

Sabah, Sheikh Jabir al-Ahmad al-Jabir al- (1928–) Emir of Kuwait from 1977. He suspended the national assembly in 1986, after mounting parliamentary criticism, ruling in a feudal, paternalistic manner. On the invasion of Kuwait by Iraq in 1990 he fled to Saudi Arabia, returning to Kuwait in March 1991. In 1992 a reconstituted national assembly was elected.

Sabbath (Hebrew *shābath*, 'to rest') the seventh day of the week, commanded by God in the Old Testament as a sacred day of rest; in Judaism, from sunset Friday to sunset Saturday; in Christianity, Sunday (or, in some sects, Saturday).

Sabin, Albert Bruce (1906–1993) Russian-born US microbiologist who developed a highly effective, live vaccine against polio. The earlier vaccine, developed by physicist Jonas ▷Salk, was based on heat-killed viruses. Sabin was convinced that a live form would be longer-lasting and more effective, and in 1957 he succeeded in weakening the virus so that it lost its virulence. The vaccine can be given by mouth.

Sabine member of an ancient people of central Italy, conquered by the Romans and amalgamated with them in the 3rd century BC. The so-called **rape of the Sabine women** – a mythical attempt by ▷Romulus in the early days of Rome to carry off the Sabine women to colonize the new city – is frequently depicted in art.

sable marten *Martes zibellina*, about 50 cm/20 in long and usually brown. It is native to northern Eurasian forests, but now found mainly in eastern Siberia. The sable has diminished in numbers because of its valuable fur, which has long attracted hunters. Conservation measures and sable farming have been introduced to save it from extinction.

saccharin (or **ortho-sulpho benzimide**) $C_7H_5NO_3S$ sweet, white, crystalline solid derived from coal tar and substituted for sugar. Since 1977 it has been regarded as potentially carcinogenic. Its use is not universally permitted and it has been largely replaced by other sweetening agents.

Sacco–Vanzetti case murder trial in Massachusetts, USA, 1920–21. Italian immigrants Nicola Sacco (1891–1927) and Bartolomeo Vanzetti (1888–1927) were convicted of murder during an alleged robbery. The conviction was upheld on appeal, with application for retrial denied. Prolonged controversy delayed execution until 1927. In 1977 the verdict was declared unjust because of the judge's prejudice against the accuseds' anarchist views.

Sachsen German form of ▷Saxony, a former kingdom and state of Germany.

Sackville, Thomas (1536–1608) Lord Buckhurst, 1st Earl of Dorset. English poet and politician. He collaborated with Thomas Norton on *Ferrex and Porrex* (1561), afterwards called *Gorboduc*. Written in blank verse, this was one of the earliest English tragedies. He also contributed to the influential *Mirror for Magistrates*, intended as a continuation of John ▷Lydgate's *Fall of Princes*. An influential figure in Elizabeth I's last years, he held offices of Privy Councillor, Lord Steward, and Lord Treasurer.

Sackville-West, Vita (Victoria Mary) (1892–1962) English writer. Her novels include *The Edwardians* (1930) and *All Passion Spent* (1931); she also wrote the long pastoral poem *The Land* (1926). The fine gardens around her home at Sissinghurst, Kent, were created by her and her husband Harold ▷Nicolson.

sacrament in Christian usage, observances forming the visible sign of inward grace. In the Roman Catholic Church there are seven sacraments: baptism, Holy Communion (Eucharist or Mass), confirmation, rite of reconciliation (confession and penance), holy orders, matrimony, and the anointing of the sick.

Sacramento capital and deep-water port of ▷California, USA, 130 km/80 mi northeast of San Francisco; population (1996 est) 376,200; metropolitan area (1992) 1,563,000. Situated in Central Valley, the city lies on the Sacramento River as it curves towards San Francisco Bay. It is the commercial, manufacturing, and distribution centre for a rich irrigated farming area, and provides government, military, and tourist services. Industries include the manufacture of detergents, jet aircraft, arms, and processed foods; almonds, peaches, and pears are local agricultural specialities.

sacred cow any person, institution, or custom that is considered above criticism. The term comes from the Hindu belief that cows are sacred and must not be killed.

Sacred Thread ceremony Hindu initiation ceremony that marks the passage to maturity for boys of the upper three castes; it usually takes place between the ages of five and twelve. It is regarded as a second birth, and the castes whose males are entitled to undergo the ceremony are called 'twice born'.

Sadat, (Muhammad) Anwar (1918–1981) Egyptian politician, president 1970–81. Succeeding ▷Nasser as president in 1970, he restored morale by his handling of the Egyptian campaign in the 1973 war against Israel. In 1974 his plan for economic, social, and political reform to transform Egypt was unanimously adopted in a referendum. In 1977 he visited Israel to reconcile the two countries, and he shared the Nobel Prize for Peace in 1978 with Israeli prime minister Menachem ▷Begin for their efforts towards the Israel-Egypt peace treaty of 1979. Although feted by the West for pursuing peace with Israel, Sadat was denounced by the Arab world. He was assassinated by Islamic fundamentalists and succeeded by Hosni Mubarak.

Sadducee (Hebrew 'righteous') member of the ancient Hebrew political party and sect of ▷Judaism that formed in pre-Roman Palestine in the 1st century BC. They were the group of priestly aristocrats in Jerusalem until the final destruction of the Temple in AD 70.

Sade, Donatien Alphonse François, comte de (1740–1814) Also known as **the Marquis de Sade**. French writer. He was imprisoned for sexual offences and finally committed to an asylum. He wrote plays and novels dealing explicitly with a variety of sexual practices, including sadism, deriving pleasure or sexual excitement from inflicting pain on others.

sadism tendency to derive pleasure (usually sexual) from inflicting physical or mental pain on others. The term is derived from the Marquis de ▷Sade.

sadomasochism sexual behaviour that combines ▷sadism and ▷masochism. The term was coined 1907 by sexologist Richard von Krafft-Ebing.

Sadowa, Battle of (or **Battle of Königgrätz**) Prussian victory over the Austrian army 13 km/8 mi northwest of Hradec Kralove (German Königgrätz) 3 July 1866, ending the ▷Seven Weeks' War. It confirmed Prussian hegemony over the German states and led to the formation of the North German Confederation 1867. It is named after the nearby village of Sadowa (Czech Sadová) in the Czech Republic.

safety glass glass that does not splinter into sharp pieces when smashed. **Toughened glass** is made by heating a glass sheet and then rapidly cooling it with a blast of cold air; it shatters into rounded pieces when smashed. **Laminated glass** is a 'sandwich' of a clear plastic film between two glass sheets; when this is struck, it simply cracks, the plastic holding the glass in place.

safety lamp portable lamp designed for use in places where flammable gases such as methane may be encountered; for example, in coal mines. The electric head lamp used as a miner's working light has the bulb and contacts in protected enclosures. The flame safety lamp, now used primarily for gas detection, has the wick enclosed within a strong glass cylinder surmounted by wire gauzes. English chemist Humphrey ▷Davy (1815) and English engineer George ▷Stephenson each invented flame safety lamps.

safflower thistlelike Asian plant with large orange-yellow flowers. It is widely grown for the oil from its seeds, which is used in cooking, margarine, and paints and varnishes; the leftovers are used as cattle feed. (*Carthamus tinctorius*, family Compositae.)

saffron crocus plant belonging to the iris family, probably native to southwestern Asia, and formerly widely cultivated in Europe; also the dried orange-yellow ▷stigmas of its purple flowers, used for colouring and flavouring in cookery. (*Crocus sativus*, family Iridaceae.)

saga prose narrative written down in the 11th–13th centuries in Norway and Iceland. The sagas range from family chronicles, such as the *Landnamabok* of Ari (1067–1148), to legendary and anonymous works such as *Njal's Saga*.

Sagan, Carl Edward (1934–1996) US physicist and astronomer who has popularized astronomy through writings and broadcasts. His main research has been on planetary atmospheres. He wrote or co-wrote 27 books, which include *Broca's Brain: Reflections on the Romance of Science* (1979) and *Cosmos* (1980), based on his television series of that name.

sage perennial herb belonging to the mint family, with grey-green aromatic leaves used for flavouring in cookery. It grows up to 50 cm/20 in high and has bluish-lilac or pink flowers. (*Salvia officinalis*, family Labiatae.)

SAGE The herb sage is a native of the arid areas of southern Europe. The variety used in cooking is the nonflowering, broad-leafed sage.

Sage Kings legendary rulers of China *c.* 2800–*c.* 2200. Of the three sovereigns and five emperors based in the Huang He (Yellow River) region, Huang-tu (reigned *c.* 2697 BC) is credited with defeating the barbarians. The era has been associated with the domestication of animals, agricultural development, the gradual replacement of stone implements with bronze, and the formation of larger tribal confederacies.

Sagittarius bright zodiac constellation in the southern hemisphere, represented as an archer aiming a bow and arrow at neighbouring Scorpius. The Sun passes through Sagittarius from mid-December to mid-January, including the winter solstice, when it is farthest south of the Equator. The constellation contains many nebulae and ▷globular clusters, and open ▷star clusters. Kaus Australis and Nunki are its brightest stars. The centre of our Galaxy, the ▷Milky Way, is marked by the radio source Sagittarius A. In astrology, the dates for Sagittarius are about 22 November–21 December (see ▷precession).

sago starchy material obtained from the pith of the sago palm *Metroxylon sagu*. It forms a nutritious food and is used for manufacturing glucose and sizing textiles.

Sahara (Arabic *Sahra*, 'wilderness') largest desert in the world, occupying around 9,065,000 sq km/3,500,000 sq mi of north Africa from the Atlantic to the Nile, covering: west Egypt; part of west Sudan; large parts of Mauritania, Mali, Niger, and Chad; and southern parts of Morocco, Algeria, Tunisia, and Libya. Small areas in Algeria and Tunisia are below sea level, but it is mainly a plateau with a central mountain system, including the Ahaggar Mountains in Algeria, the Aïr Massif in Niger, and the Tibesti Massif in Chad, of which the highest peak is Emi Koussi, 3,415 m/11,208 ft.

Oases punctuate the caravan routes, now modern roads. Resources include oil and gas in the north. Satellite observations have established a pattern below the surface of dried-up rivers that existed 2 million years ago. Cave paintings confirm that 4,000 years ago running rivers and animal life existed. Satellite photos taken during the 1980s have revealed that the Sahara expands and contracts from one year to another depending on rainfall; there is no continuous expansion, as had been feared.

Sahel (Arabic *sahil* 'coast') marginal area to the south of the Sahara, from Senegal to Somalia, which experiences desert-like conditions during periods of low rainfall. The ▷desertification is partly due to climatic fluctuations but has also been caused by the pressures of a rapidly expanding population, which has led to overgrazing and the destruction of trees and scrub for fuelwood. In recent years many famines have taken place in the area.

The average rainfall in the Sahel ranges from 100 mm/4 in to 500 mm/20 in per year, but the rainfall over the past 30 years has been significantly below average. The resulting famine and disease are further aggravated by civil wars. The areas most affected are Ethiopia and the Sudan.

saiga antelope *Saiga tartarica* of eastern European and western Asian steppes and deserts. Buff-coloured, whitish in winter, it stands 75 cm/30 in at the shoulder, with a body about 1.5 m/5 ft long. Its nose is unusually large and swollen, an adaptation which may help warm and moisten the air inhaled, and keep out the desert dust. The saiga can run at 80 kph/50 mph.

Saigon former name (to 1976) of ▷Ho Chi Minh City, Vietnam.

Saigon, Battle of during the Vietnam War, battle 29 January–23 February 1968, when 5,000 Vietcong were expelled by South Vietnamese and US forces. The city was finally taken by North Vietnamese forces 30 April 1975, after South Vietnamese withdrawal from the central highlands.

sailing sport involving cruising or racing a small vessel; see ▷yachting.

saint holy man or woman respected for his or her wisdom, spirituality, and dedication to their faith. Within the Roman Catholic Church a saint is officially recognized through ▷canonization by the pope. Many saints are associated with miracles and canonization usually occurs after a thorough investigation of the lives and miracles attributed to them. For individual saints, see under forename; for example, ▷Paul, St.

In the Orthodox Church, saints are recognized by the patriarch and Holy Synod after recommendation by local churches. The term 'saint' is also used in Buddhism for individuals who have led a virtuous and holy life, such as Kūkai (774–835), also known as Kōbō Daishi, founder of the Japanese Shingon school of Buddhism.

The lives of thousands of Catholic saints have been collected by the Bollandists, a group of Belgian Jesuits. In 1970 Pope Paul VI revised the calendar of saints' days: excluded were Barbara, Catherine, Christopher, and Ursula (as probably nonexistent); optional veneration might be given to George, Januarius, Nicholas (Santa Claus), and Vitus; insertions for obligatory veneration include St Thomas More and the Uganda martyrs.

In the revised Calendar of Saints of 1970, only 58 saints were regarded as of worldwide importance. In 1980 the Church of England added 20 saints from the Post-Reformation era, including Josephine Butler, Thomas More, King Charles I, John Bunyan, and William Wilberforce.

St Albans city in Hertfordshire, England, on the River Ver, 40 km/25 mi northwest of London; population (1991) 80,400. The chief industries are electrical engineering, hosiery, clothing, information and legal services, musical instruments, and orchid culture. Printing is very important: one of the early presses set up in the late 15th century by the 'Scolemaster Printer', and his *The Book of St Albans* contains the earliest example of colour printing in England. There are the ruins of the Roman city of Verulamium on Watling Street. A Benedictine abbey was founded in 793 in honour of St Alban, and it became a cathedral in 1878. Other features include the Clock Tower (1411) in the High Street; the Royal National Rose Society headquarters and gardens; Rothamsted Park agricultural research centre; the Organ Museum of mechanical musical instruments; and the Verulamium Museum, with its collection of Roman remains.

St Andrews town in Fife, Scotland, 19 km/12 mi southeast of Dundee; population (1991) 11,100. Its university (1411) is the oldest in Scotland. It is considered to be the 'home of golf', with a famous Old Course. The Royal and Ancient Club (1754) is the ruling body of golf. There is a cathedral, founded in 1160 and consecrated in 1318.

There are six golf courses, four of which, the Old, New, Eden, and Jubilee, are owned by the Links Trust; the Old Course dates from the 16th century. The Royal and Ancient Golf Club was so named in 1834, 80 years after its inception as the Society of St Andrews Golfers.

The town is named after St Andrew, the patron saint of Scotland. There are ruins of a castle (originally built in 1200). A fragment of wall and some archways are the only remnants of a wealthy Augustinian priory which Bishop Robert founded here in 1144.

The cathedral suffered iconoclastic damage provoked by a sermon by John Knox in the town's parish church Holy Trinity in 1559. In the 9th century, St Andrews was a bishopric.

St Bartholomew's Day Massacre slaughter of ▷Huguenots (Protestants) in Paris, 24 August–17 September 1572, and until
3 October in the provinces. About 25,000 people are believed to have been killed. When ▷Catherine de' Medici's plot to have Admiral Coligny assassinated failed, she resolved to have all the Huguenot leaders killed, persuading her son Charles IX it was in the interest of public safety.

St Bernard breed of large, heavily built dog, named after the monks of Grand St Bernard Hospice, Switzerland, who kept them for finding lost travellers in the Alps and to act as guides. They are 70 cm/30 in high at the shoulder, and weigh about 70 kg/154 lb. They have pendulous ears and lips, large feet, and drooping lower eyelids. They are usually orange and white.

St Christopher–Nevis alternate form of ▷St Kitts and Nevis.

St Elmo's fire bluish, flamelike electrical discharge that sometimes occurs above ships' masts and other pointed objects or about aircraft in stormy weather. Although high voltage, it is low current and therefore harmless. St Elmo (or St Erasmus) is the patron saint of sailors.

Saint-Exupéry, Antoine Marie Roger de (1900–1944) French author and pilot. He wrote the autobiographical *Vol de nuit/Night Flight* (1931) and *Terre des hommes/Wind, Sand, and Stars* (1939). His children's book *Le Petit Prince/The Little Prince* (1943) is also an adult allegory.

Related Web site: Saint-Exupéry, Antoine Marie Roger de
http://www.estegg.com/exupery/

St George's port and capital of Grenada, on the southwest coast; population (1994 est) 30,000. The port has a well-sheltered harbour, exporting nutmeg, bananas, and rum, and is also an administrative and commercial centre. Refined sugar and alcoholic drinks are leading products and there is an established tourist industry. It was founded in 1650 by the French, and was the capital of the Windward Islands 1885–1958 (at that time a British dependency).

St Helena British island in the south Atlantic, 1,900 km/1,200 mi west of Africa, area 122 sq km/47 sq mi; population (1997) 5,644. Its capital is Jamestown, and it exports fish and timber. Ascension and Tristan da Cunha are dependencies.

St Helens, Mount volcanic mountain in Skamania County, Washington. It is located on the western flank of the Cascade Range, 56 km/35 mi east of Kelso, in the Gifford Pinchot National Forest. Dormant since 1857, it erupted on 18 May 1980, devastating an area of 600 sq km/230 sq mi, and killing 60 people; its height was reduced from 2,950 m/9,682 ft to 2,560 m/8,402 ft. The Mount St Helens National Volcanic Monument now surrounds the peak.

St Helier resort and capital of Jersey, Channel Islands; population (1991) 28,100. The 'States of Jersey', the island legislature, sits here in the *salle des états*.

St Ives fishing port and resort in Cornwall; population (1991) 10,100. Its artists' colony, founded by Walter Sickert and James Whistler, later included Naum Gabo, Barbara ▷Hepworth (a museum and sculpture gardens commemorate her), and Ben Nicholson. A branch of the Tate Gallery opened here in 1993, displaying works of art from the Tate's collection by artists connected with St Ives.

St John, Order of (or **Knights Hospitallers of St John of Jerusalem**) oldest order of Christian chivalry, named after the hospital at Jerusalem founded about 1048 by merchants of Amalfi for pilgrims, whose travel routes the knights defended from the Muslims. Today there are about 8,000 knights (male and female), and the Grand Master is the world's highest-ranking Roman Catholic lay person.

St John's port and capital of Antigua and Barbuda, on the northwest coast of Antigua; population (1992) 38,000. It exports rum, cotton, and sugar.

St John's capital and chief port of ▷Newfoundland, Canada; population (1991) 95,800, metropolitan area (1996) 177,800. Situated on the east coast of the Avalon peninsula, its deepwater harbour is connected to the Atlantic by a channel named the Narrows. St John's is the administrative, commercial, and service centre of the province. Fish-processing is the main industry; other manufactured products include textiles, fishing equipment, furniture, and machinery.

Saint-Just, Louis Antoine Léon Florelle de (1767–1794) French revolutionary. A close associate of ▷Robespierre, he became a member of the Committee of Public Safety 1793, and was guillotined with Robespierre.

St Kitts and Nevis see country box.

Saint-Laurent, Yves Henri Donat Mathieu (1936–) French fashion designer. He has had an exceptional influence on fashion in the second half of the 20th century. He began working for Christian ▷Dior 1955 and succeeded him as designer on Dior's death 1957. He established his own label in 1962 and went on to create the first 'power-dressing' looks for men and women: classic, stylish city clothes.

In 1966 Saint-Laurent established a chain of boutiques called Rive Gauche selling his ready-to-wear line. By the 1970s he had popularized a style of women's day wear that was inspired by conventionally 'masculine' garments such as blazers, trousers, and shirts. He launched a menswear collection in 1974. He continues to produce tailored, stylish designs, but his main influence was in the 1960s–70s. He retired in January 2002.

St Lawrence river in eastern North America. With the ▷Great Lakes and linking canals such as the ▷Welland Ship Canal, it forms the ▷St Lawrence Seaway, an inland route for small ocean-going ships from the Gulf of St Lawrence, an arm of the Atlantic Ocean, to ▷Thunder Bay at the head of Lake Superior; larger vessels stop at ▷Montréal. The river is 1,200 km/745 mi long and icebound for four months each year. Enormous quantities of hydroelectric power are generated along its course.

ST LAWRENCE A view of Québec, Canada's oldest city, and the St Lawrence River. It shows (right) one of the city's best known landmarks, the neo-Gothic Château Frontenac, a hotel built in 1892 and named after Count Louis de Frontenac, a 17th-century governor of the district. *Canadian Tourist Office*

St Lawrence Seaway deep-water channel and transport corridor in North America, connecting the St Lawrence River with the Great Lakes, allowing ocean-going vessels to navigate from the Atlantic Ocean to Lake Superior (3,769 km/2,342 mi). It was opened for navigation by the USA and Canada in 1959.

In the strict sense the seaway is the section from Montréal to Lake Ontario, but the name is applied generally to the whole system from the Atlantic to the Great Lakes. There are 78 ports on the seaway, which remains navigable for moderate-sized vessels for about 250 days a year.

St Louis city and riverport in Missouri, USA, on the Mississippi River; population (1996 est) 351,6000; metropolitan area (1996 est) 2,600,000. Occupying a central US location, it is a warehousing and distribution hub, and a major market for livestock, grain, wool, and lumber. The port handles oil, coal, sulphur, cement, and agricultural and manufactured goods. Products include aerospace and transport equipment, pharmaceuticals, refined oil, rubber, printed materials, and processed metals, tobacco, and food.

Related Web site: Official St Louis Visitors Guide http://www.st-louis-cvc.com/

St Lucia see country box.

St Paul capital and river port of ▷Minnesota, USA, on the Mississippi River, adjacent to ▷Minneapolis, with which it forms the Twin Cities area; population (1996 est) 259,600. Industries include printing, oil-refining, brewing, food-processing, meat-packing, and the manufacture of electronics, chemicals, plastics, and machinery. A high proportion of the population has a Scandinavian cultural background.

St Paul's Cathedral cathedral church of the City of London, the largest Protestant church in England, and a national mausoleum second only to Westminster Abbey. An earlier Norman building, which had replaced the original Saxon church, was burned down in the Great Fire of 1666. The present cathedral, designed by Christopher ▷Wren, was built from 1675 to 1711.

St Petersburg capital of the St Petersburg region, Russian Federation, at the head of the Gulf of Finland; population (1994) 4,883,000. Industries include shipbuilding, machinery, chemicals, and textiles. It was renamed **Petrograd** 1914 and was called **Leningrad** 1924–91, when its original name was restored.

Built on a low and swampy site, St Petersburg is split up by the mouths of the River Neva, which connects it with Lake Ladoga. The climate is severe. The city became a seaport when it was linked with the Baltic by a ship canal built 1875–93. It is also linked by canal and river with the Caspian and Black Seas, and in 1975 a seaway connection was completed via lakes Onega and Ladoga with the White Sea near Belomorsk, allowing naval forces to reach the Barents Sea free of NATO surveillance.

Related Web site: Saint Petersburg, Russia http://www.geocities.com/TheTropics/Shores/6751/

St Peter's Cathedral Roman Catholic cathedral church of the ▷Vatican City State, ▷Rome, built 1506–1626. It is the creation of the vision of Pope Julius II and the greatest architects of the Italian Renaissance, including Donato ▷Bramante and ▷Michelangelo. The cathedral has an internal length of 180 m/600 ft and a width at the transepts of 135 m/450 ft. The dome has an internal diameter of 42 m/137 ft and rises externally 138 m/452 ft to the crowning cross of the lantern.

St-Pierre and Miquelon territorial collectivity of France, comprising eight small islands off the south coast of Newfoundland, Canada; area St-Pierre group 26 sq km/10 sq mi; Miquelon-Langlade group 216 sq km/83 sq mi; population (1990) 6,400. The capital is St-Pierre. Industries include fishing and tourism. Cattle are raised and there is subsistence farming.

Saint-Saëns, (Charles) Camille (1835–1921) French composer, pianist, and organist. Saint-Saëns was a master of technique and a prolific composer. He wrote many lyrical Romantic pieces and symphonic poems. He is well known for the opera *Samson et Dalila* (1877), which was prohibited on the French stage until 1892, and the uncharacteristic orchestral piece *Le carnaval des animaux/The Carnival of the Animals* (1886), his most popular work.

Saint-Simon, Claude Henri de Rouvroy, comte de (1760–1825) French socialist who fought in the American Revolution and was imprisoned during the French Revolution. He advocated an atheist society ruled by technicians and industrialists in *Du système industriel/The Industrial System* (1821).

St Kitts and Nevis

ST KITTS AND NEVIS Beginning in 1690, colonists and soldiers from Britain spent more than a century fortifying the imposing military structure of Brimstone Hill Fortress on St Kitts, the walls of which are up to 3.7 m/12 ft thick. After a siege that lasted a month, it was captured by French troops in 1782, but was returned the following year. *Photodisk*

St Kitts and Nevis or St Christopher and Nevis, formerly part of Leeward Islands Federation (until 1956) country in the West Indies, in the eastern Caribbean Sea, part of the Leeward Islands.

NATIONAL NAME *Federation of St Christopher and St Nevis*
AREA 262 sq km/101 sq mi (St Kitts 168 sq km/65 sq mi, Nevis 93 sq km/36 sq mi)
CAPITAL Basseterre (on St Kitts) (and chief port)
MAJOR TOWNS/CITIES Charlestown (Nevis), Newcastle, Sandy Point Town, Dieppe Bay Town, Saint Paul
PHYSICAL FEATURES both islands are volcanic; fertile plains on coast; black beaches

Government
HEAD OF STATE Queen Elizabeth II from 1983, represented by Governor General Dr Cuthbert Montraville Sebastian from 1996
HEAD OF GOVERNMENT Denzil Douglas from 1995
POLITICAL SYSTEM liberal democracy
POLITICAL EXECUTIVE parliamentary
ADMINISTRATIVE DIVISIONS 14 parishes
ARMED FORCES army disbanded in 1981 and absorbed by Volunteer Defence Force; participates in US-sponsored Regional Security System established in 1982
DEATH PENALTY retained and used for ordinary crimes

Economy and resources
CURRENCY East Caribbean dollar
GPD (US$) 340 million (2002 est)
REAL GDP GROWTH (% change on previous year) 1.8 (2001)
GNI (US$) 293 million (2002 est)
GNI PER CAPITA (PPP) (US$) 9,780 (2002 est)

CONSUMER PRICE INFLATION 2% (2003 est)
UNEMPLOYMENT 4.5% (1996 est)
FOREIGN DEBT (US$) 204 million (2001 est)
MAJOR TRADING PARTNERS USA, UK, Trinidad and Tobago, St Vincent and the Grenadines, Canada, Barbados
INDUSTRIES electronic equipment, food and beverage processing (principally sugar and cane spirit), clothing, footwear, tourism
EXPORTS sugar, manufactures, postage stamps; sugar and sugar products accounted for approximately 20% of export earnings in 2000. Principal market: USA 72.4% (2001)
IMPORTS machinery and transport equipment, foodstuffs, basic manufactures, mineral fuels. Principal source: USA 46.2% (2001)
ARABLE LAND 22.2% (2000 est)
AGRICULTURAL PRODUCTS sugar cane, coconuts, yams, sweet potatoes, groundnuts, sweet peppers, carrots, cabbages, bananas, cotton; fishing

Population and society
POPULATION 42,000 (2003 est)
POPULATION GROWTH RATE –0.7% (2000–05)
POPULATION DENSITY (per sq km) 160 (2003 est)
URBAN POPULATION (% of total) 35 (2003 est)
AGE DISTRIBUTION (% of total population) 0–14 31%, 15–59 58%, 60+ 11% (2001 est)
ETHNIC GROUPS almost entirely of African descent
LANGUAGE English (official)

RELIGION Anglican 36%, Methodist 32%, other Protestant 8%, Roman Catholic 10%
EDUCATION (compulsory years) 12
LITERACY RATE 99% (men); 97% (women) (2003 est)
LABOUR FORCE 14.7% agriculture, 20.9% industry, 64.4% services (1994)
LIFE EXPECTANCY 68 (men); 72 (women) (2000–05)
CHILD MORTALITY RATE (under 5, per 1,000 live births) 24 (2001)

PHYSICIANS (per 1,000 people) 1.2 (1998 est)
HOSPITAL BEDS (per 1,000 people) 6.4 (1996 est)
TV SETS (per 1,000 people) 256 (1999 est)
RADIOS (per 1,000 people) 719 (1998 est)
INTERNET USERS (per 10,000 people) 1,063.8 (2002 est)
PERSONAL COMPUTER USERS (per 100 people) 19.2 (2002 est)

Chronology

1493: Visited by the explorer Christopher Columbus, after whom the main island is named, but for next two centuries the islands were left in the possession of the indigenous Caribs.

1623 and 1628: St Kitts and Nevis islands successively settled by British as their first Caribbean colony, with 2,000 Caribs brutally massacred in 1626.

1783: In the Treaty of Versailles France, which had long disputed British possession, rescinded its claims to the islands, on which sugar cane plantations developed, worked by imported African slaves.

1816: Anguilla was joined politically to the two islands.

1834: Abolition of slavery.

1871–1956: Part of the Leeward Islands Federation.

1937: Internal self-government granted.

1952: Universal adult suffrage granted.

1958–62: Part of the Federation of the West Indies.

1967: St Kitts, Nevis, and Anguilla achieved internal self-government, within the British Commonwealth, with Robert Bradshaw, Labour Party leader, as prime minister.

1970: NRP formed, calling for separation for Nevis.

1971: Anguilla returned to being a British dependency after rebelling against domination by St Kitts.

1980: People's Action Movement (PAM) and NRP centrist coalition government, led by Kennedy Simmonds, formed after inconclusive general election.

1983: Full independence was achieved within the Commonwealth.

1994: A three-week state of emergency was imposed after violent antigovernment riots by Labour Party supporters in Basseterre.

1995: Labour Party won a general election; Denzil Douglas became prime minister.

1997: Nevis withdrew from the federation.

1998: Nevis referendum on secession failed to secure support.

2000: Denzil Douglas was re-elected as prime minister.

ST PAUL'S CATHEDRAL St Paul's Cathedral survived German bombing raids during the Blitz of World War II, but its silhouette, which once dominated the London skyline, has since become lost among towering high-rise office blocks of the late 1900s. The present building, designed by Christopher Wren, replaced an earlier Norman building, which was destroyed by fire in 1666. *Archive Photos*

ST PETER'S CATHEDRAL The dome of St Peter's, Rome. In 1546 Pope Paul III commissioned Michelangelo to design and complete the dome. However, only the drum for the dome was completed by the time of Michelangelo's death in 1564, and the dome itself was only finally finished under Pope Sixtus V (1585–90). *Image Bank*

St Lucia

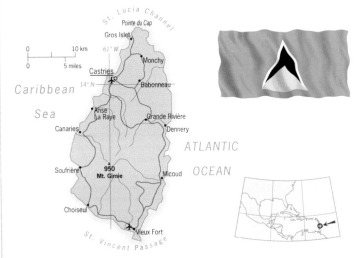

St Lucia formerly part of Windward Islands Federation (until 1960) country in the West Indies, in the eastern Caribbean Sea, one of the Windward Islands.

AREA 617 sq km/238 sq mi
CAPITAL Castries
MAJOR TOWNS/CITIES Soufrière, Vieux Fort, Choiseul, Gros Islet
MAJOR PORTS Vieux-Fort
PHYSICAL FEATURES mountainous island with fertile valleys; mainly tropical forest; volcanic peaks; Gros and Petit Pitons

Government

HEAD OF STATE Queen Elizabeth II from 1979, represented by Governor General Dr Perlette Louisy from 1997
HEAD OF GOVERNMENT Kenny Anthony from 1997
POLITICAL SYSTEM liberal democracy
POLITICAL EXECUTIVE parliamentary
ADMINISTRATIVE DIVISIONS 11 districts
ARMED FORCES none; participates in the US-sponsored Regional Security System established in 1982; police force numbers around 300
DEATH PENALTY retained and used for ordinary crimes

Economy and resources

CURRENCY East Caribbean dollar
GPD (US$) 660 million (2002 est)
REAL GDP GROWTH (% change on previous year) –5.4 (2001)
GNI (US$) 609 million (2002 est)
GNI PER CAPITA (PPP) (US$) 5,000 (2002 est)
CONSUMER PRICE INFLATION 2.3% (2003 est)
UNEMPLOYMENT 17.5% (2000)
FOREIGN DEBT (US$) 216 million (2001 est)
MAJOR TRADING PARTNERS USA, UK, Trinidad and Tobago (and other CARICOM member states), Japan, Canada, Italy
RESOURCES geothermal energy
INDUSTRIES processing of agricultural products (principally coconut oil, meal, and copra), clothing, rum, beer, and other beverages, plastics, paper and packaging, electronic assembly, tourism
EXPORTS bananas, coconut oil, cocoa beans, copra, beverages, tobacco, miscellaneous articles. Principal market: UK 55.7% (2000)
IMPORTS machinery and transport equipment, foodstuffs, basic manufactures, mineral fuels. Principal source: USA 37.5% (2000)

ST LUCIA Rising out of the sea are two forest-covered peaks, the Gros Piton (798 m/2,618 ft) and Petit Piton (750 m/2,461 ft). These volcanic cones are situated on the west coast, near the town of Soufrière, which takes its name from the nearby sulphur springs, the remains of a vast collapsed volcano. *St Lucia Tourist Board*

ARABLE LAND 8.2% (1998)
AGRICULTURAL PRODUCTS bananas, cocoa, coconuts, mangoes, citrus fruits, spices, breadfruit

Population and society

POPULATION 149,000 (2003 est)
POPULATION GROWTH RATE 1.1% (2000–05)
POPULATION DENSITY (per sq km) 240 (2003 est)
URBAN POPULATION (% of total) 38 (2003 est)

Chronology

1502: Sighted by the explorer Christopher Columbus on St Lucia's day but not settled for more than a century due to hostility of the island's Carib Indian inhabitants.
1635: Settled by French, who brought in slaves to work sugar cane plantations as the Carib community was annihilated.
1814: Ceded to Britain as a crown colony, following Treaty of Paris; African slaves brought in to work sugar cane plantations.
1834: Slavery abolished.
1860s: A major coal warehousing centre until the switch to oil and diesel fuels in 1930s.
1871–1960: Part of Windward Islands Federation.
1951: Universal adult suffrage granted.
1967: Acquired internal self-government as a West Indies associated state.
1979: Independence achieved within Commonwealth with John Compton, leader of United Workers' Party (UWP), as prime minister.
1991: Integration with other Windward Islands (Dominica, Grenada, and St Vincent) was proposed.
1993: Unrest and strikes by farmers and agricultural workers arose as a result of depressed prices for the chief cash crop, bananas.

St Vincent and the Grenadines see country box.

Sakha (formerly **Yakutia**; **Yakutsk Autonomous Soviet Socialist Republic**) autonomous republic of the Russian Federation, in eastern Siberia; area 3,103,000 sq km/1,198,100 sq mi; population (1997) 1,032,000 (50% Russians, 33% Yakuts). The capital is ▷Yakutsk. Industries include fur trapping, gold and natural gas extraction, and lumbering; there is some agriculture in the south.

Sakhalin (formerly Japanese **Karafuto** (1855–75; 1905–45)) island in the Russian Far East between the Sea of Okhotsk and the Sea of Japan, separated from the mainland of the Russian Federation by the Tatar Strait and from the northernmost island of Japan, Hokkaido, by La Pérouse Strait. Sakhalin is some 965 km/600 mi long and covers an area of 76,400 sq km/29,498 sq mi. The main town is Yuzhno-Sakhalinsk. Coal, oil, natural gas, iron ore, and gold deposits, together with extensive coniferous and mixed forests, provide the basis for mining, oil extraction, and industries producing timber, cellulose, and paper (the latter established by the Japanese). The oil that is extracted on Sakhalin is piped across the Tatar Strait to Komsomolsk-na-Amure. Fishing is also an important economic activity. Sakhalin supports limited arable (potatoes and vegetables) and dairy farming.

Sakharov, Andrei Dmitrievich (1921–1989) Soviet physicist. He was an outspoken human-rights campaigner, who with Igor Tamm developed the hydrogen bomb. He later protested against Soviet nuclear tests and was a founder of the Soviet Human Rights Committee in 1970. In 1975 he was awarded the Nobel Prize for Peace for his advocacy of human rights and disarmament. For criticizing Soviet action in Afghanistan, he was sent into internal exile 1980–86.

Sakharov was elected to the Congress of the USSR People's Deputies in 1989, where he emerged as leader of its radical reform grouping before his death later the same year.

Related Web site: Sakharov, Andrei http://www.nobel.se/peace/laureates/1975/sakharov-autobio.html

ANDREI SAKHAROV The work of Soviet physicist Andrei Sakharov laid the foundation for the development of a Soviet hydrogen bomb in the early 1950s. However, Sakharov and his wife, Yelena Bonner, campaigned for a nuclear test ban in the 1960s and so alienated the Soviet authorities. *Archive Photos*

Saki (1870–1916) Pen-name of H(ector) H(ugh) Munro. Burmese-born British writer. He produced ingeniously witty and bizarre short stories, often with surprise endings. He also wrote two novels, *The Unbearable Bassington* (1912) and *When William Came* (1913).

Sakkara (or **Saqqara**) village in Egypt, 16 km/10 mi south of Cairo, with 20 pyramids. The oldest of these (third dynasty) is the 'Step Pyramid' designed by ▷Imhotep, whose own tomb here was the nucleus of the Aesklepieion, a centre of healing in the ancient world.

> **Saki**
> *A little inaccuracy sometimes saves tons of explanation.*
> 'Comments of Moung Ka'

Sakyamuni the historical ▷Buddha, called **Shaka** in Japan (because Gautama was of the Sakya clan).

Saladin (c. 1138–1193) (Arabic in full **Salah ad-Din Yusuf ibn Ayyub**; Arabic *Salah ad-Din*, 'righteousness of the faith') Kurdish conqueror of the Kingdom of Jerusalem. Saladin believed in ▷jihad (holy war) – the Muslim equivalent of the Crusades. He conquered Syria 1174–87, and recovered Jerusalem from the Christians in 1187, causing the third ▷Crusade (1191–92). The Christian army, headed by Philip II of France and Richard (I) the Lionheart of England retook Acre in 1191, but Saladin was a brilliant general and the Third Crusade, although inflicting some defeats, achieved little. In 1192 he made peace with Richard (I) the Lionheart, left fighting alone after quarrels with his allies.

Saladin was recognized, even by his opponents, for his knightly courtesy, piety, and justice. His administration also improved communications, leaving behind a network of roads and canals, and built many citadels (castle or city strongholds).

Salamanca, Battle of during the ▷Peninsular War, victory 22 July 1812 of the British led by the Duke of Wellington over the French under Marshal Auguste Marmont. The battle took place to the south of Salamanca, 170 km/105 mi northwest of Madrid.

salamander tailed amphibian of the order Urodela. They are sometimes confused with ▷lizards, but unlike lizards they have no scales or claws. Salamanders have smooth or warty moist skin. The order includes some 300 species, arranged in nine families, found mainly in the northern hemisphere. Salamanders include hellbenders, ▷mudpuppies, ▷olms, waterdogs, sirens, mole salamanders, ▷newts, and lungless salamanders (dusky, woodland, and spring salamanders).

They eat insects and worms, and live in water or in damp areas in the northern temperate regions, mostly feeding at night

St Vincent and the Grenadines

ST VINCENT AND THE GRENADINES Among the chain of islands that make up St Vincent and the Grenadines, Bequia and Mustique are the private resorts of many of the world's rich and famous. *Corel*

St Vincent and the Grenadines country in the West Indies, in the eastern Caribbean Sea, part of the Windward Islands.

AREA 388 sq km/150 sq mi (including islets of the Northern Grenadines 43 sq km/17 sq mi)
CAPITAL Kingstown
MAJOR TOWNS/CITIES Georgetown, Châteaubelair, Layon, Dovers
PHYSICAL FEATURES volcanic mountains, thickly forested; La Soufrière volcano

Government

HEAD OF STATE Queen Elizabeth II from 1979, represented by Governor General Frederick Ballantyne from 2002
HEAD OF GOVERNMENT Ralph Gonsalves from 2001
POLITICAL SYSTEM liberal democracy
POLITICAL EXECUTIVE parliamentary
ADMINISTRATIVE DIVISIONS six parishes
ARMED FORCES none – police force only; participates in the US-sponsored Regional Security System established in 1982

DEATH PENALTY retained and used for ordinary crimes

Economy and resources

CURRENCY East Caribbean dollar
GPD (US$) 361 million (2002 est)
REAL GDP GROWTH (% change on previous year) 0.2 (2001)
GNI (US$) 329 million (2002 est)
GNI PER CAPITA (PPP) (US$) 5,100 (2002 est)
CONSUMER PRICE INFLATION 0.3% (2003 est)
UNEMPLOYMENT 20% (2002)
FOREIGN DEBT (US$) 441 million (2001 est)
MAJOR TRADING PARTNERS USA, UK, Trinidad and Tobago, Antigua and Barbuda, Barbados, Canada, Japan, St Lucia
INDUSTRIES clothing, assembly of electronic equipment, processing of agricultural products (including brewing, flour milling, rum distillation, dairy products), industrial gases, plastics, tourism
EXPORTS bananas, rice, eddoes, dasheen, sweet potatoes, flour, ginger, tannias, plantains. Principal market: UK 37.4% (2001)
IMPORTS basic manufactures, machinery and transport equipment, food and live animals, mineral fuels, chemicals, miscellaneous manufactured articles. Principal source: USA 35.9% (2001)
ARABLE LAND 9.5% (2000 est)
AGRICULTURAL PRODUCTS bananas, cocoa, citrus fruits, mangoes, avocado pears, guavas, sugar cane, vegetables, spices; world's leading producer of arrowroot starch; fishing

Population and society

POPULATION 120,000 (2003 est)
POPULATION GROWTH RATE 0.6% (2000–05)
POPULATION DENSITY (per sq km) 309 (2003 est)
URBAN POPULATION (% of total) 58 (2003 est)
AGE DISTRIBUTION (% of total population) 0–14 37%, 15–59 55%, 60+ 8% (2002 est)
ETHNIC GROUPS largely of African origin; most of the original indigenous Caribs have disappeared
LANGUAGE English (official), French patois
RELIGION Anglican, Methodist, Roman Catholic
EDUCATION not compulsory
LITERACY RATE 92% (men); 89% (women) (2003 est)
LABOUR FORCE 24.8% agriculture, 21.3% industry, 53.7% services (1991)
LIFE EXPECTANCY 73 (men); 76 (women) (2000–05)
CHILD MORTALITY RATE (under 5, per 1,000 live births) 25 (2001)

Chronology

1498: Main island visited by the explorer Christopher Columbus on St Vincent's day.
17th–18th centuries: Possession disputed by France and Britain, with fierce resistance from the indigenous Carib community.
1783: Recognized as British crown colony by Treaty of Versailles.
1795–97: Carib uprising, with French support, resulted in deportation of 5,000 to Belize and Honduras.
1834: Slavery abolished.
1902: Over 2,000 killed by the eruption of La Soufrière volcano.
1951: Universal adult suffrage granted.
1958–62: Part of West Indies Federation.
1969: Achieved internal self-government.
1979: Achieved full independence within Commonwealth.
1981: General strike against new industrial-relations legislation at a time of economic recession.
1984: James Mitchell, of the centre-right New Democratic Party (NDP) became prime minister.
2000: Mitchell was later replaced by Arnhim Eustace.
2002: Ralph Gonsalves replaced Eustace as prime minister.

and hiding during the day, and often hibernating during the winter. Fertilization is either external or internal, often taking place in water. The larvae have external gills. Some remain in the larval form, although they become sexually mature and breed; this is called neoteny. The Mexican ▷axolotl and the mud puppy *Necturus maculosus* of North America are neotenic.

In 1998, five new salamander species were discovered in tropical east-central Mexico. The species all belong to the genus *Thorius*, whose members are characterized by their smallness – some species are less than 2 cm/0.8 in length.

Salamanders include the European spotted or fire salamander *Salamandra salamandra*, black with bright yellow, orange, or red markings, and up to 20 cm/8 in long. It was falsely believed in medieval times to be immune to fire.

SALAMANDER The fire salamander is seldom far from water, preferring moist areas. The bright markings warn predators of the salamander's poisonous body secretions, which burn the mouth and eyes of an attacker.

salat the daily prayers that are one of the Five Pillars of ▷Islam.

Salazar, António de Oliveira (1889–1970) Portuguese prime minister 1932–68 who exercised a virtual dictatorship. During World War II he maintained Portuguese neutrality but fought long colonial wars in Africa (Angola and Mozambique) that impeded his country's economic development as well as that of the colonies.

Salem capital of ▷Oregon, in Marion County (of which it is administrative headquarters) and Polk County, on the Willamette River, 84 km/53 mi south of Portland; population (1996 est) 122,600. It is a distribution and processing centre for timber from the Cascades forests to the east, and fruit and vegetables from the fertile Willamette farmlands. Hi-tech goods, building materials, and textiles are also produced. It is the home of Willamette University (1844), Chemeketa Community College (1962), and the neoclassical marble capitol (1937).

Salford industrial city in Greater Manchester, northwest England, on the west bank of the River Irwell and the Manchester Ship Canal; population (1991) 80,600. Industries include engineering and the manufacture of electrical goods and textiles.

Features include the Roman Catholic Cathedral of St John (1844–48) and Salford University (1966), founded in 1896 as the Royal Technical Institute. The artist L S Lowry lived in Salford for much of his life; a new arts centre, the Lowry, opened in 2000.

SALFORD Salford Quays, Manchester, England, was redeveloped during the late 20th century. *Image Bank*

salicylic acid HOC_6H_4COOH the active chemical constituent of aspirin, an analgesic drug. The acid and its salts (salicylates) occur naturally in many plants; concentrated sources include willow bark and oil of wintergreen.

Salieri, Antonio (1750–1825) Italian composer. He taught Beethoven, Schubert, Hummel, and Liszt, and was the musical rival of Mozart at the emperor's court in Vienna, where he held the position of court composer. It has been suggested, without proof, that he poisoned Mozart.

Salinas de Gortari, Carlos (1948–) Mexican politician, president 1988–94, a member of the dominant Institutional Revolutionary Party (PRI). During his presidency he promoted economic reform, including privatization, and signed a North American Free Trade Agreement (NAFTA) with the USA and Canada in December 1992. However, he was also confronted with problems of drug trafficking and violent crime, including the murder of his nominated successor, Luis Donaldo Colosio, in 1994. He went into exile in 1995 after his brother Raúl was implicated in the assassination of another high-ranking PRI official and held in jail. It was later revealed that his brother had amassed more than $84 million in a Swiss bank account.

Salinger, J(erome) D(avid) (1919–) US writer. He wrote the classic novel of mid-20th-century adolescence *The Catcher in the Rye* (1951). He developed his lyrical Zen themes in *Franny and Zooey* (1961) and *Raise High the Roof Beam, Carpenters* and *Seymour: An Introduction* (1963), short stories about a Jewish family named Glass, after which he stopped publishing. He also wrote *For Esmé – With Love and Squalor* (1953).

Related Web site: Bananafish Home http://www.salinger.org/

Salisbury city and market town in Wiltshire, south England, on the edge of Salisbury Plain 135 km/84 mi southwest of London; population (1991) 39,300. Salisbury is an agricultural centre, and industries include brewing and engineering. The nearby Wilton Royal Carpet factory closed in 1995. The cathedral of St Mary, built 1220–66, is an example of Early English architecture; its decorated spire 123 m/404 ft is the highest in England; its clock (1386) is one of the oldest still working. The cathedral library contains one of only four copies of the *Magna Carta*.

Salisbury Plain undulating plateau between Salisbury and Devizes in Wiltshire, southwest England; area 775 sq km/300 sq mi. It rises to 235 m/770 ft in Westbury Down. Since the mid-19th century it has been a military training area. ▷Stonehenge stands on Salisbury Plain.

Salisbury, Robert Arthur Talbot Gascoyne-Cecil, 3rd Marquess of Salisbury (1830–1903) British Conservative politician. He entered the Commons in 1853 and succeeded to his title in 1868. As foreign secretary 1878–80, he took part in the Congress of Berlin, and as prime minister 1885–86, 1886–92, and 1895–1902 gave his main attention to foreign policy, remaining also as foreign secretary for most of this time.

Salisbury, Robert Cecil, 1st Earl of Salisbury, title conferred on Robert ▷Cecil, secretary of state to Elizabeth I of England.

saliva in vertebrates, an alkaline secretion from the salivary glands that aids the swallowing and digestion of food in the mouth. In mammals, it contains the enzyme amylase, which converts starch to sugar. The salivary glands of mosquitoes and other blood-sucking insects produce ▷anticoagulants.

Salk, Jonas Edward (1914–1995) US physician and microbiologist. In 1954 he developed the original vaccine that led to virtual eradication of paralytic ▷polio in industrialized countries. He was director of the Salk Institute for Biological Studies, University of California, San Diego, 1963–75.

Sallust, Gaius Sallustius Crispus (86–*c*. 34 BC) Roman historian. He served under Julius ▷Caesar in Gaul (France) and during the civil war, but retired from public life after a scandal involving his governorship of Africa. He wrote histories of the Catiline conspiracy and the Jugurthine War, as well as a Roman history of which only fragments survive.

> **Gaius Sallustius Crispus Sallust**
>
> *Everyone who wishes to rise above the lower animals should strive his hardest to avoid living all his days in obscurity.*
>
> *Catilinarian Conspiracy*, preface

salmon any of the various bony fishes of the family Salmonidae. More specifically the name is applied to several species of game fishes of the genera Salmo and Oncorhynchus of North America and Eurasia that mature in the ocean but, to spawn, return to the freshwater streams where they were born. Their normal colour is silvery with a few dark spots, but the colour changes at the spawning season.

Life cycle The spawning season is between September and January, although they occasionally spawn at other times. Once the salmon pair, the female hollows out her **redd** in the riverbed and in it deposits her orange eggs, about 6 mm/0.25 in in diameter, to be fertilized by the male. Once fertilized, the eggs are then covered with gravel by the female. The incubation period is from five weeks to five months. The young hatched fish are known as **alevins**, and when they begin feeding they are called **parr**. At about two years old, their coat becomes silvery, and they are called **smolts**. Depending on the species, they may spend up to four years at sea before returning to their home streams to spawn (at this stage called **grilse**), often overcoming great obstacles to get there and die.

As the salmon migrate up stream, their colouring changes to include greens, pinks, and blues and they increase in size, some growing to as much 1 m/ 3 ft. The jaws of the males undergo restructuring to become hook shaped to enable them to drive rival males from spawning areas. Internally, the reproductive organs increase in size in both males and females and the gut decreases to such an extent that salmon fast for their migration.

Salmon farming Salmon are increasingly farmed in cages, and 'ranched' (selectively bred, hatched, and fed before release to the sea). Stocking rivers indiscriminately with hatchery fish may destroy the precision of their homing instinct owing to interbreeding between fish originating in different rivers.

Salmon returned to the Thames, the Tyne, the Tees, the Humber, and in 1997 to Medway.

Related Web site: Salmon Page http://www.riverdale.k12.or.us/salmon.htm

Salmond, Alex(ander Elliott Anderson) (1954–) Scottish nationalist politician, leader of the Scottish National Party (SNP) 1990–2000. He joined the SNP in 1973, entering the House of Commons in 1987 as SNP member of Parliament for Banff and Buchan. Through his ability to project a moderate image, he did much as leader to improve his party's credibility, even though its proposals to make Scotland an independent member of the European Union (EU) went far beyond the limits of what the majority of Scottish electors would support. He supported the new Labour government's proposals for Scottish devolution, viewing it as a stepping-stone towards independence, and the SNP achieved 35 seats in the 1999 elections to Scotland's new parliament, becoming the main opposition to a Labour government.

salmonella any of a very varied group of bacteria, genus *Salmonella*, that colonize the intestines of humans and some animals. Some strains cause typhoid and paratyphoid fevers, while others cause salmonella ▷food poisoning, which is characterized by stomach pains, vomiting, diarrhoea, and headache. It can be fatal in elderly people, but others usually recover in a few days without antibiotics. Most cases are caused by contaminated animal products, especially poultry meat.

Related Web site: Bad Bug Book – Salmonella http://vm.cfsan.fda.gov/~mow/chap1.html

Salonika English name for ▷Thessaloniki, a port in Greece.

Salop abbreviation and former official name (1972–80) of ▷Shropshire, a county in England.

salsify (or **vegetable oyster**) hardy biennial plant native to the Mediterranean region. Its white fleshy roots and spring shoots are cooked and eaten; the roots are said to taste like oysters. (*Tragopogon porrifolius*, family Compositae.)

SALT abbreviation for ▷Strategic Arms Limitation Talks, a series of US–Soviet negotiations 1969–79.

salt in chemistry, any compound formed from an acid and a base through the replacement of all or part of the hydrogen in the acid by a metal or electropositive radical. **Common salt** is sodium chloride (see ▷salt, common).

A salt may be produced by chemical reaction between an acid and a base, or by the displacement of hydrogen from an acid by a metal. As a solid, the ions normally adopt a regular arrangement to form crystals. Some salts only form stable crystals as hydrates (when combined with water). Most inorganic salts readily dissolve in water to give an electrolyte (a solution that conducts electricity).

saltbush any of a group of drought-resistant plants belonging to the goosefoot family, especially the widespread genus *Atriplex*, used as grazing plants in arid, saline, and alkaline parts of North America, Australia, and South Africa, and the Australian and New Zealand genus *Rhagodia*. Where saltbush is the predominant vegetation, as in southwestern South Australia, the whole area is referred to as the saltbush. (Family Chenopodiaceae.)

salt, common (or **sodium chloride**) NaCl white crystalline solid, found dissolved in sea water and as rock salt (the mineral halite) in large deposits and salt domes. Common salt is used extensively in the food industry as a preservative and for flavouring, and in the chemical industry in the making of chlorine and sodium.

COMMON SALT Workers on the salt fields near the coastal city of Nha Trang on Cam Ranh Bay, Vietnam. *Image Bank*

Salt Lake City capital of ▷Utah, USA, on the River Jordan, 605 km/378 mi northwest of Denver, Colorado; population (1992) 165,900. It is the commercial centre and world capital of the Church of Jesus Christ of the Latter-day Saints (the ▷Mormon Church). Industries include mineral refining, food processing, and the manufacture of textiles, footwear, and electronic and mining equipment. Copper, silver, lead, zinc, coal, and iron mines are worked nearby. In 1995 Salt Lake City was chosen as the site for the 2002 Winter Olympic Games.

salt marsh wetland with halophytic vegetation (tolerant to sea water). Salt marshes develop around ▷estuaries and on the sheltered side of sand and shingle ▷spits. Salt marshes usually have a network of creeks and drainage channels by which tidal waters enter and leave the marsh.

saltpetre former name for potassium nitrate (KNO_3), the compound used in making gunpowder (from about 1500). It occurs naturally, being deposited during dry periods in places with warm climates, such as India.

saluki ancient breed of hunting dog resembling the greyhound. It is about 65 cm/26 in high and has a silky coat, which is usually fawn, cream, or white.

Salvador port, resort, and naval base, capital of Bahía federal unit (state), northeast Brazil, on the inner side of a peninsula separating Todos los Santos Bay from the Atlantic Ocean; population (1991) 2,075,400 (metropolitan area 3,134,900). Chief industries include oil refining, petrochemicals, and tourism; fruit, cocoa, sisal, soybeans, and petrochemical products are exported. The city is built on two distinct levels; the Cidade Alta (upper city), the site of the original settlement where there are many examples of colonial architecture, and Cidade Baixa (lower city), comprising the commercial, financial, and port district. It was the first capital of Brazil 1549–1763.

Salvador was founded in 1549 by the Portuguese as a fortification against invasion by the Dutch and French. Cultivation of sugar cane and tobacco in the surrounding region, and its situation on the trade routes of the New World, contributed to making Salvador the most important city in the Portuguese empire after Lisbon. It also became a centre for the slave trade, the workforce for the plantations having been obtained from the west coast of Africa; as a result there is a very noticeable African influence in the city to the present day.

Related Web site: Salvador, Brazil http://travel.lycos.com/Destinations/South_America/Brazil/Salvador/

Salvador, El republic in Central America; see ▷El Salvador.

Salvation Army Christian evangelical, social-service, and social-reform organization, originating in 1865 in London, England, with the work of William ▷Booth. Originally called the Christian Revival Association, it was renamed the East London Christian Mission in 1870 and from 1878 has been known as the Salvation Army, now a worldwide organization. It has military titles for its officials, is renowned for its brass bands, and its weekly journal is the *War Cry*.

Related Web site: Salvation Army http://www.salvationarmy.org/

Salyut (Russian 'salute') series of seven space stations launched by the USSR 1971–86. Salyut was cylindrical in shape, 15 m/50 ft long, and weighed 19 tonnes/21 tons. It housed two or three cosmonauts at a time, for missions lasting up to eight months.

Salyut 1 was launched 19 April 1971. It was occupied for 23 days in June 1971 by a crew of three, who died during their return to Earth when their ▷Soyuz ferry craft depressurized. In 1973 *Salyut 2* broke up in orbit before occupation. The first fully successful Salyut mission was a 14-day visit to *Salyut 3* in July 1974. In 1984–85 a team of three cosmonauts endured a record 237-day flight in *Salyut 7*. In 1986 the Salyut series was superseded by ▷*Mir*, an improved design capable of being enlarged by additional modules sent up from Earth.

Crews observed Earth and the sky, and carried out processing of materials in weightlessness. The last in the series, *Salyut 7*, crashed to Earth in February 1991, scattering debris in Argentina.

Salzburg capital of the federal state of Salzburg, west Austria, on the River Salzach; population (1995) 142,000. There are textile industries, and stock rearing, dairy farming, forestry, tourism, and the manufacture of musical instruments all contribute to the local economy. The city is dominated by the Hohensalzburg fortress (founded 1077, present buildings 1465–1519). It is the seat of an archbishopric founded by St Boniface in about 700 and has a 17th-century cathedral. It is also a conference centre. There are numerous fine Romanesque, Gothic, and baroque churches. It is the birthplace of the composer Wolfgang Amadeus Mozart and an annual music festival in August has been held here since 1920. The Mozart Museum of Sound and Film opened in 1991.

Related Web site: City of Salzburg – The Stage of the World http://www.salzburginfo.or.at/desk/frame_trailer.htm

SALZBURG The altar of St Georgskirche in Salzburg, Austria. *Image Bank*

Salzburg federal state of Austria, bounded on the northwest by Bavaria; area 7,200 sq km/2,779 sq mi; population (1994) 504,300. It lies mainly in the Salzburg Alps. Its capital is Salzburg. The chief industries are cattle rearing, dairy-farming, forestry, and tourism. It was annexed by Germany in 1938 but reunited with Austria in 1945.

Samara (formerly **Kuibyshev** (1935–91)) capital city and river port of Samara oblast (region), west-central Russian Federation; population (1996 est) 1,175,000. Samara is located on the River Volga and the main Trans-Siberian Railway, 820 km/510 mi southeast of Moscow. It is a major industrial centre, with large heavy-engineering industries (producing road vehicles and railway rolling stock), as well as chemical, oil-processing, wood-processing, and light industries.

samara in botany, a winged fruit, a type of ▷achene.

Samaria region of ancient Israel. The town of Samaria (now **Sebastiyeh**) on the west bank of the River Jordan was the capital of Israel in the 10th–8th centuries BC. It was renamed **Sebarte** in the 1st century BC by the Roman administrator Herod the Great. Extensive remains have been excavated.

Samaritan members or descendants of the colonists forced to settle in Samaria (now northern Israel) by the Assyrians after their occupation of the ancient kingdom of Israel 722 BC. Samaritans adopted a form of Judaism, but adopted only the Pentateuch, the five books of Moses of the Old Testament, and regarded their temple on Mount Gerizim as the true sanctuary.

Samaritans voluntary organization aiding those tempted to suicide or despair, established in 1953 in the UK. Groups of lay people, often consulting with psychiatrists, psychotherapists, and doctors, offer friendship and counselling to those using their emergency telephone numbers, day or night. In July 1994 the Samaritans began operating an e-mail service.

samarium hard, brittle, grey-white, metallic element of the ▷lanthanide series, symbol Sm, atomic number 62, relative atomic mass 150.4. It is widely distributed in nature and is obtained commercially from the minerals monzanite and bastnaesite. It is used only occasionally in industry, mainly as a catalyst in organic reactions. Samarium was discovered by spectroscopic analysis of the mineral samarskite and named in 1879 by French chemist Paul Lecoq de Boisbaudran (1838–1912) after its source.

Samarkand (Uzbek **Samarqand**) city in eastern Uzbekistan, capital of Samarkand wiloyat (region), near the River Zerafshan, 217 km/135 mi east of Bukhara; population (1996) 370,000. Industries include cotton-ginning, silk manufacture, production of foodstuffs, and engineering. Samarkand is one of the oldest cities in Central Asia, dating from the 3rd or 4th millennium BC. The Registan – a collection of mosques, courtyards and former Muslim theological seminaries ('madrasahs') – forms the centrepiece of the historic town. A university is situated here.

Samarra (or **Smarra**) ancient town in Iraq, on the River Tigris, 105 km/65 mi northwest of Baghdad; population (1998 est) 126,500. Founded in 836 by the Abbasid caliph Motassim, it was the Abbasid capital until 892 and is a place of pilgrimage for ▷Shiite Muslims. It is one of the largest archaeological sites in the world, and includes over 6,000 separate sites. The best preserved palace is Qasr al-Ashiq, built entirely of brick between 878 and 882.

samba Latin American ballroom dance; the music for this. Samba originated in Brazil and became popular in the West in the 1940s. There are several different samba rhythms; the ▷bossa nova is a samba-jazz fusion.

samizdat (Russian 'self-published') in the USSR and eastern Europe before the 1989 uprisings, written material circulated underground to evade state censorship; for example, reviews of Solzhenitsyn's banned novel *August 1914* (1972).

Samoa see country box.

Samoa volcanic island chain in the southwestern Pacific. It is divided into Samoa and American Samoa.

Samoa, American group of islands 4,200 km/2,610 mi south of Hawaii, administered by the USA; area 200 sq km/77 sq mi; population (1993) 52,900. The capital is Pago Pago. Exports include canned tuna, handicrafts, and copra. The main languages are Samoan and English; the principal religion is Christianity.

Related Web site: American Samoa http://www.umsl.edu/services/govdocs/wofact96/13.htm

samoyed breed of dog originating in Siberia. It weighs about 25 kg/60 lb and is 58 cm/23 in tall. It resembles a ▷chow chow, but has a more pointed face and a white or cream coat.

samphire (or **glasswort** or **sea asparagus**) perennial plant found on sea cliffs and coastlines in Europe. The aromatic, salty leaves are fleshy and sharply pointed; the flowers grow in yellow-green open clusters. Samphire is used in salads, or pickled. (*Crithmum maritimum*, family Umbelliferae.)

SAMPHIRE The true samphire native to coasts in southern England, belongs to the same family as parsley and carrot. The drab, yellowish flowers appear in profusion during the summer. *Premaphotos Wildlife*

Sampras, Pete (1971–) US tennis player. At the age of 19 years and 28 days, he became the youngest winner of the US Open in 1990. A fine server and volleyer, Sampras also won the inaugural Grand Slam Cup in Munich in 1990. In 1997 he finished at the top of the ATP men's world rankings for an unprecedented fifth consecutive year. In August 1999 he beat Ivan Lendl's all-time record of 270 weeks at the top of the ATP Tour world rankings. In 2000 he won his 7th Wimbledon men's singles title, equalling the record established by English player William Renshaw between 1882 and 1889. It was Sampras's 13th Grand Slam singles title, an unprecedented achievement in the men's game. He didn't win another tournament until 2002, when he triumphed in the US Open for the fifth time and claimed his 14th Grand Slam.

Samson (lived 11th century BC) In the Old Testament, a hero of Israel. He was renowned for exploits of strength against the Philistines. His lover Delilah had his hair, the source of his strength, cut off, as told in the Book of Judges.

Samsun Black Sea port and capital of a province of the same name in northern Turkey; situated at the mouth of the Murat River in a tobacco-growing area; population (1990) 303,900. It is the site of the ancient city of **Amisus**.

samurai (or **bushi**; Japanese 'one who serves') Japanese term for the warrior class which became the ruling military elite for almost 700 years. A samurai was an armed retainer of a *daimyō* (large landowner) with specific duties and privileges and a strict code of honour. The system was abolished in 1869.

Related Web site: History of the Japanese Samurai http://www.geocities.com/Tokyo/Temple/9577/report.html

San (formerly **Bushman**) a small group of hunter-gatherer peoples living in and around the Kalahari Desert. Their language belongs to the ▷Khoisan family.

San'a (or **Sana'a**) capital of Yemen, southwest Arabia, 320 km/200 mi north of Aden on the central plateau, 2,210 m/7,250 ft above sea level; population (1995) 972,000. A walled city, with fine mosques and traditional architecture, it is rapidly being modernized. Weaving and jewellery are local handicrafts.

San Andreas fault geological fault stretching for 1,125 km/700 mi northwest–southeast through the state of California, USA. It marks a conservative plate margin, where two plates slide past each other (see ▷plate tectonics).

Friction is created as the coastal Pacific plate moves northwest, rubbing against the American continental plate, which is moving slowly southeast. The relative movement is only about 5 cm/2 in a year, which means that Los Angeles will reach San Francisco's latitude in 10 million years. The friction caused by the tectonic movement gives rise to frequent, destructive ▷earthquakes. For example, in 1906 an earthquake originating from the fault almost destroyed San Francisco and killed about 700 people.

    Related Web site: San Andreas Fault and Bay Area http://sepwww.stanford.edu/oldsep/joe/fault_images/BayAreaSanAndreasFault.html

San Antonio (or **San Antonio de Bejar**) city in southern Texas, USA, on the **San Antonio River**; population (1996 est) 1,067,800. It is a commercial, financial, and military centre. Industries include tourism, aircraft maintenance, oil refining, and meat packing. Fort Sam Houston, four Air Force bases, the South Texas Medical Center, and the Southwest Research Center lie within the city limits and play an important part in the economy.

San Cristóbal capital of Táchira state, western Venezuela, situated 800 m/26,250 ft above sea level in the northern Andes overlooking the River Torbes, 56 km/35 mi from the Colombian border; population (1990) 220,700. It is the centre of a coffee growing region, and other products include textiles, cement, leather goods, and tobacco. San Cristóbal was founded by Spanish settlers in 1561 and stands on the ▷Pan-American Highway.

sanction economic or military measure taken by a state or number of states to enforce international law. The first use of sanctions, as a trade ▷embargo, was the attempted economic boycott of Italy 1935–36 during the Abyssinian War by the League of Nations.

Sanctorius, Sanctorius (1561–1636) Italian physiologist who pioneered the study of ▷metabolism and invented the clinical thermometer and a device for measuring pulse rate.

sanctuary (Latin *sanctuarium* 'sacred place') the holiest area of a place of worship; also a place of refuge from persecution or prosecution, usually in or near a place of worship. The custom of offering sanctuary in specific places goes back to ancient times and was widespread in Europe in the Middle Ages.

sand loose grains of rock, sized 0.0625–2.00 mm/0.0025–0.08 in in diameter, consisting most commonly of ▷quartz, but owing their varying colour to mixtures of other minerals. Sand is used in cement making, as an abrasive, in glass making, and for other purposes.

Sands are classified into marine, freshwater, glacial, and terrestrial. Some 'light' soils contain up to 50% sand. Sands may eventually consolidate into ▷sandstone.

Sand, George (1804–1876) Pen-name of Amandine Aurore Lucie Dupin. French author. Her prolific literary output was often autobiographical. In 1831 she left her husband after nine years of marriage and, while living in Paris as a writer, had love affairs with Alfred de Musset, Chopin, and others. Her first novel *Indiana* (1832) was a plea for women's right to independence.

sandalwood fragrant heartwood of any of several Asiatic and Australian trees, used for ornamental carving, in perfume, and burned as incense. (Genus *Santalum*, family Santalaceae.)

sandbar ridge of sand built up by the currents across the mouth of a river or bay. A sandbar may be entirely underwater or it may form an elongated island that breaks the surface. A sandbar stretching out from a headland is a **sand spit**.

Sandburg, Carl August (1878–1967) US poet. He worked as a farm labourer and a bricklayer, and his poetry celebrates ordinary life in the USA, as in *Chicago Poems* (1916), *The People, Yes* (1936), and *Complete Poems* (1950; Pulitzer prize). In free verse, it is reminiscent of Walt Whitman's poetry. Sandburg also wrote a monumental biography of Abraham Lincoln, *Abraham Lincoln: The Prairie Years* (1926; two volumes) and *Abraham Lincoln: The War Years* (1939; four volumes; Pulitzer prize). *Always the Young Strangers* (1953) is his autobiography.

> ### George Sand
> *What constitutes adultery is not the hour which a woman gives her lover, but the night which she afterwards spends with her husband.*
> Attributed remark

sand eel small, carnivorous fish found near the coasts of temperate seas of the northern hemisphere. Their bodies are covered with small scales, the swimbladder is absent, and they have long, sharply pointed snouts with which they bury themselves in the sand. Sand eels are in genus *Ammodytes* in the family Ammodytidae, belonging to the order Perciformes, class Osteichthyes.

sandflea another name for ▷jigger.

Samoa

Samoa formerly Western Samoa (until 1997) country in the southwest Pacific Ocean, in ▷Polynesia, northeast of Fiji Islands.

NATIONAL NAME *'O la Malo Tu To'atasi o Samoa/Independent State of Samoa*
AREA 2,830 sq km/1,092 sq mi
CAPITAL Apia (on Upolu island) (and chief port)
MAJOR TOWNS/CITIES Lalomanu, Tuasivi, Falealupo, Falelatai, Salotulafai, Taga
PHYSICAL FEATURES comprises South Pacific islands of Savai'i and Upolu, with two smaller tropical islands and uninhabited islets; mountain ranges on main islands; coral reefs; over half forested

Government

HEAD OF STATE King Malietoa Tanumafili II from 1962
HEAD OF GOVERNMENT Tuila'epa Sa'ilele Malielegaoi from 1998
POLITICAL SYSTEM liberal democracy
POLITICAL EXECUTIVE parliamentary
ADMINISTRATIVE DIVISIONS 11 districts
ARMED FORCES no standing defence forces; under Treaty of Friendship signed with New Zealand in 1962, the latter acts as sole agent in Samoa's dealings with other countries and international organizations

DEATH PENALTY retains the death penalty for ordinary crimes but can be considered abolitionist in practice

Economy and resources

CURRENCY tala, or Samoan dollar
GPD (US$) 261 million (2002)
REAL GDP GROWTH (% change on previous year) 6.5 (2001)
GNI (US$) 250 million (2002 est)
GNI PER CAPITA (PPP) (US$) 5,350 (2002 est)
CONSUMER PRICE INFLATION 3.8% (2003 est)
FOREIGN DEBT (US$) 181 million (2001 est)
MAJOR TRADING PARTNERS USA, Australia, New Zealand, Fiji, Japan, American Samoa
INDUSTRIES coconut-based products, timber, light engineering, construction materials, beer, cigarettes, clothing, leather goods, wire, tourism
EXPORTS fresh fish, coconut oil and cream, beer, cigarettes, taro, copra, cocoa, bananas, timber. Principal market: Australia 64.7% (2001)
IMPORTS food and live animals, machinery and transport equipment, mineral fuel, clothing and other manufactured goods. Principal source: USA 26.6% (2001)
ARABLE LAND 19.4% (2000 est)
AGRICULTURAL PRODUCTS coconuts, taro, copra, bananas, papayas, mangoes, pineapples, cocoa, taamu, breadfruit, maize, yams, passion fruit; livestock rearing (pigs, cattle, poultry, and goats) is important for local consumption; forest resources provide an important export commodity (47% of land was forest and woodland early 1990s)

Population and society

POPULATION 178,000 (2003 est)
POPULATION GROWTH RATE 0.3% (2000–05)
POPULATION DENSITY (per sq km) 63 (2003 est)
URBAN POPULATION (% of total) 23 (2003 est)
AGE DISTRIBUTION (% of total population) 0–14 41%, 15–59 52%, 60+ 7% (2002 est)

Chronology

c. 1000 BC: Settled by Polynesians from Tonga.
AD 950–1250: Ruled by Tongan invaders; the Matai (chiefly) system was developed.
15th century: United under the Samoan Queen Salamasina.
1722: Visited by Dutch traders.
1768: Visited by the French navigator Louis Antoine de Bougainville.
1830: Christian mission established and islanders were soon converted to Christianity.
1887–89: Samoan rebellion against German attempt to depose paramount ruler and install its own puppet regime.
1889: Under the terms of the Act of Berlin, Germany took control of the nine islands of Western Samoa, while the USA was granted American Samoa, and Britain Tonga and the Solomon Islands.
1900s: More than 2,000 Chinese brought in to work coconut plantations.
1914: Occupied by New Zealand on the outbreak of World War I.
1918: Nearly a quarter of the population died in an influenza epidemic.

ETHNIC GROUPS 93% of Samoan (Polynesian) origin; 7% Euronesian (mixed European and Polynesian), a small European minority
LANGUAGE English, Samoan (both official)

SAMOA A Samoan stamp commemorating the 21st anniversary of the South Pacific Commission. *Stanley Gibbons*

See also ▷Commonwealth, the (British); ▷League of Nations; ▷Samoa, American.

1920s: Development of nationalist movement, the Mau, and civil disobedience.
1920–61: Administered by New Zealand under League of Nations and, later, United Nations mandate.
1959: Local government established, headed by chief minister Fiame Mata'afa Mulinu'u.
1961: Referendum favoured independence.
1962: King Malietoa Tanumafili succeeded to the throne.
1962: Independence achieved within Commonwealth, with Mata'afa as prime minister, a position he retained (apart from a short break 1970–73) until his death in 1975.
1990: Universal adult suffrage was introduced and the power of Matai (elected clan leaders) reduced.
1991: Major damage was caused by 'Cyclone Val'.
1997: Name was changed officially from Western Samoa to Samoa, despite protests from American Samoa that it would undermine American Samoa's identity.
1998: Tuila'epa Sa'ilele Malielegaoi, of the HRPP, became the new prime minister.
2001: Malielegaoi was re-elected.

sandgrouse any bird of the family Pteroclidae, order Columbiformes. They look like long-tailed grouse, but are actually closely related to pigeons. They live in warm, dry areas of Europe, Asia, and Africa and have long wings, short legs and bills, a wedge shaped tail, and thick skin. They are sandy coloured and feed on vegetable matter and insects.

sand hopper (or **beachflea**) any of various small crustaceans belonging to the order Amphipeda, with laterally compressed bodies, that live in beach sand and jump like fleas. The eastern sand hopper *Orchestia agilis* of North America is about 1.3 cm/0.5 in long.

San Diego city and US naval air station, on the Pacific Ocean, and on the border of Mexico, in California, USA; population (1996 est) 1,171,100; metropolitan area (1992) 2,601,000. San Diego is linked to Tijuana, Mexico, by a 26-km/16-mi transit line (1981), popular with tourists. It is an important fishing port. Manufacturing includes aerospace and electronic equipment, metal fabrication, printing and publishing, seafood-canning, and shipbuilding. San Diego is the oldest Spanish settlement in California; a Spanish mission and fort were established here in 1769.

Related Web site: San Diego http://sandiego.about.com/citiestowns/caus/sandiego/mbody.htm

Sandinista member of a Nicaraguan left-wing organization (Sandinist National Liberation Front, FSLN) named after Augusto César Sandino, a guerrilla leader killed in 1934. It was formed in 1962 and obtained widespread support from the trade unions, the church, and the middle classes, which enabled it to overthrow the regime of General Anastasio Somoza in July 1979.

The FSLN dominated the Nicaraguan government and fought a civil war against US-backed Contra guerrillas until 1988. The FSLN was defeated in elections of 1990 by a US-backed coalition, but remained the party with the largest number of seats.

sand lizard lizard found on sandy heaths in Britain and central Europe, growing to nearly 20 cm/8 in in length. The male is brownish above, and in the spring a bright green on the flanks and belly. The female is brownish or greyish and mottled all over. They are active burrowers. The sand lizard *Lacerta agilis* is in the suborder Sauria, order Squamata, class Reptilia.

sandpiper shorebird with a long, slender bill, which is compressed and grooved at the tip. They belong to the family Scolopacidae, which includes godwits, ▷curlews, and ▷snipes, order Charadriiformes.

The **common sandpiper** *Tringa hypoleucos* is a small graceful bird about 18 cm/7 in long with a short tail. The head and back are greenish-brown with irregular markings on the plumage; underparts are white. The wingspan measures about 35 cm/14 in. It is common in the northern hemisphere except North America and is a summer migrant to Britain frequenting tidal rivers from April to September. It has a rapid and easy flight, and is a skilful swimmer and diver, feeding on worms and small insects. Its nest is usually made in a bank or tuft of grasses, though sometimes the pretty yellowish-white eggs are laid on the ground. The **green sandpiper** *T. ochropus* is a larger bird, and from a short distance appears to be black and white in colour. Its cry is extremely shrill. Other species are the **wood sandpiper** *T. glareola*, a passage migrant in Britain, and the **redshank** *T. totanus* a handsome, graceful bird, often gathering in large flocks on the coast in winter.

sandstone ▷sedimentary rocks formed from the consolidation of sand, with sand-sized grains (0.0625–2 mm/0.0025–0.08 in) in a matrix or cement. Their principal component is quartz. Sandstones are commonly permeable and porous, and may form freshwater ▷aquifers. They are mainly used as building materials.

SANDSTONE A red flag flies, a siren sounds, and there is a sudden deafening explosion as tons of sandstone turn from rock into small chunks and individual grains in a UK blasting quarry. *Image Bank*

San Francisco chief Pacific port in California, USA, on the tip of a peninsula in San Francisco Bay; population (1996 est) 735,300, metropolitan area of San Francisco and Oakland 3,686,600. The entrance channel from the Pacific to San Francisco Bay was named the Golden Gate in 1846; its strait was crossed in 1937 by the world's second-longest single-span bridge, 1,280 m/4,200 ft in length. Manufactured goods include textiles, machinery and metalware, electrical equipment, petroleum products, and pharmaceuticals. San Francisco is also a financial, trade, corporate, and diversified service centre. Tourism is a major industry. A Spanish fort (the Presidio) and the San Francisco de Asis Mission were established here in 1776. San Francisco has the largest Chinese community outside Asia.

Related Web site: Passporte! Your Complete Travel Guide to San Francisco http://bayarea.citysearch.com/San_Francisco/Hotels_and_Tourism/

SAN FRANCISCO Built in the 1930s, the San Francisco–Oakland Bay Bridge across San Francisco Bay is one of the longest combination bridges in the world and one of the great engineering feats of the 20th century. *Image Bank*

San Francisco conference conference attended by representatives from 50 nations who had declared war on Germany before March 1945; held in San Francisco, California, USA. The conference drew up the United Nations Charter, which was signed 26 June 1945.

Sanger, Frederick (1918–) English biochemist. He was awarded the Nobel Prize for Chemistry in 1958 for determining the structure of ▷insulin, and again in 1980 for work on the chemical structure of ▷genes. He was the first person to be awarded the Chemistry Prize twice.

Sanger's second Nobel prize was shared with two US scientists, Paul ▷Berg and Walter ▷Gilbert, for establishing methods of determining the sequence of nucleotides strung together along strands of ▷RNA and DNA. He also worked out the structures of various enzymes and other proteins.

Sangha in Buddhism, the monastic orders, one of the Three Treasures of Buddhism (the other two are Buddha and the teaching, or dharma).

The term Sangha is sometimes used more generally by Mahāyāna Buddhists to include all followers, including the laity.

San José capital of ▷Costa Rica, and of San José province; population (1991 est) 299,400. It is situated in the broad fertile valley of the central plateau. Products include coffee, cocoa, sugar cane, textiles, and pharmaceuticals. There is a cathedral, and the University of Costa Rica, which was founded in 1843. San José was founded in 1737 and became capital in 1823, replacing the former capital Cartago because it had a better all-year-round climate.

San José city in California, USA, in Santa Clara Valley, at the head of the southern arm of San Francisco Bay; population (1996) 838,700. It is situated at one end of 'Silicon Valley', the site of many high-technology electronic firms turning out semiconductors and other computer components. There are also electrical, aerospace, missile, rubber, metal, and machine industries, and it is a commercial and transportation centre for orchard crops and wines produced in the area.

Founded in 1777 as **El Pueblo de San José de Guadalupe**, a Spanish military supply base, it served as the state capital 1849–51.

San Juan industrial city and capital of Puerto Rico; population (1995 est) 458,000. It is a major port, exporting sugar, tobacco, coffee, and tropical fruits, mostly to the US mainland, and providing the world's busiest cruise ship base. It stands on an island joined by a bridge to the north coast of Puerto Rico. Industries include tourism, banking, metalworking, publishing, cigars, sugar, and clothing. Products include chemicals, pharmaceuticals, machine tools, electronic equipment, textiles, plastics, and rum.

San Marino see country box.

San Martín, José de (1778–1850) South American revolutionary leader. He served in the Spanish army during the Peninsular War, but after 1812 he devoted himself to the South American struggle for independence, playing a large part in the liberation of Argentina, Chile, and Peru from Spanish rule.

San Miguel de Tucumán capital of Tucumán province, northwest Argentina; situated on the Rio Sali, to the east of the Sierra de Aconquija range in the foothills of the Andes; population (1991) 473,000; metropolitan area (1992 est) 642,500. Industries include sugar mills and distilleries. It is the commercial centre of the province, and the largest city in northern Argentina. Founded in 1565, San Miguel de Tucumán was the site of the signing of the Argentine declaration of independence from Spain on 9 July 1816. There are several colonial buildings remaining in the city, including the Governor's Palace, the cathedral, and the church of San Francisco. The university was founded in 1914.

sannyasin in Hinduism, a person who has renounced worldly goods to live a life of asceticism and seek *moksha*, or liberation from reincarnation, through meditation and prayer.

San Pedro Sula main industrial and commercial city in northwest Honduras, near the Guatemalan border, capital of ▷Cortés department and the second-largest city in the country; population (1991 est) 325,900. Situated in the fertile valley of the Ulúa River, and 45 km/28 mi south of the port of Puerto Cortés, it is a trading centre and key distribution point for the north and northwest regions, which produce bananas, coffee, sugar, and timber; industries include steel, textiles, plastics, furniture, and cement. One of Central America's fastest growing cities, it was founded in 1536 by the Spaniard Pedro de Alvarado.

San Salvador capital of ▷El Salvador and of San Salvador department; situated at the foot of San Salvador volcano (2,548 m/8,360 ft) on the River Acelhuate, 48 km/30 mi from the Pacific Ocean; population (1992) 422,600. Industries include coffee, food processing, pharmaceuticals, and textiles. One-third of the country's industrial output comes from the city. Founded in 1525, it was destroyed by an earthquake in 1854 and rebuilt on the present site. It is now a modern city with architecture conditioned to seismic activity, to which the region is prone, although many buildings collapsed during a further earthquake in 1986.

sans-culotte (French 'without knee breeches') in the French Revolution, a member of the working classes, who wore trousers, as opposed to the aristocracy and bourgeoisie, who wore knee breeches. In Paris, the sans-culottes, who drew their support predominantly from apprentices, small shopkeepers, craftspeople, and the unemployed, comprised a large armed force that could be mobilized by radical politicians, for example in the ▷Jacobin seizure of power from the ▷Girondins in June 1793. Their fate was sealed by the fall of the Jacobins between 1794 and 1795.

Sanskrit the dominant classical language of the Indian subcontinent, a member of the Indo-Iranian group of the Indo-European language family, and the sacred language of Hinduism. The oldest form of Sanskrit is **Vedic**, the variety used in the *Vedas* and *Upanishads* (about 1500–700 BC).

Santa Anna, Antonio López de (*c.* 1795–1876) Mexican revolutionary. He became general and dictator of Mexico for most of the years between 1824 and 1855. He led the attack on the ▷Alamo fort in Texas in 1836.

Santa Claus another (especially American) name for ▷Father Christmas.

Santa Cruz capital of Santa Cruz department in central Bolivia, 550 km/342 mi southeast of La Paz; the second-largest city in the country; population (1992) 694,600. The surrounding area is fertile, producing sugar cane, soybeans, cotton, rice, maize, and coffee. It is a hub of transport and trade. Newly discovered oil and natural gas has led to the city's rapid development. It was founded by the Spaniard Nuflo de Chaves in 1561 as Santa Cruz de la Sierra. There is a university (founded 1880), and a cathedral.

Santa Cruz, Andrés (1792–1865) President of Bolivia 1829–34, 1839, 1841–44, and 1853–55. Strong-willed and conservative, he dabbled in political intrigue before and after his intermittent rule as dictator. He established order in the new state and increased expenditure on education and road building.

Santa Cruz de Tenerife capital of Tenerife and of the Canary Islands; population (1994) 204,000. It is a fuelling port and cable centre. Industry also includes oil refining, pharmaceuticals, and trade in fruit. Santa Cruz was bombarded by the British admirals Blake in 1657 and Nelson in 1797 (the action in which he lost his arm).

Santa Fé river port and capital of Santa Fé province, northeast Argentina, on the Salado River 153 km/95 mi north of Rosario; population (1991) 395,000. It is a leading distribution centre for the area and an export outlet for its agro-industrial and processed products. There are shipyards, and timber, cattle, and wool are exported. It has a 17th-century cathedral, several churches such as the mid-17th century Templo de Santo Domingo, and the Litoral University (founded 1919). Santa Fé was founded in 1573, and the 1853 constitution was drafted here.

Santa Fe capital of ▷New Mexico, USA, on the **Santa Fe River**, 65 km/40 mi west of Las Vegas; population (1996 est) 66,500, many Spanish-speaking. It is situated in the Rio Grande Valley, over 2,000 m/6,500 ft above sea level, on the western slopes of the Sangre de Cristo Mountains. Santa Fe is the cultural and tourist capital of the southwest, home to many artists, theatre, and opera. Precision instruments, pottery, and American Indian jewellery and textiles are produced.

Founded by the Spanish in 1610 on a prehistoric Tiwa pueblo site, it was later a trading post on the 19th-century Santa Fe Trail. Ceded to the USA in 1848, it became the territorial capital in 1851, and state capital in 1912 on New Mexico's admission to the Union.

Santayana, George (1863–1952) Born Jorge Augustín Nicolás Ruiz de Santayana. Spanish-born US philosopher and critic. He developed his philosophy based on naturalism and taught that everything has a natural basis.

Santer, Jacques (1937–) Luxembourg politician, prime minister 1984–94, and president of the European Commission 1995–99. He resigned his EC presidency along with the rest of the Commission, following a scandal over fraud and mismanagement.

Santiago capital of Chile, on the Mapocho River; population (1992) 4,385,500 (metropolitan area 5,180,800). It is the fifth largest city in South America and the country's cultural, commercial, and manufacturing centre. Industries include textiles, chemicals, and food processing. It has three universities, and several theatres, libraries, and museums.

Features Spanish colonial architecture, including the former Governors' Palace, now housing a museum; cathedral (founded 1558); Palacio de la Moneda (built 1788–1805), now the presidential palace; churches; broad avenues; skyscrapers.
History Founded by the Spaniard Pedro de Valdivia in 1541, it became the capital of Chile in 1818.
    Related Web site: Santiago http://sunsite.dcc.uchile.cl/chile/turismo/santiago.html

Santiago second-largest city in the Dominican Republic; population (1991 est) 375,000. It is a processing and trading centre for sugar, coffee, and cacao.

Santiago de Compostela capital of ▷Galicia autonomous community, in the province of La Coruña, northwest Spain; population (1991) 87,500. Textiles, chocolate, and soap are manufactured here, and there is a trade in agricultural produce. The 11th-century cathedral was reputedly built over the grave of Sant Iago el Mayor (St ▷James the Great), patron saint of Spain, and was a world-famous centre for medieval pilgrims. Santiago is the seat of an archbishop, and there is also a university, founded in 1532.

Santiago de Cuba port on the south coast of Cuba; population (1995 est) 425,000. It is the second largest city and former capital of Cuba, and is now the capital of Santiago de Cuba province. Products include sugar, rum, and cigars.

Santo Domingo capital and chief sea port of the Dominican Republic; population (1991 est) 2,055,000. Founded 1496 by Bartolomeo, brother of Christopher Columbus, it is the oldest colonial city in the Americas. Its cathedral was built 1515–40.

Santos industrial city and principal seaport in São Paulo federal unit (state), southeast Brazil, 72 km/45 mi southeast of the city of São Paulo on the Atlantic coast; population (1991) 546,600. It is the largest and most important port in Brazil, and the world's leading coffee-exporting port. There are oil refineries and chemical and steel industries. The port lies 5 km/3 mi along the Santos Channel

SANTO DOMINGO The Columbus Palace, or Alcazar Colón, in Santo Domingo in the Dominican Republic. *Image Bank*

and is surrounded by sandy beaches. The Brazilian soccer player Pelé played here for many years. Santos was founded in 1534.

San Yu, U (1919–1996) Myanmar (Burmese) politician, president 1981–88. A member of the revolutionary council that came to power in 1962, he became president in 1981 and was re-elected in 1985. He was forced to resign in July 1988, along with Ne Win, after riots in Yangon (formerly Rangoon).

Saône river in eastern France, rising in the Vosges Mountains and flowing 480 km/300 mi to join the ▷Rhône at Lyon. After rising in the Faucilles Mountains of the Vosges, it flows south past Gray, Chalon-sur-Saône, and Mâcon. The chief tributaries are the ▷Doubs and the Ognon. It is connected by canal with the rivers Loire, Seine, Meuse, Moselle, and Rhine.

San Marino

San Marino small landlocked country within northeast Italy.

NATIONAL NAME *Serenissima Repubblica di San Marino/Most Serene Republic of San Marino*
AREA 61 sq km/24 sq mi
CAPITAL San Marino
MAJOR TOWNS/CITIES Serravalle, Faetano, Fiorentino, Borgo Maggiore, Domagnano
PHYSICAL FEATURES the slope of Mount Titano

Government

HEAD OF STATE AND GOVERNMENT Giovanni Lonfernini and Valeria Ciavatta from 2003
POLITICAL SYSTEM liberal democracy
POLITICAL EXECUTIVE parliamentary
ADMINISTRATIVE DIVISIONS 12 districts

ARMED FORCES voluntary military forces and a paramilitary gendarmerie
DEATH PENALTY abolished in 1865

Economy and resources

CURRENCY euro
GPD (US$) 863 million (2001)
REAL GDP GROWTH (% change on previous year) 9% (2001)
GNI (US$) 820 million (2001)
GNI PER CAPITA (PPP) (US$) 26,960 (2001)
CONSUMER PRICE INFLATION 2% (2001)
UNEMPLOYMENT 2.6% (2001)
MAJOR TRADING PARTNERS maintains customs union with Italy (for trade data see Italy)
RESOURCES limestone and other building stone

INDUSTRIES cement, synthetic rubber, leather, textiles, ceramics, tiles, wine, chemicals, olive oil, tourism, postage stamps
EXPORTS wood machinery, chemicals, wine, olive oil, textiles, tiles, ceramics, varnishes, building stone, lime, chestnuts, hides. Principal market: Italy
IMPORTS consumer goods, raw materials, energy supply. Principal source: Italy
ARABLE LAND 16.7% (2000 est)
AGRICULTURAL PRODUCTS wheat, barley, maize, grapes, olives, fruit, vegetables; viticulture; dairy farming

Population and society

POPULATION 28,000 (2003 est)
POPULATION GROWTH RATE 1.1% (2000–05)
POPULATION DENSITY (per sq km) 452 (2003 est)
URBAN POPULATION (% of total) 91 (2003 est)

SAN MARINO A stamp from San Marino, produced for the 75th anniversary of the Universal Postal Union. *Stanley Gibbons*

AGE DISTRIBUTION (% of total population) 0–14 16%, 15–59 63%, 60+ 21% (2001 est)
ETHNIC GROUPS predominantly Italian, Sanmarinese; about 11% are foreign citizens
LANGUAGE Italian (official)
RELIGION Roman Catholic 95%
EDUCATION (compulsory years) 8
LITERACY RATE 99% (men); 98% (women) (2003 est)
LABOUR FORCE 1.4% agriculture, 38.6% industry, 60.0% services (1999)
LIFE EXPECTANCY 78 (men); 85 (women) (2001 est)

Chronology

***c.* AD 301**: Founded as a republic (the world's oldest surviving) by St Marinus and a group of Christians who settled there to escape persecution.
12th century: Self-governing commune.
1600: Statutes (constitution) provided for a parliamentary form of government, based around the Great and General Council.
1815: Independent status of the republic recognized by the Congress of Vienna.
1862: Treaty with Italy signed; independence recognized under Italy's protection.
1945–57: Communist–Socialist administration in power, eventually ousted in a bloodless 'revolution'.
1957–86: Governed by a series of left-wing and centre-left coalitions.
1971: Treaty with Italy renewed.
1992: San Marino joined the United Nations (UN).
1998: The ruling PDCS–PSS coalition remained in power after a general election.

São Paulo industrial city and capital of São Paulo federal unit (state), southeast Brazil, 72 km/45 mi northwest of its port Santos, and 400 km/249 mi southwest of Rio de Janeiro; population (1992) 9,646,200 (metropolitan area 16,567,300). It is Latin America's second-largest city after Mexico City. It is 900 m/3,000 ft above sea level, and 2° south of the Tropic of Capricorn. It is also South America's leading industrial city, producing electronics, steel, and chemicals; it has meat-packing plants and is the centre of Brazil's coffee trade. The city has a cathedral and four universities (the University of São Paulo is the largest in Brazil). The Butantã Snake Farm is a biomedical research institute for the production of antidotes for snakebite.

SÃO PAULO One of the steel-making foundries in São Paulo, Brazil. São Paulo is the centre of the country's automotive manufacturing. It was also in São Paulo that, in 1822, the Brazilians first declared their independence from Portugal. *Image Bank*

São Tomé port and capital of ▷São Tomé e Príncipe, on the northeast coast of São Tomé island, Gulf of Guinea; population (1991) 43,400. It exports sugar, cocoa, and coffee.

São Tomé and Príncipe see country box.

sap the fluids that circulate through ▷vascular plants, especially woody ones. Sap carries water and food to plant tissues. Sap contains alkaloids, protein, and starch; it can be milky (as in rubber trees), resinous (as in pines), or syrupy (as in maples).

saponification in chemistry, the ▷hydrolysis (splitting) of an ▷ester by treatment with a strong alkali, resulting in the liberation of the alcohol from which the ester had been derived and a salt of the constituent fatty acid. The process is used in the manufacture of soap.

sapphire deep-blue, transparent gem variety of the mineral ▷corundum Al$_2$O$_3$, aluminium oxide. Small amounts of iron and titanium give it its colour. A corundum gem of any colour except red (which is a ruby) can be called a sapphire; for example, yellow sapphire.

Sappho (*c.* 610–*c.* 580 BC) Greek lyric poet. A native of Lesbos and contemporary of the poet Alcaeus, she was famed for her female eroticism (hence lesbianism). The surviving fragments of her poems express a keen sense of loss, and delight in the worship of the goddess ▷Aphrodite.

Sapporo capital of ▷Hokkaido prefecture, Japan, on the Ishikari River; population (1994) 1,719,000. Industries include rubber, food processing, printing, brewing beer, and lead and zinc mining. It is a winter sports centre and was the site of the 1972 Winter Olympics. Giant figures are sculpted in ice at the annual snow festival. The city has an underground railway.

saprotroph (formerly **saprophyte**) organism that feeds on the excrement or the dead bodies or tissues of others. They include most fungi (the rest being parasites); many bacteria and protozoa; animals such as dung beetles and vultures; and a few unusual plants, including several orchids. Saprotrophs cannot make food for themselves, so they are a type of ▷heterotroph. They are useful scavengers, and in sewage farms and refuse dumps break down organic matter into nutrients easily assimilable by green plants.

Saracen ancient Greek and Roman term for an Arab, used in the Middle Ages by Europeans for all Muslims. The equivalent term used in Spain was ▷Moor.

Saragossa English spelling of ▷Zaragoza, a city and province of Spain.

Sarajevo capital of Bosnia-Herzegovina; population (1991) 526,000. Industries include engineering, brewing, chemicals, carpets, and ceramics. A Bosnian, Gavrilo Princip, assassinated Archduke ▷Franz Ferdinand here in 1914, thereby precipitating World War I. From April 1992 the city was the target of a siege by Bosnian Serb forces in their fight to carve up the newly independent republic. A United Nations ultimatum and the threat of NATO bombing led to a ceasefire February 1994 and the effective end of the siege as Serbian heavy weaponry was withdrawn from the high points surrounding the city.

Sarawak state of Malaysia, in the northwest of the island of Borneo; area 124,400 sq km/48,018 sq mi; population (1991) 1,669,000 (24 ethnic groups make up almost half this number). The capital is Kuching. Industries include timber, oil, rice, pepper, rubber, coconuts, and natural gas.

sarcoidosis chronic disease of unknown cause involving enlargement of the lymph nodes and the formation of small fleshy nodules in the lungs. It may also affect the eyes, and skin, and (rarely) other tissue. Many cases resolve spontaneously or may be successfully treated using ▷corticosteroids.

sarcoma malignant ▷tumour arising from the fat, muscles, bones, cartilage, or blood and lymph vessels and connective tissues. Sarcomas are much less common than ▷carcinomas.

sardine common name for various small fishes (▷pilchards) in the herring family.

Six species of sardine are generally recognized: five in the Pacific and Indian Oceans (*Sardinops* species) and *Sardinia pilchardus* in the Atlantic and Mediterranean. In 1998 US researchers announced, following analysis of mitochondrial DNA from the *Sardinops* species, that they were in fact probably widely dispersed regional populations of the same species, rather than different species.

The name is legally restricted in the UK, following a court ruling of 1915 in favour of an application by a French firm, to the young of the pilchard, caught off Sardinia (hence the name) and Brittany.

Sardinia (Italian **Sardegna**) mountainous island and special autonomous region of Italy, about 240 km/150 mi southwest of the Orbetello promontory in Tuscany; area 24,100 sq km/9,300 sq mi; population (1992 est) 1,651,900. It is the second-largest Mediterranean island and comprises the provinces of Cagliari, Nuoro, Oristano, and Sassari; its capital is ▷Cagliari. Cork, fruit, grain, tobacco, minerals (lead, zinc, manganese), and petrochemicals are exported. Features include the Costa Smeralda (Emerald Coast) tourist area in the northeast and *nuraghi* (fortified Bronze Age dwellings). After centuries of foreign rule, Sardinia became linked with Piedmont in 1720, and this dual kingdom became the basis of a united Italy in 1861.

Sargent, John Singer (1856–1925) US portrait painter. Born in Florence, Italy, of American parents, he studied there and in Paris, and settled in England in 1885. He quickly became a fashionable and prolific painter, though not in the sense that he flattered: he brilliantly depicted affluent late Victorian and Edwardian society, British and American. His portrait of Mme Gautreau, *Madame X* (1884; Metropolitan Museum of Art, New York), criticized for its impropriety when first shown in Paris, is one of his best-known works.

Sargent, (Harold) Malcolm (Watts) (1895–1967) English conductor. He was professor at the Royal College of Music from 1923, chief conductor of the BBC Symphony Orchestra 1950–57, and continued as conductor in chief of the annual Henry Wood promenade concerts at the Royal Albert Hall.

Sargon two Mesopotamian kings:

> **Sappho**
> *Some say a formation of horseman, infantry, / or ships is the loveliest thing on the black / earth, but I maintain it is whatever / a person loves.*
> Fragment 16: 1–4

Sargon I King of Akkad *c.* 2334–*c.* 2279 BC, and founder of the first Mesopotamian empire. Like Moses, he was said to have been found floating in a cradle on the local river, in his case the Euphrates.

Sargon II (died 705 BC) King of Assyria from 722 BC, who assumed the name of his predecessor. To keep conquered peoples from rising against him, he had whole populations moved from their homelands, including the Israelites from Samaria.

Sark one of the ▷Channel Islands, 10 km/6 mi east of Guernsey; area 5 sq km/2 sq mi; population (1991) 575.

There is no town or village. It is divided into Great and Little Sark, linked by an isthmus, and is of great natural beauty. The Seigneurie of Sark was established by Elizabeth I, the ruler being known as Seigneur/Dame, and has its own parliament, the Chief Pleas. There is no income tax or divorce, cars are forbidden, and immigration is controlled.

Sarmiento, Domingo Faustino (1811–1888) Argentina's first civilian president 1868–74, regarded as one of the most brilliant Argentines of the 19th century. An outspoken critic of the dictator Juan Manuel de ▷Rosas, Sarmiento spent many years in exile. As president, he doubled the number of schools, creating the best education system in Latin America, and encouraged the establishment of libraries and museums. He also expanded trade, extended railroad building, and encouraged immigration.

SARS acronym for Severe Acute Respiratory Syndrome. Highly infectious disease with symptoms similar to influenza, notably chills, headaches, muscle pains, a sore throat, and a high fever. Pneumonia develops as the disease progresses, and can result in death – the mortality rate is estimated by the World Health Organization (WHO) at around 15%. First identified in 2003, there is no known cure or vaccine for the disease.

SARS is caused by a type of coronavirus, which usually produces colds in humans, but severe conditions, such as pneumonia and diarrhoea in animals. The SARS virus was thought to have mutated to allow it to jump the species barrier from animals to humans. The incubation period of SARS varies but is on average between 2 and 10 days. The risk of death increases with age and the mortality rate is as high as 50% in those over 60 years of age.

The first outbreak of SARS is thought to have been near Foshan in the southern Chinese province of Guangdong in November 2002, but the disease only came to public attention in February 2003 as it rapidly spread worldwide due to the use of air travel. Over 8,000 cases and over 800 deaths from SARS have been reported globally, with China, Taiwan, and Hong Kong being the areas mainly affected.

Sartre, Jean-Paul (1905–1980) French author and philosopher. He was a leading proponent of ▷existentialism. He published his first novel, *La Nausée/Nausea* (1937), followed by the trilogy *Les Chemins de la liberté/Roads to Freedom* (1944–45) and many plays, including *Les Mouches/The Flies* (1943), *Huis clos/In Camera* (1944), and *Les Séquestrés d'Altona/The Condemned of Altona* (1960). *L'Etre et le néant/Being and Nothingness* (1943), his first major philosophical work, sets out a radical doctrine of human freedom. In the later work *Critique de la raison dialectique/Critique of Dialectical Reason* (1960) he tried to produce a fusion of existentialism and Marxism. He was awarded the Nobel Prize for Literature in 1964, which he declined.

Sartre was born in Paris, and was the long-time companion of the feminist writer Simone de ▷Beauvoir. During World War II he was a prisoner for nine months, and on his return from Germany

> **Jean-Paul Sartre**
> *I confused things with their names: that is belief.*
> The Words

JEAN-PAUL SARTRE The French author and philosopher in the 1940s. *Image Bank*

joined the Resistance. As a founder of existentialism, he edited its journal *Les Temps modernes/Modern Times*, and expressed its tenets in his novels and plays. According to Sartre, people have to create their own destiny without relying on powers higher than themselves. Awareness of this freedom takes the form of anxiety, and people therefore attempt to flee from awareness into what he terms *mauvaise foi* ('bad faith'); this is the theory he put forward in *L'Etre et le néant*. In *Les Mains sales/Crime passionel* (1948) he attacked aspects of communism while remaining generally sympathetic. In his later work Sartre became more sensitive to the social constraints on people's actions. He refused the Nobel prize for 'personal reasons', but allegedly changed his mind later, saying he wanted it for the money.

Related Web site: Sartre, Jean-Paul
http://members.aol.com/KatharenaE/private/Philo/Sartre/sartre.html

SAS abbreviation for ▷Special Air Service; also for **Scandinavian Airlines System.**

Saskatchewan (called 'Canada's breadbasket'; Cree *Kis-is-ska-tche-wan* 'swift flowing') province of west-central Canada, the middle Prairie province, bordered to the west by Alberta and to the east by Manitoba. To the north of Saskatchewan (above the 60th parallel) are the Northwest Territories, while to the south (below the 49th parallel) lie the US states of North Dakota and Montana; area 652,300 sq km/251,854 sq mi; population (1997) 1,023,500. The capital is Regina. Industries include extraction of oil, natural gas, uranium, zinc, potash, copper, and helium; and manufacture of cement, chemicals, fertilizers, and wood products. Wheat, oats, barley, rye, and flax are grown, and there is cattle rearing and dairying.

Sassanian Empire Persian empire founded AD 224 by Ardashir, a chieftain in the area of what is now Fars, in Iran, who had taken over ▷Parthia; it was named after his grandfather, Sasan. The capital was Ctesiphon, near modern ▷Baghdad, Iraq. After a rapid period of expansion, when it contested supremacy with Rome, it was destroyed in 637 by Muslim Arabs at the Battle of Qadisiya.

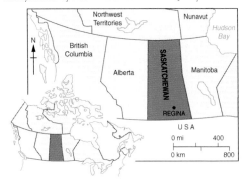

Sassau-Nguesso, Denis (1943–) Congolese socialist politician, president 1979–92 and from 1997. He progressively consolidated his position within the ruling left-wing Congolese Labour Party (PCT), at the same time as improving relations with France and the USA. In 1990, in response to public pressure, he agreed that the PCT should abandon Marxism-Leninism and that a multiparty system should be introduced. He returned to power in November 1997.

Sassoon, Siegfried Loraine (1886–1967) English poet. His anti-war poems which appeared in *The Old Huntsman* (1917), *Counter-Attack* (1918), and later volumes, were begun in the trenches during World War I and express the disillusionment of his generation. His later poetry tended towards the reflective and the spiritual. His three fictionalized autobiographical studies, including *Memoirs of a Fox-Hunting Man* (1928), *Memoirs of an Infantry Officer* (1930), and *Sherston's Progress* (1936), were published together as *The Complete Memoirs of George Sherston* (1937).

Satan a name for the ▷devil.

Satanism worship of the devil (Satan) instead of God, and the belief that doing so can bind a person to his power. The most significant ritual in Satanism is believed to be the Black Mass, a parody of the Christian Mass or Eucharist.

satellite any small body that orbits a larger one, either natural or artificial. Natural satellites that orbit planets are called moons. The first **artificial satellite**, *Sputnik 1*, was launched into orbit around the Earth by the USSR in 1957. Artificial satellites are used for scientific purposes, communications, weather forecasting, and military applications. The brightest artificial satellites can be seen by the naked eye. At any time, there are several thousand artificial satellites orbiting the Earth, including active satellites, satellites that have ended their working lives, and discarded sections of rockets. Artificial satellites eventually re-enter the Earth's atmosphere. Usually they burn up by friction, but sometimes debris falls to the Earth's surface,

> **Siegfried Sassoon**
> *Soldiers are dreamers;*
> *when the guns begin / They*
> *think of firelit homes, clean*
> *beds, and wives.*
> 'Dreamers' 1918

São Tomé and Principe

SÃO TOMÉ AND PRINCIPE This stamp displays the flag of the republic and the location of the islands. *Stanley Gibbons*

São Tomé and Príncipe country in the Gulf of Guinea, off the coast of West Africa.

NATIONAL NAME *República Democrática de São Tomé e Príncipe/Democratic Republic of São Tomé and Príncipe*
AREA 1,000 sq km/386 sq mi
CAPITAL São Tomé
MAJOR TOWNS/CITIES Santo António, Santana, Porto-Alegre, Trinidad, Neves, Santo Amaro
PHYSICAL FEATURES comprises two main islands and several smaller ones, all volcanic; thickly forested and fertile

Government

HEAD OF STATE Fradique de Menezes from 2001
HEAD OF GOVERNMENT Maria das Neves de Sousa from 2002
POLITICAL SYSTEM emergent democracy
POLITICAL EXECUTIVE limited presidency
ADMINISTRATIVE DIVISIONS six districts
ARMED FORCES no proper army; reorganization of island's armed forces (estimated at 900) and police into two separate police forces (one for public order, the other for criminal investigations) was initiated in 1992
DEATH PENALTY abolished in 1990

Economy and resources

CURRENCY dobra
GPD (US$) 50 million (2002 est)
REAL GDP GROWTH (% change on previous year) 4 (2001)
GNI (US$) 45 million (2002 est)
GNI PER CAPITA (PPP) (US$) 1,310 (2002 est)
CONSUMER PRICE INFLATION 8% (2003 est)
UNEMPLOYMENT 29.5% (1997)
FOREIGN DEBT (US$) 293 million (2001 est)
MAJOR TRADING PARTNERS Portugal, the Netherlands, USA, UK, Germany, Canada, Belgium, France, Japan, Angola
INDUSTRIES agricultural and timber processing, soft drinks, soap, textiles, beer, bricks, ceramics, shirts
EXPORTS cocoa, copra, coffee, bananas, palm oil. Principal market: the Netherlands 27.3% (2001)

IMPORTS capital goods, food and live animals, petroleum and petroleum products. Principal source: Portugal 38.9% (2001)
ARABLE LAND 4.1% (2000 est)
AGRICULTURAL PRODUCTS cocoa, coconuts, copra, bananas, palm oil, cassava, sweet potatoes, yams, coffee; fishing; forestry

Population and society

POPULATION 161,000 (2003 est)
POPULATION GROWTH RATE 1.8% (2000–05)
POPULATION DENSITY (per sq km) 167 (2003 est)
URBAN POPULATION (% of total) 49 (2003 est)
AGE DISTRIBUTION (% of total population) 0–14 47%, 15–59 47%, 60+ 6% (2002 est)
ETHNIC GROUPS predominantly African; mixed African and Portuguese origin, angolares (descendants of Angolan slaves)
LANGUAGE Portuguese (official), Fang (a Bantu language), Lungwa São Tomé (a Portuguese Creole)
RELIGION Roman Catholic 80%, animist
EDUCATION (compulsory years) 4

Chronology

1471: First visited by the Portuguese, who imported convicts and slaves to work on sugar plantations in the formerly uninhabited islands.
1522: Became a province of Portugal.
1530: Slaves successfully revolted, forcing plantation owners to flee to Brazil; thereafter became a key staging post for Congo-Americas slave trade.
19th century: Forced contract labour used to work coffee and cocoa plantations.
1953: More than 1,000 striking plantation workers gunned down by Portuguese troops.
1960: First political party formed, the forerunner of the socialist-nationalist Movement for the Liberation of São Tomé e Príncipe (MLSTP).
1974: Military coup in Portugal led to strikes, demonstrations, and army mutiny in São Tomé; thousands of Portuguese settlers fled the country.
1975: Independence achieved, with Manuel Pinto da Costa (MLSTP) as president; close links developed with communist bloc.

LITERACY RATE 86% (men); 70% women (2003 est)

1984: Formally declared a nonaligned state as economy deteriorated.
1988: Coup attempt against da Costa foiled by Angolan and East European troops.
1990: Influenced by collapse of communism in Eastern Europe, MLSTP abandoned Marxism; a new pluralist constitution was approved in a referendum.
1991: First multiparty elections.
1994: MLSTP returned to power with Carlos da Graca as prime minister.
1998: MLSTP–PSD won an absolute majority in the assembly.
2003: A coup by the armed forces led by Fernando Pereira against the elected government ended peacefully as President Menezes, backed by Nigeria, agreed to an amnesty for the mutineers and to the replacement of ministers. The political turmoil was linked reportedly to control of the country's abundant potential offshore oil resources.

as with ▷*Skylab* and *Salyut 7*. In 1997 there were 300 active artificial satellites in orbit around Earth, the majority used in communications.

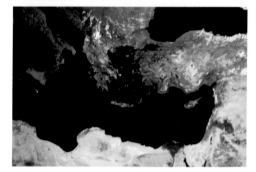

SATELLITE A photo of the central and eastern Mediterranean region, taken by an orbiting satellite. The first vehicle in the Landsat series took over 300,000 pictures of the Earth's surface between 1972 and 1978; subsequent Landsats have contributed greatly to accurate mapping of the world's remoter regions. *Image Bank*

satellite television transmission of broadcast signals through artificial communications satellites. Mainly positioned in ▷geostationary orbit, satellites have been used since the 1960s to relay television pictures around the world.

Higher-power satellites have more recently been developed to broadcast signals to cable systems or directly to people's homes.

Satie, Erik (Alfred Leslie) (1866–1925) French composer. His piano pieces, such as the three *Gymnopédies* (1888), are precise and tinged with melancholy, and parody romantic expression with surreal commentary. His aesthetic of ironic simplicity, as in the *Messe des pauvres/Poor People's Mass* (1895), acted as a nationalist antidote to the perceived excesses of German Romanticism.

Mentor of the group of composers ▷*Les Six*, Satie promoted the concept of *musique d'ameublement* ('furniture music'), anticipating the impact of radio. A commission from Diaghilev led to the ballet *Parade* (1917), with instrumentation for siren, typewriter, and steamship whistle, and he invented a new style of film music for René Clair's *Entr'acte* (1924).

satire literary or dramatic work that ridicules human pretensions or exposes social evils. Satire is related to parody in its intention to mock, but satire tends to be more subtle and to mock an attitude or a belief, whereas parody tends to mock a particular work (such as a poem) by imitating its style, often with purely comic intent.

satrap title of a provincial governor in ancient Persia. Under Darius I, the Persian Empire was divided between some 20 satraps, each owing allegiance only to the king.

SATs (abbreviations for Standard Assessment Tests; or **National Curriculum Assessments**) in the UK, formal assessment of children's educational standards. Children are assessed at the end of each Key Stage of the National Curriculum, in English and maths at 7, and English, maths, and science at 11 and 14. The vast majority take GCSE examinations at 16 at the end of Key Stage 4. Results are expressed in a series of 'levels' with the desirable outcome set at Level 2 at 7, Level 4 at 11, and Level 5 or 6 at 14. The results of the assessments are aggregated by school and the results published, although very small schools, where so few children are assessed that they might be identifiable from the results, do not have to publish their scores. The aggregated results for Local Education Authorities (LEAs) are also published. The results are used to produce comparative league tables of school and LEA performance, although teachers complain that these do not reflect the relative difficulties of children in different areas and social groups.

The government uses the results of the assessments to set targets at school, LEA, and national level. Its first objective is to ensure that 80% of 11-year-olds have reached Level 4 standard in the core National Curriculum subjects by the year 2002.

saturated compound organic compound, such as propane, that contains only single covalent bonds. Saturated organic compounds can only undergo further reaction by ▷substitution reactions, as in the production of chloropropane from propane.

saturated fatty acid ▷fatty acid in which there are no double bonds in the hydrocarbon chain.

saturated solution in physics and chemistry, a solution obtained when a solvent (liquid) can dissolve no more of a solute

(usually a solid) at a particular temperature. Normally, a slight fall in temperature causes some of the solute to crystallize out of solution. If this does not happen the phenomenon is called supercooling, and the solution is said to be supersaturated.

Saturn in astronomy, the second-largest planet in the Solar System, sixth from the Sun, and encircled by bright and easily visible equatorial rings. Viewed through a telescope it is ochre. Its polar diameter is 12,000 km/7,450 mi smaller than its equatorial diameter, a result of its fast rotation and low density, the lowest of any planet. Its mass is 95 times that of Earth, and its magnetic field 1,000 times stronger.

mean distance from the Sun 1.427 billion km/0.886 billion mi **equatorial diameter** 120,000 km/75,000 mi **rotational period** 10 hr 14 min at equator, 10 hr 40 min at higher latitudes **year** 29.46 Earth years **atmosphere** visible surface consists of swirling clouds, probably made of frozen ammonia at a temperature of −170°C/−274°F, although the markings in the clouds are not as prominent as Jupiter's. The space probes *Voyager 1* and *2* found winds reaching 1,800 kph/1,100 mph **surface** Saturn is believed to have a small core of rock and iron, encased in ice and topped by a deep layer of liquid hydrogen **satellites** 22 known moons, more than for any other planet. The largest moon, ▷Titan, has a dense atmosphere. Other satellites include Epimetheus, Janus, Pandor, and Prometheus **rings** The rings visible from Earth begin about 14,000 km/9,000 mi from the planet's cloudtops and extend out to about 76,000 km/47,000 mi. Made of small chunks of ice and rock (averaging 1 m/3.3 ft across), they are 275,000 km/170,000 mi rim to rim, but only 100 m/300 ft thick. The *Voyager* probes showed that the rings actually consist of thousands of closely spaced ringlets, looking like the grooves in a gramophone record. From Earth, Saturn's rings appear to be divided into three main sections. Ring A, the outermost, is separated from ring B, the brightest, by the Cassini division, named after its discoverer Italian astronomer Giovanni ▷Cassini (1625–1712), which is 3,000 km/2,000 mi wide; the inner, transparent ring C is also called the Crepe Ring. Each ringlet of the rings is made of a swarm of icy particles like snowballs, a few centimetres to a few metres in diameter. Outside the A ring is the narrow and faint F ring, which the *Voyagers* showed to be twisted or braided. The rings of Saturn could be the remains of a shattered moon, or they may always have existed in their present form.

Saturn (or **Saturnus**) in Roman mythology, the god of agriculture, identified by the Romans with the Greek god ▷Kronos. His period of rule was the ancient Golden Age, when he introduced social order and the arts of civilization. Saturn was dethroned by his sons Jupiter, Neptune, and Dis. At the **Saturnalia**, his festival in December, gifts were exchanged, and slaves were briefly treated as their masters' equals.

SATURN The rings of Saturn, consisting of small pieces of ice and rock. *National Aeronautical Space Agency*

Saturn rocket family of large US rockets, developed by German-born US rocket engineer Wernher von Braun (1912–1977) for the ▷Apollo project. The two-stage *Saturn IB* was used for launching Apollo spacecraft into orbit around the Earth. The three-stage *Saturn V* sent Apollo spacecraft to the Moon, and launched the ▷*Skylab* space station. The takeoff thrust of a *Saturn V* was 3.4 million kg/7.5 million lb. After Apollo and *Skylab*, the Saturn rockets were retired in favour of the ▷space shuttle.

satyagraha (Sanskrit 'insistence on truth') nonviolent resistance to British rule in India, as employed by Mahatma ▷Gandhi from 1918 to press for political reform; the idea owes much to the Russian writer Leo ▷Tolstoy.

satyr in Greek mythology, a lustful, drunken woodland creature, half man and half beast, characterized by pointed ears, two horns on the forehead, and a tail. Satyrs attended the god of wine, ▷Dionysus. They represented the vital powers of nature.

Roman writers confused the satyr with their goat-footed Italian ▷Faunus.

Saudi Arabia see country box.

Saul (lived 11th century BC) In the Old Testament, the first king of Israel. He was anointed by Samuel and warred successfully against the neighbouring Ammonites and Philistines, but fell from God's favour in his battle against the Amalekites. He became jealous and suspicious of ▷David and turned against him and Samuel. After being wounded in battle with the Philistines, in which his three sons died, he committed suicide.

sausage tree tropical African tree, which grows up to 12 m/40 ft tall and has purplish flowers. Its gourdlike fruits hang from

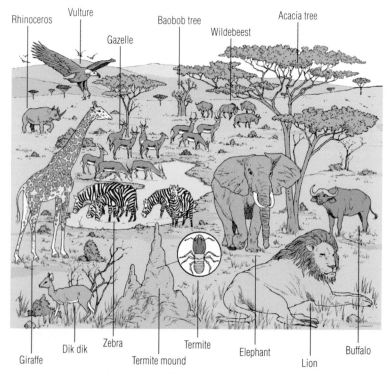

SAVANNAH Composite to show the diversity of wildlife found on the African savannah. The savannah habitat supports large herds of grazers and their large carnivorous predators.

stalks and look like thick sausages; they can be up to 60 cm/2 ft long and weigh 2–5 kg/5–12 lb. (Genus *Kigelia pinnata*, family Bignoniaceae.)

Saussure, Ferdinand de (1857–1913) Swiss language scholar, a pioneer of modern linguistics and the originator of the concept of ▷structuralism as used in linguistics, anthropology, and literary theory.

Saussure, Horace Bénédict de (1740–1799) Swiss geologist who made the earliest detailed and first-hand study of the Alps. He was a physicist at the University of Geneva. The results of his Alpine survey appeared in his classic work *Voyages des Alpes/Travels in the Alps* (1779–86).

savannah (or **savanna**) extensive open tropical grasslands, with scattered trees and shrubs. Savannahs cover large areas of Africa, North and South America, and northern Australia. The soil is acidic and sandy and generally considered suitable only as pasture for low-density grazing.

A new strain of rice suitable for savannah conditions was developed 1992. It not only grew successfully under test conditions in Colombia but also improved pasture quality so grazing numbers could be increased twentyfold.

Related Web site: Tropical Savannas CRC: Landscape Processes
http://savanna.ntu.edu.au/information/information.html

Save the Children organization established in 1919 to promote the rights of children to care, good health, material welfare, and moral, spiritual, and educational development. It operates in more than 50 Third World countries and the UK; projects include the provision of health care, education,

community development, and emergency relief. In 1997 Save the Children had an income of £78.4 million. Its headquarters are in London.

Savimbi, Jonas Malheiro (1934–) Angolan soldier and right-wing revolutionary, founder and leader of the National Union for the Total Independence of Angola (UNITA). From 1975 UNITA, under Savimbi's leadership, tried to overthrow the government. A peace agreement was signed in 1994. Savimbi rejected the offer of vice presidency in a coalition government in 1996; however, in 1998, UNITA was demilitarized and accepted as a national political party.

The struggle for independence from Portugal escalated in 1961 into a civil war. In 1966 Savimbi founded the right-wing UNITA, which he led against the left-wing People's Movement for the

Saudi Arabia

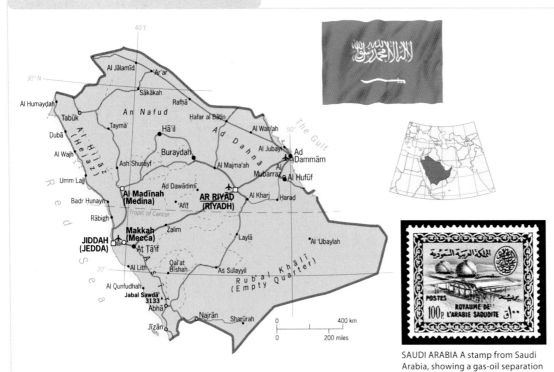

Saudi Arabia country on the Arabian peninsula, stretching from the Red Sea in the west to the Arabian Gulf in the east, bounded north by Jordan, Iraq, and Kuwait; east by Qatar and United Arab Emirates; southeast by Oman; and south by Yemen.

NATIONAL NAME *Al-Mamlaka al-'Arabiyya as-Sa'udiyya/Kingdom of Saudi Arabia*
AREA 2,200,518 sq km/849,620 sq mi
CAPITAL Riyadh
MAJOR TOWNS/CITIES Jiddah, Mecca, Medina, Ta'if, Dammam, Hofuf, Tabuk, Buraida
MAJOR PORTS Jiddah, Dammam, Jubail, Jizan, Yanbu
PHYSICAL FEATURES desert, sloping to the Gulf from a height of 2,750 m/9,000 ft in the west

Government

HEAD OF STATE AND GOVERNMENT King Fahd Ibn Abdul Aziz from 1982
POLITICAL SYSTEM absolutist
POLITICAL EXECUTIVE absolute
ADMINISTRATIVE DIVISIONS 13 provinces
ARMED FORCES 199,500; plus paramilitary forces of 15,500 (2002 est)
CONSCRIPTION military service is voluntary
DEATH PENALTY retained and used for ordinary crimes
DEFENCE SPEND (% GDP) 12 (2002 est)
EDUCATION SPEND (% GDP) 6.8 (2002 est)
HEALTH SPEND (% GDP) 5.3 (2000 est)

Economy and resources

CURRENCY riyal
GPD (US$) 186.4 billion (2002 est)
REAL GDP GROWTH (% change on previous year) 1.2 (2001)
GNI (US$) 181.1 billion (2002 est)
GNI PER CAPITA (PPP) (US$) 11,480 (2002 est)
CONSUMER PRICE INFLATION 1.1% (2003 est)
UNEMPLOYMENT 6.5% (2001)
FOREIGN DEBT (US$) 36.15 billion (2001 est)
MAJOR TRADING PARTNERS USA, Japan, Germany, South Korea, UK, France, Italy, Singapore, the Netherlands
RESOURCES petroleum, natural gas, iron ore, limestone, gypsum, marble, clay, salt, gold, uranium, copper, fish
INDUSTRIES petroleum and petroleum products, urea and ammonia fertilizers, steel, plastics, cement
EXPORTS crude and refined petroleum, petrochemicals, wheat. Principal market: USA 17.3% (2000)
IMPORTS machinery and transport equipment, foodstuffs, beverages, tobacco, chemicals and chemical products, base metals and metal manufactures, textiles and clothing. Principal source: USA 21% (2000)

Chronology

622: Muhammad began to unite Arabs in Muslim faith.
7th–8th centuries: Muslim Empire expanded, ultimately stretching from India to Spain, with Arabia itself being relegated to a subordinate part.
12th century: Decline of Muslim Empire; Arabia grew isolated and internal divisions multiplied.
13th century: Mameluke sultans of Egypt became nominal overlords of Hejaz in western Arabia.
1517: Hejaz became a nominal part of the Ottoman Empire after the Turks conquered Egypt.
18th century: Al Saud family united tribes of Nejd in central Arabia in support of the Wahhabi religious movement.
c.1830: The Al Saud established Riyadh as the Wahhabi capital.
c.1870: Turks took effective control of Hejaz and also Hasa on Persian Gulf.
late 19th century: Rival Wahhabi dynasty of Ibn Rashid became leaders of Nejd.
1902: Ibn Saud organized Bedouin revolt and regained Riyadh.
1913: Ibn Saud completed the reconquest of Hasa from Turks.
1915: Britain recognized Ibn Saud as emir of Nejd and Hasa.

ARABLE LAND 1.7% (2000 est)
AGRICULTURAL PRODUCTS wheat, barley, sorghum, millet, tomatoes, dates, watermelons, grapes; livestock (chiefly poultry) and dairy products

Population and society

POPULATION 24,217,000 (2003 est)
POPULATION GROWTH RATE 2.9% (2000–15)
POPULATION DENSITY (per sq km) 11 (2003 est)
URBAN POPULATION (% of total) 88 (2003 est)
AGE DISTRIBUTION (% of total population) 0–14 42%, 15–59 53%, 60+ 5% (2002 est)
ETHNIC GROUPS predominantly Arab; 10% Afro-Asian; over 25% non-nationals
LANGUAGE Arabic (official), English
RELIGION Sunni Muslim 85%; there is a Shiite minority
LITERACY RATE 85% (men); 70% (women) (2003 est)
LABOUR FORCE 12.2% agriculture, 23.6% industry, 64.2% services (1997 est)
LIFE EXPECTANCY 71 (men); 74 (women) (2000–05)
CHILD MORTALITY RATE (under 5, per 1,000 live births) 28 (2001)
PHYSICIANS (per 1,000 people) 1.7 (1998 est)
HOSPITAL BEDS (per 1,000 people) 2.3 (1998 est)
TV SETS (per 1,000 people) 264 (2001 est)
RADIOS (per 1,000 people) 326 (2001 est)
INTERNET USERS (per 10,000 people) 615.3 (2002 est)
PERSONAL COMPUTER USERS (per 100 people) 13.0 (2002 est)

1916–18: British-backed revolt, under aegis of Sharif Hussein of Mecca, expelled Turks from Arabia.
1919–25: Ibn Saud fought and defeated Sharif Hussein and took control of Hejaz.
1926: Proclamation of Ibn Saud as king of Hejaz and Nejd.
1932: Hejaz and Nejd renamed the United Kingdom of Saudi Arabia.
1933: Saudi Arabia allowed US-owned Standard Oil Company to prospect for oil, which was discovered in Hasa in 1938.
1939–45: Although officially neutral in World War II, Saudi Arabia received subsidies from USA and Britain.
1940s: Commercial exploitation of oil began, bringing great prosperity.
1987: Rioting by Iranian pilgrims caused 400 deaths in Mecca and a breach in diplomatic relations with Iran.
1990: Iraqi troops invaded Kuwait and massed on the Saudi Arabian border, prompting King Fahd to call for assistance from US and UK forces.
1991: Saudi Arabia fought on the Allied side against Iraq in the Gulf War.
1992: Under international pressure to move towards democracy, King Fahd formed a 'consultative council' to assist in the government of the kingdom.

SAUDI ARABIA A stamp from Saudi Arabia, showing a gas-oil separation plant. These two natural resources are vital to the country's economy.
Stanley Gibbons

Liberation of Angola (MPLA), led by Agostinho Neto. Neto, with Soviet and Cuban support, became president when independence was achieved in 1975, while UNITA, assisted by South Africa, continued its fight. A ceasefire was agreed in June 1989, but fighting continued, and the truce was abandoned after two months. A further truce was signed in May 1991. Civil war re-erupted in September 1992 following an election victory for the ruling party, a result which Savimbi disputed. Representatives of UNITA and the government signed a peace agreement in 1994.

savings unspent income, after deduction of tax, put aside through bank deposits or other financial schemes offering ▷interest to savers on their deposits. In economics a distinction is made between ▷investment, involving the purchase of capital goods, such as buying a house, and saving (where capital goods are not directly purchased; for example, buying shares as a way of earning an income).

savings and loan association (S&L) in the USA, a cooperative, mutual, savings organization that sells stock to its members. Created primarily to finance loans for home improvements, construction, and purchase, S&Ls at one time provided 40% of the funds for home purchases. In the late 1980s a crisis developed, with S&Ls making huge losses on unsecured loans. A federal bailout pledging more than $100 billion in taxpayer funds was negotiated in 1989.

Savonarola, Girolamo (1452–1498) Italian reformer, a Dominican friar and an eloquent preacher. His crusade against political and religious corruption won him popular support, and in 1494 he led a revolt in Florence that expelled the ruling Medici family and established a democratic republic. His denunciations of Pope ▷Alexander VI led to his excommunication 1497, and in 1498 he was arrested, tortured, hanged, and burned for heresy.

Savoy area of France between the Alps, Lake Geneva, and the River Rhône. A medieval duchy, it was made into the *départements* of Savoie and Haute-Savoie, in the Rhône-Alpes region.

sawfish any fish of the order Pristiformes of large, sharklike ▷rays, characterized by a flat, sawlike snout edged with teeth. The common sawfish *Pristis pectinatus*, also called the smalltooth, is more than 6 m/19 ft long. It has some 24 teeth along an elongated snout (2 m/6 ft) that can be used as a weapon.

SAWFISH Sawfishes are related to skates and rays. They use their elongated, toothed snouts to grub for molluscs and crustaceans on muddy seabeds.

sawfly any of several families of insects of the order Hymenoptera, related to bees, wasps, and ants, but lacking a 'waist' on the body. The egg-laying tube (ovipositor) of the female is surrounded by a pair of sawlike organs, which it uses to make a slit in a plant stem to lay its eggs. Horntails are closely related.

Some species have sharp ovipositors that can drill into wood, such as the black and yellow European wood wasp *Uroceras gigas*, about 4 cm/1.5 in long, which bores into conifers.

Saw Maung (1929–) Myanmar (Burmese) soldier and politician. Appointed head of the armed forces in 1985 by ▷Ne Win, he led a coup to remove Ne Win's successor, Maung Maung, in 1988 and became leader of a totalitarian 'emergency government', which remained in office despite being defeated in the May 1990 election. In April 1992 he was replaced as chair of the ruling military junta, prime minister, and commander of the armed forces by Than Shwe.

Saxe-Coburg-Gotha Saxon duchy. Albert, the Prince Consort of Britain's Queen Victoria, was a son of the 1st Duke, Ernest I (1784–1844), who was succeeded by Albert's elder brother, Ernest II (1818–1893). It remained the name of the British royal house until 1917, when it was changed to Windsor.

saxhorn family of brass musical instruments played with valves, invented in 1845 by the Belgian Adolphe Sax (1814–1894). It is played with a cup mouthpiece and made in seven different pitches, covering between them a range of some five octaves: soprano in E flat, alto in B flat (both also called flügelhorns), tenor in E flat, baritone in B flat (both also called althorns), bass in B flat (euphonium), bass tuba in E flat (bombardon), and contrabass in

B flat. They are rarely used in the orchestra, but are regular constituents of military and brass bands.

saxifrage any of a group of plants belonging to the saxifrage family, found growing in rocky, mountainous, and alpine areas in the northern hemisphere. They are low plants with groups of small white, pink, or yellow flowers. (Genus *Saxifraga*, family Saxifragaceae.)

Saxon member of a Germanic tribe once inhabiting the Danish peninsula and northern Germany. The Saxons migrated from their homelands in the early Middle Ages, under pressure from the Franks, and spread into various parts of Europe, including Britain (see ▷Anglo-Saxon). They also undertook piracy in the North Sea and the English Channel.

According to the English historian Bede, the Saxons arrived in Britain in 449, and the archaeological evidence and sparse literary sources suggest the years around 450 as marking the end of their piratical raids, and the establishment of their first settlements in southern England.

Saxony (German **Sachsen**) administrative *Land* (state) of Germany; area 17,036 sq km/6,578 sq mi; population (1995) 4,602,000. The capital is ▷Dresden. Industries include electronics, textiles, vehicles, machinery, chemicals, and coal. The region is on the plain of the River Elbe north of the Erzgebirge mountain range. Towns include Leipzig, Chemnitz, and Zwickau.

Saxony-Anhalt administrative *Land* (state) of Germany; area 20,450 sq km/7,900 sq mi; population (1995) 2,735,000. The capital is ▷Magdeburg; other towns include Halle and Dessau. Industries include chemicals, electronics, rolling stock, and footwear. Cereals and vegetables are grown.

The territory of Anhalt, named after the medieval castle of Anhalt, was divided and reunited many times before becoming a duchy. In 1952, as part of the East German region of Saxony-Anhalt, it was divided into the districts of Halle and Magdeburg. After the reunification of Germany in 1990, Saxony-Anhalt was reconstituted as one of the five new *Länder* of the Federal Republic.

saxophone member of a hybrid brass instrument family of conical bore, with a single-reed woodwind mouthpiece and keywork, invented about 1840 by Belgian instrument-maker Adolphe Sax (1814–1894). Soprano, alto, tenor, and baritone forms remain current. The soprano saxophone is usually straight; the others are characteristically curved back at the mouthpiece and have an upturned bell. Initially a concert instrument of suave tone, the saxophone was incorporated into dance bands of the 1930s and 1940s, and assumed its modern guise as a solo jazz instrument after 1945. It has a voicelike ability to bend a note.

Related Web site: International Saxophone Home Page
http://www.saxophone.org/

Sayers, Dorothy L(eigh) (1893–1957) English writer of detective fiction, playwright, and translator. Her books, which feature the detective Lord Peter Wimsey and the heroine Harriet Vane, include classics of the detective fiction genre such as *Strong Poison* (1930), *Murder Must Advertise* (1933), *The Nine Tailors* (1934), and *Gaudy Night* (1935).

Say's law in economics, the 'law of markets' formulated by Jean-Baptiste Say (1767–1832) to the effect that supply creates its own demand and that resources can never be underused.

SC abbreviation for the state of ▷South Carolina, USA.

scabies contagious infection of the skin caused by the parasitic itch mite *Sarcoptes scabiei*, which burrows under the skin to deposit eggs. Treatment is by antiparasitic creams and lotions.

SAWFLY The sawlike ovipositor of this female *Thenthredo scrophulariae* sawfly is just visible beneath the tip of the abdomen as she cuts a slit into a leaf to insert her eggs. This species is an excellent wasp mimic. *Premaphotos Wildlife*

scabious any of a group of plants belonging to the teasel family, native to Europe and Asia, with many small, usually purplish-blue flowers borne in a single head on a tall stalk. The small scabious (*S. columbaria*) and the Mediterranean sweet scabious (*S. atropurpurea*) are often cultivated. (Genus *Scabiosa*, family Dipsacaceae.)

Scafell Pike highest mountain in England, in the ▷Lake District, Cumbria, northwest England; height 978 m/3,210 ft. It is separated from Scafell (964 m/3,164 ft) by a ridge called Mickledore.

Scala, La (or **Teatro alla Scala**) the greatest Italian opera house, established in Milan in 1778. Many of Italy's finest opera composers have written for La Scala, including Puccini, Verdi, and Donizetti.

LA SCALA View of the interior of La Scala, with a range of boxes. La Scala is one of the most famous opera houses in the world. *Image Bank*

scalar quantity in mathematics and science, a quantity that has magnitude but no direction, as distinct from a ▷vector quantity, which has a direction as well as a magnitude. Temperature, mass, and volume are scalar quantities.

scale in chemistry, ▷calcium carbonate deposits that form on the inside of a kettle or boiler as a result of boiling ▷hard water.

scale in music, a sequence of pitches that establishes a key, and in some respects the character of a composition. A scale is defined by its starting note and may be ▷major or minor depending on the order of intervals. A ▷chromatic scale is the full range of 12 notes: it has no key because there is no fixed starting point.

SCALE A whole-tone scale.

scale insect any small plant-sucking insect, order Homoptera, of the superfamily Coccoidea. Some species are major pests – for example, the citrus mealy bug (genus *Pseudococcus*), which attacks citrus fruits in North America. The female is often wingless and legless, attached to a plant by the head and with the body covered with a waxy scale. The rare males are winged.

scallop any marine bivalve ▷mollusc of the family Pectinidae, with a fan-shaped shell. There are two 'ears' extending from the socketlike hinge. Scallops use water-jet propulsion to move through the water to escape predators such as starfish. The giant Pacific scallop found from Alaska to California can reach 20 cm/8 in width.

The St James's shell *Pecten jacobaeus* was used as a badge by medieval pilgrims to ▷Santiago de Compostela.

scaly anteater another name for the ▷pangolin.

Scandinavia peninsula in northwestern Europe, comprising Norway and Sweden; politically and culturally it also includes Denmark, Iceland, the Faroe Islands, and Finland. (See separate entries for all of these.)

scandium silver-white, metallic element of the ▷lanthanide series, symbol Sc, atomic number 21, relative atomic mass 44.956.

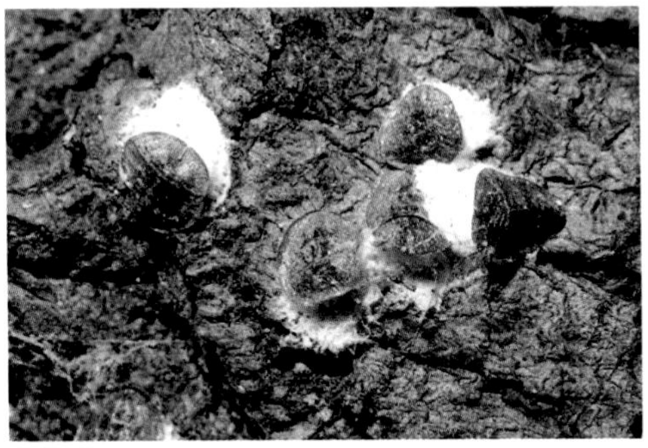

SCALE INSECT Scale insects *Pulvinaria regalis* on lime trees. *K G Preston-Mafham/Premaphotos Wildlife*

Its compounds are found widely distributed in nature, but only in minute amounts. The metal has little industrial importance.

Scandium is relatively more abundant in the Sun and other stars than on Earth. Scandium oxide (scandia) is used as a catalyst, in making crucibles and other ceramic parts, and scandium sulphate (in very dilute aqueous solution) is used in agriculture to improve seed germination.

The element was discovered and named in 1879 by Swedish chemist Lars Nilson (1840–1899) after Scandinavia, because it was found in the Scandinavian mineral euxenite.

scanner in computing, a device that can produce a digital image file of a document for input and storage in a computer. It uses technology similar to that of a photocopier. Small scanners can be passed over the document surface by hand; larger versions have a flat bed, like that of a photocopier, on which the input document is placed and scanned.

scanning in medicine, the noninvasive examination of body organs to detect abnormalities of structure or function. Detectable waves – for example, ▷ultrasound, gamma, or ▷X-rays – are passed through the part to be scanned. Their absorption pattern is recorded, analysed by computer, and displayed pictorially on a screen.

scanning electron microscope (SEM) electron microscope that produces three-dimensional images, magnified 10–200,000 times. A fine beam of electrons, focused by electromagnets, is moved, or scanned, across the specimen. Electrons reflected from the specimen are collected by a detector, giving rise to an electrical signal, which is then used to generate a point of brightness on a television-like screen. As the point moves rapidly over the screen, in phase with the scanning electron beam, an image of the specimen is built up.

scanning transmission electron microscope (STEM) electron microscope that combines features of the ▷scanning electron microscope (SEM) and the transmission electron microscope (TEM). First built in the USA in 1966, the microscope has both the SEM's contrast characteristics and lack of aberrations and the high resolution of the TEM. Magnifications of over 90 million times can be achieved, enough to image single atoms.

scapula (or **shoulder blade**) large, flat, triangular bone which lies over the second to seventh ribs on the back, forming part of the pectoral girdle, and assisting in the articulation of the arm with the chest region. Its flattened shape allows a large region for the attachment of muscles.

scarab any of a family Scarabaeidae of beetles, often brilliantly coloured, and including ▷cockchafers, June beetles, and dung beetles. The *Scarabeus sacer* was revered by the ancient Egyptians as the symbol of resurrection.

Scarborough spa and holiday resort on the North Sea coast of North Yorkshire, northern England, 56 km/35 mi northeast of York; population (1991) 38,900. It is a touring centre for the Yorkshire Moors, and is also centre for fishing. A ruined 12th-century Norman castle overlooks the town.

Scargill, Arthur (1938–) British trade-union leader. Elected president of the National Union of Miners (NUM) in 1981, he embarked on a collision course with the Conservative government of Margaret Thatcher. The damaging strike of 1984–85 split the miners' movement. In 1995, criticizing what he saw as the Labour Party's lurch to the right, he announced that he would establish a rival party, the independent Socialist Labour Party. This proved to be largely ineffectual, and made little impact in consequent elections. By 1997 membership of the NUM had fallen to 10,000.

Scarlatti, (Pietro) Alessandro (Gaspare) (1660–1725) Italian baroque composer. He was maestro di capella at the court of Naples and developed the opera form. He composed more than 100 operas, including *Tigrane* (1715), as well as church music and oratorios.

Scarlatti, (Giuseppe) Domenico (1685–1757) Italian composer. The eldest son of Alessandro ▷Scarlatti, he lived most of his life in Portugal and Spain in the service of the Queen of Spain. He wrote over 500 sonatas for harpsichord, short pieces in binary form demonstrating the new freedoms of keyboard composition and inspired by Spanish musical idioms. Scarlatti was the most celebrated harpsichordist of his time, and his music provided the foundation for modern piano technique.

scarlet fever (or **scarlatina**) acute infectious disease, especially of children, caused by the bacteria in the *Streptococcus pyogenes* group. It is marked by fever, vomiting, sore throat, and a bright red rash spreading from the upper to the lower part of the body. The rash is followed by the skin peeling in flakes. It is treated with antibiotics.

scarp and dip in geology, the two slopes which comprise an escarpment. The scarp is the steep slope and the dip is the gentle slope. Such a feature is common when sedimentary rocks are uplifted, folded, or eroded, the scarp slope cuts across the bedding planes of the sedimentary rock whilst the dip slope follows the direction of the strata. An example is Salisbury Crags in Edinburgh, Scotland.

scatter diagram (or **scattergram**) diagram whose purpose is to establish whether or not a relationship or ▷correlation exists between two variables; for example, between life expectancy and gross national product. Each observation is marked with a dot in a position that shows the value of both variables. The pattern of dots is then examined to see whether they show any underlying trend by means of a **line of best fit** (a straight line drawn so that its distance from the various points is as short as possible).

scepticism ancient philosophical view that absolute knowledge of things is ultimately unobtainable, hence the only proper attitude is to suspend judgement. Its origins lay in the teachings of the Greek philosopher Pyrrho, who maintained that peace of mind lay in renouncing all claims to knowledge.

Related Web site: Ancient Greek Scepticism http://www.utm.edu/research/iep/s/skepanci.htm

Scheele, Karl Wilhelm (1742–1786) Swedish chemist and pharmacist who isolated many elements and compounds for the first time, including oxygen, about 1772, and chlorine 1774, although he did not recognize it as an element. He showed that oxygen is involved in the respiration of plants and fish.

Scheherazade the storyteller in the *Arabian Nights.*

Schengen Group association of states, within the European Union, that in theory adhere to the ideals of the Schengen Convention, notably the abolition of passport controls at common internal borders and the strengthening of external borders. The Convention, which went into effect on a three-month trial basis in March 1995, was signed by Belgium, France, Germany, Luxembourg, and the Netherlands in June 1990; Italy in November 1990; Portugal and Spain in June 1991; Greece in November 1992; Austria in April 1995; and Denmark, Sweden, Finland, and the first two non-European Union (EU) countries, Iceland and Norway in 2001. In May 1995 several EU countries urged Italy to introduce tighter entry controls, believing that many illegal immigrants were entering the EU through Italy. The pact was renewed permanently in June 1995 by all signatories except France, which invoked a clause allowing it to continue passport checks for a further six months; in March 1996, France again refused to implement the agreement due to concerns about the risk of drugs coming in from the Netherlands.

In April 1996 five observer members were accepted: Denmark, Finland, Iceland, Norway, and Sweden. The UK has not joined the agreement because of concerns over the removal of checks against drug trafficking, terrorists, and animals with rabies.

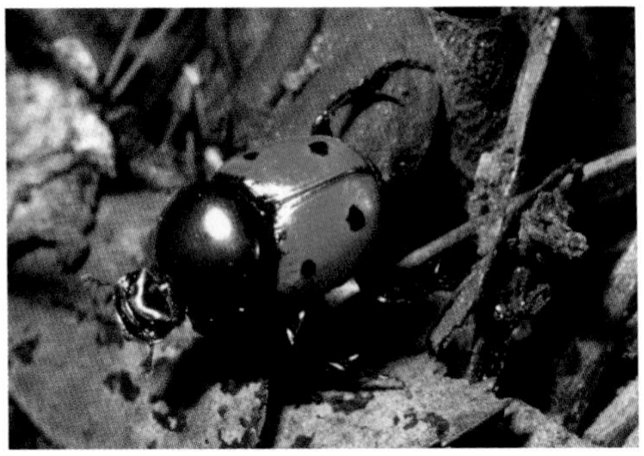

SCARAB This striking scarab beetle *Helictopleurus quadripunctatus*, from the dry forests of Madagascar, is one of many scarabs that collect and bury dung on which to rear their larvae. *Premaphotos Wildlife*

scherzo (Italian 'joke') in music, a lively piece, usually in rapid triple (3/4) time; often used for the third movement of a symphony, sonata, or quartet as a substitute for the statelier ▷minuet and trio.

Schiele, Egon (1890–1918) Austrian artist. Strongly influenced by ▷art nouveau, and in particular Gustav ▷Klimt, he developed an angular, contorted style, employing garish colours, that made him an important pioneer of ▷expressionism. His subject matter includes portraits and openly erotic nudes.

Schiller, Johann Christoph Friedrich von (1759–1805) German dramatist, poet, and historian. He wrote ▷*Sturm und Drang* ('storm and stress') verse and plays, including the dramatic trilogy *Wallenstein* (1798–99). He was an idealist, and much of his work concerns the aspiration for political freedom and the avoidance of mediocrity.

After the success of his play *Die Räuber/The Robbers* (1781), he completed the tragedies *Die Verschwörung des Fiesko zu Genua/Fiesco, or, the Genoese Conspiracy* (his first historical drama) and *Kabale und Liebe/Intrigue and Love* (1783). In 1787 he wrote his more mature blank-verse drama *Don Carlos* and the hymn 'An die Freude/Ode to Joy', later used by ▷Beethoven in his ninth symphony. As professor of history at Jena from 1789 he completed a history of the Thirty Years' War and developed a close friendship with ▷Goethe, after early antagonism. His essays on aesthetics include the piece of literary criticism *über naive und sentimentalische Dichtung/Naive and Sentimental Poetry* (1795–96). Schiller became the foremost German dramatist with his classic dramas *Wallenstein*, *Maria Stuart* (1800), *Die Jungfrau von Orleans/The Maid of Orleans* (1801), and *Wilhelm Tell/William Tell* (1804).

Related Web site: History of the Thirty Years' War http://www.catawba.k12.nc.us/books/1jcfs10.txt

schism formal split over a doctrinal difference between religious believers, as in the ▷Great Schism in the Roman Catholic Church; over the doctrine of papal infallibility, as with the Old Catholics in 1879; and over the use of the Latin Tridentine Mass in 1988.

schist ▷metamorphic rock containing ▷mica or another platy or elongate mineral, whose crystals are aligned to give a foliation (planar texture) known as schistosity. Schist may contain additional minerals such as ▷garnet.

schizocarp dry ▷fruit that develops from two or more carpels and splits, when mature, to form separate one-seeded units known as mericarps.

schizophrenia mental disorder, a psychosis of unknown origin, which can lead to profound changes in personality, behaviour, and perception, including delusions and hallucinations. It is more common in males and the early-onset form is more severe than when the illness develops in later life. Modern treatment approaches include drugs, family therapy, stress reduction, and rehabilitation.

Schizophrenia implies a severe divorce from reality in the patient's thinking. Although the causes are poorly understood, it is now recognized as an organic disease, associated with structural anomalies in the brain. There is some evidence that early trauma, either in the womb or during delivery, may play a part in causation. There is also a genetic contribution: a gene linked to schizophrenia was identified in 2000.

There is an enormous variation between countries in the symptoms of schizophrenia and in the incidence of the main forms of the disease, according to a 1997 report by American investigators. **Paranoid schizophrenia**, characterized by a feeling of persecution, is 50% more common in developed countries, whereas **catatonic schizophrenia**, characterized by total immobility, is six times more frequent in developing countries. **Hebephrenic schizophrenia**, characterized by disorganized behaviour and speech and emotional bluntness, is four times more prevalent in developed countries overall but is rare in the USA. The prevalence of schizophrenia in Europe is about two to five cases per 1,000 of the population.

Related Web site: Schizophrenia http://www.pslgroup.com/SCHIZOPHR.HTM

Schlesinger, John (Richard) (1926–2003) English film and television director. His eclectic career embraced British social conscience films of the 1960s, comedies, thrillers, and nostalgic period pieces. Early films include *Billy Liar* (1963) and *Darling* (1965). His first US film, *Midnight Cowboy* (1969) (Academy Award), was a big commercial success and was followed by *Sunday, Bloody Sunday* (1971), *Marathon Man* (1978), *Yanks* (1979), *Pacific Heights* (1990), *Eye for an Eye* (1996), and *The Next Best Thing* (2000).

Schleswig-Holstein administrative region (German *Land*) in north Germany, bounded on the north by Denmark, on the east by the Baltic Sea and Mecklenberg-West Pomerania, on the south by Lower Saxony and Hamburg, and on the west by the North Sea and the Heligoland Bight; area 15,700 sq km/6,060 sq mi; population (1995) 2,708,000. The capital is ▷Kiel. There are shipbuilding, mechanical and electrical engineering, food processing, and textile industries. There are fisheries, and cattle, sheep, pigs, and poultry are raised.

Schlüter, Poul Holmskov (1929–) Danish right-wing politician, leader of the Conservative People's Party (KF) from 1974 and prime minister 1982–93. His centre-right coalition survived the 1990 election and was reconstituted, with Liberal support. In January 1993 Schlüter resigned, accused of dishonesty over his role in an incident involving Tamil refugees. He was succeeded by Poul Nyrup Rasmussen.

Schmidt, Helmut Heinrich Waldemar (1918–) German socialist politician, member of the Social Democratic Party (SPD), chancellor of West Germany 1974–83. As chancellor, Schmidt introduced social reforms and continued Brandt's policy of Ostpolitik. With the French president Giscard d'Estaing, he instigated annual world and European economic summits. He was a firm supporter of ▷NATO and of the deployment of US nuclear missiles in West Germany during the early 1980s.

Schoenberg, Arnold Franz Walter (1874–1951) Born Arnold Franz Walter Schönberg. Austro-Hungarian composer, a US citizen from 1941. After Romantic early works such as *Verklärte Nacht/Transfigured Night* (1899) and the *Gurrelieder/Songs of Gurra* (1900–11), he experimented with ▷atonality (absence of key), producing works such as *Pierrot lunaire/Moonstruck Pierrot* (1912) for chamber ensemble and voice, before developing the ▷twelve-tone system of musical composition.

After 1918, Schoenberg wrote several neoclassical works for chamber ensembles. He taught at the Berlin State Academy 1925–33. The twelve-tone system was further developed by his pupils Alban ▷Berg and Anton ▷Webern. Driven from Germany by the Nazis, Schoenberg settled in the USA in 1933, where he influenced music scoring for films. Later works include the opera *Moses und Aron* (1932–51).

Arnold Schoenberg
Dissonances are only the more remote consonances.
Quoted in Machlis *Introduction to Contemporary Music* 1963

Scholastic Aptitude Test (SAT) in US education, national examination used as a college admissions test for high-school students. The SAT tests reasoning, maths, and use of the English language only, not knowledge of specific subjects.

scholasticism the theological and philosophical systems and methods taught in the schools of medieval Europe, especially in the 12th–14th centuries. Scholasticism tried to integrate orthodox Christian teaching with Aristotelian and some Platonic philosophy. The scholastic method involved surveying different opinions and the reasons given for them, and then attempting solutions of the problems raised, using logic and dialectic.

Schopenhauer, Arthur (1788–1860) German philosopher. His *The World as Will and Idea* (1818), inspired by Immanuel Kant and ancient Hindu philosophy, expounded an atheistic and pessimistic world view: an irrational will is considered as the inner principle of the world, producing an ever-frustrated cycle of desire, of which the only escape is aesthetic contemplation or absorption into nothingness.

Having postulated a world of suffering and disappointment, he based his ethics on compassion. His notion of an irrational force at work in humans strongly influenced both the philosopher Friedrich Nietzsche and the founder of psychiatry, Sigmund Freud. The theory also struck a responsive chord in the composer Richard Wagner, the German novelist Thomas Mann, and the English writer Thomas Hardy.

Schrödinger, Erwin (1887–1961) Austrian physicist. He advanced the study of wave mechanics to describe the behaviour of electrons in atoms. He produced in 1926 a solid mathematical explanation of the ▷quantum theory and the structure of the atom. He shared the Nobel Prize for Physics in 1933 for his work in the development of quantum mechanics.

Schrödinger's mathematical description of electron waves superseded matrix mechanics, developed in 1925 by Max ▷Born and Werner ▷Heisenberg, which also described the structure of the atom mathematically but, unlike wave mechanics, gave no picture of the atom. It was later shown that wave mechanics is equivalent to matrix mechanics.

Schubert, Franz Peter (1797–1828) Austrian composer. His ten symphonies include the incomplete eighth in B minor (the 'Unfinished') and the 'Great' in C major. He wrote chamber and piano music, including the 'Trout Quintet', and over 600 lieder (songs) combining the Romantic expression of emotion with pure melody. They include the cycles *Die schöne Müllerin/The Beautiful Maid of the Mill* (1823) and *Die Winterreise/The Winter Journey* (1827).

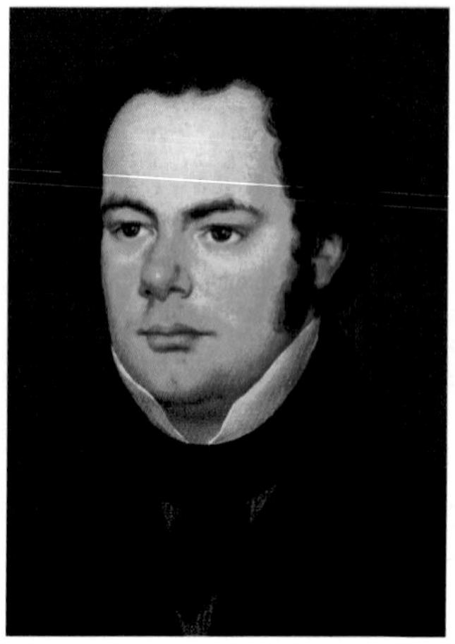
FRANZ SCHUBERT Schubert developed a unique style marked by melody and lyricism. *The Art Archive/Society Friends Music Vienna/Dagli Orti*

Schulz, Charles M(onroe) (1922–2000) US cartoonist who created the *Peanuts* strip, syndicated by United Features Syndicate from 1950. By 1999 it had become the world's most widely syndicated cartoon strip, featured in more than 2,600 newspapers in 75 countries. His characters Snoopy, Charlie Brown, Lucy, and Linus have been merchandized worldwide and featured in a 1967 musical, *You're a Good Man, Charlie Brown*, played on Broadway.

Franz Schubert
A review, however favourable, can be ridiculous at the same time if the critic lacks average intelligence, as is not seldom the case.
Letter, 1825

Schumacher, Fritz (Ernst Friedrich) (1911–1977) German economist who made his career in the UK. He believed that the increasing size of institutions, coupled with unchecked economic growth, creates a range of social and environmental problems. He argued his case in books such as *Small is Beautiful* (1973), and established the Intermediate Technology Development Group.

Schumacher studied at Oxford and held academic posts there and in the USA at Columbia in the 1930s and 1940s. After World War II he was economic adviser to the British Control Commission in Germany 1946–50 and to the UK National Coal Board 1950–70.

Related Web site: Schumacher Society http://www.oneworld.org/schumachersoc/

Schumacher, Michael (1969–) German motor-racing driver. He began his career in the Mercedes-Benz junior team; he joined the Jordan Formula 1 team in 1991, but was poached by Benetton almost immediately. He won his first Grand Prix in Belgium in 1992. Hailed by many as a gifted 'natural' driver, he won the world drivers' championship title some six times (1994, 1995, 2000, 2001, 2002, 2003). He joined Ferrari at the end of the 1995 season. In July 1998 Schumacher won the British Grand Prix for the first time and signed a new £100 million contract with Ferrari.

In October 2002 he won a record 11th race in a single season, which took his record total to 64 Grand Prix wins. His 2002 season points total of 144 was also a new record.

Schuman, Robert Jean-Baptiste Nicolas (1886–1963) French Christian-Democrat politician, prime minister 1947–48 and foreign minister 1948–55. He was a member of the post-war Mouvement Républicain Populaire (MRP). His Schuman Declaration of May 1950, drafted by Jean Monnet, outlines a scheme for pooling coal and iron-ore resources. The resultant European Coal and Steel Community, established by France, Belgium, Germany, the Netherlands, Italy and Luxembourg under the 1951 Paris Treaty, was the forerunner of the European Community (now the European Union).

Schumann, Robert Alexander (1810–1856) German composer and writer. His songs and short piano pieces portray states of emotion with great economy. Among his compositions are four symphonies, a violin concerto, a piano concerto, sonatas, and song cycles, such as *Dichterliebe/Poet's Love* (1840). Mendelssohn championed many of his works.

Schumpeter, Joseph A(lois) (1883–1950) Austrian-born US economist and sociologist. In *Capitalism, Socialism and Democracy* (1942) he contended that Western capitalism, impelled by its very success, was evolving into a form of socialism because firms would become increasingly large and their managements increasingly divorced from ownership, while social trends were undermining the traditional motives for entrepreneurial accumulation of wealth.

Schwarzenegger, Arnold (1947–) Called 'Arnie'. Austrian-born US film actor. Having starred in sword-and-sorcery films such as *Conan the Barbarian* (1982), he graduated to big-budget action movies such as *Terminator* (1984), *Predator* (1987), *Terminator II* (1991), and *True Lies* (1994). He was regarded by many to be the ultimate action hero. In 2004 he was elected Governor of California.

Schwarzkopf, Norman (1934–) Called 'Stormin' Norman'. US general. He was supreme commander of the Allied forces in the ▷Gulf War 1991. He planned and executed a blitzkrieg campaign, 'Desert Storm', sustaining remarkably few Allied casualties in the liberation of Kuwait. He was a battalion commander in the Vietnam War and deputy commander of the US invasion of Grenada in 1983.

Schwarzkopf was born in Trenton, New Jersey. A graduate of the military academy at West Point, he obtained a master's degree in guided-missile engineering. He became an infantry soldier and later a paratrooper, and did two tours of service in Vietnam, as an adviser 1965–66 and in command of an infantry battalion 1969–70. Maintaining the 28-member Arab-Western military coalition against Iraq in 1991 extended his diplomatic skills, and his success in the Gulf War made him a popular hero in the USA. He retired from the army in August 1991.

Related Web site: General H Norman Schwarzkopf Profile http://www.achievement.org/autodoc/page/sch0pro-1

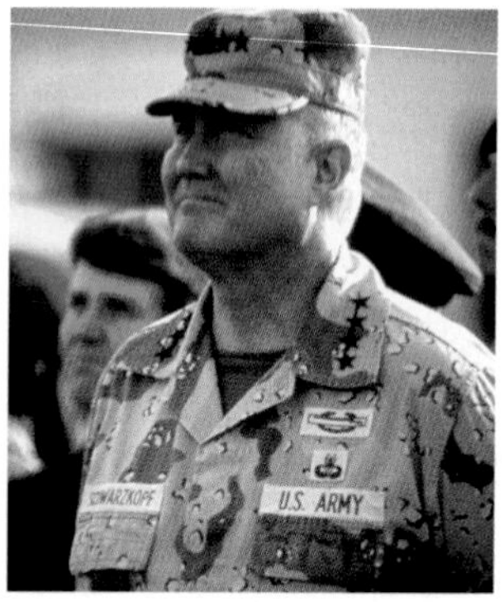

NORMAN SCHWARZKOPF A 1991 photograph shows General Norman Schwarzkopf during his command of Operation Desert Storm, the combined military campaign for the liberation of Kuwait. *Archive Photos*

Schwarzwald German name for the ▷Black Forest, a coniferous forest in Germany.

Schweitzer, Albert (1875–1965) Protestant theologian, organist, and missionary surgeon. He founded the hospital at Lambaréné in Gabon in 1913, giving organ recitals to support his work there. He wrote a life of German composer J S Bach and *Von reimarus zu Wrede/The Quest for the Historical Jesus* (1906). He was awarded the Nobel Prize for Peace in 1952 for his teaching of 'reverence for life' and for his medical and other work in Africa.

Schwerin capital of the *Land* of ▷Mecklenburg–West Pomerania, Germany, on the western shore of the lake of Schwerin; population (1995) 117,200. Products include machinery, foods, and chemicals. Formerly the capital of ▷Mecklenburg and earlier of the old republic of Mecklenburg–Schwerin, Schwerin became capital of Mecklenburg–West Pomerania with the reunification of Germany in 1990.

Schwitters, Kurt (1887–1948) German artist and poet. He was a leading member of the ▷Dada movement. His most important works are constructions and collages, which he called 'Merz', made from scraps and bric-a-brac of all kinds.

Schwyz capital of Schwyz canton, Switzerland; population (1995) 15,200. Schwyz was one of the three original cantons of the Swiss Confederation of 1291, which gave its name to the whole country in about 1450.

sciatica persistent pain in the back and down the outside of one leg, along the sciatic nerve and its branches. Causes of sciatica include inflammation of the nerve or pressure of a displaced disc on a nerve root leading out of the lower spine.

science (Latin *scientia* 'knowledge') any systematic field of study or body of knowledge that aims, through experiment, observation, and deduction, to produce reliable explanations of phenomena, with reference to the material and physical world.

History Activities such as healing, star-watching, and engineering have been practised in many societies since ancient times. Pure science, especially physics (formerly called natural philosophy), had traditionally been the main area of study for philosophers. The European scientific revolution between about 1650 and 1800 replaced speculative philosophy with a new combination of observation, experimentation, and rationality.

Philosophy of science Today, scientific research involves an interaction between tradition, experiment and observation, and deduction. The subject area called philosophy of science investigates the nature of this complex interaction, and the extent of its ability to gain access to the truth about the material world. It has long been recognized that induction from observation cannot give explanations based on logic. In the 20th century Karl ▷Popper has described scientific method as a rigorous experimental testing of a scientist's ideas or hypotheses (see ▷hypothesis). The origin and role of these ideas, and their interdependence with observation, have been examined, for example, by the US thinker Thomas S ▷Kuhn, who places them in a historical and sociological setting.

Sociology of science The sociology of science investigates how scientific theories and laws are produced, and questions the possibility of objectivity in any scientific endeavour. One controversial point of view is the replacement of scientific realism with scientific relativism, as proposed by Paul K ▷Feyerabend. Questions concerning the proper use of science and the role of science education are also restructuring this field of study.

Branches of science Science is divided into separate areas of study, such as astronomy, biology, geology, chemistry, physics, and mathematics, although more recently attempts have been made to combine traditionally separate disciplines under such headings as ▷life sciences and ▷earth sciences. These areas are usually jointly referred to as the **natural sciences**. The **physical sciences** comprise mathematics, physics, and chemistry. The application of science for practical purposes is called **technology**. **Social science** is the systematic study of human behaviour, and includes such areas as anthropology, economics, psychology, and sociology.

One area of contemporary debate is whether the social-science disciplines are actually sciences; that is, whether the study of human beings is capable of scientific precision or prediction in the same way as natural science is seen to be.

Employment in science Some 595,000 people were employed in science, technology, and mathematics in the UK in 1993; about 170,000 of them in computing.

Related Web site: Explore Science http://www.explorescience.com/activities/activity_list.cfm?categoryID=11

> **Arthur C Clarke**
> British science and science fiction writer
>
> *When a distinguished but elderly scientist states that something is possible, he is always certainly right. When he states that something is impossible, he is very probably wrong.*
>
> *Profiles of the Future*

science fiction (or **SF** or **sci-fi**) genre of fiction and film with an imaginary scientific, technological, or futuristic basis. It is sometimes held to have its roots in the works of Mary ▷Shelley, notably *Frankenstein* (1818). Often taking its ideas and concerns from current ideas in science and the social sciences, science fiction aims to shake up standard perceptions of reality.

Scientology (Latin *scire* 'to know' and Greek *logos* 'branch of learning') 'applied religious philosophy' based on dianetics, founded in California 1952 by L Ron Hubbard as the **Church of Scientology**, and claiming to 'increase man's spiritual awareness'. Its headquarters from 1984 have been in Los Angeles.

Related Web site: Scientology http://www.religioustolerance.org/scientol.htm

scilla any of a group of bulbous plants belonging to the lily family, with blue, pink, or white flowers; they include the spring ▷squill (*S. verna*). (Genus *Scilla*, family Liliaceae.)

Scilly, Isles of (or **Scilly Isles/Islands** or **Scillies**) group of 140 islands and islets lying 40 km/25 mi southwest of Land's End, England; administered by the Duchy of Cornwall; area 16 sq km/6.3 sq mi; population (1991) 2,050. The five inhabited islands are **St Mary's**, the largest, on which is Hugh Town, capital of the Scillies; **Tresco**, the second largest, with subtropical gardens; **St Martin's**, noted for its beautiful shells; **St Agnes**; and **Bryher**.

scintillation counter instrument for measuring very low levels of radiation. The radiation strikes a scintillator (a device that emits a unit of light when a charged elementary particle collides with it), whose light output is 'amplified' by a photomultiplier; the current pulses of its output are in turn counted or added by a scaler to give a numerical reading.

Scipio Aemilianus, Publius Cornelius (c. 185–129 BC) Also known as **Scipio Africanus Minor**. Roman general, the adopted grandson of Scipio Africanus Major. He destroyed Carthage in 146, and subdued Spain in 133. He was opposed to his brothers-in-law, the Gracchi (see ▷Gracchus).

Scipio, Publius Cornelius (died 211 BC) Roman general, father of Scipio Africanus Major. Elected consul in 218, during the Second ▷Punic War, he was defeated by Hannibal at Trebia and killed by the Carthaginians in Spain.

Scipio, Publius Cornelius (236–c. 183 BC) Also known as **Scipio Africanus Major**. Roman general whose tactical and strategic abilities turned the tide of the Second Punic War in 208–201 BC and established his reputation as one of Rome's greatest commanders. He defeated the Carthaginians in Spain in 210–206 BC and invaded Africa in 204 BC. At Zama in 202 BC he defeated the Carthaginian general ▷Hannibal to win the war for Rome. He adopted the name 'Africanus' in recognition of the place of his greatest victory, but he felt that his achievements had not been sufficiently rewarded and retired to his villa embittered.

sclerenchyma plant tissue whose function is to strengthen and support, composed of thick-walled cells that are heavily lignified (toughened). On maturity the cell inside dies, and only the cell walls remain.

> **Albert Szent-Györgyi**
> Hungarian-born US biochemist
>
> *Discovery consists of seeing what everybody has seen, thinking what nobody has thought.*
>
> Quoted in I G Good (ed) *The Scientist Speculates* (1962)

sclerosis any abnormal hardening of body tissues, especially the nervous system or walls of the arteries. See ▷multiple sclerosis.

Scofield, (David) Paul (1922–) English actor. His wide-ranging roles include the drunken priest in Graham Greene's *The Power and the Glory* (1956), Lear in *King Lear* (1962), Salieri in Peter Shaffer's *Amadeus* (1979), Othello (1980), and Shotov in *Heartbreak House* (1992). He appeared as Sir Thomas More in both stage and film versions of Robert Bolt's *A Man for All Seasons* (stage 1960–61, film 1966).

scoliosis lateral (sideways) deviation of the spine. It may be congenital or acquired (through bad posture, illness, or other deformity); or it may be idopathic (of unknown cause). Treatments include mechanical or surgical correction, depending on the cause.

Scopes monkey trial trial held in Dayton, Tennessee, USA, 1925. John T Scopes, a science teacher at the high school, was accused of teaching, contrary to a law of the state, Charles Darwin's theory of evolution. He was fined $100, but this was waived on a technical point. The defence counsel was Clarence Darrow and the prosecutor William Jennings Bryan.

scorched earth in warfare, the policy of burning and destroying everything that might be of use to an invading army, especially the crops in the fields. It was used to great effect in Russia in 1812 against the invasion of the French emperor Napoleon and again during World War II to hinder the advance of German forces in 1941.

scorpion any arachnid of the order Scorpiones, common in the tropics and subtropics. Scorpions have four pairs of walking legs, large pincers, and long tails ending in upcurved poisonous stings, though the venom is not usually fatal to a healthy adult human. Some species reach 25 cm/10 in. There are about 600 different species.

They are nocturnal in habit, hiding during the day beneath stones and under the loose bark of trees. The females are viviparous (producing live young), the eggs being hatched in the enlarged oviducts. Scorpions sometimes prey on each other, but their main food is the woodlouse. They seize their prey with their powerful claws or palpi. They are also able to survive for a long time without eating; one scorpion managed to survive for 17 months on a single housefly.

In 1992 a colony of scorpions *Euscorpius flavicaudis* was discovered on the Isle of Sheppey, Kent – the colony is thought to have survived there for more than 120 years.

scorpion fly any insect of the order Mecoptera. They have a characteristic downturned beak with jaws at the tip, and many males have a scorpion-like upturned tail, giving them their common name. Most feed on insects or carrion. They are an ancient group with relatively few living representatives.

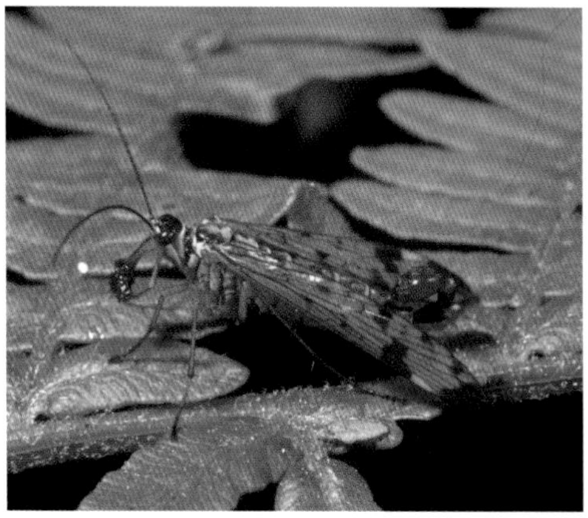

SCORPION FLY The long, down-turned beak and upturned scorpionlike genital capsule are clearly visible on this male common scorpion fly *Panorpa vulgaris*, the most widespread Eurasian species.
Premaphotos Wildlife

Scorpius bright zodiacal constellation in the southern hemisphere between ▷Libra and ▷Sagittarius, represented as a scorpion. The Sun passes briefly through Scorpius in the last week of November. The heart of the scorpion is marked by the bright red supergiant star ▷Antares. Scorpius contains rich ▷Milky Way star fields, plus the strongest ▷X-ray source in the sky, Scorpius X-1. The whole area is rich in clusters and nebulae. In astrology, the dates for Scorpius are about 24 October–21 November (see ▷precession).

Scorsese, Martin (1942–) US director, screenwriter, and producer. One of the most influential figures in modern American cinema, he has made such contemporary classics as *Mean Streets* (1973), *Taxi Driver* (1976), *Raging Bull* (1980), *GoodFellas* (1990), and *The Age of Innocence* (1993).

Many of Scorsese's films are immensely personal narratives, informed by his Italian-American Catholic background. They deal with the motifs of sin and redemption, alienation, masculine violence, and obsession, and display complex characterization, an elaborate visual style, and innovative use of popular music. Among his other films are *Alice Doesn't Live Here Anymore* (1974), *New York, New York* (1977), *The King of Comedy* (1982), *After Hours* (1985), *The Last Temptation of Christ* (1988), *Cape Fear* (1991), *Casino* (1995), and *Bringing Out the Dead* (1999), and *Gangs of New York* (2002).

From the late 1980s onwards, Scorsese became involved in the work of other film-makers. He produced *The Grifters* (1990) and *Clockers* (1995), among several others, and also performed in *Round Midnight* (1986), *Akira Kurosawa's Dreams* (1989), *Guilty by Suspicion* (1991), *Quiz Show* (1994), and *Search and Destroy* (1995). He received the American Film Institute's life achievement Award in 1997. In 1998 he was the recipient of the Billy Wilder Award for Excellence in Film Direction presented by the National Board of Review of Motion Pictures Awards.

Scot inhabitant of Scotland, part of Britain; or a person of Scottish descent. Originally the Scots were a Celtic (Gaelic) people of Northern Ireland who migrated to Scotland in the 5th century.

Scotland (Roman **Caledonia**) the northernmost part of Britain, formerly an independent country, now part of the UK.

area 78,470 sq km/30,297 sq mi **capital** Edinburgh **towns** Glasgow, Dundee, Aberdeen **features** the Highlands in the north

Scotland: Key Dates

3,000 BC	Neolithic settlements include Beaker people and Skara Brae on Orkney.
1st millennium BC	The Picts reach Scotland from mainland Europe.
1st century AD	Picts prevent Romans from penetrating far into Scotland.
122–128	Hadrian's Wall is built to keep northern tribes out of England.
500	The Scots, a Gaelic-speaking tribe from Ireland, settle in the Kingdom of Dalriada (Argyll).
563	St Columba founds the monastery on Iona and begins to convert the Picts to Christianity.
9th c.	Norsemen conquer Orkney, Shetland, Western Isles, and much of Highlands.
c.843	Kenneth McAlpin unifies the Scots and Picts to become first king of Scotland.
1040	King Duncan is murdered by Macbeth.
1263	Scots defeat Norwegian invaders at Battle of Largs.
1295	First treaty between Scotland and France (the Auld Alliance).
1296	Edward I of England invades and declares himself King of Scotland.
1297	William Wallace and Andrew Moray defeat the English at the Battle of Stirling Bridge.
1314	Robert the Bruce defeats the English at Battle of Bannockburn.
1328	Scottish independence recognized by England.
1371	Robert II becomes first king of the House of Stuart.
1513	Battle of Flodden: Scots defeated by the English and James IV killed.
1542	Mary, Queen of Scots, succeeds to throne when less than a week old.
1540s	John Knox introduces Calvinism to Scotland.
1557	The First Covenant establishes the Protestant faith in Scotland.
1567	Mary, Queen of Scots, is forced to abdicate in favour of her son, who is crowned James VI of Scotland. Mary later flees to England, where she is beheaded in 1587.
1603	Union of crowns: when Elizabeth I dies childless, James VI of Scotland becomes James I of England.
1638	Scots rebel after National Covenant condemns Charles I's changes to church ritual.
1643	Solemn League and Covenant allies the Scots with Parliament in the English Civil War.
1650	Oliver Cromwell invades and defeats the Scots at Dunbar.
1679	Presbyterian Covenanters are defeated by Episcopalians at Battle of Bothwell Brig.
1689	Jacobite victory at Killiecrankie, but rebellion against William III collapses soon after.
1692	Campbells massacre the Macdonalds at Glencoe.
1698	Unsuccessful Scottish colony founded at Darien in what is now Panama.
1707	Act of Union unites the Scottish and English Parliaments.
1715	'The Fifteen': Jacobite rebellion in support of James Edward Stuart.
1745	'The Forty-Five': Charles Edward Stuart leads Jacobite rebels as far south as Derby.
1746	Jacobites defeated at Battle of Culloden by English forces under Duke of Cumberland.
1747	Act of Prescription bans Highland costume until repeal in 1782.
c.1780–1860	Highland clearances: crofters evicted to make way for sheep.
1822	George IV makes state visit to Scotland.
1843	The Disruption: 400 ministers leave the Church of Scotland to form the Free Church of Scotland.
1885	Scottish Office created.
1886	Crofters Act provides security of tenure for crofters.
1926	Scottish Secretary upgraded to Secretary of State.
1928	National Party of Scotland forms (becomes Scottish National Party 1932).
1939	Headquarters of Scottish Office moves from London to Edinburgh.
1945	First Scottish Nationalist MP is elected.
1970s	Aberdeen becomes centre of North Sea oil development.
1979	Referendum fails to approve devolution of power to a Scottish Assembly.
1990	'Constitutional Convention' of Labour and Liberal Parties demands a Scottish Parliament.
1994	Scottish Grand Committee of MPs given additional powers.
1996	Local government reform: unitary authorities replace regional and district councils.
1997	Referendum supports plans for a Scottish Parliament and its tax-varying powers.
1999	Labour wins the most seats in the Scottish parliamentary elections but is just short of an overall majority, Donald Dewar is elected head of a coalition. The Scottish Parliament is opened by Queen Elizabeth II in July at a temporary location in Edinburgh.
2000	Donald Dewar dies. His successor is Henry McLeish.

SCOTLAND Cawdor Castle, in the heart of the Scottish Highlands, is one of the most magnificent and well-preserved strongholds in Scotland. The keep dates to the early 14th century, with the parapet and upper works being added in 1454. *Image Bank*

Scottish Monarchs 1005–1603

This table covers the period from the unification of Scotland to the union of the crowns of Scotland and England.

Reign	Name
Celtic Kings	
1005–34	Malcolm II
1034–40	Duncan I
1040–57	Macbeth
1057–93	Malcolm III Canmore
1093–94	Donald III Donalbane
1094	Duncan II
1094–97	Donald III (restored)
1097–1107	Edgar
1107–24	Alexander I
1124–53	David I
1153–65	Malcolm IV
1165–1214	William the Lion
1214–49	Alexander II
1249–86	Alexander III
1286–90	Margaret of Norway
English Domination	
1292–96	John Baliol
1296–1306	annexed to England
House of Bruce	
1306–29	Robert I the Bruce
1329–71	David II
House of Stuart	
1371–90	Robert II
1390–1406	Robert III
1406–37	James I
1437–60	James II
1460–88	James III
1488–1513	James IV
1513–42	James V
1542–67	Mary
1567–1625	James VI[1]

[1] After the union of crowns in 1603, he became James I of England.

SCOTLAND The Royal Unicorn of Holyrood Palace, Edinburgh, Scotland. *Image Bank*

(with the ▷Grampian Mountains); central Lowlands, including valleys of the Clyde and Forth, with most of the country's population and industries; Southern Uplands (including the ▷Lammermuir Hills); and islands of the Orkneys, Shetlands, and Western Isles; the world's greatest concentration of nuclear weapons are at the UK and US bases on the Clyde, near Glasgow; 8,000-year-old pinewood forests once covered 1,500,000 ha/3,706,500 acres, now reduced to 12,500 ha/30,900 acres; there were at least 104,876 ha/259,150 acres of native woodlands remaining in the Highlands in 1994, covering only 2% of the total area. The 1995 Millennium Commission award will fund the creation of the Millennium Forest, and double Scotland's forests **industry** electronics, marine and aircraft engines, oil, natural gas, chemicals, textiles, clothing, printing, paper, food processing, tourism, whisky, coal, computer industries (Scotland's 'Silicon Glen' produces over 35% of Europe's personal computers) **currency** pound sterling **population** (2000 est) 5,114,600 **languages** English; Scots, a lowland dialect (derived from Northumbrian Anglo-Saxon); Gaelic spoken by 1.3%, mainly in the Highlands **religions** Presbyterian (Church of Scotland), Roman Catholic **famous people** Robert Bruce, Walter Scott, Robert Burns, Robert Louis Stevenson, Adam Smith **government** Scotland sends 72 members to the UK Parliament at Westminster. The Local Government (Scotland) Bill of 1994 abolished the two-tier system of local government. Since 1996 there have been 32 unitary authorities. There is a differing legal system to England (see ▷Scottish law). Scots voted overwhelmingly in favour of a ▷Scottish Parliament and the beginning of devolution in a referendum held in September 1997. Scotland's last legislature vanished with the Union of 1707. The Scottish Parliament was backed by 75% of the 2.4 million people who voted in the two-question referendum and 63% agreed that it should have tax-varying powers. There was a 61.4% turnout. Elections to the 129-member assembly took place in May 1999. The Edinburgh-based Scottish Parliament and its ▷Scottish Executive have charge over most of Scotland's domestic affairs, including education, the health service, local government, and agriculture. The Executive is headed by a First Minister, who is effectively Scotland's prime minister. However, the London-based ▷Scotland Office, led by the secretary of state for Scotland, has charge of a considerable range of 'reserved matters', including defence, foreign affairs, and finance and economic policy. **Related Web site: Gateway to Scotland** http://www.geo.ed.ac.uk/home/scotland/scotland.html

Scotland Yard, New headquarters of the ▷Criminal Investigation Department (CID) of Britain's London Metropolitan Police, established in 1878. It is named from its original location in Scotland Yard, off Whitehall.

Scots language the form of the English language as traditionally spoken and written in Scotland, regarded by some scholars as a distinct language. Scots derives from the Northumbrian dialect of Anglo-Saxon or Old English, and has been a literary language since the 14th century.

Scott, (George) Gilbert (1811–1878) English architect. As the leading practical architect of the mid-19th-century Gothic Revival in England, Scott was responsible for the building or restoration of many public buildings and monuments, including the Albert Memorial (1863–72), the Foreign Office in Whitehall (1862–73), and the St Pancras Station Hotel (1868–74), all in London.

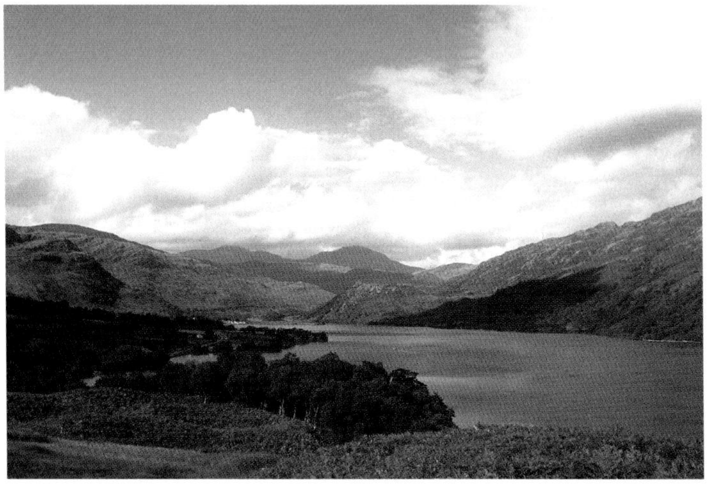

SCOTLAND Loch Lomond, western Scotland. *Corel*

Scott, Giles Gilbert (1880–1960) English architect. He was the grandson of Gilbert ▷Scott. He designed Liverpool Anglican Cathedral (begun 1903; completed 1978), Cambridge University Library (1931–34), Battersea Power Station (1932–34), and Waterloo Bridge, London (1939–45). He also designed and supervised the rebuilding of the House of Commons chamber at the Palace of Westminster in a modern Gothic style after World War II.

Scott, Paul Mark (1920–1978) English novelist. He was the author of *The Raj Quartet* consisting of *The Jewel in the Crown* (1966), *The Day of the Scorpion* (1968), *The Towers of Silence* (1972), and *A Division of the Spoils* (1975), dealing with the British Raj in India. Other novels include *Staying On* (1977), set in post-independence India, for which he won the Booker Prize.

Scott, Ridley (1939–) English film director and producer. His work includes some of the most visually spectacular and influential films of the 1980s and 1990s, such as *Alien* (1979) and *Blade Runner* (1982). Criticized for sacrificing storyline and character development in favour of ornate sets, Scott replied with *Thelma and Louise* (1991), a story of female bonding and adventure. In 2000 he released *Gladiator*, (seven Academy Awards, including Best Picture), followed by *Black Hawk Down* (2002) and *Matchstick Men* (2003).

Scott, Robert Falcon (1868–1912) Called 'Scott of the Antarctic'. English explorer who commanded two Antarctic expeditions, 1901–04 and 1910–12. On 18 January 1912 he reached the South Pole, shortly after the Norwegian Roald ▷Amundsen, but on the return journey he and his companions died in a blizzard only a few miles from their base camp. His journal was recovered and published in 1913.

Born in Devonport, he entered the navy in 1882. With Scott on the final expedition were Edward Wilson (1872–1912), Laurence ▷Oates, H R Bowers, and E Evans. The Scott Polar Research Institute in Cambridge was founded in 1920 out of funds donated by the public following Scott's death, as a memorial to him and his companions. It houses a small museum and library, and carries out research into all aspects of the Antarctic and Arctic regions.

Scott, Walter (1771–1832) Scottish novelist and poet. His first works were translations of German ballads and collections of Scottish ballads, which he followed with narrative poems of his own, such as *The Lay of the Last Minstrel* (1805), *Marmion* (1808), and *The Lady of the Lake* (1810). He gained a European reputation for his historical novels such as *Waverley* (1814), *Rob Roy* (1817), *The Heart of Midlothian* (1818), and *Ivanhoe* (1819), all published anonymously.

His last years were marked by frantic writing to pay off his debts, after the bankruptcy of the printing and publishing business of which he was a partner. He was created a baronet in 1820.

Scott exerted a strong influence on the imaginative life of his country. He stimulated an interest in Scottish history and materially affected the literary movement of his time: his unconventional manner of writing and his total freedom from the academic point of view were largely instrumental in arousing the French Romantic movement which produced such writers as Victor Hugo, Alfred de Musset, and Théophile Gautier, and such painters as Corot and Millet. Scott was also the creator of the historical novel, combining naturalness and realism with the historical and romantic element of adventure and the marvels of superstition. His influence on Honoré de Balzac was acknowledged.

Related Web site: Selected Poetry of Sir Walter Scott (1771–1832) http://www.library.utoronto.ca/utel/rp/authors/scott.html

Scottish Borders unitary authority in southeast Scotland, created in 1996 to replace the former Borders region.
area 4,733 sq km/1,827 sq mi **towns** Galashiels, Hawick, Jedburgh, Kelso, Newtown St Boswells (administrative headquarters), Peebles, Selkirk **physical** much of the west part of the area is upland (Lammermuir, Moorfoot and Pentland Hills); Broad Law (840 m/2,756 ft), near Tweedsmuir, is the highest point. The principal river, the Tweed, traverses the region west–east; its tributaries include the River Teviot. The largest loch is St Mary's, and the only substantial area of low-lying agricultural land is the Merse in the southeast, near the English border. The coast is generally precipitous **features** Walter Scott's home at Abbotsford; Field Marshal Haig and Walter Scott buried at Dryburgh Abbey; Melrose Abbey (12th century) **famous people** Mungo Park, James Hogg (Scottish poet 'the Ettrick Shepherd'), Walter Scott **industries** electronics, timber, knitwear, tweed **agriculture** sheep and cattle; cereals and root crops; fishing **population** (1996) 105,300

Scottish Executive the government of Scotland for devolved matters. The Executive comprises a First Minister and a team of Scottish ministers, including law officers, supported by civil servants. The ministers are politicians drawn from the Scottish Parliament – from the party or coalition with a majority of seats – to whom they are accountable. The Executive comprises six main functional departments: justice; health; rural affairs; development; education; and enterprise and lifelong learning. The Executive also overseas nine agencies, which include the Scottish Courts, Scottish Prison Service, Historic Scotland, and the National Archives of Scotland.

Scottish Gaelic language see ▷Gaelic language.

Scottish Gaelic literature the earliest examples of Scottish Gaelic prose belong to the period 1000–1150, but the most significant early original composition is the history of the MacDonalds in the Red and Black Books at Clanranald. The first printed book in Scottish Gaelic was a translation of Knox's Prayer Book (1567). Prose Gaelic is at its best in the folk tales, proverbs, and essays by writers such as Norman MacLeod in the 19th and Donald Lamont in the 20th century.

Scottish Gaelic poetry falls into two main categories. The older, syllabic verse was composed by professional bards. The chief sources of our knowledge of this are the Book of the Dean of Lismore (16th century), which is also the main early source for the Ossianic ballads; the panegyrics in the Books of Clanranald; and the Fernaig manuscript. Modern Scottish Gaelic stressed poetry began in the 17th century but reached its zenith during the Jacobite period with Alexander MacDonald, Duncan Macintyre, Rob Donn, and Dugald Buchanan. Only William Livingstone (1808–1870) kept alive the old nationalistic spirit in the 19th century. During and after World War II a new school emerged, including Somhairle MacGilleathain, George Campbell-Hay, and Ruaraidh MacThómais.

Scottish law the legal system of Scotland. Owing to its separate development, Scotland has a system differing from the rest of the UK, being based on ▷civil law. Its continued separate existence was guaranteed by the Act of Union with England in 1707.

Scottish Parliament devolved legislative body of Scotland. It comprises 129 members and was created by the November 1998 Scotland Act, which was passed following the Scottish electorate's overwhelming approval of government proposals in a referendum on devolution held on 11 September 1997. The first elections to the parliament were held on 6 May 1999 and the parliament opened on 1 July 1999.

Members are elected for four-year terms through a 'semi-proportional' electoral system. Seventy-three members are returned on a first-past-the-post basis from single-member constituencies, comprising Scotland's existing Westminster constituencies, with an extra seat created through dividing the Orkney and Shetland constituency into two. An additional 56 members are selected on a proportional basis from party lists based on Scotland's eight European Parliament constituencies.

The parliament has devolved law-making powers in all areas except defence, foreign affairs, the constitution, social security, company regulation, economic management, and taxation. It also has the authority to vary the basic rate of income tax in Scotland by up to 3 pence in the pound to supplement a block grant (£14.9 billion for 2000–01) to supersede the former Scottish Office budget. A First Minister (equivalent to a Scottish prime minister), with a main office in St Andrew's House, is drawn from the majority grouping within the parliament, and relevant ministers sit with their UK government counterparts at negotiating meetings in Brussels whenever Scottish interests are affected.

The parliament's temporary base is the Church of Scotland General Assembly Hall and City of Edinburgh Council buildings, at the Mound and on George IV Bridge, in Edinburgh. A permanent home is being built on the Royal Mile, next to ▷Holyrood House, designed by a team led by the Spanish architect Enric Miralles, with completion planned for 2004. The construction project has been faced by problems of spiralling costs (estimated in 2003 at more than £290 million) and slippage in the timetable.

Related Web site: Scottish Parliament http://www.scottish.parliament.uk/

Scouts worldwide youth organization that emphasizes character, citizenship, and outdoor life. It was founded (as the Boy Scouts) in England in 1908 by Robert ▷Baden-Powell. His book *Scouting for Boys* (1908) led to the incorporation in the UK of the Boy Scout Association by royal charter in 1912. There are some 25 million members of the World Organization of the Scout Movement (1998).

scrapie fatal disease of sheep and goats that attacks the central nervous system, causing deterioration of the brain cells, and leading to the characteristic staggering gait and other behavioural abnormalities, before death. It is caused by the presence of an abnormal version of the brain protein PrP and is related to ▷bovine spongiform encephalopathy, the disease of cattle known as 'mad cow disease', and Creutzfeldt–Jakob disease in humans. It is a transmissible spongiform encephalopathy.

screamer any South American marsh-dwelling bird of the family Anhimidae, order Anseriformes; there are only three species, all in the genus *Anhima*. They are about 80 cm/30 in long, with short curved beaks, long toes, dark plumage, spurs on the fronts of the wings, and a crest or horn on the head.

scree pile of rubble and sediment that collects at the foot of a mountain range or cliff. The rock fragments that form scree are usually broken off by the action of frost (▷freeze-thaw weathering).

screen dump in computing, the process of making a printed copy of the current VDU screen display. The screen dump is sometimes stored as a data file instead of being printed immediately.

screening (or **health screening**) the systematic search for evidence of a disease, or of conditions that may precede it, in people who are at risk but not suffering from any symptoms. The aim of screening is to try to limit ill health from preventable diseases that might otherwise go undetected in the early stages. Examples are hypothyroidism and phenylketonuria, for which all newborn babies in Western countries are screened; breast cancer (▷mammography) and cervical cancer; and stroke, for which high blood pressure is a known risk factor.

screw in construction, cylindrical or tapering piece of metal or plastic (or formerly wood) with a helical groove cut into it. Each turn of a screw moves it forward or backwards by a distance equal to the pitch (the spacing between neighbouring threads).

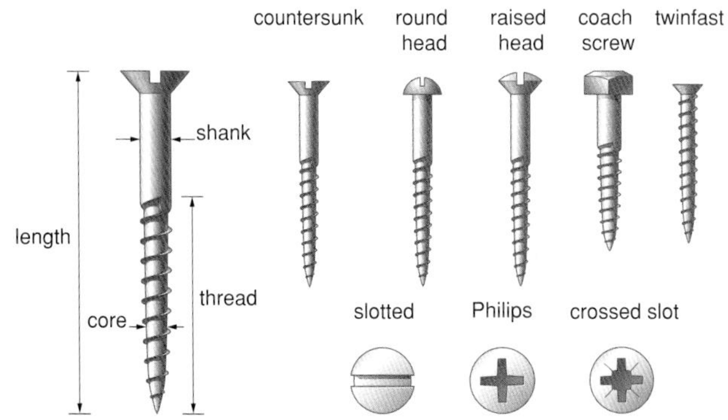

SCREW The screw heads on these different types of wood screw vary depending on the nature of the job; for example, countersunk screws are used for work where it is important that the screw head is flush to the surface.

Scriabin see ▷Skriabin.

scuba (acronym for self-contained underwater breathing apparatus) another name for ▷aqualung.
Related Web site: Welcome to Aquanaut http://www.aquanaut.com/

Scud Soviet-produced surface-to-surface ▷missile that can be armed with a nuclear, chemical, or conventional warhead. The Scud-B, deployed on a mobile launcher, was the version most commonly used by the Iraqi army in the Gulf War 1991. It is a relatively inaccurate weapon.

Scudamore, Peter Michael (1958–) British National Hunt jockey. He was champion jockey in 1982 (shared with John Francome) and from 1986 to 1992. In 1988–89 he rode a record 221 winners, a total surpassed in 1997–98 by Tony McCoy. In April 1993 he announced his retirement from the sport, with a world record 1,677 winners.

sculpture artistic shaping of materials such as wood, stone, clay, metal, and, more recently, plastic and other synthetics. The earliest prehistoric human artefacts include sculpted stone figurines, and all ancient civilizations have left behind examples of sculpture. Many indigenous cultures have maintained rich traditions of sculpture. Those of Africa (see ▷African art), South America, and the Caribbean in particular have been influential in the development of contemporary Western sculpture.

Historically, most sculpture has been religious in intent. Chinese, Japanese, and Indian sculptures are usually Buddhist or Hindu images. African, American Indian, and Oceanic sculptures reflect spirit cults and animist beliefs.

There are two main techniques traditionally employed in sculpture: **carving**, involving the cutting away of hard materials such as wood or stone to reveal an image; and **modelling**, involving the building up of an image from malleable materials, such as clay or wax, which may then be cast in bronze. In the 20th century various techniques for 'constructing' sculptures have been developed, for example metal welding and assemblage.

Ancient sculpture Egyptian and Mesopotamian sculpture took the form of monumental ▷reliefs in palace and temple decoration. Standing sculptures of the period were intended to be seen only from the front and sides. The first sculptures in the round (to be seen from all sides) were Greek. The development of vigorous poses (contrapposto) and emotional expressiveness elevated Greek sculpture to the pinnacle of artistic achievement (see ▷Phidias, ▷Praxiteles, and ▷Parthenon), and much of subsequent Western sculpture has been imitative of Greek ideals. Lifelike portrait sculpture was introduced by the Romans.

Medieval sculpture Sculpture of the medieval period is epitomized by niche figures carved in stone for churches (for example, Chartres Cathedral, France) and by delicate ivory carvings. The work of Nicola Pisano began a great tradition of Italian sculpture.

Renaissance sculpture Greek supremacy was challenged by the reintroduction of free-standing sculptures, notably Michelangelo's *David* (1501–04), and by superlative bronze casting, for example, Donatello's equestrian monument of *Gattamelata* (1447–50; Piazza del Santo, Padua). In the work of Lorenzo Ghiberti, Luca della Robbia, and Andrea del Verrocchio, figure sculpture attained a new dignity and power. The work of Benvenuto Cellini and Giovanni Bologna (1524–1608) exemplified the Mannerist style.

Pedro Berruguete, a pupil of Michelangelo, introduced the Renaissance to Spain. In France, Jean Goujon developed Mannerism. However, it was the High Renaissance style of Michelangelo that was later encouraged by Louis XIV, who commissioned numerous busts and figure groups, notably by François Girardon.

Baroque and rococo sculpture Relief rather than free-standing sculptures came to the fore. The limpid virtuosity of such sculptors as Giovanni Bernini seemed to defy the nature of the materials they used. The style was represented in France by Etienne Falconet, and in Spain by Alonso Cano.

Neoclassical sculpture Sculpture of the 18th century concentrated on smooth perfection of form and surface, notably the work of Antonio Canova. The last great exponent of sculpture in the classical tradition was Auguste Rodin. The work of Aristide Maillol and Antoine Bourdelle (1861–1929) emphasized formal qualities, rejecting both realism and Impressionism.

20th century Sculptors such as Henry Moore, Barbara Hepworth, and Jacob Epstein used traditional materials and techniques to create forms inspired by 'primitive' art and nature. The work of Amedeo Modigliani and Henri Gaudier-Brzeska also reflects such influences. Abstract sculpture was pioneered by Alexander Archipenko and Ossip Zadkine, both exponents of cubism, and Constantin Brancusi and Alberto Giacometti, who developed three-dimensional abstract forms from natural materials. Followers of the

SCULPTURE Baroque sculpture at its dramatic best in the Triton Fountain, Piazza Barberini, Rome, Italy, by the Italian painter and sculptor Gianlorenzo Bernini (1598–1680). *The Art Archive/Piazza Barberini Rome/Album/Joseph Martin*

nonrepresentational school include Jacques Lipchitz, Jean Arp, Naum Gabo and Antoine Pevsner (pioneers of Russian constructivism), Reg Butler, and Anthony Caro. Among more traditional sculptors whose work powerfully expresses the modern idiom are Marino Marini in Italy and Frank Dobson (1888–1963) in England.

Other sculptors have broken with the past entirely, rejecting both carving and modelling. Today the term sculpture applies to the mobiles of Alexander Calder, assemblages of various materials, 'environment sculpture' and ▷earthworks (pioneered by Carl André), and 'installations'.

Another development has been the sculpture garden; for example, Hakore open-air museum in Japan and the Grizedale Forest sculpture project in the Lake District, England.

scurvy disease caused by deficiency of vitamin C (ascorbic acid), which is contained in fresh vegetables and fruit. The signs are weakness and aching joints and muscles, progressing to bleeding of the gums and other spontaneous haemorrhage, and drying-up of the skin and hair. It is reversed by giving the vitamin.

scurvy grass plant found growing in salt marshes and on banks by the sea in the northern hemisphere. Shoots may grow low, or more upright, up to 50 cm/20 in, with fleshy heart-shaped lower leaves; the flowers are white and have four petals. The edible, sharp-tasting leaves are a good source of vitamin C and were formerly eaten by sailors as a cure for the disease scurvy. (*Cochlearia officinalis*, family Cruciferae.)

Scylla and Charybdis in Greek mythology, a sea monster and a whirlpool, between which ▷Odysseus had to sail. Later writers located them at the northern end of the Straits of Messina, between Sicily and Italy.

Scythia region north of the Black Sea between the Carpathian Mountains and the River Don, inhabited by the Scythians 7th–1st centuries BC. From the middle of the 4th century, they were slowly superseded by the Sarmatians. The Scythians produced ornaments and vases in gold and electrum with animal decoration. Although there is no surviving written work, there are spectacular archaeological remains, including vast royal burial mounds which often contain horse skeletons.

SD abbreviation for the state of ▷South Dakota, USA.

SDLP abbreviation for ▷Social Democratic and Labour Party, a Northern Ireland political party.

SDP abbreviation for ▷Social Democratic Party, former British political party.

sea anemone invertebrate marine animal of the phylum Cnidaria with a tubelike body attached by the base to a rock or shell. The other end has an open 'mouth' surrounded by stinging tentacles, which capture crustaceans and other small organisms. Many sea anemones are beautifully coloured, especially those in tropical waters.

seaborgium synthesized radioactive element of the ▷transactinide series, symbol Sg, atomic number 106, relative atomic mass 263. It was first synthesized 1974 in the USA and given the temporary name unnilhexium. The discovery was not confirmed until 1993. It was officially named 1997 after US nuclear chemist Glenn ▷Seaborg.

The University of California, Berkeley, bombarded californium with oxygen nuclei to get isotope 263; the Joint Institute for Nuclear Research, Dubna, Russia, bombarded lead with chromium nuclei to obtain isotopes 259 and 260.

sea cucumber any echinoderm of the class Holothuroidea with a cylindrical body that is tough-skinned, knobbed, or spiny. The size ranges from 3 cm/1.2 in to 2 m/6.6 ft. There are around 900 species, which are mostly black, brown, or olive green in colour. Sea cucumbers are sometimes called 'cotton-spinners' because of the sticky filaments they eject from the anus in self-defence.

The dried flesh of sea cucumbers is a delicacy in Japan and Taiwan, and overfishing has threatened some populations. A high density is vital to sustain a population as they reproduce by releasing sperm or ova into the water; other sea cucumbers must also be releasing sperm or ova nearby.

seafloor spreading growth of the ocean ▷crust outwards (sideways) from ocean ridges. The concept of seafloor spreading has been combined with that of continental drift and incorporated into ▷plate tectonics.

seagull see ▷gull.

sea horse any marine fish of several related genera, especially *Hippocampus*, of the family Syngnathidae, which includes the ▷pipefishes. The body is small and compressed and covered with bony plates raised into tubercles or spines. The tail is prehensile, and the tubular mouth sucks in small shellfish and larvae as food. The head and foreparts, usually carried upright, resemble those of a horse. They swim vertically and beat their fins up to 70 times a second.

Unusually for fish, sea horses are monogamous and have a relatively long courtship, from 3–7 days. The female deposits her eggs, from dozens to hundreds, in a special pouch in the male. The male fertilizes the eggs whilst they are in his pouch, and nourishes them for six weeks or so until they are finally released as young fish.

SEA HORSE The dwarf sea horse swims in an upright position, propelled by gentle movements of its dorsal fin.

seakale perennial European coastal plant with broad, fleshy leaves and white flowers; it is cultivated in Europe and the young shoots are eaten as a vegetable. (*Crambe maritima*, family Cruciferae.)

seal aquatic carnivorous mammal of the families Otariidae and Phocidae (sometimes placed in a separate order, the Pinnipedia). The eared seals or sea lions (Otariidae) have small external ears, unlike the true seals (Phocidae). Seals have a streamlined body with thick blubber for insulation, and front and hind flippers. They are able to close their nostrils as they dive, and obtain oxygen from their blood supply while under water. They feed on fish, squid, or crustaceans, and are commonly found in Arctic and Antarctic seas, but also in Mediterranean, Caribbean, and Hawaiian waters.

Related Web sites: Elephant Seals http://ourworld.compuserve.com/homepages/jaap/elepseal.htm
North Pacific Fur Seal http://www.yoto98.noaa.gov/books/seals/seals6.htm
Seal Conservation Society: The Pinnipeds http://www.greenchannel.com/tec/pinniped.htm

seal mark or impression made in a block of wax to authenticate letters and documents. Seals were used in ancient China and are still used in China, Korea, and Japan.

sea law set of laws dealing with fishing areas, ships, and navigation; see ▷maritime law.

sea lily any ▷echinoderm of the class Crinoidea. In most, the rayed, cuplike body is borne on a sessile stalk (permanently attached to a rock) and has feathery arms in multiples of five encircling the mouth. However, some sea lilies are free-swimming and unattached.

sea lion any of several genera of ▷seals of the family Otariidae (eared seals), which also includes the fur seals. These streamlined animals have large fore flippers which they use to row themselves through the water. The hind flippers can be turned beneath the body to walk on land.

There are two species of sea lion in the northern hemisphere, and three in the south. They feed on fish, squid, and crustaceans. Steller's sea lion *Eumetopias jubatus* lives in the North Pacific, large numbers breeding on the Aleutian lslands. Males may be up to 3.4 m/11 ft long, with a thick neck with a characteristic mane, and weigh up to one tonne. Females are one-third the weight. The **Californian sea lion** *Zalophus californianus* only reaches 2.3 m/7 ft, and is the species most often seen in zoos and as a 'performing seal'.

The **Australian sea lion** *Neophoca cinerea* is found only in southern Australian waters, especially on offshore islands such as Kangaroo Island. It is one of the larger sea lions; males weigh up to 300 kg/660 lb, three times as much as females, and are 2 m/6.5 ft long. The **New Zealand sea lion** *Phocarctos hookeri*, of similar size, is found mainly on Auckland Island, 322 km/200 mi south of New Zealand. It is the rarest sea lion, with only about 12,000 existing in 1998.

Related Web site: California Sea Lion http://www.seaworld.org/animal_bytes/sea_lionab.html

SEA LION South American sea lions *Otaria flavescens*. The battles for mates are intense (as the successful males will procure the majority of matings) and injuries between males may be severe. *K G Preston-Mafham/Premaphotos Wildlife*

Sealyham breed of terrier dog, named after the place in Pembrokeshire, Wales, where it originated in the 19th century as a cross between the Welsh and Jack Russell terriers. It has a coarse white coat and reaches a height of 30 cm/12 in.

sea mouse any of a genus *Aphrodite* of large marine ▷annelid worms (polychaetes), with oval bodies covered in bristles and usually found on muddy sea floors.

Seanad Éireann (Irish senate) upper house or senate of the Oireachtas (legislature) in the Republic of Ireland. It has 60 members or senators, and its term of office is up to five years, concurrent with that of the ▷Dáil (lower house of the Irish legislature). The Seanad has limited powers, being able only to delay bills; in the case of money bills, it can only refer a bill back to the Dáil. Although nominally a vocational chamber it tends to mirror the Dáil's political composition, making it even less powerful.

Of its 60 members, 43 are elected by a constituency of TDs (Teachta Dála; member of the Dáil), senators, and local councillors through the single transferable vote. These are elected from five vocational panels: agriculture, labour, language and culture, industry and commerce, and public administration. Six are elected by the graduates of two of the Republic of Ireland's universities and 11 are nominated by the Taoiseach (prime minister).

Sea Peoples unidentified seafaring warriors who may have been Achaeans, Etruscans, or ▷Philistines, who ravaged and settled the Mediterranean coasts in the 12th–13th centuries BC. They were defeated by Ramses III of Egypt 1191 BC.

seaplane aeroplane capable of taking off from, and landing on, water. There are two major types, floatplanes and flying boats. The floatplane is similar to an ordinary aeroplane but has floats in place of wheels; the flying boat has a broad hull shaped like a boat and may also have floats attached to the wing tips.

sea potato yellow-brown sea urchin *Echinocardium cordatum* covered in short spines, and found burrowing in sand from the lower shore downwards.

search engine in computing, online program to help users find information on the Internet. Commercial search engines such as AltaVista and Lycos comprise databases of documents, Usenet articles, images, and news stories, which can be searched by keying in a key word or phrase. The databases are compiled by a mixture of automated agents (spiders) and webmasters registering their sites.

searching in computing, extracting a specific item from a large body of data, such as a file or table. The method used depends on how the data are organized. For example, a binary search, which requires the data to be in sequence, involves first deciding which half of the data contains the required item, then which quarter, then which eighth, and so on until the item is found.

sea slug any of an order (Nudibranchia) of marine gastropod molluscs in which the shell is reduced or absent. The order includes some very colourful forms, especially in the tropics. They are largely carnivorous, feeding on hydroids and ▷sponges.

Most are under 2.5 cm/1 in long, and live on the sea bottom or on vegetation, although some live in open waters. Tentacles on the back help take in oxygen.

British species include the shore-living common grey sea slug *Aeolidia papillosa* up to 8 cm/3 in and the yellow sea lemon *Archidoris pseudoargus*.

sea snake one of a number of aquatic venomous snakes. Their tails are compressed laterally, and form powerful swimming organs. The eyes are extremely small, have round pupils, and the snakes are practically blind when out of water. The poison secreted by the animals is very virulent, and is used by them to kill the fish on which they feed.

season period of the year having a characteristic climate. The change in seasons is mainly due to the change in attitude of the Earth's axis in relation to the Sun, and hence the position of the Sun in the sky at a particular place. In temperate latitudes four seasons are recognized: spring, summer, autumn (fall), and winter. Tropical regions have two seasons – the wet and the dry. Monsoon areas around the Indian Ocean have three seasons: the cold, the hot, and the rainy.

The northern temperate latitudes have summer when the southern temperate latitudes have winter, and vice versa. During winter, the Sun is low in the sky and has less heating effect because of the oblique angle of incidence and because the sunlight has further to travel through the atmosphere. The differences between the seasons are more marked inland than near the coast, where the sea has a moderating effect on temperatures. In polar regions the change between summer and winter is abrupt; spring and autumn are hardly perceivable. In tropical regions, the belt of rain associated with the trade winds moves north and south with the Sun, as do the dry conditions associated with the belts of high pressure near the tropics. The monsoon's three seasons result from the influence of the Indian Ocean on the surrounding land mass of Asia in that area.

Related Web site: Earth's Seasons: Equinoxes, Solstices, Perihelion, and Aphelion http://aa.usno.navy.mil/AA/data/docs/EarthSeasons.html

seasonal adjustment in statistics, an adjustment of figures designed to take into account influences that are purely seasonal, and relevant only for a short time. The resulting figures are then thought to reflect long-term trends more accurately.

seasonal affective disorder (SAD) form of depression that occurs in winter and is relieved by the coming of spring. Its incidence decreases closer to the Equator. One type of SAD is associated with increased sleeping and appetite.

It has been suggested that SAD may be caused by changes in the secretion of melatonin, a hormone produced by the ▷pineal body in the brain. Melatonin secretion is inhibited by bright daylight.

Related Web site: Seasonal Light – SAD Home Page http://www.geocities.com/HotSprings/7061/sadhome.html#SC

sea squirt (or **tunicate**) any solitary or colonial-dwelling saclike ▷chordate of the class Ascidiacea. A pouch-shaped animal attached to a rock or other base, it draws in food-carrying water through one siphon and expels it through another after straining it through numerous gill slits. The young are free-swimming tadpole-shaped organisms, which, unlike the adults, have a notochord.

Sea squirts have transparent or translucent tunics made of cellulose. They vary in size from a few millimetres to 30 cm/12 in in length and are cylindrical, circular, or irregular in shape. Their defences against predators include sulphuric acid secretion and the accumulation of vanadium, a toxic heavy metal.

Seattle (called 'the Emerald City') port on Lake Washington, USA; the largest city in the Pacific Northwest; population (2000 est) (city) 563,400; (Greater Seattle) 3,275,800. It is the main transit point for supplies to Alaska. Industries include aerospace (it is the headquarters of the Boeing Corporation), timber, tourism, banking and insurance, paper industries, electronics, computing (Microsoft is based in adjoining Redmond), biotechnology, ocean science, shipbuilding and repair, and fishing. Coffee has been an important product since the development of the Starbucks Company in the 1970s. Trade with Japan is important.

Related Web site: Seattle http://www.ci.seattle.wa.us/

SEA URCHIN The bony skeleton of the sea urchin is often washed up in large numbers on beaches. Often sold as an ornament, it has a relatively smooth surface as the urchin's spines are quickly detached once the animal dies. *Premaphotos Wildlife*

sea urchin any of various orders of the class Echinoidea among the ▷echinoderms. They all have a globular body enclosed with plates of lime and covered with spines. Sometimes the spines are anchoring organs, and they also assist in locomotion. Sea urchins feed on seaweed and the animals frequenting them, and some are edible, as is their roe.

sea water the water of the seas and oceans, covering about 70% of the Earth's surface and comprising about 97% of the world's water (only about 3% is fresh water). Sea water contains a large amount of dissolved solids, the most abundant of which is sodium chloride (almost 3% by mass); other salts include potassium chloride, bromide, and iodide, magnesium chloride, and magnesium sulphate. It also contains a large amount of dissolved carbon dioxide, and thus acts as a carbon 'sink' that may help to reduce the greenhouse effect.

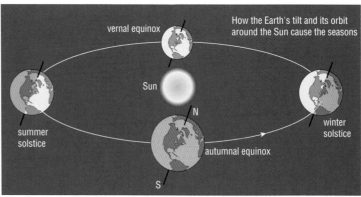

SEASON The diagram shows the cause of the seasons. As the Earth orbits the Sun, its axis of rotation always points in the same direction. This means that, during the northern hemisphere summer solstice (usually 21 June), the Sun is overhead in the northern hemisphere. At the northern hemisphere winter solstice (usually 22 December), the Sun is overhead in the southern hemisphere.

seaweed any of a vast group of simple multicellular plant forms belonging to the ▷algae and found growing in the sea, brackish estuaries, and salt marshes, from about the high-tide mark to depths of 100–200 m/300–600 ft. Many seaweeds have holdfasts (attaching them to rocks or other surfaces), stalks, and fronds, sometimes with air bladders to keep them afloat, and are green, blue-green, red, or brown.

Related Web site: Seaweed Home Page http://seaweed.ucg.ie/seaweed.html

Sebastian, St (died *c.* 258) Roman soldier. He was traditionally a member of Emperor Diocletian's bodyguard until his Christian faith was discovered. He was condemned to be killed by arrows. Feast day 20 January.

Sebastiano del Piombo (*c.* 1485–1547) Adopted name of Sebastiano Luciani. Venetian painter, he was a pupil of ▷Giorgione and developed a similar style. In 1511 he moved to Rome, where his friendship with Michelangelo (and rivalry with Raphael) inspired his finest works, such as *The Raising of Lazarus* (1517–19; National Gallery, London).

Sebastopol alternative spelling of ▷Sevastopol, a Black Sea port on the peninsula of ▷Crimea in Ukraine.

seborrhoeic eczema common skin disease affecting any sebum-(natural oil) producing area of the skin. It is thought to be caused by the yeast *Pityrosporum*, and is characterized by yellowish-red, scaly areas on the skin, and dandruff. Antidandruff shampoos are often helpful.

secant in trigonometry, the function of a given angle in a right-angled triangle, obtained by dividing the length of the hypotenuse (the longest side) by the length of the side adjacent to the angle. It is the ▷reciprocal of the ▷cosine (sec = 1/cos).

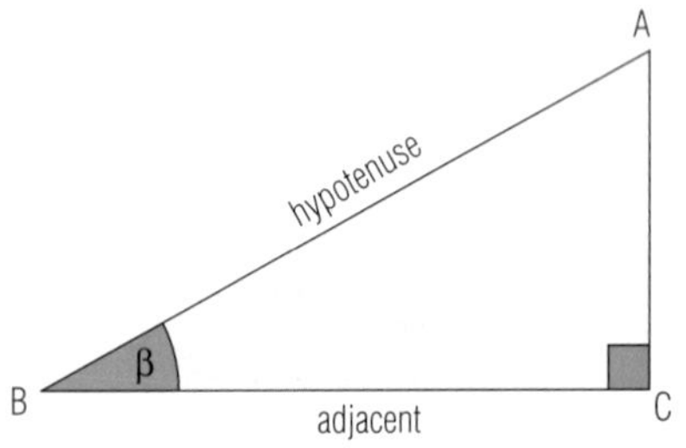

$$\text{sec(ant) } \beta = \frac{1}{\cos\beta} = \frac{\text{hypotenuse}}{\text{adjacent}} = \frac{AB}{BC}$$

SECANT The secant of an angle is a function used in the mathematical study of the triangle. If the secant of angle B is known, then the hypotenuse can be found given the length of the adjacent side, or the adjacent side can be found from the hypotenuse.

second basic SI unit (symbol sec or s) of time, one-sixtieth of a minute. It is defined as the duration of 9,192,631,770 cycles of regulation (periods of the radiation corresponding to the transition between two hyperfine levels of the ground state) of the caesium-133 isotope. In mathematics, the second is a unit (symbol ″) of angular measurement, equalling one-sixtieth of a minute, which in turn is one-sixtieth of a degree.

secondary emission in physics, an emission of electrons from the surface of certain substances when they are struck by high-speed electrons or other particles from an external source. It can be detected with a photomultiplier.

secondary growth (or **secondary thickening**) increase in diameter of the roots and stems of certain plants (notably shrubs and trees) that results from the production of new cells by the ▷cambium. It provides the plant with additional mechanical support and new conducting cells, the secondary ▷xylem and ▷phloem. Secondary growth is generally confined to ▷gymnosperms and, among the ▷angiosperms, to the dicotyledons. With just a few exceptions, the monocotyledons (grasses, lilies) exhibit only primary growth, resulting from cell division at the apical ▷meristems.

secondary sexual characteristic in biology, an external feature of an organism that is indicative of its gender (male or female), but not the reproductive organs themselves. They include facial hair in men and breasts in women, combs in cockerels, brightly coloured plumage in many male birds, and manes in male lions. In many cases, they are involved in displays and contests for mates and have evolved by ▷sexual selection. Their development is stimulated by sex hormones.

Second World War alternative name for ▷World War II, 1939–45.

secretary bird ground-hunting, long-legged, mainly grey-plumaged bird of prey *Sagittarius serpentarius*. It is about 1.2 m/4 ft tall, with an erectile head crest tipped with black. It is protected in southern Africa because it eats poisonous snakes.

It gets its name from the fact that its head crest supposedly looks like a pen behind a clerk's ear. It is the only member of the family Sagittariidae, in the same order (Falconiformes) as vultures, eagles, and hawks.

secretin ▷hormone produced by the small intestine of vertebrates that stimulates the production of digestive secretions by the pancreas and liver.

secretion in biology, any substance (normally a fluid) produced by a cell or specialized gland, for example, sweat, saliva, enzymes, and hormones. The process whereby the substance is discharged from the cell is also known as secretion.

secret police any state security force that operates internally, against political dissenters or subversives; for example, the US ▷Federal Bureau of Investigation and the UK ▷Special Branch.

secret service any government ▷intelligence organization. In the USA the Secret Service is a law-enforcement unit of the Treasury Department and provides the president's bodyguard. The secret service in Britain is concerned with the detection of offences, civil or political, committed or threatened by people who act in secrecy, and the provision of political intelligence.

secret society society with membership by invitation only, often involving initiation rites, secret rituals, and dire punishments for those who break the code. Often founded for religious reasons or mutual benefit, some have become the province of corrupt politicians or gangsters, like the ▷Mafia, ▷Ku Klux Klan, and the ▷Triad. See also ▷freemasonry.

sect small ideological group, usually religious in nature, that may have moved away from a main group, often claiming a monopoly of access to truth or salvation. Sects are usually highly exclusive. They demand strict conformity, total commitment to their code of behaviour, and complete personal involvement, sometimes to the point of rejecting mainstream society altogether in terms of attachments, names, possessions, and family.

sector in geometry, part of a circle enclosed by two radii and the arc that joins them. A **minor sector** has an angle at the centre of the circle of less than 180°. A **major sector** has an angle at the centre of the circle of more than 180°.

secularization the process through which religious thinking, practice, and institutions lose their religious and/or social significance. The concept is based on the theory, held by some sociologists, that as societies become industrialized their religious morals, values, and institutions give way to secular ones and some religious traits become common secular practices.

Securities and Investment Board UK body with the overall responsibility for policing financial dealings in the City of London. Introduced in 1987 following the deregulation process of the so-called ▷Big Bang, it acts as an umbrella organization to such self-regulating bodies as the Stock Exchange.

Security Council the most important body of the United Nations; see ▷United Nations.

sedative any drug that has a calming effect, reducing anxiety and tension.

Sedatives will induce sleep in larger doses. Examples are ▷barbiturates, ▷narcotics, and ▷benzodiazepines.

sedge any of a group of perennial grasslike plants, usually with three-cornered solid stems, common in low water or on wet and marshy ground. (Genus *Carex*, family Cyperaceae.)

Sedgemoor, Battle of in English history, a battle on 6 July 1685 in which ▷Monmouth's rebellion was crushed by the forces of James II, on a tract of marshy land 5 km/3 mi southeast of Bridgwater, Somerset.

sediment any loose material that has 'settled' – deposited from suspension in water, ice, or air, generally as the water current or wind speed decreases. Typical sediments are, in order of increasing coarseness, clay, mud, silt, sand, gravel, pebbles, cobbles, and boulders.

Sediments differ from sedimentary rocks in which deposits are fused together in a solid mass of rock by a process called ▷lithification. Pebbles are cemented into ▷conglomerates; sands become sandstones; muds become mudstones or shales; peat is transformed into coal.

sedimentary rock rock formed by the accumulation and cementation of deposits that have been laid down by water, wind, ice, or gravity. Sedimentary rocks cover more than two-thirds of the Earth's surface and comprise three major categories: clastic, chemically precipitated, and organic (or biogenic). Clastic sediments are the largest group and are composed of fragments of pre-existing rocks; they include clays, sands, and gravels.

Chemical precipitates include some limestones and evaporated deposits such as gypsum and halite (rock salt). Coal, oil shale, and limestone made of fossil material are examples of organic sedimentary rocks.

Most sedimentary rocks show distinct layering (stratification), because they are originally depositied as essentially horizontal layers.

sedition in the UK, the offence of inciting unlawful opposition to the crown and government. Unlike ▷treason, sedition does not carry the death penalty.

Seebeck effect in physics, the generation of a voltage in a circuit containing two different metals, or semiconductors, by keeping the junctions between them at different temperatures. Discovered by the German physicist Thomas Seebeck (1770–1831), it is also called the thermoelectric effect, and is the basis of the ▷thermocouple. It is the opposite of the ▷Peltier effect (in which current flow causes a temperature difference between the junctions of different metals).

seed the reproductive structure of higher plants (▷angiosperms and ▷gymnosperms). It develops from a fertilized ovule and consists of an embryo and a food store, surrounded and protected by an outer seed coat, called the testa. The food store is contained either in a specialized nutritive tissue, the ▷endosperm, or in the ▷cotyledons of the embryo itself. In angiosperms the seed is enclosed within a ▷fruit, whereas in gymnosperms it is usually naked and unprotected, once shed from the female cone.

Following ▷germination the seed develops into a new plant.

Seeds may be dispersed from the parent plant in a number of different ways. Agents of dispersal include animals, as with ▷burs and fleshy edible fruits, and wind, where the seed or fruit may be winged or plumed. Water can disperse seeds or fruits that float, and various mechanical devices may eject seeds from the fruit, as in the pods of some leguminous plants (see ▷legume).

There may be a delay in the germination of some seeds to ensure that growth occurs under favourable conditions. Most seeds remain viable for at least 15 years if dried to about 5% water and kept at −20°C/−4°F, although 20% of them will not survive this process.

seed plant any seed-bearing plant; also known as a **spermatophyte**.

The seed plants are subdivided into two classes: the ▷angiosperms, or flowering plants, and the ▷gymnosperms, principally the cycads and conifers.

Together, they comprise the major types of vegetation found on land.

segment in geometry, part of a circle cut off by a straight line or ▷chord, running from one point on the circumference to another. All angles in the same segment are equal.

seiche a pendulous movement seen in large areas of water resembling a ▷tide. It was originally observed on Lake Geneva and is created either by the wind, earth tremors or other atmospheric phenomena.

Seikan Tunnel the world's longest underwater tunnel, opened 1988, linking the Japanese islands of Hokkaido and Honshu, which are separated by the Tsungaru Strait; length 51.7 km/32.3 mi.

Seine French river rising on the Langres plateau in the *département* of Côte d'Or, 30 km/19 mi northwest of Dijon, and flowing 774 km/472 mi northwest through ▷Paris and Rouen to join the English Channel at Le Havre. It is the third longest, but economically the most important, river in the country.

seismic wave energy wave generated by an ▷earthquake or an artificial explosion. There are two types of seismic waves: **body waves** that travel through the Earth's interior, and **surface waves** that travel through the surface layers of the crust and can be felt as the shaking of the ground, as in an earthquake.

Body waves There are two types of body waves: P-waves and S-waves, so-named because they are the primary and secondary waves detected by a seismograph. **P-waves** are longitudinal waves (wave motion in the direction the wave is travelling), whose compressions and rarefactions resemble those of a sound wave. **S-waves** are transverse waves or shear waves, involving a back-and-forth shearing motion at right angles to the direction the wave is travelling (see ▷wave).

Because liquids have no resistance to shear and cannot sustain a shear wave, S-waves cannot travel through liquid material. The Earth's outer core is believed to be liquid because S-waves disappear at the mantle-core boundary, while P-waves do not.

Surface waves Surface waves travel in the surface and subsurface layers of the crust. **Rayleigh waves** travel along the free surface (the uppermost layer) of a solid material. The motion of particles is elliptical, like a water wave, creating the rolling motion often felt during an earthquake. **Love waves** are transverse waves trapped in a subsurface layer due to different densities in the rock layers above and below. They have a horizontal side-to-side shaking motion transverse (at right angles) to the direction the wave is travelling.

seismograph instrument used to record ground motion. A heavy inert weight is suspended by a spring and attached to this is a pen that is in contact with paper on a rotating drum. During an earthquake the instrument frame and drum move, causing the pen to record a zigzag line on the paper; held steady by inertia, the pen does not move.

seismology the study of ▷earthquakes, the seismic waves they produce, the processes that cause them, and the effects they have. By examining the global pattern of waves produced by an earthquake, seismologists can deduce the nature of the materials through which they have passed. This leads to an understanding of the Earth's internal structure.

On a smaller scale, artificial earthquake waves, generated by explosions or mechanical vibrators, can be used to search for subsurface features in, for example, oil or mineral exploration. Earthquake waves from underground nuclear explosions can be distinguished from natural waves by their shorter wavelength and higher frequency.

Selangor state of the Federation of Malaysia; area 7,956 sq km/ 3,071 sq mi; population (1993 est) 1,981,200. It was under British protection from 1874 and was a federated state 1895–1946. The capital was transferred to Shah Alam from Kuala Lumpur in 1973. Klang is the seat of the sultan and a centre for rubber growing and tin mining; Port Kelang (or Klang), formerly Port Swettenham, exports tin and rubber.

select committee any of several long-standing committees of the UK House of Commons, such as the Environment Committee and the Treasury and Civil Service Committee. These were intended to restore parliamentary control of the executive, improve the quality of legislation, and scrutinize public spending and the work of government departments. Select committees represent the major parliamentary reform of the 20th century, and a possible means – through their all-party membership – of avoiding the automatic repeal of one government's measures by its successor.

Related Web site: Select Committees http://www.parliament.uk/ commons/selcom/cmsel.htm

Selene in Greek mythology, the goddess of the Moon; daughter of the Titan Hyperion; and sister of the Sun god ▷Helios and ▷Eos, goddess of the dawn. In later times she was identified with ▷Artemis.

selenium (Greek *Selene* 'Moon') grey, nonmetallic element, symbol Se, atomic number 34, relative atomic mass 78.96. It belongs to the sulphur group and occurs in several allotropic forms that differ in their physical and chemical properties. It is an essential trace element in human nutrition.

Obtained from many sulphide ores and selenides, it is used as a red colouring for glass and enamel.

Because its electrical conductivity varies with the intensity of light, selenium is used extensively in photoelectric devices. It was discovered in 1817 by Swedish chemist Jöns Berzelius and named after the Moon because its properties follow those of tellurium, whose name derives from Latin *Tellus* 'Earth'.

Seleucus (I) Nicator (c. 358–281 BC) Macedonian general under ▷Alexander (III) the Great and founder of the Seleucid dynasty of Syria. After Alexander's death in 323 BC, Seleucus became governor and then, in 312 BC, ruler of Babylonia, founding the city of Seleucia on the River Tigris. He conquered Syria and had himself crowned king in 306 BC, but his expansionist policies brought him into conflict with the Ptolemies of Egypt and he was assassinated. He was succeeded by his son Antiochus I.

self-inductance (or **self-induction**) in physics, the creation of an electromotive force opposing the current. See ▷inductance.

Seljuk Empire empire of the Turkish people (converted to Islam during the 7th century) under the leadership of the invading Tatars or Seljuk Turks. The Seljuk Empire (1055–1243) included Iran, Iraq, and most of Anatolia and Syria. It was a loose confederation whose centre was in Iran, jointly ruled by members of the family and led by a great sultan exercising varying degrees of effective power. It was succeeded by the ▷Ottoman Empire.

Sellafield site of a nuclear power station on the coast of Cumbria, northwest England. It was known as **Windscale** until 1971, when the management of the site was transferred from the UK Atomic Energy Authority to British Nuclear Fuels Ltd. It reprocesses more than 1,000 tonnes of spent fuel from nuclear reactors annually. The plant is the world's greatest discharger of radioactive waste: between 1968 and 1979, 180 kg/400 lb of plutonium was discharged into the Irish Sea. According to a report by Britain's nuclear safety watchdog, the Nuclear Installations

Inspectorate (NII), published in January 1999, the storage facilities, which store 65 tonnes (25%) of the world's civilian plutonium, are in poor structural condition presenting a significant hazard risk of leakage.

Sellers, Peter (1925–1980) Stage name of Richard Henry Sellers. English comedian and film actor. He was particularly skilled at mimicry. He made his name in the innovative British radio programme *The Goon Show* (1949–60). His films include *The Ladykillers* (1955), *I'm All Right Jack* (1960), *Dr Strangelove* (1964), five *Pink Panther* films (1964–78) (as the bumbling Inspector Clouseau), and *Being There* (1979).

Selznick, David O(liver) (1902–1965) US film producer. His early work includes *King Kong, Dinner at Eight*, and *Little Women*, all 1933. His independent company, Selznick International (1935–40), made such lavish films as *Gone With the Wind* (1939), *Rebecca* (1940), and *Duel in the Sun* (1946). His last film was *A Farewell to Arms* (1957).

semantics branch of linguistics dealing with the meaning of words and sentences. Semantics asks how we can use language to express things about the real world and how the meanings of linguistic expressions can reflect people's thoughts. Semantic knowledge is **compositional**; the meaning of a sentence is based on the meanings of the words it contains and the order they appear in. For example, the sentences 'Teachers love children' and 'Children love teachers' both involve people loving other people but because of the different order of words they mean different things.

semaphore visual signalling code in which the relative positions of two movable pointers or hand-held flags stand for different letters or numbers. The system is used by ships at sea and for railway signals.

Semarang port in north Java, Indonesia; population (1995 est) 1,447,000, the capital of Java Tengah province. There are shipbuilding, fishing, and textile industries and exports include coffee, teak, sugar, tobacco, kapok, and petroleum from nearby oilfields.

Semele in Greek mythology, the daughter of Cadmus of Thebes and mother of Dionysus by Zeus. At Hera's suggestion she demanded that Zeus should appear to her in all his glory, but when he did so she was consumed by lightning.

semelparity in biology, the occurrence of a single act of reproduction during an organism's lifetime. Most semelparous species produce very large numbers of offspring when they do reproduce, and normally die soon afterwards. Examples include the Pacific salmon and the pine looper moth. Many plants are semelparous, or ▷monocarpic. Repeated reproduction is called ▷iteroparity.

semiconductor material with electrical conductivity intermediate between metals and insulators and used in a wide range of electronic devices. Certain crystalline materials, most notably silicon and germanium, have a small number of free electrons that have escaped from the bonds between the atoms. The atoms from which they have escaped possess vacancies, called holes, which are similarly able to move from atom to atom and can be regarded as positive charges. Current can be carried by both electrons (negative carriers) and holes (positive carriers). Such materials are known as **intrinsic semiconductors**.

Conductivity of a semiconductor can be enhanced by doping the material with small numbers of impurity atoms which either release free electrons (making an **n-type semiconductor** with more electrons than holes) or capture them (a **p-type semiconductor** with more holes than electrons). When p-type and n-type materials are brought together to form a p–n junction, an electrical barrier is formed which conducts current more

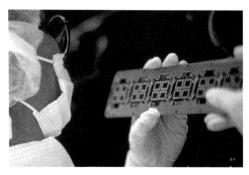

SEMICONDUCTOR Experimentation on the identification and use of semiconductors began in the late 1940s. Progress in the field enabled radios during the 1960s to lose their bulky vacuum tubes (valves) and instead use transistors. *Image Bank*

readily in one direction than the other. This is the basis of the semiconductor diode, used for rectification, and numerous other devices including ▷transistors, rectifiers, and ▷integrated circuits (silicon chips).

semiology (or **semiotics**) the study of the function of signs and symbols in human communication, both in language and by various nonlinguistic means. Beginning with the notion of the Swiss linguist Ferdinand de ▷Saussure that no word or other sign (**signifier**) is intrinsically linked with its meaning (**signified**), it was developed as a scientific discipline, especially by Claude ▷Lévi-Strauss and Roland ▷Barthes.

Related Web site: Semiotics for Beginners http://www.aber.ac.uk/ media/Documents/S4B/sem01.html

Semiramis in Greek legend, founder of ▷Nineveh (Ninua) with her husband Ninus. The legends probably originated in the deeds of two vigorous queen-mothers: **Sammuramat**, who ruled Assyria for her son Adad-nirari III from 810 to 806 BC; and **Naqi'a**, wife of Sennacherib (d. 681 BC) and mother of Esarhaddon, who administered Babylonia. Semiramis was later identified with the chief Assyrian goddess ▷Ishtar.

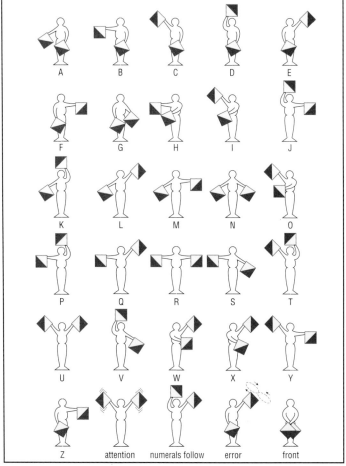

SEMAPHORE The semaphore signals for the letters of the alphabet and some special signals.

Semite any of the peoples of the Middle East originally speaking a Semitic language, and traditionally said to be descended from Shem, a son of Noah in the Bible. Ancient Semitic peoples include the Hebrews, Ammonites, Moabites, Edomites, Babylonians, Assyrians, Chaldaeans, Phoenicians, and Canaanites. The Semitic peoples founded the monotheistic religions of Judaism, Christianity, and Islam.

Semitic languages branch of the Hamito-Semitic language; see ▷Afro-Asiatic language.

Semtex plastic explosive, manufactured in the Czech Republic. It is safe to handle (it can only be ignited by a detonator) and difficult to trace, since it has no smell. It has been used by extremist groups in the Middle East and by the IRA in Northern Ireland.

Senate in ancient Rome, the 'council of elders'. Originally consisting of the heads of patrician families, it was recruited from ex-magistrates and persons who had rendered notable public service, but was periodically purged by the censors. Although nominally advisory, it controlled finance and foreign policy. Sulla doubled its size to 600.

Seneca, Lucius Annaeus (*c.* 4 BC–AD *c.* 65) Roman Stoic playwright, author of essays and nine tragedies. He was tutor to the future emperor Nero but lost favour after Nero's accession to the throne and was ordered to commit suicide. His tragedies were accepted as classical models by 16th-century dramatists.

> **Lucius Annaeus Seneca**
> *No-one can lead a happy life, or even a bearable one, without the pursuit of wisdom.*
> Letters 16

Senegal see country box.

Senegal river in West Africa, formed by the confluence of the Bafing and Bakhoy rivers and flowing 1,125 km/700 mi northwest and west to join the Atlantic Ocean near St Louis, Senegal. In 1968 the Organization of Riparian States of the River Senegal (Guinea, Mali, Mauritania, and Senegal) was formed to develop the river valley, including a dam for hydroelectric power and irrigation at Joina Falls in Mali; its headquarters is in Dakar. The river gives its name to the Republic of Senegal.

senile dementia ▷dementia associated with old age, often caused by ▷Alzheimer's disease.

Senna, Ayrton (1960–1994) Brazilian motor-racing driver. He won his first Grand Prix in Portugal in 1985 and won 41 Grand Prix in 161 starts, including a record six wins at Monaco. Senna was world champion in 1988, 1990, and 1991. He was killed at the 1994 San Marino Grand Prix at Imola.

Sennacherib (died 681 BC) King of Assyria from 705 BC. Son of ▷Sargon II, he rebuilt the city of Nineveh on a grand scale, sacked Babylon 689, and defeated Hezekiah, King of Judah, but failed to take Jerusalem. He was assassinated by his sons, and one of them, Esarhaddon, succeeded him.

sense organ any organ that an animal uses to gain information about its surroundings. All sense organs have specialized receptors (such as light receptors in the eye) and some means of translating their response into a nerve impulse that travels to the brain. The main human sense organs are the eye, which detects light and colour (different wavelengths of light); the ear, which detects sound (vibrations of the air) and gravity; the nose, which detects some of the chemical molecules in the air; and the tongue, which detects some of the chemicals in food, giving a sense of taste. There are also many small sense organs in the skin, including pain, temperature, and pressure sensors, contributing to our sense of touch.

sensitivity in biology, the ability of an organism, or part of an organism, to detect changes in the environment. All living things are capable of some sensitivity, and any change detected by an organism is called a stimulus. Plant response to stimuli (for example, light, heat, moisture) is by directional growth (▷tropism). In animals, the body cells that detect the stimuli are called ▷receptors, and these are often contained within a ▷sense organ. For example, the eye is a sense organ, within which the retina contains rod and cone cells which are receptors. The part of the body that responds to a stimulus, such as a muscle, is called an effector, and the communication of stimuli from receptors to effectors is termed 'coordination'; messages are passed from receptors to effectors either via the ▷nerves or by means of chemicals called ▷hormones. Rapid communication and response to stimuli, such as light, sound, and scent, can be essential to an animal's well-being and survival, and evolution has led to the development of highly complex mechanisms for this purpose.

Nervous systems Most animals have a nervous system that coordinates communication between stimulus and response. Nervous systems consist of special cells called neurones (see ▷nerve cell) which are fundamentally the same as other body cells in that each contains a nucleus, cytoplasm, and cell membrane. In addition, in order to receive and pass messages, they also have long thin fibres of cytoplasm extending out from the cell body termed 'nerve fibres'. The longest of these, which can be more than a metre long, are called **axons**. The shorter fibres are called **dendrites**.

Nerve nets Small animals, such as jellyfish, which do not need to coordinate complex messages between stimuli and response mechanisms, have simple nervous systems, termed 'nerve nets'. In a nerve net, each neurone is connected by fibres to adjacent neurones, so that a message received in any one part of the nervous system is relayed from neurone to neurone throughout the whole of the organism's body.

Central nervous systems The evolution of larger and more complex animals, such as humans, has necessitated the development of far more elaborate nervous systems, and most animals have a ▷central nervous system (CNS). The main difference between a simple nerve net and a central nervous system is the addition of a brain and spinal cord to coordinate and relay messages between receptors and the appropriate effectors, without involving the whole body. Thus rapid responses to specific stimuli are triggered.

sentence in law, the judgement of a court stating the punishment to be imposed following a plea of guilty or a finding of guilt by a jury. Before a sentence is imposed, the antecedents (criminal record) and any relevant reports on the defendant are made known to the judge and the defence may make a plea in mitigation of the sentence.

Seoul (or **Sŏul**) capital of ▷South Korea (Republic of Korea), near the Han River, and with its chief port at Inchon; population (2002 est) 11,153,200. Industries include engineering, textiles, food processing, electrical and electronic equipment, chemicals, and machinery.

sepal part of a flower, usually green, that surrounds and protects the flower in bud. The sepals are derived from modified leaves, and are collectively known as the ▷calyx.

Sephardi (plural **Sephardim**) Jews descended from those expelled from Spain and Portugal in the 15th century, or from those forcibly converted during the Inquisition to Christianity (Marranos). Many settled in North Africa and in the Mediterranean countries, as well as in the Netherlands, England, and Dutch colonies in the New World. Sephardim speak Ladino, a 15th-century Romance dialect, as well as the language of their nation.

Sepoy Rebellion alternative name for the ▷Indian Mutiny, a revolt of Indian soldiers against the British in India 1857–58.

sepsis general term for infectious change in the body caused by bacteria or their toxins.

September 11th Phrase commonly used in Britain to refer to the terrorist attacks on New York City and Washington, DC, on 11 September 2001 that resulted in the deaths of around 3,000 people. The work of Islamic extremists, the attacks were classed as 'an act of war' by US president George W Bush, and led to the declaration of an international ▷War on Terrorism.

septicaemia general term for any form of ▷blood poisoning.

septic shock life-threatening fall in blood pressure caused by blood poisoning (septicaemia). Toxins produced by bacteria infecting the blood induce a widespread dilation of the blood vessels throughout the body, and it is this that causes the patient's collapse (see ▷shock).

sequencing in biochemistry, determining the sequence of chemical subunits within a large molecule. Techniques for sequencing amino acids in proteins were established in the 1950s, insulin being the first for which the sequence was completed. The ▷Human Genome Project is attempting to determine the sequence of the 3 billion base pairs within human ▷DNA. In April 2003 scientists announced the completion of the mapping of the whole human genome.

sequoia either of two species of ▷conifer tree belonging to the redwood family, native to the western USA. The **redwood** (*Sequoia sempervirens*) is a long-living timber tree, and one specimen, the Howard Libbey Redwood, is the world's tallest tree at 110 m/361 ft, with a trunk circumference of 13.4 m/44 ft. The **giant sequoia** (*Sequoiadendron giganteum*) reaches up to 30 m/100 ft in circumference at the base of the trunk, and grows almost as tall as the redwood. It is also (except for the bristlecone pine) the oldest living tree, some specimens being estimated at over 3,500 years of age. (Family Taxodiaceae.)

Serb Ethnic group, found mainly in Serbia and Montenegro, but also in the neighbouring independent republics of Bosnia-Herzegovina and Croatia. Their language is generally recognized to be the same as Croat and is hence known as ▷Serbo-Croatian.

Serbia and Montenegro see country box.

Serbo-Croatian (or **Serbo-Croat**) the most widely spoken language in Yugoslavia and its former constituent republics, it is a member of the South Slavonic branch of the Indo-European family, and has over 17 million speakers.

The different dialects of Serbo-Croatian tend to be written by the Greek Orthodox Serbs in the Cyrillic script, and by the Roman Catholic Croats in the Latin script.

serfdom the legal and economic status of peasants under ▷feudalism. Serfs could not be sold like slaves, but they were not free to leave their master's estate without his permission. They had to work the lord's land without pay for a number of days every week and pay a percentage of their produce to the lord every year. They also served as soldiers in the event of conflict. Serfs also had to perform extra labour at harvest time and other busy seasons; in return they were allowed to cultivate a portion of the estate for their own benefit.

Sergius, St, of Radonezh (1314–1392) Born Barfolomay Kirillovich. Patron saint of Russia, who founded the Eastern Orthodox monastery of the Blessed Trinity near Moscow 1334. Mediator among Russian feudal princes, he inspired the victory of Dmitri, Grand Duke of Moscow, over the Tatar khan Mamai at Kulikovo, on the upper Don, in 1380.

serialism in music, a later form of the ▷twelve-tone system of composition.

series circuit electrical circuit in which the components are connected end to end, so that the current flows through them all one after the other.

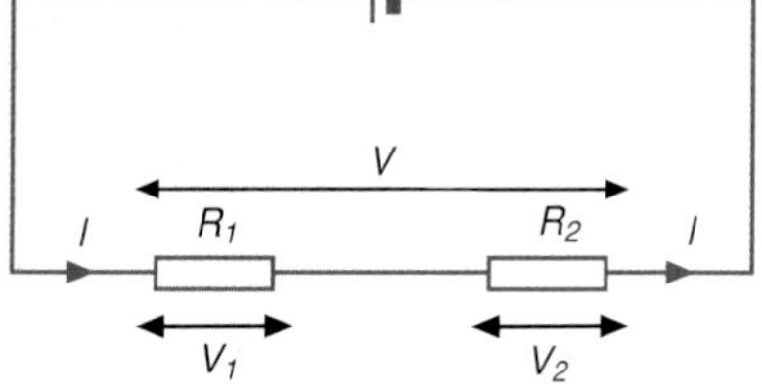

SERIES CIRCUIT In a series circuit, the components of the circuit are connected end to end, so that the current passes through each component one after the other, without division or branching into parallel circuits.

Serpens constellation on the celestial equator (see ▷celestial sphere), represented as a serpent coiled around the body of Ophiuchus. It is the only constellation divided into two halves: **Serpens Caput**, the head (on one side of Ophiuchus), and **Serpens Cauda**, the tail (on the other side). Its main feature is the Eagle nebula.

serpentine group of minerals, hydrous magnesium silicate, $Mg_3Si_2O_5(OH)_4$, occurring in soft ▷metamorphic rocks and usually dark green. The fibrous form **chrysotile** is a source of ▷asbestos; other forms are **antigorite** and **lizardite**. Serpentine minerals are formed by hydration of ultramafic rocks during metamorphism. Rare snake-patterned forms are used in ornamental carving.

serum clear fluid that separates out from clotted blood. It is blood plasma with the anticoagulant proteins removed, and contains ▷antibodies and other proteins, as well as the fats and sugars of the blood. It can be produced synthetically, and is used to protect against disease.

serval African wild cat *Felis serval*. It is a slender, long-limbed cat, about 1 m/3 ft long, with a yellowish-brown, black-spotted coat. It has large, sensitive ears, with which it locates its prey, mainly birds and rodents.

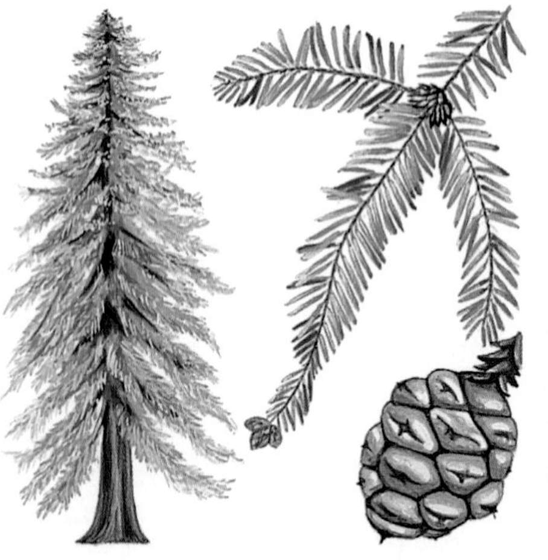

SEQUOIA The sequoia, or California redwood, is the tallest and largest tree. Twenty homes, a church, a mansion, and a bank have been built from the timber of one redwood.

service industry (or **tertiary industry**) sector of the economy that supplies services such as retailing, banking, and education.

services, armed air, sea, and land forces of a country; its ▷army, ▷navy, and ▷air force; also called the armed forces.

service tree deciduous tree (*S. domestica*) with alternate pinnate leaves (leaflets growing either side of the stem), creamy white flowers, and small, brown, edible, oval fruits, native to Europe and Asia. The European wild service tree (*S. torminalis*) has oblong rather than pointed leaflets. It is related to the ▷mountain ash. (Genus *Sorbus*, family Rosaceae.)

servomechanism automatic control system used in aircraft, motor cars, and other complex machines. A specific input, such as moving a lever or joystick, causes a specific output, such as feeding current to an electric motor that moves, for example, the rudder of the aircraft. At the same time, the position of the rudder is detected and fed back to the central control, so that small adjustments can continually be made to maintain the desired course.

sesame annual ▷herbaceous plant, probably native to Southeast Asia, and widely cultivated in India. It produces oily seeds used in cooking and soap making. (*Sesamum indicum*, family Pedaliaceae.)

Sesshū, Tōyō (1420–1506) Japanese painter. Influenced by several Chinese landscape painters, he established a tradition of realism in landscape painting that was maintained by succeeding generations of Japanese painters.

sessile in botany, a leaf, flower, or fruit that lacks a stalk and sits directly on the stem, as with the sessile acorns of certain ▷oaks. In zoology, it is an animal that normally stays in the same place, such as a barnacle or mussel. The term is also applied to the eyes of ▷crustaceans when these lack stalks and sit directly on the head.

Session, Court of one of the civil courts in Scotland; see ▷Court of Session.

Set (or **Seth** or **Setekh**) in Egyptian mythology, the god of night, the desert, and of all evils. Portrayed as a grotesque animal with long ears and a tail, Set was the murderer of his brother ▷Osiris, later ruler of the underworld.

set (or **class**) in mathematics, any collection of defined things (elements), provided the elements are distinct and that there is a rule to decide whether an element is a member of a set. It is usually denoted by a capital letter and indicated by curly brackets { }.

For example, *L* may represent the set that consists of all the letters of the alphabet. The symbol ∈ stands for 'is a member of'; thus $p \notin L$ means that *p* belongs to the set consisting of all letters, and $4 \notin L$ means that 4 does not belong to the set consisting of all letters.

Senegal

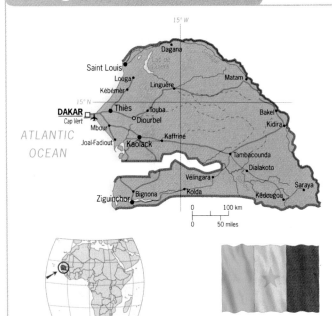

SENEGAL
Senegal wattled plovers *Vanellus senegallus* grow to 34 cm/13 in long and have distinctive bright yellow wattles at the base of the beak.
Preston-Mafham/ Premaphotos Wildlife

Senegal country in West Africa, on the Atlantic Ocean, bounded north by Mauritania, east by Mali, south by Guinea and Guinea-Bissau, and enclosing the Gambia on three sides.

NATIONAL NAME *République du Sénégal/Republic of Senegal*
AREA 196,200 sq km/75,752 sq mi
CAPITAL Dakar (and chief port)
MAJOR TOWNS/CITIES Thiès, Kaolack, Saint-Louis, Ziguinchor, Diourbel, Mbour
PHYSICAL FEATURES plains rising to hills in southeast; swamp and tropical forest in southwest; River Senegal; The Gambia forms an enclave within Senegal

Government

HEAD OF STATE Abdoulaye Wade from 2000
HEAD OF GOVERNMENT Idrissa Seck from 2002
POLITICAL SYSTEM nationalistic socialist
POLITICAL EXECUTIVE unlimited presidency
ADMINISTRATIVE DIVISIONS ten regions
ARMED FORCES 9,400; plus paramilitary forces of 5,800 (2002 est)
DEATH PENALTY retains the death penalty for ordinary crimes but can be considered abolitionist in practice; date of last known execution 1967

Economy and resources

CURRENCY franc CFA
GPD (US$) 4.9 billion (2002 est)
REAL GDP GROWTH (% change on previous year) 5.7 (2001)

GNI (US$) 4.7 billion (2002 est)
GNI PER CAPITA (PPP) (US$) 1,510 (2002 est)
CONSUMER PRICE INFLATION 2% (2003 est)
UNEMPLOYMENT 23% (urban; 2000)
FOREIGN DEBT (US$) 3.6 billion (2001 est)
MAJOR TRADING PARTNERS France, Mali, India, Italy, USA, Côte d'Ivoire, Germany, Nigeria
RESOURCES calcium phosphates, aluminium phosphates, salt, natural gas; offshore deposits of petroleum to be developed
INDUSTRIES food processing (principally fish, groundnuts, palm oil, and sugar), mining, cement, artificial fertilizer, chemicals, textiles, petroleum refining (imported petroleum), tourism
EXPORTS fresh and processed fish, phosphate products, refined petroleum products, cotton, chemicals, groundnuts and related products. Principal market: India 18.1% (2000)
IMPORTS food and live animals, machinery and transport equipment, rice, mineral fuels and lubricants (mainly crude petroleum), consumer goods, chemicals. Principal source: France 27.4% (2000)
ARABLE LAND 12.3% (2000 est)
AGRICULTURAL PRODUCTS groundnuts, cotton, millet, sorghum, rice, maize, cassava, vegetables; fishing

Population and society

POPULATION 10,095,000 (2003 est)
POPULATION GROWTH RATE 2.1% (2000–15)
POPULATION DENSITY (per sq km) 51 (2003 est)
URBAN POPULATION (% of total) 50 (2003 est)
AGE DISTRIBUTION (% of total population) 0–14 44%, 15–59 50%, 60+ 4% (2002 est)
ETHNIC GROUPS the Wolof group are the most numerous, comprising about 35% of the population; the Fulani comprise about 18%; the Serer 16%; the Diola 3%; and the Mandingo 3%
LANGUAGE French (official), Wolof, other ethnic languages
RELIGION mainly Sunni Muslim; Christian 4%, animist 1%

Chronology

10th–11th centuries: Links established with North Africa; the Tukolor community was converted to Islam.
1445: First visited by Portuguese explorers.
1659: French founded Saint-Louis as a colony.
17th–18th centuries: Export trades in slaves, gums, ivory, and gold developed by European traders.
1854–65: Interior occupied by French who checked the expansion of the Islamic Tukulor Empire; Dakar founded.
1902: Became territory of French West Africa.
1946: Became French overseas territory, with own territorial assembly and representation in French parliament.
1948: Leopold Sedar Senghor founded the Senegalese Democratic Bloc to campaign for independence.
1959: Formed Federation of Mali with French Sudan.
1960: Achieved independence and withdrew from federation. Senghor, leader of socialist Senegalese Progressive Union (UPS), became president.
1966: UPS declared only legal party.
1974: Pluralist system re-established.

EDUCATION (compulsory years) 6
LITERACY RATE 50% (men); 30% (women) (2003 est)
LABOUR FORCE 74.6% agriculture, 7.2% industry, 18.2% services (1997 est)
LIFE EXPECTANCY 51 (men); 55 (women) (2000–05)
CHILD MORTALITY RATE (under 5, per 1,000 live births) 138 (2001)
PHYSICIANS (per 1,000 people) 0.08 (1996 est)
HOSPITAL BEDS (per 1,000 people) 0.4 (1996 est)
TV SETS (per 1,000 people) 79 (2001 est)
RADIOS (per 1,000 people) 126 (2001 est)
INTERNET USERS (per 10,000 people) 107.1 (2002 est)
PERSONAL COMPUTER USERS (per 100 people) 2.0 (2002 est)

See also ▷Senghor, Léopold Sédar.

1976: UPS reconstituted as Socialist Party (PS).
1980: Troops sent to defend The Gambia against suspected Libyan invasion.
1981: Military help again sent to The Gambia to thwart coup attempt. Abdou Diouf was appointed president.
1982: Confederation of Senegambia came into effect.
1988: Mamadou Lamine Loum became prime minister.
1989: Diplomatic links with Mauritania severed after 450 died in violent clashes; over 50,000 people repatriated from both countries. Senegambia federation abandoned.
1992: Diplomatic links with Mauritania were re-established.
1993: Assembly and presidential elections were won by the ruling PS.
1998: PS won the election despite claims of fraud. Abdou Diouf became 'president for life'.
1999: A new 60-member Senate was created as Senegal's second legislative chamber.
2000: In presidential elections, Abdou Diouf lost to Abdoulaye Wade, who appointed Mustafa Niasse as his prime minister. Diouf withdrew from politics.
2002: Idrissa Seck became prime minister.

Serbia and Montenegro

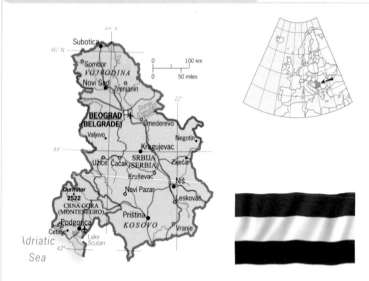

Serbia and Montenegro formerly the Federal Republic of Yugoslavia (1992–2003). From 1945 to 1992 the Republic of Yugoslavia was a federation of the republics Serbia, Montenegro, Bosnia-Herzegovina, Croatia, Slovenia, and Macedonia; the last four seceded in the period 1991–92.

NATIONAL NAME *Srbija i Crna Gora/Serbia and Montenegro*
AREA 58,300 sq km/22,509 sq mi
CAPITAL Belgrade
MAJOR TOWNS/CITIES Priština, Novi Sad, Niš, Kragujevac, Podgorica (formerly Titograd), Subotica
PHYSICAL FEATURES federation of republics of Serbia and Montenegro and two former autonomous provinces, Kosovo and Vojvodina

Government

HEAD OF STATE Svetozar Marovic from 2003
HEAD OF GOVERNMENT Vojislav Koštunica (Serbia) from 2004 and Milo Djukanovic (Montenegro) from 2003
POLITICAL SYSTEM emergent democracy
POLITICAL EXECUTIVE limited presidency
ADMINISTRATIVE DIVISIONS two republics (Serbia and Montenegro) and two nominally autonomous provinces (Kosovo and Vojvodina)
ARMED FORCES 74,500; plus paramilitary forces of 50,000 (2002 est)
DEATH PENALTY abolished in 2002

Economy and resources

CURRENCY new Yugoslav dinar
GPD (US$) 15.6 billion (2002 est)
REAL GDP GROWTH (% change on previous year) 6.2 (2001)
GNI (US$) 11.6 billion (2002 est)
GNI PER CAPITA (PPP) (US$) 2,500 (2002 est)
CONSUMER PRICE INFLATION 13.4% (2003 est)
UNEMPLOYMENT 27.5% (2001)
FOREIGN DEBT (US$) 4.7 billion (2001 est)
MAJOR TRADING PARTNERS Italy, Bosnia-Herzegovina, Russia, Germany, Macedonia, Greece
RESOURCES petroleum, natural gas, coal, copper ore, bauxite, iron ore, lead, zinc
INDUSTRIES crude steel, pig-iron, steel castings, cement, machines, passenger cars, electrical appliances, artificial fertilizers, plastics, bicycles, textiles and clothing
EXPORTS basic manufactures, machinery and transport equipment, clothing, miscellaneous manufactured articles, food and live animals. Principal market: Italy 16.3% (2001)

IMPORTS machinery and transport equipment, electrical goods, agricultural produce, mineral fuels and lubricants, basic manufactures, foodstuffs, chemicals. Principal source: Russia 14.3% (2001)
ARABLE LAND 40% (1998)
AGRICULTURAL PRODUCTS maize, sugar beet, wheat, potatoes, grapes, plums, soybeans, vegetables; livestock production declined 1991–95

Population and society

POPULATION 10,527,000 (2003 est)
POPULATION GROWTH RATE 0.1% (2000–15)
POPULATION DENSITY (per sq km) 103 (2003 est)
URBAN POPULATION (% of total) 52 (2003 est)
AGE DISTRIBUTION (% of total population) 0–14 19%, 15–59 63%, 60+ 18% (2002 est)
ETHNIC GROUPS 63% Serbs, 14% Albanian, 6% Montenegrin, 4% Hungarian, and 13% other. Serbs predominate in the republic of Serbia, where they form (excluding the autonomous areas of Kosovo and Vojvodina) 85% of the population; in Vojvodina they comprise 55% of the population. Albanians constitute 77% of the population of Kosovo; Montenegrins comprise 69% of the population of the republic of Montenegro; and Muslims predominate in the Sandzak region, which straddles the Serbian and Montenegrin borders. Since 1992 an influx of Serb refugees from Bosnia and Kosovo has increased the proportion of Serbs in Serbia, while many ethnic Hungarians have left Vojvodina, and an estimated 500,000 Albanians have left Kosovo
LANGUAGE Serbo-Croat (official), Albanian (in Kosovo)
RELIGION Serbian and Montenegrin Orthodox; Muslim in southern Serbia
EDUCATION (compulsory years) 8
LITERACY RATE 98% (men); 90% (women) (2003 est)
LABOUR FORCE 4.9% agriculture, 45.6% industry, 49.5% services (2000)
LIFE EXPECTANCY 71 (men); 76 (women) (2000–05)

See also ▷Bosnia-Herzegovina; ▷Croatia; ▷Tito.

Chronology

3rd century BC: Serbia (then known as Moesia Superior) conquered by Romans; empire was extended to Belgrade centuries later by Emperor Augustus.

6th century AD: Slavic tribes, including Serbs, Croats, and Slovenes, crossed River Danube and settled in Balkan Peninsula.

879: Serbs converted to Orthodox Church by St Cyril and St Methodius.

mid-10th–11th centuries: Serbia broke free briefly from Byzantine Empire to establish independent state.

1217: Independent Serbian kingdom re-established, reaching its height in mid-14th century under Stefan Dushan, when it controlled much of Albania and northern Greece.

1389: Serbian army defeated by Ottoman Turks at Battle of Kosovo; area became Turkish *pashalik* (province). Montenegro in southwest survived as sovereign principality. Croatia and Slovenia in northwest became part of Habsburg Empire.

18th century: Vojvodina enjoyed protection from the Austrian Habsburgs.

1815: Uprisings against Turkish rule secured autonomy for Serbia.

1878: Independence achieved as Kingdom of Serbia, after Turks defeated by Russians in war over Bulgaria.

1912–13: During Balkan Wars, Serbia expanded its territory at expense of Turkey and Bulgaria.

1918: Joined Croatia and Slovenia, formerly under Austrian Habsburg control, to form Kingdom of Serbs, Croats, and Slovenes under Serbian Peter Karageorgević (Peter I); Montenegro's citizens voted to depose their ruler, King Nicholas, and join the union.

1929: New name of Yugoslavia ('Land of the Southern Slavs') adopted; Serbian-dominated dictatorship established by King Alexander I as opposition mounted from Croatian federalists.

1934: Alexander I assassinated by a Macedonian with Croatian terrorist links; his young son Peter II succeeded, with Paul, his uncle, as regent.

1941: Following a coup by pro-Allied air-force officers, Nazi Germany invaded. Peter II fled to England. Armed resistance to German rule began, spearheaded by pro-royalist, Serbian-based Chetniks ('Army of the Fatherland'), led by Gen Draza Mihailović, and communist Partisans ('National Liberation Army'), led by Marshal Tito. An estimated 900,000 Yugoslavs died in the war, including more than 400,000 Serbs and 200,000 Croats.

1943: Provisional government formed by Tito at liberated Jajce in Bosnia.

1945: Yugoslav Federal People's Republic formed under leadership of Tito; communist constitution introduced.

1948: Split with Soviet Union after Tito objected to Soviet 'hegemonism'; expelled from Cominform.

1953: Workers' self-management principle enshrined in constitution and private farming supported; Tito became president.

1961: Nonaligned movement formed under Yugoslavia's leadership.

1971: In response to mounting separatist demands in Croatia, new system of collective and rotating leadership introduced.

1980: Tito died; collective leadership took power.

1981–82: Armed forces suppressed demonstrations in Kosovo province, southern Serbia, by Albanians demanding full republic status.

1986: Slobodan Milošević, a populist-nationalist hardliner became leader of communist party in the Serbian republic.

1988: Economic difficulties: 1,800 strikes, 250% inflation, 20% unemployment. Ethnic unrest in Montenegro and Vojvodina, and separatist demands in rich northwestern republics of Croatia and Slovenia.

1989: Reformist Croatian Ante Marković became prime minister. Ethnic riots in Kosovo province against Serbian attempt to end autonomous status of Kosovo and Vojvodina.

1990: Multiparty systems were established in the republics; Kosovo and Vojvodina were stripped of autonomy. In Croatia, Slovenia, Bosnia, and Macedonia elections brought to power noncommunist governments seeking looser confederation.

1991: Demonstrations against Serbian president Slobodan Milošević in Belgrade were crushed by riot police and tanks. Slovenia and Croatia declared their independence, resulting in clashes between federal and republican armies; Slovenia accepted a peace pact sponsored by the European Community (EC), but fighting intensified in Croatia, where Serb militias controlled over a third of the republic; Federal President Stipe Mesic and Prime Minister Marković resigned.

1992: There was an EC-brokered ceasefire in Croatia; the EC and the USA recognized Slovenia's and Croatia's independence. Bosnia-Herzegovina and Macedonia then declared their independence, and Bosnia-Herzegovina's independence was recognized by the EC and the USA. A New Federal Republic of Yugoslavia (FRY) was proclaimed by Serbia and Montenegro but not internationally recognized; international sanctions were imposed and UN membership was suspended. Ethnic Albanians proclaimed a new 'Republic of Kosovo', but it was not recognized.

1993: Pro-Milošević Zoran Lilic became Yugoslav president. There was antigovernment rioting in Belgrade. Macedonia was recognized as independent under the name of the Former Yugoslav Republic of Macedonia (FYROM). The economy was severely damaged by sanctions.

1994: A border blockade was imposed by Yugoslavia against Bosnian Serbs; sanctions were eased.

1995: Serbia played a key role in the US-brokered Dayton peace accord for Bosnia-Herzegovina and accepted the separate existence of Bosnia and Croatia.

1996: Diplomatic relations were restored between Serbia and Croatia, and UN sanctions against Serbia were lifted. Diplomatic relations were established with Bosnia-Herzegovina. There was mounting opposition to Milošević's government following its refusal to accept opposition victories in municipal elections.

1997: Milošević was elected president. The validity of Serbian presidential elections continued to be questioned. The anti-Milošević candidate was elected president of Montenegro.

1998: A Serb military offensive against ethnic Albanian separatists in Kosovo led to a refugee and humanitarian crisis. The offensive against the Kosovo Liberation Army (KLA) was condemned by the international community and NATO military intervention was threatened.

1999: Fighting continued between Serbians and Albanian separatists in Kosovo. Following the failure of efforts to reach a negotiated settlement, NATO began a bombing campaign against the Serbs; the ethnic cleansing of Kosovars by Serbs intensified and the refugee crisis in neighbouring countries worsened as ethnic Albanians fled Kosovo. President Milošević was indicted for crimes against humanity by the International War Crimes Tribunal in The Hague. A peace was agreed on NATO terms. Refugees began returning to Kosovo.

2000: Presidential elections were held in which opposition candidate Vojislav Koštunica claimed outright victory against Milošević, but the federal election commission ordered a second round of voting. The opposition claimed ballot-rigging and organized mass demonstrations throughout Yugoslavia, in the face of which Milošević conceded defeat. Koštunica appointed Zoran Zizic prime minister. The UN reinstated Yugoslavia's membership.

2001: Former president Milošević was arrested and charged with abuse of power, corruption, and fraud.

2002: The trial of former president Slobodan Milošević – the most significant war crimes trial since World War II – began in the Hague, the Netherlands. The constituent republics of Serbia and Montenegro agreed to stay together in a looser federation. Both republics were given equal powers and would have common foreign and defence policies.

2003: The Federal Republic of Yugoslavia ceased to exist as the two remaining republics of the former Yugoslav federation officially became a new constitutional entity called Serbia and Montenegro. Prime Minister Zoran Djindjic was assassinated in Belgrade. Serbia and Montenegro became the 45th member of the Council of Europe.

There are various types of sets. A **finite set** has a limited number of members, such as the letters of the alphabet; an **infinite set** has an unlimited number of members, such as all whole numbers; an **empty** or **null set** has no members, such as the number of people who have swum across the Atlantic Ocean, written as { } or Ø; a **single-element set** has only one member, such as days of the week beginning with M, written as {Monday}. **Equal sets** have the same members; for example, if W = {days of the week} and S = {Sunday, Monday, Tuesday, Wednesday, Thursday, Friday, Saturday}, it can be said that W = S. Sets with the same number of members are **equivalent sets**. Sets with some members in common are **intersecting sets**; for example, if R = {red playing cards} and F = {face cards}, then R and F share the members that are red face cards. Sets with no members in common are **disjoint sets**. Sets contained within others are **subsets**; for example, V = {vowels} is a subset of L = {letters of the alphabet}.

Sets and their interrelationships are often illustrated by a ▷Venn diagram.

Related Web site: **Beginnings of Set Theory** http://www-history.mcs. st-and.ac.uk/history/HistTopics/Beginnings_of_set_theory.html

setter any of various breeds of gun dog, called 'setters' because they were trained to crouch or 'set' on the sight of game to be pursued. They stand about 66 cm/26 in high and weigh about 25 kg/55 lb. They have a long, smooth coat, feathered tails, and spaniel-like faces.

settlement collection of dwellings forming a community. There are many different types of settlement and most owe their origin to historical and geographical factors. The growth and development of a settlement is greatly influenced by its location, site, situation, and function. Human settlements can be identified as centres that function as marketplaces, administrative centres, and social and cultural meeting places serving surrounding hinterlands. The science or study of human settlements is termed 'ekistics' (from the Greek *oikistikos* 'of or concerning settlements', and *oikos* 'a house'). Two additional study fields concerned with the development of settlements are urban geography and regional science.

Settlement, Act of in Britain following the ▷Glorious Revolution of 1688, a law passed in 1701 during the reign of King William III, designed to ensure a Protestant succession to the throne by excluding the Roman Catholic descendants of ▷James II in favour of the Protestant House of Hanover. Elizabeth II still reigns under this act.

Seurat, Georges Pierre (1859–1891) French artist. One of the major post-Impressionists, he originated, with Paul ▷Signac, the technique of ▷pointillism (painting with small dabs rather than long brushstrokes). One of his best-known works is *A Sunday Afternoon on the Island of La Grande Jatte* 1886 (Art Institute of Chicago).

At the age of 16 Seurat went to the Ecole des Beaux-Arts, showing a remarkable early proficiency in figure drawing. Artists whose work he studied closely were Delacroix, whose frescoes at St Sulpice made him realize the significance of colour; and Piero della Francesca, whose sense of formal and geometrical beauty he shared.

Although fascinated by the Impressionists' use of colour, he rejected what he considered to be their lack of form, and sought to create a perfectly ordered art based on scientific principles. His pointillism was based on scientific research on the perception of colour. One of the first major results of his new art was his *Bathers at Asnières* (1884; National Gallery, London), which combines the atmospheric effect of Impressionist painting with a new solidity of form and composition.

Sevastopol (or **Sebastopol**) Black Sea port, resort, and fortress in the ▷Crimea, Ukraine; population (1990) 361,000. It is the base of the Black Sea fleet (jointly owned by Russia and Ukraine). Industries include shipbuilding and wine making. Founded by Catherine (II) the Great in 1784, Sevastopol was successfully besieged by the English and French (October 1854–September 1855) during the Crimean War, and again in World War II by the Germans (November 1941–July 1942). On both occasions, the city was devastated. Retaken by Soviet forces in 1944, Sevastopol still remains officially a closed city, because of its naval installations.

seven deadly sins in Christian theology, the vices that are considered fundamental to all other sins: anger, avarice, envy, gluttony, lust, pride, and sloth (or dejection).

Seventh-Day Adventist (or **Adventist**) member of the Protestant religious sect of the same name. It originated in the USA in the fervent expectation of Christ's Second Coming, or advent, that swept across New York State following William Miller's prophecy that Christ would return on 22 October 1844. When this failed to come to pass, a number of Millerites, as his followers were called, reinterpreted his prophetic speculations and continued to maintain that the millennium was imminent. Adventists observe Saturday as the Sabbath and emphasize healing and diet; many are vegetarians. The sect has 36,920 organized churches and almost 8 million members in 210 countries and territories (1995).

Seven Weeks' War war 1866 between Austria and Prussia, engineered by the German chancellor ▷Bismarck. It was nominally over the possession of ▷Schleswig-Holstein, but it was actually to confirm Prussia's superseding Austria as the leading German state. The Prussian victory at the Battle of ▷Sadowa was the culmination of General von Moltke's victories.

Seven Wonders of the World in antiquity, the ▷pyramids of Egypt, the ▷Hanging Gardens of Babylon, the temple of Artemis at ▷Ephesus, the Greek sculptor Phidias' chryselephantine statue of Zeus at ▷Olympia, the Mausoleum at ▷Halicarnassus, the ▷Colossus of Rhodes, and the lighthouse on the island of Pharos in the Bay of Alexandria.

Related Web site: **Seven Wonders of the World** http://ce.eng.usf.edu/ pharos/wonders/

Seven Years' War (or **French and Indian War**) war in North America 1756–63 arising from the conflict between Austria and Prussia, and between France and Britain over colonial supremacy. Britain and Prussia defeated France, Austria, Spain, and Russia; Britain gained control of India and many of France's colonies, including Canada.

Spain ceded Florida to Britain in exchange for Cuba. Fighting against great odds, Prussia was eventually successful in becoming established as one of the great European powers. The war ended with the Treaty of Paris (1763), signed by Britain, France, and Spain.

Severn (Welsh **Hafren**) river in Britain, which rises on the slopes of Plynlimon, in Ceredigion, west Wales, and flows east and then south, finally forming a long estuary leading into the Bristol Channel; length 336 km/208 mi. The Severn is navigable for 290 km/180 mi, up to Welshpool (Trallwng) on the Welsh border. The principal towns on its course are Shrewsbury, Worcester, and Gloucester. England and South Wales are linked by two road bridges and a railway tunnel crossing the Severn. A remarkable feature of the river is a tidal wave known as the 'Severn Bore' that flows for some miles upstream and can reach a height of 2 m/6 ft.

Severus, Lucius Septimius (AD 146–211) Roman emperor 193–211. After holding various commands under the emperors ▷Marcus Aurelius and ▷Commodus, Severus was appointed commander-in-chief of the army on the Danube, in the Roman provinces, Pannonia and Illyria. After the murder of Pertinax (Roman emperor 193), he was proclaimed emperor by his troops. Severus was an able administrator. He was born in North Africa at Leptis Magna, and was the only native of Africa to become emperor. He died at York.

Seville (Spanish **Sevilla**) capital of Seville province and of the autonomous community of ▷Andalusia, southern Spain, on the River Guadalquivir, 96 km/60 mi north of Cádiz; population (2001) 708,200. Products include machinery, spirits, porcelain, pharmaceuticals, silk, and tobacco. Although 80 km/50 mi from the sea, Seville has a historically important port (now little used), and during the 16th century it had a monopoly of trade with the West Indies.

Related Web site: **Seville, Spain** http://www.sol.com/

Sèvres, Treaty of the last of the treaties that ended World War I. Negotiated between the Allied powers and the Ottoman Empire, it was finalized August 1920 but never ratified by the Turkish government.

sewage disposal the disposal of human excreta and other waterborne waste products from houses, streets, and factories. Conveyed through sewers to sewage works, sewage has to undergo a series of treatments to be acceptable for discharge into rivers or the sea, according to various local laws and ordinances. Raw sewage, or sewage that has not been treated adequately, is one serious source of water pollution and a cause of ▷eutrophication.

sewing machine apparatus for the mechanical sewing of cloth, leather, and other materials by a needle, powered by hand, treadle, or belted electric motor. The popular lockstitch machine, using a double thread, was invented independently in the USA by both Walter Hunt in 1834 and Elias Howe in 1846. Howe's machine was the basis of the machine patented in 1851 by US inventor Isaac ▷Singer.

sex determination process by which the sex of an organism is determined. In many species, the sex of an individual is dictated by the two sex chromosomes (X and Y) it receives from its parents. In mammals, some plants, and a few insects, males are XY, and females XX; in birds, reptiles, some amphibians, and butterflies the reverse is the case. In bees and wasps, males are produced from unfertilized eggs, females from fertilized eggs.

males have two different sex chromosomes X and Y

females have two similar sex chromosomes X and X

M E I O S I S

X   sperm cells   Y

X   ova   X

F E R T I L I Z A T I O N

boy XY

girl XX

SEX DETERMINATION In humans, sex is determined by the male. Sperm cells contain an X or a Y chromosome, but egg cells contain only X chromosomes. If a sperm cell carrying an X chromosome fertilizes the egg, the resulting baby will be female; if the sperm cell is carrying a Y chromosome, then the baby will be male.

GEORGES SEURAT *Une Baignade Asnières/Bathers at Asnières*, painted in 1883–84 by French artist Georges Seurat. *The Art Archive/National Gallery London*

Environmental factors can affect some fish and reptiles, such as turtles, where sex is influenced by the temperature at which the eggs develop. In 1991 it was shown that maleness is caused by a single gene, 14 base pairs long, on the Y chromosome.

Most fish have a very flexible system of sex determination, which can be affected by external factors. For example, in wrasse all individuals develop into females, but the largest individual in each area or school changes sex to become the local breeding male.

sex hormone steroid hormone produced and secreted by the gonads (testes and ovaries). Sex hormones control development and reproductive functions and influence sexual and other behaviour.

sexism belief in (or set of implicit assumptions about) the superiority of one's own sex, often accompanied by a ▷stereotype or preconceived idea about the opposite sex. Sexism may also be accompanied by ▷discrimination on the basis of sex, generally as practised by men against women.

sex linkage in genetics, the tendency for certain characteristics to occur exclusively, or predominantly, in one sex only. Human examples include red-green colour blindness and haemophilia, both found predominantly in males. In both cases, these characteristics are ▷recessive and are determined by genes on the ▷X chromosome.

Sex Pistols, the UK punk-rock group (1975–78) that became notorious under the guidance of their manager Malcolm McLaren (1946–   ). Their first singles, 'Anarchy in the UK' (1976) and 'God Save the Queen' (1977), unbridled attacks on contemporary Britain, made the Pistols into figures the media loved to hate.

sextant navigational instrument for determining latitude by measuring the angle between some heavenly body and the horizon. It was invented in 1730 by John Hadley (1682–1744) and can be used only in clear weather.

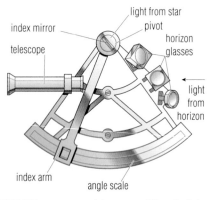

SEXTANT The geometry of the sextant. When the light from a star can be seen at the same time as light from the horizon, the angle A can be read from the position of the index arm on the angle scale.

sexually transmitted disease (STD) any disease transmitted by sexual contact, involving transfer of body fluids. STDs include not only traditional ▷venereal disease, but also a growing list of conditions, such as ▷AIDS and scabies, which are known to be spread primarily by sexual contact. Other diseases that

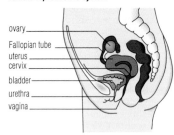

female reproductive system

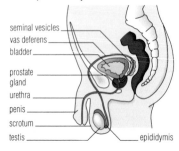

male reproductive system

SEXUAL REPRODUCTION The human reproductive organs. In the female, gametes called ova are released regularly in the ovaries after puberty. The Fallopian tubes carry the ova to the uterus or womb, in which the fetus will develop. In the male, sperm is produced inside the testes after puberty; about 10 million sperm cells are produced each day, enough to populate the world in six months. The sperm duct or vas deferens, a continuation of the epididymis, carries sperm to the urethra during ejaculation.

are transmitted sexually include viral ▷hepatitis. The WHO estimate that there are 356,000 new cases of STDs daily worldwide (1995).

sexual reproduction reproductive process in organisms that requires the union, or ▷fertilization, of gametes (such as eggs and sperm). These are usually produced by two different individuals, although self-fertilization occurs in a few ▷hermaphrodites such as tapeworms. Most organisms other than bacteria and cyanobacteria (▷blue-green algae) show some sort of sexual process. Except in some lower organisms, the gametes are of two distinct types called eggs and sperm. The organisms producing the eggs are called females, and those producing the sperm, males. The fusion of a male and female gamete produces a **zygote**, from which a new individual develops. See ▷reproduction.

The alternatives to sexual reproduction are parthenogenesis and asexual reproduction by means of ▷spores.

sexual selection process similar to ▷natural selection but relating exclusively to success in finding a mate for the purpose of sexual reproduction and producing offspring. Sexual selection occurs when one sex (usually but not always the female) invests more effort in producing young than the other. Members of the other sex compete for access to this limited resource (usually males competing for the chance to mate with females).

Seychelles see country box.

Seyfert galaxy galaxy whose small, bright centre is caused by hot gas moving at high speed around a massive central object, possibly a ▷black hole. Almost all Seyferts are spiral galaxies. They seem to be closely related

to ▷quasars, but are about 100 times fainter. They are named after their discoverer Carl Seyfert (1911–1960).

Seymour, Jane (c. 1509–1537) English noble, third wife of Henry VIII, whom she married 1536. She died soon after the birth of her son Edward VI.

Daughter of John Seymour and sister of Edward, Duke of Somerset, she was a lady-in-waiting to Henry VIII's first two wives, Catherine of Aragón and Anne Boleyn. She married Henry a few days after Anne's execution.

Sfax (Arabic **Safaqis**) port and second-largest city in Tunisia, about 240 km/150 mi southeast of Tunis; population (1994) 230,900. It is the capital of Sfax district, on the Gulf of Gabès. Products include leather, soap, and carpets; there are also salt works and phosphate workings nearby. Exports include phosphates, fertilizers, olive oil, dates, almonds, esparto grass, and sponges.

Sforza family Italian family that ruled the duchy of Milan 1450–99, 1512–15, 1521–24, and 1529–35. Its court was a centre of Renaissance culture and its rulers prominent patrons of the arts.

's-Gravenhage Dutch name for The ▷Hague.

Shaanxi (or **Shensi**) province of northwest China, bounded to the north by Inner Mongolia, to the east by Shanxi and Henan, to the south by Hubei and Sichuan, and to the west by Gansu and Ningxia Hui Autonomous Region; area 195,800 sq km/75,600 sq mi; population (1996) 35,430,000. The capital is ▷Xi'an. There are coalmining, iron, steel, textile, and aerospace industries. Wheat, maize, rice, fruit, and tea are grown.

Shackleton, Ernest Henry (1874–1922) Irish Antarctic explorer. In 1908–09, he commanded the British Antarctic expedition that reached 88° 23' S latitude, located the magnetic South Pole, and climbed Mount ▷Erebus. He was knighted in 1909.

Shackleton was a member of Scott's Antarctic expedition 1901–04, and also commanded the expedition 1914–16 to cross the Antarctic, when he had to abandon his ship, the *Endurance*, crushed in the ice of the Weddell Sea. He died on board the *Quest* on his fourth expedition 1921–22 to the Antarctic.

shad any of several marine fishes, especially the genus *Alosa*, the largest (60 cm/2 ft long and 2.7 kg/6 lb in weight) of the herring family (Clupeidae). They migrate in shoals to breed in rivers.

shadoof (or **shaduf**) machine for lifting water, consisting typically of a long, pivoted wooden pole acting as a lever, with a weight at one end. The other end is positioned over a well, for example. The shadoof was in use in ancient Egypt and is still used in Arab countries today.

> **Thomas Shadwell**
> *Every man loves what he is good at.*
> A True Widow V. i

shadow area of darkness behind an opaque object that cannot be reached by some or all of the light coming from a light source in front. Its presence may be explained in terms of light rays travelling in straight lines and being unable to bend round obstacles. A point source of light produces an umbra, a completely black shadow with sharp edges. An extended source of light produces both a central umbra and a ▷penumbra, a region of semi-darkness with blurred edges where darkness gives way to light.

shadow cabinet the chief members of the British parliamentary opposition, each of whom is responsible for commenting on the policies and performance of a government ministry.

Shadwell, Thomas (c. 1642–1692) English dramatist and poet. His plays include *Epsom-Wells* (1672) and *Bury-Fair* (1689). He was involved in a violent feud with the poet ▷Dryden, whom he attacked in *The Medal of John Bayes* (1682) (believed to be his work). Shadwell became poet laureate in 1689.

Shaftesbury (or **Shaston**) market town and agricultural centre in Dorset, southwest England, 30 km/19 mi southwest of Salisbury; population (1991) 6,200. Industries include tourism. King Alfred is said to have founded an abbey on the site in 880 (consecrated in 888); King Canute died at Shaftesbury in 1035.

Shaftesbury, Anthony Ashley Cooper, 1st Earl of Shaftesbury (1621–1683) English politician, a supporter of the Restoration of the monarchy. He became Lord Chancellor in 1672, but went into opposition in 1673 and began to organize the ▷Whig Party. He headed the Whigs' demand for the exclusion of the future James II from the succession, secured the passing of the Habeas Corpus Act of 1679, then, when accused of treason in 1681, fled to Holland. He became Baronet in 1631, Baron in 1661, and was created Earl in 1672.

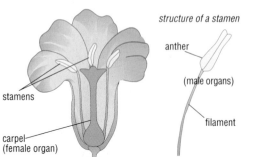

structure of a stamen

anther

(male organs)

filament

stamens

carpel (female organ)

structure of a carpel

stigma

style

ovary wall

ovule

SEXUAL REPRODUCTION Reproductive organs in flowering plants. The stamens are the male parts of the plant. Each consists of a stalklike filament topped by an anther. The anther contains four pollen sacs which burst to release tiny grains of pollen, the male sex cells. The carpels are the female reproductive parts. Each carpel has a stigma which catches the pollen grain. The style connects the stigma to the ovary. The ovary contains one or more ovules, the female sex cells. Buttercups have many ovaries; the lupin has only one.

Shaftesbury, Anthony Ashley Cooper, 7th Earl of Shaftesbury (1801–1885) British Tory politician. From 1833 he became the leader in the House of Commons of the movement to improve factory conditions. After successfully obtaining a number of factory acts, he persuaded Parliament to pass the Ten Hours Act of 1847, also known as Lord Ashley's Act. He supported legislation to improve conditions in the mines, notably the Mines Act of 1842 (forbidding the employment of women and children underground), and he secured the passage of the Lunacy Act of 1845, which improved lunatic asylums. In 1846 he persuaded Parliament to forbid the use of children as chimney sweeps.

shag waterbird *Phalacrocorax aristoclis*, order Pelecaniformes, related to the ▷cormorant. It is smaller than the cormorant, with a green tinge to its plumage and in the breeding season has a crest. Its food consists mainly of sand eels for which it dives, staying underwater for up to 54 seconds. It breeds on deeply fissured cliffs, and on rocky parts of isolated islands.

shah (more formally, **shahanshah** 'king of kings') traditional title of ancient Persian rulers, and also of those of the recent ▷Pahlavi dynasty in Iran.

Shah Jahan (1592–1666) Mogul emperor of India from 1628, under whom the dynasty reached its zenith. Succeeding his father ▷Jahangir, he extended Mogul authority into the Deccan plateau (eastern India), subjugating Ahmadnagar, Bijapur, and Golconda 1636, but lost Kandahar in the northwest to the Persians 1653. His reign marked the high point of Indo-Muslim

architecture, with Delhi being rebuilt as Shahjahanabad, while the Taj Mahal and Pearl Mosque were constructed at Agra. On falling seriously ill 1658 he was dethroned and imprisoned by his son ▷Aurangzeb.

Shahn, Ben(jamin) (1898–1969) Lithuanian-born US painter. A leading social realist, he created works which drew attention to social and political issues, such as the notorious ▷Sacco-Vanzetti case, in which two Italian anarchists living in the USA were accused of murder. He painted murals for the Rockefeller Center, New York (with the Mexican artist Diego ▷Rivera), and the Federal Security Building, Washington, 1940–42.

Shaka (or Chaka) (c. 1787–1828) Zulu chief who formed a Zulu empire in southeastern Africa. He seized power from his half-brother 1816 and then embarked on a bloody military campaign to unite the Zulu clans. He was assassinated by his two half-brothers.

Shaker member of the Christian sect of the **United Society of Believers in Christ's Second Appearing**, called Shakers because of their ecstatic trembling and shaking during worship. The movement was founded by James and Jane Wardley in England about 1747, and taken to North America in 1774 by Ann Lee (1736–1784).

Shakespeare, William (1564–1616) English dramatist and poet. He is considered the greatest English dramatist. His plays, written in blank verse with some prose, can be broadly divided into lyric plays, including *Romeo and Juliet* and A ▷*Midsummer Night's Dream*; comedies, including *The Comedy of Errors*, *As You Like It*,

SHAH JAHAN The Mogul emperor Shah Jahan in 1630. *The Art Archive*

Seychelles

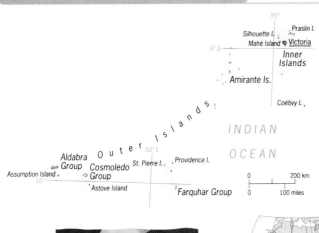

Seychelles country in the Indian Ocean, off east Africa, north of Madagascar.

NATIONAL NAME *Republic of Seychelles*
AREA 453 sq km/174 sq mi
CAPITAL Victoria (on Mahé island) (and chief port)
MAJOR TOWNS/CITIES Cascade, Port Glaud, Misere, Anse Boileau, Takamaka
PHYSICAL FEATURES comprises two distinct island groups: one, the Granitic group, concentrated, the other, the Outer or Coralline group, widely scattered; totals over 100 islands and islets

Government

HEAD OF STATE AND GOVERNMENT France-Albert René from 1977
POLITICAL SYSTEM emergent democracy
POLITICAL EXECUTIVE limited presidency
ADMINISTRATIVE DIVISIONS 23 districts
ARMED FORCES 500; plus paramilitary forces of 300 and national guard of 1,000 (2002 est)
DEATH PENALTY abolished in 1993

Economy and resources

CURRENCY Seychelles rupee
GPD (US$) 630 million (2002 est)
REAL GDP GROWTH (% change on previous year) 1 (2001)
GNI (US$) 573 million (2001)
GNI PER CAPITA (PPP) (US$) 11,150 (2001)
CONSUMER PRICE INFLATION 6% (2003 est)
UNEMPLOYMENT 1.0% (1995)
FOREIGN DEBT (US$) 16.9 billion (2001 est)
MAJOR TRADING PARTNERS UK, South Africa, France, Singapore, the Netherlands, Italy
RESOURCES guano; natural gas and metal deposits were being explored mid-1990s
INDUSTRIES food processing (including cinnamon, coconuts, and tuna canning), beer and soft drinks, petroleum refining, cigarettes, paper, metals, chemicals, wood products, paints, tourism

EXPORTS canned tuna, frozen prawns, fresh and frozen fish, shark fins, cinnamon bark, refined petroleum products. Principal market: UK 30.7% (2000)
IMPORTS machinery and transport equipment, food and live animals, petroleum and petroleum products, chemicals, basic manufactures. Principal source: South Africa 9.6% (2000)
ARABLE LAND 2.2% (2000 est)
AGRICULTURAL PRODUCTS coconuts, copra, cinnamon bark, tea, patchouli, vanilla, limes, sweet potatoes, cassava, yams, sugar cane, bananas; poultry meat and egg production are important for local consumption; fishing

Population and society

POPULATION 81,000 (2003 est)
POPULATION GROWTH RATE 1.3% (2000–05)
POPULATION DENSITY (per sq km) 178 (2003 est)
URBAN POPULATION (% of total) 66 (2003 est)
AGE DISTRIBUTION (% of total population) 0–14 28%, 15–59 62%, 60+ 10% (2002 est)
ETHNIC GROUPS predominantly Creole (of mixed African, Asian, and European

Chronology

Early 16th century: First sighted by European navigators.
1744: Became French colony.
1756: Claimed as French possession and named after an influential French family.
1770s: French colonists brought African slaves to settle the previously uninhabited islands; plantations established.
1794: Captured by British during French Revolutionary Wars.
1814: Ceded by France to Britain; incorporated as dependency of Mauritius.
1835: Slavery abolished by British, leading to influx of liberated slaves from Mauritius and Chinese and Indian immigrants.
1903: Became British crown colony, separate from Mauritius.

SEYCHELLES A squirrel fish, hiding among rocks in the reefs of the Seychelles. In recent years there has been growing concern about coral reef degradation, as tropical shallow-water marine environments come increasingly under pressure from human activities. There are approximately 27,000 ha/66,700 acres of protected marine area and reefs in the Seychelles. *Seychelles Tourist Office*

descent); small European minority (mostly French and British)
LANGUAGE Creole (an Asian, African, European mixture) (95%), English, French (all official)
RELIGION Roman Catholic 90%

1963–64: First political parties formed.
1976: Independence achieved from Britain as republic within Commonwealth, with a moderate, James Mancham, of the centre-right Seychelles Democratic Party (SDP) as president.
1977: More radical France-Albert René ousted Mancham in armed bloodless coup and took over presidency; white settlers emigrated.
1979: Nationalistic socialist Seychelles People's Progressive Front (SPPF) became sole legal party under new constitution; became nonaligned state.
1981: An attempted coup by South African mercenaries was thwarted.
1993: A new multiparty constitution was adopted. René defeated Mancham, who had returned from exile, in competitive presidential elections; SPPF won parliamentary elections.
1998: President René was re-elected. SPUP won assembly elections.

WILLIAM SHAKESPEARE An engraving from 1623 shows the English dramatist William Shakespeare in a rare, almost contemporary portrait. *Archive Photos*

Much Ado About Nothing, and *Measure For Measure*; historical plays, such as *Henry VI* (in three parts), *Richard III*, and *Henry IV* (in two parts), which often showed cynical political wisdom; and tragedies, including ▷*Hamlet*, ▷*Othello*, ▷*King Lear*, and ▷*Macbeth*. He also wrote numerous sonnets.

Born in Stratford-upon-Avon, the son of a wool dealer, he was educated at the grammar school, and in 1582 married Anne Hathaway. They had a daughter, Susanna, in 1583, and in 1585 twins, Hamnet (who died in 1596) and Judith. By 1592 Shakespeare was established in London as an actor and a dramatist, and from 1594 he was an important member of the Lord Chamberlain's Company of actors. In 1598 the Company tore down their regular playhouse, the Theatre, and used the timber to build the Globe Theatre in Southwark. Shakespeare became a 'sharer' in the venture, which entitled him to a percentage of the profits. In 1603 the Company became the King's Men. By this time Shakespeare was the leading playwright of the company and one of its business directors; he also continued to act. He retired to Stratford about 1610, where he died on 23 April 1616. He was buried in the chancel of Holy Trinity, Stratford.

Early plays In the plays written around 1589–94, Shakespeare may be regarded as a young writer learning the techniques of his art and experimenting with different forms. These include the three parts of *Henry VI*; the comedies *The Comedy of Errors*, *The* ▷*Taming of the Shrew*, and *The Two Gentlemen of Verona*; the Senecan revenge tragedy *Titus Andronicus*; and *Richard III*. About 1593 he came under the patronage of the Earl of ▷Southampton, to whom he dedicated his long poems *Venus and Adonis* (1593) and *The Rape of Lucrece* (1594); he also wrote for him the comedy *Love's Labour's Lost*, satirizing the explorer Walter Raleigh's circle, and seems to have dedicated to him his sonnets written around 1593–96, in which the mysterious 'Dark Lady' appears.

Lyric plays The lyric plays *Romeo and Juliet*, *A Midsummer Night's Dream*, and *Richard II* (which explores the relationship between the private man and the public life of the state) 1594–97 were followed by *King John* (again exploring the ironies and problems of politics) and *The* ▷*Merchant of Venice* (1596–97). The Falstaff plays of 1597–1600 – *Henry IV* (parts I and II, juxtaposing the comic world of the tavern and the dilemmas and responsibilities attending kingship and political ambition), *Henry V* (a portrait of King Hal as the ideal soldier-king), and *The Merry Wives of Windsor* (said to have been written at the request of Elizabeth I, to show Falstaff in love) – brought his fame to its height. He wrote *Julius Caesar* (1599) (anticipating the great tragedies in its concentration on a central theme and plot: the conspiracy to assassinate Caesar, and the confrontation between political rivals, in which the more ruthless win). The period ended with the lyrically witty *Much Ado About Nothing*, *As You Like It*, and ▷*Twelfth Night*, (*c.* 1598–1601).

Tragedies and late plays With *Hamlet* begins the period of the great tragedies, 1601–08: *Othello*, *King Lear*, *Macbeth*, *Timon of Athens*, ▷*Antony and Cleopatra*, and *Coriolanus* (the hero of which comes into disastrous conflict with the Roman people through his overriding sense of personal honour). This 'darker' period is also reflected in the comedies *Troilus and Cressida* (a sardonic

WILLIAM SHAKESPEARE A watercolour of the Globe Theatre, by artist G Shepherd in 1810, taken from an earlier engraving of 1638. *The Art Archive/British Museum/ Eileen Tweedy*

exploration of the concept of chivalric honour in relation to sexual conduct and the war between Greece and Troy), *All's Well That Ends Well*, and *Measure for Measure* (*c.* 1601–04). It is thought that Shakespeare was only part author of *Pericles*, which is grouped with the other plays of around 1608–11 – *Cymbeline* (set in ancient Britain, when Augustus Caesar ruled in Rome and Christ was born in Palestine), *The Winter's Tale* (a refashioning of a romance by an envious rival, Robert Greene), and *The* ▷*Tempest* – as the mature romance or 'reconciliation' plays of the end of his career. It is thought that *The Tempest* may have been based on the real-life story of William Strachey, who was shipwrecked off Bermuda in 1609. During 1613 it is thought that Shakespeare collaborated with John ▷Fletcher on *Henry VIII* (in which the theme of reconciliation and regeneration after strife is played out in historical terms, so that the young child who represents hope for the future is none other than Elizabeth I) and *The Two Noble Kinsmen*.

For the first 200 years after his death, Shakespeare's plays were frequently performed in cut or revised form (Nahum Tate's *King Lear* was given a happy ending), and it was not until the 19th century, with the critical assessment of Samuel ▷Coleridge and William ▷Hazlitt, that the original texts were restored.

Related Web site: Shakespeare Illustrated
http://www.emory.edu/ENGLISH/classes/
Shakespeare_Illustrated/Shakespeare.html

shale fine-grained and finely layered ▷sedimentary rock composed of silt and clay. It is a weak rock, splitting easily along bedding planes to form thin, even slabs (by contrast, mudstone splits into irregular flakes). Oil shale contains kerogen, a solid bituminous material that yields ▷petroleum when heated.

shallot small onion in which bulbs are clustered like garlic; it is used for cooking and in pickles. (*Allium ascalonicum*, family Liliaceae.)

shaman (Tungu *samân*) ritual leader who acts as intermediary between society and the supernatural world in many indigenous cultures of Asia, Africa, and the Americas. Also known as a **medicine man**, **seer**, or **sorcerer**, the shaman is expected to use special powers to cure illness and control good and evil spirits.

Shamir, Yitzhak Yernitsky (1915–   ) Polish-born Israeli right-wing politician; prime minister 1983–84 and 1986–92; leader of the Likud (Consolidation Party) until 1993. He was foreign minister under Menachem Begin 1980–83, and again foreign minister in Shimon ▷Peres's unity government 1984–86.

shamrock any of several leguminous plants (see ▷legume) whose leaves are divided into three leaflets, including ▷clovers. St Patrick is said to have used one to illustrate the doctrine of the Holy Trinity, and it was made the national badge of Ireland. (Family Leguminosae.)

Shan member of a people of the mountainous borderlands separating Thailand, Laos, Myanmar (Burma), and China. They are related to the ▷Laos and ▷Thais, and their language belongs to the Sino-Tibetan family.

Shakespeare's Plays	
Title	**First performed/written (approximate)**
Early Plays	
Henry VI Part I	1589–92
Henry VI Part II	1590–91
Henry VI Part III	1590–92
The Comedy of Errors	1591–93
The Taming of the Shrew	1593–94
Titus Andronicus	1593–94
The Two Gentlemen of Verona	1590–95
Love's Labour's Lost	1593–95
Romeo and Juliet	1594–95
Histories	
Richard III	1592–93
Richard II	1595–97
King John	1595–97
Henry IV Part I	1596–97
Henry IV Part II	1596–97
Henry V	1599
Roman Plays	
Julius Caesar	1599
Antony and Cleopatra	1606–07
Coriolanus	1608
The 'Great' or 'Middle' Comedies	
A Midsummer Night's Dream	1594–95
The Merchant of Venice	1596–98
Much Ado About Nothing	1598
As You Like It	1599–1600
The Merry Wives of Windsor	1597
Twelfth Night	1600–02
The Great Tragedies	
Hamlet	1601–02
Othello	1604
King Lear	1605–06
Macbeth	1606
Timon of Athens	1607–08
The 'Dark' Comedies	
Troilus and Cressida	1601–02
All's Well That Ends Well	1602–03
Measure for Measure	1604
Late Plays	
Pericles	1606–08
Cymbeline	1609–10
The Winter's Tale	1611
The Tempest	1611
Henry VIII	1613

> **William Shakespeare**
> *Let me have men about me that are fat; /*
> *Sleek-headed men and such as sleep o' nights; /*
> *Yond' Cassius has a lean and hungry look; /*
> *He thinks too much: such men are dangerous.*
> Julius Cæsar I. ii 191

> **Yitzhak Shamir**
> *Our image has undergone a change from David fighting Goliath to being Goliath.*
> On Israel, *The Observer* January 1989

Shandong (or **Shantung**) province of east China, bounded to the north by the Bohai Gulf, to the east by the Yellow Sea, to the south by Jiangsu and Anhui, and to the west by Henan and Hebei provinces; area 153,300 sq km/59,200 sq mi; population (2000 est) 90,790,000. It is one of the most densely populated provinces of China. The capital is ▷Jinan. There are coal, oil, petrochemical, engineering, and textile industries.

Cereals, cotton, peanuts, wild silk, and wine are produced.

Related Web site: Brief Introduction to Shandong Province, China
http://www.china-sd.com/

Shang dynasty Also known as **Yin dynasty**. China's first fully authenticated dynasty, *c.* 1500–*c.* 1066 BC, which saw the start of the Bronze Age. Shang rulers dominated the Huang He (Yellow River) plain of northern China, developing a complex agricultural civilization which used a written language.

Shanghai largest urban settlement and mainland port in China, in Jiangsu province, on the Huangpu and Wusong rivers, 24 km/ 15 mi from the Chang Jiang estuary; population (1999 est) 8,937,200. The municipality of Shanghai has an area of 5,800 sq km/2,239 sq mi; population (1996) 14,190,000. Shanghai is China's principal commercial and financial centre. Textiles, paper, chemicals, steel, vehicles, agricultural machinery, precision instruments, ship building, and flour are produced; other industries include vegetable oil milling and oil refining. Administratively independent of Jiangsu, Shanghai answers directly to the central government.

Shanghai is thought to be the most densely populated area in the world, with an average of 6 sq m/65 sq ft of living space and 2.2 sq m/2.6 sq yd of road per person.

SHANGHAI Shanghai night skyline, an example of a traditional style of Chinese architecture. *Image Bank*

Features Landmarks include the 16th-century Yu Yuan garden; the Ming dynasty (1368–1644) Garden of the Purple Clouds of Autumn; the Jade Buddha Temple built in 1882; the former home of the revolutionary leader ▷Sun Zhong Shan (Sun Yat-sen); the house where the First National Congress of the Communist Party of China met secretly in 1921; the house, museum, and tomb of the writer Lu Xun; the Bund, a tree-lined boulevard along the Huangpu River; and the Museum of Art and History.

History Founded as a fishing village in the 11th century, and a county town in 1292, Shanghai became significant after 1842 when it was opened to foreign trade under the Treaty of Nanjing. Much of its large foreign community lived in the International Settlement, which had its own administration. Chinese resistance to the foreign presence grew, and in 1927 the nationalist Guomindang and communist forces combined to capture the city, after which the Guomindang suppressed the communists. It was occupied by the Japanese from 1937 to 1945. When Shanghai returned to Chinese rule the International Settlement was formally ended. The city was recaptured by communist forces in May 1949.

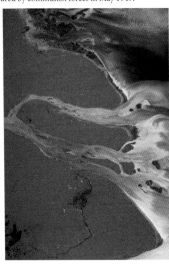

SHANGHAI A satellite image of Shanghai, China. Such images can provide useful information about the location of minerals, water sources, vegetation, and geological features. *Image Bank*

Shankar, Ravi (1920–　） Indian composer and musician. A virtuoso of the ▷sitar, he has been influential in popularizing Indian music in the West. He has composed two concertos for sitar and orchestra (1971) and (1981), and film music, including scores for Satyajit Ray's *Pather Panchali* (1955) and Richard Attenborough's *Gandhi* (1982). He also founded music schools in Bombay (now Mumbai) and Los Angeles.
　　Related Web site: Ravi Shankar Foundation http://www.ravishankar.org/

Shannon longest river in Ireland, rising 105 m/344 ft above sea level in the Cuilcagh Mountains in County Cavan, and flowing 386 km/240 mi to the Atlantic Ocean past Athlone, and through loughs Allen, Boderg, Forbes, Ree, and Derg. The estuary, which is 110 km/68 mi long and 3–16 km/2–10 mi wide, forms the northern boundary of County Limerick. The river is navigable as far as Limerick city, above which are the rapids of Doonas and Castletroy. The river is known for its salmon farms, Castleconnell being an important centre. It also has the first and largest hydroelectric scheme in the Republic of Ireland (constructed 1925–29), with hydroelectric installations at and above Ardnacrusha, 5 km/3 mi north of Limerick.

Shansi alternative transliteration of the Chinese province of ▷Shanxi.

Shantou (or **Swatow**) port and industrial city in Guangdong province, southeast China; population (1993) 610,000. It was opened as a special economic zone in 1979. Industries include food processing, and the export-oriented manufacture of clothes, shoes, and electronic goods. Other exports include timber, food products, fish, and fruit.

Shantung alternative transliteration of the Chinese province of ▷Shandong.

Shanxi (or **Shansi**) province of north China, bounded to the north by Inner Mongolia, to the east by Hebei, to the south by Henan, and to the west by Shaanxi; area 157,100 sq km/60,700 sq mi; population (1996) 31,090,000. The capital is ▷Taiyuan. There are coal, iron, machinery, mining equipment, and chemical industries. Fruit and cereals are grown, and meat is produced.

share in finance, that part of the ▷capital of a company held by a member (shareholder). Shares may be numbered and are issued as units of definite face value; shareholders are not always called on to pay the full face value of their shares, though they bind themselves to do so.

share option in finance, see ▷option.

Sharia the law of ▷Islam believed by Muslims to be based on divine revelation, and drawn from a number of sources, including the Koran, the Hadith, and the consensus of the Muslim community. Under this law, *qisās*, or retribution, allows a family to exact equal punishment on an accused; *diyat*, or blood money, is payable to a dead person's family as compensation.

shark any member of various orders of cartilaginous fishes (class Chondrichthyes), found throughout the oceans of the world. There are about 400 known species of shark. They have tough, usually grey skin covered in denticles (small toothlike scales). A shark's streamlined body has side pectoral fins, a high dorsal fin, and a forked tail with a large upper lobe. Five open gill slits are visible on each side of the generally pointed head. They shed and replace their teeth continually, even before birth. Teeth may be replaced as frequently as every week. Most sharks are fish-eaters, and a few will attack humans. They range from several feet in length to the **great white shark** *Carcharodon carcharias*, 9 m/30 ft long, and the harmless plankton-feeding **whale shark** *Rhincodon typus*, over 15 m/50 ft in length.

　　Relatively few attacks on humans lead to fatalities, and research suggests that the attacking sharks are not searching for food, but attempting to repel perceived rivals from their territory.

Endangered species An estimated 100 million sharks are killed each year for their meat, skin, and oil (basking shark). Some species, such as the great white shark, the tiger shark, and the hammerhead, are now endangered and their killing has been banned in US waters since July 1991. Other species will be protected by catch quotas. The Convention on International Trade in Endangered Species (CITES) agreed in 1994 to investigate the extent of the shark trade.

　　The fins of 90% of sharks caught are traded, almost all destined for Asia, to be made into soup. Many sharks are 'finned': the fins are sliced from live sharks, which are then thrown back to die. Finning was banned in US Atlantic waters in 1993, and by Canada in 1994. As most sharks tend to be long-lived, not reaching sexual maturity till the age of almost 30, and produce small numbers of young with a high juvenile mortality rate, they are ill-equipped to withstand high levels of fishing.

Physiology Their eyes, though lacking acuity of vision or sense of colour, are highly sensitive to light. Their sense of smell is so acute

SHARK The great white shark appears from time to time off both the Pacific and the Atlantic coasts of the USA. However, it is more common in the waters that surround the Great Barrier Reef off eastern Australia and elsewhere in the southern Pacific Ocean. *Image Bank*

SHARK A white tip reef shark, off the coast of Costa Rica. There are 400 known species of shark, ranging in length from 15 m/50 ft (the whale shark is the world's largest fish) down to 75 cm/2.5 ft (such as the dogfish, which is a type of shark). *Image Bank*

that one-third of the brain is given up to interpreting its signals; they can detect blood in the water up to 1 km/1,100 yd away. They also respond to electrical charges emanating from other animals.

　　The **basking shark** *Cetorhinus maximus* of temperate seas reaches 12 m/40 ft, but eats only marine organisms. The whale shark is the largest living fish. Sharks have remained virtually unchanged for millions of years.
　　Related Web site: Shark Research Institute http://www.sharks.org/

Sharman, Helen (1963–　） The first Briton to fly in space, chosen from 13,000 applicants for a 1991 joint UK–Soviet space flight. Sharman, a research chemist, was launched on 18 May 1991 in *Soyuz TM-12* and spent six days with Soviet cosmonauts aboard the *Mir* space station.

sharp in music, sounding higher in pitch than the indicated note value, or than expected. A sharp sign (♯) in front of a written note indicates that it is to be raised by a semitone. It is cancelled by a natural sign (♮).

Sharpe, Tom (1928–　） Born Thomas Ridley Sharpe. English satirical novelist. Sharpe uses satire and farcical plots to explore the eccentricities and social manners of the English middle classes, in works such as *Porterhouse Blue* (1973), *Blott on the Landscape* (1975), *Wilt* (1976), and *Vintage Stuff* (1982). Many of his works have been successfully adapted for television.

Sharpeville black township in South Africa, 65 km/40 mi south of Johannesburg and north of Vereeniging; 69 people were killed here when police fired on a crowd of anti-apartheid demonstrators 21 March 1960.

Shastri, Lal Bahadur (1904–1966) Indian politician, prime minister 1964–66. He campaigned for national integration, and secured a declaration of peace with Pakistan at the Tashkent peace conference in 1966.

Shatt-al-Arab ('river of Arabia') waterway formed by the confluence of the rivers ▷Euphrates and ▷Tigris; length 190 km/120 mi to the Gulf. Basra, Khorramshahr, and Abadan stand on it. Its main tributary is the Karun River.

Shaw, George Bernard (1856–1950) Irish dramatist, critic, and novelist, and an early member of the socialist ▷Fabian Society, although he resigned in 1911. His plays combine comedy with political, philosophical, and polemic aspects, aiming to make an impact on his audience's social conscience as well as their emotions. They include *Arms and the Man* (1894), *The Devil's Disciple* (1897), *Man and Superman* (1903), *Pygmalion* (1913), and *St Joan* (1923). He was awarded the Nobel Prize for Literature in 1925.

　　Shaw was born in Dublin, and went to London in 1876 to work as a critic. *Our Theatre in the Nineties* (1932) contains many of his reviews published in the *Saturday Review* between 1895 and 1898. He became a brilliant debater and supporter of the Fabians. His first play, *Widowers' Houses*, was privately produced in 1892. Attacking slum landlords, it allied him with the realistic, political, and polemical movement in the theatre, pointing to people's responsibility to improve themselves and their social environment. His first public production was *Arms and the Man*, a cynical view of war, published as one of seven plays entitled *Plays: Pleasant and Unpleasant* (1898). Also in the volume was *Mrs Warren's Profession* (1898), dealing with prostitution, which was banned until 1902. *Man and Superman* expounds his ideas of evolution by following the character of Don Juan into hell for a debate with the devil.

　　The 'anti-romantic' comedy *Pygmalion*, first performed in 1913, was written for the actor Mrs Patrick Campbell (and after Shaw's

> **George Bernard Shaw**
> *We have no more right to consume happiness without producing it than to consume wealth without producing it.*
> *Candida* I

death was converted to a musical as *My Fair Lady*). Shaw combined treatment of social issues with a comic technique that relied on brilliantly witty serio-comic dialogue and playfully ironic inversion of audience expectations about character and situation. As a result, he put himself in the vanguard of the intellectually serious and progressive English theatre, yet also became a successful popular playwright. Later plays included *Heartbreak House* (1920), about the decline of Edwardian England; *Back to Methuselah* (1922), an ambitious cycle of plays offering a view of history from human beginnings to the distant future; and the historical *St Joan* (1923), which examines the nature of religious belief.

Altogether Shaw wrote more than 50 plays and became a byword for wit. His theories were further explained in the voluminous prefaces to the plays, and in books such as *The Intelligent Woman's Guide to Capitalism, Socialism and Fascism* (1928).

Shearer, Alan (1970–) English footballer. In 1996 he was transferred to Newcastle United from Blackburn Rovers for what was then a world record fee of £15 million. A strongly-built centre-forward, he made his England debut in 1992. He retired from international football after captaining England in the 2000 European Championships. His final tally of 30 goals in 63 internationals has been bettered by only three players, Bobby ▷Charlton, Gary ▷Lineker, and Jimmy Greaves.

shearwater any sea bird of the genus *Puffinus*. All the species are oceanic, and either dark above and white below or all dark. Shearwaters are members of the same family (Procellariidae), as the diving ▷petrels, order Procellariiformes. They get their name from their habit of skimming low over the sea on still wings.

sheath another name for a ▷condom.

Sheba ancient name for southern ▷Yemen (Sha'abijah). It was once renowned for gold and spices. According to the Old Testament, its queen visited Solomon; until 1975 the Ethiopian royal house traced its descent from their union.

sheep any of several ruminant, even-toed, hoofed mammals of the family Bovidae. Wild species survive in the uplands of central and eastern Asia, North Africa, southern Europe and North America. The domesticated breeds are all classified as *Ovis aries*.

Various breeds of sheep are reared worldwide for meat, wool, milk, and cheese, and for rotation on arable land to maintain its fertility.

Domestic sheep are descended from wild sheep of the Neolithic Middle East. The original species may be extinct but was probably closely related to the surviving mouflon *O. musimom* of Sardinia and Corsica. The dozens of different breeds known across the world were developed to suit different requirements and a range of geographical and climatic conditions. Over 50 breeds of sheep evolved in the UK, but only a small proportion are still in full commercial use. They are grouped into three principal categories.

The hardy **upland** breeds, such as the Scottish Blackface and Welsh Mountain, are able to survive in a bleak, rugged environment. Lowland breeds include the **shortwool** varieties, such as the Down breeds of Hampshire and Suffolk, which are well adapted to thrive on the lush grassland of lowland areas. The Southdown, from which many of the shortwool varieties are descended, is known for its high quality mutton and fine wool. The **longwool** varieties, such as the Leicesters and Border Leicesters, were originally bred for their coarse, heavy fleeces, but are now crossed with hill-sheep flocks to produce fat lambs. In 1989 there were 41 million sheep in Britain, making Britain the main producer of lambs in Europe.

SHEEP The traditional method of shearing sheep in Australia. *Image Bank*

sheepdog any of several breeds of dog, bred originally for herding sheep. The dog now most commonly used by shepherds and farmers in Britain to tend sheep is the border collie. Non-pedigree dogs of the border collie type, though more variable in size and colour, are referred to as working sheepdogs. Other recognized British breeds are the ▷Old English and Shetland sheepdogs. Many countries have their own breeds of sheepdog, such as the Belgian sheepdog, Australian kelpie, and Hungarian puli.

sheep ked wingless insect that is an external parasite of sheep, feeding on their blood.

Sheffield industrial city and metropolitan borough on the River Don, South Yorkshire, England; population of metropolitan district (1995) 528,500. From the 12th century, iron smelting was the chief industry, and by the 14th century, Sheffield cutlery, silverware, and plate were being made. During the Industrial Revolution the iron and steel industries developed rapidly. It now produces alloys and special steels, cutlery of all kinds, permanent magnets, drills, and precision tools. Other industries include electroplating, type-founding, and the manufacture of optical glass. It is an important conference centre.

Features The parish church of St Peter and St Paul (14th–15th centuries) is the cathedral of Sheffield bishopric established in 1914. Mary Queen of Scots was imprisoned in Sheffield 1570–84, part of the time in the Norman castle, which was captured by the Parliamentarians in 1644 and subsequently destroyed. There are two art galleries (Graves Art Gallery and Mappin Art Gallery); the Ruskin museum, opened in 1877 and revived in 1985; and the Cutlers' Hall. There are also three theatres (the Crucible (1971); the Lyric, designed by W R Sprague in 1897; and the restored Lyceum, reopened in 1990) and two universities (the University of Sheffield and Sheffield Hallam University). The Sheffield Supertram, Britain's most modern light rail system, opened in 1995. The city is a touring centre for the Peak District. The Meadowhall shopping centre in the old steel works area is one of the largest shopping centres in the UK. In 1997 Sheffield was chosen as the site for the new National Sports Institute. A Millennium Gallery and Museum are to be built as part of a project to revitalize the city centre.

sheikh leader or chief of an Arab family or village; also Muslim title meaning 'religious scholar'.

Shelburne, William Petty, 2nd Earl of Shelburne (1737–1805) British Whig politician. He was an opponent of George III's American policy, and, as prime minister in 1783, he concluded peace with the USA.

shelduck duck *Tadorna tadorna* of family Anatidae, order Anseriformes. It has a dark-green head and red bill, with the rest of the plumage strikingly marked in black, white, and chestnut. The drake is about 60 cm/24 in long. Widely distributed in Europe and Asia, it lays 10–12 white eggs in rabbit burrows on sandy coasts, and is usually seen on estuary mudflats.

shelf sea relatively shallow sea, usually no deeper than 200 m/650 ft, overlying the continental shelf around the coastlines. Most fishing and marine mineral exploitations are carried out in shelf seas.

shell the hard outer covering of a wide variety of invertebrates. The covering is usually mineralized, normally with large amounts of calcium. The shell of birds' eggs is also largely made of calcium.

shellac resin derived from secretions of the ▷lac insect.

Shelley, Mary Wollstonecraft (1797–1851) Born Mary Godwin. English writer. She is best known as the author of the Gothic horror story *Frankenstein* (1818), which is considered to be the origin of modern science fiction, and her other novels include *The Last Man* (1826) and *Valperga* (1823). In 1814 she eloped to Switzerland with the poet Percy Bysshe Shelley, whom she married in 1816 on the death of his first wife Harriet. She was the daughter of Mary Wollstonecraft and William Godwin.

Shelley, Percy Bysshe (1792–1822) English lyric poet and critic. With his skill in poetic form and metre, his intellectual capacity and searching mind, his rebellious but constructive nature, and his notorious moral nonconformity, he is a commanding figure of the Romantic movement. He fought all his life against religion and for political freedom. This is reflected in his early poems such as *Queen Mab* (1813). He later wrote tragedies including *The Cenci* (1818), lyric dramas such as *Prometheus Unbound* (1820), and lyrical poems such as 'Ode to the West Wind'. He drowned while sailing in Italy.

Born near Horsham, Sussex, he was educated at Eton and University College, Oxford, where his collaboration in a pamphlet *The Necessity of Atheism* (1811) caused his expulsion. While living in London he fell in love with 16-year-old Harriet Westbrook, whom he married in 1811. He visited Ireland and Wales, writing pamphlets defending vegetarianism and political freedom, and in 1813 published privately *Queen Mab*, a poem with political freedom as its theme. Meanwhile he had become estranged from his wife and in 1814 left England with Mary Wollstonecraft Godwin, whom he married after Harriet drowned herself in 1816. *Alastor*, written in 1815, was followed by the epic *The Revolt of Islam*. By 1818 Shelley was living in Italy where he produced *The Cenci*; the satire on Wordsworth, *Peter Bell the Third* (1819); and *Prometheus Unbound*. Other works of the period are 'Ode to the West Wind' (1819); 'The Cloud' and 'The Skylark' (both 1820); 'The Sensitive Plant' and 'The Witch of Atlas'; 'Epipsychidion' and, on the death of the poet Keats, 'Adonais' (1821); the lyric drama *Hellas* (1822); and the prose *Defence of Poetry* (1821). In July 1822 Shelley was drowned while sailing near Viareggio, and his ashes were buried in Rome.

Percy Bysshe Shelley
Poets are the unacknowledged legislators of the world.
Defence of Poetry

Related Web site: Complete Poetical Works of Percy Bysshe Shelley
http://www.bartleby.com/139/index.html

shellfish popular name for molluscs and crustaceans, including the whelk and periwinkle, mussel, oyster, lobster, crab, and shrimp.

shell shock (or **combat neurosis** or **battle fatigue**) any of the various forms of mental disorder that affect soldiers exposed to heavy explosions or extreme ▷stress. Shell shock was first diagnosed during World War I.

Shensi alternative transcription of the Chinese province of ▷Shanxi.

Shenyang (or **Mukden**) capital of ▷Liaoning province, China; population (1999) 3,876,300. It is the region's main trading city, and one of China's principal metal-fabricating and machine-building centres. It was the capital of the Manchu emperors from 1625 to 1644; their tombs are nearby.

Shenzhen special economic zone on the coast of Guangdong province, south China, established in 1980 opposite Hong Kong; population (1993) 2,400,000. A poor rural area in 1979, with a population of 20,000, it grew spectacularly with the relocation of toy, textiles, and electronics factories from Hong Kong. Diverse light industries have subsequently been introduced, particularly the manufacture of chemicals and electrical goods. It is also an international financial centre, housing one of China's two stock exchanges. The zone is fenced off, and immigration strictly controlled.

Shepard, E(rnest) H(oward) (1879–1976) English illustrator and cartoonist. He worked for *Punch*, but is best remembered for his illustrations for children's classics, including A A Milne's *Winnie-the-Pooh* (1926) and Kenneth Grahame's *The Wind in the Willows* (1908).

shepherd's purse annual plant distributed worldwide in temperate zones. It is a persistent weed with white flowers followed by heart-shaped, seed-containing pouches, which give the plant its name. (*Capsella bursa-pastoris*, family Cruciferae.)

Sher, Antony (1949–) South African-born actor. A versatile performer in contemporary and classic drama, his roles include *Richard III* (1984), Shylock in *The Merchant of Venice* (1987), the title role in Peter Flannery's *Singer* (1989), Mikhail Astrov in *Uncle Vanya* (1992), Tamburlaine in Marlowe's tragedy (1992), and *Stanley* (1996), for which he won the 1997 Olivier Award for Best Actor. For television, he played Howard Kirk in Malcolm Bradbury's *The History Man* (1981). Films include *Mrs Brown* (1997).

Sheraton, Thomas (1751–1806) English designer of elegant inlaid neoclassical furniture. He was influenced by his predecessors ▷Hepplewhite and ▷Chippendale.

Sheridan, Philip Henry (1831–1888) Union general in the American ▷Civil War. Recognizing Sheridan's aggressive spirit, General Ulysses S ▷Grant gave him command of his cavalry 1864, and soon after of the Army of the Shenandoah Valley, Virginia. Sheridan laid waste to the valley, cutting off grain supplies to the Confederate armies. In the final stage of the war, Sheridan forced General Robert E ▷Lee to retreat to Appomattox Court House and surrender.

Sheridan, Richard Brinsley (1751–1816) Irish dramatist and politician, born in Dublin. His social comedies include *The*

Rivals (1775), celebrated for the character of Mrs Malaprop, whose unintentional misuse of words gave the English language the word 'malapropism', and his best-known piece, *The School for Scandal* (1777). He also wrote a burlesque, *The Critic* (1779), on the staging of inferior dramatic work. In 1776 he became lessee of the Drury Lane Theatre, London.

sheriff (Old English *scír* 'shire', *gerēfa* 'reeve') in England and Wales, the crown's chief executive officer in a county for ceremonial purposes; in Scotland, the equivalent of the English county-court judge, but also dealing with criminal cases; and in the USA the popularly elected head law-enforcement officer of a county, combining judicial authority with administrative duties.

Sherman, William Tecumseh (1820–1891) Union general in the American ▷Civil War. In 1864 he captured and burned Atlanta; continued his march eastward, to the sea, laying Georgia waste; and then drove the Confederates northward. He was US Army Chief of Staff 1869–83.

Sherpa member of a Mongolian people who originally migrated from Tibet and now live in northeastern Nepal. They are related to the Tibetans. Skilled mountaineers, they frequently work as support staff and guides for climbing expeditions.

's-Hertogenbosch (or **Den Bosch**; French **Bois-le-Duc**) capital of North Brabant province, the Netherlands, at the confluence of the Aa and Dommel rivers, 45 km/28 mi southeast of Utrecht; population (1997) 126,500. There is an important cattle market here. The Gothic cathedral, St John's, dates back to the 11th century, although it was rebuilt or extended in the 14th century. It was the birthplace of the painter Hieronymus Bosch.

Sherwood Forest hilly stretch of parkland in west Nottinghamshire, central England; area about 520 sq km/200 sq mi. Formerly an ancient royal forest extending from Nottingham to Worksop, it is associated with the legendary outlaw ▷Robin Hood. According to the Forestry Commission, Sherwood Forest is over 1,000 years old.

Shetland Islands (Old Norse **Hjaltland** 'high land' or 'Hjalte's land') islands and unitary authority off the north coast of Scotland, 80 km/50 mi northeast of the Orkney Islands, an important centre of the North Sea oil industry, and the most northerly part of the UK.

   area 1,452 sq km/560 sq mi   **towns** Lerwick (administrative headquarters), on Mainland, largest of 12 inhabited islands   **physical** the 100 islands are mostly bleak, hilly, and clad in moorland. The climate is moist, cool, and windy; in summer there is almost perpetual daylight, whilst winter days are very short. On clear winter nights, the aurora borealis ('northern lights') can frequently be seen in the sky   **industries** processed fish, handknits from Fair Isle and Unst, herring fishing, salmon farming, cattle and sheep farming; large oil and gas fields west of Shetland; Europe's largest oil port is Sullom Voe, Mainland; production at Foinaven oilfield, the first to be developed in Atlantic waters; tourism   **population** (1996) 22,500   **history** dialect derived from Norse, the islands having been a Norse dependency from the 9th century until 1472 when they were annexed by Scotland

Shevardnadze, Edvard Amvrosievich (1928–) Georgian politician, Soviet foreign minister 1985–91, head of the state of Georgia from 1992. A supporter of Mikhail ▷Gorbachev, he was first secretary of the Georgian Communist Party from 1972 and an advocate of economic reform. In 1985 he became a member of the Politburo, working for détente and disarmament. In July 1991 he resigned from the Soviet Communist Party (CPSU) and, along with other reformers and leading democrats, established the Democratic Reform Movement. In March 1992 he was chosen as chair of Georgia's ruling military council, and in October was elected speaker of parliament (equivalent to president). He survived assassination attempts in 1995 and in 1998, and was re-elected to a second term as president in 2000.

Shiah see ▷Shiite.

shiatsu in alternative medicine, Japanese method of massage derived from ▷acupuncture and sometimes referred to as 'acupressure', which treats organic or physiological dysfunctions by applying finger or palm pressure to parts of the body remote from the affected part.

shield in geology, alternative name for ▷craton, the ancient core of a continent.

shield in technology, any material used to reduce the amount of radiation (electrostatic, electromagnetic, heat, nuclear) reaching from one region of space to another, or any material used as a protection against falling debris, as in tunnelling.

Electrical conductors are used for electrostatic shields, soft iron for electromagnetic shields, and poor conductors of heat for heat shields. Heavy materials, such as lead, and concrete are used for protection against X-rays and nuclear radiation. See also ▷biological shield and ▷heat shield.

Shi Huangdi (or **Shih Huang Ti**) (*c.* 259–*c.* 210 BC) Emperor of China. He succeeded to the throne of the state of Qin 246 BC and had reunited China as an empire by 228 BC. He burned almost all existing books in 213 to destroy ties with the past; rebuilt the ▷Great Wall of China; and was buried in Xi'an, Shaanxi province, in a tomb complex guarded by 10,000 life-size terracotta warriors (excavated in the 1980s). He had so overextended his power that the dynasty and the empire collapsed with the death of his weak successor in 207.

   Related Web site: About Shi Huangdi http://library.thinkquest.org/23295/media/bmpic/qshe.htm

SHI HUANGDI Life-sized terracotta soldiers form an army of figures in the 3rd-century BC tomb of the emperor Shi Huangdi. As the first ruler of China to call himself emperor, Shi Huangdi was buried surrounded by signs of his wealth and power. Excavations at Xi'an, China, in the 1980s revealed the huge tomb. *Image Bank*

Shiite (or **Shiah**) member of a sect of ▷Islam that believes that ▷Ali was ▷Muhammad's first true successor. The Shiites are doctrinally opposed to the Sunni Muslims. They developed their own law differing only in minor directions, such as inheritance and the status of women. In Shi'ism, the clergy are empowered to intervene between God and humans, whereas among the Sunni, the relationship with God is direct and the clergy serve as advisers.

   The Shiites are prominent in Iran, the Lebanon, and Indo-Pakistan, and are also found in Iraq and Bahrain.

   Related Web site: Shi'ite Encyclopedia http://www.al-islam.org/encyclopedia/

Shijiazhuang (or **Shihchiachuang**) capital of ▷Hebei province, China, at the foot of the Taihang Mountains; population (1993) 1,210,000. It is a major railway junction and agricultural distribution point. Industries include printing, light engineering, and the manufacture of chemicals, petrochemicals, and electronics.

Shikoku smallest of the four main islands of Japan, south of Honshu, east of Kyushu; area 18,800 sq km/7,250 sq mi; population (1995) 4,183,000. The island consists of four prefectures, Kagawa, Tokushima, Ehime, and Kochi. The chief towns are Matsuyama and Takamatsu. The population is largely concentrated in the small coastal plains which front the Inland Sea. Products include rice, wheat, soybeans, sugar cane, orchard fruits, salt, and copper.

shingles common name for ▷herpes zoster, a disease characterized by infection of sensory nerves, with pain and eruption of blisters along the course of the affected nerves.

Shinto (Chinese *shin tao* 'way of the gods') the indigenous religion of Japan. It combines an empathetic oneness with natural forces and loyalty to the reigning dynasty as descendants of the Sun goddess, Amaterasu-Omikami. An aggressive nationalistic form of Shinto, known as State Shinto, was developed under the Emperor Meiji (1868–1912) and remained official until 1945, when it was discarded.

   Related Web site: Shinto – The Way of the Gods http://www.trincoll.edu/~tj/tj4.4.96/articles/cover.html

ship large seagoing vessel. The Greeks, Phoenicians, Romans, and Vikings used ships extensively for trade, exploration, and warfare. The 14th century was the era of European exploration by sailing ship, largely aided by the invention of the compass. In the 15th century Britain's Royal Navy was first formed, but in the 16th–19th centuries Spanish and Dutch fleets dominated the shipping lanes of both the Atlantic and Pacific.

   The ultimate sailing ships, the fast US and British tea clippers, were built in the 19th century. Also in the 19th century, iron was first used for some shipbuilding instead of wood. Steam-propelled ships of the late 19th century were followed by compound engine and turbine-propelled vessels from the early 20th century. See picture on p. 866.

   Related Web site: Hellsmouth Diving and Shipwreck site http://www.hellsmouth.co.uk/

SHIP A ship in dry dock at Port Glasgow, Scotland. Dry docks are used to check and make repairs to a ship's exterior, as well as for building new ships. Glasgow has one of the largest dry docks in Europe. *Image Bank*

Shipley, Jenny (1952–) New Zealand right-of-centre politician, prime minister 1997–99. She joined the conservative National Party at the age of 23 and, after a spell as a local councillor, was elected to the House of Representatives in 1987. When the National Party came to power in 1990, Shipley entered Jim ▷Bolger's government as minister of social welfare and women's affairs 1990–93, health and women's affairs 1993–94, and minister of transport and state services 1996–97. She provoked controversy through benefit-cutting and introducing an internal market into the health service.

Shiraz ancient walled city of southern Iran, the capital of Fars province, on the highway from Tehran to Bushire; population (1991) 965,000. Grain, rice, pulses, tobacco, gum tragacanth, clarified butter, wine, wool, skins, and carpets are the main products, as well as cotton goods, glass, attar of roses, and inlaid craftwork. There are many mosques. The tombs of the poets Sa'di and Hafiz are on the outskirts of the city.

shire administrative area formed in Britain for the purpose of raising taxes in Anglo-Saxon times. By AD 1000 most of southern England had been divided into shires with fortified strongholds at their centres. The Midland counties of England are still known as the **Shires**; for example Derbyshire, Nottinghamshire, and Staffordshire.

Shiva alternative spelling of ▷Siva, Hindu god.

shock in medicine, circulatory failure marked by a sudden fall of blood pressure and resulting in pallor, sweating, fast (but weak) pulse, and sometimes complete collapse. Causes include disease, injury, and psychological trauma.

   In shock, the blood pressure falls below that necessary to supply the tissues of the body, especially the brain. Treatment depends on the cause. Rest is needed, and, in the case of severe blood loss, restoration of the normal circulating volume.

Richard Brinsley Sheridan

What I write in a hurry I always feel to be not worth reading, and what I . . . take pains with, I am sure never to finish.

Letter to David Garrick, 1778

Jo Grimond

British Liberal politician.

Scotland is a foreign country, from their point of view.

On the people in his constituency of Orkney and Shetland, who voted 'no' in the devolution referendum of 1979

Ships: Key Dates

8000–7000 BC	Reed boats are developed in Mesopotamia and Egypt; dugout canoes are used in northwest Europe.
4000–3000 BC	The Egyptians use single-masted square-rigged ships on the Nile.
1200 BC	The Phoenicians build keeled boats with hulls made of wooden planks.
1st century BC	The Chinese invent the rudder.
AD 200	The Chinese build ships with several masts.
200–300	The Arabs and Romans develop fore-and-aft rigging that allows ships to sail across the direction of the wind.
800–900	Square-rigged Viking longboats cross the North Sea to Britain, the Faroe Islands, and Iceland.
1090	The Chinese invent the magnetic compass.
1400–1500	Three-masted ships are developed in Western Europe, stimulating voyages of exploration.
1535	A group of Italians use a primitive glass diving bell to explore the wrecks of sunken ships on the bed of Lake Nemi near Rome, Italy.
1596	Visunsin, a Korean naval commander, invents the first ironclad battleship.
1620	Dutch engineer Cornelius Drebbel invents the submarine.
1775	US engineer David Bushnell builds a hand-powered submarine, *Turtle*, with buoyancy tanks.
1777	The first boat with an iron hull is built in Yorkshire, England.
1783	Frenchman Jouffroy d'Abbans builds and tests the first paddle-driven steamboat.
1787	American inventor John Fitch demonstrates the first steamboat in the western hemisphere on the Delaware River at Philadelphia, Pennsylvania.
1797	Fitch applies a screw propeller to his steamboat.
1802	Scottish engineer William Symington launches the first stern paddle-wheel steamer, the *Charlotte Dundas*.
1807	The first practical and economically successful steamboat, the *Clermont*, designed by US engineer and inventor Robert Fulton, sails between New York and Albany.
1811	Fulton designs and builds the *Chancellor Livingston*, a ship 49 m/161 ft long drawing its power from a 60-horsepower steam engine.
1819	US inventor Joseph Francis develops an 'unsinkable' lifeboat with hydrogen-filled buoyancy tanks
1823	US inventor Samuel Morey begins building the *Aunt Sallie*, a boat powered by an early form of internal-combustion engine. The vessel sinks sometime before Morey's death in 1843.
1836	The English inventor Francis Pettit Smith patents the screw propeller in the UK. Shortly afterwards, in the same year, the Swedish inventor John Ericsson also patents a screw propeller.
1837	English engineer Isambard Kingdom Brunel completes the ship *Great Western*, the first steamship built for crossing the Atlantic Ocean regularly.
1838	The Steamship *Sirius* makes the first crossing of the Atlantic under steam power alone. It travels from London to New York in 18 days. The steamship *Great Western* makes its maiden voyage later the same year, sailing from Bristol to New York in 15 days.
1845	*Great Britain*, another vessel built by Isambard Kingdom Brunel, becomes the first propeller-driven iron ship to cross the Atlantic.
1845	The first clipper ship, *Rainbow*, is launched in the USA.
1863	*Plongeur*, the first submarine powered by an air-driven engine, is launched in France.
1866	The British clippers *Taeping* and *Ariel* sail, laden with tea, from China to London in 99 days.
1883	German engineer Gottlieb Daimler constructs his first high-speed internal-combustion engine and installs it in a boat.
1897	English engineer Charles Parsons fits a steam turbine to the ship *Turbinia*, making it the fastest boat of the time.
1900	Irish-American John Philip Holland designs the first modern submarine *Holland VI*, fitted with an electric motor for underwater sailing and an internal-combustion engine for surface travel; Enrico Forlanini of Italy builds the first hydrofoil.
1902	The French ship *Petit-Pierre* becomes the first boat to be powered by a diesel engine.
1905	A US inventor, Cameron B. Waterman, patents and demonstrates the first outboard motor. In Germany, the first U-boat is launched.
1908	US inventor Elmer Ambrose Sperry patents gyrostabilization, the manipulation of gyroscopes in ships as a means of reducing roll.
1911	Elmer Ambrose Sperry patents the gyrocompass. It is first installed in a merchant ship 1919.
1912	The liner *Titanic* sinks after a collision with an iceberg in the north Atlantic on her maiden voyage. Designed with separate watertight compartments, she is considered unsinkable, but the collision produces a large gash in her side, flooding enough compartments to make it impossible for her to stay afloat.
1948	Swiss-born Belgian Auguste Piccard builds his first bathyscaphe for deep undersea exploration.
1955	The first nuclear-powered submarine, *Nautilus*, is built in the USA; the hovercraft is patented by English inventor Christopher Cockerell.
1959	The first nuclear-powered surface ship, the Soviet ice-breaker *Lenin*, is commissioned; the US *Savannah* becomes the first nuclear-powered merchant (passenger and cargo) ship.
1968	The first supertankers for the bulk transportation of oil and petroleum come into service. A regular hovercraft service across the English Channel comes into operation.
1980	Launch of the first wind-assisted commercial ship for half a century, the Japanese tanker *Shin-Aitoku-Maru*.
1983	German engineer Ortwin Fries invents a hinged ship designed to bend into a V-shape in order to scoop up oil spillages in its jaws.
1986	Launch of the ship *Windstar*. The sails on its four 62-m/204-ft masts are under the control of a computer.
1989	*Gentry Eagle* sets a record for the fastest crossing of the Atlantic in a power vessel, taking 2 days, 14 hours, and 7 minutes.
1990	*Hoverspeed Great Britain*, a wave-piercing catamaran, crosses the Atlantic in 3 days, 7 hours, and 52 minutes, setting a record for the fastest crossing by a passenger vessel. Hoverspeed also begins operating a car ferry service across the English Channel using the catamaran SeaCat. The world's largest car and passenger ferry, the *Silja Serenade*, enters service between Stockholm and Helsinki, carrying 2,500 passengers and 450 cars.
1992	The Japanese propellerless ship *Yamato* driven by magnetohydrodynamics completes its sea trials. The ship uses magnetic forces to suck in and eject sea water like a jet engine.
1997	The biggest cruise ship ever, the *Carnival Destiny*, is launched. It is as long as three football pitches, taller than the Statue of Liberty, and too wide to pass through the Panama Canal. US researchers test a new type of submersible (small submarine) with wings, which can turn, dive, and roll like an aeroplane.
2000	The English cross-Channel car-ferry company Hoverspeed ends its hovercraft service after 22 years. The decade-old SeaCat service continues.

SHIP Advertisement card from a French series issued in 1900 that was intended to illustrate the history of navigation lights at sea. This card features a contemporary idea of what a Roman bireme (a galley having two banks of oars) would have looked like with a flare on the mast and a brazier at the prow. See entry on p. 865. *The Art Archive/Dagli Orti*

shock absorber in technology, any device for absorbing the shock of sudden jarring actions or movements. Shock absorbers are used in conjunction with coil springs in most motor-vehicle suspension systems and are usually of the telescopic type, consisting of a piston in an oil-filled cylinder. The resistance to movement of the piston through the oil creates the absorbing effect.

shoebill (or **whale-headed stork**) large, grey, long-legged, swamp-dwelling African bird *Balaeniceps rex*. Up to 1.5 m/5 ft tall, it has a large wide beak 20 cm/8 in long and more than 10 cm/4 in wide, with which it scoops fish, molluscs, reptiles, and carrion out of the mud. Shoebills occupy largish territories of several square kilometres and build their nests on floating mats of vegetation, approximately 1.5 m in diameter.

shogun Japanese term for military dictator and abbreviation for '*seii tai shogun*' – 'great barbarian-conquering general'. Technically an imperial appointment, the office was treated as hereditary and was held by a series of clans, the ▷Minamoto 1192–1219, the ▷Ashikaga 1336–1573, and the ▷Tokugawa 1603–1868. The shogun held legislative, judicial, and executive power.

Related Web site: Who Were the Shoguns? http://www.jinjapan.org/kidsweb/japan/i/q8.html

Sholes, Christopher Latham (1819–1890) American printer and newspaper editor who, in 1867, invented the first practicable typewriter in association with Carlos Glidden and Samuel Soulé. In 1873, they sold their patents to Remington & Sons, a firm of gunsmiths in New York, who developed and sold the machine commercially. In 1878 Sholes developed a shift-key mechanism that made it possible to touch-type.

Shona a Bantu-speaking people of South Africa, comprising approximately 80% of the population of Zimbabwe. They also occupy the land between the Save and Pungure rivers in Mozambique, and smaller groups are found in South Africa, Botswana, and Zambia. The Shona are mainly farmers, living in scattered villages. The Shona language belongs to the Niger-Congo family.

shoot in botany, the parts of a ▷vascular plant growing above ground, comprising a stem bearing leaves, buds, and flowers. The shoot develops from the ▷plumule of the embryo.

shooting star another name for a ▷meteor.

SHOEBILL The shoebill (also known as the shoe-billed stork or whale-headed stork) is native to the upper reaches of the White Nile in Uganda. It has a little tuft of feathers at the back of its head, and a huge, hooked bill. Despite its size and clumsiness, it settles in trees to roost at night. *Image Bank*

shop steward trade-union representative in a 'shop', or department of a factory, elected by his or her fellow workers. Shop stewards are unpaid and usually conduct union business in their own time. They recruit for the union, inspect contribution cards, and report grievances to the district committee. They represent their members' interests to employers through the process of ▷collective bargaining.

short circuit unintended direct connection between two points in an electrical circuit. ▷Resistance is proportional to the length of wire through which current flows. By bypassing the rest of the circuit, the short circuit has low resistance and a large current flows through it. This may cause the circuit to overheat dangerously.

shorthand any system of rapid writing, such as the abbreviations practised by the Greeks and Romans. The first perfecter of an entirely phonetic system was Isaac ▷Pitman, by which system speeds of about 300 words a minute are said to be attainable.

Short Parliament the English Parliament that was summoned by ▷Charles I on 13 April 1640 to raise funds for his war against the Scots. It was succeeded later in the year by the ▷Long Parliament.

When it became clear that the parliament opposed the war and would not grant him any money, he dissolved it on 5 May and arrested some of its leaders.

short-sightedness nontechnical term for ▷myopia.

short story short work of prose fiction, usually consisting of between 500 and 10,000 words, which typically either sets up and resolves a single narrative point or depicts a mood or an atmosphere.

Shostakovich, Dmitri Dmitrievich (1906–1975) Russian composer. His music is tonal, expressive, and sometimes highly dramatic; it was not always to official Soviet taste. He wrote 15 symphonies, chamber and film music, ballets, and operas, the latter including *Lady Macbeth of the Mtsensk District* in 1934, which was suppressed as 'too divorced from the proletariat', but revived as *Katerina Izmaylova* in 1963. His symphonies are among the greatest of the 20th century.

His son Maxim (1938–), a conductor, defected to the West after his father's death.

Related Web site: Shostakovichiana http://www.siue.edu/~aho/musov/dmitri.html

shot put (or **putting the shot**) in athletics, the sport of throwing (or putting) overhand from the shoulder a metal ball (or shot). Standard shot weights are 7.26 kg/16 lb for men and 4 kg/8.8 lb for women.

Related Web site: Shot Put http://www.geocities.com/Colosseum/8682/shot.htm

shoveler fresh-water duck *Anas clypeata*, family Anatidae, order Anseriformes, so named after its long and broad flattened beak used for filtering out small organisms from sand and mud. The male has a green head, white and brown body plumage, black and white wings, greyish bill, orange feet, and can grow up to 50 cm/20 in long. The female is speckled brown. Spending the summer in northern Europe or North America, it winters further south.

Shrapnel, Henry (1761–1842) British army officer who invented shells containing bullets, to increase the spread of casualties, first used in 1804; hence the word **shrapnel** to describe shell fragments.

shrew insectivorous mammal of the family Soricidae, order Insectivora, found in the Americas and Eurasia. It is mouselike, but with a long nose and pointed teeth. Its high metabolic rate means that it must eat almost constantly.

The **common shrew** *Sorex araneus* is about 7.5 cm/3 in long with a long, supple, pointed snout bearing numerous stiff hairs projecting beyond the lower jaw; its fur is reddish-grey above and greyish beneath. It has glands which secrete a strong, unpleasant odour as a means of defence. It feeds on insects, worms, and often on members of its own kind killed after a fight.

Related Web site: Shrew(-ists) Site http://members.vienna.at/shrew/index.html

Shrewsbury market town on the River Severn, Shropshire, England, 244 km/152 mi northwest of London; population (1991) 64,200. It is the administrative headquarters of Shropshire. There are service industries and light manufacturing, and tourism is important. To the east at Wroxeter is the site of the Roman city of **Viroconium**.

shrike (or **butcher-bird**) bird of the family Laniidae, of which there are over 70 species, living mostly in Africa, but also in Eurasia and North America. They often impale insects and small vertebrates on thorns. They can grow to 35 cm/14 in long, have grey, black, or brown plumage, sharply clawed feet, and hooked beaks.

SHRIKE Shrikes are often referred to as 'butcher birds' because of their habit of impaling their prey on thorns in a gruesome larder.

shrimp crustacean related to the ▷prawn. It has a cylindrical, semi-transparent body, with ten jointed legs. Some shrimps grow as large as 25 cm/10 in long.

The European common shrimp *Crangon vulgaris* is greenish, translucent, has its first pair of legs ending in pincers, possesses no rostrum (the beaklike structure which extends forwards from the head in some crustaceans), and has comparatively shorter antennae than the prawn.

Synalpheus regalis, a shrimp that lives within sponges in the coral reefs of Belize, was discovered in 1996 to live in social colonies with a structure resembling that of social insects, such as ants. All are the offspring of a single reproductive female; care of young is cooperative; and larger individuals act to defend the colony.

Shropshire county of western England, which has contained the unitary authority of Telford and Wrekin since April 1998. Sometimes abbreviated to **Salop**, Shropshire was officially known by this name from 1974 until local protest reversed the decision in 1980.

area 3,490 sq km/1,347 sq mi **towns** ▷Shrewsbury (administrative headquarters), Ludlow, Oswestry **physical** Shropshire is bisected, on the Welsh border, northwest–southeast by the River Severn; River Teme; Ellesmere (47 ha/116 acres), the largest of several lakes; the Clee Hills rise to about 610 m/1,800 ft (Brown Clee) in the southwest **features** Ironbridge Gorge open-air museum of industrial archaeology, with the Iron Bridge (1779), the world's first cast-iron bridge; Market Drayton is famous for its gingerbread, and Wem for its sweet peas **agriculture** cereals (barley, oats, wheat), sugar beet, mangolds (a root vegetable used for cattle feed), vegetables (turnips, swedes), sheep and cattle; dairy farming; forestry **industries** brick making; engineering; limestone; manufacturing: machine tools, agricultural implements (Shrewsbury, Market Drayton, Prees, Whitchurch, Ellesmere), carpets and radio receivers (Bridgnorth), clocks (Whitchurch); Shropshire is the principal iron-producing county of England **population** (1996) 421,200 **famous people** Charles Darwin, A E Housman, Wilfred Owen, Gordon Richards

shrub perennial woody plant that typically produces several separate stems, at or near ground level, rather than the single trunk of most trees. A shrub is usually smaller than a tree, but there is no clear distinction between large shrubs and small trees.

Shushkevich, Stanislav (1934–) Belorussian politician, president 1991–94. He was elected to parliament as a nationalist 'reform communist' in 1990 and played a key role in the creation of the Commonwealth of Independent States (CIS) as the successor to the USSR. A supporter of free-market reforms, he opposed the alignment of Belarus's economic and foreign policy with that of neighbouring Russia.

sial in geochemistry and geophysics, the substance of the Earth's continental ▷crust, as distinct from the ▷sima of the ocean crust. The name, now used rarely, is derived from **si**lica and **al**umina, its two main chemical constituents. Sial is often rich in granite.

siamang the largest ▷gibbon *Symphalangus syndactylus*, native to Malaysia and Sumatra. Siamangs have a large throat pouch to amplify the voice, making the territorial 'song' extremely loud.

Siamese fighting fish beautiful freshwater fish noted for its colour and elaborate behavioural displays. The male builds a nest of bubbles and looks after the eggs. The Siamese fighting fish *Betta splendens* is in family Belontidae, order Perciformes, class Osteichthyes.

Sian alternative transliteration of ▷Xi'an, capital of Shaanxi province, China.

Sibelius, Jean Julius Christian (1865–1957) Finnish composer. His works include nationalistic symphonic poems such as *En saga* (1893) and *Finlandia* (1900), a violin concerto (1904), and seven symphonies. In 1940 he abruptly ceased composing and spent the rest of his life as a recluse. Restoration of many works to their original state has helped to dispel his conservative image and reveal unexpectedly radical features.

Related Web site: Sibelius, Jean http://w3.rz-berlin.mpg.de/cmp/sibelius.html

Siberia Asian region of Russia, extending from the Ural Mountains to the Pacific Ocean; area 12,050,000 sq km/4,650,000 sq mi. Hydroelectric power is generated from the rivers Lena, Ob, and Yenisey; forestry and agriculture are practised. There are vast mineral resources, including coal (in the Kuznetsk Basin), gold, diamonds, oil, natural gas, iron, copper, nickel, and cobalt.

Sibyl in Roman mythology, one of many priestesses who prophesied under a deity's direct inspiration; most notably the Sibyl of Cumae, near Naples. A priestess of ▷Apollo, she guided ▷Aeneas to Hades, and offered to sell nine collections of prophecies, the **Sibylline Books**, to the legendary king of Rome, ▷Tarquinius Superbus. The price was too high, but after she had destroyed all but three, he bought those surviving for the initial sum. They were kept in the Capitol for consultation in emergency by order of the Senate.

Sichuan (or **Szechwan**; 'four rivers') province of central China, bounded to the north by Qinghai, Gansu, and Shaanxi; to the east by Hubei and Hunan; to the south by Guizhou and Yunnan; and to the west by Tibet; area 539,000 sq km/208,000 sq mi; population (1996) 84,300,000. The capital is ▷Chengdu. There are coal, natural gas, iron ore, salt brine, textile, engineering, and electronics industries. Rice, wheat, and maize are grown.

Sicily (Italian **Sicilia**) the largest Mediterranean island and an autonomous region of Italy, divided from the Italian mainland by the Strait of Messina; area 25,700 sq km/9,920 sq mi; population (2001) 4,866,200. It consists of nine provinces: Agrigento, Caltanissetta, Catania, Enna, Messina, Palermo, Ragusa, Syracuse, and Trapani; its capital is Palermo. Exports include Marsala wine, olives, citrus, refined oil and petrochemicals, pharmaceuticals, potash, asphalt, and marble. The region also incorporates the islands of ▷Lipari, Egadi, Ustica, and ▷Pantelleria. Etna, 3,323 m/10,906 ft high, is the highest volcano in Europe; its last major eruption was in 1993.

History Conquered by most of the major powers of the ancient world, Sicily flourished under the Greeks who colonized the island during the 8th–5th centuries BC. It was invaded by Carthage and became part of the Roman Empire (241 BC–AD 476). In the Middle Ages it was ruled successively by the Arabs; the Normans (1059–1194), who established the **Kingdom of the Two Sicilies** (Sicily and the southern part of Italy); the German emperors; and then the Angevins, until the popular revolt known as the **Sicilian Vespers** in 1282.

Spanish rule was invited and continued in varying forms, with a temporary displacement of the Spanish Bourbons by Napoleon I, until ▷Garibaldi's invasion in 1860 resulted in the two Sicilies being united with Italy in 1861. In World War II Sicily was the launch point for the Allied invasion of Italy in 1943.

sick building syndrome malaise diagnosed in the early 1980s among office workers and thought to be caused by such pollutants as formaldehyde (from furniture and insulating materials), benzene (from paint), and the solvent trichloroethene, concentrated in air-conditioned buildings. Symptoms include headache, sore throat, tiredness, colds, and flu. Studies have found that it can cause a 40% drop in productivity and a 30% rise in absenteeism.

Sickert, Walter Richard (1860–1942) English artist. His works, broadly Impressionist in style, capture subtleties of tone and light, often with a melancholic atmosphere, their most familiar subjects being the rather shabby cityscapes and domestic and music-hall interiors of late Victorian and Edwardian London. *Ennui* (*c.* 1913; Tate Gallery, London) is a typical interior painting. His work inspired the ▷Camden Town Group.

Sickert learned his craft from James Whistler in London and then from Degas in Paris. Though often described as an Impressionist, he was only so to the same limited extent as Degas, constructing pictures from swift notes made on the spot, and never painting in the open air.

He worked in Dieppe from 1885 to 1905, with occasional visits to Venice, and produced music-hall paintings and views of Venice and Dieppe in dark, rich tones. In his 'Camden Town' period (1905–14), he explored the back rooms and dingy streets of North

London. His zest for urban life and his personality drew together a group of younger artists who formed the nucleus of the Camden Town Group, which played a leading role in bringing post-Impressionism into English art.

sickle-cell disease (or **sickle-cell anaemia**) hereditary chronic blood disorder common among people of black African descent; also found in the eastern Mediterranean, parts of the Persian Gulf, and in northeastern India. It is characterized by distortion and fragility of the red blood cells, which are lost too rapidly from the circulation. This often results in ▷anaemia.

People with this disease have abnormal red blood cells (sickle cells), containing a defective ▷haemoglobin. The presence of sickle cells in the blood is called **sicklemia**.

The disease is caused by a recessive allele. Those with two copies of the allele suffer debilitating anaemia; those with a single copy paired with the normal allele, suffer with only mild anaemia and have a degree of protection against ▷malaria because fewer normal red blood cells are available to the parasites for infection.

In the USA there were approximately 65,000 African-Americans suffering from sickle-cell disease in 1996; there were about 5,500 British sufferers. Worldwide, 100,000 babies are born with the disease annually. Those born in developing countries are unlikely to survive for long.

Bone marrow transplantation can provide a cure, but the risks (a fatality rate of 10% and a complications rate of 20%) are so great that it is only an option for the severely ill. US researchers announced in April 1995 that patients treated with a drug called hydroxyurea showed a reduction in the number of sickle cells. The drug works by reducing the amount of defective haemoglobin produced, and reviving the production of fetal haemoglobin. Fetal haemoglobin is not affected by sickling.

Siddons, Sarah (1755–1831) Born Sarah Kemble. English actor. Her majestic presence made her suited to tragic and heroic roles such as Lady Macbeth, Zara in Congreve's *The Mourning Bride*, and Constance in *King John*.

sidewinder rattlesnake *Crotalus cerastes* that lives in the deserts of the southwestern USA and Mexico, and moves by throwing its coils into a sideways 'jump' across the sand. It can grow up to 75 cm/30 in long.

Sidney, Philip (1554–1586) English poet. He wrote the sonnet sequence *Astrophel and Stella* (1591), *Arcadia* (1590), a prose romance, and *Apologie for Poetrie* (1595). Politically, Sidney became a charismatic, but hardly powerful, figure supporting a 'forward' foreign policy that would help the Protestant Netherlands against the Spanish.

Sidney was born in Penshurst, Kent. Educated at Christ Church, Oxford, he rounded off his education by a tour around Europe in the company of Hubert Languet. He entered Parliament in 1581, and was knighted in 1583. In 1585 he was made governor of Vlissingen in the Netherlands, and died at Zutphen, fulfilling his desire of fighting the Spanish.

> **Philip Sidney**
> *Who shoots at the mid-day sun, though he be sure he shall never hit the mark; yet as sure he is he shall shoot higher than who aims but at a bush.*
> Arcadia II

Sidney's reputation, which was high among a few writers and politicians (like Edmund ▷Spenser) in his life, increased immeasurably after his death. He provided the nearest thing the English Calvinists had to a martyr for their cause; his life was mythologized by Fulke Greville.

Related Web site: Sidney, Sir Philip http://www.luminarium.org/renlit/sidney.htm

SIDS acronym for sudden infant death syndrome, the technical name for ▷cot death.

Siegfried legendary Germanic and Norse hero. His story, which may contain some historical elements, occurs in the German *Nibelungenlied/Song of the Nibelung* and in the Norse *Elder* or *Poetic* ▷*Edda* and the prose *Völsunga Saga* (in the last two works, the hero is known as Sigurd).

Siegfried wins Brunhild for his liege lord and marries his sister, but is eventually killed in the intrigues that follow.

He is the hero of the last two operas in Wagner's *The Ring of the Nibelung* cycle.

Siegfried Line in World War I, a defensive line established in 1917 by the Germans in France, really a subdivision of the main ▷Hindenburg Line; in World War II, the Allies' name for the West Wall, a German defensive line established along its western frontier, from the Netherlands to Switzerland.

siemens SI unit (symbol S) of electrical conductance, the reciprocal of the ▷resistance of an electrical circuit. One siemens equals one ampere per volt. It was formerly called the mho or reciprocal ohm.

Siena (ancient **Saena Julia**) town in Tuscany, Italy, about 50 km/31 mi south of Florence; population (1990) 57,700. Founded by the Etruscans, it has medieval sculpture including works in the 13th-century unfinished Gothic cathedral by Niccolo Pisano and Donatello, and many examples of the Sienese school of painting that flourished from the 13th to the 16th centuries. The *Palio* ('banner', in reference to the prize) is a dramatic and dangerous horse race in the main square, held annually (2 July and 16 August) since the Middle Ages.

Sierra Leone see country box.

Sierra Madre chief mountain system of Mexico, consisting of three ranges, the Sierra Madre Oriental, the Sierra Madre del Sur, and the Sierra Madre Occidental, enclosing the central plateau of the country; highest Citlaltepetl 5,700 m/18,700 ft. The Sierra Madre del Sur ('of the south') runs along the southwest Pacific coast.

Sierra Nevada mountain range of southern Spain, mainly in the province of Granada, but also extending east into Almería. The highest point is Mulhacén (3,481 m/11,425 ft high). It has several winter sports resorts; the main centre is Sol y Nieve.

Sierra Nevada mountain range in eastern California, extending for about 640 km/400 mi, with a general ridge line at over 2,500 m/8,202 ft. Its highest point is Mount Whitney, which rises to 4,418 m/14,500 ft. The Sierra Nevada includes the King's Canyon, ▷Yosemite, and Sequoia national parks.

sievert SI unit (symbol Sv) of radiation dose equivalent. It replaces the rem (1 Sv equals 100 rem). Some types of radiation do more damage than others for the same absorbed dose – for example, an absorbed dose of alpha radiation causes 20 times as much biological damage as the same dose of beta radiation. The equivalent dose in sieverts is equal to the absorbed dose of radiation in grays multiplied by the relative biological effectiveness. Humans can absorb up to 0.25 Sv without immediate ill effects; 1 Sv may produce radiation sickness; and more than 8 Sv causes death.

Sigismund (1368–1437) Holy Roman Emperor from 1411, king of Hungary 1387–1437, and king of Bohemia 1419–37. Sigismund's reign was overshadowed by two religious issues: the Great Schism and the agitation of the reformer John ▷Huss. Sigismund demonstrated his ability as a European leader in working to end the schism by arranging the Council of Constance in 1414–18; his weakness was manifest in his continual failure to suppress the ▷Hussites.

The younger son of the house of Luxemburg, Sigismund owed his conglomeration of lands to his father's foresight and his brother's incompetence. Married to the daughter of Lewis of Hungary, Sigismund inherited that kingdom on his father-in-law's death, though in the following years he faced repeated revolts. Meanwhile, his elder brother Wenceslas (1361–1419) had failed to impress as Holy Roman Emperor or king of Bohemia, being given to heavy drinking rather than high politics. Wenceslas was deposed as emperor in 1400 and was eventually succeeded by Sigismund. On Wenceslas's death in 1419, Sigismund also inherited Bohemia – a poisoned chalice, as Wenceslas had failed to deal with the Hussites. He convened and presided over the Council of Constance 1414–18, where he promised protection to the religious reformer John ▷Huss, but imprisoned him after his condemnation for heresy and acquiesced in his burning in 1415. After unsuccessful crusades against his subjects, Sigismund found the door opened to his second kingdom by the actions of another council of the church, that at Basel.

Signac, Paul (1863–1935) French artist. Associated with ▷Seurat in the development of ▷pointillism, he is best known for his landscapes and seascapes painted in mosaic-like blocks of pure colour. One of his most striking works is his *Portrait of Félix Fénéon* (1980; J Logan Collection, New York).

signal any sign, gesture, sound, or action that conveys information.

Examples include the use of flags (▷semaphore), light (traffic and railway signals), radio telephony, radio telegraphy (▷Morse code), and electricity (telecommunications and computer networks).

Sigurd hero of Norse legend; see ▷Siegfried.

Sihanouk, Norodom (1922–) Cambodian politician, king 1941–55 and from 1993. He was prime minister 1955–70, when his government was overthrown in a military coup led by Lon Nol. With ▷Pol Pot's resistance front, he overthrew Lon Nol in 1975 and again became prime minister 1975–76, when he was forced to resign by the ▷Khmer Rouge. He returned from exile in November 1991 under the auspices of a United Nations-brokered peace settlement to head a coalition intended to comprise all Cambodia's warring factions (the Khmer Rouge, however, continued fighting). He was re-elected king after the 1993 elections, in which the royalist party won a majority; in 1996, however, it was announced that he was suffering from a brain tumour and might abdicate. In October 1997, three months after a successful coup by communists, he left for China and his return was uncertain. In March 1998 he pardoned his son, prince Norodom Ranariddh, who had been sentenced to 30 years' imprisonment for smuggling arms and colluding with the Khmer Rouge.

Educated in Vietnam and Paris, he was elected king of Cambodia in 1941. He abdicated in 1955 in favour of his father, founded the Popular Socialist Community, and governed as prime minister 1955–70.

After he was deposed in 1970, Sihanouk established a government in exile in Beijing and formed a joint resistance front with Pol Pot. This movement succeeded in overthrowing Lon Nol in April 1975 and Sihanouk was reappointed head of state, but was forced to resign in April 1976 by the communist Khmer Rouge leadership. Based in North Korea, he became the recognized head of the Democratic Kampuchea government in exile in 1982, leading a coalition of three groups opposing the Vietnamese-installed government. International peace conferences aimed at negotiating a settlement repeatedly broke down, fighting intensified, and the Khmer Rouge succeeded in taking some important provincial capitals.

A peace agreement was eventually signed in Paris on 23 October 1991. On his return from exile, Sihanouk called for an international trial of the leaders of the Khmer Rouge on charges of genocide. His son, Prince Norodom Ranariddh, became prime minister in July 1993. In October 1993 Sihanouk was crowned king under a new constitution providing for an elected monarch with limited powers. During 1994 there were a number of attempted coups against him, led by his close relatives.

Sikhism religion professed by 14 million Indians, living mainly in the Punjab. Sikhism was founded by Nanak (1469–*c.* 1539). Sikhs believe in a single God who is the immortal creator of the universe and who has never been incarnate in any form, and in the equality of all human beings; Sikhism is strongly opposed to caste divisions.

Their holy book is the *Guru Granth Sahib*. Guru Gobind Singh (1666–1708) instituted the *Khanda-di-Pahul*, the baptism of the sword, and established the Khalsa ('pure'), the company of the faithful. The Khalsa wear the five Ks: *kes*, long hair; *kangha*, a comb; *kirpan*, a sword; *kachh*, short trousers; and *kara*, a steel bracelet. Sikh men take the last name 'Singh' ('lion') and women 'Kaur' ('princess').

Related Web site: Sikhism Home Page http://www.sikhs.org/

Sikh Wars two wars in India between the Sikhs and the British:

The **First Sikh War 1845–46** followed an invasion of British India by Punjabi Sikhs. The Sikhs were defeated and part of their territory annexed.

The **Second Sikh War 1848–49** arose from a Sikh revolt in Multan. They were defeated, and the British annexed the Punjab.

Si-Kiang alternative transliteration of ▷Xi Jiang, a Chinese river.

Sikkim (or **Denjong**) upland state of northeast India, bounded by Nepal to the west, Bhutan to the east, Tibet (China) to the north and West Bengal state to the south; area 7,299 sq km/2,818 sq mi; population (2001 est) 540,500 sq mi. The capital is Gangtok. Industries include carpets, textiles, cigarettes, and food processing. Cardamom, tea, grain, fruit, and soybeans are grown, and livestock is raised.

Sikorski, Władysław Eugeniusz (1881–1943) Polish general and politician; prime minister 1922–23, and 1939–43 in the Polish government in exile in London during World War II. He was killed in an aeroplane crash near Gibraltar in controversial circumstances.

Together with Józef ▷Piłsudski he fought for the restoration of an independent Poland during World War I. As a result of his opposition to the military coup of 1926 he was denied a military appointment. Instead, he concentrated on studying military strategy and wrote a number of books based on his analysis of the French wartime experiences. In September 1939 he left Poland for Paris where, after a bitter contest with supporters of the pre-war regime, he formed a government in exile committed to close military cooperation with France and the UK. After the fall of France he moved to London. In July 1941, strongly supported by the UK prime minister Winston Churchill, he signed a controversial agreement for military cooperation with the USSR, which evoked strong opposition from within the Polish army in the UK and in the USSR. Following Sikorski's death, the Polish government in exile lost its sense of direction and its influence declined.

Sikorsky, Igor Ivan (1889–1972) Ukrainian-born US engineer. He built the first successful Helicopter in 1939 (commercially produced from 1943). His first biplane flew in 1910, and in 1929 he began to construct multi-engined flying boats.

The first helicopter was followed by a whole series of production designs using one, then two, piston engines. During the late 1950s piston engines were replaced by the newly developed gas-turbine engines.

Silayev, Ivan Stepanovich (1930–) Soviet politician, prime minister of the USSR August–December 1991.

A member of the Communist Party 1959–91 and of its Central Committee 1981–91, Silayev emerged as a reformer in 1990, founding the Democratic Reform Movement (with former foreign minister ▷Shevardnadze).

silencer (North American **muffler**) device in the exhaust system of cars and motorcycles. Gases leave the engine at supersonic speeds, and the exhaust system and silencer are designed to slow them down, thereby silencing them.

Silesia region of Europe that has long been disputed because of its geographical position, mineral resources, and industrial potential; now in Poland and the Czech Republic with metallurgical industries and a coalfield in Polish Silesia. Dispute began in the 17th century with claims on the area by both Austria and Prussia. It was seized by Prussia's Frederick the Great, which started the War of the ▷Austrian Succession; this was finally recognized by Austria in 1763, after the Seven Years' War. After World War I, it was divided in 1919 among newly formed Czechoslovakia, revived Poland, and Germany, which retained the largest part. In 1945, after World War II, all German Silesia east of the Oder-Neisse line was transferred to Polish administration; about 10 million inhabitants of German origin, both there and in Czechoslovak Silesia, were expelled.

silhouette profile or shadow portrait filled in with black or a dark colour. A common pictorial technique in Europe in the late 18th and early 19th centuries, it was named after Etienne de Silhouette (1709–1767), a French finance minister who made paper cut-outs as a hobby.

silica silicon dioxide, SiO₂, the composition of the most common mineral group, of which the most familiar form is quartz. Other silica forms are ▷chalcedony, chert, opal, tridymite, and cristobalite.

Common sand consists largely of silica in the form of quartz.

silicate one of a group of minerals containing silicon and oxygen in tetrahedral units of SiO_4, bound together in various ways to form specific structural types. Silicates are the chief rock-forming minerals. Most rocks are composed, wholly or in part, of silicates (the main exception being limestones). Glass is a manufactured complex polysilicate material in which other elements (boron in borosilicate glass) have been incorporated.

silicon (Latin *silex* 'flint') brittle, nonmetallic element, symbol Si, atomic number 14, relative atomic mass 28.086. It is the

---

Sierra Leone

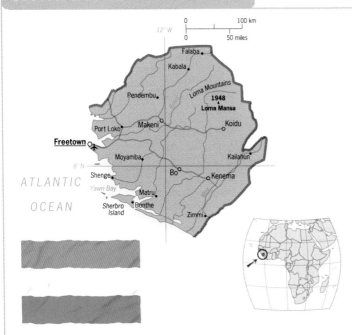

Sierra Leone country in West Africa, on the Atlantic Ocean, bounded north and east by Guinea and southeast by Liberia.

NATIONAL NAME *Republic of Sierra Leone*
AREA 71,740 sq km/27,698 sq mi
CAPITAL Freetown
MAJOR TOWNS/CITIES Koidu, Bo, Kenema, Makeni, Marampa
MAJOR PORTS Bonthe-Sherbro
PHYSICAL FEATURES mountains in east; hills and forest; coastal mangrove swamps

Government

HEAD OF STATE AND GOVERNMENT Ahmad Tejan Kabbah from 1996
POLITICAL SYSTEM transitional
POLITICAL EXECUTIVE transitional
ADMINISTRATIVE DIVISIONS four regions comprising 12 districts
ARMED FORCES 13,000 (2002 est)
DEATH PENALTY retained and used for ordinary crimes

Economy and resources

CURRENCY leone
GPD (US$) 789 million (2002 est)
REAL GDP GROWTH (% change on previous year) 5 (2001)
GNI (US$) 725 million (2002 est)
GNI PER CAPITA (PPP) (US$) 490 (2002 est)
CONSUMER PRICE INFLATION 3.5% (2003 est)
FOREIGN DEBT (US$) 1.1 billion (2001 est)

MAJOR TRADING PARTNERS Greece, UK, Belgium, USA, the Netherlands
RESOURCES gold, diamonds, bauxite, rutile (titanium dioxide)
INDUSTRIES palm oil and other agro-based industries, rice mills, textiles, mining, sawn timber, furniture making
EXPORTS diamonds, rutile, bauxite, gold, coffee, cocoa beans. Principal market: Greece 32.1% (2001)
IMPORTS consumer goods, fuel and lubricants, machinery and transport equipment, food and live animals, basic manufactures, chemicals. Principal source: UK 25.3% (2001)
ARABLE LAND 6.8% (2000 est)
AGRICULTURAL PRODUCTS rice, cassava, palm oil, coffee, cocoa, bananas; cattle production

Population and society

POPULATION 4,971,000 (2003 est)
POPULATION GROWTH RATE 2.1% (2000–15)
POPULATION DENSITY (per sq km) 69 (2003 est)
URBAN POPULATION (% of total) 39 (2003 est)
AGE DISTRIBUTION (% of total population) 0–14 45%, 15–59 50%, 60+ 5% (2002 est)
ETHNIC GROUPS 20 ethnic groups, 3 of which (the Mende, Temne, and Limbe) comprise

almost 70% of the population; 10% Creole (descendants of freed Jamaican slaves)
LANGUAGE English (official), Krio (a Creole language), Mende, Limba, Temne
RELIGION animist 45%, Muslim 44%, Protestant 8%, Roman Catholic 3%
EDUCATION not compulsory
LITERACY RATE 51% (men); 23% (women) (2000 est)
LABOUR FORCE 63.8% agriculture, 14% industry, 22.2% services (1997 est)
LIFE EXPECTANCY 33 (men); 36 (women) (2000–05)
CHILD MORTALITY RATE (under 5, per 1,000 live births) 316 (2001)
PHYSICIANS (per 1,000 people) 0.1 (1998 est)
HOSPITAL BEDS (per 1,000 people) 0.4 (1998 est)
TV SETS (per 1,000 people) 79 (2001 est)
RADIOS (per 1,000 people) 126 (2001 est)
INTERNET USERS (per 10,000 people) 16.2 (2002 est)

SIERRA LEONE A diamond dominates this stamp from Sierra Leone. The first Sierra Leonean diamond was found in 1930 and the industry has since flourished.
Stanley Gibbons

Chronology

15th century: Mende, Temne, and Fulani peoples moved from Senegal into region formerly populated by Bulom, Krim, and Gola peoples. The Portuguese, who named the area Serra Lyoa, established a coastal fort, trading manufactured goods for slaves and ivory.

17th century: English trading posts established on Bund and York islands.

1787–92: English abolitionists and philanthropists bought land to establish settlement for liberated and runaway African slaves (including 1,000 rescued from Canada), known as Freetown.

1808: Became a British colony and Freetown a base for British naval operations against slave trade, after Parliament declared it illegal.

1896: Hinterland conquered and declared British protectorate.

1951: First political party, Sierra Leone People's Party (SLPP), formed by Dr Milton Margai, who became 'leader of government business', in 1953.

1961: Independence achieved within Commonwealth, with Margai as prime minister.

1965: Free-trade area pact signed with Guinea, Liberia, and the Côte d'Ivoire.

1967: Election won by All People's Congress (APC), led by Siaka Stevens, but disputed by army, who set up National Reformation Council and forced governor general to leave the country.

1968: Army revolt brought back Stevens as prime minister.

1971: New constitution made Sierra Leone a republic, with Stevens as president.

1978: New constitution made APC the only legal party.

1985: Stevens retired and was succeeded as president and APC leader by Maj-Gen Joseph Momoh.

1991: A referendum endorsed multiparty politics and new constitution. A Liberian-based rebel group began guerrilla activities.

1992: President Momoh was overthrown by the military, and party politics were suspended as the National Provisional Ruling Council was established under Capt Valentine Strasser.

1995: The ban on political parties was lifted.

1996: Ahmad Tejan Kabbah became president after multiparty elections.

1997: President Kabbah's civilian government was ousted in a bloody coup. Maj Johnny Paul Koroma seized the presidency and the Revolutionary Council was formed.

1998: A Nigerian-led peacekeeping force drove out Maj Koroma's junta; Kabbah returned from exile.

1999: Fighting between government and rebel forces continued. Diplomatic efforts were spearheaded by the Organization of African Unity; a ceasefire and peace agreement were reached with rebels, and in November the first unit of what would become a 6,000-strong United Nations (UN) peacekeeping force arrived in Sierra Leone.

2000: As rebel activity continued, the UN force was increased to 11,000, the largest UN force in operation. Some UN peacekeepers were besieged by rebels but most were released and the remainder freed by UN troops. In August, 11 British soldiers were captured. Five were later released and the remaining six rescued in September. The government and rebels signed a 30-day truce.

2001: Fighting between the Guinean army and Sierra Leonean rebels left 170,000 refugees trapped in southern Guinea.

2002: Peaceful presidential and parliamentary elections were held after a decade of civil war. Kabbah was returned to power after ongoing armed conflict between the deposed government (with British military backing) and the rebel Revolutionary United Front (RUF).

second-most abundant element (after oxygen) in the Earth's crust and occurs in amorphous and crystalline forms. In nature it is found only in combination with other elements, chiefly with oxygen in silica (silicon dioxide, SiO_2) and the silicates. These form the mineral ▷quartz, which makes up most sands, gravels, and beaches.

Pottery glazes and glassmaking are based on the use of silica sands and date from prehistory. Today the crystalline form of silicon is used as a deoxidizing and hardening agent in steel, and has become the basis of the electronics industry because of its ▷semiconductor properties, being used to make 'silicon chips' for microprocessors.

The element was isolated by Swedish chemist Jöns Berzelius in 1823, having been named in 1817 by Scottish chemist Thomas Thomson by analogy with boron and carbon because of its chemical resemblance to these elements.

silicon chip ▷integrated circuit with microscopically small electrical components on a piece of silicon crystal only a few millimetres square.

One chip may contain more than a million components. A chip is mounted in a rectangular plastic package and linked via gold wires to metal pins, so that it can be connected to a printed circuit board for use in electronic devices, such as computers, calculators, television sets, car dashboards, and domestic appliances.

Silicon Valley nickname given to a region of southern California, approximately 32 km/20 mi long, between Palo Alto and San Jose. It is the site of many high-technology electronic firms, whose prosperity is based on the silicon chip. Silicon Valley faces increasing competition from companies in Asia.

Related Web site: Silicon Valley http://www.internetvalley.com/introduction.html

silicosis chronic disease of miners and stone cutters who inhale ▷silica dust, which makes the lung tissues fibrous and less capable of aerating the blood. It is a form of ▷pneumoconiosis.

Silk Road ancient and medieval overland route of about 6,400 km/4,000 mi by which silk was brought from China to Europe in return for trade goods; it ran west via the Gobi Desert, Samarkand, and Antioch to Mediterranean ports in Greece, Italy, the Middle East, and Egypt. Buddhism came to China via this route, which was superseded from the 16th century by sea trade.

silk-screen printing (or **serigraphy**) method of ▷printing based on stencilling. It can be used to print on most surfaces, including paper, plastic, cloth, and wood. An impermeable stencil (either paper or photosensitized gelatin plate) is attached to a finely meshed silk screen that has been stretched on a wooden frame, so that the ink passes through to the area beneath only where an image is required. The design can also be painted directly on the screen with varnish. A series of screens can be used to add successive layers of colour to the design.

silkworm usually the larva of the **common silkworm moth** *Bombyx mori*. After hatching from the egg and maturing on the leaves of white mulberry trees (or a synthetic substitute), it spins a protective cocoon of fine silk thread 275 m/900 ft long. To keep the thread intact, the moth is killed before emerging from the cocoon, and several threads are combined to form the commercial silk thread woven into textiles.

Other moths produce different fibres, such as **tussah** from *Antheraea mylitta*. The raising of silkworms is called **sericulture** and began in China in about 2000 BC. Chromosome engineering and artificial selection practised in Japan have led to the development of different types of silkworm for different fibres.

SILKWORM Despite its name, the silkworm is in fact the larva of a moth.

SILKWORM Silkworms feeding on mulberry leaves, forming part of the process of silk production in China. *Image Bank*

sill sheet of igneous rock created by the intrusion of magma (molten rock) between layers of pre-existing rock. (A ▷dyke, by contrast, is formed when magma cuts *across* layers of rock.) An example of a sill in the UK is the Great Whin Sill, which forms the ridge along which Hadrian's Wall was built.

Sillitoe, Alan (1928–) English novelist. He wrote *Saturday Night and Sunday Morning* (1958) about a working-class man in Nottingham, Sillitoe's home town. *The Loneliness of the Long Distance Runner* is the title story of a collection of short stories published in 1959.

silt sediment intermediate in coarseness between clay and sand; its grains have a diameter of 0.002–0.02 mm/0.00008–0.0008 in. Silt is usually deposited in rivers, and so the term is often used generically to mean a river deposit, as in the silting-up of a channel.

Silurian Period period of geological time 439–409 million years ago, the third period of the Palaeozoic era. Silurian sediments are mostly marine and consist of shales and limestone. Luxuriant reefs were built by coral-like organisms. The first land plants began to evolve during this period, and there were many ostracoderms (armoured jawless fishes). The first jawed fishes (called acanthodians) also appeared.

silver white, lustrous, extremely malleable and ductile, metallic element, symbol Ag (from Latin *argentum*), atomic number 47, relative atomic mass 107.868. It occurs in nature in ores and as a free metal; the chief ores are sulphides, from which the metal is extracted by smelting with lead. It is one of the best metallic conductors of both heat and electricity; its most useful compounds are the chloride and bromide, which darken on exposure to light and are the basis of photographic emulsions.

Silver is used ornamentally, for jewellery and tableware, for coinage, in electroplating, electrical contacts, and dentistry, and as a solder. It has been mined since prehistory; its name is an ancient non-Indo-European one, *silubr*, borrowed by the Germanic branch as *silber*.

silverfish wingless insect, a type of ▷bristletail.

silverpoint drawing instrument consisting of silver wire encased in a holder, used on paper prepared with opaque white. An example of silverpoint is Dürer's *Self-portrait* (1484; Albertina, Vienna).

sima in geochemistry and geophysics, the substance of the Earth's oceanic ▷crust, as distinct from the ▷sial of the continental crust. The name, now used rarely, is derived from **si**lica and **ma**gnesia, its two main chemical constituents.

Simenon, Georges Joseph Christian (1903–1989) Belgian crime writer. Initially a pulp fiction writer, in 1931 he created Inspector Maigret of the Paris Sûreté who appeared in a series of detective novels.

simile (Latin 'likeness') ▷figure of speech that in English uses the conjunctions *like* and *as* to express comparisons between two things of different kinds ('run like the devil'; 'as deaf as a post'). It is sometimes confused with ▷metaphor. The simile makes an explicit comparison, while the metaphor's comparison is implicit.

Simon, (Marvin) Neil (1927–) US dramatist and screenwriter. His stage plays (which were made into films) include the wryly comic *Barefoot in the Park* (1963; filmed 1967), *The Odd Couple* (1965; filmed 1968), and *The Sunshine Boys* (1972; filmed 1975), and the more serious, autobiographical trilogy *Brighton Beach Memoirs* (1983; filmed 1986), *Biloxi Blues* (1985; filmed 1988), and *Broadway Bound* (1986; filmed 1991). Similarly autobiographical is his play *Proposals*, first staged in 1997.

Simon, Paul (1942–) US pop singer and songwriter. In a folk-rock duo with Art Garfunkel, he had such hits as 'Mrs Robinson' (1968) and 'Bridge Over Troubled Water' (1970). Simon's solo work includes the critically acclaimed album *Graceland* (1986), for which he drew on Cajun and African music.

The success of *Graceland* and subsequent tours involving African musicians helped to bring world music to international attention, but Simon had always had an eclectic ear and had, for example, as early as 1971 used reggae rhythm on the song 'Mother and Child Reunion' and a Latin beat on 'Me and Julio Down by the Schoolyard'. A Brazilian drumming group, Olodum, featured on his album *The Rhythm of the Saints* (1990). In 1998 he produced his first Broadway musical *The Capeman*. He was inducted into the Rock and Roll Hall of Fame in the USA with Garfunkel in 1990 and as a soloist in 2001.

Simone Martini (*c.* 1284–1344) Italian painter. A master of the Sienese school, he was a pupil of ▷Duccio and continued the bright colours and graceful linear patterns of Sienese painting while introducing a fresh element of naturalism. Among his most important works are the *Maestà* (1315) in the Town Hall of Siena and the *Annunciation* (1333; Uffizi, Florence).

simony in the Christian church, the buying and selling of church preferments, now usually regarded as a sin. First condemned 451, it remained widespread until the Reformation.

Simplon Pass (Italian **Sempione**) Alpine pass Switzerland–Italy. The road was built by Napoleon 1800–05; the Simplon Tunnel, built in 1906, is 19.8 km/12.3 mi, one of Europe's longest.

Simpson, Wallis Warfield, Duchess of Windsor (1896–1986) US socialite, twice divorced. She married ▷Edward VIII 1937, who abdicated in order to marry her. He was given the title Duke of Windsor by his brother, George VI, who succeeded him.

Simpson Desert desert area in Australia, chiefly in Northern Territory; area 145,000 sq km/56,000 sq mi. The desert was named after a president of the South Australian Geographical Society who financed its exploration.

simultaneous equations in mathematics, one of two or more algebraic equations that contain two or more unknown quantities that may have a unique solution. For example, in the case of two linear equations with two unknown variables, such as:

(i) $x + 3y = 6$

and

(ii) $3y - 2x = 4$

the solution will be those unique values of x and y that are valid for both equations. Linear simultaneous equations can be solved by using algebraic manipulation to eliminate one of the variables, ▷coordinate geometry, or matrices (see ▷matrix).

sin transgression of the will of God or the gods, as revealed in the moral code laid down by a particular religion. In Roman Catholic theology, a distinction is made between **mortal sins**, which, if unforgiven, result in damnation, and **venial sins**, which are less serious. In Islam, the one unforgivable sin is **shirk**, denial that Allah is the only god.

Sinai Egyptian peninsula, largely desert, at the head of the Red Sea; area 65,000 sq km/25,000 sq mi. Resources include oil, natural gas, manganese, and coal; irrigation water from the River Nile is carried under the Suez Canal. The main towns are Al-Arish (the capital of South Sinai governorate) and Al-Tur (capital of North Sinai governorate). It is the ancient source of turquoise. Tourism is of increasing importance.

Sinai, Battle of battle 6–24 October 1973 during the Yom Kippur War between Israel and Egypt. It was one of the longest tank battles in history. Israeli troops crossed the Suez Canal 16 October, cutting off the Egyptian 3rd Army.

Sinai, Mount (or **Horeb**) mountain near the tip of the Sinai Peninsula; height 2,285 m/7,500 ft. According to the Old Testament this is where ▷Moses received the Ten Commandments from God. Its identity is not absolutely certain, but it is traditionally thought to be Jebel Musa ('Mountain of Moses').

Sinan (1489–1588) Ottoman architect. He was chief architect to Suleiman the Magnificent from 1538. Among the hundreds of buildings he designed are the Suleimaniye mosque complex in Istanbul 1551–58 and the Selimiye mosque in Adrinople (now Edirne) 1569–74.

Sinatra, Frank (Francis Albert) (1915–1998) US singer and film actor. Celebrated for his phrasing and emotion, especially on love ballads, he was particularly associated with the song 'My Way'. His films included *From Here to Eternity* (1953), for which he won an Academy Award, *Some Came Running* (1959), and the political thriller *The Manchurian Candidate* (1963).

Sinatra returned to recording in the 1950s with a contract with Capitol that marked the heyday of his recording career. He enjoyed a string of popular successes, many of them orchestrated by Nelson Riddle (1921–1985). It was a musical partnership that would pioneer the LP album and produce classics such as 'Come Fly With Me', 'In the Wee Small Hours', and 'Songs for Swingin' Lovers'. In the cinema, Sinatra also had several hit musical films such as *Guys and Dolls* (1955), *High Society* (1956), and *Pal Joey* (1957).

By the 1960s Sinatra had gathered around himself a coterie of friends and fellow-performers, who became known as the 'rat pack' and included Dean Martin, Sammy Davis Jr, and Peter Lawford. Together they made several films, including *Oceans 11* (1960).

Related Web site: Sinatra, Frank http://members.aol.com/jillywest/

Sind province of southeast Pakistan, mainly in the Indus delta; area 140,914 sq km/54,393 sq mi; population (1993 est) 28,930,000. The capital and chief port is ▷Karachi. Industries include shipbuilding, cement, textiles, and foundries; salt is mined. Wheat, rice, cotton, barley, oilseeds, and vegetables are grown; red Sindhi cattle, buffaloes, and camels are raised.

Sindhi the majority ethnic group living in the Pakistani province of Sind. The Sindhi language is spoken by about 15 million people. Since the partition of India and Pakistan 1947, large numbers of Urdu-speaking refugees have moved into the region from India, especially into the capital, Karachi.

sine in trigonometry, a function of an angle in a right-angled triangle which is defined as the ratio of the length of the side opposite the angle to the length of the hypotenuse (the longest side).

Various properties in physics vary sinusoidally; that is, they can be represented diagrammatically by a sine wave (a graph obtained by plotting values of angles against the values of their sines). Examples include simple harmonic motion, such as the way alternating current (AC) electricity varies with time.

sine rule in trigonometry, a rule that relates the sides and angles of a triangle, stating that the ratio of the length of each side and the sine of the angle opposite is constant (twice the radius of the circumscribing circle). If the sides of a triangle are a, b, and c, and the angles opposite are A, B, and C, respectively, then the sine rule may be expressed as

$$\frac{a}{\sin A} = \frac{b}{\sin B} = \frac{c}{\sin C}$$

sinfonietta orchestral work that is of a shorter, lighter nature than a ▷symphony, for example Leoš ▷Janáček's *Sinfonietta* (1926). It is also the name for a small-scale orchestra specializing in such works, for example the London Sinfonietta.

Singapore (Sanskrit *Singa pura* 'city of the lion') see country box.

Singapore City capital of Singapore, on the southeast coast of the island of Singapore; population (2000 est) 3,151,300. Major industries include trade, shipping, banking, electronics, shipbuilding, and oil refining. Formerly a British colonial town, it was occupied by Japanese forces during World War II.

Singer, Isaac Bashevis (1904–1991) Polish-born US novelist and short-story writer. He lived in the USA from 1935. His works, written in Yiddish, often portray traditional Jewish life in Poland and the USA, and the loneliness of old age. They include *The Family Moskat* (1950) and *Gimpel the Fool and Other Stories* (1957). He was awarded the Nobel Prize for Literature in 1978.

Written in an often magical storytelling style, his works combine a deep psychological insight with dramatic and visual impact. Many of his novels were written for serialization in New York Yiddish newspapers. Among his works are *The Slave* (1960), *Shosha* (1978), *Old Love* (1979), *Lost in America* (1981), *The Image and Other Stories* (1985), and *The Death of Methuselah* (1988). He also wrote plays and books for children.

Singer, Isaac Merrit (1811–1875) US inventor of domestic and industrial sewing machines. Within a few years of opening his first factory in 1851, he became the world's largest sewing-machine manufacturer (despite infringing the patent of Elias Howe), and by the late 1860s more than 100,000 Singer sewing machines were in use in the USA alone.

Singh, Gobind Sikh guru; see ▷Gobind Singh.

Singh, Vishwanath Pratap (1931–) Indian politician, prime minister 1989–90. As a member of the Congress (I) Party, he held ministerial posts under Indira Gandhi and Rajiv Gandhi, and from 1984 led an anti-corruption drive. When he unearthed an arms-sales scandal in 1988, he was ousted from the government and party and formed a broad-based opposition alliance, the ▷Janata Dal, which won the November 1989 election. Mounting caste and communal conflict split the Janata Dal and forced him out of office in November 1990.

Single European Act act signed in 1986 (and in force from July 1987) to establish a ▷single European market, defined as an area without frontiers in which free movement of goods, services, people, and capital is ensured.

The act was the first major revision of the treaties of ▷Rome. It provided for greater involvement of the ▷European Parliament in the decision-making process, and the introduction of qualified majority voting in the Council of Ministers (now the Council of the European Union) for some policy areas. In addition, it included provisions concerning collaboration in research and development and in environmental policy.

single European currency (former name for 'the euro') new common currency, known as the euro, introduced by 11 of the 15 member states of the European Union, as part of the European Monetary Union (EMU), which began in January 1999. States joining the EMU agreed conversion rates for their currencies during 1998, and between 1999 and 2002 there was a three-year transitional period, during which national currencies continued to exist for normal transactions. In January 2002 euro banknotes and coins were introduced and from July 2002 national notes and coins were to cease to be legal tender in the participating states. A European Central Bank (ECB) was established in June 1999 to control interest rates. The new euro, supporting a combined GDP for the Euro-11 which will equal that of the USA, will soon become a rival to the dollar as the world's pre-eminent currency. The participating states are Austria, Belgium, Finland, France, Germany, Ireland, Italy, Luxembourg, the Netherlands, Portugal, and Spain.

single European market single market within the ▷European Union. Established under the ▷Single European Act, it was the core of the process of European economic integration, involving the removal of obstacles to the free movement of goods, services, people, and captial between member states of the EU. It covers, among other benefits, the elimination of customs barriers, the liberalization of capital movements, the opening of public procurement markets, and the mutual recognition of professional qualifications. It came into effect on 1 January 1993.

singularity in astrophysics, the point in ▷space-time at which the known laws of physics break down. Singularity is predicted to exist at the centre of a black hole, where infinite gravitational forces compress the infalling mass of a collapsing star to infinite density. It is also thought, according to the Big Bang model of the origin of the universe, to be the point from which the expansion of the universe began.

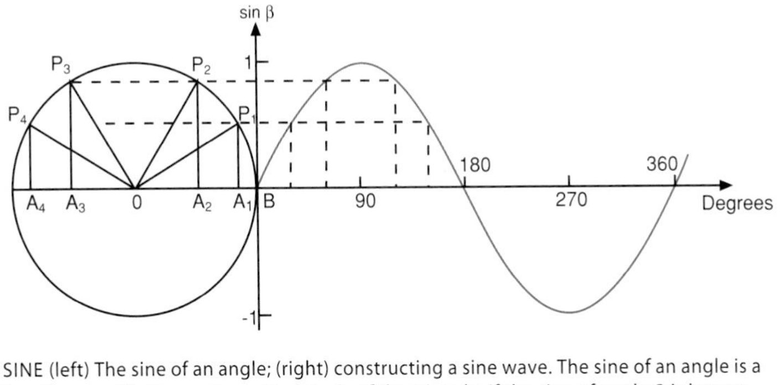

SINE (left) The sine of an angle; (right) constructing a sine wave. The sine of an angle is a function used in the mathematical study of the triangle. If the sine of angle β is known, then the hypotenuse can be found given the length of the opposite side, or the opposite side can be found from the hypotenuse. Within a circle of unit radius (left), the height P_1A_1 equals the sine of angle P_1OA_1. This fact and the equalities below the circle allow a sine curve to be drawn, as on the right.

Sinhalese the majority ethnic group of Sri Lanka (70% of the population). Sinhalese is the official language of Sri Lanka; it belongs to the Indo-Iranian branch of the Indo-European family, and is written in a script derived from the Indian Pali form. The Sinhalese are Buddhists. Since 1971 they have been involved in a violent struggle with the Tamil minority, who are seeking independence.

The Veddas of the central highlands are thought to be the descendants of the original inhabitants of Sri Lanka. Around 550 BC the island was invaded by Aryans from the mainland, though it seems likely that these people had already become mixed with the Dravidian inhabitants of southern India. The name Sinhalese is derived from the lion, **sinha**, symbol which occurs in the legends of origin.

Buddhism was flourishing by the 3rd century BC and during the 5th century AD the Sinhalese began to keep a Buddhist chronicle. Their script is based on the Indian Pali form. The Hīnayāna (Lesser Vehicle) Buddhists of Sri Lanka have had an impact on Southeast Asian religion, especially in Myanmar. During the 11th century there were Tamil incursions and by the time of the arrival of the Portuguese the Tamils were firmly established in the north. Today there is a large Tamil minority especially around Jaffna. There are also mixed populations, the descendants of islanders who married European seafarers, and small Arab communities along the coast. Trading and fishing remain important activities in coastal regions, while further inland rice is cultivated in irrigated fields.

Sining alternative transliteration of ▷Xining, capital of Qinghai province, China.

Sinn Fein (Gaelic 'we ourselves') Irish political party founded in 1905, whose aim is the creation of a united republican Ireland. The driving political force behind Irish nationalism between 1916 and 1921, Sinn Fein returned to prominence with the outbreak of violence ('the Troubles') in ▷Northern Ireland in the late 1960s, when it split into 'Provisional' and 'Official' wings at the same time as the ▷Irish Republican Army (IRA), with which it is closely associated. From the late 1970s 'Provisional' Sinn Fein assumed a more active political role, putting up candidates to stand in local and national elections. Sinn Fein won two seats in the 1997 UK general election and one seat in the 1997 Irish general election. Gerry ▷Adams became party president in 1978. Sinn Fein participated in the multiparty negotiations (known as the Stormont Talks) and became a signatory of the agreement reached on Good Friday, 10 April 1998. The party gained 17.6% of votes in the June 1998 elections to the 108-seat Belfast assembly. In September a historic meeting between Gerry Adams and the Ulster Unionist leader, David Trimble, took place at Stormont; Sinn Fein also agreed to appoint a contact with the international body overseeing the decommissioning of arms – the party's chief negotiator, Martin McGuinness.

Sinn Fein was founded by Arthur Griffith (1872–1922). Éamon ▷de Valera became its president in 1917. Sinn Fein MPs won a majority of the Irish seats in the 1918 UK general election, set up a secessionist Dáil (Irish parliament) in Dublin, and declared Irish independence in January 1919. The party split over the 1921 Anglo-Irish Treaty which created the Irish Free State and partitioned Ireland. The refusal of a section of Sinn Fein, led by de Valera, to accept the terms of the treaty, led to armed conflict between his followers and the forces of the new Free State. In the aftermath of the Irish Civil War, Sinn Fein pursued a policy of abstention from the Dáil. The party rapidly declined in importance after Éamon de Valera resigned the presidency of Sinn Fein to form his new ▷Fianna Fáil party in 1926.

SINN FEIN Fighting rebel Sinn Fein members, Dublin, 1922. *Art Archive*

Sino-Japanese Wars two wars waged by Japan against China 1894–95 and 1931–45 to expand to the mainland. Territory gained in the First Sino-Japanese War (Korea) and in the 1930s (Manchuria, Shanghai) was returned at the end of World War II.

Sino-Tibetan languages group of languages spoken in Southeast Asia. This group covers a large area, and includes Chinese and Burmese, both of which have numerous dialects. Some classifications include the Tai group of languages (including Thai and Lao) in the Sino-Tibetan family.

Sinuiju (or **Siniju**) capital of North Pyongan province, near the mouth of the Yalu River, North Korea; population (1998 est) 349,500. The city lies on the Yellow Sea. It was founded in 1910,

becoming important after the 1910 completion of a bridge over the Yalu linking it with Dandong in China. Sinuiju continues to be a major centre of rail transport between North Korea and China. Industries include paper, chemicals, alcohol distillation, and soya-bean processing.

sinusitis painful inflammation of one of the sinuses, or air spaces, that surround the nasal passages. Most cases clear with antibiotics and nasal decongestants, but some require surgical drainage.

Sinusitis most frequently involves the maxillary sinuses, within the cheek bones, producing pain around the eyes, toothache, and a nasal discharge.

Sioux (or **Lakota**, **Dakota**, or **Nakota**; Chippewa 'enemies') member of the largest group of American Indian ▷Plains Indians, numbering about 103,000 (1990) in the USA and 60,000 in Canada (1991), and now living on reservations in North and South Dakota and Nebraska, and scattered throughout the country. Their language belongs to the Macro-Siouan family.

siphon tube in the form of an inverted U with unequal arms. When it is filled with liquid and the shorter arm is placed in a tank or reservoir, liquid flows out of the longer arm provided that its exit is below the level of the surface of the liquid in the tank.

Siraj-ud-Daula (1728–1757) Nawab of Bengal, India, from April 1756. He captured Calcutta from the British in June 1756 and

Singapore

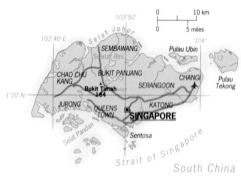

SINGAPORE The city of Singapore has a skyline of tall skyscrapers above its busy docks. Singapore's wealth has helped to build one of the most modern cities in the East. The rich variety of cultures in the city is reflected in the large number of theatres, concert halls, museums, and art galleries. *Corel*

Singapore formerly part of Straits Settlement (1826–1942), part of the Federation of Malaysia (1963–65) country in southeast Asia, off the tip of the Malay Peninsula.

NATIONAL NAME *Repablik Singapura/Republic of Singapore*
AREA 622 sq km/240 sq mi
CAPITAL Singapore City
PHYSICAL FEATURES comprises Singapore Island, low and flat, and 57 small islands; Singapore Island is joined to the mainland by causeway across Strait of Johore

Government

HEAD OF STATE Sellapan Ramanathan Nathan from 1999
HEAD OF GOVERNMENT Goh Chok Tong from 1990
POLITICAL SYSTEM liberal democracy
POLITICAL EXECUTIVE parliamentary
ADMINISTRATIVE DIVISIONS none
ARMED FORCES 60,500 (2002 est)
CONSCRIPTION 24–30 months
DEATH PENALTY retained and used for ordinary crimes
DEFENCE SPEND (% GDP) 5.2 (2002 est)
EDUCATION SPEND (% GDP) 3.1 (2001 est)
HEALTH SPEND (% GDP) 3.5 (2000 est)

Economy and resources

CURRENCY Singapore dollar
GPD (US$) 87 billion (2002 est)
REAL GDP GROWTH (% change on previous year) –2 (2001)
GNI (US$) 86.2 billion (2002 est)
GNI PER CAPITA (PPP) (US$) 23,090 (2002 est)
CONSUMER PRICE INFLATION 1% (2003 est)
UNEMPLOYMENT 3.3% (2001)
FOREIGN DEBT (US$) 240 million (2001 est)
MAJOR TRADING PARTNERS Malaysia, Japan, USA, Hong Kong, Thailand, Taiwan, Germany, China, Saudi Arabia
RESOURCES granite

INDUSTRIES electrical machinery (particularly radios and televisions), petroleum refining and petroleum products, transport equipment (especially shipbuilding), chemicals, metal products, machinery, food processing, clothing, finance and business services, tourism
EXPORTS electrical and nonelectrical machinery, transport equipment, petroleum products, chemicals, rubber, foodstuffs, clothing, metal products, iron and steel, orchids and other plants, aquarium fish. Principal market: Malaysia 17.3% (2001)
IMPORTS electrical and nonelectrical equipment, crude petroleum, transport equipment, chemicals, food and live animals, textiles, scientific and optical instruments, paper and paper products. Principal source: Malaysia 17.3% (2001)
ARABLE LAND 1.6% (2000 est)
AGRICULTURAL PRODUCTS vegetables, plants, orchids; poultry and fish production

Population and society

POPULATION 4,253,000 (2003 est)
POPULATION GROWTH RATE 1.3% (2000–15)
POPULATION DENSITY (per sq km) 6,882 (2003 est)
URBAN POPULATION (% of total) 100 (2003 est)
AGE DISTRIBUTION (% of total population) 0–14 21%, 15–59 68%, 60+ 11% (2002 est)
ETHNIC GROUPS 77% of Chinese ethnic descent, predominantly Hokkien, Teochew, and Cantonese; 14% Malay; 7% Indian, chiefly Tamil
LANGUAGE Malay, Mandarin Chinese, Tamil, English (all official), other Indian languages, Chinese dialects

RELIGION Buddhist, Taoist, Muslim, Hindu, Christian
EDUCATION (compulsory years) 6
LITERACY RATE 97% (men); 90% (women) (2003 est)
LABOUR FORCE 0.3% agriculture, 28.5% industry, 71.2% services (1999)
LIFE EXPECTANCY 76 (men); 80 (women) (2000–05)
CHILD MORTALITY RATE (under 5, per 1,000 live births) 4 (2001)

PHYSICIANS (per 1,000 people) 1.6 (1998 est)
HOSPITAL BEDS (per 1,000 people) 3.1 (1996 est)
TV SETS (per 1,000 people) 300 (2001 est)
RADIOS (per 1,000 people) 672 (2001 est)
INTERNET USERS (per 10,000 people) 5,396.6 (2002 est)
PERSONAL COMPUTER USERS (per 100 people) 50.8 (2002 est)

Chronology

12th century: First trading settlement established on Singapore Island.

14th century: Settlement destroyed, probably by Javanese Empire of Mahapahit.

1819: Stamford Raffles of British East India Company obtained Singapore from sultan of Johore.

1826: Straits Settlements formed from British possessions of Singapore, Penang, and Malacca ruled by governor of Bengal.

1832: Singapore became capital of Straits Settlements; the port prospered, attracting Chinese and Indian immigrants.

1851: Responsibility for Straits Settlements fell to governor general of India.

1858: British government, through the India Office, took over administration of Straits Settlements.

1867: Straits Settlements became crown colony of British Empire.

1922: Singapore chosen as principal British military base in Far East.

1942: Japan captured Singapore, taking 70,000 British and Australian prisoners.

1945: British rule restored after defeat of Japan.

1946: Singapore became separate crown colony.

1959: Internal self-government achieved as State of Singapore with Lee Kuan Yew (PAP) as prime minister.

1960s: Rapid development as leading commercial and financial centre.

1963: Singapore combined with Federation of Malaya, Sabah, and Sarawak to form Federation of Malaysia.

1965: Became independent republic after withdrawing from Federation of Malaysia in protest at alleged discrimination against ethnic Chinese.

1971: Last remaining British military bases closed.

1984: Two opposition members elected to national assembly for first time.

1988: Ruling PAP won all but one of available assembly seats; increasingly authoritarian rule.

1990: Lee Kuan Yew retired from the premiership after 31 years and was succeeded by Goh Chok Tong.

1996: Constitutional change was introduced, allowing better representation of minority races.

1997: The PAP, led by Prime Minister Goh Chok Tong, won a general election.

1998: Pay cuts were introduced as Singapore slipped into recession for the first time in 13 years.

1999: After all other candidates were screened out of the election, Sellapan Ramanathan Nathan, the government's candidate, became the new president.

imprisoned some of the British in the ▷Black Hole of Calcutta (a small room in which a number of them died), but was defeated in 1757 by Robert ▷Clive, and lost Bengal to the British at the Battle of Plassey. He was killed in his capital, Murshidabad.

siren in Greek mythology, a sea ▷nymph, half woman and half bird, who lured sailors to shipwreck along rocky coasts with her irresistable singing, before devouring them. ▷Odysseus, on the advice of the enchantress ▷Circe, tied himself to the mast of his ship in order to hear the sirens safely, and plugged his crew's ears with wax.

Sirius (or **the Dog Star** or **Alpha Canis Majoris**) brightest star in the night sky, 8.6 light years from the Sun in the constellation ▷Canis Major. Sirius is a double star: Sirius A is a white star with a mass 2.3 times that of the Sun, a diameter 1.8 times that of the Sun, and a true luminosity of 23 Suns. It is orbited every 50 years by a ▷white dwarf, Sirius B, also known as the Pup.

Sirius B is an eighth-magnitude companion which is sometimes known as 'the Dark Companion' as it was first detected in the 19th century by German astronomer Friedrich ▷Bessel from its gravitational effect on the proper motion of Sirius A. 'Dog Star' is the alternative name for Sirius, dating back to ancient Egypt. The unpleasantness of the hot summer season known as the 'dog days' was attributed to the influence of Sirius being in conjunction with the Sun. It was seen for the first time in 1862 but it was only in the 1920s that it was recognized as the first known example of a white dwarf.

sirocco hot, normally dry and dust-laden wind that blows from the deserts of North Africa across the Mediterranean into southern Europe. It occurs mainly in the spring. The name 'sirocco' is also applied to any hot oppressive wind.

sisal strong fibre made from various species of ▷agave, such as *Agave sisalina*.

siskin North American finch *Carduelis pinus* with yellow markings or greenish-yellow bird *Carduelis spinus* about 12 cm/5 in long, found in Eurasia. They are members of the finch family Fringillidae, order Passeriformes.

Sisley, Alfred (1839–1899) French Impressionist painter, born in Paris of English parents. Lyrical and harmonious, his landscapes are distinctive for their lightness of touch and subtlety of tone. Among his works are *The Square at Argenteuil* (1872) and *The Canal* (1872) (both in the Louvre, Paris).

Sistine Chapel principal chapel in the Vatican, Rome, begun under Pope Sixtus IV in 1473 by Giovanni del Dolci, and decorated by (among others) Michelangelo. The voting of the cardinals at the election of a new pope takes place in the Sistine Chapel.

Sisulu, Walter Max Ulyate (1912–) South African civil-rights activist, deputy president of the African National Congress (ANC). In 1964 he became, with Nelson Mandela, one of the first full-time secretaries general of the ANC. He was imprisoned following the 1964 Rivonia Trial for opposition to the apartheid system and released in 1989, at the age of 77, as a gesture of reform by President F W ▷de Klerk. In 1991, when Mandela became ANC president, Sisulu became his deputy.

Sisyphus in Greek mythology, a king of Corinth who was condemned to ▷Tartarus, a region of the underworld for the wicked. As punishment for his evil life, he was forced to roll a huge stone uphill for eternity; it always fell back before he could reach the top.

Sita in Hinduism, the wife of Rama, an avatar (manifestation) of the god Vishnu; a character in the *Rāmāyana* epic, characterized by chastity and kindness.

sitar (Hindi, from Persian *seh tar*, 'three strings') a long-necked lute used mainly in North Indian (Hindustani) music. Modern sitars have 6 or 7 playing strings (several of which are used mainly for drone and rhythmic punctuation) and 12 or more sympathetic strings; some have a small gourd resonator attached to the upper end of the neck. The best-known solo concert instrument in the tradition, where it is usually accompanied by the tabla drum pair, the sitar is also well known outside India.

sitatunga herbivorous antelope *Tragelaphus spekei* found in several swamp regions in Central Africa. Its hooves are long and splayed to help progress on soft surfaces. It grows to about 1.2 m/4 ft high at the shoulder; the male has thick horns up to 90 cm/3 ft long.

site of special scientific interest (SSSI) in the UK, land that has been identified as having animals, plants, or geological features that need to be protected and conserved. From 1991 these sites were designated and administered by English Nature, Scottish Natural Heritage, and the Countryside Council for Wales.

Sitting Bull (c. 1834–1890) Sioux **Tatanka Iyotake**, 'Sitting Buffalo Bull'. American Indian chief of the Hunkpapa Sioux during the Plains Wars of 1865–90, the battle between the ▷Plains Indians and the USA. In 1868 Sitting Bull agreed to ▷Sioux resettlement in North and South Dakota, but when gold was discovered in the Black Hills region, miners and the US army invaded Sioux territory. With the treaty broken, Sitting Bull led the Sioux against Lt-Col ▷Custer at the Battle of the ▷Little Bighorn, Montana, in 1876.

Sitting Bull was pursued by the US Army and forced to flee to Canada. He was allowed to return in 1881, and he toured in the Wild West show of 'Buffalo Bill' ▷Cody. He settled in South Dakota on the Standing Rock Reservation and was killed by Red Tomahawk, a Sioux police officer, during his arrest on suspicion of involvement in Indian agitations. His death represented one of the final acts of the defeat of the freedom and traditional way of life of the Plains Indians.

Related Web site: Sitting Bull – In Memory http://www.dickshovel.com/sittingbull.html

SITTING BULL Native American chief of the Dakota Sioux, led the defeat of General Custer at the Battle of Little Bighorn on 25 June, 1876 in Montana, USA *Archive Photos*

situationism in ethics, the doctrine that any action may be good or bad depending on its context or situation. Situationists argue that no moral rule can apply in all situations and that what may be wrong in most cases may be right if the end is sufficiently good. In general, situationists believe moral attitudes are more important than moral rules.

Sitwell, Edith (Louisa) (1887–1964) English poet, biographer, and critic. Her verse has an imaginative and rhythmic intensity. Her series of poems *Facade* (1922) was performed as recitations to the specially written music of William ▷Walton (1923).

SI units (French *Système International d'Unités*) standard system of scientific units used by scientists worldwide. Originally proposed in 1960, it replaces the ▷m.k.s., ▷c.g.s., and ▷f.p.s. systems. It is based on seven basic units: the metre (m) for length, kilogram (kg) for mass, second (s) for time, ampere (A) for electrical current, kelvin (K) for temperature, mole (mol) for amount of substance, and candela (cd) for luminosity.

Siva (or **Shiva**; Sanskrit 'propitious') in Hinduism, the third chief god (with Brahma and Vishnu). As Mahadeva (great lord), he is the creator, symbolized by the phallic *lingam*, who restores what as Mahakala he destroys. He is often sculpted as Nataraja, performing his fruitful cosmic dance.

His consort or female principle (*sakti*) is Parvati, otherwise known as Durga or Kali.

Six Counties the six counties that form Northern Ireland: Antrim, Armagh, Down, Fermanagh, Londonderry, and Tyrone.

Six-Day War another name for the third ▷Arab–Israeli War.

Six, Les group of French 20th-century composers; see ▷*Les Six*.

Sjælland (or **Zealand**) main island of Denmark, on which Copenhagen is situated; area 7,000 sq km/2,700 sq mi; population (1995) 2,157,700. It is low-lying with an irregular coastline. The chief industry is dairy farming.

skate any of several species of flatfish of the ray group. The common skate *Raja batis* is up to 1.8 m/6 ft long and greyish, with black specks. Its egg cases ('mermaids' purses') are often washed ashore by the tide.

skateboard single flexible board mounted on wheels and steerable by weight positioning. As a land alternative to surfing, skateboards developed in California in the 1960s and became a worldwide craze in the 1970s. Skateboarding is practised in urban environments and has enjoyed a revival since the late 1980s.

Related Web site: Skateboarding.com http://www.skateboarding.com/

skating self-propulsion on ice by means of bladed skates, or on other surfaces by skates with small rollers (wheels of wood, metal, or plastic).

The chief competitive ice-skating events are figure skating, for singles or pairs, ice-dancing, and simple speed skating. The first world ice-skating championships were held in 1896.

Related Web site: Figure Skating Page http://frog.simplenet.com/skateweb/

skeleton the rigid or semirigid framework that supports and gives form to an animal's body, protects its internal organs, and provides anchorage points for its muscles. The skeleton may be composed of bone and cartilage (vertebrates), chitin (arthropods), calcium carbonate (molluscs and other invertebrates), or silica (many protists). The human skeleton is composed of 206 bones, with the ▷vertebral column (spine) forming the central supporting structure.

A skeleton may be internal, forming an ▷endoskeleton, or external, forming an ▷exoskeleton, as in the shells of insects or crabs. Another type of skeleton, found in invertebrates such as earthworms, is the **hydrostatic skeleton**. This gains partial rigidity from fluid enclosed within a body cavity. Because the fluid cannot be compressed, contraction of one part of the body results in extension of another part, giving peristaltic motion.

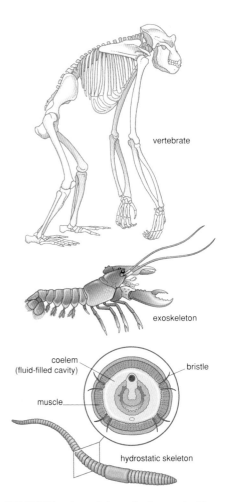

SKELETON Vertebrate skeletons (top) are made of bone and cartilage and provide a scaffold for the flesh. Only in certain parts (for example the skull and the rib cage) are organs encased totally. A gorilla is shown here. Invertebrates may have an exoskeleton, made of chitin, as in insects and crustacea, such as the lobster (middle). The exoskeleton totally encases the animal and is periodically moulted to allow growth. Molluscs, worms, and other 'soft' invertebrates have a hydrostatic 'skeleton' that supports the body and facilitates locomotion. A cross-section of the fluid-filled cavity of an earthworm is shown below.

skiing self-propulsion on snow by means of elongated runners (skis) for the feet, slightly bent upward at the tip. It is a popular recreational sport, as cross-country ski touring or as downhill runs on mountain trails; events include downhill; slalom, in which a series of turns between flags have to be negotiated; cross-country racing; and ski jumping, when jumps of over 150 m/490 ft are achieved from ramps up to 90 m/295 ft high. Speed-skiing uses skis approximately one-third longer and wider than normal with which speeds of up to 200 kph/125 mph have been recorded. Recently, **snowboarding** (or monoboarding), the use of a single, very broad ski, similar to a surf board, used with the feet facing the front and placed together, has become increasingly popular.

SKIING A cross-country skier in the Dolomites, Italy. *Image Bank*

skin the covering of the body of a vertebrate. In mammals, the outer layer (epidermis) is dead and its cells are constantly being rubbed away and replaced from below; it helps to protect the body from infection and to prevent dehydration. The lower layer (dermis) contains blood vessels, nerves, hair roots, and sweat and sebaceous glands, and is supported by a network of fibrous and elastic cells. The medical speciality concerned with skin diseases is called dermatology.

Skin grafting is the repair of injured skin by placing pieces of skin, taken from elsewhere on the body, over the injured area.

skink lizard of the family Scincidae, a large family of about 700 species found throughout the tropics and subtropics. The body is usually long and the legs are reduced. Some skinks are legless and rather snakelike. Many are good burrowers, or can 'swim' through sand, like the **sandfish** genus *Scincus* of North Africa. Some skinks lay eggs, others bear live young.

Skinks include the **three-toed skink** *Chalcides chalcides* of southern Europe and northwest Africa, up to 40 cm/16 in long, of which half is tail, and the **stump-tailed skink** *Tiliqua rugosa* of Australia, which stores fat in its triangular tail, looks the same at either end, and feeds on fruit as well as small animals. A new skink genus was identified in the rainforest of the Philippine Islands and described in 1997. There are two species of **moist forest skink** *Parvoscinus*. They lack external ear openings and females have only one oviduct and lay a single egg.

Skinner, B(urrhus) F(rederic) (1904–1990) US psychologist. He was a radical behaviourist who rejected mental concepts, seeing the organism as a 'black box' where internal processes are not significant in predicting behaviour. He studied operant conditioning (influencing behaviour patterns by reward or punishment) and held that behaviour is shaped and maintained by its consequences.

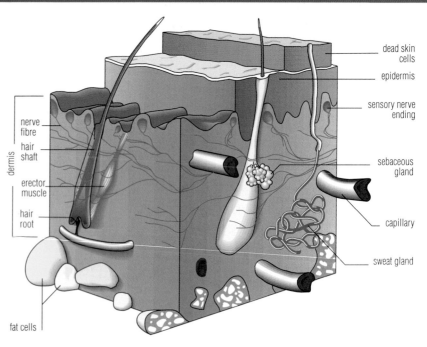

SKIN The skin of an adult man covers about 1.9 sq m/20 sq ft; a woman's skin covers about 1.6 sq m/17 sq ft. During our lifetime, we shed about 18 kg/40 lb of skin.

Skopje capital and industrial city of Macedonia; population (1991) 563,300. Industries include iron, steel, chromium mining, and food processing.

History It stands on the site of an ancient town destroyed by an earthquake in the 5th century. The city was taken in 1282 by the Serbian king Milutin, who made it his capital, and in 1392 by the Turks, when it became part of the Ottoman Empire. Captured by Serbia during the Balkan Wars of 1912–13, it became part of Yugoslavia in 1929. Again destroyed by an earthquake 1963, Skopje was rebuilt on a safer site nearby.

Skriabin (or Scriabin), **Aleksandr Nikolaievich** (1872–1915) Russian composer and pianist. His visionary tone poems such as *Prometheus* (1911), and symphonies such as *Divine Poem* (1903), employed unusual scales and harmonies.

skua dark-coloured gull-like seabird, living in Arctic and Antarctic waters. Skuas can grow up to 60 cm/2 ft long, with long, well-developed wings and short, stout legs; in colour they are greyish above and white below. They are aggressive scavengers, and seldom fish for themselves but force gulls to disgorge their catch, and also eat chicks of other birds. Skuas are in the family Stercorariidae, order Charadriiformes.

skull in vertebrates, the collection of flat and irregularly shaped bones (or cartilage) that enclose the brain and the organs of sight, hearing, and smell, and provide support for the jaws. In most

mammals, the skull consists of 22 bones joined by fibrous immobile joints called sutures. The floor of the skull is pierced by a large hole (*foramen magnum*) for the spinal cord and a number of smaller apertures through which other nerves and blood vessels pass.

The skull comprises the cranium (brain case) and the bones of the face, which include the upper jaw, enclosing the sinuses, and form the framework for the nose, eyes, and the roof of the mouth cavity. The lower jaw is hinged to the middle of the skull at its lower edge. The opening to the middle ear is located near the jaw hinge. The plate at the back of the head is jointed at its lower edge with the upper section of the spine. Inside, the skull has various shallow cavities into which fit different parts of the brain.

skunk North American mammal of the weasel family. The common skunk *Mephitis mephitis* has a long, arched body, short legs, a bushy tail, and black fur with white streaks on the back. In self-defence, it discharges a foul-smelling fluid.

Related Web site: Skunk and Opossum Page http://granicus.if.org/~firmiss/m-d.html

Skye largest island of the Inner ▷Hebrides, Highland region, off the west coast of Scotland; area 1,740 sq km/672 sq mi; population (2000 est) 12,000. It is separated from the mainland to the southeast by the Sound of Sleat and by the islands of Raasay and Scalpay to the northeast. The chief port and town is Portree. The economy is based on crofting, craft industries, tourism, and livestock. The **Skye Bridge**, a privately financed toll bridge to Kyleakin on the island from the Kyle of Lochalsh, was completed in 1995.

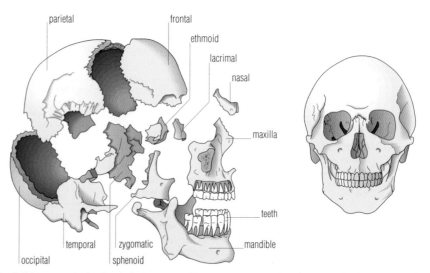

SKULL The skull is a protective box for the brain, eyes, and hearing organs. It is also a framework for the teeth and flesh of the face. The cranium has eight bones: occipital, two temporal, two parietal, frontal, sphenoid, and ethmoid. The face has 14 bones, the main ones being two maxillae, two nasal, two zygoma, two lacrimal, and the mandible.

Skylab US space station, launched 14 May 1973, made from the adapted upper stage of a Saturn V rocket. At 75 tonnes/82.5 tons, it was the heaviest object ever put into space, and was 25.6 m/84 ft long. *Skylab* contained a workshop for carrying out experiments in weightlessness, an observatory for monitoring the Sun, and cameras for photographing the Earth's surface.

Damaged during launch, it had to be repaired by the first crew of astronauts. Three crews, each of three astronauts, occupied *Skylab* for periods of up to 84 days, at that time a record duration for human spaceflight. *Skylab* finally fell to Earth on 11 July 1979, dropping debris on Western Australia.

skylark a type of ▷lark.

skyscraper building so tall that it appears to 'scrape the sky', developed 1868 in New York, USA, where land prices were high and the geology allowed such methods of construction. Skyscrapers are now found in cities throughout the world. The world's tallest free-standing structure is the CN (Canadian National) Tower, Toronto, at 553 m/1,815 ft.

slag in chemistry, the molten mass of impurities that is produced in the smelting or refining of metals.

slaked lime in chemistry, common name for ▷calcium hydroxide.

slander spoken defamatory statement; if written, or broadcast on radio or television, it constitutes ▷libel.

slash and burn simple agricultural method whereby natural vegetation is cut and burned, and the clearing then farmed for a few years until the soil loses its fertility, whereupon farmers move on and leave the area to regrow. Although this is possible with a small, widely dispersed population, it becomes unsustainable with more people and is now a cause of ▷deforestation.

slate fine-grained, usually grey metamorphic rock that splits readily into thin slabs along its ▷cleavage planes. It is the metamorphic equivalent of ▷shale.

Slav (or **Slavonian**, or **Slowene**, or **Slowane**; *Slawa* or *Slowo*, 'articulate') member of an Indo-European people in central and Eastern Europe, the Balkans, and parts of northern Asia, speaking closely related ▷Slavonic languages, some written in the Cyrillic and some in the Roman alphabet. The ancestors of the Slavs are believed to have included the Sarmatians and ▷Scythians. Moving west from central Asia, they settled in eastern and southeastern Europe during the 2nd and 3rd millennia BC.

slavery the enforced servitude of one person (a slave) to another or one group to another. A slave has no personal rights and is the property of another person through birth, purchase, or capture. Slavery goes back to prehistoric times but declined in Europe after the fall of the Roman Empire. During the imperialism of Spain, Portugal, and Britain in the 16th to 18th centuries and in the American South in the 17th to 19th centuries, slavery became a mainstay of an agricultural factory economy, with millions of Africans sold to work on plantations in North and South America. Millions more died in the process, but the profits from this trade were enormous. Slavery was abolished in the ▷British Empire in 1833 and in the USA at the end of the Civil War (1863–65), but continues illegally in some countries.

Related Web sites: Affirmative Action: a Timeline http://www.auaa.org/timeline/index.html
African Slave Trade and European Imperialism http://www.cocc.edu/cagatucci/classes/hum211/timelines/htimeline3.htm

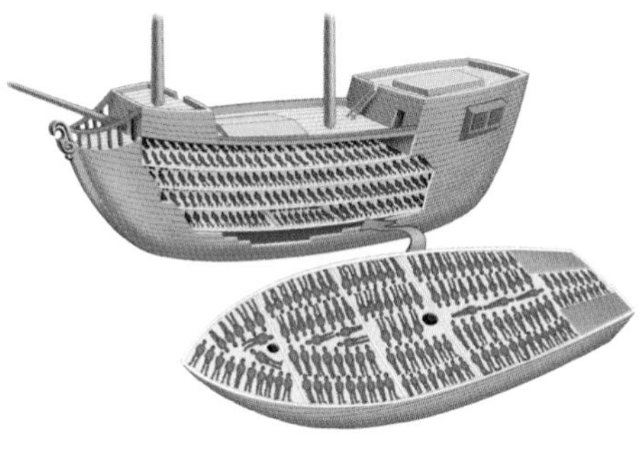

SLAVERY Thousands of slaves died during transportation. They were kept chained up in excessively cramped conditions without sufficient food, water, or exercise, throughout the long Atlantic voyage to the Americas and West Indies.

Slavonia region of eastern Croatia bounded by the Sava, Drava, and Danube rivers; Osijek is the largest town. Eastern and western Slavonia declared themselves autonomous provinces of Serbia following Croatia's declaration of independence from Yugoslavia 1991, and the region was the scene of fierce fighting between Croatian forces and Serb-dominated Yugoslav federal troops 1991–92. After the ceasefire 1992, 10,000 UN troops were deployed in eastern and western Slavonia and contested Krajina. Rebel Serbs in Croatia agreed November 1995 to return the region of eastern Slavonia to Croatian control.

Slavonic languages (or **Slavic languages**) branch of the Indo-European language family spoken in central and Eastern Europe, the Balkans, and parts of northern Asia. The family comprises the **southern group** (Slovene, Serbo-Croatian, Macedonian, and Bulgarian); the **western group** (Czech and Slovak, Sorbian in Germany, and Polish and its related dialects); and the **eastern group** (Russian, Ukrainian, and Belorussian).

SLD abbreviation for ▷Social and Liberal Democrats, British political party.

sleep state of natural unconsciousness and activity that occurs at regular intervals in most mammals and birds, though there is considerable variation in the amount of time spent sleeping. Sleep differs from hibernation in that it occurs daily rather than seasonally, and involves less drastic reductions in metabolism. The function of sleep is unclear. People deprived of sleep become irritable, uncoordinated, forgetful, hallucinatory, and even psychotic.

In humans, sleep is linked with hormone levels and specific brain electrical activity, including delta waves, quite different from the brain's waking activity. REM (rapid eye movement) phases, associated with dreams, occur at regular intervals during sleep, when the eyes move rapidly beneath closed lids.

Species that do not have distinct periods of sleep (most invertebrates and fishes, for example) have short intervals of reduced activity throughout a given 24-hour period. Extensive periods of sleep may have developed to make animals inconspicuous at times when they would be vulnerable to predators.

US researchers into REM sleep showed in 1998 that platypuses experience more REM (dream) sleep than any other animal. It had previously been thought that dreaming had evolved only in placental mammals.

sleeping pill any ▷sedative that induces sleep; in small doses, such drugs may relieve anxiety.

sleeping sickness infectious disease of tropical Africa, a form of ▷trypanosomiasis. Early symptoms include fever, headache, and chills, followed by ▷anaemia and joint pains. Later, the disease attacks the central nervous system, causing drowsiness, lethargy, and, if left untreated, death. Sleeping sickness is caused by either of two trypanosomes, *Trypanosoma gambiense* or *T. rhodesiense*. Control is by eradication of the tsetse fly, which transmits the disease to humans. Out of the 1 million people in Africa who become infected with the sleeping sickness, 100,000 people die each year from the disease, it was reported in August 2000.

slide rule mathematical instrument with pairs of logarithmic sliding scales, used for rapid calculations, including multiplication, division, and the extraction of square roots. It has been largely superseded by the electronic calculator.

Sligo county of the Republic of Ireland, in the province of Connacht, situated on the Atlantic coast of northwest Ireland; county town Sligo; area 1,800 sq km/695 sq mi; population (1996) 55,800. Limestone mountains rise behind a boggy coastal plain. There is some mineral wealth, including barytes, coal, lead, and copper. Agricultural activity includes cattle farming and dairy farming. The other principal town is Ballymote.

Slim, William Joseph, 1st Viscount Slim (1891–1970) British field marshal in World War II. He served in the North Africa campaign 1941 then commanded the 1st Burma Corps 1942–45, stemming the Japanese invasion of India, and then forcing them out of Burma (now Myanmar) in 1945. He was governor general of Australia 1953–60. He was created a KCB in 1944 and a Viscount in 1960.

> **William Slim**
> *In a battle nothing is ever as good or as bad as the first reports of excited men would have it.*
> *Unofficial History*

slime mould (or **myxomycete**) extraordinary organism that shows some features of ▷fungus and some of ▷protozoa. Slime moulds are not closely related to any other group, although they are often classed, for convenience, with the fungi. There are two kinds, cellular slime moulds and plasmodial slime moulds, differing in their complex life cycles.

Cellular slime moulds go through a phase of living as single cells, looking like amoebae, and feed by engulfing the bacteria found in rotting wood, dung, or damp soil. When a food supply is exhausted, up to 100,000 of these amoebae form into a colony resembling a single sluglike animal and migrate to a fresh source of bacteria. The colony then takes on the aspect of a fungus, and forms long-stalked fruiting bodies which release spores. These germinate to release amoebae, which repeat the life cycle.

Plasmodial slime moulds have a more complex life cycle involving sexual reproduction. They form a slimy mass of protoplasm with no internal cell walls, which slowly spreads over the bark or branches of trees.

Related Web site: Myxo Web http://www.wvonline.com/myxo/

Sloane, Hans (1660–1753) British physician, born at Killyleagh in County Down, Ireland (now Northern Ireland). He settled in London, and in 1721 founded the Chelsea Physic Garden. He was president of the Royal College of Physicians 1719–35, and in 1727 succeeded the physicist Isaac ▷Newton as president of the Royal Society, a post he occupied until 1740. Sloane can be credited with introducing the scientific method into medicine. His library, which he bequeathed to the nation, formed the nucleus of the British Museum. He was created 1st baronet by Queen Anne in 1716.

sloe fruit of the ▷blackthorn bush.

SLOE The blueish bloom on the fruit of the blackthorn is characteristic, although eventually washed off by the rain. *Premaphotos Wildlife*

slogan catchphrase of a type commonly used in advertising and politics. A slogan needs to be short and memorable. Wordplay and puns are often used in slogans ('Go to work on an egg' in the UK and 'It takes a licking and keeps on ticking' in the USA).

sloth slow-moving South American mammal, about 70 cm/2.5 ft long, family Bradypodidae, order Edentata. Sloths are greyish brown and have small rounded heads, rudimentary tails, and prolonged forelimbs. Each foot has long curved claws adapted to clinging upside down from trees. On the ground the animals cannot walk, but drag themselves along. They are vegetarian.

The hair is brown, long, coarse and shaggy. An alga lives in it, and in damp weather turns the hair green, which helps the animal to blend in with its leafy background. Sloths are nocturnal animals. They usually live alone in the treetops, eating leaves. They give birth to one young at a time, which spends its first few weeks clinging to its mother's hair.

Slough industrial town and unitary authority in southern England, near Windsor, 32 km/20 west of London; it was part of the county of Berkshire to April 1998.

area 28 sq km/11 sq mi **features** the home of astronomer William Herschel is now a museum; the history of the town is recorded in Slough Museum **industries** pharmaceuticals, electronics, engineering, aviation support services, and the manufacture of chocolate, paint, and power tools; a trading estate was developed here in the 1920s, the first of its kind to be established in England **population** (1996) 105,000

Slovakia one of the two republics that formed the Federative Republic of Czechoslovakia. Settled in the 5th–6th centuries by Slavs; it was occupied by the Magyars in the 10th century, and was part of the kingdom of Hungary until 1918, when it became a province of Czechoslovakia. Slovakia was a puppet state under German domination 1939–45, and was abolished as an administrative division in 1949. Its capital and chief town was Bratislava. It was re-established as a sovereign state, the ▷Slovak Republic, after the break-up of Czechoslovakia in 1993.

Slovak literature The literature of the Slovak republic and people. Slovakian emerged as a literary language only in the

Slovak Republic

SLOVAK REPUBLIC Rural Slovak Republic, long linked with the Czech Republic, has its own official language, developed from many dialects. The language is related to Czech, Polish, and Moravian, but as part of a movement for independence in the early 20th century, a distinctive written Slovak language was created. *Leonardo.com*

Slovak Republic formerly Czechoslovakia (with the Czech Republic) (1918–93) landlocked country in central Europe, bounded north by Poland, east by the Ukraine, south by Hungary, west by Austria, and northwest by the Czech Republic.

NATIONAL NAME *Slovenská Republika/Slovak Republic*
AREA 49,035 sq km/18,932 sq mi
CAPITAL Bratislava
MAJOR TOWNS/CITIES Košice, Nitra, Prešov, Banská Bystrica, Zilina, Trnava, Martin
PHYSICAL FEATURES Western range of Carpathian Mountains, including Tatra and Beskids in north; Danube plain in south; numerous lakes and mineral springs

Government

HEAD OF STATE Rudolf Schuster from 1999
HEAD OF GOVERNMENT Mikulas Dzurinda from 1998
POLITICAL SYSTEM emergent democracy
POLITICAL EXECUTIVE parliamentary
ADMINISTRATIVE DIVISIONS eight regions and 79 districts
ARMED FORCES 26,200 (2002 est)
CONSCRIPTION military service is compulsory for six months
DEATH PENALTY abolished in 1990
DEFENCE SPEND (% GDP) 2 (2002 est)
EDUCATION SPEND (% GDP) 4.2 (2001 est)
HEALTH SPEND (% GDP) 5.9 (2000 est)

Economy and resources

CURRENCY Slovak koruna (based on Czechoslovak koruna)
GPD (US$) 23.7 billion (2002 est)
REAL GDP GROWTH (% change on previous year) 3.3 (2001)
GNI (US$) 21.4 billion (2002 est)
GNI PER CAPITA (PPP) (US$) 12,190 (2002 est)
CONSUMER PRICE INFLATION 8.8% (2003 est)
UNEMPLOYMENT 18.3% (2001)
FOREIGN DEBT (US$) 6.7 billion (2001 est)
MAJOR TRADING PARTNERS Germany, Czech Republic, Russia, Austria, Hungary, Italy, Poland
RESOURCES brown coal, lignite, copper, zinc, lead, iron ore, magnesite

INDUSTRIES chemicals, pharmaceuticals, heavy engineering, munitions, mining, textiles, clothing, glass, leather, footwear, construction materials, televisions, transport equipment (cars, lorries, and motorcycles)
EXPORTS basic manufactures, machinery and transport equipment, miscellaneous manufactured articles. Principal market: Germany 26.8% (2000)
IMPORTS machinery and transport equipment, mineral fuels and lubricants, basic manufactures, chemicals and related products. Principal source: Germany 25.1% (2000)
ARABLE LAND 30.4% (2000 est)
AGRICULTURAL PRODUCTS wheat and other grains, sugar beet, potatoes and other vegetables; livestock rearing (cattle, pigs, and poultry)

Population and society

POPULATION 5,402,000 (2003 est)
POPULATION GROWTH RATE 0.0% (2000–15)
POPULATION DENSITY (per sq km) 110 (2003 est)
URBAN POPULATION (% of total) 58 (2003 est)
AGE DISTRIBUTION (% of total population) 0–14 18%, 15–59 66%, 60+ 16% (2002 est)
ETHNIC GROUPS 86% ethnic Slovak, 11% ethnic Hungarian (Magyar), 2% Romany; small Czech, Moravian, Silesian, and Ukrainian communities
LANGUAGE Slovak (official), Hungarian, Czech, other ethnic languages
RELIGION Roman Catholic (over 50%), Lutheran, Reformist, Orthodox, atheist 10%
EDUCATION (compulsory years) 9
LITERACY RATE 99% (men); 99% (women) (2003 est)
LABOUR FORCE 7.4% agriculture, 38.4% industry, 54.2% services (1999)
LIFE EXPECTANCY 70 (men); 78 (women) (2000–05)

CHILD MORTALITY RATE (under 5, per 1,000 live births) 9 (2001)
PHYSICIANS (per 1,000 people) 3.5 (1998 est)
HOSPITAL BEDS (per 1,000 people) 7.1 (1998 est)
TV SETS (per 1,000 people) 407 (2001 est)
RADIOS (per 1,000 people) 965 (2001 est)

INTERNET USERS (per 10,000 people) 1,604.4 (2002 est)
PERSONAL COMPUTER USERS (per 100 people) 18.0 (2002 est)

See also ▷Austro-Hungarian Empire; ▷Czechsolvakia; ▷Czech Republic.

Chronology

9th century: Part of kingdom of Greater Moravia, in Czech lands to west, founded by Slavic Prince Sviatopluk; Christianity adopted.

906: Came under Magyar (Hungarian) domination and adopted Roman Catholicism.

1526: Came under Austrian Habsburg rule.

1867: With creation of dual Austro-Hungarian monarchy, came under separate Hungarian rule; policy of forced Magyarization stimulated a revival of Slovak national consciousness.

1918: Austro-Hungarian Empire dismembered; Slovaks joined Czechs to form independent state of Czechoslovakia. Slovak-born Tomas Masaryk remained president until 1935, but political and economic power became concentrated in Czech lands.

1939: Germany annexed Czechoslovakia, which became Axis puppet state under the Slovak autonomist leader Monsignor Jozef Tiso; Jews persecuted.

1944: Popular revolt against German rule ('Slovak Uprising').

1945: Liberated from German rule by Soviet troops; Czechoslovakia re-established.

1948: Communists assumed power in Czechoslovakia.

1950s: Heavy industry introduced into previously rural Slovakia; Slovak nationalism and Catholic Church forcibly suppressed.

1968–69: 'Prague Spring' political reforms introduced by Slovak-born Communist Party leader Alexander Dubček; Warsaw Pact forces invaded Czechoslovakia to stamp out reforms; Slovak Socialist Republic, with autonomy over local affairs, created under new federal constitution.

1989: Prodemocracy demonstrations in Bratislava; new political parties, including centre-left People Against Violence (PAV), formed and legalized;

Communist Party stripped of powers; new government formed, with ex-dissident playwright Václav Havel as president.

1990: Slovak nationalists polled strongly in multiparty elections, with Vladimir Meciar (PAV) becoming prime minister.

1991: There was increasing Slovak separatism as the economy deteriorated. Meciar formed a PAV splinter group, Movement for a Democratic Slovakia (HZDS), pledging greater autonomy for Slovakia. Pro-Meciar rallies in Bratislava followed his dismissal.

1992: Meciar returned to power following an electoral victory for the HZDS. Slovak parliament's declaration of sovereignty led to Havel's resignation.

1993: The Slovak Republic joined the United Nations (UN) and Council of Europe as a sovereign state, with Meciar as prime minister and Michal Kovac, formerly of HZDS, as president.

1994: The Slovak Republic joined NATO's 'Partnership for Peace' programme.

1995: A Treaty of Friendship and Cooperation was signed with Hungary.

1996: An anti-Meciar coalition, the Slovak Democratic Coalition, was formed, comprising five opposition parties.

1997: A referendum on NATO membership and presidential elections was declared invalid after confusion over voting papers.

1998: Presidential powers were assumed by Meciar after failure to elect new president. The national council chair, Ivan Gasparovič, became acting head of state. Meciar stepped down as prime minister after the opposition Slovak Democratic Coalition (SDC) polled strongly in a general election. A new SDC-led coalition was formed under Mikulas Dzurinda. The koruna was devalued by 6%.

1999: Dzurinda formed a new coalition. Meciar was arrested on charges of corruption.

2004: The Slovak Republic was set to join the EU 1 May.

18th century. It served as a medium for literary patriots such as L'udovít Štur, and came of age in the 20th century in fine lyric poetry such as that of Ivan Krasko, a Symbolist, and Vojtech Mihálik.

Slovak Republic (or **Slovakia**) see country box.

Slovene member of the southern ▷Slav people of Slovenia and parts of the Alpine provinces of Styria and Carinthia in Austria, and Gorizia and Carniola in Italy. Formerly under ▷Hapsburg rule, they united with the Serbs and Croats to form the state of Yugoslavia after World War II. There are 1.5–2 million speakers of Slovene, a language belonging to the South Slavonic branch of the Indo-European family. The Slovenes use the Roman alphabet and the majority belong to the Roman Catholic Church.

Slovenia (or **Slovenija**) see country box.

slow-worm harmless species of lizard *Anguis fragilis*, once common in Europe, now a protected species in Britain. Superficially resembling a snake, it is distinguished by its small mouth and movable eyelids. It is about 30 cm/1 ft long, and eats worms and slugs.

SLR abbreviation for **single-lens reflex**, a type of ▷camera in which the image can be seen through the lens before a picture is taken.

slug soft-bodied land-living gastropod (type of ▷mollusc) related to the snails, but without a shell, or with a much reduced shell. All slugs have a protective coat of slime and a distinctive head with protruding tentacles. The eyes are at the end of the tentacles, which are also used to smell and locate food. Slugs eat dead animal matter and plants; some species are carnivorous and eat other slugs, snails,

and earthworms. Slugs are hermaphrodite (having both male and female organs). They can fertilize themselves, but usually mate with another. Slugs can live for up to three years, and are invertebrates (animals without backbones).

Behaviour Water can quickly be lost from the slug's body, so, to prevent drying out, slugs normally come out to feed only at night or when it is wet. During dry weather they shelter in crevices, hide under rocks or go underground. The slug moves by gliding its flattened body (foot) over the ground, leaving a slimy mucus trail.

Types of slug Land slugs belong to two groups, the roundbacks and the keeled slugs. Roundbacks, such as the slugs found in gardens, are usually about 2–3cm/0.7–1 in long and have soft fleshy sausage-shaped bodies. Keeled slugs, such as the great grey slug, are usually longer, growing up to 20 cm/6.4 in long, and they have a ridge or keel along their backs.

Slovenia

Slovenia country in south-central Europe, bounded north by Austria, east by Hungary, west by Italy, and south by Croatia.

NATIONAL NAME *Republika Slovenija/Republic of Slovenia*
AREA 20,251 sq km/7,818 sq mi
CAPITAL Ljubljana
MAJOR TOWNS/CITIES Maribor, Kranj, Celje, Velenje, Koper, Novo Mesto
MAJOR PORTS Koper
PHYSICAL FEATURES mountainous; Sava and Drava rivers

Government

HEAD OF STATE Janez Drnovšek from 2002
HEAD OF GOVERNMENT Anton Rop from 2002
POLITICAL SYSTEM emergent democracy
POLITICAL EXECUTIVE dual executive
ADMINISTRATIVE DIVISIONS 192 municipalities of which 11 are urban municipalities
ARMED FORCES 9,000; plus a paramilitary police force of 4,500 (2002 est)
CONSCRIPTION military service is compulsory for seven months (conscription to end in 2004)
DEATH PENALTY abolished in 1989
DEFENCE SPEND (% GDP) 1.5 (2002 est)
EDUCATION SPEND (% GDP) 5.2 (1999)
HEALTH SPEND (% GDP) 8.6 (2000 est)

Economy and resources

CURRENCY tolar
GPD (US$) 21.1 billion (2002 est)
REAL GDP GROWTH (% change on previous year) 3 (2001)

GNI (US$) 19.6 billion (2002 est)
GNI PER CAPITA (PPP) (US$) 17,690 (2002 est)
CONSUMER PRICE INFLATION 5.7% (2003 est)
UNEMPLOYMENT 11.6% (2001)
FOREIGN DEBT (US$) 5.9 billion (2001 est)
MAJOR TRADING PARTNERS Germany, Italy, Croatia, France, Austria, EU
RESOURCES coal, lead, zinc; small reserves/deposits of natural gas, petroleum, salt, uranium
INDUSTRIES metallurgy, furniture making, sports equipment, electrical equipment, food processing, textiles, paper and paper products, chemicals, wood and wood products
EXPORTS raw materials, semi-finished goods, machinery, electric motors, transport equipment, foodstuffs, clothing, pharmaceuticals, cosmetics. Principal market: Germany 26.2% (2001)
IMPORTS machinery and transport equipment, raw materials, semi-finished goods, foodstuffs, chemicals, miscellaneous manufactured articles, mineral fuels and lubricants. Principal source: Germany 19.2% (2001)
ARABLE LAND 8.6% (2000 est)
AGRICULTURAL PRODUCTS wheat, maize, sugar beet, potatoes, cabbage, fruits (especially grapes); forest resources (approximately 45% of total land area was forest in 1994)

SLOVENIA These buildings are built in the Venetian Gothic style, but are in fact in Slovenia. Italy's Friuli-Venezia Giulia region is on the western border of Slovenia, and in the southwest part of its coastline lies along the Gulf of Venice. *Image Bank*

Population and society

POPULATION 1,984,000 (2003 est)
POPULATION GROWTH RATE –0.2% (2000–15)
POPULATION DENSITY (per sq km) 98 (2003 est)
URBAN POPULATION (% of total) 49 (2003 est)
AGE DISTRIBUTION (% of total population) 0–14 15%, 15–59 65%, 60+ 20% (2002 est)
ETHNIC GROUPS 89% of Slovene origin, 3% ethnic Croat, 2% Serb; small Italian, Hungarian, and Albanian communities
LANGUAGE Slovene (related to Serbo-Croat; official), Hungarian, Italian
RELIGION Roman Catholic 70%; Eastern Orthodox, Lutheran, Muslim
EDUCATION (compulsory years) 8
LITERACY RATE 99% (men); 99% (women) (2003 est)
LABOUR FORCE 10.8% agriculture, 37.8% industry, 51.4% services (1999)
LIFE EXPECTANCY 73 (men); 80 (women) (2000–05)
CHILD MORTALITY RATE (under 5, per 1,000 live births) 5 (2001)

Chronology

1st century BC: Came under Roman rule.
AD 395: In the division of the Roman Empire, stayed in the west, along with Croatia and Bosnia.
6th century: Settled by the Slovene South Slavs.
7th century: Adopted Christianity as Roman Catholics.
8th–9th centuries: Under successive rule of Franks and dukes of Bavaria.
907–55: Came under Hungarian domination.
1335: Absorbed in Austro-Hungarian Habsburg Empire, as part of Austrian crownlands of Carniola, Styria, and Carinthia.
1848: Slovene struggle for independence began.
1918: On collapse of Habsburg Empire, Slovenia united with Serbia, Croatia, and Montenegro to form the 'Kingdom of Serbs, Croats and Slovenes', under Serbian Karageorgevic dynasty.
1929: Kingdom became known as Yugoslavia.
1941–45: Occupied by Nazi Germany and Italy during World War II; anti-Nazi Slovene Liberation Front formed and became allies of Marshal Tito's communist-led Partisans.
1945: Slovenia became a constituent republic of the Yugoslav Socialist Federal Republic.
mid-1980s: The Slovenian Communist Party liberalized itself and agreed to free elections. Yugoslav counterintelligence (KOV) began repression.

HOSPITAL BEDS (per 1,000 people) 5.7 (1998 est)
TV SETS (per 1,000 people) 367 (2001 est)
RADIOS (per 1,000 people) 405 (2001 est)
INTERNET USERS (per 10,000 people) 4,008.0 (2002 est)
PERSONAL COMPUTER USERS (per 100 people) 30.1 (2002 est)

See also ▷Austro-Hungarian Empire; ▷Croatia; ▷Serbia and Montenegro.

1989: The constitution was changed to allow secession from the federation.
1990: A Nationalist Democratic Opposition of Slovenia (DEMOS) coalition secured victory in the first multiparty parliamentary elections; Milan Kučan, a reform communist, became president. Sovereignty was declared. Independence was overwhelmingly approved in a referendum.
1991: Slovenia seceded from the Yugoslav federation; 100 people were killed after the Yugoslav federal army intervened; a ceasefire brokered by the EC brought the withdrawal of the Yugoslav army.
1992: Janez Drnovšek, a centrist Liberal Democrat, was appointed prime minister; independence was recognized by the EC and the USA. Slovenia was admitted into the United Nations (UN).
1997: A new government was formed by the ruling LDS, led by Prime Minister Janez Drnovšek. President Kučan was re-elected. The European Union (EU) agreed to open membership talks with Slovenia.
2000: A right-wing coalition government, led by Andrej Bajuk, took office. The coalition broke down over whether to move away from the system of election by proportional representation. New elections were won by a centre-left coalition led by former prime minister, Janez Drnovšek.
2004: Slovenia was set to join the EU 1 May.

Classification Slugs belong to the animal phylum Mollusca (molluscs), class Gastropoda (slugs and snails). There are over 40,000 species of gastropod and most land and freshwater slugs belong to a group called the pulmonates. The great number of land species include the common garden slug (*Arion hortensis*) and the great grey slug (*Limax maximus*).

The grey field slug *Deroceras reticulatum* is a common British species, and a pest to crops and garden plants.

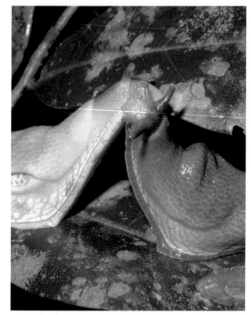

SLUG A number of slugs, such as this giant *Trichotoxon* species from Kenya, engage in an elaborate courtship ritual, caressing and mouthing one another's faces before eventually mating. *Premaphotos Wildlife*

Sluis, Battle of (or **Sluys**) 1340 naval victory for England over France which marked the beginning of the Hundred Years' War. England took control of the English Channel and seized 200 great ships from the French navy of Philip IV; there were 30,000 French casualties.

slump in the business or trade cycle, the period of time when the economy is in depression, unemployment is very high, and ▷national income is well below its full employment level. In the UK, the economy experienced a slump in the 1930s (the Great Depression), in 1980–81, and 1990–92.

Sluter, Claus (*c.* 1380–1406) Netherlandish sculptor, in the service of Philip the Bold of Burgundy. He was active in Dijon (France) and at the Charterhouse in nearby Champinol. For the latter, he worked on the *Well of Moses* about 1395–1403 (now in the grounds of a hospital in Dijon) and the kneeling mourners, or *pleurants*, for the tomb of his patron (Dijon Museum and Cleveland Museum, Ohio), commissioned by Philip the Bold himself but completed under John the Fearless. His style, with its attention to human featues, was continued at the Burgundian court by his nephew, Claus de Werve.

small arms one of the two main divisions of firearms: guns that can be carried by hand. The first small arms were portable handguns in use in the late 14th century, supported on the ground and ignited by hand. Today's small arms range from breech-loading single-shot rifles and shotguns to sophisticated automatic and semiautomatic weapons.

smallpox acute, highly contagious viral disease, marked by aches, fever, vomiting, and skin eruptions leaving pitted scars. Widespread vaccination programmes have wiped out this often fatal disease.

Smallpox was probably first brought to Europe by the returning crusaders, and as sea travel developed it was carried to the New World by explorers and settlers. It was common in Europe until the development of vaccination by Edward ▷Jenner about 1800, and remained so in Asia, where a virulent form of the disease (*variola major*) was fatal to 30% of victims until the World Health Organization (WHO) campaign from 1967, which resulted in its virtual disappearance by 1980. The campaign was estimated to have cost $300 million/£200 million, and was the organization's biggest health success to date.

When the disease was still common, a number of measures were used to stop an outbreak: victims were isolated, and doctors tried to

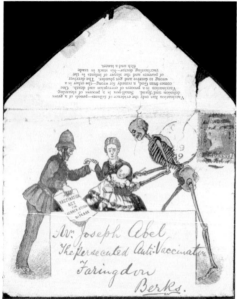

SMALLPOX A protest envelope is shown, dated 1859, denouncing the introduction, in 1853, of compulsory vaccination against smallpox in Britain. Public outcry against the enforced governmental measure had remained vociferous for a number of years. Expressed pictorially on the front of the envelope, the protest continues as outraged text on the flap. *The Art Archive/Private Collection/ Eileen Tweedy*

trace and vaccinate anyone who had been in contact with victims, while also keeping them apart from the public at large. The population exposed to risk were also vaccinated, and infected houses and contagious material were disinfected. Vaccination of known contacts within a day or two of their exposure to infection made any attack less severe. Vaccination before infection provided immediate and complete immunity for about two or three years, and a lesser degree of immunity for many years, if not for life.

The introduction of compulsory vaccination in 1853, together with improved preventive health measures, the introduction of port health inspection of seafarers and others arriving in the country, and increasing medical knowledge of the nature of infections led gradually to the stamping out of smallpox in the UK. Vaccination ceased to be compulsory in 1948.

Smart, Christopher (1722–1771) English poet. In 1756 he was confined to an asylum, where he wrote *A Song to David* 1763 and *Jubilate Agno/Rejoice in the Lamb* (not published until 1939), the latter appreciated today for its surrealism.

smart card plastic card with an embedded microprocessor and memory. It can store, for example, personal data, identification, and bank-account details, to enable it to be used as a credit or debit card. The card can be loaded with credits, which are then spent electronically, and reloaded as needed. Possible other uses range from hotel door 'keys' to passports.

The smart card was invented by French journalist Juan Moreno in 1974. Smart cards now have as much computing power as the leading personal computers of 1990.

smart drug any drug or combination of nutrients (vitamins, amino acids, minerals, and sometimes herbs) said to enhance the functioning of the brain, increase mental energy, lengthen the span of attention, and improve the memory. As yet there is no scientific evidence to suggest that these drugs have any significant effect on healthy people.

smart weapon programmable bomb or missile that can be guided to its target by laser technology, TV homing technology, or terrain-contour matching (TERCOM). A smart weapon relies on its pinpoint accuracy to destroy a target rather than on the size of its warhead.

smell sense that responds to chemical molecules in the air. It works by having receptors for particular chemical groups, into which the airborne chemicals must fit to trigger a message to the brain.

Related Web site: Mystery of Smell http://www.hhmi.org/senses/d/ d110.htm

SMELTING At a smelting plant in Asturias, Spain, molten metal is being poured into a mould. *Image Bank*

smelt small fish, usually marine, although some species are freshwater.

They occur in Europe and North America. The most common European smelt is the sparling *Osmerus eperlanus*.

smelting processing a metallic ore in a furnace to produce the metal. Oxide ores such as iron ore are smelted with coke (carbon), which reduces the ore into metal and also provides fuel for the process.

A substance such as limestone is often added during smelting to facilitate the melting process and to form a slag, which dissolves many of the impurities present.

Smetana, Bedřich (1824–1884) Bohemian composer. He established a Czech nationalist style in, for example, the operas *Prodaná Nevěsta/The Bartered Bride* (1866) and *Dalibor* (1868), and the symphonic suite *Má Vlast/My Country* (1875–80). He conducted at the National Theatre of Prague 1866–74.

Related Web site: Smetana, Bedrich http://www.hnh.com/composer/ smetana.htm

Smith, Adam (1723–1790) Scottish economist. He is often regarded as the founder of political economy. His *The Wealth of Nations* (1776) defined national wealth in terms of consumable goods and the labour that produces them, rather than in terms of bullion, as prevailing economic theories assumed. The ultimate cause of economic growth is explained by the division of labour – dividing a production process into several repetitive operations, each carried out by different workers, is more efficient. Smith advocated the free working of individual enterprise, and the necessity of 'free trade'.

> **Adam Smith**
> *The propensity to truck, barter and exchange one thing for another . . . is common to all men, and is to be found in no other race of animals.*
> The Wealth of Nations I. i ch. 2

Born in Kirkcaldy, he was professor of moral philosophy at Glasgow 1752–63. In *Theory of Moral Sentiments* (1759), Smith argued that the correct way to discern the morally right is to ask what a hypothetical impartial spectator would regard as fitting or proper.

The Adam Smith Institute, an organization which studies economic trends, is named after him.

Related Web site: Adam Smith: Excerpt from The Wealth of Nations: Regarding the Cost of Empire http://odur.let.rug.nl/~usa/D/ 1776-1800/adamsmith/wealth02.htm

Smith, Bessie (Elizabeth) (1894–1937) US jazz and blues singer. Known as the 'Empress of the Blues', she established herself in the 1920s after she was discovered by Columbia Records. She made over 150 recordings accompanied by such greats as Louis Armstrong and Benny Goodman.

Smith, David (Roland) (1906–1965) US sculptor and painter. His large openwork metal abstracts made a lasting impact on sculpture after 1945. *Cubi XXVII* (1965; Guggenheim Museum, New York) is typical of his late work.

Smith, Ian (Douglas) (1919–) Rhodesian politician. He was a founder of the Rhodesian Front in 1962 and prime minister 1964–79. In 1965 he made a unilateral declaration of Rhodesia's independence and, despite UN sanctions, maintained his regime with tenacity.

In 1979 he was succeeded as prime minister by Bishop Abel Muzorewa, when the country was renamed Zimbabwe. He was suspended from the Zimbabwe parliament in April 1987 and resigned in May as head of the white opposition party. In 1992 he helped found a new opposition party, the United Front.

Smith, John (1580–1631) English colonist. After an adventurous early life he took part in the colonization of Virginia, acting as president of the North American colony 1608–09. He explored New England in 1614, which he named, and published pamphlets on America and an autobiography. His trade with the Indians may have kept the colonists alive in the early years.

JOHN SMITH English explorer John Smith was captured during an expedition through Indian territory but was saved by Pocahontas, daughter of Chief Powhatan, who secured his release. *Philip Sauvain Picture Collection*

Smith, John Maynard British biologist, see ▷Maynard Smith.

Smith, Joseph (1805–1844) US founder of the ▷Mormon religious sect.

Smith, Maggie (Margaret Natalie Cross) (1934–) English actor. She has a commanding presence, and delivers throwaway lines in a fluting voice. Her films include *The Prime of Miss Jean Brodie* (1969) (Academy Award), *California Suite* (1978), *A Private Function* (1984), *A Room with a View* and *The Lonely Passion of Judith Hearne* (both 1987), *Sister Act* (1992), *Richard III* (1995), and *Washington Square* (1997). She was created a DBE in 1990.

Smith, Stevie (Florence Margaret) (1902–1971) English poet and novelist. She made her debut with *Novel on Yellow Paper* (1936). She wrote nine volumes of eccentrically direct verse illustrated with her equally eccentric line drawings, including *Not Waving but Drowning* (1957), and two more novels.

Smith, William (1769–1839) English geologist. He produced the first geological maps of England and Wales, setting the pattern for stratigraphical geology. Often called the founder of stratigraphical geology, he determined the succession of English strata across the whole country, from the Carboniferous up to the Cretaceous. He also established their fossil specimens.

Working as a canal engineer, he observed while supervising excavations that different beds of rock could be identified by their fossils, and so established the basis of stratigraphy.

Smithson, Alison Margaret (born Alison Margaret Gill; 1928–1993) and **Peter Denham** (1923–). English architects, teachers, and theorists. They are known for their development in the 1950s and 1960s of the style known as Brutalism, for example, Hunstanton School, Norfolk, England (1950–52). Notable among their other designs are the Economist Building, London, England (1964), Robin Hood Gardens, London (1968–72), and the Garden Building at St Hilda's College, Oxford, England (1970).

smog natural fog containing impurities, mainly nitrogen oxides (NO_x) and volatile organic compounds (VOCs) from domestic fires, industrial furnaces, certain power stations, and internal-combustion engines (petrol or diesel). It can cause substantial illness and loss of life, particularly among chronic bronchitics, and damage to wildlife.

smokeless fuel fuel that does not give off any smoke when burned, because all the carbon is fully oxidized to carbon dioxide (CO_2). Natural gas, oil, and coke are smokeless fuels.

smoking inhaling the fumes from burning substances, generally ▷tobacco in the form of cigarettes. The practice is habit-forming and dangerous to health, since carbon monoxide and other toxic materials result from the combustion process. A direct link between lung cancer and tobacco smoking was established in 1950; the habit is also linked to respiratory and coronary heart diseases. In the West, smoking is now forbidden in many public places because even **passive smoking** – breathing in fumes from other people's cigarettes – can be harmful. Some illegal drugs, such as ▷crack and ▷opium, are also smoked.

In June 1997 the US tobacco industry agreed a settlement with the US government of US$368 billion. Payments will be spread over 25 years and the money will fund the treatment of smoking-related illnesses and settle lawsuits against the industry. The deal also limited tobacco advertising. In 1998, 46 US states signed a further deal with 4 major tobacco companies, agreeing that the companies would pay US$206 billion to cover the cost of treating smoking-related illnesses.

Health risks In the UK in 1988 33% of men and 30% of women were smokers (a decrease on the 1972 figures of 52% and 41%). UK figures in 1991 showed that smoking kills around 113,000 people per year from related diseases, more than the entire number of deaths from road accidents, drug misuse, AIDS, and alcohol put together. Approximately 50% of smokers die as a result of smoking-related diseases, while a study of smoking in British male doctors 1951–94 indicated that the death rate in middle age was three times higher for smokers than for those who have never smoked. The National Health Service spends up to £500 million a year caring for people with severe illnesses directly related to smoking.

Manufacturers have attempted to filter out harmful substances such as tar and nicotine, and to use milder tobaccos, and governments have carried out extensive antismoking advertising campaigns. In the UK and the USA all cigarette packaging must carry a government health warning, and television advertising of cigarettes is forbidden.

Passive smoking UK and Australian studies in 1991 showed that passive smoking is a cause of lung cancer. In the USA the Environmental Protection Agency estimated in 1994 that 30,000 nonsmokers die annually as a result of passive smoking. Cigarette smoke contains at least 40 known ▷carcinogens. US research in 1994 showed that one carcinogen, found only in tobacco products, can be detected in the urine of nonsmokers after exposure for 90 minutes to conditions typical of a smoky room. In 1996 US research indicated that 88% of US nonsmokers have detectable levels of the nicotine breakdown product cotinine in their blood.

Children whose parents smoke suffer an increased risk of asthma and respiratory infections. A UK study in 1996 into the smoking habits of parents whose children have died of cancer concluded that the fathers were more likely to have been heavy smokers. However, as the mothers' smoking habits seemed to have little influence, the researchers concluded that the cancers arose not as a result of passive smoking by the children, but because of mutations within the fathers' sperm.

Related Web site: Action on Smoking and Health (ASH)
http://www.ash.org.uk/

Smollett, Tobias George (1721–1771) Scottish novelist. He wrote the picaresque novels *Roderick Random* (1748), *Peregrine Pickle* (1751), *Ferdinand Count Fathom* (1753), *Sir Launcelot Greaves* (1760–62), and *Humphrey Clinker* (1771). His novels are full of gusto and vivid characterization.

smooth snake common nonvenomous snake found in southern and central Europe. It grows to a length of 60 cm/24 in, and it is brownish-red or grey in colour, with dark-brown spots along its back. It is ovoviviparous, producing live young that free themselves from their shells immediately. The smooth snake *Coronella austriaca* is in family Colubridae, suborder Serpentes, order Squamata, class Reptilia.

smuggling illegal import or export of prohibited goods or the evasion of customs duties on dutiable goods. Smuggling has a long tradition in most border and coastal regions; goods smuggled include tobacco, spirits, diamonds, gold, and illegal drugs.

Restrictions on imports, originally a means of preventing debasement of coinage (for example, in 14th-century England), were later used for raising revenue, mainly on luxury goods, and led to a flourishing period of smuggling during the 18th century in such goods as wine, brandy, tea, tobacco, and lace. Until the mid-19th century the islanders of Scilly, UK, poor in natural resources, thought little of the round trip to France in their long boats to bring back contraband.

smut in botany, any of a group of parasitic fungi (see ▷fungus) that infect flowering plants, particularly cereal grasses. (Order Ustilaginales.)

Smuts, Jan Christian (1870–1950) South African politician and soldier; prime minister 1919–24 and 1939–48. He supported the Allies in both world wars and was a member of the British imperial war cabinet 1917–18.

Smyrna ancient city near the modern Turkish port of ▷Izmir. The earliest remains date from the 3rd millennium BC, and excavations have revealed that by the 8th century BC the city had a circuit of defensive walls. This is one of the earliest signs of the revival of Greek culture after the collapse of the ▷Mycenaean civilization.

snail air-breathing gastropod mollusc with a spiral shell. There are thousands of species, on land and in water. The typical snails of the genus *Helix* have two species in Europe. The common garden snail *H. aspersa* is very destructive to plants.

> ### Stevie Smith
> *I was much too far out all my life / And not waving but drowning.*
> 'Not Waving but Drowning'

SNAIL The European white-lipped or garden snail *Cepaea hortensis* is a typical gastropod, having a coiled shell, a single extending foot, and two pairs of retractable sensory tentacles. The visceral mass comprising the main body organs remains permanently within the protection of the shell. *Premaphotos Wildlife*

Snails are hermaphrodite and, before mating, produce a mucus covered calcerous 'love dart' that pierces the skin of their mate. The mucus contains a pheromone that makes the female reproductive canal less hostile to sperm.

The Roman snail *H. pomatia* is 'corralled' for the gourmet food market. Overcollection has depleted the population. The French eat as much as 5 kg/11 lb of snails a head each year.

Snake (formerly **Lewis**) river in northwest USA, the largest tributary of the Columbia River; 1,670 km/1,038 mi in length. Rising as the South Fork in a lake 2,375 m/7,790 ft above sea-level in the ▷Yellowstone National Park, Wyoming, it flows southwest through Idaho, turning north to form the border of Idaho between Oregon and then Washington, and joining the Columbia near Pasco. Its course travels 65 km/40 mi through the 2,400 m/7,874 ft-deep Hell's Canyon, one of the deepest gorges in the world.

snake reptile of the suborder Serpentes of the order Squamata, which also includes lizards. Snakes are characterized by an elongated limbless body, possibly evolved because of subterranean ancestors. However, a team of US and Israeli palaeontologists rediscovered a fossil collection in 1996 which suggested that snakes evolved from sea-dwelling predators.

One of the striking internal modifications is the absence or greatly reduced size of the left lung. The skin is covered in scales, which are markedly wider underneath where they form. There are 3,000 species found in the tropical and temperate zones, but none in New Zealand, Ireland, Iceland, and near the poles. Only three species are found in Britain: the adder, smooth snake, and grass snake.

Locomotion In all except a few species, scales are an essential aid to locomotion. A snake is helpless on glass where scales can effect no 'grip' on the surface; progression may be undulant, 'concertina', or creeping, or a combination of these.

Senses Detailed vision is limited at a distance, though movement is immediately seen; hearing is restricted to ground vibrations (sound waves are not perceived); the sense of touch is acute; besides the sense of smell through the nasal passages, the flickering tongue picks up airborne particles which are then passed to special organs in the mouth for investigation; and some (rattlesnakes) have a cavity between eye and nostril which is sensitive to infrared rays (useful in locating warm-blooded prey in the dark).

Reproduction Some are oviparous and others ovoviviparous, that is, the eggs are retained in the oviducts until development is complete; in both cases the young are immediately self-sufficient.

Species The majority of snakes belong to the Colubridae family, and are chiefly harmless, such as the common grass snake of Europe, but this family includes the deadly African boomslang *Dispholidus typus*. The venomous families include the Elapidae, comprising the true ▷cobras, the New World coral snakes, and the Australian taipan, copper-head, and death adder; the Viperidae (see ▷viper); and the Hydrophiidae, aquatic sea-snakes.

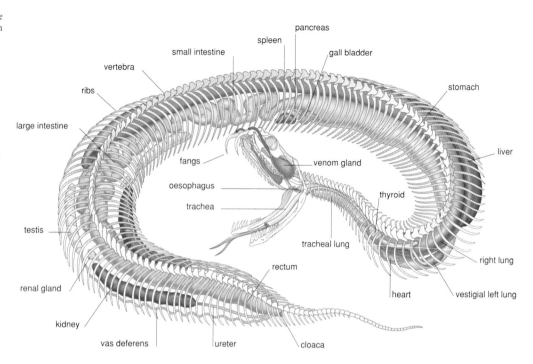

SNAKE The anatomy of a snake (male). A snake's skeleton contains over 400 spinal bones. Its internal organs lie in the linear body cavity enclosed by the ribs.

Among the more primitive snakes are the Boidae, which still show links with lizards and include the boa constrictor, anaconda, and python. These kill by constriction but their victims are usually comparatively small animals.

All snakes are carnivorous, and often camouflaged for better concealment in hunting as well as for their own protection.

Treatment of snakebite There are 50,000–100,000 deaths from snake bites worldwide annually, it was announced in September 2000. The serums used to treat snakebites are called antivenins. Antivenins are produced by injecting animals (horses and sheep are used) with venom, extracting their blood, now containing antibodies to the venom, and removing the red blood cells. However, in addition to the desired venom antibodies, many other antibodies and proteins are contained within the serum. These often cause 'serum sickness' in the patient, as a result of a severe allergenic reaction.

As antivenins are expensive to prepare and store, and specific to one snake species, experiments have been carried out using more widely valid treatments, for example, trypsin, a powerful protein-degrading enzyme, effective against the cobra/mamba group.

In 1993 Japanese and Brazilian researchers independently identified a protein in the blood of a venomous snake that neutralizes its own venom. In laboratory tests in Australia, this protein, named *Notechis scutatus* inhibitor (NSI) after the tiger snake from the whose blood it was isolated, was effective against the venom of six other snakes.

Related Web site: Slithering Snakes http://www2.excite.sfu.ca/pgm/students/alex_reid/snakes/MAINPAGE.HTM

snakebird (or **darter**) water bird of genus *Anhinga*, related to the cormorant and pelican, forming the family Anhingidae, order Pelecaniformes. They swim in lakes, rivers, or seas with only the head on the long neck showing above water, moving sinuously, then darting forward to seize a fish, the neck vertebrae being specially adapted for flexibility. The snakebirds are widely distributed throughout Central and South America, South Asia, and Australia, and vary little in colour.

snake fly elongate insect found in wooded regions, among flowers or tree-trunks. More than 80 species are known.

snapdragon perennial ▷herbaceous plant belonging to the figwort family, with spikes of brightly coloured two-lipped flowers. (*Antirrhinum majus*, family Scrophulariaceae.)

Related Web site: Snapdragon http://www.gardenguides.com/flowers/annuals/snapdrag.htm

snapper one of a number of tropical, carnivorous fish, about 60 cm/24 in or more in length. Many are red, but the species come in many colours. They are valuable edible fishes, especially the red snapper *Lutjanus blackfordi*. Snappers are in the family Lutjanidae of order Perciformes, class Osteichthyes.

Snell's law of refraction in optics, the rule that when a ray of light passes from one medium to another, the sine of the angle of incidence divided by the sine of the angle of refraction is equal to the ratio of the indices of refraction in the two media. For a ray passing from medium 1 to medium 2: $n_2/n_1 = \sin i/\sin r$ where n_1 and n_2 are the refractive indices of the two media. The law was devised by the Dutch physicist, Willebrord Snell.

snipe marsh bird of the family Scolopacidae, order Charadriiformes closely related to the ▷woodcock. Snipes use their long, straight bills to probe marshy ground for worms, insects, and molluscs. Their nests are made on the grass, and they lay four eggs.

snooker indoor game derived from ▷billiards (via pool). It is played with 22 balls: 15 red, one each of yellow, green, brown, blue, pink, and black, and one white cueball. A tapered pole (cue) is used to move the balls across the table. Red balls are worth one point when sunk, while the coloured balls have ascending values from two points for the yellow to seven points for the black.

The world professional championship was first held in 1927. The world amateur championship was first held in 1963. A snooker World Cup team event was inaugurated at Bangkok, Thailand, in 1996. The International Olympic Committee recognized snooker as an Olympic sport in 1998; snooker is likely to make its Olympic debut at the Athens games in 2004.

Related Web site: Snooker Net http://www.snookernet.com/

snoring loud noise during sleep made by vibration of the soft palate (the rear part of the roof of the mouth), caused by streams of air entering the nose and mouth at the same time. It is most common when the nose is partially blocked.

SNAKE A flying tree-snake from southeast Asia. These snakes are able to glide through the air for short distances by adjusting their ventral scales and making their bellies concave. *Image Bank*

SNAPPER Snapper fish are found in abundance throughout the tropics, such as this one in the Tuamotu Islands of French Polynesia. *Image Bank*

snowboarding art of riding across snow standing on a snowboard, a wide single ski resembling a small surf board, with bindings to secure the feet. Snowboards can be ridden at speed on downhill runs and slalom courses, as in Alpine skiing, or used to perform jumps and other manoeuvres, a discipline known as freestyle or halfpipe riding (a halfpipe being a banked course carved out of snow).

SNOWBOARDING Snowboarding in Colorado, USA. *Image Bank*

Snowdon (Welsh **Eryri**) highest mountain in Wales, 1,085 m/3,560 ft above sea level. Situated 16 km/10 mi southeast of the Menai Strait, it consists of a cluster of five peaks. At the foot of Snowdon are the Llanberis, Aberglaslyn, and Rhyd-ddu passes. A rack railway ascends to the summit from Llanberis. ▷Snowdonia, the surrounding mountain range, was made a national park in 1951. It covers 2,188 sq km/845 sq mi of mountain, lakes, and forest land.

Snowdonia mountainous region of north Wales, comprising three massifs above 1,000 m/3,280 ft divided by the passes of Llanberis and Nant Ffrancon: ▷Snowdon (Welsh *Yr Wddfa*), the Glyders, and the Carnedds (including Carnedd Dafydd and Carnedd Llewelyn). Snowdonia was designated a National Park in 1951. The park area of 2,188 sq km/845 sq mi dominates Gwynedd and extends eastwards into Conwy county borough.

snowdrop small bulbous European plant; its white bell-shaped hanging flowers, tinged with green, are among the first to appear in early spring. (*Galanthus nivalis*, family Amaryllidaceae.)

SNOWDROP Snowdrops flower in the early spring when snow may still be on the ground in the woodlands and shrubland of Europe. The small drooping flowers hang about 15 cm/6 in above the ground. They have six petals, the three inner ones having a green patch.

snow leopard a type of ▷leopard.

Snowy Mountains range in the Australian Alps, chiefly in New South Wales, near which the **Snowy River** rises; both river and mountains are known for a hydroelectric and irrigation system.

Soane, John (1753–1837) English architect. His refined neoclassical designs anticipated contemporary taste. Soane was a master of the established conventions of classical architecture, he also developed a highly individual style based on an elegantly mannered interpretation of neoclassicism. He designed his own house in Lincoln's Inn Fields, London (1812–13), now **Sir John Soane's Museum**, which he bequeathed to the nation in 1835, together with his collection of antiques, architectural elements and casts, papers, and drawings. Little remains of his extensive work at the Bank of England, London (rebuilt 1930–40).

Related Web site: Sir John Soane's Museum http://www.soane.org/

soap mixture of the sodium salts of various ▷fatty acids: palmitic, stearic, and oleic acid. It is made by the action of sodium hydroxide (caustic soda) or potassium hydroxide (caustic potash) on fats of animal or vegetable origin. Soap makes grease and dirt disperse in water in a similar manner to a ▷detergent.

Soap was mentioned by Galen in the 2nd century for washing the body, although the Romans seem to have washed with a mixture of sand and oil. Soap was manufactured in Britain from the 14th century, but better-quality soap was imported from Castile or Venice. The Soapmakers' Company, London, was incorporated in 1638. Soap was taxed in England from the time of Cromwell in the 17th century to 1853.

soapstone compact, massive form of impure ▷talc.

Soares, Mario Alberto Nobre Lopes (1924–) Portuguese socialist politician, president 1986–96. Exiled in 1970, he returned to Portugal in 1974, and, as leader of the Portuguese Socialist Party, was prime minister 1976–78. He resigned as party leader in 1980, but in 1986 he was elected Portugal's first socialist president.

Sobers, Garry (Garfield St Auburn) (1936–) West Indian Test cricketer, arguably the world's finest ever all-rounder. He held the world individual record for the highest Test innings with 365 not out, until beaten by Brian Lara in 1994. He played county cricket for Nottinghamshire and, in a match against Glamorgan at Swansea in 1968, he became the first cricketer to score six sixes in an over in first-class cricket. He played for the West Indies on 93 occasions, and was captain 39 times. He was knighted for services to cricket in 1975.

Sobieski, John alternative name for ▷John III, king of Poland.

Social and Liberal Democrats official name for the British political party formed in 1988 from the former Liberal Party and most of the Social Democratic Party. The common name for the party is the ▷Liberal Democrats.

social behaviour in zoology, behaviour concerned with altering the behaviour of other individuals of the same species. Social behaviour allows animals to live harmoniously in groups by establishing hierarchies of dominance to discourage disabling fighting. It may be aggressive or submissive (for example, cowering and other signals of appeasement), or designed to establish bonds (such as social grooming or preening).

Social Chapter chapter of the 1991 ▷Maastricht Treaty on European Union relating to social policy. It required European Community (EC) member states to adopt common social policies and was intended to implement the Community Charter of Fundamental Social Rights, which was adopted by 11 EC member states, but opposed by British prime minister Margaret Thatcher, at a summit meeting in Strasbourg in December 1989.

In the face of continued UK opposition, member states were given freedom of choice over whether or not to adopt it; only the UK declined to sign up to it at the time. However, Tony Blair's Labour government signed it in 1997.

social contract the idea that government authority derives originally from an agreement between ruler and ruled in which the former agrees to provide order in return for obedience from the latter. It has been used to support both absolutism (Thomas ▷Hobbes) and democracy (John ▷Locke, Jean-Jacques ▷Rousseau).

social costs and benefits in economics, the costs and benefits to society as a whole that result from economic decisions. These include private costs (the financial cost of production incurred by firms) and benefits (the profits made by firms and the value to people of consuming goods and services) and external costs and benefits (affecting those not directly involved in production or consumption); pollution is one of the external costs.

social Darwinism see ▷Darwinism, social.

social democracy political ideology or belief in the gradual evolution of a democratic ▷socialism within existing political structures. The earliest was the German *Sozialdemokratische Partei* (SPD), now one of the two main German parties, which had been created in 1875 by the amalgamation of other groups including August Bebel's earlier German Social Democratic Workers' Party, founded in 1869. Parties along the lines of the German model were founded in the last two decades of the 19th century in a number of countries, including Austria, Belgium, the Netherlands, Hungary, Poland, and Russia. The British Labour Party is in the social democratic tradition.

Social Democratic and Labour Party (SDLP) Northern Ireland left-of-centre political party, formed in 1970. It aims ultimately at Irish unification, but has distanced itself from violent tactics, adopting a constitutional, conciliatory role. Its leader, John Hume, played a key role in the negotiations which ended in the 1998 Good Friday Agreement on power-sharing. It secured 24 of the 108 seats in the new Northern Ireland Assembly, elected in June 1998; the party's deputy leader, Seamus Mallon, was voted deputy first minister (to Ulster Unionist David Trimble) by the first meeting of the Assembly.

Social Democratic Federation (SDF) in British history, a socialist society, founded as the Democratic Federation in 1881 and renamed in 1884. It was led by H M Hyndman (1842–1921), a former conservative journalist and stockbroker who claimed Karl ▷Marx as his inspiration without obtaining recognition from his mentor. In 1911 it became the British Socialist Party.

Social Democratic Party (SDP) British centrist political party 1981–90, formed by members of Parliament who resigned from the Labour Party. The 1983 and 1987 general elections were fought in alliance with the Liberal Party as the **Liberal/SDP Alliance**. A merger of the two parties was voted for by the SDP in 1987, and the new party became the ▷Social and Liberal Democrats, leaving a rump SDP that folded in 1990.

social history branch of history that documents the living and working conditions of people rather than affairs of state. In recent years, television programmes, books, and museums have helped to give social history a wide appeal.

socialism movement aiming to establish a classless society by substituting public for private ownership of the means of production, distribution, and exchange. The term has been used to describe positions as widely apart as anarchism and social democracy. Socialist ideas appeared in classical times; in early Christianity; among later Christian sects such as the ▷Anabaptists and ▷Diggers; and, in the 18th and early 19th centuries, were put forward as systematic political aims by Jean-Jacques Rousseau, Claude Saint-Simon, François Fourier, and Robert Owen, among others. See also Karl ▷Marx and Friedrich ▷Engels.

'socialism in one country' concept proposed by the Soviet dictator Stalin in 1924. In contrast to Leon Trotsky's theory of permanent revolution, Stalin suggested that the emphasis be changed away from promoting revolutions abroad to the idea of building socialism, economically and politically, in the USSR without help from other countries.

socialist realism officially approved type of art in the former USSR and other communist countries; in line with communist doctrine, art was expected to educate and inspire the people with optimistic works extolling the virtues of work and patriotism, but in effect it was mainly devoted to glorifying the state. In Soviet Russia, as in other totalitarian countries, the government controlled all artistic organizations, and all forms of artistic experimentation were seen as a sign of decadent Western influence. Although the term is used mainly with reference to painting, it can apply to literature and music.

socialization process, beginning in childhood, by which a person becomes a member of a society, learning its norms, customs, laws, and ways of living. The main agents of socialization are the family, school, peer groups, work, religion, and the mass media. The main methods of socialization are direct instruction, rewards and punishment, imitation, experimentation, role play, and interaction.

social mobility movement of groups and individuals up and down the social scale in a classed society. The extent or range of social mobility varies in different societies. Individual social mobility may occur through education, marriage, talent, and so on; group mobility usually occurs through change in the occupational structure caused by new technological or economic developments.

social realism in painting, art that realistically depicts subjects of social concern, such as poverty and deprivation. Those described as social realists include: in the USA, members of the ▷Ashcan School and Ben Shahn; in the UK, the 'kitchen-sink group', for example John Bratby; and in Mexico, the muralists José Orozco and Diego Rivera.

social science the group of academic disciplines that investigate how and why people behave the way they do, as individuals and in groups. The term originated with the 19th-century French thinker Auguste ▷Comte. The academic social sciences are generally listed as sociology, economics, anthropology, political science, and psychology.

social security state provision of financial aid to alleviate poverty. The term 'social security' was first applied officially in the USA, in the Social Security Act of 1935. In Britain it was first used officially in 1944, and following the ▷Beveridge Report of 1942 a series of acts was passed from 1945 to widen the scope of social security. Basic entitlements of those paying National Insurance contributions in Britain include an old-age pension, unemployment benefit (known as jobseeker's allowance from October 1996), widow's pension, incapacity benefit, and payment during a period of sickness in one's working life (Statutory Sick Pay). Other benefits, which are non-contributory, include family credit, ▷income support, child benefit, and attendance allowance for those looking after sick or disabled people. It was announced in the March 1998 budget that family credit and the disabled working allowance would be replaced from October 1999 by a working families tax credit and disabled persons tax credit, to be administered by the Inland Revenue.

Society Islands (French **Archipel de la Société**) archipelago in ▷French Polynesia, divided into the Windward Islands and the Leeward Islands; area 1,685 sq km/650 sq mi; population (1995 est) 178,000. The administrative headquarters is Papeete on ▷Tahiti. The **Windward Islands** (French **Iles du Vent**) have an area of 1,200 sq km/460 sq mi and a population (1995 est) of 151,000. They comprise Tahiti, Moorea (area 132 sq km/51 sq mi), Maio (or Tubuai Manu; 9 sq km/3.5 sq mi), and the smaller Tetiaroa and Mehetia. The **Leeward Islands** (French **Iles sous le Vent**) have an area of 404 sq km/156 sq mi and a population of 27,000 (1995 est). They comprise the volcanic islands of Raiatea (including the main town of Uturoa), Huahine, Bora-Bora, Maupiti, Tahaa, and four small atolls. The islands were named after the ▷Royal Society by Captain Cook, who visited them in 1769. Claimed by France in 1768, the group became a French protectorate in 1843, and a colony in 1880. Products include copra, phosphates, mother-of-pearl, and vanilla.

SOCIETY ISLANDS Moorea Island is part of French Polynesia. It is situated 19 km/12 mi west of the island of Tahiti and is the second largest island (after Tahiti) in the Windward group of the Society Islands. *Image Bank*

Society of Jesus official name of the Roman Catholic order commonly known as the ▷Jesuits.

Socinianism 17th-century Christian belief that rejects such traditional doctrines as the Trinity and original sin, named after **Socinus**, the Latinized name of Lelio Francesco Maria Sozzini (1525–1562), Italian Protestant theologian. It is an early form of ▷Unitarianism.

sociobiology study of the biological basis of all social behaviour, including the application of population genetics to the evolution of behaviour. It builds on the concept of ▷inclusive fitness, contained in the notion of the 'selfish gene'. Contrary to some popular interpretations, it does not assume that all behaviour is genetically determined.

sociology systematic study of the origin and constitution of human society, in particular of social order and social change, social conflict and social problems. It studies institutions such as the family, law, and the church, as well as concepts such as norm, role, and culture. Sociology attempts to study people in their social environment according to certain underlying moral, philosophical, and political codes of behaviour.

> **Socrates**
> *Nothing can harm a good man, either in life or after death.*
> Quoted in Plato *Apology* 42

Socrates (*c.* 469–399 BC) Athenian philosopher. He wrote nothing but was immortalized in the dialogues of his pupil Plato. In his desire to combat the scepticism of the ▷sophists, Socrates asserted the possibility of genuine knowledge. In ethics, he put forward the view that the good person never knowingly does wrong. True knowledge emerges through dialogue and systematic questioning and an abandoning of uncritical claims to knowledge.

The effect of Socrates' teaching was disruptive since he opposed tyranny. Accused in 399 on charges of impiety and corruption of youth, he was condemned by the Athenian authorities to die by drinking hemlock, which he is said to have taken willingly.

Related Web site: Last Days of Socrates http://socrates.clarke.edu/

Socratic method method of teaching used by Socrates, in which he aimed to guide pupils to clear thinking on ethics and politics by asking questions and then exposing their inconsistencies in cross-examination. This method was effective against the ▷sophists.

Soddy, Frederick (1877–1956) English physical chemist who pioneered research into atomic disintegration and coined the term ▷isotope. He was awarded the Nobel Prize for Chemistry in 1921 for investigating the origin and nature of isotopes.

sodium soft, waxlike, silver-white, metallic element, symbol Na (from Latin *natrium*), atomic number 11, relative atomic mass 22.989. It is one of the ▷alkali metals and has a very low density, being light enough to float on water. It is the sixth-most abundant element (the fourth-most abundant metal) in the Earth's crust. Sodium is highly reactive, oxidizing rapidly when exposed to air and reacting violently with water. Its most familiar compound is sodium chloride (common salt), which occurs naturally in the oceans and in salt deposits left by dried-up ancient seas.

Other sodium compounds used industrially include sodium hydroxide (caustic soda, NaOH), sodium carbonate (washing soda, Na_2CO_3) and hydrogencarbonate (sodium bicarbonate, $NaHCO_3$), sodium nitrate (saltpetre, $NaNO_3$, used as a fertilizer), and sodium thiosulphate (hypo, $Na_2S_2O_3$, used as a photographic fixer). Thousands of tons of these are manufactured annually. Sodium metal is used to a limited extent in spectroscopy, in discharge lamps, and alloyed with potassium as a heat-transfer medium in nuclear reactors.

It was isolated from caustic soda in 1807 by English chemist Humphry Davy.

sodium chloride (or **common salt** or **table salt**) NaCl white, crystalline compound found widely in nature. It is a typical ionic solid with a high melting point (801°C/1,474°F); it is soluble in water, insoluble in organic solvents, and is a strong electrolyte when molten or in aqueous solution. Found in concentrated deposits, it is widely used in the food industry as a flavouring and preservative, and in the chemical industry in the manufacture of sodium, chlorine, and sodium carbonate.

sodium hydroxide (or **caustic soda**) NaOH the commonest alkali. The solid and the solution are corrosive. It is used to neutralize acids, in the manufacture of soap, and in oven cleaners. It is prepared industrially from sodium chloride by the ▷electrolysis of concentrated brine.

Sodom and Gomorrah two ancient cities in the Dead Sea area of the Middle East, recorded in the Old Testament (Genesis) as being destroyed by fire and brimstone for their wickedness.

Sofia (or **Sofiya**) capital of Bulgaria since 1878; population (1991) 1,221,000. Industries include textiles, rubber, machinery, and electrical equipment. It lies at the foot of the Vitosha Mountains.

History Sofia was of great importance in Roman times, when it was known as Serdica, especially under the emperor Constantine in the 4th century AD. As part of the Byzantine Empire, it was of strategic importance as it was on the road linking Constantinople and Belgrade. It was captured by the Turks 1382 and became part of the Ottoman Empire until chosen as capital of the newly independent state of Bulgaria in 1878.

Features 4th-century rotunda of St George's church; ruins of Serdica; 6th-century church of Sveta Sofia; 13th-century Boyana church; Banya bashi mosque (1576); Alexsandar Nevski memorial church (1924); mausoleum of Georgi Dimitrov (1949).

soft currency vulnerable currency that tends to fall in value on foreign-exchange markets because of political or economic uncertainty.

Governments are unwilling to hold soft currencies in their foreign-exchange reserves, preferring strong or hard currencies, which are easily convertible.

software in computing, a collection of programs and procedures for making a computer perform a specific task, as opposed to ▷hardware, the physical components of a computer system. Software is created by programmers and is either distributed on a suitable medium, such as the ▷floppy disk, or built into the computer in the form of ▷firmware. Examples of software include ▷operating systems, ▷compilers, and applications such as payroll or word processing programs. No computer can function without some form of software.

To function, computers need two types of software: application software and systems software. **Application software**, such as a payroll system or a ▷word processor, is designed for the benefit of the end user. **Systems software** performs tasks related to the operation and performance of the computer system itself. For example, a systems program might control the operation of the display screen, or control and organize backing storage.

soft water water that contains very few dissolved metal ions such as calcium (Ca^{2+}) or magnesium (Mg^{2+}). It lathers easily with soap, and no ▷scale is formed inside kettles or boilers. It has been found that the incidence of heart disease is higher in soft-water areas.

softwood any coniferous tree (see ▷conifer), or the wood from it. In general this type of wood is softer and easier to work, but in some cases less durable, than wood from flowering (or angiosperm) trees.

soil loose covering of broken rocky material and decaying organic matter overlying the bedrock of the Earth's surface. It is comprised of minerals, organic matter (called ▷humus) derived from decomposed plants and organisms, living organisms, air, and water. Soils differ according to climate, parent material, rainfall, relief of the bedrock, and the proportion of organic material. The study of soils is **pedology**.

A soil can be described in terms of its **soil profile**, that is, a vertical cross-section from ground-level to the bedrock on which the soils sits. The profile is divided into layers called horizons. The A horizon, or topsoil, is the uppermost layer, consisting primarily of humus and living organisms and some mineral material. Most soluble material has been leached from this layer or washed down to the B horizon. The B horizon, or subsoil, is the layer where most of the nutrients accumulate and is enriched in clay minerals. The C horizon is the layer of weathered parent material at the base of the soil.

Two common soils are the ▷podzol and the **chernozem** soil. The podzol is common in coniferous forest regions where precipitation exceeds evaporation. The A horizon consists of a very thin litter of organic material producing a poor humus. Needles take a long time to decompose. The relatively heavy precipitation causes ▷leaching of minerals, as nutrients are washed downwards.

Chernozem soils are found in grassland regions, where evaporation exceeds precipitation. The A horizon is rich in humus due to decomposition of a thick litter of dead grass at the surface. Minerals and moisture migrate upward due to evaporation, leaving the B and A horizons enriched.

The organic content of soil is widely variable, ranging from zero in some desert soils to almost 100% in peats.

Soils influence the type of agriculture employed in a particular region – light well-drained soils favour arable farming, whereas heavy clay soils give rise to lush pasture land.

soil creep gradual movement of soil down a slope in response to gravity. This eventually results in a mass downward movement of soil on the slope.

soil depletion decrease in soil quality over time. Causes include loss of nutrients caused by overfarming, erosion by wind, and chemical imbalances caused by acid rain.

soil erosion the wearing away and redistribution of the Earth's soil layer.

It is caused by the action of water, wind, and ice, and also by improper methods of ▷agriculture. If unchecked, soil erosion results in the formation of deserts (▷desertification). It has been estimated that 20% of the world's cultivated topsoil was lost between 1950 and 1990.

If the rate of erosion exceeds the rate of soil formation (from rock and decomposing organic matter), then the land will become infertile. The removal of forests (▷deforestation) or other vegetation often leads to serious soil erosion, because plant roots

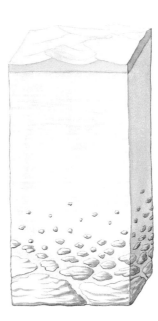

SOIL
Common
types of
soil profile.

chernozem   podzol   desert   rainforest

bind soil, and without them the soil is free to wash or blow away, as in the American ▷dust bowl. The effect is worse on hillsides, and there has been devastating loss of soil where forests have been cleared from mountainsides, as in Madagascar.

Improved agricultural practices such as contour ploughing are needed to combat soil erosion. Windbreaks, such as hedges or strips planted with coarse grass, are valuable, and organic farming can reduce soil erosion by as much as 75%.

Soil degradation and erosion are becoming as serious as the loss of the rainforest. It is estimated that more than 10% of the world's soil lost a large amount of its natural fertility during the latter half of the 20th century. Some of the worst losses are in Europe, where 17% of the soil is damaged by human activity such as mechanized farming and fallout from acid rain. Mexico and Central America have 24% of soil highly degraded, mostly as a result of deforestation.

soil mechanics branch of engineering that studies the nature and properties of the soil. Soil is investigated during construction work to ensure that it has the mechanical properties necessary to support the foundations of dams, bridges, and roads.

Sokoto state in Nigeria, established 1976; capital Sokoto; area 102,500 sq km/39,565 sq mi; population (1991) 4,392,400. It was an Islamic ▷Fula sultanate from the 16th century until occupied by the British in 1903.

sol ▷colloid of very small solid particles dispersed in a liquid that retains the physical properties of a liquid.

solan goose another name for the ▷gannet.

solar energy energy derived from the Sun's radiation. The amount of energy falling on just 1 sq km/0.3861 sq mi is about 4,000 megawatts, enough to heat and light a small town. In one second the Sun gives off 13 million times more energy than all the electricity used in the USA in one year. **Solar heaters** have industrial or domestic uses. They usually consist of a black (heat-absorbing) panel containing pipes through which air or water, heated by the Sun, is circulated, either by thermal ▷convection or by a pump.

Solar energy may also be harnessed indirectly using **solar cells** (photovoltaic cells) made of panels of ▷semiconductor material (usually silicon), which generate electricity when illuminated by sunlight. Although it is difficult to generate a high output from solar energy compared to sources such as nuclear or fossil fuels, it is a major nonpolluting and renewable energy source used as far north as Scandinavia as well as in the southwestern USA and in Mediterranean countries.

Related Web sites: One Life for Solar Power http://www.xs4all.nl/~solomon/
Solar Energy: Basic Facts http://www.brookes.ac.uk/other/uk-ises/facts.htm

solar flare brilliant eruption on the Sun above a ▷sunspot, thought to be caused by release of magnetic energy. Flares reach maximum brightness within a few minutes, then fade away over about an hour. They eject a burst of atomic particles into space at up to 1,000 kps/600 mps. When these particles reach Earth they can cause radio blackouts, disruptions of the Earth's magnetic field, and ▷aurorae.

solar pond natural or artificial 'pond', such as the Dead Sea, in which salt becomes more soluble in the Sun's heat. Water at the bottom becomes saltier and hotter, and is insulated by the less salty water layer at the top. Temperatures at the bottom reach about 100°C/212°F and can be used to generate electricity.

solar radiation radiation given off by the Sun, consisting mainly of visible light, ▷ultraviolet radiation, and ▷infrared radiation, although the whole spectrum of ▷electromagnetic waves is present, from radio waves to X-rays. High-energy charged particles, such as electrons, are also emitted, especially from solar ▷flares. When these reach the Earth, they cause magnetic storms (disruptions of the Earth's magnetic field), which interfere with radio communications.

Solar System the ▷Sun (a star) and all the bodies orbiting it: the nine ▷planets (Mercury, Venus, Earth, Mars, Jupiter, Saturn, Uranus, Neptune, and Pluto), their moons, the asteroids, and the comets. The Sun contains 99.86% of the mass of the Solar System.

The Solar System gives every indication of being a strongly unified system having a common origin and development. It is isolated in space; all the planets go round the Sun in orbits that are nearly circular and coplanar, and in the same direction as the Sun itself rotates; moreover this same pattern is continued in the regular system of satellites that accompany Jupiter, Saturn, and Uranus. It is thought to have formed by condensation from a cloud of gas and dust in space about 4.6 billion years ago.

Related Web sites: Solar System Live http://www.fourmilab.ch/solar/solar.html
Space Telescope Electronic Information Service http://www.stsci.edu/

solar wind stream of atomic particles, mostly protons and electrons, from the Sun's corona, flowing outwards at speeds of between 300 kps/200 mps and 1,000 kps/600 mps.

The fastest streams come from 'holes' in the Sun's corona that lie over areas where no surface activity occurs. The solar wind pushes the gas of comets' tails away from the Sun, and 'gusts' in the solar wind cause geomagnetic disturbances and aurorae on Earth.

solder any of various alloys used when melted for joining metals such as copper, its common alloys (brass and bronze), and tin-plated steel, as used for making food cans.

soldier beetle reddish beetle with soft, black elytra (wing cases) and a black patch and black legs. It reaches a length of 15 mm/0.5 in and can be found in the daytime during the months of April to July on field, garden, and forest plants. It feeds particularly on aphids.

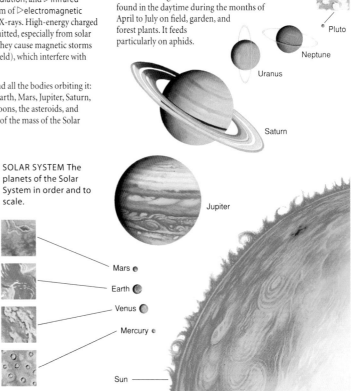

SOLAR SYSTEM The planets of the Solar System in order and to scale.

Pluto
Neptune
Uranus
Saturn
Jupiter
Mars
Earth
Venus
Mercury
Sun

Its larvae are black, and are to be found in the soil or among moss. The soldier beetle is in family Cantharidae, order Coleoptera, class Insecta, phylum Arthropoda.

sole flatfish found in temperate and tropical waters. The **common sole** *Solea solea*, also called **Dover sole**, is found in the southern seas of northwestern Europe. Up to 50 cm/20 in long, it is a prized food fish, as is the **sand** or **French sole** *Pegusa lascaris* further south.

solenodon rare insectivorous shrewlike mammal, genus *Solenodon*. There are two species, one each on Cuba and Hispaniola. They are about 30 cm/12 in long with a 25 cm/10 in naked tail, shaggy hair, long, pointed snouts, and strong claws, and they produce venomous saliva. They are slow-moving, come out mostly at night, and eat insects, worms, and other invertebrate animals. They are threatened with extinction owing to introduced predators.

solenoid coil of wire, usually cylindrical, in which a magnetic field is created by passing an electric current through it (see ▷electromagnet). This field can be used to move an iron rod placed on its axis. Mechanical valves attached to the rod can be operated by switching the current on or off, so converting electrical energy into mechanical energy. Solenoids are used to relay energy from the battery of a car to the starter motor by means of the ignition switch.

Solent, the channel between the coast of Hampshire, southern England, and the Isle of ▷Wight. It is a yachting centre.

Solferino, Battle of Napoleon III's victory over the Austrians 1859 at a village near Verona, northern Italy, 8 km/5 mi south of Lake Garda.

solicitor in the UK, a member of one of the two branches of the English legal profession, the other being a ▷barrister.

A solicitor is a lawyer who provides all-round legal services (making wills, winding up estates, conveyancing, divorce, and litigation). A solicitor cannot appear at High Court level, but must brief a barrister on behalf of his or her client. Solicitors may become circuit judges and recorders.

Solicitor General in the UK, a law officer of the crown, deputy to the ▷Attorney General, a political appointee with ministerial rank.

solid in physics, a state of matter that holds its own shape (as opposed to a liquid, which takes up the shape of its container, or a gas, which totally fills its container). According to ▷kinetic theory, the atoms or molecules in a solid are not free to move but merely vibrate about fixed positions, such as those in crystal lattices.

Solidarity (Polish **Solidarność**) national confederation of independent trade unions in Poland, formed under the leadership of Lech ▷Wałęsa September 1980. An illegal organization from 1981 to 1989, it was then elected to head the Polish government. Divisions soon emerged in the leadership and in 1990 its political wing began to fragment (Wałęsa resigned as chairman in December of that year). In the September 1993 elections Solidarity gained less than 5% of the popular vote but, in September 1997, under the leadership of Marian Krzaklewski, Solidarity Electoral Action (AWS) won 34% of the vote and led the subsequent coalition government with Jerzy Buzek as prime minister.

solid-state circuit electronic circuit where all the components (resistors, capacitors, transistors, and diodes) and interconnections are made at the same time, and by the same processes, in or on one piece of single-crystal silicon. The small size of this construction accounts for its use in electronics for space vehicles and aircraft.

solifluction the downhill movement of topsoil that has become saturated with water. Solifluction is common in periglacial environments (those bordering glacial areas) during the summer months, when the frozen topsoil melts to form an unstable soggy mass. This may then flow slowly downhill under gravity to form a **solifluction lobe** (a tonguelike feature).

solipsism in philosophy, a view that maintains that the self is the only thing that can be known to exist. It is an extreme form of ▷scepticism. The solipsist sees himself or herself as the only individual in existence, assuming other people to be a reflection of his or her own consciousness.

Related Web site: Solipsism and the Problem of Other Minds http://www.utm.edu/research/iep/s/solipsis.htm

Solomon (*c.* 974–*c.* 922 BC) In the Old Testament, third king of Israel, son of David by Bathsheba. During a peaceful reign, he was famed for his wisdom and his alliances with Egypt and Phoenicia. The much later biblical Proverbs, Ecclesiastes, and Song of Songs are attributed to him. He built the temple in Jerusalem with the aid of heavy taxation and forced labour, resulting in the revolt of northern Israel.

The so-called **King Solomon's Mines** at Aqaba, Jordan (copper and iron), are of later date.

Solomon Islands see country box.

Solomon's seal any of a group of perennial plants belonging to the lily family, native to Europe and found growing in moist, shady woodland areas. They have drooping bell-like white or greenish-white flowers which appear just above the point where the leaves join the arching stems, followed by blue or black berries. (Genus *Polygonatum*, family Liliaceae.)

Solon (*c.* 638–*c.* 558 BC) Athenian statesman. As one of the chief magistrates about 594 BC, he carried out the cancellation of all debts from which land or liberty was the security and the revision of the constitution that laid the foundations of Athenian democracy. He was one of the Seven Sages of Greece.

solstice either of the days on which the Sun is farthest north or south of the celestial equator each year. The **summer solstice**, when the Sun is farthest north, occurs around 21 June; the **winter solstice** around 22 December.

Solti, Georg (1912–1997) Born György Stern. Hungarian-born British conductor. He was music director at the Royal Opera House, Covent Garden, London 1961–71, and director of the Chicago Symphony Orchestra 1969–91. He was also principal conductor of the London Philharmonic Orchestra 1979–83. He made more than 250 recordings, including 45 operas, throughout his recording career and was honoured with 32 Grammy awards – more than any other artist. He was made a KBE in 1971.

solubility measure of the amount of solute (usually a solid or gas) that will dissolve in a given amount of solvent (usually a liquid) at a particular temperature. Solubility may be expressed as grams of solute per 100 grams of solvent or, for a gas, in parts per million (ppm) of solvent.

solute substance that is dissolved in another substance (see ▷solution).

solution two or more substances mixed to form a single, homogenous phase. One of the substances is the **solvent** and the others (**solutes**) are said to be dissolved in it.

The constituents of a solution may be solid, liquid, or gaseous. The solvent is normally the substance that is present in greatest quantity; however, if one of the constituents is a liquid this is considered to be the solvent even if it is not the major substance.

solution (or **dissolution**) in earth science, the process by which the minerals in a rock are dissolved in water. Solution is one of the processes of ▷erosion as well as ▷weathering (in which the dissolution of rock occurs without transport of the dissolved material). An example of this is when weakly acidic rainfall dissolves calcite.

solvent substance, usually a liquid, that will dissolve another substance (see ▷solution). Although the commonest solvent is water, in popular use the term refers to low-boiling-point organic liquids, which are harmful if used in a confined space. They can give rise to respiratory problems, liver damage, and neurological complaints.

Typical organic solvents are petroleum distillates (in glues), xylol (in paints), alcohols (for synthetic and natural resins such as shellac), esters (in lacquers, including nail varnish), ketones (in cellulose lacquers and resins), and chlorinated hydrocarbons (as paint stripper and dry-cleaning fluids). The fumes of some solvents, when inhaled (▷glue-sniffing), affect mood and perception. In addition to damaging the brain and lungs, repeated inhalation of solvent from a plastic bag can cause death by asphyxia.

Solway Firth inlet of the Irish Sea, formed by the estuaries of the rivers Eden and Esk, at the western end of the border between England and Scotland, separating Cumbria in England from Dumfries and Galloway in Scotland. Solway Firth is in part the estuary of the River Esk, and in part an inlet of the Irish Sea.

Solyman I alternative spelling of ▷Suleiman, Ottoman sultan.

Solzhenitsyn, Alexander Isayevich (1918–) Russian novelist. He became a US citizen in 1974. He was in prison and exile 1945–57 for anti-Stalinist comments. Much of his writing is semi-autobiographical and highly critical of the system, including *One Day in the Life of Ivan Denisovich* (1962), which deals with the labour camps under Stalin, and *The Gulag Archipelago* (1973), an exposé of the whole Soviet labour-camp network. This led to his expulsion from the USSR in 1974. He was awarded the Nobel Prize for Literature in 1970.

Other works include *The First Circle* and *Cancer Ward*, (both 1968), and his historical novel *August 1914* (1971). His autobiography, *The Oak and the Calf*, appeared in 1980. He has adopted a Christian position, and his criticism of Western materialism is also stringent. In 1991, cleared of the original charges of treason, he returned to Russia.

Related Web site: Solzhenitsyn, Alexander http://members.aol.com/KatharenaE/private/Alsolz/alsolz.html

> **Alexander Solzhenitsyn**
>
> *You only have power over people as long as you don't take everything away from them. But when you've robbed a man of everything he's no longer in your power - he's free again.*
>
> The First Circle

soma intoxicating drink made from the fermented sap of the *Asclepias acida* plant, used in Indian religious ritual as a sacrifice to the gods. Its consumption also constituted the central rite in Zoroastrian ritual, where it was known as *haoma*. Some have argued that the plant was in fact a hallucogenic mushroom.

Somali member of a group of East African peoples from the Horn of Africa. Although the majority of Somalis live in the Somali Republic, there are minorities in Ethiopia and Kenya. Primarily nomadic pastoralists and traders, they live in families, grouped in clans, under an elective or hereditary chieftain. They are mainly Sunni Muslims. Their Cushitic language belongs to the Hamitic branch of the Afro-Asiatic family.

Somalia see country box.

Somaliland region of Somali-speaking peoples in eastern Africa including the former British Somaliland Protectorate (established 1887) and Italian Somaliland (made a colony 1927, conquered by Britain 1941, and administered by Britain until 1950) – which both became independent in 1960 as the Somali Democratic Republic, the official name for ▷Somalia – and former French Somaliland, which was established in 1888, became known as the Territory of the Afars and Issas in 1967, and became independent as ▷Djibouti in 1977.

Somerset county of southwest England.

area 3,460 sq km/1,336 sq mi **towns** ▷Taunton (administrative headquarters); Bridgwater, Frome, Glastonbury, Wells, Yeovil; Burnham-on-Sea, Minehead (coastal resorts) **physical** rivers Avon, Axe, Brue, Exe, Parret (the principal river), and Yeo; marshy coastline on the Bristol Channel; Mendip Hills; Quantock Hills; Exmoor; Blackdown Hills **features** Cheddar Gorge and Wookey Hole, a series of limestone caves where Stone Age flint implements and bones of extinct animals have been found; Glastonbury Tor **agriculture** apples; dairy farming; cereals (wheat, barley, oats), vegetables (turnips, mangolds (a root vegetable used as animal feed)); cider; cattle and sheep rearing; willows (withies) for wickerwork **industries** agricultural implements; Bath-bricks (manufactured at Bridgwater from the sand of the Parret); chemicals; dairy products (including Cheddar cheese); engineering; food processing; helicopters; leather; mineral working (iron, lead, zinc); stone quarrying (slate); textiles; tourism **population** (1996) 482,600 **famous people** Roger Bacon, Ernest Bevin, Arthur C Clarke, Henry Fielding, John Locke, John Pym

Somerset, Edward Seymour, 1st Duke of Somerset (*c.* 1506–1552) English politician. Created Earl of Hertford after Henry VIII's marriage to his sister Jane, he became Duke of Somerset and protector (regent) for Edward VI in 1547. His attempt to check ▷enclosure (the transfer of land from common to private ownership) offended landowners and his moderation in religion upset the Protestants. Knighted in 1523, viscount in 1536, earl in 1537, he was eventually beheaded on a treason charge in 1552.

Somme river in northern France, on which Amiens and Abbeville stand; length 245 km/152 mi. It rises in Aisne *département* near St Quentin and flows west through Somme *département* to the English Channel near St Valéry-sur-Somme. It is connected by canal with the Oise and the Schelde (French Escaut). Its tributaries include the rivers Ancre and Avre.

Some of the heaviest fighting of World War I took place on the banks of the Somme, especially in July–November 1916 (see ▷Somme, Battle of the).

Somme, Battle of the Allied offensive in World War I during July–November 1916 on the River Somme in northern France, during which severe losses were suffered by both sides. It was planned by the Marshal of France, Joseph Joffre, and UK commander-in-chief Douglas Haig; the Allies lost over 600,000 soldiers and advanced 13 km/8 mi. It was the first battle in which tanks were used. The German offensive around St Quentin during March–April 1918 is sometimes called the Second Battle of the Somme.

Somoza Debayle, Anastasio (1925–1980) Nicaraguan soldier and politician, president 1967–72 and 1974–79. The second son of Anastasio ▷Somoza García, he succeeded his brother Luis Somoza Debayle as president of Nicaragua in 1967, to head an even more oppressive and corrupt regime, characterized by tightened press censorship and rising popular discontent as the economic situation deteriorated. He was removed by Sandinista guerrillas in 1979 and assassinated in Paraguay in 1980.

Somoza García, Anastasio (1896–1956) Nicaraguan soldier and politician, president 1937–47 and 1950–56. As head of the Nicaraguan army, he deposed President Juan Bautista Sacasa, his uncle, in 1936 and assumed the presidency the following year, ruling as a virtual dictator from 1937 until his assassination in 1956. He exiled most of his political opponents and amassed a considerable fortune in land and businesses. Members of his family retained control of the country until 1979, when they were overthrown by popular forces.

sonar (acronym for sound navigation and ranging) method of locating underwater objects by the reflection of ultrasonic waves. The time taken for an acoustic beam to travel to the object and back to the source enables the distance to be found since the velocity of sound in water is known. Sonar devices, or **echo sounders**, were developed in 1920, and are the commonest means of underwater navigation.

The process is similar to that used in ▷radar. During and after World War I, the Allies developed and perfected an apparatus for detecting the presence of enemy U-boats beneath the sea surface by the use of ultrasonic echoes. It was originally named ASDIC, from the initials of the Allied Submarine Detection Investigation Committee responsible for its development, but in 1963 the name was changed to sonar.

sonata (Italian 'sounded') in music, an essay in instrumental composition for a solo player or a small ensemble and consisting of a single movement or series of movements. The name signifies that the work is not beholden to a text or existing dance form, but is self-sufficient.

sonata form in music, a method determining the structure of a movement, typically divided into exposition, development, and recapitulation sections. It introduced the new possibility of open and continuous development to an 18th-century music previously limited to closed dance routines. It developed initially in the instrumental ▷sonata, from which it took its name, even though its use extended throughout all genres; it is also particularly associated with the first movement of a work, giving the alternative name of **first movement form**.

son et lumière (French 'sound and light') outdoor night-time dramatization of the history of a notable building, monument, or town, using theatrical lighting effects, sound effects, music, and narration; it was invented by Paul Robert Houdin, curator of the Château de Chambord, France, and the first show was held here 1952.

song a setting of words to music for one or more singers, with or without instrumental accompaniment. Song may be sacred, for example a psalm, motet, or cantata, or secular, for example a folk song or ballad. In verse song, the text changes in mood while the music remains the same; in ▷lied and other forms of art song, the music changes in response to the emotional development of the text.

Related Web site: International Lyrics Server http://www.lyrics.ch

song cycle sequence of songs related in mood and sung as a group, used by romantic composers such as Franz Schubert, Robert Schumann, and Hugo Wolf.

Song dynasty (or **Sung dynasty**) (lived 10th–13th centuries) Chinese imperial family ruling from 960 to 1279, founded by northern general Taizu or Zhao Kuangyin (928–76). A distinction is conventionally made between the Northern Song period (960–1126), when the capital was at Kaifeng, and Southern Song (1127–1279), when it was at Hangzhou (Hangchow). A stable

---

Solomon Islands

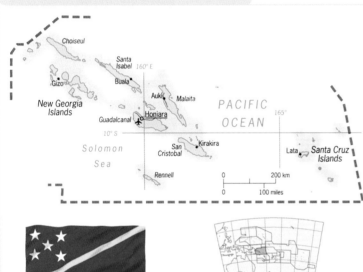

SOLOMON ISLANDS The Melanesian peoples of the Solomon Islands have a long cultural history. These Aliki children are wearing traditional dress, and learn about their heritage through stories and songs. *Corel*

Solomon Islands country in the southwest Pacific Ocean, east of New Guinea, comprising many hundreds of islands, the largest of which is Guadalcanal.

AREA 27,600 sq km/10,656 sq mi
CAPITAL Honiara (on Guadalcanal island) (and chief port)
MAJOR TOWNS/CITIES Gizo, Auki, Kirakira, Buala
MAJOR PORTS Yandina
PHYSICAL FEATURES comprises all but the northernmost islands (which belong to Papua New Guinea) of a Melanesian archipelago stretching nearly 1,500 km/900 mi. The largest is Guadalcanal (area 6,500 sq km/2,510 sq mi); others are Malaita, San Cristobal, New Georgia, Santa Isabel, Choiseul; mainly mountainous and forested

Government

HEAD OF STATE Queen Elizabeth II from 1978, represented by Governor General John Lapli from 1999
HEAD OF GOVERNMENT Allan Kemakeza from 2001
POLITICAL SYSTEM emergent democracy
POLITICAL EXECUTIVE parliamentary
ADMINISTRATIVE DIVISIONS nine provinces and the Honiara municipal authority
ARMED FORCES no standing army; 80-strong marine wing of police force (1998)
DEATH PENALTY laws do not provide for the death penalty for any crime

Economy and resources

CURRENCY Solomon Island dollar
GPD (US$) 240 million (2002 est)
REAL GDP GROWTH (% change on previous year) –14.3 (2001)
GNI (US$) 254 million (2002 est)
GNI PER CAPITA (PPP) (US$) 1,520 (2002 est)
CONSUMER PRICE INFLATION 8.1% (2003 est)
FOREIGN DEBT (US$) 176 million (2001 est)
MAJOR TRADING PARTNERS Australia, Japan, UK, New Zealand, Singapore, China, South Korea, USA
RESOURCES bauxite, phosphates, gold, silver, copper, lead, zinc, cobalt, asbestos, nickel
INDUSTRIES food processing (mainly palm oil and rice milling, fish, and coconut-based products), saw milling, logging, tobacco, furniture, handicrafts, boats, clothing, tourism
EXPORTS timber, fish products, oil palm products, copra, cocoa, coconut oil. Principal market: Japan 19.8% (2001)
IMPORTS rice, machinery and transport equipment, meat preparations, refined sugar, mineral fuels, basic manufactures, construction materials. Principal source: Australia 29.3% (2001)
ARABLE LAND 1.5% (2000 est)
AGRICULTURAL PRODUCTS coconuts, cocoa, rice, cassava, sweet potatoes, yam, taro, banana, palm oil; livestock rearing (pigs and cattle); fishing, sea shells, and seaweed farming; forestry

Population and society

POPULATION 477,000 (2003 est)
POPULATION GROWTH RATE 3.3% (2000–05)
POPULATION DENSITY (per sq km) 17 (2003 est)
URBAN POPULATION (% of total) 21 (2003 est)
AGE DISTRIBUTION (% of total population) 0–14 45%, 15–59 51%, 60+ 4% (2002 est)
ETHNIC GROUPS 93% Melanesian, 4% Polynesian, 1.5% Micronesian, 0.7% European, 0.2% Chinese
LANGUAGE English (official), pidgin English, more than 80 Melanesian dialects (85%), Papuan and Polynesian languages
RELIGION more than 80% Christian; Anglican 34%, Roman Catholic 19%, South Sea Evangelical, other Protestant, animist 5%
EDUCATION not compulsory
LITERACY RATE 77% (men); 75% (women) (2003 est)
LABOUR FORCE 26.8% agriculture, 11.7% industry, 61.5% services (1999)
LIFE EXPECTANCY 68 (men); 71 (women) (2000–05)

See also ▷Australasia and Oceania; ▷Pacific Islands.

Chronology

1568: The islands, rumoured in South America to be the legendary gold-rich 'Islands of Solomon', were first sighted by Spanish navigator Alvaro de Mendana, journeying from Peru.
1595 and 1606: Unsuccessful Spanish efforts to settle the islands, which had long been peopled by Melanesians.
later 18th century: Visited again by Europeans.
1840s: Christian missions established.
1870s: Development of copra export trade and shipment of islanders to work on sugar cane plantations in Australia and Fiji Islands.
1886: Northern Solomon Islands became German protectorate.
1893: Southern Solomon Islands placed under British protection.
1899: Germany ceded Solomon Islands possessions to Britain in return for British recognition of its claims to Western Samoa.
1900: Unified British Solomon Islands Protectorate formed and placed under jurisdiction of Western Pacific High Commission (WPHC), with its headquarters in Fiji Islands.
1942–43: Occupied by Japan. Site of fierce fighting, especially on Guadalcanal, which was recaptured by US forces, with the loss of 21,000 Japanese and 5,000 US troops.
1943–50: Development of Marching Rule (Ma'asina Ruru) cargo cult populist movement on Malaita island, campaigning for self-rule.
1945: Headquarters of WPHC moved to Honiara.
1960: Legislative and executive councils established by constitution.
1974: Became substantially self-governing, with Solomon Mamaloni of centre-left People's Progressive Party (PPP) as chief minister.
1976: Became fully self-governing, with Peter Kenilorea of right-of-centre Solomon Islands United Party (SIUPA) as chief minister.
1978: Independence achieved from Britain within Commonwealth.
1988: The Solomon Islands joined Vanuatu and Papua New Guinea to form the Spearhead Group, to preserve Melanesian cultural traditions.
1997: Bartholomew Ulufa'alu was elected prime minister.
1998: Ulufa'alu's Alliance for Change government narrowly survived a no-confidence vote.
2000: A military coup, led by rebel leader, Andrew Nori, forced the resignation of Ulufa'alu. The former opposition leader, Mannesseh Sogavare, became prime minister. A peace treaty was signed by rival ethnic militias in October.
2001: The Central Bank warned that the country was on the verge of economic collapse.
2003: A 2,300-strong Australian-led international peacekeeping force arrived to restore order and government authority.

government was supported by a thoroughly centralized administration. The dynasty was eventually ended by Mongol invasion.

Songhai Empire former kingdom of northwestern Africa, founded in the 8th century, which developed into a powerful Muslim empire under the rule of Sonni Ali (reigned 1464–92). It superseded the ▷Mali Empire and extended its territory, occupying an area that included parts of present-day Guinea, Burkina Faso, Senegal, Gambia, Mali, Mauritania, Niger, and Nigeria. In 1591 it was invaded and overthrown by Morocco.

sonic boom noise like a thunderclap that occurs when an aircraft passes through the ▷sound barrier, or begins to travel faster than the speed of sound. It happens when the cone-shaped shock wave caused by the plane touches the ground.

Sonic Youth US rock group formed in New York in 1981. Their use of detuned guitars, dissonance, and distortion, combined with a chilling melodic sense, made them one of the most influential bands of the decade. Albums include *Bad Moon Rising* (1985) and *Daydream Nation* (1988). Albums in the 1990s include *Goo* (1990), *Dirty* (1992), and *Washing Machine* (1995).

sonnet fourteen-line poem of Italian origin introduced to England by Thomas ▷Wyatt in the form used by Petrarch (rhyming *abba abba cdcdcd* or *cdecde*) and followed by Milton and Wordsworth; Shakespeare used the form *abab cdcd efef gg*.

Sons of Liberty in American colonial history, the name adopted by those colonists opposing the ▷Stamp Act of 1765. Merchants, lawyers, farmers, artisans, and labourers joined what was an early instance of concerted resistance to British rule, causing the repeal of the act in March 1766.

Somalia

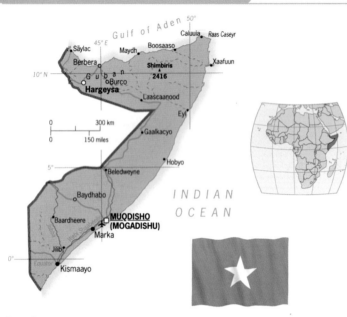

SOMALIA Somalian famine victims line up for food.
© David Turnley/CORBIS

RELIGION Sunni Muslim; small Christian community, mainly Roman Catholic
EDUCATION (compulsory years) 8
LITERACY RATE 36% (men); 14% (women) (1995 est)
LABOUR FORCE 71.1% agriculture, 9.1% industry, 19.8% services (2000)
LIFE EXPECTANCY 46 (men); 50 (women) (2000–05)
CHILD MORTALITY RATE (under 5, per 1,000 live births) 225 (2001)
PHYSICIANS (per 1,000 people) 0.04 (1998 est)
HOSPITAL BEDS (per 1,000 people) 0.8 (1998 est)
TV SETS (per 1,000 people) 14 (2001 est)
RADIOS (per 1,000 people) 60 (2001 est)
INTERNET USERS (per 10,000 people) 0.01 (2001 est)

See also ▷British Somaliland; ▷Italian Somaliland.

Somalia country in northeast Africa (the Horn of Africa), on the Indian Ocean, bounded northwest by Djibouti, west by Ethiopia, and southwest by Kenya.

NATIONAL NAME *Jamhuuriyadda Soomaaliya/Republic of Somalia*
AREA 637,700 sq km/246,215 sq mi
CAPITAL Mogadishu (and chief port)
MAJOR TOWNS/CITIES Hargeysa, Berbera, Kismaayo, Marka
MAJOR PORTS Berbera, Marka, Kismaayo
PHYSICAL FEATURES mainly flat, with hills in north

Government

HEAD OF STATE Abdiqasim Salad Hassan from 2000
HEAD OF GOVERNMENT Hasan Abshir Farah from 2001
POLITICAL SYSTEM military
POLITICAL EXECUTIVE military
ADMINISTRATIVE DIVISIONS 18 regions
ARMED FORCES no active army; following 1991 revolution, national forces have yet to be formed (2002)
DEATH PENALTY retained and used for ordinary crimes
DEFENCE SPEND (% GDP) 4 (2002 est)
HEALTH SPEND (% GDP) 1.3 (2000 est)

Economy and resources

CURRENCY Somali shilling
GPD (US$) 4.6 billion (2001)
CONSUMER PRICE INFLATION 20% (2002)
FOREIGN DEBT (US$) 2.3 billion (2001 est)
MAJOR TRADING PARTNERS Saudi Arabia, Djibouti, Kenya, Italy, United Arab Emirates, Yemen, Brazil, India, Pakistan
RESOURCES chromium, coal, salt, tin, zinc, copper, gypsum, manganese, iron ore,

uranium, gold, silver; deposits of petroleum and natural gas have been discovered but remain unexploited
INDUSTRIES food processing (especially sugar refining), textiles, petroleum refining, processing of hides and skins
EXPORTS livestock, skins and hides, bananas, fish and fish products, myrrh. Principal market: Saudi Arabia 32% (2001)
IMPORTS petroleum, fertilizers, foodstuffs, machinery and parts, manufacturing raw materials. Principal source: Djibouti 28% (2001)
ARABLE LAND 1.7% (2000 est)
AGRICULTURAL PRODUCTS bananas, sugar cane, maize, sorghum, grapefruit, seed cotton; agriculture is based on livestock rearing (cattle, sheep, goats, and camels) – 80% of the population depend on this activity

Population and society

POPULATION 9,890,000 (2003 est)
POPULATION GROWTH RATE 3.2% (2000–15)
POPULATION DENSITY (per sq km) 16 (2003 est)
URBAN POPULATION (% of total) 29 (2003 est)
AGE DISTRIBUTION (% of total population) 0–14 48%, 15–59 48%, 60+ 4% (2002 est)
ETHNIC GROUPS 98% indigenous Somali (about 84% Hamitic and 14% Bantu); population is divided into around 100 clans
LANGUAGE Somali, Arabic (both official), Italian, English

Chronology

8th–10th centuries: Arab ancestors of Somali clan families migrated to the region and introduced Sunni Islam; coastal trading cities, including Mogadishu, were formed by Arabian immigrants and developed into sultanates.

11th–14th century: Southward and westward movement of Somalis and Islamization of Christian Ethiopian interior.

early 16th century: Portuguese contacts with coastal region.

1820s: First British contacts with northern Somalia.

1884–87: British protectorate of Somaliland established in north.

1889: Italian protectorate of Somalia established in south.

1927: Italian Somalia became a colony and part of Italian East Africa from 1936.

1941: Italian Somalia occupied by Britain during World War I.

1943: Somali Youth League (SYL) formed as nationalist party.

1950: Italy resumed control over Italian Somalia under UN trusteeship.

1960: Independence achieved from Italy and Britain as Somalia, with Aden Abdullah Osman as president.

1963: Border dispute with Kenya; diplomatic relations broken with Britain for five years.

1969: President Ibrahim Egal assassinated in army coup led by Maj-Gen Muhammad Siad Barre; constitution suspended, political parties banned, Supreme Revolutionary Council set up, and socialist-Islamic state formed.

1972: 20,000 died in severe drought.

1978: Defeated in eight-month war with Ethiopia fought on behalf of Somali guerrillas in Ogaden to the southwest. Armed insurrection began in north and hundreds of thousands became refugees.

1979: New constitution for socialist one-party state dominated by Somali Revolutionary Socialist Party (SRSP).

1982: The antigovernment Ethiopian-backed Somali National Movement (SNM) was formed in the north, followed by oppressive countermeasures by the government.

late 1980s: Guerrilla activity increased in the north as the civil war intensified.

1991: Mogadishu was captured by rebels; Ali Mahdi Muhammad took control of the north of the town, and General Aidid took control of the south; free elections were promised. The secession of northeast Somalia, as the Somaliland Republic, was announced but not recognized internationally.

1992: There was widespread famine. Western food-aid convoys were hijacked by 'warlords'. United Nations (UN) peacekeeping troops, led by US Marines, were sent in to protect relief operations.

1993: Leaders of armed factions (except the Somaliland-based faction) agreed to a federal system of government. US-led UN forces destroyed the headquarters of warlord General Aidid after the killing of Pakistani peacekeepers.

1994: Ali Mahdi Muhammad and Aidid signed a truce. Most Western peacekeeping troops were withdrawn, but clan-based fighting continued.

1996: Aidid was killed in renewed faction fighting; his son Hussein Aidid succeeded him as interim president.

1998: A peace plan was agreed.

1999: In June the Ethiopian army, supporting opponents of Aidid, invaded Somalia.

2000: The four-month Somali reconciliation conference in Djibouti ended in August after the new transitional parliament elected Abdulkassim Salat Hassan as Somalia's first civilian president since civil war broke out nine years earlier.

Sontag, Susan (1933–) US critic, novelist, and screenwriter. Her novel *The Benefactor* appeared in 1963, and she established herself as a critic with the influential cultural essays of 'Against Interpretation' (1966) and 'Styles of Radical Will' (1969). More recent studies, showing the influence of French structuralism, are *On Photography* (1976) and the powerful *Illness as Metaphor* (1978) and *Aids and its Metaphors* (1989). Her novels include *In America* (2000), which won the 2000 National Book Award.

Susan Sontag
Much of modern art is devoted to lowering the threshold of what is terrible. By getting us used to what, formerly, we could not bear to see or hear, because it was too shocking, painful, or embarrassing, art changes morals.

On Photography, 'America, Seen Through Photographs, Darkly'

Soochow alternative transliteration of the Chinese city of ▷Suzhou.

Sophia, Electress of Hanover (1630–1714) Twelfth child of Frederick V, elector palatine of the Rhine and king of Bohemia, and Elizabeth, daughter of James I of England. She married the elector of Hannover in 1658. Widowed in 1698, she was recognized in the succession to the English throne in 1701, and when Queen Anne died without issue in 1714, her son George I founded the Hanoverian dynasty.

sophist (Greek *sophistes* 'wise man') in ancient Greece, one of a group of 5th-century BC itinerant lecturers on culture, rhetoric, and politics. Sceptical about the possibility of achieving genuine knowledge, they applied bogus reasoning and were concerned with winning arguments rather than establishing the truth. ▷Plato regarded them as dishonest and **sophistry** came to mean fallacious reasoning. In the 2nd century AD the term was linked to the art of public speaking.
Related Web site: Sophists http://www.utm.edu/research/iep/s/ sophists.htm

Sophocles (c. 496–406 BC) Athenian dramatist. He is credited with having developed tragedy by introducing a third actor and scene-painting, and ranked with ▷Aeschylus and ▷Euripides as one of the three great tragedians. He wrote some 120 plays, of which seven tragedies survive. These are *Antigone* (443 BC), *Oedipus the King* (429), *Electra* (410), *Ajax*, *Trachiniae*, *Philoctetes* (409 BC), and *Oedipus at Colonus* (401; produced after his death).

Sophocles lived in Athens when the city was ruled by Pericles, a period of great prosperity; he was a devout man, and assumed public office. A regular winner of dramatic competitions, he first defeated Aeschylus at the age of 27. In his tragedies heroic determination leads directly to violence unless, as in *Philoctetes* and *Oedipus at Colonus*, it contains an element of resignation. Among his other works are a lost treatise on the chorus, and a large surviving fragment of one of his satyr-dramas, *Ichneutai*.
Related Web site: Works by Sophocles http://classics.mit.edu/Browse/ browse-Sophocles.html

---

Sophocles
None love the messenger who brings bad news.
Antigone

---

soprano the highest range of the female voice, stretching from around D4 (the D above middle C) to A6. Some operatic roles require the extended upper range of a ▷coloratura soprano, reaching to around F6, for example Kiri ▷Te Kanawa. Some instruments use the prefix soprano for those models that sound in the compass of the soprano voice.

Sopwith, Thomas Octave Murdoch (1888–1989) English designer of the Sopwith Camel biplane, used in World War I, and joint developer of the Hawker Hurricane fighter plane used in World War II. He was knighted in 1953.

sorbic acid $CH_3CH=CHCH=CHCOOH$ tasteless acid found in the fruit of the mountain ash (genus *Sorbus*) and prepared synthetically. It is widely used in the preservation of food – for example, cider, wine, soft drinks, animal feeds, bread, and cheese.

Sorbonne common name for the University of Paris, originally a theological institute founded 1253 by Robert de Sorbon, chaplain to Louis IX.

Sorel, Georges Eugène (1847–1922) French philosopher who believed that socialism could only come about through a general strike; his theory of the need for a 'myth' to sway the body of the people was used by fascists.

Sørensen, Søren Peter Lauritz (1868–1939) Danish chemist who in 1909 introduced the concept of using the ▷pH scale as a measure of the acidity of a solution. On Sørensen's scale, still used today, a pH of 7 is neutral; higher numbers represent alkalinity, and lower numbers acidity.

sorghum (or **great millet** or **Guinea corn**) any of a group of ▷cereal grasses native to Africa but cultivated widely in India, China, the USA, and southern Europe. The seeds are used for making bread. ▷Durra is a member of the genus. (Genus *Sorghum*.)

sorrel (Old French *sur* 'sour') any of several plants belonging to the buckwheat family. *R. acetosa* is grown for its bitter salad leaves. ▷Dock plants are of the same genus. (Genus *Rumex*, family Polygonaceae.)

sorting in computing, arranging data in sequence. When sorting a collection, or file, of data made up of several different fields, one must be chosen as the **key field** used to establish the correct sequence. For example, the data in a company's mailing list might include fields for each customer's first names, surname, address, and telephone number. For most purposes the company would wish the records to be sorted alphabetically by surname; therefore, the surname field would be chosen as the key field.

sorus in ferns, a group of sporangia, the reproductive structures that produce ▷spores. They occur on the lower surface of fern fronds.

SORUS Heaps of bright yellow spore-producing sporangia grouped to form sori are clearly visible beneath this frond of common polypody fern. *Premaphotos Wildlife*

SOS internationally recognized distress signal, using letters of the ▷Morse code (... – – – ...).

Sōseki, Natsume (1867–1916) Pen-name of Natsume Kinnosuke. Japanese novelist. His works are deep psychological studies of urban intellectual lives. Strongly influenced by English literature, his later works are somewhat reminiscent of Henry James; for example, the unfinished *Meian/Light and Darkness* (1916). Sōseki is regarded as one of Japan's greatest writers.

Sotho a large ethnic group in southern Africa, numbering about 7 million (1987) and living mainly in Botswana, Lesotho, and South Africa. The Sotho are predominantly farmers, living in small village groups. They speak a variety of closely related languages belonging to the Bantu branch of the Niger-Congo family. With English, Sotho is the official language of Lesotho.

soul according to many religions, an intangible part of a human being that survives the death of the physical body. Judaism,

SORGHUM Sorghum is a type of grass that was originally cultivated in Africa to provide grain for animal fodder and to make flour for bread or porridge.

Christianity, and Islam all teach that at the end of the world each soul will be judged and assigned to heaven or hell on its merits.

soul music emotionally intense style of ▷rhythm and blues sung by, among others, Sam Cooke, Aretha Franklin, and Al Green (1946–). A synthesis of blues, gospel music, and jazz, it emerged in the 1950s. Sometimes all popular music made by African-Americans is labelled soul music.

sound physiological sensation received by the ear, originating in a vibration that communicates itself as a pressure variation in the air and travels in every direction, spreading out as an expanding sphere. All sound waves in air travel with a speed dependent on the temperature; under ordinary conditions, this is about 330 m/ 1,070 ft per second. The pitch of the sound depends on the number of vibrations imposed on the air per second (▷frequency), but the speed is unaffected. The loudness of a sound is dependent primarily on the amplitude of the vibration of the air.

Sound travels as a **longitudinal wave**, that is, its compressions and rarefactions are in the direction of propagation. Like other waves – light waves and water waves – sound can be reflected, diffracted, and refracted. ▷Reflection of a sound wave is heard as an echo. ▷Diffraction explains why sound can be heard round doorways. When sound is refracted (see ▷refraction), sound is bent when it passes into a denser or less dense material because sound travels faster in denser materials, such as solids and liquids. The lowest note audible to a human being has a frequency of about 20 ▷hertz (vibrations per second), and the highest one of about 20,000 Hz; the lower limit of this range varies little with the person's age, but the upper range falls steadily from adolescence onwards.
Related Web site: The Soundry http://library.thinkquest.org/19537/

sound barrier concept that the speed of sound, or sonic speed (about 1,220 kph/760 mph at sea level), constitutes a speed limit to flight through the atmosphere, since a badly designed aircraft suffers severe buffeting at near sonic speed owing to the formation of shock waves. US test pilot Chuck Yeager first flew through the 'barrier' in 1947 in a Bell X-1 rocket plane. Now, by careful design, such aircraft as Concorde can fly at supersonic speed with ease, though they create in their wake a ▷sonic boom.
Related Web site: Faster Than Sound http://www.pbs.org/wgbh/ nova/barrier/

SOUND BARRIER The Bell X-1 plane, famed as US test pilot Chuck Yeager's 'Glamorous Glennis', was the first plane to break the sound barrier. It is seen here accelerating towards Mach 1 on its epic flight on 14 October 1947. The aircraft's conical nose, modelled on the lines of a .50 calibre bullet, and the shock diamonds from its exhaust trail, can be seen. *Archive Photos*

sound synthesis the generation of sound (usually music) by electronic ▷synthesizer.

Sound, the (Swedish and Danish **øresund**) see ▷øresund.

soundtrack band at one side of a cine film on which the accompanying sound is recorded. Usually it takes the form of an optical track (a pattern of light and shade). The pattern is produced on the film when signals from the recording microphone are made to vary the intensity of a light beam. During playback, a light is shone through the track on to a photocell, which converts the pattern of light falling on it into appropriate electrical signals. These signals are then fed to loudspeakers to recreate the original sounds.

Sour (or **Tyre**) town in southwest Lebanon, about 80 km/50 mi south of Beirut, formerly a port until its harbour silted up; population (1991 est) 70,000. It stands on the site of the ancient city of the same name, a seaport of ▷Phoenicia.

source language in computing, the language in which a program is written, as opposed to ▷machine code, which is the form in which the program's instructions are carried out by the computer. Source languages are classified as either ▷high-level languages or ▷low-level languages, according to whether each notation in the source language stands for many or only one instruction in machine code.

souring change that occurs to wine on prolonged exposure to air. The ethanol in the wine is oxidized by the air (oxygen) to ethanoic acid. It is the presence of the ethanoic (acetic) acid that produces the sour taste.

$$CH_3CH_2OH_{(aq)} + O_{2(g)} \rightarrow CH_3COOH_{(aq)} + H_2O_{(l)}$$

Sousa, John Philip (1854–1932) US bandmaster and composer of marches. He wrote 'The Stars and Stripes Forever' in 1897.

sousaphone large bass ▷tuba designed to wrap round the player in a circle and having a forward-facing bell. The form was suggested by US bandmaster John Sousa. Today sousaphones are largely fabricated in lightweight fibreglass.

South Africa see country box.

South African literature the founder of South African literature in English was Thomas Pringle (1789–1834), who published lyric poetry and the prose *Narrative of a Residence in South Africa* (1834). More recent poets are Roy Campbell, Francis Carey Slater (1876–1959), Guy Butler (1918–), Sydney Clouts (1926–82), Douglas Livingstone (1932–), and Jeremy Cronin (1949–). The founder of South African fiction was Olive Schreiner, whose novel *Story of an African Farm* (1883) sought to establish the South African context as the norm rather than the exotic. Later writers of fiction include Sarah Gertrude Millin (regarded as the arch-racist of South African literature in English), Pauline Smith (1882–1959), William Plomer, Laurens van der Post, Alan Paton, Nadine Gordimer (winner of the Nobel Prize for Literature in 1991), André P Brink, and J M Coetzee. Preeminent among South Africa's playwrights is Athol Fugard.

Black South African writers include Sol Plaatje (1875–1932), author of *Mhudi* (1930), the first novel in English by a black South African; Peter Abrahams (1928–); Esk'ia Mphahlele; Lewis Nkosi; Njabulo Ndebele (1948–), and Mongane Wally Serote (1944–).

South African Wars (or **Boer Wars**) two wars between the Boers (settlers of Dutch origin) and the British; essentially fought for the gold and diamonds of the Transvaal.

The **War of 1881** was triggered by the attempt of the Boers of the ▷Transvaal to reassert the independence surrendered in 1877 in return for British aid against African peoples. The British were defeated at Majuba, and the Transvaal again became independent.

The **War of 1899–1902**, also known as the **Boer War**, was preceded by the armed Jameson Raid into the Boer Transvaal; a failed attempt, inspired by the Cape Colony prime minister Cecil Rhodes, to precipitate a revolt against Paul Kruger, the Transvaal president. The *uitlanders* (non-Boer immigrants) were still not given the vote by the Boers, negotiations failed, and the Boers invaded British territory, besieging Ladysmith, Mafeking (now Mafikeng), and Kimberley. The war ended with the Peace of Vereeniging following the Boer defeat.

Related Web site: Anglo-Boer War Museum http://www.anglo-boer.co.za/

South America fourth largest of the continents, nearly twice as large as Europe (13% of the world's land surface), extending south from ▷Central America.

area 17,864,000 sq km/6,897,000 sq mi **largest cities** (population over 3.5 million) Buenos Aires, São Paulo, Rio de Janeiro, Bogotá, Santiago, Lima, Belo Horizonte **features** Lake Titicaca (the world's highest navigable lake); La Paz (highest capital city in the world); Atacama Desert; Inca ruins at Machu Picchu; rivers include the Amazon (world's largest and second longest), Paraná, Madeira, São Francisco, Purús, Paraguay, Orinoco, Araguaia, Negro, Uruguay **physical** occupying the southern part of the landmass of the Western hemisphere, the South American continent stretches from Point Gallinas on the Caribbean coast of Colombia to Cape Horn at the southern tip of Horn Island, which lies adjacent to Tierra del Fuego; the most southerly point on the mainland is Cape Froward on the Brunswick peninsula, southern Chile; at its maximum width (5,120 km/3,200 mi) the continent stretches from Point Pariñas, Peru, in the extreme west to Point Coqueiros, just north of Recife, Brazil, in the east; five-sixths of the continent lies in the southern hemisphere and two-thirds within the tropics **population** (1996 est) 323 million. The urban population has increased rapidly since 1950, as millions of poor people have left the countryside in the hope of a better standard of living in the cities. By 1996 about 75% of the population was living in cities **language** Spanish, Portuguese (chief language in Brazil), Dutch (Suriname), French (French Guiana), American Indian languages; Hindi, Javanese, and Chinese spoken by descendants of Asian immigrants to Suriname and Guyana; a variety of Creole dialects spoken by those of African descent **religion** 90–95% Roman Catholic; local animist beliefs among Amerindians; Hindu and Muslim religions predominate among the descendants of Asian immigrants in Suriname and Guyana. **climate** the distribution of rainfall in South America is affected by three factors: (1) the areas of high pressure over the South Atlantic and the South Pacific between latitudes 20° and 40°; (2) the tropical continental region of low pressure in the Upper Amazon basin; and (3) the direction of the ocean currents which wash both east and west coasts, together with a cold current that clings to the coast along most of the west coast. The continent's summer rainfall is of a monsoonal type, but differs from that of Asia in that there is no movement outwards of high-pressure air owing to the continent being as a whole warmer than the surrounding seas during all seasons. **industries** South America produces 44% of the world's coffee (Brazil, Colombia), 22% of its cocoa (Brazil), 35% of its citrus fruit, meat (Argentina, Brazil), soybeans (Argentina, Brazil), cotton (Brazil), and linseed (Argentina); Argentina is the world's second-largest producer of sunflower seed; Brazil is the world's l argest producer of bananas, its second-largest producer of tin, and its third-largest producer of manganese, tobacco, and mangoes; Peru is the world's second-largest producer of silver; Chile is the world's largest producer of copper.

South America is a compact land mass and has a fairly regular coastline, except in southern Chile, where sunken valleys have resulted from subsidence that has left mountain peaks as islands. The continent can be divided into the following physical regions: (1) the Andes mountain system, which consists of extensive chains of parallel folded mountains, formed during the subsidence of the bed of the Pacific Ocean; they are new mountains as distinct from the ancient rocks, and contain limestones which were deposited under deep water later than the older sandstones of the eastern highlands; they show signs of crustal movement due to earthquake and volcanic action; the Andes begin as three separate ranges in the north and stretch the whole length of the west coast, approximately 7,200 km/4,500 mi; the highest peak is Cerro Aconcagua, 6,960 m/22,834 ft; the width of the Andes ranges from 40 km/25 mi in Chile to 640 km/400 mi in Bolivia; a narrow coastal belt lies between the Andes and the Pacific Ocean; (2) the uplifted remains of the old continental mass, with interior plains at an elevation of 610–1,520 m/2,000–5,000 ft, which are found in the east and northeast, in the Brazilian Highlands (half the area of Brazil) and Guiana Highlands; (3) the plain of the Orinoco River, which is an alluvial tropical lowland lying between the Venezuelan Andes and the Guiana Highlands; (4) the tropical Amazon Plain, which stretches over 3,200 km/2,000 mi from the eastern foothills of the Andes to the Atlantic Ocean, separating the Brazilian and Guiana highlands; once an inland sea, the Amazon basin was filled with sediment from highland rivers and then uplifted; the Amazon's chief tributaries are the Tocantins, Xingu, Tapajós, Madeira, Purús, Ucayali, Negro, Yapura, Napo, and Morona; it has a huge estuary 80–320 km/50–200 mi wide; (5) the Pampa-Chaco plain of Argentina, Paraguay, and Bolivia, which occupies a former bay of the Atlantic Ocean that has been filled with sediment brought down from the surrounding highlands; and (6) the Patagonian Plateau in the south, which consists of a series of terraces that rise from the Atlantic Ocean to the foothills of the Andes; glaciation, wind, and rain have dissected these terraces and created rugged land forms; the plateau is traversed by rivers including the Colorado, the Negro, and the Chubut; lakes are formed in some of the valleys by dams of residual moraines left from the ice age.

SOUTH AFRICAN WARS This cartoon (dated 1900) shows the Boer general Piet Arnoldus Cronje (1835–1911) surrendering to British forces at Paardeberg on 27 February 1900. British statesman in South Africa Cecil Rhodes is pictured, and English author and poet Rudyard Kipling appears as a reporter with a typewriter. *The Art Archive/Eileen Tweedy*

Southampton industrial city, seaport, and unitary authority in southern England, at the head of Southampton Water, 20 km/12 mi southwest of Winchester; it was part of the county of Hampshire to 1997.

area 52 sq km/20 sq mi **features** Southampton University, established in 1952; ferry link to the Isle of Wight; the port is a base for many liners, including P&O's *Oriana*; Southampton City Art Gallery; parts of the medieval town wall survive, including four of the town-wall towers, and Bargate, the elaborate old north gateway to the city; the partly Norman St Michael's Church has an 18th-century spire 50 m/164 ft high; the 14th-century Wool House now houses a maritime museum; Tudor House Museum, situated in a half-timbered 15th-century building; the hospital of God's House was originally founded in 1185 for pilgrims going either to the shrine of St Swithin at Winchester, or to Canterbury; 15th-century God's House Tower houses a museum of archaeology; Norman House and Canute's Palace are among the oldest examples of Norman domestic architecture in Britain; a memorial column marks the place of embarkation of the *Mayflower*; the headquarters of the Ordnance Survey are here **industries** marine engineering, chemicals, plastics, flour-milling, tobacco, the manufacture of cables and electrical goods, and financial services. It is a major passenger and container port. There is an oil refinery nearby at Fawley **population** (1996) 207,100 **famous people** Donald Griffin, Benny Hill, George Saintsbury, George Thomas

SOUTH AMERICA A gold pectoral (decoration or protection for the chest) from one of South America's ancient cultures, that of the Tairona in Colombia, dating from before 1500. The Tairona, and their relatives, while lacking the political abilities of the Incas or Aztecs, were a people of high culture. Although they rapidly assimilated Spanish customs, they were nevertheless soon exterminated by the invading Spaniards. *The Art Archive*

Southampton, Henry Wriothesley, 3rd Earl of Southampton (1573–1624) English courtier, patron of Shakespeare. Shakespeare dedicated *Venus and Adonis* and *The Rape of Lucrece* to him and may have addressed him in the sonnets.

South Australia state of south-central Australia, including Kangaroo Island and other islands in the Indian Ocean; bounded on the northeast by Queensland, on the east by New South Wales, on the southeast by Victoria, on the south by the Indian Ocean, and on the west by Western Australia; area 984,381 sq km/380,071 sq mi; population (1996) 1,428,000. The capital (and chief port) is ▷Adelaide. Products are meat, wool, wine, wheat, barley, almonds, oranges and other citrus fruits, and dried and canned fruit, coal, copper, uranium, silver, zinc, gold, steel, jade, slate, opals, marble, granite, household and electrical goods, vehicles, oil, and natural gas.

Related Web site: South Australian Tourist Commission http://www.tourism.sa.gov.au/

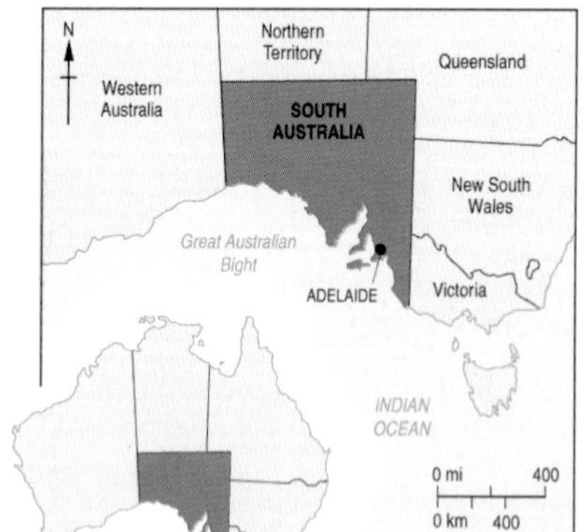

South Ayrshire unitary authority in southwest Scotland, created in 1996 from Kyle and Carrick district (1975–96), Strathclyde region.

area 1,245 sq km/480 sq mi **towns** ▷Ayr (administrative headquarters), Prestwick, Girvan, Troon, Maybole **physical** coastal plain which rises to higher ground inland (500 m/1,640 ft); rivers Ayr, Stinchar, Water of Girvan; Brown Carrick Hill (287 m/942 ft); Ailsa Craig; many beaches interspersed with cliffs and caves **features** Glasgow Prestwick Airport; Culzean Castle; Crossraguel Abbey; Royal Troon and Turnberry championship golf courses; Ayr racecourse **industries** aerospace, high technology, tourism **agriculture** fishing (Ayr), dairying, beef cattle, potatoes **population** (1996) 114,000 **history** birthplace of Robert Burns

South Africa

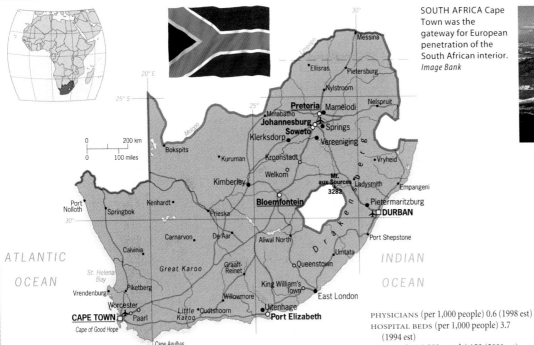

SOUTH AFRICA Cape Town was the gateway for European penetration of the South African interior. *Image Bank*

South Africa country on the southern tip of Africa, bounded north by Namibia, Botswana, and Zimbabwe and northeast by Mozambique and Swaziland.

NATIONAL NAME *Republiek van Suid-Afrika/Republic of South Africa*
AREA 1,222,081 sq km/471,845 sq mi
CAPITAL Cape Town (legislative), Pretoria (administrative), Bloemfontein (judicial)
MAJOR TOWNS/CITIES Johannesburg, Durban, Port Elizabeth, Vereeniging, Pietermaritzburg, Kimberley, Soweto, Tembisa
MAJOR PORTS Cape Town, Durban, Port Elizabeth, East London
PHYSICAL FEATURES southern end of large plateau, fringed by mountains and lowland coastal margin; Drakensberg Mountains, Table Mountain; Limpopo and Orange rivers
TERRITORIES Marion Island and Prince Edward Island in the Antarctic

Government

HEAD OF STATE AND GOVERNMENT Thabo Mbeki from 1999
POLITICAL SYSTEM emergent democracy
POLITICAL EXECUTIVE limited presidency
ADMINISTRATIVE DIVISIONS nine provinces
ARMED FORCES 60,000 (2002 est)
DEATH PENALTY abolished in 1997

Economy and resources

CURRENCY rand
GPD (US$) 104.2 billion (2002 est)
REAL GDP GROWTH (% change on previous year) 2.2 (2001)
GNI (US$) 113.5 billion (2002 est)
GNI PER CAPITA (PPP) (US$) 9,870 (2002 est)
CONSUMER PRICE INFLATION 8.5% (2003 est)
UNEMPLOYMENT 29.4% (2002)
FOREIGN DEBT (US$) 22.9 billion (2001 est)
MAJOR TRADING PARTNERS USA, UK, Germany, Italy, Japan, Switzerland
RESOURCES gold (world's largest producer), coal, platinum, iron ore, diamonds, chromium, manganese, limestone, asbestos, fluorspar, uranium, copper, lead, zinc, petroleum, natural gas
INDUSTRIES chemicals, petroleum and coal products, gold, diamonds, food processing, transport equipment, iron and steel, metal products, machinery, fertilizers, textiles, paper and paper products, clothing, wood and cork products
EXPORTS metals and metal products, gold, precious and semiprecious stones, mineral products and chemicals, natural cultured pearls, machinery and mechanical appliances, wool, maize, fruit, sugar. Principal market: USA 10.6% (2001)
IMPORTS machinery and electrical equipment, transport equipment, chemical products, mechanical appliances, textiles and clothing, vegetable products, wood, pulp, paper and paper products. Principal source: USA 13.3% (2001)
ARABLE LAND 12.1% (2000 est)
AGRICULTURAL PRODUCTS maize, sugar cane, sorghum, fruits, wheat, groundnuts, grapes, vegetables; livestock rearing, wool production

Population and society

POPULATION 45,026,000 (2003 est)
POPULATION GROWTH RATE 0.5% (2000–15)
POPULATION DENSITY (per sq km) 37 (2003 est)
URBAN POPULATION (% of total) 59 (2003 est)
AGE DISTRIBUTION (% of total population) 0–14 33%, 15–59 61%, 60+ 6% (2002 est)
ETHNIC GROUPS 77% of the population is black African, 11% white (of European descent), 9% of mixed African–European descent, and 3% Asian
LANGUAGE English, Afrikaans, Xhosa, Zulu, Sesotho (all official), other African languages
RELIGION Dutch Reformed Church and other Christian denominations 77%, Hindu 2%, Muslim 1%
EDUCATION (compulsory years) 10
LITERACY RATE 87% (men); 86% (women) (2003 est)
LABOUR FORCE 11.8% agriculture, 23.8% industry, 64.4% services (2001)
LIFE EXPECTANCY 45 (men); 51 (women) (2000–05)
CHILD MORTALITY RATE (under 5, per 1,000 live births) 71 (2001)
PHYSICIANS (per 1,000 people) 0.6 (1998 est)
HOSPITAL BEDS (per 1,000 people) 3.7 (1994 est)
TV SETS (per 1,000 people) 152 (2001 est)
RADIOS (per 1,000 people) 338 (2001 est)
INTERNET USERS (per 10,000 people) 682.0 (2002 est)
PERSONAL COMPUTER USERS (per 100 people) 7.3 (2002 est)

See also ▷African National Congress; ▷Afrikaner; ▷apartheid; ▷Mandela, Nelson; ▷South African Wars.

Chronology

1652: Dutch East India Company established colony at Cape Town as a port of call.

1795: Britain occupied Cape after France conquered the Netherlands.

1814: Britain bought Cape Town and hinterland from the Netherlands for £6 million.

1820s: Zulu people established military kingdom under Shaka.

1836–38: The Great Trek: 10,000 Dutch settlers (known as Boers, meaning 'farmers') migrated north to escape British rule.

1843: Britain established colony of Natal on east coast.

1852–54: Britain recognized Boer republics of Transvaal and Orange Free State.

1872: The Cape became self-governing colony within British Empire.

1877: Britain annexed Transvaal.

1879: Zulu War: Britain destroyed power of Zulus.

1881: First Boer War: Transvaal Boers defeated British at Majuba Hill and regained independence.

1886: Discovery of gold on Witwatersrand attracted many migrant miners (uitlanders) to Transvaal, which denied them full citizenship.

1895: Jameson Raid: uitlanders, backed by Cecil Rhodes, tried to overthrow President Paul Kruger of Transvaal.

1899–1902: Second South African War (also known as Boer War): dispute over rights of uitlanders led to conflict which ended with British annexation of Boer republics.

1907: Britain granted internal self-government to Transvaal and Orange Free State on a whites-only franchise.

1910: Cape Colony, Natal, Transvaal, and Orange Free State formed Union of South Africa, with Louis Botha as prime minister.

1912: Gen Barry Hertzog founded (Boer) Nationalist Party; ANC formed to campaign for rights of black majority.

1914: Boer revolt in Orange Free State suppressed; South African troops fought for British Empire in World War I.

1919: Jan Smuts succeeded Botha as premier; South West Africa (Namibia) became South African mandate.

1924: Hertzog became prime minister, aiming to sharpen racial segregation and loosen ties with British Empire.

1939–45: Smuts led South Africa into World War II despite neutralism of Hertzog; South African troops fought with Allies in Middle East, East Africa, and Italy.

1948: Policy of apartheid ('separateness') adopted when National Party (NP) took power under Daniel Malan; continued by his successors Johannes Strijdom 1954–58, Hendrik Verwoerd 1958–66, B J Vorster 1966–78, and P J Botha 1978–89.

1950: Entire population classified by race; Group Areas Act segregated blacks and whites; ANC responded with campaign of civil disobedience.

1960: 70 black demonstrators killed at Sharpville; ANC banned.

1961: South Africa left Commonwealth and became republic.

1964: ANC leader Nelson Mandela sentenced to life imprisonment.

1967: Terrorism Act introduced indefinite detention without trial.

1970s: Over 3 million people forcibly resettled in black 'homelands'.

1976: Over 600 killed in clashes between black protesters and security forces in Soweto.

1984: New constitution gave segregated representation to coloureds and Asians, but continued to exclude blacks.

1985: Growth of violence in black townships led to proclamation of a state of emergency.

1986: USA and Commonwealth imposed limited economic sanctions against South Africa.

1989: F W de Klerk succeeded P W Botha as president; public facilities were desegregated; many ANC activists were released.

1990: The ban on the ANC was lifted; Mandela was released; talks began between the government and the ANC; there was a daily average of 35 murders.

1991: De Klerk repealed the remaining apartheid laws; sanctions were lifted; however, there was severe fighting between the ANC and the Zulu Inkatha movement.

1993: An interim majority rule constitution was adopted; de Klerk and Mandela agreed to form a government of national unity after free elections.

1994: The ANC were victorious in the first nonracial elections; Mandela became president; Commonwealth membership was restored.

1996: De Klerk withdrew the NP from the coalition after the new constitution failed to provide for power-sharing after 1999.

1997: A new constitution was signed by President Mandela. De Klerk announced his retirement from politics.

1999: Mandela retired as state president; he was succeeded by Thabo Mbeki. ANC won assembly majority in election.

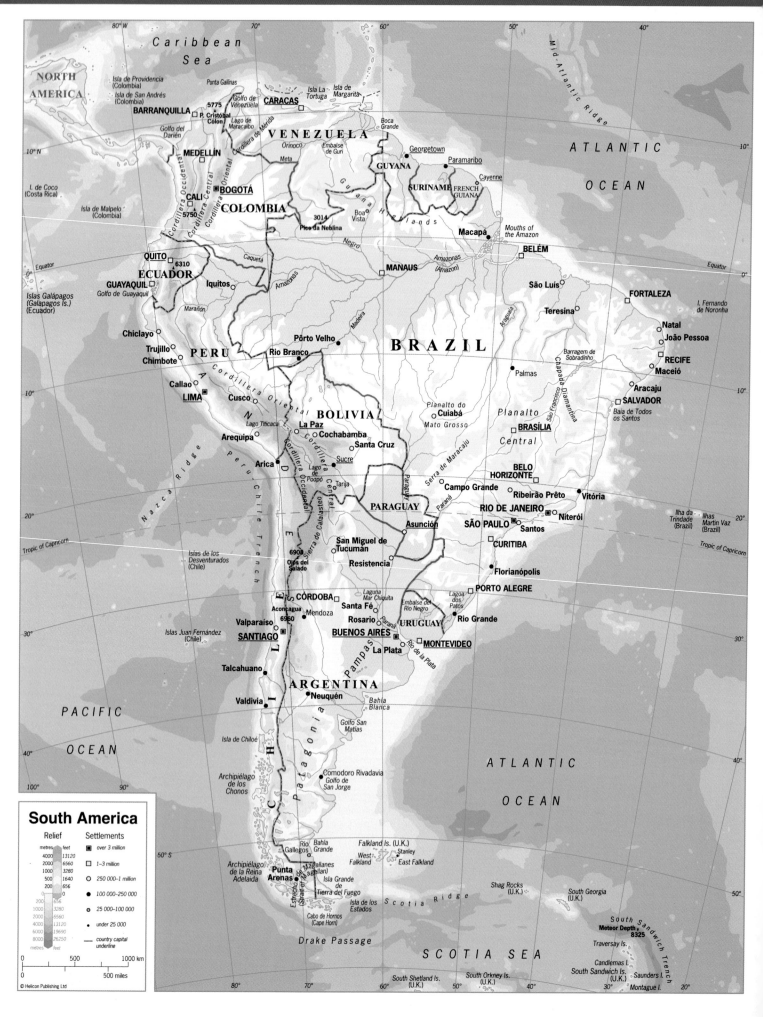

South America

Relief

metres	feet
4000	13120
2000	6560
1000	3280
500	1640
200	656
0	0
200	656
1000	3280
2000	6560
4000	13120
6000	19690
8000	26250
metres	feet

Settlements

■ over 3 million
□ 1–3 million
○ 250 000–1 million
● 100 000–250 000
◉ 25 000–100 000
• under 25 000
— country capital underline

0   500   1000 km
0   500 miles

© Helicon Publishing Ltd

South Carolina state in southeastern USA. It is nicknamed the Palmetto State. South Carolina ratified the US Constitution in 1788, becoming the 8th state to join the Union. Part of the Deep South, it is bordered to the north and east by North Carolina, to the west and south by Georgia, and to the southeast by the Atlantic Ocean. South Carolina was one of the original US plantation states, associated with slavery.

population (1995) 3,673,300 **area** 80,600 sq km/31,112 sq mi **capital** Columbia **towns and cities** Charleston, North Charleston, Greenville, Spartanburg **industries and products** tobacco, soybeans, lumber, textiles, clothing, paper, wood pulp, chemicals, nonelectrical machinery, primary and fabricated metals, tourism, leisure industry

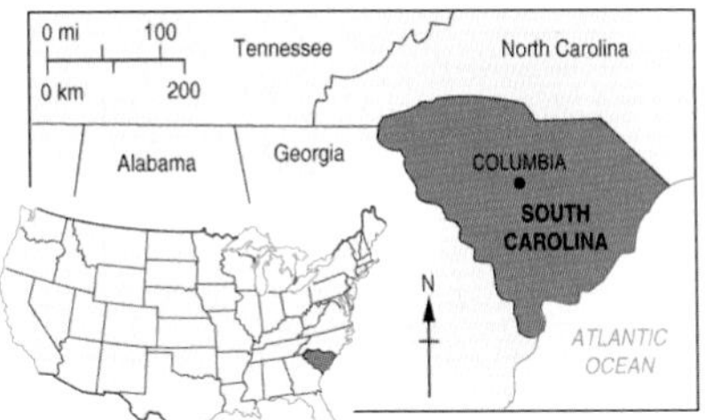

South China Sea see ▷China Sea.

South Dakota state in western USA. It is nicknamed the Coyote or Sunshine State. South Dakota was admitted to the Union in 1889 as the 40th US state. It is bordered to the north by North Dakota, to the west by Montana and Wyoming, to the south by Nebraska, and to the east by Minnesota and Iowa.

population (1995) 729,000 **area** 199,800 sq km/77,150 sq mi **capital** Pierre **towns and cities** Sioux Falls, Rapid City, Aberdeen **industries and products** cereals, hay, livestock, gold (second-largest US producer), meat products, tourism

Southeast Asia Treaty Organization (SEATO) collective military system 1954–77 established by Australia, France, New Zealand, Pakistan, the Philippines, Thailand, the UK, and the USA, with Vietnam, Cambodia, and Laos as protocol states.

After the Vietnam War, SEATO was phased out.

Southend resort and unitary authority in eastern England, on the Thames estuary, 60 km/37 mi east of London, the nearest seaside resort to London; it was part of the county of Essex to April 1998.

area 42 sq km/16 sq mi **features** a pier, 2 km/1.25 mi long, said to be the longest in the world; 11 km/7 mi of seafront, an aquarium, amusement facilities, and many public parks and gardens, including the Cliff Gardens; well known for its flowers, including carpet bedding displays and a Floral Trail Tour; nearly a third of all land in the area is managed for nature conservation, including Belfairs Wood Nature Reserve and Leigh National Nature Reserve on Two Tree Island **industries** tourism, financial services, light engineering, and boatbuilding **population** (1996) 171,000

Southern African Development Community (SADC) organization of countries in the region working together initially to reduce their economic dependence on South Africa and harmonize their economic policies, but from 1995 to promote the creation of a free-trade zone by 2000. It was established in 1980 as the **Southern African Development Coordination Conference** (SADCC), adopting its present name in 1992, and focuses on transport and communications, energy, mining, and industrial production. The member states are Angola, Botswana, Lesotho, Malawi, Mauritius, Mozambique, Namibia, South Africa, Swaziland, Tanzania, Zambia, and Zimbabwe; headquarters in Gaborone, Botswana.

Southern Alps range of mountains running the entire length of South Island, New Zealand. They are forested to the west, with scanty scrub to the east. The highest peaks are Aoraki, 3,764 m/12,349 ft, and Mount Tasman 3,498m/11,476 ft. Scenic features include gorges, glaciers, lakes, and waterfalls. Among its lakes are those at the southern end of the range: Manapouri, Te Anau, and the largest, Wakatipu, 83 km/52 mi long, which lies about 300 m/1,000 ft above sea level and has a depth of 378 m/1,242 ft. The Fiordland National Park also lies in the south of the range.

Southern Cone Common Market alternative name for ▷Mercosur.

Southerne, Thomas (1660–1746) English playwright and poet. He was the author of the tragi-comedies *Oroonoko* (1695–96) and *The Fatal Marriage* (1694).

southern lights common name for the ▷aurora australis, coloured light in southern skies.

Southern Ocean corridor linking the Pacific, Atlantic, and Indian oceans, all of which receive cold polar water from the world's largest ocean surface current, the Antarctic Circumpolar Current, which passes through the Southern Ocean.

Southern Uplands one of the three geographical divisions of Scotland, being most of the hilly Scottish borderland to the south of a geological fault line that stretches from Dunbar, East Lothian, on the North Sea to Girvan, South Ayrshire, on the Firth of Clyde. The Southern Uplands, largely formed by rocks of the Silurian and Ordovician age, are intersected by the broad valleys of the Nith and Tweed rivers.

Southey, Robert (1774–1843) English poet and author. He is sometimes regarded as one of the 'Lake poets', more because of his friendship with Samuel Taylor ▷Coleridge and William ▷Wordsworth and residence in Keswick, in the English Lake District, than for any Romantic influence in his work. In 1813 he became poet laureate, but he is better known for his *Life of Nelson* (1813) and for his letters.

> **Robert Southey**
> *Curses are like young chickens, they always come home to roost.*
> *The Curse of Kehama*, Motto

South Georgia island in the South Atlantic, a British crown colony administered, with the South Sandwich Islands, from the Falkland Islands by a commissioner; area 3,757 sq km/1,450 sq mi. The average temperature on the island is −2°C/28.4°F.

There has been no permanent population since the whaling station was abandoned in 1966. South Georgia lies 1,300 km/800 mi southeast of the Falkland Islands, of which it was a dependency until 1985. The British Antarctic Survey has a station on nearby Bird Island.

South Glamorgan (Welsh **De Morgannwg**) former county of south Wales, 1974–1996, now divided between ▷Cardiff and ▷Vale of Glamorgan unitary authorities.

South Gloucestershire unitary authority in southwest England created in 1996 from part of the former county of Avon.

area 497 sq km/192 sq mi **towns and cities** Thornbury (administrative headquarters), Patchway, Yate, Chipping Sodbury **features** River Severn borders northwest; Vale of Berkeley; Severn Road Bridge; Marshfield has one of Britain's longest village streets with 17th-century almshouses; 13th-century church of St Peter (Dyrham); late 17th century Dyrham Park Mansion **industries** agriculture and associated industries **population** (1996) 220,000

South Holland (Dutch **Zuid Holland**) low-lying coastal province of the Netherlands, bounded to the north by North Holland, to the east by Utrecht and North Brabant, to the south by Zeeland, and to the west by the North Sea; area 2,910 sq km/1,124 sq mi; population (1997) 3,344,700. The capital is ▷The Hague. There are chemical, textile, distilling, and petroleum refining industries. Bulbs are grown, and there is horticulture, livestock raising, and dairying.

SOUTHERN ALPS This range of mountains was formed by a vertical movement of the Earth's crust along the Alpine fault line. *Corel*

South Korea see country box.

South Lanarkshire unitary authority in south central Scotland, created in 1996 from three districts of Strathclyde region.

area 1,772 sq km/684 sq mi **towns** Hamilton (administrative headquarters), Lanark, Rutherglen, East Kilbride, Carluke, Cambuslang **physical** area of stark contrast: predominantly rural to the south and urban to the north. The River Clyde flows through the area. Tinto (707 m/2,320 ft) is a key landmark to the south **features** Craignethan Castle; Carstairs State Hospital, New Lanark **industries** textiles, electronics, engineering **agriculture** fruit cultivation in the valleys of the Clyde; less intensive grazing and stock rearing in the upland south; dairying around the urban core in the north **population** (1996) 307,100 **history** New Lanark village is a World Heritage Site, significant for the attempt to improve living conditions for workers and their families

South Ossetia autonomous region of the Georgian republic, part of the region of ▷Ossetia; population (1990) 99,800. It lies on the southern slopes of the Greater Caucasus mountains, mostly above 1,000 m/3,300 ft above sea level. Its capital is Tskinvali. Its rivers are used to produce hydroelectric power, and less than 10% of the land is cultivated. Cereals, vines, and fruit are grown, while the higher land is used for forestry and rearing sheep, goats, and cattle. Traditional industries produce leather goods, fur clothing, and metal objects.

South Pacific Commission (SPC) former name, until February 1998, of the ▷Pacific Community.

South Pacific Forum former name, until October 2000, of ▷Pacific Islands Forum.

South Pole the southern point where an imaginary line penetrates the Earth's surface by the axis about which it revolves; see also ▷pole and ▷Antarctica.

South Sea Bubble financial crisis in Britain in 1720. The South Sea Company, founded in 1711, which had a monopoly of trade with South America, offered in 1719 to take over more than half the national debt in return for further concessions. Its 100 shares rapidly rose to 1,000, and an orgy of speculation followed. When the 'bubble' burst, thousands were ruined.

The discovery that cabinet ministers had been guilty of corruption led to a political crisis.

Robert Walpole became prime minister, protected the royal family and members of the government from scandal, and restored financial confidence.

Related Web site: South Sea Bubble http://is.dal.ca/~dmcneil/sketch.html

South Shields manufacturing port in Tyne and Wear, northeast England, on the south side of the Tyne estuary opposite North Shields and east of Gateshead; population (1991) 82,400. Shipbuilding has declined and industries now include electrical goods, cables, chemicals, and paint.

South, the historically, the states of the USA bounded on the north by the ▷Mason–Dixon Line, the Ohio River, and the eastern and northern borders of Missouri, with an agrarian economy based on plantations worked by slaves, and which seceded from the Union in 1861, beginning the American Civil War, as the ▷Confederacy. The term is now loosely applied in a geographical and cultural sense, with Texas often regarded as part of the Southwest rather than the South.

South Yorkshire metropolitan county of northeast England, created in 1974; in 1986, most of the functions of the former county council were transferred to the metropolitan borough councils.

area 1,560 sq km/602 sq mi **towns** Barnsley, Doncaster, Rotherham, Sheffield (all administrative centres for the districts of the same name) **physical** River Don; part of Peak District National Park; the county contains a rich diversity of rural landscapes between the barren Pennine moors in the southwest and the very low, flat carr-lands (a mixture of marsh and copses) in the east **features** the Earth Centre for Environmental Research **agriculture** sheep; dairy and arable farming **industries** metal-work, coal, engineering, iron, and steel **population** (1996) 1,304,800 **famous people** Ian Botham, Arthur Scargill

Soutine, Chaïm (1893–1943) Lithuanian-born French painter. The greatest of the French expressionists, he used brilliant colours and thick, energetically applied paint to create intense, emotionally charged works, mostly landscapes and portraits. *Page Boy* (1927; Albright-Knox Art Gallery, Buffalo, New York) is typical.

sovereignty absolute authority within a given territory. The possession of sovereignty is taken to be the distinguishing feature

South Korea

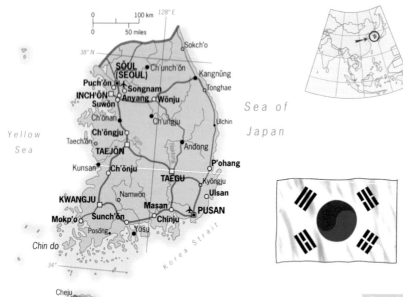

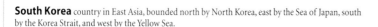

SOUTH KOREA A pavilion in the grounds of the Kyongbuk-kung Palace, Seoul, South Korea. *Corel*

South Korea country in East Asia, bounded north by North Korea, east by the Sea of Japan, south by the Korea Strait, and west by the Yellow Sea.

NATIONAL NAME *Daehan Minguk/Republic of Korea*
AREA 98,799 sq km/38,146 sq mi
CAPITAL Seoul
MAJOR TOWNS/CITIES Pusan, Taegu, Inchon, Kwangju, Taejon, Songnam
MAJOR PORTS Pusan, Inchon
PHYSICAL FEATURES southern end of a mountainous peninsula separating the Sea of Japan from the Yellow Sea

Government

HEAD OF STATE Goh Kun (acting) from 2004
HEAD OF GOVERNMENT Goh Kun from 2003
POLITICAL SYSTEM liberal democracy
POLITICAL EXECUTIVE limited presidency
ADMINISTRATIVE DIVISIONS nine provinces and seven cities with provincial status
ARMED FORCES 686,000 (2002 est)
DEATH PENALTY retained and used for ordinary crimes

Economy and resources

CURRENCY won
GPD (US$) 476.7 billion (2002 est)
REAL GDP GROWTH (% change on previous year) 3.3 (2001)
GNI (US$) 473.1 billion (2002 est)
GNI PER CAPITA (PPP) (US$) 16,480 (2002 est)
CONSUMER PRICE INFLATION 4.1% (2001)
UNEMPLOYMENT 4.1% (2001)
FOREIGN DEBT (US$) 108.5 billion (2001 est)
MAJOR TRADING PARTNERS USA, Japan, Germany, Saudi Arabia, Australia, Singapore, China, Taiwan
RESOURCES coal, iron ore, tungsten, gold, molybdenum, graphite, fluorite, natural gas, hydroelectric power, fish
INDUSTRIES electrical machinery, transport equipment (principally motor vehicles and shipbuilding), chemical products, textiles and clothing, iron and steel, electronics equipment, food processing, tourism
EXPORTS electrical machinery, textiles, clothing, footwear, telecommunications and sound equipment, chemical products, ships ('invisible export' – overseas construction work). Principal market: USA 20.7% (2001)
IMPORTS machinery and transport equipment (especially electrical machinery), petroleum

and petroleum products, grain and foodstuffs, steel, chemical products, basic manufactures. Principal source: Japan 18.9% (2001)
ARABLE LAND 17.4% (2000 est)
AGRICULTURAL PRODUCTS rice, maize, barley, potatoes, sweet potatoes, fruit; livestock (pigs and cattle)

Population and society

POPULATION 47,700,000 (2003 est)
POPULATION GROWTH RATE 0.4% (2000–15)
POPULATION DENSITY (per sq km) 482 (2003 est)
URBAN POPULATION (% of total) 84 (2003 est)
AGE DISTRIBUTION (% of total population) 0–14 20%, 15–59 68%, 60+ 12% (2002 est)
ETHNIC GROUPS with the exception of a small Nationalist Chinese minority, the population is almost entirely of Korean descent
LANGUAGE Korean (official)
RELIGION Buddhist 48%, Confucian 3%, Christian 47%, mainly Protestant; Chund Kyo (peculiar to Korea, combining elements of Shaman, Buddhist, and Christian doctrines)
EDUCATION (compulsory years) 9
LITERACY RATE 99% (men); 97% (women) (2003 est)
LABOUR FORCE 10.9% agriculture, 28.0% industry, 61.1% services (2000)
LIFE EXPECTANCY 72 (men); 79 (women) (2000–05)
CHILD MORTALITY RATE (under 5, per 1,000 live births) 5 (2001)
PHYSICIANS (per 1,000 people) 1.4 (1998 est)
HOSPITAL BEDS (per 1,000 people) 6.1 (1998 est)
TV SETS (per 1,000 people) 363 (2001 est)
RADIOS (per 1,000 people) 1,034 (2001 est)
INTERNET USERS (per 10,000 people) 5,518.9 (2002 est)
PERSONAL COMPUTER USERS (per 100 people) 55.6 (2002 est)

See also ▷Korean War; ▷North Korea; ▷Russo-Japanese War.

Chronology

2333 BC: Traditional date of founding of Korean state by Tangun (mythical son from union of bear-woman and god).

1122 BC: Ancient texts record founding of kingdom in Korea by Chinese nobleman Kija.

194 BC: Northwest Korea united under warlord, Wiman.

108 BC: Korea conquered by Chinese.

1st–7th centuries AD: Three Korean kingdoms – Koguryo, Paekche, and Silla – competed for supremacy.

668: Korean peninsula unified by Buddhist Silla kingdom; culture combining Chinese and Korean elements flourished.

935: Silla dynasty overthrown by Wang Kon of Koguryo, who founded Koryo dynasty in its place.

1258: Korea accepted overlordship of Mongol Yüan Empire.

1392: Yi dynasty founded by Gen Yi Song-gye, vassal of Chinese Ming Empire; Confucianism replaced Buddhism as official creed; extreme conservatism characterized Korean society.

1592 and 1597: Japanese invasions repulsed by Korea.

1636: Manchu invasion forced Korea to sever ties with Ming dynasty.

18th–19th centuries: Korea resisted change in political and economic life and rejected contact with Europeans.

1864: Attempts to reform government and strengthen army by Taewongun (who ruled in name of his son, King Kojong); converts to Christianity persecuted.

1873: Taewongun forced to cede power to Queen Min; reforms reversed; government authority collapsed.

1882: Chinese occupied Seoul and installed governor.

1894–95: Sino-Japanese War: Japan forced China to recognize independence of Korea; Korea fell to Japanese influence.

1904–05: Russo-Japanese War: Japan ended Russian influence in Korea.

1910: Korea formally annexed by Japan; Japanese settlers introduced modern industry and agriculture; Korean language banned.

1919: 'Samil' nationalist movement suppressed by Japanese.

1945: After defeat of Japan in World War II, Russia occupied regions of Korea north of 38th parallel (demarcation line agreed at Yalta Conference) and USA occupied regions south of it.

1948: The USSR refused to permit United Nations (UN) supervision of elections in the northern zone; the southern zone became independent as the Republic of Korea, with Syngman Rhee as president.

1950: North Korea invaded South Korea; UN forces (mainly from the USA) intervened to defend South Korea; China intervened in support of North Korea.

1953: The Korean War ended with an armistice which restored the 38th parallel; no peace treaty was agreed and US troops remained in South Korea.

1961: Military coup placed Gen Park Chung Hee in power; a major programme of industrial development began.

1972: Martial law was imposed and presidential powers increased.

1979: The government of President Choi Kyu-Hah introduced liberalizing reforms.

1979: Gen Chun Doo Hwan assumed power after anti-government riots; Korea emerged as a leading shipbuilding nation and exporter of electronic goods.

1987: The constitution was made more democratic as a result of Liberal pressure; ruling Democratic Justice Party (DJP) candidate Roh Tae Woo Was elected president amid allegations of fraud.

1988: The Olympic Games were held in Seoul.

1991: Large-scale antigovernment protests were suppressed; South Korea joined the UN.

1992: South Korea established diplomatic relations with China.

1994: The US military presence was stepped up in response to the perceived threat from North Korea.

1997: South Korea was admitted to the OECD. Kim Dae Jung, former dissident and political prisoner, became the first opposition politician to lead South Korea.

1998: Kim Dae Jung was sworn in as president, with Kim Jong Pil as prime minister. New labour laws ended lifetime employment and the financial system was opened up. More than 2,000 prisoners were released, including 74 political prisoners.

1999: Talks on possible reunification with North Korea were suspended.

2000: Kim Jong Pil resigned as prime minister and was replaced by Park Tae Joon. In elections in April, the opposition Grand National Party won a majority, Park Tae Joon resigned, and was replaced by Lee Han Dong. At the first summit meeting between the divided countries, Kim Dae Jung was welcomed by Kim Jong Il, in Pyongyang, North Korea. The two leaders came to some agreement, including a plan for South Korea to speed up economic investment in North Korea.

2002: In the worst clash between North and South Korea in three years, naval vessels fired on each other in disputed coastal waters in the Yellow Sea. The incident threatened to derail President Kim Dae Jung's policy of engagement with North Korea.

of the state, as against other forms of community. The term has an internal aspect, in that it refers to the ultimate source of authority within a state, such as a parliament or monarch, and an external aspect, where it denotes the independence of the state from any outside authority.

soviet (Russian 'council') originally a strike committee elected by Russian workers in the 1905 revolution; in 1917 these were set up by peasants, soldiers, and factory workers. The soviets sent delegates to the All-Russian Congress of Soviets to represent their opinions to a future government. They were later taken over by the ▷Bolsheviks.

Soviet Central Asia former name (to 1991) of the ▷Central Asian Republics.

Soviet Union alternative name for the former ▷Union of Soviet Socialist Republics (USSR).

Soweto (acronym for South West Township) urban settlement in South Africa, southwest of Johannesburg; population (1991) 597,000. It experienced civil unrest during the ▷apartheid regime. Industries include wood pulp and paper manufacturing.

soybean leguminous plant (see ▷legume), native to East Asia, in particular Japan and China. Originally grown as a food crop for animals, it is increasingly used for human consumption in cooking oils and margarine, as a flour, soya milk, soy sauce, or processed into tofu, miso, or textured vegetable protein (▷TVP). (*Glycine max*)

SOYBEAN The grain of the soybean plant. *Image Bank*

Soyinka, Wole (1934–) Pen-name of Akinwande Oluwole Soyinka. Nigerian author and dramatist, who founded a national theatre in Nigeria. His plays explore Yoruba myth, ritual, and culture, with the early *Swamp Dwellers* (1958) and *The Lion and the Jewel* (1959), culminating with *A Dance of the Forests* (1960), written as a tragic vision of Nigerian independence. Tragic inevitability is the theme of *Madmen and Specialists* (1970) and of *Death and the King's Horseman* (1976), but he has also written sharp satires, from *The Jero Plays* (1960 and 1973) to the indictment of African dictatorship in *A Play of Giants* (1984). His plays have also been produced in London, England, and New York. He was the first African to be awarded the Nobel Prize for Literature, in 1986. A volume of poetry, *From Zia with Love*, appeared in 1992.

Soyinka was charged with treason by the Nigerian government in March 1997 over a spate of bomb blasts in the country. Since December 1996 a series of blasts on army buses had killed three soldiers and wounded dozens more. Soyinka and 11 other dissidents were charged and if convicted would face the death penalty. Soyinka was among the four opposition figures who had fled Nigeria in 1995 to Europe and the USA. The charges would pave the way for Nigeria to try to have Soyinka extradited back home.

Soyuz (Russian 'union') Soviet (now Russian) series of spacecraft, capable of carrying up to three cosmonauts. Soyuz spacecraft consist of three parts: a rear section containing engines; the central crew compartment; and a forward compartment that gives additional room for working and living space. They are now used

Space Flight: Key Dates

1903	Russian scientist Konstantin Tsiolkovsky publishes the first practical paper on astronautics.
1926	US engineer Robert Goddard launches the first liquid-fuel rocket.
1937–45	In Germany, Wernher von Braun develops the V2 rocket.
1957	The USSR launches the first space satellite, *Sputnik 1* into Earth orbit. The USSR launches *Sputnik 2*, which carries a dog called Laika; it dies on board after seven days.
1958	*Explorer 1*, the first US satellite, discovers the Van Allen radiation belts.
1961	The USSR launches the first crewed spaceship, *Vostok 1*, on 12 April, with Soviet cosmonaut Yuri Gagarin on board. Before landing he completes a single orbit of 89.1 min at an altitude of 142–175 km/88–109 mi. On 5 May Alan B Shepard, of the USA, makes a 15-minute suborbital flight reaching an altitude of 185 km/115 mi aboard the Mercury capsule Freedom 7.
1962	US astronaut John Glenn in *Friendship 7* becomes the first US citizen to orbit the Earth. *Telstar*, a US communications satellite, sends the first live television transmission between the USA and Europe.
1963	During 16–19 June, Soviet cosmonaut Valentina Tereshkova becomes the first woman in space, making 48 orbits of the Earth in *Vostok 6*.
1965	On 18 March, Soviet cosmonaut Alexei Leonov performs the first 'space walk', outside the spacecraft *Voskhod 2*.
1967	US astronauts Virgil Grissom, Edward White, and Roger Chaffee die during a simulated countdown when a flash fire sweeps through the cabin of *Apollo 1*. Vladimir Komarov is the first person to be killed on a space mission, when his ship, *Soyuz 1* (USSR), crash-lands on the Earth.
1969	On 20 July, US astronaut Neil Armstrong of *Apollo 11* becomes the first person to walk on the Moon.
1970	The *Apollo 13* mission to the Moon is cut short after an onboard explosion; all three astronauts survive the return to Earth. *Luna 17* (USSR) is launched; its space probe, *Lunokhod*, takes photographs and makes soil analyses of the Moon's surface.
1971	The Soviet *Salyut 1*, the first orbital space station, is established; it is later visited by the *Soyuz 11* crewed spacecraft. Cosmonauts Georgi Dobrovolsky, Viktor Patsayev, and Vladislav Volkov, aboard the *Soyuz 11* mission, are the first people to die in space when their cabin depressurizes during re-entry.
1973	*Skylab 2*, the first US orbital space station, is established.
1975	The crafts *Apollo 18* of the USA and *Soyuz 19* of the USSR make a joint flight and link up in space.
1979	The European Space Agency's satellite launcher, *Ariane 1*, is launched.
1981	The first reusable crewed spacecraft, the US space shuttle *Columbia* is launched.
1983	On 18 June the US space shuttle *Challenger* carries the first five-person crew into orbit, including Sally K Ride, the first US woman in space. Later that year, the space shuttle *Columbia*, with a crew of six, launches the European experimental platform *Spacelab*.
1984	Soviet cosmonaut Svetlana Savitskaya, one of the crew of the *Soyuz T12*, becomes the first woman to walk in space.
1986	The Soviet space station *Mir* is launched into orbit and its first crew visit it. The US space shuttle *Challenger* (USA) explodes shortly after take-off, killing all seven crew members.
1988	The US shuttle programme resumes with launch of *Discovery*. The Soviet shuttle *Buran* is launched from the rocket *Energiya*. Soviet cosmonauts Musa Manarov and Vladimir Titov in the space station *Mir* complete a whole year – actually 365 days 59 min – in space.
1990	The US Hubble Space Telescope is launched from Cape Canaveral. The US space probe *Magellan*, launched in 1989, reaches Venus and begins mapping the planet in detail.
1991	5 April: The Gamma Ray Observatory is launched from the space shuttle *Atlantis* to survey the sky at gamma-ray wavelengths. On 18 May Helen Sharman, the first Briton in space, is launched with Anatoli Artsebarsky and Sergei Krikalev to *Mir* space station, returning to Earth 26 May in *Soyuz TM-11* with Viktor Afanasyev and Musa Manarov. Manarov sets a record for the longest time spent in space, 541 days, having also spent a year aboard *Mir* 1988.
1992	European satellite *Hipparcos*, launched 1989 to measure the position of 120,000 stars, fails to reach geostationary orbit and goes into a highly elliptical orbit, swooping to within 500 km/308 mi of the Earth every ten hours. The satellite is later retrieved. *LAGEOS II* (Laser Geodynamics Satellite) is released from the space shuttle *Columbia* into an orbit so stable that it will still be circling the Earth in billions of years. Astronauts aboard the space shuttle *Endeavour* successfully carry out mission to replace the Hubble Space Telescope's solar panels and repair its mirror.
1994	Japan's heavy-lifting *H-2* rocket is launched successfully, carrying an uncrewed shuttle craft.
1995	The US space shuttle *Atlantis* docks with *Mir*, exchanging crew members.
1996	4 June: the *Ariane 5* rocket disintegrates almost immediately after takeoff, destroying the four Cluster satellites.
1997	Astronauts aboard the US space shuttle *Discovery* carry out a second service mission to improve the performance of the Hubble Space Telescope. *Mir* undergoes increasing difficulties, following a collision with a cargo ship that depressurized one of its modules, *Spektr*.
1998	NASA launches the space probe *Deep Space 1* to explore interplanetary space. A Russian Proton rocket lifts *Zarya*, the first module of the International Space Station (ISS) into Earth orbit. The ISS is an international project involving 15 countries, including the USA and Russia.
1999	The Russian space agency abandons the problem-ridden *Mir* space station. The US space shuttle *Columbia* launches *Chandra* X-ray Observatory in July. The same month, US probe *Deep Space 1* flies past the recently discovered asteroid Braille. The European Space Agency launches its X-ray Multi-mirror Mission (X-MM) Observatory atop an *Ariane 5* rocket; it is later renamed Newton. A space shuttle crew aboard *Discovery* carry out another servicing mission on the Hubble Space Telescope to fix faulty gyroscopes in November. NASA loses two important Mars probes, *Mars Climate Orbiter* and *Mars Polar Lander*.
2000	The European Space Agency launches its Cluster project. A Dutch-based company, MirCorp, takes over the *Mir* space station with support from the Russian government. The first crew of scientists move into the International Space Station to begin what is hoped will be a permanent residence in space.
2001	The *Mir* space station is decommissioned and is crashed into the Pacific Ocean.

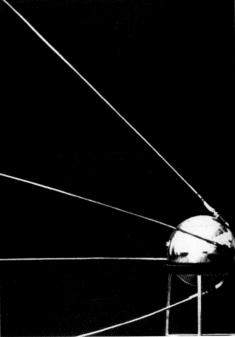

SPACE FLIGHT *Sputnik I* displayed on a stand before its launch. *Sputnik* was the first man-made object in space. *Archive Photos*

for ferrying crews up to space stations, though they were originally used for independent space flight.

Soyuz 1 crashed on its first flight in April 1967, killing the lone pilot, Vladimir Komarov. Three cosmonauts were killed in 1971 aboard *Soyuz 11*, while returning from a visit to the *Salyut 1* space station, when a faulty valve caused their cabin to lose pressure. In 1975 the Apollo–Soyuz test project resulted in a successful docking of the two spacecraft in orbit.

Spaak, Paul-Henri (1899–1972) Belgian socialist politician. From 1936 to 1966 he held office almost continuously as foreign minister or prime minister. He was an ardent advocate of international peace.

space (or **outer space**) void that exists beyond Earth's atmosphere. Above 120 km/75 mi, very little atmosphere remains, so objects can continue to move quickly without extra energy. The space between the planets is not entirely empty, but filled with the tenuous gas of the ▷solar wind as well as dust specks. See also Space Flight: Key Dates on p. 893.

Related Web site: Space.Com http://www.space.com/

space-frame in architecture, a lightweight, triangulated, structural framework, designed to be of uniform load resistance and used principally in large-span constructions, such as exhibition halls, stadia, and aircraft hangars. The Eiffel Tower, Paris, 1889, is a space-frame of riveted steel beams. A contemporary development is Buckminster Fuller's geodesic dome, a shell-like space-frame covered in plastic, plywood, or metal sheeting.

Spacelab small space station built by the European Space Agency, carried in the cargo bay of the US space shuttle, in which it remains throughout each flight, returning to Earth with the shuttle. Spacelab consists of a pressurized module in which astronauts can work, and a series of pallets, open to the vacuum of space, on which equipment is mounted. Spacelab is used for astronomy, Earth observation, and experiments utilizing the conditions of weightlessness and vacuum in orbit.

space probe any instrumented object sent beyond Earth to collect data from other parts of the Solar System and from deep space. The first probe was the Soviet *Lunik 1*, which flew past the Moon in 1959. The first successful planetary probe was the US *Mariner 2*, which flew past Venus in 1962, using ▷transfer orbit. The first space probe to leave the Solar System was *Pioneer 10* in 1983. Space probes include *Galileo, Giotto, Magellan, Mars Observer, Ulysses*, the ▷Moon probes, and the Mariner, Pioneer, Viking, and Voyager series.

space shuttle reusable crewed spacecraft. The first was launched 12 April 1981 by the USA. It was developed by NASA to reduce the cost of using space for commercial, scientific, and military purposes. After leaving its payload in space, the space-shuttle orbiter can be flown back to Earth to land on a runway, and is then available for reuse.

Four orbiters were built: *Columbia, Challenger, Discovery*, and *Atlantis. Challenger* was destroyed in a midair explosion just over a minute after its 10th launch 28 January 1986, killing all seven crew members, the result of a failure in one of the solid rocket boosters. Flights resumed with redesigned boosters in September 1988. A replacement orbiter, *Endeavour*, was built, which had its maiden flight in May 1992. At the end of the 1980s, an average of $375 million had been spent on each space-shuttle mission. On 16 January 2003 the psace stuttle Columbia lifted off from Kennedy Space Center in Florida for its 28th flight into space. On its return to earth on 1 February 2003 it broke up upon re-entering the Earth's atmosphere, killing all seven crew members. The aftermath of the tragedy was an increased focus on astronaut safety and a decrease in the number of missions that space shuttles would have to fly.

The USSR produced a shuttle of similar size and appearance to the US one. The first Soviet shuttle, *Buran*, was launched without a crew by the Energiya rocket 15 November 1988. In Japan, development of a crewless shuttle began in 1986.

The space-shuttle orbiter, the part that goes into space, is 37.2 m/122 ft long and weighs 68 metric tons/75 tons. Two to eight crew members occupy the orbiter's nose section, and missions last up to 30 days. In its cargo bay the orbiter can carry up to 29 tonnes of satellites, scientific equipment, ▷Spacelab, or military payloads. At launch, the shuttle's three main engines are fed with liquid fuel from a cylindrical tank attached to the orbiter; this tank is discarded shortly before the shuttle reaches orbit. Two additional solid-fuel boosters provide the main thrust for launch, but are jettisoned after two minutes.

Related Web site: NASA Shuttle Web http://spaceflight.nasa.gov/shuttle/index.html

space suit protective suit worn by astronauts and cosmonauts in space. It provides an insulated, air-conditioned cocoon in which people can live and work for hours at a time while outside the spacecraft. Inside the suit is a cooling garment that keeps the body at a comfortable temperature even during vigorous work. The suit provides air to breathe, and removes exhaled carbon dioxide and moisture. The suit's outer layers insulate the occupant from the extremes of hot and cold in space ($-150°C/-240°F$ in the shade to $+180°C/+350°F$ in sunlight), and from the impact of small meteorites. Some space suits have a jet-propelled backpack, which the wearer can use to move about.

space-time in physics, combination of space and time used in the theory of ▷relativity. When developing relativity, Albert Einstein showed that time was in many respects like an extra dimension (or direction) to space. Space and time can thus be considered as entwined into a single entity, rather than two separate things.

Spain see country box.

Spalato Italian name for ▷Split, a port in Croatia.

spaniel any of several breeds of small and medium-sized gundog, characterized by large, drooping ears and a wavy, long, silky coat. Spaniels are divided into two groups: those that are still working gundogs – Clumber, cocker, Irish water, springer, and Sussex – and the toy breeds that are kept as pets – including the Japanese, King Charles, papillon, and Tibetan.

Spanish inhabitants of Spain or people of Spanish descent, as well as the culture and Romance language of such persons. The standard Spanish language, Castilian, originated in the kingdoms of Castile and Aragón (Catalan and Basque languages are also spoken in Spain).

Spanish-American War brief war in 1898 between Spain and the USA over Spanish rule in Cuba and the Philippines; the complete defeat of Spain made the USA a colonial power. The

Treaty of Paris ceded the Philippines, Guam, and Puerto Rico to the USA; Cuba became independent. The USA paid $20 million to Spain. This ended Spain's colonial presence in the Americas.

The war began in Cuba when the US battleship *Maine* was blown up in Havana harbour, allegedly by the Spanish. Other engagements included the Battle of Manila Bay, in which Commander George Dewey's navy destroyed the Spanish fleet in the Philippines; and the taking of the Cuban port cities of El Caney and San Juan Heights (in which Theodore Roosevelt's regiment, the Rough Riders, was involved), destroying the Spanish fleet there.

Related Web site: Spanish-American War Centennial Web Site http://www.spanam.simplenet.com/

Spanish Monarchs from 1516

In 1516 Charles I was the first king to inherit a unified Spain. He later became Archduke of Austria and Holy Roman Emperor as Charles V.

Reign	Name
House of Habsburg	
1516–56	Charles I
1556–98	Philip II
1598–1621	Philip III
1621–65	Philip IV
1665–1700	Charles II
House of Bourbon	
1700–46	Philip V
1746–59	Ferdinand VI
1759–88	Charles III
1788–1808	Charles IV
1808	Ferdinand VII (deposed)
1808–13	Joseph Napoleon[1]
1813–33	Ferdinand VII (restored)
1833–68	Isabel II
1868–70	provisional government
1870–73	Amadeus I[2] (abdicated)
1873–74	first republic
1874–86	Alfonso XII
1886–1931	Alfonso XIII (deposed)
1975–	Juan Carlos I

[1] House of Bonaparte.
[2] House of Savoy.

SPACE SHUTTLE The vertical launch of a space shuttle from Cape Canaveral. The shuttle orbiter, its two huge fuel boosters, and its central fuel tank are clearly visible. *Corel*

SPANISH-AMERICAN WAR North Americans arriving in Cuba to oust the Spanish in the Spanish-American War, 1898. *Art Archive*

SPANISH MONARCHS *Apotheosis of the Spanish Monarchy*, one of the ceilings decorated by Italian rococo painter Giovanni Battista Tiepolo at the Royal Palace of Madrid, Spain, in 1764. Whether his subjects were from the Bible or classical mythology, Tiepolo's works were typically glorifications of his patrons – usually princes and the Catholic Church. *The Art Archive/Birmingham City Art Gallery/Eileen Tweedy*

Spain

SPAIN The El Escorial monastery and palace in Sierra de Guadarrama, Spain was built in 1563–84. It became the centre of the Spanish Empire ruled by Philip II. *Corel*

TV SETS (per 1,000 people) 598 (2001 est)
RADIOS (per 1,000 people) 330 (2001 est)
INTERNET USERS (per 10,000 people) 1,931.0 (2002 est)

See also ▷Civil War, Spanish; ▷Spanish Armada; ▷Spanish Succession, War of the.

Spain country in southwestern Europe, on the Iberian Peninsula between the Atlantic Ocean and the Mediterranean Sea, bounded north by France and west by Portugal.

NATIONAL NAME *España/Spain*
AREA 504,750 sq km/194,883 sq mi (including the Balearic and Canary islands)
CAPITAL Madrid
MAJOR TOWNS/CITIES Barcelona, Valencia, Zaragoza, Seville, Málaga, Bilbao, Las Palmas (on Gran Canarias island), Murcia, Palma (on Mallorca)
MAJOR PORTS Barcelona, Valencia, Cartagena, Málaga, Cádiz, Vigo, Santander, Bilbao
PHYSICAL FEATURES central plateau with mountain ranges, lowlands in south; rivers Ebro, Douro, Tagus, Guadiana, Guadalquivir; Iberian Plateau (Meseta); Pyrenees, Cantabrian Mountains, Andalusian Mountains, Sierra Nevada
TERRITORIES Balearic and Canary islands; in North Africa: Ceuta, Melilla, Peña d'Alhucemas, Islas Chafarinas, Peñón de Vélez de la Gomera

Government

HEAD OF STATE King Juan Carlos I from 1975
HEAD OF GOVERNMENT José Luis Rodríguez Zapatero from 2004
POLITICAL SYSTEM liberal democracy
POLITICAL EXECUTIVE parliamentary
ADMINISTRATIVE DIVISIONS 17 autonomous regions (Melilla and Ceuta are also administered as autonomous regions) and 50 provinces
ARMED FORCES 177,900 (2002 est)
DEATH PENALTY abolished in 1995

Economy and resources

CURRENCY euro (peseta until 2002)
GPD (US$) 649.8 billion (2002 est)
REAL GDP GROWTH (% change on previous year) 2.7 (2001)
GNI (US$) 594.1 billion (2002 est)
GNI PER CAPITA (PPP) (US$) 20,460 (2002 est)
CONSUMER PRICE INFLATION 2.9% (2003 est)
UNEMPLOYMENT 10.5% (2001)
MAJOR TRADING PARTNERS EU (principally France, Germany, Italy, and UK), USA, Japan, Latin America, OPEC
RESOURCES coal, lignite, anthracite, copper, iron, zinc, uranium, potassium salts

INDUSTRIES machinery, motor vehicles, textiles, footwear, chemicals, electrical appliances, wine, olive oil, fishery products, steel, cement, tourism
EXPORTS motor vehicles, machinery and electrical equipment, vegetable products, metals and their manufactures, foodstuffs, wine. Principal market: France 19.5% (2001)
IMPORTS machinery and transport equipment, electrical equipment, petroleum and petroleum products, chemicals, consumer goods. Principal source: France 16.8% (2001)
ARABLE LAND 26.7% (2000 est)
AGRICULTURAL PRODUCTS barley, wheat, sugar beet, vegetables, citrus fruit, bananas (Canary Islands), grapes, olives (Spanish olives account for 40% of the world total); fishing (one of the world's largest fishing fleets)

Population and society

POPULATION 41,060,000 (2003 est)
POPULATION GROWTH RATE –0.1% (2000–15)
POPULATION DENSITY (per sq km) 81 (2003 est)
URBAN POPULATION (% of total) 78 (2003 est)
AGE DISTRIBUTION (% of total population) 0–14 14%, 15–59 64%, 60+ 22% (2002 est)
ETHNIC GROUPS mostly of Moorish, Roman, and Carthaginian descent
LANGUAGE Spanish (Castilian; official), Basque, Catalan, Galician
RELIGION Roman Catholic 98%
EDUCATION (compulsory years) 10
LITERACY RATE 99% (men); 97% (women) (2003 est)
LABOUR FORCE 7.3% agriculture, 30.7% industry, 62.0% services (1999)
LIFE EXPECTANCY 76 (men); 83 (women) (2000–05)
CHILD MORTALITY RATE (under 5, per 1,000 live births) 6 (2001)
PHYSICIANS (per 1,000 people) 4.2 (1998 est)
HOSPITAL BEDS (per 1,000 people) 4.1 (1998 est)

Chronology

2nd century BC: Roman conquest of the Iberian peninsula, which became the province of Hispania.
5th century AD: After the fall of the Roman Empire, Iberia was overrun by Vandals and Visigoths.
711: Muslims invaded from North Africa and overthrew Visigoth kingdom.
9th century: Christians in northern Spain formed kingdoms of Asturias, Aragón, Navarre, and Léon, and county of Castile.
10th century: Abd-al-Rahman III established caliphate of Córdoba; Muslim culture at its height in Spain.
1230: Léon and Castile united under Ferdinand III, who drove the Muslims from most of southern Spain.
14th century: Spain consisted of Christian kingdoms of Castile, Aragón, and Navarre, and the Muslim emirate of Granada.
1469: Marriage of Ferdinand of Aragón and Isabella of Castile; kingdoms united on their accession in 1479.
1492: Conquest of Granada ended Muslim rule in Spain.
1494: Treaty of Tordesillas; Spain and Portugal divided newly discovered America; Spain became a world power.
1519–56: Emperor Charles V was both King of Spain and Archduke of Austria; he also ruled Naples, Sicily, and the Low Countries; Habsburgs dominant in Europe.
1555: Charles V divided his domains between Spain and Austria before retiring; Spain retained the Low Countries and southern Italy as well as South American colonies.
1568: Dutch rebelled against Spanish rule; Spain recognized independence of Dutch Republic in 1648.
1580: Philip II of Spain inherited the throne of Portugal, where Spanish rule lasted until 1640.
1588: Spanish Armada: attempt to invade England defeated.
17th century: Spanish power declined amid wars, corruption, inflation, and loss of civil and religious freedom.
1701–14: War of the Spanish Succession: allied powers fought France to prevent Philip of Bourbon inheriting throne of Spain.
1713–14: Treaties of Utrecht and Rastat: Bourbon dynasty recognized, but Spain lost Gibraltar, southern Italy, and Spanish Netherlands.
1793: Spain declared war on revolutionary France; reduced to a French client state in 1795.
1808: Napoleon installed his brother Joseph as King of Spain.

1808–14: Peninsular War: British forces played a large part in liberating Spain and restoring Bourbon dynasty.
1810–30: Spain lost control of its South American colonies.
1833–39: Carlist civil war: Don Carlos (backed by conservatives) unsuccessfully contested the succession of his niece Isabella II (backed by liberals).
1870: Offer of Spanish throne to Leopold of Hohenzollern-Sigmaringen sparked Franco-Prussian War.
1873–74: First republic ended by military coup which restored Bourbon dynasty with Alfonso XII.
1898: Spanish-American War: Spain lost Cuba and Philippines.
1923–30: Dictatorship of Gen Primo de Rivera with support of Alfonso XIII.
1931: Proclamation of Second Republic, initially dominated by anticlerical radicals and socialists.
1933: Moderates and Catholics won elections; insurrection by socialists and Catalans in 1934.
1936: Left-wing Popular Front narrowly won fresh elections; General Francisco Franco launched military rebellion.
1936–39: Spanish Civil War: Nationalists (with significant Italian and German support) defeated Republicans (with limited Soviet support); Franco became dictator of nationalist-fascist regime.
1941: Though officially neutral in World War II, Spain sent 40,000 troops to fight USSR.
1955: Spain admitted to the United Nations (UN).
1975: Death of Franco; he was succeeded by King Juan Carlos I.
1978: A referendum endorsed democratic constitution.
1982: Socialists took office under Felipe González; Spain joined the North Atlantic Treaty Organization (NATO); Basque separatist organization ETA stepped up its terrorist campaign.
1986: Spain joined the European Economic Community (EEC).
1997: 23 Basque nationalist leaders were jailed for terrorist activities.
1998: ETA announced an indefinite ceasefire. The government announced that it would begin peace talks.
2000: Prime Minister Aznar was re-elected. ETA ended its ceasefire with a bombing in Madrid, and assassinations and bombing continued throughout the year. Thirty-six suspected ETA terrorists, including its commander, were arrested in September but violence continued.
2004: In March a train in Madrid was bombed by terrorists, killing around 190 people and injuring 2,000.

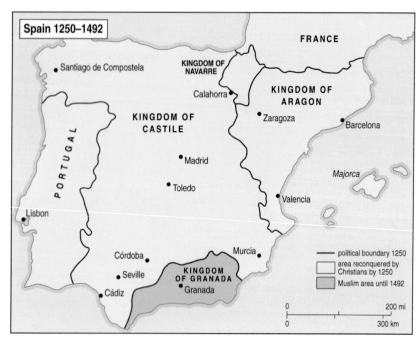

Spain 1250–1492

Spanish architecture

Spanish architecture the architecture of Spain has been influenced by both European classical and Islamic traditions.

Early Christian (5th–8th centuries) The Visigoths invaded Spain 415 and were later converted to Christianity. Their small churches, few of which remain, are indebted to Roman architecture and have parallels with the early French Romanesque style. Fine examples are San Juan de Banos 661 and San Pedro de Nave about 7th century.

Muslim (8th–15th centuries) The Muslims invaded in 711, quickly capturing most of the country. In Córdoba, the Great Mosque, a huge rectangular hall with a proliferation of columns, was begun in 786 and worked on over the next 200 years. Elsewhere in Muslim-occupied Spain architecture developed in unique response to its environment, characterized by a particularly delicate decorative style. In the fortified palaces of the Alcázar, Seville, 1350–69, and the Alhambra, Granada, built mainly 1248–1354, a vocabulary of water gardens, courtyards, colourful tilework, and elaborate stalactite decoration is used.

Romanesque (11th–12th centuries) Romanesque church building began in Cataluña from the 11th century and developed along the pilgrimage routes from France. The cathedral of Santiago de Compostela (begun about 1075) is a fine example, with its barrel-vaulted roof and huge, sculpted Pórtico de la Gloria.

Gothic (13th–16th centuries) In the 12th century, the Cistercian order brought the Gothic style to Spain and by the following century the style of northern French Gothic cathedrals had been adopted, as in Burgos Cathedral (begun 1221). The Catalan version of Gothic proved the most distinctive, introducing a high wide nave, as at Sta Maria, Barcelona (begun 1298). Later cathedrals, such as that in Seville (begun 1402), show German influence in their use of rib-vaulting but this is tempered by unique ground plans owing much to Islamic mosque architecture.

Renaissance (16th century) The Italian Renaissance reached Spain in the 16th century. The finest example of the High Renaissance is the Escorial (begun 1563), the huge palace, monastery, and church built for Phillip II, largely designed by Juan de Herrera (1530–1597). This structure is more severe than most other Spanish Renaissance architecture, which is characterized by richly decorative work in a style known as Plateresque, as in the facade of Salamanca University (1514).

Baroque (17th–18th centuries) An interest in surface decoration, reflecting the Muslim past, re-emerged in the late-17th-century Spanish variation of baroque, Churrigueresque, of which the west front of the cathedral of Santiago de Compostela (begun 1738), is a fine example. José Benito de Churriguera and Narciso Tomè (active 1715–1742) were both active in this style.

Neoclassicism (18th century) In the latter part of the 18th century a severe neoclassicism was developed in such works as the portico of Pamplona Cathedral (1783) by Ventura Rodríguez (1717–1783).

Art nouveau (late 19th–early 20th century) The industrialization of Catalan provided Spain with a distinctive late-19th-century architecture, a variation of art nouveau known as modernismo. Connected in part to a growth in Catalan nationalism, it is best represented in the works of Lluis Doménech i Montaner (1850–1923), who built the Palau de la Música Catalana 1905–08, and of Antonio Gaudí, who designed the Church of the Holy Family (begun 1883) and the Casa Milá (1905–10), both in Barcelona.

20th century Under Franco, Spain retreated from its European connections into a provincialism that was echoed in its architecture. Since the restoration of democracy numerous designers of international importance have emerged. Among these are the neoclassicist Ricardo Bofill, now practising largely in France, who built the Antigone development in Montpelier 1992, the architect and engineer Santiago Calatrava, and Rafael Moneo (1937–   ), who was the architect responsible for the Museum of Archaeology at Mérida in 1986.

Spanish Armada fleet sent by Philip II of Spain against England in 1588. Consisting of 130 ships, it sailed from Lisbon and carried on a running fight up the Channel with the English fleet of 197 small ships under Howard of Effingham and Francis ▷Drake – although only three Spanish ships were lost to the English attack. The Armada anchored off Calais but the Duke of Parma, the leader of the Spanish army, was unwilling to embark until the English fleet was defeated. The English forced the Armada to put to sea by sending in fire ships, and a general action followed off Gravelines, although only four Spanish ships were lost in the battle. What remained of the Armada escaped around the north of Scotland and west of Ireland, losing an estimated 55 ships to storm and shipwreck on the way. Only about half the original fleet returned to Spain.

The Spanish fleet had been hastily prepared – corrupt Spanish traders had supplied unseasoned barrels and poor quality equipment. The commander, the Duke of Medina Sidonia, lacked naval experience, and the fleet was a motley collection of warships, armed merchantmen, and oared galleys. The English ships were longer and narrower and, therefore, more manoeuvrable than the Spanish ships. They were also better gunned than the Spanish, although they lacked the ammunition to inflict decisive damage in battle. What really defeated the Spanish Armada was the weather.

Spanish art painting and sculpture of Spain. Spanish art has been fashioned by both European and Islamic traditions, with notable regional adaptations. Whatever the source of its influences, Spanish art has always transformed styles and given them a distinctively Spanish character.

Spanish Civil War 1936–39. See ▷Civil War, Spanish.

Spanish fly alternative name for a European blister ▷beetle *Lytta vesicatoria*, once used in powdered form as a dangerous diuretic and supposed aphrodisiac.

Spanish language member of the Romance branch of the Indo-European language family, traditionally known as Castilian and originally spoken only in northeastern Spain. As the language of the court, it has been the standard and literary language of the

Spain: Regions and Provinces

Regions and provinces	Regional capital	Area		Population (1995 est)
		sq km	sq mi	
Andalusia Almería, Cádiz, Córdoba, Granada, Huelva, Jaén, Málaga, Sevilla	Seville	87,268	33,694	7,314,600
Aragon Huesca, Teruel, Zaragoza	Zaragoza	47,669	18,405	1,205,700
Asturias	Oviedo	10,565	4,079	1,117,400
Balearic Islands	Palma de Mallorca	5,014	1,935	788,000
Basque Country Alava, Guipúzcoa, Vizcaya	Vitoria	7,261	2,803	2,130,800
Canary Islands Las Palmas, Santa Cruz de Tenerife	Las Palmas and Santa Cruz de Tenerife	7,273	2,808	1,631,500
Cantabria				
Santander	Santander	5,289	2,042	541,900
Castilla–La Mancha Albacete, Ciudad Real, Cuenca, Guadalajara, Toledo	Toledo	79,226	30589	1,730,700
Castilla–León Avila, Burgos, León, Palencia, Salamanca, Segovia, Soria, Valladolid, Zamora	Valladolid	94,147	36,350	2,584,400
Catalonia Barcelona, Gerona, Lleida, Tarragona	Barcelona	31,930	12,328	6,226,900
Extremadura Badajoz, Cáceres	Mérida	41,602	16,063	1,100,500
Galicia La Coruña, Lugo, Orense, Pontevedra	Santiagade Compostele	29,434	11,364	2,825,000
Madrid	Madrid	7,995	3,087	5,181,700
Murcia	Murcia[1]	11,317	4,369	1,110,000
Navarra	Pamplona	10,421	4,024	536,200
La Rioja	Longroñá	5,034	1,944	268,200
Valencia Alicante, Castellón, Valencia	Valencia	23,305	8,998	4,028,800
Ceuta[2]		18	7	73,100
Melilla[2]		14	5	64,700

[1] Regional parliament is in Cartagena.

[2] Spanish enclaves on the north coast of Morocco.

Spanish state since the 13th century. It is now a world language, spoken in Mexico and all South and Central American countries (except Brazil, Guyana, Suriname, and French Guiana) as well as in the Philippines, Cuba, Puerto Rico, and much of the USA.

Spanish literature prose and poetry of Spain, written in any of the country's languages. Spanish literature has roots in the 12th century, but its golden age was in the 15th–17th centuries with Miguel de Cervantes's novel ▷*Don Quixote* and the plays of Lope de Vega and Calderón de la Barca. Outstanding in the early 20th century was the playwright and poet Federico García Lorca.

Spanish Main common term for the Caribbean Sea in the 16th–17th centuries, but more properly the South American mainland between the River Orinoco and Panama.

Spanish Succession, War of the war 1701–14 of Britain, Austria, the Netherlands, Portugal, and Denmark (the Allies) against France, Spain, and Bavaria. It was caused by Louis XIV's acceptance of the Spanish throne on behalf of his grandson, Philip, in defiance of the Partition Treaty of 1700, under which it would have passed to Archduke Charles of Austria (later Holy Roman Emperor Charles VI).

Peace was made by the Treaties of Utrecht 1713 and Rastatt 1714. Philip V was recognized as king of Spain, thus founding the Spanish branch of the Bourbon dynasty. Britain received Gibraltar, Menorca, and Nova Scotia; and Austria received Belgium, Milan, and Naples.

spark chamber electronic device for recording tracks of charged subatomic particles, decay products, and rays. In combination with a stack of photographic plates, a spark chamber enables the point where an interaction has taken place to be located, to within a cubic centimetre. At its simplest, it consists of two smooth threadlike ▷electrodes that are positioned 1–2 cm/0.5–1 in apart, the space between being filled by an inert gas such as neon. Sparks jump through the gas along the ionized path created by the radiation. See ▷particle detector.

Spark, Muriel (1918–) Born Muriel Sarah Camberg. Scottish-born novelist. After writing poetry and critical and biographical works, she was encouraged to embark upon fiction after winning the *Observer* short-story competition in 1951 and her conversion to Catholicism in 1954. Many of her characters are misfits, such as feature in *The Comforters* (1957) (her first novel), *The Prime of Miss Jean Brodie* (1961), and *A Far Cry from Kensington* (1988). Blacker satire is in *Memento Mori* (1959), *Symposium* (1990), and *Realities and Dreams* (1996). *Collected Poems* appeared in 1967 and *The Collected Stories* was published in 1994. The novel *Aiding and Abetting* was published in 2000.

> **Muriel Spark**
> *The one certain way for a woman to hold a man is to leave him for religion.*
> The Comforters ch. 1

spark plug plug that produces an electric spark in the cylinder of a petrol engine to ignite the fuel mixture. It consists essentially of two electrodes insulated from one another. High-voltage (18,000 V) electricity is fed to a central electrode via the distributor. At the base of the electrode, inside the cylinder, the electricity jumps to another electrode earthed to the engine body, creating a spark.

sparrow any of a family (Passeridae) of small Old World birds of the order Passeriformes with short, thick bills, but applied particularly to the different members of the genus *Passer* in the family Ploceidae, order Passeriformes.

Many members of the New World family Emberizidae, which includes ▷warblers, orioles, and buntings, are also called sparrows; for example, the North American song sparrow *Melospize melodia*.

The **house sparrow** *Passer domesticus* has brown-black marked plumage, and a black chest and eyestripe in the male. It is inconspicuous, intelligent, and adaptable, with a cheery chirp and untidy nesting habits, using any scrap materials to hand for the nest. In diet it is omnivorous, feeding on insects and their larvae in spring and summer, and on grain in winter. The average sparrow flock size in Britain was reduced by one-third between 1970 and 1994; cats, cars, and pesticides were cited as the main culprits.

The **tree sparrow** *P. montanus*, the only other British species, is a smaller bird, found on the west coast of Scotland and in England. Tree sparrow populations have declined by 89% since the1960s. The **hedge sparrow** or ▷dunnock *Prunella modularis* is a species of Prunellidae, and is related to the nightingales and thrushes.

sparrow hawk small woodland ▷hawk *Accipiter nisus*, of the family Falconidae, order Falconiformes, found in Eurasia and North Africa. It is bluish-grey, with brown and white markings, and has a long tail and short wings. The male grows to 28 cm/11 in long, and the female to 38 cm/15 in. It hunts small birds and mice.

Sparta ancient Greek city-state in the southern Peloponnese (near Sparte), developed from Dorian settlements in the 10th century BC. The Spartans, known for their military discipline and austerity, took part in the ▷Persian and ▷Peloponnesian Wars.

Spartacist member of a group of left-wing radicals in Germany at the end of World War I, founders of the **Spartacus League**, which became the German Communist Party in 1919. The league participated in the Berlin workers' revolt of January 1919, which was suppressed by the Freikorps on the orders of the socialist government. The agitation ended with the murder of Spartacist leaders Karl ▷Liebknecht and Rosa ▷Luxemburg.

Spartacus (died 71 BC) Thracian gladiator. In 73 BC he led a revolt of gladiators and slaves in Capua, near Naples, and swept through southern Italy and Cisalpine Gaul. He was eventually caught by Roman general Crassus 71 BC. The fate of Spartacus is not known, although his followers were executed in mass crucifixions.

speakeasy bar that illegally sold alcoholic beverages during the ▷Prohibition period (1920–33) in the USA. The term is probably derived from the need to speak quickly or quietly to the doorkeeper in order to gain admission.

Speaker presiding officer charged with the preservation of order in the legislatures of various countries. In the UK the equivalent of the Speaker in the House of Lords is the Lord Chancellor; in the House of Commons the Speaker is elected for each parliament, usually on an agreed basis among the parties, but often holds the office for many years. The original appointment dates from 1377. Betty Boothroyd was the first female Speaker of the House of Commons 1992–2000.

spearmint perennial herb belonging to the mint family, with aromatic leaves and spikes of purple flowers; the leaves are used for flavouring in cookery. (*Mentha spicata*, family Labiatae.)

Special Air Service (**SAS**) specialist British regiment recruited from regiments throughout the army. It has served in Malaysia, Oman, Yemen, the Falklands, Northern Ireland, and during the 1991 Gulf War, as well as against international urban guerrillas, as in the siege of the Iranian embassy in London in 1980.

Special Branch section of the British police originally established in 1883 to deal with Irish Fenian activists. All 42 police forces in Britain now have their own Special Branches. They act as the executive arm of MI5 (British ▷intelligence) in its duty of preventing or investigating espionage, subversion, and sabotage; carry out duties at air and sea ports in respect of naturalization and immigration; and provide armed bodyguards for public figures.

special constable in the UK, a part-time volunteer who supplements local police forces as required. Special constables were established by the Special Constabulary Act 1831. They number some 16,000. They wear a police uniform and have all the powers and privileges of a regular constable, and are bound by the same duties and responsibilities. They do not specialize in a particular area of police work, for example dog-handling or traffic duty, but are allowed to go out on patrol alone once they have gained sufficient experience.

special drawing right (**SDR**) the right of a member state of the ▷International Monetary Fund to apply for money to finance its balance of payments deficit. Originally, the SDR was linked to gold and the US dollar. After 1974 SDRs were defined in terms of a 'basket' of the 16 currencies of countries doing 1% or more of the world's trade. In 1981 the SDR was simplified to a weighted average of US dollars, French francs, German marks, Japanese yen, and UK pounds sterling.

speciation emergence of a new species during evolutionary history. One cause of speciation is the geographical separation of populations of the parent species, followed by reproductive isolation and selection for different environments so that they no longer produce viable offspring when they interbreed. Other causes are ▷assortative mating and the establishment of a ▷polyploid population.

species in biology, a distinguishable group of organisms that resemble each other or consist of a few distinctive types (as in ▷polymorphism), and that can all interbreed to produce fertile offspring. Species are the lowest level in the system of biological classification.

Related species are grouped together in a genus. Within a species there are usually two or more separate ▷populations, which may in time become distinctive enough to be designated subspecies or varieties, and could eventually give rise to new species through ▷speciation. Around 1.4 million species have been identified so far, of which 750,000 are insects, 250,000 are plants, and 41,000 are vertebrates. In tropical regions there are roughly two species for each temperate-zone species. It is estimated that one species becomes extinct every day through habitat destruction.

A **native** species is a species that has existed in that country at least from prehistoric times; a **naturalized** species is one known to have been introduced by humans from another country, but which now maintains itself; while an **exotic** species is one that requires human intervention to survive.

specific gravity alternative term for ▷relative density.

specific heat capacity in physics, quantity of heat required to raise unit mass (1 kg) of a substance by one ▷kelvin (1 K). The unit of specific heat capacity in the SI system is the ▷joule per kilogram kelvin ($J\ kg^{-1}\ K^{-1}$).

specific latent heat in physics, the heat that changes the physical state of a unit mass (one kilogram) of a substance without causing any temperature change.

spectacles another name for ▷glasses, worn to correct or assist defective vision.

Spector, Phil (1940–) US record producer. He is known for the 'wall of sound', created using a large orchestra, which distinguished his work in the early 1960s with vocal groups such as the Crystals and the Ronettes. He withdrew into semi-retirement 1966 but his influence can still be heard.

spectroscopy study of spectra (see ▷spectrum) associated with atoms or molecules in solid, liquid, or gaseous phase. Spectroscopy can be used to identify unknown compounds and is an invaluable tool in science, medicine, and industry (for example, in checking the purity of drugs).

Emission spectroscopy is the study of the characteristic series of sharp lines in the spectrum produced when an ▷element is heated. Thus an unknown mixture can be analysed for its component elements. Related is **absorption spectroscopy**, dealing with atoms and molecules as they absorb energy in a characteristic way. Again, dark lines can be used for analysis. More detailed structural information can be obtained using **infrared spectroscopy** (concerned with molecular vibrations) or **nuclear magnetic resonance (NMR) spectroscopy** (concerned with interactions between adjacent atomic nuclei). **Supersonic jet laser beam spectroscopy** enables the isolation and study of clusters in the gas phase. A laser vaporizes a small sample, which is cooled in helium, and ejected into an evacuated chamber. The jet of clusters expands supersonically, cooling the clusters to near absolute zero, and stabilizing them for study in a ▷mass spectrometer.

spectrum (plural **spectra**) in physics, the pattern of frequencies or wavelengths obtained when electromagnetic radiations are separated into their constituent parts. Visible light is part of the ▷electromagnetic spectrum and most sources emit waves over a range of wavelengths that can be broken up or 'dispersed'; white light can be separated into red, orange, yellow, green, blue, indigo, and violet. The visible spectrum was first studied by Isaac ▷Newton, who showed in 1672 how white light could be broken up into different colours.

There are many types of spectra, both emission and absorption, for radiation and particles, used in ▷spectroscopy. An incandescent body gives rise to a **continuous spectrum** where the dispersed radiation is distributed uninterruptedly over a range of wavelengths. A gaseous element gives a **line spectrum** – one or more bright discrete lines at characteristic wavelengths. Molecular gases give **band spectra** in which there are groups of close-packed lines. In an **absorption spectrum** dark lines or spaces replace the characteristic bright lines of the absorbing medium. The **mass**

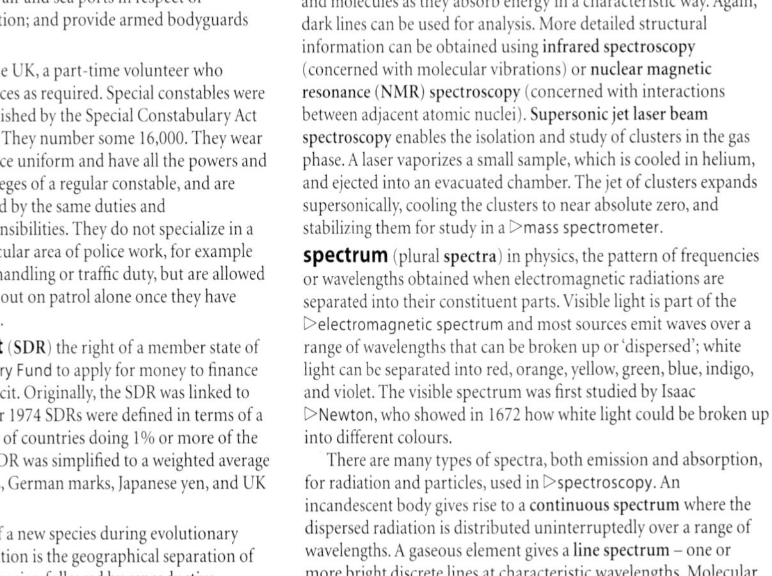

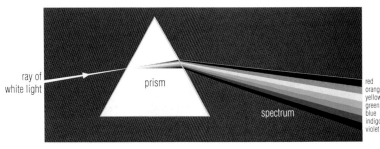

SPECTRUM A prism (a triangular block of transparent material such as plastic, glass, or silica) is used to split a ray of white light into its spectral colours.

spectrum of an element is obtained from a mass spectrometer and shows the relative proportions of its constituent ▷isotopes.

speculative action law case taken on a 'no-win, no-fee' basis, legal in the USA and Scotland, but not in England.

speech recognition (or **voice input**) in computing, any technique by which a computer can understand ordinary speech. Spoken words are divided into 'frames', each lasting about one-thirtieth of a second, which are converted to a wave form. These are then compared with a series of stored frames to determine the most likely word. Research into speech recognition started in 1938, but the technology did not become sufficiently developed for commercial applications until the late 1980s.

speech synthesis (or **voice output**) computer-based technology for generating speech. A speech synthesizer is controlled by a computer, which supplies strings of codes representing basic speech sounds (phonemes); together these make up words. Speech-synthesis applications include children's toys, car and aircraft warning systems, and talking books for the blind.

speed common name for ▷amphetamine, a stimulant drug.

speed the rate at which an object moves. The average speed v of an object may be calculated by dividing the distance s it has travelled by the time t taken to do so, and may be expressed as:

$$v = s/t$$

The usual units of speed are metres per second or kilometres per hour.

speed of light speed at which light and other ▷electromagnetic waves travel through empty space. Its value is 299,792,458 m/186,282 mi per second. The speed of light is the highest speed possible, according to the theory of ▷relativity, and its value is independent of the motion of its source and of the observer. It is impossible to accelerate any material body to this speed because it would require an infinite amount of energy.

speed of sound speed at which sound travels through a medium, such as air or water. In air at a temperature of 0°C/32°F, the speed of sound is 331 m/1,087 ft per second. At higher temperatures, the speed of sound is greater; at 18°C/64°F it is 342 m/1,123 ft per second. It is greater in liquids and solids; for example, in water it is around 1,440 m/4,724 ft per second, depending on the temperature.

speedometer instrument attached to the transmission of a vehicle by a flexible drive shaft, which indicates the speed of the vehicle in miles or kilometres per hour on a dial easily visible to the driver.

speedway sport of motorcycle racing on a dirt track. Four riders compete in each heat over four laps. A series of heats make up a match or competition. In Britain there are two leagues, the British League and the National League. World championships exist for individuals, pairs (first held in 1970), four-rider teams (first held in 1960), long-track racing, and ice speedway.

speedwell any of a group of flowering plants belonging to the snapdragon family. Of the many wild species, most are low-growing with small bluish flowers. (Genus *Veronica*, family Scrophulariaceae.)

Speer, Albert (1905–1981) German architect and minister in the Nazi government during World War II. He was appointed Hitler's architect and, like his counterparts in Fascist Italy, chose an overblown classicism to glorify the state, for example, his plan for the Berlin and Nürnberg Party Congress Grounds in 1934. He built the New Reich Chancellery, Berlin, 1938–39 (now demolished), but his designs for an increasingly megalomaniac series of buildings in a stark classical style were never realized.

As armaments minister he raised the index of arms production from 100 in January 1942 to 322 by July 1944. In the latter months of the war he concentrated on frustrating Hitler's orders for the destruction of German industry in the face of the advancing Allies. After the war, he was sentenced to 20 years' imprisonment for his employment of slave labour. His memoirs, *Inside the Third Reich* (1969), gave a highly influential account of the period, but in portraying their author as a technocrat they understated his participation in the Nazi project.

Speke, John Hanning (1827–1864) British explorer. He joined British traveller Richard ▷Burton on an African expedition in which they reached Lake Tanganyika in 1858; Speke became the first European to see Lake ▷Victoria.

speleology scientific study of caves, their origin, development, physical structure, flora, fauna, folklore, exploration, mapping, photography, cave-diving, and rescue work. **Potholing**, which involves following the course of underground rivers or streams, has become a popular sport. Speleology first developed in France in the late 19th century, where the Société de Spéléologie was founded in 1895.

Related Web site: Caves and Caving in the UK http://www.sat.dundee.ac.uk/~arb/speleo.html

Spence, Basil Urwin (1907–1976) Scottish architect. For nearly 20 years his work comprised houses, factories, theatres, and the Scottish Pavilion at the Empire Exhibition in 1938. In 1951 he won the competition for Coventry Cathedral, and in 1952 began the Nuclear Physics Building at Glasgow University. He was professor of architecture at the Royal Academy, London, from 1961 to 1968.

Spencer, Stanley (1891–1959) English painter. He was born and lived in Cookham-on-Thames, and recreated the Christian story in a Cookham setting. Typically his dreamlike compositions combine a dry, meticulously detailed, and often humorous depiction of everyday life with an elaborate religious symbolism, as in *The Resurrection, Cookham* (1924–26; Tate Gallery, London).

Spender, Stephen (Harold) (1909–1995) English poet and critic. His early poetry has a left-wing political content. With Cyril ▷Connolly he founded the magazine *Horizon* (of which he was co-editor 1939–41), and Spender was co-editor of *Encounter* 1953–66. His *Journals 1939–83* and *Collected Poems 1928–1985* were published in 1985. He was knighted in 1983.

Spengler, Oswald (1880–1936) German philosopher whose *Decline of the West* (1918) argued that civilizations go through natural cycles of growth and decay.

He was admired by the Nazis.

Oswald Spengler
Christian theology is the grandmother of Bolshevism.
Hour of Decision

Spenser, Edmund (*c.* 1552–1599) English poet. His major work is the allegorical epic *The Faerie Queene*, of which six books survive (three published in 1590 and three in 1596). Other books include *The Shepheard's Calendar* (1579), *Astrophel* (1586), the love sonnets *Amoretti*, and the marriage poem *Epithalamion* (1595).

Born in London and educated at Cambridge University, in 1580 he became secretary to Lord Grey de Wilton, Lord Deputy in Ireland and at Kilcolman Castle completed the first three books of *The Faerie Queene*. In 1598 the castle was burned down by rebels, and Spenser and his family narrowly escaped. He died in London, and was buried in Westminster Abbey.

His attitude towards the Irish problem, expressed in both book five of the *Faerie Queene* and his *View of the Present State of Ireland* was that merciless oppression was the only solution.

Related Web site: Edmund Spenser Home Page http://www.english.cam.ac.uk/spenser/main.htm

sperm (or **spermatozoon**) in biology, the male ▷gamete of animals. Each sperm cell has a head capsule containing a nucleus, a middle portion containing ▷mitochondria (which provide energy), and a long tail (flagellum). See ▷sexual reproduction.

The sperm head contains an enzyme acrosin that dissolves the ovum casing enabling the sperm to penetrate it. The discovery of a protein called protein C inhibitor (PCI) was announced by Dutch researchers in 1998. PCI blocks the activation of acrosin when sperm is stored in the epididymis until it is released by ejaculation.

In most animals, the sperm are motile, and are propelled by a long flagellum, but in some (such as crabs and lobsters) they are nonmotile. Sperm cells are produced in the testes (see ▷testis). From there they pass through the sperm ducts via the seminal vesicles and the ▷prostate gland, which produce fluids called semen that give the sperm cells energy and keep them moving after they leave the body. Hundreds of millions of sperm cells are contained in only a small amount of semen. The human sperm is 0.005 mm/0.0002 in long and can survive inside the female for 2–9 days. Mammalian sperm have receptor cells identical to some of those found in the lining of the nose. These may help in navigating towards the egg.

The term is sometimes applied to the motile male gametes (▷antherozoids) of lower plants.

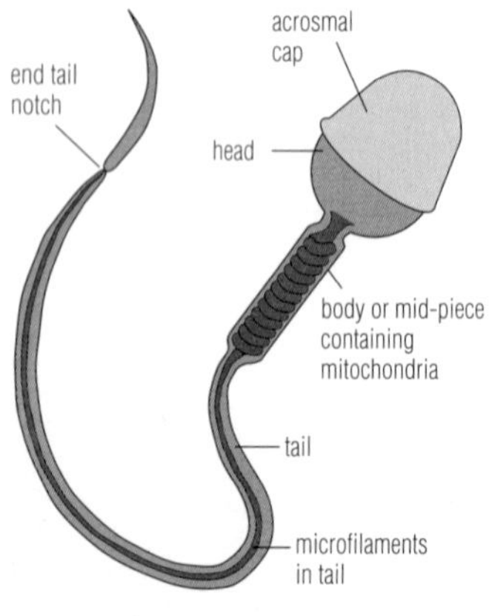

SPERM Only a single sperm is needed to fertilize an egg, or ovum, yet up to 500 million may start the journey towards the egg. Once a sperm has fertilized an egg, the egg's wall cannot be penetrated by other sperm. The unsuccessful sperm die after about three days.

spermaceti glistening waxlike substance, not a true oil, contained in the cells of the huge, almost rectangular 'case' in the head of the sperm whale, amounting to about 2.8 tonnes/3 tons. It rapidly changes in density with variations in temperature. It was formerly used in lubricants and cosmetics, but in 1980 a blend of fatty acids and esters from tallow and coconut oil was developed as a substitute.

spermatophore small capsule containing ▷sperm and other nutrients produced in invertebrates, newts, and cephalopods.

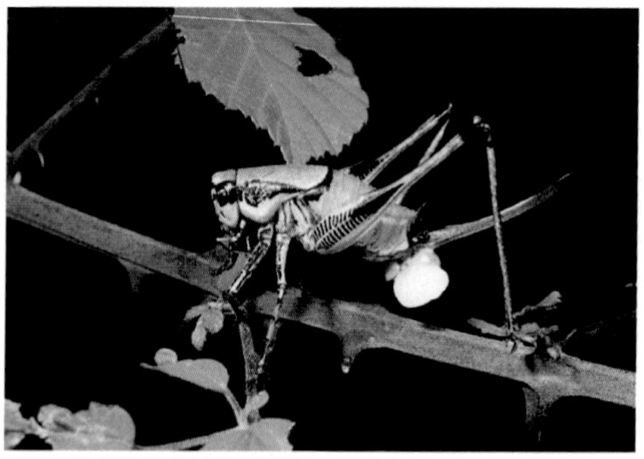

SPERMATOPHORE Female bush cricket *Eupholidoptera chabrieri* with a spermatophore. The male produces the spermatophore and deposits it in the female's cloaca during their courtship ritual. Internal fertilization can then take place. *R A Preston-Mafham/Premaphotos Wildlife*

spermatophyte in botany, another name for a ▷seed plant.

spermicide any cream, jelly, pessary, or other preparation that kills the ▷sperm cells in semen. Spermicides are used for contraceptive purposes, usually in combination with a ▷condom or ▷diaphragm. Sponges impregnated with spermicide have been developed but are not yet in widespread use. Spermicide used alone is only 75% effective in preventing pregnancy.

sphalerite mineral composed of zinc sulphide with a small proportion of iron, formula (Zn,Fe)S. It is the chief ore of zinc. Sphalerite is brown with a nonmetallic lustre unless an appreciable amount of iron is present (up to 26% by weight). Sphalerite usually occurs in ore veins in limestones, where it is often associated with galena. It crystallizes in the cubic system but does not normally form perfect cubes.

sphere in mathematics, a perfectly round object with all points on its surface the same distance from the centre. This distance is the radius of the sphere. For a sphere of radius r, the volume $V = \frac{4}{3}\pi r^3$ and the surface area $A = 4\pi r^2$.

sphincter ring of muscle, such as is found at various points in the ▷alimentary canal, that contracts and relaxes to open and close the canal and control the movement of food. The **pyloric sphincter**, at the base of the stomach, controls the release of the gastric contents into the ▷duodenum. After release the sphincter contracts, closing off the stomach. The **external anal sphincter** closes the ▷anus; the **internal anal sphincter** constricts the rectum; the **sphincter vesicae** controls the urethral orifice of the bladder. In the eye the **sphincter pupillae** contracts the pupil in response to bright light.

Sphinx mythological creature, depicted in Egyptian, Assyrian, and Greek art as a lion with a human head. The Greek **Sphinx of Thebes** was winged with a woman's breasts, and was adopted as an emblem of wisdom. She killed all those who failed to answer her riddle about which animal went on four, then two, and finally three legs: the answer being humanity (baby, adult, and old person with stick). When ▷Oedipus gave the right reply, she committed suicide.

sphygmomanometer instrument for measuring blood pressure. Consisting of an inflatable arm cuff joined by a rubber tube to a pressure-recording device (incorporating a column of mercury with a graduated scale), it is used, together with a stethoscope, to measure arterial blood pressure.

Spica (or **Alpha Virginis**) brightest star in the constellation Virgo and the 16th-brightest star in the night sky. Spica has a true luminosity of over 1,500 times that of the Sun and is 260 light years from the Sun. It is a spectroscopic binary star, the components of which orbit each other every four days.

spice any aromatic vegetable substance used as a condiment and for flavouring food. Spices are mostly obtained from tropical plants, and include pepper, nutmeg, ginger, and cinnamon. They have little food value but increase the appetite and may help digestion.

SPICE The spice market in a covered bazaar (*souk*), typical of any such market from Morocco eastwards. Emissaries from Western civilizations once travelled vast distances in order to track down the aromatic wares sold in such markets. *Image Bank*

spider any arachnid (eight-legged animal) of the order Araneae. There are about 30,000 known species, mostly a few centimetres in size, although a few tropical forms attain great size, for example, some bird-eating spiders attain a body length of 9 cm/3.5 in. Spiders produce silk, and many spin webs to trap their prey. They are found everywhere in the world except Antarctica. Many species are found in woods and dry commons; a few are aquatic. Spiders are predators; they bite their prey, releasing a powerful toxin from poison glands which causes paralysis, together with digestive juices. They then suck out the juices and soft parts.

Over 630 species of spider have been identified in Britain. One of the most familiar is the common garden spider *Araneus diadematus*, which spins webs of remarkable beauty. There are three species of house spider: *Tegenaria domestica*, *T. atrica*, both up to 2 cm/0.75 in long, and *T. parietina*, better known as the cardinal spider.

The first book devoted to spiders was *English Spiders* 1678 by Martin Lister, who described 38 species.

A species of spider which is new to Britain was discovered near Dover in 1997. Previously, the small ant-eating spider *Zodarion obscurium* had been recorded at only a small number of sites in Italy.

spider monkey species of monkey found in Central and South America. Spider monkeys have long and very flexible limbs and a long, prehensile tail that is much used in climbing. The thumb is either absent or vestigial (much reduced).

spider plant African plant belonging to the lily family. Two species (*C. comosum* and *C. elatum*) are popular house plants. They have long, narrow, variegated leaves and produce flowering shoots from which the new plants grow, hanging below the main plant. The flowers are small and white. Spider plants absorb toxins from the air and therefore help to purify the atmosphere around them. (Genus *Chlorophytum*, family Liliaceae.)

Spielberg, Steven (1947–   ) US film director, writer, and producer. Immensely popular, Spielberg's films often combine heartfelt sentimentality and a childlike sensibility. His credits include such phenomenal box-office successes as *Jaws* (1975), *Close Encounters of the Third Kind* (1977), *Raiders of the Lost Ark* (1981),

STEVEN SPIELBERG Film director Steven Spielberg working on the set of the hugely successful *Close Encounters of the Third Kind* in 1977. *Archive Photos*

ET The Extra-Terrestrial (1982), *Jurassic Park* (1992), the multi-award-winning *Schindler's List* (1993), and *Saving Private Ryan* (1998). He was the recipient of the American Film Institute's life achievement award in 1995. The US financial magazine *Forbes* listed him in 1997 as the biggest earner in showbusiness.

One of the most commercially-successful film-makers in the history of American cinema, Spielberg, with the likes of ▷Coppola, ▷Scorsese, and ▷Lucas, was one of the new generation of 'movie brats' who emerged in the late 1960s. Having worked in television, directing films such as *Duel* (1971), he made his feature film debut with *The Sugarland Express* (1974). He has also directed *Indiana Jones and the Temple of Doom* (1984), *The Color Purple* (1985), *Empire of the Sun* (1987), *Indiana Jones and the Last Crusade* (1989), *Hook* (1991), *Amistad* (1997), and *Men in Black* (1997). In 1994 he formed a partnership with David ▷Geffen and Jeffrey Katzenberg to create a new Hollywood studio called DreamWorks SKG.

> **Steven Spielberg**
> *I think that today's youth have a tendency to live in the present and work for the future – and to be totally ignorant of the past.*
> *Independent on Sunday,*
> *22 August 1999*

spikelet in botany, one of the units of a grass ▷inflorescence. It comprises a slender axis on which one or more flowers are borne.

spikenard either of two plants: a Himalayan plant belonging to the valerian family whose underground stems produce a perfume used in Eastern aromatic oils; or a North American plant of the ginseng family, with fragrant roots. (Himalayan *Nardostachys jatamansi*, family Valerianaceae; North American *Aralia racemosa*, family Araliaceae.)

spin in physics, the intrinsic angular momentum of a subatomic particle, nucleus, atom, or molecule, which continues to exist even when the particle comes to rest. A particle in a specific energy state has a particular spin, just as it has a particular electric charge and mass. According to ▷quantum theory, this is restricted to discrete and indivisible values, specified by a spin ▷quantum number. Because of its spin, a charged particle acts as a small magnet and is affected by magnetic fields.

spina bifida congenital defect in which part of the spinal cord and its membranes are exposed, due to incomplete development of the spine (vertebral column). It is a neural tube defect.

spinach annual plant belonging to the goosefoot family. It is native to Asia and widely cultivated for its leaves, which are eaten as a vegetable. (*Spinacia oleracea*, family Chenopodiaceae.)

spinal cord major component of the ▷central nervous system in vertebrates. It consists of bundles of nerves enveloped in three layers of membrane (the meninges) and is bathed in cerebrospinal fluid. The spinal cord is encased and protected by the vertebral column, lying within the vertebral canal formed by the posterior arches of successive vertebrae.

In humans, the spinal cord is about 45 cm/18 in long, extending from the bottom of the skull, where it is continuous with the medulla oblongata, only to about waist level. It consists of nerve cell bodies (grey matter) and their myelinated processes or nerve fibres (white matter). In cross-section, the grey matter is arranged in an H-shape around the central canal of the spinal cord, and it is surrounded in turn by the white matter.

Paired spinal nerves arise from the cord at each vertebra. Each is a mixed nerve, consisting of both sensory and motor nerve fibres. The sensory fibres enter the spinal cord at a dorsal root and the motor fibres enter at a ventral root. This arrangement enables the spinal cord to relay impulses coming in and out at the same level, to relay impulses going up and down the cord to other levels, and relay impulses to and from the brain. The first of these involves a **reflex arc**, by which a sensory impulse can create a very rapid, involuntary response to a particular stimulus.

spinal tap another term for ▷lumbar puncture, a medical test.

spine backbone of vertebrates. In most mammals, it contains 26 small bones called **vertebrae**, which enclose and protect the **spinal cord** (which links the peripheral nervous system to the brain). The spine articulates with the skull, ribs, and hip bones, and provides attachment for the back muscles.

In humans it is made up of individual vertebrae, separated by intervertebral discs. In the adult there are seven cervical vertebrae in the neck; twelve thoracic in the upper trunk; five lumbar in the lower back; the sacrum (consisting of five rudimentary vertebrae fused together, joined to the hipbones); and the coccyx (four vertebrae, fused into a tailbone). The human spine has four curves (front to rear), which allow for the increased size of the chest and pelvic cavities, and for a degree of spring so as to minimize jolting of the internal organs.

spinel any of a group of 'mixed oxide' minerals consisting mainly of the oxides of magnesium and aluminium, $MgAl_2O_4$ and $FeAl_2O_4$. Spinels crystallize in the cubic system, forming octahedral crystals. They are found in high-temperature igneous and metamorphic rocks. The aluminium oxide spinel contains gem varieties, such as the ruby spinels of Sri Lanka and Myanmar (Burma).

spinet 17th-century domestic keyboard instrument. It has a laterally tapered case with a single manual (keyboard) of up to a three-and-a-half octave range, having a plucking action and single strings. It was the precursor of the ▷harpsichord.

spinifex spiny grass chiefly found in Australia, growing on the coastal sand dunes. It is often planted to bind sand along the seashore. The term also refers to porcupine grass, any of a group of spiny-leaved, tussock-forming grasses of inland Australia. (Genus *Spinifex*; porcupine grass genus *Triodia*.)

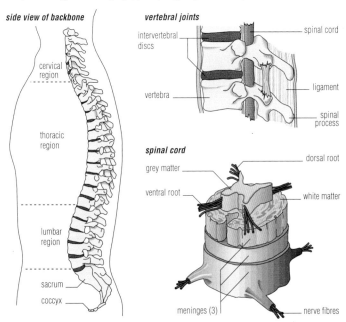

side view of backbone — cervical region, thoracic region, lumbar region, sacrum, coccyx

vertebral joints — intervertebral discs, vertebra, spinal cord, ligament, spinal process

spinal cord — grey matter, ventral root, meninges (3), dorsal root, white matter, nerve fibres

SPINE The human spine extends every night during sleep. During the day, the cartilage discs between the vertebra are squeezed when the body is in a vertical position, standing or sitting, but at night, with pressure released, the discs swell and the spine lengthens by about 8 mm/0.3 in.

spinning art of drawing out and twisting fibres (originally wool or flax) into a long thread, or yarn, by hand or machine. Synthetic fibres are extruded as a liquid through the holes of a spinneret.

Spinning was originally done by hand, then with the spinning wheel, and in about 1764 in England James ▷Hargreaves built the **spinning jenny**, a machine that could spin 8, then 16, bobbins at once. Later, Samuel ▷Crompton's **spinning mule** 1779 had a moving carriage carrying the spindles; this is still in use today.

Spinoza, Benedict (or Baruch)

(1632–1677) Dutch philosopher. He believed in a rationalistic pantheism that owed much to René ▷Descartes's mathematical appreciation of the universe. Mind and matter are two modes of an infinite substance that he called God or Nature, good and evil being relative. He was a determinist, believing that human action was motivated by self-preservation.

Ethics (1677) is his main work. *A Treatise on Religious and Political Philosophy* (1670) was the only one of his works published during his life, and was attacked by Christians. He was excommunicated by the Jewish community in Amsterdam on charges of heretical thought and practice in 1656. He was a lens-grinder by trade.

Related Web site: Spinoza, Benedict de http://www.orst.edu/instruct/phl302/philosophers/spinoza.html

> **Benedict Spinoza**
> *All things excellent are as difficult as they are rare.*
> *Ethics V. xlii*

spiny anteater alternative name for ▷echidna.

spiracle in insects, the opening of a ▷trachea, through which oxygen enters the body and carbon dioxide is expelled. In cartilaginous fishes (sharks and rays), the same name is given to a circular opening that marks the remains of the first gill slit.

spiraea any of a group of ▷herbaceous plants or shrubs, which includes many cultivated species with ornamental sprays of white or pink flowers; their delicate appearance has given rise to the popular name bridal wreath. (Genus *Spiraea*, family Rosaceae.)

spiral a plane curve formed by a point winding round a fixed point from which it distances itself at regular intervals, for example the spiral traced by a flat coil of rope. Various kinds of spirals can be generated mathematically – for example, an equiangular or logarithmic spiral (in which a tangent at any point on the curve always makes the same angle with it) and an involute. Spirals also occur in nature as a normal consequence of accelerating growth, such as the spiral shape of the shells of snails and some other molluscs.

spiritual healing (or **psychic healing**) transmission of energy from or through a healer, who may practise hand healing or absent healing through prayer or meditation.

spiritualism belief in the survival of the human personality and in communication between the living and those who have died. The spiritualist movement originated in the USA in 1848. Adherents practise **mediumship**, which claims to allow clairvoyant knowledge of distant events and spirit healing. The writer Arthur Conan ▷Doyle and the Victorian prime minister William ▷Gladstone were converts.

spit ridge of sand or shingle projecting from the land into a body of water. It is formed by the interruption of ▷longshore drift due to wave interaction with tides, currents, or a bend in the coastline. The consequent decrease in wave energy causes more material to be deposited than is transported down the coast, building up a finger of sand that points in the direction of the longshore drift. Deposition in the brackish water behind a spit may result in the formation of a ▷salt marsh.

Spitsbergen mountainous island with a deeply indented coastline, situated in the Arctic Ocean between Franz Josef Land and Greenland. It is the main island in the Norwegian archipelago of ▷Svalbard, 657 km/408 mi north of Norway, and now owned by that country; area 39,043 sq km/15,075 sq mi. Fishing, hunting, and coal mining are the chief economic activities. The Norwegian Polar Research Institute operates an all-year scientific station on the west coast. The highest point is Newtontoppen, which rises to 1,713 m/5,620 ft. The island was formerly called West Spitsbergen when part of the Svalbard archipeligo was named Spitsbergen.

spittle alternative name for ▷saliva and ▷cuckoo spit.

spittlebug alternative name for ▷froghopper.

spleen organ in vertebrates, part of the reticuloendothelial system, which helps to process ▷lymphocytes. It also regulates the number of red blood cells in circulation by destroying old cells, and stores iron. It is situated on the left side of the body, behind the stomach.

Split (Italian **Spalato**) port in Croatia, on the Adriatic coast; population (1991) 189,400. Industries include engineering, cement, and textiles.

Split was bombed during 1991 as part of Yugoslavia's blockade of the Croatian coast.

Related Web site: Celebrating 17 Centuries of the City of Split http://www.st.carnet.hr/split/

Spock, Benjamin (McLane) (1903–1998) US paediatrician and writer on child care. His *Common Sense Book of Baby and Child Care* (1946) urged less rigidity in bringing up children than had been advised by previous generations of writers on the subject, but this was misunderstood as advocating permissiveness. He was also active in the peace movement, especially during the Vietnam War.

Spode, Josiah (1754–1827) English potter. Around 1800, he developed bone porcelain (made from bone ash, china stone, and china clay), which was produced at all English factories in the 19th century. He became potter to King George III in 1806.

His father, Josiah Spode the elder (1733–1797), founded the Spode factory at Stoke-on-Trent in 1770. He succeeded to the firm in 1797, and added porcelain and, in 1805, stone-china to its production. The Spode works were taken over by W T Copeland in 1833.

Related Web site: Welcome to the Story of Spode http://www.spode.co.uk/

spoils system in the USA, the granting of offices and favours among the supporters of a party in office. The spoils system, a type of ▷patronage, was used by President Jackson in the 1830s in particular, and by Republican administrations after the Civil War. The practice remained common in the 20th century in US local government.

sponge any saclike simple invertebrate of the phylum Porifera, usually marine. A sponge has a hollow body, its cavity lined by cells bearing flagellae, whose whiplike movements keep water circulating, bringing in a stream of food particles. The body walls are strengthened with protein (as in the bath sponge) or small spikes of silica, or a framework of calcium carbonate.

Fossil sponges only 1 mm in length were found in China and described in 1998. They are estimated to be 580 million years old, the oldest discovered to date.

SPONGE A fluorescent vase sponge in the Caribbean. Sponges are enormously varied and widespread, occurring in fresh water as well as in the sea. *Cliff Nelson ARPS/Premaphotos Wildlife*

spontaneous combustion burning that is not initiated by the direct application of an external source of heat. A number of materials and chemicals, such as hay and sodium chlorate, can react with their surroundings, usually by oxidation, to produce so much internal heat that combustion results.

spooling in computing, the process in which information to be printed is stored temporarily in a file, the printing being carried out later. It is used to prevent a relatively slow printer from holding up the system at critical times, and to enable several computers or programs to share one printer.

spoonbill any of several large wading birds of the ibis family Threskiornithidae, order Ciconiiformes, characterized by a long, flat bill, dilated at the tip in the shape of a spoon. Spoonbills are white or pink, and up to 90 cm/3 ft tall. Their feet are adapted for wading, and the birds obtain their food, consisting chiefly of fish, frogs, molluscs, and crustaceans, from shallow water.

SPIRACLE The spiracles of this large *Dirphia avia* moth caterpillar from Trinidad are visible as a line of white ovals outlined with a rim. *Premaphotos Wildlife*

SPOONBILL The roseate spoonbill, native to the USA. *Image Bank*

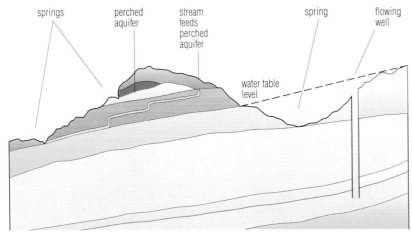

SPRING Springs occur where water-laden rock layers (aquifers) reach the surface. Water will flow from a well whose head is below the water table.

spoonerism exchange of elements in a flow of words. Usually a slip of the tongue, a spoonerism can also be contrived for comic effect (for example 'a troop of Boy Scouts' becoming 'a scoop of Boy Trouts'). William Spooner (1844–1930) gave his name to the phenomenon.

spore small reproductive or resting body, usually consisting of just one cell. Unlike a ▷gamete, it does not need to fuse with another cell in order to develop into a new organism. Spores are produced by the lower plants, most fungi, some bacteria, and certain protozoa. They are generally light and easily dispersed by wind movements.

Plant spores are haploid and are produced by the sporophyte, following ▷meiosis; see ▷alternation of generations.

sporophyte diploid spore-producing generation in the life cycle of a plant that undergoes ▷alternation of generations.

sport activity pursued for exercise or pleasure, performed individually or in a group, often involving the testing of physical capabilities and usually taking the form of a competitive game. There are many different kinds of sport, but most can be grouped into four main categories: these are athletics, which includes swimming competitions, gymnastics, and a wide range of track and field events; racing sports, which involve the use of transportation, such as horse racing, cycling, and motor racing; combat-based sports, such as judo and wrestling; and ball games, such as baseball, tennis, and football.

sprat small marine bony fish common around the British Isles. It is 7–15 cm/2.8–6 in long, with smooth scales and a prominent lower jaw. It has a sharp, toothed edge to its belly. The sprat *Clupea sprattus* is a small member of the herring genus, order Clupeiformes, class Osteichthyes.

Spratly Islands (Chinese **Nanshan Islands**) disputed group of small islands, coral reefs, and sandbars dispersed over a distance of 965 km/600 mi in the South China Sea. The islands are of strategic importance, commanding the sea passage from Japan to Singapore, and in 1976 oil was discovered.

spreadsheet in computing, a program that mimics a sheet of ruled paper, divided into columns down the page, and rows across. The user enters values into cells within the sheet, then instructs the program to perform some operation on them, such as totalling a column or finding the average of a series of numbers. Highly complex numerical analyses may be built up from these simple steps.

Columns and rows in a spreadsheet are labelled; although different programs use different methods, columns are often labelled with alpha characters, and rows with numbers. This way, each cell has its own **reference**, unique within that spreadsheet. For example, A5 would be the cell reference for the fifth row in the first column. Cells can also be grouped using references; the range H9:H30 groups together all the cells in column H between (and including) rows 9 and 30. Single references or cell ranges may be used when inputting formulae into cells.

When a cell containing a formula is copied and pasted within a spreadsheet, the formula is said to be **relative**, meaning the cell references from which it takes its values are relative to its new position. An **absolute** reference does not change.

The pages of a spreadsheet can be formatted to make them easier to read; the height of rows, the width of columns, and the typeface of the text may all be changed. Number formats may also be changed to display, for example, fractions as decimals or numbers as integers.

Spreadsheets are widely used in business for forecasting and financial control. The first spreadsheet program, Software Arts' VisiCalc, appeared in 1979. The best known include Lotus 1-2-3 and Microsoft Excel.

spring device, usually a metal coil, that returns to its original shape after being stretched or compressed. Springs are used in some machines (such as clocks) to store energy, which can be released at a controlled rate. In other machines (such as engines) they are used to close valves. In vehicle suspension systems, springs are used to cushion passengers from road shocks. These springs are used in conjuction with shock absorbers to limit their amount of travel. In bedding and upholstered furniture springs add comfort.

spring in geology, a natural flow of water from the ground, formed at the point of intersection of the water table and the ground's surface. The source of water is rain that has percolated through the overlying rocks. During its underground passage, the water may have dissolved mineral substances that may then be precipitated at the spring (hence, a mineral spring).

A spring may be continuous or intermittent, and depends on the position of the water table and the topography (surface features).

Spring, Dick (1950–) Born Richard Spring. Irish Labour Party leader from 1982. He entered into a coalition with Garret ▷FitzGerald's Fine Gael in 1982 as deputy prime minister (with the posts of minister for the environment 1982–83 and minister for energy 1983–87). In 1993 he became deputy prime minister to Albert ▷Reynolds in a Fianna Fáil–Labour Party coalition, with the post of minister for foreign affairs. He withdrew from the coalition in November 1994 in protest over a judicial appointment made by Reynolds, and the following month formed a new coalition with Fine Gael, with John Bruton as prime minister, in power until 1997.

springbok South African antelope *Antidorcas marsupialis* about 80 cm/30 in at the shoulder, with head and body 1.3 m/4 ft long. It may leap 3 m/10 ft or more in the air when startled or playing, and has a fold of skin along the middle of the back which is raised to a crest in alarm. Springboks once migrated in herds of over a million, but are now found only in small numbers where protected.

SPRINGBOK Male and female springbok look alike, with strong ridged horns.

Springsteen, Bruce (1949–) US rock singer, songwriter, and guitarist. His music combines melodies in traditional rock idiom and reflective lyrics about working-class life and the pursuit of the American dream on such albums as *Born to Run* (1975), *Born in the USA* (1984), and *Human Touch* (1992). His retrospective collection of songs, *Tracks*, was released in November 1998. He was inducted into the Rock and Roll Hall of Fame in March 1999.

Springsteen was born in New Jersey. His philanthropy is legendary – he donated thousands of dollars to women's groups in the United Kingdom in 1983 during the miners' strike, and he headlined Amnesty International's World Tour in 1988. Although Springsteen had declared himself for the Democrats, the title track from *Born in the USA* was used by the Republican party in the 1984 Presidential election. Ronald Reagan is quoted as having said, 'America's future rests in a thousand dreams inside your heart. It rests in the message of hope in the songs of a man so many young Americans admire, New Jersey's Bruce Springsteen'.

Darkness at the Edge of Town (1978), *The River* (1980), and the solo acoustic *Nebraska* (1982) reinforced his reputation as a songwriter. His vast stadium concerts with the E Street Band were marked by his ability to overcome the distance between audience and artist, making him one of rock's finest live performers.

Related Web site: Glory Days! http://www.springsteen.de/

springtail small wingless insect. The maximum size is 6 mm/0.2 in in length. Springtails are extremely widespread and can be found in soil, decaying vegetable matter, under the bark of trees, in ant and termite nests, and on the surface of fresh water. There are about 1,500 species of springtail and some species are, unusually for insects, marine.

sprite in computing, a graphics object made up of a pattern of ▷pixels (picture elements) defined by a computer programmer. Some ▷high-level languages and ▷applications programs contain routines that allow a user to define the shape, colours, and other characteristics of individual graphics objects. These objects can then be manipulated and combined to produce animated games or graphic screen displays.

spruce coniferous tree belonging to the pine family, found over much of the northern hemisphere. Pyramidal in shape, spruces have rigid, prickly needles and drooping, leathery cones. Some are important forestry trees, such as the sitka spruce (*P. sitchensis*), native to western North America, and the Norway spruce (*P. abies*), now planted widely in North America. (Genus *Picea*, family Pinaceae.)

SPRUCE Spruces are evergreen trees of the pine family. They have hard sharp needles and soft leathery cones hanging from the branches. Perhaps the most familiar is the traditional Christmas tree, the Norway spruce.

spur ridge of rock jutting out into a valley or plain. In mountainous areas rivers often flow around interlocking spurs because they are not powerful enough to erode through the spurs. Spurs may be eroded away by large and powerful glaciers to form truncated spurs.

Sputnik (Russian 'fellow traveller') series of ten Soviet Earth-orbiting satellites. *Sputnik 1* was the first artificial satellite, launched 4 October 1957. It weighed 84 kg/184 lb, with a 58 cm/23 in diameter, and carried only a simple radio transmitter which allowed scientists to track it as it orbited Earth. It burned up in the atmosphere 92 days later. Sputniks were superseded in the early 1960s by the Cosmos series.

Sputnik 2, launched 3 November 1957, weighed about 500 kg/ 1,100 lb including the dog Laika, the first living creature in space. Unfortunately, there was no way to return the dog to Earth, and it died in space. Later Sputniks were test flights of the Vostok spacecraft.

> **Bruce Springsteen**
> *Bob freed your mind in the way Elvis freed your body.*
> On Bob Dylan, in a speech, 1988

SQL (abbreviation for structured query language) high-level computer language designed for use with relational databases. Although it can be used by programmers in the same way as other languages, it is often used as a means for programs to communicate with each other. Typically, one program (called the 'client') uses SQL to request data from a database 'server'.

square in geometry, a quadrilateral (four-sided) plane figure with all sides equal and each angle a right angle. Its diagonals bisect each other at right angles. The area A of a square is the length l of one side multiplied by itself ($A = l \times l$).

Also, any quantity multiplied by itself is termed a square, represented by an ▷exponent of power 2; for example, $4 \times 4 = 4^2 = 16$ and $6.8 \times 6.8 = 6.8^2 = 46.24$.

square root in mathematics, a number that when squared (multiplied by itself) equals a given number. For example, the square root of 25 (written $\sqrt{25}$) is ± 5, because $5 \times 5 = 25$, and $(-5) \times (-5) = 25$. As an ▷exponent, a square root is represented by $\frac{1}{2}$, for example, $16^{\frac{1}{2}} = 4$.

Negative numbers (less than 0) do not have square roots that are ▷real numbers. Their roots are represented by ▷complex numbers, in which the square root of -1 is given the symbol i (that is, $\pm i^2 = -1$). Thus the square root of -4 is $\sqrt{[(-1) \times 4]} = \sqrt{-1} \times \sqrt{4} = 2i$.

squash (or **squash rackets**) racket-and-ball game usually played by two people on an enclosed court, derived from rackets. Squash became a popular sport in the 1970s and later gained competitive status. There are two forms of squash: the American form, which is played in North and some South American countries, and the English, which is played mainly in Europe and Commonwealth countries such as Pakistan, Australia, and New Zealand.

> **Related Web site: Internet Squash Federation**
> http://www.squash.org/

squatter person illegally occupying someone else's property; for example, some of the urban homeless in contemporary Britain making use of vacant houses. Squatters commit a criminal offence if they take over property where there is a 'residential occupier'; for example, by moving in while the owner is on holiday.

squill bulb-forming perennial plant belonging to the lily family, found growing in dry places near the sea in Western Europe. Cultivated species usually bear blue flowers, either singly or in clusters, at the top of the stem. (Genus *Scilla*, family Liliaceae.)

SQUILL The blue flowers of the spring squill *Scilla verna* often carpet the short grassland sward on clifftops around the coasts of western Europe. Some species are cultivated for the garden. *Premaphotos Wildlife*

squint (or **strabismus**) common condition in which one eye deviates in any direction. A squint may be convergent (with the bad eye turned inwards), divergent (outwards), or, in rare cases, vertical. A convergent squint is also called **cross-eye**.

squirrel rodent of the family Sciuridae. Squirrels are found worldwide except for Australia, Madagascar, and polar regions. Some are tree dwellers; these generally have bushy tails, and some, with membranes between their legs, are called ▷flying squirrels. Others are terrestrial, generally burrowing forms called ground squirrels; these include chipmunks, gophers, marmots, and prairie dogs.

The **red squirrel** *Sciurus vulgaris* is found throughout Europe and northern Asia. It is about 23 cm/9 in long (plus 18 cm/7 in tail), with red fur and a bushy tail. It rears its young in stick nests, or 'dreys'. Although it is less active in winter, it does not hibernate, burying nuts as a winter store. In Britain, the red squirrel has been replaced in most areas by the introduced **grey squirrel** *S. carolinensis* from North America; in 1996 there were only 160,000 red squirrels remaining, compared with 2.5 million greys.

Ground squirrels or **gophers** make networks of tunnels in open ground, and carry their food in cheek pouches.

> **Related Web site: Squirrel Place** http://www.squirrels.org/

Sr abbreviation for **senior**; **señor**.

SRAM (acronym for static random-access memory) computer memory device in the form of a silicon chip used to provide immediate access memory. SRAM is faster but more expensive than ▷DRAM (dynamic random-access memory), and does not require such frequent refreshing.

Sri Lanka see country box.

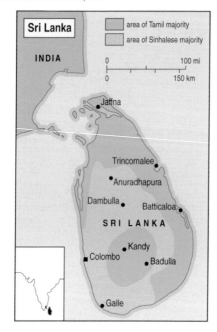

Sri Lanka

□ area of Tamil majority
□ area of Sinhalese majority

INDIA

0   100 mi
0   150 km

Jaffna
Trincomalee
Anuradhapura
Dambulla
Batticaloa
SRI LANKA
Kandy
Colombo
Badulla
Galle

Srinagar summer capital of the state of ▷Jammu and Kashmir, India, on the Jhelum River, 1,600 m/5,250 ft above sea level; population (1991) 595,000. It is a beautiful resort, intersected by waterways and wooden bridges, with numerous mosques, palaces, a fortress, and public gardens. Lake Dal to the northeast is an important tourist centre. It has carpet, papier mâché, silk, silver, and leather industries. The university of Jammu and Kashmir was established in 1948.

SS (German *Schutz-Staffel*, 'protective squadron') Nazi elite corps established 1925. Under ▷Himmler its 500,000 membership included the full-time **Waffen-SS** (armed SS), which fought in World War II, and spare-time members. The SS performed state police duties and was brutal in its treatment of the Jews and others in the concentration camps and occupied territories. It was condemned as an illegal organization at the Nuremberg Trials of war criminals.

SSSI abbreviation for ▷Site of Special Scientific Interest.

stabilizer one of a pair of fins fitted to the sides of a ship, especially one governed automatically by a ▷gyroscope mechanism, designed to reduce side-to-side rolling of the ship in rough weather.

stack in computing, a method of storing data in which the most recent item stored will be the first to be retrieved. The technique is commonly called 'last in, first out'.

stack isolated pillar of rock that has become separated from a headland by ▷coastal erosion. It is usually formed by the collapse

STACK Marsden Rock off the NE coast of England is one of many stacks around the British coastline which are home to large colonies of nesting seabirds. *Premaphotos Wildlife*

of an ▷arch. Further erosion will reduce it to a stump, which is exposed only at low tide.

Staël, Anne Louise Germaine Necker, Madame de (1766–1817) French author. She wrote semi-autobiographical novels such as *Delphine* (1802) and *Corinne* (1807), and the critical work *De l'Allemagne* (1810), on German literature. She was banished from Paris by Napoleon in 1803 because of her advocacy of political freedom.

Staffordshire county of west central England (since April 1997 Stoke-on-Trent has been a separate unitary authority).

> **area** 2,720 sq km/1,050 sq mi **towns** Stafford (administrative headquarters), Newcastle-under-Lyme, Lichfield, Tamworth, Leek, Uttoxeter **physical** largely flat, with hilly regions in the north (part of the Peak district) and southwest; River Trent and its tributaries (the Churnet, Dove, Penk, Sow, and Tame); Cannock Chase (a large open area in the middle of the county) **features** castles at Chartley, Tamworth, and Tutbury; Lichfield Cathedral; Keele University (1962); Shugborough Hall (17th century), seat of the earls of Lichfield; Staffordshire bull terriers **agriculture** dairy farming **industries** breweries (Burton-upon-Trent); china and earthenware in the ▷Potteries and the upper Trent basin (including Wedgwood and Royal Doulton); tractors and agricultural equipment (JCB construction equipment manufacturers was founded in Staffordshire in 1945, and some of its sites are still in the area); tyres (including Michelin); electrical engineering; electronics **population** (1996) 555,700 **famous people** Arnold Bennett, Clarice Cliff, David Garrick, John Jervis, Samuel Johnson, Robert Peel, Isaak Walton, Josiah Wedgwood, Peter de Wint
> **Related Web site: Stafford Borough Council** http://www.staffordbc.gov.uk/

Staffs abbreviation for ▷Staffordshire, an English county.

stag in finance, a subscriber for new ▷share issues who expects to profit from a rise in price on early trading in the shares.

stag beetle any of a number of large dark brown beetles, the males of which possess enormous mandibles, or jaws, shaped rather like the antlers of a stag. There are over 900 species within this family.

stagflation (combination of *stagnation* and *inflation*) economic condition (experienced in the USA and Europe in the 1970s) in which rapid inflation is accompanied by stagnating, even declining, output and by increasing unemployment. Its cause is often sharp increases in costs of raw materials and/or labour. It is a recently coined term to explain a condition that violates many of the suppositions of classical economics.

> **Anne, Madame de Staël**
> *Love is the whole history*
> *of a woman's life, it is but*
> *an episode in a man's.*
> 'On the Influence of the Passions'

stain in chemistry, a coloured compound that will bind to other substances. Stains are used extensively in microbiology to colour micro-organisms and in histochemistry to detect the presence and whereabouts in plant and animal tissue of substances such as fats, cellulose, and proteins.

stained glass pieces of coloured glass held in place by thin strips of metal (usually lead) to form pictures in a window. One of the great medieval arts, it developed with the increase of window space in the Gothic church, and to some extent serves the same purpose as a wall-painting, with the added richness given by translucence and the variations of light piercing through from outside.

stainless steel widely used ▷alloy of iron, chromium, and nickel that resists rusting. Its chromium content also gives it a high tensile strength. It is used for cutlery and kitchen fittings, and in surgical instruments. Stainless steel was first produced in the UK in 1913 and in Germany in 1914.

stakeholder economy an idea floated by English journalist and writer on politics and economics Will Hutton; which put forward the prospect of greater worker involvement in companies on something of the German model. In his best-selling book *The State We're In* (1996), Hutton ranged far wider than industrial democracy and called for a major review of Britain's constitution.

stalactite and stalagmite cave structures formed by the deposition of calcite dissolved in ground water. **Stalactites** grow downwards from the roofs or walls and can be icicle-shaped, straw-shaped, curtain-shaped, or formed as terraces. **Stalagmites** grow upwards from the cave floor and can be conical, fir-cone-shaped, or resemble a stack of saucers. Growing stalactites and stalagmites may meet to form a continuous column from floor to ceiling.

Stalactites are formed when ground water, hanging as a drip, loses a proportion of its carbon dioxide into the air of the cave. This reduces the amount of calcite that can be held in solution, and a

Sri Lanka

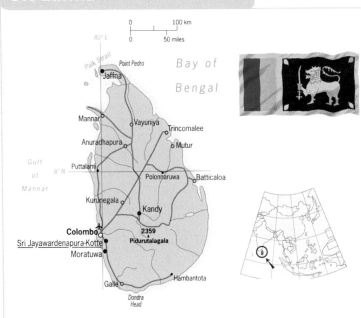

Sri Lanka formerly Ceylon (until 1972) island in the Indian Ocean, off the southeast coast of India.

NATIONAL NAME *Sri Lanka Prajatantrika Samajavadi Janarajaya/Democratic Socialist Republic of Sri Lanka*
AREA 65,610 sq km/25,332 sq mi
CAPITAL Sri Jayewardenapura Kotte
MAJOR TOWNS/CITIES Colombo, Kandy, Dehiwala-Mount Lavinia, Moratuwa, Jaffna, Kotte, Galle
MAJOR PORTS Colombo, Jaffna, Galle, Negombo, Trincomalee
PHYSICAL FEATURES flat in north and around coast; hills and mountains in south and central interior

Government

HEAD OF STATE Chandrika Bandaranaike Kumaratunga from 1994
HEAD OF GOVERNMENT Ranil Wickremesinghe from 2001
POLITICAL SYSTEM liberal democracy
POLITICAL EXECUTIVE dual executive
ADMINISTRATIVE DIVISIONS eight provinces
ARMED FORCES 157,900; plus paramilitary forces of 88,600 (2002 est)
CONSCRIPTION military service is voluntary
DEATH PENALTY retains the death penalty for ordinary crimes but can be considered abolitionist in practice; date of last known execution 1976
DEFENCE SPEND (% GDP) 3.2 (2002 est)
EDUCATION SPEND (% GDP) 3.1 (2000 est)
HEALTH SPEND (% GDP) 3.6 (2000 est)

Economy and resources

CURRENCY Sri Lankan rupee
GPD (US$) 16.4 billion (2002 est)
REAL GDP GROWTH (% change on previous year) –1.4 (2001)
GNI (US$) 15.9 billion (2002 est)
GNI PER CAPITA (PPP) (US$) 3,390 (2002 est)
CONSUMER PRICE INFLATION 6.6% (2003 est)
UNEMPLOYMENT 7.8% (2001)
FOREIGN DEBT (US$) 8.3 billion (2001 est)
MAJOR TRADING PARTNERS Japan, USA, UK, India, Germany, South Korea, Singapore, Hong Kong, Taiwan, China, Iran
RESOURCES gemstones, graphite, iron ore, monazite, rutile, uranium, iemenite sands, limestone, salt, clay

INDUSTRIES food processing, textiles, clothing, petroleum refining, leather goods, chemicals, rubber, plastics, tourism
EXPORTS clothing and textiles, tea (world's largest exporter and third-largest producer), precious and semi-precious stones, coconuts and coconut products, rubber. Principal market: USA 40% (2001)
IMPORTS machinery and transport equipment, petroleum, food and live animals, beverages, construction materials. Principal source: India 10.1% (2001)
ARABLE LAND 13.8% (2000 est)
AGRICULTURAL PRODUCTS rice, tea, rubber, coconuts; livestock rearing (cattle, buffaloes, pigs, and poultry); fishing

Population and society

POPULATION 19,065,000 (2003 est)
POPULATION GROWTH RATE 1.1% (2000–15)
POPULATION DENSITY (per sq km) 291 (2003 est)
URBAN POPULATION (% of total) 24 (2003 est)
AGE DISTRIBUTION (% of total population) 0–14 25%, 15–59 65%, 60+ 10% (2002 est)
ETHNIC GROUPS 74% Sinhalese, about 18% Tamil, and 7% Moors or Muslims (concentrated in east); the Tamil community is divided between the long-settled 'Sri Lankan Tamils' (11% of the population), who reside in northern and eastern coastal areas, and the more recent immigrant 'Indian Tamils' (7%), who settled in the Kandyan highlands during the 19th and 20th centuries
LANGUAGE Sinhala, Tamil (both official), English
RELIGION Buddhist 69%, Hindu 15%, Muslim 8%, Christian 8%
EDUCATION (compulsory years) 10
LITERACY RATE 95% (men); 90% (women) (2003 est)
LABOUR FORCE 41.6% agriculture, 22.5% industry, 35.9% services (1998)
LIFE EXPECTANCY 70 (men); 76 (women) (2000–05)
CHILD MORTALITY RATE (under 5, per 1,000 live births) 19 (2001)
PHYSICIANS (per 1,000 people) 0.4 (1999 est)

SRI LANKA A Kandyan dancer is on the left, a devil dancer on the right. Sri Lankan dance uses symbolic body movement and neat footwork to tell a story, rather than gestures and facial expressions. Its roots are in folk rituals. 'Devil' dancing has a background of exorcism and is to be found in the lowlands around Colombo, whereas Kandyan dancing flourishes in the uplands. *Image Bank*

HOSPITAL BEDS (per 1,000 people) 2.8 (1997 est)
TV SETS (per 1,000 people) 117 (2001 est)
RADIOS (per 1,000 people) 215 (2001 est)
INTERNET USERS (per 10,000 people) 105.6 (2002 est)
PERSONAL COMPUTER USERS (per 100 people) 1.3 (2002 est)

See also ▷Sinhalese; ▷Tamil; ▷Tamil Tigers.

Chronology

c. **550 BC**: Arrival of the Sinhalese, led by Vijaya, from northern India, displacing long-settled Veddas.

5th century BC: Sinhalese kingdom of Anuradhapura founded by King Pandukabaya.

c. **250–210 BC**: Buddhism, brought from India, became established in Sri Lanka.

AD 992: Downfall of Anuradhapura kingdom, defeated by South Indian Colas.

1070: Overthrow of Colas by Vijayabahu I and establishment of the Sinhalese kingdom of Polonnaruva, which survived for more than two centuries before a number of regional states arose.

late 15th century: Kingdom of Kandy established in central highlands.

1505: Arrival of Portuguese navigator Lorenço de Almeida, attracted by spice trade developed by Arab merchants who had called the island Serendip.

1597–1618: Portuguese controlled most of Sri Lanka, with the exception of Kandy.

1658: Dutch conquest of Portuguese territories.

1795–98: British conquest of Dutch territories.

1802: Treaty of Amiens recognized island as British colony of Ceylon.

1815: British won control of Kandy, becoming the first European power to rule whole island.

1830s: Immigration of south Indian Hindu Tamil labourers to work central coffee plantations.

1880s: Tea and rubber become chief cash crops after blight ended production of coffee.

1919: Formation of the Ceylon National Congress to campaign for self rule; increasing conflicts between Sinhalese majority community and Tamil minority.

1948: Ceylon achieved independence from Britain within Commonwealth, with Don Senanayake of conservative United National Party (UNP) as prime minister.

1949: Indian Tamils disenfranchised.

1956: Sinhala established as official language.

1960: Sirimavo Bandaranaike, the widow of assassinated prime minister Solomon Bandaranaike, won general election and formed an SLFP government, which nationalized oil industry.

1971: Sinhalese Marxist uprising, led by students and People's Liberation Army (JVP).

1972: Socialist Republic of Sri Lanka proclaimed; Buddhism given 'foremost place' in new state, antagonizing Tamils.

1976: Tamil United Liberation Front formed to fight for independent Tamil state ('Eelam') in north and east Sri Lanka.

1978: Presidential constitution adopted by new free-market government headed by Junius Jayawardene of UNP.

1982: Sri Jayewardenepura-Kotte designated the new national capital, replacing Colombo.

1983: Ethnic riots as Tamil guerrilla violence escalated; state of emergency imposed.

1987: President Jayawardene and Indian prime minister Rajiv Gandhi signed Colombo Accord aimed at creating new provincial councils, disarming Tamil militants ('Tamil Tigers'), and stationing 7,000-strong Indian Peace Keeping Force. Violence continued despite ceasefire policed by Indian troops.

1988: Left-wing JVP guerrillas campaigned against Indo-Sri Lankan peace pact. Prime Minister Ranasinghe Premadasa elected president.

1989: Dingiri Banda Wijetunga became prime minister. Leaders of Tamil Tigers and banned Sinhala extremist JVP assassinated.

1990: The Indian peacekeeping force was withdrawn. Violence continued, with a death toll of over a thousand a month.

1991: The Sri Lankan army killed 2,552 Tamil Tigers in the northern Jaffna region. A new party, the Democratic National United Front (DUNF), was formed by former members of UNP.

1992: Several hundred Tamil Tiger rebels were killed in an army offensive.

1993: President Premadasa was assassinated by Tamil Tiger terrorists; he was succeeded by Dingiri Banda Wijetunge.

1994: The UNP were narrowly defeated in a general election; Chandrika Kumaratunga became prime minister in an SLFP-led left-of-centre coalition. Peace talks opened with the Tamil Tigers. Kumaratunga was elected the first female president; her mother, Sirimavo Bandaranaike, became prime minister.

1995: Renewed bombing campaign by Tamil Tigers. A major offensive drove out Tamil Tigers from Jaffna city.

1996: A state of emergency was extended nationwide after Tamils bombed the capital.

1998: The Tamil Tigers were outlawed after the bombing of Sri Lanka's holiest Buddhist site. In September over 1,300 Sri Lankan soldiers and Tamil Tiger rebels died in renewed fighting in the north. In October the Tamil Tigers captured the strategic northern town of Kilinochchi, killing more than 600 government troops.

1999: The government lost a large amount of territory, including military bases, to Tamil guerrillas. In the presidential elections, Kumaratunga was re-elected, just days after she survived an attack by a Tamil suicide bomber.

2000: Terrorist activity continued, and government forces suffered their worst setback in the 17-year civil war in April when they were forced to surrender Pallai, a key military base, to Tamil guerrillas. Prime Minister Bandaranaike died two months after resigning her position because of poor health. She was replaced by Ratnasiri Wickremanayake. The Tamil Tigers announced a month-long ceasefire, but the government did not reciprocate.

2002: In an indefinite ceasefire between the government and the Tamil Tigers, mediated by the Norwegian government, the guerrilla group conceded to autonomy rather than a separate state for minority Tamils.

small trace of calcite is deposited. Successive drips build up the stalactite over many years. In stalagmite formation the calcite comes out of the solution because of agitation – the shock of a drop of water hitting the floor is sufficient to remove some calcite from the drop. The different shapes result from the splashing of the falling water.

Stalin, Joseph (1879–1953) Adopted name of Joseph Vissarionovich Djugashvili. (Russian 'steel') Soviet politician. A member of the October Revolution committee of 1917, Stalin became general secretary of the Communist Party in 1922. After ▷Lenin's death in 1924, Stalin sought to create 'socialism in one country' and clashed with ▷Trotsky, who denied the possibility of socialism inside Russia until revolution had occurred in Western Europe. Stalin won this ideological struggle by 1927, and a series of five-year plans was launched to collectivize industry and agriculture from 1928. All opposition was eliminated in the Great ▷Purge 1936–38. During World War II, Stalin intervened in the military direction of the campaigns against Nazi Germany. He managed not only to bring the USSR through the war but to help it emerge as a superpower, although only at an immense cost in human suffering to his own people. After the war, Stalin quickly turned Eastern Europe into a series of Soviet satellites and maintained an autocratic rule domestically. His role was denounced after his death by Khrushchev and other members of the Soviet regime.

Stalin was born in Georgia, the son of a shoemaker. Educated for the priesthood, he was expelled from his seminary for Marxist propaganda. He became a member of the Social Democratic Party in 1898, and joined Lenin and the Bolsheviks in 1903. He was repeatedly exiled to Siberia 1903–13. He then became a member of the Communist Party's ▷Politburo, and sat on the October Revolution committee. Stalin rapidly consolidated a powerful following (including Molotov); in 1921 he became commissar for nationalities in the Soviet government, responsible for the decree granting equal rights to all peoples of the Russian Empire, and was appointed general secretary of the Communist Party in 1922. As dictator in the 1930s, he disposed of all real and imagined enemies. His anti-Semitism caused, for example, the execution of 19 Jewish activists in 1952 for a 'Zionist conspiracy'.

Related Web site: Modern World History: Stalin
http://www.bbc.co.uk/education/modern/stalin/stalihtm.htm

JOSEPH STALIN Soviet leader Joseph Stalin, wearing a white military uniform, at the Potsdam Conference in Potsdam, Germany, 1945. *Archive Photos*

Stalingrad former name (1925–61) of the Russian city of ▷Volgograd.

Stallone, Sylvester (Enzio) (1946–) US film actor, director, and screenwriter. He became a star as the boxer in *Rocky* (1976; Academy Award for best picture), and its sequels. He wrote the screenplays for all five of the *Rocky* series, and directed three of them. Other films include *First Blood* (1982), the *Rambo* series from 1985, and the comedy *Stop! Or My Mom Will Shoot* (1992). He has also appeared in *Demolition Man* (1993) and contributed his voice to the animated film *Antz* (1998). He starred in *Get Carter* (2000), a remake of the 1970 film starring Michael Caine.

stamen male reproductive organ of a flower. The stamens are collectively referred to as the ▷androecium. A typical stamen consists of a stalk, or filament, with an anther, the pollen-bearing organ, at its apex, but in some primitive plants, such as *Magnolia*, the stamen may not be markedly differentiated.

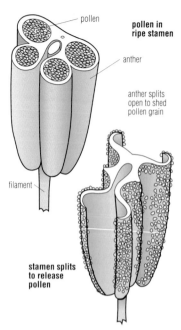

STAMEN The stamen is the male reproductive organ of a flower. It has a thin stalk called a filament with an anther at the tip. The anther contains pollen sacs, which split to release tiny grains of pollen.

Stamp Act UK act of Parliament in 1765 that sought to raise enough money from the American colonies to cover the cost of their defence.

Refusal to use the required tax stamps and a blockade of British merchant shipping in the colonies forced repeal of the act the following year. It helped to precipitate the ▷American Revolution.

The act provoked vandalism and looting in America, and the Stamp Act Congress in October 1765 (the first intercolonial congress) declared the act unconstitutional, with the slogan 'No taxation without representation', because the colonies were not represented in the British Parliament.

The act taxed (by requiring an official stamp) all publications and legal documents published in British colonies.

Related Web site: Considerations on the Propriety of Imposing Taxes in the British Colonies http://odur.let.rug.nl/~usa/D/1751-1775/stampact/consid.htm

standard atmosphere alternative term for ▷atmosphere, a unit of pressure.

standard deviation in statistics, a measure (symbol σ or *s*) of the spread of data. The deviation (difference) of each of the data items from the mean is found, and their values squared. The mean value of these squares is then calculated. The standard deviation is the square root of this mean.

Standard English form of English that in its grammar, syntax, vocabulary, and spelling system does not identify the speaker or writer with a particular geographical area or social grouping. In Britain, the accent associated with Standard English is ▷received pronunciation. All forms of slang, dialect, and grammatical deviation are non-Standard.

standard form (or **scientific notation**) method of writing numbers often used by scientists, particularly for very large or very small numbers. The numbers are written with one digit before the decimal point and multiplied by a power of 10. The number of digits given after the decimal point depends on the accuracy required. For example, the ▷speed of light is 2.9979×10^8 m/1.8628×10^5 mi per second.

standard gravity acceleration due to gravity, generally taken as 9.81274 m/32.38204 ft per second per second. See also ▷g scale.

standard illuminant any of three standard light intensities, A, B, and C, used for illumination when phenomena involving colour are measured. A is the light from a filament at 2,848K (2,575°C/4,667°F), B is noon sunlight, and C is normal daylight. B and C are defined with respect to A. Standardization is necessary because colours appear different when viewed in different lights.

standard model in physics, the modern theory of ▷elementary particles and their interactions. According to the standard model, elementary particles are classified as leptons (light particles, such as electrons), ▷hadrons (particles, such as neutrons and protons, that are formed from quarks), and gauge bosons. Leptons and hadrons interact by exchanging ▷gauge bosons, each of which is responsible for a different fundamental force: photons mediate the electromagnetic force, which affects all charged particles; gluons mediate the strong nuclear force, which affects quarks; gravitons mediate the force of gravity; and the weakons (intermediate vector bosons) mediate the weak nuclear force. See also ▷forces, fundamental, ▷quantum electrodynamics, and ▷quantum chromodynamics.

standard of living in economics, the measure of consumption and welfare of a country, community, class, or person. Individual standard-of-living expectations are heavily influenced by the income and consumption of other people in similar jobs.

standard temperature and pressure (STP) in chemistry, a standard set of conditions for experimental measurements, to enable comparisons to be made between sets of results. Standard temperature is 0°C/32°F (273K) and standard pressure 1 atmosphere (101,325 Pa).

standard volume in physics, the volume occupied by one kilogram molecule (the molecular mass in kilograms) of any gas at standard temperature and pressure. Its value is approximately 22.414 cubic metres.

standing committee committee of the UK House of Commons that examines parliamentary bills (proposed acts of Parliament) for detailed correction and amendment. The committee comprises members of Parliament from the main political parties, with a majority usually held by the government. Several standing committees may be in existence at any time, each usually created for a particular bill.

standing order in banking, an instruction (banker's order) by a depositor with the bank to pay a certain sum of money at regular intervals. In some cases, the bank may be billed by a third party such as a supplier of gas or electricity, who is authorized by the depositor to invoice the bank directly, which in turn will pay out the sum demanded (known as **direct debit**).

standing wave in physics, a wave in which the positions of ▷nodes (positions of zero vibration) and antinodes (positions of maximum vibration) do not move. Standing waves result when two similar waves travel in opposite directions through the same space.

Joseph Stalin

It will unmake our work. No greater instrument of counter-revolution and conspiracy can be imagined.

On the telephone, quoted in L D Trotsky *Life of Stalin*

Stanhope, Hester Lucy (1776–1839) English traveller who left England in 1810 to tour the east Mediterranean with Bedouins and eventually settled there. She adopted local dress and became involved in Middle Eastern politics.

Stanislavsky, Konstantin Sergeivich Alekseyev (1863–1938) Russian actor, director, and teacher of acting. He rejected the declamatory style of acting in favour of a more realistic approach, concentrating on the psychological basis for the development of character. The Actors Studio is based on his methods. As a director, he is acclaimed for his productions of the great plays of ▷Chekhov.

Stanley town on eastern Falkland, capital of the ▷Falkland Islands; population (1991) 1,557. After changing its name only once between 1843 and 1982, it was renamed five times in the space of six weeks during the Falklands War April–June 1982.

Stanley, Henry Morton (1841–1904) Adopted name of John Rowlands. Welsh-born US explorer and journalist who made four expeditions to Africa. He and David ▷Livingstone met at Ujiji in 1871 and explored Lake Tanganyika. He traced the course of the Congo River to the sea 1874–77, established the Congo Free State (Democratic Republic of Congo) 1879–84, and charted much of the interior 1887–89. GCB 1899.

Henry Morton Stanley

Dr Livingstone, I presume?

On meeting David Livingstone at Lake Tanganyika November 1871, in *How I Found Livingstone*

Stanley worked his passage over to America when he was 18. He fought on both sides in the US Civil War. He worked for the *New York Herald* from 1867, and in 1871 he was sent by the editor James Gordon Bennett (1795–1872) to find the ailing Livingstone, which he did on 10 November. From Africa he returned to the UK and was elected to Parliament in 1895.

Stansted London's third international airport, in Essex, southeast England.

Stanton, Elizabeth (1815–1902) Born Elizabeth Cady. US feminist. With Susan B ▷Anthony, she founded the National Woman Suffrage Association in 1869, the first women's movement in the USA, and was its first president. She and Anthony wrote and compiled the *History of Women's Suffrage* (1881–86). Stanton also worked for the abolition of slavery.

She organized the International Council of Women in Washington, DC. Her publications include *Degradation of Disenfranchisement* and *Solitude of Self* (1892), and in 1885 and 1898 she published a two-part feminist critique of the Bible: *The Woman's Bible*.

star luminous globe of gas, mainly hydrogen and helium, which produces its own heat and light by nuclear reactions. Although stars shine for a very long time – many billions of years – they are not eternal, and have been found to change in appearance at different stages in their lives.

The smallest mass possible for a star is about 8% that of the Sun (80 times that of ▷Jupiter), otherwise nuclear reactions do not occur. Objects with less than this critical mass shine only dimly, and are termed **brown dwarfs**. See also Studying the Stars Focus Feature on pp. 908–909.

Star: Nearest Stars

Star	Distance (light years)	Star	Distance (light years)
Proxima Centauri	4.2	UV Ceti A	8.4
Alpha Centauri A	4.3	UV Ceti B	8.4
Alpha Centauri B	4.3	Sirius A	8.6
Barnard's Star	6.0	Sirius B	8.6
Wolf 359	7.7	Ross 154	9.4
Lalande 21185	8.2	Ross 249	10.4

starch widely distributed, high-molecular-mass ▷carbohydrate, produced by plants as a food store; main dietary sources are cereals, legumes, and tubers, including potatoes. It consists of varying proportions of two ▷glucose polymers (▷polysaccharides): straight-chain (amylose) and branched (amylopectin) molecules.

Purified starch is a white powder used to stiffen textiles and paper and as a raw material for making various chemicals. It is used in the food industry as a thickening agent. Chemical treatment of starch gives rise to a range of 'modified starches' with varying properties. Hydrolysis (splitting) of starch by acid or enzymes generates a variety of 'glucose syrups' or 'liquid glucose' for use in the food industry. Complete hydrolysis of starch with acid generates the ▷monosaccharide glucose only. Incomplete hydrolysis or enzymic hydrolysis yields a mixture of glucose, maltose, and nonhydrolysed fractions called dextrins.

Star Chamber in English history, a civil and criminal court, named after the star-shaped ceiling decoration of the room in the Palace of Westminster, London, where its first meetings were held. Created in 1487 by ▷Henry VII, the Star Chamber comprised some 20 or 30 judges. It was abolished in 1641 by the ▷Long Parliament.

Starck, Philippe Patrick (1949–) French product, furniture, and interior designer. He brought French design to international attention in the 1980s with his innovative and elegant designs, notably those for a room in the Elysée Palace in 1982 and for the Café Costes in Paris in 1984.

star cluster group of related stars, usually held together by gravity. Members of a star cluster are thought to form together from one large cloud of gas in space. **Open clusters** such as the ▷Pleiades contain from a dozen to many hundreds of young stars, loosely scattered over several light years. ▷Globular clusters are larger and much more densely packed, containing perhaps 10,000–1,000,000 stars.

starfish (or **sea star**) any ▷echinoderm of the subclass Asteroidea with arms radiating from a central body. Usually there are five arms, but some species have more. They are covered with spines and small pincerlike organs. There are also a number of small tubular processes on the skin surface that assist in locomotion and respiration. Starfish are predators, and vary in size from 1.2 cm/0.5 in to 90 cm/3 ft.

Some species use their suckered tube feet to pull open the shells of bivalve molluscs, then evert their stomach to surround and digest the animal inside. The poisonous and predatory crown-of-thorns of the Pacific is very destructive to coral and severely damaged Australia's Great Barrier Reef when it multiplied prolifically in the 1960s–70s. Although it had practically disappeared by 1990, in 1996 another outbreak along the Great Barrier Reef was officially declared.

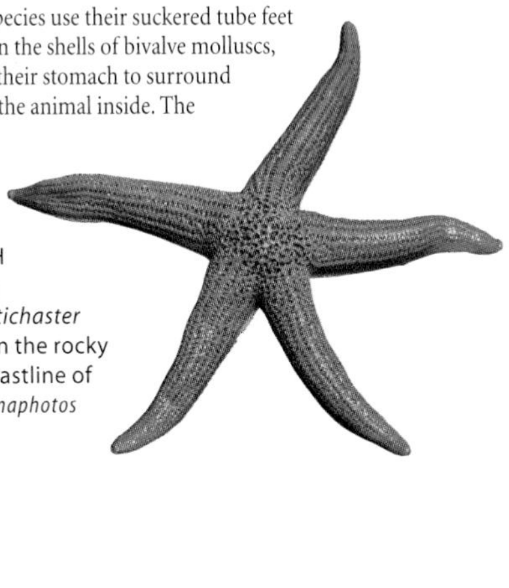

STARFISH The large starfish *Stichaster striatus* on the rocky Pacific coastline of Peru. *Premaphotos Wildlife*

Another destructive species, *Asteria amurensis*, spread round the coast of Tasmania in 1993, and could reach as far as Sydney. It is normally found only in the North Pacific and was probably introduced into Tasmania in the ballast water of a ship travelling from Japan.

star fruit fruit of the ▷carambola tree.

Stark, Freya Madeline (1893–1993) English traveller, mountaineer, and writer. Often travelling alone in dangerous territories, she described her explorations in the Middle East in many books, including *The Valley of the Assassins* (1934), *The Southern Gates of Arabia* (1936), and *A Winter in Arabia* (1940).

> **Freya Stark**
> *The great and almost only comfort about being a woman is that one can always pretend to be more stupid than one is, and no one is surprised.*
> *Valley of the Assassins*

starling any member of a large widespread Old World family (Sturnidae) of chunky, dark, generally gregarious birds of the order Passeriformes. The European starling *Sturnus vulgaris*, common in northern Eurasia, has been naturalized in North America from the late 19th century. The black, speckled plumage is glossed with green and purple. The feathers on the upper parts are tipped with buff, and the wings are greyish-black, with a reddish-brown fringe. The female is less glossy and lustrous than the male. Its own call is a bright whistle, but it is a mimic of the songs of other birds. It is about 20 cm/8 in long.

Strikingly gregarious in feeding, flight, and roosting, it often becomes a pest in large cities, where it becomes attached to certain buildings as 'dormitories', returning each night from omnivorous foraging in the countryside.

Star of David (or **Magen David**; Hebrew 'shield of David') six-pointed star (made with two equilateral triangles), a symbol of Judaism since the 17th century. It is the central motif on the flag of Israel, and, since 1897, the emblem of Zionism.

Starr, Ringo (1940–) born Richard Starkey. English rock and pop drummer with the legendary English rock group the Beatles. Starr replaced original Beatles' drummer Pete Best in 1962. He occasionally sang vocals for the group, including on 'Yellow Submarine' (1966). After the group split up in 1970, he pursued a solo musical career. He has also appeared in films and as a broadcaster on children's television, including narrating the series *Thomas the Tank Engine* 1984–96.

Star Wars popular term for the ▷Strategic Defense Initiative announced by US president Reagan in 1983.

state territory that forms its own domestic and foreign policy, acting through laws that are typically decided by a government and carried out, by force if necessary, by agents of that government. It can be argued that growth of regional international bodies such as the European Union (formerly the European Community) means that states no longer enjoy absolute sovereignty.

State Department (Department of State) US government department responsible for ▷foreign relations, headed by the secretary of state, the senior cabinet officer of the executive branch.

statement in UK education, the results of an assessment of the special educational needs of a child with physical or mental disabilities. Under the Education Act 1981, less able children are entitled to such an assessment by various professionals, to establish what their needs are and how they might be met.

States General former French parliament that consisted of three estates: nobility, clergy, and commons. First summoned in 1302, it declined in importance as the power of the crown grew. It was not called at all between 1614 and 1789 when the crown needed to institute fiscal reforms to avoid financial collapse. Once called, the demands made by the States General formed the first phase in the ▷French Revolution. States General is also the name of the Dutch parliament.

states of matter forms (solid, liquid, or gas) in which material can exist. Whether a material is solid, liquid, or gaseous depends on its temperature and the pressure on it. The transition between states takes place at definite temperatures, called melting point and boiling point.

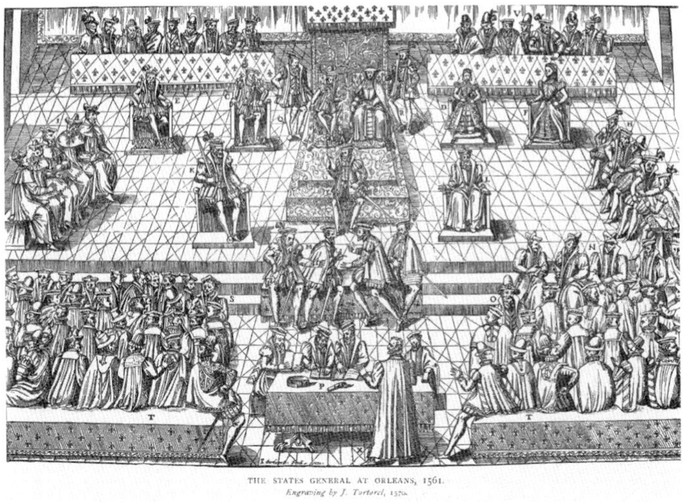

STATES GENERAL The meeting of the States General at Orleans in 1561. *Philip Sauvain Picture Collection*

states' rights interpretation of the US constitution that emphasizes the powers retained by individual states and minimizes those given to the federal government. The dividing line between state and national sovereignty was left deliberately vague in the Philadelphia convention devising the constitution 1787.

static electricity ▷electric charge that is stationary, usually acquired by a body by means of electrostatic induction or friction. Rubbing different materials can produce static electricity, as seen in the sparks produced on combing one's hair or removing a nylon shirt. In some processes static electricity is useful, as in paint spraying where the parts to be sprayed are charged with electricity of opposite polarity to that on the paint droplets, and in ▷xerography.

statics branch of mechanics concerned with the behaviour of bodies at rest and forces in equilibrium, and distinguished from ▷dynamics.

Stationery Office, His/Her Majesty's (HMSO) organization established in 1786 to supply books and stationery to British government departments, and to superintend the printing of government reports and other papers, and books and pamphlets on subjects ranging from national works of art to industrial and agricultural processes.

The corresponding establishment in the USA is the Government Printing Office.

statistics branch of mathematics concerned with the collection and interpretation of data. For example, to determine the ▷mean age of the children in a school, a statistically acceptable answer might be obtained by calculating an average based on the ages of a representative sample, consisting, for example, of a random tenth of the pupils from each class. ▷Probability is the branch of statistics dealing with predictions of events.

Mean, median, and mode The mean, median, and mode are different ways of finding a 'typical' or 'central' value of a set of data. The ▷mean is obtained by adding up all the observed values and dividing by the number of values; it is the number which is commonly used as an average value. The ▷median is the middle value, that is, the value which is exceeded by half the items in the sample. The ▷mode is the value which occurs with greatest frequency; the most common value. The mean is the most useful measure for the purposes of statistical theory. The idea of the median may be extended and a distribution can be divided into four quartiles. The first quartile is the value which is exceeded by three-quarters of the items; the second quartile is the same as the median; the third quartile is the value that is exceeded by one-quarter of the items.

Standard deviation and other measures of dispersion
The mean is a very incomplete summary of a group of observations; it is useful to know also how closely the individual members of a group approach the mean, and this is indicated by various measures of dispersion. The **range** is the difference between the maximum and minimum values of the group; it is not very satisfactory as a measure of dispersion. The **mean deviation** is the arithmetic mean of the differences between the mean and the

individual values, the differences all being taken as positive. However, the **mean deviation** also does not convey much useful information about a group of observations. The most useful measure of dispersion is the **variance**, which is the arithmetic mean of the squares of the deviations from the mean. The positive square root of the variance is called the ▷standard deviation, a measure (symbol σ or s) of the spread of data. The deviation (difference) of each of the data items from the mean is found, and their values squared. The mean value of these squares is then calculated. The standard deviation is the square root of this mean.

It is usual to standardize the measurements by working in units of the standard deviation measured from the mean of the distributions, enabling statistical theories to be generalized. A standardized distribution has a mean of zero and a standard deviation of unity. Another useful measure of dispersion is the semi-interquartile range, which is one-half of the distance between the first and third quartiles, and can be considered as the average distance of the quartiles from the median. In many typical distributions the semi-interquartile range is about two-thirds of the standard deviation and the mean deviation is about four-fifths of the standard deviation.

Applications One of the most important uses of statistical theory is in testing whether experimental data support hypotheses or not. For example, an agricultural researcher arranges for different groups of cows to be fed different diets and records the milk yields. The milk-yield data are analysed and the means and standard deviations of yields for different groups vary. The researcher can use statistical tests to assess whether the variation is of an amount that should be expected because of the natural variation in cows or whether it is larger than normal and therefore likely to be influenced by the difference in diet.

Correlation Correlation measures the degree to which two quantities are associated, in the sense that a variation in one quantity is accompanied by a predictable variation in the other. For example, if the pressure on a quantity of gas is increased then its volume decreases. If observations of pressure and volume are taken then statistical correlation analysis can be used to determine whether the volume of a gas can be completely predicted from a knowledge of the pressure on it.

status in the social sciences, an individual's social position, or the esteem in which he or she is held by others in society. Both within and between most occupations or social positions there is a status hierarchy. **Status symbols**, such as insignia of office or an expensive car, often accompany high status.

Statute of Westminster in the history of the British Empire, legislation enacted in 1931 which gave the dominions of the British Empire complete autonomy in their conduct of external affairs. It made them self-governing states whose only allegiance was to the British crown.

Stauffenberg, Claus von (1907–1944) German colonel in World War II who, in a conspiracy to assassinate Hitler (the July Plot), planted a bomb in the dictator's headquarters conference room in the Wolf's Lair at Rastenburg, East Prussia, on 20 July 1944. Hitler was merely injured, and Stauffenberg and 200 others were later executed by the Nazi regime.

Stavropol (formerly **Voroshilovsk** (1935–44)) capital city, economic and cultural centre of ▷Stavropol krai (territory) in the southwestern Russian Federation; population (1996 est) 344,000. Stavropol is located in the foothills of northwestern ▷Caucasia, at the centre of a major agricultural region. Heavy industry in the city produces automobiles, building materials, and construction equipment. There are also food, wool, and leather industries here. An important natural-gas pipeline runs from here to Moscow.

Stavropol krai (territory) in the southwestern Russian Federation; area 80,600 sq km/31,120 sq mi; population (1996) 2,667,000 (54% urban). The capital is ▷Stavropol. Wheat and sunflowers are grown, and cattle and sheep are raised. Natural gas is piped to Moscow and St Petersburg, and there are food-processing industries. There are spas and health resorts around Mineralnye Vody.

STD abbreviation for ▷sexually transmitted disease.

steady-state theory in astronomy, a rival theory to that of the ▷Big Bang, which claims that the universe has no origin but is expanding because new matter is being created continuously throughout the universe. The theory was proposed in 1948 by Austrian-born British cosmologist Hermann ▷Bondi, Austrian-born US Astronomer Thomas Gold, and English astronomer, cosmologist, and writer Fred ▷Hoyle, but it was dealt a severe blow in 1965 by the discovery of ▷cosmic background radiation (radiation left over from the formation of the universe) and is now largely rejected.

stealth technology methods used to make an aircraft as invisible as possible, primarily to radar detection but also to

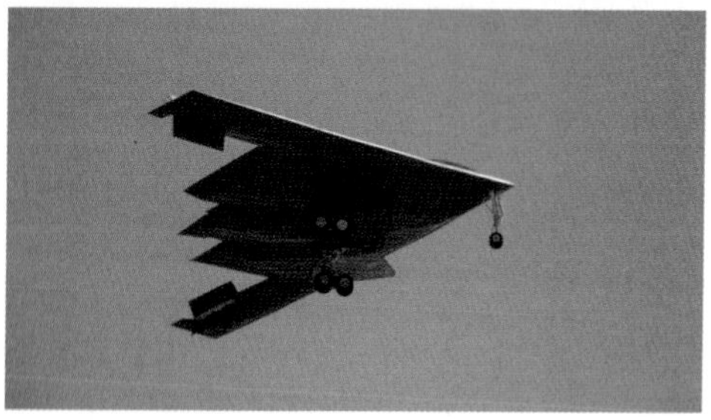

STEALTH TECHNOLOGY The B-2 stealth bomber's 'jagged wedge' profile is unmistakable in this picture. *Image Bank*

detection by visual means and heat sensors. This is achieved by a combination of aircraft-design elements: smoothing off all radar-reflecting sharp edges; covering the aircraft with radar-absorbent materials; fitting engine coverings that hide the exhaust and heat signatures of the aircraft; and other, secret technologies.

steam in chemistry, a dry, invisible gas formed by vaporizing water.

The visible cloud that normally forms in the air when water is vaporized is due to minute suspended water particles. Steam is widely used in chemical and other industrial processes and for the generation of power.

steam engine engine that uses the power of steam to produce useful work. It was the principal power source during the British Industrial Revolution in the 18th century. The first successful steam engine was built in 1712 by English inventor Thomas ▷Newcomen at Dudley, West Midlands; it was developed further by Scottish mining engineer James ▷Watt from 1769 and by English mining engineer Richard ▷Trevithick, whose high-pressure steam engine of 1802 led to the development of the steam locomotive.

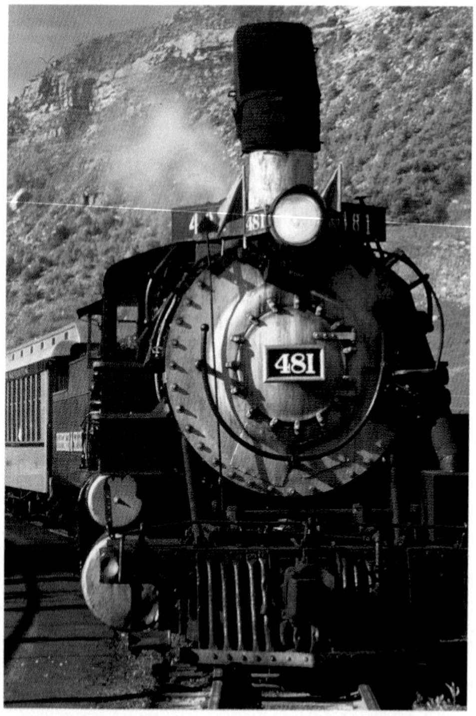

STEAM ENGINE A steam train in Durango, Colorado. The main type of locomotive in the USA until well after 1865 was known as the American Standard – it had four driving wheels and four pilot (or leading) wheels to guide it around curves. *Image Bank*

stearic acid $CH_3(CH_2)_{16}COOH$ saturated long-chain ▷fatty acid, soluble in alcohol and ether but not in water. It is found in many fats and oils, and is used to make soap and candles and as a lubricant. The salts of stearic acid are called stearates.

steel alloy or mixture of iron and up to 1.7% carbon, sometimes with other elements, such as manganese, phosphorus, sulphur, and silicon. The USA, Russia, Ukraine, and Japan are the main steel producers. Steel has innumerable uses, including ship and car manufacture, skyscraper frames, and machinery of all kinds.

Steels with only small amounts of other metals are called **carbon steels**. These steels are far stronger than pure iron, with properties varying with the composition. **Alloy steels** contain greater amounts of other metals. Low-alloy steels have less than 5% of the alloying material; high-alloy steels have more. Low-alloy steels containing up to 5% silicon with relatively little carbon have a high electrical resistance and are used in power transformers and motor or generator cores, for example. **Stainless steel** is a high-alloy steel containing at least 11% chromium. Steels with up to 20% tungsten are very hard and are used in high-speed cutting tools. About 50% of the world's steel is now made from scrap.

Steel is produced by removing impurities, such as carbon, from raw or pig iron, produced by a ▷blast furnace. The main industrial process is the ▷basic-oxygen process, in which molten pig iron and scrap steel is placed in a container lined with heat-resistant, alkaline (basic) bricks. A pipe or lance is lowered near to the surface of the molten metal and pure oxygen blown through it at high pressure. The surface of the metal is disturbed by the blast and the impurities are oxidized (burned out). The **open-hearth process** is an older steelmaking method in which molten iron and limestone are placed in a shallow bowl or hearth (see ▷open-hearth furnace). Burning oil or gas is blown over the surface of the metal, and the impurities are oxidized. High-quality steel is made in an **electric furnace**. A large electric current flows through electrodes in the furnace, melting a charge of scrap steel and iron. The quality of the steel produced can be controlled precisely because the temperature of the furnace can be maintained exactly and there are no combustion by-products to contaminate the steel. Electric furnaces are also used to refine steel, producing the extra-pure steels used, for example, in the petrochemical industry.

The steel produced is cast into ingots, which can be worked when hot by hammering (forging) or pressing between rollers to produce sheet steel. Alternatively, the **continuous-cast process**, in which the molten metal is fed into an open-ended mould cooled by water, produces an unbroken slab of steel.

Steele, Richard (1672–1729) Irish essayist, playwright, and politician. Born in Dublin, he entered the Life Guards, and then settled in London. He founded the journal *The Tatler* (1709–11), in which Joseph ▷Addison collaborated. They continued their joint work in the *Spectator* (1711–12), also founded by Steele, and *The Guardian* (1713). He also wrote plays, such as *The Conscious Lovers* (1722). In 1713 Steele was elected to Parliament. He was knighted in 1715.

Steen, Jan Havickszoon (*c.* 1626–1679) Dutch painter. He painted humorous genre scenes, mainly set in taverns or bourgeois households, as well as portraits and landscapes. An example is *The Prince's Birthday* (Rijksmuseum, Amsterdam).

Steer, Philip Wilson (1860–1942) English artist. Strongly influenced by the French Impressionists, he is known for his landscapes, such as *The Beach at Walberswick* (1890; Tate Gallery, London). He became a leader (with Walter ▷Sickert) of the English Impressionist movement and a founder-member of the New English Art Club.

Stefan–Boltzmann constant in physics, a constant relating the energy emitted by a black body (a hypothetical body that absorbs or emits all the energy falling on it) to its temperature. Its value is 5.6697×10^{-8} W m^{-2} K^{-4}.

Stefan–Boltzmann law in physics, a law that relates the energy, E, radiated away from a perfect emitter (a black body), to the temperature, T, of that body. It has the form $E = \sigma T^4$, where E is the energy radiated per unit area per second, T is the temperature, and σ is the **Stefan–Boltzmann constant**. Its value is 5.6697×10^{-8} W m^{-2} K^{-4}. The law was derived by the Austrian physicists Josef Stefan and Ludwig Boltzmann.

Stegosaurus genus of late Jurassic North American dinosaurs of the order Ornithischia. They were ungainly herbivores, with very small heads, a double row of triangular plates along the back, and spikes on the tail.

Steiermark German name for ▷Styria, a province of Austria.

Stein, Gertrude (1874–1946) US writer. She influenced authors Ernest ▷Hemingway, Sherwood Anderson, and F Scott ▷Fitzgerald with her radical prose style. Drawing on the stream-of-consciousness psychology of William James and on the geometry of Cézanne and the cubist painters in Paris, she evolved a 'continuous present' style made up of constant repetition and variation of simple phrases. Her work includes the self-portrait *The Autobiography of Alice B Toklas* (1933).

Born in Allegheny, Pennsylvania, Stein went to Paris in 1903 after medical school at Johns Hopkins University and lived there, writing and collecting art, for the rest of her life. She settled in with her brother, also a patron of the arts, and a companion/secretary, Alice B Toklas (1877–1967), and in her home she held court to a 'lost generation' of expatriate US writers and modern artists

(Picasso, Matisse, Braque, Gris). She also wrote *Three Lives* (1910), *The Making of Americans* (1925), *Composition as Explanation* (1926), *Tender Buttons* (1914), *Mrs Reynolds* (1952), and the operas (with composer Virgil Thomson) *Four Saints in Three Acts* (1929) and *The Mother of Us All* (1947). A tour of the USA in 1934 resulted in *Everybody's Autobiography* (1937).

Related Web site: Stein, Gertrude http://dept.english.upenn.edu:80/~afilreis/88/stein-bio.html

Steinbeck, John Ernst (1902–1968) US novelist. His realist novels, such as *In Dubious Battle* (1936), *Of Mice and Men* (1937), and *The Grapes of Wrath* (1939; Pulitzer prize; filmed 1940), portray agricultural life in his native California, where migrant farm labourers from the Oklahoma dust bowl struggled to survive. He was awarded the Nobel Prize for Literature in 1962.

Born in Salinas, California, Steinbeck worked as a labourer to support his writing career, and his experiences supplied him with authentic material for his books. He first achieved success with *Tortilla Flat* (1935), a humorous study of the lives of Monterey paisanos (farmers). His early naturalist works are his most critically acclaimed. Later books include *Cannery Row* (1944), *The Wayward Bus* (1947), *East of Eden* (1952), *Once There Was a War* (1958), *The Winter of Our Discontent* (1961), and *Travels with Charley* (1962).

He also wrote screenplays for films, notably *Viva Zapata!* (1952). His best-known short story is the fable 'The Pearl'.

steinbok (or **steenbok**) southern African antelope. It is reddish-brown and about 60 cm/23.5 in high at the shoulder. The steinbok *Raphicerus campestris* is in family Bovidae, in order Artiodactyla.

Steinem, Gloria (1934–) US journalist and liberal feminist. She emerged as a leading figure in the US women's movement in the late 1960s. She was also involved in radical protest campaigns against racism and the Vietnam War. She cofounded the Women's Action Alliance in 1970 and *Ms* magazine. In 1983 a collection of her articles was published as *Outrageous Acts and Everyday Rebellions*.

Gloria Steinem
I can't mate in captivity.
Attributed remark, on being asked why she has never married

Steiner, Rudolf (1861–1925) Austrian philosopher, occultist, and educationalist. He formulated his own mystic and spiritual teaching, which he called anthroposophy. This rejected materialism and aimed to develop the whole human being, intellectually, socially, and, above all, spiritually. A number of Steiner schools follow a curriculum laid down by him with a strong emphasis on the arts.

Related Web site: Rudolf Steiner Archive http://www.elib.com/Steiner/

Stella, Frank Philip (1936–) US painter. He was a pioneer of the severe, hard-edged geometric trend in abstract art that followed ▷abstract expressionism. From around 1960 he also experimented with shaped canvases.

Born in Malden, Massachusetts, he studied at Princeton University. In the late 1950s he abandoned abstract expressionism and in 1960 came to prominence when he exhibited large-scale paintings consisting of thin regular white stripes on black. From 1960 to 1962 he worked in metallic paint, again using thin stripes which repeated the non-rectangular shape of the support. Later paintings by Stella employ a wider range of colour, the choice of which emphasizes the flatness of the painting, which is then contradicted by the use of overlapping shapes.

stem main supporting axis of a plant that bears the leaves, buds, and reproductive structures; it may be simple or branched. The plant stem usually grows above ground, although some grow underground, including ▷rhizomes, ▷corms, ▷rootstocks, and ▷tubers. Stems contain a continuous vascular system that conducts water and food to and from all parts of the plant.

The point on a stem from which a leaf or leaves arise is called a node, and the space between two successive nodes is the internode. In some plants, the stem is highly modified; for example, it may form a leaf-like cladode or it may be twining (as in many climbing plants), or fleshy and swollen to store water (as in cacti and other succulents). In plants exhibiting ▷secondary growth, the stem may become woody, forming a main trunk, as in trees, or a number of branches from ground level, as in shrubs.

Stendhal (1783–1842) Pen-name of Marie Henri Beyle. French novelist. His novels *Le Rouge et le Noir/The Red and the Black* (1830) and *La Chartreuse de Parme/The Charterhouse of Parma* (1839) were pioneering works in their treatment of disguise and hypocrisy and outstanding for their psychological analysis; a review of the latter by fellow novelist ▷Balzac (1840) furthered Stendhal's reputation, but he was not fully understood during his lifetime.

His critical works include *Histoire de la peinture en Italie/History of Painting in Italy* (1817), *Rome, Naples et Florence/Rome, Naples and Florence* (1817), *Racine et Shakespeare/Racine and Shakespeare* (1823–25), and *Promenades dans Rome/A Roman Journal* (1829). His unfinished novel *Lucien Leuwen* was published in 1894. Although he shared many of the literary ideas of the Romantics, he remained fiercely independent.

Stephen (*c.* 1097–1154) King of England from 1135. A grandson of William the Conqueror, he was elected king in 1135, although he had previously recognized Henry I's daughter ▷Matilda as heiress to the throne. Matilda landed in England in 1139, and civil war disrupted the country until 1153, when Stephen acknowledged Matilda's son, Henry II, as his own heir.

Stephen's reign was a time of near-anarchy when, according to the Anglo-Saxon Chronicle, 'there was nothing but strife, evil, and robbery...the land was ruined by such doings, and men said openly that Christ and the saints slept.'

Stephen, St (lived *c.* AD 35) The first Christian martyr; he was stoned to death. Feast day 26 December.

Stephenson, George (1781–1848) English engineer. He built the first successful steam locomotive. He also invented a safety lamp independently of Humphrey ▷Davy in 1815. He was appointed engineer of the Stockton and Darlington Railway, the world's first public railway, in 1821, and of the Liverpool and Manchester Railway in 1826. In 1829 he won a prize with his locomotive *Rocket*.

Experimenting with various gradients, Stephenson found that a slope of 1 in 200, common enough on roads, reduced the haulage power of a locomotive by 50% (on a completely even surface, a tractive force of less than 5 kg/11 lb would move a tonne). Friction was virtually independent of speed. It followed that railway gradients should always be as low as possible, and cuttings, tunnels, and embankments were therefore necessary. He also advocated the use of malleable iron rails instead of cast iron. The gauge for the Stockton and Darlington Railway was set by Stephenson at 1.4 m/4 ft 8 in, which became the standard gauge for railways in most of the world.

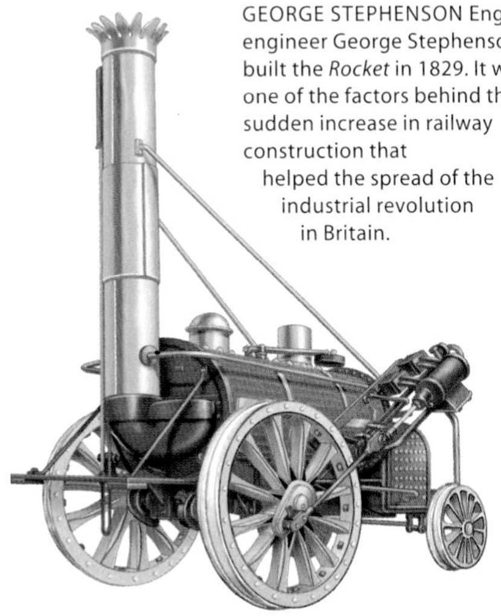

GEORGE STEPHENSON English engineer George Stephenson built the *Rocket* in 1829. It was one of the factors behind the sudden increase in railway construction that helped the spread of the industrial revolution in Britain.

Stephenson, Robert (1803–1859) English civil engineer. He constructed railway bridges such as the high-level bridge at Newcastle-upon-Tyne, England, and the Menai and Conway tubular bridges in Wales. He was the son of George ▷Stephenson.

The successful *Rocket* steam locomotive was built under his direction in 1829, as were subsequent improvements to it.

steppe the temperate grasslands of Europe and Asia. Sometimes the term refers to other temperate grasslands and semi-arid desert edges.

steradian SI unit (symbol sr) of measure of solid (three-dimensional) angles, the three-dimensional equivalent of the ▷radian. One steradian is the angle at the centre of a sphere when an area on the surface of the sphere equal to the square of the sphere's radius is joined to the centre.

stereophonic sound system of sound reproduction using two complementary channels leading to two loudspeakers, which gives a more natural depth to the sound. Stereo recording began with the introduction of two-track magnetic tape in the 1950s. See ▷hi-fi.

Robert Louis Stevenson
For my part, I travel not to go anywhere, but to go. I travel for travel's sake. The great affair is to move.
Travels with a Donkey

stereotype (Greek 'fixed impression') in sociology, a fixed, exaggerated, and preconceived description about a certain type of person, group, or society.

It is based on prejudice rather than fact, but by repetition and with time, stereotypes become fixed in people's minds, resistant to change or factual evidence to the contrary.

sterilization the killing or removal of living organisms such as bacteria and fungi. A sterile environment is necessary in medicine, food processing, and some scientific experiments. Methods include heat treatment (such as boiling), the use of chemicals (such as disinfectants), irradiation with gamma rays, and filtration. See also ▷asepsis.

sterilization any surgical operation to terminate the possibility of reproduction. In women, this is normally achieved by sealing or tying off the ▷Fallopian tubes (tubal ligation) so that fertilization can no longer take place. In men, the transmission of sperm is blocked by ▷vasectomy.

sterling silver ▷alloy containing 925 parts of silver and 75 parts of copper. The copper hardens the silver, making it more useful.

Sternberg, Josef von (1894–1969) Austrian film director. He lived in the USA from childhood. He made seven films with Marlene Dietrich, including *Der blaue Engel/The Blue Angel* (1930), *Blonde Venus* (1932), and *The Devil Is a Woman* (1935), all of which are marked by his expressive use of light and shadow.

Sterne, Laurence (1713–1768) Irish writer. Sterne was born in Clonmel, County Tipperary, and ordained in 1737. He created the comic anti-hero Tristram Shandy in *The Life and Opinions of Tristram Shandy, Gent* (1759–67). An eccentrically whimsical and bawdy novel, its associations of ideas on the philosophic principles of John Locke, and other devices, foreshadow in part some of the techniques associated with the 20th-century novel, such as stream-of-consciousness. His other works include *A Sentimental Journey through France and Italy* (1768).

Sterne became vicar of Sutton-in-the-Forest, Yorkshire, in 1738, and married Elizabeth Lumley in 1741, an unhappy union largely because of his infidelity. He had a sentimental love affair with Elizabeth Draper, recorded in his *Letters of Yorick to Eliza* (1775).

Related Web site: Life and Opinions of Tristram Shandy, Gent, The http://www.gifu-u.ac.jp/~masaru/TS/contents.html#start

steroid in biology, any of a group of cyclic, unsaturated alcohols (lipids without fatty acid components), which, like sterols, have a complex molecular structure consisting of four carbon rings. Steroids include the sex hormones, such as ▷testosterone, the corticosteroid hormones produced by the ▷adrenal gland, bile acids, and ▷cholesterol.

The term is commonly used to refer to ▷anabolic steroid. In medicine, synthetic steroids are used to treat a wide range of conditions.

Steroids are also found in plants. The most widespread are the **brassinosteroids**, necessary for normal plant growth.

sterol any of a group of solid, cyclic, unsaturated alcohols, with a complex structure that includes four carbon rings; cholesterol is an example. Steroids are derived from sterols.

stethoscope instrument used to ascertain the condition of the heart and lungs by listening to their action. It consists of two earpieces connected by flexible tubes to a small plate that is placed against the body. It was invented in 1819 in France by René Théophile Hyacinthe ▷Laënnec.

Stevens, Wallace (1879–1955) US poet. An insurance company executive, he was not recognized as a major poet until late in life. His volumes of poems include *Harmonium* (1923), *The Man with the Blue Guitar* (1937), and *Transport to Summer* (1947). *The Necessary Angel* (1951) is a collection of essays.

An elegant and philosophical poet, he won a Pulitzer prize in 1954 for his *Collected Poems*.

Stevenson, Robert Louis Balfour (1850–1894) Scottish novelist and poet. He wrote the adventure stories *Treasure Island* (1883), *Kidnapped* (1886), and *The Master of Ballantrae* (1889), notable for their characterization as well as their action. He was a master also of shorter fiction such as *The Strange Case of Dr Jekyll and Mr Hyde* (1886), and of stories of the supernatural such as *Thrawn Janet* (1881). In depth of character and power, his unfinished novel *Weir of Hermiston* might have exceeded all his other works. *A Child's Garden of Verses* (1885) is a collection of nostalgic poetry reflecting childhood.

Related Web site: Selected Poems by Robert Louis Stevenson http://www.library.utoronto.ca/utel/rp/authors/stvnsnrl.html

Studying the Stars

by Richard James

People have been interested in astronomy since civilization began. In the classical Greek era, Aristarchus estimated the distances to the Sun and Moon, Eratosthenes measured the size of the Earth, and Hipparchus detected the precession of its rotation axis. But until 1781, only five planets, in addition to the Earth, were known: Mercury, Venus, Mars, Jupiter, and Saturn. In the 17th century, Johannes Kepler worked out three laws governing planetary motion from data collected by Tycho Brahe. Galileo's introduction of the telescope to astronomy started an explosion in our knowledge. William Herschel discovered a sixth planet, Uranus, in 1781, and small perturbations of the orbit of Uranus led to the discovery of Neptune and subsequently Pluto. In the 20th century, the *Voyager* spacecraft visited Jupiter, Saturn, Uranus, and Neptune, obtaining a wealth of new data. Rings were discovered around Jupiter and Uranus, superb pictures were obtained of the rings of Saturn, and additional satellites were found around the planets.

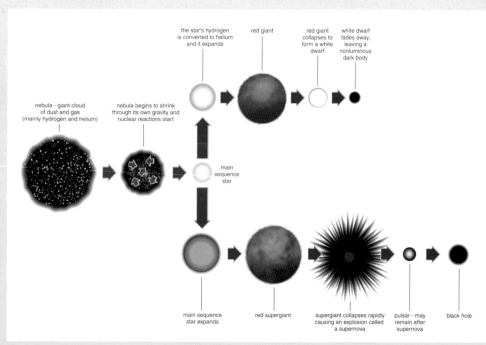

the star's hydrogen is converted to helium and it expands

red giant

red giant collapses to form a white dwarf

white dwarf fades away, leaving a nonluminous dark body

nebula - giant cloud of dust and gas (mainly hydrogen and helium)

nebula begins to shrink through its own gravity and nuclear reactions start

main sequence star

main sequence star expands

red supergiant

supergiant collapses rapidly causing an explosion called a supernova

pulsar - may remain after supernova

black hole

THE LIFE CYCLE OF A STAR New stars are being formed all the time when nebulae (giant clouds of dust and gas) contract due to the action of gravity. As the star contracts and heats up, eventually nuclear reactions begin and the star becomes a main sequence star. If the star is less than 1.2 times the mass of the Sun, it eventually forms a white dwarf that finally fades to a dark body. If it is a massive star, then the main sequence star expands to become a red supergiant that eventually explodes as a supernova. It leaves part of the core as a neutron star (pulsar), or as a black hole if the mass of the collapsing supernova core is three times greater than the Sun.

stars

Stars vary in mass, brightness, and energy output, called 'luminosity'. Even a small telescope reveals a multitude of stars too faint to be seen with the naked eye. If we compare other stars to the Sun, we find that luminosities can be anywhere from 1,000 times less to 100,000 times greater than that of the Sun, and masses between 10 times less and 60 times greater. Surface temperatures vary between 3,000 and 50,000 K, as compared with the sun at 5,770 K. (Astronomers give temperatures on the Kelvin (K) scale. The zero of the Centigrade scale (or 32° Fahrenheit) is at 273.15 K.)

The energy radiated by stars comes mainly from fusion of light atomic nuclei into heavy nuclei, a process that releases energy. Of this energy, 90% comes from the fusion (or burning) of hydrogen (which forms helium), and this is the source for most of a star's life. Burning is quickest at the centre of a star and eventually uses all the hydrogen there, leaving a helium core. After that, burning takes place in a shell around the core. As this happens, the star expands rapidly, while its core becomes hot and dense. Eventually the helium burns, forming carbon, oxygen, and neon. Heavier elements may be produced later on.

death of a star: supernovae, neutron stars, and black holes

Many stars exhaust their nuclear fuel and become **white dwarfs**. These have radii of a few thousand kilometres and central densities up to 1,000 tonnes per cubic centimetre. They continue to glow with thermal energy, but they slowly cool down. Some stars are too massive to become white dwarfs. Instead, their central regions collapse, causing a supernova explosion which, for a short time, is as bright as an entire galaxy. The outer layers are ejected, leaving a remnant behind. This type of explosion was seen by Chinese astronomers in 1054 in the constellation of the Crab. Today we can see the remnant of this explosion, which is a **neutron star** surrounded by a hot nebula (a cloud of dust and gas). A neutron star has a radius of just a few kilometres and is 100,000 times more dense than a white dwarf. This one spins rapidly and has a powerful magnetic field, a combination which generates pulses of radiation 30 times a second. Such objects are called **pulsars**. The interval between pulses is remarkably constant and is usually between a few milliseconds and several seconds. After a supernova explosion, some remnants are too massive to form neutron stars and collapse to become **black holes**. Black holes are so dense that their gravitational fields are too strong for even light to escape, and so they cannot be seen directly.

developments in technology

Our knowledge of the universe was accelerated in the 19th century with the introduction of photography and **spectroscopy**. Spectroscopy is the analysis of electromagnetic radiation, which includes light, into different **wavelengths**. Radio telescopes built after World War II extended observation to a new wavelength range and enabled the discovery of several new classes of astronomical object, such as pulsars. Currently, observations use almost all wavelengths from the very long radio waves to the very short gamma rays. Ground-based observations are hampered by the atmosphere, which smears images and is opaque to important wavelength bands, such as the ultraviolet. Instruments in orbit, notably the Hubble Space Telescope, reveal detail invisible from the ground. Terrestrial observations have found massive planets in orbits around nearby stars but techniques are not yet sufficiently sensitive to detect planetary satellites.

Milky Way

Stars gather into groups, called **galaxies**, held together by gravity. The Sun is part of the Milky Way, which appeared to our ancestors as a diffuse band of light across the sky. Galileo's telescope resolved it into a multitude of faint stars. They form the shape of a disc, which has a radius exceeding 40,000 light years and a thickness of 2,000 light years. Around the disc there is a halo of old stars in the shape of a sphere. The disc rotates slowly, rotating faster towards the centre. The sun is about 25,000 light years from the centre and takes 200 million years to circle it. The rotation provides a centrifugal force that balances the Milky Way's gravitational field in the disc plane, thus supporting the disc structure.

In the disc there are dusty clouds with temperatures between 10 and 40 K. Inside these clouds hydrogen and other elements form simple molecules. The clouds are denser than most gas clouds and are the regions where stars are forming now.

galaxies

The Milky Way is one of several thousand million galaxies in the Universe and is typical of large disc galaxies. Galaxies vary considerably in appearance. Some, but not all, have spiral arms. Some are irregular in shape and contain a lot of gas. Some galaxies appear elliptical in the sky and consist of old stars. Some abnormal galaxies have bright sources at the centre that can outshine the rest of the system. These are believed to be black holes, between a few million and a thousand million times more massive than the Sun. The light comes from gas compressed and heated as it falls into the hole; astronomers often see jets of gas emerging from the centre of the galaxy. There is evidence that massive black holes exist at the centres of many, possibly all, galaxies.

Galaxies are not isolated. The Milky Way and the nearby Andromeda galaxy are the principal members of a small local cluster. The Milky Way also has satellite galaxies, the most conspicuous of which are the two small, irregular Magellanic Clouds. Astronomers have identified many clusters of galaxies beyond our local group. Collisions can occur between galaxies in a cluster with spectacular results. One example of this occurring is the Cartwheel galaxy, thought to have been produced by the transit of a small elliptical galaxy through the disc of the larger galaxy. Other groups of galaxies have conspicuous bridges and tails produced by tidal effects during collisions.

dark matter

Measurements of the rotation of disc galaxies show that the gravity from the visible material is insufficient to hold the stars in circular orbits,

ASTROLABE A French mariner using an astrolabe to fix the position of a star, from a vellum manuscript of Jacques Devaulx (1583; Bibliothèque Nationale, Paris, France). The mariner's astrolabe was introduced in the mid 15th-century, but did not see general use until the beginning of the 16th century. It was supplanted by the sextant in the 18th century. © The Art Archive/Dagli Orti

A SMALL REMNANT OF A SUPERNOVA pictured by the Hubble Space Telescope in 1993. Named the Cygnus Loop supernova, the explosion approximately 15,000 years ago resulted in a colossal blast wave that heated and compressed the interstellar gas it collided with, causing it to glow. Although the supernova is 2,600 light-years away, the Hubble Space Telescope has been able to capture the glowing remains of the star as a high-resolution image. *J J Hester Arizona State University, NASA*

especially in the outer regions. This is one indication that the universe contains unseen '**dark matter**', – matter that does not emit any radiation. We know very little about dark matter, but experiments to detect it are currently in progress.

cosmology

In 1929, US astronomer Edwin Hubble showed that the universe is expanding and that distant galaxies move away from us with a speed proportional to their distance. The obvious explanation for the expansion is the **Big Bang** model, the theory that the universe has expanded from a dense initial state. The theory implies the existence of background radiation left over from the initial explosion. This radiation was discovered by Penzias and Wilson in 1965 and led to general acceptance of the Big Bang theory.

We would expect the expansion to be decelerated by gravity, but recent evidence suggests that it is accelerating instead. There is a vigorous debate about

the soundness of the results and their implications. The distribution of galaxies also provides evidence for how the universe is built and how it came into existence. They are found in clusters, superclusters, filaments, and sheets, separated by large voids. Numerical simulations, using the most powerful computers available, have examined a variety of cosmological models. The most promising show a filamentary structure resembling that found observationally, but much work remains to be done before we can be confident that we understand the universe.

The 20th century saw tremendous progress in our understanding of the universe, arising from observational and theoretical developments and the availability of powerful computers. There is no sign that progress is slowing down. Powerful telescopes are being built, new satellite observations are planned, and technical development is rapid. Great as our progress has been, many problems remain unsolved and await the attention of future astronomers.

Stewart, James (Maitland) (1908–1997) US film actor. He was noted for his awkward, almost bemused screen presence, his hesitant, drawling delivery, and, in many of his film roles, his embodiment of traditional American values and ideals. His films included *Mr Smith Goes to Washington* (1939), *The Philadelphia Story* (1940), for which he won an Academy Award, and *It's a Wonderful Life* (1946).

stick insect insect of the order Phasmida, closely resembling a stick or twig. The eggs mimic plant seeds. Many species are wingless. The longest reach a length of 30 cm/1 ft. Fossilized eggs were identified in 1995, and are thought to be around 44 million years old.

Related Web site: Stick Insect http://www.ex.ac.uk/bugclub/sticks.html

STICK INSECT The Brazilian *Phibalosoma phyllinum*, which is 30 cm/1 ft long, spends the day resting in cryptic pose in trees and bushes. Stick insects do not always rest among twigs. Many species from tropical rainforests rest on top of large leaves such as palms, where they resemble a fallen twig. *Premaphotos Wildlife*

stickleback any fish of the family Gasterosteidae, found in marine and fresh waters of the northern hemisphere. It has a long body that can grow to 18 cm/7 in. The spines along a stickleback's back take the place of the first dorsal fin, and can be raised to make the fish difficult to eat for predators. After the eggs have been laid the female takes no part in rearing the young: the male builds a nest for the eggs, which he then guards and rears for the first two weeks.

The common three-spined stickleback *Gasterosteus aculeatus*, up to 10 cm/4 in, is found in freshwater habitats and also in brackish estuaries.

Stieglitz, Alfred (1864–1946) US photographer. After forming the multimedia Photo-Secession Group with Edward Steichen in New York (1902), he started up the magazine *Camera Work* (1902–17). Through exhibitions at his gallery '291' he helped to establish photography as an art form. In 1924 he married the painter Georgia O'Keeffe, who was the model in many of his photographs. His cloud series, the portraits of O'Keeffe, and his studies of New York City, are his most famous works.

stigma in a flower, the surface at the tip of a ▷carpel that receives the ▷pollen. It often has short outgrowths, flaps, or hairs to trap pollen and may produce a sticky secretion to which the grains adhere.

Stijl, De (Dutch 'the style') influential movement in art, architecture, and design founded 1917 in the Netherlands. Attempting to bring art and design together in a single coherent system, the members of De Stijl developed an austere simplification of style, based on simple geometrical shapes and primary colour. Its best-known member was the abstract painter Piet ▷Mondrian. The group's main theorist and publicist was Theo van Doesburg (1883–1931), and his death in 1931 effectively marked its end.

still life in painting and other visual arts, a depiction of inanimate objects, such as flowers, fruit, or tableware. Pictures of dead animals are also embraced by the term. Still-life painting was popular among the ancient Greeks and Romans (who also made still-life mosaics), but thereafter it was sidelined in European art for centuries, as art was overwhelmingly devoted to religious subjects during the Middle Ages. It reappeared during the Renaissance and became established as a distinctive branch of painting in the 17th century, flourishing first in the Netherlands, where the Reformation had discouraged religious imagery and artists were seeking new subjects.

Early examples often combine a delight in the appearance of things with religious or moral symbolism. Flowers, for example, can always refer to the frailty and brief span of human life, because flowers quickly fade and die. In the same vein, a *vanitas* (Latin for 'emptiness' or 'worthlessness') is a particular type of still life consisting entirely of objects stressing the shortness of life: a skull, a candle, flower petals, and so on. In spite of the popularity of such symbolism, in the history of art still life was regarded as the lowest branch of painting for centuries, requiring only the skill of copying rather than creative imagination. This attitude was common until the 19th century, when people began to be more interested in how a picture was painted than what it represented, and since then many great artists have devoted a good deal of time to still life, which enabled them to concentrate on formal problems. Paul Cézanne, for example, was particularly suited to still life as he was a very slow worker, and it was also the favourite subject of the cubists.

STILL LIFE *British Plums*, a still life by English watercolour painter William Henry Hunt. *The Art Archive/JFB*

Stilwell, Joseph Warren (1883–1946) Called 'Vinegar Joe'. US general in World War II. In 1942 he became US military representative in China, when he commanded the Chinese forces cooperating with the British (with whom he quarrelled) in Burma (now Myanmar). He later commanded all US forces in China, Burma, and India until recalled to the USA in 1944 after differences over nationalist policy with the ▷Guomindang (nationalist) leader Chiang Kai-shek. Subsequently he commanded the US 10th Army on the Japanese island of Okinawa.

stimulant any substance that acts on the brain to increase alertness and activity; for example, ▷amphetamine. When given to children, stimulants may have a paradoxical, calming effect. Stimulants cause liver damage, are habit-forming, have limited therapeutic value, and are now prescribed only to treat narcolepsy and severe obesity.

Sting (1951–) Stage name of Gordon Sumner. English pop singer, songwriter, bass player, and actor. As a member of the trio the Police (1977–83), he had UK number-one hits with 'Message in a Bottle' (1979), 'Walking on the Moon' (1979), and 'Every Breath You Take' (1983). 'Don't Stand So Close to Me' was the best-selling single in the UK in 1980. In his solo career he has often drawn on jazz, as on the albums *The Dream of Blue Turtles* (1985), *Nothing Like the Sun* (1987), and *Soul Cages* (1991). His album *Brand New Day* appeared in 1999. He won a 2001 Grammy for Male Pop Vocal Performance for the song 'She Walks this Earth (Soberana Rosa)'.

stingray cartilaginous fish that is a species of ▷ray.

stinkhorn any of a group of foul-smelling European fungi (see ▷fungus), especially *P. impudicus*; they first appear on the surface as white balls. (Genus *Phallus*, order Phallales.)

stinkwood any of various trees with unpleasant-smelling wood. The South African tree *O. bullata* has offensive-smelling wood when newly felled, but fine, durable timber used for furniture. Another stinkwood is *G. augusta* from tropical America. (Genera *Ocotea*, family Lauraceae; *Gustavia*.)

Stirling unitary authority in central Scotland, created in 1996 from Stirling district, Central region.

area 2,196 sq km/848 sq mi **towns** Dunblane, ▷Stirling (administrative headquarters), Aberfoyle **physical** mountainous to the north, including the forested Trossachs, and the open moorland north and west of Breadalbane, within the flood plain of the River Forth to the south around Sterling. The area contains many famous Scottish lochs (Tay, Katrine, Lomond) and Scotland's only lake (Lake of Menteith). Peaks include Ben More (1,174 m/3,852 ft) and Ben Venue (727 m/2,385 ft) **features** Bannockburn Heritage Centre; Stirling Castle (most visited paid attraction in Scotland outside Edinburgh) **industries** tourism, light engineering **agriculture** forestry and stock rearing in the uplands, while in the lowlands some of the richest agricultural lands in Scotland may be found, including the Carse of Gowrie **population** (1996) 82,000 **history** William Wallace won battle of Stirling Bridge in 1297; English defeated at Bannockburn by Robert the Bruce in 1314; battle at Sheriffmuir in 1715 between Jacobites and Hanoverians

Stirling administrative headquarters of Stirling unitary authority, Scotland, on the River Forth, 43 km/27 mi northeast of Glasgow; population (1991) 30,500. Industries include the manufacture of agricultural machinery, textiles, chemicals, and carpets. The Stirling skyline is noted for its castle, which guarded a key crossing of the river, and the (William) Wallace Monument, erected in 1870 to commemorate the Scots' victory of the English at nearby **Stirling Bridge** in 1297. Edward I of England (in raising a Scottish siege of the town) went into battle at Bannockburn in 1314 and was defeated by Robert I (the Bruce), in the Scots' greatest victory over the English.

Stirling, James Frazer (1926–1992) Scottish architect. He was possibly the most influential of his generation. While in partnership with James Gowan (1924–), he designed an influential housing estate at Ham Common, Richmond (1958), and the Leicester University Engineering Building (1959–63) in a constructivist vein. He later adopted a more eclectic approach, exemplified in his considered masterpiece, the Staatsgalerie, Stuttgart, Germany (1977–83), which blended constructivism, modernism, and several strands of classicism. He also designed the Clore Gallery (1980–86) extension to the Tate Gallery, London. He was knighted in 1983.

Stirling engine A hot-air external combustion engine invented by Scottish priest Robert Stirling 1816. The engine operates by adapting to the fact that the air in its cylinders heats up when it is compressed and cools when it expands. The engine will operate on any fuel, is nonpolluting and relatively quiet. It was used fairly widely in the 19th century before the appearance of small, powerful, and reliable electric motors. Attempts have also been made in recent times to use Stirling's engine to power a variety of machines.

stoat carnivorous mammal *Mustela erminea* of the northern hemisphere, in the weasel family, about 37 cm/15 in long including the black-tipped tail. It has a long body and a flattened head. The upper parts and tail are red-brown, and the underparts are white. In the colder regions, the coat turns white (ermine) in winter. Its young are called kits.

The stoat is an efficient predator, killing its prey (typically rodents and rabbits) by biting the back of the neck. It needs to consume the equivalent of almost a third of its body weight each day. Females are about half the size of males, and males and females live in separate territories. Stoats live in Europe, Asia, and North America; they have been introduced to New Zealand.

stock in botany, any of a group of ▷herbaceous plants commonly grown as garden ornamentals. Many cultivated varieties, including simple-stemmed, queen's, and ten-week stocks, have been derived from the wild stock (*M. incana*); night-scented (or evening) stock (*M. bicornis*) becomes aromatic at night. (Genus *Matthiola*, family Cruciferae.)

stock in finance, the UK term for the fully paid-up capital of a company. It is bought and sold by subscribers not in units or shares, but in terms of its current cash value. In US usage the term stock generally means an ordinary share. See also ▷stocks and shares.

stock exchange institution for the buying and selling of stocks and shares (securities). The world's largest stock exchanges are London, New York (Wall Street), and Tokyo. The oldest stock exchanges are Antwerp (1460), Hamburg (1558), Amsterdam (1602), New York (1790), and London (1801). The former division on the London Stock Exchange between brokers (who bought shares from jobbers to sell to the public) and jobbers (who sold them only to brokers on commission, the 'jobbers' turn') was abolished in 1986.

Related Web site: London Stock Exchange http://www.londonstockexchange.com/
Stockmarket – the UK's Personal Finance Web Site http://www.moneyworld.co.uk/stocks/index.html

Karlheinz Stockhausen
What is modern today will be tradition tomorrow.
Notes on Telemusik 1966

Stockhausen, Karlheinz (1928–) German composer of avant-garde music. He has continued to explore new musical sounds and compositional techniques since the 1950s. His major works include *Gesang der Jünglinge* (1956), *Kontakte* (1960) (electronic music), and *Sirius* (1977).

Since 1977 all his works have been part of *LICHT*, a cycle of seven musical ceremonies intended for performance on the evenings of a week. He has completed *Donnerstag* (1980), *Samstag* (1984), *Montag* (1988), and *Dienstag* (1992). Earlier works include *Klavierstücke I–XIV* (1952–85), *Momente* (1961–64), and *Mikrophonie I* (1964).

Stockholm capital and industrial port of Sweden; population (1994 est) 703,600. It is built on a number of islands. Industries include engineering, brewing, electrical goods, paper, textiles, and pottery.

A network of bridges links the islands and the mainland; an underground railway was completed in 1957. The 18th-century royal palace stands on the site of the 13th-century fortress that defended the trading settlements of Lake Mälar, around which the town first developed. The old town is well preserved and has a church (1264). The town hall was designed by Ragnar Östberg 1923. The new city has been developed since 1950 with contemporary architecture. Most of Sweden's educational institutions are in Stockholm (including the ▷Nobel Institute). The warship *Wasa* (built for King Gustavus Adolphus, 69 m/75 yd long and 52 m/57 yd high), which sank in the harbour 1628, was raised in 1961 and is preserved in a museum.

During the 17th century, the city was the capital of Sweden's Baltic empire.

Related Web site: Stockholm http://travel.excite.com/show/?loc=2693

Stockport town in Greater Manchester, northwest England, 10 km/6 mi southeast of Manchester; population (1991) 130,800. The rivers Tame and Goyt join here to form the Mersey. Formerly important in the textile industry, Stockport now manufactures electrical machinery, paper, plastics, hats, and some cotton textiles; other industries include electronics, chemicals, and engineering.

stocks and shares investment holdings (securities) in private or public undertakings. Although distinctions have become blurred, in the UK stock usually means fixed-interest securities – for example, those issued by central and local government – while ▷shares represent a stake in the ownership of a trading company which, if they are ordinary shares, yield to the owner dividends reflecting the success of the company. In the USA the term stock generally signifies what in the UK is an ordinary share.

Stockton-on-Tees unitary authority in northeast England created in 1996 from part of the former county of Cleveland.

area 200 sq km/77 sq mi **towns and cities** ▷Stockton-on-Tees (administrative headquarters), Billingham, Yarm, Longnewton **features** River Tees forms east border; Tees Barrage; Yarm viaduct; Preston Hall Museum and Park (Stockton); Castlegate Quay (Stockton) includes full-scale replica of *HMS Endeavour* **industries** chemicals, polythene film, light and heavy engineering, insulation products, plastics, electronics **population** (1996) 176,600

Stockton-on-Tees town, port, and administrative headquarters of ▷Stockton-on-Tees metropolitan borough, on the River Tees, 5 km/3 mi west of Middlesbrough, northeast England; population (1991) 82,400. There are ship-repairing, steel, and chemical industries. It was the starting point for the Stockton–Darlington railway, the world's first passenger railway, which opened in 1825.

Stoicism (Greek *stoa* 'porch') Greek school of philosophy, founded about 300 BC by Zeno of Citium. The Stoics were pantheistic materialists who believed that happiness lay in accepting the law of the universe. They emphasized human brotherhood, denounced slavery, and were internationalist. The name is derived from the porch on which Zeno taught.

Related Web site: Stoicism http://www.utm.edu/research/iep/s/stoicism.htm

Stoke-on-Trent city and unitary authority in central England, on the River Trent, 23 km/14 mi north of Stafford; it was part of the county of Staffordshire to 1997.

area 93 sq km/36 sq mi **features** the Gladstone Pottery Museum is a working pottery museum **industries** it is the heart of the ▷Potteries, a major ceramic centre, and the largest clayware producer in the world; the ceramics factories of ▷Minton, ▷Wedgwood, Spode, and Royal Doulton are all based here. Other industries include the manufacture of steel, chemicals, engineering machinery, paper, rubber, and tyres. Michelin has its headquarters in the town **population** (1996) 254,200 **famous people** Arnold Bennett, John Wain, Robbie Williams **history** Stoke was formed in 1910 from Burslem, Hanley, Longton, Stoke-upon-Trent, Fenton, and Tunstall

STOL (acronym for **short takeoff and landing**) aircraft fitted with special devices on the wings (such as sucking flaps) that increase aerodynamic lift at low speeds. Small passenger and freight STOL craft may become common with the demand for small airports, especially in difficult terrain.

stolon in botany, a type of ▷runner.

stoma (plural **stomata**) in botany, a pore in the epidermis of a plant. Each stoma is surrounded by a pair of guard cells that are crescent-shaped when the stoma is open but can collapse to an oval shape, thus closing off the opening between them. Stomata allow the exchange of carbon dioxide and oxygen (needed for

▷photosynthesis and ▷respiration) between the internal tissues of the plant and the outside atmosphere. They are also the main route by which water is lost from the plant, and they can be closed to conserve water, the movements being controlled by changes in turgidity of the guard cells.

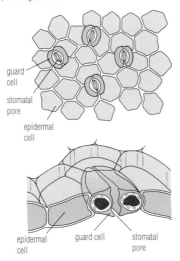

guard cell
stomatal pore
epidermal cell

epidermal cell
guard cell
stomatal pore

STOMA The stomata, tiny openings in the epidermis of a plant, are surrounded by pairs of crescent-shaped cells, called guard cells. The guard cells open and close the stoma by changing shape.

stomach the first cavity in the digestive system of animals. In mammals it is a bag of muscle situated just below the diaphragm. Food enters it from the oesophagus, is digested by the acid and ▷enzymes secreted by the stomach lining, and then passes into the duodenum. Some plant-eating mammals have multichambered stomachs that harbour bacteria in one of the chambers to assist in the digestion of ▷cellulose. The gizzard is part of the stomach in birds.

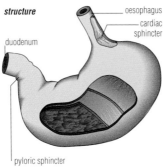

structure
oesophagus
cardiac sphincter
duodenum
pyloric sphincter

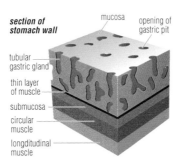

section of stomach wall
mucosa
opening of gastric pit
tubular gastric gland
thin layer of muscle
submucosa
circular muscle
longtitudinal muscle

STOMACH The human stomach can hold about 1.5 l/2.6 pt of liquid. The digestive juices are acidic enough to dissolve metal. To avoid damage, the cells of the stomach lining are replaced quickly – 500,000 cells are replaced every minute, and the whole stomach lining every three days.

stone (plural **stone**) imperial unit (abbreviation st) of mass. One stone is 14 pounds (6.35 kg).

Stone Age the developmental stage of humans in ▷prehistory before the use of metals, when tools and weapons were made chiefly of stone, especially flint. The Stone Age is subdivided into the Old or **Palaeolithic**, when flint implements were simply chipped into shape; the Middle or **Mesolithic**; and the New or **Neolithic**, when

implements were ground and polished. Palaeolithic people were hunters and gatherers; by the Neolithic period people were taking the first steps in agriculture, the domestication of animals, weaving, and pottery.

Recent research has been largely directed towards the relationship of the Palaeolithic period to ▷geochronology (the measurement of geological time) and to the clarification of an absolute chronology based upon geology. The economic aspects of the Neolithic cultures have attracted as much attention as the typology of the implements and pottery, and the study of chambered tombs.

stonechat small insectivorous ▷thrush *Saxicola torquata*, family Muscicapidae, order Passeriformes, frequently found in Eurasia and Africa on open land with bushes. The male has a black head and throat, tawny breast, and dark back; the female is browner. It is about 13 cm/5 in long.

stonecrop any of a group of plants belonging to the orpine family, succulent herbs with fleshy leaves and clusters of red, yellow, or white starlike flowers. Stonecrops are characteristic of dry, rocky places and some grow on walls. (Genus *Sedum*, family Crassulaceae.)

stonefish any of a family (Synanceiidae) of tropical marine bony fishes with venomous spines and bodies resembling encrusted rocks.

STONEFISH Stonefish in a Kenyan rockpool. Its colouring makes it difficult to see, as it lies half concealed in rock crevices. *K G Preston-Mafham/Premaphotos Wildlife*

stonefly any insect of the order Plecoptera, with a long tail and antennae and two pairs of membranous wings. Stoneflies live near fresh water. There are over 1,300 species.

Stonehenge (Old English 'hanging stones') megalithic monument on Salisbury Plain, 3 km/1.9 mi west of Amesbury in Wiltshire, England. The site developed over various periods from a simple henge (earthwork circle and ditch), dating from about 3000 BC, to a complex stone structure, from about 2100 BC, which included a circle of 30 upright stones, their tops linked by lintel stones to form a continuous circle about 30 m/100 ft across.

Within this sarsen **peristyle** was a horseshoe arrangement of five sarsen **trilithons** (two uprights plus a lintel, set as five separate entities), and the so-called 'Altar Stone' – an upright pillar – on the axis of the horseshoe at the open, northeast end, which faces in the direction of the rising sun. A further horseshoe and circle within the sarsen peristyle were constructed from bluestone relocated from previous outer circles.

It has been suggested that Stonehenge was constructed as an observatory.

Local sandstone, or sarsen, was used for the uprights, which measure 5.5 by 2 m/18 by 7 ft and weigh some 26 tonnes each. The bluestone was transported from the Prescelly Mountains, Pembrokeshire, Wales.

Stonehenge is one of a number of prehistoric structures on Salisbury Plain, including about 400 round ▷barrows (burial mounds), Durrington Walls (once a structure similar to that in Avebury), Woodhenge (a monument once consisting of great wooden posts), and the **Cursus** (a pair of banked ditches, about 100 m/300 ft apart, which run straight for some 3 km/2 mi; dated 4th millennium BC). The purpose of these is unknown but may have been ritual.

Although Stonehenge is far older than Druidism, an annual Druid ceremony is held there at the summer solstice. At that time it is also a spiritual focus for many people with a nomadic way of life, who on several consecutive midsummers in the 1980s and 1990s were forcibly kept from Stonehenge by police.

Related Web site: Stonehenge http://www.anima.demon.co.uk/stones/england/stonehen/index.html

Stopes, Marie Charlotte Carmichael (1880–1958) Scottish birth-control campaigner. With her second husband H V Roe (1878–1949), an aircraft manufacturer, she founded Britain's first birth-control clinic in London in 1921. In her best-selling manual *Married Love* (1918) she urged women to enjoy sexual intercourse within their marriage, a revolutionary view for the time. She also wrote plays and verse.

Stoppard, Tom (1937–) Born Thomas Straussler. Czechoslovak-born British dramatist. His works use wit and wordplay to explore logical and philosophical ideas. His play *Rosencrantz and Guildenstern are Dead* (1967) was followed by comedies including *The Real Inspector Hound* (1968), *Jumpers* (1972), *Travesties* (1974), *Dirty Linen* (1976), *The Real Thing* (1982), *Hapgood* (1988), *Arcadia* (1993), and *Indian Ink* (1995). He has also written for radio, television, and the cinema.

He shared the Best Screenplay award (with Marc Norman) for *Shakespeare in Love* in the 1998 New York Film Critics Circle Awards. The screenplay also received the 1999 Golden Globe award.

Related Web site: 'Rosencrantz and Guildenstern Are Dead – Aspects of the Human Condition' http://yosh.gimp.org/~saji/stoppard.html

> **Tom Stoppard**
> *Eternity's a terrible thought. I mean, where's it all going to end?*
> Rosencrantz and Guildenstern Are Dead II

stork any of the 17 species of the Ciconiidae, a family of long-legged, long-necked wading birds with long, powerful wings, and long conical bills used for spearing prey. Some species grow up to 1.5 m/5 ft tall. Species include the Eurasian white stork *Ciconia ciconia*, which is encouraged to build on rooftops as a luck and fertility symbol. It feeds on reptiles, small mammals, and insects. Its plumage is greyish white, its quills and longest feathers on the wing coverts black, and the beak and legs red. It migrates to Africa in winter. The jabiru *Jabiru mycteria* of the Americas is up to 1.5 m/5 ft high, and is white plumaged, with a black and red head. In the black stork *C. nigra*, the upper surface is black and the lower parts are white. It is widely found in southern and central Europe, Asia, and parts of Africa. The adjutant bird, ▷ibis, ▷heron, and ▷spoonbill are related birds.

STORK Openbill storks *Anastomus oscitans* at their nest site in India. *K G Preston-Mafham/Premaphotos Wildlife*

Stormont suburb 8 km/5 mi east of Belfast, Northern Ireland. It is the site of the new Northern Ireland Assembly, elected as a result of the Good Friday agreement in 1998 and functioning from 1999 when some powers were transferred back to Northern Ireland from Westminster. It was previously the seat of the government of Northern Ireland 1921–72.

storm surge abnormally high tide brought about by a combination of a deep atmospheric depression (very low pressure) over a shallow sea area, high spring tides, and winds blowing from the appropriate direction. A storm surge can cause severe flooding of lowland coastal regions and river estuaries.

Stowe, Harriet Elizabeth Beecher (1811–1896) US suffragist, abolitionist, and author. Her antislavery novel *Uncle Tom's Cabin* was first published serially 1851–52. The inspiration came to her in a vision 1848, and the book brought immediate success.

Strabo (c. 63 BC–AD c. 24) Greek geographer and historian who travelled widely to collect first-hand material for his *Geography*.

Strachey, (Giles) Lytton (1880–1932) English critic and biographer. He was a member of the ▷Bloomsbury Group of writers and artists. His *Landmarks in French Literature* was written in 1912. The mocking and witty treatment of Cardinal Manning, Florence Nightingale, Thomas Arnold, and General Gordon in *Eminent Victorians* (1918) won him recognition. His biography of *Queen Victoria* (1921) was more affectionate.

> **Harriet Beecher Stowe**
> *'Do you know who made you?' 'Nobody, as I knows on,' said the child, with a short laugh.... 'I 'spect I grow'd.'*
> Uncle Tom's Cabin

Stradivari, Antonio (c. 1644–1737) (Latin **Stradivarius**) Italian stringed instrument maker, generally considered the greatest of all violin makers. He produced more than 1,100 instruments from his family workshops, over 600 of which survive; they have achieved the status (and sale-room prices) of works of art.

Strafford, Thomas Wentworth, 1st Earl of Strafford (1593–1641) English politician. He was originally an opponent of ▷Charles I, but from 1628 he was on the Royalist side. He ruled despotically as Lord Deputy of Ireland 1632–39, when he returned to England as Charles's chief adviser and received an earldom. He was impeached in 1640 by Parliament, abandoned by Charles as a scapegoat, and beheaded. He was knighted in 1611, became Baron in 1628, and created Earl in 1640.

Straits Settlements former province of the ▷East India Company 1826–58, a British crown colony 1867–1946; it comprised Singapore, Malacca, Penang, Cocos Islands, Christmas Island, and Labuan.

Strasberg, Lee (1901–1982) Born Israel Strassberg. US actor and artistic director of the Actors Studio from 1948. He developed Method acting from ▷Stanislavsky's system; pupils have included Marlon Brando, Paul Newman, Julie Harris, Kim Hunter, Geraldine Page, Al Pacino, and Robert De Niro.

Strasbourg (German **Strassburg**) administrative centre of the Bas-Rhin *département* and of ▷Alsace region, northeast France, situated near the German border on the River Ill, 3 km/1.9 mi west of the Rhine near its confluence with the Rhine–Rhône and Rhine and Marne canals; population (1999) 264,000, conurbation (2000 est) 652,300. Industries include car manufacture, tobacco, printing and publishing, and preserves. The town was selected as the headquarters for the ▷Council of Europe in 1949, and sessions of the European Parliament alternate between here and Luxembourg. It has an 11th–15th-century cathedral.

Related Web site: Strasbourg Online http://www.strasbourg.com/index.html

strata (singular **stratum**) layers or ▷beds of sedimentary rock.

THOMAS STRAFFORD The execution of the Earl of Strafford, Charles I's chief adviser, on Tower Hill, in 1641 after an etching by Wenceslaus Hollar. Upon hearing that Charles had signed his death warrant at parliament's insistence, Strafford famously commented 'Put not your trust in princes'. *Philip Sauvain Picture Collection*

HARRIET BEECHER STOWE A poster for Harriet Beecher Stowe's antislavery novel *Uncle Tom's Cabin* (1851–52). The book was hugely popular and is thought to have had a major influence on swaying public opinion against slavery. This poster appeared in 1860, a year before the American Civil War began. *Archive Photos*

Strategic Air Command (SAC) the headquarters commanding all US land-based strategic missile and bomber forces. It is located in Colorado in an underground complex with an instant communications link to the president of the USA.

Strategic Arms Limitation Talks (SALT) series of US-Soviet discussions 1969–79 aimed at reducing the rate of nuclear-arms build-up (as opposed to ▷disarmament, which would reduce the number of weapons, as discussed in ▷Strategic Arms Reduction Talks [START]). The accords of the 1970s sought primarily to prevent the growth of nuclear arsenals.

Strategic Arms Reduction Talks (START) phase in peace discussions dealing with ▷disarmament, initially involving the USA and the Soviet Union, from 1992 the USA and Russia, and from 1993 Belarus and the Ukraine.

It began with talks in Geneva, Switzerland, in 1983, leading to the signing of the ▷Intermediate Nuclear Forces Treaty in 1987. In 1989 proposals for reductions in conventional weapons were added to the agenda. As the Cold War drew to a close from 1989, negotiations moved rapidly. Reductions of about 30% in strategic nuclear weapons systems were agreed in Moscow in July 1991 (START) and more significant cuts were agreed in January 1993 (START II); the latter treaty was ratified by the US Senate in January 1996. Russia's Duma ratified START II in April 2000. just following the inauguration of Russian President Vladimir Putin. Under the treaty, which applies to inter-continental rockets, the USA and Russia will both halve their stocks of atomic warheads to between 3,000 and 3,500 each by 2007. A START III treaty, currently being negotiated, would increase arms reduction even further.

Related Web site: START II Treaty Fact Sheet http://www.state.gov/www/regions/nis/russia_start2_treaty.html

Strategic Defense Initiative (SDI or **Star Wars**) US programme (1983–93) to explore the technical feasibility of developing a comprehensive defence system against incoming nuclear missiles, based in part outside the Earth's atmosphere. The programme was started by President Ronald Reagan in March 1983, and was overseen by the Strategic Defence Initiative Organization (SDIO). In May 1993, the SDIO changed its name to the Ballistic Missile Defence Organization (BMDO), to reflect its focus on defence against short-range rather than long-range missiles. SDI lives on today in the less ambitious National Missile Defence (NMD) programme.

strategy, military the planning of warfare. **Grand strategy** requires both political and military input and designs the overall war effort at national level. Planning for a campaign at army-group level or above is **strategy** proper. **Operational strategy** involves military planning at corps, divisional, and brigade level. **Tactics** is the art of warfare at unit level and below; that is, the disposition of relatively small numbers of soldiers over relatively small distances.

Stratford-upon-Avon market town on the River Avon, in Warwickshire, England, 35 km/22 mi southeast of Birmingham; population (1991) 22,200. It is the birthplace of William ▷Shakespeare and has the Royal Shakespeare Theatre (1932), the Swan Theatre, and The Other Place. Stratford receives over 2 million tourists a year. Industries include canning, aluminium ware, and boat building.

Related Web site: Shakespeare's Stratford http://www.stratford.co.uk/

stratosphere that part of the atmosphere 10–40 km/6–25 mi from the Earth's surface, where the temperature slowly rises from a low of −55°C/−67°F to around 0°C/32°F. The air is rarefied and at around 25 km/15 mi much ▷ozone is concentrated.

Strauss, Richard (Georg) (1864–1949) German composer and conductor. He followed the German Romantic tradition but had a strongly personal style, characterized by his bold, colourful orchestration. He first wrote tone poems such as *Don Juan* (1889), *Till Eulenspiegel's Merry Pranks* (1895), and *Also sprach Zarathustra/Thus Spake Zarathustra* (1896). He then moved on to opera with *Salome* (1905) and *Elektra* (1909), both of which have elements of polytonality. He reverted to a more traditional style with *Der Rosenkavalier/The Knight of the Rose* (1909–10).

Stravinsky, Igor Fyodorovich (1882–1971) Russian composer, later of French (1934) and US (1945) nationality. He studied under ▷Rimsky-Korsakov and wrote the music for the Diaghilev ballets *The Firebird* (1910), *Petrushka* (1911), and *The Rite of Spring* (1913), which were controversial at the time for their unorthodox rhythms and harmonies. His works also include symphonies, concertos (for violin and piano), chamber music, and operas; for example, *The Rake's Progress* (1951) and *The Flood* (1962).

Along with Schoenberg, Stravinsky was the most important composer of the early 20th century, who determined more than any others the course of music for the following 50 years. His versatile work ranges from his neoclassical ballet *Pulcinella* (1920) to the choral-orchestral *Symphony of Psalms* (1930). He later made use of serial techniques in such works as the *Canticum Sacrum* (1955) and the ballet *Agon* (1953–57).

strawberry low-growing perennial plant widely cultivated for its red, fleshy fruits, which are rich in vitamin C. Commercial cultivated forms bear one crop of fruit in summer, with the berries resting on a bed of straw to protect them from the damp soil, and multiply by runners. The flowers are normally white, although pink-flowering varieties are cultivated as ornamentals. (Genus *Fragaria*, family Rosaceae.)

William Butler
English physician

Doubtless God could have made a better berry but doubtless God never did.

Of the strawberry, in Izaak Walton's *Compleat Angler*

streamlining shaping a body so that it offers the least resistance when travelling through a medium such as air or water. Aircraft, for example, must be carefully streamlined to reduce air resistance, or drag.

stream of consciousness narrative technique in which a writer presents directly the uninterrupted flow of a character's thoughts, impressions, and feelings, without the conventional devices of dialogue and description. It first came to be widely used in the early 20th century. Leading exponents have included the novelists Virginia Woolf, James Joyce, and William Faulkner.

Streep, Meryl (Mary Louise) (1949–) US actor. She has played strong character roles, portrayed with emotionally dramatic intensity, in such films as *The Deer Hunter* (1978), *Kramer vs Kramer* (1979, Academy Award for Best Supporting Actress), *The French Lieutenant's Woman* (1981), *Sophie's Choice* (1982, Academy Award), *Out of Africa* (1985), and *The Hours* (2002).

Streisand, Barbra (Joan) (1942–) US singer and actor. She became a film star in *Funny Girl* (1968; for which she received an Academy Award). Her subsequent films include *What's Up Doc?* (1972), *The Way We Were* (1973), and *A Star Is Born* (1979). She directed, produced, and starred in *Yentl* (1983) and *Prince of Tides* (1991).

streptomycin antibiotic drug discovered in 1944, active against a wide range of bacterial infections.

stress in psychology, any event or situation that makes heightened demands on a person's mental or emotional resources. Stress can be caused by overwork, anxiety about exams, money, job security, unemployment, bereavement, poor relationships, marriage breakdown, sexual difficulties, poor living or working conditions, and constant exposure to loud noise.

Many changes that are apparently 'for the better', such as being promoted at work, going to a new school, moving to a new house, and getting married, are also a source of stress. Stress can cause, or aggravate, physical illnesses, among them psoriasis, eczema, asthma, and stomach and mouth ulcers. Apart from removing the source of stress, acquiring some control over it and learning to relax when possible are the best responses.

stress and strain in the science of materials, measures of the deforming force applied to a body (stress) and of the resulting change in its shape (strain). For a perfectly elastic material, stress is proportional to strain (▷Hooke's law).

stridulatory organs in insects, organs that produce sound when rubbed together. Crickets rub their wings together, but grasshoppers rub a hind leg against a wing. Stridulation is thought to be used for attracting mates, but may also serve to mark territory.

strike the compass direction of a horizontal line on a planar structural surface, such as a fault plane, bedding plane, or the trend of a structural feature, such as the axis of a fold. Strike is 90° from dip.

strike stoppage of work by employees, often as members of a trade union, to obtain or resist change in wages, hours, or conditions. A **lockout** is a weapon of an employer to thwart or enforce such change by preventing employees from working. Another measure is **work to rule**, when production is virtually brought to a halt by strict observance of union rules.

STRIKE Strikers in the USA during the 1960s. *Image Bank*

Strindberg, (Johan) August (1849–1912) Swedish dramatist and novelist. His plays are in a variety of styles including historical dramas, symbolic dramas (the two-part *Dödsdansen/The Dance of Death* (1901)), and 'chamber plays' such as *Spöksonaten/The Ghost [Spook] Sonata* (1907). *Fadren/The Father* (1887) and *Fröken Julie/Miss Julie* (1888) are among his best-known works.

Born in Stockholm, he lived mainly abroad after 1883, having been unsuccessfully prosecuted for blasphemy in 1884 following publication of his short stories *Giftas/Marrying*. His life was stormy and his work has been criticized for its hostile attitude to women, but he is regarded as one of Sweden's greatest writers.

His prose works include the satirical novel *Röda rummet/The Red Room* (1879), about bohemian life in Stockholm, and the autobiography *Tjänstekvinnans son/The Son of a Servant* (1886).

string quartet ▷chamber music ensemble consisting of two violins, viola, and cello; or the music written for such a group. The 18th-century successor to the domestic viol consort, the string quartet with its stronger and more rustic tone formed the basis of the symphony orchestra. Important composers for the string quartet include Haydn (more than 80 string quartets), Mozart (27), Schubert (20), Beethoven (17), Bartók (6), and Shostakovich (15).

stroboscope instrument for studying continuous periodic motion by using light flashing at the same frequency as that of the motion; for example, rotating machinery can be optically 'stopped' by illuminating it with a stroboscope flashing at the exact rate of rotation.

Stroessner, Alfredo (1912–) Paraguayan military dictator and president 1954–89. As head of the armed forces from 1951, he seized power from President Federico Chávez in a coup in 1954, sponsored by the right-wing ruling Colorado Party. Accused by his opponents of harsh repression, his regime spent heavily on the military to preserve his authority. Despite criticisms of his government's civil-rights record, he was re-elected seven times and remained in office until ousted in an army-led coup in 1989, after which he gained asylum in Brazil.

Stroheim, Erich von (1885–1957) Adopted name of Erich Oswald Stroheim. Austrian actor and director. In Hollywood from 1914, he was successful as an actor in villainous roles. His career as a director, which produced films such as *Foolish Wives* (1922), was wrecked by his extravagance (*Greed* (1923)) and he returned to acting in such films as *La grande Illusion* (1937) and *Sunset Boulevard* (1950).

stroke (or **cerebrovascular accident** or **apoplexy**) interruption of the blood supply to part of the brain due to a sudden bleed in the brain (cerebral haemorrhage) or ▷embolism or ▷thrombosis. Strokes vary in severity from producing almost no symptoms to proving rapidly fatal. In between are those (often recurring) that leave a wide range of impaired function, depending on the size and location of the event.

Strokes involving the right side of the brain, for example, produce weakness of the left side of the body. Some affect speech. Around 80% of strokes are **ischaemic strokes**, caused by a blood clot blocking an artery transporting blood to the brain. Transient ischaemic attacks, or 'mini-strokes', with effects lasting only briefly (less than 24 hours), require investigation to try to forestall the possibility of a subsequent full-blown stroke.

The disease of the arteries that predisposes to stroke is atherosclerosis. High blood pressure (▷hypertension) is also a precipitating factor – a worldwide study in 1995 estimated that high blood pressure before middle age gives a tenfold increase in the chance of having a stroke later in life.

Strokes can sometimes be prevented by surgery (as in the case of some ▷aneurysms), or by use of ▷anticoagulant drugs or vitamin E or daily aspirin to minimize the risk of stroke due to blood clots. According to the results of a US trial announced in December 1995, the clot-buster drug tPA, if administered within three hours of a stroke, can cut the number of stroke victims experiencing lasting disability by 50%. The best predictor of strokes among older people may be an echogram (sonogram) of carotid arteries.

Related Web site: Brain Basics: Preventing Stroke http://www.ninds.nih.gov/patients/disorder/stroke/strokepr.htm

stromatolite mound produced in shallow water by mats of algae that trap mud particles. Another mat grows on the trapped mud layer and this traps another layer of mud and so on. The stromatolite grows to heights of a metre or so. They are uncommon today but their fossils are among the earliest evidence for living things – over 2,000 million years old.

Stromboli Italian island in the Tyrrhenian Sea, one of the ▷Lipari Islands; area 12 sq km/5 sq mi. It has an active volcano, 926 m/3,039 ft high. The island produces Malmsey wine and capers.

strong nuclear force one of the four fundamental ▷forces of nature, the other three being the gravitational force or gravity, the electromagnetic force, and the weak nuclear force. The strong nuclear force was first described by the Japanese physicist Hideki Yukawa in 1935. It is the strongest of all the forces, acts only over very small distances within the nucleus of the atom (10^{-13} cm), and is responsible for binding together ▷quarks to form ▷hadrons, and for binding together protons and neutrons in the atomic nucleus. The particle that is the carrier of the strong nuclear force is the ▷gluon, of which there are eight kinds, each with zero mass and zero charge.

strontium soft, ductile, pale-yellow, metallic element, symbol Sr, atomic number 38, relative atomic mass 87.62. It is one of the ▷alkaline-earth metals, widely distributed in small quantities only as a sulphate or carbonate. Strontium salts burn with a red flame and are used in fireworks and signal flares.

The radioactive isotopes Sr-89 and Sr-90 (half-life 25 years) are some of the most dangerous products of the nuclear industry; they are fission products in nuclear explosions and in the reactors of nuclear power plants. Strontium is chemically similar to calcium and deposits in bones and other tissues, where the radioactivity is damaging. The element was named in 1808 by English chemist Humphry Davy, who isolated it by electrolysis, after Strontian, a mining location in Scotland where it was first found.

strophanthus any of a group of tropical plants belonging to the dogbane family, native to Africa and Asia. Seeds of the handsome climber *S. gratus* yield a poison, strophantin, which is used on arrowheads in hunting, and in medicine as a heart stimulant. (Genus *Strophanthus*, family Apocynaceae.)

structuralism 20th-century philosophical movement that has influenced such areas as linguistics, anthropology, and literary criticism. Inspired by the work of the Swiss linguist Ferdinand de Saussure, structuralists believe that objects should be analysed as systems of relations, rather than as positive entities.

structured programming in computing, the process of writing a program in small, independent parts. This makes it easier to control a program's development and to design and test its individual component parts. Structured programs are built up from units called **modules**, which normally correspond to single ▷procedures or ▷functions. Some programming languages, such as Pascal and Modula-2, are better suited to structured programming than others.

strychnine $C_{21}H_{22}O_2N_2$ bitter-tasting, poisonous alkaloid. It is a poison that causes violent muscular spasms, and is usually obtained by powdering the seeds of plants of the genus *Strychnos* (for example *S. nux vomica*). Curare is a related drug.

Stuart (or Stewart) royal family that inherited the Scottish throne in 1371 and the English throne in 1603, holding it until 1714, when Queen Anne died without heirs; the house of Stuart was succeeded by the house of ▷Hanover. The claimants to the British throne James Francis Edward Stuart (the 'Old Pretender', son of the deposed James VII of Scotland and II of England) and his son Charles Edward Stuart (the 'Young Pretender') both attempted unsuccessful invasions of England in support of their claims, in 1715 and 1745 (see ▷Jacobites).

Stubbs, George (1724–1806) English artist. He is renowned for his paintings of horses, such as *Mares and Foals* (about 1763; Tate Gallery, London). After the publication of his book of engravings *The Anatomy of the Horse* (1766), he was widely commissioned as an animal painter. The dramatic *Lion Attacking a Horse* (1770; Yale University Art Gallery, New Haven, Connecticut) and the peaceful *Reapers* (1786; Tate Gallery, London) show the variety of mood in his painting.

GEORGE STUBBS *A Lion Attacking a Horse*, painted by English painter George Stubbs in 1770. Stubbs has been considered as nothing more than a horse painter, and was often ignored by art critics, but the power of this painting is seen in the anguished face of the horse, and the terror created by the lion's attack. *The Art Archive/ Tate Gallery London*

stucco durable plaster finish for exterior walls, composed of sand and lime. In the 18th and 19th centuries stucco was used extensively to add dignity to brick buildings, by giving the illusion that they were built of stone. The stucco would be moulded, coursed, or coloured to imitate ashlar ▷masonry. John ▷Nash used stucco to create the illusory stone palaces that surround Regents Park, London (begun 1811).

stupa domed structure built to house a Buddhist or Jain relic. The stupa originated in India around 1000 BC from burial monuments and is usually a hemisphere crowned by a spire. In the Far East the stupa developed into the ▷pagoda.

sturgeon any of a family of large, primitive, bony fishes with five rows of bony plates, small sucking mouths, and chin barbels used for exploring the bottom of the water for prey.

Sturmabteilung (SA; German 'storm section') German militia, also known as **Brownshirts**, of the ▷Nazi Party, established in 1921 under the leadership of Ernst ▷Röhm, in charge of physical training and political indoctrination.

Sturm und Drang (German 'storm and stress') German early Romantic movement in literature and music, from about 1775,

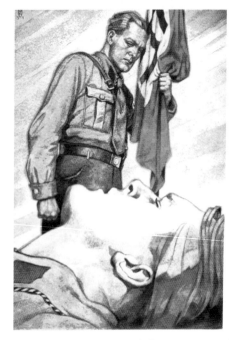

STURMABTEILUNG Nazi propaganda depicting a martyred member of the *Sturmabteilung*, or SA, the armed and uniformed branch of the Nazi party in 1930s Germany. *Philip Sauvain Picture Collection*

concerned with the depiction of extravagant passions. Writers associated with the movement include Johann Gottfried von Herder, Johann Wolfgang von Goethe, and Friedrich von Schiller. The name is taken from a play by Friedrich von Klinger in 1776.

Stuttgart capital of Baden-Württemberg, on the River Neckar, Germany; population (1995) 587,000. Industries include the manufacture of vehicles, electronics, mechanical and electrical engineering, precision instruments, foodstuffs, textiles, papermaking and publishing; it is a fruit-growing and wine-producing centre. There are two universities. Stuttgart was founded in the 10th century.

    Related Web site: Stuttgart City Guide http://www.stgt.com/ stuttgart/homee.htm

style in flowers, the part of the ▷carpel bearing the ▷stigma at its tip. In some flowers it is very short or completely lacking, while in others it may be long and slender, positioning the stigma in the most effective place to receive the pollen.

Styria (German **Steiermark**) Alpine state of southeast Austria, bordered on the east by Hungary and on the south by Slovenia; area 16,400 sq km/6,330 sq mi; population (1994) 1,202,700. Its capital is Graz, and its industries include iron, steel, vehicles, electrical goods, electronics, computers, and engineering. A large proportion

of the population is engaged in agriculture. An independent state from 1056 until it passed to the ▷Habsburgs in the 13th century, it was annexed by Germany in 1938.

Styx (Greek 'hateful') in Greek mythology, the river surrounding ▷Hades, the underworld. When an oath was sworn by Styx, its waters were taken to seal the promise. Gods who broke such a vow suffered a year's unconsciousness and nine years' exile, while to mortal transgressors its waters were deadly poison. The tradition may have derived from some form of trial by ordeal.

subatomic particle in physics, a particle that is smaller than an atom. Such particles may be indivisible ▷elementary particles, such as the ▷electron and ▷quark, or they may be composites, such as the ▷proton, ▷neutron, and ▷alpha particle. See also ▷particle physics.

subduction zone region where two plates of the Earth's rigid lithosphere collide, and one plate descends below the other into the weaker asthenosphere. Subduction results in the formation of ocean trenches, most of which encircle the Pacific Ocean.

    Ocean trenches are usually associated with volcanic ▷island arcs and deep-focus earthquakes (more than 300 km/185 mi below the surface), both the result of disturbances caused by the plate subduction.

sub judice (Latin 'under a judge') of judicial proceedings, not yet decided by a court of law or judge. As long as a matter is sub judice all discussion is prohibited elsewhere.

sublimation in chemistry, the conversion of a solid to vapour without passing through the liquid phase.

    Sublimation depends on the fact that the boiling-point of the solid substance is lower than its melting-point at atmospheric pressure. Thus by increasing pressure, a substance which sublimes can be made to go through a liquid stage before passing into the vapour state.

    Some substances that do not sublime at atmospheric pressure can be made to do so at low pressures. This is the principle of freeze-drying, during which ice sublimes at low pressure.

submarine underwater warship. The first underwater boat was constructed in 1620 for James I of England by the Dutch scientist Cornelius van Drebbel (1572–1633). A naval submarine, or submersible torpedo boat, the *Gymnote*, was launched by France in 1888. The conventional submarine of World War I was driven by diesel engine on the surface and by battery-powered electric motors underwater. The diesel engine also drove a generator that produced electricity to charge the batteries.

History In the 1760s the American David Bushnell (1742–1824) designed a submarine called *Turtle* for attacking British ships, and in 1800 Robert Fulton designed a submarine called *Nautilus* for Napoleon for the same purpose. John P Holland, an Irish emigrant to the USA, designed a submarine in about 1875, which was used by both the US and the British navies at the turn of the century. Submarine warfare was established as a distinct form of naval tactics during World War I and submarines, from the ocean-going vessels to the midget type, played a vital role in both world wars. In particular, German U-boats caused great difficulty to Allied merchant shipping, until the radio codes were broken in 1942.

Nuclear submarines In 1954 the USA launched the first nuclear-powered submarine, the *Nautilus*. The US nuclear submarine *Ohio*, in service from 1981, is 170 m/560 ft long and carries 24 Trident missiles, each with 12 independently targetable nuclear warheads. The nuclear warheads on US submarines have a range that is being extended to 11,000 km/6,750 mi. Three Vanguard-class Trident missile-carrying submarines, which when armed will each wield more firepower than was used in the whole of World War II, were built in the 1990s in the UK. Operating depth is usually up to 300 m/ 1,000 ft, and nuclear-powered speeds of 30 knots (55 kph/ 34 mph) are reached. As in all nuclear submarines, propulsion is by steam turbine driving a propeller. The steam is raised using the heat given off by the nuclear reactor (see ▷nuclear energy).

In oceanography, salvage, and pipe-laying, smaller submarines called **submersibles** are used. They are also being developed for tourism.

STUPA Buddhist *stupas* (domed edifices) on a hillside in Bayinhot, China. Buddhism reached China before AD 100 and developed there under the influence of Taoism and Confucianism. *Image Bank*

subpoena (Latin 'under penalty') in law, an order requiring someone who might not otherwise come forward of his or her own volition to give evidence before a court or judicial official at a specific time and place. A witness who fails to comply with a subpoena is in ▷contempt of court.

subsidiarity devolution of decision-making within the European Union from the centre to the lowest level possible. Since the signing of the ▷Maastricht Treaty on European union 1991, which affirms that, wherever possible, decisions should be 'taken as closely as possible to the citizens', subsidiarity has been widely debated as a means of countering trends towards excessive centralization.

subsidiary in business, a company that is legally controlled by another company having 50% or more of its shares.

subsidy government payment or concession granted to a state or private company, or an individual. A subsidy may be provided to keep prices down, to stimulate the market for a particular product, or because it is perceived to be in the public interest.

substitution reaction in chemistry, the replacement of one atom or ▷functional group in an organic molecule by another.

substrate in biochemistry, a compound or mixture of compounds acted on by an enzyme. The term also refers to a substance such as ▷agar that provides the nutrients for the metabolism of micro-organisms. Since the enzyme systems of micro-organisms regulate their metabolism, the essential meaning is the same.

succession in ecology, a series of changes that occur in the structure and composition of the vegetation in a given area from the time it is first colonized by plants (**primary succession**), or after it has been disturbed by fire, flood, or clearing (**secondary succession**).

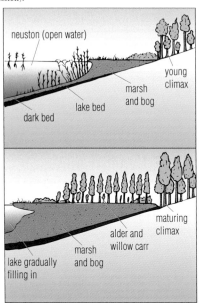

SUCCESSION The succession of plant types along a lake. As the lake gradually fills in, a mature climax community of trees forms inland from the shore. Extending out from the shore, a series of plant communities can be discerned with small, rapidly growing species closest to the shore.

Succot (or **Sukkoth**) in Judaism, a harvest festival celebrated in October, also known as the **Feast of Booths**, which commemorates the time when the Israelites lived in the wilderness during the Exodus from Egypt. As a reminder of the shelters used in the wilderness, huts are built and used for eating and sleeping during the seven days of the festival.

succulent plant thick, fleshy plant that stores water in its tissues; for example, cacti and stonecrops *Sedum*. Succulents live either in areas where water is very scarce, such as deserts, or in places where it is not easily obtainable because of the high concentrations of salts in the soil, as in salt marshes. Many desert plants are ▷xerophytes.

Suceava capital of Suceava county, northern Romania; population (1993) 116,000. Industries include textiles and lumber. It was a former centre of pilgrimage and capital of Moldavia 1388–1564.

sucker fish another name for ▷remora.

suckering in plants, reproduction by new shoots (suckers) arising from an existing root system rather than from seed. Plants that produce suckers include elm, dandelion, and members of the rose family.

Sucre legal capital and seat of the judiciary of Bolivia, also capital of Chuquisaca department; population (1992) 131,000. It stands on the central plateau in the Andes at an altitude of 2,840 m/9,320 ft. It is the commercial centre for the surrounding agricultural area and has an oil refinery.

Sucre was founded in 1538 as La Plata. From 1559 it was the Spanish centre of the Charcas region (stretching from southern Peru to Rio de la Plata in Argentina). In 1776, new territorial divisions resulted in the city's name being changed to Chuquisaca. It was given its present name on 6 August 1825 in honour of Antonio José de Sucre, the first president of the new republic. The cathedral dates from 1553, and the University of San Francisco Xavier (founded 1624) is probably the oldest in South America. The first revolt against Spanish rule in South America began here on 25 May 1809.

Sucre, Antonio José de (1795–1830) South American revolutionary leader. As chief lieutenant of Simón ▷Bolívar, he won several battles in freeing the colonies of Ecuador and Bolivia from Spanish rule, and in 1826 became president of Bolivia. After a mutiny by the army and invasion by Peru, he resigned in 1828 and was assassinated in 1830 on his way to join Bolívar.

sucrose (or **cane sugar** or **beet sugar**) $C_{12}H_{22}O_{11}$ a sugar found in the pith of sugar cane and in sugar beets. It is popularly known as ▷sugar.

Sucrose is a disaccharide sugar, each of its molecules being made up of two simple sugar (monosaccharide) units: glucose and fructose.

Sudan see country box.

sudden infant death syndrome (SIDS) in medicine, the technical term for ▷cot death.

Sudeten mountainous region in northeast Bohemia, Czech Republic, extending eastwards along the border with Poland. Sudeten was annexed by Germany under the ▷Munich Agreement 1938; it was returned to Czechoslovakia in 1945.

Germany and the Czech Republic sought to bury decades of mutual antagonism in January 1997 by signing a joint declaration aimed at drawing a line under the vexed issue of the Sudetenland. Germany apologized for the suffering caused during the Nazi occupation. For their part, the Czechs expressed regret over the 'injustices' that took place during the expulsion of more than 2.5 million Sudetenland Germans after World War II. It took over two years to reach agreement.

Suetonius, Gaius Suetonius Tranquillus (c. AD 69–c. 140) Roman historian. He was the author of *Lives of the Caesars* (Julius Caesar to Domitian).

Suez (Arabic **El Suweis**) port at the Red Sea terminus of the Suez Canal, 120 km/75 mi east of Cairo; population (1994) 458,000. Industries include oil refining and the manufacture of fertilizers. Port Ibrahim, 3 km/1.8 mi south of Suez, lies at the entrance to the canal. It was reconstructed in 1979 after the ▷Arab-Israeli Wars.

Suez Canal artificial waterway from Port Said to Suez, linking the Mediterranean and Red Seas; 160 km/100 mi long. It separates Africa from Asia and provides the shortest eastwards sea route from Europe. It was opened in 1869, nationalized in 1956, blocked by Egypt during the Arab-Israeli War in 1967, and not reopened until 1975.

The French Suez Canal Company was formed in 1858 to execute the scheme of Ferdinand de Lesseps. The canal was opened in 1869, and in 1875 British prime minister ▷Disraeli acquired a major shareholding for Britain from the khedive of Egypt. The 1888 Convention of Constantinople opened it to all nations. The Suez

Canal was administered by a company with offices in Paris controlled by a council of 33 (10 of them British) until 1956 when it was forcibly nationalized by President ▷Nasser of Egypt. The new Damietta port complex on the Mediterranean at the mouth of the canal was inaugurated in 1986. The port is designed to handle 16 million tonnes of cargo.

Related Web site: Suez 1956 http://history.acusd.edu/gen/text/suez.html

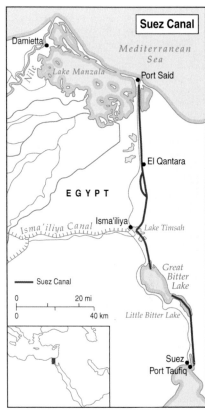

Suez Crisis military confrontation from October to December 1956 following the nationalization of the Suez Canal by President Nasser of Egypt. In an attempt to reassert international control of the canal, Israel launched an attack, after which British and French troops landed. Widespread international censure forced the withdrawal of the British and French. The crisis resulted in the resignation of British prime minister Anthony ▷Eden.

At a London conference of maritime powers the Australian prime minister Robert Menzies was appointed to negotiate a settlement in Cairo. His mission was unsuccessful. The military intervention met Soviet protest and considerable domestic opposition, and the USA did not support it. ▷Cold War politics came into play during the Suez Crisis, and the UK and France found themselves unable to act independently of the USA in a way that they could have done before World War II. British, French, and Australian relations with the USA were greatly strained during this period. The USSR was seeking to extend its influence in Africa at the time and saw Egypt as a key country with which it could establish friendly relations. The support given to Egypt by the Soviets during the Suez Crisis increased their influence in the region, and this was sealed during the 1960s when the USSR provided much of the funding for the Aswan High Dam project in Egypt. The Suez Crisis, therefore, had a significant role in the Cold War as well as in the conflict between Egypt and the former colonial powers of Britain and France.

See also ▷United Kingdom, the Suez Crisis; ▷Egypt, towards the Suez Crisis and Suez and the Second Arab–Israeli War; and ▷Israel, the Suez Crisis and the Second Arab–Israeli War.

Related Web site: 1956 – The Suez Crisis and the Peacekeeping Debut http://www.screen.com/mnet/eng/med/class/teamedia/peace/Part1/P1_11.htm

SUEZ CANAL An artificial waterway reaching from Port Said to Suez, the Suez Canal links the Mediterranean and the Red Sea and was originally opened in 1869. *Image Bank*

Suffolk county of eastern England.
area 3,800 sq km/1,467 sq mi **towns** ▷Ipswich (administrative headquarters), Aldeburgh, Beccles, Bury St Edmunds, Felixstowe, Lowestoft, Sudbury, Southwold **physical** undulating lowlands in the south and west; flat coastline; rivers Waveney (the boundary with Norfolk), Alde, Deben, Orwell, Stour (the boundary with Essex), Little Ouse; part of the Norfolk Broads **features** Minsmere marshland bird reserve, near Aldeburgh; the Sandlings (heathlands and birds); bloodstock rearing and horse racing at

Newmarket; ▷Sutton Hoo (7th-century ship burial); Sizewell B, Britain's first pressurized-water nuclear reactor plant; Aldeburgh Festival, held every June at Snape Maltings **agriculture** cereals (barley, oats, wheat), sugar beet; cattle, sheep, and pig rearing; fishing (for which Lowestoft is the main centre) **industries** agricultural machinery; chemicals; coconut matting; electronics; fertilizers; food processing; motor vehicle components; North Sea oil and gas exploration; printing; telecommunications research; silk; timber; brewing

population (1996) 661,600 **famous people** Benjamin Britten, John Constable, George Crabbe, Thomas Gainsborough, Elizabeth Garrett Anderson

suffragette woman fighting for the right to vote. In the UK, the repeated defeat in Parliament of women's suffrage bills, introduced by supporters of the ▷women's movement between 1886 and 1911, led to the launch of a militant campaign in 1906 by Emmeline ▷Pankhurst and her daughters, founders of the ▷Women's Social

Sudan

SUDAN A stamp from Sudan showing a postman transported by camel. *Stanley Gibbons*

the north and black Africans (52%) in the south; Beja (6%), foreigners (2%)
LANGUAGE Arabic (51%) (official), 100 local languages
RELIGION Sunni Muslim 70%; also animist 25%, and Christian 5%
EDUCATION (compulsory years) 6
LITERACY RATE 72% (men); 50% (women) (2003 est)
LABOUR FORCE 61.1% agriculture, 9.2% industry, 29.7% services (2000)
LIFE EXPECTANCY 54 (men); 57 (women) (2000–05)
CHILD MORTALITY RATE (under 5, per 1,000 live births) 107 (2001)
PHYSICIANS (per 1,000 people) 0.1 (1998 est)
HOSPITAL BEDS (per 1,000 people) 1.2 (1994 est)
TV SETS (per 1,000 people) 386 (2001 est)
RADIOS (per 1,000 people) 466 (2001 est)
INTERNET USERS (per 10,000 people) 25.8 (2002 est)
PERSONAL COMPUTER USERS (per 100 people) 0.6 (2002 est)

See also ▷Khartoum; ▷Nubia.

Sudan country in northeast Africa, bounded north by Egypt, northeast by the Red Sea, east by Ethiopia and Eritrea, south by Kenya, Uganda, and Congo (formerly Zaire), west by the Central African Republic and Chad, and northwest by Libya. It is the largest country in Africa.

NATIONAL NAME *Al-Jumhuryyat es-Sudan/Republic of Sudan*
AREA 2,505,800 sq km/967,489 sq mi
CAPITAL Khartoum
MAJOR TOWNS/CITIES Omdurman, Port Sudan, Juba, Wad Medani, El Obeid, Kassala, al-Qadarif, Nyala
MAJOR PORTS Port Sudan
PHYSICAL FEATURES fertile Nile valley separates Libyan Desert in west from high rocky Nubian Desert in east

Government

HEAD OF STATE AND GOVERNMENT Gen Omar Hassan Ahmed al-Bashir from 1989
POLITICAL SYSTEM military
POLITICAL EXECUTIVE military
ADMINISTRATIVE DIVISIONS 26 states
ARMED FORCES 117,000 (2002 est)
CONSCRIPTION military service is compulsory for two years (men 18–30)
DEATH PENALTY retained and used for ordinary crimes
DEFENCE SPEND (% GDP) 4.9 (2002 est)
EDUCATION SPEND (% GDP) 1.4 (1997)
HEALTH SPEND (% GDP) 4.7 (2000 est)

Economy and resources

CURRENCY Sudanese dinar
GPD (US$) 13.5 billion (2002 est)
REAL GDP GROWTH (% change on previous year) 5.3 (2001)
GNI (US$) 11.5 billion (2002 est)
GNI PER CAPITA (PPP) (US$) 1,690 (2002 est)
CONSUMER PRICE INFLATION 5% (2003 est)
UNEMPLOYMENT 5% (2001)

FOREIGN DEBT (US$) 9.04 billion (2001 est)
MAJOR TRADING PARTNERS China, Saudi Arabia, Germany, UK, France, Japan
RESOURCES petroleum, marble, mica, chromite, gypsum, gold, graphite, sulphur, iron, manganese, zinc, fluorspar, talc, limestone, dolomite, pumice
INDUSTRIES food processing (especially sugar refining), textiles, cement, petroleum refining, hides and skins
EXPORTS cotton, sesame seed, gum arabic, sorghum, livestock, hides and skins. Principal market: China 49.3% (2001)
IMPORTS basic manufacture, crude materials (mainly petroleum and petroleum products), foodstuffs, machinery and equipment. Principal source: China 11.9% (2001)
ARABLE LAND 6.8% (2000 est)
AGRICULTURAL PRODUCTS sorghum, sugar cane, groundnuts, cotton, millet, wheat, sesame, fruits; livestock rearing (cattle, sheep, goats, and poultry)

Population and society

POPULATION 33,610,000 (2003 est)
POPULATION GROWTH RATE 2.0% (2000–15)
POPULATION DENSITY (per sq km) 13 (2003 est)
URBAN POPULATION (% of total) 39 (2003 est)
AGE DISTRIBUTION (% of total population) 0–14 40%, 15–59 54%, 60+ 6% (2002 est)
ETHNIC GROUPS over 50 ethnic groups and almost 600 subgroups; the population is broadly distributed between Arabs (39%) in

Chronology

c. **600 BC–AD 350**: Meroë, near Khartoum, was capital of the Nubian Empire, which covered southern Egypt and northern Sudan.

6th century: Converted to Coptic Christianity.

7th century: Islam first introduced by Arab invaders, but did not spread widely until the 15th century.

16th–18th centuries: Arab-African Fur and Fung Empires established in central and northern Sudan.

1820: Invaded by Muhammad Ali and brought under Egyptian control.

1881–85: Revolt led to capture of Khartoum by Sheik Muhammad Ahmed, a self-proclaimed Mahdi ('messiah'), and the killing of British general Charles Gordon.

1898: Anglo-Egyptian offensive led by Lord Kitchener subdued Mahdi revolt at Battle of Omdurman in which 20,000 Sudanese died.

1899: Sudan administered as Anglo-Egyptian condominium.

1923: White Flag League formed by Sudanese nationalists in north; British instituted policy of reducing contact between northern and southern Sudan, with the aim that the south would eventually become part of federation of eastern African states.

1955: Civil war between the dominant Arab Muslim north and black African Christian and animist south broke out.

1956: Sudan achieved independence from Britain and Egypt as a republic.

1958: Military coup replaced civilian government with Supreme Council of the Armed Forces.

1964: Civilian rule reinstated after October Revolution of student demonstrations.

1969: Coup led by Col Gaafar Mohammed al-Nimeri abolished political institutions and concentrated power in a leftist Revolutionary Command Council.

1971: Nimeri confirmed as president and the Sudanese Socialist Union (SSU) declared the only legal party by a new constitution.

1972: Plans to form Federation of Arab Republics, comprising Sudan, Egypt, and Syria, abandoned due to internal opposition. To end 17-year-long civil war, Nimeri agreed to give south greater autonomy.

1974: National assembly established.

1980: Country reorganized into six regions, each with own assembly and effective autonomy.

1983: Shari'a (Islamic law) imposed. Sudan People's Liberation Movement (SPLM) formed in south as civil war broke out again.

1985: Nimeri deposed in a bloodless coup led by Gen Swar al-Dahab.

1986: Coalition government formed after general election, with Sadiq al-Mahdi, great-grandson of the Mahdi, as prime minister.

1987: Civil war with Sudan People's Liberation Army (SPLA); drought and famine in south and refugee influx from Ethiopa and Chad.

1988: A peace pact was signed with SPLA, but fighting continued.

1989: Al-Mahdi was overthrown in a coup led by Islamic fundamentalist Gen Omar Hassan Ahmed el-Bashir. All political activity was suspended.

1991: A federal system was introduced, with division of the country into nine states as the civil war continued.

1998: Civil war continued between the SPLA and the Islamist government. There was famine in the south. The USA launched a missile attack on a suspected chemical weapons-producing site in retaliation for bombings of US embassies in Nairobi and Dar es Salaam. There was a temporary ceasefire by the SPLA.

1999: Multiparty politics were reintroduced. Steps to restore diplomatic ties with Uganda were taken when in December an agreement was signed to attempt to end rebel wars across the mutual border by ceasing to support rebel factions in the other's country. In late December the president declared a state of emergency and dissolved parliament.

2000: President Bashir dismissed his entire cabinet in January, but then reappointed key ministers. In Khartoum, women were banned from working in public places where they might meet men.

2001: Elections re-established a parliament and confirmed Bashir in power, but were boycotted by opposition parties.

2002: The Islamic government and the SPLA agreed a framework for ending the ongoing civil war.

and Political Union (WSPU). In 1918 women were granted limited franchise; in 1928 it was extended to all women over 21.

SUFFRAGETTE Suffragettes marching for equal rights in London, England, in 1910. *Archive Photos*

Sufism mystical movement of ▷Islam that originated in the 8th century. Sufis believe that deep intuition is the only real guide to knowledge. The movement has a strong strain of asceticism. The name derives from Arabic *suf*, a rough woollen robe worn as an indication of disregard for material things. There are a number of groups or brotherhoods within Sufism, each with its own method of meditative practice, one of which is the whirling dance of the ▷dervishes.

> **Related Web site: 'What Sufism Is'** http://www.sufism.org/books/livinex.html

sugar (or **sucrose**) sweet, soluble, crystalline carbohydrate found in the pith of sugar cane and in sugar beet. It is a **disaccharide** sugar, each of its molecules being made up of two simple-sugar (**monosaccharide**) units: glucose and fructose. Sugar is easily digested and forms a major source of energy in humans, being used in cooking and in the food industry as a sweetener and, in high concentrations, as a preservative. A high consumption is associated with obesity and tooth decay. In the UK, sucrose may not be used in baby foods.

Sugar, Alan Michael (1947–) British entrepreneur, founder in 1968 of the Amstrad electronics company, which holds a strong position in the European consumer electronics and personal-computer market. In 1985 he introduced a complete word-processing system at the price of £399. Subsequent models consolidated his success internationally.

sugar cane large tropical grass *Saccharum officinarum*, in the family Gramineae, one of the world's main sources of ▷sugar. Plants reach 3–4 m/10–13 ft in height and have thick, solid stems up to 7 cm/2.5 in diameter that yield a sugary juice when crushed. Sugar cane is native to Southeast Asia; it was taken to the Americas by European settlers, and is now cultivated in moist tropical and subtropical regions worldwide.

sugar maple eastern North American ▷maple tree.

Suharto, Thojib I (1921–) Indonesian politician and general. He was president from 1967–98. His authoritarian rule met with domestic opposition from the left, but the Indonesian economy enjoyed significant growth until 1997. He was re-elected in 1973, 1978, 1983, 1988, 1993, and, unopposed, in March 1998. This was despite his deteriorating health and the country's economy being weakened by a sharp decline in value of the Indonesian currency (the rupiah), which had provoked student unrest and food riots. After mounting civil unrest reached a critical point, on 21 May 1998 he handed over the presidency to the vice-president, Bacharuddin Jusuf Habibie.

suicide the act of intentionally killing oneself; also someone who does this. The frequency of attempted suicide is 20 times higher than actual suicide. Three times more women than men attempt suicide, and three times more men succeed. Men tend to use more violent methods like gunshot wounds to the head; women are more likely to take an overdose. Over 6,000 people in the USA use handguns to kill themselves each year. The highest suicide rate for both sexes is in the over-75 age group. Hungary has the highest suicide rate in this age category at 108 per 100,000 (1992). Suicide among people aged 18–24, suicide is the third leading cause of death after accident and homicide.

Sui dynasty Chinese ruling family 581–618 which reunited China after the strife of the ▷Three Kingdoms era. There were two Sui emperors: Yang Qien (Yang Chien, 541–604), and Yangdi (Yang-ti, ruled 605–17). Though short-lived, the Sui re-established strong centralized government, rebuilding the ▷Great Wall and digging canals which later formed part of the Grand Canal system. The Sui capital was Chang'an.

suite in baroque music, a set of contrasting instrumental pieces based on dance forms, known by their French names as allemande, bourrée, courante, gavotte, gigue, minuet, musette, passepied, rigaudon, sarabande, and so on. The term refers in more recent usage to a concert arrangement of set pieces from an extended ballet or stage composition, such as Tchaikovsky's *Nutcracker Suite* (1891–92). Igor Stravinsky's suite from *The Soldier's Tale* (1920) incorporates a tango, waltz, and ragtime.

Sukarno, Achmed (1901–1970) Indonesian nationalist, president 1945–67. During World War II he cooperated in the local administration set up by the Japanese, replacing Dutch rule. After the war he became the first president of the new Indonesian republic, becoming president-for-life in 1966; he was ousted by ▷Suharto.

Sulawesi (formerly **Celebes**) island in eastern Indonesia, one of the Sunda Islands; area (with dependent islands) 190,000 sq km/73,000 sq mi; population (1995 est) 13,756,000. This mountainous and forested island lies off the coast of eastern Borneo. Minerals such as copra, nickel, coal, asphalt, mica, sulphur and salt are among the products.

Suleiman (or **Solyman**) (*c.* 1494–1566) Ottoman sultan from 1520, known as **the Magnificent** and **the Lawgiver**. Under his rule, the Ottoman Empire flourished and reached its largest extent. He made conquests in the Balkans, the Mediterranean, Persia, and North Africa, but was defeated at Vienna in 1529 and Valletta (on Malta) in 1565. He was a patron of the arts, a poet, and an administrator.

Suleiman captured Belgrade in 1521, the Mediterranean island of Rhodes in 1522, defeated the Hungarians at Mohács in 1526, and was halted in his advance into Europe only by his failure to take Vienna, capital of the Austro-Hungarian Empire, after a siege from September to October 1529. In 1534 he turned more successfully against Persia, and then in campaigns against the Arab world took almost all of North Africa and the Red Sea port of Aden. Only the ▷Knights of Malta inflicted severe defeat on both his army and fleet when he tried to take Valletta in 1565.

Triumphzug des Sultans Suleiman

SULEIMAN A woodcarving by Domenico de'Franceschi 1565 showing a triumphant procession of the Ottoman sultan Suleiman the Magnificent. The Ottoman Empire made many conquests under Suleiman's rule. *Philip Sauvain Picture Collection*

Sulla, Publius Cornelius (138 BC–78 BC) Roman general and dictator. He was elected consul in 88 BC after defeating the Samnites several times during the Italian Social War. In the same year, Marius tried to deprive him of the command against the king of Pontus, Mithridates (VI) Eupator (120–60 BC). Sulla's unprecedented response was to march on Rome, executing or putting to flight his rivals. His campaign against Mithridates ended successfully in 85 BC, and Sulla returned to Italy in 83 where his opponents had raised armies against him. Sulla defeated them in 82 and massacred all his opponents. After holding supreme power as dictator and carrying out a series of political reforms, he retired to private life in 80 BC.

Sullivan, Arthur Seymour (1842–1900) English composer. He wrote operettas in collaboration with William Gilbert, including *HMS Pinafore* (1878), *The Pirates of Penzance* (1879), and *The Mikado* (1885). Their partnership broke down in 1896. Sullivan also composed serious instrumental, choral, and operatic works – for example, the opera *Ivanhoe* (1890) – which he valued more highly than the operettas.

Other Gilbert and Sullivan operettas include *Patience* (which ridiculed the Aesthetic Movement) (1881), *The Yeomen of the Guard* (1888), and *The Gondoliers* (1889).

Sullivan, Louis Henry (1856–1924) US architect. He was a leader of the Chicago School and an early developer of the ▷skyscraper. His skyscrapers include the Wainwright Building, St Louis (1890); the Guaranty Building, Buffalo (1894); and the Carson, Pirie, and Scott Store, Chicago (1899). He was the teacher of Frank Lloyd ▷Wright.

sulphate SO_4^{2-} salt or ester derived from sulphuric acid. Most sulphates are water soluble (the exceptions are lead, calcium, strontium, and barium sulphates), and require a very high temperature to decompose them.

The commonest sulphates seen in the laboratory are copper(II) sulphate ($CuSO_4$), iron(II) sulphate ($FeSO_4$), and aluminium sulphate ($Al_2(SO_4)_3$). The ion is detected in solution by using barium chloride or barium nitrate to precipitate the insoluble sulphate.

sulphide compound of sulphur and another element in which sulphur is the more electronegative element (see ▷electronegativity). Sulphides occur in a number of minerals. Some of the more volatile sulphides have extremely unpleasant odours (hydrogen sulphide smells of bad eggs).

sulphite SO_3^{2-} salt or ester derived from sulphurous acid.

sulphonamide any of a group of compounds containing the chemical group sulphonamide (SO_2NH_2) or its derivatives, which were, and still are in some cases, used to treat bacterial diseases. Sulphadiazine ($C_{10}H_{10}N_4O_2S$) is an example.

Sulphonamide was the first commercially available antibacterial drug, the forerunner of a range of similar drugs. Toxicity and increasing resistance have limited their use chiefly to the treatment of urinary-tract infection.

sulphur brittle, pale-yellow, nonmetallic element, symbol S, atomic number 16, relative atomic mass 32.064. It occurs in three allotropic forms: two crystalline (called rhombic and monoclinic, following the arrangements of the atoms within the crystals) and one amorphous. It burns in air with a blue flame and a stifling odour. Insoluble in water but soluble in carbon disulphide, it is a good electrical insulator. Sulphur is widely used in the manufacture of sulphuric acid (used to treat phosphate rock to make fertilizers) and in making paper, matches, gunpowder and fireworks, in vulcanizing rubber, and in medicines and insecticides.

It is found abundantly in nature in volcanic regions combined with both metals and nonmetals, and also in its elemental form as a crystalline solid. It is a constituent of proteins, and has been known since ancient times.

SULPHUR A worker in a sulphur quarry, on the Indonesian island of Java. *Image Bank*

Between 20 and 50 million tonnes of sulphur are returned from the oceans to the atmosphere every year in the form of dimethyl sulphide (DMS), the gas that gives sea air its bracing smell. DMS is a breakdown product of a salt produced by marine algae to maintain their osmotic balance (see ▷osmosis). Human activity releases about 80 million tonnes of sulphur.

Sulphur is an essential plant nutrient and, according to German research in 1995, reductions in European sulphur emissions have resulted in an increase in sulphur deficiency diseases in crops and other plants, in particular members of the *Brassica* family, especially oilseed rape.

sulphur dioxide SO_2 pungent gas produced by burning sulphur in air or oxygen. It is widely used for disinfecting food vessels and equipment, and as a preservative in some food products. It occurs in industrial flue gases and is a major cause of ▷acid rain.

sulphuric acid (or **oil of vitriol**) H_2SO_4 a dense, viscous, colourless liquid that is extremely corrosive. It gives out heat when added to water and can cause severe burns. Sulphuric acid is used extensively in the chemical industry, in the refining of petrol, and in the manufacture of fertilizers, detergents, explosives, and dyes. It forms the acid component of car batteries.

In the UK more than 2 million tonnes of sulphuric acid are produced each year.

sulphurous acid H_2SO_3 solution of sulphur dioxide (SO_2) in water. It is a weak acid.

Sulu Archipelago group of about 870 islands off southwest Mindanao in the Philippines, between the Sulawesi and Sulu seas; area 2,700 sq km/1,042 sq mi; population (1990 est) 698,200. The capital is Jolo, on the island (the largest) of the same name. Until 1940 the islands were an autonomous sultanate.

Sumatra (or **Sumatera**) second-largest island of Indonesia, one of the Sunda Islands; area 473,600 sq km/182,800 sq mi, length 1,760 km/1,094 mi, width 400 km/250 mi; population (1995 est) 40,343,000. About a third of the area, mainly in the southeast, is permanently waterlogged. The highest part is in the west where, at Gunung Kerinci, the Bukit Barisan volcanic mountain range reaches 3,805 m/12,483 ft. East of the range is a wide plain; both are heavily forested. Products include rubber, rice, tobacco, tea, timber, tin, petroleum, bauxite, gold, natural gas, coffee and pepper.

SUMATRA The hot and humid climate on Sumatra encourages rich vegetation and animal life, and the surrounding waters provide a natural habitat for many species of sea life including this colourful example of gorgon. *Image Bank*

Sumerian civilization the world's earliest civilization, dating from about 3500 BC and located at the confluence of the Tigris and Euphrates rivers in lower Mesopotamia (present-day Iraq). It was a city-state with priests as secular rulers. After 2300 BC, Sumer declined.

Sumerian culture was based on the taxation of the surplus produced by agricultural villagers to support the urban ruling class and its public-works programme, which included state-controlled irrigation. Cities included ▷Lagash, ▷Eridu, and ▷Ur. Centralized control over the region (an empire) was first asserted by neighbouring Akkad, about 2300 BC. Trade with Egypt and the Indus valley may have influenced the formation of the ancient civilizations there.

summer time practice introduced in the UK in 1916 whereby legal time from spring to autumn is an hour in advance of Greenwich Mean Time.

Continental Europe 'puts the clock back' a month earlier than the UK in autumn. British summer time was permanently in force February 1940–October 1945 and February 1968–October 1971. Double summer time (2 hours in advance) was in force during the summers of 1941–45 and 1947.

In North America the practice is known as **daylight saving time**.

summit (or **summit conference**) in international diplomacy, a personal meeting between heads of state to settle international crises and other matters of general concern. 'Summit' was first used in this sense by Winston Churchill in 1950, although it could be applied to the meetings between himself, Roosevelt, and Stalin at Tehran and Yalta during World War II. During the ▷Cold War, the term 'superpower summit' was applied to meetings between the Soviet Union's Communist Party leader and the US president.

summons in law, a court order officially delivered, requiring someone to appear in court on a certain date.

Sumner, James (Batcheller) (1887–1955) US biochemist. Sumner shared the Nobel Prize for Chemistry in 1946 with John Northrop and Wendell Stanley for his work in 1926 when he succeeded in crystallizing the enzyme urease and demonstrating its protein nature.

sumo wrestling national sport of Japan. Fighters of larger than average size (rarely less than 130 kg/21 st or 285 lb) try to push, pull, or throw each other out of a circular ring.

Sun the ▷star at the centre of the Solar System. Its diameter is 1.4 million/865,000 mi; its temperature at the surface is about 5,800K/5,530°C/9,986°F, and at the centre 15 million K/about 15 million°C/about 27 million°F. It is composed of about 70% hydrogen and 30% helium, with other elements making up less than 1%. The Sun's energy is generated by nuclear fusion reactions that turn hydrogen into helium at its centre. The gas core is far denser than mercury or lead on Earth. The Sun is about 4.6 billion years old, with a predicted lifetime of 10 billion years.

At the end of its life, it will expand to become a ▷red giant the size of Mars's orbit, then shrink to become a ▷white dwarf. The Sun spins on its axis every 25 days near its equator, but more slowly towards its poles. Its rotation can be followed by watching the passage of dark ▷sunspots across its disc. Sometimes bright eruptions called ▷flares occur near sunspots. Above the Sun's ▷photosphere (its visible surface which emits light and heat) lies a layer of thinner gas called the ▷chromosphere, visible only by means of special instruments or at eclipses. Tongues of gas called ▷prominences extend from the chromosphere into the corona, a halo of hot, tenuous gas surrounding the Sun. Gas boiling from the corona streams outwards through the Solar System, forming the ▷solar wind. Activity on the Sun, including sunspots, flares, and prominences, waxes and wanes during the **solar cycle**, which peaks every 11 years or so, and seems to be connected with the solar magnetic field.

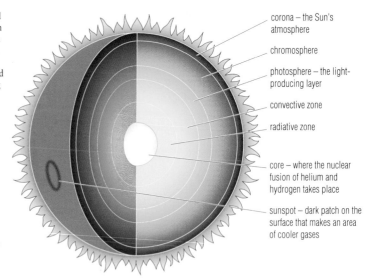

corona – the Sun's atmosphere

chromosphere

photosphere – the light-producing layer

convective zone

radiative zone

core – where the nuclear fusion of helium and hydrogen takes place

sunspot – dark patch on the surface that makes an area of cooler gases

SUN The structure of the Sun. Nuclear reactions at the core release vast amounts of energy in the form of light and heat that radiate out to the photosphere and corona. Surges of glowing gas rise as prominences from the surface of the Sun and cooler areas, known as sunspots, appear as dark patches on the giant star's surface.

Sunda Islands islands west of Maluku (Moluccas), in the Malay Archipelago, the greater number belonging to Indonesia. They are so named because they lie largely on the Indonesian extension of the Sunda continental shelf. The **Greater Sundas** include Borneo, Java (including the small island of Madura), Sumatra, Sulawesi, and Belitung. The **Lesser Sundas** (Indonesian *Nusa Tenggara*) are all Indonesian and include Bali, Lombok, Flores, Sumba, Sumbawa, and Timor.

Sundanese the second-largest ethnic group in the Republic of Indonesia. There are more than 20 million speakers of Sundanese, a member of the western branch of the Austronesian family. Like their neighbours, the Javanese, the Sundanese are predominantly Muslim.

They are known for their performing arts, especially *jaipongan* dance traditions, and distinctive batik fabrics.

Sunday trading buying and selling on Sunday; this was banned in the UK by the Shops Act 1950, but the ban may have been in breach of Article 30 of the Treaty of Rome as amounting to an unlawful restraint on the free movement of goods. Following the defeat of a bill to enable widespread Sunday trading in April 1986, compromise legislation was introduced in 1994 in Britain which allowed shops to open but restricted larger stores (over 280 sq m/3,014 ft) to a maximum of six hours. Shops in Scotland, where Sunday trading is fully deregulated, retained the right to open at any time.

Sunderland, Robert Spencer, 2nd Earl of Sunderland (1640–1702) English politician, a sceptical intriguer who converted to Roman Catholicism to secure his place under James II, and then reverted with the political tide. In 1688 he fled to Holland (disguised as a woman), where he made himself invaluable to the future William III. Now a Whig, he advised the new king to adopt the system, which still prevails, of choosing the government from the dominant party in the Commons. He was created an Earl in 1643.

sundew any of a group of insectivorous plants found growing in bogs; sticky hairs on the leaves catch and digest insects that land on them. (Genus *Drosera*, family Droseraceae.)

sundial instrument measuring time by means of a shadow cast by the Sun. Almost completely superseded by the proliferation of clocks, it survives ornamentally in gardens. The dial is marked with the hours at graduated distances, and a style or gnomon (parallel to Earth's axis and pointing to the north) casts the shadow.

sunfish marine fish *Mola mola* with a disc-shaped body 3 m/10 ft long found in all temperate and tropical oceans. The term also applies to fish of the North American freshwater Centrarchidae family, which have compressed, almost circular bodies, up to 80 cm/30 in long, and are nestbuilders and avid predators.

sunflower tall, thick-stemmed plant with a large, single, yellow-petalled flower, belonging to the daisy family. The common or giant sunflower (*H. annuus*), probably native to Mexico, can grow up to 4.5 m/15 ft high. It is commercially cultivated in central Europe, the

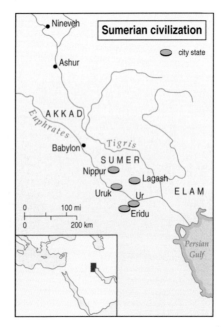

Nineveh

Sumerian civilization

Ashur

● city state

AKKAD

Euphrates

Babylon

Tigris

SUMER

Nippur

Lagash

Uruk

Ur

Eridu

ELAM

0 ___ 100 mi

0 ___ 200 km

Persian Gulf

USA, Russia, Ukraine, and Australia for the oil-bearing seeds that ripen in the central disc of the flower head; sunflower oil is widely used as a cooking oil and in margarine. (Genus *Helianthus*, family Compositae.)

Related Web site: Growing Sunflowers http://jstait.addr.com/~jstait/sunflowers/howto.htm

SUNFLOWER The large flower head, holding the oil-bearing seeds, can measure up to 30 cm/12 in across, and turns throughout the day in order to face toward the sun. *Image Bank*

sungrebe (or **finfoot**) any one of several species of tropical waterbird in the family Heliornithidae. Sungrebes have an elongated body with a long neck and short legs with lobed toes. The bill is pointed and the plumage drab. They feed on fish, amphibians, invertebrates, seeds, and leaves.

Sunni member of the larger of the two main sects of ▷Islam, with about 680 million adherents. Sunni Muslims believe that the first three caliphs were all legitimate successors of the prophet Muhammad, and that guidance on belief and life should come from the Koran and the Hadith, and from the Shari'a, not from a human authority or spiritual leader. Imams in Sunni Islam are educated lay teachers of the faith and prayer leaders.

sunshine recorder device for recording the hours of sunlight during a day. The **Campbell-Stokes sunshine recorder** consists of a glass sphere that focuses the sun's rays on a graduated paper strip. A track is burned along the strip corresponding to the time that the Sun is shining.

sunspot dark patch on the surface of the Sun, actually an area of cooler gas, thought to be caused by strong magnetic fields that block the outward flow of heat to the Sun's surface. Sunspots consist of a dark central **umbra**, about 4,000 K (3,700°C/6,700°F), and a lighter surrounding **penumbra**, about 5,500 K (5,200°C/9,400°F). They last from several days to over a month, ranging in size from 2,000 km/1,250 mi to groups stretching for over 100,000 km/62,000 mi.

Sunspots are more common during active periods in the Sun's magnetic cycle, when they are sometimes accompanied by nearby ▷flares. The number of sunspots visible at a given time varies from none to over 100, in a cycle averaging 11 years. There was a lull in sunspot activity, known as the Maunder minimum, 1645–1715, that coincided with a cold spell in Europe.

Sun Yat-sen Wade-Giles transliteration of ▷Sun Zhong Shan.

Sun Zhong Shan (or Sun Yat-sen) (1867–1925) Chinese revolutionary leader. He was the founder of the Kuomintang (▷Guomindang, nationalist party) in 1894, and provisional president of the Republic of China 1912 after playing a vital part in deposing the emperor. He was president of a breakaway government from 1921.

After many years in exile he returned to China during the 1911 revolution that overthrew the Manchu dynasty. In an effort to bring unity to China, he resigned as provisional president in 1912 in favour of the military leader Yuan Shikai. As a result of Yuan's increasingly dictatorial methods, Sun established an independent republic in southern China based in Canton in 1921. He was criticized for lack of organizational ability, but his 'three people's principles' of nationalism, democracy, and social reform are accepted by both the nationalists and the Chinese communists.

Between 1916 and Sun's death in 1925, his southern-based nationalist regime contended for supremacy with northern-based warlords and from the early 1920s received support from the Soviet Union and the new Chinese Communist Party (CCP). He failed in his goal of securing national reunification, which was left to be achieved, briefly, by his successor, Jiang Jie Shi (Chiang Kai-shek).

Related Web site: Fundamentals Of National Reconstruction http://acc6.its.brooklyn.cuny.edu/~phalsall/texts/sunyat.html

superactinide any of a theoretical series of superheavy, radioactive elements, starting with atomic number 113, that extend beyond the ▷transactinide series in the periodic table. They do not occur in nature and none has yet been synthesized.

Super Bowl US professional American Football championship, inaugurated in 1967. It is the annual end-of-season contest between the American Football Conference (AFC) and the National Football Conference (NFC) champions.

superbug popular name given to an infectious bacterium that has developed resistance to most or all known antibiotics.

Methicillin-resistant *Staphylococcus aureus* (MRSA) is a superbug that causes problems in many hospitals. So far outbreaks of MRSA, which can cause temporary closure of operating rooms and intensive care units, have been met with vancomycin, a 'last resort' antibiotic normally reserved for life-threatening infections. But in the spring of 1997, the Japanese reported the most convincing evidence yet of the appearance of vancomycin-resistant strains.

In 1998 US researchers successfully synthesized the last-resort antibiotic vancomycin. This should also make it possible to synthesize slightly altered versions of the drug with which to treat vancomycin-resistant bacteria. In 2000 the US Food and Drug Administration approved a new type of antibiotic to fight superbugs resistant to other treatments. Zyvox has proved effective for bacteria which are resistant to vancomycin and methicillin. It works by halting bacteria from multiplying earlier than other antibiotics do by stopping the production of proteins needed for the bacteria's growth.

supercomputer fastest, most powerful type of computer, with speeds measured in gigaflops (billions of floating-point calculations per second), or, at the higher end, in teraflops (trillions of floating-point calculations per second).

To achieve these extraordinary speeds, supercomputers use many processors working together and techniques such as cooling processors down to nearly ▷absolute zero temperature, so that their components conduct electricity many times faster than normal. Supercomputers are used in weather forecasting, fluid dynamics, and aerodynamics. Manufacturers include Cray Research, Fujitsu, and NEC.

In November 2003, 248 of the world's 500 most powerful supercomputers were located in the USA, 33 in Japan, and 142 in Europe (with 33 in the UK). In 1992 Fujitsu announced the launch of the first computer capable of performing 300 billion calculations a second. In 1996 University of Tokyo researchers presented a computer able to perform 1.08 trillion floating-point operations per second.

superconductivity in physics, increase in electrical conductivity at low temperatures. The resistance of some metals and metallic compounds decreases uniformly with decreasing temperature until at a critical temperature (the superconducting point), within a few degrees of absolute zero (0 K/−273.15°C/−459.67°F), the resistance suddenly falls to zero.

Some metals, such as platinum and copper, do not become superconductive; as the temperature decreases, their resistance decreases to a certain point but then rises again. Superconductivity can be nullified by the application of a large magnetic field. In the superconducting state, an electric current will continue indefinitely once started, provided that the material remains below the superconducting point. In 1986 IBM researchers achieved superconductivity with some ceramics at −243°C/−405°F), opening up the possibility of **'high-temperature'** superconductivity; Paul Chu at the University of Houston, Texas, achieved superconductivity at −179°C/−290°F, a temperature that can be sustained using liquid nitrogen. Researchers are now trying to find a material that will be superconducting at room temperature.

SUN ZHONG SHAN A portrait of Sun Zhong Shan (or Sun Yat-Sen), political philosopher and founder of modern China, 1910s. *Archive Photos*

supercooling the cooling of a liquid below its freezing point without freezing taking place; or the cooling of a ▷saturated solution without crystallization taking place, to form a supersaturated solution. In both cases supercooling is possible because of the lack of solid particles around which crystals can form. Crystallization rapidly follows the introduction of a small crystal (seed) or agitation of the supercooled solution.

superego in Freudian psychology, the element of the human mind concerned with the ideal, responsible for ethics and self-imposed standards of behaviour. It is characterized as a form of conscience, restraining the ▷ego, and responsible for feelings of guilt when the moral code is broken.

superfluid fluid that flows without viscosity or friction and has a very high thermal conductivity. Liquid helium at temperatures below 2 K (−271°C/−456°F) is a superfluid: it shows unexpected behaviour; for instance, it flows uphill in apparent defiance of gravity and, if placed in a container, will flow up the sides and escape.

supergiant largest and most luminous type of star known, with a diameter of up to 1,000 times that of the Sun and apparent magnitudes of between 0.4 and 1.3. Supergiants are likely to become ▷supernovae.

superheterodyne receiver the most widely used type of radio receiver, in which the incoming signal is mixed with a signal of fixed frequency generated within the receiver circuits. The resulting signal, called the intermediate-frequency (i.f.) signal, has a frequency between that of the incoming signal and the internal signal. The intermediate frequency is near the optimum frequency of the amplifier to which the i.f. signal is passed.

Superior, Lake largest and deepest of the ▷Great Lakes and the largest freshwater lake in the world; area 82,100 sq km/31,700 sq mi. Extending east–west for 616 km/385 mi, it reaches a maximum width of 260 km/163 mi and depth of 407 m/1,335 ft. The lake is bordered by the Canadian province of Ontario and the US states of Minnesota, Wisconsin, and Michigan. As the westernmost of the Great Lakes, Superior is at the western end of the ▷St Lawrence Seaway.

supernova explosive death of a star, which temporarily attains a brightness of 100 million Suns or more, so that it can shine as brilliantly as a small galaxy for a few days or weeks. Very approximately, it is thought that a supernova explodes in a large galaxy about once every 100 years. Many supernovae – astronomers estimate some 50% – remain undetected because of obscuring by interstellar dust.

The name 'supernova' was coined in 1934 by Swiss Astronomer Fritz Zwicky and German-born US astronomer Walter Baade. Zwicky was also responsible for the division into types I and II. **Type I** supernovae are thought to occur in ▷binary star systems, in which gas from one star falls on to a ▷white dwarf, causing it to explode. **Type II** supernovae occur in stars ten or more times as massive as the Sun, which suffer runaway internal nuclear reactions at the ends of their lives, leading to explosions. These are thought to leave behind ▷neutron stars and ▷black holes. Gas ejected by such an explosion causes an expanding radio source, such as the ▷Crab nebula. Supernovae are thought to be the main source of elements heavier than hydrogen and helium.

superpower state that through disproportionate military or economic strength can dominate smaller nations. The term was used to describe the USA and the USSR from the end of World War II, when they emerged as significantly stronger than all other countries. With the collapse of the Soviet Union in 1991, the USA is, arguably, now the world's sole superpower.

supersaturation in chemistry, the state of a solution that has a higher concentration of ▷solute than would normally be obtained in a ▷saturated solution.

supersonic speed speed greater than that at which sound travels, measured in ▷Mach numbers. In dry air at 0°C/32°F, sound travels at about 1,170 kph/727 mph, but decreases its speed with altitude until, at 12,000 m/39,000 ft, it is only 1,060 kph/658 mph.

When an aircraft passes the ▷sound barrier, shock waves are built up that give rise to ▷sonic boom, often heard at ground level. US pilot Captain Charles Yeager was the first to achieve supersonic flight, in a Bell VS-1 rocket plane on 14 October 1947.

superstring theory in physics, a mathematical theory developed in the 1980s to explain the properties of ▷elementary

particles and the forces between them (in particular, gravity and the nuclear forces) in a way that combines ▷relativity and ▷quantum theory. In string theory, the fundamental objects in the universe are not pointlike particles but extremely small stringlike objects. These objects exist in a universe of ten dimensions, but since the earliest moments of the Big Bang six of these have been compacted or 'rolled up', so that now, only three space dimensions and one dimension of time are discernible.

There are many unresolved difficulties with superstring theory, but some physicists think it may be the ultimate 'theory of everything' that explains all aspects of the universe within one framework.

supersymmetry in physics, a theory that relates the two classes of elementary particle, the ▷fermions and the ▷bosons. According to supersymmetry, each fermion particle has a boson partner particle, and vice versa. It has not been possible to marry up all the known fermions with the known bosons, and so the theory postulates the existence of other, as yet undiscovered fermions, such as the photinos (partners of the photons), gluinos (partners of the gluons), and gravitinos (partners of the gravitons). Using these ideas, it has become possible to develop a theory of gravity – called **supergravity** – that extends Einstein's work and considers the gravitational, nuclear, and electromagnetic forces to be manifestations of an underlying superforce. Supersymmetry has been incorporated into the ▷superstring theory, and appears to be a crucial ingredient in the 'theory of everything' sought by scientists.

supply in economics, the production of goods or services for a market in anticipation of an expected ▷demand. The level of supply is determined by the price of the product, the cost of production, the level of technology available for production, and the price of other goods. There is no guarantee that supply will match actual demand.

supply and demand one of the fundamental approaches to economics, which examines and compares the supply of a good with its demand (usually in the form of a graph of supply and demand curves plotted against price). For a typical good, the supply curve is upward-sloping (the higher the price, the more the manufacturer is willing to sell), while the demand curve is downward-sloping (the cheaper the good, the more demand there is for it). The point where the curves intersect is the equilibrium price at which supply equals demand.

supply-side economics school of economic thought advocating government policies that allow market forces to operate freely, such as privatization, cuts in public spending and income tax, reductions in trade-union power, and cuts in the ratio of unemployment benefits to wages. Supply-side economics developed as part of the monetarist (see ▷monetarism) critique of ▷Keynesian economics.

support environment in computing, a collection of programs (▷software) used to help people design and write other programs. At its simplest, this includes a ▷text editor (word-processing software) and a ▷compiler for translating programs into executable form; but it can also include interactive debuggers for helping to locate faults, data dictionaries for keeping track of the data used, and rapid prototyping tools for producing quick, experimental mock-ups of programs. Support environments are sometimes referred to as Integrated Development Environments (IDEs). Common examples are Microsoft Visual Studio (for C++ and Java) and Microfocus (for COB).

Supremacy, Acts of two UK acts of Parliament 1534 and 1559, which established Henry VIII and Elizabeth I respectively as head of the English church in place of the pope.

suprematism Russian abstract art movement launched in St Petersburg in 1915 by Kasimir Malevich, who was virtually its only exponent. It was the most radical abstract art movement up to this date; suprematist paintings used only a few colours and a few basic geometric shapes, such as the square, the circle, the cross, and the triangle.

Supreme Court highest US judicial tribunal, composed since 1869 of a chief justice (William Rehnquist from 1986) and eight associate justices. Appointments are made for life by the president, with the advice and consent of the Senate, and justices can be removed only by impeachment.

Related Web site: Supreme Court Opinion, 1993–1998 http://fedbbs. access.gpo.gov/court01.htm

Supremes, the US vocal group, pioneers of the Motown sound, formed 1959 in Detroit. Beginning in 1962, the group was a trio comprising, initially, Diana Ross (1944–), Mary Wilson (1944–), and Florence Ballard (1943–1976). The most successful female group of the 1960s, they had a string of pop hits beginning with 'Where Did Our Love Go?' (1964) and 'Baby Love' (1964). Diana Ross left to pursue a solo career in 1969.

Surat city and former seaport in Gujarat, west India, 25 km/15 mi from the mouth of the Tapti River; population (1991) 1,499,000. The chief industry is textiles. The main port of the Mogul empire in the 16th and 17th centuries, the first East India Company trading post in India was established here 1612. The town declined as a port until the cotton boom of the 1860s, and its railway junctions revived its importance.

surd expression containing the root of an ▷irrational number that can never be exactly expressed – for example, √3 = 1.732050808... .

surface tension in physics, the property that causes the surface of a liquid to behave as if it were covered with a weak elastic skin; this is why a needle can float on water. It is caused by the exposed surface's tendency to contract to the smallest possible area because of cohesive forces between ▷molecules at the surface. Allied phenomena include the formation of droplets, the concave profile of a meniscus, and the capillary action by which water soaks into a sponge.

surfing sport of riding on the crest of large waves while standing on a narrow, keeled surfboard, usually of light synthetic material such as fibreglass, about 1.8 m/6 ft long (or about 2.4–7 m/8–9 ft known as the Malibu), as first developed in Hawaii and Australia. Windsurfing is a recent development.

Related Web site: Waterman http://www.surfart.com/watrpage.htm

SURFING A surfer on a breaking wave in the ocean off Tahiti. *Image Bank*

surge abnormally high tide; see ▷storm surge.

surgeon fish any fish of the tropical marine family Acanthuridae. It has a flat body up to 50 cm/20 in long, is brightly coloured, and has a movable spine on each side of the tail that can be used as a weapon.

surgery branch of medicine concerned with the treatment of disease, abnormality, or injury by operation. Traditionally it has been performed by means of cutting instruments, but today a number of technologies are used to treat or remove lesions, including ultrasonic waves and laser surgery.

surgical spirit ▷ethanol to which has been added a small amount of methanol to render it unfit to drink. It is used to sterilize surfaces and to cleanse skin abrasions and sores.

Suriname (or **Surinam**) see country box.

surrealism movement in art, literature, and film that developed out of ▷Dada around 1922. Led by André ▷Breton, who produced the *Surrealist Manifesto* (1924), the surrealists were inspired by the thoughts and visions of the subconscious mind. They explored varied styles and techniques, and the movement became the dominant force in Western art between World Wars I and II.

Related Web site: Surrealism http://www.surrealist.com/

Surrey county of southern England.
area 1,660 sq km/641 sq mi towns Kingston upon Thames (administrative headquarters), Farnham, Guildford, Leatherhead, Reigate, Woking, Epsom, Dorking physical rivers Mole, Thames, and Wey; Box Hill (183 m/600 ft), Gibbet Hill (277 m/909 ft), and Leith Hill (299 m/981 ft, 5 km/3 mi south of Dorking, the highest hill in southeast England); North Downs features Kew Palace and Royal Botanic Gardens, Kew; Yehudi Menuhin School (one of four specialist music schools in England) agriculture vegetables; sheep rearing; dairy farming; horticulture industries service industries; sand and gravel quarrying; fuller's earth extraction (near Reigate) population (1996) 1,047,100 famous people Eric Clapton, John Galsworthy, Aldous Huxley, Laurence Olivier

Surrey, Henry Howard, Earl of Surrey (c. 1517–1547) English courtier and poet. With Thomas ▷Wyatt, he introduced the sonnet to England and was a pioneer of ▷blank verse. He was executed on a poorly based charge of high treason.

surrogacy practice whereby a woman is sought, and usually paid, to bear a child for an infertile couple or a single parent.

surveying the accurate measuring of the Earth's crust, or of land features or buildings. It is used to establish boundaries, and to evaluate the topography for engineering work. The measurements used are both linear and angular, and geometry and trigonometry are applied in the calculations.

Survival International organization formed in 1969 to support tribal peoples and their right to decide their own future, and to help them protect their lands, environment, and way of life. It operates in more than 60 countries worldwide. Its headquarters are in London, England.

Sūrya in Hindu mythology, the sun god, son of the sky god Indra. His daughter, also named Sūrya, is a female personification of the Sun.

suslik small Eurasian ground ▷squirrel *Citellus citellus*.

suspension mixture consisting of small solid particles dispersed in a liquid or gas, which will settle on standing. An example is milk of magnesia, which is a suspension of magnesium hydroxide in water.

Sussex former county of England, on the south coast, now divided into ▷East Sussex and ▷West Sussex.

sustainable capable of being continued indefinitely. For example, the sustainable yield of a forest is equivalent to the amount that grows back. Environmentalists made the term a catchword, in advocating the sustainable use of resources.

Sutcliff, Rosemary (1920–1992) English historical novelist. She wrote for both adults and children, and her books include *The Eagle of the Ninth* (1954), *Tristan and Iseult* (1971), and *The Road to Camlann* (1981). Her settings range from the Bronze Age to the 18th century, but her favourite period was the Roman occupation of Britain.

Sutherland, Donald (McNichol) (1934–) Canadian-born US film actor. He often appears in offbeat roles. He starred in *M.A.S.H.* (1970), and his subsequent films include *Klute* (1971), *Don't Look Now* (1973), *Ordinary People* (1980), *Revolution* (1985), *The Art of War* (2000), and *Baltic Storm* (2003). He is the father of actor Kiefer Sutherland.

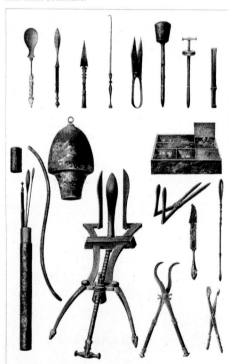

SURGERY Medical and surgical instruments excavated from the house of the surgeon at Pompeii, Italy, in a late 19th-century illustration. These are some of the best-surviving examples of a surgeon's tools from the 1st century BC, and – since innovation in surgical tools was relatively slow after the classical period – are also typical of surgical practice for nearly a millennium. Indeed, some tools, such as the vaginal speculum (bottom centre), changed little until the 20th century. Other instruments seen here include a cupping vessel for blood-letting, forceps, surgical scissors, a male catheter, and scalpels. (Bibliothèque des Arts Décoratifs, Paris). *Art Archive*

Sutherland, Graham Vivian (1903–1980) English painter, graphic artist, and designer. He was active mainly in France from the 1940s. A leading figure of the Neo-Romantic movement (1935–55), which revived the spirit of 19th-century Romanticism in a more modern idiom, he executed portraits, landscapes, and religious subjects, often using a semi-abstract style. In the late 1940s he turned increasingly to portraiture. His portrait of Winston Churchill (1954) was disliked by its subject and eventually burned on the instructions of Lady Churchill (studies survive). He was awarded the OM in 1960.

suttee Hindu custom whereby a widow committed suicide by joining her husband's funeral pyre, often under public and family pressure. Banned in the 17th century by the Mogul emperors, the custom continued even after it was made illegal under British rule in 1829. There continue to be sporadic revivals.

Sutton Hoo archaeological site in Suffolk, England, where in 1939 a Saxon ship burial was excavated. It may be the funeral monument of Raedwald, King of the East Angles, who died about 624 or 625. The jewellery, armour, and weapons discovered were placed in the British Museum, London.

Suu Kyi, Aung San (1945–   ) Myanmar (Burmese) politician and human-rights campaigner, leader of the National League for Democracy (NLD), the main opposition to the military junta. She is the daughter of former Burmese premier ▷Aung San, who fought for the country's independence. Despite Suu Kyi being

placed under house arrest in 1989, the NLD won the 1990 elections, although the junta refused to surrender power. She was awarded the Nobel Prize for Peace in 1991 in recognition of her 'nonviolent struggle for democracy and human rights' in Myanmar. Although officially released from house arrest in 1995, she was banned from resuming any leadership post within the NLD by the junta.

Her liberties continued to be restricted by the Myanmar government, which refused visas to enable her family to visit her, while Suu Kyi believed that she would be refused re-entry to her country if she was to leave. Her situation grabbed international attention in 1998, when it was announced that her husband, Oxford academic Michael Aris, whom she met when she too was at Oxford University, England, was dying of cancer. He was refused a visa and died in March 1999, having not seen his wife for two years.

In August 2000, Suu Kyi was prevented from leaving the capital, Yangon, to go a nearby town to meet members of her League. She was involved in a nine-day roadside protest after which she was put under house arrest for two weeks, as she had been held from 1989 to 1995. This latest restriction on Suu Kyi, who has not been allowed to move freely since 1989, prompted renewed international condemnation of the military government, who also searched the offices of her party, and failed to enter into dialogue with Suu Kyi, or to take any other steps towards reform.

Suzhou (or **Soochow**; formerly **Wuhsien** (1912–49)) city in Jiangsu province, China, south of the Chang Jiang River delta and east of the ▷Grand Canal; population (1994) 1,050,000. Dating from about 1000 BC, it is popularly known as the 'Venice of the East' because of its network of ancient bridges and canals. Traditional silk, embroidery, and other handicrafts have been augmented by papermaking and the production of chemicals, electronics, and telecommunications equipment.

Suzman, Helen Gavronsky (1917–   ) South African politician and human-rights activist. A university lecturer concerned about the inhumanity of the ▷apartheid system, she joined the white opposition to the ruling National Party and became a strong advocate of racial equality, respected by black communities inside and outside South Africa. In 1978 she received the United Nations Human Rights Award. She retired from active politics in 1989.

Suzuki, Zenkō (1911–   ) Japanese politician. Originally a socialist member of the Diet in 1947, he became a conservative (Liberal Democrat) in 1949, and was prime minister 1980–82.

Svalbard Norwegian archipelago in the Arctic Ocean; population (1995) 2,900 (41% being Norwegian). The main island is ▷Spitsbergen, which includes the largest town, Longyearbyen; other islands include Edgeøya, Barentsøya, Svenskøya, Nordaustlandet, Prins Karls Foreland, Wilhelmøya, Lågøya,

---

Suriname

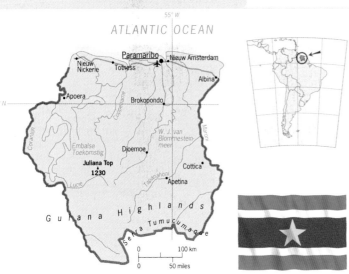

Suriname formerly Dutch Guiana (1954–75) country on the north coast of South America, bounded west by French Guiana, south by Brazil, east by Guyana, and north by the Atlantic Ocean.

NATIONAL NAME *Republiek Suriname/Republic of Suriname*
AREA 163,820 sq km/63,250 sq mi
CAPITAL Paramaribo
MAJOR TOWNS/CITIES Nieuw Nickerie, Moengo, Brokopondo, Nieuw Amsterdam, Albina, Groningen
PHYSICAL FEATURES hilly and forested, with flat and narrow coastal plain; Suriname River

Government

HEAD OF STATE Ronald Venetiaan from 2000
HEAD OF GOVERNMENT Jules Ajodhia from 2000
POLITICAL SYSTEM emergent democracy
POLITICAL EXECUTIVE limited presidency
ADMINISTRATIVE DIVISIONS ten districts
ARMED FORCES 2,000 (2002 est)
CONSCRIPTION military service is voluntary
DEATH PENALTY retains the death penalty for ordinary crimes but can be considered abolitionist in practice; date of last known execution 1982
DEFENCE SPEND (% GDP) 5 (2002 est)
EDUCATION SPEND (% GDP) 5.4 (1997 est)
HEALTH SPEND (% GDP) 9.8 (2000 est)

Economy and resources

CURRENCY Suriname guilder
GPD (US$) 895 million (2002 est)
REAL GDP GROWTH (% change on previous year) 1.9 (2001)
GNI (US$) 828 million (2002 est)
GNI PER CAPITA (PPP) (US$) 3,420 (2002 est)
CONSUMER PRICE INFLATION 20% (2003 est)
UNEMPLOYMENT 20% (2001)
FOREIGN DEBT (US$) 441 million (2001 est)
MAJOR TRADING PARTNERS USA, Norway, Trinidad and Tobago, the Netherlands, Netherlands Antilles, Brazil, Japan
RESOURCES petroleum, bauxite (one of the world's leading producers), iron ore, copper, manganese, nickel, platinum, gold, kaolin
INDUSTRIES bauxite refining and smelting, food processing, beverages, cigarettes, wood products, chemical products, cement
EXPORTS alumina, aluminium, shrimps, bananas, plantains, rice, wood and wood products. Principal market: USA 30.9% (2001)
IMPORTS raw materials and semi-manufactured goods, mineral fuels and lubricants, investment goods, foodstuffs, cars and motorcycles, textiles. Principal source: USA 58.5% (2001)

ARABLE LAND 0.4% (2000 est)
AGRICULTURAL PRODUCTS rice, citrus fruits, bananas, plantains, vegetables, coconuts, cassava, root crops, sugar cane; forest resources; commercial fishing

Population and society

POPULATION 436,000 (2003 est)
POPULATION GROWTH RATE 0.4% (2000–05)
POPULATION DENSITY (per sq km) 3 (2003 est)
URBAN POPULATION (% of total) 76 (2003 est)
AGE DISTRIBUTION (% of total population) 0–14 29%, 15–59 63%, 60+ 8% (2002 est)
ETHNIC GROUPS a wide ethnic composition, including Creoles (34%), East Indians (34%), Indonesians (15%), Africans (10%), American Indians (3%), Chinese (3%), European and others (2%)
LANGUAGE Dutch (official), Spanish, Sranan (Creole), English, Hindi, Javanese, Chinese, various tribal languages
RELIGION Christian 47%, Hindu 28%, Muslim 20%
EDUCATION (compulsory years) 11
LITERACY RATE 94% (men); 91% (women) (2001 est)
LABOUR FORCE 5.6% agriculture, 25.0% industry, 69.1% services (1998)

Chronology

AD **1593**: Visited and claimed by Spanish explorers; the name Suriname derived from the country's earliest inhabitants, the Surinen, who were driven out by other Amerindians in the 16th century.

1602: Dutch settlements established.

1651: British colony founded by settlers sent from Barbados.

1667: Became a Dutch colony, received in exchange for New Amsterdam (New York) by Treaty of Breda.

1682: Coffee and sugar cane plantations introduced, worked by imported African slaves.

1795–1802 and 1804–16: Under British rule.

1863: Slavery abolished and indentured labourers brought in from China, India, and Java.

1915: Bauxite discovered and gradually became main export.

1954: Achieved internal self-government as Dutch Guiana.

1958–69: Politics dominated by Johan Pengel, charismatic leader of the mainly Creole Suriname National Party (NPS).

SURINAME This stamp from Suriname was produced to celebrate the 50th anniversary of the discovery of large bauxite deposits, which revolutionized the economy.
Stanley Gibbons

LIFE EXPECTANCY 69 (men); 74 (women) (2000–05)
CHILD MORTALITY RATE (under 5, per 1,000 live births) 32 (2001)
PHYSICIANS (per 1,000 people) 2.5 (1998 est)
TV SETS (per 1,000 people) 153 (1997)
RADIOS (per 1,000 people) 728 (1997)
INTERNET USERS (per 10,000 people) 330.0 (2002 est)
PERSONAL COMPUTER USERS (per 100 people) 4.6 (2002 est)

1975: Independence achieved, with Dr Johan Ferrier as president and Henck Arron (NPS) as prime minister; 40% of population emigrated to the Netherlands.

1980: Arron's government overthrown in an army coup. The army replaced Ferrier with Dr Chin A Sen.

1982: The army, led by Lt Col Desi Bouterse, seized power, setting up a Revolutionary People's Front; economic aid from the Netherlands and US was cut off after opposition leaders, charged with plotting a coup, were executed.

1985: Ban on political activities lifted.

1989: Bouterse rejected a peace accord reached by President Shankar with guerrilla insurgents, the Bush Negro (descendants of escaped slaves) maroons, and vowed to continue fighting.

1991: A New Front opposition alliance won an assembly majority.

1992: A peace accord was reached with guerrilla groups.

2000: Ronald Venetiaan was chosen as president in August. He had previously been president 1991–96. Jules Ajodhia was elected prime minister.

Storøya, Danskøya, and Sørkappøya. The other main centres of population are the Russian mining settlements of Barentsburg and Grumantbyen. The total land area is 62,000 sq km/23,938 sq mi.

Svedberg, Theodor (1884–1971) Swedish chemist. In 1923 he constructed the first ultracentrifuge, a machine that allowed the rapid separation of particles by mass. This can reveal the presence of contaminants in a sample of a new protein, or distinguish between various long-chain polymers. He was awarded the Nobel Prize for Chemistry in 1926 for his investigation of dispersed systems.

Svengali person who moulds another into a performer and masterminds his or her career. The original Svengali was a character in the novel *Trilby* (1894) by George ▷Du Maurier.

Swabia (German **Schwaben**) historic region of southwestern Germany, an independent duchy in the Middle Ages. It includes Augsburg and Ulm and forms part of the *Länder* (states) of Baden-Württemberg, Bavaria, and Hessen.

Swahili (or **Kiswahili**; Arabic *sawahil* 'language of the coast') language belonging to the Bantu branch of the Niger-Congo family,

widely used in east and central Africa. Swahili originated on the East African coast as a *lingua franca* used among traders, and contains many Arabic loan words. It is an official language in Kenya and Tanzania.

swallow any bird of the family Hirundinidae of small, insect-eating birds in the order Passeriformes, with long, narrow wings, and deeply forked tails. Swallows feed while flying, capturing winged insects in the mouth, which is lined with bristles made viscid (sticky) by a salivary secretion.

Species The **common swallow** *Hirundo rustica* has a dark blue back, brown head and throat, and pinkish breast. It winters in Africa and tropical Asia, and visits Europe April–September. It feeds in flight. Two broods a year are reared in nests of mud, hair, feathers, and straw, shaped like a half-saucer and built on ledges or the rafters of barns. Other species include the **red-rumped swallow** *Cecropsis daurica* of the eastern Mediterranean, and the ▷**martins**. Swallows have declined in Britain by 43% since the late 1960s.

swamp region of low-lying land that is permanently saturated with water and usually overgrown with vegetation; for example, the

everglades of Florida, USA. A swamp often occurs where a lake has filled up with sediment and plant material. The flat surface so formed means that runoff is slow, and the water table is always close to the surface. The high humus content of swamp soil means that good agricultural soil can be obtained by draining.

swan large water bird, with a long slender neck and webbed feet, closely related to ducks and geese. The four species of swan found in the northern hemisphere are white; the three species found in the southern hemisphere are all or partly black. The male (cob) and female (pen) are similar in appearance, and they usually pair for life. They nest on or near water in every continent, except Africa and Antarctica. Swans produce a clutch of 4–6 greenish coloured eggs and their young are known as cygnets. Cygnets are covered with a grey down and only become fully feathered and able to fly after 14–16 weeks.

Swans feed mainly on aquatic plants. They are among the largest and heaviest birds that can fly and because of this require large areas of water to take off. They fly with a slow, graceful wing beat and when migrating, fly in a distinctive V-shaped flock.

Swaziland

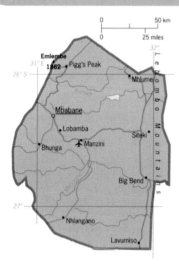

Swaziland country in southeast Africa, bounded east by Mozambique and southeast, south, west, and north by South Africa.

NATIONAL NAME *Umbuso wakaNgwane/Kingdom of Swaziland*
AREA 17,400 sq km/6,718 sq mi
CAPITAL Mbabane (administrative), Lobamba (legislative)
MAJOR TOWNS/CITIES Manzini, Big Bend, Mhlume, Havelock Mine, Nhlangano
PHYSICAL FEATURES central valley; mountains in west (Highveld); plateau in east (Lowveld and Lubombo plateau)

Government
HEAD OF STATE King Mswati III from 1986
HEAD OF GOVERNMENT Themba Dlamini from 1996
POLITICAL SYSTEM absolutist
POLITICAL EXECUTIVE absolute
ADMINISTRATIVE DIVISIONS four regions
ARMED FORCES 120,000 (2002 est)
CONSCRIPTION military service is compulsory for two years
DEATH PENALTY retained and used for ordinary crimes
DEFENCE SPEND (% GDP) 4.7 (2002 est)
EDUCATION SPEND (% GDP) 6.1 (2000 est)
HEALTH SPEND (% GDP) 4.2 (2000 est)

Economy and resources
CURRENCY lilangeni
GPD (US$) 1.2 billion (2002 est)
REAL GDP GROWTH (% change on previous year) 1.8 (2001)
GNI (US$) 1.3 billion (2002 est)
GNI PER CAPITA (PPP) (US$) 4,530 (2002 est)

CONSUMER PRICE INFLATION 9.5% (2003 est)
UNEMPLOYMENT 35% (2001)
FOREIGN DEBT (US$) 281 million (2001 est)
MAJOR TRADING PARTNERS South Africa, EU, Mozambique, Japan, USA, Singapore
RESOURCES coal, asbestos, diamonds, gold, tin, kaolin, iron ore, talc, pyrophyllite, silica
INDUSTRIES food processing, paper, textiles, wood products, beverages, metal products
EXPORTS sugar, wood pulp, cotton yarn, canned fruits, asbestos, coal, diamonds, gold. Principal market: South Africa 59.7% (2000)
IMPORTS machinery and transport equipment, minerals, fuels and lubricants, manufactured items, food and live animals. Principal source: South Africa 92.6% (2000)
ARABLE LAND 10.3% (2000 est)
AGRICULTURAL PRODUCTS sugar cane, cotton, citrus fruits, pineapples, maize, sorghum, tobacco, tomatoes, rice; livestock rearing (cattle and goats); commercial forestry

Population and society
POPULATION 1,077,000 (2003 est)
POPULATION GROWTH RATE 1.3% (2000–15)
POPULATION DENSITY (per sq km) 62 (2003 est)
URBAN POPULATION (% of total) 27 (2003 est)
AGE DISTRIBUTION (% of total population) 0–14 41%, 15–59 54%, 60+ 5% (2002 est)

ETHNIC GROUPS about 95% indigenous African, comprising the Swazi, Zulu, Tonga, and Shangaan peoples; there are European and Afro-European (Eurafrican) minorities numbering around 22,000
LANGUAGE Swazi, English (both official)
RELIGION about 60% Christian, animist
EDUCATION (compulsory years) 7
LITERACY RATE 83% (men); 81% (women) (2003 est)
LABOUR FORCE 33.6% agriculture, 22.3% industry, 44.1% services (2000)
LIFE EXPECTANCY 33 (men); 35 (women) (2000–05)
CHILD MORTALITY RATE (under 5, per 1,000 live births) 149 (2001)
PHYSICIANS (per 1,000 people) 0.2 (1998 est)
TV SETS (per 1,000 people) 128 (2001 est)
RADIOS (per 1,000 people) 162 (2001 est)
INTERNET USERS (per 10,000 people) 193.8 (2002 est)
PERSONAL COMPUTER USERS (per 100 people) 2.4 (2002 est)

SWAZILAND A photograph of a Swazi man, taken in the 1970s. The man is singing as he plays a musical bow with a gourd resonator. Traditionally a warrior race, the Swazi form the majority Bantu group of people in Swaziland in South Africa. *Archive Photos*

Chronology

Late 16th century: King Ngwane II crossed Lubombo mountains from the east and settled in southeast Swaziland; his successors established a strong centralized Swazi kingdom, dominating the long-settled Nguni and Sothi peoples.

mid-19th century: Swazi nation was ruled by the warrior King Mswati who, at the height of his power, controlled an area three times the size of the present-day state.

1882: Gold was discovered in the northwest, attracting European fortune hunters, who coerced Swazi rulers into granting land concessions.

1894: Came under joint rule of Britain and the Boer republic of Transvaal.

1903: Following the South African War, Swaziland became a special British protectorate, or High Commission territory, against South Africa's wishes.

1922: King Sobhuza II succeeded to the Swazi throne.

1968: Independence achieved within the Commonwealth, as the Kingdom of Swaziland, with King (or Ngwenyama) Sobhuza II as head of state.

1973: The king suspended the constitution, banned political activity, and assumed absolute powers after the opposition deputies had been elected to parliament.

1977: The king announced substitution of traditional tribal communities (*tinkhundla*) for the parliamentary system, arguing it was more suited to Swazi values.

1982: King Sobhuza died; his place was taken by one of his wives, Queen Dzeliwe, until his son, Prince Makhosetive, was old enough to become king.

1983: Queen Dzeliwe ousted by a younger wife, Queen Ntombi, as real power passed to the prime minister, Prince Bhekimpi Dlamini.

1986: The crown prince was formally invested as King Mswati III.

1990: Following demands for greater freedom, King Mswati called for the creation of an *indaba* (popular parliament).

1992: King Mswati approved further democratic constitutional amendments.

1993: Direct elections of *tinkhundla* candidates were held for the first time.

1996: Barnabas Sibusiso Dlamini was appointed prime minister.

2000: There was further agitation for democratic reform. When the leader of the opposition party Mario Masuku called for an end to the 27-year-old state of emergency, he was arrested for allegedly making seditious comments.

Sweden

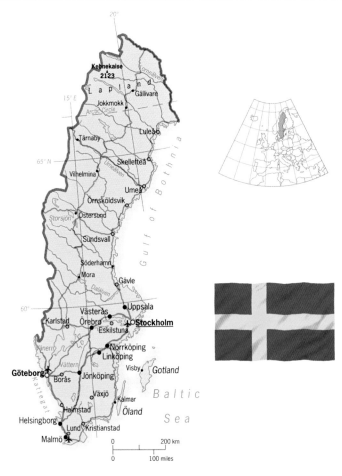

SWEDEN Kalmar Castle in Kalmar, Sweden was originally built in the 14th century. The castle survived 11 different sieges and was rebuilt by King Johan III in the 16th century in the German Renaissance style with turrets, ramparts, and a drawbridge. *Corel*

Sweden country in northern Europe, bounded west by Norway, northeast by Finland and the Gulf of Bothnia, southeast by the Baltic Sea, and southwest by the Kattegat.

NATIONAL NAME *Konungariket Sverige/Kingdom of Sweden*
AREA 450,000 sq km/173,745 sq mi
CAPITAL Stockholm
MAJOR TOWNS/CITIES Göteborg, Malmö, Uppsala, Norrköping, Västerås, Linköping, Orebro, Helsingborg
MAJOR PORTS Helsingborg, Malmö, Göteborg, Stockholm
PHYSICAL FEATURES mountains in west; plains in south; thickly forested; more than 20,000 islands off the Stockholm coast; lakes, including Vänern, Vättern, Mälaren, and Hjälmaren

Government

HEAD OF STATE King Carl XVI Gustaf from 1973
HEAD OF GOVERNMENT Göran Persson from 1996
POLITICAL SYSTEM liberal democracy
POLITICAL EXECUTIVE parliamentary
ADMINISTRATIVE DIVISIONS 24 counties
ARMED FORCES 33,900 (2002 est)
CONSCRIPTION 7–15 months (army and navy) or 8–12 months (air force)
DEATH PENALTY abolished in 1972
DEFENCE SPEND (% GDP) 1.7 (2002 est)
EDUCATION SPEND (% GDP) 7.8 (2000 est)
HEALTH SPEND (% GDP) 8.4 (2000 est)

Economy and resources

CURRENCY Swedish krona
GPD (US$) 229.8 billion (2002 est)
REAL GDP GROWTH (% change on previous year) 0.8 (2001)
GNI (US$) 221.5 billion (2002 est)

GNI PER CAPITA (PPP) (US$) 25,080 (2002 est)
CONSUMER PRICE INFLATION 1.5% (2003 est)
UNEMPLOYMENT 4% (2001)
MAJOR TRADING PARTNERS Germany, UK, Norway, USA, Denmark, France, the Netherlands, Finland
RESOURCES iron ore, uranium, copper, lead, zinc, silver, hydroelectric power, forests
INDUSTRIES motor vehicles, foodstuffs, machinery, precision equipment, iron and steel, metal products, wood products, chemicals, shipbuilding, electrical goods
EXPORTS machinery and transport equipment, forestry products (wood, pulp, and paper), motor vehicles, power-generating non-electrical machinery, chemicals, iron and steel. Principal market: Germany 10.6% (2001)
IMPORTS machinery and transport equipment, chemicals, mineral fuels and lubricants, textiles, clothing, footwear, food and live animals. Principal source: Germany 17.8% (2001)
ARABLE LAND 6.6% (2000 est)
AGRICULTURAL PRODUCTS barley, wheat, oats, potatoes, sugar beet, tame hay, oil seed; livestock and dairy products

Population and society

POPULATION 8,876,000 (2003 est)
POPULATION GROWTH RATE –0.1% (2000–15)
POPULATION DENSITY (per sq km) 20 (2003 est)
URBAN POPULATION (% of total) 83 (2003 est)

AGE DISTRIBUTION (% of total population) 0–14 17%, 15–59 60%, 60+ 23% (2002 est)
ETHNIC GROUPS predominantly of Teutonic descent, with small Saami (Lapp), Finnish, and German minorities
LANGUAGE Swedish (official), Finnish, Saami (Lapp)
RELIGION Evangelical Lutheran, Church of Sweden (established national church) 90%; Muslim, Jewish
EDUCATION (compulsory years) 9

LITERACY RATE 99% (men); 99% (women) (2003 est)
LABOUR FORCE 2.5% agriculture, 25.1% industry, 72.4% services (1999)
LIFE EXPECTANCY 78 (men); 83 (women) (2000–05)
CHILD MORTALITY RATE (under 5, per 1,000 live births) 3 (2001)
PERSONAL COMPUTER USERS (per 100 people) 62.1 (2002 est)

See also ▷Denmark; ▷Finland; ▷Norway; ▷Viking.

Chronology

8th century: Kingdom of the Svear, based near Uppsala, extended its rule across much of southern Sweden.

9th–11th centuries: Swedish Vikings raided and settled along the rivers of Russia.

c. 1000: Olaf Skötkonung, king of the Svear, adopted Christianity and united much of Sweden (except south and west coasts, which remained Danish until 16th century).

11th–13th centuries: Sweden existed as isolated kingdom under the Stenkil, Sverker, and Folkung dynasties; series of crusades incorporated Finland.

1397: Union of Kalmar: Sweden, Denmark, and Norway united under a single monarch; Sweden effectively ruled by succession of regents.

1448: Breach with Denmark: Sweden alone elected Charles VIII as king.

1523: Gustavus Vasa, leader of insurgents, became king of a fully independent Sweden.

1527: Swedish Reformation: Gustavus confiscated Church property and encouraged Lutherans.

1544: Swedish crown became hereditary in House of Vasa.

1592–1604: Sigismund Vasa, a Catholic, was king of both Sweden and Poland until ousted from Swedish throne by his Lutheran uncle Charles IX.

17th century: Sweden, a great military power under Gustavus Adolphus 1611–32, Charles X 1654–60, and Charles XI 1660–97, fought lengthy wars with Denmark, Russia, Poland, and Holy Roman Empire.

1720: Limited monarchy established; political power passed to *Riksdag* (parliament) dominated by nobles.

1721: Great Northern War ended with Sweden losing nearly all its conquests of the previous century.

1741–43: Sweden defeated in disastrous war with Russia; further conflict 1788–90.

1771–92: Gustavus III increased royal power and introduced wide-ranging reforms.

1809: Russian invaders annexed Finland; Swedish nobles staged coup and restored powers of *Riksdag*.

1810: Napoleonic marshal, Jean-Baptiste Bernadotte, elected crown prince of Sweden, as Charles XIII had no heir.

1812: Bernadotte allied Sweden with Russia against France.

1814: Treaty of Kiel: Sweden obtained Norway from Denmark.

1818–44: Bernadotte reigned in Sweden as Charles XIV John.

1846: Free enterprise established by abolition of trade guilds and monopolies.

1866: Series of liberal reforms culminated in new two-chambered *Riksdag* dominated by bureaucrats and farmers.

late 19th century: Development of large-scale forestry and iron-ore industry; neutrality adopted in foreign affairs.

1905: Union with Norway dissolved.

1907: Adoption of proportional representation and universal suffrage.

1920s: Economic boom transformed Sweden from an agricultural to an industrial economy.

1932: Social Democrat government of Per Halbin Hansson introduced radical public-works programme to combat trade slump.

1940–43: Under duress, neutral Sweden permitted limited transit of German forces through its territory.

1946–69: Social Democrat government of Tage Erlander developed comprehensive welfare state.

1959: Sweden joined European Free Trade Association.

1971: Constitution amended to create single-chamber *Riksdag*.

1975: Remaining constitutional powers of monarch removed.

1976–82: Centre–right coalition government under Prime Minister Thorbjörn Fälldin ended 44 years of Social Democrat dominance.

1991: The leader of the Moderate Party, Carl Bildt, headed up a coalition of the Moderate, Centre, Liberal, and Christian Democratic parties.

1995: Sweden became a member of the European Union.

1996: Göran Persson (SAP) became prime minister.

1998: The SAP were narrowly re-elected in a general election.

2003: Voters rejected a proposal to adopt the European Union single currency, the euro, by 56% to 42% in a referendum, despite widespread support for the move among Sweden's political establishment and industrial sector.

In England the swan is a royal bird, as it was once highly valued as food. On the Thames, at the annual 'swan-upping', the cygnets are still marked on the beak as either the property of the crown or of the two privileged City of London companies, the Dyers and Vintners.

The **mute swan** is the most common species. It is native to northern Europe and Asia, but has been introduced and is now widespread in North America. The mute swan has white feathers, black legs and a bright orange flattened bill with a black knob on the upper bill, near the eyes. It may be as long as 150 cm/5 ft in length and weigh as much as 14 kg/30 lb. It hisses loudly when angry.

Swans belong to animal phylum Chordata, class Aves (birds), order Anseriformes, family Anatidae. They belong to the genus *Cygnus*. There are seven species: the mute swan (*Cygnus olor*), the whooper swan (*C. cygnus*), Bewick's swan (*C. bewicki*), the tundra (whistling) swan (*C. columbianus*), the North American trumpeter swan (*C. buccinator*), the black swan of Australia (*C. atratus*), and the South American black-necked swan (*C. melanocoryphus*). The North American trumpeter swan is the largest, with a wingspan of 2.4 m/8 ft.

Swan, Joseph Wilson (1828–1914) English inventor of the incandescent-filament electric lamp and of bromide paper for use in developing photographs. He was knighted in 1904.

Swansea unitary authority in south Wales, created in 1996 from part of the former county of West Glamorgan.
area 377 sq km/146 sq mi **towns** ▷Swansea (administrative headquarters) **physical** River Tawe **features** Gower Peninsula (an area of outstanding natural beauty) **industries** tinplate manufacture, chemicals, oil refineries **population** (1996 est) 231,200

Swansea (Welsh **Abertawe**) port and administrative centre of ▷Swansea unitary authority, south Wales, at the mouth of the River Tawe 70 km/43 mi west of Cardiff; population (1996 est) 231,200. It is the second-largest city in Wales. It has oil refineries, chemicals, metallurgical industries, and tin plate manufacturing, and has produced stained glass since 1936.

Swansea received its first charter in 1210 and a new charter in 1655; it was made a city in 1970. The University College of Swansea, a constituent college of the University of Wales, was established here in 1920. The scientific process of refining copper ore was initiated in the Swansea region.

It is the vehicle-licensing centre of the UK.

Swanson, Gloria (*c.* 1897–1983) Stage name of Gloria Josephine Mae Svenson. US actor. A star of silent films, she became the epitome of glamour during the 1920s. She retired in 1932 but made several major comebacks. Her work includes *Sadie Thompson* (1928), *Queen Kelly* (1928; unfinished), and *Sunset Boulevard* (1950).

SWAPO (acronym for South West Africa People's Organization) organization formed 1959 in South West Africa (now ▷Namibia) to oppose South African rule. SWAPO guerrillas, led by Sam Nujoma, began attacking with support from Angola. In 1966 SWAPO was recognized by the United Nations as the legitimate government of Namibia, and won the first independent election in 1989.

swastika (Sanskrit *svasti* 'prosperity') cross in which the bars are extended at right angles in the same clockwise or anticlockwise direction. Its origin is uncertain, but it appears frequently as an ancient good-luck and religious symbol in both the Old World and the New. A swastika with clockwise bars was adopted as the emblem of the Nazi Party and incorporated into the German national flag 1935–45.

Swatow another name for the Chinese port of ▷Shantou.

Swazi member of the majority Bantu group of people in Swaziland. The Swazi are primarily engaged in cultivating and raising livestock, but many work in industries in South Africa. The Swazi language belongs to the Bantu branch of the Niger-Congo family.

Swazi kingdom South African kingdom, established by Sobhuza I (died 1839), and named after his successor Mswati (ruled 1840–75).

The kingdom was established by Sobhuza as a result of the ▷Mfecane disturbances.

Swaziland see country box.

sweat gland ▷gland within the skin of mammals that produces surface perspiration. In primates, sweat glands are distributed over the whole body, but in most other mammals they are more localized; for example, in cats and dogs they are restricted to the feet and around the face.

sweatshop workshop or factory where employees work long hours under substandard conditions for low wages. Exploitation of labour in this way is associated with unscrupulous employers, who often employ illegal immigrants or children in their labour force.

swede annual or biennial plant widely cultivated for its edible root, which is purple, white, or yellow. It is similar in taste to the turnip but is of greater food value, firmer fleshed, and can be stored for a longer time. (*Brassica napus*, family Cruciferae.)

Sweden see country box.

Swedenborg, Emanuel (1688–1772) Born Emanuel Svedberg. Swedish mystic and scientist. In *Divine Love and Wisdom* (1763), he concluded that the Last Judgement had taken place in 1757, and that the **New Church**, of which he was the prophet, had now been inaugurated. His writings are the scriptures of the sect popularly known as Swedenborgians, and his works are kept in circulation by the Swedenborg Society, London.

Swedish language member of the Germanic branch of the Indo-European language family, spoken in Sweden and Finland and closely related to Danish and Norwegian.

sweet cicely plant belonging to the carrot family, native to southern Europe; the root is eaten as a vegetable, and the aniseed-flavoured leaves are used in salads. (*Myrrhis odorata*, family Umbelliferae.)

sweet pea plant belonging to the ▷pea family.

sweet potato tropical American plant belonging to the morning-glory family; the white-orange tuberous root is used as a source of starch and alcohol and eaten as a vegetable. (*Ipomoea batatas*, family Convolvulaceae.)

sweet william biennial to perennial plant belonging to the pink family, native to southern Europe. It is grown for its fragrant red, white, and pink flowers. (*Dianthus barbatus*, family Caryophyllaceae.)

swift fast-flying, short-legged bird of the family Apodidae, order Apodiformes, of which there are about 75 species, found largely in the tropics. They are 9–23 cm/4–11 in long, with brown or grey plumage, long, pointed wings, and usually a forked tail. They are capable of flying at 110 kph/70 mph.

The nests of the **grey-rumped swiftlet** *Collocalia francica* of Borneo consist almost entirely of solidified saliva, and are harvested for bird's-nest soup. The increasing removal of nests for commercial purposes is endangering the birds.

The **common swift** *Apus apus* is about 16.5 cm/6.5 in long, dark brown with a small greyish white patch under the chin, long swept-back wings, and migrates to Europe in summer from Africa. It catches insects on the wing, and rarely perches except at the nest, even sleeping on the wing high in the air. Swifts often make colonies of nests on buildings, sticking the nest material together with saliva. They lay two or three large white eggs. An occasional visitor to Britain is the **white-bellied** or **Alpine swift** *A. melba*.

Jonathan Swift
Satire is a sort of glass, wherein beholders do generally discover everybody's face but their own.
Battle of the Books

Swift, Jonathan (1667–1745) Irish satirist and Anglican cleric. Born in Dublin, he was educated there at Trinity College, and ordained in 1694. He wrote *Gulliver's Travels* (1726), an allegory describing travel to lands inhabited by giants, miniature people, and intelligent horses. His other works include *The Tale of a Tub* (1704), attacking corruption in religion and learning; and the satirical pamphlet *A Modest Proposal* (1729); written in protest of the on-going famine in Ireland, it suggested that children of the poor should be eaten. His lucid prose style is simple and controlled and he imparted his views with fierce indignation and wit.

Swift became secretary to the diplomat William Temple (1628–1699) at Moor Park, Surrey, where his friendship with the child 'Stella' (Esther Johnson; 1681–1728) began in 1689. Returning to Ireland, he was ordained in the Church of England in 1694, and in 1699 was made a prebendary of St Patrick's, Dublin. He made contributions to the Tory paper *The Examiner*, of which he was editor 1710–11. He obtained the deanery of St Patrick in 1713. His *Journal to Stella* is a series of intimate letters (1710–13), in which he described his life in London. From about 1738 his mind began to fail.

Related Web site: Jonathan Swift Essays http://socserv2.socsci.mcmaster.ca/~econ/ugcm/3ll3/swift/index.html

swim bladder thin-walled, air-filled sac found between the gut and the spine in bony fishes. Air enters the bladder from the gut or from surrounding capillaries (see ▷capillary), and changes of air pressure within the bladder maintain buoyancy whatever the water depth.

swimming self-propulsion of the body through water. There are four strokes in competitive swimming: freestyle, breaststroke, backstroke, and butterfly. Distances of races vary between 50 and 1,500 metres. Olympic-size pools are 50 m/55 yd long and have eight lanes.

Swinburne, Algernon Charles (1837–1909) English poet. He attracted attention with the choruses of his Greek-style tragedy *Atalanta in Calydon* (1865), but he and ▷Rossetti were attacked in 1871 as leaders of 'the fleshly school of poetry', and the revolutionary politics of *Songs before Sunrise* (1871) alienated others. His verse is notable for its emotion and opulent language.

Swindon town and administrative headquarters of ▷Swindon unitary authority in southwest England, 124 km/77 mi west of London; population (1996) 170,000; it was part of the county of Wiltshire until 1997. The site of a major railway engineering works 1841–1986 on the Great Western Railway, the town has diversified since 1950 into such industries as heavy engineering, electronics, electrical manufacture, cars, and also insurance.

There is a railway museum, and the White Horse of Uffington, an ancient hill figure on the chalk downs, is nearby.

Swindon unitary authority in southwest England, created in 1997 from the former district council of Thamesdown.
area 230 sq km/89 sq mi **towns and cities** ▷Swindon (administrative headquarters); villages of Stanton, Fitzwarren, Highworth **features** River Thames forms northern border of authority; Barbury Castle, Iron Age hill fort on Marlborough Downs; Great Weatern Railway Museum and National Monuments Records Centre (Swindon) **industries** insurance, motor vehicle manufacturing, publishing, energy services, high technology industries, information technology **population** (1996) 170,000

swing wing (correctly **variable-geometry wing**) aircraft wing that can be moved during flight to provide a suitable configuration for either low-speed or high-speed flight. The British engineer Barnes Wallis developed the idea of the swing wing, first used on the US-built Northrop X-4, and since used in several aircraft, including the US F-111, F-114, and the B-1, the European Tornado, and several Soviet-built aircraft.

These craft have their wings projecting nearly at right angles for takeoff and landing and low-speed flight, and swung back for high-speed flight.

Swiss cheese plant common name for ▷monstera, a plant belonging to the arum family.

Swithun, St (or St Swithin) (*c.* 800–*c.* 862) English priest, chancellor of King Ethelwolf and bishop of Winchester from 852. According to legend, the weather on his feast day (15 July) determines the weather for the next 40 days.

Switzerland see country box.

swordfish marine bony fish *Xiphias gladius*, the only member of its family (Xiphiidae), characterized by a long swordlike beak protruding from the upper jaw. It may reach 4.5 m/15 ft in length and weigh 450 kg/1,000 lb.

sycamore deciduous tree native to Europe. The leaves are five-lobed, and the hanging clusters of flowers are followed by winged fruits. The timber is used for furniture making. (*Acer pseudoplatanus*.)

SYCAMORE The sycamore is a maple native to southern Europe but widely distributed elsewhere.

Sydenham, Thomas (1624–1689) English physician, the first person to describe measles and to recommend the use of quinine for relieving symptoms of malaria. His original reputation as the 'English Hippocrates' rested upon his belief that careful observation is more useful than speculation. His *Observationes medicae* was published in 1676.

Sydney principal port of Australia and capital of the state of ▷New South Wales; population (1996) 3,276,500. Founded in 1788, Sydney is situated on Port Jackson inlet on the southeast coast of Australia, and is built around a number of bays and inlets that form an impressive natural harbour. Industries include financial services, oil refining, engineering, electronics, and the manufacture of scientific equipment, chemicals, clothing, and furniture. Notable architectural landmarks are the Harbour Bridge, the nearby ▷Sydney Opera House, and Centre Point Tower. There are many parks, as well as coastal beaches ideal for surfing, such as Bondi and Manly. Sydney hosted the Olympic Games in the year 2000.

Originally a British penal colony, Sydney grew rapidly, especially during the gold rushes of the mid-19th century. Many of Sydney's streets follow the original wagon tracks laid down when the land was being prospected for gold.

Related Web site: Sydney Interactive Visitors Guide
http://www.visitorsguide.aust.com/~tourism/sydney/index.html

Sydney Opera House opera house designed by Danish architect Jorn Utzon, located on Bennelong Point, Sydney Harbour, and opened 1973. It is known for the billowing, white, sail-shaped shells that form the roof structure.

syenite grey, crystalline, plutonic (intrusive) ▷igneous rock, consisting of feldspar and hornblende; other minerals may also be present, including small amounts of quartz.

Switzerland

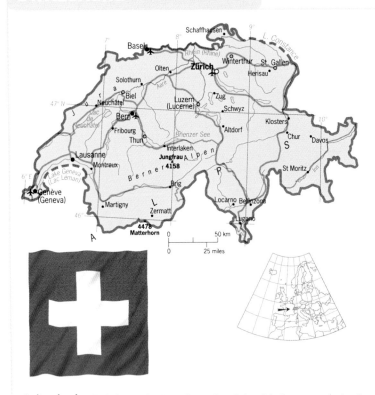

SWITZERLAND A view of Lausanne, Switzerland, showing the 13th-century Gothic cathedral of Notre-Dame. *Swiss National Tourist Office*

Switzerland landlocked country in Western Europe, bounded north by Germany, east by Austria and Liechtenstein, south by Italy, and west by France.

NATIONAL NAME *Schweizerische Eidgenossenschaft* (German)/*Confédération Suisse* (French)/ *Confederazione Svizzera* (Italian)/ *Confederaziun Svizra* (Romansch)/*Swiss Confederation*
AREA 41,300 sq km/15,945 sq mi
CAPITAL Bern
MAJOR TOWNS/CITIES Zürich, Geneva, Basel, Lausanne, Lucerne, St Gallen, Winterthur
MAJOR PORTS river port Basel (on the Rhine)
PHYSICAL FEATURES most mountainous country in Europe (Alps and Jura mountains); highest peak Dufourspitze 4,634 m/15,203 ft in Apennines

Government

HEAD OF STATE AND GOVERNMENT Joseph Deiss from 2004
GOVERNMENT liberal democracy
POLITICAL EXECUTIVE limited presidency
ADMINISTRATIVE DIVISIONS 20 cantons and six demi-cantons
ARMED FORCES 27,600 (2002 est)
DEATH PENALTY abolished in 1992

Economy and resources

CURRENCY Swiss franc
GPD (US$) 268 billion (2002 est)
REAL GDP GROWTH (% change on previous year) 0.9 (2001)
GNI (US$) 274.2 billion (2002 est)
GNI PER CAPITA (PPP) (US$) 31,250 (2002 est)

CONSUMER PRICE INFLATION –0.1% (2003 est)
UNEMPLOYMENT 1.9% (2001)
MAJOR TRADING PARTNERS EU (principally Germany, France, Italy, the Netherlands, and UK), USA, Japan
RESOURCES salt, hydroelectric power, forest
INDUSTRIES heavy engineering, machinery, precision engineering (clocks and watches), jewellery, textiles, chocolate, dairy products, cigarettes, footwear, wine, international finance and insurance services, tourism
EXPORTS pharmaceutical and chemical products, machinery and equipment, foodstuffs, precision instruments, clocks and watches, metal products. Principal market: Germany 22.2% (2001)
IMPORTS machinery and electronic devices, motor vehicles, agricultural and forestry products, vehicles, construction material, fuels and lubricants, chemicals, textiles and clothing. Principal source: Germany 32.2% (2001)
ARABLE LAND 10.4% (2000 est)
AGRICULTURAL PRODUCTS sugar beet, potatoes, wheat, apples, pears, tobacco, grapes; livestock and dairy products, notably cheese

Population and society

POPULATION 7,169,000 (2003 est)
POPULATION GROWTH RATE 0.0% (2000–15)
POPULATION DENSITY (per sq km) 174 (2003 est)

URBAN POPULATION (% of total) 67 (2003 est)
AGE DISTRIBUTION (% of total population) 0–14 16%, 15–59 62%, 60+ 22% (2002 est)
ETHNIC GROUPS German 65%, French 18%, Italian 10%, Romansch 1%
LANGUAGE German (65%), French (18%), Italian (10%), Romansch (1%) (all official)
RELIGION Roman Catholic 46%, Protestant 40%
EDUCATION (compulsory years) 8–9 (depending on canton)
LITERACY RATE 99% (men); 99% (women) (2003 est)
LABOUR FORCE 4.5% agriculture, 26.4% industry, 69.1% services (2000)

Chronology

58 BC: Celtic Helvetii tribe submitted to Roman authority after defeat by Julius Caesar.
4th century AD: Region overrun by Germanic tribes, Burgundians, and Alemannians.
7th century: Formed part of Frankish kingdom and embraced Christianity.
9th century: Included in Charlemagne's Holy Roman Empire.
12th century: Many autonomous feudal holdings developed as power of Holy Roman Empire declined.
13th century: Habsburgs became dominant as overlords of eastern Switzerland.
1291: Cantons of Schwyz, Uri, and Lower Unterwalden formed Everlasting League, a loose confederation to resist Habsburg control.
1315: Battle of Morgarten: Swiss Confederation defeated Habsburgs.
14th century: Luzern, Zürich, Basel, and other cantons joined Swiss Confederation, which became independent of Habsburgs.
1523–29: Zürich, Bern, and Basel accepted Reformation but rural cantons remained Roman Catholic.
1648: Treaty of Westphalia recognized Swiss independence from Holy Roman Empire.
1798: French invasion established Helvetic Republic, a puppet state with centralized government.

LIFE EXPECTANCY 76 (men); 82 (women) (2000–05)
CHILD MORTALITY RATE (under 5, per 1,000 live births) 6 (2001)
PHYSICIANS (per 1,000 people) 3.5 (1999 est)
HOSPITAL BEDS (per 1,000 people) 17.9 (1999 est)
TV SETS (per 1,000 people) 554 (2001 est)
RADIOS (per 1,000 people) 1,002 (2001 est)
INTERNET USERS (per 10,000 people) 3,261.8 (2002 est)
PERSONAL COMPUTER USERS (per 100 people) 58.0 (2002 est)

1803: Napoleon's Act of Mediation restored considerable autonomy to cantons.
1814: End of French domination; Switzerland reverted to loose confederation of sovereign cantons with a weak federal parliament.
1815: Great Powers recognized 'Perpetual Neutrality' of Switzerland.
1845: Seven Catholic cantons founded Sonderbund league to resist any strengthening of central government by Liberals.
1847: Federal troops defeated Sonderbund in brief civil war.
1848: New constitution introduced greater centralization; Bern chosen as capital.
1874: Powers of federal government increased; principle of referendum introduced.
late 19th century: Development of industry, railways, and tourism led to growing prosperity.
1920: League of Nations selected Geneva as its headquarters.
1960: Joined European Free Trade Association (EFTA).
1971: Women gained right to vote in federal elections.
2000: Adolf Ogi was elected president.
2001: Moritz Leuenberger replaced Ogi as president. A proposal for European Union (EU) membership was rejected in a national referendum.
2002: Switzerland became the 190th member of the United Nations (UN) after a public referendum. It maintained its traditional neutrality.

Syktyvkar (formerly **Ust Sysolsk** (1586–1930)) capital of the autonomous republic of ▷Komi, in northern central Russia, 1,100 km/684 mi northeast of Moscow; population (1990) 235,000. Situated on the Vychegda River, it has a large timber industry; other economic activities are paper milling and tanning. The city was founded in 1740 as a Russian colony, and formerly had a flourishing grain and fur trade.

syllable unit of pronunciation within a word, or as a monosyllabic word, made by a vowel or a combination of vowels and consonants. For example, the word 'competition' contains four syllables: 'com/pe/ti/tion'.

syllogism set of philosophical statements devised by Aristotle in his work on logic. It establishes the conditions under which a valid conclusion follows or does not follow by deduction from given premises. The following is an example of a valid syllogism: 'All men are mortal, Socrates is a man, therefore Socrates is mortal.'

symbiosis any close relationship between two organisms of different species, and one where both partners benefit from the association. A well-known example is the pollination relationship between insects and flowers, where the insects feed on nectar and carry pollen from one flower to another. This is sometimes known as ▷mutualism.

Symbiosis in a broader sense includes ▷commensalism, ▷parasitism, and inquilinism (one animal living in the home of another and sharing its food).

symbol in general, something that stands for something else. A symbol may be an aesthetic device or a sign used to convey information visually, thus saving time, eliminating language barriers, or overcoming illiteracy.

symbolic processor computer purpose-built to run so-called symbol-manipulation programs rather than programs involving a great deal of numerical computation. They exist principally for the ▷artificial intelligence language ▷LISP, although some have also been built to run ▷PROLOG.

Symbolism in the arts, the use of symbols as a device for concentrating or intensifying meaning. The Symbolist movement in art flourished during the last two decades of the 19th century. Symbolist painters rejected realism and Impressionism, seeking to express moods and psychological states through colour, line, and form. Their subjects were often mythological, mystical, or fantastic. Gustave Moreau was a leading Symbolist painter. Others included Pierre Puvis de Chavannes and Odilon Redon in France, Arnold Böcklin in Switzerland, Edward Burne-Jones in Britain, and Jan Theodoor Toorop in the Netherlands.

Symbolism late 19th-century movement in French poetry, which inspired a similar trend in French painting. The Symbolist poets used words for their symbolic rather than concrete meaning. Leading exponents were Paul Verlaine, Stéphane Mallarmé, and Arthur Rimbaud.

symmetry exact likeness in shape about a given line (axis), point, or plane. A figure has symmetry if one half can be rotated and/or reflected onto the other. (Symmetry preserves length, angle, but not necessarily orientation.) In a wider sense, symmetry exists if a change in the system leaves the essential features of the system unchanged; for example, reversing the sign of electric charges does not change the electrical behaviour of an arrangement of charges.

symphonic poem in music, a term originated by Franz ▷Liszt for his 13 one-movement orchestral works that interpret a story from literature or history, also used by many other composers. Richard Strauss preferred the term 'tone poem'.

symphony abstract musical composition for orchestra, traditionally in four separate but closely related movements. It developed from the smaller ▷sonata form, the Italian ▷overture, and the concerto grosso.

synagogue in Judaism, a place of worship; in the USA a synagogue is also called a temple by the non-Orthodox. As an institution it dates from the destruction of the Temple in Jerusalem in AD 70, though it had been developing from the time of the Babylonian exile as a substitute for the Temple. In antiquity it was a public meeting hall where the Torah was also read, but today it is used primarily for prayer and services. A service requires a quorum (*minyan*) of ten adult Jewish men.

synapse junction between two ▷nerve cells, or between a nerve cell and a muscle (a neuromuscular junction), across which a nerve impulse is transmitted. The two cells are separated by a narrow gap called the **synaptic cleft**. The gap is bridged by a chemical ▷neurotransmitter, released by the nerve impulse.

synchrotron particle ▷accelerator in which particles move, at increasing speed, around a hollow ring. The particles are guided around the ring by electromagnets, and accelerated by electric fields at points around the ring. Synchrotrons come in a wide range of sizes, the smallest being about 1 m/3.3 ft across while the largest is 27 km/17 mi across. The Tevatron synchrotron at ▷Fermilab is some 6 km/4 mi in circumference and accelerates protons and antiprotons to 1 TeV.

syncline geological term for a fold in the rocks of the Earth's crust in which the layers or ▷beds dip inwards, thus forming a trough-like structure with a sag in the middle. The opposite structure, with the beds arching upwards, is an ▷anticline.

syncopation in music, the deliberate upsetting of rhythm by shifting the accent to a beat that is normally unaccented.

syndicalism (French *syndicat* 'trade union') political movement in 19th-century Europe that rejected parliamentary activity in favour of direct action, culminating in a revolutionary general strike to secure worker ownership and control of industry. After 1918 syndicalism was absorbed in communism, although it continued to have an independent existence in Spain until the late 1930s.

synecdoche (Greek 'accepted together') ▷figure of speech that uses either the part to represent the whole ('There were some *new faces* at the meeting', rather than *new people*), or the whole to stand for the part ('The West Indies beat England at cricket', rather than naming the national teams in question).

synergy in medicine, the 'cooperative' action of two or more drugs, muscles, or organs; applied especially to drugs whose combined action is more powerful than their simple effects added together.

Synge, J(ohn) M(illington) (1871–1909) Irish dramatist and leading figure in the Irish literary revival of the early 20th century, born in Rathfarnham, County Dublin. His six plays, which include *In the Shadow of the Glen* (1903), *Riders to the Sea* (1904), and *The Playboy of the Western World* (1907), reflect the speech patterns of the Aran Islands and western Ireland. *The Playboy of the Western World*, Synge's best-known work, caused violent disturbances at the Abbey Theatre, Dublin, when it was first performed.

Synge, Richard Laurence Millington (1914–1994) British biochemist who improved paper ▷chromatography (a means of separating mixtures) to the point where individual amino acids could be identified. He shared the Nobel Prize for Chemistry in 1952 with his colleague Archer ▷Martin for the development in 1944 of the technique known as partition chromatography.

synovial fluid viscous colourless fluid that bathes movable joints between the bones of vertebrates. It nourishes and lubricates the ▷cartilage at the end of each bone.

syntax the structure of language; the ways in which words are ordered and combined to convey meaning. Syntax applies principally to grammar, and a grammatically correct sentence is also syntactically correct, but syntax has a wider significance.

synthesis in chemistry, the formation of a substance or compound from more elementary compounds. The synthesis of a drug can involve several stages from the initial material to the final product; the complexity of these stages is a major factor in the cost of production.

synthesizer musical device for the simulation of vocal or instrumental ▷timbre by mechanical or electro-acoustic means.

synthetic any material made from chemicals. Since the 1900s, more and more of the materials used in everyday life are synthetics, including plastics (polythene, polystyrene), ▷synthetic fibres (nylon, acrylics, polyesters), synthetic resins, and synthetic rubber. Most naturally occurring organic substances are now made synthetically, especially pharmaceuticals.

synthetic fibre fibre made by chemical processes, unknown in nature. There are two kinds. One is made from natural materials that have been chemically processed in some way; ▷rayon, for example, is made by processing the cellulose in wood pulp. The other type is the true synthetic fibre, made entirely from chemicals. ▷Nylon was the original synthetic fibre, made from chemicals obtained from petroleum (crude oil).

syphilis sexually transmitted disease caused by the spiral-shaped bacterium (spirochete) *Treponema pallidum*. Untreated, it runs its course in three stages over many years, often starting with a painless hard sore, or chancre, developing within a month on the area of infection (usually the genitals). The second stage, months later, is a rash with arthritis, hepatitis, and/or meningitis. The third stage, years later, leads eventually to paralysis, blindness, insanity, and death. The Wassermann test is a diagnostic blood test for syphilis.

Syracuse (Italian **Siracusa**) industrial port (chemicals, salt) in eastern Sicily; population (1992) 126,800. It has a cathedral and remains of temples, aqueducts, catacombs, and an amphitheatre. Founded 734 BC by the Corinthians, it became a centre of Greek culture under the elder and younger ▷Dionysius. After a three-year siege it was taken by Rome 212 BC. In AD 878 it was destroyed by the Arabs, and the rebuilt town came under Norman rule in the 11th century.

Syria see country box.

Syriac language ancient Semitic language, originally the Aramaic dialect spoken in and around Edessa (now in Turkey) and widely used in western Asia from about 700 BC to AD 700. From the 3rd to 7th centuries it was a Christian liturgical and literary language.

syringa common, but not technically accurate, name for the ▷mock orange. The genus *Syringa* includes ▷lilacs, and is not related to the mock orange.

Système International d'Unités official French name for ▷SI units.

systemic in medicine, relating to or affecting the body as a whole. A systemic disease is one where the effects are present throughout the body, as opposed to local disease, such as ▷conjunctivitis, which is confined to one part.

systems analysis in computing, the investigation of a business activity or clerical procedure, with a view to deciding if and how it can be computerized. The analyst discusses the existing procedures with the people involved, observes the flow of data through the business, and draws up an outline specification of the required computer system. The next step is ▷systems design. A recent system is Unified Modeling Language (UML), which is specifically designed for the analysis and design of object-oriented programming systems.

Systems analysis and design methodologies currently in use include Yourdon, SSADM (Structured Systems Analysis and Design Methodology), and Soft Systems Methodology.

systems design in computing, the detailed design of an applications package. The designer breaks the system down into component programs, and designs the required input forms, screen layouts, and printouts. Systems design forms a link between systems analysis and ▷programming.

SYNAGOGUE A Jewish synagogue in the medieval Old Town of Tbilisi, the capital of Georgia. *Corel*

systems program in computing, a program that performs a task related to the operation and performance of the computer system itself. For example, a systems program might control the operation of the display screen, or control and organize backing storage. In contrast, an ▷applications program is designed to carry out tasks for the benefit of the computer user.

Szechwan alternative spelling for the central Chinese province of ▷Sichuan.

Szent-Györgyi, Albert von Nagyrapolt (1893–1986) Hungarian-born US biochemist who was awarded a Nobel Prize for Physiology or Medicine in 1937 for his investigation of biological oxidation processes and of the action of ascorbic acid (vitamin C).

Syria

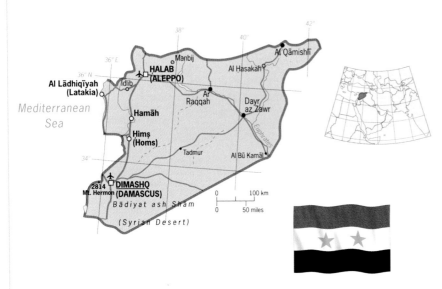

SYRIA Corridor in the crusader castle of Krak Des Chevaliers, the principal garrison of the Knights of St John (Hospitallers). It was usual for 2,000 soldiers to be garrisoned here, behind the two concentric towered walls separated by a wide moat. Built from around 1115 onwards, it was held by the Knights Hospitaller until 1271, when it was overcome by the trickery of the Mameluke sultan of Egypt, Baibars I. *Photodisk*

Syria country in western Asia, on the Mediterranean Sea, bounded to the north by Turkey, east by Iraq, south by Jordan, and southwest by Israel and Lebanon.

NATIONAL NAME *al-Jumhuriyya al-Arabiyya as-Suriyya/Syrian Arab Republic*
AREA 185,200 sq km/71,505 sq mi
CAPITAL Damascus
MAJOR TOWNS/CITIES Aleppo, Homs, Latakia, Hama, Ar Raqqah, Deir-es-Zor
MAJOR PORTS Latakia
PHYSICAL FEATURES mountains alternate with fertile plains and desert areas; Euphrates River

Government

HEAD OF STATE Bashar al-Assad from 2000
HEAD OF GOVERNMENT Naji al-Otari from 2003
POLITICAL SYSTEM nationalistic socialist
POLITICAL EXECUTIVE unlimited presidency
ADMINISTRATIVE DIVISIONS 14 provinces
ARMED FORCES 319,000; plus paramilitary forces of 108,800 (2002 est)
CONSCRIPTION 30 months
DEATH PENALTY retained and used for ordinary crimes
DEFENCE SPEND (% GDP) 10.3 (2002 est)
EDUCATION SPEND (% GDP) 4.1 (2001 est)
HEALTH SPEND (% GDP) 2.5 (2000 est)

Economy and resources

CURRENCY Syrian pound
GPD (US$) 21.9 billion (2002 est)
REAL GDP GROWTH (% change on previous year) 1.7 (2001)
GNI (US$) 19.2 billion (2002 est)
GNI PER CAPITA (PPP) (US$) 3,250 (2002 est)
CONSUMER PRICE INFLATION 2.5% (2003 est)
UNEMPLOYMENT RATE 20% (2000)
FOREIGN DEBT (US$) 16.7 billion (2001 est)
MAJOR TRADING PARTNERS Germany, Ukraine, Turkey, Italy, France, Lebanon, Japan
RESOURCES petroleum, natural gas, iron ore, phosphates, salt, gypsum, sodium chloride, bitumen
INDUSTRIES petroleum and petroleum products, coal, rubber and plastic products, textiles, clothing, leather products, tobacco, processed food
EXPORTS crude petroleum, textiles, vegetables, fruit, raw cotton, natural phosphate. Principal market: France 20.6% (2001)

IMPORTS manufactured goods, machinery and transport equipment, chemicals, crude petroleum, wheat, base metals, metal products, foodstuffs. Principal source: Italy 8.6% (2001)
ARABLE LAND 24.7% (2000 est)
AGRICULTURAL PRODUCTS cotton, wheat, barley, maize, olives, lentils, sugar beet, fruit, vegetables; livestock (principally sheep and goats)

Population and society

POPULATION 17,800,000 (2003 est)
POPULATION GROWTH RATE 2.1% (2000–15)
POPULATION DENSITY (per sq km) 96 (2003 est)
URBAN POPULATION (% of total) 52 (2003 est)
AGE DISTRIBUTION (% of total population) 0–14 39%, 15–59 56%, 60+ 5% (2002 est)
ETHNIC GROUPS predominantly Arab, with many differences in language and regional affiliations; Kurds, Armenian
LANGUAGE Arabic (89%) (official), Kurdish (6%), Armenian (3%), French, English, Aramaic, Circassian
RELIGION Sunni Muslim 74%; other Islamic sects 16%, Christian 10%
EDUCATION (compulsory years) 6
LITERACY RATE 90% (men); 64% (women) (2003 est)
LABOUR FORCE 28.4% agriculture, 27.3% industry, 44.3% services (1999)
LIFE EXPECTANCY 71 (men); 73 (women) (2000–05)
CHILD MORTALITY RATE (under 5, per 1,000 live births) 28 (2001)
PHYSICIANS (per 1,000 people) 1.4 (1998 est)
HOSPITAL BEDS (per 1,000 people) 1.5 (1998 est)
TV SETS (per 1,000 people) 64 (2001 est)
RADIOS (per 1,000 people) 276 (2001 est)
INTERNET USERS (per 10,000 people) 129.1 (2002 est)
PERSONAL COMPUTER USERS (per 100 people) 1.9 (2002 est)

See also ▷Assad, Hafez al; ▷Ba'ath Party; ▷Druze.

Chronology

c.1750 BC: Syria became part of Babylonian Empire; during the next millennium it was successively conquered by Hittites, Assyrians, Chaldeans, and Persians.
333 BC: Alexander the Great of Macedonia conquered Persia and Syria.
301 BC: Seleucus I, one of the generals of Alexander the Great, founded the kingdom of Syria, which the Seleucid dynasty ruled for over 200 years.
64 BC: Syria became part of Roman Empire.
4th century AD: After division of Roman Empire, Syria came under Byzantine rule.
634: Arabs conquered most of Syria and introduced Islam.
661–750: Damascus was the capital of Muslim Empire.
1055: Seljuk Turks overran Syria.
1095–99: First Crusade established Latin states on Syrian coast.
13th century: Mameluke sultans of Egypt took control.
1516: Ottoman Turks conquered Syria.
1831: Egyptians led by Mehemet Ali drove out Turks.
1840: Turkish rule restored; Syria opened up to European trade.
late 19th century: French firms built ports, roads, and railways in Syria.
1916: Sykes-Picot Agreement: secret Anglo-French deal to partition Turkish Empire allotted Syria to France.
1918: British expelled Turks with help of Arab revolt.
1919: Syrian national congress called for independence under Emir Faisal and opposed transfer to French rule.
1920: Syria became League of Nations protectorate, administered by France.
1925: People's Party founded to campaign for independence and national unity; insurrection by Druze religious sect against French control.
1936: France promised independence within three years, but martial law imposed in 1939.
1941: British forces ousted Vichy French regime in Damascus and occupied Syria in conjunction with Free French.
1944: Syrian independence proclaimed but French military resisted transfer of power.
1946: Syria achieved effective independence when French forces withdrew.
1948–49: Arab–Israeli War: Syria joined unsuccessful invasion of newly independent Israel.

1958: Syria and Egypt merged to form United Arab Republic (UAR).
1959: USSR agreed to give financial and technical aid to Syria.
1961: Syria seceded from UAR.
1964: Ba'ath Socialist Party established military dictatorship.
1967: Six-Day War: Syria lost Golan Heights to Israel.
1970–71: Syria invaded Jordan in support of Palestinian guerrillas.
1971: Hafez al-Assad was elected president.
1973: Yom Kippur War: Syrian attack on Israel repulsed.
1976: Start of Syrian military intervention in Lebanese civil war.
1978: Syria opposed peace deal between Egypt and Israel.
1986: Britain broke off diplomatic relations, accusing Syria of involvement in international terrorism.
1990: Diplomatic links with Britain were restored.
1991: Syria contributed troops to a US-led coalition in the Gulf War against Iraq. A US Middle East peace plan was approved by Assad.
1994: Israel offered a partial withdrawal from the Golan Heights in return for peace, but Syria remained sceptical.
1995: A security framework agreement was made with Israel. 1,200 political prisoners, including members of the banned Muslim Brotherhood, were released to commemorate the 25th anniversary of President Assad's seizure of power.
1996: Syria re-deployed armed forces in southern Lebanon.
1997: Three border points with Iraq, closed since 1980, were re-opened.
1998: Relations with Israel deteriorated after Israeli forces seized land cultivated by Arab farmers in the Golan heights.
1999: Amnesty International charged Syrian authorities with human rights abuses and called for the release of over 300 political prisoners. Peace talks with Israel over Lebanon and the Golan Heights resumed after a break of three years. Relations with Iraq were normalized.
2000: Further peace talks were held with Israel, and Israel withdrew from the Golan Heights. President Assad appointed Muhammad Mustafa Miro as prime minister. President Assad died in June, and his son Bashar became president. The Iraq-Syria border re-opened.
2001: Syria signed a free-trade accord with Iraq.
2003: In parliamentary elections the ruling National Progressive Front retained its constitutionally mandated majority.

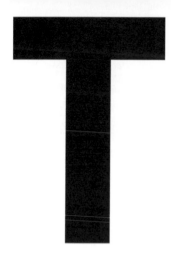

T

Table Bay wide bay on the north coast of the Cape of Good Hope, South Africa, on which Cape Town stands. It is overlooked by Table Mountain.

table tennis (or **ping pong**) indoor game played on a rectangular table by two or four players. It was developed in Britain in about 1880 and derived from lawn tennis. World championships were first held in 1926.

taboo (Polynesian *tabu*, 'that contact would profane') prohibition applied to magical and religious objects. In psychology and the social sciences the term refers to practices that are generally prohibited because of religious or social pressures; for example, ▷incest is forbidden in most societies.

Tachisme (French 'blotting, staining') French style of abstract painting current in the 1940s and 1950s, the European equivalent to ▷abstract expressionism. Breaking free from the restraints of ▷cubism, the Tachistes adopted a novel, spontaneous approach to brushwork, typified by all-over blotches of impastoed colour and dribbled paint, or swirling calligraphy applied straight from the tube, as in the work of Georges Mathieu. The terms **L'Art Informel**, meaning gestural or ▷action painting, and **abstraction lyrique** ('lyrical abstraction') are also used to describe the style.

tachograph combined speedometer and clock that records a vehicle's speed and the length of time the vehicle is moving or stationary. It is used to monitor a lorry driver's working hours.

Tacitus, Publius Cornelius (AD 55–c. 120) Roman historian. A public orator in Rome, he was consul under Nerva 97–98 and proconsul of Asia 112–113. He wrote histories of the Roman empire, *Annales* and *Historiae*, covering the years 14–68 and 69–97 respectively. He also wrote a *Life of Agricola* in 97 (he married Agricola's daughter in 77) and a description of the Germanic tribes, *Germania* in 98.

Related Web site: Works by P Cornelius Tacitus http://classics.mit. edu/Browse/browse-Tacitus.html

Taegu third-largest city in South Korea, situated between Seoul and Pusan; population (1995 est) 2,331,000. Nearby is the Haeinsa Temple (dating from 802), one of the country's largest monasteries and repository of the *Triptaka Koreana*, a collection of 80,000 wood blocks on which the Buddhist scriptures are carved. Grain, fruit, textiles, and tobacco are produced.

Taejon (Korean 'large rice paddy') capital of South Chungchong province, central South Korea; population (1995 est) 1,111,000. Korea's tallest standing Buddha and oldest wooden building are found northeast of the city at Popchusa in the Mount Songnisan National Park.

tae kwon do Korean ▷martial art similar to ▷karate, which includes punching and kicking. It was included in the 1988 Olympic Games as a demonstration sport, and became a full medal discipline at the Sydney 2000 Olympic Games.

taffeta (Persian 'spun') light, plain-weave fabric with a high lustre, originally silk but today also manufactured from artificial fibres.

Taft, William Howard (1857–1930) 27th president of the USA 1909–13, a Republican. He was secretary of war 1904–08 in Theodore Roosevelt's administration, but as president his conservatism provoked Roosevelt to stand against him in the 1912 election. Taft served as chief justice of the Supreme Court 1921–30.

Born in Cincinnati, Ohio, Taft graduated from Yale University and Cincinnati Law School. He was appointed US solicitor general in 1890 and became a federal circuit court judge in 1892. His first interest was always the judiciary, although he accepted a post as governor of the Philippines and took responsibility for the construction of the ▷Panama Canal. His single term as president was characterized by struggles against progressives, although he prosecuted more trusts than had his predecessor. As chief justice of the Supreme Court, he supported a minimum wage.

Related Web site: William Howard Taft – Twenty-seventh President 1909–1913 http://www.whitehouse.gov/WH/glimpse/presidents/html/wt27.html

Tagalog the majority ethnic group living around Manila on the island of Luzon, in the Philippines, who number about 10 million (1988). The Tagalog live by fishing and trading. In its standardized form, known as Pilipino, Tagalog is the official language of the Philippines, and belongs to the Western branch of the Austronesian family. The Tagalog religion is a mixture of animism, Christianity, and Islam.

tagging, electronic long-distance monitoring of the movements of people charged with or convicted of a crime, thus enabling them to be detained in their homes rather than in prison.

Tagore, Rabindranath (1861–1941) Bengali Indian writer. He translated into English his own verse *Gitanjali/Song Offerings* (1912) and his verse play *Chitra* (1896). He was awarded the Nobel Prize for Literature in 1913.

An ardent nationalist and advocate of social reform, he resigned his knighthood as a gesture of protest against British repression in India.

Related Web site: 'Gitanjali' http://etext.lib.virginia.edu/etcbin/browse-mixed-new?id=TagGita&tag=public&images=images/modeng&data=/texts/english/modeng/parsed

RABINDRANATH TAGORE A photograph from the 1920s shows Indian philosopher and poet Rabindranath Tagore with Albert Einstein (on the left). *Archive Photos*

Tagus (Spanish **Tajo**, Portuguese **Tejo**) river in Spain and Portugal; length 1,007 km/626 mi. It rises in the Sierra de Albarracín, Spain, on the border between the provinces of Cuenca and Teruel. It flows west past Toledo and Alcántara, then follows the Spanish-Portuguese frontier for 50 km/31 mi, and crosses Portugal to the Atlantic Ocean at Lisbon.

Tahiti largest of the Society Islands, in ▷French Polynesia; area 1,042 sq km/402 sq mi; population (1996) 150,700. Its capital is Papeete. The volcano, Orohena, reaches 2,237 m/7,339 ft, and much of the soil is volcanic, producing coconuts, sugar cane, and vanilla. Tourism is increasingly important as a source of revenue. Captain James ▷Cook observed the transit of Venus across the sun during a visit to Tahiti in 1769. It came under French control in 1843 and became a colony in 1880. Paul ▷Gauguin, French painter, lived here 1891–93, painting many pictures of local people.

Related Web site: Tahiti http://tahiti.com/

Tai member of any of the groups of Southeast Asian peoples who speak Tai languages, all of which belong to the Sino-Tibetan language family. There are over 60 million speakers, the majority of whom live in Thailand. Tai peoples are also found in southwestern China, northwestern Myanmar (Burma), Laos, and North Vietnam.

T'ai Chi series of 108 complex, slow-motion movements, each named (for example, the White Crane Spreads Its Wings) and designed to ensure effective circulation of the **chi**, or intrinsic energy of the universe, through the mind and body. It derives partly from the Shaolin ▷martial arts of China and partly from ▷Taoism.

taiga (or **boreal forest**) Russian name for the forest zone south of the ▷tundra, found across the northern hemisphere. Here, dense

forests of conifers (spruces and hemlocks), birches, and poplars occupy glaciated regions punctuated with cold lakes, streams, bogs, and marshes. Winters are prolonged and very cold, but the summer is warm enough to promote dense growth.

The varied fauna and flora are in delicate balance because the conditions of life are so precarious. This ecology is threatened by mining, forestry, and pipeline construction.

taipan species of small-headed cobra *Oxyuranus scutellatus*, found in northeastern Australia and New Guinea. It is about 3 m/10 ft long, and has a brown back and yellow belly. Its venom is fatal within minutes.

Taipei (or **Taibei**) capital and commercial centre of Taiwan; population (1995) 2,639,300. Industries include electronics, plastics, textiles, and machinery. The National Palace Museum (1965) houses the world's greatest collection of Chinese art, brought here from the mainland in 1948.

Taiping Rebellion popular revolt 1850–64 that undermined China's Qing dynasty (see ▷Manchu). By 1853 the rebels had secured control over much of the central and lower Chang Jiang valley region, instituting radical, populist land reforms. Civil war continued until 1864, when the Taipings, weakened by internal dissension, were overcome by the provincial Hunan army of ▷Zeng Guofan and the Ever-Victorious Army, led by American F T Ward and British soldier Charles ▷Gordon.

Related Web site: Taiping Rebellion 1851–64 http://www-chaos.umd.edu/history/modern2.html#taiping

Taira (also known as **Heike**) in Japanese history, a military clan prominent in the 10th to 12th centuries and dominant at court 1159–85. Their destruction by their rivals, the ▷Minamoto, in 1185 is the subject of the 13th-century literary classic *Heike Monogatari/The Tale of the Heike*.

Taiwan see country box. Taiwan is not recognized by a number of countries.

Taiyuan capital of ▷Shanxi province, north China, on the River Fen He; population (1994) 2,086,300. Lying in a rich coal and iron-mining district, it is one of the most important centres of heavy industry in the north; heavy and agricultural machinery, iron, steel, and textiles are produced. It is the seat of Shanxi University.

Taizé ecumenical Christian community based in the village of that name in southeastern France. Founded in 1940 by Swiss theologian Roger Schutz, it has been a communal centre for young Christians since the 1960s.

Tajik (or **Tadzhik**) member of the majority ethnic group in Tajikistan. Tajiks also live in Afghanistan and parts of Pakistan and western China. The Tajiki language belongs to the West Iranian sub-branch of the Indo-European family, and is similar to Farsi; it is written in the Cyrillic script. The Tajiks have long been associated with neighbouring Turkic peoples and their language contains Altaic loan words. The majority of the Tajik people are Sunni Muslims; there is a Shiite minority in Afghanistan.

Tajikistan (formerly **Tadzhikistan**, to 1991) see country box.

Taj Mahal white marble mausoleum built 1630–53 on the River Yamuna near Agra, India. Erected by Shah Jahan to the memory of his favourite wife, it is a celebrated example of Indo-Islamic architecture, the fusion of Muslim and Hindu styles.

Related Web site: Taj Mahal http://www.erols.com/zenithco/tajmahal.html

Tajo Spanish name for the River ▷Tagus.

takahe flightless bird *Porphyrio mantelli* of the rail family, order Gruiformes, native to New Zealand. It is about 60 cm/2 ft tall and weighs just over 2 kg/4.4 lb, with blue and green plumage and a red bill. The takahe was thought to have become extinct at the end of

TAKAHE The takahe, native to New Zealand, was once thought to be extinct, but now its habitat is protected and numbers are gradually increasing. In 1995 there were approximately 180 birds.

Related Web site: Works by P Cornelius Tacitus http://classics.mit. edu/Browse/browse-Tacitus.html

> **Publius Cornelius Tacitus**
> *I shall write without anger or bias.*
> *Annals* bk 1, ch. 1

TAIWAN Memorial to the Chinese leader of the nationalist Guomindang (Kuomintang), in Taipeh, Taiwan. *Image Bank*

Taiwan not recognized by the UN: (formerly Formosa, until 1949) country in east Asia, officially the Republic of China, occupying the island of Taiwan between the East China Sea and the South China Sea, separated from the coast of China by the Taiwan Strait.

NATIONAL NAME *Chung-hua Min-kuo/Republic of China*
AREA 36,179 sq km/13,968 sq mi
CAPITAL Taipei
MAJOR TOWNS/CITIES Kaohsiung, Taichung, Tainan, Panchiao, Chungho, Sanchung
MAJOR PORTS Kaohsiung, Keelung
PHYSICAL FEATURES island (formerly Formosa) off People's Republic of China; mountainous, with lowlands in west; Penghu (Pescadores), Jinmen (Quemoy), Mazu (Matsu) islands

Government

HEAD OF STATE Chen Shui-bian from 2000
HEAD OF GOVERNMENT Yu Shyi-kun from 2002
POLITICAL SYSTEM emergent democracy
POLITICAL EXECUTIVE limited presidency
ADMINISTRATIVE DIVISIONS 16 counties, five municipalities, and two special municipalities (Taipei and Kaohsiung)
ARMED FORCES 370,000; plus paramilitary forces of 26,700 and reserves of 1,657,500 (2002 est)
CONSCRIPTION military service is compulsory for 20 months
DEATH PENALTY retained and used for ordinary crimes
DEFENCE SPEND (% GDP) 2.7 (2002 est)
EDUCATION SPEND (% GDP) 2.4 (2000 est)
HEALTH SPEND (% GDP) 5.4 (2000 est)

Economy and resources

CURRENCY New Taiwan dollar
GPD (US$) 278.2 billion (2002 est)

REAL GDP GROWTH (% change on previous year) −2.2 (2001)
GNI (US$) 286.8 billion (2002 est)
GNI PER CAPITA (PPP) (US$) 22,650 (2002 est)
CONSUMER PRICE INFLATION 0.7% (2003 est)
UNEMPLOYMENT 4.6% (2001)
FOREIGN DEBT (US$) 31.7 billion (2001 est)
MAJOR TRADING PARTNERS USA, Japan, Hong Kong, Germany, Singapore, the Netherlands, Malaysia, Indonesia, South Korea, Australia
RESOURCES coal, copper, marble, dolomite; small reserves of petroleum and natural gas
INDUSTRIES electronics, plastic and rubber goods, textiles and clothing, base metals, vehicles, aircraft, ships, footwear, cement, fertilizers, paper
EXPORTS electronic products, base metals and metal articles, textiles and clothing, machinery, information and communication products, plastic and rubber products, vehicles and transport equipment, footwear, headwear, umbrellas, toys, games, sports equipment. Principal market: USA 22.5% (2001)
IMPORTS machinery and transport equipment, basic manufactures, chemicals, base metals and metal articles, minerals, textile products, crude petroleum, plastics, precision instruments, clocks and watches, musical instruments. Principal source: Japan 24.1% (2001)
ARABLE LAND 24% (1998)
AGRICULTURAL PRODUCTS rice, tea, bananas, pineapples, sugar cane, maize, sweet potatoes, soybeans, peanuts; fishing; forest resources

Population and society

POPULATION 22,500,000 (2002 est)
POPULATION GROWTH RATE 1.0% (1995–2000)
POPULATION DENSITY (per sq km) 620 (2002 est)
URBAN POPULATION (% of total) 80 (2000 est)
AGE DISTRIBUTION (% of total population) 0–14 21%, 15–59 68%, 60+ 11% (2001 est)
ETHNIC GROUPS 98% Han Chinese and 2% aboriginal by descent; around 84% are Taiwan-born and 14% are 'mainlanders'
LANGUAGE Chinese (dialects include Mandarin (official), Min, and Hakka)
RELIGION officially atheist; Buddhist 23%, Taoist 18%, I-Kuan Tao 4%, Christian 3%, Confucian and other 3%
EDUCATION (compulsory years) 9

See also ▷China; ▷Guomindang; ▷Sino-Japanese Wars.

LITERACY RATE 97% (men); 95% (women) (2003 est)
LABOUR FORCE 9.6% agriculture, 28.5% industry, 61.9% services (1997)
LIFE EXPECTANCY 74 (men); 80 (women) (2001 est)
CHILD MORTALITY RATE (under 5, per 1,000 live births) 7 (1997 est)
PHYSICIANS (per 1,000 people) 1.54 (2001 est)
HOSPITAL BEDS (per 1,000 people) 5.7 (2001 est)
TV SETS (per 1,000 people) 362 (1996)
RADIOS (per 1,000 people) 744 (1994)
INTERNET USERS (per 10,000 people) 3,825.1 (2002 est)
PERSONAL COMPUTER USERS (per 100 people) 39.6 (2002 est)

Chronology

7th century AD: Island occupied by aboriginal community of Malayan descent; immigration of Chinese from mainland began, but remained limited before 15th century.

1517: Sighted by Portuguese vessels en route to Japan and named Ilha Formosa ('beautiful island').

1624: Occupied and controlled by Dutch.

1662: Dutch defeated by Chinese Ming general, Cheng Ch'eng-kung (Koxinga), whose family came to rule Formosa for a short period.

1683: Annexed by China's rulers, the Manchu Qing.

1786: Major rebellion against Chinese rule.

1860: Ports opened to Western trade.

1895: Ceded 'in perpetuity' to Japan under Treaty of Shominoseki at end of Sino-Japanese war.

1945: Recovered by China's Nationalist Guomindang government at end of World War II.

1947: Rebellion against Chinese rule brutally suppressed.

1949: Flight of Nationalist government, led by Generalissimo Jiang Jie Shi (Chiang Kai-shek), to Taiwan after Chinese communist revolution. They retained the designation of Republic of China (ROC), claiming to be the legitimate government for all China, and were recognized by USA and United Nations (UN). Taiwan replaced Formosa as the name of the country.

1950s onwards: Rapid economic growth as Taiwan became a successful export-orientated Newly Industrializing Country (NIC).

1954: US–Taiwanese mutual defence treaty.

1971: Expulsion from UN as USA adopted new policy of détente towards communist China.

1972: Commencement of legislature elections as a programme of gradual democratization and Taiwanization was launched by the mainlander-dominated Guomindang.

1975: President Jiang Jie Shi died; replaced as Guomindang leader by his son, Jiang Ching-kuo.

1979: USA severed diplomatic relations and annulled the 1954 security pact.

1986: Centrist Democratic Progressive Party (DPP) formed as opposition to nationalist Guomindang.

1987: Martial law lifted; opposition parties legalized; press restrictions lifted.

1988: President Jiang Ching-kuo died; replaced by Taiwanese-born Lee Teng-hui.

1990: Chinese-born Guomindang members became a minority in parliament.

1991: President Lee Teng-hui declared an end to the civil war with China. The constitution was amended. Guomindang won a landslide victory in elections to the new National Assembly, the 'superparliament'.

1993: A cooperation pact was signed with China.

1996: Lee Teng-hui was elected president in the first ever Chinese democratic elections.

1997: The government narrowly survived a no-confidence motion. Vincent Siew became prime minister.

1998: President Lee Teng-hui announced that reunion with mainland China was impossible until Beijing adopted democracy. The ruling Guomindang increased its majority in parliamentary and local elections.

2000: Despite threats of invasion from China if Taiwan made moves towards independence, a pro-independence president, Chen Shui-bian, was elected, who appointed a member of the former government, Tang Fei, as prime minister. Tang Fei was replaced by Chang Chun-hsiung after he resigned in October.

2001: Taiwan partially lifted its 52-year ban on direct trade and communications with China.

the 19th century, but in 1948 small numbers were rediscovered in the tussock grass of a mountain valley on South Island.

Takao Japanese name for ▷Kaohsiung, a city on the west coast of Taiwan.

takeover in business, the acquisition by one company of a sufficient number of shares in another company to have effective control of that company – usually 51%, although a controlling stake may be as little as 30%.

Takeshita, Noboru (1924–2000) Japanese conservative politician. Elected to parliament as a Liberal Democratic Party (LDP) deputy in 1958, he became president of the LDP and prime minister in 1987. He and members of his administration were shown in the ▷Recruit scandal to have been involved in insider trading and he resigned in 1989.

Talbot, William Henry Fox (1800–1877) English pioneer of photography. He invented the paper-based ▷calotype process in 1841, the first negative/positive method. Talbot made photograms several years before Louis Daguerre's invention was announced.

talc $Mg_3Si_4O_{10}(OH)_2$, mineral, hydrous magnesium silicate. It occurs in tabular crystals, but the massive impure form, known as **steatite** or **soapstone**, is more common. It is formed by the alteration of magnesium compounds and is usually found in metamorphic rocks. Talc is very soft, ranked 1 on the Mohs scale of hardness. It is used in powdered form in cosmetics, lubricants, and as an additive in paper manufacture.

Talgai skull cranium of a pre-adult male, dating from 10,000–20,000 years ago, found at Talgai station, southern Queensland, Australia. It was one of the earliest human

archaeological finds in Australia, having been made in 1886. Its significance was not realized, however, until the work of Edgeworth David and others after 1914. The skull is large with heavy eyebrow ridges and cheekbones.

Talibaan ('the Seekers') Afghan political and religious military force which seized control of southern and central Afghanistan, including the country's capital, Kabul, in September 1996. An Islamic regime was imposed, and by the end of 1996 the Talibaan controlled two-thirds of the country. In 1997 the Talibaan changed the country's official name to the Islamic Emirate of Afghanistan. The Talibaan receives financial support from Saudi Arabia, but the regime was, as of mid-1998, recognized by only three states: Saudi Arabia, the United Arab Emirates, and Pakistan. In September 2000 the Talibaan claimed to control 95% of Afghanistan and declared

Tajikistan

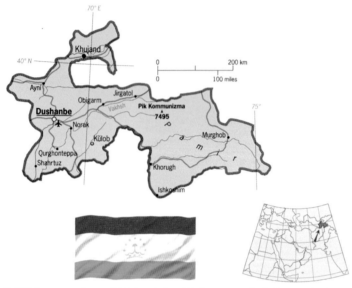

TAJIKISTAN
These yurts are on the Karakoram Highway where it traverses the Pamir plateau in Tajikistan.
Image Bank

RELIGION Sunni Muslim; small Russian Orthodox and Jewish communities
EDUCATION (compulsory years) 9
LITERACY RATE 99% (men); 99% (women) (2003 est)
LABOUR FORCE 46.1% agriculture, 17.4% industry, 36.5% services (1997)
LIFE EXPECTANCY 66 (men); 71 (women) (2000–05)
CHILD MORTALITY RATE (under 5, per 1,000 live births) 72 (2001)

PHYSICIANS (per 1,000 people) 2 (1998 est)
HOSPITAL BEDS (per 1,000 people) 8.9 (1996 est)
TV SETS (per 1,000 people) 328 (1999)
RADIOS (per 1,000 people) 142 (1997)
INTERNET USERS (per 10,000 people) 5.5 (2002 est)

See also ▷Russia; ▷Union of Soviet Socialist Republics.

Tajikistan country in central Asia, bounded north by Kyrgyzstan and Uzbekistan, east by China, and south by Afghanistan and Pakistan.

NATIONAL NAME *Jumhurii Tojikston/Republic of Tajikistan*
AREA 143,100 sq km/55,250 sq mi
CAPITAL Dushanbe
MAJOR TOWNS/CITIES Khojand, Qurghonteppa, Kulob, Uroteppa, Kofarnihon
PHYSICAL FEATURES mountainous, more than half of its territory lying above 3,000 m/10,000 ft; huge mountain glaciers, which are the source of many rapid rivers

Government

HEAD OF STATE Imamali Rakhmanov from 1994
HEAD OF GOVERNMENT Akil Akilov from 1999
POLITICAL SYSTEM authoritarian nationalist
POLITICAL EXECUTIVE unlimited presidency
ADMINISTRATIVE DIVISIONS two provinces and one autonomous region (Gornyi Badakhstan)
ARMED FORCES 6,000; plus paramilitary forces of 1,200 (2002 est)
DEATH PENALTY retained and used for ordinary crimes

Economy and resources

CURRENCY Tajik rouble
GPD (US$) 1.2 billion (2002 est)
REAL GDP GROWTH (% change on previous year) 10.3 (2001)
GNI (US$) 1.2 billion (2002 est)
GNI PER CAPITA (PPP) (US$) 900 (2002 est)
CONSUMER PRICE INFLATION 9.5% (2003 est)
UNEMPLOYMENT 30% (2001)
FOREIGN DEBT (US$) 891 million (2001 est)

MAJOR TRADING PARTNERS Uzbekistan, the Netherlands, Switzerland, Russia, UK, Kazakhstan, Ukraine
RESOURCES coal, aluminium, lead, zinc, iron, tin, uranium, radium, arsenic, bismuth, gold, mica, asbestos, lapis lazuli; small reserves of petroleum and natural gas
INDUSTRIES mining, aluminium production, engineering, food processing, textiles (including silk), carpet making, clothing, footwear, fertilizers
EXPORTS aluminium, electricity, cotton lint. Principal market: Russia 30% (2000)
IMPORTS industrial products and machinery (principally for aluminium plants), unprocessed agricultural products, food and beverages, petroleum and chemical products, natural gas, consumer goods. Principal source: Uzbekistan 27% (2000)
ARABLE LAND 5.2% (2000 est)
AGRICULTURAL PRODUCTS cotton, jute, rice, millet, fruit, vegetables; livestock rearing (cattle, sheep, goats, and pigs)

Population and society

POPULATION 6,245,000 (2003 est)
POPULATION GROWTH RATE 1.5% (2000–15)
POPULATION DENSITY (per sq km) 44 (2003 est)
URBAN POPULATION (% of total) 28 (2003 est)
AGE DISTRIBUTION (% of total population) 0–14 37%, 15–59 56%, 60+ 7% (2002 est)
ETHNIC GROUPS 62% ethnic Tajik, 24% Uzbek, 8% ethnic Russian, 1% Tatar, 1% Kyrgyz, and 1% Ukrainian
LANGUAGE Tajik (related to Farsi; official), Russian

Chronology

c. 330: Formed an eastern part of empire of Alexander the Great of Macedonia.

8th century: Tajiks established as distinct ethnic group, with semi-independent territories under the tutelage of the Uzbeks, to the west; spread of Islam.

13th century: Conquered by Genghis Khan and became part of Mongol Empire.

1860–1900: Northern Tajikistan came under tsarist Russian rule, while the south was annexed by Emirate of Bukhara, to the west.

1917–18: Attempts to establish Soviet control after Bolshevik revolution in Russia resisted initially by armed guerrillas (basmachi).

1921: Became part of Turkestan Soviet Socialist Autonomous Republic.

1924: Tajik Autonomous Soviet Socialist Republic formed.

1929: Became constituent republic of Soviet Union (USSR).

1930s: Stalinist era of collectivization led to widespread repression of Tajiks.

1978: 13,000 participated in anti-Russian riots.

late 1980s: Resurgence in Tajik consciousness, stimulated by the *glasnost* initiative of Soviet leader Mikhail Gorbachev.

1989: Rastokhez ('Revival') Popular Front established and Tajik declared state language. New mosques constructed.

1990: Violent interethnic Tajik–Armenian clashes in Dushanbe; a state of emergency was imposed.

1991: President Kakhar Makhkamov, local communist leader since 1985, was forced to resign after supporting the failed anti-Gorbachev coup in Moscow. Independence was declared. Rakhman Nabiyev, communist leader 1982–85, was elected president. Joined new Commonwealth of Independent States (CIS).

1992: Joined Muslim Economic Cooperation Organization, the Conference on Security and Cooperation in Europe (CSCE; now the Organization on Security and Cooperation in Europe, OSCE), and the United Nations (UN). Violent demonstrations by Islamic and prodemocracy groups forced Nabiyev to resign. Civil war between pro- and anti-Nabiyev forces claimed 20,000 lives, made 600,000 refugees, and wrecked the economy. Imamali Rakhmanov, a communist sympathetic to Nabiyev, took over as head of state.

1993: Government forces regained control of most of the country. CIS peacekeeping forces were drafted in to patrol the border with Afghanistan, the base of the pro-Islamic rebels.

1994: A ceasefire was agreed. Rakhmanov was popularly elected president under a new constitution.

1995: Parliamentary elections were won by Rakhmanov's supporters. There was renewed fighting on the Afghan border.

1996: Pro-Islamic rebels captured towns in the southwest. There was a UN-sponsored ceasefire between government and pro-Islamic rebels.

1997: A four-stage peace plan was signed. There was a peace accord with the Islamic rebel group the United Tajik Opposition (UTO).

1998: Members of UTO were appointed to the government as part of a peace plan. The UN military observer mission (UNMOT) suspended its operations, following the killing of four UN workers. More than 200 people were killed in clashes in Leninabad between the army and rebel forces loyal to the renegade Tajik army commander Col Makhmud Khudoberdiyev; the deputy leader of the Islamic-led UTO, Ali Akbar Turadzhonzada, was appointed first deputy prime minister.

1999: President Rakhmanov was popularly re-elected and appointed Akil Akilov as his prime minister.

that it deserved international recognition as the country's government.

Talien alternative transliteration of ▷Dalian, a port in Liaoning province, China.

Taliesin (lived *c.* 550) Legendary Welsh poet, a bard at the court of the king of Rheged in Scotland. Taliesin allegedly died at Taliesin (named after him) in Dyfed, Wales.

Tallahassee (Cree 'old town') capital of ▷Florida, USA; population (1996 est) 136,800. It is an agricultural and lumbering centre, trading in cotton, tobacco, and cattle. Industries include publishing, food-processing, and the manufacture of forest products, building materials, and textiles.

Talleyrand-Périgord, Charles Maurice de (1754–1838) French politician and diplomat. As bishop of Autun 1789–91 he supported moderate reform during the ▷French Revolution, was excommunicated by the pope, and fled to the USA during the Reign of Terror (persecution of anti-revolutionaries). He returned and became foreign minister under the Directory 1797–99 and under Napoleon 1799–1807. He represented France at the Congress of ▷Vienna 1814–15.

Tallinn (German **Reval**; Russian **Revel**) naval port and capital of Estonia, 300 km/186 mi west of St Petersburg on the Gulf of Finland; population (1990) 505,100. Industries include the manufacture of electrical and oil-drilling machinery, textiles, and paper production. It is a major cultural centre, containing the Estonian Academy of Sciences and a number of polytechnic, arts, and other institutes. Founded as a Danish fortress in 1219, Tallinn was a member of the ▷Hanseatic League throughout the Middle Ages; it came under the control of the ▷Teutonic Knights in 1346, Sweden in 1561, and Russia in 1750. It was occupied by German forces in both World Wars, and suffered widespread damage.

Many historic buildings remain in the city, including Vyshgorod Castle (13th–14th century) and the Town Hall (14th–15th century). Tallinn is also a centre for yachting.

Tallis, Thomas (*c.* 1505–1585) English composer. He was a master of ▷counterpoint, and has become best known for his elaborate and ingenious 40-part motet *Spem in alium non habui* (*c.* 1573). His works also include *Tallis's Canon* ('Glory to thee my God this night') (1567), and a collection of 34 motets, *Cantiones sacrae* (1575), of which 16 are by Tallis and 18 by Byrd.

Talmud the two most important works of post-biblical Jewish literature. The Babylonian and the Palestinian (or Jerusalem) Talmud provide a compilation of ancient Jewish law and tradition. The Babylonian Talmud was edited at the end of the 5th century AD and is the more authoritative version for later Judaism; both Talmuds are written in a mix of Hebrew and Aramaic. They contain the commentary (*gemara*) on the ▷Mishnah (early rabbinical commentaries compiled about AD 200), and the material can be generally divided into *halakhah*, consisting of legal and ritual matters, and *aggadah* (or *haggadah*), concerned with ethical, theological, and folklorist matters.

    Related Web site: Babylonian Talmud http://www.ucalgary.ca/~elsegal/TalmudPage.html

tamandua tree-living toothless anteater *Tamandua tetradactyla* found in tropical forests and tree savannah from southern Mexico to Brazil. About 56 cm/1.8 ft long with a prehensile tail of equal length, it uses its strong foreclaws to break into nests of tree ants and termites, which it licks up with its narrow tongue.

tamarack coniferous tree native to boggy soils in North America, where it is used for timber. It is a type of larch. (*Larix laricina*, family Pinaceae.)

tamarind evergreen tropical tree native to the Old World, with pinnate leaves (leaflets either side of the stem) and reddish-yellow flowers, followed by pods. The pulp surrounding the seeds is used in medicine and as a flavouring. (*Tamarindus indica*, family Leguminosae.)

tamarisk any of a group of small trees or shrubs that flourish in warm, salty, desert regions of Europe and Asia where no other vegetation is found. The common tamarisk *T. gallica*, which grows in European coastal areas, has small, scalelike leaves on feathery branches and produces spikes of small pink flowers. (Genus *Tamarix*, family Tamaricaceae.)

Tamayo, Rufino (1899–1991) Mexican painter and printmaker. His work, nurtured by both European modernism and pre-Columbian indigenous art, demonstrates a clear break with the rhetoric and pictorialism of the preceding generation of Mexican muralists. His mainly easel-sized paintings, with their vibrant colours and cryptic, semi-abstract figures, display strong cubist, expressionist, and surrealist elements, as in *Women Reaching for the Moon* (1946; Cleveland Museum of Art, Cleveland, Ohio).

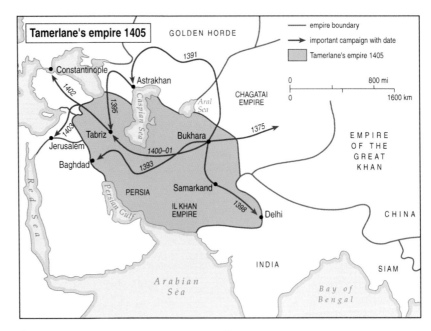

Tambo, Oliver (1917–1993) South African nationalist politician, in exile 1960–90, president of the ▷African National Congress (ANC) 1977–91. Because of poor health, he was given the honorary post of national chair in July 1991, and Nelson ▷Mandela resumed the ANC presidency.

tambourine musical percussion instrument of ancient origin, almost unchanged since Roman times, consisting of a shallow frame drum with a single skin and loosely set jingles in the rim which add their noise when the drum skin is struck or rubbed, or sound separately when the instrument is shaken.

Tamerlane (or **Timur Leng** or **Timur the Lame**) (1335–1405) Turco-Mongol ruler of Samarkand, in Uzbekistan, from 1369 who conquered Persia, Azerbaijan, Armenia, and Georgia. He defeated the ▷Golden Horde in 1395, sacked Delhi in 1398, invaded Syria and Anatolia, and captured the Ottoman sultan Bayezid I (*c.* 1360–1403) in Ankara in 1402; he died invading China.

Tamerlane claimed to be a descendant of the Mongol leader Genghis Khan, and was the great-grandfather of Babur (1483–1530), founder of the Mogul Empire of India. His descendants ruled Persia.

Tamil the majority ethnic group living in the Indian state of Tamil Nadu (formerly Madras). Tamils also live in southern India, northern Sri Lanka, Malaysia, Singapore, and South Africa, totalling 35–55 million worldwide. Tamil belongs to the Dravidian family of languages; written records in Tamil date from the 3rd century BC. The 3 million Tamils in ▷Sri Lanka are predominantly Hindu, unlike the Sinhalese, the majority group there, who are mainly Buddhist. The **Tamil Tigers**, the most prominent of the various Tamil groups, are attempting to create a separate homeland in northern Sri Lanka through both political and military means.

Tamil Hinduism traditional form of Hinduism found in southern India, particularly in Tamil Nadu, where the invasions and political upheavals of northern India had little influence. The important centres of Tamil Hinduism are Rameshvaram, dedicated to Shiva; Shrirangam, dedicated to Vishnu; and Madurai, dedicated to Meenakshi, the wife of Shiva. Tamil temple architecture is characterized by towering *gopurams*, or temple gateways.

Tamil Nadu (formerly **Madras State** (until 1968)) state of southeast India, bounded on the north by Karnataka and Andhra Pradesh, on the west by Kerala, and on the east and south by the Bay of Bengal and the Indian Ocean; area 130,100 sq km/50,200 sq mi; population (2001 est) 64,158,000. The capital is ▷Chennai (formerly Madras). There are cotton, leather, and sugar-refining industries. Tea, coffee, spices, sugar cane, and coconuts are grown.

Tammany Hall Democratic Party organization in New York. It originated in 1789 as the Society of St Tammany, named after the building in which they met. It was dominant from 1800 until the 1930s and gained a reputation for corruption and rule by bosses; its domination was broken by Mayor ▷La Guardia in the 1930s and Mayor Koch in the 1970s.

Tammuz (or **Thammuz**) in Sumerian mythology, a vegetation god representing the decay and growth of natural life; he died at midsummer and was rescued from the underworld the following spring by his lover ▷Ishtar. His cult spread over Babylonia, Syria, Phoenicia, and Palestine. He was possibly identified with the Egyptian ▷Osiris and the Greek ▷Adonis.

Tampere (Swedish **Tammerfors**) city in southwestern Finland; population (1994) 179,000, metropolitan area 258,000. Industries include textiles, paper, footwear, and turbines. It is the second-largest city in Finland.

Tanabata (Japanese 'star festival') festival celebrated annually on 7 July, introduced to Japan from China in the 8th century. It is dedicated to Altair and Vega, two stars in the constellations Aquila and Lyra respectively, separated by the Milky Way. According to legend they represent two star-crossed lovers allowed by the gods to meet on that night.

tanager New World bird of the family Emberizidae, order Passeriformes. There are about 230 species in forests of Central and South America, all brilliantly coloured. They are 10–20 cm/4–8 in long, with plump bodies and conical beaks. The tanagers of North America all belong to the genus *Piranga*.

Tana, Lake lake on the north central plateau of Amhara, Ethiopia, 1,800 m/5,900 ft above sea level; area 3,600 sq km/1,390 sq mi. It is about 75 km/47 mi long and 70 km/43 mi wide. The Blue Nile, the source of which lies just above Lake Tana, leaves the lake via the Tisisat Falls, where it is harnessed for hydroelectric power.

Tandy, Jessica (1909–1994) English film and theatre actor. One of the greatest classical theatre actors of her day, she played all the major Shakespearean heroines, including Ophelia alongside John Gielgud's Hamlet in 1934. She won an Academy Award for the film *Driving Miss Daisy* (1989). She was created a DBE in 1990.

JESSICA TANDY English actor Jessica Tandy and her husband, Canadian-born actor Hume Cronyn, attending the Academy Awards ceremony in 1992. *Image Bank*

Tanganyika, Lake lake 772 m/2,534 ft above sea level in the Great Rift Valley, East Africa, with the Democratic Republic of Congo to the west, Zambia to the south, and Tanzania and Burundi to the east. It is about 645 km/400 mi long, with an area of about 31,000 sq km/12,000 sq mi, and is the deepest lake (1,435 m/ 4,710 ft) in Africa, and the second-deepest freshwater lake in the world. The mountains around its shores rise to about 2,700 m/ 8,860 ft. The chief ports on the lake are Bujumbura (Burundi), Kigoma (Tanzania), and Kalémié (Democratic Republic of Congo).

Tang dynasty the greatest of China's imperial dynasties, which ruled from 618 to 907. Founded by the ▷Sui official Li Yuan (566–635), it extended Chinese authority into central Asia, Tibet, Korea, and Annam, establishing what was then the world's largest empire. The dynasty's peak was reached during the reign of Emperor Minghuang or Hsuan-tsung (712–56).

The Tang dynasty set up a centralized administrative system based on the ▷Han examination model. Buddhism continued to spread and the arts and science flourished. Printing was invented, gunpowder first used, and seaborne and overland trade and cultural contacts were widened.

Related Web site: Tang Dynasty Poems http://zhongwen.com/tangshi.htm

Tange, Kenzo (1913–) Japanese modernist architect. His works include the National Gymnasium, Tokyo, for the 1964 Olympics with its vast catenary steel roof, and the crescent-shaped city of Abuja, which replaced Lagos as the capital of Nigeria in 1992. In 1991 he completed the 70-storey City Hall, Tokyo – Japan's tallest building.

tangent in geometry, a straight line that touches a curve and gives the gradient of the curve at the point of contact. At a maximum, minimum, or point of inflection, the tangent to a curve has zero gradient. Also, in trigonometry, a function of an acute angle in a right-angled triangle, defined as the ratio of the length of the side opposite the angle to the length of the side adjacent to it; a way of expressing the gradient of a line.

tangerine small type of ▷orange.

Tangier (or **Tangiers** or **Tanger**; Arabic **Tanjah**) port in north Morocco, on the Strait of Gibraltar, 58 km/36 mi southwest of Gibraltar; population (urban area, 1994) 497,100. Cigarette manufacturing is the most important industry, and there are fisheries, market gardens, and preserving industries. It is the northern terminus of the Tangier–Fès railway. It was a Phoenician trading centre in the 15th century BC. Captured by the Portuguese in 1471, it passed to England in 1662 as part of the dowry of Catherine of Braganza, but was abandoned in 1684, and later became a lair of Barbary Coast pirates. From 1923 Tangier and a small surrounding enclave became an international zone, administered by Spain 1940–45. In 1956 it was transferred to independent Morocco and became a free port in 1962.

tango dance for couples, the music for which was developed in Argentina during the early 20th century. The dance consists of two long steps followed by two short steps then one long step, using stylized body positions. The music is in moderately slow duple time (2/4) and employs syncopated rhythms. Similar to the habanera, from which it evolved, the tango consists of two balanced sections, the second usually in the ▷dominant key or the relative minor of the first section. William Walton uses a tango in his suite *Facade* (1923).

Tanguy, Yves (1900–1955) French painter. He lived in the USA from 1939. A leading surrealist, he created dreamlike desert landscapes peopled by metallic, semi-abstract forms casting long shadows. Self-taught, Tanguy was first inspired to paint by the works of Chirico and in 1925 he joined the surrealist movement.

Tanizaki, Jun-ichirō (1886–1965) Japanese novelist. His works include a version of ▷Murasaki's *The Tale of Genji* (1939–41), *The Makioka Sisters* in three volumes (1943–48), and *The Key* (1956).

tank armoured fighting vehicle that runs on tracks and is fitted with weapons systems capable of defeating other tanks and destroying life and property. The term was originally a code name for the first effective tracked and armoured fighting vehicle, invented by the British soldier and scholar Ernest Swinton, and first used in the Battle of the Somme in 1916.

A tank consists of a body or hull of thick steel, on which are mounted machine guns and a larger gun. The hull contains the crew (usually consisting of a commander, driver, and one or two soldiers), engine, radio, fuel tanks, and ammunition. The tank travels on caterpillar tracks that enable it to cross rough ground and debris. It is known today as an MBT (main battle tank).

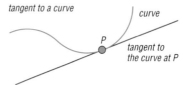

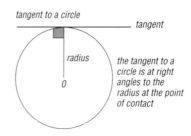

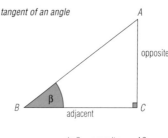

$$\text{tangent } \beta = \frac{\sin \beta}{\cos \beta} = \frac{\text{opposite}}{\text{adjacent}} = \frac{AC}{BC}$$

TANGENT The tangent of an angle is a mathematical function used in the study of right-angled triangles. If the tangent of an angle β is known, then the length of the opposite side can be found given the length of the adjacent side, or vice versa.

tannic acid (or **tannin**) $C_{14}H_{10}O_9$ yellow astringent substance, composed of several ▷phenol rings, occurring in the bark, wood, roots, fruits, and galls (growths) of certain trees, such as the oak. It precipitates gelatin to give an insoluble compound used in the manufacture of leather from hides (tanning).

tanning treating animal skins to preserve them and make them into leather. In vegetable tanning, the prepared skins are soaked in tannic acid. Chrome tanning, which is much quicker, uses solutions of chromium salts.

tansy perennial herb belonging to the daisy family, native to Europe. The yellow flower heads grow in clusters on stalks up to 120 cm/4 ft tall, and the aromatic leaves are used in cookery. (*Tanacetum vulgare*, family Compositae.)

tantalum hard, ductile, lustrous, grey-white, metallic element, symbol Ta, atomic number 73, relative atomic mass 180.948. It occurs with niobium in tantalite and other minerals. It can be drawn into wire with a very high melting point and great tenacity, useful for lamp filaments subject to vibration. It is also used in

alloys, for corrosion-resistant laboratory apparatus and chemical equipment, as a catalyst in manufacturing synthetic rubber, in tools and instruments, and in rectifiers and capacitors.

It was discovered and named in 1802 by Swedish chemist Anders Ekeberg (1767–1813) after the mythological Greek character Tantalos.

Tantalus in Greek mythology, a king of Lydia, son of Zeus, and father of Pelops and Niobe. He offended the gods by divulging their secrets and serving them human flesh at a banquet. His crimes were punished in ▷Tartarus (a part of the underworld for the wicked) by the provision of food and drink he could not reach. The word 'tantalize' derives from his torment.

Tantrism forms of Hinduism and Buddhism that emphasize the division of the universe into male and female forces which maintain its unity by their interaction. Tantric Hinduism is associated with magical and sexual yoga practices that imitate the union of Siva and Sakti, as described in scriptures known as the *Tantras*. In Buddhism, the *Tantras* are texts attributed to the Buddha, describing magical ritual methods of attaining enlightenment.

Tanzania see country box.

Taoiseach (plural **Taoisigh**) Irish title for the prime minister of the Republic of Ireland. The Taoiseach has broadly similar powers to the UK prime minister.

Taoism Chinese philosophical system, traditionally founded by the Chinese philosopher Lao Zi in the 6th century BC. He is also attributed authorship of the scriptures, *Tao Te Ching*, although these were apparently compiled in the 3rd century BC. The 'tao' or 'way' denotes the hidden principle of the universe, and less stress is laid on good deeds than on harmonious interaction with the environment, which automatically ensures right behaviour. The magical side of Taoism is illustrated by the *I Ching* or *Book of Changes*, a book of divination.

Beliefs The universe is believed to be kept in balance by the opposing forces of yin and yang that operate in dynamic tension between themselves. Yin is female and watery: the force in the Moon and rain which reaches its peak in the winter; yang is masculine and solid: the force in the Sun and earth which reaches its peak in the summer. The interaction of yin and yang is believed to shape all life.

This magical, ritualistic aspect of Taoism developed from the 2nd century AD and was largely responsible for its popular growth; it stresses physical immortality, which was attempted by means ranging from dietary regulation and fasting to alchemy. By the 3rd century, worship of gods had begun to appear, including that of the stove god Tsao Chun. From the 4th century, rivalry between Taoists and Mahāyāna Buddhists was strong in China, leading to persecution of one religion by the other; this was resolved by mutual assimilation, and Taoism developed monastic communities similar to those of the Buddhists.

Taoist texts record the tradition of mental and physical discipline, and methods to use in healing, exorcism, and the quest for immortality. The second major work was that of Zhuangzi (c. 389–286 BC), *The Way of Zhuangzi*.

Related Web site: Brief Introduction to Taoism http://www.geocities.com/HotSprings/2426/Ttaointro.html

tap dancing rapid step dance, derived from clog dancing. Its main characteristic is the tapping of toes and heels accentuated by steel taps affixed to the shoes. It was popularized in vaudeville and in 1930s films by such dancers as Fred Astaire and Bill 'Bojangles' Robinson.

tape recording, magnetic method of recording electric signals on a layer of iron oxide, or other magnetic material, coating a thin plastic tape. The electrical signals from the microphone are fed to the electromagnetic recording head, which magnetizes the tape in accordance with the frequency and amplitude of the original signal. The impulses may be audio (for sound recording), video (for television), or data (for computer). For playback, the tape is passed over the same, or another, head to convert magnetic into electrical signals, which are then amplified for reproduction. Tapes are easily demagnetized (erased) for reuse, and come in cassette, cartridge, or reel form.

TANK A German soldier in a tank surrendering to the British infantry in World War II. *Archive Photos*

tapestry ornamental woven textile used for wall hangings, furniture, and curtains. The tapestry design is threaded into the warp with various shades of yarn. The great European centres of tapestry weaving were in Belgium, France, and England. See illustration on page 934.

tapeworm any of various parasitic flatworms of the class Cestoda. They lack digestive and sense organs, can reach 15 m/50 ft in length, and attach themselves to the host's intestines by means of hooks and suckers. Tapeworms are made up of hundreds of individual segments, each of which develops into a functional hermaphroditic reproductive unit capable of producing numerous eggs. The larvae of tapeworms usually reach humans in imperfectly cooked meat or fish, causing anaemia and intestinal disorders.

tapir any of the odd-toed hoofed mammals (perissodactyls) of the single genus *Tapirus*, now constituting the family Tapiridae. There are four species living in the American and Malaysian tropics. They reach 1 m/3 ft at the shoulder and weigh up to 350 kg/770 lb. Their survival is in danger because of destruction of the forests.

Tapirs have thick, hairy, black skin, short tails, and short trunks. They are vegetarian, harmless, and shy. They are related to the ▷rhinoceros, and slightly more distantly to the horse.

The **Malaysian tapir** *T. indicus* is black with a large white patch on the back and hindquarters. The three South American species are dark to reddish brown; the **Brazilian tapir** *T. terrestris* is the most widespread. **Baird's tapir** *T. bairdii* is rare and found only in Central America.

The **mountain tapir** *T. pinchaque* is the rarest tapir (fewer than 2,500 remaining), and is found only in the northern Andes. It

Tanzania

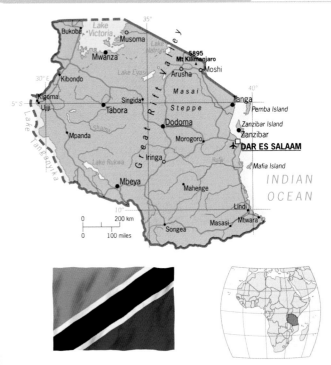

TANZANIA A woman from the Mangati tribe in Tanzania. *Image Bank*

POPULATION GROWTH RATE 1.8% (2000–15)
POPULATION DENSITY (per sq km) 39 (2003 est)
URBAN POPULATION (% of total) 35 (2003 est)
AGE DISTRIBUTION (% of total population) 0–14 44%, 15–59 52%, 60+ 4% (2002 est)
ETHNIC GROUPS 99% of the population are Africans, ethnically classified as Bantu, and distributed among over 130 tribes; main tribes are Bantu, Nilotic, Nilo-Hamitic, Khoisan, and Iraqwi
LANGUAGE Kiswahili, English (both official), Arabic (in Zanzibar), many local languages
RELIGION Muslim, Christian, traditional religions
EDUCATION (compulsory years) 7
LITERACY RATE 86% (men); 71% (women) (2003 est)
LABOUR FORCE 80.4% agriculture, 6.5% industry, 13.1% services (2000)
LIFE EXPECTANCY 43 (men); 44 (women) (2000–05)
CHILD MORTALITY RATE (under 5, per 1,000 live births) 165 (2001)
PHYSICIANS (per 1,000 people) 0.04 (1996 est)
HOSPITAL BEDS (per 1,000 people) 0.9 (1994 est)
TV SETS (per 1,000 people) 42 (2001 est)
RADIOS (per 1,000 people) 406 (2001 est)
INTERNET USERS (per 10,000 people) 23.1 (2002 est)
PERSONAL COMPUTER USERS (per 100 people) 0.4 (2002 est)

See also ▷Nyerere, Julius; ▷Zanzibar.

Tanzania (formerly Tanganyika, until 1964) country in east Africa, bounded to the north by Uganda and Kenya; south by Mozambique, Malawi, and Zambia; west by Congo (formerly Zaire), Burundi, and Rwanda; and east by the Indian Ocean.

NATIONAL NAME *Jamhuri ya Muungano wa Tanzania*/United Republic of Tanzania
AREA 945,000 sq km/364,864 sq mi
CAPITAL Dodoma (official), Dar es Salaam (administrative)
MAJOR TOWNS/CITIES Zanzibar, Mwanza, Mbeya, Tanga, Morogoro
MAJOR PORTS Dar es Salaam
PHYSICAL FEATURES central plateau; lakes in north and west; coastal plains; lakes Victoria, Tanganyika, and Nyasa; half the country is forested; comprises islands of Zanzibar and Pemba; Mount Kilimanjaro, 5,895 m/19,340 ft, the highest peak in Africa; Olduvai Gorge; Ngorongoro Crater, 14.5 km/9 mi across, 762 m/2,500 ft deep

Government

HEAD OF STATE Benjamin Mkapa from 1995
HEAD OF GOVERNMENT Frederick Sumaye from 1995
POLITICAL SYSTEM emergent democracy
POLITICAL EXECUTIVE limited presidency
ADMINISTRATIVE DIVISIONS 27 regions
ARMED FORCES 27,000 (2002 est)
CONSCRIPTION two years
DEATH PENALTY retained and used for ordinary crimes
DEFENCE SPEND (% GDP) 1.5 (2002 est)
EDUCATION SPEND (% GDP) 3.4 (1999)
HEALTH SPEND (% GDP) 5.1 (2000 est)

Economy and resources

CURRENCY Tanzanian shilling
GPD (US$) 9.4 billion (2002 est)
REAL GDP GROWTH (% change on previous year) 5.6 (2001)
GNI (US$) 9.6 billion (2002 est)
GNI PER CAPITA (PPP) (US$) 550 (2002 est)
CONSUMER PRICE INFLATION 4.2% (2003 est)
FOREIGN DEBT (US$) 5.5 billion (2001 est)
MAJOR TRADING PARTNERS India, UK, Germany, South Africa, Japan, the Netherlands, Kenya, Malaysia
RESOURCES diamonds, other gemstones, gold, salt, phosphates, coal, gypsum, tin, kaolin (exploration for petroleum in progress)
INDUSTRIES food processing, textiles, cigarette production, pulp and paper, petroleum refining, diamonds, cement, brewing, fertilizers, clothing, footwear, pharmaceuticals, electrical goods, metalworking, vehicle assembly
EXPORTS minerals, coffee beans, raw cotton, tobacco, tea, cloves, cashew nuts, petroleum products. Principal market: India 15.4% (2001)
IMPORTS machinery and transport equipment, crude petroleum and petroleum products, construction materials, foodstuffs, consumer goods. Principal source: South Africa 13.7% (2001)
ARABLE LAND 4.5% (2000 est)
AGRICULTURAL PRODUCTS coffee, cotton, tobacco, cloves, tea, cashew nuts, sisal, pyrethrum, sugar cane, coconuts, cardamoms

Population and society

POPULATION 36,977,000 (2003 est)

Chronology

8th century: Growth of city states along coast after settlement by Arabs from Oman.

1499: Portuguese navigator Vasco da Gama visited island of Zanzibar.

16th century: Portuguese occupied Zanzibar, defeated coastal states, and exerted spasmodic control over them.

1699: Portuguese ousted from Zanzibar by Arabs of Oman.

18th century: Sultan of Oman reasserted Arab overlordship of East African coast, which became subordinate to Zanzibar.

1744–1837: Revolt of ruler of Mombasa against Oman spanned 93 years until final victory of Oman.

1822: Moresby Treaty: Britain recognized regional dominance of Zanzibar, but protested against the slave trade.

1840: Sultan Seyyid bin Sultan moved his capital from Oman to Zanzibar; trade in slaves and ivory flourished.

1861: Sultanates of Zanzibar and Oman separated on death of Seyyid.

19th century: Europeans started to explore inland, closely followed by Christian missionaries.

1884: German Colonization Society began to acquire territory on mainland in defiance of Zanzibar.

1890: Britain obtained protectorate over Zanzibar, abolished slave trade, and recognized German claims to mainland.

1897: German East Africa formally established as colony.

1905–06: Maji Maji revolt suppressed by German troops.

1916: Conquest of German East Africa by British and South African forces, led by Gen Jan Smuts.

1919: Most of German East Africa became British League of Nations mandate of Tanganyika.

1946: Britain continued to govern Tanganyika as United Nations (UN) trusteeship.

1954: Julius Nyerere organized the Tanganyikan African National Union (TANU) to campaign for independence.

1961–62: Tanganyika achieved independence from Britain with Nyerere as prime minister, and became a republic in 1962 with Nyerere as president.

1963: Zanzibar achieved independence.

1964: Arab-dominated sultanate of Zanzibar overthrown by Afro-Shirazi Party in violent revolution; Zanzibar merged with Tanganyika to form United Republic of Tanzania.

1967: East African Community (EAC) formed by Tanzania, Kenya, and Uganda; Nyerere pledged to build socialist state.

1974: Dodama was designated the new national capital, replacing Dar es Salaam.

1977: Revolutionary Party of Tanzania (CCM) proclaimed as only legal party; EAC dissolved.

1979: Tanzanian troops intervened in Uganda to help overthrow President Idi Amin.

1992: Multiparty politics were permitted.

1995: Benjamin Mkapa of CCM was elected president.

1998: A bomb exploded at the US embassy in Dar es Salaam, killing 6 people and injuring 60; an anti-American Islamic group claimed responsibility.

1999: Tanzania withdrew from Africa's largest trading block, the Common Market for Eastern and Southern Africa. In October, the country's founder, Julius Nyerere, died.

2000: President Mkapa and the CCM were re-elected.

2001: Violence broke out between opposition supporters and troops on Zanzibar after the elections had been partially rerun following claims of corruption.

TAPESTRY *The Pastoral*, a Flemish tapestry from early 16th-century Tournai, depicting a woodcutter. *The Art Archive/Victoria and Albert Museum London*

weighs 150–200 kg/330–440 lb and is about 80 cm/32 in tall. It is mainly solitary except when breeding. The gestation period is 13 months and the single young remains with the mother for 18 months. Mountain tapirs are strong swimmers.

taproot in botany, a single, robust, main ▷root that is derived from the embryonic root, or ▷radicle, and grows vertically downwards, often to considerable depth. Taproots are often modified for food storage and are common in biennial plants such as the carrot *Daucus carota*, where they act as ▷perennating organs.

tar dark brown or black viscous liquid obtained by the destructive distillation of coal, shale, and wood. Tars consist of a mixture of hydrocarbons, acids, and bases. Creosote and ▷paraffin are produced from wood tar. See also ▷coal tar.

Tara Hill (or **Hill of Tara**) ancient religious and political centre in County Meath, Republic of Ireland. A national monument, and depicted in a 7th-century *Life of St Patrick* as the 'capital of the Irish', Tara Hill was the site of a palace and was the coronation place of many Irish kings. Its heyday was in the 3rd century AD, and the site was still in use in the 10th century. St ▷Patrick, patron saint of Ireland, preached here. Some tumuli and earthworks remain, and the pillar stone, reputed to be the coronation stone, can still be seen on the summit. In 1843 it was the venue for a meeting held by Daniel O'Connell, 'the Liberator', following the launch of his campaign for the repeal of the Act of Union (1801) in 1841.

tarantella southern Italian dance in very fast compound time (6/8); also a piece of music composed for, or in the rhythm of, this dance. It is commonly believed to be named after the tarantula spider which was (incorrectly) thought to cause tarantism (hysterical ailment), at one time epidemic in the southern Italian town of Taranto, the cure for which was thought to involve wild dancing. The dance became popular during the 19th century, several composers writing tarantellas employing a perpetuum mobile in order to generate intense energy. Examples include those by Chopin, Liszt, and Weber.

Taranto (Greek **Tarantum**) naval base and port in Apulia region, southeast Italy, on the Gulf of Taranto, 80 km/50 mi southeast of Bari; population (1992) 230,200. It is an important commercial centre, and its steelworks are part of the new industrial complex of southern Italy. There are chemical and oil-refining industries, and oyster and mussel fisheries. It was founded in the 8th century BC by ▷Sparta, and was captured by the Romans in 272 BC.

tarantula wolf spider *Lycosa tarantula* (family Lycosidae) with a 2.5 cm/1 in body. It spins no web, relying on its speed in hunting to catch its prey. The name 'tarantula' is also used for any of the numerous large, hairy spiders of the family Theraphosidae, with large poison fangs, native to the southwestern USA and tropical America.

The theraphosid *Aphonopelma* has a body length of 5 cm/2 in and a leg span of 12.5 cm/5 in. They are no more poisonous than other spiders of similar size. They burrow in the ground and catch their prey by pouncing on it and not by means of a web.

In the Middle Ages, the wolf spider's bite was thought to cause hysterical ailments or **tarantism** for which dancing was the cure, hence the name 'tarantula' and its popular association with the dance 'tarantella'.

TARANTULA The mygalomorph bird-eating spider *Stichoplastus incei* and related species are generally described as tarantulas. *Premaphotos Wildlife*

The tarantula was originally named after the town of Taranto in Puglia, Italy, where tarantism was at one time epidemic.
Related Web site: American Tarantula Society http://atshq.org/

tariff tax or duty placed on goods when they are imported into a country or trading bloc (such as the European Union) from outside. The aim of tariffs is to reduce imports by making them more expensive.

Tarkington, (Newton) Booth (1869–1946) US novelist. His novels for young people, which include *Penrod* (1914), are classics. He was among the best-selling authors of the early 20th century with works such as *Monsieur Beaucaire* (1900) and novels of the Midwest, including *The Magnificent Ambersons* (1918) (filmed in 1942 by Orson Welles).

Tarkovsky, Andrei Arsenyevich (1932–1986) Soviet film director. His work is characterized by an epic style combined with intense spirituality. His films include *Solaris* (1972), *Zerkalo/Mirror* (1975), *Stalker* (1979), and *Offret/The Sacrifice* (1986).

Tarleton, Richard (died 1588) Elizabethan theatrical clown, the most celebrated clown of his time. A member of the Queen's Men theatre company from 1583, he was renowned for the jig, a doggerel song-and-dance routine, and for his extempore humour, which influenced some of the characters in Shakespeare's plays.

tarot cards fortune-telling aid consisting of 78 cards: the 56 **minor arcana** in four suits (resembling playing cards) and the **major arcana**, 22 cards with densely symbolic illustrations that have links with astrology and the ▷kabbala.

tarpon large silver-sided fish *Tarpon atlanticus* of the family Megalopidae. It reaches 2 m/6 ft and may weigh 135 kg/300 lb. It lives in warm western Atlantic waters.

Tarquinius Superbus (lived 6th century BC) Called 'Tarquin the Proud'. Last king of Rome 534–510 BC. He abolished certain rights of Romans, and made the city powerful. According to legend, he was deposed when his son Sextus raped ▷Lucretia.

tarragon perennial bushy herb belonging to the daisy family, native to the Old World. It grows up to 1.5 m/5 ft tall and has narrow leaves and small green-white flower heads arranged in

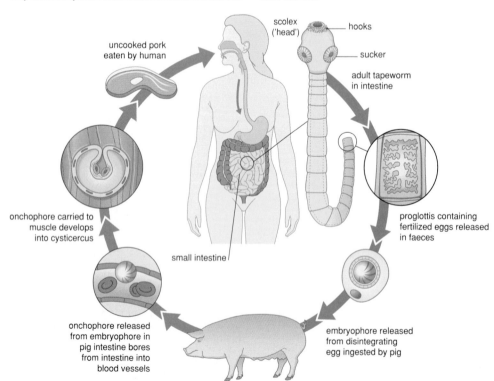

TAPEWORM The life cycle of the pork tapeworm *Taenia solium*. If a person eats pork from an infected pig that has not been properly cooked, the cysticercus attaches to the intestine and develops into an adult tapeworm. The tapeworm is a hermaphrodite and fertilizes itself, releasing proglottis, each of which may contain as many as 40,000 embryos encased in separate capsules. If the embryos are eaten by a pig, they bore from the pig's intestine into the bloodstream which carries them to the muscles, where they may be eaten by a human and the cycle continues.

TARRAGON Tarragon is a bushy perennial with narrow green leaves and small green-white flowers in July and August. It is one of the subtlest of herbs, going well with foods of delicate flavour.

groups. Tarragon contains an aromatic oil; its leaves are used to flavour salads, pickles, and tartar sauce. It is closely related to wormwood. (*Artemisia dracunculus*, family Compositae.)

Tarragona port and capital of Tarragona province in Cataluña, northeast Spain, at the mouth of the Francoli River on the Mediterranean coast; population (1991) 110,000. Industries include petrochemicals, pharmaceuticals, and electrical goods. It has a cathedral and Roman remains, including an aqueduct and amphitheatre.

tarsier any of three species of the prosimian primates, genus *Tarsius*, of the East Indies and the Philippines. These survivors of early primates are about the size of a rat with thick, light-brown fur, very large eyes, long feet and hands, and a long naked tail. They are nocturnal, arboreal, and eat insects and lizards.

tartan woollen cloth woven in specific chequered patterns individual to Scottish clans, with stripes of different widths and colours crisscrossing on a coloured background; it is used in making skirts, kilts, trousers, and other articles of clothing.

TARSIER Spectral tarsier *Tarsius spectrum* at night in the rainforest of Sulawesi, Indonesia. *Ken Preston-Mafham/Premaphotos Wildlife*

Tartar variant spelling of ▷Tatar, member of a Turkic people now living mainly in the autonomous region of Tatarstan, Russia.

tartaric acid HOOC(CHOH)$_2$COOH organic acid present in vegetable tissues and fruit juices in the form of salts of potassium, calcium, and magnesium. It is used in carbonated drinks and baking powders.

Tartarus in Greek mythology, a part of ▷Hades, the underworld, where the wicked were punished.

tartrazine (**E102**) yellow food colouring produced synthetically from petroleum. Many people are allergic to foods containing it. Typical effects are skin disorders and respiratory problems. It has been shown to have an adverse effect on hyperactive children.

Tartu (German **Dorpat**; Russian **Yurev**) city in Estonia, 150 km/93 mi southeast of Tallinn and 50 km/31 mi west of Lake Peipus; population (1990) 115,400. Industries include light engineering, food processing, and lumber. Founded by Russians in 1030, it was a stronghold of the ▷Teutonic Knights from 1224 onwards. Tartu was captured by Russia in 1558 and subsequently held by Sweden and Poland, but returned to Russian control in 1704. It was occupied by German forces in both World Wars.

Tasaday an indigenous people of the rainforests of Mindanao in the ▷Philippines, contacted in the 1960s. Some anthropologists doubt their claim to leading a hunter-gatherer way of life.

Tashkent (Uzbek **Toshkent**) capital of ▷Uzbekistan and of Tashkent wiloyat (region), located in the western foothills of the Tien Shan mountain range and in the valley of the River Chirchiq. With a population (1996) of some 2,300,000, it is the largest city in Central Asia. It is an important transit centre for the region; there is an international airport terminal here. Industrial activity includes the manufacture of mining machinery, chemicals, textiles, and leather goods. Tashkent suffered severe damage in an earthquake in 1966, but was rapidly rebuilt.

Tasman, Abel Janszoon (1603–1659) Dutch navigator. In 1642, he was the first European to see Tasmania. He also made the first European sightings of New Zealand, Tonga, and the Fiji Islands.

Tasmania (formerly **Van Diemen's Land** (1642–1856)) island in the Indian Ocean, southeast of Australia, separated from the mainland by Bass Strait; state of Australia; area about 68,000 sq km/26,000 sq mi; population (1996) 459,700. The capital is ▷Hobart. Products include wool, dairy products, apples and other fruit, processed foods, timber, paper, iron, tungsten, copper, silver, coal, and cement.

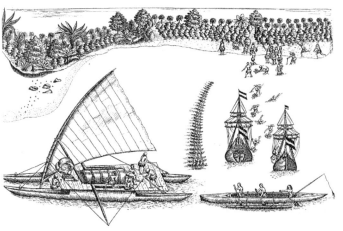

ABEL TASMAN A drawing depicting the arrival in the Fiji Islands of Dutch explorer Abel Tasman. *Philip Sauvain Picture Collection*

Territory Tasmania is the smallest of the Australian states. Over 50 islands are administered by Tasmania. The main ones are the Furneaux group, at the eastern end of Bass Strait, including Flinders Island, Cape Barren Island, and Clarke Island; Chappell Islands and the Kent group, at the eastern end of Bass Strait; the Hunter Islands, including King Island, at the western end of Bass Strait; Bruny Island and Maria Island, off the south and southeast coasts; and the uninhabited, subarctic, volcanic Macquarie Island.

Related Web site: Interactive Tour of Tasmania http://www.tased.edu.au/tot/index.html

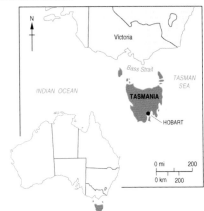

Tasmanian devil carnivorous marsupial *Sarcophilus harrisii*, in the same family (Dasyuridae) as native 'cats'. It is about 65 cm/2.1 ft long with a 25 cm/10 in bushy tail. It has a large head, strong teeth, and is blackish with white patches on the chest and hind parts. It is nocturnal, carnivorous, and can be ferocious when cornered. It has recently become extinct in Australia and survives only in remote parts of Tasmania.

Related Web site: Tasmanian Devil http://www.schoolworld.asn.au/species/tasdevil.html

TASMANIAN DEVIL The Tasmanian devil, despite its name, is not particularly aggressive – it is more likely to scavenge for dead animals than to attack living ones. Nevertheless, it has powerful jaws, capable of crushing large bones.

Tasmanian wolf (or **Tasmanian tiger** or **thylacine**) carnivorous marsupial *Thylacinus cynocephalus*, in the family Dasyuridae. It is doglike in appearance with a long tail, characteristic dark stripes on back and hindquarters, and measures nearly 2 m/6 ft from nose to tail tip. It was hunted to probable extinction in the 1930s, the last known Tasmanian wolf dying in

Hobart Zoo, Tasmania, in 1936, but there are still occasional unconfirmed reports of sightings, both on the Australian mainland and in the Tasmanian mountains, its last known habitat.

A team of scientists at the Australian Museum, Sydney, has extracted DNA from a preserved Tasmanian wolf pup as the first stage in an attempt to recreate the extinct marsupial. The leader of the project and head of evolutionary biology at the Australian Museum, Dr Don Colgan, gave the project, at its outset in 2000, only an 8–10% chance of success. It would be the first cloning of an animal from dead DNA.

Tasman Sea part of the ▷Pacific Ocean between southeast Australia and northwest New Zealand. It is named after the Dutch explorer Abel Tasman.

Tasso, Torquato (1544–1595) Italian poet. He was the author of the romantic epic poem of the First Crusade *Gerusalemme liberata/Jerusalem Delivered* completed by 1575 and first published in 1581, which he revised as *Gerusalemme conquistata/Jerusalem Conquered*, published in 1593.

taste sense that detects some of the chemical constituents of food. The human ▷tongue can distinguish four basic tastes (sweet, sour, bitter, and salty) but it is supplemented by the sense of smell. What we refer to as taste is really a composite sense made up of both taste and smell. In 2000, US researchers confirmed the existence of the fifth taste, 'umami', which was first proposed in the early 19th century by Japanese researcher Kikunae Ikeda. Umami is now called L-glutamate and a specific molecule receptor for it has been identified in taste buds.

Tatar (or **Tartar**) member of a Turkic people, the descendants of the mixed Mongol and Turkic followers of ▷Genghis Khan. The Tatars now live mainly in the Russian autonomous republic of Tatarstan, western Siberia, Turkmenistan, and Uzbekistan (where they were deported from the Crimea in 1944). There are over 5 million speakers of the Tatar language, which belongs to the Turkic branch of the Altaic family.

Tatarstan (formerly **Tatar Autonomous Republic**) autonomous republic in the eastern Russian Federation; area 68,000 sq km/26,255 sq mi; population (1990) 3,658,000 (48% Tatars, 43% Russian). The capital is ▷Kazan. There are oil, natural gas, chemical, textile, and timber industries; and there is arable and dairy farming.

Tate, Nahum (1652–1715) Irish poet. Tate was born in Dublin, and educated there at Trinity College before moving to London. He wrote an adaptation of Shakespeare's *King Lear* with a happy ending, entitled *The History of King Lear* (1681). He wrote the libretto for Purcell's *Dido and Aeneas*; he also produced *A New Version of the Psalms* (1696); his hymn 'While Shepherds Watched Their Flocks by Night' appeared in the *Supplement* (1703). He became British poet laureate in 1692.

Tate Gallery art gallery in London, housing British art from the late 16th century and international art from 1810. Endowed by the sugar merchant Henry Tate (1819–1899), it was opened in 1897. A Liverpool branch of the Tate Gallery opened in 1988, and the St Ives extension in 1993. In 2000, an initiative began to split the gallery thematically into two. The current site was relaunched in March 2000 as Tate Britain, aiming to become a national gallery of British art – Tate's original intention. Tate Modern opened in May 2000 at the former Bankside power station, London, displaying the Tate collection of international 20th and 21st century art.

Tati, Jacques (1908–1982) Stage name of Jacques Tatischeff. French comic actor, director, and writer. He portrayed Monsieur Hulot, the embodiment of polite opposition to modern mechanization, in a series of films, beginning with *Les Vacances de M Hulot/Monsieur Hulot's Holiday* (1953) and including *Mon Oncle/My Uncle* (1959) and *Playtime* (1968).

Tatlin, Vladimir (Yevgrapovich) (1885–1953) Russian artist. He was a cofounder of ▷constructivism. After encountering cubism in Paris in 1913, he evolved his first constructivist works, using such materials as glass, metal, plaster, and wood to create totally abstract sculptures, some of which were meant to be suspended in the air. He worked as a stage designer 1933–52.

Tatra Mountains range in central Europe, extending for about 65 km/40 mi along the Polish-Slovakian border; the highest part of the central ▷Carpathian Mountains.

tatting lacework in cotton, made since medieval times by knotting and looping a single thread with a small shuttle.

Tatum, Art(hur) (1910–1956) US jazz pianist. He is considered among the most technically brilliant of jazz pianists and his technique and chromatic harmonies influenced many musicians, such as Oscar Peterson. He worked mainly as a soloist in the 1930s and improvised with the guitarist Tiny Grimes in a trio from 1943.

tau ▷elementary particle with the same electric charge as the electron but a mass nearly double that of a proton. It has a lifetime of around 3×10^{-13} seconds and belongs to the ▷lepton family of particles – those which interact via the electromagnetic, weak nuclear, and gravitational forces, but not the strong nuclear force.

Taunton market town and administrative headquarters of ▷Somerset, southwest England, 50 km/31 mi northeast of Exeter, on the River Tone; population (1991) 56,400. Products include cider, leather, optical instruments, computer software, aeronautical instruments, and concrete; other industries include light engineering, and there is a weekly cattle market. Taunton is the main market centre for west Somerset and east Devon. The remains of Taunton Castle include the Elizabethan hall in which Judge ▷Jeffreys held his Bloody Assizes in 1685 after the Duke of Monmouth's rebellion.

Taupo, Lake largest lake in New Zealand, in central North Island; area 620 sq km/239 sq mi. It is 357 m/1,170 ft above sea level, maximum depth 159 m/522 ft. The lake is in a volcanic area of hot springs and is the source of the Waikato River. The lake and its tributary rivers attract tourists and anglers.

Taurus conspicuous zodiacal constellation in the northern hemisphere near ▷Orion, represented as a bull. The Sun passes through Taurus from mid-May to late June. In astrology, the dates for Taurus are between about 20 April and 20 May (see ▷precession).

The V-shaped Hyades open ▷star cluster forms the bull's head, with ▷Aldebaran as the red eye. The ▷Pleiades open cluster is in the shoulder. Taurus also contains the ▷Crab nebula, the remnants of the supernova of AD 1054, which is a strong radio and X-ray source and the location of one of the first ▷pulsars to be discovered.

Tavener, John Kenneth (1944–   ) English composer. He has written austere vocal works, including the dramatic cantata *The Whale* (1968) and the opera *Thérèse* (1979). *The Protecting Veil*, composed in 1987 for cello and strings alone, became a best-selling classical recording. Recent works include *Vlepondas* for soprano, bass and cello, and *Feast of Feasts* for chorus, both 1996. His *Song for Athene* was played at the funeral of Diana, Princess of Wales.

Taverner, John (c. 1495–1545) English organist and composer. He wrote masses and motets in polyphonic style, showing great contrapuntal skill, but as a Protestant renounced his art. He was imprisoned in 1528 for heresy, and, as an agent of Thomas Cromwell, assisted in the dissolution of the monasteries.

taxation raising of money from individuals and organizations by the state in order to pay for the goods and services it provides. Taxation can be **direct** (a deduction from income) or **indirect** (added to the purchase price of goods or services, that is, a tax on consumption). The standard form of indirect taxation in Europe is **value-added tax (VAT)**. **Income tax** is the most common form of direct taxation.

The proportions of direct and indirect taxation in the total tax revenue vary widely from country to country. By varying the effect of a tax on the richer and poorer members of society, a government can attempt to redistribute wealth from the richer to the poorer, both by taxing the rich more severely and by returning some of the collected wealth in the form of **benefits**. A **progressive** tax is one that falls proportionally more on the rich; most income taxes, for example, have higher rates for those with higher incomes. **regressive** tax, on the other hand, affects the poor proportionally more than the rich.

In Britain, income tax is collected by the Inland Revenue, as are the other direct taxes, namely **corporation tax** on company profits; **capital gains tax**, introduced to prevent the use of capital as untaxed income in 1961; and **inheritance tax** (which replaced capital transfer tax). The UK has a high proportion of direct taxation compared, for example, with the USA which has a higher proportion of indirect taxation.

VAT is based on the French TVA (*taxe sur la valeur ajoutée*), and was introduced in the UK in 1973. It is paid on the value added to any goods or services at each particular stage of the process of production or distribution and, although collected by traders at each stage, it is in effect a tax on consumer expenditure. In some states of the USA a similar result is achieved by a **sales tax** deducted by the retailer at the point of sale. In the UK, a ▷council tax, based on property values, is the form of taxation that pays for local government spending. It replaced the unpopular **poll tax** or community charge of 1989–93, levied on each person of voting age.

In other countries, including the USA, there are local property taxes or a local income tax. In Britain taxes are also levied on tobacco, wine, beer, and petrol, in the form of **excise duties**.

The UK tax system has been criticized in many respects; alternatives include an **expenditure tax**, which would be imposed only on income spent, and the **tax-credit system** under which all are guaranteed an income bolstered as necessary by social-security benefits, taxation beginning only above that level, hence eliminating the 'poverty trap', by which the unemployed receiving state benefits may have a net loss in income if they take employment at a low wage.

Related Web site: Inland Revenue and National Insurance Contributions Office http://www.inlandrevenue.gov.uk

tax avoidance conducting of financial affairs in such a way as to keep tax liability to a minimum within the law.

tax evasion failure to meet tax liabilities by illegal action, such as not declaring income. Tax evasion is a criminal offence.

tax haven country or state where taxes are much lower than elsewhere. Tax havens are often used by companies from different countries that register in the tax haven in order to avoid paying tax. Any business transacted is treated as completely confidential. Tax havens include the Channel Islands, Switzerland, Bermuda, the Bahamas, and Liberia.

taxis (plural **taxes**; or **tactic movement**) in botany, the movement of a single cell, such as a bacterium, protozoan, single-celled alga, or gamete, in response to an external stimulus. A movement directed towards the stimulus is described as positive taxis, and away from it as negative taxis. The alga *Chlamydomonas*, for example, demonstrates positive **phototaxis** by swimming towards a light source to increase the rate of photosynthesis.

Chemotaxis is a response to a chemical stimulus, as seen in many bacteria that move towards higher concentrations of nutrients.

taxonomy another name for the ▷classification of living organisms.

Tay longest river in Scotland; length 193 km/120 mi, it flows northeast through **Loch Tay**, then east and southeast past Perth to the **Firth of Tay**, crossed at Dundee by the **Tay Bridge**, before joining the North Sea. The Tay has salmon fisheries; its main tributaries are the Tummel, Isla, and Earn, Braan, and Almond.

Taylor, A(lan) J(ohn) P(ercivale) (1906–1990) English historian and television lecturer. His books include *The Struggle for Mastery in Europe 1848–1918* (1954), *The Origins of the Second World War* (1961), and *English History 1914–1945* (1965).

Taylor, Elizabeth (Rosemond) (1932–   ) English-born US actor. She graduated from juvenile leads to dramatic roles, becoming one of the most glamorous stars of the 1950s and 1960s. Her films include *National Velvet* (1944), *Cat on a Hot Tin Roof* (1958), *Butterfield 8* (1960; Academy Award), *Cleopatra* (1963), and *Who's Afraid of Virginia Woolf?* (1966; Academy Award).

Taylor, Robert (1714–1788) English Neo-Palladian architect and sculptor. He was immensely successful during his lifetime, although little of his work has survived. Stone Building in Lincoln's Inn Fields, London (1775), is the finest extant example.

ELIZABETH TAYLOR Elizabeth Taylor and her husband Richard Burton in costume between scenes on the set of *Becket*, in 1964. *Archive Photos*

Taylor, Zachary (1784–1850) 12th president of the USA 1849–50. A veteran of the War of 1812 and a hero of the Mexican War 1846–48, he was nominated for the presidency by the Whigs in 1848 and was elected, but died less than one-and-a-half years into his term. He was succeeded by Vice-President Millard Fillmore.

Tay–Sachs disease inherited disorder, due to a defective gene, causing an enzyme deficiency that leads to blindness, retardation, and death in infancy. It is most common in people of Eastern European Jewish descent.

TB abbreviation for the infectious disease ▷tuberculosis.

Tbilisi (formerly **Tiflis**) capital and cultural centre of ▷Georgia, located on the Kura River in the ▷Caucasus Mountains; population (1996) 1,200,000. It is a major economic, transportation and industrial centre. Industries include the manufacture of textiles, machinery, ceramics, and tobacco. In the lead-up to the collapse of the USSR in 1989 and Georgian independence, the city was the scene of bloody clashes between Russian security forces and nationalist demonstrators.

Related Web site: Tbilisi – The Warm Heart of Georgia http://www. parliament.ge/~nino/tbilis/tbilisi.html

T cell (or **T lymphocyte**) immune cell (see ▷immunity and ▷lymphocyte) that plays several roles in the body's defences. T cells are so called because they mature in the ▷thymus.

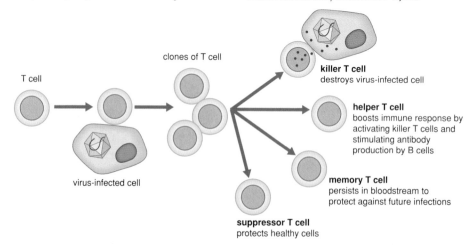

T CELL T cells, a type of lymphocyte (white blood cell), have an important role in the body's immune system. When a T cell encounters an invading virus it begins to divide, forming four different types of T cell, each with a different function. Killer T cells destroy cells that have become infected with the virus by lysis. Helper T cells activate more killer T cells and also stimulate B cells to begin antibody production (unlike B cells, T cells do not produce antibodies to destroy invading pathogens). Suppressor T cells protect healthy cells from viral attack and memory T cells persist in the bloodstream to guard against re-infection.

Tchaikovsky, Pyotr Il'yich (1840–1893) Russian composer. He successfully united western European influences with native Russian fervour and emotion, and was the first Russian composer to establish a reputation with Western audiences. His strong sense of melody, personal expression, and brilliant orchestration are clear throughout his many Romantic works, which include six symphonies, three piano concertos, a violin concerto, operas (including *Eugene Onegin* (1879)), ballets (including *The Nutcracker* (1891–92)), orchestral fantasies (including *Romeo and Juliet* (1870)), and chamber and vocal music.

tea evergreen shrub or small tree whose fermented, dried leaves are soaked in hot water to make a refreshing drink, also called tea. Known in China as early as 2737 BC, tea was first brought to Europe AD 1610 and rapidly became a popular drink. In 1823 the shrub was found growing wild in northern India, and plantations were later established in Assam and Sri Lanka; producers today include Africa, South America, Georgia, Azerbaijan, Indonesia, and Iran. (*Camellia sinensis*, family Theaceae.)

TEA In Sri Lanka, climatic and soil conditions are such that the picking of leaves from tea bushes (which reach maturity after three years) can continue all year round. Elsewhere – other than in tropical India – picking is generally seasonal, and the taste of the tea differs according to the season. *Image Bank*

teak tropical Asian timber tree with yellowish wood used in furniture and shipbuilding. (*Tectona grandis*, family Verbenaceae.)

teal any of various small, short-necked dabbling ducks of the genus *Anas*, order Anseriformes, but particularly *A. crecca*. The male is dusky grey; its tail feathers ashy grey; the crown of its head deep cinnamon or chestnut; its eye is surrounded by a black band, glossed with green or purple, which unites on the nape; its wing markings are black and white; and its bill is black. The female is mottled brown. The total length is about 35cm/14 in.

Teapot Dome Scandal US political scandal that revealed the corruption of President ▷Harding's administration. It centred on the leasing of naval oil reserves in 1921 at Teapot Dome, Wyoming, without competitive bidding, as a result of bribing the secretary of the interior, Albert B Fall. Fall was tried and imprisoned in 1929.

tear gas any of various volatile gases that produce irritation and watering of the eyes, used by police against crowds and used in chemical warfare. The gas is delivered in pressurized, liquid-filled canisters or grenades, thrown by hand or launched from a specially adapted rifle. Gases (such as Mace) cause violent coughing and blinding tears, which pass when the victim breathes fresh air, but there are no lasting effects.

teasel upright prickly biennial herb, native to Europe and Asia. It grows up to 1.5 m/5 ft tall, has prickly stems and leaves, and a large prickly head of purple flowers. The dry, spiny seed heads were once used industrially to tease or fluff up the surface fibres of cloth. (*Dipsacus fullonum*, family Dipsacaceae.)

Related Web site: Teazles http://www.botanical.com/botanical/mgmh/t/teazle09.html

tea tree shrub or small tree native to Australia and New Zealand. It is thought that some species of tea tree were used by the explorer Captain Cook to brew tea; it was used in the first years of settlement for this purpose. (Genus *Leptospermum*, family Myrtaceae.)

technetium (Greek *technetos* 'artificial') silver-grey, radioactive, metallic element, symbol Tc, atomic number 43, relative atomic mass 98.906. It occurs in nature only in extremely minute amounts, produced as a fission product from uranium in ▷pitchblende and other uranium ores. Its longest-lived isotope, Tc-99, has a half-life of 216,000 years. It is a superconductor and is used as a hardener in steel alloys and as a medical tracer.

It was synthesized in 1937 (named in 1947) by Italian physicists Carlo Perrier and Emilio Segrè, who bombarded molybdenum with deuterons, looking to fill a missing spot in the ▷periodic table of the elements (at that time it was considered not to occur in nature). It was later isolated in large amounts from the fission product debris of uranium fuel in nuclear reactors.

Technicolor trade name for a film colour process using three separate negatives of blue, green, and red images. It was invented by Daniel F Comstock and Herbert T Kalmus in the USA in 1922, and became the most commonly used colour process for cinematography.

techno dance music in minimalist style played on electronic instruments, created with extensive use of studio technology for a futuristic, machine-made sound, sometimes with sampled soul vocals. The German band Kraftwerk (formed in 1970) is an early example, and Germany continued to produce some of the best techno records in the 1990s.

technology the use of tools, power, and materials, generally for the purposes of production. Almost every human process for getting food and shelter depends on complex technological systems, which have been developed over a 3-million-year period. Significant milestones include the advent of the ▷steam engine in 1712, the introduction of ▷electricity and the ▷internal combustion engine in the mid-1870s, and recent developments in communications, ▷electronics, and the nuclear and space industries. The **advanced technology** (highly automated and specialized) on which modern industrialized society depends is frequently contrasted with the **low technology** (labour-intensive and unspecialized) that characterizes some developing countries. ▷Intermediate technology is an attempt to adapt scientifically advanced inventions to less developed areas by using local materials and methods of manufacture. **Appropriate technology** refers to simple and small-scale tools and machinery of use to developing countries.

Related Web site: Technology Summary http://www.yahoo.com/headlines/compute/

> **Max Frisch**
> Swiss dramatist
>
> *Technology . . . the knack of so arranging the world that we don't have to experience it.*
>
> In D J Boorstin *The Image*

tectonics in geology, the study of the movements of rocks on the Earth's surface. On a small scale tectonics involves the formation of ▷folds and ▷faults, but on a large scale ▷plate tectonics deals with the movement of the Earth's surface as a whole.

Tecumseh (1768–1813) American Indian chief of the Shawnee. He attempted to unite the Indian peoples from Canada to Florida against the encroachment of white settlers, but the defeat of his brother **Tenskwatawa**, 'the Prophet', at the battle of Tippecanoe in November 1811 by W H Harrison, governor of the Indiana Territory, largely destroyed the confederacy built up by Tecumseh.

He was commissioned a brigadier general in the British army during the War of 1812, and died in battle.

Tedder, Arthur William (1890–1967) 1st Baron Tedder. UK marshal of the Royal Air Force in World War II. As deputy supreme commander under US general Eisenhower 1943–45, he was largely responsible for the initial success of the 1944 Normandy landings. He was made a KCB in 1942, and became a baron in 1946.

Tees river flowing from the Pennines in Cumbria, northwest England, to the North Sea via Tees Bay, Middlesbrough unitary authority, in northeast England; length 130 km/80 mi. Its port, Teesport, handles in excess of 42 million tonnes per annum, with port trade mainly chemical-related.

TEASEL The pale purple flowers of the teasel attract numerous butterflies, bees, and hoverflies during the summer. The dead seed heads persist through the winter. Numerous small insects are often drowned in the miniature pools that collect in the deep troughs formed by the leaf bases, and it is possible that the plant absorbs some of its nutrients this way. *Premaphotos Wildlife*

Teesside industrial area at the mouth of the River Tees, northeast England; population (1994 est) 323,000. It includes the towns of ▷Stockton-on-Tees, ▷Middlesbrough, Billingham, and Thornaby. There are high-technology industries, as well as petrochemicals, electronics, steelmaking, and plastics. The area includes an oil-fuel terminal and the main North Sea natural gas terminal.

tefillin (or **phylacteries**) in Judaism, two small leather boxes containing scrolls from the Torah, that are strapped to the left arm and the forehead by Jewish men for daily prayer.

Teflon trade name for polytetrafluoroethene (PTFE), a tough, waxlike, heat-resistant plastic used for coating nonstick cookware and in gaskets and bearings.

Tegucigalpa capital of ▷Honduras; situated at an altitude of 975 m/3,199 ft in the highlands of south-central Honduras, on the River Choluteca at the foot of the extinct El Pichacho volcano; population (1991 est) 670,100. Industries include textiles, chemicals, and food-processing, mostly for domestic consumption. It was founded by the Spanish in the 16th century as a gold-and silver-mining centre, and became capital in 1880 (the former capital was Comayagua). Tocontín international airport is 6 km/4 mi to the south. The city has some fine colonial architecture including an 18th-century cathedral, and the church of Saint Francis, completed in 1592.

Tehran (or **Teheran**) capital of Iran; population (1991) 6,475,500. Industries include textiles, chemicals, engineering, and tobacco. It is built at an average altitude of 1,220 m/3,937 ft on a slope running south from the Elburz Mountains.

Features Landmarks include the Sepahsolar Mosque and library; the Gulistan Palace (the former royal residence); the Iran Bastan Museum; the Shahyad Tower, a symbol of modern Iran; the Borj-e azadi monument commemorating the 2,500th anniversary of the Persian Empire; and the tomb of Ayatollah Khomeini.

History It was founded in the 12th century and made the capital in 1788 by Muhammad Shah. Much of the city was rebuilt in the 1920s and 1930s.

Teilhard de Chardin, Pierre (1881–1955) French Jesuit theologian, palaeontologist, and philosopher. He developed a creative synthesis of nature and religion, based on his fieldwork and fossil studies. Publication of his *Le Phénomène humain/The Phenomenon of Man*, written 1938–40, was delayed (owing to his unorthodox views) until after his death by the embargo of his superiors. He saw humanity as being in a constant process of evolution, moving towards a perfect spiritual state.

Tej Bahadur (1621–1675) Indian religious leader, ninth guru (teacher) of Sikhism 1664–75, executed for refusing to renounce his faith.

Tejo Portuguese name for the River ▷Tagus.

Te Kanawa, Kiri Janette (1944–) New Zealand soprano. Te Kanawa's first major role was the Countess in Mozart's *The Marriage of Figaro* at Covent Garden, London, in 1971. Her voice combines the purity and intensity of the upper range with an extended lower range of great richness and resonance. Apart from classical roles, she has also featured popular music in her repertoire, such as the 1984 recording of Leonard Bernstein's *West Side Story*.

tektite (from Greek *tektos* 'molten') small, rounded glassy stone, found in certain regions of the Earth, such as Australasia. Tektites are probably the scattered drops of molten rock thrown out by the impact of a large ▷meteorite.

Tel Aviv-Yafo (or **Tel Aviv-Jaffa**) city in Israel, situated on the coast of Sharon Plain, 77 km/48 mi northwest of Jerusalem; population (1995) 355,900. Industries include textiles, chemicals, sugar, printing, publishing, and tourism. Tel Aviv was founded in 1909 as a Jewish residential area in the Arab town of ▷Jaffa, with which it was combined in 1949; their ports were superseded in 1965 by Ashdod to the south. During the ▷Gulf War of 1991, Tel Aviv became a target for Iraqi missiles as part of Saddam Hussein's strategy to break up the Arab alliance against him. It is regarded by the UN as the capital of Israel.

telecommunications communications over a distance, generally by electronic means. Long-distance voice communication was pioneered in 1876 by Scottish scientist Alexander Graham Bell when he invented the telephone. Today it is possible to communicate internationally by telephone cable or by satellite or microwave link, with over 100,000 simultaneous conversations and several television channels being carried by the latest satellites.

TELECOMMUNICATIONS Telegraph operators in a 'cable room' during the late 1950s or early 1960s. At this time, telegrams were encoded as perforations on tape. The tape was fed into a machine that read the perforations and sent them as signals down a land line. A receiver at the far end reprocessed the message back onto tape. A telephone operator would then ring the intended recipient and read out the message. *Image Bank*

telegraphy transmission of messages along wires by means of electrical signals. The first modern form of telecommunication, it now uses printers for the transmission and receipt of messages. Telex is an international telegraphy network.

TELEGRAPHY A telegraph receiver invented by the British physicist Charles Wheatstone in about 1840. In addition to the telegraph, Wheatstone also invented the rheostat (variable electrical resistor), and carried out experiments in underwater telegraphy. *The Art Archive/Science Museum London*

Telemachus in Greek mythology, son of ▷Odysseus and ▷Penelope. He was a child when his father set out for the Trojan wars. In Homer's *Odyssey*, he attempted to control his mother's suitors while his father was believed dead, but on Odysseus' return after 20 years, he helped him to kill them, with the support of the goddess ▷Athena.

Telemann, Georg Philipp (1681–1767) German baroque composer, organist, and conductor. He was the best-known German composer of his time with a contemporary reputation much greater than Johann Sebastian Bach's. His prolific output of concertos for both new and old instruments, including violin, viola da gamba, recorder, flute, oboe, trumpet, horn, and bassoon, represents a methodical and fastidious investigation into the tonal resonances and structure of the new baroque orchestra, research which was noted by Bach. Other works include 25 operas, numerous sacred cantatas, and instrumental fantasias.

Teleostei dominant superorder within the class Osteichthyes (bony fish), consisting of the 'modern' fish, such as the herring, salmon, catfish, eels, and anglerfish. This is the largest group of living vertebrates with more than 20,000 species known.

telepathy 'the communication of impressions of any kind from one mind to another, independently of the recognized channels of sense', as defined by the English essayist F W H Myers (1843–1901), cofounder in 1882 of the Psychical Research Society, who coined the term. It is a form of ▷extrasensory perception.

telephone instrument for communicating by voice along wires, developed by Scottish inventor Alexander Graham ▷Bell in 1876. The transmitter (mouthpiece) consists of a carbon microphone, with a diaphragm that vibrates when a person speaks into it. The diaphragm vibrations compress grains of carbon to a greater or lesser extent, altering their resistance to an electric current passing through them. This sets up variable electrical signals, which travel along the telephone lines to the receiver of the person being called.

There they cause the magnetism of an electromagnet to vary, making a diaphragm above the electromagnet vibrate and give out sound waves, which mirror those that entered the mouthpiece originally.

telephone tapping (or **telephone bugging**) listening in on a telephone conversation, without the knowledge of the participants; in the UK and the USA this is a criminal offence if done without a warrant or the consent of the person concerned.

teleprinter (or **teletypewriter**) transmitting and receiving device used in telecommunications to handle coded messages. Teleprinters are automatic typewriters keyed telegraphically to convert typed words into electrical signals (using a five-unit Baudot code, see ▷baud) at the transmitting end, and signals into typed words at the receiving end.

telescope optical instrument that magnifies images of faint and distant objects; any device for collecting and focusing light and other forms of electromagnetic radiation. A telescope with a large aperture, or opening, can distinguish finer detail and fainter objects than one with a small aperture. The **refracting telescope** uses lenses, and the **reflecting telescope** uses mirrors. A third type, the catadioptric telescope, is a combination of lenses and mirrors. See also ▷radio telescope.

Refractor In a refractor, light is collected by a ▷lens called the **object glass** or **objective**, which focuses light down a tube, forming an image magnified by an **eyepiece**. Invention of the refractor is attributed to a Dutch optician, Hans ▷Lippershey, in 1608. Hearing of the invention in 1609, ▷Galileo quickly constructed one for himself and went on to produce a succession of such instruments which he used from 1610 onwards for astronomical observations. The largest refracting telescope in the world, at ▷Yerkes Observatory, Willimas Bay, Wisconsin, has an aperture of 102 cm/40 in.

Reflector In a reflector, light is collected and focused by a concave mirror. The first reflector was built about 1670 by Isaac ▷Newton. Large mirrors are cheaper to make and easier to mount than large lenses, so all the largest telescopes are reflectors. The largest reflector with a single mirror, 6 m/236 in, is at ▷Zelenchukskaya, Russia. Telescopes with larger apertures composed of numerous smaller segments have been built, such as the Keck Telescopes on Mauna Kea. A **multiple-mirror telescope** was installed on Mount Hopkins, Arizona, USA, in 1979. It originally consisted of six mirrors of 1.8 m/72 in aperture, which performed like a single 4.5-m/176-in mirror. The six mirrors were replaced in 1996 by a single 6.5-m/21.3-ft mirror. **Schmidt telescopes** are used for taking wide-field photographs of the sky. They have a main mirror plus a thin lens at the front of the tube to increase the field of view.

The **liquid-mirror telescope** is a reflecting telescope constructed with a rotating mercury mirror. In 1995 NASA completed a 3-m/9.8-ft liquid mirror telescope at its Orbital Debris Observatory in New Mexico, USA.

Telescopes in space Large telescopes can now be placed in orbit above the distorting effects of the Earth's atmosphere. Telescopes in space have been used to study infrared, ultraviolet, and X-ray radiation that does not penetrate the atmosphere but carries much information about the births, lives, and deaths of stars and galaxies.

TELEPHONE Telephone operators connecting calls in the 1940s. Before automatic exchanges were invented, all calls went through a manual exchange system. A light on a switchboard alerted an operator that someone wished to place a call, and the operator plugged an electrical cable into a jack corresponding to the caller requesting service, which allowed the caller and operator to converse. The operator then plugged an adjacent cable into the called-party's jack, and operated an electrical switch to connect the caller to the called-party's telephone. *Archive Photos*

The 2.4-m/94-in ▷Hubble Space Telescope, launched in 1990, can see the sky more clearly than can any telescope on Earth. In 1996 an X-ray telescope was under development by UK, US, and Australian astronomers, based on the structure of a lobster's eye, which has thousands of square tubes reflecting light onto the retina. The $6.4 million Lobster Eye telescope will contain millions of tubes 10–20 micrometres across and is intended for use on a satellite. It is currently under technological development and it is hoped to launch the telescope by 2005.

NASA launched the Far Ultraviolet Spectroscopic Explorer, and Earth-orbiting telescope, in June 1999.

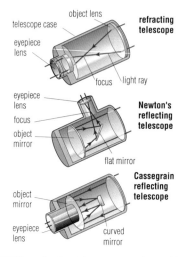

TELESCOPE The refracting telescope uses a large objective lens to gather light and form an image which the smaller eyepiece lens magnifies. A reflecting telescope uses a mirror to gather light.

teletext broadcast system of displaying information on a television screen. The information – typically covering news, entertainment, sport, and finance – is constantly updated. Teletext is a form of ▷videotext, pioneered in Britain by the British Broadcasting Corporation (BBC) with Ceefax and by Independent Television (ITN) with Teletext.

televangelist in North America, a fundamentalist Christian minister, often of a Pentecostal church, who hosts a television show and solicits donations from viewers. Well-known televangelists include Jim Bakker, convicted in 1989 of fraudulent misuse of donations, and Jimmy Swaggart.

television (TV) reproduction of visual images at a distance using radio waves. For transmission, a television camera converts the pattern of light it takes in into a pattern of electrical charges. This is scanned line by line by a beam of electrons from an electron gun, resulting in variable electrical signals that represent the picture. These signals are combined with a radio carrier wave and broadcast as electromagnetic waves. The TV aerial picks up the wave and feeds it to the receiver (TV set). This separates out the vision signals, which pass to a cathode-ray tube where a beam of electrons is made to scan across the screen line by line, mirroring the action of the electron gun in the TV camera. The result is a recreation of the pattern of light that entered the camera.

telex (acronym for teleprinter exchange) international telecommunications network that handles telegraph messages in the form of coded signals. It uses ▷teleprinters for transmitting and receiving, and makes use of land lines (cables) and radio and satellite links to make connections between subscribers.

Telford, Thomas (1757–1834) Scottish civil engineer. He opened up northern Scotland by building ▷roads and waterways. He constructed many aqueducts and ▷canals, including the ▷Caledonian Canal (1802–23), and erected the Menai road suspension bridge between Wales and Anglesey (1819–26), a type of structure scarcely tried previously in the UK. In Scotland he constructed over 1,600 km/1,000 mi of road and 1,200 bridges, churches, and harbours.

In 1786 Telford was appointed official surveyor to the county of Shropshire. There he built three bridges over the River Severn, among other structures. He also rebuilt many Roman roads to meet the need for faster travel, copying, to some extent, Roman road design – a foundation of large tapered stones, covered with a thick

1878	English engineer William Crookes invents the Crookes tube, which produces cathode rays.
1884	German inventor Paul Nipkow builds a mechanical scanning device, the Nipkow disc, a rotating disc with a spiral pattern of holes in it.
1897	German inventor Karl Ferdinand Braun modifies the Crookes tube to produce the ancestor of the TV receiver picture tube. In his evacuated tube, a beam of cathode rays (electrons), guided by electromagnetic fields, forms a picture on a fluorescent screen.
1906	Russian engineer Boris Rosing begins to experiment with the Nipkow disc and cathode-ray tube, eventually succeeding in transmitting some crude TV pictures.
1919	US inventor Charles Francis Jenkins patents a television system using prismatic rings.
1923	Russian-born US engineer Vladimir Zworykin invents the first electronic camera tube, the iconoscope.
1926	English inventor John Logie Baird demonstrates a workable TV system, using mechanical scanning by Nipkow disc.
1928	Baird demonstrates colour TV.
1929	The British Broadcasting Corporation (BBC) begins broadcasting experimental TV programmes, using Baird's system.
1931	US physicist Allen Balcom Du Mont perfects the first practical, low-cost cathode-ray tube.
1936	The BBC begins regular broadcasting from Alexandra Palace, London, using a high-definition all-electronic system developed by EMI. This marks the end of the BBC's usage of Baird's system.
1938	Allen Balcom Du Mont manufactures the first all-electronic receiver to be marketed in the USA. It uses a huge 35 cm/14 in cathode ray tube.

1939	The National Broadcasting Company (NBC) begins the first regular television broadcasting service in the USA.
1940	Experimental colour TV transmission begins in the USA, as the Columbia Broadcasting System (CBS) in New York City makes colour broadcasts using a semi-mechanical method called the 'field sequential system'.
Late 1940s	Cable television, also known as community antenna television (CATV) begins in the USA.
1953	Successful colour TV transmissions begin in the USA, using the NTSC (National Television Systems Committee) system. This system is used today throughout the American continents and Japan.
1956	The first videotape recorder is produced in California by the Ampex Corporation.
1950s	Two systems for transmitting colour television are introduced in Europe. Germany brings in the phase-alternate line (PAL) system, which is later adopted in the UK and most of Western Europe, Africa, Asia, and Australia. France introduces *Sequentiel coleur à mémoir* (SECAM), a system that becomes the standard there and in Eastern Europe and the Middle East.
1962	TV signals are transmitted across the Atlantic via the Telstar satellite.
1970	The first video disc system is announced by Decca in Britain and AEG-Telefunken in Germany.
1973	The BBC and Independent Television in the UK introduce the world's first teletext systems, Ceefax and Oracle, respectively.
1975	Sony introduces a domestic videocassette tape-recorder system, Betamax. The UK Post Office (now British Telecom) announces the Prestel viewdata system.
1979	Matsushita in Japan develops a pocket-sized, flat-screen TV set, using a liquid-crystal display.

1986	Data broadcasting using digital techniques is developed; an enhancement of teletext is produced.
1989	The Japanese begin broadcasting high-definition television; satellite television is introduced in the UK.
1990	The BBC introduces a digital stereo sound system (NICAM); MAC, a European system allowing greater picture definition, more data, and sound tracks, is introduced.
1992	All-digital high-definition television is demonstrated in the USA.
1993	A worldwide standard for digital television is agreed at a meeting of manufacturers and broadcasters in Sydney, Australia. The Japanese electronics company NEC announces the development of a flat thin screen that produces full-colour high resolution pictures, without a cathode-ray tube. 'Sport' television glasses go on sale in the USA, enabling the wearer to watch television while walking.
1995	The US House of Representatives votes in favour of including a chip in all TV sets that will allow parents to block out programmes that they consider unsuitable for their children.
1998	A select committee report recommends that the British government set 2010 as the latest date for closing down the analogue network. All non-digital television receivers from that date will need a set-top box or adaptor.
1999	Multi-channel digital television broadcasting, launched in late 1998, becomes widely available to the public in the UK. The chief service providers are Sky, providing a digital service via satellite, and ONdigital, supplying digital television through existing terrestrial aerials.
2000	Digital TV service providers begin marketing limited Internet (Web browsing and e-mail) services via television. Digital TV providers and cable companies also begin selling 'movies-on-demand'. In the UK, digital TV is expected to supersede analogue TV by 2006.

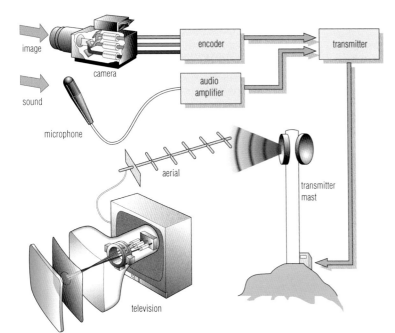

TELEVISION A simplified block diagram of a complete colour television system – transmitting and receiving. The camera separates the picture into three colours – red, blue, green – by using filters and different camera tubes for each colour. The audio signal is produced separately from the video signal. Both signals are transmitted from the same aerial using a special coupling device called a diplexer. There are four sections in the receiver: the aerial, the tuners, the decoders, and the display. As in the transmitter, the audio and video signals are processed separately. The signals are amplified at various points.

atomic mass 127.60. Chemically it is similar to sulphur and selenium, and it is considered one of the sulphur group. It occurs naturally in telluride minerals, and is used in colouring glass blue-brown, in the electrolytic refining of zinc, in electronics, and as a catalyst in refining petroleum.

It was discovered in 1782 by the Austrian mineralogist Franz Müller (1740–1825), and named in 1798 by the German chemist Martin Klaproth.

Its strength and hardness are greatly increased by the addition of 0.1% lead; in this form it is used for pipes and cable sheaths.

Tellus in Roman mythology, the goddess of the Earth, identified with a number of other agricultural gods and celebrations.

Telstar US communications satellite, launched on 10 July 1962, which relayed the first live television transmissions between the USA and Europe. *Telstar* orbited the Earth every 2.63 hours, and so had to be tracked by ground stations, unlike the geostationary satellites of today.

Telugu language spoken in southeastern India. It is the official language of Andhra Pradesh, and is also spoken in Malaysia, giving a total number of speakers of around 50 million. Written records in Telugu date from the 7th century AD. Telugu belongs to the Dravidian family.

temp. abbreviation for temperature; temporary.

tempera painting medium in which powdered pigments are mixed with a water-soluble binding agent such as egg yolk. Tempera is noted for its strong, translucent colours. A form of tempera was used in ancient Egypt, and egg tempera was the foremost medium for panel painting in late Medieval and early Renaissance Europe. It was gradually superseded by oils from the late 15th century onwards.

temperament in music, a system of tuning ('tempering') the ▷pitches of a mode or ▷scale whereby ▷intervals are lessened or enlarged, away from the 'natural'. In folk music this is done to preserve its emotional or ritual meaning; in Western music to allow a measure of freedom in changing key. Johann Sebastian Bach composed *The Well-Tempered Clavier*, a sequence of 48 preludes and fugues in every key of the ▷chromatic scale, to demonstrate the superior versatility of tempered tuning.

layer of broken stones and a surface of gravel. Telford built roads in Scotland, and also the London–Holyhead road (1815–1830). His roads were expensive, but extremely hard-wearing.

As engineer to the Ellesmere Canal Company from 1793, Telford was responsible for the building of aqueducts over the Ceirog and Dee valleys in Wales, using a new method of construction consisting of troughs made from cast-iron plates and fixed in masonry. He also built the Birmingham and Liverpool Junction Canal, and the Gotha Canal in Sweden.

In 1963 the new town of Telford, Shropshire, 32 km/20 mi northwest of Birmingham, was named after him.

Telford and Wrekin unitary authority in west England, created in 1998 from part of Shropshire.
area 291 sq km/112 sq mi **towns and cities** Telford (administrative headquarters), Newport **features** The Wrekin, isolated hill (407 m/1,334 ft); Ironbridge Gorge (World Heritage Site) includes world's first iron bridge, built across the River Severn in 1779 by Abraham Darby, and Ironbridge Gorge Museum Trust (seven industrial history museums including Museum of the River, Museum of Iron, Blists Hill Open Air Museum, Coalport China Museum) **industries** iron founding, agriculture, dairy farming, food processing, confectionery, audio and tape manufacture, electronic tools and equipment, vehicle

parts, plastics, clothing manufacture, information technology
population (1996) 144,600

Tell, William (German **Wilhelm Tell**) legendary 14th-century Swiss archer, said to have refused to salute the Habsburg badge at Altdorf on Lake Lucerne. Sentenced to shoot an apple from his son's head, he did so, then shot the tyrannical Austrian ruler Gessler, symbolizing his people's refusal to submit to external authority.

Tell el Amarna site of the ancient Egyptian capital ▷Akhetaton. The Amarna tablets were found there.

Teller, Edward (1908–2003) Hungarian-born US physicist known as the father of the ▷hydrogen bomb (H-bomb). He worked on the Manhattan Project developing the fission bomb – the first atomic bomb 1942–46, and on the fusion, or hydrogen, bomb 1946–52. Vigorous in his promotion of nuclear weapons and in his opposition to communism, he was, in the 1980s, one of the leading advocates of the Star Wars programme (the ▷Strategic Defense Initiative).

tellurium (Latin *Tellus* 'Earth') silver-white, semi-metallic (▷metalloid) element, symbol Te, atomic number 52, relative

temperance movement societies dedicated to curtailing the consumption of alcohol by total prohibition, local restriction, or encouragement of declarations of personal abstinence ('the pledge'). Temperance movements were first set up in the USA, Ireland, and Scotland, then in northern England in the 1830s.

temperature degree or intensity of heat of an object and the condition that determines whether it will transfer heat to another object or receive heat from it, according to the laws of ▷thermodynamics. The temperature of an object is a measure of the average kinetic energy possessed by the atoms or molecules of which it is composed. The SI unit of temperature is the kelvin (symbol K) used with the Kelvin scale. Other measures of temperature in common use are the Celsius scale and the Fahrenheit scale..

> Related Web site: Explanation of Temperature Related Theories
> http://www.unidata.ucar.edu/staff/blynds/tmp.html

tempering heat treatment for improving the properties of metals, often used for steel alloys. The metal is heated to a certain temperature and then cooled suddenly in a water or oil bath.

Templars (or **Knights Templar** or **Order of Poor Knights of Christ and of the Temple of Solomon**) military religious order founded in Jerusalem 1119–20 to protect pilgrims travelling to the Holy Land. They played an important part in the ▷Crusades of the 12th and 13th centuries. Innocent II placed them under direct papal authority in 1139, and their international links allowed them to adapt to the 13th-century decline of the Crusader states by becoming Europe's bankers. The Templars' independence, power, and wealth, rather than their alleged heresy, probably motivated ▷Philip IV of France, helped by the Avignon pope Clement V, to suppress the order in 1307–14.

> Related Web site: Poor Fellow Soldiers of Christ and the Temple of
> Solomon http://www.xyz.org/templars/indexr.html

Temple, Shirley (1928–) US actor who became the most successful child star of the 1930s. The charming, curly-haired, dimpled tot's films include *Bright Eyes* (1934), in which she sang 'On the Good Ship Lollipop'; *Little Miss Marker* (1934); *Curly Top* (1935); *The Little Colonel* (1935); *Captain January* (1936); *Heidi* (1937); *Rebecca of Sunnybrook Farm* (1938); and *The Little Princess* (1939). She is now a US ambassador.

SHIRLEY TEMPLE The child actress and box-office star of the 1930s. *Archive Photos*

Temple Bar former western gateway of the City of London, between Fleet Street and the Strand (site marked by a stone griffin); the heads of traitors were formerly displayed above it on spikes. It was rebuilt by Christopher Wren in 1672, and moved to Theobald's Park, Hertfordshire, in 1878.

Temple of Jerusalem centre of Jewish national worship in Jerusalem, Israel, in both ancient and modern times, situated on

Temple Mount. The **Wailing Wall** is the surviving part of the western wall of the enclosure of Herod's Temple. Since the destruction of the Temple in AD 70, Jews have gone there to pray and to mourn their dispersion and the loss of their homeland.

tempo (Italian 'time') in music, the speed at which a piece should be played. One way of indicating the tempo of a piece of music is to give a metronome marking, which states the number of beats per minute; for example, 'crotchet = 60' means that there should be 60 crotchet beats to the minute. Modern electronic metronomes measure tempo very accurately, but performers often change or even ignore metronome markings, playing at a tempo that suits their interpretation of the music.

Temuco capital of Araucanía region, south-central Chile, situated to the north of the Lake District on the River Cautín, 675 km/420 mi south of Santiago; population (1992) 240,900. Cereals, timber, and apples are produced in the surrounding region, and industries include coal mining, and the manufacture of steel and textiles. It is a market town for the Mapuche Indians, who trade their produce and crafts. The great majority of them live in the forest land around Temuco. Founded in 1881, the city is the gateway to the Lake District region.

tench European freshwater bony fish *Tinca tinca*, a member of the carp family, now established in North America. It is about 45 cm/ 18 in long, weighs 2 kg/4.5 lb, and is coloured olive-green above and grey beneath. The scales are small and there is a barbel at each side of the mouth.

Tench, Watkin (c. 1759–1833) English-born military officer and author in Australia. He arrived in New South Wales with the First Fleet in command of a detachment of marines. While in the colony he discovered the Nepean River and recorded the life of the settlement in a daily journal. This was published in two volumes *Narrative of the Expedition to Botany Bay, with an Account of New South Wales* and *Complete Account of the Settlement at Port Jackson* (1793).

Ten Commandments in the Old Testament, the laws given by God to the Hebrew leader Moses on Mount Sinai, engraved on two tablets of stone.

They form the basis of Jewish and Christian moral codes; the 'tablets of the Law' given to Moses are also mentioned in the Koran. The giving of the Ten Commandments is celebrated in the Jewish festival of *Shavuot* (see ▷Pentecost).

> Related Web site: Commandments of God http://www.newadvent.
> org/cathen/04153a.htm

tendon (or **sinew**) in vertebrates, a cord of very strong, fibrous connective tissue that joins muscle to bone. Tendons are largely composed of bundles of fibres made of the protein collagen, and because of their inelasticity are very efficient at transforming muscle power into movement.

tendril in botany, a slender, threadlike structure that supports a climbing plant by coiling around suitable supports, such as the stems and branches of other plants. It may be a modified stem, leaf, leaflet, flower, leaf stalk, or stipule (a small appendage on either side of the leaf stalk), and may be simple or branched. The tendrils of Virginia creeper *Parthenocissus quinquefolia* are modified flower heads with suckerlike pads at the end that stick to walls, while those of the grapevine *Vitis* grow away from the light and thus enter dark crevices where they expand to anchor the plant firmly.

Tenerife largest of the ▷Canary Islands, in the province of Santa Cruz de Tenerife, Spain; area 2,060 sq km/795 sq mi; population (1991) 706,900. Fruit and vegetables are produced, especially bananas and tomatoes, and the island is a popular tourist resort. Santa Cruz is the main town here, and Pico de Teide, an active volcano, is the highest peak in Spain (3,713 m/12,186 ft high).

Teng Hsiao-ping alternative spelling of ▷Deng Xiaoping, Chinese politician.

Teniers, David (1610–1690) Called 'the Younger'. Flemish painter. He is best known for his scenes of peasant life, full of vitality, inspired by Adriaen Brouwer. His works were immensely popular and he became court painter to Archduke Leopold Wilhelm, governor of the Netherlands, in Brussels.

Tennessee state in eastern central USA. It is nicknamed the Volunteer State. Tennessee was admitted to the Union in 1796 as the 16th US state. It is bordered to the east by North Carolina, to the south by Georgia, Alabama, and Mississippi, to the west by Arkansas and Missouri, across the Mississippi River, and to the north by Kentucky and Virginia. Historically, Tennessee was a plantation state, associated with slavery. Culturally, it is one of the centres of country music.

> **population** (1995) 5,256,100 **area** 109,200 sq km/42,151 sq mi
> **capital** Nashville **towns and cities** Memphis, Knoxville, Chattanooga, Clarksville **industries and products** cereals, cotton, tobacco, soybeans, livestock, timber, coal, zinc, copper, chemicals, power generation, automobiles, aluminium, music industry, tourism

Tennessee Valley Authority (**TVA**) US government corporation founded in 1933 to develop the Tennessee River basin (an area of some 104,000 sq km/40,000 sq mi) by building hydroelectric power stations, producing and distributing fertilizers, and similar activities. The TVA was associated with President F D Roosevelt's ▷New Deal, promoting economic growth by government investment.

Tenniel, John (1820–1914) English illustrator and cartoonist. He is known for his cartoons for *Punch* magazine and for his illustrations for Lewis Carroll's *Alice's Adventures in Wonderland* (1865) and *Through the Looking-Glass* (1872). He was knighted in 1893.

tennis racket-and-ball game invented towards the end of the 19th century. Although played on different surfaces (grass, wood, shale, clay, concrete), it is also called 'lawn tennis'.

The aim of the two or four players (in singles or doubles matches) is to strike the ball into the prescribed area of the court, with oval-headed rackets (strung with gut or nylon), in such a way that it cannot be returned. The game is won by those first winning four points (called 15, 30, 40, game), unless both sides reach 40 (deuce), when two consecutive points are needed to win.

A set is won by winning six games with a margin of two over opponents, although a tie-break system operates at six games to each side (or in some cases eight) except in the final set. A match lasts a maximum of five sets for men, three for women. .

Tennyson, Alfred (1809–1892) 1st Baron Tennyson. English poet. He was poet laureate 1850–92. His verse has a majestic, musical quality, and few poets have surpassed his precision and delicacy of language. His works include 'The Lady of Shalott' (1833), 'The Lotus Eaters' (1833), 'Ulysses' (1842), 'Break, Break, Break' (1842), and 'The Charge of the Light Brigade' (1854); the longer narratives *Locksley Hall* (1832) and *Maud* (1855); the elegy *In Memoriam* (1850); and a long series of poems on the Arthurian legends, *The Idylls of the King* (1859–89).

He was born in Somersby, Lincolnshire, and educated at Cambridge. An unhappy childhood and youth may account for his remarkable sensitivity and melancholia in later years. The death of English writer Arthur Hallam (a close friend during his years at Cambridge) in 1833 prompted the elegiac sequence *In Memoriam*, which grew over the years into a record of spiritual conflict and a confession of faith; it was finally published (anonymously) in 1850, the year in which he succeeded Wordsworth as poet laureate and married Emily Sellwood (1811–1889). He was made a peer in 1884.

Tennyson's poetry is characterized by a wide range of interests; an intense sympathy with the deepest feelings and aspirations of humanity; an exquisite sense of beauty; and a marvellous power of vivid and minute description, often achieved by a single phrase, and heightened by the perfect matching of sense and sound.

Related Web site: Tennyson, Alfred Lord http://landow.stg.brown.edu/victorian/tennyson/tennyov.html

> **Alfred Tennyson**
> *The woods decay, the woods decay and fall, / The vapours weep their burthen to the ground, / Man comes and tills the field and lies beneath, / And after many a summer dies the swan.*
> *Tithonus*

Tenochtitlán capital of the Mexican ▷Aztecs. It was founded *c.* 1325 on an island among the lakes that occupied much of the Valley of Mexico, on the site of modern Mexico City. Its population reached about 150,000. Spanish conquistador Hernán ▷Cortés met Aztec ruler ▷Montezuma here in November 1519. Welcomed as guests, the Spaniards captured Montezuma and forced him to recognize the sovereignty of ▷Charles V. Cortés destroyed Tenochtitlán in 1521 and rebuilt it as a Spanish colonial city.

tenor the highest range of adult male singing voice when not using ▷falsetto, approximately C3–A5. It is the preferred voice for operatic heroic roles. Exponents are Luciano ▷Pavarotti and Placido ▷Domingo. It is also used as a prefix for models of instruments that sound in the same compass, for example tenor saxophone.

tenpin bowling indoor sport popular in North America and Britain. As in skittles, the object is to bowl a ball down an alley at pins (ten as opposed to nine). The game is usually between two players or teams. A game of tenpins is made up of ten 'frames'. The frame is the bowler's turn to play and in each frame he or she may bowl twice. One point is scored for each pin knocked down, with bonus points for knocking all ten pins down in either one ball or two. The player or team making the greater score wins.

Related Web site: Tenpin World http://www.shef.ac.uk/~sutbc/

Tenzing Norgay (1914–1986) Called 'Sherpa Tenzing'. Nepalese mountaineer. In 1953 he was the first, with Edmund Hillary, to reach the summit of Mount Everest.

Teotihuacán huge ancient city in central Mexico, founded about 300 BC, about 32 km/20 mi north of modern Mexico City. Known as the 'metropolis of the gods', it reached its zenith in the 5th–6th centuries AD. As a religious centre of Mesoamerica, it contained two great pyramids and the temple of ▷Quetzalcoatl. It is one of the best-excavated archaeological sites in Mexico.

teratogen any substance or agent that can induce deformities in the fetus if absorbed by the mother during pregnancy. Teratogens include some drugs (notably alcohol and thalidomide), other chemicals, certain disease organisms, and radioactivity.

terbium soft, silver-grey, metallic element of the ▷lanthanide series, symbol Tb, atomic number 65, relative atomic mass 158.925. It occurs in gadolinite and other ores, with yttrium and ytterbium, and is used in lasers, semiconductors, and television tubes. It was named in 1843 by Swedish chemist Carl Mosander (1797–1858) for the town of Ytterby, Sweden, where it was first found.

Terence (*c.* 190–*c.* 159 BC) Born Publius Terentius Afer. Roman dramatist. Born in Carthage, he was taken as a slave to Rome where he was freed and came under the patronage of the Roman general Scipio Africanus Minor. His surviving six comedies (including *The Eunuch* (161 BC)) are subtly characterized and based on Greek models. They were widely read and performed during the Middle Ages and the Renaissance.

Teresa, St (1515–1582) Spanish mystic who founded an order of nuns in 1562. She was subject to fainting fits, during which she saw visions. She wrote *The Way to Perfection* (1583) and an autobiography, *Life of the Mother Teresa of Jesus* (1611). In 1622 she was canonized, and in 1970 was made the first female Doctor of the Church. She was born in Avila.

Teresa, Mother (1910–1997) Born Agnes Gonxha Bojaxhiu. Roman Catholic nun who devoted her life to working among the sick and poor of Calcutta, India. She established the Missionaries of Charity, now a multinational organization with 517 centres around the world. More than 4,000 nuns staff the Missionaries of Charity orphanages, Aids hospices, mental homes and basic medical clinics, alongside numerous volunteers. Mother Teresa was awarded the Nobel Prize for Peace in 1979 for her help with the destitute in India.

Related Web site: Mother Teresa http://www.gargaro.com/mother_teresa/

terminal in computing, a device consisting of a keyboard and display screen (▷VDU) to enable the operator to communicate with the computer. The terminal may be physically attached to the computer or linked to it by a telephone line (remote terminal). A 'dumb' terminal has no processor of its own, whereas an 'intelligent' terminal has its own processor and takes some of the processing load away from the main computer.

terminal moraine linear, slightly curved ridge of rocky debris deposited at the front end, or snout, of a glacier. It represents the furthest point of advance of a glacier, being formed when deposited material (till), which was pushed ahead of the snout as it advanced, became left behind as the glacier retreated.

terminal voltage the potential difference (pd) or voltage across the terminals of a power supply, such as a battery of cells. When the supply is not connected in circuit its terminal voltage is the same as its ▷electromotive force (emf); however, as soon as it begins to supply current to a circuit its terminal voltage falls because some electric potential energy is lost in driving current against the supply's own internal resistance. As the current flowing in the circuit is increased the terminal voltage of the supply falls.

termite any member of the insect order Isoptera. Termites are soft-bodied social insects living in large colonies which include one or more queens (of relatively enormous size and producing an egg every two seconds), much smaller kings, and still smaller soldiers, workers, and immature forms. Termites build galleried nests of soil particles that may be 6 m/20 ft high.

Termites may dispose of a quarter of the vegetation litter of an area, and their fondness for wood (as in houses and other buildings) brings them into conflict with humans. The wood is broken down in their stomachs by numerous micro-organisms living in ▷symbiosis with their hosts. Some species construct adjustable air vents in their nests, and one species moistens the inside of the nest with water to keep it cool. One group of African termites, the Macrotermitinae, constructs fungus gardens, within the nest, by infecting its own faeces with a special fungus that digests the faeces and renders them edible. Fossilized termite nests found in Arizona, USA, have been estimated to be about 220 million years old.

Termites in the rainforest mostly excavate huge underground nests and feed on rotting vegetation. In one UK study in Cameroon (1993–98) soil-dwelling termites, many of which were discovered to be new species, were found to have a greater biomass than any other animal group.

Related Web site: Formosan Termite http://www.llbrewton.com/termite.htm

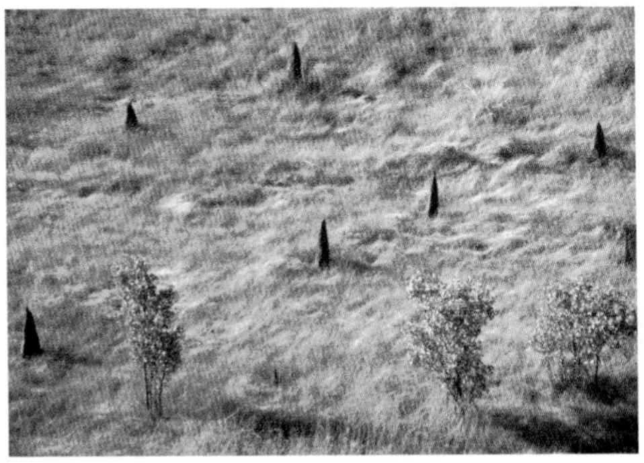

TERMITE The *Amitermes meridionalis* termite of Kakadu, Northern Territory, Australia, builds wedge-shaped mounds, called compass or magnetic mounds. The long axis of the mound is always aligned north–south, while the broad side faces east–west (the orientation probably serves to regulate the temperature of the mound). Termites of some species can live for 60–70 years. *Image Bank*

terms of trade in international trade, the ratio of export prices to import prices. An improvement in the terms of trade (there is an increase in the value of the ratio) should mean that the country is better off, having to give foreigners fewer exports for the same number of imports as before. ▷Devaluation of the currency leads to a deterioration of the terms of trade.

tern any of various lightly built seabirds in the gull family Laridae, order Charadriiformes, with pointed wings and bill, and usually a forked tail. Terns plunge-dive after aquatic prey. They are 20–50 cm/8–20 in long, and usually coloured in combinations of white and black. They are extensively distributed, especially in temperate climates.

Species The common tern *Sterna hirundo* has white underparts, grey upper wings, and a black crown on its head. The **Arctic tern** *Sterna paradisea* migrates from northern parts of Greenland, North America, and Europe to the Antarctic, thereby ensuring most of its life is spent in daylight. The **Antarctic tern** *Sterna vittata* has a striking blood-red beak; it does not migrate.

A number of species occur in Britain, in addition to the common and Arctic terns. They are the **Sandwich tern** *S. sandvicensis*, the **little tern** *S. albifrons*, and the **roseate tern** *S. dougallii*.

terracotta (Italian 'baked earth') brownish-red baked clay, usually unglazed, used in building, sculpture, and pottery. The term is specifically applied to small figures or figurines, such as those found at Tanagra in central Greece. Excavations at Xi'an, China, have revealed life-size terracotta figures of the army of the Emperor Shi Huangdi dating from the 3rd century BC.

Terragni, Giuseppe (1904–1942) Italian architect. He was largely responsible for introducing the ▷Modern Movement to Italy. As a leading member of **Gruppo 7**, he advocated a return to the principles of rationalism, inciting widespread opposition from the orthodox architectural establishment. Notable among his designs are the Novecomum block of flats, Como (1927), and his masterpiece, the Casa del Fascio, Como (1932–36), a crystalline white cube, devoid of ornament but clearly exhibiting its structure.

terrane in geology, a tract of land with a distinct geological character. The term **exotic terrane** is commonly used to describe a rock mass that has a very different history from others near by. The exotic terranes of the Western ▷Cordillera of North America represent old island chains that have been brought to the North American continent by the movements of plate tectonics, and welded to its edge.

terrapin member of some species of the order Chelonia (▷turtles and ▷tortoises). Terrapins are small to medium-sized, aquatic or semi-aquatic, and are found widely in temperate zones. They are omnivorous, but generally eat aquatic animals. Some species are in danger of extinction owing to collection for the pet trade; most of the animals collected die in transit.

Species include the **diamondback terrapin** *Malaclemys terrapin* of the eastern USA, the **yellow-bellied terrapin**, and the **red-eared terrapin** *Pseudemys scripta elegans*.

terrier any of various breeds of highly intelligent, active dogs. They are usually small. Types include the bull, cairn, fox, Irish, Scottish, Sealyham, Skye, and Yorkshire terriers. They were originally bred for hunting rabbits and following quarry such as foxes down into burrows.

The small Parson Jack Russell terrier was recognized by the Kennel Club in 1990 as a variant of the fox terrier.

Territorial Army British force of volunteer soldiers, created from volunteer regiments (incorporated in 1872) as the **Territorial Force** in 1908. It was raised and administered by county associations, and intended primarily for home defence. It was renamed the Territorial Army in 1922. Merged with the Regular Army in World War II, it was revived in 1947, and replaced by a smaller, more highly trained Territorial and Army Volunteer Reserve, again renamed the Territorial Army in 1979.

territorial behaviour in biology, any behaviour that serves to exclude other members of the same species from a fixed area or ▷territory. It may involve aggressively driving out intruders, marking the boundary (with dung piles or secretions from special scent glands), conspicuous visual displays, characteristic songs, or loud calls.

territorial waters area of sea over which the adjoining coastal state claims territorial rights. This is most commonly a distance of 22.2 km/12 nautical mi from the coast, but, increasingly, states claim fishing and other rights up to 370 km/200 mi.

territory in animal behaviour, a fixed area from which an animal or group of animals excludes other members of the same species. Animals may hold territories for many different reasons; for example, to provide a constant food supply, to monopolize potential mates, or to ensure access to refuges or nest sites.

The size of a territory depends in part on its function: some nesting and mating territories may be only a few square metres, whereas feeding territories may be as large as hundreds of square kilometres.

terrorism systematic violence in the furtherance of political aims, often by small ▷guerrilla groups.

Forms of terrorism Terrorist groups include those dedicated to a political programme for their country, usually involving the overthrow of the regime: communist and fascist terrorists fall into this category. Systematic violence used to press a single-issue cause, such as anti-abortionism or animal rights, may also be seen as terrorism. Terrorism may also be directed by an ethnic majority against a minority ruling group (as in South Africa or the former Rhodesia) or against an occupying force (as with Afghan resistance to Soviet occupation). Terrorist organizations which represent the interests of an ethnic group in a particular region are often separatist (though they may also be anti-separatist).

Left-wing revolutionary groups have included the ▷Baader-Meinhof gang in Germany or the ▷Red Brigades in Italy, and bomb attacks in Italy in 1980 and the UK in 1999 have been attributed to right-wing elements. Terrorists representing ethnic groups or peoples have included Palestinian, ▷Kurdish, and ▷Kosovan Albanian groups.

In English law, under the Prevention of Terrorism Act 1984, people arrested may be detained for 48 hours; the secretary of state can extend the period of detention for a maximum of five further days. This procedure, which results in the holding of those suspected of terrorism for up to seven days with no judicial control, was condemned as unlawful by the European Court of Human Rights in 1988. By 1991, 18,000 people had been detained but only 250 were charged with offences.

Terror, Reign of phase of the ▷French Revolution when the ▷Jacobins were in power (October 1793 to July 1794) under ▷Robespierre and began systematically to murder their political opponents. The Terror was at its height in the early months of 1794. Across France, it is thought that between 17,000 and 40,000 people were executed, mainly by guillotine, until public indignation rose and Robespierre was overthrown and guillotined in July 1794.

The Reign of Terror began with the Jacobin seizure of power from the more moderate ▷Girondins in June 1793. The Committee of Public Safety, with Robespierre at the helm, assumed dictatorial powers and liquidated anyone regarded as a threat to the state. One of the most prominent of the Terror's victims was the revolutionary minister of justice Georges ▷Danton.

Terry, (Alice) Ellen (1847–1928) English actor. She was leading lady to Henry ▷Irving from 1878. She excelled in Shakespearean roles, such as Ophelia in *Hamlet*. She was a correspondent of longstanding with the dramatist George Bernard Shaw. She was awarded the GCBE in 1925.

tertiary in the Roman Catholic Church, a member of a 'third order' (see under ▷holy orders); a lay person who, while marrying and following a normal employment, attempts to live in accordance with a modified version of the rule of one of the religious orders. The first such order was founded by St ▷Francis in 1221.

Tertiary period period of geological time 65 to 1.64 million years ago, divided into five epochs: Palaeocene, Eocene, Oligocene, Miocene, and Pliocene. During the Tertiary period, mammals took over all the ecological niches left vacant by the extinction of the dinosaurs, and became the prevalent land animals. The continents took on their present positions, and climatic and vegetation zones as we know them became established. Within the geological time column the Tertiary follows the Cretaceous period and is succeeded by the Quaternary period.

Tertullian, Quintus Septimius Florens (*c*. AD 155–*c*. 222) Carthaginian theologian, one of the so-called Fathers of the Church and the first major Christian writer in Latin. He became a leading exponent of ▷Montanism.

Terylene trade name for a synthetic polyester fibre produced by the chemicals company ICI. It is made by polymerizing ethylene glycol and terephthalic acid. Cloth made from Terylene keeps its shape after washing and is hard-wearing.

tesla SI unit (symbol T) of ▷magnetic flux density. One tesla represents a flux density of one ▷weber per square metre, or 10^4 ▷gauss. It is named after the Croatian-born US physicist Nikola Tesla.

Tesla, Nikola (1856–1943) Serbian-born US physicist and electrical engineer who invented fluorescent lighting, the Tesla induction motor (1882–87), and the Tesla coil, and developed the ▷alternating current (AC) electrical supply system.

testa the outer coat of a seed, formed after fertilization of the ovule. It has a protective function and is usually hard and dry. In some cases the coat is adapted to aid dispersal, for example by being hairy. Humans have found uses for many types of testa, including the fibre of the cotton seed.

Test Ban Treaty agreement signed by the USA, the USSR, and the UK on 5 August 1963 contracting to test nuclear weapons only underground. In the following two years 90 other nations signed the treaty, the only major nonsignatories being France and China, which continued underwater and ground-level tests. In January 1996 France announced the ending of its test programme, and supported the implementation of a universal test ban.

test data data designed to test whether a new computer program is functioning correctly. The test data are carefully chosen to ensure that all possible branches of the program are tested. The expected results of running the data are written down and are then compared with the actual results obtained using the program.

testis (plural **testes**) the organ that produces ▷sperm in male (and hermaphrodite) animals. In vertebrates it is one of a pair of oval structures that are usually internal, but in mammals (other than elephants and marine mammals), the paired testes (or testicles) descend from the body cavity during development, to hang outside the abdomen in a scrotal sac. The testes also secrete the male sex hormone ▷androgen.

testosterone in vertebrates, hormone secreted chiefly by the testes, but also by the ovaries and the cortex of the adrenal glands. It promotes the development of secondary sexual characteristics in males. In animals with a breeding season, the onset of breeding behaviour is accompanied by a rise in the level of testosterone in the blood.

tetanus (or **lockjaw**) acute disease caused by the toxin of the bacillus *Clostridium tetani*, which usually enters the body through a wound. The bacterium is chiefly found in richly manured soil. Untreated, in seven to ten days tetanus produces muscular spasm and rigidity of the jaw spreading to other parts of the body, convulsions, and death. There is a vaccine, and the disease may be treatable with tetanus antitoxin and antibiotics.

Tethys in Greek mythology, one of the ▷Titans; a daughter of Uranus and Gaia; and the wife of the sea god ▷Oceanus, by whom she was the mother of over three thousand children: the river gods, oceanids (▷nymphs of the open sea), and the waves.

Tethys Sea sea that in the Mesozoic era separated ▷Laurasia from ▷Gondwanaland. The formation of the Alpine fold mountains caused the sea to separate into the Mediterranean, the Black, the Caspian, and the Aral seas.

Tet Offensive in the Vietnam War, a prolonged attack mounted by the Vietcong against Saigon (now Ho Chi Minh City) and other South Vietnamese cities and hamlets (including the US Marine base at Khe Sanh), which began on 30 January 1968. Although the Vietcong were finally forced to withdraw, the Tet Offensive brought into question the ability of the South Vietnamese army and their US allies to win the war and added fuel to the antiwar movement in both the USA and Australia. From this political perspective, the Tet Offensive might be considered the watershed of the Vietnam War.

tetra any of various brightly coloured tropical freshwater bony fishes of the family Characidae, formerly placed in the genus *Tetragonopterus*. Tetras are found mainly in tropical South America, and also in Africa.

tetrachloromethane (or **carbon tetrachloride**) CCl_4 chlorinated organic compound that is a very efficient solvent for fats and greases, and was at one time the main constituent of household dry-cleaning fluids and of fire extinguishers used with electrical and petrol fires. Its use became restricted after it was discovered to be carcinogenic and it has now been largely removed from educational and industrial laboratories.

tetracycline one of a group of antibiotic compounds having in common the four-ring structure of chlortetracycline, the first member of the group to be isolated. They are prepared synthetically or obtained from certain bacteria of the genus *Streptomyces*. They are broad-spectrum antibiotics, effective against a wide range of disease-causing bacteria.

tetraethyl lead $Pb(C_2H_5)_4$ compound added to leaded petrol as a component of antiknock to increase the efficiency of combustion in car engines. It is a colourless liquid that is insoluble in water but soluble in organic solvents such as benzene, ethanol, and petrol.

tetrahedron (plural **tetrahedra**) in geometry, a solid figure (▷polyhedron) with four triangular faces; that is, a ▷pyramid on a triangular base. A regular tetrahedron has equilateral triangles as its faces.

In chemistry and crystallography, tetrahedra describe the shapes of some molecules and crystals; for example, the carbon atoms in a crystal of diamond are arranged in space as a set of interconnected regular tetrahedra.

tetrapod (Greek 'four-legged') type of ▷vertebrate. The group includes mammals, birds, reptiles, and amphibians. Birds are included because they evolved from four-legged ancestors, the forelimbs having become modified to form wings. Even snakes are tetrapods, because they are descended from four-legged reptiles.

William Makepeace Thackeray

'Tis not the dying for a faith that's so hard . . . every man of every nation has done that – 'tis the living up to it that is difficult.

History of Henry Esmond bk 1, ch. 6

Teutonic Knight member of a German Christian military order, the **Knights of the Teutonic Order**, founded in 1190 by Hermann of Salza in Palestine. They crusaded against the pagan Prussians and Lithuanians from 1228 and controlled Prussia until the 16th century. Their capital was Marienburg (now Malbork, Poland).

Texas state in southwestern USA. It is nicknamed the Lone Star State. Texas was admitted to the Union in 1845 as the 28th US state. One of the Great Plains states, it is bordered to the east by Louisiana, to the northeast by Arkansas, to the north by Oklahoma, to the west by New Mexico, to the southwest by the Mexican states of Chihuahua, Coahuil, Nuevo Léon, and Tamaulipas, and to the southeast by the Gulf of Mexico. Texas is the largest state in the lower 48 US states.

population (1995) 18,724,000 **area** 691,200 sq km/266,803 sq mi **capital** Austin **towns and cities** Houston, Dallas, Fort Worth, San Antonio, El Paso, Corpus Christi, Lubbock **industries and products** rice, cotton, sorghum, wheat, hay, livestock, shrimps, meat products, lumber, wood and paper products, petroleum (nearly one-third of US production), natural gas, sulphur, salt, uranium, chemicals, petrochemicals, nonelectrical machinery, fabricated metal products, transportation equipment, electric and electronic equipment, aerospace equipment, computer and high-tech machinery, finance sector, tourism **famous people** James Bowie, George Bush, O Henry, Buddy Holly, Sam Houston, Howard Hughes, Lyndon Johnson, Janis Joplin, Katherine Anne Porter, Patrick Swayze, Tina Turner, Bob Wills.

Related Web site: Texas-American Relations, 1838–1846
http://www.yale.edu/lawweb/avalon/texmenu.htm

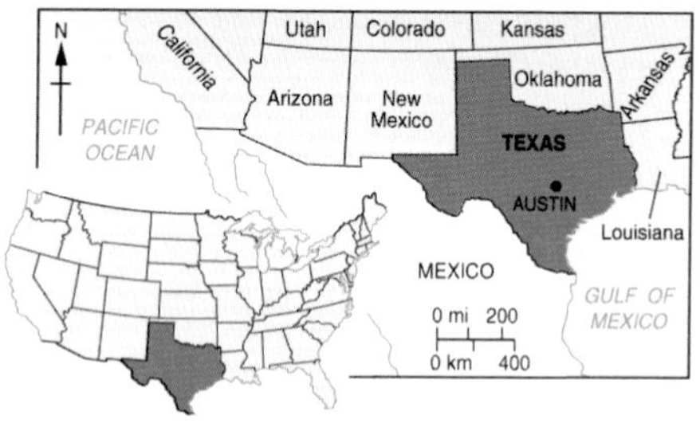

Texel (or **Tessel**) largest and southernmost of the ▷Frisian Islands, in North Holland province, the Netherlands; area 190 sq km/73 sq mi; population (1997) 13,300. It is separated from the mainland by the 4 km/2.5 mi wide Marsdiep channel and is reached by boat from Den Helder. Den Burg is the chief settlement. Local industries include tourism, fishing and farming. Texel sheep are kept for their wool and cheese. The northern part of the island is called Eierland (Egg Land) because it is a good breeding ground for thousands of birds.

Tex-Mex mix of Texan and Mexican cultural elements in the southwest USA and Mexico; specifically, accordion-based dance music originating in Texas among the ethnic Mexican community. The accordionist Flaco Jimenez and the band Los Lobos, among others, have popularized the genre beyond Texas.

text editor in computing, a program that allows the user to edit text on the screen and to store it in a file. Text editors are similar to ▷word processors, except that they lack the ability to format text into paragraphs and pages and to apply different typefaces and styles.

textile (Latin *texere* 'to weave') woven fabric; formerly a material woven from natural spun thread, now loosely extended to machine knits and spun-bonded fabrics (in which a web of fibre is created and then fuse-bonded by passing it through controlled heat).

Thackeray, William Makepeace (1811–1863) English novelist and essayist. He was a regular contributor to *Fraser's Magazine* and *Punch*. His first novel was *Vanity Fair* (1847–48), significant for the breadth of its canvas as well as for the depth of the characterization. This was followed by *Pendennis* (1848), *Henry Esmond* (1852) (and its sequel *The Virginians* (1857–59)), and *The Newcomes* (1853–55), in which Thackeray's tendency to sentimentality is most marked.

The son of an East India Company official, he was educated at Cambridge University. He studied law, and then art in Paris, before ultimately becoming a journalist in London. Other works include *The Book of Snobs* (1848) and the fairy tale *The Rose and the Ring* (1855).

Related Web site: Vanity Fair http://www.catawba.k12.nc.us/books/vfair10.txt

Thai the majority ethnic group living in Thailand and northern Myanmar (Burma). Thai peoples also live in southwestern China, Laos, and North Vietnam. They speak Tai languages, all of which belong to the Sino-Tibetan language family. There are over 60 million speakers, the majority of whom live in Thailand. Most Thais are Buddhists, but the traditional belief in spirits, phi, remains.

Thailand (formerly **Siam** (to 1939 and 1945–49)) see country box.

Thaïs (lived 4th century BC) Greek courtesan, mistress of Alexander the Great and later wife of ▷Ptolemy I, king of Egypt. She allegedly instigated the burning of ▷Persepolis.

thalassaemia (or **Cooley's anaemia**) any of a group of chronic hereditary blood disorders that are widespread in the Mediterranean countries, Africa, the Far East, and the Middle East.

Thailand

Thailand (formerly Siam, until 1939 and 1945–49) country in southeast Asia on the Gulf of Siam, bounded east by Laos and Cambodia, south by Malaysia, and west by Myanmar (Burma).

NATIONAL NAME *Ratcha Anachak Thai/Kingdom of Thailand*
AREA 513,115 sq km/198,113 sq mi
CAPITAL Bangkok (and chief port)
MAJOR TOWNS/CITIES Chiang Mai, Hat Yai, Khon Kaen, Songkhla, Nakhon Ratchasima, Nonthaburi, Udon Thani
MAJOR PORTS Nakhon Sawan
PHYSICAL FEATURES mountainous, semi-arid plateau in northeast, fertile central region, tropical isthmus in south; rivers Chao Phraya, Mekong, and Salween

Government

HEAD OF STATE King Bhumibol Adulyadej from 1946
HEAD OF GOVERNMENT Thaksin Shinawatra from 2001
POLITICAL SYSTEM emergent democracy
POLITICAL EXECUTIVE parliamentary
ADMINISTRATIVE DIVISIONS 73 provinces
ARMED FORCES 306,000 (2002 est)
DEATH PENALTY retained and used for ordinary crimes

Economy and resources

CURRENCY baht
GPD (US$) 126.4 billion (2002 est)
REAL GDP GROWTH (% change on previous year) 1.9 (2001)
GNI (US$) 122.2 billion (2002 est)
GNI PER CAPITA (PPP) (US$) 6,680 (2002 est)
CONSUMER PRICE INFLATION 1.7% (2003 est)
UNEMPLOYMENT 3.3% (2001)
FOREIGN DEBT (US$) 61.02 billion (2001 est)
MAJOR TRADING PARTNERS Japan, USA, Singapore, Germany, Malaysia, Hong Kong, the Netherlands

RESOURCES tin ore, lignite, gypsum, antimony, manganese, copper, tungsten, lead, gold, zinc, silver, rubies, sapphires, natural gas, petroleum, fish
INDUSTRIES textiles and clothing, electronics, electrical goods, cement, petroleum refining, sugar refining, motor vehicles, agricultural products, beverages, tobacco, metals and metal products, plastics, furniture, tourism
EXPORTS machinery and mechanical appliances, textiles and clothing, electronic goods, rice, rubber, gemstones, sugar, cassava (tapioca), fish (especially prawns), chemicals. Principal market: USA 22.2% (2001)
IMPORTS petroleum and petroleum products, electrical machinery, chemicals, iron and steel, non-electronic machinery, consumer goods. Principal source: Japan 22.4% (2001)
ARABLE LAND 28.8% (2000 est)
AGRICULTURAL PRODUCTS rice, cassava, rubber, sugar cane, maize, kenat (a jute-like fibre), tobacco, coconuts; fishing (especially prawns) and livestock (mainly buffaloes, cattle, pigs, and poultry)

Population and society

POPULATION 62,833,000 (2003 est)
POPULATION GROWTH RATE 0.8% (2000–15)
POPULATION DENSITY (per sq km) 122 (2003 est)
URBAN POPULATION (% of total) 20 (2003 est)
AGE DISTRIBUTION (% of total population) 0–14 26%, 15–59 66%, 60+ 8% (2002 est)
ETHNIC GROUPS 75% of the population is of Thai descent; 14% ethnic Chinese, one-third of whom live in Bangkok; Thai Malays constitute the next largest minority, followed by hill tribes; a substantial Kampuchean (Khmer) refugee community resides in border camps
LANGUAGE Thai, Chinese (both official), English, Lao, Malay, Khmer
RELIGION Buddhist 95%; Muslim 5%
EDUCATION (compulsory years) 6
LITERACY RATE 97% (men); 95% (women) (2003 est)
LABOUR FORCE 48.5% agriculture, 18.4% industry, 33.1% services (1999)
LIFE EXPECTANCY 65 (men); 74 (women) (2000–05)
CHILD MORTALITY RATE (under 5, per 1,000 live births) 28 (2001)
PHYSICIANS (per 1,000 people) 0.4 (1998 est)
HOSPITAL BEDS (per 1,000 people) 2 (1998 est)
TV SETS (per 1,000 people) 300 (2001 est)
RADIOS (per 1,000 people) 235 (2001 est)
INTERNET USERS (per 10,000 people) 775.6 (2002 est)
PERSONAL COMPUTER USERS (per 100 people) 4.0 (2002 est)

See also ▷Buddhism; ▷Bhumibol Adulyadej.

Chronology

13th century: Siamese (Thai) people migrated south and settled in valley of Chao Phraya River in Khmer Empire.

1238: Siamese ousted Khmer governors and formed new kingdom based at Sukhothai.

14th and 15th centuries: Siamese expanded at expense of declining Khmer Empire.

1350: Siamese capital moved to Ayatthaya (which also became name of kingdom).

1511: Portuguese traders first reached Siam.

1569: Conquest of Ayatthaya by Burmese ended years of rivalry and conflict.

1589: Siamese regained independence under King Naresuan.

17th century: Foreign trade under royal monopoly developed with Chinese, Japanese, and Europeans.

1690s: Siam expelled European military advisers and missionaries and adopted policy of isolation.

1767: Burmese invaders destroyed city of Ayatthaya, massacred ruling families, and withdrew, leaving Siam in a state of anarchy.

1782: Reunification of Siam after civil war under Gen Phraya Chakri, who founded new capital at Bangkok and proclaimed himself King Rama I.

1824–51: King Rama III reopened Siam to European diplomats and missionaries.

1851–68: King Mongkut employed European advisers to help modernize the government, legal system, and army.

1856: Royal monopoly on foreign trade ended.

1868–1910: King Chulalongkorn continued modernization and developed railway network using Chinese immigrant labour; Siam became major exporter of rice.

1896: Anglo-French agreement recognized Siam as independent buffer state between British Burma and French Indo-China.

1932: Bloodless coup forced King Rama VII to grant a constitution with a mixed civilian-military government.

1939: Siam changed its name to Thailand (briefly reverting to Siam 1945–49).

1941: Japanese invaded; Thailand became puppet ally of Japan under Field Marshal Phibun Songkhram.

1945: Japanese withdrawal; Thailand compelled to return territory taken from Laos, Cambodia, and Malaya.

1947: Phibun regained power in military coup, reducing monarch to figurehead; Thailand adopted strongly pro-American foreign policy.

1955: Political parties and free speech introduced.

1957: State of emergency declared; Phibun deposed in bloodless coup; military dictatorship continued under Gen Sarit Thanarat (1957–63) and Gen Thanom Kittikachorn (1963–73).

1967–72: Thai troops fought in alliance with USA in Vietnam War.

1973: Military government overthrown by student riots.

1974: Adoption of democratic constitution, followed by civilian coalition government.

1976: Military reassumed control in response to mounting strikes and political violence.

1978: Gen Kriangsak Chomanan introduced constitution with mixed civilian–military government.

1980: Gen Prem Tinsulanonda assumed power.

1983: Prem relinquished army office to head civilian government; martial law maintained.

1988: Chatichai Choonhavan succeeded Prem as prime minister.

1991: A military coup imposed a new military-oriented constitution despite mass protests.

1992: A general election produced a five-party coalition; riots forced Prime Minister Suchinda Kraprayoon to flee; Chuan Leekpai formed a new coalition government.

1995–96: The ruling coalition collapsed. A general election in 1996 resulted in a new six-party coalition led by Chavalit Yongchaiyudh.

1997: A major financial crisis led to the floating of currency. An austerity rescue plan was agreed with the International Monetary Fund (IMF). Chuan Leekpai was re-elected prime minister.

1998: Repatriation of foreign workers commenced, as the economy contracted sharply due to the rescue plan. The opposition Chart Patthana party was brought into the coalition government of Chuan Leekpai.

2001: The Thai Rak Thai party won general elections, but failed to achieve an absolute majority. Thaksin Shinawatra became prime minister.

THAILAND A stamp from Thailand produced in celebration of the Buddhist religious festival Asalhapuga Day. This was the day when Buddha gave his first sermon, when the order of Sangha was initiated, and when the religion was founded. *Stanley Gibbons*

They are characterized by an abnormality of the red blood cells and bone marrow, with enlargement of the spleen. The genes responsible are carried by about 100 million people worldwide. The diseases can be diagnosed prenatally.

Thalberg, Irving (Grant) (1899–1936) US film-production executive. At the age of 20 he was head of production at Universal Pictures, and in 1924 he became production supervisor of the newly formed ▷Metro-Goldwyn-Mayer (MGM). He was responsible for such prestige films as *Ben Hur* (1926) and *Mutiny on the Bounty* (1935). With Louis B Mayer, he built up MGM into one of the biggest Hollywood studios of the 1930s.

Thales (*c.* 624–*c.* 547 BC) Also known as *Thales of Miletus*. Greek philosopher and scientist. He made advances in geometry, predicted an eclipse of the Sun in 585 BC, and, as a philosophical materialist, theorized that water was the first principle of all things. He speculated that the Earth floated on water, and so proposed an explanation for earthquakes. He lived in Miletus in Asia Minor.

thallium (Greek *thallos* 'young green shoot') soft, bluish-white, malleable, metallic element, symbol Tl, atomic number 81, relative atomic mass 204.38. It is a poor conductor of electricity. Its compounds are poisonous and are used as insecticides and rodent poisons; some are used in the optical-glass and infrared-glass industries and in photocells.

Discovered spectroscopically by its green line, thallium was isolated and named by William Crookes in 1861.

thallus any plant body that is not divided into true leaves, stems, and roots. It is often thin and flattened, as in the body of a seaweed, lichen, or liverwort, and the gametophyte generation (prothallus) of a fern.

Thames river in south England, flowing through London; length 338 km/210 mi. The longest river in England, it rises in the Cotswold Hills above Cirencester and is tidal as far as Teddington. Below London there is protection from flooding by means of the **Thames Barrier** (1982). The headstreams unite at Lechlade.

Thanet, Isle of northeast corner of Kent, southeast England, bounded by the North Sea at the Thames estuary, and the rivers Stour and Wantsum. It was an island until the 16th century, and includes the coastal resorts of Broadstairs, ▷Margate, and Ramsgate. Traditionally a cereal-growing area, it has now become a major area for the cultivation of vegetables. In addition to agriculture, industries include toymaking, signmaking, and plastics.

Thanksgiving (or **Thanksgiving Day**) national holiday in the USA (fourth Thursday in November) and Canada (second Monday in October), first celebrated by the Pilgrim settlers in Massachusetts after their first harvest in 1621.

    Related Web site: Thanksgiving on the Net – Welcome http://www.holidays.net/thanksgiving/

THANKSGIVING Following its discovery by Europeans, the American continent was inhabited in the 1500s by both white settlers and American Indians. In the USA today, this racial mix is remembered at Thanksgiving, originally celebrated, as in this illustration, with a meal of local foods. *Archive Photos*

Thant, U (1909–1974) Burmese diplomat, secretary general of the United Nations 1962–71. He helped to resolve the US–Soviet crisis over the Soviet installation of missiles in Cuba, and he made the controversial decision to withdraw the UN peacekeeping force from the Egypt–Israel border in 1967 (see ▷Arab-Israeli Wars).

Tharp, Twyla (1941–) US modern-dance choreographer and dancer. A phenomenal success in the 1970s, Tharp's work both entertains and challenges audiences with her ability to create serious and beautifully constructed ballets with an often amusing or flippant veneer. Reflecting her eclectic training, she has fused many dance styles including ballet, jazz, modern, tap, and

avant-garde dance. Her works, frequently to set to popular music, include *Eight Jelly Rolls* (1971), *Deuce Coupe* (1973) (music by the Beach Boys), and *Push Comes to Shove* (1976) with Mikhail Baryshnikov, which was one of the most popular works of the decade.

Thatcher, Margaret Hilda (1925–) Baroness Thatcher; born Margaret Hilda Roberts. British Conservative politician, prime minister 1979–90. She was education minister 1970–74 and Conservative Party leader 1975–90. In 1982 she sent British troops to recapture the Falkland Islands from Argentina. She confronted trade-union power during the miners' strike 1984–85, sold off majority stakes in many public utilities to the private sector, and reduced the influence of local government through such measures as the abolition of metropolitan councils, the control of expenditure through 'rate-capping', and the introduction of the community charge, or ▷poll tax, in 1989. In 1990, splits in the cabinet over the issues of Europe and consensus government forced her resignation. An astute parliamentary tactician, she tolerated little disagreement, either from the opposition or from within her own party.

Thatcher was the most influential peacetime Conservative prime minister of the 20th century. She claimed to have 'rolled back the frontiers of the state' by reducing income-tax rates, selling off council houses, and allowing for greater individual choice in areas such as education. However, such initiatives often resulted paradoxically in greater central government control. She left the opposition Labour Party in disarray, and forced it to a fundamental review of its policies. Her vindictiveness against the left was revealed in her crusade against local councils, which she pursued at the cost of a concern for social equity. In 1991, after three months of relative quiescence on the back benches, she made it evident that she intended to remain an active voice in domestic and international politics. She was created a life peer in 1992. Her first speech in the House of Lords was an attack on the government's policies.

Since leaving public office, she has devoted herself to the development of her individual philosophy through the 'Thatcher Foundation'.

    Related Web site: Biography of Lady Margaret Thatcher http://www.uu.edu/front/features/front/fall98/mtbio.htm

Thatcherism political outlook comprising a belief in the efficacy of market forces, the need for strong central government, and a conviction that self-help is preferable to reliance on the state, combined with a strong element of ▷nationalism. The ideology is associated with the former UK premier Margaret ▷Thatcher, but stems from an individualist view found in Britain's 19th-century Liberal and 20th-century Conservative parties, and is no longer confined to Britain. Since leaving public office, Baroness Thatcher has established her own 'Foundation'.

theatre a place or building in which dramatic performances for an audience take place; these include ▷drama, dancing, music, ▷mime, ▷opera, ▷ballet, and ▷puppets. Theatre history can be traced to Egyptian religious ritualistic drama as long ago as 3200 BC. The first known European theatres were in Greece from about 600 BC.

The earliest theatres were natural amphitheatres. By the Hellenistic period came the development of the stage, a raised platform on which the action took place. In medieval times, temporary stages of wood and canvas, one for every scene, were set up in churches and market squares for the performance of mimes and ▷miracle plays. With the Renaissance came the creation of

THEATRE A performance of Verdi's popular dramatic opera *Aïda* at the Kirov Theatre, St Petersburg. The opera was written in 1871 to commemorate the opening of the Suez Canal, and was first performed in Cairo. *Corel*

scenic illusion, with the actors appearing within a proscenium arch; in the 19th century the introduction of the curtain and interior lighting further heightened this illusion. In the 20th century, alternative types of theatre were developed, including open stage, thrust stage, theatre-in-the-round, and studio theatre.

Famous theatre companies include the ▷Comédie Française in Paris (founded by Louis XIV in 1690 and given a permanent home in 1792), the first national theatre. The Living Theater was founded in New York in 1947 by Julian Beck and Judith Malina. In Britain the ▷National Theatre company was established in 1963; other national theatres exist in Stockholm, Moscow, Athens, Copenhagen, Vienna, Warsaw, and elsewhere.

    Related Web site: Theatre Arts Library http://www.perspicacity.com/elactheatre/index.html

theatre-in-the-round theatrical performance that has the audience watching from all sides. In a reaction to the picture-frame stage of the 19th century, a movement began in the mid-20th century to design theatres with the performing area placed centrally in the auditorium. Notable examples are the Arena Stage in Washington, DC, USA (1961) and the Royal Exchange in Manchester, England (1976).

Thebes Greek name of an ancient city (Niut-Amen) in Upper Egypt, on the Nile. Probably founded under the first dynasty, it was the centre of the worship of Amen, and the Egyptian capital under the New Kingdom from about 1550 BC. Temple ruins survive near the villages of Karnak and Luxor, and in the nearby **Valley of the Kings** are buried the 18th to 20th dynasty kings, including Tutankhamen and Amenhotep III.

    Related Web site: Theban Mapping Project http://www.kv5.com/intro.html

Thebes capital of Boeotia in ancient Greece. In the Peloponnesian War it was allied with Sparta against Athens. For a short time after 371 BC when Thebes defeated Sparta at Leuctra, it was the most powerful state in Greece. Alexander the Great destroyed it in 336 BC and although it was restored, it never regained its former power.

ANCIENT EGYPTIAN WALL-PAINTINGS IN A TOMB AT THEBES Circa 1380 BC

THEBES Ancient Egyptian wall paintings in a tomb at Thebes from about 1380 BC. *Philip Sauvain Picture Collection*

theism belief in the existence of gods, but more specifically in that of a single personal God, at once immanent (active) in the created world and transcendent (separate) from it.

Themis in Greek mythology, one of the ▷Titans, the daughter of Uranus and Gaia. She was the personification of law and order.

Themistocles (*c.* 524–*c.* 460 BC) Athenian admiral and politician. His success in persuading the Athenians to build a navy is credited with saving Greece from Persian conquest. During the Persian War, he fought with distinction in the battles of Artemisium and Salamis in 480 BC. After the war he pursued an anti-Spartan line which got him ostracized, possibly in 471. Some years later he fled to Asia Minor where he died.

theocracy political system run by priests, as was once found in Tibet. In practical terms it means a system where religious values determine political decisions. The closest modern example have been Iran during the period when Ayatollah Khomeini was its religious leader, 1979–89, and Afghanistan, since the Talibaan came to power in 1996. The term was coined by the historian ▷Josephus in the 1st century AD.

theodolite instrument for the measurement of horizontal and vertical angles, used in surveying. It consists of a small telescope

Theatre: Key Events

c. 3200 BC	Beginnings of Egyptian religious drama, essentially ritualistic.
c. 600	Choral performances (dithyrambs) form the beginnings of Greek tragedy.
500–300	Great age of Greek drama which includes tragedy, comedy, and satyr plays (grotesque farce).
468	Sophocles' first victory at the Athens festival. His use of a third actor alters the course of the tragic form.
458	Aeschylus' Oresteia first performed.
c. 425–388	Comedies of Aristophanes including The Birds (414), Lysistrata (411), and The Frogs (405). In tragedy the importance of the chorus diminishes under Euripides, author of The Bacchae (c. 405).
c. 320	Menander's 'New Comedy' of social manners develops.
c. 240 BC–AD 100	Emergence of Roman drama, adapted from Greek originals. Plautus, Terence, and Seneca are the main dramatists.
c. AD 400	Kālidāsa's Sakuntalā marks the height of Sanskrit drama in India.
c. 1250–1500	European mystery (or miracle) plays flourish, first in the churches and later in marketplaces.
c. 1375	Nō (Noh) drama develops in Japan.
c. 1495	Everyman, the best known of all the morality plays, is first performed.
1525–1750	Italian commedia dell'arte troupes perform popular, improvised comedies; they are to have a large influence on Molière and on English harlequinade and pantomime.
c. 1540	Nicholas Udall writes Ralph Roister Doister, the first English comedy.
c. 1576	The first English playhouse, The Theatre, is built by James Burbage in London.
c. 1587	Christopher Marlowe's play Tamburlaine the Great marks the beginning of the great age of Elizabethan and Jacobean drama in England.
c. 1588	Thomas Kyd's play The Spanish Tragedy is the first of the 'revenge' tragedies.
c. 1590–1612	Shakespeare's greatest plays, including Hamlet and King Lear, are written.
1604	Inigo Jones designs The Masque of Blackness for James I, written by Ben Jonson.
c. 1614	Lope de Vega's Fuenteovejuna marks the Spanish renaissance in drama.
1636	Pierre Corneille's Le Cid establishes classical tragedy in France.
1642	An act of Parliament closes all English theatres.
1660	With the restoration of Charles II to the English throne, dramatic performances recommence. The first professional actor appears as Desdemona in Shakespeare's Othello.
1664	Molière's Tartuffe is banned for five years by religious factions.
1667	Jean Racine's first success, Andromaque, is staged.
1680	The Comédie Française is formed by Louis XIV.
1700	William Congreve, the greatest exponent of Restoration comedy, writes The Way of the World.
1716	The first known American theatre is built in Williamsburg, Virginia.
1728	John Gay's The Beggar's Opera is first performed.
1737	The Stage Licensing Act in England requires all plays to be approved by the Lord Chamberlain before performance.
1773	In England, Oliver Goldsmith's She Stoops to Conquer and Richard Sheridan's The Rivals (1775) establish the 'comedy of manners'. Goethe's Götz von Berlichingen is the first Sturm und Drang play (literally, storm and stress).
1781	Friedrich Schiller's Die Räuber/The Robbers.
1784	Beaumarchais' Le Mariage de Figaro/The Marriage of Figaro (written 1778) is first performed.
1830	Victor Hugo's Hernani causes riots in Paris. His work marks the beginning of a new Romantic drama.
1879	Henrik Ibsen's A Doll's House is an early example of realism in European theatre.
1888	August Strindberg writes Miss Julie.
1893	George Bernard Shaw writes Mrs Warren's Profession (banned until 1902 because it deals with prostitution).
1895	Oscar Wilde's comedy The Importance of Being Earnest is performed.
1896	The first performance of Anton Chekhov's The Seagull fails. Alfred Jarry's Ubu Roi, a forerunner of surrealism, is produced in Paris.
1904	Chekhov's The Cherry Orchard. The Academy of Dramatic Art (Royal Academy of Dramatic Art from 1920) is founded in London to train young actors.
1919	The Theater Guild is founded in the USA to perform new less commercial plays.
1920	Beyond the Horizon, Eugene O'Neill's first play, marks the beginning of serious theatre in the USA.
1921	Luigi Pirandello's Six Characters in Search of an Author introduces themes of the individual and exploration of reality and appearance.
1927	Show Boat, composed by Jerome Kern with libretto by Oscar Hammerstein II, lays the foundations of the US musical.
1928	Bertolt Brecht's Die Dreigroschenoper/The Threepenny Opera with score by Kurt Weill; other political satires by Karel Čapek and Elmer Rice.
1930s	US social-protest plays of Clifford Odets, Lillian Hellman, Thornton Wilder, and William Saroyan are produced.
1935	T S Eliot's Murder in the Cathedral is performed.
1935–39	WPA Federal Theater Project in the USA is active.
1938	Publication of Antonin Artaud's Theatre and Its Double.
1943	The first of the Rodgers and Hammerstein musicals, Oklahoma!, opens.
1944	Jean-Paul Sartre's Huis Clos/In Camera; Jean Anouilh's Antigone.
post-1945	Resurgence of German-language theatre, including Wolfgang Borchert, Max Frisch, Friedrich Dürrenmatt, and Peter Weiss.
1947	Tennessee Williams' A Streetcar Named Desire. First Edinburgh Festival, Scotland, with fringe theatre events.
1949	Bertolt Brecht and Helene Weigel founds the Berliner Ensemble in East Germany.
1953	Arthur Miller's The Crucible opened in the USA; En attendant Godot/Waiting for Godot by Samuel Beckett exemplifies the Theatre of the Absurd.
1956	The English Stage Company is formed at the Royal Court Theatre. John Osborne's Look Back in Anger is included in its first season.
1957	Leonard Bernstein's West Side Story opens in New York.
1960	Harold Pinter's The Caretaker is produced in London.
1960s	Off-off-Broadway theatre, a more daring and experimental type of drama, begins to develop in New York.
1961	The Royal Shakespeare Company is formed in the UK under the directorship of Peter Hall.
1963–64	The UK National Theatre Company is formed at the Old Vic under the directorship of Laurence Olivier.
1964	Théâtre du Soleil, directed by Ariane Mnouchkine, is founded in Paris.
1967	Athol Fugard founds the Serpent Players as an integrated company in Port Elizabeth, South Africa; success in the USA of Hair, the first of the 'rock' musicals; Tom Stoppard's Rosencrantz and Guildenstern are Dead is produced in London.
1968	Abolition of the legal requirement to obtain official approval before staging a performance in the UK.
1970	Peter Brook founds his international company, the International Centre for Theatre Research, in Paris; first festival of Chicano theatre in the USA.
1972	Sam Shepard's The Tooth of Crime is performed in London.
1974	Athol Fugard's Statements After an Arrest under the Immorality Act is performed in London.
1975	A Chorus Line, to become the longest-running musical, opens in New York; Tadeusz Kantor's Dead Class is produced in Poland.
1980	Howard Brenton's The Romans in Britain leads in the UK to a private prosecution of the director for obscenity; David Edgar's The Life and Times of Nicholas Nickleby is performed in London.
1985	Peter Brook's first production of The Mahabharata is produced at the Avignon Festival.
1987	The Japanese Ninagawa Company perform Shakespeare's Macbeth in London.
1989	Discovery of the remains of the 16th-century Rose and Globe theatres, London.
1992	Ariane Mnouchkine's production of Les Atrides opens in Paris and the UK; Robert Wilson's production of Alice opens in Germany.
1993	Construction of the new Globe Theatre, a replica of the Elizabethan Globe Playhouse, begins in London, approximately 183 m/600 ft from the site of the original Globe.
1995	The National Lottery in the UK begins to distribute millions of pounds to the theatre. However, most is allocated to the large prestigious concerns, and many small and medium-scale touring companies are left disappointed.
1996	The Prologue Season at the new Globe Theatre in London opened with The Two Gentlemen of Verona.
1998	Many Hollywood stars appear in London stage productions, including Liam Neeson, Kevin Spacey, and Juliet Binoche.

THEATRE The English actor Alec Guinness, in the role of the Welsh poet Dylan Thomas, being interviewed by the US television talk-show host Ed Sullivan in June 1964. *Image Bank*

---

mounted so as to move on two graduated circles, one horizontal and the other vertical, while its axes pass through the centre of the circles. See also ▷triangulation.

Theodora (c. 508–548) Byzantine empress from 527. She was originally the mistress of Emperor Justinian before marrying him in 525. She earned a reputation for charity, courage, and championing the rights of women.

Theodoric the Great (c. 455–526) King of the Ostrogoths 471–526. He led the Ostrogoths from the Danube frontier regions of the Roman Empire to conquer Italy, where he established a peaceful and prosperous kingdom. Although remembered for his benevolent rule in later years, Theodoric was ruthless in his efforts to attain power. He had no strong successor and his kingdom eventually became part of the Byzantine Empire of Justinian.

Theodosius (I) the Great (c. AD 346–395) Roman emperor. Appointed emperor of the East in 379, he fought against the ▷Goths successfully, and established Christianity throughout the region. He invaded Italy in 393, restoring unity to the empire, and died in Milan. He was buried in Constantinople.

theology study of God or gods, either by reasoned deduction from the natural world (natural theology) or through divine revelation (revealed theology), as in the scriptures of Christianity, Islam, or other religions.

Related Web site: World Scripture http://unification.net/ws/

Theophrastus (c. 372–c. 287 BC) Greek philosopher, regarded as the founder of botany. A pupil of Aristotle, Theophrastus took over the leadership of his school in 323 BC, consolidating its reputation. Of his extensive writings, surviving work is mainly on scientific topics, but includes the Characters, a series of caricatures which may have influenced the comic dramatist ▷Menander.

theorbo musical instrument, a bass ▷lute or archlute developed around 1500 and incorporating dual sets of strings, a set of freely vibrating bass strings for plucking with the thumb in addition to five to seven courses over a fretted fingerboard. It survived to form part of the Italian baroque orchestra from about 1700.

theorem mathematical proposition that can be deduced by logic from a set of axioms (basic facts that are taken to be true without proof). Advanced mathematics consists almost entirely of theorems and proofs, but even at a simple level theorems are important.

theory in science, a set of ideas, concepts, principles, or methods used to explain a wide set of observed facts. Among the major theories of science are ▷relativity, ▷quantum theory, ▷evolution, and ▷plate tectonics.

theosophy any religious or philosophical system based on intuitive insight into the nature of the divine, but especially that of the Theosophical Society, founded in New York in 1875 by Madame Blavatsky and H S Olcott. It was based on Hindu ideas of ▷karma and ▷reincarnation, with ▷nirvana as the eventual aim.

Theravāda one of the two major forms of ▷Buddhism, common in Southeast Asia (Sri Lanka, Thailand, Cambodia, and Myanmar); the other is the later Mahāyāna.

Related Web site: What is Theravada Buddhism? http://www.accesstoinsight.org/theravada.html

Thérèse of Lisieux, St (1873–1897) Born Thérèse Martin. French saint. She was born in Alençon, and entered a Carmelite convent in Lisieux at 15, where her holy life induced her superior to ask her to write her spiritual autobiography. She advocated the 'Little Way of Goodness' in small things in everyday life, and became known as the 'Little Flower of Jesus'. She died of tuberculosis and was canonized in 1925.

therm unit of energy defined as 10^5 British thermal units; equivalent to 1.055×10^8 J. It is no longer in scientific use.

thermal conductivity in physics, the ability of a substance to conduct heat. Good thermal conductors, like good electrical conductors, are generally materials with many free electrons (such as metals).

Thermal conductivity is expressed in units of joules per second per metre per kelvin ($J\ s^{-1}\ m^{-1}\ K^{-1}$). For a block of material of cross-sectional area a and length l, with temperatures T_1 and T_2 at its end faces, the thermal conductivity λ equals $Hl/at(T_2 - T_1)$, where H is the amount of heat transferred in time t.

thermal reactor nuclear reactor in which the neutrons released by fission of uranium-235 nuclei are slowed down in order to increase their chances of being captured by other uranium-235 nuclei, and so induce further fission. The material (commonly graphite or heavy water) responsible for doing so is called a **moderator**. When the fast newly-emitted neutrons collide with the nuclei of the moderator's atoms, some of their kinetic energy is lost and their speed is reduced. Those that have been slowed down to a speed that matches the thermal (heat) energy of the surrounding material are called **thermal neutrons**, and it is these that are most likely to induce fission and ensure the continuation of the chain reaction. See ▷nuclear reactor and ▷nuclear energy.

thermic lance cutting tool consisting of a tube of mild steel, enclosing tightly packed small steel rods and fed with oxygen. On ignition, temperatures above 3,000°C/5,400°F are produced and the thermic lance becomes its own sustaining fuel. It rapidly penetrates walls and a 23-cm/9-in steel door can be cut through in less than 30 seconds.

thermite process method used in incendiary devices and welding operations. It uses a powdered mixture of aluminium and (usually) iron oxide, which, when ignited, gives out enormous heat. The oxide is reduced to iron, which is molten at the high temperatures produced. This can be used to make a weld. The process was discovered in 1895 by German chemist Hans Goldschmidt (1861–1923).

thermocouple electric temperature measuring device consisting of a circuit having two wires made of different metals welded together at their ends. A current flows in the circuit when the two junctions are maintained at different temperatures (▷Seebeck effect). The electromotive force generated – measured by a millivoltmeter – is proportional to the temperature difference.

thermodynamics branch of physics dealing with the transformation of heat into and from other forms of energy. It is the basis of the study of the efficient working of engines, such as the steam and internal-combustion engines. The three laws of thermodynamics are: (1) energy can be neither created nor destroyed, heat and mechanical work being mutually convertible; (2) it is impossible for an unaided self-acting machine to convey heat from one body to another at a higher temperature; and (3) it is impossible by any procedure, no matter how idealized, to reduce any system to the ▷absolute zero of temperature (0 K/−273.15°C/−459.67°F) in a finite number of operations. Put into mathematical form, these laws have widespread applications in physics and chemistry.

thermography photographic recording of heat patterns. It is used medically as an imaging technique to identify 'hot spots' in the body – for example, tumours, where cells are more active than usual. Thermography was developed in the 1970s and 1980s by the military to assist night vision by detecting the body heat of an enemy or the hot engine of a tank. It uses detectors sensitive to infrared (heat) radiation.

thermometer instrument for measuring temperature. There are many types, designed to measure different temperature ranges to varying degrees of accuracy. Each makes use of a different physical effect of temperature. Expansion of a liquid is employed in common **liquid-in-glass thermometers**, such as those containing mercury or alcohol. The more accurate **gas thermometer** uses the effect of temperature on the pressure of a gas held at constant volume. A **resistance thermometer** takes advantage of the change in resistance of a conductor (such as a platinum wire) with variation in temperature. Another electrical thermometer is the ▷thermocouple. Mechanically, temperature change can be indicated by the change in curvature of a **bimetallic strip** (as commonly used in a ▷thermostat).

thermopile instrument for measuring radiant heat, consisting of a number of ▷thermocouples connected in series with alternate junctions exposed to the radiation. The current generated (measured by an ▷ammeter) is proportional to the radiation falling on the device.

Thermopylae, Battle of battle between the Greeks under the Spartan king Leonidas and the invading Persians under Xerxes I. They clashed at the narrow mountain pass of Thermopylae, leading from Thessaly to Locrish in central Greece. Although the Greeks were defeated, the heroism of those who fought to the last against the Persians boosted Greek morale.

thermoset type of ▷plastic that remains rigid when set, and does not soften with heating. Thermosets have this property because the long-chain polymer molecules cross-link with each other to give a rigid structure. Examples include Bakelite, resins, melamine, and urea–formaldehyde resins.

thermosphere layer in the Earth's ▷atmosphere above the mesosphere and below the exosphere. Its lower level is about 80 km/50 mi above the ground, but its upper level is undefined. The ionosphere is located in the thermosphere. In the thermosphere the temperature rises with increasing height to several thousand degrees Celsius. However, because of the thinness of the air, very little heat is actually present.

thermostat temperature-controlling device that makes use of feedback. It employs a temperature sensor (often a bimetallic strip) to operate a switch or valve to control electricity or fuel supply. Thermostats are used in central heating, ovens, and car engines.

Theroux, Paul Edward (1941–) US novelist and travel writer. His works include the novels *Saint Jack* (1973), *The Mosquito Coast* (1981), *Doctor Slaughter* (1984), *Chicago Loop* (1990), *Kowloon Tong* (1997), and *The Stranger at the Palazzo d'Oro* (2003). His accounts of his travels by train, notable for their sharp depiction of the socio-economic divides, include *The Great Railway Bazaar* (1975), *The Old Patagonian Express* (1979), *The Kingdom by the Sea* (1983), *Riding the Iron Rooster* (1988), and *Fresh-Air Fiend: Travel Writings 1985–2000* (2000).

thesaurus (Greek 'treasure') extensive collection of synonyms or words with related meaning. Thesaurus compilers include Francis ▷Bacon, Comenius, and Peter Mark ▷Roget, whose work was published in 1852.

Theseus in Greek mythology, a hero of ▷Attica, who was believed to have united the states of the area under a constitutional government in Athens. He killed the monstrous ▷Minotaur with the aid of ▷Ariadne, fought the ▷Amazons, and took part in the expedition of the ▷Argonauts.

Thesiger, Wilfred Patrick (1910–) English explorer and writer. His travels and military adventures in Abyssinia (now Ethiopia and Eritrea), North Africa, and Arabia are recounted in a number of books, including *Arabian Sands* (1959), *Desert, Marsh and Mountain* (1979), and the autobiographical *The Life of My Choice* (1987).

Thespis (lived 6th century BC) Greek poet. He is said to have introduced the first actor into dramatic performances (previously presented by choruses only), hence the word **thespian** for an actor. He is also said to have invented tragedy and to have introduced the wearing of linen masks.

Thessaloníki (English **Salonika**) port in Macedonia, northeastern Greece, at the head of the Gulf of Thessaloniki; the second-largest city in Greece; population (1991) 378,000. Industries include textiles, shipbuilding, chemicals, brewing, and tanning. It was founded from Corinth by the Romans in 315 BC as **Thessalonica** (to whose inhabitants St Paul addressed two epistles), captured by the Saracens in AD 904 and by the Turks in 1430, and restored to Greece in 1912.

Thessaly (Greek **Thessalia**) region of eastern central Greece, on the Aegean; area 13,904 sq km/5,368 sq mi; population (1991) 731,200. It is a major area of cereal production. It was an independent state in ancient Greece and later formed part of the Roman province of ▷Macedonia. It was Turkish from the 14th century until incorporated in Greece in 1881.

Thetford Mines town in south Québec, Canada, and the site of the world's largest asbestos deposits; population (1991) 17,300. It is situated on the River Bécancour, in the Notre Dame Mountains, 80 km/50 mi south of Québec. Thetford Mines is a regional service and mining centre. Dairying, sawmilling, and diverse manufactures also contribute to the local economy.

Thetis in Greek mythology, the most beautiful ▷Nereid (a sea goddess), and mother of ▷Achilles. She dipped the baby in the ▷Styx, rendering him invulnerable except for the heel which she held. In Homer's *Iliad* she also gave Achilles armour forged by Hephaestus. Fated to have a son more powerful than his father, she was married by the gods against her will to a mortal, Peleus.

thiamine (or **vitamin B_1**) a water-soluble vitamin of the B complex. It is found in seeds and grain. Its absence from the diet causes the disease ▷beriberi.

Thibault, Jacques Anatole François French writer who wrote as Anatole ▷France.

Thimphu capital of ▷Bhutan, lying on the River Raidak at an altitude of 2,000 m/7,000 ft; population (2001 est) 48,300. It is the main marketing centre for agricultural goods produced in the surrounding valley and on terraced hill slopes, including rice, maize, and wheat. Power is supplied by a hydroelectric station (1966), and industries include sawmilling, wood products, and food processing.

third estate (or *tiers état*) in pre-revolutionary France, the order of society comprising the common people as distinct from members of the first (noble) or the second (clerical) estates. All three met collectively as the ▷States General.

Third Reich (or **Third Empire**) Germany during the years of Adolf ▷Hitler's dictatorship after 1933. Hitler and the ▷Nazis wanted to place their government into the history of Germany for both historical precedent and legitimacy. The idea of the Third Reich was based on the existence of two previous German empires: the medieval ▷Holy Roman Empire, and the second empire of 1871 to 1918.

The term was coined by the German writer Moeller van den Bruck (1876–1925) in the 1920s and was used by the Nazis.

Third World (or **developing world**) those countries that are less developed than the industrialized free-market countries of the West (First World) and the industrialized former communist countries (Second World). Third World countries are the poorest, as measured by their income per head of population, and are concentrated in Asia, Africa, and Latin America.

The early 1970s saw the beginnings of attempts by Third World countries to act together in confronting the powerful industrialized countries over such matters as the level of prices of primary products, with the nations regarding themselves as a group that had been exploited in the past by the developed nations and that had a right to catch up with them (see ▷nonaligned movement).

Related Web site: Project Hope http://www.projhope.org/

Thirteen Colonies 13 American colonies that signed the ▷Declaration of Independence from Britain in 1776. Led by George ▷Washington, the Continental Army defeated the British army in the ▷American Revolution 1776–81 to become the original 13 United States of America: Connecticut, Delaware, Georgia, Maryland, Massachusetts, New Hampshire, New Jersey, New York, North Carolina, Pennsylvania, Rhode Island, South Carolina, and Virginia. They were united first under the Articles of ▷Confederation and from 1789, the US ▷constitution.

38th parallel demarcation line between North (People's Democratic Republic of) and South (Republic of) Korea, agreed at the Yalta Conference in 1945 and largely unaltered by the Korean War 1950–53.

Thirty-Nine Articles set of articles of faith defining the doctrine of the Anglican Church; see under ▷Anglican Communion.

Thirty Years' War major war 1618–48 in central Europe. Beginning as a German conflict between Protestants and Catholics, it was gradually transformed into a struggle to determine whether the ruling Austrian Habsburg family could gain control of all

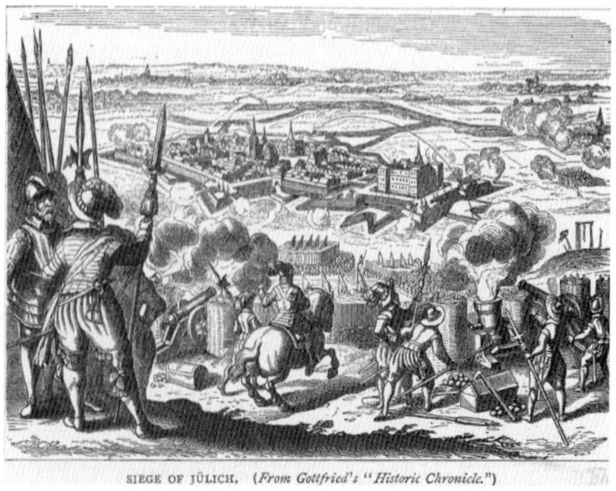
SIEGE OF JÜLICH. (From Gottfried's "Historic Chronicle.")

THIRTY YEARS' WAR The siege of Jülich in the Thirty Years' War. *Philip Sauvain Picture Collection*

Germany. The war caused serious economic and demographic problems in central Europe. Under the **Peace of Westphalia** the German states were granted their sovereignty and the emperor retained only nominal control.

Thirty Years' War 1618–48

majority religion
- Catholic
- Calvinist
- Lutheran
- Orthodox

SWEDEN
DENMARK
BRANDENBURG
POLAND
UNITED PROVINCES
Magdeburg
Breitenfeld 1631 ✗ ✗ Lützen 1632
HOLY
ROMAN
BOHEMIA
White Mountain 1620
EMPIRE
✗ Prague
✗ Nördlingen 1634
AUSTRIA
FRANCE
PAPAL STATES
OTTOMAN EMPIRE
Adriatic Sea
0   200 mi
0   300 km

Thiruvananthapuram (formerly **Trivandrum**) capital of ▷Kerala, southwest India; population (1991) 524,000. It has chemical, textile, and rubber industries, and there is an international airport. Formerly the capital of the princely state of Travancore, it has many palaces, an old fort, and a shrine.

thistle any of a group of prickly plants with spiny stems, soft cottony purple flower heads, and deeply indented leaves with prickly edges. The thistle is the national emblem of Scotland. (Genera include *Carduus, Carlina, Onopordum*, and *Cirsium*; family Compositae.)

Thistle, Order of the Scottish order of ▷knighthood.

Thomas, St (died AD 53) In the New Testament, one of the 12 Apostles, said to have preached in southern India, hence the ancient churches there were referred to as the 'Christians of St Thomas'. He is not the author of the Gospel of St Thomas, the Gnostic collection of Jesus' sayings.

Thomas, Clarence (1948–) US Supreme Court justice from 1991. Born in Savannah, Georgia, he received a law degree from Yale University Law School in 1974. President Reagan appointed him head of the civil-rights division of the department of education in 1981 and the head of the Equal Employment Opportunities Commission in 1982. In 1990 President Bush appointed him a justice on the US Court of Appeals. It was widely believed that his Republican views and opposition to abortion, rather than his legal experience, led to his nomination to the Supreme Court the following year. He was not supported by the National Association for the Advancement of Colored People, which would normally back a black nominee. Thomas was accused of sexual harassment by former colleague Anita Hill, but was confirmed by the Senate by 52 votes to 48, the narrowest margin for any nominee to the Supreme Court in the 20th century.

Thomas, Dylan Marlais (1914–1953) Welsh poet. His poems, characterized by complex imagery and a strong musicality, include the celebration of his 30th birthday 'Poem in October' and the evocation of his youth 'Fern Hill' (1946). His 'play for voices' *Under Milk Wood* (1954) describes with humour and compassion a day in the life of the residents of a small Welsh fishing village, Llareggub. The short stories of *Portrait of the Artist as a Young Dog* (1940) are autobiographical.

He was born in Swansea, the son of the English teacher at the local grammar school where he was educated. He worked as a reporter on the *South Wales Evening Post*, then became a journalist in London and published his first volume *Eighteen Poems* in 1934. He returned periodically to Wales, to the village of Laugharne, from 1938, with his wife Caitlin (born Macnamara, 1913–1994), moving

into the Boat House in 1949. Here he wrote most of *Under Milk Wood*, several major poems, and some short stories. He collapsed and died during a lecture tour of the USA.

Thomas, Michael Tilson (1944–) US conductor and pianist. He was appointed principal conductor of the London Symphony Orchestra in 1988. An enthusiastic proponent of 'authentic' restorations of modern repertoire, he has championed US composers. He has made first recordings of Steve Reich's *The Desert Music* (1983), the complete symphonies of Charles Ives, and a reconstruction of George Gershwin's original *Rhapsody in Blue*.

Thomas, R(onald) S(tuart) (1913–2000) Welsh poet. His verse contrasts traditional Welsh values with encroaching 'English' sterility. His poems, including *The Stones of the Field* (1946), *Song at the Year's Turning* (1955), and *Laboratories of the Spirit* (1975), excel at the portrayal of the wild beauty of the Welsh landscape and the religious spirit that the harshness of life there engenders. His *Collected Poems* appeared in 1993.

Thomas à Kempis (c. 1380–1471) Adopted name of Thomas Hämmerken. German Augustinian monk, author of *De Imitatio Christi/Imitation of Christ* (1441), a devotional handbook of the *devotio moderna*. The work proved quickly popular, being translated into Dutch and French.

Thomism in philosophy, the method and approach of Thomas ▷Aquinas. Neo-Thomists apply this philosophical method to contemporary problems. It is a form of scholasticism.

Thompson, Alice original name of the English writer Alice ▷Meynell.

Thompson, Emma (1959–) English actor. She has worked in cinema, theatre, and television, ranging from song-and-dance to Shakespeare, often playing variations on the independent woman. She won an Academy Award for her performance in *Howards End* (1992) and another for her film adaptation (1995) of Jane Austen's novel *Sense and Sensibility*, in which she also played the role of Elinor.

Thompson, Hunter Stockton (1939–) US writer and journalist. A proponent of the New Journalism school of reporting, which made the writer an essential component of the story, Thompson mythologized himself as the outrageous Doctor Gonzo in his political journalism of the 1960s. These articles were mainly published in *Rolling Stone* magazine. An acute observer of the decadence and depravity in American life, he wrote such books as *Hell's Angels* (1966), *Fear and Loathing on the Campaign Trail '72* (1973), and the reportage novel *Fear and Loathing in Las Vegas* (1971). His first ever novel, *The Rum Diary*, written in 1959, was first published in 1998.

Thompson, Jack (John Payne) (1940–) Australian television and film actor. He came to prominence in the television series *Spyforce* (1971–72). His films include *Sunday Too Far Away* (1975), *Breaker Morant* (1980), *The Man from Snowy River* (1982) and *Merry Christmas, Mr Lawrence* (1983).

Thomson, George Paget (1892–1975) English physicist who shared the Nobel Prize for Physics in 1937 for his work on ▷interference phenomena in the scattering of electrons by crystals which helped to confirm the wavelike nature of particles. He was knighted in 1943.

DYLAN THOMAS Dylan Thomas, photographed here in the 1950s, was recognized from the publication of his first book, *Eighteen Poems* (1934), to be an original and eloquent poet. His readings of his own work, in both the UK and the USA, brought his poems to a wider audience. *Archive Photos*

In the USA, C J Davisson made the same discovery independently, earlier the same year, using a different method.

Thomson, J(oseph) J(ohn) (1856–1940) English physicist. He discovered the ▷electron in 1897. His work inaugurated the electrical theory of the atom, and his elucidation of positive rays and their application to an analysis of neon led to the discovery of ▷isotopes. He was awarded the Nobel Prize for Physics in 1906 for his theoretical and experimental work on the conduction of electricity by gases. He was knighted in 1908.

Using magnetic and electric fields to deflect positive rays, Thomson found in 1912 that ions of neon gas are deflected by different amounts, indicating that they consist of a mixture of ions with different charge-to-mass ratios. English chemist Frederick ▷Soddy had earlier proposed the existence of isotopes and Thomson proved this idea correct when he identified, also in 1912, the isotope neon-22. This work was continued by his student Francis Aston.

Thor in Norse and Teutonic mythology, the god of thunder (his hammer), represented as a man of enormous strength defending humanity against demons and the frost giants. He was the son of Odin and Freya, and one of the Aesir (warrior gods). Thursday is named after him.

thorax in four-limbed vertebrates, the part of the body containing the heart and lungs, and protected by the ribcage; in arthropods, the middle part of the body, between the head and abdomen.

In mammals the thorax is separated from the abdomen by the muscular diaphragm. In insects the thorax bears the legs and wings. The thorax of spiders and crustaceans, such as lobsters, is fused with the head, to form the cephalothorax.

Thoreau, Henry David (1817–1862) US author. One of the most influential figures of 19th-century US literature, he is best known for his vigorous defence of individualism and the simple life. His work *Walden, or Life in the Woods* (1854) stimulated the back-to-nature movement, and he completed some 30 volumes based on his daily nature walks. His essay 'Civil Disobedience' (1849), prompted by his refusal to pay taxes, advocated peaceful resistance to unjust laws and had a wide impact, even in the 20th century.

thorium dark-grey, radioactive, metallic element of the ▷actinide series, symbol Th, atomic number 90, relative atomic mass 232.038. It occurs throughout the world in small quantities in minerals such as thorite and is widely distributed in monazite beach sands. It is one of three fissile elements (the others are uranium and plutonium), and its longest-lived isotope has a half-life of 1.39×10^{10} years. Thorium is used to strengthen alloys. It was discovered by Jöns Berzelius in 1828 and was named by him after the Norse god Thor.

thorn apple (or **jimson weed**) annual plant belonging to the nightshade family, native to America and naturalized worldwide. It grows to 2 m/6 ft in northern temperate and subtropical areas and has white or violet trumpet-shaped flowers followed by capsulelike fruits that split to release black seeds. All parts of the plant are poisonous. (*Datura stramonium*, family Solanaceae.)

THORN APPLE Although most thorn apples are the fruit of the jimson weed, they are also produced by other species of *Datura*, such as this *D. discolor* from California. *Premaphotos Wildlife*

thoroughbred horse bred for racing purposes. All racehorses are thoroughbreds, and all are direct descendants of one of three stallions imported into Britain during the 17th and 18th centuries: the Darley Arabian, Byerley Turk, and Godolphin Barb.

Thoth (Greek **Hermes Trismegistos**) in Egyptian mythology, the god of wisdom, learning, and magic. Inventor of ▷hieroglyphic writing, he was the patron of scribes, and associated with the Moon, whose phases were used for reckoning. He was represented as a dog-faced baboon or as a scribe with the head of an ibis; the bird was sacred to him.

Thousand Islands group of about 1,700 islands in the upper St Lawrence River, on the border between Canada and the USA. Most of them are in Ontario, Canada; the rest are in the US state of New York. Some are in Canada's St Lawrence Islands National Park; many of the others are privately owned. The largest is Wolfe Island in Ontario, 127 sq km/49 sq mi. Tourism and resort trade have been important to the islands' economy since the early 19th century.

Thrace (Greek **Thráki**) ancient region of the Balkans, southeastern Europe, formed by parts of modern Greece and Bulgaria. It was held successively by the Greeks, Persians, Macedonians, and Romans.

threadworm kind of ▷nematode.

Three Kingdoms period in Chinese history from 220 to 581, an era of disruptive, intermittent warfare between three powers. Sometimes the term is used to cover only the period 220 to 280 following the end of the ▷Han dynasty when the Wei, Shu, and Wu fought for supremacy.

Three Mile Island island in the Shenandoah River near Harrisburg, Pennsylvania. It is the site of a nuclear power station which was put out of action following a serious accident in March 1979. Opposition to nuclear power in the USA was reinforced after this accident and safety standards reassessed.

threshold population in geography, the minimum number of people necessary before a particular good or service will be provided in an area. Typically a low-order shop (such as a grocer or newsagent) may require only 800 or so customers, whereas a higher-order store such as Marks and Spencer may need a threshold of 70,000 to be profitable, and a university may need 350,000 to be viable.

thrift (or **sea pink**) any of several perennial low-growing coastal plants. The common sea pink *A. maritima* occurs in clumps on seashores and cliffs throughout Europe. The leaves are small and linear and the dense round heads of pink flowers rise on straight stems. (Genus *Armeria*, family Plumbaginaceae.)

thrips any of a number of tiny insects of the order Thysanoptera, usually with feathery wings. Many of the 3,000 species live in flowers and suck their juices, causing damage and spreading disease. Others eat fungi, decaying matter, or smaller insects.

throat in human anatomy, the passage that leads from the back of the nose and mouth to the ▷trachea and ▷oesophagus. It includes the ▷pharynx and the ▷larynx, the latter being at the top of the trachea. The word 'throat' is also used to mean the front part of the neck, both in humans and other vertebrates, for example, in describing the plumage of birds. In engineering, it is any narrowing entry, such as the throat of a carburettor.

thrombosis condition in which a blood clot forms in a vein or artery, causing loss of circulation to the area served by the vessel. If it breaks away, it often travels to the lungs, causing pulmonary embolism.

thrush any bird of the large family Turdidae, order Passeriformes, found worldwide and known for their song. Thrushes are usually brown with speckles of other colours. They are 12–30 cm/5–12 in long.

The **song thrush** *Turdus philomelos* is 23 cm/9 in long, brown above and with a paler throat and breast speckled with dark brown. Slightly larger is the **mistle thrush** *T. viscivorus*, so-called because of its habit of defending a clump of mistletoe during the winter to use as a food store. It is also nicknamed the stormcock because it often sings before and during wild, wet weather. Song thrushes have declined in Britain by 73% and mistle thrushes by 39% since the late 1960s. North American species include the **hermit thrush** *Catharus guttatus*, the **wood thrush** *Hylocichla mustelina*, and the **American robin** *T. migratorius*.

thrush infection usually of the mouth (particularly in infants), but also sometimes of the vagina, caused by a yeastlike fungus (▷*Candida*). It is seen as white patches on the mucous membranes.

Related Web site: Candidiasis http://www.projinf.org/fs/candida.html

Thucydides (c. 455 BC–c. 400 BC) Athenian historian. He was briefly a general during the ▷Peloponnesian War with Sparta, but as a result of his failure to save Amphipolis from the Spartan

THRUSH The mistle thrush *Turdus viscivorus*. *Premaphotos Wildlife*

general Brasidas, he was banished from Athens in 424. His *History of the Peloponnesian War* gives a detailed account of the conflict to 411.

thug originally a member of a Hindu sect who strangled travellers as sacrifices to ▷Kali, the goddess of destruction. The sect was suppressed in about 1830.

Thule Greek and Roman name for the most northerly land known, originally used by the explorer Pytheas to refer to land he discovered six days after leaving the northern coast of Britain. It has been identified with the Shetlands, the Orkneys, Iceland, and Scandinavia.

thulium soft, silver-white, malleable and ductile, metallic element of the ▷lanthanide series, symbol Tm, atomic number 69, relative atomic mass 168.94. It is the least abundant of the rare earth metals, and was first found in gadolinite and various other minerals. It is used in arc lighting.

The X-ray-emitting isotope Tm-170 is used in portable X-ray units. Thulium was named by French chemist Paul Lecoq de Boisbaudran in 1886 after the northland, Thule.

thunderstorm severe storm of very heavy rain, thunder, and is ▷lightning. Thunderstorms are usually caused by the intense heating of the ground surface during summer. The warm air rises rapidly to form tall cumulonimbus clouds with a characteristic anvil-shaped top. Electrical charges accumulate in the clouds and are discharged to the ground as flashes of lightning. Air in the path of lightning becomes heated and expands rapidly, creating shock waves that are heard as a crash or rumble of thunder.

Thurber, James Grover (1894–1961) US humorist. His short stories, written mainly for the *New Yorker* magazine, include 'The Secret Life of Walter Mitty' (1932). His doodle drawings include fanciful impressions of dogs.

Thuringia administrative region (German *Land*) in central Germany, bounded on the north by Saxony-Anhalt and Lower Saxony, on the east by Saxony, on the south by Bavaria, and on the west by Hesse; area 15,482 sq km/5,978 sq mi; population (1995) 2,684,000. The capital is Erfurt. There are machine tool, optical instrument, steel, vehicle, ceramic, electronics, glassware, and timber industries. Wheat, maize, and sugar beet are grown.

Thurrock unitary authority in eastern England, created in 1998 from part of Essex.

area 163 sq km/63 sq mi towns and cities Grays (administrative headquarters), Purfleet, Tilbury, Chadwell, St Mary, Stanford-le-Hope, Corringham, South Ockendon features located on north bank of River Thames; Holehaven Creek forms eastern border of authority; Tilbury Marshes; Mucking Marshes; Dartford Tunnel and Queen Elizabeth II bridge have northern approach through Thurrock; 17th-century Tilbury Fort, with three moats; Alexandra Lake; Lakeside shopping centre industries oil refineries, power station at west Tilbury Marshes, sand and gravel extraction, cement works, soap, margarine, timber products population (1996) 130,600

Thutmose four kings (pharaohs) of ancient Egypt of the 18th dynasty, including:

Thutmose I (or **Thothmes I**) King (pharaoh) of ancient Egypt, reigned c. 1493–c. 1482 BC. He campaigned in Syria.

Thutmose III (or **Thothmes III**) King (pharaoh) of ancient Egypt, reigned c. 1479–c. 1426 BC. He extended the empire to the River Euphrates, and conquered Nubia. He was a grandson of ▷Thutmose I.

Thyestes in Greek mythology, the son of Pelops and brother of Atreus. His rivalry with Atreus for the kingship of Mycenae was continued by their sons, Aegisthus and Agamemnon.

thylacine another name for the ▷Tasmanian wolf.

thyme any of several herbs belonging to the mint family. Garden thyme *T. vulgaris*, native to the Mediterranean, grows to 30 cm/1 ft high and has small leaves and pinkish flowers. Its aromatic leaves are used for seasoning in cookery. (Genus *Thymus*, family Labiatae.)

THYME The wild thyme *Thymus drucei* is widespread in western Europe and the British Isles, often forming a dense fragrant mat on downs, heaths, and coastal dunes. It produces masses of tiny pink flowers from May to August. *Premaphotos Wildlife*

thymus organ in vertebrates, situated in the upper chest cavity in humans. The thymus processes ▷lymphocyte cells to produce T-lymphocytes (T denotes 'thymus-derived'), which are responsible for binding to specific invading organisms and killing them or rendering them harmless.

thyristor type of ▷rectifier, an electronic device that conducts electricity in one direction only. The thyristor is composed of layers of ▷semiconductor material sandwiched between two electrodes called the anode and cathode. The current can be switched on by using a third electrode called the gate.

thyroid ▷endocrine gland of vertebrates, situated in the neck in front of the trachea. It secretes several hormones, principally thyroxine, an iodine-containing hormone that stimulates growth, metabolism, and other functions of the body. The thyroid gland may be thought of as the regulator gland of the body's metabolic rate. If it is overactive, as in ▷hyperthyroidism, the sufferer feels hot and sweaty, has an increased heart rate, diarrhoea, and weight loss. Conversely, an underactive thyroid leads to myxoedema, a condition characterized by sensitivity to the cold, constipation, and weight gain. In infants, an underactive thyroid leads to cretinism, a form of mental retardation.

thyrotoxicosis synonym for ▷hyperthyroidism.

Tiahuanaco (or **Tihuanaco**) site of a city in Bolivia 24 km/15 mi south of Lake Titicaca in the Andes. It gave its name to the 8th–14th-century civilizations found in Peru and Bolivia that preceded the Inca. The Tiahuanco were responsible for many of the roads originally thought to have been built by the Inca.

Tiananmen Square (Chinese 'Square of Heavenly Peace') paved open space in central Beijing (Peking), China, the largest public square in the world (area 0.4 sq km/0.14 sq mi). On 3–4 June 1989 more than 1,000 unarmed protesters were killed by government troops in a massacre that crushed China's emerging prodemocracy movement.

Related Web site: Tiananmen – 1989 http://www.christusrex.org/www1/sdc/tiananmen.html

TIANANMEN SQUARE It was from here that Mao Zedong declared the founding of the People's Republic of China on 1 October 1949. His portrait hangs above the gate. *Image Bank*

Tianjin (or **Tientsin**) city and special municipality in Hebei province, north China; municipality area 4,000 sq km/1,544 sq mi; city population (1994) 5,894,900, municipality (1996) 9,480,000. One of four municipalities administered directly from Beijing, it includes the city of Tianjin and the port of Tanggu. An industrial and commercial centre, its handmade silk and wool carpets are renowned. Dagang oilfield lies nearby. Tianjin was opened to foreign trade in 1860 and was occupied by the Japanese in 1937.

Tiber (Italian **Tevere**; Latin **Tiberis**) river in Italy that flows through Rome; its length from its source in the Apennines to the Tyrrhenian Sea is 400 km/250 mi. It is Italy's third longest river.

Tiberias, Lake (or **Sea of Galilee** or **Lake of Gennesaret**; Hebrew **Yam Kinneret**) lake in north Israel, 210 m/689 ft below sea level, into which the River ▷Jordan flows; area 170 sq km/66 sq mi. The first Israeli ▷kibbutz (cooperative settlement) was founded nearby in 1909.

Tiberius (42 BC–AD 37) Born Tiberius Claudius Nero. Roman emperor, the stepson, adopted son, and successor of Augustus from AD 14. He was a cautious ruler whose reign was marred by the heavy incident of trials for treason or conspiracy. Tiberius fell under the influence of Sejanus who encouraged the emperor's fear of assassination and was instrumental in Tiberius' departure from Rome to Caprae (Capri). He never returned to Rome.

Tibet autonomous region of southwestern China (Pinyin form **Xizang**); area 1,221,600 sq km/471,700 sq mi; population (1993 est) 2,290,000 (many Chinese have settled in Tibet; 2 million Tibetans live in China outside Tibet). The capital is ▷Lhasa. Although Tibet has its own People's Government and People's Congress, Tibetan nationalists regard the province as being under colonial rule. The controlling force in Tibet is the Communist Party of China, represented locally by First Secretary Wu Jinghua from 1985. There is a government-in-exile in Dharmsala, Himachal Pradesh, India, where the ▷Dalai Lama lives. The religion in the region is traditionally ▷Lamaism (a form of Mahāyāna Buddhism).

Tibet occupies a barren plateau bounded to the south and southwest by the Himalayas and north by the Kunlun Mountains, traversed west to east by the Bukamagna, Karakoram, and other mountain ranges, and having an average elevation of 4,000–4,500 m/13,000–15,000 ft. The Sutlej, Brahmaputra, and Indus rivers rise in Tibet, which has numerous lakes, many of which are salty. The ▷yak is the main domestic animal.

Industries include wool, borax, salt, horn, musk, herbs, furs, gold, iron pyrites, lapis lazuli, mercury, textiles, chemicals, and agricultural machinery. Tibet has the largest uranium reserves in the world: uranium processing and extraction is causing pollution, and human and animal birth deformities.

History Tibet was an independent kingdom from the 5th century AD. It came under nominal Chinese rule in about 1700.

From 1910–13 the capital, Lhasa, was occupied by Chinese troops, after which independence was re-established. China invaded Tibet in 1949, signing a treaty in May 1950 which recognized Chinese sovereignty but Tibetan local autonomy. The Chinese People's Liberation Army (PLA) controlled Tibet 1951–59, although the Dalai Lama remained as nominal spiritual and temporal head of state. In response to repeated breaches by the Chinese of the 1950 agreement, including forcing the monks (who formed 25% of the population) out of the monasteries, in 1959 a Tibetan uprising spread from bordering regions to Lhasa and was supported by Tibet's local government. The rebellion was suppressed by the PLA, prompting the Dalai Lama and 9,000 Tibetans to flee to India. The Chinese proceeded to dissolve the Tibet local government, abolish serfdom, collectivize agriculture, and suppress Lamaism. In 1965 Tibet became an autonomous region of China. Chinese rule continued to be resented, however, and the economy languished.

Related Web site: Tibet in the 20th Century http://www.tibetinfo.net/tibet-file/chronol.htm

Tibetan a Mongolian people inhabiting Tibet who practise a form of Mahāyāna Buddhism, introduced in the 7th century. Since China's Cultural Revolution 1966–68, refugee communities have formed in India and Nepal. The Tibetan language belongs to the Sino-Tibetan language family.

Tibetan mastiff large breed of dog regarded as the ancestor of many present breeds. It is a very powerful animal with a long black or black and tan coat. It is about 71 cm/28 in in height and 60 kg/132 lb in weight.

tibia the anterior of the pair of bones in the leg between the ankle and the knee. In humans, the tibia is the shinbone. It articulates with the ▷femur above to form the knee joint, the ▷fibula externally at its upper and lower ends, and with the talus below, forming the ankle joint.

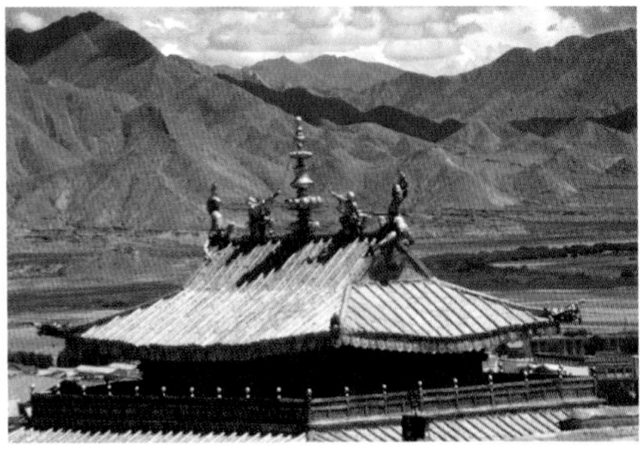

TIBET The gilded roof of Tashilumpo Monastery, Xigaze, Tibet. The monastery is the former home of the Panchen Lama, second in the lamaist hierarchy to the Dalai Lama. The Panchen Lama, a supporter of Chinese policy in Tibet, moved to Beijing in 1965. *Corel*

tick any of the arachnid family Ixodoidae, order Acarina, of large bloodsucking mites. They have flat bodies protected by horny shields. Many carry and transmit diseases to mammals (including humans) and birds.

Life cycle During part of their existence they parasitize animals and birds, for which they have developed a rostrum or beak composed of two barbed harpoons above and a dart below. Their eggs are laid on rough herbage and hatch into white six-legged larvae, which climb up the legs of passing animals and in some species complete their life history on the animal's skin, but in others return to the grass for a period, dropping from the host when engorged with blood.

Ticks cause irritation and anaemia, and can also transmit ▷typhus, Lyme disease, rickettsia, and relapsing fever.

tidal energy energy derived from the tides. The tides mainly gain their potential energy from the gravitational forces acting between the Earth and the Moon. If water is trapped at a high level during high tide, perhaps by means of a barrage across an estuary, it may then be gradually released and its associated gravitational potential energy exploited to drive turbines and generate electricity. Several schemes have been proposed for the Bristol Channel, in southwestern England, but environmental concerns as well as construction costs have so far prevented any decision from being taken.

tidal wave common name for a ▷tsunami.

tide the rhythmic rise and fall of the sea level in the Earth's oceans and their inlets and estuaries due to the gravitational attraction of the Moon and, to a lesser extent, the Sun, affecting regions of the Earth unequally as it rotates. Water on the side of the Earth nearest the Moon feels the Moon's pull and accumulates directly below the Moon producing high tide.

High tide occurs at intervals of 12 hr 24 min 30 sec. The maximum high tides, or spring tides, occur at or near new and full Moon when the Moon and Sun are in line and exert the greatest combined gravitational pull. Lower high tides, or neap tides, occur when the Moon is in its first or third quarter and the Moon and Sun are at right angles to each other.

Gravitational tides – the pull of nearby groups of stars – have been observed to affect the galaxies.

Tiepolo, Giovanni Battista (Giambattista) (1696–1770) Italian painter. He was one of the first exponents of Italian rococo and created monumental decorative schemes in palaces and churches in northeastern Italy, southwestern Germany, and Madrid. His style is light-hearted, his colours light and warm, and he made great play with illusion.

Tierra del Fuego island group separated from the southern extremity of South America by the Strait of Magellan; Cape Horn is at the southernmost point. There are oil, natural gas, and sheep farming industries. Tourism is also important. The largest island is Tierra del Fuego, or **Isla Grande**, with an area of 48,100 sq km/18,571 sq mi; half of this island, and the islands west of it, belong to Chile, and form part of the Magallanes region, the capital and chief town of which is Punta Arenas. The eastern part of the archipelago belongs to Argentina, forming the federal district of Tierra del Fuego; its capital, Ushuaia, is the world's most southerly town.

Tiffany, Louis Comfort (1848–1933) US artist and glassmaker. He was the son of Charles Louis Tiffany, who founded Tiffany and Company, the New York City jewellers. He produced stained-glass windows, iridescent Favrile (from Latin *faber* 'craftsman') glass, and lampshades in the art nouveau style. He used glass that contained oxides of iron and other elements to produce rich colours.

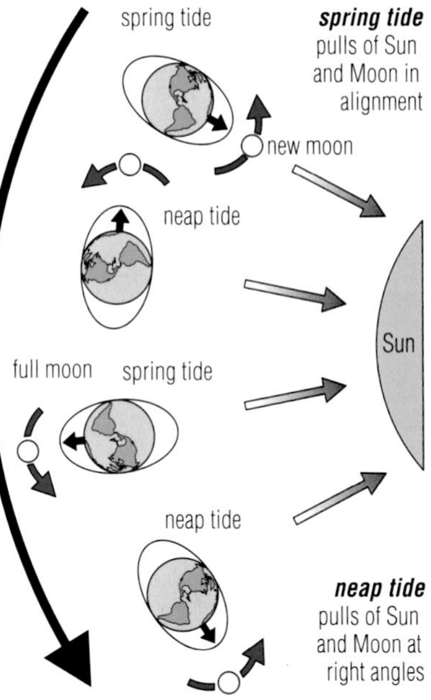

TIDE The gravitational pull of the Moon is the main cause of the tides. Water on the side of the Earth nearest the Moon feels the Moon's pull and accumulates directly under the Moon. When the Sun and the Moon are in line, at new and full moon, the gravitational pull of Sun and Moon are in line and produce a high spring tide. When the Sun and Moon are at right angles, lower neap tides occur.

tiger largest of the great cats, *Panthera tigris* (family Felidae, order Carnivora), formerly found in much of central and South Asia, from Siberia south to Sumatra, but nearing extinction (5,000 in 1997) because of hunting and the high prices paid for the pelt, as well as the destruction of its natural habitat.

The male tiger can grow to 3.6 m/12 ft long, while the female averages about 2.6 m/8.5 ft. It weighs up to 300 kg/660 lb, and has a yellow-orange coat with black stripes. Tigers are solitary, and largely nocturnal. They will eat carrion, but generally kill for themselves. Their food consists mainly of deer, antelopes, and smaller animals, but they sometimes kill wild boar. Human-eating tigers are rare and are the result of weakened powers or shortage of game.

Related Web site: Bengal Tiger http://www.seaworld.org/animal_bytes/tigerab.html

tiger beetle brightly coloured beetle with long legs and antennae. The most striking feature is their large eyes. Most adult tiger beetles are in shades of blue, bronze, or green, with yellow or white markings. They are typically found on sand or dry soils. Some 2,000 species have been recorded, mostly in the tropics.

Tigré a people of northern Ethiopia. The Tigré language is spoken by about 2.5 million people; it belongs to the southeastern Semitic branch of the Afro-Asiatic (Hamito-Semitic) family. **Tigrinya** is a closely related language spoken slightly to the south.

Tigré (or **Tigray**) region in the northern highlands of Ethiopia; area 65,900 sq km/25,444 sq mi; population (1995 est) 3,307,000. The chief town is Mek'elē. A mountainous region in the west; the highest point is Mokada, rising to 2295 m/7529 ft. The east of the region is much lower; some of the Danakil Depression is below sea level. Most of the population live by cultivation in the south and by nomadic herding in the north, but the area suffers from periodic severe droughts. In 1978 a guerrilla group known as the Tigré People's Liberation Front (TPLF) began fighting for regional autonomy. In 1989 government troops were forced from the province, and the TPLF advanced towards Addis Ababa, playing the key role in the fall of the Ethiopian government in May 1991.

Tigris (Arabic **Dijla**) river flowing through Turkey and Iraq (see also ▷Mesopotamia), joining the ▷Euphrates 80 km/50 mi northwest of Basra, where it forms the ▷Shatt-al-Arab; length 1,600 km/1,000 mi.

Tihuanaco alternative spelling of ▷Tiahuanaco, an ancient Bolivian city.

Tijuana city and resort in northwestern Mexico; population (1995 est) 824,000. It is on the Pacific Ocean in the state of Baja California Norte. The border with the USA at Tijuana and ▷San Diego is believed to be the busiest frontier in the world and there is a considerable tourist trade, for which local horse and dog racing, bullfighting and casinos are attractions.

till (or **boulder clay**) deposit of clay, mud, gravel, and boulders left by a ▷glacier. It is unsorted, with all sizes of fragments mixed up together, and shows no stratification; that is, it does not form clear layers or ▷beds.

Tilly, Jan Tserklaes, Count von Tilly (1559–1632) Flemish commander of the army of the Catholic League and imperial forces in the ▷Thirty Years' War. Notorious for his storming of Magdeburg, East Germany in 1631, he was defeated by the Swedish king Gustavus Adolphus at Breitenfeld and at the River Lech in southwestern Germany, where he was mortally wounded.

tilt-rotor aircraft type of vertical takeoff aircraft, also called a convertiplane.

timber wood used in construction, furniture, and paper pulp. **Hardwoods** include tropical mahogany, teak, ebony, rosewood, temperate oak, elm, beech, and eucalyptus. All except eucalyptus are slow-growing, and world supplies are almost exhausted. **Softwoods** comprise the ▷conifers (pine, fir, spruce, and larch), which are quick to grow and easy to work but inferior in quality of grain. **White woods** include ash, birch, and sycamore; all have light-coloured timber, are fast-growing, and can be used as veneers on cheaper timber.

TIMBER The mill pictured is at Fideris in Switzerland. Timber is processed for commercial use either by pulping in readiness for making into paper or by sawing into planks of varying length and thickness for building and furniture making. Bark that is stripped off and not pulped may be recycled as garden mulch. *Image Bank*

timbre (French 'tone') in music, the tone colour, or quality of tone, of a particular ▷sound. Different instruments playing a note at the same ▷pitch have different sound qualities, and it is the timbre that enables the listener to distinguish the sound of, for example, a trumpet from that of a violin. The tone quality of a sound depends on several things, including its waveform, the strength of its ▷harmonics, and its attack and decay – the 'shape' of the sound. The study of the elements of sound quality is part of the science of acoustics.

time continuous passage of existence, recorded by division into hours, minutes, and seconds. Formerly the measurement of time was based on the Earth's rotation on its axis, but this was found to be irregular. Therefore the second, the standard ▷SI unit of time, was redefined in 1956 in terms of the Earth's annual orbit of the Sun, and in 1967 in terms of a radiation pattern of the element caesium.

time and motion study process of analysis applied to a job or number of jobs to check the efficiency of the work method, equipment used, and the worker. Its findings are used to improve performance.

Times Beach town in Missouri, USA, that accidentally became contaminated with ▷dioxin, and was bought by the Environmental Protection Agency in 1983 for cleansing.

time-sharing in computing, a way of enabling several users to access the same computer at the same time. The computer rapidly switches between user ▷terminals and programs, allowing each user to work as if he or she had sole use of the system.

Timişoara capital of Timiş county, western Romania; population (1993) 325,000. Industries include electrical engineering, chemicals, pharmaceuticals, textiles, food processing, metal, and footwear. The revolt against the Ceauşescu regime began here in December 1989 when demonstrators prevented the arrest and deportation of a popular Protestant minister who was promoting the rights of ethnic Hungarians. This soon led to large prodemocracy rallies.

Related Web site: Timişoara Home Page http://timisoara.com/ timisoara/timisoara.html

Timon Athenian of the age of ▷Pericles notorious for his misanthropy, which was reported and elaborated by classical authors, and became the subject of the play by ▷Shakespeare.

Timor largest and most easterly of the Lesser Sunda Islands, part of Indonesia; area 33,610 sq km/12,973 sq mi. Its indigenous people were the Atoni; successive migrants have included the Malay, Melanesian, Chinese, Arab, and Gujerati.

The Dutch were established in Kupang in 1613, with the Portuguese in the north and east. Portugal established a colonial administration in Timor in 1702, but the claim was disputed by the Dutch, as well as by the Timorese, who frequently rebelled. Timor was divided into **West Timor** and ▷East Timor by treaties of 1859 and 1913 and subjected to Dutch and Portuguese control respectively; during World War II both parts were occupied by Japan. West Timor (capital Kupang) became part of Indonesia in 1949. East Timor (capital Dili) comprises the enclave on the northwest coast, and the islands of Atauro and Jaco. It was seized by Indonesia in 1975, and became an Indonesian province in 1976 (East Timor is the English name for the Indonesian province of Timor Timur). The annexation was not recognized by the United Nations (UN), and guerrilla warfare by local people seeking independence continued. In August 1999, despite a six-month campaign of violence and intimidation, the people of East Timor turned out in overwhelming numbers to vote in favour of the referendum on independence. Violence perpetrated by Indonesians and pro-Indonesian Timorese led to the imposition of martial law and the creation of hundreds of thousands of refugees escaping violence. Australian, British, and New Zealand troops formed the biggest military operation to be launched in the area since World War II, and by the end of September 1999, an estimated 20,000 displaced East Timorese had returned to Dili. The new Indonesian government of Abdurrahman Wahid in November 1999 agreed unanimously to let the province of East Timor become independent of Indonesian rule, as thousands of refugees from the west of the island made their way back home. Evidence of atrocities continued to be discovered, and UN peacekeeping forces were dispatched to the area. After three members of the UN refugee agency (UNHCR) in West Timor were killed on 7 September 2000 by militiamen who were detaining in the area 120,000 refugees from breakaway East Timor, international and local relief workers were evacuated from West Timor. The UN warned that, because of their departure, thousands of refugees were left helpless and would soon run out of food. Indonesia rejected a UN mission to investigate the killings, and promised to disarm militias who were threatening the refugee camps. One of the militia leaders, Eurico Guterres, was arrested in Indonesia in October 2000. He was alleged to have been responsible for violence in East Timor in 1999, and subsequently, attacks against the West Timorese refugee camps.

Products include coffee, maize, rice, and coconuts.

Timur i Leng alternative spelling of ▷Tamerlane, Mongol ruler.

tin soft, silver-white, malleable and somewhat ductile, metallic element, symbol Sn (from Latin *stannum*), atomic number 50, relative atomic mass 118.69. Tin exhibits ▷allotropy, having three forms: the familiar lustrous metallic form above 13.2°C/55.8°F; a brittle form above 161°C/321.8°F; and a grey powder form below 13.2°C/55.8°F (commonly called tin pest or tin disease). The metal is quite soft (slightly harder than lead) and can be rolled, pressed, or hammered into extremely thin sheets; it has a low melting point. In nature it occurs rarely as a free metal. It resists corrosion and is therefore used for coating and plating other metals.

Tin and copper smelted together form the oldest desired alloy, bronze; since the Bronze Age (3500 BC) that alloy has been the basis of both useful and decorative materials. Tin is also alloyed with metals other than copper to make solder and pewter. It was recognized as an element by Antoine Lavoisier, but the name is very old and comes from the Germanic form *zinn*. The mines of

manufactured boards · **softwoods** · **hardwoods**

plywood · hardboard · chipboard · blockboard · MDF

spruce · parana pine · scots pine · western red cedar

ash · mahogany · walnut · beech · oak · teak · elm

TIMBER Types of hard and soft woods and also manufactured boards, such as chipboard and MDF. Hardwoods come from broadleaf trees and softwoods from evergreens.

Cornwall were the principal Western source of tin until the 19th century, when rich deposits were found in South America, Africa, South-East Asia, and Australia. Tin production is concentrated in Malaysia, Indonesia, Brazil, and Bolivia.

In Cornwall, the last surviving tin mine in the UK, and Europe, closed in 1998. The closure of this mine, in South Crofty, near Camborne, once the largest tin mine in the world, marked the end of a long battle to save Cornwall's most distinctive industry, which during its heyday in the 19th century employed 30,000 people and spread through 400 mines. The decision was largely due to the falling price of tin on the world market.

TIN An old tin mine in St Agnes, Cornwall, England. Tin mining used to be a major industry in Cornwall; in the 19th century there were over 400 mines. Richer deposits were then discovered overseas, where local labour costs were negligible; this, combined with a fall in the market price of tin worldwide in the 1980s, led to the closure of the last tin mine in Cornwall (and Europe) in 1998. *Image Bank*

tinamou fowl-like bird of the family Tinamidae, in the South American order Tinamiformes, of which there are some 45 species. They are up to 40 cm/16 in long, and their drab colour provides good camouflage. They are excellent runners but poor flyers and are thought to be related to the ▷ratites (flightless birds). Tinamous are mainly vegetarian, but sometimes eat insects. They escape predators by remaining still or by burrowing through dense cover.

Tinbergen, Jan (1903–1994) Dutch economist. He shared the Nobel Prize for Economics in 1969 with Ragnar ▷Frisch for his work on ▷econometrics (the mathematical-statistical expression of economic theory).

Tinbergen, Niko(laas) (1907–1988) Dutch-born British zoologist who was awarded a Nobel Prize for Physiology or Medicine in 1973 for his work in animal behaviour patterns. He specialized in the study of instinctive behaviour in animals, and was one of the founders of ▷ethology, the scientific study of animal behaviour in natural surroundings. He shared the prize with Konrad ▷Lorenz (with whom he worked on several projects) and Karl von Frisch.

Tinbergen investigated other aspects of animal behaviour, such as learning, and also studied human behaviour, particularly aggression, which he believed to be an inherited instinct that developed when humans changed from being predominantly herbivorous to being hunting carnivores.

tinnitus in medicine, constant buzzing or ringing in the ears. The phenomenon may originate from prolonged exposure to noisy conditions (drilling, machinery, or loud music) or from damage to or disease of the middle or inner ear. The victim may become overwhelmed by the relentless noise in the head.

In some cases there is a hum at a frequency of about 40 Hz, which resembles that heard by people troubled by environmental hum but may include whistles and other noises resembling a machine workshop. Being in a place where external noises drown the internal ones gives some relief, and devices may be worn that create pleasant, soothing sounds to override them.

Approximately 20% of Europeans and North Americans will experience tinnitus at some period in their lives. Treatment often involves counselling and teaching the sufferer how to cope with the noise.

Objective tinnitus is a very rare form in which other people can also hear the noises. This may be caused by muscle spasms in the inner ear or throat, or abnormal resonance of the eardrum and ossicles.

Related Web site: Tinnitus http://www.deafblind.com/tinnitus.html

tin ore mineral from which tin is extracted, principally cassiterite, SnO_2. The world's chief producers are Malaysia, Thailand, and Bolivia.

tinplate milled steel coated with tin, the metal used for most 'tin' cans. The steel provides the strength, and the tin provides the corrosion resistance, ensuring that the food inside is not contaminated. Tinplate may be made by ▷electroplating or by dipping in a bath of molten tin.

Tintagel village resort on the coast of north Cornwall, southwest England. There are castle ruins, and legend has it that King Arthur was born and held court here.

Tintoretto (1518–1594) Adopted name of Jacopo Robusti. Venetian painter who produced portraits and religious works of great intensity. Outstanding among his many works is a series of religious works in the Scuola di S Rocco in Venice (1564–88), the dramatic figures lit by a flickering, unearthly light, the space around them distorted into long perspectives. Among his best-known works is *St George and the Dragon* (*c.*1570; National Gallery, London).

He was born in Venice, the son of a dyer, hence the name Tintoretto ('little dyer'). He studied under ▷Titian, and was strongly influenced by ▷Michelangelo: it is commonly claimed that his motto was 'Michelangelo's drawing, and Titian's colour'. His works are characterized by broad and dramatic composition, fine draughtsmanship, and a superb use of colour, the scenes spectacularly lit and full of movement.

His works include the *Miracle of St Mark Rescuing a Slave* (1548; Accademia, Venice); his lives of Christ and the Virgin for the Scuola di S Rocco (including the vast *Christ before Pilate* and *The Last Supper*); his *Paradise* (1588), for the Doge's Palace; his *St George and the Dragon*, which demonstrates his characteristic originality in depicting figures in rushing movement; and *The Origin of the Milky Way* (after 1570; National Gallery, London), one of the finest of his allegories.

He also painted a large number of portraits, such as the *Doge Mocenigo* (Accademia, Venice), *Self-Portrait* (Louvre, Paris), and *Vincenzo Morosini* (National Gallery, London). Other works, apart from his religious works on a decorative scale, include *Susanna and the Elders* (Accademia, Vienna).

Tipperary county of the Republic of Ireland, in the province of Munster, divided into North and South Ridings; county town Clonmel; area 4,255 sq km/1,643 sq mi; population (1996) 133,500. It includes part of the Golden Vale, a fertile dairy-farming region. Agriculture is the chief industry; barley and oats are the main crops, but potatoes and turnips are also grown. Cattle are reared in large numbers, and there are flour mills and butter factories. There is also horse and greyhound breeding. Other main towns are Cahir, Carrick-on-Suir, Cashel, Templemore, Tipperary, Thurles, Nenagh, and Roscrea. Major tourist attractions in the county include the Rock of Cashel and Cahir Castle.

Tippett, Michael (Kemp) (1905–1998) English composer. With Benjamin Britten, he became the foremost English composer of his generation. His works include the operas *The Midsummer Marriage* (1952), *The Knot Garden* (1970), and *New Year* (1989); four symphonies; *Songs for Ariel* (1962); and choral music, including *The Mask of Time* (1982).

Tipu Sultan (*c.* 1750–1799) Sultan of Mysore (now Karnataka) in southwestern India from the death of his father, ▷Hyder Ali in 1782. He died of wounds when his capital, Seringapatam, was captured by the British. His rocket brigade led Sir William Congreve (1772–1828) to develop the weapon for use in the ▷Napoleonic Wars.

Tirana (or **Tiranë**) capital (since 1920) of Albania; population (1991) 251,000. Industries include metallurgy, cotton textiles, soap, and cigarettes. It was founded in the early 17th century by Turks when part of the Ottoman Empire. Although the city is now largely composed of recent buildings, some older districts and mosques have been preserved.

Tirol federal state of Austria; area 12,600 sq km/4,864 sq mi; population (1995) 655,200. Its capital is Innsbruck, and it produces diesel engines, optical instruments, and hydroelectric power. Tirol was formerly a province (from 1363) of the Austrian Empire, divided in 1919 between Austria and Italy (see ▷Trentino–Alto Adige).

Tissot, James (Joseph Jacques) (1836–1902) French painter. He is best known for detailed depictions of Victorian high society during a ten-year stay in England, as in *Ball on Shipboard* (1874; Tate Gallery, London).

tissue in biology, any kind of cellular fabric that occurs in an organism's body. Several kinds of tissue can usually be distinguished, each consisting of cells of a particular kind bound together by cell walls (in plants) or extracellular matrix (in animals). Thus, nerve and muscle are different kinds of tissue in animals, as are ▷parenchyma and ▷sclerenchyma in plants.

tissue culture process by which cells from a plant or animal are removed from the organism and grown under controlled conditions in a sterile medium containing all the necessary nutrients. Tissue culture can provide information on cell growth and differentiation, and is also used in plant propagation and drug production.

tissue plasminogen activator (tPA) naturally occurring substance in the body tissues that activates the enzyme plasmin that is able to dissolve blood clots. Human tPA, produced in bacteria by genetic engineering, has, like streptokinase, been used to dissolve blood clots in the coronary arteries of heart attack victims. It has been shown to be more effective than streptokinase when used in conjunction with heparin, but it is much more expensive.

tit (or **titmouse**) any of 65 species of insectivorous, acrobatic bird of the family Paridae, order Passeriformes. Tits are 8–20 cm/3–8 in long and have grey or black plumage, often with blue or yellow markings. They are found in Eurasia and Africa, and also in North America, where they are called **chickadees**.

Species British species are all insect-eaters and include the **blue tit** *Parus caeruleus*, often seen in gardens. Its prevailing colour is blue, with green above, and a black throat. The **coal tit** *P. ater* has a black head, with a white patch on the nape. The **great tit** *P. major* is about 15 cm/6 in long and is yellow on the back, breast, and sides, with grey wings and tail, and black head and throat. The **marsh tit** *P. palustris* and the **willow tit** *P. montanus* resemble the coal tit except for the latter's white nape and white spots on the wings. The **long-tailed tit** *Aegithalos caudatus* is about 13 cm/5 in long, and has prolonged, graduated black tail feathers.

The **bearded tit** *Panurus biarmicus* is not a true tit. It is found mainly in Norfolk and the male is about 15 cm/6 in long, light red, with a tuft of black feathers on either side of its head.

TIT The blue tit is common in gardens throughout the year in the British Isles and across Europe as far east as Iran. *Premaphotos Wildlife*

Titan in astronomy, the largest moon of the planet Saturn, with a diameter of 5,150 km/3,200 mi and a mean distance from Saturn of 1,222,000 km/759,000 mi. It was discovered in 1655 by Dutch mathematician and astronomer Christiaan ▷Huygens, and is the second-largest moon in the Solar System (Ganymede, of Jupiter, is larger).

Titan is the only moon in the Solar System with a substantial atmosphere (mostly nitrogen), topped with smoggy orange clouds that obscure the surface, which may be covered with liquid ethane lakes. Its surface atmospheric pressure is greater than Earth's. Radar signals suggest that Titan has dry land as well as oceans (among the planets, only Earth has both in the Solar System).

Titan in Greek mythology, any of the giant children of ▷Uranus, the primeval sky god, and ▷Gaia, goddess of the Earth, whose six sons and six daughters included ▷Kronos, ▷Rhea, ▷Themis, and

▷Oceanus. Kronos and Rhea were in turn the parents of Zeus, who ousted his father as ruler of the world.

Titanic British passenger liner, supposedly unsinkable, that struck an iceberg and sank off the Grand Banks of Newfoundland on its first voyage on 14–15 April 1912; estimates of the number of lives lost, largely due to inadequate provision of lifeboats, vary between 1,503 and 1,517. In 1985 it was located by robot submarine 4 km/2.5 mi down in an ocean canyon, preserved by the cold environment, and in 1987 salvage operations began.

In August 1996 salvage divers eased a 15-tonne section of the liner's steel hull away from the sea floor and raised it more than 2 mi/3.2 km from the seabed using flotation balloons. The high-tech expedition appeared to be on the verge of success when the balloons lost pressure and the liner returned to the ocean floor. By 1996, the cost of the project to raise the wreck stood at $5 million/£3.3 million.

The results of the first ultrasonic scan of the front of the *Titanic*, much of which is buried in mud, showed that a series of six short slits was the only damage inflicted on the ship by the iceberg, and not, as has always been thought, a gaping 91 m/300 ft gash. The total area of openings was found to be only about 1.1 or 1.2 sq m/12 or 13 sq ft. The unexpected discovery, which emerged from an expedition to the seabed by a team of scientists and engineers in August 1996, will force a re-writing of the countless histories of the disaster. Although small, the gaps would have been roughly 6 m/20 ft below the water line. The high pressure would have forced the ocean through the holes fast enough to flood the ship with about 39,000 tonnes of water before it finally went down.

Some historians condemned the expedition as a form of grave-robbing, arguing that the wreck should be left on the sea bed as a memorial to those who lost their lives, and a reminder. RMS Titanic Inc, which owns salvage rights to the wreck, claimed it was simply trying to preserve a piece of history.

Related Web site: RMS Titanic, Inc http://www.titanic-online.com/

titanium strong, lightweight, silver-grey, metallic element, symbol Ti, atomic number 22, relative atomic mass 47.90. The ninth-most abundant element in the Earth's crust, its compounds occur in practically all igneous rocks and their sedimentary deposits. It is very strong and resistant to corrosion, so it is used in building high-speed aircraft and spacecraft; it is also widely used in making alloys, as it unites with almost every metal except copper and aluminium. Titanium oxide is used in high-grade white pigments.

Titanium bonds with bone in a process called **osseointegration**. As the body does not react to the titanium it is valuable for permanent implants such as prostheses.

The element was discovered in 1791 by English mineralogist William Gregor (1761–1817) and was named by German chemist Martin Klaproth in 1796 after the Titans, the giants of Greek mythology. It was not obtained in pure form until 1925.

titanium ore any mineral from which titanium is extracted, principally ilmenite ($FeTiO_3$) and rutile (TiO_2). Brazil, India, and Canada are major producers. Both these ore minerals are found either in rock formations or concentrated in heavy mineral sands.

Titan rocket family of US space rockets, developed from the Titan intercontinental missile. Two-stage Titan rockets launched the ▷Gemini crewed missions. More powerful Titans, with additional stages and strap-on boosters, were used to launch spy satellites and space probes, including the ▷Viking and ▷Voyager probes and *Mars Observer*.

tithe formerly, payment exacted from the inhabitants of a parish for the maintenance of the church and its incumbent; some religious groups continue the practice by giving 10% of members' incomes to charity.

It was originally the grant of a tenth of all agricultural produce made to priests in Hebrew society. In the Middle Ages the tithe was adopted as a tax in kind paid to the local parish church, usually for the support of the incumbent, and stored in a special tithe barn; as such, it survived into contemporary times in Europe and Britain. In Protestant countries, these payments were often appropriated by lay landlords.

In Britain in the 19th century a rent charge was substituted. By the Tithe Commutation Act of 1836, tithes were abolished and replaced by 'redemption annuities' payable to the crown, government stock being issued to tithe-owners.

Titian (*c.* 1487–1576) Italian **Tiziano Vecellio**. Italian painter. He was one of the greatest artists of the High Renaissance. During his long career he was court painter to Charles V, Holy Roman Emperor, and to his son, Philip II of Spain. He produced a vast number of portraits, religious paintings, and mythological scenes, including *Bacchus and Ariadne* (1520–23; National Gallery, London) and *Venus and Adonis* (1554; Prado, Madrid).

The most famous of his early works are *Flora* (*c.* 1515; Uffizi, Florence), the so-called *Sacred and Profane Love* (*c.* 1516; Borghese, Rome), *Man with a Glove* (*c.* 1520; Louvre, Paris), and *Christ and the Tribute Money* (Gemäldegalerie Alter Meister, Dresden). After about 1518 his reputation rose rapidly, and the great religious works *The Assumption of the Virgin* (Church of the Frari, Venice) and *The Entombment* (Louvre, Paris) belong to this period.

In 1533 he was introduced to the Emperor Charles V, who sat for his portrait. The admiration of Charles V and his successor, Philip II, for Titian accounts for the presence of so many of his masterpieces in the imperial collections and the Prado, Madrid. Titian was now internationally famous, and European rulers competed for his 'poetical compositions' or *poesie* (as he termed his mythological scenes with their sumptuous nude figures) and for his portraits.

He worked in a number of centres: in Venice, where in 1537 he painted his *Battle of Cadore* (destroyed by fire in 1577); in Milan, where in 1541 he was with the emperor; in Rome, in 1545, at the invitation of the pope; and in Augsburg, in 1548, where he painted Philip of Spain. From this time onwards he painted mainly in Venice, producing late works profound in feeling and characterized by remarkable developments in technique. He died of the plague; his son and assistant **Orazio** died in the same epidemic. Velázquez, Rubens, and Poussin are among the many great artists inspired by Titian's achievement.

Titicaca, Lake lake in the Andes, 3,810 m/12,500 ft above sea level and 1,220 m/4,000 ft above the treeline; area 8,300 sq km/3,200 sq mi, the largest lake in South America, and the world's highest navigable body of water. It is divided between Bolivia (port at Guaqui) and Peru (ports at Puno (principal port) and Huancane). The lake is fed by several streams which originate in the snow-capped surrounding mountains. The lake contains enormous frogs, which are farmed, the legs being an edible delicacy, and there is some trout farming. The herding of alpacas and llamas is also common. It is one of the few places in the world where reed boats are still made by the Uru tribal peoples (Lake Tana in Ethiopia is another). The lake is also used for irrigation.

Tito (1892–1980) Adopted name of Josip Broz. Yugoslav communist politician, in effective control of Yugoslavia from 1943. In World War II he organized the National Liberation Army to carry on guerrilla warfare against the German invasion in 1941, and was created marshal in 1943. As prime minister 1945–53 and president from 1953, he followed a foreign policy of 'positive neutralism'.

Born in Croatia, Tito served in the Austrian army during World War I, was captured by the Russians, and fought in the Red Army during the civil wars. Returning to Yugoslavia in 1923, he became prominent as a communist and during World War II as ▷partisan leader against the Nazis. In 1943 he established a provisional government and gained Allied recognition (previously given to the ▷Chetniks) in 1944, and with Soviet help proclaimed the federal republic in 1945. As prime minister, he settled the Yugoslav minorities question on a federal basis, and in 1953 took the newly created post of president (for life from 1974). In 1948 he was criticized by the USSR and other communist countries for his successful system of decentralized profit-sharing workers' councils, and became a leader of the ▷nonaligned movement.

titration in analytical chemistry, a technique to find the concentration of one compound in a solution by determining how much of it will react with a known amount of another compound in solution.

Titus (AD 39–81) Born Titus Flavius Vespasianus. Roman emperor from AD 79. Eldest son of ▷Vespasian, he captured Jerusalem in 70 to end the Jewish revolt in Roman Palestine. He completed the Colosseum, and helped to mitigate the suffering from the eruption of Vesuvius in 79, which destroyed Pompeii and Herculaneum.

Tivoli (ancient **Tibur**) town in Lazio, Italy, 25 km/15 mi northeast of Rome, Italy; population (1990) 55,000. It has the remains of Hadrian's Villa, with gardens; and the Villa d'Este, with Renaissance gardens laid out in 1549 for Cardinal Ippolito d'Este. Wine is produced, and travertine (a decorative building stone) is quarried locally.

Tlatelolco, Treaty of international agreement signed in 1967 in Tlatelolco, Mexico, prohibiting nuclear weapons in Latin America.

Tlingit member of an ▷American Indian people living on the west coast of southern Alaska and northern British Columbia and numbering about 14,000 (1990). The Tlingit are known for their dugout canoes, their potlatch ceremonies, where food and gifts are distributed to guests in order to gain status, and their carved wooden 'totem' poles representing their family crests, and which show such animals as the raven, whale, octopus, beaver, bear, wolf, and the mythical Thunderbird. Their language belongs to the Na-Dene branch of the the Athabaskan language family.

TN abbreviation for the state of ▷Tennessee, USA.

TNT abbreviation for **trinitrotoluene**, $CH_3C_6H_2(NO_2)_3$, a powerful high explosive. It is a yellow solid, prepared in several isomeric forms from ▷toluene by using sulphuric and nitric acids.

toad any of the more terrestrial warty-skinned members of the tailless amphibians (order Anura). The name commonly refers to members of the genus *Bufo*, family Bufonidae, which are found worldwide, except for Australia (where the marine or ▷cane toad *B. marinus* has been introduced), Madagascar, and Antarctica. They differ from ▷frogs chiefly by the total absence of teeth, and in certain other anatomical features.

Toads may grow up to 25 cm/10 in long. They live in cool, moist places and lay their eggs in water. The eggs are laid not in a mass as with frogs, but in long strings. The common toad *B. bufo* of Europe and Asia has a rough, usually dark-brown skin in which there are glands secreting a poisonous fluid that makes it unattractive as food for other animals; it needs this protection because its usual progress is a slow, ungainly crawl. European toads have a size range of 2–25 cm/0.8–10 in. They live mostly on land, are active at night, and hibernate in burrows during the winter. Breeding takes place in winter and the eggs are laid in spring. The animals migrate large distances (up to 1.5 km/1 mi) from their land quarters to suitable breeding waters.

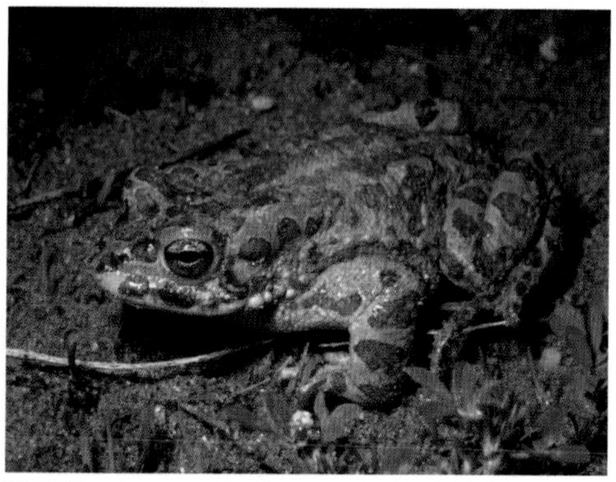

TOAD Toads are among the commonest amphibians. This striking green toad *Bufo viridis* is distributed in a number of habitats in the east Mediterranean area, such as these coastal sand flats. *Premaphotos Wildlife*

toadflax any of a group of small plants belonging to the snapdragon family, native to Western Europe and Asia. Toadflaxes have spurred, two-lipped flowers, commonly purple or yellow, and grow 20–80 cm/8–32 in tall. (Genus *Linaria*, family Scrophulariaceae.)

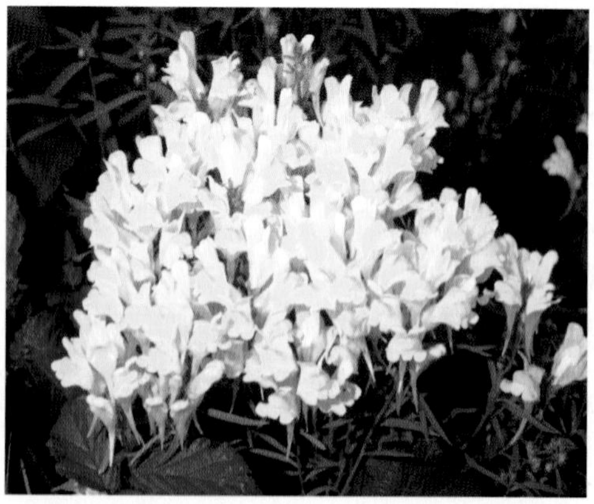

TOADFLAX Common toadflax *Linaria vulgaris* is frequent on grassy riverbanks, roadsides, and waste ground almost throughout the British Isles and across Europe east to the Altai Mountains. It is naturalized in the USA. Pollination is only by large bumblebees powerful enough to force open the hinge on the two-lipped flowers. *Premaphotos Wildlife*

toadstool common name for many umbrella-shaped fruiting bodies of fungi (see ▷fungus). The term is normally applied to those that are inedible or poisonous.

tobacco any of a group of large-leaved plants belonging to the nightshade family, native to tropical parts of the Americas. The species *N. tabacum* is widely cultivated in warm, dry climates for use in cigars and cigarettes, and in powdered form as snuff. (Genus *Nicotiana*, family Solanaceae.)

Related Web site: Nicotiana Tobacum http://www.nnlm.nlm.nih.gov/pnr/uwmhg/species.html

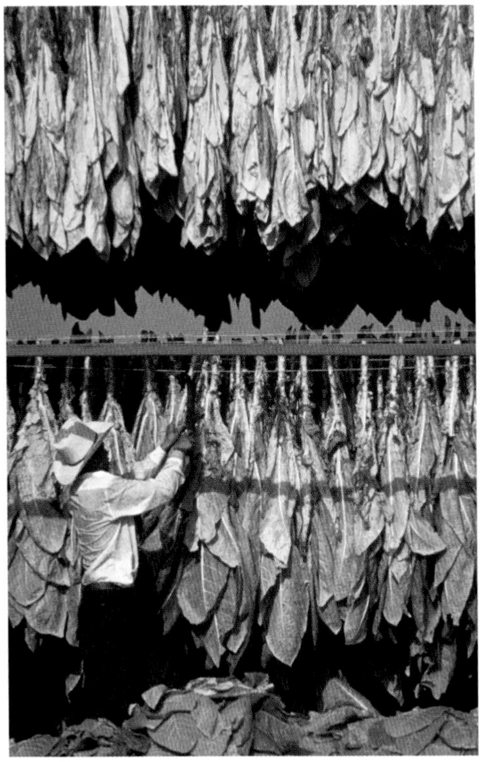

TOBACCO Drying or 'curing' of tobacco in Chiapas, in the far south of Mexico. *Image Bank*

Tobago island in the West Indies; part of the republic of ▷Trinidad and Tobago.

tocopherol (or **vitamin E**) fat-soluble chemical found in vegetable oils. Deficiency of tocopherol leads to multiple adverse effects on health. In rats, vitamin E deficiency has been shown to cause sterility.

Tocqueville, Alexis Charles Henri Clérel de (1805–1859) French politician, sociologist, and historian. He was the author of the first analytical study of the strengths and weaknesses of US society, *De la Démocratie en Amérique/Democracy in America* (1835). He also wrote a penetrating description of France before the Revolution, *L'Ancien Régime et la Révolution/The Old Regime and the Revolution* (1856).

tog unit of measure of thermal insulation used in the textile trade; a light summer suit provides 1.0 tog.

Togliatti (or **Tolyatti**; formerly **Stavropol**) port on the River ▷Volga in the Samara oblast of western central Russia, 65 km/40 mi northwest of the city of Samara; population (1990) 642,000. Togliatti is the principal centre for Russian car manufacture; the Volga automobile works here began production in 1970. Other industries include ship repair and food processing, and the production of synthetic rubber, chemicals and fertilizers, electrical goods, and cement. Following flooding and the construction of the Kuybyshev Reservoir in the 1950s, the city was relocated and in 1964 was renamed in honour of the Italian communist leader Palmiro Togliatti.

Togo see country box.

toilet place where waste products from the body are excreted. Simple latrines, with sewers to carry away waste, have been found in the Indus Valley and ancient Babylon; the medieval garderobe is essentially the same, even though flushing lavatories had been known to Roman civilizations.

Tōjō, Hideki (1884–1948) Japanese general and premier 1941–44 during World War II. Promoted to chief of staff of Japan's Guangdong army in Manchuria in 1937, he served as minister for war 1940–41 where he was responsible for negotiating the tripartite Axis alliance with Germany and Italy in 1940. He was held responsible for defeats in the Pacific in 1944 and forced to resign. After Japan's defeat, he was hanged as a war criminal.

Tokugawa military family which controlled Japan as ▷shoguns from 1603 to 1868. **Tokugawa Ieyasu** (1542–1616) was the Japanese general and politician who established the Tokugawa shogunate. The Tokugawa were feudal lords who ruled about one-quarter of Japan. Undermined by increasing foreign incursions, they were overthrown by an attack of provincial forces from Chōshū, Satsuma, and Tosa, who restored the ▷Meiji emperor to power.

Tokyo capital of Japan, on Honshu island; population (2000 est) 8,130,000. It is Japan's main cultural, financial and industrial centre (engineering, chemicals, textiles, electrical goods).

Founded in the 16th century as **Yedo** (or **Edo**), it was renamed when the emperor moved his court here from Kyoto in 1868. By the end of the 18th century, Yedo, with 1 million people, was the largest city in the world. An earthquake in 1923 killed 58,000 people and destroyed much of the city, which was again severely damaged by Allied bombing in World War II when 60% of Tokyo's housing was destroyed; US firebomb raids of 1945 were particularly destructive with over 100,000 people killed in just one night of bombing on 9 March. The subsequent rebuilding has made it into one of the world's most modern cities.

Features include the Imperial Palace, National Diet (parliament), Asakusa Kannon Temple (7th century; rebuilt after World War II), National Theatre, National Museum and other art collections, Tokyo University (1877), Tokyo Disneyland, and the National Athletic Stadium. The Sumida River delta separates the city from its suburb of Honjo.

Related Web site: Tokyo http://www.pandemic.com/tokyo/

Tokyo trials war-crimes trials 1946–48 of Japan's wartime leaders, held during the Allied occupation after World War II. Former prime minister Tōjō was among the seven sentenced to death by an international tribunal, while 16 were given life imprisonment. Political considerations allowed Emperor ▷Hirohito (Shōwa) to escape trial.

Toledo capital of Toledo province in Castilla–La Mancha, central Spain, built on a rock above the River Tagus; population (1990) 60,700. It was the capital of the Visigoth kingdom 534–711 (see ▷Goth), then became a Moorish city, and was the Castilian capital from 1085–1560. Knives, silks, and ceramics are manufactured here. There is a Gothic cathedral (13th–17th centuries) and several churches which preserve paintings by El Greco. The alcazar (fortified palace) was rebuilt after the successful Nationalist defence of Toledo in the Spanish Civil War (1936–39) and became a Nationalist shrine.

Toledo inland port in Ohio, USA, at the mouth of the Maumee River on Lake Erie, 153 km/96 mi west of Cleveland; population (1996 est) 317,610. It is an oil- and gas-pipeline terminus, and a shipping centre for coal, iron-ore, vehicle parts, and grain. Industries include oil-refining, shipbuilding, food-processing, and the manufacture of cars, electrical goods, steel, and glass. A French fort was built in 1700, but permanent settlement did not begin until after the War of 1812.

Tolkien, J(ohn) R(onald) R(euel) (1892–1973) English writer and scholar. To express his theological and philosophical beliefs, and as a vehicle for his linguistic scholarship, he created a complete mythological world of 'Middle Earth', on which he drew for his children's fantasy *The Hobbit* (1937), and the trilogy *The Lord of the Rings* (1954–55), nominated in a UK bookselling chain's survey in 1997 as the 'greatest book of the 20th century'. His work developed a cult following in the 1960s and had many imitators. At Oxford University he was professor of Anglo-Saxon from 1925–45 and Merton professor of English from 1945–59.

Tolpuddle Martyrs six farm labourers of Tolpuddle, a village in Dorset, southwest England, who were transported to Australia in 1834. The labourers had formed a union on the advice of the Grand National Consolidated Trades Union (GNCTU) to try to prevent their wages being reduced. Entry into their 'union' involved a payment of a shilling (5p), and swearing before a picture of a skeleton never to tell anyone the union's secrets. Local magistrates used an old law to convict them for 'administering unlawful oaths'. The severity of the punishment destroyed the GNCTU. After nationwide agitation, the labourers were pardoned two years later. They returned to England and all but one migrated to Canada.

Related Web site: Tolpuddle http://www.dorset-cc.gov.uk/tolpudd.htm

Tolstoy, Leo Nikolaievich (1828–1910) Russian novelist. He wrote *War and Peace* 1863–69 and *Anna Karenina* 1873–77. He was offended by the materialism of Western Europe and in the 1860s and 1870s he became a pioneer of 'free education'. From 1880 he underwent a profound spiritual crisis and took up various moral positions, including passive resistance to evil, rejection of authority (religious or civil) and private ownership, and a return to basic mystical Christianity. He was excommunicated by the Orthodox Church, and his later works were banned.

His first published work was *Childhood* (1852), the first part of the trilogy that was completed with *Boyhood* (1854) and *Youth* (1857). *Tales from Sevastopol* was published in 1856; later books illustrating and disseminating the personal philosophy he developed after his crisis include *What I Believe* (1883), *The Kreutzer Sonata* (1889), and the novel *Resurrection* (1900). His desire to give up his property and live as a peasant disrupted his family and he finally fled his home and died of pneumonia at the railway station in Astapovo. As a writer he has had considerable influence on subsequent literature, but as a thinker he has proved much less influential; his only great disciple in his philosophy of nonresistance to evil was Mahatma ▷Gandhi.

Related Web site: Tolstoy Library http://www.tolstoy.org/

Toltec ('builder') member of an ancient American Indian people who ruled much of Mexico and Central America in the 10th–12th centuries, with their capital and religious centre at ▷Tula or Tollán, northeast of Mexico City. They also occupied and extended the ancient Maya city of ▷Chichen Itzá in Yucatán. After the fall of the Toltecs the Aztecs took over much of their former territory, except for the regions regained by the Maya.

toluene (or **methyl benzene**) $C_6H_5CH_3$ colourless, inflammable liquid, insoluble in water, derived from petroleum. It is used as a solvent, in aircraft fuels, in preparing phenol (carbolic acid, used in making resins for adhesives, pharmaceuticals, and as a disinfectant), and the powerful high explosive ▷TNT.

tomato annual plant belonging to the nightshade family, native to South America. It is widely cultivated for its shiny, round, red fruit containing many seeds (technically a berry), which is widely used in salads and cooking. (*Lycopersicon esculentum*, family Solanaceae.)

Related Web site: Tomatoes http://www.homegrowntomatoes.com/tomato.htm

Tombouctou (or **Timbuktu**) town in Mali, near the most northerly point on the Niger River; population (1996) 20,500 (town); (1987) 453,000 (region). It was a Tuareg camel caravan centre on the fringe of the Sahara from the 11th century. Since 1960 the area surrounding the town has become increasingly arid, and the former canal link with the River Niger is dry. Products include salt.

Tombstone former silver-mining town in the desert of southeastern Arizona, USA. The gunfight at the OK Corral, with deputy marshal Wyatt Earp, his brothers, and 'Doc' Holliday against the Clanton gang, took place here on 26 October 1881.

tomography the technique of using X-rays or ultrasound waves to procure images of structures deep within the body for diagnostic purposes. In modern medical imaging there are several techniques, such as the ▷CAT scan (computerized axial tomography).

ton imperial unit of mass. The **long ton**, used in the UK, is 1,016 kg/2,240 lb; the **short ton**, used in the USA, is 907 kg/2,000 lb. The **metric ton** or **tonne** is 1,000 kg/2,205 lb.

ton in shipping, unit of volume equal to 2.83 cubic metres/100 cubic feet. **Gross tonnage** is the total internal volume of a ship in tons; **net register tonnage** is the volume used for carrying cargo or passengers. **Displacement tonnage** is the weight of the vessel, in terms of the number of imperial tons of seawater displaced when the ship is loaded to its load line; it is used to describe warships.

tonality in music, a sense of ▷key orientation in relation to form, for example the step pattern of a dance as expressed by corresponding changes of direction from a tonic or 'home' key to a related key. Most popular and folk music worldwide recognizes an underlying tonality or reference pitch against which the movement of a melody can be clearly heard. The opposite of tonality is ▷atonality.

Tone, (Theobald) Wolfe (1763–1798) Irish nationalist, prominent in the revolutionary society of the ▷United Irishmen. In 1798 he accompanied the French invasion of Ireland and was captured and condemned to death, but slit his own throat in prison.

tone poem in music, an alternative name for ▷symphonic poem, or a similar piece for smaller forces.

Tonga see country box.

tongue in tetrapod vertebrates, a muscular organ usually attached to the floor of the mouth. It has a thick root attached to a U-shaped bone (hyoid), and is covered with a ▷mucous membrane containing nerves and taste buds. It is the main organ of taste. The tongue directs food to the teeth and into the throat for chewing and swallowing. In humans, it is crucial for speech; in other animals, for lapping up water and for grooming, among other functions. In some animals, such as frogs, it can be flipped forwards to catch insects; in others, such as anteaters, it serves to reach for food found in deep holes.

tonic in music, the key note of a ▷scale (for example, the note C in the scale of C major), or the 'home key' in a composition (for example, the chord of C major in a composition in the same key).

Tonkin (or **Tongking**) former region of Vietnam, on the China Sea; area 103,500 sq km/39,950 sq mi. Under Chinese rule from 111 BC, Tonkin became independent AD 939 and remained self-governing until the 19th century. A part of French Indochina 1885–1946, capital Hanoi, it was part of North Vietnam from 1954 and was merged into Vietnam after the Vietnam War.

Tonkin Gulf Incident clash that triggered US entry into the Vietnam War in August 1964. Two US destroyers (USS *C Turner Joy* and USS *Maddox*) reported that they were fired on by North Vietnamese torpedo boats. It is unclear whether hostile shots were actually fired, but the reported attack was taken as a pretext for making air raids against North Vietnam. On 7 August the US Congress passed the **Tonkin Gulf Resolution**, which formed the basis for the considerable increase in US military involvement in the Vietnam War.

tonne the metric ton of 1,000 kg/2,204.6 lb; equivalent to 0.9842 of an imperial ▷ton.

tonsillitis inflammation of the ▷tonsils.

tonsils in higher vertebrates, masses of lymphoid tissue situated at the back of the mouth and throat (palatine tonsils), and on the rear surface of the tongue (lingual tonsils). The tonsils contain many ▷lymphocytes and are part of the body's defence system against infection.

The ▷adenoids are sometimes called pharyngeal tonsils.

Tonton Macoute member of a private army of death squads on Haiti. The Tontons Macoutes were initially organized by François ▷Duvalier, president of Haiti 1957–71, and continued to terrorize the population under his successor J C Duvalier. It is alleged that the organization continued to operate after Duvalier's exile to France.

Togo

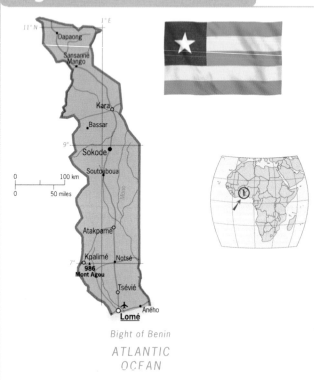

TOGO The people of Togo follow traditional methods of farming, live in villages of round thatched houses built of adobe or mud brick, and sell their produce in local markets. *Corel*

Togo (formerly Togoland, until 1956) country in West Africa, on the Atlantic Ocean, bounded north by Burkina Faso, east by Benin, and west by Ghana.

NATIONAL NAME *République Togolaise/Togolese Republic*
AREA 56,800 sq km/21,930 sq mi
CAPITAL Lomé
MAJOR TOWNS/CITIES Sokodé, Palimé, Kara, Atakpamé, Bassar, Tsévié
PHYSICAL FEATURES two savannah plains, divided by range of hills northeast–southwest; coastal lagoons and marsh; Mono Tableland, Oti Plateau, Oti River

Government

HEAD OF STATE Etienne Gnassingbé Eyadéma from 1967
HEAD OF GOVERNMENT Koffi Sama from 2002
POLITICAL SYSTEM emergent democracy
POLITICAL EXECUTIVE limited presidency
ADMINISTRATIVE DIVISIONS five regions
ARMED FORCES 9,500 (2002 est)
CONSCRIPTION military service is by selective conscription for two years
DEATH PENALTY retains the death penalty for ordinary crimes, but can be considered abolitionist in practice
DEFENCE SPEND (% GDP) 1.8 (2002 est)
EDUCATION SPEND (% GDP) 4.8 (2001 est)
HEALTH SPEND (% GDP) 2.8 (2000 est)

Economy and resources

CURRENCY franc CFA
GPD (US$) 1.4 billion (2002 est)

REAL GDP GROWTH (% change on previous year) 5.4 (2001)
GNI (US$) 1.3 billion (2002 est)
GNI PER CAPITA (PPP) (US$) 1,430 (2002 est)
CONSUMER PRICE INFLATION 4.3% (2003 est)
FOREIGN DEBT (US$) 1.4 billion (2001 est)
MAJOR TRADING PARTNERS Nigeria, Benin, Ghana, China, France, Colombia, Côte d'Ivoire
RESOURCES phosphates, limestone, marble, deposits of iron ore, manganese, chromite, peat; exploration for petroleum and uranium was under way in the early 1990s
INDUSTRIES processing of phosphates, steel rolling, cement, textiles, processing of agricultural products, beer, soft drinks
EXPORTS re-exports, phosphates (mainly calcium phosphates), ginned cotton, green coffee, cocoa beans. Principal market: Benin 13% (2001)
IMPORTS petroleum products, machinery and transport equipment, cotton yarn and fabrics, cigarettes, antibiotics, food (especially cereals) and live animals, chemicals, beverages. Principal source: Ghana 35% (2001)
ARABLE LAND 46.1% (2000 est)
AGRICULTURAL PRODUCTS cotton, cocoa, coffee, oil palm, yams, cassava, maize, millet, sorghum

Population and society

POPULATION 4,909,000 (2003 est)
POPULATION GROWTH RATE 1.9% (2000–15)
POPULATION DENSITY (per sq km) 86 (2003 est)
URBAN POPULATION (% of total) 35 (2003 est)
AGE DISTRIBUTION (% of total population) 0–14 44%, 15–59 51%, 60+ 5% (2002 est)
ETHNIC GROUPS predominantly of Sudanese Hamitic origin in the north, and black African in the south; they are distributed among 37 different ethnic groups. There are three main ethnic groups: the Ewe, Mina, and Outchi in the south, the Akposso-Adele in the central region, and the Kabre in the north. There are also European, Syrian, and Lebanese minorities
LANGUAGE French (official), Ewe, Kabre, Gurma, other local languages

RELIGION animist about 50%, Catholic and Protestant 35%, Muslim 15%
EDUCATION (compulsory years) 6
LITERACY RATE 75% (men); 47% (women) (2003 est)
LABOUR FORCE 60.3% agriculture, 11.8% industry, 27.9% services (1999)
LIFE EXPECTANCY 48 (men); 51 (women) (2000–05)
CHILD MORTALITY RATE (under 5, per 1,000 live births) 141 (2001)
PHYSICIANS (per 1,000 people) 0.8 (1998 est)
HOSPITAL BEDS (per 1,000 people) 5.1 (1998 est)
TV SETS (per 1,000 people) 37 (2001 est)
RADIOS (per 1,000 people) 265 (2001 est)
INTERNET USERS (per 10,000 people) 398.6 (2002 est)
PERSONAL COMPUTER USERS (per 100 people) 3.0 (2002 est)

Chronology

15th–17th centuries: Formerly dominated by Kwa peoples in southwest and Gur-speaking Voltaic peoples in north, Ewe clans immigrated from Nigeria and the Ane (Mina) from Ghana and the Côte d'Ivoire.

18th century: Coastal area held by Danes.

1847: Arrival of German missionaries.

1884–1914: Togoland was a German protectorate until captured by Anglo-French forces; cocoa and cotton plantations developed, using forced labour.

1922: Divided between Britain and France under League of Nations mandate.

1946: Continued under United Nations trusteeship.

1957: British Togoland, comprising one-third of the area and situated in the west, integrated with Ghana, following a referendum.

1956: French Togoland voted to become an autonomous republic within the French union. The new Togolese Republic achieved internal self-government.

1960: French Togoland, situated in the east, achieved full independence from France as the Republic of Togo with Sylvanus Olympio, leader of the United Togolese (UP) party, as head of state.

1967: Lt-Gen Etienne Gnassingbé Eyadéma became president in a bloodless coup; political parties were banned.

1969: Assembly of the Togolese People (RPT) formed by Eyadéma as the sole legal political party.

1975: EEC Lomé convention signed in Lomé, establishing trade links with developing countries.

1977: An assassination plot against Eyadéma, allegedly involving the Olympio family, was thwarted.

1979: Eyadéma returned in election. Further EEC Lomé convention signed.

1986: Attempted coup failed and situation stabilized with help of French troops.

1990: There were casualties as violent antigovernment demonstrations in Lomé were suppressed; Eyadéma relegalized political parties.

1991: Eyadéma was forced to call a national conference that limited the president's powers, and elected Joseph Kokou Koffigoh head of an interim government. Three attempts by Eyadéma's troops to unseat the government failed.

1992: There were strikes in southern Togo. A referendum showed overwhelming support for multiparty politics. A new constitution was adopted.

1993: Eyadéma won the first multiparty presidential elections amid widespread opposition.

1994: An antigovernment coup was foiled. The opposition CAR polled strongly in assembly elections. Eyadéma appointed Edem Kodjo of the minority UTD prime minister.

1998: President Eyadéma was re-elected.

2002: Koffi Sama was appointed prime minister.

Tony award annual award by the League of New York Theaters to dramatists, performers, and technicians in ▷Broadway plays. It is named after the US actor and producer Antoinette Perry (1888–1946).

tooth in vertebrates, one of a set of hard, bonelike structures in the mouth, used for biting and chewing food, and in defence and aggression. In humans, the first set (20 milk teeth) appear from age six months to two and a half years. The permanent ▷dentition replaces these from the sixth year onwards, the wisdom teeth (third molars) sometimes not appearing until the age of 25 or 30. Adults have 32 teeth: two incisors, one canine (eye tooth), two premolars, and three molars on each side of each jaw. Each tooth consists of an enamel coat (hardened calcium deposits), dentine (a thick, bonelike layer), and an inner pulp cavity, housing nerves and blood vessels. Mammalian teeth have roots surrounded by cementum, which fuses them into their sockets in the jawbones.

The neck of the tooth is covered by the gum, while the enamel-covered crown protrudes above the gum line.

The chief diseases of teeth are misplacements resulting from defect or disturbance of the tooth-germs before birth, eruption out of their proper places, and caries (decay).

A genetically engineered protein able to stimulate the recovery of tooth tissue in decayed teeth was undergoing trials in 1993.

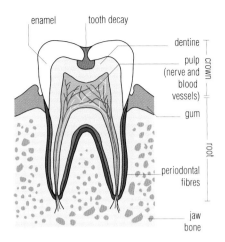
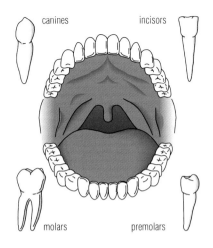

TOOTH Adults have 32 teeth: two incisors, one canine, two premolars, and three molars on each side of each jaw. Each tooth has three parts: crown, neck, and root. The crown consists of a dense layer of mineral, the enamel, surrounding hard dentine with a soft centre, the pulp.

Tonga

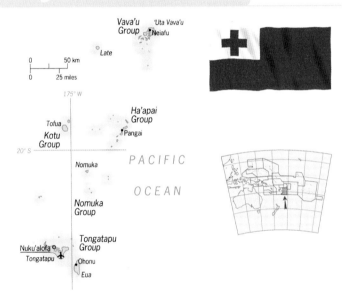

TONGA The Houma blowholes in Tonga. Tonga has a predominantly Polynesian population who inhabit a group of over a hundred Pacific islands. Most of their livelihood is gained from the sea, though farmers also grow coconut and export the oil. *Corel*

Tonga (or Friendly Islands) country in the southwest Pacific Ocean, in ▷Polynesia.

NATIONAL NAME *Pule'anga Fakatu'i 'o Tonga/Kingdom of Tonga*
AREA 750 sq km/290 sq mi
CAPITAL Nuku'alofa (on Tongatapu island)
MAJOR TOWNS/CITIES Neiafu, Haveloloto, Vaini, Tofoa-Koloua
PHYSICAL FEATURES three groups of islands in southwest Pacific, mostly coral formations, but actively volcanic in west; of the 170 islands in the Tonga group, 36 are inhabited

Government

HEAD OF STATE King Taufa'ahau Tupou IV from 1965
HEAD OF GOVERNMENT Prince Lavaka Ata Ulukalala from 2000
POLITICAL SYSTEM absolutist
POLITICAL EXECUTIVE absolute
ADMINISTRATIVE DIVISIONS five divisions comprising 23 districts
ARMED FORCES 125-strong naval force
DEATH PENALTY retains the death penalty for ordinary crimes but can be considered abolitionist in practice; date of last known execution 1982

Economy and resources

CURRENCY pa'anga, or Tongan dollar
GPD (US$) 136 million (2002 est)
REAL GDP GROWTH (% change on previous year) 3 (2001)
GNI (US$) 143 million (2002 est)
GNI PER CAPITA (PPP) (US$) 6,340 (2002 est)
CONSUMER PRICE INFLATION 3.1% (2003 est)
UNEMPLOYMENT 13.3% (1996)
FOREIGN DEBT (US$) 59 million (2001 est)
MAJOR TRADING PARTNERS New Zealand, Japan, Australia, Fiji Islands, USA, UK
INDUSTRIES concrete blocks, small excavators, clothing, coconut oil, furniture, textiles, handicrafts, sports equipment (including small boats), brewing, sandalwood processing, tourism
EXPORTS fish, vanilla beans, pumpkins, coconut oil and other coconut products, watermelons, knitted clothes, cassava, yams, sweet potatoes, footwear. Principal market: Japan 42.3% (2001)
IMPORTS food, beverages and tobacco, basic manufactures, machinery and transport equipment, mineral fuels. Principal source: New Zealand 32.6% (2001)

ARABLE LAND 24% (2000 est)
AGRICULTURAL PRODUCTS coconuts, copra, cassava, vanilla, pumpkins, yams, taro, sweet potatoes, watermelons, tomatoes, lemons and limes, oranges, groundnuts, breadfruit; livestock rearing (pigs, goats, poultry, and cattle); fishing

Population and society

POPULATION 104,000 (2003 est)
POPULATION GROWTH RATE 0.4% (2000–05)
POPULATION DENSITY (per sq km) 139 (2003 est)

URBAN POPULATION (% of total) 33 (2003 est)
AGE DISTRIBUTION (% of total population) 0–14 24%, 15–59 67%, 60+ 9% (2001 est)
ETHNIC GROUPS 98% of Tongan ethnic origin, a Polynesian group with a small mixture of Melanesian; the remainder is European and part-European
LANGUAGE Tongan (official), English
RELIGION mainly Free Wesleyan Church; Roman Catholic, Anglican
EDUCATION (compulsory years) 8

See also ▷Australasia and Oceania.

Chronology

c. **1000 BC**: Settled by Polynesian immigrants from the Fiji Islands.
c. **AD 950**: The legendary Aho'eitu became the first hereditary Tongan king (Tu'i Tonga).
13th–14th centuries: Tu'i Tonga kingdom at the height of its power.
1643: Visited by the Dutch navigator, Abel Tasman.
1773: Islands visited by British navigator Capt James Cook, who named them the 'Friendly Islands'.
1826: Methodist mission established.
1831: Tongan dynasty founded by a Christian convert and chief of Ha'apai, Prince Taufa'ahau Tupou, who became king 14 years later.
1845–93: Reign of King George Tupou I, during which the country was reunited after half a century of civil war; Christianity was spread and a modern constitution adopted in 1875.
1900: Friendship ('Protectorate') treaty signed between King George Tupou II and Britain,

establishing British control over defence and foreign affairs, but leaving internal political affairs under Tongan control.
1918: Queen Salote Tupou III ascended the throne.
1965: Queen Salote died; she was succeeded by her son, King Taufa'ahau Tupou IV, who had been prime minister since 1949.
1970: Tonga achieved independence from Britain, but remained within the Commonwealth.
1991: Baron Vaea was appointed prime minister.
1993: Six prodemocracy candidates were elected. There were calls for reform of absolutist power.
1996: A prodemocracy movement led by the People's Party won a majority of the 'commoner' seats in the legislative assembly. Prodemocracy campaigner Akilisi Pohiva was released after a month's imprisonment.
2000: Upon the retirement of Prime Minister Baron Vaea, he was replaced by Prince Ulakalala Lavaka Ata.

topaz mineral, aluminium fluorosilicate, $Al_2(F_2SiO_4)$. It is usually yellow, but pink if it has been heated, and is used as a gemstone when transparent. It ranks 8 on the Mohs scale of hardness.

tope slender shark *Galeorhinus galeus* ranging through temperate and tropical seas. Dark grey above and white beneath, it reaches 2 m/6 ft in length. The young are born well-formed, sometimes 40 at a time.

Topeka capital of ▷Kansas, USA, on the Kansas River, 85 km/53 mi west of Kansas City; population (1996 est) 119,660. It is an agricultural centre for eastern Kansas, trading in wheat and cattle. Manufactured products include processed foods, printed materials, and rubber and metal goods.

topiary clipping of trees and shrubs into ornamental shapes, originated by the Romans in the 1st century and revived in the 16th–17th centuries in formal European and American gardens.

topography the surface shape and composition of the landscape, comprising both natural and artificial features, and its study. Topographical features include the relief and contours of the land; the distribution of mountains, valleys, and human settlements; and the patterns of rivers, roads, and railways.

topology in computing, the arrangement of devices in a ▷network. The most common is the ▷bus topology, where all the computers are interconnected using a single, open-ended cable. Most modern network solutions use either a ring or bus layout, but with physical characteristics that resemble a star layout.

topology branch of geometry that deals with those properties of a figure that remain unchanged even when the figure is transformed (bent, stretched) – for example, when a square painted on a rubber sheet is deformed by distorting the sheet.

Topology has scientific applications, as in the study of turbulence in flowing fluids.

The topological theory, proposed in 1880, that only four colours are required in order to produce a map in which no two adjoining countries have the same colour, inspired extensive research, and was proved in 1972 by Kenneth Appel and Wolfgang Haken.

The map of the London Underground system is an example of the topological representation of a network; connectivity (the way the lines join together) is preserved, but shape and size are not.

Related Web site: Topology in Mathematics http://www-history.mcs.st-and.ac.uk/~history/HistTopics/Topology_in_mathematics.html

tor isolated mass of rock, often granite, left upstanding on a hilltop after the surrounding rock has been broken down. Weathering takes place along the joints in the rock, reducing the outcrop into a mass of rounded blocks.

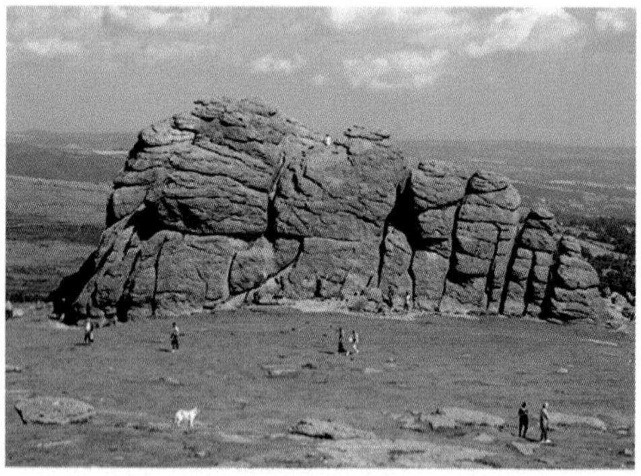

TOR Hay Tor on Dartmoor, England. The surrounding boulders clearly show where the rock has been weathered. *Dr Rod Preston-Mafham/Premaphotos Wildlife*

Torah in ▷Judaism, the first five books of the Hebrew Bible (Christian Old Testament). It contains a traditional history of the world from the Creation to the death of Moses; it also includes the Hebrew people's covenant with their one God, rules for religious observance, and guidelines for social conduct, including the Ten Commandments.

Torbay urban area and unitary authority in southwest England created in April 1998 from part of the county of Devon.

area 627 sq km/242 sq mi **towns and cities** Torquay (administrative headquarters), Paignton, Brixham **features** Tor Bay; English Channel coast; 23 beaches including Goodrington Sands; Oldway Mansion (Paignton) modelled partly on Versailles; 12th-century Torre Abbey (Torquay); replica of Drake's *Golden Hind* (Brixham); Abbey Mansion (17th/18th century); Paignton Zoo **industries** tourism, fishing, electronics, radio equipment, iron founding, horticultural products **population** (1996) 128,000

Tordesillas, Treaty of agreement reached in 1494 when Castile and Portugal divided the uncharted world between themselves. An imaginary line was drawn 370 leagues west of the Azores and the Cape Verde Islands, with Castile receiving all lands discovered to the west, and Portugal those to the east.

Torfaen unitary authority in south Wales, created in 1996 from part of the former county of Gwent.

area 98 sq km/38 sq mi **towns** Pontypool (administrative headquarters), Cwmbran (the first new town in Wales) **physical** Coity Mountain in the north, River Afon Llwyd **industries** advanced electronics, automotive, engineering **population** (1996) 90,700

Torino Italian name for the city of ▷Turin.

tornado extremely violent revolving storm with swirling, funnel-shaped clouds, caused by a rising column of warm air propelled by strong wind. A tornado can rise to a great height, but with a diameter of only a few hundred metres or less. Tornadoes move with wind speeds of 160–480 kph/100–300 mph, destroying everything in their path. They are common in the central USA and Australia.

Related Web site: Tornado Project Online http://www.tornadoproject.com/

Toronto (Huron 'place of meeting') port and capital of ▷Ontario, Canada, at the mouths of the Humber and Don rivers on Lake Ontario; population (1999 est) 2,529,300, metropolitan area (1996) 4,444,700. It is a major shipping point on the ▷St Lawrence Seaway, and Canada's main financial, business, commercial, and manufacturing centre. Industries include shipbuilding, food-processing, publishing, and the production of fabricated metals, aircraft, farm machinery, cars, chemicals, and clothing. It is also a tourist and cultural centre, with theatres and a film industry.

A French fort was established in 1749, and the site became the provincial capital in 1793; it was known until 1834 as York.

Related Web site: Toronto Star City Search http://www.starcitysearch.com/

torpedo (or **electric ray**) any species of the order Torpediniformes of mainly tropical rays (cartilaginous fishes), whose electric organs between the pectoral fin and the head can give a powerful shock. They can grow to 180 cm/6 ft in length.

torpedo self-propelled underwater missile, invented 1866 by English engineer Robert Whitehead. Modern torpedoes are homing missiles; some resemble mines in that they lie on the seabed until activated by the acoustic signal of a passing ship. A television camera enables them to be remotely controlled, and in the final stage of attack they lock on to the radar or sonar signals of the target ship.

torque (or **torc**) prehistoric neck-ring ornament usually made of gold. They are found during the Bronze and Iron Age periods in Britain, Ireland, and northwestern Europe, particularly in Celtic cultures, where they exemplify the fine design of ▷Celtic art.

torque turning effect of force on an object. A turbine produces a torque that turns an electricity generator in a power station. Torque is measured by multiplying the force by its perpendicular distance from the turning point.

Torquemada, Tomás de (1420–1498) Spanish Dominican monk, confessor to Queen Isabella I. In 1483 he revived the ▷Inquisition on her behalf, and at least 2,000 'heretics' were burned; Torquemada also expelled the Jews from Spain 1492, with a resultant decline of the economy.

torr unit of pressure equal to 1/760 of an ▷atmosphere, used mainly in high-vacuum technology.

Torremolinos tourist resort on the Costa del Sol between Málaga and Algeciras in Andalusia, southern Spain; population (1991) 31,700. There is a wine museum and a modern congress and exhibition centre.

Torres Strait channel between the Arafura Sea and the Coral Sea, separating the island of New Guinea from Cape York on the northern tip of Queensland, Australia; width 130 km/80 mi. The strait is scattered with reefs and small islands.

Torricelli, Evangelista (1608–1647) Italian physicist who established the existence of atmospheric pressure and devised the mercury ▷barometer in 1644.

torsion in physics, the state of strain set up in a twisted material; for example, when a thread, wire, or rod is twisted, the torsion set up in the material tends to return the material to its original state. The **torsion balance**, a sensitive device for measuring small gravitational or magnetic forces, or electric charges, balances these against the restoring force set up by them in a torsion suspension.

tort in law, a wrongful act for which someone can be sued for damages in a civil court. It includes such acts as libel, trespass, injury done to someone (whether intentionally or by negligence), and inducement to break a contract (although breach of contract itself is not a tort).

tortoise reptile of the order Chelonia, family Testudinidae, with the body enclosed in a hard shell. Tortoises are related to the ▷terrapins and ▷turtles, and range in length from 10 cm/4 in to 150 cm/5 ft. The shell consists of a curved upper carapace and flattened lower plastron joined at the sides; it is generally more domed than that of turtles. The head and limbs are withdrawn into it when the tortoise is in danger. Most land tortoises are herbivorous, feeding on plant material, and have no teeth. The mouth forms a sharp-edged beak. They occur in the warmer regions of all continents except Australia. Tortoises have been known to live for 150 years.

The sex of a tortoise is difficult to determine, except when the female is on heat. Mating can last up to five hours. Eggs are laid in warm earth in great numbers, and are not incubated by the mother.

Best known in the pet trade is the small **spur-thighed tortoise** *Testudo graeca*, found in Asia Minor, the Balkans, and North Africa. It was extensively exported, often in appalling conditions, until the 1980s, when strict regulations were introduced to prevent its probable extinction. The **giant tortoises** of the Galapagos in the Pacific and the Seychelles in the Indian Ocean may reach a length of 150 cm/5 ft and weigh over 225 kg/500 lbs, and can yield about 90 kg/200 lbs of meat; hence its almost complete extermination by sailors in passing ships.

Tortoiseshell is the semi-transparent shell of the hawksbill turtle.

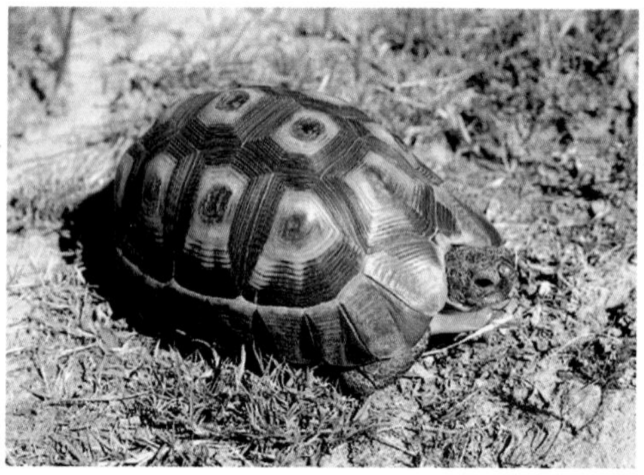

TORTOISE An angulate tortoise *Chersina angulata*. *K G Preston-Mafham/Premaphotos Wildlife*

tortoise beetle leaf-feeding beetle usually found in the tropics. The outer margins of its wing covers and the prothorax (shield) are drawn out to form a convex shield a bit like the outline of a tortoise. They are often brilliantly coloured with a metallic sheen.

torture infliction of bodily pain to extort evidence or confession. In the 20th century torture is widely (though, in most countries, unofficially) used. The human-rights organization ▷Amnesty International investigates and publicizes the use of torture on prisoners of conscience.

Tory Party the forerunner of the British ▷Conservative Party about 1680–1830. It was the party of the squire and parson, as opposed to the Whigs (supported by the trading classes and Nonconformists). The name is still applied colloquially to the Conservative Party. In the USA a Tory was an opponent of the break with Britain in the American Revolution 1775–83.

total internal reflection the complete reflection of a beam of light that occurs from the surface of an optically 'less dense' material. For example, a beam from an underwater light source can be reflected from the surface of the water, rather than escaping through the surface. Total internal reflection can only happen if a light beam hits a surface at an angle greater than the critical angle for that particular pair of materials.

totalitarianism government control of all activities within a country, overtly political or otherwise, as in fascist or communist dictatorships. Examples of totalitarian regimes are Italy under Benito ▷Mussolini 1922–45; Germany under Adolf ▷Hitler 1933–45; the USSR under Joseph ▷Stalin from the 1930s until his death in 1953; and more recently Romania under Nicolae ▷Ceauşescu 1974–89.

totalizator (or **Tote**) system of betting on racehorses or greyhounds. All money received is divided in equal shares among winning ticket owners, less expenses. It was first introduced 1928; see ▷betting.

totemism (Algonquin Indian 'mark of my family') the belief in individual or clan kinship with an animal, plant, or object. This totem is sacred to those concerned, and they are forbidden to eat or desecrate it; marriage within the clan is usually forbidden.

Totemism occurs among Pacific Islanders and Australian Aborigines, and was formerly prevalent throughout Europe, Africa, and Asia. Most American Indian societies had totems as well.

TOTEMISM Totem poles are carved and painted logs, placed upright, made by native Indians of northwest USA and Canada. The poles are decorated according to the function of the pole – for instance, it can serve as a grave marker, or depict a family legend. *Image Bank*

Tottenham district of the Greater London borough of Haringey.

toucan any South and Central American forest-dwelling bird of the genus *Ramphastos*, family Ramphastidae, order Piciformes. Toucans have very large, brilliantly coloured beaks and often handsome plumage. They live in small flocks and eat fruits, seeds, and insects. They nest in holes in trees, where the female lays 2–4 eggs; both parents care for the eggs and young. There are 37 species, ranging from 30 cm/1 ft to 60cm/2ft in size.

In the true toucans the ground colour of the plumage is generally black; the throat, breast and rump are adorned with yellow, red and white; the body is short and thick; the tail is rounded or even and can be turned up over the back when the bird goes to roost. The largest are about 60 cm/24 in long.

TOUCAN The toucan has a large, brightly coloured bill, which is very light and strong, being constructed of honeycomb material.

touch sensation produced by specialized nerve endings in the skin. Some respond to light pressure, others to heavy pressure. Temperature detection may also contribute to the overall sensation of touch. Many animals, such as nocturnal ones, rely on touch more than humans do. Some have specialized organs of touch that project from the body, such as whiskers or antennae.

touch screen in computing, an input device allowing the user to communicate with the computer by touching a display screen with a finger. In this way, the user can point to a required ▷menu option or item of data. Touch screens are used less widely than other pointing devices such as the ▷mouse or ▷joystick. A typical application is in public houses, where sales staff simply need to touch the items sold on the screen; a total is displayed for the customer, while the computing system connected to the screen calculates remaining stock levels.

touch sensor in a computer-controlled ▷robot, a device used to give the robot a sense of touch, allowing it to manipulate delicate objects or move automatically about a room. Touch sensors provide the feedback necessary for the robot to adjust the force of its movements and the pressure of its grip. The main types include the strain gauge and the microswitch.

Toulon port and administrative centre of Var *département*, southeast France, on the Mediterranean Sea, 48 km/30 mi southeast of Marseille; population (1990) 170,200, conurbation 437,000. It is the chief Mediterranean naval station of France. Industries include oil refining, marine engineering, armaments, chemicals, furniture, and clothing. There is a university. Toulon was the Roman **Telo Martius**, became the seat of a bishopric in the 6th century and was made a port by Henry IV. During World War II the French fleet was scuttled here (1942) to avoid it passing into German control.

Toulouse administrative centre of Haute-Garonne *département* in southwest France, 200 km/125 mi southeast of Bordeaux on the River Garonne; population (1990) 365,900, conurbation 650,000. It is the fourth city of France, a centre of communications, and the seat of an archbishopric and a university, founded in 1229. The town is a marketing, publishing, and banking centre, and its chief industries are textiles, chemicals, metallurgical goods, and aircraft construction; Concorde was built here. It has also become a major European centre of scientific research, especially in aerospace, electronics, data processing, and agriculture.

Features Toulouse is known as *la ville rose* ('the pink city') because most of the buildings are made from red brick. The old abbey church of St Sernin is probably the finest Romanesque church in France. It was the church of the Jacobins and belonged to a monastery founded in 1216. The cathedral of St Etienne is 11th–17th-century. The town's main square is the Place du Capitole, and the Pont Neuf, a 16th-century bridge, joins Toulouse to the western suburb of St Cyprien, southwest of which is the new town of Le Mirail ('The Miracle'), built to house 100,000 people. There are museums, art galleries, and libraries.

Related Web site: Welcome to Toulouse http://www.cict.fr/toulouse/EBienvenue.html

TOULOUSE An illustration depicting the siege of Toulouse 1218, led by Simon de Montfort against the Albigenses, a Christian sect whose anti-Catholic stance provoked de Montfort's crusade against them. *Philip Sauvain Picture Collection*

Toulouse-Lautrec, Henri (Marie Raymond de)

(1864–1901) French artist. He was active in Paris, where he painted entertainers and prostitutes in a style characterized by strong colours, bold design, and brilliant technical skill. From 1891 his lithographic posters were a great success, skilfully executed and yet retaining the spontaneous character of sketches. His later work was to prove vital to the development of ▷poster art.

Career His main activity as an artist belongs to the decade 1885–95, when his life revolved round Montmartre, Paris. At home in society of every kind, he drew and observed in the cafés, cabarets, and brothels. In a sanatorium 1899–1901, he drew and painted from memory the series *Au Cirque*.

Style He was influenced by Edgar ▷Degas, and brilliantly adapted the design and technique of the Japanese print to his own purpose in colour lithography. His posters for the Moulin Rouge and other venues are classics of their kind. Oil diluted with petrol and used on board, giving a matt effect, was a favoured medium, enabling him to sketch swiftly and vividly in paint, but it is in drawings and lithographs that he is unique. He was interested neither in light nor form as such, but in the intensity of mood and expression that he conveyed.

Related Web site: Toulouse-Lautrec, Henri de http://sunsite.unc.edu/wm/paint/auth/toulouse-lautrec/

touraco (or **turaco**) any fruit-eating African bird of the family Musophagidae, order Cuculiformes. They have a small high bill, notched and serrated mandibles, a long tail, erectile crest, and short, rounded wings. The largest are 70 cm/28 in long.

Tour de France French road race for professional cyclists held annually over approximately 4,800 km/3,000 mi of primarily French roads. The race takes about three weeks to complete and the route varies each year, often taking in adjoining countries, but always ending in Paris. A separate stage is held every day, and the overall leader at the end of each stage wears the coveted 'yellow jersey' (French *maillot jaune*).

Related Web site: Tour de France http://www.letour.fr/

tourmaline hard, brittle mineral, a complex silicate of various metals, but mainly sodium aluminium borosilicate.

Tournai (Flemish **Doornik**) town and railway junction in Hainaut province, Belgium, on the River Schelde, 43 km/27 mi northeast of Mons; population (1997) 67,900. Industries include carpets, textiles, pottery, cement, and leather. There are freestone and limestone quarries. It stands on the site of a Roman relay post and has a Romanesque and Gothic cathedral (11th–14th centuries) with the oldest belfry in the country.

tournament in medieval England, martial competition between knights. Until the accession of the Stuarts to the English throne, chivalric contests were a feature of court life. Jousting and hand-to-hand combat took place, and a lord might dedicate himself to one of the ladies present. In the early part of his reign, Henry VIII participated in tournaments personally, much to the consternation of his counsellors.

Tours administrative centre of Indre-et-Loire *département* in Centre region, west-central France, on the River Loire 200 km/125 mi southwest of Paris; population (1990) 133,400, conurbation 282,000. It manufactures chemicals, textiles, machinery, and electrical goods, and has a trade in agricultural produce, fruit, wine, and spirits. It is an ancient city and was capital of the former province of Touraine. Tours became the seat of the French government for four days in 1940 during World War II.

Toussaint L'Ouverture, Pierre Dominique (c. 1743–

1803) Haitian revolutionary leader, born a slave. He joined the insurrection of 1791 against the French colonizers and was made governor by the revolutionary French government. He expelled the Spanish and British, but when the French emperor Napoleon reimposed slavery he revolted, was captured, and died in prison in France. In 1983 his remains were returned to Haiti.

Tower Bridge bridge over the River ▷Thames in London, England, between the Tower of London and Bermondsey. Designed by Horace Jones and John Wolfe Barry, it was built in 1886–94. The central span between two towers consists of two drawbridges which can be raised to allow vessels to pass to and from the Pool of London.

TOWER BRIDGE Tower Bridge, on the River Thames, London, England. *Image Bank*

Tower Hamlets inner borough of east Greater London. It includes the districts of Limehouse, Spitalfields, Bethnal Green, ▷Wapping, Poplar, Stepney, and the Isle of Dogs; population (1991) 161,100. Large parts of the borough's dockland areas have been redeveloped for business and residential use. The Tower of London, the ▷Docklands redevelopment area (including ▷Canary Wharf); and ▷Billingsgate fish market are features of the borough.

Tower of London fortress on the bank of the River Thames to the east of the City of London, England. William (I) the Conqueror established a camp here immediately after his coronation in 1066, and in 1078 Gundulf of Bec, Bishop of Rochester, began building the White Tower on the site of British and Roman fortifications. It is the centrepiece of the fortress and probably the finest and best-preserved Norman keep in existence. It is surrounded by two strong walls and a ditch, now dry, and was for centuries a royal residence and the principal state prison.

Today it is a barracks, an armoury, and a museum. In 1994 the crown jewels, traditionally kept in a bunker in the keep, were moved to a specially designed showcase, the Jewel House, situated above ground level.

Townshend, Charles (1725–1767) British politician, chancellor of the Exchequer 1766–67. The **Townshend Acts**, designed to assert Britain's traditional authority over its colonies, resulted in widespread resistance. Among other things they levied taxes on imports (such as tea, glass, and paper) into the North American colonies. Opposition in the colonies to taxation without representation (see ▷Stamp Act) precipitated the American Revolution.

toxaemia another term for ▷blood poisoning; **toxaemia of pregnancy** is another term for ▷pre-eclampsia.

toxic shock syndrome rare condition marked by rapid onset of fever, vomiting, and low blood pressure, sometimes leading to death. It is caused by a toxin of the bacterium *Staphylococcus aureus*, normally harmlessly present in the body. It is seen most often in young women using tampons during menstruation.

toxic syndrome fatal disease for which the causes are not confirmed. In an outbreak in Spain in the early 1980s, more than 20,000 people became ill and 600–700 died.

toxic waste ▷hazardous waste, especially when it has been dumped.

toxin any poison produced by another living organism (usually a bacterium) that can damage the living body. In vertebrates, toxins are broken down by ▷enzyme action, mainly in the liver.

toxoplasmosis disease transmitted to humans by animals, often in pigeon or cat excrement, or in undercooked meat. It causes flulike symptoms and damages the central nervous system, eyes, and visceral organs. It is caused by a protozoan, *Toxoplasma gondii*. Congenital toxoplasmosis, transmitted from an infected mother to her unborn child, can lead to blindness and retardation.

Toynbee, Arnold (1852–1883) English economic historian who coined the term 'industrial revolution' in his 'Lectures on the Industrial Revolution', published in 1884.

Toyotomi, Hideyoshi (1537–1598) Adopted name of Kinoshita Tōkichirō. Japanese warlord, one of the three military leaders who unified Japan in the 16th century (Momoyama period). Successful military campaigns and alliances gave him control of central and southwestern Japan by 1587 and eastern Japan by 1590. His invasion of Korea 1592–98 was, however, defeated.

HIDEYOSHI TOYOTOMI A popular print depicting Hideyoshi Toyotomi, a Japanese feudal lord and samurai (Japanese warrior). *The Art Archive*

trace element chemical element necessary in minute quantities for the health of a plant or animal. For example, magnesium, which

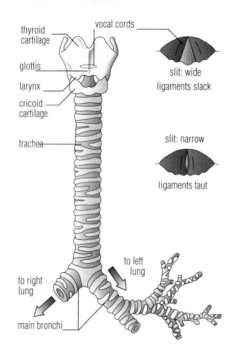

TRACHEA The larynx, or voice box, lies at the entrance to the trachea. The two vocal cords are membranes that normally remain open and still. When they are drawn together, the passage of air makes them vibrate and produce sounds.

occurs in chlorophyll, is essential to photosynthesis, and iodine is needed by the thyroid gland of mammals for making hormones that control growth and body chemistry.

tracer in science, a small quantity of a radioactive ▷isotope (form of an element) used to follow the path of a chemical reaction or a physical or biological process. The location (and possibly concentration) of the tracer is usually detected by using a Geiger–Muller counter.

trachea tube that forms an airway in air-breathing animals. In land-living ▷vertebrates, including humans, it is also known as the **windpipe** and runs from the larynx to the upper part of the chest. Its diameter is about 1.5 cm/0.6 in and its length 10 cm/4 in. It is strong and flexible, and reinforced by rings of ▷cartilage. In the upper chest, the trachea branches into two tubes: the left and right bronchi, which enter the lungs. Insects have a branching network of tubes called tracheae, which conduct air from holes (▷spiracles) in the body surface to all the body tissues. The finest branches of the tracheae are called tracheoles.

Some spiders also have tracheae but, unlike insects, they possess gill-like lungs (book lungs) and rely on their circulatory system to transport gases throughout the body.

tracheotomy (or **tracheostomy**) surgical opening in the windpipe (trachea), usually created for the insertion of a tube to enable the patient to breathe. It is done either to bypass an airway impaired by disease or injury, or to safeguard it during surgery or a prolonged period of mechanical ventilation.

trachoma chronic eye infection, resembling severe ▷conjunctivitis. The conjunctiva becomes inflamed, with scarring and formation of pus, and there may be damage to the cornea. It is caused by a viruslike organism (▷chlamydia), and is a disease of dry tropical regions. Although it responds well to antibiotics, numerically it remains the biggest single cause of blindness worldwide. In 1999 there were 146 million people suffering with trachoma worldwide, mostly in developing countries.

Tractarianism another name for the ▷Oxford Movement, 19th-century movement for Catholic revival within the Church of England.

Tracy, Spencer (1900–1967) US actor. He was distinguished for his understated, seemingly effortless, natural performances. His films include *Captains Courageous* (1937) and *Boys' Town* (1938) (for both of which he won Academy Awards), and he starred with Katharine ▷Hepburn in nine films, including *Adam's Rib* (1949) and *Guess Who's Coming to Dinner* (1967), his final appearance.

trade description description of the characteristics of goods, including their quality, quantity, and fitness for the purpose for which they are required. Under the Trade Descriptions Acts 1968 and 1972, making a false trade description is a criminal offence in English law.

Tradescant, John (1570–*c*. 1638) English gardener and botanist who travelled widely in Europe and is thought to have introduced the cos lettuce to England from the Greek island of that name. He was appointed gardener to Charles I and was succeeded by his son, **John Tradescant the Younger** (1608–1662). The younger Tradescant undertook three plant-collecting trips to Virginia in North America.

tradescantia any of a group of plants native to North and Central America, with variegated or striped leaves. The spiderwort *T. virginiana* is a cultivated garden plant; the wandering jew *T. albiflora* is a common house plant, with green oval leaves tinged with pink, purple or silver-striped. They are named after English botanist John ▷Tradescant the Younger. (Genus *Tradescantia*, family Commelinaceae.)

Trades Union Congress (TUC) voluntary organization of trade unions, founded in the UK in 1868, in which delegates of affiliated unions meet annually to consider matters affecting their members. In 1997 there were 67 affiliated unions, with an aggregate membership of 6 million.

trade union organization of workers that exists to promote and defend the interests of its members, to achieve improved working conditions, and to undertake collective bargaining (negotiating on the behalf of members, the employees) with employers. Attitudes of government to unions and of unions to management vary greatly from country to country. Probably the most effective trade union system is that of Sweden, and the most internationally known is the Polish ▷Solidarity.

Trade unions are particularly concerned with pay, working conditions, job security, and redundancy. Four types of trade union are often distinguished: general unions (covering all skilled and semi-skilled workers), craft unions (comprising those performing a specific type of work, for example electricians or printers), industrial unions (covering workers in one industry or trade, for example steel or car workers), and white-collar unions (covering those in clerical/administrative jobs). Unions may also be affiliated to a larger organization which negotiates with the government, for example the ▷Trades Union Congress in the UK and the ▷American Federation of Labor and Congress of Industrial Organizations in the USA.

Trade-union members in a place of work elect a ▷shop steward to represent them and their concerns to the management. Trade unions also employ full-time trade-union officers who tend to cover a geographical area. Top trade-union officials must be elected by a secret ballot of members.

Unions negotiate with employers over any differences they may have. Both parties may invite an outside body such as the ▷Advisory, Conciliation and Arbitration Service (ACAS) to conciliate or arbitrate in an industrial dispute. Alternatively, trade-union members may take industrial action, going on strike or working to rule, for example. In continental Europe, particularly France, where syndicalism was influential (the practise of transferring the ownership and control of production to the trade unions), the use of direct action in the form of a general strike directed against the government, has been more typical than in the UK.

Trade unions try to get a larger share of the profits of their members' labour allocated to the workers rather than to management and shareholders. In economics, it can be shown that in a free market, assuming normal supply and demand curves for labour, a trade union that raises wages above the equilibrium wage will cause unemployment. However, many labour markets are not free and there is no direct link between trade-union membership and the level of unemployment in an industry or in the economy. Moreover, some contest that trade unions prevent the exploitation of workers by employers whose only goal is to minimize the cost of labour used in the production process. In Sweden, where around 75% of the workforce are union members, conflicts of unions within an industry (demarcation disputes) are largely eliminated, and unions and employers cooperate freely.

trade unionism, international worldwide cooperation between unions. In 1973 a European Trade Union Confederation was established, with a membership of 29 million, and there is an International Labour Organization, established in 1919 and affiliated to the United Nations from 1945, which formulates standards for labour and social conditions. Other organizations are the International Confederation of Free Trade Unions (1949) – which includes the American Federation of Labor and Congress of Industrial Organizations and the UK Trades Union Congress – and the World Federation of Trade Unions (1945).

trade wind prevailing wind that blows towards the Equator from the northeast and southeast. Trade winds are caused by hot air rising at the Equator and the consequent movement of air from north and south to take its place. The winds are deflected towards the west because of the Earth's west-to-east rotation.

The unpredictable calms known as the ▷doldrums lie at their convergence.

The trade-wind belts move north and south about 5° with the seasons. The name is derived from the obsolete expression '*blow trade*' meaning to blow regularly, which indicates the trade winds' importance to navigation in the days of cargo-carrying sailing ships.

trading standards department local authority department responsible for enforcing consumer legislation. Trading standards departments are responsible for checking garages to ensure that, under the ▷Weights and Measures Act 1963, the right amount of petrol is given from the pumps. They check any premises preparing or serving food because under the Food and Drugs Act 1955 food sold must be fit for human consumption. They also enforce the Trade Descriptions Act 1968.

Trafalgar, Battle of during the ▷Napoleonic Wars, victory of the British fleet, commanded by Admiral Horatio ▷Nelson, over a combined French and Spanish fleet on 21 October 1805; Nelson was mortally wounded during the action. The victory laid the foundation for British naval supremacy throughout the 19th century. It is named after Cape Trafalgar, a low headland in southwest Spain, near the western entrance to the Straits of Gibraltar.

tragedy in the ▷theatre, a play dealing with a serious theme, traditionally one in which a character meets disaster as a result either of personal failings or circumstances beyond his or her control. Historically the classical view of tragedy, as expressed by the Greek tragedians Aeschylus, Euripides, and Sophocles, and the Roman tragedian Seneca, has been predominant in the Western tradition. In the 20th century tragedies dealing with exalted or heroic figures in an elevated manner have virtually died out. Tragedy has been replaced by dramas with 'tragic' implications or overtones, as in the work of Ibsen, O'Neill, Tennessee Williams, and Osborne, for example, or by the problem plays of Pirandello, Brecht, and Beckett.

Quentin Crisp
English writer
Whenever we confront an unbridled desire we are surely in the presence of a tragedy-in-the-making.
Manners from Heaven

tragicomedy drama that contains elements of tragedy and comedy; for example, Shakespeare's 'reconciliation' plays, such as *The Winter's Tale*, which reach a tragic climax but then lighten to a happy conclusion. A tragicomedy is the usual form for plays in the tradition of the Theatre of the ▷Absurd, such as Samuel ▷Beckett's *En attendant Godot/Waiting for Godot* (1952) and Tom ▷Stoppard's *Rosencrantz and Guildenstern are Dead* (1967).

tragopan any of several species of bird of the genus *Tragopan*, a short-tailed pheasant living in wet forests along the southern Himalayas. Tragopans are brilliantly coloured with arrays of spots, long crown feathers and two blue erectile crests. All have been reduced in numbers by destruction of their habitat. The western tragopan is the rarest, as a result of extensive deforestation.

Traherne, Thomas (c. 1637–1674) English Christian mystic, religious poet, and essayist. His lyric poetry was not published until 1903, and his prose *Centuries of Meditations* until 1908.

Trail of Tears route traversed by 16,000 ▷Cherokee in 1838 from their ancestral lands in North Carolina, Georgia, Tennessee, and Alabama to ▷Indian Territory under the ▷Indian Removal Act of 1830. Held initially in stockades by the US army, they were forced to march under military escort nearly 1,600 km/1,000 mi in winter with little food; over 4,000 died from disease, hunger, and exposure. The Trail of Tears became a national monument in 1987.

Training Agency UK government-sponsored organization responsible for retraining of unemployed workers. Founded as the **Manpower Services Commission** in 1974, the organization has operated such schemes as the Training Opportunities Scheme (TOPS) (1974), the Youth Opportunities Programme (YOP) (1978), the Youth Training Scheme (YTS) (1983), and the Technical and Vocational Initiative (TVEI) (1983).

Trajan (AD 52–117) Born Marcus Ulpius Trajanus. Roman emperor from AD 98. He conquered Dacia (Romania) in 101–07 and much of ▷Parthia in 113–17, bringing the empire to its greatest extent.

trampolining gymnastics performed on a sprung canvas sheet which allows the performer to reach great heights before landing again. Marks are gained for carrying out difficult manoeuvres. Synchronized trampolining and tumbling are also popular forms of the sport.

tranquillizer common name for any drug for reducing anxiety or tension (anxiolytic), such as ▷benzodi-azepines, barbiturates,

antidepressants, and beta-blockers. The use of drugs to control anxiety is becoming much less popular, because most of the drugs available are capable of inducing dependence.

transactinide element any of a series of eight radioactive, metallic elements with atomic numbers that extend beyond the ▷actinide series, those from 104 (rutherfordium) to 111 (unununium). They are grouped because of their expected chemical similarities (they are all bivalent), the properties differing only slightly with atomic number. All have ▷half-lives that measure less than two minutes.

Trans-Alaskan Pipeline one of the world's greatest civil engineering projects, the construction of a pipeline to carry petroleum (crude oil) 1,285 km/800 mi from northern Alaska to the ice-free port of Valdez. It was completed in 1977 after three years' work and much criticism by ecologists. In 1997 the Pipeline delivered more than 20% of US oil production.

Trans-Amazonian Highway (or **Transamazonica**) road in Brazil, linking Recife in the east with the provinces of Rondonia, Amazonas, and Acre in the west.

Transcaucasia geographical region south of the Caucasus Mountains, encompassing the independent states of ▷Armenia, ▷Azerbaijan, and ▷Georgia; it is bounded by the Caucasus Mountains in the north, the frontier with Turkey and Iran in the south, and the Black and Caspian Seas in the west and east respectively. Transcaucasia covers a total area of 186,100 sq km/71,853 sq mi.

transcendentalism philosophy inaugurated in the 18th century by the German philosopher Immanuel Kant. As opposed to metaphysics in the traditional sense, transcendental philosophy is concerned with the conditions of possibility of experience, rather than the nature of being. It seeks to show the necessary structure of our 'point of view' on the world.

transcendental meditation (TM) technique of focusing the mind, based in part on Hindu meditation. Meditators are given a mantra (a special word or phrase) to repeat over and over in the mind; such meditation is believed to benefit the practitioner by relieving stress and inducing a feeling of wellbeing and relaxation. It was introduced to the West by Maharishi Mahesh Yogi and popularized by the ▷Beatles in the late 1960s.

transcription in living cells, the process by which the information for the synthesis of a protein is transferred from the ▷DNA strand on which it is carried to the messenger ▷RNA strand involved in the actual synthesis.

Trans-Dniester region of northeastern ▷Moldova, lying between the River Dniester and the Ukraine, and largely inhabited by ethnic Slavs (Russians and Ukrainians). The main city in the region is Tiraspol. In the early 1990s, Trans-Dniester was the scene

TRAJAN Roman citizens salute Roman Emperor Trajan in a replica relief from Trajan's Column from AD 113. The 30 m/98 ft column stands in Trajan's Forum in Rome, Italy. *The Art Archive/Victoria and Albert Museum London/Eileen Tweedy*

of violent agitation for a separate state; it was granted special autonomous status in the new Moldovan constitution of 1994.

transducer device that converts one form of energy into another. For example, a thermistor is a transducer that converts heat into an electrical voltage, and an electric motor is a transducer that converts an electrical voltage into mechanical energy. Transducers are important components in many types of sensor, converting the physical quantity to be measured into a proportional voltage signal.

transfer orbit elliptical path followed by a spacecraft moving from one orbit to another, designed to save fuel although at the expense of a longer journey time.

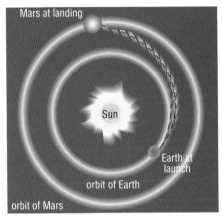

TRANSFER ORBIT The transfer orbit used by a spacecraft when travelling from Earth to Mars.

transformation in mathematics, a mapping or ▷function, especially one which causes a change of shape or position in a geometric figure. Reflection, rotation, enlargement, and translation are the main geometrical transformations.

transformational grammar theory of language structure initiated by the US linguist Noam ▷Chomsky, which proposes that below the actual phrases and sentences of a language (its **surface structure**) there lies a more basic layer (its **deep structure**), which is processed by various transformational rules when we speak and write.

transformer device in which, by electromagnetic induction, an alternating current (AC) of one voltage is transformed to another

TRANSFORMER Transformers in a power-generating plant. The purpose of such transformers is to increase the voltage generated (usually around 25,000 volts) to 400,000 volts or more in order that the power can be transmitted long-distance via the national grid system without a critical loss in voltage. *Image Bank*

voltage, without change of ▷frequency. Transformers are widely used in electrical apparatus of all kinds, and in particular in power transmission where high voltages and low currents are utilized.

A transformer has two coils, a primary for the input and a secondary for the output, wound on a common iron core. The ratio of the primary to the secondary voltages is directly proportional to the number of turns in the primary and secondary coils; the ratio of the current, is inversely proportional.

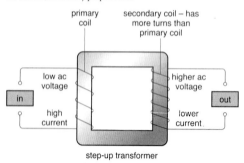

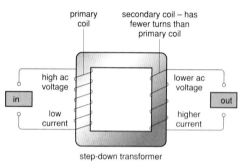

TRANSFORMER A step-up transformer increases voltage and has more turns on the secondary coil than on the primary. A step-down transformer decreases voltage and has more turns on the primary coil than on the secondary.

transfusion intravenous delivery of blood or blood products (plasma, red cells) into a patient's circulation to make up for deficiencies due to disease, injury, or surgical intervention.

Cross-matching is carried out to ensure the patient receives the right blood group. Because of worries about blood-borne disease, there is a growing interest in autologous transfusion with units of the patient's own blood 'donated' over the weeks before an operation.

Blood is rarely transfused whole. Blood cells and platelets are separated and resuspended in solution. Plasma can be frozen and is used to treat clotting deficiencies.

Blood transfusion, first successfully pioneered in humans in 1818, remained highly risky until the discovery of blood groups, by Austrian-born immunologist Karl ▷Landsteiner in 1900, which indicated the need for compatibility of donated blood.

transistor solid-state electronic component, made of ▷semiconductor material, with three or more ▷electrodes, that can regulate a current passing through it. A transistor can act as an amplifier, ▷oscillator, ▷photocell, or switch, and (unlike earlier thermionic valves) usually operates on a very small amount of power. Transistors commonly consist of a tiny sandwich of ▷germanium or ▷silicon, alternate layers having different electrical properties because they are impregnated with minute amounts of different impurities.

A crystal of pure germanium or silicon would act as an insulator (nonconductor). By introducing impurities in the form of atoms of other materials (for example, boron, arsenic, or indium) in minute amounts, the layers may be made either **n-type**, having an excess of electrons, or **p-type**, having a deficiency of electrons. This enables electrons to flow from one layer to another in one direction only. Transistors have had a great impact on the electronics industry, and thousands of millions are now made each year. They perform many of the functions of the thermionic valve, but have the advantages of greater reliability, long life, compactness, and instantaneous action, no warming-up period being necessary. They are widely used in most electronic equipment, including portable radios and televisions, computers, and satellites, and are the basis of the ▷integrated circuit (silicon chip). They were invented at Bell Telephone Laboratories in the USA in 1948 by John ▷Bardeen and Walter Brattain, developing the work of William Shockley.

transistor–transistor logic (TTL) in computing, the type of integrated circuit most commonly used in building electronic products. In TTL chips the bipolar transistors are directly connected (usually collector to base). In mass-produced items, large numbers of TTL chips are commonly replaced by a small number of uncommitted logic arrays (ULAs), or logic gate arrays.

transit in astronomy, the passage of a smaller object across the visible disc of a larger one. Transits of the inferior planets occur when they pass directly between the Earth and the Sun, and are seen as tiny dark spots against the Sun's disc.

transition metal any of a group of metallic elements that have incomplete inner electron shells and exhibit variable valency – for example, cobalt, copper, iron, and molybdenum. They are excellent conductors of electricity, and generally form highly coloured compounds.

Transkei former independent homeland ▷Black National State within South Africa, part of Eastern Cape Province from 1994; area 43,808 sq km/16,914 sq mi. Its capital was Umtata. It became self-governing in 1963, and achieved full independence in 1976, but this was not recognized outside South Africa. The largest of South Africa's homelands, it extended northwest from the Great Kei River, on the coast of Cape Province, to the border of Natal.

translation in living cells, the process by which proteins are synthesized. During translation, the information coded as a sequence of nucleotides in messenger ▷RNA is transformed into a sequence of amino acids in a peptide chain. The process involves the 'translation' of the ▷genetic code. See also ▷transcription.

transmigration of souls another name for ▷reincarnation.

transparency in photography, a picture on slide film. This captures the original in a positive image (direct reversal) and can be used for projection or printing on positive-to-positive print material, for example by the Cibachrome or Kodak R-type process.

transpiration the loss of water from a plant by evaporation. Most water is lost from the leaves through pores known as ▷stomata, whose primary function is to allow ▷gas exchange between the plant's internal tissues and the atmosphere. Transpiration from the leaf surfaces causes a continuous upward flow of water from the roots via the ▷xylem, which is known as the transpiration stream.

A single maize plant has been estimated to transpire 245 l/54 gal of water in one growing season.

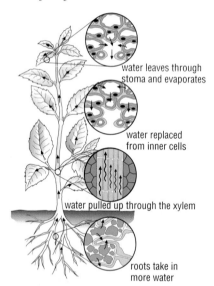

water leaves through stoma and evaporates

water replaced from inner cells

water pulled up through the xylem

roots take in more water

TRANSPIRATION The loss of water from a plant by evaporation is known as transpiration. Most of the water is lost through the surface openings, or stomata, on the leaves. The evaporation produces what is known as the transpiration stream, a tension that draws water up from the roots through the xylem, water-carrying vessels in the stem.

transplant in medicine, the transfer of a tissue or organ from one human being to another or from one part of the body to another (skin grafting). In most organ transplants, the operation is for life-saving purposes, although the immune system tends to reject foreign tissue. Careful matching and immunosuppressive drugs must be used, but these are not always successful.

Corneal grafting, which may restore sight to a diseased or damaged eye, was pioneered in 1905, and is the oldest successful human transplant procedure. Of the internal organs, kidneys were first transplanted successfully in the early 1950s and remain most in demand. Modern transplantation also encompasses the heart, lungs, liver, pancreatic tissue, bone, and bone-marrow.

Most transplant material is taken from cadaver donors, usually those suffering death of the ▷brainstem, or from frozen tissue banks. In rare cases, kidneys, corneas, and part of the liver may be obtained from living donors. Besides the shortage of donated material, the main problem facing transplant surgeons is rejection of the donated organ by the recipient's body. The 1990 Nobel Prize for Medicine or Physiology was awarded to two US surgeons, Donnall Thomas and Joseph Murray, for their pioneering work on organ and tissue transplantation.

The first experiments to use genetically altered animal organs in humans were given US government approval in July 1995 – genetically altered pig livers were attached to the circulatory systems of patients who were near death or whose livers had failed. Need for the tests had arisen due to a shortage of human organs available for transplant.

In 1999 US researchers found that patients awaiting liver transplants could be kept alive by regular infusions of frozen liver cells. These cells are readily available as they can be taken from damaged livers unsuitable for whole-organ donation. One patient suffering acute liver failure made a full recovery after the cell infusions. Even very damaged livers may be capable of some regeneration.

Under the UK transplant code of practice 1979 covering the use of material from a donor, two doctors (independent of the transplant team and clinically independent of each other) must certify that the donor is brainstem dead.

Related Web site: Transplantation and Donation http://www. transweb.org/default.htm

Transport and General Workers' Union (TGWU) UK trade union founded in 1921 by the amalgamation of a number of dockers' and road-transport workers' unions, previously associated in the Transport Workers' Federation. With more than 900,000 members, it ranks behind the public employers' union, UNISON, as the second-largest trade union in Britain.

transportation punishment of sending convicted persons to overseas territories to serve their sentences. It was introduced in England towards the end of the 17th century and although it was abolished in 1857 after many thousands had been transported, mostly to Australia, sentences of penal servitude continued to be partly carried out in Western Australia up until 1867. Transportation was used for punishment of criminals by France until 1938.

transsexual person who identifies himself or herself completely with the opposite sex, believing that the wrong sex was assigned at birth. Unlike **transvestites**, who desire to dress in clothes traditionally worn by the opposite sex, transsexuals think and feel emotionally in a way typically considered appropriate to members of the opposite sex, and may undergo surgery to modify external sexual characteristics.

Trans-Siberian Railway the world's longest single-service railway, connecting the cities of European Russia with Omsk, Novosibirsk, Irkutsk, and Khabarovsk, and terminating at Nakhodka on the Pacific coast east of Vladivostok. The line was built between 1891 and 1915, and has a total length of 9,289 km/ 5,772 mi, from Moscow to Vladivostok.

Related Web site: Across Russia on the Trans-Siberian Railroad http://www.ego.net/tlogue/xsib/index.htm

transubstantiation in Christian theology, the doctrine that the whole substance of the bread and wine changes into the substance of the body and blood of Jesus when consecrated in the ▷Eucharist.

transuranic element (or **transuranium element**) chemical element with an atomic number of 93 or more – that is, with a greater number of protons in the nucleus than has uranium. All transuranic elements are radioactive. Neptunium and plutonium are found in nature; the others are synthesized in nuclear reactions.

Transvaal former province of northeast South Africa to 1994, when it was divided into Mpumalanga, Northern, and Gauteng provinces. It bordered Zimbabwe to the north, Botswana to the northwest, and Swaziland and Mozambique to the east. It was settled by *Voortrekkers*, Boers who left Cape Colony in the Great Trek from 1831. Independence was recognized by Britain in 1852, until the settlers' difficulties with the conquered Zulus led to British annexation in 1877. It was made a British colony after the South African War 1899–1902, and in 1910 became a province of the Union of South Africa.

transverse wave ▷wave in which the displacement of the medium's particles, or in electromagnetic waves, the direction of the electric and magnetic fields, is at right angles to the direction of travel of the wave motion.

Transylvania mountainous area of central and northwestern Romania, bounded to the south by the Transylvanian Alps (an extension of the ▷Carpathian Mountains). Formerly a principality, with its capital at Cluj-Napoca, it was part of Hungary from about

1000 until its people voted to unite with Romania 1918. In a 1996 treaty Hungary renounced its claims on Transylvania.

TRANSYLVANIA A rural scene in Transylvania, home of the vampire legends. *Image Bank*

trapezium (US **trapezoid**) in geometry, a four-sided plane figure (quadrilateral) with two of its sides parallel. If the parallel sides have lengths a and b and the perpendicular distance between them is h (the height of the trapezium), its area $A = \frac{1}{2} h(a + b)$.

An isosceles trapezium has its sloping sides equal, is symmetrical about a line drawn through the midpoints of its parallel sides, and has equal base angles.

Trappist member of a Roman Catholic order of monks and nuns, renowned for the strictness of their rule, which includes the maintenance of silence, manual labour, and a vegetarian diet. The order was founded 1664 at La Trappe, in Normandy, France, by Armand de Rancé (1626–1700) as a reformed version of the ▷Cistercian order.

travel sickness nausea and vomiting caused by the motion of cars, boats, or other forms of transport. Constant vibration and movement may stimulate changes in the fluid of the semicircular canals (responsible for balance) of the inner ear, to which the individual fails to adapt, and to which are added visual and psychological factors. Some proprietary remedies contain ▷antihistamine drugs.

treason act of betrayal, in particular against the sovereign or the state to which the offender owes allegiance.

In the USA, treason is defined in the constitution as the crime of 'levying war against [the USA], or adhering to their enemies, giving them aid and comfort'. Congress has the power to declare the punishment for treason.

Treason is punishable in Britain by death. It includes: plotting the wounding or death of the sovereign or his or her spouse or heir; levying war against the sovereign in his or her realm; and giving aid or comfort to the sovereign's enemies in wartime. During World War II, treachery (aiding enemy forces or impeding the crown) was punishable by death, whether or not the offender owed allegiance to the crown. Sixteen spies (not normally capable of treason, though liable to be shot in the field) were convicted under these provisions. William Joyce (Lord Haw-Haw), although a US citizen, was executed for treason because he carried a British passport when he went to Germany in 1939.

treasure trove in England, any gold or silver, plate or bullion, found concealed in a house or the ground, the owner being unknown. Normally, treasure originally hidden, and not abandoned, belongs to the crown, but if the treasure was casually lost or intentionally abandoned, the first finder is entitled to it against all but the true owner. Objects buried with no intention of recovering them, for example in a burial mound, do not rank as treasure trove, and belong to the owner of the ground.

Treasury UK government department established in 1612 to collect and manage the public revenue and coordinate national economic policy. Technically, the prime minister is the first lord of the Treasury, but the chancellor of the Exchequer is the acting financial head.

Treasury bill in Britain, borrowing by the government in the form of a promissory note to repay the bearer 91 days from the date of issue; such bills represent a flexible and relatively cheap way for the government to borrow money for immediate needs.

treaty port port in Asia where the Western powers had special commercial privileges in the 19th century. As a result of the enforced unequal treaties, treaty ports were established mainly in China, from 1842; and Japan, from 1854 to 1899. Foreigners living in 'concessions' in the ports were not subject to local taxes or laws.

On the eve of the republican revolution in 1911 there were more than 50 treaty ports in China, mainly on the eastern seaboard and along the Chang Jiang River. They were dynamic focuses for Westernization and industrialization. Although resented by the ▷Guomindang (nationalist) government, foreign privileges in the treaty ports lasted until 1943.

tree perennial plant with a woody stem, usually a single stem (trunk), made up of ▷wood and protected by an outer layer of ▷bark. It absorbs water through a ▷root system. There is no clear dividing line between shrubs and trees, but sometimes a minimum achievable height of 6 m/20 ft is used to define a tree.

Angiosperms A treelike form has evolved independently many times in different groups of plants. Among the ▷angiosperms, or flowering plants, most trees are ▷dicotyledons. This group includes trees such as oak, beech, ash, chestnut, lime and maple, and they are often referred to as broad-leaved trees because their leaves are broader than those of conifers, such as pine and spruce. In temperate regions angiosperm trees are mostly ▷deciduous (that is, they lose their leaves in winter), but in the tropics most angiosperm trees are evergreen. There are fewer trees among the ▷monocotyledons, but the palms and bamboos (some of which are treelike) belong to this group.

Gymnosperms The ▷gymnosperms include many trees and they are classified into four orders: Cycadales (including cycads and sago palms), Coniferales (the conifers), Ginkgoales (including only one living species, the ginkgo, or maidenhair tree), and Taxales (including yews). Apart from the ginkgo and the larches (conifers), most gymnosperm trees are evergreen.

Tree ferns There are also a few living trees in the ▷pteridophyte group, known as tree ferns. In the swamp forests of the Carboniferous era, 300 million years ago, there were giant treelike horsetails and club mosses in addition to the tree ferns.

Oldest trees The world's oldest living trees are found in the Pacific forest of North America, some more than 2,000 years old.

Conservation According to a 1998 report by the World Conservation Monitoring Centre (WCMC) and the ▷World Conservation Union, approximately 8,750 tree species (around 10% of all known tree species) are in danger of extinction. In the 20th century 77 species became extinct and 7 more species were reduced to fewer than a dozen specimens.

Roots The great storm of October 1987 destroyed some 15 million trees in Britain, and showed that large roots are less significant than those of 10 cm/4 in diameter or less. If enough of these are cut, the tree dies or falls.

Related Web site: Wonderful World of Trees http://www.domtar.com/arbre/english/start.htm

TREE The monkey-puzzle tree is the nearest living example of the trees of the Carboniferous period, about 300 million years ago, which gave us our coal. Its name derives from the belief that monkeys have difficulty climbing it.

TREFOIL This red clover *Trifolium pratense* clearly shows how the leaves are divided into three leaflets, from which the name trefoil is derived. *Premaphotos Wildlife*

Tree, Herbert Draper Beerbohm (1853–1917) English actor and theatre manager. Noted for his lavish Shakespeare productions, he was founder of the Royal Academy of Dramatic Art (RADA). He was the half-brother of Max ▷Beerbohm. He was knighted in 1909.

tree creeper small, short-legged bird of the family Certhiidae, which spirals with a mouselike movement up tree trunks searching for food with its thin down-curved beak.

tree diagram in probability theory, a branching diagram consisting only of arcs and nodes (but not loops curving back on themselves), which is used to establish probabilities.

tree-frog about 600 species of the amphibian family Hylidae, order Anura. They are widely distributed, especially in the USA. The common tree-frog *Hyla arborea* is about 2.5 cm/1 in long, bright leaf-green above and white underneath, and possesses some powers of colour change. The male can croak loudly by means of a distensible throat sac. The digits bear adhesive discs, with which it readily climbs.

trefoil any of several ▷clover plants of a group belonging to the pea family, the leaves of which are divided into three leaflets. The name is also used for other plants with leaves divided into three lobes. (Genus *Trifolium*, family Leguminosae.)

trematode parasitic flatworm with an oval non-segmented body, of the class Trematoda, including the ▷fluke.

tremor minor ▷earthquake.

Trent third longest river of England; length 275 km/170 mi. Rising in the south Pennines (at Norton in the Moors) by the Staffordshire–Cheshire border, it flows south and then northeast through Derbyshire, along the county boundary of Leicestershire, and through Nottinghamshire and Lincolnshire, joining the Ouse east of Goole to form the Humber estuary, and entering the North Sea below Spurn Head. Its drainage basin covers more than 10,000 sq km/4,000 sq mi. Main tributaries are the Churnet, Dove, and Derwent.

Trent, Council of conference held 1545–63 by the Roman Catholic Church at Trento, northern Italy, initiating the so-called ▷Counter-Reformation; see also ▷Reformation.

Related Web site: Council of Trent http://www.newadvent.org/cathen/15030c.htm

Trentino-Alto Adige (formerly **Venezia Tridentina**) autonomous region of northern Italy, comprising the provinces of Bolzano and Trento; area 13,600 sq km/5,250 sq mi; population (1992 est) 896,700. Its chief towns are Trento (the capital) in the Italian-speaking southern area, and Bolzano (Bozen) in the northern German-speaking area of South Tirol (the region was Austrian until ceded to Italy in 1919 in the settlement following World War I). Wine, fruit, dairy products, and timber are produced. Paper, chemical, and metal industries use hydroelectric power.

Trento (German **Trient**; ancient **Tridentum**) capital of Trentino-Alto Adige region, Italy, on the Adige River and the Brenner Pass route, 160 km/100 mi northeast of Milan; population (1992)

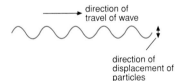

TRANSVERSE WAVE The diagram illustrates the motion of a transverse wave. Light waves are examples of transverse waves: they undulate at right angles to the direction of travel and are characterized by alternating crests and troughs. Simple water waves, such as the ripples produced when a stone is dropped into a pond, are also examples of transverse waves.

101,500. Industries include the manufacture of electrical goods, cement, agricultural machinery, chemicals, and processed foods and beverages. The Council of ▷Trent was held here from 1545 to 1563.

Trenton capital of ▷New Jersey, USA, on the Delaware River, 50 km/31 km northeast of Philadelphia; population (1996 est) 85,400. Trenton is the head of navigation on the Delaware, which forms the New Jersey–Philadelphia state border. Industries include metalworking, food-processing, and the manufacture of car parts, steel cable, rubber, and ceramics.

trespass going on to the land of another without authority. In law, a landowner has the right to eject a trespasser by the use of reasonable force and can sue for any damage caused.

Trevithick, Richard (1771–1833) English engineer, constructor of a steam road locomotive in 1801, the first to carry passengers, and probably the first steam engine to run on rails in 1804.

Triad secret society, founded in China as a Buddhist cult AD 36. It became known as the Triad because the triangle played a significant part in the initiation ceremony. Today it is reputed to be involved in organized crime (drugs, gambling, prostitution) among overseas Chinese. Its headquarters are alleged to be in Hong Kong.

trial in law, the determination of an accused person's innocence or guilt by means of the judicial examination of the issues of the case in accordance with the law of the land. The two parties in a trial, the defendant and plaintiff, or their counsels, put forward their cases and question the witnesses; on the basis of this evidence the jury or other tribunal body decides on the innocence or guilt of the defendant.

trial by ordeal in the Middle Ages, a test of guilt or innocence; see ▷ordeal, trial by.

triangle in geometry, a three-sided plane figure, the sum of whose interior angles is 180°. Triangles can be classified by the relative lengths of their sides. A **scalene triangle** has three sides of unequal length; an **isosceles triangle** has at least two equal sides; an **equilateral triangle** has three equal sides (and three equal angles of 60°).

A **right-angled triangle** has one angle of 90°. If the length of one side of a triangle is l and the perpendicular distance from that side to the opposite corner is h (the height or altitude of the triangle), its area $A = \frac{1}{2} lh$.

triangulation technique used in surveying and navigation to determine distances, using the properties of the triangle. To begin, surveyors measure a certain length exactly to provide a base line. From each end of this line they then measure the angle to a distant point, using a ▷theodolite. They now have a triangle in which they know the length of one side and the two adjacent angles. By simple trigonometry they can work out the lengths of the other two sides.

Triassic Period period of geological time 245–208 million years ago, the first period of the Mesozoic era. The present continents were fused together in the form of the world continent ▷Pangaea. Triassic sediments contain remains of early dinosaurs and other animals now extinct. By late Triassic times, the first mammals had evolved.

There was a mass extinction of 95% of plants at the end of the Triassic possibly caused by rising temperatures.

The climate was generally dry; desert sandstones are typical Triassic rocks.

triathlon test of stamina involving three sports: swimming 3.8 km/2.4 mi, cycling 180 km/112 mi, and running a marathon 42.195 km/26 mi 385 yd, each one immediately following the last.

tribunal strictly, a court of justice, but used in English law for a body appointed by the government to arbitrate in disputes, or investigate certain matters. Tribunals usually consist of a lawyer as chair, sitting with two lay assessors.

tribune Roman magistrate of ▷plebeian family, elected annually to defend the interests of the common people; only two were originally chosen in the early 5th century BC, but there were later ten. They could veto the decisions of any other magistrate.

triceratops any of a genus *Triceratops* of massive, horned dinosaurs of the order Ornithischia. They had three horns and a neck frill and were up to 8 m/25 ft long; they lived in the Cretaceous period.

trichloromethane technical name for ▷chloroform.

tricolour (French *tricolore*) any flag or similar made up of three colours. The French national flag has three vertical bands of red, white, and blue. The red and blue were the colours of Paris and the white represented the royal house of Bourbon. The flag was first adopted on 17 July 1789, three days after the storming of the Bastille during the French Revolution. The Russian tricolour, introduced in 1991, is red, white, and blue.

tricuspid valve flap of tissue situated on the right side of the ▷heart between the atrium and the ventricle. It prevents blood flowing backwards when the ventricle contracts.

Trident nuclear missile deployed on certain US nuclear-powered submarines and in the 1990s also being installed on four UK submarines. Each missile has eight warheads (MIRVs) and each of the four submarines will have 16 Trident D-5 missiles. The Trident replaced the earlier Polaris and Poseidon missiles.

Trieste (Slovenian **Trst**; ancient **Tergeste**) port in Friuli-Venezia Giulia, Italy, on the Adriatic coast, opposite Venice; population (1992) 228,400, including a large Slovene minority. It is the largest seaport on the Adriatic, extending for 13 km/8 mi along the Gulf of Trieste. There are large shipyards, and an oil pipeline linked with refineries in Germany and Austria. It is the site of the International Centre for Theoretical Physics, established in 1964.

triggerfish any marine bony fish of the family Balistidae, with a laterally compressed body, up to 60 cm/2 ft long, and a deep belly. They have small mouths but strong jaws and teeth. The first spine on the dorsal fin locks into an erect position, allowing them to fasten themselves securely in crevices for protection; it can only be moved by depressing the smaller third ('trigger') spine.

trigger plant any of a group of grasslike plants, with most species occurring in Australia. Flowers of the trigger plant are fertilized by insects trapped by a touch-sensitive column within the flower. In struggling to free themselves, the insects become covered in pollen, which they then spread to other flowers after escaping. (Genus *Stylidium*, family Stylidiaceae.)

triglyceride chemical name for ▷fat comprising three fatty acids reacted with a glycerol.

trigonometry branch of mathematics that solves problems relating to plane and spherical triangles. Its principles are based on the fixed proportions of sides for a particular angle in a right-angled triangle, the simplest of which are known as the ▷sine, ▷cosine, and ▷tangent (so-called trigonometrical ratios). Trigonometry is of practical importance in navigation, surveying, and simple harmonic motion in physics.

Using trigonometry, it is possible to calculate the lengths of the sides and the sizes of the angles of a right-angled triangle as long as one angle and the length of one side are known, or the lengths of two sides. The longest side, which is always opposite to the right angle, is called the **hypotenuse**. The other sides are named depending on their position relating to the angle that is to be found or used: the side opposite this angle is always termed **opposite** and that adjacent is the **adjacent**. So the following trigonometrical ratios are used:

$$\text{sine} = \frac{\text{opposite}}{\text{hypotenuse}} \qquad \text{cosine} = \frac{\text{adjacent}}{\text{hypotenuse}}$$

$$\text{tangent} = \frac{\text{opposite}}{\text{adjacent}}$$

Related Web site: Trigonometric Functions http://www-history.mcs.st-and.ac.uk/history/HistTopics/Trigonometric_functions.html

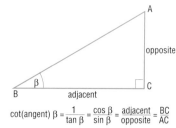

$$\cot(\text{angent}) \beta = \frac{1}{\tan \beta} = \frac{\cos \beta}{\sin \beta} = \frac{\text{adjacent}}{\text{opposite}} = \frac{BC}{AC}$$

TRIGONOMETRY The cotangent of angle β is equal to the ratio of the length of the adjacent side to the length of the opposite side.

trillium any of a group of perennial herbaceous woodland plants belonging to the lily family, native to Asia and North America. They have a circle, or whorl, of three leaves around the stem, at the end of which the single flower has three green ▷sepals and three usually maroon or white petals. The nodding trillium *T. cernuum* ranges across most of the eastern half of North America. (Genus *Trillium*, family Liliaceae.)

trilobite any of a large class (Trilobita) of extinct, marine, invertebrate arthropods of the Palaeozoic era, with a flattened, oval body, 1–65 cm/0.4–26 in long. The hard-shelled body was divided by two deep furrows into three lobes. Some were burrowers, others were swimming and floating forms. Their worldwide distribution, many species, and the immense quantities of their remains make them useful in geological dating.

There were more than 1,500 genera of trilobites, which existed for about 300 million years. They disappeared 250 million years ago, probably due to the evolution of new predators. According to a 1997 study of fossils by a US palaeontologist, the trilobite moulted its body segments individually; thus moulting may have taken several days increasing vulnerability. The largest trilobite found was 70 cm/28 in long, and lived 445 million years ago, in what is now Hudson Bay, Canada. It was discovered by Canadian palaeontologists in 2000.

Trimble, David (1944–) Northern Ireland politician, leader of the ▷Ulster Unionist party (or Official Unionist Party, OUP) from 1995 and Northern Ireland's first minister 1998–2001. Representing the Upper Bann constituency in the House of Commons from 1990, he won the leadership of the OUP in August 1995, when James ▷Molyneaux decided to retire at the age of 75. Trimble shared the Nobel Prize for Peace in 1998 with John ▷Hume for their efforts to find a peaceful solution to the conflict in

---

Equilateral triangle: all the sides are the same length; all the angles are equal to 60°

Isosceles triangle: two sides and two angles are the same

Scalene triangle: all the sides and angles are different

Acute-angle triangle: each angle is acute (less than 90°)

Obtuse-angle triangle: one angle is obtuse (more than 90°)

Right-angle triangle: one angle is 90°, the hypotenuse is the side opposite the right angle

hypotenuse

Area of triangle = 1/2 lh

Triangles are congruent if corresponding sides and corresponding angles are equal

Similar triangles have corresponding angles that are equal; they therefore have the same shape

TRIANGLE Types of triangle.

David Trimble

A ceasefire is a ceasefire is a ceasefire. You are not on ceasefire when you are shooting people.

On Northern Ireland Secretary Mo Mowlam's ruling that the IRA ceasefire was still intact. *Daily Telegraph*, 27 August 1999

Northern Ireland, and was one of the leading negotiators in the creation of a cross-community government in Belfast which met for the first time in December 1999 as powers were devolved to the province by the British government.

Trimble, originally seen as a hardliner and not likely to move easily into Molyneaux's seat, proved to be more flexible and tolerant than had been predicted. Following his election as OUP leader, he sought to give an impetus to the Northern Ireland peace process, meeting UK prime minister John Major, Irish taoiseach John Bruton, and US president Bill Clinton. Still emphasizing the need for the Irish Republican Army (IRA) to decommission its weaponry, he nevertheless suggested a route to all-party talks through elections, although this proposal was opposed by republican spokespersons.

He accepted the 1998 Good Friday Agreement on power-sharing, which was rejected by the more extreme Democratic Unionist Party, led by Ian Paisley, and the United Kingdom Unionist Party, led by Robert McCartney. He was chosen as Northern Ireland's first minister after the newly elected Northern Ireland Assembly met in June 1998, and seemed determined to make the peace agreement work. In the first meeting between Unionist and Republican leaders for several generations he met the president of Sinn Fein, Gerry Adams, at Stormont in September 1998. His determination to make a success of the power-sharing Northern Ireland Assembly was underlined when, after the Assembly's powers had been suspended following the failure of the IRA to begin decommissioning of arms, Trimble persuaded his Ulster Unionist party to return to the Assembly in exchange for another IRA initiative on decommissioning.

Trimurti the Hindu triad of gods, representing the Absolute Spirit in its three aspects: Brahma, personifying creation; Vishnu, preservation; and Siva, destruction.

Trinidad city in the province of Sancti Spíritus on the south coast of Cuba, in the West Indies, 282 km/175 mi southeast of Havana; population (1994 est) 38,000. It is one of the oldest towns in Cuba, founded by Diego de Velázquez in 1514. Sugar is cultivated in the surrounding area, fishing is important, as is cigar and cigarette manufacturing, but the economy of the city is based mainly on tourism.

Trinidad and Tobago see country box.

Trinitarianism belief in the Christian Trinity.

Trinity in Christianity, the union of three persons – Father, Son, and Holy Ghost/Spirit – in one godhead. The precise meaning of the doctrine has been the cause of unending dispute, and was the chief cause of the split between the Eastern Orthodox and Roman Catholic churches. **Trinity Sunday** occurs on the Sunday after Pentecost (Whitsun).

Tripitaka (sanskrit 'three baskets') the canonical texts of Theravāda Buddhism, divided into three parts: the **Vinaya-pitaka**, containing the rules governing the monastic community; the **Sūtra-pitaka**, a collection of scriptures recording the teachings of the Buddha; and **Abhidharma-pitaka**, a collection of Buddhist philosophical writings.

Triple Alliance pact from 1882 between Germany, Austria-Hungary, and Italy to offset the power of Russia and France. It was last renewed 1912, but during World War I Italy's initial neutrality

gradually changed and it denounced the alliance 1915. The term also refers to other alliances: 1668 – England, Holland, and Sweden; 1717 – Britain, Holland, and France (joined 1718 by Austria); 1788 – Britain, Prussia, and Holland; 1795 – Britain, Russia, and Austria.

Triple Entente alliance of Britain, France, and Russia 1907–17. In 1911 this became a military alliance and formed the basis of the Allied powers in World War I against the Central Powers, Germany and Austria-Hungary.

triple jump track and field event in athletics comprising a hop, step, and jump sequence from a takeoff board into a sandpit landing area measuring 8 m/26.25 ft (minimum) in length. The takeoff board is usually 13 m/42.65 ft from the landing area. Each competitor has six trials and the winner is the one who covers the longest distance.

triple nose-leaf bat one of many threatened bats in Africa, *Triaenops persicus* is found scattered along much of the coastal regions of East Africa and faces threats from disturbance of the caves in which it breeds. Tourism development, resulting in disturbance to coral caves which the bats inhabit, is a particular problem.

Tripoli (Arabic **Tarabolus al-Gharb**) capital and chief port of Libya, on the Mediterranean coast, 600 km/373 west of Benghazi; population (1996 est) 990,000. Products include olive oil, fruit, fish, and textiles; industries include oil refining and food processing. Tripoli was founded about the 7th century BC by Phoenicians from Oea (now Tripoli in Lebanon). It was a base for the Axis powers during World War II. In 1986 it was bombed by the US Air Force in retaliation for international guerrilla activity.

Trinidad and Tobago

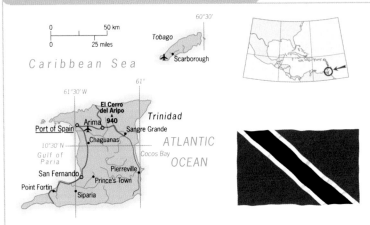

Trinidad and Tobago country in the West Indies, off the coast of Venezuela.

NATIONAL NAME *Republic of Trinidad and Tobago*
AREA 5,130 sq km/1,980 sq mi (Trinidad 4,828 sq km/1,864 sq mi and Tobago 300 sq km/ 115 sq mi)
CAPITAL Port-of-Spain (and chief port)
MAJOR TOWNS/CITIES San Fernando, Arima, Point Fortin
MAJOR PORTS Scarborough, Point Lisas
PHYSICAL FEATURES comprises two main islands and some smaller ones in Caribbean Sea; coastal swamps and hills east–west

Government

HEAD OF STATE Maxwell Richards from 2003
HEAD OF GOVERNMENT Patrick Manning from 2001
POLITICAL SYSTEM liberal democracy
POLITICAL EXECUTIVE parliamentary
ADMINISTRATIVE DIVISIONS eight counties, three municipalities, and one ward (Tobago)
ARMED FORCES 2,700 (2002 est)
DEATH PENALTY retained and used for ordinary crimes

Economy and resources

CURRENCY Trinidad and Tobago dollar
GPD (US$) 9.4 billion (2002 est)
REAL GDP GROWTH (% change on previous year) 3.7 (2001)

GNI (US$) 8.6 billion (2002 est)
GNI PER CAPITA (PPP) (US$) 8,680 (2002 est)
CONSUMER PRICE INFLATION 3.5% (2003 est)
UNEMPLOYMENT 10.8% (2001)
FOREIGN DEBT (US$) 4.9 billion (2001 est)
MAJOR TRADING PARTNERS USA, Venezuela, UK, Germany, Canada, Barbados, Colombia, Jamaica, Guyana, Netherlands Antilles
RESOURCES petroleum, natural gas, asphalt (world's largest deposits of natural asphalt)
INDUSTRIES petroleum refining, food processing, iron and steel, beverages, chemicals, cement, beer, cigarettes, motor vehicles, paper, printing and publishing, tourism (third-largest source of foreign exchange)
EXPORTS mineral fuels and lubricants, chemicals, basic manufactures, food. Principal market: USA 38.8% (2000)
IMPORTS raw materials and intermediate goods, machinery and transport equipment, manufactured goods, mineral fuel products, food and live animals, consumer goods. Principal source: USA 35.4% (2000)
ARABLE LAND 14.6% (2000 est)
AGRICULTURAL PRODUCTS sugar cane, coffee, cocoa, citrus fruits; fishing

Population and society

POPULATION 1,303,000 (2003 est)
POPULATION GROWTH RATE 0.8% (2000–15)
POPULATION DENSITY (per sq km) 254 (2003 est)
URBAN POPULATION (% of total) 75 (2003 est)
AGE DISTRIBUTION (% of total population) 0–14 23%, 15–59 67%, 60+ 10% (2002 est)
ETHNIC GROUPS the two main ethnic groups are Africans (40%) and East Indians (40%); 18% are mixed, and there are also European, Afro-European, and Chinese minorities. The original Carib population has largely disappeared
LANGUAGE English (official), Hindi, French, Spanish
RELIGION Roman Catholic 33%, Hindu 25%, Anglican 15%, Muslim 6%, Presbyterian 4%
EDUCATION (compulsory years) 7
LITERACY RATE 99% (men); 98% (women) (2003 est)
LABOUR FORCE 8.1% agriculture, 28.2% industry, 63.6% services (1998)
LIFE EXPECTANCY 68 (men); 74 (women) (2000–05)

Chronology

1498: Visited by the explorer Christopher Columbus, who named Trinidad after the three peaks at its southeastern tip and Tobago after the local form of tobacco pipe. Carib and Arawak Indians comprised the indigenous community.
1532: Trinidad colonized by Spain.
1630s: Tobago settled by Dutch, who introduced sugar-cane growing.
1797: Trinidad captured by Britain and ceded by Spain five years later under Treaty of Amiens.
1814: Tobago ceded to Britain by France.
1834: Abolition of slavery resulted in indentured labourers being brought in from India, rather than Africa, to work sugar plantations.
1889: Trinidad and Tobago amalgamated as a British colony.
1956: The People's National Movement (PNM) founded by Eric Williams, a moderate nationalist.
1958–62: Part of West Indies Federation.
1959: Achieved internal self-government, with Williams as chief minister.

TRINIDAD AND TOBAGO This stamp shows a copper-rumped hummingbird. *Stanley Gibbons*

CHILD MORTALITY RATE (under 5, per 1,000 live births) 20 (2001)
PHYSICIANS (per 1,000 people) 0.8 (1998 est)
HOSPITAL BEDS (per 1,000 people) 5.1 (1998 est)
TV SETS (per 1,000 people) 340 (2001 est)
RADIOS (per 1,000 people) 532 (2001 est)
INTERNET USERS (per 10,000 people) 1,060.3 (2002 est)
PERSONAL COMPUTER USERS (per 100 people) 8.0 (2002 est)

See also ▷Arawak; ▷Carib.

1962: Independence achieved within Commonwealth, with Williams as prime minister.
1970: Army mutiny and violent Black Power riots directed against minority East Indian population; state of emergency imposed for two years.
1976: Became a republic, with former Governor General Ellis Clarke as president and Williams as prime minister.
1986: Tobago-based National Alliance for Reconstruction (NAR), headed by A N R Robinson, won the general election.
1990: An attempted antigovernment coup by Islamic fundamentalists was foiled.
1991: A general election resulted in victory for PNM, with Patrick Manning as prime minister.
1995: The UNC and PNM tied in general election; a UNC–NAR coalition was formed, led by Basdeo Panday.
1997: Former Prime Minister Robinson was elected president.
2000: The UNC won an absolute majority in parliamentary elections.

Tripura hill state of northeast India since 1972, formerly a princely state, between Bangladesh and Assam; area 10,500 sq km/4,050 sq mi; population (2001 est) 3,631,000. The capital is Agartala. Steel, jute, timber, and rubber are produced, and rice, millet, maize, fruit, cotton, tea, and sugar cane are grown.

trireme (Anglicized Latin 'three-oared') ancient Greek warship with three banks of oars. They were used at the Battle of Salamis and by the Romans until the 4th century AD.

Tristan (or **Tristram**) legendary Celtic hero of a tragic romance. He fell in love with Isolde, the bride he was sent to win for his uncle King Mark of Cornwall. The story became part of the Arthurian cycle and is the subject of Richard Wagner's opera *Tristan und Isolde* (1865).

tritium radioactive isotope of hydrogen, three times as heavy as ordinary hydrogen, consisting of one proton and two neutrons. It has a half-life of 12.5 years.

Triton in astronomy, the largest of Neptune's moons. It has a diameter of 2,700 km/1,680 mi, and orbits Neptune every 5.88 days in a retrograde (east to west) direction at a distance of 54,000 km/220,162 mi. It takes the same time to rotate about its own axis as it does to make one revolution of Neptune.

Triton in Greek mythology, a merman sea god with the lower body of a dolphin; the son of ▷Poseidon and the sea goddess Amphitrite. Traditionally, he is shown blowing on a conch shell to raise or calm a storm.

triumvir one of a group of three administrators sharing power in ancient Rome, as in the **First Triumvirate** 60 BC: Caesar, Pompey, Crassus; and **Second Triumvirate** 43 BC: Augustus, Antony, and Lepidus.

Trobriand Islands group of coral islands in the Solomon Sea, forming part of the province of Milne Bay, Papua New Guinea; chief town Losuia; area 440 sq km/170 sq mi.

troglodyte ancient Greek term for a cave dweller, designating certain pastoral peoples of the Caucasus, Ethiopia, and the southern Red Sea coast of Egypt.

trogon (Greek *trogein* 'to gnaw') any species of the family Trogonidae, order Trogoniformes, of tropical birds, up to 50 cm/1.7 ft long, with resplendent plumage, living in the Americas, Africa, and Asia. They are primarily birds of forest or woodland, living in trees. Their diet consists mainly of insects and other arthropods, and sometimes berries and other fruit. Most striking is the ▷quetzal.

troilite FeS, probable mineral of the Earth's core, abundant in meteorites.

Trojan in computing, a program that looks as though it will do something entertaining or useful but actually does something unhelpful, such as reformatting the user's hard disk. Trojans are named after the Trojan horse in Greek mythology. A virus is not a Trojan, but inserting a virus into another program – such as virus checker – would make that program a Trojan.

Trojan horse seemingly innocuous but treacherous gift from an enemy. In Greek mythology, during the siege of Troy, an enormous wooden horse was left by the Greek army outside the gates of the city. The Greeks had sailed away as if they had retreated. The Trojans, believing the horse to be a religious offering, brought it into the city. Greek soldiers then emerged from their hiding place within the hollow horse and opened the city gates to enable the rest of the Greek army to enter and capture the city.

Trollope, Anthony (1815–1882) English novelist. He delineated provincial English middle-class society in a series of novels set in or around the imaginary cathedral city of Barchester. *The Warden* (1855) began the series, which includes *Barchester Towers* (1857), *Doctor Thorne* (1858), and *The Last Chronicle of Barset* (1867). His political novels include *Can You Forgive Her?* (1864), *Phineas Finn* (1867–69), and *The Prime Minister* (1875–76).

trombone brass wind instrument of mainly cylindrical bore, incorporating a movable slide which allows a continuous glissando (slide) in pitch over a span of half an octave. The longer the tube length, the lower the note. All the notes of the chromatic scale are therefore available by placing the slide in any of seven basic positions, and blowing a harmonic series of notes built upon each basic note.

trompe l'oeil (French 'deceives the eye') painting that gives a convincing illusion of three-dimensional reality. As an artistic technique, it has been in common use in most stylistic periods in the West, originating in classical Greek art.

Tromsø fishing port and largest town in northwest Norway, on Tromsø Island, and capital of the county of Troms; population (1991) 51,300. A church was founded here in the 13th century and the town grew up around it. Today the town trades in fish and fish products and is used as a base for Arctic expeditions.

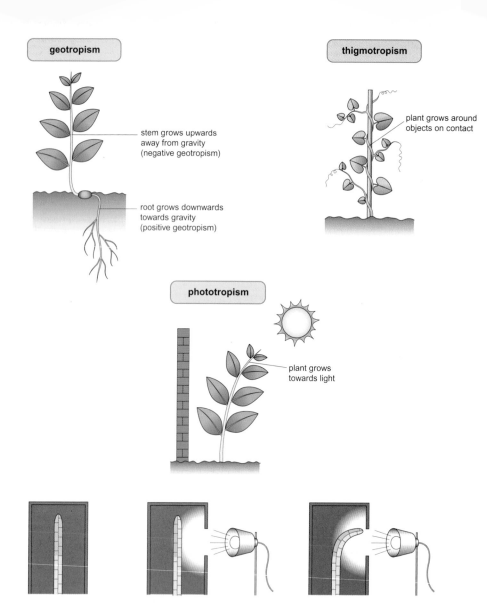

geotropism

stem grows upwards away from gravity (negative geotropism)

root grows downwards towards gravity (positive geotropism)

thigmotropism

plant grows around objects on contact

phototropism

plant grows towards light

in darkness, auxin, a plant hormone that regulates stem and root-growth, is evenly concentrated around shoot tip

light shining on one side of the shoot causes auxin to be destroyed on that side but remains present on darker side

auxin causes cells on darker side to elongate and shoot bends, thus growing towards the light

ANTHONY TROLLOPE The English novelist Anthony Trollope wrote more than 50 works. His 'Barsetshire' novels describe the lives of clergymen, from the richest to the poorest. *The Art Archive/Garrick Club*

TROPISM Tropisms are plant movements in response to external stimuli. Geotropism is the movement in response to gravity, either towards it in most root systems (positive geotropism), or away as in most stems (negative geotropism). Most plants exhibit positive phototropism and grow towards light. Thigmotropism is found in most climbing plants.

Trondheim fishing port, and county town of Sor-Trondelag, Norway, at the mouth of the Nid on Trondheim Fjord, 135 km/84 mi northeast of Kristiansund; population (1996) 135,900. It has canning, textile, margarine and soap industries. Originally called Nidaros, it was the medieval capital of Norway. Norwegian kings are crowned in the cathedral (1066–93), which is one of the most celebrated in Scandinavia. Trondheim was occupied by the Germans 1940–45 and used as a U-boat base, and the town was frequently bombed by the Allies.

tropical cyclone another term for ▷hurricane.

tropical disease any illness found mainly in hot climates. The most significant tropical diseases worldwide are ▷malaria, ▷leishmaniasis, ▷sleeping sickness, lymphatic filiarasis, and schistosomiasis. Other major scourges are ▷Chagas's disease, ▷leprosy, and river blindness. Malaria kills about 1.5 million people each year, and produces chronic anaemia and tiredness in 100 times as many, while schistosomiasis is responsible for 1 million deaths a year. All the main tropical diseases are potentially curable, but the facilities for diagnosis and treatment are rarely adequate in the countries where they occur.

tropics the area between the tropics of Cancer and Capricorn, defined by the parallels of latitude approximately 23°30′ north and south of the Equator. They are the limits of the area of Earth's surface in which the Sun can be directly overhead. The mean monthly temperature is over 20°C/68°F.

Climates within the tropics lie in parallel bands. Along the Equator is the ▷intertropical convergence zone, characterized by high temperatures and year-round heavy rainfall. Tropical rainforests are found here. Along the tropics themselves lie the tropical high-pressure zones, characterized by descending dry air and desert conditions. Between these, the conditions vary seasonally between wet and dry, producing the tropical grasslands.

tropism (or **tropic movement**) the directional growth of a plant, or part of a plant, in response to an external stimulus such as gravity or light. If the movement is directed towards the stimulus it is described as positive; if away from it, it is negative. **Geotropism** for example, the response of plants to gravity, causes the root (positively geotropic) to grow downwards, and the stem (negatively geotropic) to grow upwards.

troposphere lower part of the Earth's ▷atmosphere extending about 10.5 km/6.5 mi from the Earth's surface, in which temperature decreases with height to about −60°C/−76°F except in local layers of temperature inversion. The **tropopause** is the upper boundary of the troposphere, above which the temperature increases slowly with height within the atmosphere. All of the Earth's weather takes place within the troposphere.

Trotsky, Leon (1879–1940) Adopted name of Lev Davidovitch Bronstein. Russian revolutionary. He joined the Bolshevik party and took a leading part in the seizure of power in 1917 and in raising the Red Army that fought the Civil War 1918–20. In the struggle for power that followed ▷Lenin's death in 1924, ▷Stalin defeated Trotsky, and this and other differences with the Communist Party led to his exile in 1929. He settled in Mexico, where he was assassinated at Stalin's instigation. Trotsky believed in world revolution and in permanent revolution (see ▷Trotskyism), and was an uncompromising, if liberal, idealist.

Trotsky was isolated by Stalin, who used the opposition to Trotsky's belief that socialist revolution had to be exported by the USSR to the rest of the world, as well as the personal feud between Trotsky and Grigory ▷Zinovyev, head of the communist ▷International, to oust him. Trotsky was left without support and lost his power in the party. Trotsky had been described as capable but arrogant by Lenin, and it was this perceived arrogance and intellectual capacity that made him unpopular with many of the other Bolshevik leaders after Lenin's death in 1924. Stalin was then able to use Trotsky's ideas for the rapid industrialization of the Soviet Union through five-year plans, despite attacking the idea when Trotsky promoted it before his exile from Russia.

Trotsky became a Marxist in the 1890s and was imprisoned and exiled for opposition to the tsarist regime. He lived in Western Europe from 1902 until the 1905 revolution,when he was again imprisoned but escaped to live in exile until 1917, when he returned to Russia and joined the Bolsheviks. Although as a young man Trotsky admired Lenin, when he worked with him organizing the revolution of 1917, he objected to Lenin's dictatorial ways. He was second in command until Lenin's death, and was minister for foreign affairs 1917–18 and minister for war 1918–January 1925. Trotsky's brilliant organizational skills and inspirational leadership of the Red Army gained victory for the Bolsheviks over the White Russian tsarists in the ▷Russian civil war (1918–21), although the Bolsheviks controlled only one third of the country and suffered attack from abroad. In exile in Mexico, he was killed with an ice pick. Official Soviet recognition of responsibility for his assassination through the secret service came in 1989.

Related Web site: Leon Trotsky Internet Archive http://www.marxists.org/archive/trotsky/index.htm

Trotskyism form of Marxism advocated by Leon Trotsky. Its central concept is that of **permanent revolution**. In his view a proletarian revolution, leading to a socialist society, could not be achieved in isolation, so it would be necessary to spark off further revolutions throughout Europe and ultimately worldwide. This was in direct opposition to the Stalinist view that socialism should be built and consolidated within individual countries.

trotting another name for the sport of ▷harness racing.

troubadour (French, from Provençal *trobador* [from Latin *tropus*]) poet-musician of Provence and southern France in the 12th–13th centuries. The troubadours originated a type of lyric poetry devoted to themes of courtly love and the idealization of women and to glorifying the chivalric ideals of the period. Little is known of their music, which was passed down orally.

trout any of various bony fishes in the salmon family, popular for sport and food, usually speckled and found mainly in fresh water. They are native to the northern hemisphere. Trout have thick bodies and blunt heads, and vary in colour. The common trout *Salmo trutta* is widely distributed in Europe, occurring in British fresh and coastal waters. Sea trout are generally silvery and river trout olive-brown, both with spotted fins and sides.

In the USA, the name 'trout' is given to various species, notably to the rainbow trout *S. gairdneri*, which has been naturalized in many other countries.

Troy (or **Ilium**) ancient city in Asia Minor (modern Hissarlik in Turkey), just south of the Dardanelles. It has a long and complex history dating from about 3000 BC to AD 1200. In 1820 the city was identified as Troy, the site of the legendary ten-year Trojan War described in Homer's epic *Iliad*, but its actual name is unknown.

Nine cities found one beneath another were originally excavated by Heinrich Schliemann 1874–90. The first fortifications appeared on the site in the Early Bronze Age. These were a stone wall with a mudbrick battlement and a gate protected by flanking towers. By the Middle Bronze Age the defences had been enlarged and required at least four gateways, two of which were protected by towers. Recent research suggests that the seventh, sacked and burned about 1270 BC, is probably the Homeric Troy. The city and its defences were rebuilt, but suffered a similar fate about 1050 BC. These two destructions, of Troy VI and VIII respectively, have been suggested as the sack of the city in the Trojan War related by the Greek poet Homer. The city of Ilium was built on the same site in the 7th century BC, and survived to the Roman period.

Related Web site: Trojan War http://www-lib.haifa.ac.il/www/art/troyan.html

Harry S Truman
The buck stops here.
Sign on his presidential desk

Troyes administrative centre of the *département* of Aube in the Champagne-Ardenne region of northeast France, situated on the River Seine 150 km/93 mi southeast of Paris; population (1990) 60,800, conurbation 120,000. The town has an agricultural market, but is also an industrial city manufacturing textiles, machinery and foodstuffs. The hosiery industry remains important. The **Treaty of Troyes** signed by Henry V of England and Charles VI in 1420 recognized Henry as heir to the French throne.

troy system system of units used for precious metals and gems. The pound troy (0.37 kg) consists of 12 ounces (each of 120 carats) or 5,760 grains (each equal to 65 mg).

Trudeau, Pierre Elliott (1919–2000) Canadian Liberal politician. He was prime minister 1968–79 and 1980–84. In 1980, he was re-elected by a landslide on a platform opposing Québec separatism, and the Québec independence movement was later defeated in a referendum. He repatriated the constitution from the UK in1982, but by 1984 had so lost support that he resigned.

Irving Layton
Canadian writer
In Pierre Elliot Trudeau Canada has at last produced a political leader worthy of assassination.
The Whole Bloody Bird

PIERRE TRUDEAU The former prime minister of Canada. *Archive Photos*

Truffaut, François (1932–1984) French New Wave film director and actor. A romantic and intensely humane film-maker, he wrote and directed a series of semi-autobiographical films starring Jean-Pierre Léaud, beginning with *Les Quatre Cent Coups/The 400 Blows* (1959). His other films include *Jules et Jim* (1961), *Fahrenheit 451* (1966), *L'Enfant sauvage/The Wild Child* (1970), and *La Nuit américaine/Day for Night* (1973; Academy Award).

truffle any of a group of underground fungi (see ▷fungus), certain of which are highly valued as edible delicacies; in particular, the species *Tuber melanosporum*, generally found growing under oak trees. It is native to the Périgord region of France but is cultivated in other areas as well. It is rounded, blackish-brown, externally covered with warts, and has blackish flesh. (Order Tuberales.)

Trujillo city in northwestern Peru, with its port at Salaverry, capital of the department of La Libertad; population (1993) 509,300. Industries include engineering, copper, sugar milling, vehicle assembly and trade in agricultural produce.

Truk Islands group of about 55 volcanic islands surrounded by a coral reef in the eastern Caroline islands of the western Pacific, forming one of the four states of the Federated States of Micronesia. Fish and copra are the main products.

Truman, Harry S (1884–1972) 33rd president of the USA 1945–53, a Democrat. In January 1945 he became vice-president to Franklin D Roosevelt, and president when Roosevelt died in April that year. He used the atomic bomb against Japan to end World War II, launched the ▷Marshall Plan to restore Western Europe's post-war economy, and nurtured the European Community (now the European Union) and NATO (including the rearmament of West Germany).

Born in Lamar, Missouri, he farmed his parents' land near Independence for 12 years. Soon after the USA entered World War I, Truman joined the army and served in France. In 1922 he was elected judge of the Jackson County court. He became a senator in 1934, and was selected as Roosevelt's last vice-president. As president, Truman took part in the ▷Potsdam Conference of July 1945. In 1947 he initiated the Truman Doctrine, a policy for helping countries threatened by, or anxious to resist, communism.

In 1948 he was elected as president for a second term in a surprise victory over Thomas Dewey (1902–1971), governor of New York. At home, he had difficulty converting the economy back to peacetime conditions, and failed to prevent witch-hunts on suspected communists such as Alger ▷Hiss. In Korea, he intervened when the South was invaded by the Korea in 1950, supplying US forces to join UN forces under General ▷MacArthur, but sacked MacArthur when the general's policy conflicted with UN aims and threatened to start World War III. Truman's decision not to enter Chinese territory, betrayed by the double agent Kim Philby, led to China's entry into the Korean War. His policy of containment of Soviet expansionism initiated the long ▷Cold War with the Soviet Union. Truman retired to Independence, Missouri.

Related Web site: Harry S Truman Presidential Library & Museum http://www.trumanlibrary.org/

Truman Doctrine US president Harry Truman's 1947 dictum that the USA would 'support free peoples who are resisting attempted subjugation by armed minorities or by outside pressures'. It was used to justify sending a counterinsurgency military mission to Greece after World War II and sending US troops abroad (for example, to Korea). See also ▷United States of America, **the Truman Doctrine**.

trumpet member of an ancient family of lip-reed instruments existing worldwide in a variety of forms and materials, and forming part of the brass section in a modern orchestra. Its distinguishing features are a generally cylindrical bore and straight or coiled shape, producing a penetrating tone of stable pitch for signalling and ceremonial use. Valve trumpets were introduced around 1820, giving access to the full range of chromatic pitches.

trumpeter any South American bird of the genus *Psophia*, family Psophiidae, order Gruiformes, up to 50 cm/20 in tall, related to the cranes. Trumpeters have long legs, a short bill, and dark plumage. The trumpeter ▷swan is unrelated.

truncation error in computing, an ▷error that occurs when a decimal result is cut off (truncated) after the maximum number of places allowed by the computer's level of accuracy.

Truro market town in ▷Cornwall, England, and administrative headquarters of the county, on the River Truro, a branch of the Fal, 14 km/9 mi north of Falmouth; population (1991) 19,000. It is a business centre.

trust arrangement whereby a person or group of people (the trustee or trustees) hold property for others (the beneficiaries) entitled to the beneficial interest. A trust can be a legal arrangement under which A is empowered to administer property belonging to B for the benefit of C. A and B may be the same person; B and C may not.

Trustee, Public in England, an official empowered to act as executor and trustee, either alone or with others, of the estate of anyone who appoints him or her. In 1986 powers were extended to cover, among other things, the affairs of mentally ill patients.

trust territory country or area placed within the United Nations trusteeship system and, as such, administered by a UN member state on the UN's behalf. A trust territory could be one of three types: one administered under a mandate given by the UN, or its predecessor, the League of Nations; a territory which was removed from an enemy state, namely Germany, Italy, or Japan, at the end of World War II; or a territory which had been placed voluntarily within the trusteeship system by a member state responsible for its administration. The last territory remaining under the UN trusteeship system, the Republic of ▷Palau, became independent in 1994.

Truth, Sojourner (c. 1797–1883) Adopted name of Isabella Baumfree, later Isabella Van Wagener. US antislavery and women's-suffrage campaigner. Born a slave, she ran away and became involved with religious groups. In 1843 she was 'commanded in a vision' to adopt the name Sojourner Truth. She published an autobiography, *The Narrative of Sojourner Truth*, in 1850.

trypanosomiasis any of several debilitating long-term diseases caused by a trypanosome (protozoan of the genus *Trypanosoma*). They include sleeping sickness in Africa, transmitted by the bites of ▷tsetse flies, and ▷Chagas's disease in Central and South America, spread by assassin bugs.

trypsin an enzyme in the vertebrate gut responsible for the digestion of protein molecules. It is secreted by the pancreas but in an inactive form known as trypsinogen. Activation into working trypsin occurs only in the small intestine, owing to the action of another enzyme enterokinase, secreted by the wall of the duodenum. Unlike the digestive enzyme pepsin, found in the stomach, trypsin does not require an acid environment.

Ts'ao Chan alternative transcription of Chinese novelist ▷Cao Chan.

tsar Russian imperial title in use from 1547 to 1721, derived from the Latin *caesar*, the title of the Roman emperors.

tsetse fly any of a number of blood-feeding African flies of the genus *Glossina*, some of which transmit the disease nagana to cattle and sleeping sickness to human beings. Tsetse flies may grow up to 1.5 cm/0.6 in long.

tsunami (Japanese 'harbour wave') ocean wave generated by vertical movements of the sea floor resulting from ▷earthquakes or volcanic activity or large submarine landslides. Unlike waves generated by surface winds, the entire depth of water is involved in the wave motion of a tsunami. In the open ocean the tsunami takes the form of several successive waves, rarely in excess of 1 m/3 ft in height but travelling at speeds of 650–800 kph/400–500 mph. In the coastal shallows tsunamis slow down and build up producing huge swells over 15 m/45 ft high in some cases and over 30 m/90 ft in rare instances. The waves sweep inland causing great loss of life and property.

Before each wave there may be a sudden withdrawal of water from the beach. Used synonymously with tsunami, the popular term 'tidal wave' is misleading: tsunamis are not caused by the gravitational forces that affect ▷tides.

Related Web site: Tsunami! http://www.geophys.washington.edu/tsunami/intro.html

Tswana member of the majority ethnic group living in Botswana. The Tswana are divided into four subgroups: the Bakwena, Bamangwato, Bangwaketse, and Batawana. The Tswana language belongs to the Bantu branch of the Niger-Congo family.

Tuamotu Archipelago two parallel ranges of 78 atolls, part of ▷French Polynesia; area 690 sq km/266 sq mi; population (1996) 15,370, including the ▷Gambier Islands to the east. The atolls stretch 2,100 km/1,300 mi north and east of the Society Islands. The administrative headquarters is Apataki. This archipelago is made up of the largest group of coral atolls in the world. The largest atoll is Rangiroa, the most significant is Hao; they produce pearl shell and copra. Spanish explorers landed 1606, and the islands were annexed by France in 1881. France conducted nuclear test explosions at the Mururoa and Fangataufa atolls between 1966 and 1996 (46 above ground and 147 below).

Tuareg (plural **Tuareg**; Arabic *tawarek* 'God-forsaken') member of one of a group of eight nomadic peoples, mainly stock breeders, from west and central Sahara and Sahel (Algeria, Libya, Mali, Niger, and Burkina Faso). Their language, Tamashek, belongs to the Berber branch of the Hamito-Semitic family and is spoken by 500,000–850,000 people. Many are Muslims.

tuatara lizardlike reptile of the genus *Sphenodon*. It grows up to 70 cm/2.3 ft long, is greenish black, and has a spiny crest down its back. On the top of its head is the ▷pineal body, or so-called 'third eye', linked to the brain, which probably acts as a kind of light meter. It has remained unchanged for 220 million years, and is the sole survivor of the reptilian order Rhynchocephalia. It has an average life span of 60 years and reaches sexual maturity for a decade. It lays eggs in burrows that it shares with seabirds, and has the longest incubation period of all reptiles (up to 15 months).

tuba member of a family of valved lip-reed brass instruments of conical bore and deep, mellow tone, introduced around 1830 as bass members of the orchestra brass section and the brass band. The tuba is surprisingly agile and delicate for its size and pitch, qualities exploited by Berlioz, Ravel, and Vaughan Williams.

tuber swollen region of an underground stem or root, usually modified for storing food. The potato is a **stem tuber**, as shown by the presence of terminal and lateral buds, the 'eyes' of the potato. **Root tubers**, for example dahlias, developed from adventitious roots (growing from the stem, not from other roots) lack these. Both types of tuber can give rise to new individuals and so provide a means of ▷vegetative reproduction.

tuberculosis (**TB**; formerly known as **consumption** or **phthisis**) infectious disease caused by the bacillus *Mycobacterium tuberculosis*. It takes several forms, of which pulmonary tuberculosis is by far the most common. A vaccine, ▷BCG, was developed around 1920 and the first anti-tuberculosis drug, streptomycin, in 1944. The bacterium is mostly kept in check by the body's immune system; about 5% of those infected develop the disease. Treatment of patients with a combination of anti-TB medicines for 6–8 months produces a cure rate of 80%. In 1999 there were 8 million new cases of TB and 2 million deaths. Only 5% of cases are in developed countries. Worldwide there are 16 million people with TB and 2 billion (a third of the global population) are infected with *Mycobacterium tuberculosis*.

In pulmonary TB, a patch of inflammation develops in the lung, with formation of an abscess. Often, this heals spontaneously, leaving only scar tissue. The dangers are of rapid spread through both lungs (what used to be called 'galloping consumption') or the development of miliary tuberculosis (spreading in the bloodstream to other sites) or tuberculous ▷meningitis.

Over the last 15 years there has been a sharp resurgence in countries where the disease was in decline. The increase has been most marked in deprived inner city areas, particularly in the USA, and here there is a clear link between TB and HIV, the virus which causes AIDS. TB is the main cause of death in HIV positive individuals.

According to a World Health Organization (WHO) report in 1995, TB is responsible for more than a quarter of all adult deaths in developing countries; worldwide there are 20 million with the disease and approximately 1.9 billion infected with the TB bacterium but not displaying symptoms. TB caused around 3.1 million deaths during 1995.

The last decade has seen the spread of drug-resistant strains of the TB bacterium. Many strains are now resistant to the two frontline drugs, isoniazid and rifampicin, and some are multi-drug resistant (MDR). Rare until its recent appearance in the USA, MDR TB is now spreading through a number of developing countries. It is untreatable and many of its victims have died. According to a 1996 WHO estimate there may be as many as 50 million people worldwide with the drug-resistant form of TB (Britain had its first case in 1995).

In Britain in 1992 there were 5,861 notified cases of TB.

tuberose Mexican flowering plant belonging to the ▷agave family, grown as a sweet-smelling greenhouse plant. It has spikes of scented white flowers like lilies. (*Polianthes tuberosa*, family Agavaceae.)

Tubman, Harriet Ross (1821–1913) US abolitionist. Born a slave in Maryland, she escaped to Philadelphia (where ▷slavery was outlawed) 1849. She set up the ▷Underground Railroad, a secret network of sympathizers, to help slaves escape to the North and Canada. During the American ▷Civil War she spied for the Union army. She spoke against slavery and for women's rights, and founded schools for emancipated slaves after the Civil War.

Tubuai Islands (or **Austral Islands**) chain of volcanic islands and reefs 1,300 km/800 mi long in ▷French Polynesia, south of the Society Islands; area 148 sq km/57 sq mi; population (1996) 6,600. The main settlement is Mataura on Tubuai. They were visited by Capt Cook 1777 and annexed by France 1880. The chief products are copra and coffee.

TUC abbreviation for ▷Trades Union Congress.

Tucson (Papago 'foot of the mountain') city in southeast Arizona, USA, on the Santa Cruz and Rillito rivers, 105 km/66 mi north of the Mexican border; population (1996 est) 449,000. It stands 760m/2,500 ft above sea level in the Sonora Desert; the Santa Catalina Mountains rise to about 2,750 m/9,000 ft to the northeast. The area's winter sports and mild, dry, sunny winter climate have made the city a popular winter residence and resort. Industries include copper-smelting, and the manufacture of aircraft and electronics. Cotton and cattle are marketed and processed from the surrounding irrigated agricultural area.

tucu-tuco any member of the genus *Ctenomys*, a burrowing South American rodent about 20 cm/8 in long with a 7 cm/3 in tail. It has a large head, sensitive ears, and enormous incisor teeth.

Tudjman, Franjo (1922–1999) Croatian nationalist leader and historian, president from 1990. As leader of the centre-right Croatian Democratic Union (CDU), he led the fight for Croatian independence. During the 1991–92 civil war, his troops were hampered by lack of arms and the military superiority of the Serb-dominated federal army, but Croatia's independence was recognized following a successful United Nations-negotiated ceasefire in January 1992. Tudjman was re-elected in August 1992 and again in October 1995. Despite suffering from stomach cancer, he was re-elected president in June 1997. He died in December 1999 while still president.

Tudor dynasty English dynasty 1485–1603, founded by Henry VII, who became king by overthrowing Richard III (the last of the York dynasty) at the Battle of Bosworth. Henry VII reigned from 1485 to 1509, and was succeeded by Henry VIII (reigned 1509–47); Edward VI (reigned 1547–53); Mary (reigned 1553–58); and Elizabeth I (reigned 1558–1603). Elizabeth died childless and the throne of England passed to her cousin James VI of Scotland, who thus became James I of England and the first of the Stuart line.

The dynasty was descended from the Welsh adventurer Owen Tudor (c. 1400–1461), who fought on the Lancastrian side in the ▷Wars of the Roses. Owen Tudor later became the second husband of Catherine of Valois (widow of Henry V of England). Their son Edmund, Earl of Richmond, married Margaret Beaufort (1443–1509), the great-granddaughter of ▷John of Gaunt, who was the fourth son of Edward III. Henry VII, the founder of the Tudor dynasty, was the son of Edmund, Earl of Richmond and Margaret Beaufort.

The dynasty's symbol, the Tudor Rose, combines the red and white roses of the Lancastrian and Yorkist houses, and symbolizes the union of the two factions which was cemented by Henry VII in January 1486 when he married Elizabeth of York, the eldest daughter of Edward IV.

tufa (or **travertine**) soft, porous, ▷limestone rock, white in colour, deposited from solution from carbonate-saturated ground water around hot springs and in caves.

Tukano an indigenous Native South American people of the Vaupés region on the Colombian-Brazilian border, numbering approximately 2,000. An estimated 12,000 speak languages related to Tukano. The other main Tukanoan groups are Bara, Barasana, Cubeo, Desana, and Makuna.

Tukulor empire Muslim theocracy founded by al-Hajj 'Umar (c. 1797–1864). Stretching from western Sudan to Senegal, it flourished for most of the 19th century, but its power was sapped by continuous internal disorder.

Tula city in the Russian Federation and capital of the Tula oblast, situated on the River Upa, 193 km/121 mi south of Moscow; population (1990) 543,000. Its traditional industries are the manufacture of firearms and samovars (Russian tea urns). The city also produces iron and steel, chemicals, agricultural equipment, and machine tools.

Tula (or **Tollan**) ancient city of the Toltec civilization in central Mexico, 65 km/40 mi northwest of Mexico City, which flourished from about 750 to 1168. At its height, it is thought to have housed a population of around 40,000. The modern town of Tula de Allende is nearby.

tulip any of a group of spring-flowering bulbous plants belonging to the lily family, usually with single goblet-shaped flowers on the end of an upright stem and narrow oval leaves with pointed ends. Tulips come in a large range of shapes, sizes, and colours and are widely cultivated as a garden flower. (Genus *Tulipa*, family Liliaceae.)

Related Web site: Tulip Book http://www.bib.wau.nl/tulips/

tumour overproduction of cells in a specific area of the body, often leading to a swelling or lump. Tumours are classified as **benign** or **malignant** (see ▷cancer). Benign tumours grow more slowly, do not invade surrounding tissues, do not spread to other parts of the body, and do not usually recur after removal. However, benign tumours can be dangerous in areas such as the brain. The most familiar types of benign tumour are warts on the skin. In some cases, there is no sharp dividing line between benign and malignant tumours.

tuna any of various large marine bony fishes of the mackerel family, especially the genus *Thunnus*, popular as food and game. **Albacore** *T. alalunga*, **bluefin tuna** *T. thynnus*, and **yellowfin tuna** *T. albacares* are commercially important.

Tuna fish gather in shoals and migrate inshore to breed, where they are caught in large numbers. The increasing use by Pacific tuna fishers of enormous driftnets, which kill dolphins, turtles, and other marine creatures as well as catching the fish, has caused protests by environmentalists; tins labelled 'dolphin-friendly' contain tuna not caught by driftnets. Thailand is a major tuna-importing and canning country.

Overfishing is causing a reduction in tuna stocks around the world. In spite of the introduction of quotas in Australia in the 1980s, the country's catch of southern bluefin tuna in 1990–91 was 5,000 tonnes – the lowest since 1962, and the species could be in danger of extinction. Tuna stocks in the Atlantic declined by almost 90% during 1970–92.

Tuna may grow up to 2.5 m/8ft long and weigh 200 kg/440 lbs. **Skipjack** or **bonito tuna** *Euthynnus pelamis* is one of the most commercially important species, and is the species most commonly sold in tins in the UK. It is a small tuna, growing up to 1 m/3 ft long.

Tunbridge Wells, Royal spa and commuter town in Kent, southeast England, between London and Hastings; population (1991) 60,300. It has a light industrial estate. The town developed after the discovery of iron-rich springs here in 1606. The **Pantiles** or shopping parade (paved with tiles in the reign of Queen Anne), was a fashionable resort; visited by Queen Victoria, the town has been named 'Royal' since 1909.

tundra region of high latitude almost devoid of trees, resulting from the presence of ▷permafrost. The vegetation consists mostly of grasses, sedges, heather, mosses, and lichens. Tundra stretches in a continuous belt across northern North America and Eurasia. Tundra is also used to describe similar conditions at high altitudes.

The term was originally applied to the topography of part of northern Russia, but is now used for all such regions.

TUNDRA A typical tundra environment in Greenland, with a glacier visible in the background. *Image Bank*

tungsten (Swedish *tung sten* 'heavy stone') hard, heavy, grey-white, metallic element, symbol W (from German *Wolfram*), atomic number 74, relative atomic mass 183.85. It occurs in the minerals wolframite, scheelite, and hubertite. It has the highest melting point of any metal (3,410°C/6,170°F) and is added to steel to make it harder, stronger, and more elastic; its other uses include high-speed cutting tools, electrical elements, and thermionic couplings. Its salts are used in the paint and tanning industries.

Tungsten was first recognized in 1781 by Swedish chemist Karl Scheele in the ore scheelite. It was isolated in 1783 by Spanish chemists Fausto D'Elhuyar (1755–1833) and his brother Juan José (1754–1796).

tungsten ore either of the two main minerals, wolframite (FeMn)WO$_4$ and scheelite, CaWO$_4$, from which tungsten is extracted. Most of the world's tungsten reserves are in China, but the main suppliers are Bolivia, Australia, Canada, and the USA.

Tunguska Event explosion at Tunguska, central Siberia, Russia, in June 1908, which devastated around 6,500 sq km/

2,500 sq mi of forest. It is thought to have been caused by either a cometary nucleus or a fragment of ▷Encke's comet about 200 m/660 ft across, or possibly an asteroid. The magnitude of the explosion was equivalent to an atom bomb (10–20 megatons) and produced a colossal shock wave; a bright falling object was seen 600 km/375 mi away and was heard up to 1,000 km/625 mi away.

tunicate any marine ▷chordate of the subphylum Tunicata (Urochordata), for example the ▷sea squirt. Tunicates have transparent or translucent tunics made of cellulose. They vary in size from a few millimetres to 30 cm/1 ft in length, and are cylindrical, circular, or irregular in shape. There are more than 1,000 species.

Tunis capital and chief port of Tunisia; population (1994) 674,100. Industries include chemicals, textiles, engineering, lead smelting, and distilling. Velvets, silks, linen, and fez caps are also manufactured. Exports include phosphates, iron ore, fruit, and vegetables. Founded by the Arabs, it was captured by the Turks in 1533, then occupied by the French in 1881 and by the Axis powers 1942–43. The ruins of ancient ▷Carthage are to the northeast.

Tunisia see country box.

Tunja capital of the Andean department of Boyacá, east-central Colombia, 2,800 m/9,200 ft above sea level; population (1992) 112,000. It is the centre of an agricultural and mining community, and linked to Bogotá by railway. One of the oldest cities in Colombia, Tunja was formerly the seat of the Chibcha Indian kings. The Spanish refounded a city here in 1539 on the site of Hunza, the ancient Muisca Indian seat. In 1818 Simón Bolívar defeated Spanish Royalists near Tunja. Industries include agriculture and mining. Many colonial buildings remain or have been restored, including the church of Santo Domingo (begun in 1594), and the Santa Clara Chapel (1580), now a museum.

tunnel passageway through a mountain, under a body of water, or underground. Tunnelling is a significant branch of civil engineering in both mining and transport. The difficulties naturally increase with the size, length, and depth of tunnel, but with the mechanical appliances now available no serious limitations are imposed. Granite or other hard rock presents little difficulty to modern power drills. In recent years there have been notable developments in linings (for example, concrete segments and steel liner plates), and in the use of rotary diggers and cutters and explosives.

tunny another name for ▷tuna.

turbine engine in which steam, water, gas, or air (see ▷windmill) is made to spin a rotating shaft by pushing on angled blades, like a fan. Turbines are among the most powerful machines. Steam turbines are used to drive generators in power stations and ships' propellers; water turbines spin the generators in hydroelectric power plants; and gas turbines (as jet engines; see ▷jet propulsion) power most aircraft and drive machines in industry.

TURBINE A range of turbines in Umatilla, Oregon, USA. *Image Bank*

turbocharger turbine-driven device fitted to engines to force more air into the cylinders, producing extra power. The turbocharger consists of a 'blower', or compressor, driven by a turbine, which in most units is driven by the exhaust gases leaving the engine.

turbofan jet engine of the type used by most airliners, so called because of its huge front fan. The fan sends air not only into the engine for combustion but also around the engine for additional thrust. This results in a faster and more fuel-efficient propulsive jet (see ▷jet propulsion).

turbojet jet engine that derives its thrust from a jet of hot exhaust gases. Pure turbojets can be very powerful but use a lot of fuel.

turbot any of various flatfishes of the flounder group prized as food, especially *Scophthalmus maximus* found in European waters. It grows up to 1 m/3 ft long and weighs up to 14 kg/30 lb. It is brownish above and whitish underneath.

Turgenev, Ivan Sergeievich (1818–1883) Russian writer. He is notable for poetic realism, pessimism, and skill in characterization. His works include the play *A Month in the Country* (1849), and the novels *A Nest of Gentlefolk* (1858), *Fathers and Sons* (1862), and *Virgin Soil* (1877). His series *A Sportsman's Sketches* (1852) criticized serfdom.

Turin (Italian **Torino**; ancient **Augusta Taurinorum**) capital of Piedmont, northwest Italy, at the confluence of the rivers Po and Dora Riparia; population (1992) 952,700. It stands at the foot of the Alps, commanding road and rail routes between France and Italy. Iron, steel, cars, silk and other textiles, fashion goods, chocolate, and wine are produced. There is a university (1404), and a 15th-century cathedral. Turin was the first capital of united Italy (1861–64).

History Turin was a duchy of the Lombards and became important after the union of Savoy and Piedmont in 1416. It was in French hands in the early 16th century, and its growth as a major city began in 1559 when Emanuele Filiberto chose it as the capital of the House of Savoy, with Italian as the official language. In 1706 Prince Eugène defeated a French army besieging the city, thus ensuring the survival of the Savoy duchy. It was annexed to France after the Battle of Marengo in 1800, became capital of the Kingdom of Sardinia from 1814 to 1860, and was the organizing centre of the reunification of Italy.

Turing, Alan Mathison (1912–1954) English mathematician and logician. In 1936 he described a 'universal computing machine' that could theoretically be programmed to solve any problem capable of solution by a specially designed machine. This concept, now called the Turing machine, foreshadowed the digital computer.

Turin shroud ancient piece of linen bearing the image of a body, claimed to be that of Jesus. Independent tests carried out in 1988 by scientists in Switzerland, the USA, and the UK showed that the cloth of the shroud dated from between 1260 and 1390. The shroud, property of the pope, is kept in Turin Cathedral, Italy. A more detailed 20-year study published in 1997 revealed that the shroud was made, around 1325, by daubing a man in red ochre paint and then wrapping him tightly in the linen sheet. Vermillion paint was then splashed on the head and wrists to suggest blood stains. Why it was made, and by whom, remains a mystery.

Turk (or **Turkic**) member of any of the Turkic-speaking peoples of Asia and Europe, especially the principal ethnic group of Turkey. Turkic languages belong to the Altaic family and include Uzbek, Ottoman, Turkish, Azeri, Turkoman, Tatar, Kirghiz, and Yakut. The ancestors of the Turks were pastoral nomads in central Asia. Islam was introduced during the 7th century.

Turkana, Lake (formerly **Lake Rudolf** (until 1979)) lake in the Great Rift Valley, 375 m/1,230 ft above sea level, with its northernmost end in Ethiopia and the rest in Kenya; area 8,000 sq km/3,100 sq mi. It is saline, and shrinking by evaporation. Its shores were an early human hunting ground, and valuable remains have been found that are accurately datable because of undisturbed stratification.

Turkestan historical area of Central Asia extending from the Caspian Sea in the west to the Gobi desert in the east. It is now divided among Kazakhstan, Kyrgyzstan, Tajikistan, Turkmenistan, Uzbekistan, Afghanistan (Northeast province), and China (part of Xinjiang Uygur province). It formerly covered an area of some 2,600,000 sq km/1,003,680 sq mi; its principal cities were ▷Tashkent, ▷Samarkand, and ▷Bukhara.

Turkey see country box.

turkey any of several large game birds of the pheasant family, Meleagrididae, order Galliformes, native to the Americas. The wild turkey *Meleagris galloparvo* reaches a length of 1.3 m/4.3 ft, and is native to North and Central American woodlands. The domesticated turkey derives from the wild species. Turkeys in the

TURKEY The common turkey, native to wooded country in the USA and Mexico, is a strong flier over short distances. It roosts in trees but feeds on the ground, eating nuts, seeds, and berries, as well as insects and small reptiles.

wild lay a single clutch of 12 eggs every spring, whereas domestic turkeys lay 120 over 27 weeks. Wild turkeys weigh up to 10 kg/22 lb; domestic turkeys up to 30 kg/66 lb. The ocellated turkey *Agriocharis ocellata* is found in Central America; it has eyespots on the tail.

The domesticated turkey was introduced to Europe in the 16th century. Since World War II, it has been intensively bred, in the same way as the chicken. It is gregarious, except at breeding time.

turkish bath bathing that involves exposure to warm air and steam, followed by massage and cold-water immersion. Originating from Roman and East Indian traditions, the concept was introduced to Western Europe by the Crusaders but only became popular when hot water could be supplied in sufficient quantities.

Turkish language language of central and West Asia, the national language of Turkey. It belongs to the Altaic language family. Varieties of Turkish are spoken in northwestern Iran and several of the Central Asian Republics, and all have been influenced by Arabic and Persian. Originally written in Arabic script, it has been written within Turkey in a variant of the Roman alphabet since 1928.

Turkish literature for centuries Turkish literature was based on Persian models, but under ▷Suleiman the Great (1494–1566) the Golden Age began, of which the poet Fuzuli (died 1563) is the great exemplar, and continued in the following century with the great poet satirist Nef'i of Erzerum (died 1635) and others. In the 19th century, mainly under French influence, Turkish writers adopted Western literary forms such as the novel. Ibrahim Shinasi Effendi (1826–1871), poet and prose writer, was one of those who made use of French models. Effendi was cofounder of the New School with Mehmed Namik Kemal (1840–1880), poet and author

Tunisia

TUNISIA The northern coast of Tunisia, seen here from the fort at Hanammet, is only 137 km/85 mi south of Sicily. *Leonardo.com*

Tunisia country in North Africa, on the Mediterranean Sea, bounded southeast by Libya and west by Algeria.

NATIONAL NAME *Al-Jumhuriyya at-Tunisiyya/Tunisian Republic*
AREA 164,150 sq km/63,378 sq mi
CAPITAL Tunis (and chief port)
MAJOR TOWNS/CITIES Sfax, L'Ariana, Bizerte, Gabès, Sousse, Kairouan, Ettadhamen
MAJOR PORTS Sfax, Sousse, Bizerte
PHYSICAL FEATURES arable and forested land in north graduates towards desert in south; fertile island of Jerba, linked to mainland by causeway (identified with island of lotus-eaters); Shott el Jerid salt lakes

Government

HEAD OF STATE Zine el-Abidine Ben Ali from 1987
HEAD OF GOVERNMENT Muhammad Ghannouchi from 1999
POLITICAL SYSTEM nationalistic socialist
POLITICAL EXECUTIVE unlimited presidency
ADMINISTRATIVE DIVISIONS 23 governorates
ARMED FORCES 35,000; plus paramilitary forces of 12,000 (2002 est)
DEATH PENALTY retained and used for ordinary crimes

Economy and resources

CURRENCY Tunisian dinar
GPD (US$) 21.2 billion (2002 est)
REAL GDP GROWTH (% change on previous year) 4.9 (2001)
GNI (US$) 19.6 billion (2002 est)
GNI PER CAPITA (PPP) (US$) 6,280 (2002 est)

CONSUMER PRICE INFLATION 3.3% (2003 est)
UNEMPLOYMENT 15% (2001)
FOREIGN DEBT (US$) 12.4 billion (2001 est)
MAJOR TRADING PARTNERS France, Italy, Germany, Belgium, USA, Spain, the Netherlands, UK
RESOURCES petroleum, natural gas, phosphates, iron, zinc, lead, aluminium fluoride, fluorspar, sea salt
INDUSTRIES processing of agricultural and mineral products (including superphosphate and phosphoric acid), textiles and clothing, machinery, chemicals, paper, wood, motor vehicles, radio and television sets, tourism
EXPORTS textiles and clothing, electrical equipment, crude petroleum, phosphates and fertilizers, electricity, gas, water, olive oil, fruit, leather and shoes, fishery products. Principal market: France 28.8% (2001)
IMPORTS machinery, textiles, food (mainly cereals, dairy produce, meat, and sugar) and live animals, petroleum and petroleum products, vehicles, cycles, tractors. Principal source: France: 28% (2001)
ARABLE LAND 18.7% (2000 est)
AGRICULTURAL PRODUCTS wheat, barley, olives, citrus fruits, dates, almonds, grapes, melons, apples, apricots and other fruits, chickpeas, sugar beet, tobacco; fishing

Population and society

POPULATION 9,832,000 (2003 est)
POPULATION GROWTH RATE 1.3% (2000–15)
POPULATION DENSITY (per sq km) 60 (2003 est)
URBAN POPULATION (% of total) 67 (2003 est)

AGE DISTRIBUTION (% of total population) 0–14 28%, 15–59 64%, 60+ 8% (2002 est)
ETHNIC GROUPS about 10% of the population is Arab; the remainder are of Berber-Arab descent. There are small Jewish and French communities
LANGUAGE Arabic (official), French
RELIGION Sunni Muslim (state religion); Jewish and Christian minorities
EDUCATION (compulsory years) 9
LITERACY RATE 84% (men); 64% (women) (2003 est)
LABOUR FORCE 22.4% agriculture, 33.2% industry, 44.4% services (1999)
LIFE EXPECTANCY 68 (men); 73 (women)

(2000–05)
CHILD MORTALITY RATE (under 5, per 1,000 live births) 27 (2001)
PHYSICIANS (per 1,000 people) 0.7 (1998 est)
HOSPITAL BEDS (per 1,000 people) 1.7 (1998 est)
TV SETS (per 1,000 people) 198 (2001 est)
RADIOS (per 1,000 people) 158 (1999)
INTERNET USERS (per 10,000 people) 515.0 (2002 est)
PERSONAL COMPUTER USERS (per 100 people) 3.1 (2002 est)

See also ▷Bourguiba, Habib; ▷Carthage.

Chronology

814 BC: Phoenician emigrants from Tyre, in Lebanon, founded Carthage, near modern Tunis, as a trading post. By 6th century BC Carthaginian kingdom dominated western Mediterranean.

146 BC: Carthage destroyed by Punic Wars with Rome, which began in 264 BC; Carthage became part of Rome's African province.

AD 533: Came under control of Byzantine Empire.

7th century: Invaded by Arabs, who introduced Islam. Succession of Islamic dynasties followed, including Aghlabids (9th century), Fatimids (10th century), and Almohads (12th century).

1574: Became part of Islamic Turkish Ottoman Empire and a base for 'Barbary Pirates' who operated against European shipping until 19th century.

1705: Husayn Bey founded local dynasty, which held power under rule of Ottomans.

early 19th century: Ahmad Bey launched programme of economic modernization, which nearly bankrupted the country.

1881: Became French protectorate, with bey retaining local power.

1920: Destour (Constitution) Party, named after the original Tunisian constitution of 1861, founded to campaign for equal Tunisian participation in French-dominated government.

1934: Habib Bourguiba founded a radical splinter party, the Neo-Destour Party, to spearhead the nationalist movement.

1942–43: Brief German occupation during World War II.

1956: Independence achieved as monarchy under bey, with Bourguiba as prime minister.

1957: Bey deposed; Tunisia became one-party republic with Bourguiba as president.

1975: Bourguiba made president for life.

1979: Headquarters for Arab League moved to Tunis after Egypt signed Camp David Accords with Israel.

1981: Multiparty elections held, as a sign of political liberalization, but were won by Bourguiba's Destourian Socialist Party (DSP).

1982: Allowed Palestine Liberation Organization (PLO) to use Tunis for its headquarters.

1985: Diplomatic relations with Libya severed; Israel attacked PLO headquarters.

1987: Zine el-Abidine Ben Ali, the new prime minister, declared Bourguiba (now aged 84) incompetent for government and seized power as president.

1988: 2,000 political prisoners freed; privatization initiative. Diplomatic relations with Libya restored. DSP renamed RCD.

1990: The Arab League's headquarters returned to Cairo, Egypt.

1991: There was opposition to US actions during the Gulf War, and a crackdown on religious fundamentalists.

1992: Human-rights transgressions provoked Western criticism.

1994: Ben Ali and the RCD were re-elected. The PLO transferred its headquarters to Gaza City in Palestine.

1999: In the country's first ever 'competitive' presidential elections, Ben Ali was re-elected president. Muhammad Ghannouchi was elected prime minister.

Turkey

TURKEY Spices for sale in the market at Ankara, the capital of Turkey. *Corel*

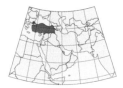

Turkey country between the Black Sea to the north and the Mediterranean Sea to the south, bounded to the east by Armenia, Georgia, and Iran, to the southeast by Iraq and Syria, to the west by Greece and the Aegean Sea, and to the northwest by Bulgaria.

NATIONAL NAME *Türkiye Cumhuriyeti/Republic of Turkey*
AREA 779,500 sq km/300,964 sq mi
CAPITAL Ankara
MAJOR TOWNS/CITIES Istanbul, Izmir, Adana, Bursa, Gaziantep, Konya, Mersin, Antalya
MAJOR PORTS Istanbul and Izmir
PHYSICAL FEATURES central plateau surrounded by mountains, partly in Europe (Thrace) and partly in Asia (Anatolia); Bosporus and Dardanelles; Mount Ararat (highest peak Great Ararat, 5,137 m/16,854 ft); Taurus Mountains in southwest (highest peak Kaldi Dag, 3,734 m/12,255 ft); sources of rivers Euphrates and Tigris in east

Government

HEAD OF STATE Ahmet Necdet Sezer from 2000
HEAD OF GOVERNMENT Recep Erdogan from 2003
POLITICAL SYSTEM liberal democracy
POLITICAL EXECUTIVE parliamentary
ADMINISTRATIVE DIVISIONS 80 provinces
ARMED FORCES 514,800 (2002 est)
DEATH PENALTY abolished for ordinary crimes in 2001; laws provide for the death penalty for exceptional crimes, such as crimes committed in wartime

Economy and resources

CURRENCY Turkish lira
GPD (US$) 182.2 billion (2002 est)
REAL GDP GROWTH (% change on previous year) –7.5 (2001)
GNI (US$) 174 billion (2002 est)
GNI PER CAPITA (PPP) (US$) 6,120 (2002 est)
CONSUMER PRICE INFLATION 20.8% (2003 est)
UNEMPLOYMENT 8.5% (2001)
FOREIGN DEBT (US$) 98.3 billion (2001 est)
MAJOR TRADING PARTNERS Germany, USA, Italy, France, UK, Russia, EU
RESOURCES chromium, copper, mercury, antimony, borax, coal, petroleum, natural gas, iron ore, salt
INDUSTRIES textiles, food processing, petroleum refining, coal, iron and steel, industrial chemicals, tourism

EXPORTS textiles and clothing, metals, motor vehicles and parts, agricultural products and foodstuffs (including figs, nuts, and dried fruit), tobacco, beverages, leather, glass, refined petroleum and petroleum products. Principal market: Germany 17.2% (2001)
IMPORTS machinery, construction material, motor vehicles, consumer goods, metals, crude petroleum, iron and steel, chemical products, fertilizer, livestock. Principal source: Germany 12.9% (2001)
ARABLE LAND 31.4% (2000 est)
AGRICULTURAL PRODUCTS barley, wheat, maize, sunflower and other oilseeds, sugar beet, potatoes, tea (world's fifth-largest producer), olives, fruits, tobacco

Population and society

POPULATION 71,325,000 (2003 est)
POPULATION GROWTH RATE 1.2% (2000–15)
POPULATION DENSITY (per sq km) 92 (2003 est)
URBAN POPULATION (% of total) 67 (2003 est)
AGE DISTRIBUTION (% of total population) 0–14 30%, 15–59 61%, 60+ 9% (2002 est)
ETHNIC GROUPS over 90% of the population are Turks, although only about 5% are of Turkic or Western Mongoloid descent; most are descended from earlier conquerors, such as the Greeks; about 8% Kurds
LANGUAGE Turkish (official), Kurdish, Arabic
RELIGION Sunni Muslim 99%; Orthodox, Armenian churches
EDUCATION (compulsory years) 5
LITERACY RATE 94% (men); 79% (women) (2003 est)
LABOUR FORCE 45.8% agriculture, 20.5% industry, 33.7% services (1999)
LIFE EXPECTANCY 68 (men); 73 (women) (2000–05)
CHILD MORTALITY RATE (under 5, per 1,000 live births) 43 (2001)
PHYSICIANS (per 1,000 people) 1.3 (1999 est)
HOSPITAL BEDS (per 1,000 people) 2.6 (1999 est)

See also ▷Atatürk, Kemal; ▷Balkan Wars; ▷Cyprus; ▷Istanbul; ▷Ottoman Empire.

Chronology

1st century BC: Asia Minor became part of Roman Empire, later passing to Byzantine Empire.

6th century AD: Turkic peoples spread from Mongolia into Turkestan, where they adopted Islam.

1055: Seljuk Turks captured Baghdad; their leader Tughrul took the title of sultan.

1071: Battle of Manzikert: Seljuk Turks defeated Byzantines and conquered Asia Minor.

13th century: Ottoman Turks, driven west by Mongols, became vassals of Seljuk Turks.

c. 1299: Osman I founded small Ottoman kingdom, which quickly displaced Seljuks to include all Asia Minor.

1354: Ottoman Turks captured Gallipoli and began their conquests in Europe.

1389: Battle of Kossovo: Turks defeated Serbs to take control of most of Balkan peninsula.

1453: Constantinople, capital of Byzantine Empire, fell to the Turks; became capital of Ottoman Empire as Istanbul.

16th century: Ottoman Empire reached its zenith under Suleiman the Magnificent 1520–66; Turks conquered Egypt, Syria, Arabia, Mesopotamia, Tripoli, Cyprus, and most of Hungary.

1683: Failure of Siege of Vienna marked the start of the decline of the Ottoman Empire.

1699: Treaty of Karlowitz: Turks forced out of Hungary by Austrians.

1774: Treaty of Kuchuk Kainarji: Russia drove Turks from Crimea and won the right to intervene on behalf of Christian subjects of the sultan.

19th century: 'The Eastern Question': Ottoman weakness caused intense rivalry between powers to shape future of Near East.

1821–29: Greek war of independence: Greeks defeated Turks with help of Russia, Britain, and France.

1854–56: Crimean War: Britain and France fought to defend Ottoman Empire from further pressure by Russians.

1877–78: Russo-Turkish War ended with Treaty of Berlin and withdrawal of Turks from Bulgaria.

1908: Young Turk revolution forced sultan to grant constitution; start of political modernization.

1911–12: Italo-Turkish War: Turkey lost Tripoli (Libya).

1912–13: Balkan War: Greece, Serbia, and Bulgaria expelled Turks from Macedonia and Albania.

1914: Ottoman Empire entered World War I on German side.

1919: Following Turkish defeat, Mustapha Kemal launched nationalist revolt to resist foreign encroachments.

1920: Treaty of Sèvres partitioned Ottoman Empire, leaving no part of Turkey fully independent.

1922: Kemal, having defied Allies, expelled Greeks, French, and Italians from Asia Minor; sultanate abolished.

1923: Treaty of Lausanne recognized Turkish independence; secular republic established by Kemal, who imposed rapid Westernization.

1935: Kemal adopted surname Atatürk ('Father of the Turks').

1938: Death of Kemal Atatürk; succeeded as president by Ismet Inönü.

1950: First free elections won by opposition Democratic Party; Adnan Menderes became prime minister.

1952: Turkey became a member of NATO.

1960: Military coup led by Gen Cemal Gürsel deposed Menderes, who was executed in 1961.

1961: Inönü returned as prime minister; politics dominated by the issue of Cyprus.

1965: Justice Party came to power under Suleyman Demirel.

1971–73: Prompted by strikes and student unrest, the army imposed military rule.

1974: Turkey invaded northern Cyprus.

1980–83: Political violence led to further military rule.

1984: Kurds began guerrilla war in a quest for greater autonomy.

1989: Application to join European Community rejected.

1990–91: Turkey joined the UN coalition against Iraq in the Gulf War.

1995: Turkish offensives against Kurdish bases in northern Iraq; the Islamicist Welfare Party won the largest number of seats in general election.

1997: Plans were agreed for the curbing of Muslim fundamentalism. Mesut Yilmaz was appointed prime minister. An agreement was reached with Greece on the peaceful resolution of disputes.

1998: The Islamic Welfare Party (RP) was banned by Constitutional Court, and regrouped as the Virtue Party (FP).

1999: Bülent Ecevit became prime minister. Ecevit's ruling centre-left party won the majority of seats in the general election. Turkey suffered two devastating earthquakes, causing extensive loss of life and structural damage. At a European Union (EU) summit, Turkey was at last declared an EU candidate, but to become a full member would first have to settle its territorial dispute with Greece and satisfy EU human rights regulations.

2000: Judeg Ahmet Necdet Sezer was inaugurated as president. He urged reform to push Turkey closer to EU membership.

2003: Suicide bombings at two synagogues in Istanbul, Turkey, killed at least 25 people and injured over 300. Suicide bombers also targeted the British consulate and the local headquarters of the UK-based bank HSBC, killing 30 people including the British consul Roger Short and injuring over 450. Islamic extremists with links to the al-Qaeda international terrorist network were thought responsible.

of the revolutionary play *Vatan/The Fatherland*, which led to his exile by the sultan. Unlike these, the poet Tevfik Fikret (1867–1915) turned rather to Persian and Arabic than to native sources for his vocabulary. The poet Mehmed Akif (1873–1936) was the author of the words of the Turkish national anthem; other distinguished modern writers include the novelist and satirist Refik Halit (1888–1965), the traditionalist poet Yahya Kemal (1884–1958), and the realist novelist Orhan Kemal (1914–1970). The work of the contemporary poet and novelist Yashar Kemal (1923–) describes the hard life of the peasant (*Memed, My Hawk* (1955) and *The Wind from the Plain* (1961)).

Turkmenistan see country box.

Turkoman (or **Turkman**; plural **Turkomen**) member of the majority ethnic group in Turkmenistan. They live to the east of the Caspian Sea, around the Kara Kum Desert, and along the borders of Afghanistan, Iraq, Syria, Turkey, and Iran. Their language belongs to the Turkic branch of the Altaic family and is closely related to the language of Turkey.

Turks and Caicos Islands British crown colony in the West Indies, the southeastern archipelago of the Bahamas; area 430 sq km/166 sq mi; population (1990 est) 12,400 (90% of African descent). The capital is Cockburn Town on Grand Turk. Exports include crayfish and conch (flesh and shell); tourism is important,

the main tourist island is Providenciales. The main languages are English and French Creole. The principal religion is Christian.
Related Web site: Turks and Caicos Gateway http://www.turksandcaicos.tc/

Turku (Swedish **Åbo**) port in southwestern Finland, near the mouth of the River Aura, on the Gulf of Bothnia; population (1992) 160,000. Industries include shipbuilding, engineering, textiles, and food processing. It was the capital of Finland until 1812.
Related Web site: Turku – Åbo – Typky http://www.turku.fi/english/index.html

turmeric perennial plant belonging to the ginger family, native to India and the East Indies; also the ground powder from its tuberous rhizomes (underground stems), used in curries to give a yellow colour and as a dyestuff. (*Curcuma longa*, family Zingiberaceae.)

Turner, Joseph Mallord William (1775–1851) English painter. He was one of the most original artists of his day. He travelled widely in Europe, and his landscapes became increasingly Romantic, with the subject often transformed in scale and flooded with brilliant, hazy light. Many later works anticipate Impressionism, for example *Rain, Steam and Speed* (1844; National Gallery, London).

TURKS AND CAICOS ISLANDS The beach at Cockburn Town, capital of the Turks and Caicos Islands. *Image Bank*

Turkmenistan

Turkmenistan country in central Asia, bounded north by Kazakhstan and Uzbekistan, west by the Caspian Sea, and south by Iran and Afghanistan.

NATIONAL NAME
Türkmenistan/Turkmenistan
AREA 488,100 sq km/188,455 sq mi
CAPITAL Ashgabat
MAJOR TOWNS/CITIES Chärjew, Mary, Nebitdag, Dashhowuz, Turkmenbashi
MAJOR PORTS Turkmenbashi
PHYSICAL
about 90% of land is desert including the Kara Kum 'Black Sands' desert (area 310,800 sq km/120,000 sq mi)

Government

HEAD OF STATE AND GOVERNMENT Saparmurad Niyazov from 1990
POLITICAL SYSTEM authoritarian nationalist
POLITICAL EXECUTIVE unlimited presidency
ADMINISTRATIVE DIVISIONS five regions
ARMED FORCES 17,500 (2002 est)
CONSCRIPTION military service is compulsory for 24 months
DEATH PENALTY abolished in 1999
DEFENCE SPEND (% GDP) 0.8 (2002 est)
HEALTH SPEND (% GDP) 5.4 (2000 est)

Economy and resources

CURRENCY manat
GPD (US$) 7.7 billion (2002 est)
REAL GDP GROWTH (% change on previous year) 20.5 (2001)
GNI (US$) 6.7 billion (2002 est)
GNI PER CAPITA (PPP) (US$) 4,570 (2002 est)
CONSUMER PRICE INFLATION 14% (2003 est)
UNEMPLOYMENT 19% (1999)
FOREIGN DEBT (US$) 2.5 billion (2001 est)
MAJOR TRADING PARTNERS Ukraine, Uzbekistan, Turkey, Russia, Iran, Italy, United Arab Emirates, France
RESOURCES petroleum, natural gas, coal, sulphur, magnesium, iodine-bromine, sodium sulphate and different types of salt
INDUSTRIES mining, petroleum refining, energy generation, textiles, chemicals, cement, mineral fertilizer, footwear
EXPORTS natural gas, cotton yarn, electric energy, petroleum and petroleum products. Principal market: Ukraine 46% (2001)
IMPORTS machinery and metalwork, light industrial products, processed food,

agricultural products. Principal source: Uzbekistan 29.1% (2001)
ARABLE LAND 3.5% (2000 est)

Population and society

POPULATION 4,867,000 (2003 est)
POPULATION GROWTH RATE 1.3% (2000–15)
POPULATION DENSITY (per sq km) 10 (2003 est)
URBAN POPULATION (% of total) 45 (2003 est)
AGE DISTRIBUTION (% of total population) 0–14 36%, 15–59 58%, 60+ 6% (2002 est)
ETHNIC GROUPS 77% ethnic Turkmen, 7% ethnic Russian, 9% Uzbek, 3% Kazakh, 1% Ukrainian, Armenian, Azeri, and Tartar
LANGUAGE Turkmen (a Turkic language; official), Russian, Uzbek, other regional languages
RELIGION Sunni Muslim
EDUCATION (compulsory years) 9
LITERACY RATE 99% (men); 98% (women) (2003 est)
LABOUR FORCE 44% agriculture, 19% industry, 37% services (1996)

Chronology

6th century BC: Part of the Persian Empire of Cyrus the Great.
4th century BC: Part of the empire of Alexander the Great of Macedonia.
7th century: Spread of Islam into Transcaspian region, followed by Arab rule from 8th century.
10th–13th centuries: Immigration from northeast by nomadic Oghuz Seljuk and Mongol tribes, whose Turkic-speaking descendants now dominate the country; conquest by Genghis Khan.
16th century: Came under dominance of Persia, to the south.
1869–81: Fell under control of tsarist Russia after 150,000 Turkmen were killed in Battle of Gok Tepe in 1881; became part of Russia's Turkestan Governor-Generalship.
1916: Turkmen revolted violently against Russian rule; autonomous Transcaspian government formed after Russian Revolution of 1917.
1919: Brought back under Russian control following invasion by the Soviet Red Army.
1921: Part of Turkestan Soviet Socialist Autonomous Republic.
1925: Became constituent republic of USSR.
1920s–30s: Soviet programme of agricultural collectivization and secularization provoked sporadic guerrilla resistance and popular uprisings.

TURKMENISTAN A stamp from Turkmenistan featuring traditional musical instruments. *Stanley Gibbons*

LIFE EXPECTANCY 64 (men); 70 (women) (2000–05)
CHILD MORTALITY RATE (under 5, per 1,000 live births) 99 (2001)
PHYSICIANS (per 1,000 people) 3 (1998 est)
HOSPITAL BEDS (per 1,000 people) 11.2 (1998 est)
TV SETS (per 1,000 people) 198 (1999 est)
RADIOS (per 1,000 people) 289 (1998 est)
INTERNET USERS (per 10,000 people) 16.6 (2002 est)

See also ▷Russia; ▷Union of Soviet Socialist Republics.

1960–67: Lenin Kara-Kum Canal built, leading to dramatic expansion in cotton production in previously semidesert region.
1985: Saparmurad Niyazov replaced Muhammad Gapusov, local communist leader since 1971, whose regime had been viewed as corrupt.
1989: Stimulated by the *glasnost* initiative of reformist Soviet leader Mikhail Gorbachev, Agzybirlik 'popular front' formed by Turkmen intellectuals.
1990: Economic and political sovereignty was declared. Niyazov was elected state president.
1991: Niyazov initially supported an attempted anti-Gorbachev coup in Moscow. Independence was later declared; Turkmenistan joined the new Commonwealth of Independent States (CIS).
1992: Joined the Muslim Economic Cooperation Organization and the United Nations; a new constitution was adopted.
1993: A new currency, the manat, was introduced and a programme of cautious economic reform introduced, with foreign investment in the country's huge oil and gas reserves encouraged. The economy continued to contract.
1994: A nationwide referendum overwhelmingly backed Niyazov's presidency.
2002: Niyazov survived an assassination attempt. It was alleged that four former government ministers and officials were behind the attack.

J M W TURNER *The Shipwreck*, by J M W Turner, is an early work, from 1805, but already deals with one of his most important themes. In the storm and the lowering clouds it is possible to anticipate the later Turners, with their almost impressionistic swirling brushstrokes of light and colour. *The Art Archive/Tate Gallery London*

A precocious talent, Turner entered the Royal Academy schools in 1789. In 1792 he made the first of several European tours from which numerous watercolour sketches survive. His early oil paintings show Dutch influence (such as that of van de Velde), but by the 1800s he had begun to paint landscapes in the 'Grand Manner', reflecting the Italianate influences of ▷Claude Lorrain and Richard ▷Wilson.

Many of his most dramatic works are set in Europe or at sea, for example, *Shipwreck* (1805), *Snowstorm: Hannibal Crossing the Alps* (1812), and *Destruction of Sodom* (1805), all at the Tate Gallery, London; and *The Slave Ship* (1839; Museum of Fine Arts, Boston, Massachusetts). Turner was also devoted to literary themes and mythologies, such as *Ulysses Deriding Polyphemus* (1829; Tate Gallery, London).

His use of colour was enhanced by trips to Italy (1919, 1828, 1835, and 1840), and his brushwork became increasingly free, allowing him to capture both the subtlest effects of light and atmosphere and also the most violent forces of nature. Although encouraged by the portraitist Thomas Lawrence and others early in his career, he failed to achieve recognition, and it was not until he was championed by the critic John ▷Ruskin in *Modern Painters* (1843) that his originality was fully appreciated.

In his old age he lived as a recluse in Chelsea, London, under an assumed name. He died there, leaving to the nation more than 300 paintings, nearly 20,000 watercolours, and over 19,000 drawings. In 1987 the Clore Gallery extension to the Tate Gallery, London, was opened to display his bequest.

Turner, Tina (1940–) Adopted name of Annie Mae Bullock. US rhythm-and-blues singer and film actor. She recorded 1960–76 with her husband **Ike Turner** (1931–). Their collaborations include *River Deep, Mountain High* (1966), produced by Phil ▷Spector, and *Workin' Together* (1970). After separating from her husband, she went on to achieve success as a solo artist, recording such albums as *Private Dancer* (1984), *Break Every Rule* (1986), *Wildest Dreams* (1997), and *Twenty-Four Seven* (2000). She also established a reputation as a highly accomplished live performer.

Turner Prize annual prize established in 1984 to encourage discussion about new developments in contemporary British art. £20,000 is awarded to a British artist under the age of 50 for an outstanding exhibition or other presentation of his or her work in the preceding 12 months; the winner is usually announced in November or early December. The Turner Prize has often attracted criticism for not celebrating what is traditionally considered to be art.

turnip biennial plant widely cultivated in temperate regions for its edible white- or yellow-fleshed root and young leaves, which are used as a green vegetable. Closely allied to it is the ▷swede (*B. napus*). (*Brassica rapa*, family Cruciferae.)

turnover in finance, the value of sales of a business organization over a period of time. For example, if a shop sells 10,000 items in a week at an average price of £2 each, then its weekly turnover is £20,000. The ▷profit of a company is not only affected by the total turnover but also by the rate of turnover.

turnstone any small wading shorebirds of the genus *Arenaria*, order Charadriiformes, especially the ruddy turnstone *A. interpres*, which breeds in the Arctic and migrates to the southern hemisphere. It is seen on rocky beaches, turning over stones for small crustaceans and insects. It is about 23 cm/9 in long and has a summer plumage of black and chestnut above, white below; it is duller in winter.

turpentine solution of resins distilled from the sap of conifers, used in varnish and as a paint solvent but now largely replaced by ▷white spirit.

Turpin, Dick (Richard) (1705–1739) English highwayman. The son of an innkeeper, he turned to highway robbery, cattle-thieving, and smuggling, and was hanged at York, England.

His legendary ride from London to York on his mare Black Bess is probably based on one of about 305 km/190 mi from Gad's Hill to York completed in 15 hours in 1676 by highwayman John Nevison (1639–1684).

turquoise mineral, hydrous basic copper aluminium phosphate, $CuAl_6(PO_4)_4(OH)_8 5H_2O$. Blue-green, blue, or green, it is a gemstone. Turquoise is found in Australia, Egypt, Ethiopia, France, Germany, Iran, Turkestan, Mexico, and southwestern USA. It was originally introduced into Europe through Turkey, from which its name is derived.

turtle small computer-controlled wheeled robot. The turtle's movements are determined by programs written by a computer user, typically using the high-level programming language ▷LOGO.

turtle freshwater or marine reptile whose body is protected by a shell. Turtles are related to tortoises, and some species can grow to a length of up to 2.5 m/8 ft. Turtles often travel long distances to lay their eggs on the beaches where they were born. Many species have suffered through destruction of their breeding sites as well as being hunted for food and their shells. Unlike tortoises, turtles cannot retract their heads into their shells.

Marine turtles are generally herbivores, feeding mainly on sea grasses. Freshwater turtles eat a range of animals including worms, frogs, and fish. They are excellent swimmers, having legs that are modified to oarlike flippers but which make them awkward on land. The shell is more streamlined and lighter than that of the tortoise.

Species include the **green turtle** *Chelonia mydas*; the **loggerhead** *Caretta caretta*; the **giant leathery** or **leatherback turtle** *Dermochelys coriacea*, which can weigh half a tonne and grow up to 2.5 m/8 ft; and the **hawksbill** *Eretmochelys imbricata*, which is hunted for its shell which provides tortoiseshell, used in jewellery and ornaments, and is now endangered. Other turtles suffer because their eggs are taken by collectors and their breeding sites are regularly destroyed, often for tourist developments. The world's rarest turtle is the **Kemp's ridley**, which breeds only at a single site in the Gulf of Mexico. The total population is less than 10,000 (1998).

A new species of turtle was discovered in Mexico in 1997. It has been named *Kinosternon chimalhuaca*.

Only two (loggerheads and leatherbacks) of the seven species of sea turtle are seen regularly in British waters.

Related Web site: Turtles http://www.turtles.org

Mark Twain

A classic – something that everybody wants to have read and nobody wants to read.

Quoting Professor Caleb Winchester in a speech at the Nineteenth Century Club, New York City, 20 November 1900

TURTLE A female Pacific ridley turtle *Lepidochelys olivacea* covering her nest on a Costa Rican beach. *K G Preston-Mafham/Premaphotos Wildlife*

Tuscany (Italian **Toscana**; Roman **Etruria**) region of north central Italy, on the west coast, comprising the provinces of Massa e Carrara, Arezzo, Florence, Grosseto, Livorno, Lucca, Pisa, Pistoia, and Siena; area 23,000 sq km/8,878 sq mi; population (1992 est) 3,528,700. Its capital is ▷Florence, and cities include Pisa, Livorno, and Siena. The area is mainly agricultural, producing cereals, wine (Chianti hills), olives (Lucca) and tobacco (plain of Arno); it also has mining of lignite (upper Arno) and iron (Elba) and marble quarries (Carrara, Apuan Alps). The Tuscan dialect has been adopted as the standard form of Italian.

Tussaud, Madame (1761–1850) Born Anne Marie Grosholtz. French wax-modeller. In 1802 she established an exhibition of wax models of celebrities in London. It was destroyed by fire 1925, but reopened 1928.

Tutankhamen King (pharaoh) of ancient Egypt of the 18th dynasty, about 1333–1323 BC. A son of Akhenaton (also called Amenhotep IV), he was about 11 at his accession. In 1922 his tomb was discovered by the British archaeologists Lord Carnarvon and Howard Carter in the Valley of the Kings at Luxor, almost untouched by tomb robbers. The contents included many works of art and his solid-gold coffin, which are now displayed in a Cairo museum.

Tutsi member of a minority ethnic group living in Rwanda and Burundi. They have politically dominated the ▷Hutu majority and the Twa (or ▷Pygmies) since their arrival in the area in the 14th century. In Burundi, positions of power were monopolized by the Tutsis, who carried out massacres in response to Hutu rebellions, notably 1972 and 1988. In Rwanda, where the balance of power is more even, Tutsis were massacred in their thousands by Hutu militia during the 1994 civil war.

Tutu, Desmond Mpilo (1931–) South African priest, Anglican archbishop of Cape Town 1986–96 and general secretary of the South African Council of Churches 1979–84. One of the leading figures in the struggle against ▷apartheid in the Republic of South Africa, he was awarded the Nobel Prize for Peace in 1984 for encouraging peaceful reconciliation between the black and white communities.

In November 1995 Tutu was named as the head of the Truth and Reconciliation Commission, a commission set up in June 1995 by Nelson Mandela to investigate abuses by both government and opposition groups during the apartheid era.

Tuva (or **Tyva**) republic in the southern Russian Federation; area 170,500 sq km/65,830 sq mi; population (1996) 309,000 (49% urban) (64% Tyvans). The capital is Kyzyl. There are coal and mineral mining, woodworking, and food-processing industries; sheep, goats, and cattle are raised.

Tuvalu see country box.

TVP (abbreviation for texturized vegetable protein) meat substitute usually made from soybeans. In manufacture, the soybean solids (what remains after oil has been removed) are ground finely and mixed with a binder to form a sticky mixture. This is forced through a spinneret and extruded into fibres, which are treated with salts and flavourings, wound into hanks, and then chopped up to resemble meat chunks.

Twa ethnic group comprising 1% of the populations of Burundi and Rwanda. The Twa are the aboriginal inhabitants of the region. They are a pygmoid people, and live as nomadic hunter-gatherers in the forests.

Twain, Mark (1835–1910) Pen-name of Samuel Langhorne Clemens. US writer. He established his reputation with the comic masterpiece *The Innocents Abroad* (1869) and two classic American novels, in dialect, *The Adventures of Tom Sawyer* (1876) and *The Adventures of Huckleberry Finn* (1885). He also wrote satire, as in *A Connecticut Yankee at King Arthur's Court* (1889). He is recognized as one of America's finest and most characteristic writers.

Early works From 1857, he was employed as a riverboat pilot on the Mississippi until the boats stopped running on the outbreak of the Civil War in 1861. He then moved west, taking a job as city editor of a Nevada newspaper. There he began to write under the pseudonym 'Mark Twain' (the call of pilots when taking soundings, meaning 'two fathoms'). The tale 'The Celebrated Jumping Frog of Calaveras County' was his first success. After a trip by boat to Palestine, he wrote *The Innocents Abroad.*

Mature works *Huckleberry Finn* is Twain's masterpiece, for its use of the vernacular, vivid characterization and descriptions, and its theme, underlying the humour, of man's inhumanity to man. He also wrote *Roughing It* (1872), *The Gilded Age* (1873), *Old Times on the Mississippi* (1875), *A Tramp Abroad* (1880), *The Prince and the Pauper* (1882), *Life on the Mississippi* (1883), *Pudd'nhead Wilson* (1894), and *Personal Recollections of Joan of Arc* (1896).

Related Web site: Mark Twain in His Times http://etext.virginia.edu/railton/index2.html

Tweed river rising in the Tweedsmuir Hills, 10 km/6 mi north of Moffat, southwest Scottish Borders, Scotland, and entering the North Sea at Berwick-upon-Tweed, Northumberland; length 156 km/97 mi. It flows in a northeasterly direction, and from

TWELVE-TONE SYSTEM A passage from Schoenberg's 'Waltz' (*5 Piano Pieces* op.23); the numbers represent the particular sequence of notes in the note-row.

Coldstream until near Berwick-upon-Tweed it forms the border between England and Scotland.

tweed cloth made of woollen yarn, usually of several shades, but in its original form without a regular pattern and woven on a hand loom in the more remote parts of Ireland, Wales, and Scotland, UK.

Twelver member of a Shiite Muslim sect who believes that the 12th imam (Islamic leader) did not die, but is waiting to return towards the end of the world as the Mahdi, the 'rightly guided one', to establish a reign of peace and justice on Earth.

Twelve Tables in ancient Rome, the earliest law code, drawn from religious and secular custom. It was published on tablets of bronze or wood at the Roman ▷forum *c.* 450 BC, and though these were destroyed in the sack of Rome by Celts 387 BC, the code survived to have influence into the later Republic.

twelve-tone system (or **twelve-note system**) method of musical composition invented by Arnold ▷Schoenberg about 1921 in which all 12 notes of the ▷chromatic scale are arranged in a particular order of the composer's choice, without repeating any of the notes. Such an arrangement is called a 'series' or 'tone row'. The initial series may be transposed, divided, and otherwise mutated to provide a complete resource for all melodic and harmonic material in a work.

twill one of the basic cloth structures, characterized by a diagonal line on the face of the fabric. Variations in structure include herringbone weaves. Denim, gabardine, serge, and some flannels and tweeds are examples of twill fabrics.

twin one of two young produced from a single pregnancy. Human twins may be genetically identical (monozygotic), having been formed from a single fertilized egg that splits into two cells, both of which became implanted. Nonidentical (fraternal or dizygotic) twins are formed when two eggs are fertilized at the same time.

two-stroke cycle operating cycle for internal combustion piston engines. The engine cycle is completed after just two strokes (up or down) of the piston, which distinguishes it from the more common ▷four-stroke cycle. Power mowers and lightweight motorcycles use two-stroke petrol engines, which are cheaper and simpler than four-strokes.

Related Web site: How Two-Stroke Expansion Chambers Work
http://www.motorcycle.com/
mo/mcnuts/em-pipes.html

TX abbreviation for the state of ▷Texas, USA.

Tyche personification of Chance in classical Greek thought, whose cult developed in the Hellenistic and Roman periods, when it was identified with that of the Roman Fortuna.

Tyler, John (1790–1862) 10th president of the USA 1841–45, succeeding William H ▷Harrison, who died after only a month in office. Tyler's government negotiated the Webster–Ashburton Treaty, which settled the Maine–New Brunswick boundary dispute in Canada in 1842, and annexed Texas in 1845.

Tyler, Wat (died 1381) English leader of the ▷Peasants' Revolt of 1381. He was probably born in Kent or Essex, and may have served in the French wars. After taking Canterbury, he led the peasant army to Blackheath, outside London, and went on to invade the city. King Richard II met the rebels at Mile End and promised to redress their grievances, which included the imposition of a poll tax. At a further conference at Smithfield, London, Tyler was murdered.

Ned Rorem
American composer

The twelve-toners behave as if music should be seen and not heard.

Paris Diary, 1966

Tyndale, William (*c.* 1492–1536) English translator of the Bible. The printing of his New Testament was begun in Cologne in 1525 and, after he had been forced to flee, completed in Worms. Tyndale introduced some of the most familiar phrases to the English language, such as 'filthy lucre', and 'God forbid'. He was strangled and burned as a heretic at Vilvorde in Belgium.

Tyne river of northeast England formed by the union of the North Tyne (rising in the Cheviot Hills) and South Tyne (rising near Cross Fell in Cumbria) near Hexham, Northumberland, and reaching the North Sea at Tynemouth; length 72 km/45 mi. Kielder Water (1980) in the North Tyne Valley is Europe's largest artificial lake, 12 km/7.5 mi long and 0.8 km/0.5 mi wide, and supplies the industries of Tyneside, Wearside, and Teesside. As well as functioning as a reservoir, it is a major resource for recreational use.

Tyne and Wear metropolitan county of northeast England, created in 1974; in 1986, most of the functions of the former county council were transferred to the metropolitan borough councils.
area 540 sq km/208 sq mi **towns and cities** Newcastle upon Tyne, Gateshead, Sunderland (administrative centres for the districts of the same name), South Shields (administrative centre of South Tyneside district), North Shields (administrative centre of North Tyneside district) **physical** rivers: Tyne and Wear **features** part of ▷Hadrian's Wall; Newcastle and Gateshead, linked with each other and with the coast on both sides by the Tyne and Wear Metro (a light

Tuvalu

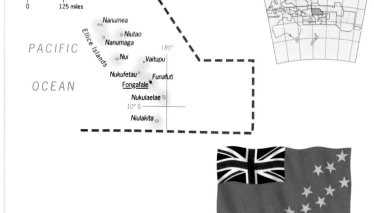

especially in the phosphate industry on Nauru

EXPORTS copra, handicrafts, garments, stamps, fisheries licences. Principal market: Belgium 22.8% (2000)

IMPORTS food and live animals, beverages, tobacco, consumer goods, machinery and transport equipment, mineral fuels. Principal source: Fiji 58.6% (2000)

AGRICULTURAL PRODUCTS coconuts, pulaka, taro, papayas, screw-pine (pandanus), bananas; livestock rearing (pigs, poultry, and goats); honey production and fishing

Population and society

POPULATION 11,000 (2003 est)
POPULATION GROWTH RATE 1.3% (2000–05)
POPULATION DENSITY (per sq km) 408 (2003 est)

TUVALU A traditionally-built beach hut on Tuvalu. *Stanley Gibbons*

URBAN POPULATION (% of total) 55 (2003 est)
EDUCATION (compulsory years) 9
LITERACY RATE 93% (1997 est)
LIFE EXPECTANCY 65 (men); 69 (women) (2001 est)

See also ▷Australasia and Oceania; ▷Kiribati.

Tuvalu country in the southwest Pacific Ocean; formerly (until 1978) the Ellice Islands; part of ▷Polynesia.

NATIONAL NAME *Fakavae Aliki-Malo i Tuvalu/Constitutional Monarchy of Tuvalu*
AREA 25 sq km/9.6 sq mi
CAPITAL Fongafale (on Funafuti atoll)
PHYSICAL FEATURES nine low coral atolls forming a chain of 579 km/650 mi in the Southwest Pacific

Government

HEAD OF STATE Queen Elizabeth II from 1978, represented by Governor General Faimalaga Luka from 2003
HEAD OF GOVERNMENT Saufatu Sopoanga from 2002
POLITICAL SYSTEM liberal democracy
POLITICAL EXECUTIVE parliamentary
ADMINISTRATIVE DIVISIONS one town council and eight island councils

ARMED FORCES no standing defence force
DEATH PENALTY laws do not provide for the death penalty for any crime

Economy and resources

CURRENCY Australian dollar
GPD (US$) 13.6 million (2001)
REAL GDP GROWTH (% change on previous year) 3 (2001)
GNI (US$) 15 million (2001)
GNI PER CAPITA (PPP) (US$) 1,300 (2001)
CONSUMER PRICE INFLATION 1.8% (2001)
MAJOR TRADING PARTNERS Belgium, Australia, Fiji, New Zealand, EU
INDUSTRIES processing of agricultural products (principally coconuts), soap, handicrafts, tourism; a large source of income is from Tuvaluans working abroad,

Chronology

c. **300 BC**: First settled by Polynesian peoples.
16th century: Invaded and occupied by Samoans.
1765: Islands first reached by Europeans.
1850–75: Population decimated by European slave traders capturing Tuvaluans to work in South America and by exposure to European diseases.
1856: The four southern islands, including Funafuti, claimed by USA.
1865: Christian mission established.
1877: Came under control of British Western Pacific High Commission (WPHC), with its headquarters in the Fiji Islands.
1892: Known as the Ellice Islands, they were joined with Gilbert Islands (now Kiribati) to form a British protectorate.
1916: Gilbert and Ellice Islands colony formed.
1942–43: Became a base for US airforce operations when Japan occupied the Gilbert Islands during World War II.
1975: Following a referendum, the predominantly Melanesian-peopled Ellice Islands, fearing domination by Micronesian-peopled Gilbert Islands in an independent state, were granted separate status.
1978: Independence achieved within Commonwealth, with Toaripi Lauti as prime minister; reverted to former name Tuvalu ('eight standing together').
1979: The USA signed a friendship treaty, relinquishing its claim to the four southern atolls in return for continued access to military bases.
1986: Islanders rejected proposal for republican status.
1995: The union flag was removed from the national flag, presaging a move towards republican status.
1999: Ionatana Ionatana became prime minister.
2000: Entered the United Nations.
2002: Saufatu Sopoanga became prime minister,

railway using existing suburban lines, extending 54 km/34 mi); Tyneside International Film Festival **industries** once a centre of heavy industry, Tyne and Wear's industry is now being redeveloped and diversified, with car manufacturing on Wearside, electronics, offshore technology (floating production vessels), automobile components, pharmaceuticals, and computers **population** (1996) 1,127,300 **famous people** Thomas Bewick, Harry Patterson ('Jack Higgins'), Robert Stephenson

Tynwald parliament of the Isle of ▷Man.

typesetting means by which text, or copy, is prepared for ▷printing, now usually carried out by using specialized computer programs.

typewriter keyboard machine that produces characters on paper. The earliest known typewriter design was patented by Henry Mills in England in 1714. However, the first practical typewriter was built in 1867 in Milwaukee, Wisconsin, USA, by Christopher Sholes, Carlos Glidden, and Samuel Soulé. By 1873 Remington and Sons, US gunmakers, had produced under contract the first typing machines for sale and in 1878 they patented the first with lower-case as well as upper-case (capital) letters. Typewriters are being superseded by word processors.

Related Web site: QWERTY Connection (Typewriter) http://home.earthlink.net/~dcrehr/

typhoid fever acute infectious disease of the digestive tract, caused by the bacterium *Salmonella typhi*, and usually contracted through a contaminated water supply. It is characterized by bowel haemorrhage and damage to the spleen. Treatment is with antibiotics.

The symptoms begin 10–14 days after ingestion and include fever, headache, cough, constipation, and rash. The combined TAB vaccine protects both against typhoid and the milder, related condition known as **paratyphoid fever.**

A strain of typhoid fever emerged in the late 1990s in Tajikistan, that was resistant to all known antibiotics.

typhoon violent revolving storm, a ▷hurricane in the western Pacific Ocean.

typhus any one of a group of infectious diseases caused by bacteria transmitted by lice, fleas, mites, and ticks. Symptoms include fever, headache, and rash. The most serious form is epidemic typhus, which also affects the brain, heart, lungs, and kidneys and is associated with insanitary overcrowded conditions. Treatment is by antibiotics.

typography design and layout of the printed word. Typography began with the invention of writing and developed as printing spread throughout Europe after the invention of metal moveable type by Johann ▷Gutenberg about 1440. Hundreds of variations have followed since, but the basic design of the Frenchman Nicholas Jensen (about 1420–1480), with a few modifications, is still the ordinary ('roman') type used in printing.

Typography, for centuries the domain of engravers and printers, is now a computerized process, carried out by using specialist software.

Tyr in Norse and Teutonic mythology, the god of battles, whom the Anglo-Saxons called Týw, hence 'Tuesday'. He was a member of the Aesir (principal warrior gods).

tyrannosaurus any of a genus *Tyrannosaurus* of gigantic flesh-eating ▷dinosaurs, order Saurischia, that lived in North America and Asia about 70 million years ago. They had two feet, were up to 15 m/50 ft long, 6.5 m/20 ft tall, weighed 10 tonnes, and had teeth 15 cm/6 in long.

Only a few whole skeletons are known; the most complete was discovered in 1989 in Hell Creek, Montana, and preserved in the Museum of the Rockies, Bozeman, Montana, USA.

Two distinct body types have been discovered for tyrannosaurs, indicating that one, the larger more robust form is female, as it has a wider pelvis. Estimates for the speed at which tyrannosaurs could run down their prey ranges from about 25 kph to 36 kph, but as only single footprints have only been found to date, this is impossible to verify.

US archaeologists proved in February 1997 that tyrannosaurs had a biting force of 1,400 kg/3,000 lb, by analysing bite marks in the fossil skeleton of a triceratops and using these to create replica teeth. They then measured the force necessary to reproduce the marks in a cow skeleton using the replica teeth.

tyre inflatable rubber hoop fitted round the rims of bicycle, car, and other road-vehicle wheels. The first pneumatic rubber tyre was patented in 1845 by the Scottish engineer Robert William Thomson (1822–73), but it was the Scottish inventor John Boyd Dunlop of Belfast who independently reinvented pneumatic tyres for use with bicycles in 1888–89. The rubber for car tyres is hardened by ▷vulcanization.

Tyrol variant spelling of ▷Tirol, a state of Austria.

Tyrone county of Northern Ireland.
    area 3,160 sq km/1,220 sq mi **towns and cities** Omagh (county town), Dungannon, Strabane, Cookstown **physical** rivers: Derg, Blackwater, Foyle; Lough Neagh; Sperrin Mountains **features** Neolithic graves and stone circles, notably at Beaghmore, west of Cookstown; Ulster History Park, north of Omagh; heritage centres in several villages, describing the linen industry; linen polishing demonstrations at Wellbrook Beetling Mill; Peatlands Park, east of Dungannon, preserving an ancient Irish bog; family home of the US president Woodrow Wilson at Dergalt, near Strabane; Ulster-American Folk Park, north of Omagh **industries** mainly agricultural: barley, flax, potatoes, turnips, cattle, sheep, brick making, linen, hosiery, shirts **population** (1991) 158,500
    Related Web site: County Tyrone http://www.interknowledge.com/northern-ireland/ukityr00.htm

Tyrrhenian Sea arm of the Mediterranean Sea surrounded by mainland Italy, Sicily, Sardinia, Corsica, and the Ligurian Sea. It is connected to the Ionian Sea through the Straits of Messina. Islands include Elba, Ustica, Capri, Stromboli, and the Lipari Islands. It has a deep seabed plain reaching a maximum depth of 3,620 m/11,876 ft.

Tyva alternative name for ▷Tuva in the Russian Federation.

Tzu-Hsi alternative transliteration of ▷Zi Xi, dowager empress of China.

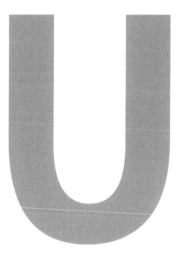

U2 Irish rock group formed in Dublin, Republic of Ireland, in 1977. U2 became one of the most popular and successful rock bands of the 1980s and 1990s, managing to sustain their fan base throughout two decades by clever reinvention. The group are known for combining their music with political messages, for example in 'Sunday, Bloody Sunday' (1983) about the conflict in Northern Ireland. The album *The Joshua Tree* (1987) propelled the band to super-stardom, and the band continued to release highly successful and critically acclaimed albums, including *Achtung Baby* in 1992, *Zooropa* in 1993, *Pop* (1997), and *All That You Can't Leave Behind* (2001). Their song 'Beautiful Day' won two Grammy Awards in 2001.

Related Web site: U2 Zone http://www.theu2zone.com/

U-2 US military reconnaissance aeroplane, used in secret flights over the USSR from 1956 to photograph military installations. In 1960 a U-2 was shot down over the USSR and the pilot, Gary Powers, was captured and imprisoned. He was exchanged for a US-held Soviet agent two years later.

uakari any of several rare South American monkeys of the genus *Cacajao*. There are three species, all with bald faces and long fur. About 55 cm/1.8 ft long in head and body, and with a comparatively short 15 cm/6 in tail, they rarely leap, but are good climbers, remaining in the tops of the trees in swampy forests and feeding largely on fruit. The black uakari is in danger of extinction because it is found in such small numbers already, and the forests where it lives are fast being destroyed.

UAKARI The bald uakari lives in the treetops of west Brazil, and seldom descends to the ground. It is very agile, although it rarely leaps, since it lacks a long tail to use as a counterbalance. The three species of uakari are the only New World monkeys to have short tails.

UCAS (acronym for the Universities and Colleges Admissions Service) central applications service for full-time undergraduate higher-education courses in the UK. Candidates can apply through UCAS for up to six courses at various institutions, and the applications and the responses from the universities and colleges concerned are coordinated through the applications service.

Uccello, Paolo (1397–1475) Adopted name of Paolo di Dono. Florentine painter. He was one of the first to experiment with perspective, though his love of detail, decorative colour, and graceful line remains traditional. His works include *St George and the Dragon* (c. 1460, National Gallery, London) and *A Hunt* (c. 1460, Ashmolean Museum, Oxford).

Udmurt (or **Udmurtiya**; Russian **Udmurtskaya**) autonomous republic in central Russian Federation, north of Tatarstan and northwest of Bashkortostan; area 42,100 sq km/16,200 sq mi; population (1990) 1,619,000 (59% Russian, 31% Udmurt, 7% Tatar). The capital is Izhevsk. There are timber, peat, quartz, tool and machine manufacturing, oil, and hydroelectric power generation industries. Flax and potatoes are grown.

Ufa capital of ▷Bashkortostan, central Russian Federation, located on the River Belaya, in the western Urals; population (1990) 1,094,000. Ufa is situated near the Tuymazy and Ishimbay fields in the Volga–Ural oil region, and is a centre for oil refining and the production of petrochemicals. One of the main manufacturing cities of the Urals, its industries include aerospace technology, electronic engineering, distilling, and lumbering.

Uffizi art gallery in Florence, Italy. Built by ▷Vasari in the 16th century as government offices, it was opened as a gallery 1765. Its collection, based on that of the Medici family, is one of the finest in Europe.

UFO abbreviation for ▷unidentified flying object.

Uganda see country box.

Ugarit ancient trading-city kingdom (modern **Ras Shamra**) on the Syrian coast. It was excavated by the French archaeologist Claude Schaeffer (1898–1982) from 1929, with finds dating from about 7000 to about 1300 BC, including the earliest known alphabet.

UHF (abbreviation for ultra high frequency) referring to radio waves of very short wavelength, used, for example, for television broadcasting.

Uigur (or **Uygur**) member of a Turkic people living in northwestern China, Uzbekistan, Kazakhstan, and Kyrgyzstan; they form about 80% of the population of the Chinese province of Xinjiang Uygur. There are about 5 million speakers of Uigur, a language belonging to the Turkic branch of the Altaic family; it is the official language of the province.

UIGUR Uigur (or Uygur) people herding cattle in the Gobi Desert. The Uigurs are a Turkic Muslim group, one of 13 recognized ethnic minorities in the autonomous region of Xinjiang Uygur, China. *Image Bank*

Ujung Pandang (formerly **Macassar** (until 1973); or **Makassar**) chief port (trading in coffee, rubber, copra, and spices) on Sulawesi, Indonesia, with fishing and food-processing industries; population (1990) 913,200. It was established by Dutch traders in 1607.

UK abbreviation for the ▷United Kingdom.

ukiyo-e (Japanese 'pictures of the floating world') Japanese colour print depicting scenes from everyday life, the dominant art form in 18th- and 19th-century Japan. Aiming to satisfy the tastes of the increasingly affluent merchant classes, ukiyo-e artists employed bright colours and strong designs, made possible by improvements in block printing, and featured actors, prostitutes, and landscapes among their favoured subjects; over a quarter of all the illustrated ukiyo-e works produced were erotic works. ▷Hiroshige, ▷Utamaro, ▷Hokusai, and Suzuki were leading exponents. The flat decorative colour and lively designs of ukiyo-e prints were later to influence many prominent French avant-garde artists.

Ukraine see country box.

Ukrainian the majority ethnic group living in Ukraine; there are minorities in Siberian Russia, Kazakhstan, Poland, Slovakia, and Romania. There are 40–45 million speakers of Ukrainian, a member of the East Slavonic branch of the Indo-European family, closely related to Russian. Ukrainian-speaking communities are also found in Canada and the USA.

ukulele musical instrument, a small four-stringed Hawaiian guitar, of Portuguese origin. It is easy to play; music for ukulele is written in a form of tablature showing finger positions on a chart of the fingerboard.

Ulaanbaatar (or **Ulan Bator**; formerly **Urga** (until 1924)) capital and largest city of ▷Mongolia, lying to the north in the valley of the River Tuul in the Khenti Mountains; population (1997 est) 627,300. Industries include machine tools, pharmaceuticals, carpets, textiles, footwear, meat packing, brewing and distilling, especially of vodka. It is the centre of Mongolia's road and rail network and is connected to the Trans-Siberian and Chinese railways.

Ulan Bator alternative spelling of Ulaanbaatar, the capital of Mongolia.

ulcer any persistent breach in a body surface (skin or mucous membrane). It may be caused by infection, irritation, or tumour and is often inflamed. Common ulcers include aphthous (mouth), gastric (stomach), duodenal, decubitus ulcers (pressure sores), and those complicating varicose veins.

Treatment of ulcers depends on the site. Drugs are the first line of attack against peptic ulcers (those in the digestive tract), though surgery may become necessary. Bleeding stomach ulcers can be repaired without an operation by the use of endoscopy: a flexible fibre-optic tube is passed into the stomach and under direct vision fine instruments are used to repair the tissues.

ulna one of the two bones found in the lower limb of the tetrapod (four-limbed) vertebrate. It articulates with the shorter radius and humerus (upper arm bone) at one end and with the radius and wrist bones at the other.

Ulster a former kingdom and province in the north of Ireland, annexed by England in 1461. From Jacobean times it was a centre of English, and later Scottish, settlement on land confiscated from its owners; divided in 1921 into Northern Ireland (counties Antrim, Armagh, Down, Fermanagh, Londonderry, and Tyrone) and the Republic of Ireland (counties Cavan, Donegal, and Monaghan).

Ulster Defence Association (UDA) Northern Ireland Protestant paramilitary organization responsible for a number of sectarian killings. Fanatically loyalist, it established a paramilitary wing (the Ulster Freedom Fighters) to combat the ▷Irish Republican Army (IRA) on its own terms and by its own methods. No political party has acknowledged any links with the UDA. In 1994, following a cessation of military activities by the IRA, the UDA, along with other Protestant paramilitary organizations, declared a ceasefire.

Ulster Freedom Fighters (UFF) paramilitary wing of the ▷Ulster Defence Association.

Ulster Unionist Party (or **Official Unionist Party** (OUP)) the largest political party in ▷Northern Ireland. Right-of-centre in orientation, it advocates equality for Northern Ireland within the UK and opposes union with the Republic of Ireland. The party has the broadest support of any Ulster party, and has consistently won a large proportion of parliamentary and local seats. Its central organization, dating from 1905, is formally called the Ulster Unionist Council. Its leader from 1995 is David ▷Trimble. It secured 28 of the 108 seats in the new Northern Ireland Assembly, elected in June 1998, and Trimble was elected Northern Ireland's first minister at the Assembly's first meeting on 1 July.

Related Web site: Ulster Unionist Party http://www.uup.org/

Ultra abbreviation of **Ultra Secret**, term used by the British in World War II from spring 1940 to denote intelligence gained by deciphering German signals from the Enigma code-making machine.

ultrasonics branch of physics dealing with the theory and application of ultrasound: sound waves occurring at frequencies too high to be heard by the human ear (that is, above about 20 kHz).

The earliest practical application of ultrasonics was the detection of submarines during World War I by reflecting pulses of sound from them (see ▷sonar). Similar principles are now used in industry for nondestructive testing of materials and in medicine to produce images of internal organs and developing fetuses (▷ultrasound scanning). High-power ultrasound can be used for cleaning, welding plastics, and destroying kidney stones without surgery.

ultrasound scanning (or **ultrasonography**) in medicine, the use of ultrasonic pressure waves to create a diagnostic image. It is a safe, noninvasive technique that often eliminates the need for exploratory surgery.

Related Web site: Obstetric Ultrasound http://www.ob-ultrasound.net

ultraviolet astronomy study of cosmic ultraviolet emissions using artificial satellites. The USA launched a series of satellites for this purpose, receiving the first useful data in 1968. Only a tiny percentage of solar ultraviolet radiation penetrates the atmosphere, this being the less dangerous longer-wavelength ultraviolet. The dangerous shorter-wavelength radiation is absorbed by gases in the ozone layer high in the Earth's upper atmosphere.

ultraviolet radiation electromagnetic radiation invisible to the human eye, of wavelengths from about 400 to 4 nm (where the ▷X-ray range begins). Physiologically, ultraviolet radiation is extremely powerful, producing sunburn and causing the formation of vitamin D in the skin.

Related Web site: Effects of Ultraviolet Radiation on Plants and Marine Organisms http://pooh.chem.wm.edu/chemWWW/courses/chem105/projects/group2/page7.html

Ulysses Roman name for ▷Odysseus.

Umar (c. 581–644) Muslim caliph (civic and religious leader of Islam) in 634–44, succeeding Abu Bakr. He laid the foundations of a regular, organized Muslim army, employing the brilliant Khalid ibn al-Walid to lead his armies in battle, and conquered Syria, Palestine, Egypt, and Persia. He was murdered by a Persian slave. The Mosque of Omar in Jerusalem is attributed to him.

Uganda

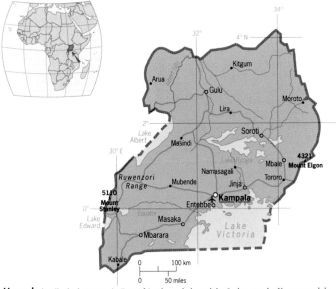

Uganda landlocked country in East Africa, bounded north by Sudan, east by Kenya, south by Tanzania and Rwanda, and west by the Democratic Republic of Congo (formerly Zaire).

NATIONAL NAME *Republic of Uganda*
AREA 236,600 sq km/91,351 sq mi
CAPITAL Kampala
MAJOR TOWNS/CITIES Jinja, Mbale, Entebbe, Masaka, Mbarara, Soroti
PHYSICAL FEATURES plateau with mountains in west (Ruwenzori Range, with Mount Margherita, 5,110 m/16,765 ft); forest and grassland; 18% is lakes, rivers, and wetlands (Owen Falls on White Nile where it leaves Lake Victoria; Lake Albert in west); arid in northwest

Government

HEAD OF STATE Yoweri Museveni from 1986
HEAD OF GOVERNMENT Apolo Nsibambi from 1999
POLITICAL SYSTEM authoritarian nationalist
POLITICAL EXECUTIVE unlimited presidency
ADMINISTRATIVE DIVISIONS 39 districts, grouped in four geographical regions
ARMED FORCES 55,000 (2002 est)
DEATH PENALTY retained and used for ordinary crimes

Economy and resources

CURRENCY Ugandan new shilling
GPD (US$) 5.9 billion (2002 est)
REAL GDP GROWTH (% change on previous year) 5.2 (2001)
GNI (US$) 5.9 billion (2002 est)
GNI PER CAPITA (PPP) (US$) 1,320 (2002 est)
CONSUMER PRICE INFLATION 1% (2003 est)
FOREIGN DEBT (US$) 3.6 billion (2001 est)
MAJOR TRADING PARTNERS Kenya, Spain, UK, Germany, the Netherlands, India, South Africa, Belgium, Japan
RESOURCES copper, apatite, limestone; believed to possess the world's second-largest deposit of gold (which began to be exploited again in the mid-1990s); also reserves of phosphate, magnetite, tin,

tungsten, beryllium, bismuth, asbestos, graphite
INDUSTRIES processing of agricultural products, brewing, vehicle assembly, textiles, cement, soap, fertilizers, footwear, metal products, paints, batteries, matches
EXPORTS coffee, cotton, tea, gold, tobacco, oil seeds and oleaginous fruit; fish and fish products, textiles. Principal market: Germany 12% (2000)
IMPORTS machinery and transport equipment, basic manufactures, petroleum and petroleum products, chemicals, miscellaneous manufactured articles, iron and steel. Principal source: Kenya 41% (2000)
ARABLE LAND 25.7% (2000 est)
AGRICULTURAL PRODUCTS coffee, cotton, tea, maize, tobacco, sugar cane, cocoa, horticulture, plantains, cassava, sweet potatoes, millet, sorghum, beans, groundnuts, rice; livestock rearing (cattle, goats, sheep, and poultry); freshwater fishing

Population and society

POPULATION 25,827,000 (2003 est)
POPULATION GROWTH RATE 2.4% (2000–15)
POPULATION DENSITY (per sq km) 109 (2003 est)
URBAN POPULATION (% of total) 15 (2003 est)
AGE DISTRIBUTION (% of total population) 0–14 49%, 15–59 47%, 60+ 4% (2002 est)
ETHNIC GROUPS about 40 different peoples concentrated into three main groups; the Bantu (the most numerous), the Nilotics, and the Nilo-Hamites; there are also Rwandan, Sudanese, Zairean, and Kenyan minorities
LANGUAGE English (official), Kiswahili, other Bantu and Nilotic languages
RELIGION Christian 65%, animist 20%, Muslim 15%

EDUCATION not compulsory
LITERACY RATE 79% (men); 60% (women) (2003 est)
LABOUR FORCE 80% agriculture, 5% industry, 15% services (2000)
LIFE EXPECTANCY 45 (men); 47 (women) (2000–05)
CHILD MORTALITY RATE (under 5, per 1,000 live births) 124 (2001)
PHYSICIANS (per 1,000 people) 0.04 (1994 est)
HOSPITAL BEDS (per 1,000 people) 0.9 (1993 est)
TV SETS (per 1,000 people) 28 (1999 est)
RADIOS (per 1,000 people) 127 (1998)
INTERNET USERS (per 10,000 people) 28.3 (2002 est)
PERSONAL COMPUTER USERS (per 100 people) 0.3 (2002 est)

See also ▷Amin, Idi; ▷Buganda.

Chronology

16th century: Bunyoro kingdom founded by immigrants from southeastern Sudan.

17th century: Rise of kingdom of Buganda people, which became particularly powerful from 17th century.

mid-19th century: Arabs, trading ivory and slaves, reached Uganda; first visits by European explorers and Christian missionaries.

1885–87: Uganda Martyrs: Christians persecuted by Buganda ruler, Mwanga.

1890: Royal Charter granted to British East African Company, a trading company whose agent, Frederick Lugard, concluded treaties with local rulers, including the Buganda and the western states of Ankole and Toro.

1894: British protectorate established, with Buganda retaining some autonomy under its traditional prince (Kabaka) and other resistance being crushed.

1904: Cotton growing introduced by Buganda peasants.

1958: Internal self-government granted.

1962: Independence achieved from Britain, within Commonwealth, with Milton Obote of Uganda People's Congress (UPC) as prime minister.

1963: Proclaimed federal republic with King Mutesa II (of Buganda) as president and Obote as prime minister.

1966: King Mutesa, who opposed creation of a one-party state, ousted in coup led by Obote, who ended federal status and became executive president.

1969: All opposition parties banned after assassination attempt on Obote; key enterprises nationalized.

1971: Obote overthrown in army coup led by Maj-Gen Idi Amin Dada; constitution suspended and ruthlessly dictatorial regime established; nearly 49,000 Ugandan Asians expelled; over 300,000 opponents of regime killed.

UGANDA Small-scale coffee farmers in Uganda laying out their coffee beans to dry in front of their houses. *Ken Preston-Mafham/Premaphotos Wildlife*

1976: Relations with Kenya strained by Amin's claims to parts of Kenya.

1979: After annexing part of Tanzania, Amin forced to leave the country by opponents backed by Tanzanian troops. Provisional government set up.

1978–79: Fighting broke out against Tanzanian troops.

1980: Provisional government overthrown by army. Elections held and Milton Obote returned to power.

1985: After opposition by pro-Lule National Resistance Army (NRA), and indiscipline in army, Obote ousted by Gen Tito Okello; constitution suspended; power-sharing agreement entered into with NRA leader Yoweri Museveni.

1986: Museveni became president, heading broad-based coalition government.

1993: The King of Buganda was reinstated as formal monarch, in the person of Ronald Muwenda Mutebi II.

1996: A landslide victory was won by Museveni in the first direct presidential elections.

1997: Allied Democratic Forces (ADF) led uprisings by rebels.

1999: The leaders of Uganda and Sudan signed an agreement to bring an end to rebel wars across their mutual border by ceasing to support rebel factions in the other's country. President Museveni appointed Apolo Nsibambi as prime minister.

2000: Rebels attacked towns in northern Uganda and fought the Ugandan army along the border with Congo. A fire at the headquarters of the Restoration of the Ten Commandments of God cult in western Uganda killed up to 500 people. It was later discovered the cult leaders had engaged in mass murder. An outbreak of the ebola virus killed 160 people between September and December.

2001: President Museveni was re-elected, despite allegations of electoral fraud.

Ukraine

UKRAINE This stamp from the Ukraine celebrates the traditional harvest festival, and depicts the rural community gathering in the harvest. *Stanley Gibbons*

See also ▷Chernobyl; ▷Commonwealth of Independent States; ▷Crimea; ▷Union of Soviet Socialist Republics.

Ukraine country in eastern central Europe, bounded to the east by Russia, north by Belarus, south by Moldova, Romania, and the Black Sea, and west by Poland, the Slovak Republic, and Hungary.

NATIONAL NAME *Ukrayina/Ukraine*
AREA 603,700 sq km/233,088 sq mi
CAPITAL Kiev
MAJOR TOWNS/CITIES Kharkov, Donetsk, Dnipropetrovs'k, Lviv, Krivoy Rog, Zaporizhzhya, Odessa
PHYSICAL FEATURES Russian plain; Carpathian and Crimean Mountains; rivers: Dnieper (with the Dnieper dam 1932), Donetz, Bug

Government

HEAD OF STATE Leonid Kuchma from 1994
HEAD OF GOVERNMENT Viktor Yanukovych from 2002
POLITICAL SYSTEM emergent democracy
POLITICAL EXECUTIVE limited presidency
ADMINISTRATIVE DIVISIONS 24 provinces, one autonomous republic (Crimea), and two metropolitan areas (Kiev and Sevastopol)
ARMED FORCES 302,300 (2002 est)
CONSCRIPTION 18 months (army and air force) or two years (navy)
DEATH PENALTY abolished in 1999
DEFENCE SPEND (% GDP) 2.2 (2002 est)
EDUCATION SPEND (% GDP) 4.7 (2001 est)
HEALTH SPEND (% GDP) 4.1 (2000 est)

Economy and resources

CURRENCY hryvna
GPD (US$) 41.4 billion (2002 est)
REAL GDP GROWTH (% change on previous year) 9.1 (2001)
GNI (US$) 37.7 billion (2002 est)
GNI PER CAPITA (PPP) (US$) 4,650 (2002 est)
CONSUMER PRICE INFLATION 5% (2003 est)
UNEMPLOYMENT 3.9% (2001)
FOREIGN DEBT (US$) 7.04 billion (2001 est)
MAJOR TRADING PARTNERS Russia, Germany, Turkey, Turkmenistan, USA, Italy, China, Poland
RESOURCES coal, iron ore, crude oil, natural gas, salt, chemicals, brown coal, alabaster, gypsum, mercury, titanium
INDUSTRIES metallurgy, mechanical engineering, chemicals, machinery products
EXPORTS non-precious metals, machinery and equipment, food, beverages, agriculture products, coal, oil, various minerals. Principal market: Russia 21.5% (2001)

IMPORTS mineral fuels, machine-building components, chemicals and chemical products. Principal source: Russia 34.4% (2001)
ARABLE LAND 56.2% (2000 est)
AGRICULTURAL PRODUCTS wheat, buckwheat, sugar beet, potatoes, fruit and vegetables, sunflowers, cotton, flax, tobacco, hops; animal husbandry accounts for more than 50% of agricultural activity

Population and society

POPULATION 48,523,000 (2003 est)
POPULATION GROWTH RATE −0.6% (2000–15)
POPULATION DENSITY (per sq km) 80 (2003 est)
URBAN POPULATION (% of total) 68 (2003 est)
AGE DISTRIBUTION (% of total population) 0–14 17%, 15–59 62%, 60+ 21% (2002 est)
ETHNIC GROUPS 73% of the population is of Ukrainian descent; 22% ethnic Russian; 1% Jewish; 4% other races including Belorussian, Moldovan, Hungarian, Bulgarian, Polish and Crimean Tatar
LANGUAGE Ukrainian (a Slavonic language; official), Russian (also official in Crimea), other regional languages
RELIGION traditionally Ukrainian Orthodox; also Ukrainian Catholic; small Protestant, Jewish, and Muslim communities
EDUCATION (compulsory years) 8 (7–15 age limit)
LITERACY RATE 99% (men); 99% (women) (2003 est)
LABOUR FORCE 26.4% agriculture, 26.2% industry, 47.4% services (1999)
LIFE EXPECTANCY 65 (men); 75 (women) (2000–05)
CHILD MORTALITY RATE (under 5, per 1,000 live births) 20 (2001)
PHYSICIANS (per 1,000 people) 3 (1998 est)
HOSPITAL BEDS (per 1,000 people) 11.8 (1998 est)
TV SETS (per 1,000 people) 456 (2001 est)
RADIOS (per 1,000 people) 889 (2001 est)
INTERNET USERS (per 10,000 people) 199.5 (2002 est)
PERSONAL COMPUTER USERS (per 100 people) 1.9 (2002 est)

Chronology

9th century: Rus' people established state centred on Kiev and adopted Eastern Orthodox Christianity 988.

1199: Reunification of southern Rus' lands, after period of fragmentation, under Prince Daniel of Galicia-Volhynia.

13th century: Mongol-Tatar Golden Horde sacked Kiev and destroyed Rus' state.

14th century: Poland annexed Galicia; Lithuania absorbed Volhynia and expelled Tatars; Ukraine peasants became serfs of Polish and Lithuanian nobles.

1569: Poland and Lithuania formed single state; clergy of Ukraine formed Uniate Church, which recognized papal authority but retained Orthodox rites, to avoid Catholic persecution.

16th and 17th centuries: Runaway serfs known as Cossacks ('outlaws') formed autonomous community in eastern borderlands.

1648: Cossack revolt led by Gen Bogdan Khmelnitsky drove out Poles from central Ukraine; Khmelnitsky accepted Russian protectorate in 1654.

1660–90: 'Epoch of Ruins': Ukraine devastated by civil war and invasions by Russians, Poles, and Turks; Poland regained western Ukraine.

1687: Gen Ivan Mazepa entered into alliance with Sweden in effort to regain Cossack autonomy from Russia.

1709: Battle of Poltava: Russian victory over Swedes ended hopes of Cossack independence.

1772–95: Partition of Poland: Austria annexed Galicia, Russian annexations included Volhynia.

1846–47: Attempt to promote Ukrainian national culture through formation of Cyril and Methodius Society.

1899: Revolutionary Ukrainian Party founded.

1917: Revolutionary parliament (Rada), proclaimed Ukrainian autonomy within a federal Russia.

1918: Ukraine declared full independence; civil war ensued between Rada (backed by Germans) and Reds (backed by Russian Bolsheviks).

1919: Galicia united with Ukraine; conflict escalated between Ukrainian nationalists, Bolsheviks, anarchists, White Russians, and Poles.

1921: Treaty of Riga: Russia and Poland partitioned Ukraine.

1921–22: Several million people perished in famine.

1922: Ukrainian Soviet Socialist Republic (Ukrainian SSR) became part of Union of Soviet Socialist Republics (USSR).

1932–33: Enforced collectivization of agriculture caused another catastrophic famine with more than 7.5 million deaths.

1939: USSR annexed eastern Poland and added Galicia-Volhynia to Ukrainian SSR.

1940: USSR seized northern Bukhovina from Romania and added it to Ukrainian SSR.

1941–44: Germany occupied Ukraine; many Ukrainians collaborated; millions of Ukrainians and Ukrainian Jews were enslaved and exterminated by Nazis.

1945: USSR annexed Ruthenia from Czechoslovakia and added it to Ukrainian SSR, which became a nominal member of the United Nations (UN).

1946: Uniate Church forcibly merged with Russian Orthodox Church.

1954: Crimea transferred from Russian Federation to Ukrainian SSR.

1986: Major environmental disaster caused by explosion of nuclear reactor at Chernobyl, north of Kiev.

1989: Rukh (nationalist movement) established as political party; ban on Uniate Church lifted.

1990: Ukraine declared its sovereignty under President Leonid Kravchuk, leader of the CP.

1991: Ukraine declared its independence from USSR; President Kravchuk left the CP; Ukraine joined the newly formed Commonwealth of Independent States (CIS).

1992: Crimean sovereignty was declared but then rescinded.

1994: Election gains were made by radical nationalists in western Ukraine and by Russian unionists in eastern Ukraine; Leonid Kuchma succeeded Kravchuk as president.

1996: A new constitution replaced the Soviet system, making the presidency stronger; remaining nuclear warheads were returned to Russia for destruction; a new currency was introduced.

1997: New government appointments were made to speed economic reform. A treaty of friendship was signed with Russia, solving the issue of the Russian Black Sea fleet. A loan of $750 million from the International Monetary Fund (IMF) was approved.

1998: The communists won the largest number of seats in parliamentary elections, but fell short of an absolute majority. The value of the hryvnya fell by over 50% against the US dollar after the neighbouring Russian currency crisis. The government survived a no-confidence vote tabled by left-wing factions that opposed the government's economic program.

1999: Viktor A Yushchenko became prime minister.

2001: Protests in Kiev called for Kuchma's resignation on grounds of corruption and mismanagement.

Umayyad dynasty Arabian dynasty of the Islamic Empire who reigned as caliphs (civic and religious leaders of Islam) from 661 to 750, when they were overthrown by Abbasids. A member of the family, Abd al-Rahmam, escaped to Spain and in 756 assumed the title of Emir of Córdoba. His dynasty, which took the title of caliph in 929, ruled in Córdoba until the early 11th century.

Umberto two kings of Italy:

Umberto I (1844–1900) King of Italy from 1878, who joined the Triple Alliance 1882 with Germany and Austria-Hungary; his colonial ventures included the defeat at Ādwa, Abyssinia, 1896. He was assassinated by an anarchist.

Umberto II (1904–1983) King of Italy May–June 1946. When his father ▷Victor Emmanuel III abdicated in May 1946, he was proclaimed king, and ruled 9 May–13 June 1946. He was forced to abdicate as the monarchy's collusion in the rise of fascism made him highly unpopular, and a referendum decided in favour of a republic. He retired to Portugal, where he died.

umbilical cord connection between the ▷embryo and the ▷placenta of placental mammals. It has one vein and two arteries, transporting oxygen and nutrients to the developing young, and removing waste products. At birth, the connection between the young and the placenta is no longer necessary. The umbilical cord drops off or is severed, leaving a scar called the navel.

umbrella bird any of three species of bird of tropical South and Central America, family Cotingidae, order Passeriformes, about 45 cm/18 in long. The Amazonian species *Cephalopterus ornatus*, the **ornate umbrella bird**, has an inflatable wattle at the neck to amplify its humming call, and in display elevates a long crest (12 cm/4 in) lying above the bill so that it rises umbrella-like above the head. These features are less noticeable in the female, which is brownish, while the male is blue-black.

umbrella tree tree native to Queensland and the Northern Territory, Australia, with large shiny leaves each made up of leaflets arranged like an open hand, and small raspberrylike clusters of red flowers at the ends of branches. It is common as an indoor plant in many countries. (*Schefflera actinophylla*.)

Umbria mountainous region of Italy in the central Apennines, including the provinces of Perugia and Terni; area 8,500 sq km/3,281 sq mi; population (1992 est) 815,000. Its capital is ▷Perugia, and the River Tiber rises in the region. Industries include textiles, chemicals, and metalworking. Wine is produced (Orvieto), and tobacco, grain, and olives (Lake Trasimene) are grown. This is the home of the Umbrian school of artists, including Raphael.

UN abbreviation for ▷United Nations.

uncertainty principle (or **indeterminacy principle**) in quantum mechanics, the principle that it is impossible to know with unlimited accuracy the position and momentum of a particle. The principle arises because in order to locate a particle exactly, an observer must bounce light (in the form of a ▷photon) off the particle, which must alter its position in an unpredictable way.

It was established by German physicist Werner ▷Heisenberg, and gave a theoretical limit to the precision with which a particle's momentum and position can be measured simultaneously: the more accurately the one is determined, the more uncertainty there is in the other.

Uncle Sam nickname for the US government. It was coined during the War of 1812 by opponents of US policy. It was probably derived from the initials 'US' placed on government property.

unconformity surface of erosion or nondeposition eventually overlain by younger ▷sedimentary rock strata and preserved in the geologic record. A surface where the ▷beds above and below lie at different angles is called an **angular unconformity**. The boundary between older igneous or metamorphic rocks that are truncated by erosion and later covered by younger sedimentary rocks is called a **nonconformity**.

unconscious in psychoanalysis, a part of the personality of which the individual is unaware, and which contains impulses or urges that are held back, or repressed, from conscious awareness.

underground (US **subway**) rail service that runs underground. The first underground line in the world was in London, opened in 1863; it was essentially a roofed-in trench. The London Underground is still the longest underground system, with over 400 km/250 mi of routes. Many large cities throughout the world have similar systems, and Moscow's underground, the Metro, handles up to 6.5 million passengers a day.

Related Web site: Going Underground http://victorian.fortunecity.com/finsbury/254/

Underground Railroad in US history, a network established in the North before the American ▷Civil War to provide sanctuary and assistance for escaped black slaves. Safe houses, transport facilities, and 'conductors' existed to lead the slaves to safety in the North and Canada, although the number of fugitives who secured their freedom by these means is uncertain.

undernourishment condition that results from consuming too little food over a period of time. Like **malnutrition** – the result of a diet that is lacking in certain nutrients (such as protein or vitamins) – undernourishment is common in poor countries. Both lead to a reduction in mental and physical efficiency, a lowering of resistance to disease in general, and often to deficiency diseases such as beriberi or anaemia. In the Third World, lack of adequate food is a common cause of death.

unemployment lack of paid employment. The unemployed are usually defined as those out of work who are available for and actively seeking work. Unemployment is measured either as a total or as a percentage of those who are available for work, known as the working population, or labour force. Periods of widespread unemployment in Europe and the USA in the 20th century include 1929–1930s, and the years since the mid-1970s. According to a report released by the UN's International Labour Organization November 1995, nearly 1 billion people, about 30% of the global workforce, were out of work or underemployed. The reduction in job opportunities was attributed to lower growth rates in industrialized countries since 1973, and the failure of most developing nations to recover fully from the economic crisis of the early 1980s. The ILO contended that despite increasing worldwide competition, the 1996 jobless figures were neither politically nor socially sustainable. Unemployment in industrialized countries (the members of the ▷Organization for Economic Cooperation and Development (OECD)) in 1995 averaged 7.5%, and in the European Union (EU) 11.1%. Within the OECD group the country with the lowest percentage of unemployed in 1995 was Japan (3%) and the highest was Spain (22.6%).

UNESCO (acronym for United Nations Educational, Scientific, and Cultural Organization) specialized agency of the United Nations, established in 1946, to promote international cooperation in education, science, and culture, with its headquarters in Paris.

Related Web site: United Nations Educational, Scientific, and Cultural Organization http://www.unesco.org/

unfair dismissal sacking of an employee unfairly. Under the terms of the UK Employment Acts, this means the unreasonable dismissal of someone who has been in continuous employment for a period of two years; that is, dismissal on grounds not in accordance with the codes of disciplinary practice and procedures prepared by ▷ACAS. Dismissed employees may take their case to an industrial tribunal for adjudication.

ungulate general name for any hoofed mammal. Included are the odd-toed ungulates (perissodactyls) and the even-toed ungulates (artiodactyls), along with subungulates such as elephants.

Uniate Church any of the ▷Orthodox Churches that accept the Catholic faith and the supremacy of the pope and are in full communion with the Roman Catholic Church, but retain their own liturgy and separate organization.

> **Italo Calvino**
> Italian writer and critic
>
> *The unconscious is the ocean of the unsayable, of what has been expelled from the land of language, removed as a result of ancient prohibitions.*
>
> 'Cybernetics and Ghosts' lecture, Turin November 1969, published in *The Literature Machine*

UNICEF acronym for **United Nations International Children's Emergency Fund**, a specialized agency of the ▷United Nations.

unicellular organism animal or plant consisting of a single cell. Most are invisible without a microscope but a few, such as the giant ▷amoeba, may be visible to the naked eye. The main groups of unicellular organisms are bacteria, protozoa, unicellular algae, and unicellular fungi or yeasts. Some become disease-causing agents, ▷pathogens.

unicorn mythical animal referred to by classical writers, said to live in India and resembling a horse, but with one spiralled horn growing from the forehead.

unidentified flying object (UFO) any light or object seen in the sky whose immediate identity is not apparent. Despite unsubstantiated claims, there is no evidence that UFOs are alien spacecraft. On investigation, the vast majority of sightings turn out to have been of natural or identifiable objects, notably bright stars and planets, meteors, aircraft, and satellites, or to have been perpetrated by pranksters. The term **flying saucer** was coined in 1947.

Related Web sites: Bufora Online (UFOs) http://www.bufora.org.uk/
SETI Institute http://www.seti-inst.edu/

Unification Church (or **Moonies**) church founded in Korea 1954 by the Reverend Sun Myung ▷Moon. The number of members (often called 'moonies') is about 200,000 worldwide. The theology unites Christian and Taoist ideas and is based on Moon's book *Divine Principle*, which teaches that the original purpose of creation was to set up a perfect family, in a perfect relationship with God.

Related Web site: Unification Church http://www.religioustolerance.org/unificat.htm

unified field theory in physics, the theory that attempts to explain the four fundamental forces (strong nuclear, weak nuclear, electromagnetic, and gravity) in terms of a single unified force (see ▷particle physics).

Research was begun by Albert Einstein, and by 1971 a theory developed by US physicists Steven Weinberg and Sheldon Glashow, Pakistani physicist Abdus Salam, and others, had demonstrated the link between the weak and electromagnetic forces. The next stage is to develop a theory (called the ▷grand unified theory) that combines the strong nuclear force with the electroweak force. The final stage will be to incorporate gravity into the scheme. Work on the ▷superstring theory indicates that this may be the ultimate 'theory of everything'.

uniformitarianism in geology, the principle that processes that can be seen to occur on the Earth's surface today are the same as those that have occurred throughout geological time. For example, desert sandstones containing sand-dune structures must have been formed under conditions similar to those present in deserts today. The principle was formulated by Scottish geologists James ▷Hutton and expounded by Charles ▷Lyell.

unilateralism in politics, support for **unilateral nuclear disarmament**: scrapping a country's nuclear weapons without waiting for other countries to agree to do so at the same time.

Union, Acts of act of Parliament of 1707 that brought about the union of England and Scotland; that of 1801 united England and Ireland.

The 1707 act, which abolished the Scottish parliament, decreed that 16 elected peers and 45 members of the House of Commons should represent Scotland at Westminster, but that the Scottish legal system and Presbyterian Church should remain separate. The 1801 act amalgamated the Irish and British parliaments, securing for Ireland a representation of 32 peers and 100 members. Irish representation was later increased to 103; but, since the creation of the independent Irish Free State in 1922 (now the Republic of Ireland), only the British province of Northern Ireland returns members to Westminster.

Related Web sites: A Brief History Of Wales: The Act Of Union http://britannia.com/wales/whist6.html
Queen Anne And The 1707 Act Of Union http://www.highlanderweb.co.uk/wallace/anne.htm

union flag British national flag. It is popularly called the **Union Jack**, although, strictly speaking, this applies only when it is flown on the jackstaff of a warship.

Union Movement British political group. Founded as the **New Party** by Oswald ▷Mosley and a number of Labour members of Parliament in 1931, it developed into the **British Union of Fascists** in 1932. In 1940 the organization was declared illegal and its leaders interned, but it was revived as the Union Movement in 1948, characterized by racist doctrines including anti-Semitism.

An attempt by the 'blackshirts' to march through the East End of London in 1936 led to prohibition of the wearing of such political uniforms.

Union of Soviet Socialist Republics (USSR) former country in northern Asia and Eastern Europe that reverted to independent states in 1991; see ▷Armenia, ▷Azerbaijan, ▷Belarus, ▷Estonia, ▷Georgia, ▷Kazakhstan, ▷Kyrgyzstan, ▷Latvia, ▷Lithuania, ▷Moldova, ▷Russian Federation, ▷Tajikistan, ▷Turkmenistan, ▷Ukraine, and ▷Uzbekistan.

History Following the Bolshevik (communist) October Revolution of 1917, and the victory of the Bolsheviks in the subsequent civil war, the Union of Soviet Socialist Republics was formed in 1922, and a constitution adopted in 1923.

The economic policy of war communism had involved the seizure of private businesses, the nationalization of industry, and the appropriation of food supplies. Disaffection among those who had supported the communists during the civil war found expression in strikes and rebellions, such as the Kronstadt uprising. In response ▷Lenin proclaimed the New Economic Policy (NEP) in 1921, which made concessions to peasants, private enterprise, and consumers.

Stalin Following Lenin's death in 1924 and having ousted his opponents, Stalin adopted the policy of 'socialism in one country', turning his back on Trotsky's ideals of exporting the revolution abroad. The country was transformed by the forced collectivization of agriculture and by industrial growth. However, millions died in the Ukraine and Kazakhstan famine of 1932–34.

Stalin also launched the so-called cultural revolution. Political purges which had begun during the 1920s grew in scale after 1934,

The successor republics to the Soviet Union

from which time Stalin ruled as unlimited dictator. Opposition among his own followers precipitated the universal terror of the Great Purge of 1937–38, which marked the culmination of the communist totalitarian dictatorship. In all, between 1934 and 1938, some 10 million political opponents, Communist Party members, government officials, army officers, and members of minority nationalities were executed or deported to labour camps.

In 1939 Stalin unexpectedly concluded a nonaggression pact with Hitler (the Ribbentrop–Molotov pact). This enabled the latter to attack Poland, which led to the outbreak of World War II.

The Soviet Union started the Russo–Finnish War by attacking Finland in December 1939 (for which it was branded as an aggressor and expelled from the League of Nations), but the determined resistance of the Finns compelled Stalin to give up his intention of annexing the whole of Finland.

The USSR in World War II Despite the nonaggression pact, Hitler invaded the USSR in June 1941. Britain and the USA immediately offered assistance to the USSR, which joined the anti-Hitler Allies.

The German armies rapidly scored great successes in the USSR, whose army had been weakened by the purging of the officer corps in 1937–38. The country was at first deeply divided in its attitude to the war: many saw in the USSR's defeat a means of liberation from communism, and were even prepared to fight on the side of the invaders. However the brutality of German policy in the occupied areas produced a swing in popular opinion against the Germans.

The war was now fought by the USSR as a second 'patriotic war' (the first had been against Napoleon in 1812). After the Allied victory in Europe the Soviet Union took part in the last stage of the war against Japan.

The Cold War As a result of World War II the USSR not only retained all the territory annexed during the period of the Stalin–Hitler pact, but acquired new territories, including much of East Prussia from Germany, and the Kuril Islands and the whole of Sakhalin from Japan. The pressure of the occupying Red Army facilitated the establishment of communist regimes in the countries of central, eastern, and southeast Europe, Manchuria, and North Korea.

This was a clear violation of the rights of self-determination that had been agreed to by the Allies at the Yalta and Potsdam Conferences, and under the Atlantic Charter and the post-war peace treaties. However, from the Soviet point of view, having suffered 20 million casualties in World War II, the establishment of buffer states between itself and its potential enemies appeared to be a strategic necessity.

The creation of Soviet-sponsored satellite states – together with Stalin's intransigence towards the Western Allies and apparently aggressive designs on Turkey and Iran – split the wartime Allies and led to the formation of two great ideological power blocs, the communist bloc led by the USSR and the capitalist bloc led by the USA. At this time the USSR was also providing indirect support to

anticolonial movements in southeast Asia. All this marked the beginning of the Cold War, which was to continue until 1990.

Internally the post-war period was characterized by the suppression of the comparative freedom of the war years and the restoration of conformity, particularly in the cultural field. This period was marked by mass deportations, xenophobia, and anti-Semitism.

De-Stalinization When Stalin died in 1953 he was succeeded by the collective leadership of his closest collaborators. De-Stalinization started immediately after Stalin's death out of the necessity for his successors to appear different from the late despot. The main policy was the scope and pace of change. It proceeded intermittently under the pressure of reviving public opinion. Many propaganda fictions of the Stalin era were exposed and dropped, including that of Stalin himself as the wise and benevolent leader.

Unrest in the Soviet satellite states culminated in the Hungarian revolution of 1956, which was suppressed by Soviet forces. In the USSR itself there had been strikes and uprisings in the main labour camp areas in 1953–55, and a radical reformist opposition arose among the intelligentsia (led by the Moscow writers), as did a revolutionary trend among students. ▷Khrushchev and his successors in the Central Committee of the Communist Party were torn between tightening the screws and slowing down the process of de-Stalinization, and the necessity of initiating more reforms and making more concessions in response to pressure from below.

Externally, the tentative Soviet policy was to relax tension with the USA and the West in the interests of a stable peace, a halt to the dangerous inflation of the military budget, and economic cooperation in the interests of a peaceful, if not ideological coexistence. This foreign policy was, however, conditional on both the internal and the external political situations. Thus the stabilized internal position of 1959 enabled Khrushchev to ease the pressure on West Berlin that had been exerted in the previous year. The renewal of détente policy, coupled with the halting of nuclear aid to China in 1958, led to the eruption of the Sino-Soviet split, which became public and increasingly bitter from 1961.

Pressure on West Berlin was renewed in 1960–61 after the shooting down of a US U-2 reconnaissance plane over Soviet territory. The building of the Berlin Wall in 1961 further increased East–West tension.

When the reckless Soviet attempt of 1962 to install missiles in Cuba failed, bringing the world to the brink of nuclear war, Khrushchev renewed his policy of détente with the West and in 1963 signed a partial nuclear test-ban treaty with the USA and Britain. At the same time, exasperated by trying to compromise with the Chinese, he virtually courted a final split with them.

Brezhnev Khrushchev's handling of foreign affairs, together with a series of poor harvests in overcropped Kazakhstan, were among the reasons for the bloodless coup mounted by his colleagues against Khrushchev in October 1964. The two key figures were Leonid Brezhnev, who became the first secretary of the party (1964–82),

and Alexei Kosygin, who became prime minister (1964–80). The new collective leadership had a strongly conservative bent, and immediately abandoned Khrushchev's reforms. Priority was now given to the expansion and modernization of the Soviet armed forces, including the creation of a naval force with global reach. This, coupled with the Warsaw Pact invasion of Czechoslovakia in 1968 (see ▷Prague Spring), resulted in a renewal of the Cold War 1964–70. In defence of the invasion of Czechoslovakia, the Brezhnev Doctrine was enunciated, which proclaimed the right of the USSR to intervene to 'preserve socialism' in Eastern Europe. During the later 1960s Leonid Brezhnev emerged as the dominant figure. He governed in a cautious and consensual manner and became state president in May 1977. Brezhnev began to meet frequently with Western leaders in the 1970s. Détente was sought with the USA (in spite of the latter's involvement in Vietnam), and attempts were made to forge new links with China, with whom a number of trade agreements were signed.

The landmarks of this period were the SALT I and SALT II Soviet–US arms-limitation agreements of 1972 and 1979 (see ▷Strategic Arms Limitation Talks) and the Helsinki Accord of 1975, which brought Western recognition of the post-war division of Eastern Europe. Success in a proposed Soviet–US trade agreement to last for the rest of the century eluded the two parties to it, but US withdrawal from Vietnam in 1973 removed a major source of friction. A treaty between the USSR and the USA controlling underground nuclear explosions for non-military purposes was signed in May 1976, and an agreement was signed in May 1977 for cooperation between the USA and the USSR on the exploitation and use of outer space for peaceful purposes. This replaced an earlier (1972) agreement.

Another cultural thaw within the USSR resulted in the emergence of a vocal dissident movement. The political and military influence of the USSR was extended into Africa with the establishment of new communist governments in Mozambique (1974), Angola and Ethiopia (1975), and South Yemen (1978). The détente era was brought to an end by the Soviet invasion of Afghanistan in December 1979 and the Polish crisis of 1980–81. The final years of the Brezhnev administration were ones of hardening policy, mounting corruption, and economic stagnation.

Andropov and Chernenko Yuri Andropov, the former KGB chief, was elected CPSU leader on Brezhnev's death in November 1982 and began energetically to introduce a series of radical economic reforms. He launched a campaign against corrupt and complacent party and state bureaucrats. These measures had a perceptible impact on the Soviet economy during 1983, but when Andropov died in February 1984 he was succeeded by the cautious Chernenko. Chernenko held power as a stop-gap leader for 13 months, his sole initiative being a renewed search for détente with the USA that was rejected by the hardline Reagan administration.

Gorbachev's 'market socialism' On Chernenko's death in March 1985, power was transferred to a new generation led by Mikhail ▷Gorbachev who introduced a number of reforms. He began to free farmers and factory managers from bureaucratic interference and to increase material incentives in a 'market socialist' manner. He restructured party and state bureaucracies and replaced cautious Brezhnevites with ambitious technocrats. Gorbachev made explicit his renunciation of the 'Brezhnev doctrine' in 1989 and his commitment to *glasnost* ('openness').

These changes were not lost on the opposition leaders in the Baltic republics or on communist deputies in the newly assertive Soviet Parliament. Lithuania declared it would permit free elections, then the Lithuanian Communist Party declared its independence from Moscow. By January 1990 Gorbachev was faced with growing calls for secession from the Soviet Union, and was forced to reconsider his earlier opposition to a multiparty system in the USSR itself. He was also provoked to declare a state of emergency and despatch troops to quell warfare between Armenians and Azeris in the enclave of Nagorno-Karabakh in Azerbaijan.

Détente renewed Working with Edvard Shevardnadze, the foreign minister, Gorbachev made skilful use of the foreign media to put the case against the US Strategic Defense Initiative and nuclear testing. He met US president Reagan in Geneva and Reykjavik in November 1985 and October 1986, and, at the Washington summit of December 1987, he concluded a treaty designed to eliminate medium-range intermediate nuclear forces (INF) from European soil. This treaty was ratified at the Moscow summit of May–June 1988. As part of the new détente initiative, the USSR also withdrew all its troops from Afghanistan in February 1989 and made broad cutbacks in the size of its conventional forces in 1989–90.

Glasnost and perestroika Gorbachev pressed for an acceleration (*uskoreniye*) of his domestic, economic, and political programme of restructuring (*perestroika*) from 1987, but faced growing opposition both from conservatives grouped around Ligachev and radicals led by Boris Yeltsin. Gorbachev's *glasnost* policy helped fan growing nationalist demands for secession among the republics of the Baltic and Transcaucasia. A new 'super-legislature', the Congress of the USSR People's Deputies (CUPD), was created, from which a full-time working parliament was subsequently to be elected, headed by a state president with increased powers.

The members of this CUPD were to be chosen in competition with one another. The authority of the local soviets was enhanced and their structures made more democratic, while, in the economic sphere, it was agreed to reintroduce private leasehold farming, reform the price system, and allow part-time private enterprise in the service and small-scale industry sectors.

'Socialist pluralism' The June 1988 reforms constituted the most fundamental reordering of the Soviet policy since the 'Stalinist departure' of 1928, entailing the creation of a new type of 'socialist democracy', as well as a new mixed economic system. In May 1989, the CUPD elected Gorbachev as its chair, and thus as state president. Gorbachev sanctioned the establishment of non-communist and 'reform communist' governments elsewhere in Eastern Europe. This led to the ruling regimes of Poland, Czechoslovakia, and Romania being overthrown in a wave of 'people's power'. Responding to these developments in February 1990, the CPSU Central Committee agreed to create a new directly elected state executive presidency on US and French models. In March 1990, the Soviet Parliament authorized private ownership of the means of production, forbidden since the 1920s. Further constitutional amendments made in 1990 supported the right of self-determination, including secession of republics, and ended the CPSU's monopoly of power.

The end of Cold War In their December 1989 summit meeting in Malta, Gorbachev and US president Bush declared an end to the Cold War, opening the possibility of most-favoured-nation trading status with the USA, membership of General Agreement on Tariffs and Trade (GATT), and an influx of Western investment.

Moves towards independence in the republics Throughout 1990 the political and economic situation deteriorated. In pluralist elections held at local and republic levels, anticommunist, nationalist, and radical deputies polled strongly, particularly in the Baltic republics and cities. Their new governments issued declarations of republican sovereignty and, in the case of the Baltics, independence. These Moscow refused to recognize, and imposed a temporary economic blockade on Lithuania. As the year progressed, a 'war of laws' developed between the centre and the republics, who kept back funds (leading to a worsening federal budget deficit), and the system of central economic planning and resource distribution began to break down. As a consequence, with crime and labour unrest also increasing, the USSR's national income fell by at least 4% during 1990 and was to decline by a further 15% during 1991. Indeed, despite a bumper, but ill-collected, harvest, mounting food shortages led to rationing and an emergency international airlift of food aid during the winter of 1990–91.

The break-up of the CPSU The CPSU also began to fracture during 1990 as a result of nationalist challenges within the republics and divisions among conservatives (grouped in the Soyuz and Communists for Russia bodies), liberals (Communists for Democracy), and radicals (Democratic Platform) over the direction and pace of economic and political reform. A split was formalized at the 28th CPSU Congress in July 1990, when Boris Yeltsin, the new indirectly elected president of the RSFSR, and Gavriil Popov and Anatoly Sobchak, radical mayors of Moscow and Leningrad (St Petersburg), resigned their party memberships. Earlier, in the RSFSR, a new Russian Communist Party had been formed. In December 1990, concerned at the gathering pace of economic and political disintegration and ethnic strife, Gorbachev persuaded the Soviet parliament to vote him increased emergency presidential powers and approve a new federalized political structure.

The proposed new Union Treaty In April 1991, a pact aimed at achieving stable relations between the federal and republic governments and concerned with economic reform (price liberalization, progressive privatization, and the control of political strikes) was signed by the presidents of nine republics; the Baltic states, Armenia, Georgia, and Moldova refused to sign. Two months later, the draft of a new Union Treaty, entailing a much greater devolution of authority and the establishment of a new two-chamber federal legislature and a directly elected executive president, was also approved by nine republics.

In July 1991, Gorbachev's standing was further enhanced by his attendance, as an invited guest, at the Group of Seven (G7) summit of the leaders of the chief industrialized Western countries, held in London, and the signing, in Moscow, of a Strategic Arms Reduction Treaty (START), to reduce the number of US and Soviet long-range nuclear missiles. At home, however, Boris Yeltsin, who was popularly elected as the RSFR's president in June 1991, pressed for even greater reform and in July 1991 Communist Party cells were banned from operating in factories, farms, and government offices in the Russian Republic. In the same month a Democratic Reform Movement was formed by Edvard Shevardnadze, Alexander Yakovlev, and the mayors of Moscow and Leningrad, Anatoly Sobchak and Gavriil Popov.

The abortive anti-Gorbachev coup These liberal–radical initiatives raised disquiet among CPSU conservatives and in June 1991 Prime Minister Pavlov unsuccessfully attempted to persuade the Soviet parliament to vote him extra powers. Two months later, on Monday 19 August 1991, a day before the new Union Treaty was to be signed, an attempted coup was launched by a reactionary alliance of leaders of the Communist Party, the KGB, and the armed forces. It was declared in the early hours of the morning that President Gorbachev was ill and that Vice-President Gennady Yanayev would take over as president, as part of an eight-person emergency committee. (*Continued on p. 982*)

The committee assumed control over radio and television, banned demonstrations and all but eight newspapers, imposed a curfew, and sent tanks into Moscow. They failed, however, to arrest the Russian president Boris Yeltsin, who defiantly stood out as head of a democratic 'opposition state' based at the Russian parliament. Yeltsin called for a general strike and the reinstatement of President Gorbachev. Having failed to wrest control of the parliament and win either international or unionwide acknowledgement of the change of regime, and having endured large demonstrations of protest, the coup disintegrated. The leaders of the coup were arrested and President Gorbachev was reinstated. There were 15 fatalities during the crisis.

The aftermath of the coup In the wake of the failed coup, established communist structures, as well as the Soviet Union itself, rapidly disintegrated, faced by a popular backlash. Forced by pressure exerted by the public and by Boris Yeltsin, Gorbachev instituted a succession of far-reaching reforms, which effectively sounded the death knell of Soviet communism and resulted in the fracturing of the union and its subsequent refounding on a much changed and truncated basis.

The republics declare independence The attempted coup also speeded up dissolution of the Soviet Union. During the coup, when Red Army tanks were sent into their capitals with orders to seize radio and television stations, the Estonian and Latvian parliaments followed the earlier example of Lithuania and declared independence. After the coup the largely conservative-communist controlled republics of Azerbaijan, Belarus, and Uzbekistan, as well as the key republic of Ukraine, also joined the Baltic states, Georgia, Moldova, and Armenia in declaring their independence. Their governments acted partly in the hope of shoring up their authority and privileges and partly because they feared Russian domination of the existing USSR and possible future territorial disputes.

New Union Treaty signed At an emergency session of the Congress of People's Deputies, the Soviet Union was partially salvaged through the creation of a new loose confederation, or 'Union of Sovereign States', though with the armed forces retained under a single military command. Ten republics – the three Baltic states, Georgia, and Moldova being the exceptions – declared a willingness to sign this agreement.

The Congress also voted on 5 September 1991 to establish a new system of government in which it would be abolished and its powers would be assumed by a revamped, two-chamber supreme soviet. It also acknowledged the rights of republics to secede, opening the way for President Gorbachev to recognize formally the independence of the Baltic states by decree (6 September 1991).

Decentralization and new realities The possibility of forging a new, decentralized union receded as 1991 progressed. Concerned at the accumulation of political and economic authority by Russia, several of the republics began to seek full independence. Participation in the new supreme soviet and state council was patchy, their gatherings attracting members from, at most, ten republics. Although a declaration of intent to maintain a 'common economic zone' of interrepublican free trade and to uphold existing factory ties was initialled in October 1991, along with a civic and interethnic accord, the republics proved unable to agree on specific details of a proposed new economic and political union.

As a consequence, President Gorbachev occupied the position of a figurehead leader, possessing little real authority and the pre-eminent leader in the new USSR, governing significantly from the former office of the CPSU Politburo, was Russia's president, Boris Yeltsin. In November 1991, the Russian Republic took over control of the Soviet money supply and exchange rate, and began implementing a market-centred economic reform programme. On 14 November preliminary agreement was reached on the formation of a new 'Union of Sovereign States', but in a subsequent meeting on 25 November the republican delegations that attended refused to initial the treaty.

The CIS replaces the USSR The growing power of the individual republics became apparent in late November when the Group of Seven (G7) industrial countries reached a Soviet debt-deferral agreement with the USSR and included eight of the republics as signatories. On 8 December 1991 the most powerful of the republics – Russia, Belarus, and Ukraine – agreed to form the Commonwealth of Independent States (CIS), a development denounced by Gorbachev. By mid-December, the five Central Asian republics (Kazakhstan, Kyrgyzstan, Tajikistan, Turkmenistan, and Uzbekistan) had announced that they would join the CIS, and Gorbachev had agreed on a transfer of power from the centralized government to the CIS. The remaining republics (Armenia, Azerbaijan, and Moldova) except Georgia, torn by civil war, joined the others in signing agreements on 21 December to establish the commonwealth, formally designated an alliance of independent states. The formal dissolution of the USSR came on 25 December 1991 when Gorbachev resigned as president.

Related Web site: Internal Workings of the Soviet System
http://sunsite.unc.edu/expo/soviet.exhibit/intro1.html

UNISON Britain's largest trade union with 1,368,796 members (1998): 966,370 female, and 402,426 male. It was formed on 1 July 1993 by the merging of the National Union of Public Employees (NUPE), the Confederation of Health Service Employees, and the National Local Government Officers Association (NALGO).

unit standard quantity in relation to which other quantities are measured. There have been many systems of units. Some ancient units, such as the day, the foot, and the pound, are still in use. ▷SI units, the latest version of the metric system, are widely used in science.

UNITA acronym for **Uniao Nacional para a Independencia Total de Angola** (National Union for the Total Independence of Angola), Angolan nationalist movement founded by Jonas ▷Savimbi in 1966. Backed by South Africa, UNITA continued to wage guerrilla warfare against the ruling People's Movement for the Liberation of Angola (MPLA) after the latter gained control of the country in 1976. A peace agreement was signed in May 1991, but fighting recommenced in September 1992, after Savimbi disputed an election victory for the ruling party, and escalated into a bloody civil war in 1993. A peace agreement was signed in 1994. Savimbi later turned down the vice-presidency in a coalition government. In 1998 UNITA was demilitarized and formally legalized.

Unitarianism a Christian denomination that rejects the orthodox doctrine of the Trinity, asserts the fatherhood of God and the brotherhood of humanity, and gives a pre-eminent position to Jesus as a religious teacher, while denying his divinity.

unitary authority administrative unit of Great Britain. Since 1996 the two-tier structure of local government has ceased to exist in Scotland and Wales, and in some parts of England, and has been replaced by unitary authorities, responsible for all local government services.

United Arab Emirates see country box.

United Arab Republic union formed in 1958, broken in 1961, between ▷Egypt and ▷Syria. Egypt continued to use the name after the break up until 1971.

United Irishmen society formed in 1791 by Wolfe ▷Tone to campaign for parliamentary reform in Ireland. It later became a secret revolutionary group.

United Kingdom (UK) see country box.

United Nations (UN) association of states for international peace, security, and cooperation, with its headquarters in New York. The UN was established in 1945 by 51 states as a successor to the ▷League of Nations, and has played a role in many areas, such as refugees, development assistance, disaster relief, cultural cooperation, and peacekeeping. Its membership in 1996 stood at 185 states, and the total proposed budget for 1995–96 (raised by the member states) was $2,600 million supporting more than 50,000 staff. Kofi Annan became secretary general in 1997 and in January 1998 Louise Frechette was elected its first deputy secretary general. There are six official working languages: English, French, Russian,

Spanish, Chinese, and Arabic. The name 'United Nations' was coined by the US president Franklin D Roosevelt.

The principal institutions are the General Assembly, the Security Council, the Economic and Social Council, the Trusteeship Council, all based in New York; and the International Court of Justice in The Hague, Netherlands. At a July 1998 UN conference in Rome, attended by 160 countries, a treaty was agreed to set up a permanent international criminal court to try individuals accused of war crimes, genocide, and crimes against humanity.

The UN operates many specialized agencies, involved either in promoting communication between states (such as the International Telecommunication Union, ITU), or concerned with welfare of states, such as the World Health Organization (WHO), the UN Educational, Scientific and Cultural Organization (UNESCO), and the International Bank for Reconstruction and Development (World Bank). Much of the work of the specialized

welfare agencies concerns the developing countries, and consists mainly of research and field work. However, they also provide international standards relevant to all countries in their respective fields. Though autonomous, the specialized agencies are related to the UN by special arrangements and work with the UN and each other through the coordinating machinery of the Economic and Social Council. In its peacekeeping role, acting in pursuance of Security Council resolutions, the UN has had mixed success. The number of peacekeeping operations increased from 1 between 1975–85 to 25 between 1985–95; in 1995 its 65,000 peacekeepers cost a total of $2 billion. The UN has always suffered from a lack of adequate and independent funds and forces. In 1996, owed $3 billion by its members (two-thirds by the USA and Russia), the cash-strapped UN was forced to slash many programmes and cut staff by 10%; in the same year, UN forces were largely replaced by NATO units. (*continued on p. 982*)

UNITED NATIONS United Nations (UN) Headquarters in Geneva, Switzerland. *Image Bank*

United Arab Emirates

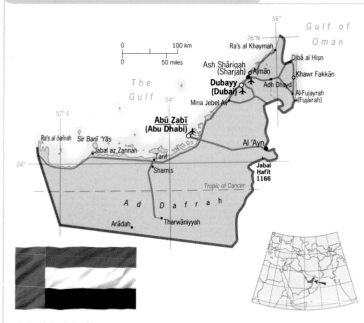

UNITED ARAB EMIRATES A clothing market in Abu Dhabi, capital of the United Arab Emirates. While traditional Arab dress is still worn, Western clothes are eagerly bought by the younger generation, especially in the city. *Corel*

United Arab Emirates (formerly Trucial States, until 1968), Federation of Arab Emirates (with Bahrain and Qatar) (1968–71) federation in southwest Asia, on the Arabian Gulf, bounded northwest by Qatar, southwest by Saudi Arabia, and southeast by Oman.

NATIONAL NAME *Dawlat Imarat al-'Arabiyya al Muttahida/State of the Arab Emirates* (UAE)
AREA 83,657 sq km/32,299 sq mi
CAPITAL Abu Dhabi
MAJOR TOWNS/CITIES Dubai, Sharjah, Ras al Khaimah, Ajman, Al 'Ayn
MAJOR PORTS Dubai
PHYSICAL FEATURES desert and flat coastal plain; mountains in east

Government

HEAD OF STATE Sheikh Zayed bin Sultan al-Nahayan of Abu Dhabi from 1971
HEAD OF GOVERNMENT Sheikh Maktum bin Rashid al-Maktum of Dubai from 1990
SUPREME COUNCIL OF RULERS
Abu Dhabi Sheikh Zayed bin Sultan al-Nahayan, president (1966); *Ajman* Sheikh Humaid bin Rashid al-Nuami (1981); *Dubai* Sheikh Maktoum bin Rashid al-Maktoum (1990); *Fujairah* Sheikh Hamad bin Muhammad al-Sharqi (1974); *Ras al Khaimah* Sheikh Saqr bin Muhammad al-Quasimi (1948); *Sharjah* Sheikh Sultan bin Muhammad al-Quasimi (1972); *Umm al Qaiwain* Sheikh Rashid bin Ahmad al-Mu'alla (1981)
POLITICAL SYSTEM absolutist
POLITICAL EXECUTIVE absolute
ADMINISTRATIVE DIVISIONS seven emirates
ARMED FORCES 41,500 (2002 est)
DEATH PENALTY retained and used for ordinary crimes

Economy and resources

CURRENCY UAE dirham
GPD (US$) 67.4 billion (2002 est)
REAL GDP GROWTH (% change on previous year) 1.3 (2001)
GNI (US$) 65 billion (2001)
GNI PER CAPITA (PPP) (US$) 20,620 (2001)
CONSUMER PRICE INFLATION 2.9% (2003 est)
FOREIGN DEBT (US$) 17.8 billion (2001 est)
MAJOR TRADING PARTNERS Japan, USA, UK, India, Singapore, South Korea, Italy
RESOURCES petroleum and natural gas
INDUSTRIES petroleum production and refining, gas handling, petrochemicals and other petroleum products, aluminium products, cable, cement, chemicals, fertilizers, rolled steel, plastics, tools, clothing
EXPORTS crude petroleum, natural gas, re-exports (mainly machinery and transport equipment). Principal market: Japan 31.1% (2001)
IMPORTS machinery and transport equipment, food and live animals, consumer goods, fuels and lubricants, chemicals, basic manufactures. Principal source: Japan 6.9% (2001)
ARABLE LAND 0.7% (2000 est)
AGRICULTURAL PRODUCTS dates, tomatoes, aubergines, other vegetables and fruits; livestock rearing; fishing

Population and society

POPULATION 2,995,000 (2003 est)
POPULATION GROWTH RATE 1.8% (2000–15)
POPULATION DENSITY (per sq km) 36 (2003 est)
URBAN POPULATION (% of total) 88 (2003 est)
AGE DISTRIBUTION (% of total population) 0–14 25%, 15–59 69%, 60+ 6% (2002 est)
ETHNIC GROUPS 75% non-Arab immigrants, mainly Iranians, Indians, and Pakistanis; about 25% Arabs (UAE nationals)
LANGUAGE Arabic (official), Farsi, Hindi, Urdu, English
RELIGION Muslim 96% (of which 80% Sunni); Christian, Hindu
EDUCATION (compulsory years) 6
LITERACY RATE 76% (men); 81% (women) (2003 est)

Chronology

7th century AD: Islam introduced.

early 16th century: Portuguese established trading contacts with Persian Gulf states.

18th century: Rise of trade and seafaring among Qawasim and Bani Yas, respectively in Ras al Khaimah and Sharjah in north and Abu Dhabi and Dubai in desert of south. Emirates' current ruling families are descended from these peoples.

early 19th century: Britain signed treaties ('truces') with local rulers, ensuring that British shipping through the Gulf was free from 'pirate' attacks and bringing Emirates under British protection.

1892: Trucial Sheiks signed Exclusive Agreements with Britain, agreeing not to cede, sell, or mortgage territory to another power.

1952: Trucial Council established by seven sheikdoms of Abu Dhabi, Ajman, Dubai, Fujairah, Ras al Khaimah, Sharjah, and Umm al Qawain, with a view to later forming a federation.

1958: Large-scale exploitation of oil reserves led to rapid economic progress.

1968: Britain's announcement that it would remove its forces from the Persian Gulf by 1971 led to an abortive attempt to arrange federation between seven Trucial States and Bahrain and Qatar.

LABOUR FORCE 7.6% agriculture, 34.5% industry, 57.9% services (1997); 91% of workforce were non-UAE nationals (2001)
LIFE EXPECTANCY 73 (men); 77 (women) (2000–05)
CHILD MORTALITY RATE (under 5, per 1,000 live births) 9 (2001)
PHYSICIANS (per 1,000 people) 1.8 (1999 est)
HOSPITAL BEDS (per 1,000 people) 2.6 (1999 est)
TV SETS (per 1,000 people) 252 (2001 est)
RADIOS (per 1,000 people) 345 (1998)
INTERNET USERS (per 10,000 people) 3,673.8 (2002 est)
PERSONAL COMPUTER USERS (per 100 people) 14.1 (2002 est)

See also ▷Abu Dhabi; ▷Arabia.

1971: Bahrain and Qatar ceded from the Federation of Arab Emirates, which was dissolved. Six Trucial States formed the United Arab Emirates, with the ruler of Abu Dhabi, Sheikh Zayed, as president. A provisional constitution was adopted. The UAE joined the Arab League and the United Nations (UN).

1972: Seventh state, Ras al Khaimah, joined the federation.

1976: Sheikh Zayed threatened to relinquish presidency unless progress towards centralization became more rapid.

1985: Diplomatic and economic links with the Soviet Union and China were established.

1987: Diplomatic relations with Egypt were restored.

1990: Sheikh Maktum bin Rashid al-Maktum of Dubai was appointed prime minister.

1990–91: UAE opposed the Iraqi invasion of Kuwait, and UAE troops fought as part of the UN coalition.

1991: The Bank of Commerce and Credit International (BCCI), partly owned and controlled by Abu Dhabi's ruler Zayed bin Sultan al-Nahayan, collapsed at a cost to the UAE of $10 billion.

1992: There was a border dispute with Iran.

1994: Abu Dhabi agreed to pay BCCI creditors $1.8 billion.

United Kingdom

UNITED KINGDOM St Paul's Cathedral, London, England. Incredibly, the building survived a blitz of incendiary bombs during World War II. *Corel*

United Kingdom country in northwest Europe off the coast of France, consisting of England, Scotland, Wales, and Northern Ireland.

NATIONAL NAME *United Kingdom of Great Britain and Northern Ireland* (UK)
AREA 244,100 sq km/94,247 sq mi
CAPITAL London
MAJOR TOWNS/CITIES Birmingham, Glasgow, Leeds, Sheffield, Liverpool, Manchester, Edinburgh, Bradford, Bristol, Coventry, Belfast, Cardiff
MAJOR PORTS London, Grimsby, Southampton, Liverpool
PHYSICAL FEATURES became separated from European continent in about 6000 BC; rolling landscape, increasingly mountainous towards the north, with Grampian Mountains in Scotland, Pennines in northern England, Cambrian Mountains in Wales; rivers include Thames, Severn, and Spey
TERRITORIES Anguilla, Bermuda, British Antarctic Territory, British Indian Ocean Territory, British Virgin Islands, Cayman Islands, Falkland Islands, Gibraltar, Montserrat, Pitcairn Islands, St Helena and Dependencies (Ascension, Tristan da Cunha), South Georgia, South Sandwich Islands, Turks and Caicos Islands; the Channel Islands and the Isle of Man are not part of the UK but are direct dependencies of the crown

Government

HEAD OF STATE Queen Elizabeth II from 1952
HEAD OF GOVERNMENT Tony Blair from 1997
POLITICAL SYSTEM liberal democracy
POLITICAL EXECUTIVE parliamentary
ADMINISTRATIVE DIVISIONS England: 34 non-metropolitan counties, 46 unitary authorities, 6 metropolitan counties, (with 36 metropolitan boroughs), 32 London boroughs, and the Corporation of London; Scotland: 9 regions, 29 unitary authorities, and 3 island authorities (from 1996); Wales: 9 counties and 22 unitary authorities/county boroughs (from 1996); Northern Ireland: 26 districts within 6 geographical counties
ARMED FORCES 210,400 (2002 est)
CONSCRIPTION military service is voluntary
DEATH PENALTY abolished in 1965, except for treason and piracy; abolished completely in 1998
DEFENCE SPEND (% GDP) 2.4 (2002 est)
EDUCATION SPEND (% GDP) 4.5 (2000 est)
HEALTH SPEND (% GDP) 7.3 (2000 est)

Economy and resources

CURRENCY pound sterling
GPD (US$) 1,552.4 billion (2002 est)
REAL GDP GROWTH (% change on previous year) 2 (2001)
GNI (US$) 1,486.2 billion (2002 est)
GNI PER CAPITA (PPP) (US$) 25,870 (2002 est)
CONSUMER PRICE INFLATION 2.8% (2003 est)
UNEMPLOYMENT 5% (2001)
MAJOR TRADING PARTNERS USA, Germany, France, the Netherlands, Japan, Ireland, EU
RESOURCES coal, limestone, crude petroleum, natural gas, tin, iron, salt, sand and gravel
INDUSTRIES machinery and transport equipment, steel, metals and metal products, food processing, shipbuilding, aircraft, petroleum and gas extraction, electronics and communications, chemicals and chemical products, business and financial services, tourism
EXPORTS industrial and electrical machinery, automatic data-processing equipment, motor vehicles, petroleum, chemicals, finished and semi-finished manufactured products, agricultural products and foodstuffs. Principal market: USA 15.4% (2001)
IMPORTS industrial and electrical machinery, motor vehicles, food and live animals, petroleum, automatic data processing equipment, consumer goods, textiles, paper, paper board. Principal source: USA 13.2% (2001)
ARABLE LAND 24.4% (2000 est)
AGRICULTURAL PRODUCTS wheat, barley, potatoes, sugar beet, fruit, vegetables; livestock rearing (chiefly poultry and cattle), animal products, fishing

Population and society

POPULATION 59,251,000 (2003 est)
POPULATION GROWTH RATE 0.0% (2000–15)
POPULATION DENSITY (per sq km) 243 (2003 est)
URBAN POPULATION (% of total) 90 (2003 est)
AGE DISTRIBUTION (% of total population) 0–14 19%, 15–59 60%, 60+ 21% (2002 est)
ETHNIC GROUPS 81.5% English; 9.6% Scots; 2.4% Irish; 1.9% Welsh; about 5% West Indian, Asian, African, and other ethnic minorities
LANGUAGE English (official), Welsh (also official in Wales), Gaelic
RELIGION about 46% Church of England (established church); other Protestant denominations, Roman Catholic, Muslim, Jewish, Hindu, Sikh
EDUCATION (compulsory years) 11
LITERACY RATE 99% (men); 99% (women) (2003 est)
LABOUR FORCE 1.5% agriculture, 25.4% industry, 73.1% services (2000)
LIFE EXPECTANCY 76 (men); 81 (women) (2000–05)
CHILD MORTALITY RATE (under 5, per 1,000 live births) 7 (2001)
PHYSICIANS (per 1,000 people) 1.8 (1998 est)
HOSPITAL BEDS (per 1,000 people) 4.1 (1998 est)
TV SETS (per 1,000 people) 950 (2001 est)
RADIOS (per 1,000 people) 1,446 (2001 est)
INTERNET USERS (per 10,000 people) 4,061.7 (2002 est)
PERSONAL COMPUTER USERS (per 100 people) 40.6 (2002 est)

See also ▷Britain, ancient; ▷British Empire; ▷England; ▷Industrial Revolution; ▷Ireland, Northern; ▷Roman Britain; ▷Scotland; ▷Wales.

Chronology

c. 400–200 BC: British Isles conquered by Celts.

55–54 BC: Romans led by Julius Caesar raided Britain.

AD 43–60: Romans conquered England and Wales, which formed the province of Britannia; Picts stopped them penetrating further north.

5th–7th centuries: After Romans withdrew, Anglo-Saxons overran most of England and formed kingdoms, including Wessex, Northumbria, and Mercia; Wales was stronghold of Celts.

500: The Scots, a Gaelic-speaking tribe from Ireland, settled in the kingdom of Dalriada (Argyll).

5th–6th centuries: British Isles converted to Christianity.

829: King Egbert of Wessex accepted as overlord of all England.

c. 843: Kenneth McAlpin unified Scots and Picts to become the first king of Scotland.

9th–11th centuries: Vikings raided the British Isles, conquering north and east England and northern Scotland.

1066: Normans led by William I defeated Anglo-Saxons at Battle of Hastings and conquered England.

12th–13th centuries: Anglo-Norman adventurers conquered much of Ireland, but effective English rule remained limited to area around Dublin.

1215: King John of England forced to sign Magna Carta, which placed limits on royal powers.

1265: Simon de Montfort summoned the first English parliament in which the towns were represented.

1284: Edward I of England invaded Scotland; Scots defeated English at Battle of Stirling Bridge in 1297.

1314: Robert the Bruce led Scots to victory over English at Battle of Bannockburn; England recognized Scottish independence in 1328.

1455–85: Wars of the Roses: House of York and House of Lancaster disputed English throne.

1513: Battle of Flodden: Scots defeated by English; James IV of Scotland killed.

(continued overleaf)

1529: Henry VIII founded Church of England after break with Rome; Reformation effective in England and Wales, but not in Ireland.

1536–43: Acts of Union united Wales with England, with one law, one parliament, and one official language.

1541: Irish parliament recognized Henry VIII of England as king of Ireland.

1557: First Covenant established Protestant faith in Scotland.

1603: Union of crowns: James VI of Scotland became James I of England also.

1607: First successful English colony in Virginia marked the start of three centuries of overseas expansion.

1610: James I established plantation of Ulster in Northern Ireland with Protestant settlers from England and Scotland.

1642–52: English Civil War between king and Parliament, with Scottish intervention and Irish rebellion, resulted in victory for Parliament.

1649: Execution of Charles I; Oliver Cromwell appointed Lord Protector in 1653; monarchy restored in 1660.

1689: 'Glorious Revolution' confirmed power of Parliament; replacement of James II by William III resisted by Scottish Highlanders and Catholic Irish.

1707: Act of Union between England and Scotland created United Kingdom of Great Britain, governed by a single parliament.

1721–42: Cabinet government developed under Robert Walpole, in effect the first prime minister.

1745: 'The Forty-Five': rebellion of Scottish Highlanders in support of Jacobite pretender to throne; defeated 1746.

c. **1760–1850**: Industrial Revolution: Britain became the first industrial nation in the world.

1775–83: American Revolution: Britain lost 13 American colonies; empire continued to expand in Canada, India, and Australia.

1793–1815: Britain at war with revolutionary France, except for 1802–03.

1800: Act of Union created United Kingdom of Great Britain and Ireland, governed by a single parliament; effective 1801.

1832: Great Reform Act extended franchise; further extensions in 1867, 1884, 1918, and 1928.

1846: Repeal of Corn Laws reflected shift of power from landowners to industrialists.

1870: Home Rule Party formed to campaign for restoration of separate Irish parliament.

1880–90s: Rapid expansion of British Empire in Africa.

1906–14: Liberal governments introduced social reforms and curbed the power of the House of Lords.

1914–18: The UK played a leading part in World War I; the British Empire expanded in Middle East.

1919–21: The Anglo-Irish war ended with the secession of southern Ireland as the Irish Free State; Ulster remained within the United Kingdom of Great Britain and Northern Ireland with some powers devolved to a Northern Irish parliament.

1924: The first Labour government was led by Ramsay MacDonald.

1926: A general strike arose from a coal dispute. Equality of status was recognized between the UK and Dominions of the British Commonwealth.

1931: A National Government coalition was formed to face a growing economic crisis; unemployment reached 3 million.

1939–45: The UK played a leading part in World War II.

1945–51: The Labour government of Clement Attlee created the welfare state and nationalized major industries.

1947–71: Decolonization brought about the end of the British Empire.

1969: Start of the Troubles in Northern Ireland; the Northern Irish Parliament was suspended in 1972.

1973: The UK joined the EEC.

1979–90: The Conservative government of Margaret Thatcher pursued radical free-market economic policies.

1982: The Falklands War with Argentina over the disputed sovereignty of the Falkland Islands cost more than a thousand lives but ended with the UK retaining control of the islands.

1983: Coal pits were closed and the miners went on strike.

1991: British troops took part in a US-led war against Iraq under a United Nations (UN) umbrella. Following the economic successes of the 1980s there was a period of severe economic recession and unemployment.

1993: A peace proposal for Northern Ireland, the Downing Street Declaration, was issued jointly with the Irish government.

1994: The IRA and Protestant paramilitary declared a ceasefire in Northern Ireland.

1996: The IRA renewed its bombing campaign in London.

1997: The Labour Party won a landslide election victory; Tony Blair became prime minister. Blair launched a new Anglo-Irish peace initiative. Blair met with Sinn Fein leader Gerry Adams; all-party peace talks began in Northern Ireland. Scotland and Wales voted in favour of devolution. Princess Diana was killed in a car crash.

1998: A historic multiparty agreement (the 'Good Friday Agreement') was reached on the future of Northern Ireland; a peace plan was approved by referenda in Northern Ireland and the Irish Republic.

1999: The Scottish Parliament and the Welsh Assembly opened, with Labour the largest party in both. The IRA agreed to begin decommissioning discussions and a coalition government was established.

2000: After it was revealed that there had been no arms handover by the IRA, the Secretary of State for Northern Ireland suspended the Northern Ireland Assembly. After the IRA agreed to put its weapons out of use, Northern Ireland's power sharing executive resumed work.

2001: Tony Blair re-elected as prime minister. David Trimble resigned as first minister for Northern Ireland.

2002: Queen Elizabeth II completed 50 years as monarch, and the Queen Mother died. The devolved administration in Northern Ireland was suspended and direct rule imposed by British government. The IRA subsequently broke off contact with the international body overseeing terrorist arms decommissioning.

2003: Despite public and Labour Party opposition, the UK launched military action in Iraq with the USA in March. The government was damaged by allegations by the BBC (British Broadcasting Corporation) that it exaggerated intelligence information about Iraq's weapons programmes to justify going to war. Elections to the Northern Ireland Assembly were held despite the continuing suspension of the devolved administration, the hardline Democratic Unionist Party and Sinn Fein made gains at the expense of more moderate parties.

United Kingdom and Ireland – local government divisions

ENGLAND

BA	BATH AND NE SOMERSET
BE	BEDFORDSHIRE
BL	BLACKPOOL
BN	BOURNEMOUTH
BR	BRACKNELL FOREST
BT	BRISTOL
BU	BUCKINGHAMSHIRE
DA	DARLINGTON
DC	DERBY CITY
GR	GREATER MANCHESTER
HA	HALTON
HE	HERTFORDSHIRE
LC	LEICESTER CITY
LE	LEICESTERSHIRE
LU	LUTON
ME	MEDWAY TOWNS
MK	MILTON KEYNES
NH	NORTHAMPTONSHIRE
NL	NORTH LINCOLNSHIRE
NS	NORTH SOMERSET
NT	NOTTINGHAMSHIRE
PB	PETERBOROUGH
PL	PLYMOUTH
PO	POOLE
PT	PORTSMOUTH
R	READING
RU	RUTLAND
S	SLOUGH
SG	SOUTH GLOUCESTERSHIRE
SO	SOUTHAMPTON
SS	STOCKTON-ON-TEES
ST	STOKE-ON-TRENT
SU	SOUTHEND
SW	SWINDON
TW	TELFORD AND WREKIN
WA	WARRINGTON
WC	WARWICKSHIRE
WK	WEST BERKSHIRE
WM	WEST MIDLANDS
WN	WINDSOR AND MAIDENHEAD
WO	WOKINGHAM
WR	WORCESTERSHIRE

SCOTLAND

CE	CITY OF EDINBURGH
CL	CLACKMANNANSHIRE
EA	EAST AYRSHIRE
ED	EAST DUNBARTONSHIRE
ER	EAST RENFREWSHIRE
FA	FALKIRK
GC	GLASGOW CITY
IN	INVERCLYDE
MI	MIDLOTHIAN
NL	NORTH LANARKSHIRE
RE	RENFREWSHIRE
SL	SOUTH LANARKSHIRE
WD	WEST DUNBARTONSHIRE
WL	WEST LOTHIAN

NORTHERN IRELAND

A	ANTRIM
AD	ARDS
AR	ARMAGH
BA	BALLYMENA
BL	BALLYMONEY
BN	BANBRIDGE
BT	BELFAST
C	CARRICKFERGUS
CA	CASTLEREAGH
CL	COLERAINE
CO	COOKSTOWN
CR	CRAIGAVON
DE	DERRY
DO	DOWN
DU	DUNGANNON
FE	FERMANAGH
LA	LARNE
LI	LIMAVADY
L	LISBURN
MA	MAGHERAFELT
MO	MOYLE
N	NEWTOWNABBEY
NM	NEWRY AND MOURNE
NO	NORTH DOWN
OM	OMAGH
ST	STRABANE

WALES

BG	BLAENAU GWENT
BR	BRIDGEND
CA	CAERPHILLY
CF	CARDIFF
DE	DENBIGHSHIRE
FL	FLINTSHIRE
MO	MONMOUTHSHIRE
MT	MERTHYR TYDFIL
NE	NEATH PORT TALBOT
NP	NEWPORT
RC	RHONDDA CYNON TAFF
SW	SWANSEA
TO	TORFAEN
VG	VALE OF GLAMORGAN
WR	WREXHAM

(*continued from p. 980*)

In September 1997 the media magnate Ted Turner donated $1 billion to the UN, to be paid over ten years.

The USA regularly (often alone or nearly so) votes against General Assembly resolutions on aggression, international law, human-rights abuses, and disarmament, and has exercised its veto on the Security Council more times than any other member (the UK is second, France a distant third).

Britain's contribution to the UN 1995–96 was $130 million.

Related Web site: United Nations Home Page http://www.un.org/

United Provinces federation of states in the northern Netherlands 1579–1795, comprising Holland, Zeeland, Friesland, Gelderland, Utrecht, Overijssel, and Groningen. Established by the Union of ▷Utrecht, its aim was to assert independence from the Spanish crown. See ▷Netherlands.

United States architecture little survives of early indigenous American architecture, although the early settlers in each region recorded the house and village styles of the local Indians. The most notable prehistoric remains are the cliff dwellings in the Southwest. Archaeologists have also discovered traces of structures associated with the moundbuilding peoples in the Mississippi river valley. Subsequent architectural forms are those that came with colonizers from European cultures, those adapted to American conditions and social development, and, most recently, those that were developed and innovated by American architects.

United States art painting and sculpture in the USA from colonial times to the present. The unspoiled landscapes romantically depicted in the 18th and 19th centuries gave way to realistic city scenes in the 20th. Modern movements have flourished in the USA, among them ▷abstract expressionism and ▷pop art.

United States literature early US literature falls into two distinct periods: **colonial writing** of the 1600s–1770s, largely dominated by the Puritans, and

Sovereigns of England and the United Kingdom from 899

Edward the Elder made the first major advances towards the unification of England under one sovereign and established the ascendancy of his dynasty.

Reign	Name	Relationship
West Saxon Kings		
899–924	Edward the Elder	son of Alfred the Great
924–39	Athelstan	son of Edward the Elder
939–46	Edmund	half-brother of Athelstan
946–55	Edred	brother of Edmund
955–59	Edwy	son of Edmund
959–75	Edgar	brother of Edwy
975–78	Edward the Martyr	son of Edgar
978–1016	Ethelred (II) the Unready	son of Edgar
1016	Edmund Ironside	son of Ethelred (II) the Unready
Danish Kings		
1016–35	Canute	son of Sweyn I of Denmark who conquered England in 1013
1035–40	Harold I	son of Canute
1040–42	Hardicanute	son of Canute
West Saxon Kings (restored)		
1042–66	Edward the Confessor	son of Ethelred (II) the Unready
1066	Harold II	son of Godwin
Norman Kings		
1066–87	William I	illegitimate son of Duke Robert the Devil
1087–1100	William II	son of William I
1100–35	Henry I	son of William I
1135–54	Stephen	grandson of William II
House of Plantagenet		
1154–89	Henry II	son of Matilda (daughter of Henry I)
1189–99	Richard I	son of Henry II
1199–1216	John	son of Henry II
1216–72	Henry III	son of John
1272–1307	Edward I	son of Henry III
1307–27	Edward II	son of Edward I
1327–77	Edward III	son of Edward II
1377–99	Richard II	son of the Black Prince
House of Lancaster		
1399–1413	Henry IV	son of John of Gaunt
1413–22	Henry V	son of Henry IV
1422–61, 1470–71	Henry VI	son of Henry V
House of York		
1461–70, 1471–83	Edward IV	son of Richard, Duke of York
1483	Edward V	son of Edward IV
1483–85	Richard III	brother of Edward IV
House of Tudor		
1485–1509	Henry VII	son of Edmund Tudor, Earl of Richmond
1509–47	Henry VIII	son of Henry VII
1547–53	Edward VI	son of Henry VIII
1553–58	Mary I	daughter of Henry VIII
1558–1603	Elizabeth I	daughter of Henry VIII
House of Stuart		
1603–25	James I	great-grandson of Margaret (daughter of Henry VII)
1625–49	Charles I	son of James I
1649–60	the Commonwealth	
House of Stuart (restored)		
1660–85	Charles II	son of Charles I
1685–88	James II	son of Charles I
1689–1702	William III and Mary	son of Mary (daughter of Charles I); daughter of James II
1702–14	Anne	daughter of James II
House of Hanover		
1714–27	George I	son of Sophia (granddaughter of James I)
1727–60	George II	son of George I
1760–1820	George III	son of Frederick (son of George II)
1820–30	George IV (regent 1811–20)	son of George III
1830–37	William IV	son of George III
1837–1901	Victoria	daughter of Edward (son of George III)
House of Saxe-Coburg		
1901–10	Edward VII	son of Victoria
House of Windsor		
1910–36	George V	son of Edward VII
1936	Edward VIII	son of George V
1936–52	George VI	son of George V
1952–	Elizabeth II	daughter of George VI

post-Revolutionary literature from the 1780s, when the ideal of US literature developed, and poetry, fiction, and drama began to evolve on national principles. Early 19th-century **Romanticism** contrasted sharply with the social realism of subsequent **post-Civil War** writing. 20th-century US writers continued the trend towards realism, as well as developing various forms of modernist experimentation.
Related Web site: American Verse Project
http://www.hti.umich.edu/english/amverse/

United States of America
(USA) see country box.

unit trust company that invests its clients' funds in other companies. The units it issues represent holdings of shares, which means unit shareholders have a wider spread of capital than if they bought shares on the stock market.
Related Web site: PR Newswire
http://www.prnewswire.com/

universal in philosophy, a property that is instantiated by all the individual things of a specific class: for example, all red things instantiate 'redness'. Many philosophical debates have centred on the status of universals, including the medieval debate between nominalism and ▷realism.

universal indicator in chemistry, a mixture of ▷pH indicators, used to gauge the acidity or alkalinity of a solution. Each component changes colour at a different pH value, and so the indicator is capable of displaying a range of colours, according to the pH of the test solution, from red (at pH 1, strong acid) through green (neutral) to purple (at pH 13, strong alkali).

universal joint flexible coupling used to join rotating shafts; for example, the drive shaft in a car. In a typical universal joint the ends of the shafts to be joined end in U-shaped yokes. They dovetail into each other and pivot flexibly about an X-shaped spider. This construction allows side-to-side and up-and-down movement, while still transmitting rotary motion.

universe all of space and its contents, the study of which is called ▷cosmology. The universe is thought to be between 10 billion and 20 billion years old, and is mostly empty space, dotted with ▷galaxies for as far as telescopes can see. The most distant detected galaxies and ▷quasars lie 10 billion light years or more from Earth, and are moving farther apart as the universe expands. Several theories attempt to explain how the universe came into being and evolved; for example, the ▷Big Bang theory of an expanding universe originating in a single explosive event, and the contradictory ▷steady-state theory. Apart from those galaxies within the Local Group, all the galaxies we see display ▷red shifts in their spectra, indicating that they are moving away from us. The farther we look into space, the greater are the observed red shifts, which implies that the more distant galaxies are receding at ever greater speeds.
This observation led to the theory of an expanding universe, first proposed in 1929 by US astronomer Edwin ▷Hubble, and to Hubble's law, which states that the speed with which one galaxy moves away from another is proportional to its distance from it. Current data suggest that the galaxies are moving apart at a rate of 50–100 kps/30–60 mps for every million ▷parsecs of distance.
Related Web site: British Interplanetary Society http://www.bis-spaceflight.com

> **Israel Zangwill**
> English writer
>
> *America is God's Crucible, the great Melting-Pot where all the races of Europe are melting and reforming! . . . God is making the American.*
>
> *The Melting Pot*

university institution of higher learning for those who have completed primary and secondary education.
Europe's oldest universities The first European university was Salerno in Italy, established in the 9th century, followed by Bologna, Paris, Oxford, Cambridge, and Montpellier in the 12th century and Salamanca and Toulouse in the 13th century. The universities of Prague, Vienna, Heidelberg, and Cologne were established in the 14th century as well as many French universities, including those at Avignon, Orléans, Cahors, Grenoble, Angers, and Orange. The universities of Aix, Dole, Poitiers, Caen, Nantes, Besançon, Bourges, and Bordeaux were established in the 15th century. St Andrew's, the first Scottish university, was founded in 1411, and Trinity College, Dublin, in 1591.
Recent British universities In the UK, a number of universities were founded in the 19th and earlier 20th centuries, mainly in the large cities (London 1836, Manchester 1851, Wales 1893, Liverpool 1903, Bristol 1909, and Reading 1926). These became known as the 'redbrick' universities, as opposed to the ancient stone of Oxford and Cambridge. After World War II, many more universities were founded, among them Nottingham in 1948 and Exeter in 1955, and were nicknamed, from their modernist buildings, the 'plate-glass' universities. In the 1960s seven new universities were established on greenfield sites, including Sussex and York. Seven colleges of advanced technology were given university status. In 1992 the polytechnics and some colleges of higher education already awarding degrees also became universities.
University students, UK The number of university students in the UK almost doubled after the expansion of the 1960s to stand at 303,000 in 1991. There was an even greater increase in degree-level students in the public-sector colleges, which educated more graduates than the universities.
The more generous funding of traditional universities was phased out and a joint funding council established. Research is funded separately from teaching, and the new universities have gained access to research funds for the first time.
In 1997 the government announced major changes in the system of students' funding: the introduction of tuition fees and the abolition of maintenance grants.
Oldest US universities The USA has both state universities (funded by the individual states) and private universities. The oldest universities in the USA are all private: Harvard 1636, William and Mary 1693, Yale 1701, Pennsylvania 1741, and Princeton 1746.
New types of universities Recent innovations include universities serving international areas; for example, the Middle East Technical University (1961) in Ankara, Turkey, supported by the United Nations; the United Nations University in Tokyo (1974); and the British ▷Open University (1969). The Open University has been widely copied; for example, in the National University Consortium set up in the USA in 1980.

Unix multiuser ▷operating system designed for mid-range computers but also used on workstations, mainframes, and supercomputers.
Unix was developed by AT&T's Bell Laboratories in the USA during the late 1960s, using the programming language ▷C. It could therefore run on any machine with a C compiler, so ensuring its wide portability. Its wide range of functions and flexibility, together with the fact that it was available free 1976–1983, have made it widely used by universities and in commercial software.
In the 1990s, AT&T's Unix System Laboratories was taken over by Novell, which later sold it to the Santa Cruz Operation.

unleaded petrol petrol manufactured without the addition of antiknock. It has a slightly lower octane rating than leaded petrol, but has the advantage of not polluting the atmosphere with lead compounds. Many cars can be converted to run on unleaded petrol by altering the timing of the engine, and most new cars are designed to do so. Cars fitted with a ▷catalytic converter must use unleaded fuel.

Unrepresented Nations' and Peoples' Organization (UNPO) international association founded in 1991 to represent ethnic and minority groups unrecognized by the United Nations and to defend the right to self-determination of oppressed peoples around the world. The founding charter was signed by representatives of Tibet, the Kurds, Turkestan, Armenia, Estonia, Georgia, the Volga region, the Crimea, the Greek minority in Albania, North American Indians, Australian Aborigines, West

(continued on p. 988)

The American Revolution

by Ian Derbyshire

The American Revolution can be seen as simply the breakaway of the American colonists from the British colonial empire, achieved, after an eight-year war, at the Treaty of Paris in 1783. But a broader view reveals a far-reaching revolution in the social, political, and economic order, which began before and continued after the military conflict and independence. In the course of this revolution, America threw off its subordinate role as a colony of Britain – a country governed by a hereditary monarchy and a parliamentary system corrupted by court patronage – and became the world's first modern political regime.

settlement of North America

Permanent English settlements were founded in North America in 1607, at Jamestown, on the Chesapeake Bay, Virginia, and in 1620, at Plymouth, in Massachusetts, by Puritan Pilgrim refugees. By the end of the century 12 colonies had been established, and in 1733 Georgia, founded to resettle imprisoned debtors, became the 13th. These Thirteen Colonies stretched 2,000 km/1,200 mi along the east coast. Resistance from native Americans made settlement inland more difficult, and nowhere did the settlers penetrate more than 300 km/190 mi from the coast. Nevertheless, by the third quarter of the 18th century there were nearly three million American colonists. In the south they had established a thriving economy, based on tobacco plantations worked by black slaves, and in the north a largely self-sufficient economy based on farming, crafts, and fishing. Constraints on trade were imposed by the Navigation Acts, making America economically dependent on Britain. However, with abundant land and low taxes, the colonies were one of the most prosperous communities in the world and, although there was a powerful and wealthy trading and landowning elite, American society was relatively egalitarian. America's remoteness from Britain made it possible for colonists to establish influential local representative assemblies, and these attracted politicians who were influenced by radical, anti-monarchist thinking.

seeds of unrest

By 1763, following success against France and Spain in the Seven Years' War (known in America as the French and Indian War), Britain had extended its influence to Canada in the north and Florida in the south, and appeared to have gained complete control of North America. However, this prolonged global conflict placed a huge strain on the British economy, doubling the national debt to £130 million. This prompted the British government to rethink imperial policy and reorganize and rationalize the administration of America on more centralized lines, with a permanent standing army and professional administration paid for by taxing the colonists. A series of measures was introduced in 1763–75 in support of this programme. This antagonized the colonies' elites, who feared that Britain intended to curb their autonomy and suppress their local assemblies. The gulf between British and American outlooks and interests began to widen. Initially, Americans responded with acts of disobedience, carried out by patriotic gangs known as the Sons of Liberty. In 1775 this escalated into armed conflict and, from 1776, became a demand for independence, drawing committed support from a third of the colonists and unspoken agreement from many more.

Declaration of Independence

Before hostilities had begun, in September 1774 delegates from 12 of the Thirteen Colonies had met in Philadelphia in a Continental Congress to protest against the British measures, known collectively as the Intolerable Acts. The Second Continental Congress (May 1775–March 1781), at which all 13 colonies were represented, became an adhoc government and eventually framed the Articles of Confederation. These delegated a restricted number of functions to a small federal, or national, legislature, but most powers were retained by the states. The revolt against the British rule took the form of a rebellion by individual colonies united in self-interest, rather than a concerted national uprising.

The first military engagements of the American War of Independence took place in April 1775 at Lexington and Concord, Massachusetts. British troops were sent to seize illegal military stores near Boston and arrest rebel leaders John Hancock and Samuel Adams; they were attacked by armed farmers – the Minutemen Militia – and forced to retreat. Further engagements followed in May at Fort Ticonderoga, New York, won by the Americans, and in June at Bunker Hill, Massachusetts, won by the British.

BRITISH REINFORCEMENTS arriving at Boston, USA in an engraving by Paul Revere. Revere carried the news of the British approach to Lexington and Concord, where the hostilities began. © *Philip Sauvain Picture Collection*

DECLARATION OF INDEPENDENCE In this 1776 painting by John Trumb, members of the American Congress step forward to sign their names to the declaration, which set down the reasons for their break with the British crown. Most members signed on 2 August or later, but 4 July 1776 is remembered as the day on which Congress first adopted the declaration.
© Archive Photos

On 4 July 1776, the colonists formally issued a Declaration of Independence, drafted by Thomas Jefferson (who became the third US president, 1801–09), and revised by Benjamin Franklin and John Adams (who became the second US president 1797–1801). The war escalated, as large numbers of British Redcoat troops, supported by German mercenaries, were sent across the Atlantic.

British overconfidence and American victory

The British anticipated swift success in the more densely populated north, where early fighting was concentrated. They were disappointed, however, since they had overestimated the extent of American loyalist support they would receive. In addition, they were hampered by overextended supply lines, and were fighting in unfamiliar terrain. Facing them were highly motivated American 'Patriot' troops led by able commanders, notably George Washington (later the first US president 1789–97), a veteran of the French and Indian Wars, who adopted novel guerrilla tactics. These contributed to a crucial early defeat of the British, in October 1777, at Saratoga Springs, New York, when British general John Burgoyne was forced to surrender. This downturn in Britain's fortunes persuaded France, followed later by the Spanish and the Dutch, to form a military alliance with the American colonists in February 1778. The alliance provided the Americans with vital naval support and distracted British forces.

From 1778, after the Americans had rejected an offer of peace negotiations, the British campaign moved south. They enjoyed initial successes at Savannah, Georgia, and Charleston, South Carolina,

but from early 1781 the tide began to turn. On 19 October 1781, besieged by 17,000 American and French troops, and blockaded by the French navy, Lord Charles Cornwallis surrendered ignominiously at Yorktown, Virginia. This decisive defeat destroyed Britain's will to continue the struggle. Hostilities formally ceased in February 1783 and on 3 September 1783, at the Treaty of Paris, Britain formally recognized America's independence and its rights to the American interior. The last British troops left New York in November 1783.

adoption of the Constitution of 1787

After the war, the looseness of the federation of colonies contributed towards political instability. Prompted by the nationally minded professional and gentry elite, known as the Federalists, 55 delegates from 12 states met at Philadelphia in May 1787 to draft a new constitution. The leading Federalist, James Madison (who became the fourth US president 1809–17) put forward the Virginia Plan for a stronger central government. Eventually, following a compromise with anti-Federalist regional interests, a constitution was adopted by the Thirteen Colonies between 1787 and 1790, providing for the sharing of power between the individual states and a federal government. This government was to be a powerful national legislature, a two-chamber Congress with a directly elected lower house; a relatively weak executive (the president) who was indirectly elected until after 1804; and an independent judiciary. Powers were deliberately balanced between the three. Post-revolutionary America became the United States of America, a federal republic based on representative democracy, in which three-quarters of

adult males had the right to vote and civil rights were enshrined in the 1791 Bill of Rights. The American Revolution had extended over nearly 30 years.

repercussions of the American Revolution

For Britain, the loss of its American empire was humiliating, but the effects were surprisingly short-lived. Lord North, the British prime minister, was immediately toppled, but national resurgence was swift. Over the next half century a new, larger, and more tightly controlled 'Second British Empire' was established, centred on India, and embracing a quarter of the world's population. Meanwhile, although economic ties with the new United States remained close, the colonists were free to harness the rich natural resources of the continent's vast interior, and to develop its own shipping and modern industries.

The deeper consequences of the American Revolution were related to political ideology. The United States, with its representative republican democracy, provided a blueprint for future political developments both in Europe and in colonial Spanish America. With its rhetorical emphasis on people's intrinsic equality and rights, the Revolution has inspired liberals and radicals down the centuries, from the French Revolution and early 19th-century anti-colonial revolts in Haiti, Venezuela, and Colombia through to the abortive pro-democracy demonstrations that took place in Tiananmen Square, Beijing, China in 1989. However, not until 1920 and 1964, when the franchise was finally extended to women and southern blacks respectively, could America claim to have fully completed its democratic revolution.

United States of America

Population and society

AGRICULTURAL PRODUCTS hay, potatoes, maize, wheat, barley, oats, sugar beet, soybeans, citrus and other fruit, cotton, tobacco; livestock (principally cattle, pigs, and poultry)

POPULATION 294,043,000 (2003 est)
POPULATION GROWTH RATE 0.8% (2000–15)
POPULATION DENSITY (per sq km) 31 (2003 est)
URBAN POPULATION (% of total) 78 (2003 est)
AGE DISTRIBUTION (% of total population) 0–14 21%, 15–59 63%, 60+ 16% (2002 est)
ETHNIC GROUPS approximately three-quarters of the population are of European origin, including 29% who trace their descent from Britain and Ireland, 8% from Germany, 5% from Italy, and 3% each from Scandinavia and Poland; approximately 83% are white (of which over 11% are Hispanic), 13% black, 4% Asian and Pacific Islanders, and about 1% American Indians, Eskimos, and Aleuts (1998); African-Americans form about a third of the population of the states of the 'Deep South', namely Alabama, Georgia, Louisiana, Mississippi, and South Carolina
LANGUAGE English, Spanish
RELIGION Protestant 58%; Roman Catholic 28%; atheist 10%; Jewish 2%; other 4% (1998)
EDUCATION (compulsory years) 10
LITERACY RATE 99% (men); 99% (women) (2003 est)
LABOUR FORCE 2.6% agriculture, 22.9% industry, 74.5% services (2002)
LIFE EXPECTANCY 74 (men); 80 (women) (2000–05)
CHILD MORTALITY RATE (under 5, per 1,000 live births) 8 (2001)
PHYSICIANS (per 1,000 people) 2.8 (1998 est)
HOSPITAL BEDS (per 1,000 people) 3.6 (1998 est)
TV SETS (per 1,000 people) 844 (1999)
RADIOS (per 1,000 people) 2,146 (1997)
INTERNET USERS (per 10,000 people) 5,375.1 (2002 est)
PERSONAL COMPUTER USERS (per 100 people) 65.9 (2002 est)

See also ▷American Indian; ▷American Revolution; ▷Civil War, American; ▷Vietnam War; The American Revolution Focus Feature on pp. 984–985.

United States of America country in North America, extending from the Atlantic Ocean in the east to the Pacific Ocean in the west, bounded north by Canada and south by Mexico, and including the outlying states of Alaska and Hawaii.

NATIONAL NAME *United States of America* (USA)
AREA 9,826,632 sq km/3,794,084 sq mi
CAPITAL Washington, DC
MAJOR TOWNS/CITIES New York, Los Angeles, Chicago, Philadelphia, Detroit, San Francisco, Dallas, San Diego, San Antonio, Houston, Boston, Phoenix, Indianapolis, Honolulu, San José
PHYSICAL FEATURES topography and vegetation from tropical (Hawaii) to arctic (Alaska); mountain ranges parallel with east and west coasts; the Rocky Mountains separate rivers emptying into the Pacific from those flowing into the Gulf of Mexico; Great Lakes in north; rivers include Hudson, Mississippi, Missouri, Colorado, Columbia, Snake, Rio Grande, Ohio
TERRITORIES the commonwealths of Puerto Rico and Northern Marianas; Guam, the US Virgin Islands, American Samoa, Wake Island, Midway Islands, Johnston Atoll, Baker Island, Howland Island, Jarvis Island, Kingman Reef, Navassa Island, Palmyra Island

Government

HEAD OF STATE AND GOVERNMENT George W Bush from 2001
POLITICAL SYSTEM liberal democracy
POLITICAL EXECUTIVE limited presidency

ADMINISTRATIVE DIVISIONS 50 states and one district (District of Columbia)
ARMED FORCES 1,414,000 (2002 est)
CONSCRIPTION military service is voluntary
DEATH PENALTY retained and used for ordinary crimes
DEFENCE SPEND (% GDP) 3.3 (2002 est)
EDUCATION SPEND (% GDP) 4.8 (2001 est)
HEALTH SPEND (% GDP) 13 (2000 est)

Economy and resources

CURRENCY US dollar
GPD (US$) 10,416.8 billion (2002 est)
REAL GDP GROWTH (% change on previous year) 1.2 (2001)
GNI (US$) 10,110.1 billion (2002 est)
GNI PER CAPITA (PPP) (US$) 35,060 (2002 est)
CONSUMER PRICE INFLATION 2.3% (2003 est)
UNEMPLOYMENT 4.8% (2001)
MAJOR TRADING PARTNERS Canada, Japan, Mexico, EU (principally UK, Germany, and France), China, Taiwan, South Korea
RESOURCES coal (world's largest producer), copper, iron, bauxite, mercury, silver, gold, nickel, zinc, tungsten, uranium, phosphate, petroleum, natural gas, timber
INDUSTRIES machinery, petroleum refining and products, food processing, motor vehicles, pig iron and steel, chemical

products, electrical goods, metal products, printing and publishing, fertilizers, cement
EXPORTS machinery, motor vehicles, agricultural products and foodstuffs, aircraft, weapons, chemicals, electronics. Principal market: Canada 22.7% (2001)
IMPORTS machinery and transport equipment, crude and partly refined petroleum, office machinery, textiles and clothing. Principal source: Canada 18.9% (2001)
ARABLE LAND 19.3% (2000 est)

UNITED STATES OF AMERICA The mid-town skyline of New York, USA. *Corel*

United States of America (cont.)

Chronology

c.15,000 BC: First evidence of human occupation in North America.

1513: Ponce de Léon of Spain explored Florida in search of the Fountain of Youth; Francisco Coronado explored southwest region of North America 1540–42.

1565: Spanish founded St Augustine (Florida), the first permanent European settlement in North America.

1585: Sir Walter Raleigh tried to establish an English colony on Roanoke Island in what he called Virginia.

1607: English colonists founded Jamestown, Virginia, and began growing tobacco.

1620: The Pilgrim Fathers founded Plymouth Colony (near Cape Cod); other English Puritans followed them to New England.

1624: Dutch formed colony of New Netherlands; Swedes formed New Sweden in 1638; both taken by England in 1664.

17th–18th centuries: Millions of Africans were sold into slavery on American cotton and tobacco plantations.

1733: Georgia became thirteenth British colony on east coast.

1763: British victory over France in Seven Years' War secured territory as far west as Mississippi River.

1765: British first attempted to levy tax in American colonies with Stamp Act; protest forced repeal in 1767.

1773: 'Boston Tea Party': colonists boarded ships and threw cargoes of tea into sea in protest at import duty.

1774: British closed Boston harbour and billeted troops in Massachusetts; colonists formed First Continental Congress.

1775: American Revolution: colonies raised Continental Army led by George Washington to fight against British rule.

1776: American colonies declared independence; France and Spain supported them in a war with Britain.

1781: Americans defeated British at Battle of Yorktown; rebel states formed loose confederation, codified in Articles of Confederation.

1783: Treaty of Paris: Britain accepted loss of colonies.

1787: 'Founding Fathers' devised new constitution for United States of America.

1789: Washington elected first president of USA.

1791: Bill of Rights guaranteed individual freedom.

1803: Louisiana Purchase: France sold former Spanish lands between Mississippi River and Rocky Mountains to USA.

1812–14: War with Britain arose from dispute over blockade rights during Napoleonic Wars.

1819: USA bought Florida from Spain.

19th century: Mass immigration from Europe; settlers moved westwards, crushing Indian resistance and claiming 'manifest destiny' of USA to control North America. By end of century, the number of states in the Union had increased from 17 to 45.

1846–48: Mexican War: Mexico ceded vast territory to USA.

1854: Kansas–Nebraska Act heightened controversy over slavery in southern states; abolitionists formed Republican Party.

1860: Abraham Lincoln (Republican) elected president.

1861: Civil war broke out after 11 southern states, wishing to retain slavery, seceded from USA and formed the Confederate States of America under Jefferson Davis.

1865: USA defeated Confederacy; slavery abolished; President Lincoln assassinated.

1867: Alaska bought from Russia.

1869: Railway linked east and west coasts; rapid growth of industry and agriculture 1870–1920 made USA very rich.

1876: Sioux Indians defeated US troops at Little Big Horn; Indians finally defeated at Wounded Knee in 1890.

1898: Spanish–American War: USA gained Puerto Rico and Guam; also Philippines (until 1946) and Cuba (until 1901); USA annexed Hawaii.

1917–18: USA intervened in World War I; President Woodrow Wilson took leading part in peace negotiations in 1919, but USA rejected membership of League of Nations.

1920: Women received right to vote; sale of alcohol prohibited, until 1933.

1924: American Indians made citizens of USA by Congress.

1929: 'Wall Street Crash': stock market collapse led to Great Depression with 13 million unemployed by 1933.

1933: President Franklin Roosevelt launched the 'New Deal' with public works to rescue the economy.

1941: Japanese attacked US fleet at Pearl Harbor, Hawaii; USA declared war on Japan; Germany declared war on USA, which henceforth played a leading part in World War II.

1945: USA ended war in Pacific by dropping two atomic bombs on Hiroshima and Nagasaki, Japan.

1947: 'Truman Doctrine' pledged US aid for nations threatened by communism; start of Cold War between USA and USSR.

1950–53: US forces engaged in Korean War.

1954: Racial segregation in schools deemed unconstitutional; start of campaign to secure civil rights for black Americans.

1962: Cuban missile crisis: USA forced USSR to withdraw nuclear weapons from Cuba.

1963: President Kennedy assassinated.

1964–68: President Lyndon Johnson introduced the 'Great Society' programme of civil-rights and welfare measures.

1961–75: USA involved in Vietnam War.

1969: US astronaut Neil Armstrong was first person on the Moon.

1974: 'Watergate' scandal: evidence of domestic political espionage compelled President Richard Nixon to resign.

1979–80: Iran held US diplomats hostage, humiliating President Jimmy Carter.

1981–89: Tax-cutting policies of President Ronald Reagan led to large federal budget deficit.

1986: 'Irangate' scandal: secret US arms sales to Iran illegally funded Contra guerrillas in Nicaragua.

1990: President George Bush declared an end to the Cold War.

1991: USA played leading part in expelling Iraqi forces from Kuwait in the Gulf War.

1992: Democrat Bill Clinton won presidential elections, beginning his term of office in 1993.

1996: US launched missile attacks on Iraq in response to Hussein's incursions into Kurdish safe havens.

1998: The House of Representatives voted to impeach Clinton on the grounds of perjury and obstruction of justice, due to his misleading the public about his relationship with a White House intern. Clinton was acquitted in 1999. In response to bombings of US embassies in Tanzania and Kenya by an Islamic group, the US bombed suspected sites in Afghanistan and Sudan.

1999: US forces led NATO air strikes against Yugoslavia in protest against Serb violence against ethnic Albanians in Kosovo.

2001: Republican George W Bush was inaugurated as president. On 11 September, Islamic extremists hijacked civil airliners and flew them into the twin towers of the World Trade Center, both of which later collapsed, and the Pentagon in Washington, DC. Around 3,000 people were killed. US forces began to congregate around Afghanistan, where Osama bin Laden, the chief suspect, was thought to be hiding. The world economy suffered a large setback.

2002: The US government adopted an increasingly threatening stance towards the regime of Iraqi president Saddam Hussein over the latter's alleged development of weapons of mass destruction and its continuing exclusion of UN weapons inspectors. The threat of war prompted international concern, and an estimated 100,000 people attended an anti-war demonstration in Washington, DC – the largest such demonstration in the US since the Vietnam War.

2003: The US and the UK went to war with Iraq and brought to an end the presidency of Saddam Hussein.

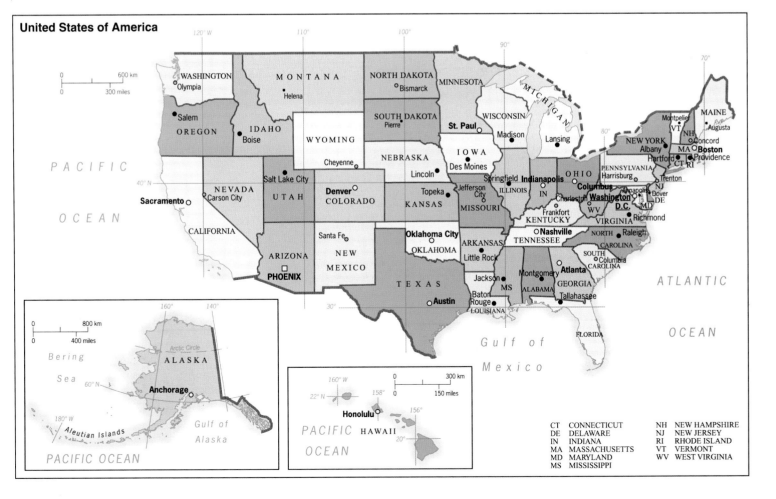

United States of America

CT CONNECTICUT   NH NEW HAMPSHIRE
DE DELAWARE   NJ NEW JERSEY
IN INDIANA   RI RHODE ISLAND
MA MASSACHUSETTS   VT VERMONT
MD MARYLAND   WV WEST VIRGINIA
MS MISSISSIPPI

United States of America: States

State	Nickname(s)	Abbreviation	Capital	Area sq km	Area sq mi	Population (1998)	Joined the union
Alabama	Heart of Dixie/Camellia State	AL	Montgomery	134,700	51,994	4,352,000	1819
Alaska	Mainland State/The Last Frontier	AK	Juneau	1,531,100	591,005	614,000	1959
Arizona	Grand Canyon State/Apache State	AZ	Phoenix	294,100	113,523	4,669,000	1912
Arkansas	Bear State/Land of Opportunity	AR	Little Rock	137,800	53,191	2,538,000	1836
California	Golden State	CA	Sacramento	411,100	158,685	32,667,000	1850
Colorado	Centennial State	CO	Denver	269,700	104,104	3,971,000	1876
Connecticut	Constitution State/Nutmeg State	CT	Hartford	13,000	5018	3,274,000	1788
Delaware	First State/Diamond State	DE	Dover	5,300	2,046	744,000	1787
Florida	Sunshine State/Everglade State	FL	Tallahassee	152,000	58,672	14,916,000	1845
Georgia	Empire State of the South/ Peach State	GA	Atlanta	152,600	58,904	7,642,000	1788
Hawaii	Aloha State	HI	Honolulu	16,800	6,485	1,193,000	1959
Idaho	Gem State	ID	Boise	216,500	83,569	1,229,000	1890
Illinois	Inland Empire/Prairie State/ Land of Lincoln	IL	Springfield	146,100	56,395	12,045,000	1818
Indiana	Hoosier State	IN	Indianapolis	93,700	36,168	5,899,000	1816
Iowa	Hawkeye State/Corn State	IA	Des Moines	145,800	56,279	2,862,000	1846
Kansas	Sunflower State/Jayhawker State	KS	Topeka	213,200	82,295	2,629,000	1861
Kentucky	Bluegrass State	KY	Frankfort	104,700	40,414	3,936,000	1792
Louisiana	Pelican State/Sugar State/ Creole State	LA	Baton Rouge	135,900	52,457	4,369,000	1792
Maine	Pine Tree State	ME	Augusta	86,200	33,273	1,244,000	1812
Maryland	Old Line State/Free State	MD	Annapolis	31,600	12,198	5,135,000	1788
Massachusetts	Bay State/Old Colony	MA	Boston	21,500	8,299	6,147,000	1788
Michigan	Great Lakes State/Wolverine State	MI	Lansing	151,600	58,518	9,817,000	1837
Minnesota	North Star State/Gopher State	MN	St Paul	218,700	84,418	4,725,000	1858
Mississippi	Magnolia State	MS	Jackson	123,600	47,710	2,752,000	1817
Missouri	Show Me State/Bullion State	MO	Jefferson City	180,600	69,712	5,439,000	1821
Montana	Treasure State/Big Sky Country	MT	Helena	381,200	147,143	880,000	1889
Nebraska	Cornhusker State/Beef State	NE	Lincoln	200,400	77,354	1,663,000	1867
Nevada	Sagebrush State/Silver State/ Battleborn State	NV	Carson City	286,400	110,550	1,747,000	1864
New Hampshire	Granite State	NH	Concord	24,000	9,264	1,185,000	1788
New Jersey	Garden State	NJ	Trenton	20,200	7,797	8,115,000	1787
New Mexico	Land of Enchantment/Sunshine State	NM	Santa Fé	315,000	121,590	1,737,000	1912
New York	Empire State	NY	Albany	127,200	49,099	18,175,000	1788
North Carolina	Tar Heel State/Old North State	NC	Raleigh	136,400	52,650	7,546,000	1789
North Dakota	Peace Garden State	ND	Bismarck	183,100	70,677	638,000	1889
Ohio	Buckeye State	OH	Columbus	107,100	41,341	11,209,000	1803
Oklahoma	Sooner State	OK	Oklahoma City	181,100	69,905	3,347,000	1907
Oregon	Beaver State/Sunset State	OR	Salem	251,500	97,079	3,282,000	1859
Pennsylvania	Keystone State	PA	Harrisburg	117,400	45,316	12,001,000	1787
Rhode Island	Little Rhody/Ocean State	RI	Providence	3,100	1,197	988,000	1790
South Carolina	Palmetto State	SC	Columbia	80,600	31,112	3,836,000	1788
South Dakota	Coyote State/Mount Rushmore State	SD	Pierre	199,800	77,123	738,000	1889
Tennessee	Volunteer State	TN	Nashville	109,200	42,151	5,431,000	1796
Texas	Lone Star State	TX	Austin	691,200	266,803	19,760,000	1845
Utah	Beehive State/Mormon State	UT	Salt Lake City	219,900	84,881	2,100,000	1896
Vermont	Green Mountain State	VT	Montpelier	24,900	9,611	591,000	1791
Virginia	Old Dominion State/Mother of Presidents	VA	Richmond	105,600	40,762	6,791,000	1788
Washington	Evergreen State/Chinook State	WA	Olympia	176,700	68,206	5,689,000	1889
West Virginia	Mountain State/Panhandle State	WV	Charleston	62,900	24,279	1,811,000	1863
Wisconsin	Badger State/America's Dairyland	WI	Madison	145,500	56,163	5,224,000	1848
Wyoming	Equality State	WY	Cheyenne	253,400	97,812	481,000	1890
District of Columbia (Federal District)	–	DC	Washington	180	69	523,000	*

*established by Act of Congress 1790–91

(*continued from p. 983*)
Irians, West Papuans, the minorities of the Cordillera in the Philippines, and the non-Chinese in Taiwan. UNPO is based in the Netherlands and its general secretary is Michael Van Walt van Praag.

unsaturated compound chemical compound in which two adjacent atoms are linked by a double or triple covalent bond.

Examples are ▷alkenes and ▷alkynes, where the two adjacent atoms are both carbon, and ▷ketones, where the unsaturation exists between atoms of different elements (carbon and oxygen). The laboratory test for unsaturated compounds is the addition of bromine water; if the test substance is unsaturated, the bromine water will be decolorized.

unsaturated solution solution that is capable of dissolving more solute than it already contains at the same temperature.

untouchable (or **harijan**) member of the lowest Indian ▷caste, formerly forbidden to be touched by members of the other castes.

ununnilium synthesized radioactive element of the ▷transactinide series, symbol Uun, atomic number 110, relative atomic mass 269. It was discovered in October 1994, detected for a millisecond, at the GSI heavy-ion cyclotron, Darmstadt, Germany, while lead atoms were bombarded with nickel atoms.

unununium synthesized radioactive element of the ▷transactinide series, symbol Uuu, atomic number 111, relative atomic mass 272. It was detected at the GSI heavy-ion cyclotron, Darmstadt, Germany, in December 1994, when bismuth-209 was bombarded with nickel.

Unzen active volcano on the Shimbara peninsula, Kyushu island, Japan, opposite the city of Kumamoto. Its eruption in June 1991 led to the evacuation of 10,000 people. It is the main feature of Unzen-Amakusa National Park. The highest peak, Fugendake, is 1,359 m/4,459 ft high. There have been hot springs in the area since the 8th century and wild azaleas (*miyamakirishima*) grow locally.

Upanishad one of a collection of Hindu sacred treatises, written in Sanskrit, connected with the ▷Vedas but composed later, about 800–200 BC. Metaphysical and ethical, their doctrine equated the atman (self) with the Brahman (supreme spirit) – *'Tat tvam asi'* ('Thou art that') – and developed the theory of the transmigration of souls.

Related Web site: Vedas and Upanishads http://www.san.beck.org/EC7-Vedas.html

Updike, John Hoyer (1932–) US writer. Associated with the *New Yorker* magazine from 1955, he soon established a reputation for polished prose, poetry, and criticism. His novels include *The Poorhouse Fair* (1959), *The Centaur* (1963), *Couples* (1968), *The Witches of Eastwick* (1984), *Roger's Version* (1986), and *S.* (1988), and deal with the tensions and frustrations of contemporary US middle-class life and their effects on love and marriage. Updike was awarded the Medal for Distinguished Contribution to American Letters in the 1998 National Book Awards. In 2000 he published a book of literary criticism, *More Matter: Essays and Criticism*.

Updike was born in Shillington, Pennsylvania, and graduated from Harvard University. Two characters recur in his novels: the former basketball player 'Rabbit' Angstrom, who matures in the series *Rabbit, Run* (1960), *Rabbit Redux* (1971), *Rabbit is Rich* (1981, Pulitzer prize), and *Rabbit at Rest* (1990, Pulitzer prize); and the novelist Henry Bech, who appears in *Bech: A Book* (1970) and *Bech is Back* (1982). Other novels by Updike include *Of the Farm* (1965), *A Month of Sundays* (1972), *Marry Me* (1976), *The Coup* (1978), *Memories of the Ford Administration* (1992), *Toward the End of Time* (1997), and *Gertrude and Claudius* (2000). His short-story collections include *The Same Door* (1959), *Pigeon Feathers* (1962), *Museums and Women* (1972), and *Problems* (1979). His body of work includes essay collections, such as *Hugging the Shore* (1983), and the play *Buchanan Dying* (1974).

Upper Austria (German **Oberösterreich**) mountainous federal state of Austria, drained by the Danube, and bordered on the north by the Czech Republic and on the west by Bavaria; area 12,000 sq km/4,632 sq mi; population (1995) 1,385,500. Its capital is Linz and the main towns are Steyr and Wels. Agricultural products include fruit, wine, sugar beet, and grain. There are reserves of oil, and salt and lignite are mined. Textiles, chemicals, and metal and electronic goods are manufactured. The population density is the highest of all the provinces except Vienna.

Upper Volta former name (to 1984) of ▷Burkina Faso.

Uppsala city in Sweden, northwest of Stockholm; population (1994) 181,200. Industries include engineering and pharmaceuticals. The university was founded 1477; there are Viking relics and a Gothic cathedral. The botanist Carolus Linnaeus lived here.

Ur ancient city of the ▷Sumerian civilization, in modern Iraq. Excavations by the British archaeologist Leonard Woolley show that it was inhabited from about 3500 BC. He discovered evidence of a flood that may have inspired the *Epic of* ▷*Gilgamesh* as well as the biblical account, and remains of ziggurats, or step pyramids.

Ural Mountains (Russian **Ural'skiy Khrebet**) mountain system extending for over 2,000 km/1,242 mi from the Arctic Ocean to the Caspian Sea, and traditionally regarded as separating Europe from Asia. The highest peak is Naradnaya, 1,894 m/6,214 ft. The mountains hold vast mineral wealth.

uraninite uranium oxide, UO_2, an ore mineral of uranium, also known as **pitchblende** when occurring in massive form. It is black or brownish-black, very dense, and radioactive. It occurs in veins and as massive crusts, usually associated with granite rocks.

uranium hard, lustrous, silver-white, malleable and ductile, radioactive, metallic element of the ▷actinide series, symbol U, atomic number 92, relative atomic mass 238.029. It is the most abundant radioactive element in the Earth's crust, its decay giving rise to essentially all radioactive elements in nature; its final decay product is the stable element lead. Uranium combines readily with most elements to form compounds that are extremely poisonous. The chief ore is ▷pitchblende, in which the element was discovered by German chemist Martin Klaproth in 1789; he named it after the planet Uranus, which had been discovered in 1781.

Small amounts of certain compounds containing uranium have been used in the ceramics industry to make orange-yellow glazes and as mordants in dyeing; however, this practice was discontinued when the dangerous effects of radiation became known.

Uranium is one of three fissile elements (the others are thorium and plutonium). It was long considered to be the element with the highest atomic number to occur in nature. The isotopes U-238 and U-235 have been used to help determine the age of the Earth.

Uranium-238, which comprises about 99% of all naturally occurring uranium, has a half-life of 4.51×10^9 years. Because of its abundance, it is the isotope from which fissile plutonium is produced in breeder ▷nuclear reactors. The fissile isotope U-235 has a half-life of 7.13×10^8 years and comprises about 0.7% of naturally occurring uranium; it is used directly as a fuel for nuclear reactors and in the manufacture of nuclear weapons.

Many countries mine uranium; large deposits are found in Canada, the USA, Australia, and South Africa.
Related Web site: What is Uranium? http://www.uic.com.au/uran.htm

uranium ore material from which uranium is extracted, often a complex mixture of minerals. The main ore is uraninite (or pitchblende), UO_2, which is commonly found with sulphide minerals. The USA, Canada, and South Africa are the main producers in the West.

Uranus seventh planet from the Sun, discovered by German-born British astronomer William ▷Herschel in 1781. It is twice as far out as the sixth planet, Saturn. Uranus has a mass 14.5 times that of Earth. The spin axis of Uranus is tilted at 98°, so that one pole points towards the Sun, giving extreme seasons.

> **mean distance from the Sun** 2.9 billion km/1.8 billion mi **equatorial diameter** 50,800 km/31,600 mi **rotation period** 17.2 hr **year** 84 Earth years **atmosphere** deep atmosphere composed mainly of hydrogen and helium **surface** composed primarily of rock and various ices with only about 15% hydrogen and helium, but may also contain heavier elements, which might account for Uranus's mean density being higher than Saturn's **satellites** 17 moons (two discovered in 1997); 11 thin rings around the planet's equator were discovered in 1977. **rings** 11 rings, composed of rock and dust, around the planet's equator, were detected by the US space probe *Voyager 2*. The rings are charcoal black and may be debris of former 'moonlets' that have broken up. The ring furthest from the planet centre (51,000 km/31,800 mi), Epsilon, is 100 km/62 mi at its widest point. In 1995, US astronomers determined that the ring particles contained long-chain hydrocarbons. Looking at the brightest region of Epsilon, they were also able to calculate the precession of Uranus as 264 days, the fastest known precession in the Solar System. Uranus has a peculiar magnetic field, in that it is tilted at 60° to the axis of spin, and is displaced about a third of the way from the planet's centre to its surface. Uranus spins from east to west, the opposite of the other planets, with the exception of Venus and possibly Pluto. The rotation rate of the atmosphere varies with latitude, from about 16 hours in mid-southern latitudes to longer than 17 hours at the equator. The space probe *Voyager 2* detected 11 rings, composed of rock and dust, around the planet's equator, and found 10 small moons in addition to the 5 visible from Earth. Titania, the largest moon, has a diameter of 1,580 km/980 mi. The rings are charcoal black, and may be debris of former 'moonlets' that have broken up.

Uranus in Greek mythology, the primeval sky god, whose name means 'Heaven'. He was responsible for both the sunshine and the rain, and was the son and husband of ▷Gaia, the goddess of the Earth. Uranus and Gaia were the parents of ▷Kronos and his fellow ▷Titans, the one-eyed giant Cyclops, and the 100-handed Hecatoncheires.

Urban six popes, including:

Urban II (*c.* 1042–1099) Pope 1088–99. He launched the First ▷Crusade at the Council of Clermont in France 1095.

Urban VIII, Maffeo Barberini (1568–1644) Pope 1623–44. His policies during the ▷Thirty Years' War were designed more to maintain the balance of forces in Europe and prevent one side from dominating the papacy than to further the ▷Counter-Reformation. He extended the papal dominions and improved their defences. During his papacy, ▷Galileo was summoned in 1633 to recant the theories that the Vatican condemned as heretical.

urbanization process by which the proportion of a population living in or around towns and cities increases through migration and natural increase as the agricultural population decreases. The growth of urban concentrations in the USA and Europe is a relatively recent phenomenon, dating back only about 150 years to the beginning of the Industrial Revolution (although the world's first cities were built more than 5,000 years ago). The UN Population Fund reported in 1996 that within ten years the majority of the world's population would be living in urban conglomerations. Almost all urban growth will occur in the developing world, spawning ten large cities a year.

Urdu language member of the Indo-Iranian branch of the Indo-European language family, related to Hindi and written not in Devanagari but in Arabic script. Urdu is strongly influenced by Farsi (Persian) and Arabic. It is the official language of Pakistan and is used by Muslims in India.

urea $CO(NH_2)_2$ waste product formed in the mammalian liver when nitrogen compounds are broken down. It is filtered from the blood by the kidneys, and stored in the bladder as urine prior to release. When purified, it is a white, crystalline solid. In industry it is used to make urea-formaldehyde plastics (or resins), pharmaceuticals, and fertilizers.

ureter tube connecting the kidney to the bladder. Its wall contains fibres of smooth muscle whose contractions aid the movement of urine out of the kidney.

urethra in mammals, a tube connecting the bladder to the exterior. It carries urine and, in males, semen.

Urey, Harold Clayton (1893–1981) US chemist. In 1932 he isolated ▷heavy water and was awarded the Nobel Prize for Chemistry in 1934 for his discovery of ▷deuterium (heavy hydrogen).

urial (or **Punjab wild sheep** or **shapu**) wild sheep that ranges from sea level near the Caspian Sea to 4,200 m/13,860 ft in Tibet. The male has massive horns up to 1 m/3.3 ft long. The urial *Ovis vignei* is in family Bovidae, in order Artiodactyla.

uric acid $C_5H_4N_4O_3$ nitrogen-containing waste substance, formed from the breakdown of food and body protein.

It is only slightly soluble in water. Uric acid is the normal means by which most land animals that develop in a shell (birds, reptiles, insects, and land gastropods) deposit their waste products. The young are unable to get rid of their excretory products while in the shell and therefore store them in this insoluble form.

Humans and other primates produce some uric acid as well as urea, the normal nitrogenous waste product of mammals, adult amphibians, and many marine fishes. If formed in excess and not excreted, uric acid may be deposited in sharp crystals in the joints and other tissues, causing gout; or it may form stones (calculi) in the kidneys or bladder.

urinary system system of organs that removes nitrogenous waste products and excess water from the bodies of animals. In vertebrates, it consists of a pair of kidneys, which produce urine; ureters, which drain the kidneys; and (in bony fishes, amphibians, some reptiles, and mammals) a bladder that stores the urine before its discharge. In mammals, the urine is expelled through the urethra; in other vertebrates, the urine drains into a common excretory chamber called a ▷cloaca, and the urine is not discharged separately.

urine amber-coloured fluid filtered out by the kidneys from the blood. It contains excess water, salts, proteins, waste products in the form of urea, a pigment, and some acid.

Urquiza, Justo José de (1801–1870) Argentine president 1854–60, regarded as the organizer of the Argentine nation. Governor of Entre Ríos from 1841, he set up a progressive administration. Supported by Brazil and Uruguay, he defeated the unpopular dictator Juan Manuel de ▷Rosas in the Battle of Caseros 1852. As president he fostered internal economic development and created the Argentine Confederation 1853 which united the country's provinces, but he failed to bring Buenos Aires into it.

Ursa Major (Latin 'Great Bear') third-largest constellation in the sky, in the north polar region. Its seven brightest stars make up the familiar shape or asterism of the **Big Dipper** or **Plough**. The second star of the handle of the dipper, called Mizar, has a companion star, Alcor.

Two stars forming the far side of the dipper bowl act as pointers to the north pole star, ▷Polaris. Dubhe, one of them, is the constellation's brightest star.

Ursa Minor (Latin 'Little Bear') small constellation of the northern hemisphere, popularly known as the Little Dipper. It is shaped like a dipper, with the bright north pole star ▷Polaris at the end of the handle.

Two other bright stars in this group, Beta and Gamma Ursae Minoris, are called 'the Guards' or 'the Guardians of the Pole'. The constellation also contains the orange subgiant Kochab, about 95 light years from Earth.

urticaria (or **nettle rash** or **hives**) irritant skin condition characterized by itching, burning, stinging, and the spontaneous appearance of raised patches of skin. Treatment is usually by ▷antihistamines or steroids taken orally or applied as lotions. Its causes are varied and include allergy and stress.

Uruguay see country box.

Urumqi (or **Urumchi** or **Wulumuqi**; formerly **Dihau** (until 1953)) industrial city and capital of Xinjiang Uygur Autonomous Region, northwest China, on the Urumqi River, at the northern foot of the Tian Shan Mountains; population (1994) 1,240,000. Industries include oil-refining, food-processing, brewing, and the manfuacture of cotton textiles, cement, iron, steel, plastics, and agricultural equipment.

USA official abbreviation for ▷United States of America; US Army.

user ID (contraction of user identification) name or nickname that identifies the user of a computer system or network.

user interface in computing, the procedures and methods through which the user operates a program. These might include ▷menus, input forms, error messages, and keyboard procedures. A ▷graphical user interface (GUI or WIMP) is one that makes use of icons (small pictures) and allows the user to make menu selections with a mouse.

A **command line interface** is a character-based interface in which a prompt is displayed on the screen at which the user types a command, followed by carriage return, at which point the command, if valid, is executed. An example of a command line interface is the **DOS** prompt.

A **menu-driven interface** presents various options to the user in the form of a list, from which commands may be selected. Types of menu include the **menu bar**, which displays the top level options available to the user as a single line across the top of the screen; selecting one of these options displays a **pull-down** menu. Programs such as Microsoft Word use menus in this way.

In a **graphical user interface** programs and files appear as icons (small pictures), user options are selected from pull-down menus, and data is displayed in windows (rectangular areas), which the operator can manipulate in various ways. The operator uses a pointing device, typically a ▷mouse, to make selections and initiate actions.

The study of the ways in which people interact with computers is a subbranch of ergonomics. It aims to make it easier for people to use computers effectively and comfortably, and has become a focus of research for many national and international programmes.

Ushant (French **Ouessant**) French island 18 km/11 mi west of Brittany, area 15 sq km/6 sq mi, off which the British admiral Richard Howe defeated the French navy 1794 on 'the Glorious First of June'. The chief town is Lampaul.

Ushuaia southernmost town in the world, at the tip of Tierra del Fuego, Argentina, less than 1,000 km/620 mi from Antarctica; population (1991) 29,700. It is a free port and naval base. Industries include lumbering, sheeprearing, and fishing.

USSR abbreviation for the former ▷Union of Soviet Socialist Republics.

Ustaše Croatian nationalist terrorist organization founded 1929 and led by Ante Pavelić against the Yugoslav state. During World War II, it collaborated with the Nazis and killed thousands of Serbs, Romanies, and Jews. It also carried out deportations and forced conversions to Roman Catholicism in its attempt to create a 'unified' Croatian state.

usury former term for charging interest on a loan of money. In medieval times, usury was held to be a sin, and Christians were forbidden to lend (although not to borrow).

UT abbreviation for ▷Utah, a state of the USA.

Utah state in western USA. It is nicknamed the Beehive State or the Mormon State. Utah was admitted to the Union in 1896 as the 45th US state. One of the Mountain States, it is bordered to the east by Colorado, to the north by Wyoming, to the west by Nevada, and to the south by Arizona. At the 'Four Corners', in the southeast, it also touches New Mexico.

> **population** (1995) 1,951,400 **area** 219,900 sq km/84,881 sq mi **capital** Salt Lake City **towns and cities** Provo, Ogden, West Valley City **industries and products** wool, gold, silver, copper, coal, oil, potash, salt, steel, aerospace and military-dependent industries, tourism
> **Related Web site: Great Gallery of Horseshoe Canyon** http://www.apogeephoto.com/mag1-6/mag2-4rh.shtml

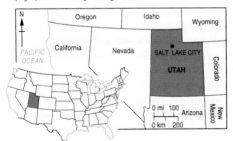

Utamaro, Kitagawa (1753–1806) Japanese colour-print artist of the ▷ukiyo-e school. He is known for his muted colour prints of women engaged in everyday activities, including informal studies of prostitutes.

UTC abbreviation for **coordinated universal time**, the standard measurement of ▷time.

uterus hollow muscular organ of female mammals, located between the bladder and rectum, and connected to the Fallopian tubes above and the vagina below. The embryo develops within the uterus, and in placental mammals is attached to it after implantation via the ▷placenta and umbilical cord. The lining of the uterus changes during the ▷menstrual cycle. In humans and other higher primates, it is a single structure, but in other mammals it is paired.

The outer wall of the uterus is composed of smooth muscle, capable of powerful contractions (induced by hormones) during childbirth.

U Thant Burmese diplomat; see ▷Thant U.

Uthman (*c.* 574–656) Third caliph (leader of the Islamic Empire) from 644, a son-in-law of the prophet Muhammad. Under his rule the Arabs became a naval power and extended their rule to North Africa and Cyprus, but Uthman's personal weaknesses led to his assassination. He was responsible for the compilation of the authoritative version of the Koran, the sacred book of Islam.

Uthman I another name for the Turkish sultan ▷Osman I.

utilitarianism philosophical theory of ethics outlined by the philosopher Jeremy ▷Bentham and developed by John Stuart Mill. According to utilitarianism, an action is morally right if it has consequences that lead to happiness, and wrong if it brings about the reverse. Thus society should aim for the greatest happiness of the greatest number.

utility program in computing, a systems program designed to perform a specific task related to the operation of the computer when requested to do so by the computer user.

Utopia (Greek 'no place') any ideal state in literature, named after philosopher Thomas More's ideal commonwealth in his book *Utopia* 1516. Other versions include Plato's *Republic*, Francis Bacon's *New Atlantis*, and *City of the Sun* by the Italian Tommaso Campanella (1568–1639). Utopias are a common subject in ▷science fiction. See also ▷dystopia.

Utrecht province of the Netherlands, lying southeast of Amsterdam, and south of the IJsselmeer, on the Kromme Rijn (Crooked Rhine); area 1,330 sq km/514 sq mi; population (1997)

1,079,400. The capital is Utrecht. Industries include petrochemicals, textiles, electrical goods, engineering, steelworks, railway workshops, and furniture. Fruit, vegetables, and cereals are grown, and there is livestock raising and dairying.

Utrecht, Treaty of treaty signed 1713 that ended the War of the ▷Spanish Succession. Philip V was recognized as the legitimate king of Spain, thus founding the Spanish branch of the Bourbon dynasty and ending the French king Louis XIV's attempts at expansion; the Netherlands, Milan, and Naples were ceded to Austria; Britain gained Gibraltar; the duchy of Savoy was granted Sicily.

Uruguay

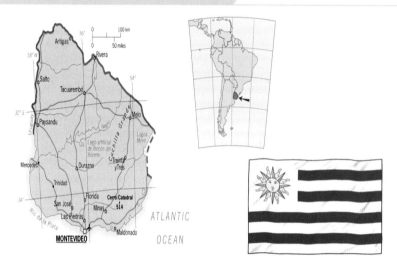

URUGUAY The government palace in Montevideo. The city was founded in 1726 by the governor of Buenos Aires, Bruno Mauricio de Zabala. It was a garrison town, placed here to defend against potential advances by the Portuguese in Brazil. Merchants began to flourish by the end of the colonial period, and today the port of Montevideo handles most of the foreign trade of Uruguay. *Photodisk*

Uruguay country in South America, on the Atlantic coast, bounded north by Brazil and west by Argentina.

NATIONAL NAME *República Oriental del Uruguay/Eastern Republic of Uruguay*
AREA 176,200 sq km/68,030 sq mi
CAPITAL Montevideo
MAJOR TOWNS/CITIES Salto, Paysandú, Las Piedras, Rivera, Tacuarembó
PHYSICAL FEATURES grassy plains (pampas) and low hills; rivers Negro, Uruguay, Río de la Plata

Government

HEAD OF STATE AND GOVERNMENT Jorge Batlle Ibáñez from 2000
POLITICAL SYSTEM liberal democracy
POLITICAL EXECUTIVE limited presidency
ADMINISTRATIVE DIVISIONS 19 departments
ARMED FORCES 23,900 (2002 est)
DEATH PENALTY abolished in 1907

Economy and resources

CURRENCY Uruguayan peso
GPD (US$) 12.3 billion (2002 est)
REAL GDP GROWTH (% change on previous year) −3.1 (2001)
GNI (US$) 14.8 billion (2002 est)
GNI PER CAPITA (PPP) (US$) 12,010 (2002 est)
CONSUMER PRICE INFLATION 27.9% (2003 est)
UNEMPLOYMENT 15.3% (2001)
FOREIGN DEBT (US$) 15.6 billion (2001 est)
MAJOR TRADING PARTNERS Brazil, Argentina, USA, Italy, Germany, Paraguay, France
RESOURCES small-scale extraction of building materials, industrial minerals, semi-precious stones; gold deposits are being developed
INDUSTRIES food processing, textiles and clothing, beverages, cement, chemicals, light engineering and transport equipment, leather products

EXPORTS textiles, meat (chiefly beef), live animals and by-products (mainly hides and leather products), rice, food and beverages, mineral products. Principal market: Brazil 23.8% (2001)
IMPORTS machinery and appliances, transport equipment, chemical products, petroleum and petroleum products, agricultural products. Principal source: Argentina 23% (2001)
ARABLE LAND 7.4% (2000 est)
AGRICULTURAL PRODUCTS rice, sugar cane, sugar beet, wheat, potatoes, barley, maize, sorghum; livestock rearing (sheep and cattle) is traditionally country's major economic activity – exports of animals, meat, skins, and hides accounted for 42% of total export revenue in 2000

Population and society

POPULATION 3,415,000 (2003 est)
POPULATION GROWTH RATE 0.6% (2000–15)
POPULATION DENSITY (per sq km) 19 (2003 est)
URBAN POPULATION (% of total) 93 (2003 est)
AGE DISTRIBUTION (% of total population) 0–14 25%, 15–59 58%, 60+ 17% (2002 est)
ETHNIC GROUPS predominantly of European descent: about 54% Spanish, 22% Italian, with minorities from other European countries; about 8% mestizo, 4% black
LANGUAGE Spanish (official), Brazilero (a mixture of Spanish and Portuguese)
RELIGION mainly Roman Catholic
EDUCATION (compulsory years) 6
LITERACY RATE 97% (men); 98% (women) (2003 est)
LABOUR FORCE 3.9% agriculture, 25.2% industry, 70.9% services (1999)
LIFE EXPECTANCY 72 (men); 79 (women) (2000–05)

CHILD MORTALITY RATE (under 5, per 1,000 live births) 16 (2001)
PHYSICIANS (per 1,000 people) 3.7 (1997 est)
HOSPITAL BEDS (per 1,000 people) 4.4 (1997 est)

Chronology

1516: Río de la Plata visited by Spanish navigator Juan Diaz de Solis, who was killed by native Charrua Amerindians. This discouraged European settlement for more than a century.

1680: Portuguese from Brazil founded Nova Colonia do Sacramento on Río de la Plata estuary.

1726: Spanish established fortress at Montevideo and wrested control over Uruguay from Portugal, with much of the Amerindian population being killed.

1776: Became part of Viceroyalty of La Plata, with capital at Buenos Aires.

1808: With Spanish monarchy overthrown by Napoleon Bonaparte, La Plata Viceroyalty became autonomous, but Montevideo remained loyal to Spanish Crown and rebelled against Buenos Aires control.

1815: Dictator José Gervasio Artigas overthrew Spanish and Buenos Aires control.

1820: Artigas ousted by Brazil, which disputed control of Uruguay with Argentina.

1825: Independence declared after fight led by Juan Antonio Lavalleja.

1828: Independence recognized by country's neighbours.

1836: Civil war between Reds and Whites, after which Colorado and Blanco parties were named.

1840: Merino sheep introduced by British traders, who later established meat processing factories for export trade.

1865–70: Fought successfully alongside Argentina and Brazil in war against Paraguay.

1903: After period of military rule, José Battle y Ordonez, a progressive from centre-left Colorado

TV SETS (per 1,000 people) 530 (2001 est)
PERSONAL COMPUTER USERS (per 100 people) 11.0 (2002 est)

See also ▷Buenos Aires.

Party, became president. As president 1903–07 and 1911–15, he gave women the franchise and created an advanced welfare state as a successful ranching economy developed.

1930: First constitution adopted, but period of military dictatorship followed during Depression period.

1958: After 93 years out of power, the right-of-centre Blanco Party returned to power.

1967: The Colorado Party were in power, with Jorge Pacheco Areco as president. A period of labour unrest and urban guerrilla activity by left-wing Tupamaros.

1972: Juan María Bordaberry Arocena of the Colorado Party became president.

1973: Parliament dissolved and Bordaberry shared power with military dictatorship, which crushed Tupamaros and banned left-wing groups.

1976: Bordaberry deposed by army; Dr Aparicio Méndez Manfredini became president.

1981: Gen Grigorio Alvárez Armellino became new military ruler.

1984: Violent antigovernment protests after ten years of repressive rule and deteriorating economy.

1985: Agreement reached between army and political leaders for return to constitutional government and freeing of political prisoners.

1986: Government of national accord established under President Sanguinetti.

1992: The public voted against privatization in a national referendum.

2000: Jorge Batlle Ibáñez, of the Colorado Party, was elected president.

Utrecht, Union of in 1579, the union of seven provinces of the northern Netherlands – Holland, Zeeland, Friesland, Groningen, Utrecht, Gelderland, and Overijssel – that, as the United Provinces, became the basis of opposition to the Spanish crown and the foundation of the present-day Dutch state.

Utrillo, Maurice (1883–1955) French artist. A self-taught painter, he was first influenced by the Impressionists, but soon developed a distinctive, almost naive style characterized by his subtle use of pale tones and muted colours. He painted views of his native Paris, many depicting Montmartre.

Uttar Pradesh state of north India, bordered by Nepal and China to the northeast, and Indian states to the south and west; area

294,400 sq km/113,638 sq mi; population (2001 est) 164,346,000. The capital is ▷Lucknow. Industries include the production of sugar, oil, textiles, leatherwork, cement, chemicals, coal, silica, and handicrafts (Varanasi, Lucknow). Wheat, rice, millet, barley, sugar cane, groundnuts, peas, cotton, oilseed, potatoes and fruit are grown, and there is livestock raising.

Uttaranchal state of north India, situated at the foot of the Himalayas and bordered by Himachal Pradesh and Uttar Pradesh; area 51,125 sq km/19,739 sq mi; population (2001 est) 8,115,000. It was carved from Uttar Pradesh and was incorporated in November 2000. The capital is ▷Dehra Dun. Nanda Devi, one of the highest peaks in India at 7,817m/25,645 ft, is located in the Region. Many

rivers originate in Uttaranchal including the Ganges and Yamuna. The state's principal industry is tourism. Other industries include forest production, a developing herbal pharmaceutical industry, and hydroelectric power. Grains and horticulture crops such as apple, orange, pear, grapes, peach, plum, apricot, mango, and guava are also produced.

Uzbek (or **Uzbeg**) member of the majority ethnic group (almost 70%) living in Uzbekistan. Minorities live in Turkmenistan, Tajikistan, Kazakhstan, and Afghanistan and include ▷Turkomen, ▷Tatars, ▷Armenians, Kazakhs, and Kirghiz.

Uzbekistan see country box.

Uzbekistan

Uzbekistan country in central Asia, bounded north by Kazakhstan and the Aral Sea, east by Kyrgyzstan and Tajikistan, south by Afghanistan, and west by Turkmenistan.

NATIONAL NAME *Özbekiston Respublikasi/Republic of Uzbekistan*
AREA 447,400 sq km/172,741 sq mi
CAPITAL Tashkent
MAJOR TOWNS/CITIES Samarkand, Bukhara, Namangan, Andijon, Nukus, Qarshi
PHYSICAL FEATURES oases in deserts; rivers: Amu Darya; Syr Darya; Fergana Valley; rich in mineral deposits

Government

HEAD OF STATE Islam Karimov from 1990
HEAD OF GOVERNMENT Shavkat Mirziyayev from 2003
POLITICAL SYSTEM authoritarian nationalist
POLITICAL EXECUTIVE unlimited presidency
ADMINISTRATIVE DIVISIONS 12 regions and one autonomous republic (Karakalpakstan)
ARMED FORCES 52,000 (2002 est)
CONSCRIPTION military service is compulsory for 12 months
DEATH PENALTY retained and used for ordinary crimes
DEFENCE SPEND (% GDP) 2.9 (2002 est)
EDUCATION SPEND (% GDP) 7.7 (1999)
HEALTH SPEND (% GDP) 3.7 (2000 est)

Economy and resources

CURRENCY som
GDP (US$) 9.7 billion (2002 est)
REAL GDP GROWTH (% change on previous year) 4.5 (2001)
GNI (US$) 11.5 billion (2002 est)
GNI PER CAPITA (PPP) (US$) 1,590 (2002 est)
CONSUMER PRICE INFLATION 21.1% (2003 est)
UNEMPLOYMENT 0.5% (2001 est; true level believed to be considerably higher)
FOREIGN DEBT (US$) 4.2 billion (2001 est)
MAJOR TRADING PARTNERS Russia, Switzerland, South Korea, UK, Germany,

Belgium, USA, Kazakhstan, Turkey, Tajikistan
RESOURCES petroleum, natural gas, coal, gold (world's seventh-largest producer), silver, uranium (world's fourth-largest producer), copper, lead, zinc, tungsten
INDUSTRIES processing of agricultural and mineral raw materials, agricultural machinery, chemical products, metallurgy, cement, mineral fertilizer, paper, textiles, footwear, electrical appliances
EXPORTS cotton fibre, textiles, machinery, food and energy products, gold. Principal market: Russia 16.7% (2000)
IMPORTS machinery and equipment, light industrial goods, food and raw materials, chemicals, plastics. Principal source: Russia 15.8% (2000)
ARABLE LAND 10.8% (2000 est)
AGRICULTURAL PRODUCTS cotton (among the world's five largest producers), grain, potatoes, vegetables, fruit and berries; livestock rearing; silkworm breeding

Population and society

POPULATION 26,093,000 (2003 est)
POPULATION GROWTH RATE 1.3% (2000–15)
POPULATION DENSITY (per sq km) 58 (2003 est)
URBAN POPULATION (% of total) 37 (2003 est)
AGE DISTRIBUTION (% of total population) 0–14 34%, 15–59 59%, 60+ 7% (2002 est)
ETHNIC GROUPS 75% Uzbek, 7% ethnic Russian, 5% Tajik, 4% Kazakh; remaining 9% include Tatar, Karalkalpak, and Korean
LANGUAGE Uzbek (a Turkic language; official), Russian, Tajik
RELIGION predominantly Sunni Muslim; small Wahhabi, Sufi, and Orthodox Christian communities
EDUCATION (compulsory years) 9
LITERACY RATE 99% (men); 99% (women) (2003 est)

UZBEKISTAN Ethnic Uzbekistani people, like this woman in Termez on the Afghan border, keep alive Uzbekistan's long history and tradition. *Corel*

LABOUR FORCE 41% agriculture, 13% industry, 46% services (2000)
LIFE EXPECTANCY 67 (men); 73 (women) (2000–05)
CHILD MORTALITY RATE (under 5, per 1,000 live births) 68 (2001)
PHYSICIANS (per 1,000 people) 3.1 (1998 est)
HOSPITAL BEDS (per 1,000 people) 8.3 (1998 est)
TV SETS (per 1,000 people) 276 (2001 est)
RADIOS (per 1,000 people) 465 (1997)
INTERNET USERS (per 10,000 people) 108.7 (2002 est)

See also ▷Bukhara; ▷Genghis Khan; ▷Samarkand; ▷Union of Soviet Socialist Republics.

Chronology

6th century BC: Part of the Persian Empire of Cyrus the Great.

4th century BC: Part of the empire of Alexander the Great of Macedonia.

1st century BC: Samarkand (Maracanda) developed as transit point on strategic Silk Road trading route between China and Europe.

7th century: City of Tashkent founded; spread of Islam.

12th century: Tashkent taken by Turks; Khorezm (Khiva), in northwest, became centre of large Central Asian polity, stretching from Caspian Sea to Samarkand in the east.

13th–14th centuries: Conquered by Genghis Khan and became part of Mongol Empire, with Samarkand serving as capital for Tamerlane.

18th–19th centuries: Dominated by independent emirates and khanates (chiefdoms) of Bukhara in southwest, Kokand in east, and Samarkand in centre.

1865–67: Tashkent was taken by Russia and made capital of Governor-Generalship of Turkestan.

1868–76: Tsarist Russia annexed emirate of Bukhara (1868); and khanates of Samarkand (1868), Khiva (1873), and Kokand (1876).

1917: Following Bolshevik revolution in Russia, Tashkent soviet ('people's council') established, which deposed the emir of Bukhara and other khans in 1920.

1918–22: Mosques closed and Muslim clergy persecuted as part of secularization drive by new communist rulers, despite nationalist guerrilla (basmachi) resistance.

1921: Part of Turkestan Soviet Socialist Autonomous Republic.

1925: Became constituent republic of USSR.

1930s: Skilled ethnic Russians immigrated into urban centres as industries developed.

1944: About 160,000 Meskhetian Turks forcibly transported from their native Georgia to Uzbekistan by Soviet dictator Joseph Stalin.

1950s–80s: Major irrigation projects stimulated cotton production, but led to desiccation of Aral Sea.

late 1980s: Upsurge in Islamic consciousness stimulated by *glasnost* initiative of Soviet Union's reformist leader Mikhail Gorbachev.

1989: Birlik ('Unity'), nationalist movement, formed. Violent attacks on Meskhetian and other minority communities in Fergana Valley.

1990: Economic and political sovereignty was declared by the increasingly nationalist UCP, led by Islam Karimov, who became president.

1991: An attempted anti-Gorbachev coup by conservatives in Moscow was initially supported by President Karimov. Independence was declared. Uzbekistan joined the new Commonwealth of Independent States (CIS); Karimov was re-elected president.

1992: There were violent food riots in Tashkent. Uzbekistan joined the Economic Cooperation Organization and the United Nations (UN). A new constitution was adopted.

1993: There was a crackdown on Islamic fundamentalists as the economy deteriorated.

1994: Economic, military, and social union was forged with Kazakhstan and Kyrgyzstan, and an economic integration treaty was signed with Russia. Links with Turkey were strengthened and foreign inward investment encouraged.

1995: The ruling PDP (formerly UCP) won a general election, from which the opposition was banned from participating, and Otkir Sultonov was appointed prime minister. Karimov's tenure as president was extended for a further five-year term by national referendum.

1996: An agreement was made with Kazakhstan and Kyrgyzstan to create a single economic market.

1998: A treaty of eternal friendship and deepening economic cooperation was signed with Kazakhstan.

1999: Uzbekistan threatened to end participation in a regional security treaty, accusing Russia of seeking to integrate the former Soviet republics into a superstate.

2000: President Islam Karimov was re-elected. Islamist rebels crossed into the country from Afghanistan via Tajikistan, reportedly seeking to create an Islamic state in east Uzbekistan.

V Roman numeral for **five**; in physics, symbol for ▷volt.

v in physics, symbol for ▷velocity.

V1, V2 (German *Vergeltungswaffe* 'revenge weapons') German flying bombs of World War II, launched against Britain in 1944 and 1945. The V1, also called the **doodlebug** and **buzz bomb**, was an uncrewed monoplane carrying a bomb, powered by a simple kind of jet engine called a pulse jet. The V2, a rocket bomb with a preset guidance system, was the first long-range ballistic ▷missile. It was 14 m/47 ft long, carried a 1-tonne warhead, and hit its target at a speed of 5,000 kph/3,000 mph.

VA abbreviation for the state of ▷Virginia, USA.

Vaal river in South Africa, the chief tributary of the Orange River. It rises in the Drakensberg mountain range, on the border of Swaziland, and is 805 km/500 mi long.

vaccine any preparation of modified pathogens (viruses or bacteria) that is introduced into the body, usually either orally or by a hypodermic syringe, to induce the specific ▷antibody reaction that produces ▷immunity against a particular disease.

vacuole in biology, a fluid-filled, membrane-bound cavity inside a cell. It may be a reservoir for fluids that the cell will secrete to the outside, or may be filled with excretory products or essential nutrients that the cell needs to store. Plant cells usually have a large central vacuole containing sap (sugar and salts in solution) which serves both as a store of food and as a key factor in maintaining turgor. In amoebae (single-celled animals), vacuoles are the sites of digestion of engulfed food particles.

vacuum in general, a region completely empty of matter; in physics, any enclosure in which the gas pressure is considerably less than atmospheric pressure (101,325 pascals).

vacuum cleaner cleaning device invented in 1901 by the Scot Hubert Cecil Booth. Having seen an ineffective dust-blowing machine, he reversed the process so that his machine (originally on wheels, and operated from the street by means of tubes running into the house) operated by suction.

vacuum flask (or **Dewar flask** or **Thermos flask**) container for keeping things either hot or cold. It has two silvered glass walls with a vacuum between them, in a metal or plastic outer case. This design reduces the three forms of heat transfer: radiation (prevented by the silvering), conduction, and convection (both prevented by the vacuum). A vacuum flask is therefore equally efficient at keeping cold liquids cold or hot liquids hot. It was invented by the British scientist James Dewar in about 1872, to store liquefied gases.

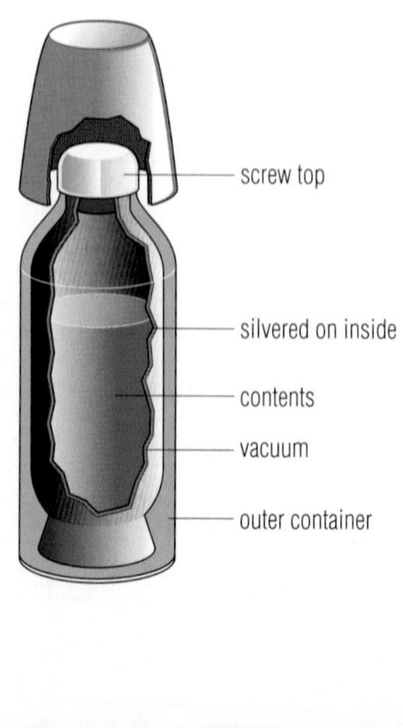

VACUUM FLASK The vacuum flask allows no heat to escape from or enter into its contents. It has double walls with a vacuum between to prevent heat loss by conduction. Radiation is prevented by silvering the walls.

Vaduz capital of the European principality of Liechtenstein; population (1995) 5,100. The economic base is now tourism and financial services. It trades in wine, fruit, and vegetables. Above the town stands the castle of the ruling prince.

vagina the lower part of the reproductive tract in female mammals, linking the uterus to the exterior. It admits the penis during sexual intercourse, and is the birth canal down which the baby passes during delivery.

Valdemar alternative spelling of Waldemar, four kings of Denmark.

Valdivia, Pedro de (*c.* 1497–1554) Spanish explorer who travelled to Venezuela about 1530 and accompanied Francisco ▷Pizarro on his second expedition to Peru. He then went south into Chile, where he founded the cities of Santiago in 1541 and Valdivia in 1544. In 1552 he crossed the Andes to explore the Negro River. He was killed by Araucanian Indians.

valence electron in chemistry, an electron in the outermost shell of an ▷atom. It is the valence electrons that are involved in the formation of ionic and covalent bonds (see ▷molecule). The number of electrons in this outermost shell represents the maximum possible valence for many elements and matches the number of the group that the element occupies in the ▷periodic table of the elements.

Valencia city and capital of Valencia province in the ▷Valencian Community, eastern Spain, on the estuary of the Guadalaviar River; population (1991) 752,900. It is the centre of a very rich agricultural plain noted for the high quality of its citrus fruits, particularly oranges; industries include textiles, chemicals, ship repair, and wine.

Valencian Community (Spanish **Comunidad Valenciana**) autonomous community of western Spain, comprising the provinces of Alicante, Castellón, and Valencia; area 23,307 sq km/8,999 sq mi; population (2001 est) 4,202,600. There is a rich agricultural area on the coastal plain, producing oranges, and rice, and industries include iron and steel production and car manufacture. The capital is ▷Valencia.

valency in chemistry, the measure of an element's ability to combine with other elements, expressed as the number of atoms of hydrogen (or any other standard univalent element) capable of uniting with (or replacing) its atoms. The number of electrons in the outermost shell of the atom dictates the combining ability of an element.

The elements are described as uni-, di-, tri-, and tetravalent when they unite with one, two, three, and four univalent atoms respectively. Some elements have **variable valency**: for example, nitrogen and phosphorus have a valency of both three and five. The valency of oxygen is two: hence the formula for water, H_2O (hydrogen being univalent).

Valentine, St According to tradition, a bishop of Terni martyred in Rome, now omitted from the calendar of saints' days as probably nonexistent. His festival was 14 February, but the custom of sending 'valentines' to a loved one on that day seems to have arisen because the day accidentally coincided with the Roman mid-February festival of ▷Lupercalia.

Related Web site: Valentine's Day http://www.holidays.net/amore/story.html

Valentino, Rudolph (1895–1926) Adopted name of Rodolfo Alfonso Guglielmi di Valentina d'Antonguolla. Italian-born US film actor and dancer. He was the archetypal romantic lover of the Hollywood silent era. His screen debut was in 1919, but his first starring role was in *The Four Horsemen of the Apocalypse* (1921). His subsequent films include *The Sheik* (1921) and *Blood and Sand* (1922).

Vale of Glamorgan unitary authority in south Wales, created in 1996 from parts of the former counties of Mid Glamorgan and South Glamorgan.

area 337 sq km/130 sq mi **towns** Barry (administrative headquarters), Penarth **physical** lowland area **agriculture** sheep farming, varied agriculture **population** (1996) 119,500

Valera, Éamon de Irish politician; see ▷de Valera.

valerian any of a group of perennial plants native to the northern hemisphere, with clustered heads of fragrant tubular flowers in red, white, or pink. The root of the common valerian or garden heliotrope *V. officinalis* is used in medicine to relieve wind and to soothe or calm patients. (Genera *Valeriana* and *Centranthus*, family Valerianaceae.)

Valhalla in Norse mythology, the golden hall in ▷Odin's palace in ▷Asgard, where he feasted with the souls of half those heroes killed in battle (*valr*) chosen by his female attendants, the ▷Valkyries; the remainder celebrated in Sessrumnir with ▷Freya, goddess of love and war.

validation in computing, the process of checking input data to ensure that it is complete, accurate, and reasonable. Although it would be impossible to guarantee that only valid data are entered into a computer, a suitable combination of validation checks should ensure that most errors are detected.

Valkyrie (Old Norse *valr* 'slain', *kjosa* 'choose') in Norse mythology, any of the female attendants of ▷Odin. They directed the course of battles and selected the most valiant warriors to die; half being escorted to ▷Valhalla, and the remainder to Sessrumnir, the hall of ▷Freya.

Valladolid capital of Valladolid province, in Castilla–León, Spain; population (1994) 328,400. Industries include food processing, textiles, engineering, and vehicle manufacture. It has a university (founded in 1346) and a 16th-century cathedral.

Valle d'Aosta autonomous region of northwest Italy, in the Alps; area 3,300 sq km/1,274 sq mi; population (1992 est) 117,200, many of whom are French-speaking. Its capital is Aosta. Wine and livestock are produced, and industries include the manufacture of special steels and textiles, and the production of hydroelectricity; tourism is also important.

Valletta capital and port of Malta; population (1995) 9,129 (inner harbour area 102,600).

Valley Forge site in Pennsylvania 32 km/20 mi northwest of Philadelphia, USA, where George ▷Washington's army spent the winter of 1777–78 in great hardship during the ▷American Revolution.

Of the 10,000 men there, 2,500 died of disease and the rest suffered from lack of rations and other supplies; many deserted.

Valley of Ten Thousand Smokes valley in southwestern Alaska, on the Alaska Peninsula, where in 1912 Mount Katmai erupted in one of the largest volcanic explosions ever known, although without loss of human life since the area was uninhabited. The valley was filled with ash to a depth of 200 m/660 ft. It was dedicated as the Katmai National Monument in 1918. Thousands of fissures on the valley floor continue to emit steam and gases.

Valley of the Kings burial place of ancient kings opposite ▷Thebes, Egypt, on the left bank of the Nile. It was established as a royal cemetery during the reign of Thotmes I (*c.* 1500 BC) and abandoned during the reign of Ramses XI (*c.* 1100 BC).

Valmy, Battle of during the French ▷Revolutionary Wars, comprehensive French victory over the Prussians 20 September 1792, near Valmy, a French village about 55 km/35 mi southwest of Reims. This forthright defeat of a powerful army by the previously despised revolutionary forces set the seal upon the authority of the revolutionary French government.

Valois branch of the Capetian dynasty, originally counts of Valois (see Hugh ▷Capet) in France, members of which occupied the French throne from Philip VI (1328) to Henry III (1589).

Valparaíso industrial port, naval base, and capital of Valparaiso region, central Chile, situated on a broad bay on the Pacific coast at the foot of a spur of hills, 120 km/75 mi northwest of Santiago; population (1992) 276,700. It is Chile's major port and second-largest city, an administrative centre, and the seat of the Chilean parliament. Both the law courts and the new National Congress are located here. Industries include textiles, chemicals, oil, sugar refining, and leather goods. Fruit and mining products are exported. It is the seat of the Chilean Naval Academy.

value added in economics, the difference between the cost of producing something and the price at which it is sold. Added value is the basis of VAT or ▷value-added tax, a tax on the value added at each stage of the production process of a commodity.

value-added tax (VAT) tax on goods and services applied at each stage of the production of a commodity, and charged only on the value added at that stage. Although collected from traders at each stage, it is in effect a tax on consumer expenditure. In some states of the USA a similar result is achieved by a **sales tax** added by the retailer at the point of sale.

valve in animals, a structure for controlling the direction of the blood flow. In humans and other vertebrates, the contractions of the beating heart cause the correct blood flow into the arteries because a series of valves prevents back flow. Diseased valves, detected as 'heart murmurs', have decreased efficiency. The tendency for low-pressure venous blood to collect at the base of limbs under the influence of gravity is counteracted by a series of small valves within the veins. It was the existence of these valves that prompted the 17th-century physician William Harvey to suggest that the blood circulated around the body.

valve (or **electron tube**) in electronics, a glass tube containing gas at low pressure, which is used to control the flow of electricity in a circuit. The electron tube valve was invented by US radio engineer Lee de Forest (1873–1961). Three or more metal electrodes are inset into the tube. By varying the voltage on one of them, called the **grid electrode**, the current through the valve can be controlled, and the valve can act as an amplifier.

Valves have been replaced for most applications by ▷transistors. However, they are still used in high-power transmitters and amplifiers, and in some hi-fi systems.

valvular heart disease damage to the heart valves, leading to either narrowing of the valve orifice when it is open (stenosis) or leaking through the valve when it is closed (regurgitation).

vampire (Hungarian *vampir* (and similar forms in other Slavonic languages) in Hungarian and Slavonic folklore, an 'undead' corpse that sleeps in its coffin by day and sucks the blood of the living by night, often in the form of a bat. ▷Dracula is a vampire in popular fiction, based on the creation of Bram Stoker.

vampire bat South and Central American bat of the family Desmodontidae, of which there are three species. The **common vampire** *Desmodus rotundus* is found from northern Mexico to central Argentina; its head and body grow to 9 cm/3.5 in. Vampire bats feed on the blood of birds and mammals; they slice a piece of skin from a sleeping animal with their sharp incisor teeth and lap up the flowing blood. They chiefly approach their prey by flying low then crawling and leaping.

Vampire bats feed on all kinds of mammals including horses, cattle, and occasionally humans. The bite is painless and the loss of blood is small (about 1 cubic cm/0.06 cubic in); the victim seldom comes to any harm. Vampire bats are intelligent and among the few mammals to show altruistic behaviour (they adopt orphans and help other bats in need).

The other species are *Diaemus youngi*, the **white-winged vampire**, and *Diphylla ecaudata*, the **hairy-legged vampire**.

VAMPIRE BAT The vampire bat is the only mammal to live as a parasite. It alights a few feet away from its victim and walks forwards on all fours. A small cut is made with its incisor teeth on a hairless part of the victim's body and the bat feeds on the oozing blood. Although the loss of blood is not severe, the bat may transmit serious diseases, such as rabies, to its victim.

vanadium silver-white, malleable and ductile, metallic element, symbol V, atomic number 23, relative atomic mass 50.942. It occurs in certain iron, lead, and uranium ores and is widely distributed in small quantities in igneous and sedimentary rocks. It is used to make steel alloys, to which it adds tensile strength.

Spanish mineralogist Andrés del Rio (1764–1849) and Swedish chemist Nils Sefström (1787–1845) discovered vanadium independently, the former in 1801 and the latter in 1831. Del Rio named it 'erythronium', but was persuaded by other chemists that he had not in fact discovered a new element; Sefström gave it its present name, after the Norse goddess of love and beauty, Vanadis (or Freya).

Van Allen radiation belts two zones of charged particles around the Earth's magnetosphere, discovered in 1958 by US physicist James Van Allen. The atomic particles come from the Earth's upper atmosphere and the ▷solar wind, and are trapped by the Earth's magnetic field. The inner belt lies 1,000–5,000 km/620–3,100 mi above the Equator, and contains ▷protons and ▷electrons. The outer belt lies 15,000–25,000 km/9,300–15,500 mi above the Equator, but is lower around the magnetic poles. It contains mostly electrons from the solar wind.

The Van Allen belts are hazardous to astronauts, and interfere with electronic equipment on satellites.

Vanbrugh, John (1664–1726) English baroque architect, dramatist, and soldier. Although entirely untrained as an architect, he designed the huge mansions of Castle Howard (1699–1726), Blenheim (1705–16; completed by Nicholas Hawksmoor 1722–25), Seaton Delaval (1720–29), and many others, as well as much of Greenwich Hospital (1718 onwards). He also wrote the comic dramas *The Relapse* (1696) and *The Provok'd Wife* (1697).

> **John Vanbrugh**
> *Love, like fortune, turns upon a wheel, and is very much given to rising and falling.*
> *False Friends* I. i

Van Buren, Martin (1782–1862) 8th president of the USA 1837–41, a Democrat, who had helped establish the ▷Democratic Party. He was secretary of state 1829–31, minister to Britain 1831–33, vice-president 1833–37, and president during the Panic of 1837, the worst US economic crisis until that time, caused by land speculation in the West. Refusing to intervene, he advocated the establishment of an independent treasury, one not linked to the federal government, worsening the depression and losing the 1840 election.

Vance, Cyrus Roberts (1917–) US Democratic politician, secretary of state 1977–80. He was United Nations negotiator in the peace talks on ▷Bosnia-Herzegovina 1992–93, resigning from the post due to ill health. Together with European Community negotiator David Owen, he devised the Vance–Owen peace plan for dividing the republic into ten semi-autonomous provinces. The plan was rejected by the Bosnian Serbs.

Vancouver chief Pacific seaport of Canada, on the mainland of British Columbia; population (2001 est) 582,000; metropolitan area (2000 est) 2,078,800. A major commercial, distribution, and tourist centre, it is the terminus of trans-continental rail and road routes, and a 1,144-km/715-mi pipeline from the Alberta oilfields. Industries include oil-refining, engineering, shipbuilding, fishing and fish-canning, brewing, timber-milling, and the manufacture of aircraft, pulp and paper, and textiles.

Surveyed in 1792 by George ▷Vancouver, the site was settled as Gastown by 1867, became Granville in 1870, and was renamed on incorporation in 1886, having been chosen as the terminus of the Canadian Pacific Railroad. It is Canada's third-largest metropolitan area.

In 1989 Vancouver had an ethnic Chinese population of 140,000, and this was rapidly augmented by thousands of immigrants from Hong Kong.

Related Web site: Vancouver – Spectacular by Nature http://www.tourism-vancouver.org/

Vancouver, George (1757–1798) English navigator who made extensive exploration of the west coast of North America.

The city of Vancouver was named after him. He accompanied James ▷Cook on two voyages, and served in the West Indies. He also surveyed parts of Australia, New Zealand, Tahiti, and Hawaii.

Vancouver Island island off the west coast of Canada, part of British Columbia, separated from the mainland by the straits of Juan de Fuca, Haro, Georgia, Johnstone, and Queen Charlotte Sound; area 32,136 sq km/12,404 sq mi. Industries include coal, timber, fish, and tourism. Fruit is grown, and there is dairying.

Vandal member of a Germanic people related to the ▷Goths. In the 5th century AD the Vandals invaded Roman ▷Gaul and Spain, many settling in Andalusia (formerly Vandalitia) and others reaching North Africa 429. They sacked Rome 455 but were defeated by Belisarius, general of the emperor Justinian, in the 6th century.

van de Graaff generator electrostatic generator capable of producing a voltage of over a million volts. It consists of a continuous vertical conveyor belt that carries electrostatic charges (resulting from friction) up to a large hollow sphere supported on an insulated stand. The lower end of the belt is earthed, so that charge accumulates on the sphere. The size of the voltage built up in air depends on the radius of the sphere, but can be increased by enclosing the generator in an inert atmosphere, such as nitrogen.

van der Waals' law modified form of the ▷gas laws that includes corrections for the non-ideal behaviour of real gases (the molecules of ideal gases occupy no space and exert no forces on each other). It is named after Dutch physicist J D van der Waals (1837–1923).

The equation derived from the law states that:

$$\left(P + \frac{a}{V^2}\right)\left(V - b\right) = RT$$

where P, V, and T are the pressure, volume, and temperature (in kelvin) of the gas, respectively; R is the ▷gas constant; and a and b are constants for that particular gas.

van Diemen, Anthony Dutch admiral, see ▷Diemen, Anthony van.

van Dyck, Anthony Flemish painter; see ▷Dyck, Anthony van.

Vane, Henry (1613–1662) English politician. In 1640 he was elected a member of the ▷Long Parliament, and was knighted in the same year. He was prominent in the impeachment of Archbishop ▷Laud and from 1643–53 was in effect the civilian head of the Parliamentary government. At the Restoration of the monarchy he was executed.

Vänern largest lake in Sweden, area 5,550 sq km/2,140 sq mi. Karlstad, Vänersborg, Lidköping, and Mariestad are on its banks.

van Eyck, Jan Flemish painter; see ▷Eyck, Jan van.

van Gogh, Vincent Dutch painter; see ▷Gogh, Vincent van.

Van Morrison Northern Irish singer, songwriter, and saxophonist; see ▷Morrison, Van.

Vanguard early series of US Earth-orbiting satellites and their associated rocket launcher. *Vanguard 1* was the second US satellite, launched on 17 March 1958 by the three-stage Vanguard rocket. Tracking of its orbit revealed that the Earth is slightly pear-shaped. The series ended in September 1959 with *Vanguard 3*.

vanilla any of a group of climbing orchids native to tropical America but cultivated elsewhere, with large, fragrant white or yellow flowers. The dried and fermented fruit, or podlike capsules, of the species *V. planifolia* are the source of the vanilla flavouring used in cookery and baking. (Genus *Vanilla*.)

van't Hoff, Jacobus Henricus (1852–1911) Dutch physical chemist. He explained the 'asymmetric' carbon atom occurring in optically active compounds. His greatest work – the concept of chemical affinity as the maximum work obtainable from a reaction – was shown with measurements of osmotic and gas pressures, and reversible electrical cells. He was the first person to be awarded the Nobel Prize for Chemistry in 1901 for his study of the laws of chemical dynamics and osmotic pressure.

Vanuatu see country box.

vapour one of the three states of matter (see also ▷solid and ▷liquid). The molecules in a vapour move randomly and are far apart, the distance between them, and therefore the volume of the vapour, being limited only by the walls of any vessel in which they might be contained. A vapour differs from a ▷gas only in that a vapour can be liquefied by increased pressure, whereas a gas cannot unless its temperature is lowered below its critical temperature; it then becomes a vapour and may be liquefied.

vapour density density of a gas, expressed as the ▷mass of a given volume of the gas divided by the mass of an equal volume of a reference gas (such as hydrogen or air) at the same temperature and pressure. If the reference gas is hydrogen, it is equal to half the relative molecular weight (mass) of the gas.

vapour pressure pressure of a vapour given off by (evaporated from) a liquid or solid, caused by atoms or molecules continuously escaping from its surface. In an enclosed space, a maximum value is reached when the number of particles leaving the surface is in equilibrium with those returning to it; this is known as the **saturated vapour pressure** or **equilibrium vapour pressure**.

Var river in southern France, rising on the Col de la Cayolle (2,326 m/7,631 ft) in the Maritime Alps, in the *département* of Alpes-Maritimes, and flowing generally southeast for 130 km/81 mi into the Mediterranean near Nice. It gives its name to the Var *département* in the Provence-Alpes-Côte d'Azur region.

Varanasi (or **Benares** or **Banaras**) city in Uttar Pradesh, India, one of the seven holy cities of Hinduism, on the River Ganges; population (2001 est) 1,211,700. There are 1,500 golden shrines, and a 5 km/3 mi frontage to the Ganges with sacred stairways (ghats) for purification by bathing. Varanasi is also a sacred centre of ▷Jainism, ▷Sikhism, and ▷Buddhism: Buddha came to Varanasi from Gaya and is believed to have preached in the Deer Park. One-third of its inhabitants are Muslim.

Varangian (Old Norse, *varan* 'to swear') member of the Byzantine imperial guard founded in 988 by Vladimir of Kiev (955–1015), which lasted until the fall of Constantinople in 1453. The name (meaning 'the sworn') came to be used for a widespread Swedish Viking people in eastern Europe and the Balkans.

Vargas, Getúlio Dornelles (1883–1954) Brazilian president 1930–45 and 1951–54. Following his presidential election failure in 1930, he overthrew the republic and in 1937 set up a totalitarian, profascist state known as the Estado Novo. Ousted by a military coup in 1945, he returned as president in 1951 with the support of the labour movement but, amid mounting opposition and political scandal, committed suicide in 1954.

Vargas Llosa, (Jorge) Mario (Pedro) (1936–) Peruvian novelist and politician. He wrote *La ciudad y los perros/The Time of the Hero* (1963) and *La guerra del fin del mundo/The War at the End of the World* (1982). In the course of his political career, Vargos Llosa began as a communist and turned to the right; he ran unsuccessfully for the presidency in 1990, when he was defeated by Alberto Fujimori.

variable in computing, a quantity that can take different values. Variables can be used to represent different items of data in the course of a program.

variable in mathematics, a changing quantity (one that can take various values), as opposed to a ▷constant. For example, in the algebraic expression $y = 4x^3 + 2$, the variables are x and y, whereas 4 and 2 are constants.

A variable may be dependent or independent. Thus if y is a ▷function of x, written $y = f(x)$, such that $y = 4x^3 + 2$, the domain of the function includes all values of the **independent variable** x while the range (or co-domain) of the function is defined by the values of the **dependent variable** y.

variable star in astronomy, a star whose brightness changes, either regularly or irregularly, over a period ranging from a few hours to months or years. The ▷Cepheid variables regularly expand and contract in size every few days or weeks.

Stars that change in size and brightness at less precise intervals include **long-period variables**, such as the red giant ▷Mira in the constellation ▷Cetus (period about 331 days), and **irregular variables**, such as some red supergiants. **Eruptive variables** emit sudden outbursts of light. Some suffer flares on their surfaces, while others, such as a ▷nova, result from transfer of gas between a close pair of stars. A ▷supernova is the explosive death of a star. In an ▷eclipsing binary, the variation is due not to any change in the star itself, but to the periodic eclipse of a star by a close companion. The different types of variability are closely related to different stages of stellar evolution.

varicose veins (or **varicosis**) condition in which the veins become swollen and twisted. The veins of the legs are most often affected; other vulnerable sites include the rectum (▷haemorrhoids) and testes.

variegation description of plant leaves or stems that exhibit patches of different colours. The term is usually applied to plants that show white, cream, or yellow on their leaves, caused by areas of tissue that lack the green pigment ▷chlorophyll. Variegated plants are bred for their decorative value, but they are often considerably weaker than the normal, uniformly green plant. Many will not breed true and require ▷vegetative reproduction.

varve in geology, a pair of thin sedimentary beds, one coarse and one fine, representing a cycle of thaw followed by an interval of freezing, in lakes of glacial regions.

Vasa dynasty Swedish royal house founded by ▷Gustavus Vasa. He liberated his country from Danish rule 1520–23 and put down local uprisings of nobles and peasants. By 1544 he was secure enough to make his title hereditary. His grandson, ▷Gustavus Adolphus, became king 1611 and led the armies of the Protestant princes in the ▷Thirty Years' War until his death. The dynasty ended 1809 when Gustavus IV was deposed by a revolution and replaced by his uncle Charles XIII. With no heir to the throne, the crown was offered 1810 to one of Napoleon's generals, Bernadotte, who became King Charles John until his death in 1844.

VARIEGATION This elder tree *Sambucus nigra* exhibits clumps of variegated leaves among a majority of normal leaves. Usually an accident in nature, variegation is encouraged in some ornamentals. *Premaphotos Wildlife*

Vanuatu

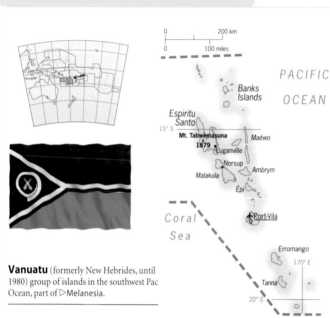

Vanuatu (formerly New Hebrides, until 1980) group of islands in the southwest Pac Ocean, part of ▷Melanesia.

NATIONAL NAME *Ripablik blong Vanuatu/République de Vanuatu/Republic of Vanuatu*
AREA 14,800 sq km/5,714 sq mi
CAPITAL Port-Vila (on Efate island) (and chief port)
MAJOR TOWNS/CITIES Luganville (on Espíritu Santo)
MAJOR PORTS Santo
PHYSICAL FEATURES comprises around 70 inhabited islands, including Espíritu Santo, Malekula, and Efate; densely forested, mountainous; three active volcanoes; cyclones on average twice a year

Government

HEAD OF STATE John Bani from 1999
HEAD OF GOVERNMENT Edward Natapei from 2001
POLITICAL SYSTEM liberal democracy
POLITICAL EXECUTIVE parliamentary
ADMINISTRATIVE DIVISIONS six provinces
ARMED FORCES no standing defence force; paramilitary force of about 300 and police naval service of about 50 (2003 est)
DEATH PENALTY laws do not provide for the death penalty for any crime
EDUCATION SPEND (% GDP) 7.3 (2001 est)
HEALTH SPEND (% GDP) 3.9 (2000 est)

Economy and resources

CURRENCY vatu
GPD (US$) 234 million (2002)
REAL GDP GROWTH (% change on previous year) –0.5 (2001)
GNI (US$) 221 million (2002 est)
GNI PER CAPITA (PPP) (US$) 2,770 (2002 est)
CONSUMER PRICE INFLATION 4% (2003 est)
FOREIGN DEBT (US$) 153 million (2001 est)
MAJOR TRADING PARTNERS Indonesia, Japan, Australia, Thailand, Singapore, Germany
RESOURCES manganese; gold, copper, and large deposits of petroleum have been discovered but have hitherto remained unexploited
INDUSTRIES processing of agricultural products (chiefly copra, meat canning, fish freezing, saw milling), soft drinks, building materials, furniture, aluminium, tourism, offshore banking, shipping registry
EXPORTS timber, copra, beef, cocoa, shells. Principal market: Indonesia 34.8% (2001)
IMPORTS machinery and transport equipment, food and live animals, basic manufactures, miscellaneous manufactured articles, mineral fuels, chemicals, beverages, tobacco. Principal source: Japan 26.1% (2001)

ARABLE LAND 2.5% (2000 est)
AGRICULTURAL PRODUCTS coconuts and copra, cocoa, coffee, yams, taro, cassava, breadfruit, squash and other vegetables, bananas; livestock rearing (cattle, pigs, goats, and poultry); forest resources

Population and society

POPULATION 212,000 (2003 est)
POPULATION GROWTH RATE 2.5% (2000–05)
POPULATION DENSITY (per sq km) 17 (2003 est)
URBAN POPULATION (% of total) 23 (2003 est)
AGE DISTRIBUTION (% of total population) 0–14 41%, 15–59 54%, 60+ 5% (2002 est)
ETHNIC GROUPS 94% Melanesian, 4% European or mixed European, 2% Chinese, Vietnamese, or other Pacific islanders
LANGUAGE Bislama (82%), English, French (all official)
RELIGION Christian 80%, animist about 8%

See also ▷Australasia and Oceania.

Chronology

1606: First visited by Portuguese navigator Pedro Fernandez de Queiras, who named the islands Espíritu Santo.

1774: Visited by British navigator Capt James Cook, who named them the New Hebrides, after the Scottish island.

1830s: European merchants attracted to islands by sandalwood trade. Christian missionaries arrived, but many were attacked by the indigenous Melanesians who, in turn, were ravaged by exposure to European diseases.

later 19th century: Britain and France disputed control; islanders were shipped to Australia, the Fiji Islands, Samoa, and New Caledonia to work as plantation labourers.

1906: The islands were jointly administered by France and Britain as the Condominium of the New Hebrides.

1963: Indigenous Na-Griamel (NG) political grouping formed on Espíritu Santo to campaign against European acquisition of more than a third of the land area.

1975: A representative assembly was established following pressure from the VP, formed in 1972 by English-speaking Melanesian Protestants.

1978: A government of national unity was formed, with Father Gerard Leymang as chief minister.

VANUATU A market in Vanuatu. *Corel*

1980: A revolt on the island of Espíritu Santo by French settlers and pro-NG plantation workers delayed independence but it was achieved within the Commonwealth, with George Kalkoa (adopted name Sokomanu) as president and left-of-centre Father Walter Lini (VP) as prime minister.

1988: The dismissal of Lini by Sokomanu led to Sokomanu's arrest for treason. Lini was later reinstated.

1991: Lini was voted out by party members and replaced by Donald Kalpokas. A general election produced a coalition government of the Francophone Union of Moderate Parties (UMP) and Lini's new National United Party (NUP) under Maxime Carlot Korman.

1993: A cyclone caused extensive damage.

1995: The governing UMP–NUP coalition won a general election, but Serge Vohor of the VP-dominated Unity Front became prime minister in place of Carlot Korman.

1996: The VP, led by Donald Kalpokas, joined the governing coalition.

1997: Prime Minister Vohor formed a new coalition. The legislature was dissolved and new elections called after a no-confidence motion against Vohor.

1998: A two-week state of emergency followed rioting in the capital.

1999: John Bernard Bani was elected president.

Vasarely, Victor (1908–1997) Hungarian **Viktor Vásárhelyi**. Hungarian-born French artist. He was one of the leading exponents of ▷op art. In the 1940s he developed precise geometric compositions, full of visual puzzles and effects of movement, which he created with complex arrangements of hard-edged geometric shapes and subtle variations in colours.

Vasari, Giorgio (1511–1574) Italian art historian, architect, and painter. He is best known for *Le vite de' più eccelenti architetti, pittori, et sculteri italiani/The Lives of the Most Excellent Italian Architects, Painters, and Sculptors* (1550; enlarged 1568), which provides an invaluable source of information on Italian Renaissance artists. His most important architectural work was the Uffizi Palace, Florence (now an art gallery).

Vasco da Gama Portuguese navigator; see ▷Gama.

vascular bundle in botany, strand of primary conducting tissue (a 'vein') in vascular plants, consisting mainly of water-conducting tissues, metaxylem and protoxylem, which together make up the primary ▷xylem, and nutrient-conducting tissue, ▷phloem. It extends from the roots to the stems and leaves. Typically the phloem is situated nearest to the epidermis and the xylem towards the centre of the bundle. In plants exhibiting ▷secondary growth, the xylem and phloem are separated by a thin layer of vascular ▷cambium, which gives rise to new conducting tissues.

vascular plant plant containing vascular bundles. ▷Pteridophytes (ferns, horsetails, and club mosses), ▷gymnosperms (conifers and cycads), and ▷angiosperms (flowering plants) are all vascular plants.

vas deferens in male vertebrates, a tube conducting sperm from the testis to the urethra. The sperm is carried in a fluid secreted by various glands, and can be transported very rapidly when the smooth muscle in the wall of the vas deferens undergoes rhythmic contraction, as in sexual intercourse.

vasectomy male sterilization; an operation to cut and tie the ducts (see ▷vas deferens) that carry sperm from the testes to the penis. Vasectomy does not affect sexual performance, but the semen produced at ejaculation no longer contains sperm.

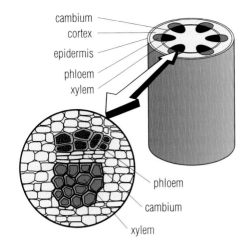

cambium
cortex
epidermis
phloem
xylem

phloem
cambium
xylem

VASCULAR BUNDLE The fluid-carrying tissue of most plants is normally arranged in units called vascular bundles. The vascular tissue is of two types: xylem and phloem. The xylem carries water up through the plant; the phloem distributes food made in the leaves to all parts of the plant.

vassal in medieval Europe, a person who paid feudal homage to a superior lord (see ▷feudalism), and who promised military service and advice in return for a grant of land. The term was used from the 9th century.

Vassar, Matthew (1792–1868) British-born US entrepreneur and educational philanthropist. A proponent of higher education for women, he endowed Vassar Female College in Poughkeepsie, New York, 1861. The school opened 1865 with a full college curriculum and became one of the finest women's educational institutions in the USA.

Vassiliou, Georgios Vassos (1931–) Greek-Cypriot politician and entrepreneur, president of Cyprus 1988–93. A self-made millionaire, he entered politics as an independent and in 1988 won the presidency, with Communist Party support. He subsequently, with United Nations help, tried to heal the rift between the Greek and Turkish communities, but was unsuccessful. In the February 1993 presidential elections he was narrowly defeated by Glafkos Clerides.

VAT abbreviation for ▷value-added tax.

Vatican City State see country box.

Vatican Council either of two Roman Catholic ecumenical councils called by Pope Pius IX 1869 (which met 1870) and by Pope John XXIII 1959 (which met 1962). These councils deliberated over elements of church policy.
    Related Web site: II Vatican Council http://www.vatican.va/archive/hist_councils/ii_vatican_council/index.htm

Vaucluse mountain range in southeast France, part of the Provence Alps east of Avignon, rising to 1,242 m/4,075 ft. It gives its name to the *département* of Vaucluse. The Italian poet Petrarch lived in the Vale of Vaucluse from 1337 to 1353.

Vaughan Williams, Ralph (1872–1958) English composer. His style was tonal and often evocative of the English countryside through the use of folk themes. Among his works are the orchestral *Fantasia on a Theme by Thomas Tallis* (1910); the opera *Sir John in Love* (1929), featuring the Elizabethan song 'Greensleeves'; and nine symphonies (1909–57).
    Related Web site: Ralph Vaughan Williams Web Page http://www.cs.qub.ac.uk/~J.Collis/RVW.html

vault in architecture, a continuous arch of brick, stone, or concrete, forming a self-supporting roof over a building or part of a building; also a vaulted structure, for example under a street pavement. See picture on p. 996.

VDU abbreviation for ▷visual display unit.

vector graphics computer graphics that are stored in the computer memory by using geometric formulas. Vector graphics can be transformed (enlarged, rotated, stretched, and so on)

Vatican City State

Vatican City State sovereign area within the city of Rome, Italy.

See also ▷John Paul II; ▷Lateran Treaties; ▷Roman Catholicism.

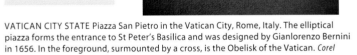

VATICAN CITY STATE Piazza San Pietro in the Vatican City, Rome, Italy. The elliptical piazza forms the entrance to St Peter's Basilica and was designed by Gianlorenzo Bernini in 1656. In the foreground, surmounted by a cross, is the Obelisk of the Vatican. *Corel*

NATIONAL NAME *Stato della Città del Vaticano/Vatican City State*
AREA 0.4 sq km/0.2 sq mi
PHYSICAL FEATURES forms an enclave in the heart of Rome, Italy

Government

HEAD OF STATE John Paul II from 1978
HEAD OF GOVERNMENT Cardinal Angelo Sodano from 1990
POLITICAL SYSTEM theocratic
POLITICAL EXECUTIVE theocratic
DEATH PENALTY abolished in 1969

Economy and resources

CURRENCY euro
GPD see Italy
REAL GDP GROWTH (% change on previous year) see Italy

GNI (US$) see Italy
GNI PER CAPITA (PPP) see Italy
INDUSTRIES the Vatican has three main sources of income: the Istituto per le Opere di Religione, 'Peter's pence' (voluntary contributions), and interest on investments managed by the Administration of the Patrimony of the Holy See

Population and society

POPULATION 1,000 (2003 est)
POPULATION DENSITY (per sq km) 1,784 (2003 est)
URBAN POPULATION (% of total) 100 (2003 est)
LANGUAGE Latin (official), Italian
RELIGION Roman Catholic
LITERACY RATE see Italy
LIFE EXPECTANCY see Italy

Chronology

AD 64: Death of St Peter, a Christian martyr who, by legend, was killed in Rome and became regarded as the first bishop of Rome. The Pope, as head of the Roman Catholic Church, is viewed as the spiritual descendent of St Peter.

756: The Pope became temporal ruler of the Papal States, which stretched across central Italy, centred around Rome.

11th–13th centuries: Under Gregory VII and Innocent III the papacy enjoyed its greatest temporal power.

1377: After seven decades in which the papacy was based in Avignon (France), Rome once again became the headquarters for the Pope, with the Vatican Palace becoming the official residence.

1860: Umbria, Marche, and much of Emilia Romagna which, along with Lazio formed the Papal States, were annexed by the new unified Italian state.

1870: First Vatican Council defined as a matter of faith the absolute primacy of the Pope and the infallibility of his pronouncements on 'matters of faith and morals'.

1870–71: French forces, which had been protecting the Pope, were withdrawn, allowing Italian nationalist forces to capture Rome, which became the capital of Italy; Pope Pius IX retreated into the Vatican Palace, from which no Pope was to emerge until 1929.

1929: The Lateran Agreement, signed by the Italian fascist leader Benito Mussolini and Pope Pius XI, restored full sovereign jurisdiction over the Vatican City State to the bishopric of Rome (Holy See) and declared the new state to be a neutral and inviolable territory.

1947: A new Italian constitution confirmed the sovereignty of the Vatican City State.

1962: The Second Vatican Council was called by Pope John XXIII.

1978: John Paul II became the first non-Italian pope for more than 400 years.

1985: A new concordat was signed under which Roman Catholicism ceased to be Italy's state religion.

1992: Relations with East European states were restored.

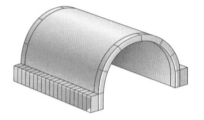

barrel vault (Romanesque)

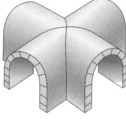

groin vault (late Romanesque)

rib vault (late Romanesque and early Gothic)

fan vault (Gothic)

VAULT Some of the many different types of vault. See entry on p. 995.

without loss of picture resolution. It is also possible to select and transform any of the components of a vector-graphics display because each is separately defined in the computer memory. In these respects vector graphics are superior to ▷raster graphics. Vector graphics are typically used for drawing applications, allowing the user to create and modify technical diagrams such as designs for houses or cars.

vector quantity any physical quantity that has both magnitude and direction (such as the velocity or acceleration of an object) as distinct from ▷scalar quantity (such as speed, density, or mass), which has magnitude but no direction. A vector is represented either geometrically by an arrow whose length corresponds to its magnitude and points in an appropriate direction, or by two or three numbers representing the magnitude of its components. Vectors can be added graphically by constructing a parallelogram

of vectors (such as the ▷parallelogram of forces commonly employed in physics and engineering).

Veda (Sanskrit 'divine knowledge') the most sacred of the Hindu scriptures, hymns written in an old form of Sanskrit; the oldest may date from 1500 or 2000 BC. The four main collections are: the *Rig-veda* (hymns and praises); *Yajur-Veda* (prayers and sacrificial formulae); *Sâma-Veda* (tunes and chants); and *Atharva-Veda*, or Veda of the Atharvans, the officiating priests at the sacrifices.

Vedānta (Sanskrit 'knowledge's end') school of Hindu philosophy that developed the teachings of the *Upanishads*. One of its teachers was Samkara, who lived in southern India in the 8th century AD and is generally regarded as a manifestation of Siva. He taught that there is only one reality, Brahman, and that knowledge of Brahman leads finally to *moksha*, or liberation from reincarnation.

VE Day (abbreviation for Victory in Europe Day) anniversary of the surrender of Germany at the end of ▷World War II, 8 May 1945. The day is celebrated as a commemoration of the victory of the Allied powers in the European theatre. The war continued in the Pacific theatre until Japan's surrender on 15 August which is marked by VJ Day.

Vedda (Sinhalese 'hunter') member of any of the aboriginal peoples of Sri Lanka, who occupied the island before the arrival of the Aryans about 550 BC. Formerly cave-dwelling hunter-gatherers, they have now almost died out or merged with the dominant Sinhalese and Tamil populations. They speak a Sinhalese language, belonging to the Indo-European family.

Vega (or **Alpha Lyrae**) brightest star in the constellation ▷Lyra and the fifth-brightest star in the night sky. It is a blue-white star, 25 light years from the Sun, with a true luminosity 50 times that of the Sun.

In 1983 the Infrared Astronomy Satellite (IRAS) discovered a ring of dust around Vega, possibly a disc from which a planetary system is forming.

Vega, Lope Felix de (Carpio) (1562–1635) Spanish poet and dramatist. He was one of the founders of modern Spanish drama. He wrote epics, pastorals, odes, sonnets, novels, and over 500 plays (of which 426 are still in existence), mostly tragicomedies. He set out his views on drama in *Arte nuevo de hacer comedias/The New Art of Writing Plays* (1609), in which he defended his innovations while reaffirming the classical forms. *Fuenteovejuna* (*c.* 1614) has been acclaimed as the first proletarian drama.

vegetative reproduction type of ▷asexual reproduction in plants that relies not on spores, but on multicellular structures formed by the parent plant. Some of the main types are ▷stolons and runners, gemmae, ▷bulbils, sucker shoots produced from roots (such as in the creeping thistle *Cirsium arvense*), ▷tubers, ▷bulbs, ▷corms, and ▷rhizomes. Vegetative reproduction has long been exploited in horticulture and agriculture, with various methods employed to multiply stocks of plants.

vein in animals with a circulatory system, any vessel that carries blood from the body to the heart. Veins contain valves that prevent the blood from running back when moving against gravity. They carry blood at low pressure, so their walls are thinner than those of arteries. They always carry deoxygenated blood, with the exception of the **pulmonary vein**, leading from the lungs to the heart in birds and mammals, which carries newly oxygenated blood. The term is also used more loosely for any system of channels that strengthens living tissues and supplies them with nutrients – for example, leaf veins (see ▷vascular bundle), and the veins in insects' wings.

Vela bright constellation of the southern hemisphere near Carina, represented as the sails of a ship. It contains large wisps of gas – called the Gum nebula after its discoverer, the Australian astronomer Colin Gum (1924–1960) – believed to be the remains of one or more ▷supernovae. Vela also contains the second optical ▷pulsar (a pulsar that flashes at a visible wavelength) to be discovered.

Velázquez, Diego Rodríguez de Silva y (1599–1660) Spanish painter. One of the outstanding artists of the 17th century, he was court painter to Philip IV in Madrid, where he produced many portraits of the royal family as well as occasional religious paintings, genre scenes, and other works. Notable among his portraits is *Las Meninas/The Maids of Honour* (1656; Prado, Madrid), while *Women Frying Eggs* (1618; National Gallery of Scotland, Edinburgh) is a typical genre scene.

veldt subtropical grassland in South Africa, equivalent to the ▷Pampas of South America.

velocity speed of an object in a given direction. Velocity is a ▷vector quantity, since its direction is important as well as its magnitude (or speed).

The velocity at any instant of a particle travelling in a curved path is in the direction of the tangent to the path at the instant considered. The velocity v of an object travelling in a fixed direction may be calculated by dividing the distance s it has travelled by the time t taken to do so, and may be expressed as:

$$v = s/t$$

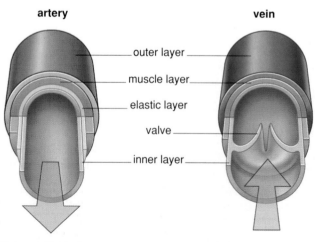

artery

vein

outer layer

muscle layer

elastic layer

valve

inner layer

VEIN Cross-sections of an artery and a vein. Arteries have thicker walls than veins as they have to withstand a higher blood pressure than do veins. Veins have valves to prevent blood from flowing backwards.

velvet fabric of silk, cotton, nylon, or other textile, with a short, thick pile. Utrecht in the Netherlands and Genoa, Italy, are traditional centres of manufacture. It is woven on a double loom, then cut between the centre pile to form velvet nap.

vena cava either of the two great veins of the trunk, returning deoxygenated blood to the right atrium of the ▷heart. The **superior vena cava**, beginning where the arches of the two innominate veins join high in the chest, receives blood from the head, neck, chest, and arms; the **inferior vena cava**, arising from the junction of the right and left common iliac veins, receives blood from all parts of the body below the diaphragm.

Venda former independent homeland ▷Black National State within South Africa, independent from 1979 (but not recognized by the United Nations) until 1994 when it was re-integrated into South Africa, in Northern Province; area 6,500 sq km/2,510 sq mi. Towns and cities include Makwarela, Makhade, and Sibasa. Its main industries are coal, copper, graphite, and construction stone. Luvenda and English are spoken here.

Vendée , La river in western France, rising near the village of La Châtaigneraie and flowing 72 km/45 mi to join the Sèvre Niortaise 11 km/7 mi east of the Bay of Biscay.

veneer thin layers of fine wood applied to the surface of furniture made with a coarser or cheaper wood. Veneer has been widely used from the second half of the 17th century.

venereal disease (**VD**) any disease mainly transmitted by sexual contact, although commonly the term is used specifically for gonorrhoea and syphilis, both occurring worldwide, and chancroid ('soft sore') and lymphogranuloma venerum, seen mostly in the tropics. The term ▷sexually transmitted disease (STD) is more often used to encompass a growing list of conditions passed on primarily, but not exclusively, by sexual contact.

Veneto region of northeast Italy, comprising the provinces of Belluno, Padua, Treviso, Rovigo, Venice, and Vicenza; area 18,400 sq km/7,102 sq mi; population (1992 est) 4,395,300. Its capital is ▷Venice, and towns include Padua, Verona, and Vicenza. The Veneto forms part of the north Italian plain, with the delta of the River Po; it includes part of the Alps and Dolomites, and Lake Garda. Products include cereals, fruit, vegetables, wine, tobacco, chemicals, ships, and textiles.

Venezia Italian form of ▷Venice, a city, port, and naval base on the Adriatic Sea.

Venezuela see country box.

Venice (Italian **Venezia**) city, port, and naval base on the northeast coast of Italy; population (2001 est) 266,200. It is the capital of Veneto region.

The old city is built on piles on low-lying islands in a salt-water lagoon, sheltered from the Adriatic Sea by the Lido and other small strips of land. There are about 150 canals crossed by some 400 bridges. Apart from tourism (it draws 8 million tourists a year), industries include glass, jewellery, textiles, and lace. Venice was an independent trading republic from the 10th century, ruled by a doge, or chief magistrate, and was one of the centres of the Italian Renaissance. It was renowned as a centre of early publishing; 15% of all printed books before 1500 were printed in Venice.

Features It is now connected with the mainland and its industrial suburb, Mestre, by road and rail viaduct. The Grand Canal divides the city and is crossed by the Rialto Bridge; transport is by traditional gondola or *vaporetto* (water bus).

St Mark's Square has the 11th-century Byzantine cathedral of S Marco, the 9th–16th-century campanile (rebuilt in 1902), and the 14th–15th-century Gothic Doge's Palace (linked to the former state prison by the 17th-century Bridge of Sighs). The nearby Lido is a

VENICE A carnival is held in Venice, Italy, before Lent, which usually begins in February. Another festival that Venetians enjoy is the annual Feast of the Redeemer, in July, when lighted boats fill the canals throughout the night to commemorate the city's deliverance from the plague in 1575. *Image Bank*

bathing resort. The **Venetian School** of artists includes the Bellinis, Carpaccio, Giorgione, Titian, Tintoretto, and Veronese. The Venetian Carnival is held annually at the end of February, with spectacular costumes and masks. Venice's opera house, La Fenice, considered to be one of the city's most beautiful monuments, was destroyed by fire in January 1996.

History In 1991 archaeologist Ernesto Canal established that the city was founded by the Romans in the 1st century AD; it was previously thought to have been founded by mainlanders fleeing from the Barbarians in AD 421. Venice became a wealthy independent trading republic in the 10th century, stretching by the mid-15th century to the Alps and including Crete. It was governed by an aristocratic oligarchy, the Council of Ten, and a senate, which appointed the doge 697–1797. Venice helped defeat the Ottoman Empire in the naval Battle of Lepanto (1571) but the republic was overthrown by Napoleon I in 1797. It passed to Austria in 1815 but finally became part of the Kingdom of Italy in 1866.

> Related Web site: History of Venice http://www.doge.it/storia/storiai.htm

veni, vidi, vici (Latin 'I came, I saw, I conquered') Julius Caesar's description of his victory over King Pharnaces II (63–47 BC) at Zela in 47 BC.

Venn diagram in mathematics, a diagram representing a ▷set or sets and the logical relationships between them. The sets are drawn as circles. An area of overlap between two circles (sets) contains elements that are common to both sets, and thus represents a third set. Circles that do not overlap represent sets with no elements in common (disjoint sets). The method is named after the English logician John Venn.

ventral surface the front of an animal. In vertebrates, the side furthest from the backbone; in invertebrates, the side closest to the ground. The positioning of the main nerve pathways on the ventral side is a characteristic of invertebrates.

ventricle in zoology, either of the two lower chambers of the heart that force blood to circulate by contraction of their muscular walls. The term also refers to any of four cavities within the brain in which cerebrospinal fluid is produced.

venture capital (or **risk capital**) money put up by investors such as merchant banks to fund a new company or the expansion of an established company. The organization providing the money receives a share of the company's equity and seeks to make a profit by rapid growth in the value of its stake, as a result of expansion by the start-up company or 'venture'.

Venus in Roman mythology, the goddess of love and beauty, equivalent to the Greek ▷Aphrodite. The patricians of Rome claimed descendance from her son, the Trojan prince ▷Aeneas, and she was consequently venerated as the guardian of the Roman people. Venus was also worshipped as a goddess of military victory and patroness of spring.

Venus second planet from the Sun. It can approach Earth to within 38 million km/24 million mi, closer than any other planet. Its mass is 0.82 that of Earth. Venus rotates on its axis more slowly than any other planet, from east to west, the opposite direction to the other planets (except Uranus and possibly Pluto).

The first artificial object to hit another planet was the Soviet probe *Venera 3*, which crashed on Venus on 1 March 1966. Later Venera probes parachuted down through the atmosphere and landed successfully on its surface, analysing surface material and sending back information and pictures. In December 1978 a US Pioneer Venus probe went into orbit around the planet and mapped most of its surface by radar, which penetrates clouds. In 1992 the US space probe *Magellan* mapped 99% of the planet's surface to a resolution of 100 m/ 330 ft.

The largest highland area is Aphrodite Terra near the equator, half the size of Africa. The highest mountains are on the northern highland region of Ishtar Terra, where the massif of Maxwell Montes rises to 10,600 m/35,000 ft above the average surface level. The highland areas on Venus were formed by volcanoes.

Venus has an ion-packed tail 45 million km/28 million mi in length that stretches away from the Sun and is caused by the bombardment of the ions in Venus's upper atmosphere by the solar wind. It was first discovered in the late 1970s but it was not until 1997 that the Solar Heliospheric Observatory (SOHO) revealed its immense length.

mean distance from the Sun 108.2 million km/67.2 million mi **equatorial diameter** 12,100 km/7,500 mi **rotation period** 243 Earth days **year** 225 Earth days **atmosphere** Venus is shrouded by clouds of sulphuric acid droplets that sweep across the planet from east to west every four days. The atmosphere is almost entirely carbon dioxide, which traps the Sun's heat by the ▷greenhouse effect and raises the planet's surface temperature to 480°C/900°F, with an atmospheric pressure of 90 times that at the surface of the Earth. **surface** consists mainly of silicate rock and may have an interior structure similar to that of Earth: an iron–nickel core, a ▷mantle composed of rocks made of more mafic rocks (rocks made of one or more

ferromagnesian, dark-coloured minerals), and a thin siliceous outer ▷crust. The surface is dotted with deep impact craters. Some of Venus's volcanoes may still be active. **satellites** no moons

Venus flytrap insectivorous plant belonging to the sundew family, native to the southeastern USA. Its leaves have two hinged surfaces that rapidly close together to trap any insect which brushes against the sensitive leaf hairs; digestive juices then break down the insect body so that it can be absorbed by the plant. (*Dionaea muscipula*, family Droseraceae.)

Veracruz port (trading in coffee, tobacco, and vanilla) in eastern Mexico, on the Gulf of Mexico; population (1990) 328,600. Products include chemicals, sisal, and textiles. It was founded by the Spanish conquistador Hernán Cortés as Villa Nueva de la Vera Cruz ('new town of the true cross') on a nearby site in 1519 and transferred to its present site in 1599.

verbena any of a group of plants containing about 100 species, mostly found in the American tropics. The leaves are fragrant and the tubular flowers are arranged in close spikes in colours ranging from white to rose, violet, and purple. The garden verbena is a hybrid annual. (Genus *Verbena*, family Verbenaceae.)

VERBENA *Verbena elegans* is one of numerous verbenas which occur in the deserts of the southwest USA and Mexico. They flower in profusion after heavy rains. *Premaphotos Wildlife*

Vercingetorix (died 46 BC) Gallic chieftain. Leader of a revolt of all the tribes of Gaul against the Romans 52 BC; he lost, was captured, displayed in Julius Caesar's triumph 46 BC, and later executed. This ended the Gallic resistance to Roman rule.

Verdi, Giuseppe Fortunino Francesco (1813–1901) Italian opera composer of the Romantic period. He took his native operatic style to new heights of dramatic expression. In 1842 he wrote the opera *Nabucco*, followed by *Ernani* in 1844 and *Rigoletto*

GIUSEPPE VERDI This score cover of the opera *Aida* dates from before 1880. The libretto was originally written in French by C du Locle, but the pictured edition is an Italian translation by A Ghislanzoni. *The Art Archive/Mander & Mitcheson Theatre Col/Eileen Tweedy*

Venezuela

Venezuela country in northern South America, on the Caribbean Sea, bounded east by Guyana, south by Brazil, and west by Colombia.

NATIONAL NAME *República de Venezuela/Republic of Venezuala*
AREA 912,100 sq km/352,161 sq mi
CAPITAL Caracas
MAJOR TOWNS/CITIES Maracaibo, Maracay, Barquisimeto, Valencia, Ciudad Guayana, Petare
MAJOR PORTS Maracaibo
PHYSICAL FEATURES Andes Mountains and Lake Maracaibo in northwest; central plains (llanos); delta of River Orinoco in east; Guiana Highlands in southeast

Government

HEAD OF STATE AND GOVERNMENT Hugo Chávez Frías from 1999
POLITICAL SYSTEM liberal democracy
POLITICAL EXECUTIVE limited presidency
ADMINISTRATIVE DIVISIONS 23 states and one federally controlled area
ARMED FORCES 82,300 (2002 est)
CONSCRIPTION military service is by selective conscription for 30 months
DEATH PENALTY abolished in 1863
DEFENCE SPEND (% GDP) 1.3 (2002 est)

EDUCATION SPEND (% GDP) 4.9 (1999)
HEALTH SPEND (% GDP) 4.7 (2000 est)

Economy and resources

CURRENCY bolivar
GPD (US$) 93.3 billion (2002 est)
REAL GDP GROWTH (% change on previous year) 2.7 (2001)
GNI (US$) 102.6 billion (2002 est)
GNI PER CAPITA (PPP) (US$) 5,080 (2002 est)
CONSUMER PRICE INFLATION 37.5% (2003 est)
UNEMPLOYMENT 13.3% (2001)
FOREIGN DEBT (US$) 31.8 billion (2001 est)
MAJOR TRADING PARTNERS USA, Colombia, Brazil, Japan, Germany, Italy, Canada, Cuba, Mexico
RESOURCES petroleum, natural gas, aluminium, iron ore, coal, diamonds, gold, zinc, copper, silver, lead, phosphates, manganese, titanium
INDUSTRIES refined petroleum products, metals (mainly aluminium, steel and pig-iron), food products, chemicals, fertilizers, cement, paper, vehicles

VENEZUELA As a result of oil revenues, Venezuela has become one of South America's richest countries. It has been able to expand into industrial development that, in turn, has paid for important modernization. Yet the country still has its peaceful side, as can be seen in this picture of pelicans at Puerto-la-Cruz. *Corel*

EXPORTS petroleum and petroleum products, metals (mainly aluminium, gold, and iron ore), natural gas, chemicals, cement, plastics, fish, shellfish, processed fish. Principal market: USA 50% (2001)
IMPORTS machinery and transport equipment, chemicals, food and live animals, basic manufactures, crude materials. Principal source: USA 33.8% (2001)
ARABLE LAND 2.8% (2000 est)
AGRICULTURAL PRODUCTS coffee, cocoa, sugar cane, bananas, maize, rice, plantains, oranges, sorghum, cassava, wheat, tobacco, cotton, beans, sisal; livestock rearing (cattle)

Population and society

POPULATION 25,699,000 (2003 est)

Chronology

1st millennium BC: Beginnings of settled agriculture.
AD 1498–99: Visited by explorers Christopher Columbus and Alonso de Ojeda, at which time the principal indigenous Indian communities were the Caribs, Arawaks, and Chibchas; it was named Venezuela ('little Venice') since the coastal Indians lived in stilted thatched houses.
1521: Spanish settlement established on the northeast coast and was ruled by Spain from Santo Domingo (Dominican Republic).
1567: Caracas founded by Diego de Losada.
1739: Became part of newly created Spanish Viceroyalty of New Granada, with capital at Bogotá (Colombia), but, lacking gold mines, retained great autonomy.
1749: First rebellion against Spanish colonial rule.
1806: Rebellion against Spain, led by Francisco Miranda.
1811–12: First Venezuelan Republic declared by patriots, taking advantage of Napoleon Bonaparte's invasion of Spain, but Spanish Royalist forces re-established their authority.
1813–14: The Venezuelan, Simón Bolívar, 'El Libertador' (the Liberator), created another briefly independent republic, before being forced to withdraw to Colombia.
1821: After the battle of Carabobo, Venezuelan independence achieved within Republic of Gran Colombia (which also comprised Colombia, Ecuador, and Panama).
1829: Became separate state of Venezuela after leaving Republic of Gran Colombia.
1830–48: Gen José Antonio Páez, the first of a series of caudillos (military leaders), established political stability.
1870–88: Antonio Guzmán Blanco ruled as benevolent liberal–conservative dictator, modernizing infrastructure and developing agriculture (notably coffee) and education.
1899: International arbitration tribunal found in favour of British Guiana (Guyana) in long-running dispute over border with Venezuela.
1902: Ports blockaded by British, Italian, and German navies as a result of Venezuela's failure to repay loans.
1908–35: Harsh rule of dictator Juan Vicente Gómez, during which period Venezuela became world's largest exporter of oil, which had been discovered in 1910.

POPULATION GROWTH RATE 1.5% (2000–15)
POPULATION DENSITY (per sq km) 28 (2003 est)
URBAN POPULATION (% of total) 88 (2003 est)
AGE DISTRIBUTION (% of total population) 0–14 33%, 15–59 60%, 60+ 7% (2002 est)
ETHNIC GROUPS 67% mestizos (of Spanish-American and American-Indian descent), 21% Europeans, 10% Africans, 2% Indians
LANGUAGE Spanish (official), Indian languages (2%)
RELIGION Roman Catholic 92%
EDUCATION (compulsory years) 10
LITERACY RATE 94% (men); 93% (women) (2003 est)
LABOUR FORCE 13% agriculture, 23% industry, 64% services (1997 est)
LIFE EXPECTANCY 71 (men); 77 (women) (2000–05)
CHILD MORTALITY RATE (under 5, per 1,000 live births) 22 (2001)
PERSONAL COMPUTER USERS (per 100 people) 6.1 (2002 est)

See also ▷Arawak; ▷Bolívar, Simón; ▷Carib.

1947: First truly democratic elections held, but the new president, Rómulo Gallegos, was removed within eight months by the military in the person of Col Marcos Pérez Jimenez.
1958: Overthrow of Pérez and establishment of an enduring civilian democracy, headed by left-wing Romulo Betancourt of Democratic Action Party (AD).
1964: Dr Raúl Leoni (AD) became president in first-ever constitutional handover of civilian power.
1974: Carlos Andrés Pérez (AD) became president, with economy remaining buoyant through oil revenues. Oil and iron industries nationalized.
1984: Social pact established between government, trade unions, and business; national debt rescheduled as oil revenues plummetted.
1987: Widespread social unrest triggered by inflation; student demonstrators shot by police.
1989: An economic austerity programme was instigated. Price increases triggered riots known as 'Caracazo'; 300 people were killed. Martial law was declared and a general strike followed. Elections were boycotted by opposition groups.
1992: An attempted antigovernment coup failed, at a cost of 120 lives.
1996: Former President Carlos Andrés Pérez was found guilty on corruption charges and imprisoned.
1999: Hugo Chávez was inaugurated as president. Flooding and mudslides swamped Venezuela's Caribbean coast in late December, resulting in death tolls as high as 30,000, at least 150,000 homeless civilians from 23,000 destroyed homes, 70,000 evacuees, and 96,000 damaged homes.
2000: Despite a shrinking economy, Hugo Chávez was re-elected as president, pledging to redistribute oil wealth from the rich to the poor. He later took a leading role in persuading the Organization of Petroleum-Exporting Countries (OPEC) to restrict world oil production to force up prices. In November, Chávez was given powers to legislate on certain issues by decree.
2003: A two-month opposition-led strike against the government of left-wing President Hugo Chavez crumbled as private-sector workers returned to work. However, the country's political and economic situation remained unstable.

in 1851. Other works include *Il trovatore* and *La traviata* (both 1853), *Aïda* (1871), and the masterpieces of his old age, *Otello* (1887) and *Falstaff* (1893). His *Requiem* (1874) commemorates the poet and novelist Alessandro Manzoni.

Verdi's music is essentially Italian in character, and owes nothing to Wagnerian influences, although in his late works (*Otello* and *Falstaff*) he developed a more continuous, orchestrally dominated texture and dramatic structure. During the mid-1800s, Verdi became a symbol of Italy's fight for independence from Austria, frequently finding himself in conflict with the Austrian authorities, who felt that his operas encouraged Italian nationalism.

verdigris green-blue coating of copper ethanoate that forms naturally on copper, bronze, and brass. It is an irritating, poisonous compound made by treating copper with ethanoic acid, and was formerly used in wood preservatives, antifouling compositions, and green paints.

Verdun fortress town in northeast France in the *département* of the Meuse, 280 km/174 mi east of Paris. During World War I it became a symbol of French resistance and was the centre of a series of bitterly fought actions between French and German forces, finally being recaptured September 1918.

Vergil alternative spelling of ▷Virgil, Roman poet.

verification in computing, the process of checking that data being input to a computer has been accurately copied from a source document.

This may be done visually, by checking the original copy of the data against the copy shown on the VDU screen. A more thorough method is to enter the data twice, using two different keyboard operators, and then to check the two sets of input copies against each other. The checking is normally carried out by the computer itself, any differences between the two copies being reported for correction by one of the keyboard operators.

Verlaine, Paul Marie (1844–1896) French lyric poet. He was acknowledged as the leader of the Symbolist poets (see ▷Symbolism). His volumes of verse, strongly influenced by the poets Charles ▷Baudelaire and Arthur ▷Rimbaud, include *Poèmes saturniens/Saturnine Poems* (1866), *Fêtes galantes/Amorous Entertainments* (1869), and *Romances sans paroles/Songs without Words* (1874). In 1873 he was imprisoned for shooting and wounding Rimbaud. His later works reflect his attempts to lead a reformed life.

Vermeer, Jan (1632–1675) Dutch painter, active in Delft. He painted quiet, everyday scenes that are characterized by an almost abstract simplicity, subtle colour harmonies, and a remarkable ability to suggest the fall of light on objects. Examples are *The Lacemaker* (c. 1655; Louvre, Paris) and *Maidservant Pouring Milk* (c. 1658; Rijksmuseum, Amsterdam).

Vermeer is remarkable among Dutch painters for the stress he places not on the subject of a picture but its formal qualities: the balance and simplicity of design, colour harmonies, and the subtleties of texture, tone, and light. Italian influence can be seen in his early work, for example *Diana and her Nymphs* (c. 1655; Mauritshuis, The Hague) and *The Courtesan* (1656; Gemäldegalerie Alter Meister, Dresden), but a totally independent – totally Dutch – vision appears in such landscapes as the *View of Delft* (1658–60; Mauritshuis, The Hague) and *The Little Street* (Rijksmuseum, Amsterdam), works which convey an astonishing sense of physical immediacy (Vermeer may well have used a ▷camera obscura).

The interiors for which he is best known – transcending the delicacy and brilliance of Pieter de Hooch, Gerard Terborch, and Gabriel Metsu – include *Lady Standing at the Virginals* (National Gallery, London), *The Painter's Studio* (Kunsthistorisches Museum, Vienna), *Girl with a Turban* (Mauritshuis, The Hague), and *A Woman Weighing Pearls* (National Gallery of Art, Washington, DC).

     Related Web site: Vermeer, Jan http://www.oir.ucf.edu/wm/paint/auth/vermeer/

Vermont state in northeastern USA. It is nicknamed the Green Mountain State. Vermont was admitted to the Union in 1791 as the 14th US state. It is bordered to the north by Québec, Canada, to the east by New Hampshire, to the south by Massachusetts, and to the west by New York.

population (1995) 584,800   **area** 24,900 sq km/9,611 sq mi
capital Montpelier   **towns and cities** Burlington, Rutland, Barre
industries and products apples, maple syrup, dairy products, china clay, granite, marble, slate, business machines, paper and allied products, computers and high-tech manufacturing, tourism, leisure industry

vernal equinox see ▷equinox.

Verne, Jules (1828–1905) French author. He wrote tales of adventure that anticipated future scientific developments: *Five Weeks in a Balloon* (1862), *Journey to the Centre of the Earth* (1864), *Twenty Thousand Leagues under the Sea* (1870), and *Around the World in Eighty Days* (1873).

     Related Web site: Journey to the Centre of the Earth http://www. math.technion.ac.il/~rl/JulesVerne/vt/c_earth

Verona town in Veneto, Italy, on the Adige River, 100 km/62 west of Venice; population (1992) 255,500. It lies at the junction of the Brenner Pass road with the Venice–Milan motorway. Industries include printing, engineering, and the manufacture of paper, plastics, furniture, and pasta. It is one of Italy's main marketing centres for fruit and vegetables.

VERONA The Roman amphitheatre at Verona, Italy. *Philip Sauvain Picture Collection*

Veronese, Paolo (Paolo Caliari) (c. 1528–1588) Italian painter, born in Verona. He was the pupil of Antonio Badile, but also learned from the study of Titian and ▷Tintoretto. Some part of his youth was spent in the shop of his brother Antonio, who dealt in the embroidery and rich fabrics that were to play an important decorative part in his painting. From 1555 he lived in Venice, producing those huge decorative compositions with their representation of splendid architecture and crowds of luxuriously dressed figures for which he is famous.

He was active mainly in Venice. He specialized in grand decorative schemes, such as his ceilings in the Doge's Palace, noted for their rich colouring, broad composition, *trompe l'oeil* effects, and inventive detail. Religious, mythological, historical, or allegorical, his paintings – usually of banquets and scenes of pageantry – celebrated the power and splendour of Venice.

Verrocchio, Andrea del (c. 1435–1488) Adopted name of Andrea di Cione. Florentine sculptor, painter, and goldsmith. He ran a large workshop in Florence and received commissions from the Medici family. His works include the vigorous equestrian statue of *Bartolommeo Colleoni* (begun about 1480; Campo SS Giovanni e Paolo, Venice) and the painting *The Baptism of Christ* (c. 1470; Uffizi, Florence).

verruca growth on the skin; see ▷wart.

Versace, Gianni (1946–1997) Italian fashion designer. He was one of the new school of Milan-based Italian designers who dominated the fashion world during the 1980s and 1990s. Versace founded his own business and presented a menswear collection in 1978. He diversified into women's wear, accessories, perfumes, furs, and costumes for opera, theatre, and ballet, using simple shapes and strong colours to create provocative clothing. His work was frequently criticized by fashion pundits for its gaudy vulgarity and its predilection for elements of sadomasochist bondage and leather. He was shot dead in 1997.

Versailles administrative centre of the *département* of Yvelines in northern France, situated 18 km/11 mi southwest of Paris; population (1990) 91,000. From 1678 to 1769 Versailles was the principal residence of the kings of France until 1793, and the seat of government from 1682 to 1789. The city grew up around the palace of Louis XIV, built between 1661 and 1687 on the site of Louis XIII's hunting lodge. Within the palace park are two small châteaux, Le Grand Trianon, built for Louis XIV, and Le Petit Trianon, built for Louis XV.

TREATY OF VERSAILLES Allied leaders pictured after signing the Treaty of Versailles, 28 June 1919. US president Woodrow Wilson is seen with the British and French prime ministers, David Lloyd George and Georges Clémenceau, leaving the palace of Versailles on the outskirts of Paris, France. *Archive Photos*

Versailles, Treaty of peace treaty after World War I between the Allies and Germany, signed on 28 June 1919. It established the ▷League of Nations, an international organization intended to solve disputes by arbitration. Germany surrendered Alsace-Lorraine to France, and large areas in the east to Poland, and made smaller cessions to Czechoslovakia, Lithuania, Belgium, and Denmark. The Rhineland was demilitarized, German rearmament was restricted, and Germany agreed to pay reparations for war damage. The treaty was never ratified by the USA, which made a separate peace with Germany and Austria in 1921. The terms of Versailles and its reshaping of Europe contributed to the outbreak of ▷World War II.

verse arrangement of words in a rhythmic pattern, which may depend on the length of syllables (as in Greek or Latin verse), or on stress, as in English. Classical Greek verse depended upon quantity, a long syllable being regarded as occupying twice the time taken up by a short syllable.

vertebral column the backbone, giving support to an animal and protecting its spinal cord. It is made up of a series of bones or vertebrae running from the skull to the tail, with a central canal containing the nerve fibres of the spinal cord. In tetrapods the vertebrae show some specialization with the shape of the bones varying according to position. In the chest region the upper or thoracic vertebrae are shaped to form connections to the ribs. The backbone is only slightly flexible to give adequate rigidity to the animal structure.

vertebrate any animal with a backbone. The 41,000 species of vertebrates include mammals, birds, reptiles, amphibians, and fishes. They include most of the larger animals, but in terms of numbers of species are only a tiny proportion of the world's animals. The zoological taxonomic group Vertebrata is a subgroup of the ▷phylum Chordata.

A giant fossil conodont (an eel-like organism from the Cambrian period) was discovered in South Africa in 1995, and is believed to be one of the first vertebrates. Conodonts evolved 520 million years ago, predating the earliest fish by about 50 million years.

vertex (plural **vertices**) in geometry, a point shared by three or more sides of a solid figure; the point farthest from a figure's base; or the point of intersection of two sides of a plane figure or the two rays of an angle.

vertigo dizziness; a whirling sensation accompanied by a loss of any feeling of contact with the ground. It may be due to temporary disturbance of the sense of balance (as in spinning for too long on one spot), psychological reasons, disease such as ▷labyrinthitis, or intoxication.

Very Large Array (VLA) largest and most complex single-site radio telescope in the world. It is located on the Plains of San Augustine, 80 km/50 mi west of Socorro, New Mexico. It consists of 27 dish antennae, each 25 m/82 ft in diameter, arranged along three equally spaced arms forming a Y-shaped array. Two of the arms are

21 km/13 mi long, and the third, to the north, is 19 km/11.8 mi long. The dishes are mounted on railway tracks enabling the configuration and size of the array to be altered as required.

Vesalius, Andreas (1514–1564) Belgian physician who revolutionized anatomy by performing postmortem dissections and making use of illustrations to teach anatomy. Vesalius upset the authority of ▷Galen, and his book – the first real textbook of anatomy – marked the beginning of biology as a science.

Vespasian (9–79AD) Also known as **Titus Flavius Vespasianus**. Roman emperor from AD 69. Proclaimed emperor by his soldiers while he was campaigning in Palestine, he reorganized the eastern provinces, and was a capable administrator. He was responsible for the construction of the Colosseum in Rome, which was completed by his son ▷Titus.

As the legate of the 2nd Legion (*Legio II Augusta*), he took part in the invasion of Britain in AD 43 by Claudius, playing a distinguished role in the Roman victory at the Medway. He then led his legion in an independent command to conquer much of southwestern England. In AD 66–67 the emperor Nero sent him to suppress the Jewish rebellion. He reconquered Galilee through a series of hard-fought sieges, capturing the cities of Jotopata, Gamala, and Gischala and accepting the defection of Sepphoris. During campaigns in 68–69, he suppressed Samaria and much of Judaea before the war to determine Nero's successor demanded his attention. He left his son Titus to complete the Jewish War, then consolidated his position in Egypt and sent an army to Italy. The civil war was decided in Vespasian's favour by the actions of his subordinate commanders, without his having to participate in a single battle.

Vespucci, Amerigo (1454–1512) Florentine merchant. The Americas were named after him as a result of the widespread circulation of his accounts of his explorations. His accounts of the voyage from 1499 to 1501 include descriptions of places he could not possibly have reached (the Pacific Ocean, British Columbia, Antarctica).

Vesta in Roman mythology, the goddess of the hearth, equivalent with the Greek Hestia. In Rome, the sacred flame in her shrine at the Forum represented the spirit of the community, and was kept constantly alight by the six **Vestal Virgins**.

Vesterålen island group off northwest Norway.

vestigial organ in biology, an organ that remains in diminished form after it has ceased to have any significant function in the adult organism. In humans, the appendix is vestigial, having once had a digestive function in our ancestors.

Vestmannaeyjar small group of islands off the south coast of Iceland. The volcanic island of Surtsey emerged from the ocean in 1963, and in 1973 the volcano Helgafell erupted, causing the population of 5,200 to be temporarily evacuated and adding 2.5 sq km/1 sq mi to the islands' area. Heimaey, the largest of the islands, is one of Iceland's chief fishing ports.

Vesuvius (Italian **Vesuvio**) active volcano in Campania, Italy, 15 km/9 mi southeast of Naples, Italy; height 1,277 m/4,190 ft. In AD 79 it destroyed the cities of Pompeii, Herculaneum, and Stabiae.

Vesuvius is a composite ▷volcano at the **convergent plate margin** where the African plate is subducting beneath the Eurasian plate. Its lava is ▷andesite in composition and consequently very viscous, giving rise to explosive eruptions. Vesuvius is comprised of two cones. Monte Somma, the remnant of a massive wall which once enclosed a huge cone in prehistoric times, is now a semicircular girdle of cliff to the north and east, separated from the main eruptive cone by the valley of Atrio di Cavallo. Layers of lava, scoriae, ashes, and pumice make up the mountain.

The surprising fertility of the volcano's slopes, especially for the cultivation of grapes and production of 'Lacrimae Christi' wine, explains why the environs of Vesuvius remain densely populated in spite of the constant threat of eruption.

Eruptions The eruption on 24 August AD 79 ended a dormant period so long that the volcano had been presumed extinct. During the eruptions of 472 and 1631 particles of dust are said to have landed in Constantinople (modern Istanbul). Other years of great activity were 1794, 1822, 1855, 1871, 1906, 1929, and 1944. There has been no eruption since 1944.

Related Web site: Vesuvius, Italy http://volcano.und.nodak.edu/vwdocs/volc_images/img_vesuvius.html

Veterans Day in the USA, the name adopted in 1954 for ▷Armistice Day and from 1971 observed by most states on 11 November. The equivalent in the UK and Canada is ▷Remembrance Sunday.

veto (Latin 'I forbid') exercise by a sovereign, branch of legislature, or other political power, of the right to prevent the enactment or operation of a law, or the taking of some course of action.

VHF (abbreviation for very high frequency) referring to radio waves that have very short wavelengths (10 m–1 m). They are used for interference-free FM transmissions (see ▷frequency modulation). VHF transmitters have a relatively short range because the waves cannot be reflected over the horizon like longer radio waves.

VI abbreviation for ▷Vancouver Island, off the west coast of Canada.

VI abbreviation for ▷Virgin Islands, in the West Indies.

vibraphone electrophonic percussion instrument resembling a ▷xylophone but with metal keys. Electrically driven discs spin within resonating tubes under each key to add a tremulant effect that can be controlled in length with a foot pedal.

vibrato in music, a rapid fluctuation of pitch for dynamic and expressive effect. It is distinct from a tremolo, which is a fluctuation in intensity of the same note.

> **Queen Victoria**
> *He speaks to Me as if I was a public meeting.*
> On her prime minister, Gladstone

viburnum any of a group of small trees or shrubs belonging to the honeysuckle family, found in temperate and subtropical regions, including the wayfaring tree, the laurustinus, and the guelder rose of Europe and Asia, and the North American blackhaws and arrowwoods. (Genus *Viburnum*, family Caprifoliaceae.)

Vichy government in World War II, the right-wing government of unoccupied France after the country's defeat by the Germans in June 1940, named after the spa town of Vichy, France, where the national assembly was based under Prime Minister Pétain until the liberation in 1944. **Vichy France** was that part of France not occupied by German troops until November 1942. Authoritarian and collaborationist, the Vichy regime cooperated with the Germans even after they had moved to the unoccupied zone in November 1942. It imprisoned some 135,000 people, interned another 70,000, deported some 76,000 Jews, and sent 650,000 French workers to Germany.

Vico, Giambattista (Giovanni Battista) (1668–1744) Italian philosopher, considered the founder of the modern philosophy of history. He argued that we can understand history more adequately than nature, since it is we who have made it. He believed that the study of language, ritual, and myth was a way of understanding earlier societies. His cyclical theory of history (the birth, development, and decline of human societies) was put forward in *New Science* (1725).

Victor Emmanuel three kings of Italy, including:

Victor Emmanuel II (1820–1878) First king of united Italy from 1861. He became king of Sardinia on the abdication of his father Charles Albert 1849. In 1855 he allied Sardinia with France and the UK in the Crimean War. In 1859 in alliance with the French he defeated the Austrians and annexed Lombardy. By 1860 most of Italy had come under his rule, and in 1861 he was proclaimed king of Italy. In 1870 he made Rome his capital.

Victor Emmanuel III (1869–1947) King of Italy from the assassination of his father, Umberto I, in 1900. He acquiesced in the Fascist regime of Mussolini from 1922 and, after the dictator's fall in 1943, relinquished power to his son Umberto II, who cooperated with the Allies. Victor Emmanuel formally abdicated in 1946.

Victoria state of southeast Australia; bounded on the north and northeast by New South Wales, from which it is separated by the River Murray; on the west by South Australia; and on the south and southeast by the Southern Ocean, Bass Strait, and the Pacific Ocean; area 227,600 sq km/87,876 sq mi; population (1996) 4,373,500.

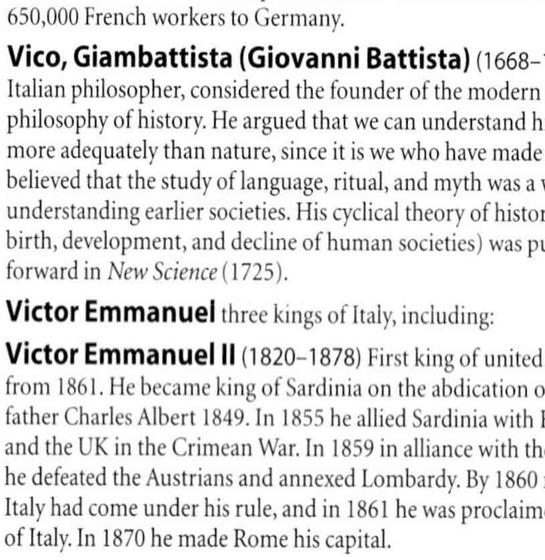

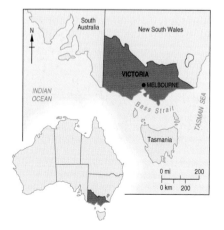

The capital is ▷Melbourne. Produce includes wool, beef, dairy products, tobacco, wheat, wine, dried fruit, orchard fruits, and vegetables. Gold, brown coal, gypsum, kaolin, and bauxite are mined, and there are oil, natural gas, electronics, food processing, chemical, pharmaceutical, machinery, car, textile, wine, aquaculture, wool, and building material industries.

Victoria port and capital of ▷British Columbia, Canada, on the southeastern tip of Vancouver Island, overlooking the Strait of Juan de Fuca, 132 km/83 mi west of mainland Vancouver; population (1991) 21,200, metropolitan area (1996) 313,400. It is a manufacturing, tourist, and retirement centre, and has a naval base. Industries include shipbuilding, food-processing, sawmilling, fishing, and the manufacture of chemicals, clothing, and furniture.

Victoria (1819–1901) Queen of the UK from 1837, when she succeeded her uncle William IV, and Empress of India from 1877. In 1840 she married Prince ▷Albert of Saxe-Coburg and Gotha. Her relations with her prime ministers ranged from the affectionate (Melbourne and Disraeli) to the stormy (Peel, Palmerston, and Gladstone). Her golden jubilee in 1887 and diamond jubilee in 1897 marked a waning of republican sentiment, which had developed with her withdrawal from public life on Albert's death in 1861.

The only child of Edward, Duke of Kent, fourth son of George III, she was born on 24 May 1819 at Kensington Palace, London. She and Albert had four sons and five daughters. After Albert's death she lived mainly in retirement. Nevertheless, she kept control of affairs, refusing the Prince of Wales (Edward VII) any active role. From 1848 she regularly visited the Scottish Highlands, where she had a house at Balmoral built to Prince Albert's designs. She died at Osborne House, her home in the Isle of Wight, on 22 January 1901, and was buried at Windsor.

Related Web site: Queen Victoria http://www.spartacus.schoolnet.co.uk/PRvictoria.htm

Victoria and Albert Museum museum of decorative arts in South Kensington, London, founded in 1852. It houses prints, paintings, and temporary exhibitions, as well as one of the largest collections of decorative arts in the world.

Victoria Cross British decoration for conspicuous bravery in wartime, instituted by Queen Victoria in 1856.

Victoria Falls (or **Mosi-oa-tunya** 'smoke that thunders') waterfall on the River Zambezi, on the Zambia–Zimbabwe border. The river is 1,700 m/5,580 ft wide and drops 120 m/400 ft to flow through a gorge 30 m/100 ft wide. The falls were named after Queen Victoria by the Scottish explorer David Livingstone in 1855.

VICTORIA FALLS The Victoria Falls on the River Zambezi, on the Zambia–Zimbabwe border, are 120 m/400 ft high. The falls were named after Queen Victoria by the explorer David Livingstone, but the local African name for them is *Mosi-oa-tunya*, 'smoke that thunders'. *Image Bank*

Victoria, Lake (or **Victoria Nyanza**) largest lake in Africa and third-largest freshwater lake in the world; area over 68,800 sq km/26,560 sq mi; length 410 km/255 mi; average depth 80 m/260 ft. It lies on the Equator at an altitude of 1,136 m/3,728 ft, bounded by Uganda, Kenya, and Tanzania. It is a source of the River Nile.

The British explorer John Hanning Speke was the first European to see the lake in 1858, recognizing it as source of the White Nile; he named it after Queen Victoria.

Victorian style of architecture, furnituremaking, and decorative art covering the reign of Queen Victoria, from 1837 to 1901. The era was influenced by significant industrial and urban development, and the massive expansion of the ▷British Empire.

Victorian style was often very ornate, markedly so in architecture, where there was more than one 'revival' of earlier styles, beginning with a lengthy competition between the **classic** and **Gothic** schools. Gothic Revival drew on the original Gothic architecture of medieval times. The Gothic boom had begun in 1818, when Parliament voted a million pounds for building 214 new Anglican churches. No fewer than 174 of them were constructed in a Gothic or near-Gothic style, and for nearly a century, most churches in England were Gothic in design. Despite the popularity of extravagant decoration, Renaissance or classic styles were also favoured for public buildings, examples being St George's Hall, Liverpool (1815), and Birmingham Town Hall (1832–50).

Many people, such as John ▷Ruskin, believed in designing objects and architecture primarily for their function, and not for mere appearance. Increasing mass production by machines threatened the existence of craft skills, and encouraged the development of the ▷Arts and Crafts Movement, with its nostalgia for the medieval way of life. In the last quarter of the century there were revivals of **Jacobean** and finally of **Queen Anne** architecture.

vicuna ▷ruminant mammal *Lama vicugna* of the camel family that lives in herds on the Andean plateau. It can run at speeds of 50 kph/30 mph. It has good eyesight, fair hearing, and a poor sense of smell. Hunted close to extinction for its meat and soft brown fur, which was used in textile manufacture, the vicuna is now a protected species. Its populations are increasing thanks to strict conservation measures; by 1996 they had reached 100,000–200,000. The vicuna is listed on ▷CITES Appendix 2 (vulnerable).

It is related to the ▷alpaca, the ▷guanaco, and the ▷llama.

VICUNA
The vicuna lives in small herds of 6–12 females with a lone male. The male keeps watch, uttering a shrill whistle at the least sign of danger, and acts to protect the retreating herd.

Vidal, Gore (1925–) Born Eugene Luther Vidal. US writer and critic. Much of his fiction deals satirically with history and politics and includes the novels *Myra Breckinridge* (1968), *Burr* (1973), *Empire* (1987), *The Smithsonian Institution* (1998), and *The Golden Age* (2000). He has written plays and screenplays, including *Suddenly Last Summer* (1958), and essays, such as 'Armageddon?' (1987). His autobiography *Palimpsest* appeared in 1995.

video camera (or **camcorder**) portable television camera that records moving pictures electronically on magnetic tape. It produces an electrical output signal corresponding to rapid line-by-line scanning of the field of view. The output is recorded on video cassette and is played back on a television screen via a video cassette recorder.

video cassette recorder (VCR) device for recording on and playing back video cassettes; see ▷videotape recorder.

video disk disk with pictures and sounds recorded on it, played back by laser. The video disk is a type of ▷compact disc.

video game electronic game played on a visual-display screen or, by means of special additional or built-in components, on the screen of a television set. The first commercially sold was a simple bat-and-ball game developed in the USA in 1972, but complex variants are now available in colour and with special sound effects.

videotape recorder (VTR) device for recording pictures and sound on cassettes or spools of magnetic tape. The first commercial VTR was launched in 1956 for the television broadcasting industry, but from the late 1970s cheaper models developed for home use, to record broadcast programmes for future viewing and to view rented or owned video cassettes of commercial films.

videotext system in which information (text and simple pictures) is displayed on a television (video) screen. There are two basic systems, known as ▷teletext and ▷viewdata. In the teletext system information is broadcast with the ordinary television signals, whereas in the viewdata system information is relayed to the screen from a central data bank via the telephone network.

Both systems require the use of a television receiver (or a connected VTR) with special decoder.

Vienna (German **Wien**) capital of Austria, on the River Danube at the foot of the Wiener Wald (Vienna Woods); population (1995) 1,531,200. Although within the territory of Lower Austria, it is a separate province. Industries include engineering, electrical goods, electronics, clothing, precision and musical instruments, and beer. It is a major cultural and tourist centre.

The United Nations City (1979) houses the United Nations Industrial Development Organization (UNIDO), the International Atomic Energy Agency (IAEA), and the Organization of Petroleum Exporting Countries (OPEC).

Features Renaissance and baroque architecture; St Stephen's Cathedral (12th–16th centuries); the Hofburg (the Hapsburgs' imperial palace dating from the 13th century), which was severely damaged by fire in 1992; the 18th-century royal palaces of Schönbrunn and Belvedere, with formal gardens; the opera house (reopened in 1955 after a disastrous fire in 1945); the ferris wheel in the Prater park; the Steiner House (1910) by Adolf Loos; and several notable collections of paintings. Vienna is known for its theatre and opera. In 2000, a new interactive music museum, Haus der Musik (House of Music), was opened. Sigmund Freud's home is a museum, and there is a university, built in 1365, with a renowned medical faculty. It is the seat of a Roman Catholic archbishop and a Protestant bishop. A memorial to the Holocaust, designed by Rachel Whiteread, is built on the *Judenplatz*, the site of the city's oldest synagogue.

History Vienna was the capital of the Austro-Hungarian Empire 1278–1918 and the commercial centre of eastern Europe. The old city walls were replaced by a wide street, the Ringstrasse, in 1860. After much destruction in World War II the city was divided into US, British, French, and Soviet occupation zones 1945–55. Vienna is associated with the waltzes of Johann Strauss, as well as the music of Haydn, Mozart, Beethoven, Brahms, Schubert, and Mahler, and the development of atonal music. Also figuring in Vienna's cultural history were the Vienna Sezession group of painters and the philosophical Vienna Circle; psychoanalysis originated here.

Related Web site: Vienna http://www.info-austria.net

Vienna, Congress of international conference held from 1814 to 1815 which agreed the settlement of Europe after the Napoleonic Wars. National representatives included the Austrian foreign minister Metternich, Alexander I of Russia, the British foreign secretary Castlereagh and military commander Wellington, and the French politician Talleyrand.

Its final act created a kingdom of the Netherlands, a German confederation of 39 states, Lombardy-Venetia subject to Austria, and the kingdom of Poland. Monarchs were restored in Spain, Naples, Piedmont, Tuscany, and Modena; Louis XVIII was confirmed king of France.

Vientiane (Lao **Vieng Chan**) capital, largest city, and chief port of Laos, lying in the north on the Mekong River on the border with Thailand; population (2002 est) 189,600; conurbation 528,100. Vientiane's strategic position on one of the main waterways of southeast Asia has helped it to become a centre for government, commerce, and religion for over a millennium. Noted for its pagodas, canals, and houses on stilts, it is situated in a rich agricultural area and is a trading centre for forest products and textiles. The Temple of the Heavy Buddha, the Pratuxai triumphal arch, and the Black Stupa are here. The Great Sacred Stupa to the northeast of the city is the most important national monument in Laos.

Vietnam see country box.

Vietnamese inhabitants of Vietnam; people of Vietnamese culture or descent. The Vietnamese comprise approximately 90% of the population. Most Vietnamese live in the fertile valleys of the Red and Mekong rivers. Vietnamese is an Austro-Asiatic language.

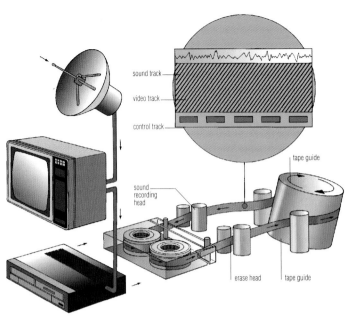

sound track
video track
control track
tape guide
sound recording head
erase head
tape guide

VIDEO CASSETTE RECORDER Home video recorders use 12.65-mm/0.5-in wide tape. A series of rollers guides the tape past the recording and erase heads in the recorder. The sloping video head records the picture as a diagonal pattern across the tape. This enables more information to be held on the tape. The sound track runs along the edge of the tape.

Vietnam War (1954–75) war between communist North Vietnam and US-backed South Vietnam, in which North Vietnam aimed to conquer South Vietnam and unite the country as a communist state; the USA, in supporting the South against the North, aimed to prevent the spread of communism in Southeast Asia. Some 200,000 South Vietnamese soldiers, 1 million North Vietnamese soldiers, and 500,000 civilians were killed; 56,555 US soldiers were killed 1961–75, a fifth of them by their own troops. The war destroyed 50% of the country's forest cover and 20% of agricultural land. Cambodia, a neutral neighbour, was bombed by the USA 1969–75, with 1 million killed or wounded. At the end of the war North and South Vietnam were reunited as a socialist republic.

Following the division of French Indochina into North and South Vietnam and the Vietnamese defeat of the French in 1954, US involvement in Southeast Asia grew through the SEATO pact.

US OUT OF VIETNAM

for life on earth

NATIONAL STUDENT ANTI-WAR CONFERENCE, CLEVELAND, OHIO, FEBRUARY 13, 14, 15, 1970

VIETNAM WAR A 1970s anti-Vietnam War poster by Jacqueline Styles. *The Art Archive/Library of Congress/ Eileen Tweedy*

Vietnam

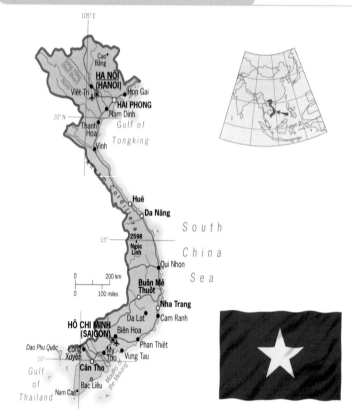

VIETNAM Market gardens on the outskirts of Nha Trang, on Cam Ranh Bay, Vietnam. Such privately owned operations have been permitted since 1986, and actively encouraged since 1998. *Image Bank*

Vietnam (formerly part of French Indo-China, 1884–1945), communist Democratic Republic of Vietnam (in north) (1945–75), non-communist Republic of Vietnam (in south) (1949–75) country in Southeast Asia, on the South China Sea, bounded north by China and west by Cambodia and Laos.

NATIONAL NAME Công-hòa xã-hôi chu-nghia Viêt Nam/Socialist Republic of Vietnam
AREA 329,600 sq km/127,258 sq mi
CAPITAL Hanoi
MAJOR TOWNS/CITIES Ho Chi Minh City (formerly Saigon), Haiphong, Da Nang, Can Tho, Nha Trang, Bien Hoa, Hué
MAJOR PORTS Ho Chi Minh City (formerly Saigon), Da Nang, Haiphong
PHYSICAL FEATURES Red River and Mekong deltas, centre of cultivation and population; tropical rainforest; mountainous in north and northwest

Government

HEAD OF STATE Tran Duc Luong from 1997
HEAD OF GOVERNMENT Phan Van Khai from 1997
POLITICAL SYSTEM communist
POLITICAL EXECUTIVE communist
ADMINISTRATIVE DIVISIONS 60 provinces and a city under central government
ARMED FORCES 484,000; plus paramilitary forces of 40,000 and about 3 million reserves (2002 est)
DEATH PENALTY retained and used for ordinary crimes

Economy and resources

CURRENCY dong
GPD (US$) 35.1 billion (2002 est)
REAL GDP GROWTH (% change on previous year) 6.8 (2001)
GNI (US$) 34.9 billion (2002 est)
GNI PER CAPITA (PPP) (US$) 2,240 (2002 est)
CONSUMER PRICE INFLATION 3.8% (2003 est)
UNEMPLOYMENT 6% (2002)
FOREIGN DEBT (US$) 9.7 billion (2001 est)
MAJOR TRADING PARTNERS Singapore, Japan, China, South Korea, USA, Thailand, Australia, Germany, France

RESOURCES petroleum, coal, tin, zinc, iron, antimony, chromium, phosphate, apatite, bauxite
INDUSTRIES food processing, chemicals, machinery, textiles, beer, glass and glassware, cigarettes, crude steel, cement, fertilizers, tourism (steady growth in the early 1990s)
EXPORTS crude petroleum, rice (leading exporter), textiles and garments, footwear, coal, coffee, marine products, handicrafts, light industrial goods, rubber, nuts, tea, tin. Principal market: Japan 17.1% (2001)
IMPORTS cloth and fabric, petroleum products, machinery and spare parts, steel, computers and electronic goods, artificial fertilizers, basic manufactures, consumer goods. Principal source: Singapore 13.6% (2001)
ARABLE LAND 17.7% (2000 est)
AGRICULTURAL PRODUCTS rice (world's fifth-largest producer), coffee, tea, rubber, cotton, groundnuts, sugar cane, coconuts; livestock rearing; fishing

Population and society

POPULATION 81,377,000 (2003 est)
POPULATION GROWTH RATE 1.2% (2000–15)
POPULATION DENSITY (per sq km) 245 (2003 est)
URBAN POPULATION (% of total) 25 (2003 est)
AGE DISTRIBUTION (% of total population) 0–14 32%, 15–59 61%, 60+ 7% (2002 est)
ETHNIC GROUPS 84% Viet (also known as Kinh), 2% Chinese, 2% Khmer, 8% consists of more than 50 minority nationalities, including the Hmong, Meo, Muong, Nung, Tay, Thai, and Tho tribal groups
LANGUAGE Vietnamese (official), French, English, Khmer, Chinese, local languages
RELIGION mainly Buddhist; Christian, mainly Roman Catholic (8–10%); Taoist, Confucian, Hos Hoa, and Cao Dai sects

VIETNAM WAR US rescue fliers during the Vietnam War.
Archive Photos

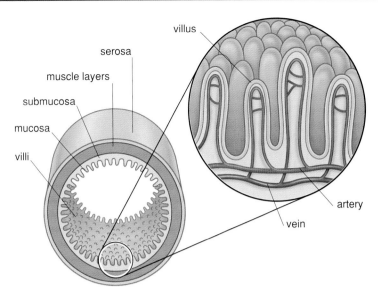

VILLUS A cross-section of the small intestine showing the villi and their blood supply. There are hundreds of villi for every square millimetre of the small intestine (itself 5 m/16 ft in length).

Noncommunist South Vietnam was viewed, in the context of the 1950s and the ▷Cold War, as a bulwark against the spread of communism throughout Southeast Asia. Advisers and military aid were dispatched to the region at increasing levels because of the so-called domino theory, which contended that the fall of South Vietnam would precipitate the collapse of neighbouring states. The USA spent $141 billion on aid to the South Vietnamese government, but corruption and inefficiency led the USA to assume ever greater responsibility for the war effort, until 1 million US combat troops were engaged.

In the USA, the draft, the high war casualties, and the undeclared nature of the war resulted in growing domestic resistance, which caused social unrest and forced President Lyndon Johnson to abandon re-election plans. President Richard Nixon first expanded the war to Laos and Cambodia but finally phased out US involvement; his national security adviser Henry Kissinger negotiated a peace treaty in 1973 with North Vietnam, which soon conquered South Vietnam and united the nation.

Although US forces were never militarily defeated, Vietnam was considered a most humiliating political defeat for the USA.

viewdata system of displaying information on a television screen in which the information is extracted from a computer data bank and transmitted via the telephone lines. It is one form of ▷videotext. British Telecom (then part of the General Post Office) developed the first viewdata system, Prestel, 1975–79. Similar systems are used in other countries. Users have access to a large store of information, presented on the screen in the form of 'pages'.

vigilante in US history, originally a member of a 'vigilance committee', a self-appointed group to maintain public order in the absence of organized authority, especially in Western frontier communities.

Vijayanagar the capital of the last extensive Hindu empire in India between the 14th and 17th centuries, situated on the River Tungabhadra, southern India. The empire attained its peak under the warrior Krishna Deva Raya (reigned 1509–65), when the city had an estimated population of 500,000. Thereafter it came under repeated attack by the Deccani Muslim kingdoms of Ahmadnagar, Bijapur, and Golconda.

Viking (or **Norseman**) the inhabitants of Scandinavia in the period 800–1100. They traded with, and raided, much of Europe, and often settled there. In their narrow, shallow-draught, highly manoeuvrable longships, the Vikings penetrated far inland along rivers. They plundered for gold and land, and were equally energetic as colonists – with colonies stretching from North America to central Russia – and as traders, with main trading posts at Birka (near Stockholm) and Hedeby (near Schleswig). The Vikings had a sophisticated literary culture, with ▷sagas and runic inscriptions, and an organized system of government with an assembly ('thing'). Their kings and chieftains were buried with their ships, together with their possessions.

In France the Vikings were given ▷Normandy. Under Sweyn I they conquered England (where they were known as 'Danes') in 1013, and his son Canute was king of England as well as Denmark and Norway. In the east they established the first Russian state and founded ▷Novgorod. They reached the Byzantine Empire in the south, and in the west sailed to Ireland, and Iceland; Greenland was visited by ▷Eric the Red, and North America, by his son Leif Ericsson who named it 'Vinland'. As ▷'Normans' they achieved a second conquest of England in 1066.

Related Web site: World of the Vikings http://www.pastforward.co.uk/vikings/index.html

Viking art sculpture and design of the Vikings, dating from the 8th to 11th century. Viking artists are known for woodcarving and finely wrought personal ornaments in gold and silver, and for an intricate interlacing decorative style similar to that found in ▷Celtic art. A dragonlike creature, known as the 'Great Beast', is a recurring motif.

Viking probes two US space probes to Mars, each one consisting of an orbiter and a lander. They were launched on 20 August and 9 September 1975. They transmitted colour pictures and analysed the soil.

Villehardouin, Geoffroy de (*c.* 1160–*c.* 1213) French historian. He was the first to write in the French language. He was a leader of the Fourth ▷Crusade, of which his *Conquest of Constantinople* (*c.* 1209) is an account.

villein a peasant who, under the ▷feudal system of land tenure that prevailed in Europe in the Middle Ages, gave dues and services to a lord in exchange for land. Villeins were not slaves, and were named as freemen and freewomen in medieval documents, but they were not free. They and their land and possessions belonged to the lord of the manor. They were not free to leave the manor, and they were subject to a large number of obligations required by the lord, including work on the lord's demesne two or three days a week, additional work at harvest, and the payment of manorial dues. In many places they also had to pay for the right to brew ale, bake bread, and grind corn at the lord's mill.

At the time of the ▷Domesday Book (1087) the villeins were the most numerous element in the English population, providing the labour force for the manors. Their social position declined until, by the early 14th century, their personal and legal status was close to that of slaves. After the mid-14th century, as the effects of the ▷Black Death led to a severe labour shortage, their status improved. By the 15th century villeinage had been supplanted by

VIKING A 9th-century picture, on stone, of a Viking ship. This image was found on the Swedish island of Gotland, in the Baltic Sea. *The Art Archive/Historiska Museet Stockholm/Dagli Orti*

a system of free tenure and labour in England, but it continued in France until 1789. Life for a medieval villein was undoutedly hard, as shown in documents such as 'Pierce the Plowman's Crede' (*c.* 1394) and picture sources such as the Luttrell Psalter (1340).

Villeneuve, Jacques (1971–   ) Canadian racing driver. The son of the Formula 1 driver Gilles Villeneuve, he rose to prominence in 1995 when he won the Indy Car World Series and the Indianapolis 500. Two years later, driving for Williams, he became the first Canadian to win the Formula 1 World Drivers' Championship. In 1999 he left Williams for the new British American Racing (BAR) team.

Villon, François (1431–*c.* 1465) French poet. He used satiric humour, pathos, and irony in works like *Petit Testament* or *Louis* (1456) and *Grand Testament* (1461) (the latter includes the 'Ballade des dames du temps jadis/Ballad of the Ladies of Former Times'), both of which are mock wills bequeathing absurd or obscene possessions. His *Ballades en jargon* are written in lowlife argot.

villus (plural **villi**) small fingerlike projection extending into the interior of the small intestine and increasing the absorptive area of the intestinal wall. Digested nutrients, including sugars and amino acids, pass into the villi and are carried away by the circulating blood.

Vilnius (German **Wilna**; Russian **Vilna**; Polish **Wilno**) capital of Lithuania, situated on the River Neris; population (1991) 593,000. Vilnius is an important railway crossroads and commercial centre. Its industries include electrical engineering, woodworking, and the manufacture of textiles, chemicals, and foodstuffs.

From a small 10th-century settlement, Vilnius became the Lithuanian capital in 1323. It came under Polish control from 1569 until Russian annexation in 1795, when it was the residence of the governor-general of the Lithuanian and Belorussian provinces. In the 17th–19th centuries, it was the principal centre of Jewish culture in Europe. Claimed by both Poland and Lithuania after World War I, it was occupied by the Soviets in 1918 and immediately transferred to independent Lithuania. However, Poland reoccupied it later that year, and it remained in Polish hands until annexation by the USSR in 1939. Nazi occupation forces (1941–44) exterminated the city's Jewish population. After recapture by the Red Army, it was made capital of the Lithuanian SSR. The city was the focal point of Lithuania's agitation for independence from the USSR (1989–91), and became the country's capital when independence was achieved in 1991.

Vimy Ridge hill in northern France, taken in World War I by Canadian troops during the battle of Arras, April 1917, at the cost of 11,285 lives. It is a spur of the ridge of Notre Dame de Lorette, 8 km/5 mi northeast of Arras.

Vincennes the University of Paris VIII, usually known as Vincennes after the suburb of eastern Paris where it was founded 1970 (following the 1968 student rebellion) for blue-collar workers. By 1980, it had 32,000 students. In June 1980, it was moved to the industrial suburb of St-Denis.

vincristine ▷alkaloid extracted from the blue periwinkle plant *Vinca rosea*. Developed as an anticancer agent, it has revolutionized the treatment of childhood acute leukaemias; it is also included in ▷chemotherapy regimens for some lymphomas (cancers arising in the lymph tissues) and lung and breast cancers. Side effects, such as nerve damage and loss of hair, are severe but usually reversible.

vine (or **grapevine**) any of a group of climbing woody plants, especially *V. vinifera*, native to Asia Minor and cultivated from antiquity. The fruits (grapes) are eaten or made into wine or other fermented drinks; dried fruits of certain varieties are known as raisins and currants. Many other species of climbing plant are also called vines. (Genus *Vitis*, family Vitaceae.)

VINE A vineyard in autumn, in Napa Valley, California, USA. *Image Bank*

Vinland Norse name for the area of North America, probably the coast of Nova Scotia or New England, which the Norse adventurer and explorer Leif Ericsson visited about 1000. It was named after the wild grapes that grew there and is celebrated in an important Norse saga.

Vinson Massif highest point in ▷Antarctica, rising to 5,140 m/16,863 ft in the Ellsworth Mountains.

viol member of a Renaissance family of bowed six-stringed musical instruments with flat backs, fretted fingerboards, and narrow shoulders that flourished particularly in England about 1540–1700, before their role was taken by the violins. Normally performing as an ensemble or consort, their repertoire is a development of ▷madrigal style with idiomatic decoration.

viola bowed, stringed musical instrument, the alto member of the ▷violin family. Its four strings are tuned C3, G3, D4, and A5. With its dark, vibrant tone, it is often used for music of reflective character, as in Stravinsky's *Elegy* (1944) or Britten's *Lachrymae* (1950). Its principal function is harmonic in string quartets and orchestras. Concertos have been written for the viola by composers such as Telemann, Berlioz, Walton, Hindemith, and Bartók.

violet any of a group of perennial ▷herbaceous plants found in temperate regions; they have heart-shaped leaves and mauve, blue, or white five-petalled flowers, for example the dog violet *V. canina*, found on sandy heaths, and the fragrant sweet violet *V. odorata*. A ▷pansy is a kind of violet. (Genus *Viola*, family Violaceae.)

violin bowed, four-stringed musical instrument, the smallest and highest pitched (treble) of the violin family. The strings are tuned in fifths (G3, D4, A5, and E5).

Related Web site: Catgut Acoustical Society http://www.marymt.edu/~cas/

Violin Making by Hans Johannsson http://www.centrum.is/hansi/

VIOLIN The open strings of the violin.

violin family family of bowed stringed instruments developed in 17th-century Italy, which eventually superseded the viols and formed the basis of the modern orchestra. There are four instruments: violin, viola, cello (or violoncello), and the double bass which is descended from the bass viol (or violone).

violoncello full name of the ▷cello.

viper any front-fanged venomous snake of the family Viperidae. Vipers range in size from 30 cm/1 ft to 3 m/10 ft, and often have diamond or jagged markings. Most give birth to live young.

There are 150 species of viper. The true vipers, subfamily Viperinae, abundant in Africa and southwestern Asia, include the ▷adder *Vipera berus*, the African puff adder *Bitis arietans*, and the horned viper of North Africa *Cerastes cornutus*. The second subfamily Crotalinae includes the mostly New World pit vipers, such as ▷rattlesnakes and copperheads of the Americas, which have a heat-sensitive pit between each eye and nostril.

Virgil (70–19 BC) Born Publius Vergilius Maro. Roman poet. He wrote the *Eclogues* (37 BC), a series of pastoral poems; the *Georgics* (30 BC), four books on the art of farming; and his epic masterpiece, the *Aeneid* (30–19 BC). He was patronized by Maecenas on behalf of Octavian (later the emperor Augustus).

Born near Mantua, Virgil was educated in Cremona and Mediolanum (Milan), and later studied philosophy and rhetoric at Rome. He wrote his second work, the *Georgics*, in honour of his new patron, Maecenas, to whom he introduced ▷Horace.

He passed much of his later life at Naples and devoted the last decade of it to the composition of the *Aeneid*, often considered the most important poem in Latin literature. In 19 BC Virgil went to Greece and caught a fever while visiting the ruins of Megara. Returning to Italy, he died soon after landing at Brundisium. The *Aeneid*, which he had wanted destroyed, was published by his executors on the order of the emperor Augustus.

Later Christian adaptations of his work, in particular of the prophetic *Fourth Eclogue*, greatly enhanced his mystical status in the Middle Ages, resulting in his adoption by ▷Dante as his guide to the underworld in the *Divine Comedy*.

Related Web site: Vergil Project http://vergil.classics.upenn.edu/

Virgin UK company founded and owned by Richard Branson. Branson started Virgin in 1969 as a mail-order business and the first Virgin record store opened in 1971. The company developed quickly, diversifying from retailing records to the airline business, then to radio, operating rail franchises, and offering financial services.

virginal plucked stringed keyboard instrument of the 16th and 17th centuries, often called 'virginals' or 'a pair of virginals' in England, where the term was applied to any quilled keyboard instrument well into the 17th century. The virginal is rectangular or polygonal in shape and is distinguished from the ▷harpsichord and ▷spinet by its strings being set at right angles to the keys, rather than parallel with them.

Virginia state in eastern USA. It is nicknamed Old Dominion. Officially known as the **Commonwealth of Virginia**, it ratified the US Constitution in 1788, becoming the 10th US state. It is bordered to the north by Maryland and the District of Columbia, to the west by Kentucky and West Virginia, and to the south by North Carolina and Tennessee. In the east it occupies the southern tip of the Delmarva Peninsula and is bordered by the Atlantic Ocean. Virginia was the northeasternmost state of the Confederacy.

population (1995) 6,618,400 **area** 105,600 sq km/40,762 sq mi **capital** Richmond **towns and cities** Norfolk, Virginia Beach, Newport News, Hampton, Chesapeake, Portsmouth **industries and products** sweet potatoes, maize, tobacco, apples, peanuts, coal, ships, lorries, paper, chemicals, processed food, textiles, tourism, leisure industry

Virginia creeper (or **woodbine**) eastern North American climbing vine belonging to the grape family, having tendrils, palmately compound leaves (made up of leaflets arranged like an open hand), green flower clusters, and blue berries eaten by many birds but inedible to humans. (*Parthenocissus quinquefolia*, family Vitaceae.)

Virgin Islands group of about 100 small islands, northernmost of the Leeward Islands in the Antilles, West Indies. Tourism is the main industry.

They comprise the **US Virgin Islands** St Thomas (with the capital, Charlotte Amalie), St Croix, St John, and about 50 small islets; area 350 sq km/135 sq mi; population (1990) 101,800; and the **British Virgin Islands** Tortola (with the capital, Road Town), Virgin Gorda, Anegada, and Jost van Dykes, and about 40 islets (11 islands are inhabited); area 150 sq km/58 sq mi; population (1991) 16,100.

The US Virgin Islands were purchased from Denmark in 1917, and form an 'unincorporated territory'. The British Virgin Islands were taken over from the Dutch by British settlers in 1666, and have partial internal self-government.

Virgo zodiacal constellation of the northern hemisphere, the second-largest in the sky. It is represented as a maiden holding an ear of wheat, marked by first-magnitude ▷Spica, Virgo's brightest star. The Sun passes through Virgo from late September to the end of October. In astrology, the dates for Virgo are between about 23 August and 22 September (see ▷precession).

Virgo contains the nearest large cluster of galaxies to us, 50 million light years away, consisting of about 3,000 galaxies centred on the giant elliptical galaxy M87. Also in Virgo is the nearest ▷quasar, 3C 273, an estimated 3 billion light years away.

virtual in computing, without physical existence. Most computers have ▷virtual memory, making their immediate-access memory seem larger than it is. ▷Virtual reality is a computer simulation of a whole physical environment.

virtual memory in computing, a technique whereby a portion of the computer backing storage, or external, ▷memory is used as an extension of its immediate-access, or internal, memory. The contents of an area of the immediate-access memory are stored on, say, a hard disk while they are not needed, and brought back into main memory when required.

VIOLIN One of the greatest skills in the art of violin-making is to achieve perfect gradation in the thickness across the curved wooden surfaces that comprise the two main elements, the 'belly' and the 'back'. The classic shape of the violin is as functional as it is traditional and aesthetic. *Image Bank*

VIPER This palm viper is a native of Sri Lanka. *Image Bank*

virtual reality advanced form of computer simulation, in which a participant has the illusion of being part of an artificial environment. The participant views the environment through two tiny television screens (one for each eye) built into a visor. Sensors detect movements of the participant's head or body, causing the apparent viewing position to change. Gloves (datagloves) fitted with sensors may be worn, which allow the participant seemingly to pick up and move objects in the environment.

The technology is still under development but is expected to have widespread applications; for example, in military and surgical training, architecture, and home entertainment.

virus in computing, a piece of ▷software that can replicate and transfer itself from one computer to another, without the user being aware of it. Some viruses are relatively harmless, but others can damage or destroy data.

virus infectious particle consisting of a core of nucleic acid (DNA or RNA) enclosed in a protein shell. Viruses are acellular and able to function and reproduce only if they can invade a living cell to use the cell's system to replicate themselves. In the process they may disrupt or alter the host cell's own DNA. The healthy human body reacts by producing an antiviral protein, ▷interferon, which prevents the infection spreading to adjacent cells.

There are around 5,000 species of virus known to science (1998), though there may be as many as 0.5 million actually in existence.

Many viruses mutate continuously so that the host's body has little chance of developing permanent resistance; others transfer between species, with the new host similarly unable to develop resistance. The viruses that cause ▷AIDS and ▷Lassa fever are both thought to have 'jumped' to humans from other mammalian hosts.

Among diseases caused by viruses are canine distemper, chickenpox, common cold, herpes, influenza, rabies, smallpox, yellow fever, AIDS, and many plant diseases. Recent evidence implicates viruses in the development of some forms of cancer (see ▷oncogenes). **Bacteriophages** are viruses that infect bacterial cells.

Retroviruses are of special interest because they have an RNA genome and can produce DNA from this RNA by a process called reverse transcription.

Viroids, discovered in 1971, are even smaller than viruses; they consist of a single strand of nucleic acid with no protein coat. They may cause stunting in plants and some rare diseases in animals, including humans.

It is debatable whether viruses and viroids are truly living organisms, since they are incapable of an independent existence. Outside the cell of another organism they remain completely inert. The origin of viruses is also unclear, but it is believed that they are degenerate forms of life, derived from cellular organisms, or pieces of nucleic acid that have broken away from the genome of some higher organism and taken up a parasitic existence.

Antiviral drugs are difficult to develop because viruses replicate by using the genetic machinery of host cells, so that drugs tend to affect the host cell as well as the virus. Acyclovir (used against the herpes group of diseases) is one of the few drugs so far developed that is successfully selective in its action. It is converted to its active form by an enzyme that is specific to the virus, and it then specifically inhibits viral replication. Some viruses have shown developing resistance to the few antiviral drugs available.

Viruses have recently been found to be very abundant in seas and lakes, with between 5 and 10 million per millilitre of water at most sites tested, but up to 250 million per millilitre in one polluted lake. These viruses infect bacteria and, possibly, single-celled algae. They may play a crucial role in controlling the survival of bacteria and algae in the plankton.

Visby historic town and bishopric on the Swedish island of Gotland in the Baltic that became the centre of the German ▷Hanseatic League.

viscacha Argentine Pampas and scrubland-dwelling rodent *Lagostomus maximus* of the chinchilla family. It is up to 70 cm/2.2 ft long with a 20 cm/8 in tail, and weighs 7 kg/15 lb. It is grey and black and has a large head and small ears. Viscachas live in warrens of up to 30 individuals. They are usually nocturnal and feed on grasses, roots, and seeds.

Visconti dukes and rulers of Milan 1277–1447. They originated as north Italian feudal lords who attained dominance over the city as a result of alliance with the Holy Roman Emperors. Despite papal opposition, by the mid-14th century they ruled 15 other major towns in northern Italy. The duchy was claimed by the ▷Sforzas in 1450.

viscose yellowish, syrupy solution made by treating cellulose with sodium hydroxide and carbon disulphide. The solution is then

regenerated as continuous filament for the making of ▷rayon and as cellophane.

viscosity in physics, the resistance of a fluid to flow, caused by its internal friction, which makes it resist flowing past a solid surface or other layers of the fluid. It applies to the motion of an object moving through a fluid as well as the motion of a fluid passing by an object.

Fluids such as pitch, treacle, and heavy oils are highly viscous; for the purposes of calculation, many fluids in physics are considered to be perfect, or nonviscous.

viscount (medieval Latin *vicecomes* 'in place of a count/earl') in the UK ▷peerage, the fourth degree of nobility, between earl and baron.

Vishnu in Hinduism, the second in the triad of gods (with Brahma and Siva) representing three aspects of the supreme spirit. He is the **Preserver**, and is believed to have assumed human appearance in nine *avatāra*s, or incarnations, in such forms as Rama and Krishna. His worshippers are the Vaishnavas.

Visigoth member of the western branch of the ▷Goths, an East Germanic people.

vision defect any abnormality of the eye that causes less-than-perfect sight. Common defects are short-sightedness or ▷myopia; long-sightedness or ▷hypermetropia; lack of ▷accommodation or presbyopia; and ▷astigmatism. Other eye defects include colour blindness.

Vistula (Polish **Wisła**) river in Poland that rises in the Carpathian Mountains and runs northwest to the Baltic Sea at Gdańsk; length 1,090 km/677 mi.

It is heavily polluted, carrying into the Baltic every year large quantities of industrial and agricultural waste, including phosphorus, oil, nitrogen, mercury, cadmium, and zinc.

visual display unit (VDU) computer terminal consisting of a keyboard for input data and a screen for displaying output. The oldest and most popular type of VDU screen is the ▷cathode-ray tube (CRT), which uses essentially the same technology as a television screen. Other types use plasma display technology and ▷liquid-crystal displays.

Screen resolution (the quality of the display) is dependent on the number of ▷pixels used; the smaller the pixel, the higher the resolution. Within the limits of the resolution supported by the screen itself, the display quality can be altered by the user to suit particular applications.

In the same way, the number of **screen colours** supported by a VDU can be selected by the user.

vitamin any of various chemically unrelated organic compounds that are necessary in small quantities for the normal functioning of the human body. Many act as coenzymes, small molecules that enable ▷enzymes to function effectively. Vitamins must be supplied by the diet because the body cannot make them. They are normally present in adequate amounts in a balanced diet. Deficiency of a vitamin may lead to a metabolic disorder ('deficiency disease'), which can be remedied by sufficient intake of the vitamin. They are generally classified as **water-soluble** (B and C) or **fat-soluble** (A, D, E, and K). See separate entries for individual vitamins, also ▷nicotinic acid, ▷folic acid, and ▷pantothenic acid.

Scurvy (the result of vitamin C deficiency) was observed at least 3,500 years ago, and sailors from the 1600s were given fresh sprouting cereals or citrus-fruit juices to prevent or cure it. The concept of scurvy as a deficiency disease, however, caused by the absence of a specific substance, emerged later. In the 1890s a Dutch doctor, Christiaan Eijkman, discovered that he could cure hens suffering from a condition like beriberi by feeding them on whole-grain, rather than polished, rice. In 1912 Casimir ▷Funk, a Polish-born biochemist, had proposed the existence of what he called 'vitamines' (vital amines), but it was not fully established until about 1915 that several deficiency diseases were preventable and curable by extracts from certain foods. By then it was known that two groups of factors were involved, one being water-soluble and present, for example, in yeast, rice-polishings, and wheat germ, and the other being fat-soluble and present in egg yolk, butter, and fish-liver oils. The water-soluble substance, known to be effective against beriberi, was named vitamin B. The fat-soluble vitamin complex was at first called vitamin A. As a result of analytical techniques these have been subsequently separated into their various components, and others have been discovered.

Megavitamin therapy has yielded at best unproven effects; some vitamins (A, for example) are extremely toxic in high doses.

Other animals may also need vitamins, but not necessarily the same ones. For example, choline, which humans can synthesize, is essential to rats and some birds, which cannot produce sufficient for themselves.

vitamin A another name for ▷retinol.

vitamin B₁ another name for ▷thiamine.

vitamin B₆ another name for ▷pyridoxine.

vitamin B₁₂ another name for ▷cyanocobalamin.

vitamin B₂ another name for ▷riboflavin.

vitamin C another name for ▷ascorbic acid.

vitamin D another name for ▷cholecalciferol.

vitamin E another name for ▷tocopherol.

vitamin H another name for ▷biotin.

vitamin K another name for ▷phytomenadione.

vitreous humour transparent jellylike substance behind the lens of the vertebrate ▷eye. It gives rigidity to the spherical form of the eye and allows light to pass through to the retina.

vitriol any of a number of sulphate salts. Blue, green, and white vitriols are copper, ferrous, and zinc sulphate, respectively.

Oil of vitriol is sulphuric acid.

Vitruvius (lived 1st century BC) Born Marcus Vitruvius Pollio. Roman architect. His ten-volume interpretation of Roman architecture, *De architectura*, provided an impetus for the Renaissance; it was first printed in Rome in 1486. Although often obscure, his writings have had a lasting influence on Western perceptions of classical architecture, mainly through the work of Leon Battista Alberti, and later Raphael and Palladio.

Vitus, St (lived early 4th century) Christian saint, perhaps Sicilian, who was martyred in Rome early in the 4th century. Feast day 15 June.

Vivaldi, Antonio Lucio (1678–1741) Italian baroque composer, violinist, and conductor. One of the most prolific composers of his day, he was particularly influential through his concertos, several of which were transcribed by Johann Sebastian Bach. He wrote 23 symphonies; 75 sonatas; over 400 concertos, including *The Four Seasons* (1725) for violin and orchestra; over 40 operas; and much sacred music. His work was largely neglected until the 1930s.

viviparous in animals, a method of reproduction in which the embryo develops inside the body of the female from which it gains nourishment (in contrast to ▷oviparous and ▷ovoviviparous). Vivipary is best developed in placental mammals, but also occurs in some arthropods, fishes, amphibians, and reptiles that have placentalike structures. In plants, it is the formation of young plantlets or bulbils instead of flowers. The term also describes seeds that germinate prematurely, before falling from the parent plant.

vivisection literally, cutting into a living animal. Used originally to mean experimental surgery or dissection practised on a live subject, the term is often used by ▷antivivisection campaigners to include any experiment on animals, surgical or otherwise.

Britain's 1876 Cruelty to Animals Act was the world's first legislation specifically to protect laboratory animals. In November 1998 the Home Office announced that testing cosmetics and their ingredients on animals is to be banned. Only three British companies were still holding testing permits for animal-tested cosmetics in 1998, and the number of animals used in such tests in 1997 was 1,319 out of the 2.6 million tests that took place overall.

Vladimir I (956–1015) Also known as **St Vladimir of Kiev**. Russian saint, prince of Novgorod, and grand duke of Kiev. Converted to Christianity 988, he married Anna, Christian sister of the Byzantine emperor Basil II, and established the Byzantine rite of Orthodox Christianity as the Russian national faith.

Vladivostok city on the western shore of the Sea of Japan, on a peninsula extending into Peter the Great Bay; population (1996 est) 627,000. It is the capital of the Primorski (Maritime) Krai of the Russian Federation, and one of the most important economic and cultural centres of the Russian Far East, where it is the largest city. Vladivostok is a terminus of the Trans-Siberian Railway (9,224 km/5,732 mi from Moscow) and the Northern Sea Route, centre of communications for the Pacific territories, the largest Russian port on the Pacific, and the chief base of the Pacific Fleet. The port is kept open by icebreakers during winter.

There are engineering works, shipyards, and factories manufacturing mining equipment in the city, along with major fishing and whaling industries. Since the collapse of communism in 1991, there has also been considerable development of financial, business, and other services. Vladivostok is a cultural and educational centre, containing a branch of the Russian Academy of Sciences and the Far Eastern University (founded in 1899 as Oriental Institute, university from 1920). The city was founded as a Russian port in 1860, has been a town since 1880, and became regional capital in 1888; it rapidly developed as a free port (handling supplies for the Russian Far East and in transit from Manchuria), naval base and fortress, and had a pronounced international character until the 1930s. In both world wars it was used for Allied supplies. During 1918–22 it saw Allied occupation under Japanese leadership, and various pro- and anti-Bolshevik governments. The city is home to a large Chinese population.

vocal cords the paired folds, ridges, or cords of tissue within a mammal's larynx, and a bird's syrinx. Air constricted between the folds or membranes makes them vibrate, producing sounds. Muscles in the larynx change the pitch of the sounds produced, by adjusting the tension of the vocal cords.

voiceprint graph produced by a sound spectograph showing frequency and intensity changes in the human voice when visually recorded. It enables individual speech characteristics to be determined.

First used as evidence in criminal trials in the USA in 1966, voiceprints were banned in 1974 by the US Court of Appeal as 'not yet sufficiently accepted by scientists'.

Vojvodina autonomous province in northern Serbia, Yugoslavia, 1945–1990; area 21,500 sq km/8,299 sq mi; population (1991) 2,012,500, including 1,110,000 Serbs and 390,000 Hungarians, as well as Croat, Slovak, Romanian, and Ukrainian minorities. Its capital is Novi Sad. In September 1990 Serbia effectively stripped Vojvodina of its autonomous status, causing antigovernment and anticommunist riots in early 1991.

volatile in chemistry, term describing a substance that readily passes from the liquid to the vapour phase. Volatile substances have a high ▷vapour pressure.

volatile memory in computing, ▷memory that loses its contents when the power supply to the computer is disconnected.

volcanic rock another name for ▷extrusive rock, igneous rock formed on the Earth's surface.

volcano crack in the Earth's crust through which hot magma (molten rock) and gases well up. The magma is termed lava when it reaches the surface. A volcanic mountain, usually cone shaped with a crater on top, is formed around the opening, or vent, by the build-up of solidified lava and ashes (rock fragments). Most volcanoes arise on plate margins (see ▷plate tectonics), where the movements of plates generate magma or allow it to rise from the mantle beneath. However, a number are found far from plate-margin activity, on 'hot spots' where the Earth's crust is thin.

There are two main types of volcano:

Composite volcanoes, such as ▷Stromboli and ▷Vesuvius in Italy, are found at destructive plate margins (areas where plates are being pushed together), usually in association with island arcs and coastal mountain chains. The magma is mostly derived from plate material and is rich in silica. This makes a very stiff lava such as andesite, which solidifies rapidly to form a high, steep-sided volcanic mountain. The magma often clogs the volcanic vent, causing violent eruptions as the blockage is blasted free, as in the eruption of ▷Mount St Helens, USA, in 1980. The crater may collapse to form a ▷caldera.

Shield volcanoes, such as ▷Mauna Loa in Hawaii, are found along the rift valleys and ocean ridges of constructive plate margins (areas where plates are moving apart), and also over hot spots. The magma is derived from the Earth's mantle and is quite free-flowing. The lava formed from this magma – usually basalt – flows for some distance over the surface before it sets and so forms broad low volcanoes. The lava of a shield volcano is not ejected violently but simply flows over the crater rim.

The type of volcanic activity is also governed by the age of the volcano. The first stages of an eruption are usually vigorous as the magma forces its way to the surface. As the pressure drops and the vents become established, the main phase of activity begins, composite volcanoes giving pyroclastic debris and shield volcanoes giving lava flows. When the pressure from below ceases, due to exhaustion of the magma chamber, activity wanes and is confined to the emission of gases and in time this also ceases. The volcano then enters a period of quiescence, after which activity may resume after a period of days, years, or even thousands of years. Only when the root zones of a volcano have been exposed by erosion can a volcano be said to be truly extinct.

Many volcanoes are submarine and occur along mid-ocean ridges. The chief terrestrial volcanic regions are around the Pacific rim (Cape Horn to Alaska); the central Andes of Chile (with the world's highest active volcano, Guallatiri, 6,063 m/19,892 ft); North Island, New Zealand; Hawaii; Japan; and Antarctica. There are more than 1,300 potentially active volcanoes on Earth. Volcanism has helped shape other members of the Solar System, including the Moon, Mars, Venus, and Jupiter's moon Io.

Related Web site: Volcanoes http://www.learner.org/exhibits/volcanoes/

vole any of various rodents of the family Cricetidae, subfamily Microtinae, distributed over Europe, Asia, and North America, and related to hamsters and lemmings. They are characterized by stout bodies and short tails. They have brown or grey fur, and blunt noses, and some species reach a length of 30 cm/12 in. They feed on grasses, seeds, aquatic plants, and insects. Many show remarkable fluctuations in numbers over 3–4 year cycles.

The most common genus is *Microtus*, which includes 45 species distributed across North America and Eurasia.

British species include the **water vole** or **water 'rat'** *Arvicola terrestris*, brownish above and grey-white below, which makes a burrow in riverbanks; and the **field** or **short-tailed vole** *Microtus agrestis*.

Water vole numbers in Britain drastically declined 1990–95. During a study of those sites along the Thames historically occupied by water voles, 73% were still inhabited in 1990 compared with only 23% in 1995. In December 1995 the water vole was listed on the UK's Biodiversity Action Plan, signalling increased investment in its conservation. Since 1998, water voles have been protected in the UK under the Wildlife and Countryside Act of 1981.

Volga (ancient **Rha**) longest river in Europe, entirely within the territory of the Russian Federation. The Volga has a total length 3,685 km/2,290 mi, 3,540 km/2,200 mi of which are navigable. It rises in the Valdai plateau northwest of Moscow, and flows into the Caspian Sea 88 km/55 mi below the city of Astrakhan. The Volga basin drains most of the central and eastern parts of European Russia, its total drainage area being 1,360,000 sq km/525,100 sq mi.

Volgograd (formerly **Tsaritsyn** (until 1925) and **Stalingrad** (1925–61)) industrial city in southwest Russian Federation, on the River Volga; population (1994) 1,000,000. Industries include the manufacture of metal goods and machinery, sawmilling, and oil refining.

volleyball indoor and outdoor team game played on a court between two teams of six players each. A net is placed across the centre of the court, and players hit the ball with their hands over it, the aim being to ground it in the opponents' court.

volt SI unit of electromotive force or electric potential (see ▷potential, electric), symbol V. A small battery has a potential of 1.5 volts, whilst a high-tension transmission line may carry up to 765,000 volts. The domestic electricity supply in the UK is 230 volts (lowered from 240 volts in 1995); it is 110 volts in the USA.

Volta main river in ▷Ghana, about 1,600 km/1,000 mi long, with two main upper branches, the Black and White Volta. It has been dammed at Akosombo to provide power.

Volta, Alessandro Giuseppe Antonio Anastasio (1745–1827) Count Volta. Italian physicist who invented the first electric cell (the voltaic pile, in 1800), the electrophorus (an early electrostatic generator, in 1775), and an ▷electroscope.

voltage commonly used term for ▷potential difference (pd) or ▷electromotive force (emf).

voltage amplifier electronic device that increases an input signal in the form of a voltage or ▷potential difference, delivering an output signal that is larger than the input by a specified ratio.

Voltaire (1694–1778) Pen-name of François-Marie Arouet. French writer. He is the embodiment of the 18th-century ▷Enlightenment. He wrote histories, books of political analysis and philosophy, essays on science and literature, plays, poetry, and the satirical fable *Candide* (1759), his best-known work.

A trenchant satirist of social and political evils, he was often forced to flee from his enemies and was twice imprisoned. His works include *Lettres philosophiques sur les Anglais/Philosophical Letters on the English* (1733) (essays in favour of English ways, thought, and political practice), *Le Siècle de Louis XIV/The Age of Louis XIV* (1751), and *Dictionnaire philosophique/Philosophical Dictionary* (1764).

Voltaire was born in Paris, the son of a notary, and used his pen-name from 1718. He was twice imprisoned in the Bastille and exiled from Paris 1716–26 for libellous political verse. *Oedipe/Oedipus*, his first essay in tragedy, was staged in 1718. While in England 1726–29 he dedicated an epic poem on Henry IV, *La Henriade/The Henriade*, to Queen Caroline, and on returning to France published the successful *Histoire de Charles XII/History of Charles XII* in 1731, and produced the play *Zaïre* in 1732.

He took refuge with his lover, the Marquise de Châtelet, at Cirey in Champagne, where he wrote the play *Mérope* (1743) and much of *Le Siècle de Louis XIV*. Among his other works are histories of Peter the Great, Louis XV, and India; the satirical tale *Zadig* (1748); *La Pucelle/The Maid* (1755), on Joan of Arc; and the tragedy *Irène* (1778). From 1751 to 1753 he stayed at the court of Frederick II (the Great) of Prussia, who had long been an admirer, but the association ended in deep enmity. From 1754 he established himself near Geneva, and after 1758 at Ferney, just across the French border.

Related Web site: Philosophical Dictionary by Voltaire http://history.hanover.edu/texts/voltaire/volindex.htm

> **Voltaire**
> *If God did not exist, it would be necessary to invent him.*
> *Épîtres*

voltmeter instrument for measuring the ▷potential difference (voltage) between two points in a circuit. It should not be confused with an ▷ammeter, which measures current. A voltmeter has a high internal resistance (so that it passes only a small current), and is connected in parallel with the component across which potential difference is to be measured – that is, the current divides and passes through both the voltmeter and the component at the same time.

volume in geometry, the space occupied by a three-dimensional solid object. A prism (such as a cube) or a cylinder has a volume equal to the area of the base multiplied by the height. For a pyramid or cone, the volume is equal to one-third of the area of the base multiplied by the perpendicular height. The volume of a sphere is equal to $\frac{4}{3} \times \pi r^3$, where r is the radius. Volumes of irregular solids may be calculated by the technique of ▷integration.

volumetric analysis procedure used for determining the concentration of a solution. A known volume of a solution of unknown concentration is reacted with a solution of known concentration (standard). The standard solution is delivered from a burette so the volume added is known. This technique is known as ▷titration. Often an indicator is used to show when the correct proportions have reacted. This procedure is used for acid–base, ▷redox, and certain other reactions involving solutions.

von Braun, Wernher Magnus Maximilian (1912–1977) German rocket engineer responsible for Germany's rocket development programme in World War II (▷V1 and V2) and later worked for the space agency ▷NASA in the USA. He also invented the ▷Saturn rocket (*Saturn V*) that sent the ▷Apollo spacecraft to the Moon in 1969.

Von Neumann, John (or Johann) (1903–1957) Hungarian-born US scientist and mathematician, a pioneer of computer design. He invented his 'rings of operators' (called **Von Neumann algebras**) in the late 1930s, and also contributed to set theory, game theory, quantum mechanics, cybernetics (with his theory of self-reproducing automata, called **Von Neumann machines**), and the development of the atomic and hydrogen bombs.

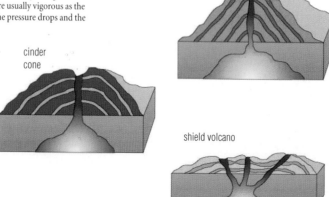

VOLCANO There are two main types of volcano, but three distinctive cone shapes. Composite volcanoes emit a stiff, rapidly solidifying lava which forms high, steep-sided cones. Volcanoes that regularly throw out ash build up flatter domes known as cinder cones. The lava from a shield volcano is not ejected violently, flowing over the crater rim forming a broad low profile.

composite volcano

cinder cone

shield volcano

Vonnegut, Kurt, Jr (1922–) US writer. His early works, *Player Piano* (1952) and *The Sirens of Titan* (1959), used the science fiction genre to explore issues of technological and historical control. He turned to more experimental methods with his highly acclaimed, popular success *Slaughterhouse-Five* (1969), a novel that mixed a world of fantasy with the author's experience of the fire-bombing of Dresden, Germany, during World War II. His later novels, marked by a bittersweet spirit of absurdist anarchy and folksy fatalism, include *Breakfast of Champions* (1973), *Slapstick* (1976), *Jailbird* (1979), *Deadeye Dick* (1982), *Galapagos* (1985), *Hocus Pocus* (1990), *The Face* (1992), and *Timequake* (1997).

KURT VONNEGUT A portrait of US author Kurt Vonnegut. *Archive Photos*

voodoo set of magical beliefs and practices, followed in some parts of Africa, South America, and the West Indies, especially Haiti. It arose in the 17th century on slave plantations as a combination of Roman Catholicism and West African religious traditions; believers retain membership in the Roman Catholic Church. It was once practiced in New Orleans and other areas of southern USA by African-Americans. Beliefs include the existence of **loa**, spirits who closely involve themselves in human affairs, and some of whose identities mesh with those of Christian saints. The loa are invoked by the priest (*houngan*) or priestess (*manbo*) at ceremonies, during which members of the congregation become possessed by the spirits and go into a trance.

 Related Web site: Vodou (Voodoo) http://members.aol.com/racine125/index1.html

Vorarlberg (German 'in front of the Arlberg') Alpine federal state of Austria, bounded on the north by Bavaria, on the west by Lake Constance, the Rhine, and Liechtenstein, on the east by north Tirol, and on the south by Switzerland; area 2,600 sq km/1,004 sq mi; population (1994) 342,500. Its capital is Bregenz. It is the most industrialized province of Austria, producing textiles, clothing, and crafts. Forestry, dairy-farming, and fruit-growing are the main agricultural occupations. Tourism is important. There are several hydroelectric stations.

Voronezh river port and capital of Voronezh oblast (region), in the western Russian Federation; population (1996 est) 909,000. Voronezh is situated 290 km/180 mi northeast of Kharkov on the Voronezh River 18 km/11 mi west of its confluence with the Don. It stands at the centre of the black soil (*chernozem*) region, which has high agricultural yields. The city has important manufacturing industries, for example engineering works (producing agricultural and food industry equipment, excavators, and diesel motors) and chemical plants (manufacturing synthetic rubber and pharmaceuticals). Other products include building materials and foodstuffs.

Vosges mountain range in eastern France near the Franco-German frontier between the *départements* of Haut-Rhin and Vosges, 250 km/155 mi in length and rising to its highest point at the Ballon de Guebwiller (1,422 m/4,667 ft). The Vosges forms the western edge of the Rhine rift valley. It gives its name to the *département* of Vosges. The Vosges is separated from the Jura Mountains to the south by the Belfort Gap.

vote expression of opinion by ▷ballot, show of hands, or other means. In systems that employ direct vote, the ▷plebiscite and ▷referendum are fundamental mechanisms. In parliamentary elections the results can be calculated in a number of ways. The main electoral systems are:

 simple plurality or **first past the post**, with single-member constituencies (USA, UK, India, Canada); **absolute majority**, achieved for example by the **alternative vote**, where the voter, in single-member constituencies, chooses a candidate by marking preferences (Australia), or by the **second ballot**, where, if a clear decision is not reached immediately, a second ballot is held (France, Egypt); ▷**proportional representation**, achieved for example by the **party list** system (Israel, most countries of Western Europe, and several in South America), the **additional member** system or AMS (Germany), the **single transferable vote** (Ireland and Malta), and the **limited vote** (Japan's upper house and Liechtenstein). Revised voting systems were adopted by Italy and New Zealand 1993, in which both houses were elected by a combination of simple majority voting and proportional representation on the AMS model. In Japan AMS was adopted for the lower house in 1994.

Vranitzky, Franz (1937–) Austrian socialist politician, federal chancellor 1986–97. A banker, he entered the political arena through the moderate, left-of-centre Socialist Party of Austria (SPÖ), and became minister of finance in 1984. He succeeded Fred Sinowatz as federal chancellor in 1986, heading an SPÖ-ÖVP (Austrian People's Party) coalition, which was returned in the October 1994 and December 1995 general elections. He resigned in January 1997.

Vries, Hugo (Marie) de (1848–1935) Dutch botanist who conducted important research on osmosis in plant cells and was a pioneer in the study of plant evolution. His work led to the rediscovery of Austrian biologist Gregor ▷Mendel's laws and the discovery of spontaneously occurring ▷mutations.

V-shaped valley river valley with a V-shaped cross-section. Such valleys are usually found near the source of a river, where the steeper gradient means that there is a great deal of corrasion (grinding away by rock particles) along the stream bed and erosion cuts downwards more than it does sideways. However, a V-shaped valley may also be formed in the lower course of a river when its powers of downward erosion become renewed by a fall in sea level, a rise in land level, or the capture of another river.

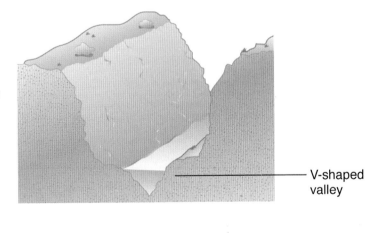

V-shaped valley

V-SHAPED VALLEY Cross section of a V-shaped valley. V-shaped valleys are formed through erosion by water.

VT abbreviation for ▷Vermont, a state of the USA.

Vuillard, (Jean) Edouard (1868–1940) French painter and printmaker. He was a founding member of *les Nabis*, and is noted for his decorative paintings of intimate domestic interiors with figures and for his brilliantly coloured lithographs.

Vukovar river port in Croatia at the junction of the rivers Vuka and Danube, 32 km/20 mi southeast of Osijek; population (1991) 44,600. Industries include foodstuffs manufacture, fishing, and agricultural trade. In 1991 the town resisted three months of siege by the Serb-dominated Yugoslav army before capitulating.

 It suffered the severest damage inflicted to any European city since the bombing of Dresden during World War II.

Vulcan (or **Vulcanus**) in Roman mythology, the god of fire and destruction, later identified with the Greek god ▷Hephaestus.

vulcanization technique for hardening rubber by heating and chemically combining it with sulphur. The process also makes the rubber stronger and more elastic. If the sulphur content is increased to as much as 30%, the product is the inelastic solid known as ebonite. More expensive alternatives to sulphur, such as selenium and tellurium, are used to vulcanize rubber for specialized products such as vehicle tyres. The process was discovered accidentally by US inventor Charles ▷Goodyear in 1839 and patented in 1844.

Vulgate (Latin 'common') the Latin translation of the Bible produced by St Jerome in the 4th century.

vulture any of various carrion-eating birds of prey in the order Falconiformes, with naked heads and necks, strong hooked bills, and keen senses of sight and smell. Vultures are up to 1 m/3.3 ft long, with wingspans of up to 3.7 m/12 ft. The plumage is usually dark, and the head brightly coloured.

 The vulture's eyes are adapted to give an overall view with a magnifying area in the centre, enabling it to locate possible food sources and see the exact site in detail.

VULTURE There are 15 species of vulture in Africa, Asia, and Europe, with a further seven species in America.

W

W in physics, symbol for **watt**.

WA abbreviation for ▷Washington, a state of the USA.

wadi in arid regions of the Middle East, a steep-sided valley containing an intermittent stream that flows in the wet season.

Wafd (Arabic 'deputation') the main Egyptian nationalist party between World Wars I and II. Under Nahas Pasha it formed a number of governments in the 1920s and 1930s. Dismissed by King Farouk in 1938, it was reinstated by the British in 1941. The party's pro-British stance weakened its claim to lead the nationalist movement, and the party was again dismissed by Farouk in 1952, shortly before his own deposition. Wafd was banned in January 1953.

Wagenfeld, Wilhelm (1900–1990) German architect and industrial designer. A graduate of the ▷Bauhaus design school in Weimar, Germany, Wagenfeld went on to become one of the country's leading proponents of the machine style (a geometric, undecorated style deemed appropriate for industrial products) in the areas of metal and glass goods.

Wagner, Otto (1841–1918) Viennese architect. Initially working in the art nouveau style, for example the Vienna Stadtbahn 1894–97, he later rejected ornament for rationalism, as in the Post Office Savings Bank, Vienna, 1904–06. He influenced such Viennese architects as Josef Hoffmann, Adolf Loos, and Joseph Olbrich.

> **Richard Wagner**
> *Where the speech of men stops short, then the art of music begins.*
> A Happy Evening

Wagner, (Wilhelm) Richard (1813–1883) German opera composer. He revolutionized the 19th-century conception of opera, envisaging it as a wholly new art form in which musical, poetic, and scenic elements should be unified through such devices as the ▷leitmotif. His operas include *Tannhäuser* (1845) *Lohengrin* (1848), and *Tristan und Isolde* (1865). In 1872 he founded the Festival Theatre in Bayreuth; his masterpiece *Der Ring des Nibelungen/The Ring of the Nibelung*, a sequence of four operas, was first performed there in 1876. His last work, *Parsifal*, was produced in 1882.

Wagner's early career was as director of the Magdeburg Theatre, where he unsuccessfully produced his first opera *Das Liebesverbot/Forbidden Love* (1836). He lived in Paris 1839–42 and conducted the Dresden Opera House 1842–48. He fled Germany to escape arrest for his part in the 1848 revolution, but in 1861 was allowed to return. He won the favour of Ludwig II of Bavaria in 1864 and was thus able to set up the Festival Theatre. The Bayreuth tradition was continued by his wife Cosima (1837–1930; Liszt's daughter, whom he married after her divorce from Hans von Bülow); by his son Siegfried Wagner (1869–1930), a composer of operas such as *Der Bärenhäuter*; and by later descendants.
Related Web site: Richard Wagner Archive http://www.utu.fi/~hansalmi/wagner.spml

Wagner, Robert (1910–1991) US Democratic politician, mayor of New York City 1954–65. He demolished slum areas, built public housing, and was instrumental in introducing members of ethnic minorities into City Hall.

Wagner, Robert F(erdinand) (1877–1953) US Democratic senator 1927–49, a leading figure in the development of welfare provision in the USA, especially in the ▷New Deal era. He helped draft much new legislation, including the National Industrial Recovery Act 1933, the Social Security Act 1936, and the National Labor Relations Act 1935, known as the Wagner Act.

Wagram, Battle of during the Napoleonic Wars, decisive French victory 6 July 1809 over the Austrians led by the Archduke Charles near Wagram, an Austrian village 18 km/11 mi northeast of Vienna. Austria was forced to concede general defeat to Napoleon.

wagtail slim, narrow-billed bird of the genus *Motacilla*, in the family Motacillidae, order Passeriformes, about 18 cm/7 in long, with a characteristic flicking movement of the tail. There are about 30 species, found mostly in Eurasia and Africa.

British species include the **pied wagtail** *M. alba* with black, grey, and white plumage, the **grey wagtail** *M. cinerae* and, a summer visitor, the **yellow wagtail** *M. flava*. There are numerous subspecies and varieties of the yellow wagtail with a very complicated taxonomy. There are also several subspecies of the pied wagtail. Yellow wagtails have declined in Britain by 31% since the late 1960s.

Wahabi puritanical Saudi Islamic sect founded by Muhammad ibn-Abd-al-Wahab (1703–1792), which regards all other sects as heretical. By the early 20th century it had spread throughout the Arabian peninsula; it still remains the official ideology of the Saudi Arabian kingdom.

Wailing Wall (or (in Judaism) **Western Wall**) the remaining part of the ▷Temple in Jerusalem, a sacred site of pilgrimage and prayer for Jews. There they offer prayers either aloud ('wailing') or on pieces of paper placed between the stones of the wall.

Wain, John (Barrington) (1925–1994) English poet and novelist. His first novel, *Hurry on Down* (1953), expresses the radical political views of the ▷Angry Young Men of the 1950s. He published several volumes of witty and ironic verse, collected in *Poems 1949–79* (1981), and was professor of poetry at Oxford University from 1973–80.

Wain was born in Stoke-on-Trent, north Staffordshire, and studied at Oxford. He lectured in English literature at Reading University from 1947–55, then worked as a freelance writer and lecturer or visiting academic. He achieved fame with his first novel; others include *Living in the Present* (1955), *The Contenders* (1958), *The Young Visitors* (1965), and the mid-20th-century Oxford saga comprising *Where the Rivers Meet* (1988), *Comedies* (1990), and *Hungry Generations* (1994). His short stories are collected in *Nuncle* (1960), *Death of the Hind Legs* (1966), *The Life Guard* (1971), and *King Caliban* (1978). Volumes of his verse include *A Word Carved on a Sill* (1956) and *Feng* (1975). He also wrote several important critical studies, including *Essays on Literature and Ideas* (1963) and *Samuel Johnson* (1974).

Wainwright, Alfred (1907–1991) English walker and author of guidebooks. His first articles appeared in 1955 in a local paper and he eventually produced over 40 meticulously detailed books, including volumes on the Lake District, Pennine Way, and other areas of northern England.

Waite, Terry (1939–   ) Born Terence Hardy Waite. English religious adviser to the archbishop of Canterbury (then Dr Robert ▷Runcie) 1980–87. As the archbishop's special envoy, Waite

RICHARD WAGNER This portrait of German opera composer Richard Wagner is by an unknown artist. *The Art Archive/Society Friends Music Vienna/Dagli Orti*

WAILING WALL The Wailing Wall, the only remaining part of the Jewish Temple of biblical times, stands below the Muslim shrine of the Dome of the Rock, Jerusalem. *Image Bank*

disappeared on 20 January 1987 while engaged in secret negotiations to free European hostages in Beirut, Lebanon. He was taken hostage by an Islamic group and released on 18 November 1991. His kidnapping followed six conversations he held with US agent Oliver ▷North, who appeared to be hoping to find a way to release US hostages through Waite.

TERRY WAITE Terry Waite, former religious adviser to the archbishop of Canterbury. *Archive Photos*

Waits, Tom (1949–   ) US singer, songwriter, musician, and actor, with a characteristic gravelly voice. His songs typically deal with urban street life and have jazz-tinged arrangements, as on *Rain Dogs* (1985). He has written music for and acted in several films, including Jim Jarmusch's *Down by Law* (1986). He also appeared in *Short Cuts* (1993).

Wajda, Andrzej (1926–) Polish film and theatre director. He was one of the most important figures in European cinema after World War II. His films have great intensity and are frequently concerned with the predicament and disillusion of individuals caught up in political events. They include *Ashes and Diamonds* (1958), *Man of Marble* (1977), *Man of Iron* (1981), *Danton* (1982), and *Korczak* (1990).

Wakefield industrial city in West Yorkshire, northern England, on the River Calder, south of Leeds; population (1991) 73,600. Industries include chemicals, machine tools, wool textiles, coal mining, and the manufacture of clothing, wire-rope, and sheet metal. Lancastrian forces defeated and killed Richard of York here in 1460, during the Wars of the ▷Roses. The National Coal Mining Museum is here.

Waksman, Selman Abraham (1888–1973) Ukrainian-born US biochemist who was awarded a Nobel Prize for Physiology or Medicine in 1952 for his discovery of streptomycin, the first antibiotic effective against tuberculosis. He coined the word 'antibiotic' for bacteria-killing chemicals derived from micro-organisms.

Walachia alternative spelling of ▷Wallachia, part of Romania.

Walcheren island in ▷Zeeland province, the Netherlands, in the estuary of the River Schelde; area 200 sq km/80 sq mi. The capital is ▷Middelburg. Industries include shipbuilding, engineering, and petrochemicals. There is dairying, and sugar beet and root vegetables are grown.

Walcott, Derek Walton (1930–) St Lucian writer, poet, and playwright. His work fuses Caribbean and European, classical and contemporary elements, and deals with the divisions within colonial society and his own search for cultural identity. His works include the long poem *Omeros* (1990), and his adaptation for the stage of Homer's *Odyssey* (1992); his *Collected Poems* were published in 1986. He was awarded the Nobel Prize for Literature in 1992. His biography of French impressionist painter Pissarro, *Tiepolo's Hound*, was published in 2000.

Waldenses (or **Waldensians** or **Vaudois**) Protestant religious sect, founded in about 1170 by Peter Waldo, a merchant of Lyons. They were allied to the ▷Albigenses. They lived in voluntary poverty, refused to take oaths or take part in war, and later rejected the doctrines of transubstantiation, purgatory, and the invocation of saints. Although subjected to persecution until the 17th century, they spread in France, Germany, and Italy, and still survive in Piedmont.

Waldheim, Kurt (1918–) Austrian politician and diplomat, president 1986–92. He was secretary general of the United Nations 1972–81, having been Austria's representative there 1964–68 and 1970–71.

He was elected president in spite of revelations that during World War II he had been an intelligence officer in an army unit responsible for transporting Jews to death camps. His election therefore led to some diplomatic isolation of Austria, and in 1991 he announced that he would not run for re-election.

Waldsterben (German 'forest death') tree decline related to air pollution, common throughout the industrialized world. It appears to be caused by a mixture of pollutants; the precise chemical mix varies between locations, but it includes acid rain, ozone, sulphur dioxide, and nitrogen oxides.

Wales (Welsh **Cymru**) Principality of; constituent part of the UK, in the west between the British Channel and the Irish Sea.

 area 20,780 sq km/8,020 sq mi **capital** Cardiff **towns and cities** Swansea, Wrexham, Newport, Carmarthen **features** Snowdonia Mountains (Snowdon 1,085 m/3,560 ft, the highest point in England and Wales) in the northwest and in the southeast the Black Mountains, Brecon Beacons, and Black Forest ranges; rivers Severn, Wye, Usk, and Dee **industries** traditional industries have declined, but varied modern and high-technology ventures are being developed. There are oil refineries and open-cast coal mining. The last deep coal mine in north Wales closed in 1996. Wales has the largest concentration of Japanese-owned plants in the UK. It also has the highest density of sheep in the world and a dairy industry; tourism is important **currency** pound sterling **population** (1993 est) 2,906,000 **language** English, 19% Welsh-speaking **religion** Nonconformist Protestant denominations; Roman Catholic minority **government** returns 40 members to the UK Parliament; in April 1996, the eight counties were replaced by 22 county and county borough unitary authorities; devolved National Assembly for Wales (approved by referendum in 1997) has sat in Cardiff since 1999
 Related Web site: Brief History of Wales http://www.britannia.com/wales/whist.html

Wałęsa, Lech (1943–) Polish trade union leader, president of Poland 1990–95. One of the founding members of the ▷Solidarity free-trade-union movement, which emerged to challenge the

communist government during strikes in the Gdańsk shipyards in August 1980. Wałęsa led the movement to become a national force. He was awarded the Nobel Prize for Peace in 1983 for his work with the Solidarity movement. After his election as president, he gradually became estranged from Solidarity. In 1997 he formed a Christian Democratic party, which was, however, unlikely to make a significant impact on Polish political life.

A brilliant orator and negotiator, as an electrician at the Lenin Shipyard in Gdańsk, Wałęsa became a trade-union organizer and led a series of strikes in 1970 and 1976. In August 1980 he successfully challenged the government to improve working conditions and grant political concessions. After the imposition of martial law in December 1981 he was interned. A devout Catholic, he obtained the support of the Church hierarchy in his negotiations with the authorities.

In 1990 he became president but lost his power base due to his apparent inability to work with the freely elected parliament and

> ### Lech Wałęsa
> *If I don't work hard, I will go to hell, and we already have Stalin and Lenin very well placed there, so they may torture me.*
>
> *Newsweek* (1999); on his leadership of the Solidarity movement.

Wales: Sovereigns and Princes 844–1282

844–78	Rhodri the Great
878–916	Anarawd
915–50	Hywel Dda (Hywel the Good)
950–79	Iago ab Idwal
979–85	Hywel ab Ieuaf (Hywel the Bad)
985–86	Cadwallon
986–99	Maredudd ab Owain ap Hywel Dda
999–1008	Cynan ap Hywel ab Ieuaf
1018–23	Llywelyn ap Seisyll
1023–39	Iago ab Idwal ap Meurig
1039–63	Gruffydd ap Llywelyn ap Seisyll
1063–75	Bleddyn ap Cynfyn
1075–81	Trahaern ap Caradog
1081–1137	Gruffydd ap Cynan ab Iago
1137–70	Owain Gwynedd
1170–94	Dafydd ab Owain Gwynedd
1194–1240	Llywelyn Fawr (Llywelyn the Great)
1240–46	Dafydd ap Llywelyn
1246–82	Llywellyn ap Gruffydd ap Llywellyn

Wales: Key Dates

For ancient history, see also ▷Britain, ancient.

c. 400 BC	Wales is occupied by Celts from central Europe.
AD 50–60	Wales becomes part of the Roman Empire.
c. 200	Christianity is adopted.
c. 450–600	Wales becomes the chief Celtic stronghold in the west since the Saxons invaded and settled in southern Britain. The Celtic tribes unite against England.
8th century	The Welsh frontier is pushed back to Offa's Dyke.
9th–11th centuries	Vikings raid the coasts. At this time Wales is divided into small states organized on a clan basis, although princes such as Rhodri (844–878), Howel the Good (c. 904–949), and Griffith ap Llewelyn (1039–1063) temporarily unite the country.
11th–12th centuries	The continual pressure on Wales from the Normans across the English border is resisted, notably by Llewelyn I and II.
1277	Edward I of England is accepted as overlord by the Welsh.
1284	Edward I completes the conquest of Wales that is begun by the Normans.
1294	A revolt against English rule is put down by Edward I.
1350–1500	Welsh nationalist uprisings against the English take place; the most notable is that led by Owen Glendower.
1485	Henry Tudor, a Welshman, becomes Henry VII of England.
1536–43	Acts of Union unite England and Wales after conquest under Henry VIII. Wales sends representatives to the English Parliament; English law is established in Wales; English becomes the official language.
18th century	The evangelical revival makes religious Nonconformism a powerful factor in Welsh life. A strong coal and iron industry develops in the south.
19th century	The miners and ironworkers are militant supporters of Chartism, and Wales becomes a stronghold of trade unionism and socialism.
1893	The University of Wales is founded.
1920s–30s	Wales suffers from industrial depression; unemployment reaches 21% in 1937, and a considerable exodus of population takes place.
post-1945	The nationalist movement grows and there is a revival of the Welsh language, earlier suppressed or discouraged.
1966	Plaid Cymru, the Welsh National Party, returns its first member to Westminster.
1969	Prince Charles is formally inducted as Prince of Wales.
1974	Local government is reorganized into eight large counties.
1979	A referendum rejects a proposal for limited home rule.
1988	A bombing campaign against estate agents selling Welsh properties to English buyers is launched by nationalists.
1996	The last deep coal mine is finally closed. Local government is reorganized into 22 counties and county boroughs.
1997	A referendum endorses devolution proposals by a narrow margin of 50.3%.
1999	The Labour Party wins the most seats but fails to secure a majority in the elections for the National Assembly (Cynulliad Cenedlaethol), which is formally opened by Queen Elizabeth II.

See also ▷United Kingdom.

WALES A winter view of Llyn Ogwen, North Wales. The lake is in the upper section of the Nant Ffrancon valley, in Snowdonia National Park. *Image Bank*

conflicts with previous allies and advisers, most notably Tadeusz ▷Mazowiecki. In 1995 he was defeated in the presidential elections by the Social Democrat Aleksander Kwaśniewski. Although he continues to take an active part in Poland's political life, his influence is not significant. The leader of the Solidarity trade union, Marian Krzaklewski, effectively blocked all Wałęsa's efforts to use it as a springboard for further involvement in the country's politics.

Wales, Church in the Welsh Anglican Church, independent from the ▷Church of England.

Wales, Prince of title conferred on the eldest son of the UK's sovereign. Prince ▷Charles was invested as 21st prince of Wales at Caernarfon in 1969 by his mother, Elizabeth II.

walkabout Australian Aboriginal term for a nomadic ritual return into the bush by an urbanized Aboriginal; also used more casually for any similar excursion.

Walker, Alice Malsenior (1944–) US poet, novelist, critic, and essay writer. She has been active in the US civil-rights movement since the 1960s and, as a black woman, wrote about the double burden of racist and sexist oppression, about colonialism, and the quest for political and spiritual recovery. Her novel *The Color Purple* (1982; filmed 1985), told in the form of letters, won a Pulitzer prize. Her other works include *Possessing the Secret of Joy* (1992), which deals passionately with female circumcision, and *By the Light of My Father's Smile* (1998) and *The Way Forward is with a Broken Heart* (2001).

She was born in Eatonton, Georgia. In 1972 she took a teaching post at Wellesley College, Massachusetts, where she founded the first women's studies course in the USA. Other novels include *The Third Life of Grange Copeland* (1970), *Meridian* (1976), and *The Temple of My Familiar* (1989). Walker's collections of poems include *Once* (1968) and *Revolutionary Petunias* (1973); her short stories and essays are collected in *Love and Trouble: Stories of Black Women* (1973) and *In Search of Our Mothers' Gardens: Womanist Prose* (1983).

Wall, Max (1908–1990) Stage name of Maxwell George Lorimer. English music-hall comedian. Towards the end of his career he appeared in starring roles as a serious actor, in John Osborne's *The Entertainer* (1974), in Harold Pinter's *The Caretaker* (1977), and in Samuel Beckett's *Waiting for Godot* (1980). In his solo comedy performances his trademark was an eccentric walk.

wallaby any of various small and medium-sized members of the ▷kangaroo family.

Wallace, Alfred Russel (1823–1913) Welsh naturalist who collected animal and plant specimens in South America and Southeast Asia, and independently arrived at a theory of evolution by natural selection similar to that proposed by Charles ▷Darwin.

Wallace, (Richard Horatio) Edgar (1875–1932) English writer of thrillers. His prolific output includes *The Four Just Men* (1905) and *The Mind of Mr J G Reeder* (1925); stories such as those in *Sanders of the River* (1911), set in Africa, and sequels; and melodramas such as *The Ringer* (1926), from his own novel *The Gaunt Stranger* (1925).

Wallace, George Corley (1919–1998) US politician; governor of Alabama 1963–67, 1971–79, and 1983–87. Wallace opposed the integration of black and white students in the 1960s. He contested the presidency in 1968 as an independent (the American Independent Party) and in 1972 campaigned for the Democratic nomination but was shot at a rally and became partly paralysed.

Wallace, Richard (1818–1890) English art collector. He inherited a valuable art collection from his father, the Marquess of Hertford, which was given in 1897 by his widow to the UK as the Wallace Collection, containing many 18th-century French paintings. He was made a baronet in 1871.

Wallace, William (1272–1305) Scottish nationalist who led a revolt against English rule in 1297, won a victory at Stirling, and assumed the title 'governor of Scotland'. ▷Edward I defeated him at Falkirk in 1298, and Wallace was captured and executed. He was styled Knight in a charter of 1298.

Wallace line imaginary line running down the Lombok Strait in Southeast Asia, between the island of Bali and the islands of Lombok and Sulawesi. It was identified by English naturalist Alfred Russel Wallace as separating the South

Asian (Oriental) and Australian biogeographical regions, each of which has its own distinctive animals.

Wallachia independent medieval principality, founded in 1290, with allegiance to Hungary until 1330 and under Turkish rule 1387–1861, when it was united with the neighbouring principality of Moldavia to form Romania.

Wallenberg, Raoul (1912–*c.* 1947) Swedish business executive who attempted to rescue several thousand Jews from German-occupied Budapest in 1944, during World War II. He was taken prisoner by the Soviet army in 1945 and was never heard from again.

Wallenstein, Albrecht Eusebius Wenzel von (1583–1634) German general who, until his defeat at Lützen in 1632, led the Habsburg armies in the Thirty Years' War. He was assassinated.

Waller, Fats (Thomas Wright) (1904–1943) US jazz pianist and composer. He had a forceful stride piano style. His songs, many of which have become jazz standards, include 'Ain't Misbehavin'' (1929), 'Honeysuckle Rose' (1929), and 'Viper's Drag' (1934).

wallflower European perennial cottage garden plant with fragrant spikes of red, orange, yellow, brown, or purple flowers in spring. (Genus *Cheiranthus cheiri*, family Cruciferae.)

Wallis and Futuna two island groups in the southwestern Pacific Ocean, an overseas territory of France; area 367 sq km/143 sq mi; population (1997 est) 14,800. The people live mostly by subsistence agriculture and farming of livestock, especially pigs and goats. Much food is imported, mainly rice, sugar and beef, as are virtually all manufactured goods. The export trade is very small, chiefly copra and handicrafts. Because of deforestation, through cutting down timber for fuel, soil erosion is a problem, especially in Futuna.

Walloon a French-speaking people of southeastern Belgium and adjacent areas of France. The name 'Walloon' is etymologically linked to 'Welsh'.

wall pressure in plants, the mechanical pressure exerted by the cell contents against the cell wall. The rigidity (turgor) of a plant often depends on the level of wall pressure found in the cells of the stem. Wall pressure falls if the plant cell loses water.

Wall Street the financial centre of the USA, a street on lower Manhattan Island, New York City, on which the New York Stock Exchange is situated; also a synonym for stock dealing in the USA. Office skyscrapers house many of the major banks, trust companies, insurance corporations, and financial institutions of the city; coffee, cotton, metal, produce, and corn exchanges are sited here. Its narrow course follows the line of a stockade wall erected by the Dutch to protect New Amsterdam in 1653.

Wall Street Crash (1929) panic selling on the New York Stock Exchange following an artificial boom from 1927 to 1929 fed by speculation. On 24 October 1929, 13 million shares changed hands, with further heavy selling on 28 October and the disposal of 16 million shares on 29 October. Many shareholders were ruined, banks and businesses failed, and in the ▷Depression that followed, unemployment rose to approximately 17 million.

The repercussions of the Wall Street Crash, experienced throughout the USA, were also felt in Europe, worsened by the

reduction of US loans. A world economic crisis followed the crash, bringing an era of depression and unemployment.

walnut deciduous tree, probably originating in southeastern Europe and now widely cultivated elsewhere. It can grow up to 30 m/100 ft high, and produces a full crop of edible nuts about 12 years after planting; the timber is used in furniture and the oil is used in cooking. (Genus *Juglans regia*, family Juglandaceae.)

WALNUT The walnut is prized for its dark timber. The wrinkled nut is contained in a hard shell which is in turn surrounded by a fleshy green layer.

Walpole, Horace (1717–1797) 4th Earl of Orford. English novelist, letter writer and politician, the son of Robert Walpole. He was a Whig member of Parliament 1741–67.

He converted his house at Strawberry Hill, Twickenham (then a separate town southwest of London), into a Gothic castle; his *The Castle of Otranto* (1764) established the genre of the Gothic, or 'romance of terror', novel. More than 4,000 of his letters have been published. He became Earl in 1791.

Walpole, Hugh (Seymour) (1884–1941) English novelist, born in New Zealand. His popular novels in many genres include *Mr Perrin and Mr Traill* (1911), *The Dark Forest* (1916), the semi-autobiographical *Jeremy* (1919) and sequels, and *Portrait of a Man with Red Hair* (1925). He also wrote the historical 'Lakeland saga' of *The Herries Chronicle* (1930–33).

Walpole, Robert (1676–1745) 1st Earl of Orford. British Whig politician, the first 'prime minister'. As First Lord of the Treasury and chancellor of the Exchequer (1715–17 and 1721–42) he encouraged trade and tried to avoid foreign disputes (until forced into the War of Jenkins' Ear with Spain in 1739).

Walpurga, St (*c.* 710–*c.* 779) English abbess who preached Christianity in Germany. **Walpurgis Night**, the eve of 1 May (one of her feast days), became associated with witches' sabbaths and other superstitions. Her feast day is 25 February.

Walras, (Marie Esprit) Léon (1834–1910) French economist. In his *Eléments d'économie politique pure* (1874–77) he attempted to develop a unified model for general equilibrium theory (a hypothetical situation in which demand equals supply in all markets). He also originated the theory of diminishing marginal utility of a good (the increased value to a person of consuming more of a product).

walrus Arctic marine carnivorous mammal *Odobenus rosmarus* of the same family (Otariidae) as the eared ▷seals. It can reach 4 m/13 ft in length, and weigh up to 1,400 kg/3,000 lb. It has webbed flippers, a bristly moustache, and large tusks. It is gregarious except at breeding time and feeds mainly on molluscs. It has been hunted for its ivory tusks, hide, and blubber; the Alaskan walrus is close to extinction.

Walruses feed continuously for days at a time, after which they rest for several days. They need to eat 2,000–6,000 shellfish a day to remain healthy. Walruses feed on fish, shellfish, and other sea invertebrates such as crabs and squid, but they will also hunt and kill seals. Their lifespan is around 40 years, with females reaching sexual maturity at about six years, and males between seven and ten years. The gestation period is 15 months and females give birth to a single calf every third year. Calves are weaned at two years.

Related Web site: Walrus http://www.seaworld.org/animal_bytes/walrusab.html

WALL STREET CRASH Panic-stricken investors on Wall Street after the stock market crash of 29 October 1929. *Archive Photos*

Walsall industrial town in West Midlands, central England, 13 km/8 mi northwest of Birmingham; population (1991) 172,600. It has a leather industry and also produces castings. Until the 1930s coal was mined here. Walsall's art gallery contains the Garman–Ryan collection, over 350 paintings including works by Jacob Epstein. The writer Jerome K Jerome was born here in 1859.

Walsingham, Francis (*c.* 1530–1590) English politician and principal secretary of state to ▷Elizabeth I from 1573 until his death. A staunch Puritan, he advocated a strong anti-Spanish foreign policy and controlled an efficient government spy network to identify and forestall Roman Catholic conspiracies against the queen. Walsingham's spies uncovered planned assassinations by Francis Throckmorton (1584) and Antony Babington (1586). His exposure of the involvement of ▷Mary Queen of Scots in the latter plot persuaded Elizabeth to order her execution. Walsingham was knighted for his services in 1577.

Walter, Hubert (died 1205) Archbishop of Canterbury 1193–1205. As justiciar (chief political and legal officer) 1193–98, he ruled England during Richard I's absence and introduced the offices of coroner and justice of the peace.

Walters, Alan Arthur (1926–) British economist and government adviser 1981–89. He became economics adviser to Prime Minister Margaret Thatcher, but his publicly stated differences with the policies of her chancellor Nigel ▷Lawson precipitated, in 1989, Lawson's resignation from the government as well as Walters' own departure. He was knighted in 1983.

Walther von der Vogelweide (*c.* 1170–1230) German poet. The greatest of the ▷Minnesingers, his songs dealt mainly with courtly love. Of noble birth, he lived in his youth at the Austrian ducal court in Vienna, adopting a wandering life after the death of his patron in 1198. His lyrics deal mostly with love, but also with religion and politics.

Arthur Ponsonby
British politician and author

When war is declared,
Truth is the first casualty.

Falsehood in Wartime, epigraph

Walton, Izaak (1593–1683) English writer. He is known for his classic fishing compendium *The Compleat Angler, or the Contemplative Man's Recreation* (1653). He also wrote lives of the poets John Donne (1658) and George Herbert (1670), and the theologian Richard Hooker (1665).

Walton, William Turner (1902–1983) English composer. Among his works are *Facade* (1923), a series of instrumental pieces designed to be played in conjunction with the recitation of surrealist poems by Edith Sitwell; the oratorio *Belshazzar's Feast* (1931); and *Variations on a Theme by Hindemith* (1963).

waltz ballroom dance in moderate triple time (3/4) that developed in Germany and Austria during the late 18th century from the Austrian *Ländler* (traditional peasants' country dance). Associated particularly with Vienna and the Strauss family, the waltz has remained popular up to the present day and has inspired composers including Chopin, Brahms, and Ravel.

Walvis Bay chief port serving Namibia, situated on the Atlantic Ocean, 275 km/171 mi southwest of Windhoek; population (1997 est) 50,000. It is the only deep-water harbour on the Namibian coast and has a fishing industry with allied trades. Because of its central coastal position, harbour, rail links, and airport, Walvis Bay now handles most of Namibia's trade. It was a detached part (area 1,100 sq km/425 sq mi) of Cape Province, South Africa, 1884–1993 (administered solely by South Africa 1922–92; from 1992 jointly by South Africa and Namibia). In 1993 South Africa waived its claim to sovereignty and control was passed to Namibia in February 1994. Walvis Bay is now part of Erongo region.

wampum cylindrical beads ground from sea shells of white and purple, woven into articles of personal adornment and also used as money by American Indians of the northeastern woodlands.

Wandering Jew in medieval legend, a Jew named Ahasuerus, said to have insulted Jesus on his way to Calvary and to have been condemned to wander the world until the Second Coming.

Wang, An (1920–1990) Chinese-born US engineer, founder in 1951 of Wang Laboratories, one of the world's largest computer companies in the 1970s. In 1948 he invented the computer memory core, the most common device used for storing computer data before the invention of the integrated circuit (chip).

WAP (acronym for wireless application protocol) initiative started in the 1990s by Unwired Planet and mobile phone manufacturers Motorola, Nokia, and Ericsson to develop a standard for delivering Web-like applications on a new generation of ▷mobile phones. It is possible to use WAP phones for e-mail and messaging, reading Web pages, shopping, booking tickets, and making other financial transactions, as well as for phone calls.

The WAP protocol has many similarities to Internet technologies. For instance, the Wireless Markup Language (WML) used to create WAP pages is very similar to HTML, which is used to create Web pages. Similarly, the WMLScript is based on JavaScript. Both WML and WMLScript are adapted and designed for a wireless environment, to address issues such as limited bandwidth and limited processing power in the mobile phone.

Andy Warhol

I paint pictures of myself to . . . I guess . . . yeah . . . to remind myself that I'm still around.

The Observer 1986

wapiti (or **elk**) species of deer *Cervus canadensis*, native to North America, Europe, and Asia, including New Zealand. It is reddish-brown in colour, about 1.5 m/5 ft at the shoulder, weighs up to 450 kg/1,000 lb, and has antlers up to 1.2 m/4 ft long. It is becoming increasingly rare, although the wapiti population in Yellowstone National Park, USA, was a thriving 25,000 in 1998. In North America, the wapiti is also called an elk.

Wapping district of the Greater London borough of ▷Tower Hamlets. The redevelopment of the London ▷Docklands began here in 1969 with work on St Katherine Dock. From the mid-1980s it has been a centre of the newspaper industry.

war act of force, usually on behalf of the state, intended to compel a declared enemy to obey the will of the other. The aim is to render the opponent incapable of further resistance by destroying its capability and will to bear arms in pursuit of its own aims. War can therefore be seen as a continuation of politics carried on with violent and destructive means, as an instrument of policy. Conversely, politics and diplomacy can be seen as attempts to avoid war.

Warbeck, Perkin (*c.* 1474–1499) Flemish pretender to the English throne. Claiming to be Richard, brother of Edward V, he led a rising against Henry VII in 1497, and was hanged after attempting to escape from the Tower of London.

War between the States another (usually Southern) name for the American ▷Civil War.

warble fly large, brownish, hairy flies, with mouthparts that are reduced or vestigial. The larva is a large maggot covered with spines. They cause myiasis (invasion of the tissues by fly larvae) in animals.

warbler any of two families of songbirds, order Passeriformes. The Old World warblers are in the family Sylviidae, while the New World warblers are members of the Parulidae.

American or wood warblers (family Parulidae) are small, insect-eating birds, often brightly coloured, such as the yellow warbler, prothonotary warbler, and dozens of others. This group is sometimes placed in the same family (Emberizidae) as sparrows and ▷orioles. Old World warblers (family Sylviidae) are typically slim and dull-plumaged above, lighter below, insectivorous, and fruit-eating, overwhelmingly represented in Eurasia and Africa. These are sometimes considered a subgroup of the same family (Muscicapidae) that includes thrushes.

Old World species, which grow up to 25 cm/10 in long, and feed on berries and insects, include the ▷**chiffchaff**, **blackcap**, **goldcrest**, ▷**willow warbler**, and the tropical long-tailed **tailorbird** *Orthotomus sutorius*, which builds a nest inside two large leaves it sews together.

Other British species include the **garden warbler** *Sylvia borin*, the **lesser whitethroat** *S. curruca*, the **grasshopper warbler** *Locustella naevia*, the **reed warbler** *Acrocephalus scirpaceus*, and the **sedge warbler** *A. schoenobaenus*. The **Dartford warbler** *Sylvia undata* is one of Britain's rarest birds.

Warburg, Otto Heinrich (1883–1970) German biochemist who was awarded a Nobel Prize for Physiology or Medicine in 1931 for the discovery of respiratory enzymes that enable cells to process oxygen. In 1923 he devised a manometer (pressure gauge) sensitive enough to measure oxygen uptake of respiring tissue. By measuring the rate at which cells absorb oxygen under differing conditions, he was able to show that enzymes called cytochromes enable cells to process oxygen.

war crime offence (such as murder of a civilian or a prisoner of war) that contravenes the internationally accepted laws governing the conduct of wars, particularly the Hague Convention of 1907 and the Geneva Convention of 1949. A key principle of the law relating to such crimes is that obedience to the orders of a superior is no defence. In practice, prosecutions are generally brought by the victorious side.

ward of court in the UK, a child whose guardian is the High Court. Any person may, by issuing proceedings, make the High Court guardian of any child within its jurisdiction. No important step in the child's life can then be taken without the court's leave.

warfarin poison that induces fatal internal bleeding in rats; neutralized with sodium hydroxide, it is used in medicine as an anticoagulant in the treatment of ▷thrombosis: it prevents blood clotting by inhibiting the action of vitamin K. It can be taken orally and begins to act several days after the initial dose.

Warhol, Andy (1928–1987) Adopted name of Andrew Warhola. US pop artist and film-maker. He made his name in 1962 with paintings of Campbell's soup cans, Coca-Cola bottles, and film stars. In his New York studio, the Factory, he and his assistants produced series of garish silk-screen prints. His films include *Chelsea Girls* (1966) and *Trash* (1970).

Warhol was born in Pittsburgh, where he studied art. In the 1950s he became a commercial artist in New York. With the breakthrough of pop art, his bizarre personality and flair for self-publicity made him a household name. He was a pioneer of multimedia events with the 'Exploding Plastic Inevitable' touring show in 1966 featuring the Velvet Underground rock group. In 1968 he was shot and nearly killed by a radical feminist, Valerie Solanas.

In the 1970s and 1980s Warhol was primarily a society portraitist, although his activities included a magazine (*Interview*) and a cable TV show.

His early silk-screen series dealt with car crashes and suicides, Marilyn Monroe, Elvis Presley, and flowers. His films, beginning with *Sleep* (1963) and ending with *Bad* (1977), have a strong improvisational and often documentary element. His books include *The Philosophy of Andy Warhol (From A to B and Back Again)* (1975) and *Popism* (1980).

Related Web site: Andy Warhol Museum Home Page http://www.warhol.org/

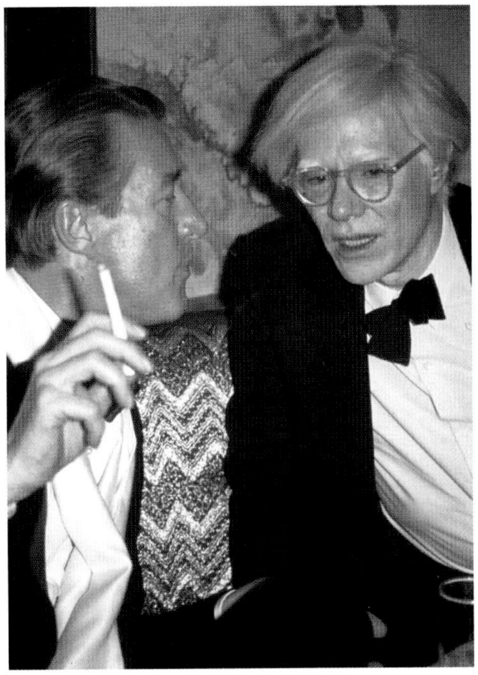

ANDY WARHOL The US pop artist Andy Warhol (right) was famous for his encouragement of younger artists.
Archive Photos

warlord in China, any of the provincial leaders who took advantage of central government weakness, after the death of the first president of republican China in 1912, to organize their own private armies and fiefdoms. They engaged in civil wars until the nationalist leader Jiang Jie Shi's (Chiang Kai-shek's) Northern Expedition against them in 1926, and they exerted power until the communists seized control under Mao Zedong in 1949.

Warner, Deborah (1959–) English theatre director. She founded the Kick Theatre company in 1980. Discarding period costume and furnished sets, she adopted an uncluttered approach to the classics, including productions of many Shakespeare plays and Sophocles' *Electra* (1989).

Warner, Rex Ernest (1905–1986) English novelist. His later novels, such as *The Young Caesar* and *Imperial Caesar* (1958–60), are based on classical themes, but he is better remembered today for his earlier works, such as *The Aerodrome* (1941), which are disturbing parables based on the political situation of the 1930s.

warning coloration in biology, an alternative term for ▷aposematic coloration.

War of 1812 war between the USA and Britain caused by British interference with US trade (shipping) as part of Britain's economic warfare against Napoleonic France. Tensions between the Americans and the British in Canada led to plans for a US invasion but these were never realized and success was limited to the capture of Detroit and a few notable naval victories. In 1814 British forces occupied Washington, DC, and burned the White House and the Capitol. A treaty signed in Ghent, Belgium, in December 1814 ended the conflict.

War Office former British government department controlling military affairs. The Board of Ordnance, which existed in the 14th century, was absorbed into the War Department after the Crimean War and the whole named the War Office. In 1964 its core became a subordinate branch of the newly established Ministry of ▷Defence.

War on Terrorism US-led international campaign against terrorist organizations, declared in response to the terrorist attacks on New York City and Washington, DC, on 11 September 2001 that killed around 3,000 people. The attacks were blamed on al-Qaeda, an international terrorist network run from Afghanistan by Saudi-born dissident Osama bin Laden. US president George W Bush rapidly assembled an international coalition to support both a crackdown on all terrorist groups and any military action against Afghanistan. After Afghanistan's ruling Taliban regime refused to hand over bin Laden to the USA, the USA led military strikes on the country on 7 October with the aim of capturing bin Laden and removing the Taliban from power. However, the war was perceived by some groups as an attack on Islam, an accusation that, although rejected by the coalition, threatened to polarize the international community.

War on Want international organization established in 1951 to support development work in the Third World and to campaign in Europe on world poverty.

War Powers Act legislation passed in 1973 restricting the US president's powers to deploy US forces abroad for combat without prior Congressional approval. The president is required to report to both Houses of Congress within 48 hours of having taken such action. Congress may then restrict the continuation of troop deployment despite any presidential veto.

Warren, Robert Penn (1905–1989) US poet and novelist. He is the only author to have received a Pulitzer prize for both prose and poetry. His work explored the moral problems of the South. His most important novel, *All the King's Men* (1946; Pulitzer prize 1947), depicts the rise and fall of a back-country demagogue modelled on the career of Huey ▷Long. He also won Pulitzer prizes for *Promises* (1968) and *Now and Then: Poems* (1976–78). He was a senior figure of the ▷New Criticism, and the first official US poet laureate 1986–88.

Warrington unitary authority in northwest England, created in 1998 from part of Cheshire.
area 176 sq km/68 sq mi **towns and cities** ▷Warrington (administrative headquarters), Lymm, Great Sankey **features** River Mersey; Manchester Ship Canal; Warrington Museum and Art Gallery includes over 1,000 paintings; Risley Moss bog and woodland with nature trails and visitors' centre **industries** chemicals, food and soft drinks processing, brewing, printing, manufacturing of clothing, leather, metal goods, timber products
population (1996) 151,000

Warrington industrial town and, from April 1998, administrative headquarters of ▷Warrington unitary authority in northwest England, on the River Mersey, 25 km/16 mi from both Liverpool and Manchester; population (1994 est) 151,000. It was part of the county of Cheshire to April 1998. Industries include the manufacture of metal goods and chemicals, brewing, iron founding, tanning, engineering, and high technology industries. A trading centre since Roman times, it was designated a ▷new town in 1968.

Warsaw (Polish **Warszawa**) capital of Poland, on the River Vistula; population (1993) 1,653,300. Industries include engineering, food processing, printing, clothing, and pharmaceuticals.
History Founded in the 13th century, it replaced Kraków as capital in 1595. Its university was founded in 1818. It was taken by the Germans after heavy fighting during World War I and following the war became capital of independent Poland. Between the mid-19th century and 1940, a third of the population were Jews. It was taken by the Germans on 27 September 1939 and its 400,000 Jews were forced to live in the city's ghetto. In 1943 there was an uprising by those who had survived; this was put down and the survivors killed. In 1944 the Polish resistance attempted to gain control of the city before the arrival of the Russian army. The Warsaw Rising, as it became known, was crushed by the Germans after nine weeks. Warsaw was finally liberated on 17 January 1945. The old city was virtually destroyed during the war but has been reconstructed.
Famous people The physicist and chemist Marie Curie was born here.

Warsaw Pact (or **Eastern European Mutual Assistance Pact**) military defensive alliance 1955–91 between the USSR and East European communist states, originally established as a response to the admission of West Germany into NATO. Its military structures and agreements were dismantled early in 1991; a political organization remained until the alliance was officially dissolved in July 1991.

warship fighting ship armed and crewed for war. The supremacy of the battleship at the beginning of the 20th century was rivalled during World War I by the development of ▷submarine attack, and was rendered obsolescent in World War II with the advent of long-range air attack. Today the largest and most important surface warships are the ▷aircraft carriers.

wart protuberance composed of a local overgrowth of skin. The common wart (*Verruca vulgaris*) is due to a virus infection.

wart hog African wild ▷pig *Phacochoerus aethiopicus*, which has a large head with a bristly mane, fleshy pads beneath the eyes, and four large tusks. It has short legs and can grow to 80 cm/2.5 ft at the shoulder.
Related Web site: Wart hog http://www.seaworld.org/animal_bytes/warthogab.html

Warton, Joseph (1722–1800) English poet and critic. His two volumes of *Odes* (1744–46) and 'Essay on the Writings and Genius of Pope' (1756–82) marked an 'anti-classical' reaction and gave an impulse to the coming Romantic movement.

Warton, Thomas Wain (1728–1790) English critic. His reputation was established with *Observations on Spenser's Faerie Queene* (1754). He was professor of poetry at Oxford 1757–67 and published the first *History of English Poetry* (1774–81). He was poet laureate from 1785.

Warwick market town, administrative headquarters of ▷Warwickshire, central England, 33 km/21 mi southeast of Birmingham, on the River Avon; population (1991) 22,300. Industries include agriculture and tourism. Founded in 914, it has many fine medieval buildings, including a 14th-century castle.

Warwick, Richard Neville, 1st or 16th Earl of Warwick (1428–1471) English politician, called **the Kingmaker**. During the Wars of the ▷Roses he fought at first on the Yorkist side against the Lancastrians, and was largely responsible for placing Edward IV on the throne. Having quarrelled with him, he restored Henry VI in 1470, but was defeated and killed by Edward at Barnet, Hertfordshire. He was made an earl in 1449.

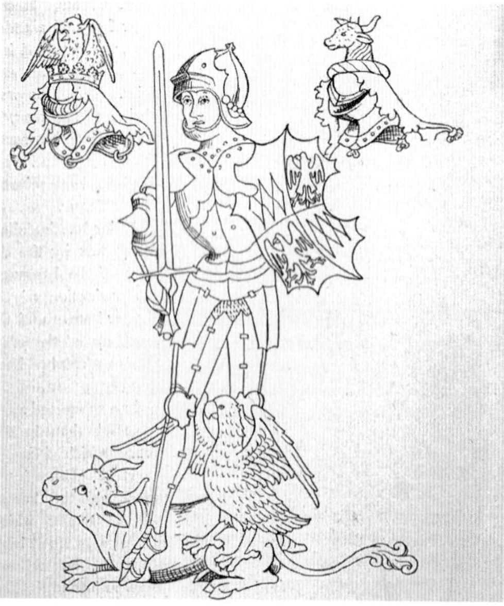

RICHARD NEVILLE Richard Neville, Earl of Warwick, known as 'the Kingmaker'. *Philip Sauvain Picture Collection*

Warwickshire county of central England.
area 1,980 sq km/764 sq mi **towns and cities** ▷Warwick (administrative headquarters), Nuneaton, Royal Leamington Spa, Rugby, Stratford-upon-Avon (the birthplace of Shakespeare) **physical** rivers Avon, Stour, and Tame; remains of the 'Forest of Arden' (portrayed by Shakespeare in *As You Like It*) **features** Kenilworth and Warwick castles; Edgehill, site of the Battle of Edgehill in 1642, during the English Civil War; annual Royal Agricultural Show held at Stoneleigh **agriculture** cereals (oats and wheat); dairy farming; fruit; market gardening **industries** cement; engineering; ironstone, and lime are worked in the east and south; motor industry; textiles; tourism **population** (1996) 500,600 **famous people** Rupert Brooke, George Eliot, William Shakespeare

Wash, the bay of the North Sea between Norfolk and Lincolnshire, eastern England; 24 km/15 mi long, 40 km/25 mi wide. The rivers Nene, Ouse, Welland, and Witham drain into the Wash. In 1992, 10,120 ha/25,000 acres of the mudflats, marshes, and sand banks on its shores were designated a national nature reserve.

washing soda $Na_2CO_3.10H_2O$ (chemical name **sodium carbonate decahydrate**) substance added to washing water to 'soften' it (see ▷hard water).

Washington town in Tyne and Wear, northeast England, 8 km/5 mi southeast of Newcastle upon Tyne, on the River Wear, designated a ▷new town in 1964; population (1991) 55,800. Industries include electronics, car assembly, and the manufacture of textiles, chemicals, and electrical goods. Beamish Open-Air Museum is nearby to the west.

Washington state in northwestern USA. It is nicknamed the Evergreen State. Washington was admitted to the Union in 1889 as the 42nd US state. It is bordered to the east by Idaho, to the south by Oregon, to the north by British Columbia, Canada, and to the west by the Pacific Ocean. Washington's Cape Alava is the westernmost point in the lower 48 US states.
population (1995) 5,430,900 (including 1.4% American Indians, mainly of the Yakima people) **area** 176,480 sq km/68,140 sq mi **capital** Olympia **towns and cities** Seattle, Spokane, Tacoma, Bellevue, Everett **industries and products** apples and other fruits, potatoes, livestock, fish and shellfish, timber, processed food, wood products, paper and allied products, aircraft and aerospace equipment, aluminium, computer software

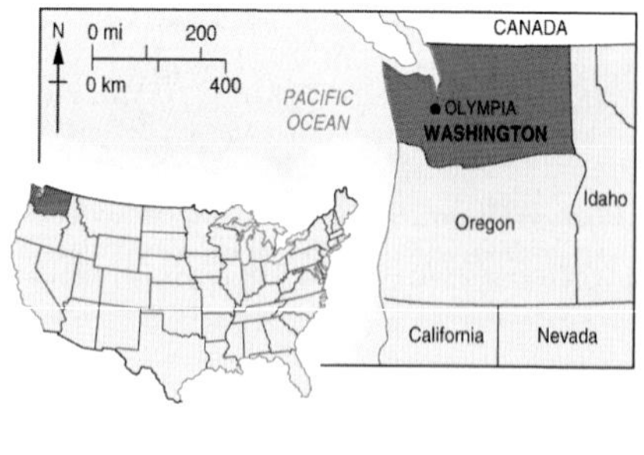

Washington, Booker T(aliaferro) (1856–1915) US educationist, pioneer in higher education for black people in the South. He was the founder and first principal of Tuskegee Institute, Alabama, in 1881, originally a training college for blacks, and now an academic institution. He maintained that economic independence was the way to achieve social equality.

Washington, George (1732–1799) commander of the American forces during the ▷American Revolution and 1st president of the USA 1789–97; known as 'the father of his country'. An experienced soldier, he had fought in campaigns against the French during the French and Indian War. He was elected to the Virginia House of Burgesses in 1759 and was a leader of the Virginia militia, gaining valuable exposure to wilderness fighting. As a strong opponent of the British government's policy, he sat in the Continental Congresses of 1774 and 1775, and on the outbreak of the ▷American Revolution was chosen commander-in-chief of the Continental army. After many setbacks, he accepted the surrender of British general Cornwallis at Yorktown in 1781.

After the war Washington retired to his Virginia estate, Mount Vernon, but in 1787 he re-entered politics as president of the Constitutional Convention in Philadelphia, and was elected US president in 1789. He attempted to draw his ministers from all factions, but his aristocratic outlook and acceptance of the fiscal policy championed by Alexander ▷Hamilton alienated his secretary of state, Thomas Jefferson, who resigned in 1793, thus creating the two-party system.

Washington was re-elected president in 1793 but refused to serve a third term, setting a precedent that stood until 1940. He died and was buried at Mount Vernon.
Related Web site: George Washington – First President 1789–1797 http://www.whitehouse.gov/WH/glimpse/presidents/html/gw1.html

Washington, DC (in full Washington, District of Columbia) capital of the ▷USA, on the Potomac River; the world's first planned national capital. It was named Washington, DC, to distinguish it from Washington state, and because it is coextensive with the ▷District of Columbia, hence DC; population (2000 est) 572,100; metropolitan area extending outside the District of Columbia (2000) 7,608,100. The District of Columbia, the federal district of the USA, is an area of 174 sq km/67 sq mi. Its site was chosen by President George Washington, and the first structures date from 1793. Washington, DC, operates the national executive, legislative, and judicial government of the USA, and is a centre for international diplomacy and finance. Federal and district government are key employers, though numbers employed in both are decreasing. Public, trade, business, and social organizations maintain a presence, as well as law and other service agencies. Tourism is a major industry.

Land for the federal district was ceded by Maryland and Virginia 1788–89. The city was designed and partly laid out by French architect Pierre L'Enfant, whose work was completed by Andrew Ellicott and Benjamin Banneker. Congress first convened in the Capitol on 1 December 1800. National monuments and buildings include the Capitol (1819–60), the Library of Congress (1886–97), the ▷Pentagon (1941–43), the ▷White House, the Supreme Court (1935), the Jefferson Memorial (1943), the Lincoln Memorial (1927), the J Edgar Hoover Federal Bureau of Investigation Building (1974), the Washington Monument (1884), the Smithsonian Institution (1849), the Vietnam Veterans Memorial (1982), and the Korean War Veterans Memorial (1995). Seven universities and numerous cultural centres are located in the city, including the National Gallery of Art, the National Air and Space Museum, and the United States Holocaust Memorial Museum (1993).

Related Web site: Washington, DC http://www.washington.org/

George Washington
I can't tell a lie, Pa; you know I can't tell a lie. I did cut it with my hatchet.

Of a prized cherry tree, attributed remark by the young George Washington in M L Weems *Life of George Washington* 10th ed ch. 2

WASP (acronym for white Anglo-Saxon Protestant) common (frequently derogatory) term to describe the white elite in US society, specifically those educated at Ivy League universities and belonging to the Episcopalian Church.

wasp any of several families of winged stinging insects of the order Hymenoptera, characterized by a thin stalk between the thorax and the abdomen. Wasps can be social or solitary. Among social wasps, the queens devote themselves to egg laying, the fertilized eggs producing female workers; the males come from unfertilized eggs and have no sting. The larvae are fed on insects, but the mature wasps feed mainly on fruit and sugar. In winter, the fertilized queens hibernate, but the other wasps die.

Of the 290 British species, only a few are true wasps, Vespidae; the rest are digger wasps. There are seven British species of social wasp in the genus *Vespa*, some nesting below ground, others in trees or bushes, the largest being the hornet; all the others are solitary.

WASP North American male cicada killer wasp sitting at a favourite vantage point in his territory awaiting passing females. The cicada killer wasp is a large solitary wasp that preys on cicadas. *Jean Preston-Mafham/Premaphotos Wildlife*

waste materials that are no longer needed and are discarded. Examples are household waste, industrial waste (which often contains toxic chemicals), medical waste (which may contain organisms that cause disease), and ▷nuclear waste (which is radioactive). By ▷recycling, some materials in waste can be reclaimed for further use. In 1990 the industrialized nations generated 2 billion tonnes of waste. In the USA, 40 tonnes of solid waste are generated annually per person, roughly twice as much as in Europe or Japan.

waste disposal depositing of waste. Methods of waste disposal vary according to the materials in the waste and include incineration, burial at designated sites, and dumping at sea. Organic waste can be treated and reused as fertilizer (see ▷sewage disposal). ▷Nuclear waste and ▷toxic waste are usually buried or dumped at sea, although this does not negate the danger.

watch portable timepiece. In the early 20th century increasing miniaturization, mass production, and convenience led to the watch moving from the pocket to the wrist. Watches were also subsequently made waterproof, antimagnetic, self-winding, and shock-resistant. In 1957 the electric watch was developed, and in the 1970s came the digital watch, which dispensed with all moving parts.

water is a chemical compound of hydrogen and oxygen elements, H_2O. It can exist as a solid (ice), liquid (water), or gas (water vapour). Water is the most common element on Earth and vital to all living organisms. It covers 70% of the Earth's surface, and provides a habitat for large numbers of aquatic organisms. It is the largest constituent of all living organisms – the human body consists of about 65% water. Pure water is a colourless, odourless, tasteless liquid which freezes at 0°C/32°F, and boils at 100°C/212°F. Natural water in the environment is never pure and always contains a variety of dissolved substances. Some 97% of the Earth's water is in the oceans; a further 2% is in the form of snow or ice, leaving only 1% available as fresh water for plants and animals. The recycling and circulation of water through the ▷biosphere is termed the **water cycle**, or 'hydrological cycle'; regulation of the water balance in organisms is termed ▷osmoregulation.

The water cycle Water occurs on the Earth's surface as standing water in oceans and lakes, as running water in rivers and streams, as rain, and as water vapour in the atmosphere. Together these sources comprise the ▷hydrosphere which is in a constant state of flux as water vapour condenses to fall as rain, and after flowing through rivers and streams into lakes and oceans is returned to the atmosphere by evaporation. And so the cycle continues. Since the hydrological cycle is a closed system, the amount of water in the Earth's hydrosphere is constant. The cycle is powered by solar radiation which provides the energy to maintain the flow through the processes of evaporation, transpiration, precipitation, and runoff.

Osmoregulation Water is very important to living organisms: it helps cells to maintain their form; as a solvent, it dissolves salts, sugars, proteins, and many other substances that are involved in metabolism and the digestion of food; it enables the transportation of bodily wastes, and the maintenance of a stable body temperature through perspiration and evaporation. But too much water can be dangerous. The process that maintains an equable balance of water content in an organism is osmoregulation. Organisms gain water in a number of ways – by ▷osmosis, in food, and by respiration. They lose water by evaporation, in urine, and by osmosis. In humans, the kidneys play a very important role in the regulation of water balance.

Water makes up 60–70% of the human body or about 40 l/70 pt of which 25 l/53 pt are inside the cells, 15 l/26 pt outside (12 l/21 pt in tissue fluid, and 3 l/5 pt in blood plasma). A loss of 4 l/7 pt may cause hallucinations; a loss of 8–10 l/14–18 pt may cause death. About 1.5 l/2.6 pt a day are lost through breathing, perspiration, and faeces, and the additional amount lost in urine is the amount needed to keep the balance between input and output. In temperate climates, people cannot survive more than five or six days without water, or two or three days in a hot environment.

A family of two adults and two children uses approximately 200 l/350 pt per day (UK figures). The British water industry was privatized in 1989, and in 1991 the UK was taken to court for failing to meet EC drinking-water standards on nitrate and pesticide levels.

Related Web sites: Clean Water – Life Depends on It http://www.ec.gc.ca/water/en/info/pubs/FS/e_FSA3.htm
Physical Properties Of Water And Ice http://www.nyu.edu/pages/mathmol/modules/water/water_student.html
Water http://www.bris.ac.uk/Depts/Chemistry/MOTM/water/water.htm

WATCH A close-up of the mechanism in an antique pocket watch. *Image Bank*

water beetle aquatic beetle with an oval, flattened, streamlined shape. The head is sunk into the thorax and the hindlegs are flattened into flippers for swimming; there is a wide variation in size within the species; they are usually dark or black in colour and the entire body has a resplendent sheen. Both the adults and larvae are entirely aquatic, and are common in still, fresh waters such as ponds and lakes. Water beetles are in family Dytiscidae, order Coleoptera, class Insecta, phylum Arthropoda.

water boatman any water ▷bug of the family Corixidae that feeds on plant debris and algae. It has a flattened body 1.5 cm/0.6 in long, with oarlike legs.

WATER BOATMAN The common backswimmer *Notonecta glauca* in a garden pond. As well as being fully aquatic, backswimmers are strong fliers and quick to colonize new ponds. *Ken Preston-Mafham/Premaphotos Wildlife*

water-borne disease disease associated with poor water supply. In the Third World four-fifths of all illness is caused by water-borne diseases, with diarrhoea being the leading cause of childhood death. Malaria, carried by mosquitoes dependent on stagnant water for breeding, affects 400 million people every year and kills 5 million. Polluted water is also a problem in industrialized nations, where industrial dumping of chemical, hazardous, and radioactive wastes causes a range of diseases from headache to cancer.

waterbuck any of several African ▷antelopes of the genus *Kobus* which usually inhabit swampy tracts and reedbeds. They vary in size from about 1.8m/6 ft to 2.1 m/7.25 ft long, are up to 1.4 m/4.5 ft tall at the shoulder, and have long brown fur. The large curved horns, normally carried only by the males, have corrugated surfaces. Some species have white patches on the buttocks. Lechwe, kor, and defassa are alternative names for some of the species.

water bug any of a number of aquatic ▷bugs where all stages of the life cycle (adult, larval, and egg) occur in the water; the eggs are usually attached to the stems or leaves of water plants. In contrast to the land bugs, which have quite distinctly noticeable antennae, the antennae of water bugs are hidden. In general, water bugs are also less brightly coloured; they are usually varying shades of black and brown, and tend to inhabit the bottom strata of ponds, lakes, and streams. They may or may not have wings. Water bugs belong to the suborder Heteroptera, order Hemiptera, class Insecta, phylum Arthropoda.

water closet (WC) alternative name for ▷toilet.

watercolour painting method of painting with pigments mixed with water, known in China as early as the 3rd century. The art as practised today began in England in the 18th century with the work of Paul Sandby and was developed by Thomas Girtin, John Sell Cotman, and J M W Turner. Other outstanding watercolourists

WATERCOLOUR PAINTING An early watercolour of 1803, entitled *Ruins of Rievaulx Abbey*, by English landscape painter John Cotman, is an example of the use of watercolour to create Romantic, atmospheric paintings. *The Art Archive/Cornelius de Vries*

were Raoul Dufy, Paul Cézanne, and John Marin. The technique of watercolour painting requires great skill since its transparency rules out overpainting.

watercress perennial aquatic plant found in Europe and Asia and cultivated for its pungent leaves which are used in salads. (Genus *Nasturtium officinale*, family Cruciferae.)

> **Related Web site: Watercress** http://www.botanical.com/botanical/mgmh/w/watcre09.html

water cycle (or **hydrological cycle**) the natural circulation of water through the upperpart of the Earth. It is a complex system involving a number of physical and chemical processes (such as ▷evaporation, ▷precipitation, and infiltration) and stores (such as rivers, oceans, and soil).

waterfall cascade of water in a river or stream. It occurs when a river flows over a bed of rock that resists erosion; weaker rocks downstream are worn away, creating a steep, vertical drop and a plunge pool into which the water falls. Over time, continuing erosion causes the waterfall to retreat upstream forming a deep valley, or ▷gorge.

water flea any aquatic crustacean in the order Cladocera, of which there are over 400 species. The commonest species is *Daphnia pulex*, used in the pet trade to feed tropical fish.

Highest Waterfalls in the World

Waterfall	Location	Total drop	
		m	ft
Angel Falls	Venezuela	979	3,212
Yosemite Falls	USA	739	2,425
Mardalsfossen–South	Norway	655	2,149
Tugela Falls	South Africa	614	2,014
Cuquenan	Venezuela	610	2,000
Sutherland	New Zealand	580	1,903
Ribbon Fall, Yosemite	USA	491	1,612
Great Karamang River Falls	Guyana	488	1,600
Mardalsfossen–North	Norway	468	1,535
Della Falls	Canada	440	1,443
Gavarnie Falls	France	422	1,385
Skjeggedal	Norway	420	1,378
Glass Falls	Brazil	404	1,325
Krimml	Austria	400	1,312
Trummelbach Falls	Switzerland	400	1,312
Takkakaw Falls	Canada	366	1,200
Silver Strand Falls, Yosemite	USA	357	1,170
Wallaman Falls	Australia	346	1,137
Wollomombi	Australia	335	1,100
Cusiana River Falls	Colombia	300	984
Giessbach	Switzerland	300	984
Skykkjedalsfossen	Norway	300	984
Staubbach	Switzerland	300	984

Waterford county of the Republic of Ireland, in the province of Munster; county town Waterford; area 1,840 sq km/710 sq mi; population (1996) 94,700. Other towns include Dungarvon, Lismore, and Tramore. The chief rivers are the Suir and the Blackwater; the Comeragh and Monavallagh mountain ranges lie in the north and centre of the county. Agriculture and dairy farming are important; wheat, barley, and vegetables are also grown. Industries include glassware, pharmaceuticals, and electronics, and there are tanneries, bacon factories, and flour mills.

waterfowl any water bird, but especially any member of the family Anatidae, which consists of ducks, geese, and swans.

water gas fuel gas consisting of a mixture of carbon monoxide and hydrogen, made by passing steam over red-hot coke. The gas was once the chief source of hydrogen for chemical syntheses such as the Haber process for making ammonia, but has been largely superseded in this and other reactions by hydrogen obtained from natural gas.

Watergate US political scandal, named after the building in Washington, DC, which housed the headquarters of the Democratic National Committee in the 1972 presidential election. Five men, hired by the Republican Committee for the Re-election of the President (popularly known as CREEP), were caught after breaking into the Watergate with complex electronic surveillance equipment. Investigations revealed that the White House was implicated in the break-in, and that there was a 'slush fund' used to finance unethical activities, including using the CIA and the Internal Revenue Service (IRS) for political ends, setting up paramilitary operations against opponents, altering and destroying evidence, and bribing defendants to lie or remain silent. In August 1974, President ▷Nixon was forced by the Supreme Court to surrender to Congress tape recordings of conversations he had held with administration officials, which indicated his complicity in a cover-up. Nixon resigned rather than face impeachment for obstruction of justice and other crimes. See also ▷United States of America, Watergate scandal.

> **Related Web site: Watergate** http://vcepolitics.com/watergate/

water glass common name for sodium metasilicate (Na_2SiO_3). It is a colourless, jellylike substance that dissolves readily in water to give a solution used for preserving eggs and fireproofing porous materials such as cloth, paper, and wood. It is also used as an adhesive for paper and cardboard and in the manufacture of soap and silica gel, a substance that absorbs moisture.

water hyacinth tropical aquatic plant belonging to the pickerelweed family. In one growing season 25 plants can produce 2 million new plants. It is liable to choke waterways, removing nutrients from the water and blocking out the sunlight, but it can be used to purify sewage-polluted water as well as in making methane gas, compost, concentrated protein, paper, and baskets. Originating in South America, it now grows in more than 50 countries. (Genus *Eichhornia crassipes*, family Pontederiaceae.)

water lily any of a group of aquatic plants belonging to the water lily family. The fleshy roots are embedded in mud and the large round leaves float on the surface of the water. The cup-shaped flowers may be white, pink, yellow, or blue. (Genera *Nymphaea* and *Nuphar*, family Nymphaeaceae.)

WATER LILY Blue- or mauve-flowered water lilies, such as this *Nymphaea stellata* from Madagascar, are common in lakes and swamps in the Old World tropics. *Premaphotos Wildlife*

Waterloo, Battle of final battle of the Napoleonic Wars on 18 June 1815 in which a coalition force of British, Prussian, and Dutch troops under the Duke of Wellington defeated Napoleon near the village of Waterloo, 13 km/8 mi south of Brussels, Belgium. Napoleon found Wellington's army isolated from his allies and began a direct offensive to smash them, but the British held on until joined by the Prussians under Marshal Gebhard von Blücher. Four days later Napoleon abdicated for the second and final time.

Wellington had 67,000 soldiers (of whom 24,000 were British, the remainder being German, Dutch, and Belgian) and Napoleon had 74,000. The French casualties numbered about 37,000; coalition casualties were similar including some 13,000 British troops.

water measurer slender long-legged wingless bug found on the water surface or on vegetation skirting the water. They are carnivorous, feeding on animals such as water fleas. They walk slowly and gracefully on the water surface using their long legs, their bodies held above the surface film. The water measurers belong to family Hydrometridae, order Hemiptera, class Insecta, phylum Arthropoda.

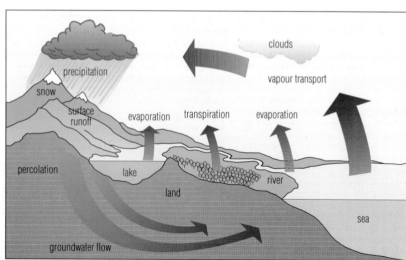

WATER CYCLE About one-third of the solar energy reaching the Earth is used in evaporating water. About 380,000 cubic km/95,000 cubic mi is evaporated each year. The entire contents of the oceans would take about one million years to pass through the water cycle.

watermelon large ▷melon belonging to the gourd family, native to tropical Africa, with a dark green rind and reddish juicy flesh studded with a large number of black seeds. It is widely cultivated in subtropical regions. (Genus *Citrullus vulgaris*, family Cucurbitaceae.)

water mill machine that harnesses the energy in flowing water to produce mechanical power, typically for milling (grinding) grain. Water from a stream is directed against the paddles of a water wheel to make it turn. Simple gearing transfers this motion to the millstones. The modern equivalent of the water wheel is the water turbine, used in ▷hydroelectric power plants.

water of crystallization water chemically bonded to a salt in its crystalline state. For example, in copper(II) sulphate, there are five moles of water per mole of copper sulphate: hence its formula is $CuSO_4.5H_2O$. This water is responsible for the colour and shape of the crystalline form. When the crystals are heated gently, the water is driven off as steam and a white powder is formed.

$$CuSO_4.5H_2O_{(s)} \rightarrow CuSO_{4(s)} + 5H_2O_{(g)}$$

water pollution any addition to fresh or sea water that disrupts biological processes or causes a health hazard. Common pollutants include nitrates, pesticides, and sewage (see ▷sewage disposal), although a huge range of industrial contaminants, such as chemical byproducts and residues created in the manufacture of various goods, also enter water – legally, accidentally, and through illegal dumping.

Related Web site: Surfers Against Sewage http://www.sas.org.uk/

WATER POLLUTION Rubbish of all kinds floating in a UK harbour. *Image Bank*

water polo water sport developed in England in 1869, originally called 'soccer-in-water'. The aim is to score goals, as in soccer, at each end of a swimming pool. It is played by teams of seven on each side (from squads of 13).

water scorpion water bug in which the first pair of legs are modified into prehensile organs for grasping prey. They are carnivorous and feed on smaller insects. The prey is held securely between their first pair of legs while the water scorpion sucks up its body fluids. Water scorpion are in family Nepidae, order Hemiptera, class Insecta, phylum Arthropoda.

water skiing water sport in which a person is towed across water on a ski or skis (wider than those used for skiing on snow), or barefoot, by means of a rope attached to a speedboat. Competitions are held for overall performances, slalom, tricks, jumping, and racing.

water softener any substance or unit that removes the hardness from water. Hardness is caused by the presence of calcium and magnesium ions, which combine with soap to form an insoluble scum, prevent lathering, and cause deposits to build up in pipes and cookware (kettle fur). A water softener replaces these ions with sodium ions, which are fully soluble and cause no scum.

waterspout funnel-shaped column of water and cloud that is drawn from the surface of the sea or a lake by a ▷tornado.

WATER SUPPLY A water recycling plant. Waste water can now be recycled, which has the effect of both reducing the demand on fresh water supplies, and decreasing river pollution by limiting the amount of effluent discharged. *Image Bank*

water supply distribution of water for domestic, municipal, or industrial consumption. Water supply in sparsely populated regions usually comes from underground water rising to the surface in natural springs, supplemented by pumps and wells. Urban sources are deep artesian wells, rivers, and reservoirs, usually formed from enlarged lakes or dammed and flooded valleys, from which water is conveyed by pipes, conduits, and aqueducts to filter beds. As water seeps through layers of shingle, gravel, and sand, harmful organisms are removed and the water is then distributed by pumping or gravitation through mains and pipes.

Water treatment Often other substances are added to the water, such as chlorine and fluoride; aluminium sulphate, a clarifying agent, is the most widely used chemical in water treatment. In towns, domestic and municipal (road washing, sewage) needs account for about 135 l/30 gal per head each day. In coastal desert areas, such as the Arabian peninsula, desalination plants remove salt from sea water. The Earth's waters, both fresh and saline, have been polluted by industrial and domestic chemicals, some of which are toxic and others radioactive (see ▷water pollution).

water table the upper level of ground water (water collected underground in porous rocks). Water that is above the water table will drain downwards; a spring forms where the water table cuts the surface of the ground. The water table rises and falls in response to rainfall and the rate at which water is extracted, for example, for irrigation and industry.

In many irrigated areas the water table is falling due to the extraction of water. Below northern China, for example, the water table is sinking at a rate of 1 m/3 ft a year. Regions with high water tables and dense industrialization have problems with ▷pollution of the water table. In the USA, New Jersey, Florida, and Louisiana have water tables contaminated by both industrial ▷wastes and saline seepage from the ocean.

Watson, James Dewey (1928–) US biologist who was awarded a Nobel Prize for Physiology or Medicine in 1962 for the discovery of the double-helical structure of DNA and determining the significance of this structure in the replication and transfer of genetic information. He shared the prize with hi co-worker Francis ▷Crick.

Crick and Watson published their work on the proposed structure of DNA in 1953, and explained how genetic information could be coded.

Related Web site: Dr James D Watson Profile http://www.achievement.org/autodoc/page/wat0pro-1

Watson, John Broadus (1878–1958) US psychologist, founder of behaviourism. He rejected introspection (observation by an individual of his or her own mental processes) and regarded psychology as the study of observable behaviour, within the scientific tradition.

watt SI unit (symbol W) of power (the rate of expenditure or consumption of energy) defined as one joule per second. A light bulb, for example, may use 40, 60, 100, or 150 watts of power; an electric heater will use several kilowatts (thousands of watts). The watt is named after the Scottish engineer James Watt.

Watt, James (1736–1819) Scottish engineer who developed the steam engine in the 1760s, making Thomas ▷Newcomen's engine vastly more efficient by cooling the used steam in a condenser separate from the main cylinder. He eventually made a double-acting machine that supplied power with both directions of the piston and developed rotary motion. He also invented devices associated with the steam engine, artistic instruments and a copying process, and devised the horsepower as a description of an engine's rate of working. The modern unit of power, the watt, is named after him.

At Glasgow University, Watt was asked to repair a small working model of Newcomen's steam engine, which was temperamental and difficult to operate without air entering the cylinder and destroying the vacuum. It was also extremely costly to run in terms of the coal required to keep a sufficient head of steam in a practical engine. In Newcomen's engine, the steam in the cylinder was condensed by a jet of water, creating a vacuum. The vacuum, in turn, was filled during the power stroke by the atmosphere pressing the piston to the bottom of the cylinder. On each stroke the cylinder was heated by the steam and cooled by the injected water, thus absorbing a tremendous amount of heat. Watt investigated the properties of steam and made measurements of boilers and pistons. He had the idea of a separate condenser (separate from the piston) that would allow the cylinder to be kept hot, and the condenser fairly cold by lagging, thus improving the thermal efficiency.

Working with manufacturer Matthew Boulton in 1782, Watt improved his machine by making it double-acting. Using a mechanical linkage known as 'parallel motion' and an extra set of valves, the engine was made to drive on both the forward and backward strokes of the piston, and a 'sun-and-planet' gear (also devised by Watt in 1781) allowed rotatory motion to be produced, which allowed the steam engine to be used to power the machines in the new factories of the Industrial Revolution. This new and highly adaptable engine was quickly adopted by cotton and woollen mills.

During the period 1775–90, Watt invented an automatic centrifugal governor, which cut off the steam when the engine began to work too quickly and turned it on again when it had slowed sufficiently. He also devised a steam engine indicator that showed steam pressure and the degree of vacuum within the cylinder. Because of the secretarial duties connected with his business, Watt invented a way of copying letters and drawings with a chemical process that was displaced only with the advent of the typewriter and photocopier.

Watt devised a rational method to rate the capability of his engines by considering the rate at which horses worked. After many experiments, he concluded that a 'horsepower' was 33,000 lb/15,000 kg raised through 1 ft/0.3 m each minute. The English-speaking world used horsepower to describe the capability of an engine until recent years.

Watteau, (Jean-)Antoine (1684–1721) French rococo painter. He developed a new category of genre painting known as the *fête galante* – fanciful scenes depicting elegantly dressed young people engaged in outdoor entertainment. One of the best-known examples is *The Embarkation for Cythera* (1717; Louvre, Paris).

wattle any of certain species of ▷acacia in Australia, where their fluffy golden flowers are the national emblem. The leathery leaves are adapted to drought conditions and avoid loss of water through ▷transpiration by turning their edges to the direct rays of the sun. Wattles are used for tanning leather and in fencing.

wattle and daub method of constructing walls consisting of upright stakes bound together with withes (strong flexible shoots or twigs, usually of willow), and covered in mud or plaster. This was the usual way of building houses in medieval Europe; it was also the traditional method used in Australia, Africa, the Middle East, and the Far East.

Watts, George Frederick (1817–1904) English painter and sculptor. Influenced by the Venetian masters, he painted biblical and classical subjects, but his fame was based largely on his moralizing allegories, such as *Hope* (1886; Tate Gallery, London). He was also a portrait painter, his works including *Gladstone* and

Tennyson (National Portrait Gallery, London). As a sculptor he executed *Physical Energy* (1904) for Cecil Rhodes's memorial in Cape Town, South Africa; a replica is in Kensington Gardens, London. He was a forerunner of Symbolism.

Watts-Dunton, Walter Theodore (1832–1914) English writer. He was the author of *Aylwin* (1898), a novel of Romany life; poems, including *The Coming of Love* (1898); and critical work, including *The Renascence of Wonder* (1901–03) and *Studies of Shakespeare* (1910).

Waugh, Evelyn (Arthur St John) (1903–1966) English novelist. His humorous social satires include *Decline and Fall* (1928), *Vile Bodies* (1930), *Scoop* (1938), and *The Loved One* (1948). He developed a serious concern with religious issues in *Brideshead Revisited* (1945) (successfully dramatized for television in the 1980s). *The Ordeal of Gilbert Pinfold* (1957) is largely autobiographical.

After World War II his writing took a more intentionally serious turn, and he produced the trilogy *Men at Arms* (1952), *Officers and Gentlemen* (1955), and *Unconditional Surrender* (1961), in which he attempted to analyse the war as a struggle between good and evil.

wave in the oceans, a ridge or swell formed by wind or other causes. The power of a wave is determined by the strength of the wind and the distance of open water over which the wind blows (the fetch). Waves are the main agents of ▷coastal erosion and deposition: sweeping away or building up beaches, creating ▷spits and berms, and wearing down cliffs by their hydraulic action and by the corrosion of the sand and shingle that they carry. A ▷tsunami (misleadingly called a 'tidal wave') is formed after a submarine earthquake.

As a wave approaches the shore it is forced to break as a result of friction with the sea bed. When it breaks on a beach, water and sediment are carried up the beach as **swash**; the water then drains back as **backwash**.

A **constructive wave** causes a net deposition of material on the shore because its swash is stronger than its backwash. Such waves tend be low and have crests that spill over gradually as they break. The backwash of a **destructive wave** is stronger than its swash, and therefore causes a net removal of material from the shore. Destructive waves are usually tall and have peaked crests that plunge downwards as they break, trapping air as they do so.

If waves strike a beach at an angle the beach material will be gradually moved along the shore (▷longshore drift), causing a deposition of material in some areas and erosion in others.

Atmospheric instability caused by the ▷greenhouse effect and global warming appears to be increasing the severity of Atlantic storms and the heights of the ocean waves. Waves in the South Atlantic are shrinking – they are on average half a metre smaller than in the mid-1980s – and those in the Northeast Atlantic have doubled in size over the last 40 years. As the height of waves affects the supply of marine food, this could affect fish stocks, and there are also implications for shipping and oil and gas rigs in the North Atlantic, which will need to be strengthened if they are to avoid damage.

Freak or 'episodic' waves form under particular weather conditions at certain times of the year, travelling long distances in the Atlantic, Indian, and Pacific oceans. They are considered responsible for the sudden disappearance, without distress calls, of many ships.

Freak waves become extremely dangerous when they reach the shallow waters of the continental shelves at 100 fathoms (180 m/ 600 ft), especially when they meet currents: for example, the Agulhas Current to the east of South Africa, and the Gulf Stream in the North Atlantic. A wave height of 34 m/112 ft has been recorded.

wave in physics, waves are oscillations that are propagated from a source. Mechanical waves require a medium through which to travel. Electromagnetic waves do not; they can travel through a vacuum. Waves carry energy but they do not transfer matter. There are two types: in a longitudinal wave, such as a sound wave, the disturbance is parallel to the wave's direction of travel; in a ▷transverse wave, such as an electromagnetic wave, it is perpendicular. The medium (for

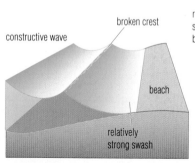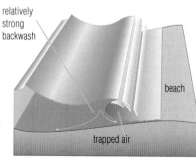

WAVE The low gentle crests of a constructive wave, with the energy of the wave flowing up the beach in a strong swash and depositing material, contrasts with the high steep crested more forceful motions of destructive waves which crash in at an angle to the beach directing all their energy into plunging waves which tear up the sand and shingle and carry it out with the strong backwash.

example the Earth, for seismic waves) is not permanently displaced by the passage of a wave. See also ▷standing wave.

Types of wave There are various ways of classifying wave types. One of these is based on the way the wave travels. In a transverse wave, the displacement of the medium is perpendicular to the direction in which the wave travels. An example of this type of wave is a mechanical wave projected along a tight string. The string moves at right angles to the wave motion. ▷Electromagnetic waves are another example of transverse waves. The directions of the electric and magnetic fields are perpendicular to the wave motion. In longitudinal waves the disturbance takes place parallel to the wave motion. A longitudinal wave consists of a series of compressions and rarefactions (states of maximum and minimum density and pressure, respectively). Such waves are always mechanical in nature and thus require a medium through which to travel. Sound waves are an example of longitudinal waves. Waves that result from a stone being dropped into water appear as a series of circles. These are called circular waves and can be generated in a ▷ripple tank for study. Waves on water that appear as a series of parallel lines are called plane waves.

Characteristics of waves All waves have a ▷wavelength. This is measured as the distance between successive crests (or successive troughs) of the wave. It is given the Greek symbol λ. The ▷frequency of a wave is the number of vibrations per second. The reciprocal of this is the wave period. This is the time taken for one complete cycle of the wave oscillation. The speed of the wave is measured by multiplying wave frequency by the wavelength.

Properties of waves When a wave moves from one medium to another (for example a light wave moving from air to glass) it moves with a different speed in the second medium. This change in speed causes it to change direction. This property is called ▷refraction. The angle of refraction depends on whether the wave is speeding up or slowing down as it changes medium. ▷Reflection occurs whenever a wave hits a barrier. The wave is sent back, or reflected, into the medium at a different angle. The angle of incidence (the angle between the ray and a perpendicular line drawn to the surface) is equal to the angle of reflection (the angle between the reflected ray and a perpendicular to the surface). See also ▷total internal reflection. An echo is the repetition of a sound wave by reflection from a surface. All waves spread slightly as they travel. This is called ▷diffraction and it occurs chiefly when a wave interacts with a solid object. The degree of diffraction depends on the relationship between the wavelength and the size of the object (or gap through which the wave travels). If the two are similar in size, diffraction occurs and the wave can be seen to spread out. Large objects cast ▷shadows because the difference between their size and the wavelength is so large that light waves are not diffracted round the object. A dark shadow results. When two or more waves meet at a point, they interact and combine to produce a resultant wave of larger or smaller amplitude (depending on whether the combining waves are in or out of phase with each other). This is called ▷interference. Transverse waves can exhibit polarization. If the oscillations of the wave take place in many different directions (all at right angles to the directions of the wave) the wave is unpolarized. If the oscillations occur in one plane only, the wave is polarized. Light, which consists of transverse waves, can be polarized.

Related Web site: Introduction to Waves http://id.mind.net/~zona/ mstm/physics/waves/waves.html/

wave-cut platform gently sloping rock surface found at the foot of a coastal cliff. Covered by water at high tide but exposed at low tide, it represents the last remnant of an eroded headland (see ▷coastal erosion).

waveguide hollow metallic tube, either empty or containing a dielectric used to guide a high-frequency electromagnetic wave (microwave) travelling within it. The wave is reflected from the internal surfaces of the guide. Waveguides are extensively used in radar systems.

wavelength the distance between successive crests of a ▷wave. The wavelength of a light wave determines its colour; red light has a wavelength of about 700 nanometres, for example. The complete range of wavelengths of electromagnetic waves is called the electromagnetic ▷spectrum.

Wavell, Archibald Percival, 1st Earl Wavell (1883–1950) British field marshal in World War II. As commander-in-chief in the Middle East, he successfully defended Egypt against Italy in July 1939 and successfully conducted the North African war against Italy 1940–41. He was transferred as commander-in-chief in India in July 1941, and became Allied Supreme Commander after Japan entered the war. He was unable to prevent Japanese advances in Malaya and Burma and Churchill became disillusioned with him. He was made viceroy of India 1943–47. He was honoured as a KCB in 1939, created Viscount in 1943, and Earl in 1947.

wave power power obtained by harnessing the energy of water waves. Various schemes have been advanced since 1973 when oil prices rose dramatically and an energy shortage threatened. In 1974 the British engineer Stephen Salter developed the duck – a floating boom, the segments of which nod up and down with the waves. The nodding motion can be used to drive pumps and spin generators. Another device, developed in Japan, uses an oscillating water column to harness wave power. A major breakthrough will be required if wave power is ever to contribute significantly to the world's energy needs, although several ideas have reached prototype stage.

Waverley, John Anderson, 1st Viscount Waverley (1882–1958) British administrator, born in Scotland. He organized civil defence for World War II, becoming home secretary and minister for home security in 1939. Anderson shelters, home outdoor air-raid shelters, were named after him. He was Chancellor of the Exchequer 1943–45. He was made a KCB in 1919, and Viscount in 1952.

wax solid fatty substance of animal, vegetable, or mineral origin.

Waxes are composed variously of ▷esters, ▷fatty acids, free ▷alcohols, and solid hydrocarbons.

Mineral waxes are obtained from petroleum and vary in hardness from the soft petroleum jelly (or petrolatum) used in ointments to the hard paraffin wax employed for making candles and waxed paper for drinks cartons.

Animal waxes include beeswax, the wool wax lanolin, and spermaceti from sperm-whale oil; they are used mainly in cosmetics, ointments, and polishes. Another animal wax is tallow, a form of suet obtained from cattle and sheep's fat, once widely used to make candles and soap. Sealing wax is made from lac or shellac, a resinous substance obtained from secretions of ▷scale insects.

Vegetable waxes, which usually occur as a waterproof coating on plants that grow in hot, arid regions, include carnauba wax (from the leaves of the carnauba palm) and candelilla wax, both of which are components of hard polishes such as car waxes.

waxbill any of a group of small, mainly African, seed-eating birds in the family Estrildidae, order Passeriformes, which also includes the grass finches of Australia. Waxbills grow to 15 cm/6 in long, are brown and grey with yellow, red, or brown markings, and have waxy-looking red or pink beaks.

They sometimes raise the young of ▷whydahs, who lay their eggs in waxbill nests.

waxwing any of several fruit-eating birds of the family Bombycillidae, order Passeriformes. They are found in the northern hemisphere. The Bohemian waxwing *Bombycilla garrulus* of North America and Eurasia is about 18 cm/7 in long, and is greyish-brown above with a reddish-chestnut crest, black streak at the eye, and variegated wings. It undertakes mass migrations in some years.

wayfaring tree European shrub belonging to the honeysuckle family, with clusters of fragrant white flowers, found on limy soils; it is naturalized in the northeastern USA. (Genus *Viburnum lantana*, family Caprifoliaceae.)

Wayne, Anthony (1745–1796) Called 'Mad Anthony'. American Revolutionary War officer and Indian fighter. He secured a treaty in 1795 that made possible the settlement of Ohio and Indiana. He built Fort Wayne, Indiana, USA.

Wayne, John (1907–1979) Called 'Duke'; stage name of Marion Michael Morrison. US actor. He played the archetypal Western hero: plain-speaking, brave, and solitary. His films include *Stagecoach* (1939), *Red River* (1948), *She Wore a Yellow Ribbon* (1949), *The Searchers* (1956), *Rio Bravo* (1959), *The Man Who Shot Liberty Valance* (1962), and *True Grit* (1969; Academy Award).

WAYFARING TREE The dainty wayfaring tree rarely reaches more than 4 m/13 ft in height. Found in many parts of Europe, in the British Isles it is a characteristic feature of downlands and bushy places on chalk and limestone in central and southern England. The fruit is a berry that first turns red and then black. *Premaphotos Wildlife*

Wayne also appeared in many war films, such as *The Sands of Iwo Jima* (1945), *In Harm's Way* (1965), and *The Green Berets* (1968). His other films include *The Quiet Man* (1952), *The High and the Mighty* (1954), and *The Shootist* (1976), his last. He was active in conservative politics.

Wazyk, Adam (1905–1982) Polish writer who made his name with *Poem for Adults* (1955), a protest against the regime that preceded the fall of the Stalinists in 1956. In 1957 he resigned with others from the Communist Party, disappointed by First Secretary Gomulka's illiberalism. He also wrote novels and plays.

weak nuclear force (or **weak interaction**) one of the four fundamental ▷forces of nature, the other three being the gravitational force or gravity, the electromagnetic force, and the strong nuclear force. It causes radioactive beta decay and other subatomic reactions. The particles that carry the weak force are called ▷weakons (or intermediate vector bosons) and comprise the positively and negatively charged W particles and the neutral Z particle.

weakon (or **intermediate vector boson**) in physics, a ▷gauge boson that carries the weak nuclear force, one of the fundamental forces of nature. There are three types of weakon, the positive and negative W particle and the neutral Z particle.

Weald, the (or **the Kent Weald**; Old English 'forest') area between the North and South Downs, England, a raised tract of forest 64 km/40 mi wide. It forms part of Kent, Sussex, Surrey, and Hampshire. Once thickly wooded, it is now an agricultural area producing fruit, hops, and vegetables. Crowborough and Wadhurst are the largest villages in the area. In the Middle Ages its timber and iron ore made it the industrial heart of England.

wealth in economics, the wealth of a nation is its stock of physical capital, human capital, and net financial capital owned overseas. Physical capital is the stock of buildings, factories, offices, machines, roads, and so on. Human capital is the workforce; not just the number of workers, but also their stock of education and training which makes them productive. Net financial capital is the difference between the money value of assets owned by foreigners in the domestic economy and the assets owned by the country abroad.

For individuals, the most significant wealth they have is themselves and their ability to generate an income by working.

After that, the largest item of wealth is likely to be their house. Possessions, money, and insurance policies are other examples of individual wealth.

weapon any implement used for attack and defence, from simple clubs, spears, and bows and arrows in prehistoric times to machine guns and nuclear bombs in modern times. The first revolution in warfare came with the invention of ▷gunpowder and the development of cannons and shoulder-held guns. Many other weapons now exist, such as grenades, shells, torpedoes, rockets, and guided missiles. The ultimate in explosive weapons are the atomic (fission) and hydrogen (fusion) bombs. They release the enormous energy produced when atoms split or fuse together (see ▷nuclear warfare). There are also chemical and bacteriological weapons, which release poisons or disease.

Wear river in northeast England; length 107 km/67 mi. From its source near Wearhead in the Pennines in County Durham, it flows eastwards along a narrow valley, Weardale, to Bishop Auckland and then northeast past Durham and Chester-le-Street, to meet the North Sea at Sunderland.

weasel any of various small, short-legged, lithe carnivorous mammals with bushy tails, especially the genus *Mustela*, found

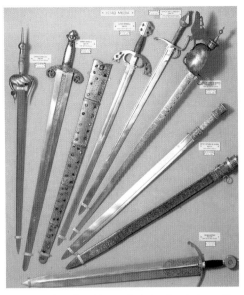

WEAPON These Spanish swords dating from between the 12th and 15th centuries show the perfection of the art of sword-making, before the development of firearms in the 16th century lessened their importance as weapons. The Spanish city of Toledo was particularly renowned for the quality of its swords. *The Art Archive/Album/Joseph Martin*

worldwide except Australia. They feed mainly on small rodents although some, like the mink *M. vison*, hunt aquatic prey. Most are 12–25 cm/5–10 in long, excluding the tail.

Included in this group are the North American long-tailed weasel, the northern hemisphere ermine or stoat, the Eurasian polecat, and the endangered North American black-footed ferret. In cold regions the coat colour of several species changes to white during the winter.

Black-footed ferrets were so close to extinction in 1987 that the entire wild population was taken into captivity. The captive population has grown from 18 then to 350 in 1998. Some have also been released back into the wild, where the population stands at between 50 and 60.

The weasel *M. nivalis* of Europe and Asia is the smallest carnivore. It feeds on mice, which it can chase into their burrows.

weather variation of atmospheric conditions at any one place over a short period of time . Such conditions include humidity, precipitation, temperature, cloud cover, visibility, and wind. Weather differs from ▷climate in that the latter is a composite of the average weather conditions of a locality or region over a long period of time (at least 30 years). ▷Meteorology is the study of short-term weather patterns and data within a circumscribed area; climatology is the study of weather over longer timescales on a zonal or global basis.

Weather forecasts Forecasts are based on current meteorological data, and predict likely weather for a particular area; they may be short-range (covering a period of one or two days), medium-range (five to seven days), or long-range (a month or so). Weather observations are made on an hourly basis at meteorological recording stations – there are more than 3,500 of these around the world. More than 140 nations participate in the exchange of weather data through the World Weather Watch programme, which is sponsored by the World Meteorological Organization (WMO), and information is distributed among the member nations by means of a worldwide communications network. Incoming data is collated at weather centres in individual countries and plotted on weather maps, or charts. The weather map uses internationally standardized symbols to indicate barometric pressure, cloud cover, wind speed and direction, precipitation, and other details reported by each recording station at a specific time. Points of equal atmospheric pressure are joined by lines called ▷isobars and from these the position and movement of weather fronts and centres of high and low pressure can be extrapolated. The charts are normally compiled on a three-hourly or six-hourly basis – the main synoptic hours are midnight, 0600, 1200 and 1800 – and predictions for future weather are drawn up on the basis of comparisons between current charts and previous charts. Additional data received from weather balloons and satellites help to complete and corroborate the picture obtained from the weather map.

weather area any of the divisions of the sea around the British Isles for the purpose of weather forecasting for shipping. The areas are used to indicate where strong or gale-force winds are expected.

weathering process by which exposed rocks are broken down on the spot by the action of rain, frost, wind, and other elements of the weather. It differs from ▷erosion in that no movement or transportation of the broken-down material takes place. Two types of weathering are recognized: physical (or mechanical) and chemical. They usually occur together.

weaver any small bird of the family Ploceidae, order Passeriformes; they are mostly about 15 cm/6 in long. The majority of weavers are African, a few Asian. The males use grasses to weave elaborate globular nests in bushes and trees. The nests are entered from beneath, and the male hangs from it calling and flapping his wings to attract a female. Their bodies are somewhat elongated and the tails long, and the prominent conical bill is very powerful. They eat insects and may eat cultivated grain. Males are often more brightly coloured than females.

Many kinds are polygamous, so build several nests, and some species build large communal nests with many chambers. One species, the red-billed African quelea *Quelea quelea*, lives and breeds in flocks numbering many thousands of individuals; the flocks migrate to follow food sources. Their destructive power can equal that of locusts.

weaving the production of ▷textile fabric by means of a loom. The basic process is the interlacing at right angles of longitudinal threads (the warp) and horizontal threads (the weft), the latter being carried across from one side of the loom to the other by a type of bobbin called a shuttle.

Webb, (Martha) Beatrice (born Potter; 1858–1943) and **Sidney James**, 1st Baron Passfield (1859–1947) English social reformers, writers, and founders of the London School of Economics and Political Science (LSE) in 1895. They were early members of the socialist ▷Fabian Society, and advocates of a radical approach to social reform. They married in 1892. They argued for social insurance in their minority report (1909) of the Poor Law Commission and wrote many influential books, including *The History of Trade Unionism* (1894), *English Local Government* (1906–29), *Decay of Capitalist Civilization* (1923), and *Soviet Communism: A New Civilization?* (1935). They founded the *New Statesman* magazine in 1913.

Webber, Andrew Lloyd English composer of musicals; see ▷Lloyd Webber.

weber SI unit (symbol Wb) of ▷magnetic flux (the magnetic field strength multiplied by the area through which the field passes). It is named after German chemist Wilhelm Weber. One weber equals 10^8 ▷maxwells.

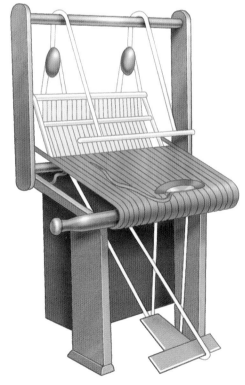

WEAVING A hand loom as used in Britain from the Middle Ages to the beginning of the industrial revolution.

Weber, Carl Maria Friedrich Ernst von (1786–1826) German composer. He established the Romantic school of opera with *Der Freischütz/The Marksman* (1821) and *Euryanthe* (1823). He was Kapellmeister (chief conductor) at Breslau 1804–06, Prague 1813–16, and Dresden in 1816. He died during a visit to London, where he produced his opera *Oberon* (1826), written for the Covent Garden Theatre.

Weber, Max (1864–1920) German sociologist, one of the founders of modern sociology. He emphasized cultural and political factors as key influences on economic development and individual behaviour.

> **Max Weber**
> *The idea of duty in one's calling prowls about in our life like the ghost of dead religious beliefs.*
> The Protestant Ethic

Webern, Anton (Friedrich Wilhelm von) (1883–1945) Austrian composer. He wrote spare, enigmatic miniatures combining a pastoral poetic with severe structural rigour. A Renaissance musical scholar, he became a pupil of Arnold ▷Schoenberg, whose 12-tone system he reinterpreted as abstract design in works such as the *Concerto for Nine Instruments* (1931–34) and the *Second Cantata* (1941–43). His constructivist aesthetic influenced the post-war generation of advanced composers.

Related Web site: Webern, Anton von http://w3.rz-berlin.mpg.de/cmp/webern.html

Webster, John (c. 1580–c. 1625) English dramatist. His reputation rests on two tragedies, *The White Devil* (1612) and *The Duchess of Malfi* (c. 1613). Though both show the preoccupation with melodramatic violence and horror typical of the Jacobean ▷revenge tragedy, they are also remarkable for their poetry and psychological insight. He collaborated with a number of other dramatists, notably with Thomas ▷Dekker on the comedy *Westward Ho* (c. 1606).

Born in London, he was the son of a tailor and was apprenticed to the same trade, becoming a freeman of the Merchant Taylors' Company in 1603. But he was also active in the theatre by 1602, working on collaborations and perhaps also acting. His first independent work was *The White Devil*, printed (and probably first performed) in 1612.

> **John Webster**
> *Is not old wine wholesomest, old pippins toothsomest, old wood burn brightest, old linen wash whitest? Old soldiers, sweethearts are surest, and old lovers are soundest.*
> Westward Hoe II. ii

Webster, Noah (1758–1843) US lexicographer whose books on grammar and spelling and *American Dictionary of the English Language* (1828) standardized US English.

Weddell, James (1787–1834) British Antarctic explorer. In 1823, he reached 75°S latitude and 35°W longitude, in the Weddell Sea, which is named after him.

Weddell Sea arm of the Southern Atlantic Ocean that cuts into the Antarctic continent southeast of Cape Horn; area 8,000,000 sq km/3,088,800 sq mi. Much of it is covered with thick pack ice for most of the year.

Wedekind, Frank (1864–1918) German dramatist. He was a forerunner of expressionism with *Frühlings Erwachen/The Awakening of Spring* (1891), and *Der Erdgeist/The Earth Spirit* (1895) and its sequel *Der Marquis von Keith. Die Büchse der Pandora/Pandora's Box* (1904) was the source for Berg's opera *Lulu*.

wedge block of triangular cross-section that can be used as a simple machine. An axe is a wedge: it splits wood by redirecting the energy of the downward blow sideways, where it exerts the force needed to split the wood.

Wedgwood, Josiah (1730–1795) English pottery manufacturer. He set up business in Staffordshire in the early 1760s to produce his agateware as well as unglazed blue or green stoneware (jasper) decorated with white neo-classical designs, using pigments of his own invention.

weever fish any of a family (Trachinidae) of marine bony fishes of the perch family, especially the genus *Trachinus*, with poison glands on the dorsal fin and gill cover that can give a painful sting. It grows up to 5 cm/2 in long, has eyes near the top of the head, and lives on sandy seabeds.

weevil any of a superfamily (Curculionoidea) of ▷beetles, usually less than 6 mm/0.25 in in length, and with a head prolonged into a downward beak, which is used for boring into plant stems and trees for feeding.

The larvae are usually white and the adults green, black, or brown. There are approximately 570 species of weevil in Britain and 40,000 known species worldwide. The grain weevil *Sitophilus granarius* is a serious pest of stored grain and the boll weevil *Anthonomus grandis* damages cotton crops.

The adult beetles of *Phyllobius* and *Polydrusus*, the common British genera, are bright green. The biscuit weevil *Stegobium paniceum* was feared by early seafarers because it would eat ship's biscuits.

Wegener, Alfred Lothar (1880–1930) German meteorologist and geophysicist whose theory of ▷continental drift, expounded in *Origin of Continents and Oceans* in 1915, was originally known as 'Wegener's hypothesis'. His ideas can now be explained in terms of ▷plate tectonics, the idea that the Earth's crust consists of a number of plates, all moving with respect to one another.

Weigel, Helene (1900–1971) Austrian actor and director. She co-founded the Berliner Ensemble with her husband Berthold ▷Brecht in 1949 and took leading roles in productions of his plays, visiting London in 1956 and 1965. She took over direction of the Ensemble after Brecht's death in 1956.

weight the force exerted on an object by ▷gravity. The weight of an object depends on its mass – the amount of material in it – and the strength of the Earth's gravitational pull, which decreases with height. Consequently, an object weighs less at the top of a mountain than at sea level. On the surface of the Moon, an object has only one-sixth of its weight on Earth, because the Moon's surface gravity is one-sixth that of the Earth.

If the mass of a body is m kilograms and the gravitational field strength is g newtons per kilogram, its weight W in newtons is given by:

$$W = mg$$

weightlessness the apparent loss in weight of a body in free fall. Astronauts in an orbiting spacecraft do not feel any weight because they are falling freely in the Earth's gravitational field. It is incorrect to attribute weightlessness to the astronauts being beyond the influence of Earth's gravity. The same phenomenon can be experienced in a falling lift or in an aircraft deliberately imitating the path of a freely falling object.

weightlifting sport of lifting the heaviest possible weight above one's head to the satisfaction of judges. In international competitions there are two standard lifts: **snatch** and **jerk**.

Related Web site: USA Weightlifting http://www.usaweightlifting.org/

weights and measures see under ▷c.g.s. system, ▷f.p.s. system, ▷m.k.s. system, ▷SI units.

Weights and Measures Act 1963 in Britain, act of Parliament which makes it illegal for businesses to give short weights or short measures to consumers. For example, it is illegal to sell a consumer half a pint of milk when it states on the carton that it contains one pint of milk. ▷Trading standards departments are responsible for enforcing the Weights and Measures Act.

Wei, Jingsheng (1951–) Chinese pro-democracy activist and essayist, imprisoned 1979–97 for attacking the Chinese communist system. He is regarded as one of China's most important political dissidents.

Weil, Simone (1909–1943) French writer who became a practising Catholic after a mystical experience in 1938. Apart from essays, her works (advocating political passivity) were posthumously published, including *Waiting for God* (1951), *The Need for Roots* (1952), and *Notebooks* (1956).

> **Simone Weil**
> *Every time I think of the crucifixion of Christ, I commit the sin of envy.*
> Letter, 1950

Weill, Kurt Julian (1900–1950) German composer; a US citizen from 1943. He wrote chamber and orchestral music and collaborated with Bertolt ▷Brecht on operas such as *Die Dreigroschenoper/The Threepenny Opera* (1928) and *Aufstieg und Fall der Stadt Mahagonny/The Rise and Fall of the City of Mahagonny* (1929), both of which attacked social corruption (*Mahagonny*, which satirized US frontier values, causing a riot at its premiere in Leipzig). He tried to evolve a new form of music theatre, using subjects with a contemporary relevance and the simplest musical means. In 1933 he left Germany, and from 1935 was in the USA, where he wrote a number of successful scores for Broadway, among them the antiwar musical *Johnny Johnson* (1936), *Knickerbocker Holiday* (1938) (including the often covered 'September Song'), and *Street Scene* (1947), based on an Elmer Rice play set in the Depression.

His musical *Love Life* (1948), with lyrics by Alan Jay Lerner, describes a typical US couple over a period of 150 years of US history, and expresses Weill's mixture of fascination and repulsion towards the 'American Dream'.

Related Web site: Kurt Weill Home Page http://www.kwf.org/

Weil's disease (or **leptospirosis**) infectious disease of animals that is occasionally transmitted to human beings, usually by contact with water contaminated with rat urine. It is characterized by acute fever, and infection may spread to the brain, liver, kidneys, and heart. It has a 10% mortality rate.

Weimar Republic constitutional republic in Germany from 1919 to 1933, which was crippled by the election of antidemocratic parties to the ▷Reichstag (parliament), and then subverted by the Nazi leader Hitler after his appointment as chancellor in 1933. It took its name from the city where in February 1919 a constituent assembly met to draw up a democratic constitution.

Weinberger, Caspar Willard (1917–) US Republican politician. He served under presidents Nixon and Ford, and was Reagan's defence secretary 1981–87.

Weir, Peter (Lindsay) (1944–) Australian film director who has worked much in the USA. His films, which range from melodramas to comedies, include the Australian *Picnic at Hanging Rock* (1975) and the US *Dead Poets Society* (1989; BAFTA award for Best Film).

Weismann, August Friedrich Leopold (1834–1914) German biologist, one of the founders of ▷genetics. He postulated that every living organism contains a special hereditary substance, the 'germ plasm', and in 1892 he proposed that changes to the body do not in turn cause an alteration of the genetic material.

This 'central dogma' of biology remains of vital importance to biologists supporting the Darwinian theory of evolution. If the genetic material can be altered only by chance mutation and recombination, then the Lamarckian view that acquired bodily changes can subsequently be inherited becomes obsolete.

Weizmann, Chaim Azriel (1874–1952) Zionist leader, the first president of Israel 1948–52. He conducted the negotiations leading up to the Balfour Declaration, by which the UK declared its support for an independent Jewish state.

Born in Motol in the Russian Empire (now Belarus), he became a naturalized British subject, and as a qualified chemist and director of the Admiralty laboratories 1916–19 discovered a process for manufacturing acetone, a solvent. He became head of the Hebrew University in Jerusalem, then in 1948 became the first president of the new republic of Israel.

Weizsäcker, Richard, Baron von (1920–) German Christian Democrat politician, president 1984–94. He began his career as a lawyer and was also active in the German Protestant church and in Christian Democratic Union party politics. He was elected to the West German Bundestag (parliament) in 1969 and served as mayor of West Berlin from 1981, before being elected federal president in 1984.

welding joining pieces of metal (or nonmetal) at faces rendered plastic or liquid by heat or pressure (or both). The principal processes today are gas and arc welding, in which the heat from a gas flame or an electric arc melts the faces to be joined. Additional 'filler metal' is usually added to the joint.

Weldon, Fay (1931–) English novelist and dramatist. Her work deals with feminist themes, often in an ironic or comic manner. Novels include *The Fat Woman's Joke* (1967), *Female Friends* (1975), *Remember Me* (1976), *Puffball* (1980), *The Life and Loves of a She-Devil* (1984) (made into a film in 1990), *The Hearts and Lives of Men* (1987), *Splitting* (1995), *Worst Fears* (1996), and *Big Women* (1998; also a television series).

Welensky, Roy (1907–1991) Born Roland Welensky. Rhodesian politician. He was instrumental in the creation in 1953 of the Central African Federation, comprising Northern Rhodesia (now Zambia), Southern Rhodesia (now Zimbabwe), and Nyasaland (now Malawi), and was prime minister 1956–63, when the federation was disbanded. His Southern Rhodesian Federal Party was defeated by Ian Smith's Rhodesian Front in 1964. In 1965, following Smith's unilateral declaration of Southern Rhodesian independence from Britain, Welensky left politics. He was knighted in 1953.

welfare state political system under which the state (rather than the individual or the private sector) has responsibility for the welfare of its citizens, providing a guaranteed minimum standard of life, and insurance against the hazards of want, disease, ignorance, squalor, and idleness. Welfare services include ▷social security, comprising provision against interruption of earnings through

WELDING The main welding techniques – gas welding and arc welding – are first documented at the end of the 19th century. *Image Bank*

sickness, injury, old age or unemployment. They take the forms of unemployment and sickness benefits, family allowances and income supplements, provided and typically financed through state insurance schemes. The services also include health and education, financed typically through taxation, and the provision of subsidized 'social housing'. Subsidized public transport, leisure facilities, public libraries, with special discounts for the elderly, unemployed, and disabled, are other non-core elements of a welfare state.

The phrase 'welfare state' was first used by Sir Alfred Zimmern in the late 1930s, to distinguish between the policies of the democracies and the 'war state' of Europe's dictators. Elements of a welfare system began to be constructed in parts of Western Europe from the late 19th century, with Germany taking the lead in 1883 with a compulsory national accident and sickness insurance law, introduced by Chancellor Otto von Bismark and financed by a state subsidy. New Zealand introduced pensions in 1898, while Austria-Hungary (late 19th century), Norway (1909), Sweden (1910), Italy, UK, and Russia (1911), introduced national health insurance. The USA followed later, with the Social Security Act of 1935. The developments came in response to political and social pressures, including the extension of voting rights. They provided minimum standards, but not to all groups in society. It was not until the early 1940s, with the UK taking the lead, that a comprehensive welfare state, covering all its elements and available to all, was established.

welfare to work programme introduced by UK ▷Labour Party's to reduce unemployment, particularly among young people, by getting them off welfare into work. In January 1998, the chancellor of the Exchequer, Gordon ▷Brown, announced a 'national crusade to end unemployment', targeting at first the under-25s, and then older people.

Welland Ship Canal waterway in south Ontario, Canada. Since 1959 it has been a part of the ▷St Lawrence Seaway, linking Lake Erie to Lake Ontario. Extending for 45 km/28 mi through the Niagara Peninsula, the modern canal (1932) carries ships over the Niagara Escarpment between Port Colborne on Lake Erie and Port Weller on Lake Ontario, which is 99 m/326 ft lower. Of its eight locks, numbers 4–6, in Thorold, are 'twin-flight', allowing one ship to be lifted as another is lowered.

Welles, (George) Orson (1915–1985) US actor, screenwriter, and film and theatre director. His first and greatest film was *Citizen Kane* (1941), which he produced, directed, and starred in. Later work includes the *films noirs The Lady from Shanghai* (1948) and

Touch of Evil (1958). As an actor, he created the character of Harry Lime in the film *The Third Man* (1949).

A child prodigy, Welles made his acting debut at 16 in Dublin, Ireland. In 1937 he founded the Mercury Theater in New York with John ▷Houseman; their repertory productions included a modern-dress version of *Julius Caesar*. Welles's realistic radio broadcast of H G Wells's *The War of the Worlds* (1938) caused panic and fear of Martian invasion in the USA. The next year he went to Hollywood. Using innovative lighting, camera angles, and movements, *Citizen Kane* is a landmark in the history of cinema. Welles's subsequent career, however, was dogged by studio interference – as on *The Magnificent Ambersons* (1942) – and he opted to work primarily in Europe, his ventures into Hollywood confined to acting roles in other people's films and a handful of directorial assignments. His films include *The Stranger* (1946), *Macbeth* (1948), *Othello* (1952), *Chimes at Midnight* (1966), and *F for Fake* (1973). He was the recipient of the American Film Institute's Life Achievement Award in 1975.

Wellesley, Richard Colley, Marquess Wellesley (1760–1842) British administrator; brother of the 1st Duke of Wellington. He was governor general of India 1798–1805, and by his victories over the Marathas of western India greatly extended the territory under British rule. He was foreign secretary 1809–12, and lord lieutenant of Ireland 1821–28 and 1833–34. He was made Baron in 1797, and Marquess in 1799.

Wellington capital and industrial port of New Zealand, in the province of the same name on North Island, on the Cook Strait; population (1996) 335,500 (urban area). Industries in the city include woollen textiles, chemicals, engineering, and electrical goods. The harbour was sighted by Captain James Cook in 1773.

Wellington, Arthur Wellesley, 1st Duke of Wellington (1769–1852) Irish-born British soldier and Tory politician. As commander in the ▷Peninsular War, he expelled the French from Spain in 1814. He defeated Napoleon Bonaparte at Quatre-Bras and Waterloo in 1815, and was a member of the Congress of Vienna. As prime minister 1828–30, he was forced to concede Roman Catholic emancipation. He was made Viscount in 1809, Earl in 1812, Marquess in 1812, and Duke in 1814.

Wellington was born in Dublin, and sat for a spell in the early 1790s in the Irish parliament as the member for Trim. He was knighted for his distinguished army service in India in the early 1800s. Wellington became a national hero for his victories of 1808–14 in the Peninsular War and as general of the allied forces ranged against Napoleon. At the Congress of Vienna, he opposed the dismemberment of France and supported restoration of the Bourbons. As prime minister he modified the Corn Laws but became unpopular for his opposition to parliamentary reform and his failure to block Catholic emancipation. Thereafter, he acted as foreign secretary 1834–35 in Peel's administration and was a member of the cabinet 1841–46. He held the office of commander in chief of the forces at various times from 1827 and for life from 1842. His London home was Apsley House, near Hyde Park.

Wells, H(erbert) G(eorge) (1866–1946) English writer. He was a pioneer of ▷science fiction with such novels as *The Time Machine* (1895) and *The War of the Worlds* (1898), which describes a Martian invasion of Earth and brought him nationwide recognition. His later novels had an anti-establishment, anticonventional humour remarkable in its day, for example *Kipps* (1905) and *Tono-Bungay* (1909). He was originally a Fabian and later became a Labour party supporter. He was a Labour candidate for London University in 1921 and 1922.

Wells was a prophet of world organization. His theme was the need for humans to impose their mastery upon their own creations and to establish benevolent systems and structures by which to rule themselves, and in pursuing this concept he became a leading advocate of social planning. A number of prophecies described in fictional works such as *The First Men in the Moon* (1901) and *The Shape of Things to Come* (1933), as well as in *The Outline of History* (1920) and other popular non-fiction works, have been fulfilled; among them, the significance of aviation, tank warfare, World War II, and the atomic bomb. He also wrote many short stories.

Related Web site: War of the Worlds, The http://www.fourmilab.ch/etexts/www/warworlds/warw.html

Welsh people of ▷Wales; see also ▷Celt. The term is thought to be derived from an old Germanic term for 'foreigner', and so linked to Walloon (Belgium) and Wallachian (Romania). It may also derive from the Latin *Volcae*, the name of a Celtic people of France.

> ### Orson Welles
> *Everybody denies I am a genius – but nobody ever called me one!*
> Quoted in Leslie Halliwell, *Filmgoer's Companion*

Welsh Assembly devolved governmental body based in Cardiff; see ▷National Assembly for Wales.

Welsh corgi breed of dog with a foxlike head and pricked ears, originally bred for cattle herding. The coat is dense, with several varieties of colouring. Corgis are about 30 cm/12 in at the shoulder, and weigh up to 12 kg/27 lb.

There are two types of corgi, the Pembrokeshire and the Cardiganshire. The Pembrokeshire has a finely textured coat, yellowish or reddish brown, or sometimes black and tan, and has almost no tail. The Cardiganshire corgi has a short, rough coat, usually red and white, and a long furry tail. Their small size is an advantage because cattle are unable to bend low enough to gore them.

Related Web site: Welsh Corgi http://www.akc.org/breeds/recbreeds/cardiga.cfm

DUKE OF WELLINGTON Wellington at the Battle of Vittoria, 21 June 1813. At this decisive battle of the Peninsular War of 1808–14, British forces under the Duke of Wellington defeated the French army of Marshal Jean-Baptiste Jourdain in northern Spain, forcing Joseph Bonaparte – who had been made king of Spain by Napoleon – to flee back to France. *Art Archive*

Welsh language (Welsh **Cymraeg**) member of the Celtic branch of the Indo-European language family, spoken chiefly in the rural north and west of Wales. Spoken by 18.7% of the Welsh population, it is the strongest of the surviving ▷Celtic languages.

Welsh has been in decline in the face of English expansion since the accession of the Welsh Henry Tudor (as Henry VII) to the throne of England in 1485. Modern Welsh, like English, is not a highly inflected language, but British, the Celtic ancestor of Welsh, was, like Latin and Anglo-Saxon, highly inflected. The continuous literature of the Welsh, from the 6th century onwards, contains the whole range of change from British to present-day Welsh. Nowadays, few Welsh people speak only Welsh; they are either bilingual or speak only English.

During the 20th century the decline of Welsh has been slowed: from about 900,000 speakers at the turn of the century, the number had shrunk to half a million in 1995. However, due to vigorous campaigning and efforts to promote the language, made by the S4C (Sianel Pedwar Cymru) television network, and the Welsh Language Society, and to some extent elsewhere in literature and the media, the numbers speaking Welsh has stabilized. According to a survey, in 1995 21% of the Welsh population spoke the national tongue; of that number, it was the mother tongue of 55%. Use of the language among young people increased as a result of its inclusion in the National Curriculum; in 1993–94, 78.4% of Welsh pupils learnt it as either first or second language.

Welsh literature the prose and poetry of Wales, written predominantly in Welsh but also, more recently, in English. Characteristic of Welsh poetry is the bardic system. In the 18th century the ▷eisteddfod (literary festival) movement brought a revival of classical forms.

> ### H G Wells
> *Human history becomes more and more a race between education and catastrophe.*
> Outline of History

Ancient literature The chief remains of early Welsh literature are contained in the Four Ancient Books of Wales – the *Black Book of Carmarthen*, the *Book of Taliesin*, the *Book of Aneirin*, and the *Red Book of Hergest* – anthologies of prose and verse of the 6th–14th centuries. The bardic system ensured the continuance of traditional conventions; most celebrated of the 12th-century bards was Cynddelw Brydydd Mawr (active 1155–1200).

Literature after the English conquest The English conquest of 1282 involved the fall of the princes who supported these bards, but after a period of decline a new school arose in South Wales with a new freedom in form and sentiment, the most celebrated poet in the 14th-century being Dafydd ap Gwilym, and in the next century the classical metrist Dafydd ap Edmwnd (active 1450–1459). With the Reformation, biblical translations were undertaken, and Morgan Llwyd (1619–1659) and Ellis Wynne (1671–1734) wrote religious prose. Popular metres resembling those of England developed – for example, the poems of Huw Morys (1622–1709).

Classical revival Goronwy Owen revived the classical poetic forms in the 18th century, and the ▷eisteddfod (literary festival) movement began: popular measures were used by the hymn writer William Williams Pantycelyn (1717–1791).

Second revival The 19th century saw few notable figures save the novelist Daniel Owen (1836–1895), but the foundation of a Welsh university and the work there of John Morris Jones (1864–1929) produced a 20th-century revival, including T Gwynn ▷Jones, W J Gruffydd (1881–1954), and R Williams Parry (1884–1956). Later writers included the poet J Kitchener Davies (1902–1952), the dramatist and poet Saunders Lewis (1893–1985), and the novelist and short-story writer Kate Roberts (1891–1985). Among writers of the period after World War II are the poets Waldo Williams (1904–1971), Euros Bowen (1904–1988), and Bobi Jones (1929–), and the novelists Islwyn Ffowc Elis (1924–), and Jane Edwards (1938–).

Welsh writers in English Those who have expressed the Welsh spirit in English include the poets Edward Thomas, Vernon Watkins (1906–67), Dylan ▷Thomas, R S ▷Thomas, and Dannie Abse (1923–), and the novelist Emyr Humphreys (1919–).

Welty, Eudora Alice (1909–2001) US novelist and short-story writer. Her works reflect life in the American South and are notable for their creation of character and accurate rendition of local dialect. Her novels include *Delta Wedding* (1946), *Losing Battles* (1970), and *The Optimist's Daughter* (1972). Her *Collected Stories* appeared in 1982.

welwitschia woody plant found in the deserts of southwestern Africa. It has a long, water-absorbent taproot and can live for up to 100 years. (Genus *Welwitschia mirabilis*, order Gnetales.)

Wembley Stadium sports ground in north London, England, completed in 1923 for the British Empire Exhibition 1924–25. It has been the scene of the annual Football Association (FA) Cup final since 1923. The 1948 Olympic Games and many concerts, including the Live Aid concert of 1985, were held here. Adjacent to the main stadium, which holds 79,000 people all seated, are the Wembley indoor arena (which holds about 10,000, depending on the event) and conference centre.

The stadium, together with its famous twin towers, was knocked down in November 2000 and is to be completely rebuilt at an estimated cost of £475 million. The new 90,000 capacity stadium, designed by a group of architects headed by Norman ▷Foster is scheduled to be ready in March 2003.

Wenceslas, St (*c.* 907–929) Duke of Bohemia. He attempted to Christianize his people and was murdered by his brother. He is patron saint of the Czech Republic and the 'good King Wenceslas' of a popular carol. Feast day 28 September.

Wends northwestern Slavonic peoples who settled east of the rivers Elbe and Saale in the 6th–8th centuries. By the 12th century most had been forcibly Christianized and absorbed by invading Germans; a few preserved their identity and survive as the Sorbs of Lusatia (eastern Germany/Poland).

werewolf in folk belief, a human being either turned into a wolf by a spell or having the ability to assume a wolf form. The symptoms of ▷porphyria may have fostered the legends.

Werner, Abraham Gottlob (1749–1817) German geologist, one of the first to classify minerals systematically. He also developed the later discarded theory of neptunism – that the Earth was initially covered by water, with every mineral in suspension; as the water receded, layers of rocks 'crystallized'.

Wesker, Arnold (1932–) English dramatist. His socialist beliefs were reflected in the successful trilogy *Chicken Soup with Barley, Roots*, and *I'm Talking About Jerusalem* (1958–60). He established a catchphrase with *Chips with Everything* (1962). His autobiography *As Much as I Dare* was published in 1994.

Wesley, Charles (1707–1788) English Methodist, brother of John ▷Wesley and one of the original Methodists at Oxford. He became a principal preacher and theologian of the Wesleyan Methodists, and wrote some 6,500 hymns.

Wesley, John (1703–1791) English founder of ▷Methodism. When the pulpits of the Church of England were closed to him and his followers, he took the gospel to the people. For 50 years he rode about the country on horseback, preaching daily, largely in the open air. His sermons became the doctrinal standard of the Wesleyan Methodist Church.

> **John Wesley**
> *Beware you be not swallowed up in books! An ounce of love is worth a pound of knowledge.*
> Quoted in R Southey *Life of Wesley* ch. 16

He was born in Epworth, Lincolnshire, where his father was the rector, and went to Oxford University together with his brother Charles, where their circle was nicknamed Methodists because of their religious observances. He was ordained in the Church of England in 1728 and returned to his Oxford college in 1729 as a tutor. In 1735 he went to Georgia, USA, as a missionary. On his return he experienced 'conversion' in 1738, and from being rigidly High Church developed into an ardent Evangelical. His *Journal* gives an intimate picture of the man and his work.

Related Web site: Selected Poetry of John Wesley (1703–1791)
http://www.library.utoronto.ca/utel/rp/authors/wesleyj.html

Wessex kingdom of the West Saxons in Britain, said to have been founded by Cerdic about AD 500, covering Hampshire, Dorset, Wiltshire, Somerset, Devon, and the former county of Berkshire. In 829 Egbert established West Saxon supremacy over all England.

Thomas ▷Hardy used the term Wessex in his novels for the southwest counties of England; drawing on England's west country, the heartland was Dorset but its outlying boundary markers were Plymouth, Bath, Oxford, and Southampton. He gave fictional names to such real places as Dorchester (Casterbridge), Salisbury (Melchester) and Bournemouth (Sandbourne), but mixed these with a sprinkling of real names such as Stonehenge, the River Frome, and Nettlecombe Tout.

Wessex, Earl of the formal title of Prince ▷Edward of the UK.

West, Benjamin (1738–1820) American neoclassical painter. A noted history painter, he was active in London from 1763 and enjoyed the patronage of George III for many years. *The Death of General Wolfe* (1770; National Gallery of Canada, Ottawa) began a vogue for painting recent historical events in contemporary costume.

West, Mae (1892–1980) US vaudeville, stage, and film actor. She wrote her own dialogue, setting herself up as a provocative sex symbol and the mistress of verbal innuendo. She appeared on Broadway in *Sex* (1926), *Drag* (1927), and *Diamond Lil* (1928), which was the basis of the film (with Cary Grant) *She Done Him Wrong* (1933).

> **Mae West**
> *Love thy neighbour – and if he happens to be tall, debonair and devastating, it will be that much easier.*
> Quoted in J Weintraub *Peel Me a Grape*

West, Nathanael (1903–1940) Pen-name of Nathan Wallenstein Weinstein. US writer. He is noted as an idiosyncratic black-humour parodist. His surrealist-influenced novels capture the absurdity and extremity of American life and the dark side of the American Dream. His most powerful novel, *The Day of the Locust* (1939), is a vivid exploration of the apocalyptic violence given release by the fantasies created by Hollywood, where West had been a screenwriter.

West, Rebecca (1892–1983) pen-name of Cicily Isabel Fairfield. English journalist and novelist, an active feminist from 1911. Her novels, of which the semi-autobiographical *The Fountain Overflows* (1956) and *The Birds Fall Down* (1966) are regarded as the best, demonstrate a social and political awareness.

> **Rebecca West**
> *There is no such thing as conversation. It is an illusion. There are intersecting monologues, that is all.*
> *There Is No Conversation*, 'The Harsh Voice' 1

West, American western frontier of the USA. Specifically the term refers to the period between 1850, when westward expansion began, and 1890, when the west coast region was settled. This was the era of the ▷gold rushes, first the California gold rush of 1848–56 and then Arizona, Colorado, Nevada, and South Dakota. It was also the time when ranchers began grazing cattle on the open range.

Cowboy legends began during this period. Many of the figures of Western novels and films were real people, such as lawmen 'Wild Bill' ▷Hickok and Wyatt Earp, and criminals such as Jesse ▷James and ▷Billy the Kid, although stories about them have on the whole been greatly exaggerated.

West African Economic Community international organization established in 1975 to end barriers in trade and to achieve cooperation in development. Members include Burkina Faso, Côte d'Ivoire, Mali, Mauritania, Niger, and Senegal; Benin and Togo have observer status.

West Bank area (5,879 sq km/2,270 sq mi) on the west bank of the River Jordan; population (1994) 1,122,900. The area was captured by Israel from Jordan in 1967; Israel refers to the area as Judaea and ▷Samaria.

The West Bank was held by the Jordanian army in 1948 at the end of the first Arab-Israeli war following the creation of the state of Israel, and was captured by Israel during the Six-Day War (5–10 June 1967). There was initially little resistance from the resident Arab Palestinian population, in part due to Israeli improvements in the standard of living, and in part lack of affinity with Jordanians in Jordan's East Bank. However, Israeli settlement of the area picked up pace in the 1980s, creating tensions and, after 1987, as the ▷Intifada (uprising) gained strength in the occupied territories, Israeli military presence increased significantly. In 1988 Jordan renounced responsibility for the West Bank, having previously recognized the main representative of Palestinians to be the Palestinian Liberation Organization (PLO).

In 1993 Israel signed an accord with the PLO, which included a phased withdrawal of Israeli troops from parts of the West Bank and the ▷Gaza Strip and limited self rule for Palestinians. However, the final status of these areas has yet to be resolved.

Related Web site: Applied Resource Institute – Jerusalem
http://www.arij.org/

West Bengal state of northeast India; area 88,700 sq km/ 34,247 sq mi; population (1994 est) 73,600,000. The capital is ▷Calcutta. Industries include jute (particularly at Hooghly industrial complex), iron and steel (at Durgapur, Asansol, based on the Raniganj coalfield), cars, locomotives, aluminium, fertilizers, chemicals, cotton, and printing. Rice, jute, tea (in Darjiling and Jalpaiguri), oilseed, sugar, pulses, and tobacco are grown, and there is fishing.

West Berkshire unitary authority in southeast England, created in 1998 from part of the former county of Berkshire.

area 705 sq km/272 sq mi **towns and cities** Newbury (administrative headquarters), Hungerford, Lambourn **features** River Kennet; River Cambourn; Kennet and Avon Canal; Snelsmore Common Country Park covers 59 ha/ 146 acres including wetland habitats; Inkpen Hill (291 m/854 ft) with Stone Age tomb and Walbury Hill (297 m/974 ft) with Iron Age fort are the highest chalk hills in England; Thatcham Moors reedbeds are designated Sites of Special Scientific Interest (SSSI); Greenham Common Women's Peace Camp has been the site of campaigning against nuclear weapons development at Greenham, Burghfield, and Aldermaston since 1981 **industries** race horse industry, agriculture, dairy cattle, pig farming (including local Berkshire pig) **population** (1996) 142,600 **famous people** Francis Baily, John Langley, George Sanger

West Dunbartonshire unitary authority in west central Scotland, created in 1996 from parts of two districts of Strathclyde region.

area 177 sq km/68 sq mi **towns** Dumbarton (administrative headquarters), Clydebank, Alexandria **physical** Leven valley and coastal land of Firth of Clyde rise toward the upland plateau of the Kilpatrick Hills **features** Dumbarton Castle **industries** whisky distilling, light manufacturing **agriculture** sheep; not significant **population** (1996) 97,800 **history** industrial area of west central Scotland, targeted by Germans and bombed in World War II; heart of ancient kingdom of Strathclyde

Related Web site: Welcome to West Dunbartonshire Council's Web Site http://www.west-dunbarton.gov.uk/

Westerlies prevailing winds from the west that occur in both hemispheres between latitudes of about 35° and 60°. Unlike the ▷trade winds, they are very variable and produce stormy weather.

Western genre of films based loosely on the history of the American ▷West and evolved from the written Western. As a genre, the Western is virtually as old as the cinema. Perhaps the foremost director of Westerns has been John ▷Ford. The genre became less popular in the 1970s, but the popularity of *Young Guns* (1988) led to a 1990s TV series based on the same theme, and *Dances with Wolves* (1990), emphasizing the American Indian perspective, won an Academy Award.

Western Australia state of Australia, bounded on the north and west by the Indian Ocean, on the east by Northern Territory and South Australia, on the south by the Southern Ocean; area

2,525,500 sq km/975,100 sq mi; population (1996) 1,726,100. The capital is ▷Perth. Products include wheat, fresh and dried fruit, beef, dairy products, wool, wine, natural gas, oil, iron, gold, nickel, diamonds, bauxite, cultured and freshwater pearls, timber, and fish. Tourism is important to the state.

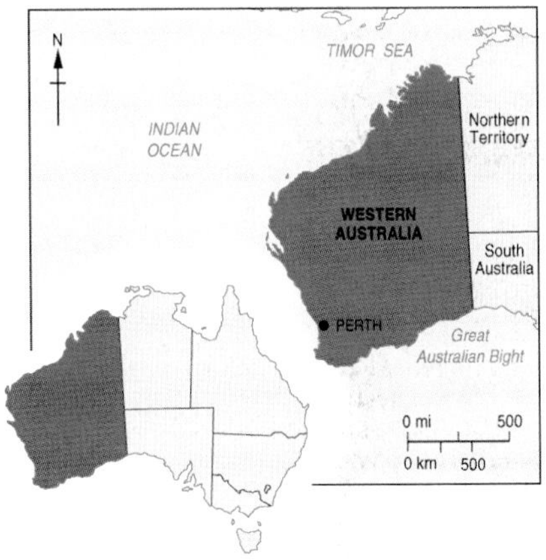

Western Cape province of the Republic of South Africa from 1994, formerly part of Cape Province; area 129,386 sq km/ 49,956 sq mi; population (1995 est) 3,721,200. The capital is ▷Cape Town. Industries include copper, oil refining, chemicals, engineering, and tourism. Fruit, wheat, and tobacco are grown, and wine is produced.

Western European Union (WEU) organization established in 1955 as a consultative forum for military issues among the Western European governments. In 2001 its members were Belgium, France, the Netherlands, Italy, Luxembourg, the UK, Germany, Spain and Portugal (from 1990), and Greece (from 1995). The Czech Republic, Hungary, Iceland, Norway, Poland, and Turkey were associate members.

Western Front battle zone in World War I between Germany and its enemies France and Britain, extending as lines of trenches from Nieuport on the Belgian coast through Ypres, Arras, Albert, Soissons, and Rheims to Verdun, constructed by both Germany and the Allies.

For over three years neither side advanced far from their defensive positions. During the period of trench warfare there were a number of significant changes. Poison gas was used by Germany at Ypres, Belgium in April 1915 and tanks were employed by Britain on the River Somme in September 1916. A German offensive in the spring of 1918 enabled its troops to reach the Marne River. However, the entry of the USA into the war in 1917 tipped the balance on the Western Front decisively in favour of the Allies. With the boost of hundreds of thousands of new troops and the increasingly fragile situation in Germany, the Allies were able to launch fresh attacks. By summer the Allies were advancing all along the front and the Germans were driven back into Belgium.

Life on the Western Front for a World War I soldier was dominated by the trenches, where conditions were water-logged and squalid. Warfare was marked by long periods of tension and inactivity punctuated by mass offensives that wreaked death and destruction on a horrifying scale but produced little result for either side.

Western Isles island administrative unitary authority area in Scotland, also known as the Outer Hebrides, including the major islands of Lewis, Harris, North and South Uist, Benbecula, and Barra.

area 3,057 sq km/1,180 sq mi **towns** Stornoway on Lewis (administrative headquarters), Castlebay, Lochboisdale, Lochmaddy, Tarbert **physical** open to the Atlantic Ocean on the west and the stormy Minch to the east, the islands are almost treeless and have extensive peat bogs. There are areas of hills and mountains on all the islands. The only fertile land is the sandy Machair on the west coast. The islands are mainly composed of the oldest rock in Britain, the Lewisian gneiss. Lewis is divided from the mainland by the Minch channel. The islands south of Lewis are divided from the Inner Hebrides by the Little Minch and the Sea of the Hebrides; uninhabited islands include St Kilda and Rockall. Harris and Lewis are often assumed to be two islands, but are linked by a narrow neck of land. **features** Callanish monolithic Stone Age circles on Lewis **industries** Harris tweed, tourism **agriculture** sheep, cattle, fishing **population** (1996) 27,800

Related Web site: Comhairle nan Eilean Siar http://www.w-isles.gov.uk/

Western Sahara (formerly **Spanish Sahara**) disputed territory in northwest Africa, bounded to the north by Morocco, to the east and south by Mauritania, and to the west by the Atlantic Ocean; area 266,800 sq km/103,000 sq mi; population (1993 est) 214,000, including indigenous Sawrawis (traditionally nomadic herders). The capital is ▷Laâyoune (Arabic *El Aaiún*). Exports include phosphates and iron ore.

History This Saharan coastal region (1,000 km/625 mi long) was designated a Spanish 'sphere of influence' in 1884 because it lies opposite the Spanish-ruled Canary Islands. On securing its independence in 1956, Morocco laid claim to and invaded this 'Spanish Sahara' territory, but was repulsed. Spanish Sahara became a Spanish province in 1958. Moroccan interest was rekindled from 1965, following the discovery of rich phosphate resources at Boukra, and within Spanish Sahara a pro-independence nationalist movement developed, spearheaded by the Popular Front for the Liberation of Saguia al Hamra and Rio de Oro (Polisario), established in 1973.

Partition After the death of the Spanish ruler General Franco, Spain withdrew and the territory was partitioned between Morocco and Mauritania in 1976. Polisario rejected this partition, declared their own independent Saharan Arab Democratic Republic (SADR), and proceeded to wage a guerrilla war, securing indirect support from Algeria and, later, Libya. By 1979 they had succeeded in their struggle against Mauritania, which withdrew from their southern sector and concluded a peace agreement with Polisario, and in 1982 the SADR was accepted as a full member of the ▷Organization of African Unity.

Defensive wall Morocco, which occupied the Mauritanian-evacuated zone, still retained control over the bulk of the territory, including the key towns and phosphate mines, which it protected with an 'electronic defensive wall' 2,500 km/1,550 mi long and defended by mines, completed in 1987. From the mid-1980s this wall was gradually extended outwards as Libya and Algeria reduced their support for Polisario and drew closer to Morocco. In 1988, Morocco and the Polisario Front agreed to United Nations-sponsored plans for a ceasefire and a referendum in Western Sahara, based on 1974 voting rolls, to decide the territory's future. However, subsequent divisions over the terms of the referendum resulted in continued fighting. The holding of the referendum was planned for the end of 1993, but was subsequently postponed after the breakdown of UN-sponsored peace talks between Morocco and the Polisario in New York; by 1995 £87.5 million had been spent and only 11,000 eligible voters identified. In 1996 Polisario threatened a resumption of fighting if the referendum was not soon held. In June 1998 it was decided to delay the referendum on the territory's future until at least February 1999. Talks were held between Morocco and Polisario in London, England, in June 2000.

Related Web site: Western Sahara Page http://www.sas.upenn.edu/African_Studies/Country_Specific/W_Sahara.html

West Germany see ▷Germany, West.

West Glamorgan (Welsh **Gorllewin Morgannwg**) former county of southwest Wales, 1974–1996, now divided into ▷Neath Port Talbot, and ▷Swansea unitary authorities.

West Indies archipelago of about 1,200 islands, dividing the Atlantic Ocean from the Gulf of Mexico and the Caribbean Sea. The islands are divided into:

Bahamas;

Greater Antilles Cuba, Hispaniola (Haiti, Dominican Republic), Jamaica, and Puerto Rico;

Lesser Antilles Aruba, Netherlands Antilles, Trinidad and Tobago, the Windward Islands (Grenada, Barbados, St Vincent, St Lucia, Martinique, Dominica, Guadeloupe), the Leeward Islands (Montserrat, Antigua, St Kitts and Nevis, Barbuda, Anguilla, St Martin, British and US Virgin Islands), and many smaller islands.

West Indies, Federation of the federal union 1958–62 comprising Antigua, Barbados, Dominica, Grenada, Jamaica, Montserrat, St Kitts and Nevis and Anguilla, St Lucia, St Vincent, and Trinidad and Tobago. This federation came to an end when first Jamaica and then Trinidad and Tobago withdrew.

Westinghouse, George (1846–1914) US inventor and founder of the Westinghouse Corporation in 1886. He patented a powerful air brake for trains in 1869, which allowed trains to run more safely with greater loads at higher speeds. In the 1880s he turned his attention to the generation of electricity. Unlike Thomas ▷Edison, Westinghouse introduced alternating current (AC) into his power stations.

West Irian former name of ▷Irian Jaya, a province of Indonesia.

West Lothian unitary authority in central Scotland, south of the Firth of Forth, which was previously a district within Lothian region (1975–96) and a county until 1974.

area 428 sq km/165 sq mi **towns** Bathgate, Linlithgow, Livingston (administrative headquarters) **physical** low-lying, undulating area through which the River Almond flows; Cairnpapple Hill **features** Linlithgow Palace; prehistoric ritual site at Cairnpapple Hill, near Torpichen **industries** electronics, engineering, coal-mining, food processing **agriculture** productive area of arable farming **population** (1996) 147,900 **history** royal connections with Linlithgow

Westmacott, Richard (1775–1856) English neoclassical sculptor. He studied under Antonio Canova in Rome, and on his return was commissioned to execute a number of monuments to politicians and heroes of the Napoleonic Wars. These include two monuments to Charles Fox, one in in Westminster Abbey and one in Bloomsbury Square, London. His bronze *Achilles* is in Hyde Park, London.

Westman Islands small group of islands off the south coast of Iceland; see ▷Vestmannaeyjar.

Westmeath county of the Republic of Ireland, in the province of Leinster; county town ▷Mullingar; area 1,760 sq km/679 sq mi; population (1996) 63,300. The rivers Brosna, Inny, and Shannon flow through the county, and its principal lakes are loughs Ree (the largest, and an extension of the River Shannon), Ennell, Owel, and Sheelin. The Royal Canal cuts through the county but is now disused. The land is low-lying, about 76 m/249 ft above sea-level, with much pasture. The main agricultural activity is cattle and dairy farming. Limestone is found, and textiles are also important. Fishing for trout is popular. Other principal towns are Athlone and Moate.

West Midlands metropolitan county of central England, created in 1974; in 1986, most of the functions of the former county council were transferred to the metropolitan borough councils.

area 900 sq km/347 sq mi **towns and cities** Birmingham, Coventry, Dudley, Solihull, Walsall, Wolverhampton (all administrative centres for districts of the same name), Oldbury (administrative centre for Sandwell) **industries** aircraft components; chemicals; coal mining; engineering; electrical equipment; glass; machine tools; motor vehicles, including Land Rover at Solihull; motor components **population** (1996) 2,642,500 **famous people** Edward Burne-Jones, Neville Chamberlain, John Curry, Francis Galton, Jerome K Jerome, Philip Larkin, John Marston, Henry Morton, Frank Whittle

Westminster, City of inner borough of central Greater London, on the north bank of the River Thames between Kensington and the City of London. It encompasses Bayswater, Belgravia, Mayfair, Paddington, Pimlico, Soho, St John's Wood, and Westminster.

Westminster Abbey Gothic church in central London, officially the Collegiate Church of St Peter. It was built from 1050 to 1745 and consecrated under Edward the Confessor in 1065. The west towers are by Nicholas ▷Hawksmoor, completed after his death in 1745. Since William I nearly all English monarchs have been crowned in the abbey, and several are buried here. Some 30 scientists, among them Isaac Newton and James Prescott, are interred or commemorated here, and many poets at Poets' Corner. In the centre of the nave is the tomb of an 'Unknown Warrior' of World War I.

WESTMINSTER ABBEY Several English and British monarchs are buried in Westminster Abbey. Nowadays only ashes are allowed; permission has to be obtained from the Dean of Westminster for all burials and monuments. People who have served the Abbey in an official capacity, such as a dean, a canon, an organist, or a Surveyor of the Fabric may be buried here. Eminent Britons from various fields may also be considered. John Masefield was buried in the Abbey in 1967 and the actor Laurence Olivier in 1991.
Image Bank

Westmorland former county in the Lake District, England, part of Cumbria from 1974.

Westphalia independent medieval duchy, incorporated in Prussia by the Congress of Vienna in 1815, and made a province in 1816 with Münster as its capital. Since 1946 it has been part of the German *Land* (region) of ▷North Rhine-Westphalia.

Westphalia, Treaty of agreement in 1648 ending the ▷Thirty Years' War. The peace marked the end of the supremacy of the Holy Roman Empire and the emergence of France as a dominant power. It recognized the sovereignty of the German states, Switzerland, and the Netherlands; Lutherans, Calvinists, and Roman Catholics were given equal rights.

West Point former fort in New York State, on the Hudson River, 80 km/50 mi north of New York City, site of the US Military Academy (commonly referred to as West Point), established 1802. Women were admitted in 1976. West Point has been a military post since 1778.

West Sussex county of southern England, created in 1974, formerly part of Sussex.

> **area** 1,990 sq km/768 sq mi **towns and cities** ▷Chichester (administrative headquarters), Crawley, Horsham, Haywards Heath, Shoreham (port); Bognor Regis, Littlehampton, Worthing (resorts) **physical** the Weald; South Downs; rivers Adur, Arun, and West Rother **features** Arundel and Bramber castles; Chichester cathedral; Goodwood House and racecourse; Petworth House (17th century); Wakehurst Place, where the Royal Botanic Gardens, Kew, have additional grounds; Uppark House (1685–90); the Weald and Downland Open Air Museum at Singleton; Fishbourne villa (important Roman site near Chichester); Selsey (reputed landing place of the South Saxons in 447); Gatwick Airport **agriculture** cereals (wheat and barley); fruit; market gardening (mainly on the coastal plain); dairy produce; forestry **industries** electronics; light engineering **population** (1996) 737,300 **famous people** Richard Cobden, William Collins, Percy Bysshe Shelley

West Virginia state in eastern central USA. It is nicknamed the Mountain State. West Virginia was admitted to the Union in 1863 as the 35th US state. It is bordered to the south and east by Virginia, to the north by Ohio, Pennsylvania, and Maryland, and to the west by Ohio and Kentucky. West Virginia is composed essentially of those Virginia counties that, unsympathetic to the plantation South, refused to join Virginia in its 1861 secession from the Union.

> **population** (1995) 1,828,100 **area** 62,900 sq km/24,279 sq mi **capital** Charleston **towns and cities** Huntington, Wheeling, Parkersburg **industries and products** apples, maize, poultry, dairy and meat products, coal, natural gas, oil, chemicals, synthetic fibres, plastics, steel, glass, pottery, tourism
> **Related Web site: West Virginia** http://wvweb.com/

Westwood, Vivienne (1941–) English fashion designer of international renown. She first attracted attention in the mid-1970s as co-owner of a shop with the rock-music entrepreneur Malcolm McLaren (1946–), which became a focus for the punk movement in London. Early in the 1980s her 'Pirate' and 'New Romantics' looks gained her international recognition.

Westwood's dramatic clothes continue to have a wide influence on the public and other designers. She has designed clothes and accessories for mail-order companies and young people's high-street fashion stores.

West Yorkshire metropolitan county of northeast England, created in 1974; in 1986, most of the functions of the former county council were transferred to the metropolitan borough councils.

> **area** 2,040 sq km/787 sq mi **towns and cities** Bradford, Leeds, Wakefield (administrative centres for districts of the same name), Halifax (administrative centre of Calderdale district), Huddersfield (administrative centre of Kirklees district) **physical** Ilkley Moor, Haworth Moor; high Pennine moorlands in the west, Vale of York to the east; rivers Aire, Calder, Colne, Wharfe **features** Haworth Parsonage; part of the Peak District National Park; British Library, Boston Spa (scientific, technical, and business documents) **industries** woollen textiles, financial services; coal mining is in decline **population** (1996) 2,109,300 **famous people** the Brontës, David Hockney, Henry Moore, J B Priestley

wet in UK politics, a derogatory term used to describe a moderate or left-wing supporter of the Conservative Party, especially those who opposed the monetary or other hardline policies of its former leader Margaret Thatcher.

weta flightless insect *Deinacrida rugosa*, 8.5 cm/3.5 in long, resembling a large grasshopper, found on offshore islands of New Zealand.

wetland permanently wet land area or habitat. Wetlands include areas of ▷marsh, fen, ▷bog, flood plain, and shallow coastal areas. Wetlands are extremely fertile. They provide warm, sheltered waters for fisheries, lush vegetation for grazing livestock, and an abundance of wildlife. Estuaries and seaweed beds are more than 16 times as productive as the open ocean.

The term is often more specifically applied to a naturally flooding area that is managed for agriculture or wildlife. A water meadow, where a river is expected to flood grazing land at least once a year thereby replenishing the soil, is a traditional example.

In the UK, the Royal Society for the Protection of Birds (RSPB) manages 2,800 hectares/7,000 acres of wetland, using sluice gates and flood-control devices to produce sanctuaries for wading birds and wild flowers.

wetted perimeter the length of that part of a river's cross-section that is in contact with the water. The wetted perimeter is used to calculate a river's hydraulic radius, a measure of its channel efficiency.

Wexford county of the Republic of Ireland, in the province of Leinster; county town ▷Wexford; area 2,350 sq km/907 sq mi; population (1996) 104,400. Wexford is one of the most intensively cultivated areas in Ireland. The main crops are wheat, barley, beet, and potatoes. Fishing is important, the main fishing port being Kilmore Quay in the south; sheep and cattle rearing are also significant, as is dairy farming. Industries include agricultural machinery and food processing. Wexford was the first part of Ireland to be colonized from England; Normans arrived in 1169. The John F Kennedy Arboretum is one of the most popular visitor attractions in the county.

Wexford seaport and county town of ▷Wexford, Republic of Ireland, on the estuary of the River Slaney; population (1996) 16,000. Industries include food processing and the manufacture of textiles, cheese, agricultural machinery, furniture, and motor vehicles. There is an annual international opera festival in October. Wexford was founded in the 9th century by Danes; it was taken by the Anglo-Normans in 1169, and besieged and devastated by Oliver Cromwell in 1649. In the Rebellion of 1798 Wexford was briefly held by Irish insurgents.

Weyden, Rogier van der (c. 1399–1464) Netherlandish artist. He was the official painter to the city of Brussels from 1436. He produced portraits and religious paintings like *The Last Judgement* (c. 1450; Hôtel-Dieu, Beaune) in a refined and elegant realist style.

whale any marine mammal of the order Cetacea. The only mammals to have adapted to living entirely in water, they have front limbs modified into flippers and no externally visible traces of hind limbs. They have horizontal tail flukes. When they surface to breathe, the hot air they breathe out condenses to form a 'spout' through the blowhole (single or double nostrils) in the top of the head. Whales are intelligent and have a complex communication system, known as 'songs'. They occur in all seas of the world.

The order is divided into two groups: the toothed whales (Odontoceti) and the baleen whales (Mysticeti). Toothed whales are predators, feeding on fish and squid. They include ▷dolphins and ▷porpoises, along with large forms such as sperm whales. The largest whales are the baleen whales, with plates of modified mucous membrane called baleen (whalebone) in the mouth; these strain the food, mainly microscopic plankton, from the water. Baleen whales include the finback and right whales, and the blue whale, the largest animal that has ever lived, of length up to 30 m/100 ft.

Whales have been hunted for hundreds of years (see ▷whaling); today they are close to extinction. Of the 11 great whale species, 7 were listed as either endangered or vulnerable in 1996. Whale-watching, as an economic alternative to whaling, generated US$121 million worldwide in 1994.

> **Related Web site: Whale Songs** http://whales.ot.com

WHALE A humpback whale breaching (leaping clear) out of the water. The humpback whale (*Megaptera novaeangliae*), an endangered species, is found principally in the North Atlantic and North Pacific Oceans. *Image Bank*

whaling the hunting of whales. Whales have been killed by humans since at least the middle ages. There were hundreds of thousands of whales at the beginning of the 20th century, but the invention of the harpoon in 1870 and improvements in ships and mechanization have led to the near-extinction of several species of whale. Commercial whaling was largely discontinued in 1986, although Norway and Japan have continued commercial whaling.

Traditional whaling areas include the coasts of Greenland and Newfoundland, but the Antarctic, in the summer months, supplies the bulk of the catch.

Practically the whole of the animal can be utilized in one form or another: whales are killed for whale oil (made from the thick layer of fat under the skin called 'blubber'), which is used as a lubricant, or for making soap, candles, and margarine; for the large reserve of oil in the head of the sperm whale, used in the leather industry; and for **ambergris**, a waxlike substance from the intestines of the sperm whale, used in making perfumes. Whalebone was used by corset manufacturers and in the brush trade; there are now synthetic substitutes for all these products. Whales have also been killed for use in petfood manufacture in the USA and Europe, and as a food in Japan. The flesh and ground bones are used as soil fertilizers.

WHALING An early 19th-century engraving by Le Breton showing the hazards of deep-sea whaling in the Southern Ocean. Before the invention of the harpoon gun, whaling was an extremely perilous occupation. *The Art Archive/Naval Museum Genoa/Dagli Orti*

Wharton, Edith Newbold

(1862–1937) Born Edith Newbold Jones. US novelist. Her work, known for its subtlety and form and influenced by her friend Henry ▷James, was mostly set in New York society. It includes *The House of Mirth* (1905), which made her reputation; the grim, uncharacteristic novel of New England *Ethan Frome* (1911); *The Custom of the Country* (1913); and *The Age of Innocence* (1920; Pulitzer prize), which was made into a film in 1993.

wheat cereal plant derived from the wild *Triticum*, a grass native to the Middle East. It is the chief cereal used in breadmaking and is widely cultivated in temperate climates suited to its growth. Wheat is killed by frost, and damp makes the grains soft, so warm, dry regions produce the most valuable grain.

WHEAT Wheat is one of the world's most important cereal crops, with millions of tons being grown each year. *Premaphotos Wildlife*

wheatear small (15 cm/6 in long) migratory bird *Oenanthe oenanthe* of the family Muscicapidae, order Passeriformes (which includes thrushes). Wheatears are found throughout the Old World and also breed in far northern parts of North America. The plumage is light grey above and white below with a buff tinge on the breast, a black face-patch, and black and white wings and tail. In flight a white patch on the lower back and tail is conspicuous. The wheatear's food consists chiefly of insects.

Wheatley, Dennis Yates (1897–1977) English thriller and adventure novelist. His works include a series dealing with black magic and occultism, but he also wrote crime novels in which the reader was invited to play the detective, as in *Murder off Miami* (1936), with real clues such as ticket stubs.

Wheatstone, Charles (1802–1875) English physicist and inventor. With William Cooke, he patented a railway telegraph in 1837, and, developing an idea of Samuel Christie (1784–1865), devised the **Wheatstone bridge**, an electrical network for measuring resistance. He also invented the concertina.

whelk any of various families of large marine snails with a thick spiral shell, especially the family Buccinidae. Whelks are scavengers, and also eat other shellfish. The largest grow to 40 cm/16 in long. Tropical species, such as the conches, can be very colourful.

WHELK Polymorphism in whelks. There are a variety of shell colours and patterns in any whelk population. *Dr Rod Preston-Mafham/Premaphotos Wildlife*

Whig Party in the UK, predecessor of the Liberal Party. The name was first used of rebel ▷Covenanters and then of those who wished to exclude James II from the English succession (as a Roman Catholic). They were in power continuously 1714–60 and pressed

for industrial and commercial development, a vigorous foreign policy, and religious toleration. During the French Revolution, the Whigs demanded parliamentary reform in Britain, and from the passing of the Reform Bill in 1832 became known as Liberals.

Whig Party in the USA, political party opposed to the autocratic presidency of Andrew ▷Jackson from 1834. The Whig presidents were W H Harrison, Taylor, and Fillmore. The party diverged over the issue of slavery: the Northern Whigs joined the Republican party and the Southern or 'Cotton' Whigs joined the Democrats. The title was taken from the British Whig Party which supported Parliament against the king. During the American Revolution, colonial patriots described themselves as Whigs, while those remaining loyal to Britain were known as Tories.

whimbrel wading bird *Numenius phaeopus*, order Charadriiformes, with a medium-sized down-curved bill, streaked brown plumage, and striped head. About 40 cm/1.3 ft long, it breeds in the Arctic, and winters in Africa, southern North America, South America, and South Asia. It is related to the ▷curlew.

whip (the whipper-in of hounds at a foxhunt) in UK politics, the member of Parliament who ensures the presence of colleagues in the party when there is to be a vote in Parliament at the end of a debate. The written appeal sent by the whips to MPs is also called a whip; this letter is underlined once, twice, or three times to indicate its importance. A **three-line whip** is the most urgent, and every MP is expected to attend and vote with their party. An MP who fails to attend may be temporarily suspended from the party, a penalty known as 'having the whip withdrawn'.

whiplash injury damage to the neck vertebrae and their attachments caused by a sudden backward jerk of the head and neck. It is most often seen in vehicle occupants as a result of the rapid deceleration experienced in a crash.

whippet breed of dog resembling a small greyhound. It grows to 56 cm/22 in at the shoulder, and 9 kg/20 lb in weight.

The whippet was developed by northern English coalminers for racing. It was probably produced by crossing a terrier and a greyhound.

Related Web site: Whippets: Born to Run http://www.sonic.net/ ~whippet

Whipple, George Hoyt (1878–1976) US physiologist who was awarded a Nobel Prize for Physiology or Medicine in 1934 for work on the treatment of pernicious anaemia by increasing the amount of liver in the diet. His research interest concerned the formation of haemoglobin in the blood. He showed that anaemic dogs, kept under restricted diets, responded well to a liver regime, and that their haemoglobin quickly regenerated. This work led to a cure for pernicious anaemia. He shared the prize with George Minot and William Murphy.

whippoorwill North American ▷nightjar *Caprimulgus vociferus*, order Caprimulgiformes, so called from its cry during the nights of its breeding season. It is about 25 cm/10 in long, mottled tawny brown in colour, with a white collar on the throat, and long, stiff bristles at the base of the bill.

whip snake (or **coachwhip**) any of the various species of nonpoisonous slender-bodied tree-dwelling snakes of the New

WHIP SNAKE Long-nosed whip snake *Ahaetulla prasinus* searching for its insect prey in the rainforest of Sulawesi, Indonesia. *Ken Preston-Mafham/Premaphotos Wildlife*

World genus *Masticophis*, family Colubridae. They are closely allied to members of the genus *Coluber* of southwestern North America, Eurasia, Australasia, and North Africa, some of which are called whip snakes in the Old World, but racers in North America.

Whip snakes grow to about 1.5 m/5 ft in length, move very quickly, and are partially tree-dwelling. They feed on rodents, small birds, lizards, sucker frogs, and insects. All lay eggs.

The European **western whip snake** *Coluber viridiflavus* is nonvenomous and lives in France and Italy. It grows to a maximum 2 m/6 ft, is fast-moving, climbing as well as sliding along the ground, and feeds on lizards, mammals, and some other snakes.

whirligig beetle aquatic steel-black beetle with an oval, flattened body. The second and third pairs of legs are exceptionally short and broad, and are used for paddling in the water. About 400 species have been recorded. The whirligig beetle is in the family Gyrinidae, order Coleoptera, class Insecta, phylum Arthropoda.

whirling disease parasitic disease of trout. The parasite *Myxobolus cerebralis* spends part of its life cycle in tubifex worms, before moving to trout where it consumes the cartilage causing eventual death. Infected fish start to swim in circles after their spines have been destroyed, hence the name.

whirlwind rapidly rotating column of air, often synonymous with a ▷tornado. On a smaller scale it produces the dust-devils seen in deserts.

whist card game for four, predecessor of ▷bridge, in which the partners try to win a majority of the 13 tricks (the highest card played being the winner of the trick).

Whistler, James Abbott McNeill (1834–1903) US painter and etcher. Active in London from 1859, he was a leading figure in the ▷Aesthetic Movement. Influenced by Japanese prints, he painted riverscapes and portraits that show subtle composition and colour harmonies, for example *Arrangement in Grey and Black: Portrait of the Painter's Mother* (1871; Musée d'Orsay, Paris).

Whistler, Rex (Reginald John) (1905–1944) English artist, illustrator, and stage designer. He painted fanciful murals, for example *In Pursuit of Rare Meats* (1926–27) in the restaurant of the Tate Gallery, London. His illustrations include editions of *Gulliver's Travels* and Hans Andersen's *Fairy Tales*.

Whitbread Literary Award annual prize of £23,000 open to writers in the UK and Ireland. Nominations are in four categories: novel, first novel, autobiography/biography, and poetry, each receiving £2,000. The overall winner receives a further £21,000. The award, which is administered by the Booksellers Association, was founded in 1971 by Whitbread, a brewery.

The Whitbread Children's Book of the Year is a separate award worth £10,000.

Whitby port and resort in North Yorkshire, northern England, on the North Sea coast, at the mouth of the River Esk, 32 km/20 mi northwest of Scarborough; population (1991) 13,800. Industries include tourism, boat building, fishing (particularly herring), and plastics. There are remains of a 13th-century abbey. Captain James Cook served his apprenticeship in Whitby and he sailed from here on his voyage to the Pacific Ocean in 1768. Bram Stoker's *Dracula* (1897) was set here.

Whitby, Synod of council summoned by King Oswy of Northumbria in 664, which decided to adopt the Roman rather than the Celtic form of Christianity for Britain.

White term denoting a counter-revolutionary, especially a member of the anticommunist forces in the Russian Civil War of 1918 to 1821. In this conflict, the Whites were led by former tsarist officers and supported by troops from foreign countries, but were eventually defeated by the Bolshevik ▷Red Army. They were named after the royalist opponents of the French Revolution, who took the white lily of the French Bourbon monarchy as their emblem.

White, E(lwyn) B(rooks) (1899–1985) US writer. He was long associated with the *New Yorker* magazine and renowned for his satire, such as *Is Sex Necessary?* (1929; with the humorist James Thurber).

White, Gilbert (1720–1793) English naturalist and cleric. He was the author of *The Natural History and Antiquities of Selborne* (1789), which records the flora and fauna of an area of Hampshire.

White, Patrick Victor Martindale (1912–1990) Australian writer. He did more than any other to put Australian literature on the international map. His partly allegorical novels explore the lives of early settlers in Australia and often deal with misfits or inarticulate people. They include *The Aunt's Story* (1948), written during his voyage back to Australia, *The Tree of Man* (1955), *Voss*

(1957), based on the ill-fated 19th-century explorer Ludwig Leichhardt, and *Riders in the Chariot* (1961), exploring suburban life. He was awarded the Nobel Prize for Literature in 1973. White became a fervent republican after the dismissal of the Gough ▷Whitlam government in 1975, returning his Order of Australia in 1976, and supported conservation causes in his later years.

White, a member of an established Australian pastoralist family, was born in London and educated in Australia and England. After graduating from Cambridge he lived and wrote in London and in 1940 joined the RAF as an intelligence officer. In the 1940s he returned to settle in Australia. *The Tree of Man* follows the lives of a pioneering family from the 1880s to the 1930s. Among his other novels are *The Vivisector* (1970), *The Eye of the Storm* (1973), *The Twyborn Affair* (1979), and his last work, *Memoirs of Many in One* (1986). As well as a novelist, he was a playwright, short-story writer, and poet. He used the Nobel prize money to establish a literary award for Australian writers deserving greater recognition. His autobiography, *Flaws in the Glass*, appeared in 1981.

White Australia Policy Australian government policy of immigration restriction, mainly aimed at non-Europeans, which began in the 1850s in an attempt to limit the number of Chinese entering the Australian goldfields and was official until 1945.

whitebait any of the fry (young) of various silvery fishes, especially ▷herring. It is also the name for a Pacific smelt *Osmerus mordax*.

whitebeam tree native to southern Europe, usually found growing on chalk or limestone. It can reach 20 m/60 ft in height. It takes its name from the dense coat of short white hairs on the underside of the leaves. (Genus *Sorbus aria*, family Rosaceae.)

white blood cell (or **leucocyte**) one of a number of different cells that play a part in the body's defences and give immunity against disease. Some (neutrophils and ▷macrophages) engulf invading micro-organisms, others kill infected cells, while ▷lymphocytes produce more specific immune responses. White blood cells are colourless, with clear or granulated cytoplasm, and are capable of independent amoeboid movement. They occur in the blood, ▷lymph, and elsewhere in the body's tissues.

Unlike mammalian red blood cells, they possess a nucleus. Human blood contains about 11,000 leucocytes to the cubic millimetre – about one to every 500 red cells.

White blood cell numbers may be reduced (leucopenia) by starvation, pernicious anaemia, and certain infections, such as typhoid and malaria. An increase in their numbers (leucocytosis) is a reaction to normal events such as digestion, exertion, and pregnancy, and to abnormal ones such as loss of blood, cancer, and most infections.

white-collar worker non-manual employee, such as an office worker or manager. With more mechanized production methods, the distinction between white- and blue-collar (manual) workers is becoming increasingly blurred.

white dwarf small, hot ▷star, the last stage in the life of a star such as the Sun. White dwarfs make up 10% of the stars in the Galaxy; most have a mass 60% of that of the Sun, but only 1% of the Sun's diameter, similar in size to the Earth. Most have surface temperatures of 8,000°C/14,400°F or more, hotter than the Sun. Yet, being so small, their overall luminosities may be less than 1% of that of the Sun. The Milky Way contains an estimated 50 billion white dwarfs.

White dwarfs consist of degenerate matter in which gravity has packed the protons and electrons together as tightly as is physically possible, so that a spoonful of it weighs several tonnes. White dwarfs are thought to be the shrunken remains of stars that have exhausted their internal energy supplies. They slowly cool and fade over billions of years.

Patrick White
Inspiration descends only in flashes, to clothe circumstances; it is not stored up in a barrel, like salt herrings, to be doled out.
Voss

whitefish any of various freshwater fishes, genera *Coregonus* and *Prosopium*, of the salmon family, found in lakes and rivers of North America and Eurasia. They include the **whitefish** *C. clupeaformis* and **cisco** *C. artedi.*

whitefly tiny four-winged insect related to aphids and scale insects. The adults barely exceed a length of 3 mm/0.12 in; their wings are dusted with a powdery white wax which they secrete. In temperate countries they may be found in glasshouses, where they are pests of plants, such as cucumber and tomato. They are widely distributed in the tropics, where they attack citrus trees. They injure the plant by feeding on the sap and excreting honeydew, which encourages sooty black mould to grow. Whiteflies are in family Aleyrodidae, order Hemiptera, class Insecta, phylum Arthropoda.

Whitehorse capital of ▷Yukon Territory, Canada, on the Yukon River; population (1996) 21,800. Situated at the junction of the Alaska and Klondike Highways, it is the centre of the region's mining and forestry industries, and an important transport focus, with air links to major Canadian and US cities, and a rail link to Skagway, Alaska. It is also the regional headquarters of the ▷Royal Canadian Mounted Police. Whitehorse was founded by prospectors during the Klondike gold rush 1897–98, when it occupied an important position at the head of navigation on the Yukon. It replaced Dawson as capital in 1953.

WHITE HOUSE The White House, Washington, DC. President George Washington, together with the city planner Pierre L'Enfant, chose the site for the new home of the federal government, and construction began in 1792. The first residents were President John Adams and his wife, in 1800. The White House is the only private residence of a head of state that is open to the public, free of charge.
Image Bank

White House official residence of the president of the USA, in Washington, DC. It is a plain three-storeyed edifice of grey sandstone, built in Italian Renaissance style 1792–99 to the designs of Philadelphia architect James Hoban, who also restored the house after it was burned by the British in 1814; it was then painted white to hide the scorches.

Whitehouse, Mary (1910–2001) British media activist. A founder of the National Viewers' and Listeners' Association, she campaigned to censor radio and television for their treatment of sex and violence.

white knight in business, a company invited by the target of a takeover bid to make a rival bid. The company invited to bid is usually one that is already on good terms with the target company.

whiteout 'fog' of grains of dry snow caused by strong winds in temperatures of between −18°C/0°F and −1°C/30°F. The uniform whiteness of the ground and air causes disorientation in humans.

White Paper in the UK and some other countries, an official document that expresses government policy on an issue. It is usually preparatory to the introduction of a parliamentary bill (a proposed act of Parliament). Its name derives from its having fewer pages than a government blue book, and therefore needing no blue paper cover.

White Russia English translation of ▷Belarus.

White Sea (Russian **Beloye More**) gulf of the Arctic Ocean on the northwest coast of Russia, on which the port of Archangel stands; area 90,000 sq km/34,750 sq mi; average depth 60 m/200 ft, maximum depth 330 m/1,082 ft. There is a warship construction base, including nuclear submarines, at Severodvinsk. The North Dvina, Mezen, and Onega rivers flow into it, and there are canal links with the Baltic, Black, and Caspian seas. In winter the bays are often ice-bound, with drifting ice offshore.

white spirit colourless liquid derived from petrol; it is used as a solvent and in paints and varnishes.

White terror general term used by socialists and Marxists to describe a right-wing counterrevolution: for example, the attempts by the Chinese Guomindang to massacre the communists 1927–31; see ▷White.

whitethroat any of several Old World warblers of the genus *Sylvia* in the family Muscicapidae, order Passeriformes. They are found in scrub, hedges, and wood clearings of Eurasia in summer, migrating to Africa in winter. They are about 14 cm/5.5 in long.

The **whitethroat** *S. communis* has reddish-brown wings; the male has a grey head, white throat, and pinkish breast, and performs an acrobatic aerial display during courtship. The **lesser whitethroat** *S. curruca* is a smaller, shyer bird and greyer in colour.

whiting predatory fish *Merlangius merlangus* common in shallow sandy northern European waters. It grows to 70 cm/2.3 ft.

Whitlam, (Edward) Gough (1916–) Australian politician, leader of the Labor Party 1967–78 and prime minister 1972–75. He ended conscription and Australia's military commitment in Vietnam, introduced the Medibank national health service, abolished university fees, expanded Aboriginal rights, attempted redistribution of wealth, raised loans to increase national ownership of industry and resources, and recognized mainland China.

Whitman, Walt(er) (1819–1892) US poet. He published *Leaves of Grass* (1855), which contains the symbolic 'Song of Myself'. It used unconventional free verse (with no rhyme or regular rhythm) and scandalized the public by its frank celebration of sexuality. His poems were often set by composers such as Hindemith, Vaughan Williams, Henze, and Delius.

Born at West Hill (Huntington, Long Island), New York, as a young man Whitman worked as a printer, teacher, and journalist. In 1865 he published *Drum-Taps*, a volume inspired by his work as an army nurse during the Civil War. *Democratic Vistas* (1871) is a collection of his prose pieces. He also wrote an elegy for Abraham Lincoln, 'When Lilacs Last in the Dooryard Bloom'd'. He preached a particularly American vision of individual freedom and human brotherhood. Such poets as Ezra Pound, Wallace Stevens, and Allen Ginsberg show his influence in their work.

Walt Whitman
I celebrate myself, and sing myself.
'Song of Myself'

Whitney, Eli (1765–1825) US inventor who in 1794 patented the cotton gin, a device for separating cotton fibre from its seeds. Also a manufacturer of firearms, he created a standardization system that was the precursor of the assembly line.

Whit Sunday Christian church festival held seven weeks after Easter, commemorating the descent of the Holy Spirit on the Apostles. The name is probably derived from the white garments worn by candidates for baptism at the festival. Whit Sunday corresponds to the Jewish festival of Shavuot (Pentecost).

Whittington, Dick (Richard) (*c.* 1358–1423) English cloth merchant who was mayor of London 1397–98, 1406–07, and 1419–20. According to legend, he came to London as a poor boy with his cat when he heard that the streets were paved with gold and silver. His cat first appears in a play about the story in 1605.

Whittle, Frank (1907–1996) English engineer. He patented the basic design for the turbojet engine in 1930. In the Royal Air Force he worked on jet propulsion 1937–46. In May 1941 the Gloster E 28/39 aircraft first flew with the Whittle jet engine. Both the German (first operational jet planes) and the US jet aircraft were built using his principles. He was knighted in 1948.

WHO acronym for ▷World Health Organization, an agency of the United Nations established to prevent the spread of diseases.

Who, the English rock group, formed in 1964, with a hard, aggressive sound, high harmonies, and a propensity for destroying their instruments on stage. Their albums include *Tommy* (1969), *Who's Next* (1971), and *Quadraphenia* (1973).

wholesale the business of selling merchandise to anyone other than the final customer. Most manufacturers or producers sell in bulk to a wholesale organization which distributes the smaller quantities required by retail outlets.

whole-tone scale in music, a scale consisting of six whole tones per octave. There are only two possible variants: the scale including the notes C–D–E–F sharp–G sharp–A sharp, and the scale including the notes D flat–E flat–F–G–A–B. In Western music the whole-tone scale became popular with Impressionist composers, including Debussy, partly because having no semitones or perfect intervals within the scale, it has no sense of tonic.

whooping cough (or **pertussis**) acute infectious disease, seen mainly in children, caused by colonization of the air passages by the bacterium *Bordetella pertussis*. There may be catarrh, mild fever, and loss of appetite, but the main symptom is violent coughing, associated with the sharp intake of breath that is the characteristic 'whoop', and often followed by vomiting and severe nose bleeds. The cough may persist for weeks.

Although debilitating, the disease is seldom serious in older children, but infants are at risk both from the illness itself and from susceptibility to other conditions, such as ▷pneumonia. During 1995, there were 355,000 deaths from whooping cough. Immunization lessens the incidence and severity of the disease: the whole cell (or 'killed') vaccine has been replaced by an acellular version, which is made up from the bacteria *Bordetella pertussis*, and has fewer side effects than its predecessor.

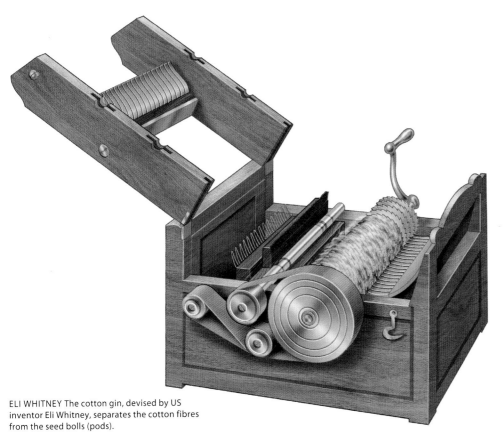

ELI WHITNEY The cotton gin, devised by US inventor Eli Whitney, separates the cotton fibres from the seed bolls (pods).

A new strain of the bacterium *Bordetella pertussis*, which had first appeared in about 1985, spread across Europe in 1997. It arose in the Netherlands and by October there were 2,785 cases there compared with 321 in 1995.

whortleberry a form of ▷bilberry.

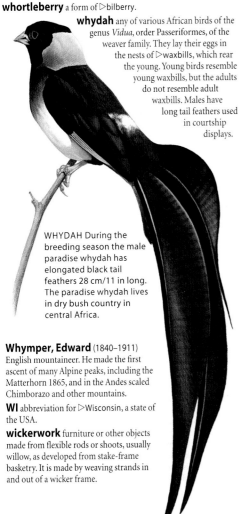

whydah any of various African birds of the genus *Vidua*, order Passeriformes, of the weaver family. They lay their eggs in the nests of ▷waxbills, which rear the young. Young birds resemble young waxbills, but the adults do not resemble adult waxbills. Males have long tail feathers used in courtship displays.

WHYDAH During the breeding season the male paradise whydah has elongated black tail feathers 28 cm/11 in long. The paradise whydah lives in dry bush country in central Africa.

Whymper, Edward (1840–1911) English mountaineer. He made the first ascent of many Alpine peaks, including the Matterhorn 1865, and in the Andes scaled Chimborazo and other mountains.

WI abbreviation for ▷Wisconsin, a state of the USA.

wickerwork furniture or other objects made from flexible rods or shoots, usually willow, as developed from stake-frame basketry. It is made by weaving strands in and out of a wicker frame.

Wicklow county of the Republic of Ireland, in the province of Leinster; county town ▷Wicklow; area 2,030 sq km/784 sq mi; population (1996) 102,700. It includes the **Wicklow Mountains**, the rivers Slaney, Avoca, Vartry, and Liffey, and the coastal resort of Bray. Other towns include Arklow, Greystones, and Baltinglass. The village of Shillelagh gave its name to rough cudgels of oak or blackthorn made there. Agriculture is important; there is livestock rearing (in particular a special breed of mountain sheep), and dairy farming. Wheat and oats are grown, and seed potatoes and bulbs are produced. Granite is mined at Aughrim and Ballyknockan.

Related Web site: Welcome to County Wicklow – The Garden of Ireland http://www.wicklow.ie/

Wicklow (Danish **Wykinglo**) resort and county town of County ▷Wicklow, Republic of Ireland, on the River Vartry, 50 km/31 mi southeast of Dublin; population (1996) 6,400.

wide-angle lens photographic lens of shorter focal length than normal, taking in a wider angle of view.

wide area network (**WAN**) in computing, a ▷network that connects computers distributed over a wide geographical area. 'Dumb' terminals or microcomputers act as workstations, which connect to remote systems via a local host computer.

Widmark, Richard (1914–) US actor. He made his film debut in *Kiss of Death* (1947) as a psychopath. He subsequently appeared in a variety of roles, including *The Alamo* (1960), *Madigan* (1968), and *Coma* (1978).

Wien German name for ▷Vienna, the capital of Austria.

Wiener, Norbert (1894–1964) US mathematician, credited with the establishment of the science of cybernetics in his book *Cybernetics* (1948). In mathematics, he laid the foundation of the study of stochastic processes (those dependent on random events), particularly ▷Brownian motion.

Wiener Werkstätte (German **Vienna Workshops**) group of artisans and artists, founded in Vienna in 1903 by Josef Hoffmann and Kolo Moser, who were both members of the Vienna ▷Sezession. They designed objects, ranging from furniture and jewellery to metal and books, in a rectilinear art nouveau style influenced by Charles Rennie ▷Mackintosh. The workshop, financed by Fritz Wärndorfer, closed in 1932.

Wien's displacement law in physics, a law of radiation stating that the wavelength carrying the maximum energy is inversely proportional to the absolute temperature of a black body:

the hotter a body is, the shorter the wavelength. It has the form $\lambda_{max}T$ = constant, where λ_{max} is the wavelength of maximum intensity and T is the temperature. The law is named after German physicist Wilhelm Wien.

Wiesel, Elie(zer) (1928–) US academic and human-rights campaigner, born in Romania. He was held in Buchenwald concentration camp during World War II, and assiduously documented wartime atrocities against the Jews in an effort to alert the world to the dangers of racism and violence. His novel *La Nuit/Night* (1956) was based on his experiences in the camps. A leading figure in human-rights campaigns, he was awarded the Nobel Prize for Peace in 1986 for his work as a writer and human-rights activist.

wigeon either of two species of dabbling duck of genus *Anas*, order Anseriformes. The **American wigeon** *A. americana*, about 48 cm/19 in long, is found along both coasts in winter and breeds inland. Males have a white-capped head and a green eye stripe.

Wight, Isle of island and unitary authority of southern England.

area area 380 sq km/147 sq mi **towns** ▷Newport (the administrative headquarters); Ryde, Sandown, Shanklin, Ventnor (all resorts) **physical** chalk cliffs and downs, and deep ravines, known locally as 'chines'; the highest point is St Boniface Down (240 m/787 ft); the Needles, a group of pointed chalk rocks up to 30 m/100 ft high in the sea to the west; the Solent, the sea channel between Hampshire and the island **features** Benedictine monastery at Quarr Abbey; Parkhurst Prison, just outside Newport; Cowes, venue of Regatta Week and headquarters of the Royal Yacht Squadron; Osborne House, built for Queen Victoria in 1845 **agriculture** fruit and vegetables grown in south of island **industries** aircraft components, electronics, marine engineering, plastics, boatbuilding, sawmills, tourism **population** (1996) 130,000 **famous people** Thomas Arnold, Robert Hooke, Alfred Tennyson **history** the Isle of Wight was called **Vectis** ('separate division') by the Romans, who conquered it in AD 43; there are Roman villas at Newport and Brading. Charles I was imprisoned (1647–48) in Carisbrooke Castle, now ruined

Wilberforce, William (1759–1833) English reformer. He was instrumental in abolishing ▷slavery in the British Empire. He entered Parliament in 1780; in 1807 his bill banning the trade in slaves from the West Indies was passed, and in 1833, largely through his efforts, slavery was eradicated throughout the empire. He died shortly before the Slavery Abolition Act was passed.

Wilberforce was a member of a humanitarian group called the Clapham Sect, which exercised considerable influence on public policy, being closely identified with Sunday schools, and the British and Foreign Bible Society, as well as the issue of slavery.

Wilde, Oscar (Fingal O'Flahertie Wills) (1854–1900) Irish writer. With his flamboyant style and quotable conversation, he dazzled London society and, on his lecture tour in 1882, the USA. He published his only novel, *The Picture of Dorian Gray*, in 1891, followed by a series of sharp comedies, including *A Woman of No Importance* (1893) and *The Importance of Being Earnest* (1895). In 1895 he was imprisoned for two years for homosexual offences; he died in exile.

Wilde was born in Dublin and studied at Dublin and Oxford, where he became known as a supporter of the Aesthetic Movement ('art for art's sake'). He published *Poems* (1881), and also wrote fairy tales and other stories, criticism, and a long, anarchic political essay 'The Soul of Man Under Socialism' (1891). His elegant social comedies include *Lady Windermere's Fan* (1892) and *An Ideal Husband* (1895). The drama *Salomé* (1893), based on the biblical character, was written in French; considered scandalous by the British censor, it was first performed in Paris in 1896 with the actor Sarah Bernhardt in the title role.

> **Oscar Wilde**
> *There is no such thing as a moral or an immoral book. Books are well written, or badly written.*
> The Picture of Dorian Gray

Among his lovers was Lord Alfred ▷Douglas, whose father provoked Wilde into a lawsuit that led to his social and financial ruin and imprisonment. The long poem *Ballad of Reading Gaol* (1898) and a letter published as *De Profundis* (1905) were written in jail to explain his side of the relationship. After his release from prison in 1897, he lived in France. He is buried in Père Lachaise cemetery, Paris. See picture on p. 1026.

Related Web sites: Complete Shorter Fiction of Oscar Wilde http://www.bibliomania.com/Fiction/wilde/stories/index.html
Poems of Oscar Wilde http://www.bartleby.com/143/index.html

wildebeest (or **gnu**) either of two species of African ▷antelope, with a cowlike face, a beard and mane, and heavy curved horns in both sexes. The body is up to 1.3 m/4.2 ft high at the shoulder and slopes away to the hindquarters. (Genus *Connochaetes*.)

The **brindled wildebeest** *C. taurinus* is silver-grey with a dark face, mane, and tail tuft, and is found from Kenya southwards.

OSCAR WILDE Irish writer Oscar Wilde. This photograph is from 1882 and is inscribed: 'For Mrs. Bigelow from her friend Oscar Wilde' See entry on p. 1025. *Archive Photos*

Wilder, Billy (Samuel) (1906–2002) Austrian-born US film director and screenwriter. His films display an acerbic wit and a cynical analysis of American society. They include the pioneering film noir *Double Indemnity* (1944), *The Lost Weekend* (1945), *Sunset Boulevard* (1950), and the comedies *Some Like It Hot* (1959) and *The Apartment* (1960).

Wilder, Thornton Niven (1897–1975) US dramatist and novelist. He won Pulitzer prizes for the novel *The Bridge of San Luis Rey* (1927) and for the plays *Our Town* (1938) and *The Skin of Our Teeth* (1942). His farce *The Matchmaker* (1954) was filmed in 1958. In 1964 it was adapted into the hit stage musical *Hello, Dolly!*, and also made into a film. His plays are overtly philosophical, they generally employ no props or scenery, and the characters often directly address the audience.

wilderness area of uninhabited land that has never been disturbed by humans, usually located some distance from towns and cities. According to estimates by US group Conservation International, 52% (90 million sq km/35 million sq mi) of the Earth's total land area was still undisturbed in 1994.

wildlife trade international trade in live plants and animals, and in wildlife products such as skins, horns, shells, and feathers. The trade has made some species virtually extinct, and whole ecosystems (for example, coral reefs) are threatened. Wildlife trade is to some extent regulated by ▷CITES (Convention on International Trade in Endangered Species).

wild type in genetics, the naturally occurring gene for a particular character that is typical of most individuals of a given species, as distinct from new genes that arise by mutation.

Wilfrid, St (634–709) Northumbrian-born bishop of York from 665. He defended the cause of the Roman Church at the Synod of ▷Whitby in 664 against that of Celtic Christianity. Feast day is 12 October.

Wilkes, John (1727–1797) British Radical politician, imprisoned for his political views; member of Parliament 1757–64 and from 1774. He championed parliamentary reform, religious tolerance, and US independence.

Wilkins, George Hubert (1888–1958) Australian polar explorer, a pioneer in the use of surveys by both aircraft and submarines. He studied engineering, learned to fly 1910, and visited both polar regions. In 1928 he flew from Barrow (Alaska) to Green Harbour (Spitsbergen), and in 1928–29 made an Antarctic flight that proved that Graham Land is an island. He also planned to reach the North Pole by submarine. He was knighted in 1928.

Wilkins, Maurice Hugh Frederick (1916–) New Zealand-born British molecular biologist who was awarded a Nobel Prize for Physiology or Medicine in 1962 with Francis ▷Crick and James ▷Watson for the discovery of the double-helical structure of DNA and of the significance of this structure in the replication and transfer of genetic information.

Wilkins began his career as a physicist working on luminescence and phosphorescence, radar, and the separation of uranium isotopes, and worked in the USA during World War II on the development of the atomic bomb. After the war he turned his attention from nuclear physics to molecular biology, and studied the genetic effects of ultrasonic waves, nucleic acids, and viruses by using ultraviolet light.

Wilkinson, Jonny (1979–) born Jonathan Wilkinson. English rugby union player and England's all-time leading points scorer. He became England's youngest international for 71 years when he made his debut in March 1998 at the age of only 18 years 301 days. Wilkinson played at centre in the 1999 Five Nations Championship, but has appeared in his favoured position of fly-half since the 1999 World Cup. He made his senior club debut with Newcastle in 1997. In April 2001, he surpassed Rob Andrew's record of 396 Test points to become England's top points scorer at the age of 21. In 2003 he helped England to win the Grand Slam in the Six Nations Championship and then played a decisive role in England's World Cup win, scoring the deciding points in the last moments of the final.

will in law, declaration of how a person wishes his or her property to be disposed of after death. It also appoints administrators of the estate (▷executors) and may contain wishes on other matters, such as place of burial or use of organs for transplant. Wills must comply with formal legal requirements of the local jurisdiction. Some US states permit people, usually the terminally ill, to specify at what stage they should be allowed to die, in living wills.

William (1982–) Born William Arthur Philip Louis. Prince of the UK, first child of the Prince and Princess of Wales.

William attended Ludgrove School, Wokingham (1990–95) and Eton College, Windsor. His first public appearance was a visit to Wales on St David's Day, aged eight years old. He studied at the University of St Andrews from 2001.

William four kings of England:

William (I) the Conqueror
(1028–1087) King of England from 25 December 1066. He was the illegitimate son of Duke Robert the Devil whom he succeeded as Duke of Normandy in 1035. Claiming that his relative King Edward the Confessor had bequeathed him the English throne, William invaded England in 1066, defeating ▷Harold (II) Godwinson at the Battle of Hastings) on 14 October 1066, and was crowned king of England.

William's coronation took place in Westminster Abbey on Christmas Day 1066. During the ▷Norman Conquest of England, he secured control of the country by ruthlessly crushing any rebellion and the construction of 50 ▷castles by 1087. He completed the establishment of the ▷feudal system in England, compiling detailed records of land and property in the ▷Domesday Book (1086), and kept the barons firmly under control. A key aspect of his policy was to gain the support of the medieval church through his archbishop of Canterbury, ▷Lanfranc. He died in Rouen after a fall from his horse and is buried in Caen, France. He was succeeded by his son William II.

After his death, one Norman monk wrote that William 'excelled in wisdom all the princes of his generation' and claimed that 'he was undaunted by danger'. The Anglo-Saxon Chronicle described him as a 'man of great wisdom and power, who surpassed in honour and strength all those who had gone before him'. It also, however, complained that William was 'a hard man...sunk in greed', who oppressed the people with castles and taxes, 'but was too relentless to care though all might hate him'.

William (II) Rufus (c. 1056–1100) Called 'William the Red'. King of England from 1087, the third son of William (I) the Conqueror. He spent most of his reign attempting to capture Normandy from his brother ▷Robert (II) Curthose , Duke of Normandy. His extortion of money led his barons to revolt and caused confrontation with Bishop Anselm. He was killed while hunting in the New Forest, Hampshire, and was succeeded by his brother Henry I.

William (III) of Orange (1650–1702) King of Great Britain and Ireland from 1688, the son of William II of Orange and Mary, daughter of the deposed James II. He was offered the English crown by the parliamentary opposition to James II. He invaded England in 1688 and in 1689 became joint sovereign with his wife, ▷Mary II. He spent much of his reign campaigning, first in Ireland, where he defeated James II at the Battle of the ▷Boyne in 1690, and later against the French in Flanders. He died childless and was succeeded by Mary's sister, Anne.

Born in the Hague, in the Netherlands, William was appointed *stadtholder* (chief magistrate) and captain-general of the Dutch forces in 1672 to resist the French invasion. He forced Louis XIV to make peace in 1678 and then concentrated on building up a European alliance against France. In 1677 he married his cousin Mary, daughter of James, Duke of York, the future James II. When invited by both Whig and Tory leaders to take the crown from James, he landed with a small force at Torbay, Devon, on 5 November 1688. James fled to France, and his Scottish and Irish supporters were defeated, respectively, at the battles of Dunkeld in 1689 and the Boyne the following year.

Related Web site: Speech Delivered by King William of England to Parliament http://odur.let.rug.nl/~usa/D/1701-1725/england/french.htm

William IV (1765–1837) King of Great Britain and Ireland from 1830, when he succeeded his brother George IV. Third son of George III, he was created Duke of Clarence in 1789, and married Adelaide of Saxe-Meiningen (1792–1849) in 1818. During the Reform Bill crisis he secured its passage by agreeing to create new peers to overcome the hostile majority in the House of Lords. He was succeeded by his niece Victoria.

William I (1797–1888) King of Prussia from 1861 and emperor of Germany from 1871; the son of Friedrich Wilhelm III. He served in the Napoleonic Wars 1814–15 and helped to crush the 1848 revolution. After he succeeded his brother Friedrich Wilhelm IV to the throne of Prussia, his policy was largely dictated by his chancellor ▷Bismarck, who secured his proclamation as emperor.

William II (1859–1941) German **Wilhelm II**. Emperor of Germany from 1888, the son of Frederick III and Victoria, daughter of Queen Victoria of Britain. In 1890 he forced Chancellor Bismarck to resign in an attempt to assert his own political authority. The result was an exacerbation of domestic and international political instability, although his personal influence declined in the 1900s. He was an enthusiastic supporter of Admiral Tirpitz's plans for naval expansion. In 1914 he first approved

---

Prince William
There's been a lot of nonsense put about by PR companies. I don't like being exploited in this way but, as I get older, it's increasingly hard to prevent.

On being linked with such showbusiness personalities as US singer Britney Spears. Interviewed by Peter Archer of the Press Association; quoted in the *Daily Telegraph*, 17 June 2000

John Wilkes
Nothing has been so obnoxious to me through life as a dead calm.

Quoted in Horace Blackley
Life of John Wilkes

JOHN WILKES British Radical politician John Wilkes. Wilkes championed the rights of the individual, but was also a notorious xenophobe who constantly ridiculed the Scots as an alien and tyrannical nation. Samuel Johnson's definition of patriotism as 'the last refuge of the scoundrel' was written with Wilkes in mind. *Philip Sauvain Picture Collection*

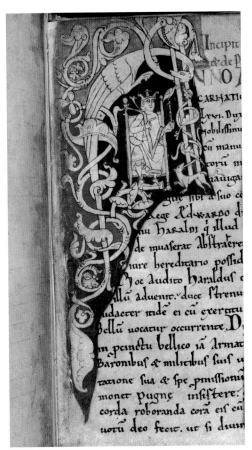

WILLIAM (I) THE CONQUEROR A detail from an 11th century manuscript showing King William I of England. *The Art Archive/British Library*

Austria's ultimatum to Serbia and then, when he realized war was inevitable, tried in vain to prevent it. In 1918 he fled to Doorn in the Netherlands after Germany's defeat and his abdication.

William I (1772–1844) King of the Netherlands 1815–40. He lived in exile during the French occupation 1795–1813 and fought against the emperor Napoleon at Jena and Wagram. The Austrian Netherlands were added to his kingdom by the Allies in 1815, but secured independence (recognized by the major European states in 1839) by the revolution of 1830. William's unpopularity led to his abdication in 1840.

William II (1792–1849) King of the Netherlands 1840–49, son of William I. He served with the British army in the Peninsular War and at Waterloo. In 1848 he averted revolution by conceding a liberal constitution.

William of Malmesbury (c. 1080–c. 1143) English historian and monk. He compiled the *Gesta regum/Deeds of the Kings* (c.1120–40) and *Historia novella*, which together formed a history of England to 1142.

William of Wykeham (c. 1323–1404) English politician, bishop of Winchester from 1367, Lord Chancellor 1367–72 and 1389–91, and founder of Winchester College (public school) 1378 and New College, Oxford 1379.

Williams, (George) Emlyn (1905–1987) Welsh actor and dramatist. His plays, in which he appeared, include *Night Must Fall* (1935) and *The Corn Is Green* (1938). He was also acclaimed for his solo performance as the author Charles Dickens. Williams gave early encouragement to the actor Richard Burton.

Williams, (Hiram) Hank (1923–1953) US country singer, songwriter, and guitarist. He was the author of dozens of country standards and one of the originators of modern country music. His songs are characteristically mournful and blues-influenced, like 'Your Cheatin' Heart' (1953), but also include the uptempo 'Jambalaya' (1952) and the proto-rockabilly 'Hey, Good-Lookin'' (1951).

Williams, Roger (c. 1603–1683) American colonist, founder of the Rhode Island colony in 1636, based on democracy and complete religious freedom. He tried to maintain good relations with the Indians of the region, although he fought against them in the Pequot War and King Philip's War.

Williams, Rowan (1950–) Archbishop of Canterbury from 2002. He is the 104th holder of the title. Dr Williams was enthroned as Bishop of Monmouth in 1992 and Archbishop of Wales in 2000.

Williams, Shirley Vivien Teresa Brittain (1930–) Baroness Williams of Crosby. British Liberal Democrat politician. She was Labour minister for prices and consumer protection 1974–76, and education and science 1976–79. She became a founder member of the Social Democrat Party (SDP) in 1981, its president in 1982, but lost her parliamentary seat in 1983. In 1988 she joined the newly merged Social and Liberal Democratic Party (SLDP). She is the daughter of the socialist writer Vera ▷Brittain. She was made a life peer in 1993.

Williams, Tennessee (Thomas Lanier) (1911–1983) US dramatist. His work is characterized by fluent dialogue and searching analysis of the psychological deficiencies of his characters. His plays, usually set in the Deep South against a background of decadence and degradation, include *The Glass Menagerie* (1945), *A Streetcar Named Desire* (1947), and *Cat on a Hot Tin Roof* (1955), the last two of which earned Pulitzer prizes.

> **Tennessee Williams**
> *We're all of us guinea pigs in the laboratory of God. Humanity is just a work in progress.*
> Camino Real

Williams, Venus (1980–) US tennis player. She turned professional aged just 14. Her unprecedented power on the court, with a serve of up to 127 mph, has changed the face of the women's game. In 2000, she won 6 out of the 10 tournaments she played in, including Wimbledon, the US Open, and the gold medal at the Sydney Olympics as part of a 35-match unbeaten run. She plays doubles with her younger sister Serena Williams and they became only the fourth pair to win all four Grand Slam tournaments when they captured the Australian open doubles title in 2001. It was Serena whom she beat in the final of the US Open when she retained her title in 2001.

Williams, William Carlos (1883–1963) US poet, essayist, and theoretician. He was associated with ▷Imagism and Objectivism. One of the most original and influential of modern poets, he is noted for advancing poetics of visual images and colloquial American rhythms, conceiving the poem as a 'field of action'. His epic, five-book poem *Patterson* (1946–58) is written in a form of free verse that combines historical documents, newspaper material, and letters, to celebrate his home town in New Jersey. *Pictures from Brueghel* (1963) won him, posthumously, a Pulitzer prize.

Williamson, Henry (1895–1977) English writer. His stories of animal life include *Tarka the Otter* (1927). He wrote the fictional 15-volume sequence *A Chronicle of Ancient Sunlight* (1951–69), and described his own experiences in three autobiographies: *The Children of Shallowford* (1939), and *A Clear Water Stream* (1958).

William the Lion (1143–1214) King of Scotland from 1165. He was captured by Henry II while invading England in 1174, and forced to do homage, but Richard I abandoned the English claim to suzerainty for a money payment in 1189. In 1209 William was forced by King John to renounce his claim to Northumberland.

William the Marshall (c. 1146–1219) 1st Earl of Pembroke. English knight, regent of England from 1216. After supporting the dying Henry II against Richard (later Richard I), he went on a crusade to Palestine, was pardoned by Richard, and was granted an earldom in 1189. On King John's death he was appointed guardian of the future Henry III, and defeated the French under Louis VIII to enable Henry to gain the throne.

William the Silent (1533–1584) Prince of Orange from 1544. Leading a revolt against Spanish rule in the Netherlands from 1573, he briefly succeeded in uniting the Catholic south and Protestant northern provinces, but the former provinces submitted to Spain while the latter formed a federation in 1579 (Union of Utrecht) which repudiated Spanish suzerainty in 1581.

WILLIAM THE SILENT An engraving of William the Silent, Prince of Orange. *Philip Sauvain Picture Collection*

Willis, Norman David (1933–) English trade union leader. A trade union official since leaving school, he was the general secretary of the Trades Union Congress (TUC) 1984–93 and president of the European TUC 1991–93.

will-o'-the-wisp light sometimes seen over marshy ground, believed to be burning gas containing methane from decaying organic matter.

willow any of a group of trees or shrubs containing over 350 species, found mostly in the northern hemisphere, flourishing in damp places. The leaves are often lance-shaped, and the male and female catkins are borne on separate trees. (Genus *Salix*, family Salicaceae.) See picture on p. 1028.

willowherb any of a group of perennial flowering plants belonging to the evening primrose family. The **rosebay willowherb** or **fireweed** *C. angustifolium* is common in woods and wasteland. It grows to 1.2 m/4 ft with tall upright spikes of red or purplish flowers. (Genera *Epilobium* and *Chamaenerion*, family Onagraceae.) See picture on p. 1028.

willow warbler bird *Phylloscopus trochilus*, family Muscicapidae, order Passeriformes. It is about 11 cm/4 in long, similar in appearance to the chiffchaff, but with a distinctive song. It is found in woods and shrubberies, and migrates from northern Eurasia to Africa.

WILLIAM (II) RUFUS Third son of William the Conqueror, William (II) Rufus is shown, in this illustration from the Stowe manuscript, seated on a throne wearing his robes of state. *The Art Archive*

willy-willy Australian Aboriginal term for a cyclonic whirlwind.

Wilson, Angus (Frank Johnstone) (1913–1991) English novelist, short-story writer, and biographer. His acidly humorous books include *Anglo-Saxon Attitudes* (1956) and *The Old Men at the Zoo* (1961). In his detailed portrayal of English society, he extracted high comedy from its social and moral grotesqueries. He was knighted in 1980.

Wilson, Colin Henry (1931–) English author. He wrote *The Outsider* (1956) and thrillers, including *Necessary Doubt* (1964). Later works, such as *Mysteries* (1978), are about the occult.

Wilson, Edward Osborne (1929–) US zoologist whose books have stimulated interest in biogeography, the study of the distribution of species, and sociobiology, the evolution of behaviour. He is a world authority on ants.

Wilson, (James) Harold (1916–1995) Baron Wilson of Rievaulx. British Labour politician, party leader from 1963, prime minister 1964–70 and 1974–76. His premiership was dominated by the issue of UK admission to membership of the European Community (now the European Union), the social contract (unofficial agreement with the trade unions), and economic difficulties.

Wilson, born in Huddersfield, West Yorkshire, studied at Jesus College, Oxford, where he gained a first-class degree in philosophy, politics, and economics. During World War II he worked as a civil servant, and in 1945 stood for Parliament and won the marginal seat of Ormskirk. Assigned by Prime Minister Clement Attlee to a junior post in the ministry of works, he progressed to become president of the Board of Trade 1947–51 (when he resigned because of social-service cuts). In 1963 he succeeded Hugh Gaitskell as Labour leader and became prime minister the following year, increasing his majority in 1966. He formed a minority government in February 1974 and achieved a majority of three in October 1974. He resigned in 1976 and was succeeded by James Callaghan. He was knighted in 1976 and made a peer in 1983.

Wilson, Richard (1714–1782) Welsh painter. His landscapes, infused with an Italianate atmosphere, are painted in a classical manner reminiscent of ▷Claude Lorrain. His work influenced the development of English landscape painting, and J M W ▷Turner in particular.

Wilson, Teddy (Theodore Shaw) (1912–1986) US bandleader and jazz pianist. He toured with Benny Goodman 1935–39 and during that period recorded in small groups with many of the best musicians of the time; some of his 1930s recordings feature the singer Billie Holiday. Wilson led a big band 1939–40 and a sextet 1940–46.

Wilson, (Thomas) Woodrow (1856–1924) 28th president of the USA 1913–21, a Democrat. He kept the USA out of World War I until 1917, and in January 1918 issued his 'Fourteen Points' as a basis for a just peace settlement.

At the peace conference in Paris he secured the inclusion of the ▷League of Nations in individual peace treaties, but these were not ratified by Congress, so the USA did not join the League. He was awarded the Nobel Prize for Peace in 1919 for his work as a founder of the League of Nations.

Wilson was born in Virginia, and became president of Princeton University in 1902. In 1910 he became governor of New Jersey. Elected president in 1912 against Theodore Roosevelt and William

> **Woodrow Wilson**
> *Democracy is not so much a form of government as a set of principles.*
> Atlantic Monthly (March 1901)

Taft, he initiated anti-trust legislation and secured valuable social reforms in his progressive 'New Freedom' programme. He strove to keep the USA neutral during World War I but the German U-boat campaign forced him to declare war in 1917. In 1919 he suffered a stroke from which he never fully recovered.

Related Web site: Woodrow Wilson – Twenty-eighth President 1913–1921
http://www.whitehouse.gov/WH/glimpse/presidents/html/ww28.html

wilting the loss of rigidity (turgor) in plants, caused by a decreasing wall pressure within the cells making up the supportive tissues. Wilting is most obvious in plants that have little or no wood.

Wiltshire county of southwest England (since April 1997 Swindon has been a separate unitary authority).

area 3,480 sq km/1,343 sq mi **towns and cities** Trowbridge (administrative headquarters), Salisbury, Wilton, Devizes, Chippenham, Warminster **physical** Marlborough Downs; Savernake Forest; rivers Kennet, Wylye, Avons (Salisbury and Bristol); Salisbury Plain (32 km/20 mi by 25 km/16 mi, lying at about 120 m/394 ft above sea-level), a military training area used since Napoleonic times **features** Longleat House (Marquess of Bath); Wilton House (Earl of Pembroke); Stourhead, with 18th-century gardens; Neolithic Stonehenge, Avebury, Silbury Hill, West Kennet Long Barrow, finest example of a long barrow in Wiltshire, dating from the 3rd millennium BC; Stonehenge, Avebury, and associated sites are a World Heritage site; Salisbury Cathedral, which has the tallest spire in Britain (123 m/404 ft) **agriculture** cereals (wheat); cattle; dairy-farming (condensed milk, cheese); pig and sheep farming **industries** brewing (Devizes); computing; electronics; engineering (Chippenham); plastics; quarrying (Portland stone); rubber (Bradford-on-Avon, Melksham); tobacco (Devizes) **population** (1996) 593,300 **famous people** Isaac Pitman, William Talbot, Christopher Wren

Wimbledon English lawn tennis centre used for international championship matches, situated in south London. There are currently 18 courts.

WIMP (acronym for windows, icons, menus, pointing device) in computing, another name for ▷graphical user interface (GUI).

Winchester cathedral city and administrative headquarters of ▷Hampshire, England, on the River Itchen, 19 km/12 mi northeast of Southampton; population (1991) 36,100. Tourism is important, and there is also light industry. Originally a Roman town, Winchester was capital of the Anglo-Saxon kingdom of Wessex, and later of England. Winchester Cathedral (1079–93) is the longest medieval church in Europe and was remodelled from Norman-Romanesque to Perpendicular Gothic under the patronage of William of Wykeham (founder of Winchester College in 1382), who is buried there, as are Saxon kings, St ▷Swithun, and the writers Izaac Walton and Jane Austen.

WIND Engineers are shown testing a propeller in a subsonic wind tunnel. Aerodynamic studies in wind tunnels have been important in solving design problems in aircraft, spacecraft, cars, boats, trains, bridges, and building structures. *Image Bank*

Winchester was a tribal centre of the Britons under the name Caer Gwent. On St Catherine's Hill can be seen the rampart and ditch made for defence by an Iron Age settlement in the 3rd century BC. Winchester was later one of the largest Roman settlements in Britain; as Venta Belgarum the town become capital of Wessex in 519, and under Alfred the Great and Canute it was the seat of government. In 827 Egbert was crowned first king of all England here. Under William the Conqueror, Winchester was declared dual capital of England with London. A medieval 'reconstruction' of Arthur's Round Table is preserved in the 13th-century hall (all that survives) of the castle.

Winchester drive in computing, an old-fashioned term for ▷hard disk.

wind the lateral movement of the Earth's atmosphere from high-pressure areas (anticyclones) to low-pressure areas (depression). Its speed is measured using an ▷anemometer or by studying its effects on, for example, trees by using the ▷Beaufort scale. Although modified by features such as land and water, there is a basic worldwide system of ▷trade winds, ▷westerlies, and polar easterlies.

A belt of low pressure (the ▷doldrums) lies along the Equator. The trade winds blow towards this from the horse latitudes (areas of high pressure at about 30° N and 30° S of the Equator), blowing from the northeast in the northern hemisphere, and from the southeast in the southern. The Westerlies (also from the horse latitudes) blow north of the Equator from the southwest and south of the Equator from the northwest.

Cold winds blow outwards from high-pressure areas at the poles. More local effects result from landmasses heating and cooling faster than the adjacent sea, producing onshore winds in the daytime and offshore winds at night.

The ▷monsoon is a seasonal wind of southern Asia, blowing from the southwest in summer and bringing the rain on which crops depend. It blows from the northeast in winter.

Famous or notorious warm winds include the **chinook** of the eastern Rocky Mountains, North America; the **föhn** of Europe's Alpine valleys; the **sirocco** (Italy)/**khamsin** (Egypt)/**sharav** (Israel), spring winds that bring warm air from the Sahara and Arabian deserts across the Mediterranean; and the **Santa Ana**, a periodic warm wind from the inland deserts that strikes the California coast.

The dry northerly **bise** (Switzerland) and the **mistral**, which strikes the Mediterranean area of France, are unpleasantly cold winds.

The fastest wind speed ever measured on earth, 512 kph/318 mph, occurred on 3 May 1999 in a tornado that struck the suburbs of Oklahoma City, Oklahoma, USA.

wind-chill factor (or **wind-chill index**) estimate of how much colder it feels when a wind is blowing. It is arrived at by combining the actual temperature and wind speed and is given as a different temperature.

Windermere largest lake in England, in the ▷Lake District, Cumbria, northwest England; length 17 km/10.5 mi; width 1.6 km/1 mi. Windermere is the principal centre of tourism in the Lake District. The town of the same name extends towards Bowness on the eastern shore of the lake.

wind farm array of windmills or ▷wind turbines used for generating electrical power. The world's largest wind farm at Altamont Pass, California, USA, consists of 6,000 wind turbines

WILLOW The willow tree is deciduous with simple leaves and small erect catkins. Willows are found throughout the world, except Australasia. See entry on p. 1027.

WILLOWHERB The great willowherb *Epilobium hirsutum* is widely distributed in Europe, Asia, and Africa, and has been introduced into North America. See entry on p. 1027. *Premaphotos Wildlife*

WIND FARM A wind farm for generating electricity in California, USA. In Britain, the majority of wind farms are to be found where the prevailing (westerly) wind is most constant, such as in Cornwall and west Wales. *Image Bank*

WIND TURBINE The wind turbine is the modern counterpart of the windmill. The rotor blades are huge – up to 100 m/330 ft across – in order to extract as much energy as possible from the wind. Inside the turbine head, gears are used to increase the speed of the turning shaft so that the electricity generation is as efficient as possible.

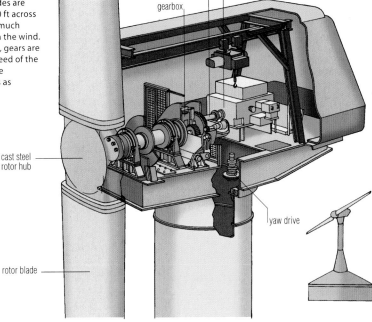

transmission shaft generator
gearbox
cast steel
rotor hub
yaw drive
rotor blade

generating 1 TWh of electricity per year. Wind farms supply about 1.5% of California's electricity needs. To produce 1,200 megawatts of electricity (an output comparable with that of a nuclear power station), a wind farm would need to occupy around 370 sq km/ 140 sq mi.

Windhoek capital of Namibia, and administrative centre of Khomas region; population (1992) 126,000. It is just north of the Tropic of Capricorn, in the Khomas Highlands, 290 km/180 mi from the west coast. It is the world centre of the karakul (breed of sheep) industry; other industries include engineering and food processing.

wind instrument musical instrument that is sounded by an airflow (the performer's breath) to make a column of air vibrate within a vented tubular resonator, sometimes activating a reed or reeds. The pitch of the note is controlled by the length of the column. Major types of wind instrument are the voice; whistles, including the recorder and flute; reed instruments, including most other woodwinds; ▷brass instruments, including horns; and free-reed instruments, such as the mouth organ.

windmill mill with sails or vanes that, by the action of wind upon them, drive machinery for grinding corn or pumping water, for example. Wind turbines, designed to use wind power on a large scale, usually have a propeller-type rotor mounted on a tall shell tower. The turbine drives a generator for producing electricity.

Windmills were used in the East in ancient times, and in Europe they were first used in Germany and the Netherlands in the 12th century. The main types of traditional windmill are the **post mill**, which is turned around a post when the direction of the wind changes, and the **tower mill**, which has a revolving turret on top. It usually has a device (fantail) that keeps the sails pointing into the wind. In the USA windmills were used by the colonists and later a light type, with steel sails supported on a long steel girder shaft, was introduced for use on farms.

window in computing, a rectangular area on the screen of a ▷graphical user interface. A window is used to display data and can be manipulated in various ways by the computer user.

Windows in computing, originally Microsoft's ▷graphical user interface (GUI) for IBM PCs and clones running ▷MS-DOS. Windows has developed into a family of operating systems that run on a wide variety of computers from pen-operated palmtop organizers to large, multi-processor computers in corporate data centres.

Windows XP Home edition is designed for homes and offices and retains maximum compatibility with programs written for the MS-DOS operating system and earlier versions of Windows. Windows XP Professional edition is designed for business use, especially on workstations and server computers, where it is seen as a rival to ▷Unix. Windows CE is a small, modular operating system

that supports a subset of the Windows applications programming interface. It is used in Pocket PCs, Windows-Based Terminals (WBTs), and consumer electronics products such as games consoles, DVD players, and television set-top boxes for Internet use. Windows XP Home is limited to Intel and x86-compatible processors but both XP Professional and CE run on a variety of chips from different manufacturers.

Windows 95, by far the most popular version, was revised three times, and in 1998 Microsoft launched an updated version called Windows 98. In February 2000, Microsoft launched Windows 2000, to replace Windows NT 4.0; it was designed to be used in local area networks. Windows 98's successor, Windows ME (Millennium Edition), was released in September 2000.
    Related Web site: Winfiles.com http://www.winfiles.com/

wind power the harnessing of wind energy to produce power. The wind has long been used as a source of energy: sailing ships and windmills are ancient inventions. After the energy crisis of the 1970s ▷wind turbines began to be used to produce electricity on a large scale.
    Related Web site: British Wind Energy Association http://www.bwea.com/

Windscale former name of ▷Sellafield, a nuclear power station in Cumbria, England.

Windsor and Maidenhead unitary authority in southeast England, created in 1998 from part of the former county of Berkshire.
    area 198 sq km/76 sq mi **towns and cities** Windsor, ▷Maidenhead (administrative headquarters) **features** River Thames; Windsor Castle, royal residence originally built by William the Conqueror; Windsor Great Park, remnant of royal hunting ground; Eton College, founded by Henry VI in 1440; Household Cavalry Museum (Windsor); Stanley Spencer (1891–1959) Gallery (Cookham on Thames); Ascot Racecourse **industries** tourism and service industries, electrical systems and components, chemicals, motor vehicle components, telecommunications, publishing, scientific equipment **population** (1996) 140,200

Windsor Castle British royal residence in Windsor, founded by William the Conqueror on the site of an earlier fortress. It includes the Perpendicular Gothic St George's Chapel and the Albert Memorial Chapel, beneath which George III, George IV, and William IV are buried. In the Home Park adjoining the castle is the Royal Mausoleum, Frogmore, where Queen Victoria and Prince Albert are buried.

Windsor, Duchess of, title of Wallis Warfield ▷Simpson.

Windsor, Duke of, title of ▷Edward VIII.

Windsor, House of official name of the British royal family since 1917, adopted in place of Saxe-Coburg-Gotha. Since 1960 those descendants of Elizabeth II not entitled to the prefix HRH (His/Her Royal Highness) have borne the surname Mountbatten-Windsor.

wind turbine windmill of advanced aerodynamic design connected to an electricity generator and used in wind-power installations. Wind turbines can be either large propeller-type rotors mounted on a tall tower, or flexible metal strips fixed to a vertical axle at top and bottom.

Windward Islands group of islands in the West Indies, forming part of the lesser ▷Antilles.

wing in biology, the modified forelimb of birds and bats, or the membranous outgrowths of the ▷exoskeleton of insects, which give the power of flight. Birds and bats have two wings. Bird wings have feathers attached to the fused digits ('fingers') and forearm bones, while bat wings consist of skin stretched between the digits. Most insects have four wings, which are strengthened by wing veins.

The wings of butterflies and moths are covered with scales. The hind pair of a fly's wings are modified to form two knoblike balancing organs (halteres).

WING Birds can fly because of the specialized shape of their wings: a rounded leading edge, flattened underneath and round on top. This aerofoil shape produces lift in the same way that an aircraft wing does. The outline of the wing is related to the speed of flight. Fast birds of prey have a streamlined shape. Larger birds, such as the eagle, have large wings with separated tip feathers which reduce drag and allow slow flight. Insect wings are not aerofoils. They push downwards to produce lift, in the same way that oars are used to push through water.

Winnipeg (called 'Gateway to the West'; Cree *win-nipuy* 'muddy water') capital of Manitoba, Canada, at the confluence of the Red and Assiniboine rivers, 65 km/40 mi south of Lake Winnipeg, 30 km/20 mi north of the US border; population (1991) 616,800, metropolitan area (1996) 676,700. It is a focus for trans-Canada and Canada–US traffic, and a market and transhipment point for wheat and other produce from the prairie provinces: Manitoba, Alberta, and Saskatchewan. Processed-foods, textiles, farming machinery, and transport equipment are manufactured. Established as Winnipeg in 1870 on the site of earlier forts, the city expanded with the arrival of the Canadian Pacific Railroad in 1881.

Related Web site: Winnipeg http://www.Tourism.Winnipeg.MB.CA/

Winnipeg, Lake (Cree *win-nipuy* 'muddy water') lake in southern Manitoba, Canada. It is a small remnant of the glacial lake Agassiz and Canada's third-largest lake, covering an area of 24,500 sq km/9,460 sq mi. Its waters are fed by the ▷Red, Saskatchewan, Winnipeg, and other rivers, draining much of the Canadian prairies. Its outflow is through the River Nelson, northeastwards to Hudson Bay.

wintergreen any of a group of plants belonging to the heath family, especially the species *G. procumbens* of northeastern North America, which creeps underground and sends up tiny shoots. Oil of wintergreen, used in treating rheumatism, is extracted from its leaves. Wintergreen is also the name for various plants belonging to the wintergreen family Pyrolaceae, including the green pipsissewa *C. maculata* of northern North America, Europe, and Asia. (Genus *Gaultheria*, family Ericaceae; also genera *Pyrola*, *Chimaphila*, *Orthilia*, and *Moneses*, family Pyrolaceae.)

Winter King, the name given to ▷Frederick V because he was king of Bohemia for one winter (1619–20).

Winter Olympics a four-yearly series of sports competitions on snow and ice, first held in 1924, and organized like the summer ▷Olympics under the auspices of the International Olympic Committee. The 2006 Games will be held in Turin, Italy.

Winterson, Jeanette (1959–) English novelist. Her autobiographical first novel *Oranges Are Not the Only Fruit* (1985), televised in 1990, humorously draws on her experiences growing up as an Evangelical Pentecostalist in Lancashire, and her subsequent realization of her homosexuality. Later novels include *Boating for Beginners* (1986), *The Passion* (1987), *Sexing the Cherry* (1989), *Written On the Body* (1992), and *Art and Lies* (1994). *Art Objects: Essays on Ecstasy and Effrontery* (1995) is a work of non-fiction.

Winter War the USSR's invasion of Finland 30 November 1939–12 March 1940, also called the Russo-Finnish War.

The USSR set up a Finnish puppet government in eastern Karelia, but their invasion forces were at first repulsed by the greatly outnumbered Finnish troops under Marshal Mannerheim. In February 1940 the Finnish lines were broken by a million-strong Soviet offensive. In the March armistice Finland ceded part of Karelia to the USSR.

wire thread of metal, made by drawing a rod through progressively smaller-diameter dies. Fine-gauge wire is used for electrical power transmission; heavier-gauge wire is used to make load-bearing cables.

wireless original name for a radio receiver. In early experiments with transmission by radio waves, notably by Italian inventor Guglielmo ▷Marconi in Britain, signals were sent in Morse code, as in telegraphy. Radio, unlike the telegraph, used no wires for transmission, and the means of communication was termed 'wireless telegraphy'.

wireworm larva of some species of ▷click beetle. Wireworms are considered agricultural pests as they attack the seeds of many crops.

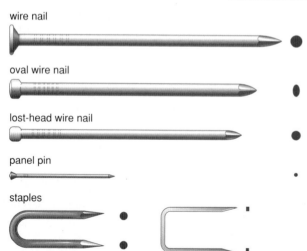
wire nail

oval wire nail

lost-head wire nail

panel pin

staples

WIRE Nails, pins, and staples are made of wire and are a quick way of joining materials together.

Wisconsin state in northern central USA. It is nicknamed the Badger State. Wisconsin was admitted to the Union in 1848 as the 30th US state. Part of the Midwest, it is bordered to the south by Illinois, to the west by Iowa and Minnesota, to the north by Lake Superior and the Upper Peninsula of Michigan, and to the east by Lake Michigan.

population (1995) 5,122,900 **area** 145,500 sq km/56,163 sq mi **capital** Madison **towns and cities** Milwaukee, Green Bay, Racine **industries and products** leading US dairy state; maize, hay, industrial and agricultural machinery, engines and turbines, precision instruments, paper products, cars and lorries, plumbing equipment, research, tourism

wisent another name for the European ▷bison.

Wishart, George (c. 1513–1546) Scottish Protestant reformer burned for heresy, who probably converted John ▷Knox.

wisteria any of a group of climbing leguminous shrubs (see ▷legume), including *W. sinensis*, native to the eastern USA and East Asia. Wisterias have hanging clusters of bluish, white, or pale mauve flowers, and pinnate leaves (leaflets on either side of the stem). They are grown against walls as ornamental plants. (Genus *Wisteria*, family Leguminosae.)

Witan (or **Witenagemot**) council of the Anglo-Saxon kings, the forerunner of Parliament, but including only royal household officials, great landowners, and top churchmen.

witchcraft the alleged possession and exercise of magical powers – **black magic** if used with evil intent, and **white magic** if benign. Its origins lie in traditional beliefs and religions. Supposed practitioners of witchcraft have often had considerable skill in, for example, herbal medicine and traditional remedies; this prompted the World Health Organization in 1976 to recommend the integration of traditional healers into the health teams of African states.

witch doctor alternative name for a ▷shaman.

witch hazel any of a group of flowering shrubs or small trees belonging to the witch hazel family, native to North America and East Asia, especially *H. virginiana*. An astringent extract prepared from the bark or leaves is used in medicine as an eye lotion and a liniment to relieve pain or stiffness. (Genus *Hamamelis*, family Hamamelidaceae.)

witch-hunt persecution of minority political opponents or socially nonconformist groups without any regard for their guilt or innocence. Witch-hunts are often accompanied by a degree of public hysteria; for example, the ▷McCarthy anticommunist hearings during the 1950s in the USA.

withdrawal in a military action, an orderly movement of forces in a rearward direction in order to occupy more favourable ground. It is voluntary and controlled, unlike a retreat.

withholding tax personal income tax on wages, salaries, dividends, or other income that is taxed at source to ensure that it reaches the tax authority. Those not liable to pay the tax can reclaim it by filing a tax return.

witness in law, a person who was present at some event (such as an accident, a crime, or the signing of a document) or has relevant special knowledge (such as a medical expert) and can be called on to give evidence in a court of law.

Wittenberg town in the state of Saxony-Anhalt, Germany, on the River Elbe, southwest of Berlin; population (1995) 52,500. Wittenberg University was founded in 1502, but transferred to Halle in 1815. The town became the cradle of the ▷Reformation in the early 16th century. The Protestant reformer

WISCONSIN Sunset over Indian Lake, Wisconsin, USA. Approximately 39% of the total surface area of the state of Wisconsin is occupied by lake water. Its two best-known lakes are Lake Michigan and Lake Superior, but there are thousands of other smaller lakes, which, other than one or two artificial reservoirs, are all the result of glacier coverage during the last Ice Age. *Image Bank*

Martin Luther preached in the Stadtkirche (in which he is buried), nailed his 95 theses to the door of the Schlosskirche in 1517, and taught Philosophy at the university.

Wittgenstein, Ludwig Josef Johann (1889–1951) Austrian philosopher. *Tractatus Logico-Philosophicus* (1922) postulated the 'picture theory' of language: that words represent things according to social agreement. He subsequently rejected this idea, and developed the idea that usage was more important than convention.

The picture theory said that it must be possible to break down a sentence into 'atomic propositions' whose elements stand for

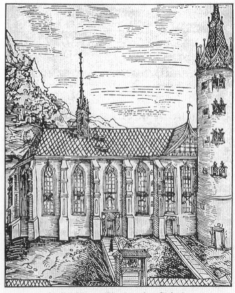

Die Schloßkirche zu Wittenberg mit der Thesentür.
Holzschnitt aus dem Wittenberger Heiligtumsbuch von Lukas Cranach d. Ä. 1509

WITTENBERG A woodcarving by Lucas Cranach of the church at Wittenberg. It was on the door of this church that Martin Luther posted his 95 theses criticizing the Roman Catholic Church in 1517. *Philip Sauvain Picture Collection*

elements of the real world. After he rejected this idea, his later philosophy developed a quite different, anthropological view of language: words are used according to different rules in a variety of human activities – different 'language games' are played with them. The traditional philosophical problems arise through the assumption that words (like 'exist' in the sentence 'Physical objects do not really exist') carry a fixed meaning with them, independent of context.

Witwatersrand (or the **Rand**; Afrikaans 'ridge of white water') economic heartland of Gauteng Province, South Africa. Its reef, which stretches nearly 100 km/60 mi, produces over half the world's gold. Gold was first found here in 1853. The chief city of the region is Johannesburg. Forming a watershed between the Vaal and the Olifant rivers, the Rand comprises a series of parallel ranges which extend 100 km/60 mi east–west and rise to 1,525–1,830 m/5,000–6,000 ft above sea level. Gold occurs in reefs that are mined at depths of up to 3,050 m/10,000 ft.

woad biennial plant native to Europe, with arrow-shaped leaves and clusters of small yellow flowers. It was formerly cultivated for a blue dye extracted from its leaves. Ancient Britons used the blue dye as a body paint in battle. (Genus *Isatis tinctoria*, family Cruciferae.)

Wodehouse, P(elham) G(renville) (1881–1975) English novelist. He became a US citizen in 1955. His humorous novels and stories portray the accident-prone world of such characters as the socialite Bertie Wooster and his invaluable and impeccable manservant Jeeves, and Lord Emsworth of Blandings Castle with his prize pig, the Empress of Blandings.

From 1906, Wodehouse also collaborated on the lyrics of Broadway musicals by Jerome Kern, Gershwin, and others. Staying in France in 1941, during World War II, he was interned by the Germans; he made some humorous broadcasts from Berlin, which were taken amiss in Britain at the time, but he was exonerated later and was knighted in 1975. His work is admired for its style, erudition, and geniality, and includes *Indiscretions of Archie* (1921), *The Clicking of Cuthbert* (1922), *The Inimitable Jeeves* (1932), and *Uncle Fred in the Springtime* (1939).
    Related Web site: P G Wodehouse Fan Club
    http://www.serv.net/~camel/wodehouse/

Woden (or **Wodan**) the foremost Anglo-Saxon god, whose Norse counterpart is ▷Odin.

Wöhler, Friedrich (1800–1882) German chemist who in 1828 became the first person to synthesize an organic compound (▷urea) from an inorganic compound (ammonium cyanate). He also devised a method in 1827 that isolated the metals aluminium, beryllium, yttrium, and titanium from their ores.

Wokingham unitary authority in southeast England, created in 1998 from part of the former county of Berkshire.
    area 179 sq km/69 sq mi **towns and cities** Wokingham (administrative headquarters), Twyford **features** River Thames forms northern border of authority; Royal Electrical and Mechanical Engineering Corps Museum (Arborfield); Swallowfield Park, house built for 2nd Earl of Clarendon in 1690; National Dairy Museum; Henley Regatta course; large areas of mixed woodland including remnants of old Royal Chase of Windsor Forest and tree-lined avenues; Finchampstead Ridges **industries** light engineering, electronics and information technology, telecommunications, computer components and software, plastics **population** (1996) 142,000

wolf any of two species of large wild dogs of the genus *Canis*. The grey or timber wolf *C. lupus*, of North America and Eurasia, is highly social, measures up to 90 cm/3 ft at the shoulder, and weighs up to 45 kg/100 lb. It has been greatly reduced in numbers except for isolated wilderness regions. The red wolf *C. rufus*, generally more slender and smaller (average weight about 15 kg/35 lb) and tawnier in colour, may not be a separate species, but a grey wolf–coyote hybrid. It used to be restricted to southern central USA, but is now thought to be extinct in the wild.

The 'prairie wolf' is another name for the ▷coyote. Wolves disappeared from England at the end of the 13th century, and from Scotland by the 17th century.
    Related Web sites: Snow Wolves http://www.pbs.org/kued/snowwolves/
    Wild Wolves http://www.pbs.org/wgbh/nova/wolves/

Wolf, Christa (1929–) German writer. She was critical of the German Democratic Republic – as in her novel *The Quest for Christa T* (1969), which was banned in East Germany – though she was supportive of Marxist ideals. She achieved recognition with her second novel, *Der geteilte Himmel/Divided Heaven* (1963), which tells the story of the conflict between Rita and Manfred: Manfred

WOAD Woad *Isatis tinctoria* is native to central and southern Europe. Though once widely cultivated in the British Isles for the blue dye extracted from its leaves, it is now rare. Its yellow flowers appear from July to August. *Premaphotos Wildlife*

decides to leave East Berlin to live in the West for greater personal and professional freedom; Rita elects to stay in East Berlin. Her other works include *Kindheitsmuster/A Model Childhood* (1976), *Till Eulenspiegel* (1972), *Parting from Phantoms: Selected Writings 1990–1994*, and *Medea* (1998).

Wolf, Hugo (Filipp Jakob) (1860–1903) Austrian composer. He wrote more than 250 *lieder* (songs), including the *Mörike-Lieder/Mörike Songs* (1888) and the two-volume *Italienisches Liederbuch/Italian Songbook* (1892, 1896).

Wolfe, James (1727–1759) English soldier. He served in Canada and commanded a victorious expedition against the French general Montcalm in Québec on the Plains of Abraham, during which both commanders were killed. The British victory established their supremacy over Canada.

Wolfe fought at the battles of Dettingen, Falkirk, and ▷Culloden. With the outbreak of the Seven Years' War (the French and Indian War in North America), he was posted to Canada and played a conspicuous part in the siege of the French stronghold of Louisburg in 1758. He was promoted to major general in 1759.

Wolfe, Thomas Clayton (1900–1938) US novelist. He is noted for the unrestrained rhetoric and emotion of his prose style. He wrote four long and hauntingly powerful autobiographical novels, mostly of the South: *Look Homeward, Angel* (1929), *Of Time and the River* (1935), *The Web and the Rock* (1939), and *You Can't Go Home Again* (1940). The last two were published posthumously.

Wolfe, Tom (1931–) Pen-name of Thomas Kennerly Wolfe, Jr. US journalist and novelist. In the 1960s he was a founder of the 'New Journalism', which brought fiction's methods to reportage. Wolfe recorded US customs and fashions in pop-style essays in, for example, *The Kandy-Kolored Tangerine-Flake Streamline Baby* (1965). His sharp social eye is applied to the New York of the 1980s in his novel *The Bonfire of the Vanities* (1988; filmed 1990).

wolfram alternative name for ▷tungsten.

WOMBAT The wombat is a powerfully built marsupial. There are three species found in Australia and one in Tasmania.

> ### Ludwig Wittgenstein
> *It is not how things are in the world that is mystical, but that it exists.*
>
> *Tractatus Logico-Philosophicus*

> ### Hugo Wolf
> *I sent him a song five years ago, and asked him to mark a cross in the score wherever he thought it was faulty . . . Brahms sent it back unread, saying, 'I don't want to make a cemetery of your composition.'*
>
> Quoted in Lochner *Fritz Kreisler* (1951)

---

wolframite iron manganese tungstate, $(Fe,Mn)WO_4$, an ore mineral of tungsten. It is dark grey with a submetallic surface lustre, and often occurs in hydrothermal veins in association with ores of tin.

Wollaston, William Hyde (1766–1828) English chemist and physicist who discovered in 1804 how to make malleable platinum. He went on to discover the new elements palladium in 1804 and rhodium in 1805. He also contributed to optics through the invention of a number of ingenious and still useful measuring instruments.

Wollongong (Aboriginal 'sound of the sea') industrial city on the coast of New South Wales, Australia, 80 km/50 mi south of Sydney; population (1996, with Port Kembla) 219,761. Wollongong, the third-largest city in New South Wales, is the main residential and business centre of the Illawarra district. Its chief industries are steel production, tourism, fishing, dairying, and the manufacture of textiles and clothing. Wollongong is situated on Australia's southern coalfield, and exports coal from its port at Port Kembla. Greater Wollongong includes Port Kembla.

Wollstonecraft, Mary (1759–1797) British feminist. She was a member of a group of radical intellectuals called the English Jacobins. Her book *A Vindication of the Rights of Women* (1792) demanded equal educational opportunities for women. She married William ▷Godwin in 1797 and died giving birth to a daughter, Mary (later Mary ▷Shelley).
    Related Web site: Vindication of the Rights of Woman, A
    http://www.bartleby.com/144/index.html

Wolof the majority ethnic group living in Senegal. There is also a Wolof minority in Gambia. There are about 2 million speakers of Wolof, a language belonging to the Niger-Congo family. The Wolof are Muslims.

Wolsey, Thomas (c. 1475–1530) English cleric and politician. In Henry VIII's service from 1509, he became archbishop of York in 1514, cardinal and lord chancellor in 1515, and began the dissolution of the monasteries.

His reluctance to further Henry's divorce from Catherine of Aragon led to his downfall in 1529. He was charged with high treason in 1530 but died before being tried.

Wolverhampton industrial town in West Midlands, central England, 20 km/12 mi northwest of Birmingham; population (1994) 256,100. Industries include metalworking, engineering, and the manufacture of chemicals, tyres, aircraft, bicycles, locks and keys, and commercial vehicles. Europe's first power station fuelled by waste tyres opened here in 1993.

The University of Wolverhampton (formerly Wolverhampton Polytechnic) was established in 1992.

wolverine *Gulo gulo*, largest land member of the weasel family (Mustelidae), found in Europe, Asia, and North America. It is stocky in build, and about 1 m/3.3 ft long. Its long, thick fur is dark brown on the back and belly and lighter on the sides. It covers food that it cannot eat with an unpleasant secretion. Destruction of habitat and trapping for its fur have greatly reduced its numbers.

womb common name for the ▷uterus.

wombat any of a family (Vombatidae) of burrowing, herbivorous marsupials, native to Tasmania and southern Australia. They are about 1 m/3.3 ft long, heavy, with a big head, short legs and tail, and coarse fur.

The two living species include the **common wombat** *Vombatus ursinus* of Tasmania and southeastern Australia, and *Lasiorhinus latifrons*, the **plains wombat** of southern Australia.
    Related Web site: Common Wombat http://www.tased.edu.au/tot/fauna/wombat.html

Women's Institute (WI) national organization with branches in many towns and villages for the 'development of community welfare and the practice of rural crafts', found in Britain and Commonwealth countries.

women's movement campaign for the rights and ▷emancipation of women, including social, political, and economic equality with men. Early European campaigners of the 17th–19th centuries fought for women's rights to own property, to have access to higher education, and to vote (see ▷suffragette). Once women's suffrage was achieved in the 20th century, the emphasis of the movement shifted to the goals of equal social and economic opportunities for women, including employment. A continuing area of concern in industrialized countries is the contradiction between the now generally accepted principle of equality and the inequalities that remain between the sexes in state policies and in everyday life. See also ▷feminism.

women's services the organized military use of women on a large scale, a 20th-century development. First, women replaced men in factories, on farms, and in noncombat tasks during wartime; they are now found in combat units in many countries, including the USA, Cuba, the UK, and Israel.

Women's Social and Political Union (WSPU) British political movement founded in 1903 by Emmeline ▷Pankhurst to organize a militant crusade for female suffrage.

Wonder, Stevie (1950–) Stage name of Steveland Judkins Morris. US pop musician, singer, and songwriter. He is associated with Motown Records, and had his first hit, 'Fingertips, Pt. 2', at the age of 13. Later hits, most of which he composed and sang, and on which he also played several instruments, include 'My Cherie Amour', 'You Are the Sunshine of My Life', 'Superstition', 'Isn't She Lovely?', and 'I Just called to Say I Love You'. Among his critically acclaimed albums are *Where I'm Coming From* (1972), *Innervisions* (1973), *Songs in the Key of Life* (1976). Later works include *Jungle Fever* (1991) and *Conversation Peace* (1995).

wood the hard tissue beneath the bark of many perennial plants; it is composed of water-conducting cells, or secondary ▷xylem, and gains its hardness and strength from deposits of ▷lignin. Hardwoods, such as oak, and **softwoods**, such as pine, have commercial value as structural material and for furniture.

Wood, Henry Joseph (1869–1944) English conductor. From 1895 until his death, he conducted the London Promenade Concerts, now named after him. He promoted a national interest in music and encouraged many young composers. As a composer he is remembered for his *Fantasia on British Sea Songs* (1905), which ends each Promenade season.

Wood, Mrs Henry (1814–1887) Born Ellen Price. English novelist who was a pioneer of the regional novel of realism. Her works include the melodramatic *East Lynne* (1861), a novel of middle-class life that sold over half a million copies; it was also dramatized repeatedly and translated into several languages. She owned and edited the magazine *Argosy*, in which she published her series of short stories, the *Johnny Ludlow Papers* (1874–87).

Wood, Natalie (1938–1981) Stage name of Natasha Gurdin. US film actor. She started out as a child star. Her films include *Miracle on 34th Street* (1947), *Rebel Without a Cause* (1955), *The Searchers* (1956), and *Bob and Carol and Ted and Alice* (1969).

woodcarving art form practised in many parts of the world since prehistoric times: for example, the northwestern Pacific coast of North America, in the form of totem poles, and West Africa, where there is a long tradition of woodcarving, notably in Nigeria. Woodcarvings survive less often than sculpture in stone or metal because of the comparative fragility of the material.

woodcock either of two species of wading birds, genus *Scolopax*, of the family Scolopacidae, which have barred plumage and long bills, and live in wet woodland areas. They belong to the long-billed section of the snipes, order Charadriiformes.

Woodcraft Folk British name for the youth organization founded in the USA as the Woodcraft League by Ernest Thompson Seton in 1902, with branches in many countries. Inspired by the ▷Scouts, it differs in that it is for mixed groups and is socialist in outlook.

woodcut print made by a woodblock in which a picture or design has been cut in relief along the grain of the wood. The woodcut is the oldest method of ▷printing, invented in China in the 5th century AD. In the Middle Ages woodcuts became popular in Europe, illustrating early printed books and broadsides.

woodland area in which trees grow more or less thickly; generally smaller than a ▷forest. Temperate climates, with four distinct seasons a year, tend to support a mixed woodland habitat, with some conifers but mostly broad-leaved and deciduous trees, shedding their leaves in autumn and regrowing them in spring. In the Mediterranean region and parts of the southern hemisphere, the trees are mostly evergreen.

Temperate woodlands grow in the zone between the cold coniferous forests and the tropical forests of the hotter climates near the Equator. They develop in areas where the closeness of the sea keeps the climate mild and moist.

Old woodland can rival tropical rainforest in the number of species it supports, but most of the species are hidden in the soil. A study in Oregon, USA, in 1991 found that the soil in a single woodland location contained 8,000 arthropod species (such as insects, mites, centipedes, and millipedes), compared with only 143 species of reptile, bird, and mammal in the woodland above.

In England in 1900, about 2.5% of land was woodland, compared to about 3.4% in the 11th century. An estimated 33% of ancient woodland has been destroyed since 1945.

WOODLOUSE The armoured segmented body is clearly visible on these *Oniscus asellus* pillbugs clustered beneath a stone, where they are often to be found. This is the commonest species in the British Isles, especially in gardens, where it may do considerable damage to tender plants. *Premaphotos Wildlife*

woodlouse crustacean of the order Isopoda. Woodlice have segmented bodies, flattened undersides, and 14 legs. The eggs are carried by the female in a pouch beneath the thorax. They often live in high densities: up to as many as 8,900 per square metre.

The hatchlings, called mancas, have only 12 legs and must moult twice before gaining their final pair of legs. Common in Britain are the genera *Oniscus* and *Porcellio*.

woodmouse (or **long-tailed field mouse**) *Apodemus sylvaticus*, rodent that lives in woodlands, hedgerows, and sometimes open fields in Britain and Europe. About 9 cm/3.5 in long, with a similar length of tail, it is yellow-brown above, white below, and has long oval ears.

It is nocturnal and feeds largely on seeds, but eats a range of foods, including some insects.

woodpecker bird of the family Picidae, order Piciformes. They are adapted for climbing up the bark of trees, and picking out insects to eat from the crevices. The feet, though very short, are usually strong; the nails are broad and crooked and the toes placed in pairs, two forward and two backward. As an additional support their tail feathers terminate in points, and are uncommonly hard. Woodpeckers have a long extensile tongue, which has muscles enabling the bird to dart it forth and to retract it again quickly. There are about 200 species worldwide.

The European **green woodpecker** or **yaffle** *Picus viridis* is green with a red crown and yellow rump, and about the size of a jay. The **greater** and **lesser spotted woodpeckers** *Dendrocopos major* and *D. minor*, also British species, have black, red, and white plumage. The **wryneck** *Jynx torquilla* is a slightly aberrant form.

Woods, Tiger (1976–) Born Eldrick Woods. US golfer. He has made a phenomenal impact on the game since 1994 when he became the youngest player, at the age of 18, to win the US Amateur Championship, the first of an unprecedented three successive titles. Previously he had won the US Junior Championship 1991–93. He turned professional in 1996, immediately becoming one of the wealthiest men in US sport as a result of endorsement deals worth US$64 million. In his first six months as a professional he won four tournaments on the US PGA circuit, then in 1997 he won the Mercedes Championships, the Honda Asian Classic (Bangkok), and the US Masters. Woods was voted the Associated Press Male Athlete of the Year in 1997 and again in 2000, becoming only the fifth golfer to win this award and the first since Lee Trevino. In February 2000, he became the first player to win six successive tournaments on the US PGA Tour since Ben Hogan in 1948. With his victory at the Masters in 2001, he became the first professional golfer to hold all four major titles at the same time.

Related Web site: 'Tiger' Woods http://www.tigerwoods.com/

Woodstock the first free rock festival, held near Bethel, New York State, USA, over three days in August 1969. It was attended by 400,000 people, and performers included the Band, Country Joe and the Fish, the Grateful Dead, Jimi Hendrix, Jefferson Airplane, and the Who. The festival was a landmark in the youth culture of the 1960s (see ▷hippie) and was recorded in the film *Woodstock* (1970).

Woodward, Robert Burns (1917–1979) US chemist who worked on synthesizing a large number of complex molecules. These included quinine in 1944, cholesterol in 1951, chlorophyll in 1960, and vitamin B_{12} in 1971. He was awarded the Nobel Prize for Chemistry in 1965 for his work in organic synthesis.

wood wasp (or **horntail**) moderately large wasp that is black or metallic blue, often with yellow bandings. The long lancelike ovipositor (egg-laying organ) of the female wood wasp is used for

WOODCUT A Japanese woodblock print of an archer firing at a target by Japanese artist Kuniyoshi. *The Art Archive/Victoria and Albert Museum London/Eileen Tweedy*

drilling holes into wood. Usually a single egg is deposited into each hole, and the larva on hatching bores through the heart wood causing much damage. The wood wasp is in the family Siricidae, suborder Symphyta, order Hymenoptera, class Insecta, phylum Arthropoda.

woodwind musical instrument from which sound is produced by blowing into a tube, causing the air within to vibrate. Woodwind instruments include those, like the flute, originally made of wood but now more commonly of metal. The saxophone, made of metal, is an honorary woodwind instrument because it is related to the clarinet. The oboe, bassoon, flute, and clarinet make up the normal woodwind section of an orchestra.

woodworm common name for the larval stage of certain wood-boring beetles. Dead or injured trees are their natural target, but they also attack structural timber and furniture.

Included are the furniture beetle *Anobium punctatum*, which attacks older timber; the powder-post beetle genus *Lyctus*, which attacks newer timber; the ▷deathwatch beetle, whose presence always coincides with fungal decay; and wood-boring ▷weevils. Special wood preservatives have been developed to combat woodworm infestation, which has markedly increased since about 1950.

Wookey Hole natural cave near Wells, Somerset, England, in which flint implements of Old Stone Age people and bones of extinct animals have been found.

Woolf, (Adeline) Virginia (1882–1941) Born (Adeline) Virginia Stephen. English novelist and critic. In novels such as *Mrs Dalloway* (1925), *To the Lighthouse* (1927), and *The Waves* (1931), she used a 'stream of consciousness' technique to render inner experience. In *A Room of One's Own* (1929) (non-fiction), *Orlando* (1928), and *The Years* (1937), she examines the importance of economic independence for women and other feminist principles.

Her first novel, *The Voyage Out* (1915), explored the tensions experienced by women who want marriage and a career. After the death of her father, Leslie Stephen, she and her siblings moved to Bloomsbury, forming the nucleus of the ▷Bloomsbury Group. She produced a succession of novels, short stories, and critical essays, included in *The Common Reader* (1925 and 1932). She was plagued by bouts of depression and committed suicide in 1941.

Related Web site: Virginia Woolf Chronology http://www.cygneis.com/woolf/vwchrono.htm

> **Virginia Woolf**
> *It is in our idleness, in our dreams, that the submerged truth sometimes comes to the top.*
> A Room of One's Own

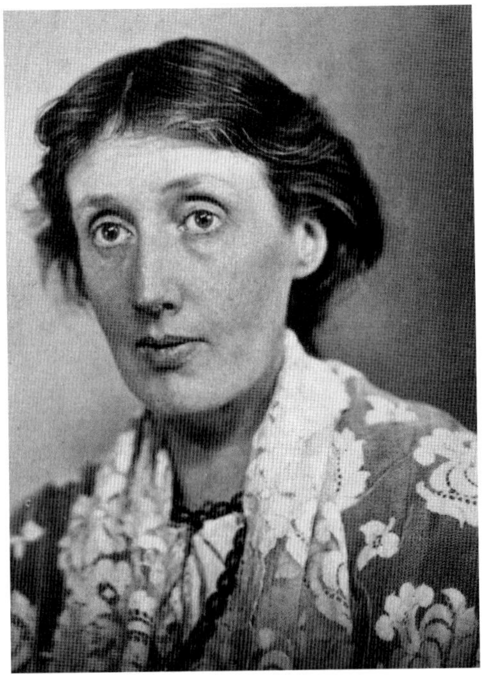

VIRGINIA WOOLF Novelist and essayist Virginia Woolf, one of the major English writers of the 20th century. *Image Bank*

woolly bear larva of the ▷carpet beetle.

Woolman, John (1720–1772) American Quaker, born in Ancocas (now Rancocas), New Jersey. He was one of the first antislavery agitators and left an important *Journal*. He supported those who refused to pay a tax levied by Pennsylvania, to conduct the French and Indian War, on the grounds that it was inconsistent with pacifist principles.

Woolworth, Frank Winfield (1852–1919) US entrepreneur. He opened his first successful 'five and dime' store in Lancaster, Pennsylvania, in 1879, and, together with his brother C S Woolworth (1856–1947), built up a chain of similar stores throughout the USA, Canada, the UK, and Europe.

Worcester cathedral city in west central England on the River Severn, and administrative headquarters of the county of ▷Worcestershire, on the River Severn, 35 km/22 mi southwest of Birmingham; population (1991) 82,700. Industries include the manufacture of shoes, Worcestershire sauce, and Royal Worcester porcelain. The cathedral dates from the 13th and 14th centuries. The birthplace of the composer Elgar at nearby Broadheath is a museum. At the **Battle of Worcester** in 1651 Oliver Cromwell defeated Charles II.

Worcestershire two-tier county of west central England. Herefordshire and Worcestershire existed as counties until 1974, when they were amalgamated to form the county of Hereford and Worcester; in 1998 this county was divided back into Worcestershire and Herefordshire, which regained their pre-1974 boundaries.

area 1,735 sq km/670 sq mi **towns and cities** ▷Worcester (administrative headquarters), Bewdley, Bromsgrove, Evesham, Kidderminster, Pershore, Stourport, Tenbury Wells **physical** Malvern Hills in the southwest (highest point Worcester Beacon 425 m/1,394 ft); rivers Severn with tributaries Stour, Teme, and Avon (running through the fertile Vale of Evesham) **features** Droitwich, once a Victorian spa, reopened its baths in 1985 (the town lies over a subterranean brine reservoir); Three Choirs Festival at Great Malvern **agriculture** cereals (oats, wheat), fruit (apples, pears), hops, vegetables; cider; much of the county is under cultivation, a large part being devoted to permanent pasture, notably for Hereford cattle **industries** carpets (Kidderminster), chemicals, engineering, food processing, needles and fishing tackle (Redditch), porcelain (Worcester), salt **population** (1996) 535,700 **famous people** Richard Baxter, Samuel Butler, Edward Elgar, A E Housman, William Langland, Francis Brett Young

Related Web site: Welcome to Worcestershire http://www.worcestershire.gov.uk

word processing input, amendment, manipulation, storage, and retrieval of text. A computer system that runs such software is known as a **word processor**. Since word-processing programs became available to microcomputers, the method has largely replaced the typewriter for producing letters or other text. Typical facilities include insert, delete, cut and paste, reformat, search and replace, copy, print, mail merge, and spelling check.

Wordsworth, Dorothy (1771–1855) English writer. She was the only sister of William ▷Wordsworth and lived with him (and later his wife) as a companion and support from 1795 until his death. Her journals describe their life in Alfoxden, Somerset (of which only a small section remains), and at Grasmere in the Lake District, and their travels, which provided inspiration and material for his poetry.

> **Dorothy Wordsworth**
> *We saw a raven very high above us. It called out, and the dome of the sky seemed to echo the sound.*
> Journals 27 July 1800

Wordsworth, William (1770–1850) English Romantic poet. In 1797 he moved with his sister Dorothy ▷Wordsworth to Somerset, where he lived near Samuel Taylor ▷Coleridge and collaborated with him on *Lyrical Ballads* (1798) (which included 'Tintern Abbey', a meditation on his response to nature). From 1799 he lived in the Lake District. His most notable individual poems were published in *Poems* (1807) (including 'Intimations of Immortality'). At intervals between then and 1839 he revised *The Prelude* (posthumously published in 1850), the first part of his uncompleted philosophical, creative, and spiritual autobiography in verse. He was appointed poet laureate in 1843.

Wordsworth was born in Cockermouth, Cumberland, and educated at Cambridge University. In 1792 he returned to England from a visit to France, having fallen in love with Annette Vallon (1766–1841), with whom he had an illegitimate daughter. In 1802 he married his cousin Mary Hutchinson (1770–1859).

A leader of the Romantic movement, Wordsworth is best known as the poet who reawakened his readers to the beauty of nature, describing the emotions and perceptive insights which natural beauty arouses in the sensitive observer. He advocated a poetry of simple feeling and the use of the language of ordinary speech, demonstrated in the unadorned simplicity of lyrics such as 'To the cuckoo' and 'I wandered lonely as a cloud'. At a deeper level, he saw himself as a philosophical poet and his nature mysticism had a strong, though diffuse, effect on his successors.

Related Web site: Complete Poetical Works of William Wordsworth http://www.bartleby.com/145/index.html

> **William Wordsworth**
> *One impulse from a vernal wood / May teach you more of man, / Of moral evil and of good, / Than all the sages can.*
> 'Tables Turned'

work in physics, a measure of the result of transferring energy from one system to another to cause an object to move. Work should not be confused with ▷energy (the capacity to do work, which is also measured in joules) or with ▷power (the rate of doing work, measured in joules per second).

worker cooperative business owned and controlled by its workers rather than outside shareholders. In some worker cooperatives each member worker has one vote at meetings, however many shares he or she owns. There are relatively few worker cooperatives in the UK; they are far more popular in Europe and Japan.

worker participation situation where workers are involved in some way with decision-making in a business organization. Worker participation can take many forms. There might be a consultative council in the company where trade unions and management meet regularly to discuss points of mutual interest. Workers can be organized in **quality circles** and meet regularly in small groups to discuss ways in which their work could be better organized.

Workers' Educational Association (WEA) British institution that aims to provide democratically controlled education for working people.

Workers' Party of Kurdistan (PKK) Kurdish guerrilla organization, active in Turkey from 1974. Initially it aimed to secure an independent Kurdish state, ▷Kurdistan, but has since modified its demands, indicating a preparedness to accept autonomy within a federal system. Responsible for many civilian deaths and bombings of private as well as government buildings, the PKK has been the subject of a prolonged and unrelenting campaign of suppression by the Turkish authorities (more than 11,000 people died in fighting between government and PKK forces 1978–94). The PKK was banned in Germany and France in 1993 after attacks on Turkish premises in those countries. The PKK turned itself into a legitimate political organization in February 2000, announcing that it renounced the armed struggle it had waged against the Turkish government for the past 15 years.

work experience the going out of pupils or students into industry to experience work for a short period of time. Typically, 15–16 year olds spend 1–2 weeks in a work experience placement. It helps them gain some understanding of the world of work and of the opportunities that might be available to them when they leave full-time education.

workhouse in the UK, a former institution to house and maintain people unable to earn their own living, established under the ▷poor law. Groups of parishes in England combined to build workhouses for the poor, the aged, the disabled, and orphaned children from about 1815 until about 1930.

Sixteenth-century poor laws made parishes responsible for helping the poor within their boundaries. The 19th-century parish poor law unions found workhouses a more cost-effective way. An act of Parliament in 1834 improved supervision of workhouses, where conditions were sometimes harsh, and a new ▷welfare legislation in the early 20th century made them redundant.

working men's club social club set up in the 19th century to cater for the education and recreation of working men. Today the clubs have few limitations on membership and are entirely social.

workstation high-performance desktop computer with strong graphics capabilities, traditionally used for engineering (▷CAD and ▷CAM), scientific research, and desktop publishing. From 1985–95, workstations were frequently based on fast RISC (reduced instruction-set computer) chips running the Unix operating system. However, the market is under attack from 'Wintel' PCs with Intel Pentium processors running Microsoft Windows NT, which are cheaper and run PC software as well as workstation programs. By 1997, four of the five leading workstation manufacturers – DEC, Hewlett-Packard, IBM, and Silicon Graphics Inc, but not Sun Microsystems – had committed to supporting NT.

work to rule industrial action whereby employees work strictly according to the legal terms of their contract of employment, usually resulting in a slowing-down of the work process.

World Bank (officially called the **International Bank for Reconstruction and Development**) specialized agency of the United Nations that borrows in the commercial market and lends on commercial terms. It was established in 1945 under the 1944 Bretton Woods agreement, which also created the International Monetary Fund (IMF). The **International Development Association** is an arm of the World Bank.

> **Related Web site: World Bank Home Page** http://www.worldbank.org/

World Council of Churches (WCC) international organization aiming to bring together diverse movements within the Christian church. Established in 1945, it has a membership of more than 100 countries and more than 300 churches. Its headquarters are located in Geneva, Switzerland.

World Cup the most prestigious competition in international soccer, organized by the sport's world governing body, Fédération Internationale de Football Association (FIFA). Similar international competitions are held in rugby union, cricket, athletics, and other sports. Most World Cup events are held every four years.

> **Related Web site: Fédération Internationale de Football Association (FIFA)** http://www.fifa.com/index.html

World Health Organization (WHO) specialized agency of the United Nations established in 1946 to prevent the spread of diseases and to eradicate them. In 1996–97 it had a budget of US$842.654 million. Its headquarters are located in Geneva, Switzerland. The WHO's greatest achievement to date has been the eradication of smallpox.

The WHO aims to eradicate seven major diseases: polio, measles, leprosy, river blindness, lymphatic filariasis (elephantiasis), Chagas' disease, and guinea worm disease. Polio is expected to be eradicated by 2005, whereas the deadline for filariasis is 2030.

In January 1998 the former Norwegian prime minister Gro Harlem ▷Brundtland became director-general of the organization and took up her director-generalship in July.

> **Related Web site: World Health Organization** http://www.who.ch/

World Intellectual Property Organization (WIPO) specialist agency of the United Nations established in 1974 to coordinate the international protection (initiated by the Paris convention in 1883) of inventions, trademarks, and industrial designs, and also literary and artistic works (as initiated by the Berne convention in 1886).

World Meteorological Organization agency, part of the United Nations since 1950, that promotes the international exchange of weather information through the establishment of a worldwide network of meteorological stations. It was founded as the International Meteorological Organization in 1873 and its headquarters are now in Geneva, Switzerland.

world music (or **roots music**) popular music which has its roots in ▷folk music, especially non-European folk music. It is usually performed by artists from the country it comes from, and has a distinct regional character. Examples are West African ▷mbalax, East African soukous, South African ▷mbaqanga, French Antillean ▷zouk, Latin American salsa and ▷lambada, and ▷Cajun music, as well as combinations of these with European folk music or rural ▷blues.

The term is sometimes used to include non-Western classical music, such as the Javanese gamelan and Spanish flamenco, or simply to describe any music other than Western classical music.

> **Related Web site: RootsWorld** http://www.rootsworld.com/rw/

World Series annual ▷baseball competition between the winning teams of the National League (NL) and American League (AL). It is a best-of-seven series played each October. The first World Series was played in 1903 (as a best-of-nine series) and the AL's Boston Pilgrims defeated the NL's Pittsburgh Pirates in eight games.

World Trade Organization (WTO) specialized agency of the United Nations, world trade monitoring body established in January 1995, on approval of the Final Act of the Uruguay round of the ▷General Agreement on Tariffs and Trade (GATT). Under the Final Act, the WTO, a permanent trading body with a status commensurate with that of the International Monetary Fund or the World Bank, effectively replaced GATT. The WTO monitors agreements to reduce barriers to trade, such as tariffs, subsidies, quotas, and regulations which discriminate against imported products.

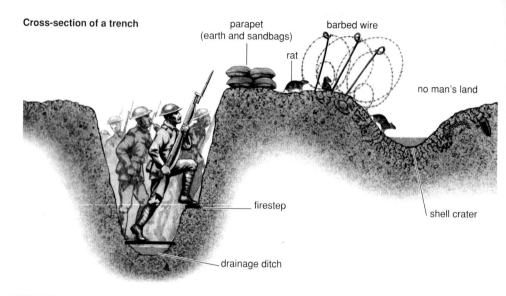

Cross-section of a trench

parapet (earth and sandbags)

barbed wire

rat

no man's land

firestep

shell crater

drainage ditch

WORLD WAR I Cross-section of a World War I trench. Conditions in the trenches were often appalling and, apart from the onslaught of enemy shot and shell, soldiers suffered numerous diseases as a result of their conditions, such as trench foot (foot rot caused by the continual damp), and trench fever and typhus (spread by body lice).

All members of GATT automatically became members of the WTO on their parliaments' ratification of the Uruguay round; new members, without exception, would have to meet the criteria established by the Uruguay round. WTO headquarters are in Geneva, Switzerland, and its director-general is Renato Ruggiero, of Italy. The organization had 129 members at the end of 1999, when China was admitted entry in exchange for allowing foreign firms access to China's markets, which would open a market of 1.3 billion consumers.

The opening of the 1999 WTO summit in Seattle, Washington, was delayed after the presence of thousands of peaceful antiglobalization protesters was overshadowed by a small number of violent protesters. A curfew and a state of civil emergency was declared by the mayor of Seattle, and America's handling of the conference was condemned by delegates attending it. By 2001, membership of WTO reached 142 countries.

> **Related Web site: World Trade Organization** http://www.wto.org/english/thewto_e/thewto_e.htm

World War I (1914–18) war between the Central European Powers (Germany, Austria-Hungary, and allies) on one side and the

Basil Liddell Hart
British military strategist

Fifty years were spent in the process of making Europe explosive. Five days were enough to detonate it.

The Real War 1914–1918 1930

WORLD SERIES US baseball player Babe Ruth, who attracted huge crowds to baseball grounds wherever he played. *Archive Photos*

WORLD WAR I A man shown in World War I infantry garb. *Image Bank*

▷Triple Entente (Britain and the British Empire, France, and Russia) and their allies, including the USA (which entered in 1917), on the other side. An estimated 10 million lives were lost and twice that number were wounded. It was fought on the eastern and western fronts, in the Middle East, in Africa, and at sea. See also World War I: Key Events on p. 1036.

> **Related Web sites: Great War and the Shaping of the 20th Century** http://www.pbs.org/greatwar/
> **Great War Statistics** http://www.d-n-a.net/users/dnetDkjs/figures.htm
> **World War I Document Archive** http://www.lib.byu.edu/~rdh/wwi/

World War II (1939–45) war between Germany, Italy, and Japan (the ▷Axis powers) on one side, and Britain, the Commonwealth, France, the USA, the USSR, and China (the ▷Allies) on the other. An estimated 55 million lives were lost (20 million of them citizens of the USSR), and 60 million people in Europe were displaced because of bombing raids. The war was fought in the Atlantic theatre (Europe, North Asfrica, and the Atlantic Ocean) and the Pacific theatre (Far East and the Pacific).

It is estimated that, during the course of the war, for every tonne of bombs dropped on the UK, 315 fell on Germany.

In 1945 Germany surrendered (May), but Japan fought on until the USA dropped atomic bombs on Hiroshima and Nagasaki (August). See also World War II: Key Events on p. 1036.

> **Related Web sites: World War II Images** http://www.earthstation1.com/wwii.html
> **World War II Timeline** http://www.historyplace.com/worldwar2/timeline/ww2time.htm

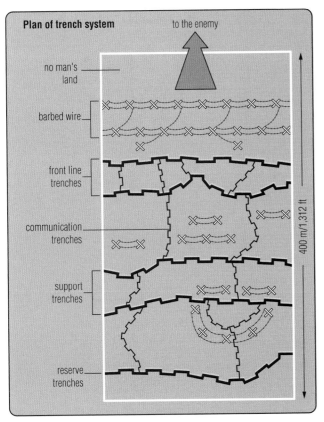

Plan of trench system

to the enemy

no man's land

barbed wire

front line trenches

communication trenches

support trenches

reserve trenches

400 m/1,312 ft

WORLD WAR I A plan of a World War I trench system. The trench system on the Western Front consisted of frontline trenches, support and reserve trenches (used to transport soldiers, equipment, and food supplies), and communication trenches, dug at an angle to the trenches facing the enemy. Soldiers were rotated so they only spent short periods at the front, where most casualties occurred, although as the war progressed and men became in shorter supply, the time at the front was often much longer.

World War II 1939–45

0　　　　500 mi
0　　　　800 km

NORWAY　ESTONIA　SWEDEN　LATVIA　LITHUANIA　DENMARK　EAST PRUSSIA　IRELAND　UNITED KINGDOM　London　NETH.　Berlin　GERMANY　POLAND　USSR　Stalingrad　BELG.　Paris　LUX.　ATLANTIC OCEAN　FRANCE　CZECHOSLOVAKIA　SWITZ.　AUSTRIA　HUNGARY　ROMANIA　VICHY FRANCE　AND.　ITALY　YUGOSLAVIA　Black Sea　PORTUGAL　SPAIN　Rome　BULGARIA　ALB.　TURKEY　GREECE　SPANISH MOROCCO　SYRIA　MOROCCO　ALGERIA　TUNISIA　Mediterranean Sea　PALESTINE　TRANS-JORDAN　El Alamein　LIBYA　EGYPT

— political boundary 1937
Axis Powers 1939
extent of Axis Powers Nov 1942
Allied Powers

World Wide Fund for Nature (WWF; formerly the **World Wildlife Fund**) international organization established in 1961 to raise funds for conservation by public appeal. Projects include conservation of particular species, for example, the tiger and giant panda, and special areas, such as the Simen Mountains, Ethiopia.

WORM (acronym for write once read many times) in computing, a storage device, similar to a ▷CD-ROM. The computer can write to the disk directly, but cannot later erase or overwrite the same area. WORMs are mainly used for archiving and backup copies.

worm any of various elongated limbless invertebrates belonging to several phyla. Worms include the ▷flatworms, such as ▷flukes and ▷tapeworms; the roundworms or ▷nematodes, such as the eelworm and the hookworm; the marine ribbon worms or nemerteans; and the segmented worms or ▷annelids.

The New Zealand flatworm *Artioposthia triangulata*, 15 cm/6 in long and weighing 2 g/0.07 oz, had by 1990 colonized every county of Northern Ireland and parts of Scotland. It can eat an ▷earthworm in 30 minutes and so destroys soil fertility.

Worms ancient city and river port in Rhineland-Palatinate, Germany, on the River Rhine, 25 km/15 mi north of Ludwigshafen; population (1995) 79,700. Industries include food processing and the manufacture of chemicals, paint, machinery, furniture, and worsted. The vineyards of the Liebfrauenkirche (14th to 15th century) produced the original Liebfraumilch wine; it is now produced by many growers around Worms. The Protestant reformer Martin Luther appeared before the **Diet** (Assembly) of **Worms** in 1521 and was declared an outlaw by the Roman Catholic Church. It is one of the oldest cities in Germany.

wormwood any of a group of plants belonging to the daisy family and mainly found in northern temperate regions, especially the aromatic herb *A. absinthium*, the leaves of which are used in the alcoholic drink absinthe. Tarragon is closely related to wormwood. (Genus *Artemisia*, family Compositae.)

worsted (from Worstead, Norfolk, where it was first made) stiff, smooth woollen fabric.

Wotton, Henry (1568–1639) English poet and diplomat under James I. He was provost of Eton College public school 1624–39. His tastes in art and architecture were influenced by his years of service in Venice, and he published *The Elements of Architecture* (1624).

Wounded Knee site on the Oglala Sioux Reservation, South Dakota, USA, of a confrontation between the US Army and American Indians on 29 December 1890; the last 'battle' of the Plains Wars. On 15 December the Hunkpapa Sioux chief ▷Sitting Bull had been killed, supposedly resisting arrest for involvement in the ▷Ghost Dance movement (rituals aimed at resumption of Indian control of North America). Sioux involved in the movement

WORLD WAR II German soldiers prepare to fire a grenade. They are on the Eastern Front, in about 1941. *Archive Photos*

WORLD WAR II The 40-cm/16-in guns of *USS Iowa* were used primarily to bombard shore positions or to protect aircraft carriers. In World War II, the increased use of aircraft reduced the need for battleships like the *USS Iowa*. *Image Bank*

World War I: Key Events

1914 June	Assassination of Archduke Franz Ferdinand of Austria, 28 June.
July	German government issues 'blank cheque' to Austria, offering support in war against Serbia. Austrian ultimatum to Serbia. Serbs accepts all but two points. Austria refuses to accept compromise and declares war. Russia begins mobilization to defend Serbian ally. Germany demands Russian demobilization.
August	Germany declares war on Russia. France mobilizes to assist Russian ally. Germans occupies Luxembourg and demands access to Belgian territory, which is refused. Germany declares war on France and invades Belgium. Britain declares war on Germany, then on Austria. Dominions within the British Empire, including Australia, are automatically involved. Battle of Tannenburg between Central Powers and Russians. Russian army encircled.
September	British and French troops halt German advance just short of Paris, and drive them back. First Battle of the Marne, and of the Aisne. Beginning of trench warfare.
October–November	First Battle of Ypres. Britain declares war on Turkey.
1915 April–May	Gallipoli offensive launched by British and dominion troops against Turkish forces. Second Battle of Ypres. First use of poison gas by Germans. Italy joins war against Austria. German submarine sinks ocean liner *Lusitania* on 7 May, later helping to bring USA into the war.
August–September	Warsaw is evacuated by the Russians. Battle of Tarnopol. Vilna is taken by the Germans. Tsar Nicholas II takes supreme control of Russian forces.
1916 January	Final evacuation of British and dominion troops from Gallipoli.
February	German offensive against Verdun begins, with huge losses for small territorial gain.
May	Naval Battle of Jutland between British and German imperial fleets ends inconclusively, but puts a stop to further German naval participation in the war.
June	Russian (Brusilov) offensive against the Ukraine begins.
July–November	First Battle of the Somme, a sustained Anglo-French offensive which wins little territory and costs a huge number of lives.
August	Hindenburg and Ludendorff take command of the German armed forces. Romania enters the war against Austria but is rapidly overrun.
September	Early tanks are used by British on Western Front.
November	Nivelle replaces Joffre as commander of French forces. Battle of the Ancre on the Western Front.
December	French complete recapture of Verdun fortifications. Austrians occupy Bucharest.
1917 February	Germany declares unrestricted submarine warfare. Russian Revolution begins and tsarist rule is overthrown.
March	British seizure of Baghdad and occupation of Persia.
March–April	Germans retreat to Siegfried Line (Arras-Soissons) on Western Front.
April–May	USA enters the war against Germany. Unsuccessful British and French offensives. Mutinies among French troops. Nivelle replaced by Pétain.
July–November	Third Ypres offensive including Battle of Passchendaele.
September	Germans occupy Riga.
October–November	Battle of Caporetto sees Italian troops defeated by Austrians.
December	Jerusalem taken by British forces under Allenby.
1918 January	US President Woodrow Wilson proclaims 'Fourteen Points' as a basis for peace settlement.
March	Treaty of Brest-Litovsk with Central Powers ends Russian participation in the war, with substantial concessions of territory and reparations. Second Battle of the Somme begins with German Spring Offensive.
July–August	Allied counter-offensive, including tank attack at Amiens, drives Germans back to the Siegfried Line.
September	Hindenburg and Ludendorff call for an armistice.
October	Armistice offered on the basis of the 'Fourteen Points'. German naval and military mutinies at Kiel and Wilhelmshaven.
November	Austria-Hungary signs armistice with Allies. Kaiser Wilhelm II of Germany goes into exile. Provisional government under social democrat Friedrich Ebert is formed. Germany agrees armistice. Fighting on Western Front stops.
1919 January	Peace conference opens at Versailles.
May	Demands are presented to Germany.
June	Germany signs peace treaty at Versailles, followed by other Central Powers: Austria (Treaty of St Germain-en-Laye, September), Bulgaria (Neuilly, November), Hungary (Trianon, June 1920), and Turkey (Sèvres, August 1920).

World War II: Key Events

1939 September	German invasion of Poland; Britain and France declare war on Germany; the USSR invades Poland; fall of Warsaw (Poland divided between Germany and USSR).
November	The USSR invades Finland.
1940 March	Soviet peace treaty with Finland.
April	Germany occupies Denmark, Norway, the Netherlands, Belgium, and Luxembourg. In Britain, a coalition government is formed under Churchill.
May	Germany outflanks the defensive French Maginot Line.
May–June	Evacuation of 337,131 Allied troops from Dunkirk, France, across the Channel to England.
June	Italy declares war on Britain and France; the Germans enter Paris; the French Prime Minister Pétain signs an armistice with Germany and moves the seat of government to Vichy.
July–October	Battle of Britain between British and German air forces.
September	Japanese invasion of French Indochina.
October	Abortive Italian invasion of Greece.
1941 April	Germany occupies Greece and Yugoslavia.
June	Germany invades the USSR; Finland declares war on the USSR.
July	The Germans enter Smolensk, USSR.
December	The Germans come within 40 km/25 mi of Moscow, with Leningrad (now St Petersburg) under siege. First Soviet counteroffensive. Japan bombs Pearl Harbor, Hawaii, and declares war on the USA and Britain. Germany and Italy declare war on the USA.
1942 January	Japanese conquest of the Philippines.
June	Naval battle of Midway, the turning point of the Pacific War.
August	German attack on Stalingrad (now Volgograd), USSR.
October–November	Battle of El Alamein in North Africa, turn of the tide for the Western Allies.
November	Soviet counteroffensive on Stalingrad.
1943 January	The Casablanca Conference issues the Allied demand of unconditional surrender; the Germans retreat from Stalingrad.
March	The USSR drives the Germans back to the River Donetz.
May	End of Axis resistance in North Africa.
July	A coup by King Victor Emmanuel and Marshal Badoglio forces Mussolini to resign.
August	Beginning of the campaign against the Japanese in Burma (now Myanmar); US Marines land on Guadalcanal, Solomon Islands.
September	Italy surrenders to the Allies; Mussolini is rescued by the Germans who set up a Republican fascist government in northern Italy; Allied landings at Salerno; the USSR retakes Smolensk.
October	Italy declares war on Germany.
November	The US Navy defeats the Japanese in the Battle of Guadalcanal.
November–December	The Allied leaders meet at the Tehran Conference.
1944 January	Allied landing in Nazi-occupied Italy: Battle of Anzio.
March	End of the German U-boat campaign in the Atlantic.
May	Fall of Monte Cassino, southern Italy.
6 June	D-day: Allied landings in Nazi-occupied and heavily defended Normandy.
July	The bomb plot by German generals against Hitler fails.
August	Romania joins the Allies.
September	Battle of Arnhem on the Rhine; Soviet armistice with Finland.
October	The Yugoslav guerrilla leader Tito and Soviets enter Belgrade.
December	German counteroffensive, Battle of the Bulge.
1945 February	The Soviets reach the German border; Yalta conference; Allied bombing campaign over Germany (Dresden destroyed); the US reconquest of the Philippines is completed; the Americans land on Iwo Jima, south of Japan.
April	Hitler commits suicide; Mussolini is captured by Italian partisans and shot.
May	Germany surrenders to the Allies.
June	US troops complete the conquest of Okinawa (one of the Japanese Ryukyu Islands).
July	The Potsdam Conference issues an Allied ultimatum to Japan.
August	Atom bombs are dropped by the USA on Hiroshima and Nagasaki; Japan surrenders.

tried to flee, including Big Foot's Miniconjou Sioux with the Hunkpapa. Big Foot's group was captured by the 7th Cavalry but during their disarmament a shot was fired leading to the gunning down of Black Foot and over 150 Sioux, half of whom were women and children, as well as 29 soldiers.

For American Indians Wounded Knee has become a symbol of US government oppression. In 1973 the militant American Indian Movement chose the site of Wounded Knee to stage a siege from 27 February to 8 May, in which they held hostages and demanded a government investigation of the Indian treaties.

Related Web site: Cankpe Opi – Wounded Knee Home Page
http://www.dickshovel.com/WKmasscre.html

W particle in physics, an ▷elementary particle, one of the weakons responsible for transmitting the ▷weak nuclear force.

wpm abbreviation for **words per minute**.

wrack any of the large brown ▷seaweeds characteristic of rocky shores. The bladder wrack *F. vesiculosus* has narrow, branched fronds up to 1 m/3.3 ft long, with oval air bladders, usually in pairs on either side of the midrib or central vein. (Genus *Fucus*.)

WRACK Bladder wrack *Fucus vesiculosus* and flat wrack *F. spiralis* often grow together to form dense mats on rocks on the middle shore around the coasts of western Europe. *Premaphotos Wildlife*

wrasse any bony fish of the family Labridae, found in temperate and tropical seas. They are slender and often brightly coloured, with a single long dorsal fin. They have elaborate courtship rituals, and some species can change their colouring and sex. Species vary in size from 5 cm/2 in to 2 m/6.5 ft.

wren any of the family Troglodytidae of small birds of the order Passeriformes, with slender, slightly curved bills, and uptilted tails.

The only Old World wren is the species *Troglodytes troglodytes* with a cocked tail, and short, rounded wings, found in Europe and northern Asia, as well as North America. Its plumage is rich reddish brown. It is about 10 cm/4 in long, has a loud trilling song, and feeds on insects and spiders. The male constructs a domed nest of moss, grass, and leaves, and additional nests are often built close at hand. It feeds almost entirely on insects. There were approximately 7 million breeding pairs in Britain in 1997.

Wren, Christopher (1632–1723) English architect. His ingenious use of a refined and sober baroque style can be seen in his best-known work, ▷St Paul's Cathedral, London (1675–1711), and in the many churches he built in London including St Mary-le-Bow, Cheapside (1670–77), and St Bride's, Fleet Street (1671–78). His other works include the Sheldonian Theatre, Oxford (1664–69), Greenwich Hospital, London (begun 1694), and Marlborough House, London (1709–10; now much altered).

Wren, P(ercival) C(hristopher)
(1875–1941) English novelist. Drawing on his experiences in the French and Indian armies, he wrote adventure novels including *Beau Geste* (1924) dealing with the Foreign Legion.

Christopher Wren

Si monumentum requiris, circumspice.

If you would see his monument, look around.

Inscription in St Paul's Cathedral, London, attributed to Wren's son

---

wrestling sport popular in ancient Egypt, Greece, and Rome, and included in the Olympics from 704 BC. The two main modern international styles are **Greco-Roman**, concentrating on above-waist holds, and **freestyle**, which allows the legs to be used to hold or trip; in both the aim is to throw the opponent to the ground.

Related Web site: World Wrestling Federation http://www.wwf.com/

Wrexham unitary authority in northeast Wales, created in 1996 from part of the former county of Clywd.

area 500 sq km/193 sq mi **towns** Wrexham (administrative headquarters), Holt, Ruabon **physical** western side is mountainous, including Ruabon Mountain; River Dee **features** Clywedog Valley, with notable countryside and industrial archaeology **industries** food manufacture, plastics, pharmaceuticals, high-technology industries **population** (1996) 123,500

Wright, Frank Lloyd
(1869–1959) US architect. He is known for 'organic architecture', in which buildings reflect their natural surroundings. From the 1890s, he developed his celebrated **prairie house** style, a series of low, spreading houses with projecting roofs. He later diversified, employing reinforced concrete to explore a variety of geometric forms. Among his buildings are his Wisconsin home, Taliesin East (1925), in prairie-house style; Falling Water, near Pittsburgh, Pennsylvania (1936), a house of cantilevered terraces straddling a waterfall; and the Guggenheim Museum, New York (1959), a spiral ramp rising from a circular plan.

Wright also designed buildings in Japan 1915–22, most notably the Imperial Hotel in Tokyo (1916). In 1938 he built his winter home in the Arizona Desert, Taliesin West, and established an architectural community there. He always designed the interiors and furnishings for his projects, to create a total environment for his patrons.

Related Web site: All-Wright Site http://www.geocities.com/SoHo/1469/flw.html

Wright, Orville
(1871–1948) and **Wilbur** (1867–1912) US inventors; brothers who pioneered piloted, powered flight. Inspired by Otto ▷Lilienthal's gliding, they perfected their piloted glider in 1902. In 1903 they built a powered machine, a 12-hp 341-kg/750-lb plane, and became the first to make a successful powered flight, near Kitty Hawk, North Carolina. Orville flew 36.6 m/120 ft in 12 seconds; Wilbur, 260 m/852 ft in 59 seconds.

Both brothers became interested in flight at early ages. They devised a wing-control system and added a rudder and a balancing tail to existing gliders. By 1903 they had built and flown a power-driven plane; they received a patent in 1906 and in 1909 set up the American Wright Corp to produce planes for the War Department. After Wilbur's death Orville did research and served on the National Advisory Committee for Aeronautics 1915–48.

Related Web site: How We Made the First Flight http://www.aero-web.org/history/wright/wright.html

ORVILLE WRIGHT A photograph of the Wright brothers, Wilbur and Orville, at Kitty Hawk, North Carolina, USA, on 17 December 1903, as their first powered glider takes off, piloted by Orville. *Archive Photos*

Wright, Joseph
(1734–1797) English painter. He was known as **Wright of Derby**, from his birthplace. He painted portraits, landscapes, and groups performing scientific experiments. His work is often dramatically lit – by fire, candlelight, or even volcanic explosion.

Wright, Richard (Nathaniel)
(1908–1960) US writer and poet. He was regarded as an inspiration by black American writers such as James Baldwin. His *Uncle Tom's Children* (1938), a collection of four stories, was highly acclaimed. In 1937 he moved to New York, New York, where he was an editor on the communist newspaper, *Daily Worker*, but the publication of *Native Son* (1940) brought him overnight fame.

writ in law, a document issued by a court requiring performance of certain actions.

write protection device on disks and tapes that provides ▷data security by allowing data to be read but not deleted, altered, or overwritten.

writing any written form of communication using a set of symbols: see ▷alphabet, ▷cuneiform, ▷hieroglyphic. The last two used ideographs (picture writing) and phonetic word symbols side by side, as does modern Chinese. Syllabic writing, as in Japanese, develops from the continued use of a symbol to represent the sound of a short word. Some 8,000-year-old inscriptions, thought to be pictographs, were found on animal bones and tortoise shells in Henan province, China, at a Neolithic site at Jiahu. They are thought to predate by 2,500 years the oldest known writing (Mesopotamian cuneiform of 3500 BC and Egyptian hieroglyphics of *c.* 3300–3200 BC).

Related Web site: Burning Press http://www.burningpress.org/bphome.html

Wrocław (formerly **Breslau**) industrial river port in Poland, on the River Oder; population (1993) 643,600. Industries include shipbuilding, engineering, textiles, and electronics. It was the capital of the German province of Lower Silesia until 1945.

wrought iron fairly pure iron containing some beads of slag, widely used for construction work before the days of cheap steel. It is strong, tough, and easy to machine. It is made in a puddling furnace, invented by Henry Colt in England in 1784. Pig iron is remelted and heated strongly in air with iron ore, burning out the carbon in the metal, leaving relatively pure iron and a slag containing impurities. The resulting pasty metal is then hammered to remove as much of the remaining slag as possible. It is still used in fences and gratings.

Wuhan river port and capital of ▷Hubei province, central China, at the confluence of the Han and Chang Jiang rivers; population (1994) 4,436,100. It was formed in 1950 as one of China's greatest industrial areas by the amalgamation of Hankou, Hanyang, and Wuchang. Iron, steel, machine tools, textiles, food and drinks, fibre optic cables, and fertilizer are manufactured.

Wuhsien alternative transliteration for ▷Suzhou, a city in Jiangsu province, China.

Wundt, Wilhelm Max (1832–1920) German physiologist who regarded psychology as the study of internal experience or consciousness. His main psychological method was introspection; he also studied sensation, perception of space and time, and reaction times.

WV abbreviation for ▷West Virginia, a state of the USA.

WY abbreviation for ▷Wyoming, a state of the USA.

Wyatt, Thomas (*c.* 1503–1542) English courtier and poet. He was employed on diplomatic missions by Henry VIII, but in 1536 was imprisoned for a time in the Tower of London, suspected of having been the lover of Henry's second wife, Anne Boleyn. Knighted in 1537 and sent on an embassy to Spain, Wyatt was again arrested in 1541 on charges of treason. Like the Earl of ▷Surrey, Wyatt experimented with Petrarchan verse forms and thus introduced the sonnet into the English language.

Wycherley, William (1640–*c.* 1716) English Restoration dramatist. His first comedy, *Love in a Wood*, won him court favour in 1671, and later bawdy works include *The Country Wife* (1675) and *The Plain Dealer* (1676).

Wycliffe (or Wyclif), **John** (*c.* 1320–1384) English religious reformer. Allying himself with the party of John of Gaunt, which was opposed to ecclesiastical influence at court, he attacked abuses in the medieval church, maintaining that the Bible rather than the church was the supreme authority. He criticized such fundamental doctrines as priestly absolution, confession, and indulgences, and set disciples to work on the first translation of the Bible into English.

FRANK LLOYD WRIGHT Portrait of the US architect Frank Lloyd Wright, who designed the Guggenheim Museum in New York, USA. He is shown here leaning against a model of the museum in 1945. *Image Bank*

Wye (Welsh **Gwy**) river in Wales and England; length 208 km/130 mi. It rises on Plynlimon in northeast Ceredigion, flows southeast and east through Powys and Hereford and Worcester, and follows the Gwent–Gloucestershire border before joining the River ▷Severn 4 km/2.5 mi south of Chepstow. It has salmon fisheries and is noted for its scenery.

Wyeth, Andrew Newell (1917–) US painter. His portraits and landscapes, usually in watercolour or tempera, are naturalistic, minutely detailed, and often convey a strong sense of the isolation of the countryside; for example, *Christina's World* (1948; Museum of Modern Art, New York).

Wyndham, John (1903–1969) Pen-name of John Wyndham Parkes Lucas Beynon Harris. English science fiction writer. He wrote *The Day of the Triffids* (1951), describing the invasion of Earth by a strange plant mutation; *The Chrysalids* (1955); and *The Midwich Cuckoos* (1957). A recurrent theme in his work is people's response to disaster, whether caused by nature, aliens, or human error.

Wyoming state in western USA. It is nicknamed the Equality State. Wyoming was admitted to the Union in 1890 as the 44th US state. One of the Mountain States, it is bordered to the east by Nebraska and South Dakota, to the north by Montana, to the west by Montana, Idaho, and Utah, and to the south by Utah and Colorado.

population (1995) 480,200 **area** 253,400 sq km/97,812 sq mi **capital** Cheyenne **towns and cities** Casper, Laramie **industries and products** oil, natural gas, sodium salts, coal, uranium, sheep, beef

WYSIWYG (acronym for what you see is what you get) in computing, a program that attempts to display on the screen a faithful representation of the final printed output. For example, a WYSIWYG ▷word processor would show actual page layout – line widths, page breaks, and the sizes and styles of type.

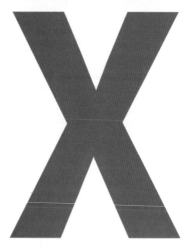

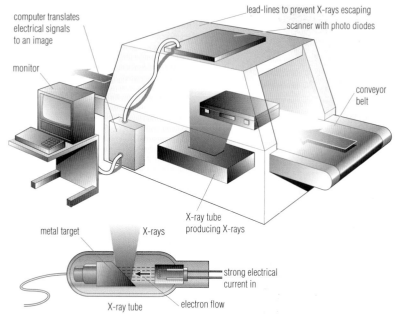

X-RAY An X-ray is generated by high-speed electrons impinging on a tungsten target. The rays pass through the specimen and on to a photographic plate or imager.

Labels: computer translates electrical signals to an image; lead-lines to prevent X-rays escaping; scanner with photo diodes; monitor; conveyor belt; X-ray tube producing X-rays; metal target; X-rays; strong electrical current in; X-ray tube; electron flow

X Roman numeral **ten**; a person or thing unknown.

x in mathematics, an unknown quantity.

xanthophyll yellow pigment in plants that, like ▷chlorophyll, is responsible for the production of carbohydrates by photosynthesis.

Xavier, St Francis (1506–1552) Spanish Jesuit missionary. He went to the Portuguese colonies in the East Indies, arriving at Goa in 1542. He was in Japan 1549–51, establishing a Christian mission that lasted for 100 years. He returned to Goa in 1552, and sailed for China, but died of fever there. He was canonized in 1622.

Related Web site: **Xavier, St Francis** http://www.newadvent.org/cathen/06233b.htm

X chromosome larger of the two sex chromosomes, the smaller being the ▷Y chromosome. These two chromosomes are involved in sex determination. Females have two X chromosomes, males have an X and a Y. Genes carried on the X chromosome produce the phenomenon of ▷sex linkage.

Early in the development of a female embryo, one of the X chromosomes becomes condensed so that most of its genes are inactivated. If this inactivation is incomplete, skeletal defects and mental retardation result.

xenon (Greek *xenos* 'stranger') colourless, odourless, gaseous, non-metallic element, symbol Xe, atomic number 54, relative atomic mass 131.30. It is grouped with the ▷inert gases and was long believed not to enter into reactions, but is now known to form some compounds, mostly with fluorine. It is a heavy gas present in very small quantities in the air (about one part in 20 million).

Xenon is used in bubble chambers, light bulbs, vacuum tubes, and lasers. It was discovered in 1898 in a residue from liquid air by Scottish chemists William Ramsay and Morris Travers.

Xenophon (*c.* 430–*c.* 350 BC) Greek soldier and writer who was a disciple of ▷Socrates (described in Xenophon's *Symposium*). He joined the Persian prince Cyrus the Younger against his brother Artaxerxes II in 401 BC, and after the Battle of Cunaxa the same year took command. His book *Anabasis* describes how he led 10,000 Greek mercenaries on a 1,600-km/1,000-mile march home across enemy territory.

> **Xenophon**
> *Prosperity creates presumption in most men, but adversity brings sobriety to all.*
> *Cyropaedia* bk 8, ch. 4

xenotransplant animal to human transplant. Animals used as organ and tissue sources include pigs and primates. Transplants carried out (with varying degrees of success) include heart, kidney, liver, bone marrow, fetal neural tissue (to treat Parkinson's disease), and fetal islet tissue (for diabetes). The first xenotransplants took place in 1964 (pig heart valves in the UK; chimpanzee kidneys in the USA).

xerography dry, electrostatic method of producing images, without the use of negatives or sensitized paper, invented in the USA by Chester Carlson in 1938 and applied in the Xerox ▷photocopier.

xerophyte plant adapted to live in dry conditions. Common adaptations to reduce the rate of ▷transpiration include a reduction of leaf size, sometimes to spines or scales; a dense covering of hairs over the leaf to trap a layer of moist air (as in edelweiss); water storage cells; sunken stomata; and permanently rolled leaves or leaves that roll up in dry weather (as in marram grass). Many desert cacti are xerophytes.

Xerxes I (*c.* 519–465 BC) Achaemenid king of Persia 486–465 BC, the son and successor of Darius (I) the Great. He suppressed Babylonian revolts in 484 and 482, then in 480, at the head of a great army supported by a fleet, he crossed the Hellespont (Dardanelles) on bridges of boats and marched through Thrace into Greece. He occupied Athens, but the Persian fleet was defeated at Salamis and Xerxes was forced to retreat. His general Mardonius remained behind, but was defeated by the Greeks at Plataea in 479 BC.

Xhosa (plural **Xhosa**) member of a Bantu people of South Africa, living mainly in the Eastern Cape province. Traditionally, the Xhosa were farmers and cattle herders, cattle having great social and religious importance to them. Their social structure is based on a monarchy. Their Bantu language belongs to the Niger-Congo family.

Xia dynasty (or Hsia dynasty) China's first legendary ruling family, *c.* 2200–*c.* 1500 BC, reputedly founded by the model emperor Yu the Great. He is believed to have controlled floods by constructing dykes. Archaeological evidence suggests that the Xia dynasty really did exist, as a Bronze Age civilization where writing was being developed, with its capital at Erlidou (Erh-li-t'ou) in Henan (Honan).

Xi'an ('western peace') industrial city and capital of ▷Shaanxi province, China, on the Wei He River; population (1993) 2,360,000. It produces chemicals, machinery, electrical and electronic equipment, aircraft, and fertilizers.

Related Web site: **Xi'an** http://www.chinapages.com/shaanxi/xian/xian.html

Xi Jiang (or Si-Kiang; 'west river') river in China, which rises in Yunnan province and flows into the South China Sea; length 1,900 km/1,200 mi. Guangzhou lies on the northern arm of its delta and the island of Hong Kong at its mouth. It is the longest river in south China.

Xining (or Sining) industrial city and capital of ▷Qinghai province, northwest China, on the Xining River; population (1994) 540,000. Products include machinery, vehicles, textiles, metals, and processed foods. For centuries Xining was a major trading centre on the caravan route to Tibet, and it is now the starting point for the modern rail and road routes into the Tibetan Plateau.

Xinjiang Uygur Autonomous Region (or **Xinjiang** or **Sinkiang Uighur Autonomous Region**) autonomous region of northwest China, bounded to the north by Kyrgyzstan, Kazakhstan, and Russia; to the east by Mongolia and Gansu; to the south by Qinghai and Tibet; and to the west by Jammu and Kashmir, Afghanistan, and Tajikistan; area 1,646,800 sq km/635,800 sq mi; population (2000 est) 19,250,000. The capital is ▷Urumqi. Industries include oil, chemicals, iron, textiles, coal, copper, and tourism. Cereals, cotton, and fruit are grown, and there is animal husbandry.

Xiongnu (or Hsiung-nu) nomadic confederacy, possibly of Turkish origin, that fought against the Chinese states in the 3rd century BC. Their power began in Mongolia in about 200 BC, but they were forced back to the Gobi Desert in 119 BC by China's Han-dynasty emperor Wudi (Wu-ti) (reigned 141–87 BC) and Qin Shi Huangdi built the Great Wall of China against them. They were eventually conquered and the survivors were employed as frontier troops.

X-ray band of electromagnetic radiation in the wavelength range 10^{-11} to 10^{-9} m (between gamma rays and ultraviolet radiation; see ▷electromagnetic waves). Applications of X-rays make use of their short wavelength (as in ▷X-ray diffraction) or their penetrating power (as in medical X-rays of internal body tissues). X-rays are dangerous and can cause cancer.

X-rays with short wavelengths pass through most body tissues, although dense areas such as bone prevent their passage, showing up as white areas on X-ray photographs. The X-rays used in ▷radiotherapy have very short wavelengths that penetrate tissues deeply and destroy them. X-rays were discovered by German experimental physicist Wilhelm Röntgen in 1895 and formerly called roentgen rays. They are produced when high-energy electrons from a heated filament cathode strike the surface of a target (usually made of tungsten) on the face of a massive heat-conducting anode, between which a high alternating voltage (about 100 kV) is applied.

X-ray astronomy detection of X-rays from intensely hot gas in the universe. Such X-rays are prevented from reaching the Earth's surface by the atmosphere, so detectors must be placed in rockets and satellites. The first celestial X-ray source, Scorpius X-1, was discovered by a rocket flight in 1962.

X-ray diffraction method of studying the atomic and molecular structure of crystalline substances by using ▷X-rays. X-rays directed at such substances spread out as they pass through the crystals owing to ▷diffraction (the slight spreading of waves around the edge of an opaque object) of the rays around the atoms. By using measurements of the position and intensity of the diffracted waves, it is possible to calculate the shape and size of the atoms in the crystal. The method has been used to study substances such as ▷DNA that are found in living material.

xylem tissue found in ▷vascular plants, whose main function is to conduct water and dissolved mineral nutrients from the roots to other parts of the plant. Xylem is composed of a number of different types of cell, and may include long, thin, usually dead cells known as tracheids; fibres (schlerenchyma); thin-walled ▷parenchyma cells; and conducting vessels.

xylophone musical ▷percussion instrument of African and Indonesian origin, consisting of a series of hardwood bars of varying lengths, each with its own distinct pitch, arranged in sequence over a resonator or resonators, and played with hard sticks. It first appeared as an orchestral instrument in Saint-Saëns's *Danse macabre* in 1874, illustrating dancing skeletons.

XYZ Affair in American history, an incident 1797–98 in which the French as represented by foreign minister ▷Talleyrand were accused of demanding a US$250,000 bribe before agreeing to negotiate with US envoys in Paris. The proposed negotiations were part of an attempt to resolve a crisis in Franco-US relations caused by the war in Europe and by French raids on American shipping. Three French agents (referred to by President John Adams in 1797 as X, Y, and Z) held secret talks with the envoys over the money. Publicity fuelled anti-French feelings in the USA and led to increased military spending.

Y

yachting pleasure cruising or racing a small and light vessel, whether sailing or power-driven. At the 1996 Olympic Games there were eight sail-driven categories: Laser, 470, Tornado, Soling, Mistral, Star, Finn, and Europe. The Laser, Mistral, Finn, and Europe are solo events; the Soling class is for three-person crews; all other classes are for crews of two. The International Sailing Federation (ISF) World Sailing Championships were inaugurated in 1994 and are held every four years. Additionally, separate world championships are held annually in each of the Olympic classes and in others such as the Melges 24 or Mumm 30.

YACHTING Sailing a schooner, hauling in sheets. *Image Bank*

Yahya Khan, Agha Muhammad (1917–1980) Pakistani president 1969–71. His mishandling of the Bangladesh separatist issue led to civil war and he was forced to resign.

yak species of cattle *Bos grunniens*, family Bovidae, which lives in wild herds at high altitudes in Tibet. It stands about 2 m/6 ft at the shoulder and has long shaggy hair on the underparts. It has large, upward-curving horns and humped shoulders. It is in danger of becoming extinct.

In the wild, the yak is brown or black, but the domesticated variety, which is half the size of the wild form, may be white. It is used for milk, meat, leather, and as a beast of burden. The yak is protected from extremes of cold by its thick coat and by the heat produced from the fermentation in progress in its stomach.

Yakutia (Russian **Yakutskaya**) former name of ▷Sakha, an autonomous republic in the Russian Federation.

Yakutsk capital, economic and cultural centre of the ▷Republic of Sakha (formerly Yakutia), eastern Siberia, Russian Federation; population (1996 est) 191,000. It is situated on the left bank of the middle Lena. The city has saw-milling, leather and shoe, and food-processing industries.

yakuza (Japanese 'good for nothing') Japanese gangster. Organized crime in Japan is highly structured, and the various syndicates between them employed some 110,000 people 1989, with a turnover of an estimated 1.5 trillion yen. The *yakuza* have been unofficially tolerated and are very powerful.

Yalta Conference strategic conference held 4–11 February 1945 in Yalta (a Soviet holiday resort in the Crimea) by the main Allied leaders in World War II. At this, the second of three key meetings between the 'Big Three' – Winston Churchill (UK), Franklin D Roosevelt (USA), and Joseph Stalin (USSR) – plans were drawn up for the final defeat and disarmament of Nazi Germany, the post-war partition of Europe (see ▷Cold War), and the foundation of the ▷United Nations.

Other matters openly discussed at Yalta included the trial of Nazi war criminals, the future border between Russia and Poland, and the composition of a post-war Polish government. In addition, a secret protocol guaranteed the entry of the USSR into hostilities against Japan once the war in Europe was over. The other major series of talks between the Allied leaders during World War II took place in Tehran, Iran (November to December 1943), and Potsdam, Germany (July to August 1945).

YALTA CONFERENCE Winston Churchill, Franklin D Roosevelt, and Josef Stalin sitting together at the Yalta Conference, on 11 February 1945. *Archive Photos*

yam any of a group of climbing plants cultivated in tropical regions; the starchy tubers (underground stems) are eaten as a vegetable. The Mexican yam (*D. composita*) contains a chemical that is used in the contraceptive pill. (Genus *Dioscorea*, family Dioscoreaceae.)

Yamato ancient name of Japan and particularly the province of western Honshu where Japanese civilization began and where the early capitals were located; also the clan from which all emperors of Japan are descended, claiming the sun-goddess as ancestor. The Yamato period is often taken as AD 539–710 (followed by the Nara period).

Yamoussoukro capital since 1983 of ▷Côte d'Ivoire; population (1995 est) 174,000. The city is in Bouaké department and lies northwest of Abidjan. The economy is based on tourism, fishing, agricultural trade and production, and petroleum

YAK A domestic yak and suckling calf in Tibet on a high plateau in the Himalayas. *Corel*

distribution to the surrounding region. Other industries include forestry and perfume manufacture.

A Roman Catholic basilica (said to be the largest church in the world) was completed in 1989 and consecrated by Pope John Paul II in September 1990.

Yanamamo (or **Yanomamo**; plural **Yanamami**) a semi-nomadic Native South American people, numbering approximately 22,000 (9,500 in northern Brazil and the rest in Venezuela), where most continue to follow their traditional way of life. The Yanamamo language belongs to the Macro-Chibcha family. In November 1991 Brazil granted the Yanamami possession of their original land, 58,395 km/36,293 sq mi on its northern border.

Yanayev, Gennady (1937–) Soviet communist politician, vice-president of the USSR 1990–91. He led the August 1991 anti-Gorbachev attempted coup, after which he was arrested and charged with treason. He was released in 1994 under an amnesty.

Yangon (formerly **Rangoon** (until 1989)) capital and chief port of Myanmar (Burma) on the Yangon River, 32 km/20 mi from the Indian Ocean; population (1998 est) 3,576,500. Industries include shipbuilding, oil refining, rice milling, and textile and pottery manufacture. Yangon is a centre of communications by road, rail, and air, as well as by river transport, and is one of the greatest rice markets in the world. The city **Dagon** was founded on the site in AD 746; it was given the name Rangoon (meaning 'end of conflict') by King Alaungpaya in 1755.

Yang Shangkun (1907–1998) Chinese communist politician. He held a senior position in the Central Committee of the Communist Party of China (CCP) 1956–66 but was demoted during the ▷Cultural Revolution. He was rehabilitated in 1978, elected to the Politburo in 1982, and served as state president 1988–93.

Yangtze-Kiang alternative transcription of ▷Chang Jiang, the longest river in China.

Yankee colloquial (often disparaging) term for an American. Outside the USA the term is applied to any American.

Yao a people living in southern China, North Vietnam, northern Laos, Thailand, and Myanmar (Burma), and numbering about 4 million (1984). The Yao language may belong to either the Sino-Tibetan or the Thai language family. The Yao incorporate elements of ancestor worship in their animist religion.

Yaoundé capital of ▷Cameroon, 210 km/130 mi east of the port of Douala; population (1991) 750,000. Industries include tourism, oil refining, food production, and textile manufacturing. It is linked by the Transcameroon railway to Douala and to Ngaoundere in the north.

yapok nocturnal ▷opossum *Chironectes minimus* found in tropical South and Central America. It is about 33 cm/1.1 ft long, with a 40 cm/1.3 ft tail. It has webbed hind feet and thick fur, and is the only aquatic marsupial. The female has a watertight pouch.

yard unit (symbol yd) of length, equivalent to 3 feet (0.9144 m).

yardang ridge formed by wind erosion from a dried-up riverbed or similar feature, as in Chad, China, Peru, and North America. On the planet Mars yardangs occur on a massive scale.

yarrow (or **milfoil**) perennial herb belonging to the daisy family, with feathery, scented leaves and flat-topped clusters of white or pink flowers. It is native to Europe and Asia. (*Achillea millefolium*, family Compositae.)

yaws contagious tropical disease common in the West Indies, West Africa, and some Pacific islands, characterized by red, raspberrylike eruptions on the face, toes, and other parts of the body, sometimes followed by lesions of the bones; these may progress to cause gross disfigurement. It is caused by a spirochete (*Treponema pertenue*), a bacterium related to the one that causes ▷syphilis. Treatment is by antibiotics.

Y chromosome smaller of the two sex chromosomes. In male mammals it occurs paired with the other type of sex chromosome (X), which carries far more genes. The Y chromosome is the smallest of all the mammalian chromosomes and is considered to be largely inert (that is, without direct effect on the physical body), apart from containing the genes that control the development of the testes. There are only 20 genes discovered so far on the human Y chromosome, much fewer than on all other human chromosomes. See also ▷sex determination.

In humans, about one in 300 males inherits two Y chromosomes at conception, making him an XYY triploid. Few if any differences from normal XY males exist in these individuals, although at one time they were thought to be emotionally unstable and abnormally aggressive. In 1989 the gene determining that a human being is male was found to occur on the X as well as on the Y chromosome; however, it is not activated in the female.

year unit of time measurement, based on the orbital period of the Earth around the Sun. The **tropical year** (also called equinoctial and solar year), from one spring ▷equinox to the next, lasts 365.2422 days. It governs the occurrence of the seasons, and is the period on which the calendar year is based. The **sidereal year** is the time taken for the Earth to complete one orbit relative to the fixed stars, and lasts 365.26 days (about 20 minutes longer than a tropical year). The difference is due to the effect of ▷precession, which slowly moves the position of the equinoxes. The **anomalistic year** is the time taken by any planet in making one complete revolution from perihelion to perihelion; for the Earth this period is about five minutes longer than the sidereal year due to the gravitational pull of the other planets. The **calendar year** consists of 365 days, with an extra day added at the end of February each leap year. **Leap years** occur in every year that is divisible by four, except that a century year is not a leap year unless it is divisible by 400. Hence 1900 was not a leap year, but 2000 was.

yeast one of various single-celled fungi (see ▷fungus) that form masses of tiny round or oval cells by budding. When placed in a sugar solution the cells multiply and convert the sugar into alcohol and carbon dioxide. Yeasts are used as fermenting agents in baking, brewing, and the making of wine and spirits. Brewer's yeast (*S. cerevisiae*) is a rich source of vitamin B. (Especially genus *Saccharomyces*; also other related genera.)

yeast artificial chromosome (YAC) fragment of ▷DNA from the human genome inserted into a yeast cell. The yeast replicates the fragment along with its own DNA. In this way the fragments are copied to be preserved in a gene library. YACs are characteristically between 250,000 and 1 million base pairs in length. A cosmid works in the same way.

Yeats, Jack Butler (1871–1957) Irish painter and illustrator. His spirited portrayals of Irish life and landscape are painted in a colourful and highly individualistic style, with vigorously worked paint, as in *Back from the Races* (1925; Tate Gallery, London). He was the brother of the poet W B ▷Yeats.

Yeats, W(illiam) B(utler) (1865–1939) Irish poet, dramatist, and scholar. He was a leader of the Irish literary revival and a founder of the ▷Abbey Theatre in Dublin. His early work was romantic and lyrical, as in the poem 'The Lake Isle of Innisfree' and the plays *The Countess Cathleen* (1892) and *The Land of Heart's Desire* (1894). His later poetry, which includes *The Wild Swans at Coole* (1917) and *The Winding Stair* (1929), was also much influenced by European and Eastern thought. He was a senator of the Irish Free State 1922–28, and was awarded the Nobel Prize for Literature in 1923.

Yeats was born into a Protestant family in Dublin and was educated both in London and Dublin. He spent much time in

W B YEATS Irish poet and dramatist W B Yeats, shown here with US-born poet T S Eliot on the right, was in 1898 one of the founders of the Irish Literary Theatre, which later became the famous Abbey Theatre in Dublin, Republic of Ireland. *Archive Photos*

England, and died in the south of France, but his most productive years were spent living in County Sligo. Following his artist father's footsteps, he first studied painting but soon turned to writing. In his early verse and poetic plays, such as *The Wind Among the Reeds* (1899), *The Wanderings of Oisin* (1889), and *Deirdre* (1907), he drew heavily on Irish legend to create allusive, sensuous imagery. Later, his work adopted a more robust, astringent style and a tighter structure, and displayed a preoccupation with public affairs, all evident in the collection *Responsibilities* (1914).

Related Web site: Yeats, W B http://www.lit.kobe-u.ac.jp/~hishika/yeats.htm

Yedo (or **Edo**) former name of ▷Tokyo, Japan, until 1868.

yeheb nut small tree found in Ethiopia and Somalia, formerly much valued for its nuts as a food source. Although cultivated as a food crop in Kenya and Sudan, it is now critically endangered in the wild and is only known to survive at three sites. Overgrazing by cattle and goats has prevented regrowth, and the taking of nuts for consumption prevents reseeding. Although reintroduction would be possible from cultivated trees, the continuing grazing pressure would make establishment unlikely without proper management. (Genus *Cordeauxia adulis*.)

yellow archangel flowering plant belonging to the mint family, found over much of Europe. It grows up to 60 cm/2 ft tall and has nettlelike leaves and rings, or whorls, of yellow flowers growing around the main stem; the lower lips of the flowers are streaked with red in early summer. (Genus *Lamiastrum galeobdolon*, family Labiatae.)

yellow fever (or **yellow jack**) acute tropical viral disease, prevalent in the Caribbean area, Brazil, and on the west coast of Africa. The yellow fever virus is an arbovirus transmitted by mosquitoes. Its symptoms include a high fever, headache, joint and muscle pains, vomiting, and yellowish skin (jaundice, possibly leading to liver failure); the heart and kidneys may also be affected. The mortality rate is 25%, with 91% of all cases occurring in Africa.

W B Yeats

I have spread my dreams under your feet; / Tread softly because you tread on my dreams.

'He Wishes for the Cloths of Heaven'

yellowhammer Eurasian bird *Emberiza citrinella* of the bunting family Emberizidae, order Passeriformes. About 16.5 cm/6.5 in long, the male has a yellow head and underside, a chestnut rump, and a brown-streaked back. The female is duller.

Yellowknife capital of ▷Northwest Territories, Canada, in Yellowknife Bay, on the northern shore of Great Slave Lake; population (1996) 17,300. It is the centre of a gold- and uranium-mining region, and the main hub of transport throughout the territories. Yellowknife was founded in 1935 after the discovery of its mineral wealth; Canada's largest gold mine lies nearby. Its name refers to the copper knives used by local Native Canadian Slavey peoples. It became the capital in 1967.

Yellow River English name for the ▷Huang He River, China.

Yellow Sea (Chinese **Huang Hai**) gulf of the Pacific Ocean between China and Korea; length approximately 1,000 km/620 mi, greatest width 700 km/435 mi; area 466,200 sq km/180,000 sq mi. To the north are the gulfs of Korea, Chihli, and Liaotung. There are many small islands to the east near the Korean coast. It receives the Huang He (Yellow River) and Chang Jiang (Yangtze Kiang), which transport yellow mud down into the shallow waters (average depth 44 m/144 ft).

Yellowstone National Park oldest US nature reserve, and largest in the lower 48 states, situated on a broad plateau in the ▷Rocky Mountains, chiefly in northwest Wyoming, but also projecting about 3 km/2 mi into southwest Montana and eastern Idaho; area 8,983 sq km/3,469 sq mi. The park contains more than 3,000 geysers and hot springs, including periodically erupting Old Faithful. Established in 1872, it is now a World Heritage Site and one of the world's greatest wildlife refuges. In 1988 naturally occurring forest fires burned 36% of the park.

Related Web site: Total Yellowstone Page http://www.yellowstone-natl-park.com/

Yeltsin, Boris Nikolayevich (1931–) Russian politician, president of the Russian Soviet Federative Socialist Republic (RSFSR) 1990–91, and president of the newly independent Russian Federation 1991–99. He directed the Federation's secession from the USSR and the formation of a new, decentralized confederation, the ▷Commonwealth of Independent States (CIS), with himself as the most powerful leader. A referendum in 1993 supported his policies of price deregulation and accelerated privatization, despite severe economic problems and civil unrest. He survived a coup attempt later the same year, but was subsequently forced to compromise on the pace of his reforms after far-right electoral gains, and lost considerable public support. He suffered two heart attacks in October and November 1995, yet still contested the June 1996 presidential elections, in which he secured re-election by defeating Communist Party leader Gennady Zyuganov in the second round run-off.

Born in Sverdlovsk (now Yekaterinburg), Yeltsin began his career in the construction industry. He joined the Communist Party of the Soviet Union (CPSU) in 1961 and became district party leader. Brought to Moscow by Mikhail Gorbachev and Nikolai Ryzhkov in 1985, he was appointed secretary for construction and then, in December 1985, Moscow party chief. His demotion to the post of first deputy chair of the State Construction Committee in November 1987 was seen as a blow to Gorbachev's ▷perestroika initiative and a victory for the conservatives grouped around Yegor Ligachev. Yeltsin was re-elected in March 1989 with an 89% share of the vote, defeating an official Communist Party candidate, and was elected to the Supreme Soviet in May 1989. A supporter of the Baltic states in their calls for greater independence, Yeltsin

YELLOWSTONE NATIONAL PARK Castle Geyser, in Yellowstone National Park, Wyoming, USA. *Image Bank*

BORIS YELTSIN Boris Yeltsin, seen here with US president Bill Clinton in 1994, came to power as Russian president in 1990. *Archive Photos*

demanded increasingly more radical economic reform. In 1990 he renounced his CPSU membership and was elected president of the RSFSR, the largest republic of the USSR. Advocating greater autonomy for the constituent republics within a federal USSR, Yeltsin prompted the Russian parliament in June 1990 to pass a decree giving the republic's laws precedence over those passed by the Soviet parliament. In April 1991, he was voted emergency powers by congress, enabling him to rule by decree, and two months later was popularly elected president.

In the abortive August 1991 coup, Yeltsin, as head of a democratic 'opposition state' based at the Russian parliament building, played a decisive role, publicly condemning the usurpers and calling for the reinstatement of President Gorbachev. As the economic situation deteriorated within Russia, Yeltsin's leadership came under increasing challenge. An attempted coup by parliamentary leaders was successfully thwarted September–October 1993, but unexpected far-right gains in assembly elections in December forced him to compromise his economic policies and rely increasingly on the support of the military.

From early 1995 he came under criticism for his apparent sanctioning of a full-scale military offensive in the breakaway republic of Chechnya. In May 1997 a peace treaty was signed with Chechnya, nevertheless war subsequently resumed, and in June 1997 a Union Treaty with Belarus committed the state to future integration.

In March 1998 Yeltsin astounded both Russia and the West by sacking the entire cabinet, and appointing as prime minister the 35-year-old fuel and energy minister Sergei Kiriyenko. The new government faced a financial crisis as the value of the rouble fell sharply by mid-1998. In late August, Yeltsin unexpectedly sacked Kiriyenko and the entire government, and sought to restore to office his trusted ally, Viktor Chernomyrdin. After the communist-dominated Duma twice refused to ratify Chernomyrdin's appointment, Yeltsin was forced to nominate Yevgeni ▷Primakov as prime minister. He sacked Primakov and his cabinet in May 1999, when the Duma debated whether to commence impeachment proceedings against him, and appointed Sergei Stepashin acting prime minister. Later that month the Duma not only decided against impeaching him but also confirmed Stepashin as prime minister. In 1999 Yeltsin was condemned by western leaders for his failure to find a political solution to the continued war against Chechnya.

Yeltsin resigned as president on 31 December 1999. Announcing that he was bowing out to give a younger generation a chance, he apologized to his country for failing to fulfil their hopes. He relinquished his power six months early to his chosen successor, Vladimir Putin, in return for receiving guarantees of immunity from any future prosecution for any of his actions in the Kremlin.

Related Web site: Yeltsin, Boris http://www.cs.indiana.edu/hyplan/dmiguse/Russian/bybio.html

Yemen see country box.

Yenisey (or **Yenisei**) one of the main rivers in Russia, rising in the Sayan Mountains in the Asian Tuva region and flowing generally north across the Siberian plain into the Arctic Ocean; length 4,100 km/2,550 mi. The Yenisey has a drainage basin of 2,580,000 sq km/996,000 sq mi. Navigable throughout almost its entire course, its chief ports are Dudinka, Igarka, and Krasnoyarsk.

yeoman in England, a small landowner who farmed his own fields – a system that formed a bridge between the break-up of feudalism and the agrarian revolution of the 18th–19th centuries.

Yeomen of the Guard
English military corps, popularly known as **Beefeaters**, the sovereign's bodyguard since the corps was founded by Henry VII in 1485. Its duties are now purely ceremonial.

Yerevan capital city, economic, and cultural centre of the independent Republic of ▷Armenia, situated in the southern Caucasus 25 km/16 mi north of the Turkish border; population (1996) 1,200,000. Yerevan stands on the Razdan River, and is a major industrial city, manufacturing machine tools, agricultural equipment, chemicals, bricks, bicycles, and wine. Other industries include the production of aluminium, plastics, and textiles, fruit canning, and distilling.

Yerevan is one of the world's most ancient cities; it was first recorded in the 7th century, and was alternately Turkish and Persian from the 15th century until ceded to Russia in 1828. The city was devastated by an earthquake in 1988.

The city was the scene of mounting inter-ethnic violence and Armenian nationalist demonstrations during the late 1980s and early 1990s onwards. These were undertaken to secure a separate Armenian state (gained in 1991), and were fanned by a dispute with neighbouring Azerbaijan over the enclave of ▷Nagorno-Karabakh.

Yerkes Observatory astronomical centre in Williams Bay, Wisconsin, USA, founded by George Hale in 1897. It houses the world's largest refracting optical ▷telescope, with a lens of diameter 102 cm/40 in.

Yersin, Alexandre Émile John (1863–1943) Swiss bacteriologist who discovered the bubonic plague bacillus in Hong Kong in 1894 and prepared a serum against it. The bacillus was discovered independently, in the same epidemic, by Japanese bacteriologist Shibasaburō ▷Kitasato, who published his results before Yersin did.

Yesenin, Sergei Aleksandrovich alternative form of ▷Esenin, Russian poet.

Yevtushenko, Yevgeny Aleksandrovich (1933–) Russian poet. He aroused controversy with his anti-Stalinist 'Stalin's Heirs' (1956), published with Khrushchev's support, and 'Babi Yar' (1961), which attacked Russian as well as Nazi anti-Semitism. His other works include the long poem *Zima Junction* (1956), the novel *Berries* (1981), and *Precocious Autobiography* (1963).

yew any of a group of evergreen coniferous trees native to the northern hemisphere. The dark green flat needlelike leaves and

YEW The yew is a slow-growing evergreen, the longest living of all European trees, probably reaching ages of 1,000 years. The seeds are enclosed in a fleshy covering called an aril which is eaten by birds; the seed itself is poisonous, as is the rest of the tree.

bright red berrylike seeds are poisonous; the wood is hard and close-grained. (Genus *Taxus*, family Taxaceae.)

Yezidi Islamic sect originating as disciples of the Sufi saint Sheikh Adi ibn Musafir (12th century). The beliefs of its adherents mingle folk traditions with Islam, also incorporating features of Judaism and Christianity (they practise circumcision and baptism), and include a cult of the Fallen Angel who has been reconciled with God. Their chief centre is near Mosul, Iraq.

Yezo (or **Ezo**) another name for ▷Hokkaido, the northernmost of the four main islands of Japan.

Yggdrasil in Norse mythology, the world tree, a sacred ash which spanned heaven and hell. It was evergreen and tended by the Norns, goddesses of past, present, and future.

Yi (plural **Yi**) member of a people living in the mountainous regions of southwestern China, northern Vietnam, Laos, Thailand, and Myanmar, totalling about 5.5 million (1987). The Yi are farmers, producing both crops and livestock, and opium as a cash crop. Traditionally they were stratified into princes, aristocrats, commoners, and debt slaves. Their language belongs to the Sino-Tibetan family; their religion is animist.

Yiddish language member of the west Germanic branch of the Indo-European language family, deriving from 13th–14th-century Rhineland German and spoken by northern, central, and eastern European Jews, who have carried it to Israel, the USA, and many other parts of the world. It is written in the Hebrew alphabet and has many dialects reflecting European areas of residence, as well as many borrowed words from Polish, Russian, Lithuanian, and other languages encountered.

Related Web site: American Variety Stage: Yiddish-Language Scripts http://lcweb2.loc.gov/ammem/vshtml/vsyid.html

yield point (or **elastic limit**) the stress beyond which a material deforms by a relatively large amount for a small increase in stretching force. Beyond this stress, the material no longer obeys ▷Hooke's law.

yin and yang (Chinese 'dark' and 'bright') the passive (characterized as feminine, negative, intuitive) and active (characterized as masculine, positive, intellectual) principles of nature. Their interaction is believed to maintain equilibrium and harmony in the universe and to be present in all things. In Taoism and Confucianism they are represented by two interlocked curved shapes within a circle, one white, one black, with a spot of the contrasting colour within the head of each.

Yinchuan capital of ▷Ningxia Hui Autonomous Region, northwest China, on the Huang He River; population (1993) 430,000. It is a trading centre for the Ningxia Plain. Industries include the manufacture of machinery, plastic products, and textiles, and the processing of wool and hides from surrounding grazing areas.

Yixian formation in palaeontology, a Chinese geological formation in the the rural province of Liaoning that is yielding a wealth of extraordinarily well-preserved fossils. The fossils date from 150 to 120 million years ago (late Jurassic or early Cretaceous) and include those of hundreds of early birds, such as *Confuciusornis*, with feathers, lizards with full skin, and mammals with hair.

YMCA abbreviation for ▷Young Men's Christian Association.

Ymir in Norse mythology, the first living being, a giant who grew from melting frost; father of the Jotuns, a race of evil giants. He was nurtured by four streams of milk from the cow Audhumla, mother of Buri, the grandfather of Odin. After Ymir was killed by Odin and his brothers, Vili and Ve, heaven and earth were created from parts of his body.

yoga (Sanskrit 'union') Hindu philosophical system attributed to Patanjali, who lived about 150 BC at Gonda, Uttar Pradesh, India. He preached mystical union with a personal deity through the practice of self-hypnosis and a rising above the senses by abstract meditation, adoption of special postures, and ascetic practices. As practised in the West, yoga is more a system of mental and physical exercise, and of induced relaxation as a means of relieving stress.

Yogi Bear cartoon-film character created for television by US animators William Hanna and Joseph Barbera. The shrewd, smiling Yogi and his accomplice Boo-Boo (a cautious cub) steal picnic baskets from tourists and generally create mischief for Mr Ranger in Jellystone Park. Yogi Bear made his US comic-book debut in 1959, and appeared in his first feature-length film *Hey There It's Yogi Bear* (1964).

Yemen

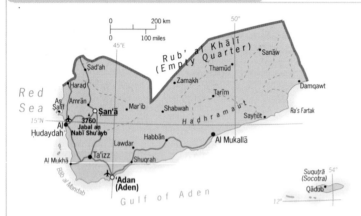

Yemen divided into North Yemen (Yemen Arab Republic) and South Yemen until 1990 country in southwest Asia, bounded north by Saudi Arabia, east by Oman, south by the Gulf of Aden, and west by the Red Sea.

NATIONAL NAME *Al-Jumhuriyya al Yamaniyya/Republic of Yemen*
AREA 531,900 sq km/205,366 sq mi
CAPITAL San'a
MAJOR TOWNS/CITIES Aden, Ta'izz, Al Mukalla, Hodeidah, Ibb, Dhamar
MAJOR PORTS Aden
PHYSICAL FEATURES hot, moist coastal plain, rising to plateau and desert

Government

HEAD OF STATE Ali Abdullah Saleh from 1990
HEAD OF GOVERNMENT Abdel Qadir Bajamal from 2001
POLITICAL SYSTEM emergent democracy
POLITICAL EXECUTIVE limited presidency
ADMINISTRATIVE DIVISIONS 17 governorates
ARMED FORCES 66,500; plus paramilitary forces of 70,000 (2002 est)
CONSCRIPTION military service is compulsory for two years
DEATH PENALTY retained and used for ordinary crimes
DEFENCE SPEND (% GDP) 5.7 (2002 est)
EDUCATION SPEND (% GDP) 10 (2001 est)
HEALTH SPEND (% GDP) 5 (2000 est)

Economy and resources

CURRENCY riyal
GPD (US$) 10.4 billion (2002 est)
REAL GDP GROWTH (% change on previous year) 3.3 (2001)
GNI (US$) 9.4 billion (2002 est)
GNI PER CAPITA (PPP) (US$) 750 (2002 est)
CONSUMER PRICE INFLATION 9% (2003 est)
UNEMPLOYMENT 30% (2001)
FOREIGN DEBT (US$) 3.8 billion (2001 est)
MAJOR TRADING PARTNERS Thailand, Saudi Arabia, China, United Arab Emirates, USA, India, France, South Korea, Kuwait
RESOURCES petroleum, natural gas, gypsum, salt; deposits of copper, gold, lead, zinc, molybdenum
INDUSTRIES petroleum refining and petroleum products, building materials, food processing, beverages, tobacco, chemical products, textiles, leather goods, metal goods
EXPORTS petroleum and petroleum products, cotton, basic manufactures, clothing, live animals, hides and skins, fish, rice, coffee. Principal market: China 19% (2000)
IMPORTS food and live animals, textiles and other manufactured consumer goods, petroleum products, cement, machinery, chemicals. Principal source: Saudi Arabia 13.8% (2000)
ARABLE LAND 2.9% (2000 est)
AGRICULTURAL PRODUCTS sorghum, sesame, millet, potatoes, tomatoes, cotton, wheat, grapes, watermelons, coffee, alfalfa, dates, bananas; livestock rearing; fishing

Population and society

POPULATION 20,010,000 (2003 est)
POPULATION GROWTH RATE 2.9% (2000–15)
POPULATION DENSITY (per sq km) 38 (2003 est)
URBAN POPULATION (% of total) 26 (2003 est)
AGE DISTRIBUTION (% of total population) 0–14 51%, 15–59 45%, 60+ 4% (2002 est)
ETHNIC GROUPS predominantly Arab; some of mixed Afro-Arab origin; small Asian and European communities
LANGUAGE Arabic (official)
RELIGION Sunni Muslim 63%, Shiite Muslim 37%
EDUCATION (compulsory years): 6 (North); 8 (South)
LITERACY RATE 70% (men); 30% (women) (2003 est)

LABOUR FORCE 53% agriculture, 10% industry, 37% services (2000)
LIFE EXPECTANCY 59 (men); 61 (women) (2000–05)
CHILD MORTALITY RATE (under 5, per 1,000 live births) 107 (2001)
PHYSICIANS (per 1,000 people) 0.2 (1998 est)
TV SETS (per 1,000 people) 286 (1999)
RADIOS (per 1,000 people) 64 (1997)
INTERNET USERS (per 10,000 people) 9.0 (2001 est)
PERSONAL COMPUTER USERS (per 100 people) 0.2 (2001 est)

See also ▷Arabia; ▷Ottoman Empire; ▷South Arabia, Federation of.

Chronology

1st millennium BC: South Yemen (Aden) divided between economically advanced Qataban and Hadramawt kingdoms.

c. 5th century BC: Qataban fell to the Sabaeans (Shebans) of North Yemen (Sana).

c. 100 BC–AD 525: All of Yemen became part of the Himyarite kingdom.

AD 628: Islam introduced.

1174–1229: Under control of Egyptian Ayyubids.

1229–1451: 'Golden age' for arts and sciences under the Rasulids, who had served as governors of Yemen under the Ayyubids.

1538: North Yemen came under control of Turkish Ottoman Empire.

1636: Ottomans left North Yemen and power fell into hands of Yemeni Imams, based on local Zaydi tribes, who also held South Yemen until 1735.

1839: Aden became a British territory. Port developed into an important ship refuelling station after opening of Suez Canal in 1869; protectorate was gradually established over 23 Sultanates inland.

1870s: The Ottomans re-established control over North Yemen.

1918: North Yemen became independent, with Imam Yahya from the Hamid al-Din family as king.

1937: Aden became a British crown colony.

1948: Imam Yahya assassinated by exiled Free Yemenis nationalist movement, but the uprising was crushed by his son, Imam Ahmad.

1959: Federation of South Arabia formed by Britain between city of Aden and feudal Sultanates (Aden Protectorate).

1962: Military coup on death of Imam Ahmad; North Yemen declared Yemen Arab Republic (YAR), with Abdullah al-Sallal as president. Civil war broke out between royalists (supported by Saudi Arabia) and republicans (supported by Egypt).

1963: Armed rebellion by National Liberation Front (NLF) began against British rule in Aden.

1967: Civil war ended with republicans victorious. Sallal deposed and replaced by Republican Council. The Independent People's Republic of South Yemen was formed after the British withdrawal from Aden. Many fled to the north as the repressive communist NLF regime took over in south.

1970: People's Republic of South Yemen renamed People's Democratic Republic of Yemen.

1971–72: War between South Yemen and YAR; union agreement brokered by Arab League signed but not kept.

1974: The pro-Saudi Col Ibrahim al-Hamadi seized power in North Yemen; Military Command Council set up.

1977: Hamadi assassinated; replaced by Col Ahmed ibn Hussein al-Ghashmi.

1978: Constituent people's assembly appointed in North Yemen and Military Command Council dissolved. Ghashmi killed by envoy from South Yemen; succeeded by Ali Abdullah Saleh. War broke out again between the two Yemens. The South Yemen president was deposed and executed; the Yemen Socialist Party (YSP) was formed in the south by communists.

1979: A ceasefire was agreed with a commitment to future union.

1986: There was civil war in South Yemen; the autocratic head of state Ali Nasser was dismissed. A new administration was formed under the more moderate Haydar Abu Bakr al-Attas, who was committed to negotiating union with the north because of the deteriorating economy in the south.

1989: A draft multiparty constitution for a single Yemen state was published.

1990: The border between the two Yemens was opened; the countries were formally united on 22 May as the Republic of Yemen. Ali Abdullah Saleh, president of North Yemen since 1978, was appointed president of the new unified Yemen.

1991: The new constitution was approved; Yemen opposed US-led operations against Iraq in the Gulf War.

1992: There were antigovernment riots.

1993: Saleh's General People's Congress (GPC) won most seats in a general election but no overall majority; a five-member presidential council was elected, including Saleh as president, YSP leader Ali Salim al-Baidh as vice-president, and Bakr al-Attas as prime minister.

1994: Fighting erupted between northern forces, led by President Saleh, and southern forces, led by Vice-president al-Baidh, as southern Yemen announced its secession. Saleh inflicted crushing defeat on al-Baidh and a new GPC coalition was appointed.

1998: A new government was headed by Abdul Ali al-Rahman al-Iryani.

1999: In the first ever popular elections for the presidency, Ali Abdullah Saleh, the president for 21 years, was successful.

2003: In parliamentary elections the General People's Congress, led by President Saleh, retained power with over two-thirds of the seats in the 301-member Assembly of Representatives.

YEMEN The Yemen is mostly a desert country, but in the hills around the capital, San'a, and in the Hadramaut to the east, there is adequate rainfall for some green trees to grow. *Corel*

Yogyakarta city in Java, Indonesia, capital 1945–1949; population (1990) 412,400. The chief industries are batik textiles, handicrafts, and tourism. It is the cultural centre of the Javanese ethnic group.

yolk store of food, mostly in the form of fats and proteins, found in the ▷eggs of many animals. It provides nourishment for the growing embryo.

yolk sac sac containing the yolk in the egg of most vertebrates. The term is also used for the membranous sac formed below the developing mammalian embryo and connected with the umbilical cord.

Yom Kippur the Jewish Day of ▷Atonement.

Yom Kippur War the surprise attack on Israel in October 1973 by Egypt and Syria; see ▷Arab-Israeli Wars; ▷Israel, **the Fourth Arab–Israeli War**; and ▷Egypt, **the Fourth Arab–Israeli War**. It is named after the Jewish national holiday on which it began, the holiest day of the Jewish year.

York cathedral and industrial city and administrative headquarters of ▷York unitary authority in northern England, on the River Ouse; population (1991) 127,700. It was the administrative headquarters of the county of North Yorkshire until 1996. Industries include tourism and the manufacture of scientific instruments, sugar, chocolate, and glass. Founded in AD 71 as the Roman provincial capital **Eboracum**, York retains many of its medieval streets and buildings and much of its 14th-century city wall; the Gothic York Minster, England's largest medieval cathedral, includes fine 15th-century stained glass. The city is visited by some 3 million tourists a year.

York unitary authority in northeast England created in 1996 from part of the county of North Yorkshire.

> **area** 271 sq km/105 sq mi **towns** ▷York (administrative headquarters) **features** River Ouse; River Fosse; York Minster –largest medieval cathedral in England, with 15th-century stained glass; York Castle and Museum; National Railway Museum; city walls built by Henry III in 13th century with 4 gates and 39 towers; Jorvik Viking Centre; the Shambles medieval streets **industries** agriculture and agricultural services, mechanical engineering, circuit boards, tourism, scientific instruments, confectionery, glass **population** (1996) 174,800 **famous people** W H Auden, Alcuin, Guy Fawkes, John Flaxman

York English dynasty founded by Richard, Duke of York (1411–60). He claimed the throne through his descent from Lionel, Duke of Clarence (1338–1368), third son of Edward III, whereas the reigning monarch, Henry VI of the rival house of Lancaster, was descended from the fourth son, John of Gaunt. The argument was fought out in the Wars of the ▷Roses. York was killed at the Battle of Wakefield in 1460, but the following year his son became King Edward IV. Edward was succeeded by his son Edward V and then by his brother Richard III, with whose death at Bosworth the line ended. The Lancastrian victor in that battle was crowned Henry VII, and consolidated his claim by marrying Edward IV's eldest daughter, Elizabeth, thus founding the House of Tudor.

York, Frederick Augustus, Duke of York (1763–1827) Second son of George III. He was an unsuccessful commander in

YORK City walls and minster, York, England. York Minster is the largest Gothic cathedral in northern Europe, and, with 128 windows in total, has the largest collection of medieval stained glass in England. Visitors can enjoy fine views over York from the central tower. *Image Bank*

Yosemite National Park

The spectacular Yosemite National Park is in the Sierra Nevada range of mountains in central California, USA. The name of the part is derived from an American-Indian word for grizzly bear. Grizzly bears are no longer found in the park, although the Californian black bear is still plentiful. The park contains the Yosemite Valley of the Merced River is 11 km/7 mi long and bordered by granite cliffs. Huge peaks, domes, and rock faces are found in and around the valley, the tallest peak being Mount Lyell which is 3,997 m/13,104 ft high. One of the most impressive features of the valley is a huge granite monolith 1,095 m/3,593 ft high called El Capitan. Yosemite Valley is also renowned for its waterfalls. Probably the best known are the Yosemite Falls (739 m/2,425 ft), the highest waterfall in North America, comprising three sections along with Ribbon Fall (491 m/1,612 ft).

The Yosemite region is composed of granite. Glaciers scoured the valley from the Merced River canyon, eroding the softer granites and creating cliff walls up to 1,220 m/4,000 ft high. Glacial lakes and meltwaters deposited silts, forming the valley floor. The calm waters of Mirror Lake are caused by its gradual silting. Other notable falls are the Nevada, Ribbon, Silver Strand, Bridalveil, and Vernal. Sites outside the main valley area are the Grand Canyon of the Tuolumne River to the north, and the Mariposa Grove containing the Grizzly Giant, a sequoia estimated to be 2,700 years old.

The Yosemite Valley was formerly inhabited by American Indian peoples, and the first Europeans to visit the area were the Mariposa Battalion in pursuit of raiding parties in 1851. It was explored by the naturalist John Muir in 1868, and made a national park by an Act of Congress in 1890.

The park has three groves of giant sequoias, with trees that are thousands of years old. The largest is Mariposa Grove, in the south of the park. It includes the famous Wawona tree, through which, in the early 1880s, a tunnel and road were cut.

YOSEMITE NATIONAL PARK The Upper Yosemite Falls cascade some 436 m/1,430 ft, but there are also many other spectacular waterfalls in the Yosemite National Park, central California, USA, amid some dazzling scenery. The name of the park derives from a local American-Indian word for a grizzly bear. *Image Bank*

the Netherlands 1793–99 and British commander-in-chief 1798–1809. He was made a duke in 1784.

Yorkshire former county in northeast England on the North Sea divided administratively into North, East, and West Ridings (thirds), but reorganized to form a number of new counties in 1974: the major part of **Cleveland** and **Humberside, North Yorkshire, South Yorkshire,** and **West Yorkshire.** Small outlying areas also went to Durham, Cumbria, Lancashire, and Greater Manchester. In 1996 Cleveland and Humberside were abolished, and a number of unitary authorities were created to replace them.

Yoruba the majority ethnic group living in southwestern Nigeria; there is a Yoruba minority in eastern Benin. They number approximately 20 million in all, and their language belongs to the Kwa branch of the Niger-Congo family. The Yoruba established powerful city states in the 15th century, known for their advanced culture which includes sculpture, art, and music.

Yosemite region in the Sierra Nevada, eastern California, USA, a national park from 1890; area 3,079 sq km/1,189 sq mi.

Yoshida, Shigeru
(1878–1967) Japanese diplomat and conservative Liberal politician who served as prime minister for most of the period 1946–54, including much of the US occupation 1945–52. Under Yoshida, Japan signed the San Francisco Peace Treaty with the USA and its allies in 1951.

Young, Brigham (1801–1877)
US ▷Mormon religious leader, born in Vermont. He joined the Mormon Church, or Church of Jesus Christ of Latter-day Saints, in 1832, and three years later was appointed an apostle. After a successful recruiting mission in Liverpool, England, he returned to the USA and, as successor of Joseph Smith (who had been murdered), led the Mormon migration to the Great Salt Lake in Utah in 1846, founded ▷Salt Lake City, and headed the colony until his death.

Young, Lester Willis (1909–1959) US tenor saxophonist and jazz composer. He was a major figure in the development of his instrument for jazz music from the 1930s and was an accompanist for the singer Billie Holiday, who gave him the nickname 'President', later shortened to 'Pres'.

Young, Neil (1945–) Canadian rock guitarist, singer, and songwriter. He lived in the USA from 1966. His high, plaintive voice and loud, abrasive guitar make his work instantly recognizable, despite abrupt changes of style throughout his career. *Rust Never Sleeps* (1979) and *Arc Weld* (1991) (both with the group Crazy Horse) are among his best work.

Young, Thomas (1773–1829) English physicist, physician, and Egyptologist who revived the wave theory of light and identified the phenomenon of ▷interference in 1801. He also established many important concepts in mechanics.

Young Ireland Irish romantic nationalist organization, centred on a group of young idealists associated with the *Nation* newspaper from 1844. They sought to create a non-sectarian spirit in an independent Ireland, and promoted Irish cultural nationalism. Young Ireland initially sided with Daniel ▷O'Connell's Repeal Association, but split over his nonviolent policies and organized a disastrous rebellion in Tipperary in 1848 led by William Smith O'Brien (1803–1864) and Thomas Meagher. Its failure destroyed Young Ireland, most of the leaders fled abroad or were transported to the penal colonies, but they left a lasting legacy in their concept of a cultural nationalism.

Young Italy Italian nationalist organization founded in 1831 by Giuseppe ▷Mazzini while in exile in Marseille. The movement, which was immediately popular, was followed the next year by Young Germany, Young Poland, and similar organizations. All the groups were linked by Mazzini in his Young Europe movement, but none achieved much practical success; attempted uprisings by Young Italy 1834 and 1844 failed miserably. It was superseded in Italy by the ▷Risorgimento.

Young Men's Christian Association (YMCA) international organization founded in 1844 by George Williams (1821–1905) in London and in 1851 in the USA. It aims at self-improvement – spiritual, intellectual, and physical.

young offender institution in the UK, establishment of detention for lawbreakers under 17 (juveniles) and 17–21 (young adults). The period of detention depends on the seriousness of the offence and on the age and sex of the offender. The institution was introduced by the Criminal Justice Act of 1988.

Young Pretender nickname of ▷Charles Edward Stuart, claimant to the Scottish and English thrones.

Young Turk member of a reformist movement of young army officers in the Ottoman Empire founded 1889. The movement was instrumental in the constitutional changes of 1908 and the abdication of Sultan Abd al-Hamid II 1909. It gained prestige during the Balkan Wars 1912–13 and encouraged Turkish links with the German empire. Its influence diminished after 1918. The term is now used for a member of any radical or rebellious faction within a party or organization.

Young Women's Christian Association (YWCA) organization for women and girls, formed in London, England, in 1887 when two organizations, both founded in 1855 – one by Emma Robarts and the other by Lady Kinnaird – combined their work. Its facilities and activities are similar to those of the Young Men's Christian Association (YMCA).

Yourcenar, Marguerite (1903–1987) Pen-name of Marguerite de Crayencour. French writer. She first gained recognition as a novelist in France in the 1930s with books such as *La Nouvelle Euridyce/The New Euridyce* (1931). Her evocation of past eras and characters, exemplified in *Les Mémoires d'Hadrien/The Memoirs of Hadrian* (1951), brought her acclaim as a historical novelist. In 1939 she settled in the USA. In 1980 she became the first woman to be elected to the French Academy.

youth culture imprecise term for the variety of subcultural phenomena associated with young people as a social group. These may oppose the norms of adult life and are often symbolized by distinctive styles of clothing and taste in music.

Youth Hostels Association (YHA) registered charity founded in Britain in 1930 to promote knowledge and care of the countryside by providing cheap overnight accommodation for young people on active holidays (such as walking or cycling). Types of accommodation range from castles to log cabins.

Youth Training Scheme (YTS) in the UK, a one- or two-year course of training and work experience for unemployed school leavers aged 16 and 17, from 1989 provided by employer-led Training and Enterprise Councils at local levels and renamed Youth Training.

Ypres, Battles of (Flemish **Ieper**) in World War I, three major battles 1914–17 between German and Allied forces near Ypres, a Belgian town in western Flanders, 40 km/25 mi south of Ostend. Neither side made much progress in any of the battles, despite heavy casualties, but the third battle in particular (also known as Passchendaele) July–November 1917 stands out as an enormous

waste of life for little return. The Menin Gate (1927) is a memorial to British soldiers lost in these battles.

Related Web site: Use of Poison Gas on the Western Front
http://www.lib.byu.edu/~rdh/wwi/1915/chlorgas.html

Ysselmeer alternative spelling of ▷IJsselmeer, a lake in the Netherlands.

YTS abbreviation for ▷Youth Training Scheme.

ytterbium soft, lustrous, silvery, malleable and ductile element of the ▷lanthanide series, symbol Yb, atomic number 70, relative atomic mass 173.04. It occurs with (and resembles) yttrium in gadolinite and other minerals, and is used in making steel and other alloys.

In 1878 Swiss chemist Jean-Charles de Marignac gave the name ytterbium (after the Swedish town of Ytterby, near where it was found) to what he believed to be a new element. French chemist Georges Urbain (1872–1938) discovered in 1907 that this was in fact a mixture of two elements: ytterbium and lutetium.

yttrium silver-grey, metallic element, symbol Y, atomic number 39, relative atomic mass 88.905. It is associated with and resembles the rare earth elements (▷lanthanides), occurring in gadolinite, xenotime, and other minerals. It is used in colour-television tubes and to reduce steel corrosion.

The name derives from the Swedish town of Ytterby, near where it was first discovered in 1788. Swedish chemist Carl Mosander (1797–1858) isolated the element in 1843.

Yuan dynasty ▷Mongol rulers of China 1279–1368 after ▷Kublai Khan defeated the Song dynasty. Much of Song China's administrative infrastructure survived and internal and foreign trade expanded. The Silk Road to the west was re-established and the Grand Canal extended north to Beijing to supply the court with grain.

Yüan Shikai (1859–1916) Chinese soldier and politician, leader of Republican China 1911–16. He assumed dictatorial powers in 1912, dissolving parliament and suppressing Sun Zhong Shan's (Sun Yat-sen's) Kuomintang (▷Guomindang). He died soon after proclaiming himself emperor.

Yucatán peninsula in Central America, divided among Mexico, Belize, and Guatemala; area 180,000 sq km/70,000 sq mi. Tropical crops are grown. It is inhabited by Maya Indians and contains the remains of their civilization.

yucca any of a group of plants belonging to the lily family, with over 40 species found in Latin America and the southwestern USA. The leaves are stiff and sword-shaped and the flowers, which grow on upright central spikes, are white and bell-shaped. (Genus *Yucca*, family Liliaceae.)

Yugoslavia Former country in the Balkans, in southeast Europe, consisting of a federation of constituent republics: Serbia, Montenegro, Bosnia-Herzegovina, Croatia, Slovenia, and Macedonia. In the period 1991–92 Bosnia-Herzegovina, Croatia,

Slovenia, and Macedonia all declared independence and seceded from the federation, leaving Serbia and Montenegro to form the Federal Republic of Yugoslavia. In 2003 the Federal Republic was renamed Serbia and Montenegro, and the name Yugoslavia became obsolete.

Yugoslav literature prose and poetry from the region historically known as Yugoslavia. There are different languages and cultural traditions, of which the most important are Serbian, Croatian, Slovene, and (more recently) Macedonian. They have in common strong oral poetic traditions.

Yukon river in North America, 3,185 km/1,979 mi long, flowing from Lake Tagish in Yukon Territory into Alaska, where it empties into the Bering Sea.

Yukon Territory (Dené *you-kon* 'great water') most northwesterly administrative division of Canada, bordered by the Beaufort Sea to the north, the Northwest Territories to the east, British Columbia to the south (below the 60th Parallel), and Alaska, USA, to the west; area 483,500 sq km/186,631 sq mi; population (1996) 31,500 (including 6,200 American Indians). The capital is ▷Whitehorse. Gold, silver, lead, coal, and zinc are mined, and oil and natural gas extracted. There is lumbering, fur-trapping, and fishing.

Yungning alternative transcription of ▷Nanning, a Chinese port.

Yunnan province of southwest China, bounded to the north by Tibet and Sichuan, to the east by Guizhou and Guangxi Zhuang Autonomous Region, to the south by Vietnam and Laos, and to the west by Myanmar (formerly Burma); area 436,200 sq km/168,373 sq mi; population (1996) 40,420,000. The capital is ▷Kunming. There are tin, copper, lead, gold, zinc, coal, salt, and cigarette industries. Rice, tea, timber, wheat, cotton, and tobacco are grown, and rubber is produced.

YWCA abbreviation for ▷Young Women's Christian Association.

Z

Zagreb industrial city (leather, linen, carpets, paper, and electrical goods) and capital of Croatia, on the Sava River; population (1991) 726,800. Zagreb was a Roman city (**Aemona**) and has a Gothic cathedral. Its university was founded in 1874. The city was damaged by bombing in October 1991 during the Croatian civil war.

Related Web site: Welcome to Zagreb http://www.tel.fer.hr/hrvatska/HRgradovi/Zagreb/Zagreb.html

Zahir Shah, Muhammad (1914–) King of Afghanistan 1933–73. Zahir, educated in Kabul and Paris, served in the government 1932–33 before being crowned king. He was overthrown in 1973 by a republican coup and went into exile. He became a symbol of national unity for the ▷Mujahedin Islamic fundamentalist resistance groups.

Zahir ud-Din Muhammad first Mogul emperor of India; see ▷Babur.

Zama, Battle of battle fought 202 BC in Numidia (now Algeria), in which the Carthaginians under Hannibal were defeated by the Romans under the younger Scipio, so ending the Second Punic War. The Carthaginians were forced to give up Spain and were also subject to harsh peace terms.

Zambezi (or **Zambesi**) river in central and southeast Africa; length 2,650 km/1,650 mi from northwest Zambia through Mozambique to the Indian Ocean, with a wide delta near Chinde. Major tributaries include the Kafue in Zambia. It is interrupted by rapids, and includes on the Zimbabwe–Zambia border the Victoria Falls (Mosi-oa-tunya) and Kariba Dam, which forms the reservoir of Lake Kariba with large fisheries. Its drainage area is about 1,347,000 sq km/520,000 sq mi.

Zambia see country box.

Zamenhof, Lazarus Ludovik (1859–1917) Polish inventor of the international language ▷Esperanto in 1887.

Zampieri, Domenico Italian baroque painter, known as ▷Domenichino.

ZANU (acronym for Zimbabwe African National Union) political organization founded in 1963 by the Reverend Ndabaningi Sithole and later led by Robert Mugabe. It was banned in 1964 by Ian Smith's Rhodesian Front government, against which it conducted a guerrilla war from Zambia until the free elections of 1980, when the ZANU Patriotic Front party, led by Mugabe, won 63% of the vote. In 1987 it merged with ▷ZAPU in preparation for making Zimbabwe a one-party state.

Zanzibar island region of Tanzania, 40 km/25 mi from the mainland, separated by the Zanzibar Channel; area 1,658 sq km/640 sq mi (80 km/50 mi long); population (1995 est) 447,000. Cloves and copra are produced. The main town is Zanzibar.

Related Web site: Zanzibar – Stone Town http://zanzibar.net/stonetow.html

Zapata, Emiliano (1879–1919) Mexican Indian revolutionary leader. He led a revolt against dictator Porfirio ▷Díaz from 1910 under the slogan 'Land and Liberty', to repossess for the indigenous Mexicans the land taken by the Spanish. By 1915 he was driven into retreat, and was assassinated in his stronghold, Morelos, by an agent of Venustiano Carranza.

Zapotec an American Indian people of southern Mexico, now numbering approximately 250,000, living mainly in Oaxaca. The Zapotec language, which belongs to the Oto-Mangean family, has nine dialects. The ancient Zapotec built the ceremonial centre of Monte Albán 1000–500 BC. They developed one of the classic Mesoamerican civilizations by AD 300, but declined under pressure from the Mixtecs from 900 until the Spanish Conquest in the 1530s.

Zappa, Frank (Francis Vincent) (1940–1993) US rock musician, bandleader, and composer. His crudely satirical songs, as in *Joe's Garage* (1980), deliberately bad taste, and complex orchestral and electronic compositions make his work hard to categorize. His group the Mothers of Invention 1965–73 was part of the 1960s avant-garde, and the Mothers' hippie parody *We're Only in It for the Money* (1967) was popular with its target.

ZAPU (acronym for Zimbabwe African People's Union) political organization founded by Joshua ▷Nkomo in 1961 and banned in 1962 by the Rhodesian government. It engaged in a guerrilla war in alliance with ▷ZANU against the Rhodesian regime until late 1979. In the 1980 elections ZAPU was defeated and was then persecuted by the ruling ZANU Patriotic Front party. In 1987 the two parties merged.

Zaragoza (English **Saragossa**) capital of Zaragoza province and of ▷Aragón autonomous community, northeast Spain, on the River Ebro; population (1994) 607,000. Industries include iron, steel, chemicals, plastics, and canned food. The medieval city walls and bridges over the River Ebro still remain, and there is a 15th-century university.

Zarathustra another name for the Persian religious leader ▷Zoroaster.

zazen formal seated meditation in Zen Buddhism. Correct posture and breathing are necessary.

Zealand another name for ▷Sjælland, the main island of Denmark, and for ▷Zeeland, a province of southwest Netherlands.

zebra black and white striped member of the horse genus *Equus* found in Africa; the stripes serve as camouflage or dazzle and confuse predators. It is about 1.5 m/5 ft high at the shoulder, with a stout body and a short, thick mane. Zebras live in family groups and herds on mountains and plains, and can run at up to 60 kph/40 mph. Males are usually solitary.

The **mountain zebra** *E. zebra* was once common in Cape Colony and Natal and still survives in parts of South Africa and Angola. It has long ears and is silvery-white with black or dark-brown markings. **Grevy's zebra** *E. grevyi*, at 1.6 m and 450 kg, is the largest member of the horse family. It has finer and clearer markings than the mountain zebra and inhabits Ethiopia and Somalia. Whereas other zebra species have a harem system, Grevy's males defend territories that females pass through to graze. The species is classified as endangered. **Burchell's** or the **common zebra** *E. burchelli* is medium in size, has white ears, a long mane, and a full tail; it roams the plains north of the Orange River in South Africa.

Related Web site: Grevy's Zebra http://www.seaworld.org/animal_bytes/grevysab.html

zebu any of a species of ▷cattle *Bos indicus* found domesticated in East Asia, India, and Africa. It is usually light-coloured, with large horns and a large fatty hump near the shoulders. It is used for pulling loads and is held by some Hindus to be sacred. There are about 30 breeds.

Zebus have been crossbred with other species of cattle in hot countries to pass on their qualities of heat tolerance and insect resistance. In the USA, they are called Brahman cattle.

Zedekiah (lived early 6th century) last king of Judah 597–586 BC. Placed on the throne by Nebuchadnezzar, he rebelled, was forced to witness his sons' execution, then was blinded and sent to Babylon. The witness to these events was the prophet Jeremiah, who describes them in the Old Testament.

Zeebrugge small Belgian ferry port on the North Sea, linked to Bruges by a canal (built 1896–1907), 14 km/9 mi long. It was occupied by the Germans in World War I and developed as a major naval base. In March 1987 it was the scene of a disaster in which over 180 passengers lost their lives when the car ferry *Herald of Free Enterprise* put to sea from Zeebrugge with its car-loading doors still open.

Zeeland province of southwest Netherlands, consisting of five islands lying in the Schelde river estuary, and the region north of the Belgian province of East Flanders; area 1,790 sq km/691 sq mi; population (1997) 368,400. The capital is ▷Middelburg. There are shipbuilding, engineering, and petrochemical industries. There is livestock raising, dairying, and cereals and potatoes are grown.

Zeffirelli, Franco (Corsi) (1923–) Italian theatre, opera and film director, and stage designer. He is associated with stylish designs and lavish productions. His films include *Romeo and Juliet* (1968), *La Traviata* (1983), *Otello* (1986), and *Hamlet* (1990).

Zeiss, Carl (1816–1888) German optician. He opened his first workshop in Jena in 1846, and in 1866 joined forces with Ernst Abbe (1840–1905) producing cameras, microscopes, and binoculars.

Zeitgeist (German 'time spirit') spirit of the age. The term was used as the title of an exhibition of neo-expressionist paintings held in Berlin in 1982.

Zelenchukskaya site of the world's largest single-mirror optical telescope, with a mirror of 6 m/19.7 ft diameter, in the Caucasus Mountains of Russia. At the same site is the RATAN 600 radio telescope, consisting of radio reflectors in a circle of 600 m/2,000 ft diameter. Both instruments are operated by the Special Astrophysical Observatory of the Russian Academy of Sciences in St Petersburg.

Zen (abbreviation of Japanese *zenna* 'quiet mind concentration') form of ▷Buddhism introduced from India to Japan via China in the 12th century. *Kōan* (paradoxical questions), intense meditation, and sudden enlightenment are elements of Zen practice. Soto Zen was spread by the priest Dōgen (1200–1253), who emphasized work, practice, discipline, and philosophical questions to discover one's Buddha-nature in the 'realization of self'.

Zenobia

Whatever must be accomplished in matters of war must be done by valour alone.

Response to the Roman demand to surrender. Quoted in *Life of Aurelian* ch. 27

Zend-Avesta sacred scriptures of ▷Zoroastrianism, today practised by the Parsees. They comprise the **Avesta** (liturgical books for the priests); the **Gathas** (the discourses and revelations of Zoroaster); and the **Zend** (commentary upon them).

Zeng Guofan (or **Tseng Kuo-fan**) (1811–1872) Chinese imperial official who played a crucial role in crushing the ▷Taiping Rebellion. He raised the Hunan army in 1852 to organize resistance to this revolt, eventually capturing Nanjing in 1864. The regional influence he acquired made him in some ways a forerunner of the 20th-century Chinese warlords.

zenith uppermost point of the celestial horizon, immediately above the observer; the ▷nadir is below, diametrically opposite. See ▷celestial sphere.

Zenobia (lived 3rd century) Queen of Palmyra AD 266–272. She assumed the crown as regent for her sons, after the death of her husband Odaenathus, and in 272 was defeated by Aurelian and taken captive to Rome. See Zenobia fact box on p. 1048.

Zeno of Citium (*c.* 335–262 BC) Greek founder of the ▷Stoic school of philosophy in Athens, about 300 BC.

Zeno of Elea (*c.* 490–*c.* 430 BC) Greek philosopher. He pointed out several paradoxes that raised 'modern' problems of space and time. For example, motion is an illusion, since an arrow in flight must occupy a determinate space at each instant, and therefore must be at rest.

Zeno of Elea

What is moving is moving neither in the place in which it is nor in the place in which it is not.

Quoted in Diogenes Laertius *Lives of the Philosophers* bk 9, ch 72

zeolite any of the hydrous aluminium silicates, also containing sodium, calcium, barium, strontium, or potassium, chiefly found in igneous rocks and characterized by a ready loss or gain of water. Zeolites are used as 'molecular sieves' to separate mixtures because they are capable of selective absorption. They have a high ion-exchange capacity and can be used to make petrol, benzene, and toluene from low-grade raw materials, such as coal and methanol.

Zephaniah, Benjamin (Obadiah Iqbal) (1958–) English poet, performer, and cultural commentator who regularly appears on television and radio in the UK. He also often performs at festivals and charity events. In 1983 he released his first poetry album, *RASTA*. Other albums include *Free South Africa* (1986), *Back to Roots* (1995), and *Belly of De Beast* (1996).

Zephaniah was born in Black River, Jamaica. He moved to England when he was two and grew up in Handsworth, Birmingham. He was frequently in trouble with the police and was sent to borstal when he was 14 years old. In 1979 he moved to London where he set up a housing cooperative and a bookshop. He published his first pamphlet of poetry, entitled *Pen Rhythm* (1980), himself. He then became involved with performance poetry, 'gigging' extensively in the UK, and articles began to appear about him in the music press.

Zephyrus in Greek mythology, the god of the west wind, husband of Iris, and father of the horses of ▷Achilles in Homer's *Iliad*.

Zeppelin, Ferdinand Adolf August Heinrich, Count von Zeppelin (1838–1917) German ▷airship pioneer. His first airship was built and tested in 1900. During World War I a number

of **zeppelins** bombed England. They were also used for luxury passenger transport but the construction of hydrogen-filled airships with rigid keels was abandoned after several disasters in the 1920s and 1930s. Zeppelin also helped to pioneer large multi-engine bomber planes.

Zermatt ski resort in the Valais (Wallis) canton, Switzerland, altitude 1,620 m/5,315 ft, at the head of the Visp valley and at the foot of the Matterhorn,; population (1990) 4,200. It lies 35 km/22 mi by rail from Visp in the Rhône valley.

Zeus in Greek mythology, the chief of the Olympian gods (Roman ▷Jupiter). He was the son of ▷Kronos, whom he overthrew; his brothers included Pluto and Poseidon, his sisters Demeter, Hestia, and Hera. As the supreme god he dispensed good and evil and was the father and ruler of all humankind, the fount of kingly power and law and order. His emblems were the thunderbolt and aegis (shield), representing the thundercloud. The colossal ivory and gold statue of the seated god, made by Phidias for the temple of Zeus in the Peloponnese, was one of the ▷Seven Wonders of the World.

Zhangjiakou (or **Changchiakow**; Mongolian **Kalgan**) historic city and trading centre in Hebei province, China, on the Great Wall, 160 km/100 mi northwest of Beijing; population (1990) 670,000. Zhangjiakou used to be an important border post between China and Mongolia on the road and railway to Ulaanbaatar; its Mongolian name means 'gate'. It developed under the Qing dynasty, and was the centre of the tea trade from China to Russia. The origin of the city lies in the forts built here in the 15th and 17th centuries as defences against Mongol incursions.

Zhao Ziyang (1919–) Chinese politician, prime minister 1980–87 and leader of the Chinese Communist Party 1987–89. His reforms included self-management and incentives for workers and factories. He lost his secretaryship and other posts after the Tiananmen Square massacre in Beijing in June 1989.

Zhejiang (or **Chekiang**) coastal province of southeast China, bounded to the north by Jiangsu, to the east by the East China Sea, to the south by Fujian, and to the west by Jiangxi and Anhui; area 101,800 sq km/39,300 sq mi; population (1996) 43,430,000. The capital is ▷Hangzhou. There are silk, chemical fibre, canning, tea-processing, and handicrafts industries. Rice, cotton, sugar, jute, maize, and timber are grown; silkworms are farmed and there is fishing. Zhejiang is the second smallest of the Chinese provinces, and densely populated. See picture on p. 1048.

Zhelev, Zhelyu (1935–) Bulgarian politician, president 1990–96. In 1989 he became head of the opposition Union Democratic Forces (UDF) coalition. He was a proponent of market-centred economic reform and social peace.

Zhengzhou (or **Chengchow**) capital of ▷Henan province, China, on the Huang He River; population (1999) 1,465,100. Industries include light engineering, food-processing, and the manufacture of chemicals, building materials, and cotton textiles.

Zambia

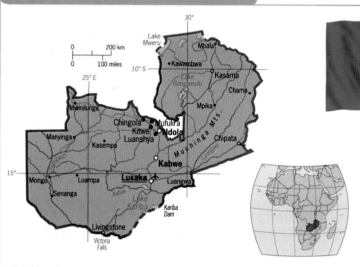

Zambia (formerly Northern Rhodesia, until 1964) landlocked country in southern central Africa, bounded north by the Democratic Republic of Congo (formerly Zaire) and Tanzania, east by Malawi, south by Mozambique, Zimbabwe, Botswana, and Namibia, and west by Angola.

NATIONAL NAME *Republic of Zambia*
AREA 752,600 sq km/290,578 sq mi
CAPITAL Lusaka
MAJOR TOWNS/CITIES Kitwe, Ndola, Kabwe, Mufulira, Chingola, Luanshya, Livingstone
PHYSICAL FEATURES forested plateau cut through by rivers; Zambezi River, Victoria Falls, Kariba Dam

Government

HEAD OF STATE AND GOVERNMENT Levy Mwanawasa from 2002
POLITICAL SYSTEM emergent democracy
POLITICAL EXECUTIVE limited presidency
ADMINISTRATIVE DIVISIONS nine provinces
ARMED FORCES 21,600; plus paramilitary forces of 1,400 (2002 est)
CONSCRIPTION military service is voluntary
DEATH PENALTY retained and used for ordinary crimes
DEFENCE SPEND (% GDP) 0.7 (2002 est)
EDUCATION SPEND (% GDP) 1.9 (1999)
HEALTH SPEND (% GDP) 5.6 (2000 est)

Economy and resources

CURRENCY Zambian kwacha
GPD (US$) 3.7 billion (2002 est)
REAL GDP GROWTH (% change on previous year) 4 (2001)
GNI (US$) 3.5 billion (2002 est)
GNI PER CAPITA (PPP) (US$) 770 (2002 est)
CONSUMER PRICE INFLATION 18.4% (2003 est)
UNEMPLOYMENT 10.3% (1999)
FOREIGN DEBT (US$) 5 billion (2001 est)

MAJOR TRADING PARTNERS South Africa, Zimbabwe, Japan, UK, Thailand, Switzerland, Malawi
RESOURCES copper, cobalt, zinc, lead, coal, gold, emeralds, amethysts and other gemstones, limestone, selenium
INDUSTRIES metallurgy (smelting and refining of copper and other metals), food canning, fertilizers, explosives, textiles, bottles, bricks, copper wire, batteries

ZAMBIA A Lozi woman sifting grain.
Image Bank

EXPORTS copper, zinc, lead, cobalt, tobacco. Principal market: South Africa 24.5% (2001)
IMPORTS petroleum, machinery and transport equipment, metals, fertilizers, electricity, basic manufactures, chemicals, food and live animals. Principal source: South Africa 65.1% (2001)
ARABLE LAND 7.1% (2000 est)
AGRICULTURAL PRODUCTS maize, sugar cane, seed cotton, tobacco, groundnuts, wheat, rice, beans, cassava, millet, sorghum, sunflower seeds, horticulture; cattle rearing

Population and society

POPULATION 10,812,000 (2003 est)
POPULATION GROWTH RATE 1.3% (2000–15)
POPULATION DENSITY (per sq km) 14 (2003 est)

Chronology

16th century: Immigration of peoples from Luba and Lunda Empires of Zaire, to the northwest, who set up small kingdoms.
late 18th century: Visited by Portuguese explorers.
19th century: Instability with immigration of Ngoni from east, Kololo from west, establishment of Bemba kingdom in north, and slave-trading activities of Portuguese and Arabs from East Africa.
1851: Visited by British missionary and explorer David Livingstone.
1889: As Northern Rhodesia, came under administration of British South Africa Company of Cecil Rhodes, and became involved in copper mining, especially from 1920s.
1924: Became a British protectorate.
1948: Northern Rhodesia African Congress (NRAC) formed by black Africans to campaign for self-rule.
1953: Became part of Central African Federation, which included South Rhodesia (Zimbabwe) and Nyasaland (Malawi).
1960: UNIP was formed by Kenneth Kaunda as a breakaway from NRAC, as African socialist body to campaign for independence and dissolution of federation dominated by South Rhodesia's white minority.
1963: The federation was dissolved and internal self-government achieved.
1964: Independence was achieved within the Commonwealth as the Republic of Zambia, with Kaunda of the UNIP as president.

URBAN POPULATION (% of total) 40 (2003 est)
AGE DISTRIBUTION (% of total population) 0–14 47%, 15–59 48%, 60+ 5% (2002 est)
ETHNIC GROUPS over 95% indigenous Africans, belonging to more than 70 different ethnic groups, including the Bantu-Botatwe and the Bemba; about 1% European
LANGUAGE English (official), Bantu languages
RELIGION about 64% Christian, animist, Hindu, Muslim
EDUCATION (compulsory years) 7
LITERACY RATE 87% (men); 75% (women) (2003 est)
LABOUR FORCE 17% agriculture, 20% industry, 63% services (1996)
LIFE EXPECTANCY 33 (men); 32 (women) (2000–05)
CHILD MORTALITY RATE (under 5, per 1,000 live births) 202 (2001)
PHYSICIANS (per 1,000 people) 0.1 (1998 est)
HOSPITAL BEDS (per 1,000 people) 2.9 (1996 est)
TV SETS (per 1,000 people) 113 (2001 est)
RADIOS (per 1,000 people) 169 (2001 est)
INTERNET USERS (per 10,000 people) 49.0 (2002 est)
PERSONAL COMPUTER USERS (per 100 people) 0.8 (2002 est)

See also ▷Kaunda, Kenneth.

later 1960s: Key enterprises were brought under state control.
1972: UNIP was declared the only legal party.
1975: The opening of the Tan-Zam railway from the Zambian copperbelt, 322 mi/200 km north of Lusaka, to port of Dar es Salaam in Tanzania, reduced Zambia's dependence on the rail route via Rhodesia (Zimbabwe) for its exports.
1976: Zambia declared its support for Patriotic Front (PF) guerrillas fighting to topple the white-dominated regime in Rhodesia (Zimbabwe).
1980: There was an unsuccessful South African-promoted coup against President Kaunda; relations with Zimbabwe improved when the PF came to power.
1985: Kaunda was elected chair of African Front Line States.
1991: A new multiparty constitution was adopted. The MMD won a landslide election victory, and its leader Frederick Chiluba became president in what was the first democratic change of government in English-speaking black Africa.
1993: A state of emergency was declared after rumours of a planned antigovernment coup. A privatization programme was launched.
1996: Kaunda was effectively barred from future elections by an amendment to the constitution.
1997: There was an abortive antigovernment coup.
1998: Former president Kaunda was placed under house arrest after alleged involvement in the antigovernment coup. Kaunda was charged but the charges were subsequently dropped.

Zenobia

Septima Zenobia married Odaenathus, the ruler of Palmyra (now Tadmur, Syria), which was an outpost of the Roman Empire. In 267 or 268, after the murder of her husband and his heir Herodes (her stepson), in which her involvement was suspected, she took power. She assumed the crown as regent for one of her own sons, Wahballat, and called herself Queen of Palmyra.

Zenobia wanted independence from Rome and within a few years she expanded her empire to include the whole of Syria; she conquered Egypt in 269 and then went on to take most of Asia Minor. In response to her military success in the East and her declaration of independence, in 271 the Roman emperor Aurelian launched an offensive against her and defeated her armies at Antioch (now Antakya, Turkey) and Emesa (now Homs, Syria). He then mounted a siege on Palmyra in which Zenobia and Wahballat were captured and taken to Rome as prisoners (272). The people of Palmyra revolted again in 273 but the Romans retaliated by destroying their city.

Zenobia and two of her sons were part of Aurelian's triumphal procession in Rome in 274. Subsequently she is thought to have married a Roman senator and to have lived the rest of her life in his villa at Tibur (now Tivoli, Italy). See entry on p. 1046.

ZENOBIA A limestone figure of Zenobia, for a short time ruler of the eastern part of the Roman Empire in the 3rd century AD. While living as a captive in Rome, she was allowed to marry a Roman senator and lived thereafter in some luxury, studying literature and participating in religious causes. *The Art Archive*

ZHEJIANG In a can factory in Anji, Zhejiang province, China, workers prepare bales of cans for shipping. See entry on p. 1047. *Image Bank*

Zhirinovsky, Vladimir (1946–) Russian politician, leader of the far-right Liberal Democratic Party of Russia (LDPR) from 1991. His strong, sometimes bizarre views, advocating the use of nuclear weapons and the restoration of the Russian empire, initially cast him as a lightweight politician. However, his ability to win third place out of six candidates in Russia's first free presidential elections in 1991, and the success of his party in winning nearly 23% of the vote and 15% of the seats in the December 1993 federal assembly elections, forced a reassessment. However, in the June 1996 presidential elections his support fell to below 6%.

Zhitomir (Ukrainian **Zhytomyr**) capital of Zhitomir oblast in western Ukraine, 125 km/78 mi west of Kiev; population (1998) 298,000. Zhitomir, on the Teterev River, is a timber and grain centre, and has furniture factories, sugar refineries, and a large brewing industry. The city was founded in the 13th century.

Zhivkov, Todor Hristo (1911–1998) Bulgarian Communist Party (BCP) leader 1954–89, prime minister 1962–71, and president 1971–89. His period in office was one of caution and conservatism. In 1990 he was charged with embezzlement during his time in office and in 1992 sentenced to seven years under house arrest. He was released in January 1997.

Zhou dynasty (or **Chou dynasty**) Chinese succession of rulers *c.* 1066–256 BC, during which cities emerged and philosophy flourished. The dynasty was established by the Zhou, a semi-nomadic people from the Wei Valley region, west of the great bend in the Huang He (Yellow River). Zhou influence waned from 403 BC, as the Warring States era began.

Zhou Enlai (or **Chou En-lai**) (1898–1976) Chinese communist politician. Zhou, a member of the Chinese Communist Party (CCP) from the 1920s, was prime minister 1949–76 and foreign minister 1949–58. He was a moderate Maoist and weathered the ▷Cultural Revolution. He played a key role in foreign affairs.

Born into a declining mandarin gentry family near Shanghai, Zhou studied in Japan and Paris, where he became a founder member of the overseas branch of the CCP. He adhered to the Moscow line of urban-based revolution in China, organizing communist cells in Shanghai and an abortive uprising in Nanchang in 1927. In 1935 Zhou supported the election of ▷Mao Zedong as CCP leader and remained a loyal ally during the next 40 years. He served as liaison officer 1937–46 between the CCP and Jiang Jie Shi's (Chiang Kai-shek's) nationalist Kuomintang (▷Guomindang) government. In 1949 he became prime minister, an office he held until his death in January 1976.

Zhou, a moderator between the opposing camps of Liu Shaoqi and Mao Zedong, restored orderly progress after the ▷Great Leap Forward (1958–60) and the Cultural Revolution (1966–69), and was the architect of the Four Modernizations programme in 1975. Abroad, Zhou sought to foster Third World unity at the Bandung Conference in 1955, averted an outright border confrontation with the USSR by negotiation with Prime Minister Kosygin in 1969, and was the principal advocate of détente with the USA during the early 1970s.

Zhubov scale scale for measuring ice coverage, developed in the USSR. The unit is the **ball**; one ball is 10% coverage, two balls 20%, and so on.

Zhu De (or **Chu The**) (1886–1976) Chinese communist military leader, 'father' and commander of the Chinese Red Army 1931–54. He devised the tactic of mobile guerrilla warfare and organized the ▷Long March to Shaanxi 1934–36. He was made a marshal in 1955.

Zhukov, Georgi Konstantinovich (1896–1974) Marshal of the USSR in World War II and minister of defence 1955–57. As chief of staff from 1941, he defended Moscow in 1941, counter-attacked at Stalingrad (now Volgograd) in 1942, organized the relief of Leningrad (now St Petersburg) in 1943, and led the offensive from the Ukraine March in 1944 which ended in the fall of Berlin.

Zia, Begum Khaleda (1945–) Bangladeshi conservative politician, prime minister 1991–96. As leader of the Bangladesh Nationalist Party (BNP) from 1984, she successfully oversaw the transition from presidential to democratic parliamentary government, but faced mounting opposition from 1994.

Zia ul-Haq, Muhammad (1924–1988) Pakistani general, in power from 1977 until his death, probably an assassination, in an aircraft explosion. He became army chief of staff in 1976, led the military coup against Zulfikar Ali ▷Bhutto in 1977, and became president in 1978. Zia introduced a fundamentalist Islamic regime and restricted political activity.

zidovudine (formerly **AZT**) antiviral drug used in the treatment of ▷AIDS. It is not a cure for AIDS but is effective in prolonging life; it does not, however, delay the onset of AIDS in people carrying the virus.

ZIFT (abbreviation for zygote inter-Fallopian transfer) modified form of ▷in vitro fertilization in which the fertilized ovum is reintroduced into the mother's ▷Fallopian tube before the ovum has undergone its first cell division. This mimics the natural processes of fertilization (which normally occurs in the Fallopian tube) and implantation more effectively than older techniques.

ziggurat in ancient Babylonia and Assyria, a step pyramid of sun-baked brick faced with glazed bricks or tiles on which stood a shrine. The Tower of Babel as described in the Bible may have been a ziggurat.

Zimbabwe (or **Great Zimbabwe**; Shona *zimbabwe* 'house of stone') extensive stone architectural ruins 27 km/17 mi southeast of Victoria in Mashonaland, Zimbabwe. The site was occupied from the 3rd century AD, but the massive stone structures date from the 10th–15th centuries AD. They were probably the work of the Shona people, who established their rule in about AD 1000 and mined minerals for trading.

Zimbabwe see country box.

zinc (Germanic *zint* 'point') hard, brittle, bluish-white, metallic element, symbol Zn, atomic number 30, relative atomic mass 65.37. The principal ore is sphalerite or zinc blende (zinc sulphide, ZnS). Zinc is hardly affected by air or moisture at ordinary temperatures; its chief uses are in alloys such as brass and in coating metals (for example, galvanized iron). Its compounds include zinc oxide, used in ointments (as an astringent) and cosmetics, paints, glass, and printing ink.

Zinc is an essential trace element in most animals; adult humans have 2–3 g/0.07–0.1 oz zinc in their bodies. There are more than 300 known enzymes that contain zinc.

Zinc has been used as a component of brass since the Bronze Age, but it was not recognized as a separate metal until 1746, when it was described by German chemist Andreas Sigismund Marggraf (1709–1782). The name derives from the shape of the crystals on smelting.

The zinc industry in Europe generates about 80,000 tons of zinc waste each year.

zinc ore mineral from which zinc is extracted, principally sphalerite (Zn,Fe)S, but also zincite, ZnO_2, and smithsonite, $ZnCO_3$, all of which occur in mineralized veins. Ores of lead and zinc often occur together, and are common worldwide; Canada, the USA, and Australia are major producers.

zinc oxide ZnO white powder, yellow when hot, that occurs in nature as the mineral zincite. It is used in paints and as an antiseptic in zinc ointment; it is the main ingredient of calamine lotion.

zinc sulphide ZnS yellow-white solid that occurs in nature as the mineral sphalerite (also called zinc blende). It is the principal ore of zinc, and is used in the manufacture of fluorescent paints.

Zinnemann, Fred(erick) (1907–1997) Austrian-born US film director, responsible for a series of liberal, moralistic, social realist narratives centred on protagonists undergoing a crisis of conscience, who ultimately feel compelled to defend their beliefs. Although Zinnemann's critical reputation has waned since the 1960s – overshadowed by the work of figures such as Orson Welles, Alfred Hitchcock, and Howard Hawks – he was highly regarded in his day, and received two Academy Awards for *From Here to Eternity* (1953) and *A Man for All Seasons* (1966).

zinnia any of a group of annual plants belonging to the daisy family, native to Mexico and South America; notably the cultivated hybrids of *Z. elegans* with brightly coloured daisylike flowers. (Genus *Zinnia*, family Compositae.)

Zinovyev, Alexander Aleksandrovich (1922–) Russian satirical writer and mathematician. He now lives in Munich, Germany. His first book *Ziyayushchie vysoty/Yawning Heights* (1976), a surreal, chaotic narrative, represents a formal negation of the socialist realist novel and the promised 'great Future' of Soviet ideology. He complicates the quasi-scientific stance of his writing by deliberate disorganization, even in his

Zimbabwe

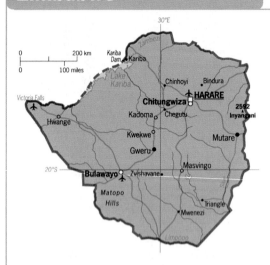

Zimbabwe (formerly Southern Rhodesia, until 1980) landlocked country in south central Africa, bounded north by Zambia, east by Mozambique, south by South Africa, and west by Botswana.

NATIONAL NAME *Republic of Zimbabwe*
AREA 390,300 sq km/150,694 sq mi
CAPITAL Harare
MAJOR TOWNS/CITIES Bulawayo, Gweru, Kwe Kwe, Mutare, Kadoma, Chitungwiza
PHYSICAL FEATURES high plateau with central high veld and mountains in east; rivers Zambezi, Limpopo; Victoria Falls

Government

HEAD OF STATE AND GOVERNMENT Robert Mugabe from 1987
POLITICAL SYSTEM nationalistic socialist
POLITICAL EXECUTIVE unlimited presidency
ADMINISTRATIVE DIVISIONS eight provinces and two cities with provincial status
ARMED FORCES 36,000; plus paramilitary forces of 21,800 (2002 est)
DEATH PENALTY retained and used for ordinary crimes

Economy and resources

CURRENCY Zimbabwe dollar
GPD (US$) 8.3 billion (2002 est)
REAL GDP GROWTH (% change on previous year) −7.3 (2001)
GNI (US$) 6.2 billion (2002 est)
GNI PER CAPITA (PPP) (US$) 2,120 (2002 est)
CONSUMER PRICE INFLATION 450% (2003 est)

UNEMPLOYMENT 6% (official figure in 2000; actual rate believed to be significantly higher)
FOREIGN DEBT (US$) 3.02 billion (2001 est)
MAJOR TRADING PARTNERS South Africa, UK, USA, Germany, Malawi, Botswana, Japan
RESOURCES gold, nickel, asbestos, coal, chromium, copper, silver, emeralds, lithium, tin, iron ore, cobalt
INDUSTRIES metal products, food processing, textiles, furniture and other wood products, chemicals, fertilizers
EXPORTS tobacco, gold, nickel, ferro-alloys, textiles and clothing, sugar, cotton lint. Principal market: South Africa 15% (2000)
IMPORTS machinery and transport equipment, basic manufactures, mineral fuels, chemicals, foodstuffs. Principal source: South Africa 36.2% (2000)
ARABLE LAND 8.3% (2000 est)
AGRICULTURAL PRODUCTS tobacco, maize, cotton, coffee, sugar cane, wheat, soybeans, groundnuts, horticulture; livestock (cattle)

Population and society

POPULATION 12,891,000 (2003 est)
POPULATION GROWTH RATE 0.7% (2000–15)
POPULATION DENSITY (per sq km) 33 (2003 est)

URBAN POPULATION (% of total) 37 (2003 est)
AGE DISTRIBUTION (% of total population) 0–14 45%, 15–59 50%, 60+ 5% (2002 est)
ETHNIC GROUPS four distinct ethnic groups: indigenous Africans (mainly Shona 71% and Ndebele 16%),who account for about 95% of the population, Europeans (mainly British), who account for about 3.5%, and Afro-Europeans and Asians, who each comprise about 0.5%
LANGUAGE English, Shona, Ndebele (all official)

Chronology

13th century: Shona people settled Mashonaland (eastern Zimbabwe), erecting stone buildings (hence name Zimbabwe, 'stone house').

15th century: Shona Empire reached its greatest extent.

16th–17th centuries: Portuguese settlers developed trade with Shona states and achieved influence over the kingdom of Mwanamutapa in northern Zimbabwe in 1629.

1837: Ndebele (or Matabele) people settled in southwest Zimbabwe after being driven north from Transvaal by Boers; Shona defeated by Ndebele led by King Mzilikazi who formed military empire based at Bulawayo.

1870: King Lobengula succeeded King Mzilikazi.

1889: Cecil Rhodes's British South Africa Company (SA Co) obtained exclusive rights to exploit mineral resources in Lobengula's domains.

1890: Creation of white colony in Mashonaland and founding of Salisbury (Harare) by Leander Starr Jameson, associate of Rhodes.

1893: Matabele War: Jameson defeated Lobengula; white settlers took control of country.

1895: Matabeleland, Mashonaland, and Zambia named Rhodesia after Cecil Rhodes.

1896: Matabele revolt suppressed.

1898: Southern Rhodesia (Zimbabwe) became British protectorate administered by BSA Co; farming, mining, and railways developed.

1922: Union with South Africa rejected by referendum among white settlers.

1923: Southern Rhodesia became self-governing colony; Africans progressively disenfranchised.

1933–53: Prime Minister Godfrey Huggins (later Lord Malvern) pursued 'White Rhodesia' policy of racial segregation.

1950s: Immigration doubled white population to around 250,000, while indigenous African population stood at around 6 million.

1953: Southern Rhodesia formed part of Federation of Rhodesia and Nyasaland.

1961: Zimbabwe African People's Union (ZAPU) formed with Joshua Nkomo as leader; declared illegal a year later.

1962: Rhodesia Front party of Winston Field took power in Southern Rhodesia, pledging to preserve white rule.

1963: Federation of Rhodesia and Nyasaland dissolved as Zambia and Malawi moved towards independence; Zimbabwe African National Union (ZANU) formed, with Robert Mugabe as secretary; declared illegal a year later.

1964: Ian Smith became prime minister; he rejected British terms for independence which required moves towards black majority rule; Nkomo and Mugabe imprisoned.

1965: Smith made unilateral declaration of independence (UDI); Britain broke off all relations.

RELIGION 50% follow a syncretic (part Christian, part indigenous beliefs) type of religion, Christian 25%, animist 24%, small Muslim minority
EDUCATION (compulsory years) 8
LITERACY RATE 94% (men); 87% (women) (2003 est)
LABOUR FORCE 26.0% agriculture, 14.6% industry, 59.4% services (2000)
LIFE EXPECTANCY 34 (men); 33 (women) (2000–05)
CHILD MORTALITY RATE (under 5, per 1,000 live births) 123 (2001)
PHYSICIANS (per 1,000 people) 0.1 (1998 est)
TV SETS (per 1,000 people) 180 (1999)
RADIOS (per 1,000 people) 362 (2001 est)
INTERNET USERS (per 10,000 people) 429.8 (2002 est)
PERSONAL COMPUTER USERS (per 100 people) 5.2 (2002 est)

See also ▷Matabeleland; ▷Mugabe, Robert; ▷Smith, Ian.

1966–68: United Nations (UN) imposed economic sanctions on Rhodesia, which still received help from South Africa and Portugal.

1969: Rhodesia declared itself a republic.

1972: Britain rejected draft independence agreement as unacceptable to African population.

1974: Nkomo and Mugabe released and jointly formed Patriotic Front to fight Smith regime in mounting civil war.

1975: Geneva Conference between British, Smith regime, and African nationalists failed to reach agreement.

1978: At height of civil war, whites were leaving Rhodesia at rate of 1,000 per month.

1979: Rhodesia became Zimbabwe-Rhodesia with new 'majority' constitution which nevertheless retained special rights for whites; Bishop Abel Muzorewa became premier; Mugabe and Nkomo rejected settlement; Lancaster House Agreement temporarily restored Rhodesia to British rule.

1980: Zimbabwe achieved independence from Britain with full transition to African majority rule; Mugabe became prime minister with Rev. Canaan Banana as president.

1984: A ZANU–PF party congress agreed to the principle of a one-party state.

1987: Mugabe combined the posts of head of state and prime minister as executive president; Nkomo became vice-president.

1989: ZANU–PF and ZAPU formally merged; the Zimbabwe Unity Movement was founded by Edgar Tekere to oppose the one-party state.

1992: The United Party was formed to oppose ZANU–PF. Mugabe declared drought and famine a national disaster.

1996: Mugabe was re-elected president.

1998: Mugabe issued new rules banning strikes and restricting political and public gatherings. There were violent antigovernment demonstrations.

2000: Veterans of the war of independence, supported by the government, began to invade and claim white-owned farms. To international and internal opposition, the government invoked special powers to seize the farms without compensation. The high court ruled Mugabe's land acquisition program illegal.

2002: The EU imposed sanctions on Mugabe and his government following the expulsion of the leader of a team monitoring the general elections. Mugabe claimed re-election as president after a campaign marred by alleged ballot rigging and intimidation of opponents. International condemnation of the result was reinforced by Zimbabwe's suspension from the Commonwealth for a year. The government ordered 2,900 white commercial farmers, whose farms had been targeted for seizure and redistribution to poor black workers, to stop work with immediate effect under threat of imprisonment. Zimbabwe faced its worst food shortage in 60 years, due to drought and violent land-reform policies.

ZIMBABWE Blasting in a gold mine in Zimbabwe. After gold production peaked in the early 20th century, the country's many mines lay dormant until the 1970s, when the rise in gold prices led to their reopening and revived gold as the country's leading export.
Image Bank

treatise *Kommunizm kak realnost/The Reality of Communism* (1981).

Zinovyev (or Zinoviev)**, Grigory Yevseyevich** (1883–1936) Russian communist politician whose name was attached to a forgery, the **Zinovyev letter**, inciting Britain's communists to rise, which helped to topple the Labour government in 1924.

Zion Jebusite (Amorites of Canaan) stronghold in Jerusalem captured by King David, and the hill on which he built the Temple, symbol of Jerusalem and of Jewish national life.

Zionism national liberation movement advocating the re-establishment of a Jewish homeland (the *Eretz Israel*) in Palestine. Here, in the 'promised land' of the Bible, its adherents called for the Jewish people to be granted a sovereign state with its capital at Jerusalem, the 'city of Zion'. The movement was founded by the Hungarian writer Theodor ▷Herzl, who in 1897 convened the First Zionist Congress in the Swiss city of Basel. Zionism was the driving force behind the creation of the state of Israel in 1948.

zip fastener fastening device used in clothing, invented in the USA by Whitcomb Judson in 1891, originally for doing up shoes. It has two sets of interlocking teeth, meshed by means of a slide that moves up and down. It became widely used in the clothing industry in the 1930s.

Zircon codename for a British signals-intelligence satellite originally intended to be launched in 1988. The revelation of the existence of the Zircon project (which had been concealed by the government), and the government's subsequent efforts to suppress a programme about it on BBC television, caused much controversy in 1987. Its intended function was to intercept radio and other signals from the USSR, Europe, and the Middle East and transmit them to the Government Communications Headquarters (GCHQ) in Cheltenham, England.

zircon zirconium silicate, $ZrSiO_4$, a mineral that occurs in small quantities in a wide range of igneous, sedimentary, and metamorphic rocks. It is very durable and is resistant to erosion and weathering. It is usually coloured brown, but can be other colours, and when transparent may be used as a gemstone.

zirconium (Germanic *zircon*, from Persian *zargun* 'golden') lustrous, greyish-white, strong, ductile, metallic element, symbol Zr, atomic number 40, relative atomic mass 91.22. It occurs in nature as the mineral zircon (zirconium silicate), from which it is obtained commercially. It is used in some ceramics, alloys for wire and filaments, steel manufacture, and nuclear reactors, where its low neutron absorption is advantageous.

It was isolated in 1824 by Swedish chemist Jöns Berzelius. The name was proposed by English chemist Humphry Davy in 1808.

zither member of a family of musical instruments consisting of one or more strings stretched over a resonating frame or soundbox, played horizontally. The modern concert zither has up to 45 strings of which five, passing over frets, are plucked with a plectrum for melody, and the remainder are plucked with the fingers for harmonic accompaniment.

Zi Xi (or Tz'u-his) (*c.* 1834–1908) Empress dowager of China. She was presented as a concubine to the emperor Xianfeng. On his death in 1861 she became regent for her young son Tongzhi (1856–1875) until 1873 and, after his death, for her nephew Guangxu (1871–1908) until 1889. A ruthless conservative, she blocked the Hundred Days' Reform launched in 1898 and assumed power again, having Guangxu imprisoned. Her policies helped deny China a peaceful transition to political and economic reform.

zodiac zone of the heavens containing the paths of the Sun, Moon, and planets. When this was devised by the ancient Greeks, only five planets were known, making the zodiac about 16° wide. In astrology, the zodiac is divided into 12 signs, each 30° in extent: Aries, Taurus, Gemini, Cancer, Leo, Virgo, Libra, Scorpio, Sagittarius, Capricorn, Aquarius, and Pisces. These do not cover the same areas of sky as the astronomical constellations.

The 12 astronomical constellations are uneven in size and do not between them cover the whole zodiac, or even the line of the ecliptic, much of which lies in the constellation of Ophiuchus.

zodiacal light cone-shaped light sometimes seen extending from the Sun along the ▷ecliptic (that is, the path that the Sun appears to follow each year as it is orbited by Earth), visible after sunset or before sunrise. It is due to thinly spread dust particles in the central plane of the Solar System. It is very faint, and requires a dark, clear sky to be seen.

Zoë (*c.* 978–1050) Byzantine empress who ruled from 1028 until 1050. She gained the title by marriage to the heir apparent Romanus III Argyrus, but was reputed to have poisoned him (1034) in order to marry her lover Michael. He died in 1041 and Zoë and her sister Theodora were proclaimed joint empresses. Rivalry led to Zoë marrying Constantine IX Monomachus with whom she reigned until her death.

Zog, Ahmed Bey Zogu (1895–1961) King of Albania 1928–39. He became prime minister of Albania in 1922, president of the republic in 1925, and proclaimed himself king in 1928. He was driven out by the Italians in 1939 and settled in the UK.

zoidogamy type of plant reproduction in which male gametes (antherozoids) swim in a film of water to the female gametes. Zoidogamy is found in algae, bryophytes, pteridophytes, and some gymnosperms (others use siphonogamy).

Zola, Émile Edouard Charles Antoine (1840–1902) French novelist and social reformer. He made his name with *Thérèse Raquin* (1867), a grim, powerful story of remorse. With *La Fortune des Rougon/The Fortune of the Rougons* (1867) he began a series of some 20 naturalistic novels collectively known as *Le Rougon-Macquart*, portraying the fortunes of a French family under the Second Empire. They include *Le Ventre de Paris/The Underbelly of Paris* (1873), *Nana* (1880), and *La Débâcle/The Debacle* (1892). In 1898 he published *J'accuse/I Accuse*, a pamphlet indicting the persecutors of Alfred ▷Dreyfus, for which he was prosecuted for libel but later pardoned.

Zola was born in Paris. He became a journalist and a clerk in the publishing house of Hachette. He wrote literary and art criticisms and published several collections of short stories, beginning with *Contes à Ninon/Stories for Ninon* (1864). Having discovered his real talent as a novelist, he produced the volumes of *Le Rougon-Macquart* steadily over a quarter of a century, proving himself a master of realism. Other titles in the series are *La Faute de l'Abbé Mouret/The Simple Priest* (1875), *L'Assommoir/Drunkard* (1878), *Germinal* (1885), *La Terre/Earth* (1888), *La Bête humaine/The Human Beast* (1890), and *L'Argent/Money* (1891). Among later novels are the trilogy *Trois Villes/Three Cities* (1894–98) (*Lourdes* (1894), *Rome* (1896), *Paris* (1898)), and *Les Quatre Evangiles/The Four Gospels* (1899–1903) (*Fécondité/Fecundity* (1899), *Travail/Work* (1902), *Vérité/Truth* (1903), and the unfinished *Justice*).

Émile Zola
J'accuse.
I accuse.
Heading of an open letter to the President of the Republic concerning the Dreyfus case, 1898

ÉMILE ZOLA A portrait of the French novelist and social reformer Émile Zola. *Archive Photos*

zombie corpse believed to be reanimated by a spirit and enslaved. The idea, widespread in Haiti, possibly arose from voodoo priests using the nerve poison tetrodotoxin (from the puffer fish) to produce a semblance of death from which the victim afterwards physically recovers. Those eating incorrectly prepared puffer fish in Japan have been similarly affected.

zone therapy alternative name for ▷reflexology.

zoo (abbreviation for zoological gardens) place where animals are kept in captivity. Originally created purely for visitor entertainment and education, zoos have become major centres for the breeding of endangered species of animals; a 1984 report identified 2,000 vertebrate species in need of such maintenance.

Notable zoos exist in New York, San Diego, Toronto, Chicago, London, Paris, Berlin, Moscow, and Beijing (Peking). Many groups object to zoos because they keep animals in unnatural conditions alien to their habitat.

Henry I started a royal menagerie at Woodstock, Oxfordshire, later transferred to the Tower of London. The Zoological Society of London was founded 1826 by Stamford Raffles in Regent's Park, London, and in 1827 the gardens were opened to members. In 1831 William IV presented the royal menagerie to the Zoological Society; the public were admitted from 1848. The name 'zoo' dates from 1867. London Zoo currently houses some 8,000 animals of over 900 species. Threatened by closure in 1991 because of falling income, the zoo was given a one-year extension to July 1992; the decision to close it was reversed in September 1992 and it is now planned to transform the zoo into a conservation park, with Whipsnade as the national collection of animals. In 1991 the number of animals in Britain's zoos totalled 35,000.

zoology branch of biology concerned with the study of animals. It includes any aspect of the study of animal form and function – description of present-day animals, the study of evolution of animal forms, ▷anatomy, ▷physiology, ▷embryology, behaviour, and geographical distribution.

zoom lens photographic lens that, by variation of focal length, allows speedy transition from long shots to close-ups.

zoonosis any infectious disease that can be transmitted to humans by other vertebrate animals. Probably the most feared example is ▷rabies. The transmitted micro-organism sometimes causes disease only in the human host, leaving the animal host unaffected.

Zoroaster (or Zarathustra) (*c.* 638–*c.* 553 BC) Persian prophet and religious teacher, founder of Zoroastrianism. Zoroaster believed that he had seen God, Ahura Mazda, in a vision. His first vision came at the age of 30 and, after initial rejection and violent attack, he converted King Vishtaspa. Subsequently, his teachings spread rapidly, becoming the official religion of the kingdom.

Zoroastrianism pre-Islamic Persian religion founded by the Persian prophet Zoroaster in the 6th century BC, and still practised by the ▷Parsees in India. The ▷Zend-Avesta are the sacred scriptures of the faith. The theology is dualistic, **Ahura Mazda** or **Ormuzd** (the good God) being perpetually in conflict with **Ahriman** (the evil God), but the former is assured of eventual victory. There are approximately 100,000 (1991) Zoroastrians worldwide; membership is restricted to those with both parents belonging to the faith.

Related Web site: Zoroastrianism http://www.religioustolerance.org/zoroastr.htm

zouk (Creole 'to party') Caribbean dance music originally created in France by musicians from the Antilles. It draws on Latin American, Haitian, and African rhythms and employs electronic synthesizers as well as ethnic drums. Zouk was developed from 1978 and is popular in Paris and parts of the West Indies.

Z particle in physics, an ▷elementary particle, one of the weakons responsible for carrying the ▷weak nuclear force.

Zsigmondy, Richard Adolf (1865–1929) Austrian-born German chemist who devised and built an ultramicroscope in 1903. The microscope's illumination was placed at right angles to the axis. (In a conventional microscope the light source is placed parallel to the instrument's axis.) Zsigmondy's arrangement made it possible to observe particles with a diameter of 10-millionth of a millimetre. He was awarded the Nobel Prize for Chemistry in 1925 for the elucidation of heterogeneity of colloids.

zucchini another name for the courgette, a type of ▷marrow.

Zuider Zee former sea inlet in the northwestern Netherlands, closed off from the North Sea by a 32-km/20-mi dyke in 1932; much of it has been reclaimed as land. The remaining lake is called the ▷IJsselmeer.

Zulu member of a group of southern African peoples mainly from Kwa Zulu-Natal, South Africa. They are traditionally agriculturalists. The Zulu language, closely related to Xhosa, belongs to the Bantu branch of the Niger-Congo family. Many Zulus are supporters of the political organization ▷Inkatha, founded by Chief ▷Buthelezi in 1975.

Zululand region in KwaZulu-Natal, South Africa, largely corresponding to the former Black National State ▷KwaZulu. The Zulus formed a powerful kingdom in the early 19th century under Shaka (died 1828) and built up an empire in Natal, displacing other peoples of southern Africa. They were defeated by the British army at Ulundi in 1879. Zululand became part of the British colony of Natal in 1897.

ZULU A Zulu woman from South Africa. The Zulu are the single largest black ethnic group in South Africa, numbering some nine million people. *Archive Photos*

Zürich city and capital of ▷Switzerland, situated at the exit of the Limmat River from Lake Zürich; population (1995) 422,700. Lying at the foot of the Alps, it is the capital of Zürich canton, the principal financial and business centre of Switzerland, and one of the world's leading international banking and insurance centres (the 'Gnomes of Zürich'). Manufactured goods include machinery, electrical goods, textiles, and printed works. It is the largest city in Switzerland.

Zweig, Stefan (1881–1942) Austrian writer. He was the author of plays, poems, and many biographies of writers (including Balzac and Dickens) and historical figures (including Marie Antoinette and Mary Stuart). He and his wife, exiles from the Nazis from 1934, despaired at what they saw as the end of civilization and culture and committed suicide in Brazil.

Zwicky, Fritz (1898–1974) Swiss astronomer. He predicted the existence of ▷neutron stars in 1934. He discovered 18 supernovae and determined that cosmic rays originate in them.

Zwingli, Ulrich (1484–1531) Swiss Protestant reformer. He was ordained a Roman Catholic priest in 1506, but by 1519 was a Reformer and led the Reformation in Switzerland with his insistence on the sole authority of the Scriptures. He was killed in a skirmish at Kappel during a war against the cantons that had not accepted the Reformation.

zwitterion ion that has both a positive and a negative charge, such as an ▷amino acid in neutral solution. For example, glycine contains both a basic amino group (NH_2) and an acidic carboxyl group (COOH); when these are both ionized in aqueous solution, the acid group loses a proton to the amino group, and the molecule is positively charged at one end and negatively charged at the other.

Zwolle capital of Overijssel province, the Netherlands, 64 km/ 40 mi northeast of Arnhem; population (1997) 101,900. There are shipbuilding, chemical, iron, cotton, brewing, distilling, and buttermaking industries. Nearby is Agnietenberg monastery, associated with Thomas à Kempis.

Zworykin, Vladimir Kosma (1889–1982) Russian-born US electronics engineer who invented a television camera tube and developed the ▷electron microscope.

zydeco dance music originating in Louisiana, USA, similar to ▷Cajun but more heavily influenced by blues and West Indian music.

zygote ▷ovum (egg) after ▷fertilization but before it undergoes cleavage to begin embryonic development.